PERFORMING ARTS BIOGRAPHY MASTER INDEX

PERFORMING ARTS BIOGRAPHY MASTER INDEX

A consolidated index to over 270,000 biographical sketches of persons living and dead, as they appear in over 100 of the principal biographical dictionaries devoted to the performing arts

Edited by Barbara McNeil
and Miranda C. Herbert

SECOND EDITION
Gale Biographical Index Series Number 5

Gale Research Company • Book Tower • Detroit, Michigan 48226

Editors: Barbara McNeil, Miranda C. Herbert

Assistant Editors: Doris Goulart, John Krol, Debra Maloy, Elizabeth Mulligan

Editorial Assistants: Ann Blake, Kim F. Cota, Dorothy Cotter, Dianna Hart, Sandra Iaderosa, Terry Lafaro, Sue Lynch, William Maher, Theresa Q. McIlrath, Paula Morgan, Jean Portfolio, Helen Rasmussen, Mildred Sherman, Joyce Stone, Sharon Wagner

Proofreaders: Barbara Brandenburg, Marie Devlin, Toni Grow

Production Supervisor-External: Carol Blanchard

Production Supervisor-Internal: Laura Bryant

Production Assistants: Tina Blakian, Louise Kava, Sharon McGilvray

Cover Design: Art Chartow

Computer photocomposition by Computer Composition Corporation, Madison Heights, Michigan

Bibliographic Note:
First edition published in 1979 under the title:
Theatre, Film and Television Biographies Master Index.

Library of Congress Cataloging in Publication Data

McNeil, Barbara.
Performing arts biography master index.

(Gale biographical index series ; no. 5)
Rev. ed. of: Theatre, film, and television biographies master index / edited by Dennis La Beau. 1st ed. c1979.
Bibliography: p.
1. Performing arts--Biography--Dictionaries--Indexes. I. Herbert, Miranda C. II. La Beau, Dennis. Theatre, film, and television biographies master index. III. Title. IV. Series.
PN1583.M37 1982 016.7902'092'2 [B] 81-20145
ISBN 0-8103-1097-X AACR2

Introduction

Performing Arts Biography Master Index, the second edition of *Theatre, Film and Television Biographies Master Index* (Gale, 1979), represents a doubling in the coverage provided by its predecessor. This index now provides more than 270,000 citations to over 100 biographical reference sources in the performing arts.

Concept and Scope

As a specialized index, *PABMI* enables the researcher to determine, without tedious searching, in which sources biographical information on an individual can be found. Thus the user can determine which edition(s) of which publication(s) to consult, or, almost as helpful, that there is no listing for a given individual in the sources indexed. In cases where *PABMI* shows multiple listings for the same person, the user is able either to choose the source which is most convenient or to locate multiple biographical sketches to compare and expand the information furnished in a single listing.

The scope of the sources indexed by *PABMI* has been greatly expanded over that of the first edition. In addition to theatre, film, and television, *PABMI* coverage now includes music, both popular and classical, dance, and other performing arts such as puppetry and magic. While the works covered are of several distinct types (biographical dictionaries, encyclopedias, filmographies, etc.), all have one common characteristic: at least a moderate amount of biographical, critical, or career-related information on individuals connected with the performing arts.

The books cited in *PABMI* are readily available and widely held in most reference collections. These books include for example the Oxford Companions to film, music, and the theatre, *The International Motion Picture Almanac, The New Grove Dictionary of Music and Musicians, Halliwell's Filmgoer's Companion,* and many more.

How to Read a Citation

Each citation gives the person's name followed by the years of birth and/or death. If a source has indicated that the dates may not be accurate, the questionable date(s) are followed by a question mark: 1980? If there is no year of birth, the death date is preceeded by a lower case *d.* The codes for the books indexed follow the dates. When a name appears in more than one edition of a reference work, the title code for the book is given only once and is followed by the edition codes only for other editions in which the name appears. If the source book has a portrait or photograph of the person this is indicated in *PABMI* by the abbreviation *[port]* after the source code. For example:

Kent, Jean 1921- *FilmAG WE, FilmEn, FilmgC, HalFC 80, IlWWBF [port] IntMPA 75,-76,-77,-78,-79,-80, WhoHol A, WhoThe 72,-77*

A list of the works indexed in *PABMI,* and the codes used to refer to them is printed on the endsheets, and complete bibliographic citations follow this introduction.

Editorial Practices

All names in an indexed work are included in *PABMI.* This is a time saver for the researcher, as there is no need to consult the work itself if the desired name is not shown in *PABMI.*

PABMI follows standard alphabetizing rules used by the Library of Congress with the exception of those pertaining to *Mac* and *Mc,* which are filed in this index strictly letter by letter. Not all source books use this method of alphabetizing; therefore, some names may have an alphabetic position in a source book different from their position in *PABMI.*

To simplify the listings, some middle names or titles have been added to citations which varied slightly when it appeared certain that the same person was indicated. If the spelling or the dates for an individual differ substantially from publication to publication, or if there is any reason to believe that more than one person is referred to by the various spellings or dates, the *PABMI* citations have retained these discrepancies:

Abbott, Bud d1974 *MotPP, WhoHol B*
Abbott, Bud 1895-1974 *CmMov, FilmEn, FilmgC, ForYSC, Funs [port], HalFC 80 [port], JoeFr [port], OxFilm, What 2 [port], WhoHrs 80 [port], WorEFlm [port]*
Abbott, Bud 1896-1974 *WhScrn 77*
Abbott, Bud 1898-1974 *MovMk [port], NotNAT B*

All the above citations refer to the same person. However, since the purpose of *PABMI* is to lead the user to biographical information in the sources indexed, not to be an authority file, the editors have made no attempt to standardize such entries. Such variations can be of importance to anyone attempting to establish biographical details about a person.

In many publications, portions of a name not used by the individual are placed in parentheses, e.g.: Charles M(onroe) Schulz. These parenthetical portions have been omitted except in those cases where the material in parentheses has been considered in alphabetizing by the source publication.

In a very few cases, extremely long names have been shortened because of typesetting limitations. For example: *Chatrain, Louis Gratien Charles Alexandre* has been shortened to:

Chatrain, Louis Gratien C Alexandre

It is believed that such editing will not affect the usefulness of individual entries.

Researchers may need to look under all possible listings for a name, especially in the cases of:

1. Names with prefixes or suffixes:

   Angeles, Victoria DeLos
   DeLosAngeles, Victoria
   LosAngeles, Victoria De

2. Spanish names which may be entered in sources under either part of the surname:

   Garcia Lorca, Federico
   Lorca, Federico Garcia

3. Chinese names which may be entered in sources in direct or inverted order, or which may be transliterated using the Pinyin spelling.

4. Names transliterated from other non-Roman alphabets:

   Chekhov, Anton Pavlovich
   Chekov, Anton
   Tchekov, Anton

5. Pseudonyms, noms de plume and stage names:

   A E
   Russell, George William

   Crosby, Bing
   Crosby, Harry Lillis

All cross references appearing in indexed publications have been retained in *PABMI* in the form of regular citations. For example, the entry in *The New Grove Dictionary of Music and Musicians*

"Damon, William *See* Daman, William" appears in *PABMI* as:

Damon, William *NewGrD 80*

Suggestions Are Welcome

Future editions of *PABMI* are planned. As their availability and usefulness become known, additional sources will be added to these new editions. The editors welcome suggestions for additional works which could be indexed, or any other comments and suggestions.

Bibliographic Key to Publication Codes for Use in Locating Sources

Code	*Book Indexed*
AmFD	*American Film Directors.* Edited by Stanley Hochman. A Library of Film Criticism. New York: Frederick Ungar Publishing Co., 1974.
AmPS	*American Popular Songs from the Revolutionary War to the Present.* Edited by David Ewen. New York: Random House, 1966. ***AmPS*** "American Popular Songs" begins on page 1 ***AmPS A*** "All-Time Best-Selling Popular Recordings" begins on page 485 ***AmPS B*** "Some American Performers of the Past and Present" begins on page 499
AmSCAP 66	*The ASCAP Biographical Dictionary of Composers, Authors and Publishers.* Third edition, 1966. Compiled and edited by The Lynn Farnol Group, Inc. New York: American Society of Composers, Authors, and Publishers, 1966.
AmSCAP 80	*ASCAP Biographical Dictionary.* Fourth edition. Compiled for the American Society of Composers, Authors and Publishers by Jaques Cattell Press. New York: R.R. Bowker Co., 1980.
Baker 78	*Baker's Biographical Dictionary of Musicians.* Sixth edition. Revised by Nicolas Slonimsky. New York: Schirmer Books, 1978.
BestMus	*The Best Musicals: From Show Boat to A Chorus Line.* Revised edition. By Arthur Jackson. New York: Crown Publishers, Inc., 1979. Biographies are found in the "Who's Who of Show and Film Music" section beginning on page 135.
BgBands 74	*The Big Bands.* Revised edition. By George T. Simon. New York: Macmillan Publishing Co., Collier Books, 1974. Use the Index to locate biographies.
BiDAmM	*Biographical Dictionary of American Music.* By Charles Eugene Claghorn. West Nyack, New York: Parker Publishing Co., Inc., 1973.
BiDFilm	*A Biographical Dictionary of Film.* By David Thomson. New York: William Morrow & Co., Inc., 1976, 1981. ***BiDFilm*** First edition, 1976 ***BiDFilm 81*** Second edition, 1981
BiE&WWA	*The Biographical Encyclopaedia and Who's Who of the American Theatre.* Edited by Walter Rigdon. New York: James H. Heineman, Inc., 1966. Revised edition published as *Notable Names in the American Theatre.* (See below.) The "Biographical Who's Who" section begins on page 227.

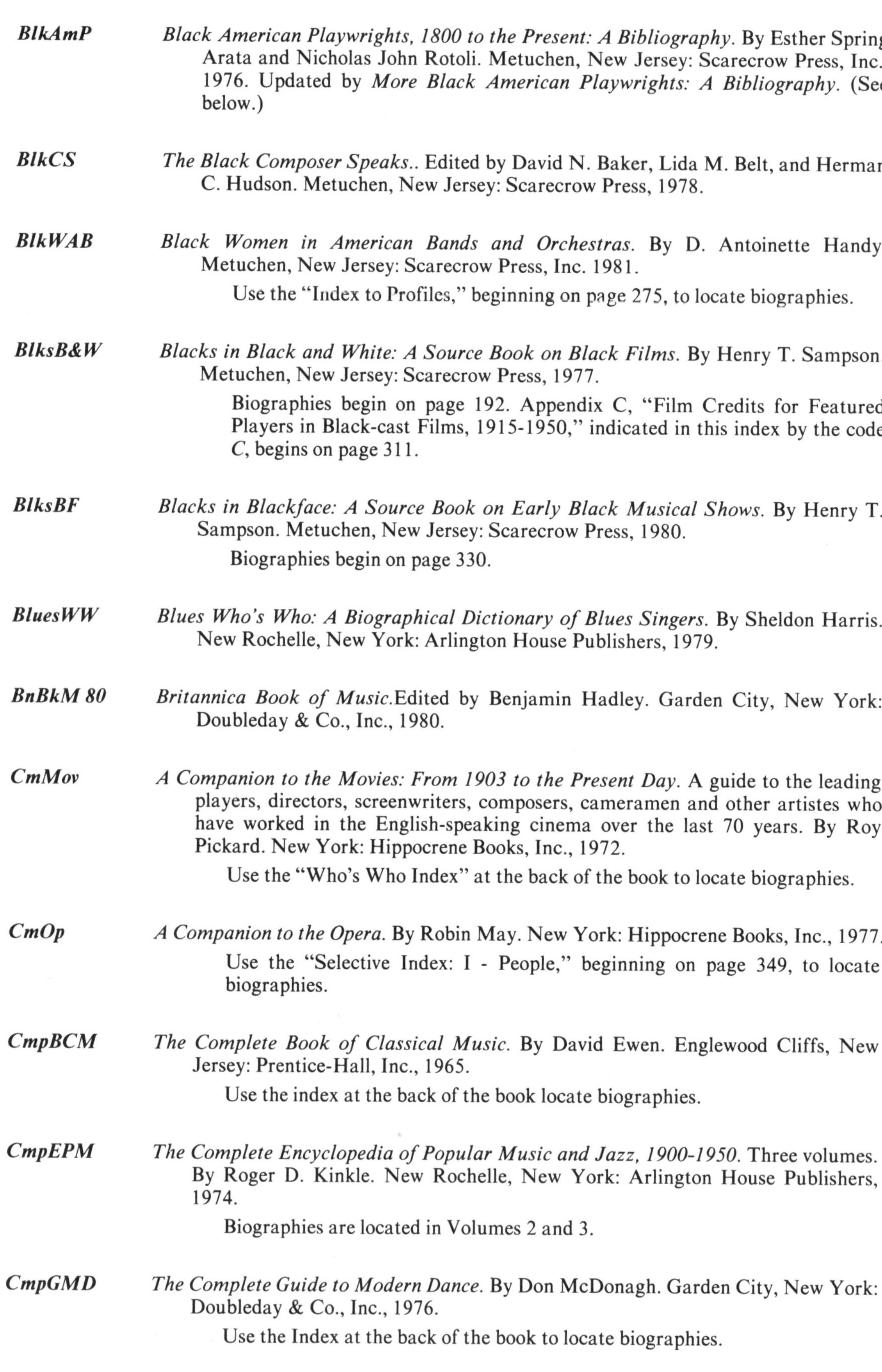

BlkAmP *Black American Playwrights, 1800 to the Present: A Bibliography.* By Esther Spring Arata and Nicholas John Rotoli. Metuchen, New Jersey: Scarecrow Press, Inc., 1976. Updated by *More Black American Playwrights: A Bibliography.* (See below.)

BlkCS *The Black Composer Speaks..* Edited by David N. Baker, Lida M. Belt, and Herman C. Hudson. Metuchen, New Jersey: Scarecrow Press, 1978.

BlkWAB *Black Women in American Bands and Orchestras.* By D. Antoinette Handy. Metuchen, New Jersey: Scarecrow Press, Inc. 1981.

Use the "Index to Profiles," beginning on page 275, to locate biographies.

BlksB&W *Blacks in Black and White: A Source Book on Black Films.* By Henry T. Sampson. Metuchen, New Jersey: Scarecrow Press, 1977.

Biographies begin on page 192. Appendix C, "Film Credits for Featured Players in Black-cast Films, 1915-1950," indicated in this index by the code *C*, begins on page 311.

BlksBF *Blacks in Blackface: A Source Book on Early Black Musical Shows.* By Henry T. Sampson. Metuchen, New Jersey: Scarecrow Press, 1980.

Biographies begin on page 330.

BluesWW *Blues Who's Who: A Biographical Dictionary of Blues Singers.* By Sheldon Harris. New Rochelle, New York: Arlington House Publishers, 1979.

BnBkM 80 *Britannica Book of Music.*Edited by Benjamin Hadley. Garden City, New York: Doubleday & Co., Inc., 1980.

CmMov *A Companion to the Movies: From 1903 to the Present Day.* A guide to the leading players, directors, screenwriters, composers, cameramen and other artistes who have worked in the English-speaking cinema over the last 70 years. By Roy Pickard. New York: Hippocrene Books, Inc., 1972.

Use the "Who's Who Index" at the back of the book to locate biographies.

CmOp *A Companion to the Opera.* By Robin May. New York: Hippocrene Books, Inc., 1977.

Use the "Selective Index: I - People," beginning on page 349, to locate biographies.

CmpBCM *The Complete Book of Classical Music.* By David Ewen. Englewood Cliffs, New Jersey: Prentice-Hall, Inc., 1965.

Use the index at the back of the book locate biographies.

CmpEPM *The Complete Encyclopedia of Popular Music and Jazz, 1900-1950.* Three volumes. By Roger D. Kinkle. New Rochelle, New York: Arlington House Publishers, 1974.

Biographies are located in Volumes 2 and 3.

CmpGMD *The Complete Guide to Modern Dance.* By Don McDonagh. Garden City, New York: Doubleday & Co., Inc., 1976.

Use the Index at the back of the book to locate biographies.

CompSN *Composers since 1900: A Biographical and Critical Guide.* Compiled and edited by David Ewen. New York: H.W. Wilson Co., 1969.

CpmDNM	*Composium Directory of New Music.* Annual index of contemporary compositions. Sedro Woolley, Washington: Crystal Musicworks: 1972, 1973, 1974, 1975, 1976, 1977, 1978, 1979, 1980.
CpmDNM 72	1972 edition
CpmDNM 73	1973 edition
CpmDNM 74	1974 edition
CpmDNM 75	1975 edition
CpmDNM 76	1976 edition
CpmDNM 77	1977 edition
CpmDNM 78	1978 edition
CpmDNM 79	1979 edition
CpmDNM 80	1980 edition

CnMD — *The Concise Encyclopedia of Modern Drama.* By Siegfried Melchinger. Translated by George Wellwarth. Edited by Henry Popkin. New York: Horizon Press, 1964.

Biographies begin on page 159. The "Additional Entries" section, indicated in this index by the code *SUP*, begins on page 287.

CnThe — *A Concise Encyclopedia of the Theatre.* By Robin May. Reading, Berkshire, England: Osprey Publishing Ltd., 1974.

Use the Index at the back of the book to locate biographies.

CnOxB — *The Concise Oxford Dictionary of Ballet.* By Horst Koegler. London: Oxford University Press, 1977.

ConAmC — *Contemporary American Composers: A Biographical Dictionary.* Compiled by E. Ruth Anderson. Boston: G.K. Hall & Co., 1976.

The Addendum, indicated in this index by the code *A*, begins on page 495.

ConAmTC — *Contemporary American Theater Critics: A Directory and Anthology of Their Works.* Compiled by M.E. Comtois and Lynn F. Miller. Metuchen, New Jersey: Scarecrow Press, Inc., 1977.

ConDr — *Contemporary Dramatists.* Edited by James Vinson. London: St. James Press; New York: St. Martin's Press, 1973, 1977.

ConDr 73	First edition, 1973
ConDr 77	Second edition, 1977, "Contemporary Dramatists" begins on page 9
ConDr 77A	Second edition, "Screen Writers" begins on page 893
ConDr 77B	Second edition, "Radio Writers" begins on page 903
ConDr 77C	Second edition, "Television Writers" begins on page 915
ConDr 77D	Second edition, "Musical Librettists" begins on page 925
ConDr 77E	Second edition, "The Theatre of the Mixed Means" begins on page 941
ConDr 77F	Second edition, Appendix begins on page 969

ConLC 16 — *Contemporary Literary Criticism.* Excerpts from criticism of the works of today's novelists, poets, playwrights, short story writers, filmmakers, and other creative writers. Volume 16. Edited by Sharon R. Gunton. Detroit: Gale Research Co., 1981.

ConMuA 80 — *Contemporary Music Almanac, 1980/81.* By Ronald Zalkind. New York: Macmillan Publishing Co., Schirmer Books, 1980.

ConMuA 80A	"Who's Who--Artists" section begins on page 157
ConMuA 80B	"Music Business Professionals" section begins on page 351

Conv 2 — *Conversations with Jazz Musicians.* Conversations series, Volume 2. Detroit: Gale Research Co., 1977.

CounME 74 — *The Country Music Encyclopedia.* By Melvin Shestack. New York: Thomas Y. Crowell Co., 1974.

The "Discography," indicated in this index by the code *A*, begins on page 325.

CreCan — *Creative Canada: A Biographical Dictionary of Twentieth-Century Creative and Performing Artists.* Compiled by the Reference Division, McPherson Library, University of Victoria, B.C. Toronto: University of Toronto Press, 1971, 1972.

CreCan 1	Volume 1, 1971
CreCan 2	Volume 2, 1972

CroCD — *Crowell's Handbook of Contemporary Drama.* By Michael Anderson, et al. New York: Thomas Y. Crowell Co., 1971.

DancEn 78 — *The Dance Encyclopedia.* Revised and enlarged edition. Compiled and edited by Anatole Chujoy and P.W. Manchester. New York: Simon and Schuster, 1978.

DcCom 77 — *The Dictionary of Composers.* Edited by Charles Osborne. London: Bodly Head, 1977.

DcCom&M 79 — *The Dictionary of Composers and Their Music: Every Listener's Companion.* Arranged chronologically and alphabetically. By Eric Gilder and June G. Port. New York: Ballantine Books, 1979.

Entries are found in Part One.

DcCM — *Dictionary of Contemporary Music.* Edited by John Vinton. New York: E.P. Dutton & Co., Inc., 1974.

This book ignores prefixes in filing surnames.

DcFM — *Dictionary of Film Makers.* By Georges Sadoul. Translated, edited, and updated by Peter Morris. Berkeley and Los Angeles: University of California Press, 1972. Originally published as *Dictionnaire des Cineastes,* 1965.

DcLB 7 — *Dictionary of Literary Biography.* Volume 7: *Twentieth-Century American Dramatists.* Two volumes. Edited by John MacNicholas. Detroit: Gale Research Co., 1981.

DcPup — *Dictionary of Puppetry.* By A.R. Philpott. Boston: Plays, Inc., 1969.

DcTwCC — *A Dictionary of Twentieth-Century Composers: 1911-1971.* By Kenneth Thompson. New York: St. Martin's Press, 1973.

The Addenda, indicated in this index by the code *A*, begins on page 659.

DrBlPA — *Directory of Blacks in the Performing Arts.* By Edward Mapp. Metuchen, New Jersey: Scarecrow Press, Inc., 1978.

EncFCWM 69 — *Encyclopedia of Folk, Country and Western Music.* By Irwin Stambler and Grelun Landon. New York: St. Martin's Press, 1969.

EncJzS 70	*The Encyclopedia of Jazz in the Seventies.* By Leonard Feather and Ira Gitler. New York: Horizon Press, 1976.
EncMT	*Encyclopaedia of the Musical Theatre.* By Stanley Green. New York: Dodd, Mead & Co., 1976.
EncWT	*The Encyclopedia of World Theater.* Translated by Estella Schmid, edited by Martin Esslin. New York: Charles Scribner's Sons, 1977. Based on *Friedrichs Theaterlexikon,* by Karl Groning and Werner Kliess.
Ent	*The Entertainers.* Edited by Clive Unger-Hamilton. New York: St. Martin's Press, 1980. Use the "Index of Entries," beginning on page 306, to locate biographies.
FamA&A	*Famous Actors and Actresses on the American Stage: Documents of American Theater History.* Two volumes. By William C. Young. New York: R.R. Bowker Co., 1975.
FilmAG WE	*Film Actors Guide: Western Europe.* By James Robert Parish. Metuchen, New Jersey: Scarecrow Press, Inc., 1977.
FilmEn	*The Film Encyclopedia.* By Ephraim Katz. New York: Thomas Y. Crowell, 1979.
Film	*Filmarama.* Compiled by John Stewart. Metuchen, New Jersey: Scarecrow Press, Inc., 1975, 1977. ***Film 1*** Volume 1: *The Formidable Years, 1893-1919,* 1975 ***Film 2*** Volume 2: *The Flaming Years, 1920-1929,* 1977
FilmgC	*The Filmgoer's Companion.* Fourth edition. By Leslie Halliwell. New York: Hill & Wang, 1974. Seventh edition published as *Halliwell's Filmgoer's Companion.* (See below.)
ForYSC	*Forty Years of Screen Credits, 1929-1969.* Two volumes. Compiled by John T. Weaver. Metuchen, New Jersey: Scarecrow Press, Inc., 1970. Entries begin on page 57.
Funs	*The Funsters.* By James Robert Parish and William T. Leonard. New Rochelle, New York: Arlington House Publishers, 1979.
GrComp	*Great Composers 1300-1900: A Biographical and Critical Guide.* Compiled and edited by David Ewen. New York: H.W. Wilson Co., 1966.
GrMovC	*The Great Movie Comedians: From Charlie Chaplin to Woody Allen.* By Leonard Maltin. New York: Crown Publishers, Inc., 1978. Use the Table of Contents to locate biographies.
HalFC 80	*Halliwell's Filmgoer's Companion.* Seventh edition. By Leslie Halliwell. New York: Granada Publishing Ltd., 1980. Fourth edition published as *The Filmgoer's Companion.* (See above.)
HolCA	*Hollywood Character Actors.* By James Robert Parish. Westport, Connecticut: Arlington House Publishers, 1978.

HolP — *Hollywood Players.* New Rochelle, New York: Arlington House Publishers, 1976.

- **HolP 30** — *The Thirties.* Edited by James Robert Parish and William T. Leonard.
- **HolP 40** — *The Forties.* Edited by James Robert Parish and Lennard DeCarl.

IlEncCM — *The Illustrated Encyclopedia of Country Music.* By Fred Dellar, Roy Thompson, and Douglas B. Green. New York: Harmony Books, 1977.

IlEncJ — *The Illustrated Encyclopedia of Jazz.* By Brian Case and Stan Britt. New York: Harmony Books, 1978.

IlEncR — *The Illustrated Encyclopedia of Rock.* Revised edition. Compiled by Nick Logan and Bob Woffinden. New York: Harmony Books, 1977?

IlWWBF — *The Illustrated Who's Who in British Films.* By Denis Gifford. London: Anchor Press, Ltd., 1978.

The "Biographical Bibliography," indicated in this index by the code *A*, begins on page 317.

IntMPA — *International Motion Picture Almanac.* Edited by Richard Gertner. New York: Quigley Publishing Co., Inc., 1975, 1976, 1977, 1978, 1979, 1980.

- **IntMPA 75** — 1975 edition
- **IntMPA 76** — 1976 edition
- **IntMPA 77** — 1977 edition
- **IntMPA 78** — 1978 edition
- **IntMPA 79** — 1979 edition
- **IntMPA 80** — 1980 edition

Biographies are found in the "Who's Who in Motion Pictures and Television" section in each volume. The listings are identical to those found in *The International Television Almanac.*

IntWWM — *International Who's Who in Music and Musicians' Directory.* Edited by Adrian Gaster. Cambridge, England: International Who's Who in Music, 1977, 1980. Distributed by Gale Research Co., Detroit, Michigan. Earlier editions published as *Who's Who in Music and Musicians' International Directory.* (See below.)

- **IntWWM 77** — Eighth edition, 1977
- **IntWWM 80** — Ninth edition, 1980

JoeFr — *Joe Franklin's Encyclopedia of Comedians.* Secaucus, New Jersey: Citadel Press, 1979.

MGM — *The MGM Stock Company: The Golden Era.* By James Robert Parish and Ronald L. Bowers. New Rochelle, New York: Arlington House, 1973.

The "Capsule Biographies of MGM Executives," indicated in this index by the code *A*, begins on page 796.

MagIlD — *Magic Illustrated Dictionary.* By Geoffrey Lamb. London: Kaye & Ward, 1979.

McGEWD — *McGraw-Hill Encyclopedia of World Drama.* An international reference work in four volumes. New York: McGraw-Hill Book Co., 1972.

MnPM — *Men of Popular Music.* By David Ewen. Chicago: Ziff-Davis Publishing Co., 1944. Reprint. Freeport, New York: Books for Libraries Press, 1972.

ModWD — *Modern World Drama: An Encyclopedia.* By Myron Matlaw. New York: E.P. Dutton & Co., Inc., 1972.

MorBAP — *More Black American Playwrights: A Bibliography.* By Esther Spring Arata. Metuchen, New Jersey: Scarecrow Press, Inc., 1978. Updates *Black American Playwrights.* (See above.)

MotPP — *Motion Picture Performers: A Bibliography of Magazine and Periodical Articles, 1900-1969.* Compiled by Mel Schuster. Metuchen, New Jersey: Scarecrow Press, Inc., 1971.

MovMk — *The Movie Makers.* By Sol Chaneles and Albert Wolsky. Secaucus, New Jersey: Derbibooks Inc., 1974.

The "Directors" section begins on page 506.

MusMk — *The Music Makers.* Edited by Clive Unger-Hamilton. New York: Harry N. Abrams, Inc., 1979.

Use the "Alphabetical List of Entries" at the front of the book to locate biographies.

MusSN — *Musicians since 1900: Performers in Concert and Opera.* Compiled and edited by David Ewen. New York: H.W. Wilson Co., 1978.

NatPD — *National Playwrights Directory.* Edited by Phyllis Johnson Kaye. Waterford, Connecticut: The O'Neill Theater Center, 1977. Distributed by Gale Research Co., Detroit, Michigan.

NewCBMT — *New Complete Book of the American Musical Theater.* By David Ewen. New York: Holt, Rinehart & Winston, 1970.

Biographies are found in the "Librettists, Lyricists and Composers" section beginning on page 607.

NewEOp 71 — *The New Encyclopedia of the Opera.* By David Ewen. New York: Hill & Wang, 1971.

NewGrD 80 — *The New Grove Dictionary of Music and Musicians.* Edited by Stanley Sadie. 20 volumes. London: Macmillan Publishers, Ltd., 1980. Distributed by Grove's Dictionaries of Music, Inc., Washington, D.C.

NewOrJ — *New Orleans Jazz: A Family Album.* Revised edition. By Al Rose and Edmond Souchon. Baton Rouge, Louisiana: Louisiana State University Press, 1978.

"Who's Who in New Orleans Jazz" section begins on page 4. The "Who's Who in New Orleans Jazz Supplement," indicated in this index by the code *SUP*, begins on page 307.

NewYTET — *The New York Times Encyclopedia of Television.* By Les Brown. New York: New York Times Book Co., Inc., 1977.

NotNAT — *Notable Names in the American Theatre.* Clifton, New Jersey: James T. White & Co., 1976. First edition published as *The Biographical Encyclopaedia and Who's Who of the American Theatre.* (See above.)

NotNAT — "Notable Names in the American Theatre" section begins on page 489

NotNAT A — "Biographical Bibliography" begins on page 309

NotNAT B "Necrology" begins on page 343

This book often alphabetizes by titles of address, e.g.: Dr., Mrs., and Sir.

OxFilm *The Oxford Companion to Film.* Edited by Liz-Anne Bawden. New York: Oxford University Press, 1976.

OxMus *The Oxford Companion to Music.* By Percy A. Scholes. 10th edition (corrected). Edited by John Owen Ward. London: Oxford University Press, 1974.

OxThe *The Oxford Companion to the Theatre.* Third edition. Edited by Phyllis Hartnoll. London: Oxford University Press, 1967.

PlP&P *Plays, Players, and Playwrights: An Illustrated History of the Theatre.* By Marion Geisinger. Updated by Peggy Marks. New York: Hart Publishing Co., Inc., 1975.

Use the Index, beginning on page 575, to locate biographies in the main section of the book. A Supplemental Index to the last chapter "The Theatre of the Seventies" begins on page 797, and is indicated in this index by the code *A*.

PopAmC *Popular American Composers: From Revolutionary Times to the Present.* A biographical and critical guide. Compiled and edited by David Ewen. New York: H.W. Wilson Co., 1962, 1972.

PopAmC	Original volume, 1962
PopAmC SUP	First Supplement, 1972
PopAmC SUPN	First Supplement, Necrology, page vi

PupTheA *The Puppet Theatre in America: A History 1524-1948.* By Paul McPharlin. With a Supplement *Puppets in America Since 1948.* By Marjorie Batchelder McPharlin. Boston: Plays, Inc., 1969.

Biographies are found in Chapter XXI "A List of Puppeteers, 1524- 1948" beginning on page 396 and in Chapter V of the Supplement "Some Careers in Puppetry," indicated in this index by the code *SUP*, beginning on page 606.

REnWD *The Reader's Encyclopedia of World Drama.* Edited by John Gassner and Edward Quinn. New York: Thomas Y. Crowell Co., 1969.

RkOn *Rock On: The Illustrated Encyclopedia of Rock n' Roll.* By Norm N. Nite. New York: Thomas Y. Crowell Co., 1974, 1978.

RkOn	Volume 1: *The Solid Gold Years,* 1974
RkOn 2	Volume 2: *The Modern Years: 1964-Present,* 1978
RkOn 2A	Volume 2: Appendix begins on page 543

Sw&Ld *Sweet and Lowdown: America's Popular Song Writers.* By Warren Craig. Metuchen, New Jersey: Scarecrow Press, Inc., 1978.

Sw&Ld A	"Before Tin Pan Alley" begins on page 15
Sw&Ld B	"Tin Pan Alley" begins on page 23
Sw&Ld C	"After Tin Pan Alley" begins on page 91

ThFT *They Had Faces Then: Super Stars, Stars and Starlets of the 1930's.* By John Springer and Jack Hamilton. Secaucus, New Jersey: Citadel Press, 1974.

TwYS *Twenty Years of Silents, 1908-1928.* Compiled by John T. Weaver. Metuchen, New Jersey: Scarecrow Press, Inc., 1971.

TwYS	"The Players" begins on page 27
TwYS A	"Directors" begins on page 407
TwYS B	"Producers" begins on page 502

Vers *The Versatiles.*A study of supporting character actors and actresses in the American motion picture, 1930-1955. By Alfred E. Twomey and Arthur F. McClure. South Brunswick, New Jersey and New York: A.S. Barnes & Co.; London: Thomas Yoseloff Ltd., 1969.

Vers A	"Biographical Section" begins on page 25
Vers B	"Non-Biographical Section" begins on page 249

What *Whatever Became of...?* By Richard Lamparski. New York: Crown Publishers, Inc., 1967-1974.

What 1	Volume One, 1967
What 2	Second Series, 1968
What 3	Third Series, 1970
What 4	Fourth Series, 1973
What 5	Fifth Series, 1974

Also printed in a paperback edition by Ace Books.

WhScrn *Who Was Who on Screen.* By Evelyn Mack Truitt. New York: R.R. Bowker Co., 1974, 1977.

WhScrn 74	First edition, 1974
WhScrn 77	Second edition, 1977

WhThe *Who Was Who in the Theatre, 1912-1976.* A biographical dictionary of actors, actresses, directors, playwrights, and producers of the English-speaking theatre. Compiled from *Who's Who in the Theatre,* Volumes 1-15, 1912-1972. Four volumes. Gale Composite Biographical Dictionary Series, Number 3. Detroit: Gale Research Co., 1978.

WhoHol *Who's Who in Hollywood, 1900-1976.* By David Ragan. New Rochelle, New York: Arlington House, 1976.

WhoHol A	"Living Players" begins on page 11
WhoHol B	"Late Players (1900-1974)" begins on page 539
WhoHol C	"Players Who Died in 1975 and 1976" begins on page 845

WhoHrs 80 *Who's Who of the Horrors and Other Fantasy Films.* The international personality encyclopedia of the fantastic film. First edition. By David J. Hogan. San Diego and New York: A.S. Barnes & Co., Inc.; London: Tantivy Press, 1980.

WhoJazz 72 *Who's Who of Jazz: Storyville to Swing Street.* By John Chilton. Philadelphia: Chilton Book Co., 1972.

WhoMus 72 *Who's Who in Music and Musicians' International Directory.* Sixth edition. New York: Hafner Publishing Co., Inc., 1972. Later editions published as *International Who's Who in Music and Musicians' Directory.*(See above.)

WhoOp 76 *Who's Who in Opera.* An international biographical directory of singers, conductors, directors, designers, and administrators. Also including profiles of 101 opera companies. Edited by Maria F. Rich. New York: Arno Press, 1976.

WhoStg 1906 *Who's Who on the Stage.* The dramatic reference book and biographical dictionary of the theatre, containing records of the careers of actors, actresses, managers, and playwrights of the American stage. Edited by Walter Browne and F.A. Austin. New York: Walter Browne & F.A. Austin, 1906.

Some entries are not in alphabetic sequence.

WhoStg 1908 *Who's Who on the Stage, 1908.* The dramatic reference book and biographical dictionary of the theatre, containing careers of actors, actresses, managers, and playwrights of the American stage. Edited by Walter Browne and E. DeRoy Koch. New York: B.W. Dodge & Co., 1908.

Some entries are not in alphabetic sequence.

WhoThe *Who's Who in the Theatre: A Biographical Record of the Contemporary Stage.* London: Pitman Publishing Ltd.; Detroit: Gale Research Co., 1972, 1977.

WhoThe 72	15th edition, compiled by John Parker, 1972.
WhoThe 77	16th edition, edited by Ian Herbert, 1977.

WomCom *Women Composers, Conductors and Musicians of the Twentieth Century: Selected Biographies.* By Jane Weiner LePage. Metuchen, New Jersey: Scarecrow Press, Inc., 1980.

WomWMM *Women Who Make Movies.* Cinema Study Series. By Sharon Smith. New York: Hopkinson & Blake, 1975.

WomWMM	"Overview" Section. Biographies can be located through the index beginning on page 299
WomWMM A	"The New Filmmakers" begins on page 145
WomWMM B	"Directory" begins on page 221

WorEFlm *The World Encyclopedia of the Film.* Edited by John M. Smith and Tim Cawkwell. New York: A. & W. Visual Library, 1972.

Author Listing for Sources Indexed

Complete bibliographic information for the following citations can be found in the *Key to Publication Codes* section of this volume.

Anderson, E. Ruth, comp. *Contemporary American Composers: A Biographical Dictionary.*

Anderson, Michael, et al. *Crowell's Handbook of Contemporary Drama.*

Arata, Esther Spring. *More Black American Playwrights: A Bibliography.*

----- and Nicholas John Rotoli. *Black American Playwrights, 1800 to the Present: A Bibliography.*

Austin, F.A. and Walter Browne, eds. *Who's Who on the Stage, 1906.*

Baker, David N., Lida M. Belt, and Herman C. Hudson, eds. *The Black Composer Speaks.*

Bawden, Liz-Anne, ed. *The Oxford Companion to Film.*

Belt, Lida M., David N. Baker, and Herman C. Hudson, eds. *The Black Composer Speaks.*

Bowers, Ronald L. and James Robert Parish. *The MGM Stock Company: The Golden Era.*

Brown, Les. *The New York Times Encyclopedia of Television.*

Browne, Walter and F.A. Austin, eds. *Who's Who on the Stage, 1906.*

----- and E. DeRoy Koch, eds. *Who's Who on the Stage, 1908.*

Britt, Stan and Brian Case. *The Illustrated Encyclopedia of Jazz.*

Case, Brian and Stan Britt. *The Illustrated Encyclopedia of Jazz.*

Cawkwell, Tim and John M. Smith, eds. *The World Encyclopedia of the Film.*

Chaneles, Sol and Albert Wolsky. *The Movie Makers.*

Chilton, John. *Who's Who of Jazz: Storyville to Swing Street.*

Chujoy, Anatole and P.W. Manchester, eds. *The Dance Encyclopedia.*

Claghorn, Charles Eugene. *Biographical Dictionary of American Music.*

Comtois, M.E. and Lynn F. Miller, comp. *Contemporary American Theater Critics: A Directory and Anthology of Their Works.*

Craig, Warren. *Sweet and Lowdown: America's Popular Song Writers.*

DeCarl, Lennard and James Robert Parish, eds. *Hollywood Players: The Forties.*

Dellar, Fred, Roy Thompson, and Douglas B. Green. *The Illustrated Encyclopedia of Country Music.*

Esslin, Martin, ed. *The Encyclopedia of World Theater.*

Ewen, David, ed. *American Popular Songs from the Revolutionary War to the Present.*

-----. *The Complete Book of Classical Music.*

-----, ed. *Composers since 1900: A Biographical and Critical Guide.*

-----, ed. *Great Composers 1300-1900: A Biographical and Critical Guide.*

-----. *Men of Popular Music.*

-----, ed. *Musicians since 1900: Performers in Concert and Opera.*

-----. *New Complete Book of the American Musical Theater.*

-----. *The New Encyclopedia of the Opera.*

-----, ed. *Popular American Composers: From Revolutionary Times to the Present.*

Feather, Leonard and Ira Gitler. *The Encyclopedia of Jazz in the Seventies.*

Franklin, Joe. *Joe Franklin's Encyclopedia of Comedians.*

Gassner, John and Edward Quinn, eds. *The Reader's Encyclopedia of World Drama.*

Gaster, Adrian, ed. *International Who's Who in Music and Musician's Directory.*

Geisinger, Marion. *Plays, Players, and Playwrights: An Illustrated History of the Theatre.*

Gertner, Richard, ed. *International Motion Picture Almanac.*

Gifford, Denis. *The Illustrated Who's Who in British Films.*

Gilder, Eric and June G. Port. *The Dictionary of Composers and Their Music: Every Listener's Companion.*

Gitler, Ira and Leonard Feather. *The Encyclopedia of Jazz in the Seventies.*

Green, Douglas B., Fred Dellar, and Roy Thompson. *The Illustrated Encyclopedia of Country Music.*

Green, Stanley. *Encyclopaedia of the Musical Theatre.*

Gunton, Sharon R., ed. *Contemporary Literary Criticism.* Volume 16.

Hadley, Benjamin, ed. *Britannica Book of Music.*

Halliwell, Leslie. *The Filmgoer's Companion.*

-----. *Halliwell's Filmgoer's Companion.*

Hamilton, Jack and John Springer. *They Had Faces Then: Super Stars, Stars and Starlets of the 1930's.*

Handy, D. Antoinette. *Black Women in American Bands and Orchestras.*

Harris, Sheldon. *Blues Who's Who: A Biographical Dictionary of Blues Singers.*

Hartnoll, Phyllis, ed. *The Oxford Companion to the Theatre.*

Herbert, Ian, ed. *Who's Who in the Theatre: A Biographical Record of the Contemporary Stage.*

Hochman, Stanley, ed. *American Film Directors.*

Hogan, David J. *Who's Who of the Horrors and Other Fantasy Films.*

Hudson, Herman C., David N. Baker, and Lida M. Belt, eds. *The Black Composer Speaks.*

Jackson, Arthur. *The Best Musicals: From Show Boat to A Chorus Line.*

Jaques Cattell Press, comp. *ASCAP Biographical Dictionary.*

Katz, Ephraim. *The Film Encyclopedia.*

Kaye, Phyllis Johnson, ed. *National Playwrights Directory.*

Kinkle, Roger D. *The Complete Encyclopedia of Popular Music and Jazz, 1900-1950.*

Koch, E. DeRoy and Walter Browne, eds. *Who's Who on the Stage, 1908.*

Koegler, Horst. *The Concise Oxford Dictionary of Ballet.*

Lamb, Geoffrey. *Magic Illustrated Dictionary.*

Lamparski, Richard. *Whatever Became of ...?*

Landon, Grelun and Irwin Stambler. *Encyclopedia of Folk, Country and Western Music.*

Leonard, William T. and James Robert Parish. *The Funsters.*

-----. *Hollywood Players: The Thirties.*

LePage, Jane Weiner. *Women Composers, Conductors and Musicians of the Twentieth Century: Selected Biographies.*

Logan, Nick and Bob Woffinden, comps. *The Illustrated Encyclopedia of Rock.*

The Lynn Farnol Group, Inc., comps. *The ASCAP Biographical Dictionary of Composers, Authors and Publishers.* Third edition, 1966.

MacNicholas, John, ed. *Dictionary of Literary Biography.* Volume 7: *Twentieth-Century American Dramatists.*

Maltin, Leonard. *The Great Movie Comedians: From Charlie Chaplin to Woody Allen.*

Manchester, P.W. and Anatole Chujoy, eds. *The Dance Encyclopedia.*

Mapp, Edward. *Directory of Blacks in the Performing Arts.*

Marks, Peggy, updater. *Plays, Players, and Playwrights: An Illustrated History of the Theatre.*

Matlaw, Myron. *Modern World Drama: An Encyclopedia.*

May, Robin. *A Companion to the Opera.*

-----. *A Concise Encyclopedia of the Theatre.*

McClure, Arthur F. and Alfred E. Twomey. *The Versatiles.*

McDonagh, Don. *The Complete Guide to Modern Dance.*

McPharlin, Marjorie Batchelder. *Puppets in America Since 1948.* Supplement to *The Puppet Theatre in America: A History 1524-1948.*

McPharlin, Paul. *The Puppet Theatre in America: A History 1524-1948.*

Melchinger, Siegfried. *The Concise Encyclopedia of Modern Drama.*

Miller, Lynn F. and M.E. Comtois, comps. *Contemporary American Theater Critics: A Directory and Anthology of Their Works.*

Morris, Peter, trans., ed., and updater. *Dictionary of Film Makers.*

Nite, Norm N. *Rock On: The Illustrated Encyclopedia of Rock n' Roll: The Modern Years, 1964-Present.*

-----. *Rock On: The Illustrated Encyclopedia of Rock n' Roll: The Solid Gold Years.*

Osborne, Charles, ed. *The Dictionary of Composers.*

Parish, James Robert. *Film Actors Guide: Western Europe.*

----- *Hollywood Character Actors.*

----- and Ronald L. Bowers. *The MGM Stock Company: The Golden Era.*

----- and Lennard DeCarl. *Hollywood Players: The Forties.*

----- and William T. Leonard. *The Funsters.*

----- and William T. Leonard. *Hollywood Players: The Thirties.*

Parker, John, comp. *Who's Who in the Theatre: A Biographical Record of the Contemporary Stage.*

Philpott, A.R. *Dictionary of Puppetry.*

Pickard, Roy. *A Companion to the Movies: From 1903 to the Present Day.*

Popkin, Henry, ed. *The Concise Encyclopedia of Modern Drama.*

Port, June G. and Eric Gilder. *The Dictionary of Composers and Their Music: Every Listener's Companion.*

Quinn, Edward and John Gassner, eds. *The Reader's Encyclopedia of World Drama.*

Ragan, David. *Who's Who in Hollywood, 1900-1976.*

The Reference Division, McPherson Library, University of Victoria, B.C., comp. *Creative Canada: A Biographical Dictionary of Twentieth-Century Creative and Performing Artists.*

Rigdon, Walter, ed. *The Biographical Encyclopaedia and Who's Who of the American Theatre.*

Rich, Maria F., ed. *Who's Who in Opera.*

Rose, Al and Edmond Souchon. *New Orleans Jazz: A Family Album.*

Rotoli, Nicholas John and Esther Spring Arata. *Black American Playwrights, 1800 to the Present: A Bibliography.*

Sadie, Stanley, ed. *The New Grove Dictionary of Music and Musicians.*

Sadoul, Georges. *Dictionary of Film Makers.*

Sampson, Henry T. *Blacks in Black and White: A Source Book on Black Films.*

-----. *Blacks in Blackface: A Source Book on Early Black Musical Shows.*

Schmid, Estella, trans. *The Encyclopedia of World Theater.*

Scholes, Percy A. *The Oxford Companion to Music.*

Schuster, Mel, comp. *Motion Picture Performers: A Bibliography of Magazine and Periodical Articles, 1900-1969.*

Shestack, Melvin. *The Country Music Encyclopedia.*

Simon, George T. *The Big Bands.*

Slonimsky, Nicolas, rev. *Baker's Biographical Dictionary of Musicians.*

Smith, John M. and Tim Cawkwell, eds. *The World Encyclopedia of the Film.*

Smith, Sharon. *Women Who Make Movies.*

Souchon, Edmond and Al Rose. *New Orleans Jazz: A Family Album.*

Springer, John and Jack Hamilton. *They Had Faces Then: Super Stars, Stars and Starlets of the 1930's.*

Stambler, Irwin and Grelun Landon. *Encyclopedia of Folk, Country and Western Music.*

Stewart, John, comp. *Filmarama: The Flaming Years, 1920-1929.*

-----. *Filmarama: The Formidable Years, 1893-1919.*

Thompson, Kenneth. *A Dictionary of Twentieth-Century Composers: 1911-1971.*

Thompson, Roy, Fred Dellar, and Douglas B. Green. *The Illustrated Encyclopedia of Country Music.*

Thomson, David. *A Biographical Dictionary of Film.*

Truitt, Evelyn Mack. *Who Was Who on Screen.*

Twomey, Alfred E. and Arthur F. McClure. *The Versatiles.*

Unger-Hamilton, Clive, ed. *The Entertainers.*

-----. *The Music Makers.*

Vinson, James, ed. *Contemporary Dramatists.*

Vinton, John, ed. *Dictionary of Contemporary Music.*

Ward, John Owen, ed. *The Oxford Companion to Music.*

Weaver, John T., comp. *Forty Years of Screen Credits, 1929-1969.*

-----. *Twenty Years of Silents, 1908-1928.*

Wellwarth, George, trans. *The Concise Encyclopedia of Modern Drama.*

Wolsky, Albert and Sol Chaneles. *The Movie Makers.*

Woffinden, Bob and Nick Logan, comps. *The Illustrated Encyclopedia of Rock.*

Young, William C. *Famous Actors and Actresses on the American Stage: Documents of American Theater History.*

Zalkind, Ronald. *Contemporary Music Almanac, 1980/81.*

No Author Given. *Composium Directory of New Music.*

-----. *Conversations with Jazz Musicians.*

-----. *McGraw-Hill Encyclopedia of World Drama.*

-----. *Notable Names in the American Theatre.*

-----. *Who Was Who in the Theatre, 1912-1976.*

-----. *Who's Who in Music and Musicians' International Directory.*

Subject Listing for Sources Indexed

Complete bibliographic information for the following citations can be found in the *Key to Publication Codes* section of this volume.

DANCE:

The Complete Guide to Modern Dance
The Concise Oxford Dictionary of Ballet
The Dance Encyclopedia

FILM:

American Film Directors
A Biographical Dictionary of Film
Blacks in Black and White: A Source Book on Black Films
A Companion to the Movies: From 1903 to the Present Day
Contemporary Literary Criticism
Dictionary of Film Makers
Film Actors Guide: Western Europe
The Film Encyclopedia
Filmarama
The Filmgoer's Companion
Forty Years of Screen Credits, 1929-1969
The Funsters
The Great Movie Comedians: From Charlie Chaplin to Woody Allen
Halliwell's Filmgoer's Companion
Hollywood Character Actors
Hollywood Players
The Illustrated Who's Who in British Films
The International Motion Picture Almanac
Joe Franklin's Encyclopedia of Comedians
The MGM Stock Company: The Golden Era
Motion Picture Performers: A Bibliography of Magazine and Periodical Articles, 1900-1969
The Movie Makers
The Oxford Companion to Film
They Had Faces Then: Super Stars, Stars and Starlets of the 1930's
Twenty Years of Silents, 1908-1928
The Versatiles: A Study of Supporting Character Actors and Actresses in the American Motion Picture, 1930-1955
Whatever Became of ...?
Who Was Who on Screen
Who's Who in Hollywood, 1900-1976
Who's Who of the Horrors and Other Fantasy Films
Women Who Make Movies
The World of Encyclopedia of the Film

MISCELLANEOUS PERFORMING ARTS:

Creative Canada: A Biographical Dictionary of Twentieth-Century Creative and Performing Artists
Dictionary of Puppetry
Directory of Blacks in the Performing Arts
The Entertainers
Joe Franklin's Encyclopedia of Comedians
Magic Illustrated Dictionary
The Puppet Theatre in America: A History 1524-1948
Whatever Became of ...?

MUSIC:

American Popular Songs from the Revolutionary War to the Present
The ASCAP Biographical Dictionary of Composers, Authors and Publishers
Baker's Biographical Dictionary of Musicians
The Best Musicals: From Show Boat to A Chorus Line
The Big Bands
Biographical Dictionary of American Music
The Black Composer Speaks
Black Women in American Bands and Orchestras
Blacks in Blackface: A Source Book on Early Black Musical Shows
Blues Who's Who: A Biographical Dictionary of Blues Singers
Britannica Book of Music
A Companion to the Opera
The Complete Book of Classical Music
The Complete Encyclopedia of Popular Music and Jazz, 1900-1950
Composers since 1900: A Biographical and Critical Guide
Composium Directory of New Music
Contemporary American Composers: A Biographical Dictionary
Contemporary Music Almanac, 1980/81
Conversations with Jazz Musicians
The Country Music Encyclopedia
The Dictionary of Composers
The Dictionary of Composers and Their Music: Every Listener's Companion
Dictionary of Contemporary Music
A Dictionary of Twentieth-Century Composers: 1911-1971
Encyclopedia of Folk, Country and Western Music
The Encyclopedia of Jazz in the Seventies
Encyclopaedia of the Musical Theatre
Great Composers 1300-1900: A Biographical and Critical Guide
The Illustrated Encyclopedia of Country Music
The Illustrated Encyclopedia of Jazz
The Illustrated Encyclopedia of Rock
International Who's Who in Music and Musicians' Directory
Men of Popular Music
The Music Makers

Musicians since 1900: Performers in Concert and Opera
New Complete Book of the American Musical Theater
The New Encyclopedia of the Opera
The New Grove Dictionary of Music and Musicians
New Orleans Jazz: A Family Album
The Oxford Companion to Music
Popular American Composers: From Revolutionary Times to the Present
Rock On: The Illustrated Encyclopedia of Rock n' Roll
Sweet and Lowdown: America's Popular Song Writers
Who's Who of Jazz: Storyville to Swing Street
Who's Who in Music and Musicians' International Directory
Who's Who in Opera
Women Composers, Conductors and Musicians of the Twentieth Century: Selected Biographies

TELEVISION:

International Motion Picture Almanac
New York Times Encyclopedia of Television

THEATER:

The Best Musicals: From Show Boat to A Chorus Line
Biographical Encyclopaedia and Who's Who of the American Theatre
Black American Playwrights, 1800 to the Present: A Bibliography
Blacks in Blackface: A Source Book on Early Black Musical Shows
The Concise Encyclopedia of Modern Drama
A Concise Encyclopedia of the Theatre
Contemporary American Theater Critics: A Directory and Anthology of Their Works
Contemporary Dramatists
Crowell's Handbook of Contemporary Drama
Dictionary of Literary Biography
Encyclopaedia of the Musical Theatre
The Encyclopedia of World Theater
Famous Actors and Actresses on the American Stage: Documents of American Theatre History
McGraw-Hill Encyclopedia of World Drama
Modern World Drama: An Encyclopedia
More Black American Playwrights: A Bibliography
National Playwrights Directory
New Complete Book of the American Musical Theater
Notable Names in the American Theatre
The Oxford Companion to the Theatre
Plays, Players, and Playwrights: An Illustrated History of the Theatre
The Reader's Encyclopedia of World Drama
Who Was Who in the Theatre, 1912-1976
Who's Who on the Stage
Who's Who in the Theatre: A Biographical Record of the Contemporary Stage

A

A Becket, Thomas *BiDAmM*
A E 1867-1935 *EncWT, PlP&P[port]*
A Kempis *NewGrD 80*
A Kempis, Jean-Florent 1635?-1711? *NewGrD 80*
A Kempis, Joannes Florentius 1635?-1711? *NewGrD 80*
A Kempis, Nicolaus 1600?-1676 *NewGrD 80*
A Kempis, Thomas 1628?-1688 *NewGrD 80*
Aabel, Hauk d1961 *NotNAT B*
Aabel, Per 1902- *Ent*
Aaberg, Philip 1949- *AmSCAP 80*
AACM *EncJzS 70*
Aadland, Beverly *What 1[port], WhoHol A*
Aaes, Erik 1899- *DcFM, FilmEn*
Aagesen, Truid *NewGrD 80*
Aaker, Lee 1943- *ForYSC*
Aakesson, Birgit *DancEn 78[port]*
Aaltonen, Erik Verner 1910- *IntWWM 80*
Aaltonen, Erkki 1910- *Baker 78*
Aanen, Greet 1947- *IntWWM 77, -80*
Aanrud, Hans 1864-1953 *NotNAT B*
Aaquist Johansen, Svend 1948- *IntWWM 77, -80*
Aaron d1052 *Baker 78*
Aaron Scotus d1052 *NewGrD 80*
Aaron, Chloe *NewYTET*
Aaron, John A d1972 *NewYTET*
Aaron, Paul *NotNAT*
Aaron, Pietro 1480?-1550? *NewGrD 80*
Aaron, Pietro 1489-1545 *Baker 78*
Aaron, Richie *ConMuA 80B*
Aarons, Al 1932- *EncJzS 70*
Aarons, Albert N 1932- *EncJzS 70*
Aarons, Alex *PlP&P*
Aarons, Alexander A 1891-1943 *NotNAT B, WhThe*
Aarons, Alfred E 1865-1936 *NotNAT B, WhThe, WhoStg 1906, -1908*
Aarons, Ruth Hughes 1918-1980 *AmSCAP 80*
Aarons, Stuart H 1910- *IntMPA 75, -76*
Aaronson, Charles S *IntMPA 75, -76*
Aaronson, Irving 1895-1963 *AmSCAP 66, -80, BgBands 74, BiDAmM, CmpEPM, NotNAT B*
Aaronson, Max *Film 1*
Aas, Ernst 1910- *IntWWM 80*
Aas, Gunnar 1947- *IntWWM 80*
Aasen, John 1887 1938 *Film 2, NotNAT B, WhScrn 77, WhoHol B*
Aav, Evald 1900-1939 *Baker 78*
Aavik, Juhan 1884- *Baker 78*
Abaco, Evaristo Felice Dall' 1675-1742 *Baker 78, NewGrD 80, OxMus*
Abaco, Giuseppe Clemens Ferdinand Dall' 1709-1805 *OxMus*
Abaco, Joseph Marie Clement Dall' 1710-1805 *Baker 78*
Abadessa, Giovanni Battista d1652? *NewGrD 80*
Abaelard, Peter *NewGrD 80*
Abag *McGEWD*
Abailard, Peter *NewGrD 80*
Abarbanel, Sam X 1914- *IntMPA 77, -76, -78, -79, -80*
Abarbanel, Sam X 1917- *IntMPA 75*
Abarbanell, Lena 1880-1963 *WhoStg 1908*
Abarbanell, Lina 1880-1963 *CmpEPM, NotNAT B, WhThe*
Abarca, Lydia 1951- *CnOxB*
Abatematteo, John Anthony 1938- *IntWWM 77*
Abatessa, Giovanni Battista d1652? *NewGrD 80*
Abba *ConMuA 80A[port], IlEncR[port], RkOn 2[port]*
Abba, Marta 1907- *WhThe*
Abba Cornaglia, Pietro 1851-1894 *NewGrD 80*
Abbadia, Natale 1792-1861 *Baker 78*
Abbado, Claudio 1933- *Baker 78, BnBkM 80, CmOp, IntWWM 77, -80, MusMk, MusSN[port], NewEOp 71, NewGrD 80, WhoMus 72, WhoOp 76*
Abbado, Marcello 1926- *Baker 78*
Abbas, Hector 1884-1942 *Film 2, WhThe*
Abbas, Khwaga Ahmad 1914- *WorEFlm*
Abbas, Khwaja Ahmad 1914- *DcFM, FilmEn*
Abbate, Carlo 1600?-1640? *NewGrD 80*
Abbatessa, Giovanni Battista *NewGrD 80*
Abbatini, Antonio Maria 1597?-1679? *Baker 78*
Abbatini, Antonio Maria 1609?-1679? *NewGrD 80*
Abbe, Charles S d1932 *Film 1, WhoHol B*
Abbe, Charles S 1859-1932 *NotNAT B*
Abbe, Charles S 1860-1932 *WhScrn 74, -77*
Abbe, Jack *Film 2*
Abbey, Alonzo Judson 1825-1887 *BiDAmM*
Abbey, Elizabeth 1946- *IntWWM 77, -80*
Abbey, Henry Edwin 1846-1896 *NotNAT B*
Abbey, Henry Eugene 1846-1896 *BiDAmM, NewEOp 71, OxThe*
Abbey, John 1785-1859 *Baker 78, NewGrD 80*
Abbey, May *Film 1*
Abbey, May Evers 1872-1952 *NotNAT B*
Abbiati, Franco 1898- *NewGrD 80*
Abbinanti, Frank 1949- *ConAmC*
Abbot, George 1562-1633 *OxMus*
Abbott, Al 1884-1962 *NotNAT B, WhScrn 74, -77*
Abbott, Anthony William 1941- *IntWWM 77, -80, WhoMus 72*
Abbott, Bess *PupTheA*
Abbott, Bessie 1877-1919 *NotNAT B*
Abbott, Bessie 1878- *WhoStg 1908*
Abbott, Bud d1974 *MotPP, WhoHol B*
Abbott, Bud 1895-1974 *CmMov, FilmEn, FilmgC, ForYSC, Funs[port], HalFC 80[port], JoeFr[port], OxFilm, What 2[port], WhoHrs 80[port], WorEFlm[port]*
Abbott, Bud 1896-1974 *WhScrn 77*
Abbott, Bud 1898-1974 *MovMk[port], NotNAT B*
Abbott, C 1726-1817 *NotNAT B*
Abbott, Charlie 1903- *AmSCAP 66, -80*
Abbott, Clara Barnes 1874-1956 *NotNAT B*
Abbott, Dolly 1887-1955 *NotNAT B*
Abbott, Dorothy d1968 *WhScrn 77, WhoHol B*
Abbott, Dorothy L 1886-1937 *NotNAT B*
Abbott, Edward B 1882-1932 *NotNAT B*
Abbott, Edward S 1914-1936 *NotNAT B*
Abbott, Emma 1850-1891 *Baker 78, BiDAmM, CmOp, NewEOp 71, NewGrD 80, NotNAT B*
Abbott, Eve *AmSCAP 80*
Abbott, Frank 1879-1957 *WhScrn 74, -77, WhoHol B*
Abbott, George *MorBAP*
Abbott, George 1887- *BiDAmM, BiE&WWA, CnThe, ConDr 73, -77, EncMT, EncWT, Ent, FilmEn, FilmgC, HalFC 80, McGEWD[port], ModWD, NewCBMT, NotNAT, -A, OxThe, PlP&P, WhoThe 72, -77, WorEFlm*
Abbott, George 1889- *BestMus, CnMD*
Abbott, Harry 1861-1942 *NotNAT B*
Abbott, James Francis 1873-1954 *WhScrn 74, -77*
Abbott, John 1905- *BiE&WWA, FilmEn, FilmgC, ForYSC, HalFC 80, MovMk, NotNAT, Vers B[port], WhThe, WhoHol A*
Abbott, John Anthony 1938- *IntWWM 77*
Abbott, Judith *BiE&WWA, NotNAT*
Abbott, Kenneth John Dearie 1919- *IntWWM 80*
Abbott, Kenneth John Dearle 1919- *WhoMus 72*
Abbott, Marion *Film 2*
Abbott, Marion 1866-1937 *NotNAT B, WhoHol B*
Abbott, Nancy Ann 1901-1964 *NotNAT B*
Abbott, Paul d1872 *NotNAT B*
Abbott, Paul James 1936- *WhoMus 72*
Abbott, Philip 1923- *FilmgC, HalFC 80*
Abbott, Philip 1924- *BiE&WWA, NotNAT, WhoHol A*
Abbott, Richard 1899- *BiE&WWA, NotNAT, WhoHol A*
Abbott, William 1789-1843 *NotNAT B, OxThe*
Abbott, Yarnell 1871-1938 *NotNAT B*
Abbott And Costello *FilmEn, ForYSC, Funs[port], GrMovC[port], JoeFr[port], MotPP*
Abbound, Phyllis *WomWMM B*
Abbrederis, Matthaus 1652?-1725? *NewGrD 80*
Abd Al-Mu'min Ibn Yusuf Ibn F Al-Urmawi *NewGrD 80*
Abd Al-Qadir d1435 *NewGrD 80*
Abdallah, Mohammad Bin *MorBAP*
Abdel-Rahim, Gamal 1924- *NewGrD 80*
Abdel-Rehim, Gamal 1924- *NewGrD 80*
Abdel-Wahab, Muhammed 1910- *NewGrD 80*
Abdias *NewGrD 80*
Abdon, Bonifacio 1876-1944 *NewGrD 80*
Abdul, Raoul 1929- *DrBlPA*
Abdul-Malik, Ahmed 1927- *BiDAmM*
Abdulhak Hamit 1852-1937 *REnWD*
Abdullah, Shakur 1940- *EncJzS 70*
Abdullah Ibn Buhaina *NewGrD 80*
Abdushelli, Zurab 1913-1957 *NotNAT B*

Abe, Chie 1940- *CnOxB*
Abe, Komei 1911- *Baker 78, NewGrD 80*
Abe, Utake *Film 1*
Abegglen, Homer N 1901- *BiE&WWA, NotNAT*
Abeille, Johann Christian Ludwig 1761-1838 *Baker 78*
Abeille, Ludwig 1761-1838 *NewGrD 80*
Abeille, Pierre-Cesar 1674?-1733? *NewGrD 80*
Abejo, Rosalina 1922- *NewGrD 80*
Abel *NewGrD 80*
Abel, Albert 1865-1937 *WhScrn 74*
Abel, Alfred 1865-1937 *NotNAT B, WhoHol B*
Abel, Alfred 1880-1937 *FilmEn, FilmgC, HalFC 80, WhScrn 77*
Abel, Alfred 1880-1939 *Film 2*
Abel, Carl Friedrich 1723-1787 *Baker 78, NewGrD 80[port]*
Abel, Christian Ferdinand 1683?-1737 *NewGrD 80*
Abel, Clamor Heinrich 1634-1696 *NewGrD 80*
Abel, David W 1914- *IntWWM 80*
Abel, David Willard 1935- *IntWWM 77*
Abel, Frederick L 1794-1820 *BiDAmM*
Abel, Jeanne *WomWMM*
Abel, Jenny 1942- *IntWWM 77, -80*
Abel, Johann Leopold 1795-1871 *NewGrD 80*
Abel, Karl Friedrich 1723-1787 *BnBkM 80, MusMk, NewGrD 80[port], OxMus*
Abel, Katharina 1856-1904 *CnOxB*
Abel, Leopold August 1718-1794 *NewGrD 80*
Abel, Lionel 1910- *CnMD, ModWD, NotNAT*
Abel, Ludwig 1834-1895 *Baker 78*
Abel, Neal 1882-1952 *NotNAT B*
Abel, Paul Louis 1926- *ConAmC*
Abel, Robert *Film 2*
Abel, Walter 1898- *BiE&WWA, FilmEn, FilmgC, ForYSC, HalFC 80, HolCA[port], IntMPA 77, -76, -78, -79, -80, MotPP, MovMk, NotNAT, Vers B[port], WhoHol A, WhoThe 72, -77*
Abel-Struth, Sigrid 1924- *IntWWM 77, -80*
Abelard, Peter 1079-1142 *NewGrD 80*
Abelard, Pierre 1079-1142 *MusMk[port]*
Abelardo, Nicanor 1893-1934 *NewGrD 80*
Abeles, Arthur 1914- *IntMPA 77, -75, -76, -78, -79, -80*
Abeles, Edward 1870-1919 *Film 1, WhScrn 77, WhoHol B*
Abeles, Edward S 1869-1919 *NotNAT B, WhThe, WhoStg 1908*
Abeles, Joseph 1911- *BiE&WWA, NotNAT*
Abell, Arthur M 1868-1958 *Baker 78*
Abell, John *NewGrD 80*
Abell, John 1652-1724 *Baker 78*
Abell, John 1653-1716? *NewGrD 80*
Abell, Kjeld 1901-1961 *CnMD, CnThe, EncWT, Ent, McGEWD[port], ModWD, OxThe, REnWD[port]*
Abello DeTorices, Benito *NewGrD 80*
Abels, Joel M 1926- *ConAmTC*
Abelson, Hope 1919- *BiE&WWA, NotNAT*
Abend, Sheldon 1929- *BiE&WWA, IntMPA 77, -75, -76, -78, -79, -80, NotNAT*
Abendroth, Hermann 1883-1956 *Baker 78, NewGrD 80*
Abendroth, Walter 1896- *Baker 78, IntWWM 77, -80*
Abene, Michael Christian Joseph 1942- *EncJzS 70*
Abene, Mike 1942- *EncJzS 70*
Aber, Adolf 1893-1960 *Baker 78, NewGrD 80*
Aber, Alice Lawson 1916- *IntWWM 77*
Aber, Johann *NewGrD 80*
Aber, Johnny *Film 2*
Abercromb, Jillian Dawn 1935- *IntWWM 80*
Abercrombie, Alexander 1949- *IntWWM 77, -80*
Abercrombie, John L 1944- *EncJzS 70*
Abercrombie, Lascelles 1881-1938 *WhThe*
Aberg, Jan Hakan 1916- *IntWWM 77*
Aberg, Kerstin 1940- *IntWWM 77, -80*
Aberg, Per Haken 1941- *IntWWM 77*
Aberg, Sivi *WhoHol A*
Abernathy, David Myles 1933- *AmSCAP 80*
Abert, Anna Amalie 1906- *Baker 78, IntWWM 77, -80, NewGrD 80*
Abert, Hermann 1871-1927 *Baker 78, NewGrD 80*
Abert, Johann Joseph 1832-1915 *Baker 78*
Abeson, Marion 1914- *AmSCAP 66, -80*
Abingdon, Earl Of 1740-1799 *NewGrD 80*
Abingdon, Henry *NewGrD 80, OxMus*
Abingdon, W B *Film 1*
Abingdon, William 1888-1959 *WhThe*
Abingdon, William L 1859-1918 *NotNAT B, WhScrn 77, WhThe, WhoHol B*
Abingdon, William L 1862-1918 *WhoStg 1906, -1908*
Abington, Frances 1731-1815 *NotNAT A, -B*
Abington, Frances 1737-1815 *CnThe, EncWT, OxThe*
Able, Will B 1923- *BiE&WWA, NotNAT*
Ableman, Paul 1927- *ConDr 73, -77*
Abler, Keith Donald 1951- *AmSCAP 80*
Ables, Richard Louis 1911- *AmSCAP 66, -80*
Abney, Don 1923- *EncJzS 70*
Abney, John Donald 1923- *BiDAmM, EncJzS 70*
Abondante, Giulio *NewGrD 80*
Abondante, Julio *NewGrD 80*
Aborn, Louis H 1912- *BiE&WWA, NotNAT*
Aborn, Milton 1864-1933 *BiDAmM, NotNAT B, WhThe*
Aborn, Sargent 1866-1956 *BiDAmM, NotNAT B*
Abos, Girolamo 1715-1760 *Baker 78, NewGrD 80*
Abosso, Girolamo 1715-1760 *NewGrD 80*
Abott, Bessie Pickens 1878-1919 *BiDAmM, WhoStg 1906*
Abouchar, Joan 1937- *BiE&WWA*
Abraham, Gerald Ernest Heal 1904- *Baker 78, IntWWM 77, -80, NewGrD 80, OxMus, WhoMus 72*
Abraham, Johnny *AmSCAP 80*
Abraham, Lars Ulrich 1922- *NewGrD 80*
Abraham, Martin, Jr. 1908- *NewOrJ[port]*
Abraham, Martin, Sr. 1886- *NewOrJ[port]*
Abraham, Max 1831-1900 *Baker 78*
Abraham, Otto 1872-1926 *Baker 78*
Abraham, Pal 1892-1960 *NewGrD 80*
Abraham, Paul 1892-1960 *Baker 78, NewGrD 80, WhThe*
Abraham, Willie 1888?- *NewOrJ*
Abrahamian, Arousiak 1890-1973 *WhScrn 77*
Abrahams, A E 1873-1966 *WhThe*
Abrahams, Derek Morris 1923- *WhoMus 72*
Abrahams, Doris Cole 1925- *WhoThe 72, -77*
Abrahams, Frank 1947- *IntWWM 77, -80*
Abrahams, Ian John 1921- *IntMPA 77, -75, -76, -78, -79, -80*
Abrahams, Maurice 1883-1931 *AmSCAP 66, -80, BiDAmM*
Abrahams, Mort 1916- *FilmEn, IntMPA 77, -75, -76, -78, -79, -80, NewYTET*
Abrahamsen, Erik 1893-1949 *NewGrD 80*
Abrahamson, Bergljot 1909- *IntWWM 80*
Abrahan *NewGrD 80*
Abram, Blanche Schwartz 1925- *IntWWM 77, -80*
Abram, Jacques 1915- *WhoMus 72*
Abramova, Anastasia Ivanovna 1902- *CnOxB, DancEn 78*
Abramovitz, Max *BiE&WWA*
Abramowitsch, Bernhard 1906- *IntWWM 77, -80*
Abramowitsch, Ruth 1907-1974 *CnOxB*
Abramowitz, David G 1950- *CpmDNM 74, -75, -76, -77, ConAmC*
Abramowitz, Jonathan 1947- *IntWWM 77, -80*
Abrams, David 1949- *IntWWM 80*
Abrams, Dolores 1927- *NotNAT*
Abrams, Harriett 1758?-1822? *NewGrD 80*
Abrams, Lee *ConMuA 80B*
Abrams, Maurie *AmSCAP 80*
Abrams, Muhal Richard 1930- *EncJzS 70, IlEncJ*
Abrams, Richard 1942- *WhoOp 76*
Abrams, Rita Jane 1943- *AmSCAP 80*
Abramsky, Alexander 1898- *Baker 78*
Abramson, Charles H 1902- *BiE&WWA, NotNAT*
Abramson, Dolores *MorBAP*
Abramson, Doris *MorBAP*
Abramson, Jean Margaret 1926- *IntWWM 77, -80*
Abramson, Robert M 1928- *AmSCAP 80, ConAmC, IntWWM 77, -80*
Abran *NewGrD 80*
Abranches, Aura d1962 *NotNAT B*
Abranyi, Cornelius 1822-1903 *Baker 78*
Abranyi, Emil 1882- *Baker 78*
Abranyi, Kornel 1822-1903 *NewGrD 80*
Abrash, Merritt 1930- *NatPD[port]*
Abravanel, Claude 1924- *IntWWM 77, -80*
Abravanel, Maurice 1903- *Baker 78, BiE&WWA, BnBkM 80, IntWWM 77, NewGrD 80, NotNAT*
Abreu, Antonio 1750?-1820? *NewGrD 80*
Abreu, Eduardo 1949- *IntWWM 77, -80, NewGrD 80*
Abreu, Jose Antonio 1939- *Baker 78*
Abreu, Maria 1916- *IntWWM 80*
Abreu, Sergio 1948- *IntWWM 77, -80, NewGrD 80*
Abril, Anton Garcia *DcCM*
Abse, Dannie 1923- *ConDr 73, -77*
Absil, Jean Nicolas Joseph 1893-1974 *Baker 78, CompSN[port], DcCM, IntWWM 77, NewGrD 80, OxMus, WhoMus 72*
Abt, Franz Wilhelm 1819-1885 *Baker 78, NewGrD 80, OxMus*
Abthorpe, Thomas *PlP&P[port]*
Abu Al-Faraj Ali Ibn Al-Husayn *NewGrD 80*
Abu Al-Faraj M Ibn Ishaq Al-Warraq Al-B *NewGrD 80*
Abu I-Salt Umayya 1068-1134 *NewGrD 80*
Abu Nasr Muhammad Ibn M Ibn Tarkhan *NewGrD 80*
Abu Saif, Salah 1915- *DcFM*
Abu Yusuf Yaqub Ibn Ishaq *NewGrD 80*
Abudu, Mungu Kimya 1948- *NatPD[port]*
Abuladze, Tenghis 1924- *DcFM*
Abundante, Giulio *NewGrD 80*
Aburto, Armando 1910-1955 *WhScrn 74, -77*
Abyndon, Henry 1420?-1497 *NewGrD 80*
Abyngdon, Henry 1420?-1497 *OxMus*
AC/DC *ConMuA 80A[port]*
Acaen *NewGrD 80*
Acaz, Mba *MorBAP*
Accademico Bizzarro Capriccioso *NewGrD 80*
Accardo, Salvatore 1941- *NewGrD 80*
Accelli, Cesare *NewGrD 80*
Accents, The *RkOn[port]*
Acciai, Giovanni 1946- *IntWWM 77, -80*
Acciaiuoli, Filippo 1637-1700 *NewGrD 80*
Accius 170?BC-086BC *Ent*
Accius, Lucius 170?BC-086BC *NotNAT B, OxThe*
Accius, Lucius 170?BC-090?BC *EncWT*
Accoluthus, Jan *NewGrD 80*
Accorambani, Agostino *NewGrD 80*
Accoramboni, Agostino 1739-1818 *NewGrD 80*
Accord, Art 1890-1931 *WhScrn 74*
Accorimbeni, Agostino 1739-1818 *NewGrD 80*
Accorimboni, Augostino 1739-1818 *NewGrD 80*
Accorrimboni, Agostino 1739-1818 *NewGrD 80*
Ace *IlEncR[port], RkOn 2[port]*
Ace, Goodman 1899- *JoeFr[port], NewYTET*
Ace, Jane 1900-1974 *WhScrn 77*
Ace, Johnny 1929-1954 *RkOn[port]*
Ace, Johnny 1932-1954 *BiDAmM*
Acelli, Cesare *NewGrD 80*
Aceves Y Lozano, Rafael 1837-1876 *NewGrD 80*
Achard, Marcel *Film 2, WhThe, WhoThe 72*
Achard, Marcel 1899-1974 *CnMD, EncWT, Ent, FilmEn, FilmgC, HalFC 80, McGEWD[port], ModWD, WorEFlm*
Achard, Marcel 1900-1974 *BiE&WWA, DcFM, NotNAT B*
Acharekar, M R 1905- *DcFM*
Achatz, Dag 1942- *WhoMus 72*
Achenbach, Max *NewGrD 80*
Acheson, Marcus Wilson, III 1905- *AmSCAP 80*
Achilles, Robert William 1937- *BiDAmM*
Achron, Isidor 1892-1948 *AmSCAP 66, -80, Baker 78, BiDAmM, ConAmC, OxMus*
Achron, Joseph 1886-1943 *AmSCAP 66, Baker 78, BiDAmM, ConAmC, NewGrD 80, OxMus*
Achsel, Wanda Margarete Gertrud *WhoMus 72*
Achte, Aino *NewGrD 80*
Achterberg, Fritz *Film 2*

Achucarro, Joaquin 1932- *IntWWM 77, 80, WhoMus 72*
Achurch, Janet 1864-1916 *CnThe, NotNAT B, OxThe, WhThe*
Acker, Dieter 1940- *NewGrD 80*
Acker, Eugene *Film 2*
Acker, Jean *Film 1, –2, TwYS*
Acker, Jean 1893-1978 *FilmEn*
Acker, Sharon *WhoHol A*
Ackere, Jules E Van 1914- *NewGrD 80*
Ackerman, Bettye 1928- *FilmgC, IntMPA 77, –76, –78, –79, –80, WhoHol A*
Ackerman, Chantal *WomWMM*
Ackerman, Floyd F 1927- *BiE&WWA*
Ackerman, Forrest J 1916- *WhoHrs 80*
Ackerman, Harry S 1912- *IntMPA 77, –76, –78, –79, –80, NewYTET*
Ackerman, Irene d1916 *NotNAT B, WhoStg 1908*
Ackerman, Konrad Ernst 1712-1771 *Ent*
Ackerman, P Dodd, Sr. d1963 *NotNAT B*
Ackerman, Paul 1908- *EncFCWM 69*
Ackerman, Walter *Film 1*
Ackerman, Walter 1881-1938 *WhScrn 74, –77, WhoHol B*
Ackermann, Bettye 1928- *HalFC 80*
Ackermann, Charlotte 1757-1774 *NotNAT B, OxThe*
Ackermann, Charlotte 1757-1775 *EncWT*
Ackermann, Dorothea 1752-1821 *EncWT, NotNAT B, OxThe*
Ackermann, Konrad Ernst 1710-1771 *NotNAT B*
Ackermann, Konrad Ernst 1712-1771 *EncWT, OxThe*
Ackermann, Otto 1909-1960 *CmOp, NewGrD 80*
Ackermann, Pavel 1935- *IntWWM 77, –80*
Ackermann, Sophia Carlotta Schroder 1714-1792 *OxThe*
Ackermann, Sophie Charlotte 1714-1793 *EncWT*
Ackermans, The *CnThe*
Ackeroyde, Samuel *NewGrD 80*
Ackers, Andrew Acquarulo 1919-1978 *AmSCAP 66, –80*
Ackland, Joss 1928- *FilmEn, FilmgC, HalFC 80, WhoThe 72, –77*
Ackland, Rodney 1908- *BiE&WWA, ConDr 73, –77, FilmEn, FilmgC, HalFC 80, IlWWBF, –A, NotNAT, –A, WhThe, WhoThe 72*
Ackles, David *IlEncR[port]*
Ackley, Alfred Henry 1887-1960 *AmSCAP 66, –80, NewGrD 80*
Ackley, Bentley D 1872-1958 *AmSCAP 66, –80, NewGrD 80*
Ackley, Edith Flack *PupTheA*
Ackman, Herman 1904- *AmSCAP 66, –80*
Ackroyd, Jack *Film 2*
Ackroyd, James E 1854-1897 *BiDAmM*
Ackte, Aino 1876-1944 *Baker 78, CmOp, NewEOp 71, NewGrD 80*
Acord, Art 1890-1931 *FilmEn, Film 1, –2, HalFC 80, TwYS, WhScrn 77, WhoHol B*
Acord, Art 1891-1931 *FilmgC*
Acorn, Milton 1923- *CreCan 2*
Acosta, Afonso Vaz De *NewGrD 80*
Acosta, Alfonso Vaz De *NewGrD 80*
Acosta, Enrique *Film 2*
Acosta, Rodolfo 1920-1974 *FilmEn, FilmgC, ForYSC, HalFC 80, WhScrn 77*
Acosta, Rudolfo 1920-1974 *WhoHol B*
Acourt, Johannes *NewGrD 80*
Acquanetta 1920- *FilmgC, WhoHol A*
Acquanetta 1921- *WhoHrs 80[port]*
Acquart, Andre 1922- *EncWT*
Acquaviva, Nicholas 1927- *AmSCAP 66*
Acres, Birt 1854-1918 *FilmEn, FilmgC, HalFC 80, IlWWBF*
Acrobats Of The Folies Bergere *Film 1*
Actman, Irving 1907-1967 *AmSCAP 66, –80, NotNAT B*
Acton, Carlo 1829-1909 *NewGrD 80*
Acton, Carol *IntWWM 77*
Acton, Charles 1829-1909 *NewGrD 80*
Acton, Charles 1914- *IntWWM 77, –80, WhoMus 72*
Acton-Bond, Acton *WhThe*
Acuff, Eddie *ForYSC*
Acuff, Eddie 1902-1956 *FilmgC, HalFC 80, MovMk*
Acuff, Eddie 1908-1956 *FilmEn, Vers B[port], WhScrn 74, –77, WhoHol B*
Acuff, Roy 1903- *BiDAmM, CmpEPM, ConMuA 80A, CounME 74[port], –74A, EncFCWM 69, IlEncCM[port], NewGrD 80*
Acuna, Judith Shaw *WomWMM B*
Ad Libs *RkOn 2A*
Ada-May *WhThe*
Adabache, Olga 1918- *CnOxB*
Adachi, Motohiko 1940- *Baker 78*
Adair, Alice *Film 2*
Adair, Frances Jeffords 1918- *AmSCAP 80*
Adair, Jack 1894-1940 *WhScrn 74, –77, WhoHol B*
Adair, James 1909- *ConAmC*
Adair, Janice *IlWWBF*
Adair, Jean d1953 *NotNAT B, WhThe*
Adair, Jean d1963 *WhoHol B*
Adair, Jean 1872-1953 *FilmgC, HalFC 80*
Adair, Jean 1873-1953 *WhScrn 74, –77*
Adair, John 1885-1952 *WhScrn 74, –77, WhoHol B*
Adair, Josephine *Film 2*
Adair, Robert 1900-1954 *WhScrn 74, –77, WhoHol B*
Adair, Robyn *Film 1*
Adair, Thomas Montgomery 1913- *AmSCAP 66, –80*
Adair, Tim *Film 2*
Adair, Tom 1913- *CmpEPM*
Adair, Yvonne 1897- *WhoMus 72*
Adair, Yvonne 1925- *BiE&WWA, NotNAT*
Adalbert Of Prague 956?-997 *NewGrD 80*
Adalbert, Max 1874-1933 *EncWT, Film 2, WhScrn 77*
Adalid Y Gurrea, Marcial Del 1826-1881 *NewGrD 80*
Adam *NewGrD 80*
Adam And Eve *DcPup*
Adam De Gevanche *NewGrD 80*
Adam De Gievenci *NewGrD 80*
Adam De Givenchi *NewGrD 80*
Adam De Givenci *NewGrD 80*
Adam De La Bassee d1286 *NewGrD 80*
Adam De La Halle 1237?-1287? *Baker 78, OxMus*
Adam De La Halle 1240?-1286? *McGEWD, MusMk, OxThe*
Adam De La Halle 1240?-1288? *BnBkM 80, EncWT*
Adam De La Halle 1245?-1285? *NewGrD 80*
Adam De St. Victor 1110?-1192? *Baker 78*
Adam Le Bossu 1240?-1288? *BnBkM 80 OxMus*
Adam Of St. Victor d1192? *NewGrD 80*
Adam The Hunchback 1240?-1288? *BnBkM 80*
Adam Von Fulda 1440?-1505 *Baker 78*
Adam Von Fulda 1445?-1505 *NewGrD 80*
Adam, Adolphe 1803-1856 *CmOp, CmpBCM, DcCom 77, DcCom&M 79, GrComp[port], MusMk, NewGrD 80*
Adam, Adolphe-Charles 1803-1856 *Baker 78, BnBkM 80, CnOxB, DancEn 78, NewEOp 71, OxMus*
Adam, Alfred 1909- *FilmEn, FilmgC, HalFC 80*
Adam, Claus 1917- *AmSCAP 80, Baker 78, ConAmC A*
Adam, Jean *NewGrD 80*
Adam, Jennifer Adele 1943- *IntWWM 80*
Adam, Jeno 1896- *Baker 78, IntWWM 77, –80, NewGrD 80*
Adam, Johann 1705?-1779 *NewGrD 80*
Adam, Ken 1921- *DcFM, FilmEn, FilmgC, HalFC 80, IntMPA 77, –76, –78, –79, –80, WhoHrs 80, WorEFlm*
Adam, Louis 1758-1848 *Baker 78*
Adam, Noelle 1933- *BiE&WWA, ForYSC*
Adam, Ronald 1896-1979 *FilmEn, FilmgC, HalFC 80, WhoThe 72, –77*
Adam, Ronald 1897- *IntMPA 77, –75, –76, –78, –79*
Adam, Theo Siegfried 1926- *Baker 78, CmOp, NewGrD 80, WhoOp 76*
Adama, Richard 1928- *CnOxB, DancEn 78[port]*
Adamany, Ken *ConMuA 80B*
Adamberger, Antonie 1791-1867 *EncWT*
Adamberger, Marie Anna *EncWT*
Adamberger, Valentin 1743-1804 *NewGrD 80*
Adamberger, Valentine *EncWT*
Adami DaBolsena, Andrea 1663-1742 *NewGrD 80*
Adamis, Michael 1929- *Baker 78, DcCM, NewGrD 80*
Adamo, Milo Angelo 1931- *AmSCAP 80*
Adamonti *NewGrD 80*
Adamov, Arthur 1908-1970 *CnMD, CnThe, CroCD, EncWT, Ent, McGEWD[port], ModWD, NotNAT B, OxThe, PlP&P, REnWD*
Adamova, Adela 1927- *DancEn 78*
Adamowska, Helenka *Film 2*
Adamowski, Joseph 1862-1930 *Baker 78, BiDAmM*
Adamowski, Timothee 1857-1943 *Baker 78*
Adamowski, Timothee 1858-1943 *BiDAmM*
Adams, Abigail d1955 *NotNAT B*
Adams, Alice Baldwin d1936 *NotNAT B*
Adams, Alton Augustus 1889- *BiDAmM*
Adams, Andrew Paul 1951- *AmSCAP 80*
Adams, Anthony Walter 1948- *AmSCAP 80*
Adams, Audri 1925- *AmSCAP 66, –80*
Adams, B M d1903 *BiDAmM*
Adams, Barbara T *PupTheA*
Adams, Beverley 1945- *FilmgC*
Adams, Beverly *WhoHol A*
Adams, Beverly 1945- *FilmEn, HalFC 80, WhoHrs 80*
Adams, Beverly 1946- *ForYSC*
Adams, Brenda Jane 1954- *IntWWM 80*
Adams, Bret 1930- *BiE&WWA, NotNAT*
Adams, Brooke 1952?- *HalFC 80, IntMPA 80*
Adams, Carolyn 1943- *CnOxB, DrBlPA*
Adams, Casey 1917- *FilmEn, FilmgC, ForYSC, HalFC 80, WhoHol A*
Adams, Charles R 1834-1900 *Baker 78, NewGrD 80*
Adams, Charles R 1843-1900 *BiDAmM*
Adams, Chris 1958- *AmSCAP 80*
Adams, Claire *Film 1, –2, TwYS*
Adams, Claire d1978 *FilmEn*
Adams, Constance 1893-1960 *WhScrn 77*
Adams, Dale *PupTheA*
Adams, David 1928- *DancEn 78*
Adams, David C *IntMPA 77, –75, –76, –78, –79, NewYTET*
Adams, David Charles 1928- *CnOxB, CreCan 1*
Adams, David Stephen 1909- *IntWWM 77, –80*
Adams, Derroll 1925- *BiDAmM, EncFCWM 69*
Adams, Diana 1926- *CnOxB, DancEn 78[port]*
Adams, Dick 1889- *WhThe*
Adams, Dolly Marie Douroux 1904- *BlkWAB, NewOrJ*
Adams, Don *JoeFr*
Adams, Donna *FilmEn*
Adams, Dorothy 1915?- *FilmgC, ForYSC, HalFC 80, WhoHol A*
Adams, Edie *BiE&WWA, MotPP, NewYTET, NotNAT, WhoHol A, WhoThe 77*
Adams, Edie 1927- *FilmEn*
Adams, Edie 1929- *FilmgC, HalFC 80, MovMk[port]*
Adams, Edie 1930- *ForYSC*
Adams, Edie 1931- *IntMPA 77, –75, –76, –78, –79, –80*
Adams, Edith 1879-1957 *WhScrn 74, –77*
Adams, Edwin 1834-1877 *FamA&A[port], NotNAT B, OxThe*
Adams, Ernest 1920- *CreCan 2*
Adams, Ernest Harry 1886-1959 *AmSCAP 66, –80, BiDAmM, ConAmC*
Adams, Ernest S 1885-1947 *WhScrn 74, –77*
Adams, Ernie S 1885-1947 *FilmEn, Film 2, WhoHol B*
Adams, Faye *RkOn*
Adams, Frances Sale d1969 *WhoHol B*
Adams, Frank R 1883-1963 *AmSCAP 66, –80, BiDAmM, NotNAT B*
Adams, Frank Steward d1964 *NotNAT B*
Adams, Franklin Pierce 1881-1960 *BiDAmM, NotNAT B*
Adams, Gene *AmSCAP 80*
Adams, George 1904- *AmSCAP 66, ConAmC*

Adams, George Rufus 1940- *EncJzS 70*
Adams, Gerald Drayson 1904?- *FilmEn, FilmgC, HalFC 80, IntMPA 77, -75, -76, -78, -79, -80*
Adams, Harry *Film 2*
Adams, Horst 1937- *Baker 78*
Adams, Howard 1909-1936 *WhScrn 74, -77, WhoHol B*
Adams, Ida d1960 *NotNAT B, WhThe*
Adams, Isabel 1856-1936 *WhScrn 77*
Adams, J T 1926- *BiDAmM*
Adams, Jack 1930- *AmSCAP 80*
Adams, James B *NewGrD 80*
Adams, Jean 1710-1765 *OxMus*
Adams, Jean Coulthard *CreCan 1*
Adams, Jeff 1936-1967 *WhScrn 77*
Adams, Jerry 1927- *NewOrJ*
Adams, Jill d1964 *NotNAT B*
Adams, Jill 1930- *FilmEn*
Adams, Jill 1931- *FilmgC, HalFC 80, WhoHol A*
Adams, Jimmie *Film 2*
Adams, Joe 1922- *DrBlPA*
Adams, Joey 1911- *BiE&WWA, JoeFr[port], NotNAT A, WhoHol A*
Adams, John 1947- *ConAmC*
Adams, John 1953- *IntWWM 80*
Adams, John Cranford 1903- *BiE&WWA*
Adams, John Greenleaf 1810-1887 *BiDAmM*
Adams, John Luther 1953- *CpmDNM 76, -78, -79*
Adams, John M 1936- *IntWWM 80*
Adams, John Tyler 1911- *BluesWW[port]*
Adams, John Wolcott 1874-1925 *WhScrn 77*
Adams, Joseph Quincy 1881-1946 *NotNAT B*
Adams, Julie *MotPP, WhoHol A*
Adams, Julie 1926- *FilmEn, FilmgC, ForYSC, HalFC 80*
Adams, Julie 1927- *WhoHrs 80[port]*
Adams, Julie 1928- *IntMPA 77, -75, -76, -78, -79, -80*
Adams, Kathryn 1894-1959 *Film 1, -2, MotPP, NotNAT B, WhScrn 74, -77, WhoHol B*
Adams, Kenneth 1916- *WhoMus 72*
Adams, Kenneth Gaither 1946- *IntWWM 77, -80*
Adams, Lawrence Vaughan 1936- *CreCan 1*
Adams, Lee 1924- *AmPS, AmSCAP 66, -80, -80, BiDAmM, BiE&WWA, EncMT, NewCBMT, NotNAT*
Adams, Leslie d1934 *WhoHol B*
Adams, Leslie 1887-1936 *NotNAT B, WhScrn 77*
Adams, Leslie 1932- *ConAmC, IntWWM 77, -80*
Adams, Lionel d1952 *Film 2, NotNAT B, WhoHol B*
Adams, Lois Irene Smith *CreCan 1*
Adams, Margie 1881-1937 *NotNAT B*
Adams, Marla *WhoHol A*
Adams, Marty *AmSCAP 80*
Adams, Mary d1973 *WhScrn 77, WhoHol B*
Adams, Maud 1950?- *FilmEn, HalFC 80, WhoHol A*
Adams, Maude 1872-1953 *CnThe, EncWT, FamA&A[port], NotNAT A, -B, OxThe, PlP&P[port], WhThe, WhoStg 1906, -1908*
Adams, Mildred *Film 1*
Adams, Miriam 1907- *WhThe*
Adams, Nathan 1783-1864 *NewGrD 80*
Adams, Nehemiah 1806-1878 *BiDAmM*
Adams, Neile *WhoHol A*
Adams, Nicholas d1935 *NotNAT B*
Adams, Nick d1968 *MotPP, WhoHol B*
Adams, Nick 1931-1968 *FilmEn, FilmgC, HalFC 80, MovMk*
Adams, Nick 1932-1968 *ForYSC, WhScrn 74, -77, WhoHrs 80[port]*
Adams, Nick 1935-1968 *NotNAT B*
Adams, Park 1930- *AmSCAP 80, BiDAmM, EncJzS 70, IntWWM 77, -80*
Adams, Paul Eugene 1922- *AmSCAP 66, -80*
Adams, Pearl G *AmSCAP 80*
Adams, Peggy *Film 1*
Adams, Pepper 1930- *EncJzS 70*
Adams, Peter *WhoHol A*
Adams, Peter D 1942- *IntWWM 77, -80*
Adams, Placide 1929- *NewOrJ*
Adams, Ritchie *AmSCAP 80*
Adams, Robert 1906- *FilmgC, HalFC 80, WhThe*
Adams, Robert 1910- *DrBlPA*
Adams, Robert K 1909- *BiE&WWA, NotNAT*
Adams, Roger 1917- *BiE&WWA, NotNAT*
Adams, Samuel Hopkins 1871-1958 *NotNAT B*
Adams, Sherman 1899- *What 3[port]*
Adams, Stanley *ConMuA 80B, WhoHol A*
Adams, Stanley 1907- *AmSCAP 66, -80, BiDAmM, BiE&WWA, CmpEPM, NotNAT, WhoMus 72*
Adams, Stanley 1910- *IntWWM 77, -80, WhoMus 72*
Adams, Stanley 1920- *ForYSC*
Adams, Stella d1961 *Film 1, -2, WhScrn 77*
Adams, Suzanne 1872-1953 *Baker 78, BiDAmM, NewEOp 71, NewGrD 80, NotNAT B, WhoStg 1906, -1908*
Adams, Thomas d1620 *NewGrD 80*
Adams, Thomas 1785-1858 *Baker 78, NewGrD 80, OxMus*
Adams, Tom 1938- *FilmgC, HalFC 80*
Adams, Tommye d1955 *WhScrn 77*
Adams, W Bridges *WhThe*
Adams, W Davenport d1904 *NotNAT B*
Adams, William David 1920- *AmSCAP 80*
Adams, William Perry 1887-1972 *WhScrn 77, WhoHol B*
Adams, Woodrow Wilson 1917- *BluesWW[port]*
Adams-Jeremiah, Dorothy Mena 1909- *WhoMus 72*
Adamski, Leon Stephen 1939- *AmSCAP 80*
Adamsky, Vladimir 1908- *IntWWM 77, -80*
Adamson, Al *WhoHrs 80*
Adamson, Dorothy *PupTheA*
Adamson, Harold 1906- *AmPS, AmSCAP 66, -80, BiDAmM, CmpEPM, NewCBMT, Sw&Ld C*
Adamson, James 1896-1956 *WhScrn 77*
Adamson, Janis-John 1924- *IntWWM 80*
Adan, Vicente *NewGrD 80*
Adani, Mariella 1934- *WhoOp 76*
Adano, Bobby *AmSCAP 80*
Adaskin, Frances James *CreCan 1*
Adaskin, Harry 1901- *CreCan 2*
Adaskin, John 1908-1964 *CreCan 2*
Adaskin, Murray 1906- *Baker 78, CreCan 1, DcCM, NewGrD 80*
Adato, Perry Miller *WomWMM A, -B*
Adcock, Eddie *EncFCWM 69*
Adcock, Edward 1938- *BiDAmM*
Addams, Augustus A d1851 *FamA&A[port]*
Addams, Charles 1913- *WhoHrs 80*
Addams, Dawn 1929- *ForYSC*
Addams, Dawn 1930- *FilmEn, FilmgC, HalFC 80, IlWWBF[port], IntMPA 77, -75, -76, -78, -79, -80, MotPP, OxFilm, WhoHol A, WhoHrs 80, WhoThe 72, -77*
Adde, Leo 1904-1942 *NewOrJ*
Adderley, Cannonball 1928-1975 *EncJzS 70, IlEncJ, MorBAP, RkOn 2[port]*
Adderley, Julian Edwin 1928-1975 *Baker 78, BiDAmM, DrBlPA, EncJzS 70*
Adderley, Nat 1931- *DrBlPA, EncJzS 70*
Adderley, Nat 1955- *EncJzS 70*
Adderley, Nathaniel 1931- *BiDAmM, EncJzS 70*
Adderley, Nathaniel, Jr. 1955- *EncJzS 70*
Addie, Fiona *IntWWM 77, -80, WhoMus 72*
Addinsell, Richard 1904-1977 *Baker 78, BiE&WWA, FilmEn, FilmgC, HalFC 80, IntMPA 77, -75, -76, -78, IntWWM 77, -80, MusMk, NewGrD 80, NotNAT, OxFilm, OxMus, WhoMus 72, WhoThe 72, -77*
Addison, Adele 1925- *DrBlPA, NewGrD 80*
Addison, Bernard 1905- *BiDAmM, CmpEPM, IlEncJ, WhoJazz 72*
Addison, Carlotta 1849-1914 *WhThe*
Addison, Errol 1901- *CnOxB, DancEn 78*
Addison, John 1766?-1844 *NewGrD 80*
Addison, John 1920- *Baker 78, BiE&WWA, CmMov, ConAmC, FilmEn, FilmgC, HalFC 80, IntMPA 77, -75, -76, -78, -79, -80, IntWWM 77, -80, NewGrD 80, NotNAT, OxFilm, OxMus, WhoMus 72*
Addison, John Mervyn 1920- *AmSCAP 80*
Addison, Joseph 1672-1719 *DcPup, EncWT, Ent[port], McGEWD[port], NewGrD 80, NotNAT B, OxMus, OxThe, PlP&P*
Addor, Ady *CnOxB, DancEn 78*
Addy, Donald Wilfred 1924- *WhoMus 72*
Addy, Wesley 1912- *FilmgC, ForYSC, HalFC 80*
Addy, Wesley 1913- *BiE&WWA, FilmEn, NotNAT, WhoHol A, WhoThe 72, -77*
Ade, George 1866-1944 *BiDAmM, EncWT, McGEWD[port], ModWD, NewCBMT, NotNAT A, -B, OxThe, WhThe, WhoStg 1906, -1908*
Adelberg-Rudow, Vivian *ConAmC*
Adelboldus d1024 *NewGrD 80*
Adelburg, August Ritter Von 1830-1873 *Baker 78, NewGrD 80*
Adell, Arthur 1894-1962 *NewGrD 80*
Adell, Ilunga 1948- *BlkAmP, MorBAP*
Adelman, Joseph A 1933- *IntMPA 78, -79, -80*
Adelman, Louis C *NatPD[port]*
Adelson, Bonnie Lynn 1944- *IntWWM 77, -80*
Adelson, Leonard Gary 1924-1972 *AmSCAP 80*
Adelstein, Milton 1925- *AmSCAP 80*
Adelung, Jakob *NewGrD 80*
Ademollo, Alessandro 1826-1891 *NewGrD 80*
Adeney, Eric *Film 1*
Adeney, Richard Gilford 1920- *NewGrD 80, WhoMus 72*
Aderer, Adolphe 1855- *WhThe*
Aderni, Vittorio 1917- *WhoMus 72*
Ades, Hawley Ward 1908- *AmSCAP 80*
Adey, Jan Cynthia 1931- *WhoMus 72*
Adgate, Andrew d1793 *BiDAmM*
Adgate, Andrew 1750?-1793 *Baker 78*
Adgate, Andrew 1762-1793 *NewGrD 80*
Adickes, Frances Wood 1889- *AmSCAP 66*
Adiny, Ada 1855?-1924 *BiDAmM*
Adix, Vern 1912- *BiE&WWA, NotNAT*
Adjani, Isabelle 1955- *FilmAG WE, FilmEn, WhoHol A*
Adjani, Isobelle 1955- *HalFC 80*
Adkins, Anthony 1949- *IntWWM 80*
Adkins, Clement John 1934- *IntWWM 77*
Adkinson, Harvey E 1934- *AmSCAP 66, -80*
Adlam, Basil G *AmSCAP 66, -80*
Adlam, Derek 1938- *NewGrD 80*
Adler, Adolph J d1961 *NotNAT B*
Adler, Allen A d1964 *NotNAT B*
Adler, Barbara Walz 1943- *IntWWM 77, -80*
Adler, Bob 1906- *IntMPA 77, -75, -76, -78, -79, -80*
Adler, Buddy d1960 *NotNAT B*
Adler, Buddy 1906-1960 *DcFM*
Adler, Buddy 1908-1960 *FilmgC, HalFC 80*
Adler, Buddy 1909-1960 *FilmEn, WorEFlm*
Adler, Clarence 1886-1969 *Baker 78, BiDAmM, ConAmC*
Adler, F Charles 1889-1959 *Baker 78*
Adler, Felix d1963 *NotNAT B*
Adler, Frances 1891-1964 *BiE&WWA, NotNAT B*
Adler, Guido 1855-1941 *Baker 78, NewGrD 80, OxMus*
Adler, Gyorgy 1789-1867 *NewGrD 80*
Adler, Henry 1915- *BiDAmM*
Adler, Hugo 1895-1955 *BiDAmM*
Adler, Hyman d1945 *NotNAT B*
Adler, Israel 1925- *NewGrD 80*
Adler, Jacob P 1855-1926 *Film 1, NotNAT B, WhScrn 77, WhThe, WhoHol B*
Adler, James R 1950- *AmSCAP 80*
Adler, Jay 1899-1978 *ForYSC, HalFC 80, WhoHol A*
Adler, Jay 1907?- *FilmgC*
Adler, Jerry *NotNAT*
Adler, Kurt 1907-1977 *Baker 78*
Adler, Kurt Herbert 1905- *Baker 78, CmOp, IntWWM 77, -80, NewEOp 71, NewGrD 80, WhoOp 76*
Adler, Larry 1914- *Baker 78, BiDAmM, BiE&WWA, FilmgC, HalFC 80, NewGrD 80, NotNAT, OxMus, What 1[port], WhoHol A, WhoMus 72*
Adler, Lawrence 1914- *NewGrD 80*
Adler, Lou *ConMuA 80B*
Adler, Luther 1903- *BiE&WWA, Ent, FilmEn, FilmgC, ForYSC, HalFC 80, HolCA[port], IntMPA 77, -75, -76, -78, -79, -80, MotPP, MovMk, NotNAT, PlP&P[port], Vers B[port], WhoHol A, WhoThe 72, -77*
Adler, Marvin S 1938- *AmSCAP 80,*

IntWWM 77
Adler, Marx Vom NewGrD 80
Adler, Maurice E 1909-1960 WorEFlm[port]
Adler, Michael ConMuA 80B
Adler, Paul ConMuA 80B
Adler, Peter Herman 1898- IntWWM 77, -80
Adler, Peter Herman 1899- Baker 78, BiDAmM, CmOp, NewEOp 71, NewGrD 80, WhoOp 76
Adler, Richard MorBAP
Adler, Richard 1921- AmSCAP 66, -80, BestMus, BiDAmM, BiE&WWA, EncMT, HalFC 80, NewGrD 80, NotNAT, PopAmC[port], PopAmC SUP, WhoThe 72, -77
Adler, Richard 1923- AmPS, NewCBMT
Adler, Samuel 1928- AmSCAP 66, -80, Baker 78, BiDAmM, CpmDNM 74, -75, -77, -79, -80, ConAmC, DcCM, IntWWM 77, -80, NewGrD 80
Adler, Sarah d1953 NotNAT B
Adler, Stella BiE&WWA, NotNAT, PlP&P, WhoHol A
Adler, Stella 1895- FilmgC, HalFC 80
Adler, Stella 1902- WhoThe 72, -77
Adler, Stella 1904- EncWT
Adler And Ross BestMus
Adlgasser, Anton Cajetan 1729-1777 Baker 78, NewGrD 80
Adlon, Louis d1947 WhScrn 74, -77, WhoHol B
Adlung, Jakob 1699-1762 Baker 78, NewGrD 80
Admetus De Aureliana NewGrD 80
Admon, Jedidiah 1894- IntWWM 80
Admon-Gorochov, Jedidiah 1894- Baker 78
Adni, Daniel 1951- IntWWM 77, -80, NewGrD 80, WhoMus 72
Adolbert, Bela 1933- WhoOp 76
Adolf, R NewGrD 80
Adolfati, Andrea 1721?-1760 NewGrD 80
Adolfi, John G 1888-1933 FilmEn, Film 1, HalFC 80, TwYS A, WhScrn 77
Adolfson, Adolf Gustaw NewGrD 80
Adolph, Heinz 1915- IntWWM 77, -80, WhoMus 72
Adolph, Johann Baptist 1657-1708 OxThe
Adolphus, Milton 1913- Baker 78, ConAmC
Adomian, Lan 1905- Baker 78, IntWWM 77
Adominan, Lan 1905- IntWWM 80
Adoree, Renee d1933 MotPP, WhoHol B
Adoree, Renee 1898-1933 BiDFilm, -81, FilmEn, Film 2, FilmgC, HalFC 80, MovMk, TwYS, WhScrn 74, -77, WorEFlm
Adoree, Renee 1902-1933 NotNAT B
Adorf, Mario 1930- FilmEn, HalFC 80
Adorian, Andrew 1908- WhoMus 72
Adorian, Paul IntMPA 77, -75, -76, -78, -79, -80
Adorjan, Andras Gyorgy 1944- IntWWM 77, -80
Adorno, Theodor W 1903-1969 Baker 78, NewGrD 80
Adreon, Franklin 1902- FilmEn
Adret, Francoise 1920- CnOxB
Adriaensen, Emanuel 1554?-1604 Baker 78, NewGrD 80
Adriaenssen, Emanuel 1554?-1604 NewGrD 80
Adrian 1903-1959 DcFM, FilmEn, FilmgC, HalFC 80
Adrian, Diane AmSCAP 66, -80
Adrian, Gilbert d1959 NotNAT B
Adrian, Iris 1913- FilmEn, FilmgC, ForYSC, HalFC 80, HolCA[port], IntMPA 77, -75, -76, -78, -79, -80, MovMk, WhoHol A
Adrian, Iris 1915- Vers A[port]
Adrian, Max 1902-1973 FilmgC, HalFC 80
Adrian, Max 1903-1973 BiE&WWA, EncMT, FilmEn, IlWWBF, NotNAT B, WhScrn 77, WhThe, WhoHol B, WhoThe 72
Adrian, Rhys ConDr 73, -77B
Adriani, Francesco 1539-1575 NewGrD 80
Adriansen, Emanuel 1554?-1604 NewGrD 80
Adrien, Martin Joseph 1767-1822 NewGrD 80
Adrienne, Jean 1905- WhThe
Adriensen, Emanuel NewGrD 80
Adrio, Adam 1901-1973 Baker 78, NewGrD 80
Adson, John d1640 NewGrD 80
Aduamoah, Andrews Lartey 1932- IntWWM 77
Adye, Oscar d1914 WhThe
Adyrkhayeva, Svetlana Dsantemirovna 1938- CnOxB
AE 1867-1935 OxThe
Aebischer, Delmer Wayne 1933- IntWWM 77
Aegidius De Zamora NewGrD 80
Aelred Of Rievaulx 1109?-1166 NewGrD 80
Aerosmith ConMuA 80A[port], IlEncR, RkOn 2[port]
Aerts, Egide 1822-1853 Baker 78
Aertsen, Hendrik 1586?-1658 NewGrD 80
Aertssens, Hendrik 1586?-1658 NewGrD 80
Aeschbacher, Adrian 1912- Baker 78, NewGrD 80
Aeschbacher, Niklaus 1917- Baker 78, IntWWM 77, -80, NewGrD 80
Aeschbacher, Walther 1901-1969 Baker 78
Aeschylus 524?BC-456?BC CnThe, McGEWD[port], REnWD
Aeschylus 525?BC-456?BC EncWT, Ent, NewEOp 71, NewGrD 80, NotNAT B, OxThe, PlP&P[port]
Aesop 620?BC-520BC DcPup
Aesopus, Claudius OxThe
Aess, Eric DcFM
Aetheria NewGrD 80
Af Malmborg, Gunilla Eva 1933- WhoOp 76
Afanassiev, Nikolai 1821-1898 Baker 78
Afanas'yev, Nikolay Yakovlevich 1821-1898 NewGrD 80
Affel, John Kweku 1936- IntWWM 77, -80
Affilard, Michel L' NewGrD 80
Affonso, Alvaro NewGrD 80
Afinogenov, Aleksander Nikolayevich 1904-1941 CnMD, McGEWD[port], ModWD
Afinogenov, Alexander 1904-1941 Ent
Afinogenov, Alexander Mikolaevich 1904-1941 NotNAT B
Afinogenov, Alexander Nikolaevich 1904-1941 EncWT, OxThe
Afonsky, Nicholas 1894-1971 BiDAmM
Afonso, Alvaro NewGrD 80
Afranio Degli Albonesi NewGrD 80
Afranio DePavia 1480-1560? Baker 78
Afranius 150?BC- Ent
Afranius, Lucius EncWT, OxThe
Afrem NewGrD 80
African Roscius OxThe
Africano, Lillian Tabeek 1935- ConAmTC
Afrique 1907-1961 NotNAT B, WhScrn 74, -77, WhoHol B
Afrouz, Novin 1942- IntWWM 80
Afton, Richard Lord IntMPA 77, -75, -76, -78, -79, -80
Afzelius, Arvid August 1785-1871 NewGrD 80
Afzelius, Bjorn Svante 1947- IntWWM 80
Agaoglu, Adalet 1929- CnThe, REnWD
Agar, Dan 1881- WhThe
Agar, Florence Leonide Charvin 1836-1891 NotNAT B
Agar, Grace Hale d1963 NotNAT B
Agar, Jane 1889-1948 WhScrn 74, -77, WhoHol B
Agar, John 1921- FilmEn, FilmgC, ForYSC, HalFC 80, IntMPA 77, -75, -76, -78, -79, -80, MotPP, What 4[port], WhoHol A, WhoHrs 80[port]
Agar-Lyons, Harry Film 2
Agate, James Evershed 1877-1947 EncWT, NotNAT A, -B, OxThe, WhThe
Agate, May 1892-1960 OxThe, WhThe
Agatea, Mario 1623?-1699 NewGrD 80
Agatharchos Ent
Agatharchos Of Samos EncWT
Agathon 447?BC-400?BC EncWT, Ent, OxThe
Agay, Denes 1911- AmSCAP 66, -80, Baker 78, CpmDNM 79, -80, ConAmC
Agazzari, Agostino 1578-1640 Baker 78, BnBkM 80, NewGrD 80
Agbenu, Victor Nicholas 1945- IntWWM 77, -80
Agee, James 1909-1955 FilmgC, HalFC 80, OxFilm, WorEFlm
Agee, James 1910-1955 FilmEn
Agee, Raymond Clinton 1930- BluesWW[port]
Ager, Laurence Mitchell 1904- IntWWM 77, -80, WhoMus 72
Ager, Milton 1893-1979 AmPS, AmSCAP 66, -80, Baker 78, BiDAmM, CmpEPM, PopAmC[port], Sw&Ld C
Agersnap, Harald 1899- IntWWM 80
Aggas, Robert 1619?-1679 OxThe
Aggere, Antonius De NewGrD 80
Agghazy, Karoly 1855-1918 NewGrD 80
Aghayan, Ray NotNAT
Agincourt, Francois D' 1680?-1758 NewGrD 80, OxMus
Agist, Dietmar De NewGrD 80
Aglie, Count Filippo D' 1604-1667 NewGrD 80
Aglie, Count Philippe D' 1604-1667 NewGrD 80
Aglio, Bartolomeo Dall' NewGrD 80
Aglione, Alessandro NewGrD 80
Agnanino, Spirito NewGrD 80
Agneletti, Giovanni Battista NewGrD 80
Agnelli, Lorenzo 1610-1674 NewGrD 80
Agnelli, Salvatore 1817-1874 NewGrD 80
Agnello, Salvatore 1817-1874 NewGrD 80
Agnesi, Maria Teresa 1720-1795 NewGrD 80
Agnew, Charlie CmpEPM
Agnew, Robert 1899- FilmEn, Film 2, ForYSC, TwYS
Agnew, Roy E 1893-1944 Baker 78, OxMus
Agnew, William Alick Talbot 1931- IntWWM 77
Agnich, Angeline PupTheA
Agnost, Frank Peter 1918- AmSCAP 80
Agobard Of Lyons 769-840 NewGrD 80
Agoglia, Esmeralda 1926- CnOxB, DancEn 78
Agosti, Guido 1901- IntWWM 77, -80, NewGrD 80, WhoMus 72
Agostinho DaCruz NewGrD 80
Agostini, Agostino d1569 NewGrD 80
Agostini, Lodovico 1534-1590 Baker 78, NewGrD 80
Agostini, Lucio 1913- CreCan 2
Agostini, Mezio 1875-1944 Baker 78
Agostini, Paolo 1583?-1629 Baker 78, NewGrD 80
Agostini, Paolo 1593-1629 MusMk
Agostini, Philippe 1910- DcFM, FilmEn, FilmgC, HalFC 80, OxFilm, WorEFlm
Agostini, Piersimone 1635?-1680 NewGrD 80
Agostini, Pietro Simone 1635?-1680 Baker 78, NewGrD 80
Agoult, Raymond A WhoMus 72
Agradoot DcFM
Agragami, Nishith Bannerjee 1924- DcFM
Agramonte, Emilio 1844-1918 BiDAmM
Agrell, Alfhild 1849-1923 OxThe
Agrell, Johan Joachim 1701-1765 Baker 78, NewGrD 80
Agren, Janet 1950- FilmAG WE
Agresta, Agostino 1575?-1617? NewGrD 80
Agricola, Alexander 1446?-1506 Baker 78, BnBkM 80, NewGrD 80, OxMus
Agricola, Benedetta Emilia 1722-1780? NewGrD 80, OxMus
Agricola, Georg Ludwig 1643-1676 NewGrD 80
Agricola, Johann Friedrich 1720-1774 Baker 78, MusMk, NewGrD 80, OxMus
Agricola, Johann Paul 1638?-1697 NewGrD 80
Agricola, Johannes 1560?-1601? NewGrD 80
Agricola, Martin 1486-1556 Baker 78, BnBkM 80, NewGrD 80, OxMus
Agricola, Rudolph 1443-1485 NewGrD 80
Agricola, Wolfgang Christoph 1600?-1659? NewGrD 80
Agronsky, Martin NewYTET
Agthe, Albrecht Wilhelm Johann 1790-1873 NewGrD 80
Agthe, Carl Christian 1762-1797 NewGrD 80
Aguado, Dionisio 1784-1849 Baker 78
Aguado, Dionysio 1784-1849 NewGrD 80
Aguglia, Mimi 1885-1970 WhScrn 74, -77, WhoHol B
Aguiar, Ernani Henrique Chaves 1950- IntWWM 77, -80
Aguiari, Lucrezia 1743-1783 NewGrD 80
Aguilar, Antonia Maria NewGrD 80
Aguilar, Emanuel Abraham 1824-1904 Baker 78
Aguilar, Gaspar De NewGrD 80
Aguilar, Maria Petra PupTheA
Aguilar, Raul Ughetti PupTheA
Aguilar, Tony WhoHol A
Aguilar-Ahumada, Miguel 1931- Baker 78, DcCM

Aguilera DeHeredia, Sebastian 1565?-1627 Baker 78, NewGrD 80
Aguirre, Diana V 1941- IntWWM 77, -80
Aguirre, Jaime Moran 1931- AmSCAP 80
Aguirre, Juan Guillermo 1950- AmSCAP 80
Aguirre, Julian 1868-1924 Baker 78, NewGrD 80
Aguirre, Manuel B 1907-1957 WhScrn 74, -77
Agujari, Lucrezia 1743-1783 Baker 78, NewGrD 80
Agus, Giuseppe 1725?-1800? NewGrD 80
Agus, Joseph 1749-1798 NewGrD 80
Agustsson, Herbert H 1926- IntWWM 77, -80, NewGrD 80
Agutter, Jenny 1952- FilmEn, FilmgC, HalFC 80, IlWWBF[port]
Agyei, Yawa Grace 1938- IntWWM 80
Aharoni, Avraham 1924- IntWWM 77, -80
Ahbez, Eden 1908- AmSCAP 66, -80, BiDAmM
Ahearn, Lillian M 1886- AmSCAP 66
Ahearne, Thomas 1906-1969 WhoHol B
Ahearne, Tom 1906-1969 WhScrn 74, -77
Ahern, Brian ConMuA 80B
Ahern, David Anthony 1947- IntWWM 77, -80, NewGrD 80
Ahern, George Film 1
Ahern, James McGEWD
Ahern, Paul ConMuA 80B
Aherne, Brian 1902- BiE&WWA, FilmEn, Film 2, FilmgC, ForYSC[port], HalFC 80, IlWWBF[port], -A, IntMPA 77, -75, -76, -78, -79, -80, MotPP, MovMk[port], NotNAT, -A, OxFilm, WhThe, WhoHol A, WhoThe 72
Aherne, Lassie Lou Film 2
Aherne, Pat 1901-1970 IlWWBF, WhoHol B
Aherne, Patrick 1901-1970 Film 2, HalFC 80, WhScrn 74, -77
Ahl, Fred Arthur 1897- AmSCAP 80
Ahlander, Thecla Ottilia 1855- WhThe
Ahlberg, Harry 1912- AmSCAP 66, -80
Ahle, Johann Georg 1651?-1706 Baker 78, NewGrD 80
Ahle, Johann Rudolf 1625-1673 Baker 78, NewGrD 80
Ahlefeldt, Countess Maria Theresia 1755-1823 NewGrD 80
Ahlen, Carl-Gunnar 1938- IntWWM 77, -80
Ahlers, Anny 1906-1933 NotNAT B, WhScrn 77, WhThe, WhoHol B
Ahlersmeyer, Matthieu 1896- NewGrD 80
Ahlert, Fred E 1892-1953 AmPS, AmSCAP 66, -80, BiDAmM, CmpEPM, NotNAT B, PopAmC[port], Sw&Ld C
Ahlert, Richard 1921- AmSCAP 80
Ahlgrimm, Isolde 1914- IntWWM 77, -80, NewGrD 80
Ahlm, Philip E 1905-1954 WhScrn 74, -77
Ahlschlager, Walter W, Sr. 1887-1965 NotNAT B
Ahlsen, Leopold 1927- CnMD, CroCD, McGEWD[port], ModWD
Ahlskog, Gunnar Mathias 1914- IntWWM 77, -80
Ahlstedt, Douglas 1945- WhoOp 76
Ahlstedt, Linda Foxx 1947- IntWWM 77, -80
Ahlstrom, David 1927- AmSCAP 80, ConAmC, IntWWM 77, -80
Ahlstrom, Jacob Niclas 1805-1857 NewGrD 80
Ahlstrom, Olof 1756-1835 NewGrD 80
Ahmad, Dorothy BlkAmP
Ahmonuel, Zyah AmSCAP 80
Ahn, Philip 1911-1978 FilmEn, FilmgC, ForYSC, HalFC 80, HolCA[port], IntMPA 77, -75, -76, -78, MovMk, Vers B[port], WhoHol A
Ahn, Yong Ku 1928- IntWWM 80
Ahna, Heinrich Karl Herman De Baker 78
Ahnell, Emil Gustave 1925- AmSCAP 80, CpmDNM 75, ConAmC
Ahnsjo, Claes Hakan 1942- IntWWM 80, WhoOp 76
Aho, Kalevi 1949- Baker 78, NewGrD 80
Ahola, Hooley 1902- WhoJazz 72
Ahonen, Leo 1939- CnOxB
Ahrendt, Carl Frederick William 1842-1909 NotNAT B
Ahrendt, Karl Frederick 1904- CpmDNM 74, ConAmC, IntWWM 77, -80, WhoMus 72
Ahrens, Carl Henry Von 1863-1936 CreCan 1
Ahrens, Henry W PupTheA
Ahrens, Joseph Johannes Clemens 1904- Baker 78, DcCM, IntWWM 77, -80, NewGrD 80
Ahrens, Sieglinde 1936- NewGrD 80
Ahrens, Thomas AmSCAP 80
Ahrold, Frank A 1931- AmSCAP 80, ConAmC
Ahronovich, Yury 1932- NewGrD 80
Ahsefjah, Bijan 1940- IntWWM 80
Aibl, Joseph Baker 78
Aiblinger, Johann Kaspar 1779-1867 Baker 78, NewGrD 80
Aich, Arnt Von d1530? NewGrD 80
Aicher, Anton 1859-1930 DcPup
Aicher, Hermann DcPup
Aichinger, Gregor 1564-1628 Baker 78, BnBkM 80, NewGrD 80
Aicken, Elinor Film 1
Aidman, Charles 1925- AmSCAP 66, BiE&WWA, ForYSC, NotNAT, WhoHol A
Aidman, Charles 1929- FilmgC, HalFC 80
Aidoo, Ama Ata 1942- ConDr 73, -77
Aiello, Salvatore 1944- CnOxB
Aigner, Engelbert 1798-1866 Baker 78
Aiguino DaBrescia, Illuminato 1520?- NewGrD 80
Aiken, Charles 1818-1882 BiDAmM
Aiken, Conrad Potter 1889-1973 CnMD, ModWD
Aiken, Frank Eugene 1840-1910 NotNAT B, WhoStg 1908
Aiken, George L 1830-1876 McGEWD[port], NotNAT B, OxThe, PlP&P, REnWD
Aiken, Kenneth 1885-1970 AmSCAP 66, ConAmC
Aiken, Larry ConMuA 80B
Aiken, Mary Film 2
Aiken, Rice 1904?- WhoJazz 72
Aiken, Vivian PupTheA
Aikin, Jesse B NewGrD 80
Aikin, W OxMus
Ailes, Roger NewYTET
Ailey, Alvin 1931- BiE&WWA, CmpGMD[port], CnOxB, DancEn 78[port], DrBlPA, NotNAT, WhoHol A
Aim, Vojtech Borivoj 1886-1972 NewGrD 80
Aimee, Anouk 1932- BiDFilm, -81, FilmAG WE[port], FilmEn, FilmgC, ForYSC, HalFC 80, MovMk[port], OxFilm, WhoHol A, WorEFlm[port]
Aimee, Anouk 1934- IntMPA 77, -75, -76, -78, -79, -80
Aimeric De Peguilhan 1175?-1230? NewGrD 80
Aimon, Francois 1779-1866 NewGrD 80
Aimos, Raymond 1889-1944 FilmEn
Ainge, Susan M WomWMM B
Ainley, Henry Hinchcliffe 1879-1945 FilmEn
Ainley, Henry Hinchliffe 1879-1945 CnThe, Film 1, -2, FilmgC, HalFC 80, IlWWBF[port], NotNAT B, OxThe, PlP&P, WhScrn 74, -77, WhThe, WhoHol B
Ainley, Richard 1910-1967 FilmEn, FilmgC, HalFC 80, NotNAT B, WhScrn 74, -77, WhThe, WhoHol B
Ainslee, Adra d1963 NotNAT B
Ainsley, Charles Film 1
Ainsley, Norman 1881-1948 WhScrn 74, -77, WhoHol B
Ainslie, Hew 1792-1878 BiDAmM
Ainsworth, Cupid Film 2
Ainsworth, Helen Shumate d1961 NotNAT B
Ainsworth, Henry 1570-1623? NewGrD 80
Ainsworth, Henry 1571-1622? OxMus
Ainsworth, Phil Film 2
Ainsworth, Sidney 1872-1922 Film 2, WhScrn 74, -77, WhoHol B
Ainsworth, Sydney 1872-1922 Film 1, -2, NotNAT B
Ainsworth, Virginia Film 2
Aiolle, Francesco Dell' NewGrD 80
Aiolli, Alamanno NewGrD 80
Aiolli, Francesco Dell' NewGrD 80
Airardus Viciliacensis NewGrD 80
Aird, Donald Bruce 1924- ConAmC
Airmet, Elliot PupTheA
Airto 1941- EncJzS 70
Aischylos NewGrD 80
Aist, Dietmar Von NewGrD 80
Aiston, Arthur C 1868-1924 NotNAT B
Aitay, Victor IntWWM 77, -80
Aitken, Frank Spottiswoode 1869-1933 WhScrn 77
Aitken, Frank Spottsworth 1869-1933 WhScrn 74
Aitken, Gene 1937- IntWWM 77
Aitken, Gordon 1928- DancEn 78
Aitken, Harry E 1870-1956 FilmEn
Aitken, Hugh 1924- AmSCAP 66, -80, Baker 78, ConAmC, IntWWM 77, -80
Aitken, John 1745-1831 BiDAmM, NewGrD 80
Aitken, Maria 1945- WhoThe 77
Aitken, Robert 1939- Baker 78, IntWWM 80, NewGrD 80
Aitken, Spottiswoode 1869-1933 FilmEn, Film 1, -2, TwYS, WhoHol B
Aitken, Webster 1908- Baker 78
Aitoff, Irene 1904- WhoMus 72
Aiuola, Francesco Dell' NewGrD 80
Ajaji, Afolabi BlkAmP
Ajamu MorBAP
Ajaye, Franklin DrBlPA
Ajolle, Francesco Dell' NewGrD 80
Akar, John J d1975 WhoHol C
Akat, Lutfu 1916- DcFM
Aked, Muriel 1887-1955 FilmEn, FilmgC, HalFC 80, NotNAT B, WhScrn 74, -77, WhThe, WhoHol B
Akeley, Carl E 1864-1926 HalFC 80
Akeman, David 1915- BiDAmM
Akens, Jewel RkOn 2A
Akerberg, Erik 1860-1938 NewGrD 80
Akerlind, Curt Ossian Nils 1912- IntWWM 77, -80
Akerman, Lucy Evelina Metcalf 1816-1874 BiDAmM
Akeroyde, Samuel 1650?-1706? Baker 78, NewGrD 80
Akers, Doris 1922- AmSCAP 80
Akers, Henry Carl Hank 1908-1967 WhScrn 74, -77
Akers, Howard E 1913- AmSCAP 66, -80, BiDAmM, IntWWM 77, -80
Akesson, Birgit 1908- CnOxB, DancEn 78
Akimenko, Feodor 1876-1945 OxMus
Akimenko, Fyodor 1876-1945 Baker 78, NewGrD 80
Akimou, Nikolai 1901-1968 NotNAT B
Akimov, Boris Borisovich 1946- CnOxB
Akimov, Nikolai Pavlovich 1901-1968 CnThe, EncWT, OxThe
Akin, Mary Film 2
Akins, Claude IntMPA 77, -76, -78, -79, -80, WhoHol A
Akins, Claude 1913- ForYSC
Akins, Claude 1918- FilmEn, FilmgC, HalFC 80
Akins, Claude 1926- Vers A[port]
Akins, Claude 1936- HolCA[port]
Akins, Zoe 1886-1958 CnMD, FilmEn, FilmgC, HalFC 80, McGEWD, ModWD, NotNAT B, OxThe, WhThe, WomWMM
Akira, Endo 1938- BiDAmM
Akiyama, Kuniharu 1929- Baker 78, DcCM
Akiyoshi, Toshiko 1929- AmSCAP 66, -80, ConAmC A, EncJzS 70
Akkerman, Jan ConMuA 80A, IlEncR
Akon, Alfred 1905- IntWWM 77, -80
Akpabot, Samuel Ekpe 1932- IntWWM 77, -80
Aksal, Sabahattin Kudret 1920- REnWD
Akses, Necil Kazim 1908- Baker 78, NewGrD 80
Akst, Albert 1890?-1958 HalFC 80
Akst, Harry 1894-1963 AmPS, AmSCAP 66, -80, BiDAmM, CmpEPM, NotNAT B, PlP&P, Sw&Ld C
Akst, Ruth Freed AmSCAP 80
Aktasheva, Irina WomWMM
Akula, Appal Raj 1930- IntWWM 77, -80
Akutagawa, Yasushi 1925- Baker 78, DcCM, NewGrD 80
Al-Amuli NewGrD 80
Al-Baghdadi NewGrD 80
Al-Farabi d950 NewGrD 80
Al-Ghazali 1058-1111 NewGrD 80

Al-Gurgani *NewGrD 80*
Al-Hasan Ibn Ahmad *NewGrD 80*
Al-Isfahani 897-967? *NewGrD 80*
Al-Jurjani 1339-1413 *NewGrD 80*
Al-Kahlil Ibn Ahmad 718?-790? *NewGrD 80*
Al-Katib *NewGrD 80*
Al-Kindi 790?-874? *NewGrD 80*
Al-Ladhiqi *NewGrD 80*
Al-Makki 800?- *NewGrD 80*
Al-Mawsili *NewGrD 80*
Al-Munajjim 856-912 *NewGrD 80*
Al-Razi, Abu Bakr 865-925 *NewGrD 80*
Al-Razi, Fakhr Al-Din 1149-1209 *NewGrD 80*
Al-Shirazi *NewGrD 80*
Al-Urmawi *NewGrD 80*
Ala, Giovanni Battista 1598?-1630? *NewGrD 80*
Ala-Konni, Erik 1911- *NewGrD 80*
Ala-Konni, Erkki 1911- *NewGrD 80*
Alabama State Collegians *BiDAmM*
Alabamians, The *BiDAmM*
Alabaster, William *PIP&P*
Alabief, Alexander 1787-1851 *OxMus*
Aladdin 1913-1970 *WhScrn 74, -77*
Alagna, Matthew 1920-1965 *AmSCAP 66, -80*
Alaimo, Chuck *RkOn*
Alaimo, Louise *WomWMM B*
Alaimo, Steve 1940- *ConMuA 80B, RkOn[port]*
Alain *NewGrD 80*
Alain De Lille 1114?-1202 *NewGrD 80*
Alain De Lisle 1114?-1202 *NewGrD 80*
Alain, Jehan 1911-1940 *Baker 78, NewGrD 80*
Alain, Marie-Claire 1926- *BnBkM 80, IntWWM 77, -80, NewGrD 80*
Alain, Olivier 1918- *NewGrD 80*
Alaire *NewGrD 80*
Alaleona, Domenico 1881-1928 *Baker 78, NewGrD 80, OxMus*
Alamani, Jo *NewGrD 80*
Alamani, Johannes *NewGrD 80*
Alamire, Petrus 1470?-1534? *NewGrD 80*
Alamire, Pierre 1470?-1534? *NewGrD 80*
Alamo, Lazaro Del 1530?-1570 *NewGrD 80*
Alamo, Tony *CmpEPM*
Alan, Buddy 1948- *CounME 74[port], -74A*
Alan, David *ConMuA 80B*
Alan, Hervey 1910- *WhoMus 72*
Alan Alan *MagIlD[port]*
Alani, Jo d1373 *NewGrD 80*
Alanus De Insulis *NewGrD 80*
Alanus, Johannes d1373 *NewGrD 80*
Alarcon, Juan Ruiz De 1581?-1639 *CnThe, OxThe*
Alarcon Y Mendoza, Juan Ruiz De 1580?-1639 *EncWT, Ent*
Alarcon Y Mendoza, Juan Ruiz Di 1588-1639 *NotNAT B*
Alard, Delphin 1815-1888 *NewGrD 80*
Alard, Jacobus 1515?-1593? *NewGrD 80*
Alard, Jacques 1515?-1593? *NewGrD 80*
Alard, Jean-Delphin 1815-1888 *Baker 78, OxMus*
Alard, Lampert 1602-1672 *NewGrD 80*
Alardi, Jacobus 1515?-1593? *NewGrD 80*
Alardi, Jacques 1515?-1593? *NewGrD 80*
Alardino, Jacobus 1515?-1593? *NewGrD 80*
Alardino, Jacques 1515?-1593? *NewGrD 80*
Alardy, Jacobus 1515?-1593? *NewGrD 80*
Alardy, Jacques 1515?-1593? *NewGrD 80*
Alarie, Amanda 1889-1965 *WhScrn 77*
Alarie, Pierrette 1921- *CreCan 1, NewGrD 80*
Alart, Jacobus *NewGrD 80*
Alart, Simon *NewGrD 80*
Alary, Jules Eugene Abraham 1814-1891 *Baker 78*
Alaupovic, Tugomir 1925- *WhoOp 76*
Alauro, Hieronymo *NewGrD 80*
Alayu, Pedro Salustiano 1904- *AmSCAP 80*
Alazraki, Benito 1923- *FilmEn, OxFilm, WorEFlm*
Alba, Alfonso Perez De d1519? *NewGrD 80*
Alba, Alonso Perez De d1519? *NewGrD 80*
Albam, Emmanuel 1922- *BiDAmM, EncJzS 70*
Albam, Manny 1922- *CmpEPM, ConAmC, EncJzS 70*
Albanes, Antonio 1938- *IntWWM 77, -80*
Albanese, Antoine 1729-1800 *NewGrD 80*
Albanese, Cecilia 1937- *WhoOp 76*
Albanese, Licia 1913- *Baker 78, CmOp, IntWWM 77, -80, MusSN[port], NewEOp 71, NewGrD 80, WhoMus 72*
Albanesi, Margharita 1899-1923 *NotNAT A*
Albanesi, Meggie 1899-1923 *Film 2, WhThe*
Albaneze, Antoine 1729-1800 *NewGrD 80*
Albani, Madame 1852- *WhoStg 1908*
Albani, Emma 1847-1930 *Baker 78, BiDAmM, CmOp, NewEOp 71, NewGrD 80[port], NotNAT B*
Albani, Marie-Louise Emma Cecile 1847-1930 *CreCan 2*
Albani, Mathias 1621-1712 *NewGrD 80*
Albani, Mattia 1621-1712 *Baker 78*
Albano, Marcello *NewGrD 80*
Albany, Joe 1924- *EncJzS 70, IlEncJ*
Albany, Joseph 1924- *BiDAmM*
Albareda, Marcian *NewGrD 80*
Albarosa, Nino 1933- *IntWWM 77, -80*
Albaugh, John W, Jr. 1867-1910 *NotNAT B, WhoStg 1906, -1908*
Albaugh, John W, Sr. 1837-1909 *NotNAT B, WhoStg 1906, -1908*
Albeck, Andy 1921- *IntMPA 79, -80*
Albee, Amos 1772- *BiDAmM*
Albee, David Lyman 1940- *IntWWM 77, -80*
Albee, Edward 1927- *CnMD*
Albee, Edward 1928- *BiDAmM, BiE&WWA, CnThe, ConDr 73, -77, CroCD, DcLB 7[port], EncWT, Ent, FilmgC, HalFC 80, McGEWD[port], ModWD, NatPD[port], NotNAT, -A, OxThe, PIP&P[port], -A, REnWD, WhoThe 72, -77*
Albee, Edward Franklin 1857-1930 *NotNAT B, OxThe*
Albee, Edward Franklin 1860-1930 *WhoStg 1908*
Albeniz, Isaac 1860-1909 *Baker 78, BnBkM 80[port], DcCom 77, DcCom&M 79, GrComp[port], MusMk, NewGrD 80[port], OxMus*
Albeniz, Mateo Perez De 1755?-1831 *Baker 78, NewGrD 80*
Albeniz, Pedro 1755?-1821 *OxMus*
Albeniz, Pedro 1795-1855 *Baker 78, OxMus*
Albeniz Y Basanta, Pedro 1795-1855 *NewGrD 80*
Alber, Erasmus 1500?-1553 *NewGrD 80*
Alberch Vila, Pere 1517-1582 *NewGrD 80*
Alberch Y Vila, Pere 1517-1582 *NewGrD 80*
Albercio Vila, Petro 1517-1582 *NewGrD 80*
Alberdi Recalde, Lope 1869-1948 *NewGrD 80*
Alberg, Mildred Freed 1920- *BiE&WWA, NewYTET, NotNAT*
Albergati, Pirro Capacelli, Conte D' 1663-1735 *Baker 78, NewGrD 80*
Alberghetti, Anna Maria 1936- *Baker 78, BiE&WWA, FilmEn, FilmgC, ForYSC, HalFC 80, IntMPA 77, -75, -76, -78, -79, -80, MotPP, MovMk, NotNAT, WhoHol A*
Alberghetti, Bernardino 1600?-1649? *NewGrD 80*
Alberghetti, Carla 1939- *BiE&WWA*
Alberghetto, Bernardino 1600?-1649? *NewGrD 80*
Alberghi, Paolo Tommaso 1716?-1785 *NewGrD 80*
Alberic Of Rheims d1141 *NewGrD 80*
Albericus Archiepiscopus Bituricensis d1141 *NewGrD 80*
Alberini, Filoteo 1865-1937 *FilmEn*
Alberni, Luis 1887-1962 *FilmEn, Film 2, FilmgC, ForYSC, HalFC 80, MotPP, MovMk, NotNAT B, Vers B[port], WhScrn 74, -77, WhoHol B*
Alberoni, Sherri *WhoHol A*
Albers, Hans 1892-1960 *EncWT, FilmAG WE, FilmEn, Film 2, FilmgC, HalFC 80, MotPP, NotNAT B, WhScrn 74, -77, WhoHol B*
Albers, John Kenneth 1924- *AmSCAP 66, -80*
Albersheim, Gerhard 1902- *Baker 78, IntWWM 77, -80, NewGrD 80*
Albert 1819-1861 *Baker 78, NewGrD 80, OxMus*
Albert, Allan 1945- *NotNAT*
Albert, Ben 1876- *WhThe*
Albert, Carolyn Faye 1937- *AmSCAP 80*
Albert, Charles Louis Napoleon D' 1809-1886 *NewGrD 80*
Albert, Dan 1890-1919 *WhScrn 77*
Albert, Don *NewOrJ[port]*
Albert, Don 1908- *WhoJazz 72*
Albert, Don 1909?- *CmpEPM*
Albert, Eddie 1908- *BiE&WWA, CmpEPM, EncMT, FilmEn, FilmgC, ForYSC, HalFC 80, HolP 30[port], IntMPA 77, -75, -76, -78, -79, -80, MotPP, MovMk[port], NotNAT, PIP&P, WhoHol A, WhoThe 77*
Albert, Edward 1951- *FilmEn, HalFC 80, IntMPA 77, -75, -76, -78, -79, -80, WhoHol A*
Albert, Eugen D' 1864-1932 *CmOp, NewGrD 80*
Albert, Eugene 1816-1890 *NewGrD 80*
Albert, Eugene D' 1864-1932 *Baker 78, BnBkM 80, CompSN[port], NewEOp 71, NewGrD 80*
Albert, Francois Decombe 1789-1865 *CnOxB*
Albert, George *ConMuA 80B*
Albert, Heinrich 1604-1651 *Baker 78, BnBkM 80, NewGrD 80*
Albert, Howard *ConMuA 80B*
Albert, J Ross 1922- *ConAmC*
Albert, Karel 1901- *Baker 78, IntWWM 77, -80, NewGrD 80, WhoMus 72*
Albert, Martin *AmSCAP 80*
Albert, Marvin H *HalFC 80*
Albert, Morris 1951- *RkOn 2[port]*
Albert, Ron *ConMuA 80B*
Albert, Stephen 1941- *AmSCAP 80, Baker 78, ConAmC, IntWWM 77, -80*
Albert, Thomas Russel 1948- *AmSCAP 80, ConAmC*
Albert, Tom 1877-1969 *NewOrJ[port]*
Albert, William 1863- *WhThe*
Albert-Lambert, Raphael 1865- *WhThe*
Albertano, Linda *WomWMM B*
Albertarelli, Francesco *NewGrD 80*
Albertazzi, Giorgio 1923- *EncWT, Ent*
Albertet De Sestairo *NewGrD 80*
Albertet De Sestaro *NewGrD 80*
Albertet De Sestarron *NewGrD 80*
Albertet De Terascon *NewGrD 80*
Alberti, Antonio Degli 1360?-1415 *NewGrD 80*
Alberti, Bob 1934- *AmSCAP 80*
Alberti, Domenico 1710?-1740 *Baker 78, BnBkM 80, MusMk, NewGrD 80*
Alberti, Fritz *Film 2*
Alberti, Gasparo 1480?-1560? *NewGrD 80[port]*
Alberti, Giuseppe Matteo 1685-1751 *NewGrD 80*
Alberti, Innocentio 1535?-1615 *NewGrD 80*
Alberti, Johann Friedrich 1642-1710 *NewGrD 80*
Alberti, Pietro *NewGrD 80*
Alberti, Rafael 1902- *CnMD, EncWT, McGEWD, ModWD*
Alberti, Solon 1889- *AmSCAP 66, ConAmC, WhoMus 72*
Albertieri, Luigi 1860?-1930 *CnOxB, DancEn 78*
Albertine, Charles 1929?- *CmpEPM*
Albertini, Albert Nicholas 1922- *AmSCAP 80*
Albertini, Giuliano *NewGrD 80*
Albertini, Ignazio 1644?-1685 *NewGrD 80*
Albertini, Joachim 1749-1812 *NewGrD 80*
Albertini, Thomas Anton 1660?-1735 *NewGrD 80*
Albertis, Gaspare De *NewGrD 80*
Alberts, Al 1922- *AmSCAP 66, -80*
Alberts, Eunice Dorothy *WhoOp 76*
Albertsen, Per 1919- *NewGrD 80*
Albertson, Arthur W 1891-1926 *WhScrn 77*
Albertson, Coit *Film 1, -2*
Albertson, Frank 1909-1964 *FilmEn, Film 2, FilmgC, ForYSC, HalFC 80, HolCA[port], MotPP, MovMk, NotNAT B, Vers A[port], WhScrn 74, -77, WhoHol B*
Albertson, Grace *WhoHol A*
Albertson, Jack *ForYSC, IntMPA 75, -76, -78, -79, -80*
Albertson, Jack 1907- *HalFC 80*
Albertson, Jack 1910- *FilmEn, FilmgC, IntMPA 77, MovMk, NotNAT,*

WhoHol A, WhoThe 77
Albertson, Lillian d1962 *NotNAT B, WhoHol B*
Albertson, Mabel *MotPP, WhoHol A*
Albertson, Mabel 1900?- *FilmgC*
Albertson, Mabel 1901- *ForYSC, HalFC 80*
Albertus Cantor *NewGrD 80*
Albertus De Bollstadt 1193?-1280 *NewGrD 80*
Albertus Magnus 1193?-1280 *NewGrD 80*
Albertus Parisiensis *NewGrD 80*
Albertus, Gaspare *NewGrD 80*
Albery, Sir Bronson James 1881-1971 *CnThe, OxThe, WhThe*
Albery, Donald Arthur Rolleston 1914- *BiE&WWA, CnThe, EncMT, NotNAT, OxThe, WhoThe 72, -77*
Albery, James 1838-1889 *NotNAT B, OxThe*
Albicastro, Henrico *OxMus*
Albicastro, Henricus *NewGrD 80*
Albicastro, Henricus d1738? *Baker 78*
Albicocco, Jean-Gabriel 1930- *FilmgC*
Albicocco, Jean-Gabriel 1936- *FilmEn*
Albicocco, Jean-Gabriel 1938- *HalFC 80*
Albin, Peter Scott 1944- *AmSCAP 80*
Albin, Roger 1920- *NewGrD 80*
Albini, Filippo 1580?-1626? *NewGrD 80*
Albini, Srecko 1869-1933 *Baker 78*
Albino, Filippo 1580?-1626? *NewGrD 80*
Albinoni, Tomaso 1671-1750 *Baker 78, OxMus*
Albinoni, Tomaso 1671-1751 *NewGrD 80*
Albinoni, Tommaso 1671-1750 *BnBkM 80, DcCom&M 79, MusMk*
Albinus, Father *NewGrD 80*
Albonesi, Afranio Degli *NewGrD 80*
Alboni, Maria Anna Marzia 1826-1894 *NewGrD 80[port]*
Alboni, Marietta 1823-1894 *Baker 78, BnBkM 80, CmOp, NewEOp 71*
Alboni, Marietta 1826-1894 *NewGrD 80[port]*
Alborea, Francesco 1691-1739 *NewGrD 80*
Alborea, Franciscello 1691-1739 *NewGrD 80*
Alborea, Francischello 1691-1739 *NewGrD 80*
Albrecht *NewGrD 80*
Albrecht, Alexander 1885-1958 *NewGrD 80*
Albrecht, Angele 1942- *CnOxB*
Albrecht, Charles 1759?-1848 *NewGrD 80*
Albrecht, Christian Frederick Ludwig 1788-1843 *NewGrD 80*
Albrecht, Elmer 1901-1959 *AmSCAP 66, -80*
Albrecht, Ernest Jacob 1937- *ConAmTC*
Albrecht, Eugen Maria 1842-1894 *NewGrD 80*
Albrecht, Evgeny Karlovich 1842-1894 *Baker 78, NewGrD 80*
Albrecht, George Alexander 1935- *IntWWM 77, -80, WhoOp 76*
Albrecht, Gerd 1934- *WhoOp 76*
Albrecht, Gerd 1935- *IntWWM 77, -80, NewGrD 80*
Albrecht, Hans 1902-1961 *Baker 78, NewGrD 80*
Albrecht, Johann Lorenz 1732-1768 *Baker 78*
Albrecht, Johann Lorenz 1732-1773 *NewGrD 80*
Albrecht, Josef 1894- *WhoMus 72*
Albrecht, Karl 1807-1863 *Baker 78, NewGrD 80*
Albrecht, Konstantin 1835-1893 *Baker 78*
Albrecht, Konstantin Karl 1836-1893 *NewGrD 80*
Albrecht, Konstantin Karlovich 1836-1893 *NewGrD 80*
Albrecht, Ludwig 1844-1899 *NewGrD 80*
Albrecht, Max 1890-1945 *Baker 78*
Albrecht, Moonyeen 1936- *ConAmC*
Albrecht, Otto Edwin 1899- *Baker 78, NewGrD 80*
Albrechtsberger, Johann Georg 1736-1809 *Baker 78, BnBkM 80, MusMk[port], NewGrD 80[port], OxMus*
Albrici, Bartolomeo 1640?-1687? *NewGrD 80*
Albrici, Vincenzo 1631-1696 *NewGrD 80*
Albright, Bob Oklahoma 1884-1971 *WhScrn 74, -77*
Albright, Charles *NewGrD 80*
Albright, Charles W *PupTheA*
Albright, H Darkes 1907- *BiE&WWA, NotNAT*
Albright, Hardie 1903-1975 *FilmEn, FilmgC, HalFC 80, HolP 30[port], MotPP, MovMk, WhScrn 77, WhThe, WhoHol C*
Albright, Hardie 1905- *ForYSC*
Albright, Janet Elaine 1933- *IntWWM 80*
Albright, Lola 1924- *MotPP*
Albright, Lola 1925- *FilmEn, FilmgC, ForYSC, HalFC 80, IntMPA 77, -75, -76, -78, -79, -80, MovMk[port], WhoHol A*
Albright, Philip H 1927- *IntWWM 77, -80*
Albright, Wally, Jr. *Film 2, WhoHol A*
Albright, William 1944- *AmSCAP 80, Baker 78, CpmDNM 72, -80, ConAmC, DcCM, NewGrD 80*
Albright, William Robert *ConAmTC*
Albritton, Sherodd *ConAmC*
Albu-Baird, Margaret Cecilia 1907- *IntWWM 80*
Albuquerque, Armando 1901- *IntWWM 77, -80*
Albutio, Joan Jacomo *NewGrD 80*
Albuzio, Giovanni Giacopo *NewGrD 80*
Alcaeus 620?BC-580?BC *NewGrD 80*
Alcaide, Chris *ForYSC, WhoHol A*
Alcaide, Mario 1927-1971 *WhoHol B*
Alcaide, Tomaz 1901-1967 *NewGrD 80*
Alcalde, Mario 1927-1971 *WhScrn 77*
Alcantra, Francisco Javier *PupTheA*
Alcaraz, Alfonso Flores D' *NewGrD 80*
Alcarotti, Giovanni Francesco 1536?-1596 *NewGrD 80*
Alcarotto, Giovanni Francesco 1536?-1596 *NewGrD 80*
Alcedo, Jose Bernardo 1788-1878 *NewGrD 80*
Alcendor, Ralph R 1926- *AmSCAP 66*
Alch, Mario 1920- *IntWWM 77, -80*
Alcman *NewGrD 80*
Alcock, Douglas 1908-1970 *WhScrn 77, WhoHol B*
Alcock, John 1715-1806 *Baker 78, NewGrD 80, OxMus*
Alcock, John 1740?-1791? *NewGrD 80*
Alcock, John 1740?-1791 *OxMus*
Alcock, Sir Walter 1861-1947 *NewGrD 80*
Alcock, Walter Galpin 1861-1947 *OxMus*
Alcoriza, Luis 1920- *FilmEn, WorEFlm*
Alcorn, Alvin Elmore 1912- *NewOrJ[port], WhoJazz 72*
Alcorn, Olive Ann *Film 2*
Alcorn, Oliver 1910- *NewOrJ*
Alcorta, Amancio 1805-1862 *NewGrD 80*
Alcott, John *FilmEn, FilmgC, HalFC 80*
Alcott, Louisa M 1832-1888 *FilmgC, HalFC 80*
Alcuin 735?-804 *NewGrD 80, OxMus*
Alcy, Jeanne D' 1865-1956 *FilmEn*
Alda, Alan 1936- *BiE&WWA, FilmEn, FilmgC, ForYSC, HalFC 80, IntMPA 77, -75, -76, -78, -79, -80, MotPP, MovMk, NewYTET, NotNAT, WhoHol A, WhoThe 72, -77*
Alda, Delyle *AmPS B*
Alda, Frances 1883-1952 *Baker 78, CmOp, MusSN[port], NewEOp 71, NewGrD 80*
Alda, Robert 1914- *BiE&WWA, CmpEPM, FilmEn, FilmgC, ForYSC, HalFC 80, HolP 40[port], IntMPA 77, -75, -76, -78, -79, -80, MotPP, MovMk[port], NotNAT, PlP&P[port], WhoHol A, WhoThe 72, -77*
Aldan, Daisy *WomWMM B*
Aldana, Jose Manuel 1758-1810 *NewGrD 80*
Alday *NewGrD 80*
Alday, Edward *NewGrD 80*
Alday, Ferdinand 1830?-1875? *NewGrD 80*
Alday, Francisque 1800?-1846? *NewGrD 80*
Alday, Francois 1761?-1835? *NewGrD 80*
Alday, Paul 1763?-1835 *NewGrD 80*
Aldaye *NewGrD 80*
Aldea, Mercedes d1954 *WhScrn 74, -77*
Aldebert, Louis J 1931- *EncJzS 70*
Aldebert, Monique 1931- *EncJzS 70*
Aldee *NewGrD 80*
Alden, Betty 1898-1948 *WhScrn 74, -77, WhoHol B*
Alden, Hortense 1903- *BiE&WWA, NotNAT, WhThe*
Alden, Joan d1968 *WhoHol B*
Alden, John d1962 *NotNAT B*
Alden, John Carver 1852-1935 *Baker 78, BiDAmM*
Alden, John Hewlett 1900- *WhoMus 72*
Alden, John W 1895- *AmSCAP 66, -80*
Alden, Joseph Reed 1886-1951 *AmSCAP 66, -80, BiDAmM*
Alden, Mary 1883-1946 *FilmEn, Film 1, -2, MotPP, NotNAT B, TwYS, WhScrn 74, -77, WhoHol B*
Alden, Norman *ForYSC, WhoHol A*
Alden, Tessie R *AmSCAP 80*
Aldenbjork, Herbert Ernfrid 1939- *IntWWM 77, -80*
Alder, Alan 1939- *CnOxB*
Alder, Cosmas 1497?-1553 *NewGrD 80*
Alderham, Joseph 1925- *AmSCAP 66*
Alderighi, Dante 1898-1968 *Baker 78*
Alderson, Anne 1925- *WhoMus 72*
Alderson, Clifton 1864-1930 *NotNAT B, WhThe*
Alderson, Erville 1883-1957 *Film 2, Vers B[port], WhScrn 74, -77, WhoHol B*
Alderson, Geoffrey 1927- *IntWWM 77, -80*
Alderson, John *ForYSC, WhoHol A*
Alderson, John 1896- *IntMPA 77, -75, -76, -78*
Alderton, John 1940- *FilmgC, HalFC 80, IlWWBF, WhoThe 72, -77*
Aldin, Arthur 1872- *WhThe*
Aldo, G R 1902-1953 *DcFM, FilmEn, FilmgC, HalFC 80, OxFilm*
Aldo, G R 1905-1953 *WorEFlm*
Aldomar, Pedro Juan *NewGrD 80*
Aldon, Mari *IntMPA 77, -75, -76, -78, -79, -80*
Aldon, Mari 1929- *FilmEn, ForYSC, WhoHol A*
Aldon, Mari 1930- *FilmgC, HalFC 80*
Aldous, Lucette 1938- *CnOxB*
Aldous, Lucette 1939- *DancEn 78*
Aldovrandin, Giuseppe Antonio Vincenzo *NewGrD 80*
Aldovrandini, Giuseppe Antonio Vincenzo *NewGrD 80*
Aldredge, Theoni V *BiE&WWA, NotNAT, WhoOp 76, WhoThe 72, -77*
Aldredge, Thomas 1928- *BiE&WWA, NotNAT*
Aldredge, Tom 1928- *WhoHol A, WhoThe 77*
Aldrich, Charles T 1872- *WhThe*
Aldrich, David Brent 1951- *AmSCAP 80*
Aldrich, Henry 1647-1710 *Baker 78, OxMus*
Aldrich, Henry 1648-1710 *NewGrD 80*
Aldrich, Kay 1919- *ForYSC*
Aldrich, Louis 1843-1901 *NotNAT B, OxThe*
Aldrich, Mariska 1881-1965 *BiDAmM, WhScrn 77*
Aldrich, Perley Dunn 1863-1933 *Baker 78, BiDAmM*
Aldrich, Putnam C 1904-1975 *Baker 78, NewGrD 80*
Aldrich, Richard 1863-1937 *Baker 78, BiDAmM, NewGrD 80, NotNAT B, OxMus*
Aldrich, Richard S 1902- *BiE&WWA, WhThe, WhoThe 72*
Aldrich, Robert 1918- *BiDFilm, -81, CmMov, DcFM, FilmEn, FilmgC, HalFC 80, IntMPA 77, -75, -76, -78, -79, -80, MovMk[port], OxFilm, WhoHrs 80, WorEFlm*
Aldrich, Thomas Bailey 1836-1907 *BiDAmM, NotNAT B*
Aldridge, Alfred 1876-1934 *WhScrn 74, -77, WhoHol B*
Aldridge, Carol Tinker 1924- *IntWWM 77, -80*
Aldridge, Donald Ray 1947- *AmSCAP 80*
Aldridge, Ira Frederick 1804-1867 *CnThe, OxThe, PlP&P[port]*
Aldridge, Ira Frederick 1807-1867 *BiDAmM, BlkAmP, DrBlPA, Ent, MorBAP, NotNAT A, -B*
Aldridge, J Tinker 1952- *IntWWM 77, -80*
Aldridge, Lorna Margaret 1922- *WhoMus 72*
Aldridge, Maisie *IntWWM 77, -80, WhoMus 72*
Aldridge, Michael 1920- *WhoThe 72, -77*
Aldridge, Robert 1738?-1793 *CnOxB*
Aldrovandi, Clelia *NewGrD 80*
Aldrovandin, Gioseffo Antonio Vincenzo 1672?-1707 *NewGrD 80*
Aldrovandin, Giuseppe Antonio Vincenzo 1672?-1707 *NewGrD 80*
Aldrovandini, Gioseffo Antonio Vincenzo 1672?-1707 *NewGrD 80*
Aldrovandini, Giuseppe 1665-1707 *Baker 78*

Aldrovandini, Giuseppe Antonio Vincenzo 1672?-1707 NewGrD 80
Aldrovandon, Gioseffo Antonio Vincenzo 1672?-1707 NewGrD 80
Aldrovandon, Giuseppe Antonio Vincenzo 1672?-1707 NewGrD 80
Aldulescu, Radu 1922- IntWWM 77, -80, NewGrD 80, WhoMus 72
Alea, Tomas Gutierrez 1928- OxFilm
Alea, Tomas Guttierrez 1928- DcFM
Alecsandri, Vasile 1821-1890 McGEWD[port], OxMus
Alectorius, Johannes NewGrD 80
Alee Film 2
Alegria, Jose Augusto 1918- NewGrD 80
Aleichem, Sholem 1859-1916 PlP&P
Aleichem, Sholom 1859-1916 NotNAT B, OxThe
Alejandro, Miguel WhoHol A
Alekan, Henri 1909- DcFM, FilmEn, FilmgC, HalFC 80, OxFilm, WorEFlm
Aleksandar, Petrovic 1927- IntWWM 80
Aleksandric, Zoran 1941- WhoOp 76
Alemann, Claudia WomWMM
Alemann, Eduardo Armando 1922- IntWWM 77, -80
Alemann, Johanna WomWMM B
Alembert, Jean-Le-Rond D' 1717-1783 Baker 78
Alembert, Jean LeRond D' 1717-1783 NewGrD 80, OxMus
Alemshah, Kourkene M 1907-1947 Baker 78
Alencar, Jose Mariniano De 1829-1877 OxThe
Alenick, Susan J 1939- AmSCAP 80
Alenikoff, Frances 1930- CnOxB, WomWMM B
Aleotti, Giovan Battista 1546-1636 EncWT, Ent
Aleotti, Giovanni Battista 1546-1636 OxThe
Aleotti, Raffaella 1570?-1646? NewGrD 80
Aleotti, Vittoria 1573?-1620? NewGrD 80
Alere NewGrD 80
Ales, Barney ConMuA 80B
Ales, Mikolas 1852-1913 DcPup
Alessandra, Caterina NewGrD 80
Alessandrescu, Alfred 1893-1959 Baker 78, NewGrD 80, OxMus
Alessandri, Felice 1747-1798 Baker 78, NewGrD 80
Alessandri, Gennaro D' NewGrD 80
Alessandri, Giulio D' NewGrD 80
Alessandrini, Goffredo 1904-1978 FilmEn
Alessandro Mantovano NewGrD 80
Alessandro Padovano NewGrD 80
Alessandro, Charles-Guillaume NewGrD 80
Alessandro, Gennaro D' NewGrD 80
Alessandro, Raffaele D' 1911-1959 Baker 78, NewGrD 80
Alessandro, Victor Nicholas 1915-1976 Baker 78, IntWWM 77, -80, NewEOp 71, WhoMus 72, WhoOp 76
Alessi, Marie-Bernadette 1951- IntWWM 77
Alette, Carl 1922- ConAmC
Aletter, Frank WhoHol A
Aletti, Vince ConMuA 80B
Alevi, Giuseppe NewGrD 80
Alexander, Meister NewGrD 80
Alexander The Great 356BC-323BC FilmgC
Alexander, A L 1906-1967 WhScrn 77
Alexander, Adolphe, Jr. 1898-1968 NewOrJ
Alexander, Adolphe, Sr. 1874-1936 NewOrJ
Alexander, Alger 1880?-1955? BluesWW[port]
Alexander, Arthur RkOn
Alexander, Arthur 1891-1969 OxMus
Alexander, Ashley Hollis 1935- IntWWM 77, -80
Alexander, Ben 1911-1969 FilmEn, Film 1, -2, FilmgC, ForYSC, HalFC 80, HolCA[port], MotPP, MovMk, TwYS, WhScrn 74, -77, WhoHol B
Alexander, C K 1923- BiE&WWA, NotNAT
Alexander, Carlos 1915- WhoOp 76
Alexander, Charles McCallom 1867-1920 NewGrD 80
Alexander, Charlie 1900- BiDAmM
Alexander, Chris 1920- WhoHol A
Alexander, Claire 1898-1927 WhScrn 74, -77, WhoHol B
Alexander, Cris 1920- BiE&WWA, NotNAT
Alexander, Dave 1938- BluesWW[port]
Alexander, David NewYTET
Alexander, Dick Film 2
Alexander, Dorothy Moses 1904- CnOxB, DancEn 78[port]
Alexander, Edward 1888-1964 Film 1, WhScrn 74, -77, WhoHol B
Alexander, Eleanor E 1925- IntWWM 77
Alexander, Elmer 1922- EncJzS 70
Alexander, Ethel Emily WhoMus 72
Alexander, Frank 1879-1937 WhScrn 74, -77, WhoHol B
Alexander, Georg 1889?-1945 Film 2, WhScrn 77
Alexander, Georg 1889-1946 FilmEn
Alexander, George 1918- AmSCAP 66
Alexander, Sir George 1858-1918 CnThe, EncWT, Ent, NotNAT A, -B, OxThe, PlP&P, WhThe, WhoStg 1908
Alexander, Gus Film 1
Alexander, Haim 1915- IntWWM 77, -80, NewGrD 80
Alexander, Heinz 1915- NewGrD 80
Alexander, James 1902-1961 WhScrn 77
Alexander, James Waddell 1804-1859 BiDAmM
Alexander, Jamie WhoHol A
Alexander, Jane 1939- FilmEn, HalFC 80, NotNAT, PlP&P A, WhoHol A, WhoThe 77
Alexander, Jane 1943- FilmgC
Alexander, Janet d1961 IlWWBF, WhThe
Alexander, Jeff 1910- AmSCAP 66, -80, ConAmC A, IntWWM 77
Alexander, Joan WhoMus 72
Alexander, Joe NewOrJ
Alexander, John 1865-1951 WhScrn 74, -77
Alexander, John 1897- BiE&WWA, FilmEn, FilmgC, HalFC 80, IntMPA 77, -75, -76, -78, -79, -80, NotNAT, Vers B[port], WhoHol B, WhoThe 72, -77
Alexander, John 1906?- ForYSC
Alexander, John 1925?- CmOp, IntWWM 80, NewGrD 80, WhoOp 76
Alexander, Josef AmSCAP 66, IntWWM 77
Alexander, Josef 1907- Baker 78
Alexander, Josef 1910- AmSCAP 80, CpmDNM 75, ConAmC, DcCM, IntWWM 80
Alexander, Joseph Addison 1809-1860 BiDAmM
Alexander, Katharine 1901- ForYSC
Alexander, Katherine 1901- BiE&WWA, FilmEn, FilmgC, HalFC 80, MovMk, NotNAT, PlP&P, ThFT[port], WhThe
Alexander, Larry 1939- AmSCAP 66, -80
Alexander, Lewis BlkAmP
Alexander, Lois A 1891-1962 WhScrn 77
Alexander, Mara 1914-1965 WhScrn 77
Alexander, Marjorie Eugene WhoMus 72
Alexander, Montgomery Bernard 1944- EncJzS 70
Alexander, Monty 1944- EncJzS 70
Alexander, Mousey 1922- EncJzS 70
Alexander, Muriel 1898-1975 Film 2, WhThe, WhoHol C
Alexander, Nick AmSCAP 80
Alexander, Perry 1895- AmSCAP 66
Alexander, Philip R 1944- ConAmC
Alexander, Queen Film 1
Alexander, Rene d1914 WhScrn 77
Alexander, Richard Film 2
Alexander, Robert NotNAT
Alexander, Robin Lynn 1951- AmSCAP 80
Alexander, Rod 1919- BiE&WWA, NotNAT
Alexander, Rod 1920- BiE&WWA, CnOxB, WhoHol A
Alexander, Rod 1925- DancEn 78
Alexander, Roland E 1935- BiDAmM
Alexander, Ronald 1917- BiE&WWA, NotNAT
Alexander, Ross 1907-1937 FilmEn, FilmgC, ForYSC, HalFC 80, NotNAT B, WhScrn 74, -77, WhoHol B
Alexander, Ross 1934- NatPD[port]
Alexander, Sara 1839-1926 WhScrn 74, -77, WhoHol B
Alexander, Suzanne d1975 WhScrn 77, WhoHol C
Alexander, Terence 1923- FilmEn, FilmgC, HalFC 80, WhoHol A, WhoThe 72, -77
Alexander, Texas BluesWW
Alexander, Van 1915- AmSCAP 66, -80, BgBands 74, BiDAmM, CmpEPM
Alexander, William P ConAmC, IntWWM 77, -80
Alexander Brothers NewGrD 80
Alexander The Great d1933 WhScrn 77
Alexanderson, Ernst F W d1975 NewYTET
Alexandra, Liana 1947- IntWWM 80
Alexandre, Charles-Guillaume 1735?-1788? NewGrD 80
Alexandre, Jacob 1804-1876 Baker 78, OxMus
Alexandre, Rene 1885-1946 Film 1, NotNAT B, WhThe
Alexandresco Film 2
Alexandri, Monsieur PupTheA
Alexandri, Vasile 1821-1890 OxMus
Alexandria, Lorez 1929- BiDAmM
Alexandrof, Anatol 1888- OxMus
Alexandrov, Alexander Vasil'yevich 1883-1946 Baker 78, NewGrD 80
Alexandrov, Anatoly 1888- Baker 78, IntWWM 77, -80, NewGrD 80
Alexandrov, Boris Alexandrovich 1905- NewGrD 80, WhoMus 72
Alexandrov, Grigori 1903- DcFM, FilmEn, Film 2, FilmgC, HalFC 80, OxFilm, WorEFlm
Alexandrova, Natalia Donatovna 1936- CnOxB
Alexandru, Tiberiu 1914- NewGrD 80
Alexanian, Diran 1881-1954 NewGrD 80
Alexeieff, Alexander 1901- WorEFlm[port]
Alexeieff, Alexandre 1901- DcFM, OxFilm
Alexenburg, Ron ConMuA 80B
Alexeyev, K NewGrD 80
Alexeyev, Konstantin Sergeyevich NewGrD 80
Alexeyeva, Ekaterina Nikolayevna 1899- NewGrD 80
Alexieff, Alexandre 1901- FilmEn, FilmgC, HalFC 80
Alexis PupTheA
Alexis 372?BC-270BC EncWT, Ent, OxThe
Alexis, Ricard 1896-1960 NewOrJ[port]
Alexius, Carl John 1928- ConAmC
Aleyn NewGrD 80
Alfano, Franco 1875-1954 NewGrD 80
Alfano, Franco 1876-1954 Baker 78, CmOp, CompSN[port], MusMk, NewEOp 71, OxMus
Alfarabi, Abu Nasr 870?-950? Baker 78
Alfaro, Keiva WhoHol A
Alfaro, Rhonda WhoHol A
Alferaki, Achilles 1846-1919 Baker 78
Alfidi, Joseph 1961- AmSCAP 66
Alfieri, Giuseppe 1630-1665 NewGrD 80
Alfieri, Pietro 1801-1863 Baker 78, NewGrD 80
Alfieri, Count Vittorio 1749-1803 CnThe, EncWT, Ent, McGEWD[port], NotNAT B, OxThe, REnWD
Alfiero, Giuseppe 1630-1665 NewGrD 80
Alfonso V 1396-1458 NewGrD 80
Alfonso X 1221-1284 NewGrD 80, OxMus
Alfonso El Sabio 1221-1284 NewGrD 80
Alfonso, Master OxMus
Alfonso, Don 1899- AmSCAP 66, -80
Alfonso, Javier 1904- NewGrD 80
Alford, Delton L 1938- AmSCAP 80
Alford, Kenneth J 1881-1945 NewGrD 80
Alford, Walter 1912- BiE&WWA, NotNAT
Alfred, Roy 1916- AmSCAP 66, -80
Alfred, William 1922- ConDr 73, -77, CroCD, McGEWD, NotNAT
Alfsen, John Martin 1902- CreCan 2
Alfven, Hugo 1872-1960 Baker 78, CompSN[port], DancEn 78, DcCom&M 79, DcCM, MusMk, NewGrD 80, OxMus
Algar, James 1912- FilmEn, IntMPA 77, -75, -76, -78, -79, -80
Algar, James 1914- DcFM, FilmgC, HalFC 80
Algaro, Gabriel 1888-1951 WhScrn 74, -77
Algaroff, Youly 1918- CnOxB, DancEn 78
Algarotti, Francesco 1712-1764 Baker 78, NewGrD 80, OxMus
Algarotti, Giovanni Francesco NewGrD 80
Algeranoff, Harcourt 1903-1967 CnOxB, DancEn 78
Algeranova, Claudie 1924- CnOxB, DancEn 78
Alghisi, Paris Francesco 1666-1733 NewGrD 80
Algier, Sidney H 1889-1945 WhScrn 74, -77, WhoHol B

Algisi, Paris Francesco 1666-1733 NewGrD 80
Algo, Julian 1899-1955 CnOxB
Algren, Nelson 1909- FilmgC, HalFC 80
Alhanko, Anneli 1953- CnOxB
Ali, Ahmed Mohamed 1915- IntWWM 80
Ali, George 1866-1947 Film 2, WhScrn 77
Ali, Jamal MorBAP
Ali, Muhammad 1939- MorBAP
Ali, Naushad 1919- IntWWM 80
Ali, Rasheid 1935- BiDAmM
Ali, Rashied 1933- DrBlPA
Ali, Rashied 1935- EncJzS 70
Ali Akbar Khan 1922- Baker 78
Ali Bongo MagIlD[port]
Ali Ibn Muhammad Al-Jurjani NewGrD 80
Aliabiev, Alexander 1787-1851 Baker 78
Aliapoulios, Paul A 1935- IntWWM 80
Alice, Mary 1941- DrBlPA
Alicoate, Charles A 1898- IntMPA 75, -76
Aliff NewGrD 80
Alin, Morris 1905- AmSCAP 66, -80, IntMPA 77, -75, -76, -78, -79, -80
Alio, Francisco 1862-1908 Baker 78
Alio Y Brea, Francisco 1862-1908 NewGrD 80
Alippi, Elias d1942 WhScrn 74, -77
Aliprandi, Bernardo 1710?-1792? Baker 78, NewGrD 80
Aliprandi, Bernardo Maria 1747-1801 NewGrD 80
Aliprandi, Bernhard Maria 1747-1801 NewGrD 80
Alis, Roman 1931- NewGrD 80
Aliseda, Jeronimo De 1548?-1591 NewGrD 80
Aliseda, Santos De d1580 NewGrD 80
Alison, Dorothy 1925- FilmgC, HalFC 80
Alison, George d1936 NotNAT B
Alison, Richard NewGrD 80, OxMus
Alister, Kathleen Cameron 1920- IntWWM 77, -80
Alive And Kicking RkOn 2A
Alix, May BluesWW[port]
Alix, May 1902- BluesWW[port]
Alix, May 1904- WhoJazz 72
Alizon OxThe
Alkaios NewGrD 80
Alkan 1813-1888 BnBkM 80
Alkan, Charles 1813-1888 MusMk
Alkan, Charles-Henri Valentin 1813-1888 Baker 78
Alkan, Charles Henry Valentin 1813-1888 OxMus
Alkan, Valentin 1813-1888 NewGrD 80[port]
Alke, Bjorn 1938- EncJzS 70
Allacci, Leone 1588-1669 NewGrD 80
Allacci, Lione 1588-1669 NewGrD 80
Allacius, Leone 1588-1669 NewGrD 80
Allacius, Lione 1588-1669 NewGrD 80
Allaire NewGrD 80
Allaire, Gaston Georges 1916- IntWWM 77, -80
Allais, Alphonse 1854-1905 Ent
Allan, Andrew Edward Fairbairn 1907- CreCan 1
Allan, Anthony 1933- IntWWM 80
Allan, David WhoMus 72
Allan, Elizabeth 1908- FilmEn, FilmgC, ForYSC, HalFC 80, IlWWBF[port], ThFT[port], WhoHol A
Allan, Esther 1914- AmSCAP 80
Allan, Hugh 1903- Film 2, TwYS
Allan, Jan 1934- EncJzS 70
Allan, Jean Mary 1899- IntWWM 80
Allan, Jed WhoHol A
Allan, Lewis AmSCAP 66, -80
Allan, Louise Rosalie 1810-1856 NotNAT B, OxThe
Allan, Marguerite 1909- Film 2, IlWWBF
Allan, Maud 1883-1956 CmpGMD[port], NotNAT A, -B, OxMus, WhThe
Allan, Maude 1883-1956 CnOxB, DancEn 78[port]
Allan, Mike AmSCAP 80
Allan, Richard Van NewGrD 80
Allan, Sandra 1943- IntWWM 77
Allan, Ted IntMPA 77, -75, -76, -78, -79, -80
Allan, Ted 1916- ConDr 73, -77
Allanbrook, Douglas Phillips 1921- AmSCAP 80, ConAmC
Alland, William 1916- FilmEn, FilmgC, HalFC 80, IntMPA 77, -75, -76, -78, -79, -80, WhoHrs 80
Allandale, Fred 1872- WhThe
Allard, Marie 1742-1802 CnOxB, DancEn 78, OxMus
Allard, Maurice 1923- NewGrD 80
Allardt, Arthur Film 1
Allasio, Marisa MotPP
Allatius, Leone NewGrD 80
Allatius, Lione NewGrD 80
Allbeury, Daisy 1885-1961 WhScrn 74, -77
Allbritton, Joe L NewYTET
Allbritton, Louise 1920-1979 FilmEn, FilmgC, ForYSC, HalFC 80, HolP 40[port], MotPP, WhoHol A
Allcock, Stephen ConAmC
Alldahl, Per-Gunnar 1943- Baker 78
Allde, Edward d1634 NewGrD 80
Alldis, John 1929- NewGrD 80, WhoMus 72
Alldrick, Donald Francis 1923- WhoMus 72
Alleborn, Al 1892-1968 WhScrn 74, -77
Allegranti, Maddalena 1754-1801? NewGrD 80
Allegret, Catherine WhoHol A
Allegret, Marc 1900-1973 BiDFilm, -81, DcFM, FilmEn, FilmgC, HalFC 80, MovMk[port], OxFilm, WhScrn 77, WorEFlm
Allegret, Yves 1907- BiDFilm, -81, DcFM, FilmEn, FilmgC, HalFC 80, MovMk[port], OxFilm, WorEFlm[port]
Allegri, Domenico 1585-1629 Baker 78, NewGrD 80
Allegri, Gregorio 1582-1652 Baker 78, MusMk, NewGrD 80, OxMus
Allegri, Lorenzo 1573?-1648 NewGrD 80
Allegro, Anita d1964 NotNAT B
Allen And Lester AmPS B
Allen, A E OxMus
Allen, A Hylton 1879- WhThe
Allen, Adrianne 1907- BiE&WWA, FilmEn, FilmgC, ForYSC, HalFC 80, IlWWBF, NotNAT, WhoHol A
Allen, Alfred 1866-1947 Film 1, -2, WhScrn 77
Allen, Allen David 1936- AmSCAP 80
Allen, Andrew Ralph 1913-1966 CreCan 1
Allen, Arthur B 1881-1947 WhScrn 74, -77, WhoHol B
Allen, Bambi d1973 WhScrn 77
Allen, Barbara Jo 1904?-1974 FilmEn, FilmgC, ForYSC, HalFC 80, WhoHol B
Allen, Barclay 1918- AmSCAP 66, -80
Allen, Benjamin Dwight 1831-1914 BiDAmM
Allen, Betty 1930- BiDAmM, DrBlPA, IntWWM 77, -80, NewGrD 80, WhoOp 76
Allen, Bob 1913?- BgBands 74, CmpEPM
Allen, Buddy ConMuA 80B
Allen, Byron 1940- BiDAmM
Allen, C J Film 2
Allen, Charles AmSCAP 80
Allen, Charles Leslie 1830-1917 NotNAT B, WhThe, WhoStg 1906, -1908
Allen, Charlie 1908- WhoJazz 72
Allen, Chesney 1893- HalFC 80
Allen, Chesney 1894- FilmgC, IlWWBF
Allen, Chesney 1896- WhThe
Allen, Corey 1934- FilmEn, FilmgC, HalFC 80, WhoHol A
Allen, Creighton 1900- AmSCAP 66, Baker 78, ConAmC
Allen, David WhoHrs 80
Allen, David Bliss 1939- AmSCAP 80
Allen, Dayton 1919- IntMPA 77, -75, -76, -78, -79, -80
Allen, Deborah 1950- DrBlPA, PlP&P A[port]
Allen, Dede 1924- FilmEn, IntMPA 77, -75, -76, -78, -79, -80, WomWMM
Allen, Dede 1925- HalFC 80
Allen, Diana Film 2
Allen, Dick AmSCAP 80, ConMuA 80B
Allen, Dorothy 1896-1970 Film 2, WhScrn 74, -77, WhoHol B
Allen, Edith Film 2
Allen, Edward Clifton 1897- BiDAmM, WhoJazz 72
Allen, Elizabeth 1916- MovMk
Allen, Elizabeth 1934- BiE&WWA, FilmEn, FilmgC, ForYSC, HalFC 80, NotNAT, WhoHol A, WhoThe 72, -77
Allen, Ethan 1882-1940 WhScrn 74, -77, WhoHol B
Allen, Fletcher B 1907- WhoJazz 72
Allen, Florence Film 2
Allen, Frank 1851- WhThe
Allen, Frank Edward 1936- IntWWM 77, -80, WhoMus 72
Allen, Fred 1894-1956 EncMT, Ent, FilmEn, FilmgC, ForYSC, HalFC 80, JoeFr[port], NewYTET, NotNAT A, -B, OxFilm, WhScrn 74, -77, WhoHol B
Allen, G Everett 1899- AmSCAP 66
Allen, George BluesWW
Allen, George Benjamin 1822-1897 Baker 78
Allen, George Nelson 1812-1877 BiDAmM
Allen, Geri A 1957- BlkWAB
Allen, Gloria WomWMM B
Allen, Gracie 1899-1964 ThFT[port]
Allen, Gracie 1902-1964 FilmEn, Film 2, FilmgC, Funs[port], HalFC 80, MotPP, MovMk, WhoHol B
Allen, Gracie 1906-1964 ForYSC, JoeFr[port], NotNAT A, -B, WhScrn 74, -77
Allen, Harold 1917- IntWWM 77, -80, WhoMus 72
Allen, Harry Film 2, PupTheA
Allen, Heman 1836-1876 BiDAmM
Allen, Henry ConMuA 80B
Allen, Henry, Jr. 1900-1967 AmSCAP 66
Allen, Henry, Jr. 1908-1967 AmSCAP 80, EncJzS 70, IlEncJ, NewGrD 80[port], NewOrJ[port]
Allen, Henry, Sr. 1877-1952 NewOrJ[port]
Allen, Henry James, Jr. 1900-1969 BiDAmM
Allen, Henry Red 1908-1967 CmpEPM
Allen, Henry Robinson 1809-1876 NewGrD 80
Allen, Herb 1913- IntMPA 77, -75, -76, -78, -79, -80
Allen, Herbert 1927- AmSCAP 66
Allen, Herbert Ethan 1929- AmSCAP 80
Allen, Hugh 1886-1966 Film 2, WhScrn 77
Allen, Sir Hugh Percy 1869-1946 Baker 78, BnBkM 80, NewGrD 80, OxMus
Allen, Inglis d1943 NotNAT B
Allen, Irving 1905- FilmEn, FilmgC, HalFC 80, IntMPA 77, -75, -76, -78, -79, -80
Allen, Irwin 1916- CmMov, FilmEn, FilmgC, HalFC 80, IntMPA 77, -75, -76, -78, -79, -80, NewYTET, WhoHrs 80
Allen, Ivan DancEn 78
Allen, Ivy M 1932- IntWWM 77, -80
Allen, J Lathrop 1815-1905? NewGrD 80
Allen, Jack 1907- WhoThe 72, -77
Allen, Jack Major Film 1
Allen, Jane 1928- IntWWM 77, -80, WhoMus 72
Allen, Jane Marie 1916-1970 WhScrn 77, WhoHol B
Allen, Jap 1899- WhoJazz 72
Allen, Jay Presson 1922- McGEWD, NotNAT, WomWMM
Allen, Jerry AmSCAP 80
Allen, Jim ConDr 73, -77C
Allen, Joe 1888-1955 WhScrn 74, -77, WhoHol B
Allen, John Piers 1912- WhoThe 77
Allen, Johnny AmPS B
Allen, Jonelle 1944- DrBlPA, WhoHol A
Allen, Joseph 1840-1917 NotNAT B
Allen, Joseph, Jr. 1918-1962 MotPP, WhScrn 74, -77, WhoHol B
Allen, Joseph, Jr. 1918-1963 NotNAT B
Allen, Joseph, Sr. 1872-1952 Film 1, -2, NotNAT B, WhScrn 74, -77, WhoHol B
Allen, Joyce Frances 1912- WhoMus 72
Allen, Joyce Herman WhoMus 72
Allen, Judith 1913- FilmEn, ForYSC, ThFT[port], WhoHol A
Allen, Kelcey 1875-1951 NotNAT B, WhThe
Allen, Lanny 1942- AmSCAP 80
Allen, Larry Dale 1947- IntWWM 77, -80
Allen, Lauri AmSCAP 80
Allen, Lee And His Band RkOn[port]
Allen, Lester 1891-1949 CmpEPM, Film 2, NotNAT B, WhScrn 74, -77, WhoHol B
Allen, Lewis 1905- FilmEn, FilmgC, HalFC 80, IntMPA 77, -75, -76, -78, -79, -80
Allen, Lewis M 1922- BiE&WWA, FilmEn, FilmgC, HalFC 80, NotNAT

Allen, Lorenzo B 1812-1872 *BiDAmM*
Allen, Louise d1909 *NotNAT B, WhoStg 1908*
Allen, Marguerite *Film 2*
Allen, Marshall 1924- *BiDAmM*
Allen, Maude d1956 *WhScrn 74, -77, WhoHol B*
Allen, Maybelle *BluesWW*
Allen, Mel 1913- *IntMPA 77, -75, -76, -78, -79, -80, NewYTET*
Allen, Morrie *AmSCAP 80*
Allen, Moses 1907- *WhoJazz 72*
Allen, Nathan Hale 1848-1925 *Baker 78, BiDAmM*
Allen, Norma *WomWMM B*
Allen, Patrick 1927- *FilmEn, FilmgC, HalFC 80, WhoHol A, WhoThe 77*
Allen, Paul Hastings 1883-1952 *Baker 78, BiDAmM, ConAmC, NewGrD 80*
Allen, Penny *WhoHol A*
Allen, Percy d1959 *NotNAT B*
Allen, Phyllis *AmPS B*
Allen, Phyllis 1861-1938 *FilmEn, Film 1, -2, TwYS, WhScrn 74, -77, WhoHol B*
Allen, Rae 1926- *BiE&WWA, NotNAT, WhoHol A, WhoThe 72, -77*
Allen, Ralph 1913-1966 *CreCan 1*
Allen, Ralph 1926- *CreCan 1*
Allen, Red 1908-1967 *EncJzS 70, WhoJazz 72*
Allen, Reginald 1905- *BiE&WWA, NotNAT*
Allen, Rex 1922- *FilmgC, ForYSC, HalFC 80, IntMPA 77, -75, -76, -78, -79, -80, WhoHol A*
Allen, Rex 1924- *BiDAmM, CmpEPM, CounME 74, -74A, EncFCWM 69, IlEncCM, RkOn*
Allen, Ricca *Film 1, -2*
Allen, Richard 1760-1831 *BiDAmM*
Allen, Richard Gould 1924- *AmSCAP 66, -80*
Allen, Rita d1968 *BiE&WWA, NotNAT B*
Allen, Robert 1906- *FilmEn, ForYSC, IntMPA 77, -75, -76, -78, -79, -80, WhoHol A*
Allen, Robert 1924- *AmPS*
Allen, Robert 1927- *AmSCAP 80*
Allen, Robert E 1920- *AmSCAP 66, -80, ConAmC*
Allen, Robert F 1928- *AmSCAP 66*
Allen, Robert I 1921- *AmSCAP 80*
Allen, Robert Thomas 1911- *CreCan 1*
Allen, Rosalie 1924- *BiDAmM, CounME 74, EncFCWM 69, IlEncCM*
Allen, Sam 1861-1934 *Film 2, WhScrn 74, -77, WhoHol B*
Allen, Sam 1909-1963 *WhoJazz 72*
Allen, Samuel 1848-1905? *NewGrD 80*
Allen, Sena *BlkAmP*
Allen, Seth *WhoHol A*
Allen, Sheila 1932- *WhoThe 72, -77*
Allen, Sian Barbara *WhoHol A*
Allen, Spencer Maurice 1902- *WhoMus 72*
Allen, Stephen Valentine Patrick William 1921- *BiDAmM*
Allen, Steve 1921- *AmSCAP 66, -80, BiE&WWA, CmpEPM, EncJzS 70, FilmEn, FilmgC, ForYSC, HalFC 80, IntMPA 77, -75, -76, -78, -79, -80, JoeFr[port], NewYTET, WhoHol A*
Allen, Stuart 1907- *CmpEPM*
Allen, Susan Ellen Hamman 1921- *IntWWM 77, -80*
Allen, Susan Westford d1944 *NotNAT B*
Allen, Terry *CmpEPM*
Allen, Tex *Film 1*
Allen, Thomas 1944- *CmOp, IntWWM 77, -80, NewGrD 80, WhoMus 72, WhoOp 76*
Allen, Vera 1897- *BiE&WWA, NotNAT, PlP&P, WhThe*
Allen, Vernon St. Clair 1906- *IntWWM 77*
Allen, Viola 1867-1948 *FamA&A[port], NotNAT B*
Allen, Viola 1869-1948 *Film 1, OxThe, WhScrn 77, WhThe, WhoHol B, WhoStg 1906, -1908*
Allen, Vivian Beaumont d1962 *NotNAT B, PlP&P*
Allen, W E *OxMus*
Allen, Warren D 1885-1964 *Baker 78*
Allen, Willi *Film 2*
Allen, William d1647 *OxThe*
Allen, William 1784-1868 *BiDAmM*
Allen, William Clyde, Jr. 1945- *AmSCAP 80*
Allen, William Francis 1830-1889 *BiDAmM*
Allen, William T 1926- *ConAmC*
Allen, Woody 1935- *BiDFilm 81, ConLC 16, FilmEn, FilmgC, ForYSC, Funs[port], GrMovC[port], HalFC 80, IntMPA 77, -75, -76, -78, -79, -80, JoeFr[port], MovMk[port], NotNAT, -A, WhoHol A, WhoHrs 80, WhoThe 77*
Allenby, Frank 1898-1953 *WhThe*
Allenby, Peggy 1905-1967 *WhThe*
Allenby, Thomas 1861-1933 *WhScrn 74, -77, WhoHol B*
Allende, Humberto 1885-1959 *CompSN[port], MusMk, OxMus*
Allende, Pedro Humberto 1885-1959 *DcCM, NewGrD 80*
Allende, Saron Humberto 1885-1959 *Baker 78*
Allende-Blin, Juan 1928- *NewGrD 80*
Allen's Brass Band Of Algiers, Louisiana *BiDAmM*
Allentuck, Max 1911- *BiE&WWA*
Aller, Eleanor 1917- *WhoMus 72*
Aller, Victor 1905- *WhoMus 72*
Allers, Franz 1905- *Baker 78, BiE&WWA, IntWWM 77, -80, NotNAT, WhoMus 72, WhoOp 76*
Allers, Fritz 1905- *BiDAmM*
Allerton, Helen 1888-1959 *WhoHol B*
Allerton, Little Helen 1888-1959 *WhScrn 74, -77*
Allesandra, Giuseppe 1865-1950 *NewOrJ[port]*
Allevi, Giuseppe 1603?-1670 *NewGrD 80*
Allevi Piacenza, Giuseppe 1603?-1670 *NewGrD 80*
Allevo, Giuseppe 1603?-1670 *NewGrD 80*
Alley, Ben d1970 *WhoHol B*
Alleyn, Edward 1566-1626 *CnThe, EncWT, Ent, NotNAT A, -B, OxThe, PlP&P*
Alleyn, George Edmund 1931- *CreCan 2*
Allgeier, Sepp 1890-1968 *FilmgC, HalFC 80*
Allgeier, Sepp 1895-1968 *FilmEn*
Allgood, Maire O'Neill 1887-1952 *OxThe*
Allgood, Sara 1883-1950 *CnThe, EncWT, FilmEn, Film 2, FilmgC, ForYSC, HalFC 80, HolCA[port], IlWWBF, MotPP, OxThe, PlP&P, Vers A[port], WhScrn 74, -77, WhThe, WhoHol B*
Allgood, Sara 1893-1950 *MovMk[port]*
Allgood, Sarah 1883-1950 *NotNAT B*
Allgood, William Thomas 1939- *ConAmC*
Allievi, Giuseppe 1603?-1670 *NewGrD 80*
Allihn, Heinrich 1841-1910 *Baker 78*
Allin, Norman 1884-1973 *CmOp, NewGrD 80, WhoMus 72*
Alline, Henry 1748-1784 *BiDAmM*
Alling, Ruth Stevenson 1892- *IntWWM 77, -80*
Allinson, Michael *BiE&WWA, NotNAT, WhoThe 77*
Allinsonne, Richard *NewGrD 80*
Allio, Rene 1921- *EncWT*
Allio, Rene 1924- *BiDFilm, -81, FilmEn, FilmgC, HalFC 80, OxFilm, WorEFlm*
Allison, Aneta Joan Northcutt 1940- *IntWWM 77*
Allison, Fran *IntMPA 77, -75, -76, -78, -79, -80, NewYTET*
Allison, Howard K, II 1948- *ConAmC*
Allison, Hughes *BlkAmP, MorBAP*
Allison, Irl 1896- *ConAmC*
Allison, John A 1914- *AmSCAP 66, -80*
Allison, Luther S 1939- *BluesWW[port]*
Allison, May 1895- *FilmEn, Film 1, -2, MotPP, TwYS, WhoHol A*
Allison, Mose John, Jr. 1927- *BiDAmM, EncJzS 70, IlEncJ*
Allison, Richard *NewGrD 80, OxMus*
Allison, Steve 1916-1969 *WhScrn 74, -77, WhoHol B*
Allister, Claud 1891-1967 *WhThe*
Allister, Claud 1891-1970 *FilmgC, HalFC 80, IlWWBF[port]*
Allister, Claud 1893-1970 *FilmEn, ForYSC, WhScrn 74, -77*
Allister, Claud 1894-1970 *WhoHol B*
Allister, Claude 1891-1970 *MovMk*
Allister, Claude 1894-1970 *Film 2*
Allister, Jean Maria 1932- *IntWWM 77, -80, WhoMus 72*
Allister, William 1919- *CreCan 2*
Allitsen, Frances *ConAmC*
Allitsen, Mary Francis 1848-1912 *NewGrD 80*
Allitt, John Stewart 1934- *IntWWM 77, -80*
Allman, Duane 1947-1971 *BiDAmM, ConMuA 80A*
Allman, Elvia *ForYSC, WhoHol A*
Allman, Gregg *ConMuA 80A*
Allman, Michael L 1911- *AmSCAP 66, -80*
Allman, Robert 1929- *WhoOp 76*
Allman Brothers *ConMuA 80A*
Allman Brothers Band, The *IlEncR, RkOn 2[port]*
Allon, Henry *OxMus*
Allon, Henry Erskine *OxMus*
Allorto, Riccardo 1921- *NewGrD 80*
Allroggen, Gerhard 1936- *IntWWM 77*
Allsebrook, Ruth *IntWWM 77, -80, WhoMus 72*
Allsop, Alfred Henry 1899- *IntWWM 80, WhoMus 72*
Allt, Wilfrid Greenhouse 1889-1969 *OxMus*
Allton, Minette 1916- *AmSCAP 66, -80*
Allured, Mackenzie 1919- *WhoMus 72*
Alluyah d847? *NewGrD 80*
Allward, Walter Seymour 1876-1955 *CreCan 1*
Allway, Kenneth Willoughby 1932- *WhoMus 72*
Allwood, Richard *NewGrD 80*
Allworth, Frank *Film 2*
Allwyn, Astrid 1909-1978 *FilmEn, FilmgC, ForYSC, HalFC 80, ThFT[port], WhoHol A*
Allyn, Alyce d1976 *WhoHol C*
Allyn, David 1923- *EncJzS 70*
Allyn, Lilly 1866-1944 *WhScrn 74, -77*
Allyn, Marilyn Ione 1946- *AmSCAP 80*
Allyson, June 1917- *BiDFilm, -81, CmpEPM, FilmEn, FilmgC, ForYSC, HalFC 80, IntMPA 77, -76, -78, -79, -80, MGM[port], MotPP, MovMk[port], WhoHol A, WorEFlm[port]*
Allyson, June 1923- *BiDAmM, IntMPA 75*
Allyson, June 1926- *OxFilm*
Allysonn, Richard *NewGrD 80*
Alm, Folke 1917- *IntWWM 80*
Alma-Tadema, Sir Lawrence 1836-1912 *NotNAT B, OxThe, PlP&P*
Almanac Singers *BiDAmM, EncFCWM 69*
Almand, Claude 1915- *BiDAmM*
Almandoz, Norberto 1893-1970 *NewGrD 80*
Almar The Clown *WhScrn 74, -77*
Almasy, Laszlo 1933- *IntWWM 77, -80*
Almaszade, Gamer 1915- *DancEn 78*
Almeida, Antonio De 1928- *NewGrD 80*
Almeida, Eumire Deodato 1942- *AmSCAP 80*
Almeida, Fernando D' 1618?-1660 *Baker 78*
Almeida, Fernando De 1600?-1660 *NewGrD 80*
Almeida, Francisco Antonio De 1702?-1755 *NewGrD 80*
Almeida, Inacio Antonio De 1760-1825 *NewGrD 80*
Almeida, John Kameaaloha 1897- *AmSCAP 80*
Almeida, Laurindo 1917- *AmSCAP 66, -80, BiDAmM, CmpEPM, EncJzS 70, IntWWM 77, -80*
Almeida, Renato 1895- *Baker 78, NewGrD 80*
Almeida Prado, Jose Antonio Rezende De 1943- *IntWWM 77, -80*
Almendros, Nestor 1930- *FilmEn, HalFC 80, OxFilm*
Almenrader, Karl 1786-1843 *Baker 78, BnBkM 80*
Almenraeder, Carl 1786-1843 *NewGrD 80*
Almeri, Giovanni Paolo 1629- *NewGrD 80*
Almerico, Tony 1905-1961 *NewOrJ*
Almgren, Tore Oscar 1935- *IntWWM 77, -80*
Almond, Claude 1915-1957 *ConAmC*
Almond, Genevieve Bujold *CreCan 1*
Almond, John 1946- *EncJzS 70*
Almond, Marsha Renee 1959- *AmSCAP 80*
Almond, Paul 1931- *CreCan 2, FilmEn, FilmgC, HalFC 80, IntMPA 77, -75, -76, -78, -79, -80*
Almorox, Juan *NewGrD 80*
Almquist, Carl Jonas Love 1793-1866 *Baker 78*
Almqvist, Carl Jonas Love 1793-1866 *NewGrD 80, OxThe*
Almroth, Greta 1888- *FilmEn*

Almroth, Grete *Film 1*
Alnaes, Eyvind 1872-1932 *Baker 78, NewGrD 80*
Alnar, Hasan Ferid 1906- *Baker 78*
Alnar, Hasan Ferit 1906- *NewGrD 80*
Aloisi, Giovanni Battista *NewGrD 80*
Aloma, Harold David 1908- *AmSCAP 66, -80*
Alomia Robles, Daniel 1871-1942 *NewGrD 80*
Aloni, Aminadav 1928- *AmSCAP 80*
Aloni, Nissim 1926- *CnThe, REnWD*
Alonso *NewGrD 80*
Alonso, Alberto 1917- *CnOxB*
Alonso, Alicia 1921- *CnOxB, DancEn 78[port]*
Alonso, Fernando 1914- *CnOxB, DancEn 78*
Alonso, Julio 1906-1955 *WhScrn 74, -77, WhoHol B*
Alonso Millan, Juan Jose 1936- *CroCD*
Alonzo, Cecil *BlkAmP, DrBlPA, MorBAP*
Alonzo, John A *FilmEn, FilmgC, HalFC 80*
Alotin, Yardena 1930- *IntWWM 77, -80, NewGrD 80*
Alov, Alexander 1923- *DcFM, FilmEn*
Aloysis *NewGrD 80*
Aloyson, Richard *NewGrD 80*
Alpaerts, Flor 1876-1954 *Baker 78, DcCM, NewGrD 80*
Alpaerts, Jef 1904-1973 *Baker 78, NewGrD 80*
Alpar, Gitta 1900- *WhThe*
Alper, Murray 1904- *ForYSC, HalFC 80, Vers B[port]*
Alperson, Edward L 1896-1969 *FilmgC, HalFC 80*
Alperson, Edward Lee, Jr. 1925- *AmSCAP 66, -80*
Alpert, David A 1929- *AmSCAP 80*
Alpert, Herb *ConMuA 80A, -80B*
Alpert, Herb 1935- *AmSCAP 80, BiDAmM, RkOn 2[port]*
Alpert, Herb 1937- *WhoHol A*
Alpert, Herb And The Tijuana Brass *RkOn[port]*
Alpert, Herman 1916- *BiDAmM*
Alpert, Mickey 1904-1965 *NotNAT B*
Alpert, Milton I 1904-1965 *AmSCAP 66, -80*
Alpert, Pauline *AmSCAP 66, -80*
Alpert, Trigger 1916- *CmpEPM*
Alphonsine 1829-1883 *NotNAT B, OxThe*
Alsager, Thomas Massa 1779-1846 *OxMus*
Alsen, Elsa 1880-1975 *Baker 78*
Alsen, Elsa 1881-1975 *Film 2, WhScrn 77, WhoHol C*
Al'shvang, Arnol'd Alexandrovich 1898-1960 *NewGrD 80*
Alsina, Carlos Roque 1941- *Baker 78, DcCM, NewGrD 80*
Alsleben, Julius 1832-1894 *Baker 78*
Alsop, Frances d1821 *BiDAmM*
Alsop, William M 1905- *WhoJazz 72*
Alsted, Johann Heinrich 1588-1638 *Baker 78, NewGrD 80*
Alstedius, Johann Heinrich 1588-1638 *NewGrD 80*
Alstedt, Johann Heinrich 1588-1638 *NewGrD 80*
Alston, John Denys *WhoMus 72*
Alston, Ovie 1906- *WhoJazz 72*
Alston, Richard 1948- *CnOxB*
Alstrup, Carl 1877-1942 *WhScrn 77*
Alswang, Ralph 1916- *BiE&WWA, NotNAT, PIP&P, WhoThe 72, -77*
Alt, Hansi 1911- *Baker 78, CpmDNM 80, IntWWM 77*
Alt, Natalie *WhThe*
Altacuria, Johannes *NewGrD 80*
Altamari, Amella 1926- *IntWWM 77*
Altar, Cevat Memduh 1902- *Baker 78*
Altem, Mademoiselle *Film 2*
Altenburg, Detlef 1947- *IntWWM 77*
Altenburg, Johann Caspar 1688-1761 *OxMus*
Altenburg, Johann Ernst 1734-1801 *Baker 78, NewGrD 80, OxMus*
Altenburg, Michael 1584-1640 *Baker 78, NewGrD 80*
Altendorf, Wolfgang 1921- *CnMD, CroCD*
Alter, Lottie *WhoStg 1906, -1908*
Alter, Louis 1902- *AmPS, AmSCAP 66, -80, BiDAmM, CmpEPM, PopAmC[port], PopAmC SUP, Sw&Ld C*
Alter, Martha 1904- *ConAmC*
Alter, Paul 1922- *AmSCAP 80*
Alterman, Joseph George 1919- *IntMPA 77, -75, -76, -78, -79, -80*
Alterman, Michael *AmSCAP 80*
Alterman, Nathan 1910-1970 *REnWD*
Altes, Ernest-Eugene 1830-1899 *Baker 78*
Altes, Joseph-Henri d1895 *Baker 78*
Altglass, Max 1886-1952 *Baker 78*
Althoff, Charles R 1890-1962 *NotNAT B, WhScrn 74, -77, WhoHol B*
Althouse, Earl F 1893-1971 *WhScrn 74, -77, WhoHol B*
Althouse, Paul 1889-1954 *Baker 78, BiDAmM, CmOp, MusSN[port], NewEOp 71*
Altieri, Paolo 1745-1820 *NewGrD 80*
Altisent Domenjo, Miguel 1898-1975 *NewGrD 80*
Altman, Adella C *ConAmC*
Altman, Arthur 1912- *AmSCAP 66, -80, CmpEPM*
Altman, Billy *ConMuA 80B*
Altman, Charles *BiE&WWA*
Altman, Elizabeth 1948- *IntWWM 77, -80*
Altman, Frieda 1904- *BiE&WWA, NotNAT, WhoHol A*
Altman, Karen *WhoOp 76*
Altman, Peter Alexander 1943- *ConAmTC*
Altman, Richard 1932- *BiE&WWA, NotNAT*
Altman, Robert *IntMPA 77, -75, -76, -78, -79, -80*
Altman, Robert 1922- *FilmgC, HalFC 80, WhoHrs 80*
Altman, Robert 1925- *BiDFilm, -81, ConLC 16, FilmEn, MovMk[port], OxFilm*
Altman, Ruth *BiE&WWA, WhThe*
Altmann, Gunter 1925- *IntWWM 80*
Altmann, Wilhelm 1862-1951 *Baker 78, NewGrD 80*
Altmeyer, Jeannine Theresa 1948- *WhoOp 76*
Altmeyer, Theo 1931- *NewGrD 80, WhoMus 72*
Altmeyer, Theodor 1931- *NewGrD 80*
Altnickol, Johann Christoph 1720?-1759 *NewGrD 80*
Altnikol, Johann Christoph 1719-1759 *Baker 78*
Altnikol, Johann Christoph 1720?-1759 *NewGrD 80*
Alton, John 1901- *FilmEn, FilmgC, HalFC 80, IntMPA 77, -75, -76, -78, -79, -80, WorEFlm*
Alton, Robert 1897-1957 *EncMT, Ent, HalFC 80*
Alton, Robert 1902-1957 *CnOxB, DancEn 78*
Alton, Robert 1903-1957 *CmMov, FilmgC, NotNAT B*
Alton, Robert 1906-1957 *FilmEn, WorEFlm*
Altrobrandino, Giuseppe Antonio Vincenzo *NewGrD 80*
Altschul, Barry 1943- *EncJzS 70*
Altschul, Mike 1945- *EncJzS 70*
Altschuler, Ernest 1922-1973 *AmSCAP 80*
Altschuler, Modest 1873-1963 *Baker 78*
Altwegg, Raffaele 1938- *IntWWM 77*
Alum, Manuel 1943- *CmpGMD, CnOxB*
Aluredus *NewGrD 80*
Alva, Alonso De d1504? *NewGrD 80*
Alva, Luigi 1927- *Baker 78, CmOp, IntWWM 77, -80, NewGrD 80, WhoMus 72, WhoOp 76*
Alva Talledo, Luis Ernesto *NewGrD 80*
Alvanos, Claire 1935- *IntWWM 77*
Alvarado, Alberto 1864-1939 *Baker 78*
Alvarado, Diego De 1570?-1643 *NewGrD 80*
Alvarado, Diogo De 1570?-1643 *NewGrD 80*
Alvarado, Don 1900-1967 *FilmgC, HalFC 80, WhScrn 74, -77*
Alvarado, Don 1904-1967 *FilmEn, Film 2, ForYSC, TwYS, WhoHol B*
Alvardo, Don 1900-1967 *MotPP, MovMk*
Alvarenga, Oneyda 1911- *NewGrD 80*
Alvares, Anthony Ignatius 1925- *WhoMus 72*
Alvares, Eduardo 1947- *WhoOp 76*
Alvares Frouvo, Joao *NewGrD 80*
Alvarez, Signor *WhoStg 1908*
Alvarez, Albert Raymond 1861-1933 *Baker 78, NewEOp 71, NotNAT B*
Alvarez, Alejandro Rodriguez *McGEWD*
Alvarez, Carmen *BiE&WWA, NotNAT*
Alvarez, Luis Manuel 1939- *IntWWM 77, -80*
Alvarez, Marguerite D' *NewEOp 71*
Alvarez, Santiago *OxFilm*
Alvarez Quintero, Joaquin 1873-1944 *EncWT, Ent, McGEWD[port], ModWD, OxThe*
Alvarez Quintero, Serafin 1871-1938 *EncWT, Ent, McGEWD[port], ModWD, OxThe*
Alvarez Solar-Quintes, Nicolas 1893-1967 *NewGrD 80*
Alvaro *NewGrD 80*
Alvars, Elias Parish *NewGrD 80*
Alvary, Lorenzo 1909- *WhoMus 72*
Alvary, Max 1856-1898 *Baker 78, CmOp, NewEOp 71, NewGrD 80*
Alveri, Giovanni Battista 1660?-1719? *NewGrD 80*
Alves, Laura 1922- *FilmAG WE[port]*
Alves DaCosta, Joaquim 1903- *FilmAG WE[port]*
Alves DaCunha, Jose Maria 1889-1956 *FilmAG WE[port]*
Alvin, Danny 1902-1958 *CmpEPM, WhoJazz 72*
Alvin, John 1917- *ForYSC, IntMPA 77, -75, -76, -78, -79, -80, WhoHol A*
Alvin, Juliette *IntWWM 77, -80, WhoMus 72*
Alvina, Anicee 1953- *FilmAG WE*
Alvis, Hayes 1907-1972 *BiDAmM, CmpEPM, EncJzS 70, WhoJazz 72*
Alvord, Robert W 1933- *IntWWM 77*
Alvsleben, Melitta *NewGrD 80*
Alvy, Theodore Bruce 1948- *AmSCAP 80*
Alwin, Karl 1891-1945 *Baker 78*
Alwood, Richard *NewGrD 80*
Alwoode, Richard *NewGrD 80*
Alwyn, Kenneth 1925- *NewGrD 80*
Alwyn, Kenneth 1928- *IntWWM 77, -80*
Alwyn, William 1905- *Baker 78, DcCom&M 79, FilmEn, FilmgC, HalFC 80, IntMPA 77, -75, -76, -78, -79, -80, IntWWM 77, -80, MusMk, NewGrD 80, OxFilm, OxMus, WhoMus 72, WorEFlm*
Alyabyev, Alexander Alexandrovich 1787-1851 *NewGrD 80*
Alyff *NewGrD 80*
Alyn, Kirk 1910- *FilmEn, What 5[port], WhoHol A*
Alyn, Kirk 1915- *WhoHrs 80[port]*
Alyoshin, Samuil 1913- *CnMD, ModWD*
Alypios *Baker 78*
Alypius *NewGrD 80*
Alzedo, Jose Bernardo *NewGrD 80*
Am Bach, Rudolf 1919- *IntWWM 77, -80*
Amacker, Frank 1890-1976 *NewOrJ[port]*
Amadei, Filippo 1670?-1729? *Baker 78, NewGrD 80*
Amadei, Michelangelo *NewGrD 80*
Amadino, Ricciardo *NewGrD 80*
Amadio, Neville 1912- *NewGrD 80*
Amadio, Pippo *NewGrD 80*
Amadis, Pietro *NewGrD 80*
Amador, Graciela *PupTheA*
Amadori, Giuseppe 1670?-1730? *NewGrD 80*
Amadori, Luis Cesar 1902- *DcFM*
Amaducci, Bruno 1925- *IntWWM 77*
Amaducci, Bruno 1935- *IntWWM 80*
Amalar 775?-850? *NewGrD 80*
Amalarius Fortunatus 775?-850? *NewGrD 80*
Amalarius Of Metz 775?-850? *NewGrD 80*
Amalbert, Emmanuel Juan *AmSCAP 80*
Amalherus 775?-850? *NewGrD 80*
Amalia Catharina, Countess Of Erbach 1640-1697 *Baker 78, NewGrD 80*
Amalia Friederike, Princess Of Saxony 1794-1870 *Baker 78*
Amanat 1816-1859 *EncWT*
Amance, Paul D' *NewGrD 80*
Amani, Nikolai 1872-1904 *Baker 78*
Amar, Licco 1891-1959 *Baker 78*
Amara, Lucine 1927- *Baker 78, MusSN[port], NewEOp 71, NewGrD 80, WhoMus 72, WhoOp 76*
Amaral, Nestor 1913-1962 *AmSCAP 66, -80*
Amarante, Estevao 1890-1952 *WhScrn 74, -77*
Amat, Joan Carlos 1572?-1642 *NewGrD 80*
Amat, Juan Carlos 1572-1642 *Baker 78*
Amateau, Rod *NewYTET*
Amateau, Rod 1923- *FilmEn, FilmgC,*

HalFC 80, IntMPA 75
Amateau, Rod 1927- IntMPA 77, -76, -78, -79, -80
Amati BnBkM 80, NewGrD 80
Amati, Andrea 1500?-1580? Baker 78
Amati, Andrea 1511?-1580? NewGrD 80
Amati, Andrea 1520?-1578? BnBkM 80
Amati, Antonio 1538?-1595? Baker 78
Amati, Antonio 1540?- NewGrD 80
Amati, Antonio 1550?-1638 BnBkM 80
Amati, Girolamo 1551-1635 BnBkM 80
Amati, Girolamo 1561?-1630 Baker 78, NewGrD 80
Amati, Girolamo 1649-1740 Baker 78, BnBkM 80, NewGrD 80
Amati, Hieronymus 1561-1630 NewGrD 80
Amati, Hieronymus 1649-1740 NewGrD 80
Amati, Nicola 1596-1684 Baker 78, NewGrD 80
Amati, Nicolaus 1596-1684 NewGrD 80
Amati, Nicolo NewGrD 80
Amati, Nicolo 1596-1684 BnBkM 80
Amati, Olga 1924- CnOxB, DancEn 78[port]
Amati, Orlanda IntWWM 77, -80
Amati Family Baker 78
Amatniek, Kathie WomWMM B
Amato, Bruno 1936- ConAmC
Amato, Giuseppe 1899-1964 FilmEn, FilmgC, HalFC 80, WhScrn 77
Amato, Pasquale 1878-1942 Baker 78, BiDAmM, MusSN[port], NewEOp 71, NewGrD 80[port], WhoHol B
Amato, Vincenzo 1629-1670 NewGrD 80
Amatucci, Paolo 1868-1935 NewGrD 80
Amaya, Carmen 1913-1963 CnOxB, DancEn 78, NotNAT B, WhScrn 74, -77, WhoHol B
Amazing Rhythm Aces ConMuA 80A, IlEncCM[port], IlEncR[port]
Ambache, Diana Bella 1948- IntWWM 77
Amber, Lili AmSCAP 80
Amber, Mabel d1945 NotNAT B
Amber, Maude d1938 NotNAT B
Amberg, George 1901-1971 CnOxB
Amberg, George H 1901-1971 DancEn 78
Amberg, Gustave 1844-1921 NotNAT B
Ambesser, Axel Von 1910- CnMD
Ambiela, Miguel De 1666?-1733 NewGrD 80
Ambient, Mark 1860-1937 NotNAT B, WhThe
Ambler, Eric 1909- FilmEn, FilmgC, HalFC 80, OxFilm
Ambler, Joss 1900-1959 FilmgC, HalFC 80, WhScrn 74, -77, WhoHol B
Ambleville, Charles D' d1637 NewGrD 80
Amboise, Jacques D' 1934- CnOxB
Amboy Dukes, The BiDAmM, ConMuA 80A
Ambrogini, Angelo McGEWD
Ambrogini Poliziano, Angelo NewGrD 80
Ambros, August Wilhelm 1816-1876 Baker 78, BnBkM 80, NewGrD 80, OxMus
Ambros, Vladimir 1890-1956 NewGrD 80
Ambros-Wiencek, Beata 1937- IntWWM 80
Ambrosch, Joseph Karl 1759-1822 NewGrD 80
Ambrose BgBands 74
Ambrose 333?-397 Baker 78
Ambrose, Saint 340?-397 NewGrD 80, OxMus
Ambrose, Bert 1897-1971 EncJzS 70, NewGrD 80
Ambrose, Bert 1897-1973 CmpEPM
Ambrose, John NewGrD 80
Ambrose, Katherine Charlotte CreCan 2
Ambrose, Kay 1914-1971 CnOxB, CreCan 2, DancEn 78
Ambrose, Robert Steele 1824-1908 BiDAmM
Ambrosetti, Flavio 1919- EncJzS 70
Ambrosetti, Franco 1941- EncJzS 70
Ambrosi, Marietta NotNAT A
Ambrosio, Alfredo D' 1871-1914 Baker 78
Ambrosio, Arturo 1869-1960 DcFM, FilmEn, OxFilm
Ambrosio, Giacomo D' NewGrD 80
Ambrosio, Giovanni NewGrD 80
Ambrosio, Jacovo D' NewGrD 80
Ambrosius, Hermann 1897- Baker 78, IntWWM 77, -80
Ambroziak, Delfina 1939- WhoOp 76
Ambruys, Honore D' NewGrD 80
Ameche, Don IntMPA 75, -76
Ameche, Don 1908- BiE&WWA, CmMov, CmpEPM, EncMT, FilmEn, FilmgC, ForYSC, HalFC 80, IntMPA 77, -78, -79, -80, MotPP, MovMk[port], WhoHol A, WhoThe 72, -77
Ameche, Don 1910- OxFilm
Amedeo, Edy Letizia 1935- WhoOp 76
Ameipsias OxThe
Ameling, Elisabeth 1938- NewGrD 80
Ameling, Elly 1938- BnBkM 80, IntWWM 77, -80, NewGrD 80, WhoMus 72
Ameller, Andre Charles Gabriel 1912- Baker 78, IntWWM 77, -80, WhoMus 72
Ameln, Konrad 1899- NewGrD 80
Amemiya, Yasukazu 1938- AmSCAP 80
Amemiya, Yasukazu 1939- IntWWM 77, -80
Amenabar, Juan 1922- DcCM, NewGrD 80
Amend, Erwin 1919- IntWWM 77, -80
Amendola, Giuseppe 1750?-1808 NewGrD 80
Amendola, Richard 1951- AmSCAP 80
Amengual, Rene 1911-1954 Baker 78, NewGrD 80
Amengual-Astaburuaga, Rene 1911-1954 DcCM
Amenreich, Bernhard 1535?-1576? NewGrD 80
Amerbach, Bonifacius 1495-1562 NewGrD 80
America BiDAmM, ConMuA 80A, IlEncR, RkOn 2[port]
American Breed, The BiDAmM, RkOn 2[port]
American Ragtime Octette BiDAmM
Amerson, Richard Manuel 1887?- BluesWW
Amerus NewGrD 80
Amerval, Eloy D' NewGrD 80
Ames, Adrienne d1947 MotPP, NotNAT B, WhoHol B
Ames, Adrienne 1907-1947 FilmEn, ThFT[port]
Ames, Adrienne 1908-1947 ForYSC
Ames, Adrienne 1909-1947 HalFC 80, WhScrn 74, -77
Ames, Ed 1927- RkOn 2[port]
Ames, Florenz 1884- WhThe
Ames, Gerald 1881-1933 FilmEn, Film 1, -2, IlWWBF[port], NotNAT B, WhScrn 74, -77, WhThe, WhoHol B
Ames, Harry 1893-1969 WhScrn 74, -77
Ames, Jimmy 1915-1965 WhScrn 74, -77
Ames, Leon 1901- WhThe
Ames, Leon 1903- BiE&WWA, FilmEn, FilmgC, ForYSC, HalFC 80, HolCA[port], IntMPA 77, -75, -76, -78, -79, -80, MGM[port], MotPP, MovMk[port], NotNAT, Vers B[port], WhoHol A
Ames, Lionel WhoHol A
Ames, Louis B 1918- IntMPA 77, -75, -76, -78, -79, -80
Ames, Michael d1972 WhoHol B
Ames, Morgan AmSCAP 80
Ames, Percy 1874-1936 Film 2, NotNAT B, WhScrn 77, WhoHol B
Ames, Rachel WhoHol A
Ames, Ramsay 1919- FilmEn, ForYSC, WhoHol A
Ames, Ramsay 1924- FilmgC, HalFC 80
Ames, Richard 1937- WhoOp 76
Ames, Robert 1889-1931 Film 2, ForYSC, NotNAT B, WhoHol B
Ames, Robert 1893-1931 WhThe
Ames, Robert 1898-1931 WhScrn 74, -77
Ames, Rosemary 1906- WhThe
Ames, Tessie BluesWW
Ames, William T 1901- ConAmC
Ames, Winthrop 1870-1937 NotNAT B
Ames, Winthrop 1871-1937 EncWT, OxThe, PlP&P, WhThe
Ames Brothers, The AmPS A, -B, BiDAmM, CmpEPM, RkOn[port]
Amess, Frederick Arthur 1909- CreCan 2
Amet, Edward H FilmEn
Ameyden, Christian 1534?-1605 NewGrD 80
Amfiteatrov, Daniele 1901- Baker 78
Amfiteatrov, Massimo 1907- NewGrD 80
Amfitheatrof, Daniele 1901- AmSCAP 66, -80, BiDAmM, ConAmC, FilmEn, FilmgC, HalFC 80, IntMPA 77, -75, -76, -78, -79, -80, IntWWM 77, -80, NewGrD 80, OxFilm, WorEFlm
Amfitheatrof, Massimo 1907- NewGrD 80
Amfitheatrov, Daniele 1901- NewGrD 80
Amherst, J H 1776-1851 NotNAT B
Amherst, Jillian 1933- IntWWM 77
Amherst, Nigel 1929- WhoMus 72
Ami DuClavier, Un NewGrD 80
Amic, Henri 1853- WhThe
Amic, Henry d1929 NotNAT B
Amicis, Anna Lucia De NewGrD 80
Amidei, Sergio 1904- DcFM, FilmEn, OxFilm
Amiel, Denys 1884- EncWT, McGEWD[port], WhThe
Amiel, Josette 1930- CnOxB, DancEn 78[port]
Amiot, Jean Joseph Marie 1718-1793 NewGrD 80
Amiot, Pere Joseph Marie 1718-1793 Baker 78
Amir, Aziza WomWMM
Amir, Nahun 1936- NewGrD 80
Amiran-Pougatchov, Emanuel 1909- IntWWM 77, -80, NewGrD 80
Amirkhanian, Charles Benjamin 1945- Baker 78, ConAmC
Amirov, Fikret Dzhamil 1922- Baker 78, NewGrD 80
Amis, John 1922- WhoMus 72
Amis, Kingsley 1922- FilmgC, HalFC 80
Amis, Lola 1930- BlkAmP
Ammann, Benno 1904- Baker 78, IntWWM 80
Ammelrooy, Willeke Van FilmAG WE
Ammerbach, Elias Nikolaus 1530?-1597 Baker 78, NewGrD 80
Ammidon, Hoyt 1909- BiE&WWA, NotNAT
Ammirati, John Lewis 1944- AmSCAP 80
Ammon, Blasius 1558-1590 Baker 78
Ammon, Blasius 1560-1590 MusMk, NewGrD 80
Ammon, Conrad NewGrD 80
Ammon, Wolfgang 1540-1589 NewGrD 80
Ammons, Albert 1907-1949 BiDAmM, CmpEPM, IlEncJ, NewGrD 80, WhoJazz 72
Ammons, Eugene 1925-1974 BiDAmM, EncJzS 70
Ammons, Gene 1925-1974 CmpEPM, EncJzS 70, IlEncJ
Ammons, Jug 1925-1974 EncJzS 70
Amner, John 1579?-1641 NewGrD 80
Amodei, Cataldo 1650?-1695? NewGrD 80
Amodio, Amedeo 1940- CnOxB
Amon, Blasius NewGrD 80
Amon, Johann 1763-1825 Baker 78
Amon, Johannes Andreas 1763-1825 NewGrD 80
Amon Duul II IlEncR
Amor, Carlos Film 2
Amores, Adelina 1883-1958 WhScrn 74, -77
Amorevoli, Angelo 1716-1798 NewGrD 80
Amorose, Anthony Alfred 1918- AmSCAP 80
Amos BluesWW
Amos, John 1939- DrBlPA, MorBAP, WhoHol A
Amos 'n' Andy JoeFr[port], What 1[port], -5[port]
Amoyal, Pierre 1949- IntWWM 77, -80
Amr Ibn Bana 820?-891 NewGrD 80
Amram, Aharon 1937- IntWWM 80
Amram, David Werner 1930- Baker 78, BiDAmM, BiE&WWA, CpmDNM 79, ConAmC, DcCM, EncJzS 70, IntWWM 77, -80, NewEOp 71, NewGrD 80, NotNAT
Amsberry, Robert Wayne 1928-1957 AmSCAP 80
Amsden, Minneola d1962 NotNAT B
Amstell, Billy 1911- IntWWM 77, WhoMus 72
Amsterdam, Chet 1926- AmSCAP 66, -80
Amsterdam, Morey WhoHol A
Amsterdam, Morey 1912- AmSCAP 66, BiDAmM, ForYSC
Amsterdam, Morey 1914- AmSCAP 80, IntMPA 77, -75, -76, -78, -79, -80, JoeFr[port]
Amuanarriz, Raul Cancio 1911-1961 WhScrn 77
Amuarriz, Raul Cancio 1911-1961 WhScrn 74
Amunarriz, Raul Cancio 1911-1961 NotNAT B
Amundrud, Lawrence 1954- IntWWM 77, -80
Amundsen, Signe 1899- IntWWM 77, -80
Amway, John C 1904- AmSCAP 66
Amy, Curtis Edward 1929- BiDAmM
Amy, George J 1903- FilmEn, HalFC 80
Amy, Gilbert 1936- Baker 78, CpmDNM 80, DcCM, NewGrD 80, WhoMus 72

Amyes, Julian 1917- *FilmgC, HalFC 80, IntMPA 77, -75, -76, -78, -79, -80*
Amzallag, Avraham 1941- *IntWWM 77, -80*
Ana, Francesco D' 1460?-1503? *NewGrD 80*
Anacker, August Ferdinand 1790-1854 *NewGrD 80*
Anacreon 570?BC-485?BC *NewGrD 80*
Anagnino, Spirito *NewGrD 80*
Anagnoson, James 1947- *IntWWM 80*
Anaguino, Spirito *NewGrD 80*
Analla, Isabel 1920-1958 *WhScrn 74, -77, WhoHol B*
Ananeotes, Michael *NewGrD 80*
Anaya, Dulce 1933- *CnOxB, DancEn 78[port]*
Ancerl, Karel 1908-1973 *Baker 78, NewGrD 80[port], WhoMus 72*
Ancey, Georges 1860 1917 *EncWT, ModWD*
Ancey, Georges 1860-1926 *NotNAT B, OxThe*
Anchieta, Juan De 1462-1523 *NewGrD 80*
Ancina, Giovanni Giovenale 1545-1604 *Baker 78*
Ancina, Giovenale 1545-1604 *NewGrD 80*
Ancliffe, Charles d1953 *NotNAT B*
Ancliffe, Charles 1880-1952 *NewGrD 80*
Ancona, Mario 1860-1931 *Baker 78, NewEOp 71, NewGrD 80*
Ancot *NewGrD 80*
Ancot, Jean 1779-1848 *Baker 78, NewGrD 80*
Ancot, Jean 1799-1829 *Baker 78, NewGrD 80*
Ancot, Louis 1803-1836 *Baker 78, NewGrD 80*
Ancot Family *Baker 78*
Anda, Geza 1921-1976 *Baker 78, BnBkM 80, NewGrD 80, WhoMus 72*
Andalina, Michael J 1925- *AmSCAP 66, -80*
Anday, Melih Cevdet 1915- *REnWD*
Andean, Richard *Film 1*
Ander, Charlotte *Film 2*
Anderberg, Carl-Olof 1914-1972 *Baker 78, NewGrD 80*
Andergast, Maria 1912- *FilmAG WE*
Anderman, Maureen *PlP&P A*
Anders, Glenn 1889- *BiE&WWA, Film 2, FilmgC, HalFC 80, NotNAT, PlP&P, WhoHol A*
Anders, Glenn 1890- *ForYSC, WhThe*
Anders, Hendrik 1657-1714 *NewGrD 80*
Anders, John Frank 1907- *AmSCAP 80*
Anders, Jorge 1939- *EncJzS 70*
Anders, Luana 1940?- *FilmEn, FilmgC, HalFC 80, WhoHol A, WhoHrs 80*
Anders, Merry 1932?- *FilmEn, FilmgC, ForYSC, HalFC 80, MotPP, WhoHrs 80[port]*
Anders, Peter 1908-1954 *CmOp, NewGrD 80*
Andersen, Anton Jorgen 1845-1926 *NewGrD 80*
Andersen, Arild 1945- *EncJzS 70*
Andersen, Arthur Olaf 1880-1958 *AmSCAP 66, -80, BiDAmM, ConAmC*
Andersen, Dennis R 1947- *NatPD[port]*
Andersen, Diane Bricault 1934- *IntWWM 77*
Andersen, Diane-Bricault 1934- *IntWWM 80*
Andersen, Elnore-Crampton 1933- *IntWWM 77*
Andersen, Eric 1943- *ConMuA 80A, IlEncR*
Andersen, Hans Christian 1805-1875 *CnOxB, DcPup, FilmgC, HalFC 80, NewEOp 71, NotNAT B*
Andersen, Harald Fridolf 1919- *IntWWM 80*
Andersen, Ib 1954- *CnOxB*
Andersen, Joachim 1847-1909 *Baker 78*
Andersen, John *Film 2*
Andersen, Karl August 1903-1970 *Baker 78*
Andersen, Karl Joachim 1847-1909 *NewGrD 80*
Andersen, Karsten 1920- *IntWWM 77, -80*
Andersen, Marjorie Elnore Crampton 1933- *IntWWM 80*
Andersen, Martin 1886- *IntWWM 77*
Andersen, Martin 1889- *IntWWM 80*
Andersen, Michael 1938- *AmSCAP 66, -80, BiDAmM, ConAmC*
Andersen, Ruth 1931- *DancEn 78*
Andersen, Werner 1930- *DancEn 78*
Andersen, Yvonne *WomWMM A, -B*
Anderson, Adeline Teresa 1933- *IntWWM 77*
Anderson, Albert 1869-1926 *BlksBF*
Anderson, Amelia *WomWMM B*
Anderson, Andy *Film 1*
Anderson, Andy 1910- *WhoJazz 72*
Anderson, Andy 1912- *NewOrJ[port]*
Anderson, Arthur 1898- *Baker 78*
Anderson, Arvid Christian *IntWWM 77*
Anderson, Audley 1885-1966 *WhScrn 77*
Anderson, Beth 1950- *ConAmC, IntWWM 77, -80*
Anderson, Beverly 1932- *BiE&WWA*
Anderson, Bibi 1935- *ForYSC, IntMPA 77, -75, -76, -78*
Anderson, Bill 1937- *CounME 74[port], -74A, EncFCWM 69, IlEncCM[port]*
Anderson, Broncho Billy 1883-1971 *CmMov*
Anderson, Bronco Billy 1882-1970 *TwYS*
Anderson, Buddy 1919- *WhoJazz 72*
Anderson, C E *Film 2*
Anderson, Cap *Film 2*
Anderson, Carl *DrBlPA, WhoHol A*
Anderson, Carl E 1892- *AmSCAP 66, -80*
Anderson, Carol Grace 1945- *AmSCAP 80*
Anderson, Cat 1916- *CmpEPM, EncJzS 70, WhoJazz 72*
Anderson, Catherine *PupTheA*
Anderson, Clair 1896-1964 *NotNAT B*
Anderson, Claire 1896-1964 *Film 1, -2, MotPP, WhScrn 74, -77, WhoHol B*
Anderson, Clinton *WhoHol A*
Anderson, Cora *Film 1*
Anderson, Dallas d1934 *NotNAT B*
Anderson, Daphne 1922- *FilmEn, FilmgC, HalFC 80, IntMPA 77, -75, -76, -78, -79, -80, WhoThe 72, -77*
Anderson, Dave *Film 1*
Anderson, Dennis 1951- *ConAmC*
Anderson, Dina *WhoHol A*
Anderson, Donna *MotPP, WhoHol A*
Anderson, Doug *PupTheA*
Anderson, Dusty *WhoHol A*
Anderson, Ed 1906- *BiDAmM*
Anderson, Eddie 1905-1977 *BlksBF, DrBlPA, FilmEn, FilmgC, ForYSC, HalFC 80, IntMPA 77, -75, -76, -78, -79, -80, JoeFr[port], MotPP, MovMk[port], What 4[port], WhoHol A*
Anderson, Edgar W 1931- *IntWWM 77*
Anderson, Edmund 1912- *AmSCAP 66, -80*
Anderson, Edwin D, Jr. 1933- *IntWWM 77, -80*
Anderson, Elisabeth *DancEn 78*
Anderson, Elizabeth Jane 1930- *BiDAmM*
Anderson, Emily 1891-1962 *Baker 78, NewGrD 80*
Anderson, Erica *WomWMM B*
Anderson, Ernest *DrBlPA, WhoHol A*
Anderson, Ernestine Irene 1928- *BiDAmM*
Anderson, Esther *DrBlPA*
Anderson, Eugene *ConAmC*
Anderson, Everett L 1900- *AmSCAP 66*
Anderson, Florence d1962 *NotNAT B*
Anderson, Frank H, Jr. 1895-1952 *AmSCAP 66, -80*
Anderson, G M 1882-1971 *FilmEn, HalFC 80, WhoHol B*
Anderson, G M 1882-1972 *FilmgC, MotPP*
Anderson, Garland 1887?-1939 *BlkAmP, DrBlPA, MorBAP, NotNAT B*
Anderson, Garland Lee 1933- *AmSCAP 80, ConAmC, IntWWM 77, -80*
Anderson, Gayle *PupTheA*
Anderson, Gene 1931-1965 *WhScrn 74, -77, WhoHol B*
Anderson, George *Film 1*
Anderson, George 1891-1948 *WhScrn 74, -77, WhoHol B*
Anderson, George Walter 1932- *ConAmTC*
Anderson, Gerry 1929- *HalFC 80, IntMPA 77, -75, -76, -78, -79, -80*
Anderson, Gia *WhoHol A*
Anderson, Gilbert M Broncho Billy 1882-1971 *WhScrn 74, -77*
Anderson, Gilbert M Broncho Billy 1883?-1971 *OxFilm, WorEFlm*
Anderson, Gilbert M Bronco Billy 1882-1970 *Film 1, -2*
Anderson, Gillian Bunshaft 1943- *IntWWM 80*
Anderson, Gordon Athol 1929- *IntWWM 80, NewGrD 80*
Anderson, Harry L 1910- *IntWWM 77, -80*
Anderson, Henry *IntMPA 77, -75, -76, -78, -79, -80*
Anderson, Herbert 1917- *ForYSC, WhoHol A*
Anderson, Horace James 1893- *WhoMus 72*
Anderson, Ian 1947- *BiDAmM*
Anderson, Ida *BlksBF*
Anderson, Ivie *AmPS B*
Anderson, Ivie 1904-1949 *IlEncJ*
Anderson, Ivie 1905-1949 *WhoJazz 72*
Anderson, Ivie 1909-1949 *WhScrn 77*
Anderson, Ivy 1904-1949 *BiDAmM, CmpEPM*
Anderson, J Grant 1897- *WhoThe 72, -77*
Anderson, Jack 1935- *CnOxB*
Anderson, James 1872-1953 *Film 2, WhScrn 74, -77, WhoHol B*
Anderson, James 1899-1965 *IlWWBF*
Anderson, James 1921-1969 *FilmEn, FilmgC, ForYSC, HalFC 80, WhScrn 74, -77, WhoHol B*
Anderson, James Granville 1946- *IntWWM 77, -80*
Anderson, James William, III 1937- *BiDAmM*
Anderson, Jay 1920- *IntWWM 80*
Anderson, Jean 1908- *FilmgC, HalFC 80*
Anderson, Jean 1923- *WhoMus 72*
Anderson, Joan d1974 *WhScrn 77*
Anderson, John *ForYSC, WhoHol A*
Anderson, John 1922- *FilmEn*
Anderson, John 1925?- *HalFC 80*
Anderson, John, Jr. 1921-1974 *EncJzS 70*
Anderson, John Hargis 1896-1943 *NotNAT B, WhThe*
Anderson, John Henry 1814-1874 *MagIlD[port], NotNAT A, -B*
Anderson, John Maxwell 1948- *AmSCAP 80*
Anderson, John Murray 1886-1954 *AmSCAP 66, -80, BiDAmM, CmpEPM, EncMT, Ent, NotNAT A, -B, WhThe*
Anderson, Joyce Giegerich 1936- *IntWWM 77*
Anderson, Judith 1898- *BiE&WWA, CnThe, EncWT, Ent, FamA&A[port], FilmEn, FilmgC, ForYSC, HalFC 80, HolCA[port], IntMPA 77, -75, -76, -78, -79, -80, MotPP, MovMk[port], NotNAT, OxFilm, OxThe, WhoHol A, WhoThe 72, -77*
Anderson, Julia 1864-1950 *NotNAT B*
Anderson, Karen 1945- *IntWWM 77, -80*
Anderson, Kenneth 1903- *IntWWM 77, -80, WhoMus 72*
Anderson, Laurie 1947- *Baker 78*
Anderson, Lawrence 1893-1939 *WhScrn 77, WhThe*
Anderson, Leona *WhoHrs 80[port]*
Anderson, Leonard Sinclair 1935- *IntWWM 77*
Anderson, Leroy 1908-1975 *AmPS, -A, AmSCAP 66, -80, Baker 78, BiDAmM, BiE&WWA, CmpEPM, ConAmC, NewGrD 80, NotNAT, PopAmC[port], PopAmC SUP, PopAmC SUPN, WhoMus 72*
Anderson, LeRoy B 1930- *IntWWM 77*
Anderson, Lillian 1881-1962 *WhScrn 77*
Anderson, Lindsay 1923- *BiDFilm, -81, DcFM, EncWT, Ent, FilmEn, FilmgC, HalFC 80, IlWWBF, -A, IntMPA 77, -75, -76, -78, -79, -80, MovMk[port], NotNAT, OxFilm, WhoThe 72, -77, WorEFlm[port]*
Anderson, Liz 1930- *CounME 74, -74A, IlEncCM*
Anderson, Lucy 1797-1878 *NewGrD 80*
Anderson, Lynn 1947- *CounME 74[port], -74A, IlEncCM[port]*
Anderson, Lynn Rene 1947- *BiDAmM, RkOn 2[port]*
Anderson, Madeline *WomWMM A, -B*
Anderson, Margaret Ann Bissell 1927- *IntWWM 77, -80*
Anderson, Margaret Monteath 1918- *WhoMus 72*
Anderson, Marian 1902- *Baker 78, BiDAmM, BnBkM 80[port], CmOp, DrBlPA, MusMk, MusSN[port], NewEOp 71, NewGrD 80, WhoMus 72*
Anderson, Marion Roberta 1892- *WhoMus 72*
Anderson, Mary 1859-1940 *FamA&A[port], Film 1, -2, MotPP, NotNAT A, -B, OxThe, WhThe, WhoStg 1906, -1908*
Anderson, Mary 1920- *FilmEn, FilmgC, HalFC 80, WhoHol A*
Anderson, Mary 1922- *ForYSC*
Anderson, Mary Beth 1954- *AmSCAP 80*
Anderson, Max 1914-1959 *FilmEn, FilmgC, HalFC 80*
Anderson, Maxwell 1888-1959 *AmSCAP 66, -80, BiDAmM, CmpEPM, CnMD,*

CnThe, CroCD, DcLB 7[port], EncMT, EncWT, Ent, FilmEn, FilmgC, HalFC 80, McGEWD[port], ModWD, NewCBMT, NotNAT A, -B, OxThe, PlP&P[port], REnWD[port], WhThe, WorEFlm[port]
Anderson, Michael 1920- BiDFilm, -81, CmMov, FilmEn, FilmgC, HalFC 80, IIWWBF, IntMPA 77, -75, -76, -78, -79, -80, MovMk[port], WhoHrs 80, WorEFlm
Anderson, Michael, Jr. 1943- FilmgC, ForYSC, HalFC 80, IntMPA 77, -75, -76, -78, -79, -80, WhoHol A
Anderson, Michael Stothart 1934- IntWWM 80
Anderson, Mignon Film 1, MotPP
Anderson, Myrtle DrBlPA
Anderson, Nellie Film 1
Anderson, Nicholas Maurice William 1941- IntWWM 77, -80
Anderson, Nicola Charlotte 1940- IntWWM 77, -80, WhoMus 72
Anderson, Norman WhoMus 72
Anderson, Odie 1943- BlkAmP
Anderson, Patrick 1915- CreCan 2
Anderson, Percy d1928 NotNAT B
Anderson, Phyllis Stohl d1956 NotNAT B
Anderson, Pink 1900-1974 BluesWW[port]
Anderson, R Alex 1894- AmSCAP 66
Anderson, Richard 1926- BiE&WWA, FilmEn, FilmgC, ForYSC, HalFC 80, IntMPA 78, -79, -80, MovMk, NotNAT, WhoHol A, WhoHrs 80
Anderson, Robert Film 1, -2
Anderson, Robert 1917- BiE&WWA, CnMD, ConDr 73, -77, CroCD, DcLB 7[port], EncWT, Ent, FilmEn, McGEWD[port], ModWD, NatPD[port], NotNAT, WhoThe 77
Anderson, Robert Alexander 1894- AmSCAP 80
Anderson, Robert Brown 1910- IntWWM 77, WhoMus 72
Anderson, Robert David 1927- IntWWM 77, -80
Anderson, Robert T 1934- WhoMus 72
Anderson, Robert Woodruff 1917- WhoThe 72
Anderson, Roland IntMPA 77, -75, -76, -78, -79, -80
Anderson, Rona 1926- FilmgC, HalFC 80, IIWWBF[port]
Anderson, Rona 1928- WhoThe 72, -77
Anderson, Ronald K 1934- IntWWM 77, -80
Anderson, Ronald Kinloch 1911- IntWWM 77, -80
Anderson, Ross 1929- IntWWM 77, -80
Anderson, Ruth 1928- Baker 78, CpmDNM 80, ConAmC
Anderson, Sherwood 1876-1941 NotNAT B
Anderson, Stig 1931- ConMuA 80B, IntWWM 77, -80
Anderson, Sylvia IntMPA 77, -75, -76, -78, -79, -80, WhoOp 76, WomWMM
Anderson, T Diane BlkAmP
Anderson, T J 1928- Baker 78
Anderson, Thomas MorBAP, WhoHol A
Anderson, Thomas 1836-1903 Baker 78
Anderson, Thomas 1906- DrBlPA
Anderson, Thomas Jefferson, Jr. 1928- BiDAmM, BlkCS[port], ConAmC, NewGrD 80
Anderson, Vernon A 1932- IntWWM 77
Anderson, W H 1882-1955 NewGrD 80
Anderson, W R 1891-1979 NewGrD 80
Anderson, Walt MorBAP
Anderson, Walter 1915- BiDAmM
Anderson, Warner 1911-1976 FilmEn, FilmgC, ForYSC, HalFC 80, HolCA[port], IntMPA 77, -75, -76, MotPP, MovMk, WhoHol A
Anderson, Warren DeWitt 1920- IntWWM 80
Anderson, William Alonzo 1916- AmSCAP 66, -80, BiDAmM, EncJzS 70
Anderson, William H 1911- IntMPA 77, -75, -76, -78, -79, -80
Anderson, William Henry 1882-1955 CreCan 2
Anderson, William Ketcham 1888-1947 BiDAmM
Anderson, William Miller 1940- IntWWM 77, -80
Anderson, William Robert 1891- OxMus, WhoMus 72
Anderson-Ivantzova, Elisabeth 1893?-1973 CnOxB
Anderssen, Alfred 1887-1940 Baker 78
Andersson, Bibi 1935- BiDFilm, -81, EncWT, Ent, FilmEn, FilmgC, HalFC 80, IntMPA 79, -80, MotPP, OxFilm, WhoHol A, WorEFlm
Andersson, Bibi 1936- MovMk[port]
Andersson, Gerd 1932- CnOxB, DancEn 78[port]
Andersson, Harriet 1932- BiDFilm, -81, FilmEn, FilmgC, HalFC 80, OxFilm, WhoHol A, WorEFlm
Andersson, Henrik 1915- IntWWM 77
Andersson, Laila Elisabeth 1941- WhoOp 76
Andersson, Nils 1864-1921 NewGrD 80
Andersson, Olaf OxMus
Andersson, Otto 1879-1969 NewGrD 80
Andersson, Per Ake 1935- WhoOp 76
Andersson, Richard 1851-1918 NewGrD 80
Anderton, Elizabeth 1938- CnOxB, DancEn 78
Andes, Keith 1920- BiE&WWA, FilmEn, FilmgC, ForYSC, HalFC 80, IntMPA 77, -75, -78, -79, -80, MotPP, NotNAT, WhoHol A
Andjaparidze, Marija WomWMM
Andon, Arma ConMuA 80B
Andor, Eva 1939- WhoOp 76
Andor, Paul WhoHol A
Andra, Anny Film 2
Andra, Fern 1893-1974 FilmEn, WhScrn 77, WhoHol B
Andrade, Adolfo 1925- CnOxB, DancEn 78
Andrade, Daniel Ray 1929- BiDAmM
Andrade, Francesco D' 1859-1921 Baker 78
Andrade, Jorge 1922- REnWD[port]
Andrade, Mario De 1893-1945 Baker 78, NewGrD 80
Andrae, Hieronymus NewGrD 80
Andre NewGrD 80
Andre, Adolf 1885-1910 Baker 78
Andre, Anton 1775-1842 Baker 78
Andre, Carl August 1806-1887 Baker 78, NewGrD 80
Andre, Charles-Louis-Joseph 1765-1839 NewGrD 80
Andre, Dean AmSCAP 80
Andre, Fabian 1910-1960 AmSCAP 66, -80
Andre, Franz 1893-1975 Baker 78, NewGrD 80
Andre, Gaby d1972 ForYSC, WhScrn 77, WhoHol B
Andre, Gwili 1908-1947 ForYSC
Andre, Gwili 1908-1959 FilmEn, MotPP, NotNAT B, WhScrn 74, -77, WhoHol B
Andre, Jean 1741-1799 NewGrD 80
Andre, Jean Baptiste 1823-1882 Baker 78, NewGrD 80
Andre, Johann 1741-1799 Baker 78, NewGrD 80
Andre, Johann Anton 1775-1842 NewGrD 80
Andre, Johann August 1817-1887 Baker 78
Andre, John 1751-1780 NotNAT B, PlP&P
Andre, Julius 1808-1880 Baker 78, NewGrD 80
Andre, Karl 1853-1914 Baker 78
Andre, Lona WhoHol A
Andre, Lona 1915- FilmEn, ThFT
Andre, Lona 1916- ForYSC
Andre, Marcel 1885- FilmEn
Andre, Maurice 1933- BnBkM 80, IntWWM 77, -80, NewGrD 80
Andre, Michel 1912- FilmEn
Andre, Victor Film 1
Andre, Wayne J 1931- AmSCAP 80, EncJzS 70
Andrea De' Servi NewGrD 80
Andrea Degli Organi NewGrD 80
Andrea Di Giovanni NewGrD 80
Andreae, Carolus d1627 NewGrD 80
Andreae, Hans 1908- IntWWM 77, -80
Andreae, Marc Edouard 1939- IntWWM 77, -80
Andreae, Volkmar 1879-1962 Baker 78, NewGrD 80, OxMus
Andreani, Henri 1872-1936 FilmEn
Andreani, Jean-Paul 1929- DancEn 78
Andreani, Jean-Paul 1930- CnOxB
Andreas Contredit NewGrD 80
Andreas De Florentia d1415? NewGrD 80[port]
Andreas, Philipoctus NewGrD 80
Andreassen, Eyvind 1945- IntWWM 80
Andreassen, Mogens Steen 1916- IntWWM 77, -80
Andree, Elfrida 1841-1929 Baker 78, NewGrD 80
Andreev, Leonid Nikolayevich 1871-1919 ModWD
Andreeva-Babakhan, Anna Misaakovna 1923- WhThe
Andreini, Francesco 1548-1624 EncWT, Ent, OxThe, PlP&P
Andreini, Giovan Battista 1579?-1654 NewGrD 80
Andreini, Giovann Battista 1578?-1654 OxThe
Andreini, Giovanni Battista 1578?-1654 EncWT
Andreini, Giovanni Battista 1579?-1654 NewGrD 80
Andreini, Isabella Canali 1562-1604 EncWT, OxThe, PlP&P
Andreini, Virginia Ramponi 1583?-1627? OxThe
Andreini, Virginia Rotari OxThe
Andreis, Josip 1909- Baker 78, IntWWM 77, -80, NewGrD 80
Andrejew, Andre 1899-1966 FilmEn
Andreoli NewGrD 80
Andreoli, Carlo 1840-1908 NewGrD 80
Andreoli, Evangelista 1810-1875 NewGrD 80
Andreoli, Guglielmo 1835-1860 NewGrD 80
Andreoli, Guglielmo 1862-1932 NewGrD 80
Andreoni, Giovanni Battista d1797 NewGrD 80
Andreozzi, Gaetano 1755-1826 NewGrD 80
Andres, Giovanni 1740-1817 NewGrD 80
Andres, Henry George 1838-1921 BiDAmM
Andres, Juan 1740-1817 NewGrD 80
Andres, Stefan 1906-1970 CnMD, CroCD, McGEWD
Andresen, Ivar 1896-1940 CmOp, NewEOp 71, NewGrD 80
Andress, Charles PupTheA
Andress, Ursula 1936- BiDFilm, -81, FilmAG WE, FilmEn, FilmgC, ForYSC, HalFC 80, IntMPA 77, -75, -76, -78, -79, -80, MotPP, MovMk, OxFilm, WhoHol A, WhoHrs 80[port], WorEFlm
Andress, Walter 1904- WhoMus 72
Andress, Will K 1938- IntWWM 77, -80
Andreva, Stella WhThe
Andrevi, Francisco 1786-1853 Baker 78
Andrevi Y Castellar, Francisco 1786-1853 NewGrD 80
Andrew Hierosolymites 660?-740? NewGrD 80
Andrew Of Crete 660?-740? NewGrD 80
Andrew Of Jerusalem 660?-740? NewGrD 80
Andrew, David S 1943- ConAmC
Andrew, Donald James Clifford 1920- IntWWM 77, -80, WhoMus 72
Andrew, M Film 2
Andrew, Milla Eugenia WhoOp 76
Andrew, Siloma H PupTheA
Andrew, Thomas 1932- CnOxB, DancEn 78
Andrewes, John Hampden 1915- IntWWM 77, -80, WhoMus 72
Andrewes, Richard Michael 1943- IntWWM 80
Andrews, Adora d1956 NotNAT B, WhoHol B
Andrews, Albert Gracia d1950 NotNAT B
Andrews, Ann 1895- BiE&WWA, NotNAT, WhThe, WhoHol A
Andrews, Anthony 1948- HalFC 80
Andrews, Bart d1969 WhScrn 77
Andrews, Bruce 1948- ConAmC
Andrews, Carroll Thomas 1918- ConAmC
Andrews, Charles NewYTET
Andrews, Curcy H, Jr. 1940- AmSCAP 80
Andrews, Dana MotPP, WhoHol A
Andrews, Dana 1909- BiDFilm, -81, FilmEn, FilmgC, HalFC 80[port], MovMk[port], OxFilm, WhoHrs 80
Andrews, Dana 1911- ForYSC
Andrews, Dana 1912- BiE&WWA, CmMov, IntMPA 77, -75, -76, -78, -79, -80, WhoThe 72, -77, WorEFlm
Andrews, Del 1903?- TwYS A
Andrews, Donald John 1929- IntWWM 77, -80
Andrews, E PupTheA
Andrews, Eamonn 1922- IntMPA 77, -75, -76, -78, -79, -80, NewYTET

Andrews, Edward IntMPA 77, -75, -76, -78, -79, -80, MotPP, WhoHol A
Andrews, Edward 1914- FilmEn, ForYSC, HolCA[port], NotNAT
Andrews, Edward 1915- FilmgC, HalFC 80
Andrews, Elizabeth 1821-1910 NotNAT B
Andrews, Ellen NewGrD 80
Andrews, Evelyn Pearl 1905- IntWWM 77
Andrews, Frank Film 2
Andrews, George 1927- ConAmC
Andrews, George Whitfield 1861-1932 BiDAmM
Andrews, H K 1904-1965 NewGrD 80
Andrews, Harry 1911- CmMov, CnThe, FilmAG WE[port], FilmEn, FilmgC, ForYSC, HalFC 80, IlWWBF, IntMPA 77, -75, -76, -78, -79, -80, MotPP, MovMk, WhoHol A, WhoThe 72, -77
Andrews, Herbert Kennedy 1904-1965 OxMus
Andrews, Hilda OxMus
Andrews, Inez DrBlPA
Andrews, J Warren 1860-1932 BiDAmM
Andrews, James William 1945- AmSCAP 80
Andrews, Julie AmPS B, IntMPA 75, -76, MotPP, PlP&P[port], WhoHol A
Andrews, Julie 1934- CmMov, FilmgC, ForYSC, HalFC 80
Andrews, Julie 1935- BiDAmM, BiDFilm, -81, BiE&WWA, EncMT, FamA&A[port], FilmEn, IntMPA 77, -78, -79, -80, MovMk[port], NotNAT, -A, OxFilm, WhThe, WhoThe 72, WorEFlm
Andrews, LaVerne 1913-1967 FilmgC, HalFC 80
Andrews, LaVerne 1915-1967 BiDAmM, FilmEn, MotPP, WhScrn 74, -77, WhoHol B
Andrews, Lee And The Hearts RkOn[port]
Andrews, Lois 1924-1968 FilmEn, FilmgC, HalFC 80, MotPP, NotNAT B, WhScrn 74, -77, WhoHol B
Andrews, Louise d1950 NotNAT B
Andrews, Lyle D d1950 NotNAT B
Andrews, Maidie WhThe
Andrews, Mark 1875-1939 AmSCAP 66, -80, ConAmC
Andrews, Maxene 1916- MotPP, WhoHol A
Andrews, Maxene 1918- BiDAmM
Andrews, Maxine 1916- FilmgC, HalFC 80
Andrews, Maxine 1918- FilmEn
Andrews, Nancy 1924- BiE&WWA, NotNAT, WhoThe 72, -77
Andrews, Orville d1968 WhScrn 74, -77
Andrews, Pamela L 1943- IntWWM 77, -80
Andrews, Patricia 1920- FilmEn
Andrews, Patti 1918- WhoHol A
Andrews, Patti 1920- ForYSC
Andrews, Patty 1918- FilmgC, HalFC 80, MotPP
Andrews, Patty 1920- BiDAmM
Andrews, Regina M BlkAmP, MorBAP
Andrews, Robert 1895- WhThe
Andrews, Robert Hardy 1903-1976 HalFC 80, IntMPA 77, -75, -76
Andrews, Roger ConAmC
Andrews, Sonny 1924- IntWWM 77
Andrews, Stanley 1892-1969 HolCA[port], Vers B[port], WhScrn 74, -77, WhoHol B
Andrews, Tige 1923?- FilmgC, HalFC 80, WhoHol A
Andrews, Tiger ForYSC
Andrews, Tod 1920-1972 BiE&WWA, ForYSC, HalFC 80, NotNAT B, WhScrn 77, WhThe, WhoHol B, WhoThe 72
Andrews Sisters, The AmPS A, -B, CmpEPM, FilmEn, FilmgC, ForYSC, HalFC 80, HolP 40[port], MotPP, MovMk[port], PlP&P A[port], What 3[port]
Andreyanova, Yelena Ivanovna 1819-1857 CnOxB, NewGrD 80
Andreyev, Boris Fedorovich 1915- FilmEn
Andreyev, Leonid 1871-1919 Ent, NewEOp 71
Andreyev, Leonid Nikolaievitch 1871-1919 NotNAT B
Andreyev, Leonid Nikolaivich 1871-1919 OxThe
Andreyev, Leonid Nikolayevich 1871-1919 CnMD, CnThe, EncWT, McGEWD[port], PlP&P, REnWD
Andreyev, Vasily Vasil'yevich 1861-1918 NewGrD 80
Andreyeva, Eleonora Evgenievna 1930- WhoOp 76
Andreyor, Yvette Film 2
Andrez, Benoit 1714-1804 NewGrD 80
Andric, Stojan 1912- IntWWM 77, -80
Andrico, Michal 1894- OxMus
Andrico, Michel 1894- DcCM
Andricu, Mihail 1894-1974 DcCM
Andricu, Mihail 1895-1974 Baker 78
Andricu, Mihail G 1894-1974 NewGrD 80
Andrien, Martin Joseph NewGrD 80
Andrienko, Kalena Cziczka 1920- IntWWM 77, -80
Andries, Jean 1798-1872 Baker 78, NewGrD 80
Andriessen NewGrD 80
Andriessen, Hendrik 1892- Baker 78, CompSN[port], IntWWM 77, NewGrD 80, OxMus
Andriessen, Henrik 1892- DcCM
Andriessen, Jurriaan 1925- Baker 78, NewGrD 80
Andriessen, Louis 1939- Baker 78, DcCM, IntWWM 77, -80, NewGrD 80
Andriessen, Willem 1887-1964 Baker 78, OxMus
Andrieu Contredit D'Arras d1248 NewGrD 80
Andrieu, F NewGrD 80
Andrieux, Francois 1759-1833 EncWT, Ent
Andriot, Lucien 1897- FilmEn, FilmgC, HalFC 80, WorEFlm[port]
Andrix, George 1932- ConAmC
Andronicus, Livius 284?BC-204BC PlP&P[port]
Andronicus, Lucius Livius 284?BC-204BC NewGrD 80, NotNAT B, OxThe
Andropediacus, Lycosthenes Psellionoros 1570?-1636? NewGrD 80
Androsky, Carol WhoHol A
Androzzo, A Bazel AmSCAP 80
Androzzo, Alma B 1912- AmSCAP 66
Andrus, Charles E, Jr. 1928- BiDAmM
Andrus, Donald George 1935- CpmDNM 78, ConAmC, IntWWM 77, -80
Andrus, Merwin 1912- NewOrJ[port]
Andzhaparidze, Vera Iulianovna 1900- OxThe
Anello, Ann Marie 1954- AmSCAP 80
Anello, John-David WhoOp 76
Aneotes, Michael NewGrD 80
Anerio, Felice 1560?-1614 Baker 78, BnBkM 80, NewGrD 80, OxMus
Anerio, Giovanni Francesco 1567?-1630 Baker 78, BnBkM 80, NewGrD 80, OxMus
Anet, Baptiste 1676-1755 Baker 78
Anet, Jean-Baptiste 1650-1710 NewGrD 80
Anet, Jean-Baptiste 1651?-1710 Baker 78
Anet, Jean-Jacques-Baptiste 1676-1755 NewGrD 80
Anette, Jean-Baptiste 1650-1710 NewGrD 80
Anfossi, Pasquale 1727-1797 Baker 78, NewGrD 80
Angas, Richard 1942- IntWWM 77, -80
Angel ConMuA 80A
Angel, Danny 1911- FilmgC, HalFC 80
Angel, Edward OxThe
Angel, Elizabeth Phyllis 1937- WhoMus 72
Angel, Heather 1909- FilmEn, FilmgC, ForYSC, HalFC 80, IlWWBF, IntMPA 77, -75, -76, -78, -79, -80, MovMk, ThFT[port], What 5[port], WhThe, WhoHol A
Angel, Suzanne WomWMM
Angela, June WhoHol A
Angeleri, Giuseppe Maria NewGrD 80
Angeles, Aimee 1880- WhoStg 1906, -1908
Angeles, Victoria DeLos 1923- Baker 78, BnBkM 80[port], MusSN[port], NewEOp 71
Angeli, Andrea D' 1868-1940 Baker 78
Angeli, Francesco Maria 1632-1697 NewGrD 80
Angeli, Pier 1932-1971 FilmEn, FilmgC, ForYSC, HalFC 80, MGM[port], MotPP, MovMk[port], WhScrn 74, -77, WhoHol B
Angelica, Maria 1933- DancEn 78
Angelieri, Giorgio NewGrD 80
Angelini, Bontempi Giovanni Andrea Baker 78
Angelini, Giovanni Andrea NewGrD 80
Angelini, Orazio NewGrD 80
Angelis, Angelo De NewGrD 80
Angell, Warren Mathewson 1907- AmSCAP 66, -80, ConAmC, IntWWM 77, -80, WhoMus 72
Angelo, Jean 1875-1933 FilmEn
Angelo, Jean 1888-1933 Film 2, WhScrn 74, -77, WhoHol B
Angelo, Louis D' 1888-1958 Baker 78
Angeloni, Carlo 1834-1901 Baker 78, NewGrD 80
Angeloni, Luigi 1759-1842 Baker 78
Angelou, Maya 1928- BlkAmP, DrBlPA, MorBAP, NotNAT A, WomWMM
Angels, The RkOn[port]
Angelus, Muriel 1909- FilmEn, FilmgC, ForYSC, HalFC 80, IlWWBF, WhThe, WhoHol A
Angelus Silesius 1624-1677 NewGrD 80
Angely, Louis 1787-1835 EncWT, Ent, NotNAT B
Anger, Kenneth 1929- HalFC 80
Anger, Kenneth 1930?- FilmgC, OxFilm
Anger, Kenneth 1932- DcFM, FilmEn, WorEFlm[port]
Angerdal, Lars Goran 1937- IntWWM 77, -80
Angerer, Paul 1927- Baker 78, DcCM, IntWWM 77, -80, NewGrD 80, WhoMus 72
Angerman, Evelyn Carlson 1927- IntWWM 77, -80
Angermann, Gerda 1933- IntWWM 77, -80
Angermuller, Rudolph Kurt 1940- IntWWM 77, -80, NewGrD 80
Angers, Avril 1922- FilmgC, HalFC 80, IntMPA 77, -75, -76, -78, -79, -80, WhoThe 72, -77
Angers, Felicite CreCan 1
Angervo, Helja WhoOp 76
Angiolini, Gasparo 1731-1803 DancEn 78, NewGrD 80
Angiolini, Gaspero 1731-1803 CnOxB, NewGrD 80
Angiolini, Pietro 1764?-1830? NewGrD 80
Angleberg, Jean-Baptiste Henri D' 1661-1747 Baker 78
Anglebert, Jean-Baptiste Henri D' 1661-1747 NewGrD 80
Anglebert, Jean Baptiste Henri D' 1661-1747 OxMus
Anglebert, Jean-Henri D' 1628?-1691 Baker 78, BnBkM 80
Anglebert, Jean Henri D' 1628?-1691 OxMus
Anglebert, Jean-Henri D' 1635-1691 MusMk, NewGrD 80
Angleria, Camillo d1630 NewGrD 80
Angles, Higini 1888-1969 Baker 78, NewGrD 80
Angles, Higinio 1888-1969 NewGrD 80
Angles, Rafael 1730-1816 NewGrD 80
Angles, Rafael 1731-1816 Baker 78
Anglesi, Domenico 1610?-1669? NewGrD 80
Anglia, Galfridus De NewGrD 80
Anglia, Robertus De NewGrD 80
Anglin, Jack 1916-1963 BiDAmM, CounME 74, EncFCWM 69
Anglin, Margaret 1876-1958 FamA&A[port], NotNAT B, OxThe, PlP&P, WhThe, WhoStg 1906, -1908
Angold, Edit 1895-1971 WhScrn 74, -77, WhoHol B
Angot, Jean 1932- WhoOp 76
Angotti, Mary Ann 1926- IntWWM 77
Angrum, Steve 1895-1961 NewOrJ
Angst, Richard 1905- FilmEn
Anguelakova, Christina Borissova 1944- WhoOp 76
Anguilar, Antonia Maria NewGrD 80
Angus, Alan 1929- WhoMus 72
Angus, John NewGrD 80
Angus, Robert OxThe
Angustini, Pietro Simone NewGrD 80
Anhalt, Edna 1914- IntMPA 77, -75, -76, -78, -79, -80, WomWMM
Anhalt, Edward 1914- FilmEn, FilmgC, HalFC 80, IntMPA 77, -75, -76, -78, -79, -80, WomWMM
Anhalt, Istvan 1919- Baker 78, CreCan 2, DcCM, NewGrD 80
Anibus, Pearl Film 1
Aniels, Arnaut D' NewGrD 80
Anievas, Agustin 1934- NewGrD 80,

WhoMus 72
Animals, The *ConMuA 80A, IlEncR[port], RkOn 2[port]*
Animuccia, Giovanni 1500?-1571 *BnBkM 80, NewGrD 80*
Animuccia, Giovanni 1514?-1571 *Baker 78*
Animuccia, Paolo 1500?-1570? *NewGrD 80*
Anisimova, Nina Alexandrovna 1909- *CnOxB, DancEn 78*
Anjos, Dionisio Dos 1638?-1709 *NewGrD 80*
Anjos DeGouvea, Simao Dos *NewGrD 80*
Anka, Paul 1941- *AmPS, -A, -B, Baker 78, BiDAmM, ConMuA 80A, CreCan 2, FilmEn, FilmgC, ForYSC, HalFC 80, MotPP, PopAmC SUP[port], RkOn[port], -2[port], WhoHol A*
Ankers, Evelyn 1918- *FilmEn, FilmgC, ForYSC, HalFC 80, HolP 40[port], IntMPA 77, -75, -76, -78, -79, -80, MotPP, MovMk[port], WhoHol A, WhoHrs 80[port]*
Ankerstjerne, Johan 1886- *DcFM, FilmEn*
Ankewich, Camille *Film 1*
Ankrom, Thelma Eileen 1931- *AmSCAP 66, -80*
Ankrum, Morris 1896-1964 *FilmEn, FilmgC, ForYSC, HalFC 80, MovMk, WhoHol B*
Ankrum, Morris 1897-1964 *HolCA[port], Vers A[port], WhScrn 77, WhoHrs 80[port]*
Ankrum, Morris 1904-1964 *WhScrn 74*
Ann, Doris *NewYTET*
Ann-Margaret 1941- *IntMPA 77, -75, -76, -78, -79*
Ann-Margret 1941- *BiDFilm, -81, FilmEn, FilmgC, ForYSC, HalFC 80, IntMPA 80, MotPP, MovMk[port], OxFilm, RkOn[port], WhoHol A*
Anna Amalia 1723-1787 *Baker 78, NewGrD 80*
Anna Amalia 1739-1807 *Baker 78, NewGrD 80*
Anna Amalie 1723-1787 *NewGrD 80*
Anna Amalie 1739-1807 *NewGrD 80*
Anna, Francesco D' *NewGrD 80*
Anna Held Girls *PlP&P[port]*
Annabella 1909- *FilmAG WE, FilmEn, Film 2, FilmgC, HalFC 80, MotPP, MovMk[port], ThFT[port], WhoHol A, WorEFlm*
Annabella 1910- *ForYSC, What 1[port]*
Annabella 1912- *WhThe*
Annabelle d1961 *Film 1, WhoHol B*
Annakin, Ken 1914- *FilmEn, FilmgC, HalFC 80, IlWWBF, MovMk[port], OxFilm, WorEFlm*
Annakin, Kenneth 1914- *IntMPA 77, -78, -79, -80*
Annals, Michael 1938- *WhoOp 76, WhoThe 72, -77*
Annand, James *Film 2*
Annand, Robert William 1923- *CreCan 1*
Annard, J *Film 1*
Annarino, John Joseph 1929- *AmSCAP 66, -80*
Anne-Marie *CreCan 2*
Annekov, Georges 1901- *FilmEn*
Annemann, Theodore 1907-1942 *MagIlD*
Annenberg, Walter H 1908- *NewYTET*
Annenkov, Georges 1901- *DcFM*
Annet, Jean-Baptiste *NewGrD 80*
Annett, Thomas 1892- *IntWWM 77*
Annette 1942- *RkOn*
Annette, Jean-Baptiste *NewGrD 80*
Annibale 1527?-1575 *Baker 78*
Annibale Padovano *NewGrD 80*
Annibali, Domenico 1705?-1779? *NewGrD 80[port]*
Annibali, Dominichino 1705?-1779? *NewGrD 80[port]*
Annis, Francesca 1944- *FilmEn, FilmgC, HalFC 80*
Annmo, Erland J 1920- *IntWWM 77, -80*
Annovazzi, Napoleone 1907- *IntWWM 77, -80, WhoMus 72, WhoOp 76*
Annuerus *NewGrD 80*
Annunciacao, Gabriel Da 1526?-1603 *NewGrD 80*
Annunzio, Gabriele D' 1863-1938 *NewEOp 71, NotNAT A, -B, OxThe, WhThe*
Anouilh, Jean 1907- *WhoThe 72, -77*
Anouilh, Jean 1910- *BiE&WWA, CnMD, CnThe, CnOxB, CroCD, DcFM, EncWT, Ent, FilmEn, FilmgC, HalFC 80, McGEWD[port], ModWD, NotNAT, -A, OxFilm, OxThe, PlP&P, REnWD[port], WorEFlm*
Anouk 1932- *WorEFlm[port]*
Anrooy, Peter Van 1879-1954 *Baker 78, NewGrD 80*
Ansalone *NewGrD 80*
Ansanus S *NewGrD 80*
Ansara, Michael *MotPP, WhoHol A*
Ansara, Michael 1922- *FilmEn, FilmgC, ForYSC, HalFC 80*
Ansara, Michael 1927- *IntMPA 77, -75, -76, -78, -79, -80*
Ansbach, Elizabeth, Margravine Of *NewGrD 80*
Anschutz, Georg 1886-1953 *NewGrD 80*
Anschutz, Heinrich 1785-1865 *EncWT*
Anschutz, Johann Andreas 1772-1856 *Baker 78*
Anschutz, Karl 1815-1870 *Baker 78, BiDAmM*
Anschutz, Ottomar 1846-1907 *DcFM, FilmEn*
Anschutz, Sonia Sylvia Carolina *IntWWM 77, -80*
Anseaume, Louis 1721?-1784 *NewGrD 80*
Ansell, John 1874-1948 *NotNAT B, WhThe*
Ansell, Mary d1950 *NotNAT B*
Ansell, Ronald William 1925- *IntWWM 77*
Anselmi, Giorgio 1386?-1443? *NewGrD 80*
Anselmi, Giuseppe 1876-1929 *NewGrD 80*
Anselmi, Rosina 1880-1965 *WhScrn 74, -77*
Anselmo *NewGrD 80*
Ansermet, Ernest 1883-1969 *Baker 78, BnBkM 80[port], CnOxB, DancEn 78, MusMk[port], MusSN[port], NewEOp 71, NewGrD 80[port]*
Anski, Sholem 1863-1920 *Ent*
Ansky 1863-1920 *OxThe*
Ansky, S 1863-1920 *CnMD, CnThe, McGEWD, ModWD, NotNAT B, REnWD*
Ansky, Scholom 1863-1920 *EncWT*
Anson, A E 1879-1936 *WhScrn 74, -77, WhThe, WhoHol B*
Anson, Albert Edward 1879-1936 *NotNAT B*
Anson, Bill 1907- *AmSCAP 66, -80*
Anson, George 1904- *AmSCAP 66, -80*
Anson, George William 1847-1920 *NotNAT B, WhThe*
Anson, H V 1894-1958 *NewGrD 80*
Anson, Hugo 1894-1958 *OxMus*
Anson, Ina *Film 2*
Anson, Laura 1892-1968 *Film 2, WhScrn 74, -77, WhoHol B*
Anson, Lura *MotPP*
Ansorge, Conrad 1862-1930 *Baker 78, NewGrD 80*
Anspach, Elizabeth, Margravine Of 1750-1828 *NewGrD 80, NotNAT B*
Anspach, Susan *FilmEn*
Anspach, Susan 1939- *HalFC 80*
Anspach, Susan 1944- *MovMk, WhoHol A*
Anspacher, Louis Kaufman 1878-1947 *NotNAT B, WhThe, WhoStg 1908*
Ansseau, Fernand 1890-1972 *NewGrD 80*
Anstee, Clive Richard 1945- *WhoMus 72*
Anstey, Albert John 1928- *IntWWM 77, -80*
Anstey, Edgar 1907- *DcFM, FilmEn, FilmgC, HalFC 80, IntMPA 77, -75, -76, -78, -79, -80, OxFilm, WorEFlm*
Anstey, F 1856-1934 *FilmgC, HalFC 80, NotNAT B, WhThe*
Anstruther, Harold *WhThe*
Antal, Istvan 1909- *IntWWM 77, -80*
Antal, Livia 1929- *IntWWM 80*
Antaramia, Anna *MorBAP*
Antegnati *NewGrD 80*
Antegnati, Bartolomeo *NewGrD 80*
Antegnati, Benedetto *NewGrD 80*
Antegnati, Costanzo 1549-1624 *Baker 78, NewGrD 80[port]*
Antegnati, Gian Battista 1500- *NewGrD 80*
Antegnati, Gian Giacomo 1501- *NewGrD 80*
Antegnati, Giovanni *NewGrD 80*
Antegnati, Graziadio 1525- *NewGrD 80*
Antegnati, Graziadio 1609- *NewGrD 80*
Antenoreo, Onofrio *NewGrD 80*
Antes, Herbert *PupTheA*
Antes, Johann 1740-1811 *NewGrD 80*
Antes, John 1740-1811 *Baker 78, BiDAmM, BnBkM 80, NewGrD 80, OxMus*
Antesberger, Gunther 1943- *IntWWM 80*
Antesignanus, Pierre *NewGrD 80*
Antheil, Georg 1900-1959 *NewGrD 80*
Antheil, George 1900-1959 *AmSCAP 66, -80, Baker 78, BiDAmM, BnBkM 80, CompSN[port], CnOxB, ConAmC, DancEn 78, DcCom&M 79, DcCM, FilmEn, HalFC 80, MusMk, NewEOp 71, NewGrD 80, NotNAT B, OxMus, WorEFlm*
Antheil, George 1900-1961 *DcFM*
Anthimos *NewGrD 80*
Anthoin, Ferdinand D' *NewGrD 80*
Anthonello De Caserta *NewGrD 80*
Anthonellus De Caserta *NewGrD 80*
Anthoni, Cristofferus *NewGrD 80*
Anthonus, Cristofferus *NewGrD 80*
Anthony And The Imperials *BiDAmM*
Anthony, Carl d1930 *NotNAT B*
Anthony, Charles 1929- *WhoOp 76*
Anthony, Cristofferus *NewGrD 80*
Anthony, Dee *ConMuA 80B*
Anthony, Earl *BlkAmP, MorBAP, NatPD[port]*
Anthony, Gordon *DancEn 78*
Anthony, Jack d1962 *NotNAT B, WhoHol B*
Anthony, Jacob 1736-1804 *NewGrD 80*
Anthony, James Raymond 1922- *IntWWM 77, -80, NewGrD 80*
Anthony, John J d1970 *What 1[port], WhoHol B*
Anthony, Joseph 1912- *BiE&WWA, FilmEn, FilmgC, HalFC 80, NotNAT, WhoHol A, WhoThe 72, -77, WorEFlm*
Anthony, Malcolm 1950- *AmSCAP 80*
Anthony, Marian 1922- *IntWWM 77, -80*
Anthony, Mary *CmpGMD*
Anthony, Muriel Louise 1912- *WhoMus 72*
Anthony, Ray 1922- *BgBands 74[port], BiDAmM, CmpEPM, ForYSC, RkOn, WhoHol A*
Anthony, Richard *AmSCAP 80*
Anthony, Tony 1937- *FilmEn, FilmgC, ForYSC, HalFC 80, IntMPA 77, -75, -76, -78, -79, -80, WhoHol A*
Anthony, Trevor 1912- *WhoMus 72*
Anthony, Vince *AmSCAP 80*
Antichi, Adam Degli *NewGrD 80*
Anticho, Andrea *NewGrD 80*
Antico, Andrea 1480?-1539? *NewGrD 80*
Antier, Marie 1687-1747 *NewGrD 80*
Antill, John Henry 1904- *Baker 78, NewGrD 80, OxMus, WhoMus 72*
Antinello, Abundio d1629? *NewGrD 80*
Antinori, Luigi *NewGrD 80*
Antiquis, A De *NewGrD 80*
Antiquis, Andrea De *NewGrD 80*
Antiquis, Giovanni Jacopo De *NewGrD 80*
Antiquo, Andrea *NewGrD 80*
Antiquus, Andrea *NewGrD 80*
Antiquus, Andreas *Baker 78*
Antiquus Episcopus Beneventinus *NewGrD 80*
Antle, Gary Wayne 1954- *AmSCAP 80*
Antoine, Andre 1857-1943 *NotNAT A, -B, WhThe*
Antoine, Andre 1858-1943 *DcFM, EncWT, Ent, FilmEn, OxFilm, OxThe*
Antoine, Andre 1859-1943 *CnThe*
Antoine, Anne-Marie 1944- *WhoOp 76*
Antoine, Bernadette 1940- *WhoOp 76*
Antoine, Ferdinand D' *NewGrD 80*
Antoine, Georges 1892-1918 *Baker 78*
Antoine, Josephine L 1908-1971 *BiDAmM*
Anton 1755-1836 *NewGrD 80*
Anton, Barbara 1936- *AmSCAP 80*
Anton, Karl 1887-1956 *Baker 78*
Anton, Max 1877-1939 *Baker 78*
Antona-Traversi, Camillo 1857- *WhThe*
Antona-Traversi, Camillo 1857-1926 *NotNAT B*
Antona-Traversi, Camillo 1857-1934 *McGEWD*
Antona-Traversi, Giannino 1860-1939 *WhThe*
Antona-Traversi Grismondi, Giannino 1860-1939 *McGEWD*
Antonelli, Abundio d1629? *NewGrD 80*
Antonelli, Angelo *NewGrD 80*
Antonelli, Francesco *NewGrD 80*
Antonelli, Giulio Cesare *NewGrD 80*

Antonelli, Laura 1941?- *FilmAG WE*
Antonelli, Luigi 1882-1942 *McGEWD*
Antonelli DaFabrica, Abundio d1629? *NewGrD 80*
Antonellio, Abundio d1629? *NewGrD 80*
Antonellus Marot De Caserta *NewGrD 80*
Antoni, Antonio D' 1801-1859 *NewGrD 80*
Antoni, Pietro Degli *NewGrD 80*
Antonicek, Theophil 1937- *NewGrD 80*
Antonii, Giovanni Battista *NewGrD 80*
Antonini, Alfredo 1901- *AmSCAP 80, ConAmC*
Antonio *NewGrD 80*
Antonio 1922- *CnOxB, DancEn 78*
Antonio Da Lucca *NewGrD 80*
Antonio Da Tempo *NewGrD 80*
Antonio De Leno *NewGrD 80*
Antonio Degli Organi *NewGrD 80*
Antonio, Juan 1945- *CnOxB*
Antonio, Lou 1934- *BiE&WWA, NotNAT, WhoHol A*
Antonioni, Michelangelo 1912- *BiDFilm, -81, DcFM, FilmEn, FilmgC, HalFC 80, MovMk[port], OxFilm, WorEFlm*
Antonioni, Michelangelo 1913- *IntMPA 77, -75, -76, -78, -79, -80*
Antoniotti, Giorgio 1692?-1776 *NewGrD 80*
Antoniotto, Giorgio 1692?-1776 *NewGrD 80*
Antoniou, Theodore 1935- *Baker 78, CpmDNM 80, DcCM, NewGrD 80*
Antoniou, Theodore 1938- *ConAmC*
Antonius De Arena *NewGrD 80*
Antonius De Civitate Austrie *NewGrD 80*
Antonius De Leno *NewGrD 80*
Antonius De Roma *NewGrD 80*
Antonius Romanus *NewGrD 80*
Antonov, Alexander *Film 2*
Antonowiczs, Ruslana *IntWWM 77*
Antonowsky, Marvin *NewYTET*
Antonowycz, Myroslau 1917- *IntWWM 77, -80*
Antonowycz, Myroslaw 1917- *NewGrD 80*
Antonowytsch, Myroslaw 1917- *NewGrD 80*
Antony, Franz Joseph 1790-1837 *Baker 78*
Antony, Hilda 1886- *WhThe*
Antony, Scott 1950- *HalFC 80, IntMPA 77, -76, -78, -79, -80*
Antoon, A J 1944- *NotNAT, PlP&P A, WhoThe 77*
Antoon, John *ConMuA 80B*
Antrim, Harry 1884-1967 *Vers B[port]*
Antrim, Harry 1895-1967 *FilmEn, ForYSC, MotPP, WhScrn 74, -77, WhoHol B*
Antrobus, John 1933- *ConDr 73, -77, EncWT, WhoThe 72, -77*
Antunes, Jorge 1942- *IntWWM 77, -80, NewGrD 80*
Antuono, Eleanor D' *CnOxB*
Anvilla, Adriano *NewGrD 80*
Anzaghi, Davide 1936- *IntWWM 77, -80*
Anzalone *NewGrD 80*
Anzalone, Andrea d1656 *NewGrD 80*
Anzalone, Francesco 1607-1657? *NewGrD 80*
Anzalone, Giacinto 1606-1656 *NewGrD 80*
Anzarut, Raymond 1912- *IntMPA 77, -75, -76, -78, -79, -80*
Anzengruber, Ludwig 1839-1889 *EncWT, McGEWD[port], NotNAT B, OxThe, REnWD*
Aoki, Tsura d1961 *WhoHol B*
Aoki, Tsuru *FilmEn*
Aoki, Tsuru d1961 *MotPP*
Aoki, Tsuru 1892-1962 *Film 1, -2, TwYS*
Aoki, Tsuru 1893-1961 *WhScrn 74, -77*
Aoyama, Yoshio *WhoOp 76*
Apel, Johann August 1771-1816 *Baker 78*
Apel, Matthaus *NewGrD 80*
Apel, Nikolas 1475?-1537 *NewGrD 80*
Apel, Willi 1893- *Baker 78, IntWWM 77, -80, NewGrD 80, OxMus*
Apell, David August Von 1754-1832 *NewGrD 80*
Apelles VonLowenstern, Matthaus *NewGrD 80*
Aperghis, Georges 1945- *Baker 78, NewGrD 80*
Apergis, Georges A 1945- *DcCM*
Apfel, Edwin R 1934- *IntMPA 77, -75, -76, -78, -79, -80*
Apfel, Ernest 1925- *IntWWM 80*
Apfel, Ernst 1925- *IntWWM 77, NewGrD 80*
Apfel, Oscar C 1874-1938 *Film 1, -2, ForYSC, HalFC 80, TwYS, -A, WhScrn 74, -77, WhoHol B*
Apfel, Oscar C 1880?-1938 *FilmEn*
Apgar, Lawrence 1907- *IntWWM 80*
Aphrem *NewGrD 80*
ApHugh, Robert 1580?-1665 *NewGrD 80*
ApHuw, Robert 1580?-1665 *NewGrD 80*
Apiarius, Mathias 1500?-1554 *NewGrD 80*
Apikian, Nevart *ConAmTC*
Apinee, Irene *CreCan 2*
ApIvor, Denis 1916- *Baker 78, IntWWM 77, -80, NewGrD 80, OxMus, WhoMus 72*
Apivor, Dennis 1916- *DancEn 78*
Aplon, Boris *WhoHol A*
Aplvor, Denis 1916- *CnOxB*
Apo, Pete *EncFCWM 69*
Apolin, Stanislav 1931- *IntWWM 77, -80*
Apolinar, Daniel George 1934- *AmSCAP 80*
Apollinaire, Guillaume 1880-1918 *CnMD, EncWT, Ent, McGEWD, ModWD, NotNAT B, REnWD*
Apollo 100 *RkOn 2[port]*
Apollodorus *OxThe*
Apollon, Dave d1972 *WhoHol B*
Apollon, Gerald *BlkAmP*
Apolloni, Giovanni Filippo 1635?-1688 *NewGrD 80*
Apolloni, Salvadore 1704?- *NewGrD 80*
Apolloni, Salvatore 1704?- *NewGrD 80*
Apollonius Of Perga *NewGrD 80*
Apolon, Uni *Film 2*
Aponte, Christopher 1950- *CnOxB*
Aponte-Ledee, Rafael 1938- *Baker 78, CpmDNM 75, DcCM*
Apostel, Hans Erich 1901-1972 *Baker 78, DcCM, NewGrD 80, WhoMus 72*
Apostle, Nicholas 1930- *IntWWM 77, -80*
Apostoleris, Harry *ConMuA 80B*
Appareti, Luigi 1924- *AmSCAP 66*
Appel, Anna 1888-1963 *NotNAT B, WhScrn 74, -77, WhoHol B*
Appel, Peter 1933- *CnOxB*
Appel, Richard Gilmore 1889-1975 *Baker 78*
Appel, Toby 1952- *IntWWM 77, -80*
Appel, Wendy *WomWMM*
Appel, Wolf Willy 1942- *WhoOp 76*
Appelbaum, Gertrude 1918- *BiE&WWA, NotNAT*
Appelboom, Max 1924- *IntMPA 79, -80*
Appeldoorn, Dina 1884-1938 *Baker 78*
Appell, Dave 1922- *AmSCAP 80*
Appell, David 1922- *AmSCAP 66*
Appell, Don *BiE&WWA, ConDr 73, -77D, NewYTET*
Appelljacks, The *RkOn*
Appelmeyer, Franz *NewGrD 80*
Appelt, Matthaus *NewGrD 80*
Appen, Karl Von 1900- *EncWT*
Appenzeller, Benedictus 1480?-1558? *Baker 78, NewGrD 80*
Apper, Elie 1933- *IntWWM 77, -80*
Apperson, Ronald R 1936- *IntWWM 77, -80*
Appert, Donald Lawrence 1953- *AmSCAP 80*
Appia, Adolph 1862-1928 *CnThe*
Appia, Adolphe 1862-1928 *EncWT, Ent, NewGrD 80, NotNAT A, -B, OxThe, PlP&P*
Appia, Edmond 1894-1961 *Baker 78, NewGrD 80*
Applebaum, Edward 1937- *Baker 78, ConAmC*
Applebaum, Louis 1918- *Baker 78, CreCan 1, DancEn 78, DcCM, NewGrD 80*
Applebaum, Stan 1922- *IntWWM 77*
Applebaum, Stan 1929- *IntWWM 80*
Applebaum, Stanley 1922- *AmSCAP 66, -80, CpmDNM 79, -80, ConAmC*
Appleby, Benjamin William 1910- *WhoMus 72*
Appleby, David P 1925- *IntWWM 77, -80*
Appleby, Dorothy 1908- *WhThe, WhoHol A*
Appleby, Thomas *NewGrD 80*
Appleby, Thomas 1886- *IntWWM 77, WhoMus 72*
Appleby, Wilfrid Morrison 1892- *WhoMus 72*
Appledorn, Mary Jeanne Van 1927- *Baker 78*
Applegarth, Jonas 1920-1965 *WhScrn 74, -77*
Applegate, Eddie *WhoHol A*
Applegate, Hazel 1886-1959 *WhScrn 74, -77, WhoHol B*
Applegate, Roy *Film 2*
Appleman, Herbert 1933- *NatPD[port]*
Appleman, Sidney Herbert 1927- *AmSCAP 80*
Appleton, Clyde R 1928- *IntWWM 77, -80*
Appleton, George J d1926 *NotNAT B*
Appleton, Jon Howard 1939- *AmSCAP 80, CpmDNM 80, ConAmC, IntWWM 77, -80*
Appleton, Thomas 1785-1872 *BiDAmM, NewGrD 80*
Applewhite, Eric Leon 1897-1973 *WhoHol B*
Applewhite, Ric 1897-1973 *WhScrn 77*
Appleyard, Beatrice 1918- *DancEn 78*
Appleyard, John David 1933- *IntWWM 77, -80*
Applin, George d1949 *NotNAT B*
Applin, Nancy Ann 1950- *IntWWM 77, -80*
Appling, Bert *Film 1*
Appling, William Thomas 1932- *IntWWM 77*
Appolini, Salvatore *NewGrD 80*
Appolloni, Gioseffo *NewGrD 80*
Appoloni, Salvatore *NewGrD 80*
Apprys, Philip *NewGrD 80*
Appunn, Anton 1839-1900 *NewGrD 80*
Appunn, Georg August Ignatius 1816-1888 *NewGrD 80*
Aprahamian, Felix 1914- *WhoMus 72*
Aprem *NewGrD 80*
ApRhys, Philip *NewGrD 80*
April, Roland 1929- *DancEn 78*
Aprile, Giuseppe 1731-1813 *Baker 78*
Aprile, Giuseppe 1732-1813 *NewGrD 80*
Apryce, Philip *NewGrD 80*
Apstein, Theodore 1918- *BiE&WWA, NotNAT*
Apted, Michael 1941- *FilmEn, HalFC 80*
Apter, Andrew William 1947- *ConAmTC*
ApThomas *OxMus*
Apthorp, William Foster 1848-1913 *Baker 78, BiDAmM, NewGrD 80*
Apuleius, Lucius 125?- *DcPup*
Aquanetta 1920- *FilmgC, HalFC 80*
Aquanus, Adam 1492?- *NewGrD 80*
Aquanus, Thomas *NewGrD 80*
Aquatones, The *RkOn*
Aquila, Marco Dall' *NewGrD 80*
Aquilano, Jacobo *NewGrD 80*
Aquilera, Bob 1895-1945 *NewOrJ*
Aquin, Hubert 1929- *CreCan 1*
Aquinas, Thomas 1224?-1274 *NewGrD 80*
Aquinas, Thomas, Saint 1226-1274 *OxMus*
Aquino, Frank Joseph 1906- *AmSCAP 80*
Aquistapace, Jean 1882-1952 *WhScrn 74, -77*
Ara, Ugo 1876-1936 *Baker 78*
Ara, Ugo Dell' 1921- *CnOxB*
Arab, John 1930- *CreCan 1*
Aradi, Maria 1944- *CnOxB*
Aragall, Giacomo 1939- *NewGrD 80, WhoOp 76*
Aragall, Jaime 1939- *NewGrD 80*
Aragon, Louis 1897- *ModWD*
Arai, Yoshiko 1949- *IntWWM 77, -80*
Araia, Francesco 1709- *NewGrD 80*
Araiz, Andres 1901- *NewGrD 80*
Araiz, Oscar 1940- *CnOxB*
Araja, Francesco 1709-1770 *Baker 78*
Arakelian, Hagop 1894- *DcFM*
Arakelian, Melvin Sam 1946- *AmSCAP 80*
Arakishvili, Dimitri Ignat'yevich 1873-1953 *NewGrD 80*
Arakishvili, Dmitri 1873-1953 *Baker 78*
Arambarri, Jesus 1902-1960 *NewGrD 80*
Arana *PupTheA*
Aranaz Y Vides, Pedro 1740?-1820 *NewGrD 80*
Aranda, Matheo De 1495?-1548 *NewGrD 80*
Aranes, Juan d1649? *NewGrD 80*
Arangi-Lombardi, Giannina 1890-1951 *NewGrD 80*
Aranha, Ray 1939- *BlkAmP, DrBlPA, MorBAP, NatPD[port]*
Arant, Everett Pierce, Jr. 1938- *IntWWM 77, -80*
Arant, Jack 1917- *AmSCAP 80*
Aranyi, Francis 1893-1966 *Baker 78*
Aranyi, Jelly D' 1895-1966 *Baker 78, NewGrD 80*
Aranyi DeHunyadvar, Jelly Eva 1895-1966 *NewGrD 80*
Arapov, Boris Alexandrovich 1905- *Baker 78, IntWWM 77, -80, NewGrD 80*
Arascione, Giovanni 1546-1600? *NewGrD 80*
Araujo, Francisco Correa De *NewGrD 80*
Araujo, Juan De 1646-1712 *NewGrD 80*

Araujo, Loipa 1943?- CnOxB
Araujo, Mozart De 1904- NewGrD 80
Araujo, Pedro De NewGrD 80
Araujo, Ruth WhoMus 72
Arauxo Baker 78
Arauxo, Francisco Correa De NewGrD 80
Arban, Jean-Baptiste 1825-1889 NewGrD 80
Arbatsky, Yury 1911-1963 Baker 78, ConAmC
Arbeau, Thoinot OxMus
Arbeau, Thoinot 1519?-1595? Baker 78, DancEn 78
Arbeau, Thoinot 1519-1596 CnOxB
Arbeau, Thoinot 1520-1595 NewGrD 80
Arbeid, Ben 1924- FilmEn, FilmgC, HalFC 80, IntMPA 77, -75, -76, -78, -79, -80
Arbello, Fernando 1907-1970 CmpEPM, WhoJazz 72
Arbenina, Stella 1887- WhThe
Arbenz, Arabella 1945-1965 WhScrn 74, -77
Arbizu, Ray Lawrence 1929- IntWWM 77, -80
Arblay, Madame D' OxMus
Arbo, Jens 1885-1944 Baker 78
Arbors, The RkOn 2[port]
Arbos, Enrique Fernandez 1863-1939 Baker 78, NewGrD 80
Arbuckle, Andrew Film 1, -2
Arbuckle, Dorothy M Fry 1910- AmSCAP 66, -80
Arbuckle, Fatty 1887-1933 GrMovC[port], JoeFr[port], WorEFlm[port]
Arbuckle, Franklin 1909- CreCan 2
Arbuckle, George Franklin CreCan 2
Arbuckle, Macklyn 1866-1931 Film 1, TwYS, WhScrn 74, -77
Arbuckle, Maclyn 1863-1931 NotNAT B
Arbuckle, Maclyn 1866-1931 Film 2, WhThe, WhoHol B
Arbuckle, Maclyn 1867-1931 WhoStg 1906, -1908
Arbuckle, Mrs. Maclyn Film 2
Arbuckle, Matthew 1828-1883 Baker 78, BiDAmM
Arbuckle, Ronnie AmSCAP 80
Arbuckle, Roscoe 1881-1932 OxFilm
Arbuckle, Roscoe 1887-1933 BiDFilm, -81, Funs[port], HalFC 80[port], NotNAT B, WorEFlm[port]
Arbuckle, Roscoe Fatty 1887-1933 FilmEn, Film 1, -2, FilmgC, MotPP, MovMk[port], TwYS, -A, WhScrn 74, -77, WhoHol B
Arbury, Guy 1907-1972 WhScrn 77
Arbusov, Alexey Nikolayevitch 1908- CnMD
Arbuthnot, John 1667-1735 Baker 78, DcPup
Arbuzov, Aleksei Nikolayevich 1908- OxThe
Arbuzov, Alexey Nikolayevich 1908- CnThe, EncWT, McGEWD, ModWD
Arcadelt, Jacob 1500?-1570? BnBkM 80
Arcadelt, Jacob 1505-1560 GrComp
Arcadelt, Jacob 1505?-1567? MusMk
Arcadelt, Jacob 1505?-1568 Baker 78
Arcadelt, Jacques 1505?-1568 NewGrD 80
Arcadelt, Jakob 1514-1568 OxMus
Arcady, Jean 1912- DcFM
Arcangelo DelLeuto NewGrD 80
Arcangelo DelLiuto NewGrD 80
Arcaro, Eddie 1916- What 1[port]
Arcaro, Flavia 1876-1937 AmPS B, NotNAT B
Arcenaux, Whitey NewOrJ
Archainbaud, George 1890-1959 FilmEn, FilmgC, HalFC 80, IntMPA 77, -75, -76, -78, -79, -80, TwYS A, WhScrn 77, WhoHol B
Archambault, Gilles 1933- CreCan 2
Archambault, Louis DeGonzague Pascal 1915- CreCan 1
Archambeau, Iwan D' 1879-1955 Baker 78
Archangelsky, Alexander 1846-1924 Baker 78, OxMus
Archard, Bernard 1922- FilmgC, HalFC 80
Archdall, Mabel Film 2
Archer, Anne 1912-1959 WhScrn 74, -77, WhoHol A
Archer, Belle 1858-1900 NotNAT B
Archer, Corliss What 5[port]
Archer, Fred R d1963 NotNAT B
Archer, Frederick 1838-1901 Baker 78, BiDAmM, NewGrD 80
Archer, Harry Film 1
Archer, Harry 1888-1960 AmSCAP 66, BiDAmM, CmpEPM, NewCBMT, NotNAT B, PopAmC
Archer, Joe WhThe
Archer, John 1915- BiE&WWA, FilmEn, FilmgC, ForYSC, HalFC 80, IntMPA 77, -75, -76, -78, -79, -80, Vers A[port], WhThe, WhoHol A
Archer, John Benjamin 1872-1954 BiDAmM
Archer, L C MorBAP
Archer, Malcolm David 1952- IntWWM 80
Archer, Nicholas NewYTET
Archer, Norman 1923- IntWWM 77, -80
Archer, Osceola 1890- DrBlPA, NotNAT
Archer, Richard Donald 1947- IntWWM 77, -80
Archer, Robert V IntMPA 78, -79, -80
Archer, Stephen Mark 1953- AmSCAP 80
Archer, Thomas d1848 NotNAT B
Archer, Tim James 1949- AmSCAP 80
Archer, Violet Balestreri 1913- Baker 78, CreCan 1, DcCM, IntWWM 77, -80, NewGrD 80
Archer, William 1856-1924 CnMD, EncWT, ModWD, NotNAT A, -B, OxThe, PlP&P, WhThe
Archerd, Army IntMPA 77, -75, -76, -78, -79, -80, WhoHol A
Archey, James H 1902-1967 BiDAmM, CmpEPM, EncJzS 70
Archey, Jimmy 1902-1967 EncJzS 70, WhoJazz 72
Archibald BluesWW
Archibald, Lord IntMPA 75
Archibald, Bruce 1933- ConAmC
Archibald, Douglas 1919- ConDr 73, -77
Archibald, James 1920- IntMPA 77, -75, -76, -78, -79, -80, IntWWM 77, -80
Archibald, Margaret Helen 1949- IntWWM 80
Archibald, Nancy WomWMM
Archibald, William 1924-1970 BiE&WWA, McGEWD, NotNAT B
Archibeque, Charlene 1935- IntWWM 77, -80
Archie Boy BluesWW
Archies, The RkOn 2[port]
Archilei, Antonio 1550?-1612 NewGrD 80
Archilei, Vittoria 1550-162-? NewGrD 80
Archilochus NewGrD 80
Archinbaud, George 1890-1959 WhScrn 74
Archipoeta 1130?-1165? NewGrD 80
Archpoet NewGrD 80
Archytas NewGrD 80
Arcipreste De Hita 1283?-1350? NewGrD 80
Arcoleo, Antonio NewGrD 80
Arct, Michal 1840-1916 NewGrD 80
Arcusa, Ramon 1936- IntWWM 80
Ardanaz, Pedro 1638-1706 NewGrD 80
Ardel NewGrD 80
Ardell, John E 1881-1949 WhScrn 74, -77
Ardelli, Norbert 1902-1972 BiDAmM
Ardemanio, Giulio Cesare 1580?-1650 NewGrD 80
Arden, Don ConMuA 80B
Arden, Eddie 1908-1952 WhScrn 74, -77
Arden, Edwin Hunter Pendleton 1864-1918 Film 1, NotNAT B, WhScrn 77, WhThe, WhoHol B, WhoStg 1906, -1908
Arden, Eve IntMPA 75, -76
Arden, Eve 1909- Funs[port]
Arden, Eve 1912- BiE&WWA, CmMov, EncMT, FilmEn, FilmgC, ForYSC, HalFC 80, IntMPA 77, -78, -79, -80, JoeFr, MotPP, MovMk, NotNAT, ThFT[port], WhoHol A, WhoThe 72, -77
Arden, Jane ConDr 73, -77
Arden, John 1930- CnMD, CnThe, ConDr 73, -77, CroCD, EncWT, Ent, McGEWD, ModWD, NotNAT, OxThe, PlP&P, REnWD, WhoThe 72, -77
Arden, Mary 1910- IntMPA 77, -75, -76, -78, -79, -80
Arden, Mildred Film 2
Arden, Robert 1921- FilmgC, HalFC 80, WhoHol A
Arden, Toni CmpEPM, RkOn
Arden, Victor 1893-1962 NotNAT B, WhScrn 74, -77
Arden, Victor 1903?- CmpEPM
Arden-Griffith, Paul 1952- IntWWM 77, -80
Ardesi, Carlo 1550?-1612? NewGrD 80
Ardesi, Giovanni Paolo NewGrD 80
Ardespin, Melchior D' 1643?-1717 NewGrD 80
Ardespine, Melchior D' 1643?-1717 NewGrD 80
Ardevol, Jose 1911- Baker 78, DcCM, NewGrD 80
Arditi, Luigi 1822-1903 Baker 78, NewGrD 80, OxMus
Ardley, Margaret Owston 1895- WhoMus 72
Ardley, Neil Richard 1937- IntWWM 77, -80
Ardoyno, Dolores 1921- WhoOp 76
Ardrey, Robert 1907- HalFC 80
Ardrey, Robert 1908- BiE&WWA, CnMD, ConDr 73, -77, FilmEn, ModWD, NotNAT, PlP&P, WhThe, WorEFlm
Area Code 615 IlEncCM, IlEncR
Arefece, Antonio NewGrD 80
Arel, Bulent 1919- Baker 78, CpmDNM 76, -79, ConAmC, DcCM, IntWWM 77, -80, NewGrD 80
Arellano, George Isidro 1923- AmSCAP 66, -80
Arellano, Juan Salvador Bautista De NewGrD 80
Aremu, Aduke MorBAP
Arena, Antonius De d1544? NewGrD 80
Arena, Giuseppe 1713-1784 NewGrD 80
Arena, Maurizio 1935- WhoOp 76
Arenas, Miguel 1902-1965 WhScrn 74, -77
Arends, Henri Joseph 1921- IntWWM 80
Arenes, Antoine De NewGrD 80
Arens, Franz Xavier 1856-1932 Baker 78, BiDAmM
Arens, Rolf-Dieter 1945- IntWWM 77, -80
Arens, Ruth WomWMM B
Arensky, Anton 1861-1906 Baker 78, BnBkM 80, GrComp, NewGrD 80
Arensky, Antony 1861-1906 DcCom&M 79, MusMk, OxMus
Arent, Arthur 1904-1972 BiE&WWA, CnMD, McGEWD, ModWD, NotNAT B
Arenzana, Manuel NewGrD 80
Aresti, Floriano NewGrD 80
Aretino, Guido OxMus
Aretino, Paolo 1508?-1584 NewGrD 80
Aretino, Pietro 1492-1556 CnThe, EncWT, Ent, McGEWD, NotNAT B, OxThe, PlP&P[port], REnWD[port]
Aretz, Isabel 1913- NewGrD 80
Arey, Wayne Film 1
Arezzo, Guido Of NewGrD 80
Arezzo, Guido D' Baker 78, OxMus
Argent ConMuA 80A, IlEncR, RkOn 2[port]
Argent, James 1927- ConAmC
Argent, Rod ConMuA 80A
Argenta, Altaulfo 1913-1958 NewGrD 80
Argenta, Ataulfo 1913-1958 Baker 78
Argentil, Ciarles NewGrD 80
Argentina d1936 NotNAT B, WhThe
Argentina, L' NewGrD 80
Argentina, La 1888-1936 DancEn 78
Argentina, La 1890-1936 CnOxB
Argentina, Imperio 1889-1962 FilmEn
Argentina, Sareno S 1917- AmSCAP 66, -80
Argentinita 1898-1945 DancEn 78[port]
Argentinita 1905-1945 NotNAT B
Argentinita, La 1895-1945 CnOxB
Argento, Dario 1943- FilmEn, FilmgC, HalFC 80, WhoHrs 80
Argento, Dominick 1927- AmSCAP 66, -80, Baker 78, BnBkM 80, CpmDNM 72, -77, -79, -80, ConAmC, DcCM, NewGrD 80
Argento, Manfredi Ruggero 1924- WhoOp 76
Argento, Pietro 1909- Baker 78
Argerich, Martha 1941- NewGrD 80, WhoMus 72
Argersinger, Charles Edward 1951- CpmDNM 80
Argese, Leonard 1942- AmSCAP 80
Argilliano, Roggerio NewGrD 80
Argilliano, Ruggiero NewGrD 80
Argir, Frederick Emmett 1943- AmSCAP 80
Argiro, James Anthony 1939- AmSCAP 80
Argov, Alexander 1914- IntWWM 77, -80
Argus, Edwin Film 2
Argyle, John F 1911- IlWWBF
Argyle, Pearl 1910-1947 CnOxB, DancEn 78
Argyle, Pearl 1910-1949 WhScrn 77, WhThe
Argyropoulos, Isaac NewGrD 80

Arhine, Moses C'Kwamenah 1934- *IntWWM 77, -80*
Ari, Carina 1897-1970 *CnOxB*
Aria, Cesare 1820-1894 *Baker 78*
Aria, Pietro *ConAmC*
Aribo *NewGrD 80*
Aribo Scholasticus *NewGrD 80*
Aribon 1000?-1078? *Baker 78*
Arick, Ron *AmSCAP 80*
Aridas, Chris William John 1947- *AmSCAP 80*
Arie, Raffaele 1922- *IntWWM 77, -80, WhoMus 72, WhoOp 76*
Arie, Raphael 1920- *CmOp, NewEOp 71*
Arien, Jan Arthur Gaston *IntWWM 77, -80*
Arienzo, Nicola D' 1842-1915 *Baker 78, NewGrD 80*
Arigoni, Giovanni Giacomo *NewGrD 80*
Arimino, Abbas De *NewGrD 80*
Arinbasarova, Natalia *WhoHol A*
Arion *NewGrD 80*
Arion, Of Lesbos 625?BC-585BC *OxThe*
Ariosti, Attilio 1666- *MusMk*
Ariosti, Attilio 1666-1729? *NewGrD 80*
Ariosti, Attilio 1666-1740? *Baker 78, OxMus*
Ariosti, Giovanni Battista 1668- *NewGrD 80*
Ariosto, Lodovico 1473-1533 *DcPup*
Ariosto, Lodovico 1474-1533 *CnThe, NewEOp 71, OxThe, REnWD[port]*
Ariosto, Ludovico 1474-1533 *EncWT, Ent, McGEWD, NewGrD 80, NotNAT B, PlP&P[port]*
Ariotobulos Eutropius *NewGrD 80*
Aristeides Kointilianos *NewGrD 80*
Aristides Quintilianus *Baker 78, BnBkM 80, NewGrD 80*
Aristophanes 445?BC-385?BC *EncWT*
Aristophanes 448?BC-385?BC *CnThe, McGEWD[port], OxThe, PlP&P[port], REnWD[port]*
Aristophanes 448?BC-388?BC *NotNAT B*
Aristophanes 450?BC-380?BC *NewEOp 71*
Aristophanes 450?BC-385?BC *DcPup, Ent, NewGrD 80*
Aristoteles 384BC-322BC *NewGrD 80*
Aristotle 384BC-322BC *Baker 78, CnThe, EncWT, NewGrD 80, NotNAT B, OxThe, PlP&P, REnWD*
Aristoxenos 354BC- *Baker 78*
Aristoxenus 375?BC- *NewGrD 80*
Arizaga, Rodolfo 1926- *Baker 78, DcCM, NewGrD 80*
Arizmendi, Fermin De 1691?-1733 *NewGrD 80*
Arizo, Miguel De 1595?-1642? *NewGrD 80*
Arizona, Johnnie 1921- *BiDAmM*
Arizona Cowboy *EncFCWM 69*
Arizona Trailblazers *BiDAmM*
Arizu, Miguel De 1595?-1642? *NewGrD 80*
Arjava, Ritva Leena 1932- *IntWWM 77, -80*
Arkansas Cotton Pickers *BiDAmM*
Arkell, Elizabeth *WhThe*
Arkell, Reginald 1882-1959 *NotNAT B, WhThe*
Arkestra *IlEncJ*
Arkhangel'sky, Alexander Andreyevich 1846-1924 *NewGrD 80*
Arkhipova, Irina 1925- *Baker 78, BnBkM 80, NewGrD 80, WhoOp 76*
Arkie The Arkansas Woodchopper 1915- *IlEncCM*
Arkin, Alan 1934- *AmSCAP 66, -80, BiDAmM, BiE&WWA, EncFCWM 69, Ent, FilmEn, FilmgC, ForYSC, HalFC 80, IntMPA 77, -75, -76, -78, -79, -80, MotPP, MovMk[port], NotNAT, WhoHol A, WhoThe 72, -77*
Arkin, David F 1906- *AmSCAP 66, -80*
Arkin, Robert B 1923- *AmSCAP 66, -80*
Arkoff, Samuel Z 1918- *FilmEn, FilmgC, HalFC 80, IntMPA 77, -75, -76, -78, -79, -80, WorEFlm*
Arkor, Andre D' 1901-1971 *NewGrD 80*
Arkus, Helena 1909- *IntWWM 77*
Arkwright, Godfrey Edward Pellen 1864-1944 *OxMus*
Arkwright, Godfrey Edward Pellew 1864-1944 *Baker 78, NewGrD 80*
Arlecchino *OxThe*
Arledge, John 1906-1947 *FilmEn, ForYSC, WhScrn 74, -77, WhoHol B*
Arledge, Roone *NewYTET*
Arlega, Sophie *Film 2*
Arlen, Betty 1904-1966 *WhScrn 77, WhoHol B*
Arlen, Harold 1905- *AmPS, AmSCAP 66, -80, Baker 78, BestMus, BiDAmM, BiE&WWA, CmpEPM, ConAmC, EncMT, EncWT, FilmEn, FilmgC, HalFC 80, IntMPA 77, -75, -76, -78, -79, -80, NewCBMT, NewGrD 80, NotNAT, OxFilm, PopAmC[port], PopAmC SUP, Sw&Ld C, WhoHrs 80, WhoThe 72, -77*
Arlen, Harold 1906- *PlP&P*
Arlen, Jeanne Burns 1917- *AmSCAP 66*
Arlen, Jerry *BiE&WWA*
Arlen, Judith 1914-1968 *WhScrn 77, WhoHol B*
Arlen, Michael 1895-1956 *NotNAT B, WhThe*
Arlen, Richard d1976 *WhoHol C*
Arlen, Richard 1898-1976 *FilmgC, HalFC 80, WhoHrs 80*
Arlen, Richard 1899-1976 *FilmEn, ForYSC, MotPP, MovMk, TwYS, What 1[port]*
Arlen, Richard 1900-1976 *Film 2, IntMPA 75, -76*
Arlen, Stephen 1913-1972 *NewGrD 80, WhThe, WhoMus 72, WhoThe 72*
Arlen, Walter 1925- *IntWWM 77, -80*
Arles, Henri D' 1870-1930 *CreCan 2*
Arless, Jean 1940?- *WhoHrs 80[port]*
Arletty 1898- *BiDFilm, -81, EncWT, Ent[port], FilmAG WE, FilmEn, FilmgC, HalFC 80, MovMk, OxFilm, WhoHol A, WorEFlm*
Arley, Cecil *Film 1*
Arley, Cecile *WhScrn 77*
Arling, Arthur E 1906- *FilmEn, FilmgC, HalFC 80, IntMPA 77, -75, -76, -78, -79, -80, WorEFlm*
Arling, Charles *Film 1*
Arling, Joyce 1911- *BiE&WWA, WhThe, WhoHol A*
Arlington, Billy 1873- *WhThe*
Arliss, Florence 1871-1950 *Film 2, HalFC 80, NotNAT B, WhScrn 74, -77, WhoHol B*
Arliss, George 1868-1946 *EncWT, FamA&A[port], FilmEn, Film 2, FilmgC, ForYSC, HalFC 80[port], MotPP, MovMk[port], NotNAT A, -B, OxFilm, OxThe, PlP&P[port], TwYS, WhScrn 74, -77, WhThe, WhoHol B, WhoStg 1908, WorEFlm*
Arliss, George 1901- *IlWWBF A*
Arliss, Leslie 1901- *FilmEn, FilmgC, HalFC 80, IlWWBF[port], WorEFlm*
Arlt, Wulf 1938- *IntWWM 77, -80, NewGrD 80*
Arluck, Elliot 1915- *AmSCAP 80*
Arma, Paul 1904- *Baker 78*
Arma, Paul 1905- *IntWWM 77, -80, NewGrD 80, WhoMus 72*
Armadottir, Katrin 1942- *IntWWM 77*
Armaganian, Lucine *NewGrD 80*
Armand, Margot *Film 2*
Armand, Teddy V 1874-1947 *WhScrn 74, -77*
Armand-Bernard, Monsieur *Film 2*
Armat, Thomas 1866-1948 *FilmEn, NotNAT B*
Armatrading, Joan 1950- *ConMuA 80A[port], IlEncR*
Armbruster, Karl 1846-1917 *Baker 78*
Armbruster, Reimundo *NewGrD 80*
Armbruster, Robert *AmSCAP 66, -80*
Armen, Kay *AmSCAP 66, -80, CmpEPM*
Armendariz, Pedro 1912-1963 *FilmEn, FilmgC, ForYSC, HalFC 80, HolCA[port], MotPP, MovMk[port], NotNAT B, WhScrn 74, -77, WhoHol B, WorEFlm*
Armendariz, Pedro, Jr. 1930- *HalFC 80*
Armenian, Raffi 1942- *IntWWM 80*
Armenreich, Bernhard *NewGrD 80*
Armentrout, Lee 1909- *AmSCAP 66, -80*
Armes, Philip 1836-1908 *Baker 78, NewGrD 80*
Armetta, Henry 1888-1945 *FilmEn, Film 2, FilmgC, ForYSC, HalFC 80, HolCA[port], MovMk, NotNAT B, TwYS, Vers A[port], WhScrn 74, -77, WhoHol B*
Armhold, Adelheid 1900- *IntWWM 80*
Armida 1913- *FilmEn, Film 2, ForYSC*
Armin, Georg 1871-1963 *Baker 78*
Armin, Robert 1568?-1611? *NotNAT B, OxThe*
Armingaud, Jules 1820-1900 *Baker 78, NewGrD 80*
Armitage, Buford 1898- *BiE&WWA*
Armitage, Merle 1893-1975 *CnOxB, DancEn 78, NotNAT A*
Armitage, Reginald Moxon *NewGrD 80*
Armitage, Walter W 1907-1953 *NotNAT B, WhScrn 74, -77, WhoHol B*
Armocida, William Francis 1922- *AmSCAP 66, -80*
Armon, William Henry 1923- *IntWWM 77, -80, WhoMus 72*
Armour, Eugene 1929- *IntWWM 77, -80*
Armour, Reginald 1905- *IntMPA 77, -75, -76, -78, -79, -80*
Armour, Thomas 1909- *CnOxB, DancEn 78*
Armour, Toby *CmpGMD*
Arms, Russell 1929- *ForYSC, RkOn, WhoHol A*
Armsby, Maurice 1932- *IntWWM 80*
Armsdorff, Andreas 1670-1699 *NewGrD 80*
Armstrong, Anthony 1897- *WhThe*
Armstrong, Barney 1870- *WhThe*
Armstrong, Billy *Film 1*
Armstrong, Clyde 1879-1937 *WhScrn 74, -77*
Armstrong, Daniel Louis 1900-1971 *BiDAmM, EncJzS 70*
Armstrong, David 1927- *IntWWM 77, -80*
Armstrong, Edwin H 1890-1954 *NotNAT B*
Armstrong, Elizabeth Audrey 1902- *WhoMus 72*
Armstrong, Gordon 1937- *IntMPA 77, -78, -79, -80*
Armstrong, Harry 1879-1951 *AmSCAP 66, -80, NotNAT B*
Armstrong, Sir Harry Gloster d1938 *NotNAT B*
Armstrong, Henry 1912- *BlksB&W C, What 5[port]*
Armstrong, Henry W 1879-1951 *BiDAmM*
Armstrong, Jack *What 4[port]*
Armstrong, Jared George 1926- *WhoMus 72*
Armstrong, John *NatPD[port]*
Armstrong, Karan *IntWWM 77, -80, WhoOp 76*
Armstrong, Kathleen Mae 1921- *CreCan 1*
Armstrong, Kay 1921- *CreCan 1*
Armstrong, Leslie Harold, II 1946- *IntWWM 77*
Armstrong, Lil 1898-1971 *DrBlPA, WhoJazz 72*
Armstrong, Lil 1902-1971 *CmpEPM, EncJzS 70*
Armstrong, Lilian Hardin 1902-1971 *EncJzS 70*
Armstrong, Lillian Hardin 1902-1971 *AmSCAP 66, -80, BlkWAB[port]*
Armstrong, Louis 1900-1971 *AmPS A, -B, AmSCAP 66, -80, Baker 78, BgBands 74[port], BnBkM 80, CmpEPM, ConAmC, DrBlPA, FilmEn, FilmgC, ForYSC, HalFC 80, IlEncJ, MnPM[port], MovMk[port], MusMk[port], NewGrD 80, NewOrJ[port], OxMus, RkOn, WhScrn 74, -77, WhoHol B*
Armstrong, Margot *Film 2*
Armstrong, Marguerite *FilmEn, Film 1, -2*
Armstrong, Ned d1961 *NotNAT B*
Armstrong, Pat *ConMuA 80B*
Armstrong, Paul 1869-1915 *NotNAT B, OxThe, WhThe, WhoStg 1908*
Armstrong, Peter McKenzie 1940- *IntWWM 77, -80*
Armstrong, Pops 1900-1971 *EncJzS 70*
Armstrong, R G 1920?- *FilmEn, FilmgC, ForYSC, HalFC 80, WhoHol A*
Armstrong, Richard 1943- *IntWWM 77, -80, WhoOp 76*
Armstrong, Robert 1890-1973 *FilmEn, FilmgC, HalFC 80, HolP 30[port], WhoHol B, WhoHrs 80[port]*
Armstrong, Robert 1896-1973 *Film 2, ForYSC, MovMk[port], TwYS, Vers B[port], WhScrn 77, WhThe*
Armstrong, Ruth G *PupTheA*
Armstrong, Satchmo 1900-1971 *EncJzS 70*
Armstrong, Sheila Ann 1942- *CmOp, IntWWM 77, NewGrD 80, WhoMus 72,*

WhoOp 76
Armstrong, Shelley *BluesWW*
Armstrong, Sinclair 1912- *AmSCAP 66, -80*
Armstrong, Suzanne *WomWMM B*
Armstrong, Sydney *WhoStg 1906, -1908*
Armstrong, Sir Thomas Henry Wait 1898- *IntWWM 77, -80, NewGrD 80, OxMus, WhoMus 72*
Armstrong, Todd 1939- *FilmgC, HalFC 80*
Armstrong, W B *PupTheA*
Armstrong, Will H 1869-1943 *NotNAT B, WhScrn 74, -77, WhoHol B*
Armstrong, Will Steven 1930-1969 *BiE&WWA, NotNAT B, WhThe*
Armstrong, William *NotNAT B*
Armstrong, William 1882-1952 *NotNAT B, OxThe, WhThe*
Armstrong, William Dawson 1868-1936 *Baker 78, BiDAmM*
Armstrong-Sexton, Sheila Ann 1942- *IntWWM 80*
Arna, Lissi d1964 *WhoHol B*
Arna, Lissy d1964 *NotNAT B, WhScrn 74, -77*
Arnaboldi, Joseph P 1920- *AmSCAP 66, -80*
Arnadottir, Katrin 1942- *IntWWM 80*
Arnall, Ellis Gibbs 1907- *IntMPA 77, -75, -76, -78, -79, -80*
Arnall, Julia 1931- *FilmgC, HalFC 80*
Arnatt, John 1917- *FilmgC, HalFC 80, WhoThe 72, -77*
Arnatt, Ronald 1930- *AmSCAP 66, -80, CpmDNM 79, ConAmC, IntWWM 77, -80*
Arnaud, Francois 1721-1784 *NewGrD 80*
Arnaud, Georges 1917- *McGEWD*
Arnaud, Leo 1904- *IntMPA 77, -75, -76, -78, -79, -80*
Arnaud, Yvonne 1890-1958 *NewGrD 80*
Arnaud, Yvonne 1892-1958 *FilmEn, FilmgC, HalFC 80, IlWWBF, NotNAT A, -B, OxThe, PlP&P, WhScrn 74, -77, WhThe, WhoHol B*
Arnaut De Mareuil *NewGrD 80*
Arnaut De Maroill *NewGrD 80*
Arnaut DeZwolle, Henri d1466 *NewGrD 80*
Arnaz, Desi *NewYTET, WhoHol A*
Arnaz, Desi 1915- *FilmgC, HalFC 80*
Arnaz, Desi 1917- *CmpEPM, FilmEn, ForYSC, IntMPA 77, -75, -76, -78, -79, -80*
Arnaz, Desi, Jr. 1951- *HalFC 80*
Arnaz, Desi, Jr. 1953- *IntMPA 77, -75, -76, -78, -79, -80, WhoHol A*
Arnaz, Lucie *HalFC 80*
Arndt, Felix 1889-1918 *AmSCAP 66, -80, BiDAmM, NotNAT B, PopAmC*
Arndt, Gunther 1907-1976 *NewGrD 80*
Arndt, Nola 1889-1977 *AmSCAP 66, -80*
Arndt-Ober, Margarethe 1885-1971 *NewGrD 80*
Arne, Cecilia *NewGrD 80*
Arne, Michael 1740?-1786 *MusMk, NewGrD 80, OxMus*
Arne, Michael 1741-1786 *Baker 78*
Arne, Peter *MotPP*
Arne, Peter 1922- *FilmEn, FilmgC, HalFC 80, IntMPA 77, -75, -76, -78, -79, -80*
Arne, Thomas Augustine 1710-1778 *BnBkM 80[port], DcCom 77[port], DcCom&M 79, MusMk, NewEOp 71, NewGrD 80[port], NotNAT B, OxMus*
Arne, Thomas Augustine 1710-1788 *Baker 78*
Arneiro, Ferreira Veiga D', Viscount 1838-1903 *Baker 78*
Arneiro, Jose Augusto Da Ferreira Veiga *NewGrD 80*
Arnell, Amy 1919?- *CmpEPM*
Arnell, Peter *IntMPA 77, -75, -76, -78, -79, -80*
Arnell, Richard 1917- *Baker 78, CompSN[port], DcCom&M 79, DcCM, IntWWM 77, -80, MusMk, NewGrD 80, OxMus*
Arnell, Robert G 1900- *IntWWM 77, -80*
Arner, Gotthard 1913- *IntWWM 77, -80*
Arness, James 1923- *FilmEn, FilmgC, ForYSC, HalFC 80, IntMPA 77, -75, -76, -78, -79, -80, MotPP, MovMk, NewYTET, WhoHol A, WhoHrs 80[port]*
Arnestad, Finn 1915- *Baker 78, NewGrD 80*
Arnet, Jan 1934- *EncJzS 70*
Arnetova, Renata 1936- *IntWWM 77, -80*
Arngrin, Stevan *WhoHol A*
Arnheim, Gus *AmPS B, BgBands 74*
Arnheim, Gus 1897-1955 *AmSCAP 66, -80, BiDAmM, CmpEPM*
Arnheim, Gus 1899-1955 *WhScrn 74, -77, WhoHol B*
Arnheim, Rudolf 1900?- *HalFC 80, OxFilm*
Arnheim, Rudolf 1904- *FilmEn*
Arnhein, Gus 1897-1955 *Film 2*
Arnic, Blaz 1901-1970 *Baker 78, NewGrD 80*
Arniches, Carlos 1866-1943 *CnMD*
Arniches Y Barrera, Carlos 1866-1943 *McGEWD[port]*
Arnim, Bettina Von *NewGrD 80*
Arno Volk *NewGrD 80*
Arno, George *AmSCAP 80*
Arno, Siegfried 1895-1975 *Film 2*
Arno, Sig 1895-1975 *BiE&WWA, FilmEn, FilmgC, ForYSC, HalFC 80, HolCA[port], MovMk[port], NotNAT B, Vers A[port], WhScrn 77, WhoHol C*
Arno, T Michael 1936- *IntWWM 77, -80*
Arnold De Lantins *NewGrD 80*
Arnold VonBruck *NewGrD 80*
Arnold, Bernard 1915- *AmSCAP 66, -80*
Arnold, Billy Boy *BluesWW*
Arnold, Byron 1901- *Baker 78, ConAmC*
Arnold, Cecile d1931 *Film 1, WhScrn 77, WhoHol B*
Arnold, Cecily *WhoMus 72*
Arnold, Corliss Richard 1926- *ConAmC*
Arnold, Danny 1925- *IntMPA 77, -75, -76, -78, -79, -80, NewYTET*
Arnold, David H 1933- *AmSCAP 80*
Arnold, David John 1951- *IntWWM 77, -80*
Arnold, Denis 1926- *NewGrD 80*
Arnold, Denis Midgley 1926- *IntWWM 77, -80, WhoMus 72*
Arnold, Dorothy *WhoHol A*
Arnold, Eddie d1962 *NotNAT B*
Arnold, Eddie 1918- *BiDAmM, WhoHol A*
Arnold, Eddy 1918- *AmPS A, -B, CmpEPM, CounME 74[port], -74A, EncFCWM 69, IlEncCM[port], IntMPA 77, -75, -76, -78, -79, -80, RkOn[port]*
Arnold, Edward d1966 *WhoHol B*
Arnold, Edward 1890-1956 *FilmEn, Film 1, FilmgC, ForYSC, HalFC 80[port], HolCA[port], MGM[port], MotPP, MovMk[port], NotNAT A, -B, Vers A[port], WhScrn 74, -77*
Arnold, Edward 1890-1957 *OxFilm*
Arnold, Eve *WomWMM A, -B*
Arnold, F T 1861-1940 *NewGrD 80*
Arnold, Frank Arthur 1944- *AmSCAP 80*
Arnold, Frank Thomas 1861-1940 *Baker 78, OxMus*
Arnold, Franz 1878-1960 *NotNAT B*
Arnold, Frederick James 1908- *WhoMus 72*
Arnold, Georg d1676 *NewGrD 80*
Arnold, Georg 1781-1848 *Baker 78*
Arnold, Gertrude *Film 2*
Arnold, Gustav 1831-1900 *Baker 78, NewGrD 80*
Arnold, Gyorgy 1781-1848 *NewGrD 80*
Arnold, Helen *Film 1*
Arnold, Horace 1937- *BiDAmM*
Arnold, Horacee 1937- *EncJzS 70*
Arnold, Hubert Eugene 1945- *CpmDNM 72, ConAmC*
Arnold, Hugh *AmSCAP 80*
Arnold, J H 1887-1956 *NewGrD 80*
Arnold, Jack d1962 *NotNAT B*
Arnold, Jack 1912- *DcFM*
Arnold, Jack 1916- *CmMov, FilmEn, FilmgC, HalFC 80, IntMPA 77, -75, -76, -78, -79, -80, MovMk[port], WhoHrs 80, WorEFlm*
Arnold, James 1901-1968 *BluesWW*
Arnold, Jeanne *WhoHol A*
Arnold, Jessie 1877-1971 *Film 2, WhScrn 77*
Arnold, Johann Gottfried 1773-1806 *Baker 78, NewGrD 80*
Arnold, John 1715?-1792 *NewGrD 80*
Arnold, John 1720-1792 *OxMus*
Arnold, John 1889- *FilmEn*
Arnold, John Henry 1887-1956 *OxMus*
Arnold, John Phillip 1944- *IntWWM 77, -80*
Arnold, Jurig Von *NewGrD 80*
Arnold, Karl 1794-1877 *Baker 78*
Arnold, Larkin *ConMuA 80B*
Arnold, Laura d1962 *NotNAT B*
Arnold, Lilian d1974 *BiE&WWA, NotNAT B*
Arnold, Lonnie 1946- *IntWWM 77*
Arnold, M Louise *PupTheA*
Arnold, Mabel 1889-1964 *WhScrn 74, -77*
Arnold, Malcolm 1912- *DancEn 78*
Arnold, Malcolm 1921- *Baker 78, CmMov, CompSN[port], CpmDNM 79, CnOxB, DcCom&M 79, DcCM, FilmEn, FilmgC, HalFC 80, IntWWM 77, -80, MusMk, NewGrD 80, OxFilm, OxMus, WhoMus 72, WorEFlm*
Arnold, Marcella 1911-1937 *WhScrn 77*
Arnold, Mary Evelyn 1906- *WhoMus 72*
Arnold, Matthew 1822-1888 *NotNAT B, OxMus, OxThe*
Arnold, Maurice 1865-1937 *Baker 78, BiDAmM*
Arnold, Phil 1909-1968 *MotPP, Vers A[port], WhScrn 74, -77, WhoHol B*
Arnold, Reggie d1963 *NotNAT B*
Arnold, Richard 1845-1918 *Baker 78, BiDAmM*
Arnold, Robert Eugene 1927- *IntWWM 77, -80*
Arnold, Samuel 1740-1802 *Baker 78, BnBkM 80, NewGrD 80[port], OxMus*
Arnold, Samuel James d1852 *NotNAT B*
Arnold, Seth 1885-1955 *NotNAT B, WhScrn 74, -77, WhoHol B*
Arnold, Stephen 1946- *WhoMus 72*
Arnold, Tom d1969 *WhThe*
Arnold, William 1935- *BluesWW[port]*
Arnold, William R 1883-1940 *WhScrn 74, -77, WhoHol B*
Arnold, Youri 1811-1898 *Baker 78*
Arnold, Yury 1811-1898 *NewGrD 80*
Arnoldo Fiamengo *NewGrD 80*
Arnoldson, Sigrid 1861-1943 *Baker 78, CmOp*
Arnoldus Flandrus *NewGrD 80*
Arnolia, Walter 1895- *NewOrJ*
Arnone, Dominick L 1920- *AmSCAP 80*
Arnone, Guglielmo 1570?-1630 *NewGrD 80*
Arnoni, Guglielmo 1570?-1630 *NewGrD 80*
Arnot, Louise d1919 *NotNAT B*
Arnott, Peter 1931- *BiE&WWA, NotNAT*
Arnoul, Francoise 1931- *BiDFilm, -81, FilmEn, FilmgC, HalFC 80, IntMPA 77, -75, -76, -78, -79, -80, WhoHol A, WorEFlm*
Arnould, Sophie 1740-1802 *Baker 78, NewEOp 71, NewGrD 80[port], NotNAT A, -B*
Arnoult, Sophie 1740-1802 *NewGrD 80[port]*
Arnoux, Alexandre 1884- *FilmEn*
Arnoux, Alexandre 1884-1973 *EncWT, McGEWD[port]*
Arnoux, Robert 1900-1964 *WhScrn 77*
Arnow, Maxwell *IntMPA 77, -75, -76, -78, -79, -80*
Arnow, Ted J *IntMPA 79, -80*
Arnschwanger, Johann Christoph 1625-1696 *NewGrD 80*
Arnshtam, Lev Oscarovish 1905- *FilmEn*
Arnst, Bobbe *Film 2*
Arnstam, Leo 1905- *DcFM*
Arnsted, Jorgen Voigt 1936- *IntWWM 80*
Arnt VonAich *NewGrD 80*
Arnt, Charles 1908- *FilmEn, FilmgC, HalFC 80, MovMk, Vers A[port], WhoHol A*
Arnulph Of St. Gilles *NewGrD 80*
Aroca Y Ortega, Jesus 1877-1935 *NewGrD 80*
Arodin, Sidney J 1901-1948 *NewOrJ, WhoJazz 72*
Aroldingen, Karin Von 1941- *CnOxB*
Arom, Simha 1930- *IntWWM 77, -80*
Aromando, Joseph S 1912- *AmSCAP 66, -80*
Aron, Pietro *NewGrD 80*
Aronoff, Frances Webber 1915- *IntWWM 77, -80*
Aronoff, Josef 1932- *IntWWM 77, -80*
Aronovsky, Sulamita 1929- *IntWWM 80*
Aronowitz, Cecil Solomon 1916-1978 *IntWWM 77, NewGrD 80, WhoMus 72*
Aronson, Boris 1899- *WhoOp 76*
Aronson, Boris 1900- *BiE&WWA, CnThe,*

NotNAT, OxThe, PlP&P, WhoThe 72, -77
Aronson, Gustaf *Film 1*
Aronson, Leah Stanley 1892- *IntWWM 77*
Aronson, Rudolph 1856-1919 *BiDAmM, NotNAT A, -B, WhoStg 1906, -1908*
Aronstein, Martin 1936- *NotNAT, WhoThe 77*
Arouet, Francois Marie *McGEWD, REnWD*
Arova, Sonia 1927- *CnOxB, DancEn 78[port]*
Arpa, Gian Leonardo Dell' 1525?-1602 *NewGrD 80*
Arpa, Gianleonardo Dell' 1525?-1602 *NewGrD 80*
Arpa, Giovan Leonardo Dell' 1525?-1602 *NewGrD 80*
Arpa, Giovanni Leonardo Dell' 1525?-1602 *NewGrD 80*
Arpa, Orazio Dell' *NewGrD 80*
Arpa, Rinaldo Dall' *NewGrD 80*
Arpin, John Francis Oscar 1936- *IntWWM 80*
Arpino, Gerald 1928- *CnOxB, DancEn 78[port]*
Arquette, Cliff 1905-1974 *AmSCAP 66, -80, JoeFr[port], WhScrn 77, WhoHol B*
Arquette, Cliff 1906-1974 *HalFC 80*
Arquier, Joseph 1763-1816 *Baker 78*
Arquimbau, Domingo 1758?-1829 *NewGrD 80*
Arrabal, F *PlP&P*
Arrabal, Fernando 1932- *CnMD, CroCD, EncWT, Ent, McGEWD, ModWD, WhoThe 72, -77*
Arrabal, Fernando 1933- *CnThe, REnWD[port]*
Arran, John 1945- *WhoMus 72*
Arrand, Dick Henry 1929- *IntWWM 77, -80*
Arras, Harry 1882-1942 *WhScrn 74, -77, WhoHol B*
Arras, Jean D' d1584 *NewGrD 80*
Arrato, Ubaldo 1897-1947 *DcFM*
Arrau *PlP&P*
Arrau, Claudio 1903- *Baker 78, BiDAmM, BnBkM 80[port], IntWWM 77, -80, MusMk, MusSN[port], NewGrD 80[port], WhoMus 72*
Arraujo, Pedro De *NewGrD 80*
Arregui, Jose Maria 1875?-1955 *NewGrD 80*
Arregui Garay, Vicente 1871-1925 *Baker 78, NewGrD 80*
Arrell, Greg F 1950- *AmSCAP 80*
Arresti, Floriano 1660?-1719 *NewGrD 80*
Arresti, Giulio Cesare 1625-1704? *NewGrD 80*
Arriaga, Juan Crisostomo 1806-1826 *Baker 78, BnBkM 80, MusMk, NewGrD 80*
Arrick, Lawrence 1928- *NotNAT*
Arrieta Y Corera, Pascual Juan Emilio 1823-1894 *Baker 78*
Arriete Y Corera, Pascual Juan Emilio 1823-1894 *NewGrD 80*
Arrieu, Claude 1903- *Baker 78, IntWWM 77, -80, NewGrD 80, WhoMus 72*
Arrigo *NewGrD 80*
Arrigo, Girolamo 1930- *Baker 78, DcCM, NewGrD 80*
Arrigo D'Ugo *NewGrD 80*
Arrigo Il Tedesco *NewGrD 80, OxMus*
Arrigoni, Carlo 1697-1744 *Baker 78, NewGrD 80*
Arrigoni, Giovanni Giacomo *NewGrD 80*
Arro, Elmar 1899- *NewGrD 80*
Arroio, Joao Marcelino 1861-1930 *NewGrD 80*
Arronge, Adolf L' 1838-1908 *Baker 78, EncWT*
Arrospide DeLaFlor, Cesar 1900- *NewGrD 80*
Arrowsmith, William 1924- *BiE&WWA, NotNAT*
Arroyo, Joao Marcellino 1861-1930 *Baker 78*
Arroyo, Martina *BnBkM 80, IntWWM 77, -80, WhoMus 72, WhoOp 76*
Arroyo, Martina 1936- *BiDAmM*
Arroyo, Martina 1937- *NewGrD 80*
Arroyo, Martina 1940- *Baker 78, MusSN[port], NewEOp 71*
Arroyo, Martino *CmOp*
Arruza, Carlos El Ciclon 1920-1966 *WhScrn 77*
Ars Nova *BiDAmM*
Arsers, Patrick Linton 1945- *IntWWM 77*
Arshawsky, Arthur *NewGrD 80*
Art Ensemble Of Chicago *EncJzS 70, IlEncJ*
Artaud, Antonin 1896?-1948 *CnThe, CroCD, EncWT, Ent[port], FilmEn, FilmgC, HalFC 80, McGEWD, ModWD, NotNAT A, -B, OxFilm, OxThe, REnWD[port], WhScrn 77, WorEFlm*
Artauld, Antonin *Film 2*
Arteaga, Esteban De 1747-1799 *Baker 78, NewGrD 80, OxMus*
Arteaga, Manuel Gaytan Y *NewGrD 80*
Arteaga, Stefano 1747-1799 *NewGrD 80*
Arteel, Freddy 1938- *IntWWM 80*
Artega, Sophia *Film 2*
Artemal, Talat 1902-1957 *WhScrn 74, -77*
Arthopius, Balthasar d1534 *NewGrD 80*
Arthur, Alfred 1844-1918 *Baker 78, BiDAmM*
Arthur, Art 1911- *IntMPA 77, -75, -76, -78, -79, -80*
Arthur, Bea *WhoHol A*
Arthur, Beatrice *BiE&WWA, EncMT, IntMPA 77, -75, -76, -78, -79, -80, NotNAT*
Arthur, Beatrice 1924- *FilmgC, HalFC 80*
Arthur, Beatrice 1926- *WhoThe 77*
Arthur, Bobb *AmSCAP 80*
Arthur, Carol 1935- *BiE&WWA, NotNAT, WhoHol A*
Arthur, Charthel 1946- *CnOxB*
Arthur, Daphne 1925- *WhThe*
Arthur, Edna Margaret Aubrey 1928- *IntWWM 77, -80, WhoMus 72*
Arthur, Edward B 1915- *IntMPA 77, -75, -76, -78, -79, -80*
Arthur, Fanny *OxMus*
Arthur, George K *MotPP*
Arthur, George K 1884-1952 *Film 2*
Arthur, George K 1899- *FilmEn, FilmgC, ForYSC, HalFC 80, IlWWBF, JoeFr, TwYS, WhoHol A*
Arthur, George K 1900- *MovMk*
Arthur, George K and Karl Dane *JoeFr*
Arthur, Hartney J 1917- *BiE&WWA*
Arthur, Helen d1939 *NotNAT B*
Arthur, Jan 1939- *ConAmC*
Arthur, Jean 1905- *BiDFilm, -81, BiE&WWA, CmMov, FilmEn, FilmgC, ForYSC, HalFC 80[port], MotPP, NotNAT, OxFilm, ThFT[port], TwYS, WhThe, WhoHol A*
Arthur, Jean 1908- *Film 2, IntMPA 77, -75, -76, -78, -79, -80, MovMk[port], WorEFlm*
Arthur, Johnny *ForYSC*
Arthur, Johnny 1883-1951 *Film 2, TwYS, WhScrn 74, -77, WhoHol B*
Arthur, Johnny 1883-1952 *FilmEn*
Arthur, Johnny 1884-1952 *Vers A[port]*
Arthur, Joseph 1848-1906 *NotNAT B*
Arthur, Julia 1869-1950 *FilmEn, Film 1, NotNAT B, PlP&P, TwYS, WhScrn 74, -77, WhThe, WhoHol B, WhoStg 1906, -1908*
Arthur, Karen *WomWMM B*
Arthur, Louise *ForYSC*
Arthur, Maureen *ForYSC, WhoHol A*
Arthur, Paul *Film 1*
Arthur, Paul 1859-1928 *NotNAT B, WhThe, WhoStg 1908*
Arthur, Robert d1929 *WhThe*
Arthur, Robert 1909- *FilmEn, FilmgC, HalFC 80, IntMPA 77, -75, -76, -78, -79, -80*
Arthur, Robert 1925- *FilmEn, FilmgC, ForYSC, HalFC 80, IntMPA 77, -75, -76, -78, -79, -80, WhoHol A*
Arthur, Robert 1928- *AmSCAP 66, -80*
Arthur, Zinn *BgBands 74*
Arthurs, George 1875-1944 *NotNAT B, WhThe*
Artigues, Albert 1907- *NewOrJ[port]*
Artman, Ruth Eleanor 1919- *AmSCAP 80*
Artocopus, Balthasar *NewGrD 80*
Artois, Armand D' *NotNAT B*
Artomius, Piotr 1552-1609 *NewGrD 80*
Artomius Grodicensis, Piotr 1552-1609 *NewGrD 80*
Artomiusz, Piotr 1552-1609 *NewGrD 80*
Artopaeus, Balthasar *NewGrD 80*
Artot, Alexandre-Joseph Montagney 1815-1845 *Baker 78, NewGrD 80*
Artot, Desiree 1835-1907 *Baker 78, CmOp, NewEOp 71, NewGrD 80*
Artot, Jean-Desire 1803-1887 *Baker 78*
Artot, Maurice Montagney 1772-1829 *Baker 78*
Artsybashev, Mikhail Petrovich 1878-1927 *CnMD, ModWD*
Artufel, Damaso *NewGrD 80*
Artus, Louis 1870- *WhThe*
Artus, March Stuttle 1931- *IntWWM 77, -80*
Artusi, Giovanni Maria 1540?-1613 *Baker 78, NewGrD 80*
Artusini, Antonio 1554?-1604? *NewGrD 80*
Artzibushev, Nikolai 1858-1937 *Baker 78*
Artzt, Alice 1943- *IntWWM 77, -80, WhoMus 72*
Artzybashev, Mikhail Petrovitch 1878-1927 *NotNAT B*
Aruhn, Britt Marie 1943- *IntWWM 80, WhoOp 76*
Arundale, Grace *WhThe*
Arundale, Sybil 1882-1965 *WhThe*
Arundel, Dennis 1898- *NewGrD 80*
Arundell, Denis 1898- *FilmgC, HalFC 80*
Arundell, Dennis 1898- *CmOp, NewEOp 71, NewGrD 80, OxMus, WhThe, WhoMus 72, WhoOp 76, WhoThe 72*
Arutiunian, Aleksander 1920- *DcCM*
Arutiunian, Alexander 1920- *Baker 78*
Arutyunyan, Alexander Grigori *NewGrD 80*
Arvan, Jan *ForYSC, WhoHol A*
Arvanitas, Georges 1931- *EncJzS 70*
Arvele, Ritva *WomWMM*
Arvey, Verna 1910- *AmSCAP 66, -80*
Arvidson, Jerker Bengt 1939- *WhoOp 76*
Arvidson, Linda 1884-1949 *FilmEn, Film 1, HalFC 80, TwYS, WhScrn 74, -77, WhoHol B*
Arvidsson, Lillemor 1942- *CnOxB*
Arvold, Alfred G 1882-1957 *NotNAT A, -B*
Arvon, Bobby *AmSCAP 80*
Arvonio, Angelo Carmen, Jr. 1948- *AmSCAP 80*
Arvonio, Robert Anthony 1941- *AmSCAP 80*
Arwyn Evans, Joan 1938- *WhoMus 72*
Arzner, Dorothy 1900-1979 *BiDFilm 81, DcFM, FilmEn, FilmgC, HalFC 80, IntMPA 77, -75, -76, -78, -79, -80, OxFilm, TwYS A, WomWMM*
Arzruni, Sahan 1943- *IntWWM 77, -80*
Asaf, George *OxMus*
Asafiev, Boris Vladimirovich 1884-1949 *Baker 78, CnOxB, DancEn 78*
Asaf'yev, Boris Vladimirovich 1884-1949 *NewGrD 80*
Asakawa, Takako 1938- *CnOxB*
Asbaje Y Ramirez DeCantillana, Juana I 1651-1695 *NotNAT B*
Asberg, Margaretha 1939- *CnOxB*
Asbjornsson, Sigurjon 1954- *IntWWM 77*
Asch, Sholem 1880-1957 *CnMD, CnThe, EncWT, McGEWD, ModWD, NotNAT B, REnWD*
Asch, Sholom 1880-1957 *OxThe*
Aschaffenburg, Walter Eugene 1927- *AmSCAP 80, Baker 78, ConAmC, IntWWM 77, -80*
Asche, Lily Brayton 1876-1953 *OxThe*
Asche, Oscar d1936 *WhoHol B*
Asche, Oscar 1871-1936 *EncMT, EncWT, OxThe, WhScrn 77, WhThe*
Asche, Oscar 1872-1936 *NotNAT A, -B*
Aschenbrenner, Christian Heinrich 1654-1732 *Baker 78, NewGrD 80*
Aschengreen, Erik 1935- *CnOxB*
Ascher, Emil 1859-1922 *AmSCAP 66, -80*
Ascher, Everett 1936- *AmSCAP 80*
Ascher, Joseph 1829-1869 *Baker 78*
Ascher, Kenneth Lee 1944- *AmSCAP 80*
Ascher, Leo 1880-1942 *Baker 78, BiDAmM*
Ascher, Ruth Jeanette 1913- *IntWWM 80*
Aschpellmayr, Franz *NewGrD 80*
Asciolla, Dino 1920- *NewGrD 80*
Asciolla, Edoardo 1920- *NewGrD 80*
Ascone, Vicente 1897- *Baker 78, DcCM, NewGrD 80*
Ascot, Rosa Garcia *NewGrD 80*
Asena, Orhan 1922- *REnWD*
Asenjo Barbieri, Francisco *NewGrD 80*
Asensio, Manola 1946- *CnOxB*
Asgeirsson, Jon 1928- *NewGrD 80*
Ash, Arty d1954 *NotNAT B*
Ash, Gail *AmSCAP 80*

Ash, Gordon d1929 *NotNAT B, WhThe*
Ash, Jerry *Film 1*
Ash, Maie 1888- *WhThe*
Ash, Marvin 1914-1974 *CmpEPM, EncJzS 70*
Ash, Paul 1891-1958 *AmSCAP 66, -80, BgBands 74, CmpEPM*
Ash, Rene 1939- *IntMPA 77, -75, -76, -78, -79, -80*
Ash, Russell 1910-1974 *WhScrn 77, WhoHol B*
Ash, Sam 1884-1951 *WhoHol B*
Ash, Samuel Howard 1884-1951 *WhScrn 74, -77*
Ashbee, Andrew 1938- *IntWWM 77, -80*
Ashbridge, Bryan 1926- *CnOxB*
Ashbridge, Bryan 1927- *DancEn 78*
Ashbrook, William 1922- *NewGrD 80*
Ashburn, Benjamin *ConMuA 80B*
Ashby, Arnold *WhoMus 72*
Ashby, Dorothy Jeanne 1932- *BiDAmM, BlkWAB*
Ashby, Hal 1936- *BiDFilm 81, FilmEn, FilmgC, HalFC 80, IntMPA 77, -75, -76, -78, -79, -80*
Ashby, Harold Kenneth 1925- *BiDAmM, EncJzS 70*
Ashby, Irving C 1920- *CmpEPM, EncJzS 70*
Ashby, Johnnie *Film 2*
Ashby, Ruth *Film 2*
Ashby, William Mobile 1889- *BlkAmP*
Ashcroft, Peggy 1907- *BiE&WWA, CnThe, EncWT, Ent, FilmEn, FilmgC, HalFC 80, IlWWBF A, NotNAT, -A, OxThe, PlP&P, WhoHol A, WhoThe 72, -77*
Ashdown, Edwin 1826-1912 *Baker 78, NewGrD 80*
Ashe, Andrew 1759?-1838 *NewGrD 80*
Ashe, Warren d1944 *WhoHol B*
Ashe, Warren d1947 *NotNAT B, WhScrn 74, -77*
Asher, Barbara Lilian 1929- *WhoMus 72*
Asher, Irving 1903- *IntMPA 77, -75, -76, -78, -79, -80*
Asher, Jack 1916- *CmMov, FilmEn, FilmgC, HalFC 80, IntMPA 77, -75, -76, -78, -79, -80*
Asher, Jane 1946- *FilmEn, FilmgC, HalFC 80, IlWWBF[port], IntMPA 79, -80, WhoHol A, WhoThe 72, -77*
Asher, Max 1880-1957 *FilmEn, Film 1, -2, MotPP, NotNAT B, WhScrn 74, -77, WhoHol B*
Asher, Peter *ConMuA 80B, IlEncR*
Asher, Richard 1917?- *ConMuA 80B*
Asher, Robert 1915- *FilmEn*
Asher, Robert 1917?- *FilmgC, HalFC 80, IlWWBF, IntMPA 77, -75, -76, -78, -79, -80*
Asher, William 1919?- *FilmEn, FilmgC, HalFC 80, NewYTET*
Asherman, Alice Cornett 1911- *AmSCAP 80*
Asherman, Edward M 1913- *AmSCAP 66, -80*
Asherman, Nat 1909- *AmSCAP 66, -80*
Ashermann, Otto 1903- *BiE&WWA*
Asherson, Renee 1920- *FilmEn, FilmgC, HalFC 80, IlWWBF[port], IntMPA 77, -75, -76, -78, -79, -80, WhoHol A, WhoThe 72, -77*
Ashewell, Thomas *NewGrD 80*
Ashfield, Robert James 1911- *IntWWM 77, -80, WhoMus 72*
Ashford, Harry d1926 *NotNAT B*
Ashford, Nickolas 1942- *AmSCAP 80*
Ashford & Simpson *ConMuA 80A[port], RkOn 2[port]*
Ashforth, Alden 1930- *ConAmC*
Ashkenasi, Shmuel 1941- *IntWWM 77, -80*
Ashkenazi, Vladimir 1937- *NewGrD 80*
Ashkenazy, Vladimir 1937- *Baker 78, BnBkM 80[port], IntWWM 77, -80, MusMk, MusSN[port], NewGrD 80, WhoMus 72*
Ashley *NewGrD 80*
Ashley, Annie d1947 *NotNAT B*
Ashley, Arthur *Film 1*
Ashley, Barbara *BiE&WWA*
Ashley, Beaulah d1965 *WhScrn 77*
Ashley, Beulah d1965 *WhScrn 74*
Ashley, C J 1773-1843 *OxMus*
Ashley, Celeste 1930- *BiE&WWA, NotNAT*
Ashley, Charles 1770-1818 *NewGrD 80*
Ashley, Charles Jane 1773-1843 *NewGrD 80*
Ashley, Clarence 1895-1967 *CounME 74, -74A*
Ashley, Derick 1901- *WhoMus 72*
Ashley, Douglas Daniels *IntWWM 80*
Ashley, Edward 1904- *FilmEn, FilmgC, ForYSC, HalFC 80, WhoHol A*
Ashley, Elizabeth 1939- *BiE&WWA, FilmEn, FilmgC, ForYSC, HalFC 80, IntMPA 77, -78, -79, -80, MovMk, NotNAT, WhoHol A, WhoThe 72, -77*
Ashley, Frank 1941- *DrBlPA*
Ashley, Helen d1954 *NotNAT B*
Ashley, Iris 1909- *WhThe*
Ashley, J d1805 *OxMus*
Ashley, John d1830 *OxMus*
Ashley, John d1834? *NewGrD 80*
Ashley, John 1734-1805 *NewGrD 80*
Ashley, John 1934- *ForYSC, IntMPA 77, -75, -76, -78, -79, -80, WhoHol A, WhoHrs 80*
Ashley, John James 1772-1815 *NewGrD 80*
Ashley, Josiah d1830 *OxMus*
Ashley, Marta *WomWMM B*
Ashley, Minnie 1875-1945 *NotNAT B, WhoStg 1906, -1908*
Ashley, Richard G 1775-1836 *NewGrD 80*
Ashley, Robert 1930- *Baker 78, ConAmC, DcCM, NewGrD 80*
Ashley, Ted 1922- *BiE&WWA, IntMPA 77, -75, -76, -78, -79, -80, NewYTET, NotNAT*
Ashley, William *BlkAmP*
Ashman, Howard Elliott 1950- *AmSCAP 80*
Ashmole, David 1949- *CnOxB*
Ashmore, Basil 1915- *WhoThe 72, -77*
Ashmore, Peter 1916- *BiE&WWA, WhThe*
Ashpole, Alfred 1892- *IntWWM 77, WhoMus 72*
Ashton, Algernon 1859-1937 *Baker 78, NewGrD 80, OxMus*
Ashton, Bob Bruce 1921- *AmSCAP 80*
Ashton, Charles *Film 2*
Ashton, Dorrit 1873-1936 *WhScrn 74, -77, WhoHol B*
Ashton, Sir Frederick 1904- *CnOxB, NewGrD 80*
Ashton, Sir Frederick 1906- *DancEn 78[port], NotNAT A, WhThe, WhoMus 72*
Ashton, Herbert *Film 2*
Ashton, Hugh *NewGrD 80*
Ashton, John Howard 1938- *AmSCAP 80, ConAmC, IntWWM 77, -80*
Ashton, Joseph Nickerson 1868-1946 *BiDAmM*
Ashton, Roy *WhoHrs 80*
Ashton, Sylvia 1880-1940 *Film 1, -2, NotNAT B, TwYS, WhScrn 74, -77, WhoHol B*
Ashton, Vera d1965 *WhScrn 74, -77*
Ashton, Winifred *McGEWD*
Ashur, Geri *WomWMM B*
Ashwander, Donald John 1929- *AmSCAP 80*
Ashwell, Lena 1872-1957 *NotNAT A, -B, OxThe, WhThe, WhoStg 1906, -1908*
Ashwell, Thomas 1478?-1513? *NewGrD 80*
Ashworth, Caleb *OxMus*
Ashworth, Charles Stewart 1777- *BiDAmM*
Ashworth, Ernie 1928- *BiDAmM, CounME 74, -74A, EncFCWM 69, IlEncCM*
Asioli, Bonifazio 1769-1832 *Baker 78, NewGrD 80*
Asioli, Francesco 1645?-1676? *NewGrD 80*
Askam, Earl 1899-1940 *WhScrn 74, -77, WhoHol B*
Askam, Perry 1898-1961 *NotNAT B, WhScrn 77*
Askan, Perry 1898-1961 *WhoHol B*
Askenase, Stefan 1896- *IntWWM 77, -80, NewGrD 80, WhoMus 72*
Asker, Bjorn 1941- *IntWWM 80, WhoOp 76*
Askew, Dennis Lee 1953- *AmSCAP 80*
Askew, Luke *WhoHol A*
Askew, R *NewGrD 80*
Askey, Arthur 1900- *FilmgC, HalFC 80, IlWWBF[port], -A[port], IntMPA 77, -75, -76, -78, -79, -80, WhoThe 72, -77*
Askin, Harry d1934 *NotNAT B*
Askin, Leon 1920?- *FilmEn, FilmgC, ForYSC, HalFC 80, WhoHol A*
Askonas, Lies 1913- *IntWWM 80, WhoMus 72*
Askue, R *NewGrD 80*
Askwith, Robin 1950- *HalFC 80*
Aslan, Gregoire 1908- *FilmEn, FilmgC, HalFC 80*
Aslan, Raoul 1890-1958 *EncWT*
Aslanian, Vahe' 1918- *IntWWM 77, -80*
Asleep At The Wheel *ConMuA 80A, IlEncCM, IlEncR*
Asmodi, Herbert 1923- *CnMD, CroCD*
Asmus, Ruth Maria 1934- *WhoOp 76*
Asmussen, Svend 1916- *CmpEPM, EncJzS 70*
Asner, Edward 1925?- *FilmgC, HalFC 80, IntMPA 77, -78, -79, -80, WhoHol A*
Asner, Edward 1929- *FilmEn*
Asola, Giammateo 1532?-1609 *NewGrD 80*
Asola, Giovanni Matteo 1530?-1609 *Baker 78*
Asola, Giovanni Matteo 1532?-1609 *NewGrD 80*
Asow, Erich H Muller Von *Baker 78*
Aspa, Mario 1799-1868 *Baker 78*
Aspelmayr, Franz 1728?-1786 *NewGrD 80*
Aspelmeier, Franz 1728?-1786 *NewGrD 80*
Aspenstrom, Werner 1918- *CnThe, CroCD, McGEWD[port], REnWD*
Asper, Frank W 1892-1973 *AmSCAP 66, -80, ConAmC A*
Aspestrand, Sigwart 1856-1941 *Baker 78*
Aspinall, Dorothea May Pryce *WhoMus 72*
Asplmayr, Franz 1728?-1786 *Baker 78, NewGrD 80*
Asplmeyr, Franz 1728?-1786 *NewGrD 80*
Asplund, John d1807 *BiDAmM*
Asproys, Jehan Simon *NewGrD 80*
Asproys, Johannes Symonis *NewGrD 80*
Aspull, George 1813-1832 *NewGrD 80*
Asquith, Anthony 1902-1968 *BiDFilm, -81, CmMov, DcFM, FilmEn, FilmgC, HalFC 80, IlWWBF, -A[port], MovMk[port], OxFilm, WhScrn 74, -77, WhThe, WorEFlm*
Asquith, Elizabeth *Film 1*
Asquith, Mary d1942 *NotNAT B*
Asriel, Andre 1922- *Baker 78, DcCM, IntWWM 80, NewGrD 80*
Asro, Gene *AmSCAP 80*
Assaly, Edmund Philip 1920- *IntWWM 77, -80*
Assandra, Caterina *NewGrD 80*
Assante, Allison 1923- *AmSCAP 80*
Asselbergs, Alphons Julianus Maria 1914- *IntWWM 77, -80*
Assembled Multitude *RkOn 2A*
Asseton, Hugo *NewGrD 80*
Asseyev, Tamara *IntMPA 79, -80, WomWMM*
Assheton, Hugo *NewGrD 80*
Asshwell, Thomas *NewGrD 80*
Assis *WomWMM*
Assisi, Ruffino D' *NewGrD 80*
Assmayer, Ignaz 1790-1862 *Baker 78*
Association, The *BiDAmM, RkOn 2[port]*
Assoucy, Charles D' *NewGrD 80*
Assunto, Frank Joseph 1932-1974 *BiDAmM, EncJzS 70, NewOrJ[port]*
Assunto, Fred J 1929-1966 *BiDAmM*
Assunto, Freddie 1929-1966 *NewOrJ[port]*
Assunto, Jac 1902- *NewOrJ[port]*
Assunto, Jacob 1905- *BiDAmM, EncJzS 70*
Assunto, Papa Jac 1905- *EncJzS 70*
Ast, Dietmar Von *NewGrD 80*
Asta *FilmEn*
Astafieva, Serafima Alexandrovna 1876-1934 *DancEn 78*
Astafieva, Serafina Alexandrovna 1876-1934 *CnOxB*
Astaire, Adele *AmPS B, CmpEPM*
Astaire, Adele 1898- *BiE&WWA, DancEn 78, EncMT, Film 1, NotNAT, PlP&P[port], WhThe*
Astaire, Adele 1899- *What 1[port]*
Astaire, Fred *AmPS B*
Astaire, Fred 1899- *AmSCAP 66, -80, BiDFilm, -81, BiE&WWA, CmMov, CmpEPM, CnOxB, DancEn 78, EncMT, EncWT, Ent[port], FilmEn, Film 1, FilmgC, ForYSC, HalFC 80, MGM[port], MotPP, MovMk[port], NewYTET, NotNAT, -A, OxFilm, PlP&P[port], WhoHol A, WhoMus 72, WorEFlm[port]*

Astaire, Fred 1900- IntMPA 77, -75, -76, -78, -79, -80, WhThe
Astangov, Mikhail 1901-1965 WhScrn 74, -77, WhoHol B
Astar, Ben WhoHol A
Astarita, Gennaro 1745?-1803? NewGrD 80
Astaritta, Gennaro 1745?-1803? NewGrD 80
Astbury, Ida Pauline 1922- IntWWM 77, -80
Aste, Dietmar Von NewGrD 80
Astell, Betty 1912- Film 2, IIWWBF
Aster, Ed AmSCAP 80
Asther, Nils MotPP
Asther, Nils 1897- FilmEn, FilmgC, ForYSC, HalFC 80, What 5[port], WhoHol A, WhoHrs 80
Asther, Nils 1901- Film 2, TwYS
Asther, Nils 1902- MovMk[port]
Astill, Gary 1955- IntWWM 80
Astin, John 1930- FilmEn, FilmgC, ForYSC, HalFC 80, IntMPA 77, -75, -76, -78, -79, -80, WhoHol A
Astin, Patty Duke HalFC 80
Astley, Edwin Thomas 1922- IntWWM 77
Astley, John WhThe
Astley, John d1821 NotNAT B
Astley, Philip 1742-1814 Ent, NotNAT B
Aston, Anthony OxThe, PlP&P
Aston, Hugh d1522 OxMus
Aston, Hugh 1480?-1522 Baker 78, MusMk
Aston, Hugh 1485?-1558 NewGrD 80
Aston, Hugh 1490?-1550? BnBkM 80
Aston, Hugo 1485?-1558 NewGrD 80
Aston, Peter George 1938- IntWWM 77, -80, NewGrD 80, WhoMus 72
Aston, Tony NotNAT A, -B
Astor, Adelaide d1951 NotNAT B
Astor, Camille Film 1, -2
Astor, Franklin O 1915- IntWWM 77, -80
Astor, Gertrude 1887-1977 FilmEn, HalFC 80
Astor, Gertrude 1889- WhoHol A
Astor, Gertrude 1906- Film 1, -2, ForYSC, TwYS
Astor, Junie 1918-1967 WhScrn 74, -77, WhoHol B
Astor, Mary 1906- BiDFilm, -81, BiE&WWA, FilmEn, Film 2, FilmgC, ForYSC, HalFC 80, IntMPA 77, -75, -76, -78, -79, -80, MGM[port], MotPP, MovMk[port], NotNAT A, OxFilm, ThFT[port], TwYS, What 4[port], WhoHol A, WorEFlm
Astor, Richard 1927- BiE&WWA, NotNAT
Astorga, Baron D' 1680-1757? OxMus
Astorga, Emanuele D' 1680-1757? Baker 78, MusMk, NewGrD 80
Astorga, Jean Oliver NewGrD 80
Astrand, Hans 1925- IntWWM 77, -80, NewGrD 80
Astredo, Humbert Allen WhoHol A
Astrin, Neal 1906- AmSCAP 66
Astruc, Alexandre 1923- BiDFilm, -81, DcFM, FilmEn, FilmgC, HalFC 80, OxFilm, WorEFlm
Astrup, Arne 1922- IntWWM 77
Astutti, Nestor Eugerio 1932- IntWWM 77, -80
Astwood, Norman BlksB&W C
Asuar, Jose Vicente 1933- Baker 78, DcCM, NewGrD 80
Asula, Giammateo NewGrD 80
Asulae, Giammateo NewGrD 80
Asvaghosa OxThe
Aswell, Thomas NewGrD 80
Atanasoff, Cyril 1941- DancEn 78
Atanasov, Georgi 1881-1931 Baker 78
Atanassoff, Cyril 1941- CnOxB
Atay, Cahit 1925- CnThe, REnWD
Atcher, Bob CounME 74A
Atcher, Bob 1914- CounME 74, EncFCWM 69, IlEncCM
Atcher, James Robert Owen 1914- BiDAmM
Atcher, Randall I 1918- BiDAmM
Atchison, David Glenn 1958- IntWWM 77
Atchison, John Bush 1840-1882 BiDAmM
Atchison, Shelby David 1912- BiDAmM
Atchley, Hooper 1887-1943 NotNAT B, WhScrn 74, -77, WhoHol B
Atchley, Samuel Lee 1945- AmSCAP 80
Atehortua, Blas Emilio 1933- NewGrD 80
Atencio, F Xavier 1919- AmSCAP 80
Ates, Roscoe MotPP
Ates, Roscoe 1892-1962 FilmEn, Film 2, FilmgC, ForYSC, HalFC 80, MovMk, WhScrn 74, -77
Ates, Roscoe 1895-1962 HolCA[port], NotNAT B, Vers A[port], WhoHol B
Ath, Andreas D' NewGrD 80
Athanasiades, Georges 1929- IntWWM 77, -80
Athanassov, Georgi 1882-1931 NewGrD 80
Athenaeus NewGrD 80
Atherton, Alice 1860-1899 NotNAT B
Atherton, Daisy d1961 NotNAT B
Atherton, David 1941- NewGrD 80
Atherton, David 1944- IntWWM 77, -80, WhoMus 72, WhoOp 76
Atherton, Ella Film 2
Atherton, Joan 1948- IntWWM 77, -80
Atherton, Percy Lee 1871-1944 Baker 78, BiDAmM, ConAmC
Atherton, Robert 1910- IntWWM 80, WhoMus 72
Atherton, William 1947- FilmEn, HalFC 80
Atherton, William 1949- IntMPA 77, -76, -78, -79, -80, WhoHol A
Athesinus, Leonardus NewGrD 80
Athey, Ralph ConAmC
Athis, Alfred 1873- WhThe
Atholl, Duke Of OxMus
Atienza, Edward 1924- BiE&WWA, NotNAT, WhoThe 72, -77
Atienza Y Pineda, Francisco De 1657?-1726 NewGrD 80
Atinsky, Jerry 1917- AmSCAP 80
Atis NewGrD 80
Atkerson, Paul 1921- AmSCAP 66, -80
Atkin, Charles 1910- BiE&WWA
Atkin, Lawrence 1907- WhoMus 72
Atkin, Nancy 1904- WhThe
Atkin, Pete And Clive James IlEncR
Atkins, Alfred 1900-1941 NotNAT B, WhScrn 74, -77
Atkins, Alvin WhoMus 72
Atkins, Boyd 1900- BiDAmM, NewOrJ, WhoJazz 72
Atkins, Chester Burton 1924- BiDAmM
Atkins, Chet 1924- ConMuA 80A, CounME 74[port], -74A, EncFCWM 69, IlEncCM[port], IlEncR
Atkins, Ed 1887- WhoJazz 72
Atkins, Eddie 1887-1926 NewOrJ
Atkins, Eileen 1934- FilmgC, HalFC 80, NotNAT, WhoHol A, WhoThe 72, -77
Atkins, Sir Ivor 1869-1953 NewGrD 80
Atkins, Ivor Algernon 1869-1953 OxMus
Atkins, James Humphrey 1912- WhoMus 72
Atkins, Jeffery MagIlD
Atkins, John d1671 NewGrD 80
Atkins, John Gordon 1933- IntWWM 77, -80, WhoMus 72
Atkins, Pervis DrBlPA
Atkins, Robert Film 1
Atkins, Robert 1886-1972 CnThe, EncWT, OxThe, PlP&P, WhScrn 77, WhThe
Atkins, Russell 1926- BlkAmP
Atkins, Terence Edward 1946- IntWWM 77, -80
Atkinson, Brooks 1894- BiE&WWA, EncWT, NotNAT, OxThe
Atkinson, Charles H d1909 NotNAT B
Atkinson, Charles M 1941- IntWWM 80
Atkinson, Clarence Frederic 1934- IntWWM 80
Atkinson, Clarence Frederick 1934- IntWWM 77
Atkinson, Condit Robert 1928- AmSCAP 80
Atkinson, David 1921- BiE&WWA, NotNAT
Atkinson, Evelyn 1900-1954 WhScrn 74, -77, WhoHol B
Atkinson, Frank 1893-1963 NotNAT B, WhScrn 74, -77, WhoHol B
Atkinson, George A 1877-1968 Film 2, WhScrn 77
Atkinson, George H d1955 NotNAT B
Atkinson, Mrs. H PupTheA
Atkinson, Harry 1866- WhThe
Atkinson, Herbert Edward 1897- WhoMus 72
Atkinson, Ione Film 2
Atkinson, J Brooks 1894- WhoThe 72, -77
Atkinson, John d1671 NewGrD 80
Atkinson, John 1835-1897 BiDAmM
Atkinson, Josephine Film 1
Atkinson, Justin Brooks 1894- ConAmTC
Atkinson, Lottie A PupTheA
Atkinson, Neville Thomas IntWWM 77, -80, WhoMus 72
Atkinson, Robert James 1922- IntWWM 77, -80
Atkinson, Robert Whitman 1868-1933 BiDAmM
Atkinson, Rosalind 1900- BiE&WWA, PlP&P, WhoThe 72, -77
Atkinson, Ted 1916- What 2[port]
Atkinson, Tom Foster 1899- WhoMus 72
Atlanta Rhythm Section, The ConMuA 80A, IlEncR, RkOn 2[port]
Atlantov, Vladimir 1939- Baker 78, NewGrD 80, WhoOp 76
Atlas 1864- WhThe
Atlas, Charles What 1[port]
Atlas, Dalia IntWWM 77, -80, WhoMus 72
Atlas, Leopold 1907-1954 NotNAT B
Atlason, Agust 1951- IntWWM 77
Atlass, H Leslie d1960 NewYTET
Atlee, Howard 1926- BiE&WWA, NotNAT
Atlwegg, Raffaele 1938- IntWWM 80
Atmar, Ann 1939-1966 WhScrn 77
Ato Episcopus Trecensis NewGrD 80
Atomic Rooster IlEncR
Ator, James Donald 1938- CpmDNM 73, ConAmC, IntWWM 77, -80
Atrash, Farid 1915?-1974 NewGrD 80
Atrio, Hermannus De NewGrD 80
Atsumi, Takayori Paul 1934- IntWWM 77, -80
Atta OxThe
Attaignant, Pierre d1552 Baker 78
Attaignant, Pierre 1480?-1550? BnBkM 80
Attaingnant, Pierre 1494?-1552? NewGrD 80
Attanasio, Donald Joseph 1938- AmSCAP 80
Attaway, Ruth BiE&WWA, DrBlPA, NotNAT, WhoHol A
Attaway, William A 1915- AmSCAP 80
Attenborough, David 1926- IntMPA 77, -75, -76, -78, -79, -80
Attenborough, Richard 1923- BiDFilm, -81, CmMov, FilmAG WE, FilmEn, FilmgC, ForYSC, HalFC 80, IlWWBF[port], IntMPA 77, -75, -76, -78, -79, -80, MotPP, MovMk[port], OxFilm, WhoHol A, WhoThe 72, -77, WorEFlm
Attenhofer, Carl 1837-1914 NewGrD 80
Attenhofer, Karl 1837-1914 Baker 78
Atterberg, Kurt 1887-1974 Baker 78, CompSN[port], DcCM, NewEOp 71, NewGrD 80, OxMus, WhoMus 72
Atterbom, Daniel Amadeus 1790-1835 OxThe
Atterbury, Luffmann 1740?-1796 NewGrD 80
Atterbury, Malcolm 1907- ForYSC, IntMPA 77, -75, -76, -78, -79, -80, WhoHol A
Atteridge, Harold Richard 1886-1938 AmSCAP 66, -80, BiDAmM, CmpEPM, NewCBMT, NotNAT B, WhThe
Attey, John d1640 NewGrD 80, OxMus
Attfield, Helen Margaret 1946- IntWWM 77, -80
Attles, Joseph E 1903- DrBlPA, NotNAT
Attwell, H M 1943- IntWWM 80
Attwell, Hugh d1621 OxThe
Attwood, Thomas 1765-1838 Baker 78, MusMk, NewGrD 80[port], OxMus
Attwooll, Hugh 1914- IntMPA 77, -75, -76, -78, -79, -80
Atwater, Barry ForYSC, WhoHol A
Atwater, Edith 1911- BiE&WWA, FilmEn, ForYSC, NotNAT, WhThe, WhoHol A, WhoThe 72
Atwater, Gladys IntMPA 77, -75, -76, -78, -79, -80
Atwell, Ben H d1951 NotNAT B
Atwell, Richard ConAmC
Atwell, Roy d1962 NotNAT B
Atwell, Roy 1878-1962 AmSCAP 66, -80, CmpEPM
Atwell, Roy 1879-1962 ForYSC
Atwell, Roy 1880-1962 Film 2, WhScrn 74, -77, WhoHol B
Atwill, Lionel 1883-1946 ForYSC
Atwill, Lionel 1885-1946 CmMov, FilmEn, Film 1, -2, FilmgC, HalFC 80, HolCA[port], MotPP, MovMk[port], NotNAT B, Vers A[port], WhScrn 74, -77, WhThe, WhoHol B, WhoHrs 80[port]

Atwood, Donna 1923?- What 4[port]
Atwood, Lorena E d1947 NotNAT B, WhoStg 1908
Atys 1715-1784 NewGrD 80
Atzmon, Moshe 1931- IntWWM 77, -80, NewGrD 80, WhoMus 72
Auber, Daniel-Francois-Esprit 1782-1871 Baker 78, BnBkM 80, CmOp, CmpBCM, CnOxB, DcCom 77[port], DcCom&M 79, GrComp[port], MusMk, NewEOp 71, NewGrD 80[port], OxMus
Auber, Francois 1782-1871 DancEn 78
Auberjonois, Rene 1940- FilmEn, FilmgC, HalFC 80, NotNAT, WhoHol A, WhoThe 72, -77
Aubert NewGrD 80
Aubert, Eric Louis 1921- IntWWM 77, -80
Aubert, Henri 1926-1971 BiDAmM
Aubert, Jacques 1689-1753 Baker 78, NewGrD 80, OxMus
Aubert, Jean-Louis 1732-1810? NewGrD 80
Aubert, Jeanne 1906- WhThe
Aubert, Lenore 1918?- FilmEn, FilmgC, ForYSC, HalFC 80, WhoHrs 80
Aubert, Louis 1720-1783? NewGrD 80
Aubert, Louis 1877-1968 CompSN[port], MusMk, OxMus
Aubert, Louis 1877-1969 DcCom&M 79
Aubert, Louis 1879-1944 DcFM
Aubert, Louis-Francois-Marie 1877-1968 Baker 78
Aubert, Olivier 1763-1830? NewGrD 80
Aubert, Roger Stephan 1913- IntWWM 77, -80
Aubery DuBoulley, Prudent-Louis 1796-1870 Baker 78, NewGrD 80
Aubeux, Louis 1917- IntWWM 77, -80
Aubignac, Francois Hedeli, Abbe D' 1604-1676 NotNAT B
Aubignac, Francois Hedelin, Abbe D' 1604-1676 EncWT, Ent, OxThe
Aubin, Tony 1907- Baker 78, NewGrD 80, WhoMus 72
Aubrey, Anne 1937- FilmgC, HalFC 80, IlWWBF[port]
Aubrey, Elizabeth 1951- IntWWM 77, -80
Aubrey, Georges 1928-1975 WhScrn 77, WhoHol C
Aubrey, James T, Jr. 1918- IntMPA 77, -75, -76, -78, -79, -80, NewYTET
Aubrey, Jimmy Film 1, -2, ForYSC, TwYS
Aubrey, Madge 1902-1970 WhThe
Aubrey, Skye 1945- FilmgC, WhoHol A
Aubrey, Will 1894-1958 WhScrn 74, -77
Aubry, Cecile 1929- FilmEn, FilmgC, HalFC 80
Aubry, Pierre 1874-1910 Baker 78, NewGrD 80
Aubuchon, Jacques 1924- ForYSC, NotNAT
Auburn, Jane Film 2
Auburn, Joy Film 2, WhScrn 74, -77
Auclair, Michel 1922- EncWT, FilmEn, FilmgC, HalFC 80
Aucoin, Bill ConMuA 80B
Auda, Antoine 1879-1964 Baker 78, NewGrD 80
Aude, Joseph 1755-1841 NotNAT B, OxThe
Audefroi Le Bastart NewGrD 80
Auden, W H 1907-1973 AmSCAP 66, BiE&WWA, CnMD, ConDr 73, FilmEn, McGEWD[port], ModWD, NewEOp 71, NewGrD 80, PlP&P, WhThe, WhoThe 72
Auden, W H 1907-1975 CmOp
Auden, Wystan Hugh 1907-1973 AmSCAP 80, BiDAmM, EncWT, Ent, OxThe
Audeoud, Susana 1919- CnOxB
Audet, Andre PupTheA
Audiard, Michel 1920- DcFM, FilmEn, FilmgC, HalFC 80, WorEFlm
Audiberti, Jacques 1899-1965 CnMD, CnThe, CroCD, EncWT, Ent[port], McGEWD[port], ModWD, OxThe, REnWD
Audiffren, Jean 1680?-1762 NewGrD 80
Audinot, Nicolas-Medard 1732-1801 NewGrD 80
Audley, Eleanor ForYSC, WhoHol A
Audley, Maxine 1920?- ForYSC
Audley, Maxine 1923- FilmEn, FilmgC, HalFC 80, WhoHol A, WhoThe 72, -77
Audran, Edmond 1840-1901 Baker 78, NewGrD 80, NotNAT B, OxMus
Audran, Edmond 1919-1951 WhScrn 74, -77, WhoHol B
Audran, Marius-Pierre 1816-1887 Baker 78
Audran, Stephane OxFilm, WhoHol A
Audran, Stephane 1933- BiDFilm, -81
Audran, Stephane 1938- FilmgC, HalFC 80, IntMPA 79, -80
Audran, Stephane 1939- FilmAG WE[port], FilmEn
Audre BiE&WWA, NotNAT
Audry, Jacqueline 1908-1977 DcFM, FilmEn, FilmgC, HalFC 80, OxFilm, WomWMM
Aue, Hartmann Von NewGrD 80
Auen, Signe d1966 FilmEn, Film 1, WhoHol B
Auer, Anna WhScrn 74, -77
Auer, Edward 1941- WhoMus 72
Auer, Florence 1880-1962 Film 1, -2, ForYSC, TwYS, WhScrn 77, WhoHol B
Auer, John H 1906- FilmEn
Auer, John H 1909-1975 FilmgC, HalFC 80, IntMPA 75, NewYTET
Auer, Leopold 1845-1930 AmSCAP 66, -80, Baker 78, BiDAmM, BnBkM 80, NewGrD 80, OxMus
Auer, Max 1880-1964 Baker 78
Auer, Mischa 1905-1967 FilmEn, Film 2, FilmgC, ForYSC, Funs[port], HalFC 80, HolCA[port], MotPP, MovMk[port], NotNAT B, TwYS, Vers A[port], What 1[port], WhScrn 74, -77, WhoHol B, WhoHrs 80
Auerbach, Arthur 1903-1957 WhScrn 74, -77
Auerbach, Artie d1957 NotNAT B
Auerbach, Cynthia 1940- IntWWM 77
Auerbach, Henry L d1916 WhScrn 77
Auerbach, Leonard BiE&WWA, NotNAT
Auerbach, Norbert T IntMPA 79, -80
Auerbach, Norman ConAmC
Auerbach-Levy, William d1961 NotNAT B
Auerhan, Chretien NewGrD 80
Auernhammer, Josepha Barbara Von 1758-1820 NewGrD 80
Auersperg, Johannes 1934- IntWWM 77, -80
Aufdemberge, Clarence T 1939- IntWWM 77, -80
Auffmann, Joseph Anton 1720?-1733? NewGrD 80
Auffschnaidter, Benedict Anton 1665?-1742 NewGrD 80
Aufmann, Joseph Anton 1720?-1733? NewGrD 80
Aufschnaiter, Benedict Anton 1665?-1742 NewGrD 80
Aufschneider, Benedict Anton 1665?-1742 NewGrD 80
Aug, Edna 1878-1938 NotNAT B
Augarde, Adrienne d1913 NotNAT B, WhThe, WhoStg 1908
Augarde, Amy 1868-1959 NotNAT B, WhThe
Augarde, Gertrude d1959 NotNAT B
Augener, George 1830-1915 Baker 78
Auger, Arleen J 1939- IntWWM 80, WhoOp 76
Auger, Brian 1939- ConMuA 80A, EncJzS 70, IlEncR[port]
Auger, Claudine 1942- FilmEn, FilmgC, HalFC 80, WhoHol A
Auger, Leslie 1925- WhoMus 72
Auger, Paul 1592?-1660 NewGrD 80
Auget, Paul 1592?-1660 NewGrD 80
Augier, Emile 1820-1889 CnThe, EncWT, Ent, McGEWD[port], OxThe, REnWD
Augier, Guillaume Victor Emile 1820-1889 NotNAT B
Augur, Munro PupTheA
August, Edwin 1883-1964 FilmEn, Film 1, -2, MotPP, NotNAT B, TwYS, WhScrn 74, -77, WhoHol B
August, Hal 1890-1918 Film 1, WhScrn 77
August, Jan 1912?- CmpEPM
August, Joseph 1890-1947 DcFM, FilmEn, FilmgC, HalFC 80, WorEFlm
August, Peter 1726-1787 NewGrD 80
Augusta, Mademoiselle 1806-1901 CnOxB DancEn 78
Augusteijn, Henri Paul 1921- IntWWM 77, -80
Augustin, George 1890- NewOrJ
Augustin, Virpi 1942- WhoOp 76
Augustine Of Hippo 354-430 NewGrD 80
Augustine, Saint OxMus
Augustine, Aurelius 354-430 Baker 78
Augustine, Daniel Schuyler 1942- AmSCAP 80
Augustine, Larry D 1940- NotNAT
Augustini, Pietro Simone NewGrD 80
Augustus Druriolanus OxThe
Augustyn, Frank 1953- CnOxB
Auld, Alexander 1836-1889 BiDAmM
Auld, George 1919- CmpEPM, IlEncJ, WhoJazz 72
Auld, Georgie 1919- AmSCAP 66, -80, BgBands 74, BiDAmM, EncJzS 70
Auld, John 1920- DancEn 78
Auld, John 1925- CnOxB
Aulen, J NewGrD 80
Auletta, Domenico 1723-1753 NewGrD 80
Auletta, Pietro 1698?-1771 NewGrD 80
Auli, Juan 1797-1869 NewGrD 80
Aulin, Ewa 1949- FilmEn, FilmgC, ForYSC, HalFC 80
Aulin, Ewa 1950- FilmAG WE
Aulin, Laura Valborg 1860-1928 NewGrD 80
Aulin, Leif 1935- IntWWM 77, -80
Aulin, Tor 1866-1914 Baker 78, MusMk, NewGrD 80, OxMus
Aulisi, Joseph G 1923- WhoThe 77
Ault, Marie 1870-1951 FilmEn, Film 2, FilmgC, HalFC 80, NotNAT B, WhScrn 74, -77, WhThe, WhoHol B
Auman, Franz Josef 1728-1797 NewGrD 80
Aumann, Franz Josef 1728-1797 NewGrD 80
Aumer, Jean 1774-1833 CnOxB
Aumon, Franz Josef 1728-1797 NewGrD 80
Aumonn, Franz Josef 1728-1797 NewGrD 80
Aumont, Jean-Pierre MotPP, WhoHol A
Aumont, Jean-Pierre 1909- FilmAG WE, FilmEn, FilmgC, ForYSC, HalFC 80, HolP 40[port], WhoThe 72, -77
Aumont, Jean-Pierre 1913- BiE&WWA, IntMPA 77, -75, -76, -78, -78, -79, -80, MovMk, NotNAT
Aumont, Tina WhoHol A
Aunt Jemima BluesWW
Aura 1946- EncJzS 70
Aura Lee 1946- EncJzS 70
Aurel, Jean 1925- FilmEn, WorEFlm
Aureli, Aurelio NewGrD 80
Aurelian Of Reome NewGrD 80
Aurelianus Reomensis Baker 78, NewGrD 80
Aurelius Augustinus NewGrD 80
Aurelius, George M 1911- IntMPA 77, -75, -76, -78, -79, -80
Aurelius, Neville NatPD[port]
Aurenche, Jean 1904- FilmEn, FilmgC, HalFC 80, WorEFlm
Auriacombe, Louis 1917- NewGrD 80
Auric, Georges 1899- Baker 78, BnBkM 80, CompSN[port], CnOxB, DancEn 78, DcCom 77, DcFM, FilmEn, FilmgC, HalFC 80, IntWWM 77, -80, MusMk, NewEOp 71, NewGrD 80, OxFilm, OxMus, WorEFlm
Auriol, Jean Baptiste d1881 NotNAT B
Auriol, Jean-George 1907-1950 OxFilm
Aurisicchio, Antonio 1710?-1781 NewGrD 80
Aurons, Alex A 1891-1943 EncMT
Aurthur, Robert Alan 1922-1978 BiE&WWA, FilmEn, FilmgC, HalFC 80, IntMPA 77, -75, -76, -78, -79, -80, NewYTET, NotNAT, WorEFlm
Aus DerOhe, Adele 1864-1937 Baker 78
Ausen, Wolfgang VonWaltersh Film 2
Auslender, Leonard Stanley 1936- ConAmC
Ausm Thal, Alexander NewGrD 80
Austen, George CreCan 1
Austen, Jane 1775-1817 HalFC 80
Auster, Andrew Howard 1950- IntWWM 77
Austin, Professor PupTheA
Austin, Albert 1882-1953 Film 1, -2, WhScrn 74, -77, WhoHol B
Austin, Anson William 1940- WhoOp 76
Austin, Arthur William 1912- IntWWM 77, -80
Austin, Billy 1896-1964 AmSCAP 66, -80
Austin, Bob ConMuA 80B
Austin, Bud IntMPA 77, -75, -76, -78, -79, -80, NewYTET
Austin, Charles 1878-1944 EncWT,

NotNAT B, OxThe, WhScrn 77, WhThe, WhoHol B
Austin, Charlotte 1933- FilmEn, FilmgC, ForYSC, HalFC 80
Austin, Claire 1918- BluesWW[port]
Austin, Cuba 1906- WhoJazz 72
Austin, Donald 1930- IntWWM 77
Austin, Dorothea 1922- IntWWM 77, -80
Austin, Elsie MorBAP
Austin, Emery M 1911- IntMPA 77, -75, -76, -78, -79, -80
Austin, Ernest 1874-1947 Baker 78, OxMus
Austin, Florence 1884-1926 Baker 78
Austin, Frances AmSCAP 80
Austin, Frank Film 2
Austin, Frederic 1872-1952 NewGrD 80, OxMus
Austin, Frederick 1872-1952 Baker 78, CmOp
Austin, Gene d1972 AmPS A, -B, WhoHol B
Austin, Gene 1900-1972 AmSCAP 66, -80, BiDAmM, CmpEPM, What 2[port]
Austin, Gene 1901-1972 WhScrn 77
Austin, George Film 2
Austin, Harold Film 2
Austin, Henry Richter 1882-1961 Baker 78
Austin, Jennie d1938 NotNAT B
Austin, Jere 1876-1927 Film 1, WhScrn 74, -77, WhoHol B
Austin, Jerry FilmgC, HalFC 80
Austin, Johanna 1853-1944 WhScrn 74, -77, WhoHol B
Austin, John 1752- NewGrD 80
Austin, John 1923- IntMPA 77, -75, -76, -78, -79, -80
Austin, John Turnell 1869-1948 Baker 78, NewGrD 80
Austin, Johnny CmpEPM
Austin, Joseph d1821 NotNAT B
Austin, Larry 1930- Baker 78, BiDAmM, ConAmC, DcCM, NewGrD 80
Austin, Leslie Film 2
Austin, Lois 1909-1957 WhScrn 77
Austin, Louis F 1930- IntWWM 80
Austin, Louis Frederick d1905 NotNAT B
Austin, Louise F 1930- IntWWM 77
Austin, Lovie 1887-1972 BiDAmM, EncJzS 70, WhoJazz 72
Austin, Lovie 1897-1972 BlkWAB, CmpEPM
Austin, Lyn 1922- BiE&WWA, NotNAT
Austin, Morris Cotter 1917- IntWWM 77
Austin, Pamela 1942- ForYSC, WhoHol A
Austin, Patricia 1950- AmSCAP 80
Austin, Ray 1915- AmSCAP 80
Austin, Richard 1903- NewGrD 80, WhoMus 72
Austin, Richard Russell 1943- IntWWM 80
Austin, Robert Edwin 1895- WhoMus 72
Austin, Sam Film 2
Austin, Sil 1929- RkOn
Austin, Stephen E 1891-1955 WhScrn 74, -77
Austin, Summer Francis WhoMus 72
Austin, Sumner Francis 1888- IntWWM 77
Austin, Terry WhoHol A
Austin, Tony 1938- AmSCAP 80
Austin, Virginia PupTheA
Austin, Vivian WhoHol A
Austin, William Film 2, ForYSC, TwYS
Austin, William W 1920- Baker 78, IntWWM 77, -80, NewGrD 80
Austral, Florence 1894-1968 Baker 78, CmOp, NewEOp 71, NewGrD 80
Australian Marie Lloyd OxThe
Austrian, Ralph Brooke 1898- IntMPA 77, -75, -76, -78, -79, -80
Autant-Lara, Claude 1903- BiDFilm, -81, DcFM, FilmEn, FilmgC, HalFC 80, IntMPA 77, -75, -76, -78, -79, -80, MovMk[port], OxFilm, WorEFlm
Auten, H William 1921- IntMPA 77, -75, -76, -78, -79, -80
Auteri Manzocchi, Salvatore 1845-1924 Baker 78
Auton, John George 1915- WhoMus 72
Autori, Franco 1903- Baker 78
Autrey, Herman 1904- AmSCAP 66, BiDAmM, CmpEPM, EncJzS 70, WhoJazz 72
Autry, Gene 1907- AmPS A, -B, AmSCAP 66, CmMov, CmpEPM, CounME 74[port], -74A, EncFCWM 69, FilmEn, FilmgC, ForYSC, HalFC 80, IlEncCM[port], IntMPA 77, -75, -76, -78, -79, -80, MotPP, MovMk, NewYTET, OxFilm, What 1[port], WhoHol A, WorEFlm
Autry, Orvon 1907- AmSCAP 80, BiDAmM
Autumnus, Johann Andreas NewGrD 80
Auvray, Jean-Claude 1942- WhoOp 76
Aux-Cousteaux, Arthur 1590?-1654? NewGrD 80
Aux-Cousteaux, Artus 1590?-1654? NewGrD 80
Auza, Atiliano 1928- NewGrD 80
Avakian, Aram HalFC 80, IntMPA 77, -76, -78, -79, -80
Avalier, Don d1973 WhScrn 77
Avalon, Frankie AmPS A, -B, ConMuA 80A, MotPP
Avalon, Frankie 1939- FilmEn, FilmgC, ForYSC, HalFC 80[port], WhoHol A, WhoHrs 80
Avalon, Frankie 1940- BiDAmM, IntMPA 77, -75, -76, -78, -79, -80, MovMk, RkOn[port]
Avancini, Nikolaus 1611-1686 EncWT, Ent
Avancinus, Nicolaus 1612-1686 OxThe
Avanzolini, Girolamo 1600?-1678? NewGrD 80
Avdeyenko, Yakov WomWMM
Avdeyeva, Larisa 1925- NewGrD 80
Avedon, Doe 1928- FilmgC, ForYSC, HalFC 80, IntMPA 77, -75, -76, -78, -79, -80, WhoHol A
Aveline, Albert 1883-1968 CnOxB, DancEn 78
Aveling, Valda 1920- IntWWM 77, -80, WhoMus 72
Avella, Giovanni D' NewGrD 80
Avellino, Alfred 1913- AmSCAP 66, -80
Avenarius, Philipp 1553?-1610? NewGrD 80
Avenary, Hanoch 1908- NewGrD 80
Avenpace NewGrD 80
Aventinus, Johannes 1477-1534 Baker 78, NewGrD 80
Aver, Phyllis Eileen 1937- WhoMus 72
Average White Band, The ConMuA 80A, IlEncR, RkOn 2[port]
Averback, Hy 1920?- HalFC 80
Averback, Hy 1925?- FilmEn, FilmgC, NewYTET
Averi, Peter Warwick 1934- IntWWM 77, -80
Averie NewGrD 80
Averill, Perry 1862-1935 BiDAmM
Averitt, William Earl 1948- ConAmC
Averkamp, Anton 1861-1934 Baker 78
Averre, Richard E 1921- ConAmC
Averroes NewGrD 80
Avery 1470?-1543? NewGrD 80
Avery, Charles Film 1
Avery, Charles 1873- TwYS A
Avery, Fred 1907- WorEFlm[port]
Avery, James Allison 1937- IntWWM 77, -80
Avery, John 1738?-1808 NewGrD 80
Avery, Joseph 1892-1955 NewOrJ
Avery, Margaret DrBlPA
Avery, Patricia 1902-1973 Film 2, WhScrn 77, WhoHol B
Avery, Phyllis 1924- BiE&WWA, ForYSC, WhoHol A
Avery, Stanley R 1879- BiDAmM
Avery, Ted ForYSC
Avery, Tex 1907- FilmgC, HalFC 80, WorEFlm
Avery, Tex 1907-1980 FilmEn
Avery, Tex 1918- DcFM
Avery, Tol 1915-1973 ForYSC, WhScrn 77, WhoHol B
Avery, Val FilmEn, WhoHol A
Avia, Jacob NewGrD 80
Avianus, Johann d1617 NewGrD 80
Avianus, Johannes d1617 NewGrD 80
Avicenna NewGrD 80
Avidom, Menahem 1908- Baker 78, DcCM, IntWWM 77, -80, NewGrD 80, OxMus
Avignone, Bertrand Di NewGrD 80
Avildsen, John G 1936- FilmgC, HalFC 80, IntMPA 77, -75, -76, -78, -79, -80
Avildsen, John G 1937?- FilmEn
Aviles, Manuel Leitao De d1630 NewGrD 80
Aviles, Vicenta WomWMM B
Aviles Lusitano, Manuel Leitao De d1630 NewGrD 80
Avilez, Manuel Leitao De d1630 NewGrD 80
Avis, Marjorie 1912- IntWWM 77, -80, WhoMus 72
Avison, Charles 1709-1770 Baker 78, BnBkM 80, MusMk, NewGrD 80[port]
Avison, Charles 1710?-1770 OxMus
Avison, John 1915- CreCan 1
Avison, John 1917- NewGrD 80
Avison, Margaret 1918- CreCan 1
Aviss, Peter Ronald Frampton 1950- IntWWM 80
Avithal, Theodor 1933- IntWWM 77, -80
Aviv, Nurith WomWMM
Avni, Tzvi Jacob 1927- Baker 78, ConAmC, DcCM, IntWWM 77, -80, NewGrD 80
Avoglio, Christina Maria NewGrD 80
Avola, Alexander Albert 1914- AmSCAP 66, -80, BiDAmM
Avolio, Christina Maria NewGrD 80
Avolo, Rosalie WhScrn 74, -77
Avon, Violet WhoHol A
Avon Comedy Four AmPS B, CmpEPM, JoeFr
Avondano, Pedro Antonio 1714?-1782 NewGrD 80
Avondano, Pietro Antonio 1714?-1782 NewGrD 80
Avorgbedor, Dan Kodzo 1952- IntWWM 80
Avos, Girolamo NewGrD 80
Avos, Giuseppe 1708-1796 NewGrD 80
Avosa, Giuseppe 1708-1796 NewGrD 80
Avosani, Orfeo NewGrD 80
Avossa, Giuseppe D' 1708-1796 Baker 78, NewGrD 80
Avosso, Girolamo NewGrD 80
Avotri, Kenneth Kafui Kwaku 1951- IntWWM 77, -80
Avrahami, Gideon 1941- CnOxB
Avramov, Eugenii 1929- Baker 78
Avril, Edwin Frank 1920- IntWWM 77, -80
Avril, Jane 1868-1942 NotNAT A
Avril, Jane 1868-1943 NotNAT B
Avril, Lloyd ConAmC
Avril, Suzanne WhThe
Avshalomoff, Aaron 1894-1965 BiDAmM
Avshalomoff, Jacob 1919- BiDAmM
Avshalomov, Aaron 1894-1965 Baker 78, ConAmC, DcCM
Avshalomov, Jacob 1919- Baker 78, ConAmC, DcCM, IntWWM 77, -80, MusMk, NewGrD 80, WhoMus 72
Aweusi, Alli BlkAmP
Ax, Emanuel 1949- Baker 78
Axarlis, Stella 1944- IntWWM 77, -80, WhoOp 76
Axelrod, David 1936- EncJzS 70
Axelrod, George 1922- BiDFilm, -81, BiE&WWA, CmMov, CnMD, ConDr 73, -77, FilmEn, FilmgC, HalFC 80, IntMPA 77, -75, -76, -78, -79, -80, McGEWD, NotNAT, OxFilm, WorEFlm
Axelrod, Jonathan 1948- IntMPA 77, -75, -76, -78, -79, -80
Axelsson, Olof Elias 1934- IntWWM 77
Axer, Erwin 1917- EncWT
Axis Sally What 2[port]
Axlerod, David 1937- AmSCAP 66, -80
Axman, Emil 1887-1949 Baker 78, NewGrD 80
Axt, William 1888-1959 AmSCAP 66, -80, ConAmC A, NotNAT B
Axton, Hoyt 1938- ConMuA 80A, IlEncCM[port], IlEncR, RkOn 2[port]
Axworthy, Geoffrey 1923- WhoThe 72, -77
Axworthy, Thomas V 1948- IntWWM 77, -80
Ayala, Adelardo Lopez De 1828-1879 NotNAT B, OxThe
Ayala, Daniel 1906-1975 Baker 78
Ayala, Robert Steven 1951- AmSCAP 80
Ayala, Siska PupTheA
Ayala-Perez, Daniel 1906-1975 DcCM
Ayala Perez, Daniel 1906-1975 NewGrD 80
Ayars, Ann ForYSC, WhoHol A
Ayars, Christine Merrick 1894- IntWWM 77
Aybar, Trudy BlkAmP
Ayckbourn, Alan 1939- ConDr 73, -77, EncWT, Ent, WhoThe 72, -77
Aye, Marion 1906-1951 WhScrn 74, WhoHol B
Aye, Maryon 1906-1951 WhScrn 77

Ayer, Nat D 1887-1952 *BiDAmM, NotNAT B, WhThe*
Ayers, Agnes 1896-1940 *NotNAT B*
Ayers, Cleo *Film 1*
Ayers, David H 1924- *BiE&WWA, NotNAT*
Ayers, Henri 1951- *IntWWM 77, -80*
Ayers, Kevin 1944- *ConMuA 80A, IlEncR*
Ayers, Lemuel 1915-1955 *NotNAT B*
Ayers, Roy E, Jr. 1940- *AmSCAP 80, BiDAmM, EncJzS 70*
Ayers, Sydney *Film 1*
Ayers, Vivian *BlkAmP, MorBAP*
Ayerton, Randle 1869-1940 *NotNAT B*
Ayestaran, Lauro 1913-1966 *NewGrD 80*
Ayesteran, Lauro 1913-1966 *Baker 78*
Ayler, Albert 1936-1970 *BiDAmM, EncJzS 70, IlEncJ, NewGrD 80[port]*
Ayler, Donald 1942- *BiDAmM*
Ayler, Ethel 1934?- *BiE&WWA, DrBlPA*
Ayler Trio, Albert *BiDAmM*
Ayles-Ransley, Gwendolen G *WhoMus 72*
Aylesworth, Arthur d1945 *ForYSC, WhoHol B*
Aylesworth, Arthur 1884-1946 *WhScrn 77*
Aylesworth, Merlin Hall d1952 *NewYTET*
Ayleward, Richard 1626-1669 *NewGrD 80*
Ayliff, Mrs. *NewGrD 80*
Ayliff, Henry Kiell d1949 *NotNAT B, WhThe*
Ayliffe, Audrey Marion *WhoMus 72*
Ayling, Marjorie 1938- *IntWWM 77, -80*
Ayling, Robert d1919 *WhScrn 77*
Aylmer, David 1933-1964 *NotNAT B, WhScrn 74, -77, WhoHol B*
Aylmer, Sir Felix 1889- *IlWWBF[port]*
Aylmer, Sir Felix 1889-1979 *BiE&WWA, EncWT, FilmEn, FilmgC, ForYSC, HalFC 80, MovMk, NotNAT, WhThe, WhoHol A, WhoThe 72*
Ayloff, Mrs. *NewGrD 80*
Ayloffe, Mrs. *NewGrD 80*
Aylott, Dave 1885-1969 *FilmEn, IlWWBF*
Aylward, Theodore 1730?-1801 *NewGrD 80*
Aylwin, Jean 1885-1964 *WhThe*
Ayme, Marcel 1902-1967 *BiE&WWA, CnMD, CnThe, EncWT, Ent, McGEWD, ModWD, NotNAT B*
Ayne VanGhizeghem *NewGrD 80*
Aynes, Edith Annette 1909- *AmSCAP 80*
Aynesworth, Allan 1864-1959 *NotNAT B*
Aynesworth, Allan 1865-1959 *WhThe*
Ayo, Felix 1933- *NewGrD 80*
Ayoub, Nicholas 1926- *EncJzS 70*
Ayoub, Nick 1926- *EncJzS 70*
Ayre, Leslie 1906- *WhoMus 72*
Ayrenhoff, Cornelius Von 1733-1819 *OxThe*
Ayrer, Jacob 1543-1605 *REnWD[port]*
Ayrer, Jakob 1543-1605 *EncWT, Ent, OxThe*
Ayres, Agnes d1940 *MotPP, TwYS, WhoHol B*
Ayres, Agnes 1896-1940 *FilmEn, Film 1, -2, FilmgC, HalFC 80, MovMk*
Ayres, Agnes 1898-1940 *WhScrn 74, -77*
Ayres, Elizabeth *PupTheA*
Ayres, Frederic 1876-1926 *Baker 78, ConAmC, NewGrD 80*
Ayres, Gerald *IntMPA 77, -75, -76, -78, -79, -80*
Ayres, Gordon *WhoHol A*
Ayres, Lemuel *PlP&P*
Ayres, Len *PupTheA*
Ayres, Lew 1908- *BiDFilm, -81, FilmEn, Film 2, FilmgC, ForYSC, HalFC 80, IntMPA 77, -75, -76, -78, -79, -80, MGM[port], MotPP, MovMk[port], OxFilm, What 3[port], WhoHol A, WorEFlm*
Ayres, Mitchell d1969 *BgBands 74*
Ayres, Mitchell 1910- *AmSCAP 80*
Ayres, Mitchell 1910-1969 *AmSCAP 66, CmpEPM*
Ayres, Mitchell 1911-1969 *WhScrn 77, WhoHol B*
Ayres, Robert 1914-1968 *FilmgC, HalFC 80, WhScrn 74, -77, WhoHol B*
Ayres, Sydney d1916 *WhScrn 77*
Ayres, Warren Joyce 1908- *AmSCAP 66, -80*
Ayrton, Edmund 1734?-1808 *Baker 78, NewGrD 80*
Ayrton, Louise *Film 2*
Ayrton, Norman 1924- *WhoThe 72, -77*
Ayrton, Randle 1869-1940 *Film 2, HalFC 80, IlWWBF, WhThe*
Ayrton, Robert d1924 *NotNAT B*
Ayrton, William 1777-1858 *Baker 78, NewGrD 80*
Ayscue, Brian Thomas 1948- *AmSCAP 80, IntWWM 80*
Ayton, Fanny 1806- *NewGrD 80*
Ayton, Vera *WhoMus 72*
Azais, Hyacinthe 1741-1795? *NewGrD 80*
Azanchevsky, Mikhail Pavlovich 1839-1881 *NewGrD 80*
Azantchevsky, Mikhail 1839-1881 *Baker 78*
Azarmi, Nassrin 1949- *WhoOp 76*
Azavedo, Francisco Correa De *NewGrD 80*
Azcarraga, Emilio d1973 *NewYTET*
Azcurra, Pedro Roberto 1940- *IntWWM 77, -80*
Azella, Paul *PupTheA*
Azevedo, Alexis-Jacob 1813-1875 *Baker 78*
Azevedo, Artur 1855-1908 *EncWT, REnWD*
Azevedo, Luiz Heitor Correa De 1905- *NewGrD 80*
Azevedo DaSilva, Fernando De d1923 *NewGrD 80*
Azkue, Resurreccion Maria De 1864-1951 *Baker 78, NewGrD 80*
Azmayparashvili, Shalva 1903- *Baker 78*
Aznavour, Charles 1924- *Baker 78, BiDAmM, FilmAG WE, FilmEn, FilmgC, ForYSC, HalFC 80, MovMk, OxFilm, WhoHol A, WorEFlm[port]*
Azoff, Irving *ConMuA 80B*
Azpiazu, Raul 1924- *AmSCAP 80*
Azpilcueta, Martin De 1491?-1586 *NewGrD 80*
Azuma, Atsuko 1939- *WhoOp 76*
Azza Gera *NewGrD 80*
Azzaiolo, Filippo *NewGrD 80*
Azzara, Bennie Anthony 1910- *AmSCAP 80*
Azzara, Candy 1912- *WhoHol A*
Azzato, Anthony *IntMPA 76*
Azzato, Anthony 1912- *IntMPA 77, -75, -78, -79, -80*
Azzolini, Acly Carlo 1913- *WhoMus 72, WhoOp 76*
Azzopardi, Francesco 1748-1809 *Baker 78*

B

B B, Jr. *BluesWW[port]*
B Bumble And The Stingers *RkOn[port]*
B T Express, The *RkOn 2[port]*
Baal, Karin 1940- *FilmAG WE*
Baaren, Kees Van 1906-1970 *Baker 78, DcCM, NewGrD 80*
Baasch, Merle Dorothy *AmSCAP 80*
Baasch, Robert Jefferson 1916- *IntWWM 77, -80*
Bab, Julius 1880-1955 *EncWT*
Babadjanyan, Arno Harutyuni 1921- *NewGrD 80*
Babadzhanian, Arno 1921- *Baker 78*
Babajanyan, Arno Arutyunovich 1921- *IntWWM 77, -80*
Babak, Renata *WhoOp 76*
Baban, Gracian 1620?-1675 *NewGrD 80*
Babanova, Maria Ivanovna 1900- *OxThe*
Babasin, Harry 1921- *BiDAmM, CmpEPM*
Babayev, Sabir 1920- *IntWWM 77, -80*
Babb, Jeffery William 1926- *IntWWM 77, -80*
Babb, Kroger 1906- *IntMPA 77, -75, -76, -78, -79, -80*
Babbage, Charles 1792-1871 *OxMus*
Babbedge, Harman Paul 1926- *WhoMus 72*
Babbi *NewGrD 80*
Babbi, Cristoforo 1745-1814 *NewGrD 80*
Babbi, Gregorio 1708-1768 *NewGrD 80*
Babbi, Gregorio 1770?-1815? *NewGrD 80*
Babbin, Jacqueline *NewYTET, WomWMM B*
Babbitt, Harry 1913- *CmpEPM, ForYSC, WhoHol A*
Babbitt, Milton Byron 1916- *Baker 78, BiDAmM, BnBkM 80, CompSN[port], CpmDNM 78, ConAmC, DcCM, IntWWM 77, -80, MusMk, NewGrD 80[port], OxMus, WhoMus 72*
Babcock, Alpheus 1785-1842 *NewGrD 80, OxMus*
Babcock, Dwight V 1909- *IntMPA 77, -75, -76, -78, -79, -80*
Babcock, Edward Chester 1913- *AmSCAP 80, NewGrD 80*
Babcock, Jeffrey *ConAmC*
Babcock, Joseph T 1932- *BiDAmM*
Babcock, Maltbie Davenport 1858-1901 *BiDAmM*
Babcock, Michael J 1940- *ConAmC*
Babcock, Theron Charles 1925- *AmSCAP 66, -80*
Babe, Angelus *Film 2*
Babe, Thomas 1941- *NatPD[port]*
Babe Ruth *IlEncR*
Babel, Isaak Emanuilovich 1894-1941? *CnMD, EncWT, McGEWD[port], ModWD*
Babel, Izaak 1894-1941? *Ent*
Babell, William 1690?-1723 *NewGrD 80, OxMus*
Baber, David M 1945- *WhoOp 76*
Baber, Joseph W 1937- *AmSCAP 80, CpmDNM 80, ConAmC*
Babic, Konstantin 1927- *Baker 78*
Babich, Herman Bernard 1917- *AmSCAP 80*
Babikian, Virginia 1930- *IntWWM 77, -80*
Babilee, Jean 1923- *CnOxB, DancEn 78[port]*
Babin, Al 1927- *NewOrJ SUP[port]*
Babin, Stanley 1932- *ConAmC*
Babin, Victor 1908-1972 *AmSCAP 66, -80, Baker 78, BiDAmM, ConAmC, NewGrD 80, WhoMus 72*
Babini, Matteo 1754-1816 *Baker 78*
Babinski, Ludwig 1909- *IntWWM 77, -80*
Babit, Hi *AmSCAP 80*
Babits, Linda 1940- *AmSCAP 66, ConAmC*
Babitz, Sol 1911- *Baker 78, NewGrD 80*
Babochkin, Boris 1904- *FilmEn*
Babou, Jean-Francois-Pascal *NewGrD 80*
Babou, Thomas 1656-1740? *NewGrD 80*
Babs, Alice 1924- *EncJzS 70*
Baburao, Pendharkar 1892- *FilmEn*
Baburao Painter 1892- *DcFM*
Baby, Lucile 1930- *IntWWM 77, -80*
Baby Ballerinas *CnOxB, DancEn 78*
Baby Blues *BluesWW[port]*
Baby Doo *BluesWW[port]*
Baby Duke *BluesWW[port]*
Baby Face *BluesWW[port]*
Baby Face Leroy *BluesWW[port]*
Baby Laurence 1921-1974 *WhScrn 77*
Baby LeRoy 1932- *FilmEn, ForYSC, MotPP, WhoHol A*
Baby Marie *WhoHol A*
Baby Peggy 1917- *FilmEn*
Baby Peggy 1918- *Film 2, What 1[port], WhoHol A*
Baby Sandy 1938- *FilmEn, What 5[port], WhoHol A*
Babys, The *ConMuA 80A[port], RkOn 2[port]*
Bac, Andre 1905- *DcFM*
Baca, Richard 1942- *IntWWM 77*
Bacal, Dave 1908- *AmSCAP 80*
Bacal, Harvey 1915- *AmSCAP 66, -80*
Bacal, Melanie Ella 1948- *AmSCAP 66*
Bacall, Lauren 1924- *BiDFilm, -81, BiE&WWA, CmMov, EncMT, FilmEn, FilmgC, ForYSC, HalFC 80, IntMPA 77, -75, -76, -78, -79, -80, MotPP, MovMk[port], NotNAT, OxFilm, WhoHol A, WhoThe 72, -77, WorEFlm[port]*
Bacarisse, Salvador 1898-1963 *Baker 78, NewGrD 80*
Baccaloni, Salvatore 1900-1969 *Baker 78, CmOp, FilmEn, HalFC 80, MusSN[port], NewEOp 71, NewGrD 80, WhScrn 74, -77, WhoHol B*
Baccaloni, Salvatore 1900-1970 *FilmgC*
Baccaloni, Salvatori 1900-1970 *ForYSC*
Baccelli, Giovanna *NewGrD 80*
Baccelli, Giovanna 1753?-1801 *CnOxB, DancEn 78*
Baccelli, Matteo Pantaleone 1690-1760? *NewGrD 80*
Bacchelli, Riccardo 1891- *CnMD*
Bacchini, Girolamo M *NewGrD 80*
Bacchius *Baker 78, NewGrD 80*
Bacchius, Johannes De d1557? *NewGrD 80*
Bacchus, Johannes De d1557? *NewGrD 80*
Bacchylides *NewGrD 80*
Bacciccia *NewGrD 80*
Baccio Fiorentino *NewGrD 80*
Baccus, Eddie 1936- *BiDAmM*
Baccusi, Ippolito 1530-1608 *Baker 78*
Baccusi, Ippolito 1550?-1609 *NewGrD 80*
Baccusii, Hippolyti 1550?-1609 *NewGrD 80*
Bacelar, Jose Gabriel 1924- *IntWWM 77, -80*
Bacevicius, Vytautas 1905- *AmSCAP 66*
Bacewicz, Grazyna 1909-1969 *Baker 78, NewGrD 80*
Bacewicz, Grazyna 1913-1969 *DcCM*
Bach *NewGrD 80, WhScrn 74, -77*
Bach, Albert 1844-1912 *Baker 78*
Bach, August Wilhelm 1796-1869 *Baker 78, NewGrD 80*
Bach, Barbara 1951- *HalFC 80*
Bach, Carl Philipp Emanuel 1714-1788 *Baker 78, BnBkM 80, CmpBCM, DcCom 77, GrComp[port], MusMk, NewGrD 80[port]*
Bach, Carl Phillip Emmanuel 1714-1788 *DcCom&M 79*
Bach, Cecilia *NewGrD 80*
Bach, Charles Ernest *NewGrD 80*
Bach, Christoph 1613-1661 *Baker 78*
Bach, Fernand d1953 *NotNAT B*
Bach, Georg Christoph 1642-1697 *Baker 78*
Bach, Hans 1604-1673 *Baker 78*
Bach, Heinrich 1615-1692 *Baker 78*
Bach, Jan Morris 1937- *AmSCAP 80, ConAmC*
Bach, Johann 1555?-1615 *NewGrD 80[port]*
Bach, Johann Ambrosius 1645-1695 *Baker 78*
Bach, Johann Bernhard 1676?-1749 *Baker 78, NewGrD 80*
Bach, Johann Christian 1735-1782 *Baker 78, BnBkM 80, DcCom 77[port], DcCom&M 79, MusMk, NewEOp 71, NewGrD 80[port], OxMus*
Bach, Johann Christoph 1642-1703 *Baker 78, MusMk, NewGrD 80, OxMus*
Bach, Johann Christoph 1645-1693 *Baker 78*
Bach, Johann Christoph 1671-1721 *Baker 78*
Bach, Johann Christoph Friedrich 1732-1795 *Baker 78, NewGrD 80, OxMus*
Bach, Johann Egidius 1645-1716 *Baker 78*
Bach, Johann Ernst 1722?-1777 *Baker 78, NewGrD 80*
Bach, Johann Ludwig 1677-1731 *Baker 78, NewGrD 80*
Bach, Johann Michael 1648?-1694 *Baker 78, NewGrD 80*
Bach, Johann Michael 1745-1820 *NewGrD 80*
Bach, Johann Nicolaus 1669-1753 *NewGrD 80*
Bach, Johann Nikolaus 1669-1753 *Baker 78*
Bach, Johann Sebastian 1685-1750 *Baker 78, BnBkM 80[port], CmpBCM, CnOxB, DcCom 77[port], DcCom&M 79, GrComp[port], MusMk[port], NewGrD 80[port], OxMus*
Bach, John Christian 1735-1782 *CmpBCM, GrComp[port]*

Bach, Karl Philipp Emanuel 1714-1788 *OxMus*
Bach, Leonhard Emil 1849-1902 *Baker 78*
Bach, Margaret Lesser *WomWMM B*
Bach, Maria 1896- *IntWWM 77, -80*
Bach, Otto 1833-1893 *OxMus*
Bach, P D Q *AmSCAP 80*
Bach, Reginald 1886-1941 *NotNAT B, WhThe*
Bach, Mrs. Rudi d1960 *WhScrn 74, -77*
Bach, Steven K 1940- *IntMPA 80*
Bach, Vincent 1890-1976 *NewGrD 80*
Bach, Wilhelm Friedemann 1710-1784 *Baker 78, BnBkM 80, CmpBCM, GrComp[port], MusMk, NewGrD 80[port], OxMus*
Bach, Wilhelm Friedrich Ernst 1759?-1845 *Baker 78, NewGrD 80*
Bachand, Treva *WomWMM B*
Bacharach, Burt *NewCBMT*
Bacharach, Burt 1928- *AmSCAP 66, Baker 78, EncMT, IlEncR, MusMk[port], PopAmC SUP[port], Sw&Ld C*
Bacharach, Burt 1929- *FilmEn, FilmgC, HalFC 80, IntWWM 77, NotNAT*
Bacharach, Burt F 1928- *AmPS, AmSCAP 80, BiDAmM, ConAmC*
Bachauer, Gina 1913-1976 *Baker 78, BnBkM 80, MusSN[port], NewGrD 80, WhoMus 72*
Bache *NewGrD 80*
Bache, Constance 1846-1903 *Baker 78, NewGrD 80, OxMus*
Bache, Francis Edward 1833-1858 *NewGrD 80, OxMus*
Bache, Walter 1842-1888 *NewGrD 80, OxMus*
Bachelar, Daniel 1574?-1610? *NewGrD 80*
Bachelbel, Johann *NewGrD 80*
Bacheler, Daniel 1574?-1610? *NewGrD 80*
Bachelet, Alfred 1864-1944 *Baker 78*
Bachelet, Jean 1894- *DcFM, FilmEn, WorEFlm*
Bachelin, Franz *IntMPA 77, -75, -76, -79, -80*
Bachelin, Franz 1938- *IntMPA 78*
Bachelor, Stephanie *ForYSC, WhoHol A*
Bachelor, Stephanie 1925?- *FilmEn*
Bachelors, The *RkOn 2[port]*
Bacherini Bartoli, Maria Adelaide 1935- *IntWWM 80*
Bachfarrt, Valentin *NewGrD 80*
Bachiler, Daniel *NewGrD 80*
Bachleda, Andrzej 1923- *IntWWM 77, -80*
Bachman, H Sherwyn 1942- *IntWWM 77*
Bachman, Jack 1917- *NewOrJ*
Bachman, Martha Jeanne 1924- *AmSCAP 80*
Bachman, Rachel Barrett 1943- *IntWWM 77*
Bachman-Turner Overdrive *ConMuA 80A, IlEncR, RkOn 2[port]*
Bachmann, Alberto Abraham 1875-1963 *Baker 78*
Bachmann, Carl Ludwig 1743-1809 *NewGrD 80*
Bachmann, Charlotte Wilhelmine Caroline 1757-1817 *NewGrD 80*
Bachmann, George Theodore, Jr. 1930- *IntWWM 77, -80*
Bachmann, Reinhard Werner 1923- *IntWWM 80*
Bachmann, Sixt 1754-1825 *NewGrD 80*
Bachmann, Werner 1923- *NewGrD 80*
Bachner, Annette *WomWMM A, -B*
Bachofen, Johann Caspar 1695-1755 *NewGrD 80*
Bachrach, Doro *WomWMM, -B*
Bachrich, Sigismund 1841-1913 *Baker 78*
Bachschmid, Anton 1728-1797 *NewGrD 80*
Bachschmidt, Anton 1728-1797 *NewGrD 80*
Bachus, Johannes De *NewGrD 80*
Bachvarova, Radka *WomWMM*
Bacilieri, Giovanni *NewGrD 80*
Bacilly, Benigne De 1625?-1690 *NewGrD 80*
Baciu, Ion 1931- *IntWWM 77, -80*
Back *Film 2*
Back, Knut 1868-1953 *Baker 78*
Back, Konrad 1749-1810 *NewGrD 80*
Back, Leon B 1912- *IntMPA 77, -75, -76, -78, -79, -80*
Back, Oskar 1879-1963 *NewGrD 80*
Back, Sven-Erik 1919- *Baker 78, DcCM, IntWWM 77, -80, NewGrD 80*
Back Door *IlEncR*
Backe, John D *NewYTET*
Backer, William Montague 1926- *AmSCAP 80*
Backer-Grondahl, Agatha Ursula 1847-1907 *OxMus*
Backer-Grondahl, Agathe *NewGrD 80*
Backer-Grondahl, Agathe 1847-1907 *Baker 78*
Backer-Grondahl, Fritjof 1885-1959 *OxMus*
Backers, Americus *NewGrD 80*
Backers, Cor 1910- *Baker 78*
Backes, Alice *WhoHol A*
Backes, Lotte 1901- *IntWWM 80*
Backhaus, Wilhelm 1884-1969 *Baker 78, BnBkM 80, MusMk, MusSN[port], NewGrD 80[port]*
Backman, Ilkka Olavi 1945- *WhoOp 76*
Backner, Arthur *Film 1*
Backner, Constance *Film 1*
Backofen, Johann Georg Heinrich 1768-1839 *NewGrD 80*
Backus, E Y d1914 *NotNAT B*
Backus, George 1858-1939 *Film 2, NotNAT B, WhScrn 74, -77, WhoHol B*
Backus, Henny *WhoHol A*
Backus, Jim 1913- *FilmEn, FilmgC, ForYSC, HalFC 80, IntMPA 77, -75, -76, -78, -79, -80, JoeFr[port] MotPP, MovMk[port], WhoHol A*
Backus, Richard 1945- *WhoThe 77*
Backvart, Valentijn *NewGrD 80*
Baclanova, Olga d1974 *MotPP, WhoHol B*
Baclanova, Olga 1896-1974 *TwYS*
Baclanova, Olga 1899-1974 *FilmEn, FilmgC, ForYSC, HalFC 80, ThFT[port], WhScrn 77, WhThe, WhoHrs 80*
Baclanova, Olga 1900-1974 *Film 2*
Baco, Roger *NewGrD 80*
Bacon *NewGrD 80*
Bacon, Bessie 1886-1952 *WhScrn 74, -77*
Bacon, David 1914-1942 *NotNAT B*
Bacon, David 1914-1943 *WhScrn 74, -77, WhoHol B*
Bacon, Denise *IntWWM 77, -80*
Bacon, Ed *ConAmTC*
Bacon, Ernst 1898- *AmSCAP 66, -80, Baker 78, BiDAmM, BnBkM 80, CpmDNM 79, ConAmC, DcCM, NewEOp 71, NewGrD 80, OxMus*
Bacon, Faith 1909-1956 *NotNAT B, WhScrn 74, -77, WhoHol B*
Bacon, Francis 1561-1626 *DcPup, NotNAT B, PlP&P[port]*
Bacon, Frank 1864-1922 *Film 1, ModWD, NotNAT B, OxThe, WhScrn 74, -77, WhThe, WhoHol B*
Bacon, Irving 1892-1965 *FilmgC, HalFC 80*
Bacon, Irving 1893-1965 *FilmEn, Film 2, ForYSC, HolCA[port], MovMk, TwYS, WhScrn 74, -77, WhoHol B*
Bacon, Irving 1904-1965 *Vers A[port]*
Bacon, Irwin *Film 2*
Bacon, Jane d1956 *NotNAT B*
Bacon, Jane 1895- *PlP&P, WhThe*
Bacon, Jane M *NewGrD 80*
Bacon, Katherine 1896- *BiDAmM*
Bacon, Leonard W 1802-1881 *BiDAmM*
Bacon, Lloyd 1889-1955 *CmMov, DcFM, MovMk[port], WorEFlm*
•**Bacon,** Lloyd 1890-1955 *BiDFilm, -81, FilmEn, Film 1, FilmgC, HalFC 80, OxFilm, TwYS A, WhScrn 74, -77, WhoHol B*
Bacon, Louis 1904-1967 *BiDAmM, WhoJazz 72*
Bacon, Louisa Mary 1800-1885 *NewGrD 80*
Bacon, Madi 1906- *IntWWM 77, -80*
Bacon, Mai 1898- *WhThe*
Bacon, Phannel d1783 *NotNAT B*
Bacon, Ralph 1934- *IntWWM 77, -80*
Bacon, Richard Mackenzie 1776-1844 *Baker 78, NewGrD 80*
Bacon, Roger 1214?-1292? *NewGrD 80*
Bacon, W Garwood, Jr. 1920- *AmSCAP 80*
Bacon, Walter Scott 1891-1973 *WhScrn 77*
Bacon Harty, Carol 1937- *IntWWM 77, -80*
Bacon-Shone, Frederic 1924- *IntWWM 80*
Bacquedano, Jose De *NewGrD 80*
Bacquier, Gabriel 1924- *CmOp, NewGrD 80, WhoOp 76*
Bacs, Ludovic 1930- *IntWWM 80*
Bacsik, Elek 1926- *EncJzS 70*
Bacso, Peter 1928- *FilmEn*
Baculis, Al 1930- *EncJzS 70*
Baculis, Alphonse 1930- *EncJzS 70*
Bacus, Lucia *WhScrn 74, -77*
Bacus Correcarius DeBononia, Johannes *NewGrD 80*
Baczynski, Stanislaw Tomasz *NewGrD 80*
Bad Company *ConMuA 80A, IlEncR, RkOn 2[port]*
Badajoz El Musico *NewGrD 80*
Badal, Janos 1927- *WorEFlm*
Badal, Jean 1927- *FilmEn, WorEFlm*
Badalamenti, Angelo Daniel 1937- *AmSCAP 80*
Badale, Andy 1937- *AmSCAP 80, IntWWM 77*
Badalla, Rosa Giacinta *NewGrD 80*
Badalli, Rosa Giacinta *NewGrD 80*
Badarzewska, Thekla 1834-1861 *Baker 78, OxMus*
Badarzewska-Baranowska, Tekla 1834-1861 *NewGrD 80*
Baddeley, Angela d1976 *PlP&P, WhoHol C*
Baddeley, Angela 1900-1976 *FilmgC*
Baddeley, Angela 1904-1976 *HalFC 80, WhoThe 72, -77*
Baddeley, Hermione *BiE&WWA, MotPP, WhoHol A*
Baddeley, Hermione 1906- *EncMT, FilmEn, FilmgC, ForYSC, HalFC 80, IlWWBF, MovMk[port], WhoThe 72, -77*
Baddeley, Hermione 1908- *Film 2, IntMPA 77, -75, -76, -78, -79, -80*
Baddeley, Robert 1732-1794 *OxThe*
Baddeley, Robert 1733-1794 *NotNAT B*
Baddeley, Sophia Snow 1745-1786 *NotNAT A, -B, OxThe*
Badel, Alan 1923- *FilmEn, FilmgC, HalFC 80, IlWWBF, WhoHol A, WhoThe 72, -77*
Badel, Allan 1923- *BiE&WWA, NotNAT*
Badel, Sarah 1943- *WhoThe 72, -77*
Baden, Conrad 1908- *Baker 78, NewGrD 80*
Baden-Semper, Nina 1945- *HalFC 80*
Bader *NewGrD 80*
Bader, Arnold *NewGrD 80*
Bader, Conrad *NewGrD 80*
Bader, Daniel 1560?-1636? *NewGrD 80*
Bader, Ernst *NewGrD 80*
Bader, Hans-Dieter 1938- *WhoOp 76*
Bader, Hans Heinrich *NewGrD 80*
Bader, Johann Gottfried *NewGrD 80*
Bader, Tobias *NewGrD 80*
Badessa, Giovanni Battista *NewGrD 80*
Badev, Georgi 1939- *NewGrD 80*
Badfinger *ConMuA 80A, IlEncR, RkOn 2[port]*
Badgely, Helen *Film 1*
Badger, Alfred G 1815-1892 *NewGrD 80*
Badger, Clarence 1880-1964 *FilmEn, FilmgC, HalFC 80, NotNAT B, TwYS A, WorEFlm*
Badger, Patricia *PupTheA*
Badham, John *HalFC 80*
Badham, Mary 1952- *FilmgC, HalFC 80, MotPP, WhoHol A*
Badham, Mary 1953- *ForYSC*
Badia, Carlo Agostino 1672-1738 *NewGrD 80*
Badia, Concepcion 1897-1975 *NewGrD 80*
Badia, Conchita 1897-1975 *NewGrD 80*
Badia, Conxita 1897-1975 *NewGrD 80*
Badie, Pete 1900-1960? *NewOrJ*
Badings, Henk 1907- *Baker 78, BnBkM 80, CompSN[port], CpmDNM 79, -80, CnOxB, DcCM, IntWWM 77, -80, MusMk, NewGrD 80, OxMus, WhoMus 72*
Badings, Vera Maria 1938- *IntWWM 77, -80*
Badini, Gerard 1931- *EncJzS 70*
Badinski, Nikolai 1937- *IntWWM 80, NewGrD 80*
Badiole, Charles *Film 2*
Badiyi, Reza S *HalFC 80*
Bado, Juan Del *NewGrD 80*
Badoaro, Giacomo 1602-1654 *NewGrD 80*
Badoaro, Iacopo 1602-1654 *NewGrD 80*
Badoer, Giacomo 1602-1654 *NewGrD 80*
Badoer, Iacopo 1602-1654 *NewGrD 80*
Badoero, Giacomo 1602-1654 *NewGrD 80*
Badoero, Iacopo 1602-1654 *NewGrD 80*
Badovero, Giacomo 1602-1654 *NewGrD 80*
Badovero, Iacopo 1602-1654 *NewGrD 80*
Badrakhan, Ahmed 1909- *DcFM*
Badura, Paul 1927- *NewGrD 80*

Badura-Skoda, Eva 1929- *IntWWM 80, NewGrD 80*
Badura-Skoda, Paul 1927- *Baker 78, BnBkM 80, IntWWM 77, -80, NewGrD 80, WhoMus 72*
Badzian, Teresa *WomWMM B*
Baeck, Sven-Erik 1919- *WhoMus 72*
Baeder, Wilhelmina *PupTheA*
Baekkelund, Kjell 1930- *IntWWM 80*
Baekvang, Peter 1941- *IntWWM 77, -80*
Baena, Lope De *NewGrD 80*
Baer, Abel 1893- *AmSCAP 66, BiDAmM, CmpEPM*
Baer, Abel 1893-1976 *AmSCAP 80*
Baer, Arthur Bugs 1886-1969 *WhScrn 77*
Baer, Buddy 1915- *FilmgC, ForYSC, HalFC 80, WhoHol A*
Baer, Bugs d1969 *WhoHol B*
Baer, Charles E 1870-1962 *AmSCAP 66, -80*
Baer, Hermanus 1902- *IntWWM 77*
Baer, Johann *NewGrD 80*
Baer, John *WhoHol A*
Baer, John G 1934- *IntMPA 78, -79, -80*
Baer, Madeleine 1928- *IntWWM 77, -80*
Baer, Max 1909-1959 *FilmEn, FilmgC, ForYSC, HalFC 80, NotNAT B, WhScrn 74, -77, WhoHol B*
Baer, Max, Jr. 1937- *HalFC 80, WhoHol A*
Baer, Parley *ForYSC, WhoHol A*
Baer, Thais 1929-1930 *WhScrn 74, -77*
Baer, Walter Karl 1928- *IntWWM 77, -80*
Baeraud, George *Film 2*
Baermann *NewGrD 80*
Baermann, Carl 1782-1842 *NewGrD 80*
Baermann, Carl 1810-1885 *NewGrD 80*
Baermann, Carl 1839-1913 *BiDAmM, NewGrD 80*
Baermann, Heinrich 1784-1847 *NewGrD 80*
Baertsoen, Jean-Claude 1923- *IntWWM 77, -80, WhoMus 72*
Baervoets, Raymond Oscar 1930- *Baker 78, IntWWM 77, -80, NewGrD 80*
Baethen, Jacob 1525?-1557? *NewGrD 80*
Baeyens, August 1895-1966 *Baker 78, NewGrD 80*
Baez, Joan 1941- *AmSCAP 80, Baker 78, BiDAmM, ConMuA 80A[port], EncFCWM 69, IlEncR[port], IntWWM 77, -80, RkOn 2[port]*
Baez, Mimi 1945- *BiDAmM*
Baffico, Giuseppe 1852-1927 *McGEWD*
Baga, Ena Rosina *WhoMus 72*
Bagalio, Alfredo S *PupTheA*
Bagati, Francesco *NewGrD 80*
Bagatti, Francesco *NewGrD 80*
Bagby, Albert Morris 1859-1941 *Baker 78*
Bagby, Doc *RkOn*
Bagdad, William d1975 *WhScrn 77, WhoHol C*
Bagdasarian, Ross d1972 *ForYSC, WhoHol B*
Bagdasarian, Ross 1919-1972 *AmSCAP 66, -80*
Bagdasarian, Ross 1920-1972 *WhScrn 77*
Bagenal, Hope *OxMus*
Bagg, Konrad *NewGrD 80*
Bagge, Charles Ernest, Baron De 1722-1791 *NewGrD 80*
Bagge, Selmar 1823-1896 *Baker 78*
Baggett, Lynne 1928-1960 *ForYSC, WhScrn 74, -77, WhoHol B*
Baggiani, Guido 1932- *Baker 78, NewGrD 80*
Baggot, King d1948 *MotPP*
Baggot, King 1874-1948 *FilmEn, WhScrn 74, -77*
Baggot, King 1880-1948 *Film 1, NotNAT B*
Baggott, King d1948 *WhoHol B*
Baggott, King 1874-1948 *ForYSC, HalFC 80*
Baggott, King 1879-1948 *FilmgC*
Baggott, King 1880-1948 *Film 2, TwYS, -A*
Baghuis, Elly 1934- *WhoMus 72*
Bagier, Guido 1888-1968 *Baker 78*
Bagin, Pavol 1933- *IntWWM 77, -80*
Bagley, Ben 1933- *BiE&WWA, EncMT, NotNAT*
Bagley, Edwin E 1857-1922 *BiDAmM*
Bagley, Eugenie *WomWMM B*
Bagley, Sam 1903-1968 *WhScrn 74, -77, WhoHol B*
Bagliani, Carlo *NewGrD 80*
Baglioni, Antonio *NewGrD 80*
Baglioni, Bruna 1947- *WhoOp 76*
Baglioni, Carnace d1770? *NewGrD 80*
Baglioni, Francesco d1770? *NewGrD 80*
Baglioni, Girolamo 1575?-1608 *NewGrD 80*
Baglioni, Luigi *NewGrD 80*
Bagnacavallo, Giuseppe Da *NewGrD 80*
Bagnall, George L 1896- *IntMPA 77, -75, -76, -78*
Bagni, Benedetto *NewGrD 80*
Bagni, John 1911-1954 *WhScrn 74, -77, WhoHol B*
Bagnius, Benedictus *NewGrD 80*
Bagnold, Enid 1889- *BiE&WWA, CnMD, ConDr 73, -77, ModWD, NotNAT, -A, PlP&P, WhoThe 72, -77*
Bagnold, Enid 1899- *EncWT*
Bagnolesi, Anna *NewGrD 80*
Bagnols, Magister Leon De *NewGrD 80*
Bagrationi, John 1768-1830 *NewGrD 80*
Baguer, Carlos 1768-1808 *NewGrD 80*
Bagwell, Wendell Lee 1930- *BiDAmM*
Bagya, Andras *IntWWM 77*
Bahati, Amirh *NatPD[port]*
Bahmann, Marianne E 1933- *ConAmC*
Bahn, Chester B d1962 *NotNAT B*
Bahner, Gert 1930- *IntWWM 77, -80*
Bahr, Hermann 1863-1934 *CnMD, EncWT, Ent, McGEWD[port], ModWD, NotNAT B, OxMus, OxThe*
Bahr, Johann *NewGrD 80*
Bahr, Johann 1610?-1670 *NewGrD 80*
Bahr, Josef 1770-1819 *NewGrD 80*
Bahr-Mildenburg, Anna 1872-1947 *CmOp, NewEOp 71, NewGrD 80[port]*
Bai, Tommaso 1660?-1714 *Baker 78, NewGrD 80*
Baiczka, Franz Xaver *NewGrD 80*
Baidanov, Georgi 1853-1927 *NewGrD 80*
Baiden, Samuel Badu 1928- *IntWWM 77*
Baierl, Helmut 1926- *CroCD, EncWT, Ent*
Baif, Jean-Antoine De 1532-1589 *Baker 78, NewGrD 80, OxMus*
Baigneres, Claude Pierre 1921- *CnOxB*
Baij, Tommaso *NewGrD 80*
Bail, Grace Shattuck 1898- *ConAmC*
Baildon, Joseph 1727?-1774 *NewGrD 80*
Bailes, Anthony James 1947- *IntWWM 77, -80*
Bailes, Walter Butler 1920- *BiDAmM*
Bailes Brothers, The *IlEncCM*
Bailey, Albert 1891-1952 *WhScrn 74, -77, WhoHol B*
Bailey, Alfred Goldsworthy 1905- *CreCan 1*
Bailey, Benny 1925- *EncJzS 70*
Bailey, Bryan 1922-1960 *NotNAT B, OxThe*
Bailey, Buster 1902-1967 *CmpEPM, EncJzS 70, IlEncJ, WhoJazz 72*
Bailey, Charity Alberta 1904-1978 *AmSCAP 80*
Bailey, Colin 1934- *EncJzS 70*
Bailey, Daniel *BiDAmM*
Bailey, Dave 1926- *EncJzS 70*
Bailey, David 1898?- *NewOrJ, WhoHol A*
Bailey, DeFord *CounME 74*
Bailey, DeFord 1899- *IlEncCM[port]*
Bailey, Derek *IlEncJ*
Bailey, Derek 1932- *EncJzS 70*
Bailey, Donald Orlando 1933- *EncJzS 70*
Bailey, Donald Orlando 1934- *BiDAmM*
Bailey, Edward Lorenz 1883-1951 *WhScrn 74, -77*
Bailey, Edwin B 1873-1950 *WhScrn 74, -77*
Bailey, Elizabeth *WomWMM B*
Bailey, Elizabeth Blitch 1939- *IntWWM 77, -80*
Bailey, Ernest Harold 1925- *BiDAmM, EncJzS 70*
Bailey, Exine Margaret Anderson 1922- *IntWWM 77, -80*
Bailey, Frankie 1859-1953 *NotNAT B, WhScrn 74, -77, WhoHol B*
Bailey, G Frederick *WhoMus 72*
Bailey, Gary *ConMuA 80B*
Bailey, Gordon 1875- *Film 1, WhThe*
Bailey, H C 1878-1961 *WhThe*
Bailey, Harry P 1912- *AmSCAP 66, -80*
Bailey, Jack *NewYTET*
Bailey, James A 1847-1906 *Ent, NotNAT B*
Bailey, Joseph W 1910- *IntMPA 77, -75, -76, -78, -79, -80*
Bailey, Leon 1931- *IntWWM 77, -80, WhoMus 72*
Bailey, Lilian *OxMus*
Bailey, Lilian 1860-1901 *NewGrD 80*
Bailey, Lynn 1942- *AmSCAP 80*
Bailey, Ma *BlksBF*
Bailey, Margery 1891-1963 *NotNAT B*
Bailey, Marie Louis 1876- *BiDAmM*
Bailey, Mildred 1907-1951 *BiDAmM, CmpEPM, IlEncJ, NewGrD 80, NotNAT B, WhoJazz 72*
Bailey, Mollie 1841-1918 *NotNAT A*
Bailey, Norman Stanley 1933- *CmOp, IntWWM 77, -80, NewGrD 80, WhoMus 72, WhoOp 76*
Bailey, Norton *Film 2*
Bailey, Parker 1902- *Baker 78, ConAmC*
Bailey, Pearl 1918- *AmPS B, AmSCAP 66, -80, BiDAmM, BiE&WWA, CmpEPM, DrBlPA, EncJzS 70, EncMT, Ent, FilmEn, FilmgC, ForYSC, HalFC 80, IntMPA 77, -75, -76, -78, -79, -80, MotPP, MovMk, NotNAT, -A, WhoHol A, WhoThe 72, -77*
Bailey, Raymond 1904- *FilmgC, HalFC 80, WhoHol A*
Bailey, Raymond 1905- *ForYSC*
Bailey, Rietta Winn *BlkAmP*
Bailey, Robert 1937- *IntWWM 77, -80*
Bailey, Roberta *BlkAmP*
Bailey, Robin 1919- *BiE&WWA, FilmgC, HalFC 80, IntMPA 77, -75, -76, -78, -79, -80, NotNAT, WhoHol A, WhoThe 72, -77*
Bailey, Ruth *BiE&WWA, NotNAT*
Bailey, Sally 1932- *DancEn 78[port]*
Bailey, Samuel David 1926- *BiDAmM, EncJzS 70*
Bailey, Teresa 1955- *IntWWM 77, -80*
Bailey, William C 1902-1967 *BiDAmM, EncJzS 70*
Bailey, William Norton 1886-1962 *Film 1, NotNAT B, WhScrn 74, -77, WhoHol B*
Bailin, Harriett 1923- *AmSCAP 66, -80*
Baillargeon, Pierre 1916-1967 *CreCan 1*
Bailleux, Antoine 1720?-1798? *NewGrD 80*
Baillie, Isobel 1895- *IntWWM 77, -80, NewGrD 80, WhoMus 72*
Baillie, Joanna 1762-1851 *NotNAT B*
Baillon, Louis De 1735?-1809? *NewGrD 80*
Baillon, Luigi De 1735?-1809? *NewGrD 80*
Baillot, Pierre 1771-1842 *NewGrD 80, OxMus*
Baillot, Pierre-Marie-Francois DeSales 1771-1842 *Baker 78*
Bailly, Henry De *NewGrD 80*
Bailly, Louis 1882-1974 *Baker 78*
Bailou, Louis De 1735?-1809? *NewGrD 80*
Bailou, Luigi De 1735?-1809? *NewGrD 80*
Bails, Benito 1730-1797 *NewGrD 80*
Baily, Anselm *NewGrD 80*
Baim, Harold *IntMPA 77, -75, -76, -78, -79, -80*
Bain, Barbara 1932- *HalFC 80*
Bain, Conrad 1923- *BiE&WWA, NotNAT, WhoHol A, WhoThe 72, -77*
Bain, Wilfred Conwell 1908- *IntWWM 77, -80, NewGrD 80*
Bainbridge, Elizabeth 1936- *CmOp, WhoOp 76*
Bainbridge, Katharine 1863- *AmSCAP 66*
Bainbridge, William d1831? *NewGrD 80*
Baines, Anthony C 1912- *Baker 78, NewGrD 80*
Baines, Beulah 1905-1930 *WhScrn 74, -77, WhoHol B*
Baines, Florence 1877-1918 *NotNAT B, WhThe*
Baines, Francis Athelstan 1917- *IntWWM 77, -80, NewGrD 80, WhoMus 72*
Baines, Rosalie Beryl 1918- *WhoMus 72*
Baines, William 1899-1922 *NewGrD 80, OxMus*
Baini, Giuseppe 1775-1844 *Baker 78, NewGrD 80*
Bainter, Fay d1968 *MotPP, WhoHol B*
Bainter, Fay 1891-1968 *ForYSC, WhScrn 74, -77, WhThe*
Bainter, Fay 1892-1968 *FilmEn, FilmgC, HalFC 80, HolCA[port], MGM[port], MovMk[port], NotNAT B, ThFT[port]*
Bainter, Fay 1893-1968 *BiE&WWA*
Bainton, Edgar Leslie 1880-1956 *Baker 78, NewGrD 80, OxMus*

Bainville, Francois 1725-1788 *NewGrD 80*
Baird, Bil 1904- *BiE&WWA, DcPup, NotNAT, PupTheA, PupTheA SUP*
Baird, Claribel 1904- *BiE&WWA*
Baird, Cora d1967 *PupTheA SUP*
Baird, Cora 1912-1967 *BiE&WWA, NotNAT B*
Baird, Cora 1913-1967 *WhScrn 74, -77*
Baird, Dorothea 1875-1933 *NotNAT B, OxThe, WhThe, WhoStg 1906, -1908*
Baird, Dorothy *WhScrn 77*
Baird, Edward Allen 1933- *WhoOp 76*
Baird, Ethel *WhThe*
Baird, Eugenie *CmpEPM*
Baird, Hugh *Film 2*
Baird, Irene Todd 1901- *CreCan 1*
Baird, James *ConAmC*
Baird, Jeanne *WhoHol A*
Baird, Jo Ann C 1927- *IntWWM 77*
Baird, John L 1886-1948 *OxMus*
Baird, John Logie d1946 *NewYTET*
Baird, John Logie 1888-1946 *DcPup*
Baird, Leah d1971 *MotPP, WhoHol B*
Baird, Leah 1887-1971 *FilmEn, Film 1, -2, TwYS*
Baird, Leah 1891-1971 *WhScrn 74, -77*
Baird, Martha 1895-1971 *Baker 78*
Baird, Nora 1900- *IntWWM 77, -80*
Baird, Stuart d1947 *NotNAT B*
Baird, Tadeusz 1928- *Baker 78, CompSN[port], DcCM, IntWWM 77, -80, NewGrD 80, OxMus, WhoMus 72*
Baird, Teddy *IntMPA 75, -76*
Baird, Teddy 1900?- *FilmgC, HalFC 80*
Bairnsfather, Bruce 1887-1959 *NotNAT A, -B*
Bairstow, Sir Edward Cuthbert 1874-1946 *Baker 78, NewGrD 80, OxMus*
Baise, Paul 1922- *IntMPA 77, -75, -76, -78, -79, -80*
Baisley, Robert William 1923- *IntWWM 77, -80*
Baj, Tommaso 1650?-1714 *NewGrD 80*
Bajalovic, Mirjana 1943- *IntWWM 77, -80*
Bajamonti, Giulio 1744-1800 *NewGrD 80*
Bajamonti, Julije 1744-1800 *NewGrD 80*
Bajer, Jiri 1925- *NewGrD 80*
Bajor, Gisi d1951 *NotNAT B*
Bajor, Gizi d1951 *WhoHol B*
Bajor, Gizi 1894-1951 *EncWT, Ent*
Bakala, Bretislav 1897-1958 *Baker 78, NewGrD 80*
Bakaleinikoff, Constantin 1898-1966 *FilmEn, FilmgC, HalFC 80*
Bakaleinikoff, Mischa d1960 *NotNAT B, WhoHrs 80*
Bakaleinikov, Vladimir Romanovitch 1885-1953 *Baker 78, ConAmC*
Bakalinsky, Adah *WomWMM B*
Bakalyan, Richard *ForYSC*
Bake, Arnold Adriaan 1899-1963 *NewGrD 80*
Baker, Alan *WhoOp 76*
Baker, Anna Willis 1860-1944 *WhScrn 74, -77*
Baker, Art 1898-1966 *FilmEn, ForYSC, HalFC 80, WhScrn 74, -77, WhoHol B*
Baker, Belle 1895-1957 *AmPS B, CmpEPM, Film 2, JoeFr, NotNAT B, WhScrn 74, -77, WhoHol B*
Baker, Benjamin A 1818-1890 *NotNAT B, OxThe*
Baker, Benjamin Franklin 1811-1889 *Baker 78, BiDAmM*
Baker, Benny 1907- *FilmEn, ForYSC, Vers B[port], WhThe, WhoHol A*
Baker, Betty Bly *Film 2*
Baker, Bob 1901-1975 *PupTheA, WhScrn 77, WhoHol C*
Baker, Bob 1914-1975 *FilmEn*
Baker, Bonnie 1918?- *CmpEPM*
Baker, Carroll *IntMPA 77, -75, -76, -78, -79, -80, MotPP, WhoHol A*
Baker, Carroll 1931- *FilmEn, FilmgC, HalFC 80, MovMk[port], WorEFlm*
Baker, Carroll 1932- *BiDFilm, -81, OxFilm*
Baker, Carroll 1935- *BiE&WWA, ForYSC*
Baker, Cassietta 1929- *AmSCAP 80*
Baker, Charles Adams 1920- *BiE&WWA*
Baker, Chesney H 1929- *BiDAmM, EncJzS 70*
Baker, Chet 1929- *EncJzS 70, IlEncJ*
Baker, Cyril 1928- *IntWWM 77*
Baker, Daniel E d1939 *NotNAT B*
Baker, David 1926- *BiE&WWA, NotNAT*
Baker, David A 1949- *ConAmC*
Baker, David Erskine d1767 *NotNAT B*
Baker, David Keith 1926- *AmSCAP 80*
Baker, David Nathaniel, Jr. 1931- *BiDAmM, BlkCS[port], ConAmC, EncJzS 70*
Baker, Diane 1938- *FilmEn, FilmgC, ForYSC, HalFC 80, MotPP, MovMk, WhoHol A*
Baker, Don 1903- *AmSCAP 66, -80*
Baker, Don 1931- *IntMPA 77, -75, -76, -78, -79, -80*
Baker, Doris *Film 2*
Baker, Dorothy 1907-1968 *BiE&WWA, NotNAT B*
Baker, Eddie 1897-1968 *TwYS A, WhScrn 74, -77, WhoHol B*
Baker, Elizabeth d1962 *WhThe*
Baker, Elsie 1893-1971 *WhScrn 74, 77*
Baker, Ernest John 1912- *WhoMus 72*
Baker, Everett B *PupTheA*
Baker, Fannie *BluesWW[port]*
Baker, Fanny *BluesWW[port]*
Baker, Fay *WhoHol A*
Baker, Floyd 1906-1943 *WhScrn 74, -77*
Baker, Frank *PupTheA*
Baker, Gene *Film 1*
Baker, George *PupTheA*
Baker, George 1768-1847 *Baker 78*
Baker, George 1885- *IntWWM 77, WhThe, WhoMus 72*
Baker, George 1929- *FilmgC, HalFC 80*
Baker, George 1931- *FilmEn, IlWWBF, IntMPA 77, -75, -76, -78, -79, -80, WhoHol A, WhoThe 72, -77*
Baker, George, Selection *RkOn 2[port]*
Baker, George D *FilmEn, TwYS A*
Baker, George Pierce 1866-1935 *EncWT, McGEWD, NotNAT A, -B, OxThe, PlP&P, WhThe*
Baker, Ginger *ConMuA 80A*
Baker, Ginger 1939- *RkOn 2[port]*
Baker, Ginger 1940- *EncJzS 70*
Baker, Harold 1914-1966 *AmSCAP 66, -80, BiDAmM, CmpEPM, EncJzS 70*
Baker, Henrietta 1837-1909 *OxThe*
Baker, Herbert 1920- *AmSCAP 66, -80*
Baker, Howard 1905- *BiE&WWA, NotNAT*
Baker, Howard George 1902- *IntWWM 77, WhoMus 72*
Baker, Hylda 1909- *FilmgC, HalFC 80*
Baker, Iris 1901- *WhThe*
Baker, Israel 1921- *NewGrD 80*
Baker, J Edwin 1914- *IntMPA 79, -80*
Baker, Jane *WomWMM*
Baker, Janet 1933- *Baker 78, BnBkM 80, CmOp[port], IntWWM 77, -80, MusMk, MusSN[port], NewGrD 80[port], WhoMus 72, WhoOp 76*
Baker, Joby *WhoHol A*
Baker, Joe Don 1943- *FilmEn, HalFC 80, IntMPA 77, -75, -76, -78, -79, -80, WhoHol A*
Baker, Josephine 1906-1975 *BiDAmM, BiE&WWA, BlksB&W C, CnOxB, DancEn 78, DrBlPA, Ent[port], FilmEn, OxFilm, WhScrn 77, WhoHol C, WhoThe 72, -77*
Baker, Julius 1915- *BnBkM 80, IntWWM 77, -80*
Baker, Kathryn June 1946- *IntWWM 77, -80*
Baker, Ken *BgBands 74*
Baker, Kenneth 1921- *EncJzS 70*
Baker, Kenny *AmPS B*
Baker, Kenny 1912- *BiDAmM, BiE&WWA, CmpEPM, FilmEn, FilmgC, ForYSC, HalFC 80, What 3[port], WhoHol A*
Baker, Kenny 1921- *CmpEPM, EncJzS 70*
Baker, Lance 1947- *WhoMus 72*
Baker, Larry 1948- *AmSCAP 80, CpmDNM 79, -80, ConAmC, IntWWM 77, -80*
Baker, Lauretta *WomWMM B*
Baker, LaVern 1929- *AmPS A, -B, RkOn[port]*
Baker, Lee 1876-1948 *Film 2, NotNAT B, WhScrn 74, -77, WhThe, WhoHol B*
Baker, Lena Amy *WhoMus 72*
Baker, Lenny *NotNAT*
Baker, Leslie F 1903- *IntMPA 77, -75, -76, -78, -79, -80*
Baker, Lewis J d1962 *NotNAT B*
Baker, Lillian *PupTheA*
Baker, Lucille McKechnie 1924- *IntWWM 77*
Baker, Marjorie 1909- *WhoMus 72*
Baker, Mark d1972 *WhoHol B*
Baker, Mark 1946- *NotNAT*
Baker, McHouston 1925- *BluesWW[port]*
Baker, Michael 1942- *Baker 78*
Baker, Nellie Bly *Film 2*
Baker, Norman D 1918- *AmSCAP 80*
Baker, Norman Louis 1941- *IntWWM 80*
Baker, Paul 1911- *BiE&WWA, NotNAT*
Baker, Percy *WhoMus 72*
Baker, Peter 1940- *EncJzS 70*
Baker, Peter Ginger 1939- *IlEncR[port]*
Baker, Phil 1896-1963 *AmSCAP 66, -80, BiDAmM, CmpEPM, HalFC 80, NotNAT B, WhoHol B*
Baker, Phil 1898-1963 *JoeFr, WhScrn 74, -77*
Baker, Philip Eldridge 1934- *CpmDNM 79, -80*
Baker, Reginald P 1896- *IntMPA 77, -75, -76, -78, -79, -80*
Baker, Richard Douglas James 1925- *IntWWM 77, -80, WhoMus 72*
Baker, Richard E 1916- *AmSCAP 66, -80*
Baker, Rick 1950- *WhoHrs 80*
Baker, Robert 1920- *IntWWM 80, WhoMus 72*
Baker, Robert A *ConAmC*
Baker, Robert Hart 1954- *AmSCAP 80*
Baker, Robert S 1916- *ConAmC, FilmEn, FilmgC, HalFC 80, IlWWBF, IntMPA 77, -75, -76, -78, -79, -80, NewGrD 80, WhoMus 72*
Baker, Ronald Cyril 1928- *WhoMus 72*
Baker, Roy 1916- *FilmEn, FilmgC, HalFC 80, IlWWBF, IntMPA 77, -75, -76, -78, -79, -80, MagIlD, WhoHrs 80, WorEFlm[port]*
Baker, Roy Thomas *ConMuA 80B*
Baker, Sam *Film 2*
Baker, Samuel 1907- *IntWWM 77, -80*
Baker, Samuel Henry 1890- *WhoMus 72*
Baker, Samuel Wensley *WhoMus 72*
Baker, Sarah 1736?-1816 *OxThe*
Baker, Shorty 1914-1966 *EncJzS 70, IlEncJ, WhoJazz 72*
Baker, Stanley *MotPP, WhoHol A*
Baker, Stanley 1927-1976 *BiDFilm, -81, CmMov, FilmEn, FilmgC, ForYSC, HalFC 80, OxFilm*
Baker, Stanley 1928-1976 *FilmAG WE[port], IlWWBF[port], -A, IntMPA 75, -76, MovMk, WorEFlm*
Baker, Tarkington d1924 *NotNAT B*
Baker, Theodore 1851-1934 *Baker 78, BiDAmM, NewGrD 80*
Baker, Tom 1941- *FilmgC, HalFC 80*
Baker, Two Ton *AmSCAP 80*
Baker, W Claude 1948- *ConAmC*
Baker, Walter Donald *WhoMus 72*
Baker, Walter William Lionel 1910- *WhoMus 72*
Baker, Wee Bonnie *AmPS B*
Baker, Wee Bonnie 1917- *What 4[port]*
Baker, William d1916 *WhScrn 77*
Baker, William Claude 1948- *AmSCAP 80*
Baker, William George Edgar 1910- *WhoMus 72*
Baker, William Stanford 1925- *AmSCAP 66, -80*
Baker, Word 1923- *BiE&WWA, NotNAT*
Baker Gurvitz Army *IlEncR*
Bakewell, William 1908- *FilmEn, Film 2, ForYSC, HalFC 80, MovMk, TwYS, WhoHol A*
Bakfark, Balint 1507-1576 *NewGrD 80*
Bakfark, Valentin 1507-1576 *Baker 78, NewGrD 80*
Bakfark, Valentine *OxMus*
Bakfark, Valentine 1507-1576 *MusMk*
Bakhrushin, Yuri Alexeievich 1896-1973 *CnOxB*
Bakhrushin, Yuri Alexeievich 1898-1973 *DancEn 78[port]*
Bakhshi, Anand Prakash 1930- *IntWWM 80*
Bakkar, Selma *WomWMM*
Bakke, Ruth 1947- *IntWWM 77, -80*
Bakkegard, Benjamin David 1951- *IntWWM 77, -80*
Bakker, Anne Johanna 1938- *IntWWM 77, -80*

Bakker, Dietrich *NewGrD 80*
Bakker, Marco 1938- *IntWWM 77, -80, WhoOp 76*
Bakkis, Georgy 1881-1938 *NewGrD 80*
Baklanov, George 1881-1938 *Baker 78*
Baklanov, George 1882-1938 *CmOp*
Baklanov, Georgy 1881-1938 *NewGrD 80*
Bakocevic, Radmila 1933- *WhoOp 76*
Baksa, Robert Frank 1938- *AmSCAP 80, CpmDNM 78, -79, -80, ConAmC*
Bakshi, Ralph *HalFC 80*
Bakshi, Ralph 1939- *FilmEn*
Bakst, Leon 1866-1924 *CnOxB, DancEn 78, EncWT, Ent, OxMus*
Bakst, Leon 1868-1924 *NotNAT A, -B*
Bakst, Ryszard 1926- *IntWWM 77, -80, WhoMus 72*
Baky, Josef Von 1902-1966 *DcFM, FilmEn*
Bal, Adrian 1925- *AmSCAP 80*
Bal, Berdella M 1928- *AmSCAP 80*
Bal Y Gay, Jesus 1905- *Baker 78, NewGrD 80*
Balaban, A J 1889-1962 *IntMPA 77, -75, -76, -78, -79, -80, NotNAT A, -B*
Balaban, Barney 1887-1971 *FilmEn, WorEFlm*
Balaban, Barney 1888-1971 *FilmgC, HalFC 80*
Balaban, Burt 1922-1965 *FilmEn, FilmgC, HalFC 80*
Balaban, Elmer *IntMPA 77, -75, -76, -78, -79, -80*
Balaban, Emanuel 1895- *DancEn 78*
Balaban, Harry 1903- *IntMPA 77, -75, -76, -78, -79, -80*
Balaban, Leonard J 1929- *EncJzS 70*
Balaban, Red 1929- *EncJzS 70*
Balabina, Feya Ivanovna 1910- *CnOxB*
Balada, Leonard 1933- *AmSCAP 80*
Balada, Leonardo 1933- *Baker 78, ConAmC, IntWWM 77, -80, NewGrD 80*
Balaguer, Juan DeSesse Y *NewGrD 80*
Balakian, Lucy Boyan 1907- *IntWWM 77, -80*
Balakiref, Mily 1837-1910 *OxMus*
Balakirev, Mily 1836?-1910 *BnBkM 80*
Balakirev, Mily 1837-1910 *Baker 78, CmpBCM, DancEn 78, DcCom 77, DcCom&M 79, GrComp[port], MusMk[port], NewGrD 80[port]*
Balamos, John *ConAmC*
Balan, George 1929- *NewGrD 80*
Balanchin, George *NewGrD 80*
Balanchine, George 1904- *Baker 78, BiE&WWA, CnOxB, DancEn 78[port], EncMT, NewGrD 80, NotNAT A, OxMus, PlP&P[port], WhoThe 72, -77*
Balanchivadze *NewGrD 80*
Balanchivadze, Andrei Melitonovich 1906- *Baker 78, IntWWM 77, -80*
Balanchivadze, Andrey 1906- *NewGrD 80*
Balanchivadze, George 1904- *NewGrD 80*
Balanchivadze, Meliton 1862-1937 *Baker 78, NewGrD 80*
Balart, Gabriel 1824-1893 *Baker 78*
Balasanian, Sergey Artem'yevich 1902- *NewGrD 80*
Balasanyan, Sergel Artemyevich 1902- *IntWWM 77, -80*
Balasaraswati *CnOxB*
Balasaraswati, Thanjavur 1918- *NewGrD 80*
Balashova, Alexandra Nicolaievna 1887- *CnOxB*
Balassa, George 1913- *IntWWM 77, -80*
Balassa, Sandor 1935- *Baker 78, IntWWM 77, -80, NewGrD 80*
Balasz, Bela 1884-1949 *FilmgC, HalFC 80*
Balasz, Bela 1885-1949 *WorEFlm*
Balatka, Hans 1825-1899 *Baker 78*
Balatka, Hans 1826-1899 *NewGrD 80*
Balatka, Hans 1827-1899 *BiDAmM*
Balay, Joan Rose 1932- *AmSCAP 80*
Balazs, Arpad 1937- *IntWWM 77, -80*
Balazs, Bela 1884-1949 *FilmEn, OxFilm*
Balazs, Frederic 1920- *ConAmC*
Balbastre, Claude-Benigne 1727-1799 *Baker 78, NewGrD 80*
Balbatre, Claude-Benigne 1727-1799 *NewGrD 80*
Balbi, Alciso *NewGrD 80*
Balbi, Aloysius *NewGrD 80*
Balbi, Aluigi *NewGrD 80*
Balbi, Alviso *NewGrD 80*
Balbi, Ignazio *NewGrD 80*
Balbi, Lodovico 1545?-1604 *Baker 78, NewGrD 80*
Balbi, Luigi *NewGrD 80*
Balbi, Melchiore 1796-1879 *Baker 78*
Balbo, G C *ConAmC*
Balch, Marston 1901- *BiE&WWA, NotNAT*
Balch, Slim d1967 *WhoHol B*
Balchin, Nigel 1908-1970 *FilmEn, FilmgC, HalFC 80*
Balcon, Jill 1925- *FilmgC, HalFC 80*
Balcon, Sir Michael 1896-1977 *BiDFilm, -81, DcFM, FilmEn, FilmgC, HalFC 80, IlWWBF A, IntMPA 77, -75, -76, -78, OxFilm, WorEFlm*
Baldan, Angelo 1753-1803 *NewGrD 80*
Baldani, Ruza 1942- *WhoMus 72, WhoOp 76*
Baldassare, Pietro 1690?- *NewGrD 80*
Baldassari, Benedetti *NewGrD 80*
Baldassari, Benedetto *NewGrD 80*
Baldassari, Pietro 1690?- *NewGrD 80*
Baldassarre, Joseph Anthony 1950- *IntWWM 77, -80*
Balde, Jacobus 1604?-1668 *NewGrD 80*
Balderston, John L 1889-1954 *CnMD, FilmgC, HalFC 80, McGEWD, ModWD, NotNAT B, WhThe*
Balderston, John L 1899-1954 *FilmEn*
Balderstone, John L 1889-1954 *CmMov*
Baldi, Antonio *NewGrD 80*
Baldi, Gian Vittorio 1930- *DcFM, WorEFlm*
Baldi, Joao Jose 1770-1816 *NewGrD 80*
Baldina, Alexandra Vasilievna 1885- *CnOxB*
Baldini, Guglielmo 1540?-1589? *NewGrD 80*
Baldini, Vittorio d1618 *NewGrD 80*
Baldock, Alice Gwendoline 1910- *WhoMus 72*
Baldoni, Tomaso *NewGrD 80*
Baldovino, Amadeo 1916- *NewGrD 80*
Baldra, Charles M 1899-1949 *WhScrn 74, -77*
Baldra, Chuck 1899-1949 *WhoHol B*
Baldradi, Bartolomeo 1645?- *NewGrD 80*
Baldrati, Bartolomeo 1645?- *NewGrD 80*
Baldridge, Richard 1926- *WhoMus 72*
Baldry, Long John 1940- *ConMuA 80A, IlEncR*
Balducci, Francesco 1579-1642 *NewGrD 80*
Baldwin, Bill *WhoHol A*
Baldwin, Catherine Janet *CreCan 2*
Baldwin, D H d1889 *BiDAmM*
Baldwin, David 1946- *ConAmC*
Baldwin, Dick *WhoHol A*
Baldwin, Doris Nellie 1898- *WhoMus 72*
Baldwin, Faith 1893-1978 *HalFC 80*
Baldwin, George d1923 *WhScrn 74, -77*
Baldwin, James 1924- *BlkAmP, ConDr 73, -77, CroCD, DcLB 7[port], EncWT, Ent[port], McGEWD[port], ModWD, MorBAP, NotNAT, -A*
Baldwin, Janet 1912- *CreCan 2*
Baldwin, John 1560?-1615 *NewGrD 80*
Baldwin, John 1940- *IntWWM 80*
Baldwin, Joseph B 1918- *BiE&WWA*
Baldwin, Kitty 1853-1934 *WhScrn 74, -77*
Baldwin, Marcia 1939- *WhoOp 76*
Baldwin, Peter *WhoHol A*
Baldwin, Ralph Lyman 1872-1943 *BiDAmM, ConAmC*
Baldwin, Russell 1913- *ConAmC*
Baldwin, Ruth Ann *WomWMM*
Baldwin, Samuel Atkinson 1862-1949 *Baker 78, BiDAmM*
Baldwin, Thomas 1753-1825 *BiDAmM*
Baldwin, Walter *Vers B[port], WhoHol A*
Baldwin, Wendy Anne 1938- *WhoMus 72*
Baldwine, John 1560?-1615 *NewGrD 80*
Baldwyn, John 1560?-1615 *NewGrD 80*
Baldwyn, Noe *NewGrD 80*
Baldwyn, Rodney Clifford 1927- *IntWWM 77, -80*
Bale, John 1495-1563 *EncWT, Ent, McGEWD, NotNAT B*
Bale, John, Bishop Of Ossory 1495-1563 *OxThe*
Balea, Ilie 1923- *IntWWM 80*
Balenda, Carla 1925- *ForYSC*
Balent, Andrew 1934- *AmSCAP 80, ConAmC, IntWWM 77*
Balentine, James *ConAmC*
Bales, Burt 1916- *EncJzS 70*
Bales, Burton F 1916- *EncJzS 70*
Bales, Dorothy Johnson 1917- *IntWWM 77, -80*
Bales, Gerald Albert 1919- *CreCan 2*
Bales, Richard 1915- *AmSCAP 66, Baker 78, BiDAmM, ConAmC*
Bales, Richard Horner 1915- *AmSCAP 80*
Bales, William 1910- *CmpGMD, CnOxB, DancEn 78*
Balestra, Reimundo *NewGrD 80*
Balestrieri, Thomas *NewGrD 80*
Balfe, Michael William 1808-1870 *Baker 78, CmOp, DcCom 77, DcCom&M 79, MusMk, NewEOp 71, NewGrD 80[port], NotNAT B, OxMus*
Balfoort, Dirk Jacobus 1886-1964 *Baker 78, NewGrD 80*
Balfour, Augustus *Film 2*
Balfour, Betty 1903- *FilmEn, Film 2, FilmgC, HalFC 80, IlWWBF[port], WhoHol A*
Balfour, Earl 1848-1930 *OxMus*
Balfour, Eva *Film 2*
Balfour, Henry Lucas 1859-1946 *Baker 78*
Balfour, Katharine *WhoHol A*
Balfour, Lorna 1913-1932 *WhScrn 74, -77, WhoHol B*
Balfour, Michael 1918- *FilmgC, HalFC 80, WhoHol A*
Balfour, Sue *Film 1*
Balfour, W *PupTheA*
Balfour, William d1964 *NotNAT B*
Balfour-Frazer, Anne *WomWMM B*
Baliani, Carlo 1680?-1747 *NewGrD 80*
Balieff, Nikita 1877-1936 *NotNAT B, OxThe, WhScrn 77, WhoHol B*
Balin, Ina 1937- *BiE&WWA, FilmEn, FilmgC, ForYSC, HalFC 80, IntMPA 77, -75, -76, -78, -79, -80, MotPP, WhoHol A*
Balin, Mireille 1909-1968 *FilmgC, HalFC 80, WhoHol B*
Balin, Mireille 1911-1968 *FilmEn, WhScrn 74, -77*
Baline, Israel *NewGrD 80*
Balino *NewGrD 80*
Balissat, Jean 1936- *IntWWM 77, -80, NewGrD 80*
Balius Y Vila, Jaime d1822 *NewGrD 80*
Balk, Howard Wesley 1932- *WhoOp 76*
Balk, Wesley *ConAmC*
Balkanska, Mimi 1902- *NewGrD 80*
Balkcom, Marion Huyett 1902- *AmSCAP 80*
Balke, Jon Georg 1955- *IntWWM 80*
Balkin, Alfred 1931- *AmSCAP 80*
Balkwill, Bryan Havell 1922- *IntWWM 77, -80, NewGrD 80, WhoMus 72, WhoOp 76*
Ball, Charles Edward *WhoMus 72*
Ball, Charles H 1931- *IntWWM 77, -80*
Ball, Christopher 1936- *IntWWM 77, -80, WhoMus 72*
Ball, Clifford Evans 1899- *IntWWM 77, -80, WhoMus 72*
Ball, Eric 1903- *WhoMus 72*
Ball, Ernest R 1878-1927 *AmPS, AmSCAP 66, -80, Baker 78, BiDAmM, CmpEPM, ConAmC, NotNAT B, PopAmC[port], Sw&Ld B*
Ball, F C *ConDr 73, -77B*
Ball, Geoffrey Stewart Morley 1925- *IntWWM 77*
Ball, George Thalben *NewGrD 80*
Ball, Grace Mary Hatfield 1905- *WhoMus 72*
Ball, J Meredith d1915 *NotNAT B*
Ball, James *NewGrD 80*
Ball, Jane *WhoHol A*
Ball, Kenny And His Jazz Band 1937- *RkOn*
Ball, Lewis d1905 *NotNAT B*
Ball, Lucille *AmPS B, IntMPA 77, -75, -76, -78, -79, -80, MotPP, NewYTET, WhoHol A*
Ball, Lucille 1910- *CmMov, CmpEPM, EncMT, FilmgC, HalFC 80, MovMk[port], OxFilm*
Ball, Lucille 1911- *BiDFilm, -81, BiE&WWA, FilmEn, Film 2, ForYSC, Funs[port], JoeFr[port], MGM[port], ThFT[port], WorEFlm*
Ball, Mel *AmSCAP 80*
Ball, Robert Hamilton 1902- *BiE&WWA, NotNAT*
Ball, Susan 1933-1955 *ForYSC, MotPP*
Ball, Suzan 1933-1955 *FilmEn, FilmgC, HalFC 80, NotNAT B, WhScrn 74, -77, WhoHol B*
Ball, Vincent *HalFC 80*

Ball, William 1931- *BiE&WWA, NotNAT, WhoThe 72, -77*
Ballabene, Gregorio 1720?-1803? *NewGrD 80*
Ballamos, William *PupTheA*
Ballantine, Carl *ForYSC, WhoHol A*
Ballantine, Christopher John 1942- *IntWWM 80*
Ballantine, E J 1888-1968 *WhScrn 74, -77, WhoHol B*
Ballantine, Edward 1886-1971 *Baker 78, BiDAmM, ConAmC, NewGrD 80*
Ballantine, Edward D 1907- *AmSCAP 66, -80*
Ballantyne, Jean *PupTheA*
Ballantyne, Nell d1959 *WhScrn 74, -77, WhoHol B*
Ballantyne, Paul 1909- *BiE&WWA, NotNAT, WhoThe 72, -77*
Ballantyne, Tanya *WomWMM*
Ballard *BnBkM 80, NewGrD 80*
Ballard, Christophe 1641-1715 *BnBkM 80, NewGrD 80*
Ballard, Christophe-Jean-Francois 1701?-1765 *BnBkM 80, NewGrD 80*
Ballard, Clint C, Jr. *AmSCAP 80*
Ballard, Elmer *Film 2*
Ballard, Francis Drake 1899-1960 *AmSCAP 66, -80*
Ballard, Frederick 1884-1957 *NotNAT B*
Ballard, Hank 1936- *AmPS B, IlEncR, RkOn[port]*
Ballard, Hank And Midnighters *AmPS A*
Ballard, Jean-Baptiste-Christophe 1663?-1750 *BnBkM 80, NewGrD 80*
Ballard, Jeremy Howard Reeves 1938- *IntWWM 80*
Ballard, Kay 1926- *HalFC 80*
Ballard, Kaye 1926- *AmPS B, BiE&WWA, EncMT, FilmEn, FilmgC, JoeFr, NotNAT, WhoHol A, WhoThe 77*
Ballard, Larry 1946- *IlEncCM*
Ballard, Louis Wayne 1931- *AmSCAP 80, Baker 78, ConAmC*
Ballard, Lucien 1908- *CmMov, DcFM, FilmEn, FilmgC, HalFC 80, IntMPA 77, -75, -76, -78, -79, -80, OxFilm, WorEFlm*
Ballard, Lucinda 1906- *NotNAT*
Ballard, Lucinda 1908- *BiE&WWA*
Ballard, Pierre 1575?-1639 *BnBkM 80, NewGrD 80*
Ballard, Pierre Robert Christophe d1812 *BnBkM 80*
Ballard, Robert 1525?-1588 *BnBkM 80, NewGrD 80*
Ballard, Robert 1575?-1650? *NewGrD 80*
Ballard, Robert 1610?-1673 *NewGrD 80*
Ballard, Robert, II *BnBkM 80*
Ballard, Robert Hudson 1913- *AmSCAP 66, -80*
Ballard, Russ *IlEncR*
Ballard Family *Baker 78*
Ballardie, Quintin *IntWWM 77, -80, WhoMus 72*
Ballarotti, Francesco 1660?-1712 *NewGrD 80*
Ballaseyus, Virginia 1893-1969 *AmSCAP 66, ConAmC*
Ballenger, Kenneth Leigh 1921- *IntWWM 77, -80*
Ballenger, Larry Desmond 1937- *AmSCAP 80*
Ballestra, Raimundo d1634 *NewGrD 80*
Ballestra, Raimundus d1634 *NewGrD 80*
Ballestra, Reimundo d1634 *NewGrD 80*
Ballet, Arthur H *NotNAT*
Balletti, Bernardino *NewGrD 80*
Ballew, Leighton M 1916- *BiE&WWA, NotNAT*
Ballew, Smith *BgBands 74*
Ballew, Smith 1900- *WhoJazz 72*
Ballew, Smith 1902- *CmpEPM, WhoHol A*
Balliani, Carlo *NewGrD 80*
Balliere DeLaisement, Denis 1729-1800 *NewGrD 80*
Ballif, Claude 1924- *Baker 78, DcCM, IntWWM 80, NewGrD 80*
Ballin, Hugo d1956 *NotNAT B*
Ballin, Hugo 1880-1956 *FilmEn*
Ballin, Mabel 1885-1958 *FilmEn, Film 1, -2, MotPP, NotNAT B, TwYS, WhScrn 74, -77, WhoHol B*
Balling, Michael 1866-1925 *Baker 78, CmOp*
Ballinger, Bertha *PupTheA*
Ballion, Luigi De *NewGrD 80*
Ballioni, Luigi De *NewGrD 80*
Ballis, Oliviero *NewGrD 80*
Ballista, Antonio 1936- *NewGrD 80*
Ballou, Esther Williamson 1915-1973 *ConAmC, NewGrD 80*
Ballou, Hosea 1771-1852 *BiDAmM*
Ballou, Marion 1871-1939 *WhScrn 74, -77, WhoHol B*
Balmain, Rollo d1920 *NotNAT B*
Balmer, Charles 1817-1892 *NewGrD 80*
Balmer, Hans 1903- *IntWWM 80*
Balmer, Luc 1898- *Baker 78, NewGrD 80*
Balogh, Endre 1954- *IntWWM 80*
Balogh, Erno 1897- *AmSCAP 66, -80, Baker 78, BiDAmM, ConAmC*
Balogh, Olga Mitana 1917- *IntWWM 80*
Baloghova, Dagmar 1929- *IntWWM 77, -80*
Balokovic, Zlatko 1895-1965 *Baker 78*
Balon, Jean 1676-1739 *CnOxB, DancEn 78*
Baloo, Sam *AmSCAP 80*
Balough, Gregor *ConAmC*
Balox, Johannes *NewGrD 80*
Balsam, Artur 1906- *AmSCAP 80, Baker 78, IntWWM 77, -80, NewGrD 80, WhoMus 72*
Balsam, Martin 1919- *BiE&WWA, FilmEn, FilmgC, ForYSC, HalFC 80, HolCA[port], IntMPA 77, -75, -76, -78, -79, -80, MotPP, MovMk[port], NotNAT, WhoHol A, WhoThe 72, -77*
Balsamino, Simone *NewGrD 80*
Balser, Ewald 1898- *HalFC 80*
Balsis, Edwardas Kosto 1919- *IntWWM 77, -80*
Balsley, Phil *EncFCWM 69*
Balsley, Philip E 1939- *BiDAmM*
Balsys, Eduardas 1919- *NewGrD 80*
Baltazar, Gabriel Ruiz, Jr. 1929- *BiDAmM*
Baltazarini *NewGrD 80*
Balter, Allan 1925- *IntMPA 77, -75, -76, -78, -79, -80*
Balter, Diane Robb *WomWMM B*
Balthrop, Carmen 1954?- *DrBlPA*
Baltor, Harold 1915- *AmSCAP 66, -80*
Baltsa, Agnes 1944- *IntWWM 77, -80, WhoOp 76*
Baltzar, Thomas 1630?-1663 *NewGrD 80*
Baltzell, Winton James 1864-1928 *Baker 78, BiDAmM*
Balucki, Michael 1837-1901 *ModWD*
Balucki, Michal 1837-1901 *EncWT*
Balzac, Honore De 1799-1850 *EncWT, Ent[port], McGEWD[port], NewGrD 80, NotNAT B, OxThe*
Balzer, Jurgen 1906-1976 *NewGrD 80*
Baмattre, Martha 1892-1970 *WhScrn 74, -77, WhoHol B*
Bambach, Paul Anton 1950- *ConAmC*
Bamber, Dennis 1947- *IntWWM 80*
Bamber, Graham Robert 1899- *IntWWM 77*
Bamber, Peter 1936- *WhoMus 72*
Bamberg, David *MagIlD*
Bamberg, David 1786-1869 *MagIlD*
Bamberg, David Tobias 1843-1914 *MagIlD*
Bamberg, Eliaser 1760-1833 *MagIlD*
Bamberg, Karl *OxMus*
Bamberg, Theodore *MagIlD*
Bamberg, Tobias 1812-1870 *MagIlD*
Bamberger, Bernice Marian 1919- *AmSCAP 80*
Bamberger, Carl 1902- *Baker 78, BiDAmM, IntWWM 77, -80, WhoMus 72*
Bamberger, David S 1940- *IntWWM 77, -80*
Bamberger, Lotte 1904- *IntWWM 77, -80*
Bamberger, Theron d1953 *NotNAT B*
Bambi, Gilberto 1925- *WhoOp 76*
Bamboschek, Giuseppe 1890-1969 *AmSCAP 66, Baker 78*
Bambridge, John 1931- *AmSCAP 80*
Bamert, Matthias 1942- *AmSCAP 80, ConAmC*
Bamester, Katherine d1919 *WhScrn 77*
Bamfi, Alfonso *NewGrD 80*
Bamford, Stephanie Catherine 1946- *IntWWM 77, -80*
Bamforth, Dennis Anthony 1935- *IntWWM 77*
Bampton, Rose 1908- *Baker 78, CmOp*
Bampton, Rose 1909- *BiDAmM, MusSN[port], NewEOp 71, NewGrD 80*
Bampton, Rose E *IntWWM 77, -80*
Bampton, Ruth 1902- *ConAmC*
Ban, Frigyes 1902- *DcFM, FilmEn*
Ban, Joan Albert 1597?-1644 *NewGrD 80*
Ban, Viorel 1920- *WhoOp 76*
Banaitis, Kazimieras Viktoras 1896-1963 *ConAmC*
Banan, Gholam-Hossein 1911- *IntWWM 77, -80*
Banaster, Gilbert 1445?-1487 *MusMk, NewGrD 80*
Banastir, Gilbert 1445?-1487 *NewGrD 80*
Banastre, Gilbert 1445?-1487 *NewGrD 80*
Banbury, Frith 1912- *WhoThe 72, -77*
Bances Y Lopez-Candamo, Francisco A 1662-1704 *McGEWD*
Banchieri, Adriano 1567-1634 *BnBkM 80*
Banchieri, Adriano 1568-1634 *Baker 78, NewGrD 80[port], OxMus*
Banchieri, Tomaso 1568-1634 *NewGrD 80[port]*
Banchz, William 1948- *ConAmC*
Banci, Giovanni *NewGrD 80*
Bancroft, Lady 1839-1921 *EncWT, NotNAT B, WhThe*
Bancroft, Anne 1931- *BiDFilm, -81, BiE&WWA, CnThe, Ent, FilmEn, FilmgC, ForYSC, HalFC 80[port], IntMPA 77, -75, -76, -78, -79, -80, MotPP, MovMk[port], NotNAT, OxFilm, WhoHol A, WhoThe 72, -77, WorEFlm*
Bancroft, B Richard 1936- *ConAmC, IntWWM 77, -80*
Bancroft, Charles 1911-1969 *WhScrn 74, -77, WhoHol B*
Bancroft, George 1882-1956 *CmMov, FilmEn, Film 2, FilmgC, ForYSC, HalFC 80, HolCA[port], MotPP, MovMk, NotNAT B, TwYS, Vers A[port], WhScrn 74, -77, WhoHol B, WorEFlm*
Bancroft, George Pleydell 1868-1956 *NotNAT A, -B, WhThe*
Bancroft, Hugh 1904- *CreCan 1*
Bancroft, James Henry 1819-1844 *BiDAmM*
Bancroft, Marie Effie Wilton 1839-1921 *CnThe, NotNAT A, OxThe, PlP&P*
Bancroft, Silas Atkins 1823-1886 *BiDAmM*
Bancroft, Sir Squire 1841-1926 *CnThe, EncWT, Ent, NotNAT A, -B, OxThe, PlP&P[port], WhThe*
Band, The *BiDAmM, ConMuA 80A, IlEncR[port], RkOn 2[port]*
Band, Albert 1924- *FilmEn, FilmgC, HalFC 80, IntMPA 77, -75, -76, -78, -79, -80*
Band, Erich 1876-1945 *Baker 78*
Band, Margaret Louise 1896- *IntWWM 77, WhoMus 72*
Band Of Pirates *BiDAmM*
Banda, Ede 1917- *IntWWM 77*
Banda, Edo 1917- *IntWWM 80*
Banderali, Davidde 1789-1849 *NewGrD 80*
Bandiera, Lodovico *NewGrD 80*
Bandini, Albert Jacovino 1916- *AmSCAP 66, -80*
Bandler, Richard M 1924- *AmSCAP 80*
Bandmann, Daniel Edward 1840-1905 *NotNAT A, -B*
Bandmann-Palmer, Mrs. d1926 *NotNAT B*
Bando, Mitsugoro d1975 *WhScrn 77*
Bando, Tsumasaburo 1898-1953 *WhScrn 74, -77*
Bandrowska-Turska, Ewa 1899- *NewGrD 80*
Bandrowski-Sas, Aleksander 1860-1913 *NewGrD 80*
Bandy, Moe *IlEncCM[port]*
Bane, Martin J 1900- *AmSCAP 66*
Banfi, Alfonso *NewGrD 80*
Banfield, Baron Raffaello De 1922- *WhoMus 72*
Bang, Herman Joachim 1857-1912 *NotNAT B*
Bang, Joy *WhoHol A*
Bang, Maia 1877-1940 *BiDAmM*
Bang, Maia 1879-1940 *Baker 78*
Bangs, Carl Oliver, III 1945- *IntWWM 77, -80*
Bangs, Frank C 1833-1908 *NotNAT B, OxThe*
Bangs, John Kendrick 1862-1922 *NotNAT B, WhThe, WhoStg 1906, -1908*
Banim, John d1842 *NotNAT B*
Banister *NewGrD 80*
Banister, Charles William 1768-1831 *Baker 78*

Banister, Henry Charles 1831-1897 *Baker 78, NewGrD 80*
Banister, Henry Joshua 1803-1847 *Baker 78*
Banister, John d1725? *NewGrD 80*
Banister, John 1625?-1679 *NewGrD 80*
Banister, John 1630-1679 *Baker 78, MusMk, OxMus*
Banister, John, Jr. 1663?-1735 *Baker 78*
Banjamin, Gladys d1948 *WhScrn 77*
Banjo Boy *BluesWW[port]*
Banjo Joe *BluesWW[port]*
Bank, Jacques 1943- *Baker 78, IntWWM 77, -80*
Bank, Mirra *WomWMM A, -B*
Bankhead, Tallulah d1968 *MotPP, PlP&P[port], WhoHol B*
Bankhead, Tallulah 1902-1965 *OxFilm*
Bankhead, Tallulah 1902-1968 *BiDFilm, -81, Film 1, -2, FilmgC, HalFC 80, ThFT[port], WhScrn 74, -77, WhoHrs 80*
Bankhead, Tallulah 1903-1968 *BiE&WWA, CnThe, EncWT, Ent[port], FamA&A[port], FilmEn, ForYSC, MovMk[port], NotNAT A, -B, WhThe, WorEFlm[port]*
Banks, B *BlkAmP*
Banks, Benjamin 1727-1795 *NewGrD 80*
Banks, Billy 1908-1967 *WhoJazz 72*
Banks, Cary Craig 1950- *AmSCAP 80*
Banks, Charles O 1899-1944 *AmSCAP 66, -80*
Banks, Don 1923- *Baker 78, DcCM, IntWWM 77, MusMk, NewGrD 80, WhoMus 72*
Banks, Eric 1932- *IntWWM 77, -80*
Banks, Estar *Film 2*
Banks, Jackie LaMonte Johnson 1945- *BlkWAB[port]*
Banks, Joe 1882?-1930? *NewOrJ*
Banks, John 1650?-1706 *NotNAT B, OxThe*
Banks, Leslie 1890-1952 *FilmAG WE, FilmEn, FilmgC, HalFC 80, IlWWBF, MovMk, NotNAT B, OxThe, WhScrn 74, -77, WhThe, WhoHol B, WhoHrs 80*
Banks, Margaret 1924- *DancEn 78*
Banks, Monty 1897-1950 *FilmEn, Film 2, FilmgC, ForYSC, HalFC 80, IlWWBF, NotNAT B, TwYS, WhScrn 74, -77, WhoHol B*
Banks, Ralph 1762-1841 *OxMus*
Banks, Robert 1930- *ConAmC*
Bankson, Budd 1916- *NotNAT A*
Bankston, Dick 1899- *BluesWW[port]*
Banky, Vilma *MotPP*
Banky, Vilma 1898- *FilmEn, ThFT[port]*
Banky, Vilma 1902- *FilmgC, HalFC 80*
Banky, Vilma 1903- *Film 2, MovMk, TwYS, WhoHol A, WorEFlm*
Bannard, Robert *WhoHol A*
Bannen, Ian 1928- *FilmAG WE, FilmEn, FilmgC, ForYSC, HalFC 80, IlWWBF, IntMPA 77, -75, -76, -78, -79, -80, MotPP, MovMk, WhoHol A, WhoThe 72, -77*
Banner, Bob 1921- *IntMPA 77, -75, -76, -78, -79, -80, NewYTET*
Banner, John 1910-1973 *FilmEn, FilmgC, ForYSC, HalFC 80, WhScrn 77, WhoHol B*
Bannerman, Celia 1946- *WhoThe 72, -77*
Bannerman, James 1902- *CreCan 1*
Bannerman, Kay 1919- *WhoThe 72, -77*
Bannerman, Kenneth 1936- *DancEn 78*
Bannerman, Margaret 1896-1976 *BiE&WWA, IlWWBF, NotNAT B, WhThe, WhoThe 72*
Bannister, Charles 1738-1804 *NotNAT B*
Bannister, Charles 1741-1804 *EncWT, OxThe*
Bannister, Harry d1961 *Film 2, WhoHol B*
Bannister, Harry 1889-1961 *WhScrn 74, -77*
Bannister, Harry 1893-1961 *NotNAT B, WhThe*
Bannister, Henry Marriott 1854-1919 *Baker 78, NewGrD 80*
Bannister, John 1760-1836 *EncWT, Ent, NotNAT A, -B, OxThe*
Bannister, Nathaniel Harrington 1813-1847 *NotNAT B, OxThe*
Bannister, Virginia *PupTheA*
Bannius, Joan Albert *NewGrD 80*
Bannon, Anthony L 1942- *ConAmTC*
Bannon, Jim 1911- *FilmEn, FilmgC, ForYSC, HalFC 80, WhoHol A*
Banos, Ricardo De 1882-1939 *DcFM*
Banovitch, Milenko 1936- *CnOxB*
Banshchikov, Gennadii Ivanovich 1943- *DcCM*
Banshchikov, Gennady 1943- *Baker 78*
Bant, George Edward 1934- *IntWWM 77, -80*
Bantau, J W 1904- *IntMPA 77, -75, -76, -78, -79, -80*
Banter, Harald 1930- *IntWWM 77, -80, WhoMus 72*
Banthim, Larry *Film 2*
Banti, Brigida Giorgi 1756?-1806 *NewGrD 80*
Banti-Giogi, Brigida 1759-1806 *Baker 78*
Bantick, John Howard 1939- *IntWWM 80*
Bantock, Sir Granville 1868-1946 *Baker 78, CompSN[port], DcCom&M 79, MusMk, NewGrD 80[port], OxMus*
Bantock, Leedham 1870-1928 *IlWWBF, NotNAT B*
Banton, Travis 1894- *DcFM, FilmEn*
Banuelas, Roberto 1931- *WhoOp 76*
Banul, Chris *ConAmC*
Banville, Theodore De 1823-1891 *Ent*
Banville, Theodore Faullain De 1823-1891 *McGEWD, NotNAT B, OxThe*
Banville, Theodore Faullin De 1823-1891 *EncWT*
Banwart, Jakob 1609-1657? *NewGrD 80*
Banyai, George 1905- *BiE&WWA*
Banzet, Janet d1970? *WhScrn 77*
Banzhaf, Max 1915- *IntMPA 77, -75, -76, -78*
Bao, Miguel Gomez d1961 *WhScrn 77*
Baptie, David 1822-1906 *NewGrD 80*
Baptista, Carlos 1900-1950 *WhScrn 77*
Baptista, Johann *NewGrD 80*
Baptiste, Albert 1872?-1931? *NewOrJ*
Baptiste, Ludwig Albert Friedrich 1700-1764? *NewGrD 80*
Baptiste, Milton *NewOrJ SUP[port]*
Baptiste, Quentin *NewOrJ*
Baptiste, Rene 1880?-1933? *NewOrJ*
Baptiste, Tink 1897-1960 *NewOrJ*
Baquedano, Jose De *NewGrD 80*
Baqueiro, Foster Geronimo 1898-1967 *NewGrD 80*
Baquet, Achille 1885-1955 *NewOrJ[port]*
Baquet, George 1883-1949 *BiDAmM, NewOrJ[port], WhoJazz 72*
Baquet, Theogene 1858?-1920? *NewOrJ*
Baquet, Theogene 1860-1920 *BiDAmM*
Bar, Jacques Jean Louis 1921- *FilmEn, FilmgC, HalFC 80, IntMPA 77, -75, -76, -78, -79, -80*
Bar-Hebraeus, Gregory *NewGrD 80*
Bar-Illan, David 1930- *MusSN[port], NewGrD 80, WhoMus 72*
Bar-Kays, The *ConMuA 80A, RkOn 2[port]*
Bar-Lev, Assaf 1936- *IntWWM 77, -80*
Bara, Theda 1890-1955 *BiDFilm, -81, FilmEn, Film 1, -2, FilmgC, HalFC 80, MotPP, MovMk[port], NotNAT B, OxFilm, TwYS, WhScrn 74, -77, WhoHol B, WorEFlm*
Barab, Seymour 1921- *AmSCAP 66, -80, CpmDNM 79, -80, ConAmC*
Barach, Daniel Paul 1931- *IntWWM 77, -80*
Baragrey, John d1975 *WhoHol C*
Baragrey, John 1918-1975 *BiE&WWA, ForYSC, NotNAT, -B*
Baragrey, John 1919-1975 *IntMPA 77, -75, -76, -78, -79, -80, WhScrn 77*
Baraka, Amiri 1934- *DcLB 7*
Baraka, Imamu Amiri 1934- *BlkAmP, ConDr 73, -77, DrBlPA, EncWT, McGEWD[port], MorBAP, NotNAT, WhoThe 77*
Baral, Robert 1910- *BiE&WWA, NotNAT*
Baralli, Raffaele 1862-1924 *NewGrD 80*
Baralli, Raffaello 1862-1924 *NewGrD 80*
Baranovic, Kresimir 1894-1975 *Baker 78, NewGrD 80*
Baranovskaya, Vera *FilmEn, Film 2*
Bararipton *NewGrD 80*
Barasch, Norman 1922- *BiE&WWA, NotNAT*
Barash, Olivia *WhoHol A*
Barati, George 1913- *Baker 78, CpmDNM 75, ConAmC, DcCM, IntWWM 77, -80*
Baratier, Jacques 1918- *DcFM, FilmEn, FilmgC, HalFC 80, WorEFlm*
Barba, Daniel Dal *NewGrD 80*
Barbacci, Rodolfo 1911- *NewGrD 80*
Barbag-Drexler, Irena 1920- *IntWWM 80*
Barbaia, Domenico 1778?-1841 *NewGrD 80*
Barbaja, Domenico 1775?-1841 *Baker 78*
Barbaja, Domenico 1778-1841 *NewEOp 71*
Barban, Harvey *Film 2*
Barbanell, Fred 1931-1959 *WhScrn 74, -77*
Barbarian, Jacques *NewGrD 80*
Barbarie, Orgue De *OxMus*
Barbarin, Isidore 1872-1960 *NewOrJ*
Barbarin, Louis 1902- *NewOrJ[port]*
Barbarin, Paul 1901-1969 *BiDAmM, CmpEPM, EncJzS 70, IlEncJ, NewOrJ[port], WhoJazz 72*
Barbarini Lupus, Manfred *NewGrD 80*
Barbarino, Bartolomeo d1617? *NewGrD 80*
Barbaro, Umberto 1902-1959 *FilmEn, OxFilm, WorEFlm*
Barbat, Percy 1883-1965 *Film 2, WhScrn 77*
Barbato, Angelo *NewGrD 80*
Barbaud, Pierre *NewGrD 80*
Barbay, Ferenc 1943- *CnOxB*
Barbe *NewGrD 80*
Barbe, Antoine d1564 *NewGrD 80*
Barbe, Antoine 1547?-1604 *NewGrD 80*
Barbe, Antoine 1573?-1636 *NewGrD 80*
Barbe, Helmut 1927- *Baker 78, DcCM, NewGrD 80*
Barbe, John 1927- *AmSCAP 80*
Barbeau, Charles Marius *CreCan 2*
Barbeau, Christian Marcel *CreCan 2*
Barbeau, Francois 1935- *CreCan 2*
Barbeau, Marcel 1925- *CreCan 2*
Barbeau, Marius 1883-1969 *Baker 78, CreCan 2, NewGrD 80*
Barbeau, Master *PupTheA*
Barbecue Bob *BluesWW[port]*
Barbee, John Henry 1905-1964 *BluesWW[port]*
Barbee, Richard 1887- *WhThe*
Barbella, Emanuele 1718-1777 *NewGrD 80*
Barber, Arnold *IntMPA 77, -75, -76, -78, -79, -80*
Barber, Benjamin Reynolds 1939- *AmSCAP 80, NatPD[port]*
Barber, Bill 1920- *EncJzS 70*
Barber, Chris 1930- *EncJzS 70, NewGrD 80, RkOn[port]*
Barber, Clarence 1903- *WhoMus 72*
Barber, Donald Christopher 1930- *EncJzS 70*
Barber, John 1932- *AmSCAP 80*
Barber, John William 1920- *EncJzS 70, IntWWM 77*
Barber, Red *NewYTET*
Barber, Robert *NewGrD 80*
Barber, Robert 1750?- *NewGrD 80*
Barber, Samuel 1910- *AmSCAP 66, -80, Baker 78, BiDAmM, BnBkM 80, CmOp, CompSN[port], CpmDNM 79, CnOxB, ConAmC, DancEn 78, DcCom 77, DcCom&M 79, DcCM, IntWWM 77, -80, MusMk, NewEOp 71, NewGrD 80[port], OxMus, WhoMus 72*
Barber, William *ConAmTC*
Barbera, Joe 1911- *FilmgC, HalFC 80*
Barbera, Jose 1874-1947 *Baker 78*
Barbera, Jose 1876-1947 *NewGrD 80*
Barbera, Joseph 1911- *FilmEn, OxFilm, WorEFlm*
Barbera, Joseph R *IntMPA 79, -80*
Barberianus, Jacobus *NewGrD 80*
Barberiis, Melchiore De *NewGrD 80*
Barberina, La 1721-1799 *CnOxB, DancEn 78*
Barberini *NewGrD 80*
Barberini, Francesco 1454-1530 *NewGrD 80*
Barberis, Mansi 1899- *IntWWM 77, -80*
Barbetta, Giulio Cesare 1540?-1603? *NewGrD 80*
Barbette 1906-1973 *WhScrn 77, WhoHol B*
Barbi, Alice 1862-1948 *Baker 78*
Barbier, Mrs. 1692?-1740? *NewGrD 80*
Barbier, George 1866-1945 *ForYSC*
Barbier, George W 1862-1945 *HolCA[port]*
Barbier, George W 1865-1945 *FilmEn, FilmgC, HalFC 80, MovMk[port], NotNAT B, Vers A[port], WhScrn 74, -77, WhoHol B*
Barbier, Guy 1924- *IntWWM 77, -80, WhoOp 76*
Barbier, Jules d1901 *NotNAT B*
Barbier, Jules 1825-1901 *NewEOp 71*

Barbier, Jules Paul 1822-1901 *Baker 78*
Barbier, Rene 1890- *Baker 78, NewGrD 80*
Barbier, Rene August Ernest 1890- *IntWWM 77, -80*
Barbieri, Carlo Emanuele 1822-1867 *NewGrD 80*
Barbieri, Carlo Emmanuele 1822-1867 *Baker 78*
Barbieri, Fedora *WhoMus 72*
Barbieri, Fedora 1919- *IntWWM 77, -80, MusSN[port]*
Barbieri, Fedora 1920- *Baker 78, CmOp, NewEOp 71, NewGrD 80, WhoOp 76*
Barbieri, Francisco Asenjo 1823-1894 *Baker 78, NewGrD 80*
Barbieri, Gato 1934- *EncJzS 70*
Barbieri, Leandro *IlEncJ*
Barbieri, Leandro 1933- *BiDAmM*
Barbieri, Leandro J 1934- *EncJzS 70*
Barbieri, Lucio 1586-1659 *NewGrD 80*
Barbieri, Luzio 1586-1659 *NewGrD 80*
Barbieri, Margaret 1947- *CnOxB*
Barbieri, Niccolo d1640? *OxThe*
Barbieri-Nini, Marianna 1820?-1887 *CmOp, NewGrD 80*
Barbiero, Michael F 1949- *AmSCAP 80*
Barbingant *NewGrD 80*
Barbini, Ernesto 1909- *CreCan 1*
Barbini, Ernesto 1911- *IntWWM 80*
Barbion, Eustachius d1556 *NewGrD 80*
Barbireau, Jacobus 1420?-1491 *NewGrD 80*
Barbireau, Jacques 1408?-1491 *Baker 78*
Barbireau, Jacques 1420?-1491 *NewGrD 80*
Barbirianus, Jacobus 1420?-1491 *NewGrD 80*
Barbirianus, Jacques 1420?-1491 *NewGrD 80*
Barbirolli, Evelyn 1911- *IntWWM 77, -80, NewGrD 80*
Barbirolli, Giovanni Battista 1899-1970 *NewGrD 80[port]*
Barbirolli, Sir John 1899-1970 *Baker 78, BnBkM 80, CmOp, MusMk, MusSN[port], NewEOp 71, NewGrD 80[port]*
Barbitonsoris *NewGrD 80*
Barblan, Guglielmo 1906-1978 *NewGrD 80, WhoMus 72*
Barblan, Otto 1860-1943 *Baker 78, NewGrD 80*
Barblan-Opienska, Lydia 1890- *IntWWM 80*
Barbor, H R 1893-1933 *NotNAT B, WhThe*
Barbosa-Lima, Carlos 1944- *IntWWM 77, -80*
Barbosa Machado, Diogo 1682-1772 *NewGrD 80*
Barbot, Joseph-Theodore-Desire 1824-1897 *Baker 78*
Barboteu, Georges-Yves 1924- *IntWWM 77, -80*
Barbour, Alan G 1933- *IntMPA 77, -75, -76, -78, -79, -80*
Barbour, Dave 1912-1965 *CmpEPM, WhScrn 77, WhoJazz 72*
Barbour, David 1912-1965 *AmSCAP 66, -80, BiDAmM*
Barbour, Edwin Wilbour d1914 *WhScrn 77*
Barbour, Florence Newell 1866-1946 *Baker 78*
Barbour, Floyd *BlkAmP*
Barbour, J Murray 1897-1970 *Baker 78, ConAmC, NewGrD 80*
Barbour, John 1937- *ConAmTC*
Barbour, Joyce 1901- *WhThe, WhoThe 72*
Barbour, Keith 1941- *AmSCAP 80*
Barbour, Malcolm 1934- *IntMPA 77, -75, -76, -78, -79, -80*
Barbour, Ross 1928- *AmSCAP 66, -80*
Barbu, Filaret 1903- *IntWWM 80*
Barca, Alessandro 1741-1814 *NewGrD 80*
Barce, Ramon 1928- *Baker 78, DcCM, NewGrD 80*
Barcelo, Randy 1946- *NotNAT*
Barcelona, Daniel 1929- *BiDAmM*
Barcewicz, Stanislaw 1858-1929 *NewGrD 80*
Barclay, Adela *Film 1*
Barclay, Arthur 1869-1943 *Baker 78*
Barclay, Delancey d1917 *WhScrn 77*
Barclay, Don 1892-1975 *Film 1, WhScrn 77, WhoHol C*
Barclay, John *WhoHol A*
Barclay, Lola *Film 1*
Barclay James Harvest *IlEncR*
Barclift, Nelson 1917- *AmSCAP 66, -80*
Barcroft, Roy 1902- *ForYSC*
Barcroft, Roy 1902-1969 *FilmEn, FilmgC, HalFC 80, HolCA[port], MotPP, Vers A[port], WhScrn 77, WhoHol B, WhoHrs 80[port]*
Bard, Ben *Film 2, ForYSC, TwYS*
Bard, Katharine *ForYSC, WhoHol A*
Bard, Maria 1901-1944 *WhScrn 74, -77*
Bard, Wilkie 1870-1944 *NotNAT B, OxThe*
Bard, Wilkie 1874- *WhThe*
Bard, Ysabelle 1889- *IntWWM 77, -80*
Barda, Antonio *Film 2*
Bardacke, Frances Lavender 1919- *ConAmTC*
Bardaisan 154-222 *NewGrD 80*
Bardd Y Brenin *NewGrD 80*
Bardella, Il *NewGrD 80*
Bardem, Juan Antonio 1922- *BiDFilm, -81, DcFM, FilmEn, FilmgC, HalFC 80, OxFilm, WorEFlm*
Bardesanes 154-222 *NewGrD 80*
Bardette, Trevor 1902- *ForYSC, Vers A[port], WhoHol A*
Bardette, Trevor 1902-1978 *FilmEn*
Bardi, Count Giovanni 1534-1612 *BnBkM 80, NewEOp 71, OxMus*
Bardi, Giovanni De' 1534-1612 *Baker 78, NewGrD 80*
Bardin, Micheline 1920- *CnOxB*
Bardin, Micheline 1926- *DancEn 78*
Bardon, Henry 1923- *WhoOp 76, WhoThe 72, -77*
Bardos, Kornel 1921- *NewGrD 80*
Bardos, Lajos 1899- *NewGrD 80*
Bardossi, Elizabeth Jane 1956- *IntWWM 77, -80*
Bardot, Brigitte *MotPP, WhoHol A*
Bardot, Brigitte 1933- *FilmgC, HalFC 80[port]*
Bardot, Brigitte 1934- *BiDFilm, -81, FilmAG WE[port], FilmEn, ForYSC, IntMPA 77, -75, -76, -78, -79, -80, MovMk[port], OxFilm, WorEFlm[port]*
Bardwell, Thomas Carew 1917- *IntWWM 77*
Bardwell, William 1915- *CpmDNM 75, IntWWM 77, -80, NewGrD 80*
Bardzinski, Jan Alan 1657-1708 *NewGrD 80*
Bare, Bobby 1935- *CounME 74[port], -74A, EncFCWM 69, IlEncCM[port], RkOn[port]*
Bare, Richard 1909- *FilmEn*
Bare, Richard L 1909?- *FilmgC, HalFC 80, IntMPA 77, -75, -76, -78, -79, -80*
Bare, Robert Joseph 1935- *BiDAmM*
Barefield, Eddie 1909- *CmpEPM, EncJzS 70, WhoJazz 72*
Barefield, Edward Emanuel 1909- *BiDAmM, EncJzS 70*
Barefield, Ora 1918- *IntWWM 77*
Barefoot Jerry *IlEncCM, IlEncR*
Barela, Margaret Mary 1946- *IntWWM 77, -80*
Baren, Harvey M 1931- *IntMPA 77, -75, -76, -78, -79, -80*
Barenboim, Daniel 1942- *Baker 78, BiDAmM, BnBkM 80, IntWWM 77, -80, MusSN[port], NewGrD 80[port], WhoMus 72*
Barer, Marshall L 1923- *AmSCAP 66, -80, BiE&WWA, EncMT, NotNAT*
Barera, Ahrodiano *NewGrD 80*
Barera, Rodiano *NewGrD 80*
Bares, Basile 1845-1902 *BiDAmM*
Baretti, Giuseppe 1719-1789 *NewGrD 80*
Bareva, Lilyana 1922- *NewGrD 80*
Barey, Pat *WomWMM B*
Bareza, Niksa 1936- *WhoOp 76*
Barford, Philip Trevelyan 1925- *IntWWM 80*
Bargagli, Girolamo 1537-1586 *McGEWD*
Bargas, Urban De *NewGrD 80*
Barge, Gillian 1940- *WhoThe 77*
Barge, Wilhelm 1836-1925 *Baker 78*
Barges, Antonino *NewGrD 80*
Barges, Antonio *NewGrD 80*
Bargiel, Woldemar 1828-1897 *Baker 78, NewGrD 80, OxMus*
Bargielski, Zbigniew 1937- *Baker 78, NewGrD 80*
Bargnani, Ottavio 1570?-1627? *NewGrD 80*
Bargues, Antonino *NewGrD 80*
Bargy, Roy d1974 *CmpEPM*
Barham, Patricia Lynn 1941- *WhoOp 76*
Bari, Gwen 1927- *AmSCAP 66, -80*
Bari, Lynn *IntMPA 75, -76, MotPP*
Bari, Lynn 1913- *FilmEn, HolP 30[port], ThFT[port]*
Bari, Lynn 1915- *FilmgC, HalFC 80, WhoHol A*
Bari, Lynn 1916- *ForYSC, MovMk[port]*
Bari, Lynn 1917- *IntMPA 77, -78, -79, -80*
Bari, Lynn 1919- *What 4[port]*
Bari, Tania 1936- *CnOxB, DancEn 78*
Barillet, Pierre 1923- *McGEWD*
Barilli, Bruno 1880-1952 *Baker 78, NewGrD 80*
Baring, Aubrey 1912- *IntMPA 77, -75, -76, -78, -79, -80*
Baring, Maurice 1874-1945 *NotNAT B, WhThe*
Baring, Norah 1907- *FilmEn, Film 2, IlWWBF[port]*
Baring-Gould, Sabine 1834-1924 *NewGrD 80, OxMus*
Barini, Giorgio 1864-1944 *Baker 78, NewGrD 80*
Bariola, Ottavio *NewGrD 80*
Barioli, Ottavio *NewGrD 80*
Bariolla, Ottavio *NewGrD 80*
Bariolus, Ottavio *NewGrD 80*
Barish, Sherlee *NewYTET*
Barishnikov, Mikhail *CnOxB*
Barison, Cesare Augusto 1887- *WhoMus 72*
Bark, Jan 1934- *Baker 78, NewGrD 80*
Barkan, Stanley Howard 1936- *AmSCAP 66*
Barkas, Geoffrey 1896- *IlWWBF, -A*
Barkauskas, Vytautas 1931- *Baker 78, DcCM*
Barkel, Charles 1898-1973 *NewGrD 80*
Barker *EncWT*
Barker, Alice *WhoMus 72*
Barker, Bradley 1883-1951 *Film 1, -2, WhScrn 74, -77, WhoHol B*
Barker, Cecil *NewYTET*
Barker, Charles Spackman 1804-1879 *NewGrD 80*
Barker, Clive 1931- *WhoThe 72, -77*
Barker, Corrine *Film 2*
Barker, Dale Willard 1920- *AmSCAP 66, -80*
Barker, Daniel 1909- *AmSCAP 80, BiDAmM, EncJzS 70*
Barker, Danny 1909- *CmpEPM, EncJzS 70, IlEncJ, NewOrJ[port], WhoJazz 72*
Barker, Enola *PupTheA*
Barker, Eric *Film 1*
Barker, Eric 1912- *FilmgC, HalFC 80, IlWWBF, -A, IntMPA 77, -75, -76, -78, -79, -80*
Barker, Ethel 1897- *WhoMus 72*
Barker, Florence 1891-1913 *Film 1, WhScrn 77*
Barker, George 1906- *WhoMus 72*
Barker, Gillian Marsha 1946- *IntWWM 77*
Barker, Harley Granville- 1877-1946 *CnThe, NotNAT A, OxThe, WhThe, WhoStg 1908*
Barker, Helen Granville- *WhThe*
Barker, Horace 1907- *WhoMus 72*
Barker, Horton 1889- *BiDAmM, EncFCWM 69*
Barker, Howard 1946- *ConDr 73, -77, WhoThe 77*
Barker, J S *MorBAP*
Barker, Jack d1950 *NotNAT B*
Barker, Jack 1922- *AmSCAP 66, -80*
Barker, James Nelson 1784-1858 *McGEWD[port], NotNAT B, OxThe, REnWD[port]*
Barker, Jess *ForYSC, MotPP*
Barker, Jess 1912- *FilmEn*
Barker, Jess 1914- *FilmgC, HalFC 80*
Barker, Jess 1915- *WhoHol A*
Barker, Joan *WhoMus 72*
Barker, John 1705?-1781 *NewGrD 80*
Barker, John Edgar 1931- *WhoMus 72, WhoOp 76*
Barker, John Stanley 1923- *WhoMus 72*
Barker, Joyce 1937- *WhoOp 76*
Barker, Lex 1919-1973 *FilmEn, FilmgC, ForYSC, HalFC 80, MotPP, MovMk, WhScrn 77, WhoHol B, WhoHrs 80*
Barker, Louisa Dupont 1913- *AmSCAP 80, BluesWW[port]*
Barker, Louise 1914?- *NewOrJ[port]*

Barker, Noelle 1928- IntWWM 77, -80, WhoMus 72
Barker, Norman IntMPA 77, -75, -76, -78, -79, -80
Barker, Philip Stanley 1913- IntWWM 77, -80, WhoMus 72
Barker, Reginald 1886-1936 TwYS A
Barker, Reginald 1886-1937 DcFM, FilmEn
Barker, Reginald 1886-1945 NotNAT B, WhScrn 74, -77
Barker, Richard d1903 NotNAT B
Barker, Robert William IntMPA 77, -75, -76, -78, -79, -80
Barker, Ronnie 1929- FilmgC, HalFC 80, WhoThe 72, -77
Barker, Ted 1926- WhoMus 72
Barker, Warren E 1923- ConAmC
Barker, Will C 1867-1951 HalFC 80
Barker, Will G 1867-1951 FilmgC, OxFilm
Barker, William George 1867-1951 DcFM, FilmEn
Barkhausen, Hans WomWMM
Barkhudaryan, Sarkis Vasilyevich 1887-1972 NewGrD 80
Barkhudaryan, Sergey Vasilyevich 1887-1972 NewGrD 80
Barkin, Elaine Radoff 1932- CpmDNM 79, -80, ConAmC, IntWWM 77, -80
Barkin, Leo 1905- CreCan 2
Barkla, Cecile Mary Cave 1922- WhoMus 72
Barkley, Deanne WomWMM
Barklie, Alice Dorothy IntWWM 77
Barkoczy, Sandor 1934- CnOxB
Barksdale, Everett 1910- BiDAmM, CmpEPM, WhoJazz 72
Barkworth, John 1858-1929 NewGrD 80
Barkworth, Peter 1929- FilmgC, HalFC 80, WhoThe 72, -77
Barlaam d1350 NewGrD 80
Barlach, Ernst Heinrich 1870-1938 CnMD, EncWT, McGEWD, ModWD, NotNAT B
Barlasca, Bernardino NewGrD 80
Barleon, Amelia Film 1
Barley, William d1614 NewGrD 80, OxMus
Barlog, Boleslaw 1906- EncWT, WhThe, WhoOp 76
Barlow, Alan 1927- WhoMus 72
Barlow, Anna Marie NatPD[port]
Barlow, Betty Marie 1920- IntWWM 77
Barlow, Billie 1862-1937 NotNAT B, WhThe
Barlow, David Frederick 1927-1975 NewGrD 80, WhoMus 72
Barlow, Fred 1881-1951 Baker 78, NewGrD 80
Barlow, H J 1892-1970 WhThe
Barlow, Harold 1915- AmSCAP 66, -80, Baker 78
Barlow, Howard 1892-1972 AmSCAP 66, Baker 78, BiDAmM, CmpEPM, ConAmC
Barlow, Jeff Film 2
Barlow, Jeremy 1939- IntWWM 77, -80
Barlow, Joel 1755-1812 BiDAmM
Barlow, John Perry 1947- AmSCAP 80
Barlow, Joyce 1910- WhoMus 72
Barlow, Kitty Film 2
Barlow, Klara 1928- WhoOp 76
Barlow, Reginald 1867-1943 Film 2, NotNAT B, WhScrn 74, -77, WhoHol B
Barlow, Samuel L M 1892- Baker 78, BiDAmM, ConAmC, NewGrD 80, WhoMus 72
Barlow, Stephen William 1954- IntWWM 77, -80
Barlow, Sybil 1902- WhoMus 72
Barlow, Sydney John 1919- WhoMus 72
Barlow, Wayne 1912- AmSCAP 66, Baker 78, BiDAmM, ConAmC, DcCM, NewGrD 80
Barlow, Wayne Brewster 1912- AmSCAP 80, CpmDNM 80
Barlow, William Film 2
Barmak, Ira 1936- AmSCAP 80
Barmann, Heinrich Joseph 1784-1847 Baker 78, OxMus
Barmann, Karl 1811-1885 Baker 78
Barmann, Karl, Jr. 1839-1913 Baker 78
Barmas, Issaye 1872-1946 Baker 78
Barmig, Johann Gotthilf 1815-1899 NewGrD 80
Barnabe, Bruno 1905- WhoThe 72, -77
Barnabee, Henry Clay 1833-1917 BiDAmM, NotNAT A, -B, WhoStg 1906, -1908
Barnabei NewGrD 80
Barnard, Mrs. OxMus
Barnard, Allan Frederic 1911- IntWWM 77
Barnard, Lady Anne OxMus
Barnard, Annie d1941 NotNAT B
Barnard, Charles d1920 NotNAT B
Barnard, Charlotte Alington 1830-1869 Baker 78, NewGrD 80
Barnard, Claribel 1830-1869 NewGrD 80
Barnard, Elizabeth 1906- WhoMus 72
Barnard, Elsie Irene 1902- WhoMus 72
Barnard, Francis ConAmC
Barnard, Howard Clive 1884- WhoMus 72
Barnard, Ivor 1887-1953 Film 2, FilmgC, HalFC 80, NotNAT B, WhThe, WhoHol B
Barnard, John OxMus
Barnard, John 1591?- NewGrD 80
Barnard, John 1681-1770 BiDAmM
Barnard, Leslie Gordon 1890-1961 CreCan 1
Barnard, Russell ConMuA 80B
Barnard, Scott 1943- CnOxB
Barnard, William 1918- ConAmC
Barnathan, Julius NewYTET
Barnay, Ludwig 1842-1924 EncWT
Barnay, Paul 1884-1960 EncWT
Barnby, Sir Joseph 1838-1896 Baker 78, BnBkM 80, NewGrD 80, OxMus
Barndorff, Bjarne 1941- IntWWM 80
Barnea, Aviasaf OxMus
Barnekow, Christian 1837-1913 Baker 78, NewGrD 80
Barnell, Nora Ely 1882-1933 WhScrn 74, -77, WhoHol B
Barnelle, Mary Beth Film 2
Barner, Juke Boy BluesWW[port]
Barnes, Al G 1862-1931 NotNAT A
Barnes, Anna Mary 1937- WhoMus 72
Barnes, Archibald George 1887- CreCan 1
Barnes, Aubrey BlkAmP
Barnes, Barnabe 1569?-1609 CnThe, REnWD
Barnes, Barnabee 1569?-1609 NotNAT B
Barnes, Barry K 1906-1965 FilmEn, FilmgC, HalFC 80, IlWWBF, WhScrn 74, -77, WhThe, WhoHol B
Barnes, Betty 1933- WhoMus 72
Barnes, Bianca WomWMM
Barnes, Bill IntMPA 80
Barnes, Billy 1927- BiE&WWA, NotNAT
Barnes, Binnie 1905- FilmEn, FilmgC, HalFC 80, HolP 30[port], MotPP, ThFT[port], What 2[port], WhThe, WhoHol A
Barnes, Binnie 1906- Film 2, IlWWBF[port], MovMk[port]
Barnes, Binnie 1908- ForYSC
Barnes, Bosby AmSCAP 80
Barnes, Charlotte Mary Sanford 1818-1863 NotNAT B, OxThe
Barnes, Christina WomWMM B
Barnes, Clifford P 1897- AmSCAP 66, -80
Barnes, Clive Alexander 1927- CnOxB, ConAmTC, DancEn 78, NotNAT, WhoThe 77
Barnes, Djuna 1892- CnMD, ConDr 73, -77
Barnes, Edna Reming 1883-1935 WhScrn 74, -77
Barnes, Edward Martin 1957- AmSCAP 80
Barnes, Edward Shippen 1887-1958 AmSCAP 66, -80, Baker 78, BiDAmM, ConAmC
Barnes, Emile 1892-1970 NewOrJ[port]
Barnes, Fae BluesWW[port]
Barnes, Faye BluesWW[port]
Barnes, Florence Pancho 1902-1975 WhScrn 77, WhoHol C
Barnes, Frank d1940 Film 2, WhScrn 74, -77, WhoHol B
Barnes, Fred 1884- WhThe
Barnes, George 1890-1949 Film 1, WhScrn 74, -77, WhoHol B
Barnes, George 1893-1953 FilmEn, FilmgC, HalFC 80, WorEFlm
Barnes, George 1921-1977 BiDAmM, CmpEPM, EncJzS 70, IlEncJ
Barnes, Gerald Linton 1935- WhoMus 72
Barnes, Grace PupTheA
Barnes, Harold Ernest 1909- WhoMus 72
Barnes, Harrison 1889-1960 NewOrJ
Barnes, Hellen 1908- AmSCAP 66, -80
Barnes, Howard 1904-1968 NotNAT B, WhThe
Barnes, Howard Lee 1918- AmSCAP 80
Barnes, J H Film 1, WhoStg 1906
Barnes, J H 1850-1925 NotNAT A, -B, WhThe
Barnes, J H 1852- WhoStg 1908
Barnes, James Charles 1949- AmSCAP 80, ConAmC
Barnes, Jessie AmSCAP 80
Barnes, Joanna 1934- FilmEn, FilmgC, ForYSC, HalFC 80, MotPP, WhoHol A
Barnes, Joe d1964 NotNAT B
Barnes, John 1761-1841 NotNAT B
Barnes, John 1904- IntWWM 80
Barnes, John Robert 1928- NewGrD 80
Barnes, Justice D Film 1
Barnes, Justus D 1862-1946 WhScrn 74, -77, WhoHol B
Barnes, Sir Kenneth Ralph 1878-1957 NotNAT A, -B, OxThe, WhThe
Barnes, Larry ConAmC
Barnes, Mabel Thomas d1962 NotNAT B
Barnes, Mac M Film 2
Barnes, Mae 1907- BiE&WWA, DrBlPA, NotNAT, WhoHol A
Barnes, Marshall 1921- ConAmC
Barnes, Milton 1931- Baker 78
Barnes, Norman John 1916- WhoMus 72
Barnes, Paul D 1901- BiDAmM
Barnes, Paul D 1902- NewOrJ[port], WhoJazz 72
Barnes, Peter 1931- ConDr 73, -77, EncWT, WhoThe 72, -77
Barnes, Ray Film 2
Barnes, Richard 1947- IntWWM 80
Barnes, Roy T d1937 WhoHol B
Barnes, Susan PupTheA
Barnes, T Roy 1880-1936 Film 2, ForYSC, TwYS
Barnes, T Roy 1880-1937 FilmEn, NotNAT B, WhScrn 74, -77
Barnes, Thomas 1785-1841 OxThe
Barnes, V L 1870-1949 Film 2, WhScrn 74, -77, WhoHol B
Barnes, Wade 1917- AmSCAP 66, -80
Barnes, Walter 1907?-1940 CmpEPM, WhoJazz 72
Barnes, Wilfred Molson 1882-1955 CreCan 1
Barnes, Will C 1858-1936 BiDAmM
Barnes, William 1927- AmSCAP 66, -80
Barnes, William E 1936- IntMPA 77, -75, -76, -78, -79
Barnes, Winifred 1894-1935 WhThe
Barnet, Boris 1902-1965 DcFM, FilmEn, Film 2, OxFilm, WorEFlm[port]
Barnet, Charles Daly 1913- BiDAmM, EncJzS 70
Barnet, Charlie 1913- AmPS B, BgBands 74[port], CmpEPM, EncJzS 70, IlEncJ, WhoJazz 72
Barnet, Chuck ConMuA 80B
Barnet, Robert Ayers 1853-1933 NotNAT B
Barnett, Alan 1926- IntMPA 77, -75, -76, -78, -79, -80
Barnett, Alice 1886- AmSCAP 66, -80, BiDAmM, ConAmC
Barnett, Battling Film 1
Barnett, Beryl 1914- AmSCAP 80
Barnett, Beverly Helene 1937- AmSCAP 80
Barnett, Bobby Glen 1936- BiDAmM
Barnett, C Z d1890 NotNAT B
Barnett, Charles Film 1
Barnett, Chester A 1885-1947 Film 1, NotNAT B, WhScrn 74, -77, WhoHol B
Barnett, David 1907- ConAmC
Barnett, George 1900- IntMPA 75
Barnett, Griff 1885-1958 WhScrn 74, -77, WhoHol B
Barnett, J J H WhoMus 72
Barnett, Jack 1920- AmSCAP 66
Barnett, Jackie AmSCAP 80
Barnett, John 1802-1890 Baker 78, NewGrD 80[port], OxMus
Barnett, John Francis 1837-1916 Baker 78, NewGrD 80, OxMus
Barnett, John Manley 1917- Baker 78
Barnett, LaQuinta R 1935- IntWWM 77
Barnett, Laurel J AmSCAP 80

Barnett, Margo *MorBAP*
Barnett, Mark Andrew 1950- *AmSCAP 80*
Barnett, Morris d1856 *NotNAT B*
Barnett, Norman 1919- *IntMPA 75, -76*
Barnett, Robert 1925- *CnOxB*
Barnett, Vince 1902-1977 *FilmEn, FilmgC, HalFC 80, MovMk, Vers A[port]*
Barnett, Vince 1903- *WhoHol A*
Barnett, Vincent 1903- *ForYSC*
Barney, Jay *BiE&WWA, NotNAT, WhoHol A*
Barnhill, James 1922- *BiE&WWA, NotNAT*
Barnhill, Joe Bob *AmSCAP 80*
Barnouw, Erik *NewYTET*
Barnowsky, Victor 1875-1952 *EncWT*
Barns, Ethel 1880-1948 *Baker 78*
Barnum, George *Film 2*
Barnum, George William d1937 *NotNAT B*
Barnum, H B *RkOn*
Barnum, H B 1936- *BiDAmM*
Barnum, Phineas Taylor 1810-1891 *CnThe, EncWT, Ent, NotNAT A, -B, OxThe*
Barocco, Dominick 1893-1970 *NewOrJ[port]*
Barocco, Joe 1891-1947 *NewOrJ[port]*
Barocco, Vincent 1878?- *NewOrJ*
Barolsky, Michael 1947- *Baker 78, IntWWM 77, -80*
Baromeo, Chase 1893- *BiDAmM*
Baron 1906-1956 *CnOxB*
Baron, Andre 1602?-1655 *OxThe*
Baron, Andre Michel 1600?-1655 *EncWT, Ent*
Baron, Auguste 1853-1938 *DcFM*
Baron, Carol Kitzes 1934- *IntWWM 80*
Baron, Ernst Gottlieb 1696-1760 *Baker 78, NewGrD 80*
Baron, Etienne 1676-1711 *OxThe*
Baron, Herman Alexander 1920- *AmSCAP 80*
Baron, Jeanne Ausoult 1625-1662 *OxThe*
Baron, Jeanne Auzoult 1625-1662 *EncWT*
Baron, John Herschel 1936- *IntWWM 77, -80*
Baron, Jonny 1925- *AmSCAP 66*
Baron, Lewis d1920 *NotNAT B*
Baron, Lita *ForYSC, WhoHol A*
Baron, Marion Weiss 1923- *AmSCAP 80*
Baron, Maurice 1889-1964 *AmSCAP 66, -80, Baker 78, ConAmC, NotNAT B*
Baron, Michael 1653?-1729 *NotNAT B*
Baron, Michel 1653-1729 *EncWT, Ent, OxThe*
Baron, Robert Alex 1920- *BiE&WWA, NotNAT*
Baron, Samuel 1925- *ConAmC, IntWWM 77, -80, NewGrD 80*
Baron, Theofil 1696-1760 *NewGrD 80*
Baron, Vic 1910- *AmSCAP 66, -80*
Baroncelli, Jacques De 1881-1951 *DcFM, FilmEn, OxFilm*
Barone, Gary 1941- *EncJzS 70*
Barone, Mark F 1952- *AmSCAP 80*
Barone, Michael Joseph 1936- *AmSCAP 80, EncJzS 70*
Barone, Mike 1936- *EncJzS 70*
Baroni *NewGrD 80*
Baroni, Adriana *NewGrD 80*
Baroni, Andreana *NewGrD 80*
Baroni, Andriana *NewGrD 80*
Baroni, Antonio *NewGrD 80*
Baroni, Catarina *NewGrD 80*
Baroni, Eleanora 1611-1670 *NewGrD 80*
Baroni, Leonora 1611-1670 *NewGrD 80*
Baroni, Lionora 1611-1670 *NewGrD 80*
Baroni, Vasco 1910- *AmSCAP 80*
Baronova, Irina 1919- *CnOxB, DancEn 78[port], WhThe*
Baronova, Irina 1922- *WhoHol A*
Baross, Jan 1943- *WomWMM B*
Baroux, Lucien 1889-1968 *WhScrn 74, -77*
Barovick, Fred *AmSCAP 66, -80, ConAmC A*
Barr, Al *ConAmC*
Barr, Albert Earl 1931- *AmSCAP 66, -80*
Barr, Anthony 1921- *AmSCAP 66, IntMPA 77, -75, -76, -78, -79, -80*
Barr, Byron 1917-1966 *FilmEn, WhScrn 77, WhoHol B*
Barr, Geoffrey 1924- *BiE&WWA*
Barr, Jeanne 1932-1967 *WhScrn 74, -77, WhoHol B*
Barr, John *ConAmC*
Barr, Michael 1927- *AmSCAP 66*
Barr, Patrick 1908- *FilmgC, HalFC 80, IlWWBF, IntMPA 77, -75, -76, -78, -79, -80, WhoHol A, WhoThe 72, -77*
Barr, Raphael 1912- *AmSCAP 80*
Barr, Raymond Arthur 1932- *IntWWM 77, -80*
Barr, Richard 1917- *BiE&WWA, NotNAT, WhoThe 72, -77*
Barr, Robin Noel 1940- *IntWWM 77, -80, WhoMus 72*
Barr, Tim *WhoHrs 80*
Barra, Jean De *NewGrD 80*
Barra, Jehan De *NewGrD 80*
Barra, Ray 1930- *CnOxB*
Barraclough, Clive 1941- *IntWWM 77*
Barraclough, Henry 1891- *AmSCAP 80*
Barraclough, Sydney d1930 *NotNAT B*
Barrae, Leonardo *NewGrD 80*
Barragan, Salvador Toscano 1872-1947 *FilmEn*
Barraine, Elsa 1910- *Baker 78, NewGrD 80, WhoMus 72*
Barranco, John, Jr. 1951- *AmSCAP 80*
Barranger, M S 1937- *NotNAT*
Barraque, Jean 1928-1973 *Baker 78, DcCM, MusMk, NewGrD 80*
Barras, Charles M 1826-1873 *NotNAT B, PlP&P[port]*
Barrat, Jean *NewGrD 80*
Barrat, Jean De *NewGrD 80*
Barrat, Jehan De *NewGrD 80*
Barrat, Robert 1891-1970 *FilmEn, FilmgC, ForYSC, HalFC 80, HolCA[port], MovMk, Vers B[port], WhScrn 74, -77, WhoHol B*
Barratt, Augustus *WhThe*
Barratt, Carol Ann 1945- *IntWWM 80*
Barratt, Clifford *IntWWM 77, -80, WhoMus 72*
Barratt, Thomas Augustin *NewGrD 80*
Barratt, Walter Augustus d1947 *NotNAT B*
Barratt, Watson 1884-1962 *NotNAT B, WhThe*
Barraud, Dany 1940- *WhoOp 76*
Barraud, George 1894- *Film 2*
Barraud, Henri 1900- *CompSN[port]*
Barraud, Henry 1900- *Baker 78, DcCM, IntWWM 77, -80, NewGrD 80, OxMus, WhoMus 72*
Barrault, Jean-Louis 1910- *BiE&WWA, CnThe, EncWT, Ent, FilmAG WE, FilmEn, FilmgC, HalFC 80, MovMk, NotNAT A, OxFilm, OxThe, WhThe, WhoHol A, WhoOp 76, WorEFlm*
Barrault, Marie-Christine 1944- *FilmEn*
Barre, Albert d1910 *NotNAT B*
Barre, Antonio *NewGrD 80*
Barre, Leonardo *NewGrD 80*
Barre, Nigel 1889- *Film 2*
Barrelhouse Sammy *BluesWW[port]*
Barrelhouse Tommy *BluesWW[port]*
Barrell, Bernard 1919- *IntWWM 77, -80, WhoMus 72*
Barrell, Joyce Howard 1917- *IntWWM 77, -80, WhoMus 72*
Barrera, Carlos Gomez 1918- *IntWWM 77, -80*
Barrera, Giulia 1942- *WhoOp 76*
Barrera, Rodiano *NewGrD 80*
Barrera Gomez, Enrique 1844-1922 *NewGrD 80*
Barrere, George *OxMus*
Barrere, Georges 1876-1944 *Baker 78, BiDAmM, BnBkM 80, MusSN[port], NewGrD 80*
Barrere, Jean 1918- *BiE&WWA*
Barrere, Paul 1948- *AmSCAP 80*
Barret, Apollon 1803-1879 *Baker 78*
Barret, Leonardo *NewGrD 80*
Barreto, Lima 1905- *FilmEn, FilmgC, HalFC 80, OxFilm*
Barreto, Victor DeLima 1905- *WorEFlm*
Barreto, Vitor DeLima 1905- *DcFM*
Barrett, Betsy Mason 1929- *IntWWM 77*
Barrett, Charles C 1871-1929 *WhScrn 74, -77*
Barrett, Claudia *ForYSC*
Barrett, Edith 1906- *WhThe*
Barrett, Edith 1907-1977 *FilmEn*
Barrett, Edith 1912-1977 *HalFC 80*
Barrett, Elizabeth Vere 1920- *WhoMus 72*
Barrett, Emma 1898- *BlkWAB[port], NewOrJ[port]*
Barrett, Emma 1905?- *BiDAmM*
Barrett, Ena Margaret 1907- *WhoMus 72*
Barrett, George 1869-1935 *NotNAT B, WhThe*
Barrett, George Edward 1849-1894 *NotNAT B, OxThe*
Barrett, Mrs. George H d1857 *NotNAT B*
Barrett, George Horton 1794-1860 *NotNAT B, OxThe*
Barrett, Harold Roger 1934- *IntWWM 77*
Barrett, Henry Michael d1872 *NotNAT B*
Barrett, Ivy Rice 1898-1962 *NotNAT B, WhScrn 74, -77, WhoHol B*
Barrett, James Lee 1929- *CmMov, FilmEn, FilmgC, HalFC 80, IntMPA 77, -75, -76, -78, -79, -80*
Barrett, Jane 1923-1969 *FilmgC, HalFC 80, WhScrn 74, -77, WhoHol B*
Barrett, Jimmie d1964 *NotNAT B*
Barrett, Joanne Lenhert 1936- *AmSCAP 80*
Barrett, John 1676?-1719 *NewGrD 80*
Barrett, Judith *WhoHol A*
Barrett, Judith 1914- *FilmEn, ForYSC*
Barrett, Laurinda *WhoHol A*
Barrett, Lawrence 1838-1891 *FamA&A[port], NotNAT A, -B, OxThe*
Barrett, Leslie *WhoHol A*
Barrett, Lester *WhThe*
Barrett, Lindsay *BlkAmP*
Barrett, Majel *WhoHol A*
Barrett, Nathan Noble 1933- *BlkAmP, NatPD[port]*
Barrett, Oscar, Jr. 1875-1941 *WhThe*
Barrett, Oscar, Jr. 1875-1943 *NotNAT B*
Barrett, Oscar, Sr. d1941 *NotNAT B*
Barrett, Pat 1889-1959 *WhScrn 77, WhoHol B*
Barrett, Ray 1926- *FilmgC, HalFC 80*
Barrett, Reginald 1861-1940 *Baker 78*
Barrett, Richard *RkOn*
Barrett, Roger L 1924- *ConAmC*
Barrett, Rona *IntMPA 78, -79, -80, NewYTET*
Barrett, Syd 1946- *ConMuA 80A, IlEncR*
Barrett, Thomas A *OxMus*
Barrett, Tony 1916-1974 *WhScrn 77, WhoHol B*
Barrett, William Alexander 1834-1891 *Baker 78, NewGrD 80*
Barrett, Wilson 1846-1904 *NotNAT B, OxThe*
Barrett, Wilson 1900- *WhThe*
Barrett-Ayres, Reginald 1920- *IntWWM 77, -80*
Barretto, Ray 1939- *RkOn*
Barri, Mario d1963 *WhScrn 74, -77, WhoHol B*
Barri, Odoardo d1920 *NotNAT B*
Barri, Steve *ConMuA 80B*
Barrie, Amanda 1939- *FilmgC, HalFC 80, WhoThe 72, -77*
Barrie, Barbara 1931- *ForYSC, NotNAT, WhoHol A, WhoThe 77*
Barrie, Eddie *Film 1*
Barrie, Elaine *WhoHol A*
Barrie, George 1912- *AmSCAP 80*
Barrie, George 1918- *IntMPA 78, -79, -80*
Barrie, Gracie 1917?- *CmpEPM*
Barrie, Sir J M 1860-1937 *HalFC 80*
Barrie, Sir James Matthew 1860-1937 *CnMD, CnThe, EncWT, Ent, FilmgC, McGEWD[port], ModWD, NotNAT A, -B, OxThe, PlP&P[port], REnWD, WhScrn 77, WhThe, WhoStg 1906, -1908*
Barrie, Mona 1909- *FilmEn, FilmgC, ForYSC, HalFC 80, IntMPA 77, -75, -76, -78, -79, -80, MovMk*
Barrie, Nigel 1889- *Film 1, -2, TwYS*
Barrie, Wendy 1912- *FilmgC, MotPP, MovMk[port], ThFT[port]*
Barrie, Wendy 1912-1978 *FilmEn, HalFC 80, IlWWBF[port]*
Barrie, Wendy 1913- *ForYSC, IntMPA 77, -75, -76, -78, WhoHol A*
Barrientos, Maria 1883-1946 *CmOp*
Barrientos, Maria 1884-1946 *Baker 78, NewEOp 71, NewGrD 80*
Barrier, Edgar 1902?-1964 *ForYSC, WhScrn 74*
Barrier, Edgar 1906-1964 *FilmEn, FilmgC, HalFC 80, MovMk*
Barrier, Edgar 1907-1964 *WhScrn 77, WhoHol B*

Bascomb, Dud 1916-1972 *CmpEPM, EncJzS 70, WhoJazz 72*
Bascomb, Paul 1910- *CmpEPM, WhoJazz 72*
Bascomb, Wilbur Odell 1916-1972 *BiDAmM, EncJzS 70*
Bascombe, Ronald D *MorBAP*
Baseggio, Lorenzo 1660?-1715? *NewGrD 80*
Basehart, Richard *IntMPA 75, -76, WhoHol A*
Basehart, Richard 1914- *FilmEn, IntMPA 77, -78, -79, -80, MovMk, WhoThe 77*
Basehart, Richard 1915- *FilmgC, ForYSC, HalFC 80, WhoHrs 80*
Basehart, Richard 1919- *BiE&WWA, NotNAT, OxFilm, WhoThe 72*
Baseheart, Richard *MotPP*
Baselli, Constantino *NewGrD 80*
Baselt, Franz Bernhard Bernd 1934- *IntWWM 77, -80*
Baselt, Fritz 1863-1931 *Baker 78*
Baseo, Francesco Antonio *NewGrD 80*
Basevi, Abramo 1818-1885 *Baker 78, NewGrD 80*
Basevi, James 1890?- *FilmEn, HalFC 80*
Baseya, Joan *NewGrD 80*
Basford, Madaline Lee d1974 *WhoHol B*
Bashful Brother Oswald *IlEncCM*
Bashkirov, Dmitry 1931- *NewGrD 80*
Bashmakov, Leonid 1927- *Baker 78, NewGrD 80*
Bashor, Wilma d1964 *NotNAT B*
Basie, Count 1904- *Baker 78, BgBands 74[port], CmpEPM, DrBlPA, EncJzS 70, IlEncJ, MusMk, NewGrD 80[port], WhoJazz 72*
Basie, William 1904- *BiDAmM, EncJzS 70, NewGrD 80[port]*
Basie, William 1906- *AmSCAP 66, -80*
Basil, Colonel De 1888-1951 *CnOxB*
Basil, The Great 329-379 *Baker 78*
Basil, W De *DancEn 78*
Basile *NewGrD 80*
Basile, Adriana 1580?-1640? *NewGrD 80*
Basile, Andreana 1580?-1640? *NewGrD 80*
Basile, Andriana 1580?-1640? *NewGrD 80*
Basile, Giambattista 1575?-1632 *NewGrD 80*
Basile, Giovanni Battista 1575?-1632 *NewGrD 80*
Basile, Jean 1932- *CreCan 1*
Basile, Joe 1889-1961 *AmSCAP 66, -80*
Basile, Lelio 1575?-1623? *NewGrD 80*
Basili, Andrea 1705-1777 *NewGrD 80*
Basili, Francesco 1767-1850 *Baker 78, NewGrD 80*
Basiliani, Carlo *NewGrD 80*
Basilicus, Ciprianus *NewGrD 80*
Basilides, Maria 1886-1946 *NewGrD 80*
Basilii, Francesco *NewGrD 80*
Basilj, Andrea 1705-1777 *NewGrD 80*
Basilj, Francesco *NewGrD 80*
Basilly, Benigne De *NewGrD 80*
Basily, Andrea 1705-1777 *NewGrD 80*
Basily, Francesco *NewGrD 80*
Basin, Adrien *NewGrD 80*
Basin, Pierre d1497 *NewGrD 80*
Basin, Simon *NewGrD 80*
Basiola, Mario 1892-1965 *Baker 78*
Basiola, Mario 1935- *WhoOp 76*
Basiron, Philippe d1497 *NewGrD 80*
Baskakov, Boris *CreCan 1*
Baskcomb, A W 1880-1939 *WhThe*
Baskcomb, Lawrence 1883-1962 *WhThe*
Baskerville, David 1918- *AmSCAP 80, IntWWM 77, -80*
Baskerville, David 1919- *AmSCAP 66, ConAmC A*
Baskett, James 1904-1948 *DrBlPA, HalFC 80, WhScrn 74, -77, WhoHol B*
Baskett, Jimmie *BlksB&W C*
Baskette, Billy 1884-1949 *AmSCAP 66, -80*
Baskette, James 1904-1948 *BlksBF*
Baskut, Cevat Fehmi 1905- *REnWD*
Basner, Veniamin Efimovich 1925- *Baker 78, NewGrD 80*
Basney, Eldon Eugene 1913- *AmSCAP 80, ConAmC*
Basquette, Lina 1907- *FilmEn, Film 1, -2, TwYS, What 4[port], WhoHol A*
Basquette, Lina 1909- *ForYSC*
Bass, Alfie 1920- *FilmgC, HalFC 80, WhoHol A*
Bass, Alfie 1921- *FilmEn, IlWWBF[port]*
Bass, Alfred 1921- *WhoThe 72, -77*
Bass, Barbara DeJong 1946- *WomWMM B*
Bass, Claude L 1935- *ConAmC*
Bass, Elaine *WomWMM B*
Bass, Fontella 1949- *RkOn 2[port]*
Bass, George Houston 1938- *BlkAmP, MorBAP, NotNAT*
Bass, Gerald H 1922- *IntWWM 77*
Bass, Jules 1935- *AmSCAP 66, -80*
Bass, Kingsley B, Jr. *BlkAmP, MorBAP*
Bass, Lee Oddis, III 1943- *EncJzS 70*
Bass, Michael T 1799-1884 *OxMus*
Bass, Mickey 1943- *EncJzS 70*
Bass, Milton Ralph 1923- *ConAmTC*
Bass, Roger 1925- *AmSCAP 66, -80*
Bass, Saul 1920- *DcFM, FilmEn, FilmgC, HalFC 80, IntMPA 77, -75, -76, -78, -79, -80, OxFilm, WorEFlm*
Bass, Sid 1913- *AmSCAP 66*
Bass, Sidney 1913- *AmSCAP 80*
Bass, Warner Seeley 1915- *AmSCAP 80, IntWWM 77, -80*
Bassani, Geronimo *Baker 78*
Bassani, Giovanni *Baker 78, NewGrD 80, OxMus*
Bassani, Giovanni Battista 1647?-1716 *Baker 78*
Bassani, Giovanni Battista 1657?-1716 *NewGrD 80, OxMus*
Bassani, Orazio 1540?-1609? *NewGrD 80*
Bassano *NewGrD 80*
Bassano, Andrew *NewGrD 80*
Bassano, Anthony *NewGrD 80*
Bassano, Augustine *NewGrD 80*
Bassano, Edward d1638 *NewGrD 80*
Bassano, Enrico 1899- *McGEWD[port]*
Bassano, Giovanni 1558?-1617 *NewGrD 80*
Bassano, Heironymo *NewGrD 80*
Bassano, Henry d1665? *NewGrD 80*
Bassano, Jerome *NewGrD 80*
Bassano, Lodovico *NewGrD 80*
Bassano, Marc Anthony *NewGrD 80*
Bassany, Lodovico *NewGrD 80*
Bassee, Adam DeLa *NewGrD 80*
Basseggio, Lorenzo *NewGrD 80*
Bassengius, Aegidius *NewGrD 80*
Bassengo, Aegidius *NewGrD 80*
Bassentin, James *NewGrD 80*
Bassere, Jo *NewGrD 80*
Basserman, Albert 1867-1952 *CnThe, FilmEn, Film 2, FilmgC, ForYSC, HalFC 80, HolCA[port], MotPP, MovMk[port], NotNAT B, Vers B[port], WhoHol B*
Basserman, Else 1878-1961 *NotNAT B, WhoHol B*
Bassermann, Albert 1865-1952 *WhScrn 74, -77*
Bassermann, Albert 1867-1952 *EncWT, Ent, OxThe*
Bassermann, August 1848-1931 *NotNAT B, OxThe*
Bassermann-Schiff, Else 1878-1961 *WhScrn 74, -77*
Basset, Serge d1917 *NotNAT B*
Bassett, Alfred Leon 1870- *WhThe*
Bassett, Franklin 1852-1915 *BiDAmM*
Bassett, Henrietta Elizabeth 1932- *IntWWM 80*
Bassett, Karolyn Wells 1892-1931 *AmSCAP 66, -80, BiDAmM, ConAmC*
Bassett, Leslie 1923- *Baker 78, BiDAmM, BnBkM 80, CompSN[port], CpmDNM 72, -78, -79, -80, ConAmC, DcCM, IntWWM 77, -80, NewGrD 80*
Bassett, Mercedes C *PupTheA*
Bassett, Phil D *PupTheA*
Bassett, Ralph Edward 1944- *IntWWM 80*
Bassett, Rip Arthur 1903- *WhoJazz 72*
Bassett, Russell 1846-1918 *Film 1, NotNAT B, WhScrn 77, WhoHol B*
Bassett, Tony 1885-1955 *WhScrn 74, -77*
Bassevi, Giacomo *Baker 78*
Bassey, Shirley 1937- *DrBlPA, HalFC 80, RkOn 2[port]*
Bassford, William Kipp 1839-1902 *Baker 78, BiDAmM*
Basshe, Em Jo *MorBAP*
Basshe, Emjo d1939 *NotNAT B*
Bassi, Amadeo 1874-1949 *Baker 78*
Bassi, Amedeo 1874-1949 *CmOp*
Bassi, Dionisio *NewGrD 80*
Bassi, Luigi 1766-1825 *Baker 78, CmOp, NewGrD 80*
Bassilly, Benigne De *NewGrD 80*
Bassin, Rose Ethel 1889- *WhoMus 72*
Bassler, Robert 1903- *FilmEn, FilmgC, HalFC 80, IntMPA 75, -76*
Bassman, George 1914- *AmSCAP 66, -80, BiDAmM, BiE&WWA*
Basso, Alberto 1931- *IntWWM 77, -80, NewGrD 80*
Basso, Gianni 1931- *EncJzS 70*
Bastaini, Vincentio *NewGrD 80*
Bastard, Jean *NewGrD 80*
Bastarda, Viola *OxMus*
Bastart, Jean *NewGrD 80*
Bastedo, Alexandra 1946- *FilmgC, HalFC 80*
Baster, Miles *WhoMus 72*
Baster-Sors, Janina 1932- *IntWWM 77, -80*
Bastia, Pascal Jean Henri Michel 1908- *WhoMus 72*
Bastiaans, Johannes Gijsbertus 1812-1875 *Baker 78, NewGrD 80*
Bastian, Don *PupTheA*
Bastian, Dudley Stuart 1939- *IntWWM 77, -80*
Bastian, Jack *Film 2*
Bastianelli, Giannotto 1883-1927 *NewGrD 80*
Bastianini, Ettore 1922-1967 *CmOp, NewGrD 80*
Bastien, Hermas 1896- *CreCan 2*
Bastin, Jules Armand 1933- *WhoOp 76*
Bastini, Vincentio 1529?-1591 *NewGrD 80*
Baston, Arthur Oliver 1917- *IntWWM 77*
Baston, J Thornton *Film 2*
Baston, Jack *Film 2*
Baston, John *Film 2, NewGrD 80*
Baston, Josquin *Baker 78, NewGrD 80*
Baszny, Jozef d1862? *NewGrD 80*
Bat The Humming-Bird *BluesWW[port]*
Bat The Hummingbird *BluesWW[port]*
Bat'ada, Judith *AmSCAP 80*
Bataille, Gabriel 1574?-1630 *BnBkM 80*
Bataille, Gabriel 1575?-1630 *NewGrD 80*
Bataille, Henri 1872-1922 *McGEWD[port]*
Bataille, Henry 1872-1922 *CnMD, EncWT, ModWD, NotNAT B, WhThe*
Bataille, Sylvie 1912- *OxFilm*
Batalof, M *Film 2*
Batalov, Alexei 1924- *WhoHol A*
Batalov, Alexei 1928- *FilmEn, WorEFlm*
Batalov, Nikolai Petrovich 1898-1937 *FilmEn*
Batalov, Nikolai Petrovich 1899-1937 *Film 2, OxThe*
Batardi, Antonio *NewGrD 80*
Batatzes, Joannes *NewGrD 80*
Batcheff, Pierre 1901-1932 *FilmEn*
Batchelar, Daniel *NewGrD 80*
Batchelder, Marjorie *DcPup, PupTheA*
Batchelder, William H 1937- *NotNAT*
Batcheller, Joseph D 1915- *BiE&WWA, NotNAT*
Batchelor, Reverend Doctor *Film 2*
Batchelor, Harry Edward 1906- *WhoMus 72*
Batchelor, Joy 1914- *DcFM, FilmEn, FilmgC, HalFC 80, IntMPA 77, -75, -76, -78, -79, -80, OxFilm, WomWMM, -B, WorEFlm*
Batchelor, Phyllis 1920- *IntWWM 77, -80*
Batchelor, Ruth 1934- *AmSCAP 80*
Batchilar, Daniel *NewGrD 80*
Bate, Humphrey 1875-1936 *IlEncCM[port]*
Bate, Jennifer Lucy 1944- *IntWWM 77, -80, WhoMus 72*
Bate, John Richard 1936- *IntWWM 77, -80, WhoMus 72*
Bate, Marie Clementina 1911- *WhoMus 72*
Bate, Philip Argall Turner 1909- *IntWWM 80, NewGrD 80*
Bate, Stanley 1912- *BiDAmM*
Bate, Stanley 1913-1959 *NewGrD 80*
Bate, Stanley Richard 1911-1959 *Baker 78, OxMus*
Bateman, Miss 1842-1917 *WhThe*
Bateman, Ellen Douglas 1844-1936 *NotNAT B, OxThe*
Bateman, Florence Golson *ConAmC*
Bateman, Mrs. H L 1823-1881 *NotNAT B*
Bateman, Hezekiah Linthicum 1812-1875 *NotNAT B, OxThe*
Bateman, Isabel Emilie 1854-1934 *NotNAT A, -B, OxThe*

Bateman, Jessie 1877-1940 *NotNAT B, WhThe*
Bateman, Kate Josephine 1842-1917 *NotNAT B*
Bateman, Kate Josephine 1843-1917 *FamA&A[port], OxThe*
Bateman, Leah 1892- *WhThe*
Bateman, Robert d1618 *NewGrD 80*
Bateman, Sidney Frances 1823-1881 *OxThe*
Bateman, Victory 1866-1926 *Film 1, -2, WhScrn 74, -77, WhoHol B, WhoStg 1906, -1908*
Bateman, Virginia Frances 1853-1940 *NotNAT B, OxThe, WhThe*
Bateman, Zillah 1900-1970 *WhThe*
Bates, Alan *IntMPA 75, -76, MotPP, PlP&P, -A[port], WhoHol A*
Bates, Alan 1930- *FilmgC, OxFilm*
Bates, Alan 1934- *BiDFilm 81, BiE&WWA, CnThe, EncWT, Ent, FilmAG WE, FilmEn, ForYSC, HalFC 80, IIWWBF[port], IntMPA 77, -78, -79, -80, MovMk[port], NotNAT, WhoThe 72, -77*
Bates, Barbara 1925-1969 *FilmEn, FilmgC, HalFC 80, MotPP, WhScrn 74, -77, WhoHol B*
Bates, Barbara 1926- *ForYSC*
Bates, Beverley *PupTheA*
Bates, Blanche 1873-1941 *FamA&A[port], Film 1, NotNAT B, OxThe, PlP&P, WhScrn 74, -77, WhThe, WhoHol B, WhoStg 1906, -1908*
Bates, Charles L 1897-1937 *AmSCAP 80*
Bates, Cuthbert Joseph 1899- *WhoMus 72*
Bates, David *ConAmC*
Bates, Deacon L J *BluesWW[port]*
Bates, Florence d1954 *MotPP, WhoHol B*
Bates, Florence 1888-1954 *FilmEn, FilmgC, HalFC 80, HolCA[port], MovMk[port], NotNAT B, WhScrn 74, -77*
Bates, Florence 1889-1954 *ForYSC*
Bates, Florence 1890-1954 *Vers A[port]*
Bates, Granville d1939 *ForYSC, WhoHol B*
Bates, Granville 1882-1940 *HalFC 80, HolCA[port], WhScrn 74, -77*
Bates, Jeanne *WhoHol A*
Bates, Joah 1740-1799 *NewGrD 80*
Bates, Joah 1741-1799 *Baker 78*
Bates, Katharine Lee 1859-1929 *OxMus*
Bates, Katherine Lee 1859-1929 *BiDAmM*
Bates, Kathleen Doyle 1948- *AmSCAP 80*
Bates, Lawson d1975 *WhoHol C*
Bates, Les 1877-1930 *Film 2, WhoHol B*
Bates, Leslie A 1877-1930 *WhScrn 74, -77*
Bates, Lulu *BiE&WWA, NotNAT*
Bates, Marie d1923 *NotNAT B*
Bates, Maxwell Bennett 1906- *CreCan 2*
Bates, Michael 1920- *WhoThe 72, -77*
Bates, Michael 1920-1978 *FilmEn*
Bates, Michael 1929-1978 *FilmgC, HalFC 80*
Bates, Peg Leg 1907- *BlksBF, DrBlPA*
Bates, Ralph 1940- *FilmEn, FilmgC, HalFC 80, WhoHrs 80*
Bates, Ronald Gordon Nudell 1924- *CreCan 1*
Bates, Sally 1907- *WhThe*
Bates, Sarah 1755?-1811 *NewGrD 80*
Bates, Thomas *NewGrD 80*
Bates, Thomas Eugene 1939- *IntWWM 77, -80*
Bates, Thorpe 1883-1958 *NotNAT B, WhThe*
Bates, Tom *Film 2*
Bates, William *Baker 78, NewGrD 80, NotNAT B*
Bateson, Thomas 1570?-1630 *Baker 78, NewGrD 80, OxMus*
Bateson, Timothy 1926- *PlP&P[port], WhoThe 72, -77*
Bath, Albert J d1964 *NotNAT B*
Bath, Hubert 1883-1945 *Baker 78, NewGrD 80, OxMus, WhThe*
Bathe, William 1564-1614 *Baker 78, NewGrD 80*
Bathenius, Jacob *NewGrD 80*
Bathori, Jane 1877-1970 *Baker 78, NewGrD 80*
Bathy, Anna 1901-1962 *NewGrD 80*
Bathyllus *EncWT, OxThe*
Bati, Luca 1550?-1608 *NewGrD 80*
Batie, Frank 1880-1949 *NotNAT B*
Batie, Franklin A 1880-1949 *WhoHol B*
Batie, Franklyn A 1880-1949 *WhScrn 77*
Batie, Jo-Ann Nellie 1939- *IntWWM 77*
Batista, Ramon Campbell *NewGrD 80*
Batiste, Antoine-Edouard 1820-1876 *Baker 78, OxMus*
Batistin *Baker 78*
Batius, Jacob *NewGrD 80*
Batka, Richard 1868-1922 *Baker 78, NewGrD 80*
Batley, Dorothy 1902- *Film 1, IIWWBF, WhThe*
Batley, Ernest G 1879-1917 *Film 1, IIWWBF, WhScrn 77*
Batley, Ethyle 1879-1917 *IIWWBF*
Baton, Charles d1754? *NewGrD 80*
Baton, Charles d1758 *OxMus*
Baton, Henri d1728? *NewGrD 80*
Baton, Henri 1710?- *OxMus*
Baton, Rene *OxMus*
Batsford, J Tucker *AmSCAP 80*
Batsford, John Frederick 1907- *WhoMus 72*
Batson, Flora 1870-1906 *BiDAmM*
Batson, George 1918- *BiE&WWA, NotNAT*
Batson, Jonathon Kingsley 1944- *AmSCAP 80*
Batson, Susan *MorBAP*
Batson, Susan 1944?- *DrBlPA*
Batstone, Philip Norman 1933- *ConAmC*
Batta, Alexandre 1816-1902 *Baker 78*
Battachon, Felix 1814-1893 *Baker 78*
Battagello, Walter Alexander 1930- *IntWWM 77*
Battaille, Charles-Aimable 1822-1872 *Baker 78, NewGrD 80*
Batteau, Dwight Wayne, Jr. 1948- *AmSCAP 80*
Batteaux, Charles *NewGrD 80*
Batten, Adrian d1637 *Baker 78*
Batten, Adrian 1585?-1637 *OxMus*
Batten, Adrian 1591-1637 *NewGrD 80*
Batten, John *Film 2*
Batten, Tom *WhoHol A*
Batteux, Charles 1713?-1780 *NewGrD 80*
Battier, Marc 1947- *IntWWM 80*
Battier, Robert 1887-1946 *WhScrn 74, -77, WhoHol B*
Battiferri, Luigi 1600?-1682? *NewGrD 80*
Battin, Adrian *NewGrD 80*
Battipaglia, Diana Mittler 1941- *IntWWM 77, -80*
Battipaglia, Victor 1940- *IntWWM 77, -80*
Battishill, Jonathan 1738-1801 *Baker 78, NewGrD 80, OxMus*
Battista, Joseph 1918- *BiDAmM*
Battista, Ludwig Albert Friedrich *NewGrD 80*
Battista, Miriam 1914- *Film 1, -2, TwYS*
Battista, Vincenzo 1823-1873 *Baker 78*
Battistini *NewGrD 80*
Battistini, Gaudenzio 1722-1800 *Baker 78, NewGrD 80*
Battistini, Giacomo 1665?-1719 *Baker 78, NewGrD 80*
Battistini, Girolamo Gaudenzio 1722-1800 *NewGrD 80[port]*
Battistini, Giuseppe 1695?-1747 *NewGrD 80*
Battistini, Mattia 1856-1928 *Baker 78, CmOp, MusSN[port], NewEOp 71, NewGrD 80[port]*
Battke, Max 1863-1916 *Baker 78*
Battle, Edgar William 1907- *AmSCAP 66, -80*
Battle, John Tucker *HalFC 80*
Battle, Puddinghead Edgar W 1907- *WhoJazz 72*
Battle, Sol 1934- *BlkAmP, MorBAP*
Battles, John 1921- *BiE&WWA, WhThe*
Battmann, Jacques-Louis 1818-1886 *Baker 78*
Batton, Desire-Alexandre 1798-1855 *Baker 78, NewGrD 80*
Battre, H *NewGrD 80*
Batts, Alfred Thomas 1900- *WhoMus 72*
Batts, Harry Vincent William 1887- *WhoMus 72*
Batts, Will 1904-1956 *BluesWW*
Battu, Pantaleon 1799-1870 *Baker 78*
Batty, Archibald 1887-1961 *NotNAT B, WhScrn 74, -77, WhThe, WhoHol B*
Batty, Peter 1931- *IntMPA 79, -80*
Battyn, Adrian *NewGrD 80*
Batu, Selahattin 1905- *REnWD*
Baty, Gaston 1885-1952 *EncWT, Ent, NotNAT B, OxThe, WhThe*
Batz, Karl 1851-1902 *Baker 78*
Bau, George 1905-1974 *WhoHrs 80*
Bau, Gordon 1907-1975 *WhoHrs 80*
Bauchens, Anne 1882-1967 *CmMov, HalFC 80, WomWMM*
Bauchspiess, Severus *NewGrD 80*
Baud-Bovy, Samuel 1906- *IntWWM 77, -80, NewGrD 80, WhoMus 72*
Baude De Rains d1397? *NewGrD 80*
Baudelaire, Charles 1821-1867 *NewGrD 80*
Baudet, Louise *Film 2*
Baudewyn, John *NewGrD 80*
Baudin, Ginette 1921-1971 *WhScrn 77*
Baudin, Henri *Film 2*
Baudiot, Charles-Nicolas 1773-1849 *Baker 78*
Baudiot, Nicolas 1773-1849 *NewGrD 80*
Baudissin, Wolf Graf Von 1789-1878 *EncWT*
Baudo, Serge 1927- *Baker 78, IntWWM 77, -80, NewGrD 80, WhoOp 76*
Baudoin, Noel *NewGrD 80*
Baudouin Des Auteus *NewGrD 80*
Baudrexel, Philipp Jakob 1627-1691 *NewGrD 80*
Baudrier, Yves 1906- *Baker 78, NewGrD 80, OxMus*
Baudron, Antoine Laurent 1742-1834 *NewGrD 80*
Bauduc, Jules 1904?- *NewOrJ[port]*
Bauduc, Ray 1909- *AmSCAP 66, BiDAmM, CmpEPM, NewOrJ[port], WhoJazz 72*
Bauduc, Raymond 1906- *AmSCAP 80*
Bauer, Billy 1915- *CmpEPM*
Bauer, Clara d1912 *BiDAmM*
Bauer, David 1918-1973 *WhScrn 77*
Bauer, Friedhold 1934- *CroCD*
Bauer, Guilherme 1940- *IntWWM 77, -80*
Bauer, Harold 1873-1951 *AmSCAP 66, Baker 78, BiDAmM, BnBkM 80, MusSN[port], NewGrD 80*
Bauer, Harry 1881-1941 *Film 1, -2*
Bauer, John *ConMuA 80B*
Bauer, Joseph Anton 1725-1808 *NewGrD 80*
Bauer, Kurt 1928- *IntWWM 77, -80*
Bauer, Ludwig *OxMus*
Bauer, Margaret 1927- *CnOxB*
Bauer, Margarete 1927- *DancEn 78[port]*
Bauer, Marion 1897-1955 *NewGrD 80*
Bauer, Marion Eugenie 1887-1955 *Baker 78, BiDAmM, CompSN[port], ConAmC, OxMus*
Bauer, Moritz 1875-1932 *Baker 78, NewGrD 80*
Bauer, Robert Paul 1950- *IntWWM 80*
Bauer, Walter Kaye 1899- *AmSCAP 80*
Bauer, William Henry 1915- *AmSCAP 66, -80, BiDAmM*
Bauer, Wolfgang 1941- *CroCD, EncWT, Ent*
Bauer, Yevgeni 188-1917 *DcFM*
Bauer, Yevgeni 1880?-1917 *FilmEn*
Bauer-Adamara *WomWMM*
Bauer-Ecsy, Leni *WhoOp 76*
Bauer-Theussl, Franz Ferdinand 1928- *WhoOp 76*
Bauerl, Paul *NewGrD 80*
Bauerle, Adolf 1786-1859 *OxThe*
Bauerle, Hermann 1869-1936 *Baker 78*
Bauernfeind, Winfried 1935- *WhoOp 76*
Bauernfeld, Eduard Von 1802-1890 *EncWT, OxThe*
Bauersfeld, Marjorie Mirandy 1890-1974 *WhScrn 77*
Bauersmith, Paula 1909- *BiE&WWA, NotNAT, WhoThe 72, -77*
Baughan, Edward Algernon 1865-1938 *NotNAT B, WhThe*
Baulard, Valerie Joyce *WhoMus 72*
Bauld, Alison 1944- *NewGrD 80*
Bauldeweyn, Noe 1480?-1530 *NewGrD 80*
Bauldeweyn, Noel 1480?-1530 *NewGrD 80*
Bauldeweyn, Nouel 1480?-1530 *NewGrD 80*
Bauldewijn, Noel 1509-1513 *Baker 78*
Baulduin, Noe 1480?-1530 *NewGrD 80*
Baulduin, Noel 1480?-1530 *NewGrD 80*
Baulduin, Nouel 1480?-1530 *NewGrD 80*
Bault, Diane Lynn 1937- *IntWWM 77, -80*
Baum, Allen *BluesWW[port]*
Baum, Bernie 1928- *AmSCAP 66*
Baum, Bernie 1929- *AmSCAP 80*
Baum, Charlie *BgBands 74*
Baum, Claude 1928- *AmSCAP 66, -80*
Baum, Mrs. H William 1882-1970 *WhScrn 74, -77*
Baum, Harry 1916-1974 *WhScrn 77,*

WhoHol B
Baum, Kurt 1908- *NewEOp 71*
Baum, L Frank 1856-1919 *HalFC 80*
Baum, Lyman Frank 1856-1919 *DcPup, FilmgC, NotNAT B, PIP&P A[port], WhoStg 1906, -1908*
Baum, Martin 1924- *BiE&WWA, IntMPA 77, -75, -76, -78, -79, -80*
Baum, Maurice 1912- *IntMPA 77, -75, -76, -78, -79, -80*
Baum, Morton 1905-1968 *NotNAT B*
Baum, Richard 1902- *NewGrD 80*
Baum, Vicki 1888-1960 *NotNAT A, -B*
Baum, Vicki 1897- *HalFC 80*
Bauman, Art 1939- *CmpGMD, CnOxB*
Bauman, Jon Ward 1939- *CpmDNM 72, -73, -77, -79, -80, ConAmC, IntWWM 77*
Bauman, Suzanne *WomWMM B*
Baumann, Georg 1554-1607 *NewGrD 80*
Baumann, Gustave *PupTheA*
Baumann, Helmut 1939- *CnOxB*
Baumann, Herbert 1925- *IntWWM 77, -80, WhoMus 72*
Baumann, Hermann 1934- *NewGrD 80*
Baumann, Max Georg 1917- *IntWWM 77, -80, NewGrD 80*
Baumbach, Adolph 1830?-1880 *BiDAmM*
Baumbach, Friedrich August 1753-1813 *Baker 78, NewGrD 80*
Baumbach, Jo Ann *WomWMM B*
Baumfelder, Friedrich 1836-1916 *Baker 78*
Baumgarten, Alexander Gottlieb 1714-1762 *NewGrD 80*
Baumgarten, Carl Friedrich 1740?-1824 *NewGrD 80*
Baumgarten, Chris 1910- *IntWWM 80*
Baumgarten, Christi 1910- *IntWWM 77*
Baumgarten, Christopher Frederick 1729?-1798 *NewGrD 80*
Baumgarten, Gotthilf Von 1741-1813 *Baker 78*
Baumgarten, Karl Friedrich 1740?-1824 *Baker 78, NewGrD 80*
Baumgarten, Samuel Christian 1729?-1798 *NewGrD 80*
Baumgartner, August 1814-1862 *Baker 78*
Baumgartner, H Leroy d1969 *ConAmC*
Baumgartner, Jean Baptiste 1723-1782 *NewGrD 80*
Baumgartner, Johann Baptist 1723-1782 *NewGrD 80*
Baumgartner, Paul 1903-1976 *NewGrD 80, WhoMus 72*
Baumgartner, Rudolf 1917- *IntWWM 77, -80, NewGrD 80*
Baumgartner, Wilhelm 1820-1867 *Baker 78, NewGrD 80*
Baumker, Wilhelm 1842-1905 *Baker 78, NewGrD 80*
Baumstone, Harold 1911- *IntMPA 77, -75, -76, -78, -79, -80*
Baumvoll, Esther Levy 1937- *WhoOp 76*
Baur *NewGrD 80*
Baur, Barthelemy 1751-1823 *NewGrD 80*
Baur, Charles-Alexis 1789- *NewGrD 80*
Baur, Elizabeth *WhoHol A*
Baur, Franklyn d1950 *CmpEPM, NotNAT B*
Baur, Harry 1880-1943 *FilmAG WE[port], FilmEn*
Baur, Harry 1881-1941 *Film 2, FilmgC, HalFC 80*
Baur, Harry 1881-1943 *NotNAT B, WhScrn 74, -77, WhoHol B, WhoHrs 80*
Baur, Jean 1719-1773? *NewGrD 80*
Baur, John William 1947- *ConAmC*
Baur, Jurg 1918- *Baker 78, DcCM, NewGrD 80*
Bausch, Ludwig Christian August 1805-1871 *Baker 78*
Bausch, Pina 1940- *CnOxB*
Baussnern, Waldemar Von 1866-1931 *Baker 78, NewGrD 80*
Baustian, Robert F 1921- *WhoOp 76*
Bausznern, Waldemar Von 1866-1931 *NewGrD 80*
Bautista, Julian 1901-1961 *Baker 78, DcCM, NewGrD 80*
Bauza, Mario 1911- *WhoJazz 72*
Bava, Mario 1914- *BiDFilm, FilmgC, HalFC 80, WorEFlm*
Bava, Mario 1914-1980 *FilmEn, WhoHrs 80*
Bavel, Zamir 1929- *IntWWM 77, -80*
Bavicchi, John Alexander 1922- *AmSCAP 66, -80, Baker 78, CpmDNM 77, -80, ConAmC*
Bavier, Frances *WhoHol A*
Bavier, Frances 1905- *ForYSC*
Bawdwine, John *NewGrD 80*
Bawn, Harry 1872- *WhThe*
Bax, Sir Arnold 1883-1953 *Baker 78, BnBkM 80, CompSN[port], DcCom 77, DcCom&M 79, DcCM, MusMk, NewGrD 80[port], OxMus*
Bax, Clifford 1886-1962 *McGEWD[port], NotNAT B, OxThe, WhThe*
Baxley, Barbara *MotPP, WhoHol A*
Baxley, Barbara 1925- *NotNAT*
Baxley, Barbara 1927- *BiE&WWA, WhoThe 72, -77*
Baxt, George *WhoHrs 80*
Baxter, Alan 1908-1976 *BiE&WWA, FilmEn, FilmgC, ForYSC, HalFC 80, MovMk, NotNAT B, WhThe, WhoThe 72*
Baxter, Alan 1911-1976 *Vers B[port]*
Baxter, Anne 1923- *BiDFilm, -81, BiE&WWA, FilmEn, FilmgC, ForYSC, HalFC 80, IntMPA 77, -75, -76, -78, -79, -80, MotPP, MovMk[port], NotNAT, WhoHol A, WhoThe 77, WorEFlm*
Baxter, Barry 1894-1922 *NotNAT B, WhThe*
Baxter, Beryl 1926- *FilmgC, HalFC 80, WhThe, WhoThe 72*
Baxter, Sir Beverley 1891-1964 *NotNAT B, WhThe*
Baxter, Billy 1926- *IntMPA 77, -75, -76, -78, -79, -80*
Baxter, Catherine Mary 1926- *WhoMus 72*
Baxter, George *Film 2*
Baxter, Glenn E 1926- *AmSCAP 66*
Baxter, Harry 1919- *IntWWM 77, WhoMus 72*
Baxter, James 1913-1964 *AmSCAP 66, -80*
Baxter, James C 1923-1969 *WhScrn 74, -77*
Baxter, James Keir 1926-1972 *ConDr 73*
Baxter, Jane 1909- *FilmEn, FilmgC, HalFC 80, IlWWBF[port], WhoHol A, WhoThe 72, -77*
Baxter, Jesse Randal 1887-1960 *NewGrD 80*
Baxter, Jimmy d1969 *WhoHol B*
Baxter, John *IntMPA 75*
Baxter, John 1896- *FilmEn*
Baxter, John 1896-1972 *FilmgC, HalFC 80, IlWWBF*
Baxter, Keith 1933- *IntMPA 77, -75, -76, -78, -79, -80, WhoHol A, WhoThe 72, -77*
Baxter, Keith 1935- *BiE&WWA, NotNAT*
Baxter, Larry 1924- *AmSCAP 66, -80*
Baxter, Les 1922- *AmPS A, -B, AmSCAP 66, BiDAmM, CmpEPM, HalFC 80, RkOn, WhoHrs 80*
Baxter, Leslie 1922- *AmSCAP 80*
Baxter, Lora 1908-1955 *NotNAT B, WhScrn 74, -77, WhoHol B*
Baxter, Lydia 1809-1874 *BiDAmM*
Baxter, Michael Frederic 1948- *WhoMus 72*
Baxter, Phil 1896-1972 *AmSCAP 66, -80, CmpEPM*
Baxter, Richard 1593-1666? *OxThe*
Baxter, Richard 1615-1691 *OxMus*
Baxter, Richard 1618- *OxThe*
Baxter, Stanley 1926- *HalFC 80, WhoThe 72, -77*
Baxter, Stanley 1928- *FilmgC, IntMPA 77, -75, -76, -78, -79, -80*
Baxter, Timothy Richard 1935- *WhoMus 72*
Baxter, Warner d1951 *MotPP, NotNAT B, WhoHol B*
Baxter, Warner 1889-1951 *FilmgC, HalFC 80*
Baxter, Warner 1891-1951 *FilmEn, WhScrn 74, -77*
Baxter, Warner 1892-1951 *BiDFilm, -81, CmMov*
Baxter, Warner 1893-1951 *Film 1, -2, ForYSC, MovMk[port], TwYS, WorEFlm*
Baxter, Warner 1893-1952 *OxFilm*
Baxter, William Hubbard, Jr. 1921- *IntWWM 77, -80*
Bay, Emmanuel 1891-1967 *Baker 78*
Bay, Howard 1912- *BiE&WWA, NotNAT, WhoThe 72, -77*
Bay, Sara 1952?- *WhoHrs 80*
Bay, Susan *WhoHol A*
Bay, Tom 1901-1933 *WhScrn 74, -77, WhoHol B*
Bay, Victor 1896- *IntWWM 77*
Bay City Rollers *ConMuA 80A, IlEncR, RkOn 2[port]*
Bayard, Carol Ann 1934- *WhoOp 76*
Baye, Nathalie 1948- *FilmEn*
Bayefsky, Aba 1923- *CreCan 1*
Bayer, Andreas 1710-1749 *NewGrD 80*
Bayer, Charles W 1893-1953 *WhScrn 74, -77*
Bayer, Johann Baptist *NewGrD 80*
Bayer, Josef 1852-1913 *Baker 78*
Bayer, Josef 1862-1913 *CnOxB*
Bayer, Joseph 1852-1913 *NewGrD 80*
Bayer, Konrad 1932-1964 *CroCD*
Bayersdorffer, Johnny 1899- *NewOrJ, WhoJazz 72*
Bayes, Nora 1880-1928 *AmPS B, AmSCAP 80, BiDAmM, CmpEPM, EncMT, FilmgC, HalFC 80, NotNAT B, WhThe*
Bayete 1951- *EncJzS 70*
Bayfield, John Heygate 1931- *WhoMus 72*
Bayfield, Peggy *Film 2*
Bayfield, Ronald 1931- *IntWWM 77*
Bayha, Charles A 1891-1957 *AmSCAP 66, -80*
Bayldon, Geoffrey 1924- *FilmgC, HalFC 80*
Bayle, Francois 1932- *Baker 78, DcCM, NewGrD 80*
Bayley, Caroline 1890- *WhThe*
Bayley, Daniel 1725?-1792 *NewGrD 80*
Bayley, Daniel 1725-1799 *BiDAmM*
Bayley, Eva *Film 1*
Bayley, Hilda d1971 *Film 2, IlWWBF, WhThe*
Baylies, Edmund 1904- *BiE&WWA, NotNAT*
Baylis, Lilian 1874-1937 *CnThe, EncWT, Ent, NotNAT A, OxMus, OxThe, WhThe*
Baylis, Lillian 1874-1937 *DancEn 78, NotNAT B*
Baylis, Nadine 1940- *CnOxB*
Baylis, Sam *PupTheA*
Bayliss, Blanche *Film 1*
Bayliss, Lillian 1874-1937 *PIP&P[port]*
Bayliss, Peter *WhoThe 72, -77*
Bayliss, Stanley Alfred 1907- *WhoMus 72*
Baylor, Hugh Murray 1913- *ConAmC*
Baylou, Luigi De *NewGrD 80*
Bayly, Anselm 1719?-1794 *NewGrD 80*
Bayly, Caroline *WhThe*
Bayly, Thomas Haynes d1839 *NotNAT B*
Bayne, Alexander *OxMus*
Bayne, Beverly 1894- *FilmEn, HalFC 80*
Bayne, Beverly 1895- *What 2[port], WhoHol A*
Bayne, Beverly 1896- *Film 1, -2, MotPP, TwYS*
Bayne, Donald S 1949- *NotNAT*
Baynes, Sydney 1879-1938 *NewGrD 80*
Baynton, Henry 1892-1951 *NotNAT B, WhThe*
Bayr, Rudolf 1919- *CnMD, CroCD*
Bayreuther, Florence Elizabeth 1917- *IntWWM 77*
Bayseitova, Kulyash Zhasimovna 1912-1957 *NewGrD 80*
Bazelaire, Paul 1886-1958 *Baker 78*
Bazelon, David L *NewYTET*
Bazelon, Irwin Allen 1922- *AmSCAP 66, -80, Baker 78, CpmDNM 74, -79, -80, ConAmC, IntWWM 77, -80*
Bazin, Andre 1918-1958 *FilmEn, FilmgC, HalFC 80, WorEFlm*
Bazin, Andre 1919-1958 *OxFilm*
Bazin, Francois-Emanuel-Joseph 1816-1878 *Baker 78, NewGrD 80*
Bazino, Francesco 1593-1660 *NewGrD 80*
Baziron, Philippe *NewGrD 80*
Bazlen, Brigid 1944- *HalFC 80*
Bazlen, Brigitte 1946- *ForYSC*
Bazley, Anthony 1936- *BiDAmM*
Bazlik, Igor 1941- *IntWWM 77, -80*
Bazlik, Miroslav 1931- *Baker 78, NewGrD 80*
Bazoon, Otis 1947- *NewOrJ SUP[port]*
Bazuky, Maya 1932- *WhoOp 76*
Bazylik, Cyprian 1535?-1600? *NewGrD 80*
Bazzani, Francesco Maria 1650?-1700? *NewGrD 80*
Bazzini, Allen B 1939- *IntMPA 77, -75, -76,*

–78, –79, –80
Bazzini, Antonio 1818-1897 *Baker 78, NewGrD 80, OxMus*
Bazzini, Francesco 1593-1660 *NewGrD 80*
Bazzini, Natale d1639 *NewGrD 80*
Bazzini, Rosily 1941- *IntMPA 77, –75, –76, –78, –79, –80*
Bazzino, Francesco 1593-1660 *NewGrD 80*
Bazzino, Natale d1639 *NewGrD 80*
Bazzle, Germaine 1932- *BlkWAB*
Be-Bop Deluxe *ConMuA 80A, IlEncR*
Beach, Albert Askew 1924- *AmSCAP 80*
Beach, Amy Marcy Cheney 1867-1944 *BiDAmM, NewGrD 80, OxMus*
Beach, Ann 1938- *WhoThe 72, –77*
Beach, Bennie 1925- *ConAmC*
Beach, Bruce C 1903- *AmSCAP 66, ConAmC*
Beach, Curtis *PupTheA*
Beach, Floyd Orion 1898- *AmSCAP 66*
Beach, Mrs. H H A 1867-1944 *AmSCAP 66, –80, Baker 78, BnBkM 80*
Beach, Henry Harris Aubrey 1844-1910 *BiDAmM*
Beach, John Parsons 1877-1953 *Baker 78, BiDAmM, ConAmC*
Beach, Perry W 1917- *ConAmC*
Beach, Rex 1877- *TwYS A*
Beach, Sandy *ConMuA 80B*
Beach, William d1926 *NotNAT B*
Beach Boys *BiDAmM, ConMuA 80A, IlEncR[port], RkOn[port]*
Beacham, Stephanie 1949- *FilmEn, FilmgC, HalFC 80, WhoHrs 80[port]*
Beacon Street Union *BiDAmM*
Beadell, Robert Morton 1925- *AmSCAP 80, ConAmC*
Beaird, Barbara *WhoHol A*
Beal, Charlie 1908- *WhoJazz 72*
Beal, Eddie 1910- *EncJzS 70, WhoJazz 72*
Beal, Frank 1864-1934 *Film 2, WhScrn 74, –77, WhoHol B*
Beal, Hilde *WhoMus 72*
Beal, John 1909- *BiE&WWA, FilmEn, FilmgC, ForYSC, HalFC 80, HolP 30[port], IntMPA 77, –75, –76, –78, –79, –80, MovMk, NotNAT, WhoHol A, WhoHrs 80[port], WhoThe 72, –77*
Beal, Joseph Carleton 1900- *AmSCAP 66, –80*
Beal, Royal d1969 *WhoHol B*
Beal, Royal 1899-1969 *BiE&WWA, NotNAT B*
Beal, Royal 1900-1969 *WhScrn 74, –77*
Beal, Scott 1890-1973 *WhScrn 77*
Beal, Tita *BlkAmP*
Bealand, Ambrose *NewGrD 80*
Bealby, George 1877-1931 *NotNAT B, WhThe*
Beale, Alan 1936- *CnOxB*
Beale, David Brooks 1945- *CpmDNM 75, ConAmC*
Beale, Everett Minot 1939- *IntWWM 77, –80*
Beale, Frederic Fleming 1876-1948 *Baker 78, ConAmC*
Beale, Frederick *OxMus*
Beale, James 1924- *ConAmC*
Beale, Thomas Willert 1828-1894 *OxMus*
Beale, William 1784-1854 *Baker 78, NewGrD 80, OxMus*
Beall, John Oliver 1942- *AmSCAP 80, CpmDNM 79, ConAmC*
Beals, Edward Roy 1929- *IntWWM 77*
Beals, Kathie Stahl *ConAmTC*
Beam, Bobbin *ConMuA 80B*
Beaman, Lottie 1900?- *BluesWW[port]*
Beament, Harold 1898- *CreCan 2*
Beament, James William Longman 1921- *IntWWM 77, –80*
Beament, Thomas Harold *CreCan 2*
Beamish, Frank 1881-1921 *WhScrn 74, –77, WhoHol B*
Beams, Mary *WomWMM B*
Bean *NewGrD 80*
Bean, Floyd R 1904-1974 *EncJzS 70, WhoJazz 72*
Bean, Hugh Cecil 1929- *IntWWM 77, –80, NewGrD 80, WhoMus 72*
Bean, Judge Roy 1823-1902 *FilmgC*
Bean, Mabel *ConAmC*
Bean, Orson 1928- *BiE&WWA, JoeFr, MotPP, NotNAT, WhoHol A, WhoThe 72, –77*
Bean, Roy 1823-1902 *HalFC 80*
Bean, Shirley Ann 1938- *IntWWM 77, –80*
Bean, Thomas Ernest 1900- *IntWWM 77, –80, WhoMus 72*
Bean, William 1927- *IntWWM 77, –80*
Beanlands, Sophia Theresa Pemberton *CreCan 1*
Bear, Mary d1972 *WhScrn 77*
Bear, Peter Ronald 1940- *IntWWM 77, –80*
Beard, John 1716?-1791 *NotNAT B, OxThe*
Beard, John 1717?-1791 *NewGrD 80[port]*
Beard, Kenneth Bernard 1927- *IntWWM 77, –80*
Beard, Leslie Lois 1950- *AmSCAP 80*
Beard, Matthew, Jr. 1925- *DrBlPA, What 5[port]*
Beard, Matthew Stymie 1925- *WhoHol A*
Beard, Paul 1901- *NewGrD 80, WhoMus 72*
Beard, Ray *Film 2*
Beard, Stymie *BlksB&W C*
Bearden, Romare H 1914- *AmSCAP 66*
Beardmore And Birchall *NewGrD 80*
Beardslee, Bethany 1927- *Baker 78, BnBkM 80, NewGrD 80*
Beardsley, Alice *WhoHol A*
Beardsley, Caroline 1860-1944 *BiDAmM*
Beardsley, Theodore S, Jr. 1930- *AmSCAP 80*
Beare *NewGrD 80*
Beare, Arthur 1875-1945 *NewGrD 80*
Beare, Charles 1937- *NewGrD 80*
Beare, John 1847-1928 *NewGrD 80*
Beare, Richard Barrington 1908- *NewGrD 80*
Beare, William Arthur 1910- *NewGrD 80*
Bearer, Elaine Louise 1947- *IntWWM 77, –80*
Bearse, Richard Stuart 1939- *AmSCAP 66, –80*
Beart, Guy 1930- *NewGrD 80*
Beasley, Byron d1927 *NotNAT B*
Beasley, Irene 1900?- *CmpEPM*
Beasley, Rule 1931- *ConAmC, IntWWM 77, –80*
Beason, Bill William 1908- *WhoJazz 72*
Beat, Janet Eveline 1937- *IntWWM 77, –80*
Beath, Betty 1932- *IntWWM 80*
Beatles, The *ConMuA 80A[port], FilmEn, FilmgC, ForYSC, HalFC 80, IlEncR[port], IlWWBF A, MotPP, MovMk[port], NewGrD 80, OxFilm, RkOn 2[port], WorEFlm[port]*
Beaton, Cecil 1902- *FilmgC, HalFC 80*
Beaton, Cecil 1904- *BiE&WWA, CnThe, CnOxB, DancEn 78, EncWT, NotNAT, –A, OxFilm, WhoThe 72, –77, WorEFlm*
Beaton, Cecil 1904-1980 *Ent, FilmEn*
Beaton, Isabella 1870-1929 *Baker 78, ConAmC*
Beaton, Mary d1962 *WhScrn 77*
Beatriz De Dia *NewGrD 80*
Beattie, Herbert 1926- *ConAmC, WhoOp 76*
Beattie, James 1735-1803 *NewGrD 80*
Beattie, Jessie Louise 1896- *CreCan 2*
Beatty, Clyde Raymond 1903-1965 *Ent, FilmEn, ForYSC, HalFC 80, WhScrn 74, –77, WhoHol B, WhoHrs 80*
Beatty, George 1895-1971 *WhScrn 74, –77, WhoHol B*
Beatty, Harcourt *WhThe*
Beatty, Harold T 1946- *AmSCAP 80*
Beatty, John William 1869-1941 *CreCan 1*
Beatty, Josephine *BluesWW[port]*
Beatty, May 1881-1945 *NotNAT B, WhScrn 74, –77, WhThe, WhoHol B*
Beatty, Morgan d1975 *NewYTET*
Beatty, Ned 1937- *FilmEn*
Beatty, Ned 1940- *HalFC 80, IntMPA 80, WhoHol A*
Beatty, Norman Paul 1924- *AmSCAP 66, –80*
Beatty, Robert 1909- *FilmAG WE, FilmEn, FilmgC, ForYSC, HalFC 80, IlWWBF[port], IntMPA 77, –75, –76, –78, –79, –80, MovMk, WhoHol A, WhoThe 72, –77*
Beatty, Roberta 1891- *WhThe*
Beatty, Talley 1923?- *CmpGMD, CnOxB, DancEn 78, DrBlPA*
Beatty, Warren *BiE&WWA, IntMPA 75, –76, MotPP, WhoHol A*
Beatty, Warren 1937- *BiDFilm, –81, FilmEn, FilmgC, ForYSC, HalFC 80, MovMk[port], OxFilm, WorEFlm*
Beatty, Warren 1938- *IntMPA 77, –78, –79, –80*
Beatty, William Alfred *WhoMus 72*
Beaty, John Richard 1932- *CreCan 1*
Beaty, Richard 1932- *CreCan 1*
Beau, Heinie 1911- *CmpEPM*
Beau, Henry John 1911- *AmSCAP 66, –80*
Beau Brummels *BiDAmM, ConMuA 80A, RkOn 2[port]*
Beau-Marks, The *RkOn*
Beaubien, Jeanine *CreCan 1*
Beaubien, Julien 1896-1947 *WhScrn 74, –77, WhoHol B*
Beaubour, Louise Pitel 1665?-1740 *OxThe*
Beaubour, Pierre Trochon De 1662-1725 *OxThe*
Beauchamp, John d1921 *NotNAT B, WhThe*
Beauchamp, Pierre 1636-1705? *CnOxB, DancEn 78, NewGrD 80*
Beauchamps, Pierre 1636-1705 *NewGrD 80*
Beauchamps, Pierre-Francois Godard De 1689-1761 *NewGrD 80*
Beauchateau *OxThe*
Beauchateau, Madeleine DePouget 1615-1683 *OxThe*
Beauchemin, Neree 1850-1931 *CreCan 2*
Beaude, Henri *CreCan 2*
Beaudet, Henri *CreCan 2*
Beaudet, Jean-Marie 1908- *CreCan 1*
Beaudet, Louise 1861-1947 *NotNAT B, WhoHol B*
Beaudet, Louise 1861-1948 *Film 1, –2, TwYS*
Beaudet, Louise 1862-1947 *WhScrn 77*
Beaudine, William d1970 *NewYTET*
Beaudine, William 1890-1970 *WhoHrs 80*
Beaudine, William 1892-1970 *FilmEn, FilmgC, HalFC 80, IlWWBF, MovMk[port], TwYS A, WhScrn 77*
Beaudry, Jacques 1929- *IntWWM 77, –80*
Beaufils, Marcel 1889- *NewGrD 80*
Beaufort, Douglas 1864-1939 *MagIlD*
Beaufort, John 1912- *ConAmTC, NotNAT, WhoThe 72, –77*
Beaugrand, Leontine 1842-1925 *CnOxB, DancEn 78*
Beauharnais, Hortense De *NewGrD 80*
Beaujoyeulx, Balthasar De 1535?-1587? *NewGrD 80*
Beaujoyeux, Balthasar De 1535?-1587? *CnOxB, DancEn 78, NewGrD 80*
Beaulaigue, Barthelemy 1543?- *NewGrD 80*
Beaulegue, Barthelemy 1543?- *NewGrD 80*
Beaulier, Simon *NewGrD 80*
Beaulieu, Andre Rosiers *NewGrD 80*
Beaulieu, Camille 1921- *AmSCAP 80*
Beaulieu, Desire 1791-1863 *NewGrD 80*
Beaulieu, Donald George 1939- *AmSCAP 80*
Beaulieu, Eustorg De 1495?-1552 *NewGrD 80*
Beaulieu, Girard De *NewGrD 80*
Beaulieu, Hector De 1495?-1552 *NewGrD 80*
Beaulieu, John 1948- *CpmDNM 73, ConAmC*
Beaulieu, Lambert De *NewGrD 80*
Beaulieu, Marie-Desire 1791-1863 *Baker 78*
Beaulieu, Maurice 1924- *CreCan 1*
Beaulieu, Paul 1888-1967 *NewOrJ*
Beaulieu, Rudolph 1900-1972 *NewOrJ*
Beaulieu, Toni *AmSCAP 80*
Beaulne, Guy 1921- *CreCan 2*
Beaumar, Constance *Film 1*
Beaumarchais, Caron De 1732-1799 *NewGrD 80, OxMus*
Beaumarchais, Pierre-Augustin Caron De 1732-1799 *BnBkM 80, CnThe, EncWT, Ent[port], McGEWD[port], NewEOp 71, NewGrD 80, NotNAT A, –B, OxThe, REnWD[port]*
Beaumenard, Rose-Perrine LeRoy 1730-1799 *OxThe*
Beaumont, Adrian 1937- *IntWWM 77, –80, WhoMus 72*
Beaumont, Charles 1929-1967 *FilmgC, HalFC 80, WhScrn 77, WhoHrs 80*
Beaumont, Charles 1930-1967 *FilmEn*
Beaumont, Cyril William 1891-1976 *CnOxB, DancEn 78[port], DcPup, OxMus, WhThe*
Beaumont, Diana Muriel 1909-1964 *NotNAT B, WhScrn 74, –77, WhThe, WhoHol B*
Beaumont, Ena *IlWWBF*
Beaumont, Etienne De, Comte 1883-1956 *CnOxB*
Beaumont, Etienne De, Comte 1885-1956 *DancEn 78*

Beaumont, Francis 1584-1616 *CnThe, EncWT, Ent, McGEWD[port], NotNAT A, -B, OxMus, OxThe, PlP&P[port], REnWD*
Beaumont, Grace *Film 2*
Beaumont, Harry d1966 *Film 1, WhoHol B*
Beaumont, Harry 1888-1966 *FilmEn, TwYS A, WhScrn 74, -77*
Beaumont, Harry 1893-1966 *CmMov, FilmgC, HalFC 80, MovMk[port]*
Beaumont, Hugh 1908-1973 *CnThe, EncMT, WhThe, WhoThe 72*
Beaumont, Hugh 1909- *FilmEn, FilmgC, ForYSC, HalFC 80, IntMPA 77, -75, -76, -78, -79, -80, WhoHol A*
Beaumont, James Lawrence 1940- *AmSCAP 66, -80*
Beaumont, John 1761-1822 *OxMus*
Beaumont, John 1902- *WhThe, WhoThe 72*
Beaumont, Lucy 1873-1937 *Film 2, TwYS, WhScrn 74, -77, WhoHol B*
Beaumont, Muriel 1881-1957 *NotNAT B, WhThe*
Beaumont, Nellie d1938 *NotNAT B*
Beaumont, Piers 1944- *CnOxB*
Beaumont, Ralph 1926- *BiE&WWA, NotNAT*
Beaumont, Roma 1914- *WhThe*
Beaumont, Rose d1938 *NotNAT B*
Beaumont, Susan 1936- *FilmgC, HalFC 80, WhoHol A*
Beaumont, Tessa 1938- *CnOxB*
Beaumont, Tom *Film 2*
Beaumont, Vertee 1889-1934 *WhScrn 74, -77*
Beaumont, Vivian *AmSCAP 80, ConAmC*
Beauplan, Marsha *Film 2*
Beaupre *OxThe*
Beaupre, Madeleine Lemoine *OxThe*
Beaupre, Marotte *OxThe*
Beauregard, Cherry Niel 1933- *IntWWM 77, -80*
Beauregard, Georges De 1920- *FilmEn*
Beausseron, Johannes *NewGrD 80*
Beauvais, Vincent De *NewGrD 80*
Beauval 1635?-1709 *EncWT, OxThe*
Beauval, Madame 1648?-1720 *Ent*
Beauval, Mademoiselle 1648?-1720 *EncWT*
Beauval, Jeanne Olivier DeBourguignon 1648?-1720 *OxThe*
Beauval, Louise 1665?-1740 *OxThe*
Beauvarlet, Henricus 1575?-1623 *NewGrD 80*
Beauvarlet-Charpentier, Jacques-Marie 1766-1834 *NewGrD 80*
Beauvarlet-Charpentier, Jean-Jacques 1734-1794 *NewGrD 80*
Beavan, P H *WhoMus 72*
Beaven, Peter Richard 1954- *IntWWM 80*
Beaver, Paul H, Jr. 1925- *ConAmC*
Beaver, Raymond Elgar 1929- *WhoMus 72*
Beaver And Krause *IlEncR*
Beavers, Clyde Winfrey 1932- *BiDAmM, CounME 74, -74A, EncFCWM 69*
Beavers, Louise d1962 *BlksB&W[port], -C, MotPP, NotNAT B, WhoHol B*
Beavers, Louise 1889-1962 *Film 2*
Beavers, Louise 1898-1962 *Vers A[port], WhScrn 74, -77*
Beavers, Louise 1902-1962 *DrBlPA, FilmEn, FilmgC, ForYSC, HalFC 80, HolP 30[port], MovMk[port], ThFT[port]*
Beazley, Samuel 1786-1851 *NotNAT B, OxThe*
Beban, George 1873-1928 *Film 1, -2, MotPP, NotNAT B, TwYS, WhScrn 74, -77, WhoHol B*
Bebderskaya, N *WomWMM*
Beber, Ambrosius *NewGrD 80*
Beberus, Virginia 1893-1964 *AmSCAP 66, -80*
Becar, Lucia 1938- *WhoOp 76*
Becaud, Francois 1927- *NewGrD 80*
Becaud, Gilbert 1927- *NewGrD 80, WhoHol A*
Becaus, Gilbert 1927- *Baker 78*
Beccari, Agostino d1598 *OxThe*
Beccatelli, Giovanni Francesco 1679-1734 *NewGrD 80*
Becce, Giuseppe 1881- *FilmEn*
Becchi, Antonio Di 1522-1568 *NewGrD 80*
Becerra, Gustavo 1925- *NewGrD 80*
Becerra-Schmidt, Gustavo 1925- *Baker 78, DcCM*
Becerril, Anthony Raymond 1945- *WhoOp 76*
Bech, Lili 1885-1939 *OxFilm, WhScrn 77*
Bech, Lily 1885-1939 *FilmEn*
Bechelli, Antonio Maria Lunarde 1932- *IntWWM 77*
Becher, Lady *OxThe*
Becher, Alfred Julius 1803-1848 *Baker 78, NewGrD 80*
Becher, Gianrico Federico 1917- *WhoOp 76*
Becher, Johannes Robert 1891-1958 *CnMD, EncWT, ModWD*
Becher, John C 1915- *BiE&WWA, NotNAT, WhoHol A*
Becher, Joseph 1821-1888 *Baker 78*
Becher, Thomas *BiE&WWA*
Becher, Ulrich 1910- *CnMD, CroCD, McGEWD[port]*
Bechet, Leonard V 1877-1952 *NewOrJ[port]*
Bechet, Sidney 1891-1959 *BiDAmM*
Bechet, Sidney 1897-1959 *Baker 78, CmpEPM, DrBlPA, IlEncJ, MusMk, NewGrD 80[port], NewOrJ[port], WhoJazz 72*
Bechgaard, Julius 1843-1917 *Baker 78*
Bechi, Gino 1913- *NewGrD 80, WhoMus 72*
Bechler, Johann Christian 1784-1857 *Baker 78, NewGrD 80*
Bechstein *NewGrD 80*
Bechstein, Carl *NewGrD 80*
Bechstein, Carl, Jr. *NewGrD 80*
Bechstein, Edwin *NewGrD 80*
Bechstein, Friedrich Wilhelm Carl 1826-1900 *NewGrD 80*
Bechstein, Karl 1826-1900 *Baker 78*
Bechtal, William 1867-1930 *Film 2*
Bechtel, William 1867-1930 *Film 1, -2, WhScrn 74, -77, WhoHol B*
Becilli, Giovanni *NewGrD 80*
Beck *NewGrD 80*
Beck, Alexander J 1922- *IntMPA 77, -75, -76, -78, -79, -80*
Beck, Anton d1563 *NewGrD 80*
Beck, Billy *WhoHol A*
Beck, Conrad 1901- *Baker 78, CompSN[port], DcCM, IntWWM 77, -80, NewGrD 80, OxMus, WhoMus 72*
Beck, Cornish *Film 1*
Beck, Danny 1904-1959 *WhScrn 74, -77, WhoHol B*
Beck, Dave 1894- *What 2[port]*
Beck, David *ConAmTC, NewGrD 80*
Beck, Dean Bryan 1928- *IntWWM 77*
Beck, E *PupTheA*
Beck, Esaias d1587 *NewGrD 80*
Beck, Francois 1734-1809 *NewGrD 80*
Beck, Franz Ignaz 1734-1809 *Baker 78, NewGrD 80*
Beck, Frederick *NewGrD 80*
Beck, Georg *NewGrD 80*
Beck, Gordon 1929- *BiE&WWA, NotNAT*
Beck, Gordon 1936- *EncJzS 70*
Beck, Gordon James 1938- *IntWWM 77, -80*
Beck, Hans *NewGrD 80*
Beck, Hans 1861-1952 *CnOxB, DancEn 78*
Beck, Harold *IntWWM 77, -80, WhoMus 72*
Beck, Heinrich 1760-1803 *OxThe*
Beck, Hermann 1929- *NewGrD 80*
Beck, J Emmett *Film 2*
Beck, Jackson *IntMPA 77, -75, -76, -78, -79, -80*
Beck, James 1932-1973 *WhScrn 77, WhoHol B*
Beck, Jean-Baptiste 1881-1943 *Baker 78, NewGrD 80*
Beck, Jeff *ConMuA 80A*
Beck, Jeff 1944- *IlEncR[port]*
Beck, Joe 1945- *EncJzS 70*
Beck, Johann Baptist 1881-1943 *NewGrD 80*
Beck, Johann H 1856-1924 *NewGrD 80*
Beck, Johann Hector *NewGrD 80*
Beck, Johann Heinrich 1856-1924 *Baker 78, BiDAmM*
Beck, Johann Nepomuk 1827-1904 *Baker 78*
Beck, John *Film 2, IntMPA 78, -79, -80, WhoHol A*
Beck, John 1944?- *HalFC 80*
Beck, John H 1933- *ConAmC*
Beck, John Ness 1930- *AmSCAP 80, Baker 78, ConAmC*
Beck, Julian 1925- *BiE&WWA, EncWT, Ent, NotNAT, -A, PlP&P, WhoThe 72, -77*
Beck, Karl 1814-1879 *Baker 78*
Beck, Karl 1850-1920 *Baker 78*
Beck, Kimberly *WhoHol A*
Beck, Mabel *Film 2*
Beck, Martha *AmSCAP 66, -80*
Beck, Martha 1900- *Baker 78*
Beck, Martha 1902- *ConAmC*
Beck, Martin 1869?-1940 *NotNAT B*
Beck, Mrs. Martin 1889- *BiE&WWA*
Beck, Meyer P *IntMPA 78*
Beck, Myer P *IntMPA 77, -75, -76, -79, -80*
Beck, Nelson C 1887-1952 *WhScrn 74, -77*
Beck, Sydney 1906- *NewGrD 80*
Beck, Theodore 1929- *CpmDNM 79, ConAmC*
Beck, Thomas Ludvigsen 1899-1963 *Baker 78*
Beck, Vincent *WhoHol A*
Beck Bogert & Appice *IlEncR*
Becke, Franz Gerhard 1937- *WhoOp 76*
Beckel, James A, Jr. 1948- *IntWWM 77*
Beckel, James Cox 1811-1880 *BiDAmM*
Becker *NewGrD 80*
Becker, Albert 1834-1899 *Baker 78*
Becker, Andreas Fred 1940- *WhoOp 76*
Becker, Bruce 1925- *BiE&WWA*
Becker, Carl F 1919- *NewGrD 80*
Becker, Carl Ferdinand 1804-1877 *NewGrD 80*
Becker, Carl G 1887-1975 *NewGrD 80*
Becker, Constantin Julius 1811-1859 *Baker 78, NewGrD 80*
Becker, Cornelius 1561-1604 *NewGrD 80*
Becker, Dietrich 1623-1679 *NewGrD 80*
Becker, F G *Film 2*
Becker, Fred *Film 2*
Becker, Garrett *PupTheA*
Becker, Georges 1834-1928 *Baker 78*
Becker, Geraldine 1955- *NewGrD 80*
Becker, Gunther 1924- *DcCM, NewGrD 80*
Becker, Gustave Louis 1861-1959 *Baker 78*
Becker, Heinz 1922- *IntWWM 77, -80, NewGrD 80*
Becker, Herbert 1933- *WhoOp 76*
Becker, Hugo 1863-1941 *Baker 78, NewGrD 80*
Becker, Jacques 1906-1960 *BiDFilm, -81, DcFM, FilmEn, FilmgC, HalFC 80, OxFilm, WhScrn 77, WorEFlm*
Becker, Jakob *NewGrD 80*
Becker, Jakob d1879 *NewGrD 80*
Becker, Jean 1833-1884 *Baker 78, NewGrD 80*
Becker, Jean 1933- *FilmEn, FilmgC, HalFC 80*
Becker, John C d1963 *NotNAT B*
Becker, John J 1886-1961 *Baker 78, BiDAmM, BnBkM 80, ConAmC, DcCM, NewGrD 80, OxMus*
Becker, Karl Ferdinand 1804-1877 *Baker 78*
Becker, Maria 1920- *EncWT, Ent*
Becker, Reinhold 1842-1924 *Baker 78*
Becker, Rene Louis 1882-1956 *Baker 78*
Becker, Rudolph Zacharias 1752-1822 *NewGrD 80*
Becker, Terry *WhoHol A*
Becker, Theodor *Film 2*
Becker, Valentin Eduard 1814-1890 *Baker 78*
Becker, Viola S *IntMPA 77, -75, -76, -78, -79, -80*
Becker, Wilhelmine Ambrosch *NewGrD 80*
Becker, William 1927- *AmSCAP 80, BiE&WWA, NotNAT*
Becker-Glauch, Irmgard 1914- *IntWWM 77, -80*
Becker-Theodore, Lee 1933- *BiE&WWA*
Beckerath, Rudolf Von 1907-1976 *NewGrD 80*
Beckerhoff, Uli 1947- *EncJzS 70*
Beckerman, Bernard 1921- *BiE&WWA, NotNAT*
Beckersache, Carl *Film 2*
Becket *AmSCAP 80*
Becket, John *WhoMus 72*
Becket, Philip d1680? *NewGrD 80*
Becket, Thomas A 1817?-1871? *BiDAmM, OxMus*
Becket, Thomas A, Jr. 1843-1918 *BiDAmM*
Beckett, Barry *ConMuA 80B*
Beckett, Fred Frederic Lee 1917-1946 *WhoJazz 72*
Beckett, Gilbert A d1856 *NotNAT B*
Beckett, James Brian 1950- *IntWWM 77, -80*

Beckett, Keith 1929- *CnOxB, DancEn 78*
Beckett, Philip d1680? *NewGrD 80*
Beckett, Samuel 1906- *BiE&WWA, CnMD, CnThe, ConDr 73, -77, CroCD, EncWT, Ent[port], McGEWD[port], ModWD, NotNAT, -A, OxThe, PlP&P, REnWD[port], WhoThe 72, -77*
Beckett, Scotty 1929-1968 *FilmEn, FilmgC, ForYSC, HalFC 80, MotPP, MovMk, NotNAT B, WhScrn 74, -77, WhoHol B*
Beckett, Sibthorpe Leopold 1920- *IntWWM 77, -80*
Beckett, Wheeler 1898- *AmSCAP 66, -80, Baker 78, ConAmC*
Beckham, Bob *RkOn*
Beckham, Emilee Ramsey 1917- *IntWWM 77*
Beckhard, Arthur J *WhThe*
Beckhelm, Paul 1906-1966 *AmSCAP 66, Baker 78, ConAmC*
Beckie, Donal Wayne 1938- *IntWWM 80*
Becking, Gustav 1894-1945 *Baker 78, NewGrD 80*
Beckingham, Charles d1731 *NotNAT B*
Beckinsale, Richard 1947-1979 *HalFC 80*
Becklenberg, Irma Elsie 1902- *AmSCAP 80*
Beckler, S R 1923- *ConAmC*
Beckler, Stanworth *CpmDNM 76*
Beckles, Terence *WhoMus 72*
Beckley, Beatrice Mary 1885- *Film 1, WhThe*
Beckley, Christine 1939- *DancEn 78*
Beckley, Tony 1932- *FilmgC, HalFC 80, WhoHol A*
Beckman, Bror 1866-1929 *NewGrD 80*
Beckman, Fokke Ph 1931- *IntWWM 80*
Beckman, Henry *WhoHol A*
Beckmann, Gustav 1883-1948 *Baker 78*
Beckmann, Johann Friedrich Gottlieb 1737-1792 *Baker 78, NewGrD 80*
Beckmann, Judith 1935- *WhoOp 76*
Beckmann, Karl *Film 2*
Beckmeier, Stephen Devinney 1948- *AmSCAP 80*
Beckstead, Joseph R 1907- *ConAmC*
Beckwith, Aaron 1914- *IntMPA 77, -75, -76*
Beckwith, Aaron 1918- *IntMPA 78, -79*
Beckwith, Bainard *Film 2*
Beckwith, John 1750-1809 *NewGrD 80*
Beckwith, John 1927- *Baker 78, CreCan 1, DcCM, IntWWM 80, NewGrD 80*
Beckwith, John Christmas 1750-1809 *Baker 78, OxMus*
Beckwith, Reginald 1908-1965 *FilmEn, FilmgC, HalFC 80, IlWWBF, MovMk, WhScrn 74, -77, WhThe, WhoHol B*
Beckwith, Robert Sterling 1931- *IntWWM 77*
Beckwith, Roger *WhScrn 74, -77*
Beclard D'Harcourt, Marguerite 1884-1964 *NewGrD 80*
Becque, Henri Francois 1837-1899 *CnThe, NotNAT B*
Becque, Henry Francois 1837-1899 *CnMD, EncWT, Ent, McGEWD[port], ModWD, OxThe, REnWD*
Becquie, A 1800-1825 *Baker 78*
Becquie, Jean-Marie 1795-1876 *Baker 78*
Becvar, Brian Francis 1954- *AmSCAP 80*
Becvarovsky, Anton Felix 1754-1823 *Baker 78*
Becvarovsky, Antonin Frantisek 1754-1823 *NewGrD 80*
Becwar, George 1917-1970 *WhScrn 77*
Beczwarzowsky, Antonin Frantisek 1754-1823 *NewGrD 80*
Bedard, Hubert 1933- *NewGrD 80*
Bedard, Jean-Baptiste 1765?-1815? *Baker 78*
Bedbrook, Gerald Stares 1907- *IntWWM 80*
Beddoe, Don 1888- *FilmEn, ForYSC, HolCA[port], WhoHol A*
Beddoe, Don 1891- *FilmgC, HalFC 80, MovMk*
Beddoe, Don 1903- *Vers A[port]*
Beddoes, Thomas Lovell 1803-1849 *NotNAT B*
Bede *NewGrD 80*
Bedeckher, Philipp Friedrich *NewGrD 80*
Bedelia, Bonnie *WhoHol A*
Bedelia, Bonnie 1946- *FilmgC, HalFC 80*
Bedelia, Bonnie 1948- *NotNAT*
Bedell, Albert Charles 1931- *AmSCAP 80*
Bedell, Lew 1919- *AmSCAP 80*
Bedell, Robert Leach 1909- *ConAmC*
Bedell, Robert Leech 1909- *AmSCAP 66*
Bedell, Stephen L 1939- *AmSCAP 80*
Bedells, Phyllis 1893- *CnOxB, DancEn 78, WhThe*
Bedford, Arthur 1668-1745 *NewGrD 80*
Bedford, Barbara *Film 2, ForYSC, TwYS*
Bedford, Barbara 1900?- *FilmEn*
Bedford, Brian 1935- *BiE&WWA, FilmgC, HalFC 80, MotPP, NotNAT, PlP&P, WhoHol A, WhoThe 72, -77*
Bedford, David 1937- *Baker 78, CpmDNM 80, DcCom&M 79, DcCM, IlEncR, IntWWM 77, -80, NewGrD 80, WhoMus 72*
Bedford, Harry d1939 *NotNAT B*
Bedford, Henry d1923 *NotNAT B*
Bedford, Herbert 1867-1945 *Baker 78, NewGrD 80, OxMus*
Bedford, Paul 1792?-1871 *NotNAT A, -B, OxThe*
Bedford, Steuart John Rudolf 1939- *IntWWM 77, -80, NewGrD 80, WhoMus 72, WhoOp 76*
Bedi, Kabir 1945- *HalFC 80*
Bedingham, John *NewGrD 80*
Bedini, Jean d1956 *NotNAT B*
Bedos DeCelles, Francis 1709-1779 *OxMus*
Bedos DeCelles, Francois 1709-1779 *Baker 78, NewGrD 80*
Bedoya, Alfonso 1904-1957 *FilmEn, FilmgC, ForYSC, HalFC 80, MovMk[port], Vers A[port], WhScrn 74, -77, WhoHol B*
Bedyngeham, Johannes d1459? *NewGrD 80*
Bedyngham, Johannes d1459? *NewGrD 80*
Bee, Joseph Thomas 1947- *AmSCAP 80*
Bee, Laurie *AmSCAP 80*
Bee, Molly 1939- *BiDAmM, CounME 74, -74A, EncFCWM 69, ForYSC, IlEncCM, WhoHol A*
Bee Gees *ConMuA 80A, IlEncR[port], RkOn 2[port]*
Beebe, Ford 1888- *FilmEn, FilmgC, HalFC 80, WhoHrs 80*
Beebe, Marjorie 1909- *Film 2*
Beech, Frances *Film 1*
Beecham, Sir Adrian 1904- *IntWWM 77, -80, WhoMus 72*
Beecham, Sir Joseph d1916 *NotNAT B, OxMus*
Beecham, Sir Thomas 1879-1961 *Baker 78, BnBkM 80[port], CmOp, DancEn 78, MusMk[port], MusSN[port], NewEOp 71, NewGrD 80[port], NotNAT B, OxMus*
Beecher, Ada 1862-1935 *WhScrn 74, -77*
Beecher, Carl Milton 1883-1968 *Baker 78, ConAmC*
Beecher, Charles 1815-1900 *BiDAmM*
Beecher, Clare Rodman 1888-1958 *AmSCAP 80*
Beecher, Henry Ward 1813-1887 *BiDAmM*
Beecher, Janet 1884-1955 *FilmEn, FilmgC, HalFC 80, HolCA[port], MotPP, MovMk, NotNAT B, ThFT[port], WhScrn 74, -77, WhThe, WhoHol B*
Beecher, Janet 1885-1955 *ForYSC*
Beecher, Johannes R 1891-1958 *CroCD*
Beecher, Sylvia *Film 2*
Beecher, William Gordon, Jr. 1904-1973 *AmSCAP 66, -80*
Beechey, Gwilym Edward 1938- *IntWWM 77, -80, WhoMus 72*
Beecke, Ignaz Von 1733-1803 *Baker 78, NewGrD 80*
Beecroft, Norma 1934- *Baker 78, DcCM*
Beecroft, Victor R 1887-1958 *WhScrn 74, -77*
Beefheart, Captain 1941- *IlEncR*
Beek, Jean Albert Adriaan Joseph 1891- *WhoMus 72*
Beekman, Bernadette *WomWMM B*
Beeks, Graydon Fisher, Jr. 1948- *IntWWM 77, -80*
Beeland, Ambrose *NewGrD 80*
Beelby, Malcolm 1907- *AmSCAP 66, -80*
Beeler, C Alan 1939- *ConAmC*
Beelitz, Claus 1938- *DancEn 78*
Beelitz, Klaus 1938- *CnOxB*
Beellaerts, Jean *Baker 78*
Beer, Anton De 1924- *IntWWM 77, -80*
Beer, Eloise *PupTheA*
Beer, Friedrich *NewGrD 80*
Beer, Jacob Liebmann *Baker 78*
Beer, Johann 1655-1700 *NewGrD 80*
Beer, Joseph 1744-1812 *Baker 78, NewGrD 80*
Beer, Max Josef 1851-1908 *Baker 78*
Beer-Hofmann, Richard 1866-1945 *CnMD, EncWT, McGEWD[port], ModWD, OxThe*
Beer-Walbrunn, Anton 1864-1929 *Baker 78, NewGrD 80*
Beerbohm, Clarence Evelyn d1917 *WhThe*
Beerbohm, Claude *Film 2*
Beerbohm, Sir Max 1872-1956 *CnMD, EncWT, ModWD, NotNAT A, -B, OxThe, WhThe*
Beerbohm Tree, Herbert 1853-1917 *Ent*
Beerbohn, Elizabeth *Film 2*
Beere, Mrs. Bernard 1856- *WhThe*
Beerman, Burton 1943- *CpmDNM 77, -79, -80, ConAmC, IntWWM 77, -80*
Beers, A A *WhoMus 72*
Beers, Adrian S *WhoMus 72*
Beers, Ethelinda Eliot 1827-1879 *BiDAmM*
Beers, Evelyne Christine Sauer 1925- *BiDAmM*
Beers, Francine *WhoHol A*
Beers, Jack *WhoHol A*
Beers, Jacques 1902-1947 *NewGrD 80*
Beers, Robert Harlan 1920-1972 *BiDAmM*
Beers Family *EncFCWM 69*
Beery, Noah 1884-1946 *CmMov, Film 1, -2, FilmgC, ForYSC, HalFC 80, MotPP, MovMk[port], OxFilm, TwYS, Vers B[port], WhScrn 74, -77, WhoHol B*
Beery, Noah, Jr. *MotPP, WhoHol A*
Beery, Noah, Jr. 1913- *Film 2, FilmgC, HalFC 80, HolCA[port]*
Beery, Noah, Jr. 1915- *FilmEn, Vers B[port]*
Beery, Noah, Jr. 1916- *ForYSC, IntMPA 77, -75, -76, -78, -79, -80, MovMk[port]*
Beery, Noah, Sr. 1883-1946 *HolCA[port], NotNAT B*
Beery, Noah, Sr. 1884-1946 *FilmEn*
Beery, Wallace 1880?-1949 *FilmgC, HalFC 80, WhoHol B*
Beery, Wallace 1881-1949 *NotNAT B*
Beery, Wallace 1885-1949 *FilmEn, WhScrn 74, -77, WhoHrs 80, WorEFlm*
Beery, Wallace 1886-1949 *BiDFilm, -81, Film 1, -2, MGM[port], MotPP, MovMk[port], OxFilm*
Beery, Wallace 1889-1949 *CmMov, ForYSC, TwYS*
Beery, William *Film 1*
Beesley, Rush 1947- *AmSCAP 80*
Beeson, Coni Irene 1930- *WomWMM A, -B*
Beeson, Jack Hamilton 1921- *AmSCAP 66, -80, Baker 78, BiDAmM, BnBkM 80, CpmDNM 74, ConAmC, DcCM, IntWWM 77, -80, NewEOp 71, NewGrD 80*
Beeson, Paul 1921- *HalFC 80*
Beeston, Christopher 1570?-1638 *NotNAT B, OxThe*
Beeston, Michael Harding 1948- *IntWWM 80*
Beeston, William 1606?-1682 *NotNAT B, OxThe, PlP&P*
Beet, Alice d1931 *NotNAT B, WhThe*
Beeth, Lola 1862-1940 *Baker 78*
Beethoven, Ludwig Van 1770-1827 *Baker 78, BnBkM 80[port], CmOp, CmpBCM, CnOxB, DancEn 78, DcCom 77[port], DcCom&M 79, GrComp[port], MusMk[port], NewEOp 71, NewGrD 80[port], OxMus*
Beezley, Neil 1917- *IntMPA 75, -76*
Beffara, Louis-Francois 1751-1838 *Baker 78*
Beffroy DeReigny, Louis-Abel 1757-1811 *NewGrD 80*
Begelman, David *IntMPA 77, -75, -76, -78, -79, -80*
Begg, Gordon *Film 2*
Begg, Heather 1932- *CmOp, IntWWM 77, -80, WhoMus 72, WhoOp 76*
Beggs, Lee 1871-1943 *Film 2, WhScrn 77*
Beggs, Malcolm Lee 1907-1956 *WhScrn 74, -77, WhoHol B*
Begin, Catherine Agnes Marie 1939- *CreCan 2*
Begin, Mireille *CreCan 1*
Beginning Of The End *RkOn 2A*
Beglarian, Grant 1927- *AmSCAP 80, Baker 78, ConAmC, DcCM, IntWWM 77, -80*

Begley, Ed 1901-1970 *BiE&WWA, FilmEn, FilmgC, ForYSC, HalFC 80, HolCA[port], MotPP, MovMk[port], NotNAT B, Vers A[port], WhScrn 74, -77, WhThe, WhoHol B*
Begley, Ed, Jr. *WhoHol A*
Begley, Martin *IntMPA 75, -76*
Begnis, Giuseppe De 1793-1849 *NewGrD 80*
Begrez, Pierre 1787-1863 *NewGrD 80*
Beh, Siew Hwa *WomWMM B*
Behague, Gerard 1937- *NewGrD 80*
Behaim, Michel 1416-1474? *NewGrD 80*
Behan, Brendan 1923-1964 *BiE&WWA, CnMD, CnThe, ConDr 77F, CroCD, EncWT, Ent[port], HalFC 80, McGEWD[port], ModWD, NotNAT A, -B, PlP&P, REnWD[port], WhThe*
Beheim, Michel 1416-1474? *Baker 78, NewGrD 80*
Behlendorf, Dieter 1930- *WhoOp 76*
Behm, Eduard 1862-1946 *Baker 78*
Behn, Aphra 1640-1689 *EncWT, Ent, McGEWD[port], NotNAT A, -B, OxThe, PlP&P*
Behn, Noel 1928- *BiE&WWA, NotNAT*
Behn-Grund, Friedl 1906- *FilmEn*
Behr, Andreas 1947- *WhoOp 76*
Behr, Franz 1837-1898 *Baker 78*
Behr, Hans-Georg 1937- *CroCD*
Behr, Jan 1911- *IntWWM 77, -80, WhoOp 76*
Behr, Johann *NewGrD 80*
Behr, Therese 1876-1959 *NewGrD 80*
Behrend, Fritz 1889- *NewGrD 80*
Behrend, Jeanne 1911- *ConAmC, NewGrD 80*
Behrend, Louise 1916- *IntWWM 77, -80*
Behrend, Siegfried 1933- *IntWWM 77, -80, NewGrD 80, WhoMus 72*
Behrend, William 1861-1940 *Baker 78*
Behrens, Frederick 1854-1938 *WhScrn 74, -77*
Behrens, Hildegard *WhoOp 76*
Behrens, Jack 1935- *AmSCAP 66, -80, Baker 78, ConAmC, IntWWM 80*
Behrens, Johan Diderik 1820-1890 *NewGrD 80*
Behrens, Richard Hermann 1925- *IntWWM 80*
Behrens, William *Film 1*
Behrenson, Doc 1893- *NewOrJ*
Behrenson, Sidney 1895?- *NewOrJ*
Behrle, Fred 1891-1941 *Film 2, WhScrn 74, -77, WhoHol B*
Behrman, David 1937- *ConAmC*
Behrman, S N 1893-1973 *BiE&WWA, CmMov, CnMD, CnThe, ConDr 73, CroCD, DcLB 7[port], FilmEn, FilmgC, HalFC 80, McGEWD[port], ModWD, NotNAT A, -B, REnWD*
Behrman, Samuel Nathan 1893-1973 *PlP&P*
Behrman, Samuel Nathaniel 1893-1973 *EncWT, Ent[port], OxThe, WhThe, WhoThe 72*
Behunin, Leslie Merrill, Jr. 1936- *AmSCAP 80*
Behymer, L E d1947 *NotNAT B*
Behymer, Minetta S d1958 *NotNAT B*
Beich, Albert 1919- *FilmgC, HalFC 80, IntMPA 77, -75, -76, -78, -79, -80*
Beiderbecke, Bix 1903-1931 *Baker 78, CmpEPM, IlEncJ, MusMk[port], NewGrD 80[port]*
Beiderbecke, Leon Bix 1903-1931 *BiDAmM, WhoJazz 72*
Beil, Johann David 1754-1794 *OxThe*
Beilby, John Frederick 1945- *IntWWM 80*
Beilenson, Gerda Maline 1903- *AmSCAP 80*
Beilschmidt, Curt 1886-1962 *Baker 78*
Beim, Norman *NatPD[port]*
Beiman, Melvyn 1932- *IntWWM 77, -80*
Bein, Albert 1902- *BiE&WWA, CnMD, ModWD, NotNAT*
Beinum, Eduard Van 1900-1959 *Baker 78*
Beinum, Eduard Van 1901-1959 *BnBkM 80, MusMk, MusSN[port]*
Beirer, Hans 1911- *IntWWM 77, -80*
Beirer, Hans 1916- *WhoOp 76*
Beissel, J Conrad 1690-1768 *NewGrD 80*
Beissel, Johann Conrad 1690-1768 *Baker 78, BiDAmM*
Beiswanger, George 1902- *CnOxB, DancEn 78*
Beitamouni, Mohammad Mujab 1937- *IntWWM 77, -80*
Beith, Sir John Hay 1876-1952 *NotNAT B*
Bejart, Armande 1642?-1700 *EncWT, Ent*
Bejart, Armande-Gresinde-Claire-E 1641-1700 *OxThe*
Bejart, Armande-Gresinde-Claire-E 1642-1700 *NotNAT B*
Bejart, Genevieve 1624-1675 *EncWT, OxThe*
Bejart, Joseph 1616?-1659 *EncWT, OxThe*
Bejart, Louis 1630-1678 *EncWT, OxThe*
Bejart, Madeleine 1618-1672 *Ent, NotNAT B, OxThe*
Bejart, Marie-Madeleine 1618-1672 *EncWT*
Bejart, Maurice 1927- *CnOxB, EncWT, WhoOp 76*
Bejart, Maurice 1928- *DancEn 78*
Bejart Family *CnThe*
Bejinariu, Mircea 1950- *IntWWM 80*
Bejtman, Vincent *IntMPA 80*
Bek, Josef 1934- *NewGrD 80*
Bek-Nazarov, Amo 1892- *DcFM*
Bekassy, Stephen 1910- *ForYSC*
Bekassy, Stephen 1915?- *FilmgC, HalFC 80*
Bekes, Andras 1927- *WhoOp 76*
Bekesy, Georg Von 1899-1972 *NewGrD 80*
Bekker, Dietrich *NewGrD 80*
Bekker, Jakov Davidovich *NewGrD 80*
Bekker, Paul 1882-1937 *Baker 78, BiDAmM, NewEOp 71, NewGrD 80*
Bekku, Sadao 1922- *Baker 78, DcCM, NewGrD 80*
Bekwark, Valentin *NewGrD 80*
Bel, Barthelemy Le *NewGrD 80*
Bel Geddes, Barbara 1922- *BiE&WWA, CnThe, EncWT, FilmEn, FilmgC, HalFC 80, IntMPA 77, -75, -76, -78, -78, -79, -80, MotPP, MovMk, NotNAT, PlP&P[port], WhoHol A, WhoThe 72, -77*
Bel Geddes, Barbara 1923- *ForYSC*
Bel Geddes, Edith Lutyens 1916- *BiE&WWA*
Bel Geddes, Edith Lutyens 1917- *NotNAT*
Bel Geddes, Norman 1893-1958 *CnThe, EncWT, Ent, PlP&P[port]*
Bela, Nicholas d1963 *Film 2, NotNAT B, WhoHol B*
Belafonte, Harold George, Jr. 1927- *AmSCAP 66, -80, BiDAmM*
Belafonte, Harry 1927- *AmPS A, -B, Baker 78, BiE&WWA, CmpEPM, DrBlPA, EncFCWM 69, FilmEn, FilmgC, ForYSC, HalFC 80, IntMPA 77, -75, -76, -78, -79, -80, MotPP, MovMk, OxFilm, RkOn[port], WhoHol A*
Belaief, Mitrofan 1836-1904 *OxMus*
Belaiev, Mitrofan 1836-1904 *Baker 78*
Belaiev, Victor 1888-1968 *Baker 78*
Belajeff, Olga *Film 2*
Belamaric, Miro 1935- *IntWWM 80*
Belan, Cliff 1921- *AmSCAP 66*
Belan, William Lee 1950- *IntWWM 77*
Belaney, Archibald Stansfeld *CreCan 1*
Belanger, Juliette *Film 2*
Belanger, Marc 1940- *IntWWM 77, -80*
Belasco, David 1853-1931 *BiDAmM, CnThe, DcLB 7[port], EncWT, McGEWD[port], OxThe, REnWD[port], WhThe*
Belasco, David 1854-1931 *Film 1*
Belasco, David 1859-1931 *Ent, ModWD, NewEOp 71, NotNAT A, -B, PlP&P[port], WhoStg 1906, -1908*
Belasco, Edward d1937 *NotNAT B*
Belasco, Frederick d1920 *BiDAmM, NotNAT B*
Belasco, Genevieve 1871-1956 *NotNAT B, WhScrn 74, -77, WhoHol B*
Belasco, Jay *Film 1*
Belasco, Keystone *AmSCAP 80*
Belasco, Leon 1902- *BgBands 74, BiE&WWA, FilmEn, Film 2, FilmgC, ForYSC, HalFC 80, Vers B[port], WhoHol A*
Belasco, Manuel *NewOrJ*
Belasco, William 1934- *IntMPA 75, -76*
Belasio, Paolo *NewGrD 80*
Belaver, Vincenzo *NewGrD 80*
Belcari, Feo 1410-1484 *McGEWD[port], OxThe*
Belcham, Henry d1917 *NotNAT B*
Belchamber, Eileen Mabel 1908- *WhoMus 72*
Belcher, Alice 1880-1939 *WhScrn 74, -77, WhoHol B*
Belcher, Cecil James 1903- *WhoMus 72*
Belcher, Charles *Film 2*
Belcher, Ernest *Film 2*
Belcher, Frank H 1869-1947 *Film 1, WhScrn 77*
Belcher, John Theodore 1937- *IntWWM 77, -80*
Belcher, Joseph 1794-1859 *BiDAmM*
Belcher, Supply 1751-1836 *Baker 78, BiDAmM*
Belcher, Supply 1752-1836 *NewGrD 80*
Belcke, F A *OxMus*
Belcke, Friedrich August 1795-1874 *Baker 78, NewGrD 80*
Belcourt, Emile *IntWWM 77, -80*
Belcourt, Emile 1926- *CmOp*
Belda, Patrick 1943-1967 *CnOxB*
Beldemandis, Prosdocimus De *NewGrD 80*
Beldini, Al 1934- *IntWWM 77*
Beldon, Edwin *WhoStg 1908*
Beldon, Eileen 1901- *WhoThe 72, -77*
Belefan, Sam *AmSCAP 80*
Belem, Antonio De 1624?-1700 *NewGrD 80*
Belew, Carl Robert 1931- *BiDAmM, CounME 74, -74A, EncFCWM 69, IlEncCM*
Belfer, Hal B *IntMPA 77, -75, -76, -78, -79, -80*
Belfer, Harold Bruce 1927- *AmSCAP 80*
Belfield, Frederick H 1901- *BiE&WWA*
Belford, Christine *WhoHol A*
Belford, David 1915- *WhoMus 72*
Belford, Hazel *Film 1*
Belfrage, Bruce 1901- *WhThe*
Belgado, Maria 1906-1969 *WhScrn 74*
Belgioioso, Baldassare De *NewGrD 80*
Belgiojoso, Baldassarino Da *DancEn 78*
Belgrave, Cynthia 1926- *DrBlPA, WhoHol A*
Beliczay, Gyula 1835-1893 *NewGrD 80*
Beliczay, Julius Von 1835-1893 *Baker 78, NewGrD 80*
Belin, Fran 1936- *IntWWM 77*
Belin, Guillaume 1500?-1568 *NewGrD 80*
Belin, Julien 1525?-1584? *NewGrD 80*
Belinfante-Dekker, Martha Suzanna Betje 1900- *IntWWM 77, -80*
Belinskii, Vissarion Grigorevich 1811-1848 *EncWT*
Belinsky, Isai 1900- *IntWWM 77, -80*
Belissen, Laurent 1693-1762 *NewGrD 80*
Belita 1923- *FilmEn*
Belita 1924- *FilmgC, HalFC 80, WhoHol A*
Belita 1925- *ForYSC*
Belitz, Joachim 1550?-1592 *NewGrD 80*
Beliy, Victor Arkadyevich 1904- *IntWWM 77, -80*
Beliy, Viktor Arkad'yevich 1904- *NewGrD 80*
Belkin, Alan Ivor 1951- *IntWWM 77, -80*
Belkin, Bestruce *Film 2*
Belkin, Jeanna 1924- *NotNAT*
Belkin, Jules *ConMuA 80B*
Belkin, Mike *ConMuA 80B*
Belknap, Daniel 1771-1815 *BiDAmM, NewGrD 80*
Bell, Lady 1851-1930 *NotNAT B*
Bell, Alistair Macready 1913- *CreCan 2*
Bell, Ann 1939- *WhoThe 72, -77*
Bell, Archie d1943 *NotNAT B*
Bell, Archie & The Drells *RkOn 2[port]*
Bell, Arnold *WhoHol A*
Bell, Arnold Craig 1911- *IntWWM 80*
Bell, Barry *ConMuA 80B*
Bell, Benny *RkOn 2A*
Bell, C Clark 1930- *AmSCAP 80*
Bell, Campton d1963 *NotNAT B*
Bell, Carey 1936- *BluesWW[port]*
Bell, Charles L 1913- *Film 2, IntMPA 75, -76*
Bell, Clarence F d1963 *NotNAT B*
Bell, Colin *Film 2*
Bell, D L *WhoMus 72*
Bell, Daniel W 1891- *BiE&WWA*
Bell, David M 1954- *IntWWM 80*
Bell, Derek Fleetwood 1923- *IntWWM 77, -80*
Bell, Diana d1965 *WhScrn 74, -77*
Bell, Digby Valentine 1849-1917 *WhoStg 1906, -1908*
Bell, Digby Valentine 1851-1917 *Film 1, NotNAT B, WhThe, WhoHol B*
Bell, Dita 1915- *AmSCAP 66*
Bell, Donald 1934- *Baker 78, CreCan 2, NewGrD 80, WhoMus 72*
Bell, Donald Munro 1934- *IntWWM 77, -80*
Bell, Edward 1905?-1960 *BluesWW*

Bell, Enid 1888- *WhThe*
Bell, Gaston 1877-1963 *Film 1, NotNAT B, WhScrn 74, -77, WhoHol B, WhoStg 1908*
Bell, Genevieve d1951 *WhScrn 74, -77, WhoHol B*
Bell, George O d1969 *WhScrn 77, WhoHol B*
Bell, Gertrude Willis 1915- *AmSCAP 80*
Bell, Graeme 1914- *CmpEPM*
Bell, Hank 1892-1950 *WhScrn 74, -77, WhoHol B*
Bell, J Raymond 1908- *IntMPA 75, -76*
Bell, James 1891-1973 *BiE&WWA, FilmEn, FilmgC, HalFC 80, MovMk, WhScrn 77, WhThe, WhoHol B*
Bell, Jeanne 1944?- *DrBlPA*
Bell, John 1745-1831 *NotNAT B, OxThe*
Bell, John 1910?-1946 *NewOrJ*
Bell, John Herbert 1926- *WhoOp 76*
Bell, John Jay 1871-1938 *NotNAT B*
Bell, John Joy 1871-1934 *OxThe*
Bell, Karina *Film 2*
Bell, Larry 1952- *ConAmC*
Bell, Laura Joyce d1904 *NotNAT B*
Bell, Leslie Richard 1906-1962 *CreCan 2, NotNAT B*
Bell, Lola d1967 *WhScrn 77*
Bell, Louise *AmSCAP 80*
Bell, Lucile Anderson *AmSCAP 66, -80*
Bell, Lucille Anderson *ConAmC*
Bell, Maggie 1945- *IlEncR*
Bell, Marie 1900- *CnThe, EncWT, Ent[port], FilmAG WE, FilmEn, Film 2, FilmgC, HalFC 80, OxFilm, WhoHol A*
Bell, Mary *WhoHol A*
Bell, Mary Hayley 1914- *BiE&WWA, NotNAT, -A, WhThe*
Bell, Mildred Blanche Elizabeth *WhoMus 72*
Bell, Monta 1891-1958 *FilmEn, FilmgC, HalFC 80, TwYS A, WhScrn 74, -77, WhoHol B*
Bell, Montana 1891-1958 *Film 1, -2*
Bell, Peter *AmSCAP 80*
Bell, Ralph W 1883-1936 *WhScrn 74, -77, WhoHol B*
Bell, Randy M 1945- *ConAmC*
Bell, Rex 1904-1962 *ForYSC*
Bell, Rex 1905-1962 *FilmEn, Film 2, FilmgC, HalFC 80, NotNAT B, WhScrn 74, -77, WhoHol B*
Bell, Rex 1907-1962 *TwYS*
Bell, Richard d1672 *NotNAT B*
Bell, Robert d1867 *NotNAT B*
Bell, Robert 1937- *WhoMus 72*
Bell, Rodney 1916-1968 *WhScrn 77*
Bell, Ruth 1907-1933 *WhScrn 74, -77*
Bell, S Aaron 1924- *IntWWM 77, -80*
Bell, Samuel Aaron 1922- *EncJzS 70*
Bell, Samuel Aaron 1934- *AmSCAP 80*
Bell, Sebastian 1941- *IntWWM 80*
Bell, Spencer *Film 2*
Bell, Stanley 1881-1952 *NotNAT B, WhThe*
Bell, Sybil Frances 1927- *IntWWM 77*
Bell, Thom *ConMuA 80B*
Bell, Tom 1932- *FilmEn, ForYSC, IntMPA 77, -75, -76, -78, -79, -80*
Bell, Tom 1933- *FilmgC, HalFC 80*
Bell, Tula *Film 1*
Bell, Vincent *RkOn 2A*
Bell, W H 1873-1946 *NewGrD 80*
Bell, William 1939- *RkOn 2[port]*
Bell, William Henry 1873-1946 *Baker 78, OxMus*
Bell, William J *NewYTET*
Bell Family *PupTheA*
Bell Notes, The *RkOn*
Bell-Smith, Frederick Martlett 1846-1923 *CreCan 2*
Bella, Jan Levoslav 1843-1936 *NewGrD 80*
Bella, Johann Leopold 1843-1936 *Baker 78, NewGrD 80*
Bella, Joseph F 1940- *NotNAT*
Bellabene, Gregorio *NewGrD 80*
Bellah, James Warner 1900-1976 *CmMov, HalFC 80*
Bellaigue, Camille 1858-1930 *Baker 78, NewGrD 80*
Bellak, Rhoda 1923- *AmSCAP 80*
Bellamann, Henry 1882-1945 *Baker 78*
Bellamente, Alan John 1937- *WhoOp 76*
Bellamy, Anne 1727?-1788 *CnThe*
Bellamy, Daniel d1788 *NotNAT B*
Bellamy, David Milton 1950- *AmSCAP 80*
Bellamy, Earl 1917- *FilmEn, FilmgC, HalFC 80, IntMPA 77, -75, -76, -78, -79, -80*
Bellamy, Franklyn 1886- *WhThe*
Bellamy, George 1866-1944 *IlWWBF, NotNAT B, WhoHol B*
Bellamy, George Anne 1727?-1788 *NotNAT A, -B, OxThe*
Bellamy, Henry Ernest d1932 *NotNAT B*
Bellamy, Madge *MotPP*
Bellamy, Madge 1900- *FilmEn, ThFT[port], WhoHol A*
Bellamy, Madge 1903- *Film 2, ForYSC, HalFC 80, MovMk, TwYS*
Bellamy, Marian Meredith 1927- *ConAmC*
Bellamy, Ralph 1904- *BiE&WWA, FilmEn, Film 2, FilmgC, HalFC 80, HolP 30[port], MotPP, MovMk[port], NotNAT, WhThe, WhoHol A, WhoHrs 80*
Bellamy, Ralph 1905- *ForYSC, IntMPA 77, -75, -76, -78, -79, -80*
Bellamy, Richard d1813 *NewGrD 80*
Bellamy, Somers *Film 2*
Bellamy, Thomas d1800 *NotNAT B*
Bellamy, Thomas 1770-1843 *NewGrD 80*
Bellamy, Thomas Ludford d1843 *NotNAT B*
Bellamy Brothers *RkOn 2[port]*
Belland, Bruce G 1936- *AmSCAP 80*
Bellanda, Lodovico *NewGrD 80*
Bellante, Dionisio d1642? *NewGrD 80*
Bellasio, Paolo 1554-1594 *Baker 78, NewGrD 80*
Bellatius, Francesco *NewGrD 80*
Bellaver, Harry 1905- *BiE&WWA, FilmgC, ForYSC, HalFC 80, NotNAT, WhoHol A*
Bell'aver, Vincenzo d1587 *NewGrD 80*
Bellavere, Vincenzo d1587 *NewGrD 80*
Bellay, Joachim Du *NewGrD 80*
Bellazza, Vincenzo 1888-1964 *CmOp*
Bellazzi, Francesco *Baker 78, NewGrD 80*
Bellazzo, Francesco *NewGrD 80*
Belle, Anne *WomWMM B*
Belle, Barbara 1922- *AmSCAP 66, -80*
Belle, Fannie *Film 2*
Belle, Jan 1552?- *NewGrD 80*
Bellecourt 1725-1778 *OxThe*
Bellefleur, Leon 1910- *CreCan 1*
Bellenfant *PupTheA*
Beller, Alex 1905- *AmSCAP 80*
Beller, Alex 1915- *AmSCAP 66*
Beller, Jackie 1916- *AmSCAP 66, -80*
Bellere, Jean 1526-1595 *Baker 78, NewGrD 80*
Bellermann *NewGrD 80*
Bellermann, Heinrich 1832-1903 *Baker 78, NewGrD 80*
Bellermann, Johann Friedrich 1795-1874 *Baker 78, NewGrD 80*
Bellermann, Johann Joachim 1754-1842 *NewGrD 80*
Bellermann, Konstantin 1696-1758 *NewGrD 80*
Bellerose 1592?-1670 *EncWT, Ent*
Bellerose 1600?-1670? *NotNAT B, OxThe*
Bellerose, Sister Cecilia 1897- *ConAmC*
Bellerose, Nicole Gassot d1680 *EncWT*
Belletti, Giovanni Battista 1813-1890 *NewGrD 80*
Belleville *OxThe*
Belleville, Anna Caroline De *NewGrD 80*
Belleville, Frederic De 1857- *WhThe*
Belleville, Jacques De *NewGrD 80*
Belleville-Oury, Caroline De *Baker 78*
Bellew, Cosmo Kyrle 1886-1948 *Film 2, NotNAT B, TwYS, WhScrn 74, -77, WhoHol B*
Bellew, Dorothy 1891- *Film 1, -2, IlWWBF*
Bellew, H Kyrle 1855-1911 *NotNAT B, WhoHol B*
Bellew, Harold Kyrle 1855-1911 *OxThe*
Bellew, Kryle 1855-1911 *Film 1*
Bellew, Kyrle 1855-1911 *WhoStg 1908*
Bellew, Kyrle 1857-1911 *FamA&A[port], WhScrn 77*
Bellew, Kyrle 1887- *WhThe*
Bellezza, Vincenzo 1888-1964 *Baker 78, NewEOp 71, NewGrD 80*
Bellfort, Joseph *IntMPA 77, -75, -76, -78, -79, -80*
Bell'Haver, Vincenzo 1530?-1857 *Baker 78, NewGrD 80*
Bellhouse, Alan Robert 1914- *IntWWM 77, -80*
Belli, Agostina 1947- *FilmAG WE[port]*
Belli, Domenico d1627 *Baker 78, NewGrD 80*
Belli, Girolamo 1552-1618? *Baker 78*
Belli, Girolamo 1552-1620? *NewGrD 80*
Belli, Giulio 1560?-1621? *Baker 78, NewGrD 80*
Belli, Remo *AmSCAP 80*
Bellido, Jose Maria 1922- *ModWD*
Bellin, Guillaume *NewGrD 80*
Bellin, Lewis Paul 1905- *AmSCAP 66, -80*
Bellin, Olga 1935- *BiE&WWA, NotNAT*
Bellincioni, Gemma 1864-1950 *Baker 78, NewEOp 71, NewGrD 80[port]*
Belline, Mary L 1920- *AmSCAP 80*
Belling, Susan *WhoOp 76*
Belling, Tom 1830?- *Ent*
Bellingan, Johannes *NewGrD 80*
Bellini, Renato 1895- *Baker 78*
Bellini, Vicenzo 1801-1835 *DcCom&M 79*
Bellini, Vincenzo 1801-1835 *Baker 78, BnBkM 80, CmOp, CmpBCM, DcCom 77[port], GrComp[port], MusMk[port], NewEOp 71, NewGrD 80[port], OxMus*
Bellinicioni, Gemma 1864-1950 *CmOp*
Bellino, Vito 1922- *AmSCAP 66, -80*
Bellinzani, Paolo Benedetto 1690?-1757 *NewGrD 80*
Bellis, Giovanni Battista De *NewGrD 80*
Bellis, Henry 1915?- *NewOrJ*
Bellis, Richard R 1946- *AmSCAP 80*
Bellison, Simeon 1883-1953 *Baker 78, NewGrD 80*
Bellissen, Laurent *NewGrD 80*
Bellman, Carl Michael 1740-1795 *Baker 78, NewGrD 80*
Bellman, Helen M *ConAmC*
Bellmann, Carl Mikael 1740-1795 *OxMus*
Bellmann, Karl Gottlieb 1772-1861 *Baker 78*
Bello DeTorices, Benito 1660?-1718? *NewGrD 80*
Bello DeTorizes, Benito 1660?-1718? *NewGrD 80*
Bello Montero, Atanasio d1847? *NewGrD 80*
Belloc, Dan 1924- *AmSCAP 66, -80*
Belloc, Teresa Giorgi 1784-1855 *Baker 78, CmOp*
Belloc-Giorgi, Teresa 1784-1855 *NewGrD 80*
Bellocchio, Marco 1939- *BiDFilm, -81, FilmEn, HalFC 80, OxFilm, WorEFlm*
Bellocchio, Marco 1940- *DcFM*
Bellochio, Marco 1940- *FilmgC*
Bellon, Yannick 1924- *DcFM, WomWMM*
Belloni, Giuseppe 1575?-1606? *NewGrD 80*
Bellonini, Edna 1903- *WhThe*
Bellosio, Anselmo 1743-1793 *NewGrD 80*
Bellotta, Francesco 1834-1907 *NewGrD 80*
Bellotti-Bon, Luigi 1820-1883 *EncWT*
Bellovacensis, Vincentius *NewGrD 80*
Bellow, Alexander 1912- *AmSCAP 66, -80, ConAmC*
Bellow, Saul 1915- *ConDr 73, -77, CroCD, NotNAT*
Bellows, Phyllis 1934- *BiE&WWA*
Belloy, Pierre-Laurent Buirette De 1727-1775 *OxThe*
Bells, The *RkOn 2[port]*
Bellsham-Revell, Roland Geoffrey 1937- *IntWWM 77*
Bellson, Louie Paul 1924- *EncJzS 70*
Bellson, Louis Paul 1924- *AmSCAP 66, -80, BiDAmM, CmpEPM, ConAmC, Conv 2[port], IlEncJ*
Bellugi, Piero 1924- *IntWWM 77, -80, NewGrD 80, WhoOp 76*
Bellville, Miriam Priscilla *IntWWM 77*
Bellwood, Bessie 1847-1896 *NotNAT B, OxThe*
Bellwood, Bessie 1860-1896 *Ent*
Belmar, Henry 1849-1931 *WhScrn 74, -77, WhoHol B*
Belmas, Xenia 1896- *IntWWM 80*
Belmondo, Jean-Paul 1933- *BiDFilm, -81, FilmAG WE[port], FilmEn, FilmgC,*

ForYSC, HalFC 80, IntMPA 77, -75, -76, -78, -79, -80, MotPP, MovMk, OxFilm, WhoHol A, WorEFlm[port]
Belmont, Baldy *Film 2*
Belmont, Bobby *PupTheA*
Belmont, Charles 1936- *FilmEn*
Belmont, Eleanor *NotNAT A*
Belmont, Gladys *Film 2*
Belmont, Joe A 1860-1930 *WhScrn 74, -77*
Belmont, John *OxMus*
Belmont, Joseph *Film 1*
Belmont, Michael 1915-1941 *WhScrn 74, -77*
Belmont, Mrs. Morgan *Film 2*
Belmont, Ralf 1892-1964 *WhScrn 77*
Belmont, Terry *WhoHol A*
Belmont, Vera *WomWMM*
Belmonte, Herman 1891-1975 *WhScrn 77, WhoHol C*
Belmonte Bermudez, Luis De 1587?-1650 *McGEWD[port]*
Belmonts, The *RkOn[port]*
Belmore, Alice d1943 *NotNAT B*
Belmore, Bertha 1882-1953 *FilmgC, HalFC 80, NotNAT B, WhScrn 74, -77, WhThe, WhoHol B*
Belmore, Daisy 1874-1954 *Film 2, NotNAT B, WhScrn 74, -77, WhoHol B*
Belmore, George d1956 *NotNAT B*
Belmore, Herbert d1952 *NotNAT B*
Belmore, Lionel 1867-1953 *FilmEn, Film 1, -2, ForYSC, NotNAT B, TwYS, WhScrn 74, -77, WhoHol B*
Belmore, Lionel 1875-1940 *FilmgC*
Belmore, Lionel 1875-1953 *HalFC 80*
Belniak, Susan Louise *WomWMM B*
Beloff, Angelina *PupTheA*
Beloin, Edmund 1910- *FilmEn, FilmgC, HalFC 80*
Belokurov, Vladimir V 1904-1973 *WhScrn 77*
Belolo, Henri *ConMuA 80B*
Belot, Adolphe d1890 *NotNAT B*
Belot, Marthe *Film 2*
Belotti, Gastone 1920- *IntWWM 77, -80*
Belsky, Igor Dmitrievich 1925- *CnOxB, DancEn 78*
Belson, Edward 1898-1975 *WhScrn 77*
Belson, Hortense Gold 1915- *AmSCAP 66, -80*
Belson, Jane *WomWMM B*
Belson, Jerry *HalFC 80, NewYTET*
Belt, Elmer 1893- *BiE&WWA, NotNAT*
Belt, James Preston, Jr. 1940- *AmSCAP 80*
Belt, Philip R 1927- *IntWWM 77, -80*
Belton, Paul D 1942- *ConAmC*
Beltrame *OxThe*
Beltran, Raymond 1892-1967 *WhScrn 77*
Beltri, Ricardo 1899-1962 *WhScrn 74, -77*
Belvin, Jesse 1933-1960 *RkOn[port]*
Belwin, Alma 1894?-1924 *NotNAT B, WhScrn 77*
Bely, Victor 1904- *Baker 78*
Belyayev, Mitrofan Petrovich 1836-1904 *NewGrD 80*
Belyayev, Viktor Mikhaylovich 1888-1968 *NewGrD 80*
Belza, Igor' Fyodorovich 1904- *Baker 78, NewGrD 80*
Beman, Nathan Sidney Smith 1785-1871 *BiDAmM*
Bemberg, Herman 1859-1931 *Baker 78*
Bemberg, Hermann-Emmanuel 1859-1931 *OxMus*
Bembo, Antonia 1670?- *Baker 78*
Bembo, Pietro 1470-1547 *NewGrD 80*
Bemetzrieder, Anton 1743?-1817? *Baker 78, NewGrD 80*
Bemis, Big Ben *AmSCAP 80*
Bemis, Connie *AmSCAP 66*
Ben, Paul 1895- *NewOrJ*
Ben-Ami, Jacob 1890- *BiE&WWA, NotNAT, WhThe*
Ben-Ari, Raikin 1904-1968 *WhScrn 74, -77, WhoHol B*
Ben-Asher *NewGrD 80*
Ben-David, Ehud 1939- *CnOxB*
Ben-Haim, Paul 1897- *Baker 78, CompSN[port], DcCM, IntWWM 80, NewGrD 80, OxMus*
Ben-Or, Nelly *IntWWM 80*
Ben-Schachar, Mordecai Enric 1926- *WhoOp 76*
Ben-Tovim, Atarah *IntWWM 80*
Ben-Veniste, Lorriane *WomWMM B*
Ben-Yohanan, Asher 1929- *IntWWM 80, NewGrD 80*
Ben Zwie, Yitzchak 1922- *IntWWM 80*
Benaceraf, Margot 1926- *WomWMM*
Benacerraf, Margot 1926- *DcFM*
Benaderet, Bea 1906-1968 *NotNAT B, WhScrn 74, -77, WhoHol B*
Benaglia, John Angelo 1938- *ConAmC, IntWWM 77, -80*
Benarby, Jim 1904?-1926? *NewOrJ*
Benas, Bertram Benjamin Baron *WhoMus 72*
Benassi, Memo 1886-1957 *WhScrn 74, -77, WhoHol B*
Benassi, Memo 1891- *Ent*
Benatzky, Ralph 1884-1957 *Baker 78, NewGrD 80, NotNAT B*
Benatzky, Ralph 1887-1957 *BiDAmM*
Benatzky, Ralph 1894-1957 *AmSCAP 66, -80*
Benaventa, Jacinto 1866-1954 *WhThe*
Benavente, Jacinte 1866-1954 *EncWT*
Benavente, Jacinto 1866-1954 *CnMD, Ent, McGEWD[port], ModWD, OxThe, PlP&P[port], REnWD*
Benavente Y Martinez, Jacinto 1866-1954 *NotNAT B*
Bencard, Johann Kaspar 1649-1720 *NewGrD 80*
Bence, John Michael 1942- *IntWWM 77, -80*
Bence, Margarethe 1930- *WhoOp 76*
Benchley, Nathaniel 1915- *BiE&WWA, NotNAT*
Benchley, Robert 1889-1945 *FilmEn, Film 2, FilmgC, ForYSC, HalFC 80, JoeFr[port], MovMk[port], NotNAT A, -B, OxFilm, OxThe, PlP&P, WhScrn 74, -77, WhThe, WhoHol B, WorEFlm*
Bencini *NewGrD 80*
Bencini, Antonio *NewGrD 80*
Bencini, Giuseppe *NewGrD 80*
Bencini, Pietro Paolo 1670?-1755 *NewGrD 80*
Bencriscutto, Frank Peter Anthony 1928- *AmSCAP 80, ConAmC, IntWWM 77*
Benda *NewGrD 80*
Benda, Anna Franziska 1728-1781 *NewGrD 80*
Benda, Frantisek 1709-1786 *NewGrD 80[port]*
Benda, Franz 1709-1786 *Baker 78, NewGrD 80[port]*
Benda, Friedrich 1745-1814 *Baker 78, NewGrD 80*
Benda, Friedrich Ernst 1749-1785 *NewGrD 80*
Benda, Friedrich Ludwig 1752-1792 *Baker 78, NewGrD 80*
Benda, Georg 1722-1795 *BnBkM 80, MusMk, NewEOp 71, NewGrD 80[port]*
Benda, Georg Anton 1722-1795 *Baker 78*
Benda, Georg Antonin 1722-1795 *OxMus*
Benda, Hans Georg 1686-1757 *NewGrD 80*
Benda, Jan Jiri 1686-1757 *NewGrD 80*
Benda, Jan Jiri 1713-1752 *NewGrD 80*
Benda, Jiri Antonin 1722-1795 *NewGrD 80[port]*
Benda, Johann 1713-1752 *NewGrD 80*
Benda, Johann Georg 1686-1757 *NewGrD 80*
Benda, Joseph 1724-1804 *NewGrD 80*
Benda, Juliane 1752-1783 *NewGrD 80*
Benda, Karl Hermann Heinrich 1748-1836 *Baker 78, NewGrD 80*
Benda, Maria Carolina 1742-1820 *NewGrD 80*
Benda, W T d1948 *Film 2*
Benda, Wladyslaw Theodor d1948 *NotNAT B*
Bendall, Ernest Alfred 1846-1924 *WhThe*
Bendel, Franz 1833-1874 *Baker 78, OxMus*
Bendeler, Johann Philipp 1654-1709 *Baker 78, NewGrD 80*
Bendeler, Salomon *NewGrD 80*
Bender, Anna Catherina 1919- *IntWWM 80*
Bender, Chief 1883-1954 *WhScrn 77*
Bender, D C 1919- *BluesWW*
Bender, Harry *Film 2*
Bender, Heinrich 1925- *WhoOp 76*
Bender, Jack E 1918- *BiE&WWA, NotNAT*
Bender, Jan O 1909- *CpmDNM 72, -77, -79, -80, ConAmC*
Bender, Joan *AmSCAP 66, -80*
Bender, Lucy *AmSCAP 80*
Bender, Milton d1964 *NotNAT B*
Bender, Mitchell Samuel 1934- *IntWWM 77*
Bender, Paul 1875-1947 *Baker 78, CmOp, NewEOp 71, NewGrD 80*
Bender, Russ 1910-1969 *WhoHrs 80[port]*
Bender, Russell 1910-1969 *WhScrn 74, -77, WhoHol B*
Bendheim, Sam, III 1935- *IntMPA 77, -75, -76, -78, -79, -80*
Bendick, Robert 1917- *IntMPA 77, -75, -76, -78, -79, -80, NewYTET*
Bendidio, Lucrezia 1547-1583? *NewGrD 80*
Bendinelli, Agostino 1550?-1598 *NewGrD 80*
Bendinelli, Agostino 1635-1703? *NewGrD 80*
Bendinelli, Cesare d1617 *NewGrD 80*
Bendinelli, Giacinto d1668 *OxThe*
Bendinello, Agostino 1550?-1598 *NewGrD 80*
Bending, Arthur 1923- *WhoMus 72*
Bendix, Doreen d1931 *NotNAT B*
Bendix, Lissen *Film 2*
Bendix, Max 1866-1945 *Baker 78, BiDAmM*
Bendix, Otto 1845-1904 *Baker 78*
Bendix, Victor Emanuel 1851-1926 *Baker 78, NewGrD 80, OxMus*
Bendix, William d1964 *MotPP, NewYTET, WhoHol B*
Bendix, William 1906-1964 *BiE&WWA, CmMov, FilmEn, FilmgC, ForYSC, HalFC 80, HolP 40[port], MovMk[port], NotNAT B, OxFilm, WhScrn 74, -77, WorEFlm*
Bendix, William 1907-1964 *CmMov*
Bendl, Karel 1838-1897 *NewGrD 80*
Bendl, Karl 1838-1897 *Baker 78*
Bendler, Salomon 1683-1724 *NewGrD 80*
Bendon, Bert d1964 *NotNAT B*
Bendow, Wilhelm *Film 2*
Bendusi, Francesco *NewGrD 80*
Benecken, Friedrich Burchard *NewGrD 80*
Benedek, Laslo 1907- *BiDFilm, -81, DcFM, FilmEn, FilmgC, HalFC 80, IntMPA 77, -75, -76, -78, -79, -80, MovMk[port], WorEFlm*
Benedek, Laszlo 1907- *OxFilm*
Benedette DiGiov Dito Benoit *NewGrD 80*
Benedetti *NewGrD 80*
Benedetti, Francesco Maria 1683-1746 *NewGrD 80*
Benedetti, Giacopone De' *NewGrD 80*
Benedetti, Gianfrancesco 1700?-1760? *NewGrD 80*
Benedetti, Piero 1585?-1649 *NewGrD 80*
Benedetti, Pietro 1585?-1649 *NewGrD 80*
Benedetto, Victor *ConMuA 80B*
Benedict Biscop 628?-690 *NewGrD 80*
Benedict Of Nursia 480?-547? *NewGrD 80*
Benedict, Saint *OxMus*
Benedict, Audrey Cecile 1901- *IntWWM 77, -80*
Benedict, Billy 1906- *ForYSC, WhoHol A*
Benedict, Billy 1917- *FilmgC, HalFC 80, HolCA[port]*
Benedict, Biscop *OxMus*
Benedict, Brooks d1968 *Film 2, WhScrn 77, WhoHol B*
Benedict, David 1923- *ConAmC*
Benedict, Dirk *IntMPA 77, -75, -76, -78, -79, -80, WhoHol A*
Benedict, Erastus Cornelius 1800-1880 *BiDAmM*
Benedict, Jean 1876-1943 *WhScrn 77*
Benedict, Sir Julius 1804-1885 *Baker 78, CmOp, MusMk, NewEOp 71, NewGrD 80, OxMus*
Benedict, Kingsley *Film 1, -2*
Benedict, Lew d1920 *NotNAT B*
Benedict, Paul 1938- *NotNAT*
Benedict, Richard 1916- *FilmgC, HalFC 80*
Benedict, Richard 1923- *FilmEn, ForYSC*
Benedict, William 1906- *FilmEn*
Benedict, William 1917- *Vers A[port]*
Benedictis DaPascarola, Giovanni Tommaso 1550?-1601? *NewGrD 80*
Benedictus A Sancto Josepho 1642?-1716 *NewGrD 80*
Benedictus De Opitiis *NewGrD 80*
Benedictus Ducis *NewGrD 80*
Benedictus, David 1938- *WhoThe 72, -77*
Benedictus, Jacobus De *NewGrD 80*
Benedictus Appenzeller *Baker 78*
Benedito Y Vives, Rafael 1885- *Baker 78*
Beneke, Tex 1914- *CmpEPM, EncJzS 70*
Beneken, Friedrich Burchard 1760-1818 *NewGrD 80*

Benell, John Thomas 1915-1940 *WhScrn 74, -77*
Benelli, Antonio Peregrino 1771-1830 *Baker 78, NewGrD 80*
Benelli, Sem 1875-1949 *NotNAT B, OxThe, PlP&P*
Benelli, Sem 1877-1949 *CnMD, McGEWD[port], ModWD, REnWD[port], WhThe*
Benelli, Ugo 1935- *CmOp, WhoMus 72, WhoOp 76*
Benenoit *NewGrD 80*
Benes, Jiri 1928- *IntWWM 80*
Benesch, Kurt 1926- *CroCD*
Benesh, Joan B 1920- *CnOxB*
Benesh, Rudolf 1916-1975 *CnOxB, DancEn 78, NewGrD 80*
Benestad, Finn 1929- *NewGrD 80*
Benet, Brenda *WhoHol A*
Benet, Harry d1948 *NotNAT B*
Benet, John *Baker 78, NewGrD 80*
Benet, Stephen Vincent 1898-1943 *NotNAT B*
Benett, John *NewGrD 80*
Benevente, Jacinto 1866-1954 *CnThe*
Beneventi, Giuseppe *NewGrD 80*
Benevento Di San Rafaele *NewGrD 80*
Benevic, Antonin *NewGrD 80*
Benevoli, Orazio 1605-1672 *Baker 78, NewGrD 80*
Benfante, Ignazio 1914- *AmSCAP 66, -80*
Benfield, Robert d1649 *OxThe*
Benfield, Warren A 1913- *IntWWM 77, -80*
Benford, Thomas P 1905- *EncJzS 70*
Benford, Tommy 1905- *EncJzS 70, WhoJazz 72*
Bengal, Richard *WhoHol A*
Benge, Elden 1904-1960 *NewGrD 80*
Benge, Wilson 1875-1955 *Film 2, WhScrn 74, -77, WhoHol B*
Benger, Sir Thomas *OxThe*
Bengraf, Joseph 1745?-1791 *NewGrD 80*
Bengtsson, Erling Blondal 1932- *IntWWM 80*
Bengtsson, Gustaf Adolf Tiburt 1886-1965 *Baker 78, NewGrD 80*
Bengtsson, Ingmar 1920- *IntWWM 77, -80, NewGrD 80*
Bengtsson, Sven-Age 1920- *IntWWM 77*
Benguerel, Xavier 1931- *Baker 78, DcCM, NewGrD 80*
BenHaim, Paul 1897- *IntWWM 77*
Benham, Arthur d1895 *NotNAT B*
Benham, Asahel 1757-1805? *NewGrD 80*
Benham, Asahel 1757-1815 *BiDAmM*
Benham, Dorothy 1910-1956 *Film 1, WhScrn 77*
Benham, Ethyle *Film 1*
Benham, Harry 1886-1969 *Film 1, -2, WhScrn 77*
Benham, Leland *Film 1*
Beni, Gimi *WhoOp 76*
Benic, Vladimir 1922- *IntWWM 77, -80, WhoMus 72*
Benigun, Johannes *NewGrD 80*
Beninate, Johnny *NewOrJ*
Beninate, Nick 1910?- *NewOrJ*
Benincori, Angelo Maria 1779-1821 *Baker 78, NewGrD 80*
Benini, Ferruccio 1854-1925 *NotNAT B, OxThe, WhThe*
Benito, Cosme Damian Jose De 1829-1888 *NewGrD 80*
Benitz, Albert 1904- *FilmEn*
Benjamin, Anton J *NewGrD 80*
Benjamin, Arthur 1893-1960 *Baker 78, CmOp, CompSN[port], DcCom&M 79, FilmgC, HalFC 80, MusMk, NewEOp 71, NewGrD 80, OxMus*
Benjamin, Bennie 1907- *AmSCAP 66, -80, CmpEPM, DrBlPA*
Benjamin, Burton *NewYTET*
Benjamin, C B d1951 *NotNAT B*
Benjamin, Joe 1919-1974 *EncJzS 70*
Benjamin, John 1868-1931 *NewGrD 80*
Benjamin, Joseph Rupert 1919-1974 *EncJzS 70*
Benjamin, Morris Edgar 1881- *WhThe*
Benjamin, Paul *BlkAmP*
Benjamin, Richard *WhoHol A*
Benjamin, Richard 1938- *FilmEn, FilmgC, HalFC 80, MovMk[port]*
Benjamin, Richard 1939- *ForYSC, IntMPA 77, -75, -76, -78, -79, -80*
Benjamin, Robert S 1909- *NewYTET*
Benjamin, S R Robert 1909- *IntMPA 80*
Benjamin, S Robert 1909- *IntMPA 77, -75, -76, -78, -79*
Benjamin, Thomas Edward 1940- *AmSCAP 80, CpmDNM 76, -79, -80, ConAmC, IntWWM 77, -80*
Benjamin, William E 1944- *Baker 78, ConAmC*
Benker, Heinz 1921- *IntWWM 77, -80*
Benko, Andras 1923- *NewGrD 80*
Benko, Andrei 1923- *NewGrD 80*
Benko, Daniel 1947- *IntWWM 77, -80*
Benko, Gregor 1944- *IntWWM 80*
Benline, Arthur J 1902- *BiE&WWA, NotNAT*
Benn, Johann 1590?-1660? *NewGrD 80*
Bennard, George 1873-1958 *AmSCAP 66, -80, Baker 78, ConAmC*
Bennati, Flavio 1935- *CnOxB*
Benner, James 1925- *IntWWM 77, -80*
Benner, Larry *PupTheA*
Benner, Lora 1907- *IntWWM 77, -80*
Benner, Lora Merle 1907- *AmSCAP 80*
Benner, Priscilla *Film 2*
Bennet, Isadora *BlkAmP*
Bennet, John *NewGrD 80, OxMus*
Bennet, John 1570?- *Baker 78*
Bennet, John 1575?- *BnBkM 80, NewGrD 80*
Bennet, Spencer Gordon 1893- *FilmEn, FilmgC, HalFC 80, IntMPA 77, -75, -76, -78, -79, -80, TwYS A*
Bennet, William 1936- *WhoMus 72*
Bennett, Al *ConMuA 80B*
Bennett, Alan 1934- *BiE&WWA, CnThe, ConDr 73, -77, Ent, NotNAT, WhoThe 72, -77*
Bennett, Alexander 1930- *CnOxB, DancEn 78*
Bennett, Alma 1889-1958 *FilmEn, HalFC 80*
Bennett, Alma 1904-1958 *Film 2, TwYS, WhScrn 77, WhoHol B*
Bennett, Arnold 1867-1931 *CnMD, EncWT, FilmgC, HalFC 80, McGEWD[port], ModWD, NewEOp 71, OxThe, WhThe*
Bennett, Barbara d1958 *NotNAT B, WhoHol B*
Bennett, Barbara 1902-1958 *Film 2, FilmgC, HalFC 80*
Bennett, Barbara 1906-1958 *FilmEn*
Bennett, Barbara 1911-1958 *WhScrn 74, -77*
Bennett, Belle 1891-1932 *FilmEn, Film 1, -2, FilmgC, ForYSC, HalFC 80, NotNAT B, TwYS, WhScrn 74, -77, WhoHol B*
Bennett, Bernard 1915- *AmSCAP 66, -80*
Bennett, Beulah Varner 1901- *IntWWM 77*
Bennett, Billie *Film 1, -2*
Bennett, Boyd *RkOn[port]*
Bennett, Bruce *IntMPA 77, -75, -76, -78, -79, -80*
Bennett, Bruce 1906- *WhoHol A*
Bennett, Bruce 1909- *FilmEn, FilmgC, ForYSC, HalFC 80, WhoHrs 80[port]*
Bennett, Bud *PupTheA*
Bennett, Charles *IntMPA 75, -76, -78, -79, -80*
Bennett, Charles d1925 *WhScrn 74, -77*
Bennett, Charles d1943 *WhoHol B*
Bennett, Charles 1891-1943 *Film 1, -2, WhScrn 74, -77*
Bennett, Charles 1899- *FilmEn, FilmgC, HalFC 80, IntMPA 77, WhThe, WorEFlm*
Bennett, Charles 1934- *CnOxB*
Bennett, Claudia *ConAmC*
Bennett, Compton 1900-1974 *FilmEn, FilmgC, HalFC 80, IlWWBF, WorEFlm*
Bennett, Constance d1964 *BiE&WWA, MotPP*
Bennett, Constance d1965 *WhoHol B, WomWMM*
Bennett, Constance 1904-1965 *FilmEn, FilmgC, HalFC 80, NotNAT B, ThFT[port]*
Bennett, Constance 1905-1965 *BiDFilm, -81, ForYSC[port], MovMk, NotNAT A, OxFilm, TwYS, WhScrn 74, -77, WorEFlm*
Bennett, Constance 1906-1965 *Film 2*
Bennett, David 1897- *AmSCAP 66, CpmDNM 80, ConAmC*
Bennett, David D 1892- *AmSCAP 80*
Bennett, Elsie Margaret 1919- *AmSCAP 66, -80*
Bennett, Enid d1969 *MotPP, WhoHol B*
Bennett, Enid 1894-1969 *Film 1, -2, TwYS*
Bennett, Enid 1895-1969 *FilmEn, ForYSC, HalFC 80, WhScrn 74, -77*
Bennett, Enoch Arnold 1867-1931 *NotNAT B*
Bennett, Faith *WhThe*
Bennett, Fran *WhoHol A*
Bennett, Fran 1935- *DrBlPA*
Bennett, Frank 1891-1957 *Film 1, WhScrn 77, WhoHol B*
Bennett, George J 1897- *AmSCAP 66, -80*
Bennett, George John d1879 *NotNAT B*
Bennett, George John 1863-1930 *Baker 78*
Bennett, Gertrude *Film 2*
Bennett, Harold Aubie 1891- *WhoMus 72*
Bennett, Harve 1930- *IntMPA 77, -75, -76, -78, -79, -80, NewYTET*
Bennett, Hugh *Film 1*
Bennett, Hywel 1944- *FilmEn, FilmgC, HalFC 80, IlWWBF, WhoHol A, WhoThe 72, -77*
Bennett, Irene *WhoMus 72*
Bennett, Isadora 1900- *CnOxB*
Bennett, J Moy *Film 2*
Bennett, Jill *WhoHol A*
Bennett, Jill 1930- *FilmgC, HalFC 80*
Bennett, Jill 1931- *CnThe, FilmEn, IlWWBF, IntMPA 77, -75, -76, -78, -79, -80, WhoThe 72, -77*
Bennett, Joan *BiE&WWA, MotPP*
Bennett, Joan 1910- *BiDFilm, -81, CmMov, FilmEn, FilmgC, ForYSC, HalFC 80, IntMPA 77, -75, -76, -78, -79, -80, MovMk[port], NotNAT A, OxFilm, ThFT[port], WhoHol A, WhoThe 72, -77, WorEFlm*
Bennett, Joan 1911- *Film 2*
Bennett, Joe 1889-1967 *WhScrn 74, -77*
Bennett, Joe And The Sparkletones *RkOn*
Bennett, John *NewGrD 80*
Bennett, John 1725?-1784 *NewGrD 80*
Bennett, John 1928- *HalFC 80*
Bennett, Johnstone 1870-1906 *NotNAT B*
Bennett, Joseph 1831-1911 *Baker 78, NewGrD 80, OxMus*
Bennett, Joseph 1869-1931 *Film 1, -2, TwYS, WhoHol B*
Bennett, Joseph 1896-1931 *WhScrn 74, -77*
Bennett, Mrs. Joseph d1943 *NotNAT B*
Bennett, Joyce W 1923- *AmSCAP 66, -80*
Bennett, Julia d1903 *NotNAT B*
Bennett, Kathryn *Film 2*
Bennett, Keith Michael 1942- *IntWWM 80*
Bennett, Lawrence Edward 1940- *IntWWM 77, -80*
Bennett, Lee 1911-1954 *CmpEPM, WhScrn 74, -77, WhoHol B*
Bennett, Leila *ThFT[port], WhThe*
Bennett, Leslie W *WhoMus 72*
Bennett, Lou 1926- *BiDAmM*
Bennett, Marjorie *ForYSC, WhoHol A*
Bennett, Martin F 1907- *IntMPA 75, -76*
Bennett, Max 1928- *AmSCAP 80, BiDAmM, CmpEPM, EncJzS 70*
Bennett, May *Film 2*
Bennett, Michael 1943- *CnOxB, ConDr 77D, EncMT, NotNAT, WhoThe 77*
Bennett, Mickey 1915-1950 *Film 2, WhScrn 74, -77, WhoHol B*
Bennett, Norman 1902- *AmSCAP 80*
Bennett, Peter 1917- *WhoThe 72, -77*
Bennett, Phil 1913- *AmSCAP 66, -80*
Bennett, Ray 1895-1957 *WhScrn 74, -77, WhoHol B*
Bennett, Red 1873-1941 *WhScrn 74, -77*
Bennett, Richard *WhoStg 1908*
Bennett, Richard 1872-1944 *FamA&A[port]*
Bennett, Richard 1873-1944 *EncWT, FilmEn, Film 1, -2, FilmgC, ForYSC, HalFC 80, NotNAT B, TwYS, Vers A[port], WhScrn 74, -77, WhThe, WhoHol B*
Bennett, Richard Rodney 1936- *Baker 78, BnBkM 80, CmOp, CompSN[port], CpmDNM 75, DcCom&M 79, DcCM, FilmEn, FilmgC, HalFC 80, IntWWM 77, -80, MusMk, NewEOp 71, NewGrD 80[port], OxMus, WhoMus 72*
Bennett, Robert Charles 1933- *ConAmC*
Bennett, Robert Joseph 1955- *AmSCAP 80*
Bennett, Robert Russell 1894- *AmSCAP 66,*

–80, Baker 78, BiDAmM, BiE&WWA, CompSN[port], CpmDNM 80, ConAmC, DcCM, IntWWM 77, –80, NewGrD 80, NotNAT, OxMus, WhoMus 72
Bennett, Roy C 1918- *AmSCAP 66, –80*
Bennett, Sam 1887-1937 *WhScrn 74, –77*
Bennett, Sanford Fillmore 1836-1898 *BiDAmM*
Bennett, Sharon Kay *WhoOp 76*
Bennett, Spencer Gordon 1893- *WhoHrs 80*
Bennett, Tommy d1943 *WhScrn 77*
Bennett, Tony 1926- *AmPS A, –B, BiDAmM, CmpEPM, EncJzS 70, RkOn[port], WhoHol A*
Bennett, Vivienne 1905- *WhoThe 72, –77*
Bennett, W I B 1936- *IntWWM 77, –80*
Bennett, Wilda 1894-1967 *CmpEPM, EncMT, WhScrn 74, –77, WhThe, WhoHol B*
Bennett, Wilda 1899- *Film 1*
Bennett, Wilhelmine 1933- *ConAmC, IntWWM 80*
Bennett, William Douglas Stilliard 1914- *WhoMus 72*
Bennett, Sir William Sterndale 1816-1875 *Baker 78, BnBkM 80, MusMk, NewGrD 80[port], OxMus*
Bennewitz, Antonin 1833-1926 *NewGrD 80*
Benning, Kathleen Agnes 1904- *WhoMus 72*
Benningsen, Lilian *WhoOp 76*
Bennion, Krista Louise 1961- *IntWWM 80*
Bennison, Andrew 1887-1942 *WhScrn 74, –77*
Bennison, Louis 1884-1929 *NotNAT B, WhScrn 74, –77, WhoHol B*
Benno, Alec Marc 1947- *AmSCAP 80*
Benny, Jack *AmPS B, IntMPA 75*
Benny, Jack 1894-1974 *BiDFilm, –81, Ent, FilmEn, Film 2, FilmgC, ForYSC, Funs[port], HalFC 80[port], JoeFr[port], MotPP, MovMk[port], NewYTET, OxFilm, PlP&P, WhScrn 77, WhoHol B, WorEFlm*
Benois, Alexander Nicolaievich 1870-1960 *CnOxB*
Benois, Alexander Nikolayevich 1870-1960 *NotNAT A, –B*
Benois, Alexandre 1870-1960 *EncWT, NewGrD 80, OxThe*
Benois, Alexandre Nikolayevich 1870-1960 *DancEn 78[port]*
Benois, Nadia *DancEn 78*
Benois, Nicola 1901- *EncWT, NewEOp 71, WhoOp 76*
Benoist, Andre 1879-1953 *Baker 78*
Benoist, Francois 1794-1878 *Baker 78, NewGrD 80, OxMus*
Benoist, Nicolaus *NewGrD 80*
Benoit *NewGrD 80, –80*
Benoit, Camille 1851-1923 *NewGrD 80*
Benoit, Jean-Christophe 1925- *IntWWM 77, –80*
Benoit, John *NewGrD 80, NewOrJ*
Benoit, Jon 1946- *CnOxB*
Benoit, Louis 1780?-1835? *BiDAmM*
Benoit, Marcelle 1921- *NewGrD 80*
Benoit, Peter 1834-1901 *Baker 78, BnBkM 80, NewGrD 80, OxMus*
Benoit, Pierre 1906- *CreCan 1*
Benoit, Real 1916- *CreCan 2*
Benoit, Real V 1945- *IntWWM 77*
Benoit, Victor *Film 1*
Benoit-Levy, Jean 1883-1959 *FilmgC, HalFC 80*
Benoit-Levy, Jean 1888-1959 *DcFM, FilmEn, IntMPA 77, –75, –76, –78, –79, MovMk[port], OxFilm, WorEFlm[port]*
Benoliel, Bernard John 1943- *CpmDNM 78, IntWWM 77, –80*
BenOr, Nelly *IntWWM 77*
Benotto Di Giovanni *NewGrD 80*
Benottus De Ferraria *NewGrD 80*
Benoy, Arthur William 1913- *WhoMus 72*
Benoyt, John *NewGrD 80*
Benrimo, J Harry 1874-1942 *WhThe*
Benrimo, Joseph Harry 1874-1942 *NotNAT B*
Benselin, Margaret Mary *IntWWM 77, –80, WhoMus 72*
Benser, J D *NewGrD 80*
Benserade, Isaac De 1612-1691 *CnOxB*
Benserade, Isaac De 1613-1691 *NewGrD 80, OxThe*
Benskin, Samuel 1922- *AmSCAP 66*
Bensley, Robert 1742-1817 *OxThe*
Bensley, Russ *NewYTET*
Benson, Lady d1946 *NotNAT B, WhThe*
Benson, Annette *Film 2*
Benson, Annette 189-?- *IlWWBF*
Benson, Arthur H 1919- *AmSCAP 66, –80*
Benson, Bruce 1951- *ConAmC*
Benson, Carol *WomWMM B*
Benson, Clifford George 1946- *IntWWM 77, –80*
Benson, Don *ConMuA 80B*
Benson, Ellsworth Harlow 1910-1964 *AmSCAP 80*
Benson, Frank 1858-1939 *EncWT*
Benson, Mrs. Frank Robert *Film 1*
Benson, Sir Frank Robert 1858-1939 *CnThe, Film 1, NotNAT A, –B, OxThe, PlP&P, WhThe*
Benson, George *ConMuA 80A[port], IlEncJ*
Benson, George 1911- *BiE&WWA, FilmgC, HalFC 80, NotNAT, WhoHol A, WhoThe 72, –77*
Benson, George 1942?- *DrBlPA*
Benson, George 1943- *BiDAmM, EncJzS 70, RkOn 2[port]*
Benson, Hamilton 1885- *NewOrJ[port]*
Benson, Hugh 1917- *IntMPA 77, –75, –76, –78, –79, –80*
Benson, Ivy *WhoMus 72*
Benson, Joan *IntWWM 77, –80*
Benson, John *WhoHol A*
Benson, John J 1915- *AmSCAP 66*
Benson, John T, Jr. 1904- *AmSCAP 80*
Benson, John William 1862-1926 *WhScrn 74, –77*
Benson, Juliette V P 1875-1962 *WhScrn 74, –77*
Benson, Leon *IntMPA 77, –75, –76, –78, –79, –80*
Benson, Lillian *WomWMM B*
Benson, Louis Fitzgerald 1855-1930 *BiDAmM*
Benson, Lucille *WhoHol A*
Benson, Martin 1918- *FilmgC, HalFC 80, WhoHol A*
Benson, May d1916 *WhScrn 77*
Benson, Nathaniel Anketell Michael 1903-1966 *CreCan 2*
Benson, Preston 1896- *WhoMus 72*
Benson, Robby *WhoHol A*
Benson, Robby 1956- *FilmEn, HalFC 80*
Benson, Robby 1957- *IntMPA 78, –79, –80*
Benson, Robin *WhoHol A*
Benson, Ruth 1873-1948 *NotNAT B, WhThe*
Benson, Sally 1897-1972 *BiE&WWA, NotNAT B, WomWMM*
Benson, Sally 1900-1972 *FilmEn*
Benson, Sandford 1914-1935 *WhScrn 74, –77*
Benson, Victor Sidney 1941- *IntWWM 77*
Benson, Warren 1924- *CpmDNM 78, –79, –80, ConAmC, NewGrD 80*
Benson, Warren Frank 1924- *AmSCAP 66, –80, IntWWM 77, –80*
Bensserade, Isaac De *DancEn 78*
Benstorp, Lars Gosta 1938- *IntWWM 77*
Bent, Buena d1957 *NotNAT B, WhThe*
Bent, Ian D 1938- *IntWWM 77, –80, NewGrD 80, WhoMus 72*
Bent, Margaret Hilda 1940- *NewGrD 80, WhoMus 72*
Bent, Marion 1879-1940 *NotNAT B, WhScrn 77*
Bent, Philip 1941-1966 *WhScrn 77*
Bent, Rosetta Case 1918- *AmSCAP 66*
Bentall, Brenda *WhoMus 72*
Bente, Matteo 1579?-1660? *NewGrD 80*
Benteen, Frederick D d1864 *BiDAmM*
Benter, Charles 1887-1964 *AmSCAP 66, –80, ConAmC A*
Benthall, Michael 1919-1974 *BiE&WWA, CnThe, NotNAT B, PlP&P, WhThe, WhoThe 72*
Bentham, Frederick *OxMus*
Bentham, Frederick 1911- *WhoThe 72, –77*
Bentham, Frederick 1916- *WhoThe 77*
Bentham, Josephine *BiE&WWA*
Benti, Matteo 1579?-1660? *NewGrD 80*
Bentine, Michael 1922- *FilmgC, HalFC 80*
Bentley, Arnold 1913- *IntWWM 77, –80, WhoMus 72*
Bentley, Beatrice *Film 2*
Bentley, Berenice Benson 1887-1971 *ConAmC*
Bentley, D B *Film 1*
Bentley, Doris d1944 *NotNAT B*
Bentley, Eric 1916- *AmSCAP 66, BiE&WWA, ConDr 77, EncWT, NotNAT, WhoThe 72*
Bentley, Gladys Alberta 1907-1960 *BluesWW[port]*
Bentley, Grendon 1877-1956 *Film 1, NotNAT B, WhThe*
Bentley, Irene d1940 *NotNAT B, WhThe, WhoHol B, WhoStg 1906, –1908*
Bentley, Irene 1904-1965 *WhScrn 77*
Bentley, John 1916- *FilmEn, FilmgC, ForYSC, HalFC 80, IlWWBF[port], IntMPA 77, –75, –76, –78, –79, –80, WhoHol A*
Bentley, Keith 1946- *IntWWM 77, –80*
Bentley, Lionel Reginald 1908- *IntWWM 77, –80, WhoMus 72*
Bentley, Muriel *CnOxB, DancEn 78*
Bentley, Richard d1782 *NotNAT B*
Bentley, Robert 1895-1958 *WhScrn 74, –77, WhoHol B*
Bentley, Spencer d1963 *NotNAT B*
Bentley, Thomas d195-? *IlWWBF*
Bentley, Thomas 1880?- *FilmgC, HalFC 80*
Bentley, Thomas 1880?-1950? *FilmEn*
Bentley, Walter d1927 *NotNAT B*
Bentley, Will 1873- *WhThe*
Bentoiu, Pascal 1927- *Baker 78, DcCM, IntWWM 77, –80, NewGrD 80*
Benton, Bessie d1917 *WhScrn 77*
Benton, Brook 1931- *AmPS A, DrBlPA, RkOn[port]*
Benton, Daniel Joseph 1945- *AmSCAP 80, CpmDNM 76*
Benton, Ernest Charles 1906- *WhoMus 72*
Benton, F R 1928- *IntWWM 77, –80*
Benton, Joseph *Baker 78*
Benton, Patricia 1907- *IntWWM 77, –80*
Benton, Pauline *PupTheA*
Benton, Rita 1920- *Baker 78, IntWWM 80, NewGrD 80*
Benton, Robert 1932- *ConDr 73, FilmEn*
Benton, Robert 1933- *ConDr 77A, IntMPA 77, –75, –76, –78, –79, –80*
Benton, Susanne *ForYSC*
Benton, Tom 1890?-1945? *NewOrJ*
Bentonelli, Joseph 1900-1975 *Baker 78*
Bentwich, Thelma *NewGrD 80*
Bentz, Cecil 1916- *ConAmC*
Bentz, Cecil William 1915- *AmSCAP 80*
Bentzon, Jogen 1871-1951 *OxMus*
Bentzon, Johan 1909- *IntWWM 77, –80*
Bentzon, Jorgen 1897-1951 *Baker 78, NewGrD 80*
Bentzon, Niels Viggo 1919- *Baker 78, DcCM, NewGrD 80, OxMus*
Benua, Alexandre Nikolayevich *NewGrD 80*
Benucci, Francesco 1745?-1824 *CmOp NewGrD 80*
Benussi, Femi 1948- *FilmAG WE*
Benvenisty, Yvonne *NewGrD 80*
Benvenuti, Arrigo 1925- *Baker 78*
Benvenuti, Giacomo 1885-1943 *Baker 78, NewGrD 80*
Benvenuti, Niccolino 1783-1867 *NewGrD 80*
Benvenuti, Nicola 1783-1867 *NewGrD 80*
Benvenuti, Tommaso 1838-1906 *Baker 78*
Beny, Roloff 1924- *CreCan 2*
Beny, Wilfred Roy *CreCan 2*
BenYohanan, Asher 1929- *IntWWM 77*
Benza, John Patrick 1947- *IntWWM 77*
Benzell, Mimi 1922-1970 *Baker 78*
Benzell, Mimi 1923-1970 *BiDAmM*
Benzell, Mimi 1924- *BiE&WWA*
Benzi, Roberto 1937- *IntWWM 77, –80, NewGrD 80, WhoMus 72, WhoOp 76*
Benzon, Otto 1856-1927 *NotNAT B, OxThe*
BenZwie, Yitzchak 1922- *IntWWM 77*
Beolco, Angelo 1502-1542 *CnThe, EncWT, NewGrD 80, OxThe, REnWD*
Ber, Alice *CreCan 1*
Beradino, John *WhoHol A*
Berain, Jean 1637-1711 *EncWT, Ent, NotNAT B, OxThe*
Berain, Jean 1638-1711 *DancEn 78*
Berain, Jean 1640-1711 *NewGrD 80*
Berain, Jean 1678-1726 *OxThe*
Berain, Jean, II 1678-1726 *DancEn 78*

Berain, Jean-Louis 1638-1711 *CnOxB*
Beranek, Leo L 1914- *NewGrD 80*
Beranek, Vratislav 1926- *IntWWM 77, -80*
Beranger, Andre 1895-1973 *FilmEn, Film 1, -2, ForYSC, TwYS, WhoHol B*
Beranger, Anne *CnOxB*
Beranger, Annie *Film 2*
Beranger, Clara d1956 *NotNAT B, WomWMM*
Beranger, George 1895-1973 *Film 1, TwYS A, WhScrn 77*
Berangere, Madame d1928 *WhScrn 74, -77*
Berard, Christian 1902-1949 *CnOxB, DancEn 78, DcFM, EncWT, Ent, NotNAT B, OxFilm, OxThe, WorEFlm*
Berard, Christian 1903-1949 *CnThe*
Berard, Jean-Antoine 1710-1772 *NewGrD 80*
Berardi, Angelo 1630-1694 *Baker 78*
Berardi, Angelo 1636?-1694 *NewGrD 80*
Berardini, Tony *ConMuA 80B*
Berardino, John 1918- *ForYSC*
Berat, Frederic 1800-1855 *Baker 78*
Berault, Charles 1798?-1836? *BiDAmM*
Berber, Ady 1915?- *WhoHrs 80[port]*
Berber, Felix 1871-1930 *Baker 78*
Berberian, Ara *IntWWM 77, -80, WhoOp 76*
Berberian, Catherine 1928- *NewGrD 80*
Berberian, Cathy *BnBkM 80, IntWWM 77, -80, WhoMus 72*
Berberian, Cathy 1925- *Baker 78*
Berberian, Cathy 1928- *NewGrD 80*
Berberian, Hratch 1927- *IntWWM 80*
Berbie, Jane 1934- *NewGrD 80, WhoOp 76*
Berbiguier, Antoine Tranquille 1782-1838 *NewGrD 80*
Berbiguier, Benoit-Tranquille 1782-1838 *Baker 78*
Berch, Jack 1907- *AmSCAP 66*
Berchem, Jachet d1580 *Baker 78*
Berchem, Jacquet De 1505?-1565? *NewGrD 80*
Berchenshaw, John *NewGrD 80*
Berckman, Evelyn 1900- *BiDAmM, ConAmC*
Bercovitch, J *WhoMus 72*
Bercutt, Max 1910- *IntMPA 77, -75, -76, -78, -79, -80*
Berczy, Gezo *Film 2*
Berd, Francoise *CreCan 1*
Berdahl, Arthur Clarence 1906- *IntWWM 77, -80*
Berdan, George *PupTheA*
Bereau, Jean-Sebastien 1934- *IntWWM 77, -80*
Beregan, Nicolo 1627-1713 *NewGrD 80*
Beregi, Oscar, Sr. 1875-1965 *Film 2, WhScrn 74, -77, WhoHol B*
Beregszaszy, Lajos 1817-1891 *NewGrD 80*
Berekétes, Petros d1720? *NewGrD 80*
Berel, Marianne *IntWWM 77*
Berenboick, Lester Willard 1921- *IntWWM 77, -80*
Berendes, M Benedicta 1927- *IntWWM 77, -80*
Berends, Hans Engel 1908- *CreCan 2*
Berendt, Rachel d1957 *NotNAT B, WhThe, WhoHol B*
Berengani, Nicolo 1627-1713 *NewGrD 80*
Berenger, F *NewGrD 80*
Berenger, Tom *IntMPA 80*
Berengerius De Orchem *NewGrD 80*
Berenguier De Palazol *NewGrD 80*
Berens, Fritz 1907- *IntWWM 77, -80*
Berens, Hermann 1826-1880 *Baker 78, NewGrD 80*
Berenson, Abe 1909- *IntMPA 75, -76*
Berenson, Marisa 1947- *HalFC 80, MovMk, WhoHol A*
Berenson, Marisa 1948- *FilmEn*
Berenstadt, Gaetano *NewGrD 80[port]*
Beresford, Miss *Film 2*
Beresford, Harry 1864-1944 *ForYSC, HalFC 80, WhScrn 74, -77, WhoHol B*
Beresford, Harry 1867-1944 *Film 2, NotNAT B, WhThe*
Beresford, Hugh *WhoOp 76*
Beresford, Marcus Walter DeLaPoer 1909- *WhoMus 72*
Beresford-Howe, Constance Elizabeth 1922- *CreCan 2*
Beretovac, Branka 1944- *WhoOp 76*
Beretta, Bonaventura *NewGrD 80*
Beretta, Caterina 1839-1911 *CnOxB*
Beretta, Francesco d1694 *NewGrD 80*
Beretta, Giovanni Battista 1819-1876 *Baker 78*
Beretta, Lodovico *NewGrD 80*
Berettari, Aurelio *NewGrD 80*
Beretti, Francesco d1694 *NewGrD 80*
Bereznicka-Pniak, Urszula 1941- *IntWWM 77, -80*
Berezovsky, Maxim Sozontovich 1745-1777 *NewGrD 80, OxMus*
Berezovsky, Maximus 1745-1777 *Baker 78*
Berezovsky, Nicolai 1900-1953 *NewGrD 80, OxMus*
Berezovsky, Nikolay 1900-1953 *NewGrD 80*
Berezowsky, Nicolai 1900-1953 *AmSCAP 66, -80, Baker 78, BiDAmM, ConAmC, DcCM, NewGrD 80*
Berezowsky, Nikolay 1900-1953 *NewGrD 80*
Berg, Adam d1610 *Baker 78, NewGrD 80*
Berg, Alban 1885-1935 *Baker 78, BnBkM 80[port], CmOp, CompSN[port], CnOxB, DcCom 77[port], DcCom&M 79, DcCM, DcTwCC, MusMk[port], NewEOp 71, NewGrD 80[port], OxMus*
Berg, Barry 1942- *NatPD[port]*
Berg, Bengt Johan Daniel 1935- *IntWWM 77, -80*
Berg, Christopher Babcock 1952- *IntWWM 77, -80*
Berg, Conrad Mathias 1785-1852 *Baker 78*
Berg, David 1892-1944 *AmSCAP 66, -80*
Berg, Dick *NewYTET*
Berg, Ellen d1906 *NotNAT B*
Berg, George 1730?-1770? *NewGrD 80*
Berg, Gertrude d1966 *NewYTET, WhoHol B*
Berg, Gertrude 1899-1966 *BiE&WWA, FilmgC, HalFC 80, JoeFr[port], NotNAT A, -B, WhThe*
Berg, Gertrude 1900-1966 *WhScrn 74, -77*
Berg, Gretchen *WomWMM*
Berg, Gunnar 1909- *Baker 78, DcCM, IntWWM 77, -80, NewGrD 80*
Berg, Harold C 1900-1973 *AmSCAP 66, -80*
Berg, Harriet *PupTheA*
Berg, Harvey M 1943- *IntMPA 79, -80*
Berg, Herbert *IntMPA 75, -76*
Berg, Jean Horton Lutz 1913- *AmSCAP 80*
Berg, Johann Von d1563 *Baker 78, NewGrD 80*
Berg, John *ConMuA 80B*
Berg, Josef 1927-1971 *Baker 78, DcCM, NewGrD 80*
Berg, Louis *IntMPA 75, -76*
Berg, Michael C d1964 *NotNAT B*
Berg, Nancy 1931- *BiE&WWA*
Berg, Natanael 1879-1957 *Baker 78, OxMus*
Berg, Natannael 1879-1957 *NewGrD 80*
Berg, Olav 1949- *IntWWM 80*
Berg, Reidun 1936- *IntWWM 80*
Berg, Richard 1949- *AmSCAP 80*
Berg, Sidney 1918- *ConAmC*
Berg, Stina 1869-1930 *WhScrn 77*
Bergaas, Mark 1951- *IntWWM 77, -80*
Bergaas, Mary Carol 1951- *IntWWM 77*
Bergamo, John J 1940- *ConAmC*
Bergamo, Petar 1930- *Baker 78, DcCM, IntWWM 77, -80, NewGrD 80*
Bergani, Nicolo *NewGrD 80*
Bergantine, Borney 1909-1954 *AmSCAP 66, -80*
Berganza, Teresa 1934- *CmOp, MusMk, MusSN[port], NewEOp 71*
Berganza, Teresa 1935- *IntWWM 77, -80, NewGrD 80[port], WhoOp 76*
Berganza, Teresa 1936- *BnBkM 80, WhoMus 72*
Bergdahl, Edith *AmSCAP 80*
Bergdahl, Victor 1878-1939 *HalFC 80*
Berge, Sigurd 1929- *Baker 78, IntWWM 80*
Bergel, John Graham 1902-1941 *NotNAT B, WhThe*
Bergell, Aaron 1943- *WhoOp 76*
Bergelson, David 1884-1952 *OxThe*
Bergen, Arthur *Film 2*
Bergen, Candice 1946- *FilmEn, FilmgC, ForYSC, HalFC 80, IntMPA 77, -75, -76, -78, -79, -80, MotPP, MovMk[port], WhoHol A*
Bergen, Edgar 1903-1978 *Ent[port], FilmEn, FilmgC, ForYSC, HalFC 80, JoeFr[port], MotPP, NewYTET, PupTheA, What 2[port], WhoHol A*
Bergen, Edgar And Charlie McCarthy *JoeFr[port]*
Bergen, Jerry *WhoHol A*
Bergen, Nella 1873-1919 *NotNAT B, WhThe, WhoStg 1906, -1908*
Bergen, Norman I 1945- *AmSCAP 80*
Bergen, Polly *IntMPA 75, -76, MotPP, WhoHol A*
Bergen, Polly 1919- *MovMk[port]*
Bergen, Polly 1929- *FilmgC, HalFC 80*
Bergen, Polly 1930- *BiE&WWA, FilmEn, ForYSC, IntMPA 77, -78, -79, -80, NotNAT*
Bergen, Stuart 1911- *NewOrJ SUP[port]*
Bergendorff, Frederick L 1944- *AmSCAP 80*
Bergenfeld, Nathan J 1935- *ConAmC*
Berger, Andreas 1584-1656 *NewGrD 80*
Berger, Arild 1941- *IntWWM 80*
Berger, Arthur 1912- *AmSCAP 80, Baker 78, BiDAmM, BnBkM 80, CpmDNM 79, -80, ConAmC, DcCM, MusMk, NewGrD 80, OxMus*
Berger, Augustin 1861-1945 *CnOxB*
Berger, Benjamin N 1896- *IntMPA 77, -75, -76, -78, -79, -80*
Berger, Bill 1928- *BiE&WWA*
Berger, Brenda Joyce 1943- *IntWWM 77*
Berger, Bror *Film 1*
Berger, Charly *Film 2*
Berger, David 1949- *ConAmC*
Berger, Erna 1900- *Baker 78, CmOp, NewEOp 71, NewGrD 80*
Berger, Francesco 1834-1933 *Baker 78, OxMus*
Berger, Georg Wilhelm 1929- *IntWWM 77, -80*
Berger, Grete *Film 1*
Berger, Helmut *IntMPA 75, -76, -78, -79, -80*
Berger, Helmut 1942?- *FilmgC, HalFC 80, IntMPA 77, WhoHol A*
Berger, Helmut 1944- *FilmAG WE, FilmEn*
Berger, Henning 1872- *WhThe*
Berger, Jean 1909- *AmSCAP 66, -80, Baker 78, CpmDNM 80, ConAmC, DcCM*
Berger, Karl Hans 1935- *EncJzS 70*
Berger, Ludwig 1777-1839 *NewGrD 80*
Berger, Ludwig 1892-1969 *FilmEn, FilmgC, HalFC 80, TwYS A*
Berger, Melvin H 1927- *IntWWM 77, -80*
Berger, Mitchel Van 1945- *IntWWM 77*
Berger, Nicole 1934-1967 *FilmgC, ForYSC, HalFC 80, WhScrn 74, -77, WhoHol B*
Berger, Nicole 1935-1967 *FilmEn*
Berger, Raimund 1917-1954 *CroCD*
Berger, Richard L *IntMPA 79, -80*
Berger, Roman 1930- *Baker 78, IntWWM 77, -80*
Berger, Rudolf 1874-1915 *Baker 78*
Berger, Senta 1941- *FilmEn, FilmgC, ForYSC, HalFC 80, MotPP, WhoHol A*
Berger, Senta 1943- *FilmAG WE*
Berger, Sidney L 1936- *NotNAT*
Berger, Theodor 1905- *Baker 78, DcCM, IntWWM 77, -80, NewGrD 80, WhoMus 72*
Berger, V Peterson 1867-1942 *OxMus*
Berger, Wilhelm 1861-1911 *Baker 78, NewGrD 80*
Berger, Wilhelm Georg 1929- *Baker 78, NewGrD 80*
Berger, William 1861-1911 *BiDAmM*
Berger-Tuna, Helmut 1942- *WhoOp 76*
Bergerac, Jacques 1927- *FilmEn, FilmgC, ForYSC, HalFC 80, IntMPA 77, -75, -76, -78, -79, -80, MotPP, WhoHol A*
Bergerac, Savinien DeCyrano De 1619-1655 *NotNAT B, OxThe*
Bergerat, Emile 1845- *WhThe*
Bergere, Ouida *FilmEn*
Bergere, Ouida d1974 *WhoHol B, WomWMM*
Bergere, Ouida 1866-1974 *Film 2*
Bergere, Ouida 1885-1974 *HalFC 80*
Bergere, Ramona 1902-1941 *WhScrn 74, -77*
Bergere, Roy 1899- *AmSCAP 66, -80*
Bergere, Valerie d1938 *WhoHol B, WhoStg 1906, -1908*
Bergere, Valerie 1867-1938 *NotNAT B*
Bergere, Valerie 1872-1938 *WhThe*
Bergere, Valerie 1875-1938 *WhScrn 74, -77*

Bergeret, Hugues *CreCan 1*
Bergeron, Suzanne 1930- *CreCan 1*
Bergersen, Baldwin 1914- *AmSCAP 66, -80, BiE&WWA, NotNAT*
Berggreen, Andreas Peter 1801-1880 *Baker 78, NewGrD 80*
Berggren, Thommy 1937- *FilmEn, FilmgC, HalFC 80, OxFilm*
Bergh, Arthur 1882-1962 *AmSCAP 66, -80, Baker 78, BiDAmM, ConAmC*
Bergh, Haakon Peder 1913-1959 *AmSCAP 80*
Bergh, Oivind 1909- *IntWWM 77, -80*
Bergh, Rudolph 1859-1924 *Baker 78*
Bergh, Sverre 1915- *IntWWM 77, -80*
Berghe, Frans VanDen *NewGrD 80*
Berghem, Jachet De *Baker 78*
Berghof, Herbert 1909- *BiE&WWA, FilmgC, HalFC 80, NotNAT, WhoHol A, WhoThe 72, -77*
Berghofer, Charles Curtis 1937- *BiDAmM*
Bergholm, Eija-Elina *WomWMM*
Bergholz, Lucas *NewGrD 80*
Berghout, Phia 1909- *NewGrD 80*
Berghout, Sophia 1909- *NewGrD 80*
Bergijk, Johannes Van *NewGrD 80*
Bergiron, Nicolas-Antoine 1690-1768 *NewGrD 80*
Bergiron DeBriou, Nicolas-Antoine 1690-1768 *NewGrD 80*
Berglas, David *MagIlD*
Berglund, Joel 1903- *CmOp, NewEOp 71, NewGrD 80*
Berglund, Paavo Allan Engelbert 1929- *IntWWM 77, -80, NewGrD 80, WhoMus 72*
Berglund, Sven 1881-1937 *DcFM, FilmEn*
Bergman, Alan 1925- *AmSCAP 66, -80*
Bergman, Barry *ConMuA 80B*
Bergman, Dewey 1900- *AmSCAP 66*
Bergman, Dewey 1902- *AmSCAP 80*
Bergman, Erik 1911- *Baker 78, DcCM, IntWWM 77, -80, NewGrD 80*
Bergman, Henry 1868-1946 *FilmEn*
Bergman, Henry 1870-1946 *Film 1, -2, FilmgC, HalFC 80, WhScrn 74, -77, WhoHol B*
Bergman, Henry 1870-1962 *NotNAT B*
Bergman, Henry Eric 1893-1958 *CreCan 2*
Bergman, Hjalmar Frederik 1883-1931 *CnMD, CnThe, EncWT, Ent, McGEWD[port], ModWD, NotNAT B, OxThe, REnWD*
Bergman, Ingmar 1918- *BiDFilm, -81, CnThe, ConLC 16, DcFM, EncWT, Ent, FilmEn, FilmgC, HalFC 80, IntMPA 77, -75, -76, -78, -79, -80, MovMk[port], OxFilm, PlP&P A[port], WhoHrs 80, WorEFlm*
Bergman, Ingmar 1919- *OxThe*
Bergman, Ingrid *MotPP, PlP&P[port], WhoHol A*
Bergman, Ingrid 1915- *BiDFilm, -81, BiE&WWA, CmMov, FilmEn, FilmgC, HalFC 80, MovMk[port], NotNAT, OxFilm, ThFT[port], WhoThe 72, -77, WorEFlm[port]*
Bergman, Ingrid 1916- *NotNAT A*
Bergman, Ingrid 1917- *ForYSC, IntMPA 77, -75, -76, -78, -79, -80*
Bergman, Janet Louise Marx 1920- *IntWWM 77, -80*
Bergman, Joel *WhoHol A*
Bergman, Jules *NewYTET*
Bergman, Lloyd Michel 1943- *AmSCAP 80*
Bergman, Marilyn Keith 1929- *AmSCAP 66, -80*
Bergman, Maurice A *IntMPA 77, -75, -76, -78*
Bergman, Nancy 1927- *AmSCAP 80*
Bergmann, Carl 1821-1876 *Baker 78, NewEOp 71, NewGrD 80*
Bergmann, Karl 1821-1876 *BiDAmM*
Bergmann, Ted 1920- *IntMPA 77, -75, -76, -78, -79, -80, NewYTET*
Bergmans, Paul Jean Etienne Charles 1868-1935 *Baker 78, NewGrD 80*
Bergna, Antonio *NewGrD 80*
Bergner, Elisabeth *What 1[port]*
Bergner, Elisabeth 1897- *EncWT, FilmAG WE*
Bergner, Elisabeth 1898- *FilmgC, HalFC 80*
Bergner, Elisabeth 1900- *BiE&WWA, Ent, FilmEn, MovMk[port], NotNAT, OxFilm, ThFT[port], WhoHol A, WhoThe 72, -77, WorEFlm*
Bergner, Elizabeth *MotPP*
Bergner, Elizabeth 1900- *Film 2, ForYSC*
Bergner, Wilhelm 1837-1907 *Baker 78*
Bergonzi *NewGrD 80*
Bergonzi, Carlo 1683?-1747 *Baker 78, NewGrD 80*
Bergonzi, Carlo 1924- *Baker 78, CmOp, IntWWM 77, -80, MusSN[port], NewEOp 71, NewGrD 80, WhoMus 72, WhoOp 76*
Bergonzi, Michel Angelo 1722?-1758? *NewGrD 80*
Bergonzi, Nicola 1746?-1796? *NewGrD 80*
Bergopzoomer, Johann Baptist 1742-1804 *OxThe*
Bergquist, Peter 1930- *IntWWM 80*
Bergsagel, John Dagfinn 1928- *IntWWM 80, NewGrD 80*
Bergsma, Deanne 1941- *CnOxB, DancEn 78*
Bergsma, William 1921- *AmSCAP 66, -80, Baker 78, BiDAmM, CompSN[port], CpmDNM 77, -79, -80, ConAmC, DcCM, NewGrD 80, OxMus*
Bergsohn, Michal 1820-1898 *NewGrD 80*
Bergson, Michael 1820-1898 *Baker 78*
Bergson, Michal 1820-1898 *NewGrD 80*
Bergstrom, Georgeina Ekstrom 1914- *IntWWM 77*
Bergstrom, Harry Lennart Yrjo 1910- *IntWWM 77*
Bergstrom, Hilda *WhThe*
Bergstrom, Hjalmar 1868-1914 *NotNAT B, OxThe*
Bergstrom-Nielsen, Carl 1952- *IntWWM 80*
Bergt, August 1771-1837 *NewGrD 80*
Bergt, Christian Gottlob August 1771-1837 *Baker 78*
Bergwald, Victor Von *NewGrD 80*
Berhard, Raymond *Film 2*
Beri, Ben d1963 *NotNAT B*
Beria, Giovanni Battista 1610?-1671? *NewGrD 80*
Berigan, Bunny d1942 *BgBands 74[port]*
Berigan, Bunny 1907-1942 *IlEncJ*
Berigan, Bunny 1908-1942 *CmpEPM, NewGrD 80, WhoJazz 72*
Berigan, Roland Bernard 1908-1942 *BiDAmM, NewGrD 80*
Beringen *NewGrD 80*
Beringen, Godefroy *NewGrD 80*
Beringen, Marcellin d1556 *NewGrD 80*
Beringer, Esme 1875-1972 *OxThe, WhThe*
Beringer, Maternus 1580-1632? *NewGrD 80*
Beringer, Oscar 1844-1922 *Baker 78, NewGrD 80, OxMus*
Beringer, Mrs. Oscar 1856-1936 *NotNAT B, WhThe*
Beringer, Vera 1879-1964 *NotNAT B, OxThe, WhThe*
Berini, Bianca *WhoOp 76*
Berio, Luciano 1923- *CompSN[port]*
Berio, Luciano 1925- *Baker 78, BnBkM 80, CpmDNM 72, CnOxB, DcCom 77, DcCom&M 79, DcCM, IntWWM 77, -80, MusMk[port], NewGrD 80[port], OxMus, WhoMus 72*
Beriosoff, Nicholas 1906- *DancEn 78*
Beriosova, Svetlana 1932- *CnOxB, DancEn 78[port]*
Beriot, Charles-Auguste De 1802-1870 *Baker 78, NewGrD 80, OxMus*
Beriot, Charles De 1802-1870 *BnBkM 80*
Beriot, Charles-Wilfrid De 1833-1914 *NewGrD 80, OxMus*
Beriot, Charles-Wilfride De 1833-1914 *Baker 78*
Beriozoff, Nicholas 1906- *CnOxB*
Beristain, Leopoldo 1883-1948 *WhScrn 74, -77, WhoHol B*
Beristain, Luis 1918-1962 *WhScrn 74, -77, WhoHol B*
Berk, Betty Jean Thomas 1915- *IntWWM 77, -80*
Berk, Dick 1939- *EncJzS 70*
Berk, Ernest 1909- *IntWWM 77, -80*
Berk, Fred 1911- *CnOxB, DancEn 78*
Berk, Lawrence 1908- *EncJzS 70*
Berk, Lew 1888- *AmSCAP 66, -80*
Berk, Maynard H 1913- *ConAmC*
Berk, Morty 1900-1955 *AmSCAP 66, -80*
Berk, Richard Alan 1939- *EncJzS 70*
Berk, Sara 1898-1975 *WhScrn 77, WhoHol C*
Berke, Miriam Levin *PupTheA*
Berke, William 1903-1958 *FilmEn*
Berke, William 1904-1958 *FilmgC, HalFC 80*
Berkeley, Arthur 1896-1962 *NotNAT B, WhScrn 74, -77, WhoHol B*
Berkeley, Ballard 1904- *FilmgC, HalFC 80, WhThe, WhoHol A*
Berkeley, Busby 1895-1976 *BiDFilm, -81, BiE&WWA, CmMov, CnOxB, DcFM, EncMT, Ent, FilmEn, FilmgC, HalFC 80, IntMPA 75, -76, MovMk[port], NotNAT A, OxFilm, What 3[port], WhoHol C, WhoThe 72, -77, WorEFlm*
Berkeley, Gertrude d1946 *Film 1, NotNAT B, WhoHol B, WhoStg 1908*
Berkeley, Sir Lennox 1903- *Baker 78, CmOp, CpmDNM 78, -79, -80, DcCom&M 79, DcCM, IntWWM 77, -80, NewEOp 71, NewGrD 80[port], OxMus, WhoMus 72*
Berkeley, Michael Fitzhardinge 1948- *IntWWM 80*
Berkeley, Reginald 1882-1936 *WhScrn 74, -77*
Berkeley, Reginald Cheyne 1890-1935 *NotNAT B, WhThe*
Berkeley, Wilma *WhThe*
Berkenhead, John L *Baker 78*
Berkenstock, James Turner 1942- *IntWWM 80*
Berkenstock, Johann Adam *NewGrD 80*
Berkes, John Patrick 1897-1951 *WhScrn 74, -77, WhoHol B*
Berkey, Ralph 1912- *BiE&WWA*
Berkov, Viktor Osipovich 1907- *NewGrD 80*
Berkowitz, Leonard *ConAmC*
Berkowitz, Ralph 1910- *Baker 78, ConAmC*
Berkowitz, Saul 1922- *ConAmC*
Berkowitz, Sol 1922- *AmSCAP 66, -80, BiE&WWA, CpmDNM 78, NotNAT*
Berkowsky, Paul B 1932- *BiE&WWA*
Berl, Christine *CpmDNM 80*
Berlanga, Luis Garcia 1921- *DcFM, FilmEn, FilmgC, HalFC 80, OxFilm, WorEFlm*
Berlatus *NewGrD 80*
Berle, Milton 1908- *AmPS B, AmSCAP 66, -80, BiDAmM, BiE&WWA, CmpEPM, EncMT, Ent, FilmEn, Film 1, -2, FilmgC, ForYSC, Funs[port], HalFC 80, IntMPA 77, -75, -76, -78, -79, -80, JoeFr[port], MovMk[port], NewYTET, NotNAT, -A, PlP&P, TwYS, WhoHol A, WhoThe 72, -77*
Berle, Sandra 1877-1954 *WhScrn 74, -77*
Berleant, Arnold 1932- *IntWWM 77, -80*
Berlein, Annie Mack d1935 *NotNAT B*
Berlengerius De Oreim *NewGrD 80*
Berley, Andre *Film 2*
Berlijn, Anton 1817-1870 *Baker 78, NewGrD 80*
Berlijn, Aron Wolf 1817-1870 *NewGrD 80*
Berlin, David 1943- *AmSCAP 80*
Berlin, David N 1943- *ConAmC*
Berlin, Edward Alan 1936- *IntWWM 80*
Berlin, Irving 1888- *AmPS, AmSCAP 66, -80, Baker 78, BestMus[port], BiDAmM, BiE&WWA, CmMov, CmpEPM, ConAmC, DcFM, EncMT, EncWT, Ent[port], FilmEn, FilmgC, HalFC 80, IntMPA 77, -75, -76, -78, -79, -80, IntWWM 77, -80, McGEWD, MnPM[port], MusMk, NewCBMT, NewGrD 80, NotNAT, -A, OxFilm, OxMus, PlP&P[port], PopAmC[port], PopAmC SUP, Sw&Ld C, WhoMus 72, WhoThe 72, -77*
Berlin, Jeannie 1949- *FilmEn, HalFC 80, WhoHol A, WomWMM*
Berlin, Johan Daniel 1714-1787 *NewGrD 80*
Berlin, Joyce *NatPD[port]*
Berlin, Richard Merrill 1947- *IntWWM 77, -80*
Berline, Byron Douglas 1944- *AmSCAP 80*
Berliner, Martin 1896-1966 *WhScrn 74, -77, WhoHol B*
Berlinger, Milton 1908- *AmSCAP 80*
Berlinger, Warren 1937- *BiE&WWA, FilmEn, FilmgC, ForYSC, HalFC 80, IntMPA 77, -75, -76, -78, -79, -80, MotPP, NotNAT, WhoHol A, WhoThe 72, -77*
Berlinski, Herman 1910- *AmSCAP 66, -80, Baker 78, ConAmC, DcCM*
Berlinski, Jacques 1913- *Baker 78*

Berlioz, Gabriel Pierre 1916- *Baker 78*
Berlioz, Hector 1803-1869 *Baker 78, BnBkM 80[port], CmOp, CmpBCM, DancEn 78, DcCom 77[port], DcCom&M 79, GrComp[port], MusMk[port], NewEOp 71, NewGrD 80[port], OxMus*
Berlioz, Louis Hector 1803-1869 *CnOxB*
Berljawsky, Joseph 1911- *IntWWM 77, -80*
Berlyn, Alfred 1860-1936 *NotNAT B, WhThe*
Berlyn, Ivan d1934 *Film 2, NotNAT B*
Berman, A L 1890- *BiE&WWA*
Berman, Al *ConMuA 80B*
Berman, Art Harry 1902-1959 *AmSCAP 66, -80*
Berman, Bart 1938- *IntWWM 77, -80*
Berman, Charles *IntMPA 77, -75, -76, -78, -79, -80*
Berman, Edward 1911- *AmSCAP 66, -80*
Berman, Eugene 1899-1972 *CnOxB, DancEn 78, EncWT, NewGrD 80*
Berman, Henry 1914- *IntMPA 75*
Berman, Karel 1919- *WhoOp 76*
Berman, Lazar 1930- *Baker 78, BnBkM 80, MusSN[port], NewGrD 80*
Berman, Mark *NatPD[port]*
Berman, Monty *IntMPA 75, -76, -78, -79, -80*
Berman, Monty 1913- *FilmgC, HalFC 80, IntMPA 77*
Berman, Monty M 1912- *IntMPA 77, -75, -76, -78, -79, -80*
Berman, Norman L 1949- *AmSCAP 80*
Berman, Pandro S 1905- *FilmEn, FilmgC, HalFC 80, IntMPA 77, -75, -76, -78, -79, -80, WorEFlm*
Berman, Saul 1924-1947 *BiDAmM*
Berman, Shelley 1920- *ForYSC*
Berman, Shelley 1924- *JoeFr[port]*
Berman, Shelley 1926- *BiE&WWA, FilmgC, HalFC 80, WhoHol A*
Berman, Shelly 1926- *NotNAT*
Berman, Sonny 1924-1947 *CmpEPM*
Bermange, Barry 1933- *ConDr 73, -77*
Bermann, Jeremias *NewGrD 80*
Bermel, Albert 1927- *ConAmTC, NatPD[port]*
Bermont, George J *AmSCAP 80*
Bermont, Georges 1901- *AmSCAP 66*
Bermudes, Pedro *NewGrD 80*
Bermudez, Pedro *NewGrD 80*
Bermudez Silva, Jesus 1884-1969 *NewGrD 80*
Bermudo, Juan 1510?-1555? *Baker 78*
Bermudo, Juan 1510?-1565? *NewGrD 80*
Bern, Julian 1911- *IntWWM 77, -80*
Bern, Paul 1889-1932 *FilmEn, FilmgC, HalFC 80, WhScrn 74, -77*
Bern, Paul 1889-1939 *TwYS A*
Berna, Elsa *Film 1*
Bernabei *NewGrD 80*
Bernabei, Ercole 1622-1687 *Baker 78, NewGrD 80*
Bernabei, Giuseppe Antonio 1649?-1732 *Baker 78, NewGrD 80*
Bernabei, Vincenzo 1660-1732? *NewGrD 80*
Bernac, Pierre 1899- *Baker 78, IntWWM 77, MusSN, NewGrD 80, WhoMus 72*
Bernacchi, Antonio Maria 1685-1756 *Baker 78, NewGrD 80[port]*
Bernadelli, Fortunato *CnOxB*
Bernai, Afonso Perea d1593 *NewGrD 80*
Bernal Goncalez, Jose *NewGrD 80*
Bernal-Jimenez, Miguel 1910-1956 *DcCM, NewGrD 80*
Bernanos, Georges 1888-1948 *CnMD, EncWT, ModWD*
Bernaola, Carmelo 1929- *NewGrD 80*
Bernard *NewGrD 80*
Bernard Of Clairvaux 1090-1153 *NewGrD 80*
Bernard, Al 1888-1949 *AmSCAP 66, -80, CmpEPM, WhScrn 74, -77*
Bernard, Annabelle *WhoOp 76*
Bernard, Anthony 1891-1963 *NewGrD 80*
Bernard, Armand *Film 2*
Bernard, Barney 1877-1924 *Film 1, -2, NotNAT B, WhScrn 74, -77, WhThe, WhoHol B*
Bernard, Barry *WhoHol A*
Bernard, Caroline Richings 1827-1882 *BiDAmM*
Bernard, Charles 1921- *IntMPA 77, -75, -76, -78, -79*
Bernard, Dick d1925 *NotNAT B, WhoHol B*
Bernard, Dorothy 1890-1955 *Film 1, -2, MotPP, NotNAT B, TwYS, WhScrn 74, -77, WhoHol B*
Bernard, Ed 1939- *DrBlPA*
Bernard, Emery *NewGrD 80*
Bernard, Emile 1843-1902 *NewGrD 80*
Bernard, Etienne 1569?-1600 *NewGrD 80*
Bernard, Felix 1897-1944 *AmSCAP 66, -80*
Bernard, Guy 1907- *DcFM*
Bernard, Harry 1878-1940 *Film 1, -2, WhScrn 74, -77, WhoHol B*
Bernard, Harry 1898- *CreCan 2*
Bernard, Ivor 1887-1953 *WhScrn 74, -77*
Bernard, James Michael 1925- *FilmgC, HalFC 80, WhoHrs 80, WhoMus 72*
Bernard, Jean Emile Auguste 1843-1902 *Baker 78*
Bernard, Jean-Jacques 1888-1972 *CnMD, CnThe, EncWT, McGEWD[port], ModWD, OxThe, WhThe*
Bernard, John 1756-1828 *FamA&A[port], OxThe*
Bernard, Josephine *Film 2*
Bernard, Judd 1927- *IntMPA 77, -75, -76, -78, -79, -80*
Bernard, Kenneth 1930- *ConDr 73, -77, NatPD, NotNAT*
Bernard, Kitty d1962 *NotNAT B*
Bernard, Leon d1935 *NotNAT B*
Bernard, Lester *Film 2*
Bernard, Lois 1898-1945 *WhScrn 74, -77*
Bernard, Marvin A 1934- *IntMPA 77, -75, -76, -78, -79, -80*
Bernard, Matvey Ivanovich 1794-1871 *NewGrD 80*
Bernard, Michelle 1928- *IntWWM 80*
Bernard, Moritz 1794-1871 *Baker 78*
Bernard, Paul d1958 *WhScrn 74, -77, WhoHol B*
Bernard, Paul 1827-1879 *Baker 78*
Bernard, Peter 1888-1960 *WhScrn 74, -77*
Bernard, Raymond 1891- *DcFM*
Bernard, Raymond 1891-1977 *FilmEn*
Bernard, Robert 1900-1971 *Baker 78, NewGrD 80*
Bernard, Rod 1940- *RkOn*
Bernard, Sam *CmpEPM*
Bernard, Sam 1863-1927 *Film 1, NotNAT B, WhScrn 74, -77, WhThe, WhoHol B, WhoStg 1906, -1908*
Bernard, Sam 1864- *ForYSC*
Bernard, Sam 1889-1950 *NotNAT B, WhScrn 74, -77, WhoHol B*
Bernard, Sophie *AmPS B*
Bernard, Stevan 1569?-1600 *NewGrD 80*
Bernard, Sylvia *Film 2*
Bernard, Tristan 1866-1947 *CnMD, EncWT, McGEWD[port], ModWD, NotNAT B, OxThe, WhThe*
Bernard, Valere *OxMus*
Bernard, W Bayle d1875 *NotNAT B*
Bernard, William Ditchburn 1904- *WhoMus 72*
Bernard-Aubert, Claude 1930- *DcFM, FilmEn, WorEFlm*
Bernard-Deschamps, Dominique 1892- *DcFM*
Bernard-Luc, Jean 1909- *McGEWD*
Bernardel *NewGrD 80*
Bernardel, Auguste Sebastien Philippe 1798-1870 *NewGrD 80*
Bernardel, Ernest Auguste 1826-1899 *NewGrD 80*
Bernardel, Gustave Adolphe 1832-1904 *NewGrD 80*
Bernardi, Bartolomeo 1660?-1732 *Baker 78, NewGrD 80*
Bernardi, Berel 1872?-1932 *NotNAT A*
Bernardi, Enrico 1838-1900 *Baker 78*
Bernardi, Francesco *Baker 78, NewGrD 80*
Bernardi, Herschel 1923- *FilmEn, FilmgC, ForYSC, NotNAT, WhoHol A*
Bernardi, Hershel 1923- *HalFC 80*
Bernardi, Mario 1930- *BiDAmM, CreCan 1, IntWWM 77, -80, NewGrD 80, WhoMus 72, WhoOp 76*
Bernardi, Nerio 1899-1971 *Film 2, WhScrn 77*
Bernardi, Stefano 1585?-1636 *NewGrD 80*
Bernardi, Stefanus *NewGrD 80*
Bernardi, Steffano 1575?-1636 *Baker 78*
Bernardi, Steffano 1585?-1636 *NewGrD 80*
Bernardic, Drago 1912- *WhoMus 72*
Bernardini, Marcello 1740?-1799? *NewGrD 80*
Bernardo, Estevan *NewGrD 80*
Bernardo, Jose Paul 1938- *ConAmC*
Bernardo, Jose Raul 1938- *IntWWM 77, -80*
Bernardo, Mane *PupTheA*
Bernardon, Joseph Felix Von *NewGrD 80*
Bernardus *NewGrD 80*
Bernart De Ventadorn 1130?-1190? *NewGrD 80*
Bernasconi, Alessio Boileau *NewGrD 80*
Bernasconi, Andrea 1706?-1784 *Baker 78, NewGrD 80*
Bernasconi, Antonia 1741?-1803? *NewGrD 80*
Bernat, Robert 1931- *ConAmC*
Bernat-Veri, Jorge Bosch *NewGrD 80*
Bernat-Veri, Jorge De 1737-1800 *NewGrD 80*
Bernathova, Eva 1932- *IntWWM 77, -80, WhoMus 72*
Bernauer, Rudolph d1953 *NotNAT B*
Bernds, Edward 1905- *FilmgC, HalFC 80*
Bernds, Edward 1911- *FilmEn, WhoHrs 80*
Berndt, Julia Helen 1905- *AmSCAP 66, -80*
Bernede, Arthur *WhThe*
Berneker, Constanz 1844-1906 *Baker 78, NewGrD 80*
Bernelinus *NewGrD 80*
Berner, Alfred 1910- *NewGrD 80*
Berner, Friedrich Wilhelm 1780-1827 *Baker 78, NewGrD 80*
Berner, Horst 1923- *IntWWM 77*
Berners, Lord 1883-1950 *Baker 78, CnOxB, DancEn 78, MusMk[port], NewGrD 80*
Berners, Gerald Hugh Tyrwhitt-Wilson 1883-1950 *OxMus*
Bernes, Mark 1912-1969 *WhScrn 74, -77, WhoHol B*
Bernet, Dietfried 1940- *WhoOp 76*
Bernet Kempers, Karel Philippus 1897-1974 *Baker 78, NewGrD 80*
Berney, Beryl *AmSCAP 66, -80*
Berney, William d1961 *NotNAT B*
Bernger Von Horheim *NewGrD 80*
Bernhagen, Roland F 1933- *NotNAT*
Bernhard DerDeutsche d1459 *Baker 78*
Bernhard, Christoph 1628-1692 *Baker 78, NewGrD 80*
Bernhard, Frank James 1937- *AmSCAP 80*
Bernhard, Harvey 1924- *IntMPA 79, -80*
Bernhard, Thomas 1931- *CroCD*
Bernhardt, Clyde Edric Barron 1905- *BluesWW[port]*
Bernhardt, Clyde Edric Barron 1908- *WhoJazz 72*
Bernhardt, Curtis 1899- *BiDFilm, -81, CmMov, DcFM, FilmEn, Film 2, FilmgC, HalFC 80, IntMPA 77, -75, -76, -78, -79, -80, MovMk[port], WorEFlm*
Bernhardt, Lewis F 1780?- *BiDAmM*
Bernhardt, Maurice d1928 *NotNAT B*
Bernhardt, Melvin *WhoThe 72, -77*
Bernhardt, Sarah 1844-1923 *EncWT, Ent[port], FamA&A[port], FilmEn, FilmgC, HalFC 80, NotNAT A, -B, OxFilm, PlP&P[port], TwYS, WhScrn 74, -77, WhoStg 1906, -1908, WorEFlm*
Bernhardt, Sarah 1845-1923 *CnThe, Film 1, -2, OxThe, WhThe, WhoHol B*
Bernhardt, Stephen 1947- *ConAmC*
Bernhart, Martha Ann 1922- *AmSCAP 80*
Bernhart, Milt 1926- *CmpEPM*
Bernheimer, Martin 1936- *Baker 78, IntWWM 77, -80*
Bernie, Ben 1891-1943 *AmPS B, AmSCAP 66, -80, BgBands 74[port], BiDAmM, CmpEPM, HalFC 80, NotNAT B, WhScrn 74, -77, WhoHol B*
Bernie, Dick d1971 *WhoHol B*
Bernier, Buddy 1910- *AmSCAP 66, -80*
Bernier, Francoys J M 1927- *CreCan 1, IntWWM 77, -80*
Bernier, Nicolas 1664-1734 *Baker 78*
Bernier, Nicolas 1665-1734 *NewGrD 80*
Bernier, Rene *OxMus*
Bernier, Rene 1905- *Baker 78, DcCM, IntWWM 80, NewGrD 80*
Bernier, Rene 1906- *WhoMus 72*
Bernikoff, Morris 1920- *AmSCAP 80*
Bernini, Gian Lorenzo 1598-1680 *Ent*
Bernini, Giovanni Lorenzo 1598-1680 *EncWT, OxThe*
Bernis, Blanche *Film 2*

Bernivici, Count 1884-1966 *WhScrn 74, -77*
Berno Augiensis d1048 *NewGrD 80*
Berno Of Reichenau d1048 *NewGrD 80*
Berno VonReichenau 970?-1048 *Baker 78*
Bernoulli, Daniel 1700-1782 *NewGrD 80*
Bernoulli, Eduard 1867-1927 *Baker 78, NewGrD 80*
Berns, Ilene *ConMuA 80B*
Berns, Larry 1908- *AmSCAP 66, -80*
Berns, Samuel D *IntMPA 77, -75, -76*
Berns, Seymour *IntMPA 77, -75, -76, -78, -79, -80*
Berns, William A *IntMPA 75*
Bernsdorff-Engelbrecht, Christiane H 1923- *IntWWM 77, -80*
Bernstein, Baron 1899- *IntMPA 77, -75, -76, -78, -79, -80*
Bernstein, Lord 1899- *FilmgC, HalFC 80*
Bernstein, Alan K 1937-1978 *AmSCAP 80*
Bernstein, Aline 1881-1955 *NotNAT B*
Bernstein, Aline 1882-1955 *OxThe, PlP&P, WhThe*
Bernstein, Arthur 1909-1964 *BiDAmM*
Bernstein, Artie 1909-1964 *CmpEPM, WhoJazz 72*
Bernstein, Bethany Harper 1944- *BlkWAB[port]*
Bernstein, Bob *IntMPA 80*
Bernstein, Cecil *IntMPA 77, -75, -76, -78, -79, -80*
Bernstein, Charles Harry 1943- *AmSCAP 80, HalFC 80*
Bernstein, David Stephen 1942- *CpmDNM 79, ConAmC*
Bernstein, Elmer 1922- *AmSCAP 66, -80, Baker 78, BiDAmM, CmMov, CmpEPM, ConAmC, DcFM, FilmEn, FilmgC, HalFC 80, IntMPA 77, -75, -76, -78, -79, -80, NewGrD 80, OxFilm, PopAmC SUP[port], WorEFlm*
Bernstein, Harry *DancEn 78*
Bernstein, Henry 1875-1953 *WhThe*
Bernstein, Henry 1876-1953 *CnMD, EncWT, McGEWD[port], ModWD, NotNAT B, OxThe*
Bernstein, Herman d1963 *NotNAT B*
Bernstein, Jack B 1937- *IntMPA 75, -76*
Bernstein, Jacob 1905- *IntWWM 77, -80*
Bernstein, Karl *BiE&WWA, NotNAT*
Bernstein, Lawrence F 1939- *NewGrD 80*
Bernstein, Leonard 1918- *AmPS, AmSCAP 66, -80, Baker 78, BestMus, BiDAmM, BiE&WWA, BnBkM 80[port], CmOp, CmpEPM, CompSN[port], CpmDNM 79, CnOxB, ConAmC, DancEn 78, DcCom 77, DcCom&M 79, DcCM, EncMT, EncWT, FilmEn, FilmgC, HalFC 80, IntWWM 77, -80, McGEWD, MusMk[port], MusSN[port], NewCBMT, NewEOp 71, NewGrD 80[port], NewYTET, NotNAT, OxFilm, OxMus, PlP&P, -A[port], PopAmC[port], PopAmC SUP, WhoMus 72, WhoOp 76, WhoThe 72, -77, WorEFlm*
Bernstein, Martin 1904- *Baker 78*
Bernstein, Morris 1916- *AmSCAP 66, -80*
Bernstein, Richard 1922- *IntMPA 77, -75, -76, -78, -79, -80*
Bernstein, Seymour Abraham 1927- *AmSCAP 80, CpmDNM 79, ConAmC, IntWWM 77, -80*
Bernstein, Sid *ConMuA 80B*
Bernstein, Sidney Lewis 1899- *FilmEn, OxFilm*
Bernstein, Sylvia 1924- *AmSCAP 66, -80*
Bernstein, Walter 1919?- *HalFC 80*
Bernstein, Walter 1920?- *FilmEn*
Bernuth, Julius Von 1830-1902 *Baker 78*
Beroff, Michel 1950- *IntWWM 77, -80, NewGrD 80, WhoMus 72*
Berolzheimer, Hobart F 1921- *BiE&WWA, NotNAT*
Berova, Olinka 1945?- *WhoHrs 80*
Berquist, Bernard H 1903-1962 *AmSCAP 66, -80*
Berr, Friedrich 1794-1838 *Baker 78, NewGrD 80*
Berr, Georges 1867-1942 *McGEWD, NotNAT B, WhThe*
Berr DeTurique, Julien 1863-1923 *WhThe*
Berr DuTurique, Julien 1863-1923 *NotNAT B*
Berra, Marco 1784-1853 *NewGrD 80*
Berre, Ferdinand 1843-1880 *Baker 78*
Berrell, George 1849-1933 *Film 2, WhScrn 77*
Berretta, Francesco *NewGrD 80*
Berri, Claude 1934- *FilmEn, FilmgC, HalFC 80*
Berry, Aileen *Film 2*
Berry, Aline 1905-1967 *WhScrn 74, -77, WhoHol B*
Berry, Arthur Nelson 1887-1945 *WhScrn 74, -77*
Berry, Bill 1930- *EncJzS 70*
Berry, Cecil Victor 1894- *WhoMus 72*
Berry, Charles Edward Anderson 1926- *BiDAmM, BluesWW[port]*
Berry, Chu 1910-1941 *CmpEPM, IlEncJ, WhoJazz 72*
Berry, Chuck *ConMuA 80A[port]*
Berry, Chuck 1926- *Baker 78, DrBlPA, NewGrD 80, RkOn[port]*
Berry, Chuck 1931- *IlEncR[port]*
Berry, Corre 1929- *IntWWM 77, -80*
Berry, David *MorBAP*
Berry, David 1943- *NatPD[port]*
Berry, David Bruce 1947- *ConAmC*
Berry, Emmett 1915- *WhoJazz 72*
Berry, Emmett 1916- *BiDAmM, CmpEPM, EncJzS 70, IlEncJ*
Berry, Eric 1913- *BiE&WWA, NotNAT, WhoHol A, WhoThe 72, -77*
Berry, Frank Joseph 1953- *AmSCAP 80*
Berry, Gillian Shelagh Sargent 1932- *WhoMus 72*
Berry, Hester Elizabeth 1929- *AmSCAP 80*
Berry, James 1883- *Film 1, WhThe*
Berry, John 1917- *BiDFilm, -81, FilmEn, FilmgC, HalFC 80, IntMPA 78, -79, -80, WorEFlm*
Berry, Jules 1883-1951 *FilmEn, FilmgC, HalFC 80, OxFilm, WhScrn 74, -77, WhoHol B*
Berry, Jules 1889-1951 *FilmAG WE, WorEFlm*
Berry, Kelley Marie *BlkAmP*
Berry, Kelly-Marie *MorBAP*
Berry, Ken 1930?- *ConMuA 80B, FilmgC, HalFC 80, WhoHol A*
Berry, Lemuel, Jr. 1946- *IntWWM 77, -80*
Berry, Leon 1910-1941 *BiDAmM*
Berry, Lillie 1905- *IntWWM 77*
Berry, Mel 1897?-1929? *NewOrJ*
Berry, Nyas d1951 *WhScrn 77*
Berry, Theodore *NewGrD 80*
Berry, Wallace 1928- *AmSCAP 80, ConAmC, NewGrD 80*
Berry, Wallace Thomas 1927- *IntWWM 77, -80, WhoMus 72*
Berry, Walter *IntWWM 77, WhoOp 76*
Berry, Walter 1929- *NewGrD 80*
Berry, William Henry 1870-1951 *WhThe, WhoHol B*
Berry, William Henry 1872-1951 *NotNAT A, -B*
Berry, William Richard 1930- *AmSCAP 80, BiDAmM, EncJzS 70*
Berry Brothers *BlksBF*
Berryman, Alice Davis *IntWWM 77, -80*
Bersa, Blagoje 1873-1934 *Baker 78*
Bersell, Michael *WhoHol A*
Bersell, Sean *WhoHol A*
Berselli, Matteo *NewGrD 80*
Bersenev, Ivan Nikolayevich 1889-1951 *OxThe*
Berson, Seweryn 1858-1917 *NewGrD 80*
Bert, Eddie 1922- *BiDAmM, CmpEPM, EncJzS 70*
Berta, Joseph Michel 1940- *IntWWM 77, -80*
Berta, Miroslav 1926- *IntWWM 77, -80*
Bertaldi, Antonio 1605-1669 *NewGrD 80*
Bertali, Antonio 1605-1669 *Baker 78, NewGrD 80*
Bertalli, Antonio 1605-1669 *NewGrD 80*
Bertalot, John 1931- *IntWWM 80, WhoMus 72*
Bertalotti, Angelo Michele 1666-1747 *NewGrD 80*
Bertani, Lelio 1550?-1620? *NewGrD 80*
Bertati, Giovanni 1735-1815? *NewGrD 80*
Bertaud, Martin 1700?-1771 *NewGrD 80*
Bertchume, Gary 1949- *ConAmC*
Berte, Charles d1908 *NotNAT B*
Berte, Harry 1857-1924 *NewGrD 80*
Berte, Heinrich 1857-1924 *Baker 78, NewGrD 80*
Berte, Heinrich 1858-1924 *NotNAT B*
Berteau, Martin 1700?-1771 *NewGrD 80*
Berteling, Theodore 1821-1890 *NewGrD 80*
Bertezen, Salvatore *NewGrD 80*
Bertha, Sandor 1843-1912 *NewGrD 80*
Berthault, Martin *NewGrD 80*
Berthaume, Isidore 1752?-1802 *NewGrD 80*
Berthaume, Julien 1752?-1802 *NewGrD 80*
Bertheaume, Isidore 1752?-1802 *Baker 78, NewGrD 80*
Bertheaume, Julien 1752?-1802 *NewGrD 80*
Berthelot, John 1942- *IntWWM 80*
Berthier, Jeanne Marie *NewGrD 80*
Berthod, Francois *NewGrD 80*
Berthold, Charlotte 1939- *IntWWM 77, -80, WhoOp 76*
Berthold, Theodor 1815-1882 *Baker 78*
Bertholdi, Madame *Film 1*
Bertholdo, Sperindio *NewGrD 80*
Bertholusius, Vincentius *NewGrD 80*
Bertholussius, Vincentius *NewGrD 80*
Berthomieu, Andre 1903-1960 *DcFM, FilmEn*
Berthulusius, Vincentius *NewGrD 80*
Berti, Carlo 1555?-1602 *NewGrD 80*
Berti, Giovanni Pietro d1638 *NewGrD 80*
Berti, Marina 1928- *HalFC 80, WhoHol A*
Berti, Zan d1638 *NewGrD 80*
Bertie, Willoughby *NewGrD 80*
Bertin, Charles 1919- *CnMD, ModWD*
Bertin, Louise-Angelique 1805-1877 *Baker 78, NewGrD 80*
Bertin, Pierre *NewGrD 80*
Bertin DeLaDoue, Thomas 1680?-1745 *NewGrD 80*
Bertinazzi, Carlin *PlP&P*
Bertinazzi, Carlo Antonio 1710-1783 *EncWT, Ent, OxThe*
Bertini, Auguste 1780-1830? *NewGrD 80*
Bertini, Benoit-Auguste 1780- *Baker 78*
Bertini, Domenico 1829-1890 *Baker 78*
Bertini, Francesca 1888- *FilmAG WE[port], FilmEn, Film 1, OxFilm*
Bertini, Gary 1927- *Baker 78, IntWWM 77, -80, NewGrD 80, WhoMus 72, WhoOp 76*
Bertini, Giuseppe 1759-1852 *NewGrD 80*
Bertini, Henri 1798-1876 *Baker 78, NewGrD 80*
Bertini, Henri Jerome 1798-1876 *OxMus*
Bertini, Salvatore 1721-1794 *NewGrD 80*
Bertinotti, Teresa 1776-1854 *NewGrD 80*
Bertl, Inge 1933- *DancEn 78*
Bertola, Giovanni Antonio *NewGrD 80*
Bertola, Giulio 1921- *WhoOp 76*
Bertolazzi, Carlo 1870-1916 *EncWT, McGEWD[port], REnWD[port], WhThe*
Bertoldi, Bertoldo Di *NewGrD 80*
Bertoldo, Sperandio 1530?-1570 *NewGrD 80*
Bertoldo, Sperindio 1530?-1570 *Baker 78, NewGrD 80*
Bertoldo, Sper'indio 1530?-1570 *NewGrD 80*
Bertoli, Giovanni Antonio *NewGrD 80*
Bertolini, Orindio *NewGrD 80*
Bertolino, Ercole Mario 1934- *IntWWM 80*
Bertolino, Mario Ercole 1934- *WhoOp 76*
Bertolli, Francesca d1767 *NewGrD 80*
Bertolotti, Bernardino 1555?-1609? *NewGrD 80*
Bertolotti, Gasparo *NewGrD 80*
Bertolucci, Bernardo 1940- *BiDFilm, -81, ConLC 16, DcFM, FilmEn, FilmgC, HalFC 80, OxFilm, WorEFlm*
Bertolucci, Bernardo 1941- *IntMPA 79, -80, MovMk[port]*
Bertolusi, Vincentius d1608 *NewGrD 80*
Bertolusi, Vincenzo d1608 *NewGrD 80*
Berton *NewGrD 80*
Berton, Adolphe 1817-1857 *NewGrD 80*
Berton, Francois 1784-1832 *NewGrD 80*
Berton, Henri 1784-1832 *NewGrD 80*
Berton, Henri-Montan 1767-1844 *Baker 78, NewGrD 80*
Berton, Pierre d1912 *NotNAT B*
Berton, Pierre Francis DeMarigny 1920- *CreCan 1*
Berton, Pierre-Montan 1727-1780 *Baker 78, NewGrD 80*

Berton, Vic 1896-1951 *BiDAmM, CmpEPM, WhoJazz 72*
Bertoncini, Gene 1937- *AmSCAP 80, EncJzS 70*
Bertoncini, Mario 1932- *NewGrD 80*
Bertone, Alfredo *Film 2*
Bertoni, Ferdinando 1725-1813 *Baker 78, NewGrD 80*
Bertouch, Georg Von 1668-1743 *NewGrD 80*
Bertouille, Gerard 1898- *Baker 78, IntWWM 77, -80, NewGrD 80*
Bertozzi, Patricia *WomWMM B*
Bertram, Arthur 1860-1955 *NotNAT B, WhThe*
Bertram, Bert *WhoHol A*
Bertram, Charles 1853-1907 *MagIID*
Bertram, Eugene 1872-1941 *NotNAT B, WhThe*
Bertram, Frank d1941 *NotNAT B, WhoHol B*
Bertram, Hans Georg 1936- *IntWWM 77, -80*
Bertram, Helen 1869- *WhoStg 1906, -1908*
Bertram, Johann 1535-1575 *NewGrD 80*
Bertram, Johannes 1535-1575 *NewGrD 80*
Bertram, Robert Fletcher 1916- *AmSCAP 66, -80*
Bertram, Vedah 1891-1912 *WhScrn 77, WhoHol B*
Bertram, William 1880-1933 *Film 2, WhScrn 77*
Bertram, William 1889- *TwYS A*
Bertran De Born 1145?-1215? *NewGrD 80*
Bertrand Di Avignone *NewGrD 80*
Bertrand, Aline 1798-1835 *Baker 78*
Bertrand, Anthoine De 1530?-1580? *NewGrD 80*
Bertrand, Antoine De 1530?-1580? *NewGrD 80*
Bertrand, Antoine De 1540?-1581? *Baker 78*
Bertrand, Buddy 1897-1956 *NewOrJ*
Bertrand, Jean-Gustave 1834-1880 *Baker 78, NewGrD 80*
Bertrand, Jimmy 1900-1960 *WhoJazz 72*
Bertrand, Mary d1955 *WhScrn 74, -77*
Bertrand, Nanon 1937- *IntWWM 80*
Bertrand, Paul 1915- *DcFM*
Bertrand, Rene *OxMus*
Bertuca, Peter Frank 1929- *IntWWM 77*
Bertucelli, Jean-Louis 1942- *FilmEn*
Bertuch, Georg Von *NewGrD 80*
Bertus, Carolus *NewGrD 80*
Beruh, Joseph 1924- *BiE&WWA, NotNAT, WhoThe 77*
Berutti, Arturo 1862-1938 *Baker 78, NewGrD 80*
Berutti, Pablo 1866-1914 *NewGrD 80*
Berval, Paul *CreCan 1*
Berwald *NewGrD 80*
Berwald, Astrid 1886- *NewGrD 80*
Berwald, August 1798-1869 *NewGrD 80*
Berwald, Christian August *Baker 78*
Berwald, Christian Friedrich Georg 1740-1825 *Baker 78, NewGrD 80*
Berwald, Franz 1796-1868 *Baker 78, BnBkM 80, DcCom 77, DcCom&M 79, MusMk, NewGrD 80[port], OxMus*
Berwald, Georg Johann Abraham 1758-1825 *NewGrD 80*
Berwald, Johan Fredrik 1787-1861 *NewGrD 80*
Berwald, Johann Friedrich 1711-1789 *NewGrD 80*
Berwald, Johann Friedrich 1787-1861 *Baker 78*
Berwald, William 1864-1948 *AmSCAP 66, -80, Baker 78*
Berwin, Isabel *Film 1*
Beryl, Edwin *Film 1*
Berze, Hugues De *NewGrD 80*
Besancourt *NewGrD 80*
Besanzoni, Gabriella 1890-1962 *Baker 78, CmOp*
Besard, Jean-Baptiste 1567?-1617? *NewGrD 80[port]*
Besard, Jean-Baptiste 1567-1625 *Baker 78*
Besardus, Joannes Baptista 1567?-1617? *NewGrD 80[port]*
Besch, Anthony John Elwyn 1924- *CmOp, WhoMus 72, WhoOp 76*
Besch, Lutz 1918- *CnMD*
Besci, Kurt 1920- *CroCD, McGEWD*
Besekirsky, Vasilly 1879- *BiDAmM*
Besekirsky, Vassili *Baker 78*
Besekow, Sam 1911- *EncWT*
Besier, Rudolf 1878-1942 *ModWD, NotNAT B, PlP&P, WhThe*
Besier, Rudolph 1878-1942 *McGEWD[port]*
Beskow, Bernhard Von 1796-1868 *OxThe*
Besler, Samuel 1574-1625 *Baker 78, NewGrD 80*
Besler, Simon 1583-1633 *NewGrD 80*
Besly, Maurice 1888-1945 *Baker 78*
Besnard, Lucien 1872- *McGEWD*
Besobrasova, Marika 1918- *CnOxB*
Besoyan, Richard 1924- *NewGrD 80*
Besoyan, Rick 1924-1970 *BiE&WWA, EncMT, NewGrD 80, NotNAT B*
Besozzi *NewGrD 80*
Besozzi, Alessandro 1702-1793 *Baker 78, NewGrD 80, -80*
Besozzi, Antonio 1714-1781 *NewGrD 80*
Besozzi, Carlo 1738-1798? *NewGrD 80*
Besozzi, Cristoforo 1661-1725 *NewGrD 80*
Besozzi, Gaetano 1727-1798 *NewGrD 80*
Besozzi, Giuseppe 1686-1760 *NewGrD 80*
Besozzi, Louis-Desire 1814-1879 *NewGrD 80*
Besozzi, Nino d1971 *WhScrn 77*
Besozzi, Paolo Girolamo 1704-1778 *NewGrD 80*
Besre, Jean 1938- *CreCan 2*
Bess, Druie R 1901- *WhoJazz 72*
Bessaraboff, Nicholas 1894-1973 *Baker 78, NewGrD 80*
Besse, Robert John 1920- *AmSCAP 66, -80*
Bessel, Vasily Vasil'yevich 1843-1907 *NewGrD 80*
Bessel, Vassili 1842-1907 *Baker 78*
Besseler, Heinrich 1900-1969 *Baker 78, NewGrD 80*
Besseling, Charles R J 1920- *IntWWM 77*
Besselink, Maria 1937- *IntWWM 77, -80*
Bessell, Ted 1926- *ForYSC, WhoHol A*
Bessems, Antoine 1809-1868 *Baker 78*
Bessent, Marie 1898-1947 *WhScrn 74, -77*
Bessenyei, Gyorgy 1747-1811 *OxThe*
Besser, Joe 1900-1972 *HalFC 80, JoeFr, WhoHol B*
Besserer, Eugenie 1870-1934 *FilmEn, Film 1, -2, ForYSC, HalFC 80, TwYS, WhScrn 74, -77, WhoHol B*
Bessette, Gerard 1920- *CreCan 1*
Bessie, Alvah *FilmgC, HalFC 80, PlP&P*
Bessie, Alvah 1904- *FilmEn*
Bessire, Antony Glenn 1949- *AmSCAP 80*
Bessmertnova, Natalia Igorievna 1941- *CnOxB*
Bessmertnova, Tatyana Igorievna 1947- *CnOxB*
Besson *NewGrD 80*
Besson, Madame d1957? *NewGrD 80*
Besson, Benno 1922- *EncWT, Ent*
Besson, Cecile *NewGrD 80*
Besson, Gabriel 1689?-1765 *NewGrD 80*
Besson, Gabriel Diaz *NewGrD 80*
Besson, Gabriel-Louis 1733-1785 *NewGrD 80*
Besson, Gustave Auguste 1820-1875 *NewGrD 80*
Besson, Marthe *NewGrD 80*
Besson, Yvette 1943- *WhoMus 72*
Bessone, Emma *CnOxB*
Bessy, Claude 1932- *CnOxB, DancEn 78*
Best, Barbara 1921- *IntMPA 77, -75, -76, -78, -79, -80*
Best, Barrie *IntWWM 77, -80*
Best, Denzil DeCosta 1917-1965 *BiDAmM, CmpEPM*
Best, Dolly 1899-1968 *WhScrn 74, -77*
Best, Edna 1900-1974 *BiE&WWA, FilmEn, Film 2, FilmgC, ForYSC, HalFC 80, IlWWBF[port], NotNAT B, ThFT[port], WhScrn 77, WhThe, WhoHol B*
Best, Harold M 1931- *ConAmC*
Best, Hubert 1952- *IntWWM 80*
Best, James 1926- *FilmEn, FilmgC, ForYSC, HalFC 80, IntMPA 77, -75, -76, -78, -79, -80, WhoHol A*
Best, Johnny 1913- *CmpEPM, WhoJazz 72*
Best, Martin 1942- *WhoMus 72*
Best, Martyn *Film 2*
Best, Richard Warner 1935- *WhoOp 76*
Best, Roger 1938- *IntWWM 77, -80*
Best, W T 1826-1897 *BnBkM 80, NewGrD 80*
Best, Warren *PupTheA*
Best, William Thomas 1826-1897 *Baker 78, OxMus*
Best, Willie 1913-1962 *HolCA[port]*
Best, Willie 1915-1962 *DrBlPA*
Best, Willie 1916-1962 *FilmEn, FilmgC, HalFC 80, NotNAT B, Vers B[port], WhScrn 74, -77, WhoHol B, WhoHrs 80*
Best, Willie 1917-1962 *ForYSC*
Bester, Elizabeth Joan 1929- *IntWWM 80*
Bestonso, Roberto 1942- *CnOxB*
Bestor, Charles 1924- *ConAmC, IntWWM 77, -80*
Bestor, Don 1889-1970 *AmSCAP 66, -80, BgBands 74, CmpEPM*
Bestourne *NewGrD 80*
Beswick, Martine 1941- *FilmgC, HalFC 80, WhoHrs 80[port]*
Betchel, William *Film 1*
Betella, Paolo *NewGrD 80*
Betenbaugh, Gordon Murray 1941- *IntWWM 77, -80*
Bethancourt, Jose 1906- *IntWWM 77*
Bethanio, Fausto *NewGrD 80*
Bethencourt, Francis 1926- *BiE&WWA, NotNAT, WhoHol A*
Bethizy, Jean Laurent De 1709-1781 *NewGrD 80*
Bethune, Conon De *NewGrD 80*
Bethune, George *PupTheA*
Bethune, George Washington 1905-1862 *BiDAmM*
Bethune, Isabel Mary *WhoMus 72*
Bethune, Thomas Greene 1849-1908 *Baker 78, BiDAmM, NewGrD 80*
Bethune, Zina *IntMPA 75, -76*
Bethune, Zina 1945- *ForYSC, IntMPA 77, WhoHol A*
Bethune, Zina 1950- *IntMPA 78, -79, -80*
Betjeman, Paul 1937- *IntWWM 77, -80*
Betley, Bozena 1940- *WhoOp 76*
Betschwarzowski, Antonin Frantisek *NewGrD 80*
Bettamy, F G d1942 *NotNAT B*
Bettelheim, Edwin Sumner 1865-1938 *NotNAT B, WhThe*
Bettella, Paolo *NewGrD 80*
Bettencourt, Blair Francis 1948- *IntWWM 77*
Bettens, Etienne 1931- *IntWWM 77, -80*
Better, Anthony *MorBAP*
Betteridge, Leslie *IntWWM 77, -80, WhoMus 72*
Betterton, Mary Sanderson d1712 *EncWT, OxThe, PlP&P*
Betterton, Thomas 1635?-1710 *CnThe, EncWT, Ent, NotNAT A, -B, OxMus, OxThe, PlP&P[port]*
Betterton, Mrs. Thomas 1647?-1712 *NotNAT B*
Bettger, Lyle 1915- *FilmEn, FilmgC, ForYSC, HalFC 80, IntMPA 77, -75, -76, -78, -79, -80, WhoHol A*
Betti, Adolfo 1873-1950 *Baker 78*
Betti, Stefano *NewGrD 80*
Betti, Ugo 1892-1953 *CnMD, CnThe, EncWT, Ent, McGEWD[port], ModWD, NotNAT B, OxThe, REnWD*
Bettinelli, Bruno 1913- *Baker 78, IntWWM 77, -80, NewGrD 80*
Bettini, Giovanni *NewGrD 80*
Bettino, Geronimo d1643? *NewGrD 80*
Bettino, Stefano *NewGrD 80*
Bettinson, Ralph 1908- *IntMPA 77, -75, -76, -78, -79, -80*
Bettis, Valerie 1920- *BiE&WWA, CmpGMD, CnOxB, DancEn 78[port], NotNAT, WhoHol A, WhoThe 72, -77*
Bettley, Cecil William 1904- *IntWWM 77*
Bettmann, Otto L 1903- *BiE&WWA, NotNAT*
Betton, George d1969 *WhoHol B*
Betts, Dickey *ConMuA 80A*
Betts, Donald *ConAmC*
Betts, Edward William 1881- *WhThe*
Betts, John 1755-1823 *NewGrD 80*
Betts, Lorne 1918- *Baker 78, CreCan 2*
Betts, William E 1856-1929 *Film 2, WhScrn 74, -77, WhoHol B*
Betty, William Henry West 1791-1874 *CnThe, EncWT, Ent, NotNAT A, -B, OxThe, PlP&P[port]*
Betulius, Sigmund *NewGrD 80*
Betz, Carl *IntMPA 75, -76, -78*
Betz, Carl 1920-1978 *FilmEn, FilmgC, HalFC 80, IntMPA 77, WhoHol A*
Betz, Carl 1921- *ForYSC*

Betz, Franz 1835-1900 *Baker 78, CmOp, NewEOp 71, NewGrD 80*
Betz, Mathew 1881-1938 *ForYSC, TwYS*
Betz, Matthew 1881-1938 *Film 2, WhScrn 74, -77, WhoHol B*
Betzner, John Fred 1908- *AmSCAP 66, -80*
Betzwarzofsky, Antonin Frantisek *NewGrD 80*
Beuerman, Lani Ann Nelson 1943- *IntWWM 77*
Beugen, Joan *WomWMM B*
Beurhaus, Friedrich 1536-1609 *NewGrD 80*
Beurle, Jurgen 1943- *Baker 78, DcCM*
Beute, Sjoerd 1942- *IntWWM 77, -80*
Beutel, Jack 1917- *WhoHol A*
Beuttner, Nicolaus d1610? *NewGrD 80*
Bevacqua, Antonio 1941- *WhoOp 76*
Bevan, Billy 1887-1957 *FilmEn, Film 1, -2, FilmgC, ForYSC, HalFC 80, MotPP, NotNAT B, OxFilm, TwYS, Vers B[port], WhoHol B*
Bevan, Billy 1897-1957 *WhScrn 74, -77*
Bevan, Clifford James 1934- *IntWWM 77, -80, WhoMus 72*
Bevan, Donald 1920- *BiE&WWA, NotNAT*
Bevan, Faith 1896- *WhThe*
Bevan, Frank 1903- *BiE&WWA*
Bevan, Isla 1910- *WhThe*
Bevan, Maurice Guy Smalman 1921- *IntWWM 77, -80, WhoMus 72*
Bevan, Roger Hugh 1918- *WhoMus 72*
Bevan, Rosalind Jane 1947- *WhoMus 72*
Bevan-Baker, John Stewart 1926- *WhoMus 72*
Bevani, Alexander *Film 2*
Bevans, Clem 1879-1963 *HolCA[port]*
Bevans, Clem 1880-1963 *FilmEn, FilmgC, ForYSC, HalFC 80, WhScrn 74, -77, WhoHol B*
Bevans, Clem 1897-1963 *Vers A[port]*
Bevans, Lionel 1884-1965 *WhScrn 74, -77*
Bevans, Philippa 1913-1968 *WhScrn 74, -77, WhoHol B*
Bevans, Philippa 1917-1968 *BiE&WWA*
Bevans, Phillippa 1913-1968 *NotNAT B*
Bevel, Charles William 1938- *AmSCAP 80*
Bevelander, Brian *ConAmC*
Bevelander, Brian Edward 1942- *CpmDNM 76*
Beveridge, Hortense *WomWMM A, -B*
Beveridge, J D 1844-1926 *NotNAT B, WhThe, WhoStg 1906, -1908*
Beveridge, Thomas Gattrell 1938- *AmSCAP 66, -80, CpmDNM 73, ConAmC*
Beveringen, Andre *NewGrD 80*
Beveringen, Andreas *NewGrD 80*
Beveringen, Andries *NewGrD 80*
Beverley, Helen *WhoHol A*
Beverley, Henry Roxby d1863 *NotNAT B*
Beverley, Hilda d1942 *NotNAT B*
Beverley, J Gray, Jr. 1935- *IntMPA 75, -76*
Beverley, Mrs. W R d1851 *NotNAT B*
Beverley, William Roxby d1842 *NotNAT B*
Beverley, William Roxby 1814?-1889 *NotNAT B, OxThe*
Beverly Hillbillies *IlEncCM*
Bevernage, Andre *NewGrD 80*
Bevernage, Andreas *NewGrD 80*
Bevernage, Andries *NewGrD 80*
Bevers, Frank *WhoMus 72*
Beversdorf, Samuel Thomas 1924- *AmSCAP 80, IntWWM 77, -80*
Beversdorf, Thomas 1924- *Baker 78, ConAmC*
Bevignani, Enrico 1841-1903 *Baker 78, NewGrD 80*
Bevilacqua, Mario 1536-1593 *NewGrD 80*
Beville, Hugh M, Jr. 1908- *IntMPA 77, -75, -76, -78, -79*
Bevin, Elway *OxMus*
Bevin, Elway 1554?-1638 *NewGrD 80*
Bevin, Elway 1560?-1640? *Baker 78*
Bevington *NewGrD 80*
Bevington, Henry *NewGrD 80*
Bevington, Martin *NewGrD 80*
Bevins, Karl A 1915- *IntWWM 80*
Bewerunge, Heinrich 1862-1923 *NewGrD 80*
Bewerunge, Henry 1862-1923 *Baker 78, NewGrD 80*
Bewes, Rodney 1937- *FilmgC, HalFC 80, WhoThe 72, -77*
Bewgintancz, Bernhard *NewGrD 80*
Bewley, Ian Howard 1928- *WhoMus 72*
Bewley, Lois 1936- *CnOxB*
Bexfield, William Richard 1824-1853 *Baker 78, NewGrD 80*
Bey, Andrew W, Jr. 1939- *EncJzS 70*
Bey, Andy 1939- *EncJzS 70*
Bey, Hannelore 1941- *CnOxB*
Bey, Iverson *BluesWW[port]*
Bey, LaRocque *DrBlPA*
Bey, Marki 1946?- *DrBlPA*
Bey, Mickey *AmSCAP 80*
Bey, Turhan 1920- *FilmEn, FilmgC, ForYSC, HalFC 80, HolP 40[port], IntMPA 77, -75, -76, -78, -79, -80, MotPP, MovMk, WhoHol A, WhoHrs 80*
Beydts, Louis 1895-1953 *Baker 78*
Beyer, Andreas *NewGrD 80*
Beyer, Charles *Film 2*
Beyer, Frank Michael 1928- *Baker 78, NewGrD 80*
Beyer, Frederick H 1926- *ConAmC*
Beyer, Howard 1929- *AmSCAP 66, ConAmC*
Beyer, Howard George 1929- *AmSCAP 80*
Beyer, Johann Baptist *NewGrD 80*
Beyer, Johann Samuel 1669-1744 *Baker 78, NewGrD 80*
Beyers, Clara *Film 1*
Beyle, Henri *NewGrD 80*
Beymer, Richard 1939- *FilmEn, FilmgC, ForYSC, HalFC 80, IntMPA 77, -75, -76, -78, -79, -80, MotPP, What 4[port], WhoHol A*
Beynon, Ivor James 1919- *IntWWM 77, -80*
Beyschlag, Adolf 1845-1914 *Baker 78*
Beza, Marcu *OxMus*
Beza, Theodore 1519-1605 *OxMus*
Bezaire, Sara *WomWMM*
Bezanson, Philip 1916- *ConAmC*
Bezdek, Jan 1896- *Baker 78*
Beze, Theodore De 1519-1605 *NewGrD 80*
Bezekirsky, Vasily Vasil'yevich 1835-1919 *NewGrD 80*
Bezekirsky, Vasily Vasil'yevich 1880-1960 *NewGrD 80*
Bezekirsky, Vassili 1835-1919 *Baker 78*
Bezekirsky, Vassili 1880-1960 *Baker 78*
Bezel, Johann Christoph *NewGrD 80*
Bezelius, Johann Christoph *NewGrD 80*
Bezetti, Victoria 1937- *WhoOp 76*
Bezrodniy, Igor Semyonovich 1930- *NewGrD 80*
Bezroundoff, Jean Basile *CreCan 1*
Bezucha, Jerzy 1949- *IntWWM 77, -80*
Bezzerides, A I *FilmEn*
Bezzerides, A I 1908- *FilmgC, HalFC 80*
Bharata *OxThe, REnWD[port]*
Bharucha, B D 1903- *IntMPA 75, -76*
Bhasa *OxThe, REnWD[port]*
Bhaskar 1930- *BiE&WWA, CnOxB, NotNAT, WhoHol A*
Bhaskar, Roy Chowdhury *DancEn 78[port]*
Bhatkhande, Vishnu Narayan 1860-1936 *NewGrD 80*
Bhatta Narayana *OxThe*
Bhavabhuti 750?- *CnThe, OxThe, REnWD*
Biabo, Giuseppe Del *NewGrD 80*
Biaggi, Girolamo Alessandro 1819-1897 *Baker 78, NewGrD 80*
Biagi, Vittorio 1941- *CnOxB*
Biagini, Henry d1944 *BgBands 74*
Bial, Rudolf 1834-1881 *Baker 78*
Bialas, Gunter 1907- *CpmDNM 78, NewGrD 80*
Biales, Albert 1929- *IntWWM 80*
Bialomizy, Stanley Frank 1934- *IntWWM 77*
Bialosky, Marshall H 1923- *AmSCAP 80, CpmDNM 76, ConAmC*
Biancardi, Nicolo Bastiano *NewGrD 80*
Bianchetti, Suzanne 1894-1936 *Film 2, WhScrn 77*
Bianchi, Andrea *NewGrD 80*
Bianchi, Antonio 1710?-1772? *NewGrD 80*
Bianchi, Antonio 1750?-1816? *NewGrD 80*
Bianchi, Antonio 1758-1817? *NewGrD 80*
Bianchi, Bianca 1855-1947 *Baker 78*
Bianchi, Caterino *NewGrD 80*
Bianchi, Charles 1901- *WhoMus 72*
Bianchi, Daniela 1942- *FilmEn, FilmgC, HalFC 80, WhoHol A*
Bianchi, Francesco 1752?-1810 *Baker 78, NewGrD 80*
Bianchi, Georgio 1904-1968 *WhScrn 74, -77*
Bianchi, Giovanni 1660?-1720? *NewGrD 80*
Bianchi, Giovanni Battista *NewGrD 80*
Bianchi, Giulio Cesare 1576?-1637? *NewGrD 80*
Bianchi, Giuseppe Francesco 1752?-1810 *NewGrD 80*
Bianchi, Lino 1920- *IntWWM 77, -80, NewGrD 80*
Bianchi, Mario *Film 1*
Bianchi, Pietro Antonio *NewGrD 80*
Bianchi, Valentina 1839-1884 *Baker 78*
Bianchiardus, Francesco *NewGrD 80*
Bianchini, Domenico 1510?-1576? *NewGrD 80*
Bianchini, Francescho *NewGrD 80*
Bianchini, Veneziano 1510?-1576? *NewGrD 80*
Bianchy, Jacobelus *NewGrD 80*
Bianciardi, Francesco 1571?-1607 *NewGrD 80*
Biancini, Ferrucio *Film 2*
Bianco, Andrea *NewGrD 80*
Bianco, Anthony 1917- *IntWWM 77, -80*
Bianco, Giovanni Battista *NewGrD 80*
Bianco, Pietro Antonio 1540?-1611 *NewGrD 80*
Bianco, Robert 1934- *AmSCAP 66, -80*
Biancolelli, Catarina 1665?-1716 *EncWT*
Biancolelli, Caterina 1665?-1716 *Ent, OxThe*
Biancolelli, Francesca Maria Apolline 1664-1747 *OxThe*
Biancolelli, Francesca Marie Apolline 1664-1747 *EncWT*
Biancolelli, Francesco d1640? *EncWT*
Biancolelli, Giuseppe Domenico 1637?-1688 *EncWT, Ent, OxThe, PlP&P[port]*
Biancolelli, Isabella Franchini d1650 *EncWT, OxThe*
Biancolelli, Orsola Cortesi 1632?-1718 *EncWT*
Biancolelli, Orsola Cortesi 1636?-1718 *OxThe*
Biancolelli, Pier Francesco 1680-1734 *EncWT, Ent*
Biancolelli, Pietro Francesco 1680-1734 *OxThe*
Biancolelli Family *CnThe*
Bianconi, Lorenzo Gennaro 1946- *IntWWM 77, -80, NewGrD 80*
Biandra, Giovanni Pietro d1633? *NewGrD 80*
Bias, Albert *Film 2*
Bias, Chester 1917-1954 *WhScrn 74, -77*
Bias, Fanny 1789-1825 *CnOxB*
Biba, Otto 1946- *IntWWM 77, -80*
Bibalo, Antonio 1922- *Baker 78, IntWWM 77, -80*
Bibas, Frank Percy 1917- *IntMPA 77, -75, -76, -78, -79, -80*
Bibb, Leon 1926?- *BiDAmM, DrBlPA*
Bibb, Leon 1935?- *EncFCWM 69*
Bibbiena *NewGrD 80*
Bibbiena, Il 1470-1520 *EncWT, Ent*
Bibbiena, Bernardo Dovizi Da 1470-1520 *OxThe, REnWD[port]*
Bibbiena, Bernardo Dovizio Da 1470-1520 *McGEWD[port]*
Bibby, Charles 1878-1917 *WhThe*
Bibby, Gillian 1945- *IntWWM 77, -80*
Bibby, Richard *ConMuA 80B*
Biber, Heinrich 1644-1704 *MusMk*
Biber, Heinrich Ignaz Franz Von 1644-1704 *Baker 78, NewGrD 80[port]*
Biber, Heinrich Johan Franz Von 1644-1704 *OxMus*
Biber, Heinrich Von 1644-1704 *BnBkM 80*
Biberian, Gilbert Emanuel 1944- *IntWWM 77, -80*
Biberman, Abner 1909-1977 *FilmEn, FilmgC, ForYSC, HalFC 80, HolCA[port], IntMPA 77, -75, -76, Vers A[port], WhoHol A*
Biberman, Herbert J 1900-1971 *DcFM, FilmEn, FilmgC, HalFC 80, OxFilm, WorEFlm*
Biberti, Leopold 1897-1969 *FilmAG WE*
Bibi, Andreas 1807-1878 *Baker 78*
Bibi, Rudolf 1832-1902 *Baker 78*
Bibiena *NewGrD 80*
Bibiena, Alessandro 1687-1769? *NotNAT B, OxThe*
Bibiena, Antonio 1700-1774 *NotNAT B, OxThe*
Bibiena, Carlo 1728-1787 *NotNAT B, OxThe*
Bibiena, Ferdinando 1657-1743 *NotNAT B, OxThe*
Bibiena, Francesco 1659-1739 *NotNAT B, OxThe*

Bibiena, Giovanni Maria 1704?-1769 *NotNAT B, OxThe*
Bibiena, Giuseppe 1696-1751 *DancEn 78*
Bibiena, Giuseppe 1696-1757 *NotNAT B, OxThe*
Bibiena Family *NotNAT A*
Bibienas Family *CnThe*
Bibl, Rudolf 1929- *WhoOp 76*
Bible, Frances L *NewEOp 71, WhoOp 76*
Bibo, Irving 1889-1962 *AmSCAP 66, -80, NotNAT B*
Biby, Edward 1885-1952 *WhScrn 74, -77, WhoHol B*
Biccilli, Giovanni 1623-1705? *NewGrD 80*
Bice, Robert d1968 *WhoHol B*
Bicilli, Giovanni 1623-1705? *NewGrD 80*
Bick, Donald A 1948- *IntWWM 80*
Bick, Jerry *IntMPA 77, 75, 76, 78, 79, -80*
Bickel, Carl S 1951- *IntWWM 77*
Bickel, Conrad *NewGrD 80*
Bickel, George L 1863-1941 *Film 2, NotNAT B, WhScrn 74, -77, WhoHol B*
Bickelhaupt, William Edward 1952- *AmSCAP 80*
Bickerstaff, Robert *WhoOp 76*
Bickerstaff, Robert Graham 1932- *IntWWM 80*
Bickerstaffe, Isaac 1735?-1812? *Ent, McGEWD, NotNAT B, OxThe*
Bickert, Ed 1932- *EncJzS 70*
Bickert, Edward Isaac 1932- *EncJzS 70*
Bickford, Charles d1967 *MotPP, WhoHol B*
Bickford, Charles 1889-1967 *FilmEn, Film 2, FilmgC, ForYSC, HalFC 80, HolP 30[port], MovMk[port], NotNAT B, OxFilm, WhScrn 74, -77*
Bickford, Charles 1891-1967 *BiDFilm, -81, BiE&WWA, WhThe, WorEFlm*
Bickham, George, Jr. 1710?-1758 *NewGrD 80*
Bicknell, Nixon S 1932- *IntWWM 77, -80*
Biczycki, Jan-Paul 1931- *WhoOp 76*
Bidart, Lycia DeBiase 1910- *IntWWM 77, -80*
Biddelman, Mark 1943- *ConAmC*
Bidder, Helen Amy 1891- *WhoMus 72*
Biddle, Baldy *Film 2*
Biddle, Craig *Film 2*
Biddlecome, Robert Edward 1930- *IntWWM 80*
Biddu Orchestra *RkOn 2[port]*
Bideau, Jean-Luc 1940- *FilmAG WE*
Bidermann *NewGrD 80*
Bidermann, David 1603-1663 *NewGrD 80*
Bidermann, Jakob 1578-1639 *EncWT, Ent, OxThe*
Bidermann, Samuel 1540?-1622 *NewGrD 80*
Bidermann, Samuel 1600-1653? *NewGrD 80*
Bideu, Lou 1919- *AmSCAP 66, -80*
Bidlo, Karel 1904- *IntWWM 77, -80*
Bidou, Henri d1943 *NotNAT B*
Bidwell, Barnaby *PlP&P*
Bie, Oscar 1864-1938 *DancEn 78, NewGrD 80*
Bie, Oskar 1864-1938 *Baker 78*
Bieber, Margarete 1879- *BiE&WWA, NotNAT*
Biechteler, Benedict 1689-1759 *NewGrD 80*
Biechteler, Ignatius 1701-1767 *NewGrD 80*
Biechteler VonGreiffenthal, Matthias S 1670?-1744? *NewGrD 80*
Biedermann, Edward Julius 1849-1933 *Baker 78, BiDAmM*
Biedermann, Joseph 1800- *OxThe*
Biegel, Erwin 1896-1954 *WhScrn 74, -77*
Biegel, Irv *ConMuA 80B*
Biego, Paolo *NewGrD 80*
Biegovitch, Jovanka 1931- *CnOxB*
Biehle, August Johannes 1870-1941 *NewGrD 80*
Biehle, Herbert 1901- *Baker 78*
Biehle, Johannes 1870-1941 *Baker 78*
Biehler, Mary *PupTheA*
Biel, Michael Von 1937- *NewGrD 80*
Bielawa, Herbert Walter 1930- *AmSCAP 80, ConAmC, IntWWM 77, -80*
Bielawski, Ludwik Augustyn 1929- *IntWWM 77, -80*
Bielek, Pal'o 1910- *DcFM*
Bieler, Andre 1896- *CreCan 2*
Bieler, Andre Charles Theodore 1938- *CreCan 1*
Bieler, Ted 1938- *CreCan 1*
Bieling, Franz Ignaz 1700?-1757 *NewGrD 80*
Bieling, Joseph Ignaz *NewGrD 80*
Bielinska, Helina *WomWMM*
Bien, Walter H 1923- *IntMPA 77, -75, -76, -78, -79, -80*
Biener, Mathias *NewGrD 80*
Bienert, Gerhard *Film 2*
Bieniecka, Wanda 1925- *IntWWM 77, -80*
Biensfeldt, Paul *Film 2*
Bienstock, Freddie *ConMuA 80B*
Bientina, Il *NewGrD 80*
Bienvenu, Florent 1568-1623 *NewGrD 80*
Bierbower, Elsie 1889-1956 *AmSCAP 80*
Bierdiajew, Walerian 1885-1956 *NewGrD 80*
Bierey, Gottlob Benedikt 1772-1840 *Baker 78, NewGrD 80*
Bierley, Paul Edmund 1926- *IntWWM 77, -80*
Bierling, Lore *WomWMM*
Bierman, Bernard 1908- *AmSCAP 66, -80*
Biermann, David Julius 1945- *IntWWM 77*
Biernacki, Nikodem 1826-1892 *NewGrD 80*
Bifetto, Francesco *NewGrD 80*
Biffetto, Francesco *NewGrD 80*
Biffi, Antonino 1666?-1773 *NewGrD 80*
Biffi, Antonio 1666?-1733 *NewGrD 80*
Biffi, Gioseffo *NewGrD 80*
Big Bill *BluesWW[port]*
Big Bloke *BluesWW[port]*
Big Bopper 1935-1959 *BiDAmM, ConMuA 80A, RkOn[port]*
Big Brother & The Holding Company *BiDAmM, ConMuA 80A, RkOn 2[port]*
Big Chief *BluesWW[port]*
Big Ed *BluesWW[port]*
Big Foot *BluesWW[port]*
Big Joe *BluesWW[port]*
Big Maceo *BluesWW[port]*
Big Mama Bev *BluesWW[port]*
Big Maybelle 1924-1972 *BluesWW[port], EncJzS 70, WhScrn 77*
Big Moose *BluesWW[port]*
Big Sister *What 4[port]*
Big Star *ConMuA 80A, IlEncR*
Big Tiny Little *AmSCAP 80*
Big Tree, Chief *Film 2*
Big Vernon *BluesWW[port]*
Big Voice *BluesWW[port]*
Big Walter *BluesWW[port]*
Big Willie *BluesWW[port]*
Bigaglia, Diogenio 1676?-1745? *NewGrD 80*
Bigard, Albany Leon 1906- *AmSCAP 80, NewOrJ[port]*
Bigard, Alec 1898- *NewOrJ*
Bigard, Barney 1906- *CmpEPM, EncJzS 70, IlEncJ, NewGrD 80*
Bigard, Emile 1890?-1935? *NewOrJ*
Bigard, Leon Albany 1906- *AmSCAP 66, BiDAmM, EncJzS 70*
Bigelow, Charles A 1862-1912 *NotNAT B, WhoStg 1908*
Bigelow, Robert Wilcox 1890-1965 *AmSCAP 66, -80*
Bigeou, Clifford *NewOrJ*
Bigeou, Esther 1895?-1936? *BluesWW[port], NewOrJ[port]*
Bigg, John 1930- *IntWWM 77, -80, WhoMus 72*
Biggar, Marjorie *WhoMus 72*
Biggers, Earl Derr 1884-1933 *FilmgC, HalFC 80, NotNAT B, WhThe*
Biggers, W Watts *AmSCAP 80*
Biggs, Ann Elizabeth 1920- *IntWWM 77, -80*
Biggs, Arthur H 1906- *BiDAmM*
Biggs, Charlene Marie 1953- *IntWWM 80*
Biggs, Claribel 1920- *IntWWM 77*
Biggs, E Power 1906-1977 *Baker 78, BnBkM 80[port], MusMk, MusSN[port], NewGrD 80*
Biggs, Edward George Power 1906- *IntWWM 77, -80, WhoMus 72*
Biggs, George B, Jr. 1929- *IntWWM 77*
Biggs, James Theran 1906- *AmSCAP 80*
Biggs, John Joseph 1932- *AmSCAP 80, CpmDNM 72, -74, -77, ConAmC*
Biggs, Lottie Lovell 1913- *AmSCAP 66*
Biggs, Richard Keys 1886-1962 *AmSCAP 66, -80, BiDAmM*
Biggs, Ronald 1893- *WhoMus 72*
Bigley, Isabel 1928- *BiE&WWA*
Bignami, Carlo 1808-1848 *Baker 78, NewGrD 80*
Bignetti, Emilio *NewGrD 80*
Bigonzi, Giuseppe *NewGrD 80*
Bigot, Sieur De *McGEWD[port]*
Bigot, Eugene 1888-1965 *NewGrD 80*
Bigot, Marie 1786-1820 *Baker 78, NewGrD 80*
Bigot, Pierre 1932- *IntWWM 80*
Bigottini, Emilie 1784-1858 *CnOxB, DancEn 78*
Bigwood, G B d1913 *NotNAT B*
Bihari, Janos 1764-1827 *NewGrD 80, OxMus*
Bije, Willy DeLa *CnOxB*
Bijvanck, Henk 1909-1969 *NewGrD 80*
Bikel, Theodore 1924- *BiDAmM, BiE&WWA, EncFCWM 69, FilmEn, FilmgC, ForYSC, HalFC 80, HolCA[port], IntWWM 77, -80, MotPP, MovMk, NotNAT, PlP&P, WhoHol A, WhoThe 72, -77*
Bikle, Charles Henry 1941- *IntWWM 77, -80*
Biland, Ambrose *NewGrD 80*
Bilbrooke, Lydia 1888- *WhThe*
Bilby, Helen Owen 1928- *AmSCAP 80*
Bilby, Kenneth W 1918- *IntMPA 77, -75, -76, -78, -79, -80, NewYTET*
Bilchick, Ruth Coleman 1904- *AmSCAP 80*
Bilder, Robert M 1911- *AmSCAP 80*
Bilder, Robert M 1913-1961 *AmSCAP 66*
Bilderback, Carolyn *WomWMM B*
Bildstein, Hieronymus 1580?-1626? *NewGrD 80*
Bildt, Paul 1885-1957 *Film 2, WhScrn 74, -77, WhoHol B*
Bilek, Ales *IntWWM 77, -80*
Bilger, David Victor 1945- *IntWWM 77, -80*
Bilgrey, Felix J 1924- *IntMPA 77, -75, -76, -78, -79, -80*
Bilham, Cecily Ethel 1916- *WhoMus 72*
Bilhaud, Paul 1854-1933 *NotNAT B, WhThe*
Bilhon, Jean De *Baker 78*
Bilik, Jerry H 1933- *AmSCAP 66, -80, ConAmC*
Bilimoria, N M 1922- *IntMPA 77, -75, -76, -78, -79, -80*
Bilinsky, B Marya *PupTheA*
Bilk, Acker *AmPS A, RkOn[port]*
Bilk, Bernard Stanley 1929- *IntWWM 77, -80*
Bill *BluesWW[port]*
Bill, Buffalo, Jr. 1902- *Film 2*
Bill, Maude *Film 2*
Bill, Teddy *Film 2*
Bill, Tony *IntMPA 76, -78, -79, -80*
Bill, Tony 1940- *FilmEn, FilmgC, HalFC 80, IntMPA 77, WhoHol A*
Bill, Tony 1941- *ForYSC*
Bill-Belotserkovsky, Vladimir Naumovich 1884-1959 *ModWD*
Bill-Belotserkovsky, Vladimir Naumovich 1885-1959 *OxThe*
Bill-Belotserkovsky, Vladimir Naumovich 1885-1970 *EncWT*
Bill-Bjelozerkowski, Vladimir 1884- *CnMD*
Billart *NewGrD 80*
Billaudot, Gerard 1911- *IntWWM 80*
Billbrew, A C H *Film 2*
Billetdoux, Francois 1927- *CnMD, CnThe, CroCD, EncWT, Ent, McGEWD[port], ModWD, REnWD[port]*
Billeter, Bernhard 1936- *IntWWM 77, -80, NewGrD 80*
Billhon, Jhan De *NewGrD 80*
Billi, Lucio *NewGrD 80*
Billing, H Chiswell 1881-1934 *WhThe*
Billinger, Richard 1893-1965 *CnMD, CroCD, McGEWD, ModWD*
Billings, Billie *Film 1*
Billings, Elmo 1913-1964 *Film 2, WhScrn 74, -77, WhoHol B*
Billings, Florence *Film 1, -2*
Billings, George A 1871-1934 *Film 2, WhScrn 74, -77, WhoHol B*
Billings, Warren K 1894- *What 2[port]*
Billings, William 1746-1800 *Baker 78, BiDAmM, BnBkM 80, NewGrD 80, NotNAT B, OxMus, PopAmC*
Billingsley, Barbara *ForYSC, WhoHol A*
Billingsley, Derrell L 1940- *AmSCAP 80*
Billingsley, Jennifer *WhoHol A*
Billingsley, William A 1922- *ConAmC*
Billington, Adeline 1825- *WhThe*
Billington, Elizabeth 1765?-1818 *Baker 78,*

CmOp, NewGrD 80[port], NotNAT B
Billington, Francelia *Film 1, MotPP*
Billington, Fred d1917 *NotNAT B*
Billington, Frederick George 1904- *WhoMus 72*
Billington, Harry George Read 1930- *IntWWM 80*
Billington, John d1904 *NotNAT B*
Billington, Mrs. John d1917 *NotNAT B*
Billington, Kevin 1933- *FilmEn, FilmgC, HalFC 80*
Billington, Michael 1939- *WhoThe 77*
Billington, Peter Bourne 1940- *WhoMus 72*
Billington, Thomas 1754-1832? *NewGrD 80*
Billitteri, Salvatore 1921- *IntMPA 77, -75, -76, -78, -79, -80*
Billon, Jan De *NewGrD 80*
Billon, Jehan De *NewGrD 80*
Billon, Jhan De *NewGrD 80*
Billon, Joannes De *NewGrD 80*
Billoups, Robert *Film 2*
Billroth, Theodor 1829-1894 *Baker 78*
Billsbury, John H d1964 *NotNAT B*
Billy And Lillie *RkOn*
Billy Joe And The Checkmates *RkOn*
Billy The Kid 1859-1881 *OxFilm*
Bilotti, Anton 1906-1963 *AmSCAP 66, -80, ConAmC*
Bilotti, John J 1916- *AmSCAP 66*
Bilowit, Ira J 1925- *BiE&WWA, NatPD[port], NotNAT*
Bilse, Benjamin 1816-1902 *Baker 78*
Bilson, George *IntMPA 77, -75, -76, -78, -79, -80*
Bilstein, Johannes 1560?-1596? *NewGrD 80*
Bilstenius, Johannes 1560?-1596? *NewGrD 80*
Bilstin, Youry 1887-1947 *Baker 78*
Bilt, Peter VanDer 1936- *NewGrD 80*
Bilton, Belle d1908 *NotNAT B*
Bilyeu, Landon 1939- *ConAmC*
Bimberg, Siegfried Wolfgang 1927- *IntWWM 77, -80*
Bimbo Jet *RkOn 2A*
Bimboni, Alberto 1882-1960 *AmSCAP 66, Baker 78, ConAmC*
Bimio, Giacomo Filippo *NewGrD 80*
Bimler, Georg Heinrich *NewGrD 80*
Binaghi, Benedetto d1619? *NewGrD 80*
Binago, Benedetto d1619? *NewGrD 80*
Binche, Gilles De 1400?-1460 *BnBkM 80*
Binchois, Gilles 1400?-1460 *Baker 78, BnBkM 80, OxMus*
Binchois, Gilles De Binch Dit 1400?-1460 *NewGrD 80[port]*
Binchois, Gilles De Binche Dit 1400?-1460 *NewGrD 80[port]*
Binchois, Gilles De Bins Dit 1400?-1460 *NewGrD 80[port]*
Binder, Abraham Wolfe 1895-1966 *AmSCAP 66, -80, Baker 78, BiDAmM, ConAmC*
Binder, Carl 1816-1860 *NewGrD 80*
Binder, Christlieb Siegmund 1723-1789 *Baker 78, NewGrD 80*
Binder, Dave 1903- *AmSCAP 80*
Binder, Fred d1963 *NotNAT B*
Binder, Karl 1816-1860 *Baker 78*
Binder, Maurice 1925- *FilmgC, HalFC 80*
Binder, Steve *NewYTET*
Binder, Sybille d1962 *NotNAT B, WhoHol B*
Binellus, Giovanni Battista *NewGrD 80*
Binellus DeGerardis, Giovanni Battista *NewGrD 80*
Binenbaum, Janco 1880-1956 *Baker 78*
Biner, Frank 1950- *AmSCAP 80*
Binet, Jean 1893-1960 *Baker 78, NewGrD 80, OxMus*
Binford, Mira *WomWMM B*
Bing, Gus 1893-1967 *WhScrn 74, -77, WhoHol B*
Bing, Herman 1889-1946 *Vers A[port]*
Bing, Herman 1889-1947 *FilmEn, Film 2, FilmgC, HalFC 80, HolCA[port], NotNAT B, WhScrn 74, -77, WhoHol B*
Bing, Herman 1898-1947 *ForYSC*
Bing, Herman 1899-1947 *MovMk[port]*
Bing, Sir Rudolf 1902- *Baker 78, IntWWM 77, -80, NewEOp 71, NewGrD 80, WhoMus 72, WhoOp 76*
Bing, Sir Rudolf 1903- *BiDAmM*
Bing, Stephen 1618?-1681 *NewGrD 80*
Binge, Ronald 1910- *IntWWM 77, -80, WhoMus 72*
Binge, Ronald 1910-1979 *NewGrD 80*
Bingham, Amelia 1869-1927 *NotNAT B, WhThe, WhoStg 1906, -1908*
Bingham, Barry 1906- *IntMPA 75, -76*
Bingham, George *WhScrn 74, -77*
Bingham, J Clarke d1962 *NotNAT B*
Bingham, John 1942- *WhoMus 72*
Bingham, Jonathan Brewster 1914- *IntWWM 77*
Bingham, Leslie d1945 *NotNAT B*
Bingham, Peter John 1935- *WhoMus 72*
Bingham, Seth 1882-1972 *AmSCAP 66, -80, Baker 78, BiDAmM, ConAmC, NewGrD 80, OxMus*
Bingham, William L, Jr. 1945- *AmSCAP 80*
Bingley, Ward 1757-1818 *OxThe*
Bini, Carlo *WhoOp 76*
Bini, Pasquale 1716-1770 *NewGrD 80*
Bini, Pasqualino 1716-1770 *NewGrD 80*
Binicki, Stanislav 1872-1942 *NewGrD 80*
Binkerd, Gordon 1916- *AmSCAP 80, Baker 78, CpmDNM 72, -74, -79, -80, ConAmC, DcCM, NewGrD 80*
Binkley, Thomas Eden 1931- *IntWWM 77, -80*
Binkley, Thurman G, Jr. 1944- *AmSCAP 80*
Binkley Brothers' Dixie Clodhoppers, The *IlEncCM*
Binkowski, Bernhard 1912- *IntWWM 80*
Binner, Margery 1908- *WhThe*
Binney, Constance 1900- *Film 1, -2, MotPP, TwYS, WhThe, WhoHol A*
Binney, Fair *TwYS*
Binney, Faire *Film 1, -2*
Binney, Malcolm 1944- *WhoMus 72*
Binney, Oliver *ConAmC*
Binney, Thomas 1798-1874 *OxMus*
Binnie, James 1938- *WhoMus 72*
Binning, Bertram Charles 1909- *CreCan 1*
Binnington, Stephen 1953- *IntWWM 80*
Binns, Edith Margaret *WhoMus 72*
Binns, Edward *IntMPA 77, -75, -76, -78, -79, -80, MotPP, WhoHol A*
Binns, Edward 1916- *ForYSC*
Binns, George H 1886-1918 *Film 1, WhScrn 77*
Binns, John 1744?-1796 *NewGrD 80*
Binns, Malcolm 1936- *IntWWM 77, -80, NewGrD 80, WhoMus 72*
Binns, Margaret *IntWWM 77, -80*
Binyon, Claude 1905-1978 *FilmEn, FilmgC, HalFC 80, IntMPA 77, -75, -76, -78*
Binyon, Larry 1908- *WhoJazz 72*
Binyon, Laurence 1869-1946 *OxThe, WhThe*
Binyon, Lawrence 1869-1946 *PlP&P*
Binyon, Robert Laurence 1869-1943 *NotNAT B*
Biondi, Giovanni Battista *NewGrD 80*
Biondi, Guy 1922- *IntMPA 77, -75, -76, -78, -79, -80*
Biondi, Ray Remo 1905- *WhoJazz 72*
Biondin *NewGrD 80*
Biondo, Rose Leonore Victoria 1931- *AmSCAP 80*
Bioni, Antonio 1698-1739? *NewGrD 80*
Biordi, Giovanni 1691-1748 *NewGrD 80*
Biot, Jean Baptiste 1774-1862 *NewGrD 80*
Biquardus *NewGrD 80*
Birabeau, Andre 1890- *CnMD, McGEWD[port], ModWD*
Biran, Tova *WomWMM*
Birch, A Cecil *IlWWBF*
Birch, Frank 1889-1956 *NotNAT B, WhThe*
Birch, John Anthony 1929- *NewGrD 80, WhoMus 72*
Birch, June Marie 1923- *WhoMus 72*
Birch, Patricia 1934?- *EncMT, NotNAT, WhoThe 77*
Birch, Paul *FilmgC*
Birch, Paul d1964 *ForYSC, WhoHol B*
Birch, Paul d1969 *WhScrn 77, WhoHrs 80[port]*
Birch, Paul 1904?- *HalFC 80*
Birch, Peter 1940- *AmSCAP 80*
Birch, Peter Hudson 1922- *AmSCAP 80*
Birch, Robert Fairfax *AmSCAP 66, -80*
Birch, Samuel d1841 *NotNAT B*
Birch, William 1918- *IntMPA 77, -75, -76, -78, -79, -80*
Birchall, Robert 1760?-1819 *NewGrD 80*
Birchall, Robert 1819- *Baker 78*
Birchall, Steven *ConAmC*
Birchard, Clarence C 1866-1946 *Baker 78*
Birchensha, John d1681 *NewGrD 80*
Bircher, John Charles 1947- *IntWWM 77, -80*
Birchfield, Benny 1937- *BiDAmM*
Birchfield, Raymond *BlkAmP*
Birck, Wenzel Raimund *NewGrD 80*
Birckenstock, Johann Adam *NewGrD 80*
Birckh, Wenzel Raimund *NewGrD 80*
Bircsak, Thusnelda A *AmSCAP 80*
Bird, Arthur 1856-1923 *Baker 78, BiDAmM, NewGrD 80*
Bird, Bernard *ConAmC*
Bird, Betty *Film 2*
Bird, Billie *WhoHol A*
Bird, Carol Henrietta 1918- *IntWWM 77, -80*
Bird, Charles *Film 2*
Bird, Charles A d1925 *NotNAT B*
Bird, Charlotte *Film 2*
Bird, Daphne Mary-Grace 1915- *WhoMus 72*
Bird, David 1907- *WhoThe 72, -77*
Bird, Elisabeth Maureen 1935- *IntWWM 77*
Bird, George T 1900-1978 *AmSCAP 66, -80*
Bird, Getty *Film 2*
Bird, Henry Richard 1842-1915 *Baker 78*
Bird, Hubert C 1939- *ConAmC, IntWWM 80*
Bird, James Edward 1950- *AmSCAP 80*
Bird, John 1936- *WhoThe 77*
Bird, Montgomery *PlP&P*
Bird, Napoleon *OxMus*
Bird, Norman 1920?- *FilmgC, HalFC 80, WhoHol A*
Bird, Richard 1894- *FilmgC, HalFC 80, IlWWBF, WhThe, WhoThe 72*
Bird, Robert Montgomery 1806-1854 *CnThe, McGEWD[port], NotNAT B, OxThe, REnWD[port]*
Bird, Theophilus 1608-1664 *NotNAT B, OxThe*
Bird, William d1624 *NotNAT B, OxThe*
Bird, William 1542?-1623 *OxMus*
Bird, William Richard 1891- *CreCan 2*
Birdt, Robert 1935- *AmSCAP 66, -80*
Birdwell, Edward Ridley 1936- *IntWWM 77, -80*
Birell, Tala 1908-1959 *FilmEn, FilmgC, ForYSC, HalFC 80, WhoHol B*
Birenbaum, Jack Abraham 1913- *IntWWM 77, -80*
Biret, Idil 1941- *IntWWM 80*
Birge, Edward Bailey *OxMus*
Birgel, Willy 1891-1974 *FilmAG WE*
Birimisa, George 1924- *ConDr 73, -77*
Biriotti, Leon 1929- *Baker 78, NewGrD 80*
Biriukov, Yuri 1908-1976 *Baker 78*
Birk, Wenzel Raimund *NewGrD 80*
Birken, Sigmund Von 1626-1681 *NewGrD 80*
Birkenhead, Susan 1935- *AmSCAP 80*
Birkenshaw, John *NewGrD 80*
Birkenstock, Johann Adam 1687-1733 *Baker 78, NewGrD 80*
Birkenstok, Johann Adam 1687-1733 *NewGrD 80*
Birkett, Michael 1929- *FilmEn, FilmgC, HalFC 80*
Birkett, Viva 1887-1934 *Film 2, NotNAT B, WhScrn 77, WhThe, WhoHol B*
Birkhead, Florence VanEck *PupTheA*
Birkin, Jane 1946- *FilmEn*
Birkin, Jane 1947- *FilmAG WE[port], WhoHol A*
Birkmeyer *CnOxB*
Birkmeyer, Adolf B *CnOxB*
Birkmeyer, Michael B 1943- *CnOxB*
Birkmeyer, Toni B 1897-1973 *CnOxB*
Birman, Serafima Germanovna 1890- *OxThe*
Birmingham, George A 1865-1950 *NotNAT B, WhThe*
Birmingham, Hugh Myers, Jr. 1929- *IntWWM 77, -80*
Birmingham, Paul A 1937- *IntMPA 77, -75, -76, -78, -79, -80*
Birmingham Sam *BluesWW[port]*
Birnbach *NewGrD 80*
Birnbach, Hanna *NewGrD 80*
Birnbach, Heinrich 1793-1879 *Baker 78*
Birnbach, Karl Joseph 1751-1805 *Baker 78*
Birnbach, Richard *NewGrD 80*
Birnbach, Richard 1883-1953 *NewGrD 80*

Birnbaum, Eduard 1855-1920 NewGrD 80
Birnbaum, Mark J 1952- ConAmC
Birney, Alfred Earle 1904- CreCan 1
Birney, David 1944- HalFC 80, IntMPA 78, -79, -80, NotNAT, WhoHol A
Birney, Earle 1904- CreCan 1
Birnie, Tessa Daphne 1934- IntWWM 80, NewGrD 80
Birnstingl, Roger 1932- IntWWM 80, WhoMus 72
Biro, Lajos 1880-1948 FilmEn, FilmgC, HalFC 80, NotNAT B, OxThe, WorEFlm[port]
Biroc, Joseph 1903- FilmEn
Biroc, Joseph F 1903- FilmgC, HalFC 80, IntMPA 77, -75, -76, -78, -79, -80, WorEFlm[port]
Birrell, Francis d1935 NotNAT B
Birri, Fernando 1925- DcFM
Birt, Daniel 1907-1955 FilmEn, FilmgC, HalFC 80, IlWWBF
Birtner, Herbert 1900-1942 NewGrD 80
Birtwistle, Harrison 1934- Baker 78, BnBkM 80, CpmDNM 80, DcCom&M 79, DcCM, IntWWM 77, -80, MusMk, NewGrD 80[port], WhoMus 72
Bisaccia, Giovanni 1815-1897 Baker 78
Biscardi, Chester 1948- CpmDNM 78, IntWWM 77, -80
Bischmann, Elwyn 1932- IntWWM 77
Bischof, Melchior 1547-1614 NewGrD 80
Bischoff, Egon 1934- CnOxB, DancEn 78
Bischoff, Georg Friedrich 1780-1841 Baker 78
Bischoff, Hans 1852-1889 Baker 78, NewGrD 80
Bischoff, Hermann 1868-1936 Baker 78
Bischoff, John W 1850-1909 BiDAmM
Bischoff, Kaspar Jakob 1823-1893 Baker 78
Bischoff, Kurt 1949- ConAmC
Bischoff, Ludwig Friedrich Christian 1794-1867 Baker 78
Bischoff, Marie Baker 78
Bischoff, Melchior 1547-1614 NewGrD 80
Bischoff, Samuel 1890-1975 FilmEn, FilmgC, HalFC 80, IntMPA 75
Biscogli, Francesco NewGrD 80
Biseghino, Giovanni NewGrD 80
Bish, Diane ConAmC
Bishoff, Donald Brian, Jr. 1936- ConAmTC
Bishop NewGrD 80
Bishop, Adelaide WhoOp 76
Bishop, Alfred 1848-1928 NotNAT B, WhThe
Bishop, Andrew BlksB&W C
Bishop, Anna Riviere 1810-1884 Baker 78, BiDAmM, NewGrD 80
Bishop, Bainbridge OxMus
Bishop, Bish Wallace Henry 1906- WhoJazz 72
Bishop, Burtus, Jr. 1905- IntMPA 75, -76
Bishop, Chester 1858-1937 WhScrn 74, -77, WhoHol B
Bishop, David 1931- NotNAT
Bishop, Detective Sergeant Film 2
Bishop, Elvin 1942- AmSCAP 80, IlEncR, RkOn 2[port]
Bishop, Frances Blackburn 1925- IntWWM 77
Bishop, George Walter 1886-1965 OxThe, WhThe
Bishop, Sir Henry Rowley 1786-1855 Baker 78, BnBkM 80, CmOp, MusMk[port], NewGrD 80[port], OxMus
Bishop, James C NewGrD 80
Bishop, Joe 1907-1976 AmSCAP 66, -80, CmpEPM, WhoJazz 72
Bishop, Joey 1918- FilmEn, FilmgC, ForYSC, HalFC 80, WhoHol A
Bishop, Joey 1919- JoeFr
Bishop, John 1665?-1737 NewGrD 80
Bishop, John Edward 1935- IntWWM 77, -80, WhoMus 72
Bishop, Julie ForYSC, MotPP
Bishop, Julie 1914- FilmEn, WhoHol A
Bishop, Julie 1917- FilmgC, HalFC 80, IntMPA 77, -75, -76, -78, -79, -80, MovMk
Bishop, Kate 1847-1923 NotNAT B, WhThe
Bishop, Marion PupTheA
Bishop, Martha 1937- IntWWM 77, -80
Bishop, Peter Frederick 1951- IntWWM 77
Bishop, Richard 1898-1956 NotNAT B, WhScrn 74, -77, WhoHol B
Bishop, Robert H, III 1916- BiE&WWA
Bishop, Ronald Taylor 1934- IntWWM 77, -80
Bishop, Stanley Walter 1910- WhoMus 72
Bishop, Stark, Jr. 1932-1945 WhScrn 74, -77
Bishop, Stephen WhoMus 72
Bishop, Stephen 1940- BiDAmM
Bishop, Stephen 1951- RkOn 2[port]
Bishop, Terry 1912- FilmEn, FilmgC, HalFC 80, IlWWBF
Bishop, Thomas Brigham 1835-1905 BiDAmM
Bishop, Walter 1905- AmSCAP 66, BiDAmM
Bishop, Walter, Jr. 1927- AmSCAP 80, BiDAmM, EncJzS 70
Bishop, Walter Francis, Sr. 1905- AmSCAP 80
Bishop, Washington Irving 1856-1889 MagIlD
Bishop, Will 1867-1944 NotNAT B, WhThe
Bishop, William d1959 MotPP, WhoHol B
Bishop, William 1917-1959 FilmEn, WhScrn 74, -77
Bishop, William 1918-1959 FilmgC, HalFC 80, NotNAT B
Bishop, William 1918-1960 ForYSC
Bishop-Kovacevich, Stephen 1940- IntWWM 77, -80, NewGrD 80
Bisiach NewGrD 80
Bisiach, Andrea 1890-1967 NewGrD 80
Bisiach, Carlo 1892-1968 NewGrD 80
Bisiach, Giacomo 1900- NewGrD 80
Bisiach, Leandro 1864-1945 NewGrD 80
Bisiach, Leandro 1904- NewGrD 80
Biskar, John L 1918- AmSCAP 66, -80
Biskup, Renate Maria 1939- WhoOp 76
Bismillah Khan 1916- Baker 78
Bispham, David Scull 1857-1921 Baker 78, BiDAmM, NewEOp 71, NewGrD 80, NotNAT B, WhoStg 1906
Bisquertt, Prospero 1881-1959 NewGrD 80
Bisschop, Ludovicus De NewGrD 80
Bissell, Keith 1912- Baker 78, CreCan 1
Bissell, Richard 1913- BiE&WWA, NotNAT
Bissell, Whit 1914?- FilmgC, HalFC 80, WhoHol A, WhoHrs 80[port]
Bissell, Whit 1919- FilmEn, ForYSC
Bisset, Jacqueline IntMPA 75, -76
Bisset, Jacqueline 1944- BiDFilm 81, FilmEn, FilmgC, ForYSC, HalFC 80, IntMPA 77, -78, -79, -80, WhoHol A
Bisset, Jacqueline 1945- MovMk
Bissett, Donald J 1930- BiE&WWA
Bissett, Jacqueline MotPP
Bissett, Margaret WhoMus 72
Bisso, Louis 1905?- NewOrJ
Bisson, Alexandre d1912 NotNAT B
Bisson, Ives 1936- WhoOp 76
Bisson, Loys NewGrD 80
Bisson, Napoleon 1923- CreCan 2, WhoOp 76
Bister, Eero Olavi 1919- IntWWM 77, -80
Biswanger, Erwin Film 2
Biteryng NewGrD 80
Bitetti, Ernesto 1943- IntWWM 77, -80, NewGrD 80
Bitgood, Roberta 1908- AmSCAP 66, -80, ConAmC
Bitner, W W Film 1
Bitsch, Marcel 1921- Baker 78, IntWWM 77, -80
Bitter, Carl Hermann 1813-1885 Baker 78, NewGrD 80
Bitter, John 1909- ConAmC, WhoMus 72
Bitter, Marietta 1904- IntWWM 77, -80
Bitti, Martino 1655?-1743 NewGrD 80
Bittman, Emil 1927- IntWWM 77, -80
Bittner, Jack 1917- NotNAT
Bittner, Julius 1874-1939 Baker 78, NewEOp 71, NewGrD 80, OxMus
Bittner, William W 1866-1918 WhScrn 77
Bittoni, Bernardo 1756-1829 NewGrD 80
Bittoni, Luigi 1753- NewGrD 80
Bittoni, Mario Gaetano 1723?-1798 NewGrD 80
Bitzel, Charles Raymond 1946- ConAmC
Bitzer, Billy 1870-1944 WorEFlm[port]
Bitzer, Billy 1872-1944 FilmEn
Bitzer, Billy 1874-1944 DcFM, FilmgC, HalFC 80, OxFilm
Biumi, Giacomo Filippo 1580?-1653 NewGrD 80
Bivens, Burke 1903-1967 AmSCAP 66, -80
Bivi, Paolo Antonio Del NewGrD 80
Bivona, Gus 1915- CmpEPM, WhoJazz 72
Bivona, Gus 1917- AmSCAP 66, BiDAmM
Bivona, S Richard 1911-1964 AmSCAP 66, -80
Bixby, Bill 1934- FilmEn, FilmgC, ForYSC, HalFC 80, IntMPA 77, -75, -76, -78, -79, -80, WhoHol A
Bixby, Jerome 1923- WhoHrs 80
Bixby, Meredith PupTheA
Bixler, Martha Harrison 1927- IntWWM 77, -80
Bizet, Charles NewGrD 80
Bizet, Georges 1838-1875 Baker 78, BnBkM 80, CmOp, CmpBCM, CnOxB, DancEn 78, DcCom 77[port], DcCom&M 79, GrComp[port], MusMk, NewEOp 71, NewGrD 80[port], NotNAT B, OxMus
Bizey, Charles NewGrD 80
Bizony, Celia 1904- IntWWM 77, -80, WhoMus 72
Bjarnason, Grimur 1955- IntWWM 80
Bjelinski, Bruno 1909- Baker 78, IntWWM 77, -80, NewGrD 80
Bjerre, Jens 1903- IntWWM 77, -80, NewGrD 80
Bjerregaard, Henrik 1792-1842 OxThe
Bjoner, Ingrid IntWWM 77, -80, WhoMus 72, WhoOp 76
Bjoner, Ingrid 1927- MusSN[port], NewGrD 80
Bjoner, Ingrid 1929- NewEOp 71
Bjoreid, Bjorg Leerstang 1925- IntWWM 77, -80
Bjork, Anita 1923- FilmEn, FilmgC, HalFC 80, MotPP, OxFilm, WhoHol A, WorEFlm[port]
Bjork, Jewel WomWMM B
Bjorkander, Nils 1893-1972 Baker 78, NewGrD 80
Bjorklund, Bjorn 1926- IntWWM 77, -80
Bjorkman, Edwin August 1866-1951 NotNAT B
Bjorlin, Ulf Stefan 1933- Baker 78, IntWWM 77, -80
Bjorling, Johan 1911-1960 NewGrD 80[port]
Bjorling, Jussi 1911-1960 Baker 78, BnBkM 80[port], CmOp, MusMk, MusSN[port], NewEOp 71, NewGrD 80[port]
Bjorling, Rolf 1928- WhoOp 76
Bjorling, Rolf Warner David 1928- IntWWM 77, -80
Bjorling, Sigurd 1907- CmOp, WhoMus 72
Bjorn, Dinna 1947- CnOxB
Bjorne, Hugh d1966 WhoHol B
Bjorne, Hugo 1886-1966 WhScrn 74, -77
Bjorneboe, Jens Ingvald 1920- CroCD
Bjornson, Bjorn 1859-1942 NotNAT B, OxThe
Bjornson, Bjorn 1859-1952 EncWT
Bjornson, Bjornstjerne 1832-1910 CnMD, CnThe, EncWT, Ent, McGEWD[port], ModWD, NotNAT B, OxThe, REnWD[port]
Bjornsson, Arni 1905- IntWWM 77, -80, NewGrD 80
Bjornsson, Fredbjorn 1926- CnOxB, DancEn 78
Bjornsson, Gunnar 1944- IntWWM 77
Bjornsson, Sigurd 1932- WhoOp 76
Bjornstrand, Gunnar 1909- FilmEn, FilmgC, HalFC 80, MovMk, OxFilm, WhoHol A, WorEFlm[port]
Blache, Alice FilmEn
Blache, Alice Guy 1873-1965 DcFM
Blache, Alice Guy 1873-1968 WomWMM
Blache, Alice Guy 1878- TwYS A
Blache, Herbert FilmEn, TwYS A, WomWMM
Blache, Jean-Baptiste 1765-1834 CnOxB
Blache, Simone WomWMM
Blacher, Boris 1903-1975 Baker 78, BnBkM 80, CmOp, CompSN[port], CpmDNM 74, CnOxB, DancEn 78, DcCM, MusMk[port], NewEOp 71, NewGrD 80, OxMus
Blacher, Deanna 1940- IntWWM 80
Blachford, Frank Edward 1879-1957 CreCan 1
Blachut, Beno 1913- CmOp, NewGrD 80, WhoOp 76
Black, Alexander F 1918- IntMPA 77, -75, -76, -78, -79, -80
Black, Alfred 1913- WhThe, WhoThe 72

Black, Allan *PupTheA*
Black, Andrew 1859-1920 *Baker 78, NewGrD 80*
Black, Ben 1889-1950 *AmSCAP 66, -80*
Black, Bill *AmPS A, Film 1, RkOn*
Black, Bill 1927-1965 *WhScrn 77*
Black, Buck *Film 2*
Black, Buddy 1918- *AmSCAP 66, -80*
Black, Charles 1903- *AmSCAP 66, -80, ConAmC*
Black, Cilla 1943- *RkOn 2[port], WhoHol A*
Black, David 1931- *BiE&WWA, NotNAT, WhoThe 72, -77*
Black, David Michael 1941- *AmSCAP 80*
Black, Donald Fisher 1941- *IntWWM 77, -80*
Black, Dorothy 1899- *WhThe*
Black, Edward William 1902- *WhoMus 72*
Black, Edwin Clair 1938- *IntWWM 80*
Black, Eugene R 1898- *BiE&WWA, NotNAT*
Black, Frank J 1894-1968 *Baker 78*
Black, Frank J 1896- *AmSCAP 66, CmpEPM, ConAmC A*
Black, Frankie *BluesWW[port]*
Black, G Howe *Film 2*
Black, George 1890-1945 *EncMT, NotNAT B, OxThe, WhThe*
Black, George 1911-1970 *WhThe*
Black, Gloria 1944- *AmSCAP 80*
Black, Gordon McCully 1913- *IntWWM 77, -80*
Black, Ira J 1943- *ConAmTC*
Black, Isaac J *MorBAP*
Black, James M 1856-1938 *BiDAmM*
Black, Jeanne 1937- *AmPS A, RkOn*
Black, Jeanne Belcher *MorBAP*
Black, Jennie Prince 1868-1945 *AmSCAP 66, -80*
Black, John *NewGrD 80*
Black, Karen *AmSCAP 80, WhoHol A*
Black, Karen 1942- *FilmEn*
Black, Karen 1943- *HalFC 80, IntMPA 77, -75, -76, -78, -79, -80, MovMk*
Black, Karen 1948- *FilmgC*
Black, Kitty 1914- *WhoThe 72, -77*
Black, Lou Thomas 1901-1965 *WhoJazz 72*
Black, Maggie 1930?- *CnOxB*
Black, Malcolm Charles Lamont 1928- *BiE&WWA, CreCan 1, NotNAT*
Black, Maurice d1938 *Film 2, WhScrn 74, -77, WhoHol B*
Black, Neal *NatPD[port]*
Black, Neil *WhoMus 72*
Black, Neil 1932- *IntWWM 77, -80, NewGrD 80*
Black, Noel 1937- *FilmEn, FilmgC, HalFC 80*
Black, Ralph 1919- *IntWWM 77, -80*
Black, Stanley 1913- *FilmEn, FilmgC, HalFC 80, IntMPA 77, -75, -76, -78, -79, -80, IntWWM 77, -80, WhoMus 72*
Black, Ted *CmpEPM*
Black, Theodore R 1906- *IntMPA 77, -75, -76, -78, -79, -80*
Black, William *Film 2*
Black, William Patton 1926-1965 *BiDAmM*
Black Ace *BluesWW[port]*
Black Arthur 1940- *EncJzS 70*
Black Artists Group *IlEncJ*
Black Experience Family *MorBAP*
Black Junior *BluesWW[port]*
Black Kangaroo *BiDAmM*
Black Muslims *BiDAmM*
Black Oak Arkansas *ConMuA 80A, IlEncR, RkOn 2[port]*
Black Patti *DrBlPA*
Black Sabbath *ConMuA 80A, IlEncR, RkOn 2[port]*
Blackburn, Andrew Stewart 1954- *IntWWM 80*
Blackburn, Aubrey 1900- *IntMPA 75*
Blackburn, Clarice *WhoHol A*
Blackburn, Dorothy *BiE&WWA, NotNAT*
Blackburn, Geoffrey Norman 1930- *IntWWM 77*
Blackburn, Harold 1925- *WhoMus 72, WhoOp 76*
Blackburn, John M 1913- *AmSCAP 80*
Blackburn, John M 1914- *AmSCAP 66*
Blackburn, Lou 1922- *BiDAmM, EncJzS 70*
Blackburn, Maurice 1914- *CreCan 2, DcFM*
Blackburn Twins, The *WhoHol A*
Blackbyrds, The *RkOn 2[port]*
Blacker, Jesse 1898- *WhoMus 72*
Blackett, Joy E 1944- *IntWWM 77, -80*
Blackford, Lottie *Film 2*
Blackford, Mary 1914-1937 *WhScrn 74, -77, WhoHol B*
Blackhall, Andrew 1535?-1609 *NewGrD 80*
Blackham, Joyce 1934- *CmOp, WhoMus 72, WhoOp 76*
Blackham, Olive *DcPup*
Blacking, John Anthony Randoll 1928- *IntWWM 77, -80*
Blackino, Yvette *WomWMM B*
Blackler, Betty 1929- *WhThe*
Blackley, Douglas *FilmEn*
Blackley, Robert R John 1936- *IntWWM 77*
Blackman, Don *WhoHol A*
Blackman, Eugene J 1922- *BiE&WWA, NotNAT*
Blackman, Fred J d1951 *NotNAT B*
Blackman, Fred J 1879- *WhThe*
Blackman, Honor 1926- *FilmAG WE, FilmEn, FilmgC, ForYSC, HalFC 80, IlWWBF[port], IntMPA 77, -75, -76, -78, -79, -80, MotPP, WhoHol A, WhoHrs 80[port], WhoThe 72, -77*
Blackman, Joan *FilmgC, WhoHol A*
Blackman, Joan 1927- *ForYSC*
Blackman, Joan 1938- *HalFC 80*
Blackman, Michael Bruce 1946- *AmSCAP 80*
Blackman, Paul Anthony 1953- *IntWWM 77, -80*
Blackmar, Armand Edward 1826-1888 *BiDAmM*
Blackmer, Sidney 1894-1973 *HolCA[port]*
Blackmer, Sidney 1895-1973 *BiE&WWA, FilmEn, Film 2, FilmgC, HalFC 80, NotNAT B, WhThe, WhoHol B, WhoHrs 80, WhoThe 72*
Blackmer, Sidney 1896-1973 *WhScrn 77*
Blackmer, Sidney 1898-1973 *ForYSC, MovMk, Vers A[port]*
Blackmon, Frederick Mosley 1947- *AmSCAP 80*
Blackmore, Carl 1904-1965 *AmSCAP 66, -80*
Blackmore, E Willard 1870-1949 *WhScrn 74, -77*
Blackmore, George Henry James 1921- *IntWWM 77, -80, WhoMus 72*
Blackmore, Peter 1909- *WhThe, WhoThe 72*
Blackmore, Ritchie 1945- *ConMuA 80A, IlEncR*
Blackshaw, Christian 1949- *IntWWM 77, -80*
Blacksmith, Henry *NewGrD 80*
Blackstone, Barbara 1919- *IntWWM 77*
Blackstone, Harry 1885-1965 *MagIlD*
Blackstone, Vivian *WomWMM B*
Blackton, Charles Stuart 1914- *Film 2*
Blackton, Greg *Film 2*
Blackton, J Stewart 1875-1941 *WorEFlm[port]*
Blackton, J Stuart 1868-1941 *FilmgC, HalFC 80*
Blackton, J Stuart 1875-1941 *FilmEn, WhScrn 77*
Blackton, J Stuart 1875-1946 *TwYS A*
Blackton, James Stuart 1875-1941 *DcFM, OxFilm*
Blackton, Jay 1909- *AmSCAP 66, -80, BiE&WWA, NotNAT*
Blackton, Marian *Film 2*
Blackton, Violet Virginia *Film 2*
Blackwell, Anna Gee 1928- *IntWWM 77, -80*
Blackwell, Carlyle d1955 *MotPP, NotNAT B, WhoHol B*
Blackwell, Carlyle 1880-1955 *Film 2*
Blackwell, Carlyle 1884-1955 *TwYS*
Blackwell, Carlyle 1888-1955 *FilmEn, Film 1, FilmgC, HalFC 80, IlWWBF, WhScrn 74, -77*
Blackwell, Carlyle, Jr. 1913-1974 *WhScrn 77, WhoHol B*
Blackwell, Derek *WhoOp 76*
Blackwell, Don *MorBAP*
Blackwell, Earl 1914- *BiE&WWA, NotNAT*
Blackwell, Ed 1927- *EncJzS 70, IlEncJ*
Blackwell, Edward B 1927- *EncJzS 70*
Blackwell, Eunice Edna 1930- *WhoMus 72*
Blackwell, Francis Hillman 1903-1962 *BluesWW[port]*
Blackwell, Glenda Rue Moseley 1940- *IntWWM 77, -80*
Blackwell, Isaac *NewGrD 80*
Blackwell, James *BlkAmP*
Blackwell, Jim *Film 2*
Blackwell, William Neal 1942- *IntWWM 77, -80*
Blackwood, Bonnie 1909-1949 *WhScrn 74, -77*
Blackwood, Cecil Stamps 1934- *BiDAmM*
Blackwood, Diana d1961 *WhScrn 74, -77*
Blackwood, Doyle J 1911- *BiDAmM*
Blackwood, Easley 1933- *AmSCAP 80, Baker 78, BiDAmM, BnBkM 80, CompSN[port], ConAmC, NewGrD 80*
Blackwood, Freda 1943- *WhoOp 76*
Blackwood, James Webre 1919- *BiDAmM*
Blackwood, James Webre, Jr. 1943- *BiDAmM*
Blackwood, William Le 1953- *AmSCAP 80*
Blade, James P 1907- *AmSCAP 66*
Bladen, Anthony William 1924- *IntWWM 77, -80*
Blades, James 1901- *IntWWM 77, -80, NewGrD 80, WhoMus 72*
Blades, Ruben 1948- *AmSCAP 80*
Blado, Antonio 1490-1567 *NewGrD 80*
Blaes, Arnold Joseph 1814-1892 *NewGrD 80*
Blaes, Elisa 1817-1878 *NewGrD 80*
Blaga, Lucian 1895-1961 *CnMD*
Blaga, Lucian 1896-1961 *EncWT*
Blagman, Norman 1926- *AmSCAP 80*
Blagoi, George 1898-1971 *WhScrn 74, -77, WhoHol B*
Blagrave, Thomas 1615?-1688 *NewGrD 80*
Blagrove, Henry Gamble 1811-1872 *Baker 78, NewGrD 80*
Blagrove, Thomas *OxThe*
Blaha, Ivo 1936- *Baker 78, IntWWM 77, -80*
Blaha-Mikes, Zaboj 1887-1957 *Baker 78*
Blahetka, Marie Leopoldine 1811-1887 *Baker 78*
Blahnik, Joel Arthur 1938- *AmSCAP 80*
Blahoslav, Jan 1523-1571 *NewGrD 80*
Blahoslav, John d1571 *OxMus*
Blaikley, David James 1846-1936 *NewGrD 80*
Blain, Albert Valdes 1921- *IntWWM 77, -80*
Blain, Gerard 1930- *FilmAG WE, FilmEn, FilmgC, HalFC 80, WhoHol A*
Blaine, Chip *AmSCAP 80*
Blaine, Eleanor G *PupTheA*
Blaine, Jerry *BgBands 74*
Blaine, Joan d1949 *WhScrn 77*
Blaine, Martin *WhoHol A*
Blaine, Rose d1974 *WhoHol B*
Blaine, Ruby *Film 2*
Blaine, Vivian *AmPS B, MotPP*
Blaine, Vivian 1921- *CmpEPM, EncMT, FilmEn, FilmgC, HalFC 80, HolP 40[port], WhoThe 77*
Blaine, Vivian 1923- *BiE&WWA, NotNAT, WhoThe 72*
Blaine, Vivian 1924- *ForYSC, IntMPA 77, -75, -76, -78, -79, -80, WhoHol A*
Blainville, Charles-Henri 1710-1770? *Baker 78*
Blainville, Charles Henri De 1710?-1777? *NewGrD 80*
Blair, Bert Alvin 1927- *IntWWM 77, -80*
Blair, Betsy 1923- *BiE&WWA, FilmEn, FilmgC, ForYSC, HalFC 80, IntMPA 77, -75, -76, -78, -79, -80, MotPP, OxFilm, WhoHol A*
Blair, Betty Woodruff 1920- *IntWWM 77, -80*
Blair, David 1932-1976 *CnOxB, DancEn 78, WhoHol C*
Blair, Dean 1932- *WhoMus 72*
Blair, Ella S 1895-1917 *WhScrn 77*
Blair, Eugenie d1922 *NotNAT B*
Blair, Frank 1915- *NewYTET*
Blair, George 1906-1970 *FilmEn, FilmgC, HalFC 80, WhoHrs 80*
Blair, Hal Keller 1915- *AmSCAP 66, -80*
Blair, Isla 1944- *WhoThe 77*
Blair, Janet 1921- *BiDAmM, BiE&WWA, CmpEPM, FilmEn, FilmgC, ForYSC, HalFC 80, HolP 40[port], IntMPA 77, -75, -76, -78, -79, -80, MotPP, MovMk, WhoHol A*
Blair, Joan *WhoHol A*
Blair, John 1943- *EncJzS 70*
Blair, Joyce 1932- *WhoThe 72, -77*
Blair, June *WhoHol A*

Blair, Larry 1935- IntMPA 77, -75, -76, -78, -79, -80
Blair, Lee L 1903-1966 WhoJazz 72
Blair, Linda 1959- FilmEn, HalFC 80, WhoHol A, WhoHrs 80[port]
Blair, Lionel 1931- WhoThe 72, -77
Blair, Mary PlP&P
Blair, Mary d1947 NotNAT B
Blair, Nicky WhoHol A
Blair, Roger Phillip Ian 1948- IntWWM 80
Blair, William 1896- BiE&WWA, NotNAT
Blais, Marie-Claire 1939- CreCan 1
Blaisdell, Charles d1930 WhoHol B
Blaisdell, Paul 1930?- WhoHrs 80
Blaisdell, William Film 2
Blaise, Adolfe Benoit d1772? NewGrD 80
Blaise, Ed 1895?-1944? NewOrJ
Blaise, Pierre 1951-1975 WhScrn 77, WhoHol C
Blaisell, Charles Big Bill 1874-1930 WhScrn 74, -77
Blaison, Thibaut De NewGrD 80
Blake, A D Film 1
Blake, Al 1877-1966 WhScrn 77
Blake, Alan AmSCAP 80
Blake, Amanda 1929- FilmEn, FilmgC, ForYSC, HalFC 80, IntMPA 77, -75, -76, -78, -79, -80, -80, WhoHol A
Blake, Anne d1973 WhScrn 77, WhoHol B
Blake, Bebe 1925- AmSCAP 66, -80
Blake, Benjamin 1751-1827 NewGrD 80
Blake, Betty 1920- BiE&WWA, NotNAT
Blake, Bobby FilmEn
Blake, Cecil Michael 1946- IntWWM 77
Blake, Charles NotNAT
Blake, Charles D 1847-1903 BiDAmM
Blake, Christopher Hugh 1949- IntWWM 80
Blake, David Leonard 1936- IntWWM 77, -80, NewGrD 80, WhoMus 72
Blake, David M 1948- IntMPA 77, -75, -76, -78, -79, -80
Blake, Dorothy Gaynor 1893- ConAmC
Blake, Eubie 1883- AmSCAP 66, -80, BlkAmP, BlksB&W C, BlksBF[port], CmpEPM, DrBlPA, EncJzS 70, EncMT, IlEncJ, MorBAP, NewGrD 80, WhoJazz 72
Blake, Frances Ann Georgina 1926- IntWWM 77, -80
Blake, George 1917-1955 AmSCAP 66, -80
Blake, George E 1775-1871 BiDAmM
Blake, George M 1912- AmSCAP 66, -80
Blake, Harry 1866- WhThe
Blake, James Hubert 1883- BiDAmM, ConAmC, EncJzS 70, NewGrD 80, WhoJazz 72
Blake, James W 1862-1935 AmSCAP 66, -80, BiDAmM
Blake, Jerry 1908-1961? CmpEPM, WhoJazz 72
Blake, Katherine 1928- FilmgC, HalFC 80
Blake, Larry WhoHol A
Blake, Leonard James 1907- WhoMus 72
Blake, Loretta Film 1
Blake, Lowell AmSCAP 80
Blake, Lucius Film 2
Blake, Madge 1900-1969 ForYSC, MotPP, WhScrn 74, -77, WhoHol B
Blake, Marie 1896- HalFC 80, MGM[port], ThFT[port], WhoHol A
Blake, Marie 1896-1978 FilmEn
Blake, Marie 1905- ForYSC
Blake, Myrtle Ann 1906- AmSCAP 66, -80
Blake, Norman 1938- IlEncCM[port]
Blake, Oliver 1905- Vers B[port]
Blake, Pamela ForYSC
Blake, Pamela 1920?- FilmEn
Blake, Paul d1960 WhScrn 74, -77, WhoHol B
Blake, Ran 1935- BiDAmM, ConAmC, EncJzS 70
Blake, Rex Etherton 1926- IntWWM 77, -80, WhoMus 72
Blake, Richard NewGrD 80
Blake, Robert WhoHol A
Blake, Robert 1933- FilmEn
Blake, Robert 1934- FilmgC, HalFC 80, MovMk
Blake, Robert 1938- ForYSC, IntMPA 77, -75, -76, -78, -79, -80
Blake, Saundra Rounette Oliver 1945- IntWWM 77
Blake, Tom Film 1, -2
Blake, Whitney WhoHol A
Blake, William OxMus
Blakeclock, Alban d1966 WhScrn 74, -77, WhoHol B
Blakeley, Colin 1930- IlWWBF
Blakeley, James 1873-1915 NotNAT B, WhThe, WhoStg 1908
Blakeley, John E 1889-1958 FilmgC, HalFC 80, IlWWBF
Blakeley, Tom 1918- FilmgC, HalFC 80
Blakelock, Denys 1901-1970 WhThe
Blakely, Bill W 1926- AmSCAP 80
Blakely, Colin 1930- CnThe, FilmEn, FilmgC, HalFC 80, PlP&P[port], WhoHol A, WhoThe 72, -77
Blakely, Don DrBlPA
Blakely, Gene 1922- BiE&WWA
Blakely, James WhoHol A
Blakely, Nora BlkAmP
Blakely, Susan 1949- HalFC 80, IntMPA 77, -76, -78, -79, -80, WhoHol A
Blakely, Susan 1950- FilmEn
Blakely, Troy ConMuA 80B
Blakeman, Virginia Louise 1949- IntWWM 77, -80
Blakemore, Erik F 1926- IntMPA 77, -75, -76
Blakemore, Michael 1928- EncWT, NotNAT, WhoThe 72, -77
Blakeney, Andrew 1898- EncJzS 70, WhoJazz 72
Blakeney, Andy 1898- EncJzS 70
Blakeney, Olive 1903-1959 WhScrn 74, -77, WhoHol B
Blaker, Charles Randolph 1943- AmSCAP 80
Blakesmit, Henry NewGrD 80
Blakey, Art 1919- BiDAmM, CmpEPM, DrBlPA, EncJzS 70, IlEncJ, NewGrD 80
Blakismet, Henry NewGrD 80
Blakiston, Clarence 1864-1943 NotNAT B, WhThe
Blakley, D Duane ConAmC
Blakley, Ronee AmSCAP 80, IlEncR, WhoHol A
Blakley, Ronee 1946- FilmEn
Blalock, Richard IntMPA 77, -75, -76, -78, -79, -80
Blam, Rafailo 1910- IntWWM 80
Blamauer, Karoline Wilhelmina NewGrD 80
Blamont, Francois Colin De 1690-1760 Baker 78
Blamont, Francois Collin De NewGrD 80
Blanc, Adolphe 1828-1885 Baker 78
Blanc, Anne-Marie 1921- FilmAG WE
Blanc, Didier Le NewGrD 80
Blanc, Ernest Marius Victor 1923- CmOp, IntWWM 77, -80, NewGrD 80, WhoOp 76
Blanc, Giuseppe 1886-1969 Baker 78, OxMus
Blanc, Jean-Pierre 1942- HalFC 80
Blanc, Johnny 1939- IntWWM 80
Blanc, Jonny 1939- NewGrD 80, WhoOp 76
Blanc, Mel 1908- AmSCAP 66, -80, FilmEn, FilmgC, HalFC 80, IntMPA 77, -75, -76, -78, -79, -80, JoeFr, WhoHol A
Blanc, Sally Film 2
Blanc-Maeterlinck, Georgette Film 2
Blancafort, Manuel 1897- Baker 78, NewGrD 80
Blancan, Peter PupTheA
Blancard, Rene 1897-1965 WhScrn 77
Blanch, Jewel Evelyn AmSCAP 80
Blanchar, Pierre 1892-1963 FilmEn, Film 2, FilmgC, HalFC 80, OxFilm
Blanchar, Pierre 1893-1963 WhScrn 74, -77
Blanchar, Pierre 1896-1963 FilmAG WE, NotNAT B, OxThe, WhoHol B
Blanchard, Barbara 1939- WhoOp 76
Blanchard, Doc 1925- WhoHol A
Blanchard, Donald F 1914- BiDAmM
Blanchard, Edward Leman 1820-1889 NotNAT B, OxThe
Blanchard, Eleanor Film 1
Blanchard, Esprit Joseph Antoine 1696-1770 NewGrD 80
Blanchard, Henri-Louis 1778-1858 Baker 78
Blanchard, Henri-Louis 1791-1858 NewGrD 80
Blanchard, Jack 1942- IlEncCM
Blanchard, Jack & Misty Morgan RkOn 2A
Blanchard, Mari 1927-1970 FilmEn, FilmgC, ForYSC, HalFC 80, WhScrn 74, -77, WhoHol B, WhoHrs 80[port]
Blanchard, Michael Kelly 1948- AmSCAP 80
Blanchard, Pierre 1896-1963 EncWT, Ent
Blanchard, Richard 1925- AmSCAP 80
Blanchard, Richard Lowell 1910- BiDAmM
Blanchard, Robert ConAmC
Blanchard, William 1769-1835 NotNAT B, OxThe
Blanchard, William Godwin 1905- AmSCAP 66, BiDAmM, ConAmC A
Blanchardus, Francesco NewGrD 80
Blanche, Ada 1862-1953 NotNAT B, WhThe
Blanche, August Theodore 1811-1868 OxThe
Blanche, Belle 1891-1963 NotNAT B, WhoStg 1908
Blanche, Francis d1974 WhoHol B
Blanche, Francis 1921- FilmEn
Blanche, Francis 1921-1974 WorEFlm[port]
Blanche, Francis 1922-1974 WhScrn 77
Blanche, Kate Film 2
Blanche, Margaret IlWWBF
Blanche, Marie 1893- WhThe
Blancher, M NewGrD 80
Blanchet NewGrD 80
Blanchet, Armand Francois Nicholas 1763-1818 NewGrD 80
Blanchet, Emile R 1877-1943 Baker 78
Blanchet, Francois Etienne d1766 NewGrD 80
Blanchet, Francois Etienne 1695-1761 NewGrD 80
Blanchet, Joseph 1724-1778 NewGrD 80
Blanchet, Nicholas 1660-1731 NewGrD 80
Blanchin, Francois NewGrD 80
Blanck, Hubert De 1856-1932 Baker 78
Blanck, Steve ConMuA 80B
Blanckenburg, Gerbrant Quirijnszoon Van NewGrD 80
Blanckenburg, Quirinus Gerbrandszoon Van NewGrD 80
Blanckenmuller, Georg 1480?- NewGrD 80
Blanckmuller, Georg 1480?- NewGrD 80
Blancks, Edward 1550?-1633 NewGrD 80
Blanco, Juan 1920- Baker 78, DcCM, WhoMus 72
Blanco, Richard M IntMPA 77, -75, -76, -78, -79, -80
Bland NewGrD 80
Bland, Alan 1897-1946 WhThe
Bland, Alexander CnOxB, DancEn 78
Bland, Billy 1932- RkOn
Bland, Bobby Blue 1930- DrBlPA, IlEncR[port], RkOn
Bland, Charles NewGrD 80
Bland, George d1807 NotNAT B, OxThe
Bland, Harcourt d1875 NotNAT B
Bland, Jack 1899- CmpEPM, WhoJazz 72
Bland, James 1798-1861 NewGrD 80, NotNAT B, OxThe
Bland, James A 1854-1911 AmPS, -B, Baker 78, BiDAmM, BlksBF, DrBlPA, NewGrD 80, NotNAT B, PopAmC[port], Sw&Ld A
Bland, John d1788 NotNAT B
Bland, John 1750?-1840? NewGrD 80
Bland, Joyce 1906-1963 WhScrn 74, -77, WhThe, WhoHol B
Bland, Maria Theresa Romanzini 1769-1838 NewGrD 80, OxThe
Bland, R Henderson d1941 Film 1, NotNAT B, WhoHol B
Bland, Robert Calvin 1930- BiDAmM, BluesWW[port]
Bland, Ronald Allan 1958- IntWWM 77
Bland, William Keith 1947- ConAmC
Blande, Edith d1923 NotNAT B
Blandford, Jeremy Richard 1943- IntWWM 77, -80
Blandford, W T H OxMus
Blandford, Walter 1864-1952 NewGrD 80
Blandford Harris, Phyllis 1907- WhoMus 72
Blandick, Clara 1880-1962 FilmEn, ThFT[port]
Blandick, Clara 1881-1962 Film 2, FilmgC, ForYSC, HalFC 80, MotPP, MovMk, NotNAT B, Vers A[port], WhScrn 74, -77, WhoHol B
Blandrati, Giovanni Pietro NewGrD 80
Blane, Marcie 1944- RkOn

Blane, Ralph 1914- *AmPS, AmSCAP 66, -80, BiDAmM, BiE&WWA, CmpEPM, EncMT, HalFC 80, IntMPA 77, -75, -76, -78, -79, -80, NotNAT*
Blane, Sally 1910- *FilmEn, Film 2, FilmgC, ForYSC, HalFC 80, MovMk, ThFT[port], TwYS, What 3[port], WhoHol A*
Blaney, Charles Edward d1944 *NotNAT B, WhThe*
Blaney, H Clay 1908-1964 *BiE&WWA*
Blaney, Harry Clay 1874- *WhoStg 1906, -1908*
Blaney, Henry Clay 1908-1964 *NotNAT B*
Blaney, May 1874-1953 *WhScrn 77*
Blaney, Norah *WhThe, WhoThe 72*
Blangini, Felice 1781-1841 *NewGrD 80*
Blangini, Giuseppe Marco Maria Felice 1781-1841 *Baker 78*
Blangsted, Folmar 1904- *HalFC 80*
Blank, Allan 1925- *CpmDNM 75, -76, -77, -78, -80, ConAmC, IntWWM 77, -80, NewGrD 80*
Blank, Edward *NewGrD 80*
Blank, Edward L 1943- *ConAmTC, IntMPA 77, -75, -76, -78, -79, -80*
Blank, Gustav 1908- *CnOxB, DancEn 78*
Blank, Jorg D 1952- *IntWWM 80*
Blank, Myron 1911- *IntMPA 77, -75, -76, -78, -79, -80*
Blanke, Edeltraud 1939- *WhoOp 76*
Blanke, Henry 1901- *FilmEn, FilmgC, HalFC 80, IntMPA 77, -75, -76, -78, -79, -80, WorEFlm[port]*
Blanke, Kate *Film 1, -2*
Blanke, Tom *Film 2*
Blanke, Toto 1939- *EncJzS 70*
Blankenburg, Gerbrand Quirijnszoon Van 1620?-1707 *NewGrD 80*
Blankenburg, Gerbrant Quirijnszoon Van 1620?-1707 *NewGrD 80*
Blankenburg, Gideon Gerbrandszoon Van 1654-1739 *NewGrD 80*
Blankenburg, Quirijn Gerbrandszoon Van 1654-1739 *NewGrD 80*
Blankenburg, Quirin Van 1654-1739 *Baker 78*
Blankenburg, Quirinus Gerbrandszoon Van 1654-1739 *NewGrD 80*
Blankenburg, Walter 1903- *IntWWM 77, -80, NewGrD 80*
Blankenheim, Toni 1922- *WhoOp 76*
Blankenheim, Walter 1926- *WhoMus 72*
Blankenship, Lyle Mark 1943- *ConAmC*
Blankenship, Wesley B 1924- *IntMPA 75, -76*
Blankenship, William Leonard 1928- *WhoOp 76*
Blankers, Laurens A 1933- *IntWWM 77, -80*
Blankes, Edward *NewGrD 80*
Blankfort, Michael 1907- *BiE&WWA, FilmEn, HalFC 80, IntMPA 77, -75, -76, -78, -79, -80, NatPD[port], NotNAT*
Blankman, George 1877-1925 *WhScrn 74, -77, WhoHol B*
Blankman, Howard Milford 1925- *AmSCAP 66, -80*
Blankner, Frederika *NatPD[port]*
Blanks, Birleanna 1889-1968 *BluesWW[port]*
Blanks, Fred Roy 1925- *IntWWM 80*
Blankshine, Robert 1948- *CnOxB*
Blankstein, Mary Freeman 1931- *IntWWM 77*
Blanq, Edward *NewGrD 80*
Blans, Patricia *WhoMus 72*
Blanter, Matvey Isaakovich 1903- *Baker 78, NewGrD 80*
Blanton, James 1921-1942 *NewGrD 80*
Blanton, Jeremy 1939- *CnOxB, CreCan 2*
Blanton, Jimmy 1918?-1942 *CmpEPM, WhoJazz 72*
Blanton, Jimmy 1921-1942 *BiDAmM, IlEncJ, NewGrD 80*
Blanzat, Anne-Marie 1944- *WhoOp 76*
Blaramberg, Pavel Ivanovich 1841-1907 *Baker 78, NewGrD 80*
Blarer, Ambrosius 1492-1564 *NewGrD 80*
Blas DeCastro, Juan *NewGrD 80*
Blasch, Robert Edward 1931- *IntWWM 77*
Blasco, Mrs. Louis *AmSCAP 80*
Blasco DeNebra, Manuel 1750-1784 *NewGrD 80*
Blasdell, Raymond Lynn 1932- *AmSCAP 80*
Blase, Pansy *PupTheA*
Blasend, Stark *OxMus*
Blaserna, Pietro 1836-1918 *Baker 78*
Blasetti, Alessandro 1900- *DcFM, FilmEn, FilmgC, HalFC 80, OxFilm, WorEFlm[port]*
Blasi, Luca *NewGrD 80*
Blasis, Carlo *OxMus*
Blasis, Carlo 1795?-1878 *DancEn 78, NewGrD 80*
Blasis, Carlo 1797-1878 *CnOxB*
Blasius *NewGrD 80*
Blasius, Frederic 1758-1829 *NewGrD 80*
Blasius, Mathieu-Frederic 1758-1829 *Baker 78*
Blasius, Matthaus 1758-1829 *NewGrD 80*
Blaska, Felix 1941- *CnOxB*
Blason, Thibaut De *NewGrD 80*
Blatas, Arbit 1910- *WhoOp 76*
Blatcher, William *Film 2*
Blatchford, William 1886-1936 *WhScrn 74, -77, WhoHol B*
Blatny, Josef 1891- *Baker 78, NewGrD 80*
Blatny, Pavel 1931- *Baker 78, DcCM, EncJzS 70, NewGrD 80*
Blatt, Edward A 1905- *BiE&WWA, FilmEn, FilmgC, HalFC 80*
Blatt, Frances 1926- *IntWWM 77*
Blatt, Frantisek Tadeas 1793-1856 *NewGrD 80*
Blatt, William Mosher *PupTheA*
Blatter, Alfred Wayne 1937- *CpmDNM 75, -79, ConAmC, IntWWM 80*
Blattmann, Hans 1922- *IntWWM 77, -80*
Blattner, Gerry 1913- *IntMPA 77, -75, -76, -78, -79, -80*
Blattner, Geza *DcPup*
Blatty, William Peter *FilmEn, FilmgC, HalFC 80, IntMPA 77, -75, -76, -78, -79, -80*
Blau, Bela d1940 *NotNAT B*
Blau, Herbert 1926- *BiE&WWA, NotNAT, PlP&P[port]*
Blau, Jeno *NewGrD 80*
Blau, Martin 1924- *IntMPA 77, -75, -76, -78, -79, -80*
Blaufuss, Walter 1883-1945 *AmSCAP 66, -80, BiDAmM*
Blaukopf, Kurt 1914- *IntWWM 77, NewGrD 80*
Blaurer, Ambrosius *NewGrD 80*
Blaustein, Julian 1913- *FilmEn, FilmgC, HalFC 80, IntMPA 77, -75, -76, -78, -79, -80, WorEFlm[port]*
Blauth, Brenno 1931- *IntWWM 77*
Blauvelt, Lillian Evans 1873-1947 *WhoStg 1906, -1908*
Blauvelt, Lillian Evans 1874-1947 *Baker 78*
Blauvert, Lillian Evans 1873-1947 *BiDAmM*
Blavet, Emile 1838- *WhThe*
Blavet, Michel 1700-1768 *NewGrD 80*
Blaydon, Richard *Film 2*
Blaylock, Travis L 1934- *BluesWW[port]*
Blayney, May 1875-1953 *NotNAT B, WhThe*
Blaze, Francois-Henri-Joseph 1784-1857 *Baker 78, NewEOp 71, NewGrD 80*
Blaze, Henri, Baron DeBury 1813-1888 *Baker 78*
Blazek, Jiri 1923- *CnOxB*
Blazek, Zdenek 1905- *Baker 78, IntWWM 77*
Blazek, Zdenek 1905-1974 *NewGrD 80*
Blazer, Walter 1918- *IntWWM 77, -80*
Blazhkov, Igor Ivanovich 1936- *Baker 78, IntWWM 77, -80*
Blazon, Thibaut De *NewGrD 80*
Bleach, Lindsay *WhoMus 72*
Blech, Hans Christian 1915- *HalFC 80*
Blech, Hans Christian 1925- *FilmAG WE*
Blech, Harry 1910- *IntWWM 77, -80, NewGrD 80, WhoMus 72*
Blech, Leo 1871-1958 *Baker 78, CmOp, NewGrD 80*
Bleckner, Jeff *WhoThe 77*
Bledsoe, Earl d1962 *NotNAT B*
Bledsoe, George 1921- *AmSCAP 66*
Bledsoe, Jules *AmPS B*
Bledsoe, Jules d1943 *WhoHol B*
Bledsoe, Jules 1898-1943 *Baker 78, DrBlPA, NotNAT B*
Bledsoe, Jules 1899-1943 *BiDAmM, ConAmC, WhScrn 74, -77*
Blees, Robert 1922- *AmSCAP 80, IntMPA 77, -75, -76, -78, -79, -80*
Blegen, Judith 1941- *Baker 78, MusSN[port], NewGrD 80*
Blegen, Judith Eyer *WhoOp 76*
Bleibtreau, Hedwig 1868-1958 *WhScrn 74, -77*
Bleibtreu, Hedwig 1868-1958 *WhoHol B*
Bleichmann, Yuly 1868-1910 *Baker 78*
Bleier, Edward 1929- *IntMPA 77, -75, -76, -78, -79, -80, NewYTET*
Bleifer, John *Film 2, WhoHol A*
Bleiman, Mikhail 1904- *DcFM*
Bleiweiss, Peter Richard 1944- *AmSCAP 80*
Blender, Leon Philip 1920- *IntMPA 77, -75, -76, -78, -79, -80*
Blendinger, Herbert 1936- *IntWWM 77, -80*
Blensfeld, Paul *Film 2*
Bleser, Robert L A 1928- *WhoOp 76*
Blessi, Manoli *NewGrD 80*
Blessing, Lynn 1938- *BiDAmM*
Blessinger, Karl 1888-1962 *Baker 78*
Blessings, Lynn Roberts 1938- *AmSCAP 80*
Bletcher, Billy 1894- *FilmEn, Film 2, WhoHol A*
Bleumers, Bart 1943- *IntWWM 77, -80*
Blevins, Scotty Lee 1954- *AmSCAP 80*
Blewitt, Jonas 1805- *NewGrD 80*
Blewitt, Jonathan 1782-1853 *Baker 78, NewGrD 80*
Bley, Carla Borg 1938- *BiDAmM, ConAmC, EncJzS 70, IlEncJ*
Bley, Maurice 1910- *BiE&WWA, NotNAT*
Bley, Paul 1932- *BiDAmM, EncJzS 70, IlEncJ*
Bleyer, Archie 1909- *BgBands 74, CmpEPM, RkOn*
Bleyer, Georg 1647-1694? *NewGrD 80*
Bleyer, Nicolaus 1591-1658 *NewGrD 80*
Bleyle, Karl 1880-1969 *Baker 78*
Blezard, William 1921- *WhoMus 72*
Blezzard, Judith Helen 1944- *IntWWM 80*
Blich, Richard *NewGrD 80*
Blick, Newton 1899-1965 *WhScrn 74, -77, WhThe, WhoHol B*
Blickhan, Charles Timothy 1945- *CpmDNM 76, ConAmC*
Blickle, Peg *PupTheA*
Blier, Bernard 1916- *FilmAG WE, FilmEn, FilmgC, HalFC 80*
Blier, Bertrand 1939- *FilmEn*
Bliesener, Ada Elizabeth Michelmann 1909- *IntWWM 77, -80*
Bligh, Elizabeth *WhoMus 72*
Blin, Roger 1907- *CnThe, EncWT, Ent*
Blind, Tom 1849-1908 *DrBlPA*
Blind Arthur *BluesWW[port]*
Blind Blake *BluesWW[port]*
Blind Boy Fuller Number 2 *BluesWW[port]*
Blind Doggie *BluesWW[port]*
Blind Faith *ConMuA 80A, IlEncR*
Blind Gary *BluesWW[port]*
Blind Gilbert 1900?- *NewOrJ*
Blind Harry *OxMus*
Blind Lemon *DrBlPA*
Blind Sammy *BluesWW[port]*
Blind Tom *Baker 78, NewGrD 80*
Blind Tom 1849-1908 *OxMus*
Blind Willie *BluesWW[port]*
Blindhamer, Adolf 1475?-1532? *NewGrD 80*
Blinkhof, Jan 1940- *WhoOp 76*
Blinn, Benjamin F 1872-1941 *WhScrn 74, -77, WhoHol B*
Blinn, Edward 1938- *AmSCAP 66*
Blinn, Genevieve d1956 *Film 1, -2, WhScrn 74, -77, WhoHol B*
Blinn, Holbrook 1872-1928 *Film 1, -2, HalFC 80, MotPP, NotNAT B, TwYS, WhScrn 74, -77, WhThe, WhoHol B, WhoStg 1906, -1908*
Blinn, Nellie Holbrook d1909 *NotNAT B*
Blinn, William *NewYTET*
Bliokh, Yakov 1895-1957 *DcFM*
Bliokh, Yalov 1895-1957 *FilmEn*
Blish, Nathaniel Pierce, Jr. 1925- *AmSCAP 80*
Bliss, Anthony Addison 1913- *BiE&WWA, WhoOp 76*
Bliss, Arthur 1891-1975 *MusMk[port]*
Bliss, Sir Arthur 1891-1975 *Baker 78, BnBkM 80, CompSN[port], CpmDNM 74, -75, CnOxB, DancEn 78, DcCom 77, DcCom&M 79, DcCM, FilmgC, HalFC 80, NewEOp 71, NewGrD 80[port], OxMus, WhoMus 72*

Bliss, Hebe d1956 *NotNAT B*
Bliss, Helena 1917- *BiE&WWA, NotNAT, WhoThe 72, -77*
Bliss, Herbert 1923-1960 *CnOxB, DancEn 78*
Bliss, John Warren 1898- *WhoMus 72*
Bliss, Milton Clay 1927- *ConAmC*
Bliss, P Paul 1872-1933 *Baker 78, ConAmC*
Bliss, Philip Paul 1838-1876 *Baker 78, BiDAmM, NewGrD 80*
Bliss, Sally Brayley *CreCan 2*
Blissett, Francis d1824 *NotNAT B*
Blitheman, John 1525?-1591 *NewGrD 80*
Blitheman, William d1591 *OxMus*
Blithman, John 1525?-1591 *NewGrD 80*
Blitz, Antonio 1810-1877 *MagIlD*
Blitz, Eugene *PupTheA*
Blitzstein, Marc 1905-1964 *AmSCAP 66, -80, Baker 78, BestMus, BiDAmM, BiE&WWA, BnBkM 80, CmOp, CompSN[port], CnMD, ConAmC, DcCM, EncMT, IntWWM 77, -80, McGEWD[port], ModWD, MusMk, NewCBMT, NewEOp 71, NewGrD 80, NotNAT B, OxMus, PIP&P*
Blizinski, Marek Bohdan 1947- *IntWWM 77, -80*
Bloch, Alexander 1881- *ConAmC, IntWWM 77, -80, WhoMus 72*
Bloch, Andre 1873-1960 *Baker 78*
Bloch, Augustyn 1929- *Baker 78, IntWWM 77, -80, NewGrD 80, WhoMus 72*
Bloch, Bertram 1892- *BiE&WWA, NotNAT*
Bloch, Ernest 1880-1959 *AmSCAP 66, -80, Baker 78, BiDAmM, BlkAmP, BnBkM 80, CompSN[port], ConAmC, DcCom 77[port], DcCom&M 79, DcCM, DcTwCC, MusMk, NewGrD 80[port], OxMus*
Bloch, Ernst 1885-1977 *NewGrD 80*
Bloch, Ray 1902- *CmpEPM*
Bloch, Raymond A 1902- *AmSCAP 66, -80, BiDAmM*
Bloch, Robert 1917- *FilmEn, FilmgC, HalFC 80, IntMPA 77, -75, -76, -78, -79, -80, WhoHrs 80*
Bloch, Sidney S 1895- *BiDAmM*
Bloch, Suzanne 1907- *Baker 78*
Block, Anita Cahn 1882-1967 *NotNAT B*
Block, Bert *BgBands 74, ConMuA 80B*
Block, Dorothy *Film 2*
Block, Frederick 1899-1945 *BiDAmM*
Block, Irving *WhoHrs 80*
Block, Martin 1903-1967 *CmpEPM*
Block, Michel *WhoMus 72*
Block, Phyllis Ray 1925- *IntWWM 80*
Block, Richard *ConMuA 80B*
Block, Richard C *NewYTET*
Block, Robert Paul 1942- *ConAmC*
Block, Sheridan *Film 1, WhoStg 1906, -1908*
Block, Steven 1928- *BiE&WWA*
Block, Will J *WhoStg 1908*
Block, Willard 1930- *IntMPA 77, -75, -76, -78, -79, -80*
Block, William J d1932 *NotNAT B*
Blocker, Dan *ForYSC*
Blocker, Dan 1928-1972 *FilmgC, HalFC 80*
Blocker, Dan 1929-1972 *WhScrn 77, WhoHol B*
Blocker, Robert Lewis 1946- *IntWWM 77, -80*
Blockland, Corneille De 1530?- *NewGrD 80*
Blockland, Cornelius 1530?- *NewGrD 80*
Blocksidge, Kathleen Mary 1904- *WhoMus 72*
Blockx, Jan 1851-1912 *Baker 78, NewGrD 80, OxMus*
Blodek, Vilem 1834-1874 *NewGrD 80*
Blodek, Wilhelm 1834-1874 *Baker 78*
Blodget, Alden S d1964 *NotNAT B*
Blodgett, Benjamin Colman 1838-1925 *Baker 78, BiDAmM*
Bloemendal, Coenraad Robert 1946- *IntWWM 80*
Blofson, Richard 1933- *BiE&WWA, NotNAT*
Blok, Aleksandr Aleksandrovich 1880-1921 *Ent, McGEWD[port], ModWD*
Blok, Alexander 1880-1921 *CnMD, EncWT*
Blom, August 1869-1942 *WorEFlm[port]*
Blom, August 1869-1947 *DcFM, FilmEn*
Blom, Eric 1888-1959 *Baker 78, NewGrD 80, OxMus*
Blomberg, Erik 1913- *DcFM, FilmEn*
Blomberg, Erik 1922- *Baker 78, IntWWM 77, -80*
Blomdahl, Karl-Birger 1916-1968 *Baker 78, BnBkM 80, CompSN[port], CnOxB, DancEn 78, DcCM, MusMk, NewEOp 71, NewGrD 80, OxMus*
Blome *NewGrD 80*
Blomfield, Derek 1920-1964 *FilmgC, HalFC 80, NotNAT B, WhScrn 77, WhThe, WhoHol B*
Blomquist, Allen 1928- *BiE&WWA, NotNAT*
Blomstedt, George *Film 2*
Blon, Franz Von 1861-1945 *Baker 78*
Blond, Susan *ConMuA 80B*
Blondal, Patricia Anne Jenkins 1926- *CreCan 1*
Blondeau, Pierre *NewGrD 80*
Blondeau, Pierre-Auguste Louis 1784-1865? *Baker 78, NewGrD 80*
Blondel De Nesle *MusMk, NewGrD 80*
Blondel, Jorge Urrutia *NewGrD 80*
Blondel, Louis-Nicolas *NewGrD 80*
Blondell, Gloria *ForYSC, WhoHol A*
Blondell, Joan *MotPP, WhoHol A*
Blondell, Joan 1909- *BiDFilm, -81, FilmgC, ForYSC, HalFC 80, MovMk[port], OxFilm, ThFT[port], WhoThe 77, WorEFlm[port]*
Blondell, Joan 1909-1979 *FilmEn*
Blondell, Joan 1912- *BiE&WWA, IntMPA 77, -75, -76, -78, -79, -80, NotNAT, WhoThe 72*
Blondell, William 1800?- *BiDAmM*
Blondi, Michel 1675-1737 *NewGrD 80*
Blondie *ConMuA 80A[port]*
Blondin 1824-1897 *Ent*
Blondy, Nicolas 1677-1747 *CnOxB*
Blonstein, Marshall *ConMuA 80B*
Blood, Adele d1936 *NotNAT B*
Blood, Denis Jeffrey 1917- *IntWWM 77, -80, WhoMus 72*
Blood, Esta 1933- *ConAmC, IntWWM 77, -80*
Blood, Esta Damesek 1933- *AmSCAP 80*
Blood Sweat And Tears *BiDAmM, ConMuA 80A[port], EncJzS 70, IlEncR, RkOn 2[port]*
Bloodgood, Clara 1870-1907 *NotNAT B*
Bloodstone *RkOn 2[port]*
Bloom, A Leon *AmSCAP 80*
Bloom, Bobby d1974 *RkOn 2[port]*
Bloom, Claire *BiE&WWA, MotPP, WhoHol A*
Bloom, Claire 1928- *OxFilm*
Bloom, Claire 1931- *BiDFilm, -81, CnThe, FilmAG WE, FilmEn, FilmgC, ForYSC, HalFC 80, IlWWBF[port], IntMPA 77, -75, -76, -78, -79, -80, MovMk[port], NotNAT, WhoHrs 80, WhoThe 72, -77, WorEFlm[port]*
Bloom, Eric 1944- *AmSCAP 80*
Bloom, Harold Jack *HalFC 80, NewYTET*
Bloom, Howard *ConMuA 80B*
Bloom, Julius 1912- *IntWWM 80*
Bloom, Larry 1914- *AmSCAP 66, -80*
Bloom, Milton 1906- *AmSCAP 66, BiDAmM, WhoJazz 72*
Bloom, Murray 1889- *AmSCAP 66*
Bloom, Murray Teigh *NatPD[port]*
Bloom, Philip 1918- *BiE&WWA*
Bloom, Robert 1908- *BnBkM 80*
Bloom, Rube 1902-1976 *AmSCAP 66, -80, CmpEPM*
Bloom, Seymour L 1911- *AmSCAP 66*
Bloom, Stephen *ConAmC*
Bloom, Vera 1898-1959 *AmSCAP 66, -80*
Bloom, Verna *IntMPA 77, -75, -76, -78, -79, -80, WhoHol A*
Bloom, William 1915- *IntMPA 77, -75, -76, -78, -79, -80*
Bloomberg, Daniel J 1905- *IntMPA 75, -76*
Bloomer, Raymond *Film 2*
Bloomer, Raymond J *Film 1*
Bloomfield, Derek 1920-1964 *WhScrn 74*
Bloomfield, Fannie *Baker 78, NewGrD 80*
Bloomfield, Michael 1943- *BluesWW[port]*
Bloomfield, Mike *ConMuA 80A, IlEncR*
Bloomfield, Robert *OxMus*
Bloomfield Zeisler, Fannie 1863-1927 *BnBkM 80*
Bloomfield-Zeisler, Fanny 1863-1955 *BiDAmM*
Bloomgarden, Kermit 1904-1976 *BiE&WWA, NotNAT B, PIP&P[port], WhoThe 72, -77*
Bloomquist, Marvin Robert 1930- *IntWWM 77*
Bloore, Ronald L 1925- *CreCan 2*
Blore, Eric d1959 *MotPP, WhoHol B*
Blore, Eric 1887-1959 *FilmEn, FilmgC, HalFC 80, HolCA[port], MovMk[port], NotNAT B, WhScrn 74, -77, WhThe*
Blore, Eric 1888-1959 *Film 2, ForYSC, Vers A[port]*
Bloss, Schmid *Film 2*
Blossom, Henry Martyn, Jr. 1866-1919 *AmPS, AmSCAP 66, -80, BiDAmM, CmpEPM, EncMT, NewCBMT, NotNAT B, Sw&Ld B, WhThe, WhoStg 1906, -1908*
Blossom, Rose *Film 2*
Blossom, Winter *Film 2*
Blount, Helon 1929- *WhoThe 77*
Blount, Jack *NewOrJ*
Blow, John 1648?-1708 *Baker 78*
Blow, John 1649-1708 *BnBkM 80, DcCom&M 79, GrComp[port], MusMk, NewGrD 80[port], OxMus*
Blow, Mark d1921 *NotNAT B*
Blow, Sydney 1878-1961 *NotNAT A, -B, WhThe*
Blowers, John 1911- *WhoJazz 72*
Blowitz, John S *IntMPA 77, -75, -76, -78, -79, -80*
Blowitz, William F d1964 *NotNAT B*
Bloym *NewGrD 80*
Blue, Ben d1975 *WhoHol C*
Blue, Ben 1900-1975 *FilmgC, HalFC 80, MovMk*
Blue, Ben 1901-1975 *FilmEn, Film 2, ForYSC, IntMPA 75, WhScrn 77*
Blue, Ben 1902-1975 *JoeFr[port], What 4[port]*
Blue, Bill Thornton 1902-1948 *WhoJazz 72*
Blue, David 1942- *IlEncR*
Blue, James 1930- *WorEFlm[port]*
Blue, Joe 1934- *BluesWW[port]*
Blue, Lu *BluesWW[port]*
Blue, Monte 1890-1963 *FilmEn, Film 1, -2, FilmgC, ForYSC, HalFC 80, MotPP, MovMk, NotNAT B, TwYS, Vers A[port], WhScrn 74, -77, WhoHol B*
Blue Belles, The *RkOn*
Blue Boys *EncFCWM 69*
Blue Cheer *BiDAmM, ConMuA 80A, RkOn 2[port]*
Blue Demon *WhoHrs 80*
Blue Haze *RkOn 2A*
Blue Jays, The *RkOn*
Blue Magic *RkOn 2[port]*
Blue Notes, The *RkOn*
Blue Oyster Cult *ConMuA 80A, IlEncR*
Blue Rhythm Band *BiDAmM*
Blue Ridge Boys *BiDAmM*
Blue Ridge Quartet *BiDAmM*
Blue Ridge Rangers *RkOn 2A*
Blue Sky Boys *BiDAmM, EncFCWM 69, IlEncCM[port]*
Blue Swede *RkOn 2[port]*
Bluefield, David *AmSCAP 80*
Bluegrass Boys *BiDAmM, EncFCWM 69*
Blues Boy *BluesWW[port]*
Blues Boy Bill *BluesWW[port]*
Blues Image, The *RkOn 2[port]*
Blues King *BluesWW[port]*
Blues Magoos *BiDAmM, ConMuA 80A, RkOn 2[port]*
Blues Man, The *BluesWW[port]*
Blues Project *BiDAmM, ConMuA 80A, IlEncR*
Blues Serenaders *BiDAmM*
Bluestone, Ed 1949- *JoeFr*
Bluette, Isa 1898-1939 *WhScrn 77*
Bluhdorn, Charles G *IntMPA 77, -75, -76, -78, -79, -80*
Blum, Anthony 1936?- *CnOxB*
Blum, Charles Martin 1945- *IntWWM 77*
Blum, Daniel 1899-1965 *NotNAT B*
Blum, Daniel 1900-1965 *BiE&WWA, FilmgC, HalFC 80*
Blum, David 1896- *IntMPA 75, -76*
Blum, Edward 1928- *BiE&WWA, NotNAT*
Blum, Ernest d1907 *NotNAT B*

Blum, Harry 1926- *AmSCAP 66, -80*
Blum, Max *PupTheA*
Blum, Max 1874-1944 *WhScrn 74, -77*
Blum, Rene 1878-1942 *CnOxB*
Blum, Rene 1884-1944 *DancEn 78[port]*
Blum, Robert 1900 *Baker 78, CpmDNM 80, DcCM, NewGrD 80*
Blum, Sam d1945 *Film 2, WhoHol B*
Blum, Sammy 1889-1945 *WhScrn 74, -77*
Blum, Stephen 1942- *IntWWM 80*
Blum, Thomas 1927- *WhoOp 76*
Blum, William 1901- *BiE&WWA*
Blumberg, Harold D 1922- *BiE&WWA*
Blumberg, Mark Eugene 1947- *AmSCAP 80*
Blume, Bernhard 1901- *CnMD, ModWD*
Blume, Clemens 1862-1932 *Baker 78, NewGrD 80*
Blume, David Nason 1931- *AmSCAP 80*
Blume, Friedrich 1893-1975 *Baker 78, NewGrD 80, OxMus*
Blume, Helmut 1914- *CreCan 2, IntWWM 80*
Blumenfeld, Fannie *NewGrD 80*
Blumenfeld, Felix 1863-1931 *Baker 78, NewGrD 80, OxMus*
Blumenfeld, Harold 1923- *AmSCAP 80, Baker 78, ConAmC, DcCM*
Blumenfeld, Joseph 1901- *IntMPA 77, -75, -76, -78, -79, -80*
Blumenschein, William Leonard 1849-1916 *Baker 78, BiDAmM*
Blumenstock, Sid *IntMPA 77, -75, -76, -78, -79, -80*
Blumental, Felicja 1915?- *NewGrD 80*
Blumenthal, Ann E *WomWMM B*
Blumenthal, Felicia 1915?- *NewGrD 80*
Blumenthal, George 1862-1943 *NotNAT A*
Blumenthal, Jacob 1829-1908 *Baker 78, OxMus*
Blumenthal, Oscar 1852-1917 *NotNAT B*
Blumenthal, Oskar 1852-1917 *EncWT*
Blumenthal, Richard M d1962 *NotNAT B*
Blumenthal, Theodore Lewis 1935- *IntWWM 77*
Blumenthal-Tamarina, Maria d1938 *NotNAT B, WhoHol B*
Blumer, Theodor 1881-1964 *Baker 78*
Blumner, Martin Traugott Wilhelm 1827-1901 *Baker 78, NewGrD 80*
Blumofe, Robert F *IntMPA 77, -75, -76, -78, -79, -80*
Blundall, John M *DcPup*
Blundell, James *NewGrD 80*
Blundell, William Thomas 1900- *IntWWM 77, -80, WhoMus 72*
Blunstone, Colin 1945- *IlEncR*
Blunt, Carroll *NewOrJ*
Bluthner *NewGrD 80*
Bluthner, Julius 1824-1910 *Baker 78, NewGrD 80*
Bly, Albert E 1892- *AmSCAP 66, -80*
Bly, Mel *ConMuA 80B*
Bly, Nellie *Film 2*
Bly, Randi Jean 1952- *IntWWM 77, -80*
Blyden, Larry 1925-1975 *BiE&WWA, FilmgC, HalFC 80, IntMPA 75, NotNAT, -B, WhScrn 77, WhoHol C, WhoThe 72, -77*
Blye, Allan And Chris Bearde *NewYTET*
Blye, Maggie *WhoHol A*
Blye, Margaret *ForYSC*
Blylods, Hillevi *WhoOp 76*
Blyndthamer, Adolf *NewGrD 80*
Blystone, John G 1892-1938 *FilmEn, FilmgC, HalFC 80, TwYS A*
Blystone, Stanley 1894-1956 *Film 2, WhScrn 77, WhoHol B*
Blyth, Alan 1929- *IntWWM 77, -80, WhoMus 72*
Blyth, Ann 1928- *CmpEPM, FilmEn, FilmgC, ForYSC[port], HalFC 80, HolP 40[port], IntMPA 77, -75, -76, -78, -79, -80, MGM[port], MotPP, MovMk, WhoHol A, WomWMM, WorEFlm[port]*
Blyth, Henry 1910- *IntMPA 77, -75, -76, -78, -79, -80*
Blyth, May 1899- *WhoMus 72*
Blyth, Sam 1744-1795 *BiDAmM*
Blyth, Samuel 1744-1795 *NewGrD 80*
Blyth-Pratt, Charles Edward 1869- *WhThe*
Blyth-Pratt, Violet *WhThe*
Blythe, Betty 1893-1972 *FilmEn, Film 1, -2, FilmgC, ForYSC, HalFC 80, MotPP, MovMk, TwYS, WhScrn 77, WhoHol B*
Blythe, Betty 1903- *What 3[port]*
Blythe, Bobby 1894- *WhThe*
Blythe, Coralie 1880-1928 *NotNAT B, WhThe*
Blythe, Erik *WhoHol A*
Blythe, Jimmy 1899?-1931 *CmpEPM*
Blythe, Jimmy 1899-1936 *BiDAmM*
Blythe, Jimmy 1901-1931 *WhoJazz 72*
Blythe, John *WhoHol A*
Blythe, John 1921- *FilmgC, HalFC 80, WhoThe 77*
Blythe, P Richard *AmSCAP 80*
Blythe, Violet *WhThe*
Blytheman, John *NewGrD 80*
Blythman, John *NewGrD 80*
Blyton, Carey 1932- *IntWWM 77, -80, NewGrD 80, WhoMus 72*
Bo Diddley *BluesWW[port]*
Boaden, James 1762-1839 *NotNAT B, OxThe*
Boag, William d1939 *NotNAT B*
Boal, Dean 1931- *IntWWM 77, -80*
Boamah, Crosby Yeboah 1928- *IntWWM 77*
Boardman, Earle M 1922- *AmSCAP 80*
Boardman, Eleanor 1898- *FilmEn, Film 2, FilmgC, HalFC 80, MotPP, MovMk, ThFT[port], TwYS, WhoHol A*
Boardman, Eleanor 1899- *ForYSC*
Boardman, Eunice 1926- *IntWWM 77*
Boardman, Herbert 1892- *ConAmC*
Boardman, Lillian d1953 *NotNAT B*
Boardman, True 1882-1918 *FilmEn, Film 1, WhScrn 77, WhoHol B*
Boardman, Virginia True 1889-1971 *FilmEn, Film 2, WhScrn 74, -77, WhoHol B*
Boas, Franz 1858-1942 *NewGrD 80*
Boasberg, Charles 1906- *IntMPA 77, -75, -76, -78, -79, -80*
Boateng, Stephen Geoffrey 1926- *IntWWM 77, -80*
Boatner, Edward H 1898- *AmSCAP 66, -80, BiDAmM, DrBlPA*
Boatrite, Harold 1932- *ConAmC*
Boatwright, Helen *Baker 78*
Boatwright, Howard Leake 1918- *AmSCAP 66, -80, Baker 78, CpmDNM 80, ConAmC, DcCM*
Boatwright, McHenry 1928- *Baker 78, DrBlPA*
Boaz, Chuck *WhoHol A*
Bob And Ray *JoeFr*
Bob B Soxx And The Blue Jeans *RkOn*
Bob Cats *BiDAmM*
Bobadilla, Pepita *WhThe*
Bobak, Bronislav Joseph 1923- *CreCan 1*
Bobak, Bruno 1923- *CreCan 1*
Bobak, Molly 1922- *CreCan 2*
Bobards, James *Film 2*
Bobbe, Jerry Alan 1949- *IntWWM 77, -80*
Bobbettes, The *RkOn*
Bobby Dee *BluesWW[port]*
Bobczynski, Michele 1946- *WomWMM B*
Bobeche 1791-1840? *OxThe*
Bobescu, Lola 1919- *NewGrD 80*
Bobillier, Marie *NewGrD 80*
Bobker, Lee R 1925- *IntMPA 75, -76*
Bobo, Willie 1934- *BiDAmM, EncJzS 70*
Bobrick, Sam 1932- *AmSCAP 66, -80*
Bobrow, Laura J 1928- *AmSCAP 80*
Bobrowicz, Jan Nepomucen 1805-1881 *NewGrD 80*
Bobs, The Two *WhThe*
Bocage 1797-1863 *EncWT, Ent, NotNAT B, OxThe*
Bocage, Charles 1895?-1963? *NewOrJ*
Bocage, Henry 1893?- *NewOrJ*
Bocage, Paul 1824-1887 *OxThe*
Bocage, Peter 1887-1967 *NewOrJ[port], WhoJazz 72*
Bocage, Pierre Francois 1797-1863 *CnThe*
Bocan *NewGrD 80*
Bocca, Laura Angela 1931- *WhoOp 76*
Boccaccini, Walter 1927- *WhoOp 76*
Boccaccio, Giovanni 1313?-1375 *DcPup, NewEOp 71, NewGrD 80*
Boccherini, Luigi 1743-1805 *Baker 78, BnBkM 80, CmpBCM, GrComp[port], MusMk, NewGrD 80[port], OxMus*
Boccherini, Luigi 1743-1806 *DcCom&M 79*
Bocci, Gildo *Film 2*
Bocham *NewGrD 80*
Bochco, Steven *NewYTET*
Bochmann, Werner 1900- *WhoMus 72*
Bochner, Lloyd 1924- *FilmgC, ForYSC, HalFC 80, WhoHol A*
Bochsa, Nicholas Charles 1789-1856 *NewGrD 80[port]*
Bochsa, Nicolas 1789-1856 *OxMus*
Bochsa, Robert 1789-1856 *Baker 78, BnBkM 80*
Bock *NewGrD 80*
Bock, Anton 1754-1815? *NewGrD 80*
Bock, Eduard d1871 *Baker 78*
Bock, Fred 1939- *AmSCAP 66, -80, ConAmC*
Bock, Gustav 1813-1863 *Baker 78*
Bock, Gustav 1882-1953 *Baker 78*
Bock, Hugo 1848-1932 *Baker 78*
Bock, Ignaz 1758-1815? *NewGrD 80*
Bock, Jerrold 1928- *NewGrD 80*
Bock, Jerry 1928- *AmPS, BestMus, BiDAmM, BiE&WWA, EncMT, HalFC 80, IntWWM 77, NewCBMT, NewGrD 80, NotNAT, PlP&P, PopAmC[port], PopAmC SUP, WhoThe 72, -77*
Bock, Lothar *NewYTET*
Bock And Harnick *BestMus*
Bockelmann, Rudolf 1892-1958 *Baker 78, CmOp, NewGrD 80*
Bockh, August 1785-1867 *Baker 78, NewGrD 80*
Bockholdt, Rudolf 1930- *NewGrD 80*
Bocklin VonBocklinsau, Franz F S A Von 1745-1813 *NewGrD 80*
Bockmann, Alfred 1905- *IntWWM 77, -80*
Bockmon, Guy Alan *ConAmC*
Bockshorn, Samuel Friedrich *NewGrD 80*
Bocquain *NewGrD 80*
Bocquam *NewGrD 80*
Bocquet, Mademoiselle d1660? *NewGrD 80*
Bocquet, Charles 1570?-1615? *NewGrD 80*
Bocquet, Florence *WomWMM*
Bocquillon-Wilhem, Guillaume Louis *NewGrD 80*
Boczkowski, Wojciech 1933- *WhoOp 76*
Boda, John 1922- *Baker 78, ConAmC*
Bodansky, Artur 1877-1939 *CmOp*
Bodanzky, Artur 1877-1939 *Baker 78, BiDAmM, MusSN[port], NewEOp 71, NewGrD 80*
Bodard, Mag 1927- *FilmgC, HalFC 80, WomWMM*
Bodart, Madame *Film 2*
Bodart, Eugen 1905- *IntWWM 77, -80*
Boddecker, Philipp Friedrich 1607-1683 *NewGrD 80*
Boddecker, Philipp Jakob 1642-1707 *NewGrD 80*
Boddey, Martin *WhoHol A*
Bode, Hannelore *WhoOp 76*
Bode, Johann Joachim Christoph 1730-1793 *NewGrD 80*
Bode, Lenore *WomWMM B*
Bode, Milton 1860-1938 *NotNAT B, WhThe*
Bode, Ralf *IntMPA 80*
Bode, Rudolf 1881-1970 *Baker 78, NewGrD 80*
Bodeen, DeWitt 1908- *CmMov, FilmEn, FilmgC, HalFC 80*
Bodel, Burman 1911-1969 *WhScrn 77, WhoHol B*
Bodel, Jean *EncWT*
Bodel, Jean d1210? *McGEWD, OxThe*
Bodel, Jehan 1165?-1209? *NewGrD 80*
Boden, Daphne 1942- *IntWWM 77, -80*
Bodenheim, Maxwell 1893-1954 *NotNAT B*
Bodenschatz, Erhard 1576-1636 *Baker 78, NewGrD 80*
Bodenstein, Nancy Marie 1940- *IntWWM 77, -80*
Bodenweiser, Gertrud 1886-1959 *DancEn 78*
Bodenwieser, Gertrud 1886-1959 *CnOxB*
Bodeo, Joan *NewGrD 80*
Boder, Gerd Wilhelm Karl 1933- *IntWWM 77, -80*
Bodey, Grace 1911- *WhoMus 72*
Bodie, Walford 1870- *WhThe*
Bodigham, Jo *NewGrD 80*
Bodin, Lars-Gunnar 1935- *Baker 78*
Bodin, Louise *CnOxB*
Bodino, Sebastian 1700?-1760? *NewGrD 80*

Bodinus, Johann August 1725-1800 *NewGrD 80*
Bodinus, Sebastian 1700?-1760? *NewGrD 80*
Bodky, Erwin 1896-1958 *Baker 78, NewGrD 80*
Bodley, Nicholas Bessaraboff *NewGrD 80*
Bodley, Seoirse 1933- *IntWWM 77, -80, NewGrD 80*
Bodner, Mark L 1956- *AmSCAP 80*
Bodner, Neal 1958- *AmSCAP 80*
Bodner, Phil 1919- *AmSCAP 66*
Bodner, Philip L 1921- *AmSCAP 80*
Bodo, Arpad 1942- *IntWWM 77, -80*
Bodoil, Jo *NewGrD 80*
Bodoyer, Rudolph 1902- *NewOrJ*
Bodsworth, Charles Frederick *CreCan 2*
Bodsworth, Fred 1918- *CreCan 2*
Body, John Stanley 1944- *IntWWM 80*
Boeck, August De 1865-1937 *NewGrD 80*
Boeck, Auguste De 1865-1937 *OxMus*
Boeck, Johann A 1917- *CroCD*
Boeck, Johann Michael 1743-1793 *OxThe*
Boeck, Orville *PupTheA*
Boedecker, Philipp Friedrich *NewGrD 80*
Boehe, Ernst 1880-1938 *Baker 78*
Boehle, William Randall 1919- *ConAmC*
Boehm, Georg *OxMus*
Boehm, Jan Szczepan 1929- *IntWWM 77, -80*
Boehm, Joseph 1795-1876 *NewGrD 80*
Boehm, Karl 1894-1981 *BiDAmM*
Boehm, Karl 1928- *FilmgC, ForYSC, HalFC 80, WhoHol A, WhoHrs 80*
Boehm, Karl Heinz 1927- *FilmEn*
Boehm, Karl-Walter 1938- *IntWWM 80*
Boehm, Mary Louise 1928- *IntWWM 77, -80*
Boehm, Sidney 1908- *FilmgC*
Boehm, Sydney 1908- *FilmEn, HalFC 80, IntMPA 77, -75, -76, -78, -79, -80, WorEFlm[port]*
Boehm, Theobald 1794-1881 *BnBkM 80, NewGrD 80, OxMus*
Boehmer, Alan *ConAmC*
Boehmer, Konrad 1941- *CpmDNM 76, IntWWM 77, -80, NewGrD 80*
Boehnlein, Frank 1945- *AmSCAP 80, ConAmC, IntWWM 77, -80*
Boekelman, Bernardus 1838-1930 *Baker 78, BiDAmM*
Boelee, Bram 1927- *IntWWM 77, -80*
Boelke, Margot *NewGrD 80*
Boelke, Walter R *NewGrD 80*
Boellmann, Leon 1862-1897 *Baker 78, DcCom&M 79, NewGrD 80, OxMus*
Boely, Alexandre Pierre Francois 1785-1858 *Baker 78, NewGrD 80, OxMus*
Boelza, Igor 1904- *Baker 78*
Boemo, Padre *OxMus*
Boen, Johannes d1367 *NewGrD 80*
Boepple, Paul 1896-1970 *Baker 78, BiDAmM*
Boer, Jan Den 1932- *IntWWM 77*
Boer, Nico 1938- *IntWWM 77, -80*
Boeringer, James Leslie 1930- *ConAmC, IntWWM 77, -80*
Boerio, Francesco Antonio *NewGrD 80*
Boerlage, Frans 1926- *WhoOp 76*
Boero, Felipe 1884-1958 *Baker 78, NewGrD 80*
Boers, Joseph Karel 1812-1896 *Baker 78*
Boesch, Rainer 1938- *NewGrD 80*
Boese, Carl 1887-1958 *FilmEn*
Boese, Joachim 1933-1971 *WhScrn 77*
Boese, Ursula 1933- *WhoOp 76*
Boesen, William 1924-1972 *WhScrn 77*
Boesing, Martha *ConAmC*
Boesing, Paul *ConAmC*
Boesmans, Philippe 1936- *Baker 78, DcCM, NewGrD 80*
Boesset, Anthoine 1586-1643 *NewGrD 80*
Boesset, Antoine 1585?-1643 *MusMk, OxMus*
Boesset, Antoine 1586-1643 *Baker 78, NewGrD 80*
Boesset, Jean-Baptiste 1614-1685 *NewGrD 80*
Boethius, Anicius Manlius Severinus 480?-524? *NewGrD 80*
Boetiger, Julia 1852-1938 *WhScrn 74, -77*
Boetius, Anicius Manlius T Severinus 480?-524 *Baker 78*
Boetler, Wade *Film 2*
Boettcher, Henry F 1903- *BiE&WWA*
Boettcher, Wilfried 1929- *IntWWM 77, NewGrD 80*
Boetticher, Budd 1916- *BiDFilm, -81, CmMov, DcFM, FilmEn, FilmgC, HalFC 80, MovMk[port], OxFilm, WorEFlm[port]*
Boetticher, Budd 1918- *IntMPA 77, -75, -76, -78, -79, -80*
Boetticher, Oscar 1916- *WorEFlm[port]*
Boetticher, Wolfgang 1914- *Baker 78, IntWWM 80, NewGrD 80*
Boeykens, Walter 1938- *IntWWM 80*
Boffety, Jean *IntMPA 77, -75, -76, -78, -79, -80*
Bogajewicz, Ireneusz 1921- *IntWWM 77, -80*
Bogan, Lucille 1897-1948 *BluesWW[port]*
Bogan, Ted 1910- *BluesWW[port]*
Boganny, Joe 1874- *WhThe*
Bogard, Carole Christine 1936- *WhoOp 76*
Bogard, Jan 1540?-1634 *NewGrD 80*
Bogard, Travis 1918- *BiE&WWA, NotNAT*
Bogarde, Dick 1921- *ForYSC*
Bogarde, Dirk *MotPP, WhoHol A*
Bogarde, Dirk 1920- *CmMov, FilmEn, FilmgC, HalFC 80, IlWWBF[port], -A, MovMk[port], WhThe, WorEFlm[port]*
Bogarde, Dirk 1921- *BiDFilm, -81, FilmAG WE[port], IntMPA 77, -75, -76, -78, -79, -80, OxFilm*
Bogart, Andrew 1874- *WhoStg 1908*
Bogart, David d1964 *NotNAT B*
Bogart, Humphrey 1899-1957 *BiDFilm, -81, CmMov, FilmEn, FilmgC, ForYSC, HalFC 80[port], MotPP, MovMk[port], OxFilm, PlP&P, WhScrn 74, -77, WhThe, WhoHol B, WhoHrs 80, WorEFlm[port]*
Bogart, Humphrey 1900-1957 *NotNAT B*
Bogart, Joyce *ConMuA 80B*
Bogart, Neil *ConMuA 80B, IntMPA 79, -80*
Bogart, Paul 1919- *FilmEn, FilmgC, IntMPA 77, -75, -76, -78, -79, -80, NewYTET*
Bogart, Paul 1925- *HalFC 80*
Bogatiryov, Anatoly Vasil'yevich 1913- *NewGrD 80*
Bogatiryov, Semyon Semyonovich 1890-1960 *NewGrD 80*
Bogatyrev, Alexander Yurievich 1949- *CnOxB*
Bogatyrev, Anatoly 1913- *Baker 78*
Bogdanoff, Rose d1957 *NotNAT B*
Bogdanov, Konstantin 1809?-1877 *CnOxB*
Bogdanov-Berezovsky, Valerian M 1903-1971 *Baker 78, NewGrD 80*
Bogdanova, Nadezhda 1836-1897 *CnOxB*
Bogdanovich, Peter 1939- *BiDFilm, -81, FilmEn, HalFC 80, IntMPA 77, -75, -76, -78, -79, -80, MovMk[port], WhoHrs 80*
Bogdanovich, Peter 1940- *OxFilm*
Bogdanovitch, Peter 1939- *FilmgC*
Bogdany, Wanda 1928- *IntWWM 77*
Bogdany-Popiel, Wanda 1928- *IntWWM 80*
Bogeaus, Benedict E 1904-1968 *FilmEn, FilmgC, HalFC 80, WorEFlm[port]*
Bogentantz, Bernhard 1494?-1527? *NewGrD 80*
Bogentanz, Bernhard 1494?-1527? *NewGrD 80*
Boggess, Gary Thomas 1952- *AmSCAP 80*
Boggetti, Victor 1895- *WhThe*
Boggio, Shelby Richard 1945- *IntWWM 77, -80*
Boggs, Dock 1898- *CounME 74, -74A, EncFCWM 69, IlEncCM*
Boggs, Jon William 1940- *IntWWM 77, -80*
Boggs, Martha Daniel 1928- *IntWWM 80*
Boggs, Moran L 1898- *BiDAmM*
Boggs, Noel Edwin 1917- *BiDAmM*
Boghen, Felice 1869-1945 *Baker 78, NewGrD 80*
Boghossian, Levon 1930- *WhoOp 76*
Bogianckino, Massimo 1922- *IntWWM 77, -80, NewGrD 80, WhoMus 72, WhoOp 76*
Bogie, Duane *NewYTET*
Bogin, Abba 1925- *NotNAT*
Bogin, Abba 1935- *IntWWM 77, -80*
Bogle, Helen 1947- *IntWWM 77*
Boglhat, Johannes De *NewGrD 80*
Boglietti, Alexander De *NewGrD 80*
Bogomolova, Liudmila 1932- *DancEn 78[port]*
Bogomolova, Ludmila Ivanovna 1932- *CnOxB*
Bogue, Merwyn *JoeFr*
Bogusch, Ronald A 1931- *AmSCAP 66*
Boguslawski, Edward 1940- *Baker 78, DcCM, IntWWM 80, NewGrD 80*
Boguslawski, Wojciech 1757-1829 *Ent, NewGrD 80, NotNAT B*
Boguslawski, Woyciech 1757-1829 *EncWT*
Bohac, Josef 1929- *Baker 78*
Bohacova, Marta 1936- *WhoOp 76*
Bohan, Edmund *IntWWM 77, -80*
Bohana, Roy 1938- *IntWWM 77, -80, WhoMus 72*
Bohanec, Mirjana *WhoOp 76*
Bohannon, E J Bo 1896-1966 *WhScrn 77*
Bohannon, Hamilton F 1942- *AmSCAP 80*
Bohannon, Steve 1947-1968 *EncJzS 70*
Bohanon, George Roland, Jr. 1937- *BiDAmM, EncJzS 70*
Bohart, James Arthur 1942- *IntWWM 77*
Bohdanowicz, Bazyli 1740-1817 *NewGrD 80*
Bohdanowicz, Michal 1779-1830 *NewGrD 80*
Bohdiewicz, Antoni 1906-1970 *OxFilm*
Boheim, Joseph Michael 1748?-1811 *NewGrD 80*
Bohem, Endre *IntMPA 77, -75, -76, -78, -79, -80*
Bohle, David *NewGrD 80*
Bohlen, Donald *ConAmC*
Bohler, Fred *Film 2*
Bohlin, Folke 1931- *IntWWM 77, -80, NewGrD 80*
Bohlmann, T H F 1865-1926 *BiDAmM*
Bohlmann, Theodor Heinrich Friedrich 1865-1931 *Baker 78*
Bohm *NewGrD 80*
Bohm, Andreas 1765-1834 *NewGrD 80*
Bohm, Anton 1807-1884 *NewGrD 80*
Bohm, Carl 1844-1920 *OxMus*
Bohm, Georg 1661-1733 *Baker 78, BnBkM 80, MusMk, NewGrD 80, OxMus*
Bohm, Johann 174-?-1792 *NewGrD 80*
Bohm, Joseph 1795-1876 *Baker 78*
Bohm, Karl 1844-1920 *Baker 78*
Bohm, Karl 1894- *CmOp*
Bohm, Karl 1894-1981 *Baker 78, BnBkM 80, IntWWM 77, -80, MusSN[port], NewEOp 71, NewGrD 80[port], WhoMus 72, WhoOp 76*
Bohm, Karl-Heinz 1928- *FilmAG WE*
Bohm, Karl-Walter 1938- *WhoOp 76*
Bohm, Karlheinz *FilmEn, MotPP*
Bohm, Moritz Anselm 1846-1896 *NewGrD 80*
Bohm, Theobald 1794-1881 *Baker 78, OxMus*
Bohman, Andrew Clive 1933- *IntWWM 77*
Bohme, Baldur 1932- *IntWWM 77, -80*
Bohme, David M 1916- *AmSCAP 66, -80*
Bohme, Erdmann Werner 1906- *IntWWM 77, -80*
Bohme, Franz Magnus 1827-1898 *Baker 78*
Bohme, Kurt 1908- *CmOp, NewGrD 80, WhoMus 72, WhoOp 76*
Bohme, Oscka *OxMus*
Bohmelt, Harald 1900- *IntWWM 77, -80, WhoMus 72*
Bohn, Elsebeth 1931- *IntWWM 77, -80*
Bohn, Emil 1839-1909 *Baker 78, NewGrD 80*
Bohn, Jack Lionel *Film 2*
Bohn, Peter 1833-1925 *Baker 78, NewGrD 80*
Bohn, Walter Morrow 1939- *AmSCAP 80*
Bohnen, Michael 1887-1965 *Baker 78, CmOp, Film 2, MusSN[port], NewEOp 71, NewGrD 80, WhScrn 77*
Bohnen, Roman 1894-1949 *FilmEn, FilmgC, ForYSC, HalFC 80, NotNAT B, PlP&P[port], WhScrn 74, -77, WhThe, WhoHol B*
Bohnen, Roman 1899-1949 *Vers A[port]*
Bohnenblust, Gottfried 1883- *OxMus*
Bohner, Gerhard 1936- *CnOxB*
Bohner, Louis 1787-1860 *NewGrD 80*
Bohner, Ludwig 1787-1860 *Baker 78, NewGrD 80*
Bohnke, Emil 1888-1928 *Baker 78*
Bohrnstedt, Wayne 1923- *AmSCAP 80*
Bohrnstedt, Wayne Rynning 1923- *ConAmC, IntWWM 77*
Boiardo, Matteomaria 1441?-1494 *DcPup*
Boice, Thomas *NewGrD 80*
Boieldieu, Adrien 1775-1834 *CmOp, NewGrD 80[port]*
Boieldieu, Adrien-Louis-Victor 1815-1883 *Baker 78*
Boieldieu, Francois 1775-1834 *DcCom&M 79, GrComp[port]*
Boieldieu, Francois-Adrein 1775-1834 *Baker 78*

Boieldieu, Francois Adrien 1775-1834 *BnBkM 80, DcCom 77[port], MusMk, NewEOp 71, OxMus*
Boieldieu, Louis 1815-1883 *NewGrD 80*
Boileau, Nicolas 1633?-1711 *NotNAT B*
Boileau, Simon *NewGrD 80*
Boileau Bernasconi, Alessio 1875-1948 *NewGrD 80*
Boileau-Despreaux, Nicolas 1636-1711 *EncWT, OxThe*
Boiles, Charles Lafayette 1932- *IntWWM 77, -80*
Boin, Henry Alphonse *NewGrD 80*
Boindin, Nicolas 1676-1751 *OxThe*
Boireau, Gerard 1919- *WhoOp 76*
Bois, Curt *ForYSC*
Bois, Curt 1900- *FilmgC, HalFC 80, WhoHol A*
Bois, Curt 1901- *EncWT, FilmEn*
Bois, Ilse *Film 2*
Bois, Rob Du 1934- *Baker 78, CpmDNM 80, NewGrD 80*
Boisdechines, Josephine 1831- *Ent*
Boise, James Warren 1930- *IntWWM 77*
Boise, Otis Bardwell 1844-1912 *Baker 78, BiDAmM*
Boisjoli, Charlotte *CreCan 2*
Boismortier, Joseph Bodin De 1689-1755 *Baker 78, NewGrD 80*
Boismortier, Joseph Bodin De 1691-1755 *BnBkM 80*
Boisrobert, Francois LeMetel De 1592-1662 *EncWT, Ent, OxThe*
Boisrobert, Francois LeNutel DeAbbe 1592-1662 *NotNAT B*
Boisrond, Michel 1921- *DcFM, FilmEn*
Boisselot, Xavier 1811-1893 *Baker 78*
Boisset, Yves 1939- *FilmEn, FilmgC, HalFC 80*
Boissonneault, Fernand Noel *CreCan 1*
Boito, Arrigo 1842-1918 *Baker 78, BnBkM 80, CmOp, -[port], CmpBCM, DcCom 77, GrComp[port], MusMk[port], NewEOp 71, NewGrD 80[port], NotNAT B, OxMus, OxThe*
Boito, Enrico 1842-1918 *NewGrD 80[port]*
Boivin *NewGrD 80*
Boivin, Francois 1693?-1733 *NewGrD 80*
Boix, Manuel Palau *NewGrD 80*
Bojangles *DancEn 78, DrBlPA*
Bojanowski, Jerzy 1936- *IntWWM 77, -80*
Bojar, Jerzy 1933- *WhoOp 76*
Bok, Josef 1890- *IntWWM 77, -80*
Bok, Mary Louise Curtis 1876-1970 *Baker 78, NewGrD 80*
Bokchenko, Luba 1941- *IntWWM 80*
Bokelund, Per 1936- *IntWWM 77, -80*
Bokemeyer, Heinrich 1679-1751 *NewGrD 80*
Boker, George Henry 1823-1890 *CnThe, McGEWD[port], NotNAT A, -B, OxThe, REnWD[port]*
Boky, Colette 1935- *WhoOp 76*
Boky, Colette 1937- *CreCan 2*
Bol, Jan *NewGrD 80*
Bol, John *NewGrD 80*
Boladian, Armen *ConMuA 80B*
Bolam, James 1937- *HalFC 80*
Bolam, James 1938- *WhoThe 72, -77*
Bolan, Marc 1947- *IlEncR[port]*
Bolan, Marc & T Rex *ConMuA 80A*
Boland, Bridget *WomWMM*
Boland, Bridget 1904- *FilmgC, HalFC 80*
Boland, Bridget 1913- *ConDr 73, -77*
Boland, Clay A 1903-1963 *AmSCAP 66, -80, CmpEPM*
Boland, Clay A, Jr. 1931- *AmSCAP 66, -80*
Boland, Eddie 1883-1935 *WhScrn 74, -77*
Boland, Eddie 1885-1935 *Film 1, -2, TwYS*
Boland, Francois 1929- *EncJzS 70*
Boland, Francy 1929- *EncJzS 70*
Boland, Mary 1880-1965 *EncMT, FilmEn, Film 1, FilmgC, Funs[port], HalFC 80, ThFT[port], WhScrn 74, -77*
Boland, Mary 1882-1965 *ForYSC, MotPP, MovMk[port], TwYS, Vers A[port], WhoHol B*
Boland, Mary 1885-1965 *BiE&WWA, NotNAT B, WhThe*
Bolanos, Cesar 1931- *NewGrD 80*
Bolar, Abe 1909- *WhoJazz 72*
Bolasni, Saul 1923- *BiE&WWA, NotNAT*
Bolck, Oskar 1837-1888 *Baker 78*
Bolcom, William 1928- *BnBkM 80*
Bolcom, William 1938- *Baker 78, CpmDNM 72, -77, -78, -80, ConAmC, DcCM, IntWWM 77, -80, NewGrD 80*
Boldemann, Laci 1921-1969 *Baker 78, NewGrD 80*
Bolden, Buddy 1868?-1931 *CmpEPM, NewGrD 80, WhoJazz 72*
Bolden, Charles 1868-1931 *BiDAmM*
Bolden, Charles 1877-1931 *NewOrJ*
Bolden, Charles Buddy 1870-1931 *MusMk*
Bolden's Band, Buddy *BiDAmM*
Bolder, Robert 1859-1937 *Film 1, -2, WhScrn 74, -77, WhoHol B*
Boldin, Dragutin 1930- *CnOxB*
Boldon, Tomaso *NewGrD 80*
Boldorini, Raquel 1943- *IntWWM 80*
Boldrey, Richard Lee 1940- *IntWWM 77, -80*
Boldt, Deborah *WomWMM*
Boleau, Simon *NewGrD 80*
Bolen, Jane Moore 1928- *IntWWM 80*
Bolen, Lin *NewYTET*
Bolender, Todd 1914- *CnOxB*
Bolender, Todd 1919- *DancEn 78*
Boles, Jim *WhoHol A*
Boles, John d1969 *BiE&WWA, MotPP, WhoHol B*
Boles, John 1890-1969 *TwYS*
Boles, John 1895-1969 *EncMT, FilmEn, Film 2, FilmgC, HalFC 80, HolP 30[port], MovMk, WhScrn 74, -77*
Boles, John 1896-1969 *NotNAT B*
Boles, John 1898-1969 *CmpEPM*
Boles, John 1900-1969 *ForYSC, What 2[port], WhThe*
Boleslavski, Richard 1889-1937 *PlP&P*
Boleslavsky, Richard 1889-1937 *BiDFilm, -81, WorEFlm[port]*
Boleslawski, Richard 1889-1937 *FilmEn, FilmgC, HalFC 80, NotNAT A, -B, WhThe, WorEFlm[port]*
Bolet, Jorge 1914- *Baker 78, BnBkM 80, IntWWM 77, -80, MusSN[port], NewGrD 80, WhoMus 72*
Bolet Tremoleda, Alberto J 1905- *WhoMus 72*
Boley, May 1882-1963 *Film 2, NotNAT B, WhScrn 74, -77, WhoHol B*
Bolger, Harry *AmPS B*
Bolger, Ray *AmPS B, WhoHol A*
Bolger, Ray 1903- *CmMov*
Bolger, Ray 1904- *BiE&WWA, CmpEPM, CnOxB, DancEn 78, EncMT, Ent, FilmEn, FilmgC, ForYSC, HalFC 80, MovMk[port], NotNAT, WhoHrs 80[port], WhoThe 72, -77*
Bolger, Ray 1906- *IntMPA 77, -75, -76, -78, -79, -80*
Bolger, Robert Bo 1937-1969 *WhScrn 77*
Bolick, Bill *EncFCWM 69*
Bolick, Bill 1917- *IlEncCM[port]*
Bolick, Earl A 1919- *BiDAmM, EncFCWM 69, IlEncCM[port]*
Bolick, William A 1917- *BiDAmM*
Bolin, Nicolai 1898- *AmSCAP 80*
Bolin, Nicolai P 1908- *AmSCAP 66, ConAmC*
Bolin, Shannon 1917- *BiE&WWA, NotNAT*
Bolin, Thomas Richard 1951-1976 *AmSCAP 80*
Bolin, Tommy d1976 *ConMuA 80A, IlEncR*
Bolkan, Florinda 1941- *FilmEn, FilmgC, HalFC 80, WhoHol A*
Boll Weenie Bill *BluesWW[port]*
Boll Weevil Bill *BluesWW[port]*
Bollard, Robert Gordon 1920-1964 *AmSCAP 80*
Bolle, James 1931- *ConAmC*
Bollengier, Albert Emile 1913- *IntMPA 75, -76*
Boller, Robert O, Sr. d1962 *NotNAT B*
Bollert, Werner 1910- *IntWWM 77, -80*
Bolling, Claude 1930- *EncJzS 70*
Bolling, Tiffany *HalFC 80, WhoHol A*
Bollinger, Anne d1962 *NotNAT B*
Bollioud-Mermet, Louis 1709-1794 *NewGrD 80*
Bollius, Daniel 1590?-1642? *NewGrD 80*
Bollon, Joseph 1915- *AmSCAP 80*
Bollow, Ludmilla *NatPD[port]*
Bollstadt, Albertus De *NewGrD 80*
Bolm, Adolf *OxMus*
Bolm, Adolph 1884-1951 *CnOxB, DancEn 78[port]*
Bolm, Adolph 1887-1951 *NotNAT B, WhThe*
Bolman, Red 1899- *NewOrJ*
Bologna, Bartolomeo Da *NewGrD 80*
Bologna, Jacopo Da *Baker 78*
Bologna, Joseph 1938- *HalFC 80, IntMPA 77, -75, -76, -78, -79, -80, NotNAT, WhoHol A, WomWMM*
Bolognese, Il *NewGrD 80*
Bolognini, Bernardo 1570?- *NewGrD 80*
Bolognini, Mauro 1923- *BiDFilm, -81, DcFM, FilmEn, WorEFlm[port]*
Bolognini, Remo E 1898- *IntWWM 77, -80*
Bolsche, Franz 1869-1935 *Baker 78*
Bolsena, Il *NewGrD 80*
Bolshakova, Natalia Dimitrievna 1943- *CnOxB*
Bolt, Carol 1941- *ConDr 77*
Bolt, Klaas 1927- *IntWWM 77, -80*
Bolt, Laurie 1893- *WhoMus 72*
Bolt, Michael Sidney 1946- *IntWWM 80*
Bolt, Robert 1924- *BiE&WWA, CnThe, ConDr 73, -77, CroCD, EncWT, Ent, FilmEn, FilmgC, HalFC 80, IntMPA 77, -78, -79, -80, McGEWD[port], ModWD, NotNAT, OxThe, REnWD[port], WhoThe 72, -77, WorEFlm[port]*
Bolte, Barbara Anne 1952- *IntWWM 80*
Bolte, Carl Eugene, Jr. 1929- *AmSCAP 66, -80*
Bolton, Betty *Film 2*
Bolton, Guy *ConDr 77D, PlP&P*
Bolton, Guy 1884- *AmSCAP 66, BestMus, BiDAmM, CmpEPM, ConDr 73, EncMT, Ent, HalFC 80, ModWD, WhoThe 72, -77*
Bolton, Guy 1885- *FilmgC*
Bolton, Guy 1885-1979 *FilmEn*
Bolton, Guy 1886- *BiE&WWA, NewCBMT, NotNAT, -A*
Bolton, Happy 1885-1928 *NewOrJ*
Bolton, Helen *Film 2*
Bolton, Jack d1962 *NotNAT B*
Bolton, Joe 1910- *IntMPA 75, -76*
Bolton, Thomas 1770?-1820? *NewGrD 80*
Bolton, Whitney 1900-1969 *BiE&WWA, NotNAT B*
Boltz, Violet Marie 1920- *AmSCAP 80*
Boluda, Gines De 1550?-1592? *NewGrD 80*
Bolvary, Geza Von 1897- *DcFM*
Bolz, Harriett *AmSCAP 80, CpmDNM 80, ConAmC, IntWWM 77, -80*
Bolzonello Zoja, Elsa 1937- *IntWWM 77, -80*
Bolzoni, Giovanni 1841-1919 *Baker 78, NewGrD 80*
Boman, Arild 1940- *IntWWM 80*
Boman, Pehr Conrad 1804-1861 *NewGrD 80*
Boman, Petter Conrad 1804-1861 *NewGrD 80*
Bombard, Lottie Gertrude 1908-1913 *WhScrn 77*
Bombardelli, Silvije 1916- *Baker 78*
Bomberger, Edward C 1933- *IntMPA 77, -75, -76, -78, -79, -80*
Bomer, Marjorie *Film 2*
Bomhard, Moritz Von 1908- *WhoOp 76*
Bomm, Urbanus Johannes 1901- *IntWWM 80*
Bommer, Johann Jakob *NewGrD 80*
Bompiani, Valentino 1898- *CnMD, McGEWD[port]*
Bomtempo, Joao Domingos 1775-1842 *Baker 78, NewGrD 80*
Bon, Francesco Augusto 1788-1858 *McGEWD[port]*
Bon, Josephus Johannes Baptizta *NewGrD 80*
Bon, Maarten 1933- *Baker 78*
Bon, Rene 1924- *CnOxB, DancEn 78*
Bon, Willem Frederik 1940- *Baker 78, NewGrD 80*
Bon, William Frederik 1940- *IntWWM 77, -80*
Bon Bon *CmpEPM*
Bon Marchier, Jean De 1520?-1570 *NewGrD 80*
Bon Voisin *NewGrD 80*
Bon Voysin *NewGrD 80*
Bona, Giovanni 1609-1674 *Baker 78, NewGrD 80*
Bona, Valerio 1560?-1620? *Baker 78, NewGrD 80*
Bonaccorsi, Alfredo 1887-1971 *NewGrD 80*
Bonachelli, Giovanni *NewGrD 80*
Bonacio, Bennie 1903-1974 *AmSCAP 66, -80*
Bonafe, Pepa *Film 1*
Bonaffino, Filippo *NewGrD 80*
Bonagionta, Giulio d1582? *NewGrD 80*

Bonagiunta, Giulio d1582? *NewGrD 80*
Bonagura, Michael John, Jr. 1953- *AmSCAP 80*
Bonaiutus Corsini *NewGrD 80*
Bonaldi, Francesco *NewGrD 80*
Bonamici, Ferdinando 1827-1905 *NewGrD 80*
Bonamico, Johann Franz *NewGrD 80*
Bonamico, Pietro *NewGrD 80*
Bonamicus, Cornelius *NewGrD 80*
Bonanni, Filippo 1638-1725 *Baker 78, NewGrD 80*
Bonano, Joseph 1904-1972 *AmSCAP 66, -80, EncJzS 70, NewOrJ[port]*
Bonano, Joseph G 1900-1972 *BiDAmM*
Bonano, Sharkey 1904-1972 *CmpEPM, EncJzS 70*
Bonano, Sharkey Joseph 1904-1972 *WhoJazz 72*
Bonanome, Franco 1938- *WhoOp 76*
Bonanova, Fortunio 1893-1969 *FilmEn, ForYSC, WhScrn 74, -77*
Bonanova, Fortunio 1896-1969 *FilmgC, HalFC 80, HolCA[port], WhoHol B*
Bonanova, Fortunio 1905-1969 *Vers B[port]*
Bonansinga, Frank 1900- *NewOrJ*
Bonaparte *NewGrD 80*
Bonaparte, Napoleon *Film 2, HalFC 80*
Bonard, Laurent *NewGrD 80*
Bonard, Nigel Ian 1946- *IntWWM 77*
Bonard Perissone, Francesco 1520?- *NewGrD 80*
Bonardi Perissone, Francesco 1520?- *NewGrD 80*
Bonardo, Iseppo *NewGrD 80*
Bonardo Perissone, Francesco 1520?- *NewGrD 80*
Bonarelli DellaRovere, Guidobaldo 1563-1608 *OxThe*
Bonart, Laurent *NewGrD 80*
Bonaventi, Giuseppe *NewGrD 80*
Bonaventura Da Brescia *NewGrD 80*
Bonaventura De Brixia *NewGrD 80*
Bonaventura, Anthony Di 1930- *Baker 78*
Bonaventura, Arnaldo 1862-1952 *Baker 78, NewGrD 80*
Bonaventura, Mario Di 1924- *Baker 78*
Bonavia, Ferruccio 1877-1950 *Baker 78, NewGrD 80*
Bonavolonta, Nino Gioacchino 1920- *WhoOp 76*
Bonawitz, Johann Heinrich 1839-1917 *Baker 78*
Bonazzi, Elaine *IntWWM 77, -80, WhoOp 76*
Bonbarde *NewGrD 80*
Bonbrest, Joseph B 1895- *AmSCAP 66, -80*
Bonci, Alessandro 1870-1940 *Baker 78, CmOp, MusSN[port], NewEOp 71, NewGrD 80*
Boncompagni, Elio 1933- *NewGrD 80, WhoOp 76*
Bond, Acton d1941 *NotNAT B, WhThe*
Bond, Anson 1914- *IntMPA 77, -75, -76, -78, -79, -80*
Bond, Bert d1964 *NotNAT B*
Bond, Brenda *Film 2*
Bond, C G 1945- *ConDr 77*
Bond, Capel 1730-1790 *NewGrD 80*
Bond, Carrie Jacobs 1862-1946 *AmPS, AmSCAP 66, Baker 78, BiDAmM, CmpEPM, MusMk, NotNAT B, PopAmC[port]*
Bond, Cyrus Whitfield 1915- *BiDAmM*
Bond, David *WhoHol A*
Bond, Derek *WhoHol A*
Bond, Derek 1919- *FilmEn, FilmgC, ForYSC, HalFC 80*
Bond, Derek 1920- *IlWWBF, IntMPA 77, -75, -76, -78, -79, -80*
Bond, Eddie J 1933- *BiDAmM*
Bond, Edward 1934- *ConDr 73, -77*
Bond, Edward 1935- *CnThe, CroCD, EncWT, Ent, NotNAT, PlP&P A[port], WhoThe 72, -77*
Bond, Frank *Film 2*
Bond, Frederic 1861-1914 *WhThe*
Bond, Frederick 1861-1914 *Film 1, NotNAT B, WhoStg 1906, -1908*
Bond, Frederick Weldon *BlkAmP*
Bond, Gary 1940- *FilmgC, HalFC 80, WhoThe 72, -77*
Bond, Graham *IlEncR[port]*
Bond, Horace J *MorBAP*
Bond, Jack 1899-1952 *WhScrn 74, -77*
Bond, James E, Jr. 1933- *BiDAmM*
Bond, Jessie 1853-1942 *NotNAT B, WhThe*
Bond, Johnny 1915- *CounME 74[port], -74A, EncFCWM 69, IlEncCM[port], RkOn*
Bond, Keith Hothersall 1929- *WhoMus 72*
Bond, Lilian 1910- *ThFT[port], WhThe*
Bond, Lillian 1910- *FilmEn, FilmgC, ForYSC, HalFC 80, WhoHol A*
Bond, Lyle 1917-1972 *WhScrn 77*
Bond, Ralph 1906- *IntMPA 77, -75, -76, -78, -79, -80*
Bond, Rudy 1913- *BiE&WWA, NotNAT, WhoHol A*
Bond, Sheila 1928- *BiE&WWA, NotNAT, WhThe, WhoHol A*
Bond, Shelly 1910- *AmSCAP 66, -80*
Bond, Sudie 1928- *BiE&WWA, NotNAT, WhoHol A, WhoThe 72, -77*
Bond, Thomas d1635 *OxThe*
Bond, Tommy 1927- *FilmEn*
Bond, Tommy Butch *WhoHol A*
Bond, Victoria 1945- *ConAmC*
Bond, Victoria 1949- *CpmDNM 76, -78, IntWWM 77, WomCom[port]*
Bond, Victoria 1950- *IntWWM 80*
Bond, Ward d1960 *MotPP, NotNAT B, WhoHol B*
Bond, Ward 1903-1960 *FilmEn, FilmgC, HalFC 80, OxFilm, WhScrn 74, -77*
Bond, Ward 1904-1960 *MovMk[port]*
Bond, Ward 1905-1960 *CmMov, Film 2, ForYSC, HolCA[port]*
Bondarchuk, Serge 1920- *MovMk[port]*
Bondarchuk, Sergei 1920- *DcFM, FilmEn, OxFilm, WhoHol A, WorEFlm[port]*
Bondartchuk, Sergei 1920- *FilmgC, HalFC 80*
Bonde, Allen 1936- *ConAmC*
Bondeville, Emmanuel 1898- *Baker 78, IntWWM 77, -80, NewGrD 80, OxMus, WhoMus 72*
Bondhill, Gertrude 1880-1960 *WhScrn 74, -77, WhoHol B*
Bondi, Alex *Film 2*
Bondi, Anna Maria 1931- *IntWWM 77, -80*
Bondi, Beulah 1892- *BiE&WWA, FilmEn, FilmgC, ForYSC, HalFC 80, HolCA[port], IntMPA 77, -75, -76, -78, -79, -80, MotPP, MovMk, NotNAT, ThFT[port], Vers A[port], What 4[port], WhThe, WhoHol A*
Bondi, Eugene B 1953- *IntWWM 77, -80*
Bondini, Pasquale 1737?-1789 *NewGrD 80*
Bondino, Ruggero 1930- *WhoOp 76*
Bondioli, Giacinto 1596-1636 *NewGrD 80*
Bondioli, Giovanni *NewGrD 80*
Bondire *Film 2*
Bondon, Jacques 1927- *Baker 78, DcCM, NewGrD 80*
Bonds, Gary U S 1939- *RkOn[port]*
Bonds, Margaret 1913-1972 *AmSCAP 66, -80, BiDAmM, ConAmC, DrBlPA*
Bonds, Son 1909-1947 *BluesWW*
Bondwin, Billy *Film 2*
Bondy, Ed 1932- *BiE&WWA*
Bone, Gene 1948- *AmSCAP 66, -80*
Bone, Harold MacPherson 1896- *ConAmTC*
Bonell, Carlos Antonio 1949- *IntWWM 77, -80*
Bonelli, Alessandro 1947- *IntWWM 77, -80*
Bonelli, Aurelio 1569?-1620? *NewGrD 80*
Bonelli, Ettore 1900- *IntWWM 77, -80*
Bonelli, Mona Modini 1903- *AmSCAP 66, -80*
Bonelli, Richard 1887- *Baker 78, MusSN[port]*
Bonelli, Richard 1894- *NewEOp 71*
Bonerz, Peter *WhoHol A*
Bonesi, Barnaba 1745?-1824 *NewGrD 80*
Boness, Clarence M 1931- *AmSCAP 66*
Bonestell, Chesley 1888- *WhoHrs 80*
Bonet, John *NewGrD 80*
Bonet, Nai *IntMPA 80*
Bonet DeParedes, Juan d1710 *NewGrD 80*
Bonetti, Carlo *NewGrD 80*
Boneventi, Giuseppe *NewGrD 80*
Bonfa, Luiz Floriano 1922- *AmSCAP 80, BiDAmM*
Bonfanti, Marietta 1847-1921 *CnOxB, DancEn 78*
Bonfichi, Paolo 1769-1840 *NewGrD 80*
Bonfilio, Paolo Antonio *NewGrD 80*
Bonfils, Helen *WhoThe 72*
Bonfils, Helen 1889-1972 *BiE&WWA, NotNAT B, WhThe*
Bonfils, Jean 1921- *NewGrD 80*
Bongini, Rafael *Film 2*
Bongiovi, Tony *ConMuA 80B*
Bonham, John 1948- *AmSCAP 80*
Bonham, Kathy *WomWMM B*
Bonhomio, Pierre 1555?-1617 *NewGrD 80*
Bonhomius, Pierre 1555?-1617 *NewGrD 80*
Bonhomme, Jean 1936- *CreCan 1, WhoMus 72*
Bonhomme, Jean Robert 1937- *WhoOp 76*
Bonhomme, Michele *WhoMus 72*
Bonhomme, Pierre 1555?-1617 *NewGrD 80*
Boni, Carmen 1904-1963 *FilmAG WE, Film 2*
Boni, Gaetano *NewGrD 80*
Boni, Guillaume d1594? *NewGrD 80*
Boniface, Mrs. George C d1883 *NotNAT B*
Boniface, George C, Jr. d1912 *NotNAT B*
Boniface, Symona 1894-1950 *WhScrn 74, -77, WhoHol B*
Bonifacio, Tina *WhoMus 72*
Bonifant, Carmen 1890-1957 *WhScrn 74, -77*
Bonillas, Myrna 1890-1959 *WhScrn 74, -77, WhoHol B*
Bonillas, Myrta *Film 2*
Bonime, Josef 1891-1959 *AmSCAP 66, -80*
Bonini, Francesco *NewGrD 80*
Bonini, Pier' Andrea *NewGrD 80*
Bonini, Pietro Andrea *NewGrD 80*
Bonini, Severo 1582-1663 *MusMk, NewGrD 80*
Bonino, Luigi 1949- *CnOxB*
Boninsegna, Celestina 1877-1947 *CmOp, NewGrD 80*
Bonis, Ferenc 1932- *IntWWM 77, -80, NewGrD 80*
Bonis, Melanie 1858-1937 *Baker 78*
Bonisolli, Franco *WhoOp 76*
Bonita 1886- *WhoStg 1908*
Boniuszko, Alicja 1937- *CnOxB*
Boniventi, Giuseppe 1670?- *NewGrD 80*
Bonizzi, Vincenzo d1630 *NewGrD 80*
Bonizzoni, Eliseo *NewGrD 80*
Bonlini, Giovanni Carlo 1673-1731 *NewGrD 80*
Bonmarche, Jean De 1520?-1570 *NewGrD 80*
Bonmarchie, Jean De 1520?-1570 *NewGrD 80*
Bonn, Ferdinand *Film 2*
Bonn, Frank 1873-1944 *WhScrn 74, -77, WhoHol B*
Bonn, Skeeter 1923- *BiDAmM*
Bonn, Walter 1889-1953 *WhScrn 74, -77, WhoHol B*
Bonnaire, Henri 1869- *WhThe*
Bonnard, Laurent *NewGrD 80*
Bonnard, Mario 1889-1965 *FilmEn, WhScrn 74, -77*
Bonnardot, Jean-Claude 1923- *DcFM*
Bonneau, Gilles Yves 1941- *ConAmC*
Bonneau, Paul 1918- *IntWWM 77, -80*
Bonnefond, Simon De *NewGrD 80*
Bonnefous, Jean-Pierre 1943- *CnOxB*
Bonnel, Pierre *NewGrD 80*
Bonnel, Pietrequin *NewGrD 80*
Bonnell, Jay *WhoHol A*
Bonnell, Lee *WhoHol A*
Bonner, Eugene MacDonald 1889- *BiDAmM, ConAmC, NewGrD 80*
Bonner, Isabel 1908-1955 *NotNAT B, WhScrn 74, -77, WhoHol B*
Bonner, Joan *WhoMus 72*
Bonner, Joe 1882-1959 *WhScrn 77, WhoHol B*
Bonner, Joe 1948- *EncJzS 70*
Bonner, Joseph Leonard 1948- *EncJzS 70*
Bonner, Marita 1905- *BlkAmP*
Bonner, Marjorie *Film 2*
Bonner, Priscella *Film 2*
Bonner, Priscilla *TwYS*
Bonner, Robert 1854-1899 *BiDAmM*
Bonner, Ronnie 1920- *AmSCAP 66, -80*
Bonner, Weldon H Philip 1932-1978 *BluesWW[port]*
Bonnet, Jacques 1644-1724 *NewGrD 80, OxMus*
Bonnet, John *NewGrD 80*
Bonnet, Joseph 1884-1944 *Baker 78, BnBkM 80*
Bonnet, Joseph Elie Georges Marie 1884-1944 *OxMus*

Bonnet, Pierre *NewGrD 80*
Bonnet-Bourdelot, Pierre *NewGrD 80*
Bonnevin, Johannes 1475?-1542 *NewGrD 80*
Bonney, Betty *CmpEPM*
Bonney, William H *OxFilm*
Bonnhorst, Carl Franz Wilhelm Von *BiDAmM*
Bonnie Lou 1926- *EncFCWM 69*
Bonnie Sisters, The *RkOn*
Bonniere, Rene 1928- *CreCan 2*
Bonno, Giuseppe 1710-1788 *OxMus*
Bonno, Giuseppe 1711-1788 *NewGrD 80*
Bonnus, Hermann 1504-1548 *NewGrD 80*
Bono, Cheryl LaPiere 1946- *BiDAmM*
Bono, Pietro *NewGrD 80*
Bono, Salvatore 1935- *BiDAmM*
Bono, Sonny *IntMPA 77, -75, -76, -78, -79, -80, WhoHol A*
Bonomi, Pierre *NewGrD 80*
Bonomo, Joe 1898- *Film 2, ForYSC, WhoHol A*
Bononcini *NewGrD 80*
Bononcini, Antonio Maria 1677-1726 *Baker 78, NewGrD 80*
Bononcini, Giovanni 1670-1747 *Baker 78, BnBkM 80, GrComp[port], MusMk, NewEOp 71, NewGrD 80[port], OxMus*
Bononcini, Giovanni Maria 1642?-1678 *Baker 78, NewGrD 80, OxMus*
Bononcini, Giovanni Maria 1678-1753 *NewGrD 80*
Bononcini, Marc Antonio 1677-1726 *OxMus*
Bononcini, Marco Antonio *Baker 78*
Bononia, Bartholomeus De *NewGrD 80*
Bonporti, Francesco Antonio 1672-1748 *Baker 78*
Bonporti, Francesco Antonio 1672?-1749 *NewGrD 80, OxMus*
Bonsall, Bessie d1963 *NotNAT B*
Bonsel, Adriaan 1918- *Baker 78, CpmDNM 76*
Bonsor, Brian 1926- *IntWWM 77, -80*
Bonsor, James 1926- *WhoMus 72*
Bonstelle, Jessie 1872-1932 *NotNAT B, OxThe*
Bontempelli, Massimo 1878-1960 *CnMD, McGEWD[port], ModWD*
Bontempi, Giovanni Andrea 1624?-1705 *Baker 78, NewGrD 80*
Bontemps, Arna 1902-1973 *BlkAmP, MorBAP*
Bontemps, Willie 1893?-1958 *NewOrJ*
Bontsema, Peter H 1897- *AmSCAP 66*
Bonucci, Alberto 1919-1969 *WhScrn 74, -77*
Bonus, Ben *WhoThe 77*
Bonvicini, Agostino d1576 *NewGrD 80*
Bonvicino, Agostino d1576 *NewGrD 80*
Bonville, Jean *NewGrD 80*
Bonvin, Ludwig 1850-1939 *Baker 78, BiDAmM*
Bonx, Nathan J 1900-1950 *AmSCAP 66, -80*
Bony, Guillaume *NewGrD 80*
Bonynge, Leta *WhoHol A*
Bonynge, Richard 1929- *CmOp*
Bonynge, Richard 1930- *CnOxB, IntWWM 77, -80, NewGrD 80, WhoMus 72, WhoOp 76*
Bonyun, Bill 1911- *EncFCWM 69*
Bonyun, William 1911- *BiDAmM*
Bonzanini, Giacomo *NewGrD 80*
Bonzo *FilmgC*
Bonzo Dog Band *ConMuA 80A, IlEncR[port]*
Boody, Charles G 1939- *IntWWM 77, -80*
Boogaarts, Jan 1934- *IntWWM 77, -80*
Boogie Bill *BluesWW[port]*
Boogie Jake *BluesWW[port]*
Boogie Man *BluesWW[port]*
Boogie Woogie Red *BluesWW[port]*
Book-Asta, George *Film 2*
Bookbinder, Paul Roy 1941- *BluesWW[port]*
Booke, Sorrell *WhoHol A*
Booke, Sorrell 1926- *FilmgC, HalFC 80*
Booke, Sorrell 1930- *FilmEn, NotNAT, WhoThe 77*
Booker, Beryl 1922- *CmpEPM*
Booker, Beryl 1923?- *BlkWAB[port]*
Booker, Beulah *Film 2*
Booker, Charlie 1925- *BluesWW*
Booker, Harry 1850-1924 *Film 1, WhScrn 74, -77, WhoHol B*
Booker, James *RkOn*
Booker, James Carroll 1939- *BluesWW[port]*
Booker, John Lee *BluesWW[port]*
Booker, Sue 1946- *WomWMM A, -B*
Booker, Walter M, Jr. 1933- *BiDAmM, EncJzS 70*
Booker T & The M G's *AmPS A BiDAmM, IlEncR, RkOn[port]*
Bookman, Leo 1932- *BiE&WWA, NotNAT*
Bookspan, Martin 1926- *IntWWM 80*
Boom, Hermanus Marinus, Van 1809-1883 *NewGrD 80*
Boom, Jan Van 1807-1872 *Baker 78*
Boom, Johan, Van 1807-1872 *NewGrD 80*
Boom, Johannes, Van 1783-1878 *NewGrD 80*
Boom, Van *NewGrD 80*
Boomtown Rats *ConMuA 80A*
Boon, Johannes *NewGrD 80*
Boon, Klaas Willem 1915- *IntWWM 77, -80*
Boon, Robert *WhoHol A*
Boone, Ashley A, Jr. 1939- *IntMPA 80*
Boone, Blind 1864- *BiDAmM*
Boone, Charles 1939- *AmSCAP 80, Baker 78, ConAmC*
Boone, Charles Eugene 1934- *AmSCAP 80, BiDAmM*
Boone, Cherry *AmSCAP 80*
Boone, Chester 1906- *WhoJazz 72*
Boone, Clara Lyle 1927- *IntWWM 80*
Boone, Daniel *RkOn 2[port]*
Boone, Daniel 1734-1820 *FilmgC, HalFC 80*
Boone, Debby 1956- *RkOn 2[port]*
Boone, Harvey G 1898-1939 *WhoJazz 72*
Boone, Leonard Coleman, II 1951- *AmSCAP 80*
Boone, Lester 1904- *WhoJazz 72*
Boone, Pat 1934- *AmPS A, -B, AmSCAP 66, -80, ConMuA 80A, FilmEn, FilmgC, ForYSC, HalFC 80, IntMPA 77, -75, -76, -78, -79, -80, MotPP, MovMk, RkOn, WhoHol A*
Boone, Paul Lowther 1913- *IntWWM 77*
Boone, Randy *WhoHol A*
Boone, Richard *IntMPA 75, -76, MotPP, WhoHol A*
Boone, Richard 1915- *CmMov, ForYSC*
Boone, Richard 1916- *FilmEn*
Boone, Richard 1917- *BiE&WWA, FilmgC, HalFC 80, IntMPA 77, -78, -79, -80, MovMk*
Boone, Richard 1930- *EncJzS 70*
Boonin, Joseph Michael 1935- *IntWWM 77, -80*
Boop, Betty *JoeFr*
Boor, Frank d1938 *NotNAT B, WhThe*
Booren, Jo VanDen 1935- *Baker 78, NewGrD 80*
Boorman, John *IntMPA 75, -76, -78, -79, -80*
Boorman, John 1933- *DcFM, FilmEn, FilmgC, HalFC 80, IntMPA 77, OxFilm, WhoHrs 80, WorEFlm[port]*
Boorman, John 1934- *BiDFilm, -81*
Boorman, Stanley Harold 1939- *WhoMus 72*
Boos, Elizabeth L 1934- *IntWWM 77, -80*
Boose, Carl 1815-1868 *NewGrD 80*
Boosey, Leslie Arthur 1887- *WhoMus 72*
Boosey, Thomas *Baker 78*
Boosey, William d1933 *NotNAT B*
Boosey & Hawkes *Baker 78*
Boot, Gladys 1890-1964 *WhScrn 74, -77, WhThe, WhoHol B*
Boote, Rosie 1878-1958 *OxThe*
Booth, Adrian 1924- *FilmEn, ForYSC, WhoHol A*
Booth, Agnes 1847-1910 *NotNAT B*
Booth, Alan 1930- *WhoMus 72*
Booth, Anthony 1937- *FilmgC, HalFC 80*
Booth, Barton 1681-1733 *EncWT, Ent, NotNAT A, -B, OxThe, PlP&P*
Booth, Bernard Joe 1928- *IntWWM 77, -80*
Booth, Blanche DeBar d1930 *NotNAT B*
Booth, Dian Atherden 1939- *IntWWM 77, -80*
Booth, Edwin Thomas 1833-1893 *CnThe, EncWT, Ent[port], FamA&A[port], NotNAT A, -B, OxThe, PlP&P[port]*
Booth, Edwina 1909-1934 *FilmEn, Film 2, FilmgC, ForYSC, HalFC 80, WhoHol A*
Booth, Elmer 1882-1915 *Film 1, WhScrn 77*
Booth, George Albert 1897- *WhoMus 72*
Booth, Harry *IlWWBF*
Booth, Helen d1971 *WhScrn 74, -77, WhoHol B*
Booth, Hope 1872-1933 *NotNAT B, WhoStg 1908*
Booth, James 1930- *FilmEn, FilmgC, HalFC 80*
Booth, James 1931- *IntMPA 77, -75, -76, -78, -79, -80*
Booth, James 1933- *IlWWBF, WhoThe 72, -77*
Booth, John Erlanger 1919- *BiE&WWA, NotNAT*
Booth, John Wilkes 1838-1865 *FamA&A[port]*
Booth, John Wilkes 1839-1865 *EncWT, Ent, NotNAT A, -B, OxThe, PlP&P*
Booth, Junius Brutus 1796-1852 *EncWT, FamA&A[port], NotNAT A, -B, OxThe, PlP&P[port]*
Booth, Junius Brutus, III d1912 *NotNAT B*
Booth, Junius Brutus, Jr. 1821-1883 *EncWT, NotNAT B, OxThe, PlP&P*
Booth, Karen *MotPP*
Booth, Karin 1923- *FilmEn, FilmgC, ForYSC, HalFC 80*
Booth, Margaret *FilmEn*
Booth, Margaret 1902?- *HalFC 80, WomWMM*
Booth, Marie *Film 1*
Booth, Nesdon d1964 *NotNAT B, WhoHol B*
Booth, Nesdon 1918-1964 *WhScrn 77*
Booth, Nesdon 1919-1964 *WhScrn 74*
Booth, Philip 1942- *IntWWM 80, WhoOp 76*
Booth, Philip Alexander 1953- *IntWWM 80*
Booth, Richard *PlP&P*
Booth, Sallie d1902 *NotNAT B*
Booth, Sarah 1794-1867 *NotNAT B*
Booth, Sheila *WomWMM A, -B*
Booth, Shirley 1907- *BiE&WWA, EncMT, FilmEn, FilmgC, ForYSC, HalFC 80, IntMPA 77, -75, -76, -78, -79, -80, MotPP, MovMk[port], NotNAT, PlP&P, WhoHol A, WhoThe 72, -77, WorEFlm[port]*
Booth, Susan Jane 1946- *IntWWM 77*
Booth, Sydney Barton 1873-1937 *EncWT, NotNAT B, OxThe*
Booth, Tony 1943- *CounME 74[port], -74A*
Booth, Walter *Film 2*
Booth, Walter R *FilmEn, IlWWBF, WhoHrs 80*
Booth, Webster 1902- *WhThe*
Booth, William 1829-1912 *OxMus*
Booth Family *NotNAT A*
Boothby, Lord 1900- *WhoMus 72*
Boothe, Clare 1903- *BiE&WWA, McGEWD, ModWD, WhThe*
Boothe, James R 1917-1976 *AmSCAP 66, -80*
Boott, Francis 1813-1904 *Baker 78, BiDAmM*
Booze, Beatrice 1920?-1975? *BluesWW[port]*
Boozer, Patricia P 1947- *ConAmC*
Bopp, Joseph Georges 1908- *IntWWM 80*
Bopp, Wilhelm 1863-1931 *Baker 78*
Boquet, Louis *CnOxB*
Boquet, Louis 1760-1782 *DancEn 78*
Bor, Edward Boris 1921- *IntWWM 77, -80, WhoMus 72*
Bor, Hilda 1910- *IntWWM 80, WhoMus 72*
Bor, Margot 1917- *IntWWM 77, -80*
Bor, Sam 1912- *WhoMus 72*
Borak, Jeffrey *ConAmTC*
Borberg, Svend 1888-1947 *CnMD*
Borbolla, Carlo 1902- *NewGrD 80*
Borbolla, Carlos 1902- *NewGrD 80*
Borbone, Nicolo *NewGrD 80*
Borboni, Nicolo *NewGrD 80*
Borboni, Paola 1900- *EncWT, Ent[port]*
Borbonius, Nicolaus 1503?- *NewGrD 80*
Borch, Gaston Louis Christopher 1871-1926 *Baker 78*
Borch, Poul 1921- *IntWWM 80*
Borchard, Adolphe 1882-1967 *Baker 78*
Borchers, Cornell 1925- *FilmEn, FilmgC, ForYSC, HalFC 80, IntMPA 77, -75, -76, -78, -79, -80, WhoHol A*
Borchers, Gladys 1891- *BiE&WWA, NotNAT*
Borchers, Gustav 1865-1913 *Baker 78*
Borchert, Brigette *Film 2*
Borchert, Wolfgang 1921-1947 *CnMD, CnThe, CroCD, EncWT, McGEWD[port], ModWD, REnWD[port]*
Borchgrevinck, Melchior 1570?-1632 *NewGrD 80*

Borchsenius, Valborg 1872-1949 *CnOxB*
Borck, Edmund Von 1906-1944 *Baker 78, NewGrD 80*
Bord, Antoine-Jean Denis 1814-1888 *NewGrD 80*
Borda, German 1935- *IntWWM 77, -80*
Bordas, Emilia F 1874-1958 *WhScrn 74, -77*
Bordas, Gyorgy 1938- *WhoOp 76*
Borde, Jean-Benjamin DeLa *Baker 78, NewGrD 80*
Borde, Percival 1922- *DrBlPA*
Borde, Seymour N *IntMPA 75, -76*
Bordeaux, Joe 1894-1950 *Film 1, WhScrn 77*
Borden, David *ConAmC*
Borden, Eddie 1888-1955 *Film 2, WhScrn 74, -77, WhoHol B*
Borden, Eugene 1897-1972 *Film 2, WhScrn 77*
Borden, Martin *Film 2*
Borden, Olive d1947 *MotPP, WhoHol B*
Borden, Olive 1906- *FilmEn*
Borden, Olive 1906-1947 *Film 2, ThFT[port], TwYS*
Borden, Olive 1907-1947 *ForYSC, HalFC 80, NotNAT B, WhScrn 74, -77*
Borden, Olive 1908?-1947 *MovMk*
Bordes, Charles 1863-1909 *Baker 78, BnBkM 80, MusMk, NewGrD 80, OxMus*
Bordes-Pene, Leontine Marie 1858-1924 *Baker 78, NewGrD 80*
Bordewijk-Roepman, Johanna 1892-1971 *NewGrD 80*
Bordier, Jules 1846-1896 *Baker 78*
Bordo, Victor Anthony 1934- *IntWWM 77*
Bordogni, Giovanni Marco 1789-1856 *Baker 78*
Bordogni, Giulio 1789-1856 *NewGrD 80*
Bordon, Eugene 1897-1972 *WhoHol B*
Bordoni, Faustina 1700-1781 *Baker 78, BnBkM 80, NewEOp 71, NewGrD 80[port], OxMus*
Bordoni, Irene *AmPS B, CmpEPM*
Bordoni, Irene 1894-1953 *Film 2, JoeFr*
Bordoni, Irene 1895-1953 *EncMT, HalFC 80, NotNAT B, WhScrn 74, -77, WhThe, WhoHol B*
Borduas, Paul-Emile 1905-1960 *CreCan 1*
Borek, Christophorus d1570? *NewGrD 80*
Borek, Krzysztof d1570? *NewGrD 80*
Borel-Clerc, Charles 1879-1959 *Baker 78*
Borell, Louis 1906-1973 *WhScrn 77, WhThe, WhoHol B*
Borelli, Alda 1882- *EncWT*
Borelli, Francesco Maria *NewGrD 80*
Borelli, Lyda 1884-1959 *FilmAG WE, FilmEn*
Borelli, Lyda 1887- *EncWT*
Borelli, Lyda 1888-1958 *WhScrn 74, -77*
Borello, Marco 1899-1966 *WhScrn 77*
Boren, Charles 1907- *IntMPA 77, -75, -76, -78*
Boreo, Emil 1885-1951 *WhScrn 74, -77, WhoHol B*
Boreo, Emile 1885-1951 *NotNAT B*
Boretti, Giovanni Antonio 1640?-1672 *NewGrD 80*
Boretz, Allen 1900- *AmSCAP 66, BiE&WWA, NatPD[port], NotNAT*
Boretz, Alvin 1919- *AmSCAP 66, -80*
Boretz, Benjamin *IntWWM 77*
Boretz, Benjamin 1934- *Baker 78, BiDAmM, ConAmC, DcCM, NewGrD 80*
Borg, Anne 1936- *CnOxB*
Borg, Conny 1938- *DancEn 78[port]*
Borg, Conny 1939- *CnOxB*
Borg, Kim 1919- *IntWWM 77, -80, NewGrD 80, WhoMus 72*
Borg, Sven Hugo *Film 2, WhoHol A*
Borg, Veda Ann 1915-1973 *FilmEn, FilmgC, ForYSC, HalFC 80, HolCA[port], MotPP, MovMk, ThFT[port], Vers A[port], WhScrn 77, WhoHol B, WhoHrs 80[port]*
Borgato, Agostino 1871-1939 *Film 2, WhScrn 74, -77, WhoHol B*
Borgato, Augustino *Film 2*
Borgato, Emilo *Film 2*
Borgatti, Giuseppe 1871-1950 *Baker 78, NewEOp 71, NewGrD 80*
Borgatti, Renata 1894- *Baker 78*
Borge, Victor 1909- *AmSCAP 66, -80, Baker 78, BiDAmM, BiE&WWA, IntMPA 77, -75, -76, -78, -79, -80, JoeFr[port], NotNAT, WhoHol A, WhoMus 72*
Borgen, Johan 1902- *CnMD*
Borgetti, Innocenzio *NewGrD 80*
Borghese, Antonio D R *NewGrD 80*
Borghese, Domenico Viglione *NewGrD 80*
Borghesi, Antonio D R *NewGrD 80*
Borghesy, Antonio D R *NewGrD 80*
Borghi, Adelaide 1829-1901 *Baker 78*
Borghi, Giovanni Battista 1738-1796 *NewGrD 80*
Borghi, Luigi 1745?-1806? *NewGrD 80*
Borgho, Cesare *NewGrD 80*
Borgia, Cesare 1476-1507 *FilmgC, HalFC 80*
Borgia, Giorgio *NewGrD 80*
Borgia, Lucretia 1480-1519 *FilmgC, HalFC 80*
Borgiani, Domenico *NewGrD 80*
Borgioli, Armando 1898-1945 *CmOp*
Borgioli, Dino 1891-1960 *Baker 78, CmOp, NewGrD 80*
Borgmann, Hans-Otto 1901-1977 *NewGrD 80*
Borgnine, Ernest *MotPP, WhoHol A*
Borgnine, Ernest 1915- *FilmgC, HalFC 80, WhoHrs 80*
Borgnine, Ernest 1917- *FilmEn, MovMk[port], OxFilm*
Borgnine, Ernest 1918- *BiDFilm, -81, ForYSC, IntMPA 77, -75, -76, -78, -79, -80, WorEFlm[port]*
Borgo, Cesare d1623 *NewGrD 80*
Borgonovo, Otello 1928- *WhoOp 76*
Borgstrom, Hilda 1871-1953 *FilmEn, Film 1, -2, WhScrn 74, -77*
Borgstrom, Hjalmar 1864-1925 *Baker 78, NewGrD 80*
Borgudd, Tommy K-E 1946- *IntWWM 77*
Borguno, Manuel 1886-1973 *NewGrD 80*
Bori, Lucrezia 1887-1960 *Baker 78, CmOp, MusSN[port], NewGrD 80*
Bori, Lucrezia 1888-1960 *BiDAmM, NewEOp 71*
Boring, Edwin *Film 1*
Borio, Josephine *Film 2*
Boris, Ruthanna 1918- *CnOxB, DancEn 78[port]*
Borishansky, Elliot 1930- *ConAmC*
Borisoff, Alexander 1902- *AmSCAP 80*
Borisoff, S *Film 2*
Borisov, Lilcho 1925- *Baker 78*
Borisova, Galina Ilinichna 1941- *WhoOp 76*
Borisova, Yulia Konstantinovna 1925- *OxThe*
Borja, Alonso Lobo De *NewGrD 80*
Borja, S Francisco De 1510-1572 *NewGrD 80*
Borja Y Gonzales DeRiancho, Lucrecia *NewGrD 80*
Borjessen, Johan 1790-1866 *OxThe*
Borjon, C E 1633-1691 *OxMus*
Borjon DeScellery, Charles-Emmanuel 1715?-1795 *NewGrD 80*
Borjon DeScellery, Pierre 1633-1691 *NewGrD 80*
Bork, Casimir Virgil 1918- *IntWWM 77*
Bork, J S *AmSCAP 80*
Borkh, Inge 1917- *CmOp, MusSN[port]*
Borkh, Inge 1921- *IntWWM 77, -80, NewEOp 71, NewGrD 80, WhoMus 72, WhoOp 76*
Borkovec, Pavel 1894-1972 *Baker 78, DcCM, NewGrD 80*
Borkowski, Bohdan 1852-1901 *NewGrD 80*
Borkowski, Marian 1934- *IntWWM 77, -80*
Borkowski, Witold 1919- *CnOxB*
Borland, Barlowe *Film 2*
Borland, Carroll 1914- *WhoHrs 80[port]*
Borland, John Ernest 1866-1937 *Baker 78, OxMus*
Borland, Rosalind Mary 1909- *WhoMus 72*
Borlasca, Bernardino 1560?- *NewGrD 80*
Borlenghi, Enzo 1908- *NewGrD 80*
Borlet *NewGrD 80*
Borlin, Jean *Film 2*
Borlin, Jean 1893-1930 *CnOxB, DancEn 78, WhThe*
Borling, Thomas 1942- *ConAmC*
Borne, Hal 1911- *AmSCAP 66, -80*
Borne, Ludwig 1786-1837 *EncWT*
Bornefeld, Helmut 1906- *DcCM, NewGrD 80*
Borner, Klaus 1929- *IntWWM 77, -80*
Bornet *NewGrD 80*
Bornet, Francois 1915- *AmSCAP 66*
Bornet, Fred 1915- *AmSCAP 80*
Bornschein, Franz Carl 1879-1948 *AmSCAP 66, -80, Baker 78, BiDAmM, ConAmC*
Bornstein, Allen *IntMPA 77, -78, -79, -80*
Bornstein, Eli 1922- *CreCan 2*
Bornyi, Lajos 1931- *IntWWM 77, -80*
Boro, Susan *WomWMM B*
Borodin, Aleksandr 1833-1887 *BnBkM 80, NotNAT B*
Borodin, Alexander 1833-1887 *Baker 78, CmOp, CmpBCM, CnOxB, DcCom 77[port], DcCom&M 79, GrComp[port], MusMk, NewEOp 71, NewGrD 80[port], OxMus*
Borodin, Alexander 1834-1887 *DancEn 78*
Borodin, Elfriede *Film 2*
Borodkin, Abram E 1906-1978 *AmSCAP 66, -80*
Boronat, Olimpia 1867-1934 *CmOp, NewGrD 80*
Boroni, Antonio 1738-1792 *NewGrD 80*
Borono, Ottavio 1590?- *NewGrD 80*
Boros, David John 1944- *ConAmC*
Boros, Ferike 1880-1951 *HalFC 80, WhScrn 74, -77, WhoHol B*
Borosini *NewGrD 80*
Borosini, Antonio 1660?-1711? *NewGrD 80*
Borosini, Francesco 1690?- *NewGrD 80[port]*
Borosini, Rosa 1693?-1740? *NewGrD 80*
Borouchoff, Israel 1929- *IntWWM 77, -80*
Borovansky, Edouard 1902-1959 *CnOxB, DancEn 78*
Borovsky, Alexander 1889-1968 *Baker 78*
Borowczyk, Walerian 1923- *BiDFilm, -81, DcFM, FilmEn, FilmgC, HalFC 80, OxFilm, WorEFlm[port]*
Borowska, Irina 1930- *CnOxB*
Borowska, Irina 1931- *DancEn 78[port]*
Borowski, Felix 1872-1956 *AmSCAP 66, -80, Baker 78, BiDAmM, ConAmC, NewGrD 80, OxMus*
Borowsky, Marvin S 1907-1969 *BiE&WWA, NotNAT B*
Borradaile, Osmond 1892?- *FilmgC, HalFC 80*
Borradaile, Osmond H 1898- *FilmEn*
Borras DePalau, Juan 1868-1953 *Baker 78*
Borrel, Eugene 1876-1962 *NewGrD 80*
Borren, Charles VanDen 1874-1966 *NewGrD 80*
Borresen, Hakon 1876-1954 *Baker 78, NewGrD 80*
Borrett, William Coates 1894- *CreCan 1*
Borri, Carlo *NewGrD 80*
Borri, Giovanni Battista *NewGrD 80*
Borri, Pasquale 1820-1884 *CnOxB*
Borris, Siegfried 1906- *Baker 78, IntWWM 77, -80, NewGrD 80*
Borro, Johann Jacob *NewGrD 80*
Borrodaile, Osmond 1892- *CmMov*
Borroff, Edith 1925- *ConAmC, IntWWM 77, -80, NewGrD 80*
Borromeo, Carlo 1538-1584 *NewGrD 80*
Borroni, Antonio *NewGrD 80*
Borrono, Pietro Paolo *NewGrD 80*
Borsai, Ilona 1924- *NewGrD 80*
Borsaro, Arcangelo *NewGrD 80*
Borsche, Dieter 1909- *FilmAG WE, HalFC 80*
Borsdorf, Emil H *WhoMus 72*
Borsdorf, Friedrich Adolf 1854-1923 *NewGrD 80*
Borso, Umberto 1923- *WhoOp 76*
Borst, David Thomas 1933- *IntWWM 77, -80*
Borst, Stephen 1944- *NotNAT*
Borstwick, Edith *Film 2*
Borthwick, A T d1943 *NotNAT B*
Bortio, Carlo *NewGrD 80*
Bortkievich, Sergei Eduardovich 1877-1952 *NewGrD 80*
Bortkiewicz, Sergei Eduardovich 1877-1952 *Baker 78, NewGrD 80*
Bortniansky, Dimitri 1751-1825 *Baker 78, OxMus*
Bortniansky, Dmitri 1752-1825 *MusMk*
Bortnyansky, Dmitry Stepanovich 1751-1825 *NewGrD 80*
Bortolotti, Mauro 1926- *NewGrD 80*
Bortolotto, Mario 1927- *Baker 78*
Bortoluzzi, Paolo 1938- *CnOxB, DancEn 78*
Borton, Robert *NewGrD 80*

Bortz, Daniel 1943- *Baker 78, IntWWM 80*
Borucinska-Zarnecka, Krystyna 1946- *IntWWM 77*
Boruff, John 1910- *BiE&WWA, NotNAT*
Borum, William 1911- *BluesWW[port]*
Borup, Lars 1944- *IntWWM 80*
Borup-Jorgensen, Axel 1924- *NewGrD 80*
Borwick, Leonard 1868-1925 *Baker 78, NewGrD 80*
Borwick, Susan Harden 1946- *IntWWM 80*
Bory, Robert 1891-1960 *NewGrD 80*
Borysenko, Elena 1948- *IntWWM 77*
Borzage, Dan d1975 *WhoHol C*
Borzage, Daniel d1975 *WhScrn 77*
Borzage, Donald Dan 1925- *AmSCAP 80*
Borzage, Frank 1893-1961 *AmFD, DcFM, OxFilm*
Borzage, Frank 1893-1962 *BiDFilm, -81, CmMov, FilmEn, Film 1, FilmgC, HalFC 80, MovMk[port], TwYS A, WhScrn 74, -77, WhoHol B, WorEFlm[port]*
Borzage, Rena d1966 *WhoHol B*
Borzio, Carlo *NewGrD 80*
Bos, Annie 1886-1975 *FilmAG WE*
Bos, Annie 1887-1975 *WhScrn 77*
Bos, Chris 1920- *IntWWM 77, -80*
Bos, Coenraad Valentyn 1875-1955 *Baker 78*
Bosabalian, Luisa Anais 1936- *WhoOp 76*
Bosakowski, Philip A 1946- *NatPD[port]*
Bosan, Alonzo 1886-1959 *DrBlPA*
Bosanquet, Caroline 1940- *IntWWM 77, -80*
Bosc, Henri *Film 2*
Bosch, Aurora 1940?- *CnOxB*
Bosch, Johann Caspar d1705 *NewGrD 80*
Bosch, Pieter Joseph VanDen 1736?-1803 *NewGrD 80*
Bosch Bernat-Veri, Jorge 1737-1800 *NewGrD 80*
Boschetti, Amina 1836-1881 *CnOxB*
Boschetti, Gerolamo *NewGrD 80*
Boschetti, Giovanni Boschetto d1622 *NewGrD 80*
Boschi, Giuseppe Maria *NewGrD 80[port]*
Boschot, Adolphe 1871-1955 *Baker 78, NewGrD 80*
Bosco, Bartolomeo 1790-1863 *MagIlD*
Bosco, Monique 1927- *CreCan 2*
Bosco, Philip 1930- *BiE&WWA, NotNAT, WhoThe 72, -77*
Bosco, Wallace *Film 2*
Boscoop, Cornelius Symonszoon *NewGrD 80*
Boscovich, Alexander Uriah 1907-1964 *Baker 78*
Bose, Bozo Sterling 1906-1958 *WhoJazz 72*
Bose, Debaki Kumar 1898- *DcFM*
Bose, Debaki Kumar 1898-1971 *FilmEn*
Bose, Fritz 1906-1975 *NewGrD 80*
Bose, Lucia 1931- *FilmAG WE, FilmEn, FilmgC, HalFC 80, WorEFlm[port]*
Bose, Maria Teresa Lapere 1932- *IntWWM 77, -80*
Bose, Nitin 1901- *DcFM*
Bose, Sterling 1906-1958 *CmpEPM*
Bose, Stirling 1906-1958 *NewOrJ[port]*
Boselli, Constantino *NewGrD 80*
Bosello, Constantino *NewGrD 80*
Bosendorfer *Baker 78*
Bosendorfer, Ignaz 1794-1859 *Baker 78*
Boshke, Nathalie 1893- *IntWWM 77, -80*
Bosillo, Nick d1964 *NotNAT B*
Bosio, Angiolina 1830-1859 *NewGrD 80*
Boskoff, George 1882-1960 *NewGrD 80*
Boskop, Cornelius Symonszoon *NewGrD 80*
Boskovich, Alexander Uriah 1907-1964 *NewGrD 80*
Boskovich, Alexander Urijah 1907-1964 *DcCM*
Boskovsky, Alfred 1913- *NewGrD 80*
Boskovsky, Willi 1909- *Baker 78, NewGrD 80*
Boskovsky, Willy 1909- *WhoMus 72*
Bosky, Marquisette *Film 2*
Bosl, Heinz 1946-1975 *CnOxB*
Bosley, Tom 1927- *BiE&WWA, FilmEn, FilmgC, HalFC 80, IntMPA 79, -80, NotNAT, WhoHol A, WhoThe 72, -77*
Bosman, Petrus 1929- *CnOxB*
Bosman, Petrus 1932- *DancEn 78*
Bosmans, Henriette 1895-1952 *Baker 78, NewGrD 80*
Bosocki, Madam *Film 2*
Bosper, Albert 1913- *CnMD*
Bosquet, Emile 1878-1958 *Baker 78*
Bosquet, Thierry F 1937- *WhoOp 76*
Boss, Yale *Film 1*
Bossak, Jerzy 1910- *DcFM, FilmEn, OxFilm*
Bossard *NewGrD 80*
Bossart *NewGrD 80*
Bosse, Carl *NewGrD 80*
Bosse, Gustave 1884-1943 *Baker 78*
Bosse-Vingard, Harriet Sofie 1878- *WhThe*
Bosseur, Jean-Yves 1947- *Baker 78*
Bossi, Costante Adolfo 1876-1953 *Baker 78*
Bossi, Enrico 1861-1925 *Baker 78, MusMk*
Bossi, Marco Enrico 1861-1925 *NewGrD 80, OxMus*
Bossi, Renzo 1883-1965 *Baker 78, NewGrD 80, OxMus*
Bossick, Bernard B 1918-1975 *WhScrn 77*
Bossinensis, Franciscus *NewGrD 80*
Bossler, Heinrich Philippe Carl 1744-1812 *NewGrD 80*
Bosso, Lucio *NewGrD 80*
Bossone, Frank 1917- *AmSCAP 80*
Bossone, Frank 1924- *AmSCAP 66*
Bossu D'Arras, Le *OxThe*
Bossy, Adan Le *NewGrD 80*
Bost, Pierre 1901- *DcFM, FilmEn, FilmgC, HalFC 80, WorEFlm[port]*
Bostan, Elizabeth *WomWMM*
Bostel, Lucas Von 1649-1716 *NewGrD 80*
Bostelmann, Otto 1907- *Baker 78*
Bostic, Earl 1913-1965 *BiDAmM, CmpEPM, DrBlPA, IlEncJ, WhoJazz 72*
Bostic, Earl 1920-1965 *RkOn[port]*
Bostic, Judith Ann 1952- *IntWWM 77*
Bostick, Calvin T 1928- *AmSCAP 66*
Bostick, Marie Robinson 1921- *AmSCAP 80*
Bostick, Robert L 1909- *IntMPA 77, -75, -76, -78, -79, -80*
Bostock, Claude W 1891- *IntMPA 77, -75, -76, -78, -79*
Bostock, Donald Ivan 1924- *WhoMus 72*
Bostock, Dorothea Willoughby 1917- *WhoMus 72*
Bostock, Edward H 1858-1940 *NotNAT A*
Bostock, Thomas H 1899- *WhThe*
Boston *ConMuA 80A[port], IlEncR, RkOn 2[port]*
Boston, Nelroy Buck 1911-1962 *NotNAT B, WhScrn 74, -77*
Bostwick, E F *Film 2*
Bostwick, Edith *Film 2*
Bosustow, Nick 1940- *IntMPA 77, -75, -76, -78, -79, -80*
Bosustow, Stephen 1911- *DcFM, FilmEn, FilmgC, HalFC 80, IntMPA 77, -75, -76, -78, -79, -80, NewYTET, OxFilm*
Bosustow, Stephen 1912- *WorEFlm[port]*
Bosustow, Tee 1938- *IntMPA 77, -75, -76, -78, -79, -80*
Boswell, Connee *AmSCAP 66, BiDAmM, WhoHol A*
Boswell, Connee 1907-1976 *AmSCAP 80, FilmEn*
Boswell, Connee 1912- *WhoJazz 72*
Boswell, Connee 1918-1976 *HalFC 80*
Boswell, Connie 1912?- *CmpEPM*
Boswell, James 1740-1795 *DcPup, OxMus*
Boswell, Martha 1905-1958 *WhScrn 74, -77, WhoHol B*
Boswell, Vet *WhoHol A*
Boswell Sisters, The *CmpEPM, ThFT[port]*
Bosworth *NewGrD 80*
Bosworth, Hobart 1867-1943 *FilmEn, Film 1, -2, FilmgC, ForYSC, HalFC 80, MotPP, MovMk, NotNAT B, TwYS, WhScrn 74, WhoHol B*
Bosworth, Hobart 1876-1943 *WhScrn 77*
Bote, Eduard *Baker 78*
Bote, Edward *NewGrD 80*
Bote & Bock *Baker 78*
Bote & Bock 1891-1943 *NewGrD 80*
Boteler, Charlotte *NewGrD 80*
Boteler, Wade 1891-1943 *FilmEn, Film 1, HalFC 80, Vers B[port], WhScrn 74, -77, WhoHol B*
Boteler, Wade 1891-1945 *Film 2, ForYSC, TwYS*
Botelero, Enrrique *NewGrD 80*
Botez, Dumitru D 1904- *IntWWM 77, -80*
Botez, Michaela Cristina 1932- *WhoOp 76*
Bothwell, John F 1921-1967 *WhScrn 74, -77, WhoHol B*
Bothwell, Johnny 1917- *BgBands 74, CmpEPM*
Botkin, Perry 1907-1973 *AmSCAP 66, -80, CmpEPM, WhScrn 77, WhoHol B*
Botkin, Perry, Jr. *HalFC 80*
Botkin, Vasily Petrovich 1812-1869 *NewGrD 80*
Botley, Betty *WomWMM*
Botnick, Bruce *ConMuA 80B*
Botoler, Charlotte *NewGrD 80*
Botsford, George 1874-1949 *AmSCAP 66, -80, BiDAmM*
Botsford, Richard *Film 2*
Botsford, Talitha 1901- *AmSCAP 66, -80*
Botsiber, Hugo 1875-1941 *Baker 78*
Botstiber, Hugo 1875-1942 *NewGrD 80*
Bott *NewGrD 80*
Bott, Alan 1894- *WhThe*
Bott, Anton 1795-1869 *NewGrD 80*
Bott, Jean Joseph 1826-1895 *Baker 78, BiDAmM, NewGrD 80*
Bott, Katharina Louise 1824-1881 *NewGrD 80*
Botta, Bergonzio Di 1489- *CnOxB, DancEn 78*
Botta, Luca 1882-1917 *Baker 78, BiDAmM*
Botta, Michael *EncFCWM 69*
Botta, Rudolf 1918- *IntWWM 77, -80*
Botta, Rudolph 1918- *WhoMus 72*
Bottaccio, Paolo *NewGrD 80*
Bottazzi, Ana Maria Trenchi De 1938- *IntWWM 77, -80*
Bottazzi, Bernardino *NewGrD 80*
Bottazzo, Pietro Silvano 1934- *WhoOp 76*
Bottcher, Eberhard Fritz 1934- *IntWWM 80*
Bottcher, Herman *Film 2*
Bottee DeToulmon, Auguste 1797-1850 *Baker 78, NewGrD 80*
Bottegari, Cosimo 1554-1620 *NewGrD 80*
Bottenberg, Wolfgang Heinz Otto 1930- *Baker 78, IntWWM 77, -80*
Bottesini, Giovanni 1821-1889 *Baker 78, BnBkM 80, NewGrD 80[port], OxMus*
Bottger, Max Lee 1930- *IntWWM 77, -80*
Bottin, Rob *WhoHrs 80*
Botting, Mary Elizabeth 1932- *IntWWM 77*
Bottini, Patrick *PupTheA*
Bottinier, Ned *PupTheA*
Bottje, Will Gay 1925- *Baker 78, ConAmC, IntWWM 77, -80*
Bottner, Barbara *WomWMM B*
Botto, Carlos 1923- *Baker 78, DcCM*
Bottome, Francis 1823-1894 *BiDAmM*
Bottomley, Gordon 1874-1948 *OxThe, PlP&P, WhThe*
Bottomley, Roland 1880-1947 *Film 1, -2, WhScrn 77, WhoHol B*
Bottomly, Gordon 1874-1948 *NotNAT B*
Bottomly, Roland d1947 *NotNAT B*
Bottoms, Joseph 1954- *HalFC 80, IntMPA 77, -75, -76, -78, -79, -80, WhoHol A*
Bottoms, Sam *WhoHol A*
Bottoms, Timothy *WhoHol A*
Bottoms, Timothy 1949- *FilmgC, HalFC 80*
Bottoms, Timothy 1950- *FilmEn, MovMk[port]*
Bottoms, Timothy 1951- *IntMPA 77, -75, -76, -78, -79, -80*
Bottrigari, Ercole 1531-1612 *Baker 78, NewGrD 80[port]*
Bottrigaro, Ercole 1531-1612 *NewGrD 80[port]*
Botvay, Karoly 1932- *IntWWM 80*
Bouber, Herman 1880- *CnMD*
Boucan *NewGrD 80*
Bouchard, Antoine 1932- *IntWWM 77, -80*
Bouchard, Joseph J 1948- *AmSCAP 80*
Bouchard, Marie Cecile 1926- *CreCan 1*
Bouchard, Mary 1912-1945 *CreCan 1*
Bouchard, Simonne Mary 1912-1945 *CreCan 1*
Bouchard, Victor 1926- *CreCan 2*
Boucher, Alexandre-Jean 1778-1861 *Baker 78, NewGrD 80*
Boucher, Andre-Pierre 1936- *CreCan 2*
Boucher, Francois 1703-1770 *EncWT, Ent, NotNAT B, OxThe*
Boucher, Pierre 1921- *CreCan 1*
Boucher, Robert 1919- *AmSCAP 66, -80*
Boucher, Victor 1879-1942 *NotNAT B, WhScrn 74, -77, WhThe*
Boucher, Vivian E 1915- *AmSCAP 66, -80*

Boucheron, Raimondo 1800-1876 *NewGrD 80*
Bouchet, Barbara 1943- *FilmAG WE, FilmEn, FilmgC, ForYSC, HalFC 80*
Bouchet, Gabriel 1937- *IntWWM 80*
Bouchet, Guillaume 1526-1606? *DcPup*
Bouchey, Willis 1895?- *ForYSC*
Bouchey, Willis 1900- *FilmgC, HalFC 80, WhoHol A*
Bouchier, Chili 1909- *FilmgC, HalFC 80, IlWWBF, WhoHol A, WhoThe 77*
Bouchier, Chili 1910- *FilmEn, Film 2*
Bouchon, Lester 1906-1962 *NewOrJ[port]*
Bouchor, Maurice 1855-1929 *DcPup*
Boucicault, Agnes Kelly Robertson 1833-1916 *EncWT, OxThe*
Boucicault, Aubrey 1868- *WhoStg 1906, -1908*
Boucicault, Aubrey 1869-1913 *NotNAT B, WhThe*
Boucicault, Dion 1820?-1890 *Ent, McGEWD[port], REnWD[port]*
Boucicault, Dion 1822-1890 *CnThe, EncWT, NotNAT A, -B, PlP&P[port]*
Boucicault, Mrs. Dion 1833-1916 *NotNAT B, WhThe*
Boucicault, Dion G 1859-1929 *NotNAT B, WhScrn 77, WhThe*
Boucicault, Dionysius George 1859-1929 *OxThe*
Boucicault, Dionysius Lardner 1822-1890 *OxThe*
Boucicault, Nina 1867-1950 *Film 2, NotNAT B, OxThe, WhScrn 77, WhThe, WhoHol B*
Boucot d1949 *WhoHol B*
Boucot, Louis 1889-1949 *WhScrn 74, -77*
Boucourechliev, Andre 1925- *Baker 78, DcCM, NewGrD 80*
Boudouris, A 1918- *IntMPA 77, -75, -76, -78, -79, -80*
Boudreau, John T 1901-1976 *AmSCAP 66, -80*
Boudreau, Robert Austin 1927- *Baker 78*
Boudreaux, Joseph *WhoHol A*
Boudwin, Jimmy *Film 2*
Boughner, Ruth *WomWMM*
Boughton, Rutland 1878-1960 *Baker 78, CmOp, MusMk, NewEOp 71, NewGrD 80, NotNAT B, OxMus, WhThe*
Boughton, Walter 1918- *BiE&WWA, NotNAT*
Bouhy, Jacques-Joseph-Andre 1848-1929 *Baker 78, NewGrD 80, OxMus*
Boukoff, Yuri 1923- *WhoMus 72*
Boul, Jan *NewGrD 80*
Boul, John *NewGrD 80*
Boulanger, Charlie *BgBands 74*
Boulanger, Daniel 1922- *FilmEn*
Boulanger, Lili 1893-1918 *Baker 78, NewGrD 80, OxMus*
Boulanger, Nadia 1887-1979 *Baker 78, BnBkM 80, DcCM, IntWWM 77, MusMk[port], NewGrD 80, OxMus, WhoMus 72*
Boulanger, Robert Francis 1940- *AmSCAP 66, -80*
Boularan, Jacques 1894?-1972 *McGEWD[port]*
Boulay, Laurence 1925- *IntWWM 80, NewGrD 80*
Bould, Beckett 1880- *WhThe*
Boulden, Edward *Film 1*
Boulder, Robert *Film 2*
Boulding, James Frederick 1915- *WhoMus 72*
Boulding, Keith Ronald Rex 1925- *IntWWM 77, -80*
Bouleau, Simon *NewGrD 80*
Boulenaz-DuPasquier, Suzanne 1922- *IntWWM 77*
Bouley, Frank *WhoHol A*
Boulez, Pierre 1925- *Baker 78, BnBkM 80[port], CmOp, CompSN[port], CnOxB, DcCom&M 79, DcCM, IntWWM 77, -80, MusMk[port], MusSN[port], NewEOp 71, NewGrD 80[port], OxMus, WhoMus 72, WhoOp 76*
Boulle, Pierre 1912- *WhoHrs 80*
Boulnois, Joseph 1884-1918 *Baker 78*
Boulos, Joseph T 1935- *AmSCAP 66*
Boult, Sir Adrian 1889- *BnBkM 80, MusMk[port], MusSN[port], NewGrD 80[port]*
Boult, Adrian Cedric 1889- *IntWWM 77, -80, OxMus*
Boult, Sir Adrian Cedric 1889- *Baker 78, WhoMus 72*
Boulter, Edward Wallace 1942- *IntWWM 77*
Boulter, Rosalyn 1916- *WhThe*
Boulting, Ingrid 1947- *HalFC 80, WhoHol A*
Boulting, John 1913- *BiDFilm, -81, CmMov, DcFM, FilmEn, FilmgC, HalFC 80, IlWWBF, IntMPA 77, -75, -76, -78, -79, -80, OxFilm, WorEFlm[port]*
Boulting, John 1914- *MovMk[port]*
Boulting, Roy 1913- *BiDFilm, -81, CmMov, DcFM, FilmEn, FilmgC, HalFC 80, IlWWBF, IntMPA 77, -75, -76, -78, -79, -80, OxFilm, WorEFlm[port]*
Boulting, Roy 1914- *MovMk[port]*
Boulton, David *FilmgC, HalFC 80*
Boulton, Derek Nelson Cyril 1927- *WhoMus 72*
Boulton, Guy Pelham 1890- *WhThe*
Boulton, Sir Harold Edwin 1859-1935 *OxMus*
Boulton, John 1909- *IntWWM 77, -80*
Boulton, Matthew 1893-1962 *WhScrn 77, WhoHol B*
Boulton, Michael 1930- *DancEn 78*
Bouma, Robert Warner, Sr. 1921- *IntWWM 77*
Bouquet, Marie Theresa 1939- *IntWWM 80*
Bouquet, Marie Therese 1939- *IntWWM 77*
Bouquet, Michel 1926- *FilmAG WE, FilmEn, OxFilm*
Bour, Ernest 1913- *NewGrD 80*
Bourber, Aaf 1885-1974 *FilmAG WE*
Bourbon *NewGrD 80*
Bourbon, Nicolaus *NewGrD 80*
Bourchier, Arthur 1863-1927 *Film 1, NotNAT B, OxThe, WhThe, WhoHol B*
Bourde, Andre Jean 1921- *IntWWM 77, -80*
Bourdelle, Thomy *Film 2*
Bourdelot *NewGrD 80*
Bourdelot, Jacques Bonnet 1644-1724 *NewGrD 80*
Bourdelot, Pierre 1610-1685 *NewGrD 80*
Bourdelot, Pierre Bonnet- 1638-1708 *NewGrD 80*
Bourdet, Edouard 1877-1945 *OxThe*
Bourdet, Edouard 1887-1945 *CnMD, EncWT, McGEWD[port], ModWD, NotNAT B*
Bourdin, Roger 1900-1974 *CmOp, NewGrD 80, WhoMus 72*
Bourdon, Rosario 1889-1961 *AmSCAP 66, -80*
Bourgault-Ducoudray, Louis-Albert 1840-1910 *Baker 78, NewGrD 80*
Bourgault-Ducoudray, Louis Albert 1840-1910 *OxMus*
Bourgeau, Joseph 1891-1970 *NewOrJ*
Bourgeois, Derek David 1941- *IntWWM 77, -80, NewGrD 80, WhoMus 72*
Bourgeois, Gerard 1874-1944 *DcFM*
Bourgeois, Joseph 1676-1751? *NewGrD 80*
Bourgeois, Lois 1510?-1561? *NewGrD 80*
Bourgeois, Louis 1510?-1561? *NewGrD 80*
Bourgeois, Loys *OxMus*
Bourgeois, Loys 1510?- *NewGrD 80*
Bourgeois, Loys 1510?-1561? *Baker 78*
Bourgeois, Martin *NewGrD 80*
Bourgeois, Mary Alice 1943- *AmSCAP 80*
Bourgeois, Milton Vernon 1937- *AmSCAP 80*
Bourgeois, Thomas-Louis 1676-1751? *NewGrD 80*
Bourgeois, Wilfred S 1907- *NewOrJ*
Bourget, Paul 1852-1935 *EncWT, NotNAT B, WhThe*
Bourgholtzer, Frank *NewYTET*
Bourgignon, Serge 1928- *FilmgC, HalFC 80*
Bourgoin, Georges 1913- *FilmEn*
Bourgoin, Jean 1913- *DcFM, FilmEn, WorEFlm[port]*
Bourgoin, Yves 1913- *FilmEn, WorEFlm[port]*
Bourgois *NewGrD 80*
Bourgoys, Loys *NewGrD 80*
Bourguignon *NewGrD 80*
Bourguignon, Francis De 1890-1961 *Baker 78, NewGrD 80*
Bourguignon, Serge 1928- *DcFM, FilmEn*
Bourguignon, Serge 1929- *WorEFlm[port]*
Bourinot, Arthur Stanley 1893- *CreCan 2*
Bourke, Fan 1886-1959 *WhScrn 74, -77, WhoHol B*
Bourke, Rory Michael 1942- *AmSCAP 80*
Bourke, Sonny *NewGrD 80*
Bourke, Walter 1945- *CnOxB*
Bourligueux, Guy 1935- *NewGrD 80*
Bourligueux, Guy Charles Corentin Jean 1935- *IntWWM 77, -80*
Bourman, Anatole 1888-1962 *DancEn 78*
Bourman, Frank 1934- *CnOxB*
Bourmeister, Vladimir Pavlovich 1904-1971 *CnOxB, DancEn 78*
Bourne, Adeline *Film 1, WhThe*
Bourne, Bramwell Bernard 1945- *IntWWM 77, -80*
Bourne, Iris *IntWWM 77, -80, WhoMus 72*
Bourne, St. Clair 1943- *DrBlPA*
Bourne, St. Claire *MorBAP*
Bourne, William Payne 1936-1972 *WhScrn 77*
Bourneuf, Philip 1912- *BiE&WWA, ForYSC, HalFC 80, NotNAT, WhoHol A, WhoThe 72, -77*
Bournonville *NewGrD 80*
Bournonville, Antoine 1760-1843 *CnOxB, DancEn 78*
Bournonville, August 1805-1879 *CnOxB, DancEn 78*
Bournonville, Jacques De 1675?-1753? *NewGrD 80*
Bournonville, Jean De 1585?-1632 *NewGrD 80*
Bournonville, Valentin De 1610?-1663? *NewGrD 80*
Boursault, Edme 1638-1701 *EncWT, Ent, McGEWD, OxThe*
Bourseiller, Antoine 1930- *EncWT*
Bourton, Robert John 1942- *IntWWM 77, -80*
Bourvil d1976 *NotNAT B*
Bourvil 1913-1970 *WhScrn 74, -77, WhoHol B*
Bourvil 1917- *ForYSC*
Bourvil 1917-1970 *FilmAG WE, FilmEn, FilmgC, HalFC 80, OxFilm, WorEFlm[port]*
Bouschet, Jan *OxThe*
Bousquet, Georges 1818-1854 *Baker 78*
Bousset, Jean-Baptiste 1662-1725 *NewGrD 80*
Bousset, Rene Drouard De 1703-1760 *NewGrD 80*
Bouteiller, Jean Le *NewGrD 80*
Bouteiller, Louis 1648-1724? *NewGrD 80*
Bouteiller, Pierre 1645?- *NewGrD 80*
Bouteillier, Pierre 1645?- *NewGrD 80*
Boutelje, Phil 1895-1979 *AmSCAP 66, -80*
Boutellier, Pierre 1645?- *NewGrD 80*
Boutmy *NewGrD 80*
Boutmy, Charles Joseph 1697-1779 *NewGrD 80*
Boutmy, Guillaume 1723-1791 *NewGrD 80*
Boutmy, Jean-Joseph 1725-1782 *NewGrD 80*
Boutmy, Josse 1697-1779 *Baker 78, NewGrD 80*
Boutmy, Laurent-Francois 1756-1838 *NewGrD 80*
Boutnikoff, Ivan 1893- *AmSCAP 66, -80*
Boutnikov, Ivan 1893- *DancEn 78*
Bouton, Betty *Film 2*
Bouton, Jim *WhoHol A*
Boutry, Roger 1932- *Baker 78, NewGrD 80*
Bouvard, Francois 1683?-1760 *NewGrD 80*
Bouvart, Francois 1683?-1760 *NewGrD 80*
Bouvet, Charles 1858-1935 *Baker 78, NewGrD 80*
Bouvier, Helene 1905- *WhoMus 72*
Bouville, Jean *NewGrD 80*
Bouwmeester, Louis 1842- *WhThe*
Bouwmeester, Louis 1842-1925 *Ent[port]*
Bouwmeester, Theo 1871-1956 *IlWWBF*
Bouzignac, Guillaume 1592?-1641? *Baker 78, NewGrD 80*
Bova, Basil A 1919- *AmSCAP 66, -80*
Bova, Joseph 1924- *BiE&WWA, NotNAT, WhoHol A, WhoThe 72, -77*
Bovasso, Julie 1930- *BiE&WWA, ConDr 73, -77, NotNAT, WhoHol A, WhoThe 72, -77*
Boven, Arlette Van 1942- *CnOxB*
Bovery, Jules 1808-1868 *Baker 78*
Bovet, Guy 1942- *IntWWM 77, -80*
Bovet, Joseph 1879-1951 *NewGrD 80*
Bovicelli, Giovanni Battista *NewGrD 80*
Bovill, C H 1878-1918 *WhThe*
Bovina, Giuseppe Maria *NewGrD 80*
Bovio, Angelo 1824-1909 *NewGrD 80*
Bovt, Violetta Trofimova 1927- *CnOxB, DancEn 78*
Bovy, Berthe 1887- *WhThe*

Bovy, Vina 1900- *Baker 78, NewEOp 71, NewGrD 80*
Bovy-Lysberg, Charles-Samuel 1821-1873 *Baker 78, NewGrD 80*
Bow, Clara d1965 *MotPP, WhoHol B, WomWMM*
Bow, Clara 1904-1965 *Film 2, ThFT[port], TwYS*
Bow, Clara 1905-1965 *BiDFilm, -81, FilmEn, FilmgC, ForYSC, HalFC 80[port], MovMk[port], OxFilm, WhScrn 74, -77, WorEFlm[port]*
Bowden, Charles 1913- *BiE&WWA, NotNAT, WhoThe 72, -77*
Bowden, Christina Mary 1908- *AmSCAP 80*
Bowden, Christine M 1908- *AmSCAP 66*
Bowden, Dorris 1915- *ThFT[port]*
Bowden, Mary Lucas Williams 1928- *IntWWM 77, -80*
Bowden, Pamela *IntWWM 77, -80, WhoMus 72*
Bowden, Richard George 1944- *AmSCAP 80*
Bowder, Jerry L 1928- *ConAmC*
Bowdler, Thomas 1754-1825 *NotNAT B*
Bowdon, Dorris 1915- *HalFC 80, WhoHol A*
Bowe, Rosemarie *ForYSC, WhoHol A*
Bowen, Edward *OxMus*
Bowen, Edwin York 1884-1961 *Baker 78*
Bowen, Eli 1844?- *Ent*
Bowen, Eugene Everett 1950- *ConAmC*
Bowen, Frances C 1905- *BiE&WWA*
Bowen, James 1682?-1702? *NewGrD 80*
Bowen, Jemmy 1682?-1702? *NewGrD 80*
Bowen, Jimmy 1937- *RkOn[port]*
Bowen, John 1924- *CnThe, ConDr 73, -77, CroCD, MorBAP, WhoThe 72, -77*
Bowen, John G 1896- *AmSCAP 66, -80*
Bowen, Kenneth John 1932- *IntWWM 77, -80, WhoMus 72*
Bowen, Roger *WhoHol A*
Bowen, Ruth 1930- *DrBlPA*
Bowen, William Meirion 1940- *IntWWM 77, -80*
Bowen, York 1884-1961 *NewGrD 80, OxMus*
Bower, Dallas 1907- *FilmgC, HalFC 80, IntMPA 77, -75, -76, -78, -79, -80*
Bower, John Dykes 1905- *NewGrD 80, OxMus*
Bower, Marian d1945 *NotNAT B, WhThe*
Bower, Maurice L 1922- *AmSCAP 66, -80*
Bower, Robert *Film 1*
Bower, Roger 1904- *IntMPA 78, -79, -80*
Bower, Roger 1908- *IntMPA 77, -75, -76*
Bowering, George Harry 1935- *CreCan 1*
Bowers, Bryan Benson 1940- *AmSCAP 80*
Bowers, D P d1857 *NotNAT B*
Bowers, Mrs. D P d1895 *NotNAT B*
Bowers, Faubion 1917- *BiE&WWA, NotNAT*
Bowers, Frederick V 1874-1961 *AmSCAP 66, -80, BiDAmM*
Bowers, Jane Meredith 1936- *IntWWM 77, -80*
Bowers, John 1891-1936 *Film 1, -2, TwYS*
Bowers, John 1899-1936 *FilmEn, WhScrn 74, -77, WhoHol B*
Bowers, Katherine Harbison 1904- *IntWWM 77*
Bowers, Lally 1917- *WhoThe 72, -77*
Bowers, Lyle 1896-1943 *WhScrn 74, -77*
Bowers, Robert Hood 1877-1941 *AmSCAP 66, -80, Baker 78, ConAmC, NotNAT B, WhThe*
Bowers, Robin Hood 1877-1941 *CmpEPM*
Bowers, Thomas J 1836-1885 *BiDAmM*
Bowers, Viola d1962 *NotNAT B*
Bowers, William 1916- *AmSCAP 80, FilmEn, FilmgC, HalFC 80, IntMPA 77, -75, -76, -78, -79, -80*
Bowers-Broadbent, Christopher Joseph 1945- *IntWWM 77, -80, WhoMus 72*
Bowery Boys, The *FilmgC, JoeFr*
Bowes, Alice d1969 *WhThe*
Bowes, Cliff *Film 1*
Bowes, Edward 1874-1946 *BiDAmM*
Bowes, Karen Laila 1948- *CreCan 1*
Bowes, Lawrence A *Film 1*
Bowes, Major Edward 1874-1946 *NotNAT B, WhScrn 74, -77, WhoHol B*
Bowes, Margie 1941- *BiDAmM, EncFCWM 69*
Bowes, Thomas J 1948- *AmSCAP 80*
Bowie, David 1947- *ConMuA 80A, HalFC 80, IlEncR[port], RkOn 2[port], WhoHol A*
Bowie, David 1949?- *WhoHrs 80*
Bowie, Edgar William Lorimer Ormond 1926- *IntWWM 77, -80*
Bowie, Jim 1796-1836 *FilmgC, HalFC 80*
Bowie, Les 1913-1979 *HalFC 80*
Bowie, Les 1920?-1979 *WhoHrs 80*
Bowie, Lester 1941- *EncJzS 70, IlEncJ*
Bowie, Walter Russell 1882-1969 *BiDAmM*
Bowin, James *NewGrD 80*
Bowkett, Sidney d1937 *NotNAT B*
Bowkun, Helena 1951- *IntWWM 80*
Bowkun, Julia 1954- *IntWWM 80*
Bowkun, Sandra 1954- *IntWWM 80*
Bowle, Raphe *NewGrD 80*
Bowles, Anthony Philip 1931- *IntWWM 77, -80*
Bowles, David Graham Alexander 1945- *IntWWM 77, -80*
Bowles, Edmund Addison 1925- *IntWWM 77, -80*
Bowles, Frank *Film 2*
Bowles, Jane 1917- *BiE&WWA*
Bowles, Paul 1909- *DancEn 78*
Bowles, Paul 1910- *AmSCAP 66, -80, BiE&WWA, ConAmC, IntWWM 77, -80, NewGrD 80, NotNAT*
Bowles, Paul Frederic 1910- *Baker 78, BiDAmM, OxMus*
Bowles, Richard William 1918- *AmSCAP 66, -80, ConAmC*
Bowles, Russell 1909- *WhoJazz 72*
Bowley, Alfred Louis 1899- *WhoMus 72*
Bowley, Flora Juliet *WhoStg 1906, -1908*
Bowling, F Lee 1909- *IntWWM 80*
Bowlly, Al 1898-1941 *CmpEPM*
Bowman, Brooks 1913-1937 *AmSCAP 66, -80*
Bowman, Carl 1913- *ConAmC*
Bowman, Dave 1914-1964 *CmpEPM, WhoJazz 72*
Bowman, David Samuel 1940- *IntWWM 77, -80*
Bowman, David W 1914-1964 *BiDAmM*
Bowman, Don 1937- *CounME 74, -74A, EncFCWM 69, IlEncCM*
Bowman, Donald 1937- *BiDAmM*
Bowman, Edgar Morris 1848-1913 *BiDAmM*
Bowman, Edward Morris 1848-1913 *Baker 78*
Bowman, Euday L 1887-1949 *AmSCAP 66, -80, BiDAmM*
Bowman, Henry *NewGrD 80*
Bowman, James Thomas 1941- *CmOp, IntWWM 77, -80, NewGrD 80, WhoMus 72, WhoOp 76*
Bowman, John 1660?-1739 *NewGrD 80*
Bowman, Judith Ann 1944- *IntWWM 77*
Bowman, Laura *BlksB&W C*
Bowman, Laura 1881-1957 *DrBlPA, NotNAT A, -B, WhScrn 77*
Bowman, Laura 1889-1957 *BlksBF[port]*
Bowman, Lee *MotPP*
Bowman, Lee 1910- *FilmgC, HalFC 80*
Bowman, Lee 1914- *BiE&WWA, ForYSC, IntMPA 77, -75, -76, -78, -79, -80, MovMk, What 5[port], WhoHol A*
Bowman, Lee 1914-1979 *FilmEn*
Bowman, Lewis Edward 1886-1961 *WhScrn 77*
Bowman, Lionel 1919- *NewGrD 80*
Bowman, Nellie 1878- *WhThe*
Bowman, Palmer 1883-1933 *WhScrn 74, -77, WhoHol B*
Bowman, Patricia 1908- *CnOxB, DancEn 78[port], Film 2*
Bowman, Pierre L 1944- *ConAmTC*
Bowman, Robert 1925- *IntWWM 80*
Bowman, Ross 1926- *BiE&WWA*
Bowman, Walter P 1910- *BiE&WWA, NotNAT*
Bowman, Wayne 1914- *BiE&WWA, NotNAT*
Bowman, William J *Film 1*
Bowmer, Angus L 1904- *BiE&WWA, NotNAT*
Bown, Edwin John 1905- *WhoMus 72*
Bown, Patricia Anne 1931- *BlkWAB, EncJzS 70*
Bown, Patti 1931- *EncJzS 70*
Bowne, Owen O d1963 *NotNAT B*
Boworth, Arthur Edward 1858-1923 *NewGrD 80*
Bowyer, Frederick d1936 *NotNAT B*
Bowyer, Michael d1645 *OxThe*
Bowyer, Sheila Grace 1931- *WhoMus 72*
Box, Betty 1920- *FilmEn, FilmgC, HalFC 80, IntMPA 77, 75, 76, -78, -79, -80, WomWMM*
Box, Charles *OxMus*
Box, Euel 1928- *AmSCAP 80*
Box, Harold Elton 1903- *WhoMus 72*
Box, John 1920- *FilmEn, FilmgC, HalFC 80*
Box, Joy *WomWMM*
Box, Muriel 1905- *FilmEn, FilmgC, HalFC 80, IlWWBF, -A, WomWMM*
Box, Sydney 1907- *FilmEn, FilmgC, HalFC 80*
Box Tops, The *ConMuA 80A, RkOn 2[port]*
Boxberg, Christian Ludwig 1670-1729 *NewGrD 80*
Boxer, John *WhoHol A*
Boxer, John 1909- *WhoThe 72, -77*
Boxtops *BiDAmM*
Boy Monachus, Hugo *NewGrD 80*
Boyadgieva, Lada *WomWMM*
Boyadjian, Hayg 1938- *AmSCAP 80, CpmDNM 80, ConAmC*
Boyajian, Aram *NewYTET*
Boyar, Ben A 1895-1964 *BiE&WWA*
Boyar, Benjamin A 1895-1964 *NotNAT B*
Boyar, Monica *BiE&WWA*
Boyar, Sully *WhoHol A*
Boyars, Albert 1924- *IntMPA 77, -75, -76, -78, -79, -80*
Boyarsky, Konstantin Fyodorovich 1915-1974 *CnOxB*
Boyartchikov, Nicolai Nicolaievich 1935- *CnOxB*
Boyce, Allen Edward 1938- *IntWWM 77*
Boyce, Bruce 1910- *WhoMus 72*
Boyce, Jack 1885-1923 *WhScrn 74, -77*
Boyce, John Barrington 1927- *WhoMus 72*
Boyce, Merel David 1922- *IntWWM 77, -80*
Boyce, Thomas *NewGrD 80*
Boyce, Tommy 1944- *RkOn 2[port]*
Boyce, William 1710-1779 *BnBkM 80, DcCom&M 79, GrComp[port], MusMk[port], OxMus*
Boyce, William 1711-1779 *Baker 78, DcCom 77, NewGrD 80[port]*
Boychuk, Albert 1915- *IntWWM 77, -80*
Boyd, Alfred *PupTheA*
Boyd, Anne Elizabeth 1946- *IntWWM 77, -80, NewGrD 80*
Boyd, Betty *Film 2, WhoHol A*
Boyd, Betty Sue Meinecke 1940- *IntWWM 77*
Boyd, Bill 1898- *ForYSC*
Boyd, Bill 1910- *IlEncCM[port]*
Boyd, Bill 1911?- *EncFCWM 69*
Boyd, Blanche Deedee 1889-1959 *WhScrn 74, -77*
Boyd, Bonita Kerry 1949- *IntWWM 77*
Boyd, Charles N 1875-1937 *Baker 78, BiDAmM*
Boyd, David Tod 1924- *WhoMus 72*
Boyd, Dorothy 1907- *Film 2, IlWWBF*
Boyd, Edward Riley 1914- *BluesWW[port]*
Boyd, Elisse *AmSCAP 66, BiE&WWA*
Boyd, Elsie Thompson 1904- *AmSCAP 66*
Boyd, Ernie *BluesWW[port]*
Boyd, Frank M 1863- *WhThe*
Boyd, Franklyn 1925- *IntWWM 80*
Boyd, George 1904-1931? *NewOrJ*
Boyd, Heather Lilian Elaine 1932- *IntWWM 80*
Boyd, Jack 1932- *AmSCAP 80, ConAmC, IntWWM 77, -80*
Boyd, Jimmy *AmPS A, ForYSC, WhoHol A*
Boyd, Joe 1942- *IlEncR*
Boyd, Malcolm *IntWWM 77, -80*
Boyd, Marilynn *Film 2*
Boyd, Mildred *Film 2*
Boyd, Mullen *AmSCAP 80*
Boyd, Richard 1937- *BiE&WWA*
Boyd, Robert *BluesWW[port]*
Boyd, Rodney C 1943- *IntWWM 77, -80*
Boyd, Sam, Jr. 1915- *BiE&WWA, NotNAT*
Boyd, Sheila *PupTheA*
Boyd, Stephen 1928-1977 *CmMov, FilmAG WE, FilmEn, FilmgC, ForYSC, HalFC 80, IlWWBF, IntMPA 77, -75, -76, MotPP, MovMk[port], WhoHol A, WorEFlm[port]*

Boyd, William d1972 MotPP, NewYTET, WhoHol B
Boyd, William 1890-1935 HalFC 80
Boyd, William 1895-1972 FilmgC, HalFC 80, What 2[port], WhScrn 77
Boyd, William 1898-1972 CmMov, FilmEn, Film 1, -2, MovMk[port], OxFilm, TwYS
Boyd, William 1911- BiDAmM
Boyd, William Henry 1890-1935 NotNAT B
Boyd, William Stage 1890-1935 FilmgC, WhScrn 74, -77, WhoHol B
Boyd, Wynn Leo 1902- AmSCAP 66, -80, ConAmC
Boydell, Brian 1917- IntWWM 77, -80, NewGrD 80
Boyden, David Dodge 1910- Baker 78, IntWWM 77, -80, NewGrD 80, OxMus, WhoMus 72
Boyell, Richard S 1923- AmSCAP 80
Boyer NewGrD 80
Boyer, Anita CmpEPM
Boyer, Charles 1897-1978 FilmAG WE[port], FilmEn, MovMk[port], OxFilm, WorEFlm[port]
Boyer, Charles 1899-1978 BiDFilm, -81, CmMov, Film 2, FilmgC, ForYSC[port], HalFC 80[port], IntMPA 77, -75, -76, -78, MotPP, WhThe, WhoHol A, WhoThe 72
Boyer, Charles Scott 1947- AmSCAP 80
Boyer, Eleanor Anderson WomWMM B
Boyer, Francois 1920- DcFM, FilmEn
Boyer, Jean 1600?-1648? NewGrD 80
Boyer, Jean 1901-1965 FilmEn
Boyer, John Jay 1945- IntWWM 77
Boyer, Pascal 1743-1794 NewGrD 80
Boyer, Phil IntMPA 77, -75, -76, -78, -79, -80
Boyer, Rachel d1935 NotNAT B
Boyer, Royce 1934- IntWWM 77
Boyes, Thomas NewGrD 80
Boyett, Bob IntMPA 78, -79
Boyett, Robert IntMPA 80
Boyington, Pappy 1912- What 5[port]
Boykan, Martin 1931- Baker 78, CpmDNM 80, ConAmC
Boykin, A Helen 1904- ConAmC
Boylan, John ConMuA 80B
Boylan, Mary WhoHol A
Boyle, Billy 1945- WhoThe 77
Boyle, Bobbi AmSCAP 80
Boyle, Catherine 1929- FilmgC, HalFC 80
Boyle, Charles P CmMov
Boyle, Diana 1954- IntWWM 80
Boyle, E Roger 1907- BiE&WWA, NotNAT
Boyle, George Frederick 1886-1948 AmSCAP 66, -80, Baker 78, BiDAmM, ConAmC A, NewGrD 80
Boyle, Harry Joseph 1915- CreCan 2, NewYTET
Boyle, Hugh 1916- IntWWM 77, -80
Boyle, Jack ConMuA 80B
Boyle, John Film 1
Boyle, Joseph C 1890- TwYS A
Boyle, Peter IntMPA 77, -75, -76, -78, -79, -80, WhoHol A
Boyle, Peter 1933- FilmEn, FilmgC, HalFC 80, WhoHrs 80[port]
Boyle, Peter 1936- MovMk[port]
Boyle, Ray 1925- BiE&WWA
Boyle, Robert FilmEn, FilmgC, HalFC 80, WorEFlm[port]
Boyle, Robert Wilson 1945- WhoMus 72
Boyle, Roger 1621-1679 NotNAT B, OxThe
Boyle, Rory David Alasdair 1951- IntWWM 80
Boyle, William 1853-1923 EncWT, McGEWD, NotNAT B, OxThe, WhThe
Boyle, William Neal IntMPA 77, -75, -76, -78, -79, -80
Boyleau, Simon NewGrD 80
Boyleu, Simon NewGrD 80
Boyne, Clifton 1874-1945 WhThe
Boyne, Leonard 1853-1920 NotNAT B, WhThe
Boyne, Sunny 1883-1966 WhScrn 74, -77, WhoHol B
Boynton, Charles Ted 1921-1968 WhScrn 77
Boys, Thomas NewGrD 80
Boysen, Bjorn Fougner 1943- IntWWM 77, -80
Boyt, John 1921- BiE&WWA, NotNAT
Boytler, Arcady 1895- DcFM
Boyton, Betty Film 2
Boyvin NewGrD 80
Boyvin, Jacques 1649?-1706 NewGrD 80
Boyvin, Jean NewGrD 80
Bozan, Jan Josef 1644-1716 NewGrD 80
Bozay, Attila 1939- Baker 78, DcCM, NewGrD 80
Bozeman, George L, Jr. 1936- IntWWM 77, -80
Bozic, Darijan 1933- Baker 78, IntWWM 77, -80, NewGrD 80
Bozic, Wolfgang 1947- WhoOp 76
Bozicevich, Ronald 1948- IntWWM 77, -80
Bozo, Little WhScrn 74, -77
Bozyk, Max 1899-1970 WhScrn 77, WhoHol B
Bozza, Eugene 1905- Baker 78, CpmDNM 80, NewGrD 80, WhoMus 72
Bozzacchi, Giuseppina 1853-1870 CnOxB, DancEn 78
Bozzi, Paolo 1550?-1628? NewGrD 80
Bozzoni, Max 1917- CnOxB
Bozzuffi, Marcel 1929- FilmEn
Bozzuffi, Marcel 1937- HalFC 80
Braban, Harvey 1883- Film 2, WhThe
Brabant NewGrD 80
Brabants, Jeanne 1920- CnOxB
Brabec, Jeffrey Joseph 1943- AmSCAP 80
Brabin, Charles 1883-1957 FilmgC, HalFC 80
Brabin, Charles J 1882-1957 WhScrn 77
Brabin, Charles J 1883-1957 FilmEn
Brabin, Charles J 1883-1959 TwYS A
Brabourne, Lord 1924- IntMPA 77, -75, -76, -78, -79, -80
Brabourne, John 1924- FilmgC, HalFC 80
Bracali, Giampaolo 1941- ConAmC, IntWWM 77, -80
Braccini, Luigi 1755?-1791 NewGrD 80
Braccini, Roberto 1755?-1791 NewGrD 80
Bracco, Roberto d1943 NotNAT B
Bracco, Roberto 1861-1943 CnThe, McGEWD[port], ModWD, REnWD[port]
Bracco, Roberto 1862-1943 OxThe
Bracco, Roberto 1863-1943 WhThe
Brace, Norman C 1892-1954 WhScrn 74, WhoHol B
Bracefield, Hilary Maxwell 1938- IntWWM 80
Bracegirdle, Anne 1663?-1748 CnThe, NotNAT B, PlP&P[port]
Bracegirdle, Anne 1673?-1748 OxThe
Bracegirdle, Anne 1674?-1748 EncWT, Ent
Bracesco, Renzo 1888- NewGrD 80
Bracey, Clara T 1847-1941 WhScrn 77, WhoHol B
Bracey, Ishmon 1901-1970 BluesWW[port]
Bracey, Sidney 1877-1942 FilmEn, WhScrn 74, -77, WhoHol B
Brachius, Georg NewGrD 80
Brachius, Jorg NewGrD 80
Bracho, Julio 190-?- DcFM
Brachrogge, Hans d1638? NewGrD 80
Brachvogel, Albert 1824-1878 OxMus
Brack, Georg NewGrD 80
Brack, Jorg NewGrD 80
Brackeen, Joanne 1938- EncJzS 70
Bracken, Bertram TwYS A
Bracken, Eddie 1920- BiE&WWA, FilmEn, FilmgC, ForYSC, HalFC 80, HolP 40[port], IntMPA 77, -75, -76, -78, -79, -80, MotPP, MovMk, NotNAT, WhoHol A, WhoThe 72, -77
Brackenridge, Hugh Henry 1748-1816 NotNAT B, OxThe
Brackett, Charles 1892-1969 CmMov, FilmEn, FilmgC, HalFC 80, NotNAT B, WorEFlm[port]
Brackett, Leigh 1915-1978 FilmEn
Brackett, Leigh 1918-1978 CmMov, FilmgC, HalFC 80, WomWMM
Brackman, George 1922- AmSCAP 80
Brackman, Jacob 1943- AmSCAP 80
Brackman, Marie L d1963 NotNAT B
Braconnier, Jean d1512 NewGrD 80
Bracquet, Gilles NewGrD 80
Bracy, Clara T 1847-1941 Film 1, WhScrn 74
Bracy, Katherine Branfield 1938- IntWWM 77, -80
Bracy, Sidney 1882-1941 FilmEn, Film 1, -2, ForYSC, TwYS
Brada, Ede 1879-1953 CnOxB
Brada, Rezso 1906-1948 CnOxB
Bradburn, Samuel 1751-1816 OxMus
Bradbury, Allan WhoHol A
Bradbury, Colin 1933- IntWWM 77, -80, WhoMus 72
Bradbury, Ernest 1919- WhoMus 72
Bradbury, James, Jr. 1894- Film 2, TwYS
Bradbury, James, Sr. 1857-1940 Film 2, NotNAT B, TwYS, WhScrn 74, -77, WhThe, WhoHol B
Bradbury, John 1944- IntWWM 77, -80, WhoMus 72
Bradbury, Kitty Film 2
Bradbury, Ray 1920- CmMov, FilmgC, HalFC 80, WhoHrs 80
Bradbury, Ray 1922- WorEFlm[port]
Bradbury, Robert North TwYS A
Bradbury, Robert North 1885?- FilmEn
Bradbury, Robert North, Jr. FilmEn
Bradbury, W B OxMus
Bradbury, William Batchelder 1816-1868 Baker 78, BiDAmM, NewGrD 80
Braddell, Maurice Film 2
Braddock, James J What 1[port]
Braddy, Pauline 1922- BlkWAB[port]
Brade, William 1560-1630 NewGrD 80, OxMus
Bradel, John F d1962 NotNAT B
Braden, Bernard 1916- CreCan 2, FilmgC, HalFC 80, WhThe, WhoThe 72
Braden, Edward Allen 1863- WhoStg 1906
Braden, Frank d1962 NotNAT B
Braden, John Stuart 1946- AmSCAP 80
Braden, Waldo W 1911- BiE&WWA, NotNAT
Braden, William 1939- IntMPA 80
Braden, William 1940- IntMPA 79
Bradfield, W Louis 1866-1919 WhThe
Bradford, Alex 1927- DrBlPA
Bradford, Andrew 1686-1742 BiDAmM
Bradford, Benjamin 1925- NatPD[port]
Bradford, Bobby Lee 1934- EncJzS 70, IlEncJ, IntWWM 77
Bradford, Charles Avery 1873-1926 WhScrn 74, -77
Bradford, Clea Annah Ethell 1936- BiDAmM
Bradford, Glenn Dale 1932- AmSCAP 80
Bradford, James C 1885-1941 AmSCAP 66
Bradford, James M d1933 NotNAT B
Bradford, John OxMus
Bradford, John Milton 1919- AmSCAP 80
Bradford, Lane 1923-1973 ForYSC, WhScrn 77, WhoHol B
Bradford, Marshall 1896-1971 WhScrn 74, -77, WhoHol B
Bradford, Perry 1890?- BlksBF[port]
Bradford, Perry 1893-1970 AmSCAP 66, BiDAmM, CmpEPM, EncJzS 70
Bradford, Perry 1895-1970 WhoJazz 72
Bradford, Peter 1919- IntMPA 77, -75, -76, -78, -79, -80
Bradford, Richard WhoHol A
Bradford, Roark 1896-1948 AmSCAP 66, -80, PlP&P
Bradford, Sylvester 1937- AmSCAP 66
Bradford, Sylvester Henry 1942- AmSCAP 80
Bradford, Vera Florence WhoMus 72
Bradford, Virginia Film 2
Bradford, William AmSCAP 80
Bradin, Jean Film 2
Bradley, Amanda d1916 WhScrn 77
Bradley, Benjamin R 1898-1950 WhScrn 74, -77
Bradley, Betty d1973 WhoHol B
Bradley, Betty 1920- CmpEPM
Bradley, Bill 1921- IntMPA 77, -75, -76, -78, -79, -80
Bradley, Buddy 1908- WhThe
Bradley, Buddy 1913- BiE&WWA
Bradley, Claire WomWMM B
Bradley, David 1919- HalFC 80, WhoHrs 80
Bradley, David 1920- FilmEn, OxFilm, WorEFlm[port]
Bradley, Edson P 1907- AmSCAP 66
Bradley, Estelle Film 2
Bradley, Frederick Archibald 1908- IntWWM 77, WhoMus 72
Bradley, Grace 1913- FilmEn, ForYSC, ThFT[port], WhoHol A
Bradley, H Dennis d1934 NotNAT B
Bradley, Harold Ray 1926- BiDAmM

Bradley, Harry C 1869-1947 *WhScrn 74, –77, WhoHol B*
Bradley, Ian Leonard 1925- *IntWWM 77, –80*
Bradley, James *PupTheA*
Bradley, Jan 1944- *RkOn*
Bradley, Jerry *ConMuA 80B*
Bradley, Leo Herman 1938- *AmSCAP 80*
Bradley, Leonora d1935 *NotNAT B*
Bradley, Leslie *WhoHol A*
Bradley, Lilian Trimble 1875- *WhThe*
Bradley, Lionel 1898-1953 *DancEn 78*
Bradley, Lisa 1941- *CnOxB, DancEn 78[port]*
Bradley, Lovyss 1906-1969 *WhScrn 74, –77, WhoHol B*
Bradley, Malcolm *Film 2*
Bradley, Milus L 1927- *AmSCAP 80*
Bradley, Oscar d1948 *NotNAT B*
Bradley, Owen 1915- *IlEncCM*
Bradley, Ruth *ConAmC*
Bradley, Sandra Wentworth *WomWMM B*
Bradley, Truman 1905-1974 *ForYSC, NewYTET, WhScrn 77, WhoHol B*
Bradley, Velma *BluesWW[port]*
Bradley, Victor 1917- *WhoMus 72*
Bradley, Will 1912- *BgBands 74[port], CmpEPM, WhoJazz 72*
Bradna, Olympe 1920- *FilmEn, FilmgC, ForYSC, HalFC 80, MotPP, ThFT[port], WhoHol A*
Bradnum, Frederick *ConDr 73, –77B*
Bradshaw, David 1937- *IntWWM 77, –80*
Bradshaw, Eunice 1893-1973 *WhScrn 77, WhoHol B*
Bradshaw, Fanny 1897-1973 *NotNAT B*
Bradshaw, Fanny 1900- *BiE&WWA*
Bradshaw, Leslie Glen 1934- *AmSCAP 80*
Bradshaw, Lionel M 1892-1918 *WhScrn 77*
Bradshaw, Merrill Kay 1929- *AmSCAP 80, CpmDNM 80, ConAmC, IntWWM 77, –80*
Bradshaw, Murray C 1930- *IntWWM 77, –80*
Bradshaw, Myron Carlton 1908-1958 *AmSCAP 80*
Bradshaw, Richard James 1944- *IntWWM 77, –80, WhoMus 72*
Bradshaw, Susan 1931- *WhoMus 72*
Bradshaw, Tiny 1905-1958 *IlEncJ, WhoJazz 72*
Bradshaw, William A *WhoMus 72*
Bradsky, Wenzel Theodor 1833-1881 *Baker 78*
Bradstreet, Ann *OxMus*
Bradt, Clifton E d1961 *NotNAT B*
Brady, Al *ConMuA 80B*
Brady, Alice d1939 *MotPP, WhoHol B*
Brady, Alice 1892-1939 *FilmEn, HalFC 80, HolCA[port], MovMk, NotNAT B, OxThe, ThFT[port], TwYS, Vers A[port], WhScrn 74, –77, WhThe*
Brady, Alice 1893-1939 *Film 1, –2, FilmgC, ForYSC*
Brady, Bessie 1882-1912 *BlksBF*
Brady, Ed 1889-1942 *TwYS*
Brady, Edward 1889-1942 *Film 2, WhoHol B*
Brady, Edward J 1888-1942 *WhScrn 74, –77*
Brady, Edwin J 1889-1942 *Film 1, –2*
Brady, Frank L 1914- *IntMPA 77, –75, –76, –78, –79, –80*
Brady, Fred 1912-1961 *WhScrn 77*
Brady, Grace George 1879-1961 *OxThe*
Brady, Hugh d1921 *NotNAT B*
Brady, Kathleen Mary 1905- *IntWWM 77, WhoMus 72*
Brady, Kathleen Teresa 1934- *IntWWM 80*
Brady, Leo B 1917- *BiE&WWA, NotNAT*
Brady, Nicholas 1659-1726 *OxMus*
Brady, Pat 1914-1972 *BiDAmM, FilmEn, WhScrn 77, WhoHol B*
Brady, Philip *Film 2*
Brady, Scott 1924- *FilmEn, FilmgC, ForYSC, HalFC 80, HolP 40[port], IntMPA 77, –75, –76, –78, –79, –80, MotPP, WhoHol A, WhoHrs 80*
Brady, Stumpy Floyd Maurice 1910- *WhoJazz 72*
Brady, Terence 1939- *WhoThe 72, –77*
Brady, Veronica 1890-1964 *NotNAT B, WhThe*
Brady, W A 1865-1950 *WhoStg 1906, –1908*
Brady, William A 1863-1950 *NotNAT A, –B, OxThe, WhThe*
Brady, William A, Jr. 1900-1935 *NotNAT B, WhThe*
Brae, June 1917- *CnOxB, DancEn 78*
Brae, June 1918- *WhThe*
Braeden, Eric *HalFC 80, WhoHol A*
Braedon, Eric *ForYSC*
Braein, Edvard Fliflet 1924-1976 *Baker 78, NewGrD 80*
Braem, Thuring Lukas 1944- *IntWWM 77, –80*
Braeunich, Johann Michael *NewGrD 80*
Braeunig, Johann Michael *NewGrD 80*
Braff, Reuben 1927- *BiDAmM, EncJzS 70*
Braff, Ruby 1927- *CmpEPM, EncJzS 70, IlEncJ, MusMk*
Braga, Eurico 1894-1962 *NotNAT B, WhScrn 74, –77*
Braga, Francisco 1868-1945 *Baker 78, NewGrD 80*
Braga, Gaetano 1829-1907 *Baker 78, NewGrD 80*
Braga, Henriqueta Rosa Fernandes 1909- *IntWWM 77, –80*
Braga, Robert 1915- *IntWWM 80*
Braga-Santos, Joly 1924- *Baker 78, DcCM, NewGrD 80*
Bragaglia, Anton 1890-1960 *Ent*
Bragaglia, Anton Giulio 1890-1960 *EncWT*
Bragaglia, Carlo Ludovico 1894- *WorEFlm[port]*
Bragaglia, Marinella *WhThe*
Bragaldi *PupTheA*
Bragard, Roger 1903- *Baker 78*
Bragdon, Claude Fayette 1866-1946 *NotNAT A, –B*
Bragg, Bernard 1928- *NotNAT A*
Bragg, Dobby *BluesWW[port]*
Bragg, Don 1935- *What 4[port]*
Bragg, Glyn Robert 1944- *WhoMus 72*
Braggins, Daphne Elizabeth *WhoMus 72*
Braggiotti, Francesca *WhoHol A*
Braggiotti, Mario 1909- *AmSCAP 66, –80, ConAmC*
Bragin, Jack 1936- *IntWWM 77*
Braglia, Onorato *NewGrD 80*
Braham, David 1838-1905 *AmPS, BiDAmM, NewCBMT, NewGrD 80, NotNAT B, PopAmC, Sw&Ld B*
Braham, David and Edward Harrigan *Sw&Ld B*
Braham, Harry 1874-1923 *NotNAT B, WhScrn 74, –77, WhoHol B*
Braham, Horace 1893-1955 *NotNAT B, WhScrn 74, –77, WhThe, WhoHol B*
Braham, John 1774-1856 *Baker 78, CmOp, NewEOp 71, NewGrD 80[port], OxMus*
Braham, Leonora 1853-1931 *WhThe*
Braham, Lionel 1879-1947 *Film 1, –2, NotNAT B, WhScrn 74, –77, WhThe, WhoHol B*
Braham, Philip 1881-1934 *NotNAT B, WhThe*
Braham Brothers *PupTheA*
Brahe, May Hanna *OxMus*
Brahm, John 1893- *FilmEn, FilmgC, HalFC 80, IntMPA 77, –75, –76, –78, –79, WorEFlm[port]*
Brahm, John 1898- *BiDFilm, –81*
Brahm, Otto 1856-1912 *EncWT, Ent, NotNAT A, –B, OxThe*
Brahms, Caryl 1901- *CnOxB, ConDr 73, –77D, DancEn 78, WhoThe 72, –77*
Brahms, Johannes 1833-1897 *Baker 78, BnBkM 80[port], CmpBCM, CnOxB, DancEn 78, DcCom 77[port], DcCom&M 79, GrComp[port], MusMk[port], NewGrD 80, OxMus*
Brahn, Lux 1946- *IntWWM 77, –80*
Braidon, Thomas *Film 2*
Braidwood, Frank *Film 2*
Brailoiu, Constantin 1893-1958 *Baker 78, NewGrD 80*
Brailovsky, Alexander 1896-1976 *NewGrD 80*
Brailowsky, Alexander 1896-1976 *Baker 78, BnBkM 80, MusSN[port], NewGrD 80, WhoMus 72*
Brailsford, Clive Robert 1945- *IntWWM 80*
Brain *NewGrD 80*
Brain, Alfred 1885-1966 *NewGrD 80*
Brain, Aubrey 1893-1955 *Baker 78, NewGrD 80*
Brain, Cornelia 1937- *IntWWM 77*
Brain, Dennis 1921-1957 *Baker 78, BnBkM 80, MusMk, NewGrD 80[port]*
Brain, Gary Clifford Dennis 1943- *IntWWM 80*
Brain, Leonard 1915-1975 *NewGrD 80, WhoMus 72*
Brainard, John Gardiner Calkins 1796-1828 *BiDAmM*
Brainard, Paul Henry 1928- *IntWWM 77, –80, NewGrD 80*
Brainard, Silas 1814-1871 *BiDAmM*
Braine, Robert 1896-1940 *Baker 78, BiDAmM, ConAmC*
Brainin, Jerome 1916- *AmSCAP 66, –80*
Brainin, Norbert 1923- *IntWWM 77, –80, WhoMus 72*
Braith, George 1939- *BiDAmM*
Braithewaite, Shirley *PupTheA*
Braithwaite, John Victor Maxwell *CreCan 2*
Braithwaite, Lilian 1871-1948 *WhScrn 74, WhoHol B*
Braithwaite, Lilian 1873-1948 *CnThe, HalFC 80, IlWWBF, OxThe, WhScrn 77, WhThe*
Braithwaite, Lillian 1873-1948 *Film 2, NotNAT B, PlP&P*
Braithwaite, Max 1911- *CreCan 2*
Braithwaite, Nicholas 1939- *WhoOp 76*
Braithwaite, Nicholas Paul Dallon 1939- *IntWWM 77, –80, NewGrD 80*
Braithwaite, Sam Hartley 1883-1947 *Baker 78*
Braithwaite, Warwick 1896-1971 *NewGrD 80*
Braithwaite, Warwick 1898-1971 *Baker 78, CmOp*
Braitstein, Marcel 1935- *CreCan 2*
Brakhage, Stan 1933- *DcFM, FilmEn, HalFC 80, OxFilm, WhoHrs 80, WorEFlm[port]*
Brakkher, Georg *NewGrD 80*
Brakstad, Anna 1944- *IntWWM 80*
Bram, Marjorie 1919- *IntWWM 80*
Bramall, Eric *DcPup*
Braman, Wallis D *ConAmC*
Brambach, Caspar Joseph 1833-1902 *Baker 78*
Brambach, Wilhelm 1841-1932 *Baker 78*
Brambell, Wilfrid 1912- *FilmgC, HalFC 80, IntMPA 77, –75, –76, –78, –79, –80, WhoThe 72, –77*
Brambilla *CmOp, NewGrD 80*
Brambilla, Giuseppina 1819-1903 *NewGrD 80*
Brambilla, Marietta 1807-1875 *Baker 78, CmOp, NewGrD 80*
Brambilla, Paolo 1787-1838 *Baker 78*
Brambilla, Teresa 1813-1895 *Baker 78, CmOp, NewGrD 80*
Brambilla, Teresina 1845-1921 *CmOp*
Brambilla-Ponchielli, Teresa 1845-1921 *NewGrD 80*
Bramble, A V d195-? *IlWWBF*
Bramble, A V 1880?-1963 *FilmEn, FilmgC, HalFC 80*
Brambrick, Gertrude *Film 1*
Brameley, Richard *NewGrD 80*
Bramley, Flora *Film 2, WhoHol A*
Bramley, John *NewGrD 80*
Bramley, Natalie *WhoMus 72*
Bramley, Raymond 1891- *BiE&WWA, NotNAT, WhoHol A*
Bramley, William *WhoHol A*
Brammer, Sheila Elizabeth 1952- *IntWWM 80*
Bramsen, Ludvig Ernst 1910- *IntWWM 77, –80*
Bramson, Danny *ConMuA 80B*
Bramson, Karen d1936 *NotNAT B*
Bramson, Sam d1962 *NotNAT B*
Bramston, Richard 1485?-1554 *NewGrD 80*
Branberger, Jan 1877-1952 *NewGrD 80*
Brancaccio, Antonio 1813-1846 *Baker 78*
Brancati, Vitaliano 1907-1954 *McGEWD*
Branch, Charlie *AmSCAP 80*
Branch, Eileen 1911- *WhThe*
Branch, Harold *ConAmC*
Branch, Sarah 1938- *FilmgC, HalFC 80*
Branch, William Blackwell 1927- *BlkAmP, DrBlPA, MorBAP*
Branch, William Earl 1951- *BluesWW[port]*
Branche, Charles-Antoine 1722- *NewGrD 80*
Branche, Lewis W 1927- *ConAmTC*
Branciforte, Girolamo 1560?-1620? *NewGrD 80*
Branciforte, Hyeronimo 1560?-1620? *NewGrD 80*

Branciforti, Girolamo 1560?-1620? *NewGrD 80*
Branciforti, Hyeronimo 1560?-1620? *NewGrD 80*
Branco, Jose Mario 1942- *IntWWM 80*
Brancour, Rene 1862-1948 *Baker 78*
Brancusi, Petre 1928- *NewGrD 80*
Brand, Adolph Johannes 1934- *EncJzS 70*
Brand, Barbarina d1854 *NotNAT B*
Brand, Dollar 1934- *EncJzS 70, IlEncJ*
Brand, Geoffrey Edward 1926- *IntWWM 77, -80*
Brand, Hannah d1821 *NotNAT B*
Brand, Jan *NewGrD 80*
Brand, Louise *PupTheA*
Brand, Max 1892-1944 *FilmgC, HalFC 80*
Brand, Max 1896- *Baker 78, BiDAmM, ConAmC, IntWWM 77, -80*
Brand, Michael *NewGrD 80*
Brand, Myra Jean Friesen 1936- *IntWWM 77, -80*
Brand, Neville *MotPP, WhoHol A*
Brand, Neville 1920- *FilmgC, HalFC 80*
Brand, Neville 1921- *FilmEn, ForYSC, IntMPA 77, -75, -76, -78, -79, -80*
Brand, Oscar 1920- *BiDAmM, EncFCWM 69, NatPD[port], NotNAT*
Brand, Oswald d1909 *NotNAT B*
Brand, Phoebe 1907- *BiE&WWA, NotNAT, PlP&P[port]*
Brand, Robert 1934- *WhoOp 76*
Brand X *ConMuA 80A*
Brandane, John 1869-1947 *OxThe*
Brandeis, Frederick 1832-1899 *Baker 78*
Brandeis, Frederick 1835-1899 *BiDAmM*
Brandeis, Ruth *WhoHol A*
Brandenstein, Johann Konrad 1695?-1757 *NewGrD 80*
Brander, Allen *Film 2*
Brandes, Edvard 1847-1931 *OxThe*
Brandes, Esther Charlotte Henrietta 1746-1784 *OxThe*
Brandes, Georg Morris Cohen 1842-1927 *NotNAT B, OxThe*
Brandes, Johann Christian 1735-1799 *OxThe*
Brandes, Marthe 1862-1930 *NotNAT B, WhThe*
Brandes, Minna 1765-1788 *OxThe*
Brandewine-Montgomery, Kandeda Rachel 1940- *AmSCAP 80*
Brandin, L M *OxMus*
Brandl, Johann Evangelist 1760-1837 *Baker 78*
Brandman, Israel 1901- *IntWWM 80*
Brando, Jocelyn *IntMPA 75, -76, -78, -79, -80*
Brando, Jocelyn 1919- *FilmgC, ForYSC, HalFC 80, IntMPA 77, MotPP, WhoHol A*
Brando, Marlon 1924- *BiDFilm, -81, BiE&WWA, Ent, FilmEn, FilmgC, ForYSC, HalFC 80, IntMPA 77, -75, -76, -78, -79, -80, MotPP, MovMk[port], NotNAT A, OxFilm, PlP&P[port], WhoHol A, WhoHrs 80, WorEFlm[port]*
Brandon, Arthur F 1925-1975 *WhScrn 77*
Brandon, Dickie *Film 2*
Brandon, Dolores 1917-1959 *WhScrn 74, -77*
Brandon, Dorothy *WhThe*
Brandon, Florence 1879-1961 *WhScrn 74, -77*
Brandon, Francis 1886-1924 *WhScrn 77*
Brandon, George 1924- *ConAmC*
Brandon, Heather 1931- *IntWWM 80*
Brandon, Henry 1910- *FilmgC, HalFC 80, WhoHol A, WhoHrs 80*
Brandon, Henry 1912- *FilmEn, ForYSC, HolCA[port]*
Brandon, Jocelyn d1948 *NotNAT B*
Brandon, Johnny *NatPD[port]*
Brandon, Liane 1939- *WomWMM A, -B*
Brandon, Mary *Film 2*
Brandon, Michael *WhoHol A*
Brandon, Peter 1926- *BiE&WWA, NotNAT*
Brandon, Richard *PupTheA*
Brandon, Seymour 1945- *AmSCAP 80*
Brandon, Sy 1945- *ConAmC*
Brandon-Thomas, Amy d1974 *WhoHol B*
Brandon-Thomas, Amy Marguerite 1890- *WhThe*
Brandon-Thomas, Jevan 1898- *WhThe, WhoThe 72*
Brands, X *WhoHol A*
Brands X *ForYSC*
Brandse, Wilhelmus Cornelis 1933- *IntWWM 77, -80*
Brandstaetter, Roman 1906- *ModWD*
Brandstatter, Roman 1906- *CnMD*
Brandstatter-Elmitt, Pauline 1932- *WhoMus 72*
Brandt, Aleksander *NewGrD 80*
Brandt, Alvin 1922- *BiE&WWA, NotNAT*
Brandt, Barbara Jean 1942- *WhoOp 76*
Brandt, Carolyn 1940?- *WhoHrs 80*
Brandt, Charles 1864-1924 *Film 1, WhScrn 77*
Brandt, Dorothea 1896- *ConAmC*
Brandt, Eddie 1924- *AmSCAP 66*
Brandt, Edward August 1924- *AmSCAP 80*
Brandt, George 1916-1963 *NotNAT B*
Brandt, Hans Henrik 1944- *IntWWM 80*
Brandt, Ivan 1903- *WhThe*
Brandt, Jan *NewGrD 80*
Brandt, Janet *IntMPA 79, -80*
Brandt, Jerome 1937- *IntWWM 77, -80*
Brandt, Jobst Vom 1517-1570 *Baker 78, NewGrD 80*
Brandt, Jodocus Vom 1517-1570 *NewGrD 80*
Brandt, Jost Vom 1517-1570 *NewGrD 80*
Brandt, Louise 1877-1959 *WhScrn 74, -77, WhoHol B*
Brandt, Marianne 1842-1921 *Baker 78, NewGrD 80*
Brandt, Mathile *Film 2*
Brandt, Michel 1934- *IntWWM 77, -80*
Brandt, Noah 1858-1925 *Baker 78*
Brandt, Pamela Robin 1947- *AmSCAP 80*
Brandt, Richard Paul 1927- *IntMPA 77, -75, -76, -78, -79, -80*
Brandt, Walter *Film 2*
Brandt, William Edward 1920- *ConAmC*
Brandtner, Fritz 1896- *CreCan 2*
Brandts Buys *NewGrD 80*
Brandts Buys, Cornelis 1757-1831 *NewGrD 80*
Brandts Buys, Cornelis Alexander 1812-1890 *NewGrD 80*
Brandts Buys, Hans 1905-1959 *NewGrD 80*
Brandts Buys, Henri Francois Robert 1850-1905 *NewGrD 80*
Brandts-Buys, Jan 1868-1933 *Baker 78*
Brandts Buys, Jan Willem Frans 1868-1939 *NewGrD 80*
Brandts Buys, Johan 1905-1959 *NewGrD 80*
Brandts Buys, Ludwig Felix 1847-1917 *NewGrD 80*
Brandts Buys, Marius Adrianus 1840-1911 *NewGrD 80*
Brandts Buys, Marius Adrianus 1874-1944 *NewGrD 80*
Brandukov, Anatol 1856-1930 *Baker 78*
Brandukov, Anatoly Andreyevich 1856-1930 *NewGrD 80*
Brandus Posnaniensis *NewGrD 80*
Brandwynne, Nat 1910- *AmSCAP 66, BgBands 74, CmpEPM*
Brandy, Howard 1929- *IntMPA 77, -75, -76, -78, -79, -80*
Branen, Jeff T 1872-1927 *AmSCAP 66, -80*
Brangjolica, Ivo 1928- *IntWWM 80*
Branion, Antonio *Film 2*
Branisteanu, Horiana 1942- *WhoOp 76*
Brann, Paul 1873-1955 *DcPup*
Brannenburger, Reinmar Der *NewGrD 80*
Branner, Hans Christian 1903-1966 *CnMD*
Brannigan, Owen 1908-1973 *CmOp, NewGrD 80, WhoMus 72*
Brannigan, Owen 1909-1973 *WhScrn 77*
Branning, Grace 1912- *ConAmC*
Brannon, Bob *AmSCAP 80*
Brannon, Fred C *WhoHrs 80*
Brannum, Hugh 1910- *AmSCAP 80, IntMPA 77, -75, -76, -78, -79, -80*
Brano, Roscoe *AmSCAP 80*
Bransby Williams *OxThe*
Branscombe, Arthur d1924 *NotNAT B*
Branscombe, Gena 1881-1977 *AmSCAP 80, Baker 78, BiDAmM, ConAmC, NewGrD 80, OxMus*
Branscombe, Gina 1881- *AmSCAP 66*
Branscombe, Peter John 1929- *IntWWM 80*
Branscome, Lilly *Film 1*
Bransford, Mallory Watkins 1912- *IntWWM 77, -80*
Branson, David 1909- *IntWWM 77, -80, NewGrD 80*
Branson, Walter E *IntMPA 77, -75, -76, -78, -79, -80*
Brant, Henry 1913- *AmSCAP 80, BnBkM 80, CompSN[port], ConAmC, DcCM, NewGrD 80*
Brant, Henry Drefuss 1913- *BiDAmM*
Brant, Henry Dreyfus 1913- *Baker 78, CpmDNM 79, MusMk*
Brant, Ira 1921- *AmSCAP 66, -80*
Brant, Jan 1554-1602 *NewGrD 80*
Brant, Jobst Vom *NewGrD 80*
Brant, Per 1714-1767 *NewGrD 80*
Brantford, Albert *Film 2*
Brantford, Mickey 1911- *IlWWBF*
Brantford, Mickey 1912- *Film 2*
Branzell, Karin 1891-1974 *Baker 78, CmOp, MusSN[port], NewEOp 71, NewGrD 80*
Braque, Georges 1882-1963 *CnOxB, DancEn 78, EncWT*
Braquet, Gilles *NewGrD 80*
Brasaola, Aulo 1915- *WhoOp 76*
Brasart, Jean *NewGrD 80*
Braschowanowa, Lada 1929- *IntWWM 80*
Brascia, John *WhoHol A*
Brasfield, Rod d1958 *WhScrn 77*
Brashear, Janice Marie 1941- *AmSCAP 80*
Brashear, Oscar 1944- *EncJzS 70*
Brashovanov, Stoyan 1888-1956 *NewGrD 80*
Brashovanova, Lada 1929- *NewGrD 80*
Brasil, Arthur 1949- *IntWWM 80*
Braslau, Sophie 1892-1935 *Baker 78, BiDAmM, MusSN[port], NewEOp 71*
Brasloff, Stanley H 1930- *IntMPA 77, -75, -76, -78, -79, -80*
Brasmer, William 1921- *BiE&WWA, NotNAT*
Brasolini, Domenico *NewGrD 80*
Brass, Tinto 1933- *WorEFlm[port]*
Brass Company *EncJzS 70*
Brass Construction *RkOn 2[port]*
Brass Ring *RkOn 2A*
Brassard, Francois 1908- *CreCan 1*
Brassart, Johannes *NewGrD 80*
Brasselle, Keefe 1923- *AmSCAP 66, FilmEn, FilmgC, ForYSC, HalFC 80, IntMPA 77, -75, -76, -78, -79, -80, MotPP, NewYTET, WhoHol A*
Brassens, Georges 1921- *IntWWM 77, -80, WhoMus 72*
Brasseur, Albert Jules 1862-1932 *NotNAT B, WhThe*
Brasseur, Claude 1936- *FilmAG WE, FilmEn*
Brasseur, Jules d1890 *NotNAT B*
Brasseur, Pierre 1903-1972 *FilmEn, Film 2, FilmgC, HalFC 80, MovMk, WhScrn 77, WorEFlm[port]*
Brasseur, Pierre 1905-1972 *BiDFilm, -81, CnThe, EncWT, Ent, FilmAG WE, OxFilm, WhoHol B*
Brassicanus, Johannes 1570?-1634 *NewGrD 80*
Brassin *NewGrD 80*
Brassin, Gerhard 1844-1885? *NewGrD 80*
Brassin, Leopold 1843-1890 *Baker 78, NewGrD 80*
Brassin, Louis 1840-1884 *Baker 78, NewGrD 80*
Brassolini, Domenico *NewGrD 80*
Braswell, Charles 1925-1974 *WhScrn 77, WhoHol B*
Braswell, John *ConAmC*
Bratanov, Ivan 1920-1968 *WhScrn 77*
Bratel, Ulrich 1495?-1545? *NewGrD 80*
Brathwayt, Raymond *Film 2*
Bratman, Carroll Charles 1906- *AmSCAP 80*
Bratt, C Griffith 1914- *ConAmC, IntWWM 77, -80*
Brattle, Thomas 1658-1713 *BiDAmM*
Bratton, John Walter 1867-1947 *AmSCAP 66, -80, BiDAmM, CmpEPM, NotNAT B, WhoStg 1906, -1908*
Bratu, Alexandru 1918- *AmSCAP 80*
Bratu, Emma 1910- *AmSCAP 80*
Brau, Alexis R 1921- *AmSCAP 66, -80*
Braud, Wellman 1891- *BiDAmM*
Braud, Wellman 1891-1966 *EncJzS 70, WhoJazz 72*
Braud, Wellman 1891-1967 *NewOrJ[port]*
Braudo, Eugen 1882-1939 *Baker 78*
Braudo, Isay 1896-1970 *NewGrD 80*
Brauel, Henning 1940- *Baker 78*
Brauer, Dieter 1935- *IntWWM 77, -80*

Brauer, Ferenc 1799-1871 *NewGrD 80*
Brauer, James Leonard 1938- *ConAmC*
Brauer, LeRoy 1902- *IntMPA 77, -75, -76, -78, -79, -80*
Brauer, Lucia *DancEn 78*
Brault, Michel 1928- *CreCan 1, OxFilm, WorEFlm[port]*
Braun *NewGrD 80*
Braun, Alexander 1930- *AmSCAP 80*
Braun, Anton 1729-1798 *NewGrD 80*
Braun, Arthur David 1952- *AmSCAP 80*
Braun, Billy 1892-1974 *NewOrJ*
Braun, Bob 1929- *RkOn*
Braun, Carl 1885-1960 *Baker 78*
Braun, Carl Anton Philipp 1788-1835 *NewGrD 80*
Braun, David *ConMuA 80B*
Braun, Edgar J *IntWWM 80*
Braun, Felix 1885-1973 *CnMD, CroCD*
Braun, Gustl 1931- *WhoOp 76*
Braun, Jean *NewGrD 80*
Braun, Johann 1753-1811 *NewGrD 80*
Braun, Johann Friedrich 1758-1824 *NewGrD 80*
Braun, Johann Georg 1656-1687 *NewGrD 80*
Braun, Johann Georg Franz *NewGrD 80*
Braun, John F d1939 *BiDAmM*
Braun, Matitiahu 1940- *BiDAmM*
Braun, Mattias 1933- *CnMD*
Braun, Moriz 1765-1828 *NewGrD 80*
Braun, Paul d1940 *PupTheA*
Braun, Peter Michael 1936- *Baker 78, DcCM, IntWWM 77, NewGrD 80*
Braun, Peter Micheal 1936- *IntWWM 80*
Braun, Richard William 1926- *AmSCAP 80*
Braun, Victor Conrad *WhoOp 76*
Braun, Victor Conrad 1935- *CmOp, CreCan 1, NewGrD 80*
Braun, Volker 1939- *CroCD*
Braun, Werner 1926- *NewGrD 80*
Braun, Wilhelm *Baker 78*
Braun, Wilhelm Theodor Johannes 1796-1867 *NewGrD 80*
Braun, Yehezkiel 1922- *NewGrD 80*
Braunagel, Jack D 1912- *IntMPA 77, -75, -76, -78, -79, -80*
Braunberger, Pierre 1905- *DcFM, FilmEn, OxFilm*
Braunfels, Walter 1882-1954 *Baker 78, NewEOp 71, NewGrD 80, OxMus*
Braunich, Johann Michael *NewGrD 80*
Brauninger, Eva J 1931- *IntWWM 77, -80*
Brauninger, James Edward 1927- *IntWWM 77, -80*
Braunlich, Helmut 1929- *ConAmC*
Braunstein, Alan R 1947- *AmSCAP 80*
Braunsweg, Julian 1897- *CnOxB*
Braupner, Jan *NewGrD 80*
Braupner, Vaclav *NewGrD 80*
Braupner, Venceslaus *NewGrD 80*
Braus, Dorothea Marcella *IntWWM 77, -80, WhoMus 72*
Brausewetter, Hans *Film 2*
Brauss, Helmut F 1930- *IntWWM 77, -80*
Brautigam, Helmut 1914-1942 *NewGrD 80*
Brautmer, Jan *NewGrD 80*
Brautmer, Vaclav *NewGrD 80*
Brautmer, Venceslaus *NewGrD 80*
Brautner, Jan *NewGrD 80*
Brautner, Vaclav *NewGrD 80*
Brautner, Venceslaus *NewGrD 80*
Braver, Billy *JoeFr*
Braverman, Charles 1944- *IntMPA 77, -75, -76, -78, -79, -80*
Braverman, Chuck *NewYTET*
Braverman, Millicent *IntMPA 77, -75, -76, -78, -79, -80*
Braverman, Roy M 1954- *AmSCAP 80*
Bravin, Steven Kirk 1954- *AmSCAP 80*
Bravington, Eric Arthur 1920- *WhoMus 72*
Bravnicar, Matija 1897- *Baker 78, IntWWM 77, -80, NewGrD 80*
Bravo, Jaime 1932-1970 *WhoHol B*
Bravo, Jamie 1932-1970 *WhScrn 74, -77*
Bravusi, Paolo 1586-1630 *NewGrD 80*
Brawn, John P *Film 1*
Brawn, John P 1869-1943 *WhScrn 74, -77*
Brawner, Kenneth Roy 1944- *AmSCAP 80*
Braxton, Anthony 1945- *ConAmC, EncJzS 70, IlEncJ*
Bray, Helen *Film 1*
Bray, John 1782-1822 *BiDAmM*
Bray, John F 1906-1955 *WhScrn 74, -77, WhoHol B*
Bray, John Randolph 1879- *IntMPA 77, -75, -76, -78, -79, WorEFlm[port]*
Bray, John Randolph 1879-1978 *FilmEn*
Bray, Lew 1907- *IntMPA 77, -75, -76, -78*
Bray, Mabel E 1878- *IntWWM 77*
Bray, Paul, Jr. *IntMPA 77, -75, -76, -78, -79, -80*
Bray, Robert 1917- *FilmEn, FilmgC, ForYSC, HalFC 80, WhoHol A*
Bray, Roger 1944- *IntWWM 80*
Bray, Yvonne De 1889- *WhThe*
Bray, Yvonne De 1899-1954 *FilmEn*
Brayfield, George d1968 *WhScrn 77, WhoHol B*
Brayley, Sally 1937- *CreCan 2*
Brayssing, Gregoire *NewGrD 80*
Brayssing, Gregor *NewGrD 80*
Brayton, Lily 1876-1953 *NotNAT B, OxThe, WhScrn 77, WhThe*
Brazda, Jan 1917- *WhoOp 76*
Brazhnikov, Maxim Viktorovich 1904-1973 *NewGrD 80*
Brazlee, Harrison 1888-1954 *NewOrJ*
Brazos Valley Boys *BiDAmM, EncFCWM 69*
Brazzi, Lidia *ForYSC, WhoHol A*
Brazzi, Rossano 1916- *CmMov, FilmEn, FilmgC, HalFC 80, IntMPA 77, -75, -76, -78, -79, -80, MotPP, MovMk, WhoHol A*
Brazzi, Rossano 1917- *FilmAG WE*
Brazzi, Rossano 1918- *ForYSC*
Brdecka, Jiri 1917- *DcFM, FilmEn, WorEFlm[port]*
Breacher, Harold 1910- *IntMPA 77, -75, -76, -78, -79, -80*
Bread *IlEncR, RkOn 2[port]*
Breakell, John William *WhoMus 72*
Breakston, George 1920-1973 *FilmEn, WhScrn 77, WhoHol B*
Breakston, George 1922-1973 *FilmgC, HalFC 80*
Breakston, George 1923- *ForYSC*
Breakwell, George W 1931- *IntWWM 77, -80*
Bream, Julian 1933- *BnBkM 80, IntWWM 77, -80, MusMk[port], MusSN[port], NewGrD 80[port], WhoMus 72*
Breamer, Sylvia 1896-1943 *Film 1, -2, TwYS*
Breamer, Sylvia 1903-1943 *MotPP, WhScrn 74, -77, WhoHol B*
Brearley, Audrey Mabel 1912- *WhoMus 72*
Brearley, Denis H R 1907- *WhoMus 72*
Brearley, John Sebastian 1939- *WhoMus 72*
Breau, Harold 1916- *BiDAmM*
Breau, Lenny 1941- *EncJzS 70*
Breau, Leonard 1941- *EncJzS 70*
Breau, Louis 1893-1928 *AmSCAP 66, -80*
Breaux, Marc *BiE&WWA, NotNAT*
Breaux, McNeal 1916- *NewOrJ*
Breazul, Professor *OxMus*
Breazul, George 1887-1961 *Baker 78, NewGrD 80*
Brebis, Johannes *NewGrD 80*
Brebos *NewGrD 80*
Brecher, Egon 1885-1946 *Film 2, NotNAT B, WhScrn 74, -77, WhThe, WhoHol B*
Brecher, Gustav 1879-1940 *Baker 78*
Brecher, Irving 1914- *FilmEn, FilmgC, HalFC 80, IntMPA 77, -75, -76, -78, -79, -80*
Brecher, Leo *IntMPA 77, -75, -76, -78, -79, -80*
Brecht, Bert *OxMus*
Brecht, Bertold 1898-1956 *PlP&P*
Brecht, Bertolt 1898-1956 *CnMD, CnThe, CroCD, DcFM, DcPup, EncWT, Ent[port], FilmEn, FilmgC, HalFC 80, McGEWD[port], ModWD, NewEOp 71, NewGrD 80, NotNAT A, -B, OxFilm, OxThe, REnWD[port], WorEFlm[port]*
Brecht, George *ConDr 73, -77E*
Brecht, Joyce Southard 1932- *IntWWM 77*
Brechtel, Franz Joachim 1554?-1593 *NewGrD 80*
Brechtl, Franz Joachim 1554-1593 *NewGrD 80*
Brechtle, Franz Joachim 1554-1593 *NewGrD 80*
Breck, Carrie Ellis 1855-1934 *AmSCAP 66, -80, BiDAmM*
Breck, Peter *WhoHol A*
Breck, Peter 1929- *ForYSC*
Breck, Peter 1930- *HalFC 80*
Brecker, Fred *Film 2*
Brecker, Mike 1949- *EncJzS 70*
Brecker, Randy 1945- *EncJzS 70*
Breckner, Gary 1896-1945 *WhScrn 77*
Brecknock, John Leighton 1937- *WhoOp 76*
Brecourt 1638-1685 *OxThe*
Brecourt, Guillaume Marcoureau, Sieur De 1638-1685 *EncWT, Ent*
Bredemann, Dan *ConAmC*
Bredemers, Henry 1472?-1522 *NewGrD 80*
Bredemeyer, Reiner 1929- *NewGrD 80*
Bredeniers, Henry 1472?-1522 *NewGrD 80*
Bredero, Gerbrand A 1585-1618 *CnThe, Ent, OxThe, REnWD[port]*
Brediceanu, Mihai 1920- *IntWWM 80*
Brediceanu, Tiberiu 1877-1968 *Baker 78, NewGrD 80*
Bredow, Erwin 1921?- *DancEn 78*
Bredt, Douglas *PupTheA*
Bredt, James *AmSCAP 80*
Bree, Jean Bernard Van 1801-1857 *Baker 78*
Bree, Johannes Bernardus Van 1801-1857 *NewGrD 80*
Bree, Peter 1949- *IntWWM 80*
Breeden, Harold Leon 1921- *BiDAmM, EncJzS 70*
Breeden, John *Film 2*
Breeden, Leon *Conv 2[port]*
Breen, Bobby 1927-1972 *AmPS B, CmpEPM, FilmEn, FilmgC, ForYSC, HalFC 80, What 1[port], WhoHol A*
Breen, Harry *Film 1*
Breen, Helen 1902- *WhThe*
Breen, Hurley Red 1913-1963 *WhScrn 74, -77*
Breen, Joseph 1890-1965 *FilmgC, HalFC 80*
Breen, Margaret d1960 *WhScrn 74, -77, WhoHol B*
Breen, Mary *WhoHol A*
Breen, May Singhi *AmSCAP 66, -80, CmpEPM*
Breen, Richard L 1919-1967 *FilmEn, FilmgC, HalFC 80, WorEFlm[port]*
Breen, Robert 1914- *BiE&WWA, NotNAT*
Breer, Robert 1926- *WorEFlm[port]*
Brees, Bud 1921- *AmSCAP 66, -80*
Breese, Edmond 1871-1936 *MovMk*
Breese, Edmund 1870-1936 *WhoStg 1908*
Breese, Edmund 1871-1935 *Film 1, -2, ForYSC, TwYS*
Breese, Edmund 1871-1936 *NotNAT B, WhScrn 74, -77, WhThe, WhoHol B, WhoStg 1906*
Breese, Lou *BgBands 74, CmpEPM*
Breese, Pamela Margaret 1927- *WhoMus 72*
Breeskin, Barnee 1910- *AmSCAP 66, -80*
Breething, Ethel Mary 1895- *WhoMus 72*
Breeze, Lou d1969 *WhoHol B*
Bregi, Hugues De *NewGrD 80*
Bregman, Martin *IntMPA 77, -78, -79, -80*
Bregman, Robert J 1943- *IntWWM 77, -80*
Bregmer, Sylvia *Film 2*
Bregni, Paolo 1937- *WhoOp 76*
Bregvadze, Boris Jakovlevich 1926- *CnOxB, DancEn 78*
Brehm, Alvin 1925- *AmSCAP 80, Baker 78, CpmDNM 79, ConAmC*
Brehme, Hans 1904-1957 *Baker 78, NewGrD 80*
Brehy, Hercule-Pierre 1673?-1737 *NewGrD 80*
Brehy, Pierre-Hercule 1673?-1737 *NewGrD 80*
Breig, Werner 1932- *NewGrD 80*
Breil, Joseph Carl 1870-1926 *Baker 78, BiDAmM, ConAmC*
Breisach, Paul 1896-1952 *NewEOp 71*
Breisiger, Peter *NewGrD 80*
Breit, Harvey 1909-1968 *NotNAT B*
Breit, Harvey 1913- *BiE&WWA*
Breitenbacher, Antonin 1874-1937 *NewGrD 80*
Breitenfeld, Paul *NewGrD 80*
Breitengraser, Wilhelm 1495?-1542 *NewGrD 80*
Breitenstrater, Hans *Film 2*
Breithaupt, Rudolf Maria 1873-1945 *Baker 78*
Breitkopf & Hartel *Baker 78*
Breitkopf, Bernhard Christoph 1695-1777 *Baker 78*

Breitkopf, Christoph Gottlob 1750-1800 *Baker 78*
Breitkopf, Johann Gottlob Immanuel 1719-1794 *Baker 78*
Brel, Jacques 1929-1978 *NewGrD 80, WhoHol A*
Brelet, Gisele 1915-1973 *NewGrD 80*
Brema, Marie 1856-1925 *Baker 78, CmOp, NewGrD 80*
Bremberger, Reinmar Der *NewGrD 80*
Bremen, Leonard *WhoHol A*
Bremer, Claus 1924- *EncWT*
Bremer, Lucille *ForYSC*
Bremer, Lucille 1922- *FilmgC, HalFC 80*
Bremer, Lucille 1923- *FilmEn, MGM[port], WhoHol A*
Bremers, Beverly *RkOn 2A*
Bremmer, Joseph 1918- *IntMPA 75, -76*
Bremner, James d1780 *BiDAmM*
Bremner, Robert 1713?-1789 *NewGrD 80*
Bremner, Robert 1720-1789 *OxMus*
Bremond, Francois 1844-1925 *NewGrD 80*
Bren, Robert J *IntMPA 77, -75, -76, -78, -79, -80*
Brenaa, Hans 1910- *CnOxB, DancEn 78*
Brencke, Dieter 1938- *WhoOp 76*
Brenda & The Tabulations *RkOn 2[port]*
Brendel, Alfred 1931- *Baker 78, BiDAmM, BnBkM 80[port], IntWWM 77, -80, NewGrD 80[port], WhoMus 72*
Brendel, El d1964 *NotNAT B*
Brendel, El 1890-1964 *FilmEn, WhScrn 74, -77*
Brendel, El 1891-1964 *FilmgC, ForYSC, HalFC 80, JoeFr[port], Vers A[port], WhoHol B*
Brendel, El 1896-1964 *MovMk*
Brendel, El 1898-1964 *Film 2, TwYS*
Brendel, Karl Franz 1811-1868 *Baker 78, NewGrD 80*
Brendel, Wolfgang *WhoOp 76*
Brendler, Eduard 1800-1831 *NewGrD 80*
Brendler, Franz Friedrich 1800-1831 *NewGrD 80*
Brendlin, Andre 1911-1934 *WhScrn 74, -77*
Brendner, Johann Joseph Ignaz *NewGrD 80*
Brendtner, Johann Joseph Ignaz *NewGrD 80*
Breneman, Tom 1902-1948 *WhScrn 74, -77, WhoHol B*
Brenet, Michel 1858-1918 *Baker 78, NewGrD 80, OxMus*
Brengola, Riccardo 1917- *NewGrD 80*
Breni, Tomaso 1603-1650? *NewGrD 80*
Brennan, Dennis *Film 2*
Brennan, Eileen 1935- *BiE&WWA, FilmEn, HalFC 80, IntMPA 77, -75, -76, -78, -79, -80, NotNAT, WhoHol A*
Brennan, Frederick Hazlitt d1962 *NotNAT B*
Brennan, J Keirn 1873-1948 *AmPS, AmSCAP 66, -80, BiDAmM, CmpEPM, NotNAT B*
Brennan, James Alexander 1885-1956 *AmSCAP 66, -80*
Brennan, Jay d1961 *NotNAT B*
Brennan, John 1911- *WhoMus 72*
Brennan, John E 1865-1940 *WhScrn 77*
Brennan, Johnny *Film 1*
Brennan, Joseph *Film 2*
Brennan, Michael 1912- *FilmgC, HalFC 80, WhoHol A*
Brennan, Robert 1892-1940 *WhScrn 74, -77*
Brennan, Teri *WhoHol A*
Brennan, Terry *IntMPA 75, -76*
Brennan, Walter 1894-1974 *BiDFilm, -81, CmMov, FilmEn, Film 2, FilmgC, ForYSC, HalFC 80, HolCA[port], IntMPA 75, MotPP, MovMk[port], OxFilm, RkOn, TwYS, Vers A[port], WhScrn 77, WhoHol B, WorEFlm[port]*
Brenneberger, Reinmar Der *NewGrD 80*
Brennecke, Wilfried 1926- *NewGrD 80*
Brenneis, Gerd *WhoOp 76*
Brenner, Alfred *BlkAmP*
Brenner, David *JoeFr*
Brenner, Georg *NewGrD 80*
Brenner, Jerry *ConMuA 80B*
Brenner, Joseph 1918- *IntMPA 77, -75, -76, -78, -79, -80*
Brenner, Jules *HalFC 80*
Brenner, Mary Louise E 1948- *AmSCAP 80*
Brenner, Peter 1930- *WhoOp 76*
Brenner, Raymond 1927- *AmSCAP 66, -80*
Brenner, Rosamond Drooker 1931- *IntWWM 77, -80*
Brenner, Selma Hautzik 1912- *AmSCAP 66, -80*
Brenner, Walter 1906- *AmSCAP 66, ConAmC*
Brenner, Walter 1906-1969 *AmSCAP 80*
Brenner, William B 1899- *IntMPA 75*
Brenntner, Johann Joseph Ignaz *NewGrD 80*
Brenon, Herbert 1880-1958 *DcFM, FilmEn, Film 1, FilmgC, HalFC 80, IlWWBF, TwYS A, WhScrn 74, -77, WhoHol B, WorEFlm[port]*
Brenon, Juliet *Film 2*
Brent, Charlotte 1735?-1802 *NewGrD 80*
Brent, Earl Karl 1914-1977 *AmSCAP 66, -80*
Brent, Eve 1930- *FilmgC, ForYSC, HalFC 80, WhoHol A*
Brent, Evelyn 1899-1975 *FilmEn, Film 1, -2, FilmgC, ForYSC, HalFC 80, IlWWBF, MotPP, MovMk[port], ThFT[port], TwYS, What 3[port], WhScrn 77, WhoHol C*
Brent, George 1904- *What 4[port], WhoHol A*
Brent, George 1904-1979 *CmMov, FilmEn, FilmgC, ForYSC, HalFC 80, IntMPA 77, -75, -76, -78, -79, MotPP, MovMk*
Brent, Harry 1904- *AmSCAP 66*
Brent, John *OxMus*
Brent, Romney 1902-1976 *BiE&WWA, FilmEn, FilmgC, ForYSC, HalFC 80, NotNAT, PlP&P, WhThe, WhoHol A, WhoThe 72*
Brent-Smith, Alexander 1889-1950 *Baker 78*
Brenta, Gaston 1902-1969 *Baker 78, NewGrD 80, OxMus*
Brentano, Bettina 1785-1859 *NewGrD 80*
Brentano, Clemens 1778-1842 *NewGrD 80*
Brentano, Elisabeth 1785-1859 *NewGrD 80*
Brentano, Felix d1961 *NotNAT B*
Brentano, Lowell d1950 *NotNAT B*
Brentano VonArnim, Bettina 1785-1859 *NewGrD 80*
Brentano VonArnim, Elisabeth 1785-1859 *NewGrD 80*
Brentner, Johann Joseph Ignaz 1689-1742 *NewGrD 80*
Brenton, Howard 1942- *ConDr 73, -77, WhoThe 77*
Brenton, Howard 1944- *EncWT*
Breon, Edmond 1882-1951 *IlWWBF, WhThe*
Breon, Edmund 1882-1951 *FilmEn, FilmgC, HalFC 80, WhScrn 74, -77, WhoHol B*
Breon, John *PupTheA*
Brereton, Austin 1862-1922 *NotNAT B, WhThe*
Brereton, Clarence 1909-1954 *WhoJazz 72*
Brereton, Philip 1935- *IntWWM 77*
Brereton, Thomas d1722 *NotNAT B*
Brero, Giulio Cesare 1908-1973 *NewGrD 80*
Brerton, Tyrone 1894-1939 *WhScrn 74, -77, WhoHol B*
Brescianello, Giuseppe Antonio 1690?-1758 *NewGrD 80*
Bresgen, Cesar 1913- *Baker 78, CpmDNM 80, IntWWM 77, -80, NewGrD 80, WhoMus 72*
Bresil, Marguerite 1880-1923 *WhThe*
Breslau, Zane *ConMuA 80B*
Breslaur, Emil 1836-1899 *Baker 78*
Bresler, Jerome 1914- *AmSCAP 80*
Bresler, Jerry 1908-1977 *FilmEn*
Bresler, Jerry 1912-1977 *AmSCAP 66, FilmgC, HalFC 80, IntMPA 77, -75, -76, WorEFlm[port]*
Bresnan, William J *NewYTET*
Bresnick, Martin 1946- *AmSCAP 80, Baker 78, ConAmC, IntWWM 77, -80*
Bress, Hyman 1931- *CreCan 2, WhoMus 72*
Bressan, P *NewGrD 80*
Bressand, Friedrich Christian 1670?-1699 *NewGrD 80*
Bressanin, Domenico 1904- *IntWWM 77*
Bressart, Felix 1880-1949 *ForYSC, HolCA[port], WhScrn 74, -77*
Bressart, Felix 1890-1949 *FilmgC, HalFC 80*
Bressart, Felix 1892-1949 *FilmEn, Vers A[port], WhoHol B*
Bressart, Felix 1893-1949 *EncWT*
Bresslaw, Bernard 1933- *FilmgC, HalFC 80*
Bressler-Gianoli, Clotilde 1875-1912 *Baker 78*
Bresson, Robert 1907- *BiDFilm, -81, ConLC 16, DcFM, FilmEn, FilmgC, HalFC 80, MovMk[port], OxFilm, WorEFlm[port]*
Bressonelli, Giuseppe Antonio *NewGrD 80*
Bret, Gustave 1875-1969 *Baker 78*
Bretan, Nicolae 1887-1968 *Baker 78*
Bretel, Jehan 1210?-1272 *NewGrD 80*
Bretherton, David *HalFC 80*
Bretherton, Howard 1896-1969 *FilmEn, FilmgC, HalFC 80, TwYS A*
Breton, Andre 1896-1966 *ModWD, REnWD[port]*
Breton, Tomas 1850-1923 *NewGrD 80, OxMus*
Breton DeLosHerreros, Manuel 1796-1873 *McGEWD[port], NotNAT B, OxThe*
Breton Y Hernandez, Tomas 1850-1923 *Baker 78*
Bretschger, Frederick 1953- *IntWWM 80*
Brett, Angela *Film 2*
Brett, Arabella d1803 *BiDAmM, NotNAT B*
Brett, Charles Michael 1941- *IntWWM 80*
Brett, Jeremy 1933- *ForYSC*
Brett, Jeremy 1935- *FilmgC, HalFC 80, WhoHol A, WhoThe 72, -77*
Brett, Philip 1937- *IntWWM 77, -80, NewGrD 80*
Brett, Stanley 1879-1923 *NotNAT B, WhThe*
Brettel, Colette *Film 2*
Brettingham Smith, Jolyon 1949- *IntWWM 77, -80*
Breuder, W Edward 1911- *AmSCAP 66, -80*
Breuenich, Johann Michael *NewGrD 80*
Breuer, Ernest H 1886- *AmSCAP 66, -80*
Breuer, Franz Josef 1914- *IntWWM 77*
Breuer, Hans 1868-1929 *Baker 78*
Breuer, Harry 1901- *AmSCAP 80*
Breuer, Janos 1932- *IntWWM 77, -80*
Breuer, Marcel 1902- *PlP&P*
Breuer, Peter 1946- *CnOxB*
Breuker, Willem 1944- *NewGrD 80*
Breul, Elisabeth 1936- *WhoOp 76*
Breunich, Johann Michael *NewGrD 80*
Breunig, Johann Michael *NewGrD 80*
Breuning, Moritz Gerhard Von 1813-1892 *Baker 78*
Breval, Jean Baptiste 1756-1825 *OxMus*
Breval, Jean-Baptiste Sebastien 1753-1823 *NewGrD 80*
Breval, Lucienne 1869-1935 *Baker 78, NewEOp 71, NewGrD 80*
Brevi, Giovanni Battista 1650?-1725? *NewGrD 80*
Brevik, Tor 1932- *Baker 78*
Breville, Pierre De 1861-1949 *NewGrD 80*
Breville, Pierre-Onfroy De 1861-1949 *Baker 78, OxMus*
Brewer, Alfred Herbert 1865-1928 *OxMus*
Brewer, Sir Alfred Herbert 1865-1928 *Baker 78*
Brewer, Bruce 1944- *WhoOp 76*
Brewer, George E, Jr. 1899-1968 *BiE&WWA, NotNAT B*
Brewer, Sir Herbert 1865-1928 *NewGrD 80*
Brewer, James 1921- *BluesWW[port]*
Brewer, John Hyatt 1856-1931 *Baker 78, BiDAmM*
Brewer, Leigh Richmond 1839-1916 *BiDAmM*
Brewer, Linda Judd 1945- *IntWWM 80*
Brewer, Monte 1934-1942 *WhScrn 74, -77, WhoHol B*
Brewer, Richard H 1921- *ConAmC*
Brewer, Roy M 1909- *IntMPA 77, -75, -76, -78, -79, -80*
Brewer, Teresa *AmPS A, -B*
Brewer, Teresa 1931- *AmSCAP 66, CmpEPM, EncJzS 70, RkOn, WhoHol A*
Brewer, Teresa 1932- *AmSCAP 80*
Brewer, Teresa 1937- *BiDAmM*
Brewer, Theresa 1931- *EncJzS 70*
Brewer, Thomas 1611-1660? *NewGrD 80*
Brewer, Virginia 1943- *IntWWM 77, -80*
Brewer, William Gordon 1901- *WhoMus 72*
Brewer & Shipley *RkOn 2[port]*
Brewster *NewGrD 80*
Brewster, Carol *ForYSC*
Brewster, Sir David 1781-1868 *MagIlD*

Brewster, Diane *ForYSC*
Brewster, Elizabeth Winifred 1922- *CreCan 1*
Brewster, Margaret *WhoHol A*
Brewster, Townsend 1924- *NatPD[port]*
Brewster, W Herbert 1899- *NewGrD 80*
Brewster-Jones, Hooper 1887-1949 *NewGrD 80*
Brexner, Edeltraud 1927- *CnOxB, DancEn 78[port]*
Breyttengraserus, Guilielmus *NewGrD 80*
Breznikar, Joseph John 1950- *IntWWM 77, -80*
Brialy, Claude 1933- *WorEFlm[port]*
Brialy, Jean-Claude 1933- *FilmAG WE[port], FilmEn, FilmgC, HalFC 80, MovMk, WhoHol A*
Brian, Albertus *NewGrD 80*
Brian, David 1914- *FilmEn, FilmgC, ForYSC, HalFC 80, IntMPA 77, -75, -76, -78, -79, -80, MotPP, WhoHol A*
Brian, Donald *AmPS B*
Brian, Donald 1871-1948 *WhScrn 74, -77*
Brian, Donald 1875-1948 *CmpEPM, Film 1*
Brian, Donald 1877-1948 *EncMT, NotNAT B, WhThe, WhoHol B, WhoStg 1908*
Brian, Havergal 1876-1972 *Baker 78, MusMk[port], NewGrD 80, OxMus*
Brian, Mary 1908- *FilmEn, Film 2, FilmgC, ForYSC, HalFC 80, HolP 30[port], MovMk, ThFT[port], TwYS, What 4[port], WhoHol A*
Briansky, Oleg 1929- *CnOxB, DancEn 78*
Briant, Denis *NewGrD 80*
Briant, George Hamilton 1922-1946 *WhScrn 74, -77*
Briant, Shane 1946- *HalFC 80, WhoHrs 80*
Brianza, Carlotta 1867-1930 *CnOxB, DancEn 78*
Briard, Etienne *Baker 78, NewGrD 80*
Bricceltti, Thomas Gaetano 1936- *IntWWM 80*
Briccetti, Thomas B 1936- *AmSCAP 66, -80, Baker 78, ConAmC*
Briccetti, Thomas Gaetano 1936- *IntWWM 77*
Briccialdi, Giulio 1818-1881 *Baker 78, NewGrD 80*
Brice, Betty 1892-1935 *WhScrn 77*
Brice, Betty 1896-1935 *Film 2, WhScrn 74, WhoHol B*
Brice, Carol 1918- *DrBlPA, NotNAT*
Brice, Carol 1920- *BiE&WWA*
Brice, Edgar Pinder 1905- *WhoMus 72*
Brice, Elizabeth d1965 *AmPS B, CmpEPM*
Brice, Fanny 1891-1951 *AmPS B, BiDAmM, CmpEPM, EncMT, EncWT, Ent[port], FamA&A[port], FilmEn, Film 2, FilmgC, ForYSC, Funs[port], HalFC 80, JoeFr[port], MovMk, NotNAT A, -B, OxFilm, PlP&P[port], ThFT[port], WhScrn 74, -77, WhThe, WhoHol B*
Brice, Jean Anne 1938- *WhoMus 72*
Brice, Monte d1962 *NotNAT B*
Brice, Monte 1895- *TwYS A*
Brice, Rosetta *Film 1, MotPP*
Briceno, Luis De *NewGrD 80*
Brick *RkOn 2[port]*
Brickell, Beth *WhoHol A*
Brickell, Richard *PupTheA*
Bricken, Carl Ernest 1898-1971 *Baker 78, ConAmC*
Bricken, Carl Ernst 1898- *BiDAmM*
Bricker, Betty 1890-1954 *WhScrn 74, -77, WhoHol B*
Bricker, Herschel 1905- *NotNAT*
Bricker, Hershel 1905- *BiE&WWA*
Bricker, John W 1893- *What 1[port]*
Brickert, Carlton 1891-1943 *WhScrn 74, -77, WhoHol B*
Brickley, Charles E 1891-1949 *WhScrn 77*
Brickman, Joel Ira 1946- *AmSCAP 80, ConAmC, IntWWM 77, -80*
Brickman, Miriam 1933- *IntWWM 77, -80*
Brickner, Roy 1904- *IntMPA 77, -75, -76, -78, -79, -80*
Bricktop 1894- *DrBlPA*
Brico, Antonia 1902- *Baker 78, WomCom[port]*
Bricusse, Leslie 1931- *EncMT, FilmEn, FilmgC, HalFC 80, IntWWM 77, NotNAT*
Bricusse, Leslie 1933- *BestMus*
Bricusse And Newley *BestMus*
Bridcut, John Creighton 1952- *IntWWM 77, -80*
Bridel, Bedrich *NewGrD 80*
Bridge, Al 1891-1957 *HalFC 80, Vers B[port]*
Bridge, Alan 1891-1957 *WhScrn 77*
Bridge, Frank 1879-1941 *Baker 78, BnBkM 80, DcCom&M 79, DcCM, MusMk, NewGrD 80[port], OxMus*
Bridge, Sir Frederick 1844-1924 *NewGrD 80, OxMus*
Bridge, Geoffrey Stuart 1936- *IntWWM 80*
Bridge, Jean Ann 1936- *IntWWM 77, -80*
Bridge, Sir John Frederick 1844-1924 *Baker 78*
Bridge, Joseph Cox 1853-1929 *Baker 78, OxMus*
Bridge, Loie 1890-1974 *WhScrn 77*
Bridge, Peggy *PupTheA*
Bridge, Peter 1925- *WhoThe 72, -77*
Bridge, Richard d1758 *NewGrD 80*
Bridge, Tom W 1909- *IntMPA 75, -76*
Bridges, Alan 1927- *FilmEn, FilmgC, HalFC 80*
Bridges, Beau *WhoHol A*
Bridges, Beau 1941- *FilmEn, FilmgC, ForYSC, HalFC 80, IntMPA 77, -75, -76, -78, -79, -80*
Bridges, Beau 1942- *MovMk[port]*
Bridges, Ethel 1897- *AmSCAP 66, -80*
Bridges, Henry 1908- *OxMus, WhoJazz 72*
Bridges, James *FilmEn, IntMPA 77, -75, -76, -78, -79, -80*
Bridges, James 1928?- *HalFC 80*
Bridges, Jeff 1949- *FilmEn*
Bridges, Jeff 1950- *FilmgC, HalFC 80, MovMk, WhoHol A*
Bridges, Jeff 1951- *IntMPA 77, -75, -76, -78, -79, -80*
Bridges, John *OxThe*
Bridges, Lloyd 1913- *FilmEn, FilmgC, ForYSC, HalFC 80, IntMPA 77, -75, -76, -78, -79, -80, MotPP, MovMk[port], WhoHol A, WhoHrs 80*
Bridges, Lou 1917- *AmSCAP 66*
Bridges, Otis Cornelius 1916- *AmSCAP 66, -80*
Bridges, Richard d1758 *NewGrD 80*
Bridges, Robert 1844-1930 *OxMus*
Bridges, Thomas Whitney 1930- *IntWWM 77, -80*
Bridges-Adams, William 1889-1965 *BiE&WWA, WhThe*
Bridgetower, George Auguste Polgreen 1780-1860 *Baker 78*
Bridgetower, George Augustus Polgreen 1780-1860 *OxMus*
Bridgetower, George Polgreen 1779?-1860 *BiDAmM, NewGrD 80*
Bridgewater, Cecil Vernon 1942- *AmSCAP 80, EncJzS 70*
Bridgewater, Dee Dee 1950- *DrBlPA, EncJzS 70*
Bridgewater, Denise 1950- *EncJzS 70*
Bridgewater, Leslie 1893- *WhThe, WhoThe 72*
Bridgman, Nanie 1907- *NewGrD 80*
Bridie, James 1888-1951 *CnMD, CnThe, CroCD, EncWT, Ent, HalFC 80, McGEWD[port], ModWD, NotNAT A, -B, OxThe, PlP&P, REnWD[port], WhThe, WorEFlm[port]*
Briece, Jack 1945- *ConAmC*
Brief, Henry 1924- *ConMuA 80B, IntWWM 77*
Briegel, George F 1890- *AmSCAP 66, -80*
Briegel, James 1914- *IntWWM 77*
Briegel, Wolfgang Carl 1626-1712 *Baker 78, NewGrD 80*
Briel, Marie 1896- *BiDAmM*
Brien, Alan 1925- *WhoThe 72, -77*
Brien, Anja *WomWMM*
Brien, Lige *IntMPA 77, -75, -76, -78, -79, -80*
Brien, Roger 1910- *CreCan 1*
Brier, Percy 1885-1970 *NewGrD 80*
Briercliffe, Nellie d1966 *WhThe*
Brierley, David 1936- *WhoThe 77*
Briers, Richard 1934- *FilmgC, WhoThe 72, -77*
Briesc, Gerd *Film 2*
Briesger, Peter *NewGrD 80*
Brieux, Eugene 1858-1932 *CnMD, CnThe, McGEWD[port], ModWD, NotNAT B, OxThe, REnWD[port], WhThe*
Brigden, Frederick Henry 1871-1956 *CreCan 1*
Briggs, Arthur 1901- *WhoJazz 72*
Briggs, David *ConMuA 80B*
Briggs, Donald *WhoHol A*
Briggs, G Wright 1916- *AmSCAP 66, BiDAmM, ConAmC*
Briggs, George Wallace 1875-1959 *BiDAmM*
Briggs, George Wright, Jr. 1910- *AmSCAP 80*
Briggs, H B *OxMus*
Briggs, Hal 1881-1925 *WhScrn 77*
Briggs, Harlan 1880-1952 *FilmEn, ForYSC, HalFC 80, NotNAT B, Vers A[port], WhScrn 74, -77, WhoHol B*
Briggs, Harold 1915- *WhoMus 72*
Briggs, Hedley 1907-1968 *DancEn 78, WhThe*
Briggs, Howard 1942- *IntWWM 80*
Briggs, John Stewart 1948- *IntWWM 80*
Briggs, Johnny 1935- *HalFC 80*
Briggs, Lillian *RkOn[port]*
Briggs, Matt 1883-1962 *NotNAT B, WhScrn 74, -77, WhoHol B*
Briggs, Norma *WomWMM B*
Briggs, Oscar 1877-1928 *WhScrn 74, -77, WhoHol B*
Briggs, Pete 1904- *WhoJazz 72*
Briggs, Ralph 1901- *ConAmC*
Briggs, Wallace Neal 1914- *BiE&WWA, NotNAT*
Briggs, William A 1915- *BiE&WWA, NotNAT*
Briggs, Winifred G *PupTheA*
Brigham, William Stanhope 1938- *BiE&WWA*
Brighouse, Harold 1882-1958 *CnMD, CnThe, McGEWD[port], ModWD, NotNAT B, OxThe, WhThe*
Bright, Alma Louie *IntWWM 80, WhoMus 72*
Bright, Ann 1943- *IntWWM 77*
Bright, Clive John 1930- *WhoMus 72*
Bright, Delbert 1913- *WhoJazz 72*
Bright, Dudley 1953- *WhoMus 72*
Bright, Houston 1916- *AmSCAP 66, -80, BiDAmM, ConAmC*
Bright, Richard *WhoHol A*
Bright, Richard S 1936- *IntMPA 80*
Bright, Robert *WhoHol A*
Bright, Ronnell Lovelace 1930- *AmSCAP 66, -80, BiDAmM, EncJzS 70*
Bright, Sol Kekipi 1909- *AmSCAP 80*
Bright, Sol Kekipi 1919- *AmSCAP 66*
Brightman, Homer H *IntMPA 77, -75, -76, -78, -79, -80*
Brightman, Stanley 1888-1961 *WhThe*
Brightmore, C V *WhoMus 72*
Brighton, Albert 1876-1911 *WhScrn 77*
Brigido, Odemar 1941- *IntWWM 77, -80*
Brignola, Nicholas Thomas 1936- *BiDAmM*
Brignole, Rosa 1908- *AmSCAP 80*
Brignone, Giuseppe *EncWT*
Brignone, Guido *EncWT*
Brignone, Lilla 1913- *EncWT, Ent*
Brignone, Mercedes *Film 1*
Brigode, Ace d1960 *CmpEPM*
Brihuega, Bernaldino De *NewGrD 80*
Brilioth, Helge 1931- *IntWWM 80, NewGrD 80, WhoOp 76*
Brill, Joan Rothman 1930- *IntWWM 77, -80*
Brill, Marty *JoeFr, WhoHol A*
Brill, Patti 1923-1963 *WhScrn 77*
Brillstein, Bernie *ConMuA 80B*
Brim, Grace 1924?- *BluesWW[port]*
Brim, John 1922- *BluesWW[port]*
Brim, Mrs. John *BluesWW[port]*
Brimer, Michael 1933- *NewGrD 80*
Brimhall, John 1928- *AmSCAP 66, -80*
Brimle, Richard *NewGrD 80*
Brimlei, John 1502?-1576 *NewGrD 80*
Brimley, John 1502?-1576 *NewGrD 80*
Brimmer, Son *BluesWW[port]*
Brinck, Eva *IntWWM 77, -80*
Brinckerhoff, Burt 1936- *BiE&WWA, NotNAT*
Brinckman, Nan *ForYSC*
Brind, Richard d1718 *NewGrD 80*
Brind, Tessa *FilmEn, WhoHol A*
Brind'Amour, Yvette 1918- *CreCan 1*
Brindeau, Jeanne *Film 2*
Brindel, Bernard 1912- *ConAmC, IntWWM 77, -80*
Brindle, Reginald Smith 1917- *DcCM, IntWWM 77, -80, NewGrD 80,*

WhoMus 72
Brindley, Charles *Film 1*
Brindley, Gerry H 1935- *IntWWM 80*
Brindley, Giles 1926- *NewGrD 80*
Brindley, Madge d1968 *WhScrn 77*
Brindmour, George 1870-1941 *WhScrn 74, -77*
Brindus, Nicolae 1935- *Baker 78*
Brine, Mark Vincent 1948- *AmSCAP 80*
Brinegar, Paul *ForYSC, WhoHol A*
Briner, Andres 1923- *IntWWM 77, -80, NewGrD 80*
Bring, Lou *BgBands 74*
Brings, Allen Stephen 1934- *AmSCAP 80, CpmDNM 76, -77, -78, -79, -80, ConAmC, IntWWM 80*
Bringuer, Estela 1931 *ConAmC*
Brink, Elga *Film 2*
Brink, Philip *ConAmC*
Brinkley, David 1920- *IntMPA 77, -76, -78, -79, -80, NewYTET*
Brinkley, John *ForYSC*
Brinkley, Neil *Film 2*
Brinkman, Dolores *Film 2*
Brinkman, Ernest 1872-1938 *WhScrn 74, -77*
Brinkmann, Reinhold 1934- *IntWWM 77, -80, NewGrD 80*
Brinnen, Gerald Alexander 1932- *WhoMus 72*
Brinsley Schwarz *ConMuA 80A, IlEncR*
Brinsmead, John 1814-1908 *Baker 78*
Brinson, Peter 1923- *CnOxB, DancEn 78*
Brinson, Rosemary Greene 1917- *AmSCAP 66, -80*
Brion, Francoise 1934- *FilmAG WE*
Brioschi, Antonio *NewGrD 80*
Briou, Nicolas-Antoine Bergiron De *NewGrD 80*
Briquet *NewGrD 80*
Briquet, Jean 1864-1936 *NotNAT B*
Brisbane, Arthur *Film 2*
Briscoe, Chesley 1900- *AmSCAP 66*
Briscoe, Gerald 1923- *WhoMus 72*
Briscoe, Lottie d1950 *NotNAT B, WhoHol B*
Briscoe, Lottie 1881-1950 *WhScrn 74, -77*
Briscoe, Lottie 1883-1950 *Film 1*
Brisiensis, Preponitus *NewGrD 80*
Briskin, Barney 1893- *IntMPA 77, -75, -76, -78, -79*
Briskin, Irving 1903- *IntMPA 77, -75, -76, -78, -79, -80*
Briskin, Mort *IntMPA 77, -76, -78, -79, -80*
Brislee, Freda *WhoMus 72*
Brisman, Heskel 1923- *AmSCAP 80, CpmDNM 78, ConAmC*
Brissac, Virginia *ForYSC, HalFC 80, WhoHol A*
Brissac, Virginia 1895?-1979 *FilmEn*
Brissia, Melchior De *NewGrD 80*
Brisson, Carl d1958 *WhoHol B*
Brisson, Carl 1893-1958 *IlWWBF[port], WhScrn 74, -77*
Brisson, Carl 1895-1958 *EncMT, FilmEn, FilmgC, HalFC 80, NotNAT B, WhThe*
Brisson, Carl 1897-1958 *Film 2*
Brisson, Cleo 1894-1975 *WhScrn 77*
Brisson, Frederick 1912- *FilmEn*
Brisson, Frederick 1913- *BiE&WWA, IntMPA 77, -75, -76, -78, -79, -80, NotNAT, WhoThe 72, -77*
Brisson, Frederick 1915?- *FilmgC, HalFC 80*
Brister, Robert S 1889-1945 *WhScrn 74, -77, WhoHol B*
Bristol, Johnny *DrBlPA, RkOn 2[port]*
Bristol, Margaret *AmSCAP 66, -80*
Bristow, Charles 1928- *WhoThe 72, -77*
Bristow, Daniel LeRoy 1924- *IntWWM 77, -80*
Bristow, G F *OxMus*
Bristow, George Frederick 1825-1898 *Baker 78, BiDAmM, NewGrD 80*
Bristow, William Richard 1803-1867 *BiDAmM*
Britain, Radie 1903- *Baker 78, BiDAmM, ConAmC, WomCom[port]*
Britain, Radie 1904- *AmSCAP 66*
Britain, Radie 1906- *WhoMus 72*
Britain, Radie 1908- *AmSCAP 80, CpmDNM 76, -77, -78, -79, IntWWM 77, -80*
Britannicus *CreCan 2*
Brito, Amparo 1950- *CnOxB*
Brito, Estevao De 1575?-1641 *NewGrD 80*
Brito, Phil 1915- *AmSCAP 66, CmpEPM*
Britt, Addy 1891-1938 *AmSCAP 66, -80*
Britt, Ben *AmSCAP 80*
Britt, Elton 1912-1972 *CmpEPM, WhScrn 77*
Britt, Elton 1913- *AmSCAP 66, -80, BiDAmM*
Britt, Elton 1917- *CounME 74A, EncFCWM 69*
Britt, Elton 1917-1972 *CounME 74, IlEncCM[port]*
Britt, Horace 1881-1971 *Baker 78, BiDAmM*
Britt, Leo 1908- *IntMPA 75*
Britt, May 1933- *FilmEn, FilmgC, ForYSC, HalFC 80, MotPP, WhoHol A*
Britt, Patrick Eugene 1940- *AmSCAP 80*
Brittain, Donald Code 1928- *CreCan 2*
Brittain, Miller Gore 1912-1968 *CreCan 2*
Britten, Benjamin 1913-1976 *Baker 78, BnBkM 80[port], CmOp[port], CompSN[port], CnOxB, DancEn 78, DcCom 77[port], DcCom&M 79, DcCM, IntWWM 77, MusMk[port], NewEOp 71, NewGrD 80[port], OxFilm, OxMus, WhoMus 72*
Britten, David Ralph 1953- *IntWWM 80*
Britton, Allen Perdue 1914- *IntWWM 80*
Britton, Barbara *IntMPA 77, -75, -76, -78, -79, -80, MotPP*
Britton, Barbara 1919- *HolP 40[port]*
Britton, Barbara 1919-1980 *FilmEn*
Britton, Barbara 1920- *FilmgC, ForYSC, HalFC 80, WhoHol A*
Britton, Barbara 1923- *MovMk*
Britton, Clifton d1963 *NotNAT B*
Britton, David James 1942- *IntWWM 77, -80*
Britton, Donald 1919- *IntWWM 77, -80*
Britton, Donald 1929- *CnOxB, DancEn 78*
Britton, Donald 1937- *WhoOp 76*
Britton, Dorothy Guyver 1922- *ConAmC*
Britton, Edna *Film 1*
Britton, Ethel 1915-1972 *WhScrn 77, WhoHol B*
Britton, Frank And Milt *BgBands 74*
Britton, Harry 1878-1958 *CreCan 1*
Britton, Hutin 1876-1965 *Film 1, -2, OxThe, WhThe*
Britton, Joe 1905- *WhoJazz 72*
Britton, Keith 1919-1970 *WhScrn 77*
Britton, Lilian *WhoStg 1908*
Britton, Melba Logue 1926- *IntWWM 77*
Britton, Milt 1894-1948 *WhScrn 74, -77, WhoHol B*
Britton, Noel Eric John 1915- *IntWWM 80*
Britton, Pamela 1923-1974 *ForYSC, HalFC 80, MotPP, WhScrn 77, WhoHol B*
Britton, Ronnie *AmSCAP 80*
Britton, Sherry 1924- *What 4[port]*
Britton, Thomas 1644-1714 *MusMk[port], NewGrD 80, OxMus*
Britton, Tony 1924- *FilmEn, IlWWBF, IntMPA 77, -75, -76, -78, -79, -80, WhoHol A, WhoThe 72, -77*
Britton, Tony 1925- *FilmgC, HalFC 80*
Brivio, Giuseppe Ferdinando d1758? *NewGrD 80*
Brix, Herman *FilmEn, ForYSC, WhoHol A*
Brixel, Eugen Johann Carl 1939- *IntWWM 77, -80*
Brixi *NewGrD 80*
Brixi, Frantisek Xaver 1732-1771 *NewGrD 80*
Brixi, Franz Xaver 1732-1771 *Baker 78, NewGrD 80*
Brixi, Jan Josef 1712?-1762 *NewGrD 80*
Brixi, Jeronym 1738-1803 *NewGrD 80*
Brixi, Simon 1693-1735 *NewGrD 80*
Brixi, Vaclav Norbert 1738-1803 *NewGrD 80*
Brixi, Viktorin 1716-1803 *NewGrD 80*
Brixides, Jan 1712?-1772? *NewGrD 80*
Brixiensis, Giovanni Battista *NewGrD 80*
Brixiensis, Prepositus *NewGrD 80*
Brizard, Jean-Baptiste 1721-1791 *OxThe*
Brizeno, Luis De *NewGrD 80*
Brkanovic, Ivan 1906- *Baker 78, NewGrD 80*
Brncic, Gabriel 1942- *DcCM, NewGrD 80*
Brncic Isaza, Gabriel 1942- *IntWWM 77*
Broad, Kid *Film 2*
Broadbent, Alan 1947- *AmSCAP 80, EncJzS 70*
Broadhurst, Cecil Arthur 1908- *AmSCAP 66, -80*
Broadhurst, George Howells 1866-1952 *ModWD, NotNAT B, OxThe, WhThe*
Broadhurst, Thomas W d1936 *NotNAT B*
Broadley, Edward d1947 *WhScrn 77*
Broadway, Richard d1760 *NewGrD 80*
Broadwood, Henry John Tschudi d1911 *Baker 78*
Broadwood, James Shudi 1772-1851 *Baker 78*
Broadwood, John *OxMus*
Broadwood, John 1732-1812 *Baker 78, OxMus*
Broadwood, Lucy Etheldred 1858-1929 *NewGrD 80, OxMus*
Broadwood, Thomas *Baker 78*
Broadwood & Sons *Baker 78*
Broca, Philippe De 1933- *FilmEn*
Broca, Philippe De 1935- *DcFM*
Brocarte, Antonio DeLaCruz d1716? *NewGrD 80*
Brocco, Giovanni *NewGrD 80*
Brocco, Nicolo *NewGrD 80*
Brocco, Peter *ForYSC, WhoHol A*
Broccoli, Albert R 1909- *FilmEn, FilmgC, HalFC 80, IntMPA 77, -75, -76, -78, -79, -80, WhoHrs 80*
Broche, Charles 1752-1803 *Baker 78, NewGrD 80*
Brochet, Henri 1898-1952 *OxThe*
Brochier, Antoine *NewGrD 80*
Brochu, Andre 1942- *CreCan 2*
Brock, Baby Dorothy *Film 2*
Brock, Blanche Kerr 1888-1958 *AmSCAP 66, -80, ConAmC*
Brock, Charles *ConAmTC*
Brock, Dorothy *Film 2*
Brock, Douglas H 1950- *IntWWM 77*
Brock, Karena 1942- *CnOxB*
Brock, Karl 1930- *WhoOp 76*
Brock, Peggi 1916- *IntWWM 77, -80, WhoMus 72*
Brock, Petr 1932- *IntWWM 77, -80*
Brock, Tony d1924 *WhScrn 77*
Brock, Virgil P 1887- *AmSCAP 66, -80*
Brockband, Harrison d1947 *NotNAT B*
Brockes, Barthold Heinrich 1680-1747 *NewGrD 80*
Brockett, O G 1923- *BiE&WWA, NotNAT*
Brockett, Timothy C 1922- *AmSCAP 66*
Brockhaus, H Alfred 1930- *IntWWM 77, -80*
Brockhaus, Heinz Alfred 1930- *NewGrD 80*
Brockhaus, Max 1867-1957 *NewGrD 80*
Brockland, Corneille De *NewGrD 80*
Brockland, Cornelius *NewGrD 80*
Brocklebank, Arthur 1930- *IntWWM 80*
Brocklebank, George Frederick Arthur 1930- *WhoMus 72*
Brocklehurst, John Brian *IntWWM 77, -80, WhoMus 72*
Brockless, Brian 1926- *IntWWM 80, WhoMus 72*
Brockman, Harry 1904-1972 *BiDAmM*
Brockman, James 1886-1967 *AmSCAP 66, -80, BiDAmM*
Brockman, Jane E 1949- *ConAmC*
Brockman, Susan *WomWMM B*
Brockman, Thomas 1922- *IntWWM 77, -80*
Brockmann *Film 2*
Brockmann, Johann Franz Hieronymus 1745-1812 *OxThe*
Brockpahler, Renate 1927- *IntWWM 77, -80*
Brockshorn, Samuel Friedrich *NewGrD 80*
Brockt, Johannes 1901- *WhoMus 72*
Brockway, Althea *PupTheA*
Brockway, Howard A 1870-1951 *Baker 78, BiDAmM, ConAmC, NewGrD 80*
Brockway, Jennie M 1886- *AmSCAP 66, -80*
Brockway, Oliver M W 1946- *IntWWM 77, -80*
Brockway, Peter 1931- *WhoMus 72*
Brockwell, Billie *Film 1*
Brockwell, Gladys d1929 *MotPP, WhoHol B*
Brockwell, Gladys 1893-1930 *Film 1, -2, TwYS*
Brockwell, Gladys 1894-1929 *FilmEn, ForYSC, WhScrn 74, -77*
Brod, Max 1884-1968 *Baker 78, McGEWD[port], NewEOp 71, NewGrD 80*
Brodacki, Krystian Wladyslaw Szymon 1937- *IntWWM 77, -80*
Brodal, Jon Eilif *IntWWM 80*
Brodax, Albert P 1926- *AmSCAP 80*

Brode, Douglas Isaac 1943- ConAmTC
Broder, Dick ConMuA 80B
Broder, Jane BiE&WWA
Broder, Nathan 1905-1967 Baker 78, NewGrD 80
Broder, Teodor 1933- IntWWM 77, -80, NewGrD 80
Broderick, Golda Avril 1919- IntWWM 80
Broderick, Helen d1959 MotPP, WhoHol B
Broderick, Helen 1890-1959 FilmgC, HalFC 80
Broderick, Helen 1891-1959 EncMT, FilmEn, Film 2, ForYSC, HolCA[port], MovMk[port], NotNAT B, ThFT[port], Vers A[port], WhScrn 74, -77, WhThe
Broderick, James IntMPA 79, -80
Broderick, James 1929- NotNAT, WhoHol A
Broderick, James 1930- HalFC 80
Broderick, Johnny 1901-1977 AmSCAP 66, -80
Broderip NewGrD 80
Broderip, Edmund 1727?-1779 NewGrD 80
Broderip, Francis Fane 1750?-1807 NewGrD 80
Broderip, John 1719-1770 NewGrD 80
Broderip, Robert 1758?-1808 NewGrD 80
Broderip, William 1683-1727 NewGrD 80
Brodie, Buster 1886-1948 Film 2, WhScrn 74, -77, WhoHol B
Brodie, Steve 1919- FilmEn, FilmgC, ForYSC, HalFC 80, WhoHol A
Brodie And Middleton DcPup
Brodin, Lena Birgitta Elise 1941- IntWWM 80
Brodin, Norbert 1897-1970 FilmEn
Brodine, Norbert 1893-1970 HalFC 80
Brodine, Norbert 1895?-1970 FilmgC
Brodine, Norbert 1897- WorEFlm[port]
Brodkin, Herbert 1912- IntMPA 77, -75, -76, -78, -79, -80, NewYTET
Brodney, Oscar 1905- FilmgC, HalFC 80, IntMPA 77, -75, -76, -78, -79, -80
Brodney, Oscar 1907- FilmEn
Brodshaug, Melvin 1900- IntMPA 77, -75, -76, -78, -79, -80
Brodsky, Adolf 1851-1929 Baker 78
Brodsky, Adolph 1851-1929 NewGrD 80
Brodsky, Jack IntMPA 77, -75, -76, -78, -79, -80
Brodsky, Vera Baker 78
Brodszky, Nicholas 1905- CmpEPM, FilmgC, HalFC 80
Brody, Ann 1884-1944 WhScrn 74, -77
Brody, Ann 1894-1944 Film 2, ForYSC, WhoHol B
Brody, Anna 1894-1944 Film 1, TwYS
Brody, David S 1955- AmSCAP 80
Brody, Elaine 1923- IntWWM 77, -80
Brody, Estelle 1904- FilmEn, Film 2, IlWWBF[port]
Brody, Joshua 1916- ConAmC
Brody, Murray Lee 1909- AmSCAP 66, -80
Brody, Sarmad 1941- CpmDNM 72
Brody, Selma Ruth 1926- AmSCAP 80
Brody Singers OxThe
Broeder, Ray 1898- BiE&WWA, NotNAT
Broege, Timothy 1947- ConAmC
Broekman, David 1902-1958 Baker 78, ConAmC
Broekman, David Hendrines 1899-1958 AmSCAP 80
Broekman, David Hendrines 1902-1958 AmSCAP 66
Broekstra, Hendrik Jan 1924- IntWWM 80
Brofsky, Howard 1927- IntWWM 77, -80
Brogden, Gwendoline 1891- WhThe
Brogi, Renato 1873-1924 Baker 78
Brogna, Joseph, Jr. 1926- IntWWM 77
Brognoligo, Orazio 1577?-1623 NewGrD 80
Brognonico, Orazio 1577?-1623 NewGrD 80
Brogue, Roslyn 1919- Baker 78, CpmDNM 75, ConAmC
Brohn, William David 1933- AmSCAP 80
Broido, Arnold Peace 1920- IntWWM 77, -80
Broidy, Steve 1905- IntMPA 77, -75, -76, -78, -79, -80
Broier, Antoine NewGrD 80
Brojer, Robert 1919- IntWWM 77, -80
Brokaw, Charles 1898-1975 WhScrn 77, WhoHol C
Brokaw, Norman R 1927- IntMPA 77, -75, -76, -78, -79, -80
Brokaw, Tom IntMPA 78, -79, -80, NewYTET
Broke, Charles Frederick Tucker 1883-1946 NotNAT B
Brolin, James IntMPA 77, -75, -76, WhoHol A
Brolin, James 1940- FilmEn, HalFC 80, MovMk, WhoHrs 80
Brolin, James 1941- FilmgC
Brolin, James 1942- IntMPA 78, -79, -80
Brollo, Bartolomeo NewGrD 80
Brollo, Bartolomeus NewGrD 80
Brolo, Bartolomeo NewGrD 80
Brolo, Bartolomeus NewGrD 80
Brom, Gustav 1921- EncJzS 70
Broma, Carleton AmSCAP 80
Broman, K Natanael 1887- OxMus
Broman, Natanael 1887-1966 Baker 78
Broman, Sten 1902- Baker 78, MusMk, NewGrD 80
Bromberg, David 1945- AmSCAP 80, ConMuA 80A, IlEncR, IntWWM 77
Bromberg, Edward J MotPP
Bromberg, J Edward 1903-1951 FilmEn, FilmgC, ForYSC, HalFC 80, HolCA[port], MovMk, NotNAT B, PlP&P, WhScrn 74, -77, WhoHol B
Bromberg, J Edward 1904-1951 Vers A[port], WhThe
Bromberger, Herve 1918- FilmEn, FilmgC, HalFC 80
Brome, Alexander d1666 NotNAT B
Brome, Richard 1590?-1652? CnThe, McGEWD, REnWD[port]
Brome, Richard 1590?-1653 NotNAT B, OxThe
Bromfield, Edward, Jr. 1723-1806 BiDAmM
Bromfield, John 1922- FilmEn, FilmgC, ForYSC, HalFC 80, IntMPA 77, -75, -76, -78, -79, -80, MotPP, WhoHol A
Bromfield, Louis 1896-1956 NotNAT B
Bromhead, Michael 1924- IntMPA 77, -75, -76, -78, -79, -80
Bromhead, Ralph S 1906- IntMPA 77, -75, -76, -78, -79, -80
Bromiley, Dorothy 1935- FilmgC, HalFC 80
Bromilow, Peter WhoHol A
Bromley, Bob PupTheA, PupTheA SUP
Bromley, Brian 1942- WhoMus 72
Bromley, Nellie d1939 NotNAT B
Bromley, Sheila 1911- ForYSC, ThFT[port], WhoHol A
Bromley-Davenport, Arthur 1867-1946 NotNAT B, WhThe
Brommel, Antoine NewGrD 80
Bron, Eleanor IntMPA 75, -76, -78, -79, -80
Bron, Eleanor 1934- FilmEn, FilmgC, HalFC 80, IntMPA 77, WhoHol A, WhoThe 77
Bron, Eleanor 1939?- ForYSC
Bronarski, Ludwik 1890-1975 NewGrD 80
Broncho Billy MotPP, OxFilm
Bronckhorst, Arnold Matthias NewGrD 80
Brondfield, Jerome 1913- IntMPA 77, -75, -76, -78, -79, -80
Broneau, Helen Film 2
Bronnemuller, Elias 1666?-1762? NewGrD 80
Bronnen, Arnolt 1895-1959 CnMD, CroCD, EncWT, Ent, McGEWD, ModWD
Bronner, Edwin 1926- BiE&WWA, NotNAT
Bronner, Georg 1667-1720 NewGrD 80
Bronner, Jurgen 1667-1720 NewGrD 80
Bronner, Robert WorEFlm[port]
Brons, Carel 1931- Baker 78, NewGrD 80
Bronsart VonSchellendorf, Hans 1830-1913 Baker 78, NewGrD 80
Bronsart VonSchellendorf, Ingeborg 1840-1913 Baker 78
Bronson, Benjamin 1896- AmSCAP 66
Bronson, Bertrand Harris 1902- IntWWM 80
Bronson, Betty 1906-1971 FilmEn, Film 2, FilmgC, ForYSC, HalFC 80, MotPP, MovMk, ThFT[port], TwYS, WhScrn 74, WhoHol B
Bronson, Betty 1907-1971 What 3[port], WhScrn 77
Bronson, Charles WhoHol A
Bronson, Charles 1920- BiDFilm 81, ForYSC, IntMPA 77, -75, -76, -78, -79, -80, MovMk
Bronson, Charles 1921- FilmEn
Bronson, Charles 1922- FilmgC, HalFC 80, WhoHrs 80
Bronson, Lillian 1902- ForYSC, HalFC 80, Vers A[port], WhoHol A
Bronson, Menzo Frank 1928- AmSCAP 80
Bronson, Michael 1938- WhoOp 76
Bronstein, Robert 1934- WhoMus 72
Bronston, Samuel IntMPA 75, -76, -78, -79, -80
Bronston, Samuel 1909- FilmEn, WorEFlm[port]
Bronston, Samuel 1910- CmMov, DcFM, FilmgC, HalFC 80, IntMPA 77
Bronte, Charlotte 1816-1855 FilmgC, HalFC 80, NotNAT B
Bronte, Emily 1818-1848 FilmgC, HalFC 80
Bronte, Jean Film 2
Brook, Barry S 1918- AmSCAP 66, -80, IntWWM 77, -80, NewGrD 80
Brook, Clive 1886-1974 What 4[port]
Brook, Clive 1887-1974 FilmAG WE, FilmEn, FilmgC, HalFC 80, IlWWBF[port], MotPP, MovMk, WhScrn 77, WhThe, WhoHol B, WhoThe 72, WorEFlm[port]
Brook, Clive 1891-1974 BiDFilm, -81, Film 2, ForYSC, TwYS
Brook, Faith 1922- FilmgC, HalFC 80, WhoThe 72, -77
Brook, Gwendolyn Giffen 1930- IntWWM 77
Brook, Helen Film 2
Brook, Hugh Film 2
Brook, Lesley 1916- FilmgC, HalFC 80, IlWWBF[port]
Brook, Lesley 1917- WhThe
Brook, Lyndon 1926- FilmgC, HalFC 80
Brook, Olive Film 2
Brook, Peter 1925- BiDFilm, -81, BiE&WWA, CmOp, CnThe, CroCD, DcFM, EncWT, Ent, FilmEn, FilmgC, HalFC 80, IlWWBF, -A, MovMk[port], NewGrD 80, NotNAT, -A, OxFilm, OxThe, PlP&P[port], WhoMus 72, WhoOp 76, WhoThe 72, -77, WorEFlm[port]
Brook, Sara WhoThe 77
Brook-Jones, Elwyn 1911-1962 FilmgC, HalFC 80, NotNAT B, WhScrn 74, -77, WhThe, WhoHol B
Brooke, Claude 1853-1933 Film 2, WhScrn 74, -77, WhoHol B
Brooke, Clifford 1872-1951 WhScrn 74, -77, WhoHol B
Brooke, Cynthia 1875-1949 NotNAT B, WhThe
Brooke, Mrs. E H d1915 WhThe
Brooke, Emily d1953 NotNAT B, WhThe
Brooke, Frances d1789 NotNAT B
Brooke, Gustavus Vaughan 1818-1860 NotNAT A, -B
Brooke, Gustavus Vaughan 1818-1866 OxThe
Brooke, Gwydion 1912- NewGrD 80
Brooke, H Sullivan d1923 NotNAT B
Brooke, Harold 1910- WhoThe 72, -77
Brooke, Henry 1703-1783 NotNAT B
Brooke, Hillary IntMPA 75
Brooke, Hillary 1914- FilmEn, What 5[port], WhoHol A
Brooke, Hillary 1916- FilmgC, ForYSC, HalFC 80, MovMk
Brooke, Iris 1908- BiE&WWA, NotNAT
Brooke, Ken MagIlD
Brooke, Myra 1865-1944 WhScrn 74, -77
Brooke, Peter R 1921- IntMPA 77, -75, -76
Brooke, Peter R 1929- IntMPA 78, -79, -80
Brooke, Ralph 1920-1963 WhScrn 77
Brooke, Sarah WhThe
Brooke, Tyler 1891-1943 Film 2, ForYSC TwYS, WhScrn 74, -77, WhoHol B
Brooke, VanDyke FilmEn
Brooke, VanDyke d1921 Film 1, -2, TwYS, WhScrn 77
Brooke, Walter ForYSC, WhoHol A
Brooker, Bertram Richard 1888-1955 CreCan 1
Brookes, Charles Film 1
Brookes, Jacqueline 1930- BiE&WWA, NotNAT, WhoThe 72, -77
Brookes, Oliver 1922- WhoMus 72
Brookfield, Charles Hallam Elton 1857-1913 NotNAT B, WhThe
Brookfield, Sydney F d1916 NotNAT B

Brooking, Dorothea 1916- *IntMPA 77, –75, –76, –78, –79, –80*
Brooking, Eleunid Mair Howard 1921- *WhoMus 72*
Brooklyn Bridge, The *RkOn 2[port]*
Brookmeyer, Bob 1929- *CmpEPM, EncJzS 70, IlEncJ*
Brookmeyer, Robert 1929- *BiDAmM, EncJzS 70*
Brooks, Alan 1888-1936 *Film 2, WhScrn 74, –77, WhoHol B*
Brooks, Anne Sooy 1911- *AmSCAP 66*
Brooks, Charles Timothy 1813-1883 *BiDAmM*
Brooks, Charlotte K *BlkAmP*
Brooks, Clarence 1895?- *BlksB&W[port], –C, DrBlPA*
Brooks, David 1920- *BiE&WWA, NotNAT*
Brooks, Dick *IntMPA 77, –75, –76, –78, –79, –80*
Brooks, Donald 1928- *BiE&WWA, NotNAT*
Brooks, Donnie *RkOn*
Brooks, Dudley Alonzo 1913- *AmSCAP 80*
Brooks, Elkie *IlEncR*
Brooks, Elston *ConAmTC*
Brooks, Foster *JoeFr*
Brooks, Fred *AmSCAP 80*
Brooks, Garnet James 1936- *WhoOp 76*
Brooks, Geraldine 1925- *BiE&WWA, FilmgC, ForYSC, HolP 40[port], IntMPA 77, –75, –76, NotNAT A, WhoHol A*
Brooks, Geraldine 1925-1977 *FilmEn, HalFC 80*
Brooks, Mrs. Gorham *OxMus*
Brooks, Hank d1925 *WhScrn 74, –77, WhoHol B*
Brooks, Harry 1895-1970 *AmSCAP 66, –80, BiDAmM*
Brooks, Harvey *AmSCAP 80*
Brooks, Harvey O 1898-1968 *WhoJazz 72*
Brooks, Harvey Oliver 1899- *AmSCAP 66, –80*
Brooks, Hazel *WhoHol A*
Brooks, Iris *WhoHol A*
Brooks, Jack 1912- *AmPS, AmSCAP 66, –80, BiDAmM*
Brooks, James L And Allan Burns *NewYTET*
Brooks, Jean 1916- *FilmEn*
Brooks, Jean 1921- *FilmgC, HalFC 80*
Brooks, Jennie *BluesWW[port]*
Brooks, Jess Lee 1894-1944 *WhScrn 74, –77, WhoHol B*
Brooks, Jesse Lee *BlksB&W C*
Brooks, Joe *NewOrJ*
Brooks, John Benson 1917- *AmSCAP 66, –80, Baker 78, ConAmC*
Brooks, Joseph *IntMPA 79, –80*
Brooks, Joseph 1938- *AmSCAP 80*
Brooks, Laurence *AmPS B*
Brooks, Lawrence 1912- *BiE&WWA, NotNAT*
Brooks, Leslie 1922- *FilmEn, FilmgC, ForYSC, HalFC 80, WhoHol A*
Brooks, Leslie Gene 1936- *IntWWM 77*
Brooks, Lonnie 1933- *BluesWW[port]*
Brooks, Louise *MotPP*
Brooks, Louise 1900- *Film 2, FilmgC, MovMk, WorEFlm[port]*
Brooks, Louise 1905- *ForYSC, WhoHol A*
Brooks, Louise 1906- *BiDFilm, –81, FilmEn, HalFC 80, OxFilm, ThFT[port], TwYS, What 3[port]*
Brooks, Lucius *BlksB&W C*
Brooks, Marion *Film 1*
Brooks, Marion 1874-1914 *BlksBF*
Brooks, Mary *WhoHol A*
Brooks, May K d1963 *NotNAT B*
Brooks, Mel *BiE&WWA, IntMPA 75, –76, NewYTET*
Brooks, Mel 1926- *BiDFilm 81, FilmEn, IntMPA 77, –78, –79, –80, JoeFr[port], MovMk[port]*
Brooks, Mel 1927- *HalFC 80*
Brooks, Mel 1928- *FilmgC, WhoHrs 80[port]*
Brooks, Nigel James 1928- *IntWWM 77*
Brooks, Norman 1928?- *CmpEPM*
Brooks, Patricia Anne 1937- *NewGrD 80, WhoOp 76*
Brooks, Pauline 1913-1967 *WhScrn 74, –77, WhoHol B*
Brooks, Phillips 1835-1893 *BiDAmM*
Brooks, Phyllis 1914- *FilmEn, FilmgC, ForYSC, HalFC 80, ThFT[port], WhoHol A*
Brooks, Rand 1918- *FilmEn*
Brooks, Rand 1918-1967 *FilmgC, ForYSC, HalFC 80, WhoHol A*
Brooks, Randy d1967 *BgBands 74[port]*
Brooks, Randy 1917-1967 *CmpEPM*
Brooks, Randy 1918-1967 *WhScrn 74, –77, WhoHol B*
Brooks, Ray 1939- *FilmEn, FilmgC, HalFC 80*
Brooks, Richard 1912- *AmFD, BiDFilm, –81, ConDr 73, –77A, DcFM, FilmEn, FilmgC, HalFC 80, IntMPA 77, –75, –76, –78, –79, –80, MovMk[port], OxFilm, WorEFlm[port]*
Brooks, Richard Allman 1940- *AmSCAP 80*
Brooks, Richard James 1942- *ConAmC*
Brooks, Roy *Film 2*
Brooks, Roy 1938- *EncJzS 70*
Brooks, Shelton *BlksB&W, –C*
Brooks, Shelton 1886-1975 *AmPS, AmSCAP 66, –80, BiDAmM, CmpEPM, JoeFr, PopAmC, PopAmC SUPN*
Brooks, Shelton 1896-1975 *BlksBF*
Brooks, Shirley d1874 *NotNAT B*
Brooks, Thor L *IntMPA 77, –75, –76, –78, –79, –80*
Brooks, Valerie *AmSCAP 80*
Brooks, Virginia *WomWMM B*
Brooks, Virginia Fox *WhThe*
Brooks, William 1943- *ConAmC*
Brooks, William Lupton 1900- *WhoMus 72*
Brooks, Wilson d1967 *WhoHol B*
Broome, Barbara Cummings *MorBAP*
Broome, Oliver 1935- *WhoMus 72*
Broome, William Edward 1868-1932 *Baker 78*
Broomsley, Big Bill *BluesWW[port]*
Broones, Martin 1892- *AmSCAP 66, WhThe*
Broones, Martin 1903-1971 *AmSCAP 80*
Broonzy, Big Bill 1893-1958 *BiDAmM, CmpEPM, IlEncJ, NewGrD 80*
Broonzy, Big Bill 1898?-1958 *EncFCWM 69*
Broonzy, William Lee Conley 1893-1958 *BluesWW[port]*
Brophy, Brigid 1929- *ConDr 73, –77*
Brophy, Ed 1895-1960 *ForYSC, HolCA[port], WhoHol B*
Brophy, Edward 1895-1960 *Film 2, FilmgC, MotPP, NotNAT B, WhScrn 74, –77*
Brophy, Edward 1900-1960 *MovMk[port], Vers A[port]*
Brophy, Edward S 1895-1960 *FilmEn, HalFC 80*
Broqua, Alfonso 1876-1946 *Baker 78, NewGrD 80*
Bros Y Bertomeu, Juan 1776?-1852 *NewGrD 80*
Brosa, Antonio 1894-1979 *NewGrD 80, WhoMus 72*
Brosca, Riccardo 1698?-1756 *NewGrD 80*
Brosch, Barry A 1942- *ConAmC*
Brosche, Gunter 1939- *NewGrD 80*
Broschi, Carlo *Baker 78, BnBkM 80, NewGrD 80*
Broschi, Riccardo 1698?-1756 *NewGrD 80*
Broscius, Jan 1585-1652 *NewGrD 80*
Brosh, Thomas 1946- *CpmDNM 73, –74, –76, –77, –78, –79, ConAmC*
Brosig, Egon 1890-1961 *WhScrn 74, –77*
Brosig, Moritz 1815-1887 *Baker 78*
Broske, Octavia *Film 2*
Brosmann, Antonin 1731-1798 *NewGrD 80*
Brosmann, Damasus 1731-1798 *NewGrD 80*
Brossard, Noel-Matthieu 1789- *Baker 78*
Brossard, Sebastien De 1655-1730 *Baker 78, NewGrD 80, OxMus*
Brosses, Charles De 1709-1777 *Baker 78, OxMus*
Brosset, Yvonne 1935- *CnOxB, DancEn 78*
Brost, Raymond *NewGrD 80*
Broster, Eileen 1935- *IntWWM 80, WhoMus 72*
Broszkiewicz, Jerzy 1922- *CroCD, ModWD*
Brother Blues *BluesWW[port]*
Brother Bones *WhScrn 77*
Brother George *BluesWW[port]*
Brother Joshua *BluesWW[port]*
Brotherhood, The *BiDAmM*
Brotherhood, William *Film 1*
Brotherhood Of Man *RkOn 2A*
Brothers, Cassandra F *WhoHol A*
Brothers, Joyce 1928- *NewYTET*
Brothers, Lester D 1945- *IntWWM 80*
Brothers Four, The *BiDAmM, EncFCWM 69, RkOn[port]*
Brothers Johnson, The *RkOn 2[port]*
Brotherson, Eric 1911- *WhoThe 72, –77*
Brothwood, Constance Edna 1925- *IntWWM 77, –80*
Brott, Alexander 1915- *Baker 78, CreCan 2, DcCM, IntWWM 80, NewGrD 80*
Brott, Boris 1944- *CreCan 1, IntWWM 77, –80, NewGrD 80*
Brott, Charlotte *CreCan 2*
Brott, Denis 1950- *IntWWM 77, –80*
Brott, Lotte *CreCan 2*
Brotzmann, Peter 1941- *EncJzS 70*
Brouck, Jacob De *NewGrD 80*
Broude, Alexander 1909- *NewGrD 80*
Broude Brothers *NewGrD 80*
Brouett, Albert *WhThe*
Brough, Fanny Whiteside 1854-1914 *NotNAT B, OxThe, WhThe*
Brough, George *CreCan 1, IntWWM 77, –80*
Brough, John Stuart 1907- *WhoMus 72*
Brough, Lionel 1836-1900 *NotNAT B, OxThe*
Brough, Mary 1863-1934 *Film 2, FilmgC, HalFC 80, IlWWBF[port], NotNAT B, OxThe, WhScrn 74, –77, WhThe, WhoHol B*
Brough, Robert d1906 *NotNAT B*
Brough, Mrs. Robert d1932 *NotNAT B, WhThe*
Brough, Robert Barnabas 1828-1860 *NotNAT B, OxThe*
Brough, Sydney 1868-1911 *NotNAT B, OxThe*
Brough, William 1826-1870 *NotNAT B, OxThe*
Brougham, John 1810-1880 *FamA&A[port], NotNAT B, OxThe, PlP&P*
Broughton, James *WorEFlm[port]*
Broughton, Jessie 1885- *WhThe*
Broughton, Philip F 1893- *AmSCAP 66, –80*
Broughton, Phyllis d1926 *WhThe*
Broughton, Simon J d1964 *NotNAT B*
Brouillon-Lacombe, Louis *Baker 78*
Brouk, Joanna 1949- *ConAmC*
Broumas, John G 1917- *IntMPA 77, –75, –76, –78, –79, –80*
Broun, Heywood 1888-1939 *NotNAT B, WhThe*
Broun, Heywood Hale 1918- *BiE&WWA, NotNAT, –A, PlP&P*
Brouncker, William 1620-1684 *NewGrD 80*
Brounckerd, William 1620-1684 *NewGrD 80*
Brouno, Guillelmo *NewGrD 80*
Brouno, Guillermo *NewGrD 80*
Brounoff, Platon 1863-1924 *Baker 78*
Brounoff, Platon 1869-1924 *BiDAmM*
Broussard, Theo *NewOrJ*
Brouwenstijn, Gre 1915- *CmOp, NewGrD 80, WhoMus 72*
Brouwer, Leo 1939- *NewGrD 80*
Browder, Earl 1891- *What 3[port]*
Browder, Robert *Film 2*
Brower, Cecil *EncFCWM 69*
Brower, Leo 1939- *Baker 78, DcCM*
Brower, Otto 1895-1946 *Film 2, TwYS A, WhScrn 74, –77, WhoHol B*
Brower, Robert 1850-1934 *Film 2, TwYS, WhScrn 77*
Brown, A M 1941- *WhoMus 72*
Brown, A Seymour 1885-1947 *AmSCAP 66, –80*
Brown, Ada 1889-1950 *WhoJazz 72*
Brown, Ada 1890-1950 *BluesWW[port]*
Brown, Adeline E *AmSCAP 66*
Brown, Al 1934- *RkOn[port]*
Brown, Al W 1884-1924 *AmSCAP 66, –80*
Brown, Alan Martin 1941- *IntWWM 77, –80*
Brown, Albert O d1945 *NotNAT B*
Brown, Alice *NewGrD 80*
Brown, Allanson G Y 1902- *IntWWM 77*
Brown, Amanda *BluesWW[port]*
Brown, Amy Louise 1930- *IntWWM 77*
Brown, Andrew 1900-1960 *WhoJazz 72*
Brown, Andrew 1937- *BluesWW[port]*
Brown, Anne 1915- *DrBlPA, PlP&P[port]*
Brown, Anthony John 1950- *CpmDNM 75, –76*
Brown, Arrow *MorBAP*

Brown, Arthur *IlEncR[port]*
Brown, Arthur Lawrence 1877-1954 *BiDAmM*
Brown, Arvin 1940- *NotNAT*
Brown, Athaleen Elizabeth 1908- *AmSCAP 66, -80*
Brown, Audrey Alexandra 1904- *CreCan 2*
Brown, B S *BlkAmP*
Brown, Barbara *WomWMM B*
Brown, Barbara d1975 *WhScrn 77, WhoHol C*
Brown, Barbara 1907- *ForYSC*
Brown, Barnetta 1859-1938 *AmSCAP 66, -80*
Brown, Barry *IntMPA 77, -75, -76, -78, WhoHol A*
Brown, Bartholomew 1772-1854 *BiDAmM, NewGrD 80*
Brown, Basil Hector 1909- *WhoMus 72*
Brown, Beatrice 1917- *IntWWM 77, -80*
Brown, Bernard 1914- *WhoMus 72*
Brown, Bernard Lionel 1946- *AmSCAP 80*
Brown, Bertrand 1888-1964 *AmSCAP 66, -80, NotNAT B*
Brown, Beryl Edith 1905- *IntWWM 80*
Brown, Bessie 1895?- *BluesWW[port]*
Brown, Beth *AmSCAP 66*
Brown, Betsy *PupTheA SUP*
Brown, Blair 1952- *HalFC 80*
Brown, Bly 1898-1950 *WhScrn 74, -77*
Brown, Bonnie Gean 1938- *BiDAmM, EncFCWM 69*
Brown, Boyce 1910-1959 *WhoJazz 72*
Brown, Bradley Scott 1955- *AmSCAP 80*
Brown, Buster 1911-1976 *BluesWW[port]*
Brown, Buster 1914- *RkOn*
Brown, Buster B *AmSCAP 80*
Brown, Carolyn 1927- *CnOxB, DancEn 78*
Brown, Carrie Clarke Ward d1926 *NotNAT B*
Brown, Cecil M *BlkAmP, MorBAP*
Brown, Chamberlain d1955 *NotNAT B*
Brown, Charles 1920- *BluesWW[port]*
Brown, Charles D d1948 *Film 2, NotNAT B, WhoHol B*
Brown, Charles D 1887-1948 *FilmEn, Film 1, FilmgC, HalFC 80, WhScrn 74, -77*
Brown, Charles D 1888-1948 *Vers B[port]*
Brown, Charles E d1947 *PupTheA*
Brown, Chelsea *DrBlPA*
Brown, Chocolate *BluesWW[port]*
Brown, Christine 1930- *IntWWM 77, -80*
Brown, Christopher Roland 1943- *IntWWM 77, -80, NewGrD 80, WhoMus 72*
Brown, Clarence 1890- *AmFD, BiDFilm, -81, CmMov, DcFM, FilmEn, FilmgC, HalFC 80, IntMPA 77, -75, -76, -78, -79, -80, MovMk[port], OxFilm, TwYS A, WorEFlm[port]*
Brown, Clarence 1924- *BluesWW[port]*
Brown, Clark d1943 *NotNAT B*
Brown, Clemmon May *ConAmC*
Brown, Cleo 1909- *WhoJazz 72*
Brown, Cleo Patra 1907- *BlkWAB*
Brown, Clifford 1930-1956 *BiDAmM, CmpEPM, IlEncJ, NewGrD 80*
Brown, Colin Stewart 1944- *IntWWM 80*
Brown, David 1916- *FilmEn, IntMPA 77, -75, -76, -78, -79, -80*
Brown, David Auldon 1943- *ConAmC*
Brown, David Clifford 1929- *IntWWM 77, -80, NewGrD 80, WhoMus 72*
Brown, David Paul 1795-1875 *NotNAT B*
Brown, Dean 1940- *WhoOp 76*
Brown, Dean Hollamby 1896- *WhoMus 72*
Brown, DeMarcus 1900- *BiE&WWA, NotNAT*
Brown, Donna *MorBAP*
Brown, Dorothy *Film 2, WhoHol A*
Brown, Dusty 1929- *BluesWW[port]*
Brown, E Brenda 1925- *IntWWM 77*
Brown, Earle 1926- *Baker 78, BiDAmM, BnBkM 80, ConAmC, DcCom&M 79, DcCM, IntWWM 77, -80, NewGrD 80, WhoMus 72*
Brown, Ed *HalFC 80*
Brown, Eddy 1895-1974 *Baker 78, BiDAmM*
Brown, Edward *Film 1*
Brown, Edwin *Film 2*
Brown, Elizabeth 1929- *IntWWM 77*
Brown, Elizabeth Bouldin 1901- *ConAmC*
Brown, Elizabeth VanNess 1902- *ConAmC*
Brown, Eunice F 1917- *AmSCAP 80*
Brown, Everett *DrBlPA*
Brown, Firman H, Jr. 1926- *BiE&WWA*
Brown, Fleming 1926- *BiDAmM, EncFCWM 69*
Brown, Ford Madox *PlP&P*
Brown, Forman 1901- *AmSCAP 66, -80, PupTheA*
Brown, Frank Edwin 1908- *WhoMus 72*
Brown, Frank W 1926- *IntWWM 77*
Brown, Frankie *EncFCWM 69*
Brown, Fred *Film 1*
Brown, Gabriel 1910?-1972? *BluesWW*
Brown, Garnett, Jr. 1936- *BiDAmM, EncJzS 70*
Brown, Gatemouth *BluesWW[port]*
Brown, Gavin William 1925- *IntWWM 77, -80, WhoMus 72*
Brown, Gene 1928- *AmSCAP 66, -80*
Brown, Georg Stanford 1943- *DrBlPA, WhoHol A*
Brown, George 1913- *FilmgC, HalFC 80, IntMPA 77, -75, -76, -78, -79, -80*
Brown, George Anderson d1920 *NotNAT B*
Brown, George Murray 1880-1960 *AmSCAP 66, -80*
Brown, George R 1910- *AmSCAP 66, -80*
Brown, Georgia 1933- *BiE&WWA, FilmEn, FilmgC, HalFC 80, NotNAT, WhoHol A, WhoThe 72, -77*
Brown, Gerald *IntWWM 77, -80*
Brown, Gerald 1936- *EncJzS 70*
Brown, Gertrude Sweeney 1909- *IntWWM 77*
Brown, Gilmor d1960 *NotNAT A, PlP&P*
Brown, Gilmorn d1960 *NotNAT B*
Brown, Glenn J 1900-1960 *AmSCAP 66, -80*
Brown, Graham 1924- *DrBlPA*
Brown, Gwen *WomWMM B*
Brown, Gwethalyn Graham Erichsen *CreCan 1*
Brown, Hal *Film 1*
Brown, Halbert *Film 2*
Brown, Harold 1909- *IntWWM 77, -80*
Brown, Harry d1966 *WhoHol B*
Brown, Harry 1917- *CmMov, FilmEn, FilmgC, HalFC 80, IntMPA 77, -75, -76, -78, -79, -80*
Brown, Harry Joe 1890-1972 *FilmEn, TwYS A*
Brown, Harry Joe 1892-1972 *FilmgC, HalFC 80*
Brown, Harry Joe 1893-1972 *WorEFlm[port]*
Brown, Harry W 1918-1966 *WhScrn 77*
Brown, Helen 1902- *BiE&WWA*
Brown, Helen Mina 1916-1974 *WhScrn 77*
Brown, Helen W d1974 *WhoHol B*
Brown, Henry 1899- *IntMPA 77, -75, -76, -78, -79, -80*
Brown, Henry 1906- *BluesWW, WhoJazz 72*
Brown, Himan 1910- *IntMPA 77, -75, -76, -78, -79, -80*
Brown, Howard C 1901- *IntMPA 77, -75, -76, -78, -79, -80*
Brown, Howard Fuller 1920- *IntWWM 77, -80*
Brown, Howard Mayer 1930- *Baker 78, IntWWM 77, -80, NewGrD 80*
Brown, Hylo 1920- *BiDAmM*
Brown, Ida G 1900?- *BluesWW[port]*
Brown, Irving 1922- *BiE&WWA, NotNAT*
Brown, Ivor 1891-1974 *BiE&WWA, EncWT, OxThe, WhThe, WhoThe 72*
Brown, J C *BluesWW[port]*
Brown, J E 1937- *CpmDNM 78, ConAmC*
Brown, J Harold 1909- *BiDAmM*
Brown, Jack Martin 1946- *AmSCAP 80*
Brown, James *BlkAmP, ConMuA 80A[port]*
Brown, James 1862-1914 *NewGrD 80*
Brown, James 1880?-1922? *NewOrJ*
Brown, James 1920- *FilmEn, FilmgC, ForYSC, HalFC 80, MotPP, WhoHol A*
Brown, James 1928- *BiDAmM, RkOn*
Brown, James 1929- *WhoMus 72*
Brown, James 1933- *DrBlPA, IlEncR[port]*
Brown, James B 1945- *AmSCAP 80*
Brown, James Clifford 1923- *WhoMus 72*
Brown, James Duff 1862-1914 *Baker 78*
Brown, James Edward 1937- *CpmDNM 76*
Brown, James Gopsill 1929- *IntWWM 80*
Brown, James Murray 1913- *IntWWM 77, -80, WhoMus 72*
Brown, James Nelson *BlkAmP, MorBAP*
Brown, James Ostend 1906-1963 *BiDAmM*
Brown, James William 1928- *IntWWM 77, -80*
Brown, Jasmin Alexandra Thalia Jane 1952- *IntWWM 80*
Brown, Jean Patricia *WomWMM B*
Brown, Jerry Leonard 1944- *AmSCAP 80*
Brown, Jewel Hazel 1937- *BiDAmM*
Brown, Jim *ConMuA 80B, IntMPA 75, -76, MorBAP, MotPP, WhoHol A*
Brown, Jim 1933- *ForYSC*
Brown, Jim 1935- *DrBlPA, FilmEn*
Brown, Jim 1936- *FilmgC, HalFC 80, IntMPA 77, -78, -79, -80, MovMk[port]*
Brown, Jim Ed *EncFCWM 69*
Brown, Jim Ed 1934- *CounME 74[port], -74A, IlEncCM[port]*
Brown, Jim Edward 1934- *BiDAmM*
Brown, Joe *Film 2*
Brown, Joe 1941- *FilmgC, HalFC 80*
Brown, Joe, Jr. *WhoHol A*
Brown, Joe E d1973 *GrMovC[port]*
Brown, Joe E 1891-1973 *FilmgC*
Brown, Joe E 1892-1973 *BiE&WWA, EncMT, FilmEn, Film 2, ForYSC, Funs[port], HalFC 80, JoeFr[port], MotPP, MovMk, NotNAT A, OxFilm, What 2[port], WhScrn 77, WhThe, WhoHol B, WhoThe 72*
Brown, John d1957 *WhScrn 77*
Brown, John 1715-1766 *Baker 78, NewGrD 80*
Brown, John Benjamin Peabody 1906- *WhoJazz 72*
Brown, John Clive Anthony 1947- *IntWWM 77*
Brown, John Edwin 1892- *Film 2, TwYS*
Brown, John Henry 1902- *BluesWW[port]*
Brown, John Hullah 1875- *OxMus*
Brown, John Mack 1904-1974 *FilmgC, HalFC 80, MotPP, MovMk[port]*
Brown, John Mason 1900-1969 *BiE&WWA, NotNAT A, -B, OxThe, PlP&P*
Brown, John Moulder 1951- *FilmgC, HalFC 80*
Brown, John Newton 1803-1868 *BiDAmM*
Brown, John Russell 1923- *WhoThe 72, -77*
Brown, Johnny *DrBlPA, WhoHol A*
Brown, Johnny 1880?-1935? *NewOrJ*
Brown, Johnny Mack 1904- *ForYSC, What 3[port]*
Brown, Johnny Mack 1904-1974 *CmMov, FilmEn, Film 2, TwYS, WhoHol B*
Brown, Johnny Mack 1904-1975 *WhScrn 77*
Brown, Jonathan Bruce 1952- *AmSCAP 80, CpmDNM 76*
Brown, Josephine *Film 2*
Brown, Joyce 1920- *BlkWAB*
Brown, Julia *Film 2*
Brown, Karl 1895?- *FilmEn*
Brown, Karl 1897- *HalFC 80*
Brown, Kay 1902- *BiE&WWA*
Brown, Keith 1933- *IntWWM 77, -80*
Brown, Keith Crosby 1885-1948 *AmSCAP 66, -80, ConAmC*
Brown, Kelly 1928- *BiE&WWA, CnOxB, DancEn 78, NotNAT*
Brown, Kenneth H 1936- *ConDr 73, -77*
Brown, Kenneth H 1937?- *NatPD[port], NotNAT, PlP&P*
Brown, L Slade 1922- *BiE&WWA, NotNAT*
Brown, Lawrence 1905- *BiDAmM, CmpEPM, EncJzS 70, IlEncJ*
Brown, Lawrence 1907- *WhoJazz 72*
Brown, Lennox John 1934- *BlkAmP, MorBAP, NatPD[port]*
Brown, Leon Ford 1918- *IntWWM 77, -80*
Brown, Les 1912- *AmPS A, -B, AmSCAP 66, BgBands 74[port], CmpEPM, EncJzS 70*
Brown, Lester Raymond 1912- *AmSCAP 80, BiDAmM, EncJzS 70*
Brown, Lew 1893- *Sw&Ld C, WhoHol A*
Brown, Lew 1893-1958 *AmPS, AmSCAP 66, -80, BiDAmM, CmpEPM, EncMT, NewCBMT, NotNAT B*
Brown, Lewis Doyle 1908- *WhoMus 72*
Brown, Lillian 1885-1969 *BluesWW[port]*
Brown, Lionel d1964 *NotNAT B*
Brown, Lottie *BluesWW[port]*
Brown, Louis 1912- *AmSCAP 80*
Brown, Lucille *Film 1*
Brown, Lucy 1913-1971 *BiDAmM*
Brown, Lyman C d1961 *NotNAT B*
Brown, Malcolm Hamrick 1929- *IntWWM 77, -80*

Brown, Marcia *WomWMM B*
Brown, Margaret Wise 1910-1952 *AmSCAP 66, -80*
Brown, Marion 1935- *BiDAmM, EncJzS 70, IlEncJ*
Brown, Marshall Richard 1920- *AmSCAP 66, -80, BiDAmM, EncJzS 70*
Brown, Martin 1885-1936 *NotNAT B*
Brown, Maurice 1905- *AmSCAP 80*
Brown, Maurice John Edwin 1906-1975 *AmSCAP 66, NewGrD 80*
Brown, Maxine 1932- *BiDAmM, DrBlPA, EncFCWM 69, RkOn*
Brown, Maxine Velena 1897-1956 *WhScrn 77*
Brown, Melaine Vadas 1956- *IntWWM 80*
Brown, Melville 1888-1938 *TwYS A, WhScrn 74, -77*
Brown, Merton 1913- *Baker 78*
Brown, Mildred A 1919- *IntWWM 77*
Brown, Milton *Film 1*
Brown, Milton 1903- *IlEncCM*
Brown, Myrna Weeks 1937- *IntWWM 77*
Brown, Myrne Weeks 1937- *IntWWM 80*
Brown, Nacio, Jr. 1921- *AmSCAP 66*
Brown, Nacio Herb 1896-1964 *AmPS, AmSCAP 66, -80, Baker 78, BestMus, BiDAmM, CmpEPM, FilmEn, Film 2, FilmgC, HalFC 80, NewGrD 80, NotNAT B, PopAmC[port], PopAmC SUP, Sw&Ld C*
Brown, Nacio Herb, Jr. 1921- *AmSCAP 80*
Brown, Nappy *RkOn*
Brown, Nathan 1807-1886 *BiDAmM*
Brown, Nathaniel S 1921- *AmSCAP 80*
Brown, Newel Kay 1932- *CpmDNM 79, -80, ConAmC*
Brown, Norman d1969 *BiDAmM*
Brown, Olive 1922- *BluesWW[port], EncJzS 70*
Brown, Oren Lathrop 1909- *IntWWM 80*
Brown, Oscar, Jr. 1926- *BiDAmM, BlkAmP, DrBlPA, MorBAP*
Brown, Pamela 1917-1975 *BiE&WWA, FilmEn, FilmgC, ForYSC, HalFC 80, NotNAT B, OxFilm, PlP&P, WhScrn 77, WhoHol C*
Brown, Pamela 1924- *IntMPA 75, -76*
Brown, Patricia *BlkAmP*
Brown, Patricia Anne 1945- *IntWWM 80*
Brown, Paul D 1920- *AmSCAP 80*
Brown, Peggy *Film 2*
Brown, Pete 1906-1963 *CmpEPM, IlEncJ, WhoJazz 72*
Brown, Pete 1940- *IlEncR*
Brown, Peter *ForYSC, WhoHol A*
Brown, Phil 1916?-1973 *FilmgC, HalFC 80, WhScrn 77, WhoHol B*
Brown, Philip *WhoHol A*
Brown, Phoebe 1783-1861 *BiDAmM*
Brown, Phyllis E *WhoMus 72*
Brown, Polly *RkOn 2[port]*
Brown, Ray 1892?-1940? *NewOrJ*
Brown, Ray 1926- *CmpEPM, DrBlPA*
Brown, Ray 1946- *EncJzS 70*
Brown, Ray Francis 1897- *BiDAmM*
Brown, Raymond 1880-1939 *WhScrn 74, -77, WhoHol B*
Brown, Raymond 1920- *IntWWM 77, -80*
Brown, Raymond Harry 1946- *AmSCAP 80, EncJzS 70*
Brown, Raymond Kenneth 1928- *WhoMus 72*
Brown, Raymond Matthews 1926- *BiDAmM, EncJzS 70*
Brown, Raymond Shannon, II 1952- *AmSCAP 80*
Brown, Rayner 1912- *AmSCAP 80, Baker 78, CpmDNM 76, -78, IntWWM 77, -80*
Brown, Raynor 1912- *CpmDNM 73, -79, ConAmC*
Brown, Reed, Jr. d1962 *NotNAT B*
Brown, Rex P *ConAmC*
Brown, Rhozier T *MorBAP*
Brown, Richard *NewGrD 80*
Brown, Richard 1880?-1937 *BluesWW[port]*
Brown, Richard Earl 1947- *CpmDNM 74, -75, ConAmC*
Brown, Richard Peyron 1936- *NotNAT*
Brown, Richard S 1947- *IntWWM 77, -80*
Brown, Robert 1910-1966 *BluesWW[port]*
Brown, Robert 1918?- *FilmgC, HalFC 80*
Brown, Robert 1927-1975 *BluesWW*
Brown, Roderick Langmere Haig Haig- *CreCan 1*
Brown, Roger William 1936- *AmSCAP 80*
Brown, Ronald C 1911-1962 *WhScrn 74, -77*
Brown, Roscoe Lee 1925- *BlkAmP, MorBAP*
Brown, Rosemary 1917- *NewGrD 80*
Brown, Rosemary Eleanor 1938- *WhoMus 72*
Brown, Rowland 1900-1963 *FilmEn*
Brown, Rowland 1901-1963 *FilmgC, HalFC 80*
Brown, Roy James 1925- *BluesWW[port]*
Brown, Russ 1892-1964 *WhScrn 74, -77, WhoHol B*
Brown, Ruth 1923- *IntWWM 77*
Brown, Ruth 1928- *DrBlPA, EncJzS 70, RkOn[port]*
Brown, Sam 1939- *EncJzS 70*
Brown, Samuel Franklin, III 1947- *AmSCAP 80*
Brown, Samuel T 1939- *EncJzS 70*
Brown, Sandy 1929-1975 *IlEncJ*
Brown, Sarah *PupTheA*
Brown, Sebastian Hubert 1903- *WhoMus 72*
Brown, Sedley d1928 *NotNAT B*
Brown, Seymour 1885-1947 *BiDAmM*
Brown, Sheila Eileen Norah 1931- *WhoMus 72*
Brown, Sidney 1894-1968 *NewOrJ*
Brown, Sonny 1936- *EncJzS 70*
Brown, Stephen Butler 1945- *IntWWM 77, -80*
Brown, Steve 1890?-1965 *NewOrJ[port], WhoJazz 72*
Brown, Susan Barbara Comstra 1949- *IntWWM 77, -80*
Brown, T Allston d1918 *NotNAT B*
Brown, Ted Allan 1945- *AmSCAP 80*
Brown, Thomas Alfred 1932- *AmSCAP 80, ConAmC*
Brown, Thomas Patrick 1945- *IntWWM 77*
Brown, Timothy 1937- *DrBlPA*
Brown, Timothy Charles 1946- *IntWWM 77, -80*
Brown, Tom 1868-1919 *BlksBF[port]*
Brown, Tom 1878?-1918? *NewOrJ[port]*
Brown, Tom 1888-1958 *NewOrJ[port], WhoJazz 72*
Brown, Tom 1913- *FilmEn, Film 2, FilmgC, ForYSC, HalFC 80, IntMPA 77, -75, -76, -78, -79, -80, MovMk, TwYS, Vers B[port], What 5[port], WhoHol A*
Brown, Tommy *BluesWW[port]*
Brown, Toni 1938- *BiDAmM*
Brown, Tony 1933- *DrBlPA*
Brown, Trisha *CmpGMD[port]*
Brown, Troy, Jr. d1944 *WhScrn 77*
Brown, Vanessa 1928- *FilmEn, FilmgC, ForYSC, HalFC 80, MotPP, WhoHol A*
Brown, Vernon 1907- *CmpEPM, WhoJazz 72*
Brown, Vida 1922- *CnOxB, DancEn 78*
Brown, Vincent Urbonavich 1916- *WhoMus 72*
Brown, Vincent Urbonavich 1947- *WhoMus 72*
Brown, Virginia *Film 2*
Brown, W H *Film 1, -2*
Brown, Wally d1961 *NotNAT B*
Brown, Wally 1898-1961 *FilmgC, HalFC 80*
Brown, Wally 1904-1961 *ForYSC, Vers B[port], WhScrn 74, -77, WhoHol B*
Brown, Walter 1917?-1956? *BluesWW[port]*
Brown, Walter Earl 1928- *AmSCAP 66, -80*
Brown, Wesley *MorBAP*
Brown, Wilfred 1921-1971 *NewGrD 80*
Brown, Willard S 1909-1967 *WhoJazz 72*
Brown, Willet Henry *IntMPA 77, -75, -76, -78, -79, -80*
Brown, William *Film 1, NewGrD 80*
Brown, William 1784- *Baker 78*
Brown, William 1918-1975 *NewOrJ*
Brown, William 1928- *BiDAmM*
Brown, William 1932- *WhoMus 72*
Brown, William Albert 1938- *WhoOp 76*
Brown, William F 1928- *AmSCAP 66, -80, ConDr 77D, MorBAP, NatPD[port]*
Brown, William H, Jr. *IntMPA 77, -75, -76, -78, -79, -80*
Brown, William Wells 1884- *BlkAmP, MorBAP*
Brown, Willie Lee 1900-1952 *BluesWW*
Brown, Winnie *MotPP*
Brown-Potter, Mrs. James 1859-1936 *NotNAT B, OxThe*
Browne, Bradford *AmSCAP 66, -80*
Browne, Coral 1913- *BiE&WWA, FilmEn, FilmgC, HalFC 80, MotPP, MovMk, NotNAT, WhoHol A, WhoThe 72, -77*
Browne, Diane Gail 1954- *AmSCAP 80*
Browne, Donald Kurtz, Jr. 1946- *ConAmC*
Browne, E Martin 1900- *BiE&WWA, NotNAT, OxThe, WhoThe 72, -77*
Browne, Earle 1872-1944 *WhScrn 74, -77, WhoHol B*
Browne, Elliott Martin 1900- *Ent*
Browne, Ernest D 1900- *AmSCAP 66*
Browne, Gwendolen Anne *WhoMus 72*
Browne, Harry C *Film 2*
Browne, Irene 1891-1965 *BiE&WWA, FilmgC, HalFC 80, WhoHol B*
Browne, Irene 1893-1965 *Film 2, ThFT[port], WhScrn 74, -77*
Browne, J Edwin *Film 2*
Browne, Jackson *ConMuA 80A[port]*
Browne, Jackson 1948- *AmSCAP 80, IlEncR[port]*
Browne, Jackson 1950- *RkOn 2[port]*
Browne, John *NewGrD 80*
Browne, John Lewis 1864-1933 *Baker 78*
Browne, John Lewis 1866-1933 *AmSCAP 66, -80*
Browne, Kathie *WhoHol A*
Browne, Kathryn *Film 1*
Browne, Martin 1900- *EncWT*
Browne, Maurice 1881-1955 *EncWT, ModWD, NotNAT A, -B, OxThe*
Browne, Murray 1907- *IntWWM 77, -80*
Browne, Patricia Wilkins 1950- *BlkAmP*
Browne, Philip 1933- *AmSCAP 80, ConAmC*
Browne, Porter Emerson 1879-1934 *NotNAT B*
Browne, Raymond A 1871-1922 *AmSCAP 66, -80*
Browne, Richard *NewGrD 80*
Browne, Richard d1710 *NewGrD 80*
Browne, Richard 1630?-1664 *NewGrD 80*
Browne, Richmond 1934- *AmSCAP 80, ConAmC*
Browne, Robert *OxThe*
Browne, Robert 1550?-1633? *OxMus*
Browne, Roscoe Lee 1925- *BiE&WWA, DrBlPA, FilmgC, HalFC 80, IntMPA 77, -75, -76, -78, -79, -80, NotNAT, WhoHol A, WhoThe 72, -77*
Browne, Roscoe Lee 1930?- *FilmEn*
Browne, Sandra 1947- *IntWWM 80*
Browne, Sylvia Theresa 1943- *AmSCAP 80*
Browne, Theodore *BlkAmP, MorBAP*
Browne, Toby 1909- *WhoJazz 72*
Browne, W Graham 1870-1937 *Film 1, NotNAT B, WhScrn 77, WhoHol B*
Browne, Walter 1856-1911 *NotNAT B, WhoStg 1908*
Browne, William Charles Denis 1888-1915 *NewGrD 80*
Browne, Wynyard Barry d1964 *NotNAT B*
Brownee, Zing *AmSCAP 80*
Brownell, Barbara *WhoHol A*
Brownell, Peleg Franklin 1856-1946 *CreCan 2*
Brownell, William Edward *AmSCAP 80*
Brownie *NewGrD 80*
Browning, Alan David Jeffrey 1955- *IntWWM 80*
Browning, Alice C *MorBAP*
Browning, Carl Anthony 1938- *IntWWM 77*
Browning, Edith d1926 *NotNAT B*
Browning, Francesca Alsing 1905- *IntWWM 80*
Browning, Harry 1895- *IntMPA 75, -76*
Browning, Ivan Harold 1891- *BlksBF*
Browning, Jean *NewGrD 80*
Browning, John 1933- *Baker 78, BnBkM 80, IntWWM 77, -80, MusSN[port], NewGrD 80, WhoMus 72*
Browning, Kirk 1921- *IntMPA 77, -75, -76, -78, -79, -80, NewYTET*
Browning, Mortimer 1891-1953 *AmSCAP 66, -80, BiDAmM, ConAmC*
Browning, Ricou 1930- *FilmgC, HalFC 80, NewYTET, WhoHrs 80*
Browning, Robert 1812-1889 *CnThe, DcPup, EncWT, McGEWD[port], OxMus, OxThe, PlP&P, REnWD[port]*
Browning, Susan 1941- *WhoThe 77*
Browning, Tod 1880-1962 *TwYS A*
Browning, Tod 1882-1962 *AmFD, BiDFilm, -81, CmMov, ConLC 16, DcFM, FilmEn,*

Film 1, FilmgC, HalFC 80, MovMk[port], OxFilm, WhScrn 77, WhoHrs 80[port], WorEFlm[port]
Browning, William E d1930 WhScrn 74, -77, WhoHol B
Brownlee, Frank 1874-1948 Film 1, -2, WhScrn 77
Brownlee, John 1900-1969 Baker 78, CmOp
Brownlee, John 1901-1969 BiDAmM, BiE&WWA, NewEOp 71, NewGrD 80
Brownlee, Norman 1896-1967 NewOrJ
Brownlow, George Watson 1902- WhoMus 72
Brownlow, Kevin 1938- FilmgC, HalFC 80, IlWWBF, OxFilm
Brownridge, Angela Mary 1944- IntWWM 77, -80, WhoMus 72
Browns, The AmPS A, BiDAmM, EncFCWM 69, IlEncCM[port], RkOn
Brown's Ferry Four BiDAmM
Brownson, Oliver NewGrD 80
Brownstein, Samuel Hyman 1905- AmSCAP 80
Brownstone, Joseph 1920- BiE&WWA
Brownsville ConMuA 80A
Brownsville Station ConMuA 80A, RkOn 2[port]
Brox Sisters, The Film 2
Broyde, Ruth WomWMM
Broza, Elliot Lawrence AmSCAP 80
Brozek, Jan NewGrD 80
Brozen, Michael 1934- AmSCAP 80, ConAmC, IntWWM 77, -80
Bruand, Aristide 1851-1925 NewGrD 80
Bruant, Aristide 1851-1925 Ent[port], NewGrD 80
Brubaker, Robert WhoHol A
Brubeck, Chris 1952- BiDAmM, EncJzS 70
Brubeck, Daniel 1955- EncJzS 70
Brubeck, Danny 1955- EncJzS 70
Brubeck, Darius BiDAmM
Brubeck, Dave 1920- Baker 78, CmpEPM, EncJzS 70, IlEncJ, MusMk[port], NewGrD 80, RkOn[port]
Brubeck, David Darius 1947- EncJzS 70
Brubeck, David Warren 1920- BiDAmM, ConAmC, EncJzS 70, IntWWM 77, -80
Brubeck, Howard 1916- Baker 78, ConAmC
Bruce, Angela WomWMM
Bruce, Belle d1960 Film 1, WhScrn 77, WhoHol B
Bruce, Betty 1920-1974 WhScrn 77, WhoHol B
Bruce, Betty 1925-1974 BiE&WWA, NotNAT B
Bruce, Beverly d1925 WhScrn 74, -77, WhoHol B
Bruce, Billy Film 2
Bruce, Brenda WhoHol A, WhoThe 72, -77
Bruce, Brenda 1918- FilmgC, HalFC 80
Bruce, Brenda 1922- IntMPA 77, -75, -76, -78, -79, -80
Bruce, Carol 1919- BiE&WWA, CmpEPM, EncMT, NotNAT, WhoHol A, WhoThe 72, -77
Bruce, Charles Tory 1906- CreCan 1
Bruce, Christopher 1945- CnOxB
Bruce, Clifford 1885-1919 Film 1, -2, WhScrn 77
Bruce, David 1914-1976 FilmEn, FilmgC, ForYSC, HalFC 80, IntMPA 75, -76, MotPP, WhoHrs 80[port]
Bruce, Denny ConMuA 80B
Bruce, Ed IlEncCM[port]
Bruce, Edgar K 1893- WhoThe 72
Bruce, F Neely 1944- IntWWM 77, -80
Bruce, Gary AmSCAP 80
Bruce, George 1898- FilmEn, IntMPA 77, -75, -76, -78, -79, -80
Bruce, Geraldine d1953 NotNAT B
Bruce, Jack 1943- EncJzS 70, IlEncR
Bruce, John Symon Asher 1943- EncJzS 70
Bruce, Kate 1858-1946 Film 1, -2, TwYS, WhScrn 77
Bruce, Lenny d1966 ConMuA 80A
Bruce, Lenny 1924-1966 JoeFr[port]
Bruce, Lenny 1925-1966 Ent[port]
Bruce, Lenny 1926-1966 WhScrn 77, WhoHrs 80
Bruce, Margaret 1943- IntWWM 80
Bruce, Marjorie Thelma 1948- IntWWM 77
Bruce, Michael Film 2
Bruce, Neely 1944- ConAmC
Bruce, Nigel 1895-1953 FilmEn, Film 2, FilmgC, ForYSC, HalFC 80, HolCA[port], MotPP, MovMk[port], NotNAT B, Vers A[port], WhScrn 74, -77, WhoHol B, WhoHrs 80[port]
Bruce, Nigel 1895-1954 CmMov
Bruce, Paul d1971 WhScrn 74, -77, WhoHol B
Bruce, Raymon R 1934- NatPD[port]
Bruce, Rhonda 1937- WhoMus 72
Bruce, Richard BlkAmP, MorBAP
Bruce, Robert 1915- AmSCAP 66
Bruce, Shelley WhoHol A
Bruce, Tonie Edgar WhScrn 74, -77
Bruce, Tony d1937 NotNAT B, WhoHol B
Bruce, Virginia 1910- FilmEn, Film 2, FilmgC, ForYSC, HalFC 80, MGM[port], MotPP, MovMk[port], ThFT[port], What 2[port], WhoHol A
Bruce-Payne, David Malcolm 1945- IntWWM 77, -80
Bruch, Max 1838-1920 Baker 78, BnBkM 80, CmpBCM, DcCom 77, DcCom&M 79, GrComp[port], MusMk, NewEOp 71, NewGrD 80, OxMus
Bruchesi, Jean 1901- CreCan 1
Bruchollerie, Monique DeLa 1915-1972 Baker 78
Bruci, Rudolf 1917- Baker 78, NewGrD 80
Bruck, Arnold Von 1470?-1554 Baker 78
Bruck, Arnold Von 1500?-1554 NewGrD 80
Bruck, Charles 1911- NewGrD 80, WhoMus 72
Brucken-Fock, Emil Von 1857-1944 Baker 78
Brucken-Fock, Gerard Van 1859-1935 OxMus
Brucken-Fock, Gerard Von 1859-1935 Baker 78, NewGrD 80
Bruckler, Hugo 1845-1871 Baker 78
Bruckman, Clyde 1894-1955 FilmEn, WorEFlm[port]
Bruckman, Clyde 1895-1955 FilmgC, HalFC 80
Bruckner, Anton 1824-1896 Baker 78, BnBkM 80[port], CmpBCM, DcCom 77[port], DcCom&M 79, GrComp[port], MusMk, NewGrD 80[port], OxMus
Bruckner, Ferdinand 1891-1958 CnMD, EncWT, Ent, McGEWD[port], ModWD, NotNAT B, OxThe
Bruckner, Friedrich 1891-1958 CroCD
Bruckner, Johannes 1730-1786 OxThe
Bruckner, Milt 1915- WhoJazz 72
Bruckner, Sidney Thomas 1914- IntMPA 77, -75, -76, -78, -79, -80
Bruckner-Ruggeberg, Wilhelm 1906- NewGrD 80
Bruderhans, Zdenek 1934- IntWWM 80
Brudieu, Jean 1520?-1591 BnBkM 80
Brudieu, Joan 1520?-1591 BnBkM 80, NewGrD 80
Brue, Steve 1904-1944 NewOrJ[port]
Brueggen, Frans 1934- IntWWM 77, -80, NewGrD 80, WhoMus 72
Brues, Otto 1897-1967 CnMD, ModWD
Brueys, David-Augustin De 1640-1723 McGEWD, OxThe
Bruford, Bill ConMuA 80A
Bruford, Rose Elizabeth 1904- WhoThe 72, -77
Bruge, George NewGrD 80
Bruggeman, George 1904-1967 WhScrn 77
Bruggemann, Kurt 1908- IntWWM 77, -80, NewGrD 80
Bruggemann, W 1936- IntWWM 80
Bruggen, Frans 1934- BnBkM 80, NewGrD 80
Brugger, Roger Werner 1942- IntWWM 77, -80
Bruggerman, George d1967 WhoHol B
Brugiensis, Arnoldus NewGrD 80
Brugier, Antoine NewGrD 80
Brugk, Hans Melchior 1909- IntWWM 77, NewGrD 80
Brugk, Hans Melchoir 1909- IntWWM 80
Brugnoli, Amalia 1810?- CnOxB
Brugnoli, Attilio 1880-1937 Baker 78, NewGrD 80
Bruguera, Juan Bautista NewGrD 80
Bruhier, Antoine NewGrD 80
Bruhl, Hans Moritz, Count Of 1736-1809 NewGrD 80
Bruhl Of Martinskirche, Count Of 1736-1809 NewGrD 80
Bruhn, Christian 1934- IntWWM 77, -80
Bruhn, Erik 1928- CnOxB, DancEn 78[port]
Bruhn, Nikolaus 1665?-1697 OxMus
Bruhns, Friedrich Nicolaus NewGrD 80
Bruhns, George Frederick William 1874-1963 AmSCAP 66, ConAmC
Bruhns, Nicolaus 1665-1697 Baker 78, NewGrD 80
Bruins, Theo 1929- NewGrD 80
Brukenfeld, Dick 1933- ConAmTC
Brule, Andre Film 1
Brule, Gace NewGrD 80
Brulin, Tone 1926- EncWT
Brull, Ignaz 1846-1907 Baker 78, NewEOp 71, NewGrD 80, OxMus
Brum, Oscar DaSilveira 1926- IntWWM 77, -80
Brumberg, Valentina 1899- DcFM, WomWMM
Brumberg, Zenajeda 1900- WomWMM
Brumberg, Zinaida 1900- DcFM
Brumby, Colin 1933- Baker 78, NewGrD 80, WhoMus 72
Brumel, Antoine 1460?-1515? NewGrD 80
Brumel, Antoine 1460-1520 Baker 78
Brumel, Antoine 1460?-1525? BnBkM 80
Brumel, Jacques NewGrD 80
Brumen, Denis NewGrD 80, -80
Brument, Denis NewGrD 80, -80
Brumentus, Denis NewGrD 80
Brumley, Tom EncFCWM 69
Brumley, Tom 1935- IlEncCM
Brummel, Antoine NewGrD 80
Brummell, Beau 1778-1840 FilmgC, HalFC 80
Brun, Alphonse 1888-1963 Baker 78
Brun, Fritz 1878-1959 Baker 78, NewGrD 80
Brun, Herbert 1918- Baker 78, CpmDNM 77, ConAmC, DcCM
Brun, Jean NewGrD 80
Brun, Jean Le NewGrD 80
Brun, Joseph WorEFlm[port]
Brun, Nordahl 1745-1816 OxThe
Bruna, Pablo 1611?-1679 NewGrD 80
Brunckhorst, Andreas Matthias 1670-1725 NewGrD 80
Brunckhorst, Arnold Matthias 1670-1725 NewGrD 80
Brunckhorst, Arnoldy Matthias 1670-1725 NewGrD 80
Brunclik, Milos PupTheA
Brundage, Bertha 1860-1939 WhScrn 74, -77, WhoHol B
Brundage, Mathilde 1871-1939 Film 1, WhScrn 77
Brundage, Matilde Film 2
Brundy, Walter 1883?-1941 NewOrJ
Brune, Adolf Gerhard 1870-1935 Baker 78
Bruneau, Alfred 1857-1934 Baker 78, BnBkM 80, NewEOp 71, NewGrD 80, OxMus
Bruneau, Kittie 1929- CreCan 1
Brunel De Tours NewGrD 80
Brunel, Adrian 1892-1958 FilmEn, Film 2, FilmgC, HalFC 80, IlWWBF, -A
Brunel, Antoine NewGrD 80
Brunel, Jacques d1564 NewGrD 80
Brunelle, Philip Charles 1943- IntWWM 77, -80
Brunelleschi, Filippo 1377-1446 OxThe
Brunelli, Antonio 1575?-1630 Baker 78, NewGrD 80
Brunelli, Domenico NewGrD 80
Brunelli, Louis Jean 1925- AmSCAP 66, -80, ConAmC
Brunello, Jacques NewGrD 80
Bruner, Cliff 1915- IlEncCM[port]
Bruner, Richard W 1926- NatPD[port]
Brunerye, Mare 1935- IntWWM 80
Brunet, Pierre NewGrD 80
Bruneti, Caetano NewGrD 80
Bruneti, Cayetano NewGrD 80
Bruneti, Gaetano NewGrD 80
Brunette, Fritzi 1890-1943 WhScrn 74, -77, WhoHol B
Brunette, Fritzi 1894-1943 Film 1, -2, TwYS
Brunette, Fritzie 1890-1943 FilmEn

Brunetti *NewGrD 80*
Brunetti, Antonio 1735?-1786 *NewGrD 80*
Brunetti, Antonio 1767?- *NewGrD 80*
Brunetti, Argentina *WhoHol A*
Brunetti, Caetano 1744-1798 *NewGrD 80*
Brunetti, Cayetano 1744-1798 *NewGrD 80*
Brunetti, Domenico 1580?-1646 *Baker 78, NewGrD 80*
Brunetti, Gaetano 1744-1798 *Baker 78, NewGrD 80*
Brunetti, Giovan Gualberto 1706-1787 *NewGrD 80*
Brunetti, Giovanni *NewGrD 80*
Brunetti, Giuseppe 1735?- *NewGrD 80*
Brunetti, Miro 1908-1966 *WhScrn 77*
Brung, Jean Le *NewGrD 80*
Bruni, Antonio Bartolomeo 1757-1821 *NewGrD 80*
Bruni, Antonio Bartolomeo 1759-1821 *Baker 78*
Bruni, Francesco Caletti *NewGrD 80*
Brunies, Albert 1900- *NewOrJ[port]*
Brunies, Albert 1914-1955 *NewOrJ[port]*
Brunies, George 1902-1974 *NewOrJ[port]*
Brunies, Henry 1882?- *NewOrJ*
Brunies, Merritt 1895-1973 *NewOrJ[port]*
Brunies, Richard 1889-1960 *NewOrJ[port]*
Brunies Brothers Of New Orleans *BiDAmM*
Bruning, Albert d1929 *NotNAT B*
Bruning, Earl H, Jr. 1943- *IntWWM 77*
Bruning, Francesca 1907- *BiE&WWA, NotNAT*
Brunious, John 1920-1976 *NewOrJ[port]*
Brunis, Georg 1900-1974 *CmpEPM, EncJzS 70, IlEncJ, WhoJazz 72*
Brunis, George 1902- *BiDAmM*
Brunius, Jacques 1906-1967 *FilmgC, HalFC 80, OxFilm, WhScrn 77*
Brunius, John W 1884-1937 *DcFM, FilmEn, WhScrn 77*
Brunius, Pauline *WomWMM*
Brunkard, William *NewGrD 80*
Brunmuller, Elias *NewGrD 80*
Brunn *NewGrD 80*
Brunnemuller, Elias *NewGrD 80*
Brunnemullerus, Elias *NewGrD 80*
Brunner, Adolf 1901- *NewGrD 80*
Brunner, Barbara Jeanne 1914- *AmSCAP 80*
Brunner, Francis Rudolf 1899- *AmSCAP 80*
Brunner, Gerhard 1939- *CnOxB*
Brunner, Robert F 1938- *AmSCAP 66, -80*
Brunner, Ulric *OxMus*
Brunns, Julia d1927 *WhoHol B*
Bruno, Giordano 1548-1600 *McGEWD[port], OxThe, REnWD[port]*
Bruno, Giovanni Battista Caletti Di *NewGrD 80*
Bruno, Guillelmo *NewGrD 80*
Bruno, Guillermo *NewGrD 80*
Bruno, James 1917- *AmSCAP 66*
Bruno, Jennie *Film 2*
Bruno, Joann *BlkAmP*
Bruno, Joanna Mary *WhoOp 76*
Bruno, Joanne *IntWWM 77, -80, MorBAP*
Bruno-Ruby, Jane *WomWMM*
Brunold, Paul 1875-1948 *Baker 78, NewGrD 80*
Brunot, Andre 1880-1973 *WhScrn 77, WhoHol B*
Bruns, Edna d1960 *NotNAT B*
Bruns, George E 1914- *AmSCAP 80*
Bruns, Heiner 1935- *WhoOp 76*
Bruns, Julia 1895-1927 *NotNAT B*
Brunskill, Muriel 1899- *IntWWM 77*
Brunskill, Muriel 1900- *WhoMus 72*
Brunsma, Donna Louise 1932- *IntWWM 77, -80*
Brunson, Doris *BlkAmP*
Brunswick, Mark 1902-1971 *Baker 78, BiDAmM, ConAmC, DcCM, NewGrD 80*
Brunton, Ann 1768-1808 *NotNAT B*
Brunton, Anne 1769-1808 *OxThe*
Brunton, Garland Lewis d1975 *WhoHol C*
Brunton, John 1741-1822 *NotNAT B, OxThe*
Brunton, John 1775-1848 *OxThe*
Brunton, John 1775-1849 *NotNAT B*
Brunton, Louisa 1779-1860 *NotNAT B, OxThe*
Brunton, William *Film 1*
Brunvoll, Gunnar Arne 1924- *WhoOp 76*
Bruolo, Bartolomeo *NewGrD 80*
Brusa, Francesco 1700?-1768? *NewGrD 80*
Bruscambille *OxThe*
Bruscantini, Sesto 1919- *Baker 78, CmOp, IntWWM 77, -80, NewGrD 80, WhoMus 72, WhoOp 76*
Bruschi, Giulio *NewGrD 80*
Brusey, James Gregory 1912- *WhoMus 72*
Brush, Mrs. Clinton E 1911- *BiE&WWA*
Brush, Clinton E, III 1911- *BiE&WWA*
Brush, Ruth Damaris *AmSCAP 80*
Brush, Ruth J 1910- *AmSCAP 66, ConAmC*
Brusilovsky, Evgeny Grigor'yevich 1905- *Baker 78, NewGrD 80*
Brusilow, Anshel 1928- *NewGrD 80*
Bruski, Natalio 1906- *IntMPA 77, -75, -76, -78, -79, -80*
Bruskin, Perry 1916- *BiE&WWA*
Bruson, Renato 1936- *NewGrD 80, WhoOp 76*
Brusse, Kees 1925- *FilmAG WE*
Brusseau, William E 1926- *IntMPA 77, -75, -76, -78, -79, -80*
Brussel, Tiburtius Van *NewGrD 80*
Brusselmans, Michel 1886-1960 *Baker 78, NewGrD 80*
Brusser *NewGrD 80*
Brust, Alfred 1891-1934 *ModWD*
Brustad, Bjarne 1895-1978 *Baker 78, NewGrD 80*
Brustein, Robert 1927- *BiE&WWA, NotNAT, WhoThe 72, -77*
Bruster *NewGrD 80*
Brusters *NewGrD 80*
Bruun, Mogens Erik Soelberg 1923- *IntWWM 77, -80*
Bruun Olsen, Ernst 1923- *CroCD*
Bruyck, Karl Debrois Van 1828-1902 *Baker 78*
Bruynel, Ton 1934- *Baker 78, DcCM, NewGrD 80*
Bruyr, Jose 1889- *NewGrD 80*
Bruzdowicz, Joanna 1943- *Baker 78*
Bruzdowicz-Tittel, Joanna 1943- *IntWWM 77, -80*
Bryan, Albertus *NewGrD 80*
Bryan, Alfred d1958 *Sw&Ld C*
Bryan, Alfred 1871-1948 *AmPS*
Bryan, Alfred 1871-1958 *AmSCAP 66, -80, BiDAmM, CmpEPM*
Bryan, Arthur Q 1899-1959 *WhScrn 74, -77, WhoHol B*
Bryan, Charles Faulkner 1911-1955 *AmSCAP 66, -80, BiDAmM, ConAmC, EncFCWM 69*
Bryan, Dora *IntMPA 77, -75, -76, -78, -79, -80, WhoHol A*
Bryan, Dora 1923- *FilmgC, HalFC 80*
Bryan, Dora 1924- *EncMT, FilmEn, IlWWBF[port], WhoThe 72, -77*
Bryan, George 1910-1969 *WhScrn 77, WhoHol B*
Bryan, Hal 1891-1948 *NotNAT B*
Bryan, Herbert George d1948 *NotNAT B*
Bryan, Jackson Lee 1909-1964 *WhScrn 74, -77*
Bryan, Jane 1918- *FilmEn, FilmgC, ForYSC, HalFC 80, MotPP, ThFT[port], What 5[port], WhoHol A*
Bryan, John 1911-1969 *DcFM, FilmEn, FilmgC, HalFC 80*
Bryan, John Howard 1952- *IntWWM 80*
Bryan, Mike 1916-1972 *EncJzS 70, WhoJazz 72*
Bryan, Ruth *Film 1*
Bryan, Ruth Jennings *WomWMM*
Bryan, Vincent *CmpEPM*
Bryan, Vincent 1883-1937 *BiDAmM*
Bryan-Turner, Edward Lorimer 1925- *IntWWM 77, -80*
Bryans, Rudy 1945?- *CnOxB*
Bryant, Allan C 1931- *Baker 78, ConAmC*
Bryant, Anita *AmPS A, -B*
Bryant, Anita 1940- *RkOn[port]*
Bryant, Anita 1941- *BiDAmM*
Bryant, Anne Marie 1937- *AmSCAP 80*
Bryant, Ardie 1929- *AmSCAP 80*
Bryant, Beulah 1918- *BluesWW[port]*
Bryant, Billy *NotNAT A*
Bryant, Bobby 1934- *EncJzS 70*
Bryant, Boudleaux 1920- *BiDAmM, EncFCWM 69, IlEncCM, PopAmC SUP[port]*
Bryant, Carolyn 1944- *IntWWM 77, -80*
Bryant, Celia Mae 1913- *IntWWM 77, -80*
Bryant, Charles 1879-1948 *FilmEn, NotNAT B, WhScrn 74, -77, WhoHol B, WomWMM*
Bryant, Charles 1887-1948 *Film 1, -2, TwYS*
Bryant, Clifford Lisle 1933- *AmSCAP 80*
Bryant, Dan 1833-1875 *BiDAmM, NewGrD 80, NotNAT B*
Bryant, Felice 1925- *EncFCWM 69, IlEncCM*
Bryant, Frederick James, Jr. 1942- *BlkAmP*
Bryant, Gilmore Ward 1859-1946 *BiDAmM*
Bryant, Hazel 1939- *BlkAmP, DrBlPA*
Bryant, Ivy 1925- *BiDAmM*
Bryant, J V 1889-1924 *NotNAT B*
Bryant, James *Film 1*
Bryant, John *WhoHol A*
Bryant, Joyce 1927?- *DrBlPA*
Bryant, Kay *Film 2*
Bryant, Margaret C 1908- *BiE&WWA*
Bryant, Mary 1936- *BiE&WWA, NotNAT*
Bryant, Michael 1928- *FilmEn, FilmgC, HalFC 80, WhoThe 72, -77*
Bryant, Nana 1888-1955 *FilmEn, FilmgC, HalFC 80, MovMk, NotNAT B, Vers A[port], WhScrn 74, -77, WhoHol B*
Bryant, Nana 1895-1955 *ForYSC*
Bryant, Paul C 1933- *BiDAmM*
Bryant, Raphael 1931- *BiDAmM, EncJzS 70*
Bryant, Ray 1931- *EncJzS 70, RkOn*
Bryant, Raymond 1908- *IntWWM 77, -80*
Bryant, Robin d1976 *WhoHol C*
Bryant, Royal G 1929- *EncJzS 70*
Bryant, Rusty 1929- *EncJzS 70, RkOn*
Bryant, Ruth Audrey 1918- *IntWWM 77, -80, WhoMus 72*
Bryant, Thomas Hoyt 1908- *BiDAmM*
Bryant, William Cullen 1794-1878 *BiDAmM*
Bryant, William Steven 1908-1964 *AmSCAP 80, BiDAmM*
Bryant, Willie 1908-1964 *AmSCAP 66, BgBands 74, CmpEPM, DrBlPA, NotNAT B, WhoJazz 72*
Bryar, Claudia *WhoHol A*
Bryar, Paul 1910- *Vers B[port], WhoHol A*
Bryars, Charles Alan 1915- *WhoMus 72*
Bryars, Gavin 1943- *NewGrD 80*
Bryce, Alex 1905- *IlWWBF*
Bryce, Owen 1920- *IntWWM 77, -80, WhoMus 72*
Bryden, Beryl 1926- *EncJzS 70*
Bryden, Bill 1942- *WhoThe 77*
Bryden, John Carrick McClure 1947- *IntWWM 77, -80*
Bryden, John Rennie 1913- *IntWWM 80*
Bryden, Ronald 1927- *WhoThe 72, -77*
Brydon, Roderick 1939- *IntWWM 77, -80, WhoMus 72*
Brydon, Wilson P 1918- *AmSCAP 66, -80*
Brydone, Alfred *Film 1*
Brydson, John Callis 1900- *IntWWM 77, -80, WhoMus 72*
Bryennius, Manuel *Baker 78, NewGrD 80*
Brygeman, William d1524 *NewGrD 80*
Brylawski, Julian A 1882- *IntMPA 75, -76*
Brymer, Jack 1915- *IntWWM 77, -80, NewGrD 80, WhoMus 72*
Brymm, James Tim 1881-1946 *BiDAmM*
Brymn, J Tim 1881-1946 *AmSCAP 66, -80*
Brymner, William 1855-1925 *CreCan 2*
Bryn-Jones, Delme 1934- *CmOp, IntWWM 77, -80, WhoMus 72, WhoOp 76*
Bryn-Julson, Phyllis 1945- *NewGrD 80*
Bryne, Albert 1621?-1671 *NewGrD 80*
Bryne, Albertus 1621?-1671 *NewGrD 80*
Brynner, Yul *AmPS B, BiE&WWA, IntMPA 77, -75, -76, -78, -79, -80, MotPP, PlP&P[port], WhoHol A*
Brynner, Yul 1915- *BiDFilm, -81, CmMov, EncMT, FilmEn, FilmgC, ForYSC, HalFC 80[port], MovMk[port], WhoHrs 80[port], WorEFlm[port]*
Brynner, Yul 1916- *CmMov, OxFilm*
Bryon, Charles Anthony 1919- *IntMPA 80*
Bryson, Arthur *Film 2*
Bryson, Betty *WhoHol A*
Bryson, E J 1915- *IntMPA 77, -75, -76, -78, -79, -80*
Bryson, Ernest 1867-1942 *Baker 78*
Bryson, Evelyn Mary 1939- *WhoOp 76*

Bryson, Winifred Film 2, TwYS
Bryssiger, Peter NewGrD 80
Brysson, John d1818 NewGrD 80
Brzeski, Andrzej Tadeusz 1944- IntWWM 77
Brzezicka-Niemotko, Krystyna 1938- IntWWM 77
Brzezina, Antoni d1831 NewGrD 80
Brzowski, Josef 1803-1888 NewGrD 80
Brzozowska, Natalia WomWMM
Bua, Gene WhoHol A
Buazzelli, Tino 1922- EncWT, Ent[port]
Bubak, Bohdan 1946- IntWWM 77, -80
Bubak, Josef 1902- IntWWM 77, -80
Bubalo, Rudolph Daniel 1927- AmSCAP 80, ConAmC
Bubble Puppy RkOn 2[port]
Bubbles, John 1902- AmPS B, DrBlPA, PlP&P[port], What 5[port]
Bubenik, Kvetoslav 1922- WhoOp 76
Bubniuk, Irena Olga 1928- IntWWM 77
Bucaenus, Paulus NewGrD 80
Bucalossi, Brigata d1924 NotNAT B
Bucalossi, Ernest d1933 NotNAT B
Bucalossi, Procida d1918 NotNAT B
Bucchi, Valentino 1916-1976 Baker 78, DcCM, NewGrD 80, WhoMus 72
Bucchianti, Giovanni Pietro 1608-1627? NewGrD 80
Bucci, Jane 1929- IntWWM 77, -80
Bucci, Mark 1924- Baker 78, ConAmC, DcCM
Buccola, Guy Film 2
Bucellanito, Auritius NewGrD 80
Bucellanito, Nicolaus De NewGrD 80
Bucenus, Paulus NewGrD 80
Buch, Hans Joachim 1935- IntWWM 80
Buchan, Annabelle Whitford d1961 NotNAT B
Buchan, David 1903- WhoMus 72
Buchan, John NewGrD 80
Buchan, John 1875-1940 FilmgC, HalFC 80
Buchanan, Annabel 1889- BiDAmM
Buchanan, Annabel Morris 1888- AmSCAP 66, ConAmC
Buchanan, Charles L d1962 NotNAT B
Buchanan, Claud Film 2
Buchanan, Cynthia NatPD[port]
Buchanan, Dorothy Quita 1945- IntWWM 77, -80
Buchanan, Edgar 1902-1979 CmMov, FilmgC, HalFC 80, IntMPA 77, -75, -76, -78, -79, MotPP, MovMk, WhoHol A
Buchanan, Edgar 1903-1979 FilmEn, ForYSC, HolCA[port]
Buchanan, Edward L 1918- ConAmC
Buchanan, Jack 1890-1957 CnThe
Buchanan, Jack 1891-1957 CmpEPM, EncMT, FilmAG WE, FilmEn, Film 1, -2, FilmgC, ForYSC, HalFC 80[port], IlWWBF[port], -A, MotPP, NotNAT B, OxFilm, WhScrn 74, -77, WhoHol B
Buchanan, James Gilbert 1917- BiDAmM
Buchanan, Larry WhoHrs 80
Buchanan, Meg d1970 WhScrn 77
Buchanan, Patrick J NewYTET
Buchanan, Robert d1901 NotNAT B
Buchanan, Roy IlEncR
Buchanan, Stuart 1894-1974 WhScrn 77
Buchanan, Thompson 1877-1937 NotNAT B
Buchanan, Virginia d1931 NotNAT B
Buchanan And Goodman RkOn
Buchannan, Patricia WomWMM B
Buchardo, Carlos Lopez NewGrD 80
Bucharoff, Simon 1881-1955 AmSCAP 66, Baker 78, ConAmC
Buchbinder, Rudolf 1946- WhoMus 72
Bucher, Josef 1929- IntWWM 77, -80
Bucher, Karl 1847-1930 Baker 78
Bucherer, Wilhelmine 1919- IntWWM 77
Buchholz, Horst 1932- FilmAG WE[port], FilmEn
Buchholz, Horst 1933- BiE&WWA, FilmgC, ForYSC, HalFC 80, IntMPA 77, -75, -76, -78, -79, -80, MotPP, MovMk, WhoHol A, WorEFlm[port]
Buchma, Ambrose Film 2
Buchman, Sidney 1902-1975 FilmEn, FilmgC, HalFC 80, IntMPA 75, WorEFlm[port]
Buchmayer, Richard 1856-1934 Baker 78
Buchner, Alexandr 1911- NewGrD 80
Buchner, August 1591-1661 NewGrD 80
Buchner, Georg 1813-1837 CnThe, EncWT, Ent, McGEWD[port], NewEOp 71, NotNAT B, OxThe, PlP&P[port], REnWD[port]
Buchner, Hans 1483-1538? Baker 78, NewGrD 80
Buchner, Philipp Friedrich 1614-1669 Baker 78, NewGrD 80
Buchome, Ferose 1922- IntWWM 77, -80
Buchowetzki, Dimitri 1885-1932 FilmEn
Buchowetzki, Dimitri 1895-1932 DcFM
Buchowetzki, Dmitri 1895-1932 BiDFilm, -81
Buchowetzski, Dimitri 1895-1932 TwYS A
Bucht, Gunnar 1927- Baker 78, DcCM, IntWWM 77, -80, NewGrD 80
Buchtel, Forrest Lawrence 1899- AmSCAP 66, -80, ConAmC, IntWWM 77, -80
Buchtger, Fritz 1903- Baker 78, DcCM
Buchwald, Theo 1902-1960 NewGrD 80
Bucil, Milan Bohumil 1936- IntWWM 77, -80
Buciuceanu, Iulia 1934- WhoOp 76
Buck DrBlPA
Buck, Carlton C 1907- AmSCAP 66, -80
Buck, Charles Stary 1928- AmSCAP 66, -80
Buck, David 1936- WhoThe 72, -77
Buck, David L 1937- IntWWM 77, -80
Buck, Dudley 1839-1909 Baker 78, BiDAmM, NewGrD 80, OxMus
Buck, Dudley 1869-1941 Baker 78, OxMus
Buck, Edward Eugene 1885-1957 BiDAmM
Buck, Elizabeth 1912-1934 WhScrn 74, -77
Buck, Ford d1955 WhScrn 74, -77, WhoHol B
Buck, Frank 1888-1950 FilmEn, FilmgC, ForYSC, HalFC 80, WhScrn 74, -77, WhoHol B
Buck, Gene 1885-1957 AmPS, AmSCAP 66, -80, CmpEPM, EncMT, NewCBMT, NotNAT B, Sw&Ld B
Buck, Sir George OxThe
Buck, Inez 1890-1957 NotNAT B, WhScrn 74, -77, WhoHol B
Buck, Jack NewYTET
Buck, Jules 1917- FilmEn, FilmgC, HalFC 80, IntMPA 77, -75, -76, -78, -79, -80
Buck, Lawrence AmSCAP 80
Buck, Nell Roy Film 2
Buck, Ole 1945- IntWWM 77, -80, NewGrD 80
Buck, Pearl S 1892-1973 BiE&WWA, FilmgC, HalFC 80
Buck, Sir Percy Carter 1871-1947 Baker 78, NewGrD 80, OxMus
Buck, Richard Henry 1870-1956 AmSCAP 66, -80, BiDAmM
Buck, Wayne Richard 1948- IntWWM 77, -80
Buck, Zechariah 1798-1879 NewGrD 80, OxMus
Buck And Bubbles BlksB&W C
Buckaroos, The BiDAmM, EncFCWM 69
Bucken, Ernst 1884-1949 Baker 78, NewGrD 80
Buckham, Bernard d1963 NotNAT B
Buckham, Hazel Film 1
Buckingham, Francis Walter WhoMus 72
Buckingham, Geoffrey MagIID
Buckingham, George Villiers, Duke Of 1628-1687 OxThe
Buckingham, Lillian Film 1
Buckingham, Robert WhoHol A
Buckinghams, The BiDAmM, RkOn 2[port]
Buckland, Warwick IlWWBF
Buckle, Richard 1916- CnOxB, DancEn 78
Buckler, Ernest 1908- CreCan 2
Buckler, Hugh 1870-1936 NotNAT B, WhScrn 77, WhoHol B
Buckler, John 1896-1936 NotNAT B, WhScrn 77, WhoHol B
Buckley, Annie d1916 NotNAT B, WhoStg 1908
Buckley, Charles T d1920 NotNAT B
Buckley, Dorothy Pike 1911- ConAmC, IntWWM 77
Buckley, Emerson 1916- IntWWM 77, -80, NewEOp 71, WhoOp 76
Buckley, F Rauson d1943 NotNAT B
Buckley, Floyd 1874-1956 Film 1, NotNAT B, WhScrn 74, -77, WhoHol B
Buckley, Geoffrey 1930- IntWWM 77, -80, WhoMus 72
Buckley, Hal WhoHol A
Buckley, Helen Dallam 1899- BiDAmM
Buckley, Joseph 1875-1930 WhScrn 74, -77
Buckley, Lord 1905- IlEncR
Buckley, Mary Henderson 1912- IntWWM 77, -80
Buckley, May 1880- WhoStg 1906, -1908
Buckley, R Bishop 1810?-1867 BiDAmM
Buckley, Robert Allen 1949- WhoOp 76
Buckley, Sara WhoMus 72
Buckley, Tim 1947-1975 ConMuA 80A, IlEncR[port]
Buckley, Timothy Charles, III 1947-1975 AmSCAP 80
Buckley, William Film 2
Buckman, Rosana 1880?-1948 CmOp
Buckman, Rosina 1880?-1948 NewGrD 80
Bucknall, Joan 1923- WhoMus 72
Bucknell, Bruce PupTheA
Buckner, Barbara WomWMM B
Buckner, John Edward 1909- BiDAmM, EncJzS 70
Buckner, Milt 1915- Baker 78, CmpEPM, EncJzS 70
Buckner, Milton 1915- EncJzS 70
Buckner, Robert 1906- FilmEn
Buckner, Robert H 1906- FilmgC, HalFC 80, IntMPA 77, -75, -76, -78, -79, -80
Buckner, Ted 1913-1976 EncJzS 70, WhoJazz 72
Buckner, Teddy 1909- CmpEPM, EncJzS 70, WhoJazz 72
Buckner, Theodore Guy 1913-1976 EncJzS 70
Buckstone, J C 1858-1924 NotNAT B
Buckstone, John Baldwin 1802-1879 NotNAT B, OxThe
Buckstone, Roland 1862-1922 Film 1
Buckstone, Rowland 1860-1922 NotNAT B
Buckstone, Rowland 1861-1922 WhoStg 1906, -1908
Buckton, Florence PlP&P
Buckton, Roger Malcolm 1939- WhoMus 72
Buckwitz, Harry 1904- EncWT, Ent
Bucky, Frida Sarsen AmSCAP 66
Bucquet, Harold S 1891-1946 FilmEn, FilmgC, HalFC 80, WhScrn 74, -77
Buczek, Barbara 1940- NewGrD 80
Buczkowski, Leonard 1900-1966 FilmEn, OxFilm
Buczynski, Walter 1933- Baker 78
Bud And Travis RkOn
Budarin, Vadim Andreyevich 1942- CnOxB
Budashkin, Nicolai 1910- Baker 78
Budashkin, Nikolai Pavlovich 1910- IntWWM 77, -80
Budd, Harold 1936- Baker 78, ConAmC, DcCM
Budd, John W 1923- AmSCAP 66
Budd, Roy 1949- HalFC 80
Budde, Elmar 1935- NewGrD 80
Budde, Kurt 1894- IntWWM 77
Budden, Julian Medforth 1924- IntWWM 77, -80, NewGrD 80
Budden, Roy Thomas 1913- IntWWM 77, -80, WhoMus 72
Buddy Boy BluesWW[port]
Budge, Donald What 1[port]
Budge, George Henry William WhoMus 72
Budge, Melba Cornwell 1898- IntWWM 77
Budgie IlEncR
Budimer, Dennis Matthew 1938- BiDAmM
Budimir, Dennis Matthew 1938- EncJzS 70
Budka, Harry H 1913- AmSCAP 66, -80
Budka, Mildred Livesay 1912- AmSCAP 66, -80
Budreckas, Ladislaus 1905- ConAmC
Budriunus, Bronius 1909- ConAmC
Budwig, Monty 1929- BiDAmM, EncJzS 70
Buebendorf, Francis 1912- ConAmC
Bueche, Gregory A 1903- AmSCAP 66, ConAmC A
Buechenberg, Matheus d1628 NewGrD 80
Buechenberg, Matteo d1628 NewGrD 80
Buechman, Charles E 1943- IntWWM 77
Buechner, Nelson Ernest 1931- IntWWM 77
Buehler, Anne PupTheA
Buehler, Arthur d1962 NotNAT B
Buehrer, Urs 1942- IntWWM 80
Buel, Christoph 1574-1631 NewGrD 80

Buell, Harriett Eugenia 1834-1910 *BiDAmM*
Buell, John 1927- *CreCan 1*
Buelow, George J 1929- *NewGrD 80*
Buenaventura, Alfredo Santos 1929- *NewGrD 80*
Buenaventura, Antonio 1904- *NewGrD 80*
Buencamino, Francisco 1883-1972 *NewGrD 80*
Buerkle, Russell C 1915- *AmSCAP 66, -80*
Buero Vallejo, Antonio 1916- *CnMD, CroCD, McGEWD[port], ModWD*
Buesst, Aylmer 1883-1970 *NewGrD 80*
Buesst, Jill Helen 1928- *WhoMus 72*
Buetel, Jack 1917- *FilmEn, FilmgC, ForYSC, HalFC 80*
Bufano, Remo 1894-1948 *DcPup, NotNAT B, PupTheA*
Buff, Iva Moore 1932- *IntWWM 77, -80*
Buffalo Bill 1846-1917 *OxFilm, OxThe*
Buffalo Bill, Jr. d1961 *ForYSC, TwYS, WhoHol B*
Buffalo Bill, Jr. 1902- *FilmEn*
Buffalo Springfield *BiDAmM, ConMuA 80A, IlEncR, RkOn 2[port]*
Buffano, Jules 1897-1960 *AmSCAP 80*
Buffardin, Pierre-Gabriel 1690?-1768 *NewGrD 80*
Buffett, Jimmy *ConMuA 80A, CounME 74[port], -74A*
Buffett, Jimmy 1946- *RkOn 2[port]*
Buffett, Jimmy 1947- *IlEncCM[port]*
Buffett, Jimmy 1948- *IlEncR*
Buffham, Charles Allen 1940- *ConAmC*
Buffington, Don 1907- *AmSCAP 66, -80*
Buffington, Sam d1960 *WhScrn 77*
Buffkins, Archie Lee *ConAmC*
Bufman, Zev 1930- *BiE&WWA, WhoThe 72, -77*
Buford, George 1929- *BluesWW[port]*
Bugatch, Samuel 1898- *AmSCAP 66, -80, ConAmC*
Buggert, Robert W 1918- *ConAmC*
Bughardt, George *Film 2*
Bughici, Dumitru 1921- *Baker 78, IntWWM 77, -80, NewGrD 80*
Buglhat, Johannes De *NewGrD 80*
Bugnet, Georges 1879- *CreCan 2*
Bugos, Keith Richard 1948- *AmSCAP 80*
Buhel, Christoph *NewGrD 80*
Buhl, Joseph David 1781- *NewGrD 80*
Buhler, Franz 1760-1823 *Baker 78*
Buhler, Richard 1876-1925 *Film 1, NotNAT B, WhScrn 77, WhoHol B*
Buhler, William *Film 1*
Buhlig, Richard 1880-1952 *Baker 78, BiDAmM*
Buhmler, Georg Heinrich *NewGrD 80*
Buhrer, Urs 1942- *IntWWM 77*
Buhrman, Albert John, Jr. 1915- *AmSCAP 66, -80*
Buhrman, Bert *ConAmC*
Buhrmann, Max *DcPup*
Buhs, Martha *CreCan 1*
Buie, Buddy *ConMuA 80B*
Buina, Giuseppe Maria 1680?-1739 *NewGrD 80*
Buini, Giuseppe Maria 1680?-1739 *NewGrD 80*
Buini, Matteo *NewGrD 80*
Buisson, Du *NewGrD 80*
Buissonneau, Paul 1926- *CreCan 2*
Buissons, Des *NewGrD 80*
Bujanska, Maria 1943- *WhoMus 72*
Bujarski, Zbigniew 1933- *IntWWM 77, -80, NewGrD 80*
Bujold, Genevieve 1942- *FilmEn, FilmgC, ForYSC, HalFC 80, IntMPA 77, -75, -76, -78, -79, -80, WhoHol A, WhoHrs 80[port]*
Bujold, Genevieve 1943- *CreCan 1*
Bujold, Genevieve 1945- *BiDFilm 81*
Bujones, Fernando 1955- *CnOxB*
Buka, Donald 1921- *ForYSC, WhoHol A*
Buketoff, Igor 1915- *AmSCAP 80, Baker 78, IntWWM 77, -80, WhoMus 72*
Bukofzer, Manfred F 1910-1955 *Baker 78, BiDAmM, NewGrD 80, OxMus*
Bukojemska, Ewa Maria 1949- *IntWWM 77, -80*
Bukovac, Paula 1935- *WhoOp 76*
Bukureshtliev, Angel 1870-1951 *NewGrD 80*
Bul, Christoph *NewGrD 80*
Bul, Jan 1562?-1628 *NewGrD 80, -80*
Bul, John 1562?-1628 *NewGrD 80, -80*
Bulajic, Veljko 1928- *FilmEn*
Bulajic, Velko 1928- *DcFM*
Bulandra, Lucia Sturdza 1873-1961 *OxThe*
Bulant, Antoine *NewGrD 80*
Bulatoff, Paul 1948- *IntWWM 77, -80*
Bulfinch, Charles 1763-1844 *NotNAT B*
Bulfinch, Stephen Greenleaf 1809-1870 *BiDAmM*
Bulgakov, Barbara *BiE&WWA, NotNAT*
Bulgakov, Leo 1889-1948 *NotNAT B, PlP&P, WhScrn 74, -77, WhoHol B*
Bulgakov, Michael Afanasyev 1891-1940 *OxThe*
Bulgakov, Mikhail 1891-1940 *CnMD, CnThe, Ent, ModWD*
Bulgakov, Mikhail Afanasyev 1891-1940 *NotNAT B*
Bulgakov, Mikhail Afanasyevich 1891-1940 *EncWT, McGEWD, REnWD[port]*
Bulger, Harry d1926 *NotNAT B*
Bulhat, Johannes De *NewGrD 80*
Bulifant, Joyce *WhoHol A*
Bulkin, Kelly Lynn 1957- *AmSCAP 80*
Bulkin, Leslie Ann 1959- *AmSCAP 80*
Bull, Amos 1744-1805? *BiDAmM*
Bull, Charles Edward *Film 2*
Bull, Christoph *NewGrD 80*
Bull, Jan 1562?-1628 *NewGrD 80*
Bull, John 1562-1628 *Baker 78, BnBkM 80, CmpBCM, GrComp[port], MusMk[port], NewGrD 80, OxMus*
Bull, John 1563-1628 *DcCom&M 79*
Bull, Ole 1810-1880 *BnBkM 80, NewGrD 80[port]*
Bull, Ole Borneman 1810-1880 *OxMus, OxThe*
Bull, Ole Bornemann 1810-1880 *Baker 78*
Bull, Peter 1912- *BiE&WWA, FilmEn, FilmgC, ForYSC, HalFC 80, IlWWBF A, MotPP, NotNAT, -A, PlP&P[port], WhoHol A, WhoThe 72*
Bull, Sandy *ConMuA 80A*
Bull, Storm 1913- *IntWWM 77, -80*
Bull, William *NewGrD 80*
Bull Cow *BluesWW[port]*
Bullandt, Antoine 1750?-1821 *NewGrD 80*
Bullant, Antoine 1750?-1821 *NewGrD 80*
Bullanto, Antoine 1750?-1821 *NewGrD 80*
Bullard, Alan 1947- *IntWWM 77, -80*
Bullard, Bob 1927- *ConAmC*
Bullard, Frederick Field 1864-1904 *Baker 78, BiDAmM*
Bullard, Gene 1937- *WhoOp 76*
Bullault, Antoine 1750?-1821 *NewGrD 80*
Bullen, Leonard *CreCan 1*
Buller, John 1927- *NewGrD 80*
Bullerian *NewGrD 80*
Bullerian, Eddy 1886-1943 *NewGrD 80*
Bullerian, Hans 1885-1948 *NewGrD 80*
Bullerian, Rudolf 1856-1911 *NewGrD 80*
Bullerjahn, Curt *Film 2*
Bullett, Jesse *ConMuA 80B*
Bulley, Erith Lillie Dulce 1913- *IntWWM 77*
Bullington, James Wiley 1933- *AmSCAP 80*
Bullins, Ed *CroCD, MorBAP*
Bullins, Ed 1934- *NotNAT*
Bullins, Ed 1935- *BlkAmP, ConDr 73, -77, DcLB 7[port], DrBlPA, EncWT, Ent, PlP&P A[port], WhoThe 77*
Bullis, Thomas 1627-1708 *NewGrD 80*
Bullis, Thomas 1657?-1712 *NewGrD 80*
Bullman, Barick *NewGrD 80*
Bullock, Boris *Film 2*
Bullock, Chick 1904?- *CmpEPM*
Bullock, Chick 1908- *WhoJazz 72*
Bullock, Christopher d1724 *NotNAT B, PlP&P*
Bullock, Dick d1971 *WhScrn 77*
Bullock, Sir Ernest 1890-1979 *IntWWM 77, -80, NewGrD 80, OxMus, WhoMus 72*
Bullock, John Malcolm 1867-1938 *NotNAT B*
Bullock, Walter 1907-1953 *AmSCAP 66, -80, CmpEPM*
Bullock, William John *PupTheA*
Bullock, William Joseph 1943- *IntWWM 77, -80*
Bullough, John Frank 1928- *IntWWM 77, -80*
Bulman, Barack *NewGrD 80*
Bulman, Barick *NewGrD 80*
Bulman, Baruck *NewGrD 80*
Bulnes, Esmee 1900- *CnOxB, DancEn 78*
Buloff, Joseph 1907- *BiE&WWA, NotNAT, WhoHol A, WhoThe 72, -77*
Bulow, Hans Von 1830-1894 *Baker 78, BnBkM 80[port], CmOp, MusMk, NewEOp 71, NewGrD 80[port], OxMus*
Bulow, Virginia *PupTheA*
Bulterijs, Nini 1929- *NewGrD 80*
Bulthaupt, Heinrich 1849-1905 *Baker 78*
Bultitude, Arthur R 1908- *NewGrD 80*
Bulwer-Lytton, Edward George E Lytton 1803-1873 *McGEWD[port], NotNAT A, -B, OxThe, PlP&P*
Bulwer-Lytton, Edward George Earle 1803-1873 *EncWT, NewEOp 71*
Bumble Bee Slim *BluesWW[port]*
Bumbry, Grace 1937- *Baker 78, CmOp, DrBlPA, IntWWM 77, -80, MusSN[port], NewEOp 71, NewGrD 80, WhoMus 72, WhoOp 76*
Bumbulis-Mellins, Valija 1937- *IntWWM 77, -80*
Bumler, Georg Heinrich 1669-1745 *NewGrD 80*
Bummeler, Georg Heinrich 1669-1745 *NewGrD 80*
Bummler, Georg Heinrich 1669-1745 *NewGrD 80*
Bump, Edmond 1877-1938 *WhScrn 74, -77*
Bumpas, Bob 1911-1959 *WhoHol B*
Bumpas, H W Bob 1911-1959 *WhScrn 74, -77*
Bumpus, Mary Francis *NewGrD 80*
Buna, Roy Peter 1951- *IntWWM 80*
Bunaldi, Francesco *NewGrD 80*
Bunce, Alan 1903-1965 *BiE&WWA, ForYSC, WhScrn 74, -77, WhoHol B*
Bunce, Corajane Diane *ConAmC A*
Bunce, Oliver Bell 1828-1890 *NotNAT B*
Bunch, Boyd 1889- *AmSCAP 66, -80*
Bunch, John L, Jr. 1921- *AmSCAP 80, BiDAmM, EncJzS 70, IntWWM 77*
Bunch, Meribeth A 1938- *IntWWM 77, -80*
Buncie, Joseph Michael 1934- *AmSCAP 80*
Bundel, Raymond *Film 1*
Bundy, Beverly C 1929- *IntWWM 77*
Bundy, Brooke *WhoHol A*
Bundy, Eve M 1910- *AmSCAP 66, -80*
Bundy, Frank 1908- *IntMPA 77, -75, -76, -78, -79, -80*
Bundy, May Sutton 1887- *What 5[port]*
Bundy, Rudy H 1907- *AmSCAP 80*
Bunger, Reid 1935- *WhoOp 76*
Bunger, Richard 1942- *CpmDNM 80, ConAmC*
Bunger, Richard Joseph 1942- *Baker 78, IntWWM 77, -80*
Bungert, August 1845-1915 *Baker 78, NewGrD 80*
Bungoro, Yoshida *DcPup*
Bunin, Hope *PupTheA*
Bunin, Louis *PupTheA*
Bunin, Maury *PupTheA*
Bunin, Revol Samuilovich 1924- *NewGrD 80*
Bunin, Vladimir 1908-1970 *Baker 78*
Bunje *CreCan 2*
Bunke, Jerome Samuel 1945- *IntWWM 77, -80*
Bunke, Joan Elizabeth 1934- *ConAmTC*
Bunke, Ralph *Film 2*
Bunker, Larry 1928- *CmpEPM, EncJzS 70*
Bunker, Lawrence Benjamin 1928- *BiDAmM, EncJzS 70*
Bunker, Ralph 1889-1966 *WhScrn 74, -77, WhoHol B*
Bunn, Alden 1924-1977 *BluesWW[port]*
Bunn, Alfred 1798-1860 *CnThe, NotNAT B, OxThe*
Bunn, Frank George 1909- *WhoMus 72*
Bunn, Margaret Agnes Somerville 1799-1883 *OxThe*
Bunn, Teddy 1909- *BiDAmM, CmpEPM, IlEncJ, WhoJazz 72*
Bunnage, Avis *WhoThe 72, -77*
Bunnett, Edward 1834-1923 *Baker 78*
Bunney, Allan Walter 1905- *WhoMus 72*
Bunney, Herrick 1915- *IntWWM 77, -80, WhoMus 72*
Bunning, Herbert 1863-1937 *Baker 78*
Bunnus, Hermann *NewGrD 80*
Bunny, George 1870-1952 *Film 2, WhScrn 74, -77, WhoHol B*
Bunny, John 1863-1915 *FilmEn, Film 1, FilmgC, HalFC 80, JoeFr[port], MotPP,*

NotNAT B, TwYS, WhScrn 77, WhoHol B
Bunston, Herbert 1874-1935 *Film 2, WhScrn 74, -77, WhoHol B*
Bunting, Edward 1773-1843 *Baker 78, NewGrD 80, OxMus*
Bunton, Margaret Rachel 1905- *AmSCAP 80*
Bunuel, Luis 1900- *BiDFilm, -81, ConLC 16, DcFM, FilmEn, FilmgC, HalFC 80, IntMPA 77, -75, -76, -78, -79, -80, MovMk[port], OxFilm, WhoHrs 80, WorEFlm[port]*
Bunyan, John 1628-1688 *DcPup, NewEOp 71, OxMus*
Bunzel, Gertrude *DancEn 78*
Buona, Valerio *NewGrD 80*
Buonamente, Giovanni Battista d1642 *NewGrD 80*
Buonamente, Giovanni Battista d1643 *Baker 78*
Buonamici, Giuseppe 1846-1914 *Baker 78, NewGrD 80*
Buonanni, Filippo *NewGrD 80*
Buonaparte *NewGrD 80*
Buonarotti, Michelangelo 1568-1642 *McGEWD[port]*
Buonavita, Antonio d1606? *NewGrD 80*
Buongiorno, Crescenzo 1864-1903 *Baker 78*
Buoni, Giorgio d1693? *NewGrD 80*
Buono, Giovan Pietro Del *NewGrD 80*
Buono, Victor *MotPP, WhoHol A*
Buono, Victor 1938- *FilmEn, FilmgC, ForYSC, HalFC 80, HolCA[port], MovMk[port], WhoHrs 80[port]*
Buono, Victor 1939- *IntMPA 77, -75, -76, -78, -79, -80*
Buononcini *Baker 78, NewEOp 71, NewGrD 80*
Buontalenti, Bernardo 1531-1608 *NewGrD 80*
Buontalenti, Bernardo 1536-1608 *EncWT, OxThe*
Buontempo, Joao Domingos *NewGrD 80*
Buquor, Robert 1935-1966 *WhScrn 77*
Burada, Teodor T 1839-1923 *NewGrD 80*
Burada, Theodor 1839-1923 *Baker 78*
Bural, Nemai Chand 1930- *IntWWM 77, -80*
Burani, Michelette 1882-1957 *Film 2, NotNAT B, WhScrn 74, -77, WhoHol B*
Burbadge, Cuthbert 1566?-1636 *NotNAT B*
Burbadge, James 1530?-1597 *NotNAT B*
Burbage, Cuthbert 1566?-1636 *EncWT, OxThe, PlP&P*
Burbage, James 1530?-1597 *EncWT, Ent, OxThe, PlP&P[port]*
Burbage, Richard 1567?-1619 *CnThe, EncWT, Ent[port], NotNAT A, -B, OxThe, PlP&P[port]*
Burbank, Albert 1902-1976 *NewOrJ[port], WhoJazz 72*
Burbank, Goldie 1880-1954 *WhScrn 74, -77*
Burbeck, Frank d1930 *NotNAT B*
Burbridge, Edward 1933- *DrBlPA, WhoThe 77*
Burbure, Leon-Philippe-Marie 1812-1889 *NewGrD 80*
Burbure DeWesembeek, Leon-P-Marie 1812-1889 *Baker 78, NewGrD 80*
Burch, Betty Evans 1888-1956 *WhScrn 74, -77*
Burch, Dean 1927- *NewYTET*
Burch, Helen *Film 2*
Burch, John 1896-1969 *WhScrn 74, -77, WhoHol B*
Burch, Robert William 1929- *IntWWM 77, -80*
Burcham, Wayne 1943- *ConAmC*
Burchard, Johannes *NewGrD 80*
Burchard, Udalricus 1484?- *NewGrD 80*
Burchard, Ulrich 1484?- *NewGrD 80*
Burchardi, Udalricus 1484?- *NewGrD 80*
Burchardi, Ulrich 1484?- *NewGrD 80*
Burchardt, Elsa *Film 2*
Burchenal, Elizabeth d1959 *DancEn 78*
Burchiella *NewGrD 80*
Burchill, James 1936- *WhoMus 72*
Burci, Nicolaus *NewGrD 80*
Burck, Joachim A 1546-1610 *Baker 78, NewGrD 80*
Burckard, Johannes 1445?-1506 *NewGrD 80*
Burco, Ferruccio 1939-1965 *Baker 78*
Burda, Antonin 1902- *IntWWM 77, -80*
Burda, Pavel 1942- *IntWWM 77, -80*
Burdach, Konrad 1859-1936 *NewGrD 80*
Burden, Hugh 1913- *FilmgC, HalFC 80, WhoHol A, WhoThe 72, -77*
Burden, James H 1923- *CpmDNM 80*
Burden, John Harold 1921- *IntWWM 80, WhoMus 72*
Burdet, Jacques 1905- *NewGrD 80*
Burdett, George Albert 1856-1943 *BiDAmM*
Burdette, Eugene 1900-1968 *AmSCAP 66, -80*
Burdette, Jack *Film 2*
Burdette, Winston *NewYTET*
Burdge, Gordon 1906-1975 *AmSCAP 66, -80*
Burdick, Rose *Film 2*
Burdine, W B, Jr. *MorBAP*
Burdon, Albert 1903- *IlWWBF*
Burdon, Eric 1941- *IlEncR[port]*
Burel, Leonce-Henri 1892- *WorEFlm[port]*
Burel, Leonce-Henry 1892- *DcFM, FilmEn*
Burell, John *NewGrD 80*
Bures, Miloslav 1930- *IntWWM 77*
Burette *NewGrD 80*
Burette, Bernard *NewGrD 80*
Burette, Claude *NewGrD 80*
Burette, Pierre-Jean 1665-1747 *Baker 78, NewGrD 80*
Burfield, Joan *FilmEn*
Burg, Eugen *Film 2*
Burgan, Arthur 1923- *IntWWM 80*
Burgate, R De *NewGrD 80*
Burgdorf, James Alan 1953- *AmSCAP 80*
Burge, David R 1930- *ConAmC, NewGrD 80*
Burge, Stuart 1918- *FilmEn, FilmgC, HalFC 80, WhoThe 72, -77*
Burger, Bernard 1932- *IntWWM 77, -80*
Burger, Corky *ConMuA 80B*
Burger, David Mark 1950- *AmSCAP 80*
Burger, Germain Gerard 1900- *IlWWBF*
Burger, Gottfried August 1748-1795 *OxMus*
Burger, H A S 1913- *IntWWM 77*
Burger, Henry 1915- *IntMPA 77, -75, -76, -78, -79, -80*
Burger, Hester Aletta Sophia 1913- *IntWWM 80*
Burger, Jack 1925- *AmSCAP 66, -80*
Burger, Samuel *ConMuA 80B*
Burgess, Anthony 1917- *Baker 78*
Burgess, Cool *AmPS B*
Burgess, Daniel Lawrence 1946- *AmSCAP 80*
Burgess, Dorothy 1907-1961 *FilmEn, Film 2, ForYSC, ThFT[port], WhScrn 77, WhoHol B*
Burgess, Gary Ellsworth 1938- *WhoOp 76*
Burgess, George 1809-1866 *BiDAmM*
Burgess, Grayston 1932- *IntWWM 77, -80, WhoMus 72*
Burgess, Hazel 1910-1973 *WhScrn 77*
Burgess, Helen 1918-1937 *WhScrn 74, -77, WhoHol B*
Burgess, Lord *AmSCAP 80*
Burgess, Nat *ConMuA 80B*
Burgess, Neil 1846-1910 *NotNAT B, WhoStg 1908*
Burgess, Russell Brian 1931- *IntWWM 77, WhoMus 72*
Burgess, William 1867-1948 *WhScrn 77*
Burgess, Wilma 1939- *BiDAmM, EncFCWM 69, IlEncCM*
Burggraf, Waldfried *McGEWD[port]*
Burgh, Steven Lawrence 1950- *AmSCAP 80*
Burghardt, Arthur N 1947?- *BlkAmP, DrBlPA*
Burghardt, Hans-Georg 1909- *IntWWM 77, -80*
Burghauser, Jarmil Michael 1921- *IntWWM 77, -80, NewGrD 80, WhoMus 72*
Burgher, Fairfax 1897-1965 *WhScrn 77*
Burghersh, Lord John Fane 1784-1859 *NewGrD 80*
Burgho, Cesare *NewGrD 80*
Burghoff, Gary *AmSCAP 80, WhoHol A*
Burgie, Irving 1924- *AmSCAP 66, -80, DrBlPA, MorBAP*
Burgin, Richard 1892- *Baker 78*
Burgio, Frances 1917- *AmSCAP 80*
Burgk, Joachim A *NewGrD 80*
Burgmuller, Friedrich 1804-1874 *CnOxB*
Burgmuller, Johann August Franz 1766-1824 *Baker 78, NewGrD 80*
Burgmuller, Johann Friedrich Franz 1806-1874 *Baker 78, OxMus*
Burgmuller, Norbert 1810-1836 *Baker 78, NewGrD 80, OxMus*
Burgo, Cesare *NewGrD 80*
Burgon, Geoffrey 1941- *IntWWM 77, -80, WhoMus 72*
Burgos, Rafael Fruhbeck De *NewGrD 80*
Burgoyne, John 1722-1792 *NotNAT B, PlP&P*
Burgoyne, Ollie 1885- *BlksBF*
Burgoyne, Robert H 1920- *AmSCAP 80*
Burgstahler, Elton E 1924- *AmSCAP 80, ConAmC*
Burgstaller, Alois 1871-1945 *Baker 78, BiDAmM*
Burgund, Ann *WomWMM B*
Burhaus, Hope *PupTheA*
Buri, Bernard De *NewGrD 80*
Burian, Emil Frantisek 1904-1959 *Baker 78, DcCM, EncWT, NewGrD 80, OxThe*
Burian, Jarka M 1927- *BiE&WWA, NotNAT*
Burian, Karel 1870-1924 *CmOp, NewGrD 80*
Burian, Karel Vladimir 1923- *IntWWM 77, -80*
Burian, Karl 1870-1924 *Baker 78*
Burian, Vlasta 1891-1962 *WhScrn 74, -77*
Burk, John Daly d1808 *NotNAT B*
Burk, John N 1891-1967 *Baker 78*
Burk, Robert 1908-1940 *AmSCAP 66*
Burkart, Arnold Emil 1927- *IntWWM 77*
Burke Of Thomond *NewGrD 80*
Burke, Alfred 1918- *FilmgC, HalFC 80, IntMPA 77, -78, -79, -80, WhoThe 77*
Burke, Billie d1970 *MotPP, WhoHol B*
Burke, Billie 1884-1970 *BiE&WWA, OxFilm*
Burke, Billie 1885-1970 *BiDAmM, FilmEn, FilmgC, ForYSC, HalFC 80, MGM[port], MovMk[port], NotNAT A, ThFT[port], TwYS, Vers B[port], WhScrn 74, -77, WhoHrs 80[port]*
Burke, Billie 1886-1970 *Film 1, -2, NotNAT B, WhoStg 1906, -1908*
Burke, Charles 1822-1854 *NotNAT B, OxThe*
Burke, Darlene Landry Harris *IntWWM 77*
Burke, David 1934- *WhoThe 77*
Burke, Dermot 1948- *CnOxB*
Burke, Ed 1906- *WhoJazz 72*
Burke, Edmund 1876-1970 *NewGrD 80*
Burke, Georgia 1906- *BiE&WWA, DrBlPA, NotNAT*
Burke, J Francis 1914- *AmSCAP 66*
Burke, J Frank 1867-1918 *Film 1, WhScrn 77*
Burke, James d1968 *ForYSC, MotPP, Vers B[port], WhScrn 74, WhoHol B*
Burke, James 1886-1968 *FilmEn, WhScrn 77*
Burke, James 1898-1968 *FilmgC, HalFC 80*
Burke, Joanne *WomWMM*
Burke, Joe 1884-1950 *BiDAmM, CmpEPM, Film 2*
Burke, Johnny *Sw&Ld C*
Burke, Johnny 1908-1964 *AmPS, AmSCAP 66, -80, BiDAmM, BiE&WWA, CmpEPM, FilmEn, Film 2, FilmgC, HalFC 80, NotNAT B*
Burke, Johnny 1908-1969 *ConAmC A*
Burke, Joseph *Film 1, -2*
Burke, Joseph 1884-1942 *WhScrn 77*
Burke, Joseph A 1884-1950 *AmPS, AmSCAP 66, -80, Sw&Ld C*
Burke, Joseph Francis 1914-1950 *AmSCAP 80*
Burke, Kathleen 1913- *HalFC 80, ThFT[port], WhoHrs 80*
Burke, Lee *AmSCAP 80*
Burke, Lionel DeCourcey 1927- *IntWWM 77*
Burke, Loretto 1922- *ConAmC*
Burke, Marian 1940- *IntWWM 77*
Burke, Marie 1894- *FilmgC, HalFC 80, WhoThe 72*
Burke, Marie R *Film 2*
Burke, Martin Teasdale 1908- *IntWWM 77, -80, WhoMus 72*
Burke, Myra d1944 *NotNAT B*
Burke, Patricia 1917- *FilmgC, HalFC 80, IlWWBF, IntMPA 77, -75, -76, -78, -79, -80, WhoThe 72, -77*
Burke, Paul 1926- *FilmEn, FilmgC, ForYSC, HalFC 80, IntMPA 77, -75, -76, -78, -79, -80, WhoHol A*
Burke, Paul 1941- *IntWWM 77, -80*
Burke, Raymond N 1904- *NewOrJ[port], WhoJazz 72*
Burke, Richard N 1947- *ConAmC*
Burke, Solomon 1935- *RkOn[port]*
Burke, Sonny 1914- *BgBands 74[port], CmpEPM*

Burke, Thomas 1890-1969 NewGrD 80
Burke, Thomas F d1941 WhScrn 74, -77
Burke, Tom 1890-1969 NewGrD 80
Burke, Walter ForYSC, WhoHol A
Burkett, Harold Brent 1939- BiDAmM
Burkhanov, Mutal 1916- NewGrD 80
Burkhanov, Mutavakkil 1916- NewGrD 80
Burkhard, Charles d1927 WhScrn 77
Burkhard, Leonard A 1911- AmSCAP 66, -80
Burkhard, Paul 1911-1977 Baker 78, NewGrD 80
Burkhard, Willy 1900-1955 Baker 78, CompSN[port], DcCM, NewGrD 80, OxMus
Burkhardt, Max 1871-1934 Baker 78
Burkhart, Herman Peter 1921- IntWWM 77, -80
Burkhart, Kent ConMuA 80B
Burkley, Bruce Hunsiker ConAmC
Burko, Louis 1932- IntWWM 77, -80
Burks, J Cooper 1919- IntMPA 77, -75, -76, -78, -79, -80
Burks, Robert 1910-1968 CmMov, FilmEn, FilmgC, HalFC 80, WorEFlm[port]
Burlando, Claude 1918-1938 WhScrn 74, -77
Burlas, Ladislav 1927- Baker 78
Burlasca, Bernardino NewGrD 80
Burle Marx, Walter 1902- NewGrD 80
Burleigh, Alston BlksBF
Burleigh, Bertram Film 2
Burleigh, Bertram 1893- IlWWBF
Burleigh, Cecil 1885- AmSCAP 66, -80, Baker 78, BiDAmM, ConAmC, IntWWM 77, -80, OxMus, WhoMus 72
Burleigh, Harry T 1866-1949 DrBlPA
Burleigh, Harry T 1886-1949 AmSCAP 66, -80
Burleigh, Henry Thacker 1866-1949 Baker 78, BiDAmM, BnBkM 80, NewGrD 80, OxMus
Burleigh, Mary Lou NewGrD 80
Burleith, William Henry 1812-1871 BiDAmM
Burles, Charles 1936- IntWWM 77, -80, WhoOp 76
Burley, George Joseph 1939- ConAmTC
Burlin, Natalie Curtis 1875-1921 BiDAmM
Burlingame, Lloyd WhoThe 77
Burlini, Antonio NewGrD 80
Burlinson, John J, Jr. 1930- IntMPA 77, -75, -76, -78, -79, -80
Burlo, Josephine Film 2
Burmaster, Augusta 1860-1934 Film 1, WhScrn 77
Burmeister, Annelies 1930- NewGrD 80
Burmeister, Augusta Film 2
Burmeister, Joachim 1564-1629 Baker 78, NewGrD 80
Burmeister, Richard 1860-1944 Baker 78, BiDAmM
Burmester, Willy 1869-1933 Baker 78
Burn, Frederick Henry IntWWM 80
Burn, John Paul 1928- WhoMus 72
Burnaby, Anne 1922- IntMPA 77, -75, -76, -78
Burnaby, Dave 1881-1949 WhScrn 77
Burnaby, Davy 1881-1949 Film 2, FilmgC, HalFC 80, IlWWBF, WhScrn 74, WhoHol B
Burnaby, G Davy 1881-1949 NotNAT B
Burnacini, Giovanni 1605?-1655 EncWT, NewGrD 80
Burnacini, Giovanni 1605?-1656 OxThe
Burnacini, Lodovico Ottavio 1636-1707 NotNAT B, OxThe
Burnacini, Ludovico Ottavio 1636-1707 EncWT, Ent, NewGrD 80
Burnand, Sir Francis Cowley 1836-1917 NotNAT B, OxThe
Burnap, Uzziah C 1834-1900 BiDAmM
Burnau, Suanna Jeannette Flake 1938- IntWWM 77, -80
Burne, Gary 1934- CnOxB, DancEn 78
Burne, Nancy 1913-1954 WhScrn 74, -77, WhoHol B
Burne-Hones, Sir Edward PlP&P
Burnell, Buster d1964 NotNAT B
Burness, John Frederick 1933- IntWWM 80
Burness, Les CmpEPM
Burness, Pete 1910- FilmEn, FilmgC, HalFC 80
Burness, Peter 1910- DcFM
Burnet, Bob 1912- WhoJazz 72
Burnet, Dana d1962 NotNAT B
Burnett, Al 1906-1973 WhScrn 77
Burnett, Avery NewGrD 80
Burnett, Carol 1933- EncMT, FilmEn, JoeFr[port], WhoHol A, WhoThe 77
Burnett, Carol 1934- FilmgC, ForYSC, HalFC 80, WhoThe 72
Burnett, Carol 1935- BiDAmM, BiE&WWA, IntMPA 75
Burnett, Carol 1936- IntMPA 77, -76, -78, -79, -80
Burnett, Chester Arthur 1910-1976 BiDAmM, BluesWW[port]
Burnett, Duncan NewGrD 80
Burnett, Ernie 1884-1959 AmSCAP 66, -80, BiDAmM
Burnett, Frances Hodgson 1849-1924 HalFC 80, NotNAT B, PlP&P, WhoStg 1906, -1908
Burnett, Harry PupTheA
Burnett, Joe 1927- BiDAmM
Burnett, June 1914- AmSCAP 66
Burnett, Richard Leslie 1932- WhoMus 72
Burnett, W R 1899- CmMov, FilmEn, FilmgC, HalFC 80, IntMPA 77, -75, -76, -78, -79, -80, WorEFlm[port]
Burnette, Dorsey 1932- RkOn[port]
Burnette, John Franklin 1900- IntWWM 77
Burnette, Johnny 1934-1964 RkOn[port]
Burnette, Lester Alvin 1911-1967 BiDAmM, MovMk
Burnette, Lester Alvin 1912-1967 Vers A[port]
Burnette, Smiley 1911-1967 FilmEn, FilmgC, HalFC 80, MotPP, WhScrn 74, -77, WhoHol B
Burnette, Smiley 1912-1967 ForYSC
Burney, Charles 1726-1814 Baker 78, BnBkM 80, MusMk, NewGrD 80[port], OxMus
Burney, Hal 1900-1933 WhScrn 74, -77
Burney, Oriel Riviere 1899- WhoMus 72
Burnford, Sheila Every 1918- CreCan 2
Burnham, Andrew 1948- IntWWM 80
Burnham, Beatrice Film 2
Burnham, Cardon Vern 1927- AmSCAP 80, ConAmC
Burnham, Charles C d1938 NotNAT B
Burnham, Nicholas 1860-1925 Film 2, WhScrn 77
Burnham, Robertus De NewGrD 80
Burnim, Kalman A 1928- NotNAT
Burno, Rinaldo NewGrD 80
Burns, Alan Raymond 1936- WhoOp 76
Burns, Anne K d1968 NotNAT B
Burns, Annelu 1889-1942 AmSCAP 66, -80
Burns, Bart WhoHol A
Burns, Billy 1904-1963 WhoJazz 72
Burns, Bob 1892-1956 ForYSC
Burns, Bob 1893-1956 FilmEn, FilmgC, HalFC 80[port], WhoHol B
Burns, Bob Bazooka 1893-1956 WhScrn 74, -77
Burns, Bobby Film 2
Burns, Carol WomWMM B
Burns, Catherine 1945- FilmEn, HalFC 80, WhoHol A
Burns, Chalmers 1906- WhoMus 72
Burns, Dave 1924- EncJzS 70
Burns, David 1901-1971 WhScrn 74, -77, WhoHol B
Burns, David 1902- WhoThe 72
Burns, David 1902-1970 FilmgC
Burns, David 1902-1971 BiE&WWA, EncMT, FilmEn, HalFC 80, NotNAT B
Burns, David 1924- EncJzS 70
Burns, Dorothy WhScrn 77
Burns, Ed 1892- FilmEn
Burns, Eddie d1957 WhScrn 77
Burns, Eddie 1892- FilmEn, Film 2
Burns, Eddie 1928- BluesWW[port]
Burns, Edmund 1892- FilmEn, Film 1, -2, ForYSC, TwYS, WhoHol A
Burns, Edward 1892- FilmEn, Film 2
Burns, Eileen WhoHol A
Burns, Fred Film 1, -2
Burns, Fred d1955 WhoHol B
Burns, Fred 1878-1955 FilmEn
Burns, George 1896- Ent, FilmEn, Film 2, FilmgC, ForYSC, Funs[port], HalFC 80, IntMPA 77, -75, -76, -78, -79, -80, JoeFr[port], MotPP, MovMk[port], NotNAT A, WhoHol A, WhoHrs 80
Burns, George And Gracie Allen ForYSC, JoeFr[port]
Burns, Harry 1884-1939 WhScrn 74, -77, WhoHol B
Burns, Harry 1885-1948 WhScrn 74, -77, WhoHol B
Burns, Irving 1914-1968 WhScrn 74, -77, WhoHol B
Burns, James d1975 WhScrn 77, WhoHol C
Burns, James F 1898-1960 AmSCAP 66, -80
Burns, James Michael 1930- IntWWM 77
Burns, Jerry d1962 NotNAT B
Burns, Joan WhoMus 72
Burns, Joseph W 1908- AmSCAP 80
Burns, Kenneth C 1920- BiDAmM, EncFCWM 69
Burns, Lorene Byrnes PupTheA
Burns, Lulu WhScrn 74, -77
Burns, Mark 1936- FilmEn
Burns, Mark 1937- FilmgC, HalFC 80
Burns, Michael 1947- FilmEn, ForYSC, WhoHol A
Burns, Nat 1887-1962 NotNAT B, WhScrn 74, -77, WhoHol B
Burns, Neal 1892-1962 Film 1, -2, TwYS
Burns, Paul Film 2
Burns, Paul E 1881-1967 ForYSC, WhScrn 74, -77
Burns, Paul E 1889-1967 Vers B[port], WhoHol B
Burns, Ralph 1922- AmSCAP 66, -80, BiDAmM, BiE&WWA, CmpEPM
Burns, Robert Film 1, -2
Burns, Robert d1947 WhScrn 77
Burns, Robert 1759-1796 NewGrD 80, OxMus
Burns, Robert Bobby TwYS
Burns, Robert E 1885-1957 WhScrn 77, WhoHol B
Burns, Robert Patrick 1929-1955 WhScrn 74, -77
Burns, Robin PupTheA
Burns, Ronnie 1935- ForYSC, WhoHol A
Burns, Sandy 1884- BlksBF[port]
Burns, Stephen Johnson 1954- AmSCAP 80
Burns, William John 1861-1932 WhScrn 77
Burns And Allen AmPS B, MotPP
Burnside, R H 1870-1952 AmSCAP 66, -80, CmpEPM, EncMT, NotNAT B
Burnside, William W, Jr. d1976 WhoHol C
Burnstein, George CreCan 1
Burnsworth, Charles Carl 1931- IntWWM 77, -80
Burnup, Peter d1964 NotNAT B
Buroni, Antonio NewGrD 80
Burr, Courtney d1961 NotNAT B
Burr, Donald 1907- BiE&WWA, NotNAT
Burr, Doris WhoMus 72
Burr, Edmund d1975 WhScrn 77, WhoHol C
Burr, Eugene d1940 Film 2, WhScrn 77
Burr, Henry CmpEPM
Burr, Marilyn 1933- CnOxB, DancEn 78
Burr, Raymond 1917- BiDFilm, -81, FilmEn, FilmgC, ForYSC, HalFC 80, HolCA[port], IntMPA 77, -75, -76, -78, -79, -80, MotPP, MovMk[port], NewYTET, WhoHol A, WhoHrs 80, WorEFlm[port]
Burr, Robert WhoThe 77
Burr, Willard, Jr. 1852-1915 Baker 78, BiDAmM
Burr, William Orndoff 1932- AmSCAP 80
Burra, Edward 1905- CnOxB, DancEn 78
Burrell, Boz 1946- AmSCAP 80
Burrell, Dave 1940- EncJzS 70
Burrell, George Film 1, -2
Burrell, Herman Davis, II 1940- EncJzS 70
Burrell, Kenneth Earl 1931- BiDAmM, EncJzS 70
Burrell, Kenny 1931- AmSCAP 66, -80, DrBlPA, EncJzS 70, IlEncJ
Burrell, Mary 1850-1898 OxMus
Burrell, Sheila 1922- WhoThe 72, -77
Burrell, Walter, Jr. 1944- DrBlPA
Burrell-Davis, Derek 1918- IntMPA 77, -75, -76, -78, -79, -80
Burrella, Tony NewOrJ
Burress, William Film 1
Burrian, Carl NewGrD 80
Burril, Mary BlkAmP
Burrill, Chris WomWMM A, -B

Burrill, Mary *MorBAP*
Burrill, Timothy 1931- *IntMPA 77, -75, -76, -78, -79, -80*
Burris, Andrew *BlkAmP*
Burris, Harvey *BlksBF*
Burris, J C 1928- *BluesWW[port]*
Burris-Meyer, Harold 1902- *BiE&WWA, NotNAT*
Burritt, Lloyd 1940- *Baker 78*
Burritt, William Nelson 1852-1929 *BiDAmM*
Burroni, Antonio *NewGrD 80*
Burrough, Tom 1869-1929 *WhScrn 77*
Burroughs, Bob Lloyd 1937- *AmSCAP 66, -80, ConAmC*
Burroughs, Charles *MorBAP*
Burroughs, Earl S 1940- *AmSCAP 80*
Burroughs, Edgar Rice 1875-1950 *FilmgC, HalFC 80, WhoHrs 80*
Burroughs, Eric d1960 *WhScrn 74, -77, WhoHol B*
Burroughs, James *Film 2*
Burroughs, Marie 1866- *WhoStg 1906, -1908*
Burroughs, Mouse 1911-1950 *WhoJazz 72*
Burroughs, Robert C 1923- *BiE&WWA, NotNAT*
Burrowes, James d1926 *NotNAT B*
Burrowes, John Freckleton 1787-1852 *Baker 78, NewGrD 80*
Burrowes, Norma Elizabeth 1944- *IntWWM 77, -80, NewGrD 80, WhoMus 72, WhoOp 76*
Burrows, Abe 1910- *AmSCAP 66, -80, BestMus, BiE&WWA, ConDr 73, -77, EncMT, Ent, FilmgC, HalFC 80, ModWD, NewCBMT, NotNAT, WhoThe 72, -77*
Burrows, Abram S 1910- *BiDAmM*
Burrows, David 1930- *IntWWM 77, -80*
Burrows, Don 1928- *EncJzS 70*
Burrows, Donald Ivan 1930- *IntWWM 80*
Burrows, Donald James 1945- *IntWWM 77, -80*
Burrows, Donald Vernon 1928- *EncJzS 70*
Burrows, James Stuart 1933- *IntWWM 80*
Burrows, John 1941- *IntWWM 77, -80*
Burrows, John 1945- *ConDr 77*
Burrows, John H 1924- *IntMPA 77, -75, -76, -78, -79, -80*
Burrows, Stuart 1933- *CmOp, NewGrD 80, WhoMus 72, WhoOp 76*
Burrows, Vinie 1928- *DrBlPA, MorBAP*
Burrud, Bill 1924- *NewYTET*
Burrud, Bill 1925- *IntMPA 77, -75, -76, -78, -79, -80, WhoHol A*
Burrud, William 1925- *ForYSC*
Burry, Lloyd Noah French 1929- *IntWWM 80*
Burry, Solen d1953 *NotNAT B*
Burse, Charlie 1901-1965 *BluesWW[port]*
Bursey, Rosetta 1912- *WhoMus 72*
Burstein, John 1949- *AmSCAP 80*
Burstein, Lillian *AmSCAP 80*
Burstyn, Ellen 1932- *BiDFilm 81, FilmEn, HalFC 80, IntMPA 77, -76, -78, -79, -80, MovMk, WhoHol A, WomWMM*
Burstyn, Neil *WhoHol A*
Burt, Amanda M 1916- *IntWWM 77, -80*
Burt, Bates Gilbert 1878-1948 *BiDAmM*
Burt, Benjamin Hapgood 1882-1950 *AmSCAP 66, -80*
Burt, Charles Aycock 1943- *ConAmC*
Burt, Francis 1926- *Baker 78, DcCM, IntWWM 80, NewGrD 80*
Burt, Frank A d1964 *NotNAT A, -B*
Burt, Frederic 1876-1943 *WhScrn 74, -77*
Burt, Frederick 1876-1943 *NotNAT B, WhoHol B*
Burt, George 1929- *ConAmC*
Burt, Harriet 1885-1935 *NotNAT B, WhoStg 1908*
Burt, Laura 1872-1952 *NotNAT B, WhScrn 77*
Burt, Laura 1882- *WhoStg 1906, -1908*
Burt, Margaret *Film 2*
Burt, Nathaniel Clark 1825-1874 *BiDAmM*
Burt, Nellie *Film 1*
Burt, Virginia M 1919- *ConAmC*
Burt, Warren 1949- *ConAmC*
Burt, William P 1873-1955 *Film 2, NotNAT B, WhScrn 74, -77, WhoHol B*
Burtch, Mervyn Arthur *WhoMus 72*
Burte, Hermann 1879-1960 *ModWD*
Burtenshaw, Leonard John 1931- *IntWWM 77*
Burtenshaw, Leonard John 1941- *IntWWM 80*
Burth, Jurg 1944- *CnOxB*
Burtis, James 1893-1939 *WhScrn 77*
Burtius, Nicolaus 1445?- *Baker 78*
Burtius, Nicolaus 1450?-1518? *NewGrD 80*
Burtnett, Earl 1896-1936 *AmSCAP 66, -80, CmpEPM*
Burton, Averie *NewGrD 80*
Burton, Avery *NewGrD 80*
Burton, Barbara 1950- *IntWWM 77, -80*
Burton, Barbara J 1948- *BlkWAB[port]*
Burton, Bernard *IntMPA 77, -75, -76, -78, -79, -80*
Burton, Charlotte 1882-1942 *Film 1, MotPP, WhScrn 74, -77, WhoHol B*
Burton, Clarence 1882-1933 *Film 1, -2, ForYSC, TwYS, WhScrn 74, -77, WhoHol B*
Burton, David *NewGrD 80*
Burton, David 1890- *FilmEn*
Burton, Davy *NewGrD 80*
Burton, Edward J 1926- *AmSCAP 80, NatPD[port]*
Burton, Eldin 1913- *AmSCAP 66, -80, ConAmC*
Burton, Ethel *Film 1*
Burton, Frances *WomWMM B*
Burton, Frederick 1871-1957 *Film 1, -2, WhScrn 74, -77*
Burton, Frederick Russell 1861-1909 *Baker 78, BiDAmM*
Burton, Gary 1943- *BiDAmM, EncJzS 70, IlEncJ*
Burton, George H 1900-1955 *WhScrn 74, -77, WhoHol B*
Burton, James *IlEncR*
Burton, James L 1934- *IntWWM 77*
Burton, Jim *ConAmC*
Burton, John *Film 1*
Burton, John 1730-1782 *NewGrD 80*
Burton, Joleen *ConMuA 80B*
Burton, Joseph R 1928- *AmSCAP 80*
Burton, Julian *WhoHol A*
Burton, Langhorne 1872-1949 *Film 1, -2, IlWWBF[port], NotNAT B*
Burton, Margaret 1924- *IntMPA 77, -75, -76, -78, -79, -80, WhoHol A*
Burton, Michael Arthur Edgar *WhoMus 72*
Burton, Nat 1901-1945 *AmSCAP 66, -80*
Burton, Ned 1850?-1922 *Film 2, WhScrn 74, -77, WhoHol B*
Burton, Nigel Mark 1947- *IntWWM 80*
Burton, Percy 1878-1948 *NotNAT A, -B*
Burton, Philip 1904- *BiE&WWA, NotNAT, -A*
Burton, Richard 1925- *BiDFilm, -81, BiE&WWA, CmMov, CnThe, EncMT, EncWT, Ent, FilmAG WE[port], FilmEn, FilmgC, ForYSC, HalFC 80, IlWWBF, -A, IntMPA 77, -75, -76, -78, -79, -80, MotPP, MovMk[port], NotNAT, -A, OxFilm, WhoHol A, WhoThe 72, -77, WorEFlm[port]*
Burton, Robert d1955 *NotNAT B*
Burton, Robert d1962 *WhoHol B*
Burton, Robert 1820-1892 *NewGrD 80*
Burton, Robert 1895-1964 *WhScrn 77*
Burton, Robert Jay 1914-1965 *EncFCWM 69*
Burton, Robert William 1936- *IntWWM 77*
Burton, Stephen Douglas 1943- *AmSCAP 80, ConAmC*
Burton, Thomas Eldin 1913- *IntWWM 77, -80*
Burton, Val 1899- *AmSCAP 66, CmpEPM*
Burton, Valentine 1900- *AmSCAP 80*
Burton, Wendell *HalFC 80*
Burton, William Evans 1804-1860 *FamA&A[port], NotNAT A, -B, OxThe*
Burton, William H 1845-1926 *Film 1, NotNAT B, WhScrn 74, -77, WhoHol B*
Burton, William Ron 1934- *EncJzS 70*
Burton-Nickson, Keith 1925- *WhoMus 72*
Burtwell, Frederick d1948 *NotNAT B*
Burwell, Clifford R 1898-1976 *AmSCAP 66, -80*
Bury, Arthur 1913- *WhoMus 72*
Bury, Bernard De 1720-1785 *NewGrD 80*
Bury, Edward 1919- *Baker 78*
Bury, John 1925- *CnThe, EncWT, NotNAT, WhoOp 76, WhoThe 72, -77*
Burzio, Nicolaus *NewGrD 80*
Bus, Gervais De *NewGrD 80*
Busatti, Cherubino d1644 *NewGrD 80*
Busatus, Cherubino d1644 *NewGrD 80*
Busby, Amy 1872-1957 *NotNAT B, WhScrn 77*
Busby, Gerald 1935- *AmSCAP 80, IntWWM 77, -80*
Busby, Joan *IntWWM 77, -80*
Busby, Thomas 1755-1838 *Baker 78, NewGrD 80, OxMus*
Busca, Lodovico *NewGrD 80*
Buscaglione, Fred 1921-1960 *WhScrn 74, -77*
Busch, Adolf 1891-1952 *Baker 78, BiDAmM, BnBkM 80, ConAmC, MusSN[port], NewGrD 80, OxMus*
Busch, Carl 1862-1943 *Baker 78, BiDAmM*
Busch, Ernst 1900-1980 *EncWT, Ent*
Busch, Fritz 1890-1951 *Baker 78, BnBkM 80, CmOp, MusMk, MusSN[port], NewEOp 71, NewGrD 80[port], OxMus*
Busch, Gudrun 1930- *IntWWM 77, -80*
Busch, Hans Peter 1914- *IntWWM 77, -80, NewEOp 71*
Busch, Hermann 1897- *Baker 78, NewGrD 80, OxMus*
Busch, Mae d1946 *MotPP*
Busch, Mae 1891-1946 *WhScrn 74, -77, WhoHol B*
Busch, Mae 1895-1944 *ForYSC, TwYS*
Busch, Mae 1895-1946 *ThFT[port]*
Busch, Mae 1897-1946 *FilmEn, Film 1, -2, FilmgC, HalFC 80, MovMk*
Busch, Mae 1902-1946 *NotNAT B*
Busch, Niven 1903- *CmMov, FilmEn, FilmgC, HalFC 80, IntMPA 77, -75, -76, -78, -79, -80, WorEFlm[port]*
Busch, Otto 1901- *IntWWM 77, -80*
Busch, William 1901-1945 *Baker 78, NewGrD 80*
Buschkotter, Wilhelm 1887-1967 *Baker 78*
Buschner, Johannes *NewGrD 80*
Buschop, Cornelis Symonszoon d1573 *NewGrD 80*
Buschop, Cornelius Symonszoon d1573 *NewGrD 80*
Buscop, Cornelis Symonszoon d1573 *NewGrD 80*
Buscop, Cornelius Symonszoon d1573 *NewGrD 80*
Busenello, Giovanni Francesco 1598-1659 *NewGrD 80*
Buset, Martin 1565?-1618 *NewGrD 80*
Busey, Bernice Bland 1918- *AmSCAP 66*
Busfield, Winifred *WhoMus 72*
Bush, Adrian John 1944- *IntWWM 77, -80*
Bush, Alan 1900- *Baker 78, CmOp, DcCM, IntWWM 77, -80, MusMk, NewGrD 80[port], OxMus, WhoMus 72*
Bush, Anita 1883?-1974 *BlksB&W, -C, DrBlPA, NotNAT B, WhScrn 77*
Bush, Billy Green *HalFC 80, WhoHol A*
Bush, Dick 1931- *HalFC 80*
Bush, Frances Cleveland d1967 *WhoHol B*
Bush, Frank d1927 *NotNAT B*
Bush, Geoffrey 1920- *Baker 78, IntWWM 77, -80, NewGrD 80, WhoMus 72*
Bush, George 1858-1937 *WhScrn 74, -77, WhoHol B*
Bush, Georgia Ann 1920- *IntWWM 77*
Bush, Gordon 1943- *ConAmC*
Bush, Grace E 1884- *AmSCAP 66, ConAmC*
Bush, Irving R 1930- *ConAmC*
Bush, Jack Hamilton 1909- *CreCan 1*
Bush, Johnny 1935- *CounME 74, -74A, IlEncCM[port]*
Bush, Kenneth R *Film 2*
Bush, Lennie 1927- *EncJzS 70*
Bush, Leonard Walter 1927- *EncJzS 70*
Bush, Louis F 1910-1979 *AmSCAP 66, -80*
Bush, Michael 1932- *IntWWM 77, -80, WhoMus 72*
Bush, Milton Louis 1925- *IntWWM 80*
Bush, Noreen 1905- *CnOxB*
Bush, Norman 1933- *DrBlPA*
Bush, Pauline 1886-1969 *Film 1, -2, MotPP, WhScrn 77*
Bush, Renee *Film 2*
Bush, Roy *MorBAP*

Bush-Fekete, Ladislas 1898- *CnMD*
Bush-Fekete, Leslie 1896- *BiE&WWA*
Bushby, Ranken 1926- *WhoMus 72*
Bushe, Joseph M *PupTheA*
Bushell, Anthony 1904- *FilmEn, Film 2, FilmgC, ForYSC, HalFC 80, IlWWBF, WhoHol A*
Bushell, Garvin Payne 1902- *CmpEPM, WhoJazz 72*
Bushkin, Joe 1916- *BiDAmM, CmpEPM, EncJzS 70, WhoJazz 72*
Bushkin, Joseph 1916- *AmSCAP 66, -80*
Bushler, Herb 1939- *EncJzS 70*
Bushman, Francis X 1883-1966 *FilmEn, Film 2, FilmgC, ForYSC, HalFC 80, MotPP, MovMk, OxFilm, TwYS, WhScrn 74, -77, WhoHol B, WhoHrs 80*
Bushman, Francis X 1885-1966 *Film 1*
Bushman, Francis X, Jr. 1903- *Film 2, ForYSC, TwYS*
Bushman, Ralph E *Film 2*
Bushong, Margaret *PupTheA*
Bushouse, M David 1941- *IntWWM 80*
Busi, Alessandro 1833-1895 *Baker 78*
Businello, Gian Francesco *NewGrD 80*
Businello, Giovanni Francesco *NewGrD 80*
Businger, Toni 1934- *WhoOp 76*
Buskin, David 1943- *AmSCAP 80*
Buskirk, Bessie *Film 1*
Busley, Jessie 1869-1950 *NotNAT B, WhScrn 74, -77, WhoHol B*
Busnach, William d1907 *NotNAT B*
Busnois, Antoine 1430?-1492 *Baker 78, BnBkM 80, NewGrD 80, OxMus*
Busnois, Antoine De 1430?-1492 *MusMk*
Busoni, Ferruccio 1866-1924 *Baker 78, BnBkM 80[port], CompSN[port], DcCom 77[port], DcCom&M 79, DcCM, DcTwCC, -A, MusMk, NewEOp 71, NewGrD 80[port], OxMus*
Busoni, Ferrucio 1866-1924 *CmOp*
Busquets, Joaquin 1875-1942 *WhScrn 74, -77*
Buss, Harry *IlWWBF*
Buss, Howard J 1951- *AmSCAP 80*
Bussani, Dorothea 1763- *NewGrD 80*
Bussani, Francesco 1743- *NewGrD 80*
Busscher, Henri De *NewGrD 80*
Busschop, Cornelius Symonszoon *NewGrD 80*
Busschop, Jules-Auguste-Guillaume 1810-1896 *Baker 78*
Busse, Burkhard 1932- *IntWWM 77*
Busse, Henry 1894-1955 *AmSCAP 66, -80, BgBands 74[port], CmpEPM*
Bussell, Jan *DcPup*
Bussell, Reginald *WhoMus 72*
Busser, Henri-Paul 1872-1973 *Baker 78, NewGrD 80, WhoMus 72*
Bussetto, Giovanni Maria Del *NewGrD 80*
Bussey, Hank 1891-1971 *WhScrn 74, -77*
Bussi, Francesco 1926- *IntWWM 77, -80, NewGrD 80*
Bussi, Solange *WomWMM*
Bussieres, Raymond 1907- *FilmEn, FilmgC, HalFC 80*
Bussler, Ludwig 1838-1900 *Baker 78*
Bussotti, Sylvano 1931- *Baker 78, DcCM, NewGrD 80[port], WhoMus 72*
Bustabo, Guila 1919- *Baker 78*
Bustanti, Linda Maria 1951- *IntWWM 77, -80*
Bustelli, Giuseppe d1781? *NewGrD 80*
Buster, Budd 1891-1965 *WhScrn 77, WhoHol B*
Bustini, Alessandro 1876-1970 *Baker 78*
Buston, Jean 1680?-1731 *NewGrD 80*
Bustos, German Eduardo 1938- *WhoOp 76*
Buswell, James Oliver 1946- *IntWWM 80, NewGrD 80*
Butcher, Dwight 1911-1978 *AmSCAP 66, -80, BiDAmM*
Butcher, Ernest 1885-1965 *FilmgC, HalFC 80, WhScrn 74, -77, WhoHol B*
Butcher, James W, Jr. *BlkAmP, MorBAP*
Butcher, Jane Elizabeth 1908- *IntWWM 77*
Butcher, Vernon 1909- *WhoMus 72*
Bute, Earl Of 1713-1792 *OxMus*
Bute, Mary Ellen *WomWMM*
Buterne, Charles *NewGrD 80*
Buterne, Jean-Baptiste 1650?-1727 *NewGrD 80*
Buthner, Crato *NewGrD 80*
Buthnerus, Crato *NewGrD 80*
Buths, Julius 1851-1920 *Baker 78, NewGrD 80*
Buti, Carlo 1902-1963 *NotNAT B, WhScrn 74, -77*
Buti, Francesco 1682- *NewGrD 80*
Butina, Roman 1937- *IntWWM 77, -80*
Butland, William *Film 2*
Butler, A L 1933- *AmSCAP 80*
Butler, Alexander *FilmEn, IlWWBF*
Butler, Alice Augarde 1868-1919 *NotNAT B, WhoStg 1908*
Butler, Antonia *WhoMus 72*
Butler, Artie *HalFC 80*
Butler, Bill *FilmEn, HalFC 80*
Butler, C 1559-1647 *OxMus*
Butler, Carl Roberts 1927- *BiDAmM, CounME 74[port], -74A, EncFCWM 69, IlEncCM*
Butler, Charles d1920 *NotNAT B, WhoHol B*
Butler, Charles 1560?-1647 *NewGrD 80*
Butler, Charles Francis 1946- *AmSCAP 80*
Butler, Charlotte 1660?-1692? *NewGrD 80*
Butler, David *IntMPA 77, -75, -76, -78, -79*
Butler, David 1894-1979 *BiDFilm, -81, CmMov, FilmEn, Film 1, -2, FilmgC, HalFC 80, MovMk[port], TwYS, WhoHol A, WorEFlm[port]*
Butler, David 1895-1979 *TwYS A*
Butler, David Henry 1953- *IntWWM 77*
Butler, Daws 1916- *IntMPA 77, -75, -76, -78, -79, -80*
Butler, Douglas Lamar 1944- *IntWWM 77, -80*
Butler, E *MorBAP*
Butler, Eddie 1888-1944 *WhScrn 74, -77*
Butler, Eugene Sanders 1935- *AmSCAP 80, CpmDNM 74, -79, ConAmC*
Butler, Frank 1890-1967 *FilmEn, Film 2, FilmgC, HalFC 80, WhScrn 74, -77, WhoHol B*
Butler, Frank 1928- *BiDAmM, EncJzS 70*
Butler, Frank R *Film 2*
Butler, Fred J *Film 1, -2, TwYS*
Butler, Fred J 1867- *WhoStg 1908*
Butler, George *Film 2*
Butler, George 1936- *BluesWW[port], ConMuA 80B*
Butler, Henry d1652 *NewGrD 80*
Butler, Henry Willis 1919- *AmSCAP 80, WhoOp 76*
Butler, Horacio *PupTheA*
Butler, Horacio 1897- *DancEn 78*
Butler, Hugo 1914-1968 *FilmEn, WorEFlm[port]*
Butler, Jack 1909- *WhoJazz 72*
Butler, Jack 1924- *AmSCAP 66, -80, ConAmC A*
Butler, James 1921-1945 *WhScrn 74, -77*
Butler, James H 1908- *BiE&WWA, NotNAT*
Butler, Jerry 1939- *AmSCAP 80, DrBlPA, RkOn*
Butler, Jerry 1940- *BiDAmM*
Butler, Jimmie d1945 *WhoHol B*
Butler, Joan *WhoMus 72*
Butler, John 1920- *BiE&WWA, CmpGMD, CnOxB, DancEn 78[port], WhoMus 72*
Butler, John A 1884-1967 *WhScrn 77, WhoHol B*
Butler, Joseph 1907- *NewOrJ[port]*
Butler, Lois 1912- *ConAmC*
Butler, Louise d1958 *WhScrn 74, -77*
Butler, Mark H 1949- *IntWWM 77, -80*
Butler, Michael 1944- *HalFC 80*
Butler, Murray *PupTheA*
Butler, O'Brien 1870?-1915 *Baker 78*
Butler, Pearl *CounME 74[port], -74A, EncFCWM 69, IlEncCM*
Butler, Priscilla Kate *WhoMus 72*
Butler, Rachel Barton d1920 *NotNAT B*
Butler, Richard William 1844-1928 *NotNAT B*
Butler, Ron *ConAmTC*
Butler, Roy d1973 *WhoHol B*
Butler, Royal 1895-1973 *WhScrn 77*
Butler, Samuel d1945 *NotNAT B*
Butler, Samuel 1835-1902 *NewGrD 80, OxMus*
Butler, Suzanne Louise 1919- *CreCan 2*
Butler, Thomas Hamly 1755?-1823 *NewGrD 80*
Butler, Tommy *MorBAP*
Butler, William H 1903- *IntWWM 77*
Butler, William J Daddy 1860-1927 *Film 1, WhScrn 74, -77, WhoHol B*
Butlin, Jan 1940- *WhoThe 77*
Butlin, Roger John 1935- *WhoOp 76*
Butner, Crato 1616-1679 *NewGrD 80*
Butor, Michel 1926- *NewGrD 80*
Butova *PlP&P[port]*
Butskoy, Anatoly Konstantinovich 1892-1965 *NewGrD 80*
Butsova, Hilda 1897?-1976 *CnOxB, DancEn 78*
Butt, Alfred 1878-1962 *EncMT*
Butt, Clara 1872-1936 *NewGrD 80[port]*
Butt, Clara 1873-1936 *Baker 78, MusMk[port], OxMus*
Butt, David 1936- *IntWWM 77, -80*
Butt, James Baseden 1929- *IntWWM 77, -80, WhoMus 72*
Butt, Johnny *Film 2*
Butt, Johnny 1930- *IlWWBF*
Butt, Lawson *Film 2*
Butt, Thelma *AmSCAP 66*
Butt, Valerie 1938- *IntWWM 77*
Butt, W Lawson *Film 1*
Butterbeans And Susie *BlksBF[port]*
Butterfield, Billy 1917- *BgBands 74[port], BiDAmM, CmpEPM, EncJzS 70, IlEncJ, WhoJazz 72*
Butterfield, Charles William 1917- *EncJzS 70*
Butterfield, Don 1923- *BiDAmM*
Butterfield, Elizabeth *IntMPA 77, -76, -78, -79, -80*
Butterfield, Erskine 1913-1961 *CmpEPM, WhoJazz 72*
Butterfield, Everett d1925 *NotNAT B*
Butterfield, Herb 1896-1957 *ForYSC, WhoHol B*
Butterfield, Herbert 1896-1957 *WhScrn 74, -77*
Butterfield, James A 1837-1891 *BiDAmM*
Butterfield, Paul *ConMuA 80A*
Butterfield, Paul 1941- *BiDAmM*
Butterfield, Paul 1942- *BluesWW[port], IlEncR[port]*
Butterley, Nigel 1935- *Baker 78, DcCM, IntWWM 77, -80, NewGrD 80*
Butterworth, Arthur Eckersley 1923- *IntWWM 77, -80, NewGrD 80, WhoMus 72*
Butterworth, Charles d1946 *MotPP, WhoHol B*
Butterworth, Charles 1896-1946 *FilmEn, FilmgC, ForYSC, HalFC 80, HolCA[port], NotNAT B, WhScrn 74, -77*
Butterworth, Charles 1897-1946 *Film 2, MovMk[port], Vers A[port]*
Butterworth, David Neil 1934- *IntWWM 77, -80, WhoMus 72*
Butterworth, Donna 1956- *FilmgC, HalFC 80*
Butterworth, Ernest *Film 2*
Butterworth, F *Film 1*
Butterworth, George 1885-1916 *Baker 78, DcCom&M 79, MusMk, NewGrD 80, OxMus*
Butterworth, Hezekiah 1839-1905 *BiDAmM*
Butterworth, Ian Christopher 1940- *WhoMus 72*
Butterworth, Joe *Film 2*
Butterworth, Peter 1919-1979 *HalFC 80*
Butterworth, Peter 1923?- *FilmgC*
Butterworth, Walter T 1893-1962 *NotNAT B, WhScrn 74, -77, WhoHol B*
Butterworth, William Jesse, Jr. 1952- *AmSCAP 80*
Butti, Enrico Annibale 1868-1912 *McGEWD*
Buttigieg, Raymond Francis 1955- *AmSCAP 80*
Butting, Max 1888-1976 *Baker 78, DcCM, NewGrD 80*
Buttino, Alfred Nicholas 1938- *WhoOp 76*
Buttner, Erhard 1592-1625 *NewGrD 80*
Buttner, Hieronim *NewGrD 80*
Buttolph, David 1902- *AmSCAP 66, -80, -80, CmMov, ConAmC, FilmEn, HalFC 80, IntMPA 77, -75, -76, -78, -79, -80*
Button, Dick 1929- *BiE&WWA, What 4[port], WhoHol A*
Buttons, Red *MotPP, NewYTET, WhoHol A*
Buttons, Red 1918- *FilmgC, HalFC 80*
Buttons, Red 1919- *AmSCAP 66, -80, FilmEn, ForYSC, IntMPA 77, -75, -76, -78, -79, -80, JoeFr, MovMk, RkOn[port]*

Buttram, Pat *ForYSC, NewYTET, WhoHol A*
Buttress, Edward Crossley 1910- *IntWWM 77, -80, WhoMus 72*
Buttrey, John 1931- *IntWWM 77, -80*
Butts, Billy *Film 2*
Butts, Carrol Maxton 1924-1980 *AmSCAP 80, ConAmC*
Butts, James H 1917- *EncJzS 70*
Butts, Jimmy 1917- *EncJzS 70, WhoJazz 72*
Butts, R Dale 1910- *AmSCAP 66, -80, IntMPA 77, -75, -76, -78, -79, -80*
Butts Band, The *IlEncR*
Buttstett, Franz Vollrath 1735-1814 *Baker 78, NewGrD 80*
Buttstett, Johann Heinrich 1666-1727 *Baker 78, NewGrD 80*
Buttykay, Akos 1871-1935 *Baker 78*
Buttykay, Akos 1871-1936 *NewGrD 80*
Butumkin, Gregory *Film 2*
Buus, Jacques 1500?-1565 *Baker 78, NewGrD 80*
Buus, Jakob 1500?-1565 *NewGrD 80*
Buxbaum, James M *IntMPA 77, -75, -76, -78, -79, -80*
Buxtehude, Diderik 1637-1707 *DcCom 77*
Buxtehude, Dietrich 1637-1707 *Baker 78, BnBkM 80, CmpBCM, DcCom&M 79, GrComp, MusMk, NewGrD 80, OxMus*
Buxton, Anne Elizabeth 1936- *WhoMus 72*
Buxton, Frank *NewYTET*
Buxton, Roger K *PupTheA*
Buyniski, Raymond John 1939- *CpmDNM 72, -73, -74, -76, ConAmC*
Buys, Cornelis *NewGrD 80*
Buys, Peter 1881-1964 *AmSCAP 66, ConAmC*
Buysse, Cyriel 1859-1932 *ModWD*
Buysson, Du *NewGrD 80*
Buyukas, George 1898- *AmSCAP 66*
Buzario, Antonio *OxThe*
Buzea, Ion 1934- *WhoMus 72, WhoOp 76*
Buzo, Alexander 1944- *ConDr 77, WhoThe 77*
Buzzanca, Lando *FilmAG WE*
Buzzati, Dino 1906-1972 *CnMD, CroCD, EncWT, Ent*
Buzzatti, Dino 1907- *CnThe*
Buzzell, Eddie 1897- *Film 2, WhoHol A*
Buzzell, Eddie 1900- *CmpEPM*
Buzzell, Edward 1897- *FilmEn, FilmgC, HalFC 80, MovMk[port]*
Buzzell, Edward 1900- *AmSCAP 66, -80*
Buzzell, Edward 1907- *IntMPA 77, -75, -76, -78, -79, -80*
Buzzi, Pietro d1921 *WhScrn 74, -77*
Buzzi-Peccia, Arturo 1854-1943 *AmSCAP 66, -80, Baker 78, BiDAmM*
Buzzolla, Antonio 1815-1871 *Baker 78, NewGrD 80*
Byard, Herbert 1912- *WhoMus 72*
Byard, Jaki 1922- *EncJzS 70*
Byard, John A, Jr. 1922- *BiDAmM, ConAmC, EncJzS 70*
Byas, Carlos Wesley 1912-1972 *BiDAmM, EncJzS 70*
Byas, Don 1912-1972 *CmpEPM, EncJzS 70, IlEncJ, WhoJazz 72*
Bybee, Ariel 1943- *WhoOp 76*
Bye, Frederick Edward 1901- *WhoMus 72*
Bye, Willy DeLa 1934- *CnOxB*
Byer, Charles *Film 2*
Byerley, Vivienne *WhoThe 72, -77*
Byers, Billy 1927- *CmpEPM, EncJzS 70*
Byers, Harold 1944- *IntWWM 80*
Byers, Joy *AmSCAP 80*
Byers, Mervyn John 1924- *IntWWM 77*
Byers, Reginald Sydney 1934- *WhoOp 76*
Byers, Roxana *ConAmC*
Byers, William Mitchell 1927- *BiDAmM, EncJzS 70*
Byfield *NewGrD 80*
Byfield, Jack Allen 1902- *WhoMus 72*
Byfield, John *NewGrD 80*
Byfield, John d1774 *NewGrD 80*
Byfield, John d1799 *NewGrD 80*
Byfield, John 1694?-1756 *NewGrD 80*
Byford, Roy 1873-1939 *Film 2, NotNAT B, WhScrn 74, -77, WhoHol B*
Bygraves, Max 1922- *FilmEn, FilmgC, HalFC 80, IlWWBF[port], -A, IntMPA 77, -75, 76, -78, -79, -80, WhoHol A*
Byington, Spring 1886-1971 *HolCA[port]*
Byington, Spring 1893-1971 *BiE&WWA, FilmEn, FilmgC, ForYSC, HalFC 80, MGM[port], MotPP, MovMk[port], NewYTET, ThFT[port], What 3[port], WhScrn 74, -77, WhoHol B*
Byington, Spring 1898-1971 *Vers A[port]*
Byland, Ambrose *NewGrD 80*
Byles, Bobby 1931-1969 *WhScrn 74, -77, WhoHol B*
Byles, Edward *WhoMus 72*
Byles, Nathan 1706-1788 *BiDAmM*
Byng, Douglas 1893- *EncMT, WhoThe 72, -77*
Bynner, Witter 1881-1968 *NotNAT B*
Bynum, Raymond Tapley 1906- *IntWWM 80*
Byram, John 1901- *BiE&WWA, NotNAT*
Byram, Marian 1904- *BiE&WWA, NotNAT*
Byram, Ronald d1919 *Film 1, WhScrn 77*
Byrd, Caruth C 1942- *IntMPA 77, -75, -76, -78, -79, -80*
Byrd, Charles L 1925- *BiDAmM, EncJzS 70*
Byrd, Charlie 1925- *AmSCAP 80, CmpEPM, EncJzS 70, IlEncJ*
Byrd, DeReath Irene *BlkAmP*
Byrd, Donald 1932- *BiDAmM, DrBlPA, EncJzS 70, IlEncJ*
Byrd, Gene 1933- *BiDAmM*
Byrd, Jerry 1920- *IlEncCM*
Byrd, Jerry Lester 1920- *BiDAmM*
Byrd, John *IntMPA 77, -75, -76, -78, -79, -80*
Byrd, Ralph 1909-1952 *FilmEn, FilmgC, ForYSC, HalFC 80, WhScrn 74, -77, WhoHol B, WhoHrs 80*
Byrd, Roy 1918- *BluesWW[port]*
Byrd, Sam 1908-1955 *NotNAT B*
Byrd, William 1542?-1623? *OxMus*
Byrd, William 1543-1623 *Baker 78, BnBkM 80[port], CmpBCM, DcCom 77[port], DcCom&M 79, GrComp[port], MusMk[port], NewGrD 80*
Byrde, William 1542?-1623? *OxMus*
Byrds, The *BiDAmM, ConMuA 80A, IlEncCM, IlEncR[port], RkOn 2[port]*
Byrens, Myer 1840-1933 *WhScrn 74, -77*
Byrne, Andrew William Arthur 1925- *IntWWM 77, -80, WhoMus 72*
Byrne, Betsy *Film 2*
Byrne, Bill 1942- *EncJzS 70*
Byrne, Bobby 1918- *BgBands 74[port], CmpEPM*
Byrne, Bridget *WomWMM*
Byrne, David 1952- *AmSCAP 80*
Byrne, Eddie 1911- *FilmEn, FilmgC, HalFC 80, IntMPA 77, -75, -76, -78, -79, -80, WhoHol A*
Byrne, Francis M 1875-1923 *NotNAT B, WhoStg 1908*
Byrne, James A d1927 *NotNAT B*
Byrne, Patsy 1933- *WhoThe 72, -77*
Byrne, Peter 1928- *WhoThe 72, -77*
Byrne, Peter 1932- *IntWWM 77, -80, WhoMus 72*
Byrne, Rosalind *Film 2*
Byrne, William E, Jr. 1942- *EncJzS 70*
Byrnes, Ed *AmPS A*
Byrnes, Edd 1933- *FilmEn, FilmgC, ForYSC, HalFC 80, WhoHol A*
Byrnes, Edward 1911- *ForYSC*
Byrnes, Edward 1933- *IntMPA 77, -75, -76, -78, -79, -80, MotPP*
Byrnes, Edward 1938- *RkOn[port]*
Byrnes, James F 1879- *What 3[port]*
Byrnes, Nancy Rosenbluth 1915-1962 *WhScrn 74, -77*
Byroade, George 1883-1975 *WhScrn 77*
Byron, Lord 1788-1824 *HalFC 80, OxMus*
Byron, Al 1932- *AmSCAP 66, -80*
Byron, Alex 1932- *IntWWM 77*
Byron, Arthur William 1872-1943 *FilmEn, HalFC 80, HolCA[port], NotNAT B, PlP&P, WhScrn 74, -77, WhoHol B, WhoStg 1906, -1908*
Byron, Charles Anthony 1919- *IntMPA 77, -75, -76, -78, -79*
Byron, Eva *Film 2*
Byron, Lord George Gordon 1788-1824 *CnThe, EncWT, McGEWD[port], NewEOp 71, NewGrD 80, NotNAT B, OxThe, REnWD[port]*
Byron, Henrietta d1924 *NotNAT B*
Byron, Henry James 1834-1884 *EncWT, Ent, NotNAT B, OxThe, PlP&P*
Byron, Jack *Film 2*
Byron, Jean *WhoHol A*
Byron, Jean 1930?- *WhoHrs 80[port]*
Byron, Kate d1920 *NotNAT B*
Byron, Kathleen 1922- *FilmEn, FilmgC, HalFC 80, IlWWBF, IntMPA 77, -75, -76, -78, -79, -80, WhoHol A*
Byron, Katy 1918-1970 *WhScrn 77*
Byron, Marion 1910- *ThFT[port]*
Byron, Marion 1911- *Film 2*
Byron, Oliver Doud 1842-1920 *NotNAT B, WhoStg 1906, -1908*
Byron, Paul 1891-1959 *WhScrn 74, -77, WhoHol B*
Byron, Peanut *Film 2*
Byron, Richard 1908-1969 *AmSCAP 66, -80*
Byron, Roy d1943 *Film 2, WhoHol B*
Byron, Royal James 1887-1943 *WhScrn 74, -77*
Byron, Walter 1899-1972 *HalFC 80*
Byron, Walter 1901-1972 *FilmEn, Film 2, FilmgC, ForYSC, WhoHol B*
Byron, Ward 1910- *IntMPA 77, -75, -76, -78, -79, -80*
Byrum, John 1947- *IntMPA 77, -78, -79, -80*
Bystrom, Oscar Fredrik Bernadotte 1821-1909 *NewGrD 80*
Bystrom, Walter E 1894-1969 *WhScrn 74, -77*
Bystry, Viliam *NewGrD 80*
Bytell, Walter *Film 1*
Bytering *NewGrD 80*
Byteryng, Thomas *NewGrD 80*
Bytner, Crato *NewGrD 80*
Byttering *NewGrD 80*
Bytteryng *NewGrD 80*
Byzantios, Petros d1808 *NewGrD 80*

C

Caamano, Roberto 1923- *Baker 78, DcCM, IntWWM 77, –80, NewGrD 80*
Caan, James *WhoHol A*
Caan, James 1938- *FilmgC, ForYSC, HalFC 80*
Caan, James 1939- *FilmEn, IntMPA 77, –75, –76, –78, –78, –79, –80, MovMk[port]*
Caaron *AmSCAP 80*
Caba, Eduardo 1890-1953 *Baker 78*
Cabal, Robert *WhoHol A*
Cabal, Roberto *ForYSC*
Cabali, F *PupTheA*
Caballe, Montserrat 1933- *BnBkM 80, CmOp, IntWWM 80, MusMk, MusSN[port], NewEOp 71, NewGrD 80[port], WhoMus 72, WhoOp 76*
Caballero, M F 1835-1906 *NewGrD 80*
Caballone, Gaspare *NewGrD 80*
Caballone, Michele 1692-1740 *NewGrD 80*
Cabalone, Michele 1692-1740 *NewGrD 80*
Cabanillas, Juan Bautista Jose 1644?-1712 *NewGrD 80*
Cabanilles, Juan Bautista Jose 1644?-1712 *Baker 78, BnBkM 80, NewGrD 80*
Cabanne, Christy 1888-1950 *FilmEn*
Cabanne, Christy William 1888-1950 *DcFM, FilmgC, HalFC 80, WhoHol B*
Cabanne, William Christy 1888-1950 *TwYS A, WhScrn 74, –77*
Cabanowski, Marek 1935- *IntWWM 77*
Cabauy, Henry 1936- *IntWWM 77*
Cabbane, Christy W 1888-1950 *Film 1*
Cabbilai *NewGrD 80*
Cabdueill, Pons De *NewGrD 80*
Cabecon *NewGrD 80*
Cabecon, Agustin De *NewGrD 80*
Cabecon, Antonio De 1508?-1566 *BnBkM 80*
Cabecon, Antonio De 1510-1566 *NewGrD 80*
Cabecon, Hernando De 1541-1602 *NewGrD 80*
Cabecon, Juan De 1510?-1566 *NewGrD 80*
Cabel, Marie 1827-1885 *NewGrD 80*
Cabeliamo, Peter *NewGrD 80*
Cabeliau *NewGrD 80*
Cabellone, Gaspare *NewGrD 80*
Cabezon *NewGrD 80*
Cabezon, Agustin De *NewGrD 80*
Cabezon, Antonio De 1500-1566 *MusMk*
Cabezon, Antonio De 1508?-1566 *BnBkM 80*
Cabezon, Antonio De 1510-1566 *Baker 78, NewGrD 80*
Cabezon, Hernando De 1541?-1602 *NewGrD 80*
Cabezon, Juan De 1510?-1566 *NewGrD 80*
Cabilliau *NewGrD 80*
Cable, Howard Reid 1920- *CreCan 1, IntWWM 77, –80*
Cables, George Andrew 1944- *EncJzS 70*
Cabo, Francisco Javier 1768-1832 *NewGrD 80*
Cabo, Louise *Film 2*
Cabot, Bruce 1904-1972 *FilmEn, FilmgC, HalFC 80, HolP 30[port], MotPP, WhScrn 77, WhoHol B, WhoHrs 80[port]*
Cabot, Bruce 1905-1972 *ForYSC, MovMk[port]*
Cabot, Eliot 1899-1938 *NotNAT B, WhThe*
Cabot, Elliott *Film 2*
Cabot, Sebastian 1918-1977 *FilmEn, FilmgC, ForYSC, HalFC 80, MotPP, MovMk, WhoHol A*
Cabot, Susan 1927- *FilmEn, FilmgC, ForYSC, HalFC 80, WhoHol A, WhoHrs 80[port]*
Cabus, Peter Noel 1923- *WhoMus 72*
Cacavas, John 1930- *AmSCAP 66, –80, ConAmC*
Caccialanza, Gisella 1914- *CnOxB, DancEn 78[port]*
Caccini *NewGrD 80*
Caccini, Francesca 1587-1640? *Baker 78, NewGrD 80*
Caccini, Giulio 1545-1618 *MusMk, NewGrD 80*
Caccini, Giulio 1546-1618 *GrComp*
Caccini, Giulio 1550?-1610 *OxMus*
Caccini, Giulio 1550?-1618 *Baker 78, BnBkM 80*
Caccini, Guilio 1546-1618 *NewEOp 71*
Caccini, Orazio *NewGrD 80*
Caccini, Settimia 1591-1638? *NewGrD 80*
Caceres, Ernest 1911-1971 *EncJzS 70*
Caceres, Ernie 1911-1971 *BiDAmM, CmpEPM, EncJzS 70, WhoJazz 72*
Caceres, Oscar 1928- *IntWWM 77, –80*
Cachino, Giulio *NewGrD 80*
Cacioppo, George 1926- *ConAmC*
Cacioppo, George 1927- *Baker 78*
Caciuleanu, Gheorge 1947- *CnOxB*
Cacoyannis, Michael 1922- *BiDFilm, –81, DcFM, FilmEn, FilmgC, HalFC 80, IntMPA 77, –75, –76, –78, –79, –80, MovMk[port], NotNAT, OxFilm, WorEFlm[port]*
Cactus *IlEncR*
Caddigan, Jack J 1879-1952 *AmSCAP 66, –80*
Caddy, Ian Graham 1947- *IntWWM 77, –80*
Cade, Rose *Film 2*
Cadeac, Pierre *NewGrD 80*
Cadell, Jean 1884-1967 *Film 2, FilmgC, HalFC 80, IntMPA 77, –75, –76, –78, –79, –80, PlP&P, WhScrn 74, –77, WhThe, WhoHol B*
Cadener, Johann *NewGrD 80*
Cadenhead, Elizabeth Margaret Gay 1936- *IntWWM 80*
Cadets, The *RkOn[port]*
Cadillac Jake *BluesWW[port]*
Cadillacs, The *RkOn[port]*
Cadman, Charles Wakefield 1881-1946 *AmSCAP 66, –80, Baker 78, BiDAmM, BnBkM 80, CmpEPM, CompSN[port], ConAmC, NewEOp 71, NewGrD 80, OxMus*
Cadman, Ethel 1886- *WhThe*
Cadmus, Paul 1906- *DancEn 78*
Cadner, Johann d1639 *NewGrD 80*
Caduff, Sylvia 1937- *Baker 78*
Caduff, Sylvia 1938- *IntWWM 77, –80*
Cady, Calvin Brainerd 1851-1928 *Baker 78, BiDAmM, NewGrD 80*
Cady, Frank *ForYSC, WhoHol A*
Cadzow, Dorothy *ConAmC*
Cadzow, Joan 1929- *CnOxB*
Caecilius Statius 219?BC-168BC *CnThe, OxThe, REnWD[port]*
Caelius Sedulius *NewGrD 80*
Caen, Arnold *NewGrD 80*
Caesar, Adolph *MorBAP*
Caesar, Irving 1895- *AmPS, AmSCAP 66, –80, BestMus, BiDAmM, BiE&WWA, CmpEPM, EncMT, HalFC 80, IntMPA 77, –75, –76, –78, –79, –80, NewCBMT, NotNAT, Sw&Ld C, WhoThe 77*
Caesar, Johann Martin *NewGrD 80*
Caesar, Johann Melchior 1648?-1692 *NewGrD 80*
Caesar, Lois Towles *BlkWAB[port]*
Caesar, Shirley 1939- *DrBlPA*
Caesar, Sid 1922- *AmSCAP 66, –80, BiE&WWA, EncMT, Ent, FilmEn, FilmgC, ForYSC, HalFC 80, IntMPA 77, –75, –76, –78, –79, –80, JoeFr[port], MovMk, NewYTET, WhoHol A, WhoThe 72, –77*
Caesar, Vic *AmSCAP 80*
Caesar, William *NewGrD 80*
Caewardine, John *NewGrD 80*
Cafarellino 1710-1783 *NewGrD 80*
Cafariello 1710-1783 *NewGrD 80*
Cafaro, Pasquale 1716?-1787 *Baker 78, NewGrD 80*
Caffagni, Mirko 1934- *IntWWM 77, –80*
Caffarelli 1703-1783 *OxMus*
Caffarelli 1710-1783 *Baker 78, CmOp, NewEOp 71, NewGrD 80*
Caffarelli, Filippo 1891- *WhoMus 72*
Caffey, H David 1950- *CpmDNM 80*
Caffey, Howard David 1950- *AmSCAP 80*
Caffi, Francesco 1778-1874 *Baker 78, NewGrD 80*
Caffi, Tommaso Bernardo *NewGrD 80*
Caffiat, Philippe-Auguste 1712-1777 *NewGrD 80*
Caffiat, Philippe-Joseph 1712-1777 *NewGrD 80*
Caffiaux, Philippe-Auguste 1712-1777 *NewGrD 80*
Caffiaux, Philippe-Joseph 1712-1777 *NewGrD 80*
Cagan, Sermet 1929- *CnThe, REnWD[port]*
Cagan, Steven *ConAmC*
Cage, James 1894-1975? *BluesWW*
Cage, John 1912- *AmSCAP 66, –80, Baker 78, BnBkM 80, CompSN[port], CpmDNM 77, CnOxB, ConAmC, ConDr 73, –77E, DancEn 78, DcCom&M 79, DcCM, IntWWM 77, –80, MusMk[port], NewGrD 80[port], OxMus, WhoMus 72*
Cage, John Milton, Jr. 1912- *BiDAmM*
Cage, Ruth 1923- *BiE&WWA, NotNAT*
Caggiano, Rosemary 1938- *AmSCAP 80*
Cagle, Buddy 1936- *BiDAmM, EncFCWM 69*
Cagliostro, Count Alessandro Di 1743-1795 *Ent, MagIlD*
Cagnazzi, Maffeo *NewGrD 80*

Cagney, James *MotPP, PlP&P*
Cagney, James 1899- *Ent, FilmEn, FilmgC, HalFC 80, What 4[port], WhoHol A, WhoHrs 80, WorEFlm[port]*
Cagney, James 1904- *BiDFilm, -81, BiE&WWA, CmMov, Film 2, ForYSC, IntMPA 77, -75, -76, -78, -79, -80, MovMk[port], OxFilm*
Cagney, Jeanne 1919- *BiE&WWA, FilmgC, ForYSC, HalFC 80, IntMPA 77, -75, -76, -78, -79, -80, MotPP, NotNAT, WhThe, WhoHol A*
Cagney, William J 1902- *FilmgC, HalFC 80, IntMPA 77, -75, -76, -78, -79, -80*
Cagnolatti, Ernie 1911- *NewOrJ*
Cagnoni, Antonio 1828-1896 *Baker 78, NewGrD 80*
Cahen, Albert 1846-1903 *NewGrD 80*
Cahen, Oscar 1916-1956 *CreCan 2*
Cahen D'Anvers 1846-1903 *NewGrD 80*
Cahier, Charles, Madame 1870-1951 *Baker 78, NewEOp 71*
Cahier, Charles, Madame 1875-1951 *BiDAmM*
Cahill, Frank E, III 1932- *IntMPA 77, -75, -76, -78, -79*
Cahill, Frank E, Jr. *IntMPA 77, -76, -78, -79, -80*
Cahill, Lilly 1886-1955 *WhScrn 74, -77*
Cahill, Lily 1886-1955 *Film 1, NotNAT B, WhThe, WhoHol B*
Cahill, Marie d1933 *AmPS B, WhThe, WhoHol B, WhoStg 1906, -1908*
Cahill, Marie 1870-1933 *BiDAmM, CmpEPM, EncMT, NotNAT B*
Cahill, Marie 1871-1933 *Film 1*
Cahill, Marie 1874-1933 *WhScrn 74, -77*
Cahill, Teresa Mary 1944- *CmOp, IntWWM 77, -80, WhoOp 76*
Cahill, Thaddeus 1867-1934 *OxMus*
Cahill, Thomas M 1889-1953 *WhScrn 74, -77*
Cahlman, Robert 1924- *BiE&WWA, NotNAT*
Cahman d1699 *NewGrD 80*
Cahn, Dana d1973 *WhoHol B*
Cahn, Edward L 1899-1963 *FilmEn, FilmgC, HalFC 80, WhoHrs 80*
Cahn, Irving W 1903- *ConAmTC*
Cahn, Julius d1921 *NotNAT B*
Cahn, Sammy 1913- *AmPS, AmSCAP 66, -80, Baker 78, BestMus, BiDAmM, CmpEPM, EncMT, FilmEn, FilmgC, HalFC 80, IntMPA 77, -75, -76, -78, -79, -80, NewCBMT, NotNAT, -A, Sw&Ld C, WhoThe 77*
Cahn-Speyer, Rudolf 1881-1940 *Baker 78*
Cahoon, Millian Benedict 1860-1951 *WhScrn 74, -77*
Cahusac *NewGrD 80*
Cahusac, Louis De 1700-1759 *CnOxB*
Cahusac, Louis De 1706-1759 *DancEn 78*
Cahusac, Thomas *NewGrD 80*
Cahusac, Thomas d1798 *NewGrD 80*
Cahusac, William Maurice *NewGrD 80*
Cahuzac, Louis 1880-1960 *NewGrD 80*
Caiani, Joe 1929- *AmSCAP 66*
Caianu, Ioan 1627-1698 *NewGrD 80*
Caianu, Joan 1627-1698 *NewGrD 80*
Caianu, Joannes 1627-1698 *NewGrD 80*
Caianu, Johannes 1627-1698 *NewGrD 80*
Caiazza, Nick 1914- *WhoJazz 72*
Caietain, Fabrice Marin *NewGrD 80*
Caifabri, Giovanni Battista *NewGrD 80*
Caignet, Denis d1625 *NewGrD 80*
Caigniez, Louis-Charles 1762-1842 *EncWT, Ent*
Cail, Harold L d1968 *NotNAT B*
Caillavet, Gaston Arman De 1869-1915 *McGEWD, NotNAT B*
Caillavet, Gaston De 1869-1915 *EncWT*
Caillet, Lucien 1891- *Baker 78, ConAmC*
Cailliet, Lucien 1891- *AmSCAP 80*
Cailliet, Lucien 1897- *AmSCAP 66*
Caillou, Alan *WhoHol A*
Cailloux, Andre 1920- *CreCan 2*
Caimi, Florentino J 1943- *IntWWM 77, -80*
Caimo, Gioseppe 1545?-1584? *NewGrD 80*
Cain, Brother *BlkAmP, MorBAP*
Cain, Andrew *OxThe*
Cain, David 1941- *IntWWM 77, -80*
Cain, Dominic 1925- *WhoMus 72*
Cain, Henri 1857- *WhThe*
Cain, Jackie 1928- *CmpEPM, EncJzS 70*
Cain, Jacqueline Ruth 1928- *BiDAmM, EncJzS 70*
Cain, James 1942- *ConAmC*
Cain, James M 1892-1977 *BiE&WWA, FilmgC, HalFC 80, NotNAT*
Cain, James Nelson 1930- *IntWWM 77, -80*
Cain, Joe Jack 1929- *AmSCAP 80*
Cain, Noble 1896-1977 *AmSCAP 66, -80, ConAmC A*
Cain, Patrick J d1949 *NotNAT B*
Cain, Perry 1929- *BluesWW*
Cain, Robert 1887-1954 *Film 1, -2, MotPP, NotNAT B, WhScrn 74, -77, WhoHol B*
Cain, Sugar *IntMPA 77, -76, -78, -79, -80, WomWMM B*
Cain, Ted 1904- *IntMPA 75*
Caine, Derwent Hall 1892- *Film 1, WhThe*
Caine, Georgia 1876-1964 *CmpEPM, FilmEn, ForYSC, NotNAT B, WhScrn 74, -77, WhoHol B*
Caine, Sir Hall 1853-1931 *NotNAT B, WhThe, WhoStg 1908*
Caine, Henry 1888-1962 *WhThe*
Caine, Howard *WhoHol A*
Caine, Lily Hall d1914 *WhThe*
Caine, Michael 1933- *BiDFilm, -81, CmMov, FilmAG WE[port], FilmEn, FilmgC, ForYSC, HalFC 80, IlWWBF[port], -A, IntMPA 77, -75, -76, -78, -79, -80, MotPP, MovMk[port], OxFilm, WhoHol A, WorEFlm[port]*
Caiola, Al 1920- *AmSCAP 66, -80, RkOn[port]*
Caiola, Alexander Emil 1920- *BiDAmM*
Caioni, Ioan *NewGrD 80*
Caioni, Joan *NewGrD 80*
Caioni, Joannes *NewGrD 80*
Caioni, Johannes *NewGrD 80*
Caird, George 1950- *IntWWM 80*
Cairnes, Sally 1920-1965 *WhScrn 74, -77*
Cairns, Angus d1975 *WhoHol C*
Cairns, Dallas *Film 2*
Cairns, David 1926- *NewGrD 80*
Caiserman, Ghitta 1923- *CreCan 1*
Caiserman-Roth, Ghitta 1923- *CreCan 1*
Caits, Joe 1889-1957 *WhoHol B*
Caits, Joseph 1889-1957 *WhScrn 74, -77*
Caix, De *NewGrD 80*
Caix, Barthelemy De 1716- *NewGrD 80*
Caix, Francois-Joseph De d1751? *NewGrD 80*
Caix, Marie-Anne Ursule De 1715-1751 *NewGrD 80*
Caix, Paul De 1717?- *NewGrD 80*
Caix D'Hervelois, Louis De 1670?-1760? *NewGrD 80, OxMus*
Caix D'Hervelois, Louis De 1680?-1760 *Baker 78*
Cajati, Mario 1902- *AmSCAP 66*
Cajetan, Fabrice Marin *NewGrD 80*
Cajoni, Joan *NewGrD 80*
Cakste, Aija 1924- *IntWWM 77, -80*
Calabrese, Anthony 1938- *NatPD[port]*
Calabresi, Oreste 1857- *WhThe*
Calabro, John A 1909- *AmSCAP 80*
Calabro, Louis 1926- *AmSCAP 66, -80, CpmDNM 72, ConAmC, DcCM*
Calado, Joaquim Antonio DaSilva 1848-1880 *NewGrD 80*
Calagni, Ann Curtis *WomWMM B*
Calamai, Clara 1915- *FilmAG WE, FilmEn, OxFilm*
Calame, Blaise 1922- *IntWWM 77, -80, WhoMus 72*
Calamity, Jane 1848?-1903 *HalFC 80*
Calamity Jane 1852?-1903 *OxFilm*
Caland, Elisabeth 1862-1929 *Baker 78*
Calandra, Nicola *NewGrD 80*
Calandria, Nicola *NewGrD 80*
Calandro, Nicola *NewGrD 80*
Calcano, Jose Antonio 1900- *NewGrD 80*
Caldara, Antonio 1670-1736 *Baker 78, MusMk, NewEOp 71, NewGrD 80[port], OxMus*
Caldara, Orme d1925 *Film 1, NotNAT B, WhoHol B*
Caldenbach, Christoph *NewGrD 80*
Calder, David Lewis 1945- *IntWWM 80*
Calder, Ethan 1922- *ConAmTC*
Calder, King 1900-1964 *NotNAT B, WhScrn 74, -77, WhoHol B*
Calder, Melvyn George 1920- *IntWWM 77*
Calder, Ronald Sim 1912- *WhoMus 72*
Calder-Marshall, Anna 1947- *WhoThe 77*
Calder-Marshall, Anna 1949- *FilmgC, HalFC 80*
Calderisi, David 1940- *WhoThe 72, -77*
Calderon, George 1868- *WhThe*
Calderon, Ian 1948- *NotNAT*
Calderon, Pasqual *PupTheA*
Calderon DeLaBarca, Pedro 1600-1681 *CnThe, EncWT, Ent[port], McGEWD[port], NewEOp 71, NewGrD 80, NotNAT B, OxMus, OxThe, REnWD[port]*
Caldicot, Richard 1908- *WhoThe 77*
Caldicott, Alfred James 1842-1897 *Baker 78*
Caldo, Joseffi *PupTheA*
Caldwell, Albert 1903- *BiDAmM, EncJzS 70*
Caldwell, Anne 1867-1936 *AmPS, AmSCAP 66, CmpEPM, EncMT, NewCBMT, NotNAT B, WhThe*
Caldwell, Ben *BlkAmP, DrBlPA, MorBAP*
Caldwell, Betty *Film 2*
Caldwell, Bruce 1941- *IntWWM 77, -80*
Caldwell, Erskine 1903- *FilmgC, HalFC 80, PlP&P[port]*
Caldwell, Gloria 1933- *AmSCAP 80*
Caldwell, Happy 1903- *EncJzS 70, WhoJazz 72*
Caldwell, Henry d1961 *NotNAT B*
Caldwell, Jack d1944 *WhScrn 77*
Caldwell, John Anthony 1938- *IntWWM 80, NewGrD 80*
Caldwell, Marianne d1933 *WhThe*
Caldwell, Mary Elizabeth 1909- *AmSCAP 66, -80, ConAmC*
Caldwell, Minna d1969 *WhoHol B*
Caldwell, Orville 1896-1967 *BiE&WWA, Film 1, -2, ForYSC, TwYS, WhScrn 74, -77, WhoHol B*
Caldwell, Sarah 1924- *Baker 78, MusSN[port], NewGrD 80*
Caldwell, Sarah 1928- *WhoOp 76*
Caldwell, Virginia *Film 1*
Caldwell, William *NewGrD 80*
Caldwell, Zoe *PlP&P[port], -A[port]*
Caldwell, Zoe 1933- *NotNAT*
Caldwell, Zoe 1934- *WhoThe 72, -77*
Cale, J J *ConMuA 80A, IlEncR*
Cale, John *AmSCAP 80, ConMuA 80A, IlEncR*
Cale, Johnny 1909- *AmSCAP 66*
Caleb, Frank 1940- *WhoOp 76*
Calef, Henri 1910- *FilmEn*
Calegari *NewGrD 80*
Calegari, Antonio 1757-1828 *Baker 78, NewGrD 80*
Calegari, Cornelia *NewGrD 80*
Calegari, Francesco Antonio 1656-1742 *NewGrD 80*
Calegari, Giuseppe 1750?-1812 *NewGrD 80*
Calegari, Isabella *NewGrD 80*
Calegari, Luigi Antonio 1780?-1849 *NewGrD 80*
Calegari, Maria Cattarina 1644-1662? *NewGrD 80*
Caleo, Michael Angelo 1902-1968 *AmSCAP 80*
Cales, Claude 1934- *WhoOp 76*
Calestani, Girolamo *NewGrD 80*
Calestani, Vincenzio 1589- *NewGrD 80*
Calestani, Vincenzo 1589- *NewGrD 80*
Caletti, Francesco *NewGrD 80*
Caletti, Giovanni Battista 1577-1642? *NewGrD 80*
Caletti DiBruno, Giovanni Battista 1577-1642? *NewGrD 80*
Caletto, Francesco *NewGrD 80*
Caletto, Giovanni Battista 1577-1642? *NewGrD 80*
Calfan, Nicole 1947- *FilmEn*
Calhern, Louis 1895-1956 *BiDFilm, FamA&A[port], FilmEn, Film 2, FilmgC, ForYSC, HalFC 80, HolCA[port], MGM[port], MotPP, MovMk[port], NotNAT B, OxFilm, PlP&P, Vers A[port], WhScrn 74, -77, WhThe, WhoHol B*
Calhoon, Barbara *WomWMM B*
Calhoun, Alice 1903-1966 *Film 1, -2, TwYS*
Calhoun, Alice 1904-1966 *FilmEn, WhScrn 74, -77, WhoHol B*

Calhoun, Eddie 1921- *BiDAmM*
Calhoun, Eleanor d1957 *NotNAT B*
Calhoun, Jeanne *Film 2*
Calhoun, Kathleen *Film 2*
Calhoun, Mister *BluesWW[port]*
Calhoun, Pat *Film 2*
Calhoun, Robert 1930- *BiE&WWA, NotNAT*
Calhoun, Rory *MotPP*
Calhoun, Rory 1922- *FilmEn, FilmgC, ForYSC, HalFC 80, MovMk[port], WhoHol A*
Calhoun, Rory 1923- *IntMPA 77, -75, -76, -78, -79, -80*
Cali, Giovan Battista 1590?-1605? *NewGrD 80*
Calicott, Joe *BluesWW[port]*
Calier, Manuel *NewOrJ*
Califano, Giovanni Battista 1550?- *NewGrD 80*
Caligan, Woodrow W 1913- *AmSCAP 66*
Caligari, Francesco Antonio *NewGrD 80*
Caliman, Hadley 1932- *EncJzS 70*
Calisch, Edith Lindeman 1898- *AmSCAP 80*
Calista, Lelio *NewGrD 80*
Calker, Darrell W 1905-1964 *AmSCAP 66, -80, ConAmC A*
Calkin *NewGrD 80*
Calkin, George 1829-1911 *NewGrD 80, OxMus*
Calkin, James 1786-1862 *NewGrD 80, OxMus*
Calkin, James Joseph 1813-1868 *OxMus*
Calkin, John Baptiste 1827-1905 *Baker 78, NewGrD 80, OxMus*
Calkin, Joseph 1781-1846 *NewGrD 80, OxMus*
Calkin, Joseph 1816-1874 *OxMus*
Calkin, Joseph George *OxMus*
Call, Audrey 1905- *AmSCAP 80*
Call, Charles W 1916- *IntMPA 77, -75, -76, -78, -79, -80*
Call, Frank Oliver 1878-1956 *CreCan 1*
Call, John 1907-1973 *WhScrn 77, WhoHol B*
Call, Leonhard Von 1767-1815 *NewGrD 80*
Callaci, Gloria *WomWMM B*
Callado, Joaquim Antonin De Silva *NewGrD 80*
Callaerts, Joseph 1838-1901 *Baker 78*
Callaghan, Domini 1923- *DancEn 78*
Callaghan, Jean 1942- *IntWWM 80*
Callaghan, Morley Edward 1903- *CreCan 2*
Callahan, Andrew J *Film 2*
Callahan, Billy 1911-1964 *NotNAT B, WhScrn 74, -77*
Callahan, Bobby d1938 *WhoHol B*
Callahan, Charles S 1891-1964 *WhScrn 74, -77*
Callahan, Chuck d1964 *WhoHol B*
Callahan, J Will 1874-1946 *AmSCAP 66, -80, BiDAmM*
Callahan, James Patrick 1942- *ConAmC, IntWWM 77, -80, WhoHol A*
Callahan, Joseph *Film 1*
Callahan, Marie Joan 1906- *AmSCAP 66, -80*
Callahan, Robert 1896-1938 *WhScrn 74, -77*
Callahan Brothers, The *IlEncCM*
Callam, D *Film 1*
Callan, Michael 1935- *FilmEn, FilmgC, ForYSC, HalFC 80, IntMPA 77, -75, -76, -78, -79, -80, MotPP, WhoHol A*
Callas, Charlie *JoeFr, WhoHol A*
Callas, Maria 1923-1977 *Baker 78, BiDAmM, BnBkM 80[port], CmOp[port], IntWWM 77, MusMk[port], NewGrD 80[port], WhoHol A, WhoMus 72*
Callas, Maria 1924-1977 *HalFC 80, MusSN[port]*
Callas, Maria Meneghini 1923- *NewEOp 71*
Callaway, Ann Marie 1949- *CpmDNM 80*
Callaway, Frank Adams 1919- *IntWWM 77, -80, NewGrD 80*
Callaway, Paul 1909- *Baker 78, BiDAmM, BiE&WWA, ConAmC, NewGrD 80, NotNAT, WhoOp 76*
Callaway, Scott Chatoney 1916- *IntWWM 77*
Callcott, John Wall 1766-1821 *Baker 78, NewGrD 80, OxMus*
Callcott, William Hutchins 1807-1882 *OxMus*
Callegari *NewGrD 80*
Callegari, Francesco Antonio *NewGrD 80*
Calleia, Joseph 1897-1975 *BiE&WWA, FilmEn, FilmgC, ForYSC, HolCA[port], MovMk, WhScrn 77, WhThe, WhoHol C*
Calleia, Joseph 1897-1976 *HalFC 80*
Calleia, Joseph 1898- *Vers A[port]*
Calleja, Gomez Rafael 1874-1938 *Baker 78*
Callelo, Charles *ConMuA 80B*
Callender, Charles R 1911- *AmSCAP 80*
Callender, George 1918- *AmSCAP 66, -80, BiDAmM, EncJzS 70*
Callender, Red 1918- *CmpEPM, EncJzS 70, WhoJazz 72*
Calley, John 1930- *IntMPA 77, -75, -76, -78, -79, -80*
Callicott, Joe 1901?-1969? *BluesWW*
Callicutt, Joe *BluesWW[port]*
Callido, Gaetano 1727-1813 *NewGrD 80*
Calliga, George *Film 2*
Calligan, Edward O d1962 *NotNAT B*
Calligaris, Sergio 1941- *Baker 78*
Callinet, Francois 1754-1820 *Baker 78*
Callinet, Louis 1786-1845 *Baker 78, NewGrD 80*
Callinicos, Constantine 1913- *AmSCAP 66, -80*
Callipides *OxThe*
Callis, Clifford *Film 1*
Callis, David 1888-1934 *Film 2, WhScrn 74, -77, WhoHol B*
Callison, Jo Ann 1938- *AmSCAP 80*
Calliste, Lester A, Jr. 1947- *NewOrJ SUP[port]*
Callot, Jacques 1592-1622 *EncWT*
Callot, Jacques 1592-1635 *NotNAT B*
Callow, Everett C *IntMPA 77, -75, -76, -78, -79, -80*
Calloway, Blanche 1904- *WhoJazz 72*
Calloway, Blanche Dorothea 1903?-1978 *BlkWAB[port]*
Calloway, Cab *AmPS B, BgBands 74[port]*
Calloway, Cab 1907- *AmSCAP 66, -80, Baker 78, BlksB&W[port], -C, CmpEPM, DrBlPA, Ent[port], FilmgC, HalFC 80, IlEncJ, NewGrD 80, WhoHol A, WhoJazz 72, WhoThe 77*
Calloway, Cab 1908- *MovMk*
Calloway, Cabell 1907- *BiDAmM, NewGrD 80*
Calloway, Kirk 1960- *DrBlPA*
Calloway, Northern J *DrBlPA*
Calman, Montague 1917- *WhoMus 72*
Calmettes, Andre 1861-1942 *DcFM, FilmEn*
Calmo, Andrea 1509?-1561? *OxThe*
Calmo, Andrea 1509?-1571 *NewGrD 80*
Calmour, Alfred C *WhThe*
Calonne, Jacques 1930- *IntWWM 77, -80*
Calori, Angiola 1732-1790? *NewGrD 80*
Calsabigi, Ranieri De *NewGrD 80*
Calsabigi, Raniero De *NewGrD 80*
Caltabiano, Sebastiano 1899- *WhoMus 72*
Calthorp, Donald 1888-1940 *Film 1*
Calthrop, David d1940 *WhoHol B*
Calthrop, Dion Clayton 1878-1937 *NotNAT B, WhThe*
Calthrop, Donald 1888-1940 *FilmEn, Film 2, FilmgC, HalFC 80, IlWWBF[port], NotNAT B, WhScrn 74, -77, WhThe*
Calthrop, Gladys E *WhThe*
Calve, Emma 1858-1942 *Baker 78, BiDAmM, BnBkM 80, CmOp, MusSN[port], NewEOp 71, NewGrD 80[port]*
Calve, Emma 1864- *WhoStg 1906, -1908*
Calvert, Adelaide Helen 1837-1921 *EncWT, NotNAT A, -B, OxThe*
Calvert, Catherine d1971 *Film 1, -2, MotPP, TwYS, WhoHol B*
Calvert, Catherine 1890-1971 *WhThe*
Calvert, Catherine 1891-1971 *FilmEn, WhScrn 74, -77*
Calvert, Cecil G 1871- *WhThe*
Calvert, Charles 1828-1879 *EncWT, IlWWBF, NotNAT B, OxThe*
Calvert, Mrs. Charles 1837-1921 *Film 1, WhThe*
Calvert, E H 1873-1941 *FilmEn, ForYSC, WhoHol B*
Calvert, E H 1890- *Film 1, -2, TwYS*
Calvert, Elisha H 1873-1941 *WhScrn 74, -77*
Calvert, John *ForYSC, MagIlD*
Calvert, Louis 1859-1923 *EncWT, Film 1, NotNAT B, OxThe, WhScrn 77, WhThe*
Calvert, Morley Frederick 1928- *IntWWM 80*
Calvert, Patricia 1908- *WhThe*
Calvert, Phyllis *MotPP*
Calvert, Phyllis 1915- *CmMov, FilmAG WE, FilmEn, FilmgC, ForYSC, HalFC 80, IlWWBF[port], MovMk, OxFilm, WhoHol A, WhoThe 72, -77*
Calvert, Phyllis 1917- *IntMPA 77, -75, -76, -78, -79, -80*
Calvesi, Vincenzo *NewGrD 80*
Calvet, Corinne *IntMPA 77, -75, -76, -78, -79, -80, MotPP*
Calvet, Corinne 1925- *FilmEn, FilmgC, ForYSC, HalFC 80, What 3[port], WhoHol A*
Calvet, Corinne 1926- *MovMk*
Calvet, Emma 1858-1942 *NewGrD 80[port]*
Calvet, Rosa Emma 1858-1942 *BnBkM 80*
Calvez, Gabriel *NewGrD 80*
Calvi, Carlo *NewGrD 80*
Calvi, Lorenzo *NewGrD 80*
Calvin, Henry 1918-1975 *ForYSC, HalFC 80, WhScrn 77, WhoHol C*
Calvin, Jean 1509-1564 *NewGrD 80*
Calvin, John 1509-1564 *OxMus*
Calvin, Susan *ConAmC*
Calvisius, Sethus 1556-1615 *Baker 78, NewGrD 80*
Calvo Sotelo, Joaquin 1905- *CroCD, McGEWD[port], ModWD*
Calvocoressi, Michel-Dimitri 1877-1944 *Baker 78, DancEn 78, NewGrD 80*
Calvoer, Caspar 1650-1725 *NewGrD 80*
Calvor, Caspar 1650-1725 *NewGrD 80*
Calzabigi, Ranieri *BnBkM 80*
Calzabigi, Ranieri 1714-1795 *CmOp*
Calzabigi, Ranieri Da 1714-1795 *NewEOp 71, OxThe*
Calzabigi, Ranieri De 1714-1795 *NewGrD 80*
Calzabigi, Ranieri Di 1714-1795 *Baker 78*
Calzabigi, Raniero De 1714-1795 *NewGrD 80, OxMus*
Calzada, Alba 1945- *CnOxB*
Camagno *NewGrD 80*
Camajani, Giovanni 1915- *IntWWM 77, -80*
Camani, Adriana 1936- *WhoOp 76*
Camara Cascudo, Luiz Da *NewGrD 80*
Camarata, Salvador 1913- *AmSCAP 66, -80*
Camarata, Toots 1913- *CmpEPM*
Camarella, Giovanni Battista *NewGrD 80*
Camargo, La *NewGrD 80*
Camargo, Ignacio *NewGrD 80*
Camargo, Marie Anne DeCupis De 1710-1770 *CnOxB, DancEn 78, NotNAT B*
Camargo, Miguel Gomez *NewGrD 80*
Camargo Guarnieri, Mozart *DcCM*
Camatero, Ippolito *NewGrD 80*
Cambefort, Jean De 1605?-1661 *NewGrD 80*
Cambern, May Hogan *AmSCAP 66, -80*
Cambert, Robert 1627?-1677 *NewGrD 80*
Cambert, Robert 1628?-1677 *Baker 78, BnBkM 80, DancEn 78, NewEOp 71, OxMus*
Cambini, Giovanni Giuseppe 1746-1825 *Baker 78*
Cambini, Giuseppe Maria 1746-1825 *NewGrD 80*
Cambio, Perissone *NewGrD 80*
Cambissa, Giorgio 1921- *IntWWM 80*
Cambrensis, Giraldus *NewGrD 80*
Cambridge, Ed *DrBlPA*
Cambridge, Godfrey *MotPP, WhoHol A*
Cambridge, Godfrey 1929-1976 *HalFC 80, OxFilm*
Cambridge, Godfrey 1933-1976 *DrBlPA, FilmEn, FilmgC, IntMPA 77, -75, -76, JoeFr, MovMk[port], NotNAT*
Camden, Anthony J 1938- *IntWWM 77, -80, WhoMus 72*
Camden, Archibald 1888-1979 *NewGrD 80*
Camden, Archie 1888-1979 *NewGrD 80, WhoMus 72*
Camden, Dorothea *Film 1*
Camden, Helen Joyce *WhoMus 72*
Camden, Kerrison Hamilton 1936- *WhoMus 72*
Camel *IlEncR*
Camelia, Muriel 1913-1925 *WhScrn 74, -77, WhoHol B*
Cameraco *NewGrD 80*
Cameracy *NewGrD 80*
Camerarius, Leonhard *NewGrD 80*
Camerata Singers And Symphony Orchestra *BiDAmM*
Camere, Manuel *Film 2*
Camerini, Carlo *WhoMus 72*
Camerini, Mario 1895- *DcFM, FilmEn,*

FilmgC, HalFC 80, OxFilm, WorEFlm[port]
Camerlo, Louis *NewGrD 80*
Camerlochner, Placidus Cajetan Von 1718-1782 *NewGrD 80*
Camerloher, Placidus Cajetan Von 1718-1782 *NewGrD 80*
Camero, Candido 1921- *AmSCAP 80, BiDAmM*
Cameron, Alan 1900-1972 *AmSCAP 66, -80*
Cameron, Alexander 1922- *IntWWM 77, -80, WhoMus 72*
Cameron, Alexandra Esther 1910- *IntWWM 80*
Cameron, Archie Andre 1957- *IntWWM 77, -80*
Cameron, Barbara Marie 1928- *AmSCAP 80*
Cameron, Basil 1884-1975 *Baker 78, NewGrD 80, WhoMus 72*
Cameron, Beatrice 1868-1940 *NotNAT B, OxThe*
Cameron, Bruce 1910-1959 *WhScrn 74, -77*
Cameron, Donald 1889-1955 *Film 1, MotPP, NotNAT B, WhScrn 74, -77, WhThe, WhoHol B*
Cameron, Douglas *WhoMus 72*
Cameron, Earl 1917- *DrBlPA*
Cameron, Earl 1925- *FilmgC, HalFC 80, IlWWBF[port]*
Cameron, Fiona *WhoMus 72*
Cameron, Gene d1928 *Film 2, WhScrn 74, -77, WhoHol B*
Cameron, Hugh 1879-1941 *Film 2, NotNAT B, WhScrn 77, WhoHol B*
Cameron, Jack *Film 2*
Cameron, Jay 1928- *BiDAmM*
Cameron, Joanna *IntMPA 78, -79, -80*
Cameron, John 1944- *HalFC 80, IntWWM 77, -77, -80*
Cameron, John Ewen 1920- *WhoMus 72*
Cameron, Kathryn d1954 *NotNAT B*
Cameron, Kenneth Neill 1908- *NatPD[port]*
Cameron, Richard 1943- *CpmDNM 72*
Cameron, Rod *MotPP*
Cameron, Rod 1910- *FilmEn, FilmgC, HalFC 80*
Cameron, Rod 1912- *CmMov, ForYSC, HolP 40[port], IntMPA 77, -75, -76, -78, -79, -80, WhoHol A*
Cameron, Rudolph 1894-1958 *Film 1, -2, WhScrn 77*
Cameron, Sheila 1909- *WhoMus 72*
Cameron, Violet 1862-1919 *WhThe*
Cametti, Alberto 1871-1935 *Baker 78, NewGrD 80*
Camidge *NewGrD 80*
Camidge, John 1734?-1803 *NewGrD 80*
Camidge, John 1735-1803 *OxMus*
Camidge, John 1790-1850 *OxMus*
Camidge, John 1790-1859 *NewGrD 80*
Camidge, John 1853-1939 *OxMus*
Camidge, Matthew 1758-1844 *Baker 78, OxMus*
Camidge, Matthew 1764?-1844 *NewGrD 80*
Camidge, Thomas Simpson 1828-1912 *OxMus*
Camilieri, Lorenzo 1878-1956 *NewGrD 80*
Camilleri, Charles 1931- *IntWWM 77, -80, NewGrD 80, WhoMus 72*
Camilli, Camillus 1704?-1754 *NewGrD 80*
Camillo, Marvin Felix *PlP&P A[port]*
Caminelli, Antonio 1436-1502 *OxThe*
Cammarano, Salvatore 1801-1852 *Baker 78, CmOp, NewEOp 71, NewGrD 80*
Cammarota, Lionello 1941- *IntWWM 80*
Cammarota, Robert Michael 1949- *IntWWM 77, -80*
Cammell, Antonin *NewGrD 80*
Cammerarius, Leonhard *NewGrD 80*
Cammerer, Leonhard *NewGrD 80*
Cammerhof, Johann Friedrich 1721-1751 *BiDAmM*
Cammerlocher, Placidus Cajetan Von *NewGrD 80*
Camoes, Luis De *OxThe, REnWD*
Camp, Clem 1898?-1968 *NewOrJ[port]*
Camp, Hamid Hamilton 1934- *AmSCAP 80*
Camp, Hamilton *WhoHol A*
Camp, Joe 1940- *FilmEn*
Camp, John Spencer 1858-1946 *Baker 78*
Camp, Max W 1935- *IntWWM 77, -80*
Camp, Shep 1882-1929 *WhoHol B*
Camp, Sheppard 1882-1929 *WhScrn 74, -77*
Campa, Gustavo 1863-1934 *NewGrD 80*
Campagnoli, Bartolomeo 1751-1827 *NewGrD 80*
Campagnoli, Bartolommeo 1751-1827 *Baker 78*
Campana, Fabio 1819-1882 *Baker 78, NewGrD 80*
Campana, Francesca d1665 *NewGrD 80*
Campanari, Giuseppe *Film 1*
Campanari, Giuseppe 1855-1927 *Baker 78, NewEOp 71*
Campanari, Leandro 1857-1939 *Baker 78, BiDAmM*
Campanella, Bruno Carmelo 1943- *WhoOp 76*
Campanella, Frank *ForYSC, WhoHol A*
Campanella, Joseph 1927- *BiE&WWA, FilmgC, HalFC 80, NotNAT, WhoHol A*
Campanella, Michele 1947- *IntWWM 80, NewGrD 80*
Campanella, Roy *ForYSC*
Campanile, Peter Benjamin 1928- *AmSCAP 80*
Campanini, Barbara *CnOxB*
Campanini, Cleofonte 1860-1919 *Baker 78, BiDAmM, CmOp, MusSN[port], NewEOp 71, NewGrD 80, NotNAT B*
Campanini, Italo 1845-1896 *Baker 78, NewEOp 71, NewGrD 80*
Campanus, Jan 1572-1622 *NewGrD 80*
Campbell, Professor *PupTheA*
Campbell, Alan 1905-1963 *AmSCAP 80, WhScrn 74, -77*
Campbell, Alexander 1764-1824 *NewGrD 80*
Campbell, Aline *Baker 78*
Campbell, Archie 1914- *BiDAmM, CounME 74[port], -74A, EncFCWM 69, IlEncCM[port]*
Campbell, Arthur 1890?- *NewOrJ*
Campbell, Arthur 1922- *ConAmC*
Campbell, Bartley 1843-1888 *NotNAT B, OxThe*
Campbell, Beatrice 1923- *FilmgC, HalFC 80, WhoHol A*
Campbell, Beatrice 1924- *ForYSC, IlWWBF*
Campbell, Betty *Film 2*
Campbell, Catherine *WhoMus 72*
Campbell, Charles d1964 *NotNAT B*
Campbell, Charles Joseph 1930- *ConAmC*
Campbell, Chester *PupTheA*
Campbell, Colin d1966 *Film 1, -2, WhoHol B*
Campbell, Colin 1880?- *FilmEn*
Campbell, Colin 1883-1966 *ForYSC, HalFC 80, WhScrn 74, -77*
Campbell, Colin 1888-1966 *TwYS A*
Campbell, Colin 1940?- *HalFC 80*
Campbell, Daisy *Film 2*
Campbell, David 1953- *IntWWM 80*
Campbell, Desmond 1894- *WhoMus 72*
Campbell, Dick 1903- *DrBlPA, MorBAP*
Campbell, Douglas 1910- *IntWWM 77*
Campbell, Douglas 1922- *BiE&WWA, CnThe, CreCan 1, NotNAT, WhoThe 72, -77*
Campbell, Eric d1917 *TwYS, WhoHol B*
Campbell, Eric 1870-1917 *FilmEn, Film 1*
Campbell, Eric 1878-1917 *FilmgC, HalFC 80*
Campbell, Eric 1879-1917 *WhScrn 77*
Campbell, Eva *Film 1*
Campbell, Frances d1948 *NotNAT B*
Campbell, Francis Joseph 1832-1914 *BiDAmM*
Campbell, Frank 1847-1934 *WhScrn 74, -77, WhoHol B*
Campbell, Frank Carter 1916- *IntWWM 80, NewGrD 80*
Campbell, Geraldine *PupTheA*
Campbell, Glen *IntMPA 77, -75, -76, -78, -79, -80, WhoHol A*
Campbell, Glen 1935- *FilmEn, FilmgC, ForYSC, HalFC 80*
Campbell, Glen 1936- *CounME 74[port], -74A, IlEncCM[port], RkOn*
Campbell, Glen 1937- *BiDAmM*
Campbell, Glen 1938- *EncFCWM 69, IlEncR*
Campbell, Grace MacLennan Grant 1895-1963 *CreCan 1*
Campbell, Henry C 1926- *AmSCAP 66, -80, ConAmC*
Campbell, Herbert 1844-1904 *BlkAmP, MorBAP, NotNAT B, OxThe, PlP&P*
Campbell, Ivar 1904- *IlWWBF*
Campbell, James 1906- *BluesWW, CmpEPM*
Campbell, Jim *WhoHol A*
Campbell, Jimmy 1903-1967 *BiDAmM*
Campbell, Jo-Ann 1938- *RkOn[port]*
Campbell, John B 1856-1938 *BiDAmM*
Campbell, John Coleman 1935- *IntWWM 77, -80*
Campbell, Judy 1916- *FilmgC, HalFC 80, IlWWBF, WhoHol A, WhoThe 72, -77*
Campbell, Kenneth 1922- *IntWWM 80*
Campbell, Lewisson 1924- *IntWWM 80*
Campbell, Lily Bess 1883- *BiE&WWA*
Campbell, Louise 1915- *FilmEn, ForYSC, WhoHol A*
Campbell, Mae E *IntMPA 79, -80*
Campbell, Margaret *IntWWM 77*
Campbell, Margaret 1873-1939 *Film 2, WhScrn 74, -77*
Campbell, Margaret 1894- *WhThe*
Campbell, Margaret Jane 1957- *IntWWM 80*
Campbell, Margaret Jean *IntWWM 80*
Campbell, Michael Rector 1944- *AmSCAP 80*
Campbell, Milton James 1934- *BluesWW[port]*
Campbell, Norman *NewYTET*
Campbell, Olive *OxMus*
Campbell, Patrick 1907- *FilmgC, HalFC 80*
Campbell, Mrs. Patrick 1865-1940 *CnThe, EncWT, Ent, FamA&A[port], FilmEn, FilmgC, HalFC 80, NotNAT A, -B, OxFilm, OxThe, PlP&P[port], ThFT[port], WhScrn 74, -77, WhThe, WhoHol B*
Campbell, Mrs. Patrick 1867-1940 *WhoStg 1906, -1908*
Campbell, Mrs. Patrick 1886-1940 *WhThe*
Campbell, Patton 1926- *BiE&WWA, NotNAT, WhoOp 76, WhoThe 72, -77*
Campbell, Paul *AmSCAP 80*
Campbell, Ralph *BlkAmP*
Campbell, Richard Gene 1932- *IntWWM 80*
Campbell, Robert Gordon 1922- *IntWWM 80*
Campbell, Robert Maurice 1922- *IntMPA 77, -75, -76, -78, -79, -80*
Campbell, Robert Myron 1944- *AmSCAP 80*
Campbell, S Brunson 1884- *BiDAmM*
Campbell, Shawn *WhoHol A*
Campbell, Sidney Scholfield 1909- *WhoMus 72*
Campbell, Sylvester 1938- *CnOxB*
Campbell, Thomas Gordon 1954- *CpmDNM 80*
Campbell, Violet d1970 *WhoHol B*
Campbell, Violet 1892-1970 *WhThe*
Campbell, Violet 1893-1970 *WhScrn 74, -77*
Campbell, Webster 1893-1972 *FilmEn, Film 1, -2, WhScrn 77, WhoHol B*
Campbell, Wilfred 1858-1918 *CreCan 2*
Campbell, William 1926- *FilmEn, FilmgC, ForYSC, HalFC 80, IntMPA 77, -75, -76, -78, -79, -80, MotPP, WhoHol A, WhoHrs 80*
Campbell, William Alexander 1913- *IntWWM 77, -80*
Campbell, William Wilfred *CreCan 2*
Campbell Batista, Ramon 1911- *NewGrD 80*
Campbell-Tipton, Louis 1877-1921 *Baker 78, BiDAmM, ConAmC*
Campbell-Watson, Frank 1898- *AmSCAP 66, Baker 78, ConAmC*
Campeau, Frank 1864-1943 *FilmEn, Film 1, -2, ForYSC, NotNAT B, TwYS, WhScrn 74, -77, WhoHol B*
Campeau, George *WhoHol A*
Campen, Jacob Van *OxThe*
Campenhout, Francois Van 1779-1848 *Baker 78, OxMus*
Campenhout, Francois Van 1799-1848 *NewGrD 80*
Campesius, Domenico *NewGrD 80*
Campey, Dorothea *WhoMus 72*
Campey, Fay *WhoMus 72*
Campey, George 1915- *IntMPA 75, -76*
Campey, Rosalind *WhoMus 72*
Camphuysen, Dirk Rafaelszoon 1586?-1627 *NewGrD 80*
Camphuysen, Theodorus Rafaelszoon 1586?-1627 *NewGrD 80*
Campian, Thomas *NewGrD 80*
Campian, Thomas 1562-1620 *DcCom&M 79*
Campian, Thomas 1567-1620 *MusMk, OxMus*
Campioli *NewGrD 80*
Campion *NewGrD 80*
Campion, Charles Antoine *NewGrD 80*
Campion, Cyril 1894-1961 *WhThe*
Campion, Francois 1686?-1748 *NewGrD 80*

Campion, Thomas 1562-1620 DcCom&M 79
Campion, Thomas 1567-1620 Baker 78, NewGrD 80, OxMus, OxThe
Campione, Carlo Antonio 1720-1788 NewGrD 80
Campioni, Carlo Antonio 1720-1788 Baker 78, NewGrD 80
Campis, Henrico De NewGrD 80
Campise, Anthony S 1943- EncJzS 70
Campise, Tony 1943- EncJzS 70
Campisi, Domenico 1588-1641 NewGrD 80
Campistron, Jean Galbert De 1656-1723 CnThe, Ent, OxThe, REnWD[port]
Campistron, Jean Gualbert De 1656-1723 EncWT
Camplin, R S IntMPA 77, -75, -76, -78, -79, -80
Camplin, William Michael 1947- AmSCAP 80
Campo, Conrado Del 1878-1953 NewGrD 80
Campo, Conrado Del 1879-1953 OxMus
Campo, Frank Philip 1927- AmSCAP 80, CpmDNM 72, -78, -79, -80, ConAmC
Campo, Murphy 1935- NewOrJ SUP[port]
Campo, Pupi BgBands 74
Campo Y Zabaleta, Conrado Del 1879-1953 Baker 78
Campogalliani, Carlo 1885- FilmEn
Campoli, Alfredo 1906- IntWWM 77, -80, NewGrD 80, WhoMus 72
Campora, Guiseppe 1925- WhoOp 76
Camporese, Violante 1785-1839 NewGrD 80
Campos, Anisia IntWWM 77, -80
Campos, Rafael ForYSC, WhoHol A
Campos, Ruben M 1876-1945 NewGrD 80
Campos, Victor WhoHol A
Campos-Parsi, Hector 1922- Baker 78, NewGrD 80
Campra, Andre 1660-1744 Baker 78, BnBkM 80, CnOxB, DancEn 78, MusMk, NewEOp 71, NewGrD 80[port], OxMus
Campra, Joseph 1662-1744 NewGrD 80
Camps, Pompeyo 1924- Baker 78
Campton, David 1924- ConDr 73, -77, CroCD, EncWT, McGEWD
Camryn, Walter 1903- DancEn 78
Camus, Albert 1913-1960 CnMD, CnThe, CroCD, EncWT, Ent, McGEWD[port], ModWD, NotNAT A, -B, OxThe, REnWD[port]
Camus, Marcel 1912- DcFM, FilmEn, FilmgC, HalFC 80, OxFilm, WorEFlm[port]
Camus, Raoul F 1930- IntWWM 80
Camussi, Ezio 1877-1956 Baker 78
Can ConMuA 80A, IlEncR
Canada, Richard 1942- AmSCAP 80
Canaday, Veronica AmSCAP 80
Canal, Marguerite 1890-1978 NewGrD 80
Canale, Floriano 1550?- NewGrD 80
Canale, Gianna Maria 1927- FilmEn, FilmgC, HalFC 80, IntMPA 77, -75, -76, -78, -79, -80, WhoHol A
Canaletto 1734-1780 DancEn 78
Canali, Floriano 1550?- NewGrD 80
Canalis, Floriano 1550?- NewGrD 80
Canarina, John Baptiste 1934- IntWWM 77, -80, WhoMus 72
Canary, David ForYSC, WhoHol A
Canavas, Jean-Baptiste 1713-1784 NewGrD 80
Canavas, Joseph 1714?-1776 NewGrD 80
Canavasso, Jean-Baptiste 1713-1784 NewGrD 80
Canavasso, Joseph 1714?-1776 NewGrD 80
Canazzi, Antonio NewGrD 80
Canby, Edward Tatnall 1912- ConAmC
Canby, Vincent 1924- IntMPA 77, -75, -76, -78, -79, -80
Cancelmo, Joe 1897- AmSCAP 66
Cancineo, Michelangelo 1550?- NewGrD 80
Cancino, Michelangelo 1550?- NewGrD 80
Candael, Karel 1883-1948 NewGrD 80
Candeille, Julie 1767-1834 NewGrD 80
Candeille, Pierre Joseph 1744-1827 NewGrD 80
Candido 1921- AmSCAP 80, BiDAmM, EncJzS 70
Candido, Candy 1905?- CmpEPM
Candido, Candy 1913?- NewOrJ
Candido, Serafino NewGrD 80
Candler, Doc PupTheA
Candler, Peter 1926- BiE&WWA, NotNAT
Candlyn, T F H 1892-1964 ConAmC
Candlyn, T Frederick H 1892-1964 AmSCAP 66, -80, BiDAmM
Candoli, Conte 1927- CmpEPM
Candoli, Pete 1923- CmpEPM, EncJzS 70
Candoli, Secondo 1927- BiDAmM, EncJzS 70
Candoli, Walter Joseph 1923- BiDAmM, EncJzS 70
Candonio, Floriano NewGrD 80
Candor, John 1944- WhoMus 72
Candullo, Joe CmpEPM
Candy, Mary AmSCAP 80
Candy & The Kisses RkOn 2A
Cane, Andrew OxThe
Cane, Charles 1899-1973 WhScrn 77, WhoHol B
Cane, Marvin ConMuA 80B
Canetti, Elias 1905- CnMD, CroCD, EncWT
Canetty-Clarke, Janet Constance 1935- IntWWM 80
Canfield, Alyce IntMPA 77, -75, -76, -78, -79, -80
Canfield, Cass 1897- BiE&WWA
Canfield, Curtis 1903- BiE&WWA, NotNAT
Canfield, Josephine Elizabeth 1902- IntWWM 77
Canfield, Mary Grace WhoHol A
Canfield, William F d1925 NotNAT B, WhScrn 77
Cangalovic, Miroslav Mihail 1921- WhoOp 76
Cangiasi, Giovanni Antonio d1614? NewGrD 80
Caniglia, Maria 1905-1979 NewGrD 80, WhoMus 72
Caniglia, Maria 1906-1979 CmOp
Canino, Bruno 1935- NewGrD 80
Caninus De Peraga De Padua NewGrD 80
Canis, Cornelius 1510?-1561 NewGrD 80
Canis DeHondt, Cornelius 1510?-1561 NewGrD 80
Canis D'Hondt, Cornelius 1510?-1561 NewGrD 80
Canizares, Jose De 1676-1750 McGEWD
Cankar, Ivan 1876-1918 CnMD
Cannabich NewGrD 80
Cannabich, Carl 1771?-1806 NewGrD 80
Cannabich, Christian 1731-1798 Baker 78, MusMk, NewGrD 80[port], OxMus
Cannabich, Johann Christian d1798 CnOxB
Cannabich, Martin Friedrich 1675?-1759? NewGrD 80
Cannan, Denis 1919- ConDr 73, -77, CroCD, WhoThe 72, -77
Cannan, Dennis 1919- EncWT
Cannan, Gerald Frank 1922- AmSCAP 80
Cannan, Gilbert 1884-1955 NotNAT B, WhThe
Cannarile, Antonietta WhoOp 76
Canne-Meijer, Cora 1929- NewGrD 80, WhoOp 76
Canned Heat BiDAmM, ConMuA 80A, IlEncR[port], RkOn 2[port]
Cannibal & The Headhunters RkOn 2[port]
Cannicciari, Pompeo 1670-1744 NewGrD 80
Canning, Thomas 1911- ConAmC
Canning, Victor 1911- HalFC 80
Cannon, Ace 1934- RkOn
Cannon, Beekman Cox 1911- Baker 78
Cannon, Dwight W 1932- ConAmC, IntWWM 77, -80
Cannon, Dyan IntMPA 75, -76, WhoHol A
Cannon, Dyan 1937- IntMPA 77, -78, -79, -80, MovMk
Cannon, Dyan 1938- FilmgC, HalFC 80
Cannon, Dyan 1939- FilmEn
Cannon, Esma d1972 HalFC 80
Cannon, Freddie AmPS A
Cannon, Freddy 1940- AmSCAP 80, RkOn[port]
Cannon, Gus 1883- BiDAmM, BluesWW[port]
Cannon, Hughie 1877-1912 BiDAmM
Cannon, J D 1922- BiE&WWA, FilmgC, HalFC 80, NotNAT, WhoHol A
Cannon, Jack Philip 1929- IntWWM 80, WhoMus 72
Cannon, Judy 1938- IntMPA 77, -75, -76, -78, -79, -80
Cannon, Marion Hilda Cecilia WhoMus 72
Cannon, Maurice Film 2
Cannon, Murray Franklin 1947- AmSCAP 80
Cannon, Norman Film 2
Cannon, Philip 1929- Baker 78, NewGrD 80
Cannon, Pomeray Film 2
Cannon, Raymond Film 1, -2
Cannon, Robert 1901-1964 DcFM, FilmEn, FilmgC, HalFC 80
Cannon, Robert 1910-1964 WorEFlm[port]
Cannon, William 1937- IntMPA 77, -75, -76, -78, -79, -80
Cannon, William Frederick 1904- WhoMus 72
Cano, Antonio 1937- CnOxB
Cano, Edward, Jr. 1927- AmSCAP 66, -80
Canobbio, Carlo 1741-1822 NewGrD 80
Canosa, Michael Raymond 1920- AmSCAP 66, -80
Canova, Diana HalFC 80
Canova, Judy 1916- AmPS B, BiDAmM, CmpEPM, FilmEn, FilmgC, ForYSC, Funs[port], HalFC 80, IlEncCM, IntMPA 77, -75, -76, -78, -79, -80, JoeFr[port], MotPP, MovMk[port], What 1[port], WhoHol A
Canova, Zeke WhoHol A
Canova DaMilano, Francesco NewGrD 80
Cansino, Eduardo 1895-1968 WhScrn 77
Cansino, Eduardo, Jr. 1920-1974 WhScrn 77, WhoHol B
Cansino, Gabriel d1963 NotNAT B
Cansler, Loman 1924- BiDAmM, EncFCWM 69
Cantagrel, Gilles 1937- IntWWM 80
Cantagrel, Marc 1879-1960 DcFM
Cantelli, Guido 1920-1956 Baker 78, BnBkM 80, CmOp, MusSN[port], NewGrD 80
Cantelo, Miss 1760?-1831 NewGrD 80
Cantelo, April 1928- NewGrD 80
Canteloube, Joseph 1879-1957 BnBkM 80, MusMk, NewGrD 80
Canteloube DeMalaret, Marie-Joseph 1879-1957 Baker 78
Cantemir, Prince Demetrius 1673-1723 OxMus
Cantemir, Dimitrie 1673-1723 NewGrD 80
Canter, Henriette WhoMus 72
Canter, Lynn WhScrn 77
Canter, Robin 1952- IntWWM 80
Canti, Giovanni NewGrD 80
Cantin, Bertin NewGrD 80
Cantin, Jean-Baptiste NewGrD 80
Cantinflas MotPP, WhoHol A
Cantinflas 1911- FilmEn, FilmgC, ForYSC, HalFC 80, OxFilm
Cantinflas 1917- MovMk
Cantino, Paolo NewGrD 80
Canton, Arthur H IntMPA 77, -75, -76, -78, -79, -80
Canton, Don 1915- AmSCAP 66
Canton, Donald 1915- AmSCAP 80
Cantone, Serafino NewGrD 80
Cantone, Vito PupTheA
Cantoni, Serafino NewGrD 80
Cantor, Arthur 1920- BiE&WWA, NotNAT, WhoThe 72, -77
Cantor, Charles 1898-1966 WhScrn 74, -77, WhoHol B
Cantor, Eddie d1964 AmPS A, -B, MotPP, NewYTET, PlP&P, WhoHol B
Cantor, Eddie 1892-1964 AmSCAP 66, -80, BiDAmM, BiE&WWA, CmpEPM, EncMT, Ent, FilmEn, Film 2, FilmgC, ForYSC, Funs[port], HalFC 80, JoeFr[port], MovMk[port], NotNAT B, TwYS, WhScrn 74, -77, WhThe
Cantor, Eddie 1893-1964 NotNAT A, OxFilm, WorEFlm[port]
Cantor, Herman 1896-1953 WhScrn 74, -77
Cantor, Ida 1892-1962 WhScrn 77
Cantor, Joseph 1913- IntWWM 77, -80
Cantor, Montague 1909- IntWWM 77, -80
Cantor, Nat 1897-1956 NotNAT B, WhScrn 74, -77
Cantos, Josef Ignacio PupTheA
Cantow, Roberta WomWMM B
Cantrell, Byron 1919- AmSCAP 80, ConAmC
Cantrell, Derrick Edward 1926- IntWWM 77, -80, WhoMus 72
Cantrick, Robert B 1917- ConAmC
Cantu, Willie EncFCWM 69
Cantway, Fred R 1883-1939 WhScrn 74, -77
Canty, Marietta 1906?- DrBlPA, HalFC 80, Vers B[port]

Canudo, Ricciotto 1879-1923 *FilmEn*
Canuel, Ivan 1935- *CreCan 1*
Canuti, Giovanni Antonio 1680?-1739 *NewGrD 80*
Canutt, Yakima 1895- *CmMov, FilmEn, Film 2, FilmgC, ForYSC, HalFC 80, IntMPA 77, -75, -76, -78, -79, -80, OxFilm, TwYS, WhoHol A, WorEFlm[port]*
Canzoneri, Tony d1959 *WhScrn 77*
Capalbo, Carmen 1925- *BiE&WWA, NotNAT*
Capaldi, Jim 1944- *IlEncR, RkOn 2[port]*
Capanna, Robert 1952- *AmSCAP 80*
Capano, Frank X 1899-1956 *AmSCAP 66, -80*
Capdenat, Philippe 1934- *NewGrD 80*
Capdevielle, Pierre 1906-1969 *Baker 78, NewGrD 80*
Capdeville, Constanca 1937- *NewGrD 80*
Capdoil, Pons De *NewGrD 80*
Capdoilh, Pons De *NewGrD 80*
Capduch, Pons De *NewGrD 80*
Capdueil, Pons De *NewGrD 80*
Capduelh, Pons De *NewGrD 80*
Capduill, Pons De *NewGrD 80*
Capduoill, Pons De *NewGrD 80*
Cape, Judith *CreCan 1*
Cape, Safford 1906-1973 *Baker 78, NewGrD 80*
Capecchi, Renato 1923- *CmOp, NewGrD 80, WhoOp 76*
Capece, Alessandro d1636 *NewGrD 80*
Capece Minutolo, Irma 1940- *WhoOp 76*
Capek *PlP&P[port]*
Capek, Josef 1887-1927 *DcPup, NotNAT B*
Capek, Josef 1887-1945 *CnThe, EncWT, REnWD[port]*
Capek, Karel 1890-1938 *CnMD, CnThe, EncWT, Ent, McGEWD[port], ModWD, NotNAT B, OxThe, REnWD[port], WhThe*
Capek, Karel 1890-1939 *DcPup*
Capel, Sharon *BlkAmP*
Capell, Manfred *WhoOp 76*
Capell, Richard 1885-1954 *Baker 78, NewGrD 80, OxMus*
Capella, Giovanni Maria 1648-1726 *NewGrD 80*
Capella, Martianus Minneus Felix *NewGrD 80*
Capellan, Richard Victor 1943- *AmSCAP 80*
Capellani, Albert 1870-1931 *DcFM, FilmEn, FilmgC, HalFC 80*
Capellani, Albert 1874-1931 *TwYS A*
Capellani, Paul *Film 1*
Capellen, George 1869-1934 *Baker 78*
Capeller, Tamara *DancEn 78*
Capelli, Dante *Film 1*
Capelli, David August Von *NewGrD 80*
Capelli, Giovanni Maria 1648-1726 *NewGrD 80*
Capellini, Carlo -1683 *NewGrD 80*
Capellini, Michelangelo 1598?-1627 *NewGrD 80*
Capello, Giovanni Francesco *NewGrD 80*
Capers, Virginia 1925- *DrBlPA, NotNAT, PlP&P A[port], WhoHol A*
Caperton, Florence Tait 1886- *ConAmC*
Capet, Lucien 1873-1928 *Baker 78, NewGrD 80*
Capey, Bertram Joseph 1921- *WhoMus 72*
Capi, Adrien *NewGrD 80*
Capi DeCamargo *NewGrD 80*
Capillas, Francisco Lopez *NewGrD 80*
Capilupi, Gemignano 1573?-1616 *NewGrD 80*
Capilupi, Geminiano 1573?-1616 *NewGrD 80*
Capirola, Vincenzo 1474- *NewGrD 80*
Capitanelli, Arnold Joseph, Jr. 1932- *AmSCAP 80*
Capitols, The *RkOn 2[port]*
Caplan, Harry 1908- *IntMPA 77, -75, -76, -78, -79, -80*
Caplan, Rupert 1896- *CreCan 2*
Caplat, Moran Victor Hingston 1916- *WhoMus 72, WhoOp 76*
Caplet, Andre 1878-1925 *Baker 78, NewGrD 80, OxMus*
Capli, Erdogan 1926- *AmSCAP 66*
Caplin, Gertrude 1921- *BiE&WWA, NotNAT*
Capmany I Farres, Aurelio 1868-1954 *NewGrD 80*
Capobianco, Tito 1931- *IntWWM 77, -80, WhoOp 76*
Capocci, Alessandro *NewGrD 80*
Capocci, Filippo 1840-1911 *NewGrD 80*
Capocci, Gaetano 1811-1898 *Baker 78, NewGrD 80*
Capoianu, Dumitru 1929- *Baker 78, NewGrD 80*
Capollini, Michelangelo *NewGrD 80*
Capolongo, Paul 1940- *WhoMus 72*
Capon, William 1757-1827 *NotNAT B, OxThe, PlP&P*
Capone, Al 1899-1947 *FilmgC, HalFC 80, OxFilm*
Caporale, Andrea *NewGrD 80*
Caporale, Fred 1953- *AmSCAP 80*
Capote, Truman *ConDr 77D, WhoHol A*
Capote, Truman 1924- *AmSCAP 66, -80, BiE&WWA, CnMD, ConDr 73, FilmEn, ModWD, NotNAT*
Capote, Truman 1925- *FilmgC, HalFC 80, OxFilm*
Capoul, Joseph-Amedee-Victor 1839-1924 *Baker 78*
Capozzi, Alberto *Film 1*
Capozzi, Alberto 1886-1945 *FilmEn*
Capp, Bartold d1636 *NewGrD 80*
Capp, Frank 1931- *EncJzS 70*
Cappa, Giofredo 1644-1717 *NewGrD 80*
Cappelli, Amy Spencer 1904- *AmSCAP 66, -80*
Cappelli, Bartolomeo *NewGrD 80*
Cappelli, Carlo Alberto 1907- *WhoOp 76*
Cappelli, Giovanni Maria *NewGrD 80*
Cappellini, Phillip Thomas 1930- *AmSCAP 80*
Cappellini, Pietro Paolo *NewGrD 80*
Cappello, Bartolomeo *NewGrD 80*
Cappi *NewGrD 80*
Cappi, Adrien *NewGrD 80*
Cappi, Giovanni 1765-1815 *NewGrD 80*
Cappi, Pietro *NewGrD 80*
Cappi DeCamargo *NewGrD 80*
Capponi, Gino Angelo 1607?-1688 *NewGrD 80*
Capponius, Ginus Angelus 1607?-1688 *NewGrD 80*
Capps, Ferald Buell, Jr. 1943- *IntWWM 77, -80*
Capps, William 1941- *IntWWM 77, -80*
Cappuccilli, Piero 1929- *NewGrD 80, WhoOp 76*
Cappucilli, Piero 1927- *CmOp*
Cappy, Adrien *NewGrD 80*
Cappy, Ted *BiE&WWA, NotNAT*
Capra, Frank 1897- *AmFD, BiDFilm, -81, CmMov, ConLC 16, DcFM, FilmEn, FilmgC, HalFC 80, IntMPA 77, -75, -76, -78, -79, -80, MovMk[port], OxFilm, TwYS A, WhoHrs 80, WorEFlm[port]*
Capranica, Matteo 1708-1776? *NewGrD 80*
Capranico, Matteo 1708-1776? *NewGrD 80*
Capraro, Angelo 1910-1963 *NewOrJ[port]*
Capraro, Joe 1903- *NewOrJ*
Capri, Ahna *WhoHol A*
Capri, Anna 1944- *ForYSC*
Caprice, June 1899-1936 *FilmEn, Film 1, -2, MotPP, NotNAT B, TwYS, WhScrn 74, -77, WhoHol B*
Capricornus, Samuel Friedrich 1628-1665 *NewGrD 80[port]*
Caprioli, Carlo *NewGrD 80*
Caprioli, Giovanni Paolo d1627? *NewGrD 80*
Caprioli, Vittorio 1921- *FilmAG WE[port], WorEFlm[port]*
Capris, The *RkOn*
Caproli, Carlo 1615?-1695? *NewGrD 80*
Caproli, Jacopo *NewGrD 80*
Capron, Henri *Baker 78, NewGrD 80*
Capron, Nicolas 1740?-1784 *NewGrD 80*
Capsir, Mercedes 1895?-1969 *NewGrD 80*
Captain & Tenille, The *ConMuA 80A*
Captain & Tennille, The *RkOn 2[port]*
Captain Beefheart *ConMuA 80A*
Captain Beefheart And His Magic Band *BiDAmM*
Captain Midnight *What 5[port]*
Captain Stubby And The Buccaneers *BiDAmM*
Captain Video *What 4[port]*
Capua, Marcello Da *NewGrD 80*
Capua, Rinaldo Di *NewGrD 80*
Capuana, Franco 1894-1969 *Baker 78, CmOp, NewGrD 80*
Capuana, Franco 1896- *IntWWM 77, -80*
Capuana, Luigi 1839-1915 *McGEWD[port]*
Capuana, Mario d1649? *NewGrD 80*
Capucci, Giuseppe Antonio *NewGrD 80*
Capucine 1933- *FilmEn, FilmgC, ForYSC, HalFC 80, IntMPA 77, -75, -76, -78, -79, -80, MotPP, MovMk[port], WhoHol A*
Capurso, Alexander 1910- *IntWWM 77, -80*
Capus, Alfred 1858-1922 *CnMD, McGEWD, ModWD, NotNAT B, WhThe*
Caputi, Giovanni Battista *NewGrD 80*
Caputi, Manilio *NewGrD 80*
Caputo, George 1916- *IntMPA 77, -75, -76, -78, -79, -80*
Capuzzi, Giuseppe Antonio 1755-1818 *NewGrD 80*
Capy, Adrien 1571?-1639? *NewGrD 80*
Cara, Irene 1959- *DrBlPA*
Cara, Marchetto 1470?-1525? *NewGrD 80*
Cara, Marchettus 1470?-1525? *NewGrD 80*
Cara, Marco 1470?-1525? *NewGrD 80*
Cara, Marcus 1470?-1525? *NewGrD 80*
Carabella, Ezio 1891-1964 *Baker 78*
Carabetta, Frank Louis 1944- *AmSCAP 66, -80*
Carabo-Cone, Madeleine 1915- *IntWWM 77, -80*
Caracciolo, Franco 1920- *NewGrD 80*
Caracciolo, Luigi 1847-1887 *Baker 78*
Caracciolo, Paolo 1560?- *NewGrD 80*
Caradori-Allan, Maria 1800-1865 *NewGrD 80*
Carafa, Michel 1787-1872 *NewGrD 80*
Carafa, Michele 1787-1872 *NewGrD 80*
Carafa DeColobrano, Michele Enrico 1787-1872 *Baker 78*
Caraffe, Charles-Placide 1730?-1756 *NewGrD 80*
Caragiale, Ion Luca 1852-1912 *CnMD, EncWT, McGEWD[port]*
Caramba, La 1751-1787 *NewGrD 80*
Caramia, Giacinto 1923- *WhoMus 72*
Caramuel, Jan 1606-1682 *NewGrD 80*
Caramuel, Juan 1606-1682 *NewGrD 80*
Caran D'Ache 1858-1909 *DcPup*
Caranda, Michael J 1918- *AmSCAP 66, -80*
Carapella, Tommaso 1654?-1736 *NewGrD 80*
Carapetyan, Armen 1908- *Baker 78, IntWWM 77, -80, NewGrD 80, OxMus*
Carapezza, Paolo Emilio 1937- *IntWWM 77, -80*
Carasali, Odoardo *NewGrD 80*
Carasaus *NewGrD 80*
Carastathis, Nicholas Sam 1922- *AmSCAP 80*
Caratelli, Sebastian 1913- *IntWWM 77, -80*
Caravan *ConMuA 80A, IlEncR*
Caravan, Ronald L 1946- *CpmDNM 76, -77*
Caravelles, The *RkOn*
Carawan, Guy 1927- *BiDAmM, EncFCWM 69*
Carazo, Castro 1895- *AmSCAP 66, -80*
Carballido, Emilio 1925- *CroCD*
Carbasse, Louise *Film 1*
Carber, Robert *NewGrD 80*
Carberry, Joe *PlP&P A[port]*
Carbonara, Gerard 1886-1959 *AmSCAP 66, -80, ConAmC*
Carbonchi, Antonio *NewGrD 80*
Carbone, Anthony 1930?- *WhoHrs 80[port]*
Carbone, Antony *WhoHol A*
Carbone, Giuseppe 1939- *CnOxB*
Carbone, Vincenzo 1907- *WhoMus 72*
Carbonnaux, Norbert 1918- *DcFM*
Carbonneau, Rene 1930- *CreCan 1*
Carbotte, Gabrielle Roy *CreCan 2*
Carbrey, John d1962 *NotNAT B*
Carcani, Giacomo 1734-1820? *NewGrD 80*
Carcani, Gioseffo 1703-1779 *NewGrD 80*
Carcani, Giuseppe 1703-1779 *NewGrD 80*
Carcano, Giacomo 1734-1820? *NewGrD 80*
Carcano, Gioseffo 1703-1779 *NewGrD 80*
Carcano, Giuseppe 1703-1779 *NewGrD 80*
Carcassi *NewGrD 80*
Carcassi, Lorenzo *NewGrD 80*
Carcassi, Tomaso *NewGrD 80*
Carchillon, Thomas *NewGrD 80*
Card, June 1942- *IntWWM 77, -80, WhoOp 76*
Card, Kathryn 1893-1964 *ForYSC, NotNAT B, WhScrn 74, -77, WhoHol B*
Card, Virginia 1918- *AmSCAP 66*
Cardan, Jerome 1501-1576 *NewGrD 80*
Cardano, Girolamo 1501-1576 *DcPup*
Cardanus, Hieronymous 1501-1576 *NewGrD 80*

Cardarelli, Francesco 1630-1700 *NewGrD 80*
Carden, Allen D 1792-1857 *NewGrD 80*
Carden, Joan Maralyn *WhoOp 76*
Cardenal, Peire *NewGrD 80*
Cardenas, Elizabeth Anne 1948- *IntWWM 77*
Cardenas, Elsa *ForYSC*
Carder, Emmeline d1961 *NotNAT B*
Carder, Richard Cameron 1917- *AmSCAP 80*
Carder, Richard Holland 1942- *IntWWM 77, -80*
Cardew, Cornelius 1936- *Baker 78, DcCM, IntWWM 77, -80, MusMk, NewGrD 80, WhoMus 72*
Cardi, Pat *WhoHol A*
Cardiff, Jack 1914- *BiDFilm, -81, CmMov, DcFM, FilmEn, FilmgC, HalFC 80, IlWWBF, IntMPA 77, -75, -76, -78, -79, -80, OxFilm, WorEFlm[port]*
Cardilli, Jacopo Antonio *NewGrD 80*
Cardinaal, Carlos 1948- *IntWWM 77, -80*
Cardinale, Claudia 1939- *BiDFilm, -81, FilmAG WE[port], FilmEn, FilmgC, ForYSC, HalFC 80, IntMPA 77, -75, -76, -78, -79, -80, MotPP, MovMk[port], OxFilm, WhoHol A, WorEFlm[port]*
Cardine, Eugene 1905- *NewGrD 80*
Cardini 1899-1973 *MagIlD*
Cardini, George 1913- *AmSCAP 66, -80*
Cardnell, Valerie Flora *IntWWM 77, -80, WhoMus 72*
Cardon, Jean-Baptiste 1732-1788 *NewGrD 80*
Cardon, Jean-Baptiste 1760-1803 *NewGrD 80*
Cardon, Jean-Guillain 1732-1788 *NewGrD 80*
Cardona, Rene *WhoHrs 80*
Cardoni, Frank 1940- *AmSCAP 66*
Cardoni, Jean-Baptiste 1732-1788 *NewGrD 80*
Cardoni, Jean-Guillain 1732-1788 *NewGrD 80*
Cardoni, Mary 1938- *AmSCAP 66*
Cardonne, Jean-Baptiste 1730-1792? *NewGrD 80*
Cardonne, Philibert 1730-1792? *NewGrD 80*
Cardoso, Lindembergue 1939- *DcCM, NewGrD 80*
Cardoso, Manuel 1566-1650 *NewGrD 80*
Cardoso, Rui 1939- *EncJzS 70*
Cardot 1380-1470 *NewGrD 80*
Cardus, Ana 1943- *CnOxB, DancEn 78*
Cardus, Sir Neville 1889-1975 *Baker 78, NewGrD 80, OxMus, WhoMus 72*
Cardwell, Albert C 1921-1954 *WhScrn 74*
Cardwell, James 1921-1954 *WhScrn 77, WhoHol B*
Carell, Annette d1967 *WhScrn 74, -77, WhoHol B*
Carelli, Gabor Paul 1915- *WhoMus 72*
Carelsen, Fie 1890-1975 *WhScrn 77*
Carere, Christine 1930- *FilmAG WE, FilmEn, FilmgC, ForYSC, HalFC 80, WhoHol A*
Caresana, Cristoforo 1640?-1709 *NewGrD 80*
Carestini, Giovanni 1705?-1760? *NewEOp 71, NewGrD 80[port]*
Carette 1897-1966 *FilmgC, HalFC 80, WhScrn 74, -77, WhoHol B*
Carette, Julien 1897-1966 *BiDFilm, -81, FilmEn, OxFilm, WorEFlm[port]*
Carette, Louis *McGEWD[port]*
Carew, Arthur Edmund 1894-1937 *FilmEn, Film 1, TwYS, WhScrn 74, -77, WhoHol B*
Carew, Arthur Edward 1894-1937 *HalFC 80*
Carew, Helen *BiE&WWA, NotNAT*
Carew, James 1876-1938 *Film 1, -2, IlWWBF, NotNAT B, WhScrn 74, -77, WhThe, WhoHol B, WhoStg 1908*
Carew, Leslie 1908- *IntWWM 77*
Carew, Michael B 1951- *ConAmC*
Carew, Ora 1893-1955 *FilmEn, Film 1, -2, MotPP, NotNAT B, TwYS, WhScrn 74, -77, WhoHol B*
Carewe, Andrew *Film 2*
Carewe, Arthur Edmund 1894-1937 *Film 2*
Carewe, Edwin 1883-1940 *FilmEn, Film 1, -2, FilmgC, HalFC 80, TwYS, -A, WhScrn 74, -77, WhoHol B*
Carewe, John Maurice Foxall 1933- *IntWWM 77, -80, WhoMus 72*
Carewe, Millicent *Film 2*
Carewe, Rita 1908-1955 *Film 2, TwYS, WhScrn 74, WhoHol B*
Carey, Bill 1916- *AmSCAP 66*
Carey, Bruce 1876-1960 *Baker 78*
Carey, Bruce Anderson 1877- *BiDAmM*
Carey, David 1926- *AmSCAP 66, -80, ConAmC*
Carey, Denis 1909- *BiE&WWA, NotNAT, WhoThe 72, -77*
Carey, Denis 1926- *CnOxB*
Carey, Eleanor 1852- *WhoStg 1908*
Carey, Francis Clive Savill 1883-1968 *Baker 78*
Carey, George Saville d1807 *NotNAT B*
Carey, Gerald Vernon 1936- *IntWWM 77, -80*
Carey, Harry 1875-1947 *Film 1, -2*
Carey, Harry 1878-1947 *FilmEn, FilmgC, ForYSC, HalFC 80, MotPP, MovMk[port], NotNAT B, TwYS, Vers A[port], WhScrn 74, -77, WhoHol B, WorEFlm[port]*
Carey, Harry 1880-1947 *CmMov, HolCA[port]*
Carey, Harry, Jr. 1921- *CmMov, FilmEn, FilmgC, ForYSC, HalFC 80, IntMPA 77, -76, -78, -79, -80, MovMk[port], WhoHol A*
Carey, Henry 1687?-1743 *Baker 78, MusMk*
Carey, Henry 1688-1743 *OxMus*
Carey, Henry 1689?-1743 *NewGrD 80*
Carey, Henry 1690-1743 *NotNAT B*
Carey, Jack 1889?-1935? *NewOrJ[port]*
Carey, Joseph A d1964 *NotNAT B*
Carey, Josie 1930- *AmSCAP 66, -80*
Carey, Joyce *IntMPA 77, -75, -76, -78, -79, -80, WhoHol A*
Carey, Joyce 1898- *FilmEn, FilmgC, HalFC 80, MovMk, OxFilm, WhoThe 72, -77*
Carey, Joyce 1905- *BiE&WWA, NotNAT*
Carey, Leonard 1893- *FilmgC, HalFC 80*
Carey, Lew *AmSCAP 80*
Carey, Macdonald 1913- *BiE&WWA*
Carey, MacDonald 1913- *FilmEn*
Carey, Macdonald 1913- *FilmgC, ForYSC, HalFC 80, HolP 40[port], IntMPA 77, -75, -76, -78, -79, -80, MotPP, MovMk[port], WhoHol A*
Carey, Matthew 1770?-1830 *BiDAmM*
Carey, Michele *WhoHol A*
Carey, Mutt 1891-1948 *CmpEPM, WhoJazz 72*
Carey, Mutt 1902-1948 *BiDAmM*
Carey, Olive Deering *ForYSC, WhoHol A*
Carey, Patrick 1916- *OxFilm*
Carey, Phil 1925- *FilmEn, FilmgC, IntMPA 77, -75, -76, -78, -79, -80, MotPP*
Carey, Philip 1925- *ForYSC, HalFC 80, WhoHol A*
Carey, Thomas 1891-1948 *NewOrJ[port]*
Carey, Thomas 1904-1972 *BiE&WWA, NotNAT B*
Carey, Thomas 1937- *WhoOp 76*
Carey, Thomas Devore 1931- *IntWWM 77*
Carey, Timothy 1925?- *FilmEn, FilmgC, HalFC 80*
Carey, William D 1916- *AmSCAP 80*
Carfagno, Edward C *HalFC 80*
Carfagno, Simon Albert 1906- *ConAmC, IntWWM 77, -80*
Carfax, Bruce 1905-1970 *WhThe*
Carfi, Anahi 1946- *IntWWM 77, -80*
Carges, Wilhelm *NewGrD 80*
Cargill, Henson 1941- *CounME 74[port], -74A, IlEncCM[port], RkOn 2[port]*
Cargill, Patrick 1918- *FilmgC, HalFC 80, WhoHol A, WhoThe 72, -77*
Carhart, James L 1843-1937 *NotNAT B, WhoStg 1908*
Cariaga, Marvellee *WhoOp 76*
Caridis, Miltiades 1923- *IntWWM 77, -80, WhoMus 72*
Carillo, Frank 1950- *AmSCAP 80*
Carillo, Mario *Film 2*
Carini, Nina 1932- *WhoOp 76*
Cariou, Len 1939- *NotNAT, WhoThe 72, -77*
Caris, Nick *ConMuA 80B*
Carisi, John E 1922- *BiDAmM, EncJzS 70*
Carisi, Johnny 1922- *EncJzS 70*
Carisio, Giovanni 1627?-1687 *NewGrD 80*
Carissimi, Giacomo 1605-1674 *Baker 78, BnBkM 80, CmpBCM, GrComp, MusMk, NewGrD 80, OxMus*
Cariteo I *NewGrD 80*
Carl And Minoka *PupTheA*
Carl, Joseph Michael 1955- *AmSCAP 80*
Carl, Karl 1789-1854 *OxThe*
Carl, M Roger *Film 2*
Carl, Renee *Film 2, WomWMM*
Carl, Roger *Film 2*
Carl, William Crane 1865-1936 *Baker 78, BiDAmM*
Carlay, Johannes *NewGrD 80*
Carlberg, Hilbur *Film 2*
Carle, C E 1899- *IntMPA 77, -75, -76, -78, -79*
Carle, Frankie 1903- *AmPS B, AmSCAP 66, -80, BgBands 74[port], BiDAmM, CmpEPM, WhoHol A*
Carle, Gilles 1929- *CreCan 1*
Carle, Richard 1871-1941 *CmpEPM, FilmEn, Film 2, FilmgC, ForYSC, HalFC 80, HolCA[port], NotNAT B, TwYS, Vers A[port], WhScrn 74, -77, WhThe, WhoHol B, WhoStg 1906, -1908*
Carle, Richard 1876-1941 *MovMk*
Carlen *NewGrD 80*
Carlen, Felix 1734- *NewGrD 80*
Carlen, Franz Josef 1779-1845 *NewGrD 80*
Carlen, Gregor 1819-1869 *NewGrD 80*
Carlen, Heinrich 1885-1957 *NewGrD 80*
Carlen, Johann Josef Conrad 1849-1926 *NewGrD 80*
Carlen, Matthaus 1691-1749 *NewGrD 80*
Carlerii, Jacobus *NewGrD 80*
Carles, Romeo 1896-1971 *WhScrn 77*
Carles Y Amat, Joan *NewGrD 80*
Carleton, Claire 1913- *ForYSC, WhThe, WhoHol A*
Carleton, George 1885-1950 *WhScrn 74, -77, WhoHol B*
Carleton, Henry *Film 1*
Carleton, Henry Guy 1851-1910 *WhoStg 1906, -1908*
Carleton, Henry Guy 1856-1910 *NotNAT B*
Carleton, Lloyd B 1872-1933 *Film 1, WhScrn 74, -77, WhoHol B*
Carleton, Marjorie d1964 *NotNAT B*
Carleton, Nicholas 1570?-1575 *NewGrD 80*
Carleton, Robert Louis 1896-1956 *AmSCAP 66, -80*
Carleton, Will C 1871-1941 *WhScrn 74, -77*
Carleton, William P 1873-1947 *Film 2, WhScrn 74, -77, WhoHol B*
Carleton, William T 1859-1930 *Film 1, -2, WhScrn 77*
Carlevaro, Abel Julio 1918- *AmSCAP 80, IntWWM 77, -80*
Carley, Karleen *AmSCAP 66*
Carli *NewGrD 80*
Carli, Antonio Francesco *NewGrD 80*
Carli, Didi 1943?- *CnOxB*
Carli, Girolamo 1530?-1602? *NewGrD 80*
Carli, Raphael *NewGrD 80*
Carlid, Gote 1920-1953 *Baker 78, NewGrD 80*
Carlidge, William 1910- *IntMPA 77, -75, -76, -78, -79, -80*
Carlie, Edward 1878-1938 *WhScrn 74, -77, WhoHol B*
Carlier, Crespin d1640? *NewGrD 80*
Carlier, Jehan Le *NewGrD 80*
Carlier, Madeleine *WhThe*
Carlile, James d1691 *NotNAT B*
Carlile, Tom *IntMPA 79, -80*
Carlin *OxThe*
Carlin, George *JoeFr, WhoHol A*
Carlin, Lynn 1930- *FilmgC, HalFC 80, WhoHol A*
Carlin, Steve *NewYTET*
Carliner, L Diane 1936- *IntWWM 77*
Carliner, Mark *NewYTET*
Carling, Foster G 1898- *AmSCAP 66*
Carlino, Giangiacomo *NewGrD 80*
Carlino, Giovanni Giacomo *NewGrD 80*
Carlino, Lewis John 1932- *ConDr 73, -77, HalFC 80, IntMPA 77, -75, -76, -78, -79, -80, NewYTET, NotNAT*
Carlisle, Alexandra 1886-1936 *NotNAT B, WhScrn 74, -77, WhThe, WhoHol B*
Carlisle, Bill 1908- *CounME 74, -74A, EncFCWM 69, IlEncCM[port]*
Carlisle, Cliff 1904- *EncFCWM 69, IlEncCM[port]*
Carlisle, Clifford Raymond 1904- *BiDAmM, CounME 74*

Carlisle, George F 1911- *BiDAmM*
Carlisle, Jack *Film 2*
Carlisle, Kitty *WhoHol A*
Carlisle, Kitty 1914- *CmpEPM, EncMT, FilmEn, ForYSC, ThFT[port], WhoThe 72, -77*
Carlisle, Kitty 1915- *BiE&WWA, FilmgC, HalFC 80, NotNAT*
Carlisle, Margaret 1905- *WhThe*
Carlisle, Mary 1912- *FilmEn, FilmgC, ForYSC, HalFC 80, MotPP, MovMk, ThFT[port], What 3[port], WhoHol A*
Carlisle, Peggy *Film 2*
Carlisle, Richard 1879- *ForYSC*
Carlisle, Rita *Film 2*
Carlisle, Robert 1906- *IntMPA 77, -75, -76, -78, -79, -80*
Carlisle, Sybil 1871- *WhThe*
Carlisle, Una Mae 1918-1956 *CmpEPM, WhoJazz 72*
Carlisle, William 1908- *BiDAmM, NewYTET*
Carlisles *EncFCWM 69*
Carlisles, The *CounME 74*
Carllile, Kenneth Ray 1931- *BiDAmM*
Carlo, Hieronymo *NewGrD 80*
Carlo, Johnny *AmSCAP 80*
Carlo, Monte 1883- *AmSCAP 66, -80, BiE&WWA*
Carlo DelViolino *NewGrD 80*
Carlo-Rim 1905- *DcFM, FilmEn, FilmgC, HalFC 80*
Carlone, Francis Nunzio 1903- *AmSCAP 80*
Carlos, Walter 1939- *ConAmC*
Carlsen, Henning 1927- *FilmEn, OxFilm, WorEFlm[port]*
Carlsen, John A 1915- *WhThe, WhoMus 72*
Carlson, Carolyn 1943- *CnOxB*
Carlson, Frank L 1914- *BiDAmM*
Carlson, Frankie 1914- *CmpEPM*
Carlson, Harry A 1904- *AmSCAP 66, -80*
Carlson, June 1924- *FilmEn, ForYSC*
Carlson, Karen *WhoHol A*
Carlson, Lenus Jesse 1945- *IntWWM 77, -80, WhoOp 76*
Carlson, Lilian 1936- *IntWWM 77, -80*
Carlson, Myrtle *PupTheA*
Carlson, Paul Bollinger 1932- *IntWWM 77, -80*
Carlson, Richard *IntMPA 77, -75, -76, -78, MotPP*
Carlson, Richard 1912-1977 *FilmEn, FilmgC, HalFC 80[port], MovMk, WhoHrs 80[port]*
Carlson, Richard 1914- *ForYSC, WhoHol A*
Carlson, Steve *ForYSC, WhoHol A*
Carlson, Veronica 1944- *HalFC 80*
Carlson, Veronica 1945- *FilmgC, IlWWBF, WhoHol A, WhoHrs 80*
Carlsruhe *NewGrD 80*
Carlstedt, Jan 1926- *Baker 78, DcCM, IntWWM 80, NewGrD 80*
Carlsten, Rune 1893- *FilmEn*
Carlton 1880- *WhThe*
Carlton, Anita 1933- *IntWWM 77, -80*
Carlton, Barbara *Film 1*
Carlton, Carl *RkOn 2[port]*
Carlton, Jack 1910- *AmSCAP 80*
Carlton, Kathleen d1964 *NotNAT B*
Carlton, Larry Eugene 1948- *AmSCAP 80, EncJzS 70*
Carlton, Nicholas *OxMus*
Carlton, Richard 1558?-1638? *NewGrD 80, OxMus*
Carlton, Richard 1919- *IntMPA 77, -75, -76, -78, -79, -80*
Carlton, William Probert *Film 1*
Carluccio Di Pamfilio *NewGrD 80*
Carlye, Grace *Film 2*
Carlyle, Aileen *AmSCAP 66, -80*
Carlyle, David *FilmEn*
Carlyle, Florence 1864-1923 *CreCan 2*
Carlyle, Francis *Film 1*
Carlyle, Helen 1893-1933 *WhScrn 74, -77, WhoHol B*
Carlyle, Joan 1931- *CmOp, IntWWM 77, -80, NewGrD 80, WhoMus 72*
Carlyle, Joan 1933- *WhoOp 76*
Carlyle, Richard *ForYSC, WhoHol A*
Carlyle, Richard 1879-1942 *Film 1, -2, TwYS, WhScrn 74, -77, WhoHol B*
Carlyle, Russ 1914- *AmSCAP 66, -80*
Carlyle, Russ 1921- *CmpEPM*
Carlyle, Sidney *Film 2*
Carlyle, Thomas *OxMus*
Carmack, Murray 1920- *IntWWM 77, -80*
Carmagnole Dancers, The *Film 2*
Carman, Bliss 1861-1929 *CreCan 1*
Carman, Ofelia 1909- *IntWWM 80*
Carman, William Bliss 1861-1929 *CreCan 1*
Carme, Pamela 1902- *WhThe*
Carmel, Dov 1933- *IntWWM 80*
Carmel, Roger C 1929- *FilmgC, HalFC 80, WhoHol A*
Carmelitus, Frater *NewGrD 80*
Carmen, Eric 1949- *ConMuA 80A, IlEncR, RkOn 2[port]*
Carmen, Jean *WhoHol A*
Carmen, Jewel *Film 1, -2, TwYS*
Carmen, Johannes *NewGrD 80*
Carmen, Marina 1942- *IntWWM 77, -80*
Carmena Y Millan, Luis 1845-1904 *NewGrD 80*
Carmi, Maria 1880-1957 *Film 1, WhScrn 74, -77*
Carmichael, Franklin 1890-1945 *CreCan 2*
Carmichael, Hoagey 1899- *WorEFlm[port]*
Carmichael, Hoagland 1899- *BiDAmM, NewGrD 80*
Carmichael, Hoagy 1889- *What 3[port]*
Carmichael, Hoagy 1897- *ConAmC*
Carmichael, Hoagy 1899- *AmPS, AmSCAP 66, Baker 78, CmpEPM, FilmEn, FilmgC, ForYSC, HalFC 80, IntMPA 77, -75, -76, -78, -79, -80, MotPP, MovMk, NewGrD 80, OxFilm, PopAmC[port], PopAmC SUP, Sw&Ld C, WhoHol A, WhoMus 72*
Carmichael, Howard Hoagland 1899- *AmSCAP 80*
Carmichael, Ian 1920- *CmMov, EncMT, FilmAG WE, FilmEn, FilmgC, HalFC 80, IlWWBF[port], IntMPA 77, -75, -76, -78, -79, -80, WhoHol A, WhoThe 72, -77*
Carmichael, James *ConMuA 80B*
Carmichael, Margaret McMillan 1906- *WhoMus 72*
Carmichael, Mary Grant 1851-1935 *Baker 78*
Carmichael, Myra d1974 *WhScrn 77, WhoHol B*
Carmichael, Neva 1907- *IntWWM 77*
Carmichael, Ralph R 1927- *AmSCAP 80*
Carmichael, Sheila Mary Stoddart *WhoMus 72*
Carmigchelt, Henk W 1933- *IntWWM 77, -80*
Carmignani, Gherardo Macarini *NewGrD 80*
Carminati, Tulio *AmPS B*
Carminati, Tulio 1894-1971 *TwYS*
Carminati, Tullio d1971 *FilmEn*
Carminati, Tullio 1894-1971 *CmpEPM, Film 2, FilmgC, ForYSC, HalFC 80, MovMk, WhScrn 74, -77, WhThe, WhoHol B*
Carminati, Tullio 1895-1971 *FilmAG WE[port]*
Carmine, Teodoro Del *NewGrD 80*
Carmines, Al 1936- *ConDr 77D, NotNAT, WhoThe 77*
Carmines, Alvin A 1938- *ConAmC*
Carmines, Alvin Allison 1936- *AmSCAP 80*
Carmirelli, Giuseppina 1914- *NewGrD 80*
Carmirelli, Pina 1914- *NewGrD 80, WhoMus 72*
Carmo, The Great 1881-1944 *MagIlD*
Carmody, Jay *BiE&WWA*
Carmona, Norberto 1925- *WhoOp 76*
Carmona, Paul Bernard 1947- *ConAmC*
Carn, Doug 1948- *EncJzS 70*
Carnahan, Suzanne d1952 *FilmEn, WhoHol B*
Carne, Judy 1939- *FilmgC, HalFC 80, WhoHol A*
Carne, Marcel 1903- *FilmgC, HalFC 80*
Carne, Marcel 1909- *BiDFilm, -81, DcFM, FilmEn, MovMk[port], OxFilm, WorEFlm[port]*
Carnefresca *NewGrD 80*
Carner, Mosco 1904- *Baker 78, IntWWM 77, -80, NewGrD 80, OxMus*
Carnera, Primo 1906-1967 *WhScrn 77, WhoHol B, WhoHrs 80*
Carnera, Primo 1907- *What 1[port]*
Carnes, Josef R 1903- *AmSCAP 66*
Carnevale, Carmen R *PupTheA*
Carney, Alan 1911-1973 *FilmgC, HalFC 80, Vers A[port], WhScrn 77, WhoHol B*
Carney, Art 1918- *BiE&WWA, FilmEn, FilmgC, HalFC 80, IntMPA 77, -75, -76, -78, -79, -80, JoeFr[port], NewYTET, NotNAT, WhoHol A, WhoThe 72, -77*
Carney, Augustus *FilmEn, Film 1*
Carney, Daniel *Film 2*
Carney, David *ConAmC*
Carney, Don 1897-1954 *WhScrn 74, -77*
Carney, Frank 1904- *BiE&WWA, NotNAT*
Carney, Fred 1914- *IntMPA 77, -75, -76, -78, -79, -80*
Carney, George d1948 *WhoHol B*
Carney, George 1887-1947 *FilmgC, HalFC 80, IlWWBF, WhScrn 74, -77, WhThe*
Carney, Harry 1910-1974 *Baker 78, BiDAmM, CmpEPM, EncJzS 70, IlEncJ, NewGrD 80, WhScrn 77, WhoJazz 72*
Carney, Julia Abigail 1823-1908 *BiDAmM*
Carney, Kate 1868-1950 *OxThe*
Carney, Kate 1869-1950 *NotNAT B*
Carney, Kate 1870- *WhThe*
Carney, Richard E 1923- *AmSCAP 66, -80*
Carneyro, Claudio 1895-1963 *Baker 78, DcCM, NewGrD 80*
Carnicer, Ramon 1789-1855 *Baker 78, NewGrD 80*
Carno, Zita *ConAmC*
Carnovsky, Morris *MotPP, PlP&P[port], WhoHol A*
Carnovsky, Morris 1897- *BiE&WWA, FamA&A[port], HolCA[port], MovMk, NotNAT, WhoThe 72, -77*
Carnovsky, Morris 1898- *CnThe, FilmEn, FilmgC, ForYSC, HalFC 80, IntMPA 77, -75, -76, -78*
Carnow, Howard N 1912- *IntMPA 77, -75, -76, -78, -79, -80*
Carns, Roscoe *Film 2*
Caro, Annibale 1507-1566 *McGEWD[port]*
Caro, Warren 1907- *BiE&WWA, NotNAT, WhoThe 77*
Caro DeBoesi, Jose Antonio 1750?-1814 *NewGrD 80*
Carol, Cindy *WhoHol A*
Carol, Diane 1940-1966 *WhScrn 77*
Carol, Gary *AmSCAP 80*
Carol, John 1910-1968 *WhScrn 77*
Carol, Martine d1967 *MotPP, WhoHol B*
Carol, Martine 1921-1967 *ForYSC, MovMk, WhScrn 74, -77*
Carol, Martine 1922-1967 *BiDFilm, -81, FilmAG WE, FilmEn, FilmgC, HalFC 80, OxFilm, WorEFlm[port]*
Carol, Marty *AmSCAP 80*
Carol, Sue 1907- *FilmEn, FilmgC, HalFC 80, MotPP, ThFT[port]*
Carol, Sue 1908- *Film 2, ForYSC, MovMk, TwYS, What 5[port], WhoHol A*
Carol-Berard 1881-1942 *Baker 78*
Carolan, John *WhoMus 72*
Carolan, Turlough 1670-1738 *Baker 78, NewGrD 80*
Caroli, Angelo Antonio 1701-1778 *NewGrD 80*
Carolin, Martha *AmSCAP 80*
Carolina Mountaineers *BiDAmM*
Carolina Slim *BluesWW[port]*
Caroll, Ann 1911- *IntWWM 77, -80*
Caroll, Evelyn *AmSCAP 66, -80*
Carollo, Antonino 1935- *WhoOp 76*
Carolsfeld, Ludwig Schnorr Von *NewGrD 80*
Caron, Cecile *WhThe*
Caron, Firmin *NewGrD 80*
Caron, Irma *Film 2*
Caron, Leon Francis Victor 1850-1905 *NewGrD 80*
Caron, Leslie *AmPS B*
Caron, Leslie 1931- *BiDFilm, -81, CmMov, CnOxB, DancEn 78, FilmEn, FilmgC, HalFC 80, IntMPA 77, -75, -76, -78, -79, -80, MGM[port], MotPP, MovMk[port], OxFilm, WhThe, WhoHol A, WorEFlm[port]*
Caron, Leslie 1932- *ForYSC*
Caron, Marguerite *WhThe*
Caron, Patricia *Film 2*
Caron, Paul 1874-1941 *CreCan 1*
Caron, Philippe *Baker 78, NewGrD 80*
Caron, Pierre Augustin 1875-1952 *McGEWD[port]*
Caron, Rose 1857-1930 *Baker 78*
Carosio, Margherita 1908- *CmOp,*

NewGrD 80
Caroso, Fabritio DancEn 78, OxMus
Caroso, Fabritio 1527?-1605? NewGrD 80
Caroso, Fabritio 1553?- CnOxB
Carotenuto, Mario 1915- FilmAG WE
Carotenuto, Memmo 1908- FilmAG WE
Caroubel, Nicolas Francisque 1594-1642? NewGrD 80
Caroubel, Pierre Francisque d1611 NewGrD 80
Carozza, Giovanni Dominico NewGrD 80
Carpani, Giovanni Antonio NewGrD 80
Carpani, Giovanni Battista NewGrD 80
Carpani, Giuseppe 1752-1825 Baker 78, NewGrD 80
Carpenter, Alicia 1930- AmSCAP 80
Carpenter, Betty Film 2
Carpenter, Billy Film 1
Carpenter, Carleton 1926- AmSCAP 66, -80, BiE&WWA, FilmEn, FilmgC, ForYSC, HalFC 80, IntMPA 77, -75, -76, -78, -79, -80, MotPP, NotNAT, WhoHol A, WhoThe 77
Carpenter, Charles E 1912- AmSCAP 66, -80
Carpenter, Constance 1906- BiE&WWA, NotNAT, WhoHol A, WhoThe 72, -77
Carpenter, Denny ConMuA 80B
Carpenter, Edward Childs 1872-1950 NotNAT B, WhThe
Carpenter, Elliot J 1894- AmSCAP 66, -80
Carpenter, Francis Film 1
Carpenter, Freddie 1908- WhoThe 72, -77
Carpenter, Gary 1951- IntWWM 77, -80
Carpenter, Gloria 1927-1958 WhScrn 74, -77
Carpenter, Horace B 1875-1945 Film 1, WhScrn 74, -77, WhoHol B
Carpenter, Howard R 1919- ConAmC
Carpenter, Hoyle D 1909- IntWWM 77, -80
Carpenter, Imogen 1918- AmSCAP 80
Carpenter, Imogen 1919- AmSCAP 66
Carpenter, Jean Film 2
Carpenter, Jeanne Film 2
Carpenter, John WhoHol A
Carpenter, John 1948- BiDFilm 81, HalFC 80, WhoHrs 80
Carpenter, John Alden 1876-1951 AmSCAP 66, -80, Baker 78, BiDAmM, BnBkM 80, CompSN[port], ConAmC, DancEn 78, DcCom&M 79, MusMk, NewGrD 80, OxMus
Carpenter, Juanita Robins 1923- AmSCAP 80
Carpenter, Kurt 1948- ConAmC
Carpenter, Maud d1967 WhThe
Carpenter, Merta Film 1
Carpenter, Nan Cooke 1912- IntWWM 80
Carpenter, Paul 1921-1964 FilmgC, HalFC 80, IlWWBF[port], NotNAT B, WhScrn 74, -77, WhoHol B
Carpenter, Peter Film 2
Carpenter, Richard Lynn 1946- AmSCAP 80
Carpenter, Robert L 1927- IntMPA 79, -80
Carpenter, Stephen Lisby 1943- AmSCAP 80
Carpenter, Thelma 1922- BiE&WWA, CmpEPM, DrBlPA, NotNAT
Carpenter, Thomas H 1927- IntWWM 77, -80
Carpenter, William Film 1
Carpenter, Wingie 1898- WhoJazz 72
Carpenters, The BiDAmM, ConMuA 80A, IlEncR[port], RkOn 2[port]
Carpentier, Alejo 1904- NewGrD 80
Carpentier, Georges 1894-1975 Film 2, What 1[port], WhScrn 77, WhoHol C
Carpentras 1470?-1548 Baker 78, NewGrD 80
Carpiani, Giovanni Luca NewGrD 80
Carpitella, Diego 1924- NewGrD 80
Carr, Alan IntMPA 79, -80
Carr, Albert Lee 1929- ConAmC
Carr, Alexander 1878-1946 FilmEn, Film 2, ForYSC, NotNAT B, WhScrn 74, -77, WhThe, WhoHol B
Carr, Alexander 1880- WhoStg 1908
Carr, Arnold 1931- IntMPA 77, -75, -76, -78, -79, -80
Carr, Arthur 1908- Baker 78, ConAmC
Carr, Benjamin 1768-1831 Baker 78, BiDAmM, NewGrD 80
Carr, Benjamin 1769-1831 OxMus
Carr, Bruno 1928- BiDAmM
Carr, Bud ConMuA 80B
Carr, Cameron Film 1, -2
Carr, Cameron 1876- IlWWBF
Carr, Carlina 1932- WhoMus 72
Carr, Cathy 1936- RkOn
Carr, Colin Michael 1957- IntWWM 80
Carr, Darleen WhoHol A
Carr, Donna Faye 1945- WhoMus 72
Carr, Edwin 1926- NewGrD 80
Carr, Emily 1871-1945 CreCan 1
Carr, Eugenie Waddell 1946- ConAmTC
Carr, F Osmond 1858-1916 WhThe
Carr, Fatty Film 2
Carr, Frank Osmond 1858-1916 Baker 78
Carr, George d1962 WhThe
Carr, Georgia 1925-1971 WhScrn 74, -77, WhoHol B
Carr, Geraldine 1917-1954 WhScrn 74, -77, WhoHol B
Carr, Gertrude d1969 WhoHol B
Carr, Ginna 1937-1972 WhScrn 77
Carr, Gunter Lee BluesWW[port]
Carr, Howard 1880-1960 Baker 78, WhThe
Carr, Ian 1933- EncJzS 70, IntWWM 77, -80
Carr, Jack d1951 WhScrn 77
Carr, Jack d1967 WhoHol B
Carr, Jack 1899-1968 WhScrn 77
Carr, Jane 1909-1957 FilmgC, HalFC 80, NotNAT B, WhScrn 74, -77, WhThe, WhoHol B
Carr, Jay ConAmTC
Carr, Jennifer Elizabeth 1935- IntWWM 77, -80, WhoMus 72
Carr, Jimmie Film 2
Carr, Joe AmSCAP 80
Carr, Joe Fingers 1910- CmpEPM, RkOn
Carr, John DcPup, NewGrD 80
Carr, John Dickson 1905-1977 HalFC 80
Carr, Joseph 1739-1819 BiDAmM, NewGrD 80
Carr, Joseph William Comyns 1849-1916 NotNAT B, WhThe
Carr, Lawrence 1916-1969 BiE&WWA, WhThe, WhoHol B, WhoThe 72
Carr, Leon 1910-1976 AmSCAP 66, -80
Carr, Leroy 1899-1935 BiDAmM
Carr, Leroy 1905-1935 BluesWW[port], CmpEPM, IlEncJ, NewGrD 80
Carr, Louella Film 2
Carr, Mac E 1906- IntWWM 77
Carr, Margie 1900- AmSCAP 66
Carr, Martin 1932- IntMPA 77, -75, -76, -78, -79, -80, NewYTET
Carr, Mary 1874-1973 FilmEn, Film 1, -2, FilmgC, ForYSC, HalFC 80, MovMk, TwYS, WhScrn 77, WhoHol B
Carr, May Beth Film 2
Carr, Michael CmpEPM, ConAmC
Carr, Michael 1900-1968 WhScrn 77
Carr, Michael Carmichael PupTheA
Carr, Nat 1886-1944 Film 2, ForYSC, WhScrn 74, -77, WhoHol B
Carr, Patrick ConMuA 80B
Carr, Paul WhoHol A
Carr, Peck 1900- WhoJazz 72
Carr, Percy 1865-1926 Film 2, WhScrn 74, -77, WhoHol B
Carr, Philip d1969 WhoHol B
Carr, Philip 1874-1957 NotNAT B, WhThe
Carr, Richard NewGrD 80
Carr, Roberta AmSCAP 80
Carr, Rosemary Film 2
Carr, Sade 1889-1940 WhScrn 74, -77, WhoHol B
Carr, Sandra Beatrice AmSCAP 80
Carr, Son NewOrJ
Carr, Stephen Film 2
Carr, Thomas 1780-1849 BiDAmM
Carr, Thomas 1907- FilmEn, FilmgC, HalFC 80, IntMPA 77, -75, -76, -78, -79, -80
Carr, Tommy 1907- WhoHrs 80
Carr, Vikki 1941- RkOn 2[port]
Carr, William 1867-1937 Film 2, WhScrn 74, -77, WhoHol B
Carr-Boyd, Ann Kirsten 1938- IntWWM 77, -80
Carr-Cook, Madge 1856-1933 NotNAT B, WhThe
Carra, Lawrence 1909- BiE&WWA, NotNAT
Carra DeVaux, Baron 1867-1953? NewGrD 80
Carradine, David 1936- FilmEn, ForYSC
Carradine, David 1940- FilmgC, HalFC 80, IntMPA 77, -75, -76, -78, -79, -80, MotPP, WhoHol A
Carradine, John 1906- BiE&WWA, CmMov, FilmEn, FilmgC, ForYSC, HalFC 80, HolCA[port], MotPP, MovMk[port], OxFilm, Vers A[port], WhoHol A, WhoHrs 80[port], WhoThe 72, -77, WorEFlm[port]
Carradine, John 1908- IntMPA 77, -75, -76, -78, -79, -80
Carradine, Keith IntMPA 77, -75, -76, -78, -79, -80, WhoHol A
Carradine, Keith 1950- RkOn 2[port]
Carradine, Keith 1951- FilmEn, HalFC 80
Carradine, Keith Ian 1949- AmSCAP 80
Carradine, Robert WhoHol A
Carradine, Robert 1954- FilmEn
Carradine, William 1896?-1958? BluesWW
Carrado, Gino Film 2
Carragan, Martha Beck ConAmC
Carranza, Gustavo Eduardo 1897-1975 Baker 78
Carrara, Michele NewGrD 80
Carraro, Tino 1910- EncWT
Carras, Nicholas S 1922- AmSCAP 66, -80
Carraud, Michel-Gaston 1864-1920 Baker 78, NewGrD 80
Carre, Albert 1852-1938 Baker 78, NewEOp 71, NotNAT B, WhThe
Carre, Antoine NewGrD 80
Carre, Bartlett A 1897-1971 WhScrn 74, -77, WhoHol B
Carre, Ben 1883-1978 HalFC 80
Carre, Fabrice 1855- WhThe
Carre, Marguerite 1880-1947 CmOp, NewGrD 80
Carre, Michel d1872 NotNAT B
Carre, Michel 1865- WhThe
Carreau, Margaret 1899- AmSCAP 66, -80, ConAmC
Carreira, Antonio 1525?-1589? NewGrD 80
Carrel, Danny 1935- FilmEn
Carrel, Dany 1935- FilmAG WE
Carrell, James P 1787-1854 NewGrD 80
Carrell, Ruth AmSCAP 80
Carreno, Cayetano 1774-1836 NewGrD 80
Carreno, Inocente 1919- Baker 78, NewGrD 80
Carreno, Teresa 1853-1917 Baker 78, BiDAmM, BnBkM 80, MusSN[port], NewGrD 80[port]
Carrera, Barbara WhoHol A
Carrera, Barbara 1945?- FilmEn
Carrera Y Lanchares, Pedro NewGrD 80
Carreras, Sir James IntMPA 75, -76, -78, -79, -80
Carreras, Sir James 1900- HalFC 80
Carreras, Sir James 1910- FilmgC, IntMPA 77, WhoHrs 80
Carreras, Jose 1946- CmOp, IntWWM 80, NewGrD 80, WhoOp 76
Carreras, Michael 1927- FilmEn, FilmgC, HalFC 80, IlWWBF, IntMPA 77, -75, -76, -78, -79, -80, WhoHrs 80
Carretta, Jerry 1915- AmSCAP 66, -80
Carretti, Giuseppe Maria 1690-1774 NewGrD 80
Carretto, Galeotto Del OxThe
Carricart, Robert WhoHol A
Carrick, Edward 1905- FilmgC, HalFC 80, WhThe
Carrick, Hartley 1881-1929 NotNAT B, WhThe
Carrickson, S B Film 2
Carrico, Charles 1888-1967 WhScrn 74, -77
Carrier, Albert WhoHol A
Carrier, Loran ConAmC
Carrier, Louis-Georges 1927- CreCan 2
Carrier, Roch 1938- CreCan 2
Carriere, Jean-Claude 1931- FilmEn, HalFC 80, OxFilm
Carriere, Mathieu 1950- FilmAG WE, FilmEn
Carrigan, Thomas J 1886-1941 Film 1, -2, NotNAT B, WhScrn 74, -77, WhoHol B
Carril, Hugo Del 1912- DcFM
Carrill, Repe MorBAP
Carrillo, Cely WhoHol A
Carrillo, Julian 1875-1965 Baker 78, DcCM, NewGrD 80, OxMus
Carrillo, Leo d1961 MotPP, WhThe,

WhoHol B
Carrillo, Leo 1880-1961 FilmEn, FilmgC, ForYSC, HalFC 80, MovMk[port]
Carrillo, Leo 1881-1961 Film 2, HolCA[port], NotNAT B, WhScrn 77
Carrilo, Leo 1881-1961 WhScrn 74
Carrington, Ethel 1889-1962 WhThe
Carrington, Evelyn 1876-1942 Film 2, NotNAT B, WhScrn 74, -77, WhoHol B
Carrington, Frank d1975 WhoHol C
Carrington, Frank 1901-1975 BiE&WWA, NotNAT B
Carrington, Frank 1902-1975 WhScrn 77
Carrington, Helen 1895-1963 WhScrn 74, -77, WhoHol B
Carrington, Jean 1918- IntWWM 77, -80
Carrington, Katherine d1953 NotNAT B
Carrington, Murray 1885-1941 Film 1, NotNAT B, WhThe
Carrington, Philip Rodney 1948- IntWWM 77, -80
Carrington, Simon Robert 1942- IntWWM 77, -80, WhoMus 72
Carrington, Terri Lyne 1965- BlkWAB[port]
Carrion, Jeronimo De 1666?-1721 NewGrD 80
Carrison, Clifford Thomas 1946- AmSCAP 80
Carritt, R Graham 1892- IntWWM 77, -80, WhoMus 72
Carrodus, Constance WhoMus 72
Carrodus, John Tiplady 1836-1895 Baker 78, NewGrD 80
Carroll And Dietrich PupTheA
Carroll, Adam 1897- AmSCAP 66
Carroll, Albert d1956 NotNAT B
Carroll, Albert 1880?- NewOrJ
Carroll, Andrea 1946- RkOn
Carroll, Barbara 1925- AmSCAP 66, -80, CmpEPM
Carroll, Bob AmSCAP 80
Carroll, Bob 1905-1952 WhoJazz 72
Carroll, Bob 1918- CmpEPM
Carroll, Carroll 1902- AmSCAP 66, -80, IntMPA 77, -75, -76, -78, -79, -80
Carroll, Charles Michael 1921- IntWWM 77, -80
Carroll, David 1913- RkOn[port]
Carroll, Diahann 1935- AmPS B, BiDAmM, BiE&WWA, DrBlPA, EncMT, FilmEn, FilmgC, ForYSC, HalFC 80, MotPP, NotNAT, WhoHol A, WomWMM
Carroll, Earl 1892-1948 NotNAT B
Carroll, Earl 1893-1948 AmSCAP 66, -80, CmpEPM, EncMT, OxThe, PlP&P[port], WhScrn 77, WhThe
Carroll, Elisabeth 1937- CnOxB, DancEn 78
Carroll, Frank M 1928- ConAmC
Carroll, Garnet H d1964 NotNAT B
Carroll, Gene 1898- AmSCAP 66
Carroll, George ConMuA 80B
Carroll, Georgia WhoHol A
Carroll, Georgia Lillian 1914- AmSCAP 66, BiDAmM
Carroll, Gordon 1928- FilmEn, IntMPA 77, -75, -76, -78, -79, -80
Carroll, Harry 1892-1962 AmPS, AmSCAP 66, -80, BiDAmM, CmpEPM, NotNAT B, PopAmC[port], PopAmC SUP
Carroll, Helena BiE&WWA, NotNAT
Carroll, Ida Gertrude WhoMus 72
Carroll, Irv 1907- AmSCAP 66
Carroll, J Robert 1927- ConAmC
Carroll, James P 1787-1854 BiDAmM
Carroll, Janice WhoHol A
Carroll, Jeanne 1931- BluesWW[port]
Carroll, Jimmy 1913-1972 AmSCAP 66, -80, BiDAmM
Carroll, Joan 1932- HalFC 80
Carroll, Joe 1919- BiDAmM
Carroll, John MotPP
Carroll, John 1905- What 4[port]
Carroll, John 1905-1979 FilmEn
Carroll, John 1907- Film 2
Carroll, John 1908-1979 FilmgC, HalFC 80, MovMk, WhoHol A
Carroll, John 1913- CmpEPM, ForYSC, MGM[port]
Carroll, June AmSCAP 66, -80, BiE&WWA, NotNAT, WhoHol A
Carroll, Kevin Alphonsus 1929- IntWWM 77
Carroll, Laurie 1935- IntMPA 77, -75, -76, -78, -79, -80
Carroll, Lawrence W d1963 NotNAT B
Carroll, Leo G 1892-1972 BiE&WWA, CmMov, FilmEn, FilmgC, ForYSC, HalFC 80, HolCA[port], MotPP, MovMk[port], NotNAT B, Vers A[port], WhScrn 77, WhThe, WhoHol B, WhoHrs 80[port]
Carroll, Lewis 1832-1898 DcPup, FilmgC, HalFC 80
Carroll, Madeleine 1906- BiDFilm, -81, BiE&WWA, FilmAG WE, FilmEn, Film 2, FilmgC, ForYSC, HalFC 80[port], IlWWBF[port], IntMPA 77, -75, -76, -78, -79, -80, MotPP, MovMk[port], OxFilm, ThFT[port], What 2[port], WhThe, WhoHol A, WorEFlm[port]
Carroll, Moon Film 2
Carroll, Nancy d1965 MotPP, WhoHol B, WomWMM
Carroll, Nancy 1904-1965 FilmEn, ThFT[port]
Carroll, Nancy 1905-1965 Film 2, FilmgC, ForYSC, HalFC 80, TwYS
Carroll, Nancy 1906-1965 CmpEPM, MovMk, WhScrn 74, -77, WhThe
Carroll, Nancy 1909-1965 BiE&WWA, NotNAT B
Carroll, Pat 1927- BiE&WWA, ForYSC, IntMPA 77, -75, -76, -78, -79, -80, NotNAT, WhoHol A
Carroll, Patricia WhoMus 72
Carroll, Patrick Francis 1902-1965 BiE&WWA, NotNAT B
Carroll, Paul Vincent 1900-1968 BiE&WWA, CnMD, CnThe, EncWT, Ent, McGEWD[port], ModWD, NotNAT B, OxThe, PlP&P, REnWD[port], WhThe
Carroll, Richard AmSCAP 80
Carroll, Richard Field 1865-1925 NotNAT B, WhoStg 1908
Carroll, Sidney NewYTET
Carroll, Sydney W 1877-1958 NotNAT B, OxThe, WhThe
Carroll, Taylor Film 2
Carroll, Vinnette 1922- BiE&WWA, BlkAmP, DrBlPA, MorBAP, NotNAT, WhoThe 72, -77
Carroll, Walter 1869-1955 Baker 78, OxMus
Carroll, William A 1876-1928 Film 1, -2, WhScrn 74, -77, WhoHol B
Carron, Arthur 1900-1967 CmOp, NewGrD 80
Carron, Elisabeth WhoOp 76
Carron, George 1930-1970 WhScrn 74, -77
Carrone, Giovanni NewGrD 80
Carrozza, Giovanni Domenico NewGrD 80
Carrozza, Giovanni Dominico NewGrD 80
Carruthers, Bill NewYTET
Carruthers, Bruce C 1901-1954 WhScrn 74, -77
Carruthers, Jock 1910-1971 WhoJazz 72
Carruthers, John Baker 78
Carry, George Dorman 1915-1970 EncJzS 70
Carry, Scoops 1915-1970 EncJzS 70, WhoJazz 72
Cars ConMuA 80A[port]
Carse, Adam 1878-1958 Baker 78, NewGrD 80, OxMus
Carsey, Mary 1938-1973 WhScrn 77, WhoHol B
Carson PupTheA
Carson, Charles 1885- FilmgC, HalFC 80, WhoHol A, WhoThe 72, -77
Carson, Charles L d1901 NotNAT B
Carson, Mrs. Charles L d1919 WhThe
Carson, Clarice WhoOp 76
Carson, Doris 1910- WhThe
Carson, Fiddlin' John d1935 CounME 74
Carson, Fiddling John 1868-1949 IlEncCM
Carson, Frances 1895- BiE&WWA, WhThe
Carson, Jack 1910-1963 CmpEPM, FilmEn, FilmgC, ForYSC, HalFC 80, HolP 40[port], JoeFr, MotPP, MovMk[port], NotNAT B, OxFilm, WhScrn 74, -77, WhoHol B
Carson, James 1918- BiDAmM
Carson, James B 1885-1958 WhScrn 74, -77, WhoHol B
Carson, Jeannie IntMPA 77, -75, -76, -78, -79, -80, MotPP, WhoHol A
Carson, Jeannie 1928- FilmgC, HalFC 80
Carson, Jeannie 1929- BiE&WWA, ForYSC, WhoThe 72, -77
Carson, John 1927- HalFC 80
Carson, John David WhoHol A
Carson, Johnny 1925- IntMPA 77, -75, -76, -78, -79, -80, JoeFr[port], NewYTET
Carson, Ken 1914- AmSCAP 80
Carson, Kit RkOn
Carson, Kit 1809-1868 FilmgC, HalFC 80, OxFilm
Carson, Lionel 1873-1937 WhThe
Carson, Lionel 1875-1937 NotNAT B
Carson, Martha 1921- BiDAmM, CounME 74, -74A, EncFCWM 69, IlEncCM
Carson, Mindy AmPS B
Carson, Mindy 1926- BiE&WWA
Carson, Mindy 1927- CmpEPM, RkOn
Carson, Murray 1865-1917 WhThe, WhoStg 1906, -1908
Carson, Nelson 1917- BluesWW
Carson, Robert ForYSC, IntMPA 77, -75, -76, -78, -79, -80, MorBAP, WhoHol A
Carson, S Murray 1865-1917 NotNAT B
Carson, Sally 1926- BiDAmM
Carson, Sunset 1922- FilmEn, ForYSC, MotPP, WhoHol A
Carson, William G B 1891- BiE&WWA, NotNAT
Carstairs, John Paddy 1910-1970 FilmEn, IlWWBF[port], -A, OxFilm
Carstairs, John Paddy 1912-1970 HalFC 80
Carstairs, John Paddy 1912-1971 FilmgC
Carsten, Peter 1929- HalFC 80
Carstensen, Vern 1914- IntMPA 77, -75, -76, -78, -79, -80
Carswell, Ian Barton 1931- WhoMus 72
Cartan, Jean 1906-1932 Baker 78, NewGrD 80, OxMus
Cartari, Giuliano 1536?-1613 NewGrD 80
Carte, Mrs. D'Oyly d1948 WhThe
Carte, R D'Oyly 1844-1901 OxMus
Carte, Richard D'Oyly 1844-1901 Baker 78, BnBkM 80, NewGrD 80
Carte, Rupert D'Oyly WhThe
Cartellieri, Carmen Film 2
Carten, Audrey 1900- WhThe
Carter, A P EncFCWM 69
Carter, A P d1960 CounME 74
Carter, Alan 1920- CnOxB, DancEn 78
Carter, Alexander Scott 1881- CreCan 2
Carter, Alvin Pleasant 1897?-1960 BiDAmM
Carter, Andrew Roger 1939- IntWWM 77
Carter, Anita Ina 1934- BiDAmM, EncFCWM 69
Carter, Ann 1936- HalFC 80
Carter, Annabel Thompson 1912- IntWWM 77
Carter, Ben MorBAP
Carter, Ben 1911-1946 WhScrn 77
Carter, Ben 1911-1947 HalFC 80, Vers A[port], WhoHol B
Carter, Ben 1912-1946 DrBlPA
Carter, Ben 1937- AmSCAP 80
Carter, Bennett Lester 1907- AmSCAP 66, -80, BiDAmM, EncJzS 70
Carter, Benny 1907- BgBands 74[port], CmpEPM, DrBlPA, EncJzS 70, IlEncJ, MusMk, NewGrD 80, WhoJazz 72
Carter, Betty 1930- BiDAmM, DrBlPA, EncJzS 70
Carter, Bill 1936- DancEn 78
Carter, Bo BluesWW[port]
Carter, Boake d1944 WhScrn 77
Carter, Bob 1922- CmpEPM
Carter, Buddy 1870?- NewOrJ
Carter, Bunny BluesWW[port]
Carter, Calvert 1859-1932 Film 2, WhoHol B
Carter, Calvin Film 1
Carter, Captain Film 2
Carter, Carlu DancEn 78
Carter, Charles 1926- ConAmC
Carter, Charles, Jr. 1939- EncJzS 70
Carter, Charles Calvert 1859-1932 WhScrn 74, -77
Carter, Charles Edward 1926- AmSCAP 80
Carter, Charles Joseph 1874-1936 MagIlD
Carter, Charlie BluesWW[port]
Carter, Chuck 1939- EncJzS 70
Carter, Clarence 1936- RkOn 2[port]
Carter, Desmond d1939 EncMT, NotNAT B, WhThe

Carter, Dixie *WomWMM B*
Carter, Elizabeth *WomWMM*
Carter, Elliott Cook, Jr. 1908- *Baker 78, BiDAmM, BnBkM 80, CompSN[port], ConAmC, DcCM, IntWWM 77, -80, MusMk, NewGrD 80[port], OxMus, WhoMus 72*
Carter, Ernest Trow 1866-1953 *Baker 78, BiDAmM*
Carter, Everett 1919- *AmSCAP 80*
Carter, Frank d1920 *WhScrn 74, -77, WhoHol B*
Carter, Fred F 1933- *EncFCWM 69*
Carter, Frederick 1900-1970 *WhThe*
Carter, Frederick George 1913- *WhoMus 72*
Carter, H Everett 1919- *AmSCAP 66*
Carter, Harry *Film 1, -2*
Carter, Hayward Hayes 1947- *AmSCAP 80*
Carter, Helen *EncFCWM 69*
Carter, Helena *MotPP*
Carter, Helena 1923- *FilmEn, FilmgC, ForYSC, HalFC 80*
Carter, Hubert *Film 2*
Carter, Hubert d1934 *WhThe*
Carter, Jack *DancEn 78*
Carter, Jack 1922- *HalFC 80*
Carter, Jack 1923- *CnOxB, IntMPA 77, -75, -76, -78, -79, -80, JoeFr[port], WhoHol A*
Carter, Jan-Broberg 1951- *AmSCAP 80*
Carter, Janis 1917- *FilmEn, ForYSC*
Carter, Janis 1921- *FilmgC, HalFC 80, MotPP, WhoHol A*
Carter, Jean *BlkAmP*
Carter, Joe 1927- *BluesWW[port]*
Carter, John *ConAmC, ConMuA 80B*
Carter, John 1927- *AmSCAP 80*
Carter, John D *BlkAmP*
Carter, John Wallace 1929- *AmSCAP 80, EncJzS 70*
Carter, June 1929- *BiDAmM, CounME 74, EncFCWM 69, IlEncCM[port], WhoHol A*
Carter, Leslie d1921 *NotNAT B*
Carter, Mrs. Leslie 1862-1937 *FamA&A[port], Film 1, FilmgC, HalFC 80, NotNAT B, OxThe, PlP&P, TwYS, WhScrn 74, -77, WhThe, WhoHol B, WhoStg 1906, -1908*
Carter, Lincoln J d1926 *NotNAT B*
Carter, Lonnie 1942- *ConDr 73, -77, NatPD[port]*
Carter, Louise 1875-1957 *ForYSC, WhScrn 74, -77, WhoHol B*
Carter, Lynda *IntMPA 79, -80*
Carter, Lynne *WhoHol A*
Carter, M Rosemary *IntWWM 77*
Carter, Margaret *WhThe*
Carter, Mark *CreCan 1*
Carter, Maurice 1913- *IntMPA 77, -75, -76, -78, -79, -80*
Carter, Maxine Goodman 1927- *IntWWM 77*
Carter, Mother Maybelle 1909- *BiDAmM, CounME 74, EncFCWM 69, IlEncCM[port]*
Carter, Mel 1943- *RkOn*
Carter, Monte 1886-1950 *WhScrn 74, -77, WhoHol B*
Carter, Nan *Film 1*
Carter, Nell 1894-1965 *WhThe*
Carter, Nelson *BluesWW[port]*
Carter, Nick *What 5[port]*
Carter, Peter John Burnett 1935- *WhoMus 72*
Carter, Ralph 1961- *DrBlPA*
Carter, Ray 1908- *AmSCAP 66, -80*
Carter, Richard *AmSCAP 66, Film 2, NewGrD 80*
Carter, Richard C 1919- *IntMPA 77, -78*
Carter, Richard Gordon 1918- *WhoMus 72*
Carter, Ron 1937- *EncJzS 70*
Carter, Ronald Levin 1937- *BiDAmM, EncJzS 70*
Carter, Sara *EncFCWM 69*
Carter, Sara 1899- *CounME 74*
Carter, Sarah 1898- *BiDAmM*
Carter, Steve 1929- *BlkAmP, MorBAP, NatPD[port]*
Carter, Terry *DrBlPA, WhoHol A*
Carter, Thomas 1740?-1804 *NewGrD 80*
Carter, Thomas 1769-1800 *NewGrD 80*
Carter, Tracy 1940- *IntMPA 77, -75, -76, -78, -79, -80*
Carter, Wilf 1904- *BiDAmM, CmpEPM, CounME 74, -74A, EncFCWM 69, IlEncCM[port]*
Carter, William 1936- *CnOxB*
Carter, William R 1908-1976 *AmSCAP 66, -80*
Carter-Edwards, James 1840-1930 *WhThe*
Carter Family *CmpEPM, CounME 74[port], -74A, EncFCWM 69, IlEncCM[port], NewGrD 80*
Carteret, Anna 1942- *WhoThe 72, -77*
Carteri, Rosanna 1930- *CmOp*
Cartford, Gerhard Malling 1923- *IntWWM 77, -80*
Carthusensis, Johannes *NewGrD 80*
Cartier, Anthoinne *NewGrD 80*
Cartier, Antoine *NewGrD 80*
Cartier, Inez Gibson 1918-1970 *WhScrn 74, -77*
Cartier, J B 1765-1841 *OxMus*
Cartier, Jean-Baptiste 1765-1841 *Baker 78, NewGrD 80*
Cartier, Michel 1932- *CreCan 2*
Cartier, Rudolph 1908- *IntMPA 77, -75, -76, -78, -79, -80*
Cartier-Bresson, Henri 1908- *DcFM, OxFilm, WorEFlm[port]*
Cartledge, Lucy Amelia 1956- *IntWWM 80*
Carton, Gwen *Film 2*
Carton, Harold *Film 2*
Carton, Katherine Mackenzie Compton 1853-1928 *OxThe*
Carton, Pauline d1974 *Film 2, WhoHol B*
Carton, Pauline 1884-1974 *FilmAG WE*
Carton, Pauline 1885-1974 *WhScrn 77*
Carton, Pauline 1888-1974 *OxFilm*
Carton, R C 1853-1928 *WhThe*
Carton, R Claude 1854-1928 *WhoStg 1906, -1908*
Carton, Richard Claude 1853-1928 *NotNAT B*
Carton, Richard Claude 1856-1928 *OxThe*
Cartwright, Angela 1952- *ForYSC, WhoHol A*
Cartwright, Charles 1855-1916 *NotNAT B, WhThe, WhoStg 1908*
Cartwright, Donald 1925- *WhoMus 72*
Cartwright, Patricia *IntWWM 80*
Cartwright, Peggy 1912- *WhThe*
Cartwright, Peggy 1915- *Film 2*
Cartwright, Peter 1785-1872 *BiDAmM*
Cartwright, Veronica *ForYSC, WhoHol A*
Cartwright, William 1611-1643 *OxThe, REnWD[port]*
Carucci, James 1942- *IntWWM 77, -80*
Carulli, Ferdinando 1770-1841 *Baker 78, NewGrD 80*
Carus, Emma 1879-1927 *AmPS B, NotNAT B, WhThe, WhoStg 1906, -1908*
Carus, Louis 1927- *IntWWM 77, -80, WhoMus 72*
Carusi, Gaetano 1773?- *BiDAmM*
Carusio, Luigi *NewGrD 80*
Caruso, Anthony 1889-1973 *AmSCAP 80*
Caruso, Anthony 1913?- *FilmgC, ForYSC, HalFC 80, MovMk[port], Vers A[port], WhoHol A*
Caruso, Anthony 1915?- *FilmEn*
Caruso, Enrico 1873-1921 *Baker 78, BiDAmM, BnBkM 80[port], CmOp[port], Film 1, FilmgC, HalFC 80, MusMk, MusSN[port], NewEOp 71, NewGrD 80[port], OxMus, TwYS, WhScrn 74, -77, WhoHol B*
Caruso, Giuseppe *NewGrD 80*
Caruso, John *ConAmC*
Caruso, Lodovico 1754-1822 *NewGrD 80*
Caruso, Luigi 1754-1822 *NewGrD 80*
Carvaille, Leon *NewGrD 80*
Carvajal, Armando 1893- *NewGrD 80*
Carvajal, Carlos 1931- *CnOxB*
Carvalho, Caroline 1827-1895 *NewGrD 80*
Carvalho, Dinora 1908- *IntWWM 77, -80*
Carvalho, Dinora De 1905- *NewGrD 80*
Carvalho, Eleazar 1912- *Baker 78*
Carvalho, Eleazar De 1915- *MusMk*
Carvalho, Joao DeSousa 1745-1798 *NewGrD 80*
Carvalho, Leon 1825-1897 *Baker 78, NewEOp 71, NewGrD 80*
Carvalho, Raul De *FilmAG WE*
Carvalho, Reginaldo 1932- *IntWWM 77, -80*
Carvalho, Rui De *FilmAG WE*
Carvalho, Urban Farrington 1939- *AmSCAP 80*
Carvalho-Miolan, Caroline-Marie-Felix 1827-1895 *Baker 78*
Carver, Miss *Film 1*
Carver, Gilman Marston 1952- *AmSCAP 80*
Carver, James 1932- *NotNAT*
Carver, Johnny 1940- *CounME 74, -74A, IlEncCM[port]*
Carver, Kathryn 1906-1947 *Film 2, NotNAT B, TwYS, WhScrn 74, -77, WhoHol B*
Carver, Louise d1956 *MotPP, NotNAT B, WhoHol B*
Carver, Louise 1868-1956 *FilmgC*
Carver, Louise 1869-1956 *ForYSC, WhScrn 74, -77*
Carver, Louise 1875-1956 *Film 1, -2, TwYS*
Carver, Louise 1898-1956 *HalFC 80*
Carver, Lynn 1909-1955 *HalFC 80, WhScrn 74, -77*
Carver, Lynne 1909-1955 *MotPP, NotNAT B, WhoHol B*
Carver, Lynne 1917-1955 *FilmEn, ForYSC*
Carver, Marilyn Joan Cassei 1934- *IntWWM 77*
Carver, Mary *PlP&P[port]*
Carver, Norman 1899- *BiE&WWA, NotNAT*
Carver, Robert *OxMus*
Carver, Robert 1487?-1546? *Baker 78, BnBkM 80, MusMk*
Carver, Robert 1490?-1546? *NewGrD 80*
Carver, Tina *ForYSC*
Carver, Wayman 1905-1967 *EncJzS 70, IlEncJ, WhoJazz 72*
Carvil, Bert Forrest 1880- *WhoStg 1908*
Carvil, Harry 1880- *WhoStg 1908*
Carvill, Henry d1941 *Film 2, NotNAT B, WhoHol B*
Carvin, Michael 1944- *EncJzS 70*
Carwarden, John d1660? *NewGrD 80*
Carwithen, Dulcie Doreen *WhoMus 72*
Cary, Alice 1820-1871 *BiDAmM*
Cary, Annie Louise 1841-1921 *Baker 78, NewEOp 71, NewGrD 80*
Cary, Annie Louise 1842-1921 *BiDAmM*
Cary, Bob 1940- *IntWWM 80*
Cary, Christopher *WhoHol A*
Cary, Clara *BluesWW[port]*
Cary, Dick 1916- *CmpEPM, EncJzS 70, WhoJazz 72*
Cary, Falkland L 1897- *WhoThe 72, -77*
Cary, Jim *Film 2*
Cary, Phoebe 1824-1871 *BiDAmM*
Cary, Richard Durant 1916- *AmSCAP 66, BiDAmM, EncJzS 70*
Cary, Tristram Ogilvie 1925- *DcCM, IntWWM 77, -80, NewGrD 80, WhoMus 72*
Caryll, Ivan d1921 *WhThe*
Caryll, Ivan 1860-1921 *EncMT, NewCBMT*
Caryll, Ivan 1861-1921 *AmPS, BiDAmM, CmpEPM, NewGrD 80, NotNAT B, PopAmC[port]*
Carzebski, Adam *NewGrD 80*
Carzou, Jean 1907- *DancEn 78*
Casa, Lisa Della *NewGrD 80*
Casa Loma *BgBands 74, BiDAmM*
Casabona, Francisco 1894- *Baker 78*
Casadesus *NewGrD 80*
Casadesus, Francis 1870-1954 *NewGrD 80*
Casadesus, Francois Louis 1870-1954 *Baker 78, NewGrD 80*
Casadesus, Gabrielle 1901- *NewGrD 80*
Casadesus, Gaby 1901- *Baker 78, IntWWM 77, -80, NewGrD 80*
Casadesus, Henri 1879-1947 *Baker 78, NewGrD 80*
Casadesus, Jean 1927-1972 *Baker 78, BiDAmM, NewGrD 80*
Casadesus, Jean-Claude 1935- *NewGrD 80*
Casadesus, Luis 1850-1919 *NewGrD 80*
Casadesus, Marcel 1882-1914 *NewGrD 80*
Casadesus, Marius Robert Max 1892- *Baker 78, IntWWM 77, -80, NewGrD 80, OxMus, WhoMus 72*
Casadesus, Mathilde 1921-1965 *WhScrn 74, -77, WhoHol B*
Casadesus, Robert 1899-1972 *Baker 78, BnBkM 80[port], MusSN[port], NewGrD 80, WhoMus 72*

Casadesus, Robert-Guillaume 1878-1940 NewGrD 80
Casadesus, Robert Marcel 1899-1972 BiDAmM
Casado, Germinal 1934- CnOxB, DancEn 78
Casady, Richard R PupTheA
Casajuana, Maria Film 2
Casal Y Chapi, Enrique 1909- NewGrD 80
Casalbigi, Ranieri De NewGrD 80
Casalbigi, Raniero De NewGrD 80
Casale, Michael 1949- NatPD[port]
Casaleggio, Giovanni 1880-1955 WhScrn 74, -77
Casali, Giovanni Battista 1715?-1792 NewGrD 80
Casali, Lodovico 1575?-1647 NewGrD 80
Casalini, Angelo BiE&WWA
Casals, Pablo 1876-1973 AmSCAP 66, -80, Baker 78, BiDAmM, BnBkM 80[port], MusSN[port], NewGrD 80[port], WhScrn 77, WhoMus 72
Casals, Pau 1876-1973 MusMk, OxMus
Casals, Paul 1876-1973 NewGrD 80[port]
Casals Mantovani, Margherita 1928- WhoOp 76
Casamorata, Luigi Ferdinando 1807-1881 NewGrD 80
Casamorata, Luigi Fernando 1807-1881 Baker 78
Casanave, Charles L, Jr. 1917- IntMPA 75, -76
Casanave, Chester F 1919- IntMPA 77, -75, -76, -78, -79
Casanova, Andre 1919- Baker 78, DcCM, NewGrD 80
Casanova, Felipe 1898- AmSCAP 66, -80
Casanova, Jimmy 1920- AmSCAP 66
Casanova DeSeingalt, Giovanni Jacopo 1725-1798 NewEOp 71
Casanovas, Jose 1924- NewGrD 80
Casanovas, Narciso 1747-1799 Baker 78, NewGrD 80
Casanoves, Narcis 1747-1799 NewGrD 80
Casapietra-Kegel, Celestina 1939- WhoOp 76
Casares, Maria 1922- CnThe, EncWT, Ent[port], FilmAG WE, FilmEn, FilmgC, HalFC 80, MotPP, OxFilm, WhoHol A, WorEFlm[port]
Casarini, Domenica NewGrD 80
Casarini, Gianfranco 1940- WhoOp 76
Casartelli, Gabrielle 1910- WhThe
Casati, Filago 1590?-1657? NewGrD 80
Casati, Gasparo 1610?-1641 NewGrD 80
Casati, Geronimo 1590?-1657? NewGrD 80
Casati, Giovanni 1811-1895 CnOxB
Casati, Girolamo 1590?-1657? NewGrD 80
Casati, Teodoro 1625?-1688? NewGrD 80
Casavant OxMus
Casavola, Franco 1891-1955 Baker 78, NewGrD 80
Casazza, Elvira 1887-1965 NewGrD 80
Cascades, The RkOn
Cascarino, Romeo 1922- AmSCAP 66, -80, ConAmC, IntWWM 77, -80
Caschindorff, Stephan NewGrD 80
Cascio, Salvatore PupTheA
Casciolini, Claudio 1697-1760 NewGrD 80
Cascudo, Luiz DaCamara 1898- NewGrD 80
Case, Anna 1889- BiDAmM, Film 1, WhoHol A
Case, Dwight ConMuA 80B
Case, Frank 1877-1946 NotNAT A
Case, Helen Film 1
Case, James 1932- ConAmC
Case, John 1539?-1600 NewGrD 80
Case, Justin AmSCAP 80
Case, Nelson IntMPA 77, -75, -76, -78, -79, -80
Case, Paul 1895-1933 WhScrn 74, -77
Case, Russ 1912-1964 CmpEPM
Case, Russell D 1912-1964 AmSCAP 66, -80
Caseda, Diego De NewGrD 80
Casei, Nedda 1935- WhoOp 76
Casella d1300? NewGrD 80
Casella, Alberto 1891- McGEWD
Casella, Alfredo 1883-1947 Baker 78, BnBkM 80, CompSN[port], CnOxB, DcCom&M 79, DcCM, MusMk, NewEOp 71, NewGrD 80[port], OxMus
Casella, Pietro Baker 78
Casella, Pietro d1300? OxMus
Casella, Pietro 1769?-1843 NewGrD 80
Casellas, Jaime 1690-1764 NewGrD 80
Casellato, Renzo 1936- WhoOp 76
Casellato Lamberti, Giorgio 1938- WhoOp 76
Caselli, Ernest Film 1
Caselli, Lamar 1921- IntMPA 77, -75, -76, -78, -79, -80
Casentini, Marsilio 1576-1651 NewGrD 80
Casentini, Silao 1540?-1594 NewGrD 80
Caserini, Mario 1874-1920 DcFM, FilmEn, OxFilm
Caserio, Jesse 1918- AmSCAP 66
Caserta, Anthonello De NewGrD 80
Caserta, Philippus De NewGrD 80
Casey, Al 1915- CmpEPM, WhoJazz 72
Casey, Albert Aloysius 1915- BiDAmM
Casey, Bernie 1939- DrBlPA, WhoHol A
Casey, Bob 1909- NewOrJ, WhoJazz 72
Casey, Claude 1912- AmSCAP 66, -80
Casey, Dolores 1917-1945 WhScrn 74, -77, WhoHol B
Casey, Floyd 1900-1967 WhoJazz 72
Casey, John McGEWD[port]
Casey, Kenneth 1899-1965 AmSCAP 66, -80, Film 1, WhScrn 74, -77, WhoHol B
Casey, Lawrence WhoHol A
Casey, Michael ConDr 77D
Casey, Pat d1962 NotNAT B
Casey, Rosemary 1904- BiE&WWA, NotNAT
Casey, Stuart F 1896-1948 WhScrn 74, -77, WhoHol B
Casey, Sue WhoHol A
Casey, Virginia B 1913- IntWWM 77
Casey, Warren 1935- AmSCAP 80
Casey, Wesley Eugene 1933- AmSCAP 66, -80
Cash, Alvin & The Crawlers RkOn 2[port]
Cash, Bruce Richard 1947- IntWWM 77
Cash, John R 1932- BiDAmM, NewGrD 80
Cash, Johnny 1932- Baker 78, ConMuA 80A[port], CounME 74[port], -74A, EncFCWM 69, FilmgC, HalFC 80, IlEncCM[port], IlEncR[port], NewGrD 80, PopAmC SUP[port], RkOn[port], WhoHol A
Cash, June WomWMM
Cash, Louise 1939- IntWWM 77, -80
Cash, Morny WhThe
Cash, Rosalind WhoHol A
Cash, Rosalind 1938- DrBlPA, FilmEn, WhoThe 77
Cash, Rosalind 1945- FilmgC, HalFC 80
Cash, Thomas R 1940- BiDAmM
Cash, Tommy 1940- CounME 74[port], -74A, IlEncCM[port]
Cash, William F 1880?-1963 NotNAT B, WhScrn 74, -77, WhoHol B
Cashel, Oliver d1747 NotNAT B
Casher, Izadore 1887-1948 WhScrn 77
Cashier, Isidore Film 2
Cashman, Betty BiE&WWA, NotNAT
Cashman, Harry Film 1
Cashman, Harry d1912 WhScrn 77
Cashman, Terry AmSCAP 80, ConMuA 80B
Cashman & West RkOn 2[port]
Cashmore, Donald 1926- IntWWM 77, -80, WhoMus 72
Casilli, Gioseppe 1580?- NewGrD 80
Casimir, Joe 1902?- NewOrJ[port]
Casimir, John 1898-1963 NewOrJ[port]
Casimiri, Raffaele Casimiro 1880-1943 Baker 78, NewGrD 80
Casimiro DaSilva, Joaquim 1808-1862 NewGrD 80
Casimiro Junior, Joaquim 1808-1862 NewGrD 80
Casini, Giovanni Maria 1652-1719 Baker 78, NewGrD 80
Casinos RkOn 2[port]
Caskel, Christoph 1932- NewGrD 80
Casken, John 1949- NewGrD 80
Casler, Herman Film 1
Caso, Fernando H 1943- IntWWM 77, -80
Casolani, Leonardo NewGrD 80
Casolaro, Hugo A 1914- IntMPA 77, -75, -76, -78, -79
Cason, Barbara WhoHol A
Cason, James E 1939- AmSCAP 80
Cason, John d1961 WhScrn 77
Casona, Alejandro 1903-1965 CnMD, CroCD, EncWT, Ent, McGEWD[port], ModWD
Casoni, Bianca Maria WhoOp 76
Casoni, Biancamaria WhoMus 72
Caspar, Adam 1590?-1665? NewGrD 80
Caspari NewGrD 80
Casparini NewGrD 80
Casparini, Adam Horacy 1676-1745 NewGrD 80
Casparini, Eugen 1623-1706 NewGrD 80
Caspary, Vera 1899- HalFC 80
Caspary, Vera 1904- BiE&WWA, FilmEn, FilmgC, NotNAT, WorEFlm[port]
Caspersen, Karen Film 2
Cass, Guy 1921-1959 WhScrn 74, -77
Cass, Henry 1902- FilmEn, FilmgC, HalFC 80, IlWWBF, PlP&P, WhoThe 72, -77
Cass, Maurice 1884-1954 FilmEn, FilmgC, HalFC 80, Vers B[port], WhScrn 74, -77, WhoHol B
Cass, Peggy MotPP, WhoHol A
Cass, Peggy 1924- FilmEn, WhoThe 72, -77
Cass, Peggy 1926- BiE&WWA, ForYSC, NotNAT
Cass, Ray WhoHol A
Cass, Ronald 1923- WhoThe 72, -77
Cass-Beggs, Barbara 1904- IntWWM 77
Cass Country Boys, The IlEncCM
Cassado, Gaspar 1897-1966 Baker 78, NewGrD 80
Cassado, Joaquin 1867-1926 Baker 78, NewGrD 80
Cassady, James 1869-1928 Film 1, WhScrn 77
Cassagne, Joseph La NewGrD 80
Cassandre 1901- EncWT
Cassandre, A M 1901- DancEn 78
Cassandre, Alexandre M 1901-1967 CnOxB
Cassani, Giuseppe NewGrD 80
Cassard, Jules 1890- NewOrJ
Cassard, Leo 1892?-1972 NewOrJ
Cassavant, Nina Film 2
Cassavetes, John 1929- AmFD, BiDFilm, -81, ConDr 73, -77A, DcFM, FilmEn, FilmgC, ForYSC, HalFC 80, IntMPA 77, -75, -76, -78, -79, -80, MotPP, MovMk[port], OxFilm, WhoHol A, WorEFlm[port]
Casseda, Diego De NewGrD 80
Cassel, Irwin M 1886-1971 AmSCAP 66, -80, BiDAmM
Cassel, Jean-Pierre 1932- FilmAG WE[port], FilmEn, FilmgC, HalFC 80, IntMPA 77, -76, -78, -79, -80, MovMk, OxFilm, WhoHol A, WorEFlm[port]
Cassel, John Walter 1910- NewEOp 71
Cassel, Marwin S 1925- AmSCAP 80
Cassel, Seymour FilmEn, WhoHol A
Cassel, Sid 1897-1960 WhScrn 74, -77, WhoHol B
Cassel, Walter John 1920- WhoOp 76
Cassell, Pete d1953 IlEncCM
Cassell, Wally ForYSC, WhoHol A
Cassellas, Jaime NewGrD 80
Cassells, Ian McIntosh 1945- IntWWM 77, -80
Cassels-Brown, Alastair K 1927- ConAmC
Casserley, Lawrence 1941- WhoMus 72
Cassett, Boyd 1911- AmSCAP 80
Casseus, Frantz Gabriel 1921- AmSCAP 80
Cassey, Charles R 1933- AmSCAP 66, -80
Cassidy, Ajax JoeFr
Cassidy, Bill 1876-1943 WhScrn 74, -77, WhoHol B
Cassidy, Claudia 1905?- BiE&WWA, ConAmTC, NotNAT
Cassidy, David 1950- AmSCAP 80, IlEncR, RkOn 2[port]
Cassidy, Donald Raymond 1934- AmSCAP 80
Cassidy, Ed 1893-1968 WhScrn 74, -77, WhoHol B
Cassidy, Edward ForYSC
Cassidy, Ellen Film 1, -2
Cassidy, J Rice d1927 NotNAT B
Cassidy, Jack d1976 WhoHol A
Cassidy, Jack 1925-1976 EncMT
Cassidy, Jack 1926-1976 FilmgC, HalFC 80
Cassidy, Jack 1927-1976 BiE&WWA, FilmEn, NotNAT, WhoThe 72, -77
Cassidy, Joanna 1944- FilmEn, HalFC 80, WhoHol A
Cassidy, Shaun IntMPA 79, -80
Cassidy, Shaun 1958- AmSCAP 80
Cassidy, Shaun 1959- RkOn 2[port]
Cassidy, Ted 1932-1979 HalFC 80

Cassilly, Richard 1927- *CmOp, NewGrD 80, WhoOp 76*
Cassily, Richard 1927- *IntWWM 80*
Cassin, James Joseph, Jr. 1926- *AmSCAP 80*
Cassinari, John 1920- *AmSCAP 66, -80*
Cassinella, Ricardo 1936- *WhoOp 76*
Cassinelli, Dolores *Film 1, -2, TwYS*
Cassiodorus, Magnus Aurelianus 485?-580? *NewGrD 80*
Cassiodorus, Magnus Aurelius 485?-580? *Baker 78*
Cassirer, Fritz 1871-1926 *Baker 78, NewGrD 80*
Cassity, Ellen *Film 2*
Cassjuana, Maria *Film 2*
Cassler, G Winston 1906- *ConAmC*
Casson, Alfred Joseph 1898- *CreCan 2*
Casson, Ann 1915- *CnThe, WhThe*
Casson, Christopher 1912- *WhThe*
Casson, John 1909- *WhThe*
Casson, Sir Lewis 1875-1969 *BiE&WWA, EncWT, NotNAT A, -B, OxThe, PlP&P, WhThe, WhoHol B*
Casson, Sir Lewis 1875-1970 *CnThe*
Casson, Sir Lewis 1876-1969 *WhScrn 74, -77*
Casson, Louis d1950 *NotNAT B*
Casson, Mary 1914- *WhThe*
Casson, Thomas 1842-1910 *NewGrD 80*
Cassone, Michael, Jr. 1938- *AmSCAP 80*
Casstevens, Mark 1949- *AmSCAP 80*
Cassuto, Alvaro Leon 1938- *Baker 78, DcCM, IntWWM 77, -80, NewGrD 80*
Castagna, Bruna 1905- *Baker 78*
Castagna, Bruna 1908- *MusSN[port], NewEOp 71*
Castagna, Joe 1934-1970 *WhScrn 77*
Castagneri, Marie-Anne 1722-1787 *NewGrD 80*
Castagnetta, Grace Sharp 1912- *IntWWM 77, WhoMus 72*
Castagnone, Riccardo 1906- *Baker 78*
Castaign, Johnny 1912-1972 *NewOrJ*
Castaldi, Alfonso 1874-1942 *Baker 78*
Castaldi, Bellerofonte 1580?-1649 *NewGrD 80*
Castaldi, Paolo 1930- *NewGrD 80*
Castaldo, Joseph F 1927- *AmSCAP 66, -80, Baker 78, ConAmC*
Castan, Count Armand De *Baker 78*
Castaneda, Daniel 1899- *NewGrD 80*
Castaways, The *RkOn 2[port]*
Castel, Jose *NewGrD 80*
Castel, Louis-Bertrand 1688-1757 *Baker 78, NewGrD 80*
Castel, Nico 1931- *IntWWM 80, WhoOp 76*
Castelain, Jean *NewGrD 80*
Castell, Antonio 1911- *IntMPA 77, -75, -76, -78, -79, -80*
Castell, Eva Millicent 1921- *WhoMus 72*
Castell, Michele 1945- *BluesWW*
Castellan, Jeanne Anais 1819-1858? *CmOp, NewGrD 80*
Castelland, Laura *WhoMus 72*
Castellani, Brute *Film 2*
Castellani, Renato 1913- *DcFM, FilmEn, FilmgC, HalFC 80, OxFilm, WorEFlm[port]*
Castellano, Richard *WhoHol A*
Castellano, Richard 1931- *FilmgC, HalFC 80*
Castellano, Richard 1933- *FilmEn*
Castellano, Richard S 1933- *IntMPA 77, -75, -76, -78, -79, -80*
Castellanos, Evencio 1915- *NewGrD 80*
Castellanos, Gonzalo 1926- *NewGrD 80*
Castellanos, Pablo 1917- *NewGrD 80*
Castellanus, Petrus *NewGrD 80*
Castelli, Ignaz Franz 1781-1862 *Baker 78*
Castelli, Ottaviano 1642- *NewGrD 80*
Castello, Dario *NewGrD 80*
Castells, The *RkOn*
Castellucci, Louis Stanislaus 1897- *AmSCAP 80*
Castellucci, Stella 1930- *AmSCAP 80*
Castelmary 1834-1897 *Baker 78, BiDAmM*
Castelnovate, Lucio *NewGrD 80*
Castelnovato, Lucio *NewGrD 80*
Castelnuovo, Nino 1937- *FilmgC, HalFC 80, WhoHol A*
Castelnuovo-Tedesco, Mario 1895-1968 *AmSCAP 66, -80, Baker 78, BiDAmM, BnBkM 80, CompSN[port], ConAmC, DcCom&M 79, DcCM, HalFC 80, MusMk, NewEOp 71, NewGrD 80, OxMus*
Castelo, Julieta 1914- *FilmAG WE[port]*
Castendorfer, Stephan *NewGrD 80*
Castera, Rene D'Avezac 1873-1955 *Baker 78*
Casterede, Jacques 1926- *NewGrD 80*
Casti, Giambattista 1724-1803 *NewGrD 80*
Castigliola, Angelo J 1924- *NewOrJ*
Castiglioni, Iphigene 1901-1963 *WhScrn 74, -77*
Castiglioni, Iphigenia d1963 *WhoHol B*
Castiglioni, Niccolo 1932- *Baker 78, DcCM, NewGrD 80*
Castigloni, Iphigenie 1901-1963 *FilmEn*
Castil-Blaze 1784-1857 *Baker 78, CnOxB, NewEOp 71, NewGrD 80*
Castile, Lynn 1898-1975 *WhScrn 77*
Castileti, Jean *NewGrD 80*
Castilla, Alberto 1883-1937 *Baker 78*
Castilleja, Pedro Fernandez De *NewGrD 80*
Castillo, Bernardo Clavijo Del *NewGrD 80*
Castillo, Diego Del 1544?-1601 *NewGrD 80*
Castillo, Emilio 1950- *AmSCAP 80*
Castillo, Fructos Del *NewGrD 80*
Castillo, Javier 1933- *ConAmC*
Castillo, Jesus 1877-1946 *NewGrD 80*
Castillo, Manuel 1930- *NewGrD 80*
Castillo, Marvin P 1936- *AmSCAP 80*
Castillo, Ricardo 1894-1967 *NewGrD 80*
Castillon, Alexis 1838-1873 *Baker 78, NewGrD 80, OxMus*
Castle, Betty d1962 *NotNAT B*
Castle, Don 1917-1966 *WhScrn 74, -77*
Castle, Don 1919-1966 *FilmgC, HalFC 80, WhoHol B*
Castle, Egerton 1858-1920 *NotNAT B*
Castle, Harry *Film 2*
Castle, Irene *AmSCAP 80, CmpEPM, CnOxB, DancEn 78, HalFC 80*
Castle, Irene 1892-1969 *NotNAT B*
Castle, Irene 1893- *What 1[port]*
Castle, Irene 1893-1968 *Film 2, OxFilm*
Castle, Irene 1893-1969 *EncMT, Film 1, FilmgC, PlP&P, TwYS, WhScrn 74, -77, WhoHol B*
Castle, Irene 1894-1969 *BiDAmM*
Castle, Irene And Vernon *AmPS B*
Castle, John 1940- *HalFC 80, WhoThe 72, -77*
Castle, Joyce 1944- *WhoOp 76*
Castle, Lee 1915- *BgBands 74[port], CmpEPM, WhoJazz 72*
Castle, Lillian 1865-1959 *WhScrn 74, -77, WhoHol B*
Castle, Mary 1931- *FilmEn, FilmgC, ForYSC, HalFC 80, WhoHol A*
Castle, Nicholas 1910- *AmSCAP 66, -80*
Castle, Nick 1910-1968 *FilmEn, FilmgC, HalFC 80, WhScrn 74, -77, WhoHol B*
Castle, Patrick *ConAmC*
Castle, Peggie 1926-1973 *WhoHrs 80[port]*
Castle, Peggie 1927-1973 *FilmEn, FilmgC, ForYSC, HalFC 80*
Castle, Peggy 1926-1973 *WhScrn 77, WhoHol B*
Castle, Robert *Film 2*
Castle, Roy 1933- *HalFC 80*
Castle, Vernon d1918 *CmpEPM, CnOxB, HalFC 80, PlP&P[port], WhoHol B*
Castle, Vernon 1885-1918 *Film 1, FilmgC, OxFilm*
Castle, Vernon 1887-1918 *DancEn 78, EncMT, NotNAT B, WhScrn 77*
Castle, Walter H 1905- *IntMPA 77, -75, -76, -78, -79, -80*
Castle, William 1914-1977 *FilmEn, FilmgC, HalFC 80, IntMPA 77, -75, -76, NewYTET, WhoHrs 80, WorEFlm[port]*
Castleberry, Pleasant Box 1932- *IntWWM 77*
Castleman, Charles Martin 1941- *IntWWM 77, -80, NewGrD 80, WhoMus 72*
Castleman, Jeffry Alan 1946- *EncJzS 70*
Castlemayne, Lady 1641-1704 *DcPup*
Castleton, Barbara 1896- *Film 1, -2, TwYS*
Caston, Leonard 1917- *BluesWW[port]*
Caston, Saul 1901- *Baker 78*
Castor, Jimmy *RkOn 2[port]*
Castrillon, Maria Teresa 1935- *IntWWM 80*
Castro *NewGrD 80*
Castro, Armando 1904-1961 *AmSCAP 66, -80*
Castro, Esteban Salas Y *NewGrD 80*
Castro, Fidel *WhoHol A*
Castro, Jean De 1540?-1600? *NewGrD 80*
Castro, Jean De 1540?-1611? *Baker 78*
Castro, Joe 1927- *EncJzS 70*
Castro, Jose Maria 1892-1964 *Baker 78, NewGrD 80, OxMus*
Castro, Joseph 1927- *BiDAmM, EncJzS 70*
Castro, Juan Blas De 1560?-1631 *NewGrD 80*
Castro, Juan Jose 1895-1968 *Baker 78, DancEn 78, DcCM, NewGrD 80, OxMus*
Castro, Luis Arnoldo 1902- *NewGrD 80*
Castro, Ricardo 1864-1907 *Baker 78*
Castro, Steven 1864-1952 *WhScrn 74, -77*
Castro, Washington 1909- *Baker 78, NewGrD 80, OxMus*
Castro Herrera, Ricardo 1864-1907 *NewGrD 80*
Castro Neves, Oscar 1940- *EncJzS 70*
Castro Y Bellvis, Guillen De 1569-1631 *EncWT, Ent, McGEWD, OxThe*
Castro Y Bellvis, Guillende 1569-1631 *NotNAT B*
Castro Y Malagaray, Juan De 1572?-1632 *NewGrD 80*
Castro Y Mallagaray, Juan De 1572?-1632 *NewGrD 80*
Castrovillari, Daniele Da *NewGrD 80*
Castrucci, Pietro 1679-1752 *Baker 78, NewGrD 80*
Casuals, The *RkOn*
Casulana, Maddalena 1540?- *NewGrD 80*
Casulani, Leonardo *NewGrD 80*
Caswall, Edward 1814-1878 *OxMus*
Caswell, Kenneth 1917- *IntWWM 77, -80, WhoMus 72*
Caswell, Oscar Charles 1913- *AmSCAP 66, -80*
Cat-Iron *BluesWW[port]*
Cat Mother And The All Night Newsboys *BiDAmM, IlEncR, RkOn 2[port]*
Cata, Alfonso 1937- *CnOxB*
Catala, Muriel 1952- *FilmAG WE*
Catalani, Alfredo 1854-1893 *Baker 78, CmOp, DcCom&M 79, GrComp[port], NewEOp 71, NewGrD 80[port], OxMus*
Catalani, Angelica 1780-1845 *OxMus*
Catalani, Angelica 1780-1849 *Baker 78, CmOp, NewEOp 71, NewGrD 80[port]*
Catalani, Ottaviano d1644? *NewGrD 80*
Catalani, Ottavio d1644? *NewGrD 80*
Catalano, Ottaviano d1644? *NewGrD 80*
Catalano, Ottavio d1644? *NewGrD 80*
Catalano, Thomas J 1933- *AmSCAP 66*
Cataldi-Tassoni, Walter 1921- *WhoOp 76*
Cataldo, Salvatore Di *NewGrD 80*
Catania, Ugo 1913- *WhoMus 72*
Catanzaro, Innocentio DiPaula Di *NewGrD 80*
Catanzaro, Tony 1946- *CnOxB*
Catch, Jack *NewGrD 80*
Catchapaw, Dorothy Deane Johnson 1912- *AmSCAP 80*
Cate Brothers *IlEncR*
Catel, Charles-Simon 1773-1830 *Baker 78, NewGrD 80*
Catelain, Jacques *Film 2*
Catelani, Angelo 1811-1866 *Baker 78, NewGrD 80*
Catelinet, Philip *ConAmC*
Catenacci, Gian Domenico *NewGrD 80*
Cates, George 1911- *AmSCAP 66, -80, RkOn[port]*
Cates, Gilbert 1934- *BiE&WWA, HalFC 80, IntMPA 77, -75, -76, -78, -79, -80, NewYTET, NotNAT*
Cates, Joseph 1924- *BiE&WWA, NewYTET, NotNAT*
Cates, Madlyn *WhoHol A*
Cates, Sidney 1900?-1968 *NewOrJ*
Cathala, Jean *NewGrD 80*
Cathalas, Jean *NewGrD 80*
Cathcart, Allen 1938- *WhoOp 76*
Cathcart, David Paul 1949- *IntWWM 77, -80*
Cathcart, Dick 1924- *CmpEPM*
Cathelas, Jean *NewGrD 80*
Catherine De'Medici 1519-1589 *OxMus*
Catherine The Great 1762-1798 *HalFC 80*
Catherine, Philip 1942- *EncJzS 70*
Cathy Jean And The Roommates *RkOn*
Catizone, Joseph 1902-1973 *AmSCAP 66, -80*
Catjuice Charley *BluesWW[port]*
Catlett, Big Sid 1910-1951 *IlEncJ, NewGrD 80,*

WhoJazz 72
Catlett, George James 1933- *BiDAmM*
Catlett, Joseph Thomas, Jr. 1953- *AmSCAP 80*
Catlett, Sid 1910-1951 *CmpEPM, NewGrD 80*
Catlett, Sidney 1910-1951 *BiDAmM, NewGrD 80*
Catlett, Walter 1889-1960 *AmPS B, EncMT, FilmEn, Film 2, FilmgC, ForYSC, HalFC 80, HolCA[port], MotPP, MovMk[port], NotNAT B, Vers A[port], WhScrn 74, -77, WhThe, WhoHol B*
Catley, Anne 1745-1789 *NewGrD 80*
Catley, Gwen 1911- *WhoMus 72*
Catlin, George 1777-1852 *NewGrD 80*
Catling, Darrel 1909- *IlWWBF*
Catling, Thomas 1838-1920 *WhThe*
Catlow, John Rolf Aldred 1940- *IntWWM 77, -80*
Cato 1875- *NewOrJ*
Cato, Adam *NewOrJ*
Cato, Big 1869?- *NewOrJ*
Cato, Diomedes 1570?-1607? *NewGrD 80*
Catoire, George 1861-1926 *OxMus*
Catoire, Georgy 1861-1926 *Baker 78, NewGrD 80*
Caton, Edward 1900- *CnOxB, DancEn 78*
Cator, Peter *ConDr 77B*
Catron, John H 1916- *AmSCAP 66, -80*
Catrufo, Gioseffo 1771-1851 *NewGrD 80*
Catrufo, Giuseppe 1771-1851 *NewGrD 80*
Catsos, Nicholas A 1912- *AmSCAP 80*
Cattani, Lorenzo d1713 *NewGrD 80*
Cattenacci, Gian Domenico d1800? *NewGrD 80*
Catterall, Arthur 1893-1943 *NewGrD 80*
Catterson, Pat *CmpGMD*
Cattin, Giulio 1929- *IntWWM 77, -80*
Cattini, Umberto 1922- *WhoOp 76*
Cattle, Harry *Film 2*
Cattley, Cyril 1876-1937 *WhThe*
Catto, Max 1907- *FilmgC, HalFC 80, WhThe*
Catts, Frances Austin 1914- *AmSCAP 80*
Catullus, Gaius Valerius 084?BC-054?BC *NewGrD 80*
Catunda, Eunice 1915- *NewGrD 80*
Caturla, Alejandro Garcia 1906-1940 *Baker 78, DcCM, NewGrD 80, OxMus*
Cau, Jean 1925- *CnMD*
Caubisens, Henri *BiE&WWA*
Cauchie, Maurice 1882-1963 *Baker 78, NewGrD 80*
Caudella, Edoardo 1841-1924 *Baker 78*
Caudella, Eduard 1841-1924 *NewGrD 80*
Caudella, Edward *OxMus*
Caudle, Theresa 1957- *IntWWM 77, -80*
Caufield, Marie Celene *WomWMM B*
Cauleray, Jean *NewGrD 80*
Caulery, Jean *NewGrD 80*
Cauley, Geoffrey 1942- *CnOxB*
Caulfield, Joan 1922- *FilmEn, FilmgC, ForYSC, HalFC 80, IntMPA 77, -75, -76, -78, -79, -80, MotPP, WhoHol A*
Caulfield, Sandra Lee 1954- *AmSCAP 80*
Caulkins, Rufus d1935 *WhScrn 74, -77*
Caulson, Roy *Film 2*
Caunce, John 1911- *WhoMus 72*
Caupain, Ernoul *NewGrD 80*
Caurroy, Eustache Du *Baker 78, NewGrD 80*
Caurroy, Francois Eustache Du 1549-1609 *OxMus*
Caus, Salomon De 1576?-1626 *NewGrD 80, OxMus*
Causer, Bob *CmpEPM*
Causinus, Arnoldus 1510?-1548? *NewGrD 80*
Causley, Ed *MorBAP*
Caussin, Ernold 1510?-1548? *NewGrD 80*
Caussin, Nicolas 1580-1651 *OxThe*
Causton, Thomas 1520?-1569 *NewGrD 80*
Caustun, Thomas 1520?-1569 *NewGrD 80, OxMus*
Caute, David 1936- *ConDr 73, -77*
Cautelay, Guillaume *NewGrD 80*
Cauvin, Andre 1907- *DcFM*
Cauvin, Jean *NewGrD 80*
Cava, Carlo 1928- *WhoOp 76*
Cavacchio, Giovanni 1556?-1626 *NewGrD 80*
Cavacchioli, Enrico 1885-1954 *McGEWD*
Cavaccio, Giovanni 1556-1626 *Baker 78, NewGrD 80*
Cavaille-Col, Aristide 1811-1899 *OxMus*
Cavaille-Coll, Aristide 1811-1899 *Baker 78, NewGrD 80*
Cavalcanti, Alberto 1897- *BiDFilm, -81, DcFM, FilmEn, FilmgC, HalFC 80, IlWWBF, IntMPA 77, -75, -76, -78, -79, -80, MovMk[port], OxFilm, WorEFlm[port]*
Cavalcanti, Nastor DeHollanda 1949- *IntWWM 77*
Cavalcanti, Nestor DeHollanda 1949- *IntWWM 80*
Cavalier, Alain 1931- *FilmEn, WorEFlm[port]*
Cavalier DuLuth *NewGrD 80*
Cavaliere, Emilio Del 1550?-1602 *BnBkM 80*
Cavaliere, Felix A 1942- *AmSCAP 80*
Cavaliere, Pietro 1939- *IntWWM 77*
Cavalieri, Catarina 1760-1801 *NewGrD 80*
Cavalieri, Emilio De' 1550?-1602 *BnBkM 80, CmpBCM, MusMk, NewEOp 71, NewGrD 80*
Cavalieri, Emilio Del 1550?-1602 *Baker 78, GrComp*
Cavalieri, Emilio Di 1550?-1602 *OxMus*
Cavalieri, Katharina 1760-1801 *Baker 78, CmOp*
Cavalieri, Lina 1874-1944 *Baker 78, FilmAG WE, Film 1, -2, MusSN[port], NewEOp 71, NewGrD 80, TwYS, WhScrn 77, WhoHol B*
Cavalieri, Paolo 1560?-1613 *NewGrD 80*
Cavallari, Ascanio *NewGrD 80*
Cavallari, Girolamo *NewGrD 80*
Cavallaro, Carmen 1913- *AmSCAP 66, -80, BgBands 74[port], BiDAmM, CmpEPM*
Cavallaro, Jeanne Fisher *WomWMM B*
Cavallazzi, Malvina 1924- *CnOxB, DancEn 78*
Cavalli, Francesco 1602-1676 *BnBkM 80, GrComp, NewEOp 71, NewGrD 80*
Cavalli, Pier Francesco 1602-1676 *Baker 78, CmOp*
Cavalli, Pietro Francesco 1602-1676 *DcCom 77, MusMk, OxMus*
Cavalli, Tony 1937- *AmSCAP 80*
Cavalliere, Giovanni Filippo *NewGrD 80*
Cavallini, Ernesto 1807-1874 *NewGrD 80*
Cavallo, Robert *ConMuA 80B*
Cavallos, Francisco De *NewGrD 80*
Cavallos, Rodrigo De *NewGrD 80*
Cavan, Allan *Film 2*
Cavanagh, Lilian d1932 *WhThe*
Cavanagh, Paul 1895- *Vers A[port], WhThe*
Cavanagh, Paul 1895-1959 *FilmEn, Film 2, ForYSC, WhoHol B*
Cavanagh, Paul 1895-1960 *MovMk[port]*
Cavanagh, Paul 1895-1964 *FilmgC, HalFC 80, HolCA[port], WhScrn 77, WhoHrs 80*
Cavanaugh, Bob 1902- *AmSCAP 66*
Cavanaugh, Dave *CmpEPM*
Cavanaugh, Helene *Film 2*
Cavanaugh, Hobart d1950 *Film 2, NotNAT B, WhoHol B*
Cavanaugh, Hobart 1886-1950 *FilmEn, FilmgC, HalFC 80, Vers A[port]*
Cavanaugh, Hobart 1887-1950 *ForYSC, MovMk, WhScrn 74, -77*
Cavanaugh, Hobart 1896-1950 *HolCA[port]*
Cavanaugh, James d1967 *AmSCAP 66, -80, CmpEPM*
Cavanaugh, Page 1922- *AmSCAP 66, -80, CmpEPM*
Cavanaugh, Robert Barnes 1902- *AmSCAP 80*
Cavanaugh, Thomas Martin 1946- *AmSCAP 80*
Cavanaugh, Walter Page 1922- *BiDAmM*
Cavanaugh, William *Film 1, -2*
Cavani, Liliana 1936- *FilmEn, HalFC 80, WomWMM*
Cavaniglia, Fernando 1920- *WhoOp 76*
Cavanillas, Juan Bautista Jose *NewGrD 80*
Cavanilles, Juan Bautista Jose *NewGrD 80*
Cavanna, Elise 1902-1963 *NotNAT B, WhScrn 74, -77, WhoHol B*
Cavanna, Elsie *Film 2*
Cavanni, Francesco *NewGrD 80*
Cavarra, Robert N 1934- *IntWWM 77, -80*
Cavatone, Pietro d1586? *NewGrD 80*
Cavatoni, Pietro d1586? *NewGrD 80*
Cavazzi, Juliette Augustina Sysak *CreCan 2*
Cavazzio, Giovanni *NewGrD 80*
Cavazzoni, Girolamo 1520?-1560 *Baker 78*
Cavazzoni, Girolamo 1525?-1577? *NewGrD 80*
Cavazzoni, Marco Antonio 1490?-1560? *NewGrD 80*
Cavazzoni, Marco Antonio 1490?-1570? *Baker 78*
Cavdarski, Vanco 1930- *IntWWM 77, -80*
Cave, Jay 1932- *BiDAmM*
Cave, Joe Arnold 1823-1912 *OxThe*
Cave, John d1664 *NewGrD 80*
Cave, Michael 1944- *ConAmC, IntWWM 77, -80*
Cavedagna, Vincenzo 1740?-1824 *NewGrD 80*
Cavelti, Elsa *WhoMus 72*
Caven, Allan 1880-1941 *WhScrn 74, -77, WhoHol B*
Cavender, Glen W 1884-1962 *Film 1, WhScrn 74, -77, WhoHol B*
Cavender, Glenn W 1884-1962 *Film 2, NotNAT B*
Cavendish, Ada 1847-1895 *NotNAT B*
Cavendish, David 1891-1960 *WhScrn 74, -77, WhoHol B*
Cavendish, Michael 1565-1628 *NewGrD 80, OxMus*
Cavendish, Milly *AmPS B*
Cavens, Fred 1882-1962 *CmMov, Film 2, WhScrn 77*
Cavett, Denise Betty 1929- *WhoMus 72*
Cavett, Dick 1937- *IntMPA 77, -75, -76, -78, -79, -80, NewYTET*
Cavett, Frank 1907-1973 *FilmEn*
Cavett, Morgan A 1944- *AmSCAP 80*
Cavi, Filippo Da *NewGrD 80*
Caviani, Ronald 1931- *ConAmC*
Caviano, Ray *ConMuA 80B*
Cavicchi, Adriano 1934- *NewGrD 80*
Cavin, Jess *Film 2*
Cavin, Mile 1936- *IntWWM 77, -80*
Cavos, Catterino 1775-1840 *Baker 78*
Cavos, Catterino 1776-1840 *NewGrD 80*
Cawarden, Sir Thomas *OxThe*
Cawley, Robert Mason 1925- *AmSCAP 80*
Cawood, Elizabeth Marion 1941- *IntWWM 77, -80*
Cawthorn, Joseph 1867-1949 *CmpEPM, EncMT, Film 2, NotNAT B, TwYS, WhThe, WhoHol B*
Cawthorn, Joseph 1868-1949 *ForYSC, HalFC 80, WhScrn 74, -77, WhoStg 1906, -1908*
Cawthorne, Ann *WomWMM*
Cawthorne, Peter *Film 2*
Cawthra, David Michael 1933- *WhoMus 72*
Cawthron, Janie M 1888-1975 *AmSCAP 66, -80*
Caxton, William 1422?-1491 *OxMus*
Cayatte, Andre 1909- *BiDFilm, -81, DcFM, FilmEn, FilmgC, HalFC 80, OxFilm, WorEFlm[port]*
Cayre, Stan *ConMuA 80B*
Cayrol, Jean 1911- *DcFM, OxFilm, WorEFlm[port]*
Cayton, William D'Arcy 1918- *AmSCAP 80*
Cayvan, Georgia 1857-1906 *FamA&A[port]*
Cayvan, Georgia 1858-1906 *NotNAT B*
Cayzer, A *WhoMus 72*
Caza, Francesco *NewGrD 80*
Cazale, John 1936-1978 *HalFC 80, PlP&P[port], WhoHol A*
Cazalet, Peter 1934- *CnOxB*
Cazalis, Henri 1840-1909 *OxMus*
Cazden, Norman 1914- *Baker 78, BiDAmM, CpmDNM 73, -74, -79, ConAmC, DcCM, NewGrD 80*
Cazeaux, Isabelle Anne-Marie 1926- *IntWWM 77, -80, NewGrD 80*
Cazenuve, Paul d1925 *Film 2, WhScrn 74, -77, WhoHol B*
Cazzati, Maurizio 1620?-1677 *NewGrD 80*
Ceballos, Francisco De *NewGrD 80*
Ceballos, Rodrigo De 1530?-1591 *NewGrD 80*
Cebotari, Maria 1910-1949 *Baker 78, CmOp, NewEOp 71, NewGrD 80*
Cebron, Jean 1938- *CnOxB, DancEn 78[port]*
Ceccarelli, Odoardo 1605?-1668 *NewGrD 80*
Ceccarelli, Vincenzo 1889-1969 *WhScrn 74, -77*
Ceccato, Aldo 1934- *Baker 78, IntWWM 77, -80, MusSN[port], NewGrD 80, WhoMus 72, WhoOp 76*
Cecchele, Gianfranco 1940- *WhoOp 76*

Cecchelli, Carlo NewGrD 80
Cecchetti, Enrico 1847-1928 WhThe
Cecchetti, Enrico 1850-1928 CnOxB, DancEn 78[port], NotNAT B
Cecchi, Emilio 1884-1966 DcFM
Cecchi, Giovan Maria 1518-1587 Ent, McGEWD
Cecchi, Giovanni Maria 1518-1587 EncWT, OxThe
Cecchi D'Amico, Suso 1914- DcFM, HalFC 80, OxFilm, WomWMM, WorEFlm[port]
Cecchi De'Amico, Suso 1914- FilmEn
Cecchini, Angelo NewGrD 80
Cecchini, Orsola OxThe
Cecchini, Penelope C 1943- IntWWM 80
Cecchini, Pier Maria 1575-1645 EncWT, Ent, OxThe
Cecchini, Tomaso 1580?-1644 NewGrD 80
Cecchino, Tomaso 1580?-1644 NewGrD 80
Cecconi-Bates, Augusta 1933- IntWWM 77, -80
Cecere, Carlo 1706-1761 NewGrD 80
Cech, Gisela 1945- CnOxB
Cechus De Florentia NewGrD 80
Cecil, Edward 1888-1940 Film 1, -2, WhScrn 74, -77, WhoHol B
Cecil, Henry 1902- WhoThe 72, -77
Cecil, Jonathan 1939- HalFC 80
Cecil, Mary 1885-1940 WhScrn 74, -77, WhoHol B
Cecil, Nora 1879- Film 1, -2, ForYSC, TwYS, Vers B[port]
Cecil, Sylvia 1906- WhThe
Cecilia NewGrD 80[port]
Cecilia, Saint OxMus
Cedar, Dayna d1974 WhScrn 77
Cedar, Ivan d1937 WhScrn 77
Cederberg, Eva Margareta 1929- IntWWM 77
Cederborg, Gucken Film 2
Cederlof, Rolf Tore 1937- WhoOp 76
Cederstrom, Ellen Film 2
Cedmark, Jan R H 1943- IntWWM 77
Ceely, Robert Paige 1930- Baker 78, CpmDNM 78, -79, ConAmC
Cegani, Elisa 1911- FilmAG WE
Cehanovsky, George 1892- Baker 78
Cekalski, Eugeniusz WomWMM
Celani NewGrD 80
Celano NewGrD 80
Celansky, Ludvik Vitezslav 1870-1931 Baker 78
Celeste, Madame 1811-1882 CnOxB, DancEn 78
Celeste, Celine 1814-1882 NotNAT B, OxThe
Celeste, Olga 1887-1969 WhScrn 74, -77
Celestin, Jack 1894- WhThe
Celestin, Oscar 1884-1954 BiDAmM, NewOrJ[port]
Celestin, Papa 1884-1954 CmpEPM, WhoJazz 72
Celestini, Eligio 1739-1812 NewGrD 80
Celestino, Eligio 1739-1812 NewGrD 80
Celi, Adolfo 1922- FilmAG WE, FilmEn, FilmgC, ForYSC, HalFC 80, WhoHol A
Celibidache, Sergiu 1912- Baker 78, NewGrD 80
Celis, Frits 1929- Baker 78
Celis, Fritz 1929- IntWWM 77, -80
Cella, Theodore 1897-1960 BiDAmM
Cellarius, Simon 1500?-1544 NewGrD 80
Cellavenia, Francesco NewGrD 80
Celles, Francois Bedos De NewGrD 80
Celletti, Rodolfo 1917- NewGrD 80
Celli, Faith 1888-1942 NotNAT B, WhThe
Celli, Frank H 1842-1904 NewGrD 80
Celli, Vincenzo DancEn 78
Cellier, Alexandre 1883-1968 NewGrD 80
Cellier, Alfred 1844-1891 Baker 78, NewGrD 80, NotNAT B, OxMus
Cellier, Antoinette 1913- WhThe
Cellier, Frank 1884-1948 FilmgC, HalFC 80, NotNAT B, WhScrn 74, -77, WhThe, WhoHol B
Cellier, Jacques d1620? NewGrD 80
Cellini, Benvenuto 1500-1571 NewEOp 71
Cellos, The RkOn
Celona, John Anthony 1947- ConAmC
Celoniat, Ignazio 1740?-1784 NewGrD 80
Celoniati, Ignazio 1740?-1784 NewGrD 80
Celoniatti, Ignazio 1740?-1784 NewGrD 80
Celonieti, Ignazio 1740?-1784 NewGrD 80
Celonietto, Ignazio 1740?-1784 NewGrD 80
Celtis, Conradus Protucius 1459-1508 NewGrD 80
Cemino, Donato NewGrD 80
Cenci, Giuseppe d1616 NewGrD 80
Cenci, Lodovico 1615-1648 NewGrD 80
Cendrars, Blaise 1887-1961 OxFilm
Censorinus NewGrD 80
Centlivre, Susanna 1667-1723 EncWT
Centlivre, Susannah 1667?-1723 Ent, McGEWD[port], NotNAT B, OxThe
Centobie, Leonard 1915- NewOrJ[port]
Cerale, Luigia 1859-1937 CnOxB
Cerato, Il NewGrD 80
Cerbus, Paul 1919- AmSCAP 66, -80
Cere, Edvige C AmSCAP 80
Cere, Mindie A 1910-1968 AmSCAP 66, -80
Ceremuga, Josef 1930- Baker 78
Cererols, Joan 1618-1676 Baker 78, NewGrD 80
Ceresini, Giovanni 1584-1659? NewGrD 80
Cerf, Bennett 1898- BiE&WWA, PlP&P
Cerha, Friedrich 1926- Baker 78, DcCM, NewGrD 80
Cerilli, Francisco NewGrD 80
Cerito, Ada WhThe
Cerito, Fanny 1817-1909 DancEn 78
Cermak, Jan Frantisek 1923- IntWWM 77
Cernauskas, Kathryn Birute 1948- IntWWM 77, -80
Cerney, Todd David 1953- AmSCAP 80
Cernik, Josef 1880-1969 NewGrD 80
Cernohorsky, Bohuslav 1684-1742 Baker 78, NewGrD 80, OxMus
Cernusak, Gracian 1882-1961 Baker 78, NewGrD 80
Cerny, Berthe WhThe
Cerny, Jaromir 1939- NewGrD 80
Cerny, Jiri NewGrD 80
Cerny, Ladislav 1891-1975 Baker 78, NewGrD 80
Cerny, Miroslav K 1924- NewGrD 80
Cerny, William Joseph 1928- IntWWM 77, -80
Ceroli, Nick 1939- AmSCAP 80, BiDAmM, EncJzS 70
Cerone, Domenico Pietro 1566?-1625 Baker 78
Cerone, Pietro 1566-1625 NewGrD 80
Cerqueira, Juan De NewGrD 80
Cerquetti, Anita 1931- CmOp
Cerrato, Scipione 1551?-1633? NewGrD 80
Cerreto, Scipione 1551-1632? Baker 78
Cerri, Cacilie 1872-1931 CnOxB
Cerrito, Fanny 1817-1909 CnOxB, NewGrD 80
Cerrito, Fanny 1821-1899 NotNAT B
Certon, Pierre 1510?-1572 Baker 78, NewGrD 80, OxMus
Ceruti, Giovanni Baptista 1755?-1817? NewGrD 80
Ceruti, Roque 1683?-1760 NewGrD 80
Cervantes 1547-1616 OxMus
Cervantes, A J ConMuA 80B
Cervantes, Ignacio 1847-1905 Baker 78, NewGrD 80
Cervantes, Miguel De 1547-1616 CnThe, McGEWD[port], NewEOp 71, NewGrD 80, REnWD[port]
Cervantes Saavedra, Miguel De 1547-1616 DcPup, EncWT, Ent, NotNAT B, OxThe
Cerveau, Pierre NewGrD 80
Cervello, Jorge 1935- NewGrD 80
Cervena, Sona WhoOp 76
Cervenka, Jan WhoMus 72
Cervenkova, Thea WomWMM
Cerveny, Vaclav Frantisek 1819-1896 NewGrD 80
Cerveny, Wenzel Franz 1819-1896 Baker 78
Cervera, Juan Francisco 1575?- NewGrD 80
Cervetti, Sergio 1940- Baker 78, ConAmC, IntWWM 80
Cervetti, Sergio 1941- DcCM, NewGrD 80
Cervetto, Giacobbe Basevi 1682?-1783 NewGrD 80
Cervetto, Giacomo 1682?-1783 Baker 78
Cervetto, James 1747?-1837 NewGrD 80
Cervi, Gino 1901-1974 EncWT, Ent, FilmAG WE, FilmEn, FilmgC, ForYSC, HalFC 80, MovMk, OxFilm, WhScrn 77, WhoHol B
Cervin, Helle 1943- IntWWM 77, -80
Cervin, Henrik 1934- IntWWM 77, -80
Cervo, Barnaba NewGrD 80
Cervo, Elda 1933- WhoOp 76
Cervone, D Donald 1932- ConAmC
Cesaire, Aime 1913- CnMD, CroCD, EncWT, REnWD[port]
Cesana, Bartolomeo Mutis, Count of NewGrD 80
Cesana, Otto 1899- AmSCAP 80, Baker 78, ConAmC A
Cesana, Otto 1905- AmSCAP 66
Cesana, Renzo 1907-1970 WhScrn 74, -77, WhoHol B
Cesana, Renzo 1917- AmSCAP 66, -80
Cesar, M d1921 WhScrn 74, -77
Cesare, Gian Martino 1590?-1667 NewGrD 80
Cesare, Giovanni Martino 1590?-1667 NewGrD 80
Cesari, Gaetano 1870-1934 Baker 78, NewGrD 80
Cesarini, Carlo Francesco 1664?-1730? NewGrD 80
Cesario, Victor Louis 1931- AmSCAP 80
Cesaris, Johannes NewGrD 80
Cesena, Giovanni Battista NewGrD 80
Cesena, Peregrinus NewGrD 80
Cesi, Beniamino 1845-1907 Baker 78
Cesi, Pietro NewGrD 80
Cesis, Sulpitia NewGrD 80
Cesti, Antonio 1623?-1669 NewGrD 80
Cesti, Marc' Antonio 1623-1669 Baker 78, NewEOp 71
Cesti, Marc'Antonio 1623-1669 GrComp
Cesti, Marcantonio 1623-1669 OxMus
Cesti, Pietro Antonio 1623-1669 BnBkM 80, CmOp, MusMk, NewGrD 80
Cesti, Remigio 1635?-1717? NewGrD 80
Ceuallos, Rodrigo De NewGrD 80
Ceulemans, Yvon Constant Jean 1905- IntWWM 77, -80
Cevallos, Francisco De NewGrD 80
Cevenini, Camillo 1607?-1676 NewGrD 80
Cevetillo, Lou 1945- ConAmTC
Cezar, Corneliu 1937- Baker 78, IntWWM 80
Chabanceau DeLaBarre NewGrD 80
Chabanon, Michel-Paul-Guy De 1729?-1792 NewGrD 80
Chabot, Cecile 1907- CreCan 1
Chaboukiani, Vakhtang Mikhailovich 1910- CnOxB
Chabran, Carlo Francesco NewGrD 80
Chabran, Gaetano NewGrD 80
Chabrier, Alexis Emmanuel 1841-1894 CnOxB, DancEn 78
Chabrier, Emanuel 1841-1894 DcCom&M 79
Chabrier, Emmanuel 1841-1894 Baker 78, BnBkM 80, CmOp, CmpBCM, DcCom 77, GrComp[port], MusMk, NewEOp 71, NewGrD 80[port], OxMus
Chabrier, Marcel 1888-1946 WhScrn 74, -77
Chabrol, Claude 1930- BiDFilm, -81, ConLC 16, DcFM, FilmEn, FilmgC, HalFC 80, IntMPA 77, -75, -76, -78, -79, -80, MovMk[port], OxFilm, WorEFlm[port]
Chabukiani, Vakhtang 1910- DancEn 78[port]
Chachkes, Maurice 1907-1964 AmSCAP 80
Chacksfield, Frank IntWWM 77, -80, WhoMus 72
Chad And Jeremy BiDAmM, ConMuA 80A, RkOn 2[port]
Chadabe, Joel 1938- AmSCAP 80, CpmDNM 75, ConAmC
Chadbon, Tom 1946- WhoThe 72, -77
Chadwick, Clive Film 2
Chadwick, Cyril Film 2, ForYSC, TwYS
Chadwick, Eric 1928- IntWWM 77, -80, WhoMus 72
Chadwick, Florence 1918- What 5[port]
Chadwick, George 1854-1931 CompSN[port]
Chadwick, George Whitefield 1854-1931 Baker 78, BnBkM 80, NewGrD 80, OxMus
Chadwick, George Whitfield 1854-1931 BiDAmM
Chadwick, Helene 1897-1940 FilmEn, Film 1, -2, MotPP, TwYS, WhScrn 74, -77, WhoHol B
Chadwick, John White 1840-1904 BiDAmM
Chaffe, John 1939- NewOrJ SUP[port]

Chaffee, George *CnOxB, DancEn 78*
Chaffee, Joan *WomWMM B*
Chaffey, Don 1917- *FilmEn, FilmgC, HalFC 80, IIWWBF, IntMPA 77, -78, -79, -80, WhoHrs 80*
Chaffin, Lucien Gates 1846-1927 *Baker 78*
Chagall, Marc 1887- *CnOxB, DancEn 78, EncWT*
Chagnon, Jack *Film 1*
Chagoll, Lydia 1931- *CnOxB*
Chagrin, Francis 1905-1972 *FilmgC, HalFC 80, NewGrD 80, WhoMus 72*
Chagrin, Julian 1940- *WhoThe 72, -77*
Chahin, Myra 1946- *IntWWM 77, -80*
Chai, Nakyong Tjong 1933- *IntWWM 77, -80*
Chaikin, Joseph 1935- *EncWT, Ent, NotNAT, WhoThe 77*
Chaikin, Jules 1934- *AmSCAP 80*
Chaikin, William E 1919- *IntMPA 77, -75, -76, -78, -79, -80*
Chaikovsky *Baker 78*
Chaikovsky, Boris Alexandrovich 1925- *DcCM, IntWWM 77, -80*
Chaikovsky, Pyotr Il'yich *NewGrD 80*
Chailley, Jacques 1910- *Baker 78, IntWWM 80, NewGrD 80, WhoMus 72*
Chaillou De Pesstain d1336? *NewGrD 80*
Chailly, Luciano 1920- *Baker 78, IntWWM 77, -80, NewGrD 80, WhoOp 76*
Chailly, Riccardo 1953- *IntWWM 80, WhoOp 76*
Chain, Leslie *AmSCAP 80*
Chaine, Pierre *WhThe*
Chaires, Nestor d1971 *WhoHol B*
Chairmen Of The Board, The *RkOn 2[port]*
Chaitkin, David 1938- *AmSCAP 80, CpmDNM 80, ConAmC*
Chaix, Charles 1885-1973 *Baker 78*
Chajes, Julius 1910- *AmSCAP 66, -80, Baker 78, BiDAmM, ConAmC*
Chakachas *RkOn 2A*
Chakeres, Michael H *IntMPA 77, -75, -76, -78, -79, -80*
Chakiris, George *MotPP, WhoHol A*
Chakiris, George 1933- *FilmEn, FilmgC, ForYSC, HalFC 80*
Chakiris, George 1934- *IntMPA 77, -75, -76, -78, -79, -80, MovMk*
Chakmakjian, Alan *NewGrD 80*
Chakolouny *Film 2*
Chalabala, Zdenek 1899-1962 *NewGrD 80*
Chalayev, Shirvani 1936- *NewGrD 80*
Chaliapin, Fedor, Jr. *Film 2*
Chaliapin, Feodor 1873-1938 *Baker 78, BnBkM 80[port], CmOp, FilmgC, HalFC 80, MusMk, MusSN[port], NewEOp 71, OxFilm, OxMus, WhScrn 74, -77, WhoHol B*
Chaliapin, Fyodor Ivanovich *NewGrD 80*
Chalif, Louis H 1876-1948 *CnOxB, DancEn 78*
Chalk, Sarah Slay 1935- *AmSCAP 80*
Challee, William 1912- *Vers A[port], WhoHol A*
Challen *NewGrD 80*
Challen, Charles H *NewGrD 80*
Challener, Frederick Sproston 1869-1959 *CreCan 1*
Challenger, Percy *Film 1, -2*
Challenger, Rudy 1928- *DrBlPA*
Challenor, Bromley 1884-1935 *WhThe*
Challier *NewGrD 80*
Challier, Carl August d1871 *NewGrD 80*
Challier, Ernest 1843-1914 *NewGrD 80*
Challier, Willibald 1849-1926 *NewGrD 80*
Challis, Bill 1904- *CmpEPM, WhoJazz 72*
Challis, Christopher 1919- *FilmEn, FilmgC, HalFC 80, WorEFlm[port]*
Challis, Eileen Mary *WhoMus 72*
Challis, John 1907-1974 *NewGrD 80*
Challis, Philip *WhoMus 72*
Challoner, Neville Butler 1784-1835? *NewGrD 80*
Challupper, Joseph 1911- *IntWWM 77, -80*
Chalmers, Bruce Abernethy 1915- *WhoOp 76*
Chalmers, Patrick 1940- *IntMPA 80*
Chalmers, Thomas 1884-1966 *BiE&WWA, NotNAT B*
Chalmers, Thomas 1890-1966 *Film 2, WhScrn 74, -77, WhoHol B*
Chaloff, Serge 1923-1957 *CmpEPM, IlEncJ, NewGrD 80*
Chalon, Alfred Edouard 1780-1860 *CnOxB*
Chalzel, Leo 1901-1953 *NotNAT B, WhScrn 74, -77, WhThe, WhoHol B*
Chamatero, Hippolito 1535?-1592? *NewGrD 80*
Chamatero, Ippolito 1535?-1592? *NewGrD 80*
Chamattero Di Negri, Hippolito 1535?-1592? *NewGrD 80*
Chamattero Di Negri, Ippolito 1535?-1592? *NewGrD 80*
Chamberlain, Cyril 1909- *FilmgC, HalFC 80*
Chamberlain, David Wayne 1944- *AmSCAP 80*
Chamberlain, George 1891- *WhThe*
Chamberlain, Houston Stewart 1855-1927 *Baker 78, NewGrD 80*
Chamberlain, Howland *WhoHol A*
Chamberlain, Richard 1935- *FilmEn, FilmgC, ForYSC, HalFC 80, IntMPA 77, -75, -76, -78, -79, -80, MotPP, MovMk[port], RkOn, WhoHol A, WhoThe 77*
Chamberlain, Roy S 1907- *AmSCAP 66, -80*
Chamberland, Paul 1939- *CreCan 2*
Chamberlin, Frank 1870-1935 *WhScrn 74, -77*
Chamberlin, Ione 1880- *WhoStg 1908*
Chamberlin, Riley C 1854-1917 *WhScrn 77, WhoHol B*
Chamberlin, Ward B, Jr. *NewYTET*
Chamberlin, William Francis 1939- *ConAmC*
Chambers, C Haddon 1860-1921 *WhoStg 1908*
Chambers, Charles Haddon 1860-1921 *NotNAT B, WhThe*
Chambers, Colin 1933- *IntWWM 80, WhoMus 72*
Chambers, Elmer 1897-1952 *WhoJazz 72*
Chambers, Emma *WhThe*
Chambers, Ernest A 1928- *AmSCAP 66, -80*
Chambers, Everett 1926- *IntMPA 77, -75, -76, -78, -79, -80, NewYTET*
Chambers, H Kellett 1867-1935 *WhThe*
Chambers, Haddon 1861- *WhoStg 1906*
Chambers, Henderson Charles 1908-1967 *BiDAmM, EncJzS 70, WhoJazz 72*
Chambers, Henry Alban 1902- *WhoMus 72*
Chambers, Henry Kellett 1867-1935 *NotNAT B*
Chambers, J Wheaton 1888-1958 *WhScrn 74, -77*
Chambers, Jack *CreCan 2*
Chambers, Jane *NatPD[port]*
Chambers, Joe 1942- *EncJzS 70, IntWWM 77*
Chambers, John 1924- *WhoHrs 80*
Chambers, John 1931- *CreCan 2*
Chambers, John 1936- *WhoMus 72*
Chambers, Joseph Arthur 1942- *BiDAmM, ConAmC, EncJzS 70*
Chambers, Kathleen *Film 2*
Chambers, Kellett 1867-1935 *WhoStg 1906, -1908*
Chambers, Lyster d1947 *NotNAT B*
Chambers, Margaret d1965 *Film 2, WhScrn 74, -77, WhoHol B*
Chambers, Marie 1889-1933 *Film 1, -2, WhScrn 74, -77, WhoHol B*
Chambers, Marilyn *WhoHol A*
Chambers, Martin 1944- *WhoOp 76*
Chambers, Norma d1953 *NotNAT B*
Chambers, Paul Laurence Dunbar, Jr. 1935-1969 *BiDAmM, EncJzS 70*
Chambers, Ralph 1892-1968 *NotNAT B, WhScrn 77, WhoHol B*
Chambers, Robert 1802-1871 *DcPup*
Chambers, Stephen A 1940- *Baker 78, BiDAmM, ConAmC*
Chambers, Tig 1880?-1950 *NewOrJ*
Chambers, Wheaton 1888-1958 *WhoHol B*
Chambers, William 1910- *BiE&WWA, NotNAT*
Chambers Brothers, The *BiDAmM, ConMuA 80A, RkOn 2[port]*
Chamblee, James Monroe 1935- *IntWWM 80*
Chambonnieres, Jacques 1602-1672? *MusMk*
Chambonnieres, Jacques Champion 1601?-1672 *Baker 78, NewGrD 80*
Chambonnieres, Jacques Champion De 1602?-1672 *BnBkM 80, OxMus*
Chambray, Louis Francois, Marquis of 1737-1807 *NewGrD 80*
Chamie, Tatiana *CnOxB*
Chamier, Francis *Film 1*
Chaminade, Cecile 1857-1944 *Baker 78, BnBkM 80, DcCom&M 79, MusMk, NewGrD 80, OxMus*
Chamlee, Mario 1892-1966 *Baker 78*
Chamlee, Mario 1892-1967 *BiDAmM*
Chamlee, Ruth Miller *WhoMus 72*
Champagne, Claude 1891-1965 *Baker 78, CreCan 2, DcCM, NewGrD 80*
Champagne, Gilles Maurice Herve 1929- *IntWWM 77*
Champagne Charlie *OxThe*
Champein, Stanislas 1753-1830 *Baker 78, NewGrD 80*
Champion *NewGrD 80*
Champion, George *Film 1*
Champion, Gower *DancEn 78, IntMPA 75, -76, MotPP*
Champion, Gower 1920- *CnOxB, EncMT, WhoThe 72, -77*
Champion, Gower 1921- *BiE&WWA, CmMov, FilmgC, ForYSC, HalFC 80, IntMPA 77, -78, -79, -80, MGM[port], MovMk, NotNAT, WhoHol A, WorEFlm[port]*
Champion, Gower 1921-1980 *FilmEn*
Champion, Harry 1866-1942 *Ent[port], NotNAT B, OxThe, WhThe*
Champion, Jacques *Baker 78, NewGrD 80*
Champion, Jacques d1535? *NewGrD 80*
Champion, Jacques 1555?-1642 *NewGrD 80*
Champion, Jehan-Nicolas 1620?-1662? *NewGrD 80*
Champion, John C 1923- *IntMPA 77, -75, -76, -78, -79, -80*
Champion, Marge *DancEn 78, IntMPA 77, -75, -76, -78, -79, -80, MotPP*
Champion, Marge 1919- *WhoHol A*
Champion, Marge 1921- *FilmEn*
Champion, Marge 1923- *CmMov, FilmgC, HalFC 80, MGM[port], MovMk*
Champion, Marge 1925- *BiE&WWA, ForYSC, NotNAT*
Champion, Nicolas *NewGrD 80*
Champion, Nicolas 1620?-1662? *NewGrD 80*
Champion, Thomas d1580? *NewGrD 80*
Champions *MotPP*
Champlain, Yves *FilmEn*
Champlin, Charles D 1926- *IntMPA 77, -75, -76, -78, -79, -80*
Champlin, E E *PupTheA*
Champlin, John Denison 1834-1915 *BiDAmM*
Champlin, William Bradford 1947- *AmSCAP 80*
Champmesle, Charles Chevillet 1642-1701 *EncWT, Ent, NotNAT B, OxThe*
Champmesle, Marie Desmares 1642-1698 *EncWT, Ent, NotNAT B, OxThe*
Champnes, Samuel 1732?-1803 *NewGrD 80*
Champness, Samuel 1732?-1803 *NewGrD 80*
Champneys, Samuel 1732?-1803 *NewGrD 80*
Champs, The *RkOn*
Chan, Mary Elizabeth 1940- *IntWWM 80*
Chan, Oie d1967 *WhoHol B*
Chan, Mrs. Pon Y 1870-1958 *WhScrn 74, -77*
Chan, Timothy Tai-Wah 1945- *IntWWM 77, -80*
Chance, Anna 1884-1943 *WhScrn 74, -77, WhoHol B*
Chance, David *AmSCAP 80*
Chance, Frank 1879-1924 *WhScrn 77*
Chance, John Barnes 1932-1972 *AmSCAP 80, CpmDNM 72, ConAmC*
Chance, Josephine LaRue 1920- *IntWWM 77*
Chance, Larry *ForYSC*
Chance, Nancy Laird 1931- *AmSCAP 80, CpmDNM 75, -76, -78, ConAmC, IntWWM 77, -80*
Chance, Naomi 1930-1964 *FilmgC, ForYSC, HalFC 80, IIWWBF, WhoHol B*
Chancellor, Betty *WhThe*
Chancellor, John 1927- *IntMPA 77, -76, -78, -79, -80, NewYTET*
Chancellor, Joyce 1906- *WhThe*
Chancerel, Leon Louis 1886-1965 *EncWT, OxThe*
Chancy, Francois De d1656 *NewGrD 80*
Chandler, Anna 1887-1957 *WhScrn 74, -77, WhoHol B*
Chandler, Chick 1905- *FilmEn, FilmgC, ForYSC, HalFC 80, IntMPA 77, -75, -76, -78, -79, -80, MovMk, WhoHol A*
Chandler, Dede 1866?-1925 *NewOrJ*

Chandler, Edward *Film 2*
Chandler, Gene 1937- *AmPS A, RkOn*
Chandler, George *MotPP*
Chandler, George 1902- *FilmEn, Film 2, FilmgC, ForYSC, HalFC 80, HolCA[port], TwYS, Vers A[port], WhoHol A*
Chandler, George 1905- *MovMk*
Chandler, Helen 1906-1965 *FilmEn, HolP 30[port], ThFT[port], WhScrn 74, –77, WhoHol B, WhoHrs 80*
Chandler, Helen 1909-1965 *BiE&WWA, Film 2, ForYSC, NotNAT B, WhThe*
Chandler, Helen 1909-1968 *FilmgC, HalFC 80, MovMk*
Chandler, James *WhoHol A*
Chandler, James Robert 1860-1950 *WhScrn 74, –77, WhoHol B*
Chandler, Jeff 1918-1961 *AmSCAP 66, –80, BiDFilm, –81, CmMov, FilmEn, FilmgC, ForYSC, HalFC 80, MotPP, MovMk[port], NotNAT B, OxFilm, WhScrn 74, –77, WhoHol B, WorEFlm[port]*
Chandler, John Davis 1937- *FilmgC, HalFC 80, WhoHol A*
Chandler, Karen *AmPS A, CmpEPM*
Chandler, Lane 1899-1972 *FilmEn, Film 2, ForYSC, TwYS, WhoHol B*
Chandler, Len 1935- *BiDAmM, EncFCWM 69*
Chandler, Mary 1911- *IntWWM 77, WhoMus 72*
Chandler, Mary 1912- *IntWWM 80*
Chandler, Mimi *WhoHol A*
Chandler, Pat 1922- *AmSCAP 66, –80*
Chandler, Raymond 1888-1959 *DcFM, FilmEn, FilmgC, HalFC 80, OxFilm, WorEFlm[port]*
Chandler, Raymond 1889-1962 *CmMov*
Chandler, S 1760- *BiDAmM*
Chandor, Henry *NewGrD 80*
Chandos, Duke Of 1673-1744 *OxMus*
Chandos, John *WhoHol A*
Chaney, Chubby 1918-1936 *WhoHol B*
Chaney, Frances *WhoHol A*
Chaney, Frances 1889-1967 *WhScrn 77*
Chaney, Harold *IntWWM 77, –80*
Chaney, Lon 1883-1930 *CmMov, FilmEn, Film 1, –2, FilmgC, HalFC 80, MotPP, MovMk[port], NotNAT B, TwYS, WhScrn 74, –77, WhoHol B, WhoHrs 80[port], WorEFlm[port]*
Chaney, Lon 1886-1930 *BiDFilm, –81, OxFilm*
Chaney, Lon, Jr. 1900-1973 *WhoHol B*
Chaney, Lon, Jr. 1905-1973 *WhScrn 77*
Chaney, Lon, Jr. 1906-1973 *FilmEn, FilmgC, HalFC 80[port], Vers A[port], WhoHrs 80[port]*
Chaney, Lon, Jr. 1907-1973 *MovMk[port]*
Chaney, Lon, Jr. 1912-1973 *CmMov*
Chaney, Lon, Jr. 1915-1973 *ForYSC, OxFilm*
Chaney, Norman Chubby 1918-1936 *Film 2, WhScrn 74, –77*
Chaney, Stewart 1910-1969 *BiE&WWA, NotNAT B, PlP&P, WhThe*
Chanfrau, Mrs. F S 1837-1909 *NotNAT B*
Chanfrau, Francis S 1824-1884 *FamA&A[port], NotNAT B*
Chanfrau, Frank S 1824-1884 *OxThe*
Chanfrau, Henrietta Baker 1837-1909 *OxThe*
Chang And Eng 1811-1874 *Ent*
Chang, G Gordon 1951- *ConAmC*
Chang, King Hoo *Film 2*
Chang, Tisa *WhoHol A*
Chang, Wah 1925?- *WhoHrs 80*
Chang, Yung-Kai James 1947- *IntWWM 80*
Changar, Myra *WomWMM*
Changar, Myrna Harrison *WomWMM B*
Changas, Estelle *WomWMM B*
Chanler, Theodore Ward 1902-1961 *Baker 78, BiDAmM, ConAmC, DcCM, NewGrD 80*
Channel, Bruce *AmPS A, RkOn*
Channels, The *RkOn[port]*
Channey, Jean De 1480?-1540? *NewGrD 80*
Channing, Carol *AmPS B*
Channing, Carol 1921- *BiE&WWA, CmpEPM, EncMT, FamA&A[port], FilmEn, FilmgC, ForYSC, HalFC 80, JoeFr[port], MotPP, NotNAT, WhoHol A, WhoThe 72, –77*
Channing, Carol 1923- *BiDAmM*
Channing, Stockard *IntMPA 77, –78, –79, –80, WhoHol A*
Channing, Stockard 1944- *FilmEn*
Channon, Merlin 1924- *WhoMus 72*
Channon, Michael David Huddleston 1939- *IntWWM 77, –80*
Channon, Thomas *OxMus*
Chanot *NewGrD 80*
Chanot, Francois 1787-1823 *NewGrD 80*
Chanot, Francois 1788-1825 *Baker 78*
Chanot, Georges 1801-1873 *NewGrD 80*
Chanot, Georges 1831-1893 *NewGrD 80*
Chanot, Georges-Adolphe 1855-1911 *NewGrD 80*
Chanot, Joseph *NewGrD 80*
Chanot, Joseph-Anthony 1865-1936 *NewGrD 80*
Chansi, Francois De *NewGrD 80*
Chanslor, Roy d1964 *NotNAT B*
Chant, Michael H 1945- *DcCM*
Chantavoine, Jean 1877-1952 *Baker 78, NewGrD 80*
Chantays, The *RkOn*
Chantels, The *RkOn[port]*
Chanters, The *RkOn*
Chanticleer, Raven 1933- *DrBlPA*
Chantilly, Mademoiselle *NewGrD 80*
Chao, Mei-Pa 1907- *IntWWM 77*
Chao, Mel-Pa 1907- *WhoMus 72*
Chapdoill, Pons De *NewGrD 80*
Chapel, Eugenia d1964 *NotNAT B*
Chapelet, Francis 1934- *NewGrD 80*
Chapelle, Jacques DeLa *NewGrD 80*
Chapelle, Pola *WomWMM B*
Chapender, Martin 1876?-1905 *MagIlD*
Chapi, Ruperto 1851-1909 *NewGrD 80*
Chapi Y Lorente, Ruperto 1851-1909 *Baker 78*
Chapin, Alice 1858-1934 *Film 2, NotNAT B, WhScrn 77, WhoHol B*
Chapin, Amzi 1768-1835 *BiDAmM*
Chapin, Benjamin 1875-1918 *Film 1, WhScrn 77*
Chapin, Billy 1943- *ForYSC, HalFC 80*
Chapin, Edwin Hubbell 1814-1880 *BiDAmM*
Chapin, Harold 1886-1915 *CnMD, ModWD, NotNAT A, –B, WhThe*
Chapin, Harry 1942- *AmSCAP 80, ConMuA 80A, IlEncR, RkOn 2[port]*
Chapin, Jacques *Film 2*
Chapin, Louis LeBourgeois 1918- *ConAmTC, WhoThe 72, –77*
Chapin, Lucius 1760-1842 *BiDAmM*
Chapin, Michael *ForYSC*
Chapin, Schuyler Garrison 1923- *IntWWM 77, –80, WhoOp 76*
Chapin, Slocum 1913- *IntMPA 77, –75, –76, –78, –79, –80*
Chaplin, Alice *Film 2*
Chaplin, Charles 1889-1977 *AmFD, BiDFilm, –81, CmMov, ConLC 16, DcFM, FilmgC, Funs[port], HalFC 80[port], IntMPA 77, –75, –76, –78, MotPP, MovMk[port], OxFilm, WhThe, WhoHol A, WorEFlm[port]*
Chaplin, Charles, Jr. 1925-1968 *FilmEn, ForYSC, WhScrn 74, –77, WhoHol B*
Chaplin, Charles S 1911- *IntMPA 77, –75, –76, –78, –79, –80*
Chaplin, Charlie 1889-1977 *ConDr 73, –77A, FilmEn, Film 1, –2, ForYSC, GrMovC[port], JoeFr[port], TwYS, –A*
Chaplin, Geraldine 1944- *BiDFilm 81, FilmAG WE, FilmEn, FilmgC, ForYSC, HalFC 80, IntMPA 80, MotPP, WhoHol A*
Chaplin, Lita Grey 1908- *What 5[port]*
Chaplin, Marian Wood 1914- *AmSCAP 66, –80*
Chaplin, Mildred Harris *Film 2*
Chaplin, Saul 1912- *AmSCAP 66, –80, BestMus, BiDAmM, CmMov, CmpEPM, FilmEn, FilmgC, HalFC 80, IntMPA 77, –75, –76, –78, –79, –80, OxFilm*
Chaplin, Sidney 1885-1965 *Film 2*
Chaplin, Syd 1885-1965 *FilmEn, Film 1, –2, FilmgC, HalFC 80*
Chaplin, Sydney 1885-1965 *Film 2, MotPP, TwYS, WhScrn 74, –77, WhoHol B*
Chaplin, Sydney 1926- *BiE&WWA, EncMT, FilmEn, FilmgC, ForYSC, HalFC 80, MotPP, NotNAT, WhoHol A*
Chapman, Ben *WhoHrs 80*
Chapman, Blanche 1851-1941 *NotNAT B, WhScrn 74, –77, WhoHol B*
Chapman, Charles *Film 1*
Chapman, Christopher 1927- *CreCan 1*
Chapman, Clive 1930- *IntWWM 80*
Chapman, Constance 1912- *WhoThe 72, –77*
Chapman, Dianne Hughes 1942- *BlkWAB[port]*
Chapman, Edward 1901-1977 *FilmgC, HalFC 80, IlWWBF, MovMk, WhThe, WhoThe 72*
Chapman, Edward Thomas 1902- *WhoMus 72*
Chapman, Edythe 1863-1948 *FilmEn, Film 1, –2, ForYSC, NotNAT B, TwYS, WhScrn 74, –77, WhoHol B*
Chapman, Ernest Walter 1914- *IntWWM 77, –80, WhoMus 72*
Chapman, George 1559?-1634 *CnThe, EncWT, NotNAT B, OxMus, REnWD[port]*
Chapman, George 1560?-1634 *Ent[port], McGEWD[port], OxThe, PlP&P*
Chapman, Gilbert W 1902- *BiE&WWA*
Chapman, Henry 1822-1865 *NotNAT B*
Chapman, J Vincent *DcPup*
Chapman, Janice Lesley 1938- *WhoOp 76*
Chapman, John 1900-1972 *BiE&WWA, NotNAT B, WhoThe 72*
Chapman, John Peter Ford 1928- *IntWWM 80*
Chapman, John R 1927- *WhoThe 72, –77*
Chapman, Joyce 1909- *WhoMus 72*
Chapman, Leonard *Film 2*
Chapman, Lonny 1920- *BiE&WWA, NotNAT, WhoHol A*
Chapman, Louise 1938- *WhoMus 72*
Chapman, Marcia *Film 2*
Chapman, Marguerite *MotPP*
Chapman, Marguerite 1916- *FilmgC, HalFC 80, WhoHrs 80[port]*
Chapman, Marguerite 1920- *FilmEn, ForYSC, WhoHol A*
Chapman, Marguerite 1921- *HolP 40[port]*
Chapman, Mary Helen 1943- *IntWWM 77*
Chapman, Mercedes *PupTheA*
Chapman, Michael *IntMPA 80*
Chapman, Michael 1941- *IlEncR*
Chapman, Mike *ConMuA 80B*
Chapman, Ned *Film 1*
Chapman, Neil 1933- *IntWWM 77, –80*
Chapman, Paul Rutledge 1948- *IntWWM 77, –80*
Chapman, Richard *WhoHol A*
Chapman, Robert H 1919- *BiE&WWA, NotNAT*
Chapman, Roger E 1916- *ConAmC*
Chapman, Tedwell 1917- *IntMPA 77, –75, –76, –78, –79, –80*
Chapman, Thomas H 1896-1969 *WhScrn 74, –77*
Chapman, Walter Lynn 1913- *AmSCAP 66, –80*
Chapman, William *Film 2, WhoOp 76*
Chapman, William 1764-1839 *NotNAT B, OxThe*
Chapman, William 1850-1917 *CreCan 2*
Chapman, William Rogers 1855-1935 *Baker 78, BiDAmM*
Chapman Whitney *IlEncR*
Chappell *NewGrD 80*
Chappell, Annette 1929- *CnOxB, DancEn 78*
Chappell, Dorothy *Film 2*
Chappell, Frank *NewGrD 80*
Chappell, Herbert 1934- *ConAmC, IntWWM 77, –80*
Chappell, Ruth Ellison 1942- *IntWWM 80*
Chappell, S Arthur 1834-1904 *Baker 78*
Chappell, T Stanley d1933 *Baker 78*
Chappell, Thomas Patey 1819-1902 *Baker 78*
Chappell, William 1809-1888 *Baker 78, BnBkM 80, OxMus*
Chappell, William 1908- *CnOxB, DancEn 78, EncMT, WhoThe 72, –77*
Chappell And Company *Baker 78*
Chappelle, Frederick W 1895- *WhThe*
Chappelle, Kathleen 1898- *WhoMus 72*
Chapple, Stanley 1900- *Baker 78, IntWWM 77, –80, WhoMus 72*
Chapple, Wendy Wood *WomWMM A, –B*
Chappuzeau, Samuel 1625-1701 *OxThe*
Chapteul, Pons De *NewGrD 80*

Chapuis, Auguste 1858-1933 *Baker 78, NewGrD 80*
Chapuis, Auguste Paul Jean Baptiste 1868-1933 *OxMus*
Chapuis, Michel 1930- *BnBkM 80, NewGrD 80*
Char, Friedrich Ernst 1865-1932 *Baker 78*
Charalambous, Andreas 1940- *IntWWM 77, -80*
Charbeneau, Oscar d1915 *WhScrn 77*
Charbonneau, Christine 1944- *CreCan 1*
Charbonneau, Helene 1894- *CreCan 2*
Charbonneau, Jean 1875-1960 *CreCan 1*
Charbonneau, Robert 1911-1967 *CreCan 2*
Charbonnier, Pierre 1897- *FilmEn*
Chard, Geoffrey William 1930- *IntWWM 77, -80, WhoMus 72, WhoOp 76*
Chard, George William 1765-1849 *NewGrD 80*
Chardavoine, Jean 1538-1580? *NewGrD 80*
Chardavoine, Jehan 1538-1580? *NewGrD 80*
Chardavoyne, Jean 1538-1580? *NewGrD 80*
Chardavoyne, Jehan 1538-1580? *NewGrD 80*
Chardin, Louis Armand 1755-1793 *NewGrD 80*
Chardini, Louis Armand 1755-1793 *NewGrD 80*
Chardiny, Louis Armand 1755-1793 *NewGrD 80*
Chardon De Croisilles *NewGrD 80*
Chardon, Yves 1902- *CpmDNM 76, IntWWM 77, -80*
Charell, Erich 1895-1974 *FilmEn*
Charell, Erik 1895- *DcFM, WhThe*
Chari, V K N 1913- *IntMPA 77, -75, -76, -78, -79, -80*
Charig, Phil 1902-1960 *AmSCAP 66, -80, BiDAmM, NotNAT B*
Charig, Philip 1902-1960 *EncMT*
Charioteers, The *CmpEPM*
Charisse, Cyd *MotPP, WhoHol A*
Charisse, Cyd 1921- *BiDFilm, -81, FilmEn, FilmgC, HalFC 80, MGM[port]*
Charisse, Cyd 1922- *WorEFlm[port]*
Charisse, Cyd 1923- *CmMov, CnOxB, DancEn 78, ForYSC, IntMPA 77, -75, -76, -78, -79, -80, MovMk[port]*
Charisse, Cyd 1924- *OxFilm*
Charite *NewGrD 80*
Chariteo, Il *NewGrD 80*
Charity *AmSCAP 80*
Charity, Pernell 1920- *BluesWW[port]*
Charke, Richard 1709?-1737 *NewGrD 80*
Charkovsky, Willis 1918- *AmSCAP 66, -80, ConAmC A*
Charland, Ainse *Film 2*
Charland, Alme *Film 2*
Charlap, Mark *BiE&WWA*
Charlap, Morris 1928- *AmSCAP 66, -80*
Charlatans *ConMuA 80A*
Charle, Gustav *Film 2*
Charlemagne 742?-814 *DcPup*
Charlemagne 743-814 *OxMus*
Charlent, Gertie *WhoOp 76*
Charles 1705?- *NewGrD 80*
Charles I 1600-1649 *OxMus*
Charles II 1630-1685 *OxMus*
Charles V *NewGrD 80, OxMus*
Charles VI *OxMus*
Charles D'Argentille *NewGrD 80*
Charles V, King Of Spain 1500-1558 *OxMus*
Charles The Great *OxMus*
Charles, Arthur M *PupTheA*
Charles, Bobby *IlEncR*
Charles, Dick 1919- *AmSCAP 66, -80*
Charles, Ernest 1895- *AmSCAP 66, -80, Baker 78, BiDAmM, ConAmC, WhoMus 72*
Charles, Ezzard 1921- *What 2[port]*
Charles, Fred d1904 *NotNAT B*
Charles, Henry *BluesWW[port]*
Charles, Hippolyte 1891- *NewOrJ*
Charles, Jesse 1900-1975 *NewOrJ*
Charles, Jimmy 1942- *RkOn*
Charles, John *Film 1*
Charles, Lewis *WhoHol A*
Charles, Maria 1929- *IntMPA 77, -75, -76, -78, -79, -80*
Charles, Marta Evans *BlkAmP*
Charles, Marte Evans *MorBAP*
Charles, Michael d1967 *WhoHol B*
Charles, Morgan 1894-1958 *Ent*
Charles, Norman *MorBAP*
Charles, Norman 1935- *AmSCAP 80*
Charles, Pamela 1932- *WhoThe 72, -77*
Charles, Ray *AmPS A, -B, ConMuA 80A*
Charles, Ray 1918- *AmSCAP 66, -80, BiDAmM*
Charles, Ray 1930- *Baker 78, BiDAmM, BluesWW[port], DrBlPA, IlEncR[port], NewGrD 80, RkOn[port]*
Charles, Ray 1932- *EncJzS 70, IlEncJ*
Charles, Roosevelt 1919- *BiDAmM, EncFCWM 69*
Charles, Rosalind *Film 2*
Charles, S Robin 1951- *IntWWM 80*
Charles, Teddy 1928- *BiDAmM, CmpEPM, NewGrD 80*
Charles, Thomas *NewGrD 80*
Charleson, Leslie *WhoHol A*
Charleson, Mary 1885-1968 *Film 1, -2, TwYS*
Charleson, Mary 1893-1961 *MotPP, NotNAT B, WhScrn 77*
Charlesworth, Florence M 1885- *AmSCAP 66, -80*
Charlesworth, John 1935-1960 *FilmgC, HalFC 80, WhScrn 74, -77, WhoHol B*
Charlesworth, Marigold 1926- *CreCan 1*
Charley, John *Film 1*
Charlia, Georges *Film 2*
Charlier, Monsieur *Film 2*
Charlier, Gilles *NewGrD 80*
Charlier DeGerson, Jean *NewGrD 80*
Charlip, Remy 1929- *CmpGMD[port], CnOxB*
Charlita *WhoHol A*
Charloff, Aaron 1941- *IntWWM 80*
Charlot, Andre 1882-1956 *CnThe, EncMT, HalFC 80, NotNAT B, WhScrn 77, WhThe*
Charlton, Andrew 1928- *AmSCAP 80, ConAmC*
Charlton, Christopher H 1883-1963 *MagIlD*
Charlton, David 1946- *IntWWM 80*
Charlton, Harold C d1954 *NotNAT B*
Charlton, Maryette *WomWMM B*
Charlton, Melville 1883- *BiDAmM*
Charmoli, Tony *NewYTET*
Charms, The *RkOn*
Charnasse, Helene Renee 1926- *IntWWM 77, -80, NewGrD 80*
Charney, Kim *ForYSC*
Charnin, Martin 1934- *AmSCAP 66, -80, BiE&WWA, NewYTET, NotNAT, WhoThe 72, -77*
Charnley, Michael 1927- *CnOxB, DancEn 78*
Charny, Suzanne *WhoHol A*
Charon, Jacques 1920-1975 *EncWT, Ent, PlP&P, WhScrn 77, WhoHol C*
Charpentier *NewGrD 80*
Charpentier, Gabriel 1925- *CreCan 2, NewGrD 80*
Charpentier, Gaston L G 1912- *IntMPA 77, -75, -76, -78, -79, -80*
Charpentier, Gustave 1860-1956 *Baker 78, BnBkM 80, CmOp, CompSN[port], DcCom&M 79, MusMk, NewEOp 71, NewGrD 80, NotNAT B, OxMus*
Charpentier, Jacques 1933- *Baker 78, CpmDNM 80, NewGrD 80*
Charpentier, Marc-Antoine 1634-1704 *BnBkM 80, GrComp, MusMk, NewEOp 71*
Charpentier, Marc-Antoine 1636?-1704 *Baker 78, OxMus*
Charpentier, Marc-Antoine 1645?-1704 *NewGrD 80*
Charpentier, Raymond 1880-1960 *Baker 78, NewGrD 80*
Charpin, Fernand 1887-1944 *OxFilm*
Charrat, Janine 1924- *CnOxB, DancEn 78[port]*
Charrel, Erik 1894-1974 *HalFC 80*
Charrell, Erik 1895- *WorEFlm[port]*
Charren, Peggy *NewYTET*
Charrier, Jacques 1936- *FilmAG WE, FilmEn, WhoHol A*
Charriere, Henri 1907-1973 *WhScrn 77*
Charry, Michael 1933- *IntWWM 77, -80, WhoOp 76*
Charsky, Boris 1893-1956 *Film 2, WhScrn 74, -77, WhoHol B*
Chart, Henry Nye 1868-1934 *WhThe*
Charteris, Leslie 1907- *FilmgC, HalFC 80, IntMPA 77, -75, -76, -78, -79, -80*
Charteris, Richard 1948- *IntWWM 77, -80*
Charters, Murray R 1943- *IntWWM 77, -80*
Charters, Spencer d1943 *ForYSC*
Charters, Spencer 1875-1943 *FilmEn, HolCA[port], NotNAT B, Vers B[port], WhScrn 74, -77, WhoHol B*
Charters, Spencer 1878-1943 *Film 2, FilmgC, HalFC 80, MovMk*
Chartoff, Robert *FilmEn, IntMPA 77, -75, -76, -78, -79, -80*
Charton-Demeur, Anne 1824-1892 *NewGrD 80*
Charton-Demeur, Arsene 1824-1892 *NewGrD 80*
Chartrain, Nicolas-Joseph 1740?-1793 *NewGrD 80*
Charts, The *RkOn*
Charvay, Robert 1858- *WhThe*
Charvein, Denise *WomWMM*
Charvet, Jehan *NewGrD 80*
Chase, Albert *Film 2*
Chase, Alida 1951- *CnOxB*
Chase, Allen *CpmDNM 74, ConAmC*
Chase, Annazette *DrBlPA*
Chase, Arline 1900-1926 *WhScrn 74, -77, WhoHol B*
Chase, Barrie *FilmEn*
Chase, Barrie 1934- *ForYSC, WhoHol A*
Chase, Bill 1935-1974 *EncJzS 70*
Chase, Borden *CmMov*
Chase, Borden 1899?-1971 *FilmgC, HalFC 80*
Chase, Borden 1900-1971 *FilmEn, WorEFlm[port]*
Chase, Brandon *IntMPA 77, -75, -76, -78, -79, -80*
Chase, Bud *Film 1*
Chase, Charley 1893-1940 *Funs[port], GrMovC[port], JoeFr[port], MotPP, OxFilm, TwYS, WhScrn 74, -77, WhoHol B, WhoHrs 80, WorEFlm[port]*
Chase, Charley 1893-1961 *ForYSC*
Chase, Charlie 1893-1940 *FilmEn, Film 1, -2, FilmgC, HalFC 80*
Chase, Chevy 1949- *HalFC 80, IntMPA 79, -80, NewYTET*
Chase, Colin 1886-1937 *Film 2, WhScrn 74, -77, WhoHol B*
Chase, Doris Totten 1923- *WomWMM B*
Chase, Edna 1888- *WhoStg 1906, -1908*
Chase, George Washington 1890-1918 *WhScrn 77*
Chase, Gilbert 1906- *Baker 78, NewGrD 80*
Chase, Hal 1883-1947 *WhScrn 77*
Chase, Ilka d1978 *BiE&WWA, MotPP, NotNAT*
Chase, Ilka 1900-1978 *FamA&A[port], FilmgC, HalFC 80*
Chase, Ilka 1903-1978 *FilmEn, ThFT[port]*
Chase, Ilka 1905-1978 *Film 2, ForYSC, IntMPA 77, -75, -76, -78, -79, -80, MovMk, NotNAT A, WhoHol A, WhoThe 72, -77*
Chase, J Newell 1904-1955 *AmSCAP 66, -80*
Chase, James Hadley 1906- *HalFC 80*
Chase, Joseph Russell 1922- *IntWWM 77, -80*
Chase, Lucia 1907- *CnOxB, DancEn 78[port]*
Chase, Marian *AmPS B*
Chase, Mary 1907- *BiE&WWA, CnMD, ConDr 73, -77, EncWT, McGEWD, ModWD, NotNAT, PlP&P, WhoThe 77*
Chase, Newell 1904-1955 *ConAmC A*
Chase, Pauline 1885-1962 *NotNAT B, WhThe, WhoStg 1908*
Chase, Ronald 1934- *WhoOp 76*
Chase, Samuel *NewOrJ*
Chase, Stanley 1928- *BiE&WWA, NotNAT*
Chase, Stephanie Ann 1957- *IntWWM 77, -80*
Chase, Stephen *WhoHol A*
Chase, Todd *ConMuA 80B*
Chase, William B d1948 *NotNAT B*
Chaseman, Joel 1926- *IntMPA 80, NewYTET*
Chasen, Dave 1899-1973 *WhScrn 77*
Chasen, Heather 1927- *WhoThe 72, -77*
Chasey, Leslie Arthur John 1912- *WhoMus 72*
Chasins, Abram 1903- *AmSCAP 66, -80, Baker 78, BiDAmM, ConAmC, IntWWM 77, -80, NewGrD 80, OxMus, WhoMus 72*
Chasman, David 1925- *IntMPA 77, -75, -76, -78, -79, -80*

Chassa *NewGrD 80*
Chastain, Don *WhoHol A*
Chastain, Tilfer Earl 1923- *AmSCAP 80*
Chastelain De Couci 1165?-1203 *NewGrD 80*
Chastelain, Jean 1490?-1578 *NewGrD 80*
Chasteleyn, Jean *NewGrD 80*
Chastellain, Jean *NewGrD 80*
Chastillon, Guillaume De 1550?-1610 *NewGrD 80*
Chateauclair, Wilfred *CreCan 2*
Chateauminors, Alphonse *OxMus*
Chatelain, Didier *IntMPA 78, -79, -80*
Chatelet, Jean Guyot De *NewGrD 80*
Chater, Geoffrey 1921- *WhoThe 72, -77*
Chatfield, Philip 1927- *CnOxB, DancEn 78*
Chatham, Pitt d1923 *NotNAT B*
Chatham, Rhys *ConAmC*
Chatkin, Stanley A 1928- *IntMPA 75*
Chatman, Bo *BluesWW[port]*
Chatman, Peter 1915- *BiDAmM, BluesWW[port]*
Chatman, Sam *BluesWW[port]*
Chatman, Stephen 1950- *ConAmC*
Chatmon, Armenter 1893-1964 *BluesWW[port]*
Chatmon, Sam 1897- *BluesWW[port]*
Chatrian, Louis Gratien C Alexandre 1826-1890 *NotNAT B*
Chattaway, Jay A 1946- *AmSCAP 80*
Chattaway, Thurland 1872-1947 *AmSCAP 66, -80, CmpEPM*
Chatterjee, Pabitra Narayan 1918- *IntWWM 77, -80*
Chatterton, Ruth 1893-1961 *BiDFilm, -81, CmMov, FilmEn, Film 2, FilmgC, HalFC 80, MotPP, MovMk[port], NotNAT B, ThFT[port], WhScrn 74, -77, WhThe, WhoHol B, WomWMM*
Chatterton, Ruth 1894-1961 *ForYSC*
Chatterton, Thomas 1881-1952 *Film 1, WhScrn 74, -77, WhoHol B*
Chatton, Sydney 1918-1966 *WhScrn 74, -77, WhoHol B*
Chatwin, Margaret d1937 *WhThe*
Chatzidakis, Manos 1925- *IntWWM 77, -80*
Chaucer, Geoffrey 1340?-1400 *DcPup, NewEOp 71, OxMus*
Chaucer, Geoffrey 1343?-1400 *NewGrD 80*
Chaudet, Louis 1884- *TwYS A*
Chaudet, Mary 1920- *AmSCAP 66, -80*
Chaudhri, Amin Qamar 1936- *IntMPA 80*
Chaudhri, Amin Qamar 1938- *IntMPA 77, -75, -76, -78, -79*
Chaumet, William 1842-1903 *Baker 78*
Chaumont, Celine d1926 *NotNAT B*
Chaumont, Lambert 1630?-1712 *NewGrD 80*
Chaumont, Segundo 1871-1929 *FilmEn*
Chaun, Frantisek 1921- *Baker 78, IntWWM 77, -80, NewGrD 80*
Chauncey, Anthony *MorBAP*
Chauncey, Harrell Cordell *MorBAP*
Chaussat, Genevieve 1941- *CnOxB*
Chausson, Ernest 1855-1899 *Baker 78, BnBkM 80, CmpBCM, CnOxB, DancEn 78, DcCom 77, DcCom&M 79, GrComp[port], MusMk, NewGrD 80[port], OxMus*
Chautard, Emile 1881-1934 *DcFM, FilmEn, Film 1, -2, ForYSC, TwYS, WhScrn 74, -77, WhoHol B*
Chautard, Emile 1892-1964 *TwYS A*
Chauvel, Charles E 1897-1959 *FilmgC, HalFC 80, OxFilm, WhScrn 74, -77*
Chauvenet, Virginia d1949 *NotNAT B*
Chauvet, Charles-Alexis 1837-1871 *Baker 78*
Chauvet, Guy-Jacques 1933- *NewGrD 80, WhoOp 76*
Chauvin, Lilyan *WhoHol A*
Chauvin, Louis 1883-1908 *BiDAmM*
Chauvire, Yvette 1917- *CnOxB, DancEn 78[port]*
Chauvon, Francois *NewGrD 80*
Chavanne, Irene Von 1868-1938 *Baker 78*
Chavarri *NewGrD 80*
Chavarri, Eduardo Lopez 1871-1970 *Baker 78*
Chavarria *NewGrD 80*
Chavez, Carlos 1899-1978 *AmSCAP 66, -80, Baker 78, BnBkM 80, CompSN[port], CpmDNM 75, DancEn 78, DcCom&M 79, DcCM, IntWWM 77, -80, MusMk, NewGrD 80[port], OxMus, WhoMus 72*
Chavez, Edmund M 1926- *NotNAT*
Chaycesel, Hubert *NewGrD 80*
Chayefsky, Paddy 1923- *AmSCAP 66, -80, BiE&WWA, CnMD, CnThe, ConDr 73, -77, CroCD, DcFM, DcLB 7[port], EncWT, FilmEn, IntMPA 77, -75, -76, -78, -79, -80, McGEWD, ModWD, NotNAT, OxFilm, PlP&P, WhoThe 72, -77, WorEFlm[port]*
Chayevsky, Paddy 1923- *FilmgC, HalFC 80, NewYTET*
Chaykovsky, Boris Alexandrovich 1925- *NewGrD 80*
Chaykovsky, Pytor Il'yich *NewGrD 80*
Chaynee, Jean De 1540?-1577 *NewGrD 80*
Chaynes, Charles 1925- *Baker 78*
Chazanoff, Daniel 1923- *IntWWM 77, -80*
Cheadle, William George 1938- *IntWWM 77, -80*
Cheap Trick *ConMuA 80A[port]*
Cheatham, Adolphus Anthony 1905- *EncJzS 70*
Cheatham, Catharine Smiley 1864-1946 *BiDAmM*
Cheatham, Doc 1905- *CmpEPM, EncJzS 70, IlEncJ, WhoJazz 72*
Cheatham, Jack 1894-1971 *WhScrn 77*
Cheatham, Kitty d1946 *NotNAT B, WhoStg 1906, -1908*
Cheatle, Esther *PupTheA*
Chebat, Georges *Film 2*
Checchi, Andrea 1916-1974 *FilmAG WE, FilmEn, WhScrn 77, WhoHol B*
Checco, Al *WhoHol A*
Chechin *NewGrD 80*
Check, John Felix 1921- *AmSCAP 80*
Checker, Chubby 1941- *AmPS A, -B, AmSCAP 66, BiDAmM, ConMuA 80A, DrBlPA, FilmgC, HalFC 80, RkOn[port], WhoHol A*
Checker, Maurice John 1933- *IntWWM 77, -80*
Checkmates, Ltd, The *RkOn 2[port]*
Chedeville *NewGrD 80*
Chedeville, Esprit Philippe 1696-1762 *NewGrD 80, OxMus*
Chedeville, Nicholas 1705-1782 *OxMus*
Chedeville, Nicolas 1705-1782 *NewGrD 80*
Chedeville, Pierre 1694-1725 *NewGrD 80, OxMus*
Cheech And Chong *ConMuA 80A, IlEncR, JoeFr[port], RkOn 2[port]*
Cheers, The *RkOn*
Cheeseman, James Russell 1937- *AmSCAP 80*
Cheeseman, Peter 1932- *EncWT, WhoThe 72, -77*
Cheetham, John Everett 1939- *AmSCAP 80, CpmDNM 80, ConAmC, NewGrD 80*
Cheever, George Barrell 1807-1890 *BiDAmM*
Chef Milani 1892-1965 *WhScrn 77*
Chefe, Jack 1894-1975 *WhoHol C*
Chefee, Jack 1894-1975 *Film 2, TwYS, WhScrn 77*
Cheiffetz, Hyman 1901- *AmSCAP 66*
Chein, Louis 1636?-1694 *NewGrD 80*
Cheirel, Jeanne 1868-1934 *WhScrn 74*
Cheirel, Jeanne 1869-1934 *WhScrn 77*
Cheirel, Micheline *WhoHol A*
Chekhov, Anton Pavlovich 1860-1904 *CnMD, CnThe, DcPup, EncWT, Ent, McGEWD[port], ModWD, NewGrD 80, NotNAT A, -B, OxThe, PlP&P[port], -A[port], REnWD[port]*
Chekhov, Michael 1891-1955 *FilmEn, FilmgC, HalFC 80, MotPP, NotNAT B, OxThe, WhScrn 74, -77, WhThe, WhoHol B*
Chekhov, Olga Knipper 1869-1959 *OxThe*
Chekhova, Olga 1869-1959 *WomWMM*
Chekov, Anton 1860-1904 *NewEOp 71*
Chekova, Olga 1869-1959 *Film 2*
Chelard, Hippolyte-Andre-Baptiste 1789-1861 *Baker 78, NewGrD 80*
Cheler, Fortunato 1686?-1757 *NewGrD 80*
Chelius, Oskar Von 1859-1923 *Baker 78*
Chelleri, Fortunato 1686?-1757 *NewGrD 80*
Chelleri, Fortunato 1690-1757 *Baker 78*
Chelton, Nick 1946- *WhoThe 77*
Chementi, Margherita *NewGrD 80*
Chemin-Petit, Hans 1902- *Baker 78, DcCM, IntWWM 77, -80, NewGrD 80*
Chempin, Beryl Margaret *IntWWM 80, WhoMus 72*
Chemyn, Nicolas *NewGrD 80*
Chen, Betty *WomWMM B*
Chen, Fu-Yen 1940- *IntWWM 77, -80*
Chenal, Pierre 1903- *DcFM, FilmEn, FilmgC, HalFC 80*
Chenault, Lawrence E 1877- *BlksB&W, -C, BlksBF[port], DrBlPA*
Chenchikova, Olga 1956- *CnOxB*
Chene, Dixie *Film 1*
Chene, Ethel d1972 *WhoHol B*
Chenette, Edward Stephen 1885-1963 *AmSCAP 80*
Chenette, Edward Stephen 1895-1963 *AmSCAP 66, ConAmC A*
Chenette, Louis Fred 1931- *IntWWM 77, -80*
Chenette, Maude Johnson Howe 1887- *AmSCAP 80*
Chenevillet, Pierre *NewGrD 80*
Chenevillet, Pierre *NewGrD 80*
Cheney, Amy Marcy *NewGrD 80*
Cheney, Sheldon 1886- *BiE&WWA, NotNAT, WhThe*
Cheney, Timothy 1913- *ConAmC*
Ch'eng, Chang-Keng 1812-1880? *NewGrD 80*
Chenier, Clifton 1925- *BluesWW[port]*
Chenier, Louise *WomWMM*
Chenier, Marie-Joseph 1764-1811 *EncWT, Ent, NotNAT B, OxThe*
Chenis, Patti-Lee *WomWMM B*
Chenneviere, Daniel *DcCM, NewGrD 80*
Chenoweth, Wilbur 1899- *AmSCAP 66, -80, Baker 78, ConAmC, IntWWM 77, -80, WhoMus 72*
Chenylle-Proctor, Stuart John 1934- *IntWWM 80*
Cher 1946- *IlEncR, IntMPA 77, -76, -78, -79, -80, NewYTET, WhoHol A*
Cherbuliez, Antoine-Elisee 1888-1964 *Baker 78, NewGrD 80*
Cherbury, Lord Herbert Of *NewGrD 80*
Cherdak, Jeanne Sylvia 1915- *AmSCAP 66, -80*
Cherepnin *Baker 78, NewGrD 80*
Cheri, Rose 1824-1861 *EncWT, OxThe*
Cherici, Sebastiano 1642?-1703? *NewGrD 80*
Cherico, Eugene V 1935- *BiDAmM, EncJzS 70*
Cherico, Gene 1935- *EncJzS 70*
Cherie, Eddie 1889-1941 *NewOrJ*
Cherin, Robert 1936- *BiE&WWA*
Cherkasov, Nikolai 1903-1966 *OxFilm, WhThe, WorEFlm[port]*
Cherkassky, Shura 1911- *Baker 78, IntWWM 77, -80, NewGrD 80, WhoMus 72*
Cherkassov, Nicolai 1903-1966 *FilmgC, HalFC 80*
Cherkassov, Nikolai 1903-1966 *FilmEn, WhScrn 74, -77, WhoHol B*
Cherkose, Eddie *AmSCAP 80*
Cherll, Giovanni Gasparo *NewGrD 80*
Chermak, Cy 1929- *IntMPA 80, NewYTET*
Cherney, Boris E 1921- *AmSCAP 66, -80*
Cherney, Brian 1942- *Baker 78*
Cherniavsky, Josef 1895-1959 *AmSCAP 66, -80, ConAmC A*
Chernis, Jay 1906- *AmSCAP 66, -80, CpmDNM 76*
Chernuck, Dorothy *BiE&WWA, NotNAT*
Cherokee County Boys *BiDAmM*
Cheron, Andre *Film 2*
Cheron, Andre 1695-1766 *NewGrD 80*
Cherrell, Gwen 1926- *WhoThe 72, -77*
Cherrill, Virginia 1908- *FilmEn, FilmgC, ForYSC, HalFC 80, MotPP, MovMk, ThFT[port], TwYS, WhoHol A*
Cherrington, Meta Miles Robson 1921- *IntWWM 77, -80*
Cherrington, Ruth *Film 2*
Cherry, Addie d1942 *NotNAT B*
Cherry, Andrew 1762-1812 *NotNAT B, OxMus*
Cherry, Charles 1872-1931 *NotNAT B, WhThe, WhoHol B, WhoStg 1906, -1908*
Cherry, Don *CmpEPM*
Cherry, Don 1924- *RkOn[port]*
Cherry, Don 1936- *DrBlPA, EncJzS 70, IlEncJ, NewGrD 80[port]*

Cherry, Donald E 1936- *BiDAmM, EncJzS 70*
Cherry, Effie d1944 *NotNAT B*
Cherry, Ellen d1934 *NotNAT B*
Cherry, Helen 1915- *FilmgC, HalFC 80, IlWWBF, WhThe, WhoHol A*
Cherry, Jessie d1903 *NotNAT B*
Cherry, Kalman 1937- *IntWWM 77, -80*
Cherry, Kate *Film 2*
Cherry, Lizzie d1936 *NotNAT B*
Cherry, Malcolm 1878-1925 *NotNAT B*
Cherry, Milton 1908- *ConAmC*
Cherry, Philip 1923- *IntWWM 77, -80*
Cherry, Wal 1932- *WhoThe 77*
Cherryman, Rex 1898-1928 *Film 2, NotNAT B, WhScrn 74, -77, WhoHol B*
Chertok, Harvey 1932- *IntMPA 77, -75, -76, -78, -79, -80*
Chertok, Jack *IntMPA 77, -75, -76, -78, -79, -80, NewYTET*
Chertok, Pearl 1918- *ConAmC*
Cherubini, Luigi 1760-1842 *Baker 78, BnBkM 80, CmOp, CmpBCM, DcCom 77[port], DcCom&M 79, GrComp[port], MusMk, NewGrD 80[port]*
Cherubini, Maria Luigi 1760-1842 *NewEOp 71, OxMus*
Chesebro, George 1888-1959 *FilmEn, Film 1, WhScrn 77, WhoHol B*
Chesebro, George 1890-1959 *Film 2, ForYSC*
Cheshire, Harry V Pappy 1892-1968 *WhScrn 77, WhoHol B*
Cheshire, John Brian 1937- *IntWWM 77, -80*
Cheshire, Roger James 1948- *IntWWM 77*
Cheskin, Irving W 1915- *BiE&WWA, NotNAT, WhoThe 77*
Cheslock, Louis 1898- *AmSCAP 80, Baker 78, ConAmC, IntWWM 77, -80, WhoMus 72*
Cheslock, Louis 1899- *BiDAmM, NewGrD 80*
Chesnais, Jacques *DcPup*
Chesnais, Pierre Louis 1924- *IntWWM 77, -80*
Chesney, Arthur 1882-1949 *Film 2, NotNAT B, WhScrn 74, -77, WhThe, WhoHol B*
Chesnokov, Pavel Grigor'yevich 1877-1944 *NewGrD 80*
Chesse, Ralph *PupTheA, PupTheA SUP*
Chessler, Deborah *AmSCAP 66*
Chessler, Shirley 1923- *AmSCAP 80*
Chester, A Lucy *WhoMus 72*
Chester, Alfred *BlksB&W, -C*
Chester, Alma 1871-1953 *WhScrn 74, -77, WhoHol B*
Chester, Betty 1895-1943 *WhThe*
Chester, Bob 1908- *BgBands 74[port], CmpEPM*
Chester, Brock 1947-1971 *WhScrn 74, -77*
Chester, Mrs. George Randolph *WomWMM*
Chester, Giraud *NewYTET*
Chester, Hal E 1921- *FilmgC, HalFC 80, IntMPA 77, -75, -76, -78, -79, -80*
Chester, J *OxMus*
Chester, John *NewGrD 80*
Chester, Robert T 1908- *AmSCAP 66, -80, BiDAmM*
Chester, Russell Elliott 1892- *WhoMus 72*
Chester, Samuel K d1921 *NotNAT B*
Chester, Slick 1900- *DrBlPA*
Chester, Virginia *Film 1*
Chester, W *OxMus*
Chester, William *NewGrD 80*
Chester, William Sidell 1865-1900 *BiDAmM*
Chesterfield, Lord 1694-1773 *OxMus*
Chesterman, David 1920- *WhoMus 72*
Chesterman, Edmund Daniel 1904- *WhoMus 72*
Chesterman, Henry David 1920- *IntWWM 77, -80*
Chesterton, G K 1874-1936 *HalFC 80*
Chesterton, Gilbert Keith 1874-1936 *DcPup, NotNAT B*
Chesworth, John 1930- *CnOxB, DancEn 78*
Chetham, John 1700?-1746 *NewGrD 80*
Chetham-Strode, Warren 1897- *WhThe*
Chetkin, Leonard 1928- *AmSCAP 66*
Chettle, Henry 1560?-1607? *CnThe, NotNAT B, OxThe, REnWD[port]*
Chetwood, William Rufus d1766 *NotNAT B*
Chetwoode, Robert *NewGrD 80*
Chetwyn, Robert 1933- *WhoThe 72, -77*
Chetwynd, Lionel 1940- *IntMPA 77, -75, -76, -78, -79, -80*
Cheung, Louie *Film 2*
Chevalier *NewGrD 80*
Chevalier, Albert 1861-1923 *NotNAT A, -B, OxThe, PlP&P, WhScrn 77, WhThe, WhoStg 1908*
Chevalier, Antoine Louis 1770-1823 *BiDAmM*
Chevalier, Georges 1934- *WhoOp 76*
Chevalier, Gus d1947 *NotNAT B*
Chevalier, Marcelle *WhThe*
Chevalier, Maurice *AmPS B*
Chevalier, Maurice 1887-1972 *CmMov, ForYSC*
Chevalier, Maurice 1888-1972 *BiDFilm, -81, BiE&WWA, CmpEPM, Ent[port], FilmEn, Film 1, -2, FilmgC, HalFC 80, MotPP, MovMk[port], NotNAT B, OxFilm, OxThe, WhScrn 77, WhThe, WhoHol B, WhoThe 72, WorEFlm[port]*
Chevalier, Maurice 1888-1973 *EncWT*
Chevalier, Maurice 1889-1972 *FilmAG WE, NotNAT A*
Chevalier, May d1940 *NotNAT B*
Chevalier DeSaint Georges, Joseph B 1739-1799 *DrBlPA*
Chevallay, Annie *WomWMM*
Chevallier *NewGrD 80*
Chevardiere, Louis Balthazard DeLa *NewGrD 80*
Cheve, Emile Joseph Maurice 1804-1864 *Baker 78, NewGrD 80, OxMus*
Chevez, Julius 1908- *NewOrJ[port]*
Chevillard, Camille 1859-1923 *Baker 78, NewGrD 80*
Chevillard, Pierre Alexandre Francois 1811-1877 *NewGrD 80*
Chevreuille, Raymond 1901-1976 *Baker 78, DcCM, NewGrD 80, WhoMus 72*
Chevrier, Andre Gaston Paul 1904- *WhoMus 72*
Chevtchenko, Tania *DancEn 78*
Chew, Frank *Film 2*
Chew, Virgilia *WhoHol A*
Cheyette, Irving 1904- *AmSCAP 80, IntWWM 77, -80*
Cheyney, Peter 1896-1951 *FilmgC, HalFC 80*
Chezy, Helmina Von 1783-1856 *NewGrD 80*
Chezy, Wilhelmina Christiane Von 1783-1856 *NewGrD 80, OxMus*
Chi, Greta *WhoHol A*
Chi-Lites, The *IlEncR, RkOn 2[port]*
Chiabrano, Carlo Francesco 1723- *NewGrD 80*
Chiabrano, Gaetano *NewGrD 80*
Chiabrera, Gabriello 1552-1638 *NewGrD 80*
Chiaffarelli, Alberte 1884-1945 *AmSCAP 66*
Chianco, Bernard V 1932- *AmSCAP 80*
Chiang, Ching *WomWMM*
Chianti, Armand *ConMuA 80B*
Chiantia, Sal *ConMuA 80B*
Chiara, Maria 1942- *CmOp, WhoOp 76*
Chiarelli, Luigi 1880-1947 *EncWT, Ent, McGEWD[port], ModWD*
Chiarelli, Luigi 1884-1947 *OxThe, REnWD[port]*
Chiarelli, Luigi 1886-1947 *CnMD*
Chiari, Giuseppe 1926- *Baker 78, DcCM, NewGrD 80*
Chiari, Mario 1909- *FilmEn, FilmgC, HalFC 80, WorEFlm[port]*
Chiari, Walter 1924- *FilmEn, FilmgC, HalFC 80, WhoHol A*
Chiarini, Luigi 1900- *DcFM, IntMPA 75, -76, OxFilm*
Chiarini, Luigi 1900-1975 *FilmEn*
Chiarini, Pietro d1765? *NewGrD 80*
Chiaromonte, Francesco 1809-1886 *Baker 78*
Chiasson, Warren 1934- *AmSCAP 66, -80, EncJzS 70*
Chiaula, Mauro 1544?-1603? *NewGrD 80*
Chiaula, Maurus Panhormita 1544?-1603? *NewGrD 80*
Chiaureli, Mikhail 1894- *DcFM, FilmEn*
Chiavelloni, Vincenzo *NewGrD 80*
Chiba, Kaoru 1928- *IntWWM 77, -80*
Chiboust, Noel Christian 1909- *WhoMus 72*
Chic *RkOn 2[port]*
Chicago *BiDAmM, ConMuA 80A, EncJzS 70, IlEncR, RkOn 2[port]*
Chicago, Judy 1939- *WomWMM B*
Chicago Bill *BluesWW[port]*
Chicago Blues Band *BiDAmM*
Chicago Bob *BluesWW[port]*
Chicago Sunny Boy *BluesWW[port]*
Chichester, Emily *Film 1, -2*
Chichester, George Forrest 1915- *AmSCAP 80*
Chichkova, Ludmilla *WomWMM*
Chicken Shack *IlEncR*
Chickering *NewGrD 80*
Chickering, Jonas 1798-1853 *Baker 78, BiDAmM, NewGrD 80*
Chickering, Joseph Cooper 1917- *AmSCAP 80*
Chidell, Anthony Derek 1942- *IntWWM 77, -80*
Chidester, L W 1906- *AmSCAP 66*
Chidester, Lawrence William 1906- *AmSCAP 80, WhoMus 72*
Chief Big Tree *ForYSC*
Chief Black Hawk d1975 *WhScrn 77, WhoHol C*
Chief Jack 1877-1943 *WhScrn 74, -77, WhoHol B*
Chief John Big Tree 1865-1967 *WhScrn 74, -77, WhoHol B*
Chief Many Treaties 1875-1948 *WhScrn 74, -77, WhoHol B*
Chief Nipo Strongheart 1891-1966 *WhScrn 74, -77*
Chief Standing Bear d1939 *WhScrn 77*
Chief Thundercloud 1889-1955 *HalFC 80, WhScrn 74, -77, WhoHol B*
Chief Thundercloud 1898-1967 *HalFC 80, WhScrn 74, -77, WhoHol B*
Chief Thundercloud 1899?-1955? *ForYSC*
Chief Yowlachie 1891-1966 *WhScrn 77, WhoHol B*
Chieftains, The *IlEncR*
Chierici, Sebastiano *NewGrD 80*
Chierisy *NewGrD 80*
Chiesa, Ivo 1920- *EncWT*
Chiesa, Melchiorre *NewGrD 80*
Chiffons, The *RkOn*
Chignell, Robert 1882-1939 *Baker 78*
Chihara, Paul 1938- *AmSCAP 80, Baker 78, CpmDNM 80, ConAmC, NewGrD 80*
Chikada, Tadashi 1919- *IntMPA 77, -75, -76, -78, -79, -80*
Chikamatsu Monzaemon 1653-1724 *DcPup*
Chikamatsu Monzaemon 1653-1725 *CnThe, McGEWD, REnWD[port]*
Chikamatsu, Monzaemon 1653-1725 *EncWT*
Chikamatsu, Monzayemon 1653?-1724 *NotNAT B*
Chilcot, Thomas 1700?-1766 *NewGrD 80*
Chilcott, Barbara *CreCan 1*
Chilcott, Nancie Marion *WhoMus 72*
Child, Abigail *WomWMM A, -B*
Child, Francis J 1825-1896 *BiDAmM, EncFCWM 69, OxMus*
Child, Harold Hannyngton 1869-1945 *NotNAT B, WhThe*
Child, Philip Albert 1898- *CreCan 2*
Child, William 1606-1697 *Baker 78, NewGrD 80[port], OxMus*
Childe *NewGrD 80*
Childe, Ann *NewGrD 80*
Childers, Marion 1926- *BiDAmM*
Childers, Naomi d1964 *MotPP, NotNAT B, WhoHol B*
Childers, Naomi 1892-1964 *FilmEn, Film 1, -2, TwYS*
Childers, Naomi 1893-1964 *WhScrn 74, -77*
Childre, Lew 1901- *IlEncCM*
Children Of God, The *BiDAmM*
Childress, Alice 1920- *BlkAmP, ConDr 77, DcLB 7[port], DrBlPA, MorBAP, NotNAT, PlP&P A[port]*
Childress, Alvin *BlkAmP, BlksB&W, -C, DrBlPA, MorBAP, NotNAT*
Childress, Lillian Hannah 1893- *AmSCAP 80*
Childs, Barney 1926- *Baker 78, CpmDNM 73, -77, ConAmC, DcCM, IntWWM 77, -80, NewGrD 80*
Childs, Elsie *WhoMus 72*
Childs, Gilbert d1931 *NotNAT B, WhThe, WhoHol B*
Childs, Gordon Bliss 1927- *IntWWM 77, -80*
Childs, Harold *ConMuA 80B*
Childs, Lucinda *CmpGMD[port]*
Childs, Monroe 1891-1963 *WhScrn 74, -77*
Childs, Reggie *BgBands 74, CmpEPM*
Childs, Valerie *WhoMus 72*
Chiles, Linden *ForYSC, WhoHol A*

Chiles, Lois 1950- *HalFC 80, WhoHol A*
Chilese, Bastian *NewGrD 80*
Chilesotti, Oscar 1848-1916 *Baker 78, NewGrD 80*
Chilingirian, Levon 1948- *IntWWM 77, -80*
Chilmead, Edmund 1610-1654 *NewGrD 80, OxMus*
Chilston *NewGrD 80*
Chilton, T E 1929- *IntMPA 77, -75, -76, -78, -79, -80*
Chilvers, Marguerita 1925- *IntWWM 77*
Chimbamul *BlkAmP*
Chimenti, Margherita *NewGrD 80*
Chimes, The *RkOn*
Chimes, John William 1953- *IntWWM 80*
Chin, Elizabeth Mae 1938- *IntMPA 79, -80*
Chin, Frank *NatPD[port]*
Chin, Tsai 1938?- *FilmgC, HalFC 80*
Chinelli, Giovanni Battista 1610-1677 *NewGrD 80*
Ching, Ling Foo 1854- *MagIlD*
Ching, William *WhoHol A*
Ching, William 1912- *FilmgC, HalFC 80*
Ching, William 1913- *ForYSC, IntMPA 77, -75, -76, -78, -79, -80, Vers B[port]*
Chini, Tarcisio 1936- *IntWWM 77, -80*
Chinich, Jesse 1921- *IntMPA 77, -75, -76, -78, -79, -80*
Chinlund, Jennifer *WomWMM B*
Chinlund, Phyllis *WomWMM A, -B*
Chinn, Nicky *ConMuA 80B*
Chinn, Richard Lee 1942- *IntWWM 77*
Chinnappa, P U d1951 *WhScrn 77*
Chinoy, Helen Krich 1922- *BiE&WWA, NotNAT*
Chinzer, Giovanni 1700?-1749? *NewGrD 80*
Chiocchio, Fernande *CreCan 2*
Chiocchiolo, Antonio 1680?-1706? *NewGrD 80*
Chioccioli, Antonio 1680?-1706? *NewGrD 80*
Chiochiolo, Antonio 1680?-1706? *NewGrD 80*
Chiodi, Buono d1783 *NewGrD 80*
Chiodino, Giovanni Battista *NewGrD 80*
Chionides *OxThe*
Chiozzotto *NewGrD 80*
Chiphe, Leppaigne *BlkAmP*
Chipmunks, The *RkOn*
Chipolone, Nunzio 1922- *AmSCAP 80*
Chipp, Edmund Thomas 1823-1886 *OxMus*
Chipre *NewGrD 80*
Chiprut, Elliot 1944- *AmSCAP 80*
Chirbury, R *NewGrD 80*
Chirello, George Shorty 1897-1963 *WhScrn 74, -77, WhoHol B*
Chirescu, Ioan D 1889- *NewGrD 80*
Chirgwin, George H 1854-1922 *OxThe, WhThe*
Chiriac, Mircea 1919- *Baker 78*
Chiriaeff, Ludmilla 1924- *CnOxB, CreCan 1, DancEn 78[port]*
Chirico, Andrea De *NewGrD 80*
Chirico, Giorgio De 1888-1974 *EncWT*
Chirico, Giorgio Di 1888- *CnOxB, DancEn 78*
Chirskov, Boris 1904- *DcFM*
Chishko, Oles' Semyonovich 1895- *NewGrD 80*
Chisholm, Audrey *WhoMus 72*
Chisholm, Earle *BlkAmP*
Chisholm, Erik 1904-1965 *Baker 78, NewEOp 71, NewGrD 80, OxMus*
Chisholm, George 1915- *EncJzS 70, IlEncJ, IntWWM 77*
Chisholm, Robert 1898-1960 *NotNAT B, WhThe, WhoHol B*
Chisolm, Mary B *PupTheA*
Chissell, Joan Olive 1919- *IntWWM 77, -80, NewGrD 80, WhoMus 72*
Chissell, Noble 1910- *IntMPA 77, -75, -76, -78, -79, -80, WhoHol A*
Chistyakov, A *Film 2*
Chiti, Girolamo 1679-1759 *NewGrD 80*
Chittison, Herman 1909-1967 *BiDAmM, CmpEPM, EncJzS 70, WhScrn 74, -77, WhoJazz 72*
Chiu, Yee-Ha 1938- *WhoMus 72*
Chivers, Alan 1918- *IntMPA 77, -75, -76, -78, -79, -80*
Chivers, Thomas Holley 1807-1858 *BiDAmM*
Chivot, Henri d1897 *NotNAT B*
Chivvis, Chic 1884-1963 *WhScrn 74, -77, WhoHol B*
Chkeidze, Revas 1926- *DcFM*
Chladek, Rosalia 1905- *CnOxB, DancEn 78[port]*
Chladni, Ernest Florens Friedrich 1756-1827 *Baker 78*
Chladni, Ernst 1756-1827 *NewGrD 80*
Chlubna, Osvald 1893-1971 *Baker 78, NewGrD 80*
Chlumberg, Hans 1897-1930 *CnMD, McGEWD, ModWD*
Chmara, Grigory *Film 2*
Chmara-Zaczkiewicz, Ewa Barbara 1933- *IntWWM 77, -80*
Chmielewski, Stephen 1947- *CpmDNM 79*
Choate, Edward 1908-1975 *BiE&WWA, NotNAT, -B*
Choate, Robert B, Jr. *NewYTET*
Chobanian, Loris Ohannes 1933- *AmSCAP 80, CpmDNM 73, -74, -76, -77, -78, -79, ConAmC*
Chock, Ping Ing Kwok 1941- *IntWWM 77*
Chocolate Brown *BluesWW[port]*
Chocolate-Coloured Coon *OxThe*
Chodorov, Edward *WhThe*
Chodorov, Edward 1904- *CnMD, FilmEn, FilmgC, HalFC 80, ModWD*
Chodorov, Edward 1914- *BiE&WWA, IntMPA 77, -75, -76, -78, -79, -80, NotNAT*
Chodorov, Jerome 1911- *BiE&WWA, ConDr 73, -77D, FilmEn, FilmgC, HalFC 80, McGEWD, ModWD, NatPD[port], NewCBMT, NotNAT, WhoThe 72, -77*
Chodos, Gabriel 1939- *IntWWM 77, -80*
Chodowiecki, Daniel Nicolas 1726-1801 *EncWT*
Chodura, Frantisek 1906- *IntWWM 77, -80*
Choerilus *OxThe*
Choir, The *RkOn 2[port]*
Chollet, Jean Baptiste 1798-1892 *NewGrD 80*
Cholmondeley, Archer *Baker 78*
Chome, Maryse Ingrid *WhoMus 72*
Chomette, Henri 1891-1941 *OxFilm*
Chomette, Henri 1896-1941 *FilmEn*
Chominski, Jozef Michal 1906- *NewGrD 80*
Chomon, Segundo De 1871-1929 *DcFM, FilmEn, OxFilm*
Chomon, Sogon De 1871-1929 *FilmEn*
Chomsky, Marvin J *HalFC 80, IntMPA 77, -76, -78, -79, -80, NewYTET*
Chong, Thomas 1938- *AmSCAP 80*
Chong, Tommy 1940- *JoeFr[port]*
Chookasian, Lili *WhoOp 76*
Chooluck, Leon 1920- *IntMPA 77, -75, -76, -78, -79, -80*
Chop, Max 1862-1929 *Baker 78*
Chopin, Frederic 1810-1849 *Baker 78, BnBkM 80[port], CmpBCM, DancEn 78, DcCom 77[port], DcCom&M 79, GrComp[port], MusMk[port], NewGrD 80[port], NotNAT B, OxMus*
Chopin, Fryderyk Franciszek 1810-1849 *NewGrD 80[port]*
Chopin, Fryderyk Frantizek 1810-1849 *CnOxB*
Chopin, Rene 1885-1953 *CreCan 2*
Chopra, Joyce *WomWMM A, -B*
Choquette, Adrienne 1915- *CreCan 1*
Choquette, Ernest 1862-1941 *CreCan 2*
Choquette, Robert 1905- *CreCan 1*
Chorasselt *NewGrD 80*
Chorbajian, John 1936- *Baker 78, CpmDNM 80, ConAmC*
Chordettes *AmPS A, -B, RkOn[port]*
Chords, The *RkOn[port]*
Chorell, Walentin 1912- *CroCD, REnWD[port]*
Chorley, Henry Fothergill 1808-1872 *Baker 78, NewGrD 80, OxMus*
Choron, Alexandre Etienne 1771-1834 *Baker 78, NewGrD 80*
Chorpenning, Ruth 1905- *WhThe*
Chorzempa, Daniel 1944- *NewGrD 80, WhoMus 72*
Chorzempa, Daniel Walter 1948- *IntWWM 77, -80*
Choset, Charles 1940- *AmSCAP 80*
Choset, Franklin 1934- *WhoOp 76*
Chottin, Alexis 1891- *NewGrD 80*
Chotzinoff, Samuel 1889-1964 *Baker 78, BiDAmM, NotNAT B*
Chou, En-Lai, Madame *WomWMM*
Chou, Wen-Chung 1923- *Baker 78, BiDAmM, ConAmC, DcCM, NewGrD 80*
Choudens *NewGrD 80*
Choudens, Antoine De 1825-1888 *NewGrD 80*
Choudens, Antony *NewGrD 80*
Choudens, Paul d1925 *NewGrD 80*
Chouinard, Joseph Jerod 1926- *IntWWM 80*
Chouquet, Adolphe-Gustave 1819-1886 *Baker 78*
Chouquet, Gustave 1819-1886 *NewGrD 80*
Choureau, Etchika 1923- *FilmgC, ForYSC, HalFC 80, WhoHol A*
Choureau, Etchika 1933- *FilmEn*
Chouret, Nicole Denise 1947- *CnOxB*
Chouteau, Yvonne 1929- *CnOxB, DancEn 78*
Choveaux, Nicholas *IntWWM 77, -80, WhoMus 72*
Chow, David *WhoHol A*
Chow, Raymond *IntMPA 79, -80*
Chowdhury, Salil 1923- *IntWWM 77, -80*
Chramer, Fredrik *PupTheA*
Chrestien, Gilles-Louis 1754-1811 *NewGrD 80*
Chrestien, Jean-Baptiste 1728?-1760 *NewGrD 80*
Chrestien, Louis-Gilles 1754-1811 *NewGrD 80*
Chretien De Troyes *NewGrD 80*
Chretien, Gilles-Louis 1754-1811 *NewGrD 80*
Chretien, Henri 1879-1956 *DcFM, FilmEn, FilmgC, HalFC 80, OxFilm, WorEFlm[port]*
Chretien, Hippolyte *NewGrD 80*
Chretien, Jean-Baptiste 1728?-1760 *NewGrD 80*
Chretien, Louis-Gilles 1754-1811 *NewGrD 80*
Chrimes, Pamela 1923- *DancEn 78*
Chrippes, Peter Gordon Charles 1945- *IntWWM 77, -80*
Chris, Marilyn *WhoHol A*
Chrisman, H Ed 1914- *IntMPA 77, -75, -76, -78, -79, -80*
Chrisman, Pat *Film 1, -2*
Chrismann, Franz Xaver 1726-1795 *NewGrD 80*
Chrismanni, Franz Xaver 1726-1795 *NewGrD 80*
Christ, Mayme *PupTheA*
Christ, William B 1919- *IntWWM 80*
Christelius, Bartholomeus 1624-1701 *NewGrD 80*
Christenius, Johann 1565?-1626 *NewGrD 80*
Christensen, Anker 1899- *IntWWM 80*
Christensen, Axel W 1881- *BiDAmM*
Christensen, Benjamin 1879-1959 *BiDFilm, -81, DcFM, FilmEn, Film 2, FilmgC, HalFC 80, OxFilm, WhScrn 77, WorEFlm[port]*
Christensen, Dieter 1932- *IntWWM 77, -80, NewGrD 80*
Christensen, Harold 1904- *CnOxB, DancEn 78[port]*
Christensen, Helge Ploug 1918- *IntWWM 80*
Christensen, James Harlan 1935- *AmSCAP 80*
Christensen, Jon 1943- *EncJzS 70*
Christensen, Lew 1906- *BiE&WWA*
Christensen, Lew 1909- *CnOxB, DancEn 78[port]*
Christensen, Mary *Film 2*
Christensen, Robert Currier 1943- *WhoOp 76*
Christensen, Siegfried 1907- *NewOrJ SUP[port]*
Christensen, William F 1902- *BiE&WWA, CnOxB, DancEn 78[port]*
Christensen Brothers *CnOxB*
Christgau, Robert *ConMuA 80B*
Christiakov, A P *Film 2*
Christian IV 1577-1648 *NewGrD 80*
Christian, Beverly M Jones 1927- *IntWWM 77*
Christian, Bobby 1911- *AmSCAP 66, -80, ConMuA 80B*
Christian, Buddy 1895-1958 *WhoJazz 72*
Christian, Charles 1886-1964 *NewOrJ*
Christian, Charles 1916?-1942 *NewGrD 80*
Christian, Charlie 1916?-1942 *CmpEPM, NewGrD 80, WhoJazz 72*
Christian, Charlie 1917-1942 *BiDAmM*
Christian, Charlie 1919-1942 *IlEncJ, MusMk*
Christian, David *AmSCAP 80*
Christian, Emile Joseph 1895-1973 *EncJzS 70, NewOrJ[port], WhoJazz 72*
Christian, Frank 1887-1973 *NewOrJ*
Christian, Hans 1929- *WhoOp 76*
Christian, John 1884-1950 *WhScrn 74, -77*

Christian, Judith Anne 1955- *IntWWM 80*
Christian, Linda *MotPP, WhoHol A*
Christian, Linda 1923- *FilmEn, FilmgC, HalFC 80*
Christian, Linda 1924- *IntMPA 77, -75, -76, -78, -79, -80, What 3[port]*
Christian, Linda 1925- *ForYSC*
Christian, Mary *Film 2*
Christian, Michael *WhoHol A*
Christian, Narcisse J 1895?- *NewOrJ*
Christian, Paul 1917- *FilmEn, ForYSC, HalFC 80, WhoHol A*
Christian, Robert 1939- *DrBlPA*
Christian, Susan Hendrick 1954- *IntWWM 80*
Christian-Jaque 1904- *BiDFilm, -81, DcFM, FilmEn, FilmgC, HalFC 80, OxFilm, WorEFlm[port]*
Christian Troubadours *BiDAmM*
Christiani, Adolf Friedrich 1836-1885 *Baker 78*
Christiani, Stefano 1768-1835? *BiDAmM*
Christianissimus *NewGrD 80*
Christiano, Eleanor Irene 1912-1932 *WhScrn 77*
Christians, George 1869-1921 *Film 2, WhoHol B*
Christians, Mady 1900-1951 *FilmEn, FilmgC, HalFC 80, MotPP, MovMk, NotNAT B, ThFT[port], WhScrn 74, -77, WhThe, WhoHol B*
Christians, Mady 1900-1952 *FilmAG WE*
Christians, Mady 1900-1959 *Film 2, ForYSC*
Christians, Margarete *Film 1*
Christians, Rudolph 1869-1921 *Film 2, WhScrn 74, -77*
Christiansen, Asger Lund 1927- *IntWWM 77, -80*
Christiansen, Benjamin *FilmEn*
Christiansen, Benjamin 1879-1959 *FilmEn, TwYS A*
Christiansen, F Melius 1871-1955 *BiDAmM, ConAmC*
Christiansen, Fredrik Melius 1871-1955 *Baker 78*
Christiansen, Henning 1932- *NewGrD 80*
Christiansen, James 1931- *IntWWM 77, -80*
Christiansen, Larry A 1941- *ConAmC*
Christiansen, Olaf Christian 1901- *Baker 78, WhoMus 72*
Christiansen, Paul 1914- *ConAmC*
Christiansen, Rasmus *Film 2*
Christiansen, Richard Dean 1931- *ConAmTC*
Christiansen, Robert W *IntMPA 79, -80*
Christiansen, Robert W & Rick Rosenberg *NewYTET*
Christiansen-Fernald, Beverly J 1936- *IntWWM 77, -80*
Christianus, Johannes *NewGrD 80*
Christie *RkOn 2[port]*
Christie, Agatha 1890-1976 *BiE&WWA, CnThe, ConDr 73, -77, EncWT, PlP&P, WhoThe 72, -77*
Christie, Agatha 1891-1976 *Ent, FilmgC, HalFC 80*
Christie, Al 1886-1951 *DcFM, FilmEn, FilmgC, HalFC 80, NotNAT B, TwYS B*
Christie, Amalie 1913- *IntWWM 80*
Christie, Audrey 1912- *BiE&WWA, ForYSC, HalFC 80, NotNAT, WhoHol A, WhoThe 72, -77*
Christie, Campbell 1893-1963 *WhThe*
Christie, Catherine *IntWWM 77, -80*
Christie, Charles H d1955 *NotNAT B*
Christie, Dorothy *Film 2*
Christie, Dorothy 1896- *WhThe*
Christie, George 1873-1949 *NotNAT B, WhScrn 77, WhThe*
Christie, George 1934- *IntWWM 77, -80*
Christie, George W L *WhoMus 72*
Christie, Howard J 1912- *FilmgC, HalFC 80, IntMPA 77, -75, -76, -78, -79, -80*
Christie, Ivan *Film 2*
Christie, John 1882-1962 *NewEOp 71, NewGrD 80, NotNAT B, OxMus*
Christie, Julie *MotPP, WhoHol A*
Christie, Julie 1940- *FilmAG WE, FilmgC, HalFC 80, MovMk[port], OxFilm, WhoHrs 80[port]*
Christie, Julie 1941- *BiDFilm, -81, FilmEn, ForYSC, IlWWBF[port], IntMPA 77, -75, -76, -78, -79, -80, WorEFlm[port]*
Christie, Lou 1943- *RkOn[port]*
Christie, Lyn 1928- *EncJzS 70*
Christie, Lyndon Van 1928- *EncJzS 70, IntWWM 77*
Christie, Nan 1948- *WhoMus 72, WhoOp 76*
Christie, Ronald Keith 1931- *EncJzS 70*
Christie, Winifred 1882-1965 *Baker 78, OxMus*
Christina 1626-1689 *NewGrD 80*
Christina Alexandra 1626-1689 *NewGrD 80*
Christine, John Ellwood *PupTheA*
Christine, Lillian *Film 2*
Christine, Virginia *IntMPA 77, -75, -76, -78, -79, -80*
Christine, Virginia 1917- *FilmgC, HalFC 80*
Christine, Virginia 1920- *WhoHol A*
Christlieb, Pete 1945- *EncJzS 70*
Christlieb, Peter 1945- *EncJzS 70*
Christman, Marion H 1902- *AmSCAP 66*
Christmann, Johann Friedrich 1752-1817 *NewGrD 80*
Christo, Luiz De 1625-1693 *NewGrD 80*
Christoff, Boris 1914- *Baker 78, MusSN[port]*
Christoff, Boris 1918- *BnBkM 80, CmOp[port], NewEOp 71, NewGrD 80[port]*
Christoff, Boris 1919- *IntWWM 77, MusMk, WhoMus 72, WhoOp 76*
Christoff, Dimiter 1933- *Baker 78*
Christopher, Berrie *AmSCAP 80*
Christopher, Cyril Stanley 1897- *Baker 78, IntWWM 77, WhoMus 72*
Christopher, Dennis *AmSCAP 80*
Christopher, Don *AmSCAP 80*
Christopher, George Addison 1910- *IntWWM 77*
Christopher, Jordan 1938- *ForYSC*
Christopher, Jordan 1941- *IntMPA 77, -75, -76, -78, -79, -80, MotPP, WhoHol A*
Christopher, May 1912- *AmSCAP 66*
Christopher, Milbourne *MagIlD*
Christopher, Robert *ForYSC*
Christopher, Russell Lewis 1930- *WhoOp 76*
Christopherson, Larry Lee 1937- *IntWWM 77, -80*
Christoskov, Peter 1917- *Baker 78*
Christou, Jani 1926-1970 *Baker 78, NewGrD 80[port]*
Christou, Yannis 1926-1970 *DcCM*
Christout, Marie-Francoise 1925- *CnOxB*
Christov, Dobri 1875-1941 *Baker 78*
Christy, Ann *MotPP*
Christy, Ann 1905- *ForYSC, WhoHol A*
Christy, Ann 1909- *Film 2, TwYS*
Christy, Bill 1925-1946 *WhScrn 74, -77, WhoHol B*
Christy, Dorothy 1906- *FilmEn, ForYSC*
Christy, Ed *AmPS B*
Christy, Edwin P 1815-1862 *Baker 78, BiDAmM, NewGrD 80, NotNAT B*
Christy, Eileen *ForYSC*
Christy, Floyd d1962 *NotNAT B*
Christy, Ivan 1888-1949 *WhScrn 74, -77, WhoHol B*
Christy, June 1925- *BiDAmM, CmpEPM, EncJzS 70*
Christy, Ken 1895-1962 *ForYSC, NotNAT B, WhScrn 74, -77, WhoHol B*
Christy, Lya *Film 2*
Christy, Suzanne 1904- *FilmAG WE*
Christy Minstrels *OxThe*
Chronegk, Ludwig 1837-1891 *OxThe*
Chrysalis *BiDAmM*
Chrysander, Friedrich 1826-1901 *NewGrD 80*
Chrysander, Karl Franz Friedrich 1826-1901 *Baker 78, BnBkM 80, OxMus*
Chrysanthos Of Madytos 1770?-1843 *Baker 78*
Chrysanthos Of Madytos 1770?-1846 *NewGrD 80*
Chrysaphes, Manuel *NewGrD 80*
Chrysogonos Gevicenus, Andrea *NewGrD 80*
Chrysogonus Gevicenus, Andrea *NewGrD 80*
Chrysoponos Gevicenus, Andrea *NewGrD 80*
Chrysoponos Gevicesis, Andrea *NewGrD 80*
Chrysoponus Gevicenus, Andrea *NewGrD 80*
Chrysostom, John 344?-407 *NewGrD 80*
Chryst, Dorothea 1940- *WhoOp 76*
Chryst, Gary 1949- *CnOxB*
Chrystal, William Adamson 1931- *ConAmC*
Chrystall, Belle 1910- *IlWWBF[port]*
Chrystall, Belle 1911- *HalFC 80*
Chu, Shih-Ling *DcFM*
Chuang, Marisa Yuen 1943- *IntWWM 77, -80*
Chubby Checker *AmSCAP 80*
Chuchro, Josef 1931- *IntWWM 77, -80, NewGrD 80*
Chuck Wagon Gang *BiDAmM*
Chudleigh, Arthur 1858-1932 *WhThe*
Chueca, Federico 1846-1908 *Baker 78, NewGrD 80*
Chugayev, Alexander Georgiyevich 1924- *NewGrD 80*
Chugg, Clarence Richard 1902- *WhoMus 72*
Chujoy, Anatole 1894-1969 *CnOxB, DancEn 78*
Chukhadjian, Tigran 1837-1898 *NewGrD 80*
Chukhrai, Grigori 1921- *FilmEn, WorEFlm[port]*
Chukrai, Grigori 1920- *FilmgC, HalFC 80*
Chukrai, Grigori 1921- *DcFM, OxFilm*
Chulaki, Mikhail Ivanovich 1908- *IntWWM 77, -80, NewGrD 80*
Chun-Wilson, Seoung Lee 1931- *IntWWM 77, -80*
Chung, Kyung-Wha 1948- *IntWWM 77, -80, NewGrD 80*
Chung, Ling Soo 1861-1918 *MagIlD[port], WhThe*
Chung, Myung-Wha 1944- *IntWWM 77, -80*
Chung, Myung-Whun 1953- *IntWWM 77, -80*
Church, Edna E *IntWWM 77*
Church, Esme 1893-1972 *WhScrn 77, WhThe*
Church, Eugene 1938- *RkOn*
Church, Frederick *Film 1*
Church, John *OxMus*
Church, John 1675-1741 *NewGrD 80, OxMus*
Church, John 1834-1890 *BiDAmM*
Church, Sandra *BiE&WWA, NotNAT, WhoHol A*
Church, Stanley *WhoHol A*
Church, Tony 1930- *WhoThe 72, -77*
Churchill, Allen 1911- *BiE&WWA*
Churchill, Berton 1876-1940 *FilmEn, Film 2, FilmgC, ForYSC, HalFC 80, HolCA[port], NotNAT B, Vers A[port], WhScrn 74, -77, WhThe, WhoHol B*
Churchill, Berton 1876-1946 *MovMk*
Churchill, Caryl 1938- *ConDr 73, -77*
Churchill, Charles d1764 *NotNAT B*
Churchill, Diana 1913- *FilmgC, HalFC 80, WhThe, WhoHol A, WhoThe 72*
Churchill, Diana 1919- *IlWWBF*
Churchill, Donald 1930- *ConDr 73, -77C, FilmgC, HalFC 80*
Churchill, Frank E 1901-1942 *AmSCAP 66, -80, BiDAmM, CmpEPM*
Churchill, Joan *WomWMM B*
Churchill, John 1920- *IntWWM 77, -80, WhoMus 72*
Churchill, Marguerite 1909- *FilmEn, ThFT[port], WhoHol A*
Churchill, Marguerite 1910- *Film 2, FilmgC, ForYSC, HalFC 80, WhThe*
Churchill, Ruth *Film 1*
Churchill, Sarah *WhoHol A*
Churchill, Sarah 1914- *FilmEn, FilmgC, ForYSC, HalFC 80, IlWWBF, WhoThe 72, -77*
Churchill, Sarah 1916- *IntMPA 77, -75, -76, -78, -79, -80*
Churchill, Savannah 1919-1974 *BiDAmM, CmpEPM, DrBlPA, EncJzS 70*
Churchill, Winston 1871-1947 *NotNAT B, WhThe*
Churchill, Sir Winston Spencer 1874-1965 *FilmgC, HalFC 80, OxFilm*
Churgin, Bathia Dina 1928- *IntWWM 80, NewGrD 80*
Chusid, Martin 1925- *NewGrD 80*
Chustrovius, Johannes d1605 *NewGrD 80*
Chute, Marchette 1909- *BiE&WWA, NotNAT*
Chuvelyov, Ivan *Film 2*
Chvala, Emanuel 1851-1924 *Baker 78, NewGrD 80*
Chwalek, Jan 1930- *IntWWM 77, -80*
Chwatal, Franz Xaver 1808-1879 *Baker 78*
Chybinski, Adolf 1880-1952 *Baker 78, NewGrD 80*
Chylinska, Teresa 1931- *IntWWM 77, -80*
Chylinski, Andrzej *NewGrD 80*

Chym, Carl NewGrD 80
Chyrbury, Robert NewGrD 80
Chytilova, Vera 1929- FilmEn, OxFilm, WomWMM, WorEFlm[port]
Ciabrano, Gaetano NewGrD 80
Ciaffi Ricagno, Luisella 1933- WhoOp 76
Ciamaga, Gustav 1930- Baker 78
Ciampi, Francesco 1690?-1764? NewGrD 80
Ciampi, Vincenzo 1719?-1762 NewGrD 80
Ciampi, Yves 1921- DcFM, FilmEn, WorEFlm[port]
Cianchettini, Pio 1799-1851 NewGrD 80
Cianchettini, Veronica NewGrD 80
Cianelli, Alma 1892-1968 WhScrn 74, -77
Cianelli, Eduardo 1887-1969 MotPP, WhScrn 74, -77
Ciani, Dino 1941- IntWWM 77, -80, WhoMus 72
Ciani, Dino 1941-1974 NewGrD 80
Ciani, Suzanne Elizabeth 1946- AmSCAP 80
Ciannelli, Alma d1968 WhoHol B
Ciannelli, Eduardo 1884-1969 MovMk[port]
Ciannelli, Eduardo 1887-1969 FilmgC, HalFC 80, WhoHol B
Ciannelli, Eduardo 1888-1969 HolCA[port]
Ciannelli, Eduardo 1889-1969 FilmEn
Ciannelli, Eduardo 1891-1969 ForYSC, Vers A[port]
Ciannelli, Lewis E 1923- IntMPA 77, -75, -76, -78, -79, -80
Ciarcia, John 1940- AmSCAP 66, -80
Ciarles Argentil NewGrD 80
Ciatrano, Carlo Francesco NewGrD 80
Ciatrano, Gaetano NewGrD 80
Ciaula, Mauro NewGrD 80
Cibber, Mrs. OxMus
Cibber, Charlotte 1713-1760 EncWT, Ent, NotNAT A, -B, OxThe
Cibber, Colley 1671-1757 CnThe, EncWT, Ent[port], McGEWD, NotNAT A, -B, OxMus, OxThe, PlP&P[port], REnWD[port]
Cibber, Susanna Maria Arne 1714-1766 EncWT, NewGrD 80, NotNAT B, OxThe
Cibber, Susannah Maria Arne 1714-1766 NotNAT A, PlP&P
Cibber, Theophilus 1703-1758 EncWT, Ent, NotNAT B, OxThe
Cibot, Noel NewGrD 80
Cicalello, Joseph 1908- AmSCAP 66
Cicalello, Joseph 1909- AmSCAP 80
Cicatello, Frank Domenick 1911- AmSCAP 80
Ciccarello, Nuntio 1585?-1611? NewGrD 80
Ciccolini, Aldo 1925- Baker 78, BnBkM 80, IntWWM 77, -80, NewGrD 80, WhoMus 72
Ciceri, Charles PlP&P
Ciceri, Pierre-Luc-Charles 1782-1868 CnOxB, NewGrD 80
Cicero PlP&P[port]
Cicero, Marcus Tullius 106BC-043BC NewGrD 80
Cichy, Theodora WomWMM B
Cicogna, Countess Marina WomWMM
Cicognini, Alessandro 1906- DcFM, FilmEn, FilmgC, HalFC 80
Cicognini, Giacinto Andrea 1606-1651 NewGrD 80
Cicognini, Giacinto Andrea 1606-1660 OxThe
Cicognini, Jacopo 1577-1633 NewGrD 80
Ciconia, Jean 1335?-1411 Baker 78
Ciconia, Johannes 1335?-1411 NewGrD 80
Cidoni, Jomar WhoHol A
Cieco, Il NewGrD 80
Cieplinski, Jan 1900-1972 CnOxB, DancEn 78
Ciera, Ippolito NewGrD 80
Cifra, Antonio 1584-1619 OxMus
Cifra, Antonio 1584-1629 Baker 78, MusMk, NewGrD 80
Cifuentes, Pedro d1769? NewGrD 80
Ciglic, Zvonimir 1921- IntWWM 77, -80, NewGrD 80
Cigna, Gina 1900- Baker 78, CmOp, NewEOp 71, NewGrD 80
Cihelnikova, Marta 1942- WhoOp 76
Cikker, Jan 1911- Baker 78, DcCM, IntWWM 77, -80, NewGrD 80
Cilea, Francesco 1866-1950 Baker 78, BnBkM 80, CmOp, DcCom 77, DcCom&M 79, MusMk, NewEOp 71, NewGrD 80, OxMus
Cilensek, Johann 1913- NewGrD 80
Cilento, Diane MotPP, WhoHol A, WhoThe 72, -77
Cilento, Diane 1932- ForYSC
Cilento, Diane 1933- BiE&WWA, FilmAG WE, FilmEn, FilmgC, HalFC 80, IlWWBF[port], MovMk, NotNAT
Cilento, Diane 1934- IntMPA 77, -75, -76, -78, -79, -80
Cilke, Robert H 1941- IntWWM 77
Cillario, Carlo Felice WhoOp 76
Cillavenia, Francesco NewGrD 80
Cima NewGrD 80
Cima, Alex 1946- AmSCAP 80
Cima, Andrea NewGrD 80
Cima, Giovanni Battista NewGrD 80
Cima, Giovanni Paolo 1570?- Baker 78, NewGrD 80
Cima, Tullio NewGrD 80
Cimador, Giambattista 1761-1805 NewGrD 80
Cimador, Giovanni Battista 1761-1805 NewGrD 80
Cimador, J B 1761-1805 NewGrD 80
Cimadoro, Giambattista 1761-1805 NewGrD 80
Cimadoro, Giovanni Battista 1761-1805 Baker 78
Cimara, Pietro 1887-1967 Baker 78
Cimarosa, Domenico 1749-1801 Baker 78, BnBkM 80, CmOp, CmpBCM, DcCom 77, DcCom&M 79, GrComp[port], MusMk, NewEOp 71, NewGrD 80[port], OxMus
Cimarron Boys BiDAmM, EncFCWM 69
Cimaszewski, Tadeusz 1936- IntWWM 77, -80
Cimatore, Michele 1510?-1587? NewGrD 80
Cimber, Matt 1936- BiE&WWA, NotNAT
Cimbrelius, Bengt Ivar 1922- IntWWM 77, -80
Cimello, Giovan Tomaso 1500?-1579? NewGrD 80
Cimello, Tomaso 1500?-1579? NewGrD 80
Cimeno, Donato NewGrD 80
Cimino, Donato NewGrD 80
Cimino, Michael 1940- HalFC 80
Cimino, Michael 1943- ConLC 16, FilmEn, IntMPA 77, -75, -76, -78, -79, -80
Cimze, Janis 1814-1881 NewGrD 80
Cina, Albert I 1896- AmSCAP 66, -80
Cinader, Robert A NewYTET
Cines, Eugene AmSCAP 80
Cingros, Marian 1918- IntWWM 77
Cini, Giovanni Battista d1586 McGEWD
Cino, Joe 1931-1967 NotNAT B
Cinquemano, Paul 1893- NewOrJ
Cinquevalli, Paul 1859-1918 NotNAT B, OxThe, WhThe
Cinthio, Il OxThe
Cinthio, Giambattista Giraldi McGEWD
Cinti-Damoreau, Laure 1801-1863 NewGrD 80
Cintolesi, Ottavio 1924- CnOxB
Ciobanu, Gheorghe 1909- IntWWM 77, -80, NewGrD 80
Cioffari, Richard J 1943- IntWWM 77, -80
Cioffi, Charles HalFC 80, WhoHol A
Ciolli, Augusta 1901-1967 WhScrn 77
Ciompi, Giorgio 1918- IntWWM 77, -80
Cioni, Renato 1929- NewEOp 71, WhoOp 76
Cioni, Renato 1931- CmOp
Cioroiu, Alexandru Sorin 1941- AmSCAP 80
Ciortea, Tudor 1903- Baker 78, DcCM, IntWWM 77, -80, NewGrD 80
Cipes, J H 1926- IntMPA 75, -76, -78, -79, -80
Cipolla, Francesco NewGrD 80
Cipollini, Gaetano 1851-1935 Baker 78
Cipra, Milo 1906- Baker 78, NewGrD 80
Ciprianus Sieradensis NewGrD 80
Circelli, Michele 1920- IntWWM 77, -80
Circus Maximus BiDAmM
Cirillo, Francesco 1623-1667? NewGrD 80
Cirillo, Michael 1903-1968 WhScrn 77
Cirillo, Tony 1910-1968 WhScrn 77
Cirillo, Wallace Joseph 1927- BiDAmM, EncJzS 70
Cirillo, Wally 1927- EncJzS 70
Cirino, Giulio 1880-1970 Baker 78
Cirker, Mitchell d1953 NotNAT B
Cirlerus, Stephanus NewGrD 80
Cirone, Anthony J 1941- AmSCAP 80, CpmDNM 79, -80, ConAmC, IntWWM 77, -80
Cirot, Noel NewGrD 80
Cirri, Giovanni Battista 1724-1808 NewGrD 80
Ciruelo, Pedro d1548 NewGrD 80
Cirullo, Giovanni Antonio NewGrD 80
Cisar, Miroslav 1929- IntWWM 77, -80
Cisilino, Siro 1903- NewGrD 80
Cisneros, Eleanora De 1878-1934 Baker 78, NewEOp 71
Cisney, Marcella BiE&WWA, NotNAT
Cisoing, Jaque De NewGrD 80
Citkowitz, Israel 1909-1974 Baker 78, BiDAmM, ConAmC, NewGrD 80
Citron, Michele WomWMM B
Citron, Phil ConMuA 80B
Citron, Pierre 1919- IntWWM 77, -80, NewGrD 80
Cittanti, Eduardo 1926- WhoOp 76
City Boy ConMuA 80A
Ciuciura, Leoncjusz 1930- Baker 78, IntWWM 77, -80, NewGrD 80
Ciulei, Liviu 1923- DcFM
Ciuntu, Paul 1866-1918 NewGrD 80
Ciurlionis, Mikolajus 1875-1911 Baker 78, NewGrD 80
Ciurlionyte, Jadvyga 1899- NewGrD 80
Cius, Anthony B, Jr. 1938- ConAmC
Cividale, Antonio Da NewGrD 80
Civil, Alan 1929- Baker 78, BnBkM 80, IntWWM 77, -80, NewGrD 80, WhoMus 72
Civita, Giacomo De NewGrD 80
Civitate Austrie, Antonius De NewGrD 80
Claassen, Arthur 1859-1920 Baker 78, BiDAmM
Clabon, Krzysztof NewGrD 80
Clabonius, Christophorus NewGrD 80
Claflin, Avery 1898- Baker 78, BiDAmM, ConAmC
Clagett, Manning 1913- IntMPA 77, -75, -76, -78, -79, -80
Clagget, Charles 1740-1795? NewGrD 80, OxMus
Clagget, Walter 1741?-1798 NewGrD 80
Claggett, Walter 1741?-1798 NewGrD 80
Claggitt, Walter 1741?-1798 NewGrD 80
Claghorn, Senator JoeFr
Clair, Ethlyne 1908- TwYS, WhoHol A
Clair, Mavis 1916- WhThe
Clair, Rene 1898- BiDFilm, -81, DcFM, FilmEn, Film 2, FilmgC, HalFC 80, IntMPA 77, -75, -76, -78, -79, -80, MovMk[port], OxFilm, WorEFlm
Claire, Bernice 1907- FilmEn, Film 2, ThFT[port]
Claire, Bernice 1911- ForYSC
Claire, Ethlyne 1908- Film 2
Claire, Gertrude 1852-1928 Film 1, -2, TwYS, WhScrn 74, -77, WhoHol B
Claire, Helen 1906-1974 WhScrn 77, WhoHol B
Claire, Helen 1911-1974 BiE&WWA, NotNAT B, WhThe
Claire, Ina AmPS B, MotPP
Claire, Ina 1892- EncMT, FilmEn, Film 1, -2, FilmgC, ForYSC, HalFC 80, ThFT[port], WhoHol A
Claire, Ina 1893- CmpEPM
Claire, Ina 1895- BiE&WWA, EncWT, FamA&A[port], NotNAT, What 2[port], WhThe
Claire, Jean 1920- NewGrD 80
Claire, Ludi 1922- BiE&WWA, NotNAT
Claire, Marion ForYSC
Clairon, Mademoiselle 1723-1803 EncWT
Clairon, Claire-Josephe-H L DeLaTude 1723-1803 OxThe
Clairon, Hyppolite 1723-1803 NotNAT A
Clairon, Hyppolyte 1723-1803 NotNAT B
Clama, Renee 1908- IlWWBF
Clampett, Bob AmSCAP 80, NewYTET
Clampett, Sody 1931- AmSCAP 80
Clampin, Ailsa Rose 1952- IntWWM 80
Clancy, Deirdre 1943- WhoThe 77
Clancy, George Film 1
Clancy, James 1912- BiE&WWA, NotNAT
Clancy, Liam EncFCWM 69
Clancy, Patrick EncFCWM 69
Clancy, Thomas BiDAmM
Clancy, Tom EncFCWM 69
Clancy Brothers EncFCWM 69

Clanton, Jimmy 1940- *AmPS A, RkOn[port]*
Clanton, Ralph 1914- *ForYSC, WhoThe 77*
Clanton, Rony *DrBlPA*
Clapham, Charlie d1959 *NotNAT B*
Clapham, John 1908- *IntWWM 77, -80, NewGrD 80, WhoMus 72*
Clapham, Leonard d1963 *Film 1, -2, WhoHol B*
Clapisson, Antoine Louis 1808-1866 *MusMk, OxMus*
Clapisson, Louis 1808-1866 *NewGrD 80*
Clapp, Charles 1899-1962 *AmSCAP 66, -80, NotNAT B*
Clapp, Charles Edwin, Jr. d1957 *NotNAT B*
Clapp, Deborah Gail 1954- *AmSCAP 80*
Clapp, Henry Austin 1841-1904 *NotNAT A*
Clapp, Lois Steele 1940- *IntWWM 77, -80*
Clapp, Philip Greeley 1888-1954 *Baker 78, BiDAmM, ConAmC, NewGrD 80*
Clapp, Stephen H 1939- *IntWWM 77, -80*
Clapper, Bernie *ConMuA 80B*
Clapton, Eric 1945- *ConMuA 80A[port], IlEncR[port], RkOn 2[port]*
Clar, Arden 1915- *AmSCAP 66, -80*
Clarance, Arthur 1883-1956 *WhScrn 74, -77*
Clare, Beatrix 1922- *IntWWM 77, -80, WhoMus 72*
Clare, Derek John 1923- *IntWWM 77, -80, WhoMus 72*
Clare, Madelyn 1894-1975 *WhScrn 77, WhoHol C*
Clare, Mary 1894-1970 *FilmEn, Film 2, FilmgC, HalFC 80, IlWWBF, WhScrn 74, -77, WhThe, WhoHol B*
Clare, Maurice 1914- *IntWWM 77, -80*
Clare, Phyllis 1908-1947 *NotNAT B, WhScrn 77, WhoHol B*
Clare, Renee 1920- *IntWWM 77, -80*
Clare, Sidney 1892-1972 *AmSCAP 66, -80, BiDAmM, CmpEPM*
Clare, Thomas Truitt 1924- *AmSCAP 66, -80*
Clare, Tom 1876- *WhThe*
Claremont, N H *PupTheA*
Clarence 1960-1969 *WhScrn 77*
Clarence, O B 1870-1955 *FilmgC, HalFC 80, NotNAT A, -B, WhScrn 74, -77, WhThe, WhoHol B*
Clarendon, Hal *Film 2*
Clarendon, J Hayden 1879- *WhoStg 1908*
Clarens, Henry F 1860-1928 *WhScrn 74, -77*
Claretie, Jules 1840-1913 *NotNAT B*
Clarges, Berner *Film 1*
Clarges, Verner 1848-1911 *WhScrn 77, WhoHol B*
Clari, Giovanni Carlo Maria 1677-1754 *Baker 78, NewGrD 80*
Claribel *Baker 78, NewGrD 80, OxMus*
Clarida, Orville Clifton 1910- *AmSCAP 66, -80*
Claridge, Gay *BgBands 74*
Claridge, Norman 1903- *WhoThe 72, -77*
Clarion, Mademoiselle 1723-1803 *Ent*
Clariond, Aime 1894-1960 *WhScrn 77*
Clark, Mr. *Film 2*
Clark, Aaron Warren 1858-1894 *NewOrJ*
Clark, Alexander 1834-1879 *BiDAmM*
Clark, Alexander 1901- *BiE&WWA, NotNAT, WhoHol A*
Clark, Alfred *WhThe*
Clark, Algeria Junius 1901- *BiDAmM*
Clark, Allan 1907- *AmSCAP 66, -80*
Clark, Amy Ashmore 1882-1954 *AmSCAP 66, -80*
Clark, Andrew *Film 2*
Clark, Andrew J 1903-1960 *WhScrn 74, -77*
Clark, Andy 1903-1960 *Film 1, -2, WhoHol B*
Clark, Barrett H 1890-1953 *NotNAT B, WhThe*
Clark, Barry 1946- *WhoMus 72*
Clark, Bill d1973 *WhScrn 77*
Clark, Bobby *CmpEPM*
Clark, Bobby 1888-1960 *EncMT, Ent, Film 2, FilmgC, HalFC 80, JoeFr, NotNAT A, -B, WhScrn 74, -77, WhThe, WhoHol B*
Clark, Bobby 1888-1962 *ForYSC*
Clark, Brian *ConDr 77C*
Clark, Bridgetta *Film 2*
Clark, Buddy 1911-1949 *NotNAT B, WhScrn 77, WhoHol B*
Clark, Buddy 1912-1949 *CmpEPM*
Clark, Buddy 1929- *EncJzS 70*
Clark, Candy 1949- *FilmEn, HalFC 80, IntMPA 77, -75, -76, -78, -79, -80, WhoHol A*
Clark, Catherine Anthony Smith 1892- *CreCan 1*
Clark, Charlene K 1945- *BlkWAB*
Clark, Charles Dow 1870-1959 *Film 2, NotNAT B, WhScrn 74, -77, WhoHol B*
Clark, Charles E 1945-1969 *EncJzS 70*
Clark, Charlie A 1948- *AmSCAP 80*
Clark, China Debra 1949- *BlkAmP, MorBAP, NatPD[port]*
Clark, Claudine 1941- *RkOn*
Clark, Cliff 1893-1953 *FilmgC, HalFC 80, Vers B[port], WhScrn 74, -77, WhoHol B*
Clark, Conrad Yeatis 1931-1963 *BiDAmM*
Clark, Cuthbert 1869-1953 *NotNAT B*
Clark, Dane 1913- *FilmEn, FilmgC, ForYSC, HalFC 80, MotPP, MovMk, WhoHol A*
Clark, Dane 1915- *HolP 40[port], IntMPA 77, -75, -76, -78, -79, -80*
Clark, Dave, Five *ConMuA 80A, RkOn 2[port]*
Clark, Dee 1938- *RkOn[port]*
Clark, Dian Manners *AmSCAP 66*
Clark, Dick 1929- *CmpEPM, ConMuA 80B, FilmEn, ForYSC, IntMPA 77, -75, -76, -78, -79, -80, NewYTET, WhoHol A*
Clark, Donald Eugene 1931- *IntWWM 77*
Clark, Dowling *Film 2*
Clark, E Holman 1864-1925 *NotNAT B, WhThe*
Clark, Ed d1954 *WhoHol B*
Clark, Eddie 1879-1954 *WhScrn 74, -77*
Clark, Edward 1878-1954 *AmSCAP 66, -80*
Clark, Edward 1888-1962 *Baker 78*
Clark, Edwin A 1871- *Film 1, WhoStg 1908*
Clark, Ernest 1912- *FilmgC, HalFC 80, WhoThe 72, -77*
Clark, Estelle *Film 2*
Clark, Ethel 1916-1964 *NotNAT B, WhScrn 74, -77, WhoHol B*
Clark, F Donald 1913- *BiE&WWA, NotNAT*
Clark, Frances Elliott 1860-1958 *OxMus*
Clark, Frances Oman 1908- *IntWWM 77, -80*
Clark, Frank *Film 1*
Clark, Frank d1945 *WhScrn 77*
Clark, Frank J 1922- *AmSCAP 66*
Clark, Fred 1914-1968 *BiE&WWA, FilmEn, FilmgC, ForYSC, HalFC 80, HolCA[port], MotPP, MovMk, NotNAT B, Vers A[port], WhScrn 74, -77, WhThe, WhoHol B*
Clark, Frederick Horace 1861-1917 *BiDAmM*
Clark, Frederick Scotson 1840-1883 *Baker 78, NewGrD 80, OxMus*
Clark, G Fletcher *PupTheA*
Clark, Garnett 1914-1938 *WhoJazz 72*
Clark, Gene 1941- *IlEncR*
Clark, Gene Emmet 1910- *AmSCAP 66*
Clark, Glen Arlen 1948- *AmSCAP 80*
Clark, Gregory 1892- *CreCan 1*
Clark, Guy 1941- *IlEncCM[port]*
Clark, Guy Charles 1941- *AmSCAP 80*
Clark, Harold Ronald 1924- *IntWWM 77, -80, WhoMus 72*
Clark, Harry *Film 2*
Clark, Harry 1911-1956 *NotNAT B, WhScrn 77, WhoHol B*
Clark, Harvey 1886-1938 *Film 2, WhScrn 74, -77, WhoHol B*
Clark, Helen 1895-1974 *WhScrn 77*
Clark, Herbert *Film 2*
Clark, Hugh d1653 *OxThe*
Clark, Ivan-John d1967 *WhScrn 77*
Clark, J Bunker 1931- *IntWWM 77, -80*
Clark, Jack *Film 1*
Clark, Jack J 1887-1947 *WhoHol B*
Clark, Jackie *AmSCAP 66*
Clark, James B *FilmEn, FilmgC, HalFC 80*
Clark, James Earl 1925- *IntWWM 77*
Clark, James John, III 1941- *IntWWM 80*
Clark, Jane 1928- *IntWWM 80*
Clark, Jeremiah *NewGrD 80*
Clark, Jim 1931- *FilmgC, HalFC 80*
Clark, Jimmy d1972 *WhoHol B*
Clark, Joe 1935- *IntWWM 77*
Clark, John J 1877-1947 *Film 2, WhScrn 74, -77*
Clark, John L 1907- *IntMPA 77, -75, -76, -78, -79, -80*
Clark, John Pepper 1935- *ConDr 73, -77, ModWD, REnWD[port]*
Clark, John R, Jr. 1915- *IntMPA 77, -75, -76, -78, -79, -80*
Clark, John Richard 1932- *WhoThe 77*
Clark, Johnny 1916-1967 *AmSCAP 66, WhScrn 74, -77, WhoHol B*
Clark, Joseph 1894-1960 *NewOrJ[port]*
Clark, Joseph L 1951- *IntWWM 77*
Clark, June 1900-1963 *WhoJazz 72*
Clark, June 1933- *IntWWM 77, -80*
Clark, June Doris 1933- *WhoMus 72*
Clark, Ken 1912- *ForYSC, HalFC 80, WhoHol A*
Clark, Kendall 1912- *BiE&WWA, NotNAT*
Clark, Kenneth 1899- *IntMPA 77, -75, -76, -78, -79, -80*
Clark, Lord Kenneth Mackenzie Clark *IntMPA 75*
Clark, Kenneth Sherman 1882-1943 *AmSCAP 66, -80*
Clark, Les 1907-1959 *WhScrn 74, -77, WhoHol B*
Clark, Lester Leroy 1905-1959 *AmSCAP 80*
Clark, Lon *WhoHol A*
Clark, Mahlon 1923- *CmpEPM*
Clark, Marguerite d1940 *MotPP, WhoHol B, WhoStg 1906, -1908*
Clark, Marguerite 1882-1940 *TwYS*
Clark, Marguerite 1883-1940 *FilmEn, Film 1, -2, FilmgC, HalFC 80*
Clark, Marguerite 1887-1940 *CmpEPM, NotNAT B, WhScrn 74, -77, WhThe*
Clark, Marie *PupTheA*
Clark, Marilyn *WhoHol A*
Clark, Marjory 1900- *WhThe*
Clark, Marlene *DrBlPA*
Clark, Melville 1850-1918 *Baker 78*
Clark, Melville Antone 1883-1953 *Baker 78*
Clark, Merrill Ross 1951- *ConAmC*
Clark, Michele d1972 *NewYTET*
Clark, Mike *ConMuA 80B*
Clark, Norman 1887- *BiE&WWA*
Clark, Paraskeva 1898- *CreCan 1*
Clark, Patricia 1929- *IntWWM 77, -80, WhoMus 72*
Clark, Paul 1927-1960 *WhScrn 74, -77, WhoHol B, WhoMus 72*
Clark, Peggy 1915- *BiE&WWA, NotNAT*
Clark, Perceval *WhThe*
Clark, Petula 1932- *FilmAG WE, FilmEn, FilmgC, ForYSC, HalFC 80, IlWWBF[port], IntMPA 77, -75, -76, -78, -79, -80, MotPP, MovMk, WhoHol A*
Clark, Petula 1933- *RkOn 2[port]*
Clark, Petula 1934- *BiDAmM*
Clark, Philip *ConAmC*
Clark, Raymond *WhoMus 72*
Clark, Raymond LeRoy 1917- *BiDAmM*
Clark, Richard 1780-1856 *OxMus*
Clark, Richard 1929- *BiDAmM*
Clark, Robert 1905- *FilmgC, HalFC 80, IntMPA 77, -75, -76, -78, -79, -80*
Clark, Robert Keyes 1925- *ConAmC*
Clark, Robert Keys 1925- *AmSCAP 80, CpmDNM 78*
Clark, Rogie 1917- *AmSCAP 66, ConAmC*
Clark, Ronald 1933- *AmSCAP 66*
Clark, Rose Francis Langdon d1962 *NotNAT B*
Clark, Roy 1933- *BiDAmM, CounME 74[port], EncFCWM 69, IlEncCM[port], RkOn 2[port]*
Clark, Roy Linwood 1933- *CounME 74A*
Clark, Samuel H 1914- *IntMPA 77, -75, -76, -78, -79, -80*
Clark, Sanford *RkOn*
Clark, Sondra Rae Scholder 1941- *IntWWM 77, -80*
Clark, Spencer W 1908- *WhoJazz 72*
Clark, Susan 1940- *FilmEn, FilmgC, ForYSC, HalFC 80, IntMPA 77, -75, -76, -78, -79, -80, WhoHol A*
Clark, Susan Hansen *WomWMM B*
Clark, T Sealey d1909 *NotNAT B*
Clark, Terrell Lee 1946- *AmSCAP 80*
Clark, Thomas Sidney 1949- *ConAmC*
Clark, Trilby *Film 2, IlWWBF*
Clark, Wallis d1961 *WhoHol B*
Clark, Wallis 1888-1961 *NotNAT B, WhThe*

Clark, Wallis 1889-1961 *Vers B[port], WhScrn 74, -77*
Clark, Walter, Jr. 1929- *EncJzS 70*
Clark, Walter E, Jr. *NatPD[port]*
Clark, Westcott *Film 2*
Clark, William Charles Sydney 1946- *IntWWM 77, -80*
Clark, William T d1925 *NotNAT B*
Clark, Willis Gaylord 1810-1841 *BiDAmM*
Clark, Yodeling Slim 1917- *IlEncCM*
Clark And McCullough *JoeFr*
Clarke, Adam 1762-1832 *OxMus*
Clarke, Allan *ConMuA 80A*
Clarke, Andrew Henry Alan 1954- *IntWWM 80*
Clarke, Angela *ForYSC, WhoHol A*
Clarke, Arthur C 1917- *WhoHrs 80*
Clarke, Austin 1896-1974 *CnMD SUP*
Clarke, Betty Ross *Film 2, WhScrn 77*
Clarke, Buck 1932- *BiDAmM*
Clarke, Buddy *BgBands 74*
Clarke, C Downing *Film 2*
Clarke, Charles G 1889- *FilmEn*
Clarke, Charles G 1899- *IntMPA 77, -75, -76, -78, -79, -80, WorEFlm*
Clarke, Creston 1865-1910 *NotNAT B, WhoStg 1906, -1908*
Clarke, Cuthbert 1869-1953 *WhThe*
Clarke, David 1908- *BiE&WWA, NatPD[port], NotNAT, WhoHol A*
Clarke, Douglas 1893-1962 *OxMus*
Clarke, Downing George d1930 *WhScrn 74, -77, WhoHol B*
Clarke, Frederick Robert Charles 1931- *IntWWM 77, -80*
Clarke, Gage 1900-1964 *WhScrn 77*
Clarke, Garry E 1943- *ConAmC*
Clarke, Gary 1935?- *WhoHrs 80[port]*
Clarke, George *Film 1*
Clarke, George 1840-1900 *NotNAT B*
Clarke, George 1840-1906 *WhoStg 1906, -1908*
Clarke, George 1886-1946 *NotNAT B, WhThe*
Clarke, George F 1911- *WhoJazz 72*
Clarke, George Frederick 1883- *CreCan 2*
Clarke, Gordon 1940- *IntWWM 77*
Clarke, Gordon B 1907-1972 *WhScrn 77, WhoHol B*
Clarke, Gordon Wilfred 1930- *WhoMus 72*
Clarke, Grant 1891-1931 *AmPS, AmSCAP 66, -80, BiDAmM, CmpEPM, Sw&Ld C*
Clarke, H Saville d1893 *NotNAT B*
Clarke, Hamilton 1840-1912 *NewGrD 80*
Clarke, Harold Richard 1914- *IntWWM 77, -80, WhoMus 72*
Clarke, Harry Corson d1923 *NotNAT B, WhoStg 1906, -1908*
Clarke, Harvey *Film 2*
Clarke, Henry Leland 1907- *Baker 78, ConAmC, DcCM, NewGrD 80*
Clarke, Herbert Lincoln 1867-1945 *AmSCAP 66, -80, BiDAmM, NewGrD 80*
Clarke, Hugh Archibald 1839-1927 *Baker 78, BiDAmM, NewGrD 80*
Clarke, J I C 1846-1925 *NotNAT A, -B*
Clarke, J Laurence 1900- *WhoMus 72*
Clarke, James Freeman 1810-1888 *BiDAmM*
Clarke, James Hamilton Smee 1840-1912 *Baker 78*
Clarke, James P 1807?-1877 *NewGrD 80*
Clarke, James Paton 1808-1877 *Baker 78*
Clarke, Jeremiah 1670?-1707 *OxMus*
Clarke, Jeremiah 1673?-1707 *Baker 78, MusMk*
Clarke, Jeremiah 1674?-1707 *BnBkM 80, NewGrD 80*
Clarke, Jeremiah 1743?-1809 *NewGrD 80*
Clarke, Joan *WhoMus 72*
Clarke, John *WhoHol A*
Clarke, John 1770-1836 *Baker 78, NewGrD 80*
Clarke, John Sleeper 1833-1899 *NotNAT B, OxThe*
Clarke, Kenneth Spearman 1914- *BiDAmM, EncJzS 70*
Clarke, Kenny 1914- *CmpEPM, EncJzS 70, NewGrD 80*
Clarke, Klook 1914- *EncJzS 70*
Clarke, Laurence G 1928- *ConAmC*
Clarke, Mae *MotPP*
Clarke, Mae 1907- *FilmEn, HolP 30[port], ThFT[port], WhThe*
Clarke, Mae 1910- *Film 2, FilmgC, ForYSC, HalFC 80, What 4[port], WhoHol A, WhoHrs 80[port]*
Clarke, Mae 1916- *MovMk[port]*
Clarke, Mary 1923- *CnOxB, DancEn 78*
Clarke, Mary Alice *BlkWAB*
Clarke, Nigel 1895- *WhThe*
Clarke, Paul 1947-1976 *CnOxB*
Clarke, Pete 1911- *WhoJazz 72*
Clarke, Rebecca 1886- *AmSCAP 66, Baker 78, ConAmC, NewGrD 80, OxMus*
Clarke, Redfield *Film 2*
Clarke, Richard *WhoHol A*
Clarke, Robert 1920- *ForYSC, WhoHol A, WhoHrs 80[port]*
Clarke, Robert Coningsby 1879-1934 *Baker 78*
Clarke, Rosemary 1921- *CpmDNM 75, -79, -80, ConAmC*
Clarke, Sir Rupert 1865-1926 *WhThe*
Clarke, Sebastian *BlkAmP*
Clarke, Shirley 1925- *ConLC 16, DcFM, FilmEn, FilmgC, HalFC 80, OxFilm, WomWMM, WorEFlm*
Clarke, Stanley 1951- *ConMuA 80A, EncJzS 70, IlEncJ*
Clarke, Stephen 1735?-1797 *NewGrD 80, OxMus*
Clarke, Stephen Lionel 1951- *IntWWM 80*
Clarke, T E B 1907- *CmMov, ConDr 73, -77A, DcFM, FilmEn, FilmgC, HalFC 80, IlWWBF A, OxFilm, WorEFlm*
Clarke, Terence Michael 1944- *BiDAmM, EncJzS 70*
Clarke, Terry 1944- *EncJzS 70, IntWWM 80*
Clarke, Thatcher 1937- *CnOxB*
Clarke, Tom *ConDr 73, -77C*
Clarke, Wescott B *Film 2*
Clarke, Wilfred d1945 *NotNAT B*
Clarke, William 1775?-1820 *NewGrD 80*
Clarke, William Horatio 1840-1913 *Baker 78, BiDAmM*
Clarke, William Hutchinson 1865- *WhoStg 1908*
Clarke-Smith, D A 1888-1959 *FilmgC, HalFC 80, WhScrn 74, -77, WhoHol B*
Clarke-Smith, Douglas A 1888-1959 *WhThe*
Clarke-Whitfeld, John 1770-1836 *NewGrD 80, OxMus*
Clarkson, Geoffrey 1914- *AmSCAP 66, -80, CmpEPM*
Clarkson, Harry F 1882-1959 *AmSCAP 66, -80*
Clarkson, Joan 1903- *WhThe*
Clarkson, Willie 1861-1934 *Film 1, WhThe*
Claro, Samuel 1934- *NewGrD 80*
Claro-Valdes, Samuel 1934- *IntWWM 77, -80*
Clarus, Max 1852-1916 *Baker 78*
Clary, Charles 1873-1931 *Film 1, -2, WhScrn 77*
Clary, Robert 1926- *BiE&WWA, WhoHol A*
Clary, Salone Theodore 1939- *AmSCAP 80*
Clash, The *ConMuA 80A, IlEncR*
Classics, The *RkOn[port]*
Claty, Charles *Film 2*
Claude De Sermisy *NewGrD 80*
Claude, Toby *Film 2*
Claudel, Paul 1868-1955 *CnMD, CnThe, EncWT, Ent, McGEWD[port], ModWD, NewEOp 71, NewGrD 80, NotNAT A, -B, OxThe, PlP&P[port], REnWD[port], WhThe*
Clauder, Joseph 1586-1653 *NewGrD 80*
Clauderus, Joseph 1586-1653 *NewGrD 80*
Claudin 1528-1600 *NewGrD 80, OxMus*
Claudin LeJeune *Baker 78*
Claudius Caesar Drusus Germanicus *NewGrD 80*
Claudius, Dane 1874-1946 *WhScrn 74, -77, WhoHol B*
Claughton, Susan *WhThe*
Claus, Hugo 1929- *CnMD, EncWT, ModWD*
Clausen, Alf H 1941- *AmSCAP 80*
Clausen, Bruce Edward 1948- *IntWWM 80*
Clausen, Svend 1893-1961 *CnMD*
Clausen, Thomas 1949- *IntWWM 77*
Clausetti, Eugenie 1905- *IntWWM 77, -80*
Clausetti, Eugenio 1905- *WhoMus 72*
Clausi, Anthony 1948- *AmSCAP 80*
Clauson, William 1930- *AmSCAP 80*
Clauss, Heinz 1935- *CnOxB*
Claussen, Joy 1938- *BiE&WWA*
Claussen, Julia 1879-1941 *Baker 78, NewEOp 71*
Claux, Johannes 1530?-1573 *NewGrD 80*
Clave, Anselmo 1824-1874 *NewGrD 80*
Clave, Antoni 1913- *CnOxB, DancEn 78*
Clave, Jose Anselmo 1824-1874 *Baker 78*
Clavel, Antoinette Cecile *NewGrD 80*
Clavel, Maurice 1918- *CnMD*
Clavell, James *IntMPA 75*
Clavell, James 1922- *FilmgC, HalFC 80*
Clavell, James 1924- *FilmEn, WorEFlm*
Clavell, Richard J 1932- *WhoOp 76*
Claver, Bob *NewYTET*
Claver, Robert E 1928- *AmSCAP 66*
Claverie, Michele 1939- *WhoOp 76*
Clavie, Leopold-Charles 1904- *IntWWM 77, -80*
Clavier, Josette 1933- *CnOxB*
Clavijo DelCastillo, Bernardo 1549?-1626? *NewGrD 80*
Clavius, Christoph 1538?-1612 *NewGrD 80*
Clavius, Christophorus 1538?-1612 *NewGrD 80*
Claxton, Andrew Edgar Kyle 1950- *IntWWM 80*
Claxton, Erie *AmSCAP 80*
Claxton, Kate 1848-1924 *FamA&A[port], OxThe*
Claxton, Kate 1850-1924 *NotNAT B*
Claxton, Leslie Edward Mitchell 1910- *WhoMus 72*
Claxton, Rozelle 1913- *WhoJazz 72*
Claxton, William F *NewYTET*
Clay, Buriel, II 1943- *BlkAmP, MorBAP*
Clay, Carl B 1951- *AmSCAP 80*
Clay, Carolyn Elizabeth 1948- *ConAmTC*
Clay, Cecil d1920 *NotNAT B*
Clay, Charles *OxMus*
Clay, Charles 1906- *CreCan 1*
Clay, Frederic 1838-1889 *Baker 78, NewGrD 80*
Clay, Frederick Emes 1838-1889 *OxMus*
Clay, Shirley 1902-1951 *BiDAmM, WhoJazz 72*
Clay, Sonny 1899- *WhoJazz 72*
Clay, Tom *RkOn 2A*
Clayburgh, Jill 1944- *FilmEn*
Clayburgh, Jill 1945- *HalFC 80, IntMPA 78, -79, -80, WhoHol A*
Clayden, Pauline 1922- *CnOxB, DancEn 78*
Claypoole, Edward B 1883-1952 *AmSCAP 66, -80*
Clayre, Alasdair 1935- *WhoMus 72*
Clayton, Arthur *Film 2*
Clayton, Bessie d1948 *NotNAT B*
Clayton, Buck 1911- *CmpEPM, DrBlPA, EncJzS 70, IlEncJ, WhoJazz 72*
Clayton, Buck 1912- *AmSCAP 66*
Clayton, Dick *WhoHol A*
Clayton, Donald 1890-1964 *WhScrn 77*
Clayton, Eddie *Film 2*
Clayton, Edith 1897- *BiDAmM*
Clayton, Edward *Film 2*
Clayton, Ethel 1884-1966 *FilmEn, Film 1, -2, ForYSC, HalFC 80, MotPP, TwYS, WhScrn 74, -77, WhoHol B*
Clayton, Gilbert 1860-1950 *Film 2, WhScrn 77*
Clayton, Hazel 1886-1963 *NotNAT B, WhScrn 74, -77, WhoHol B*
Clayton, Heather Mary 1932- *WhoMus 72*
Clayton, Herbert 1876-1931 *NotNAT B, WhThe*
Clayton, Herbert Kenneth 1920- *IntWWM 80, WhoMus 72*
Clayton, Ja *IntMPA 79*
Clayton, Jack 1921- *BiDFilm, -81, DcFM, FilmEn, FilmgC, HalFC 80, IlWWBF, IntMPA 77, -75, -76, -78, -79, -80, MovMk[port], OxFilm, WhoHrs 80, WorEFlm*
Clayton, James 1902-1963 *NewOrJ[port]*
Clayton, Jan 1917- *BiE&WWA, EncMT, IntMPA 77, -75, -76, -78, -80, NotNAT, WhoHol A*
Clayton, Jane *WhoHol A*
Clayton, Lou 1887-1950 *NotNAT B, WhScrn 74, -77, WhoHol B*
Clayton, Marguerite *MotPP*
Clayton, Marguerite 1894?-1968 *WhScrn 77*

Clayton, Marguerite 1896- *FilmEn, Film 1, -2, TwYS*
Clayton, Norman John 1903- *NewGrD 80*
Clayton, Paul 1933- *BiDAmM, EncFCWM 69*
Clayton, Peter Joe 1898-1947 *BluesWW[port]*
Clayton, Steve *AmSCAP 80*
Clayton, Thomas 1660?-1730? *NewGrD 80*
Clayton, Una *WhoStg 1908*
Clayton, Wilbur 1912- *BiDAmM*
Clayton, Wilbur Dorsey 1911- *AmSCAP 80, EncJzS 70*
Clayton, William, Jr. 1897- *BlksB&W, -C*
Clayworth, June *WhoHol A*
Cleall, Charles 1927- *IntWWM 77, -80, WhoMus 72*
Cleander *OxThe*
Clearwater, Eddy 1935- *BluesWW[port]*
Cleary, Chip 1910- *IntMPA 77, -75, -76, -78, -79, -80*
Cleary, Leo Thomas 1895-1955 *WhScrn 74, -77, WhoHol B*
Cleary, Michael *Film 2*
Cleary, Michael H 1902-1954 *AmSCAP 66, -80, CmpEPM*
Cleary, Peggy 1892-1972 *WhScrn 77, WhoHol B*
Cleary, Ruth *AmSCAP 66, -80*
Cleary, Mrs. Vincent *PupTheA*
Cleather, Gordon 1872- *WhThe*
Cleave, Arthur *Film 1*
Cleave, Arthur 1884- *WhThe*
Cleave, Van *WhoHrs 80*
Cleaver, Sylvia 1926- *WhoMus 72*
Cleaver, William Emrys 1904- *WhoMus 72*
Clebanoff, Herman 1917- *AmSCAP 66, -80*
Cleemann, Friedrich 1770?-1825 *NewGrD 80*
Cleese, John 1939- *FilmgC, HalFC 80*
Cleeve, Stewart Montagu *IntWWM 77, -80, WhoMus 72*
Clef Club Orchestra *BiDAmM*
Cleftones, The *RkOn[port]*
Clegg, Cy *Film 2*
Clegg, R *WhoMus 72*
Clegg, Valce V 1888-1947 *WhScrn 74, -77, WhoHol B*
Cleghorn, John H 1909- *IntMPA 77, -75, -76, -78*
Cleighton, Peter *BluesWW*
Clelland, Lamond 1921- *IntWWM 77, -80, WhoMus 72*
Clem, Edward *NewOrJ*
Clem, Johann Gottlob *NewGrD 80*
Cleman, Majel *Film 2*
Cleman, Thomas J 1941- *ConAmC*
Clemencic, Rene 1928- *NewGrD 80*
Clemens 1510?-1556? *NewGrD 80*
Clemens, Albert *BluesWW*
Clemens, Benjamin S 1790?-1854 *BiDAmM*
Clemens, Brian 1931- *FilmgC, HalFC 80, IntMPA 77, -75, -76, -78, -79, -80, WhoHrs 80*
Clemens, Charles Edwin 1858-1923 *Baker 78*
Clemens, Clara 1874-1921 *BiDAmM*
Clemens, Earl L 1925- *IntWWM 77, -80*
Clemens, Hans 1890-1958 *Baker 78*
Clemens, Jacobus 1510?-1556? *Baker 78*
Clemens, Jacobus 1510?-1557 *MusMk*
Clemens, Johann Georg *NewGrD 80*
Clemens, LeRoy 1889- *Film 2, WhThe*
Clemens, William 1905- *FilmEn, FilmgC, HalFC 80*
Clemens Non Papa 1510?-1556? *OxMus*
Clemens Non Papa, Jacobus 1510?-1558? *BnBkM 80*
Clement IX, Pope *NewGrD 80*
Clement, Andries 1943- *IntWWM 77, -80*
Clement, Charles-Francois 1720?-1782? *NewGrD 80*
Clement, Clay 1888-1956 *NotNAT B, WhScrn 74, -77, WhThe, WhoHol B*
Clement, Dick 1937- *FilmEn, FilmgC, HalFC 80*
Clement, Donald 1941-1970 *WhScrn 74, -77, WhoHol B*
Clement, Doris *AmSCAP 80*
Clement, Edmond 1867-1928 *Baker 78, NewEOp 71*
Clement, Elfrida *WhThe*
Clement, Eloise *Film 1*
Clement, Felix 1822-1885 *Baker 78, NewGrD 80*
Clement, Frank d1937 *NotNAT B*
Clement, Franz 1780-1842 *Baker 78, NewGrD 80*
Clement, Jack 1932- *IlEncCM*
Clement, Jacob *NewGrD 80*
Clement, Jacobus *Baker 78*
Clement, Jacques 1510?-1558? *BnBkM 80*
Clement, Johann Georg 1710?-1794 *NewGrD 80*
Clement, Rene 1913- *BiDFilm, -81, DcFM, FilmEn, FilmgC, HalFC 80, MovMk[port], OxFilm, WorEFlm*
Clement-Cart, Marianne 1929- *IntWWM 77, -80*
Clement-Scott, Joan 1907-1969 *WhThe*
Clement-Scott, Margaret *WhThe*
Clemente, Steve *Film 1, -2*
Clementi, Aldo 1925- *Baker 78, DcCM, NewGrD 80*
Clementi, Johann Georg *NewGrD 80*
Clementi, Marjorie Doris 1927- *WhoMus 72*
Clementi, Mutius Philippus V F Xaverius 1752-1832 *NewGrD 80[port]*
Clementi, Muzio 1752-1832 *Baker 78, BnBkM 80[port], DcCom&M 79, GrComp[port], MusMk, NewGrD 80[port], OxMus*
Clementi, Pierre 1942- *FilmAG WE, FilmEn*
Clemento, Steve *Film 2*
Clements, Charles Edwin 1858-1933 *BiDAmM*
Clements, Charles Henry 1898- *WhoMus 72*
Clements, Colin d1948 *NotNAT B*
Clements, Dudley 1889-1947 *NotNAT B, WhScrn 77, WhoHol B*
Clements, Gwen R Sikes 1934- *IntWWM 77*
Clements, Heather Anne 1945- *WhoMus 72*
Clements, Sir John 1910- *CnThe, EncWT, Ent, FilmEn, FilmgC, HalFC 80, IlWWBF, PlP&P, WhoHol A, WhoThe 72, -77*
Clements, Joy *WhoOp 76*
Clements, Miriam *WhThe*
Clements, Otis 1926- *AmSCAP 66, -80*
Clements, Otis 1928- *ConAmC*
Clements, Paul D 1947- *AmSCAP 80*
Clements, Stanley 1926- *FilmEn, FilmgC, ForYSC, HalFC 80, Vers B[port], WhoHol A, WhoHrs 80*
Clements, Vassar *EncFCWM 69*
Clements, Vassar 1928- *IlEncCM[port]*
Clements, Zeke 1911- *IlEncCM[port]*
Clemm, Johann Gottlob *NewGrD 80*
Clemm, John 1690-1762 *Baker 78, BiDAmM, OxMus*
Clemons, James K 1883-1950 *WhScrn 74, -77, WhoHol B*
Clendenin, W Ritchie, Jr. 1943- *IntWWM 77*
Clendenin, William Ritchie, Sr. 1917- *IntWWM 77, -80*
Cleobury, Nicholas Randall 1950- *IntWWM 77, -80*
Cleobury, Stephen John 1948- *IntWWM 77, -80*
Cleonides *Baker 78, NewGrD 80*
Cleopatra 069BC-030BC *HalFC 80*
Clerambault *NewGrD 80*
Clerambault, Cesar-Francois-Nicolas d1760 *NewGrD 80*
Clerambault, Dominique 1644?-1704 *NewGrD 80*
Clerambault, Evrard Dominique 1710?-1790 *NewGrD 80*
Clerambault, Louis Nicholas 1676-1749 *BnBkM 80, OxMus*
Clerambault, Louis Nicolas 1676-1749 *Baker 78, MusMk, NewGrD 80[port]*
Clerc, Jean-Pantaleon Le *NewGrD 80*
Clercx, Suzanne 1910- *Baker 78*
Clercx-Lejeune, Suzanne 1910- *NewGrD 80*
Clereau, Pierre *Baker 78, NewGrD 80*
Clerget, Paul 1867-1935 *Film 1, -2, WhScrn 74, -77, WhoHol B*
Clerice, Justin 1863-1908 *Baker 78*
Clerici, Giovanni *NewGrD 80*
Clerici, Sebastiano *NewGrD 80*
Clerico, Francesco 1755?-1833? *CnOxB*
Clerico, Paolo 1518-1562? *NewGrD 80*
Clerk, Jeremiah *NewGrD 80*
Cless, Johann *NewGrD 80*
Cless, Rod 1907-1944 *CmpEPM, IlEncJ, WhoJazz 72*
Cleva, Fausto 1902-1971 *Baker 78, BiDAmM, BnBkM 80, CmOp, MusSN[port], NewEOp 71, NewGrD 80, WhoMus 72*
Cleva, Maria Angela *WhoOp 76*
Cleve, Halfdan 1879-1951 *Baker 78, NewGrD 80*
Cleve, Johannes De 1528?-1582 *NewGrD 80*
Cleveland, Anna 1880-1954 *WhScrn 77*
Cleveland, Charles Dexter 1802-1869 *BiDAmM, MorBAP*
Cleveland, George d1957 *MotPP, NotNAT B, WhoHol B*
Cleveland, George 1883-1957 *ForYSC, HolCA[port], WhScrn 74, -77*
Cleveland, George 1886-1957 *FilmEn, FilmgC, HalFC 80, Vers A[port]*
Cleveland, George 1886-1965 *MovMk*
Cleveland, James 1926- *EncJzS 70*
Cleveland, James 1931- *DrBlPA*
Cleveland, James 1932- *NewGrD 80*
Cleveland, James Milton 1926- *BiDAmM*
Cleveland, Jimmy 1926- *CmpEPM, EncJzS 70*
Cleveland, Robert R 1921- *AmSCAP 80*
Cleveland, William H, Jr. *PupTheA*
Cleveland Singers *BiDAmM*
Clewing, Carl *Film 1, -2*
Clewlow, F D d1957 *NotNAT B*
Clibano, Hieronimus De d1504? *NewGrD 80*
Clibano, Jacobus De *NewGrD 80*
Clibano, Jerome De d1504? *NewGrD 80*
Clibano, Jherome De d1504? *NewGrD 80*
Clibano, Jheronimo De d1504? *NewGrD 80*
Clibano, Nicasio De d1497 *NewGrD 80*
Clibano, Nicasius De d1497 *NewGrD 80*
Clibano, Nicolas De d1497 *NewGrD 80*
Clibano, Nycasius De d1497 *NewGrD 80*
Cliburn, Harvey Lavan 1934- *BiDAmM*
Cliburn, Van 1934- *Baker 78, BnBkM 80, IntWWM 77, -80, MusMk, MusSN[port], NewGrD 80, WhoMus 72*
Clickner, Susan Fisher 1934- *IntWWM 77, -80*
Clicquot *Baker 78, NewGrD 80*
Clicquot, Claude Francois 1762-1801 *NewGrD 80*
Clicquot, Francois-Henri 1732-1790 *Baker 78, NewGrD 80*
Clicquot, Jean-Baptiste 1678-1744 *Baker 78*
Clicquot, Jean-Baptiste 1678-1746 *NewGrD 80*
Clicquot, Louis-Alexandre 1680?-1760 *Baker 78*
Clicquot, Louis-Alexandre 1684?-1760 *NewGrD 80*
Clicquot, Robert 1645?-1719 *Baker 78, NewGrD 80*
Cliff, Charles Joseph 1912- *AmSCAP 66, -80*
Cliff, Daisy *BluesWW*
Cliff, Jimmy 1948- *ConMuA 80A, DrBlPA, IlEncR, RkOn 2[port]*
Cliff, Laddie 1891-1937 *EncMT, HalFC 80, NotNAT B, WhScrn 74, -77, WhThe, WhoHol B*
Cliffe, Frederic 1857-1931 *NewGrD 80*
Cliffe, Frederick 1857-1931 *Baker 78*
Cliffe, H Cooper 1862-1939 *Film 1, -2, NotNAT B, WhScrn 74, -77, WhThe, WhoHol B, WhoStg 1908*
Cliffe, Percy Eric *WhoMus 72*
Clifford, Buzz 1942- *RkOn[port]*
Clifford, Camille *WhThe*
Clifford, Charles d1943 *NotNAT B*
Clifford, Daphne Monica 1926- *IntWWM 77, -80, WhoMus 72*
Clifford, Doug R 1945- *AmSCAP 80*
Clifford, Gordon 1902-1968 *AmSCAP 66, -80, NotNAT B*
Clifford, Jack 1880-1956 *ForYSC, NotNAT B, WhScrn 74, -77, WhoHol B*
Clifford, James 1622-1698 *NewGrD 80, OxMus*
Clifford, John 1947- *CnOxB*
Clifford, John William 1918- *AmSCAP 80*
Clifford, Kathleen *Film 1, -2*
Clifford, Kathleen d1963 *NotNAT B*
Clifford, Kathleen 1887-1962 *WhScrn 74, -77, WhThe, WhoHol B*
Clifford, Larry d1955 *WhScrn 77*
Clifford, Margaret Ellen 1908- *BiE&WWA*
Clifford, Mary Angela 1932- *WhoMus 72*
Clifford, Mike 1943- *RkOn[port]*
Clifford, Robert William 1921- *WhoMus 72*

Clifford, Ruth 1900- *FilmEn, Film 1, -2, ForYSC, TwYS, WhoHol A*
Clifford, Mrs. W K d1929 *NotNAT B, WhThe*
Clifford, William d1941 *Film 1, -2, WhoHol B*
Clifford, William 1878-1941 *WhScrn 77*
Clifford-Smith, Ronald Herbert *WhoMus 72*
Cliffon, William 1877-1941 *WhScrn 74*
Clift, Denison 1892-1961 *FilmEn*
Clift, Denison 1893- *IntMPA 77, -75, -76, -78, -79, -80*
Clift, Denison 1894- *IlWWBF*
Clift, Dennis Richard 1919- *IntWWM 77, -80, WhoMus 72*
Clift, Ernest Paul 1881-1963 *WhThe*
Clift, Montgomery 1920-1966 *BiDFilm, -81, BiE&WWA, CmMov, FilmEn, FilmgC, HalFC 80, MotPP, MovMk, NotNAT B, OxFilm, WhScrn 74, -77, WhThe, WhoHol B, WorEFlm*
Clift, Montgomery 1921-1966 *ForYSC*
Clifton, Arthur 1784-1832 *BiDAmM*
Clifton, Bernard 1902-1970 *WhThe*
Clifton, Bill 1931- *BiDAmM, IlEncCM[port]*
Clifton, Chalmers 1889-1966 *Baker 78, BiDAmM, ConAmC*
Clifton, Elmer d1949 *NotNAT B, WhoHol B, WomWMM*
Clifton, Elmer 1890-1947 *Film 2*
Clifton, Elmer 1890-1949 *Film 1, FilmgC, HalFC 80, TwYS A*
Clifton, Elmer 1892-1949 *FilmEn*
Clifton, Elmer 1893-1949 *WhScrn 74, -77*
Clifton, Elmer 1895-1947 *TwYS*
Clifton, Emma *Film 1*
Clifton, Geoffrey 1920- *WhoMus 72*
Clifton, Harry 1832-1872 *OxThe*
Clifton, Herbert 1884-1947 *WhScrn 74, -77, WhoHol B*
Clifton, John *AmSCAP 80*
Clifton, Josephine d1847 *NotNAT B*
Clifton, Michelle Gamm 1944- *WomWMM B*
Clifton, William 1800?-1870? *BiDAmM*
Clifton, William John *NewGrD 80*
Clifton-James, M E 1898-1963 *WhScrn 77*
Climax *RkOn 2[port]*
Climax Blues Band *ConMuA 80A, IlEncR, RkOn 2[port]*
Climen, J De *NewGrD 80*
Climenhaga, Joel Ray 1922- *BiE&WWA, NotNAT*
Climmons, Artie *BlkAmP, MorBAP*
Clinch, Peter Gladstone 1930- *IntWWM 80*
Cline, Brady *Film 2*
Cline, Eddie 1892-1948 *WorEFlm*
Cline, Eddie 1892-1961 *FilmEn, TwYS A, WhScrn 74, -77, WhoHol B*
Cline, Edward 1892-1961 *DcFM, Film 1, -2, FilmgC, HalFC 80, MovMk[port]*
Cline, George *Film 2*
Cline, Maggie 1857-1934 *AmPS B, NotNAT B*
Cline, Patsy 1932-1963 *BiDAmM, CounME 74[port], -74A, EncFCWM 69, IlEncCM[port], RkOn*
Cline, Robert *Film 2*
Clingher, Teodoro d1602 *NewGrD 80*
Clinio, Teodoro d1602 *NewGrD 80*
Clint, H O'Reilly 1900-1961 *AmSCAP 66, -80*
Clinton, Edward J 1948- *NatPD[port]*
Clinton, Francis Gordon 1912- *IntWWM 77, -80, WhoMus 72*
Clinton, Geoffrey *Film 2*
Clinton, George *ConMuA 80B*
Clinton, George Arthur 1850-1913 *NewGrD 80*
Clinton, Kate d1935 *NotNAT B*
Clinton, Larry 1909- *AmPS B, AmSCAP 66, -80, BgBands 74[port], CmpEPM, WhoJazz 72*
Clippinger, David Alva 1860-1938 *Baker 78*
Clipsham, Olive 1904- *WhoMus 72*
Clique *RkOn 2A*
Cliques, The *RkOn*
Cliquet, Henri 1894-1963 *NewGrD 80*
Cliquet-Pleyel, Henri 1894-1963 *NewGrD 80*
Cliquot *NewGrD 80*
Clisbee, Ethel *Film 1*
Clitheroe, Jimmy 1923-1973 *WhScrn 77*
Cliutmas, Harry F d1964 *NotNAT B*
Clive, Catherine 1711-1785 *NewGrD 80[port]*
Clive, Colin 1898-1937 *CmMov, FilmEn, FilmgC, ForYSC, HalFC 80, MovMk, PlP&P, WhScrn 74, -77, WhoHol B, WhoHrs 80[port]*
Clive, Colin 1900-1937 *FilmAG WE, NotNAT B, WhThe*
Clive, David J 1923- *BiE&WWA*
Clive, E E 1879-1940 *FilmEn, FilmgC, HalFC 80, MovMk*
Clive, E E 1880-1940 *HolCA[port], Vers A[port], WhoHol B*
Clive, E E 1898-1937 *ForYSC*
Clive, E E 1898-1940 *WhScrn 74, -77*
Clive, Edward E d1940 *NotNAT B*
Clive, Henry 1883-1960 *Film 1, WhScrn 74, -77, WhoHol B*
Clive, Kitty 1711-1785 *CnThe, EncWT, Ent, NewGrD 80[port], NotNAT A, -B, OxThe, PlP&P*
Clive, Vincent d1943 *WhThe*
Cload, Julia 1946- *IntWWM 77, -80, WhoMus 72*
Cloche, Maurice 1907- *DcFM, FilmEn, FilmgC, HalFC 80*
Clodius, Christian 1647-1717 *NewGrD 80*
Cloerec, Rene 1911- *DcFM, WhoMus 72*
Cloke, Olive *WhoMus 72*
Clokey, Joseph Waddel 1890-1960 *AmSCAP 80*
Clokey, Joseph Waddel 1890-1961 *AmSCAP 66*
Clokey, Joseph Waddell 1890-1960 *Baker 78*
Clokey, Joseph Waddell 1890-1961 *BiDAmM, ConAmC*
Clonblough, G Butler *FilmEn*
Clonbough, G Butler *Film 1*
Clonebaugh, G Butler d1943 *WhoHol B*
Cloninger, Ralph *Film 2*
Clooney, Betty 1930?- *CmpEPM*
Clooney, Rosemary 1928- *AmPS A, -B, BiDAmM, CmpEPM, FilmEn, FilmgC, ForYSC, HalFC 80, RkOn[port], WhoHol A, WhoMus 72*
Cloquet, Ghislain 1924- *WorEFlm*
Clore, Leon *IntMPA 77, -75, -76, -78, -79, -80*
Clork, Harry *IntMPA 77, -75, -76, -78, -79, -80*
Close, Iva *Film 2*
Close, Ivy 1890-1968 *IlWWBF[port], WhScrn 74, -77*
Close, Ivy 1893- *Film 1, -2*
Close, Ivy 1893-1968 *FilmEn*
Close, John d1964 *WhScrn 77*
Close, Roy M *ConAmTC*
Closser, Louise 1872- *WhThe*
Closson, Ernest 1870-1950 *Baker 78, NewGrD 80*
Closson, Herman 1901- *ModWD*
Clothier, William H 1903- *CmMov, FilmEn, FilmgC, HalFC 80, WorEFlm*
Clottu, Dagmar 1952- *IntWWM 77, -80*
Cloud, Lee V 1950- *IntWWM 80*
Clough, Inez *BlksBF*
Clough, John Francis 1952- *IntWWM 77*
Clough, Kathleen 1904- *WhoMus 72*
Clough-Leighter, Henry 1874-1956 *Baker 78*
Clough-Leiter, Henry 1874-1956 *BiDAmM, ConAmC, NewGrD 80*
Clouse, Robert *HalFC 80*
Clouse, Rose 1865- *BiDAmM*
Clouser, James 1935- *CnOxB, CreCan 1, DancEn 78*
Clouser, Lionel Randolph 1910-1942 *AmSCAP 80*
Cloussnitzer, Paul *OxMus*
Cloutier, Albert 1902-1965 *CreCan 2*
Cloutier, Cecile 1930- *CreCan 1*
Cloutier, Eugene 1921- *CreCan 1*
Cloutier, Maurice E 1933- *AmSCAP 66, -80*
Cloutier, Suzanne 1927- *FilmEn, FilmgC, HalFC 80, WhoHol A*
Clouzot, H G *IntMPA 75, -76*
Clouzot, Henri-Georges 1907-1977 *BiDFilm, -81, DcFM, FilmEn, FilmgC, HalFC 80, IntMPA 77, MovMk[port], OxFilm, WhoHrs 80, WorEFlm*
Clouzot, Vera 1921-1960 *FilmgC, HalFC 80, WhScrn 74, WhoHol B*
Clouzout, Vera d1960 *WhScrn 77*
Clovelly, Cecil 1891-1965 *Film 2, WhScrn 74, -77, WhoHol B*
Clover, David Alexander 1930- *IntMPA 79, -80, WhoMus 72*
Clovers, The *RkOn[port]*
Clow, Jo Ellen Thompson 1948- *IntWWM 80*
Cloward, Robert Louis 1934- *AmSCAP 66*
Clower, Jerry 1926- *IlEncCM[port]*
Clowes, Richard 1900- *WhThe*
Clubley, John Sherwood d1964 *NotNAT B*
Cluchey, Rick 1933- *ConDr 77*
Cluer, John d1728 *Baker 78, NewGrD 80*
Clug, A Stephen 1929- *IntMPA 80*
Clugston, H M *Film 2*
Clunes, Alec S 1912-1970 *FilmgC, HalFC 80, NotNAT A, -B, WhScrn 77, WhThe, WhoHol B*
Clunes, Alex 1913-1970 *WhScrn 74*
Clurman, Harold 1901- *BiE&WWA, CnThe, ConAmTC, FilmgC, HalFC 80, NotNAT, -A, OxThe, PlP&P[port], WhoThe 72, -77, WorEFlm*
Clurman, Harold Edgar 1901- *EncWT*
Clustine, Ivan 1862-1941 *CnOxB, DancEn 78*
Clute, Chester 1891-1956 *FilmEn, FilmgC, ForYSC, HalFC 80, Vers B[port], WhScrn 74, -77, WhoHol B*
Clute, Sidney *WhoHol A*
Clutsam, George H 1866-1951 *Baker 78*
Clutterbuck, Ursular Kant 1929- *WhoMus 72*
Clutton, Cecil 1909- *NewGrD 80*
Clutyens, Andre 1905-1967 *CmOp*
Cluytens, Andre 1905-1967 *Baker 78, BnBkM 80, MusSN[port], NewEOp 71, NewGrD 80*
Cluzeau-Mortet, Luis 1889-1957 *Baker 78, NewGrD 80*
Clyde, Andy 1872-1967 *ForYSC*
Clyde, Andy 1892-1967 *FilmEn, Film 2, FilmgC, HalFC 80, HolCA[port], MotPP, TwYS, Vers A[port], WhScrn 74, -77, WhoHol B*
Clyde, David 1855-1945 *WhScrn 74, -77, WhoHol B*
Clyde, Jean 1889-1962 *NotNAT B, WhScrn 74, -77, WhoHol B*
Clyde, June 1909- *FilmEn, Film 2, ForYSC, ThFT[port], WhoHol A*
Clyde, Thomas 1949- *IntMPA 77, -75, -76, -78, -79, -80*
Clymer, Beth 1887-1952 *WhScrn 74, -77*
Clyne, Lionel 1908- *IntMPA 77, -75, -76, -78, -79, -80*
Clyne, Malcolm Edward 1943- *IntWWM 77, -80*
Cnattingius, Claes Magnus 1933- *IntWWM 80*
Coad, Joyce Marie *Film 2*
Coad, Oral Sumner 1887- *NotNAT*
Coakley, Marion *Film 2, WhThe*
Coakley, Patty *Film 2*
Coakley, Tom *CmpEPM*
Coalter, Frazer *Film 2*
Coan, Nonee Edward 1910- *AmSCAP 66, -80*
Coasters, The *AmPS A, BiDAmM, IlEncR, RkOn[port]*
Coates, Albert 1882-1953 *Baker 78, BnBkM 80, CmOp, MusSN[port], NewEOp 71, NewGrD 80, OxMus*
Coates, Anne V 1925- *HalFC 80, WomWMM*
Coates, Carolyn 1930- *WhoHol A, WhoThe 72, -77*
Coates, Carroll 1929- *AmSCAP 80*
Coates, Dale Young 1942- *IntWWM 77, -80*
Coates, Douglas Marsden 1898- *WhoMus 72*
Coates, Edith 1908- *CmOp, IntWWM 77, -80, NewGrD 80, WhoMus 72*
Coates, Eric 1886-1957 *Baker 78, DcCM, MusMk, NewGrD 80, OxMus*
Coates, Franklin *Film 2*
Coates, Gloria Kannenberg 1938- *CpmDNM 75, ConAmC, IntWWM 77, -80*
Coates, John 1865-1941 *Baker 78, CmOp, MusSN[port], NewGrD 80, OxMus*
Coates, John Francis, Jr. 1938- *EncJzS 70*
Coates, Leon 1937- *IntWWM 77, -80*
Coates, Lulu *BlksBF*
Coates, Paul 1921-1968 *WhScrn 77*
Coates, Philip Duncan 1937- *IntWWM 77*
Coates, Phyllis *ForYSC, WhoHol A*
Coates, Phyllis 1927?- *WhoHrs 80[port]*
Coates, Robert 1772-1848 *OxThe*
Coates, Tamara 1928- *IntWWM 77, -80,*

WhoMus 72
Coates, William David D 1916- *IntMPA 77, -75, -76, -78, -79*
Coats, Gordon Telfer 1930- *WhoOp 76*
Coats, R Roy 1898- *AmSCAP 66, -80*
Cob, James d1697 *NewGrD 80*
Cobb, A Willard 1929- *IntWWM 77, -80*
Cobb, Alice *PupTheA*
Cobb, Arnett Cleophus 1918- *CmpEPM, DrBlPA, EncJzS 70, IlEncJ, WhoJazz 72*
Cobb, Charles H, Jr. 1937- *IntWWM 77*
Cobb, Clifford *Film 2*
Cobb, David Alan 1930- *IntWWM 77, -80*
Cobb, Donald Lorain 1936- *CpmDNM 80*
Cobb, Edmund 1892-1974 *FilmEn, Film 1, -2, ForYSC, TwYS, Vers A[port], WhScrn 77, WhoHol B*
Cobb, George L 1886-1942 *AmSCAP 66, -80*
Cobb, Grover C d1975 *NewYTET*
Cobb, Hazel 1892-1973 *ConAmC*
Cobb, Irvin S 1876-1944 *FilmEn, Film 1, HalFC 80, NotNAT B, WhScrn 74, -77, WhoHol B*
Cobb, Irvin S 1877-1944 *ForYSC*
Cobb, James d1697 *NewGrD 80*
Cobb, Jimmy 1929- *EncJzS 70*
Cobb, Joe Fat 1917- *Film 2*
Cobb, Joe Wheezer *WhoHol A*
Cobb, Joey 1917- *TwYS*
Cobb, John *NewGrD 80*
Cobb, Joyce Renee 1945- *BlkWAB[port]*
Cobb, Junie 1896- *WhoJazz 72*
Cobb, Lee J 1911-1976 *BiDFilm, -81, BiE&WWA, CmMov, Ent, FamA&A[port], FilmEn, FilmgC, ForYSC, HalFC 80, HolCA[port], IntMPA 75, -76, MotPP, MovMk[port], NotNAT B, OxFilm, PlP&P[port], WhThe, WhoHol C, WorEFlm[port]*
Cobb, Margaret Evelyn 1918- *IntWWM 77, -80, WhoMus 72*
Cobb, Otis *PupTheA*
Cobb, Thomas *NewGrD 80*
Cobb, Ty 1886-1961 *WhScrn 77*
Cobb, Tyrone Jennings 1924- *AmSCAP 80*
Cobb, Wilbur James 1929- *BiDAmM, EncJzS 70*
Cobb, Will D 1876-1930 *AmPS, AmSCAP 66, -80, BiDAmM, CmpEPM, Sw&Ld B*
Cobbe, Hugh Michael Thomas 1942- *IntWWM 77, -80*
Cobbett, Walter Willson 1847-1937 *OxMus*
Cobbett, Walter Wilson 1847-1937 *Baker 78, NewGrD 80*
Cobbold, William 1560-1639 *NewGrD 80, OxMus*
Cobbs, Willie 1940- *BluesWW*
Cobelli, Giuseppina 1898-1948 *NewGrD 80*
Coben, Cy 1919- *AmSCAP 66, -80*
Coberg, Johann Anton 1649?-1708 *NewGrD 80*
Cobey, Louis 1897-1972 *AmSCAP 66, -80*
Cobey, Philip Sheridan 1910- *IntMPA 77, -75, -76, -78, -79*
Cobham, Billy *ConMuA 80A*
Cobham, Billy 1944- *EncJzS 70, IlEncR*
Cobham, Billy 1947?- *DrBlPA*
Cobham, William C 1944- *EncJzS 70*
Cobhold, William *NewGrD 80*
Cobine, Albert Stewart 1929- *ConAmC*
Coble, James William 1930- *IntWWM 77*
Cobley, Martin Howard 1944- *IntWWM 80*
Cobold, William *NewGrD 80*
Coborn, Charles 1852-1945 *FilmgC, HalFC 80, WhScrn 77, WhThe*
Coborn, Charlie 1852-1945 *NotNAT B, OxThe*
Cobos, Antonia *DancEn 78*
Cobos, Henry Diaz 1931- *IntWWM 77, -80*
Coburn, Bob *ConMuA 80B*
Coburn, Charles 1877-1961 *BiDFilm, -81, EncWT, FilmEn, FilmgC, ForYSC, HalFC 80, HolCA[port], MotPP, MovMk[port], NotNAT B, OxFilm, OxThe, Vers A[port], WhScrn 74, -77, WhThe, WhoHol B, WorEFlm*
Coburn, Dorothy *Film 2*
Coburn, Frederick Simpson 1871-1960 *CreCan 2*
Coburn, Gladys *Film 2*
Coburn, Ivah Wills 1882-1937 *EncWT, NotNAT B, OxThe*
Coburn, James 1928- *BiDFilm, -81, FilmEn, FilmgC, ForYSC, HalFC 80[port], IntMPA 77, -75, -76, -78, -79, -80, MotPP, MovMk, OxFilm, WhoHol A, WorEFlm*
Coburn, Jolly *BgBands 74, CmpEPM*
Coburn, Kathleen Hazel 1905- *CreCan 2*
Coburn, Richard 1886-1952 *AmSCAP 66, -80, BiDAmM*
Coburn, William James 1913- *AmSCAP 80*
Coca, Imogene *IntMPA 77, -75, -76, -78, -79, -80, NewYTET, WhoHol A*
Coca, Imogene 1908- *EncMT, ForYSC, HalFC 80, WhoThe 77*
Coca, Imogene 1909- *BiE&WWA, FilmgC, JoeFr, NotNAT, WhoThe 72*
Cocaine d1973? *WhScrn 77*
Cocchi, Claudio d1632? *NewGrD 80*
Cocchi, Gioacchino 1715?-1804 *Baker 78*
Cocchi, Gioacchino 1720?-1788? *NewGrD 80*
Cocchi, John 1939- *IntMPA 77, -75, -76, -78, -79, -80*
Coccia, Aurelio *Film 2*
Coccia, Carlo 1782-1873 *Baker 78, NewGrD 80*
Coccia, Maria Rosa 1759-1833 *NewGrD 80*
Cocciola, Giovanni Battista *NewGrD 80*
Cocea, Alice 1899- *WhThe*
Coceicao, Roque Da *NewGrD 80*
Coceycao, Diego Da *NewGrD 80*
Cochem, Martin Von *NewGrD 80*
Cochereau, Jacques 1680?-1734 *NewGrD 80*
Cochereau, Pierre 1924- *IntWWM 77, NewGrD 80, WhoMus 72*
Cochise 1818?-1874 *HalFC 80*
Cochlaeus, Johannes 1479-1552 *Baker 78, NewGrD 80*
Cochran, C B 1872-1951 *EncWT, NotNAT A*
Cochran, Sir Charles Blake 1872-1951 *EncMT, Ent, NotNAT B, OxThe, WhThe*
Cochran, Sir Charles Blake 1873-1951 *CnThe*
Cochran, Eddie d1960 *ConMuA 80A, IlEncR[port]*
Cochran, Eddie 1929-1960 *WhScrn 77*
Cochran, Eddie 1938-1960 *BiDAmM, RkOn[port]*
Cochran, Hank 1935- *CounME 74, -74A, EncFCWM 69, IlEncCM[port]*
Cochran, Henry 1935- *BiDAmM*
Cochran, J Paul 1946- *CpmDNM 76, -77, -78*
Cochran, Jean Kathleen 1928- *IntWWM 77, -80*
Cochran, Marsha Rabe 1948- *ConAmTC*
Cochran, Ron 1912- *IntMPA 77, -75, -76, -78, -79, -80*
Cochran, Steve 1917-1965 *BiE&WWA, FilmEn, FilmgC, ForYSC, HalFC 80, HolP 40[port], MotPP, MovMk, WhScrn 74, -77, WhoHol B, WorEFlm*
Cochran, Todd *EncJzS 70*
Cochran, William *WhoOp 76*
Cochrane, Frank 1882-1962 *NotNAT B, WhScrn 74, -77, WhThe, WhoHol B*
Cochrane, Talie *AmSCAP 80*
Cochrane, William Cecil Macvicar 1914- *WhoMus 72*
Cock, Lilian Mary 1910- *WhoMus 72*
Cock, Richard Alan Charles 1949- *IntWWM 77, -80*
Cock, Symon 1489-1562 *NewGrD 80*
Cockburn, Alicia 1712?-1794 *OxMus*
Cockburn, Catherine d1749 *NotNAT B*
Cockburn, John M d1964 *NotNAT B*
Cockelberg, Louis J 1880-1962 *WhScrn 74, -77*
Cocker, Joe 1944- *ConMuA 80A[port], IlEncR, RkOn 2[port]*
Cockerill, John T *WhoMus 72*
Cockerill, M B *WhoMus 72*
Cockney Rebel *IlEncR*
Cocks, Arthur Lincoln *Baker 78*
Cocks, Rena *WhoMus 72*
Cocks, Riquardus *NewGrD 80*
Cocks, Robert 1798-1887 *Baker 78, NewGrD 80*
Cocks, Robert Macfarlane *Baker 78*
Cocks, Stroud Lincoln *Baker 78*
Cocks And Company *Baker 78*
Cockshott, Gerald Wilfred 1915- *Baker 78, IntWWM 77, WhoMus 72*
Cockx, Riquardus *NewGrD 80*
Coclico, Adrianus Petit 1499?-1562 *NewGrD 80*
Coclico, Adrianus Petit 1500?-1563 *Baker 78*
Coclico, Adrien Petit 1500-1563 *MusMk*
Coco 1900-1974 *Ent*
Coco, James *IntMPA 75, -76, PlP&P[port], WhoHol A*
Coco, James 1928- *FilmgC, HalFC 80*
Coco, James 1929- *FilmEn, IntMPA 77, -78, -79, -80, WhoThe 77*
Coco, James 1930- *NotNAT, WhoThe 72*
Cocteau, Jean 1889-1963 *BiDFilm, -81, CnMD, CnThe, CnOxB, ConLC 16, DancEn 78, DcFM, EncWT, Ent[port], FilmEn, FilmgC, HalFC 80, McGEWD[port], ModWD, MovMk[port], NewGrD 80, NotNAT B, OxFilm, OxThe, REnWD[port], WhScrn 77, WhThe, WhoHrs 80, WorEFlm*
Cocteau, Jean 1891-1963 *NewEOp 71, NotNAT A*
Cocx, Jan 1630?-1678 *NewGrD 80*
Codax, Martin *NewGrD 80*
Codaz, Martin *NewGrD 80*
Code, Grant Hyde 1896-1974 *WhScrn 77, WhoHol B*
Codecasa, Teresa *NewGrD 80*
Codee, Ann 1890-1961 *FilmEn, FilmgC, ForYSC, HalFC 80, MovMk, WhScrn 74, -77, WhoHol B*
Coderre, Emile 1893-1970 *CreCan 2*
Codian, Michael 1915- *AmSCAP 66, -80*
Codling, Bess *BlkAmP*
Codman, Richard *PupTheA*
Codman, Stephen 1796?-1852 *NewGrD 80*
Codmans, The *DcPup*
Codreanu, Petre 1933- *WhoOp 76*
Codrington, Ann 1895- *WhThe*
Codron, Michael 1930- *WhoThe 72, -77*
Cody, Albert *Film 2*
Cody, Bill, Sr. 1891-1948 *FilmEn, ForYSC, NotNAT B, WhScrn 74, -77, WhoHol B*
Cody, Buffalo Bill 1846-1917 *Ent, WhoHol B*
Cody, Emmett F 1920-1960 *WhScrn 77*
Cody, Ethel d1957 *NotNAT B, WhoHol B*
Cody, Frank *ConMuA 80B*
Cody, Harry 1896-1956 *WhScrn 74, -77, WhoHol B*
Cody, Hiram Alfred 1872-1948 *CreCan 2*
Cody, Iron Eyes 1914- *ForYSC, MotPP, WhoHol A*
Cody, Iron Eyes 1916- *FilmEn*
Cody, Kathleen *WhoHol A*
Cody, Lew d1934 *MotPP, WhoHol B*
Cody, Lew 1884-1934 *FilmEn, Film 1, -2, FilmgC, HalFC 80, MovMk[port], TwYS*
Cody, Lew 1885-1934 *ForYSC*
Cody, Lew 1887-1934 *NotNAT B, WhScrn 74, -77*
Cody, Maurice *WhoMus 72*
Cody, Philip 1945- *AmSCAP 80*
Cody, Robert O 1928- *ConAmC*
Cody, William 1891-1948 *Film 1, -2*
Cody, William Frederick 1846-1917 *FilmgC, HalFC 80, NotNAT B, OxFilm, OxThe, WhScrn 77*
Cody, William Frederick 1913- *AmSCAP 80*
Coe, Anthony George 1934- *EncJzS 70*
Coe, Barry 1934- *FilmgC, ForYSC, HalFC 80, WhoHol A*
Coe, David Allan *IlEncCM[port]*
Coe, Donald G 1914- *IntMPA 77, -75, -76, -78, -79, -80*
Coe, Fred 1914-1979 *BiE&WWA, FilmEn, FilmgC, HalFC 80, IntMPA 77, -75, -76, -78, -79, NewYTET, NotNAT, WhoThe 72, -77*
Coe, Kelvin 1946- *CnOxB*
Coe, Kenton 1932- *ConAmC*
Coe, Peter 1929- *BiE&WWA, FilmgC, ForYSC, HalFC 80, NotNAT, WhoHol A, WhoThe 72, -77*
Coe, Richard L 1916- *BiE&WWA, IntMPA 77, -75, -76, -78, -79, -80, NotNAT*
Coe, Richard Livingston 1916- *ConAmTC*
Coe, Rose *Film 2*
Coe, Tony 1934- *EncJzS 70*
Coe, Vivian *WhoHol A*
Coedel, Lucien 1905-1947 *WhScrn 74, -77, WhoHol B*
Coelen, Lambert *NewGrD 80*

Coelho, Manuel Rodrigues NewGrD 80
Coelho, Peter 1906- IntWWM 77, -80
Coelho, Rui 1892- NewGrD 80
Coelho, Ruy 1891- Baker 78
Coelho, Ruy 1892- DcCM
Coelho, Terrye Lynn 1952- AmSCAP 80
Coelho Maciel, Emanuel 1935- IntWWM 77, -80
Coelho Neto, Marcos 1750?-1823 NewGrD 80
Coello Y Ochoa, Antonio 1611-1652 McGEWD
Coen, Franklin HalFC 80
Coen, Guido IntMPA 77, -75, -76, -78, -79, -80
Coen, Massimo 1933- IntWWM 77, -80
Coenen NewGrD 80
Coenen, Frans 1826-1904 NewGrD 80
Coenen, Franz 1826-1904 Baker 78
Coenen, Johannes Meinardus 1824-1899 Baker 78
Coenen, Johannes Meinardus 1825-1899 NewGrD 80
Coenen, Louis 1834-1900 NewGrD 80
Coenen, Louis 1856-1904 NewGrD 80
Coenen, Ludovicus 1797-1873 NewGrD 80
Coenen, Paul Franz 1908- IntWWM 77, -80
Coenen, Willem 1837-1918 Baker 78, NewGrD 80, OxMus
Coerne, Louis Adolphe 1870-1922 Baker 78, BiDAmM, ConAmC, NewGrD 80, OxMus
Coertse, Mimi 1932- WhoMus 72
Coertse, Mimi 1934- WhoOp 76
Coeuroy, Andre 1891- Baker 78, NewGrD 80
Cofalik, Antoni 1940- IntWWM 80
Coferati, Matteo 1638-1703 NewGrD 80
Coffee, Lenore Film 2, WomWMM
Coffee, Lenore J 1900?- FilmEn
Coffel, Clarence M 1900- AmSCAP 66
Coffer, Jack 1939-1967 WhScrn 74, -77
Coffey, Charles d1745 NewGrD 80, OxMus
Coffey, Clark Film 2
Coffey, Denise 1936- WhoThe 72, -77
Coffey, Dennis & The Detroit Guitar Band RkOn 2A
Coffey, John 1909-1944 WhScrn 74, -77
Coffin, Berton 1910- IntWWM 77, -80
Coffin, C Hayden 1862-1935 NotNAT A, -B, WhThe
Coffin, Hank 1904-1966 WhScrn 74, -77, WhoHol B
Coffin, Henry Sloane 1877-1954 BiDAmM
Coffin, Tristam HalFC 80
Coffin, Tristram ForYSC, WhoHol A, WhoHrs 80[port]
Coffman, Steven BlkAmP
Coffyn, Frank Film 2
Coffyn, Pauline Film 2
Cogan, Alma 1933-1966 WhScrn 77
Cogan, David J 1923- BiE&WWA, NotNAT
Cogan, Fanny Hay 1866-1929 WhScrn 74, -77, WhoHol B
Cogan, Philip 1748-1833 Baker 78, NewGrD 80
Cogan, Robert David 1930- ConAmC
Cogane, Nelson 1902- AmSCAP 66, -80
Cogdell, Josephine 1901-1969 WhScrn 74, -77, WhoHol B
Cogert, Jed d1961 NotNAT B
Coggin, C Elwood 1914- AmSCAP 80, ConAmC
Coggins, Alan 1932- IntWWM 77, -80
Coggins, Willis Robert 1926- IntWWM 77, -80
Coghill, Harry MacLeod 1944- IntWWM 77, -80
Coghill, Joy 1926- CreCan 2
Coghill, Nevill 1899- ConDr 73, -77D, WhoThe 77
Coghill, Neville 1899- WhoThe 72
Coghlan, Charles F d1972 WhScrn 77
Coghlan, Charles F 1841-1899 NotNAT B
Coghlan, Charles F 1842-1899 OxThe, PlP&P
Coghlan, Gertrude 1879-1952 WhThe
Coghlan, Gertrude Evelyn 1876-1952 NotNAT B, WhoStg 1906, -1908
Coghlan, Junior 1916- FilmgC, HalFC 80
Coghlan, Junior 1917- FilmEn, Film 2, ForYSC, TwYS, WhoHol A
Coghlan, Katherine 1889-1965 WhScrn 74, -77, WhoHol B
Coghlan, Rosalind d1937 NotNAT B
Coghlan, Rose d1932 PlP&P, WhoHol B
Coghlan, Rose 1850-1932 WhScrn 74, -77, WhThe
Coghlan, Rose 1851-1932 FamA&A[port], NotNAT B, OxThe
Coghlan, Rose 1853-1932 Film 1, -2, WhoStg 1906, -1908
Cogill, Barbara CreCan 1
Cogill, Bobs CreCan 1
Cogill, Zema Barbara CreCan 1
Cogley, Nicholas 1869-1936 WhScrn 74, -77
Cogley, Nick 1869-1936 Film 1, -2, TwYS, WhoHol B
Cognazzo, Roberto 1943- IntWWM 77, -80
Cogswell, Frederick William 1917- CreCan 2
Cohan, Agnes Merrill d1972 WhoHol B
Cohan, Charles 1886- WhThe
Cohan, George M 1878-1942 AmPS, -B, AmSCAP 66, -80, Baker 78, BestMus, BiDAmM, CmpEPM, CnMD, EncMT, EncWT, Ent, FamA&A[port], FilmEn, Film 1, FilmgC, HalFC 80, McGEWD[port], ModWD, NewCBMT, NewGrD 80, NotNAT A, -B, OxThe, PlP&P, PopAmC[port], PopAmC SUP, Sw&Ld B, TwYS, WhScrn 74, -77, WhThe, WhoHol B, WhoStg 1906, -1908
Cohan, George M 1879-1942 CnThe
Cohan, Georgette 1900- WhThe
Cohan, Helen WhoHol A
Cohan, Helen Frances Costigan 1854-1928 NotNAT B
Cohan, Jere J 1848-1917 NotNAT B
Cohan, Josephine 1876-1916 NotNAT B
Cohan, Robert 1925- CnOxB, DancEn 78
Cohan, Ronnie ConMuA 80B
Cohen, Albert 1929- IntWWM 77, -80, NewGrD 80
Cohen, Alexander 1884-1953 NewGrD 80
Cohen, Alexander H 1920- BiE&WWA, EncMT, NotNAT, WhoThe 72, -77
Cohen, Allen Laurence NatPD[port]
Cohen, Av Shalom 1928- AmSCAP 66, -80
Cohen, Charles 1912- AmSCAP 80, IntMPA 77, -75, -76, -78, -79, -80
Cohen, Daniel AmSCAP 80
Cohen, David 1927- AmSCAP 66, CpmDNM 78, ConAmC
Cohen, Edward M 1940- ConAmC, NatPD[port]
Cohen, Edwin Greines 1934- AmSCAP 80
Cohen, Ellis A 1945- IntMPA 77, -76, -78, -79, -80
Cohen, Eta IntWWM 77, -80, WhoMus 72
Cohen, Fred 1939- AmSCAP 66
Cohen, Frederic 1904-1967 CnOxB, DancEn 78
Cohen, Frederick 1904-1967 BiE&WWA, NotNAT B
Cohen, Fritz DancEn 78
Cohen, Gustave 1879-1958 OxThe
Cohen, Harriet 1895-1967 Baker 78, MusSN[port], NewGrD 80
Cohen, Harry L 1891- WhThe
Cohen, Herman IntMPA 75
Cohen, Herman 1928- FilmgC, HalFC 80, IntMPA 77, -76, -78, -79, -80, WhoHrs 80
Cohen, Janelle WomWMM
Cohen, Jerome D 1936- AmSCAP 80, ConAmC
Cohen, Joe ConMuA 80B
Cohen, John 1932- BiDAmM, ConMuA 80B, EncFCWM 69, IntWWM 77
Cohen, Joseph 1918- AmSCAP 66, -80
Cohen, Joseph M 1917- AmSCAP 66, -80, ConAmC
Cohen, Jules-Emile-David 1835-1901 Baker 78
Cohen, Katie d1946 NotNAT B
Cohen, Kip 1940- BiE&WWA
Cohen, Lane Nathan 1951- AmSCAP 80
Cohen, Larry HalFC 80, WhoHrs 80
Cohen, Leonard 1933- BiDAmM
Cohen, Leonard 1934- ConMuA 80A, CreCan 1, IlEncR[port]
Cohen, Louis 1894-1956 NewGrD 80
Cohen, Marcia 1937- CpmDNM 80
Cohen, Martin B 1923- BiE&WWA, NotNAT
Cohen, Maxi M WomWMM B
Cohen, Meyer AmPS B
Cohen, Michael ConAmC
Cohen, Mickey 1913- What 5[port]
Cohen, Mildred PupTheA
Cohen, Milton E IntMPA 77, -75, -76, -78, -79, -80
Cohen, Myron JoeFr
Cohen, Nathan 1905- IntMPA 77, -75, -76, -78, -79, -80
Cohen, Nathan 1923-1971 BiE&WWA, CreCan 1
Cohen, Norm 1936- IntWWM 77, -80
Cohen, Norman 1936- FilmEn, FilmgC, HalFC 80, IlWWBF
Cohen, Octavus Roy 1891-1959 NotNAT B
Cohen, Oscar ConMuA 80B
Cohen, Raymond 1919- IntWWM 77, -80, NewGrD 80, WhoMus 72
Cohen, Rob IntMPA 79, -80
Cohen, Robert 1959- IntWWM 80
Cohen, Sammy Film 2
Cohen, Sara B d1963 NotNAT B
Cohen, Selma Jeanne 1920- BiE&WWA, CnOxB, DancEn 78, NotNAT
Cohen, Sheldon 1933- AmSCAP 66, -80
Cohen, Sol B 1891- AmSCAP 66, -80, ConAmC
Cohen, Theodore PupTheA
Cohen, Ze'eva 1940- CnOxB
Cohill, William Film 1
Cohl, Emile 1857-1938 DcFM, FilmEn, Film 1, FilmgC, HalFC 80, OxFilm, WorEFlm
Cohl, Michael ConMuA 80B
Cohn, Al 1925- AmSCAP 66, -80, CmpEPM, EncJzS 70, IlEncJ
Cohn, Alvin Gilbert 1925- BiDAmM, EncJzS 70
Cohn, Arthur 1910- AmSCAP 66, -80, Baker 78, BiDAmM, ConAmC, DcCM, NewGrD 80
Cohn, Arthur 1928- FilmgC, HalFC 80
Cohn, Bennett 1894- TwYS A
Cohn, George Thomas 1925- BiDAmM, EncJzS 70
Cohn, Gregory Phil 1919- AmSCAP 66, -80
Cohn, Harry 1891-1958 BiDFilm 81, FilmEn, FilmgC, HalFC 80, NotNAT A, -B, OxFilm, TwYS B, WorEFlm
Cohn, Heinrich Baker 78
Cohn, Jack FilmEn
Cohn, James 1928- AmSCAP 66, -80, CpmDNM 75, ConAmC, IntWWM 77, -80
Cohn, Janet BiE&WWA
Cohn, John ConAmC
Cohn, Judith WomWMM B
Cohn, Julia 1902-1975 WhScrn 77, WhoHol C
Cohn, Marvin ConMuA 80B
Cohn, Robert 1920- IntMPA 77, -75, -76, -78, -79, -80
Cohn, Sidra Gay 1937- NatPD[port]
Cohn, Sonny 1925- EncJzS 70
Cohn, Stephen AmSCAP 80
Cohn, Stewart 1921- AmSCAP 66, -80
Cohn, Zinky Augustus 1908-1952 WhoJazz 72
Cohon, Baruch Joseph 1926- AmSCAP 80
Coignet, Horace 1735-1821 NewGrD 80
Coipeau, Charles NewGrD 80
Cokayne, Sir Aston d1684 NotNAT B
Coke, Peter 1913- WhThe, WhoThe 72
Coke, Richard d1955 NotNAT B
Coke, Roger Sacheverell 1912- WhoMus 72
Coke-Jephcott, Norman 1893-1962 ConAmC
Coker, Charles Mitchell 1927- BiDAmM, EncJzS 70
Coker, Dolo 1927- EncJzS 70
Coker, Henry 1919- BiDAmM, CmpEPM, EncJzS 70
Coker, Henry L 1919- WhoJazz 72
Coker, Jerry 1932- BiDAmM
Coker, Paul Thomas 1959- IntWWM 80
Coker, Wilson 1928- AmSCAP 66, ConAmC
Cola Ianno, Giuseppe NewGrD 80
Colaiaco, Alfred James 1913- AmSCAP 80
Colaianni, Giuseppe NewGrD 80
Colalillo, Martha 1944- WhoOp 76
Colamosca, Frank O 1910- AmSCAP 66, -80
Colanzi, Richard P 1929- AmSCAP 66, -80
Colar, George 1908- NewOrJ[port]
Colart Le Boutellier NewGrD 80
Colas, Monsieur Film 2

Colasanti, Veniero 1910- WhoOp 76
Colasse, Pascal 1649-1709 Baker 78, NewGrD 80
Colbentson, Oliver 1927- IntWWM 77, -80
Colberg, Christoph Loeffelholz Von NewGrD 80
Colbert, Claudette MotPP, PIP&P, WomWMM
Colbert, Claudette 1905- BiDFilm, -81, BiE&WWA, FilmEn, Film 2, FilmgC, ForYSC[port], HalFC 80[port], OxFilm, ThFT[port], WhoHol A, WhoThe 72, -77, WorEFlm[port]
Colbert, Claudette 1907- IntMPA 77, -75, -76, -78, -79, -80, MovMk[port]
Colbert, Robert WhoHol A
Colbert, Warren Ernest 1929- AmSCAP 80
Colbin, Rod 1923- BiE&WWA, NotNAT
Colbourne, Maurice 1894-1965 WhThe
Colbran, Isabel 1785-1845 NewGrD 80
Colbran, Isabella 1785-1845 CmOp, NewEOp 71, NewGrD 80
Colbron, Grace Isabel d1943 NotNAT B, WhThe
Colburn, Carrie 1859-1932 WhScrn 74, -77, WhoHol B
Colburn, George 1878-1921 Baker 78, ConAmC
Colby, Anita 1914- FilmEn, ForYSC, MotPP, What 5[port], WhoHol A
Colby, Barbara 1940-1975 WhScrn 77, WhoHol C
Colby, Elinor PupTheA
Colby, Ethel 1908- BiE&WWA, IntMPA 77, -75, -76, -78, -79, -80, NotNAT
Colby, Herbert 1839-1911 WhScrn 77
Colby, Michael Elihu 1951- AmSCAP 80
Colby, Paul ConMuA 80B
Colby, Robert AmSCAP 66, -80
Colby, Vineta 1922- ConAmTC
Colcock, Erroll Hay AmSCAP 66
Colcord, Lincoln 1883-1947 BiDAmM
Colcord, Mabel 1872-1952 WhScrn 74, -77, WhoHol B
Cold, Ulrik 1939- IntWWM 77, -80, NewGrD 80
Colder, Ben AmSCAP 80, EncFCWM 69, IlEncCM
Colding-Jorgensen, Birgit 1939- IntWWM 77, -80
Colding-Jorgensen, Henrik 1944- IntWWM 77, -80, NewGrD 80
Coldwell, Goldie Film 1
Cole, Alonzo Deen d1971 WhoHol B
Cole, Benjamin NewGrD 80
Cole, Bob CmpEPM, MorBAP
Cole, Bob 1863-1911 Sw&Ld B
Cole, Bob 1869-1912 NotNAT B
Cole, Bobby ConMuA 80B
Cole, Brian 1944-1972 WhScrn 77
Cole, Buddy 1916-1964 CmpEPM, WhScrn 77
Cole, Carol 1944- DrBlPA
Cole, Corinne WhoHol A
Cole, Cozy 1909- CmpEPM, DrBlPA, EncJzS 70, IlEncJ, WhoJazz 72
Cole, Cozy 1928- RkOn[port]
Cole, Dennis 1943- ForYSC, WhoHol A
Cole, Edith 1870-1927 WhThe
Cole, Edward C 1904- BiE&WWA, NotNAT
Cole, Edwin LeMar 1916-1964 BiDAmM
Cole, Elmer Francis Wyatt 1938- IntWWM 77, -80
Cole, Elmertha Butler 1905- IntWWM 77, -80
Cole, Frances Elaine 1937- BlkWAB[port]
Cole, Frank AmSCAP 80
Cole, Franklin 1909- AmSCAP 66
Cole, Fred 1901-1964 WhScrn 74, -77, WhoHol B
Cole, George 1925- ConAmC, FilmEn, FilmgC, HalFC 80, IlWWBF[port], IntMPA 77, -75, -76, -78, -79, -80, WhoHol A, WhoThe 72, -77
Cole, George Burt 1905- AmSCAP 80
Cole, George L PupTheA
Cole, Gerald E 1917- ConAmC
Cole, Helen West 1911- IntWWM 77
Cole, Howard 1913- IntWWM 77, -80
Cole, Hugo 1917- NewGrD 80, WhoMus 72
Cole, Jack CmpGMD
Cole, Jack 1913-1974 CnOxB, DancEn 78
Cole, Jack 1914-1974 BiE&WWA, CmMov, EncMT, FilmEn, FilmgC, HalFC 80, NotNAT B, WhScrn 77, WhoHol B, WorEFlm
Cole, James Film 1
Cole, John 1774-1855 BiDAmM, NewGrD 80
Cole, Johnny d1974 WhScrn 77
Cole, June Lawrence 1903-1960 WhoJazz 72
Cole, Lester 1900-1962 WhScrn 74, -77, WhoHol B
Cole, Marie Keith 1914-1975 WhoHol C
Cole, Mary Keith 1914-1975 WhScrn 77
Cole, Michael WhoHol A
Cole, Nancy PupTheA SUP
Cole, Nat 1917-1969 BiDAmM
Cole, Nat King AmPS A, -B
Cole, Nat King 1917-1965 Baker 78, CmpEPM, MusMk[port], NewGrD 80, WhoJazz 72
Cole, Nat King 1919-1965 AmSCAP 66, DrBlPA, FilmEn, FilmgC, HalFC 80, IlEncJ, MovMk, NewYTET, RkOn[port], WhScrn 74, -77, WhoHol B
Cole, Nat King 1919-1966 ForYSC
Cole, Natalie 1950- ConMuA 80A[port], DrBlPA, RkOn 2[port]
Cole, Nathaniel Adams 1919-1965 AmSCAP 80
Cole, Olena J 1926- AmSCAP 80
Cole, Olivia DrBlPA
Cole, Robert 1863-1911 BiDAmM
Cole, Robert 1869-1911 BlkAmP, DrBlPA
Cole, Robert L 1915- AmSCAP 66, -80
Cole, Rossetter Gleason 1866-1952 Baker 78, BiDAmM
Cole, Rupert 1909- WhoJazz 72
Cole, Samuel Winkley 1848- BiDAmM
Cole, Sara Rochester 1930- IntWWM 77
Cole, Sidney 1908- IntMPA 77, -75, -76, -78, -79, -80
Cole, Sidney Robert 1865-1937 Baker 78
Cole, Slim Film 1, -2
Cole, Tina WhoHol A
Cole, Toby 1916- BiE&WWA, NotNAT
Cole, Tom MorBAP
Cole, Ulric 1905- AmSCAP 66, -80, Baker 78, BiDAmM, ConAmC
Cole, Vincent L 1946- ConAmC, IntWWM 80
Cole, Ward K 1922- IntWWM 80
Cole, Wendell 1914- BiE&WWA, NotNAT
Cole, William 1909- NewGrD 80, WhoMus 72
Cole, William Charles 1909- IntWWM 80
Cole, William R 1909- BiDAmM, EncJzS 70
Cole, Zaida MorBAP
Cole And Johnson AmPS B
Colean, Chuck 1908-1971 WhScrn 74, -77
Colebault, Jacques NewGrD 80
Colebrooke, Janet Mildred 1942- IntWWM 77, -80, WhoMus 72
Coleburn, Catherine Film 2
Coleby, A E d1930 IlWWBF[port]
Coleby, Geoffrey 1921- WhoMus 72
Coleby, Wilfred T 1865- WhThe
Colee, Forest R 1893-1962 WhScrn 77
Coleman, Mrs. PIP&P
Coleman, Bill 1904- CmpEPM, EncJzS 70, IlEncJ, WhoJazz 72
Coleman, Brian Robert 1944- IntWWM 77, -80
Coleman, Burl C 1896-1950 BluesWW
Coleman, Carole d1964 NotNAT B
Coleman, Charles OxMus
Coleman, Charles 1605?-1664 NewGrD 80
Coleman, Charles 1885-1951 FilmEn, Film 2, FilmgC, HalFC 80, HolCA[port], MovMk, Vers A[port], WhScrn 74, -77, WhoHol B
Coleman, Cherrie Film 1
Coleman, Claudia 1889-1938 WhScrn 74, -77, WhoHol B
Coleman, Cy 1929- AmPS, AmSCAP 66, -80, BestMus, BiE&WWA, EncMT, HalFC 80, NewCBMT, NewGrD 80, NotNAT, PopAmC SUP[port]
Coleman, Dabney WhoHol A
Coleman, Deborah 1919- BiE&WWA
Coleman, Delle WomWMM
Coleman, Don Film 2
Coleman, Earl 1925- BiDAmM, EncJzS 70
Coleman, Edward d1669 NewGrD 80
Coleman, Emil BgBands 74
Coleman, Emil 1893-1965 WhScrn 74, -77, WhoHol B
Coleman, Emil 1894- CmpEPM
Coleman, Emily DancEn 78
Coleman, Fanny 1840-1919 WhThe
Coleman, Fay R 1918- BiE&WWA, NotNAT
Coleman, Fay Ross PupTheA
Coleman, Frank J Film 1
Coleman, George 1935- BiDAmM, EncJzS 70
Coleman, Henry 1888-1965 OxMus
Coleman, Henry, Jr. 1938- ConAmC
Coleman, Herbert 1927- AmSCAP 80
Coleman, Jack Lambert 1920- AmSCAP 80, IntWWM 77
Coleman, Jim Film 2
Coleman, John 1831-1904 NotNAT A, -B
Coleman, Lonnie 1920- BiE&WWA, NotNAT
Coleman, Mabel Film 2
Coleman, Majel Film 2
Coleman, Major Film 2
Coleman, Margret WhoHol A
Coleman, Michael 1940- CnOxB
Coleman, Nancy IntMPA 77, -75, -76, -78, -79, -80, MotPP
Coleman, Nancy 1914- BiE&WWA, ForYSC, WhoHol A
Coleman, Nancy 1917- FilmEn, FilmgC, HalFC 80, NotNAT
Coleman, Nelly BluesWW
Coleman, Ornette 1930- AmSCAP 66, -80, Baker 78, BiDAmM, BnBkM 80, ConAmC, DrBlPA, EncJzS 70, IlEncJ, NewGrD 80
Coleman, Patricia 1930- AmSCAP 80
Coleman, Raft BlkAmP
Coleman, Randolph 1937- CpmDNM 77, -78
Coleman, Randolph E 1937- ConAmC
Coleman, Richard E 1933- AmSCAP 66, -80
Coleman, Robert, Jr. 1900- BiE&WWA, WhThe
Coleman, Ruth AmSCAP 80
Coleman, Shepard 1924- BiE&WWA, NotNAT
Coleman, Thomas 1897-1959 WhScrn 74, -77
Coleman, Vincent Film 2
Coleman, Wanda BlkAmP
Coleman, Warren R 1901-1968 NotNAT B, WhScrn 74, -77, WhoHol B
Coleman, Willette WomWMM B
Coleman, William Johnson 1904- BiDAmM, EncJzS 70
Coleman, William S E 1926- NotNAT
Coler, Martin NewGrD 80
Coleridge, Amy d1951 NotNAT B
Coleridge, Arthur 1830-1913 NewGrD 80
Coleridge, Eric C WhoMus 72
Coleridge, Ethel 1883- WhThe
Coleridge, Samuel Taylor 1772-1834 DcPup, EncWT, NotNAT B, OxMus, OxThe
Coleridge, Sylvia 1909- WhoThe 77
Coleridge, Sylvia 1912- WhoThe 72
Coleridge-Taylor, Avril Gwendolen 1903- BlkWAB[port], IntWWM 77, -80, WhoMus 72
Coleridge-Taylor, Samuel 1875-1912 Baker 78, BnBkM 80, CompSN[port], DcCom&M 79, DrBlPA, MusMk[port], NewGrD 80, OxMus
Colerus, David NewGrD 80
Coles, Charles BlksBF
Coles, Erostine BlkAmP, MorBAP
Coles, George 1792-1858 BiDAmM
Coles, Harry Montague 1919- IntWWM 77
Coles, Honi DrBlPA
Coles, Jack 1914- WhoMus 72
Coles, James 1943- IntWWM 80
Coles, John 1926- EncJzS 70
Coles, Johnny 1926- BiDAmM, EncJzS 70
Coles, Nathaniel Adams NewGrD 80
Coles, Russell 1909-1960 WhScrn 74, -77
Coles, Zaida 1933- DrBlPA
Colesworthy, Daniel C 1810-1893 BiDAmM
Colette 1873-1954 EncWT, FilmEn, FilmgC, HalFC 80, NotNAT B, OxFilm
Colette, Sidonie Gabrielle 1873-1954 DcPup
Coletti, Agostino Bonaventura 1675?-1752 NewGrD 80
Coletti, Filippo 1811-1894 NewGrD 80
Coley, Frederick Benjamin 1906- WhoMus 72
Coley, Thomas WhoHol A
Colf, Dorritt Licht ConAmC

Colfach, Elsa *WomWMM*
Colgan, James 1710?-1772 *NewGrD 80*
Colgon, James 1710?-1772 *NewGrD 80*
Colgrass, Michael 1932- *AmSCAP 80, Baker 78, ConAmC, DcCM, NewGrD 80*
Colic, Dragutin 1907- *IntWWM 80*
Colicchio, Ralph 1896- *AmSCAP 66, -80*
Colicos, John 1928- *CreCan 1, FilmgC, HalFC 80, NotNAT, WhoThe 77*
Colijns, Jean-Baptiste *NewGrD 80*
Colin Muset *NewGrD 80*
Colin, Georges *WhThe*
Colin, Georges Emile 1921- *IntWWM 77, -80, WhoMus 72*
Colin, Guilielmo *NewGrD 80*
Colin, Jean 1905- *FilmgC, HalFC 80, WhThe, WhoHol A*
Colin, Jeanne 1924- *IntWWM 77, -80*
Colin, Lotte *WomWMM*
Colin, Pierre *NewGrD 80*
Colin, Ralph *NewYTET*
Colin, Sid 1920- *HalFC 80*
Colin DeBlamont, Francois *NewGrD 80*
Colini-Cosgrave, Ilona *WhoMus 72*
Colista, Lelio 1629-1680 *NewGrD 80*
Colizzi, Johann Andreas 1740?- *NewGrD 80*
Coll, Antonio Martin Y *NewGrD 80*
Coll, David 1947- *CnOxB*
Coll, Owen G 1879-1960 *WhScrn 74, -77*
Colla, Giuseppe 1731-1806 *NewGrD 80*
Colla, Richard A *HalFC 80*
Colla, Richard J *FilmgC*
Collaer, Paul 1891- *Baker 78, NewGrD 80, WhoMus 72*
Collan, Karl 1828-1871 *NewGrD 80*
Collangettes, Xavier Maurice 1860-1943 *NewGrD 80*
Collard *Baker 78*
Collard, Edward *NewGrD 80*
Collard, Frederick William 1772?-1860 *NewGrD 80*
Collard, Jean-Philippe 1948- *IntWWM 80*
Collard, William Frederick 1776?-1866 *NewGrD 80*
Collasse, Pascal 1649?-1709 *NewGrD 80*
Collasse, Paschal 1649?-1709 *NewGrD 80*
Collasse, Pasquier 1649?-1709 *NewGrD 80*
Collazo, Bobby 1915- *AmSCAP 80*
Collazo, Bobby 1916- *AmSCAP 66*
Colle, Charles 1709-1783 *EncWT, Ent, OxThe*
Colleano, Bonar 1923-1958 *NotNAT B, WhThe*
Colleano, Bonar 1924-1958 *FilmEn, FilmgC, ForYSC, HalFC 80, IlWWBF, MotPP, WhScrn 74, -77, WhoHol B*
Colleano, Bonar, Sr. d1957 *NotNAT B*
Collen, Jean McIntyre 1943- *IntWWM 80*
Coller, Jerome Thomas 1929- *ConAmC*
Coller, Percy E B 1895- *BiDAmM*
Colleran, Bill *IntMPA 77, -75, -76, -78, -79, -80*
Colleran, William A *NewYTET*
Colleran, William Martin 1929- *WhoMus 72*
Colles, H C 1879-1943 *NewGrD 80*
Colles, Harry 1879-1943 *NewGrD 80*
Colles, Henry Cope 1879-1943 *Baker 78, OxMus*
Collet, Henri 1885-1951 *Baker 78, NewGrD 80*
Collet, Richard 1885-1946 *WhThe*
Collet, Wilfred Robert 1905- *WhoMus 72*
Collett, John *OxMus*
Collette, Buddy 1921- *CmpEPM, EncJzS 70*
Collette, Buddy 1922- *Baker 78*
Collette, Charles 1842-1924 *WhThe*
Collette, Joannes M J F B 1918- *IntWWM 77, -80*
Collette, William Marcell 1921- *AmSCAP 66, -80, BiDAmM, ConAmC, EncJzS 70*
Colley, Don Pedro *DrBlPA*
Colli, Tonino Delli *FilmEn*
Collie, Bennadetta *PupTheA*
Collie, Biff 1926- *EncFCWM 69*
Collie, Hiram Abiff 1926- *BiDAmM*
Collie, Kelsey *BlkAmP, MorBAP*
Collier, Alan Caswell 1911- *CreCan 1*
Collier, Buster 1900- *Film 2*
Collier, Charles R 1935- *IntWWM 77, -80*
Collier, Constance d1955 *MotPP, PlP&P, WhoHol B*
Collier, Constance 1875-1955 *HolCA[port], ThFT[port]*
Collier, Constance 1878-1955 *EncWT, FilmEn, Film 1, -2, FilmgC, ForYSC, HalFC 80, MovMk[port], NotNAT A, -B, OxThe, TwYS, WhScrn 74, -77, WhThe*
Collier, Constance 1880-1955 *Vers A[port]*
Collier, Corlu 1927- *IntWWM 77, -80*
Collier, Derek 1929- *IntWWM 77, -80, WhoMus 72*
Collier, Gaylan Jane 1924- *BiE&WWA, NotNAT*
Collier, Graham 1937- *EncJzS 70, WhoMus 72*
Collier, J Walter d1920 *NotNAT B*
Collier, Jeremy 1650-1726 *NotNAT B*
Collier, Jeremy 1656-1726 *OxThe*
Collier, John 1901- *FilmgC, HalFC 80*
Collier, John Payne 1789-1883 *NotNAT B, OxThe*
Collier, Lesley 1947- *CnOxB*
Collier, Lizzie Hudson d1924 *NotNAT B*
Collier, Lois 1919- *FilmEn, ForYSC, WhoHol A*
Collier, Marie 1927-1971 *CmOp[port], NewGrD 80, WhoMus 72*
Collier, Mary Ann 1810-1866 *BiDAmM*
Collier, Patience 1910- *WhoThe 72, -77*
Collier, Ron 1930- *CreCan 2, EncJzS 70*
Collier, Ronald 1930- *Baker 78*
Collier, Sherlee d1972 *WhoHol B*
Collier, Simone *BlkAmP*
Collier, Thomas W 1948- *AmSCAP 80*
Collier, William 1866-1944 *FilmEn, HalFC 80*
Collier, William, Jr. 1900- *Film 2, TwYS*
Collier, William, Jr. 1902- *FilmEn, ForYSC*
Collier, William, Jr. 1903- *Film 1*
Collier, William, Sr. 1866-1944 *Film 1, -2, FilmgC, ForYSC, MovMk, NotNAT B, WhScrn 74, -77, WhThe*
Collier, William, Sr. 1868-1944 *WhoHol B, WhoStg 1906, -1908*
Collier, William E 1924- *AmSCAP 66*
Collin, Darja 1902-1967 *CnOxB*
Collin, John 1931- *FilmgC, HalFC 80*
Collin, Reginald *IntMPA 79, -80*
Collin-Barbie DuBocage, Louis *McGEWD*
Collin DeBlamont, Francois 1690-1760 *NewGrD 80*
Collinge, Christina Hamilton 1910- *WhoMus 72*
Collinge, Patricia 1892-1974 *HolCA[port]*
Collinge, Patricia 1893-1974 *HalFC 80*
Collinge, Patricia 1894-1974 *BiE&WWA, FilmEn, FilmgC, ForYSC, NotNAT B, OxFilm, Vers B[port], WhScrn 77, WhThe, WhoHol B*
Collinge, Robert J 1928- *WhoOp 76*
Collingham, G G d1923 *NotNAT B*
Collingham, Kenneth Roy Victor *WhoMus 72*
Collings, Ann *WhoHol A*
Collings, Blanche d1968 *WhoHol B*
Collings, David 1940- *HalFC 80*
Collings, Marcia Vivien Helen 1940- *IntWWM 80*
Collingwood, Charles 1917- *NewYTET*
Collingwood, Laurence 1887- *CmOp*
Collingwood, Lawrance 1887- *Baker 78, IntWWM 77, NewGrD 80, OxMus, WhoMus 72*
Collingwood, Monica *WomWMM*
Collins, A Greville 1896- *WhThe*
Collins, Aaron 1930- *AmSCAP 80*
Collins, Adrian Anthony 1937- *IntWWM 77*
Collins, Albert 1932- *BluesWW[port]*
Collins, Alf *FilmEn, IlWWBF*
Collins, Alfred *DcFM*
Collins, Allen Frederick 1915- *BiE&WWA, NotNAT*
Collins, Anne 1943- *IntWWM 77, -80, WhoOp 76*
Collins, Anthony 1892- *OxMus*
Collins, Anthony 1893-1963 *NewGrD 80*
Collins, Anthony 1893-1964 *HalFC 80*
Collins, Arthur 1863- *CmpEPM, WhThe*
Collins, Barry 1941- *ConDr 77*
Collins, Beatrice Helen 1918- *IntWWM 77*
Collins, Bert d1962 *NotNAT B*
Collins, Blanche M 1910-1968 *WhScrn 77*
Collins, Booker 1914- *WhoJazz 72*
Collins, Burt 1931- *EncJzS 70*
Collins, Burton I 1931- *EncJzS 70*
Collins, C E 1873-1951 *WhScrn 77*
Collins, C Pat *Film 2*
Collins, Carrie Beatrice Holloway 1930- *AmSCAP 80, IntWWM 77*
Collins, Charles d1964 *NotNAT B*
Collins, Charles 1904- *WhThe*
Collins, Charles Frederick 1916- *IntWWM 77, -80, WhoMus 72*
Collins, Cora Sue 1927- *FilmEn, HalFC 80, ThFT[port]*
Collins, Cora Sue 1929- *ForYSC*
Collins, Daniel d1964 *NotNAT B*
Collins, Dorothy *PlP&P A[port]*
Collins, Dorothy 1926- *BiDAmM, What 3[port]*
Collins, Dorothy 1927?- *CmpEPM*
Collins, Eddie 1884-1940 *FilmEn, FilmgC, HalFC 80, Vers B[port], WhScrn 74, -77, WhoHol B*
Collins, Eddy 1866-1916 *WhScrn 77*
Collins, Edwin J *IlWWBF*
Collins, Ethel D W *PupTheA*
Collins, Frances *IntWWM 77, -80, WhoMus 72*
Collins, Frank 1878-1957 *NotNAT B, WhThe*
Collins, G Pat 1895-1959 *WhScrn 74, -77*
Collins, Gail *AmSCAP 80*
Collins, Gary *WhoHol A*
Collins, George Pat 1895-1959 *WhoHol B*
Collins, H B 1870-1941 *NewGrD 80*
Collins, Hal 1920- *IntMPA 77, -75, -76, -78, -79, -80, NewYTET*
Collins, Horace 1875-1964 *WhThe*
Collins, Jack *WhoHol A*
Collins, Jackie *WhoHol A*
Collins, Janet 1917- *CnOxB, DancEn 78, DrBlPA*
Collins, Joan 1933- *FilmAG WE[port], FilmEn, FilmgC, ForYSC, HalFC 80, IlWWBF[port], -A, IntMPA 77, -75, -76, -78, -79, -80, MotPP, MovMk, WhoHol A, WhoHrs 80[port]*
Collins, John d1808 *NotNAT B*
Collins, John Elbert 1913- *BiDAmM, CmpEPM, EncJzS 70, WhoJazz 72*
Collins, Jose 1887-1958 *AmPS B, EncMT, Film 1, NotNAT B, OxThe, WhScrn 74, -77, WhThe, WhoHol B*
Collins, Joyce Louise 1930- *AmSCAP 80, BiDAmM*
Collins, Judy 1939- *AmSCAP 80, BiDAmM, ConMuA 80A[port], EncFCWM 69, IlEncR[port], RkOn 2[port]*
Collins, Kathleen *Film 2*
Collins, Kenneth 1935- *WhoOp 76*
Collins, Larry *EncFCWM 69*
Collins, Larry 1944- *AmSCAP 80*
Collins, Lawrence Albert 1944- *BiDAmM*
Collins, Lawrencine May 1942- *BiDAmM*
Collins, Lee 1901-1960 *BiDAmM, CmpEPM, IlEncJ, NewOrJ[port], WhoJazz 72*
Collins, LeRoy *NewYTET*
Collins, Lewis D 1899-1954 *FilmEn*
Collins, Lorrie *EncFCWM 69*
Collins, Lottie 1866-1910 *Ent, NotNAT B, OxMus, OxThe*
Collins, Louis Bo 1932- *BluesWW[port]*
Collins, Mae *Film 2*
Collins, Mary Sharacio *WomWMM B*
Collins, May d1955 *NotNAT B, WhoHol B*
Collins, Monte, Sr. *Film 2*
Collins, Monte F, Jr. 1898-1951 *Film 2, WhScrn 74, -77, WhoHol B*
Collins, Norman 1907- *IntMPA 77, -75, -76, -78, -79, -80*
Collins, Pamela 1948-1974 *WhScrn 77*
Collins, Pat 1935- *IntMPA 77, -75, -76, -78, -79, -80*
Collins, Pauline 1940- *WhoThe 72, -77*
Collins, Ray d1965 *MotPP, WhoHol B*
Collins, Ray 1888-1965 *FilmEn*
Collins, Ray 1889-1965 *HolCA[port], NotNAT B*
Collins, Ray 1890-1965 *FilmgC, ForYSC, HalFC 80, MovMk, Vers A[port], WhScrn 74, -77*
Collins, Richard Lee 1922- *IntWWM 77, -80*
Collins, Robert John *WhoMus 72*

Collins, Rosamond May Lissant 1934- *WhoMus 72*
Collins, Rudolph Alexander 1934- *BiDAmM, EncJzS 70*
Collins, Rudy 1934- *EncJzS 70*
Collins, Russell 1897-1965 *BiE&WWA, FilmEn, FilmgC, ForYSC, HalFC 80, NotNAT B, PlP&P, WhScrn 74, -77, WhThe, WhoHol B*
Collins, S D J 1907-1947 *WhScrn 74, -77, WhoHol B*
Collins, Sam 1826-1865 *NotNAT B, OxThe*
Collins, Samuel 1887-1949 *BluesWW*
Collins, Sewell 1876-1934 *NotNAT B, WhThe*
Collins, Shad 1910- *CmpEPM, WhoJazz 72*
Collins, Stephen *IntMPA 80*
Collins, Susan 1950- *AmSCAP 80*
Collins, Susan Trieste *WomWMM B*
Collins, Ted d1964 *NotNAT B*
Collins, Thomas William 1935- *ConAmC, IntWWM 77*
Collins, Tom d1973 *BluesWW, WhScrn 77, WhoHol B*
Collins, Tommy 1930- *BiDAmM, EncFCWM 69, IlEncCM*
Collins, Una d1964 *NotNAT B*
Collins, Verne Edman 1935- *IntWWM 77, -80*
Collins, Wallace 1858-1944? *NewOrJ[port]*
Collins, Walter Stowe 1926- *IntWWM 77, -80*
Collins, Wilkie 1824-1889 *HalFC 80, NotNAT B, PlP&P*
Collins, Will 1893-1968 *AmSCAP 66, -80*
Collins, William B *ConAmTC, ConMuA 80B*
Collins, Winnie 1896- *WhThe*
Collins Kids *EncFCWM 69*
Collinson, Francis 1898- *IntWWM 77, -80, WhoMus 72*
Collinson, Julian Carson 1944- *IntWWM 77, -80*
Collinson, Laurence Henry 1925- *ConDr 73, -77*
Collinson, Madeleine 1952?- *WhoHrs 80*
Collinson, Mary 1952?- *WhoHrs 80*
Collinson, Peter 1936- *FilmEn, IntMPA 77, -75, -76, -78, -79, -80*
Collinson, Peter 1938- *FilmgC, HalFC 80, IlWWBF*
Collinus, Matthaeus 1516-1566 *NewGrD 80*
Collis, Hainricus *NewGrD 80*
Collis, Peter Evan 1947- *IntWWM 77, -80*
Collison, Wilson 1892-1941 *WhThe*
Collison, Wilson 1893-1941 *NotNAT B*
Collisson, Winifred Mercy *WhoMus 72*
Collom, Steve Donald 1944- *AmSCAP 80*
Collot, Serge 1923- *IntWWM 80*
Collum, Herbert 1914- *NewGrD 80*
Collum, John 1926-1962 *NotNAT B, WhScrn 74, -77, WhoHol B*
Collyer, Bud *NewYTET*
Collyer, Dan d1918 *NotNAT B*
Collyer, June 1907-1968 *FilmEn, Film 2, FilmgC, ForYSC, HalFC 80, NotNAT B, ThFT[port], TwYS, WhScrn 74, -77, WhoHol B*
Collymore, Valerie 1942- *BlkWAB*
Colmagro, Gianluigi 1929- *WhoOp 76*
Colman, Booth *WhoHol A*
Colman, Charles *NewGrD 80*
Colman, George 1732-1794 *EncWT, Ent, McGEWD[port], NotNAT A, -B, OxThe, PlP&P[port]*
Colman, George, Jr. *CreCan 2*
Colman, George, Jr. 1762-1836 *EncWT, NotNAT A, -B, OxThe*
Colman, Irene 1915-1975 *WhScrn 77*
Colman, Maria Logan 1770-1844 *OxThe*
Colman, Ronald 1891-1958 *BiDFilm, -81, FilmEn, Film 1, -2, FilmgC, ForYSC, HalFC 80[port], IlWWBF, -A, MotPP, MovMk[port], NotNAT B, OxFilm, TwYS, WhScrn 74, -77, WhThe, WhoHol B, WorEFlm*
Colman, Ronald 1891-1959 *CmMov*
Colmans, Edward *WhoHol A*
Colobrano, Michele Enrico Carafa De *Baker 78*
Cologne, Franco Of *NewGrD 80*
Colomba, Giovanni Battista Innocenzo 1717-1793 *EncWT*
Colombani, Oratio 1550?-1595? *NewGrD 80*
Colombi, Giovanni Antonio *NewGrD 80*
Colombi, Giovanni Bernardo *NewGrD 80*
Colombi, Giuseppe 1635-1694 *NewGrD 80*
Colombier, Marie 1842?-1910 *NotNAT B, OxThe*
Colombini, Francesco 1573-163-? *NewGrD 80*
Colombo, Albert Carl 1888-1954 *AmSCAP 80*
Colombo, Giovanni Antonio *NewGrD 80*
Colombo, Giovanni Bernardo *NewGrD 80*
Colombo, John Robert 1936- *CreCan 2*
Colombo, Pierre 1914- *NewGrD 80*
Colombo, Russ 1908-1934 *Film 2*
Colombo, Scipio 1910- *WhoMus 72, WhoOp 76*
Colombo, Vera 1931- *CnOxB, DancEn 78*
Colomby, Bobby 1944- *EncJzS 70*
Colomby, Robert Wayne 1944- *EncJzS 70*
Colon, Fernando 1488-1539 *NewGrD 80*
Colon, Jenny 1808-1842 *OxThe*
Colon, Miriam 1945- *ForYSC, NotNAT, WhoHol A, WhoThe 77*
Colonna, Fabio 1580?-1650? *NewGrD 80*
Colonna, Giovanni Ambrosio *NewGrD 80*
Colonna, Giovanni Pablo 1640?-1695 *OxMus*
Colonna, Giovanni Paolo 1637-1695 *Baker 78, NewGrD 80*
Colonna, Jerry 1903- *FilmgC, HalFC 80[port]*
Colonna, Jerry 1904- *AmSCAP 66, -80, BiDAmM, FilmEn, ForYSC, JoeFr[port], MovMk, WhoHol A*
Colonna, Jerry 1905- *What 3[port]*
Colonna, Pompeo *NewGrD 80*
Colonne, Edouard 1838-1910 *Baker 78, BnBkM 80, NewGrD 80[port], OxMus*
Colonne, Judas 1838-1910 *NewGrD 80[port]*
Colonnello, Attilio 1931- *WhoOp 76*
Colony, Alfred T d1964 *NotNAT B*
Colosimo, Enrico 1924- *WhoOp 76*
Colosse, M *Film 2*
Colosseum *IlEncR*
Colpi, Henri 1912- *DcFM*
Colpi, Henri 1921- *FilmEn, FilmgC, HalFC 80, OxFilm, WorEFlm*
Colquhoun, Neil 1929- *IntWWM 77, -80*
Colson, Andree 1924- *IntWWM 77, -80, WhoMus 72*
Colson, William Wilder 1945- *ConAmC, IntWWM 77, -80*
Colson-Haig, S *CreCan 2*
Colson-Malleville, Marie *WomWMM*
Colt, Alvin 1915- *BiE&WWA, NotNAT, WhoThe 72, -77*
Colt, Alvin 1916- *DancEn 78*
Colt, Ethel Barrymore 1912- *NotNAT*
Colta, Charles J *PupTheA*
Colta, Mimi *PupTheA*
Coltart, James M 1903- *IntMPA 75*
Coltellini, Celeste 1760-1829 *NewGrD 80*
Coltellini, Marco 1719-1777 *NewGrD 80*
Colter, Jessi 1947- *IlEncCM[port], RkOn 2[port]*
Colton, John B 1889-1946 *McGEWD, NotNAT B, WhThe*
Colton, Scott *ForYSC*
Coltrane, Alice 1937- *BlkWAB, EncJzS 70, IlEncJ*
Coltrane, Chi 1948- *AmSCAP 80, RkOn 2[port]*
Coltrane, John 1926-1967 *Baker 78, BiDAmM, DrBlPA, EncJzS 70, IlEncJ, NewGrD 80[port], NotNAT B*
Colts, The *RkOn*
Colum, Padraic 1881-1972 *AmSCAP 66, -80, CnMD, McGEWD[port], ModWD, NotNAT A, OxThe, PlP&P[port], REnWD[port]*
Columbo, Russ 1908-1934 *BgBands 74, BiDAmM, CmpEPM, FilmEn, FilmgC, ForYSC, HalFC 80, WhScrn 74, -77, WhoHol B*
Columbro, Mary Electa 1934- *IntWWM 77, -80*
Columbus, Chris 1903- *WhoJazz 72*
Columbus, Ferdinand *NewGrD 80*
Colver, Nathaniel 1794-1870 *BiDAmM*
Colvig, Vance 1892-1967 *FilmgC, HalFC 80, WhScrn 74, -77, WhoHol B*
Colville, Alex 1920- *CreCan 1*
Colville, David Alexander 1920- *CreCan 1*
Colville, John *IntMPA 77, -76, -78, -79, -80*
Colville, Robin 1945- *IntWWM 77, -80*
Colville, Thomas Louis 1941- *IntWWM 77*
Colvin, Gilly *Film 2*
Colvin, Mrs. James E 1923- *IntWWM 77*
Colvin, Marion *Film 2*
Colvin, William *Film 2*
Colwell, Ralph Johnson 1937- *AmSCAP 80*
Colwell, Richard 1930- *IntWWM 77, -80*
Colwell-Winfield Blues Band *BiDAmM*
Colyer, Ken 1928- *EncJzS 70*
Colyns, Jean-Baptiste 1834-1902 *NewGrD 80*
Colzani, Anselmo 1918- *CmOp, WhoOp 76*
Coma, Annibale 1550?-1598? *NewGrD 80*
Coma, Antonio *NewGrD 80*
Coma, Giacomo *NewGrD 80*
Coman, Nicolae 1936- *IntWWM 80*
Comanche, Laurence Tex 1908-1932 *WhScrn 74, -77*
Comandini, Adele *WomWMM*
Comanedo, Flaminio 1570?-1619? *NewGrD 80*
Comant, Mathilda 1888-1938 *WhScrn 74, -77*
Comardo, Carlo *PupTheA*
Comathiere, A B *BlksB&W, -C*
Combarieu, Jules 1859-1916 *Baker 78, NewGrD 80*
Combe, Boyce *Film 1, -2*
Combe, Edouard 1866-1942 *Baker 78, NewGrD 80*
Comber, Bobbie 1886-1942 *WhThe*
Comber, Bobbie 1890-1942 *WhScrn 74, -77*
Comberiate, Josephine Bertolini 1917- *AmSCAP 80*
Combermere, Edward 1888- *WhThe*
Comberousse, Alexis De 1793-1862 *OxThe*
Combes, Jean 1904- *CnOxB*
Combs, F Michael 1943- *ConAmC*
Combs, Gilbert Raynolds 1863-1934 *Baker 78, BiDAmM*
Combs, Jackie *Film 2*
Combs, Ronald *ConAmC*
Combs, Sheila G 1950- *IntWWM 80*
Comden, Betty *AmSCAP 66, BiE&WWA, ConDr 77D, IntMPA 77, -75, -76, -78, -79, -80, WomWMM*
Comden, Betty 1915- *AmPS, BiDAmM, CmpEPM, EncMT, NewCBMT*
Comden, Betty 1916- *CmMov, OxFilm, WorEFlm*
Comden, Betty 1918- *BestMus, FilmgC, HalFC 80*
Comden, Betty 1919- *AmSCAP 80, ConDr 73, FilmEn, NotNAT, WhoThe 72, -77*
Comden And Green *BestMus*
Comegys, Kathleen 1895- *BiE&WWA, NotNAT, WhoHol A*
Comelin, Jean-Paul 1939- *CnOxB*
Comella, Luciano Francisco 1751-1812 *OxThe*
Comelli, Attilio d1925 *NotNAT B*
Comencini, Luigi 1916- *DcFM, FilmEn, FilmgC, HalFC 80, WorEFlm*
Comenius, Johann Amos *NewGrD 80*
Comer, Anjanette 1942- *FilmEn, FilmgC, ForYSC, HalFC 80, MotPP, WhoHol A*
Comer, Carolyn Jane 1937- *AmSCAP 80*
Comer, Thomas 1790-1862 *BiDAmM*
Comerford, Maurice d1903 *NotNAT B*
Comes, Count *NewOrJ[port]*
Comes, Bartholomaeus *NewGrD 80*
Comes, Juan Bautista 1568-1643 *Baker 78, OxMus*
Comes, Juan Bautista 1582-1643 *NewGrD 80*
Comes, Liviu 1918- *IntWWM 77, -80*
Comes, Pietro *NewGrD 80*
Comettant, Jean-Pierre-Oscar 1819-1898 *Baker 78*
Comettant, Oscar 1819-1898 *NewGrD 80*
Comfort, Abraham 1931- *IntWWM 80*
Comfort, Charles Fraser 1900- *CreCan 2*
Comfort, Lance 1908-1966 *FilmgC, HalFC 80*
Comfort, Lance 1908-1967 *FilmEn, IlWWBF*
Comi, Paul *WhoHol A*
Comingore, Dorothy 1913-1971 *FilmgC, HalFC 80*
Comingore, Dorothy 1918-1971 *FilmEn, ForYSC, WhScrn 74, -77, WhoHol B*
Comings, George Francis 1931- *IntWWM 77, -80*
Comini, Raiberto 1907- *AmSCAP 66*
Comisel, Emilia 1913- *IntWWM 80*
Comissiona, Sergiu 1928- *Baker 78, BnBkM 80, IntWWM 77, -80,*

MusSN[port], NewGrD 80, WhoMus 72, WhoOp 76
Comley, Nora Mabel 1921- WhoMus 72
Commander, Maurice David 1948- AmSCAP 80
Commander Cody ConMuA 80A
Commander Cody & His Lost Planet Airmen IlEncCM[port], RkOn 2[port]
Commander Cody & The Lost Planet Airmen IlEncR
Commandon, Jean 1877- DcFM, OxFilm
Comment, Constance WomWMM B
Commer, Franz 1813-1887 Baker 78, NewGrD 80
Commerford, Thomas 1855-1920 Film 1, WhScrn 77
Commette, Edouard 1883-1967 Baker 78
Commire, Anne NatPD[port]
Commodores, The IlEncR, RkOn 2[port]
Commuck, Thomas 1805-1855 NewGrD 80
Como, Bill 1925- CnOxB
Como, Franca 1937- WhoOp 76
Como, Perry AmPS A, -B, IntMPA 75, -76, -78, -79, -80
Como, Perry 1912- BiDAmM, CmpEPM, FilmEn, FilmgC, HalFC 80, IntMPA 77, NewYTET, RkOn[port], WhoHol A
Como, Perry 1913- ForYSC, WhoMus 72
Comont, M Film 2
Comont, Mathilde d1938 Film 2, WhoHol B
Comont, Nattie Film 2
Compan, Le Sieur CnOxB
Compan, Honore d1798? NewGrD 80
Companeez, Jacques 1906-1956 FilmEn
Companeez, Nina WomWMM
Companeez, Nina 1938- FilmEn
Compenius NewGrD 80
Compenius, Adolph d1650 NewGrD 80
Compenius, Esaias d1617 NewGrD 80
Compenius, Heinrich d1611 NewGrD 80
Compenius, Heinrich d1631 NewGrD 80
Compenius, Jakob d1602 NewGrD 80
Compenius, Johann Heinrich d1642 NewGrD 80
Compenius, Ludwig d1671 NewGrD 80
Compenius, Timotheus NewGrD 80
Compere, Loyset d1518 OxMus
Compere, Loyset 1445?-1518 NewGrD 80
Compere, Loyset 1450?-1518 Baker 78, BnBkM 80
Compson, Betty 1896-1974 HalFC 80
Compson, Betty 1897-1974 FilmEn, Film 1, -2, FilmgC, ForYSC, MotPP, MovMk[port], ThFT[port], TwYS, What 2[port], WhScrn 77, WhoHol B
Compson, John d1913 Film 1, WhoHol B
Compton, Betty 1907-1944 NotNAT B, WhScrn 74, -77, WhoHol B
Compton, Edward 1854-1918 EncWT, NotNAT B, OxThe, WhThe
Compton, Mrs. Edward 1853-1940 NotNAT B, WhThe
Compton, Fay 1894-1978 BiE&WWA, EncWT, FilmAG WE[port], FilmEn, Film 1, -2, FilmgC, HalFC 80, IlWWBF[port], NotNAT, -A, OxThe, PlP&P[port], WhThe, WhoHol A, WhoThe 72
Compton, Fay 1895-1978 CnThe
Compton, Forrest WhoHol A
Compton, Francis 1885-1964 BiE&WWA, NotNAT B, WhScrn 74, -77, WhoHol B
Compton, Harry J 1947- AmSCAP 80
Compton, Henry 1805-1877 EncWT, NotNAT A, -B, OxThe
Compton, J Glover 1884-1964 WhoJazz 72
Compton, John Haywood 1876-1957 NewGrD 80
Compton, Joyce ForYSC, IntMPA 77, -75, -76, -78, -79, -80, MotPP, What 3[port], WhoHol A
Compton, Joyce 1907- FilmEn, Film 2, FilmgC, HalFC 80, MovMk
Compton, Joyce 1908- ThFT[port]
Compton, Juleen WomWMM A, -B
Compton, Juliette Film 2
Compton, Juliette 1902- IlWWBF
Compton, Katherine 1858-1928 EncWT
Compton, Katherine Mackenzie 1853-1928 NotNAT B, WhThe
Compton, Lacy Wilford 1916- AmSCAP 80
Compton, Madge d1970 WhThe
Compton, Sydney d1938 NotNAT B
Compton, Viola 1886-1971 WhScrn 77, WhThe, WhoHol B
Compton, Virginia Frances Bateman 1853-1940 OxThe
Compton Brothers IlEncCM
Comstock, Anthony B 1844-1915 NotNAT B
Comstock, Bobby 1943- RkOn
Comstock, F Ray 1880-1949 EncMT, NotNAT B, WhThe
Comstock, Frank G 1922- AmSCAP 66, -80, CmpEPM
Comstock, Nanette 1873-1942 NotNAT B, WhThe, WhoStg 1908
Comstock, Oscar Franklin 1865-1944 BiDAmM
Comstock, William Collins 1924- AmSCAP 66, -80
Comtois, Ulysse 1931- CreCan 1
Conan, Laure 1845-1924 CreCan 1
Conant, H Weston PupTheA
Conant, Isabel Pope 1901- IntWWM 77, -80, NewGrD 80
Conant, Robert 1928- IntWWM 77, -80
Conati, Marcello 1938- IntWWM 77, -80
Conaway, Donald F BiE&WWA
Conaway, Sterling Bruce 1898- WhoJazz 72
Concarini, Vittoria NewGrD 80
Conceicao, Diego Da NewGrD 80
Conceicao, Roque Da NewGrD 80
Conchita d1940 NotNAT B
Conci, Noretta 1931- WhoMus 72
Concone, Giuseppe 1801-1861 Baker 78, NewGrD 80
Conde, Johnny 1895-1960 WhScrn 74, -77
Conde, Rita WhoHol A
Condell, Henry 1556?-1627 Ent, NotNAT B, OxThe
Condell, Henry 1757-1824 NewGrD 80
Condoli, Conte 1927- EncJzS 70
Condon, Albert Edwin 1904-1973 AmSCAP 80, BiDAmM, EncJzS 70
Condon, Albert Edwin 1905-1973 AmSCAP 66
Condon, David ForYSC
Condon, Denis Francis 1933- IntWWM 80
Condon, Eddie 1904-1973 MusMk
Condon, Eddie 1905- WhoJazz 72
Condon, Eddie 1905-1973 CmpEPM, IlEncJ, WhoMus 72
Condon, Jackie Film 1
Condon, Jackie 1913- Film 2
Condon, Jackie 1923- TwYS
Condos, Steve WhoHol A
Cone, Edward T 1917- Baker 78, ConAmC, DcCM, IntWWM 77, -80, NewGrD 80, WhoMus 72
Cone, Fairfax M d1977 NewYTET
Cone, Mike Zets 1910-1969 WhScrn 74, -77, WhoHol B
Conegliano, Emmanuele NewGrD 80
Conelly, Claire NewGrD 80
Conely, James Hannon, Jr. 1938- AmSCAP 80
Cones, Nancy Ford WomWMM
Conesa, Marie Film 1
Conetta, Lewis D 1927- AmSCAP 80
Confalonieri, Giulio 1896-1972 Baker 78, NewGrD 80
Confer, Robert 1931- AmSCAP 66
Conforti, Giovanni Battista NewGrD 80
Conforti, Giovanni Luca 1560?-1607? Baker 78, NewGrD 80
Conforti, Nicola 1718-1788? NewGrD 80
Conforto, Nicola 1718-1788? NewGrD 80
Confrey, Edward 1895-1971 BiDAmM
Confrey, Edward E 1895-1971 AmSCAP 66, -80, ConAmC
Confrey, Zez 1895-1971 Baker 78
Confrey, Zez 1895-1972 CmpEPM
Conga, Stu AmSCAP 80
Congdon, James WhoHol A
Congreve, William 1670-1729 CnThe, EncWT, Ent, McGEWD[port], NewGrD 80, NotNAT A, -B, OxThe, PlP&P[port], REnWD[port]
Coning, Servaas De NewGrD 80
Conkey, Ithamar 1815-1867 BiDAmM
Conkey, Thomas d1927 NotNAT B
Conkle, E P 1899- BiE&WWA, CnMD, ModWD, NotNAT
Conklin, Charles Heine 1880-1959 FilmEn
Conklin, Charles Heinie 1880-1959 Film 1, -2, TwYS, WhScrn 74, -77
Conklin, Chester 1886-1971 JoeFr, OxFilm, TwYS
Conklin, Chester 1888-1971 FilmEn, Film 1, -2, FilmgC, ForYSC, HalFC 80, MotPP, MovMk[port], What 1[port], WhScrn 74, -77, WhoHol B
Conklin, Heinie 1880-1959 ForYSC, HalFC 80, WhoHol B
Conklin, John Marshall 1937- WhoOp 76
Conklin, Peggy 1910- FilmEn, ThFT[port]
Conklin, Peggy 1912- BiE&WWA, NotNAT, WhThe, WhoHol A, WhoThe 72
Conklin, William 1877-1935 Film 1, -2, TwYS, WhScrn 74, -77, WhoHol B
Conklin, William 1887-1935 FilmEn
Conkling, Charles A d1964 NotNAT B
Conlan, Frank d1955 NotNAT B, WhoHol B
Conley, Arthur 1946- RkOn 2[port]
Conley, Arthur 1947- BiDAmM
Conley, Darlene WhoHol A
Conley, David 1930- ConAmC
Conley, Dick 1920- IntMPA 77, -75, -76, -78, -79, -80
Conley, Earl Thomas 1941- AmSCAP 80
Conley, Harry J 1885-1975 WhScrn 77
Conley, John 1934- ConAmC
Conley, Larry 1895-1960 AmSCAP 66, -80
Conley, Lige 1899-1937 Film 2, WhScrn 74, -77, WhoHol B
Conley, Lloyd Edgar 1924- AmSCAP 80, CpmDNM 80, ConAmC
Conley, Sandra 1943- CnOxB
Conley, William Bing d1962 WhScrn 77
Conlin, Jimmy 1884-1962 FilmEn, HalFC 80, NotNAT B, Vers A[port], WhScrn 74, -77, WhoHol B
Conlin, Jimmy 1885-1962 FilmgC, ForYSC
Conlin, Ray, Sr. d1964 NotNAT B
Conlon, Alfred Sanford PupTheA
Conlon, Francis Film 2
Conlon, James 1950- FilmEn, WhoOp 76
Conn, Billy 1917- What 2[port]
Conn, Charles Gerard 1844-1931 BiDAmM, NewGrD 80
Conn, Chester 1896- AmSCAP 66, -80
Conn, Irving 1898-1961 AmSCAP 66, -80, BiDAmM
Conn, Mervin 1920- AmSCAP 80
Conn, Robert A 1926- IntMPA 77, -75, -76, -78, -79, -80
Conn, Stewart 1936- ConDr 73, -77
Connah, Geoffrey Hall 1924- IntWWM 77, -80
Connecticut Yankees BiDAmM
Connell, Barbara WomWMM
Connell, David D NewYTET
Connell, F Norreys 1874-1948 NotNAT B, WhThe
Connell, Gordon 1923- BiE&WWA, NotNAT
Connell, Harold W PupTheA
Connell, Howard 1912- AmSCAP 66, -80
Connell, Jane 1925- BiE&WWA, NotNAT, WhoHol A, WhoThe 72, -77
Connell, Leigh 1926- BiE&WWA, NotNAT, PlP&P
Connell, Richard 1893-1949 HalFC 80
Connell, Thelma WomWMM
Connell, Will, Jr. 1938- EncJzS 70
Connelly, Bobby 1909-1922 Film 1, -2, WhScrn 74, -77, WhoHol B
Connelly, Christopher WhoHol A
Connelly, E J Film 2
Connelly, Edward J 1855-1928 Film 1, -2, NotNAT B, TwYS, WhScrn 74, -77, WhThe, WhoHol B
Connelly, Edwin 1873-1931 Film 2
Connelly, Erwin 1873-1931 Film 2, WhScrn 74, -77, WhoHol B
Connelly, Jane d1925 Film 2, WhScrn 74, -77, WhoHol B
Connelly, Marc 1890- BiDAmM, BiE&WWA, CnMD, CnThe, ConDr 73, -77, DcFM, DcLB 7[port], EncWT, Ent, FilmEn, McGEWD[port], ModWD, NotNAT, -A, OxThe, PlP&P, REnWD[port], WhoHol A, WhoThe 72, -77
Connelly, One-Eye Film 2
Connelly, Paul V 1923- IntMPA 77, -75, -76, -78, -79, -80

Connelly, Reg *CmpEPM*
Conner, Betty *WhoHol A*
Conner, Bruce 1933- *FilmEn*
Conner, David Allen 1936- *AmSCAP 80*
Conner, E S 1809-1891 *NotNAT B*
Conner, Nadine 1914- *NewEOp 71*
Conner, William James 1951- *IntWWM 77, -80*
Conners, Barry 1883-1933 *NotNAT B, WhThe*
Conners, Gene 1930- *EncJzS 70*
Conners, Mighty Flea 1930- *EncJzS 70*
Connery, Neil 1938- *FilmgC, HalFC 80, WhoHol A*
Connery, Sean 1930- *BiDFilm, -81, CmMov, FilmAG WE, FilmEn, FilmgC, ForYSC, HalFC 80, IIWWBF[port], -A, IntMPA 77, -75, -76, -78, 79, -80, MotPP, MovMk[port], OxFilm, WhoHol A, WhoHrs 80, WorEFlm*
Conness, Robert 1868-1941 *NotNAT B, WhScrn 77*
Conniff, Ray 1916- *BiDAmM, CmpEPM, EncJzS 70, RkOn, WhoJazz 72*
Connock, Kenneth Danby 1922- *WhoMus 72*
Connolly, Billy 1942- *IlEncR*
Connolly, Bobby 1895-1944 *EncMT, NotNAT B*
Connolly, Ernest 1890- *WhoMus 72*
Connolly, Jack *Film 1*
Connolly, Justin Riveagh 1933- *Baker 78, IntWWM 77, -80, NewGrD 80, WhoMus 72*
Connolly, Martha Nixon Taugher 1939- *IntWWM 80*
Connolly, Martha Nixon Tougher 1939- *IntWWM 77*
Connolly, Michael d1911 *NotNAT B*
Connolly, Norma *WhoHol A*
Connolly, Sadie *WhoStg 1908*
Connolly, Walter 1887-1940 *FilmEn, FilmgC, ForYSC, HalFC 80, HolCA[port], MotPP, MovMk, NotNAT B, OxFilm, WhScrn 74, -77, WhThe, WhoHol B*
Connolly, Walter 1888-1940 *Vers A[port]*
Connor, Chris 1927- *BiDAmM, CmpEPM, EncJzS 70*
Connor, Chris 1930- *RkOn*
Connor, Edric *WhoMus 72*
Connor, Edric 1915-1968 *FilmgC, HalFC 80, WhScrn 74, -77, WhoHol B*
Connor, Edward d1932 *WhScrn 74, WhoHol B*
Connor, Joseph P 1895-1952 *AmSCAP 80*
Connor, Kenneth 1918- *FilmgC, HalFC 80, IntMPA 77, -75, -76, -78, -79, -80, WhoHol A*
Connor, Kevin 1940?- *FilmEn, WhoHrs 80*
Connor, Laura 1946- *CnOxB*
Connor, Pierre Norman 1895-1952 *AmSCAP 66*
Connor, Ralph 1860-1937 *CreCan 1*
Connor, Tommie 1904- *WhoMus 72*
Connor, Whitfield 1916- *BiE&WWA, NotNAT, WhoHol A*
Connors, Ann-Marie 1951- *IntWWM 80*
Connors, Bill 1949- *EncJzS 70*
Connors, Buck *MotPP*
Connors, Charles 1930- *BiDAmM*
Connors, Chuck *MotPP, WhoHol A*
Connors, Chuck 1921- *FilmEn, FilmgC, ForYSC, HalFC 80*
Connors, Chuck 1924- *IntMPA 77, -75, -76, -78, -79, -80*
Connors, Eddie *Film 2*
Connors, Edgar d1934 *BlksBF*
Connors, Michael 1925- *FilmEn, FilmgC, ForYSC, HalFC 80*
Connors, Mike 1925- *IntMPA 77, -75, -76, -78, -79, -80, MotPP, WhoHol A, WhoHrs 80*
Connors, Norman 1947- *EncJzS 70*
Connors, Norman 1948- *RkOn 2[port]*
Connors, Sharon *WhoHol A*
Connors, William A 1949- *EncJzS 70*
Conomos, Dimitri Emmanuel 1947- *IntWWM 80*
Conon De Bethune 1160?-1220? *NewGrD 80*
Cononovici, Magdalena 1937- *WhoOp 76*
Conor, Harry d1931 *AmPS B, NotNAT B*
Conover, Teresa Maxwell *Film 2*
Conover, Willis Clark, Jr. 1920- *EncJzS 70*
Conquest, Arthur 1875-1945 *NotNAT B, OxThe, WhThe*
Conquest, Benjamin Oliver 1805-1872 *NotNAT B, OxThe*
Conquest, Fred 1870-1941 *NotNAT B, WhThe*
Conquest, Fred 1871-1941 *OxThe*
Conquest, George 1858-1926 *NotNAT B, OxThe, WhThe*
Conquest, George Augustus 1837-1901 *NotNAT B, OxThe*
Conquest, Ida 1870-1937 *WhoStg 1908*
Conquest, Ida 1876-1937 *NotNAT B, WhThe*
Conquet, John Henry 1927- *AmSCAP 66, -80*
Conrad Von Zabern d1481? *NewGrD 80*
Conrad, Beverly Grant *WomWMM B*
Conrad, Charles *ConMuA 80B*
Conrad, Con 1891-1938 *AmPS, AmSCAP 66, -80, BiDAmM, CmpEPM, FilmEn, Film 2, NotNAT B, PopAmC, Sw&Ld C, WhThe*
Conrad, Eddie 1891-1941 *Film 2, WhScrn 74, -77, WhoHol B*
Conrad, Eugene J d1964 *NotNAT B*
Conrad, Ferdinand 1912- *NewGrD 80*
Conrad, Hugh *AmSCAP 80*
Conrad, Jess 1940- *FilmgC, HalFC 80*
Conrad, Joseph 1857-1924 *CnMD, FilmgC, HalFC 80, ModWD*
Conrad, Karen 1919- *CnOxB, DancEn 78[port]*
Conrad, Michael *WhoHol A*
Conrad, Robert 1935- *FilmEn, FilmgC, HalFC 80, IntMPA 77, -75, -76, -78, -79, -80, WhoHol A*
Conrad, Robert Taylor 1810-1858 *McGEWD, NotNAT B, PlP&P*
Conrad, Tony 1940- *ConAmC*
Conrad, William *IntMPA 77, -75, -76, -78, -79, -80, NewYTET, WhoHol A*
Conrad, William 1920- *AmSCAP 80, FilmEn, FilmgC, ForYSC, HalFC 80, HolCA[port]*
Conrad, William 1923- *MovMk*
Conradi, August 1821-1873 *Baker 78, NewGrD 80*
Conradi, Gottfried 1820-1896 *NewGrD 80*
Conradi, Johann Georg d1699 *NewGrD 80*
Conradi, Johann Melchior 1675-1756 *NewGrD 80*
Conradi, Paul *Film 2*
Conradus De Pistoja *NewGrD 80*
Conradus De Zabernia d1481? *NewGrD 80*
Conrat Von Wertzeburc *NewGrD 80*
Conreid, Hans 1917- *NotNAT, WhoHrs 80[port]*
Conried, Hans 1917- *FilmEn, FilmgC, ForYSC, HalFC 80, HolCA[port], MotPP, MovMk[port], WhoHol A, WhoThe 77*
Conried, Heinrich 1848-1909 *Baker 78*
Conried, Heinrich 1855-1909 *NewEOp 71, NotNAT A, WhoStg 1906, -1908*
Conroy, Frank 1890-1964 *FilmEn, FilmgC, HalFC 80, HolCA[port], MovMk, NotNAT B, PlP&P, Vers A[port], WhScrn 74, -77, WhThe, WhoHol B*
Conroy, Thom 1911-1971 *WhScrn 74, -77, WhoHol B*
Conroy, Thomas 1924- *IntMPA 77, -75, -76, -78, -79, -80*
Cons, Emma 1838-1912 *PlP&P*
Conseil, Jean 1498-1535 *NewGrD 80*
Conseulla, Senorita *Film 2*
Considine, John *WhoHol A*
Considine, John W, Jr. 1898- *FilmEn*
Considine, Tim 1941- *ForYSC, WhoHol A*
Consilium, Johannes *NewGrD 80*
Consoli, Marc-Antonio 1941- *CpmDNM 78, -80, ConAmC*
Consoni, Giovanni Battista 1706-1765? *NewGrD 80*
Consoni, Giuseppe Antonio 1710?-1765 *NewGrD 80*
Constable, John Robert 1934- *IntWWM 77, -80, WhoMus 72*
Constance *NewGrD 80*
Constanduros, Mabel d1957 *NotNAT A, -B, WhThe, WhoHol B*
Constans Brawe d1481 *NewGrD 80*
Constans Breeu d1481 *NewGrD 80*
Constans Breuwe d1481 *NewGrD 80*
Constans De Languebroek d1481 *NewGrD 80*
Constans De Trecht d1481 *NewGrD 80*
Constant, Franz 1910- *Baker 78, CpmDNM 80*
Constant, Marius 1925- *Baker 78, CnOxB, IntWWM 77, -80, NewGrD 80, WhoMus 72*
Constant, Marius 1926- *DcCM*
Constant, Max d1943 *WhScrn 74, -77, WhoHol B*
Constant, Yvonne 1935- *BiE&WWA, ConAmTC*
Constanten, Thomas Charles 1944- *AmSCAP 80*
Constantin *PlP&P*
Constantin, Louis 1585?-1657 *NewGrD 80*
Constantin, Michel *WhoHol A*
Constantin, Mila *Film 2*
Constantin, Rudolf 1935- *IntWWM 80*
Constantin-Weyer, Maurice 1881-1964 *CreCan 2*
Constantine VII Porphyrogennetus d959 *NewGrD 80*
Constantine, Eddie 1917- *FilmAG WE, FilmEn, FilmgC, HalFC 80, MotPP, OxFilm, WhoHrs 80, WorEFlm*
Constantine, Michael 1927- *BiE&WWA, FilmgC, HalFC 80, WhoHol A*
Constantineau, Gilles 1933- *CreCan 2*
Constantinescu, Dan 1931- *Baker 78, DcCM, IntWWM 77, -80*
Constantinescu, Mihai 1926- *IntWWM 80*
Constantinescu, Nicolae 1938- *WhoOp 76*
Constantinescu, Paul 1909-1963 *Baker 78, NewGrD 80*
Constantini, Livia *NewGrD 80*
Constantini, Nino *Film 2*
Constantinides, Constantine Dinos 1929- *ConAmC*
Constantinides, Dinos Demetrios 1929- *AmSCAP 80, CpmDNM 75, -78, -79, -80, IntWWM 77, -80*
Constantinidis, Yannis 1903- *DcCM, NewGrD 80*
Constantino, Joseph George 1931- *AmSCAP 80*
Constanz, Hans Von *NewGrD 80*
Consuella, Senorita *Film 2*
Consuelo, Beatriz *CnOxB, DancEn 78*
Consumer Rapport *RkOn 2[port]*
Contant, Alexis 1858-1918 *CreCan 2, NewGrD 80*
Contarini, Marco 1632-1689 *NewGrD 80*
Contat, Louise-Francoise 1760-1813 *EncWT, Ent, OxThe*
Conte, Il *NewGrD 80*
Conte, Donald J 1941- *IntMPA 77, -75, -76, -78, -79*
Conte, John *ForYSC, IntMPA 75, -76, -78, -79, -80*
Conte, John 1915- *BiE&WWA, IntMPA 77, WhThe*
Conte, Michel 1932- *CreCan 2, DancEn 78*
Conte, Richard d1975 *MotPP, WhoHol C*
Conte, Richard 1911-1975 *HalFC 80*
Conte, Richard 1914-1975 *FilmEn, FilmgC, ForYSC, HolP 40[port], IntMPA 75, WhScrn 77, WorEFlm*
Conte, Richard 1915-1975 *MovMk[port]*
Conte, Richard 1919-1975 *CmMov*
Contestabile, Emma 1928- *WhoMus 72*
Conti, Albert 1887-1967 *FilmEn, Film 2, ForYSC, TwYS, WhScrn 74, -77, WhoHol B*
Conti, Bill *HalFC 80*
Conti, Bill 1940- *RkOn 2[port]*
Conti, Bill 1943- *IntMPA 80*
Conti, Carlo 1796-1868 *Baker 78, NewGrD 80*
Conti, Dick *AmSCAP 80*
Conti, Francesco Bartolomeo 1681-1732 *Baker 78, NewGrD 80*
Conti, Giacomo 1754-1805 *NewGrD 80*
Conti, Gioacchino 1714-1761 *NewGrD 80[port]*
Conti, Ignazio Maria 1699-1759 *NewGrD 80*
Conti, Italia 1874-1946 *EncWT, NotNAT A, -B, OxThe, WhThe*
Conti, Jacques 1754-1805 *NewGrD 80*
Conti, Lorenzo 1680?-1740? *NewGrD 80*
Conti, Louise *Film 2*
Conti, Niccolo *NewGrD 80*
Conti, Nicola *NewGrD 80*
Contiguglia, John Joseph 1927- *WhoMus 72*

Contiguglia, Richard 1937- *WhoMus 72*
Contilli, Gino 1907-1978 *Baker 78, NewGrD 80*
Contino, Dick 1930- *What 3[port], WhoHol A*
Contino, Giovanni 1513?-1574? *NewGrD 80*
Contino, Joan 1513?-1574? *NewGrD 80*
Contours *AmPS A*
Contours, The *RkOn*
Contredit D'Arras, Andrieu *NewGrD 80*
Contreras, Frank Rodriguez 1942- *IntWWM 77, -80*
Contreras, Gloria 1934- *CnOxB*
Contreras, Jose Rozo *NewGrD 80*
Contreras, Joseph *NewGrD 80*
Contreras, Salvador 1912- *NewGrD 80*
Conus, George 1862-1933 *OxMus*
Conus, Georgi 1862-1933 *Baker 78*
Conus, Julius 1869-1942 *Baker 78*
Conus, Sergei 1902- *Baker 78*
Converse, Charles Crozat 1832-1918 *Baker 78, BiDAmM*
Converse, Frank 1938- *HalFC 80, IntMPA 77, -76, -78, -79, -80, WhoHol A*
Converse, Frank 1939- *ForYSC*
Converse, Frederick Shepherd 1871-1940 *AmSCAP 66, -80, Baker 78, BiDAmM, CompSN[port], ConAmC, NewEOp 71, NewGrD 80, OxMus*
Converse, Peggy *ForYSC, WhoHol A*
Converse, Thelma *Film 2*
Conversi, Girolamo *NewGrD 80*
Conville, David 1929- *WhoThe 72, -77*
Conville, Robert *Film 1*
Convy, Bert *WhoHol A*
Convy, Bert 1934- *WhoThe 72, -77*
Convy, Bert 1936- *BiE&WWA, NotNAT*
Conway, Booth *Film 2*
Conway, Curt 1915-1974 *BiE&WWA, NotNAT B, WhScrn 77, WhoHol B*
Conway, Frederick Bartlett 1819-1874 *NotNAT B, OxThe*
Conway, Gary 1938- *FilmgC, HalFC 80, IntMPA 78, -79, -80, WhoHol A, WhoHrs 80*
Conway, Harold 1906- *WhThe*
Conway, Hugh d1885 *NotNAT B*
Conway, Jack d1951 *WhScrn 74, -77, WhoHol B*
Conway, Jack 1887-1952 *CmMov, DcFM, FilmEn, Film 1, FilmgC, HalFC 80, MovMk[port], NotNAT B, TwYS A, WhScrn 74, -77, WhoHol B, WorEFlm*
Conway, John Ashby 1905- *BiE&WWA, NotNAT, PupTheA*
Conway, Joseph 1889?-1959 *WhScrn 74, -77*
Conway, Kevin *IntMPA 79, -80*
Conway, Lionel *ConMuA 80B*
Conway, Martin *Film 2*
Conway, Mel *BlkAmP, MorBAP*
Conway, Minnie 1854-1896 *NotNAT B, OxThe*
Conway, Morgan *WhoHol A*
Conway, Morgan 1903- *FilmEn*
Conway, Pat *ForYSC, WhoHol A*
Conway, Russ *WhoHol A*
Conway, Sarah Crocker 1834-1875 *NotNAT B, OxThe*
Conway, Shirl 1916- *BiE&WWA, IntMPA 77, -75, -76, -78, -79, -80, NotNAT, WhoHol A*
Conway, Tim 1933- *FilmEn, ForYSC, IntMPA 77, -76, -78, -79, -80, NewYTET, WhoHol A*
Conway, Tom 1904-1967 *FilmEn, FilmgC, ForYSC, HalFC 80, HolP 40[port], MotPP, MovMk, WhScrn 74, -77, WhoHol B, WhoHrs 80*
Conway, William Augustus 1789-1828 *NotNAT B, OxThe*
Conwell, Carolyn *WhoHol A*
Conyers, Darcy 1919-1973 *FilmgC, HalFC 80*
Conyers, D'Arcy 1919-1973 *IlWWBF*
Conyers, David 1945- *IntWWM 80*
Conyers, Joseph d1920 *NotNAT B*
Conyngham, Barry 1944- *Baker 78, DcCM, IntWWM 80, NewGrD 80*
Conyngham, Fred 1909- *IlWWBF, WhThe*
Conz, Bernhard 1906- *WhoOp 76*
Conzelmann, Curt 1919- *IntWWM 77, -80*
Cooder, Ry 1947- *ConMuA 80A[port], IlEncCM[port], IlEncR*
Coogan, Gene B d1972 *WhScrn 77*
Coogan, Jack, Sr. 1880-1935 *Film 2, WhScrn 77*
Coogan, Jackie *MotPP*
Coogan, Jackie 1914- *FilmEn, FilmgC, ForYSC, HalFC 80, IntMPA 77, -75, -76, -78, -79, -80, MovMk[port], OxFilm, TwYS, WhoHol A*
Coogan, Jackie 1915- *Film 1, -2*
Coogan, Robert 1925- *ForYSC, WhoHol A*
Cook, Al 1882-1935 *WhScrn 74, -77, WhoHol B*
Cook, Alfred Melville 1912- *WhoMus 72*
Cook, Ann 1888?-1962 *NewOrJ[port]*
Cook, Ann 1903-1962 *BluesWW[port]*
Cook, Barbara 1927- *BiE&WWA, EncMT, NotNAT, WhoThe 72, -77*
Cook, Bart 1949- *CnOxB*
Cook, Bramwell William Harold 1922- *WhoMus 72*
Cook, Brian Rayner 1945- *IntWWM 77, -80, NewGrD 80*
Cook, Carole *WhoHol A*
Cook, Caroline Frances *Film 2*
Cook, Charles Emerson d1941 *NotNAT B*
Cook, Clyde 1891- *FilmEn, Film 1, -2, ForYSC, TwYS*
Cook, Deborah 1938- *IntWWM 77, -80, WhoOp 76*
Cook, Donald 1900-1961 *FilmEn, FilmgC, HalFC 80*
Cook, Donald 1900-1967 *MovMk*
Cook, Donald 1901-1961 *ForYSC, HolP 30[port], MotPP, NotNAT B, WhScrn 74, -77, WhThe, WhoHol B*
Cook, Douglas 1929- *NotNAT*
Cook, E T 1880-1953 *NewGrD 80*
Cook, Edna Evelyn 1907- *WhoMus 72*
Cook, Edward Dutton 1829-1883 *NotNAT B, OxThe*
Cook, Elisha, Jr. *WhoHol A*
Cook, Elisha, Jr. 1902- *CmMov, FilmgC, HalFC 80, HolCA[port], MovMk, WhThe, WhoHrs 80*
Cook, Elisha, Jr. 1906- *BiE&WWA, FilmEn, ForYSC, NotNAT, WorEFlm[port]*
Cook, Elisha, Jr. 1907- *CmMov, IntMPA 77, -75, -76, -78, -79, -80, OxFilm, Vers B[port]*
Cook, Ethyle 1880-1949 *WhScrn 77*
Cook, Fielder 1923- *FilmEn, FilmgC, HalFC 80, IntMPA 77, -75, -76, -78, -79, -80, NewYTET*
Cook, Fred *WhoHol A*
Cook, George Cram 1873-1924 *CnMD, ModWD, NotNAT B*
Cook, Herman 1934- *BiDAmM, EncJzS 70*
Cook, Ira Leigh 1916- *AmSCAP 66, -80*
Cook, J David 1927- *ConAmTC*
Cook, Jean *IntWWM 80*
Cook, Jeanne *WhoOp 76*
Cook, Joe 1890-1959 *AmPS B, CmpEPM, EncMT, JoeFr[port], NotNAT B, WhScrn 77, WhThe, WhoHol B*
Cook, John *Film 1*
Cook, John 1923- *BiDAmM, ConAmC, NewGrD 80*
Cook, John Russell 1911-1964 *NotNAT B*
Cook, Josephine Mary 1952- *IntWWM 80*
Cook, Junior 1934- *EncJzS 70*
Cook, Keith Linwood 1951- *IntWWM 80*
Cook, Ken 1914-1963 *NotNAT B, WhScrn 74, -77*
Cook, Kwenam David 1922- *IntMPA 77, -75, -76, -78, -79, -80*
Cook, Lawrence *DrBlPA*
Cook, Lillian 1898-1918 *WhScrn 77*
Cook, Lucius 1891-1952 *WhScrn 77*
Cook, Madge Carr 1856-1933 *NotNAT B*
Cook, Martha Ann 1807-1874 *BiDAmM*
Cook, Mary d1944 *WhScrn 74, -77*
Cook, Mary Lou d1944 *WhoHol B*
Cook, May A 1870- *BiDAmM*
Cook, Melville 1912- *IntWWM 77, -80*
Cook, Michael 1933- *ConDr 77*
Cook, Nadine *PupTheA*
Cook, Nigel Cyril John 1949- *WhoMus 72*
Cook, Olivia 1913- *BlkWAB[port]*
Cook, Peter 1937- *BiE&WWA, FilmEn, FilmgC, ForYSC, HalFC 80, NotNAT, WhoHol A, WhoThe 77*
Cook, Peter Francis 1923- *ConAmC, IntWWM 77, -80*
Cook, Richard G 1929- *ConAmC*
Cook, Richard Leonard, Jr. *AmSCAP 80*
Cook, Ross 1898-1930 *WhScrn 74, -77*
Cook, Russell Sturgis 1811-1864 *BiDAmM*
Cook, S N *MorBAP*
Cook, Shorty *AmSCAP 80*
Cook, Thomas Aynsley 1831?-1894 *NewGrD 80*
Cook, Tommy *ForYSC, WhoHol A*
Cook, Tommy 1930- *FilmEn*
Cook, W Mercer 1903- *AmSCAP 66, -80*
Cook, Warren 1879-1939 *Film 1, -2, WhScrn 74, -77*
Cook, Wayne Evans 1939- *IntWWM 77, -80*
Cook, Will Marion 1865-1944 *BlksBF[port]*
Cook, Will Marion 1869-1944 *AmSCAP 66, -80, BiDAmM, BlkAmP, CmpEPM, DrBlPA, MorBAP, NewGrD 80, NotNAT B*
Cook, Zale Edward 1942- *IntMPA 78, -79, -80*
Cook-MacDonald, Linda 1947- *WhoOp 76*
Cooke, Al *Film 2, TwYS*
Cooke, Alexander d1614 *NotNAT B*
Cooke, Alistair 1908- *IntMPA 77, -75, -76, -78, -79, -80, NewYTET*
Cooke, Anthony John 1931- *IntWWM 80, WhoMus 72*
Cooke, Arnold 1906- *Baker 78, CpmDNM 79, IntWWM 77, -80, NewGrD 80, OxMus, WhoMus 72*
Cooke, Baldwin *Film 2*
Cooke, Beach 1898-1948 *Film 2, WhoHol B*
Cooke, Benjamin 1695?-1743? *NewGrD 80*
Cooke, Benjamin 1734-1793 *Baker 78, NewGrD 80, OxMus*
Cooke, Charles L 1891-1958 *AmSCAP 66, -80, BiDAmM*
Cooke, Deryck 1919-1976 *Baker 78, IntWWM 77, NewGrD 80, WhoMus 72*
Cooke, Doc 1891-1958 *WhoJazz 72*
Cooke, Eddie d1942 *NotNAT B*
Cooke, Esther Louise 1929- *BlkWAB*
Cooke, Frank *Film 2*
Cooke, George Alfred 1825-1905 *MagIlD*
Cooke, George Frederick 1756-1811 *CnThe*
Cooke, George Frederick 1756-1812 *FamA&A[port], NotNAT A, -B, OxThe, PlP&P[port]*
Cooke, Harry d1958 *NotNAT B*
Cooke, Henry 1615?-1672 *NewGrD 80*
Cooke, Henry 1616?-1672 *BnBkM 80, OxMus*
Cooke, J d1419 *NewGrD 80*
Cooke, Jack Kent 1912- *AmSCAP 80, NewYTET*
Cooke, James Francis 1875-1960 *AmSCAP 66, -80, Baker 78, BiDAmM, ConAmC*
Cooke, James Patrick 1944- *AmSCAP 80*
Cooke, John William 1930- *IntWWM 77, -80, WhoMus 72*
Cooke, Kerrison 1943- *CnOxB*
Cooke, Margaret 1911- *WhoMus 72*
Cooke, Marjorie Benton d1920 *NotNAT B*
Cooke, Matthew 1761?-1829 *NewGrD 80*
Cooke, Maxwell Joseph Lorimer 1924- *IntWWM 77, -80*
Cooke, Nelson 1924- *IntWWM 77, -80, WhoMus 72*
Cooke, Ray *Film 2*
Cooke, Richard P 1904- *BiE&WWA, NotNAT*
Cooke, Robert *NewGrD 80*
Cooke, Sam 1935-1964 *AmPS A, -B, BiDAmM, ConMuA 80A, DrBlPA, IlEncR, RkOn[port], WhoHol B*
Cooke, Stanley 1868-1931 *Film 2, WhThe*
Cooke, Stephen Beach 1898-1948 *WhScrn 74, -77*
Cooke, Thomas d1756 *NotNAT B*
Cooke, Thomas Coffin d1939 *NotNAT B*
Cooke, Thomas Potter 1786-1864 *NotNAT B, OxThe*
Cooke, Thomas Simpson 1782-1848 *Baker 78, NewGrD 80, OxMus*
Cooke, Tom 1782-1848 *NewGrD 80*
Cooke, Warren 1897-1939 *WhoHol B*
Cooker, John Lee *BluesWW, EncFCWM 69*

Cookies, The *RkOn*
Cookman, Anthony Victor 1894-1962 *NotNAT B, OxThe, WhThe*
Cooksey, Curtis 1892-1962 *BlkAmP, Film 2, ForYSC, NotNAT B, WhScrn 74, -77, WhoHol B*
Cookson, Georgina *WhThe, WhoThe 72*
Cookson, Peter *WhoHol A*
Cookson, Peter 1913- *BiE&WWA, NotNAT*
Cookson, S A d1947 *Film 1, NotNAT B*
Cool, Harold 1890-1949 *AmSCAP 66, -80*
Cool, Harry 1913- *CmpEPM*
Cool Papa *BluesWW*
Coolen, Lambert 1585?-1654 *NewGrD 80*
Cooley, Alex *ConMuA 80B*
Cooley, Carleton 1898- *ConAmC*
Cooley, Charles 1903-1960 *WhScrn 74, -77, WhoHol B*
Cooley, Eddie And The Dimples *RkOn*
Cooley, Frank L 1870-1941 *Film 2, WhScrn 74, -77, WhoHol B*
Cooley, Hallam 1888- *Film 1, -2, TwYS*
Cooley, Hallam 1895- *ForYSC*
Cooley, Isabelle *DrBlPA*
Cooley, James R 1880-1948 *Film 1, -2, WhScrn 74, -77, WhoHol B*
Cooley, Spade d1972 *CmpEPM*
Cooley, Spade 1910-1969 *Baker 78, CounME 74, ForYSC, IlEncCM[port], WhScrn 74, -77, WhoHol B*
Cooley, Willard *Film 1, -2*
Coolidge, Mrs. E S 1864-1953 *OxMus*
Coolidge, Elizabeth Sprague 1864-1953 *Baker 78, CnOxB, DancEn 78, NewGrD 80*
Coolidge, Martha *WomWMM, -A, -B*
Coolidge, Peggy Stuart 1913- *AmSCAP 66, -80, ConAmC*
Coolidge, Philip 1908-1967 *BiE&WWA, NotNAT B, WhScrn 74, -77, WhoHol B*
Coolidge, Philip 1909-1967 *ForYSC*
Coolidge, Richard Ard 1929- *CpmDNM 80, ConAmC, IntWWM 77, -80*
Coolidge, Rita *ConMuA 80A[port]*
Coolidge, Rita 1944- *IlEncCM[port], IlEncR*
Coolidge, Rita 1945- *BiDAmM, RkOn 2[port]*
Coolidge, Walt *PupTheA*
Cools, Eugene 1877-1936 *Baker 78*
Coolsma, Hans 1919- *NewGrD 80*
Coolsma, Johannis 1919- *NewGrD 80*
Coolus, Romain 1868-1952 *McGEWD, WhThe*
Coombe, Carol 1911-1966 *WhScrn 77, WhThe, WhoHol B*
Coombs, Charles Whitney 1859-1940 *AmSCAP 66, -80, Baker 78, BiDAmM*
Coombs, Edith Grace 1890- *CreCan 1*
Coombs, Guy *Film 1*
Coombs, Harry *ConMuA 80B*
Coombs, Jack d1939 *PupTheA*
Coombs, Jack 1883-1957 *WhScrn 77*
Coombs, Jackie *Film 2*
Coombs, John Martin 1929- *IntWWM 77, -80, WhoMus 72*
Coombs, Thelma Hughes 1907- *IntWWM 77*
Coomes, Thomas William 1946- *AmSCAP 80*
Coon, Carleton 1894-1932 *CmpEPM*
Coon Creek Girls, The *IlEncCM*
Coon-Sanders Orchestra, The *BgBands 74[port], CmpEPM*
Coonan, Dorothy *WhoHol A*
Cooney, Joan Ganz 1929- *NewYTET*
Cooney, Ray 1932- *WhoThe 72, -77*
Cooninck, Servaas De *NewGrD 80*
Coons, Johnny 1917-1975 *WhScrn 77*
Coop, Colin d1937 *NotNAT B*
Coop, Denys 1920- *FilmEn, FilmgC, HalFC 80*
Cooper, Alice 1948- *ConMuA 80A[port], IlEncR[port], RkOn 2[port]*
Cooper, Alice, Group *RkOn 2[port]*
Cooper, Anthony Kemble 1908- *BiE&WWA, NotNAT, WhThe, WhoThe 72*
Cooper, Arthur Melbourne 1872-1962 *IlWWBF*
Cooper, Ashley 1882-1952 *NotNAT B, WhScrn 74, -77, WhoHol B*
Cooper, Ben *IntMPA 75, -76, -78, -79, -80*
Cooper, Ben 1930- *FilmgC, HalFC 80, IntMPA 77, MotPP, WhoHol A*
Cooper, Ben 1932- *FilmEn, ForYSC*
Cooper, Bigelow *Film 1, -2*
Cooper, Bob 1925- *BiDAmM, CmpEPM, EncJzS 70*
Cooper, Bud 1899- *AmSCAP 66*
Cooper, Budge *WomWMM*
Cooper, Buster 1929- *EncJzS 70*
Cooper, Charles Kemble d1923 *NotNAT B*
Cooper, Cheryl *AmSCAP 66*
Cooper, Clancy d1975 *WhScrn 77, WhoHol C*
Cooper, Claude 1881-1932 *Film 1, WhScrn 74, -77, WhoHol B*
Cooper, Clifford d1895 *NotNAT B*
Cooper, Mrs. Clifford 1823-1895 *NotNAT B*
Cooper, Daley 1872- *WhThe*
Cooper, David 1952- *AmSCAP 80*
Cooper, David Edwin 1944- *IntWWM 77, -80*
Cooper, David Shearer 1922- *ConAmC, IntWWM 77*
Cooper, Diana 1892- *NotNAT A*
Cooper, Earl *Film 1*
Cooper, Edna Mae *Film 1, -2*
Cooper, Edward d1956 *NotNAT B, WhScrn 77, WhoHol B*
Cooper, Edward 1903- *IntMPA 77, -75, -76, -78, -79, -80*
Cooper, Edward 1925- *AmSCAP 66, -80*
Cooper, Edwin *WhoHol A*
Cooper, Emil 1877-1960 *Baker 78, CmOp, NewEOp 71, NewGrD 80*
Cooper, Emil 1879-1960 *BiDAmM*
Cooper, Enid 1902- *WhThe*
Cooper, Evelyne Love *AmSCAP 66, -80*
Cooper, F B *Film 1*
Cooper, Frances d1872 *NotNAT B*
Cooper, Frank *BiE&WWA*
Cooper, Frank Kemble 1857-1918 *NotNAT B, WhThe*
Cooper, Frederick 1890-1945 *Film 2, HalFC 80, NotNAT B, WhThe, WhoHol B*
Cooper, G Melville 1896- *WhThe, WhoThe 72*
Cooper, Gary 1901-1961 *BiDFilm, -81, CmMov, FilmEn, Film 2, FilmgC, ForYSC, HalFC 80, MotPP, MovMk[port], NotNAT B, OxFilm, TwYS, WhScrn 74, -77, WhoHol B, WorEFlm*
Cooper, Gaze 1895- *IntWWM 77*
Cooper, George 1820-1876 *Baker 78*
Cooper, George 1840-1927 *BiDAmM*
Cooper, George 1891- *Film 1, -2, TwYS*
Cooper, George 1892-1943 *ForYSC, WhScrn 77*
Cooper, George 1929- *BiDAmM, EncJzS 70*
Cooper, George A *WhoHol A*
Cooper, George A 1894-1947 *IlWWBF*
Cooper, George A 1913- *MovMk*
Cooper, George A 1916- *FilmgC, HalFC 80*
Cooper, Georgia 1882-1968 *WhScrn 74, -77*
Cooper, Georgie 1882-1968 *WhoHol B*
Cooper, Giles 1918-1966 *ConDr 77F, CroCD, EncWT, NotNAT B, WhThe*
Cooper, Gladys 1888-1971 *BiE&WWA, CnThe, EncWT, Ent[port], FilmAG WE, FilmEn, Film 1, -2, FilmgC, ForYSC, HalFC 80, IlWWBF[port], -A, MGM[port], MotPP, MovMk[port], Vers A[port], WhScrn 74, -77, WhThe, WhoHol B, WhoThe 72*
Cooper, Gladys 1889-1971 *NotNAT A, -B*
Cooper, Greta Kemble *WhThe*
Cooper, Hal 1923- *IntMPA 77, -75, -76, -78, -79, -80*
Cooper, Hal David 1944- *IntWWM 77*
Cooper, Harold 1924- *NewOrJ*
Cooper, Harry 1882-1957 *WhScrn 74, -77*
Cooper, Harry R 1903-1961 *WhoJazz 72*
Cooper, Herman E *BiE&WWA*
Cooper, Imogen 1949- *IntWWM 77, -80*
Cooper, Jack *Film 2*
Cooper, Jackie *MotPP, NewYTET, WhoHol A*
Cooper, Jackie 1921- *FilmEn, FilmgC, HalFC 80, IntMPA 75*
Cooper, Jackie 1922- *BiDAmM, BiE&WWA, Film 2, ForYSC, IntMPA 77, -76, -78, -79, -80, MGM[port], MovMk[port]*
Cooper, James Fenimore 1789-1851 *FilmgC, HalFC 80*
Cooper, Jay *ConMuA 80B*
Cooper, Jeanne *WhoHol A*
Cooper, Jerome 1946- *EncJzS 70*
Cooper, Jerry *CmpEPM*
Cooper, John *ConAmC, NewGrD 80, OxMus*
Cooper, John Craig 1925- *AmSCAP 66, -80, ConAmC A*
Cooper, John Harris 1933- *IntWWM 77, -80*
Cooper, Joseph 1912- *IntWWM 77, -80, WhoMus 72*
Cooper, Kenneth 1941- *Baker 78*
Cooper, Kent 1880-1965 *AmSCAP 66, -80*
Cooper, Lawrence 1946- *IntWWM 80*
Cooper, Les *RkOn*
Cooper, Lester *AmSCAP 80*
Cooper, Lewis Hugh 1920- *IntWWM 77, -80*
Cooper, Lillian Kemble 1891- *WhThe*
Cooper, Lindsay 1951- *IntWWM 77, -80*
Cooper, Louis Budd 1899- *AmSCAP 80*
Cooper, Marcus F 1902- *IntMPA 75, -76*
Cooper, Margaret d1922 *NotNAT B*
Cooper, Margaret Gernon *WhThe*
Cooper, Marilyn 1935- *BiE&WWA*
Cooper, Mark *ConMuA 80B*
Cooper, Martin DuPre 1910- *Baker 78, IntWWM 77, -80, NewGrD 80, OxMus*
Cooper, Melville 1896-1973 *BiE&WWA, FilmEn, FilmgC, ForYSC, HalFC 80, HolCA[port], MovMk[port], NotNAT B, Vers A[port], WhScrn 77, WhoHol B*
Cooper, Meriam C 1893-1973 *TwYS A*
Cooper, Merian C 1893-1973 *BiDFilm, -81, DcFM, FilmEn, FilmgC, HalFC 80, WhScrn 77, WhoHrs 80, WorEFlm*
Cooper, Merian C 1894-1973 *OxFilm*
Cooper, Milton 1929- *IntWWM 77*
Cooper, Miriam 1893-1976 *FilmEn, WhoHol A*
Cooper, Miriam 1894-1976 *Film 1, -2, TwYS*
Cooper, Paul 1926- *AmSCAP 80, Baker 78, CpmDNM 78, ConAmC, NewGrD 80*
Cooper, Peter Douglas 1918- *IntWWM 77, -80*
Cooper, Ralph *BlksB&W[port], -C, DrBlPA*
Cooper, Richard 1893-1947 *IlWWBF, NotNAT B, WhThe, WhoHol B*
Cooper, Robert William 1925- *AmSCAP 66, -80, NewGrD 80*
Cooper, Rose Marie 1937- *AmSCAP 66, -80, ConAmC*
Cooper, Rosemary *Film 2*
Cooper, Sandra Ranee 1952- *AmSCAP 80*
Cooper, Sidney 1918- *AmSCAP 66, -80*
Cooper, Stoney 1918- *BiDAmM, EncFCWM 69*
Cooper, Stoney 1918-1977 *CounME 74, IlEncCM[port]*
Cooper, Ted *BlkAmP, MorBAP*
Cooper, Terence *WhoHol A*
Cooper, Tex 1877-1951 *WhScrn 74, -77, WhoHol B*
Cooper, Thelma Lou 1936- *IntWWM 77*
Cooper, Theodore Gleston 1939- *NotNAT*
Cooper, Thomas Abthorpe 1776-1849 *FamA&A[port], NotNAT B, OxThe, PlP&P*
Cooper, Tommy 1921- *IntMPA 77, -75, -76, -78, -79, -80*
Cooper, Violet Kemble 1886-1961 *FilmgC, ForYSC, HalFC 80*
Cooper, Violet Kemble 1889-1961 *NotNAT B, WhThe*
Cooper, W M *NewGrD 80*
Cooper, Walter Thomas Gaze 1895- *IntWWM 80, WhoMus 72*
Cooper, Wilkie 1911- *FilmEn, FilmgC, HalFC 80*
Cooper, William B 1920- *ConAmC*
Cooper, Wilma Lee 1921- *BiDAmM, CounME 74, EncFCWM 69, IlEncCM[port]*
Cooper, Wilma Lee And Stoney *CounME 74A*
Cooper, Zack *AmSCAP 80*
Cooperman, Alvin 1923- *IntMPA 77, -75, -76, -78, -79, -80, NewYTET*
Cooperman, Mort *ConMuA 80B*
Coopersmith, Harry 1902?- *AmSCAP 66*
Coopersmith, J M 1903-1968 *NewGrD 80*
Coopersmith, Jacob Maurice 1903- *AmSCAP 66, -80, Baker 78*
Coors, Joseph *NewYTET*
Coot *BluesWW*
Coote, Bernard *IntMPA 77, -75, -76, -78, -79, -80*

Coote, Bert 1867-1938 *NotNAT B*
Coote, Bert 1868-1938 *WhScrn 74, -77, WhThe*
Coote, Robert 1909- *BiE&WWA, FilmEn, FilmgC, ForYSC, HalFC 80, MotPP, MovMk, NotNAT, Vers B[port], WhoHol A, WhoThe 72, -77*
Cooter, Hubert Brian Edmund 1904- *WhoMus 72*
Cootes, Louise *WhoMus 72*
Coots *BluesWW[port]*
Coots, J Fred 1897- *AmPS, AmSCAP 66, BiDAmM, BiE&WWA, CmpEPM, EncMT, NewCBMT, NotNAT, PopAmC[port], Sw&Ld C*
Coots, John Frederick 1897- *AmSCAP 80*
Coover, James B 1925- *IntWWM 77, -80, NewGrD 80*
Copage, Marc 1962- *DrBlPA*
Copani, Peter 1942- *AmSCAP 80, NatPD[port]*
Copas, Cowboy *AmPS A*
Copas, Cowboy 1913-1963 *CounME 74, -74A, EncFCWM 69, IlEncCM*
Copas, Cowboy 1914-1963 *WhScrn 77*
Copas, Lloyd Estel 1913-1963 *BiDAmM*
Cope, David Howell 1941- *AmSCAP 80, CpmDNM 72, -77, ConAmC, IntWWM 77, -80*
Cope, David M 1941- *CpmDNM 76*
Cope, Hilary Lucy 1928- *WhoMus 72*
Cope, Kenneth 1931- *FilmgC, HalFC 80*
Copeau, Jacques 1878-1949 *CnThe, NotNAT B, WhThe*
Copeau, Jacques 1879-1949 *CnMD, EncWT, Ent, McGEWD[port], ModWD, OxThe, PlP&P, WhScrn 77*
Copeland, Alan R 1926- *AmSCAP 80*
Copeland, Allan 1926- *AmSCAP 66*
Copeland, Benjamin 1855-1940 *BiDAmM*
Copeland, George 1882-1971 *BiDAmM*
Copeland, Isabella d1912 *NotNAT B*
Copeland, Joan 1922- *BiE&WWA, NotNAT, WhoHol A, WhoThe 72, -77*
Copeland, Julia Viola 1916- *AmSCAP 66*
Copeland, Kenneth Thomas 1908- *IntWWM 77, -80*
Copeland, Mary Dowell d1963 *NotNAT B*
Copeland, Nicholas W 1895-1940 *WhScrn 74, -77*
Copeland, Nick d1940 *WhoHol B*
Copeland, Ray M 1926- *BiDAmM, EncJzS 70*
Copenhagen, A *AmSCAP 80*
Copenhaver, Laura 1868-1940 *BiDAmM*
Coperario 1575?-1626 *Baker 78*
Coperario, John *NewGrD 80*
Coperario, John 1570?-1626 *OxMus*
Coperario, John 1575?-1626 *MusMk*
Copes, V Earle 1920- *CpmDNM 74, ConAmC*
Copinus, Alessandro *NewGrD 80*
Copland, Aaron 1900- *AmSCAP 66, -80, Baker 78, BiDAmM, BnBkM 80[port], CmOp, CompSN[port], CpmDNM 74, -79, -80, CnOxB, ConAmC, DancEn 78, DcCom 77[port], DcCom&M 79, DcCM, FilmEn, FilmgC, HalFC 80, IntWWM 77, -80, MusMk[port], NewEOp 71, NewGrD 80[port], OxFilm, OxMus, WhoMus 72, WorEFlm*
Copland, Robert *DancEn 78*
Copland, Thomas d1945 *NewOrJ*
Copley, Ian Alfred 1926- *WhoMus 72*
Copley, John Michael 1933- *CmOp, WhoOp 76*
Copley, Peter 1915- *FilmgC, HalFC 80, WhoHol A, WhoThe 72, -77*
Copley, R Evan 1930- *ConAmC*
Coppa, Joe *Film 2*
Coppee, Francois Edouard Joachim 1842-1908 *CnMD, McGEWD[port], ModWD, NotNAT B*
Coppel, Alec 1910-1972 *BiE&WWA, FilmgC, HalFC 80, WhThe*
Coppen, Hazel 1925-1975 *WhScrn 77*
Coppens, Claude A 1936- *IntWWM 77, -80, NewGrD 80*
Coppersmith, Barbara C 1928- *AmSCAP 80*
Copperwheat, Winifred *WhoMus 72*
Coppet, Edward J De 1855-1916 *Baker 78*
Coppini, Alessandro 1465?-1527 *NewGrD 80*
Coppini, Alexander 1465?-1527 *NewGrD 80*
Coppinus, Alessandro 1465?-1527 *NewGrD 80*
Coppinus, Alexander 1465?-1527 *NewGrD 80*
Coppola, Anton 1917- *WhoOp 76*
Coppola, Anton 1918- *BiE&WWA, NotNAT*
Coppola, Carmine 1910- *AmSCAP 66, ConAmC A*
Coppola, Carmine 1912- *CpmDNM 76, -77, IntWWM 77, -80*
Coppola, Don *ConAmC*
Coppola, Francis Ford 1933- *ConLC 16, OxFilm*
Coppola, Francis Ford 1939- *BiDFilm, -81, FilmEn, FilmgC, HalFC 80, IntMPA 77, -75, -76, -78, -79, -80, MovMk[port], WorEFlm*
Coppola, Piero 1888-1971 *Baker 78, NewGrD 80*
Coppola, Pietro Antonio 1793-1877 *Baker 78, NewGrD 80*
Coppola, Talia *FilmEn, WhoHol A*
Coppolla, Francis Ford 1939- *WhoHrs 80*
Coprario, Giovanni 1570?-1626 *NewGrD 80*
Coprario, John 1570?-1626 *NewGrD 80*
Copus, Caspar *NewGrD 80*
Coquard, Arthur 1846-1910 *Baker 78, NewGrD 80*
Coquelin *PlP&P*
Coquelin, Benoit Constant 1841-1909 *NotNAT B, WhoHol B*
Coquelin, Constant-Benoit 1841-1909 *CnThe, EncWT, Ent, OxThe*
Coquelin, Ernest-Alexandre-Honore 1848-1909 *EncWT, NotNAT B, OxThe*
Coquelin, Jean 1865-1944 *EncWT, NotNAT B, OxThe, WhThe, WhoHol B*
Coquelin, Jean-Paul 1924- *EncWT*
Coquet, Odile 1932- *IntWWM 77, -80*
Coquille, Robert 1911- *NewOrJ[port]*
Coquillon, John *FilmgC, HalFC 80*
Coradigni, Francesco *NewGrD 80*
Coradini, Francesco *NewGrD 80*
Coradini, Nicolo *NewGrD 80*
Coralli, Jean 1779-1854 *CnOxB, DancEn 78*
Coralli, Vera *CnOxB*
Coram 1883- *WhThe*
Corazza, Remy 1933- *WhoOp 76*
Corb, Mortimer G 1917- *BiDAmM*
Corb, Morty G 1917- *AmSCAP 66, -80*
Corbe, Eduardo 1878-1967 *WhScrn 77*
Corbeil, Claude 1940- *CreCan 1*
Corbeil, Claude 1942- *WhoOp 76*
Corbet, August 1907-1964 *NewGrD 80*
Corbet, Ben *Film 2*
Corbett, Ben 1892-1961 *Film 1, WhScrn 74, -77*
Corbett, Benny 1892-1961 *WhoHol B*
Corbett, Cecil *ConMuA 80B*
Corbett, Duane 1924- *AmSCAP 80*
Corbett, Glenn 1929- *FilmgC, HalFC 80, WhoHol A*
Corbett, Glenn 1934- *FilmEn, ForYSC*
Corbett, Gretchen 1947- *WhoThe 77*
Corbett, Harry H 1925- *DcPup, FilmEn, FilmgC, HalFC 80, IlWWBF, IntMPA 77, -75, -76, -78, -79, -80, WhoThe 72, -77*
Corbett, James J 1866-1933 *NotNAT B, WhoStg 1906, -1908*
Corbett, James J 1867-1933 *Film 1, -2, WhScrn 74, -77, WhoHol B*
Corbett, Leonora d1960 *WhoHol B*
Corbett, Leonora 1907-1960 *FilmgC, HalFC 80*
Corbett, Leonora 1908-1960 *NotNAT B, WhScrn 74, -77, WhThe*
Corbett, Mary 1926-1974 *WhScrn 77*
Corbett, Richard Dean 1942- *ConAmC*
Corbett, Ronnie 1930- *HalFC 80*
Corbett, Ronnie 1933- *FilmgC*
Corbett, Stanley *FilmEn*
Corbett, Thalberg 1864- *WhThe*
Corbett, William 1675?-1748 *NewGrD 80, OxMus*
Corbett, William D *Film 2*
Corbetta, Francesco 1615?-1681 *NewGrD 80*
Corbetta, Jerry Anthiny 1947- *AmSCAP 80*
Corbette, Francisque 1615?-1681 *NewGrD 80*
Corbin, Clayton 1928- *DrBlPA*
Corbin, Frank G M 1925- *IntMPA 75, -76*
Corbin, Gladys *MotPP*
Corbin, John 1870-1959 *NotNAT B, WhThe*
Corbin, Solange 1903-1973 *NewGrD 80*
Corbin, Virginia Lee 1910-1942 *Film 1, -2, WhScrn 74, -77, WhoHol B*
Corbin, Virginia Lee 1912- *TwYS*
Corbisieri, Francesco 1730?-1802? *NewGrD 80*
Corbisiero, Antonio 1720-1790 *NewGrD 80*
Corbisiero, Francesco 1730?-1802? *NewGrD 80*
Corbitt, Gretchen Johnson 1920- *IntWWM 77, -80*
Corboz, Michel Jules 1934- *IntWWM 77, -80, NewGrD 80*
Corbrand, William *NewGrD 80*
Corbronde, William *NewGrD 80*
Corbucci, Sergio 1926- *FilmEn*
Corbucci, Sergio 1927- *FilmgC, HalFC 80*
Corbus DePadua, Jacobus *NewGrD 80*
Corby, Ellen 1913- *FilmEn, FilmgC, ForYSC, HalFC 80, MovMk, Vers A[port], WhoHol A*
Corby, Ellen 1914- *HolCA[port]*
Corcoran, Brian 1951- *WhoHol A*
Corcoran, Corky 1924- *CmpEPM, EncJzS 70*
Corcoran, Donna *ForYSC*
Corcoran, Donna 1942- *WhoHol A*
Corcoran, Donna 1943- *FilmEn, HalFC 80*
Corcoran, Francis 1944- *IntWWM 80*
Corcoran, Gene Patrick 1924- *BiDAmM, EncJzS 70*
Corcoran, Hugh *WhoHol A*
Corcoran, Jane *WhThe*
Corcoran, Katharine 1857-1943 *OxThe*
Corcoran, Katherine 1857-1943 *NotNAT B, PlP&P*
Corcoran, Kelly 1958- *WhoHol A*
Corcoran, Kevin 1949- *FilmEn, ForYSC, HalFC 80, WhoHol A*
Corcoran, Noreen 1943- *ForYSC, WhoHol A*
Corcoran, William *ConAmC*
Cord, Alex 1931- *FilmEn, FilmgC, ForYSC, HalFC 80, IntMPA 77, -75, -76, -78, -79, -80, MotPP, WhoHol A*
Corda, Maria *Film 2*
Corda, Michael 1921- *AmSCAP 66*
Corda, Mike 1921- *AmSCAP 80*
Cordans, Bartolomeo 1700?-1757 *NewGrD 80*
Cordasco, Gerald Michael 1952- *AmSCAP 80*
Corday, Leo 1902- *AmSCAP 66, -80*
Corday, Mara 1922- *ForYSC*
Corday, Mara 1932- *FilmEn, FilmgC, HalFC 80, WhoHol A, WhoHrs 80[port]*
Corday, Marcelle *Film 2, TwYS*
Corday, Paula 1924- *FilmEn, FilmgC, ForYSC, HalFC 80, WhoHol A*
Corday, Raymond d1956 *Film 2*
Corday, Rita 1924- *FilmEn*
Cordeilles, Charles *NewGrD 80*
Cordeiro, Joseph 1926- *IntWWM 77, -80*
Cordell, Cathleen *WhoHol A*
Cordell, Cathleen 1916- *WhThe*
Cordell, Cathleen 1917- *BiE&WWA*
Cordell, Denny *ConMuA 80B*
Cordella, Geronimo *NewGrD 80*
Cordella, Giacomo 1786-1846 *NewGrD 80*
Corden, Henry *WhoHol A*
Corder, Bruce Derrick 1921- *BiE&WWA, WhoOp 76*
Corder, Frederick 1852-1932 *Baker 78, NewGrD 80, OxMus*
Corder, Leeta 1890-1956 *WhScrn 74, -77*
Corder, Paul 1879-1942 *Baker 78*
Cordero, Ernesto 1946- *AmSCAP 80, IntWWM 77, -80*
Cordero, Roque 1917- *Baker 78, CpmDNM 75, -79, ConAmC, DcCM, DrBlPA, IntWWM 77, -80, NewGrD 80*
Cordes, Barbara 1948- *WhoOp 76*
Cordier, Baude *NewGrD 80*
Cordier, Charles 1911- *CnMD*
Cordier, Jacques 1580?-1655? *NewGrD 80*
Cordilla, Charles Joseph 1899- *NewOrJ*
Cording, Harry 1891-1954 *WhScrn 77*
Cording, Harry 1894-1954 *Film 2, Vers B[port], WhScrn 74, WhoHol B*
Cordoba, Pedro De 1881-1950 *Vers A[port]*
Cordon, Norman 1904-1964 *Baker 78, NewEOp 71*
Cordry, Donald *PupTheA*
Cordua, Beatrice 1943- *CnOxB*

Cordy, Annie 1928- *FilmAG WE, FilmEn*
Cordy, Henry 1908-1965 *WhScrn 74, -77, WhoHol B*
Cordy, Raymond 1898-1956 *FilmEn, FilmgC, HalFC 80, WhScrn 74, -77, WhoHol B*
Core, Howard A 1941- *IntWWM 77, -80*
Corea, Armando Anthony 1941- *AmSCAP 80, BiDAmM, EncJzS 70*
Corea, Chick 1941- *ConMuA 80A, EncJzS 70, IlEncJ*
Corelli, Arcangelo 1653-1713 *Baker 78, BnBkM 80[port], CmpBCM, DcCom 77[port], DcCom&M 79, GrComp[port], MusMk[port], NewGrD 80[port], OxMus*
Corelli, Franco *IntWWM 77, -80*
Corelli, Franco 1921- *NewGrD 80*
Corelli, Franco 1923- *Baker 78, BnBkM 80, CmOp, MusSN[port], NewEOp 71, WhoOp 76*
Corelli, Juan 1934- *CnOxB*
Corelli, Juan 1935- *DancEn 78*
Corelli, Marie *OxMus*
Corena, Fernando 1916- *CmOp, IntWWM 77, -80, MusSN[port], NewGrD 80, WhoOp 76*
Corena, Fernando 1923- *NewEOp 71*
Corenne, Renee 1937- *WhoOp 76*
Corey, Eugene *Film 2*
Corey, Irwin *JoeFr, -, WhoHol A*
Corey, Jeff 1914- *FilmEn, FilmgC, ForYSC, HalFC 80, IntMPA 77, -75, -76, -78, -79, -80, Vers B[port], WhoHol A*
Corey, Jill 1935- *RkOn[port]*
Corey, Joseph 1927-1972 *WhScrn 77, WhoHol B*
Corey, Wendell 1914-1968 *BiDFilm, -81, BiE&WWA, FilmEn, FilmgC, ForYSC, HalFC 80[port], HolP 40[port], MotPP, MovMk, NotNAT B, WhScrn 74, -77, WhThe, WhoHol B, WorEFlm*
Corfe *NewGrD 80*
Corfe, Arthur Thomas 1773-1863 *NewGrD 80*
Corfe, Charles 1708?-1742 *NewGrD 80*
Corfe, James 1713?- *NewGrD 80*
Corfe, Joseph 1741?-1820 *NewGrD 80*
Corfield, Greta 1912- *IntWWM 77, -80*
Corfield, John 1893- *FilmgC, HalFC 80*
Corfini, Jacopo 1540?-1591 *NewGrD 80*
Coria, Miguel Angel 1937- *Baker 78, DcCM, NewGrD 80*
Coriandoli, Francesco d1670 *NewGrD 80*
Corigliano, John 1901-1975 *Baker 78*
Corigliano, John 1938- *AmSCAP 66, -80, Baker 78, BiDAmM, CpmDNM 80, ConAmC, DcCM*
Corina, John Hubert 1928- *AmSCAP 80, ConAmC, IntWWM 77, -80*
Corinne 1873-1937 *NotNAT B, WhoStg 1908*
Corinne 1875-1937 *WhoStg 1906*
Corio, Ann *WhoHol A*
Corita, Nicasio *NewGrD 80*
Cork, Cyril Arthur 1922- *WhoMus 72*
Cork, Peter Thorrington 1926- *WhoMus 72*
Corkhill, David Thomas James 1946- *IntWWM 77, -80*
Corkine, William *NewGrD 80, OxMus*
Corkle, Francesca 1952- *CnOxB*
Corley, Catherine *PupTheA*
Corley, Dewey 1898-1974 *BluesWW[port]*
Corley, Robert d1971 *WhScrn 77*
Cormack, Barbara Villy 1903- *CreCan 2*
Corman, Gene *HalFC 80, IntMPA 77, -75, -76, -78, -79, -80, WhoHrs 80*
Corman, Roger 1926- *BiDFilm, -81, CmMov, DcFM, FilmEn, FilmgC, HalFC 80, IntMPA 77, -75, -76, -78, -79, -80, MovMk[port], OxFilm, WhoHrs 80, WorEFlm*
Cormany, Elaine 1944- *WhoOp 76*
Cormon, Nelly *Film 2*
Corn, Edward 1932- *WhoOp 76*
Corn Huskers *BiDAmM*
Cornacchioli, Giacinto 1598?-1673 *NewGrD 80*
Cornago, Johannes *NewGrD 80*
Cornazano, Antonio 1430?-1484 *NewGrD 80*
Cornazano, Antonio 1431-1500? *CnOxB*
Cornazano, Antonio 1440?- *DancEn 78*
Cornazzani, Phileno Agostino 1543?-1628 *NewGrD 80*
Cornazzano, Antonio 1430?-1484 *NewGrD 80*
Corneau, Alain 1943- *FilmEn*
Corneille, Pierre 1606-1684 *CnThe, EncWT, Ent[port], McGEWD[port], NewEOp 71, NewGrD 80, NotNAT A, -B, OxThe, PlP&P, REnWD[port]*
Corneille, Thomas 1625-1709 *Ent, McGEWD, NotNAT B, OxThe, REnWD[port]*
Cornejo, Rodolfo 1909- *NewGrD 80*
Cornelis, Evert 1884-1931 *Baker 78*
Cornelius, Corky Edward 1914-1943 *WhoJazz 72*
Cornelius, Don 1937?- *ConMuA 80B, DrBlPA*
Cornelius, Helen *IlEncCM*
Cornelius, Henry 1913-1958 *CmMov, DcFM, FilmEn, FilmgC, HalFC 80, IlWWBF, MovMk[port], OxFilm*
Cornelius, J *NewGrD 80*
Cornelius, O Henry 1913-1958 *WorEFlm*
Cornelius, Peter 1824-1874 *Baker 78, BnBkM 80, CmOp, GrComp[port], NewEOp 71, NewGrD 80[port], OxMus*
Cornelius, Peter 1865-1934 *CmOp, NewGrD 80*
Cornelius Brothers & Sister Rose, The *RkOn 2[port]*
Cornell, Charles Sydney 1902- *AmSCAP 80*
Cornell, Don *AmPS A, CmpEPM*
Cornell, Don 1921- *BiDAmM*
Cornell, Don 1924- *RkOn*
Cornell, Gwynn *WhoOp 76*
Cornell, John 1913- *BiE&WWA*
Cornell, John Henry 1828-1894 *Baker 78*
Cornell, John Henry 1838-1894 *BiDAmM*
Cornell, Jonas 1938- *WorEFlm*
Cornell, Katharine 1893-1974 *EncWT, FamA&A[port], PlP&P, WhScrn 77, WhoHol B*
Cornell, Katharine 1898-1974 *BiE&WWA, CnThe, Ent[port], NotNAT A, -B, OxThe, What 2[port], WhThe, WhoThe 72*
Cornell, Melva *Film 2*
Cornelys, Theresa 1723-1797 *NewGrD 80, OxMus*
Corner, David Gregor 1585-1648 *NewGrD 80*
Corner, James W 1919-1944 *WhScrn 74, -77, WhoHol B*
Corner, Philip Lionel 1933- *AmSCAP 80, Baker 78, ConAmC, IntWWM 77, -80*
Corner, Sally 1894-1959 *WhScrn 74, -77, WhoHol B*
Cornet, Peeter 1570?-1633 *NewGrD 80*
Cornet, Peter 1570?-1633 *NewGrD 80*
Cornet, Pierre 1570?-1633 *NewGrD 80*
Cornet, Pieter 1570?-1633 *NewGrD 80*
Cornet, Pietro 1570?-1633 *NewGrD 80*
Cornet, Severin 1530?-1582 *NewGrD 80*
Cornett, Alice 1911- *AmSCAP 66, -80*
Cornett, Ewel 1937- *AmSCAP 80*
Cornette, Victor 1795-1868 *NewGrD 80*
Cornetti, Paolo *NewGrD 80*
Cornfield, Hubert 1929- *FilmEn, FilmgC, HalFC 80, IntMPA 78, -79, -80, WorEFlm*
Cornil, Dominique 1953- *IntWWM 77, -80*
Cornish *NewGrD 80*
Cornish, John Buckley 1914- *CreCan 1*
Cornish, Roger N *NatPD[port]*
Cornish, Willie 1875-1942 *NewOrJ[port]*
Cornsweet, Harold 1918- *IntMPA 77, -75, -76, -78*
Cornthwaite, Robert *ForYSC, WhoHol A*
Cornthwaite, Robert 1917- *WhoHrs 80*
Cornuel, Jean *NewGrD 80*
Cornwall, Anne 1897- *Film 1, -2, TwYS, WhoHol A*
Cornwell, Judy 1942- *WhoThe 72, -77*
Cornyn, Stan 1933- *AmSCAP 66, ConMuA 80B*
Cornysh *NewGrD 80*
Cornysh, John *NewGrD 80*
Cornysh, William d1502? *NewGrD 80*
Cornysh, William d1523 *NewGrD 80*
Cornyshe *NewGrD 80*
Cornyshe, William d1502 *BnBkM 80*
Cornyshe, William 1468?-1523 *BnBkM 80*
Cornyshe, William 1468?-1523? *MusMk*
Cornyshe, William 1468?-1523 *OxMus*
Cornysshe *NewGrD 80*
Corona, Agostino *NewGrD 80*
Corona, Giovanni *NewGrD 80*
Coronado, Elida *WomWMM B*
Coronaro *NewGrD 80*
Coronaro, Antonio 1851-1933 *NewGrD 80*
Coronaro, Gaetano 1852-1908 *Baker 78, NewGrD 80*
Coronaro, Gellio Benevenuto 1863-1916 *NewGrD 80*
Coronaro, Gellio Benvenuto 1863-1916 *Baker 78*
Corp, Charles Leworthy *IntWWM 77, -80*
Corpora, Victor Gari 1919- *AmSCAP 80*
Corradi, Flamminio *NewGrD 80*
Corradi, Giampaolo 1930- *WhoOp 76*
Corradi, Giulio Cesare 1701d1702? *NewGrD 80*
Corradine, Tom J 1924- *IntMPA 77, -75, -76, -78, -79, -80*
Corradini, Francesco 1700?-1749? *NewGrD 80*
Corradini, Nicolo d1646 *NewGrD 80*
Corradino, Nicolo d1646 *NewGrD 80*
Corrado, Gino *Film 1, -2, ForYSC, TwYS*
Corradus De Pistoria *NewGrD 80*
Correa, Henrique Carlos 1680-1752? *NewGrD 80*
Correa, Joan *NewGrD 80*
Correa, Juan *NewGrD 80*
Correa, Julio *OxThe*
Correa, Louis Patricio 1925- *IntWWM 77, -80*
Correa, Manoel d1653 *NewGrD 80*
Correa, Manuel d1653 *NewGrD 80*
Correa DeAraujo, Francisco 1576?-1654 *NewGrD 80*
Correa DeArauxo, Francisco 1576?-1654 *Baker 78, NewGrD 80*
Correa DeAzavedo, Francisco 1576?-1654 *NewGrD 80*
Correa DeAzevedo, Luis Heitor 1905- *Baker 78*
Correa DeAzevedo, Luiz Heitor *NewGrD 80*
Correa DeAzevedo, Luiz Heitor 1905- *IntWWM 77, -80*
Correia, Fernao Gomes d1532? *NewGrD 80*
Correia, Henrique Carlos *NewGrD 80*
Correia DeOliveira, Fernando 1921- *NewGrD 80*
Correl, Gladis d1962 *NotNAT B*
Correll, Charles J 1890-1972 *JoeFr, WhScrn 77, WhoHol B*
Correll, Stephen Mungia 1949- *AmSCAP 80*
Corrette, Gaspard d1733? *NewGrD 80*
Corrette, Michel 1709-1795 *NewGrD 80, OxMus*
Correya, Joao *NewGrD 80*
Corri *NewGrD 80*
Corri, Adrienne *WhoHol A*
Corri, Adrienne 1930- *FilmEn, FilmgC, HalFC 80, IlWWBF, WhoHrs 80[port]*
Corri, Adrienne 1933- *IntMPA 77, -75, -76, -78, -79, -80*
Corri, Charles Montague 1861- *PlP&P, WhThe*
Corri, Domenico 1744-1825 *Baker 78*
Corri, Domenico 1746-1825 *NewGrD 80, OxMus*
Corri, Frances 1795?-1833? *NewGrD 80*
Corri, Haydn 1785-1860 *NewGrD 80*
Corri, Montague Philip 1784?-1849 *NewGrD 80*
Corri, Natale 1765-1822 *NewGrD 80*
Corri, Philip Anthony 1784?-1832 *NewGrD 80*
Corri, Sophia Giustina 1775-1828? *NewGrD 80*
Corrie, Joe 1894-1968 *OxThe*
Corrigan, Charles 1894-1966 *WhScrn 74, -77*
Corrigan, D'Arcy *Film 2*
Corrigan, Douglas 1907- *HalFC 80, What 1[port], WhoHol A*
Corrigan, E *Film 2*
Corrigan, Emmett d1932 *Film 2, WhoHol B*
Corrigan, Emmett 1867-1932 *WhScrn 74, -77*
Corrigan, Emmett 1868-1932 *NotNAT B, WhoStg 1908*
Corrigan, Emmett 1871-1932 *WhThe*
Corrigan, James 1871-1929 *Film 2, TwYS, WhScrn 74, -77, WhoHol B*
Corrigan, Lloyd 1900-1969 *FilmEn, Film 2, FilmgC, ForYSC, HalFC 80, MovMk, Vers B[port], WhScrn 74, -77, WhoHol B*
Corrigan, Ray 1903-1976 *HalFC 80*
Corrigan, Ray 1907-1976 *FilmEn, WhoHrs 80*
Corrigan, Ray 1909-1969 *ForYSC*
Corrigan, Ray Crash 1907- *FilmgC, WhoHol A*

Corrigan, Robert W 1927- *BiE&WWA, NotNAT*
Corrigan, Thomas J *Film 1, WhScrn 77*
Corrigan, Tom *Film 2*
Corrin, R L *PupTheA*
Corrin, Mrs. R L *PupTheA*
Corrington, Helen *PupTheA*
Corrington, Joyce *WomWMM*
Corrodi, Annelies 1935- *WhoOp 76*
Corsairs, The *RkOn*
Corsari, Franco *WhoHol A*
Corsaro, Frank 1924- *BiE&WWA, IntWWM 77, -80, NotNAT, WhoOp 76, WhoThe 72, -77*
Corsaut, Aneta *WhoHol A*
Corselli, Francesco 1702?-1778 *NewGrD 80*
Corselli, Francisco 1702?-1778 *NewGrD 80*
Corseuil, Jaques 1913- *DancEn 78*
Corsi, Bernardo d1619? *NewGrD 80*
Corsi, Giuseppe 1630-1690 *Baker 78*
Corsi, Giuseppe 1630-1690? *NewGrD 80*
Corsi, Jacopo 1560?-1604? *Baker 78, NewEOp 71*
Corsi, Jacopo 1561-1602 *NewGrD 80*
Corsini, Jacopo *NewGrD 80*
Corsini, Lorenzo *NewGrD 80*
Corso, Giuseppe *Baker 78*
Corson, Richard *BiE&WWA, NotNAT*
Cort, Bud 1950- *FilmgC, HalFC 80, MovMk, WhoHol A*
Cort, Harry Linsley d1937 *NotNAT B*
Cort, John d1929 *NotNAT B*
Cort, Lois-Alexandra Lund *IntWWM 77, -80*
Cort, Robert W *IntMPA 77, -78, -79, -80*
Corte, Andrea Della *Baker 78*
Corteccia, Francesco Bernardo 1502-1571 *Baker 78, NewGrD 80*
Cortellini, Camillo 1560?-1630 *NewGrD 80*
Cortes, Armand 1880-1948 *Film 1, -2, WhScrn 77*
Cortes, Hernando 1485-1547 *DcPup*
Cortes, Ramiro 1933- *Baker 78, ConAmC, DcCM, NewGrD 80*
Cortesa, Valentina 1924- *FilmEn, FilmgC, HalFC 80*
Cortesa, Valentina 1925- *IntMPA 77, -75, -76, -78, -79, -80, MovMk*
Cortese, Dominic 1921- *AmSCAP 80*
Cortese, Louis 1899-1976 *NewGrD 80*
Cortese, Luigi 1899-1976 *Baker 78, IntWWM 77, NewGrD 80, WhoMus 72*
Cortese, Paolo 1465-1510 *NewGrD 80*
Cortese, Valentina 1924- *FilmEn*
Cortese, Valentina 1925- *FilmAG WE, ForYSC, WhoHol A, WorEFlm*
Cortesi, Antonio 1796-1879 *CnOxB*
Cortesi, Francesco 1826-1904 *Baker 78*
Cortesi, Giulio *Film 2*
Cortesi, Mrs. Giulio *Film 2*
Cortez, Armand *Film 2*
Cortez, Dave Baby 1939- *RkOn[port]*
Cortez, Leon 1898-1970 *WhScrn 74, -77, WhoHol B*
Cortez, Ricardo 1899-1977 *FilmEn, Film 2, FilmgC, ForYSC, HalFC 80, MotPP, MovMk[port], What 2[port], WhoHol A*
Cortez, Richard 1899-1977 *TwYS*
Cortez, Stanley 1908- *FilmEn, FilmgC, HalFC 80, IntMPA 77, -75, -76, -78, -79, -80, OxFilm, WorEFlm*
Cortez, Viorica 1935- *NewGrD 80, WhoMus 72, WhoOp 76*
Corthell, Herbert 1875-1947 *Film 2, NotNAT B, WhScrn 74, -77, WhoHol B, WhoStg 1908*
Corti, Ottavio Giuseppe 1911- *IntWWM 77, -80*
Corti-Colleoni, Mario Enrico *IntWWM 77, -80, WhoMus 72*
Cortina, Raquel 1946- *IntWWM 77, -80*
Cortinas, Cesar 1890-1918 *NewGrD 80*
Cortinas, Pedro 1943- *IntWWM 80*
Cortini, Giovanna *NewGrD 80*
Cortis, Antonio 1891-1952 *CmOp, NewGrD 80*
Cortois, Jean *NewGrD 80*
Cortolezis, Fritz 1878-1934 *Baker 78, NewGrD 80*
Cortot, Alfred 1877-1962 *Baker 78, BnBkM 80[port], MusMk[port], MusSN[port], NewGrD 80[port], OxMus*
Cortrubas, Ileana *CmOp*
Corts, Antonio *NewGrD 80*
Corujo, Francisco 1909- *IntWWM 77, -80*
Corum, Alfred 1890- *WhoMus 72*
Corvinus, Christopher *NewGrD 80*
Corvinus, Johannes Michaelii *NewGrD 80*
Corvus, Valentinus *NewGrD 80*
Corwin, Betty L 1920- *AmSCAP 66*
Corwin, Bruce Conrad 1940- *IntMPA 77, -75, -76, -78, -79, -80*
Corwin, Norman 1910- *AmSCAP 66, -80, BiE&WWA, IntMPA 77, -75, -76, -78, -79, -80, NewYTET, NotNAT*
Corwin, Robert Alfred 1933- *AmSCAP 80, BiDAmM*
Corwin, Sherrill C *IntMPA 77, -75, -76, -78, -79, -80*
Cory, Eleanor Thayer 1943- *ConAmC, IntWWM 77, -80*
Cory, George 1920- *AmSCAP 66, BiDAmM, ConAmC*
Cory, George C, Jr. 1920- *AmSCAP 80*
Cory, Patrick 1910- *WhoMus 72*
Cory, Robert 1883-1955 *WhScrn 74, -77*
Coryell, Larry 1943- *ConMuA 80A, EncJzS 70*
Coryphaeus *NewGrD 80*
Cos, Joachim *DcFM*
Cosby, Bill *NewYTET, RkOn 2A, WhoHol A*
Cosby, Bill 1937- *DrBlPA, EncJzS 70, FilmEn*
Cosby, Bill 1938- *FilmgC, HalFC 80, IntMPA 77, -75, -76, -78, -79, -80, JoeFr[port]*
Cosby, Henry, Sr. 1938- *AmSCAP 80*
Cosby, William H, Jr. 1937- *EncJzS 70*
Coscarelli, Don 1952- *WhoHrs 80*
Coscia, Silvio 1899- *AmSCAP 66, -80, ConAmC, IntWWM 77, -80*
Cosell, Howard 1920- *IntMPA 79, -80, NewYTET*
Cosen, John *NewGrD 80*
Cosens, Benjamin *NewGrD 80*
Cosens, John *NewGrD 80*
Cosenza, Arthur 1924- *WhoOp 76*
Cosgrave, Jack *Film 1, -2*
Cosgrave, Luke 1862-1949 *Film 2, NotNAT A, WhScrn 74, -77, WhoHol B*
Cosgrove, John *Film 2*
Cosgrove, Robert 1900-1960 *WhScrn 74, -77*
Cosgrove, Stanley 1911- *CreCan 2*
Cosi, Liliana 1941- *CnOxB, DancEn 78*
Cosima, Renee *WomWMM*
Cosin, Benjamin *NewGrD 80*
Cosin, John 1594-1672 *NewGrD 80, OxMus*
Coslow, Sam *AmSCAP 80, Sw&Ld C*
Coslow, Sam 1902- *AmPS, AmSCAP 66, CmpEPM, FilmEn*
Coslow, Sam 1905- *IntMPA 77, -75, -76, -78, -79, -80*
Cosma, Edgar 1925- *WhoMus 72*
Cosma, Octavian Lazar 1933- *IntWWM 77, -80, NewGrD 80*
Cosma, Viorel 1923- *Baker 78, IntWWM 77, -80, NewGrD 80*
Cosmatos, George Pan 1941- *HalFC 80*
Cosme, Luiz 1908-1965 *NewGrD 80*
Cossa, Basilio *NewGrD 80*
Cossa, Dominic 1935- *IntWWM 77, -80, WhoOp 76*
Cossa, Pietro 1830-1881 *McGEWD[port], NotNAT B, OxThe*
Cossa, Vincenzo 1550?-1587? *NewGrD 80*
Cossaeus, Sophie 1893-1965 *WhScrn 74, -77*
Cossandi, Antonio *NewGrD 80*
Cossar, John Hay 1865-1935 *Film 2, WhScrn 74, -77, WhoHol B*
Cossart, Ernest 1876-1951 *FilmEn, Film 1, FilmgC, ForYSC, HalFC 80, NotNAT B, PIP&P, WhScrn 74, -77, WhThe, WhoHol B*
Cossart, Valerie 1910- *WhThe*
Cosset, Francois 1610?-1664? *NewGrD 80*
Cossette, Francois 1610?-1664? *NewGrD 80*
Cossettini, Leticia *PupTheA*
Cossettini, Olga *PupTheA*
Cossetto, Emil 1918- *Baker 78, IntWWM 77, -80, NewGrD 80*
Cossie, Tom *ConMuA 80B*
Cossins, James 1932- *FilmgC, HalFC 80*
Cossmann, Bernhard 1822-1910 *Baker 78, NewGrD 80*
Cossoni, Carlo Donato d1700 *NewGrD 80*
Cossonio, Carlo Donato d1700 *NewGrD 80*
Cossotto, Fiorenza 1935- *Baker 78, CmOp, NewGrD 80, WhoOp 76*
Cossotto, Fiorenza 1938- *IntWWM 77, -80*
Cossoul, Guilherme Antonio 1828-1880 *NewGrD 80*
Cossuino, Antonius *NewGrD 80*
Cossutta, Carlo 1932- *CmOp, NewGrD 80, WhoOp 76*
Costa *NewGrD 80*
Costa, Miss *Film 2*
Costa, Afonso Vaz Da d1642? *NewGrD 80*
Costa, Alfonso Vaz Da d1642? *NewGrD 80*
Costa, Andre Da *NewGrD 80*
Costa, Andre Da d1685 *NewGrD 80*
Costa, Anthony J 1910- *NewOrJ*
Costa, Antonio Da 1714?-1780? *NewGrD 80*
Costa, Antonio Pereyra Da d1770 *NewGrD 80*
Costa, Beatriz 1907- *FilmAG WE*
Costa, Don 1925- *AmPS A, RkOn[port]*
Costa, Eddie 1930-1962 *CmpEPM*
Costa, Edwin James 1930-1962 *BiDAmM*
Costa, Felix Jose Da 1701-1760? *NewGrD 80*
Costa, Francesco Antonio *NewGrD 80*
Costa, Francisco Da d1667 *NewGrD 80*
Costa, Francisco Eduardo Da 1819-1855 *NewGrD 80*
Costa, Francisco Pereira Da 1847-1890 *NewGrD 80*
Costa, Gasparo *NewGrD 80*
Costa, Geronimo Maria *NewGrD 80*
Costa, Giovanni Antonio *NewGrD 80*
Costa, Giovanni Maria 1581?-1656? *NewGrD 80*
Costa, Giovanni Paolo *NewGrD 80*
Costa, Helena Sa E *NewGrD 80*
Costa, Joao Alberto Rodrigues Da 1798-1870 *NewGrD 80*
Costa, Joao Evangelista Pereira Da 1798?-1832 *NewGrD 80*
Costa, John 1922- *AmSCAP 80*
Costa, Lelio *NewGrD 80*
Costa, Leonilde Moreira Sa E *NewGrD 80*
Costa, Lucile *WomWMM*
Costa, Luis 1879-1960 *NewGrD 80*
Costa, Madalena Sa E *NewGrD 80*
Costa, Margarita *NewGrD 80*
Costa, Mario 1908- *FilmEn*
Costa, Mary *WhoHol A, WhoOp 76*
Costa, Mary Pokora 1908- *IntWWM 77, -80*
Costa, Michael 1808-1884 *BnBkM 80, CmOp*
Costa, Sir Michael 1806-1884 *Baker 78*
Costa, Sir Michael 1808-1884 *NewGrD 80[port]*
Costa, Michael A 1915- *NewOrJ*
Costa, Michael Andrew Agnus 1806-1884 *OxMus*
Costa, Sir Michele Andrea Agniello 1808-1884 *NewGrD 80[port]*
Costa, Orazio 1911- *EncWT*
Costa, Pasquale *Baker 78*
Costa, Rochio *NewGrD 80*
Costa, Rodrigo Ferreira Da 1776-1825 *NewGrD 80*
Costa, Sebastiano 1876-1935 *WhScrn 74, -77*
Costa, Sebastiao Da d1696 *NewGrD 80*
Costa, Sequeira 1929- *WhoMus 72*
Costa, Sylvia Bess 1937- *WomWMM B*
Costa, Vitorino Jose Da d1750? *NewGrD 80*
Costa, William F 1920- *AmSCAP 66, -80*
Costa E Faria, Luiz Calixto Da 1679-1759? *NewGrD 80*
Costa E Silva, Francisco Da d1727 *NewGrD 80*
Costa E Silva, Jose Da 1826-1881 *NewGrD 80*
Costa-Gavras 1933- *FilmgC, HalFC 80*
Costa-Gavras, Constantin 1933- *FilmEn*
Costa-Gavras, Costi 1933- *OxFilm, WorEFlm*
Costa-Gavras, Henri 1933- *IntMPA 77, -75, -76, -78, -79, -80, MovMk[port]*
Costa-Greenspon, Muriel *WhoOp 76*
Costain, George Arthur 1901- *WhoMus 72*
Costain, Thomas Bertram 1885-1965 *CreCan 2*
Costallat d1901 *NewGrD 80*
Costantakos, Chris Anastasios 1924- *AmSCAP 80*
Costantini, Alessandro 1581?-1657 *NewGrD 80*

Costantini, Angelo 1654?-1729 *EncWT, Ent*
Costantini, Angelo 1655?-1729 *OxThe*
Costantini, Costantino 1634?-1696? *EncWT, OxThe*
Costantini, Domenica *OxThe*
Costantini, Fabio 1570?-1644 *NewGrD 80*
Costantini, Giovan Battista d1720 *OxThe*
Costantini, Livia *NewGrD 80*
Costantino, Romola 1930- *IntWWM 80*
Costanzi, Giovanni Battista 1704-1778 *NewGrD 80*
Costanzo, Fabrizio *NewGrD 80*
Costanzo, Jack J *AmSCAP 66*
Costanzo, Jack J 1924- *AmSCAP 80*
Costanzo DaCosena, Francesco *NewGrD 80*
Coste, G J DeLa *NewGrD 80*
Coste, Gabriel *NewGrD 80*
Coste, Maurice R 1875-1963 *WhScrn 74, -77*
Coste, Napoleon 1806-1883 *NewGrD 80*
Costeley, Guillaume 1530?-1606 *NewGrD 80[port]*
Costeley, Guillaume 1531-1606 *Baker 78*
Costeley, William 1531-1606 *OxMus*
Costello, Anthony *WhoHol A*
Costello, Bartley C 1871-1941 *AmSCAP 66, -80*
Costello, Carmen *Film 2*
Costello, Delmar 1906-1961 *WhScrn 77*
Costello, Diosa *WhoHol A*
Costello, Dolores 1904- *ThFT[port]*
Costello, Dolores 1905-1979 *FilmEn, Film 1, -2, FilmgC, ForYSC, HalFC 80, MotPP, MovMk, TwYS, WhoHol A*
Costello, Dolores 1906- *What 2[port]*
Costello, Don 1901-1945 *WhScrn 74, -77, WhoHol B*
Costello, Donald James, Jr. 1933- *AmSCAP 80*
Costello, Elvis *ConMuA 80A*
Costello, Helene d1957 *MotPP, NotNAT B, WhoHol B*
Costello, Helene 1903-1957 *FilmEn, Film 1, -2, ForYSC, TwYS, WhScrn 74, -77*
Costello, Helene 1904-1957 *FilmgC, HalFC 80*
Costello, Helene 1905-1957 *ThFT[port]*
Costello, John *Film 2*
Costello, Lou 1906-1959 *CmMov, FilmEn, FilmgC, Funs, HalFC 80, JoeFr[port], MotPP, MovMk, NotNAT B, OxFilm, WhScrn 74, -77, WhoHol B, WhoHrs 80[port], WorEFlm[port]*
Costello, Lou 1908-1959 *ForYSC*
Costello, Maurice 1877-1950 *FilmEn, Film 1, -2, FilmgC, HalFC 80, MotPP, NotNAT B, TwYS, WhScrn 74, -77, WhoHol B*
Costello, Mildred *Film 2*
Costello, Tom 1863- *WhThe*
Costello, Tom 1863-1943 *NotNAT B*
Costello, Tom 1863-1945 *OxThe*
Costello, Ward *WhoHol A*
Costello, William A 1898-1971 *Film 2, WhScrn 74, -77, WhoHol B*
Costenoble, Karl Ludwig 1769-1837 *EncWT*
Coster, Nicolas *WhoHol A*
Coster, Wayne Joseph 1953- *AmSCAP 80*
Costere, Edmond 1905- *IntWWM 77, -80*
Costigan, James 1928- *BiE&WWA, NewYTET, NotNAT*
Costillo, Carmen *Film 2*
Costin, William Lorne 1952- *IntWWM 80*
Costinescu, Gheorghe 1934- *ConAmC*
Costinha 1891- *FilmAG WE[port]*
Costinus Breuwe *NewGrD 80*
Cosyn, Benjamin *OxMus*
Cosyn, Benjamin 1570?-1652? *NewGrD 80*
Cosyn, John d1609? *NewGrD 80*
Cotapos, Acario 1889-1969 *Baker 78, DcCM, NewGrD 80*
Cote, Aurele DeFoy Suzor *CreCan 1*
Cotek, Pavel 1922- *Baker 78, IntWWM 77, -80*
Cotel, Morris Moshe 1943- *AmSCAP 80, ConAmC*
Cotelay, Guillaume *NewGrD 80*
Cotell, Richard *NewGrD 80*
Cotes, Ambrosio 1550?-1603 *NewGrD 80*
Cotes, Mrs. Everard 1861-1922 *CreCan 1*
Cotes, Peter 1912- *IntMPA 77, -75, -76, -78, -79, -80, WhoThe 72, -77*
Cotes, Sara Jeannette Duncan 1861-1922 *CreCan 1*
Cotner, Carl B 1916- *BiDAmM, IlEncCM*
Cotomaccio, Carlo *NewGrD 80*
Coton, A V 1906-1969 *CnOxB, DancEn 78*
Cotopouli, Marika d1954 *NotNAT B*
Cotrubas, Ileana 1939- *IntWWM 77, -80, NewGrD 80, WhoMus 72, WhoOp 76*
Cotsworth, Staats 1908- *BiE&WWA, IntMPA 77, -75, -76, -78, -79, NotNAT, WhoHol A, WhoThe 72, -77*
Cott, Ted d1973 *NewYTET*
Cottafavi, Vittorio 1914- *BiDFilm, DcFM, FilmEn, FilmgC, HalFC 80, OxFilm, WorEFlm[port]*
Cotte, Roger 1921- *NewGrD 80*
Cotten, Elizabeth 1892- *BluesWW[port]*
Cotten, Elizabeth 1893- *BiDAmM*
Cotten, Joseph 1905- *BiDFilm, -81, BiE&WWA, CmMov, FilmEn, FilmgC, ForYSC, HalFC 80, IntMPA 77, -75, -76, -78, -79, -80, MotPP, MovMk, NotNAT, OxFilm, PlP&P[port], WhoHol A, WhoHrs 80[port], WhoThe 72, -77, WorEFlm[port]*
Cottens, Victor De 1862- *WhThe*
Cotter, Hans *NewGrD 80*
Cotter, Joseph Seaman, Sr. 1861-1949 *BlkAmP, MorBAP*
Cottlow, Augusta 1878-1954 *Baker 78, BiDAmM*
Cotto, John *NewGrD 80*
Cotto DelValle, Luis 1913-1971 *WhScrn 74, -77*
Cottom, Frederick Arthur Sefton 1928- *WhoMus 72*
Cotton, Billy 1899-1969 *CmpEPM, NewGrD 80*
Cotton, Billy 1900-1969 *Film 2, WhScrn 74, -77, WhoHol B*
Cotton, Carolina *ForYSC*
Cotton, Charles d1687 *NotNAT B*
Cotton, Eric Beaumont 1916- *IntWWM 77, -80*
Cotton, Fred d1964 *WhoHol B*
Cotton, Fred Ayers 1907-1964 *NotNAT B*
Cotton, Fred Ayres 1907-1964 *WhScrn 74, -77*
Cotton, George 1903-1975 *WhScrn 77*
Cotton, James 1925- *BiDAmM*
Cotton, James 1935- *BluesWW[port]*
Cotton, John *Baker 78, NewGrD 80, OxMus*
Cotton, Larry *CmpEPM*
Cotton, Lucy 1891-1948 *Film 1, -2, NotNAT B, TwYS, WhScrn 74, -77, WhoHol B*
Cotton, Norman Paul 1945- *AmSCAP 80*
Cotton, Richardson d1916 *WhScrn 77*
Cotton, Robert F *NotNAT B*
Cotton, Walter *BlkAmP*
Cotton, Wilfred 1873- *WhThe*
Cotton, William 1899-1969 *NewGrD 80*
Cotton Blues Band, James *BiDAmM*
Cotton Pickers *BiDAmM*
Cottone, Giovanni Pietro 1540?-1593 *NewGrD 80*
Cottonius, John *NewGrD 80*
Cottrau, Teodoro 1827-1879 *Baker 78, NewGrD 80*
Cottrell, Cherry 1909- *WhThe*
Cottrell, Louis, Jr. 1911- *NewOrJ[port], WhoJazz 72*
Cottrell, Louis, Sr. 1875?-1927 *NewOrJ[port]*
Cottrell, Richard 1936- *WhoThe 72, -77*
Cottrelly, Mathilde 1851-1933 *NotNAT B*
Cotts, Campbell 1903-1964 *NotNAT B, WhScrn 77*
Cotumacci, Carlo 1709?-1785 *NewGrD 80*
Coty, Anny *Film 2*
Coty, Henri Roland 1922- *IntMPA 77, -75, -76, -78, -79, -80*
Coubier, Heinz 1905- *CnMD*
Couch, Robert *Film 2*
Couchet *NewGrD 80*
Couchet, Joannes 1612?-1655 *NewGrD 80*
Couesnon, Amedee 1850-1951 *NewGrD 80*
Couffer, Jack 1922- *FilmgC, HalFC 80*
Cougar, John *AmSCAP 80*
Coughlin, Father Charles E *What 1[port]*
Coughlin, Kevin 1945- *ForYSC*
Coughlin, Kevin 1945-1976 *WhoHol C*
Coughtry, John Graham 1931- *CreCan 1*
Couldock, Charles Walter 1815-1898 *NotNAT B, OxThe*
Couling, Vivien 1931- *IntWWM 77, -80, WhoMus 72*
Coulon *CnOxB*
Coulon, Anne-Jacqueline *CnOxB*
Coulon, Antoine-Louis 1796-1849 *CnOxB*
Coulon, Eugene *CnOxB*
Coulon, Jean-Francois 1764-1836 *CnOxB*
Couloris, George *MotPP*
Coulouris, George 1903- *BiE&WWA, FilmEn, FilmgC, ForYSC, HalFC 80, IlWWBF, MovMk[port], NotNAT, Vers A[port], WhoHol A, WhoHrs 80, WhoThe 72, -77*
Coulson, Richard 1948- *IntWWM 77, -80, WhoMus 72*
Coulson, Roy *Film 2*
Coulter, Frazer 1848-1937 *Film 1, NotNAT B, WhoStg 1906, -1908*
Coulter, Frazer 1849-1937 *WhScrn 77*
Coulter, Frazier *Film 2*
Coulter, John William 1888- *CreCan 1*
Coulter, R Scott, Jr. 1925- *ConAmC*
Coulthard, Jean 1908- *Baker 78, CreCan 1, IntWWM 77, -80, NewGrD 80*
Coulthard, William Marshall 1912- *WhoMus 72*
Counce, Curtis Lee 1926-1963 *BiDAmM, CmpEPM, IlEncJ*
Council, Floyd 1911-1976? *BluesWW[port]*
Counradi, Johann Melchior *NewGrD 80*
Counsell, John 1905- *OxThe, WhoThe 72, -77*
Count Five, The *RkOn 2[port]*
Count Rockin' Sydney *BluesWW*
Countess Ducella d1921 *WhScrn 74, -77*
Countiss, Cathrine *WhoStg 1908*
Country Boys *BiDAmM*
Country Drifters *BiDAmM*
Country Gazette *IlEncCM[port]*
Country Gentlemen *BiDAmM, CounME 74[port], -74A, EncFCWM 69, IlEncCM[port]*
Country Joe And The Fish *BiDAmM, RkOn 2[port]*
Country Kojac *AmSCAP 80*
Country Lads *BiDAmM*
Country Paul *BluesWW[port]*
Country Rhythm Boys *BiDAmM*
Coupar, Robert *NewGrD 80*
Couper, Barbara 1903- *WhThe*
Couper, Mildred 1887- *ConAmC*
Couper, Robert *NewGrD 80*
Couperin *BnBkM 80, NewGrD 80*
Couperin, Armand-Louis 1727-1789 *Baker 78, NewGrD 80*
Couperin, Charles 1638-1679 *Baker 78, BnBkM 80, NewGrD 80*
Couperin, Francois 1631?- *Baker 78*
Couperin, Francois 1631-1701 *BnBkM 80*
Couperin, Francois 1631?-1712? *NewGrD 80*
Couperin, Francois 1668-1733 *Baker 78, BnBkM 80[port], CmpBCM, CnOxB, DcCom 77[port], DcCom&M 79, GrComp[port], MusMk[port], NewGrD 80[port], OxMus*
Couperin, Francois-Gervais 1759-1826 *NewGrD 80*
Couperin, Gervais-Francois 1759-1826 *Baker 78, NewGrD 80*
Couperin, Louis 1626?-1661 *Baker 78, BnBkM 80, NewGrD 80*
Couperin, Marguerite-Antoinette 1705-1778? *NewGrD 80*
Couperin, Marguerite-Louise 1676?-1728 *NewGrD 80*
Couperin, Nicolas 1680-1748 *Baker 78, NewGrD 80*
Couperin, Pierre-Louis 1755-1789 *Baker 78, NewGrD 80*
Couperin Family *Baker 78, OxMus*
Coupillet, Nicolas *NewGrD 80*
Couppeau, Charles *NewGrD 80*
Courance, Spider Edgar 1903-1969 *WhoJazz 72*
Courant, Curt 1895?- *DcFM, FilmEn, FilmgC, HalFC 80, OxFilm, WorEFlm*
Courant, Curtis *WorEFlm*
Couraud, Marcel 1912- *NewGrD 80*
Courbes, Sieur De *NewGrD 80*
Courboin, Charles Marie 1884-1973 *Baker 78*
Courbois, Philippe *NewGrD 80*

Courcel, Nicole 1930- FilmEn, FilmgC, HalFC 80, WhoHol A
Courcelle, Francesco NewGrD 80
Couret, Gabriel 1917- WhoOp 76
Cournand, Gilberte 1913- CnOxB
Couroierie, Oede DeLa NewGrD 80
Couroupos, George 1942- NewGrD 80
Court, Alfred C 1886-1953 WhScrn 74, -77
Court, Antoine DeLa NewGrD 80
Court, Dorothy WhThe
Court, Hazel 1926- FilmEn, FilmgC, ForYSC, HalFC 80, IlWWBF[port], WhoHol A, WhoHrs 80[port]
Court, Henri DeLa NewGrD 80
Courteau, Ann McDonald 1911- IntWWM 77
Courteline, Georges 1858-1929 CnMD, CnThe, EncWT, Ent, McGEWD[port], ModWD, OxThe, PlP&P, REnWD
Courteline, Georges 1860-1929 WhThe
Courteline, Georges 1861-1929 NotNAT B
Courtenay, Tom 1937- Ent, FilmAG WE, FilmEn, FilmgC, ForYSC, HalFC 80, IlWWBF[port], IntMPA 77, -75, -76, -78, -79, -80, MotPP, MovMk[port], OxFilm, WhoHol A, WhoThe 72, -77, WorEFlm
Courtenay, William 1875-1933 Film 2, NotNAT B, WhScrn 74, -77, WhThe, WhoHol B, WhoStg 1908
Courteney, Fay d1943 NotNAT B
Courteney, Shelia Film 2
Courteville, Ralph NewGrD 80
Courteville, Raphael NewGrD 80
Courteville, Raphael d1772 NewGrD 80
Courtice, Michael 1888-1962 WorEFlm
Courtland, Jerome 1926- FilmEn, FilmgC, ForYSC, HalFC 80, IntMPA 77, -78, -79, -80, MotPP, WhoHol A
Courtleigh, Edna d1962 NotNAT B
Courtleigh, Stephen d1968 WhScrn 77
Courtleigh, William 1867-1930 NotNAT B
Courtleigh, William 1876-1930 WhoStg 1906, -1908
Courtleigh, William, Jr. 1869-1930 Film 1, -2, WhScrn 74, -77, WhThe, WhoHol B
Courtleigh, William, Sr. 1892-1918 WhScrn 77
Courtneay, Peter Film 1
Courtneay, William F 1875-1933 Film 1
Courtneidge, Charles d1935 NotNAT B
Courtneidge, Cicely 1893- EncMT, FilmAG WE, FilmgC, HalFC 80, IlWWBF[port], -A, NotNAT A, WhoHol A, WhoThe 72, -77
Courtneidge, Cicely 1893-1980 FilmEn
Courtneidge, Robert 1859-1939 EncMT, NotNAT A, -B, WhThe
Courtneidge, Mrs. Robert d1914 NotNAT B
Courtneidge, Rosaline 1903-1926 NotNAT B, WhThe
Courtney, Alan 1912-1978 AmSCAP 66, -80, CmpEPM
Courtney, C C ConDr 73, -77D
Courtney, Dan WhoHol A
Courtney, Del 1910- AmSCAP 80, BgBands 74, CmpEPM
Courtney, Fay d1941 NotNAT B
Courtney, Gordon 1895-1964 WhThe
Courtney, Inez 1908-1975 FilmEn, ForYSC, ThFT[port], WhScrn 77, WhoHol C
Courtney, John d1865 NotNAT B
Courtney, Maud 1884- WhThe
Courtney, Oscar W d1963 NotNAT B
Courtney, Oscar W 1877-1962 WhScrn 74, -77
Courtney, Pat Film 2
Courtney, Thomas 1929- BluesWW[port]
Courtney, William Leonard 1850-1928 NotNAT B, WhThe
Courtois, Jean Baker 78, NewGrD 80
Courtois, Lambert 1520?- NewGrD 80
Courtois, Leon Film 2
Courtot, Juliette Film 2
Courtot, Marguerite 1897- Film 1, -2, MotPP, TwYS
Courtoys, Jean NewGrD 80
Courtoys, Lambert 1520?- NewGrD 80
Courtright, Clyde 1885-1967 WhScrn 74, -77
Courtright, Jennie Lee Film 1
Courtright, William 1848-1933 WhScrn 74, -77
Courts, Eddy AmSCAP 80
Courtwright, William 1848-1933 Film 2, WhoHol B
Courvile, Joachim Thibault De d1581 NewGrD 80
Courville, Albert Pierre De 1887-1960 OxThe
Courville, Joachim Thibault De d1581 NewGrD 80
Courville, Thibaut De OxMus
Courvoisier, Karl 1846-1908 Baker 78, OxMus
Courvoisier, Walter 1875-1931 Baker 78, NewGrD 80
Coury, Al ConMuA 80B
Cousin, Jack 1952- IntWWM 77, -80
Cousin, Jean NewGrD 80
Cousin, Linda MorBAP
Cousin Jacques NewGrD 80
Cousin Jody d1975 WhoHol C
Cousin Jody 1914-1976 IlEncCM[port]
Cousin Joe BluesWW, NewOrJ
Cousin Joseph BluesWW
Cousineau NewGrD 80
Cousineau, Georges 1733-1800? NewGrD 80
Cousineau, Jacques-Georges 1760-1824 NewGrD 80
Cousineau, Yves CreCan 1
Cousins, John Edward 1943- IntWWM 77, -80
Cousins, M Thomas 1914-1972 AmSCAP 66, -80, ConAmC
Cousins, Malcolm Ernest 1932- WhoMus 72
Cousins, Michael Gene 1940- WhoOp 76
Coussemaker, Charles-Edmond-Henri De 1805-1876 Baker 78, NewGrD 80
Cousser, Jean Sigismond NewGrD 80
Coustaut, Manuel NewOrJ
Coustaut, Sylvester d1910? NewOrJ
Cousteau, Jacques-Yves 1910- DcFM, FilmEn, FilmgC, HalFC 80, OxFilm, WorEFlm
Cousu, Antoine De NewGrD 80
Coutard, Raoul 1924- DcFM, FilmEn, FilmgC, HalFC 80, OxFilm, WorEFlm
Coutinho, Francisco Jose 1680-1724 NewGrD 80
Coutreman NewGrD 80
Coutts, William Fisher 1889- WhoMus 72
Coutu, Jean 1925- CreCan 1
Couture, Guillaume 1851-1915 CreCan 1, NewGrD 80
Couture, Severe CreCan 1
Couzin, Sharon WomWMM A, -B
Cova, Alyrio Lima 1949- EncJzS 70
Cova, Fiorella 1936- CnOxB, DancEn 78
Covais, Jack AmSCAP 80
Covan, Deforrest 1917- BlksB&W
Covans, The Four Film 2
Covay, Don And The Goodtimers RkOn
Cove, George Netherton 1888- WhoMus 72
Covell, Roger David 1931- IntWWM 80, NewGrD 80
Coven RkOn 2[port]
Coventry, Karen Olivia 1946- IntWWM 77
Coventry, Tom Film 2
Coverdale, Miles 1488-1568 OxMus
Coverdale, Miles 1914- IntWWM 80, WhoMus 72
Coverly, Robert 1864-1944 Baker 78
Covert, John 1937- IntWWM 77, -80
Covert, Mary Ann Hunter 1936- IntWWM 77, -80
Covington, Ben 1900?-1935? BluesWW
Covington, Bruce Film 2
Covington, Ruth PupTheA
Covington, Treadwell D AmSCAP 80
Covington, Warren 1921- AmPS A, AmSCAP 66, -80, BiDAmM, CmpEPM, EncJzS 70
Covington, Z Wall Film 2
Cowan, Cathy 1929- AmSCAP 80
Cowan, Christopher Home 1908- WhoMus 72
Cowan, Jerome 1897-1972 BiE&WWA, FilmEn, FilmgC, ForYSC, HalFC 80, HolCA[port], MovMk[port], NotNAT B, Vers A[port], WhScrn 77, WhoHol B
Cowan, Joan Yarbrough 1940- IntWWM 77, -80
Cowan, Lester 1905?- FilmEn, FilmgC, HalFC 80
Cowan, Louis G d1976 NewYTET
Cowan, Lynn F 1888-1973 AmSCAP 66, -80, Film 2, WhScrn 77
Cowan, Maurice A 1891-1974 FilmgC, HalFC 80, WhThe
Cowan, Michael 1944- AmSCAP 66, -80
Cowan, Robert Holmes 1931- IntWWM 77, -80
Cowan, Rubey 1891-1957 AmSCAP 66, -80
Cowan, Sigmund Sumner 1948- IntWWM 77, -80
Cowan, Stanley Earl 1918- AmSCAP 66, -80
Cowan, Theodore IntMPA 77, -75, -76, -78, -79, -80
Cowan, Warren J IntMPA 77, -75, -76, -78, -79, -80
Coward, Helen WhoMus 72
Coward, Sir Henry 1849-1944 Baker 78, NewGrD 80, OxMus
Coward, Noel 1899- WhoThe 72
Coward, Noel 1899-1973 Baker 78, BestMus[port], BiE&WWA, CmpEPM, CnMD, CnThe, ConDr 73, CroCD, DcFM, EncMT, EncWT, Ent[port], FamA&A[port], FilmAG WE, Film 1, FilmgC, ForYSC, HalFC 80, IlWWBF[port], -A, McGEWD, ModWD, MovMk, NewGrD 80, NotNAT A, -B, OxFilm, OxThe, PlP&P[port], REnWD[port], WhScrn 77, WhThe, WhoHol B, WhoMus 72, WorEFlm
Coward, Sir Noel 1899-1973 FilmEn
Coward, Richard Anthony 1949- IntWWM 77
Cowboy Ramblers, The BiDAmM
Cowden, Irene d1961 NotNAT B
Cowden, John P NewYTET
Cowden, Robert Hapgood 1934- IntWWM 77, -80
Cowderoy, Peter Sutherland 1918- IntWWM 77, -80, WhoMus 72
Cowell, Florence 1852-1926 OxThe
Cowell, Henry 1887-1965 BnBkM 80
Cowell, Henry 1897- CpmDNM 72
Cowell, Henry 1897-1965 Baker 78, BiDAmM, CompSN[port], ConAmC, DcCM, EncFCWM 69, MusMk, NewGrD 80[port], OxMus
Cowell, Joe 1792-1863 FamA&A[port]
Cowell, John 1926- IntWWM 77
Cowell, Joseph Leathley 1792-1863 NotNAT A, -B, OxThe
Cowell, Samuel Houghton 1820-1864 NotNAT A, -B, OxThe
Cowell, Shirley Ione 1923- AmSCAP 80
Cowell, Stanley A 1941- EncJzS 70
Cowell, Sydney 1846-1925 NotNAT B, OxThe
Cowell, Sydney 1872-1941 OxThe
Cowen, Sir Frederic Hymen 1852-1935 Baker 78, NewGrD 80
Cowen, Sir Frederick Hymen 1852-1935 OxMus
Cowen, Hymen Frederick 1852-1935 NewGrD 80
Cowen, Joe AmSCAP 80
Cowen, Laurence 1865-1942 NotNAT B, WhThe
Cowen, Louis d1925 NotNAT B
Cowen, Ron 1944- ConDr 73, -77, NatPD[port]
Cowen, William Joyce d1964 NotNAT B
Cowen, William Joyce 1883-1964 HalFC 80
Cowens, Kat Herbert 1904- WhoJazz 72
Cowger, Roger Ray 1938- AmSCAP 66, -80
Cowgill, Bryan NewYTET
Cowie, Edward 1943- NewGrD 80
Cowie, Laura 1892-1969 PlP&P, WhThe
Cowie, Laure Film 1
Cowie, Leroy 1940- IntWWM 77, -80, WhoMus 72
Cowking, John 1956- IntWWM 77
Cowl, George Film 2
Cowl, Jane d1950 PlP&P, WhoHol B
Cowl, Jane 1884-1950 EncWT, Ent, FamA&A[port], NotNAT B
Cowl, Jane 1887-1950 FilmEn, WhScrn 74, -77
Cowl, Jane 1890-1950 Film 1, FilmgC, HalFC 80, WhThe
Cowl, Jane 1891-1950 ForYSC
Cowles, Cecil AmSCAP 66
Cowles, Cecil d1966 AmSCAP 80
Cowles, Cecil M 1898- BiDAmM
Cowles, Cecil Marion 1898-1968 ConAmC
Cowles, Chandler 1917- BiE&WWA, NotNAT
Cowles, Darleen 1942- ConAmC
Cowles, Eugene 1860-1948 AmPS B, BiDAmM, NotNAT B, WhoStg 1906,

–1908
Cowles, Fleur 1910- *What 4[port]*
Cowles, Jules 1878-1943 *Film 2, WhScrn 74, –77, WhoHol B*
Cowles, Mathew *WhoHol A*
Cowles, Matthew *PlP&P[port]*
Cowles, Walter Ruel 1881-1959 *Baker 78, ConAmC*
Cowley, Abraham 1618-1667 *NotNAT B, OxThe*
Cowley, Eric 1886-1948 *NotNAT B, WhThe, WhoHol B*
Cowley, Hannah 1743-1809 *EncWT, Ent, NotNAT B, OxThe*
Cowley, Hilda *Film 2*
Cowley, Richard d1619 *NotNAT B, OxThe*
Cowling, Bruce *ForYSC*
Cowling, Susan Heather 1940- *IntWWM 77*
Cowper, Clara d1917 *NotNAT B*
Cowper, John *NewGrD 80*
Cowper, Robert 1474?-1535? *NewGrD 80*
Cowper, William 1731-1800 *DcPup, OxMus*
Cowper, William C 1853-1918 *WhScrn 77*
Cowsills, The *BiDAmM, RkOn 2[port]*
Cox, Alison Mary 1956- *IntWWM 80*
Cox, Arthur *NewGrD 80*
Cox, Brian 1946- *WhoThe 77*
Cox, Christopher Christian 1816-1882 *BiDAmM*
Cox, Clifford Laird 1935- *IntWWM 77, –80*
Cox, Constance 1912- *WhoThe 72*
Cox, Constance 1915- *WhoThe 77*
Cox, David 1916- *IntWWM 77, –80, NewGrD 80*
Cox, Elford Bradley 1914- *CreCan 2*
Cox, Freddie *Film 2*
Cox, Sir Geoffrey 1910- *IntMPA 75, –76*
Cox, Harold 1905- *IntMPA 77, –75, –76, –78, –79, –80*
Cox, Ida 1889- *IlEncJ*
Cox, Ida 1889-1967 *CmpEPM, EncJzS 70, WhoJazz 72*
Cox, Ida 1889-1968 *BiDAmM*
Cox, Ida 1896-1967 *BluesWW[port]*
Cox, Irby Royce 1953- *IntWWM 77*
Cox, James M, Jr. 1903- *IntMPA 75*
Cox, James M, Jr. 1903-1974 *NewYTET*
Cox, James M, Jr. 1930-1974 *BiDAmM*
Cox, Jean 1922- *NewGrD 80*
Cox, Jean 1932- *WhoOp 76*
Cox, Jim *EncFCWM 69*
Cox, Jimmy 1882- *AmSCAP 80*
Cox, John 1935- *IntWWM 77, –80, WhoOp 76*
Cox, Joseph Mason Andrew *BlkAmP*
Cox, Kenneth A *NewYTET*
Cox, Larry 1942- *AmSCAP 66, ConMuA 80B*
Cox, Lawrence L 1942- *AmSCAP 80*
Cox, Lester Morgan 1910- *AmSCAP 66*
Cox, Nell *WomWMM A, –B*
Cox, Noel Frederick 1917- *WhoMus 72*
Cox, Olive *Film 1*
Cox, Patricia 1936- *CnOxB, DancEn 78*
Cox, Ralph 1884-1941 *AmSCAP 66, –80, ConAmC A*
Cox, Renee S 1952- *IntWWM 80*
Cox, Richard *NewGrD 80*
Cox, Robert d1655 *OxThe*
Cox, Robert 1895-1974 *WhScrn 77, WhoHol B*
Cox, Ronn 1942- *CpmDNM 74, –76, –78, ConAmC*
Cox, Ronny *WhoHol A*
Cox, Ronny 1938- *HalFC 80*
Cox, Tom 1892-1914 *WhScrn 77*
Cox, Vivian 1915- *FilmgC, HalFC 80*
Cox, W Ralph 1884-1941 *BiDAmM*
Cox, Wallace Maynard 1924-1973 *AmSCAP 80*
Cox, Wally 1924-1973 *FilmEn, FilmgC, ForYSC, JoeFr[port], NewYTET, NotNAT A, –B, WhScrn 77, WhoHol B*
Cox, Wally 1924-1976 *HalFC 80*
Cox, Walter S *PupTheA*
Cox, Winifred Spencer 1901- *WhoMus 72*
Coxe, Arthur Cleveland 1818-1896 *BiDAmM*
Coxe, Louis O 1918- *BiE&WWA, McGEWD, NotNAT*
Coxe, Nigel 1932- *IntWWM 77, WhoMus 72*
Coxe, William 1747-1828 *NewGrD 80*
Coxen, Ed 1884-1954 *WhoHol B*
Coxen, Edward Albert 1884-1954 *Film 2, WhScrn 74, –77*
Coxson, Robert 1489?-1548? *NewGrD 80*
Coxsun, Robert 1489?-1548? *NewGrD 80*
Coxwell, Jack Gordon *WhoMus 72*
Coy, A Wayne d1957 *NewYTET*
Coy, Johnnie 1921-1973 *WhScrn 77*
Coy, Johnny d1973 *MotPP, WhoHol B*
Coy, Walter 1906-1974 *WhScrn 77, WhoHol B*
Coy, Walter 1913- *ForYSC*
Coya, Simone *NewGrD 80*
Coyan, Betty 1901-1935 *WhScrn 74, –77*
Coycault, Ernest 1890- *NewOrJ*
Coycault, Jerome 1895?-1928 *NewOrJ*
Coyle, J J 1928- *NatPD[port]*
Coyle, John E d1964 *NotNAT B*
Coyle, Joseph Anthony 1946- *AmSCAP 80*
Coyle, Paul Raymond 1944- *AmSCAP 80*
Coyle, Walter V 1888-1948 *WhScrn 74, –77*
Coyne, Jeanne 1923-1973 *WhScrn 77*
Coyne, Joseph 1867-1941 *EncMT, NotNAT B, WhThe*
Coyne, Joseph 1870- *WhoStg 1908*
Coyne, Joseph Stirling d1868 *NotNAT B*
Coyne, Kevin 1944- *ConMuA 80A, IlEncR*
Coyne, Robert W 1904- *IntMPA 75*
Coyner, Lou 1931- *CpmDNM 72, ConAmC*
Coypeau, Charles *NewGrD 80*
Coyssard, Michel 1547-1623 *NewGrD 80*
Cozad, Joseph 1935- *IntWWM 77, –80*
Cozeneuve, Paul *Film 2*
Cozens, John 1906- *IntWWM 80*
Cozette, Francois *NewGrD 80*
Cozio DiSalabue, Count Ignazio A 1755-1840 *NewGrD 80*
Cozzella, Damiano 1930- *NewGrD 80*
Cozzens, Jimmy 1898?- *NewOrJ*
Cozzi, Carlo d1658? *NewGrD 80*
Cozzolani, Chiara Margarita d1653? *NewGrD 80*
Crabb, Michael 1938- *IntWWM 77, –80*
Crabbe, Armand 1883-1947 *Baker 78, NewGrD 80*
Crabbe, Armand 1884-1948 *BiDAmM*
Crabbe, Buster *IntMPA 76, –78, –79, –80*
Crabbe, Buster 1907- *FilmgC, HalFC 80[port], IntMPA 77, MotPP, WhoHol A*
Crabbe, Larry *What 1[port]*
Crabbe, Larry 1907- *FilmEn, WhoHrs 80[port]*
Crabbe, Larry 1910- *ForYSC*
Crabbe, Larry Buster *IntMPA 75*
Crabbe, Larry Buster 1907- *MovMk[port]*
Crabbe, Larry Buster 1908- *HolP 30[port]*
Crabtree, Arthur 1900- *CmMov, FilmEn, FilmgC, HalFC 80, IlWWBF, WhoHrs 80*
Crabtree, Charlotte 1847-1924 *Ent, NotNAT B, OxThe, WhoStg 1906, –1908*
Crabtree, Lotta 1847-1924 *FamA&A[port], NotNAT A*
Crabtree, Paul 1918- *AmSCAP 66, BiE&WWA, NotNAT*
Crabtree, Phillip D 1937- *IntWWM 77, –80*
Crabtree, Ray *ConAmC*
Crabtree, William Nelson 1955- *AmSCAP 80*
Crackers *DcPup*
Cracoviensis, N Z *NewGrD 80*
Craddock, Billy *CounME 74A*
Craddock, Billy 1939- *CounME 74[port], IlEncCM[port]*
Craddock, Claudia 1889-1945 *WhScrn 74, –77, WhoHol B*
Crader, Jeannine 1934- *WhoOp 76*
Craen, Nicolaus *NewGrD 80*
Crafft *NewGrD 80*
Crafft, Georg Andreas Von *NewGrD 80*
Craft, Garland 1949- *AmSCAP 80*
Craft, Lois Adele *AmSCAP 80*
Craft, Lynne d1975 *WhScrn 77*
Craft, Marcella 1880-1959 *Baker 78, BiDAmM*
Craft, Robert 1923- *Baker 78, BnBkM 80, NewGrD 80, WhoMus 72*
Craft, Virginia *Film 1*
Craft, William J 1886- *TwYS A*
Crafts, Griffin 1900-1973 *WhScrn 77, WhoHol A*
Crager, Ted J 1925- *IntWWM 77, –80*
Craggs, The *WhThe*
Cragun, Richard Allan 1944- *CnOxB*
Craig, Alec 1878-1945 *FilmgC, HalFC 80*
Craig, Alec 1885-1945 *HolCA[port], Vers A[port], WhScrn 74, –77, WhoHol B*
Craig, Blanche 1878- *Film 1, –2, TwYS*
Craig, Bob *Film 2*
Craig, Bradford Joseph 1937- *AmSCAP 80*
Craig, Burton *Film 2*
Craig, Carolyn d1970 *WhScrn 77*
Craig, Catherine *ForYSC, WhoHol A*
Craig, Charles *Film 1, –2*
Craig, Charles 1920- *NewGrD 80*
Craig, Charles 1922- *CmOp, IntWWM 77, –80, WhoMus 72*
Craig, Mrs. Charles *Film 2*
Craig, Mrs. Charles G *Film 2*
Craig, Charles James 1925- *WhoOp 76*
Craig, Dale Allan 1939- *ConAmC, IntWWM 77, –80*
Craig, David 1923- *BiE&WWA, NotNAT*
Craig, David MacLeod 1941- *IntWWM 80*
Craig, Donald Michael 1925- *AmSCAP 80*
Craig, Douglas 1916- *WhoMus 72*
Craig, Edith 1869-1947 *NotNAT A, –B, OxThe, WhThe, WhoHol B, WhoStg 1908*
Craig, Edward Gordon 1872-1966 *BiE&WWA, CnThe, EncWT, Ent, HalFC 80, NewGrD 80, NotNAT A, –B, OxFilm, WhThe*
Craig, Edward Gordon 1872-1967 *DcPup*
Craig, Frances B 1869?-1925 *WhScrn 74, –77*
Craig, Francis 1900-1966 *AmSCAP 66, –80, BgBands 74, CmpEPM*
Craig, Godfrey 1915-1941 *WhScrn 74, –77, WhoHol B*
Craig, Gordon *Film 2*
Craig, Gordon d1973 *WhoHol B*
Craig, Gordon 1872-1966 *OxThe, PlP&P*
Craig, H A L 1911-1978 *HalFC 80*
Craig, Hal *Film 2*
Craig, Hardin 1875-1968 *BiE&WWA, NotNAT B*
Craig, Helen 1912- *BiE&WWA, MotPP, NotNAT, WhoHol A, WhoThe 77*
Craig, Helen 1914- *WhoThe 72*
Craig, James 1912- *FilmEn, FilmgC, ForYSC, HalFC 80, MGM[port], MotPP, MovMk, WhoHol A*
Craig, Jimmy *AmSCAP 80*
Craig, John *WhoHol A*
Craig, John d1932 *NotNAT B, WhoHol B*
Craig, John Dixon d1946 *CreCan 1*
Craig, Juanita *PupTheA*
Craig, Leonard C D 1917- *IntWWM 80*
Craig, May 1889-1972 *WhScrn 77, WhoHol B*
Craig, Michael *WhoHol A*
Craig, Michael 1928- *FilmAG WE[port], FilmEn, FilmgC, HalFC 80, IlWWBF[port], WhoThe 77*
Craig, Michael 1929- *ForYSC, IntMPA 77, –75, –76, –78, –79, –80, WhoThe 72*
Craig, Nell 1891-1965 *FilmEn, Film 1, –2, ForYSC, TwYS, WhScrn 74, –77, WhoHol B*
Craig, Patricia 1943- *IntWWM 80*
Craig, Patricia 1947- *WhoOp 76*
Craig, R Gordon *Film 2*
Craig, Richy, Jr. d1934 *JoeFr[port]*
Craig, Richy, Jr. 1902-1933 *WhScrn 74, –77, WhoHol B*
Craig, Robert *Film 2*
Craig, Robert W *Film 2*
Craig, Sandra 1942- *CnOxB*
Craig, Stanley Herbert *IntMPA 77, –75, –76, –78, –79, –80*
Craig, Wendy 1934- *FilmEn, FilmgC, HalFC 80, WhoHol A, WhoThe 72, –77*
Craig, William C 1908- *BiE&WWA*
Craig, William James 1933- *IntWWM 77, –80*
Craig, Yvonne 1941- *FilmgC, ForYSC, HalFC 80, WhoHol A*
Craighead, David 1924- *NewGrD 80*
Craigie, Jill 1914- *FilmgC, HalFC 80, WomWMM*
Craigo, Jack *ConMuA 80B*
Crail, Helen L *PupTheA*
Crain, Harold 1911- *BiE&WWA, NotNAT*
Crain, Jeanne 1925- *BiDFilm, –81, FilmEn,*

FilmgC, ForYSC, HalFC 80, IntMPA 77, –75, –76, –78, –79, –80, MotPP, MovMk[port], WhoHol A, WorEFlm
Crain, William *DrBlPA*
Craine, Eileen 1930- *WhoMus 72*
Crais, William J 1927- *NewOrJ[port]*
Cram, James Douglas 1931- *AmSCAP 66, –80, ConAmC*
Cram, Mildred *WomWMM*
Cramer *NewGrD 80*
Cramer, Carl Friedrich 1752-1807 *NewGrD 80*
Cramer, Caspar d165-? *NewGrD 80*
Cramer, David 1590?-1666? *NewGrD 80*
Cramer, Dick 1889- *Film 2*
Cramer, Douglas S 1931- *IntMPA 77, –75, –76, NewYTET*
Cramer, Ed *ConMuA 80B*
Cramer, Edd 1924-1963 *NotNAT B, WhScrn 74, –77, WhoHol B*
Cramer, Floyd 1933- *BiDAmM, CounME 74[port], –74A, EncFCWM 69, IlEncCM[port], RkOn[port]*
Cramer, Francois 1772-1848 *NewGrD 80*
Cramer, Franz 1772-1848 *NewGrD 80, OxMus*
Cramer, Ivo 1921- *CnOxB, DancEn 78*
Cramer, Johann Baptist 1771-1858 *Baker 78, MusMk, NewGrD 80[port], OxMus*
Cramer, John Baptist 1771-1858 *BnBkM 80, NewGrD 80[port]*
Cramer, Marguerite *Film 2*
Cramer, Richard 1889-1960 *FilmEn, Film 2, ForYSC, WhScrn 77, WhoHol B*
Cramer, Rychard 1890-1960 *HalFC 80*
Cramer, Susanne 1938-1969 *WhScrn 74, –77, WhoHol B*
Cramer, Wilhelm 1745-1799 *OxMus*
Cramer, Wilhelm 1746-1799 *Baker 78, NewGrD 80*
Cramer, William Douglas 1931- *IntMPA 78, –79, –80*
Cramer Family *OxMus*
Crampton, Carline 1906- *WhoMus 72*
Crampton, Freda Henrietta Carline 1906- *IntWWM 77, –80*
Crampton, Howard *Film 1, –2*
Crandall, Edward *Film 2*
Crandell, David Miller 1914- *BiE&WWA*
Crandell, L Lee *WomWMM B*
Crandell, Robert E 1910- *ConAmC*
Crandell, Suzi *ForYSC*
Crane, Bob *IntMPA 75, –76*
Crane, Bob 1927- *ForYSC*
Crane, Bob 1928- *IntMPA 77, –78, WhoHol A*
Crane, Bob 1928-1978 *FilmEn*
Crane, Bob 1929-1978 *HalFC 80*
Crane, Cheryl 1944- *What 3[port]*
Crane, Dagne *WhoHol A*
Crane, Dean 1932- *BiE&WWA*
Crane, Dixie 1888-1936 *WhScrn 74, –77*
Crane, Doc *Film 1*
Crane, Earl *Film 2*
Crane, Edith 1865-1912 *NotNAT B, WhoStg 1908*
Crane, Ethel G d1930 *WhScrn 74, –77*
Crane, Frank *Film 1, –2*
Crane, Harry F *Film 1*
Crane, Helen *ConAmC, Film 2*
Crane, James *Film 1, –2*
Crane, Jimmie 1910- *AmSCAP 66, –80*
Crane, Joelle Wallach 1946- *CpmDNM 80, ConAmC, IntWWM 80*
Crane, John Thomas 1943- *ConAmC*
Crane, Les *NewYTET, RkOn 2A*
Crane, Mae 1925-1969 *WhScrn 74, –77, WhoHol B*
Crane, Norma 1931-1973 *WhScrn 77, WhoHol B*
Crane, Philip Miller 1930- *AmSCAP 66, –80*
Crane, Phyllis *Film 2*
Crane, Ralph 1550?-1621? *OxThe*
Crane, Richard *MotPP*
Crane, Richard 1918-1969 *FilmEn, ForYSC, WhoHrs 80[port]*
Crane, Richard 1919-1969 *HalFC 80*
Crane, Richard 1944- *WhoThe 77*
Crane, Richard O 1918-1969 *WhScrn 74, –77, WhoHol B*
Crane, Robert 1919- *ConAmC, IntWWM 80*
Crane, Shirley *WomWMM B*
Crane, Stephen *ForYSC*
Crane, Steve *WhoHol A*
Crane, Violet *Film 2*
Crane, W H 1845-1928 *WhThe*
Crane, Ward 1891-1928 *FilmEn, Film 1, –2, TwYS, WhScrn 74, –77, WhoHol B*
Crane, William d1545? *NewGrD 80*
Crane, William H 1845-1928 *FamA&A[port], Film 1, –2, NotNAT A, –B, OxThe, PlP&P, WhScrn 74, –77, WhoHol B, WhoStg 1906, –1908*
Crane, William H 1892-1957 *WhScrn 74, –77*
Cranesteyn, Gasparo *NewGrD 80*
Cranford, Thomas *NewGrD 80*
Cranford, William 1600?- *NewGrD 80*
Cranforth, William 1600?- *NewGrD 80*
Crang, John d1774 *NewGrD 80*
Cranham, Frederick John Charles *WhoMus 72*
Cranko, John 1927-1973 *CnOxB, DancEn 78, NewGrD 80*
Cranmer, Arthur 1885-1954 *NewGrD 80*
Cranmer, Damian Saint George 1943- *WhoMus 72*
Cranmer, Margaret Valerie 1945- *IntWWM 80*
Cranmer, Philip 1918- *IntWWM 77, –80, WhoMus 72*
Cranmer, Thomas 1489-1556 *OxMus*
Cranshaw, Bob 1932- *EncJzS 70*
Cranshaw, Melbourne R 1932- *BiDAmM, EncJzS 70*
Cranston, Mary *Film 1*
Cranz, Alwin 1834-1923 *NewGrD 80*
Cranz, August Heinrich *Baker 78*
Cranz, August Heinrich 1789-1870 *NewGrD 80*
Crappius, Andreas 1542?-1623 *NewGrD 80*
Cras, Jean Emile Paul 1879-1932 *Baker 78, NewGrD 80, OxMus*
Craske, Margaret 1898- *CnOxB, DancEn 78*
Crasnaru, George-Emil 1941- *IntWWM 80*
Crasnaru, Gheorghe Emil 1941- *WhoOp 76*
Crass, Franz 1928- *NewGrD 80, WhoOp 76*
Crasselius, Bartholomaus 1667-1724 *NewGrD 80*
Crasselt, Bartholomaus 1667-1724 *NewGrD 80*
Crassot, Richard 1530?- *NewGrD 80*
Crater, Allene d1957 *NotNAT B*
Crates *OxThe*
Cratinus 520?BC-423?BC *OxThe*
Crauford, J R 1847-1930 *WhThe*
Crauford, Kent *Film 2*
Cravat, Nick 1911- *FilmEn, FilmgC, ForYSC, HalFC 80, WhoHol A*
Cravat, Noel 1910-1960 *WhScrn 74, –77, WhoHol B*
Craven, Arthur Scott d1917 *NotNAT B, WhThe*
Craven, Elise 1898- *WhThe*
Craven, Elizabeth *NewGrD 80*
Craven, Frank d1945 *MotPP, WhoHol B*
Craven, Frank 1875-1945 *FilmEn, FilmgC, HalFC 80, HolCA[port], MovMk, NotNAT B, WhScrn 74, –77*
Craven, Frank 1878-1945 *Film 2, Vers A[port]*
Craven, Frank 1880-1945 *ForYSC, OxThe, WhThe*
Craven, Gemma 1950- *HalFC 80, WhoThe 77*
Craven, Gladys *IntWWM 77, WhoMus 72*
Craven, Hawes 1837-1910 *NotNAT B, OxThe*
Craven, Henry Thornton 1818-1905 *NotNAT B*
Craven, Robin 1906- *BiE&WWA, NotNAT*
Craven, Ruby d1964 *NotNAT B*
Craven, T A M *NewYTET*
Craven, Tom 1868-1919 *NotNAT B, WhThe*
Craven, Walter S *Film 1*
Craveri, Mario 1902- *FilmEn*
Crawford, Alice 1882- *Film 2, WhThe*
Crawford, Andrew 1917- *FilmgC, HalFC 80, WhoHol A*
Crawford, Anne 1920-1956 *FilmgC, HalFC 80, IlWWBF[port], NotNAT B, WhScrn 74, –77, WhThe, WhoHol B*
Crawford, Anne Margaret 1939- *IntWWM 77, –80*
Crawford, Bennie Ross, Jr. 1934- *EncJzS 70*
Crawford, Benny Ross, Jr. 1934- *BiDAmM*
Crawford, Bessie 1882-1943 *WhScrn 74, –77*
Crawford, Broderick *MotPP, WhoHol A*
Crawford, Broderick 1910- *BiDFilm, –81, FilmgC, HalFC 80, MovMk[port], OxFilm*
Crawford, Broderick 1911- *BiE&WWA, FilmEn, ForYSC, IntMPA 77, –75, –76, –78, –79, –80, WorEFlm[port]*
Crawford, Cheryl 1902- *BiE&WWA, EncMT, EncWT, NotNAT, PlP&P[port], WhoThe 72, –77*
Crawford, Christina *ForYSC, WhoHol A*
Crawford, Clifton *CmpEPM*
Crawford, Clifton 1875-1920 *NotNAT B, WhScrn 77*
Crawford, David B 1943- *AmSCAP 80*
Crawford, David Eugene 1939- *IntWWM 77, –80*
Crawford, Dawn Constance 1919- *ConAmC, IntWWM 77, –80*
Crawford, Dorothy Maude 1885- *BiE&WWA*
Crawford, Florence *Film 2*
Crawford, Forrest 1908- *WhoJazz 72*
Crawford, Francis Marion 1854-1909 *NotNAT B*
Crawford, Hank 1934- *EncJzS 70*
Crawford, Hector William 1913- *WhoMus 72*
Crawford, Holland R 1924- *BiDAmM*
Crawford, Howard Marion 1914-1969 *HalFC 80, WhScrn 74, –77*
Crawford, Jack 1847-1917 *WhScrn 77*
Crawford, Jack Randall 1878-1968 *BiE&WWA, NotNAT B*
Crawford, James 1910- *CmpEPM*
Crawford, Jesse 1895-1962 *AmSCAP 66, –80, CmpEPM, NotNAT B*
Crawford, Jimmy 1910- *BiDAmM, IlEncJ*
Crawford, Joan *MotPP, WhoHol A, WomWMM*
Crawford, Joan 1904- *CmMov*
Crawford, Joan 1904-1977 *FilmEn, WorEFlm*
Crawford, Joan 1906-1977 *BiDFilm, –81, FilmgC, HalFC 80, WhoHrs 80[port]*
Crawford, Joan 1908- *Film 2, ForYSC, IntMPA 77, –75, –76, MGM[port], MovMk[port], OxFilm, ThFT[port], TwYS*
Crawford, Joanna *WomWMM*
Crawford, John *HalFC 80, WhoHol A*
Crawford, John 1931- *AmSCAP 80, CpmDNM 80, ConAmC*
Crawford, John R *ForYSC*
Crawford, Johnny 1946- *ForYSC, RkOn, WhoHol A*
Crawford, Julia *OxMus*
Crawford, Louise *ConAmC*
Crawford, Michael *IntMPA 75, –76*
Crawford, Michael 1941- *ForYSC*
Crawford, Michael 1942- *FilmAG WE[port], FilmEn, FilmgC, HalFC 80, IlWWBF, IntMPA 77, –78, –79, –80, MotPP, WhoHol A, WhoThe 77*
Crawford, Mimi d1966 *WhThe*
Crawford, Nan 1893-1975 *WhScrn 77, WhoHol C*
Crawford, Paul 1925- *NewOrJ[port]*
Crawford, Richard *Film 2*
Crawford, Robert *MorBAP*
Crawford, Robert Caldwell 1925- *NewGrD 80, WhoMus 72*
Crawford, Robert M 1899-1961 *AmSCAP 66, –80, Baker 78, ConAmC*
Crawford, Ruth Porter 1901-1953 *Baker 78, BiDAmM, NewGrD 80, OxMus, WomCom[port]*
Crawford, Sam *Film 2*
Crawford, Tad 1946- *NatPD[port]*
Crawford Seeger, Ruth Porter 1901-1953 *BnBkM 80*
Crawford-Seeger, Ruth Porter 1901-1953 *ConAmC*
Crawford Seeger, Ruth Porter 1901-1953 *DcCM*
Crawley, Budge 1911- *CreCan 1*
Crawley, Constance 1879-1919 *Film 1, WhScrn 77*
Crawley, Frank Radford 1911- *CreCan 1*
Crawley, Hazel L 1921- *NatPD[port]*
Crawley, J Sayre d1948 *NotNAT B*
Crawley, James Elvin 1931- *AmSCAP 80*
Crawley, Judith 1914- *CreCan 2*
Crawley, Sayre d1948 *WhScrn 77*
Crawley, Wilton 1900- *WhoJazz 72*
Crawshaw, Caroline 1941- *WhoMus 72*
Craxton, Harold 1885-1971 *NewGrD 80, OxMus*

Craxton, Janet 1929- IntWWM 77, -80, NewGrD 80, WhoMus 72
Cray, Kevin Earl 1922- AmSCAP 80, IntWWM 77, -80
Crayford, Helen Elizabeth 1953- IntWWM 80
Crayton, Connie Curtis 1914- BluesWW[port]
Craytor, Hallie L PupTheA
Crazy Elephant RkOn 2A
Crazy Gang, The IlWWBF[port]
Crazy Horse ConMuA 80A, IlEncR
Crazy World Of Arthur Brown, The RkOn 2[port]
Crea, Jose 1924- WhoOp 76
Creach, John 1917- EncJzS 70
Cream ConMuA 80A, IlEncR[port], RkOn 2[port]
Creamer, Alice DuBois 1915- IntWWM 77, -80
Creamer, Charles 1894-1971 WhScrn 74, -77
Creamer, David 1812-1887 BiDAmM
Creamer, Henry S 1879-1930 AmSCAP 66, -80, BiDAmM, BlkAmP, BlksBF, CmpEPM
Creamer, John WhoHol A
Crean, Robert d1974 NewYTET
Creath, Charles Cyril 1890-1951 WhoJazz 72
Creatore, Giuseppe 1871-1952 Baker 78
Creatore, Luigi 1920- AmSCAP 66, -80, ConMuA 80B
Crebillon, Prosper Jolyot De 1674-1762 CnThe, EncWT, Ent, McGEWD, NotNAT B, OxThe, REnWD[port]
Crechillon, Thomas 1480?-1557? NewGrD 80
Crecquillon, Thomas 1480?-1557 Baker 78
Crecquillon, Thomas 1480?-1557? NewGrD 80
Credan, Simone Film 2
Cree Brown, Christopher John 1953- IntWWM 80
Creed, Elizabeth Mary 1933- IntWWM 77, -80
Creed, John Edward Hodgson 1904- WhoMus 72
Creed, Kay 1940- WhoOp 76
Creed, Marcus Alan 1951- IntWWM 80
Creeden, Terry L 1949- AmSCAP 80
Creedence Clearwater Revival BiDAmM, ConMuA 80A, IlEncR, RkOn 2[port]
Creedon, Dennis 1880- WhThe
Creel, Frances d1957 NotNAT B
Crees, Eric James 1952- IntWWM 80
Crees, Kathleen Elsie 1944- IntWWM 77, -80, WhoMus 72
Cregan, David 1931- ConDr 73, -77, EncWT, WhoThe 72, -77
Cregar, Laird d1944 WhoHol B
Cregar, Laird 1913-1944 WhScrn 77
Cregar, Laird 1916-1944 CmMov, FilmEn, FilmgC, ForYSC, HalFC 80, HolP 40[port], MovMk, NotNAT B, WhoHrs 80
Cregar, Laird 1916-1945 BiDFilm, -81
Cregar, Laird 1917-1944 WhScrn 74
Creger, Bill 1900-1927 NewOrJ
Creham, Joseph d1966 Film 1
Crehan, Joseph d1966 MotPP, WhoHol B
Crehan, Joseph 1884-1966 FilmgC, ForYSC, HalFC 80, MovMk
Crehan, Joseph 1886-1966 FilmEn, Vers A[port], WhScrn 74, -77
Crehan, Thomas J 1912- IntMPA 77, -75, -76, -78
Crehore, Benjamin d1819 BiDAmM
Crehore, Benjamin 1765-1831 NewGrD 80
Crehore, Tom Oliver NatPD[port]
Creighton, Cleva WhScrn 77
Creighton, Luella Sanders Bruce 1901- CreCan 2
Creighton, Robert 1636?-1734 NewGrD 80
Creighton, Robert 1639?-1734 OxMus
Creighton, Walter R Film 1
Crema, Giovanni Maria Da NewGrD 80
Cremer, Bruno 1929- FilmEn
Cremer, W H, Jr. MagIlD
Cremonese, Ambrosio NewGrD 80
Crenna, Richard IntMPA 75, -76, MotPP, WhoHol A
Crenna, Richard 1926- FilmEn, FilmgC, ForYSC, HalFC 80
Crenna, Richard 1927- IntMPA 77, -78, -79, -80, MovMk
Crenshaw, Randel L 1955- IntWWM 77, -80
Creole Jazz Band BiDAmM
Crequillon, Thomas d1557 BnBkM 80, NewGrD 80
Cresap, Sally Williss WomWMM B
Crescendos, The AmPS A, RkOn[port]
Crescentini, Girolamo 1762-1846 Baker 78, NewEOp 71, NewGrD 80
Cresci, Orazio NewGrD 80
Creser, William 1844-1933 Baker 78
Creshevsky, Noah 1945- ConAmC
Crespel, Jean NewGrD 80
Crespi, Todd WhoHol A
Crespin, Regina 1927- NewEOp 71
Crespin, Regine 1927- Baker 78, CmOp, IntWWM 77, -80, MusSN[port], NewGrD 80[port], WhoMus 72, WhoOp 76
Crespo, Jose Film 2
Cressall, Maud 1886-1962 WhThe
Cresswell, Hubert Frank 1893- WhoMus 72
Cresswell, Lyell Richard 1944- IntWWM 77, -80
Cressy, Will M 1863-1930 NotNAT A, WhoStg 1908
Cressy, William 1863-1930 NotNAT B
Creston, Paul 1906- AmSCAP 66, -80, Baker 78, BiDAmM, BnBkM 80, CompSN[port], CpmDNM 79, ConAmC, DcCM, IntWWM 77, -80, MusMk, NewGrD 80, OxMus, WhoMus 72
Crests, The AmPS A, RkOn
Creswell, Helen d1949 NotNAT B
Cretecos, James Nicholas 1948- AmSCAP 80
Cretien De Troyes NewGrD 80
Cretien, Gilles-Louis NewGrD 80
Cretien, Jean-Baptiste NewGrD 80
Cretinetti OxFilm
Creuz 1924- WhoOp 76
Crevel, Marcus Van 1890-1974 NewGrD 80
Crevena, Alfredo DcFM
Crew, Richard Page 1941- AmSCAP 80
Crew Cuts AmPS A, -B, RkOn[port]
Crewdson, Henry Alastair Fergusson 1897- WhoMus 72
Crewdson, William Richard Inge 1932- WhoMus 72
Crewe, Bertie d1937 NotNAT B
Crewe, Bob 1931- ConMuA 80B, RkOn
Crewe, Bob, Generation RkOn 2[port]
Crews, George Norman 1946- IntWWM 80
Crews, Kay C 1901-1959 WhScrn 74, -77, WhoHol B
Crews, Laura Hope 1879-1942 FilmEn, HolCA[port], ThFT[port]
Crews, Laura Hope 1880-1942 Film 1, -2, FilmgC, ForYSC, HalFC 80, MotPP, MovMk, NotNAT B, Vers A[port], WhScrn 74, -77, WhThe, WhoHol B, WhoStg 1908
Crews, Lucile 1888- ConAmC
Creyghton, Robert 1639?-1734 NewGrD 80, OxMus
Cribari, Donna Marie 1939- AmSCAP 80
Cribari, Joe 1920- AmSCAP 66, -80
Cribbins, Bernard 1928- FilmgC, HalFC 80, WhoThe 72, -77
Cribelli, Arcangelo NewGrD 80
Crichton, Charles 1910- CmMov, DcFM, FilmEn, FilmgC, HalFC 80, IlWWBF, IntMPA 77, -75, -76, -78, -79, -80, MovMk[port], OxFilm, WorEFlm
Crichton, Kyle S 1896-1960 NotNAT B
Crichton, Madge 1881- WhThe, WhoStg 1908
Crichton, Michael 1942- FilmEn, FilmgC, HalFC 80, IntMPA 77, -75, -76, -78, -79, -80, WhoHrs 80
Crichton, Ronald 1913- WhoMus 72
Crick, Monte d1969 WhoHol B
Crickets, The AmPS A, IlEncR, RkOn
Crickmay, Anthony 1937- CnOxB
Cricquillon, Thomas NewGrD 80
Crider, Clarence W 1934- AmSCAP 80
Crighton, Robert Garry 1942- IntWWM 80
Crimi, Giulio 1885-1939 NewEOp 71
Crimmins, Dan Film 2
Crimmins, Daniel 1863-1945 WhScrn 77
Criner, John Lawrence 1898-1965 BlksB&W
Criner, Lawrence 1898-1965 BlksB&W C
Crinley, William A d1927 WhScrn 74, -77, WhoHol B
Cripanuk, Michael WhoHol A
Crippen, Katie 1895-1929 BluesWW
Cripps, Kernan 1886-1953 Film 2, WhScrn 77
Crisanius, Georgius NewGrD 80
Crisci, Oratio NewGrD 80
Criscuolo, James Michael 1930- AmSCAP 80
Crisham, Walter WhThe
Crisman, Arline C d1956 WhScrn 74, -77
Crismann, Franz Xaver NewGrD 80
Crisp, Barbara ConAmC
Crisp, Clement 1931- CnOxB
Crisp, Donald d1974 MotPP, WhoHol B
Crisp, Donald 1880-1974 BiDFilm, -81, FilmEn, FilmgC, ForYSC, HalFC 80, HolCA[port], MovMk[port], OxFilm, TwYS, -A, WhScrn 77, WorEFlm[port]
Crisp, Donald 1882-1974 CmMov, Film 1, -2, Vers A[port]
Crisp, Marie Film 2
Crisp, Samuel d1783 NotNAT B, OxMus
Crisp, Wilfred 1921- WhoMus 72
Crispi, Ida WhThe, WhoStg 1908
Crispi, Pietro Maria 1737?-1797 NewGrD 80
Crispin VanStappen NewGrD 80
Criss, Louis 1925- NotNAT
Criss, Sonny 1927- CmpEPM, EncJzS 70
Criss, William 1927- BiDAmM, EncJzS 70
Crist, Abagail P -1969 PupTheA
Crist, Bainbridge 1883-1969 AmSCAP 66, -80, Baker 78, BiDAmM, ConAmC, NewGrD 80
Crist, Judith 1922- IntMPA 77, -75, -76, -78, -79, -80
Cristal, Linda 1935- FilmEn, ForYSC
Cristal, Linda 1936- FilmgC, HalFC 80, MotPP, WhoHol A
Cristaldi, Franco 1924- FilmEn, HalFC 80, IntMPA 77, -75, -76, -78, -79, -80
Cristancho, Mauricio 1946- IntWWM 77, -80
Cristescu, Mircea-Cornel 1928- WhoMus 72
Cristiani, Lisa 1827-1853 NewGrD 80
Cristina, Ines 1875- WhThe
Cristo, Luis De NewGrD 80
Cristofer, Michael 1946- DcLB 7[port]
Cristofoli, Francesco 1932- WhoOp 76
Cristoforeanu, Florica 1887-1960 NewGrD 80
Cristofori, Bartolomeo 1655-1731 NewGrD 80, OxMus
Cristofori, Bartolommeo 1655-1731 Baker 78, MusMk
Cristoforus De Feltro NewGrD 80
Cristoforus De Monte NewGrD 80
Criswick, Mary 1945- IntWWM 77, -80
Critchfield, Edward 1919- IntMPA 77, -75, -76, -78, -79, -80
Critser, William 1928- ConAmC
Crittenden, Dwight Film 1, -2
Crittenden, T D Film 1
Critters, The BiDAmM, RkOn 2[port]
Crivellati, Cesare NewGrD 80
Crivellati, Domenico NewGrD 80
Crivelli, Arcangelo 1546-1617 NewGrD 80
Crivelli, Domenico NewGrD 80
Crivelli, Filippo 1928- WhoOp 76
Crivelli, Gaetano 1768-1836 NewGrD 80
Crivelli, Giovanni Battista d1652 NewGrD 80
Crivelli, Giovanni Battista d1682 Baker 78
Crivello, Arcangelo 1546-1617 NewGrD 80
Croatti, Francesco NewGrD 80
Croce, Arlene 1934- CnOxB
Croce, Benedetto 1866-1952 NewGrD 80
Croce, Elena NewGrD 80
Croce, Giovanni 1557?-1609 BnBkM 80, MusMk, NewGrD 80
Croce, Giovanni 1560?-1609 Baker 78
Croce, Ingrid 1947- AmSCAP 80
Croce, James Joseph 1943- AmSCAP 80
Croce, Jim d1974 ConMuA 80A[port]
Croce, Jim 1942-1973 IlEncR[port]
Croce, Jim 1943-1973 RkOn 2[port]
Crochet, Evelyne 1934- WhoMus 72
Crochet, Sharon Brandstetter 1945- IntWWM 80
Croci, Antonio d1642? NewGrD 80
Crocker, Frankie 1944?- ConMuA 80B, DrBlPA
Crocker, Harry 1893-1958 Film 2, WhScrn 77
Crocker, Henry d1937 NotNAT B
Crocker, Richard L 1927- NewGrD 80
Crocker, Roger John 1948- IntWWM 77
Crocker-King, C H 1873-1951 Film 2
Crockett, Charles B 1872-1934 Film 2,

WhScrn 74, –77
Crockett, Dave ConMuA 80B
Crockett, David AmSCAP 80
Crockett, Davy 1786-1836 FilmgC, HalFC 80, OxFilm
Crockett, Jim ConMuA 80B
Croes, Henri-Jacques De 1705-1786 Baker 78, NewGrD 80
Crofoot, Alan Paul 1929- WhoOp 76
Croft, Anne 1896-1959 NotNAT B, WhThe
Croft, Douglas WhoHrs 80
Croft, Esther WomWMM
Croft, Mary Jane WhoHol A
Croft, Michael 1922- EncWT, WhoThe 72, –77
Croft, Nita 1902- WhThe
Croft, Paddy WhoThe 77
Croft, William 1678-1727 Baker 78, BnBkM 80, MusMk, NewGrD 80[port], OxMus
Crofton, Kathleen 1902- CnOxB, DancEn 78
Crofts, William 1678-1727 NewGrD 80[port]
Croise, Hugh IlWWBF
Croisset, Francis De 1877-1937 McGEWD[port], WhThe
Croix, A Sainte- CreCan 1
Croix, Antoine NewGrD 80
Croiza, Claire 1882-1946 NewGrD 80
Croke, Wentworth 1871-1930 WhThe
Croker, Sam, Jr. 1876-1914 BlksBF
Croker, T F Dillon 1831-1912 NotNAT B, WhThe
Croker-King, C H 1873-1951 WhThe, WhoHol B
Croker-King, Charles H 1873-1951 NotNAT B
Crole OxMus
Crole-Rees, Lucy Elizabeth 1911- WhoMus 72
Croleus OxMus
Croley, Randell 1946- ConAmC
Croll, Gerhard 1927- IntWWM 80, NewGrD 80
Croly, George 1780-1860 NotNAT B
Cromarty, George Michael 1941- AmSCAP 80
Crombeen, Marc-Anton Ernst 1928- IntWWM 80
Crombie, Alonzo 1895?- NewOrJ
Crombie, Anthony John 1925- EncJzS 70
Crombie, Tony 1925- EncJzS 70
Cromie, Beatrice Florence Dickson 1946- IntWWM 77, –80
Crommelynck, Fernand 1885-1970 CnMD, Ent, McGEWD[port], ModWD, REnWD[port], WhThe
Crommelynck, Fernand 1888-1970 EncWT
Crommie, Liege Film 1, –2
Crompton, Richmal 1890-1969 HalFC 80
Crompton, Richmal 1890-1970 FilmgC
Crompton, William H 1843-1909 NotNAT B
Cromwell, John Film 2, NatPD[port]
Cromwell, John 1887-1979 BiE&WWA, NotNAT, WhoHol A, WhoThe 72, –77
Cromwell, John 1888-1979 BiDFilm, –81, CmMov, DcFM, FilmEn, FilmgC, HalFC 80, MovMk[port], OxFilm, WorEFlm
Cromwell, Link AmSCAP 80
Cromwell, Oliver 1599-1658 DcPup, OxMus, PlP&P
Cromwell, Richard 1910-1960 FilmEn, FilmgC, ForYSC, HalFC 80, HolP 30[port], MovMk[port], NotNAT B, WhScrn 74, –77, WhoHol B
Cron, John B 1923- IntMPA 77, –75, –76, –78, –79, –80
Cron, Paul 1917- IntWWM 77
Crone, Adeline Leipnik d1962 NotNAT B
Crone, Tan 1930- IntWWM 80
Cronenberg, David 1948?- WhoHrs 80
Cronenweth, Jordan HalFC 80
Croner, Daniel 1656-1740 NewGrD 80
Croner, Franz Carl Thomas 1724?-1787 NewGrD 80
Croner, Johann Nepomuk 1737?-1785 NewGrD 80
Croner DeVasconcelos, Jorge 1910-1974 NewGrD 80
Cronhamn, Johan Peter 1803-1875 NewGrD 80
Cronhamn, Jons Peter 1803-1875 NewGrD 80
Cronin, A J 1896- FilmgC, HalFC 80
Cronin, Kevin P, Jr. 1951- AmSCAP 80
Cronjager, Edward 1904-1960 CmMov, FilmEn, FilmgC, HalFC 80, WorEFlm
Cronkite, Kathy WhoHol A
Cronkite, Walter 1916- IntMPA 77, –75, –76, –78, –79, –80, NewYTET
Cronquist, Robert Lee 1929- IntWWM 77, –80
Cronyn, Hume 1911- BiE&WWA, FilmEn, FilmgC, ForYSC, HalFC 80, IntMPA 77, –75, –76, –78, –79, –80, MGM[port], MotPP, MovMk[port], NotNAT, PlP&P[port], WhoHol A, WhoThe 72, –77
Crook, John d1922 NotNAT B, WhThe
Crook, Paul 1936- WhoOp 76
Crooke, Sidney WhoMus 72
Crooker, Earle T 1899- AmSCAP 66, –80, BiDAmM
Crooks, Mack 1937- ConAmC
Crooks, Richard 1900- NewEOp 71
Crooks, Richard 1900-1972 Baker 78, BiDAmM, CmOp, MusSN[port], NewGrD 80
Croom, John Robert 1941- ConAmC
Cropper, Peter John 1945- IntWWM 80
Cropper, Roy 1898-1954 NotNAT B, WhThe
Cropper, Steve 1942- ConMuA 80A, –80B, IlEncR
Cros, Charles OxMus
Crosbie, Annette 1934- HalFC 80
Crosbie, William Perry 1947- IntWWM 77, –80
Crosby, Bing d1977 AmPS A, –B, MotPP, NewYTET
Crosby, Bing 1901-1977 BiDFilm, –81, CmMov, CmpEPM, FilmgC, HalFC 80, OxFilm
Crosby, Bing 1903-1977 Baker 78, MusMk[port], WhoMus 72
Crosby, Bing 1904-1977 AmSCAP 66, FilmEn, ForYSC, IlEncJ, IntMPA 77, –75, –76, –78, MovMk[port], NewGrD 80, WhoHol A, WorEFlm[port]
Crosby, Bob AmPS B, AmSCAP 80, BgBands 74[port]
Crosby, Bob 1913- AmSCAP 66, CmpEPM, EncJzS 70, FilmgC, ForYSC, HalFC 80, IlEncJ, IntMPA 77, –75, –76, –78, –79, –80, WhoHol A
Crosby, Brian 1933- IntWWM 77
Crosby, Cathy ForYSC, WhoHol A
Crosby, Cathy Lee WhoHol A
Crosby, David 1941- AmSCAP 80, BiDAmM, ConMuA 80A, IlEncR[port]
Crosby, Dennis 1935- ForYSC, WhoHol A
Crosby, Edward Harold d1934 NotNAT B
Crosby, Fanny Jane 1820-1915 NewGrD 80
Crosby, Floyd 1899- FilmEn, FilmgC, HalFC 80, WhoHrs 80, WorEFlm
Crosby, Floyd 1900- CmMov, OxFilm
Crosby, Frances J 1820-1915 BiDAmM
Crosby, Gary 1934- ForYSC, MotPP, WhoHol A
Crosby, George Robert 1913- BiDAmM, EncJzS 70, WhoJazz 72
Crosby, George Robert 1923- AmSCAP 80
Crosby, Harry Lillis 1904-1977 AmSCAP 80, BiDAmM, NewGrD 80
Crosby, Hazel d1964 NotNAT B
Crosby, Israel 1919-1962 BiDAmM, CmpEPM, IlEncJ, WhoJazz 72
Crosby, Jack Film 2
Crosby, John 1926- Baker 78, NewGrD 80, WhoOp 76
Crosby, Juliette Film 2
Crosby, Kathryn 1933- IntMPA 77, –75, –76, –78, –79, –80
Crosby, Lindsay 1938- ForYSC, WhoHol A
Crosby, Marshal 1883 1954 WhScrn 74, –77
Crosby, Octave 1898- NewOrJ[port]
Crosby, Phillip 1935- ForYSC, WhoHol A
Crosby, Wade 1905-1975 WhScrn 77, WhoHol C
Crosby Stills Nash & Young ConMuA 80A[port], IlEncR[port], RkOn 2[port]
Crosdale, John 1929- IntWWM 80
Crosdill, John 1755-1825 NewGrD 80
Croser, Peter 1936- WhoMus 72
Croset, Paule FilmEn, FilmgC, HalFC 80, WhoHol A
Croshaw, Christine Mary 1942- IntWWM 77, –80
Croshaw, Gertrude May 1906- WhoMus 72
Crosland, Alan 1891-1936 TwYS A
Crosland, Alan 1894-1936 BiDFilm, –81, DcFM, FilmEn, FilmgC, HalFC 80, MovMk[port], WorEFlm
Crosland, Alan, Jr. Film 2
Crosley, Lawrence E 1932- IntWWM 80
Crosman, Henrietta d1944 PlP&P, WhoHol B
Crosman, Henrietta 1861-1944 FamA&A[port], HalFC 80, HolCA[port], NotNAT B, ThFT[port], WhScrn 74, –77
Crosman, Henrietta 1865-1944 Film 1, WhThe
Crosman, Henrietta 1871-1944 WhoStg 1906, –1908
Crosman, Henriette 1865-1944 Film 2
Cross, Alfred Francis 1891-1938 WhScrn 74, –77, WhoHol B
Cross, Allen Eastman 1864-1943 BiDAmM
Cross, Benjamin 1786-1857 BiDAmM
Cross, Beverley 1931- ConDr 73, –77, WhoThe 72, –77
Cross, Chris PupTheA
Cross, Dennis WhoHol A
Cross, Douglass 1920- AmSCAP 66, –80
Cross, Else 1907- WhoMus 72
Cross, Eric 1902- FilmgC, HalFC 80
Cross, Frank Leroy 1904- AmSCAP 80
Cross, Hugh 1904- IlEncCM
Cross, Jimmie d1978 AmSCAP 66, –80
Cross, Jimmy WhoHol A
Cross, Joan 1900- CmOp, IntWWM 77, –80, NewGrD 80[port], WhoMus 72
Cross, John S d1976 NewYTET
Cross, Julian 1851-1925 WhThe
Cross, Letitia 1681?-1725? NewGrD 80
Cross, Lowell 1938- Baker 78, ConAmC, DcCM
Cross, Michael Hurley 1833-1897 BiDAmM
Cross, Milton J 1897-1975 NewEOp 71, WhScrn 77
Cross, Moses Smith 1854-1911 BiDAmM
Cross, Norma 1917- IntWWM 77, –80
Cross, Perry IntMPA 77, –75, –76, –78, –79, –80
Cross, Rhoda M Film 2
Cross, Richard Bruce 1935- WhoOp 76
Cross, Roger Meston WhoMus 72
Cross, Ronald 1929- Baker 78, ConAmC, IntWWM 77, –80
Cross, Thomas 1660?-1735? NewGrD 80
Cross, Vernon AmSCAP 80
Cross, Wellington PlP&P[port]
Cross, William Samuel 1952- IntWWM 80
Crosse, Gordon 1937- Baker 78, CmOp, DcCM, IntWWM 77, –80, NewGrD 80, OxMus, WhoMus 72
Crosse, Rupert 1927?-1973 DrBlPA, HalFC 80
Crosse, Rupert 1928-1973 WhScrn 77, WhoHol B
Crossett, David Allen 1941- ConAmTC
Crosskey, Gordon 1938- WhoMus 72
Crossland, Anthony 1931- IntWWM 77, –80
Crossley, Ada 1874-1929 Baker 78
Crossley, Paul Christopher Richard 1944- IntWWM 77, –80, NewGrD 80, WhoMus 72
Crossley, Sid 1885-1960 WhScrn 74, –77, WhoHol B
Crossley, Syd 1885-1960 Film 2, HalFC 80, IlWWBF
Crossley-Holland, Peter Charles 1916- IntWWM 77, –80, NewGrD 80, WhoMus 72
Crossley-Taylor, E W d1963 NotNAT B
Crossman, Allan ConAmC
Crossman, Henrietta 1861-1944 ForYSC
Crosswell, Anne Pearson AmSCAP 66
Crosswell, William 1804-1851 BiDAmM
Crosten, William Loran 1909- IntWWM 77, –80, WhoMus 72
Crosthwaite, Ivy 1898-1962 Film 1, WhScrn 77, WhoHol B
Croswell, Anna NotNAT
Croswell, Anne BiE&WWA
Croswell, Anne Pearson AmSCAP 80
Crotch, William 1775-1847 Baker 78, MusMk, NewGrD 80[port], OxMus
Crothers, Benjamin Sherman 1910- AmSCAP 80
Crothers, Bert 1937- AmSCAP 80
Crothers, J Frances PupTheA

Crothers, Rachel 1878-1958 *CnMD, CnThe, DcLB 7[port], FilmgC, HalFC 80, McGEWD[port], ModWD, NotNAT B, OxThe, REnWD[port], WhThe, WomWMM*
Crothers, Scatman 1910- *DrBlPA, WhoHol A*
Crothers, Sherman 1910- *AmSCAP 66*
Crothers, Shirley Evans *AmSCAP 80*
Crotte, Nicolas DeLa *NewGrD 80*
Crotti, Archangelo *NewGrD 80*
Crotti, Francesco *NewGrD 80*
Crotty, Michael 1950- *ConAmC*
Crouch, Andrae Edward 1942- *AmSCAP 80, NewGrD 80*
Crouch, Anna Maria 1763-1805 *NewGrD 80*
Crouch, Frederick Nicholls 1808-1896 *Baker 78, NewGrD 80, OxMus*
Crouch, Frederick W Nichols 1808-1896 *BiDAmM*
Crouch, Jack H 1918- *BiE&WWA, NotNAT*
Crouch, Margaret Cecelia Long 1937- *IntWWM 77, -80*
Crouch, Orville 1912- *IntMPA 75, -76*
Crouch, Stanley 1945- *EncJzS 70*
Crouch, Worth 1917-1943 *WhScrn 74, -77*
Crouse, Lindsay *IntMPA 78, -79, -80*
Crouse, Russel 1893-1966 *BiE&WWA, CnThe, EncMT, EncWT, HalFC 80, McGEWD, ModWD, NewCBMT, NotNAT B, WhThe*
Crouse, Russell 1893-1966 *BiDAmM*
Crow *RkOn 2A*
Crow, Todd 1945- *IntWWM 77, -80*
Crow, William Orval 1927- *BiDAmM*
Crow Bait, Ophelia Mae *AmSCAP 80*
Crowden, Graham 1922- *PlP&P, WhoThe 72, -77*
Crowder, Jack *DrBlPA*
Crowder, Laurin Peyton 1927- *IntWWM 77*
Crowder, Robert Henry 1912- *WhoJazz 72*
Crowe, Cameron *ConMuA 80B*
Crowe, Eyre Alexander 1947- *IntWWM 77, -80*
Crowe, Gillian 1934- *BiE&WWA*
Crowe, Peter Russell 1942- *IntWWM 77, -80*
Crowell, Arthur *Film 2*
Crowell, Bubbles *Film 2*
Crowell, Burt 1873-1946 *WhScrn 74, -77*
Crowell, Joseph *Film 2*
Crowell, Josephine d1929 *Film 1, -2, TwYS*
Crowest, Frederick J 1850-1927 *Baker 78*
Crowley, Alice Lewisohn *BiE&WWA*
Crowley, Anne *WhoMus 72*
Crowley, Kathleen 1930- *ForYSC, WhoHol A*
Crowley, Kathleen 1931- *FilmEn*
Crowley, Mart 1935- *ConDr 77, DcLB 7[port], McGEWD, NatPD[port], NotNAT, WhoThe 77*
Crowley, Matt *WhoHol A*
Crowley, Pat 1929- *FilmgC, HalFC 80, MotPP*
Crowley, Pat 1933- *FilmEn*
Crowley, Patricia 1933- *ForYSC, WhoHol A*
Crowley, Peter *ConMuA 80B*
Crowley, Robert 1518?-1588 *OxMus*
Crowley, Robert Dennis 1921- *ConAmC*
Crown, Alfred W 1913- *IntMPA 77, -75, -76, -78, -79, -80*
Crown, Helen Barbara 1951- *IntWWM 80*
Crown Jewels, The *BiDAmM*
Crowne, John 1640?-1703? *McGEWD, OxThe*
Crowne, John 1640?-1710? *NotNAT B*
Crowne, John 1640?-1712 *NewGrD 80*
Crows, The *RkOn[port]*
Crowson, Lamar *WhoMus 72*
Crowther, Bosley *IntMPA 77, -75, -76, -78, -79, -80*
Crowther, Cecile Marguerite *WhoMus 72*
Crowther, Leslie 1933- *WhoThe 72, -77*
Croxford, Eileen 1924- *IntWWM 77, -80, WhoMus 72*
Croxton, Arthur 1868- *WhThe*
Croy, Homer 1883-1965 *WhScrn 77*
Croydon, John 1907- *IntMPA 77, -75, -76, -78, -79, -80*
Crozet, Simone *WomWMM*
Crozier, Catharine 1914- *NewGrD 80, WhoMus 72*
Crozier, David E 1863-1935 *BiDAmM*
Crozier, Eric John 1914- *CmOp, NewEOp 71, WhoMus 72*
Crozier, James Alvin 1951- *AmSCAP 80*
Crozier, Nancy *NewGrD 80*
Cruchon, Pierre 1908- *WhoMus 72*
Crudup, Arthur 1905-1974 *BluesWW[port]*
Crudup, Carl W *DrBlPA*
Crudup, Percy Lee *BluesWW*
Crudux, Art *BluesWW*
Cruea, Edmond D 1918- *IntMPA 79, -80*
Cruft, Adrian 1921- *IntWWM 77, -80, NewGrD 80, WhoMus 72*
Cruft, Eugene John *WhoMus 72*
Cruft, Eugene John 1887-1976 *NewGrD 80*
Cruft, John Herbert 1914- *WhoMus 72*
Cruger, Johann 1598-1662 *Baker 78, BnBkM 80, OxMus*
Cruger, Johannes 1598-1662 *NewGrD 80*
Cruger, Pancratius 1546-1615? *NewGrD 80*
Cruickshank, Alistair Urquhart 1909- *IntWWM 80, WhoMus 72*
Cruickshank, Andrew 1907- *FilmgC, HalFC 80, PlP&P, WhoHol A, WhoThe 72, -77*
Cruickshank, Gladys 1902- *WhThe*
Cruikshank, A Stewart 1877-1949 *WhThe*
Cruikshank, George 1792-1878 *DcPup*
Cruikshank, Sally *WomWMM B*
Cruikshank, Stewart 1908-1966 *WhThe*
Cruikshanks, Charles 1844-1928 *WhThe*
Crum, Dorothy Edith 1944- *IntWWM 77, -80*
Crum, George 1926- *DancEn 78*
Crum, Simon *IlEncCM*
Crum, Simon 1899- *EncFCWM 69[port]*
Crumb, Earl 1899- *NewOrJ[port]*
Crumb, George 1929- *Baker 78, BnBkM 80, CpmDNM 72, -79, CnOxB, ConAmC, DcCM, IntWWM 77, -80, MusMk, NewGrD 80*
Crumb, Sarah F *PupTheA*
Crumbley, Elmer E 1908- *WhoJazz 72*
Crume, Camilla 1874-1952 *WhScrn 74, -77*
Crumit, Frank *AmPS B*
Crumit, Frank 1888-1943 *NotNAT B*
Crumit, Frank 1889-1943 *AmSCAP 66, -80, BiDAmM, CmpEPM, EncMT*
Crummles, Vincent *OxThe*
Crump, Arthur *BluesWW[port]*
Crump, Frank 1903-1957 *NewOrJ*
Crump, Jesse 1906- *BluesWW*
Crump, Peter Norman 1928- *WhoMus 72*
Crunden-White, Paul William 1937- *WhoMus 72*
Crusaders, The *ConMuA 80A, EncJzS 70, IlEncR, RkOn 2[port]*
Crusell, Bernhard Henrik 1775-1838 *NewGrD 80*
Crusius, Johann *NewGrD 80*
Cruster, Aud 1889-1938 *WhScrn 74, -77, WhoHol B*
Crusto, Manuel 1918- *NewOrJ SUP[port]*
Crutcher, Jay Leroy 1951- *AmSCAP 80*
Crutchfield, Edmund Allday 1943- *IntWWM 77, -80*
Crutchfield, Kevin 1953- *AmSCAP 80*
Crutchley, Rosalie 1921- *FilmgC, HalFC 80, WhThe, WhoHol A, WhoThe 72*
Crute, Sally 1886-1971 *Film 1, -2, WhScrn 74, -77, WhoHol B*
Cruttwell, Hugh 1918- *WhoThe 72, -77*
Cruvelli, Jeanne Sophie Charlotte 1826-1907 *NewGrD 80*
Cruwell, Jeanne Sophie Charlotte 1826-1907 *NewGrD 80*
Crux, June Roper *CreCan 1*
Cruz, Agostinho Da 1590?-1632? *NewGrD 80*
Cruz, Domingo Santa *DcCM*
Cruz, Filipe Da 1603?-1668? *NewGrD 80*
Cruz, Ivo 1901- *Baker 78, DcCM, IntWWM 77, -80, NewGrD 80*
Cruz, Ramon DeLa 1731-1794 *McGEWD[port]*
Cruz, Richard H 1929- *IntWWM 77, -80*
Cruz, Sor Juana Ines DeLa 1648?-1695 *CnThe, REnWD[port]*
Cruz, Sor Juana Ines DeLa 1651-1695 *OxThe*
Cruz Brocarte, Antonio DeLa *NewGrD 80*
Cruz Cano Y Olmedilla, Ramon F DeLa 1731-1794 *OxThe*
Cruz-Romo, Gilda *IntWWM 80, WhoOp 76*
Cruze, James d1942 *WhoHol B, WomWMM*
Cruze, James 1884-1942 *AmFD, BiDFilm, -81, CmMov, DcFM, FilmEn, Film 1, FilmgC, HalFC 80, MovMk[port], NotNAT B, OxFilm, TwYS A, WorEFlm*
Cruze, James 1894-1942 *WhScrn 74, -77*
Cruze, Mae 1891-1965 *WhScrn 74, -77, WhoHol B*
Cruzon, Virginia *WhoHol A*
Cryan' Shames, The *RkOn 2[port]*
Cryer, David 1936- *NotNAT, WhoThe 77*
Cryer, Gretchen *ConDr 73, -77D*
Cryin' Red *BluesWW*
Crystal, Lester *NewYTET*
Crystals, The *RkOn[port]*
Csaba, Janos 1938- *IntWWM 77, -80*
Csaba, Jerry L 1940- *IntWWM 77, -80*
Csanyi, Janos 1931- *WhoOp 76*
Csarnoy, Katalin 1948- *CnOxB*
Csatkai, Endre 1896-1970 *NewGrD 80*
Cselenyi, Jozsef 1928- *CreCan 2*
Csermak, Antal Gyorgy 1774?-1822 *NewGrD 80*
Csiky, Boldizsar 1937- *Baker 78, IntWWM 80, NewGrD 80*
Csiky, Gergely 1842-1891 *McGEWD[port], OxThe*
Csokor, Franz Theodor 1885-1969 *CnMD, CroCD, EncWT, McGEWD[port], ModWD*
Csokor, Franz Theodor 1891-1969 *OxThe*
Csomasz Toth, Kalman 1902- *NewGrD 80*
Ctesibius *Baker 78, NewGrD 80*
Cubbage, John 1937- *ConAmC*
Cuber, Ronald Edward 1941- *EncJzS 70*
Cuber, Ronnie 1941- *EncJzS 70*
Cubiles, Jose 1894-1971 *Baker 78*
Cubillo DeAragon, Alvaro 1596?-1661 *McGEWD*
Cubr, Antonin 1904- *IntWWM 77, -80*
Cuccaro, Costanza *WhoOp 76*
Cucchi, Claudina 1834?-1913 *CnOxB*
Cucchi, Claudine 1838-1913 *DancEn 78*
Cucciolla, Ricardo 1932- *FilmgC, HalFC 80*
Cuchetti, Richard Frank 1937- *AmSCAP 80*
Cucinotta, Robert Edward 1949- *AmSCAP 80*
Cuckston, Alan George 1940- *IntWWM 77, -80, WhoMus 72*
Cuclin, Dimitri 1885- *Baker 78*
Cuclin, Dimitrie 1885- *NewGrD 80*
Cucu, Gheorghe 1882-1932 *NewGrD 80*
Cucuel, Georges 1884-1918 *NewGrD 80*
Cudworth, C L 1908- *WhoMus 72*
Cudworth, Charles Leonard 1908- *IntWWM 77*
Cudworth, Charles Leonard 1908-1977 *Baker 78, NewGrD 80*
Cuellar Y Altarriba, Ramon Felix 1777-1833 *NewGrD 80*
Cuenca, Pedro Fernandez d1940 *NotNAT B*
Cuenod, Hughes 1902- *WhoMus 72*
Cuenod, Hugues 1902- *Baker 78, BnBkM 80, CmOp, IntWWM 77, NewGrD 80*
Cuenot, Yves 1951- *IntWWM 77, -80*
Cueto, German *PupTheA*
Cueto, Lola *PupTheA*
Cueva, Juan DeLa 1550?-1610? *McGEWD[port], OxThe*
Cueva, Juan DeLa 1550?-1615? *NotNAT B*
Cuevas, Francisca Pulido 1861- *PupTheA*
Cuevas, George, Marquis De 1885-1961 *CnOxB*
Cuff Links, The *RkOn 2[port]*
Cuffee, Edward Emerson 1902-1959 *WhoJazz 72*
Cugat, Carmen d1967 *WhoHol B*
Cugat, Xavier 1900- *AmPS B, Baker 78, BgBands 74[port], BiDAmM, CmpEPM, FilmEn, FilmgC, ForYSC, HalFC 80, WhoHol A*
Cugley, Ian 1945- *Baker 78, DcCM, IntWWM 77, -80, NewGrD 80*
Cui, Cesar 1835-1918 *Baker 78, BnBkM 80, CmOp, DcCom&M 79, GrComp[port], MusMk, NewEOp 71, NewGrD 80[port], OxMus*
Cuka, Frances 1936- *WhoThe 72, -77*
Cukor, George 1899- *AmFD, BiDFilm, -81, BiE&WWA, CmMov, DcFM, FilmEn, FilmgC, HalFC 80, IntMPA 77, -75, -76, -78, -79, -80, MovMk[port], NewYTET, OxFilm, WorEFlm*
Culbertson, Alexander 1894-1944 *Baker 78*
Culbertson, Earl 1897- *AmSCAP 66*

Culbertson, Melvin W 1946- *IntWWM 77, -80*
Culbertson, Roy Frederich 1946- *AmSCAP 80*
Culbreath, Edward Blake 1941- *IntWWM 77, -80*
Culder, Mary *Film 2*
Culkin, John *NewYTET*
Cull, Howard *Film 2*
Cull, Robert M 1949- *AmSCAP 80*
Cullaz, Albert 1941- *EncJzS 70*
Cullaz, Alby 1941- *EncJzS 70*
Cullaz, Pierre 1935- *EncJzS 70*
Cullberg, Birgit 1908- *CnOxB, DancEn 78[port]*
Cullen, Antony John 1930- *WhoMus 72*
Cullen, Arthur *Film 2*
Cullen, Bill 1920- *IntMPA 77, -75, -76, -78, -79, -80, NewYTET*
Cullen, Countee 1903-1946 *BlkAmP, DrBlPA, MorBAP*
Cullen, Edward 1899- *BiE&WWA*
Cullen, Edward L d1964 *NotNAT B*
Cullen, James F *Film 2*
Cullen, James V 1938- *IntMPA 77, -75, -76, -78, -79, -80*
Cullen, John Gavin 1936- *IntWWM 80, WhoMus 72*
Cullen, Maurice Galbraith 1866-1934 *CreCan 2*
Culley, Frederick 1879-1942 *NotNAT B, WhThe, WhoHol B*
Culley, Wendell Philips 1906- *WhoJazz 72*
Cullinan, Ralph d1950 *NotNAT B*
Cullington, Margaret 1891-1925 *Film 2, WhScrn 74, -77, WhoHol B*
Cullman, Howard S 1891-1972 *BiE&WWA, NotNAT B*
Cullman, Marguerite *BiE&WWA, NotNAT*
Cullum, John 1930- *EncMT, NotNAT, WhoHol A, WhoThe 77*
Cully, Wendell Philips 1906- *BiDAmM*
Cully, Zara *DrBlPA*
Culmell, Joaquin Nin *DcCM*
Culp, Julia 1880-1970 *Baker 78, MusSN[port], NewGrD 80*
Culp, Robert *IntMPA 75, -76*
Culp, Robert 1930- *FilmEn, FilmgC, HalFC 80, IntMPA 77, -78, -79, -80, MotPP, WhoHol A*
Culp, Robert 1931- *ForYSC*
Culpepper, Edward J 1903-1979 *AmSCAP 66, -80*
Culshaw, John Royds 1924- *IntWWM 77, -80, NewGrD 80, WhoMus 72*
Culver, D Jay 1902- *BiE&WWA*
Culver, David Jay 1902-1968 *NotNAT B*
Culver, Roland 1900- *BiE&WWA, FilmEn, FilmgC, ForYSC, HalFC 80, IlWWBF, IntMPA 77, -75, -76, -78, -79, -80, MovMk, NotNAT, WhoHol A, WhoThe 72, -77*
Culver, Rolland Pierce 1908- *BiDAmM*
Culverwell, Andrew Robert 1944- *AmSCAP 80*
Culwick, James C 1845-1907 *Baker 78*
Cumali, Necati 1921- *REnWD[port]*
Cumberland, Alan 1945- *WhoMus 72*
Cumberland, Gerald 1879-1926 *NotNAT B, WhThe*
Cumberland, Gerald 1881-1926 *Baker 78*
Cumberland, John d1866 *NotNAT B*
Cumberland, John 1880- *Film 1, WhThe*
Cumberland, Richard 1732-1811 *EncWT, McGEWD[port], NotNAT B, OxThe, PlP&P*
Cumberland Ridge Runners, The *IlEncCM*
Cumberworth, Starling A 1915- *Baker 78, ConAmC*
Cumbo, Clarissa Wilhelmina 1903- *BlkWAB[port]*
Cumbuka, Ji-Tu *DrBlPA*
Cummerford, Tom *Film 1*
Cumming, Dorothy *Film 2*
Cumming, Richard 1928- *AmSCAP 66, -80, ConAmC*
Cumming, Ruth 1904-1967 *WhScrn 74, -77*
Cummings, Bob 1910- *BiE&WWA, IntMPA 77, -75, -76, -78, -79, -80, WorEFlm[port]*
Cummings, Burton 1947- *ConMuA 80A, RkOn 2[port]*
Cummings, Claudia 1941- *WhoOp 76*
Cummings, Constance 1910- *BiE&WWA, CnThe, FilmEn, FilmgC, ForYSC, HalFC 80, HolP 30[port], IlWWBF, IntMPA 77, -75, -76, -78, -79, -80, MotPP, MovMk[port], NotNAT, ThFT[port], WhoHol A, WhoThe 72, -77*
Cummings, Diana 1941- *IntWWM 77, -80*
Cummings, Diane M 1952- *IntWWM 77, -80*
Cummings, Dorothy *Film 2, ForYSC, TwYS*
Cummings, Douglas 1946- *WhoMus 72*
Cummings, E E 1894-1962 *AmSCAP 80, CnMD, McGEWD[port], ModWD, NewGrD 80*
Cummings, Edward Estlin 1894-1962 *NotNAT B*
Cummings, Frances d1923 *WhScrn 74, -77*
Cummings, Henry 1906- *IntWWM 77, -80, WhoMus 72*
Cummings, Irving 1888-1959 *CmMov, FilmEn, Film 1, -2, FilmgC, HalFC 80, MovMk[port], TwYS, -A, WhScrn 74, -77, WhoHol B*
Cummings, Irving, Jr. *IntMPA 77, -75, -76, -78, -79, -80*
Cummings, Jack *IntMPA 77, -75, -76, -78, -79, -80*
Cummings, Jack 1900- *CmMov, FilmEn, FilmgC, HalFC 80*
Cummings, Jack 1906- *WorEFlm*
Cummings, Keith 1906- *IntWWM 77, -80, WhoMus 72*
Cummings, Patricia Hager 1924- *AmSCAP 66, -80*
Cummings, Richard 1858-1938 *Film 1, -2, WhScrn 74, -77, WhoHol B*
Cummings, Robert 1867-1949 *Film 1, WhScrn 77*
Cummings, Robert 1908- *FilmEn, FilmgC, HalFC 80, MovMk[port]*
Cummings, Robert 1910- *ForYSC, MotPP, WhoHol A, WorEFlm*
Cummings, Sandy 1913- *IntMPA 77, -75, -76, -78, -79, -80*
Cummings, Susan *ForYSC*
Cummings, Vicki d1969 *BiE&WWA, WhoHol B*
Cummings, Vicki 1913-1969 *NotNAT B, WhThe*
Cummings, Vicki 1919-1969 *WhScrn 74, -77*
Cummings, W H 1831-1915 *NewGrD 80*
Cummings, William Hayman 1831-1915 *Baker 78, OxMus*
Cummings, Winford Claude, Jr. 1919- *IntWWM 77, -80*
Cummins, Bernie *BgBands 74, CmpEPM*
Cummins, Betty 1933- *BiDAmM*
Cummins, Cecil *BlkAmP*
Cummins, Dwight W 1901- *IntMPA 77, -75, -76, -78, -79, -80*
Cummins, Evelyn 1891- *BiDAmM*
Cummins, Peggy *MotPP*
Cummins, Peggy 1925- *FilmEn, FilmgC, ForYSC, HalFC 80, IlWWBF, WhThe, WhoHol A*
Cummins, Peggy 1926- *IntMPA 77, -75, -76, -78, -79, -80*
Cummins, Richard 1936- *ConAmC*
Cumpson, John R *Film 1*
Cumpson, John R 1868-1913 *WhScrn 77*
Cunard, Grace d1967 *MotPP, WhoHol B, WomWMM*
Cunard, Grace 1893-1967 *Film 1, -2, FilmgC, HalFC 80, TwYS, WhScrn 77*
Cunard, Grace 1894-1967 *FilmEn, WhScrn 74*
Cunard, Mina *Film 1*
Cundall, C W *Film 2*
Cundari, Emilia 1933- *CreCan 2*
Cundell, Edric 1893-1961 *Baker 78, NewGrD 80, OxMus*
Cundick, Robert Milton 1926- *AmSCAP 80, ConAmC*
Cunelier *NewGrD 80*
Cuneo, Lester 1888-1925 *FilmEn, Film 1, -2, TwYS, WhScrn 77, WhoHol B*
Cuneo, Linda Boring 1945- *IntWWM 77, -80*
Cuney-Hare, Maude 1874-1936 *BlkAmP*
Cunha, Brasilio Itibere Da 1846-1913 *NewGrD 80*
Cunha, Joao Itibere Da 1869-1953 *NewGrD 80*
Cunha, Richard *WhoHrs 80*
Cuninggim, Maud 1874- *BiDAmM*
Cuningham, Juliet Elizabeth 1928- *IntWWM 77*
Cuningham, Philip 1865- *WhThe*
Cunkle, Frank 1905- *AmSCAP 80*
Cunliffe, Richard R 1906-1968 *AmSCAP 66, -80*
Cunliffe, Whit *WhThe*
Cunning, Patrick *Film 2*
Cunningham, Aloysius d1936 *WhScrn 74, -77*
Cunningham, Arthur d1955 *NotNAT B*
Cunningham, Arthur 1928- *AmSCAP 66, -80, BiDAmM, CpmDNM 80, ConAmC, DrBlPA, NewGrD 80*
Cunningham, Cecil 1888-1959 *Film 2, ForYSC, HolCA[port], ThFT[port], WhScrn 77, WhoHol B*
Cunningham, G D 1878-1948 *NewGrD 80*
Cunningham, George 1904-1962 *NotNAT B, WhScrn 74, -77, WhoHol B*
Cunningham, Glenn 1912- *What 2[port]*
Cunningham, Hallie *PupTheA*
Cunningham, James 1938- *CmpGMD[port], CnOxB*
Cunningham, Joe 1890-1943 *WhScrn 77*
Cunningham, John d1773 *NotNAT B*
Cunningham, John Collins 1950- *AmSCAP 80*
Cunningham, Juliet Elizabeth 1928- *IntWWM 80*
Cunningham, Louis Arthur 1900-1954 *CreCan 2*
Cunningham, Merce 1919- *CmpGMD[port], CnOxB, ConDr 73, -77E, DancEn 78[port]*
Cunningham, Michael Gerald 1937- *AmSCAP 80, CpmDNM 76, -77, -78, -79, ConAmC*
Cunningham, Paul 1890-1960 *AmSCAP 66, -80*
Cunningham, Phyllis Fenn *WomWMM B*
Cunningham, Robert *Film 2*
Cunningham, Robert 1866- *WhThe*
Cunningham, Mrs. Rudolph 1907- *AmSCAP 66, -80*
Cunningham, Sarah *WhoHol A*
Cunningham, Sean S *WhoHrs 80*
Cunningham, Vera *Film 1*
Cunningham, Zamah 1893-1967 *WhScrn 74, -77, WhoHol B*
Cunninghame, Agnes Jane Winifred *WhoMus 72*
Cunnington, Phillis *BiE&WWA*
Cunny, Joe *Film 2*
Cuno, Johann *NewGrD 80*
Cuny, Alain 1908- *EncWT, Ent, FilmEn, FilmgC, HalFC 80, OxFilm, WhoHol A*
Cuny, Frank 1890-1966 *NewOrJ*
Cuny, Joe *Film 1*
Cuoco, Joyce 1953- *CnOxB*
Cuomo, Edward A 1925- *AmSCAP 66*
Cuomo, James *ConAmC*
Cupers, Jean-Louis 1946- *IntWWM 77, -80*
Cupis, Ferdinand-Joseph 1684-1757 *NewGrD 80*
Cupis, Francois 1732-1808 *NewGrD 80*
Cupis, Jean-Baptiste 1711-1788 *NewGrD 80*
Cupis, Marie-Anne 1710-1770 *NewGrD 80*
Cupis DeCamargo *NewGrD 80*
Cupper, Ralph John 1954- *IntWWM 80*
Cuppett, Charles Harold 1894- *AmSCAP 66, -80, ConAmC A*
Cuppi DeCamargo *NewGrD 80*
Cuppis DeCamargo *NewGrD 80*
Curb, Mike *ConMuA 80B*
Curbelo, Fausto 1911- *AmSCAP 66, -80*
Curbishley, Bill *ConMuA 80B*
Curci, Gennaro 1888-1955 *WhScrn 77*
Curci, Giuseppe 1808-1877 *Baker 78*
Curea, Marie Brown 1931- *IntWWM 77*
Curel, Francois De 1854-1928 *CnMD, EncWT, Ent, McGEWD[port], ModWD, NotNAT B, WhThe*
Curel, Francois De 1854-1929 *OxThe*
Curess, Richard 1893- *IntWWM 80*
Curiel, Federico *WhoHrs 80*
Curioni, Alberico 1785-1875 *NewGrD 80*
Curioni, Rosa *NewGrD 80*
Curl, Langston W 1899- *WhoJazz 72*
Curless, Dick 1932- *CounME 74[port], -74A, EncFCWM 69, IlEncCM[port]*
Curless, Richard 1932- *BiDAmM*
Curletto, Giorgio Francesco 1937- *AmSCAP 80*
Curley, Miss *Film 1*

Curley, James *Film 1*
Curley, Leo 1878-1960 *WhScrn 77*
Curley, Pauline *Film 1, -2*
Curley, Wilma 1937- *CnOxB*
Curll, Edmund d1747 *NotNAT B*
Curnoe, Gregory Richard 1936- *CreCan 1*
Curnow, Allen 1911- *ConDr 73, -77*
Curnow, James Edward 1943- *AmSCAP 80*
Curnow, Robert H 1941- *ConAmC, EncJzS 70*
Curnutt, John Paul 1939- *AmSCAP 80*
Curphey, Geraldine Casterline 1921- *IntWWM 77*
Curphey, Margaret 1938- *CmOp, IntWWM 77, -80, NewGrD 80, WhoOp 76*
Currah, Brian Mason 1929- *WhoThe 72, -77*
Curran, Alvin 1938- *ConAmC*
Curran, Sir Charles *NewYTET*
Curran, Homer F d1952 *NotNAT B*
Curran, Pearl Gildersleeve 1875-1941 *AmSCAP 66, -80, Baker 78, ConAmC*
Curran, Thomas A 1880-1941 *WhScrn 74, -77, WhoHol B*
Currer-Briggs, Arthur Noel 1925- *WhoMus 72*
Currie, Clive 1877-1935 *NotNAT B, WhThe, WhoHol B*
Currie, Finlay 1878-1968 *CmMov, FilmAG WE, FilmEn, FilmgC, ForYSC, HalFC 80, IlWWBF, MotPP, MovMk, NotNAT B, Vers A[port], WhScrn 74, -77, WhThe, WhoHol B*
Currie, George *Film 2*
Currie, Glenne 1926- *ConAmTC*
Currie, John 1934- *IntWWM 77, -80, WhoMus 72*
Currie, Louise *WhoHol A*
Currie, Randolph Newell 1943- *ConAmC*
Currie, Thomas A 1929- *BiE&WWA*
Currier, Art *Film 2*
Currier, Everett Raymond 1877-1954 *BiDAmM*
Currier, Frank 1857-1928 *Film 1, -2, MotPP, NotNAT B, TwYS, WhScrn 74, -77, WhoHol B*
Currier, Ruth 1926- *CmpGMD, CnOxB, DancEn 78*
Curris, Irwin d1972 *AmSCAP 66, -80*
Currlin, Lee *NewYTET*
Curro, John Ronald 1932- *IntWWM 80*
Curry, Arthur Mansfield 1866-1953 *Baker 78, BiDAmM*
Curry, Carol Anne Isabelle 1943- *IntWWM 80*
Curry, Carrol Anne Isabelle 1943- *IntWWM 77*
Curry, Diane 1942- *IntWWM 80*
Curry, Donna Jayne 1939- *IntWWM 77, -80*
Curry, Dora Dean 1911-1931 *WhScrn 77*
Curry, Jack A 1902- *AmSCAP 66, -80*
Curry, John *Film 2*
Curry, Richard Orr 1931- *AmSCAP 66*
Curry, W Lawrence 1906-1966 *AmSCAP 66, -80, ConAmC A*
Curry-Jones, Beulah Agnes 1933- *IntWWM 77*
Curschmann, Karl Friedrich 1804-1841 *Baker 78*
Curschmann, Karl Friedrich 1805-1841 *NewGrD 80*
Cursi, Bernardo *NewGrD 80*
Cursio, Jan *AmSCAP 80*
Curson, Ted 1935- *EncJzS 70*
Curson, Theodore 1935- *BiDAmM, EncJzS 70, IntWWM 77, -80*
Curti, Franz 1854-1898 *Baker 78*
Curtin, John P 1915- *IntMPA 77, -75, -76, -78, -79, -80*
Curtin, Noel John Joseph 1918- *WhoMus 72*
Curtin, Phyllis *IntWWM 77, -80, WhoMus 72*
Curtin, Phyllis 1922- *Baker 78, MusSN[port], NewGrD 80*
Curtin, Phyllis 1927- *NewEOp 71*
Curtin, Phyllis 1930- *CmOp*
Curtis, Alan 1893-1953 *ForYSC*
Curtis, Alan 1909-1953 *FilmEn, FilmgC, HalFC 80, MotPP, NotNAT B, WhScrn 74, -77, WhoHol B*
Curtis, Alan 1934- *IntWWM 77, -80, NewGrD 80*
Curtis, Allen d1961 *NotNAT B, WhoHol B*
Curtis, Beatrice 1901-1963 *WhScrn 74, -77, WhoHol B*
Curtis, Billy *WhoHol A*
Curtis, Billy 1885-1954 *AmSCAP 66, -80*
Curtis, Billy 1911?- *WhoHrs 80*
Curtis, Chris *ConMuA 80B*
Curtis, Dan 1928- *HalFC 80, IntMPA 77, -75, -76, -78, -79, -80, NewYTET, WhoHrs 80*
Curtis, Dick 1902-1952 *FilmEn, ForYSC, Vers B[port], WhScrn 74, -77, WhoHol B*
Curtis, Eddie 1927- *AmSCAP 66, -80*
Curtis, Edgar *ConAmC*
Curtis, Eric Joseph 1899- *WhoMus 72*
Curtis, George William 1824-1892 *BiDAmM*
Curtis, H Holbrook 1856-1920 *BiDAmM*
Curtis, Jack 1880-1956 *Film 1, -2, TwYS, WhScrn 74, -77, WhoHol B*
Curtis, Jack B 1926-1970 *WhScrn 77*
Curtis, Jackie 1947- *ConDr 73, -77*
Curtis, James 1912-1970 *BluesWW[port]*
Curtis, James Gilbert 1904- *IntWWM 77, -80, WhoMus 72*
Curtis, Jamie Lee 1955?- *WhoHrs 80*
Curtis, Keene 1923- *BiE&WWA, NotNAT, WhoHol A, WhoThe 72, -77*
Curtis, Ken 1916- *CmpEPM, FilmEn, ForYSC, IntMPA 77, -75, -76, -78, -79, -80, WhoHol A, WhoHrs 80*
Curtis, King 1935-1971 *BiDAmM, ConMuA 80A, EncJzS 70, RkOn[port], WhoHol B*
Curtis, Loyal 1877-1947 *AmSCAP 66, -80*
Curtis, Mann 1911- *AmSCAP 66, -80*
Curtis, Marie *Film 1*
Curtis, Natalie 1875-1921 *Baker 78, OxMus*
Curtis, Paul J 1927- *NotNAT*
Curtis, Peter 1942- *CnOxB*
Curtis, Richard Olin 1947- *AmSCAP 80*
Curtis, Spencer M 1856-1921 *WhScrn 74, -77*
Curtis, Stanley Charles 1905- *WhoMus 72*
Curtis, Thomas B *NewYTET*
Curtis, Tony 1925- *BiDFilm, -81, CmMov, FilmEn, FilmgC, ForYSC, HalFC 80, IntMPA 77, -75, -76, -78, -79, -80, MotPP, MovMk, OxFilm, WhoHol A, WorEFlm[port]*
Curtis, Willa Pearl 1896-1970 *WhScrn 77*
Curtis-Smith, Curtis O B 1941- *CpmDNM 78, ConAmC, IntWWM 77, -80*
Curtiss, Clinton E 1930- *IntWWM 77*
Curtiss, Mina 1896- *Baker 78*
Curtiz, David d1962 *NotNAT B*
Curtiz, Michael 1888-1962 *AmFD, BiDFilm, -81, CmMov, DcFM, FilmEn, FilmgC, HalFC 80, MovMk, OxFilm, WhScrn 74, -77, WhoHrs 80, WorEFlm[port]*
Curtiz, Michael 1889-1962 *TwYS A*
Curto, Ramada d1961 *NotNAT B*
Curtois, Lambert *NewGrD 80*
Curtola, Bobby 1944- *RkOn*
Curtwright, Jorja *WhoHol A*
Curtz, Albert 1600-1671 *NewGrD 80*
Curved Air *IlEncR*
Curvin, Jonathan W 1911- *BiE&WWA, NotNAT*
Curwen *NewGrD 80*
Curwen, Annie Jessy 1845-1932 *NewGrD 80, OxMus*
Curwen, John 1816-1880 *Baker 78, NewGrD 80, OxMus*
Curwen, John 1817-1880 *BiDAmM*
Curwen, John Christopher 1911- *NewGrD 80*
Curwen, John Kenneth 1881-1935 *NewGrD 80*
Curwen, John Spencer 1847-1916 *Baker 78, NewGrD 80, OxMus*
Curwen, Patric 1884-1949 *NotNAT B, WhThe, WhoHol B*
Curwood, Bob *Film 2*
Curwood, James Oliver 1878-1927 *CreCan 1*
Curzon, Clara-Jean 1924- *AmSCAP 80*
Curzon, Clifford 1907- *Baker 78, BnBkM 80, IntWWM 77, -80, MusSN[port], NewGrD 80[port], WhoMus 72*
Curzon, Emanuel-Henri-Parent De 1861-1942 *Baker 78*
Curzon, Frank 1868-1927 *NotNAT B, WhThe*
Curzon, Frederic Ernest 1899-1973 *NewGrD 80, WhoMus 72*
Curzon, George 1896- *FilmgC*
Curzon, George 1896-1977 *HalFC 80*
Curzon, George 1898- *WhThe*
Curzon, George 1898-1976 *IlWWBF*
Curzon, Henri De 1861-1942 *NewGrD 80*
Cusack, Cyril 1910- *BiE&WWA, FilmAG WE, FilmEn, Film 1, FilmgC, ForYSC, HalFC 80, IlWWBF, IntMPA 77, -75, -76, -78, -79, -80, MovMk, NotNAT, WhoHol A, WhoThe 72, -77*
Cusack, Dymphna *WomWMM*
Cusack, Sinead 1949- *FilmgC, HalFC 80*
Cuscaden, Sarah D 1873-1954 *WhScrn 74, -77*
Cusenza, Frank Jerome 1899- *AmSCAP 66, -80, ConAmC*
Cushing, Catherine Chisholm 1874-1952 *AmSCAP 66, -80, BiDAmM, NotNAT B, WhThe*
Cushing, Charles C 1905- *ConAmC, NewGrD 80*
Cushing, Peter 1913- *CmMov, FilmAG WE, FilmEn, FilmgC, ForYSC, HalFC 80, IlWWBF[port], IntMPA 77, -75, -76, -78, -79, -80, MotPP, WhoHol A, WhoHrs 80[port], WhoThe 72, -77*
Cushing, Sidney *Film 1*
Cushing, Tom 1879-1941 *NotNAT B, WhThe*
Cushing, William Orcutt 1823-1902 *BiDAmM*
Cushings, Eileen *PupTheA*
Cushings, Wilfred *PupTheA*
Cushman, Charlotte Saunders 1816-1876 *CnThe, Ent, FamA&A[port], NotNAT A, -B, OxThe, PlP&P[port]*
Cushman, Nancy 1913- *BiE&WWA, NotNAT*
Cushman, Stephen 1938- *IntWWM 77, -80*
Cushman, Susan 1822-1859 *NotNAT B, OxThe*
Cusins, Sir William George 1833-1893 *Baker 78, NewGrD 80*
Cusmich, Mario *Film 2*
Custer, Arthur 1923- *Baker 78, ConAmC, DcCM, IntWWM 77, -80*
Custer, Bob 1898-1974 *FilmEn, Film 2, ForYSC, TwYS, WhScrn 77, WhoHol B*
Custer, Calvin 1939- *AmSCAP 80*
Custer, George Armstrong 1839-1876 *HalFC 80, OxFilm*
Custer, Laurenz 1930- *IntWWM 77, -80*
Custer, Rudolf Presber 1912- *AmSCAP 80*
Custis, George Washington Parke 1781-1857 *NotNAT B*
Custodio, Bernardino 1911- *NewGrD 80*
Custodio, Bernardino F 1914- *IntWWM 77, -80*
Cutell, Richard *NewGrD 80*
Cutelli, Count Gaetano d1944 *WhScrn 74, -77*
Cutforth, David Ecroyd 1923- *WhoMus 72*
Cuthbert, David *ConAmTC*
Cuthbert, Neil 1951- *NatPD[port]*
Cuthbertson, Allan 1921?- *FilmgC, HalFC 80*
Cuthbertson, Eric 1908- *IntWWM 77, -80*
Cuthbertson, Iain 1930- *WhoThe 72, -77*
Cuti, Donato Antonio *NewGrD 80*
Cutler, Ben *BgBands 74*
Cutler, Forest A 1914- *AmSCAP 80*
Cutler, Henry Stephen 1824-1902 *Baker 78, BiDAmM*
Cutler, Ivor 1923- *IntWWM 77, -80, WhoMus 72*
Cutler, Jesse *AmSCAP 80*
Cutler, Kate 1870-1955 *NotNAT B, WhThe, WhoHol B*
Cutler, Max 1907- *AmSCAP 80*
Cutler, Peggy d1945 *NotNAT B*
Cutler, Victoria-Diane 1953- *AmSCAP 80*
Cutler, Yosl *PupTheA*
Cutner, Sidney Benjamin 1903-1971 *AmSCAP 80*
Cutner, Solomon *NewGrD 80*
Cutshall, Cutty 1911-1968 *CmpEPM, EncJzS 70, WhoJazz 72*
Cutshall, Robert Dewees 1911-1968 *BiDAmM, EncJzS 70*
Cutter, Benjamin 1857-1910 *BiDAmM*
Cutter, Murray 1902- *AmSCAP 66, -80, ConAmC A*
Cutter, William 1801-1867 *BiDAmM*
Cutting, Francis *NewGrD 80*
Cutting, Norman Alan 1905- *WhoMus 72*
Cutting, Richard H 1912-1972 *WhScrn 77, WhoHol B*
Cutting, Sewell Sylvester 1813-1882 *BiDAmM*
Cutting, Thomas *NewGrD 80*
Cuttino, David William 1927- *IntWWM 77*

Cutts, Graham 1885-1958 *FilmEn, FilmgC, HalFC 80, IlWWBF*
Cutts, John d1692 *NewGrD 80*
Cutts, Patricia 1926-1974 *FilmgC, HalFC 80, IlWWBF, WhScrn 77, WhoHol B*
Cutts, Patricia 1931-1974 *BiE&WWA, NotNAT B*
Cutts, William M 1857-1943 *CreCan 1*
Cuvelier, Jo *NewGrD 80*
Cuvelier, Marcel *OxMus*
Cuvelier D'Arras, Jehan Le *NewGrD 80*
Cuvillier, Charles 1877-1955 *Baker 78, NewGrD 80*
Cuvillier, Charles 1879- *WhThe*
Cuvillies, Francois De 1695-1768 *EncWT*
Cuyler, Louise E 1908- *Baker 78, NewGrD 80*
Cuypers, Johannes Theodorus 1724-1808 *NewGrD 80*
Cuzzoni, Francesca 1698?-1770 *NewGrD 80[port]*
Cuzzoni, Francesca 1700?-1770 *Baker 78, BnBkM 80, NewEOp 71*
Cvejic, Biserka 1928- *WhoOp 76*
Cvetko, Dragotin 1911- *IntWWM 77, -80, NewGrD 80, WhoMus 72*
Cvjetko, Rihtman 1902- *IntWWM 77*
Cvrcek, Vaclav 1928- *IntWWM 77, -80*
Cwojdzinski, Antoni 1896- *ModWD*
Cybot, Noel d1556 *NewGrD 80*
Cybulski, Izydor Jozef *NewGrD 80*
Cybulski, Zbigniew d1967 *MotPP, WhoHol B*
Cybulski, Zbigniew 1927-1967 *FilmEn, FilmgC, HalFC 80, MovMk, OxFilm, WhScrn 74, -77*
Cybulski, Zbygniew 1928-1967 *WorEFlm[port]*
Cyera, Hippolito *NewGrD 80*
Cyera, Ippolito *NewGrD 80*
Cyerman, Claude 1947- *IntWWM 77, -80*
Cymarron *RkOn 2A*
Cymbal, Johnny *RkOn*
Cymerman, Lilian 1949- *IntWWM 77, -80*
Cynel, Samuel *NewGrD 80*
Cyprian Z Sieradza *NewGrD 80*
Cyr, Gordon Conrad 1925- *ConAmC*
Cyrano DeBergerac 1619-1655 *EncWT*
Cyrille, Andrew Charles 1939- *AmSCAP 80, EncJzS 70*
Cyrkle, The *BiDAmM, RkOn 2[port]*
Cyrquillon, Thomas *NewGrD 80*
Cyrus, Alston Becket 1949- *AmSCAP 80*
Cysarz, Rosemary Mason 1931- *WhoMus 72*
Cytron, Samuel *ConAmC*
Cytron, Warren Allen 1944- *CpmDNM 80*
Czajkowska, Teresa 1920- *IntWWM 77, -80*
Czajkowski, Michael 1939- *ConAmC*
Czakan *NewGrD 80*
Czapiewski, Bogdan Windenty 1949- *IntWWM 77, -80*
Czapinski, Kazimierz 1933- *IntWWM 80*
Czard, Georg *NewGrD 80*
Czarnecki, Harry Edward 1905- *AmSCAP 80*
Czarny, Charles 1931- *CnOxB*
Czarth, George *NewGrD 80*
Czartoryska, Princess Marcelina 1817-1894 *NewGrD 80*
Czechowicz *NewGrD 80*
Czeczot, Witold 1846-1929 *NewGrD 80*
Czeczott, Witold 1846-1929 *NewGrD 80*
Czegert, Josef *NewGrD 80*
Czekanowska, Anna 1929- *NewGrD 80*
Czernohorsky, Bohuslav Matej *NewGrD 80*
Czernohorsky, Bohuslav Matej 1684-1742 *Baker 78*
Czerny, Carl 1791-1857 *Baker 78, NewGrD 80[port], OxMus*
Czerny, Jiri *NewGrD 80*
Czerny, Joseph *NewGrD 80*
Czerny, Karl 1791-1857 *BnBkM 80, GrComp[port], MusMk*
Czerny-Stefanska, Halina 1922- *IntWWM 77, NewGrD 80, WhoMus 72*
Czerwenka, Oscar 1924- *CmOp, NewGrD 80*
Czerwenka, Oskar 1924- *WhoMus 72, WhoOp 76*
Czerwinski, Wilhelm 1837-1893 *NewGrD 80*
Czerwonky, Richard Rudolph 1886-1949 *AmSCAP 66, -80, ConAmC*
Czettel, Ladislas Philip d1949 *NotNAT B*
Cziak, Benedikt *NewGrD 80*
Czibulka, Alphons 1842-1894 *Baker 78, NewGrD 80, OxMus*
Cziffra, Georges 1921- *NewGrD 80, WhoMus 72*
Cziffra, Gyorgy 1921- *Baker 78, IntWWM 80, NewGrD 80*
Czinner, Paul 1890-1972 *BiDFilm, -81, DcFM, FilmEn, FilmgC, HalFC 80, IlWWBF, OxFilm, WorEFlm*
Czobel, Lisa 1906- *CnOxB*
Czyz, Henryk 1923- *Baker 78, IntWWM 77, -80, NewGrD 80, WhoMus 72*

D

Da-Oz, Avraham 1929- *NewGrD 80*
Da-Oz, Ram 1929- *Baker 78, IntWWM 80, NewGrD 80*
Dabbs, H R d1913 *NotNAT B*
Dable, Frances *Film 2*
Dabney, Augusta *WhoHol A*
Dabney, Ford T 1883-1958 *AmSCAP 66, -80, BiDAmM*
Dabney, Wendell Phillips 1865-1952 *BiDAmM*
Daborne, Robert d1628 *NotNAT B*
D'Abreu, Gerald Joseph 1916- *WhoMus 72*
Dabrowski, Bronislaw 1903- *EncWT*
Daca, Esteban *NewGrD 80*
D'Accone, Frank A 1931- *NewGrD 80*
Dace, Wallace *NatPD[port]*
Dach, Simon 1605-1659 *NewGrD 80*
Dachinger, Mark 1909- *IntWWM 77, -80*
Dachs, Joseph 1825-1896 *Baker 78*
Dachstein, Wolfgang 1487?-1553 *NewGrD 80*
Dachwitz, Curt 1931- *IntWWM 80*
Dacia, Mademoiselle *Film 2*
DaCosta, Joaquim *FilmAG WE*
DaCosta, Morton 1914- *BiE&WWA, FilmEn, FilmgC, HalFC 80, NotNAT, WhoThe 72, -77, WorEFlm*
DaCosta, Noel 1930- *BiDAmM, CpmDNM 79, ConAmC, DrBlPA*
DaCosta, Noel George 1929- *AmSCAP 80, BlkCS[port]*
Dactalus De Padua *NewGrD 80*
DaCunha, Jose 1889-1956 *FilmAG WE, WhScrn 74, -77*
Dadap, Jerry Amper 1935- *NewGrD 80*
Daddy Deep Throat *BluesWW*
Daddy Stovepipe *BluesWW*
Dade, Frances 1910-1968 *WhScrn 74, -77, WhoHol B*
Dade, Stephen 1909- *FilmEn, FilmgC, HalFC 80*
Dadelsen, Georg Von 1918- *NewGrD 80*
Dadmun, John W 1819-1890 *BiDAmM*
Dadswell, Pearl d1963 *NotNAT B*
Daehler, Jorg Ewald 1933- *IntWWM 77*
Daff, Alfred Edward 1902- *IntMPA 77, -75, -76, -78, -79, -80*
Daffan, Ted 1912- *CmpEPM, EncFCWM 69, IlEncCM[port]*
Daffan, Theron Eugene 1912- *BiDAmM*
Daffner, Hugo 1882-1936 *Baker 78, NewGrD 80*
Dafoe, Christopher Grannis 1936- *ConAmTC*
Dafora, Asadata 1890-1965 *BlkAmP, DancEn 78, DrBlPA, MorBAP*
Dagenais, Pierre *CreCan 1*
Dagerman, Stig 1923-1954 *CnMD, CnThe, CroCD, EncWT, McGEWD[port], ModWD, REnWD[port]*
Daget, Robert True d1975 *WhScrn 77, WhoHol C*
Daghofer, Lillitts *Film 2*
Dagincour, Francois 1684-1758 *NewGrD 80*
Dagincourt, Francois 1684-1758 *NewGrD 80*
D'Agincourt, Francois 1684-1758 *NewGrD 80*
Dagmar 1926- *JoeFr[port], NewYTET*
Dagmar, Florence *Film 1*
Dagmar, Marie d1925 *NotNAT B*
Dagmer *PupTheA*
Dagna, Jeanette *Film 2*
Dagnall, Ells 1868-1935 *WhThe*
Dagnall, Thomas C d1926 *WhThe*
D'Agostino, Albert S 1893-1970 *CmMov, FilmEn, FilmgC, HalFC 80, WhoHrs 80*
D'Agostino, Joseph D 1929- *AmSCAP 66, -80*
Dagover, Lil *Film 2*
Dagover, Lil 1894- *EncWT, TwYS*
Dagover, Lil 1897-1980 *FilmAG WE, Film 1, FilmEn, FilmgC, HalFC 80, MovMk, OxFilm, WhoHol A, WhoHrs 80 WorEFlm[port]*
Daguerre, Louis 1787-1851 *FilmgC, HalFC 80*
Daguerre, Louis 1789-1851 *FilmEn*
Daguerre, Mande 1789-1851 *DcFM*
Dagues, Pierre *NewGrD 80*
Dahdah, Robert Sarkis 1926- *AmSCAP 80*
Dahl, Arlene *MotPP, WhoHol A*
Dahl, Arlene 1924- *FilmEn, FilmgC, HalFC 80, MGM[port], MovMk[port]*
Dahl, Arlene 1925- *ForYSC, IntMPA 77, -75, -76*
Dahl, Arlene 1928- *IntMPA 78, -79, -80*
Dahl, Ingolf 1912-1970 *AmSCAP 66, -80, Baker 78, ConAmC, DcCM, NewGrD 80*
Dahl, Roald 1916- *HalFC 80, WhoHrs 80*
Dahl, Tessa *WhoHol A*
Dahl, Viking 1895-1945 *Baker 78*
Dahl Eriksen, Richard 1918- *IntWWM 80*
Dahlander, Bert 1928- *EncJzS 70*
Dahlander, Nils-Bertil 1928- *AmSCAP 80, EncJzS 70*
Dahlbeck, Eva *WhoHol A*
Dahlbeck, Eva 1920- *FilmEn, HalFC 80, OxFilm, WorEFlm*
Dahlbeck, Eva 1921- *FilmgC*
Dahler, Jorg Ewald 1933- *IntWWM 80*
Dahlgren, Fredrik August 1816-1895 *OxThe*
Dahlhart, Vernon *AmPS B*
Dahlhaus, Carl 1928- *NewGrD 80*
Dahlin, Inger Berg 1935- *IntWWM 77, -80*
Dahlquist, Lasse Lars-Erik 1910- *IntWWM 77*
Dahlstrom, Patricia Cornelia 1947- *AmSCAP 80*
Dahm, Johann Jacob d1727 *NewGrD 80*
Dahmen *NewGrD 80*
Dahmen, Arnold 1768-1829 *NewGrD 80*
Dahmen, Herman 1755-1830 *NewGrD 80*
Dahmen, Herman Jacob 1805-1881 *NewGrD 80*
Dahmen, Hubert 1812-1837 *NewGrD 80*
Dahmen, Jacob 1798-1875 *NewGrD 80*
Dahmen, Jacob Arnold Wilhelm 1871- *NewGrD 80*
Dahmen, Jan 1898- *NewGrD 80*
Dahmen, Johan Arnold 1766-1794 *NewGrD 80*
Dahmen, Johan Arnold 1805-1834 *NewGrD 80*
Dahmen, Johan Arnold 1805-1853 *NewGrD 80*
Dahmen, Johan Cornelis 1801?-1842 *NewGrD 80*
Dahmen, Johan Francis Arnold Theodor 1837-1912 *NewGrD 80*
Dahmen, Peter 1757?-1835 *NewGrD 80*
Dahmen, Pieter Wilhelm 1808-1886 *NewGrD 80*
Dahmen, Wilhelm 1731-1780 *NewGrD 80*
Dahmen, Wilhelm 1769- *NewGrD 80*
Dahmen, Wilhelm Hendrik 1797-1847 *NewGrD 80*
Dahms, Walter 1887-1973 *Baker 78*
Dahnert, Hans Karl Ulrich 1903- *IntWWM 77, -80*
Dahrouge, Raymond Anthony 1942- *AmSCAP 80*
Dai, Alima *WomWMM*
Dai, Lin 1931-1964 *NotNAT B, WhScrn 74, -77, WhoHol B*
Dai, Yona *WomWMM*
Daiken, Melanie 1945- *WhoMus 72*
Dailey, Al 1938- *EncJzS 70*
Dailey, Albert Preston 1938- *BiDAmM, EncJzS 70*
Dailey, Dan *MotPP, WhoHol A*
Dailey, Dan 1914-1978 *FilmEn, FilmgC, HalFC 80*
Dailey, Dan 1915-1978 *BiDFilm, -81, CmMov, ForYSC, WhoThe 77*
Dailey, Dan 1917- *CmpEPM, MovMk[port], WorEFlm*
Dailey, Frank *BgBands 74*
Dailey, Frank 1901?-1956 *CmpEPM*
Dailey, Irene 1920- *BiE&WWA, WhoHol A, WhoThe 72, -77*
Dailey, Irene 1930- *NotNAT*
Dailey, Joseph *Film 1*
Dailey, Peter F *AmPS B*
Dailey, Peter F 1868-1908 *NotNAT B, WhoStg 1906, -1908*
Daily, Bill *WhoHol A*
Daily, Bud *ConMuA 80B*
Daily, Don *ConMuA 80B*
Daily, Pappy 1902- *EncFCWM 69*
Daily, Pete 1911- *CmpEPM, WhoJazz 72*
Dainton, Marie 1881-1938 *NotNAT B, WhThe*
Dainton, Patricia 1930- *FilmgC, HalFC 80*
Daisey, John *PupTheA*
Daisne, Johan 1912- *ModWD*
Daix, Daisy 1930-1950 *WhScrn 74, -77*
Dakers, Lionel Frederick 1924- *IntWWM 77, -80, WhoMus 72*
D'Alamanya, Johan *NewGrD 80*
Dalayrac, Nicolas 1753-1809 *Baker 78, MusMk, NewGrD 80, -80, OxMus*
DalBarba, Daniel 1715-1801 *NewGrD 80*
DalBarba, Daniele 1715-1801 *NewGrD 80*
Dalberg, Evelyn 1939- *WhoOp 76*
Dalberg, Johann Friedrich Hugo 1760-1812 *Baker 78, NewGrD 80*
Dalberg, Baron Wolfgang Heribert Von 1750-1806 *EncWT, NotNAT B, OxThe*
D'Albert, Eugen 1864-1932 *MusMk*
D'Albert, Eugene 1864-1932 *Baker 78, BnBkM 80, NewEOp 71, OxMus*
D'Albert, Francois Joseph 1918- *IntWWM 77,*

-80
D'Albert, George d1949 *NotNAT B*
D'Albert, George 1870- *WhThe*
D'Albert, Julius 1892- *IntWWM 77, -80*
Dalbert, Suzanne *ForYSC*
Dalbert, Suzanne d1971 *WhoHol B*
Dalbert, Suzanne 1927-1970 *WhScrn 77*
Dalbrook, Sidney *Film 1*
D'Albrook, Sidney *ForYSC*
D'Albrook, Sidney 1886-1948 *Film 2, TwYS, WhScrn 77*
D'Albrook, Sydney *Film 2*
Dalby, Amy 1888?-1969 *FilmgC, HalFC 80, WhScrn 74, -77, WhoHol B*
Dalby, John Briggs 1910- *IntWWM 77, -80, WhoMus 72*
Dalby, Martin 1942- *IntWWM 77, -80, NewGrD 80, WhoMus 72*
Dalcaraz, Alfonso Flores *NewGrD 80*
Dalcroze, Emile Jacques 1865-1950 *EncWT*
Dalcroze, Emile Jaques *Baker 78*
Dalcroze, Emile Jaques 1865-1950 *DancEn 78*
Dalcroze, Jaques *CnOxB*
Dale *NewGrD 80*
Dale And Grace *RkOn[port]*
Dale, Alan *AmPS A, -B*
Dale, Alan 1861-1928 *NotNAT B, WhThe*
Dale, Alan 1926- *CmpEPM*
Dale, Anne *Film 2*
Dale, Benjamin James 1885-1943 *Baker 78, NewGrD 80, OxMus*
Dale, Bert *AmSCAP 80*
Dale, Carlotta *CmpEPM*
Dale, Charles 1881-1971 *HalFC 80, WhScrn 74, -77, WhoHol B*
Dale, Charlie 1881-1971 *Film 2*
Dale, Clifford *PupTheA*
Dale, Dana *FilmEn, WhoHol A*
Dale, Daphne 1932- *CnOxB*
Dale, Dorothy 1883-1957 *WhScrn 74, -77, WhoHol B*
Dale, Dorothy 1925-1937 *WhScrn 74, -77, WhoHol B*
Dale, Esther d1961 *MotPP, NotNAT B, WhoHol B*
Dale, Esther 1885-1961 *FilmEn, HolCA[port], ThFT[port]*
Dale, Esther 1886-1961 *FilmgC, ForYSC, HalFC 80, Vers A[port], WhScrn 74, -77*
Dale, Flora *BluesWW*
Dale, Frank Q 1911- *AmSCAP 66, -80*
Dale, Gordon Alan 1935- *IntWWM 77, -80, WhoMus 72*
Dale, Gretchen 1886- *WhoStg 1906, -1908*
Dale, Grover 1936- *BiE&WWA, NotNAT*
Dale, James *NewGrD 80*
Dale, James Littlewood 1886- *WhThe*
Dale, Jean 1904- *AmSCAP 66*
Dale, Jim 1935- *FilmEn, FilmgC, HalFC 80, IlWWBF, PlP&P A[port], WhoHol A, WhoThe 72, -77*
Dale, Jimmie 1917- *AmSCAP 66, -80*
Dale, Jimmy 1901- *AmSCAP 66, -80, CmpEPM*
Dale, Joseph 1750-1821 *NewGrD 80*
Dale, Kathleen 1895- *NewGrD 80, WhoMus 72*
Dale, Margaret 1880-1972 *Film 2, WhScrn 77, WhThe, WhoHol B, WhoStg 1908*
Dale, Margaret 1922- *CnOxB, DancEn 78, WhThe*
Dale, Margie d1962 *NotNAT B*
Dale, Mervyn *IntWWM 77, -80, WhoMus 72*
Dale, Peggy 1903-1967 *WhScrn 74, -77, WhoHol B*
Dale, Philip Leonard 1922- *WhoMus 72*
Dale, Phyllis 1914- *IntWWM 80, WhoMus 72*
Dale, Rube L *WomWMM B*
Dale, Vikki 1931- *AmSCAP 66, -80*
Dale, Virginia *ForYSC*
Dale, Virginia 1919?- *FilmEn*
Dale, William 1780?-1827? *NewGrD 80*
Dale, William Henry 1911- *IntWWM 77, -80*
Dale Roberts, Jeremy 1934- *WhoMus 72*
D'Alembert, Jean LeRond 1717-1783 *Baker 78, NewGrD 80*
Daleo, Hilaire *NewGrD 80*
Dales, John L 1907- *BiE&WWA, NotNAT*
Dales, L John 1907- *IntMPA 77, -75, -76, -78, -79, -80*
Daley, Cass 1915-1975 *CmpEPM, FilmEn, FilmgC, ForYSC, HalFC 80, HolP 40[port], MotPP, What 4[port], WhScrn 77, WhoHol C*
Daley, Guilbert A 1923- *BiE&WWA, NotNAT*
Daley, Jack 1882-1967 *WhScrn 77, WhoHol B*
Daley, Joseph Albert 1918- *BiDAmM*
Daley, Mary Patricia 1932- *BiE&WWA*
Daley, Robert *IntMPA 77, -75, -76, -78, -79, -80*
Daley, Sandy *WomWMM B*
Dalgaard, Leif 1945- *IntWWM 77, -80*
DalGaudio, Antonio *NewGrD 80*
D'Algy, Antonio *Film 2*
D'Algy, Helena *Film 2*
D'Algy, Tony *Film 2*
Dalham *NewGrD 80*
Dalhart, Vernon *AmPS A*
Dalhart, Vernon 1883-1948 *BiDAmM, CmpEPM, CounME 74, IlEncCM, NewGrD 80*
D'Alheim, Marie *Baker 78*
D'Alheim, Mariya Alexeyevna Olenina *NewGrD 80*
D'Alheim, Pierre 1862-1922 *Baker 78*
Dali, Salvador 1904- *CnOxB, DancEn 78, EncWT, FilmEn, FilmgC, HalFC 80, OxFilm, WhoHrs 80, WorEFlm*
Dalin, Olaf 1708-1763 *NotNAT B*
Dalin, Olof 1708-1763 *OxThe*
Dalio, Marcel 1900- *BiDFilm, -81, FilmEn, FilmgC, ForYSC, HalFC 80, MovMk, OxFilm, WhoHol A, WorEFlm*
Dalio, Marcel 1915- *FilmAG WE*
Dalis, Irene 1929- *CmOp, NewEOp 71*
Dalis, Irene 1930- *WhoOp 76*
Dall, Evelyn 1914?- *FilmgC, HalFC 80*
Dall, John 1918-1971 *FilmEn, FilmgC, HalFC 80, MotPP, MovMk, WhScrn 74, -77, WhoHol B*
Dall, John 1920- *ForYSC*
Dalla Casa, Girolamo d1601 *NewGrD 80*
Dalla Corte, Dario 1936- *WhoOp 76*
Dalla Gostena, Giovanni Battista *NewGrD 80*
Dalla Pergola, Domenico Evangelisti *NewGrD 80*
Dalla Rizza, Gilda 1892-1975 *CmOp, NewEOp 71, NewGrD 80*
Dalla Tavola, Antonio d1674 *NewGrD 80*
Dalla Viola *NewGrD 80*
Dalla Viola, Alfonso 1508?-1573? *NewGrD 80*
Dalla Viola, Francesco d1568 *NewGrD 80*
Dalla Volpe, Lelio *NewGrD 80*
Dall'Abaco, Evaristo Felice 1675-1742 *Baker 78, NewGrD 80*
Dall'Abaco, Giuseppe Clemens 1710-1805 *NewGrD 80*
Dall'Abaco, Joseph *Baker 78*
Dall'Abaco, Joseph-Marie-Clement 1710-1805 *NewGrD 80*
Dall'Aglio, Bartolomeo *NewGrD 80*
Dallaire, Jean-Philippe 1916-1965 *CreCan 2*
Dallam *NewGrD 80*
Dallam, George *NewGrD 80*
Dallam, Helen *AmSCAP 66, ConAmC*
Dallam, Ralph d1673 *NewGrD 80*
Dallam, Robert 1602-1665 *NewGrD 80*
Dallam, Thomas 1570?-1614? *NewGrD 80*
Dallans *NewGrD 80*
Dallapiccola, Luigi 1904-1975 *Baker 78, BiDAmM, BnBkM 80, CmOp, CompSN[port], DcCom&M 79, DcCM, MusMk[port], NewEOp 71, NewGrD 80[port], OxMus, WhoMus 72*
Dallapozza, Adolf 1940- *WhoOp 76*
Dall'Aquila, Marco 1480?-1538? *NewGrD 80*
Dall'Argine, Costantino 1842-1877 *NewGrD 80*
Dall'Arpa, Giovanni Leonardo *NewGrD 80*
Dallas, Charlene *WhoHol A*
Dallas, J J 1853-1915 *WhThe*
Dallas, Leroy 1920- *BluesWW*
Dallas, Meredith 1916- *BiE&WWA, NotNAT*
Dallas, Mitzi 1928- *AmSCAP 66, -80*
Dallas, Sonny 1931- *IntWWM 77*
Dallas, Weaver *PupTheA*
Dalle Molle, Giuseppina 1943- *WhoOp 76*
Dalle Palle, Scipione *NewGrD 80*
Dallery *NewGrD 80*
Dallery, Charles 1702-1770 *NewGrD 80*
Dallery, Louis-Paul 1797-1870 *NewGrD 80*
Dallery, Pierre 1735-1801 *NewGrD 80*
Dallery, Pierre-Francois 1764-1833 *NewGrD 80*
Dallesandro, Joe 1948- *HalFC 80, WhoHol A, WhoHrs 80*
Dalleui, Monsieur *Film 2*
Dalley-Scarlett, Robert 1887-1959 *NewGrD 80, OxMus*
Dallier, Henri 1849-1934 *NewGrD 80*
Dallimore, Maurice 1912-1973 *WhScrn 77, WhoHol B*
Dallin, Leon 1918- *AmSCAP 66, -80, ConAmC, IntWWM 77, -80*
Dallis, Thomas *NewGrD 80*
Dallo Y Lana, Miguel Mateo De 1650?-1705 *NewGrD 80*
Dall'Oglio, Domenico 1700?-1764 *NewGrD 80*
Dallow *NewGrD 80*
Dalmado, Tony 1918- *NewOrJ*
Dalmain, Jean *CreCan 2*
Dalmain, Monique Tremblay *CreCan 2*
Dalmaine, Cyril 1904- *WhoMus 72*
Dalman, Elizabeth Cameron 1934- *CnOxB*
Dalmas *NewGrD 80*
Dalmas, H J *NewGrD 80*
Dalmatoff, B 1862- *WhThe*
DalMonte, Antonietta 1893-1975 *NewGrD 80*
DalMonte, Toti 1893-1975 *Baker 78, CmOp, NewGrD 80*
Dalmores, Charles 1871-1939 *Baker 78, BiDAmM, NewEOp 71, NewGrD 80, NotNAT B, WhoStg 1908*
Daloze, Paule 1932- *IntWWM 80*
DalPane, Domenico 1630?-1694 *NewGrD 80*
DalPestrino, Giulio *NewGrD 80*
DalPozzo, Vincenzo *NewGrD 80*
Dalring, Arne 1918- *IntWWM 77, -80*
D'Alroy, Evelyn d1915 *WhThe*
Dalroy, Harry Rube 1879-1954 *WhScrn 74, -77, WhoHol B*
Dalrymple, Glenn Vogt 1934- *IntWWM 80*
Dalrymple, Ian 1903- *FilmEn*
Dalrymple, Ian Murray 1903- *FilmgC, HalFC 80, IlWWBF, IntMPA 75*
Dalrymple, Jean 1910- *BiE&WWA, EncMT, NotNAT, -A, WhoThe 72, -77*
Dalsgaard, Mogens 1942- *IntWWM 77, -80*
Dalton, Abby 1934- *ForYSC, WhoHol A*
Dalton, Audrey 1934- *FilmEn, FilmgC, ForYSC, HalFC 80, MotPP, WhoHol A*
Dalton, Charles d1942 *WhoHol B*
Dalton, Charles 1864-1942 *NotNAT B, WhThe*
Dalton, Charles 1866-1942 *WhoStg 1908*
Dalton, Doris 1910- *WhThe*
Dalton, Dorothy d1972 *MotPP, WhoHol B*
Dalton, Dorothy 1893-1972 *TwYS, WhScrn 77, WhThe*
Dalton, Dorothy 1894-1972 *FilmEn, Film 1, -2, FilmgC, HalFC 80*
Dalton, Emmet d1937 *WhScrn 77*
D'Alton, Hugo 1913- *WhoMus 72*
Dalton, Irene 1901-1934 *Film 2, WhScrn 74, -77, WhoHol B*
Dalton, James 1930- *NewGrD 80*
Dalton, Larry Randall 1946- *AmSCAP 80*
Dalton, Timothy 1944- *FilmEn, FilmgC, HalFC 80, WhoHol A*
Daltrey, Roger 1944- *HalFC 80, IlEncR[port], WhoHol A*
D'Alvarez, Marguerite 1886-1953 *NewEOp 71*
D'Alvimare, Martin-Pierre *Baker 78*
Dalvimare, Martin-Pierre 1772-1839 *Baker 78*
Dalvimare, Pierre 1772-1839 *NewGrD 80*
D'Alvimare, Pierre 1772-1839 *NewGrD 80*
Daly, Arnold 1875-1927 *Film 1, NotNAT A, -B, OxThe, PlP&P[port], WhScrn 74, -77, WhThe, WhoHol B, WhoStg 1906, -1908*
Daly, Augustin 1838-1899 *CnThe, McGEWD[port], ModWD, NotNAT A, -B, REnWD[port]*
Daly, Augustin 1839-1899 *OxThe, PlP&P[port]*
Daly, Blyth 1902- *WhThe*
Daly, Bob *Film 1*
Daly, Dan 1858-1904 *NotNAT B*
Daly, Dixie d1963 *NotNAT B*
Daly, Duke *BgBands 74*
Daly, Dutch 1848- *WhThe*
Daly, Hazel *Film 1, -2, TwYS*

Daly, Herbert 1902-1940 *WhScrn 77*
Daly, Jack d1968 *WhScrn 77*
Daly, James 1918-1978 *BiE&WWA, FilmEn, FilmgC, ForYSC, HalFC 80, IntMPA 77, -75, -76, -78, NotNAT, WhoHol A, WhoThe 72, -77*
Daly, James L 1852-1933 *WhScrn 74, -77, WhoHol B*
Daly, John 1937- *IntMPA 77, -75, -76, -78, -79, -80*
Daly, John Augustin 1838-1899 *EncWT, Ent*
Daly, John Charles *NewYTET*
Daly, Jonathan *WhoHol A*
Daly, Joseph 1891- *AmSCAP 66, -80*
Daly, Lawrence d1900 *NotNAT B*
Daly, M E *AmSCAP 80*
Daly, Mae d1962 *NotNAT B*
Daly, Marcella *Film 2*
Daly, Mark 1887-1957 *FilmgC, HalFC 80, NotNAT B, WhScrn 74, -77, WhThe, WhoHol B*
Daly, Pat 1891-1947 *WhScrn 74, -77, WhoHol B*
Daly, Robert *Film 2*
Daly, Robert A *NewYTET*
Daly, Thomas Cullen 1918- *CreCan 1*
Daly, Tom 1918- *CreCan 1*
Daly, Tyne *WhoHol A*
Daly, Warren James 1946- *EncJzS 70*
Dalya, Jacqueline *AmSCAP 80, WhoHol A*
Dalyell, Sir John Graham 1776-1851 *OxMus*
Dalza, Joan Ambrosio *NewGrD 80*
Dalzell, Allan C 1896- *BiE&WWA*
Dalzell, Lyda St. Clair d1974 *WhoHol B*
Dam, H J W d1906 *NotNAT B*
Dam, Jose Van *NewGrD 80*
Damais, Emile 1906- *IntWWM 77, -80*
Damala, Jacques d1889 *NotNAT B*
Daman, William 1540?-1591 *NewGrD 80*
Damance, Paul 1650?-1700? *NewGrD 80*
Damarati, Luciano 1942- *IntWWM 77, -80*
Damascene, Alexander d1719 *NewGrD 80*
Damase, Jean-Michel 1928- *Baker 78, CnOxB, DancEn 78, NewGrD 80, WhoMus 72*
Damato, Anthony 1927- *NatPD[port]*
D'Amato, Michael 1926- *IntWWM 80*
DAmato, Noel *WhoMus 72*
Dambis, Pauls 1936- *NewGrD 80*
Dambois, Maurice 1889-1969 *Baker 78, BiDAmM*
D'Amboise, Jacques *CnOxB*
D'Amboise, Jacques 1934- *DancEn 78[port], WhoHol A*
D'Amboise, Jacques 1935- *ForYSC*
D'Ambricourt, Adrienne d1946 *Film 2, ForYSC*
D'Ambricourt, Adrienne 1888-1957 *WhScrn 74, -77, WhoHol B*
D'Ambrose, Joseph 1938- *IntWWM 77, -80*
D'Ambruis, Honore *NewGrD 80*
Dambruis, Honore *NewGrD 80*
D'Ambruys, Honore *NewGrD 80*
Dambruys, Honore *NewGrD 80*
Damcke, Berthold 1812-1875 *Baker 78, NewGrD 80*
Damen *NewGrD 80*
Dameral, George d1936 *NotNAT B*
Damerel, Donna 1913-1941 *WhScrn 77, WhoHol B*
Damerini, Adelmo 1880-1976 *Baker 78, NewGrD 80*
Dameron, Tadd 1917-1965 *CmpEPM, IlEncJ, NewGrD 80*
Dameron, Tadley 1917-1965 *AmSCAP 66, -80, BiDAmM*
Damesek, Abbe 1904- *ConAmC*
Damett, Thomas 1389?-1437? *NewGrD 80*
Damgaard, Harry 1934- *IntWWM 77, -80*
Damgaard, John 1941- *IntWWM 80*
Damia, Ugo J 1932- *IntWWM 77*
Damiani, Damiano 1922- *FilmEn, HalFC 80, WorEFlm*
Damiani, Luciano 1923- *EncWT, WhoOp 76*
Damiano, Gerald *HalFC 80*
Damianus A Ss Trinitate *NewGrD 80*
D'Amico, Achilles Matthew 1917- *WhoOp 76*
D'Amico, Fedele 1912- *IntWWM 77, -80, NewGrD 80, WhoMus 72*
Damico, Frank James 1909- *AmSCAP 80*
D'Amico, Hank 1915-1965 *CmpEPM, WhoJazz 72*
D'Amico, Henry 1915-1965 *BiDAmM*
D'Amico, Leslee Ann 1948- *AmSCAP 80*
D'Amico, Peter David 1949- *IntWWM 80*
D'Amico, Silvio 1887-1955 *EncWT, OxThe*
D'Amico, Suso Cecchi *DcFM*
D'Amico, Suso Cecci *FilmEn*
Damion *ConMuA 80B*
Damita, Lili *Film 2, MotPP*
Damita, Lili 1901- *FilmEn, FilmgC, HalFC 80, ThFT[port]*
Damita, Lili 1904- *WhoHol A*
Damita, Lili 1906- *MovMk[port]*
Damita, Lili 1907- *ForYSC*
Damita Jo 1940- *RkOn[port]*
Damler, John *ForYSC*
Damm, Peter 1937- *IntWWM 77, -80*
Damm, Walter J d1962 *NewYTET*
Dammann, Rolf 1929- *IntWWM 80, NewGrD 80*
Damme, Jose Van *NewGrD 80*
Damned, The *IlEncR*
DaModena, Giacomo *NewGrD 80*
Damon *NewGrD 80*
Damon, Les 1909-1962 *NotNAT B, WhScrn 77, WhoHol B*
Damon, Mark 1935- *FilmgC, ForYSC, HalFC 80, MotPP, WhoHol A, WhoHrs 80*
Damon, Stuart 1937- *BiE&WWA, FilmgC, NotNAT, WhoThe 72, -77*
Damon, William *NewGrD 80, OxMus*
Damone, Vic *AmPS A, -B, IntMPA 75, -76, -78, -79, -80*
Damone, Vic 1928- *BiDAmM, CmpEPM, FilmEn, ForYSC, RkOn[port]*
Damone, Vic 1929- *FilmgC, HalFC 80, IntMPA 77, WhoHol A*
Damon's, Liz, Orient Express *RkOn 2A*
Damoreau, Etienne-Gregoire *NewGrD 80*
Damoreau, Jean-Francois *NewGrD 80*
Damoreau, Laure-Cinthie 1801-1863 *Baker 78, CmOp*
Damoreau, Laure Cinti- *NewGrD 80*
DaMotta, Jose Vianna 1868-1948 *Baker 78*
D'Amour, Rolland 1913- *CreCan 2*
Dampier, Claude 1879-1955 *IlWWBF, WhScrn 77*
Dampier, Claude 1885-1955 *FilmgC, HalFC 80, WhScrn 74, WhoHol B*
Dampierre, Marc Antoine 1676-1756 *NewGrD 80*
Damrosch *NewGrD 80*
Damrosch, Frank 1859-1937 *Baker 78, BnBkM 80, NewGrD 80*
Damrosch, Frank, Jr. 1888- *BiDAmM*
Damrosch, Frank Heino 1859-1937 *BiDAmM*
Damrosch, Leopold 1832-1885 *Baker 78, BiDAmM, BnBkM 80, CmOp, NewEOp 71, NewGrD 80*
Damrosch, Walter Johannes 1862-1950 *AmSCAP 66, -80, Baker 78, BiDAmM, BnBkM 80, NewEOp 71, NewGrD 80, NotNAT B, OxMus, WhScrn 77*
Damrosch, Walter Johnanes 1862-1950 *MusSN[port]*
Damse, Jozef 1789-1852 *NewGrD 80*
Dan, Ikuma 1924- *Baker 78, DcCM, NewGrD 80, WhoMus 72*
Dan Fog *NewGrD 80*
Dana, Barbara *WhoHol A*
Dana, Bill 1924- *AmSCAP 66, -80, JoeFr, WhoHol A*
Dana, Charles Anderson 1819-1897 *BiDAmM*
Dana, Charles Henshaw 1846-1883 *BiDAmM*
Dana, Henry 1855-1921 *NotNAT B, WhThe*
Dana, Leora 1923- *BiE&WWA, FilmEn, FilmgC, ForYSC, HalFC 80, NotNAT, WhoHol A, WhoThe 72, -77*
Dana, Mark *WhoHol A*
Dana, Mary Louise d1946 *NotNAT B*
Dana, Mary Stanley Bunce Palmer 1810-1883 *BiDAmM*
Dana, Vic 1942- *RkOn*
Dana, Viola *MotPP*
Dana, Viola 1891- *TwYS*
Dana, Viola 1897- *FilmEn, Film 1, -2, FilmgC, HalFC 80, What 5[port], WhoHol A*
Dana, Walter 1902- *ConAmC*
Dana, William Henry 1846-1916 *Baker 78, BiDAmM*
Danbe, Jules 1840-1905 *Baker 78*
Danburg, Russell L 1909- *CpmDNM 74, ConAmC*
Danby, Charles d1906 *NotNAT B*
Danby, John 1757?-1798 *NewGrD 80, OxMus*
Danby, Kenneth Edison 1940- *CreCan 2*
Danby, Nicholas Charles 1935- *IntWWM 77, -80, WhoMus 72*
Dance, Dennis Linwood Vennor 1906- *IntWWM 77, -80, WhoMus 72*
Dance, Sir George 1858-1932 *NotNAT B, OxThe*
Dance, Sir George 1865-1932 *WhThe*
Dance, William 1755-1840 *NewGrD 80*
Danchenko, Victor 1937- *IntWWM 80*
Danchenko, Vladimir Nemirovich- 1859-1943 *NotNAT B, OxThe, PlP&P*
Danckert, Werner 1900-1970 *Baker 78, NewGrD 80*
Danckerts, Ghiselin 1510?-1565? *Baker 78, NewGrD 80*
Dancla *NewGrD 80*
Dancla, Arnaud Phillipe 1819-1862 *Baker 78, NewGrD 80*
Dancla, Charles 1817-1907 *Baker 78, NewGrD 80*
Dancla, Jean Baptiste Charles 1817-1907 *OxMus*
Dancla, Laure 1824-1880 *NewGrD 80*
Dancla, Leopold 1822-1895 *NewGrD 80*
Dancla, Leopold 1823-1895 *Baker 78*
Danco, Suzanne 1911- *Baker 78, CmOp, IntWWM 77, -80, NewGrD 80, WhoMus 72*
Dancoff, Judy *WomWMM B*
Dancourt, Florent Carton 1661-1725 *CnThe, EncWT, Ent, McGEWD[port], NotNAT B, OxThe, REnWD[port]*
Dancourt, Marie-Anne-Armande 1684-1745 *EncWT, OxThe*
Dancourt, Marie-Anne-Michelle 1685-1780 *EncWT, OxThe*
Dancourt, Marie-Therese Lenoir 1663-1725 *EncWT, OxThe*
Dancuo, Mirjana 1929- *WhoOp 76*
Dancy, Edward L 1946- *AmSCAP 80*
Dancy, Jeanette *Film 2*
Dancy, Mel 1937- *DrBlPA*
Danczowska, Kaja 1949- *IntWWM 77, -80*
Dandara, Liviu 1933- *Baker 78*
Dandelot, Georges 1895-1975 *Baker 78, IntWWM 77, WhoMus 72*
Dando, Joseph 1806-1894 *NewGrD 80*
Dando, W P d1944 *NotNAT B*
Dandre, Victor E 1870-1944 *CnOxB, DancEn 78*
Dandrea, Anthony Augustine 1911- *AmSCAP 80*
D'Andrea, Franco 1941- *EncJzS 70*
D'Andrea, Tom 1909- *ForYSC, MotPP, WhoHol A*
Dandridge, Dorothy d1965 *MotPP, WhoHol B*
Dandridge, Dorothy 1922-1965 *BlksB&W[port], -C*
Dandridge, Dorothy 1923?- *DrBlPA*
Dandridge, Dorothy 1923-1965 *FilmEn, FilmgC, HalFC 80, MovMk[port], WhScrn 74, -77*
Dandridge, Dorothy 1924-1965 *ForYSC, NotNAT A*
Dandridge, Putney 1900?-1946? *CmpEPM*
Dandridge, Putney Louis 1900-1946 *WhoJazz 72*
Dandridge, Ruby 1902- *ForYSC, WhoHol A*
Dandridge, Ruby 1904- *DrBlPA*
Dandrieu, Jean-Francois 1682?-1738 *Baker 78*
Dandrieu, Jean Francois 1682-1738 *MusMk*
Dandrieu, Jean-Francois 1682?-1738 *NewGrD 80*
D'Andrieu, Jean-Francois 1682?-1738 *NewGrD 80*
Dandrieu, Jean Francois 1682-1738 *OxMus*
Dandrieu, Pierre d1733 *NewGrD 80*
Dandy, Jess 1871-1923 *NotNAT B, WhScrn 74, -77, WhoHol B*
Dane, Barbara 1927- *BiDAmM, BluesWW[port], EncFCWM 69*
Dane, Clemence 1888-1965 *BiE&WWA, CnMD, Ent, McGEWD, ModWD, NotNAT B, OxThe, WhThe*

Dane, Clemence 1890?-1965 *EncWT*
Dane, Dorothy *Film 1*
Dane, Essex d1962 *NotNAT B, WhoStg 1908*
Dane, Ethel *WhThe*
Dane, Frank *Film 2*
Dane, Jean R 1948- *IntWWM 77, -80*
Dane, Karl 1886-1934 *FilmEn, Film 1, -2, FilmgC, ForYSC, HalFC 80, JoeFr[port], MovMk, TwYS, WhScrn 74, -77, WhoHol B*
Dane, Karl 1887-1934 *NotNAT B*
Dane, Marjorie 1898- *WhThe*
Dane, Pat *ForYSC*
Daneau, Nicolas 1866-1944 *Baker 78*
Daneel, Sylvia 1931- *BiE&WWA, NotNAT*
Daneels, Francois 1921- *IntWWM 77, -80*
Danegger, Theodor 1891-1959 *WhScrn 74, -77, WhoHol B*
Danek, Adalbert *NewGrD 80*
Danek, Victor Bartholomew 1914- *IntWWM 77, -80*
Danel, J Gordon *AmSCAP 80*
Daneman, Paul 1925- *HalFC 80, PlP&P[port], WhoThe 72, -77*
Daneman, Paul 1930- *FilmgC*
Daneri, Julie 1914-1957 *WhScrn 74, -77*
Danforth, Jim 1938?- *WhoHrs 80*
Danforth, William 1867-1941 *NotNAT B, WhThe, WhoHol B*
Dangcil, Linda *WhoHol A*
D'Angelo, Beverly *IntMPA 80*
D'Angelo, Bill *NewYTET*
D'Angelo, Carlo 1919-1973 *WhScrn 77*
D'Angelo, Gianna 1929- *WhoMus 72*
D'Angelo, James 1939- *ConAmC*
D'Angelo, Nicholas Vincent 1929- *CpmDNM 72*
D'Angelo, Paul James 1941- *IntWWM 80*
Dangerfield, Rodney *JoeFr, WhoHol A*
Dangeville, Marie-Anne Botot 1714-1796 *EncWT, Ent, NotNAT B, OxThe*
D'Anglebert, Jean-Baptiste-Henri *NewGrD 80*
D'Anglebert, Jean-Henri *BnBkM 80*
D'Anglebert, Jean-Henri 1635-1691 *NewGrD 80*
Dangman, William *Film 1*
Danhauser, Adolphe-Leopold 1835-1896 *Baker 78*
Danhuser, Der *NewGrD 80*
Danias, Starr 1949- *CnOxB*
Danican *NewGrD 80*
Daniel, Arnaut 1150?-1200? *NewGrD 80*
Daniel, Billy 1912-1962 *NotNAT B, WhScrn 77*
Daniel, Cyrus 1900- *ConAmC*
Daniel, Francisco Salvador 1831-1871 *NewGrD 80*
Daniel, George d1864 *NotNAT B*
Daniel, Gloria *BlkAmP*
Daniel, Harian 1932- *IntWWM 80*
Daniel, Harlan 1932- *IntWWM 77*
Daniel, Jean 1480?-1550? *NewGrD 80*
Daniel, John *NewGrD 80*
Daniel, Oliver 1911- *Baker 78, IntWWM 77, -80*
Daniel, Pierre *CreCan 1*
Daniel, Ralph Thomas 1921- *IntWWM 77, -80*
Daniel, Rita d1951 *NotNAT B*
Daniel, Robert T 1773-1840 *BiDAmM*
Daniel, Salvador 1787-1850? *NewGrD 80*
Daniel, Salvador 1831-1871 *Baker 78*
Daniel, Samuel 1562?-1619 *NotNAT B*
Daniel, Samuel 1563?-1619 *OxThe, PlP&P, REnWD[port]*
Daniel, Sean 1939- *IntWWM 77, -80*
Daniel, Sean 1952- *IntMPA 80*
Daniel, T 1945- *NotNAT*
Daniel, Tamara *WhoHol A*
Daniel, Viora *Film 2*
Daniel-Lesur 1908- *Baker 78, DcCM, NewGrD 80*
Daniel-Lesur, J Y 1908- *IntWWM 77, -80, WhoMus 72*
Danielewski, Tad 1921- *BiE&WWA, IntMPA 77, -75, -76, -78, -79, -80*
Danieli, Fred 1917- *CnOxB, DancEn 78*
Danieli, Lucia 1929- *WhoOp 76*
Danielian, Leon 1920- *CnOxB, DancEn 78[port]*
Danielis, Daniel 1635-1696 *NewGrD 80*
Daniell, Henry 1894-1963 *CmMov, FilmEn, Film 2, FilmgC, ForYSC, HalFC 80, HolCA[port], MotPP, MovMk, NotNAT B, PlP&P[port], Vers A[port], WhScrn 74, -77, WhThe, WhoHol B, WhoHrs 80[port]*
Daniell, Timothy Jenner 1948- *IntWWM 77, -80*
Daniells, James Roy 1902- *CreCan 1*
Daniells, Roy 1902- *CreCan 1*
Danielou, Alain 1907- *Baker 78, IntWWM 77, -80, NewGrD 80*
D'Aniels, Arnaut 1150?-1200? *NewGrD 80*
Daniels, Bebe 1901-1971 *BiDFilm, -81, CmpEPM, FilmEn, Film 2, FilmgC, ForYSC, HalFC 80, IlWWBF[port], -A, MotPP, MovMk[port], NotNAT B, OxFilm, ThFT[port], TwYS, What 1[port], WhScrn 74, -77, WhThe, WhoHol B, WomWMM*
Daniels, Bebe 1909-1971 *Film 1*
Daniels, Billy 1915?- *AmPS B, CmpEPM, DrBlPA, WhoHol A*
Daniels, Charles Neil 1878-1943 *AmSCAP 80, BiDAmM*
Daniels, Charlie 1936- *RkOn 2[port]*
Daniels, Charlie 1937- *IlEncCM[port]*
Daniels, Charlie, Band *ConMuA 80A, IlEncR*
Daniels, Danny 1924- *BiE&WWA, CnOxB, DancEn 78, NotNAT*
Daniels, David 1927- *BiE&WWA, NotNAT*
Daniels, Don *AmSCAP 80*
Daniels, Donald O'Neal 1949- *AmSCAP 80*
Daniels, Eddie 1941- *EncJzS 70*
Daniels, Edward Kenneth 1941- *BiDAmM, EncJzS 70, IntWWM 77*
Daniels, Florence Nellie 1904- *WhoMus 72*
Daniels, Frank 1860-1935 *Film 1, NotNAT B, PlP&P, WhScrn 74, -77, WhThe, WhoHol B, WhoStg 1906, -1908*
Daniels, Frank Albert 1856-1935 *OxThe*
Daniels, Hank, Jr. 1919-1973 *WhScrn 77, WhoHol B*
Daniels, Harold 1903-1971 *IntMPA 77, -75, -76, -78, -79, -80, WhScrn 77*
Daniels, Lisa *ForYSC, WhoHol A*
Daniels, M L 1931- *AmSCAP 80*
Daniels, Mabel Wheeler 1878-1971 *Baker 78, BiDAmM, ConAmC, NewGrD 80, OxMus*
Daniels, Mabel Wheeler 1879- *AmSCAP 66, -80*
Daniels, Marc 1912?- *NotNAT*
Daniels, Mark *WhoHol A*
Daniels, Melvin L 1931- *ConAmC, IntWWM 77, -80*
Daniels, Mickey 1914- *Film 2, ForYSC, WhoHol A*
Daniels, Peter H B 1923- *AmSCAP 80*
Daniels, Richard *Film 2*
Daniels, Robert Laurence 1933- *ConAmTC*
Daniels, Ron *MorBAP*
Daniels, Thelma *Film 2*
Daniels, Tom *ConMuA 80B*
Daniels, Victor *WhScrn 74, -77*
Daniels, Violet *Film 2*
Daniels, Walter 1875-1928 *Film 2, WhScrn 74, -77, WhoHol B*
Daniels, William 1895-1970 *CmMov, DcFM, FilmEn, FilmgC, HalFC 80, OxFilm, WorEFlm[port]*
Daniels, William 1927- *BiE&WWA, FilmEn, ForYSC, HalFC 80, NotNAT, PlP&P, WhoHol A*
Danielson, Dale H *IntMPA 77, -75, -76, -78, -79, -80*
Danielson, Janet *ConAmC*
Daniely, Lisa 1930- *FilmgC, ForYSC, HalFC 80, WhoHol A*
Danilevich, Lev Vasil'yevich 1912- *NewGrD 80*
Danilewicz-Czeczot, Witold *NewGrD 80*
Danilin, Nikolay Mikhaylovich 1878-1945 *NewGrD 80*
Danilo, Don *WhScrn 74, -77*
Danilov, Kirsha *NewGrD 80*
Danilova, Alexandra 1906- *BiE&WWA, DancEn 78[port], What 4[port]*
Danilova, Alexandra 1907- *WhThe*
Danilova, Alexandra Dionysievna 1904- *CnOxB*
Danilova, Maria 1793-1810 *CnOxB, DancEn 78*
Danis, Aimee *WomWMM*
Danis, Ida d1921 *WhScrn 74, -77*
Danischewsky, J 1940- *IntMPA 75, -76*
Danischewsky, Monja 1911- *FilmgC, HalFC 80, IlWWBF A*
Danise, Giuseppe 1883-1963 *BiDAmM*
Danish Radio Big Band *EncJzS 70*
Danish Radio Jazzgroup *EncJzS 70*
Danjou, Jean-Louis-Felix 1812-1866 *Baker 78*
Danjuro, Ichikawa d1903 *NotNAT B*
Dank, David 1895- *BiE&WWA*
Dankevich, Konstantin Fyodorovich 1905- *Baker 78, IntWWM 77*
Dankner, Stephen 1944- *ConAmC*
Dankowski, Adalbert 1760?-1800? *NewGrD 80*
Danks, H P 1834-1903 *PopAmC[port]*
Danks, Harry 1912- *IntWWM 77, -80, WhoMus 72*
Danks, Hart Pease 1834-1903 *Baker 78, BiDAmM, NotNAT B*
Dankworth, Avril Margaret 1922- *IntWWM 77, -80, WhoMus 72*
Dankworth, John 1927- *NewGrD 80, OxFilm*
Dankworth, John Philip William 1927- *EncJzS 70, IntWWM 77, -80, WhoMus 72*
Dankworth, Johnny 1927- *CmpEPM, ConAmC, FilmgC, HalFC 80, IlEncJ, NewGrD 80*
Danleers, The *RkOn[port]*
Dann, Elias 1916- *IntWWM 80*
Dann, Harry *PupTheA*
Dann, Hollis Ellsworth 1861-1939 *BiDAmM*
Dann, Michael H *NewYTET*
D'Anna, Mario 1940- *WhoOp 76*
Dannatt, George 1915- *IntWWM 80, WhoMus 72*
Dannatt, Norman Frederick 1919- *IntWWM 80*
Dannemann, Manuel 1932- *NewGrD 80*
Danner, Blythe *FilmEn*
Danner, Blythe 1945?- *HalFC 80, IntMPA 77, -75, -76, -78, -79, -80, WhoHol A, WhoThe 77*
Danner, Christian 1757-1813 *NewGrD 80*
Danner, Harry *WhoOp 76*
Danner, Johann Georg 1722-1803 *NewGrD 80*
Dannreuther, Edward George 1844-1905 *Baker 78, NewGrD 80, OxMus*
Dannreuther, Gustav 1853-1923 *Baker 78, BiDAmM*
Dannstrom, Isidor 1812-1897 *NewGrD 80*
D'Annunzio, Gabriele 1863-1938 *CnMD, CnThe, EncWT, Ent[port], McGEWD[port], ModWD, NewEOp 71, NewGrD 80, OxThe, PlP&P, REnWD[port], WorEFlm*
D'Annunzio, Lola d1956 *NotNAT B, WhoHol B*
Danny And The Juniors *AmPS A, RkOn*
Dano, Royal 1922- *FilmEn, ForYSC, HalFC 80, HolCA[port], WhoHol A*
Danoff, Mary Catherine 1944- *AmSCAP 80*
Danoff, Sid 1920- *AmSCAP 66*
Danoff, Sidney 1920- *AmSCAP 80*
Danoff, William Thomas 1946- *AmSCAP 80*
Danon, Oscar 1913- *WhoOp 76*
Danon, Oskar 1913- *NewGrD 80*
D'Anossa, Giuseppe *NewGrD 80*
Danova, Cesare 1926- *FilmAG WE, FilmEn, FilmgC, ForYSC, HalFC 80, WhoHol A*
Danoville *NewGrD 80*
Danovschi, Oleg 1917- *CnOxB*
Danowski, Conrad John 1950- *AmSCAP 80*
Danowski, Helen K 1932- *AmSCAP 80*
Danser, John 1934- *AmSCAP 80*
Dansereau, Fernand 1928- *CreCan 2*
Dansereau, Mireille *WomWMM*
Dansey, Herbert 1870-1917 *WhScrn 77, WhThe*
Dansie, Eric Blaise Kuuyanibe 1940- *IntWWM 77, -80*
Danson, Harold L 1905- *IntMPA 77, -75, -76, -78, -79, -80*
Danson, Linda d1975 *WhScrn 77, WhoHol C*
Dant, Charles Gustave 1907- *AmSCAP 80*
Dant, June Anne 1918- *AmSCAP 80*
Dante 1882-1955 *MagIlD[port]*
Dante 1884-1955 *WhScrn 74, -77*
Dante Alighieri 1265-1321 *NewEOp 71, NewGrD 80*

Dante The Magician 1884-1955 WhoHol B
Dante, Ethel d1954 NotNAT B
Dante, Lionel 1907-1974 WhScrn 77, WhoHol B
Dante, Michael 1931- FilmgC, ForYSC, HalFC 80, WhoHol A
Dante, Michael 1935- FilmEn
Dante, Ron ConMuA 80B
Dante And The Evergreens RkOn
Dantes, Perry AmSCAP 80
Dantine, Helmut IntMPA 77, -78, -79, -80, MotPP
Dantine, Helmut 1917- FilmEn, WhoHol A
Dantine, Helmut 1918- FilmgC, ForYSC, HalFC 80, IntMPA 75, -76, MovMk
Dantis, Suzanne Film 2
Danton, Henry 1919- CnOxB, DancEn 78
Danton, Ray 1931- FilmEn, FilmgC, ForYSC, HalFC 80, IntMPA 77, -75, -76, -78, -79, -80, WhoHol A, WhoHrs 80, WorEFlm[port]
D'Antoni, Philip 1929- HalFC 80, IntMPA 77, -75, -76, -78, -79, -80, NewYTET
D'Antonio, Carmen WhoHol A
D'Antuono, Eleanor 1939- CnOxB, DancEn 78[port]
D'Antuono, Vincent Joseph 1940- AmSCAP 80
Dantzig, Rudi Van 1933- CnOxB
Danvers, Billy d1964 NotNAT B
Danvers, Johnnie 1860-1939 OxThe
Danvers, Johnny 1870-1939 NotNAT B, WhThe
Danvers-Walker, Bob IntMPA 77, -75, -76, -78, -79, -80
Danyel, John 1564-1626? NewGrD 80
Danyell, John 1560?-1630 OxMus
Danz, Frederic A 1918- IntMPA 80
Danz, Fredric A 1918- IntMPA 77, -75, -76, -78, -79
Danzi NewGrD 80
Danzi, Franz 1763-1826 Baker 78, BnBkM 80, NewGrD 80
Danzi, Franziska 1756-1791 NewGrD 80
D'Anzi, Giovanni 1906- WhoMus 72
Danzi, Innocente 1730?-1798 NewGrD 80
Danzi, Innozenz 1730?-1798 NewGrD 80
Danzi, Johann Baptist 1758- NewGrD 80
Danzi, Margarethe 1768-1800 NewGrD 80
Danzig, Dorothy AmSCAP 80
Danzig, Evelyn 1902- AmSCAP 66
Danziger, Edward HalFC 80
Danziger, Harry HalFC 80
Danziger, Howard 1938- AmSCAP 80
Danziger Brothers, The FilmgC
Da'Oud, Gary AmSCAP 80
DaPalermo, Mauro NewGrD 80
Dapeer, Harry Ellis 1911- AmSCAP 80
Dapogny, James 1940- ConAmC
DaPonte, Lorenzo 1749-1838 Baker 78, BiDAmM, NewEOp 71, NewGrD 80[port], OxMus, REnWD[port]
Daquin, Louis 1908- DcFM, FilmEn, OxFilm, WorEFlm
Daquin, Louis Claude 1694-1772 Baker 78, BnBkM 80, MusMk, NewGrD 80, OxMus
Dara, Enzo 1938- IntWWM 80, WhoOp 76
D'Aragon, Lionel Film 2, IlWWBF
D'Aranyi, Adila NewGrD 80
D'Aranyi, Yelly Baker 78
Darasse, Xavier 1934- IntWWM 77, -80, NewGrD 80
Darbaud, Monique 1924-1971 WhScrn 77
Darbellay, Etienne 1946- IntWWM 77, -80
Darby, Ike 1933- BluesWW[port]
Darby, Ken 1909- CmMov
Darby, Kenneth Lorin 1909- AmSCAP 66, -80, ConAmC A, IntWWM 77
Darby, Kim WhoHol A
Darby, Kim 1937- FilmgC
Darby, Kim 1947- HalFC 80
Darby, Kim 1948- FilmEn, ForYSC, IntMPA 77, -75, -76, -78, -79, -80
Darby, Nettie Bell Film 2
Darby, Ray 1912- AmSCAP 66, -80
Darby, Rhy Film 1
Darby, Theodore 1906- BluesWW[port]
Darbyshire, Iris 1905- WhThe
Darc, Mireille WhoHol A
Darc, Mireille 1938- FilmAG WE, FilmEn
Darc, Mireille 1939- WorEFlm
Darc, Mireille 1940- FilmgC, HalFC 80
D'Arcais, Francesco 1830-1890 NewGrD 80
Darcel, Denise 1925- FilmEn, FilmgC, ForYSC, HalFC 80, WhoHol A
Darcey-Roche, Clara Film 2
Darch, Robert Russell 1920- AmSCAP 80
D'Archambeau, Iwan Baker 78
Darciea, Edy Film 2
Darcis, Francois-Joseph 1759?-1783? NewGrD 80
D'Arcis, Francois-Joseph 1759?-1783? NewGrD 80
Darclee, Hariclea 1860-1939 NewGrD 80[port]
Darclee, Hariclea 1868?-1929 CmOp
D'Arcy, Alex 1908- FilmEn, Film 2, FilmgC, HalFC 80, WhoHol A
D'Arcy, Alexander 1908- FilmEn
D'Arcy, Alexandre 1908- FilmEn
D'Arcy, Belle d1936 NotNAT B, WhoStg 1908
D'Arcy, Camille 1879-1916 Film 1, WhScrn 77
D'Arcy, Colin 1912- AmSCAP 66
Darcy, Don 1918- CmpEPM
D'Arcy, Francois-Joseph 1759?-1783? NewGrD 80
Darcy, Georgine WhoHol A
D'Arcy, Hugh Antoine 1843-1925 BiDAmM, NotNAT B
Darcy, Robert 1910-1967 Baker 78
D'Arcy, Roy 1894-1969 FilmEn, Film 1, -2, ForYSC, TwYS, WhScrn 74, -77, WhoHol B
Darcy, Sheila WhoHol A
Darcy, Thomas F, Jr. 1895-1968 AmSCAP 66, -80, ConAmC A
Darcy, Warren Jay 1946- ConAmC
D'Arcy-Orga, Husnu Ates 1944- IntWWM 77, -80
Darden, Jack ConMuA 80B
Darden, Severn 1937- FilmgC, HalFC 80, NotNAT, WhoHol A
Dare, Daphne WhoThe 77
Dare, Doris Film 1
Dare, Dorris 1899-1927 WhScrn 74, -77, WhoHol B
Dare, Elkanah Kelsay 1782-1826 BiDAmM
Dare, Eva d1931 NotNAT B
Dare, Margaret Marie 1902- WhoMus 72
Dare, Phyllis 1890-1975 EncMT, Film 2, WhScrn 77, WhThe, WhoHol C
Dare, Richard d1964 NotNAT B, WhoHol B
Dare, Virginia d1962 NotNAT B, WhScrn 74, -77, WhoHol B
Dare, Zena 1887-1975 Film 2, WhScrn 77, WhThe, WhoHol C
Darensbourg, Joe 1906- CmpEPM, EncJzS 70, NewOrJ[port], WhoJazz 72
Darensbourg, Joe And The Dixie Flyers RkOn
Darensbourg, Joseph 1906- AmSCAP 80, BiDAmM, EncJzS 70
Darensburg, Caffrey 1880?- NewOrJ[port]
Darensburg, Percy 1882?- NewOrJ[port]
Darensburg, Willie 1885?- NewOrJ
Darewski, Herman 1883-1947 NewGrD 80, NotNAT B, WhThe
Darewski, Max 1894-1929 NotNAT B, WhThe
Dargan, Olive Tilford d1968 NotNAT B
Dargan, William T 1948- ConAmC
D'Argentille, Charles NewGrD 80
Dargies, Gautier De NewGrD 80
Dargillieres NewGrD 80
Dargillieres, Antoine 1518?-1572 NewGrD 80
Dargillieres, Roch 1559- NewGrD 80
Dargomijsky, Alexander 1813-1869 OxMus
Dargomizhsky, Alexander 1813-1869 CmOp, DcCom&M 79, MusMk, NewEOp 71, NewGrD 80[port]
Dargomyzhsky, Aleksandr 1813-1869 BnBkM 80
Dargomyzhsky, Alexander 1813-1869 Baker 78
Darian, Fred 1927- AmSCAP 66, -80
Darien, Frank, Jr. d1955 Vers B[port], WhScrn 74, -77, WhoHol B
Darigan, Emily Johnson 1947- IntWWM 77
Darin, Bobby AmPS A, -B, ConMuA 80A
Darin, Bobby 1936- AmPS, BiDAmM
Darin, Bobby 1936-1973 EncJzS 70, FilmEn, FilmgC, MotPP, MovMk, PopAmC SUP[port], PopAmC SUPN, RkOn[port], WhScrn 77, WhoHol B
Darin, Bobby 1936-1974 HalFC 80
Darin, Bobby 1937- ForYSC
Darin, Robert 1936-1973 EncJzS 70
Daring, Kevin Mason 1949- AmSCAP 80
Darion, Joe 1917- EncMT, NewCBMT
Darion, Joseph 1917- AmSCAP 66, -80
Darius, Adam 1930- CnOxB
Dark, Christopher d1971 ForYSC, WhScrn 74, -77, WhoHol B
Dark, John 1495?-1569? NewGrD 80
Dark, Michael Film 2
Dark, Sidney 1874-1947 NotNAT B, WhThe
Dark, Stanley 1874- WhoStg 1906, -1908
Dark Cloud Film 1
Dark Cloud, Beulah d1946 WhoHol B
Darkcloud, Beulah d1946 WhScrn 74, -77
Darke, Harold Edwin 1888-1976 Baker 78, IntWWM 77, NewGrD 80, OxMus, WhoMus 72
Darke, John 1495?-1569? NewGrD 80
Darkfeather, Mona Film 1
Darley, Brian Film 2
Darley, Dick IntMPA 77, -75, -76, -78, -79, -80
Darley, Francis Thomas Sully 1835?- BiDAmM
Darley, William Henry Westray 1813-1858 BiDAmM
Darling, Candy 1948-1974 WhScrn 77, WhoHol B
Darling, Denver 1909- AmSCAP 66, -80
Darling, Erik 1933- BiDAmM, EncFCWM 69
Darling, Grace 1896- Film 1, -2, TwYS
Darling, Helen Film 2
Darling, Ida 1875-1936 Film 1, -2, WhScrn 74, -77, WhoHol B
Darling, James Sands 1929- IntWWM 77
Darling, Jean 1922- Film 2, TwYS
Darling, Jean 1925- BiE&WWA, NotNAT, WhoHol A
Darling, Joan 1935- BiE&WWA, FilmEn, WhoHol A
Darling, Robert 1937- WhoOp 76
Darling, Ruth Film 1, -2
Darling, Ruth d1918 WhScrn 77
Darling, Sandra IntWWM 77, -80
Darling, William 1882- FilmEn
Darlington, William Aubrey 1890- BiE&WWA, NotNAT, OxThe, WhoThe 72, -77
Darlow, Denys 1921- IntWWM 77, -80, NewGrD 80, WhoMus 72
D'Armand, John 1935- IntWWM 77, -80
Darmanin, Joseph 1927- AmSCAP 80
Darmatow, Ossip Film 2
Darmond, Grace 1898-1963 FilmEn, Film 2, MotPP, TwYS, WhScrn 74, -77, WhoHol B
Darmond, Grace 1898-1964 Film 1
Darmont, Albert d1909 NotNAT B
Darnay, Toni WhoHol A
Darnborough, Anthony 1913- FilmgC, HalFC 80
Darnborough, Antony 1913- IntMPA 77, -75, -76, -78, -79, -80
Darnbrough, Joan May 1914- WhoMus 72
Darnell, Bill 1920- CmpEPM
Darnell, Jean 1889-1961 Film 1, WhScrn 77, WhoHol B
Darnell, Linda d1965 MotPP, WhoHol B
Darnell, Linda 1921-1965 FilmEn, FilmgC, HalFC 80, ThFT[port], WhScrn 74, -77
Darnell, Linda 1923-1965 BiDFilm, -81, ForYSC, MovMk[port], WorEFlm[port]
Darnell, Linda 1949- IntWWM 77
Darnley, Herbert d1947 NotNAT B, WhThe
Darnley, J H d1938 NotNAT B
Darnold, Blaine A 1886-1926 WhScrn 74, -77
Darnton, Charles d1950 NotNAT B
Darnton, Charles 1836-1933 Baker 78
Darnton, Christian 1905- Baker 78, NewGrD 80, WhoMus 72
Darnton, Fred Film 1
Darondeau, Benoni 1740- NewGrD 80
Darondeau, Henry 1779-1865 NewGrD 80
Darr, Jerome 1910- WhoJazz 72
Darr, Kathryn Film 2
Darr, Vondell Film 2
Darragh, Miss d1917 NotNAT B, WhThe
D'Arras, Adam NewGrD 80

D'Arrast, Harry D'Abbabie 1893-1968 FilmgC, HalFC 80
D'Arrast, Harry D'Abbadie 1893-1968 BiDFilm, -81, WorEFlm
D'Arrast, Harry D'Abbadie 1897-1968 FilmEn
Darre, Jeanne-Marie 1905- Baker 78
Darrell, Charles d1932 NotNAT B
Darrell, J Stevan 1905-1970 WhScrn 74, -77
Darrell, Johnny 1940- BiDAmM
Darrell, Maisie 1901- WhThe
Darrell, Peter 1929- CnOxB, DancEn 78, NewGrD 80
Darrell, R D 1903- IntWWM 77, -80
Darrell, Robert Donaldson 1903- Baker 78
Darrell, Robert Donaldson 1939- WhoMus 72
Darrell, Steve d1970 WhoHol B
Darren, James 1936- AmPS A, FilmEn, FilmgC, ForYSC, HalFC 80, IntMPA 77, -75, -76, -78, -79, -80, MotPP, MovMk, RkOn, WhoHol A
Darrenkamp, John David 1935- IntWWM 77, -80, WhoOp 76
Darrid, William 1923- BiE&WWA
Darrieux, Danielle 1917- BiDFilm, -81, EncWT, FilmAG WE, FilmEn, FilmgC, ForYSC, HalFC 80, IntMPA 77, -75, -76, -78, -79, -80, MotPP, MovMk[port], OxFilm, ThFT[port], WhoHol A, WorEFlm
Darrin, Diana WhoHol A
Darro, Frankie 1917-1976 FilmEn
Darro, Frankie 1917-1977 Film 2, FilmgC, HalFC 80, MovMk[port], What 4[port], WhoHol A
Darro, Frankie 1918- ForYSC, Vers B[port]
Darrow, Barbara WhoHol A
Darrow, Clarence 1857-1938 HalFC 80
Darrow, Frankie 1917- TwYS
Darrow, Henry WhoHol A
Darrow, John Film 2
Darrow, John 1907- FilmEn
Darrow, Johnny WhoHol A
D'Arrow, Philip 1945- AmSCAP 80
Darrow, Stanley 1934- ConAmC
Darry-Cowl 1925- FilmEn
Darsonval, Lycette 1912- CnOxB, DancEn 78[port]
Darst, W Glen 1896- AmSCAP 66, ConAmC
Darst, William Glen 1896- AmSCAP 80
Dart, Thurston 1921-1971 Baker 78, BnBkM 80, NewGrD 80, OxMus
D'Artega, Alfonso 1907- AmSCAP 66, -80, ConAmC A
Dartells, The RkOn
Darter, Thomas Eugene, Jr. 1949- ConAmC, IntWWM 77, -80
Darthy, Gilda WhThe
Dartigue, John 1940- IntMPA 77, -78, -79, -80
Dartnall, Gary 1937- IntMPA 77, -75, -76, -78, -79, -80
Dartos, Tunica AmSCAP 80
Darvas, Charles Film 2
Darvas, Gabor 1911- Baker 78, IntWWM 77, -80, NewGrD 80
Darvas, Jozsef 1912- CroCD
Darvas, Lili 1902-1974 NotNAT, WhScrn 77, WhoHol B
Darvas, Lili 1906- BiE&WWA, ForYSC, WhThe, WhoThe 72
Darvi, Bella d1971 WhoHol B
Darvi, Bella 1927-1971 FilmgC, HalFC 80
Darvi, Bella 1928-1971 FilmEn, ForYSC, WhScrn 74, -77
D'Arvil, Yola Film 2
D'Arville, Camille 1863-1932 NotNAT B, WhThe, WhoStg 1906, -1908
Darwell, Jane d1967 MotPP, WhoHol B
Darwell, Jane 1879-1967 FilmEn, HolCA[port], ThFT[port], Vers A[port]
Darwell, Jane 1880-1967 BiDFilm, -81, Film 1, -2, FilmgC, ForYSC, HalFC 80, MovMk[port], OxFilm, TwYS, WhScrn 74, -77, WorEFlm
Darwin, Erasmus 1731-1802 OxMus
Darwin, Glenn 1912- IntWWM 77, -80
Darwish, Sayed 1892-1923 NewGrD 80
Darwish, Sayyid 1892-1923 NewGrD 80
Daryll, Ted AmSCAP 80
Darzins, Emils 1875-1910 Baker 78, NewGrD 80
Darzins, Volfgangs 1906-1962 ConAmC
Dasch, George 1877-1955 Baker 78, ConAmC
Dasek, Rudolf 1933- EncJzS 70
Daser, Ludwig 1525?-1589 Baker 78, NewGrD 80
Dasgupta, Gautam 1949- ConAmTC
Dash, James E 1948- IntWWM 77
Dash, Julian 1916-1974 AmSCAP 66, -80
Dash, Pauly 1918-1974 WhScrn 77, WhoHol B
Dash, St. Julian Bennett 1916-1974 EncJzS 70, WhoJazz 72
Dasher, Richard Taliaferro 1923- IntWWM 80
Dasher, Richard Taliaferro 1933- IntWWM 77
Dashiell, Willard 1867-1943 WhScrn 74, -77, WhoHol B
Dashington, James J d1962 NotNAT B
Dashow, James 1944- AmSCAP 80, CpmDNM 76, ConAmC, IntWWM 77, -80
DaSilva, Antonio 1886-1971 FilmAG WE
DaSilva, Henry 1881-1947 WhScrn 74, -77
DaSilva, Howard 1909- BiE&WWA, EncMT, FilmEn, FilmgC, ForYSC, HalFC 80, IntMPA 77, -75, -76, -78, -79, -80, MovMk[port], NotNAT, PIP&P, WhoHol A, WhoThe 72, -77
DaSilva, Raul 1933- IntMPA 78, -79, -80
DaSilva Nunes, Armando CreCan 1
Dasser, Ludwig Baker 78
Dassin, Jules ConDr 73, -77A, IntMPA 77, -75, -76, -78, -79, -80, WhoHol A
Dassin, Jules 1911- BiDFilm, -81, BiE&WWA, CmMov, FilmEn, FilmgC, HalFC 80, OxFilm, WorEFlm
Dassin, Jules 1912- DcFM, MovMk[port]
Dassoucy, Charles 1605-1677 NewGrD 80
D'Assoucy, Charles 1605-1677 NewGrD 80
Dassylva, Martial 1936- ConAmTC
Dastagir, Sabu WhScrn 74, -77
Daste, Jean 1904- EncWT, FilmEn, OxFilm
Dastree, Anne WomWMM
Datas 1876- WhThe
Date, Keshavrao 1939-1971 WhScrn 74, -77
Dattari, Ghinolfo 1535?-1617 NewGrD 80
Dattaro, Ghinolfo 1535?-1617 NewGrD 80
D'Attili, Dario 1922- NewGrD 80
D'Attino, Giacomo Film 2
Datyner, Harry 1923- IntWWM 77, -80
Datyner, Henry 1917- WhoMus 72
Dau, Katharina 1950- WhoOp 76
Daub, Inge IntWWM 80
Daub Olesen, Inge IntWWM 77
D'Auban, Ernest d1941 NotNAT B
Daube, Harda 1888-1959 WhScrn 74, -77, WhoHol B
Daube, Johann Friedrich 1730?-1797 NewGrD 80
Daubenrock, Georg NewGrD 80
Daubeny, Peter 1921-1975 CnThe, EncWT, OxThe, WhThe, WhoThe 72
Dauberval, Jean 1742-1806 CnOxB, DancEn 78, NewGrD 80
Daublaine Et Callinet Baker 78
Daudet, Alphonse OxMus
Daudet, Alphonse 1840-1897 McGEWD[port], NewEOp 71, NotNAT B
Daudet, Ernest 1837-1921 NotNAT B
Daudet, Jeanette Film 2
Dauer, Johann Ernst 1746-1812 NewGrD 80
Daufel, Andre 1919-1975 WhScrn 77
Daugherty, Herschel FilmgC, HalFC 80
Daugherty, Jack d1938 Film 2, WhoHol B
Daugherty, Patrick Dale 1947- AmSCAP 80
Daughs, Eugene William 1927- ConAmC
Daukaev, Marat 1952- CnOxB
Daum, Gerda 1942- CnOxB
Daumerey, Carey Film 2
D'Aumery, Carrie Film 2
Daumery, Carry Film 2
Daumery, John 1898-1934 IlWWBF
Dauncey, Sylvanus d1912 NotNAT B
Daunch, Virginia Obenchain 1919- AmSCAP 66, -80
Dauner, Wolfgang 1935- EncJzS 70, NewGrD 80
Dauney, William 1800-1843 Baker 78, NewGrD 80, OxMus
Daunt, William 1893-1938 NotNAT B, WhThe
Dauphin NewGrD 80
Dauphin, Claude IntMPA 77, -75, -76, -78, -79, -80, MotPP, WhoHol A
Dauphin, Claude 1903-1978 FilmEn, FilmgC, ForYSC, HalFC 80, WhoThe 72, -77
Dauphin, Claude 1904- BiE&WWA, MovMk, NotNAT
Dauphin, Johann Christian NewGrD 80
Dauphin, Johann Christian 1682-1730 NewGrD 80
Dauphin, Johann Eberhard 1670?-1731 NewGrD 80
Dauphin, Johann Georg NewGrD 80
Dauphin, John Christian 1713-1772 NewGrD 80
Dauphin, Susan Helfrich 1928- ConAmTC
Dauprat, Louis-Francois 1781-1868 Baker 78, NewGrD 80
D'Auray, Jacques Film 2
Dauriac, Lionel 1847-1923 NewGrD 80
D'Auriac, Lionel 1847-1923 NewGrD 80
Dauriac, Lionel Alexandre 1847-1923 Baker 78
D'Auril, Yola Film 2
Daus, Avraham 1902-1974 NewGrD 80
Daus, Ram NewGrD 80
Daussoigne-Mehul, Louis-Joseph 1790-1875 Baker 78, NewGrD 80
Dauth, Ursula Alexandra 1949- IntWWM 80
Dauvergne, Antoine 1713-1797 Baker 78, NewGrD 80
D'Auvergne, Antoine 1713-1797 NewGrD 80
Dauvergne, Antoine 1713-1797 OxMus
Dauvilliers, Nicolas Dorne d1690 OxThe
Dauvilliers, Victoire-Francoise 1657?-1733 OxThe
Dauvray, Marise Film 2
D'Auxerre, Pierre NewGrD 80
Davalos, Richard 1930- ForYSC, MotPP, WhoHol A
Davan Wetton, Hilary John 1943- IntWWM 77, -80
Davantes, Pierre 1525-1561 NewGrD 80
Davashe, Mackay 1920-1972 NewGrD 80
Davau, Jean-Baptiste 1742-1822 NewGrD 80
Davaux, Jean-Baptiste 1742-1822 NewGrD 80
D'Avaux, Jean-Baptiste 1742-1822 NewGrD 80
Dave And Sugar IlEncCM[port]
Dave, Johnny 1898?-1943 NewOrJ
Davee, Lawrence W 1900- IntMPA 77, -75, -76, -78, -79, -80
Davel, D A OxMus
Davel, Hendrik 1940- CnOxB
Daveluy, Marie CreCan 1
Daveluy, Marie-Claire 1880-1968 CreCan 1
Daveluy, Raymond 1926- CreCan 1, NewGrD 80
Daven, Andre Film 2
Davenant, Lady PIP&P
Davenant, Charles PIP&P
Davenant, Sir William 1606-1668 CnThe, DcPup, EncWT, Ent, McGEWD[port], NewGrD 80, NotNAT A, -B, OxMus, OxThe, PIP&P[port], REnWD[port]
Davenport, A Bromley Film 2
Davenport, Alice 1853?-1936 WhScrn 77
Davenport, Alice 1864- FilmEn, Film 1, TwYS
Davenport, Alice Shepard WhoHol B
Davenport, Ann d1968 WhScrn 74, -77, WhoHol B
Davenport, Blanch Film 2
Davenport, Butler 1871-1958 NotNAT B
Davenport, Charles 1895-1955 AmSCAP 66, -80, BiDAmM
Davenport, Charles Edward 1894-1955 BluesWW[port]
Davenport, Cow Cow 1894-1955 CmpEPM, WhoJazz 72
Davenport, David N 1925- AmSCAP 66, -80, ConAmC A
Davenport, Doris 1915- HalFC 80, WhoHol A
Davenport, Dorothy 1895- Film 1, -2, HalFC 80, TwYS, WhoHol A
Davenport, Dorothy 1895-1977 FilmEn
Davenport, Edgar Longfellow 1862-1918 NotNAT B, OxThe
Davenport, Edward Loomis 1815-1877 FamA&A[port], NotNAT A, -B, OxThe
Davenport, Eva d1932 NotNAT B, WhoStg 1906, -1908
Davenport, Fanny 1860-1898 PIP&P

Davenport, Fanny Elizabeth Vining 1829-1891 *NotNAT B, OxThe*
Davenport, Fanny Lily Gypsy 1850-1898 *FamA&A[port], NotNAT B, OxThe*
Davenport, Francis William 1847-1925 *Baker 78, NewGrD 80*
Davenport, George Gosling d1814 *NotNAT B*
Davenport, Harry 1866-1949 *FilmEn, Film 1, -2, FilmgC, ForYSC, HolCA[port], MotPP, MovMk[port], NotNAT B, OxThe, Vers A[port], WhScrn 74, -77, WhThe, WhoHol B, WhoStg 1906, -1908*
Davenport, Harry 1886-1949 *HalFC 80*
Davenport, Harry J 1858-1929 *WhScrn 77*
Davenport, Harry J 1858-1949 *WhScrn 74*
Davenport, Havis 1933-1975 *WhScrn 77, WhoHol C*
Davenport, Ira 1839-1911 *MagIlD*
Davenport, Jean Margaret 1829-1903 *NotNAT B, OxThe*
Davenport, Jed *BluesWW*
Davenport, Kate 1896-1954 *WhScrn 74, -77, WhoHol B*
Davenport, Kenneth 1879-1941 *WhScrn 74, -77, WhoHol B*
Davenport, LaNoue 1922- *ConAmC, NewGrD 80*
Davenport, Lewis 1883-1916 *MagIlD*
Davenport, Marcia 1903- *Baker 78*
Davenport, Mary d1916 *NotNAT B*
Davenport, May 1856-1927 *NotNAT B, OxThe*
Davenport, Milla 1871-1936 *Film 1, -2, TwYS, WhScrn 74, -77, WhoHol B*
Davenport, Millia 1895- *BiE&WWA, NotNAT*
Davenport, Millie *Film 2*
Davenport, Nigel 1928- *FilmEn, FilmgC, HalFC 80, IlWWBF, WhoHol A, WhoThe 72, -77*
Davenport, Pembroke Mortimer 1911- *AmSCAP 66, -80, BiE&WWA, NotNAT*
Davenport, Rebecca *WomWMM B*
Davenport, Suzanne *WomWMM B*
Davenport, T D *OxThe*
Davenport, William 1841-1877 *MagIlD*
Davern, John Kenneth 1935- *EncJzS 70*
Davern, Kenny 1935- *EncJzS 70, IlEncJ*
Daverne, Gary Michiel 1939- *IntWWM 77, -80*
Daves, Delmer 1904-1977 *BiDFilm, -81, CmMov, DcFM, FilmEn, Film 2, FilmgC, HalFC 80, IntMPA 77, -75, -76, MovMk[port], OxFilm, WorEFlm*
Davesne, Pierre Just *NewGrD 80*
D'Avesne, Pierre Just *NewGrD 80*
Davesnes, Edouard *Film 1*
Davesnes, Pierre Just *NewGrD 80*
Davey, Florence *WomWMM B*
Davey, Frank 1940- *CreCan 2*
Davey, Henry 1853-1929 *Baker 78, NewGrD 80, OxMus*
Davey, Malcolm *IntWWM 77, -80, WhoMus 72*
Davey, Michael Wade 1939- *WhoMus 72*
Davey, Nuna 1902- *WhThe*
Davey, Peter 1857-1946 *NotNAT B, WhThe*
Davey, William Reginald 1895- *WhoMus 72*
Davia, Federico 1933- *WhoMus 72, WhoOp 76*
Davico, Vincenzo 1889-1969 *Baker 78, NewGrD 80*
David *NewGrD 80[port]*
David And Jonathan *RkOn 2[port]*
David Of The White Rock *OxMus*
David, Avram 1930- *ConAmC*
David, Benjamin 1896- *AmSCAP 66*
David, Clifford 1933- *BiE&WWA, NotNAT*
David, David *AmSCAP 80*
David, Felicien-Cesar 1810-1876 *Baker 78, BnBkM 80, MusMk, NewEOp 71, NewGrD 80[port], OxMus*
David, Ferdinand 1810-1873 *Baker 78, BnBkM 80, MusMk, NewGrD 80, OxMus*
David, Gary 1935- *AmSCAP 80*
David, Gyula 1913-1977 *Baker 78, IntWWM 77, -80*
David, Gyula 1913-1979 *NewGrD 80*
David, Hal *Sw&Ld C*
David, Hal 1921- *AmPS, AmSCAP 66, -80, BiDAmM, CmpEPM, EncMT, NotNAT*
David, Hans Theodore 1902-1967 *Baker 78, BiDAmM, NewGrD 80*
David, Hubert Worton 1904- *WhoMus 72*
David, James 1951- *AmSCAP 80*
David, Johann Nepomuk 1895-1977 *Baker 78, DcCM, IntWWM 77, -80, NewGrD 80, OxMus*
David, Jose 1913- *Baker 78, IntWWM 77, -80*
David, Karl Heinrich 1884-1951 *Baker 78, NewGrD 80*
David, Lee 1891-1978 *AmSCAP 66, -80*
David, Leon 1867-1962 *Baker 78*
David, Mack 1912- *AmPS, AmSCAP 66, -80, BiDAmM, BiE&WWA, CmpEPM, NotNAT, Sw&Ld C*
David, Madeline Bloom *NewYTET*
David, Meridith Bar *WomWMM B*
David, Michael *ForYSC, PlP&P A[port]*
David, Nathan *AmSCAP 80*
David, Nellie Maillard 1917- *CreCan 2*
David, Paul *ConMuA 80B*
David, Paul 1840-1932 *OxMus*
David, Samuel 1836-1895 *Baker 78*
David, Saul 1921- *HalFC 80, IntMPA 77, -75, -76, -78, -79, -80*
David, Thayer 1926-1978 *HalFC 80*
David, Thayer 1927- *NotNAT, WhoHol A*
David, Thomas Christian 1925- *IntWWM 80, NewGrD 80*
David, Vincent 1924- *AmSCAP 66, ConAmC A*
David, Will *AmSCAP 80*
David, William 1882-1965 *WhScrn 74, -77, WhoHol B*
David, Worton d1940 *NotNAT B, WhThe*
Davide, Giovanni 1790-1864 *CmOp, NewEOp 71, NewGrD 80*
Davidenko, Alexander Alexandrovich 1899-1934 *Baker 78, NewGrD 80*
Davidoff, Serafin d1975 *WhScrn 77*
Davidov, Carl 1838-1889 *Baker 78*
Davidov, Karl Yul'yevich 1838-1889 *NewGrD 80*
Davidov, Stepan Ivanovich 1777-1825 *NewGrD 80*
Davidovsky, Mario 1934- *Baker 78, BiDAmM, BnBkM 80, CpmDNM 73, ConAmC, NewGrD 80*
Davids, Heintje 1888-1975 *WhScrn 77*
Davidson, Bill 1918- *BiE&WWA*
Davidson, Bing 1939-1965 *WhScrn 74, -77*
Davidson, Bruce *IntMPA 80*
Davidson, Charles Stuart 1929- *AmSCAP 66, -80, ConAmC*
Davidson, Cliff *Film 2*
Davidson, Dore 1850-1930 *Film 1, -2, NotNAT B, WhScrn 74, -77, WhoHol B*
Davidson, Douglass Albert 1926- *AmSCAP 80*
Davidson, Duane Andrew 1934-1964 *AmSCAP 80*
Davidson, George Henry 1800?-1875 *NewGrD 80*
Davidson, Gordon 1933- *WhoThe 72, -77*
Davidson, Gordon 1934?- *NotNAT*
Davidson, Harley *AmSCAP 80*
Davidson, Harold Gibson 1893-1959 *Baker 78, ConAmC, OxMus*
Davidson, Harold P 1908- *AmSCAP 66, ConAmC A*
Davidson, Hugh 1930- *CreCan 2*
Davidson, J B *WhScrn 74*
Davidson, James *WhoHol A*
Davidson, James 1908- *CreCan 1*
Davidson, James 1942- *ForYSC*
Davidson, James B *WhScrn 77*
Davidson, James Robert 1942- *IntWWM 77, -80*
Davidson, John 1886-1968 *FilmEn, Film 1, -2, ForYSC, TwYS, WhScrn 77, WhoHol B*
Davidson, John 1886-1969 *HolCA[port]*
Davidson, John 1941- *IntMPA 77, -75, -76, -78, -79, -80, MotPP, WhoHol A*
Davidson, Joy Elaine 1940- *IntWWM 77, -80, WhoMus 72, WhoOp 76*
Davidson, Lawford *Film 2*
Davidson, Louis 1912- *IntWWM 77, -80*
Davidson, Lyle 1938- *CpmDNM 79, ConAmC*
Davidson, M *WhoMus 72*
Davidson, Maitland d1936 *NotNAT B*
Davidson, Malcolm Gordon 1891-1949 *OxMus*
Davidson, Max 1875-1946 *ForYSC, TwYS*
Davidson, Max 1875-1950 *Film 1, -2, HalFC 80, WhScrn 74, -77, WhoHol B*
Davidson, Michael 1935- *WhoOp 76*
Davidson, Milton *BiE&WWA*
Davidson, Morrey 1899- *AmSCAP 66*
Davidson, Morris 1899- *AmSCAP 80*
Davidson, Norbert R, Jr. 1940- *BlkAmP, MorBAP*
Davidson, Norma Lewis 1929- *IntWWM 77, -80*
Davidson, Peter *CreCan 1*
Davidson, Richard 1918- *BiE&WWA, NotNAT*
Davidson, Robert *AmSCAP 80*
Davidson, Russell Edward 1946- *AmSCAP 80*
Davidson, Walter 1902- *ConAmC*
Davidson, William B 1888-1947 *FilmEn, Film 1, -2, ForYSC, HolCA[port], TwYS, WhScrn 74, -77, WhoHol B*
Davidson, William P *BlkAmP*
Davidsson, Ake 1913- *NewGrD 80*
Davidt, Michael 1877-1944 *WhScrn 74, -77*
Davie, Cedric Thorpe 1913- *OxMus, WhoMus 72*
Davie, Hutch *RkOn*
Davies *NewGrD 80*
Davies, Acton 1870-1916 *NotNAT B, WhThe*
Davies, Andrew Richard 1949- *IntWWM 77, -80*
Davies, Aneurin Vaughan 1908- *WhoMus 72*
Davies, Ben 1858-1943 *Baker 78, NewGrD 80, NotNAT B, WhThe*
Davies, Betty Ann 1910-1955 *FilmgC, HalFC 80, NotNAT B, WhScrn 74, -77, WhThe, WhoHol B*
Davies, Brian 1912- *BiE&WWA*
Davies, Brian 1938- *BiE&WWA*
Davies, Cecilia 1756?-1836 *NewGrD 80*
Davies, Clara Novello *OxMus*
Davies, Cliff *ConMuA 80B*
Davies, Cyril 1932- *IlEncR*
Davies, D T Ffrangcon 1855-1918 *OxMus*
Davies, David d1920 *WhScrn 74, -77*
Davies, David 1855-1921 *BiDAmM*
Davies, David Ivor *McGEWD, NewGrD 80*
Davies, Dennis Russell 1944- *BiDAmM, BnBkM 80, NewGrD 80*
Davies, Dorothy 1899- *NewGrD 80*
Davies, E D *PupTheA*
Davies, Edna 1905- *WhThe*
Davies, Edward Harold 1867-1947 *OxMus*
Davies, Eiluned *IntWWM 80, WhoMus 72*
Davies, Evan Thomas 1878-1969 *OxMus*
Davies, Fanny 1861-1934 *Baker 78, NewGrD 80*
Davies, Ffrangcon 1925- *IntWWM 80, WhoMus 72*
Davies, Frederic Justus 1941- *IntWWM 77*
Davies, George 1891-1960 *WhScrn 74, -77*
Davies, Gerald 1915- *WhoMus 72*
Davies, Harry Parr 1914-1955 *NewGrD 80, NotNAT B, WhThe*
Davies, Hazel Anne 1937- *IntWWM 77, -80, WhoMus 72*
Davies, Henrietta Grisell Mary 1918- *WhoMus 72*
Davies, Sir Henry Walford 1869-1941 *Baker 78, OxMus*
Davies, Howard *Film 1*
Davies, Hubert Henry 1869-1917 *NotNAT B, WhThe*
Davies, Hugh 1580?-1644 *NewGrD 80*
Davies, Hugh 1943- *DcCM, NewGrD 80*
Davies, Ivor Richard 1901- *WhoMus 72*
Davies, Jack 1913- *FilmEn, FilmgC, HalFC 80, IntMPA 77, -75, -76, -78, -79, -80*
Davies, Joan *IntWWM 77, -80, WhoMus 72*
Davies, John H *OxMus*
Davies, John Hassall 1933- *WhoMus 72*
Davies, John Howard 1909-1972 *NewGrD 80*
Davies, John Howard 1939- *FilmEn, FilmgC, HalFC 80, WhoHol A*
Davies, John Huw 1935- *IntWWM 77, -80, WhoMus 72*
Davies, John Leighton 1918- *IntWWM 77, -80, WhoMus 72*
Davies, John W 1908- *IntMPA 77, -75, -76,*

–78, –79, –80
Davies, Lewis A 1911- *AmSCAP 66, –80*
Davies, Lilian 1895-1932 *NotNAT B, WhThe*
Davies, Lionel Edward 1913- *WhoMus 72*
Davies, Lyndon 1944- *IntWWM 77, –80*
Davies, Maldwyn Thomas 1950- *IntWWM 80*
Davies, Marianne 1744-1792 *NewGrD 80, OxMus*
Davies, Marion d1961 *MotPP, WhoHol B*
Davies, Marion 1897-1961 *BiDFilm, –81, FilmEn, Film 1, –2, FilmgC, HalFC 80, MGM[port], MovMk[port], NotNAT B, ThFT[port], WhThe, WorEFlm*
Davies, Marion 1898-1961 *OxFilm, WhScrn 74, –77*
Davies, Marion 1900-1961 *ForYSC, TwYS*
Davies, Marion Hall *Film 2*
Davies, Mary *NewGrD 80*
Davies, Mary 1855-1930 *NewGrD 80*
Davies, Mary Carolyn *AmSCAP 66*
Davies, Meredith 1922- *IntWWM 77, –80, NewGrD 80, WhoMus 72*
Davies, Murray 1902- *IntWWM 77, WhoMus 72*
Davies, Noel Anthony 1945- *IntWWM 77, –80, WhoOp 76*
Davies, Paul *IntMPA 79, –80*
Davies, Peter Maxwell *BnBkM 80*
Davies, Peter Maxwell 1934- *Baker 78, CmOp, CpmDNM 80, DcCom&M 79, IntWWM 77, –80, NewGrD 80[port], OxMus, WhoMus 72*
Davies, Peter Maxwell 1937- *MusMk[port]*
Davies, Peter Neville 1928- *IntWWM 77, –80, WhoMus 72*
Davies, Philippa Claire 1953- *IntWWM 80*
Davies, Phoebe *WhoStg 1906, –1908*
Davies, Reine *Film 1*
Davies, Robertson 1913- *CnThe, ConDr 73, –77, CreCan 1, McGEWD, REnWD[port]*
Davies, Roy Edward Charles 1920- *WhoMus 72*
Davies, Rupert 1916-1976 *FilmgC, HalFC 80, IntMPA 77, –75, –76, WhoHol A*
Davies, Ryland 1943- *CmOp[port], IntWWM 77, –80, NewGrD 80, WhoMus 72, WhoOp 76*
Davies, Samuel 1723-1761 *BiDAmM*
Davies, Siobhan 1950- *CnOxB*
Davies, Thomas d1785 *NotNAT B*
Davies, Tudor 1892-1958 *CmOp, NewGrD 80*
Davies, Valentine 1905- *FilmEn*
Davies, Walford 1869-1941 *BnBkM 80, MusMk, NewGrD 80*
Davies, William Benjamin 1902- *WhoMus 72*
Davies, William C 1932- *IntMPA 77, –75, –76, –78, –79, –80*
Davies, William Henry 1911- *AmSCAP 80*
Davies, William Robertson 1913- *CreCan 1*
Davies, Windsor 1930- *HalFC 80*
Davies Hibbard, Trevor 1925- *WhoMus 72*
Davignon, Grace *CreCan 2*
Davilla, Sid 1915- *NewOrJ[port]*
DaVinci, Leonardo 1452-1519 *Ent[port]*
Davion, Alexander 1929- *FilmgC, HalFC 80, WhoHol A*
Daviot, Gordon 1897-1952 *EncWT, NotNAT B, WhThe*
Davis *NewGrD 80*
Davis, Miss 1726?- *NewGrD 80*
Davis, Mr. *NewGrD 80*
Davis, Mrs. *NewGrD 80*
Davis, A I *BlkAmP*
Davis, Al *BlkAmP, MorBAP*
Davis, Alan Roger 1945- *IntWWM 80*
Davis, Albert Oliver 1920- *ConAmC, IntWWM 77, –80*
Davis, Alex *PupTheA*
Davis, Alfred 1899- *IntMPA 77, –75, –76, –78, –79, –80*
Davis, Allan 1913- *WhoThe 72, –77*
Davis, Allan 1913-1943 *WhScrn 77*
Davis, Allan Gerald 1922- *AmSCAP 66, –80, CpmDNM 76, –80, ConAmC, IntWWM 77, –80*
Davis, Allen *ConMuA 80B*
Davis, Allen, III *NatPD[port]*
Davis, Allen H 1945- *ConAmC*
Davis, Altovise *DrBlPA*
Davis, Andrew Frank 1944- *BnBkM 80, IntWWM 77, –80, NewGrD 80, WhoMus 72*
Davis, Angela R 1947- *IntWWM 77, –80*
Davis, Ann d1961 *NotNAT B*
Davis, Ann B *WhoHol A*
Davis, Anna 1890-1945 *WhScrn 74, –77*
Davis, Annette *WhoHol A*
Davis, Ariel Rual 1912- *NotNAT*
Davis, Arthur 1917- *IntMPA 77, –75, –76, –78, –79*
Davis, Arthur 1927- *IntMPA 80*
Davis, Arthur David 1934- *BiDAmM, IntWWM 77, –80*
Davis, Auguste *BiDAmM*
Davis, Barbara *WomWMM*
Davis, Barbara Chilcott *CreCan 1*
Davis, Bea *WomWMM*
Davis, Benny 1895- *AmPS, AmSCAP 66, –80, BiDAmM, CmpEPM, Sw&Ld C*
Davis, Bert Etta 1923- *BlkWAB*
Davis, Beryl 1925?- *CmpEPM*
Davis, Bette 1908- *AmPS B, BiDFilm, –81, BiE&WWA, CmMov, EncMT, FilmEn, FilmgC, ForYSC, HalFC 80[port], IntMPA 77, –75, –76, –78, –79, –80, MotPP, MovMk[port], NotNAT, –A, OxFilm, ThFT[port], WhoHol A, WhoHrs 80[port], WhoThe 77, WorEFlm[port]*
Davis, Betty Jack 1932-1953 *BiDAmM*
Davis, Bill *NewYTET*
Davis, Bill 1918- *CmpEPM*
Davis, Billy 1940- *BiDAmM*
Davis, Blevins 1903-1971 *BiE&WWA, NotNAT B*
Davis, Bob 1909- *AmSCAP 66, –80*
Davis, Bob Alabam 1910-1971 *WhScrn 74, –77*
Davis, Boyd 1885-1963 *ForYSC, NotNAT B, WhScrn 74, –77, WhThe, WhoHol B*
Davis, Buster *MorBAP*
Davis, Buster 1918- *AmSCAP 80*
Davis, Buster 1920- *AmSCAP 66, BiE&WWA, NotNAT*
Davis, Carl 1886- *BluesWW*
Davis, Carl 1936- *WhoThe 77*
Davis, Charles *WhoHol A*
Davis, Charles 1933- *BiDAmM, EncJzS 70*
Davis, Charles Belmont d1926 *NotNAT B*
Davis, Charles Wheeler 1915- *IntWWM 77, –80*
Davis, Charlotte Anne 1945- *BlkWAB*
Davis, Clifton 1945- *DrBlPA, WhoHol A*
Davis, Clive *ConMuA 80B[port]*
Davis, Colin 1927- *Baker 78, BnBkM 80, CmOp, IntWWM 77, MusMk[port], MusSN[port], NewEOp 71, NewGrD 80[port], WhoMus 72, WhoOp 76*
Davis, Conrad d1969 *WhoHol B*
Davis, Curtis Harrison 1949- *ConAmTC*
Davis, Dan *ConMuA 80B*
Davis, Danny *IlEncCM[port]*
Davis, Danny 1925- *CounME 74[port], –74A*
Davis, Danny 1929-1970 *WhScrn 74, –77*
Davis, Danny 1930- *AmSCAP 66, BiDAmM*
Davis, Danny B 1943- *IntWWM 77*
Davis, David And Lorenzo Music *NewYTET*
Davis, David H 1930- *AmSCAP 80*
Davis, Desmond 1927- *FilmgC, HalFC 80*
Davis, Desmond 1928- *FilmEn, IlWWBF, WorEFlm*
Davis, Dolly *Film 2*
Davis, Don *AmSCAP 80*
Davis, Don S 1928- *BiDAmM*
Davis, Donald 1928- *BiE&WWA, CreCan 2, NotNAT, WhoHol A*
Davis, Donald 1938- *AmSCAP 80*
Davis, Earl B 1930- *AmSCAP 80*
Davis, Eddie d1958 *NotNAT B*
Davis, Eddie 1921- *BiDAmM, CmpEPM, IlEncJ*
Davis, Eddie 1922- *EncJzS 70*
Davis, Edward d1936 *Film 1, –2, WhoHol B*
Davis, Edwards 1871-1936 *WhScrn 74, –77*
Davis, Elias And David Pollock *NewYTET*
Davis, Ellabelle 1907-1960 *DrBlPA*
Davis, Elmer d1958 *NewYTET*
Davis, Ernestine 1907- *BlkWAB[port]*
Davis, Evan 1923- *IntWWM 77, –80*
Davis, Evelyn Helen Johnson 1915- *IntWWM 77, –80*
Davis, Evelyn Marguerite Bailey 1914- *IntWWM 77, –80*
Davis, Fay 1872-1945 *NotNAT B, WhThe, WhoStg 1906, –1908*
Davis, Fitzroy 1912- *BiE&WWA, NotNAT*
Davis, Frank 1894-1970 *AmSCAP 66, –80*
Davis, Frank I 1919- *IntMPA 77, –75, –76, –78, –79, –80*
Davis, Frederick 1909- *AmSCAP 66, –80*
Davis, Freeman 1903-1974 *WhScrn 77, WhoHol B*
Davis, Gail 1925- *ForYSC, What 5[port], WhoHol A*
Davis, Garry 1922- *What 2[port]*
Davis, Gary 1896-1972 *BluesWW[port], NewGrD 80, WhScrn 77*
Davis, Genevieve 1889-1950 *AmSCAP 66, –80, ConAmC A*
Davis, George 1875?- *NewOrJ*
Davis, George 1889-1965 *Film 2, Vers B[port], WhScrn 74, –77, WhoHol B*
Davis, George Collin 1867-1929 *AmSCAP 66, –80*
Davis, George W 1914- *IntMPA 77, –75, –76, –78, –79, –80*
Davis, Gilbert 1899- *WhThe*
Davis, Ginia *WhoMus 72*
Davis, Glenn *WhoHol A*
Davis, Gregory Russell 1948- *IntWWM 77*
Davis, Gussie L 1863-1899 *BiDAmM, NewGrD 80*
Davis, H O d1964 *NotNAT B*
Davis, Hallie Flanagan 1890- *BiE&WWA*
Davis, Ham Leonard 1905-1957 *WhoJazz 72*
Davis, Harry 1874-1929 *WhScrn 74, –77, WhoHol B*
Davis, Harry E 1905-1968 *BiE&WWA, NotNAT B*
Davis, Harvey O 1915- *ConAmC*
Davis, Hazel 1907- *AmSCAP 66*
Davis, Hiram W 1825-1905 *Ent*
Davis, Houston 1914- *AmSCAP 80*
Davis, Howard 1900?- *NewOrJ[port]*
Davis, Howard 1940- *IntWWM 77, –80, WhoMus 72*
Davis, Hugh Scott 1916- *WhoMus 72*
Davis, Ivan 1932- *Baker 78, IntWWM 77, –80, NewGrD 80, WhoMus 72*
Davis, J B 1935- *WhoOp 76*
Davis, J Edward *Film 2*
Davis, J Gunnis 1874-1937 *Film 2, WhoHol B*
Davis, Jack *WhoHol A*
Davis, Jack d1968 *WhScrn 77*
Davis, Jackie *Film 2*
Davis, Jackson 1920- *AmSCAP 66*
Davis, James *ConAmTC*
Davis, James 1915- *FilmgC, HalFC 80*
Davis, James Franklin 1944- *ConAmC*
Davis, James Gunnis 1874-1937 *WhScrn 74, –77*
Davis, James Houston 1902- *BiDAmM*
Davis, Janette *CmpEPM*
Davis, Jean Reynolds 1927- *AmSCAP 66, –80, ConAmC*
Davis, Jed H 1921- *BiE&WWA, NotNAT*
Davis, Jeff 1884-1968 *WhScrn 77*
Davis, Jeff 1952- *EncJzS 70*
Davis, Jeri Turner *BlkAmP*
Davis, Jerry *NewYTET*
Davis, Jessie Bartlett *AmPS B*
Davis, Jessie Bartlett 1860-1905 *BiDAmM*
Davis, Jessie Bartlett 1861-1905 *NotNAT B*
Davis, Jim *MotPP*
Davis, Jim 1915- *FilmEn, ForYSC, WhoHol A*
Davis, Jimmie 1902- *CmpEPM, CounME 74[port], –74A, EncFCWM 69*
Davis, Jimmy *BluesWW*
Davis, Jimmy 1902- *IlEncCM*
Davis, Joan d1961 *MotPP, WhoHol B*
Davis, Joan 1906-1961 *WhThe, WhoThe 72*
Davis, Joan 1907-1961 *FilmEn, Funs[port], ThFT[port], WhScrn 74, –77*
Davis, Joan 1908-1961 *FilmgC, HalFC 80, JoeFr[port], MovMk*
Davis, Joan 1913-1961 *ForYSC, NotNAT B*
Davis, Joe 1912- *WhoThe 72, –77*
Davis, John 1773-1839 *BiDAmM*
Davis, Sir John 1906- *FilmgC, HalFC 80, IntMPA 77, –75, –76, –78, –79, –80*

Davis, John Carlyle 1878-1948 AmSCAP 66, –80, ConAmC A
Davis, John David 1867-1942 Baker 78
Davis, John Edward, Jr. 1952- AmSCAP 80
Davis, John Henry 1913- BluesWW
Davis, John Jeffrey 1944- ConAmC
Davis, John S 1935- ConAmC
Davis, Johnny 1915?- BgBands 74, CmpEPM
Davis, Jordan P 1933- IntMPA 77, –75, –76, –78, –79, –80
Davis, Joseph M 1896-1978 AmSCAP 66, –80
Davis, Karl Victor 1905-1979 AmSCAP 80, BiDAmM, ForYSC
Davis, Katherine K 1892-1980 AmSCAP 66, –80, CpmDNM 80, ConAmC
Davis, Kathleen June 1947- IntWWM 77
Davis, Keith BiE&WWA
Davis, Keith C 1951- IntWWM 77, –80
Davis, Larry 1936- BluesWW[port]
Davis, Lem Arthur 1914-1970 WhoJazz 72
Davis, Lemuel A 1914- AmSCAP 66, –80
Davis, Leonard 1915- IntWWM 77, –80
Davis, Lockjaw 1922- EncJzS 70
Davis, Lottie McNeill 1920- AmSCAP 80
Davis, Lou 1881-1961 AmSCAP 66, –80, BiDAmM
Davis, Luther 1916- BiE&WWA, NotNAT
Davis, Luther 1921- IntMPA 77, –75, –76, –78, –79, –80
Davis, Luther 1938- NatPD[port]
Davis, Mac 1942- CounME 74[port], –74A, IlEncCM[port], RkOn 2[port]
Davis, Mack 1898-1947 AmSCAP 66, –80
Davis, Margaret Munger 1908- ConAmC
Davis, Margaret Phillips 1912- BlkWAB[port]
Davis, Marilyn Johnson 1936- IntWWM 77, –80
Davis, Mark Llewellyn 1906- IntWWM 77, –80
Davis, Martin S IntMPA 77, –75, –76, –78, –79, –80
Davis, Mary ConAmC, PlP&P[port]
Davis, Mary 1650?-1698? NewGrD 80
Davis, Maxwell 1916-1970 CmpEPM
Davis, Meyer BgBands 74
Davis, Meyer 1895?- CmpEPM
Davis, Meyer 1896- BiE&WWA
Davis, Michael D 1937- IntWWM 77, –80, WhoMus 72
Davis, Mike DancEn 78
Davis, Milburn BlkAmP
Davis, Mildred 1900-1969 WhScrn 74, –77, WhoHol B
Davis, Mildred 1903-1969 Film 1, –2, TwYS
Davis, Miles ConMuA 80A[port], IlEncR
Davis, Miles 1925- MusMk[port]
Davis, Miles 1926- Baker 78, BiDAmM, CmpEPM, DrBlPA, EncJzS 70, IlEncJ, IntWWM 77, –80, NewGrD 80[port], WhoMus 72
Davis, Moll 1650?-1698? NewGrD 80
Davis, Murray CreCan 1
Davis, Nancy 1924- FilmgC, ForYSC, HalFC 80, MotPP, WhoHol A
Davis, Nathan 1937- BiDAmM, ConAmC
Davis, Nathan Tate 1937- EncJzS 70, IntWWM 77
Davis, Newnham- WhThe
Davis, Nolan 1942- BlkAmP
Davis, Norman AmSCAP 80
Davis, Ossie MorBAP
Davis, Ossie 1917- BiE&WWA, BlkAmP, ConDr 73, –77, DcLB 7[port], DrBlPA, Ent, FilmEn, FilmgC, HalFC 80, IntMPA 77, –75, –76, –78, –79, –80, MotPP, MovMk[port], NotNAT, PlP&P A[port], WhoHol A, WhoThe 72, –77
Davis, Ossie 1921- ForYSC
Davis, Owen 1874-1956 CnMD, McGEWD[port], ModWD, NotNAT A, –B, OxThe, WhThe
Davis, Owen, Jr. 1907-1949 Film 2, ForYSC, NotNAT B, WhScrn 74, –77, WhThe, WhoHol B
Davis, Ozora Stearns 1866-1931 BiDAmM
Davis, Pat 1909- CmpEPM
Davis, Paul 1925- IntMPA 77, –75, –76, –78
Davis, Paul 1948- RkOn 2[port]
Davis, Peter NewYTET
Davis, Philip Lincoln 1911- AmSCAP 66, –80
Davis, Phoebe 1865- WhThe
Davis, Pike Clifton 1895- WhoJazz 72
Davis, Quin Hall 1944- EncJzS 70
Davis, Ray C WhoThe 77
Davis, Ray Dean 1949- AmSCAP 80
Davis, Redd 1896- IlWWBF
Davis, Rex 1890- Film 2, IlWWBF
Davis, Rex 1927- IntWWM 80
Davis, Richard 1930- AmSCAP 80, BiDAmM, EncJzS 70
Davis, Richard Harding 1864-1916 NotNAT B, WhThe, WhoStg 1906, –1908
Davis, Robert WhoHol A
Davis, Roger Film 2
Davis, Roger H 1923- IntMPA 77, –75, –76, –78, –79, –80
Davis, Roquel 1942- AmSCAP 80
Davis, Rufe 1908-1974 Vers A[port], WhScrn 77, WhoHol B
Davis, Rusty AmSCAP 80
Davis, Ryrrell Film 2
Davis, Sammy AmPS B
Davis, Sammy 1881?- NewOrJ
Davis, Sammy 1885- BiDAmM
Davis, Sammy, Jr. 1925- BiDAmM, BiE&WWA, DrBlPA, EncMT, Ent, FilmEn, FilmgC, ForYSC, HalFC 80, IntMPA 77, –75, –76, –78, –79, –80, MotPP, MovMk[port], NotNAT, –A, OxFilm, RkOn, WhoHol A, WhoThe 72, –77
Davis, Sammy, Jr. 1926- BlksBF[port]
Davis, Sammy, Jr. And Will Mastin Trio BlksBF[port]
Davis, Sharon 1937- AmSCAP 80, CpmDNM 77, –78, –79, IntWWM 80
Davis, Sheila 1927- AmSCAP 66, –80
Davis, Skeeter 1931- BiDAmM, CounME 74[port], –74A, EncFCWM 69, IlEncCM[port], RkOn[port]
Davis, Spencer ConMuA 80A
Davis, Spencer, Group RkOn 2[port]
Davis, Stringer 1896-1973 FilmgC, HalFC 80, WhoHol A
Davis, Stuart 1927?- NewOrJ
Davis, Sylvia WhoHol A
Davis, Thomas L 1931- AmSCAP 80
Davis, Tom Buffen 1867-1931 NotNAT B, WhThe
Davis, Tyrone 1938- RkOn 2[port]
Davis, Walter 1912-1963? BluesWW[port]
Davis, Walter, Jr. 1932- EncJzS 70
Davis, Wild Bill 1918- EncJzS 70, WhoJazz 72
Davis, Will J WhoStg 1908
Davis, William Film 2
Davis, William A NewYTET
Davis, William Boyd 1885- WhThe
Davis, William Dwight 1949- ConAmC
Davis, William Strethen 1918- BiDAmM, EncJzS 70
Davis, Willis J d1963 NotNAT B
Davis Sisters EncFCWM 69
Davison, A T 1883-1961 NewGrD 80
Davison, Archibald Thompson 1883-1961 Baker 78, BiDAmM, ConAmC
Davison, Arthur IntWWM 77, –80, WhoMus 72
Davison, Bruce 1948- FilmgC, HalFC 80, IntMPA 77, –75, –76, –78, –79, WhoHol A
Davison, Davey WhoHol A
Davison, J W 1813-1885 NewGrD 80
Davison, James William 1813-1885 Baker 78, OxMus
Davison, John H 1930- ConAmC
Davison, June 1908- IntWWM 77
Davison, Lesley AmSCAP 66, –80
Davison, Lita 1927- AmSCAP 80
Davison, Maria d1858 NotNAT B
Davison, Nigel St. John 1929- IntWWM 80, WhoMus 72
Davison, Peter 1948- ConAmC
Davison, Sid I 1941- AmSCAP 80
Davison, Wayne Marshall 1916- AmSCAP 66
Davison, Wild Bill 1906- CmpEPM, EncJzS 70, IlEncJ, WhoJazz 72
Davison, William Edward 1906- BiDAmM, EncJzS 70
Davisson, Ananias 1780-1857 NewGrD 80
D'Avril, Yola 1907- Film 2, ForYSC, TwYS
Davy, Charles 1722?-1797 NewGrD 80
Davy, Gloria 1931- DrBlPA, NewGrD 80, WhoMus 72
Davy, John 1763-1824 Baker 78, NewGrD 80, OxMus
Davy, Richard 1465?-1507? NewGrD 80, OxMus
Davy And Blake PupTheA
Davye, John Joseph 1929- CpmDNM 75, –76, –77, ConAmC, IntWWM 77, –80
Davys, Mary NewGrD 80
Daw, Evelyn 1912-1970 FilmgC, HalFC 80, WhScrn 74, –77, WhoHol B
Daw, Marjorie 1902- FilmEn, Film 1, –2, MotPP, TwYS
Dawber, Pam IntMPA 80
Dawe, Carlton d1935 NotNAT B
Dawe, Thomas F 1881-1928 WhThe
Dawes, Edwin A MagIlD
Dawes, Francis Eric 1902- WhoMus 72
Dawes, Frank 1910- IntWWM 77, –80, WhoMus 72
Dawes, William 1942- ConAmC
Dawison, Bogumil 1818-1872 EncWT, Ent
Dawkes, Hubert 1916- WhoMus 72
Dawkins, James Henry 1936- BluesWW[port]
Dawley, Herbert M PupTheA
Dawley, J Searle TwYS A
Dawley, J Searle d1950 FilmEn
Dawn RkOn 2[port]
Dawn, Allan Film 1
Dawn, Carl PupTheA
Dawn, Dolly 1919- AmSCAP 66, CmpEPM
Dawn, Doris Film 1
Dawn, Dorothy Film 2
Dawn, Faith PupTheA
Dawn, Hazel AmPS B, MotPP, What 2[port]
Dawn, Hazel 1891- CmpEPM, EncMT, Film 1, –2, TwYS, WhThe
Dawn, Hazel 1894- BiE&WWA, NotNAT, WhoHol A
Dawn, Hazel, Jr. WhoHol A
Dawn, Isabel 1905-1966 WhScrn 74, –77, WomWMM
Dawn, Jack 1889-1956 WhoHrs 80
Dawn, Janet 1935- Film 2
Dawn, Marpessa MotPP
Dawn, Marpessa 1935- DrBlPA
Dawn, Norman 1887- TwYS A
Dawney, Michael William 1942- IntWWM 77, –80, WhoMus 72
Dawson, Alan 1929- BiDAmM, EncJzS 70
Dawson, Anna WhoThe 77
Dawson, Anthony 1916- FilmgC, HalFC 80, IntMPA 77, –75, –76, –78, –79, –80, WhoHol A
Dawson, Beatrice 1908-1976 WhoThe 72, –77
Dawson, David 1939- IntWWM 80
Dawson, Dorice 1909-1950 WhScrn 74
Dawson, Doris 1909- Film 2, TwYS, WhoHol A
Dawson, Eddie 1884-1972 NewOrJ
Dawson, Eli 1880-1960 AmSCAP 66, –80
Dawson, Forbes 1860- WhThe
Dawson, Frank 1870-1953 WhScrn 74, –77, WhoHol B
Dawson, Frederick 1868-1940 NewGrD 80
Dawson, Hal K Vers B[port], WhoHol A
Dawson, Harold Allen 1950- AmSCAP 80
Dawson, Herbert William 1890- WhoMus 72
Dawson, Ivo d1934 Film 2, NotNAT B, WhoHol B
Dawson, Jenny d1936 NotNAT B
Dawson, Joan Copeland 1917- IntWWM 77, –80
Dawson, Julian 1937- WhoMus 72
Dawson, Mark 1920- BiE&WWA, NotNAT
Dawson, Nancy Juno WhoHol A
Dawson, Peter 1882-1961 OxMus
Dawson, Ralph d1962 NotNAT B
Dawson, Ralph 1897- FilmEn
Dawson, Richard WhoHol A
Dawson, Ted 1951- Baker 78
Dawson, Thomas H NewYTET
Dawson, William Levi 1897- ConAmC
Dawson, William Levi 1898- Baker 78, BiDAmM, DrBlPA, OxMus
Dawson, William Levi 1899- NewGrD 80
Dawson-Lyell, Julian 1947- IntWWM 80
Dax, Jean Film 2
Day, Alfred 1810-1849 NewGrD 80, OxMus

Day, Alice 1905- *FilmEn, Film 2, ForYSC, TwYS, WhoHol A*
Day, Ann Trent 1948- *IntWWM 80*
Day, Anna 1884- *WhoStg 1906, -1908*
Day, Bobby 1934- *BgBands 74, RkOn*
Day, Charles Russell 1860-1900 *Baker 78*
Day, Clarence *PupTheA*
Day, Cyrus L 1900-1968 *NotNAT B*
Day, Dennis *MotPP*
Day, Dennis 1917- *BiDAmM, CmpEPM, ForYSC, WhoHol A*
Day, Dennis 1921- *FilmgC, HalFC 80*
Day, Doris *AmPS A, -B*
Day, Doris 1922- *CmpEPM*
Day, Doris 1924- *BiDAmM, BiDFilm, -81, CmMov, FilmEn, FilmgC, ForYSC, HalFC 80, IntMPA 77, -75, -76, -78, -79, -80, MotPP, MovMk[port], OxFilm, RkOn[port], WhoHol A, WorEFlm*
Day, Dorothy 1898- *BiE&WWA*
Day, Dulcie 1911-1954 *WhScrn 74, -77*
Day, Edith 1896-1971 *AmPS B, BiDAmM, CmpEPM, EncMT, Film 1, NotNAT B, WhScrn 74, -77, WhThe, WhoHol B*
Day, Eric Harrold 1915- *WhoMus 72*
Day, Frances 1908- *EncMT, Film 2, FilmgC, HalFC 80, IlWWBF, WhThe, WhoHol A*
Day, George Henry 1883- *BiDAmM*
Day, Gordon M 1918- *IntMPA 77, -75, -76, -78, -79*
Day, James *NewYTET*
Day, James F 1917- *AmSCAP 66*
Day, James K 1917- *AmSCAP 80*
Day, Jill 1932-1978 *FilmgC, HalFC 80*
Day, John 1522-1584 *NewGrD 80, NotNAT B, OxMus*
Day, John 1574-1640? *CnThe, NotNAT B, OxThe, REnWD[port]*
Day, Josette 1914-1978 *FilmEn, FilmgC, HalFC 80, WhoHol A, WhoHrs 80*
Day, Juliette d1957 *NotNAT B, WhoHol B*
Day, Laraine *MotPP*
Day, Laraine 1917- *FilmEn, FilmgC, HalFC 80, ThFT[port], What 3[port]*
Day, Laraine 1919- *ForYSC, MGM[port], MovMk[port], WhoHol A*
Day, Laraine 1920- *IntMPA 77, -75, -76, -78, -79, -80*
Day, Lynda *WhoHol A*
Day, Marceline 1907- *FilmEn, Film 2, TwYS*
Day, Marceline 1908- *ForYSC, WhoHol A*
Day, Marie L 1855-1939 *WhScrn 74, -77, WhoHol B*
Day, Marjorie *Film 2*
Day, Marjorie 1889- *WhThe*
Day, Mary *CnOxB, DancEn 78*
Day, Olga *Film 2*
Day, Ralph William 1895- *AmSCAP 66, -80*
Day, Richard *ConAmC*
Day, Richard d1973 *WhoHol B*
Day, Richard 1552-1607? *NewGrD 80*
Day, Richard 1894-1972 *FilmgC, HalFC 80*
Day, Richard 1896- *WorEFlm*
Day, Richard 1896-1972 *FilmEn*
Day, Richard Digby 1940- *WhoThe 72, -77*
Day, Richard Wrisley 1936- *ConAmTC*
Day, Robert 1922- *FilmEn, FilmgC, HalFC 80, IlWWBF, IntMPA 77, -75, -76, -78, -79, -80*
Day, Roy d1963 *NotNAT B*
Day, Rusty *AmSCAP 80*
Day, Shannon *Film 2, WhoHol A*
Day, Stanley A 1894- *AmSCAP 66*
Day, Stanley A 1894-1975 *AmSCAP 80*
Day, Susan Hartman 1949- *IntWWM 77*
Day, Tom *Film 2*
Day, Vera 1939- *IlWWBF*
Day, Vernon Alfred Francis 1935- *WhoMus 72*
Day, Yvonne 1920- *Film 2*
Dayan, Assaf *WhoHol A*
Dayan, Assaf 1945- *FilmEn*
Dayas, William Humphreys 1863-1903 *Baker 78*
Dayde, Bernard 1921- *DancEn 78*
Dayde, Bernard Helin Henri 1921- *CnOxB, WhoOp 76*
Dayde, Liane 1932- *CnOxB*
Dayde, Liane 1934- *DancEn 78[port]*
Daye, Irene 1918?-1971 *BiDAmM, CmpEPM*
Daykarhanova, Tamara 1892- *BiE&WWA, NotNAT*
Dayman, Bain, Sr. d1964 *NotNAT B*
Dayne, Blanche d1944 *NotNAT B*
Dayton, Craig *AmSCAP 80*
Dayton, Frank 1865-1924 *Film 1, WhScrn 77*
Dayton, Lewis *Film 1, -2*
Dayton, Lyman D 1941- *IntMPA 77, -75, -76, -78, -79, -80*
Dayton, Michael Owen 1948- *IntWWM 77, -80*
Daza, Esteban *NewGrD 80*
Daze, Mercedes 1892-1945 *WhScrn 74, -77, WhoHol B*
Dazey, Charles Turner 1853-1938 *NotNAT B, WhThe, WhoStg 1906, -1908*
Dazie, Mademoiselle 1882-1952 *WhThe*
Dazie, Mademoiselle 1884-1952 *NotNAT B, WhoStg 1906, -1908*
DeAbravanel, Maurice 1903- *BiDAmM*
Deacon, Mary Conner 1907- *AmSCAP 80*
Deacon, Mary Connor 1907- *AmSCAP 66, ConAmC A*
Deacon, Michael Cameron 1952- *IntWWM 77*
Deacon, Richard 1923- *FilmgC, ForYSC, HalFC 80, MotPP, WhoHol A*
Deacy, Jane *BiE&WWA*
Dead End Kids *JoeFr*
Deadeye, Sheriff *JoeFr*
Deagan, Charles 1880-1932 *WhScrn 74, -77*
Deagon, Arthur d1927 *NotNAT B*
Deagon, Arthur 1873- *WhoStg 1908*
Deahl, Robert W 1928- *IntWWM 77, -80*
DeAhna, Heinrich Karl Hermann 1835-1892 *Baker 78*
Deak, Csaba 1932- *Baker 78*
Deak, Jon 1943- *ConAmC*
Deak, Tamas 1928- *IntWWM 77, -80*
Deakin, Andrew 1822-1903 *Baker 78*
Deakin, Irving 1901-1958 *DancEn 78*
Deakin, Richard 1946- *IntWWM 77, -80*
Deal, Bill & The Rhondells *RkOn 2[port]*
DeAlba, Carlos 1925-1960 *WhScrn 74, -77*
DeAlmeida, Antonio 1928- *IntWWM 77, -80, WhoMus 72, WhoOp 76*
DeAmicis, Anna Lucia 1733?-1816 *NewGrD 80*
DeAmicis-Buonsollazzi, Anna Lucia 1733?-1816 *NewGrD 80*
Dean And Jean *RkOn*
Dean, Alexander d1939 *NotNAT B, PlP&P*
Dean, Barbara *Film 2*
Dean, Barney 1904-1954 *WhScrn 74, -77, WhoHol B*
Dean, Basil 1888-1978 *EncWT, FilmEn, Film 2, FilmgC, HalFC 80, IlWWBF, -A, ModWD, OxThe, WhThe*
Dean, Beth *DancEn 78*
Dean, Dacia *Film 2*
Dean, Dearest *AmSCAP 80*
Dean, Demas 1903- *WhoJazz 72*
Dean, Dinky *Film 2, WhoHol A*
Dean, Dizzy 1911- *What 2[port]*
Dean, Donald Wesley 1937- *BiDAmM*
Dean, Dorris *Film 2*
Dean, Eddie *IntMPA 75, -76, -78, -79, -80*
Dean, Eddie 1907- *BiDAmM, IlEncCM[port]*
Dean, Eddie 1908?- *FilmgC, ForYSC, HalFC 80, IntMPA 77, WhoHol A*
Dean, Eddie 1910?- *FilmEn*
Dean, Elisabeth *WhoMus 72*
Dean, Fabian 1930-1971 *WhScrn 74, -77, WhoHol B*
Dean, George Dixie 1916- *IntWWM 80*
Dean, Hector *Film 1*
Dean, Isabel 1918- *FilmgC, HalFC 80, WhoHol A, WhoThe 72, -77*
Dean, Ivor d1964 *WhoHol B*
Dean, Ivor 1917-1974 *WhScrn 77*
Dean, Jack 1875-1950 *Film 1, WhScrn 77, WhoHol B*
Dean, James 1931-1955 *BiDFilm, -81, FilmEn, FilmgC, ForYSC, HalFC 80, MotPP, MovMk[port], NotNAT B, OxFilm, WhScrn 74, -77, WhoHol B, WorEFlm[port]*
Dean, Jimmy 1928- *AmPS A, -B, BiDAmM, CounME 74[port], -74A, EncFCWM 69, IlEncCM[port], IntMPA 77, -75, -76, -78, -79, -80, RkOn[port], WhoHol A*
Dean, John Theodore 1934- *IntWWM 80*
Dean, John W d1950 *NotNAT B*
Dean, Julia 1830-1868 *NotNAT B, OxThe*
Dean, Julia 1830-1869 *FamA&A[port]*
Dean, Julia 1878-1952 *Film 1, FilmgC, HalFC 80, Vers B[port], WhScrn 74, -77, WhoHol B*
Dean, Julia 1878-1953 *ForYSC, TwYS*
Dean, Julia 1880-1952 *NotNAT B, WhThe*
Dean, Julie *MotPP*
Dean, Laura Sweedler 1945- *CmpGMD[port], CnOxB*
Dean, Lorene *AmSCAP 80*
Dean, Louis *Film 1*
Dean, Man Mountain 1890-1953 *WhScrn 74, -77, WhoHol B*
Dean, Man Mountain 1899-1963 *HalFC 80*
Dean, Margia *ForYSC, WhoHol A*
Dean, Mary *PupTheA*
Dean, May d1937 *WhScrn 74, -77, WhoHol B*
Dean, Nelson 1882-1923 *WhScrn 74, -77*
Dean, Peter 1911- *AmSCAP 80, BgBands 74*
Dean, Peyton *MorBAP*
Dean, Philip Hayes *BlkAmP, PlP&P A[port]*
Dean, Phillip Hayes *DrBlPA, MorBAP*
Dean, Priscilla 1896- *FilmEn, Film 1, -2, MotPP, TwYS, WhoHol A*
Dean, Ralph 1868-1923 *WhScrn 74, -77*
Dean, Robert G, Jr. 1939- *AmSCAP 80*
Dean, Rose 1892-1952 *WhScrn 74, -77*
Dean, Ruby 1887-1935 *WhScrn 74, -77*
Dean, Sherry *WhoHol A*
Dean, Stafford 1937- *CmOp, NewGrD 80, WhoOp 76*
Dean, Stafford Roderick 1937- *IntWWM 77, -80, WhoMus 72*
Dean, Talmage Whitman 1915- *ConAmC, IntWWM 77, -80*
Dean, Thomas *NewGrD 80*
Dean, Walter *ConMuA 80B*
Dean, Winton 1916- *Baker 78, NewGrD 80, OxMus, WhoMus 72*
Dean, Winton Basil 1916- *IntWWM 77, -80*
DeAna, Hugo 1949- *WhoOp 76*
DeAnda, Agustin 1935-1960 *WhScrn 74, -77*
DeAnda, Peter 1940- *BlkAmP, DrBlPA, HalFC 80, MorBAP*
Deane, Barbara 1886- *WhThe*
Deane, Basil 1928- *IntWWM 80, NewGrD 80*
Deane, Derry Ruth 1932- *WhoMus 72*
Deane, Doris 1901-1974 *WhScrn 77, WhoHol B*
Deane, Dorothy *AmSCAP 80*
Deane, Eddie V 1929- *AmSCAP 66, -80*
Deane, Hazel *Film 1, -2, TwYS*
Deane, Shirley *ForYSC*
Deane, Sidney *Film 2*
Deane, Sydney *Film 1*
Deane, Tessa *WhThe*
Deane, Thomas 1686?- *NewGrD 80*
Deane, Verna *Film 2*
Deane-Drummond, Sophia T Pemberton *CreCan 1*
DeAngelis, Angelo d1825? *NewGrD 80*
DeAngelis, Jefferson 1859-1933 *AmPS B, CmpEPM, NotNAT A, -B, WhScrn 77, WhThe, WhoStg 1906, -1908*
DeAngelis, Nazareno 1881-1962 *NewEOp 71*
DeAngelis, Nazzareno 1881-1962 *CmOp, NewGrD 80*
DeAngelis, Peter 1929- *AmSCAP 66, -80*
DeAngelis, Thomas Jefferson 1859-1933 *OxThe*
DeAngelo, Carlo d1962 *NotNAT B*
DeAnglia, John *NewGrD 80*
Deans, F Harris 1886-1961 *NotNAT B, WhThe*
Deans, Marjorie *WomWMM*
DeAntonio, Emile 1920- *FilmEn*
Dearden, Basil 1911-1971 *BiDFilm, -81, CmMov, DcFM, FilmEn, FilmgC, HalFC 80, IlWWBF, MovMk[port], OxFilm, WhoHrs 80, WorEFlm*
Dearden, Harold 1882- *WhThe*
Dearholt, Ashton *Film 1, -2*
Dearie, Blossom 1926- *EncJzS 70, IlEncJ*
Dearing, Edgar 1893-1974 *Film 2, HalFC 80, Vers B[port], WhScrn 77, WhoHol B*
Dearing, Peter 1912- *WhThe*
Dearing, Richard *NewGrD 80*
Dearly, Max 1874-1943 *NotNAT B, WhScrn 74, -77, WhoHol B*
Dearly, Max 1875-1943 *WhThe*

Dearmer, Percy 1867-1936 *OxMus*
Dearner, Mrs. Percy d1915 *NotNAT B*
Dearnley, Christopher Hugh 1930- *IntWWM 77, -80, NewGrD 80*
Dearnley, Dorothy Alice 1914- *IntWWM 77, -80*
Dearth, Harry 1876-1933 *NotNAT B, WhThe*
Deas, James Stewart 1903- *OxMus*
Deas, Stewart 1903- *WhoMus 72*
Dease, Bobby 1899-1958 *WhScrn 74, -77, WhoHol B*
Deasey, Michael Keith 1947- *IntWWM 77, -80*
Deason, David 1945- *CpmDNM 80*
Deason, William David 1945- *AmSCAP 80*
DeAspre, Jehan Simon *NewGrD 80*
DeAspre, Johannes Symonis *NewGrD 80*
Deathridge, John William 1944- *IntWWM 77, -80*
D'Eaubonne, Jean 1903-1971 *DcFM, FilmEn, WorEFlm*
DeAubry, Diane 1890-1969 *WhScrn 74, -77, WhoHol B*
Deaves, Ada d1920 *NotNAT B*
Deaves, Edwin 1809-1890? *PupTheA*
Deaves, Edwin 1889-1941 *PupTheA*
Deaves, Harry 1860?-1927 *PupTheA*
Deaves, Walter Eugene 1854-1919 *PupTheA*
Debain, Alexandre Francois 1809-1877 *Baker 78, NewGrD 80, OxMus*
Debain, Henri *Film 2*
DeBalzac, Jeanne d1930 *WhScrn 77*
DeBanfield, Raffaello 1922- *WhoOp 76*
DeBanos, Richard 1884-1939 *FilmEn*
DeBanzie, Brenda 1915- *BiE&WWA, FilmEn, FilmgC, HalFC 80, IlWWBF[port], IntMPA 77, -75, -76, -78, -79, -80, NotNAT, WhThe, WhoHol A, WhoThe 72*
DeBanzie, Lois *WhoHol A*
DeBaroncelli, Jacques *FilmEn*
DeBaroncelli, Jacques 1881-1951 *DcFM, WorEFlm*
DeBarros, Eudoxia 1937- *IntWWM 80*
DeBasil, Wassily d1951 *WhThe*
DeBasil, Wassily 1888-1951 *DancEn 78*
DeBear, Archibald 1889-1970 *WhThe*
DeBeaumarchais, Pierre-Augustin Caron *PlP&P*
DeBeck, Billy *Film 2*
DeBecker, Harold 1889-1947 *WhScrn 74, -77, WhoHol B*
DeBecker, Marie 1881-1946 *WhScrn 74, -77, WhoHol B*
DeBegnis, Giuseppe 1793-1849 *NewEOp 71*
DeBelleville, Frederic 1857-1923 *NotNAT B, WhThe, WhoStg 1906, -1908*
DeBellis, Enzo 1907- *WhoMus 72*
DeBellis, Giovanni Battista 1585?-1637? *NewGrD 80*
Debenedictis, Richard 1937- *AmSCAP 80*
Debenham, Cicely 1891-1955 *NotNAT B, WhThe*
DeBeradinis, John Arthur 1943- *ConAmC*
DeBeranger, Andre *Film 2*
DeBergerac, Cyrano *OxThe*
DeBergerac, Savinien DeCyrano 1619-1655 *Ent*
Debi, Arundhati *WomWMM*
DeBiere, Arnold 1878-1934 *MagIID*
Debin, Nat 1911- *BiE&WWA*
DeBlanc, Damita Jo 1933- *BiDAmM*
DeBlasio, Gene 1940-1971 *WhScrn 77*
DeBlasio, Ron *ConMuA 80B*
DeBlasis, James Michael 1931- *BiE&WWA, WhoOp 76*
DeBodamere, Madame *Film 2*
DeBoeck, Auguste 1865-1937 *Baker 78*
DeBoer VanRijk, Esther d1937 *NotNAT B*
Debolecki, Wojciech 1585?-1647? *NewGrD 80*
DeBord, Sharon *WhoHol A*
DeBornier, Henri d1901 *NotNAT B*
DeBosio, Gianfranco 1924- *EncWT, WorEFlm*
Debost, Michel H 1934- *BnBkM 80, WhoMus 72*
DeBourbon, Princess Marie *Film 2*
DeBoyescu, Parepa *NewGrD 80*
DeBozoky, Barbara 1871-1937 *WhScrn 77*
DeBrant, Cyr *AmSCAP 80*
Debras, Louis G M 1938- *ConAmC, IntWWM 77, -80*
DeBrassine *NewGrD 80*
DeBray, Harold 1874-1932 *WhScrn 74, -77*
DeBray, Henri 1889-1965 *WhScrn 74, -77*
DeBray, Henry 1889-1965 *WhThe*
DeBray, Yvonne *FilmEn*
DeBray, Yvonne 1889-1954 *FilmgC, HalFC 80, WhScrn 74, -77, WhoHol B*
DeBremaeker, Angele M 1893- *IntWWM 80*
DeBrest, James 1937-1973 *EncJzS 70*
DeBrest, Spanky 1937-1973 *EncJzS 70*
DeBrey, Claire *Film 1*
DeBriac, Jean *Film 2*
DeBriac Twins *Film 2*
DeBrie, Mademoiselle 1620?-1706? *EncWT*
Debrie, Andre 1880-1967 *OxFilm*
Debrie, Andre 1891-1967 *FilmEn*
DeBrie, Catherine 1620?-1706 *Ent*
DeBrie, Catherine Leclerc DuRozet 1630?-1706 *OxThe*
DeBrie, Edme Villequin 1607-1676 *EncWT, OxThe*
Debrnov, Josef *NewGrD 80*
DeBroca, Philippe *FilmEn*
DeBroca, Philippe 1920- *OxFilm*
DeBroca, Philippe 1933- *BiDFilm, -81, FilmgC, HalFC 80, IntMPA 77, -75, -76, -78, -79, -80, WorEFlm*
DeBroca, Philippe 1935- *DcFM, MovMk[port]*
DeBroda, Paulus *NewGrD 80*
DeBromhead, Jerome Andrew 1945- *IntWWM 80*
DeBroyer, Lisette *WomWMM*
DeBrulier, Nigel 1878-1948 *FilmEn, Film 1, -2, FilmgC, ForYSC, HalFC 80, HolCA[port], TwYS, WhScrn 74, -77, WhoHol B*
DeBruyn, Randall Keith 1947- *ConAmC*
Debucourt, Jean 1894-1958 *Film 2, FilmgC, HalFC 80, WhScrn 74, -77, WhoHol B*
DeBuescher, Henri 1880- *NewGrD 80*
Deburau, Charles 1829-1873 *NotNAT B, OxThe*
Deburau, Jean-Baptiste Gaspard 1796-1846 *EncWT, Ent[port], NotNAT A, -B*
Deburau, Jean-Gaspard 1796-1846 *CnThe, OxThe*
DeBurgh, Aimee d1946 *NotNAT B, WhThe*
DeBurgos, Rafael Fruhbeck *WhoMus 72*
Debuskey, Merle 1923- *BiE&WWA, NotNAT*
DeBusne, Antoine *NewGrD 80*
DeBusscher, Henri 1880- *NewGrD 80*
DeBussy *NewGrD 80*
Debussy, Claude 1862-1918 *Baker 78, BnBkM 80[port], CmOp, CmpBCM, CompSN[port], CnOxB, DcCom 77[port], DcCom&M 79, DcCM, DcPup, DcTwCC, MusMk, NewEOp 71, NewGrD 80[port], OxMus*
Decadt, Jan 1914- *Baker 78, NewGrD 80[port]*
Decadt, Jean 1914- *IntWWM 77, -80*
Decae, Henri 1915- *FilmEn, FilmgC, HalFC 80, IntMPA 79, -80, OxFilm, WorEFlm*
Decae, Henry 1915- *DcFM*
DeCaesar, Gabriel 1928- *IntMPA 77, -75, -76, -78, -79, -80*
DeCaix D'Hervelois, Louis *NewGrD 80*
DeCamp, Dot *NatPD[port]*
DeCamp, Rosemary *IntMPA 75, -76, MotPP, WhoHol A*
DeCamp, Rosemary 1913- *FilmgC, ForYSC, HalFC 80, IntMPA 77, -78, -79, -80, MovMk*
DeCamp, Rosemary 1914- *FilmEn, HolCA[port], Vers B[port]*
DeCampo, Guiseppe *Film 2*
DeCanonge, Maurice *Film 2*
Decapella *NewGrD 80*
DeCaprio, Al *IntMPA 77, -75, -76, -78, -79, -80*
DeCarlo, Rita Frances 1938- *WhoOp 76*
DeCarlo, Yvonne *MotPP, PlP&P A[port], WhoHol A*
DeCarlo, Yvonne 1922- *BiDFilm, -81, CmMov, FilmEn, FilmgC, ForYSC, HalFC 80, MovMk, WhoHrs 80, WorEFlm[port]*
DeCarlo, Yvonne 1924- *CmMov, IntMPA 77, -75, -76, -78, -79, -80*
DeCarlos, Perla Granda 1903-1973 *WhScrn 77*
DeCarlton, George *Film 1, -2*
DeCarmo, Pussy d1964 *NotNAT B*
DeCarvalho, Raul 1901- *FilmAG WE*
DeCarvalho, Rui 1926- *FilmAG WE*
DeCasalis, Jean 1897-1966 *IlWWBF A*
DeCasalis, Jeanne d1966 *WhoHol B*
DeCasalis, Jeanne 1896-1966 *FilmgC, HalFC 80*
DeCasalis, Jeanne 1897-1966 *IlWWBF, WhScrn 74, -77, WhThe*
DeCastrejon, Blanca 1916-1969 *WhScrn 77*
DeCastrejon, Blance 1916-1969 *WhScrn 74*
DeCastro, Dolores *WomWMM B*
DeCastro Sisters, The *RkOn*
Decaux, Abel 1869-1943 *NewGrD 80*
DeCecco, Disma *WhoOp 76*
DeCesare, Ruth 1923- *IntWWM 77, -80*
DeCevee, Alice 1904- *AmSCAP 66, ConAmC*
Dechario, Tony Houston 1940- *IntWWM 77, -80*
Dechevrens, Antoine 1840-1912 *Baker 78, NewGrD 80*
Deci, Josip 1904- *IntWWM 77, -80*
DeCicco, Pat *WhoHol A*
DeCimber, Joseph Valentino 1898- *AmSCAP 66, -80*
DeCisneros, Eleanora Broadfoot 1878-1934 *BiDAmM*
DeCisneros, Eleonora 1878-1934 *NotNAT B*
Decius, Nikolaus 1485?-1546? *NewGrD 80*
Decker, Diana 1926- *FilmgC, HalFC 80*
Decker, Franz-Paul 1923- *IntWWM 77, -80, WhoOp 76*
Decker, Harold Augustus 1914- *IntWWM 77, -80*
Decker, Joachim 1575?-1611 *NewGrD 80*
Decker, Johann 1598-1668 *NewGrD 80*
Decker, John 1895-1947 *WhScrn 74, -77*
Decker, Kathryn Browne d1919 *WhScrn 77*
Deckers, Eugene 1917-1977 *FilmgC, HalFC 80, WhoHol A*
Decleir, Jan *FilmAG WE*
DeCoeur, A *Film 2*
Decoeur, M Albert *Film 1*
Decoin, Henri 1896-1969 *DcFM, FilmEn, FilmgC, HalFC 80, WorEFlm*
DeCola, Felix 1906- *AmSCAP 80*
DeCola, Felix 1910- *AmSCAP 66*
DeCollibus, Nicholas 1913- *AmSCAP 80*
DeColonia, Juan *PupTheA*
Decombie, Guy d1964 *WhScrn 77*
DeConde, Syn *WhoHol A*
Deconet, Michele 1712?-1780? *NewGrD 80*
DeConynck, Romein 1925- *FilmAG WE*
DeCoppet, Edward J 1855-1916 *BiDAmM*
DeCoppett, Theodosia *WhScrn 74, -77*
DeCordoba, Pedro 1881-1950 *FilmEn, Film 1, -2, FilmgC, ForYSC, HalFC 80, MotPP, MovMk, NotNAT B, TwYS, WhScrn 74, -77, WhThe, WhoHol B, WhoHrs 80*
DeCordova, Arturo d1973 *MotPP, WhoHol B*
DeCordova, Arturo 1907-1973 *WhScrn 77*
DeCordova, Arturo 1908-1973 *FilmEn, FilmgC, ForYSC, HalFC 80*
DeCordova, Fred 1910- *NewYTET*
DeCordova, Frederick 1910- *FilmEn, FilmgC, HalFC 80, IntMPA 77, -75, -76, -78, -79, -80*
DeCordova, Leander 1878-1936 *WhScrn 77*
DeCordova, Rudolf *Film 2*
DeCordova, Rudolph 1860-1941 *NotNAT B, WhThe*
DeCormier, Robert 1922- *AmSCAP 66, -80*
DeCorsia, Ted 1903-1973 *HolCA[port]*
DeCorsia, Ted 1904-1973 *FilmEn, HalFC 80, WhScrn 77, WhoHol B*
DeCorsia, Ted 1905 *ForYSC*
DeCorsia, Ted 1906- *FilmgC*
Decorus, Volupius *NewGrD 80*
DeCosmo, Emile 1924- *AmSCAP 80*
DeCosta, Harry 1885-1964 *AmSCAP 66*
Decosta, Harry 1885-1964 *AmSCAP 80*
DeCosta, Morris 1890-1957 *WhScrn 74, -77*
Decou, Harold H 1932- *AmSCAP 80*
Decou, Patricia R 1945- *AmSCAP 80*
Decou, Walter 1890?-1966 *NewOrJ*
Decourcelle, Adrien d1892 *NotNAT B*
Decourcelle, Pierre 1856-1926 *NotNAT B, WhThe*
DeCourcy, Eric Henry 1922- *WhoMus 72*
DeCourcy, Ken *MagIID*
DeCourcy, Nanette *Film 2*

DeCourelle, Rose Marie *Film 2*
Decoursey, Nettie d1964 *NotNAT B*
DeCourville, Albert P 1887-1960 *FilmgC, HalFC 80, IlWWBF, -A, NotNAT A, -B, WhThe*
Decoust, Michel 1936- *Baker 78, NewGrD 80*
DeCoy, Robert d1975 *WhScrn 77*
DeCoy, Robert H 1920- *BlkAmP*
DeCrescenzo, Vincenzo 1875-1964 *AmSCAP 66, -80, ConAmC A*
Decreus, Camille 1876-1939 *Baker 78*
DeCrevecoeur, Jeanne *PupTheA*
DeCroisset, Francis d1937 *NotNAT B*
Decroux, Etienne 1898- *EncWT, Ent[port]*
Decroux, Maximilian *EncWT*
Decsenyi, Janos 1927- *IntWWM 77, -80, NewGrD 80*
Decsey, Ernst 1870-1941 *Baker 78, NewGrD 80*
DeCsillery, Bela *WhoMus 72*
Dectreaux, Evelyn 1902-1952 *WhScrn 74, -77*
DeCuevas, George, Marquis 1886-1961 *DancEn 78*
DeCuir, John 1918- *FilmEn, FilmgC, HalFC 80, IntMPA 77, -75, -76, -78, -79, -80*
DeCupis *NewGrD 80*
DeCurel, Francois Viscomte d1928 *NotNAT B*
DeCurtis, Antonio 1898-1967 *FilmAG WE*
DeCyr, Zel *IntMPA 77, -75, -76, -78, -79, -80*
Dede, Edmund 1829-1903 *BiDAmM, OxMus*
Dedeaux, Richard A 1940- *BlkAmP*
Dedecius, Richard 1945- *WhoMus 72*
Dedekind, Constantin Christian 1628-1715 *NewGrD 80*
Dedekind, Euricius 1554-1619 *NewGrD 80*
Dedekind, Henning 1562-1626 *NewGrD 80*
Deden, Otto 1925- *IntWWM 77, -80*
DeDenise, Fred 1912- *AmSCAP 80*
Dedi *MagIlD*
DeDica, Vittorio 1901- *ForYSC*
Dedinstev, A *Film 2*
Dedrick, Arthur 1915- *ConAmC*
Dedrick, Christopher 1947- *ConAmC*
Dedrick, Lyle F 1918- *ConAmC, EncJzS 70*
Dedrick, Matilda Farrell 1899- *IntWWM 77*
Dedrick, Rusty 1918- *CmpEPM, EncJzS 70*
Dedroit, Johnny 1892- *NewOrJ*
Dedroit, Paul 1894-1963 *NewOrJ*
Dee, Frances *MotPP, WhoHol A, WomWMM*
Dee, Frances 1907- *FilmEn, FilmgC, ForYSC, HolP 30[port], ThFT[port], What 5[port]*
Dee, Frances 1908- *HalFC 80, MovMk*
Dee, Freddie 1924-1958 *WhScrn 74, -77, WhoHol B*
Dee, Jimmy *RkOn*
Dee, Joey 1940- *BiDAmM*
Dee, Joey And Starliters *AmPS A*
Dee, Joey And The Starlighters *RkOn*
Dee, Johnny *RkOn*
Dee, Kiki 1947- *IlEncR, RkOn 2[port]*
Dee, Lenny *RkOn*
Dee, Mercy *BluesWW*
Dee, Richard 1936- *ConAmC*
Dee, Ruby *BiE&WWA, MotPP, NotNAT, WhoHol A, WomWMM*
Dee, Ruby 1923- *DrBlPA, ForYSC, HalFC 80, MorBAP, WhoThe 72, -77*
Dee, Ruby 1924- *BlksB&W[port], -C, FilmEn, FilmgC, MovMk[port]*
Dee, Sandra 1942- *FilmEn, FilmgC, ForYSC, HalFC 80, IntMPA 77, -75, -76, -78, -79, -80, MotPP, MovMk[port], WhoHol A*
Dee, Sylvia 1914-1967 *AmSCAP 66, -80*
Dee, Tommy 1940- *RkOn*
Deed, Andre 1884- *OxFilm, WhScrn 77*
Deed, Andre 1884-1938 *FilmEn*
Deeflos, Huguette *Film 2*
Deeg, Nikolaus *NewGrD 80*
Deege, Gisela 1928- *CnOxB, DancEn 78*
Deel, Sandra *WhoHol A*
Deeley, Ben 1878-1924 *Film 1, -2, WhoHol B*
Deeley, J Bernard 1878-1924 *WhScrn 74, -77*
Deeley, Michael 1931- *FilmgC, HalFC 80*
Deeley, Michael 1932- *IntMPA 77, -75, -76, -78, -79, -80*
Deems, Barrett 1914- *WhoJazz 72*
Deems, Barrett B 1913- *EncJzS 70*
Deems, James Monroe 1818-1901 *BiDAmM*
Deems, Mickey 1925- *BiE&WWA, NotNAT*
Deen, Nedra d1975 *WhScrn 77, WhoHol C, WomWMM B*
Deep Purple *BiDAmM, ConMuA 80A, IlEncR[port], RkOn 2[port]*
Deer, Alma *Film 2*
Deer, Louis *Film 2*
Deering, John d1955 *WhoHol B*
Deering, John 1905-1959 *WhScrn 74, -77*
Deering, Marda d1961 *WhoHol B*
Deering, Olive *ForYSC, NotNAT, WhoHol A, WhoThe 77*
Deering, Patricia *Film 2*
Deering, Richard 1580?-1630 *Baker 78, NewGrD 80, OxMus*
Deering, Richard Jon 1947- *IntWWM 77, -80*
Deering, Tommy 1938- *AmSCAP 66*
Deery, Jack *Film 2*
Dees, Rick *ConMuA 80B*
Dees, Rick & His Cast Of Idiots *RkOn 2[port]*
Dees, Sylvia *WomWMM B*
DeEsta *PupTheA*
Deeter, Jasper 1893-1972 *BiE&WWA, NotNAT B*
Deeter, Jasper 1895-1972 *WhScrn 77*
Deevy, Teresa d1963 *NotNAT B*
DeFabritiis, Oliviero 1902- *NewGrD 80*
DeFabritiis, Oliviero 1904- *WhoOp 76*
DeFalla, Manuel 1876-1946 *DcPup, NewEOp 71*
DeFalla, Manuel 1877-1946 *DancEn 78*
DeFas, Boris *Film 2*
DeFast, Boris *Film 2*
DeFaut, Volley 1904- *EncJzS 70, WhoJazz 72*
DeFaut, Voltaire 1904- *EncJzS 70*
Defauw, Desire 1885-1960 *Baker 78, BiDAmM, NewGrD 80*
DeFeghe, Willem *NewGrD 80*
DeFelice, Alfredo *Film 2*
DeFeraudy, Maurice *Film 2*
DeFeraudy, Maurice d1873 *NotNAT B*
DeFeraudy, Maurice 1859-1932 *WhScrn 77*
DeFerra, Giampaolo 1929- *WhoOp 76*
DeFerrari, Serafino 1824-1885 *NewGrD 80*
DeFerraris, Paolo Agostino *NewGrD 80*
DeFesch, Willem 1687-1757? *NewGrD 80[port]*
Deffayet, Daniel 1922- *IntWWM 80*
Deffes, Pierre-Louis 1819-1900 *Baker 78*
DeFilippi, Amedeo 1900- *AmSCAP 66, -80, ConAmC, IntWWM 77, -80*
DeFilippo, Eduardo 1900- *CmOp, CnMD, CnThe, CroCD, EncWT, Ent, FilmAG WE, FilmEn, HalFC 80, McGEWD[port], ModWD, OxThe, REnWD[port], WhoOp 76, WorEFlm*
DeFilippo, Peppino 1903- *EncWT, FilmAG WE, OxThe*
DeFilippo, Titina 1898-1963 *EncWT, FilmAG WE, OxThe*
DeFillippo, Eduardo 1900- *FilmgC*
DeFlers, Robert d1927 *NotNAT B*
DeFoe, Annette 1889-1960 *Film 2, WhScrn 77, WhoHol B*
Defoe, Daniel 1660?-1731 *DcPup, FilmgC, HalFC 80*
DeFoe, Louis Vincent 1869-1922 *NotNAT B, WhThe*
DeFontenoy, Diane 1878- *WhThe*
DeFoor, John W 1929- *AmSCAP 66, -80*
DeFore, Don *MotPP, WhoHol A*
DeFore, Don 1916- *BiE&WWA, NotNAT*
Defore, Don 1917- *FilmEn, FilmgC, ForYSC, HalFC 80, MovMk[port]*
DeForest, Charles 1928- *AmSCAP 66, -80*
DeForest, Hal 1862-1938 *WhScrn 74, -77, WhoHol B*
DeForest, Lee 1873-1961 *FilmEn, FilmgC, HalFC 80, NewYTET, WorEFlm*
DeForest, Marian d1935 *NotNAT B*
DeForrest, Maude 1900?- *BluesWW*
Defossez, Rene 1905- *Baker 78, NewGrD 80, WhoMus 72*
De'Franceschi *NewGrD 80*
DeFrancesco, Amada Santos-Ocampo 1927- *IntWWM 77, -80*
DeFrancesco, Louis E 1888-1974 *AmSCAP 66, -80*
DeFranco, Boniface 1923- *AmSCAP 66, -80, BiDAmM, EncJzS 70*
DeFranco, Buddy 1923- *CmpEPM, EncJzS 70, IlEncJ*
DeFranco Family, The *RkOn 2[port]*
DeFrank, Vincent 1915- *IntWWM 77, -80*
DeFrece, Lady 1864-1952 *NotNAT A*
DeFrece, Lauri 1880-1921 *WhThe*
DeFrece, Walter 1870- *WhThe*
DeFreitas, Frederico 1902- *IntWWM 80*
Defresne, August 1893- *CnMD*
DeFroment, Louis Georges Francois 1921- *IntWWM 77, -80, NewGrD 80, WhoMus 72*
Defronciaco *NewGrD 80*
DeFrumerie, Gunnar 1908- *WhoMus 72*
DeFunes, Louis *FilmEn*
DeFunes, Louis 1908- *FilmgC, HalFC 80*
DeFunes, Louis 1914- *FilmAG WE, WorEFlm*
DeGabarain, Marina 1926 *WhoMus 72*
DeGabarain, Marina 1928- *IntWWM 80*
DeGaetani, Jan 1933- *Baker 78, NewGrD 80*
DeGaetani, Thomas 1929- *BiE&WWA, DancEn 78*
DeGaetano, Michael A 1939- *IntMPA 77, -75, -76*
DeGalantha, Yekaterina 1898- *DancEn 78*
DeGante, Pedro 1500?-1572? *BiDAmM*
DeGarde, Adele *Film 1, TwYS*
Degas, Edgar Hilaire Germain 1834-1917 *CnOxB, DancEn 78*
DeGaston, Gallie 1890-1937 *BlksBF*
DeGastyne, Serge 1930- *AmSCAP 66, -80, CpmDNM 73, ConAmC*
DeGay, Sylvia *WhoMus 72*
Degelin, Emile 1926- *DcFM*
Degen, Helmut 1911- *Baker 78, IntWWM 80, NewGrD 80*
Degen, Johann 1585?-1637 *NewGrD 80*
Degener, Claire S 1928- *BiE&WWA*
DeGeorge, Carleton *Film 2*
Degermark, Pia 1949- *HalFC 80, WhoHol A*
DeGeymuller, Marguerite-Camille-Louise 1897- *IntWWM 77*
Degeyter, Pierre 1848-1932 *Baker 78*
Degeyter, Pierre 1849-1932 *OxMus*
Deggeler, Johann Caspar 1695-1776 *NewGrD 80*
Deggeller, Johann Caspar 1695-1776 *NewGrD 80*
Degiardino, Felice *NewGrD 80*
DeGiosa, Nicola 1819-1885 *NewGrD 80*
De'Giunti Modesti *NewGrD 80*
Degius, Nikolaus *NewGrD 80*
DeGivray, Claude 1933- *WorEFlm*
Degli Antoni, Giovanni Battista 1660-1696? *NewGrD 80*
Degli Antoni, Pietro 1648-1720 *NewGrD 80*
Degli Antonii, Giovanni Battista 1660-1696? *NewGrD 80*
Degli Antonii, Pietro 1648-1720 *NewGrD 80*
Degner, Erich Wolf 1858-1908 *Baker 78*
DeGoede, Nicolaas A J 1915- *IntWWM 77, -80*
DeGogorza, Emilio 1874-1949 *BiDAmM*
DeGooyer, Rijk 1925- *FilmAG WE*
DeGraaf, Gerard Albert Cornelis 1928- *IntWWM 77, -80*
DeGraaff, Rein 1942- *EncJzS 70*
Degrada, Francesco 1940- *IntWWM 77, -80, NewGrD 80*
DeGraff, Robert 1909- *AmSCAP 66, -80*
Degraffenreid, George Merl 1946- *AmSCAP 80*
DeGraft, Joe *ConDr 73, -77*
DeGrandis, Renato 1927- *DcCM*
DeGrandis, Vincenzo 1577-1646 *NewGrD 80*
DeGrandis, Vincenzo 1631-1708 *NewGrD 80*
DeGrasse, Joseph 1873-1940 *FilmEn, TwYS A, WhScrn 74, -77, WhoHol B, WomWMM*
DeGrasse, Robert 1900-1971 *FilmEn, FilmgC, HalFC 80*
DeGrasse, Sam 1875-1953 *FilmEn, Film 1, -2, ForYSC, MotPP, NotNAT B, TwYS, WhScrn 74, -77, WhoHol B*
DeGravonne, Gabriel *Film 2*
Degraw, Jimmy Dwaine 1936- *AmSCAP 80*
DeGray, Julian 1905- *IntWWM 77, -80*
DeGray, Sidney *Film 1*
DeGray, Sydney *Film 2*
DeGreef, Arthur 1862-1940 *NewGrD 80*
DeGresac, Fred d1943 *NotNAT B*
DeGroff, Etta *Film 1*
DeGroot, Cor 1914- *IntWWM 77, -80*
DeGroot, Walter 1896- *WhThe*

DeGroote, Andre 1940- *IntWWM 77, -80*
DeGroote, Hilda Maria 1945- *WhoOp 76*
DeGrunwald, Anatole 1910-1967 *FilmEn, FilmgC, HalFC 80, WorEFlm*
DeGrunwald, Dimitri 1913?- *IntMPA 77, -75, -76, -78, -79, -80*
DeGrunwald, Dmitri 1913?- *FilmgC, HalFC 80*
Degtyaryov, Stepan Anikiyevich 1766-1813 *NewGrD 80*
DeGuide, Richard 1909-1962 *Baker 78*
DeGuingand, Pierre d1964 *Film 2, WhScrn 77*
D'Egville, James Harvey 1770?-1836? *CnOxB*
DeHaan, Stefan Johannes 1921- *WhoMus 72*
DeHaas, Max 1903- *DcFM*
DeHaas, Polo 1933- *IntWWM 77*
DeHartog, Jan 1914- *BiE&WWA, CnMD, NotNAT*
DeHaven, Carter 1887-1977 *Film 1, -2, HalFC 80, IntMPA 77, -75, -76, -78, -79, TwYS*
DeHaven, Carter 1896-1977 *FilmEn*
DeHaven, Mrs. Carter 1883-1950 *Film 1, -2, TwYS, WhScrn 77, WhoHol B*
DeHaven, Flora 1883-1950 *WhScrn 77*
DeHaven, Gloria *AmPS B, MotPP, WhoHol A*
DeHaven, Gloria 1924- *CmpEPM, FilmEn, HalFC 80, MGM[port], MovMk*
DeHaven, Gloria 1925- *BiE&WWA, FilmgC, ForYSC*
DeHaven, Gloria 1926- *BiDAmM*
DeHaven, Penny 1948- *IlEncCM*
DeHavilland, Olivia 1916- *BiDFilm, -81, BiE&WWA, CmMov, FilmEn, FilmgC, ForYSC, HalFC 80[port], IntMPA 77, -75, -76, -78, -79, -80, MotPP, MovMk[port], OxFilm, ThFT[port], WhoHol A, WhoHrs 80, WorEFlm*
DeHedemann, Baroness *Film 2*
DeHeer, Hans 1927- *IntWWM 77, -80*
DeHeijo, Hortensia S *PupTheA*
Dehelly, Emile 1871- *WhThe*
DeHeman *NewGrD 80*
DeHeman, Francois d1652 *NewGrD 80*
DeHeman, Jean d1660 *NewGrD 80*
DeHeman, Louis d1645? *NewGrD 80*
DeHeman, Valeran 1584-1640 *NewGrD 80*
DeHen, Ferdinand Joseph 1933- *IntWWM 77, -80, NewGrD 80*
DeHesse, Jean-Baptiste Francois 1705-1779 *CnOxB*
DeHidalgo, Elvira 1882- *NewEOp 71*
DeHirsch, Storm *WomWMM A, -B*
Dehlavi, Hosein 1927- *IntWWM 77, -80*
Dehli, Else Synnove 1937- *WhoOp 76*
Dehmel, Richard 1863-1920 *NewGrD 80*
Dehn, Dorothy *Film 2*
Dehn, Michael d1656 *NewGrD 80*
Dehn, Paul 1912-1976 *FilmEn, FilmgC, HalFC 80, IntMPA 77, -75, -76, OxFilm, WhoThe 72, -77*
Dehn, Siegfried Wilhelm 1799-1858 *Baker 78, NewGrD 80, OxMus*
Dehne, Michael d1656 *NewGrD 80*
Dehner, John 1915- *CmMov, FilmEn, FilmgC, ForYSC, HalFC 80, HolCA[port]*
Dehnert, Edmund John 1931- *IntWWM 77, -80*
Dehni, Salah 1929- *DcFM*
Deiber *NewGrD 80*
Deiber, Paul-Emile 1925- *WhoOp 76*
Deichel *NewGrD 80*
Deichel, Anton 1662?-1712 *NewGrD 80*
Deichel, Johann Dominicus 1656?-1715? *NewGrD 80*
Deichel, Joseph Anton 1699-1778 *NewGrD 80*
Deichel, Joseph Christoph 1695-1753 *NewGrD 80*
Deichmann, Benny 1893-1939 *NewOrJ*
Deichmann, Charles 1894-1927 *NewOrJ*
Deighton, Len 1929- *HalFC 80, IntMPA 77, -75, -76, -78, -79, -80*
Deighton, Marga Ann d1971 *WhScrn 77*
Deihl, Ned Charles 1931- *IntWWM 80*
Deilich, Philipp *NewGrD 80*
Dein, Edward *IntMPA 77, -75, -76, -78, -79, -80, WhoHrs 80*
Deinl, Nikolaus 1665-1725 *NewGrD 80*
Deis, Carl 1883-1960 *Baker 78, BiDAmM, ConAmC*
Deiss, Michael 1552?- *NewGrD 80*
Deitch, Donna *WomWMM B*
Deitch, Hyman 1914- *AmSCAP 66*
Deiters, Hermann 1833-1907 *Baker 78, NewGrD 80*
Deitrich, Angela *WomWMM B*
Deitz, Gerald 1903- *AmSCAP 80*
Dejan, Harold 1909- *NewOrJ[port]*
Dejan, Leo 1911- *NewOrJ*
Dejanow, Bisser 1949- *CnOxB*
DeJardins, Silvion *Film 1*
Dejazet, Eugene 1820?-1880 *EncWT*
Dejazet, Pauline-Virginie 1798-1875 *EncWT, Ent, NotNAT B, OxThe*
Dejdler, Rochus 1779-1822 *Baker 78*
DeJesus, Louis A 1923- *AmSCAP 80*
Dejmek, Kazimierz 1924- *EncWT*
DeJohn Sisters, The *RkOn[port]*
DeJohnette, Jack 1942- *EncJzS 70*
Dejoncker, Theodore 1894-1964 *Baker 78, OxMus*
DeJong, Bettie 1933- *CnOxB*
DeJong, Conrad 1934- *AmSCAP 80, Baker 78, ConAmC*
DeJong, Marinus 1891- *Baker 78, IntWWM 77, -80, WhoMus 72*
DeJong, Willem Coenraad 1908- *IntWWM 77, -80*
DeJough, James *MorBAP*
DeJouy *NewEOp 71*
DeJudice, Caesar *NewGrD 80*
Dekany, Bela 1928- *IntWWM 77, -80*
DeKeczer, Irma *Film 2*
Dekemel, Matthew Antoine Desire 1900?-1967 *NewOrJ[port]*
DeKerekjarto, Duci 1901-1962 *WhScrn 74, -77, WhoHol B*
DeKergommeaux, Duncan Robert 1927- *CreCan 1*
Dekeukeleire, Charles 1905- *DcFM*
DeKirby, Annette *Film 2*
DeKirby, Ivar *Film 2*
Dekker, Albert d1968 *MotPP, WhoHol B*
Dekker, Albert 1900-1968 *Vers B[port]*
Dekker, Albert 1904-1968 *FilmEn, WhScrn 74, -77, WhoHrs 80[port]*
Dekker, Albert 1905-1968 *BiE&WWA, FilmgC, ForYSC, HalFC 80[port], HolCA[port], MovMk, NotNAT B, WhThe*
Dekker, Desmond 1942- *RkOn 2[port]*
Dekker, Gerard H 1931- *IntWWM 77, -80*
Dekker, Maurits Rudolph Joell 1896-1962 *CnMD*
Dekker, Rose *PupTheA*
Dekker, Thomas 1570?-1632? *DcPup, NotNAT A*
Dekker, Thomas 1570?-1641? *NotNAT B, OxMus*
Dekker, Thomas 1572?-1632? *CnThe, EncWT, Ent, McGEWD[port], OxThe, PlP&P[port], REnWD[port]*
DeKnight, Fannie Belle *Film 2*
DeKnight, Jimmy *AmSCAP 66, -80*
DeKock, Hubert 1863-1941 *WhScrn 74, -77*
DeKolta 1847-1903 *MagIlD*
DeKolta, Bautier 1845-1903 *Ent*
DeKova, Frank *ForYSC, WhoHol A*
DeKoven, Henry Louis Reginald 1859-1920 *BiDAmM, NotNAT B, OxMus*
DeKoven, Reginald 1859-1920 *AmPS, AmSCAP 66, -80, Baker 78, BnBkM 80, CmpEPM, NewCBMT, NewEOp 71, NewGrD 80, PlP&P, PopAmC[port], WhThe, WhoStg 1906, -1908*
DeKoven, Reginald 1861-1920 *EncMT*
DeKoven, Roger 1907- *BiE&WWA, NotNAT*
DeKowa, Viktor 1904-1973 *WhScrn 77*
DeKresz, Geza 1882-1959 *NewGrD 80*
DeKruif, Paul 1890- *BiE&WWA*
Del Vikings *AmPS A*
Dela, Maurice 1919- *Baker 78*
DeLaBassee, Adam *NewGrD 80*
Delaborde, Jean-Baptiste *NewGrD 80*
DeLaBye, Willy 1934- *DancEn 78*
DeLaCanal, Lolita Alva *PupTheA*
DeLaCanal, Ramon Alva *PupTheA*
DeLacey, Jack *Film 2*
DeLacey, Philippe 1917- *WhoHol A*
DeLacey, Phillipe 1917- *ForYSC, TwYS*
DeLacey, Robert *TwYS A*
DeLacour, Marcelle 1896- *IntWWM 77, -80*
DeLaCourt, Antoine 1530?-1600 *NewGrD 80*
DeLaCourt, Henri d1577 *NewGrD 80*
Delacroix, Francois *NewGrD 80*
DeLaCruz, Joe 1892-1961 *WhScrn 77*
DeLaCruze, Jimmy *Film 2*
DeLacy, Philippe 1917- *Film 2, MotPP*
DeLacy, Phillipe 1917- *Film 2*
DeLadomerszky, Thomas L 1923- *AmSCAP 80*
DeLaFarge, P *NewGrD 80*
Delafield, E M 1890-1943 *NotNAT B, WhThe*
DeLaFons *NewGrD 80*
DeLaFont *NewGrD 80*
DeLaFuente, Gita 1921- *IntWWM 77, -80, WhoMus 72*
Delage, Maurice 1879-1961 *Baker 78, NewGrD 80*
Delage, Roger 1922- *IntWWM 77, -80*
Delaharpe, Jean Francois *NewGrD 80*
DeLaHaye, Ina 1906- *WhThe, WhoThe 72*
DeLaHele, George *NewGrD 80*
DeLaHoussaye, Frank *NewOrJ*
Delair, Etienne Denis d1727? *NewGrD 80*
Delair, Paul d1894 *NotNAT B*
Delair, Suzy 1916- *FilmEn, FilmgC, HalFC 80, WhoHol A*
Delalande, Michel 1739-1812 *NewGrD 80*
DeLaLande, Michel-Richard *NewGrD 80*
Delalande, Michel-Richard 1657-1726 *Baker 78, BnBkM 80*
DeLaMain, Henry d1796 *NewGrD 80*
Delamaine, Henry d1796 *NewGrD 80*
DeLaMare, Elizabeth 1931- *WhoMus 72*
Delamare, Gil d1966 *WhScrn 74, -77*
DeLaMarre *NewGrD 80*
DeLamarter, Eric 1880-1953 *AmSCAP 66, -80, Baker 78, BiDAmM, ConAmC*
Delamont, Gordon Arthur 1918- *Baker 78, CreCan 2*
DeLaMothe, Leon 1880-1943 *Film 1, WhScrn 74, -77*
DeLaMotte, Diether 1928- *DcCM*
DeLaMotte, Marguerite d1950 *MotPP, WhoHol B*
DeLaMotte, Marguerite 1902-1950 *FilmEn, NotNAT B, TwYS*
DeLaMotte, Marguerite 1903-1950 *Film 1, -2, FilmgC, HalFC 80*
DeLaMotte, Marguriete 1902-1950 *WhScrn 74, -77*
Delancy, Henriette *Film 2*
DeLanda, Juan 1894-1968 *WhScrn 74, -77, WhoHol B*
Delandry, Frank 1888?- *NewOrJ*
Delane *PlP&P[port]*
DeLane Lea, Jacques 1931- *IntMPA 77, -75, -76, -78, -79, -80*
DeLane Lea, William 1900-1964 *FilmgC, HalFC 80*
Delaney And Bonnie *ConMuA 80A, IlEncR, RkOn 2[port]*
Delaney, Mrs. 1700-1788 *DcPup*
Delaney, Charles 1892-1959 *Film 2, ForYSC, NotNAT B, TwYS, WhScrn 74, -77, WhoHol B*
DeLaney, Charles Oliver 1925- *AmSCAP 66, -80, ConAmC*
Delaney, Eric 1924- *IntWWM 77*
Delaney, Francis Edward 1936- *AmSCAP 80*
Delaney, Iria *Film 2*
Delaney, Jack 1930-1976 *NewOrJ[port]*
Delaney, Jere A 1888-1954 *Film 2, WhScrn 74, -77, WhoHol B*
Delaney, Jerry *Film 1*
Delaney, Leo 1885-1920 *Film 1, WhScrn 77*
Delaney, Maureen 1888-1961 *NotNAT B, WhScrn 74, -77, WhoHol B*
Delaney, Robert Mills 1903-1956 *Baker 78, BiDAmM, ConAmC, NewGrD 80*
Delaney, Sean 1945- *AmSCAP 80*
Delaney, Shelagh 1939- *BiE&WWA, CnMD, ConDr 73, -77, CroCD, EncWT, Ent, HalFC 80, McGEWD, ModWD, NotNAT, PlP&P[port], WhoThe 72, -77*
Delaney, Thomas Henry 1889-1963 *BluesWW[port]*
DeLange, Daniel 1841-1918 *BiDAmM*
DeLange, Eddie 1904-1949 *AmPS, CmpEPM, WhScrn 74, -77*

DeLange, Edgar 1904-1949 *AmSCAP 66, -80, BiDAmM*
DeLange, Hans 1884- *BiDAmM*
DeLange, Herman 1851-1929 *NotNAT B, WhThe*
Delange, Herman-Francois 1715-1781 *NewGrD 80*
Delanian, Zorick *IntWWM 77, -80*
DeLannis, Johannes *NewGrD 80*
Delannoy, Henriette *Film 2*
Delannoy, Jean 1908- *DcFM, FilmEn, FilmgC, HalFC 80, IntMPA 77, -75, -76, -78, -79, -80, WorEFlm*
Delannoy, Marcel 1898-1962 *Baker 78, DcCM, NewGrD 80, OxMus*
Delano, Clothilde *Film 2*
Delano, Gwen 1882-1954 *WhScrn 74, -77*
Delano, Jack 1914- *AmSCAP 80, CpmDNM 75, ConAmC, IntWWM 77, -80*
Delano, James *Film 1*
Delanoy, Edmond d1888 *NotNAT B*
DeLanti, Stella *Film 2*
DeLantins *NewGrD 80*
Delany, Clarissa Scott 1901-1927 *BlkAmP*
Delany, Eric 1924- *WhoMus 72*
Delany, John Albert 1852-1907 *NewGrD 80*
DeLaParelle, Marion *Film 1*
DeLaPasture, Mrs. Henry 1866-1945 *NotNAT B, WhThe*
DeLaPatelliere, Denys *FilmEn*
DeLaPatelliere, Denys 1921- *FilmgC, HalFC 80, WorEFlm*
Delapierre, Andre William 1921- *IntWWM 77, -80*
DeLaPierre, Paul *NewGrD 80*
DeLaPorte, Elizabeth 1941- *IntWWM 77, -80, WhoMus 72*
DeLappe, Gemze 1921- *DancEn 78*
DeLappe, Gemze 1922- *BiE&WWA, NotNAT*
DeLara, Adelina 1872-1961 *NewGrD 80*
DeLara, Isidore 1858-1935 *Baker 78, NewEOp 71*
Delaro, Hattie *Film 1, -2*
DeLaRoche, Mazo 1879-1961 *CreCan 2, NotNAT B*
DeLaRosa, Frank 1933- *EncJzS 70*
DeLaroux, Hugues d1925 *NotNAT B*
DeLarrocha, Alicia 1923- *IntWWM 77, -80, MusSN[port], NewGrD 80, WhoMus 72*
Delarue, Allison *DancEn 78, NotNAT*
DeLaRue, Pierre *NewGrD 80*
Delas, Jose Luis 1928- *NewGrD 80*
DeLaSable, Antoine *NewGrD 80*
DeLaSagesse, Soeur Marie *CreCan 1*
DeLatere, Petit Jean 1510?-1569 *NewGrD 80*
DeLaTorre, Amadeo *PupTheA*
DeLaTour, Frances 1944- *WhoThe 77*
Delatre, Father *OxMus*
DeLatre, Petit Jan 1510?-1569 *NewGrD 80*
DeLatre, Petit Jean 1510?-1569 *NewGrD 80*
DeLatre, Petit Jehan 1510?-1569 *NewGrD 80*
DeLattre, Petit Jean 1510?-1569 *NewGrD 80*
DeLattre, Roland *OxMus*
Delaunay, Louis 1854- *WhThe*
Delaunay, Louis-Arsene 1826-1903 *EncWT, Ent, OxThe*
Delauney, Louis-Arsene 1826-1903 *NotNAT B*
Delaunoy, Didier 1937- *ConAmTC*
DeLaurentiis, Dino 1919- *BiDFilm, -81, CmMov, DcFM, FilmEn, FilmgC, HalFC 80, IntMPA 77, -75, -76, -78, -79, -80, OxFilm, WhoHrs 80, WorEFlm*
DeLauze, F *DancEn 78*
DeLavallade, Carmen 1931- *BiE&WWA, DancEn 78[port], DrBlPA, NotNAT*
Delavalle, Hugo 1935- *DancEn 78*
Delavan, E Macon 1932- *IntWWM 77, -80*
Delavan, Macon 1932- *ConAmC*
Delavan, Marlene Elizabeth McKenzie 1932- *IntWWM 77, -80*
DeLaVarre, Andre, Jr. 1934- *IntMPA 77, -75, -76, -78, -79, -80*
DeLaveaux, Teresa Maria 1940- *IntWWM 77, -80*
DeLaVega, Alfredo Gomez 1897-1958 *WhScrn 74, -77*
DeLaVega, Aurelio 1925- *DcCM*
Delavergne, Antoine-Barthelemy *NewGrD 80*
Delavigne, Casimir 1793-1843 *McGEWD*
Delavigne, Germain d1868 *NotNAT B*
Delavigne, Jean Francois Casimir 1793-1843 *NotNAT B*
DeLaViola *NewGrD 80*
Delavrancea, Barbu 1858-1918 *McGEWD[port]*
DeLay, Mel 1900-1947 *WhScrn 74, -77*
Delay, Mike 1909- *NewOrJ*
DeLay, Peggy *WomWMM B*
DelBiabo, Giuseppe *NewGrD 80*
DelBorgo, Elliot Anthony 1938- *ConAmC*
DelBuono, Gioanpietro *NewGrD 80*
DelCampo, Conrado *NewGrD 80*
DelCampo, Santiago d1963 *NotNAT B*
DelCarril, Hugo 1912- *FilmEn*
DelChitarino, Pietrobono *NewGrD 80*
DelCornetto, Ascanio *NewGrD 80*
Delcroix, Leon Charles 1880-1938 *Baker 78*
Delden, Lex Van 1919- *Baker 78, NewGrD 80*
Delderfield, George Edward 1919- *IntWWM 77, -80, WhoMus 72*
Delderfield, R F 1912- *WhThe*
Deldevez, Edme 1817-1897 *NewGrD 80*
Deldevez, Edouard-Marie-Ernest 1817-1897 *Baker 78, NewGrD 80*
Deldevez, Edward-Marie-Ernest 1817-1897 *DancEn 78*
DeLeath, Vaughn 1896-1943 *AmSCAP 66, -80, CmpEPM*
DeLeeuw, Paul 1927- *IntWWM 77, -80*
DeLeeuw, Thelma Mary 1934- *WhoMus 72*
DeLeeuw, Ton 1926- *DcCM, IntWWM 77, -80*
Delegates *RkOn 2A*
DeLegh, Kitty 1887- *WhThe*
DelEncina, Juan 1469-1529? *Ent*
DeLeo, Joseph August 1943- *IntWWM 77*
DeLeon, Aristides 1904-1954 *WhScrn 74, -77*
DeLeon, Don Pedro *Film 2*
DeLeon, Jack 1897-1956 *NotNAT B, WhThe*
DeLeon, Millie d1922 *NotNAT B*
DeLeon, Raoul 1905-1972 *WhScrn 77, WhoHol B*
DeLeon, Robert 1904-1961 *AmSCAP 66, -80*
Deleone, Carmon, Jr. 1942- *AmSCAP 80*
DeLeone, Francesco Bartolomeo 1887-1948 *AmSCAP 66, -80, Baker 78, ConAmC*
DeLerma, Dominique-Rene 1928- *IntWWM 77, -80*
Delerue, Georges 1924- *FilmgC, HalFC 80, IntMPA 77, -76, -78, -79, -80, OxFilm*
Delerue, Georges 1925- *DcFM, FilmEn, NewGrD 80, WorEFlm*
DeLetraz, Jean d1954 *NotNAT B*
Delevanti, Cyril 1887-1975 *FilmgC, WhScrn 77, WhoHol C*
Delevanti, Cyril 1887-1976 *HalFC 80*
Delevanti, Cyril 1889- *ForYSC*
Delevines, The *WhThe*
Delevoryas, Sonja Gisela Clara 1926- *IntWWM 77, -80*
Delf, Harry 1892-1964 *AmSCAP 66, NotNAT B*
Delfert, Charles *NewGrD 80*
Delfonics, The *RkOn 2[port]*
Delfont, Bernard 1909- *BiE&WWA, EncMT, IntMPA 77, -75, -76, -78, -79, -80, WhoThe 72, -77*
Delfont, Bernard 1910- *HalFC 80*
Delfosse, Georges 1869-1939 *CreCan 2*
Delfrati, Carlo 1938- *IntWWM 77, -80*
Delgadillo, Luis 1887-1962 *NewGrD 80*
Delgadillo, Luis Abraham 1887-1961 *Baker 78*
Delgado, Marcel 1900-1976 *WhoHrs 80*
Delgado, Maria 1906-1969 *WhScrn 77, WhoHol B*
Delgado, Ramon 1937- *NatPD[port]*
Delgado, Roger 1920-1973 *WhScrn 77*
DelGaudio, Antonio *NewGrD 80*
DelGiudice, Cesare 1607-1680 *NewGrD 80*
DelGiudice, Filippo 1892-1961 *FilmgC, HalFC 80, OxFilm, WorEFlm*
Delgrosso, Jean Ann 1938- *AmSCAP 80*
DelGuidice, Filippo 1892-1961 *FilmEn*
DeLiagre, Alfred, Jr. 1904- *BiE&WWA, NotNAT, WhoThe 72, -77*
Deliane, Helen *Film 1*
Delibes, Clement Philibert Leo 1836-1891 *CnOxB, DancEn 78*
Delibes, Leo 1836-1891 *Baker 78, BnBkM 80, CmOp, CmpBCM, DcCom 77, DcCom&M 79, GrComp[port], MusMk, NewEOp 71, NewGrD 80, OxMus*
Delight, June 1898-1975 *WhScrn 77, WhoHol C*
DeLigt, Ben Nicolas 1939- *IntWWM 80*
DeLigt, Thomas *IntWWM 80*
DeLiguoro, Countess Eugenio *Film 2*
DeLiguoro, Rina 1892-1966 *FilmAG WE*
DeLiguoro, Rina 1893-1966 *Film 2, WhScrn 74, -77, WhoHol B*
DeLima Y Sintiago, Emirto 1893- *WhoMus 72*
DeLimur, Jean *Film 2*
Delinger, Lawrence Ross 1937- *ConAmC*
Delinsky, Victor A 1883-1951 *WhScrn 74, -77*
Delipari, Michele *NewGrD 80*
DeLis, Jehanne 1885- *IntWWM 77, -80*
Delisa, Victor V 1924- *AmSCAP 80, IntWWM 77, -80*
Delisle, Baptiste 1868?-1920? *NewOrJ*
DeLisle, Christiane 1913- *IntWWM 77, -80*
Delisle, Louis Nelson 1885-1949 *NewOrJ[port]*
DeLisle, Rae 1947- *IntWWM 77, -80*
Delius, Frederick 1862-1934 *Baker 78, BnBkM 80, CmOp, CompSN[port], DcCom 77[port], DcCom&M 79, DcCM, DcTwCC, MusMk[port], NewEOp 71, NewGrD 80[port], OxMus*
Delius, Frederick 1863-1934 *DancEn 78*
Delius, Fritz 1862-1934 *NewGrD 80[port]*
Dell, Claudia 1910- *FilmEn, ForYSC, ThFT[port]*
Dell, Dorothy 1915-1934 *FilmEn, ThFT[port], WhScrn 74, -77, WhoHol B*
Dell, Floyd 1887-1969 *NotNAT B, PlP&P, WhThe*
Dell, Gabe *JoeFr*
Dell, Gabriel *ForYSC*
Dell, Gabriel 1919- *NotNAT*
Dell, Gabriel 1920- *HalFC 80*
Dell, Gabriel 1921- *WhoHol A*
Dell, Gabriel 1923- *WhoThe 77*
Dell, Gabriel 1930- *WhoThe 72*
Dell, Jeffrey 1899- *WhThe*
Dell, Jeffrey 1904- *FilmgC, HalFC 80, IlWWBF*
Dell, Myrna *ForYSC, WhoHol A*
Dell, Tommy *AmSCAP 80*
Della-Chiesa, Vivienne *IntMPA 77, -75, -76, -78, -79*
Della-Cioppa, Guy *NewYTET*
Della-Maria, Dominique 1769-1800 *NewGrD 80*
DellaBella, Domenico *NewGrD 80*
DellaCasa, Lisa 1919- *CmOp, MusSN[port], NewEOp 71, NewGrD 80, WhoMus 72, WhoOp 76*
DellaCasa-Debeljevic, Lisa *IntWWM 77, -80*
DellaCiaia, Azzolino Bernardino 1671-1755 *Baker 78, NewGrD 80*
DellaCiaja, Azzolino Bernardino 1671-1755 *NewGrD 80*
DellaCorte, Andrea 1883-1968 *Baker 78, NewGrD 80*
DellaFaya, Aurelio d1579 *NewGrD 80*
DellaGala, Michael D 1950- *AmSCAP 80*
DellLago, Giovanni 1490?-1543? *NewGrD 80*
DellaGostena, Giovanni Battista 1540?-1598 *NewGrD 80*
Dell'Aiolle, Francesco *NewGrD 80*
Dell'Aiula, Francesco *NewGrD 80*
Dell'Ajolle, Francesco *NewGrD 80*
DellaMaria, Pierre-Antoine-Dominique 1769-1800 *Baker 78*
Dellanoy, Marcel 1898- *DancEn 78*
DellaPergola, Edith 1918- *CreCan 1*
DellaPergola, Luciano 1910- *CreCan 1*
DellaPeruti, Carl 1947- *ConAmC*
DellaPorta, Francesco 1600?-1666 *NewGrD 80*
DellaPorta, Gasparo d1613? *NewGrD 80*
DellaPorta, Giambattista 1535-1615 *McGEWD[port]*
DellaPorta, Giambattista 1538-1613 *OxThe*
DellaPorta, Gioseppe *NewGrD 80*
DellaPorta, Giovan Battista 1535-1615 *Ent*
DellaPorta, Giovan Battista 1538-1613 *EncWT*
Dell'Ara, Ugo 1921- *DancEn 78*
Dellario, Michael Richard 1949- *AmSCAP 80*
DellaRipa, Dominic J 1921- *AmSCAP 66, -80*
Dell'Arpa, Giovanni Leonardo *NewGrD 80*
Dell'Arpa, Orazio *NewGrD 80*

DellaValle, Federico 1560?-1628 *McGEWD*
DellaValle, Pietro 1586-1652 *NewGrD 80*
DellaViola *NewGrD 80*
DellaViola, Alessandro *NewGrD 80*
DellaViola, Alexander *NewGrD 80*
DellaVolpe, Lelio *NewGrD 80*
Delle Palle, Scipione *NewGrD 80*
Delle Sedie, Enrico 1822-1907 *NewGrD 80*
Deller, Alfred 1912-1979 *Baker 78, BnBkM 80, IntWWM 77, NewGrD 80*
Deller, Florian Johann 1729-1773 *CnOxB, NewGrD 80*
Deller, Mark Damian 1938- *IntWWM 77, -80*
Dell'Era, Antonietta 1865- *DancEn 78*
Dellert, Kjerstin 1925- *WhoMus 72*
DelleSedie, Enrico 1822-1907 *Baker 78*
DelleSedie, Enrico 1824-1907 *NewEOp 71*
Delley, Jozsef 1937- *IntWWM 80*
Dellger, Michael Lawrence *AmSCAP 80*
Delli, Bertrun 1928- *IntWWM 80*
Delli Colli, Tonino 1923- *FilmEn*
Dellinger, Rudolf 1857-1910 *Baker 78, NewGrD 80*
Dello Joio, Norman 1913- *Baker 78, BiDAmM, BnBkM 80, CompSN[port], CpmDNM 73, -80, CnOxB, ConAmC, DancEn 78, DcCM, IntWWM 77, -80, NewEOp 71, NewGrD 80, OxMus*
Dell'olio, Anselma *WomWMM B*
Dell'Orefice, Giuseppe 1848-1889 *Baker 78*
Dellow, Ronald Graeme 1924- *IntWWM 77, -80*
Dells, The *RkOn[port]*
Delluc, Louis 1890-1924 *DcFM, FilmEn, OxFilm, WorEFlm*
Delluc, Louis 1892-1924 *FilmgC, HalFC 80*
Delmaine, Barry *IntMPA 77, -75, -76, -78, -79, -80*
Delman, Jacqueline 1933- *WhoMus 72*
DelMar, Claire 1901-1959 *WhScrn 74, -77, WhoHol B*
Delmar, Dezso 1891- *AmSCAP 66, Baker 78, ConAmC*
Delmar, Eddie 1886-1944 *WhScrn 74, -77*
Delmar, Herbert *Film 1*
Delmar, Kenny *WhoHol A*
DelMar, Norman Rene 1919- *Baker 78, IntWWM 77, -80, NewGrD 80, WhoMus 72*
DelMar, Pauline Elizabeth 1926- *IntWWM 77, -80*
Delmar, Thomas *Film 2*
Delmar, Vina *WomWMM*
Delmas, Jean-Francois 1861-1933 *Baker 78, NewEOp 71*
Delmas, Marc-Jean-Baptiste 1885-1931 *Baker 78, NewGrD 80*
Delmas, Suzanne *Film 2*
DelMatta, Mauro *NewGrD 80*
DelMonaco, Alfredo 1938- *ConAmC*
DelMonaco, Giancarlo 1945- *WhoOp 76*
DelMonaco, Mario 1915- *Baker 78, CmOp, MusSN[port], NewEOp 71, NewGrD 80[port], WhoOp 76*
DelMonaco, Mario 1919- *IntWWM 77, -80, WhoMus 72*
Delmonte, Jack 1889-1973 *WhScrn 77*
DelMonte, Louis J 1912- *AmSCAP 66, -80*
Delmore, Alton 1908-1964 *BiDAmM, CounME 74, EncFCWM 69*
Delmore, Lionel Alton 1940- *AmSCAP 80*
Delmore, Rabon 1910-1952 *BiDAmM, EncFCWM 69*
Delmore, Rabon 1916-1952 *CounME 74*
Delmore, Ralph d1923 *NotNAT B, WhoStg 1908*
Delmore Brothers *CmpEPM, CounME 74, -74A, EncFCWM 69, IlEncCM*
Delmotte, Roger 1925- *NewGrD 80*
Delna, Marie 1875-1932 *Baker 78*
DelNegro, Giulio Santo Pietro *NewGrD 80*
Delo, Kenneth Edward *AmSCAP 80*
Delon, Alain 1935- *BiDFilm, -81, FilmAG WE[port], FilmEn, FilmgC, ForYSC, HalFC 80, IntMPA 77, -75, -76, -78, -79, -80, MotPP, MovMk[port], OxFilm, WhoHol A, WorEFlm[port]*
Delon, Nathalie *FilmAG WE, WhoHol A*
DeLone, Peter *ConAmC*
DeLone, Richard Pierce *ConAmC*
Deloney, Thomas 1543?-1607? *OxMus*
Delores, Jean *Film 2*
DeLorez, Claire *Film 2*
Deloriea, Marybelle C 1917- *AmSCAP 80*
Delorme, Daniele 1926- *FilmAG WE, FilmEn, FilmgC, HalFC 80, OxFilm, WhoHol A*
DeLorme, Danielle 1926- *ForYSC*
Delorme, Hugues *WhThe*
DeLory, Alfred V 1930- *AmSCAP 66*
DeLosAngeles, Victoria *BnBkM 80, MusSN[port]*
DeLosAngeles, Victoria 1923- *CmOp, IntWWM 77, -80, MusMk, NewEOp 71*
DeLosAngeles, Victoria 1924- *WhoMus 72*
DeLoustal, Genevieve Marie-Louise Odette 1918- *IntWWM 80*
DeLoutherbourg, Philip James 1740-1812 *OxThe, PlP&P*
DeLoutherbourg, Philippe Jacques 1740-1812 *NotNAT B*
Delp, Ron 1946- *ConAmC*
DelPalla, Scipione *NewGrD 80*
DelPalle, Scipione *NewGrD 80*
DelPane, Domenico *NewGrD 80*
Delphin 1882-1938 *OxFilm, WhScrn 77*
Delpini *OxThe*
Delpini, Carlo d1828 *NotNAT B*
DelPomo, Francesco 1594- *NewGrD 80*
DelPrincipe, Joseph A 1932- *CpmDNM 78, -79, IntWWM 77*
DelPrincipe, Joseph A 1935- *CpmDNM 76, -77*
DelPuente, Giuseppe 1841-1900 *NewEOp 71, NewGrD 80*
DelPuerto, Diego *NewGrD 80*
DelPueyo, Eduardo *NewGrD 80*
DelRey, Pilar *ForYSC, WhoHol A*
DelRiego, Theresa *ConAmC*
DelRio, Dolores *AmPS B, Film 2, MotPP*
DelRio, Dolores 1904- *ThFT[port]*
DelRio, Dolores 1905- *BiDFilm, -81, FilmEn, Film 1, FilmgC, ForYSC, HalFC 80, IntMPA 77, -75, -76, -78, -79, -80, MovMk[port], OxFilm, TwYS, What 3[port], WhoHol A, WorEFlm*
Delrose, Harold *NewOrJ*
Delrose, Henry *NewOrJ*
DelRosso, Giovanni Maria *NewGrD 80*
Delroy, Albert *IntWWM 77, -80*
Delroy, Irene 1898- *EncMT, WhThe*
DelRuth, Hampton 1888- *TwYS A*
DelRuth, Roy 1895-1961 *BiDFilm, -81, CmMov, FilmEn, FilmgC, HalFC 80, MovMk[port], TwYS A, WhoHrs 80, WorEFlm*
Delsaert, Jules 1844-1900 *NewGrD 80*
Delsart, Jules 1844-1900 *NewGrD 80*
Delsarte, Francois 1811-1871 *CnOxB, DancEn 78, NotNAT A, PlP&P*
Delschaft, Mady *Film 2*
Delsener, Ron *ConMuA 80B*
Delsol, Paule *WomWMM*
Delson, Sue *WomWMM B*
Delta Joe *BluesWW*
Delta John *BluesWW*
Delta Rhythm Boys *BiDAmM, CmpEPM*
DelTredici, David 1937- *AmSCAP 80, Baker 78, BnBkM 80, ConAmC, DcCM, NewGrD 80*
DelTurco, Giovanni 1577-1647 *NewGrD 80*
DelTurco, Lorenzo *NewGrD 80*
Deluc, Germaine *WomWMM B*
DeLuca, Giuseppe 1876-1950 *Baker 78, BiDAmM, CmOp, MusSN[port], NewEOp 71, NewGrD 80[port]*
Deluce *NewGrD 80*
DeLuce, Nathaniel 1795?-1842 *BiDAmM*
DeLuce, Virginia 1921- *BiE&WWA, NotNAT, WhoHol A*
DeLucia, Fernando 1860-1925 *CmOp, NewGrD 80[port]*
DeLucia, Ralph Lawrence 1920- *AmSCAP 80*
Delugg, Anne Renfer 1922- *AmSCAP 66*
Delugg, Anne Renfer 1923- *AmSCAP 80*
DeLugg, Milton 1918- *AmSCAP 66, CmpEPM*
DeLugg, Milton 1921- *AmSCAP 80*
DeLuise, Dom *IntMPA 77, -75, -76, -78, -79, -80, WhoHol A*
DeLuise, Dom 1933- *FilmEn*
DeLuise, Dom 1934- *ForYSC*
DeLuise, Dom 1936- *HalFC 80*
DeLuke, Peter Faber 1930- *IntWWM 77*
DeLullo, Giorgio 1921- *EncWT, Ent, WhoOp 76*
Delune, Louis 1876-1940 *Baker 78*
DeLungo, Tony 1892- *Film 2, WhThe*
DeLussan, Zelie 1861-1949 *CmOp*
DeLussan, Zelie 1863-1949 *BiDAmM, NotNAT B, WhoStg 1908*
Delusse *NewGrD 80*
Delusse, Christophe *NewGrD 80*
Delusse, Jacques *NewGrD 80*
DeLutry, Michel 1924- *DancEn 78*
Delvair, Jeanne *Film 1*
DelVal, Jean 1892-1975 *Film 2, WhScrn 77, WhoHol C*
DelValle, Jaime 1910- *IntMPA 77, -75, -76, -78, -79, -80*
DelValle, John 1904- *IntMPA 77, -75, -76, -78, -79, -80*
DelValle, Luis Cotto *WhScrn 74, -77*
DelValle DePaz, Edgardo 1861-1920 *Baker 78*
Delvaux, Albert 1913- *Baker 78, IntWWM 77, -80, WhoMus 72*
Delvaux, Andre 1926- *BiDFilm, -81, FilmEn, FilmgC, HalFC 80, WorEFlm*
DelVescovo, Pierre Louis Emile 1929- *IntWWM 77, -80*
DelVicario, Silvio Patrick 1921- *AmSCAP 66*
Delvicario, Silvio Patrick 1921- *AmSCAP 80*
DelVikings, The *RkOn[port]*
Delvincourt, Claude 1888-1954 *Baker 78, NewGrD 80, OxMus*
DelViolino, Carlo *NewGrD 80*
DelViolino, Giovanni Battista *NewGrD 80*
Delysia, Alice 1888- *EncMT*
Delysia, Alice 1889- *CnThe, OxThe, WhThe*
Delza, Sophia *DancEn 78*
Demachi, Giuseppe 1732-1791? *NewGrD 80*
Demachy, Sieur *NewGrD 80*
DeMacq, Rene 1932- *IntWWM 77, -80*
DeMadina, Francisco 1907-1972 *AmSCAP 66, -80*
DeMaeyer, Jan Irma Maria 1949- *IntWWM 77, -80*
DeMain, Gordon 1897-1967 *Film 2, WhScrn 77*
Demaio, James Paul 1913- *AmSCAP 80*
DeMajo, Cecilia *IntWWM 77, -80*
Demant, Christoph 1567-1643 *NewGrD 80*
Demant, Leo S 1900- *IntWWM 77, -80*
Demantius, Christoph 1567-1643 *Baker 78, BnBkM 80, NewGrD 80*
DeMar, Carrie d1963 *NotNAT B*
DeMarchand, Elsa Caraffi *PupTheA*
DeMarchena-Dujarric, Enrique 1908- *DcCM*
Demarchi, Elida Maria 1945- *IntWWM 77, -80*
DeMarco, Norman 1910- *BiE&WWA*
Demarco, Rosalinda Jill *AmSCAP 80*
DeMarco, Tony 1898-1965 *WhScrn 74, -77, WhoHol B*
Demare, Lucas 1910- *DcFM*
DeMare, Rolf *Film 2*
DeMare, Rolf 1886-1964 *DancEn 78[port]*
Demarest, Anne Shannon 1919- *IntWWM 77*
Demarest, Clifford 1874-1946 *Baker 78, ConAmC*
Demarest, Drew *Film 2*
Demarest, Mary Augusta 1838-1888 *BiDAmM*
Demarest, Rube 1886-1962 *WhoHol B*
Demarest, Rubin 1886-1962 *NotNAT B, WhScrn 74, -77*
Demarest, William 1892- *FilmEn, Film 2, FilmgC, HalFC 80, IntMPA 77, -75, -76, -78, -79, -80, MotPP, MovMk[port], TwYS, Vers A[port], WhoHol A*
Demarest, William 1894- *ForYSC, HolCA[port]*
DeMarez Oyens, Gerrit H 1922- *IntWWM 77, -80*
DeMarez Oyens, Tera 1932- *IntWWM 77*
DeMarinis, Paul Michael 1948- *ConAmC*
DeMarney, Derrick 1906-1978 *FilmgC, HalFC 80, IlWWBF, IntMPA 77, -75, -76, -78, WhThe, WhoHol A*
DeMarney, Terence 1909-1971 *FilmgC, HalFC 80, IlWWBF[port], WhThe, WhoHol B*
DeMarney, Terrence 1909-1971 *WhScrn 74, -77*

Demarquez, Suzanne 1899-1965 *Baker 78*
Demars, Charles *NewGrD 80*
Demars, Helene-Louise 1736?- *NewGrD 80*
Demars, Jean Odo 1696?-1756 *NewGrD 80*
DeMarthold, Jules d1927 *NotNAT B*
DeMartin, Imelda 1936- *BiE&WWA*
DeMasi, Joseph 1904- *AmSCAP 66, -80*
DeMasi, Joseph Anthony 1935- *AmSCAP 66, -80*
DeMatteo, Donna 1941- *NatPD[port]*
Demaunde, William *NewGrD 80*
DeMaupassant *NewEOp 71*
DeMaupassant, Guy 1850-1893 *FilmgC, HalFC 80*
DeMave, Jack *WhoHol A*
DeMax, Edouard d1924 *Film 2, NotNAT B*
Dembinski, Boleslaw 1833-1914 *NewGrD 80*
Dembo, Gerald 1922- *AmSCAP 80*
Dembo, Joseph T *NewYTET*
Dembolecki, Wojciech *NewGrD 80*
Demby, Emanuel H 1919- *IntMPA 77, -75, -76, -78, -79, -80*
Demby, Jill *WomWMM B*
DeMeester, Louis *NewGrD 80*
DeMeis, Mia T C 1945- *IntWWM 77*
Demelius, Christian 1643-1711 *NewGrD 80*
DeMenasce, Jacques 1905-1960 *BiDAmM*
DeMendoza, Carlo *Film 2*
DeMendoza, Fernando Diaz d1930 *NotNAT B*
DeMenezes Bastos, Rafael Jose 1945- *IntWWM 77, -80*
Demensions, The *RkOn*
Demeny, Desiderius 1871-1937 *Baker 78*
Demeny, Georges 1850-1917 *FilmEn, OxFilm*
Demeny, Janos 1915- *NewGrD 80*
DeMerle, Lester William 1946- *EncJzS 70*
Demessieux, Jeanne 1921-1968 *Baker 78, BnBkM 80, MusMk, NewGrD 80*
Demetrakas, Johanna *WomWMM A, -B*
DeMetruis, Claude 1917- *AmSCAP 80*
Demeur, Anne Arsene 1824-1892 *CmOp, NewEOp 71*
DeMezzo, Pietro 1730?-1794? *NewGrD 80*
Demian, Vilmos 1910- *NewGrD 80*
Demian, Wilhelm 1910- *Baker 78, NewGrD 80*
Demich, Irina 1937- *ForYSC*
DeMichaele, Antoninus *NewGrD 80*
Demick, Irina 1937- *FilmgC, HalFC 80, WhoHol A*
DeMiddeleer, Jean 1909- *IntWWM 80*
Demidoff, Madame *Film 1*
Demieree, Aline 1930- *IntWWM 80*
Demierre, Aline 1930- *IntWWM 77*
DeMille, Agnes *BiE&WWA, NotNAT, WhoThe 72*
DeMille, Agnes 1905- *EncMT, WhoThe 77*
DeMille, Agnes 1908- *NotNAT A*
DeMille, Agnes 1909- *DancEn 78[port], Ent*
DeMille, Beatrice M d1923 *NotNAT B*
DeMille, Cecelia *Film 1*
DeMille, Mrs. Cecil d1960 *NotNAT B*
DeMille, Cecil B 1881-1959 *AmFD, BiDFilm, -81, CmMov, DcFM, FilmEn, FilmgC, HalFC 80, MovMk[port], NotNAT B, OxFilm, TwYS A, WhScrn 74, -77, WhThe, WhoHol B, WomWMM, WorEFlm[port]*
DeMille, Henry C 1850-1893 *NotNAT B, PlP&P[port]*
DeMille, Katherine *ForYSC*
DeMille, Katherine 1911- *FilmEn, FilmgC, HalFC 80, ThFT[port], WhoHol A*
DeMille, William C 1878-1955 *DcFM, FilmEn, FilmgC, HalFC 80, NotNAT B, TwYS A, WhScrn 74, -77, WhThe, WhoHol B*
Deming, Arthur *AmPS B*
Deming, Walter *Film 2*
Deming, Will d1926 *NotNAT B*
DeMinil, Renee d1941 *NotNAT B*
Demme, Jonathan 1944- *HalFC 80, IntMPA 80*
Demmeni, Yevgeni Sergeivitch *DcPup*
Demmers, Alex *ConMuA 80B*
Demming, Lanson F 1902- *AmSCAP 66, -80, ConAmC*
Demmler, Johann Michael 1748-1785 *NewGrD 80*
DeMol, Francoise *WomWMM*
DeMol, Pierre 1825-1899 *Baker 78*
DeMolas, Nicolas 1900-1944 *DancEn 78*
Demond, Frank 1933- *NewOrJ SUP[port]*
Demongeat, Mylene 1936- *ForYSC*
Demongeot, Mylene 1936- *FilmEn, FilmgC, HalFC 80, MotPP, WhoHol A*
DeMont, Willem Rene 1911- *WhoMus 72*
DeMonte Regali Gallus *NewGrD 80*
DeMontellano, Bernardo Ortiz *PupTheA*
DeMontherlant, Henry 1896- *WhThe, WhoThe 72*
DeMoore, Harry *Film 1*
DeMori, Enrico 1930- *WhoOp 76*
DeMoroda, Derra 1897- *DancEn 78*
Demos, Peter John 1941- *IntWWM 80*
Demoss, Lyle *IntMPA 77*
Demoss, Lyle 1907- *IntMPA 75, -76, -78, -79, -80*
DeMott, John A 1912-1975 *WhScrn 77, WhoHol C*
DeMoura Castro, Luiz Carlos 1941- *IntWWM 77, -80*
Dempsey, Clifford 1865-1938 *Film 2, NotNAT B, WhScrn 74, -77, WhoHol B*
Dempsey, Don *ConMuA 80B*
Dempsey, Gregory John 1931- *CmOp[port], NewGrD 80, WhoMus 72, WhoOp 76*
Dempsey, Jack 1895- *Film 2, WhoHol A*
Dempsey, James Clifford 1937- *BiDAmM*
Dempsey, James E 1876-1918 *AmSCAP 66, -80*
Dempsey, Thomas 1862-1947 *WhScrn 74, -77, WhoHol B*
Dempster, Austin *FilmgC, HalFC 80*
Dempster, Carol *MotPP*
Dempster, Carol 1901- *FilmgC, HalFC 80*
Dempster, Carol 1902- *FilmEn, Film 1, -2, TwYS, What 2[port], WhoHol A*
Dempster, Hugh 1900- *WhThe, WhoHol A, WhoThe 72*
Dempster, Stuart 1936- *NewGrD 80*
Dempster, William R 1809-1871 *BiDAmM*
Demus, Joerg 1928- *IntWWM 77, -80, WhoMus 72*
Demus, Jorg 1928- *BnBkM 80, NewGrD 80*
DeMusset, Alfred *NewEOp 71*
Demuth, Norman 1898-1968 *Baker 78, NewGrD 80, OxMus*
Demuth, Theodore Louis 1924- *AmSCAP 80*
Demy, Jacques 1931- *BiDFilm, -81, DcFM, FilmEn, FilmgC, HalFC 80, MovMk[port], OxFilm, WorEFlm*
Denard, Michael 1944- *CnOxB*
DeNarke, Victor 1930- *WhoMus 72*
DeNaut, George Matthews 1915- *AmSCAP 66, -80*
Denberg, Susan 1945?- *WhoHrs 80*
DenBoer, Jan 1932- *IntWWM 80*
Denbow, Stefania Bjornson 1916- *AmSCAP 80, CpmDNM 76, -77, ConAmC*
Denby, Edwin 1903- *CnOxB, DancEn 78[port]*
Dence, Phyllis Elizabeth 1905- *WhoMus 72*
Dench, Judi 1934- *FilmgC, HalFC 80, IntMPA 77, -75, -76, -78, -79, -80, WhoThe 72, -77*
Dench, Judi 1935- *CnThe*
Dench, Lily *WhoMus 72*
Dencke, Jeremiah 1725-1795 *Baker 78, NewGrD 80, OxMus*
Dencke, Jeremias 1735-1795 *BiDAmM*
Dencker-Jensen, Aksel Ingvard 1914- *IntWWM 80*
Dendrino, Gherase 1901-1973 *Baker 78*
Deneau, Sidney G *IntMPA 77, -75, -76, -78, -79, -80*
DeNeergaard, Beatrice 1908- *BiE&WWA*
DeNeergaard, Virginia *AmSCAP 66, -80*
Denefve, Jules 1814-1877 *NewGrD 80*
Denekas, Mark Raymond 1949- *IntWWM 77*
Denenholz, Reginald 1913- *BiE&WWA*
Denereaz, Alexandre 1875-1947 *Baker 78*
Denes, Oscar 1893- *WhThe*
Deneufville, Johann Jacob *NewGrD 80*
Deneuve, Catherine *MotPP, WhoHol A*
Deneuve, Catherine 1943- *BiDFilm, -81, FilmAG WE[port], FilmEn, FilmgC, ForYSC, HalFC 80, MovMk, OxFilm, WhoHrs 80, WorEFlm[port]*
Deneuve, Catherine 1945- *IntMPA 77, -75, -76, -78, -79, -80*
DeNeve *NewGrD 80*
Dengremont, Maurice 1866-1893 *Baker 78*
Denham, Isolde 1920- *WhThe*
Denham, Maurice 1909- *FilmEn, FilmgC, HalFC 80, IlWWBF[port], IntMPA 77, -75, -76, -78, -79, -80, WhoHol A, WhoThe 72, -77*
Denham, Reginald 1894- *BiE&WWA, IlWWBF, -A, NotNAT, WhoThe 72, -77*
Denham, Sergei I 1897-1970 *CnOxB, DancEn 78*
DenHertog, Gerard 1914- *IntWWM 77, -80*
Denhof, Ernst d1936 *NewGrD 80*
Denic, Miomir Alexander 1913- *WhoOp 76*
Denim, Joe *BluesWW*
Denim, Kate d1907 *NotNAT B*
DeNiro, Robert *WhoHol A*
DeNiro, Robert 1943- *FilmEn, HalFC 80, MovMk[port]*
DeNiro, Robert 1945- *BiDFilm 81, IntMPA 77, -75, -76, -78, -79, -80*
Denis *NewGrD 80*
Denis, Claude d1752? *NewGrD 80*
Denis, Claude 1544-1587 *NewGrD 80*
Denis, Didier 1947- *Baker 78*
Denis, G *NewGrD 80*
Denis, Jean *NewGrD 80*
Denis, Jean-Baptiste 1720?-1765? *NewGrD 80*
Denis, Jehan 1549-1589 *NewGrD 80*
Denis, Martin *NewGrD 80*
Denis, Michaela *WomWMM*
Denis, Philippe *NewGrD 80*
Denis, Pierre *NewGrD 80*
Denis, Pierre d1777? *NewGrD 80*
Denis, Pietro d1777? *NewGrD 80*
Denis, Robert d1589? *NewGrD 80*
Denis, Thomas d1620? *NewGrD 80*
Denis, Valentin 1916- *IntWWM 77, -80, NewGrD 80*
Denise, Patricia 1922- *CreCan 1*
Denison, Helen Lee *PupTheA*
Denison, John Law 1911- *IntWWM 77, -80, NewGrD 80, WhoMus 72*
Denison, Merrill 1893- *CreCan 1, McGEWD, REnWD[port]*
Denison, Michael 1915- *FilmEn, FilmgC, HalFC 80, IlWWBF[port], -A, IntMPA 77, -75, -76, -78, -79, -80, WhoHol A, WhoThe 72, -77*
Denison, Muriel Goggin 1885-1954 *CreCan 1*
Denisov, Edison 1929- *Baker 78, DcCM, NewGrD 80*
Denisova, Alexandra *CreCan 1*
DeNiverville, Louis *CreCan 1*
Deniz, Clare Frances 1945- *IntWWM 80*
Denize, Nadine 1943- *WhoOp 76*
Denker, Henry 1912- *BiE&WWA, CnMD SUP, NotNAT*
Denman, John 1933- *IntWWM 77, -80, WhoMus 72*
Denmark, L Kirk 1916- *BiE&WWA, NotNAT*
Dennee, Charles Frederick 1863-1946 *Baker 78, BiDAmM*
Denner *NewGrD 80*
Denner, Charles 1926- *FilmAG WE, FilmEn*
Denner, Charles 1933?- *FilmgC, HalFC 80*
Denner, Heinrich *NewGrD 80*
Denner, Jacob 1681-1735 *NewGrD 80*
Denner, Johann Christoph 1655-1707 *MusMk, NewGrD 80*
Denner, Johann Christopher *OxMus*
Denner, Johann David 1691- *NewGrD 80*
D'Ennery, Adolphe Eugene Philippe 1811-1899 *NotNAT B*
D'Ennery, Guy *Film 2*
Dennes, Eileen *Film 2*
Denni, Gwynne 1882-1949 *AmSCAP 66, -80*
Denni, Lucien 1886-1947 *AmSCAP 66, -80, BiDAmM*
Denniker, Paul 1897- *AmSCAP 66, -80*
Denning, Darryl 1939- *IntWWM 77, -80*
Denning, Frank 1909- *AmSCAP 66, -80*
Denning, Richard 1914- *FilmEn, FilmgC, HalFC 80, MotPP, MovMk, WhoHol A, WhoHrs 80[port]*
Denning, Richard 1916- *ForYSC*
Denning, Wade Fulton, Jr. 1922- *AmSCAP 66, -80*
Denning, Will H d1926 *NotNAT B*
Dennington, Arthur 1904- *WhoMus 72*
Dennis, Brian 1941- *DcCM, NewGrD 80*

Dennis, Clark 1911- *CmpEPM*
Dennis, Crystal 1893-1973 *WhScrn 77, WhoHol B*
Dennis, Danny *WhoHol A*
Dennis, Doris L *MorBAP*
Dennis, Eddie *Film 2*
Dennis, Ginny Maxey 1923- *AmSCAP 66, -80*
Dennis, Henry *OxMus*
Dennis, John *WhoHol A*
Dennis, John 1657-1734 *NotNAT B*
Dennis, Kenneth Carl 1930- *BiDAmM*
Dennis, Mark Andrew, Jr. 1949- *IntWWM 77*
Dennis, Matt 1914- *AmSCAP 66, -80, BiDAmM, CmpEPM*
Dennis, Nick *ForYSC, WhoHol A*
Dennis, Nigel 1912- *CnMD, CnThe, ConDr 73, -77, CroCD, EncWT, ModWD*
Dennis, Robert 1933- *AmSCAP 80, ConAmC*
Dennis, Russell 1916-1964 *NotNAT B, WhScrn 74, -77, WhoHol B*
Dennis, Ruth *Film 1*
Dennis, Sandy 1937- *BiE&WWA, FilmEn, FilmgC, ForYSC, HalFC 80, IntMPA 77, -75, -76, -78, -79, -80, MotPP, MovMk[port], NotNAT, WhoHol A, WhoThe 72, -77*
Dennis, Will d1914 *NotNAT B*
Dennis, Willie 1926-1965 *BiDAmM*
Dennison, Eva *Film 2*
Dennison, Frank d1964 *NotNAT B*
Dennison, Gwendolyn Elaine 1954- *AmSCAP 80*
Dennison, Peter John 1942- *IntWWM 77, -80, NewGrD 80, WhoMus 72*
Dennison, Sam 1926- *ConAmC*
Denniston, Reynolds 1881-1943 *NotNAT B, WhScrn 77*
Denny, Charles R, Jr. *NewYTET*
Denny, Ernest 1869-1943 *NotNAT B, WhThe*
Denny, Ike *WhoHol A*
Denny, J William 1935- *EncFCWM 69*
Denny, Jack 1894?-1950 *BgBands 74, CmpEPM*
Denny, James 1911-1963 *IlEncCM*
Denny, James R 1911-1963 *EncFCWM 69*
Denny, James Runciman 1908- *OxMus, WhoMus 72*
Denny, Malcolm *Film 2*
Denny, Martin 1911- *AmSCAP 66, -80, BiDAmM, RkOn*
Denny, Reginald 1891-1967 *BiE&WWA, FilmEn, Film 1, -2, FilmgC, ForYSC, HalFC 80, HolCA[port], MotPP, MovMk, NotNAT B, TwYS, Vers A[port], WhScrn 74, -77, WhThe, WhoHol B*
Denny, Sandy d1978 *ConMuA 80A, IlEncR[port]*
Denny, William D 1910- *Baker 78, ConAmC*
Denny, William Henry Leigh 1853-1915 *NotNAT B, WhThe, WhoStg 1906, -1908*
DeNobel, Felix 1907- *NewGrD 80*
DeNobili, Lila *WhoOp 76*
Denoff, Samuel 1928- *AmSCAP 66, -80*
Denola, Georges 1880?-1950 *DcFM*
DeNoon, David 1928- *AmSCAP 66*
DeNorby, Irene Jellinek *CreCan 1*
DeNormand, George *IntMPA 77, -75, -76, -78, -79, -80*
DenOuden, Peter 1948- *IntWWM 77, -80*
DeNoyer, Alfred Loring *PupTheA*
DeNoyer, Mrs. Alfred Loring *PupTheA*
Densmore, Frances 1867-1957 *Baker 78, NewGrD 80, OxMus*
Densmore, John Hopkins 1880-1943 *AmSCAP 66, -80, Baker 78, BiDAmM, ConAmC*
Densmore, John Paul 1944- *AmSCAP 80*
Denson, Seaborn M 1854-1936 *NewGrD 80*
Denss, Adrian *NewGrD 80*
Dent, Alan 1905- *WhoThe 72, -77*
Dent, Edward Joseph 1876-1957 *Baker 78, NewEOp 71, NewGrD 80, OxMus*
Dent, Lawrence *NewOrJ*
Dent, Thomas C *BlkAmP, MorBAP*
Dent, Vernon d1963 *Film 2, ForYSC, TwYS, WhoHol B*
Dent, Vernon 1894-1963 *FilmgC, HalFC 80*
Dent, Vernon 1900-1963 *WhScrn 74, -77, WhoHrs 80*
Dentay, Elizabeth Benson Guy *CreCan 2*
Dentice *NewGrD 80*
Dentice, Fabrizio 1525?-1601? *NewGrD 80*
Dentice, Luigi 1510?-1566? *NewGrD 80*
Dentice, Scipione 1560-1635? *NewGrD 80*
Denton, Crahan 1914-1966 *BiE&WWA, NotNAT, WhScrn 74, -77, WhoHol B*
Denton, Frank 1878-1945 *NotNAT B, WhThe*
Denton, George 1865-1918 *WhScrn 77*
Denton, Jack *IlWWBF*
Denton, James *AmSCAP 80*
Denton, Jon *ConAmTC*
Denton, Robert Charles 1941- *IntWWM 77*
Denton, William Lewis 1932- *IntWWM 77, -80*
Denty, Edward Thomas 1905- *WhoMus 72*
Denver, Bob 1935- *FilmgC, ForYSC, HalFC 80, WhoHol A*
Denver, Joel *ConMuA 80B*
Denver, John 1943- *AmSCAP 80, ConMuA 80A, CounME 74[port], -74A, HalFC 80, IlEncCM[port], IlEncR, RkOn 2[port]*
Denville, Alfred 1876-1955 *NotNAT B, WhThe*
DeNys, Carl Augustin Leon 1917- *IntWWM 77, -80, WhoMus 72*
Denysenko, Wlodzimierz 1931- *WhoOp 76*
Denza, Luigi 1846-1922 *Baker 78, NewGrD 80, OxMus*
Denzler, Robert 1892-1972 *Baker 78, CmOp, NewGrD 80, WhoMus 72*
Deodata, Mary *PupTheA*
Deodato *RkOn 2[port]*
Deodato, Eumir DeAlmeida 1942- *AmSCAP 80, EncJzS 70*
DeOliveira, Babi 1915- *IntWWM 80*
DeOliveira, Fernando Correa 1921- *IntWWM 77, -80*
DePachmann, Vladimir *MusSN[port]*
DePackh, Maurice 1896-1960 *AmSCAP 66, -80*
DePadua, Anthony *AmSCAP 80*
DePalma, Brian 1940- *BiDFilm 81, IntMPA 77, -76, -78, -79, -80*
DePalma, Brian 1941- *FilmEn*
DePalma, Brian 1944- *FilmgC, HalFC 80, WhoHrs 80*
DePalowski, Gaston *NotNAT B*
Depansis *NewGrD 80*
DePaolis, Alessio 1893-1964 *NewEOp 71*
Depaolis, Leone F *AmSCAP 80*
Depardieu, Gerard 1948- *FilmAG WE, FilmEn, WhoHol A*
DeParis, Sidney 1903-1967 *BiDAmM*
DeParis, Sidney 1905-1967 *CmpEPM, EncJzS 70, IlEncJ, WhoJazz 72*
DeParis, Wilbur 1900-1973 *BiDAmM, CmpEPM, EncJzS 70, WhoJazz 72*
DeParis, Wilbur 1901-1973 *WhScrn 77*
DePaschoal, Glaucio Roberto 1942- *IntWWM 77, -80*
DePasquali, Bernice d1925 *NotNAT B*
Depass, Arnold 1900?-1945? *NewOrJ*
Depass, Dave 1888?- *NewOrJ*
DePasse, Suzanne *WomWMM*
DePatie, David Hudson 1930- *AmSCAP 80*
DePaul, Gene 1919- *AmPS, AmSCAP 66, -80, BiE&WWA, CmpEPM*
DePaul, Judith 1944- *WhoOp 76*
DePaur, Leonard *AmSCAP 66, -80*
DePaur, Leonard 1915- *BiDAmM*
DePaur, Leonard 1919- *DrBlPA*
DePedery-Hunt, Dora 1913- *CreCan 1*
Depelsenaire, Jean-Marie 1914- *IntWWM 77, -80*
Depew, Joe *Film 2*
Depew, Joseph *Film 2*
Depew, Richard H 1925- *IntMPA 77, -75, -76, -78, -79, -80*
DePeyer, Adrian Christopher 1933- *IntWWM 77, -80*
DePeyer, Everard E V *WhoMus 72*
DePeyer, Gervase 1926- *BnBkM 80, IntWWM 77, -80, NewGrD 80, WhoMus 72*
DePhilippe, Edis 1917- *WhoOp 76*
Depierro, Thomas 1950- *AmSCAP 80*
De'Pietri, Antonio *NewGrD 80*
Depinet, Ned E 1890- *IntMPA 75*
DePirro, Nicola 1898- *IntMPA 77, -75, -76, -78, -79*
Depkat, Gisela 1942- *IntWWM 77, -80*
DePlace, Adelaide 1945- *IntWWM 80*
DePlata, Manitas 1921- *WhoMus 72*
Depp, Harry 1886-1957 *Film 2, WhScrn 74, -77, WhoHol B*
Deppe, Hans 1898-1969 *WhScrn 74, -77*
Deppe, Ludwig 1828-1890 *Baker 78, NewGrD 80, OxMus*
Deppen, Jessie L 1881-1956 *AmSCAP 66, ConAmC A*
Deppenschmidt, Buddy 1936- *BiDAmM*
Depre, Ernest 1854- *WhThe*
DePreist, James 1936- *IntWWM 77, NewGrD 80*
DePriest, James 1936- *BiDAmM, DrBlPA, IntWWM 80*
DePue, Wallace Earl 1932- *AmSCAP 66, -80, CpmDNM 75, -76, -77, -80, ConAmC, IntWWM 77, -80*
DePutti, Lya d1932 *WhoHol B*
DePutti, Lya 1901-1931 *FilmEn, FilmgC, WhScrn 74, -77*
DePutti, Lya 1901-1932 *HalFC 80*
DePutti, Lya 1904-1931 *Film 2, TwYS*
DeQuesada, Alfonso 1918- *DancEn 78*
DeQuincey, Thomas *OxMus*
DeQuinones, Fray Cristobal d1609 *BiDAmM*
DerAbrahamian, Arousiak *WhScrn 77*
Derain, Andre 1880-1954 *CnOxB, DancEn 78*
Derain, Lucy *WomWMM*
DeRamey, Pierre *Film 2*
DeRamus, Betty *BlkAmP*
DeRathsckoff, Monsieur *PupTheA*
DeRavenne, Caroline Marie 1883-1962 *WhScrn 77, WhoHol B*
DeRavenne, Charles *Film 2*
DeRavenne, Raymond 1904-1950 *WhScrn 74, -77*
Deray, Jacques 1929- *FilmEn, FilmgC, HalFC 80, WorEFlm*
Derba, Mimi 1894-1953 *WhScrn 74, -77*
Derbigny, Arthur 1906?-1962 *NewOrJ*
Derby, Richard 1951- *ConAmC*
Dere, Jean 1886-1970 *Baker 78*
DeReede, Rien 1942- *IntWWM 77, -80*
DeReeder, Pierre 1887-1966 *AmSCAP 66*
Derek *RkOn 2[port]*
Derek, John 1926- *CmMov, FilmEn, FilmgC, ForYSC, HalFC 80, MotPP, MovMk, What 4[port], WhoHol A, WorEFlm*
Derek & The Dominoes *RkOn 2[port]*
DeRemer, Ruby *Film 1, -2, TwYS*
Deren, Maya 1908-1961 *ConLC 16, DcFM, OxFilm, WhScrn 77, WomWMM, WorEFlm*
Deren, Maya 1917-1961 *WhoHrs 80*
DeRensis, Raffaello 1879-1970 *Baker 78*
DeReszke *NewGrD 80*
DeReszke, Edouard 1853-1917 *Baker 78, BnBkM 80, CmOp, NewEOp 71, NewGrD 80[port]*
DeReszke, Jean 1850-1925 *Baker 78, BnBkM 80, CmOp[port], NewEOp 71*
DeReszke, Jean 1850-1935 *NewGrD 80[port]*
DeReszke, Josephine 1855-1891 *Baker 78, BnBkM 80, NewEOp 71, NewGrD 80*
Derey, Blanzej 1585?-1666 *NewGrD 80*
DeReyes, Consuelo 1893-1948 *NotNAT B, WhThe*
DeReyghere, Alfred J 1901- *WhoMus 72*
DeRhoda, Paulus *NewGrD 80*
DeRidder, Anton *WhoOp 76*
DeRienzo, Silvio 1909- *AmSCAP 66, -80*
Derieteanu, George 1918- *IntWWM 80*
Derigney, Louise *Film 2*
Dering, Lady *NewGrD 80*
Dering, Richard 1580?-1630 *Baker 78, BnBkM 80, MusMk, NewGrD 80*
DeRiso, Camillo *Film 2*
DeRita, Joe *ForYSC, JoeFr, MotPP, WhoHol A*
Derksen, Jan 1936- *WhoOp 76*
D'Erlanger, Baron Frederic 1868-1943 *Baker 78*
D'Erlanger, Rodolphe 1872-1932 *Baker 78*
Derman, Vergie 1942- *CnOxB*
Dermota, Anton 1910- *CmOp, IntWWM 77, -80, NewGrD 80, WhoOp 76*
Dermota, Anton 1912- *WhoMus 72*
Dern, Bruce *WhoHol A*
Dern, Bruce 1936- *FilmEn, FilmgC,*

HalFC 80, WhoHrs 80[port]
Dern, Bruce 1937- BiDFilm 81, IntMPA 77, -75, -76, -78, -79, -80
Dernesch, Helga 1939- IntWWM 77, -80, NewGrD 80, WhoOp 76
Dernesh, Helga 1939- CmOp
Dero, Al AmSCAP 80
DeRobertis, Francesco 1902-1959 DcFM, OxFilm
DeRobertis, Francesco 1903-1959 WorEFlm
Deroc, Jean 1925- CnOxB
DeRoche, Charles 1880-1952 Film 1, -2, MotPP, TwYS, WhScrn 74, -77, WhoHol B
DeRochemont, Louis 1899-1978 DcFM, FilmEn, FilmgC, HalFC 80, IntMPA 77, -75, -76, -78, -79, OxFilm, WorEFlm[port]
DeRochemont, Richard IntMPA 77, -75, -76, -78, -79, -80
DeRocher, L E 1912- BiE&WWA
DeRoet, Janette 1938- IntWWM 77, -80
DeRojas, Fernando 1465?-1541 Ent
Deroo, Maurits Alfons 1902- IntWWM 77, -80
DeRooij, Dorthy 1946- IntWWM 77, -80
DeRoos, Robert 1907- IntWWM 77, -80
DeRosa, A Film 2
DeRosa, Carmella Millie 1914- AmSCAP 66, -80
DeRosa, Clem R 1925- AmSCAP 80
DeRosa, Dario 1919- WhoMus 72
DeRosa, Pat A 1921- AmSCAP 80
DeRosas, Enrique d1948 WhScrn 74, -77
DeRose, Peter 1896-1953 NotNAT B
DeRose, Peter 1900-1953 AmPS, AmSCAP 66, -80, Baker 78, BiDAmM, CmpEPM, PopAmC[port], PopAmC SUP, Sw&Ld C
DeRosier, G Philippe 1918- WhoOp 76
Derosier, Michael Joseph 1951- AmSCAP 80
Derosier, Nicolas NewGrD 80
DeRossi, Francesco NewGrD 80
DeRossi, Giuseppe NewGrD 80
DeRoy, Harry Film 1
Derozier, Nicolas NewGrD 80
Derp, Clothilde Von 1892-1974 CnOxB
Derr, Emily IntWWM 77, -80
Derr, Richard 1917- BiE&WWA, FilmgC, ForYSC, HalFC 80, NotNAT, WhThe, WhoHol A, WhoHrs 80
Derr, Zan AmSCAP 80
Derra DeMoroda, Friderica 1897- CnOxB
Derrick NewGrD 80
Derrick, Frank John, Jr. 1913- AmSCAP 80
Derrick, Samuel d1769 NotNAT B
Derringer, Rick IlEncR
Derringer, Rick 1947- ConMuA 80A, RkOn 2[port]
Dersan, Jon AmSCAP 80
DeRue, Baby Film 1
DeRuiz, Nick F Film 2
Dervaux, Pierre 1917- NewGrD 80, WhoMus 72
Dervis, Charles Film 2
Derwent, Clarence 1884-1959 NotNAT A, -B, OxThe, WhScrn 74, -77, WhThe, WhoHol B
Derwent, Elfrida d1958 NotNAT B
Derwyn, Hal 1914- CmpEPM
Dery, Gabriella 1935- WhoOp 76
Dery, Tibor 1894- CroCD
DeRycke, Antonius NewGrD 80
DeRyke, DeLores 1929- IntWWM 77, -80
Derzhinskaya, Xeniya Georgiyevna 1889-1951 NewGrD 80
DeSabata NewEOp 71
DeSabata, Victor MusSN[port]
DeSabata, Victor 1892-1967 CmOp, NewGrD 80[port]
Desabaye, Mark d1837 BiDAmM
DeSai, V H d1950? WhScrn 77
Desaides, Nicholas NewGrD 80
Desailly, Jean 1920- FilmAG WE, FilmEn, FilmgC, HalFC 80, WorEFlm[port]
DeSales, Francis ForYSC, WhoHol A
DeSamora, Juan PupTheA
DeSanctis, Alfredo WhThe
DeSanti, Angelo 1847-1922 NewGrD 80
DeSantis NewGrD 80
DeSantis, Alberto 1876-1968 NewGrD 80
DeSantis, Emidio 1893- AmSCAP 66, -80, ConAmC A
Desantis, Ernest 1892- AmSCAP 80
DeSantis, Giuseppe 1917- DcFM, FilmEn, FilmgC, HalFC 80, IntMPA 77, -75, -76, -78, -79, -80, OxFilm, WorEFlm
DeSantis, Joe 1909- FilmgC, HalFC 80, NotNAT, Vers A[port], WhoHol A
DeSantis, Joseph 1909- ForYSC
DeSantis, Pasqalino FilmEn
DeSantis, Pietro Giovanni 1822-1914 NewGrD 80
DeSantis, Renato 1901-1974 NewGrD 80
DeSaram, Rohan 1939- NewGrD 80
Desargus, Xavier 1768?-1832 NewGrD 80
DeSarigny, Peter 1911- FilmgC, HalFC 80
Desarthis, Robert DcPup
Desarzens, Victor 1908- NewGrD 80
Desauglers, Marc-Antoine 1742-1793 NewGrD 80
Desaulniers, Gonzalve 1863-1934 CreCan 2
DesAutels, Van 1911-1968 WhScrn 74, -77, WhoHol B
DeSaxe, Chretien-Charles NewGrD 80
DeSaxe, Rudolph 1905-1958 AmSCAP 80
DeSaxe, Serena AmSCAP 80
Desbiens, Francine WomWMM
DesBordes NewGrD 80
Desborough, Philip 1883- WhThe
DesBuissons NewGrD 80
Desbuissons, Michael NewGrD 80
Desby, Frank 1922- IntWWM 77, -80
Descartes, Rene 1596-1650 NewGrD 80
Descaves, Lucien 1861-1949 McGEWD, WhThe
DeSchaap, Philip 1911- IntMPA 77, -75, -76, -78, -79, -80
Deschamps, Emile 1791-1871 NewGrD 80
Descher, Sandy 1948- WhoHrs 80[port]
Desclee, Aimee-Olympe 1836-1874 NotNAT B, OxThe
Desclos, Jeanne Film 2
Descombey, Michel 1930- CnOxB, DancEn 78
Desderi, Ettore 1892-1974 Baker 78
Desdunes, Clarence 1896-1934? NewOrJ
DeSegurola, Andre d1953 ForYSC
DeSegurola, Andre 1875-1953 Film 2
DeSegurola, Andreas 1875-1953 WhScrn 74, -77
DeSegurola, Andres 1874-1953 Baker 78
DeSegurola, Andres 1875-1953 TwYS, WhoHol B
Deseine, Mademoiselle d1759 NotNAT B, OxThe
DeSelincourt, Hugh 1878-1951 NotNAT B, WhThe
Deses, Greta WomWMM
DeSeta, Vittorio 1923- DcFM, FilmEn, FilmgC, HalFC 80, OxFilm, WorEFlm
Desfis, Angelo 1888-1950 WhScrn 74, -77
Desfontaines, Henri 1876- WhThe
DesGranges, Louis Anthony 1935- AmSCAP 80
DeShannon, Jackie 1944- AmSCAP 80, RkOn
Deshayes DancEn 78, NewGrD 80
Deshayes, Andre Jean-Jacques 1777-1846 CnOxB, DancEn 78, NewGrD 80
Deshayes, Paul d1891 NotNAT B
Deshayes, Pierre Louis NewGrD 80
DesHayes, Prosper-Didier d1815 NewGrD 80
Deshays, Prosper-Didier d1815 NewGrD 80
Deshevov, Vladimir Mikhaylovich 1889-1955 Baker 78, NewGrD 80
Deshon, Florence Film 2
Deshon, Florence 1894-1922 WhScrn 77
Deshon, Florence 1898?- WhoHol B
DeSica, Gennaro WhoOp 76
DeSica, Vittorio 1901-1974 FilmAG WE, HalFC 80, OxFilm, WhScrn 77
DeSica, Vittorio 1902-1974 BiDFilm, -81, DcFM, FilmEn, FilmgC, IntMPA 75, MovMk[port], WhoHol B, WorEFlm[port]
Desideri, Girolamo 1635?- NewGrD 80
DeSignori, Giocondo 1915- IntWWM 77, -80
Desilets, Alphonse 1888-1956 CreCan 2
Desilets, Guy 1928- CreCan 1
DeSilva, Andreas 1475?- NewGrD 80
DeSilva, David 1936- BiE&WWA
DeSilva, Frank 1890-1968 NotNAT B, WhScrn 74, -77
DeSilva, Fred Film 2
DeSilva, N 1868-1949 WhThe
DeSilva, Nina 1868-1949 NotNAT B
Desiron, Marcel 1913- WhoOp 76
Desjardins, Marie-Catherine-Hortense 1632-1683 NotNAT B, OxThe
Desjardins, Maxime WhThe
Desjardins, Maxine Film 2
Deslandres, Adolphe-Edouard-Marie 1840-1911 Baker 78
Deslaw, Eugene 1900- DcFM
Deslins, Joannes NewGrD 80
Deslins, Johann NewGrD 80
Deslius, Joannes NewGrD 80
Deslius, Johann NewGrD 80
Deslouges, Philippe d1920 NewGrD 80
Deslys, Gaby d1920 AmPS B
Deslys, Gaby 1883?-1920 CmpEPM
Deslys, Gaby 1884-1920 Film 1, NotNAT B, OxThe, WhScrn 74, -77, WhThe, WhoHol B
Deslys, Kay Film 2
Desmarais, Henry 1661-1741 NewGrD 80
DesMarais, Paul 1920- Baker 78, ConAmC, DcCM, NewGrD 80
Desmarchais, Rex 1908- CreCan 1
Desmares, Charlotte 1682-1753 OxThe
Desmares, Nicolas 1645?-1714 OxThe
Desmarest, Henry 1661-1741 NewGrD 80
Desmarestz, Henry 1661-1741 NewGrD 80
Desmarets, Henri 1661-1741 Baker 78
Desmarets, Henri 1662?-1741 MusMk
Desmarets, Henry 1661-1741 NewGrD 80
Desmarets DeSaint-Sorlin, Jean 1595-1676 CnThe, Ent, REnWD[port]
Desmaretz DeSaint-Sorlin, Jean 1595-1676 McGEWD, OxThe
Desmasures, Laurent 1714-1778 NewGrD 80
Desmazures, Laurent 1714-1778 NewGrD 80
DeSmet, Monique Henriette M Antoinette 1925- IntWWM 77, -80
DeSmet, Robin John 1935- IntWWM 77, -80, WhoMus 72
Desmond, Astra 1893-1973 NewGrD 80, WhoMus 72
Desmond, Cleo 1888-1958 BlksB&W, -C
Desmond, Dagmar Film 2
Desmond, Eric Film 1
Desmond, Ethel 1874-1949 WhScrn 74, -77
Desmond, Florence WhoHol A
Desmond, Florence 1905- FilmgC, HalFC 80, IlWWBF, -A, NotNAT A, WhThe
Desmond, Florence 1907- EncMT
Desmond, Gary Christopher 1948- IntWWM 77, -80
Desmond, Johnny AmPS B, WhoHol A
Desmond, Johnny 1920- CmpEPM
Desmond, Johnny 1923- ForYSC, IntMPA 77, -75, -76, -78, -79, -80
Desmond, Johnny 1925- AmSCAP 66, BiDAmM
Desmond, Lucille 1894-1936 WhScrn 74, -77
Desmond, Paul 1924-1977 Baker 78, BiDAmM, CmpEPM, EncJzS 70, NewGrD 80
Desmond, William 1878-1949 FilmEn, Film 1, -2, FilmgC, ForYSC, HalFC 80, MotPP, NotNAT B, TwYS, WhScrn 74, -77, WhoHol B
Desmond And Desmond PupTheA
Desmonde, Jerry 1908-1967 FilmgC, HalFC 80, WhScrn 74, -77, WhoHol B
Desni, Tamara 1913- FilmgC, HalFC 80, IlWWBF[port], WhoHol A
Desni, Xenia Film 2
Desny, Ivan 1922- FilmEn, FilmgC, HalFC 80, WhoHol A
Desoeillets, Mademoiselle 1621-1670 OxThe
DeSolla, Rachel d1920 NotNAT B
DeSolliers, Jean 1916- IntWWM 77, -80
DeSomery, Gene David 1948- ConAmC
Desormerie, Leopold-Bastien 1740?-1810? NewGrD 80
Desormery, Leopold-Bastien 1740?-1810? NewGrD 80
Desormiere, Roger 1898-1963 Baker 78, CmOp, NewEOp 71, NewGrD 80
DeSoto, Henry 1888-1963 WhScrn 77
DeSousa, Filipe 1927- NewGrD 80
DeSousa, May 1882-1948 NotNAT B
DeSousa, May 1887-1948 WhThe
DeSouza, Camilla 1941- WhoMus 72
DeSouza, Edward 1933- FilmgC, HalFC 80
DeSouza, Joao Jose Pereira 1934- EncJzS 70

DeSouza, Raimundo Nonato 1938- *IntWWM 80*
DeSouza Salvador, Aecio 1906- *IntWWM 80*
Despalj, Pavle 1934- *Baker 78, NewGrD 80*
Despic, Dejan 1930- *IntWWM 77, -80*
Despins, Jean-Paul 1935- *IntWWM 77, -80*
Desplanes, Jean-Antoine *NewGrD 80*
Despo *WhoHol A*
Desportes, Philippe 1546-1606 *NewGrD 80*
Desportes, Yvonne 1907- *NewGrD 80*
Despreaux, Jean-Etienne 1748-1820 *CnOxB*
Despreaux, Jean Etienne 1748-1820 *DancEn 78*
Despreaux, Jean-Etienne 1748-1820 *NewGrD 80*
Despreaux, Louis Felix 1746-1813 *NewGrD 80*
Despres, Alain *CreCan 1*
DesPres, Josquin *BnBkM 80*
Despres, Suzanne 1875-1951 *NotNAT B, WhThe, WhoHol B*
Desprez, Frank 1853-1916 *NotNAT B, WhThe*
DesPrez, Josquin 1440?-1521 *Baker 78, NewGrD 80*
Desprez, Louis-Jean 1742-1804 *NewGrD 80*
Despuig, Guillermo *NewGrD 80*
Desquesnes, Jean *NewGrD 80*
Desrat, G *DancEn 78*
Desrochers, Alfred 1901- *CreCan 1*
Desrochers, Joseph Alfred Houle 1901- *CreCan 1*
Desroches, Francis 1895- *CreCan 2*
Desroches, Michel 1942- *IntWWM 77*
Desrosiers, Leo-Paul 1896-1967 *CreCan 2*
Dessart, Professor *PupTheA*
Dessau, Bernhard 1861-1923 *Baker 78*
Dessau, Paul 1894-1979 *Baker 78, BnBkM 80, DcCM, EncWT, IntWWM 77, NewGrD 80, WhoMus 72*
Dessauer, Josef 1798-1876 *NewGrD 80*
Dessauer, Joseph 1798-1876 *Baker 78, NewGrD 80*
DesSerres, Marthe *CreCan 2*
Dessler, Wolfgang Christoph 1660-1722 *NewGrD 80*
Dessoff, Felix Otto 1835-1892 *Baker 78*
Dessoff, Margarethe 1874-1944 *Baker 78*
DeStafini, Helen 1880-1938 *WhScrn 74, -77*
Deste, Luli 1902-1951 *WhScrn 74, -77, WhoHol B*
DeStefano, Filippo Joseph *WhoOp 76*
DeStern, Ana Biro *PupTheA*
DeStern, Emilio *PupTheA*
D'Esterre, Madame *Film 2*
Destine, Jean-Leon 1925- *DancEn 78*
Destine, Jean-Leon 1928- *DrBlPA*
Destinn, Emmy 1878-1930 *Baker 78, BnBkM 80, CmOp, MusSN[port], NewEOp 71, NewGrD 80[port], WhScrn 77*
Destinnova, Ema 1878-1930 *NewGrD 80[port]*
Destouches 1680-1754 *REnWD[port]*
Destouches, Andre Cardinal 1672-1749 *Baker 78, BnBkM 80, NewGrD 80, OxMus*
Destouches, Franz Von 1772-1844 *Baker 78, NewGrD 80*
Destouches, Philippe Nericault 1680-1754 *CnThe, EncWT, Ent, McGEWD, NotNAT B, OxThe*
DeStoutz, Edmond 1920- *IntWWM 80*
Destranges, Louis Augustin E Rouille 1863-1915 *Baker 78, NewGrD 80*
DesUrlis *OxThe*
Desvallieres, Maurice 1857-1926 *NotNAT B, WhThe*
Desvigne, Sidney 1893-1959 *NewOrJ*
Desvignes, Sidney 1893-1959 *WhoJazz 72*
Deswert, Jules 1843-1891 *Baker 78*
Desy, Victor *CreCan 1*
DeSylva, B G d1950 *AmSCAP 80*
Desylva, B G d1950 *Sw&Ld C*
DeSylva, B G 1895-1950 *AmSCAP 66, BestMus, EncMT, WhThe*
DeSylva, B G 1896-1950 *NotNAT B*
DeSylva, Bud 1895-1950 *AmPS*
DeSylva, Buddy 1895-1950 *CmpEPM, HalFC 80*
DeSylva, George Gard 1895-1950 *AmSCAP 80, BiDAmM*
DeSylva Brown And Henderson *BestMus NewCBMT*
Deszczynski, Jozef 1781-1844 *NewGrD 80*
Deszner, Salomea 1759-1806 *NewGrD 80*
Desznier, Gerhard *NewGrD 80*
DeTar, Vernon 1905- *BiDAmM*
Detcher, Abi 1932-1957 *DancEn 78*
DeTedla, Al *AmSCAP 80*
DeTellier, Mariette 1891-1957 *WhScrn 74, -77, WhoHol B*
Detergents, The *RkOn 2[port]*
Detheridge, Joseph 1898- *WhoMus 72*
Dethick, John *WhoMus 72*
Dethier, Edouard 1885-1962 *BiDAmM*
Dethier, Edouard 1886-1962 *Baker 78*
Dethier, Gaston Marie 1875-1958 *Baker 78, BiDAmM*
DeThier, Henry *NewGrD 80*
DeTitta, Arthur A 1904- *IntMPA 77, -75, -76, -78, -79, -80*
DeTolly, Deena d1976 *WhoHol C*
DeTomasi, Giuseppe 1934- *WhoOp 76*
Detoni, Dubravko 1937- *Baker 78, IntWWM 77, -80, NewGrD 80*
DeTonnancour, Jacques *CreCan 2*
DeTorices, Benito Bello *NewGrD 80*
DeToth, Andre *IntMPA 77, -75, -76, -78, -79, -80*
DeToth, Andre 1900- *CmMov, FilmEn, MovMk[port]*
DeToth, Andre 1910- *WorEFlm*
DeToth, Andre 1912- *FilmgC, HalFC 80*
DeToth, Andre 1913- *BiDFilm, -81*
Detoy, Charles 1897- *BiE&WWA*
Detrekoy, Bela 1925- *IntWWM 77, -80*
DeTroffeis, Ruggier *NewGrD 80*
Detroit Emeralds, The *RkOn 2[port]*
Detroit Junior *BluesWW*
Detroit Red *BluesWW*
Dett, R Nathaniel 1882-1943 *Baker 78*
Dett, Robert Nathaniel 1882-1943 *AmSCAP 66, -80, BiDAmM, ConAmC, DrBlPA, NewGrD 80, OxMus*
Dettmer, Roger 1927- *Baker 78, BiE&WWA, ConAmTC, IntWWM 77, NotNAT*
Dettmer, Roger Christian 1927- *IntWWM 80*
Deuchar, James 1930- *EncJzS 70*
Deuel, Peter *ForYSC*
Deulich, Philipp *NewGrD 80*
Deus, Filipe DaMadre De *NewGrD 80*
Deus, Michael *NewGrD 80*
Deutch, Murray *ConMuA 80B*
Deutchmeister, Henri *FilmEn*
Deutekom, Cristina *CmOp*
Deutekom, Cristina 1932- *NewGrD 80*
Deutekom, Cristina 1935- *WhoOp 76*
Deutlich, Jeremias *NewGrD 80*
Deutsch, Adolph 1897- *AmSCAP 66,—80, CmpEPM, ConAmC, IntMPA 75,—76,—77, —78,—79,—80*
Deutsch, Adolph 1897-1979 *HalFC 80*
Deutsch, Adolph 1897-1980 *FilmEn*
Deutsch, Armand S 1913- *BiE&WWA, IntMPA 77, -75, -76, -78, -79, -80*
Deutsch, Benoit-Leon 1892- *WhThe*
Deutsch, David 1926- *FilmgC, HalFC 80, IntMPA 77, -75, -76, -78, -79, -80*
Deutsch, Elizabeth Veronica Wells 1915- *AmSCAP 80*
Deutsch, Emery 1907- *AmPS B, AmSCAP 66, -80, BgBands 74, CmpEPM*
Deutsch, Ernest 1891-1969 *WhoHol B*
Deutsch, Ernst 1890-1969 *HalFC 80*
Deutsch, Ernst 1891-1969 *Film 2, WhScrn 74, -77*
Deutsch, Gregory Paul 1952- *AmSCAP 66*
Deutsch, Helen 1906- *AmSCAP 66, -80, IntMPA 77, -75, -76, -78, -79, -80, WomWMM*
Deutsch, Herbert Arnold 1932- *AmSCAP 80, ConAmC, IntWWM 80*
Deutsch, Leonhard 1887-1951 *BiDAmM*
Deutsch, Lou 1898-1968 *WhScrn 77, WhoHol B*
Deutsch, Max 1892- *NewGrD 80*
Deutsch, Otto Erich 1883-1967 *Baker 78, NewGrD 80*
Deutsch, Otto Erich 1883-1968 *OxMus*
Deutschendorf, Henry John, Jr. 1943- *AmSCAP 80*
DeVahl, Anders 1869- *WhThe*
Deval, Jacques d1972 *PlP&P*
Deval, Jacques 1890-1972 *BiE&WWA, EncWT, ModWD, NotNAT B*
Deval, Jacques 1893-1972 *CnMD*
Deval, Jacques 1894-1972 *McGEWD[port]*
Deval, Jacques 1895-1972 *WhThe*
DeValasco, Mercedes *Film 2*
DeValdez, Carlos J 1894-1939 *WhScrn 74, -77, WhoHol B*
DeVale, Sue Carole 1942- *IntWWM 77, -80*
DeValois, Ninette 1898- *CnOxB, DancEn 78[port], PlP&P, WhThe*
Devan, William Carrolle *NewGrD 80*
Devane, William 1938?- *FilmEn, HalFC 80, WhoHol A*
Devant, David 1863-1941 *WhThe*
Devant, David 1868-1941 *MagIlD*
DeVarney, Emil *Film 1*
DeVaron, Lorna Cooke 1921- *IntWWM 77, -80*
DeVasionellos Correa, Sergio 1934- *IntWWM 77, -80*
Devaty, Antonin 1903- *IntWWM 77, -80*
DeVaughn, William 1948- *RkOn 2[port]*
DeVaull, Billie *Film 2*
DeVaull, William P 1871-1945 *Film 1, WhScrn 74, -77, WhoHol B*
Devaux, Richard *CreCan 2*
Devcic, Natko 1914- *Baker 78, DcCM, NewGrD 80*
DeVeaux, Alex *MorBAP*
DeVeaux, Alexis 1948- *NatPD[port]*
DeVeg, Willem *NewGrD 80*
DeVega, Henry 1930- *EncJzS 70*
Devenport, Frank Perry 1920- *AmSCAP 80*
Devenson, Rosemary *CreCan 2*
DeVera, Cris 1925-1974 *WhScrn 77*
Deverall, Maurice Frederick 1916- *WhoMus 72*
DeVerdier, Anton *Film 2*
Devere, Arthur 1883-1961 *WhScrn 74, -77*
Devere, Arthur 1894-1961 *FilmAG WE*
DeVere, Chester *PupTheA*
DeVere, Daisy *Film 1*
Devere, Francesca 1891-1952 *NotNAT B, WhScrn 74, -77, WhoHol B*
DeVere, George F d1910 *NotNAT B*
Devere, Harry *Film 2*
Devere, Margaret 1889-1918 *WhScrn 77*
Devere, Sam *AmPS B*
Devereaux, Jack 1882-1958 *NotNAT B, WhScrn 74, -77, WhoHol B*
Devereaux, Louise Drew d1954 *NotNAT B*
Devereaux, Richmond *AmSCAP 80*
Deverell, John W 1880-1965 *WhScrn 77, WhThe*
Devereux, William d1945 *NotNAT B, WhThe*
DeVernon, Frank 1845-1923 *WhScrn 74, -77, WhoHol B*
DeVesa, Leonardo *Film 2*
Deveson, Rosemary 1922?- *CreCan 2*
DeVestel, Guy d1973 *WhScrn 77*
Devhrys, Rachel *Film 2*
Devi, Kamala *ForYSC, WhoHol A*
Devi, Prova d1952 *WhScrn 77*
Devi, Ragini *DancEn 78*
Devi, Ritha 1934- *CnOxB*
Devi, Seeta *Film 2*
Devi, Susheela 1930- *IntWWM 77, -80*
Devich, Sandor 1935- *IntWWM 80*
Devienne, Francois 1759-1803 *Baker 78, NewGrD 80[port]*
DeVienne, Lucie 1902- *CreCan 1*
Devigna, Antoine d1499? *NewGrD 80*
DeVigne, Antoine d1499? *NewGrD 80*
DeVilbiss, Robert *Film 2*
Deville, Michel 1931- *BiDFilm, -81, DcFM, FilmEn, FilmgC, HalFC 80, WorEFlm*
DeVilliers *OxThe*
DeVilliers, Dirk Izak Catoggia 1920- *IntWWM 77*
DeVilliers, Dirk Izak Catoggio 1920- *IntWWM 80*
Devil's Daddy-In-Law *BluesWW*
Devil's Son-In-Law *BluesWW[port]*
Devine, Andy 1905-1977 *CmMov, FilmEn, Film 2, FilmgC, ForYSC, HalFC 80, HolCA[port], IntMPA 77, -75, -76, MotPP, MovMk[port], OxFilm, TwYS, What 2[port], WhoHol A*
Devine, George 1901-1966 *CnThe*
Devine, George 1910-1965 *OxThe, PlP&P*

Devine, George 1910-1966 *BiE&WWA, CroCD, EncWT, NotNAT B, WhScrn 77, WhThe*
DeVine, J Lawrence 1935- *ConAmTC*
Devine, Jerry *Film 2*
Devine, John *Film 2*
DeVine, Lawrence 1935- *NotNAT*
DeVinea, Antoine d1499? *NewGrD 80*
DeVinna, Clyde 1892-1953 *FilmEn, FilmgC, HalFC 80*
Devinny, Darey Grant 1943- *AmSCAP 80*
Devirian, Diana Lynn Armstrong 1944- *IntWWM 77, -80*
DeVita, Luciano 1929- *WhoOp 76*
DeVito, Albert 1919- *AmSCAP 66, CpmDNM 80, ConAmC*
DeVito, Albert Kenneth 1919- *AmSCAP 80*
DeVito, Don *ConMuA 80B*
DeVito, Gioconda 1907- *Baker 78, IntWWM 77, -80, NewGrD 80, WhoMus 72*
Devlin, Joe A 1899-1973 *WhScrn 77, WhoHol B*
Devlin, Michael Coles 1942- *WhoOp 76*
Devlin, William 1911- *WhThe*
Devo *ConMuA 80A*
DeVocht, Lodewijk 1887-1977 *Baker 78*
Devoe, Bert 1884-1930 *WhScrn 74, -77, WhoHol B*
Devoe, Dale 1951- *AmSCAP 80*
DeVoe, Robert Alan 1928- *ConAmC*
DeVoght, Carl *Film 2*
DeVogt, Carl *Film 1*
DeVol, Frank *HalFC 80*
DeVol, Frank 1911- *AmSCAP 66, -80, CmpEPM*
DeVoll, Calvin Joseph 1886-1970 *AmSCAP 66, -80*
DeVolt, Artiss 1907- *IntWWM 77, -80, WhoMus 72*
Devolt, Charlotte *IntWWM 77, -80, WhoMus 72*
Devon, Laura 1940- *FilmgC, ForYSC, HalFC 80*
Devon, Richard *ForYSC, WhoHol A*
Devon, Richard 1920?- *WhoHrs 80[port]*
Devore, Dorothy 1899-1976 *FilmEn*
Devore, Dorothy 1901- *Film 1, -2, TwYS, WhoHol A*
Devore, Gaston 1859- *WhThe*
Devore, Jesse *MorBAP*
DeVorzon, Barry & Perry Botkin, Jr. *RkOn 2[port]*
Devotions, The *RkOn 2[port]*
Devoto, Daniel 1916- *NewGrD 80*
DeVoto, Mark Bernard 1940- *ConAmC, DcCM*
Devoyod, Suzanne *WomWMM*
Devreese, Frederic 1929- *Baker 78, NewGrD 80*
Devreese, Godefroid 1893-1972 *Baker 78*
Devreese, Godfried 1893-1972 *NewGrD 80*
Devrient, Eduard 1801-1877 *Baker 78, EncWT, Ent, NewGrD 80, NotNAT B, OxThe*
Devrient, Emil 1803-1872 *EncWT, Ent, NotNAT B, OxThe*
Devrient, Friedrich Philipp 1827-1871 *EncWT*
Devrient, Hans 1878-1927 *OxThe*
Devrient, Karl 1797-1872 *EncWT, NotNAT B, OxThe*
Devrient, Ludvig 1784-1832 *Ent*
Devrient, Ludwig 1784-1832 *CnThe, EncWT, NotNAT B, OxThe*
Devrient, Max 1857-1929 *EncWT, Ent, NotNAT B, OxThe*
Devrient, Otto 1838-1894 *EncWT, NotNAT B, OxThe*
DeVries, Han Libbe 1941- *IntWWM 77*
DeVries, Han Samuel 1941- *IntWWM 80*
DeVries, Henri *Film 1*
DeVries, Henry *WhThe*
Devries, Herman 1858-1949 *Baker 78*
DeVries, John 1915- *AmSCAP 66, -80*
DeVries, Leo Gerrit Herman 1924- *IntWWM 77, -80*
DeVries, Peter 1910- *BiE&WWA, NotNAT*
DeVries Robbe, Willem Arnold 1902- *IntWWM 77, -80*
Devroye, Theodore Joseph 1804-1873 *NewGrD 80*
Devry, Elaine 1935- *HalFC 80*
DeVry, William C 1908- *IntMPA 77, -75, -76, -78, -79*
DeWaart, Edo 1941- *IntWWM 77, -80, MusSN, NewGrD 80, WhoOp 76*
Dewaere, Patrick 1947- *FilmEn*
Dewar, Allison *AmSCAP 80*
Dewar, Ted Royal 1904- *AmSCAP 80*
DeWarfaz, George 1889-1966 *WhThe*
Dewdney, Selwyn Hanington 1909- *CreCan 2*
Dewdrop, Daddy *RkOn 2[port]*
Dewell, Michael 1931- *BiE&WWA, NotNAT, WhoThe 77*
Dewever, Jean 1927- *WorEFlm*
Dewey, Arthur *Film 2*
Dewey, Earl S 1881-1950 *WhScrn 74, -77, WhoHol B*
Dewey, Elmer 1884-1954 *WhScrn 74, -77, WhoHol B*
Dewey, Ethelyn A *PupTheA*
Dewey, Priscilla B *NatPD[port]*
Dewey, Ray F 1933- *AmSCAP 80*
Dewey, Thomas E 1902- *What 2[port]*
Dewey, W Margaret V 1927- *WhoMus 72*
Dewhurst, Coleen 1926- *CnThe*
Dewhurst, Colleen 1926- *BiE&WWA, Ent, FilmEn, ForYSC, HalFC 80, MovMk[port], NotNAT, PlP&P A[port], WhoHol A, WhoThe 72, -77*
Dewhurst, George *Film 1, -2*
Dewhurst, George W *IlWWBF*
Dewhurst, Jonathan d1913 *NotNAT B*
Dewhurst, Keith 1931- *ConDr 73, -77*
Dewhurst, Olive G M 1934- *WhoMus 72*
Dewhurst, William 1888-1937 *WhScrn 74, -77, WhoHol B*
DeWild, Gene 1929- *BiE&WWA*
DeWilde, Brandon 1942-1972 *BiE&WWA, FilmEn, FilmgC, ForYSC, HalFC 80, MotPP, MovMk[port], NotNAT B, OxFilm, WhScrn 77, WhoHol B*
DeWilde, Frederic 1914- *BiE&WWA*
DeWinat, Hal *MorBAP*
DeWindt, Hal *BlkAmP*
Dewinsky, Lucie *CreCan 1*
DeWinton, Albert *Film 2*
DeWinton, Alice *WhThe*
DeWit, Jacqueline *ForYSC, WhoHol A*
DeWitt, Allan *CmpEPM*
DeWitt, Elizabeth *Film 1*
DeWitt, Fay 1935- *BiE&WWA, NotNAT*
DeWitt, Jennings *Film 2*
DeWitt, Johann *PlP&P[port]*
DeWitt, Lew C 1938- *BiDAmM, EncFCWM 69*
DeWitt, Louis *WhoHrs 80*
DeWolfe, Billy d1974 *BiE&WWA, MotPP, WhoHol B*
DeWolfe, Billy 1905-1974 *ForYSC, Vers B[port]*
DeWolfe, Billy 1907-1974 *FilmEn, FilmgC, HalFC 80, HolP 40[port], MovMk[port], NotNAT B, WhScrn 77, WhThe, WhoThe 72*
DeWolfe, Elsie Anderson 1865-1950 *Film 2, NotNAT A, -B, WhThe, WhoStg 1906, -1908*
DeWolfe, John 1786-1862 *BiDAmM*
DeWolff, Francis 1913- *HalFC 80*
DeWonck, Philippe M G J C 1945- *IntWWM 77*
Dews, Peter 1929- *NotNAT, WhoThe 77*
Dewsbury, Ralph d1921 *IlWWBF*
DeXandoval, Guerrero *Film 2*
Dexter, Al 1902- *AmPS A, -B, BiDAmM, CmpEPM, EncFCWM 69*
Dexter, Al 1905- *CounME 74, -74A, IlEncCM[port]*
Dexter, Alan *WhoHol A*
Dexter, Anthony 1919- *FilmEn, FilmgC, ForYSC, HalFC 80, MotPP, WhoHrs 80*
Dexter, Aubrey 1898-1958 *NotNAT B, WhThe, WhoHol B*
Dexter, Benning 1915- *IntWWM 77, -80*
Dexter, Brad 1917- *FilmEn, ForYSC, WhoHol A*
Dexter, Brad 1922- *FilmgC, HalFC 80*
Dexter, Elliot 1870-1941 *Film 1, NotNAT B*
Dexter, Elliott 1870-1941 *FilmEn, Film 2, TwYS, WhScrn 74, -77, WhoHol B*
Dexter, Harold 1920- *IntWWM 80, WhoMus 72*
Dexter, Henry Martyn 1821-1890 *BiDAmM*
Dexter, John *PlP&P A[port], WhoThe 72, -77*
Dexter, John 1925- *CmOp, CnThe, EncWT, Ent, NotNAT, WhoOp 76*
Dexter, John 1935- *FilmEn, FilmgC, HalFC 80*
Dexter, Maury 1927- *FilmEn, FilmgC, HalFC 80*
Dexter, Maury 1928?- *WhoHrs 80*
Dexter, Von *WhoHrs 80*
Dexter, William *MagIID*
Dey, Larry 1910- *AmSCAP 66, -80*
Dey, Manju *WomWMM*
Dey, Susan *IntMPA 79, -80, WhoHol A*
Deybrook, L M 1910-1976 *AmSCAP 80*
Deyers, Lien *Film 2*
DeYllanes, Johannes *NewGrD 80*
Deyo, Felix 1888-1959 *Baker 78, ConAmC*
Deyo, Ruth Lynda 1884-1960 *Baker 78, ConAmC*
DeYoung, Dennis *AmSCAP 80*
DeYoung, Lynden E 1923- *ConAmC, IntWWM 80*
Deyton, Camilla Hill 1952- *IntWWM 80*
DeYzarduy, Madame *Film 2*
DeZaides, Nicolas 1740?-1792 *NewGrD 80*
Dezais, Joseph *NewGrD 80*
Dezede, Nicolas 1740?-1792 *Baker 78, NewGrD 80*
Dezedes, Nicolas 1740?-1792 *NewGrD 80*
Dezel, Albert 1900- *IntMPA 77, -75, -76, -78, -79, -80*
DeZoete, Beryl d1962 *DancEn 78*
DeZurich Sisters *IlEncCM[port]*
D'Haese, Iwein Lydia Roeland 1932- *IntWWM 77, -80*
D'Harcourt, Eugene 1859-1918 *NewGrD 80*
D'Harcourt, Marguerite Beclard *NewGrD 80*
Dharma, Buck *AmSCAP 80*
Dheigh, Khigh 1910- *HalFC 80*
Dhelfer, Charles *NewGrD 80*
D'Helfert, Charles *NewGrD 80*
Dhelia, France d1964 *WhScrn 77*
D'Helpher, Charles *NewGrD 80*
Dhepley, Ruth *Film 2*
Dhery, Robert 1921- *BiE&WWA, FilmEn, FilmgC, HalFC 80, NotNAT*
Dhiegh, Khigh *WhoHol A*
D'Hoedt, Henri-Georges 1885-1936 *Baker 78*
D'Hooghe, Clement 1899-1951 *NewGrD 80*
D'Hooghe, Kamiel Frans Marie 1929- *IntWWM 77, -80, WhoMus 72*
Dia, Beatriz De *NewGrD 80*
Dia, Dick 1917- *AmSCAP 66, -80*
Diabelli, Anton 1781-1858 *Baker 78, BnBkM 80, NewGrD 80*
Diabelli, Antonio 1781-1858 *OxMus*
Diablos, The *RkOn*
Diack, John Michael 1869-1946 *Baker 78*
Diaconescu, Florin 1942- *WhoOp 76*
Diaghilef, Serge 1872-1929 *OxMus*
Diaghileff, Serge Pavolich 1872-1929 *WhThe*
Diaghileff, Sergey Pavlovich *NewGrD 80*
Diaghilev, Serge Pavlovich 1872-1929 *CnOxB, DancEn 78[port], OxThe*
Diaghilev, Sergei Pavlovich 1872-1929 *Baker 78, DcPup, NewEOp 71*
Diaghilev, Sergey Pavlovich *BnBkM 80, NewGrD 80*
Diakov, Anton 1934- *WhoOp 76*
Dial, Auzie Russell 1900- *BlkWAB[port]*
Dial, Harry 1907- *WhoJazz 72*
Dial, Patterson *Film 2*
Diamand, Peter 1913- *NewGrD 80*
Diamant, Lincoln 1923- *IntMPA 77, -75, -76, -78, -79, -80*
Diamant-Berger, Henri 1895- *DcFM, FilmEn*
Diamante, Juan Bautista 1625-1687 *McGEWD*
Diamond, Arline 1928- *ConAmC*
Diamond, Bernard 1918- *IntMPA 77, -75, -76, -78, -79, -80*
Diamond, Cliff *AmSCAP 80*
Diamond, Dave *AmSCAP 80*
Diamond, David Leo 1915- *AmSCAP 66, -80, Baker 78, BiDAmM, BnBkM 80, CompSN[port], ConAmC, DcCom&M 79, DcCM, IntWWM 77, -80, NewGrD 80, OxMus, WhoMus 72*

Diamond, Don *WhoHol A*
Diamond, Dorothy Florence 1910- *AmSCAP 80*
Diamond, Eileen *IntWWM 80*
Diamond, I A L *CmMov*
Diamond, I A L 1915- *FilmgC, HalFC 80*
Diamond, I A L 1920- *FilmEn, IntMPA 77, -75, -76, -78, -79, -80, OxFilm, WorEFlm[port]*
Diamond, Isidore 1920- *AmSCAP 80*
Diamond, Joel *AmSCAP 80*
Diamond, Joseph E 1944- *AmSCAP 80*
Diamond, Leo 1915-1966 *AmSCAP 66, -80*
Diamond, Leo G 1907- *AmSCAP 66, -80*
Diamond, Lillian d1962 *NotNAT B*
Diamond, Margaret 1916- *WhoThe 72, -77*
Diamond, Neil *ConMuA 80A[port]*
Diamond, Neil 1941- *AmSCAP 80, IlEncR[port], RkOn 2[port]*
Diamond, Neil 1942- *BiDAmM*
Diamond, Stuart Samuel 1950- *ConAmC*
Diamond, William d1812 *NotNAT B*
Diamond, William 1913?- *BluesWW[port]*
Diamonds, The *AmPS A, RkOn*
Dianda, Hilda 1925- *Baker 78, DcCM, NewGrD 80*
Dianin, Sergei 1888-1968 *Baker 78*
Dianov, Anton 1882-1939 *Baker 78*
Diante, Denny *ConMuA 80B*
Dias Velasco, Nicolao *NewGrD 80*
Diasio, Daniel Joseph 1941- *AmSCAP 80*
Diaz, Alirio 1923- *IntWWM 77, -80, NewGrD 80*
Diaz, Cirilo Grassi 1883- *DancEn 78*
Diaz, Eugene 1837-1901 *Baker 78*
Diaz, Felix Guerrero *NewGrD 80*
Diaz, Gaspar *NewGrD 80*
Diaz, Horace 1906?- *NewOrJ[port]*
Diaz, Jorge 1930- *CroCD*
Diaz, Justino 1940- *IntWWM 77, -80, NewEOp 71, NewGrD 80, WhoOp 76*
Diaz, Rafaelo 1884-1943 *Baker 78*
Diaz, Rudy *WhoHol A*
Diaz Besson, Gabriel 1590?-1638 *NewGrD 80*
Dibble, Pater Davis 1927- *ConAmTC*
Dibden, Charles *ConAmC*
Dibdin, Charles 1745-1814 *Baker 78, DcPup, Ent, MusMk, NewGrD 80[port], NotNAT A, -B, OxMus, OxThe*
Dibdin, Charles Isaac Mungo Pitt 1768-1833 *NotNAT A, -B, OxMus, OxThe*
Dibdin, Henry Edward 1813-1866 *OxMus*
Dibdin, Thomas John Pitt 1771-1841 *NotNAT A, -B, OxMus, OxThe, PlP&P*
Dibelius, Ulrich 1924- *NewGrD 80*
DiBello, Victor 1933- *IntWWM 80*
DiBenedetta, Marie *Film 2*
Dibley, Mary *Film 2*
DiBona, Giovanni *NewGrD 80*
DiBona, Linda 1948- *CnOxB*
DiBonaventura, Anthony 1929- *Baker 78, WhoMus 72*
DiBonaventura, Mario *Baker 78*
DiBonaventura, Sam 1923- *AmSCAP 66, -80*
DiCapua, Eduardo 1864-1917 *Baker 78*
Dicenta, Joaquin 1860- *WhThe*
Dicenta, Manuel 1904-1974 *WhScrn 77, WhoHol B*
Dicenta Y Benedicto, Joaquin 1863-1917 *McGEWD*
Dicenzo, Panfilo Anthony 1949- *AmSCAP 80*
DiCesare, Fred Peter 1948- *IntWWM 77*
DiCesare, Pat *ConMuA 80B*
Dicey, William *NewGrD 80*
DiChiera, David 1935- *ConAmC, IntWWM 77, -80*
Dichler, Josef 1912- *WhoMus 72*
Dichler-Sedlacek, Erika 1929- *IntWWM 80*
Dichter, Misha 1945- *Baker 78, MusSN[port], NewGrD 80*
Dick And Deedee *RkOn[port]*
Dick, C S Cotsford d1911 *NotNAT B*
Dick, Dorothy 1900- *AmSCAP 66, -80*
Dick, Douglas 1920- *FilmgC, ForYSC, HalFC 80, WhoHol A*
Dick, Eleanor 1918- *IntWWM 77*
Dick, Eleanor 1922- *IntWWM 80*
Dick, Marcel 1898- *AmSCAP 66, -80, Baker 78, ConAmC*
Dick, Robert 1950- *ConAmC*
Dickens, C Stafford 1896-1967 *WhThe*
Dickens, Charles 1812-1870 *DcPup, FilmgC, HalFC 80, MagIlD, NewEOp 71, NotNAT B, OxFilm, OxMus, OxThe, PlP&P*
Dickens, Jimmy 1925- *BiDAmM*
Dickens, Little Jimmy 1925- *CounME 74, -74A, EncFCWM 69, IlEncCM[port], RkOn 2[port]*
Dickenson, James William 1940- *IntWWM 80*
Dickenson, Jean 1914- *CreCan 2*
Dickenson, Jennie *Film 1*
Dickenson, Margaret *WomWMM B*
Dickenson, Vic 1906- *CmpEPM, IlEncJ*
Dickenson, Victor 1906- *BiDAmM, EncJzS 70, WhoJazz 72*
Dickerson, Beech 1935?- *WhoHrs 80*
Dickerson, Bernard Francis *IntWWM 77, -80*
Dickerson, Carlton Monroe 1949- *IntWWM 77*
Dickerson, Carroll 1895-1957 *WhoJazz 72*
Dickerson, Charles L 1928- *IntWWM 77, -80*
Dickerson, Dudley d1968 *WhoHol B*
Dickerson, Dwight Lowell 1944- *EncJzS 70*
Dickerson, Glenda *BlkAmP, MorBAP*
Dickerson, Henry 1906-1968 *WhScrn 77*
Dickerson, Milton *Film 2*
Dickerson, Roger 1934- *AmSCAP 80, CpmDNM 75, ConAmC*
Dickerson, Roger Quincey 1898-1951 *WhoJazz 72*
Dickerson, Walt 1931- *BiDAmM*
Dickey, Dan Benjamin 1949- *AmSCAP 80*
Dickey, James 1923- *Conv 1[port]*
Dickey, Mark 1885- *BiDAmM, ConAmC*
Dickey, Paul d1933 *Film 2, WhoHol B*
Dickey, Paul 1884-1933 *WhThe*
Dickey, Paul 1885-1933 *NotNAT B, WhScrn 74, -77*
Dickey, Richard Scott 1956- *AmSCAP 80*
Dickie, Brian James 1941- *WhoMus 72, WhoOp 76*
Dickie, Murray 1924- *CmOp, IntWWM 77, -80, NewGrD 80, WhoMus 72, WhoOp 76*
Dickie, William Payne 1914- *IntWWM 77, -80, WhoMus 72*
Dickieson, George William 1912- *IntWWM 77, -80*
Dickinson, A E F 1899-1978 *NewGrD 80*
Dickinson, Alan Edgar Frederic 1899-1978 *IntWWM 77*
Dickinson, Angie *IntMPA 75, -76, MotPP, WhoHol A*
Dickinson, Angie 1931- *BiDFilm, -81, FilmEn, FilmgC, ForYSC, HalFC 80, WorEFlm*
Dickinson, Angie 1936- *IntMPA 77, -78, -79, -80, MovMk[port]*
Dickinson, Charles Albert 1849-1906 *BiDAmM*
Dickinson, Clarence 1873- *AmSCAP 66*
Dickinson, Clarence 1873-1969 *AmSCAP 80, Baker 78, BiDAmM, ConAmC, NewGrD 80, WhoMus 72*
Dickinson, Desmond 1902- *FilmEn, FilmgC, HalFC 80, IntMPA 77, -75, -76, -78, -79, -80*
Dickinson, Don *PupTheA*
Dickinson, Dorothy Helen 1941- *IntWWM 80*
Dickinson, Edward 1853-1946 *Baker 78*
Dickinson, Genevieve 1909- *BiE&WWA, NotNAT*
Dickinson, George Sherman 1888-1964 *Baker 78, NewGrD 80*
Dickinson, Glen, Jr. 1914- *IntMPA 77, -76, -78, -79, -80*
Dickinson, Hal 1914-1970 *WhScrn 77, WhoHol B*
Dickinson, Harold H, Jr. 1913- *AmSCAP 66, -80*
Dickinson, Helen Adell 1875-1957 *AmSCAP 66, -80, Baker 78*
Dickinson, Homer 1890-1959 *WhScrn 74, -77*
Dickinson, John 1732-1808 *BiDAmM*
Dickinson, June McWade 1924- *AmSCAP 66, -80*
Dickinson, Maggie d1949 *NotNAT B*
Dickinson, Meriel 1940- *IntWWM 77, -80, WhoMus 72*
Dickinson, Milton *Film 2*
Dickinson, Peter 1934- *Baker 78, IntWWM 77, -80, NewGrD 80, WhoMus 72*
Dickinson, Robert Preston 1924- *IntMPA 77, -75, -76, -78, -79, -80*
Dickinson, Thorold 1903- *BiDFilm, -81, DcFM, FilmEn, FilmgC, HalFC 80, IlWWBF, IntMPA 77, -75, -76, -78, -79, -80, OxFilm, WorEFlm*
Dickison, Maria Bobrowska 1902- *AmSCAP 66*
Dickreiter, Michael 1942- *IntWWM 77, -80*
Dickson, Charles 1921- *CnOxB, DancEn 78*
Dickson, Deborah *WomWMM B*
Dickson, Donald 1911-1972 *WhScrn 77*
Dickson, Dorothy 1896- *EncMT, WhThe*
Dickson, Dorothy 1900- *BiE&WWA, NotNAT*
Dickson, Dorothy 1902- *Film 1, -2, FilmgC, HalFC 80, WhoHol A*
Dickson, Gloria d1945 *MotPP, NotNAT B, WhoHol B*
Dickson, Gloria 1916-1944 *ForYSC*
Dickson, Gloria 1916-1945 *FilmEn, HalFC 80, WhScrn 74, -77*
Dickson, Gloria 1917-1945 *ThFT[port]*
Dickson, Hester Mary Campbell 1924- *IntWWM 77, -80*
Dickson, Ivey 1919- *IntWWM 77, -80, WhoMus 72*
Dickson, Joan 1921- *IntWWM 77, -80, NewGrD 80, WhoMus 72*
Dickson, Joy Irvine Margaret 1923- *WhoMus 72*
Dickson, Katharine Joan Balfour 1921- *IntWWM 77*
Dickson, Katherine Joan Balfour 1921- *IntWWM 80, WhoMus 72*
Dickson, Lamont d1944 *NotNAT B, WhoHol B*
Dickson, LaRue 1901- *AmSCAP 66, -80*
Dickson, Lydia 1878-1928 *Film 2, NotNAT B, WhScrn 74, -77, WhoHol B*
Dickson, Paul 1920- *FilmEn, FilmgC, HalFC 80, IlWWBF*
Dickson, William Kennedy Laurie 1860-1935 *FilmEn, Film 1, OxFilm, WorEFlm*
Dickson, William Kennedy Laurie 1860-1937 *DcFM*
Dictators *ConMuA 80A*
Didacus A Portu *NewGrD 80*
Diddley, Bo *ConMuA 80A*
Diddley, Bo 1928- *BiDAmM, BluesWW, DrBlPA, IlEncR, MusMk, RkOn[port]*
Didelot, Charles Louis 1767-1836 *DancEn 78[port]*
Didelot, Charles Louis 1767-1837 *CnOxB, NewGrD 80*
Diderot, Denis 1713-1784 *Baker 78, CnThe, EncWT, Ent[port], McGEWD[port], NewGrD 80, NotNAT B, OxMus, OxThe, REnWD[port]*
Didier, Laura Gambardella 1933- *WhoOp 76*
Didion, Joan *WomWMM*
DiDomenica, Robert 1927- *Baker 78, CpmDNM 80, ConAmC*
Didrickson, Babe 1914-1956 *WhScrn 77*
Didrickson, Luther Norman 1938- *IntWWM 77, -80*
Didring, Ernst 1868-1931 *NotNAT B, OxThe, WhThe*
Didur, Adam 1874-1946 *NewGrD 80*
Didur, Adamo 1874-1946 *Baker 78, MusSN[port], NewEOp 71*
Didway, Ernest 1872-1939 *WhScrn 74, -77*
Didymus 063BC- *Baker 78, NewGrD 80*
Die Asta *WhScrn 77*
Diebel, Wendel H 1914- *ConAmC*
Diebel, Wendel Hobard 1914- *IntWWM 80*
Diebel, Wendel Hobart 1914- *IntWWM 77*
Diebold, Jerome C 1909- *IntMPA 77, -75, -76, -78, -79, -80*
Dieden, Claes 1942- *IntWWM 77*
Diederichs, Yann 1952- *IntWWM 80*
Dieffopruchar *NewGrD 80*
Dieffoprukhar *NewGrD 80*
Diegelmann, Wilhelm *Film 1, -2*
Diehl, Karl Ludwig 1897-1958 *WhScrn 74, -77*
Diehl, Walter F 1907- *IntMPA 79, -80*
Diekema, Willis Alcott 1892- *AmSCAP 80*
Dieken, Sandra *DancEn 78*
Diemente, Edward 1923- *AmSCAP 80, CpmDNM 77, ConAmC, IntWWM 77, -80*

Diemente, Edward 1926- *CpmDNM 76*
Diemer, Emma Lou 1927- *AmSCAP 66, -80, CpmDNM 74, -77, -78, -79, ConAmC, IntWWM 77, -80, WomCom[port]*
Diemer, Louis 1843-1919 *Baker 78, BnBkM 80, NewGrD 80*
Dienel, Otto 1839-1905 *Baker 78*
Diener, Joan 1934- *BiE&WWA, EncMT, IntMPA 77, -75, -76, -78, -79, -80, NotNAT, WhoThe 72, -77*
Dieni, John 1924- *AmSCAP 66, -80*
Dieni, Joseph 1923- *AmSCAP 66, -80*
Dienis, Jean-Claude 1941- *CnOxB*
Dientrans, Pete 1882?- *NewOrJ*
Diepenbrock, Alphons 1862-1921 *Baker 78, MusMk, NewGrD 80*
Diepenbrock, Alphonse 1862-1921 *OxMus*
Diercks, John Henry 1927- *AmSCAP 80, ConAmC*
Dieren, Bernard Van 1884-1936 *Baker 78, MusMk, OxMus*
Dieren, Bernard Van 1887-1936 *NewGrD 80*
Dierkes, John 1905-1975 *HalFC 80*
Dierkes, John 1906?-1975 *ForYSC*
Dierkes, John 1908-1975 *FilmgC, WhScrn 77, WhoHol C*
Dierkop, Charles *WhoHol A*
Dierks, Dieter *ConMuA 80B*
Dierlam, Robert J 1917- *BiE&WWA, NotNAT*
Diers, Hank 1931- *BiE&WWA, NotNAT*
Dies, Albert Christoph 1755-1822 *NewGrD 80*
Dies, Martin 1901- *What 1[port]*
Diesel, Gustav 1900-1948 *Film 2, WhScrn 74, -77*
Diesel, Leota *BiE&WWA, NotNAT*
Diesener, Gerhard *NewGrD 80*
Diesneer, Gerhard *NewGrD 80*
Diesner, Gerhard *NewGrD 80*
Diessener, Gerhard *NewGrD 80*
Diessl, Gustav 1900-1948 *WhoHol B*
Diestal, Edith *Film 1*
Diet, Edmond-Marie 1854-1924 *Baker 78*
Dieter, Christian Ludwig 1757-1822 *NewGrD 80*
Dieterich, Georg *NewGrD 80*
Dieterich, Sixt 1493?-1548 *NewGrD 80*
Dieterich, Sixtus 1493?-1548 *NewGrD 80*
Dieterich, Xistus 1493?-1548 *NewGrD 80*
Dieterle, Eugene *Film 2*
Dieterle, Til *AmSCAP 66, -80*
Dieterle, Wilhelm 1893-1973 *BiDFilm, -81*
Dieterle, William 1893- *DcFM, MovMk[port], WorEFlm*
Dieterle, William 1893-1972 *CmMov, FilmEn, FilmgC, HalFC 80, OxFilm, WhScrn 77, WhoHrs 80*
Dieterle, William 1893-1973 *AmFD, BiDFilm, -81*
Dieterle, William 1894-1973 *Film 2*
Dieterle, William 1899-1972 *EncWT*
Diethelm, Caspar 1926- *IntWWM 77, -80*
Diether, Jack 1919- *Baker 78*
Dietmar Von Aist d1171? *NewGrD 80*
Dietrich, Albert Hermann 1829-1908 *Baker 78, NewGrD 80*
Dietrich, Antonia *Film 2*
Dietrich, Daniel P 1944- *NotNAT*
Dietrich, Georg 1525-1598 *NewGrD 80*
Dietrich, John E 1913- *BiE&WWA, NotNAT*
Dietrich, Karl 1927- *IntWWM 80*
Dietrich, Marlene *AmPS B, MotPP, WhoHol A*
Dietrich, Marlene 1900- *Film 2, WhoThe 77*
Dietrich, Marlene 1901- *BiDAmM, BiDFilm, -81, Ent[port], FilmAG WE, FilmEn, HalFC 80, MovMk[port], NewGrD 80, ThFT[port], WorEFlm[port]*
Dietrich, Marlene 1902- *CmMov, EncWT, FilmgC, ForYSC, OxFilm, TwYS*
Dietrich, Marlene 1904- *CmMov, CmpEPM, IntMPA 77, -75, -76, -78, -79, -80*
Dietrich, Oskar 1888- *IntWWM 77, -80*
Dietrich, Sixt 1493?-1548 *NewGrD 80*
Dietrich, Sixtus 1492?-1548 *Baker 78*
Dietrich, Sixtus 1493?-1548 *NewGrD 80*
Dietrich, Tina *Film 2*
Dietrich, Xistus 1493?-1548 *NewGrD 80*
Dietricus *NewGrD 80*
Dietsch, Louis 1808-1865 *NewGrD 80*
Dietsch, Pierre-Louis-Philippe 1808-1865 *Baker 78, NewEOp 71*
Diettenhofer, Giuseppe 1743?-1799? *NewGrD 80*
Diettenhofer, Joseph 1743?-1799? *NewGrD 80*
Dietz, Anton Ferdinand *NewGrD 80*
Dietz, Hanns-Bertold 1929- *NewGrD 80*
Dietz, Howard 1896- *AmPS, AmSCAP 66, -80, BestMus, BiDAmM, BiE&WWA, CmpEPM, ConDr 73, -77D, EncMT, FilmEn, FilmgC, HalFC 80, ModWD, NewCBMT, NotNAT, -A, PlP&P[port], Sw&Ld C, WhoThe 72, -77*
Dietz, Johann Christian 1773-1849 *NewGrD 80*
Dietz, Johann Christian 1804?-1888 *NewGrD 80*
Dietz, Linda d1920 *NotNAT B*
Dietz, Louis *NewGrD 80*
Dietz, Max 1857-1928 *Baker 78*
Dietz, Norman C 1919- *ConAmC*
Dietz, Robert James 1928- *IntWWM 77*
Dietzch, Louis *NewGrD 80*
Dietzenschmidt, Anton 1893-1955 *CnMD*
Dieu Donne, Albert *Film 1*
Dieudonne, M d1922 *NotNAT B*
Dieupart, Charles 1667?-1740? *NewGrD 80*
Dieupart, Francois 1670?-1740? *Baker 78*
Diez, Johann Sebastian 1720-1753? *NewGrD 80*
Difenderfer, John 1866-1933 *PupTheA*
Diffen, Ray 1922- *BiE&WWA, NotNAT*
Differing, Anton 1918- *ForYSC*
Diffring, Anton 1918- *FilmEn, FilmgC, HalFC 80, IntMPA 77, -75, -76, -78, -79, -80, WhoHol A, WhoHrs 80[port]*
DiFilippi, Arturo 1894-1972 *BiDAmM*
Difrancesco, Burnadette 1944- *AmSCAP 80*
Difrancesco, Joseph 1942- *AmSCAP 80*
DiFranco, Loretta Elizabeth 1942- *WhoOp 76*
DiGaetano, Adam 1907-1966 *WhScrn 77*
DiGangi, Jim *IntMPA 75, -76*
Digby, Desmond Ward 1933- *WhoOp 76*
Digby, Freda Ruby 1890- *WhoMus 72*
Digges, Dudley d1947 *PlP&P, WhoHol B*
Digges, Dudley 1879-1947 *Film 2, FilmgC, ForYSC, HalFC 80, HolCA[port], MovMk, NotNAT B, OxThe, WhScrn 74, -77, WhThe*
Digges, Dudley 1880-1947 *FamA&A[port]*
Digges, Dudley West 1720-1786 *NotNAT A, -B, OxThe*
Diggins, Peggy *WhoHol B*
Diggle, Roland 1887-1954 *AmSCAP 66, -80, BiDAmM, ConAmC A*
Diggs, John *WhoHol A*
Diggs, Leonard Lee 1939- *IntWWM 77, -80*
Dight, Leonard 1913- *WhoMus 72*
Dighton, John 1909- *FilmgC, HalFC 80, WhoThe 72, -77*
DiGiacomo, Frank *ConAmC*
DiGiacomo, Salvatore 1860-1934 *McGEWD[port], NewGrD 80*
DiGiovanni, Edoardo *CreCan 2, NewGrD 80*
Digiovanni, Rocco 1924- *AmSCAP 80*
DiGirolamo, Joseph 1942- *IntWWM 80*
DiGiuseppe, Enrico 1938- *WhoOp 76*
DiGiuseppe, Severino 1919- *AmSCAP 80*
Dignam, Basil 1905-1979 *FilmgC, HalFC 80, WhoHol A*
Dignam, Mark 1909- *FilmgC, HalFC 80, WhoHol A, WhoThe 72, -77*
Digney, John Neil 1948- *IntWWM 77, -80*
Dignon, Edmond *Film 2*
Dignum, Charles 1765?-1827 *NewGrD 80*
DiGolconda, Ligia 1884-1942 *WhScrn 74, -77*
Dijck, Jeanette Van 1925- *IntWWM 77, -80*
Dijk, Jan Van 1918- *Baker 78*
Dijk, Peter Van *CnOxB*
Dijkman, Ludert d1717 *NewGrD 80*
DiJulio, Max 1919- *AmSCAP 66, -80, ConAmC A*
Dikie, Alexei Denisovich 1889-1955 *OxThe*
Diklic, Drago 1937- *IntWWM 77*
Diktonius, Elmer 1896-1961 *NewGrD 80*
DiLanti, Stella *Film 2*
Dilday, William H, Jr. *NewYTET*
Diletsky, Nikolai 1630?-1690? *NewGrD 80*
Diletsky, Nikolay 1630?-1690? *NewGrD 80*
DiLeva, Anthony *WhoHol A*
Dilezki, Nikolai 1630?-1690? *NewGrD 80*
Dilezki, Nikolay 1630?-1690? *NewGrD 80*
Dilherr, Johann Michael 1604-1669 *NewGrD 80*
Diliberto, Pietro 1931- *WhoOp 76*
Dilkes, Neville 1930- *IntWWM 77, -80, WhoMus 72*
Dill, Max M 1878-1949 *WhScrn 77*
Dill, William L 1913- *AmSCAP 66, ConAmC*
Dill, William Leslie 1913- *AmSCAP 80*
Dillard, Bill 1911- *CmpEPM, WhoJazz 72*
Dillard, Burt 1909-1960 *WhScrn 74, -77*
Dillard, Doug *EncFCWM 69*
Dillard, Doug 1937- *CounME 74*
Dillard, Douglas Flint 1937- *AmSCAP 66, -80, BiDAmM*
Dillard, Rod *EncFCWM 69*
Dillard, Rodney 1942- *BiDAmM, CounME 74*
Dillard, William *DrBlPA*
Dillard & Clark *BiDAmM*
Dillards *CounME 74, -74A, IlEncCM[port]*
Dillards, The *BiDAmM, EncFCWM 69, IlEncR*
Dille, Denijs 1904- *NewGrD 80*
Dille, John F, Jr. *NewYTET*
Diller, Angela 1877-1968 *Baker 78*
Diller, Barry *IntMPA 77, -76, -78, -79, -80, NewYTET*
Diller, Marie *Film 2*
Diller, Phyllis 1917- *FilmEn, Film 2, FilmgC, ForYSC, Funs[port], HalFC 80, IntMPA 77, -75, -76, -78, -79, -80, JoeFr[port], MotPP, WhoHol A*
Diller, Saralu C 1930- *ConAmC*
Dilley, Harry B 1913- *WhoMus 72*
Dilley, Perry *PupTheA*
Dilliger, Johann 1593-1647 *NewGrD 80*
Dilligil, Avni 1909-1971 *WhScrn 74, -77*
Dilling, Mildred 1894- *Baker 78*
Dillinger, Johann 1593-1647 *NewGrD 80*
Dillinger, John 1903-1934 *HalFC 80, OxFilm*
Dillingham, Charles Bancroft 1868-1934 *EncMT, NotNAT B, OxThe, WhThe*
Dillion, John Webb *Film 2*
Dillman, Bradford 1930- *BiE&WWA, FilmEn, FilmgC, ForYSC, HalFC 80, IntMPA 77, -75, -76, -78, -79, -80, MotPP, MovMk[port], NotNAT, WhoHol A*
Dillon, Andrew *Film 2*
Dillon, Carmen 1908- *HalFC 80*
Dillon, Charles d1881 *NotNAT B*
Dillon, Charles E d1964 *NotNAT B*
Dillon, Clara d1898 *NotNAT B*
Dillon, Dick 1896-1961 *WhScrn 74, -77, WhoHol B*
Dillon, Eddie *Film 2, TwYS*
Dillon, Edward 1880-1933 *Film 1, -2, TwYS A, WhScrn 74, -77, WhoHol B*
Dillon, Fannie Charles 1881-1947 *AmSCAP 66, -80, Baker 78, BiDAmM, ConAmC*
Dillon, Frances d1947 *NotNAT B, WhThe*
Dillon, George Tim 1888-1965 *WhScrn 74, -77, WhoHol B*
Dillon, Henri 1912-1954 *Baker 78*
Dillon, Jack 1887-1934 *Film 1, TwYS A, WhoHol B*
Dillon, James Shaun Hamilton 1944- *IntWWM 77, WhoMus 72*
Dillon, John 1876-1937 *WhScrn 74, WhoHol B*
Dillon, John Francis 1884-1934 *WhScrn 77*
Dillon, John Francis 1887-1934 *FilmEn, HalFC 80, WhScrn 74*
Dillon, John T 1866-1937 *Film 2, WhScrn 77*
Dillon, John Webb 1877-1949 *Film 1, -2, WhScrn 74, -77, WhoHol B*
Dillon, Josephine 1884-1971 *WhScrn 77, WhoHol B*
Dillon, Melinda 1939- *BiE&WWA, IntMPA 79, -80, NotNAT*
Dillon, Paul *Film 1*
Dillon, Robert *HalFC 80*
Dillon, Robert M 1922- *ConAmC*
Dillon, Stella 1878-1934 *WhScrn 74, -77*
Dillon, Thomas Patrick 1896-1962 *NotNAT B, WhScrn 74, -77*
Dillon, Tim 1888-1965 *WhScrn 77*
Dillon, Tom d1962 *WhoHol B*
Dillon, Tom d1965 *WhoHol B*
Dillon, William A 1877-1966 *AmSCAP 66, -80, BiDAmM*
Dillon Brothers *AmPS B*

Dillow, Jean Carmen IntMPA 77, -75, -76, -78, -79, -80, WomWMM
Dills, Barbara WomWMM B
Dills, William Film 2
Dillson, Clyde 1900-1957 WhScrn 77
Dilmen, Gungor 1930- REnWD[port]
Dilorenzo, Randy Paul 1952- AmSCAP 80
DiLorenzo, Tina d1930 NotNAT B
Dilsner, Laurence AmSCAP 66, -80
Dilsner, Lawrence ConAmC
Dilson, John H 1893-1944 WhScrn 74, -77, WhoHol B
Dilthey, Wilhelm 1833-1911 NewGrD 80
Dilworth, Gordon 1913- BiE&WWA, NotNAT
Dima, Elena WhoOp 76
Dima, George OxMus
Dima, Gheorghe 1847-1925 Baker 78, NewGrD 80
DiMaggio, Francesco d1688 NewGrD 80
DiMaggio, Joe 1914- WhoHol A
DiMarzio, Matilde Film 1
Dimbleby, Richard 1913-1965 NewYTET, WhScrn 77
Dime, James Film 2
DiMeola, Al ConMuA 80A
Dimes, Bill 1895?- NewOrJ
DiMicheli, Antonino d1680 NewGrD 80
DiMinno, Daniel Gaetano 1911- AmSCAP 66, -80
Dimitrescu, Constantin 1847-1928 NewGrD 80
Dimitri, Michele WomWMM
Dimitroff, Pashanko 1924- IntWWM 77, -80
Dimitrov, Georgi 1904- NewGrD 80
Dimitrova, Anastasia Ilieva 1940- WhoOp 76
Dimler, Franz Anton 1753-1827 NewGrD 80
Dimmler, Franz Anton 1753-1827 NewGrD 80
Dimmock, Peter 1920- IntMPA 77, -75, -76, -78, -79, -80, NewYTET
Dimon, Florence Irene WhScrn 74, -77
Dimov, Bojidar 1935- Baker 78, DcCM, NewGrD 80
Dimov, Dimo 1938- NewGrD 80
Dimov, Ivan 1927- Baker 78
Dimsdale, Verna Lorraine 1936- IntWWM 77, -80
Dimucci, Dion Francis 1939- AmSCAP 80
DiMurska, Ilma 1836-1889 NewGrD 80
DiMuzio, Leonard Alan 1933- IntWWM 77
DiNapoli, Mario John 1914- AmSCAP 66, -80
DiNapoli, Raffele Film 1
DiNardo, Nicholas E 1906- AmSCAP 66, -80
DiNardo, Thomas C 1905- AmSCAP 66
D'India, Sigismondo 1582?- MusMk, NewGrD 80
D'Indy, Vincent 1851-1931 Baker 78, BnBkM 80, CmOp, MusMk, NewEOp 71, NewGrD 80, OxMus
Dine, Jim ConDr 73, -77E
Dinehart, Alan 1886-1944 FilmgC, HalFC 80, MovMk
Dinehart, Alan 1889-1944 HolCA[port], NotNAT B, WhScrn 74, -77
Dinehart, Alan 1890-1944 WhThe, WhoHol B
Dinehart, Allan 1890-1944 ForYSC
Dinehart, Mason ForYSC
Dinelli, Mel HalFC 80
Dinensen, Marie Film 2
Dinensen, Robert Film 2
Dinerstein, Norman M 1937- AmSCAP 80, ConAmC
Dines, Gordon 1911- FilmEn
Dinesen, Isak 1885-1962 WomWMM
Dinesen, Robert 1874?-1940 DcFM
Dinesen, Robert 1874-1940? FilmEn
Dingelstedt, Franz Von 1814-1881 EncWT, Ent, OxThe
Dingle, Charles 1887-1955 ForYSC
Dingle, Charles 1887-1956 FilmgC, HalFC 80, HolCA[port], MotPP, NotNAT B, Vers A[port], WhScrn 74, -77, WhoHol B
Dingle, Charles 1888-1956 MovMk
Dingle, Tom d1925 NotNAT B
Dingwall, Alexander W d1918 NotNAT B
Dinicu, Grigoras 1889-1949 Baker 78, NewGrD 80
Dinino, Louis Lee 1928- AmSCAP 80
Dinino, Vincent Rairden 1918- AmSCAP 80
Diniz, Jaime 1929- NewGrD 80
Dinkel, Wilbur 1880?-1940 NewOrJ[port]
Dinn, Freda 1910- WhoMus 72
Dinn, Winifreda Louise 1910- IntWWM 77, -80
Dinneen, Georgina L 1940- IntWWM 77, -80
Dinning, Mark 1933- AmPS A, RkOn
Dinning Sisters CmpEPM
Dino, Desi And Billy BiDAmM, RkOn 2[port]
Dino, Kenny 1942- RkOn
Dino, Paul 1939- RkOn[port]
Dino, Ralph AmSCAP 80
DiNovi, Eugene 1928- AmSCAP 66, BiDAmM
Dinovi, Eugene Salvatore 1928- AmSCAP 80
Dinsdale, Patricia Joudry CreCan 2
Dinu, Robert A 1928- AmSCAP 66, -80
Dinwiddie, Richard D 1937- IntWWM 77
Diomedes NewGrD 80
Dion AmPS A, AmSCAP 80
Dion 1939- IlEncR, RkOn[port]
Dion, Carmen AmSCAP 66
Dion, Hector Film 1, -2
Dion And The Belmonts BiDAmM, ConMuA 80A, RkOn[port]
Dione, Rose Film 1, -2, ForYSC, TwYS
Dionigi, Marco d1668? NewGrD 80
Dionne, Claire Gagnier CreCan 1
Dionne, Emelie 1934-1954 WhScrn 74, -77
Dionne, Emilie 1934-1954 WhoHol B
Dionne, Marie 1934-1970 WhScrn 74, -77, WhoHol B
Dionne Quintuplets, The 1934- What 3[port]
Dionysius Trebellianus NewGrD 80
Dior, Christian 1905-1957 NotNAT B
Diorio, Joseph Louis 1936- EncJzS 70
DiPalma, Carlo 1925- FilmEn, WorEFlm
DiPasquale, James Anthony 1941- ConAmC, IntWWM 77
DiPaula, Innocentio NewGrD 80
DiPaula DiCatanzaro, Innocentio NewGrD 80
Diphilus d290BC OxThe
DiPianduni, Osvaldo 1939- WhoOp 76
DiPietro, Rocco 1949- ConAmC
DiPirani, Eugenio 1852-1939 AmSCAP 66, -80
Dippel, Andreas 1866-1932 Baker 78, BiDAmM, NewEOp 71
Dippel, Johann Andreas 1866-1932 NotNAT B
Dipson, William D 1916- IntMPA 77, -75, -76, -78, -79, -80
Dirck Van Embden NewGrD 80
Dirck Pieterszoon NewGrD 80
Dire Straits ConMuA 80A[port]
Diringus, Richard NewGrD 80
Dirksen, Everett McKinley 1896-1969 RkOn 2A, WhScrn 77
Dirksen, Richard Wayne 1921- AmSCAP 80, ConAmC
DiRobbio, Armando 1915- AmSCAP 80
Dirt Band IlEncCM
Dirtl, Willy 1931- CnOxB, DancEn 78
Dirty Red BluesWW
Diruta, Agostino 1595?-1647? NewGrD 80
Diruta, Girolamo 1550-1610? Baker 78
Diruta, Girolamo 1554?-1610? NewGrD 80
DiSangro, Elena Film 2
Discant, Mack 1916-1961 AmSCAP 66, -80
Disco-Tex & The Sex-O-Lettes RkOn 2[port]
Disdier, Ramiro E 1927- AmSCAP 80
Disertori, Benvenuto 1887-1969 NewGrD 80
Disher, Maurice Willson 1893-1969 WhThe
Dishy, Bob NotNAT, WhoThe 77
Disineer, Gerhard NewGrD 80
Diskant, George E 1907-1965 FilmgC, HalFC 80
Dismore, Valerie Patricia 1925- IntWWM 77
Disney, Roy E 1930- IntMPA 77, -75, -76, -78, -79, -80
Disney, Walt 1901-1966 DcFM, FilmEn, FilmgC, HalFC 80, NewYTET, OxFilm, WhoHol B, WhoHrs 80, WorEFlm
Disney, Walt 1901-1968 TwYS B
Dispa, Robert Francois Joseph Louis 1929- IntWWM 77, -80
Disraeli, Benjamin 1804-1881 DcPup, FilmgC, HalFC 80
D'Israeli, Isaac 1766-1845 OxMus
Dissen, Mary ConAmTC
Dissmann, Patricia Rideout CreCan 2
DiStefano, Giuseppe 1921- Baker 78, BnBkM 80, CmOp, IntWWM 77, -80, MusSN[port], NewEOp 71, NewGrD 80, WhoOp 76
Distin NewGrD 80
Distin, George d1848 NewGrD 80
Distin, Henry 1819-1903 NewGrD 80
Distin, John 1793-1863 NewGrD 80
Distler, Hugo 1908-1942 Baker 78, DcCM, NewGrD 80
Distler, Johann Georg 1760-1799 NewGrD 80
Distler, P Antonie 1937- NotNAT
Ditfurth, Franz Wilhelm 1801-1880 NewGrD 80
Dithmar, Edward A 1854-1917 NotNAT B
Ditmars, Ivan Dale 1907- AmSCAP 80
Ditmas, Bruce 1946- EncJzS 70
Diton, Carl Rossini 1886-1962 DrBlPA
Diton, Carl Rossini 1886-1969 BiDAmM
Ditrichstein, Leo James 1865-1928 NotNAT B, WhThe, WhoStg 1906, -1908
Ditson, Oliver 1811-1888 Baker 78, BiDAmM, NewGrD 80
Ditt, Josephine 1868-1939 WhScrn 77
Dittenhaver, Sarah Louise 1901-1973 AmSCAP 66, ConAmC
Ditters, Carl 1739-1799 NewGrD 80[port]
Dittersdorf, Carl Ditters Von 1739-1799 DcCom 77, DcCom&M 79, NewGrD 80[port]
Dittersdorf, Karl Ditters Von 1739-1799 Baker 78, BnBkM 80, MusMk, NewEOp 71, OxMus
Dittersdorf, Karl Von 1739-1799 GrComp[port]
Dittert, Carlos Joao 1935- WhoOp 76
Dittmer, Luther A 1927- NewGrD 80
Dittrich, Paul-Heinz 1930- IntWWM 80, NewGrD 80
DiTursi, Mary WomWMM
Divall, Richard S 1945- IntWWM 80
DiVenanzo, Gianni 1920-1966 DcFM, FilmEn, FilmgC, HalFC 80, OxFilm, WorEFlm
DiVirgilio, Nicholas WhoMus 72
DiVirgilio, Nicolas WhoOp 76
Divitis, Antonius 1470?-1534? NewGrD 80
Divitis, Antonius 1475?- Baker 78
Dix, Audius 1668?-1719 NewGrD 80
Dix, Aureo 1668?-1719 NewGrD 80
Dix, Aureus 1668?-1719 NewGrD 80
Dix, Aurius 1668?-1719 NewGrD 80
Dix, Barbara 1944- IntWWM 77, -80
Dix, Beulah Marie 1876- WhThe, WhoStg 1908, WomWMM
Dix, Billy 1911-1973 WhScrn 77
Dix, Dorothy 1892-1970 WhThe
Dix, Lillian d1922 NotNAT B
Dix, Mae 1895-1958 WhScrn 74, -77
Dix, Richard 1894-1949 BiDFilm, -81, CmMov, FilmEn, Film 1, -2, FilmgC, HalFC 80[port], NotNAT B, TwYS, WhScrn 74, -77, WhoHrs 80
Dix, Richard 1895-1945 MovMk[port]
Dix, Richard 1895-1949 ForYSC
Dix, Richard 1898-1949 MotPP, WhoHol B
Dix, Robert ForYSC, WhoHol A
Dix, Robert Knight 1917- AmSCAP 80
Dix, William 1956- FilmgC, HalFC 80, WhoHrs 80
Dixey, Henry E 1859-1943 EncMT, Film 1, NotNAT B, WhScrn 74, -77, WhThe, WhoHol B, WhoStg 1906, -1908
Dixey, Phyllis d1964 NotNAT B
Dixie, Joe 1924- IntWWM 77
Dixie All-Stars BiDAmM
Dixie Blue Boys BiDAmM
Dixie Cups, The RkOn 2[port]
Dixie Jass Band BiDAmM
Dixie Jubilee Singers, The Film 2
Dixie Partners BiDAmM
Dixiebells, The RkOn[port]
Dixieland Band, The Sal Pace BiDAmM
Dixit d1949 WhScrn 77
Dixon, Adele 1908- WhThe
Dixon, Akua 1948- BlkWAB
Dixon, Alfred d1964 NotNAT B
Dixon, Campbell 1895-1960 NotNAT B, WhThe
Dixon, Charles Film 1
Dixon, Charlies 1898-1940 WhoJazz 72
Dixon, Charlotte L d1970 WhScrn 74, -77
Dixon, Chet PupTheA
Dixon, Cliff 1889- AmSCAP 66
Dixon, Conway 1874-1943 NotNAT B,

WhScrn 77
Dixon, David George 1938- *AmSCAP 80*
Dixon, Dean 1915- *WhoMus 72*
Dixon, Dean 1915-1976 *Baker 78, BiDAmM, DrBlPA, IntWWM 77, NewGrD 80*
Dixon, Denver 1890-1972 *WhScrn 77, WhoHol B*
Dixon, Dorsey Murdock 1897- *BiDAmM, CounME 74, -74A, EncFCWM 69*
Dixon, Eric 1930- *BiDAmM, EncJzS 70*
Dixon, Florence *Film 1, -2*
Dixon, Florence Rose 1944- *AmSCAP 80*
Dixon, Floyd 1929- *BluesWW[port]*
Dixon, George 1909- *NewGrD 80, WhoJazz 72*
Dixon, George Washington 1808-1861 *AmPS B, BiDAmM, NewGrD 80*
Dixon, Glenn *WhoHol A*
Dixon, Gloria d1945 *WhScrn 77*
Dixon, Harland d1969 *WhoHol B*
Dixon, Henry 1871-1943 *WhScrn 74, -77*
Dixon, Howard *EncFCWM 69*
Dixon, Howard 1903-1961 *BiDAmM, CounME 74*
Dixon, Ivan 1931- *DrBlPA, MovMk, WhoHol A*
Dixon, James 1928- *Baker 78*
Dixon, James 1949-1974 *WhScrn 77*
Dixon, Jean *Film 2*
Dixon, Jean 1894- *NotNAT*
Dixon, Jean 1896- *BiE&WWA, FilmEn, ThFT[port], WhThe, WhoHol A*
Dixon, Jean 1905- *ForYSC*
Dixon, Joe 1917- *CmpEPM, WhoJazz 72*
Dixon, Lawrence 1895-1970 *WhoJazz 72*
Dixon, Lee 1911-1953 *NotNAT B, WhoHol B*
Dixon, Lee 1914-1953 *WhScrn 74, -77*
Dixon, Lillian B d1962 *NotNAT B*
Dixon, Lucille 1923- *BlkWAB[port]*
Dixon, Marcia *WhoHol A*
Dixon, Marion *Film 2*
Dixon, Melvin *BlkAmP*
Dixon, Mort 1892-1956 *AmPS, AmSCAP 66, -80, BiDAmM, CmpEPM, Sw&Ld C*
Dixon, Norman 1926- *CnOxB, DancEn 78*
Dixon, Paul d1975 *NewYTET*
Dixon, Paul 1918-1974 *WhScrn 77*
Dixon, Reginald 1904- *WhoMus 72*
Dixon, Susan Jennifer 1938- *WhoMus 72*
Dixon, Thomas, Jr. 1864-1946 *FilmgC, HalFC 80, NotNAT B, WhoStg 1906, -1908*
Dixon, Vance 1895- *WhoJazz 72*
Dixon, William Robert 1925- *BiDAmM*
Dixon, Willie 1915- *BiDAmM, BluesWW[port], ConMuA 80A*
Dixon Brothers *CounME 74, EncFCWM 69*
Dixon-Smith, Frederick James John 1912- *IntWWM 77, WhoMus 72*
Dixon's Brass Band *BiDAmM*
Dizenzo, Charles 1938- *ConDr 73, -77*
Dizi, Francois Joseph 1780-1840? *NewGrD 80*
Dizi, Francois-Joseph 1780-1847 *Baker 78*
Djakonovski, Dragan 1931- *IntWWM 77, -80*
Djemil, Enyss 1917- *NewGrD 80*
Djordjevic, Mirjana 1936- *WhoOp 76*
Djordjevic, Vladimir R 1869-1938 *NewGrD 80*
D'Joseph, Jac 1919- *AmSCAP 66, -80*
Djuric-Klajn, Stana *NewGrD 80*
Dlabac, Bohumir Jan 1758-1820 *NewGrD 80*
Dlabacz, Gottfried Johann 1758-1820 *Baker 78, NewGrD 80*
D'Lower, Del 1912- *AmSCAP 80*
D'Lower, I Del 1912- *AmSCAP 66*
Dlugacz, Judith *ConMuA 80B*
D'Lugoff, Burton C 1928- *AmSCAP 66*
Dlugoraj, Albertus 1557?-1619? *NewGrD 80*
Dlugoraj, Wojciech 1557?-1619? *NewGrD 80*
Dlugoszewski, Lucia 1925- *ConAmC*
Dlugoszewski, Lucia 1931- *Baker 78, BiDAmM, CpmDNM 79, DcCM, NewGrD 80*
Dluski, Erazm 1857-1923 *NewGrD 80*
Dmitrevsky, Ivan Afanasyevich 1733-1821 *Ent, NotNAT B, OxThe*
Dmitri Of Rostov, Saint 1651-1709 *OxThe*
Dmytryk, Edward 1908- *BiDFilm, -81, CmMov, DcFM, FilmEn, FilmgC, HalFC 80, IntMPA 77, -75, -76, -78, -79, -80, MovMk[port], OxFilm, WorEFlm*
Doamekpor, Cornelius Raymond Kwame 1937- *IntWWM 77, -80*
Doane, Dorothy 1917- *AmSCAP 66, -80*
Doane, George Washington 1799-1859 *BiDAmM*
Doane, William Croswell 1832-1913 *BiDAmM*
Doane, William Howard 1832-1915 *Baker 78, BiDAmM, NewGrD 80*
Dobbelin, Carl Theophilus 1727-1793 *EncWT*
Dobbelin, Karl Theophilus 1727-1793 *Ent, OxThe*
Dobber, Johannes 1866-1921 *Baker 78*
Dobbins, Earl E 1911-1949 *WhScrn 74, -77*
Dobbins, Emeline *PupTheA*
Dobbins, Eugene David 1934- *AmSCAP 80*
Dobbins, William *ConAmC*
Dobbs, Jack Percival Baker 1922- *IntWWM 77, -80, WhoMus 72*
Dobbs, Kildare Robert Eric 1923- *CreCan 1*
Dobbs, Mattawilda 1925- *NewEOp 71*
Dobbs, Mattiwilda 1925- *CmOp, DrBlPA, IntWWM 77, -80, MusMk, MusSN[port], WhoMus 72*
Dober, Conrad K 1891-1938 *AmSCAP 80*
Dobias, Charles 1923- *IntWWM 80*
Dobias, Vaclav 1909-1978 *Baker 78, IntWWM 77, -80, NewGrD 80*
Dobie, Alan 1932- *FilmgC, HalFC 80, PlP&P[port], WhoThe 72, -77*
Dobinson, William Garry 1947- *IntWWM 77*
Dobkin, Larry *ForYSC, WhoHol A*
Dobkins, Carl, Jr. 1941- *AmPS A, RkOn[port]*
Doble, Budd d1919 *WhScrn 77*
Doble, Frances 1902-1969 *Film 2, WhScrn 77, WhThe*
Dobler, Charles 1923- *IntWWM 77, -80*
Dobler, Ludwig Leopold 1801-1864 *MagIID*
Dobneck, Johannes *NewGrD 80*
Dobos, Kalman 1931- *Baker 78, IntWWM 77, -80*
Dobos, Viorel-Constantin 1917- *IntWWM 80*
Doboujinsky, Mstislav 1875-1957 *CnOxB, DancEn 78*
Dobree, Georgina 1930- *IntWWM 77, -80, WhoMus 72*
Dobricht, Johanna Elisabeth 1692-1786 *NewGrD 80*
Dobrievich, Pierre 1931- *CnOxB*
Dobrin, George William 1936- *AmSCAP 80*
Dobrin, Lucille Rebecca 1935- *AmSCAP 80*
Dobrinski, Ingeborg 1945- *IntWWM 77*
Dobronic, Antun 1878-1955 *Baker 78*
Dobroven, Issay Alexandrovich 1894-1953 *NewGrD 80*
Dobrowen, Issai 1893-1953 *NewEOp 71*
Dobrowen, Issay 1891-1953 *Baker 78*
Dobrowen, Issay 1894-1953 *CmOp*
Dobrowolska-Gruszczynska, Maria F 1918- *IntWWM 80*
Dobrowolski, Andrzej 1921- *Baker 78, IntWWM 77, -80, NewGrD 80*
Dobrski, Julian 1811?-1886 *NewGrD 80*
Dobry, Wallace B 1933- *ConAmC*
Dobrzynski, Ignacy F 1807-1867 *OxMus*
Dobrzynski, Ignacy Feliks 1807-1867 *NewGrD 80*
Dobrzynski, Ignacy Felix 1807-1867 *Baker 78*
Dobrzynski, Jerzy 1936- *IntWWM 80*
Dobson, Edward d1925 *WhScrn 77*
Dobson, James 1923- *ForYSC, WhoHol A*
Dobson, Jane *WomWMM B*
Dobson, Jean Gabrielle Austin *IntWWM 77, -80, WhoMus 72*
Dobson, Michael 1923- *IntWWM 77, -80, WhoMus 72*
Dobson, Tamara 1947- *DrBlPA, WhoHol A*
Dobszay, Laszlo 1935- *NewGrD 80*
Dobujinsky, Mstislav 1875-1957 *OxThe*
Doche, Joseph Denis 1766-1825 *Baker 78, NewGrD 80*
Docherty, Peter 1944- *CnOxB*
Dockson, Evelyn 1888-1952 *WhScrn 74, -77, WhoHol B*
Dockstader, Lew 1856-1924 *JoeFr, OxThe, PlP&P*
Dockstader, Tod 1932- *ConAmC, DcCM*
Doctor Clayton's Buddy *BluesWW*
Doctor John *ConMuA 80A*
Doczy, Lajos 1845-1919 *OxThe*
Dodart, Denis 1634-1707 *NewGrD 80*
Dodd d1973 *NewGrD 80*
Dodd, Claire *ForYSC*
Dodd, Claire d1973 *MotPP, WhoHol B*
Dodd, Claire 1908-1973 *FilmEn, HalFC 80, MovMk[port], ThFT[port]*
Dodd, Claire 1909?-1973 *WhScrn 77*
Dodd, David Haseltine *PupTheA*
Dodd, Edward 1705-1810 *NewGrD 80*
Dodd, Elan E 1868-1935 *WhScrn 74, -77*
Dodd, Emily d1944 *NotNAT B*
Dodd, J D 1944- *AmSCAP 80*
Dodd, James *NewGrD 80*
Dodd, James William 1734-1796 *NotNAT B, OxThe*
Dodd, Jimmie 1910-1964 *AmSCAP 66, -80, WhScrn 74, -77*
Dodd, Jimmy 1910-1964 *WhoHol B*
Dodd, Jimmy 1914-1964 *ForYSC*
Dodd, John 1752-1839 *NewGrD 80*
Dodd, Joseph A *Film 2*
Dodd, Ken 1929- *WhoThe 72, -77*
Dodd, Lee Wilson 1879-1933 *NotNAT B, OxThe, WhThe*
Dodd, Neal 1878-1966 *Film 2, WhScrn 74, -77*
Dodd, Neal 1878-1969 *WhoHol B*
Dodd, Raymond Henry 1929- *WhoMus 72*
Dodd, Ruth Carrell *AmSCAP 66, -80*
Dodd, Thomas *NewGrD 80*
Dodd, Thomas J d1971 *NewYTET*
Dodd, Wilfrid E 1923- *IntMPA 77, -75, -76, -78, -79, -80*
Dodd, William 1729-1777 *OxMus*
Doddridge, Philip 1702-1751 *OxMus*
Dodds, Baby 1898-1959 *Baker 78, CmpEPM, IlEncJ, NewGrD 80, WhoJazz 72*
Dodds, Chuck 1936-1967 *WhScrn 74, -77*
Dodds, Elreta 1957- *BlkWAB*
Dodds, Jack 1927-1962 *NotNAT B, WhScrn 74, -77*
Dodds, Jamieson 1884-1942 *NotNAT B, WhThe*
Dodds, Johnny 1892-1940 *Baker 78, BiDAmM, CmpEPM, IlEncJ, NewGrD 80, NewOrJ[port], WhoJazz 72*
Dodds, Warren 1894-1959 *BiDAmM*
Dodds, Warren 1896-1959 *NewOrJ[port]*
Dodds, Warren 1898-1959 *NewGrD 80*
Dodds, William *BiE&WWA, NotNAT*
Doderer, Gerhard 1944- *IntWWM 77, -80*
Dodge, Anna *Film 2*
Dodge, Charles 1942- *Baker 78, ConAmC, DcCM, IntWWM 77, -80*
Dodge, Charles 1945- *NewGrD 80*
Dodge, Henry Irving 1861-1934 *WhThe*
Dodge, Roger 1898-1974 *WhScrn 77*
Dodge, Shirlee *BiE&WWA, NotNAT*
Dodgen, Gary Norman 1954- *AmSCAP 80*
Dodgion, Dottie 1929- *EncJzS 70*
Dodgion, Jerry 1932- *BiDAmM, EncJzS 70*
Dodgson, Jolyon 1936- *IntWWM 77, -80*
Dodgson, Stephen 1924- *NewGrD 80*
Dodimead, David 1919- *WhoThe 72, -77*
Dods, Marcus 1918- *IntWWM 77, -80, WhoMus 72*
Dodsley, James d1797 *NotNAT B*
Dodsley, Robert 1703-1764 *NotNAT B, OxThe*
Dodson, Edgar *AmSCAP 66*
Dodson, Howard J 1910-1971 *BiDAmM*
Dodson, John E 1857-1931 *NotNAT B, WhThe, WhoStg 1906, -1908*
Dodson, Milton Allen 1914- *AmSCAP 80*
Dodson, Owen 1914- *BiE&WWA, BlkAmP, DrBlPA, MorBAP, NotNAT*
Dodsworth, Charles d1920 *NotNAT B*
Dodsworth, John 1910-1964 *WhScrn 77*
Doe, Edward Niel 1926- *WhoOp 76*
Doe, John *WhoMus 72*
Doe, Paul Maurice 1931- *IntWWM 80, NewGrD 80*
Doebler, Curt 1896-1970 *Baker 78*
Doelle, Franz 1883-1965 *NewGrD 80*
Doench, Karl 1915- *WhoMus 72*
Doenhoff, Albert Von 1880-1940 *Baker 78, ConAmC*
Doerfel, Herbert 1924- *AmSCAP 66, -80*
Doerfer, John C *NewYTET*
Doerner, Armin W 1852-1924 *BiDAmM*
Doerr, Ludwig 1925- *NewGrD 80*

Doflein, Erich 1900-1977 *Baker 78, NewGrD 80*
Dogaru, Anton 1945- *IntWWM 80*
Doggett, Bill 1916- *AmPS A, CmpEPM, RkOn[port]*
Doggett, Thomas 1670?-1721 *NotNAT A, -B, OxThe, PIP&P*
Doggett, William Ballard 1916- *BiDAmM, EncJzS 70, WhoJazz 72*
Dognazzi, Francesco *NewGrD 80*
Dohanyi Lajos, Lajos *CreCan 1*
Doherty, Anthony *ConAmC*
Dohl, Friedhelm 1936- *DcCM, NewGrD 80*
Dohler, Theodor Von 1814-1856 *Baker 78, NewGrD 80, OxMus*
Dohm, Dorothy G *PupTheA*
Dohnanyi, Christoph Von 1929- *Baker 78, BnBkM 80, NewGrD 80*
Dohnanyi, Erno 1877-1960 *MusMk, NewGrD 80[port], OxMus*
Dohnanyi, Ernst Von 1877-1960 *Baker 78, BnBkM 80, CompSN[port], ConAmC, DcCom 77, DcCom&M 79, MusSN[port], NewGrD 80[port]*
Doire, Rene 1879-1959 *Baker 78*
D'Oisley, Maurice d1949 *NotNAT B*
Doisy, Marcal 1916- *IntWWM 80*
Doisy, Marcel 1916- *IntWWM 77*
Doizi DeVelasco, Nicolas 1590?-1659? *NewGrD 80*
Dokoudovsky, Vladimir 1920- *CnOxB*
Dokoudovsky, Vladimir 1922- *DancEn 78*
Dokshitser, Timofey 1921- *NewGrD 80*
Doktor, Paul Karl 1919- *Baker 78, IntWWM 77, -80, MusSN[port], NewGrD 80, WhoMus 72*
Dolan, Alida Mary 1912- *AmSCAP 80*
Dolan, Anton *Film 2*
Dolan, Diane Marie 1941- *IntWWM 77, -80*
Dolan, Harry *BlkAmP*
Dolan, Jimmie 1924- *BiDAmM, EncFCWM 69*
Dolan, Joann *WhoHol A*
Dolan, John 1929- *AmSCAP 66, -80*
Dolan, Lida 1912- *AmSCAP 66*
Dolan, Mary 1919- *BiE&WWA*
Dolan, Michael J d1954 *NotNAT B*
Dolan, Robert Emmett 1906-1972 *AmSCAP 66, -80, CmpEPM, FilmgC, HalFC 80*
Dolan, Robert Emmett 1908-1972 *BiE&WWA, FilmEn, NotNAT B*
Dolanska, Vera 1926- *IntWWM 77, -80*
Dolar, Krtitel *NewGrD 80*
Dolaro, Hattie d1941 *NotNAT B*
Dolce, Lodovico 1508-1568 *McGEWD, OxThe*
Dolcevillico, Francesco Saverio *NewGrD 80*
Doldinger, Klaus 1936- *EncJzS 70*
Dole, Nathan Haskell 1852-1935 *BiDAmM*
Dolega-Kamienski *Baker 78*
Doleman, Guy 1923- *FilmgC, HalFC 80*
Dolentz, George 1908-1963 *ForYSC*
Dolenz, George 1908-1963 *FilmgC, HalFC 80, NotNAT B, WhScrn 74, -77, WhoHol B*
Dolenz, Mickey *WhoHol A*
Doles, Johann Friedrich 1715-1797 *Baker 78, NewGrD 80, OxMus*
Dolezalek, Jan Emanuel 1780-1858 *Baker 78, NewGrD 80*
Dolge, Alfred 1848-1922 *NewGrD 80*
Dolgorukov, Prince Pavel Ivanovich 1787-1845 *NewGrD 80*
Dolgushin, Nikita Alexandrovich 1938- *CnOxB*
Doliarius, Hieronim *NewGrD 80*
Dolin, Anton 1904- *CnOxB, DancEn 78[port], WhThe*
Dolin, Boris 1903- *DcFM*
Dolin, Lynn Marie 1948- *AmSCAP 80*
Dolin, Samuel *ConAmC*
Dolin, Samuel 1917- *Baker 78, CreCan 2*
Doll, Andy Joseph 1921- *BiDAmM*
Doll, Bill 1910- *BiE&WWA, NotNAT*
Doll, Dora *WhoHol A*
Doll, Giuseppe d1774 *NewGrD 80*
Doll, Hans Peter 1925- *WhoOp 76*
Doll, Joseph d1774 *NewGrD 80*
Dollar, Jimmy 1936- *BiDAmM*
Dollar, John Washington, Jr. 1933- *BiDAmM*
Dollar, Johnny 1933- *CounME 74, -74A*
Dollar, Johnny 1936- *EncFCWM 69*
Dollar, William 1907- *CnOxB, DancEn 78*
Dollarhide, Theodore J 1948- *ConAmC*
Dolle, Charles *NewGrD 80*
Doller, Florian Johann *NewGrD 80*
Dollinger, Irving 1905- *IntMPA 77, -75, -76, -78, -79, -80*
Dolliole, Milford 1903- *NewOrJ*
Dollitz, Grete Franke 1924- *IntWWM 77, -80*
Dolly, Jennie 1892-1941 *WhThe*
Dolly, Jenny 1892-1941 *NotNAT B, WhScrn 74, -77, WhoHol B*
Dolly, Jenny 1893-1941 *HalFC 80*
Dolly, Lady 1876-1953 *WhScrn 74, -77*
Dolly, Rosie 1892-1970 *WhScrn 74, -77, WhThe, WhoHol B*
Dolly, Rosie 1893-1970 *HalFC 80*
Dolly, Rosika *BiDAmM*
Dolly, Roziska 1892- *Film 1*
Dolly, Yancsi 1892-1941 *Film 1*
Dolly Sisters *AmPS B, BiDAmM, CmpEPM, EncMT*
Dolman, Richard 1895- *WhThe*
Dolmetsch *NewGrD 80*
Dolmetsch, Arnold 1858-1940 *Baker 78, BnBkM 80, MusMk[port], NewGrD 80[port], OxMus*
Dolmetsch, Carl Frederick 1911- *IntWWM 77, -80, NewGrD 80, OxMus, WhoMus 72*
Dolmetsch, Cecile 1904- *IntWWM 77, -80, OxMus, WhoMus 72*
Dolmetsch, Helene 1878-1924 *NewGrD 80*
Dolmetsch, Jeanne-Marie 1942- *IntWWM 77, -80*
Dolmetsch, Mabel 1874-1963 *NewGrD 80, OxMus*
Dolmetsch, Marguerite Mabel 1942- *IntWWM 77, -80*
Dolmetsch, Nathalie 1905- *IntWWM 77, -80, OxMus, WhoMus 72*
Dolmetsch, Rudolph 1906-1942 *NewGrD 80, OxMus*
Dolores, Carmen 1924- *FilmAG WE*
Dolorez, Mademoiselle *Film 2*
Dolph, John M 1895-1962 *AmSCAP 66, -80*
Dolph, Norman Edward 1939- *AmSCAP 80*
Dolphy, Eric Allan 1928-1964 *BiDAmM, IlEncJ, NewGrD 80*
Dolukhanova, Zara 1918- *Baker 78, NewGrD 80*
Dolukhanova, Zarui 1918- *NewGrD 80*
Dolzhansky, Alexander Naumovich 1908-1966 *NewGrD 80*
Domaniewski, Boleslaus 1857-1925 *Baker 78*
Domaniewski, Boleslaw Marian 1857-1925 *NewGrD 80*
Domaninska, Libuse 1924- *NewGrD 80, WhoOp 76*
Domarto, Petrus De *NewGrD 80*
Domazlicky, Frantisek 1913- *IntWWM 77, -80*
Domb, Daniel 1944- *WhoMus 72*
Domberger, Georg Joseph *NewGrD 80*
Dombre, Barbara 1950-1973 *WhScrn 77*
Dombrecht, Paulus Stephanus 1948- *IntWWM 80*
Dombrowski, Stanley 1932- *IntWWM 77, -80*
Domenegino Da Piacenza d1470? *NewGrD 80*
Domenichino Da Piacenza d1470? *NewGrD 80*
Domenico Da Piacenza d1462? *CnOxB*
Domenico Da Piacenza d1470? *NewGrD 80*
Domenico Del Matta *NewGrD 80*
Domenico Ferrarese d1470? *NewGrD 80*
Domenico Of Ferrara *DancEn 78*
Domenico, Gianpaolo Di *NewGrD 80*
Domenicus Gundissalinus *NewGrD 80*
Domer, Jerry Lloyd 1938- *IntWWM 77, -80*
Domergue, Faith 1925- *FilmEn, FilmgC, ForYSC, HalFC 80, MotPP, WhoHol A, WhoHrs 80[port]*
Domgraf-Fassbaender, Willi 1897-1978 *NewEOp 71*
Domgraf-Fassbaender, Willy 1897-1978 *WhoMus 72*
Domgraf-Fassbander, Willi 1897-1978 *CmOp, NewGrD 80*
Domingo, Placido 1941- *Baker 78, BiDAmM, CmOp[port], IntWWM 77, -80, MusSN[port], NewEOp 71, NewGrD 80, WhoMus 72, WhoOp 76*
Dominguez, Beatrice d1921 *Film 2, WhScrn 74, -77, WhoHol B*
Dominguez, Joe 1894-1970 *WhScrn 77, WhoHol B*
Dominguez, Oralia 1928- *NewGrD 80, WhoMus 72*
Dominguez, Paul, Jr. 1887?- *NewOrJ*
Dominguez, Paul, Sr. 1865?- *NewOrJ*
Dominguez, Ruben 1940- *WhoOp 76*
Dominic, Zoe *CnOxB, DancEn 78*
Dominiceti, Cesare 1821-1888 *Baker 78, NewGrD 80*
Dominici, Gianpaolo Di *NewGrD 80, -80*
Dominici, Giovan Paolo Di *NewGrD 80*
Dominici, Mario *Film 2*
Dominicus De Ferraria *NewGrD 80*
Dominicus, Evelyn *Film 1*
Dominik, Alexander *NewGrD 80*
Dominique *OxThe*
Dominique Et Francoise *CnOxB*
Dominique, Albert 1909- *NewOrJ[port]*
Dominique, Anatie 1896- *BiDAmM, NewOrJ[port]*
Dominique, Carl-Axel Martinelli 1939- *IntWWM 77, -80*
Dominique, Francois *CreCan 2*
Dominique, Ivan 1928-1973 *WhScrn 77*
Dominique, Monica Anita Elisabeth 1940- *IntWWM 77*
Dominique, Natty 1896- *IlEncJ*
Dominique, Natty Anatie 1896- *WhoJazz 72*
Domino, Antoine *AmPS A*
Domino, Antoine 1928- *AmPS, BiDAmM, BluesWW[port], PopAmC SUP[port]*
Domino, Fats *AmPS B, ConMuA 80A[port]*
Domino, Fats 1928- *DrBIPA, IlEncR[port], MusMk, RkOn[port]*
Dominoes, The *BiDAmM, RkOn[port]*
Dommange, Rene Auguste Louis Henri *WhoMus 72*
Dommel-Dieny, Amy 1894- *IntWWM 77, -80*
Dommelen, Jan Van *FilmAG WE*
Dommer, Arrey Von 1828-1905 *Baker 78, NewGrD 80*
Dommett, Leonard 1928- *NewGrD 80*
Domnerus, Arne 1924- *CmpEPM, NewGrD 80*
Domnich, Heinrich 1767-1844 *NewGrD 80*
Domokos, Pal Peter 1901- *NewGrD 80*
Domsaitis, Adelheid Agathe Marie 1900- *IntWWM 77, -80*
Domurad, John J 1931- *AmSCAP 80*
Domvill, Silas *NewGrD 80*
Domville, James DeBeaujeu 1933- *CreCan 2*
Don And Dewey *RkOn*
Don, Carl *WhoHol A*
Don, David L 1867-1949 *WhScrn 77*
Don, Wesley 1892?-1934 *NewOrJ*
Don And Juan *RkOn[port]*
Don Heusser, Der *NewGrD 80*
Don Rodriquez *PupTheA*
Dona, Mariangela 1916- *NewGrD 80*
Donadio, Gaetano 1921- *WhoOp 76*
Donaghey, Frederick 1870-1937 *NotNAT B, WhoStg 1906, -1908*
Donahue, Al 1904- *BgBands 74, CmpEPM*
Donahue, Bertha Terry *ConAmC*
Donahue, Bonnie *WomWMM B*
Donahue, Elinor *ForYSC, WhoHol A*
Donahue, Jack 1892-1930 *CmpEPM, EncMT, NotNAT A, -B, WhScrn 74, -77, WhThe*
Donahue, Phil 1936- *IntMPA 80, NewYTET*
Donahue, Robert L 1931- *AmSCAP 80, ConAmC*
Donahue, Sam Koontz 1918-1974 *BgBands 74[port], BiDAmM, CmpEPM, EncJzS 70*
Donahue, Troy *MotPP, WhoHol A*
Donahue, Troy 1936- *FilmEn, FilmgC, HalFC 80*
Donahue, Troy 1937- *IntMPA 77, -75, -76, -78, -79, -80, MovMk*
Donahue, Troy 1939- *ForYSC*
Donahue, Vincent J d1976 *WhoHol C*
Donald, Barbara Kay 1942- *EncJzS 70*
Donald, Donald K *ConMuA 80B*
Donald, James 1917- *FilmEn, FilmgC, ForYSC, HalFC 80, IlWWBF, IntMPA 77, -75, -76, -78, -79, -80, WhThe, WhoHol A, WhoThe 72*
Donald, Robin 1942- *WhoOp 76*
Donalda, Pauline 1882-1970 *Baker 78, CreCan 1, NewGrD 80*
Donalda, Pauline 1884-1970 *BiDAmM*

Donaldson, Arthur 1869-1955 Film 2, NotNAT B, WhoStg 1908
Donaldson, Bo & The Heywoods RkOn 2[port]
Donaldson, Herbert 1918- AmSCAP 66
Donaldson, Herbert Franklin 1918- AmSCAP 80
Donaldson, Jack 1910-1975 WhScrn 77, WhoHol C
Donaldson, Lou 1926- BiDAmM, EncJzS 70
Donaldson, Norma DrBlPA
Donaldson, Robert Stanley 1922-1971 EncJzS 70
Donaldson, Sadie 1909- ConAmC
Donaldson, Sam NewYTET, PupTheA
Donaldson, Ted 1933- FilmgC, ForYSC, HalFC 80
Donaldson, Walter 1793?-1877 NotNAT A, -B
Donaldson, Walter 1893-1947 AmPS, AmSCAP 66, -80, BiDAmM, CmpEPM, EncMT, NewGrD 80, NotNAT B, PopAmC[port], Sw&Ld C
Donaldson, Will 1891-1954 AmSCAP 66, -80
Donat NewGrD 80
Donat, Peter 1928- BiE&WWA, NotNAT, WhoHol A
Donat, Robert 1905-1958 BiDFilm, -81, EncWT, FilmAG WE, FilmEn, FilmgC, ForYSC, HalFC 80[port], IlWWBF[port], -A, MotPP, MovMk[port], NotNAT B, OxFilm, OxThe, PlP&P, WhScrn 74, -77, WhThe, WhoHol B, WorEFlm[port]
Donat, Zdzislawa Jozefa WhoOp 76
Donath, Helen 1940- IntWWM 77, -80, NewGrD 80, WhoMus 72
Donath, Helen 1940-1967 WhoOp 76
Donath, Ludwig 1900-1967 FilmEn, FilmgC, HalFC 80, MotPP, WhScrn 74, -77, WhoHol B
Donath, Ludwig 1905- ForYSC
Donath, Ludwig 1905-1967 Vers A[port]
Donath, Ludwig 1907-1967 BiE&WWA, MovMk[port], NotNAT B, WhThe
Donati NewGrD 80
Donati, August Friedrich Wilhelm 1773-1842 NewGrD 80
Donati, Baldassare 1530?-1603 Baker 78, NewGrD 80
Donati, Bindo D'Alesso NewGrD 80
Donati, Carl Friedrich 1740-1814 NewGrD 80
Donati, Christian Gottlob 1732-1795 NewGrD 80
Donati, Christoph 1625-1706 NewGrD 80
Donati, Christoph 1659-1713 NewGrD 80
Donati, Gotthold Heinrich 1734-1799 NewGrD 80
Donati, Ignazio 1570?-1638 Baker 78
Donati, Ignazio 1575?-1638 NewGrD 80
Donati, Jean Schabacker 1926- IntWWM 77
Donati, Johann Christoph 1737-1764 NewGrD 80
Donati, Johann Christoph Gottlob 1694-1756 NewGrD 80
Donati, Johann Jacob 1715- NewGrD 80
Donati, Johannes Jacobus 1663- NewGrD 80
Donati, Maria 1902-1966 WhScrn 77
Donati, Pino 1907-1975 Baker 78
Donato Da Cascia NewGrD 80
Donato, Anthony 1909- AmSCAP 66, -80, Baker 78, ConAmC, IntWWM 77, -80
Donato, Baldassare 1525?-1603 NewGrD 80[port]
Donato, Baldassare 1530?-1603 MusMk
Donato, Baldissera 1525?-1603 NewGrD 80[port]
Donato, Michel Andre 1942- EncJzS 70
Donato DeOliveira, Joao 1934- BiDAmM
Donatoni, Franco 1927- Baker 78, DcCM, NewGrD 80, WhoMus 72
Donatus De Florentia, Magister Dominus NewGrD 80
Donaudy, Stefano 1879-1925 Baker 78
Donberger, Georg Joseph 1709-1768 NewGrD 80
Doncaster, Caryl 1923- IntMPA 77, -75, -76, -78, -79, -80
Doncastre, W De NewGrD 80
Donch, Karl 1915- WhoOp 76
Dondo, Mathurin PupTheA
Dondoni, Cesare Film 1
Donegan, Dorothy 1924- BiDAmM, BlkWAB[port], CmpEPM, DrBlPA
Donegan, Lonnie 1931- RkOn
Donehue, Vincent J 1915-1966 NotNAT B
Donehue, Vincent J 1916-1966 FilmgC, HalFC 80
Donehue, Vincent J 1920-1966 BiE&WWA, WhThe
Donelly, Henry V d1910 NotNAT B
Donen, Stanley 1924- BiDFilm, -81, CmMov, DcFM, FilmEn, FilmgC, HalFC 80, IntMPA 77, -75, -76, -78, -79, -80, MovMk, OxFilm, WorEFlm
Donenfeld, James 1917- AmSCAP 66, -80
Doner, Maurice 1905-1971 WhScrn 74, -77
Doner, Rose 1905-1926 WhScrn 74, -77
Dones, Sidney Preston BlksB&W C
Doney, John Marvin 1933- IntWWM 77
Donez, Ian 1891- AmSCAP 66
Donfrid, Johann 1585-1654 NewGrD 80
Donfrid, Johannes 1585-1650 Baker 78
Donfrid, Johannes 1585-1654 NewGrD 80
Donfried, Johann 1585-1654 NewGrD 80
Donfried, Johannes 1585-1654 NewGrD 80
Doni, Antonfrancesco 1513-1574 NewGrD 80
Doni, Antonio Francesco 1513-1574 Baker 78
Doni, Giovanni Battista 1594-1647 Baker 78
Doni, Giovanni Battista 1595-1647 NewGrD 80
Doniach, Shula WhoMus 72
Doniger, Walter 1917- FilmEn, FilmgC, HalFC 80, IntMPA 77, -75, -76, -78, -79, -80
Donington, Margaret 1909- IntWWM 77, -80, WhoMus 72
Donington, Robert 1907- Baker 78, IntWWM 77, -80, NewGrD 80, OxMus, WhoMus 72
Doniol-Valcroze, Jacques 1920- BiDFilm, -81, DcFM, FilmEn, OxFilm, WorEFlm
Donisthorpe, G Sheila 1898-1946 NotNAT A, -B, WhThe
Donizetti, Alfredo 1867-1921 Baker 78
Donizetti, Gaetano 1797-1848 Baker 78, BnBkM 80[port], CmOp, CmpBCM, CnOxB, DcCom 77[port], DcCom&M 79, GrComp[port], MusMk[port], NewEOp 71, NewGrD 80, OxMus
Donizetti, Giuseppe 1788-1856 Baker 78
Donlan, James 1889-1938 Film 2, WhScrn 74, -77, WhoHol B
Donlan, Mike Film 2
Donlan, Yolande 1920- FilmEn, FilmgC, ForYSC, HalFC 80, IlWWBF, -A, IntMPA 77, -75, -76, -78, -79, -80, WhoHol A, WhoThe 72, -77
Donleavy, J P 1926- CnMD, ConDr 73, -77, ModWD, WhoThe 72, -77
Donlevy, Brian d1972 BiE&WWA, MotPP, WhoHol B
Donlevy, Brian 1899-1972 BiDFilm, -81, FilmEn, FilmgC, HalFC 80, OxFilm, WhScrn 77, WhoHrs 80
Donlevy, Brian 1901-1972 Film 2, ForYSC, HolP 30[port]
Donlevy, Brian 1903-1972 MovMk[port], NotNAT B, WhThe
Donlin, Mike 1877-1933 Film 2, WhScrn 74, -77, WhoHol B
Donn, Jorge 1947- CnOxB
Donnay, Charles Maurice 1859-1945 NotNAT B
Donnay, Maurice 1859-1945 CnMD, McGEWD[port], ModWD, WhThe
Donnberger, Georg Joseph NewGrD 80
Donne, John 1576-1631 DcPup
Donnell, Jeff 1921- FilmEn, FilmgC, ForYSC, HalFC 80, IntMPA 77, -75, -76, -78, -79, -80, MotPP, WhoHol A
Donnell, Patrick 1916- WhoThe 72, -77
Donnelly, Andrew 1893-1955 AmSCAP 66, -80
Donnelly, Donal 1931- WhoThe 72, -77
Donnelly, Donal 1932- FilmgC, HalFC 80
Donnelly, Donald Film 2
Donnelly, Dorothy 1880-1928 AmSCAP 66, -80, BestMus, BiDAmM, CmpEPM, EncMT, Film 1, HalFC 80, NewCBMT, NotNAT B, WhThe, WhoStg 1908
Donnelly, James 1865-1937 Film 1, WhScrn 74, -77, WhoHol B
Donnelly, Leo 1878-1935 WhScrn 74, -77, WhoHol B
Donnelly, Malcolm Douglas 1943- IntWWM 80
Donnelly, Muttonleg 1912-1958 WhoJazz 72
Donnelly, Ralph E 1932- IntMPA 80
Donnelly, Ruth 1896- AmSCAP 80, BiE&WWA, FilmEn, Film 2, FilmgC, ForYSC, HalFC 80, HolCA[port], MovMk[port], NotNAT, ThFT[port], Vers A[port], What 3[port], WhoHol A
Donnelly, Vincent Paul 1941- IntWWM 77
Donnenfeld, Bernard 1926- IntMPA 77, -75, -76, -78, -79, -80
Donner, Clive IntMPA 77, -75, -76, -78, -79, -80
Donner, Clive 1920- FilmgC
Donner, Clive 1926- BiDFilm, -81, FilmEn, HalFC 80, IlWWBF, OxFilm, WhoThe 77, WorEFlm
Donner, Mrs. E R PupTheA
Donner, Henrik Otto 1939- Baker 78, DcCM, IntWWM 80, NewGrD 80
Donner, Jorn 1933- BiDFilm, -81, FilmEn, FilmgC, HalFC 80, OxFilm, WorEFlm
Donner, Maurice d1971 WhoHol B
Donner, Ral 1943- RkOn
Donner, Richard 1939?- FilmgC, HalFC 80, IntMPA 80, WhoHrs 80
Donner, Robert WhoHol A
Donner, Vyvyan WomWMM
Donnet, Jacques 1917- AmSCAP 66, -80, IntWWM 77
Donnie Film 2
Donnini, Girolamo d1752 NewGrD 80
D'Onofrio, John Francis 1917- IntWWM 77
Donoghue, Dennis BlkAmP
Donohoe, Peter Howard 1953- IntWWM 80
Donohue, Jack 1908- FilmEn, WhoThe 77
Donohue, Jack 1912- BiE&WWA, FilmgC, HalFC 80, NotNAT
Donohue, Jack 1914- IntMPA 77, -75, -76, -78, -79, -80
Donohue, Joe d1921 Film 1, WhoHol B
Donohue, Joseph 1884-1921 Film 2, WhScrn 74, -77
Donohue, Richard William 1936- IntWWM 77, -80
Donostia, Jose Antonio De 1886-1956 Baker 78, NewGrD 80
Donovan 1946- ConMuA 80A, EncFCWM 69, IlEncR, RkOn 2[port], WhoHol A
Donovan, Henry B IntMPA 78, -79, -80
Donovan, Henry B 1914- IntMPA 77, -76
Donovan, Henry B 1924- IntMPA 75
Donovan, Jack Film 2
Donovan, King 1919?- FilmgC, ForYSC, HalFC 80, WhoHol A, WhoHrs 80
Donovan, Margaret Henderlite 1925- IntWWM 77
Donovan, Michael Film 2
Donovan, Richard Frank 1891- BiDAmM
Donovan, Richard Frank 1891-1970 Baker 78, ConAmC, DcCM, NewGrD 80, OxMus
Donovan, Walter 1888-1964 AmSCAP 66, -80, NotNAT B
Donovan, Wilfred Film 2
Donovan, William Film 2
Donska, Maria 1912- WhoMus 72
Donskoi, Marc 1901- WorEFlm
Donskoi, Mark 1897- FilmgC, HalFC 80
Donskoi, Mark 1901- BiDFilm, -81, DcFM, MovMk[port], OxFilm
Donskoy, Mark 1897- FilmEn
Donskoy, Mark 1901- DcFM
Donson, Don AmSCAP 80
Dont, Jacob 1815-1888 OxMus
Dont, Jakob 1815-1888 Baker 78
Dont, Joseph Valentin 1776-1833 Baker 78
Dontchos, Patricia Ann 1946- NotNAT
Donzelli, Domenico 1790-1873 CmOp, NewEOp 71, NewGrD 80
Doo, Dickey And The Don'ts RkOn
Doobie Brothers, The ConMuA 80A[port], IlEncR, RkOn 2[port]
Doohan, James WhoHol A
Dooley, Billy 1893-1938 Film 1, -2, ForYSC, TwYS, WhScrn 74, -77, WhoHol B
Dooley, Edna Mohr 1907- AmSCAP 66, -80
Dooley, Gordon Film 2
Dooley, James d1949 NotNAT B
Dooley, John Anthony NatPD[port]

Dooley, Johnny 1887-1928 *Film 1, -2, TwYS, WhScrn 74, -77, WhoHol B*
Dooley, Phil S 1898-1967 *AmSCAP 80*
Dooley, Rae *BiE&WWA, NotNAT, WhoHol A*
Dooley, Ray 1896- *CmpEPM, EncMT, What 3[port], WhThe*
Dooley, Rosemary Margaret Stanton 1947- *IntWWM 80*
Dooley, Simmie 1881-1961 *BluesWW*
Dooley, William 1932- *IntWWM 77, -80, WhoOp 76*
Doolittle, Amos 1754-1832 *BiDAmM, NewGrD 80*
Doolittle, Eliakim 1772-1850 *BiDAmM*
Doolittle, James 1914- *BiE&WWA, NotNAT*
Doonan, George 1897-1973 *WhScrn 77*
Doonan, Patric 1925-1958 *HalFC 80*
Doonan, Patric 1927-1958 *FilmgC, WhScrn 74, WhoHol B*
Doonan, Patrick 1927-1958 *WhScrn 77*
Door, Anton 1833-1919 *Baker 78*
Doors, The *BiDAmM, ConMuA 80A[port], IlEncR[port], RkOn 2[port]*
Doorslaer, George Van 1864-1940 *Baker 78*
Doorslaer, Georges Van 1864-1940 *NewGrD 80*
Doph, Josephine *Film 2*
Doppelbauer, Josef Friedrich 1918- *IntWWM 80*
Dopper, Cornelis 1870-1939 *Baker 78, NewGrD 80*
Doppler *NewGrD 80*
Doppler, Albert Franz 1821-1883 *Baker 78*
Doppler, Arpad 1857-1927 *Baker 78, NewGrD 80*
Doppler, Ferenc 1821-1883 *NewGrD 80*
Doppler, Franz 1821-1883 *NewGrD 80*
Doppler, Karl 1825-1900 *Baker 78, NewGrD 80*
Doppler, Karoly 1825-1900 *NewGrD 80*
DoQui, Robert *DrBlPA, WhoHol A*
Dor, Karin 1936- *FilmAG WE*
D'Ora, Daisy *Film 2*
Dora, Josefine *Film 2*
Doraiswamy, V 1912- *IntMPA 77, -75, -76, -78, -79, -80*
Doraldina 1888-1936 *WhScrn 74, -77*
Doraldina, Mademoiselle 1888-1936 *TwYS*
Doralinda 1888-1936 *WhoHol B*
Doralinda, Mademoiselle 1888-1936 *Film 1, -2*
Doran, Ann *ForYSC, MotPP, WhoHol A*
Doran, Ann 1913- *FilmEn, MovMk[port]*
Doran, Ann 1914- *FilmgC, HalFC 80, WhoHrs 80*
Doran, Charles 1877-1964 *NotNAT B, WhThe*
Doran, Elsa 1915- *AmSCAP 66, -80*
Doran, J Terence 1936- *ConAmTC*
Doran, John 1807-1878 *NotNAT B*
Doran, Mary 1907- *FilmEn, Film 2, ForYSC, ThFT[port]*
Doran, Matt Higgins 1921- *AmSCAP 80, Baker 78, ConAmC*
Dorati, Antal 1906- *Baker 78, BiDAmM, BnBkM 80, CnOxB, ConAmC, DancEn 78, IntWWM 77, -80, MusMk[port], MusSN[port], NewGrD 80[port], WhoMus 72, WhoOp 76*
Dorati, Geronimo 1590-1617 *NewGrD 80*
Dorati, Girolamo 1590-1617 *NewGrD 80*
Dorati, Hieronymus 1590-1617 *NewGrD 80*
Dorati, Niccolo 1513?-1593 *NewGrD 80*
Dorati, Nicolao 1513?-1593 *NewGrD 80*
Dorati, Nicolaus 1513?-1593 *NewGrD 80*
Dorati, Nicolo 1513?-1593 *NewGrD 80*
Doratius, Geronimo 1590-1617 *NewGrD 80*
Doratius, Girolamo 1590-1617 *NewGrD 80*
Doratius, Hieronymus 1590-1617 *NewGrD 80*
D'Orazi, Attilio 1929- *WhoOp 76*
Dore, Adrienne *Film 2*
Dore, Alexander 1923- *WhoThe 72, -77*
Dore, Gustave *PlP&P*
Dore, Helen Margaret *IntWWM 77*
Dore, Philip Guy 1903- *WhoMus 72*
Doree, Doris 1909-1971 *BiDAmM*
Doret, Gustave 1866-1943 *Baker 78, NewGrD 80*
Doretto, Roberta *Film 1*
Dorety, Charles R 1898-1957 *WhScrn 74, -77, WhoHol B*
Dorety, Charley *Film 2*
Dorff, Daniel Jay 1956- *AmSCAP 80, CpmDNM 80*
Dorffel, Alfred 1821-1905 *Baker 78, NewGrD 80*
Dorfman, Helen Horn 1913-1968 *AmSCAP 80*
Dorfman, Irvin S 1924- *BiE&WWA, IntMPA 77, -75, -76, -78, -79, -80*
Dorfman, Joseph 1940- *IntWWM 80, NewGrD 80*
Dorfman, Mel 1931- *IntWWM 77*
Dorfman, Nat 1895- *BiE&WWA, NotNAT*
Dorfman, Robert S 1930- *IntMPA 77, -75, -76, -78, -79, -80*
Dorfmann, Ania 1899- *Baker 78*
Dorfmann, Robert *FilmgC, HalFC 80*
Dorfmuller, Kurt 1922- *IntWWM 77, -80*
Dorfsman, Louis *NewYTET*
D'Orgemont d1665? *OxThe*
Dorgere, Arlette *WhThe*
Dorham, Kenny 1924-1972 *CmpEPM, EncJzS 70, IlEncJ, WhScrn 77*
Dorham, McKinley Howard 1924-1972 *BiDAmM, EncJzS 70*
Doria, Al, Sr. 1899-1977 *NewOrJ*
Doria, Vera *Film 1*
Dorian, Charles 1893-1942 *Film 1, WhScrn 74, -77*
Dorian, Frederick Deutsch 1902- *Baker 78, IntWWM 77, -80, NewGrD 80*
Dorico, Valerio 1500?-1565 *NewGrD 80*
Dorimond 1628?-1664? *OxThe*
Doring, Ernest Nicholas 1877-1955 *Baker 78*
Doring, Heinrich 1834-1916 *Baker 78*
Doring, Johann Friedrich Samuel 1766-1840 *NewGrD 80*
Doris, Hubert *ConAmC*
Dority, Bryan *ConAmC*
Dorival, Georges d1939 *NotNAT B*
Dorlag, Arthur H 1922- *BiE&WWA, NotNAT*
Dorland, Retta Mae *PupTheA*
Dorleac, Francoise 1941-1967 *FilmgC, HalFC 80, MotPP, OxFilm, WhScrn 74, -77, WhoHol B*
Dorleac, Francoise 1942-1967 *FilmAG WE, FilmEn, ForYSC*
Dorman, Elizabeth *NewGrD 80*
Dorman, Harold *RkOn*
Dorman, Shirley *Film 2*
D'Orme, Aileen 1877-1939 *NotNAT B, WhThe*
Dormer, Charles *Film 2*
Dormer, Daisy 1889- *WhThe*
Dorn, Alexander 1833-1901 *Baker 78*
Dorn, Dolores 1935- *BiE&WWA, FilmgC, ForYSC, HalFC 80, NotNAT, WhoHol A*
Dorn, Heinrich 1800-1892 *Baker 78*
Dorn, Heinrich Ludwig Egmont 1804-1892 *NewGrD 80*
Dorn, Philip d1975 *MotPP, WhoHol C*
Dorn, Philip 1901-1975 *FilmEn, What 5[port]*
Dorn, Philip 1902-1975 *WhScrn 77*
Dorn, Philip 1904-1975 *ForYSC*
Dorn, Philip 1905-1975 *FilmgC, HalFC 80*
Dorn, Rudi 1926- *CreCan 1*
Dorn, Veeder Van 1946- *AmSCAP 80*
Dorn, William 1893- *AmSCAP 66*
Dornay, Jules *WhThe*
Dorne, Mary *Film 2*
Dorne, Sandra 1925- *FilmgC, HalFC 80, IlWWBF[port], WhoHol A*
Dornel, Louis-Antoine 1680?-1756? *NewGrD 80*
Dorney, Richard d1921 *NotNAT B*
Dornton, Charles d1900 *NotNAT B*
Dornya, Maria *WhoOp 76*
Doro, Grace 1912- *AmSCAP 80*
Doro, Marie d1956 *MotPP, WhoHol B, WhoStg 1908*
Doro, Marie 1881-1956 *Film 1*
Doro, Marie 1882-1956 *FilmEn, Film 2, FilmgC, HalFC 80, NotNAT B, WhScrn 74, -77, WhThe*
Doronina, Tatyana 1933- *EncWT*
Dorotheos A Bemdba *NewGrD 80*
Dorough, Robert Lrod 1923- *EncJzS 70*
Dorr, Donald 1934- *MorBAP, WhoOp 76*
Dorr, Dorothy 1867- *WhThe, WhoStg 1908*
Dorr, Julia Caroline 1825-1913 *BiDAmM*
Dorr, Lester *WhoHol A*
Dorraine, Lucy *Film 2*
Dorree, Babette Bobbie 1906-1974 *WhScrn 77*
Dorris, Gaylon Doyle 1945- *AmSCAP 80*
Dors, Diana 1931- *FilmAG WE, FilmEn, FilmgC, ForYSC, HalFC 80, IlWWBF[port], -A[port], IntMPA 77, -75, -76, -78, -79, -80, MotPP, MovMk[port], WhoHol A, WhoHrs 80[port]*
Dorsam, Paul 1941- *ConAmC, IntWWM 77, -80*
Dorsay, Edmund 1897-1959 *WhScrn 74, -77*
D'Orsay, Fifi *MotPP, WhoHol A*
D'Orsay, Fifi 1904- *FilmEn, ThFT[port], What 3[port]*
D'Orsay, Fifi 1907- *Film 2, FilmgC, ForYSC, HalFC 80, MovMk*
D'Orsay, Lawrance 1853-1931 *WhThe, WhoStg 1906, -1908*
D'Orsay, Lawrence d1931 *Film 1, -2, WhoHol B*
D'Orsay, Lawrence 1853-1931 *NotNAT B*
D'Orsay, Lawrence 1860-1931 *WhScrn 74, -77*
Dorsch, Kaethe 1889-1957 *WhScrn 74, -77*
Dorsch, Kathe 1890-1957 *EncWT, Ent*
Dorset, Earl Of *McGEWD*
Dorsey *NewGrD 80*
Dorsey, Bill Ballantine 1932- *AmSCAP 80*
Dorsey, Bob Robert 1915-1965 *WhoJazz 72*
Dorsey, Donald Merrill 1953- *AmSCAP 80*
Dorsey, Edmund d1959 *WhoHol B*
Dorsey, Georgia Tom 1899- *NewGrD 80*
Dorsey, James 1904-1957 *BiDAmM, NewGrD 80*
Dorsey, James Elno 1905- *ConAmC*
Dorsey, Jimmy 1904-1957 *AmPS A, -B, AmSCAP 66, -80, Baker 78, BgBands 74, CmpEPM, FilmgC, HalFC 80, IlEncJ, NewGrD 80, NotNAT B, RkOn, WhScrn 74, -77, WhoHol B*
Dorsey, Jimmy James 1904-1957 *WhoJazz 72*
Dorsey, John *NewYTET*
Dorsey, Lee *RkOn[port]*
Dorsey, Thomas 1905-1956 *BiDAmM, NewGrD 80*
Dorsey, Thomas Andrew 1899- *BluesWW, DrBlPA, NewGrD 80*
Dorsey, Tommy 1905-1956 *AmPS A, -B, AmSCAP 80, Baker 78, BgBands 74[port], CmpEPM, HalFC 80, IlEncJ, MusMk[port], NewGrD 80, NotNAT B, RkOn, WhScrn 74, -77, WhoHol B, WhoJazz 72*
Dorsey Brothers, The *BgBands 74[port]*
Dorsey Brothers Orchestra *CmpEPM*
Dorso, Dick *NewYTET*
Dorst, Tankred 1925- *CnMD SUP, CroCD, EncWT, Ent, McGEWD, ModWD*
Dortch, Eileen Wier *ConAmC*
Dortort, David 1916- *IntMPA 77, -75, -76, -78, -79, -80, NewYTET*
Dorumsgaard, Arne 1921- *NewGrD 80*
Dorus-Gras, Josephine 1805-1896 *NewGrD 80*
Dorus-Gras, Julie 1805-1896 *CmOp, NewGrD 80*
Doruzka, Lubomir 1924- *IntWWM 77, -80*
Dorval 1798-1849 *NotNAT B*
Dorval, Mareal *Film 2*
Dorval, Marie-Thomas Amelie 1798-1849 *EncWT, Ent*
Dorval, Marie-Thomase-Amelie 1798-1849 *OxThe*
Dorvigny 1742-1812 *NotNAT B, OxThe*
Dorward, David Campbell 1933- *IntWWM 77, -80, WhoMus 72*
Dorziat, Gabrielle 1880- *FilmgC, HalFC 80, MovMk[port], WhThe*
Dorziat, Gabrielle 1886-1979 *FilmEn*
Doscher, Doris 1882-1970 *Film 1, WhoHol B*
Dose, Helena Elisabeth Astrid *WhoOp 76*
DosPassos, John 1896-1970 *BiE&WWA, CnMD, ModWD*
Doss, Adolf Von 1823-1886 *NewGrD 80*
DosSantos, Nelson Pereira *DcFM*
Dossett, Chappell *Film 2*
Dossick, Jane *WomWMM*
Dossor, Lance 1916- *IntWWM 77, -80, WhoMus 72*
Dostal, Nico 1885- *IntWWM 80*

Dostal, Nico 1895- *Baker 78, IntWWM 77, NewGrD 80*
Doster, Robert Franklin 1935- *IntWWM 77*
Dostoievsky, Feodor 1821-1881 *NotNAT B, OxThe*
Dostoievsky, Fyodor 1821-1881 *FilmgC, HalFC 80*
Dostoyevsky, Feodor 1821-1881 *NewEOp 71*
Dostoyevsky, Fyodor 1821-1881 *EncWT, Ent, NewGrD 80*
Dotrice, Karen 1955- *FilmgC, ForYSC, HalFC 80, WhoHol A*
Dotrice, Michele 1947- *HalFC 80, WhoHol A*
Dotrice, Roy *WhoHol A*
Dotrice, Roy 1923- *FilmgC, HalFC 80*
Dotrice, Roy 1925- *WhoThe 72, -77*
Dotson, Dennis 1946- *EncJzS 70*
Dotti, Anna Vincenza *NewGrD 80*
Dottsy *IlEncCM*
Doty, Weston 1915-1934 *WhScrn 74, -77, WhoHol B*
Doty, Winston 1915-1934 *WhScrn 74, -77, WhoHol B*
Dotzauer, Friedrich 1783-1860 *Baker 78, NewGrD 80*
Dotzauer, Karl Ludwig 1811-1897 *Baker 78*
Double Exposure *RkOn 2A*
Doubleday-Pirani, Leila *WhoMus 72*
Doubler, Margaret N *DancEn 78*
Doubrava, Jaroslav 1909-1960 *Baker 78, NewGrD 80*
Doubrovska, Felia 1896- *CnOxB, DancEn 78[port]*
Doucet, Catharine 1875-1958 *NotNAT B, ThFT[port], WhoHol B*
Doucet, Catherine 1875-1958 *FilmEn, HalFC 80, WhScrn 77, WhThe*
Doucet, H Paul 1886-1928 *Film 2*
Doucet, Louis-Joseph 1874-1959 *CreCan 1*
Doucet, M Paul 1886-1928 *WhScrn 74, -77*
Doucet, Paul 1886-1928 *Film 1, WhoHol B*
Doucett, Catherine *ForYSC*
Doucette, John *ForYSC, WhoHol A*
Dougall, Ian *ConDr 73, -77B*
Dougan, Vera Wardner 1898- *IntWWM 77*
Dougherty, Anne Helena 1908- *AmSCAP 66, -80*
Dougherty, Ariel *WomWMM B*
Dougherty, Celius 1902- *AmSCAP 66, Baker 78, ConAmC*
Dougherty, Celius H 1902- *AmSCAP 80*
Dougherty, Christina Hosack 1938- *IntWWM 77, -80*
Dougherty, Dan 1897-1955 *AmSCAP 66, -80*
Dougherty, Eddie 1915- *WhoJazz 72*
Dougherty, Frances Ann *BiE&WWA, NotNAT*
Dougherty, Jack 1895-1938 *Film 2*
Dougherty, Jennie 1888- *AmSCAP 66*
Dougherty, Joseph Rymer 1949- *AmSCAP 80*
Dougherty, Virgil Jack 1895-1938 *WhScrn 74, -77*
Douglas, Al 1907- *AmSCAP 66*
Douglas, Angela 1940- *HalFC 80*
Douglas, Audrey 1926- *IntWWM 80*
Douglas, Bert 1900-1958 *AmSCAP 66, -80*
Douglas, Billy 1908- *WhoJazz 72*
Douglas, Boots *CmpEPM*
Douglas, Byron 1865-1935 *Film 2, NotNAT B, WhScrn 74, -77, WhoHol B*
Douglas, Carl *RkOn 2[port]*
Douglas, Carol 1948- *RkOn 2[port]*
Douglas, Charles 1956- *AmSCAP 80*
Douglas, Charles Winfred 1867-1944 *BiDAmM*
Douglas, Christine *PupTheA*
Douglas, Clive Martin 1903- *IntWWM 77, -80, WhoMus 72*
Douglas, Clive Martin 1903-1977 *Baker 78, NewGrD 80*
Douglas, Darrell Ramon 1930- *AmSCAP 80*
Douglas, Diana *ForYSC, WhoHol A*
Douglas, Don 1905-1945 *WhScrn 74, -77, WhoHol B*
Douglas, Donald 1905-1945 *FilmgC, HalFC 80*
Douglas, Donald 1905-1947 *Film 2, ForYSC*
Douglas, Donna 1933- *HalFC 80, MotPP, WhoHol A*
Douglas, Doris 1918-1970 *WhScrn 77, WhoHol B*
Douglas, Dorothea d1962 *NotNAT B*
Douglas, Felicity 1910- *WhoThe 72, -77*
Douglas, Gavin *OxMus*
Douglas, Gordon *IntMPA 75, -76, -78, -79, -80*
Douglas, Gordon 1909- *BiDFilm, -81, CmMov, FilmEn, FilmgC, HalFC 80, IntMPA 77, MovMk, WhoHol A, WhoHrs 80, WorEFlm[port]*
Douglas, Gordon Leslie 1910- *IntWWM 77*
Douglas, Helen Gahagan *BiE&WWA, What 1[port]*
Douglas, Helen Gahagan 1910?- *WhoHrs 80*
Douglas, Jack 1927- *ConMuA 80B, HalFC 80*
Douglas, James *WhoHol A*
Douglas, James 1932- *IntWWM 77, -80, WhoMus 72*
Douglas, James 1933- *ForYSC*
Douglas, Jeanne Pratt 1931- *IntWWM 77*
Douglas, Johnny 1922- *WhoMus 72*
Douglas, Josephine *WhoHol A*
Douglas, K C 1913-1975 *BluesWW[port]*
Douglas, Keith d1973 *WhoHol B*
Douglas, Kenneth d1923 *WhThe*
Douglas, Kent d1966 *ForYSC, WhScrn 74, -77, WhoHol B*
Douglas, Kirk *MotPP, WhoHol A*
Douglas, Kirk 1916- *BiDFilm, -81, CmMov, FilmEn, FilmgC, ForYSC, HalFC 80, MovMk[port], OxFilm, WorEFlm[port]*
Douglas, Kirk 1918- *IntMPA 77, -75, -76, -78, -79, -80*
Douglas, Kirk 1920- *BiE&WWA, NotNAT*
Douglas, Laerteas Larry 1917- *AmSCAP 80*
Douglas, Larry 1914- *BiE&WWA, NotNAT*
Douglas, Larry 1917- *AmSCAP 66, BiDAmM*
Douglas, Leal *Film 1, -2*
Douglas, Lewis W 1894- *BiE&WWA*
Douglas, Lillian *Film 2*
Douglas, Lizzie 1897-1973 *BluesWW[port]*
Douglas, Lloyd C 1877-1951 *FilmgC, HalFC 80*
Douglas, Marian *WhoHol A*
Douglas, Marie Booth d1932 *NotNAT B*
Douglas, Melvin 1901- *BiE&WWA, NotNAT*
Douglas, Melvyn 1901- *BiDFilm, -81, FamA&A[port], FilmEn, FilmgC, ForYSC, HalFC 80, IntMPA 77, -75, -76, -78, -79, -80, MGM[port], MotPP, MovMk[port], OxFilm, WhoHol A, WhoThe 72, -77, WorEFlm*
Douglas, Michael 1944- *FilmEn*
Douglas, Michael 1945- *FilmgC, HalFC 80, IntMPA 77, -75, -76, -78, -79, -80, WhoHol A*
Douglas, Mike *AmPS B, CmpEPM*
Douglas, Mike 1925- *IntMPA 79, -80, NewYTET, RkOn 2[port], WhoHol A*
Douglas, Milton 1906-1970 *WhScrn 77, WhoHol B*
Douglas, Minnie *NewGrD 80*
Douglas, Minnie 1902-1973 *BlkWAB[port]*
Douglas, Nigel *IntWWM 77, -80*
Douglas, Nigel 1934- *WhoMus 72, WhoOp 76*
Douglas, Pamela *WomWMM*
Douglas, Patrick *OxMus*
Douglas, Paul 1899-1959 *OxFilm*
Douglas, Paul 1907-1959 *BiDFilm, -81, FilmEn, FilmgC, ForYSC, HalFC 80, MotPP, MovMk[port], NotNAT B, WhScrn 74, -77, WhoHol B, WorEFlm*
Douglas, R H d1935 *NotNAT B*
Douglas, Richard d1911 *NotNAT B*
Douglas, Richard Roy 1907- *IntWWM 77, -80, WhoMus 72*
Douglas, Robert 1909- *CmMov, FilmEn, FilmgC, HalFC 80, IlWWBF, Vers A[port], WhThe*
Douglas, Robert 1910- *BiE&WWA, ForYSC, NotNAT, WhoHol A*
Douglas, Rodney K *BlkAmP*
Douglas, Ron *AmSCAP 80*
Douglas, Roy 1907- *NewGrD 80*
Douglas, Samuel Osler 1943- *ConAmC*
Douglas, Scott 1927- *CnOxB, DancEn 78[port]*
Douglas, Sharon *WhoHol A*
Douglas, Susan 1926- *ForYSC*
Douglas, Tom 1903- *Film 2, ForYSC, WhThe*
Douglas, Tommy 1911- *WhoJazz 72*
Douglas, Torrington *WhoThe 72, -77*
Douglas, Valerie *IntMPA 79, -80*
Douglas, Valerie 1938-1969 *WhScrn 77, WhoHol B*
Douglas, Wallace d1958 *WhoHol B*
Douglas, Wallace 1911- *WhoThe 72, -77*
Douglas, Wally *WhScrn 74, -77*
Douglas, Warren *ForYSC*
Douglas, William 1944- *ConAmC, OxMus*
Douglas-Hamilton, Patrick George 1950- *IntWWM 77*
Douglas Tutt, Jean Marjorie *IntWWM 77, -80*
Douglas-Williams, Eiluned *WhoMus 72*
Douglas-Williams, Eiluned 1919- *IntWWM 80*
Douglass, Albert 1864-1940 *WhThe*
Douglass, David d1786 *NotNAT B, OxThe, PlP&P*
Douglass, Mrs. David d1773 *PlP&P*
Douglass, Frederick 1817-1895 *BlkAmP*
Douglass, Harry Monroe 1916- *AmSCAP 80*
Douglass, Jane *AmSCAP 80*
Douglass, John d1874 *NotNAT B*
Douglass, John d1917 *NotNAT B*
Douglass, Joseph 1869-1935 *BiDAmM*
Douglass, Kent *FilmEn*
Douglass, Margaret d1949 *NotNAT B*
Douglass, R H *WhThe*
Douglass, Robert Satterfield 1919- *IntWWM 77, -80*
Douglass, Stephen 1921- *BiE&WWA, NotNAT, WhoThe 72, -77*
Douglass, Steven L 1945- *IntWWM 80*
Douglass, Steven L 1946- *IntWWM 77*
Douglass, Vincent 1900-1926 *NotNAT B, WhThe*
Doukan, Pierre 1927- *IntWWM 80*
Douking, Georges 1902- *EncWT*
Douliez, Paul 1905- *IntWWM 80*
Doulukhanova, Zara 1918- *WhoMus 72*
Dounias, Minos E 1900-1962 *Baker 78, NewGrD 80*
Dounis, Demetrius Constantine 1886-1954 *Baker 78*
Dourif, Brad 1950- *HalFC 80, WhoHol A*
Dourlen, Victor-Charles-Paul 1780-1864 *NewGrD 80*
Douroux Family *NewOrJ*
Dousmoulin, Joseph *NewGrD 80*
Doussant, Herbert 1931- *WhoOp 76*
Doutremont, Henri *CreCan 2*
Doutreval, Andre 1942- *CnOxB*
Douty, Nicholas 1870-1955 *BiDAmM*
Douvan-Torzow, J N *Film 2*
Douvere, Andre Alphonse Theophile 1924- *IntWWM 77, -80*
Douvillier, Suzanne Theodore d1826 *CnOxB*
Douvillier, Suzanne Theodore 1788-1826 *DancEn 78*
Douwes, Claas 1650?-1725? *NewGrD 80*
Douy, Max 1914- *DcFM, FilmEn*
DoValle, Raul Thomas Oliveira 1936- *IntWWM 77, -80*
Dove, Billie *MotPP*
Dove, Billie 1900- *FilmEn, FilmgC, ForYSC, HalFC 80, MovMk, ThFT[port]*
Dove, Billie 1903- *What 2[port]*
Dove, Billie 1904- *Film 2, TwYS, WhoHol A*
Dove, Lewis U, Jr. 1925-1965 *AmSCAP 66, -80*
Dove, Ronnie 1940- *RkOn 2[port]*
Dovells, The *RkOn*
Dover, Nancy *Film 2*
Dover, William B 1901- *IntMPA 75, -76*
Dovey, Alice 1885-1969 *AmPS B, Film 1, WhScrn 74, -77, WhThe, WhoHol B*
Dovorsko, Jess *Film 2*
DoVries, Harry *Film 2*
Dovzhenko, Alexander 1894-1956 *BiDFilm, -81, DcFM, FilmgC, HalFC 80, MovMk[port], OxFilm, WhScrn 74, -77, WomWMM, WorEFlm*
Dovzhenko, Alexander Petrovich 1894-1956 *FilmEn*
Dow, Ada d1926 *NotNAT B*
Dow, Alexander d1779 *NotNAT B*
Dow, Clara 1883-1969 *WhThe*
Dow, Daniel 1732-1783 *NewGrD 80*
Dow, Maree *WhoHol A*
Dow, Mary E *Film 2*
Dow, Pamella Elder 1941- *WhoMus 72*
Dow, Peggy 1928- *FilmEn, FilmgC, ForYSC,*

HalFC 80, MotPP, WhoHol A
Dowd, Charles 1948- *IntWWM 77, -80*
Dowd, Harrison 1897-1964 *BiE&WWA, NotNAT B, WhoHol A*
Dowd, John Andrew 1932- *ConAmC*
Dowd, Kaye *WhoHol A*
Dowd, M'el *BiE&WWA, NotNAT, WhoHol A, WhoThe 72, -77*
Dowd, Nancy Ellen *WomWMM B*
Dowd, Ronald 1914- *CmOp, IntWWM 77, -80, NewGrD 80, WhoMus 72*
Dowd, Tom *ConMuA 80B, IlEncR*
Dowd, William 1922- *NewGrD 80*
Dowdall, Ann 1928- *WhoMus 72*
Dowdeswell, Reginald Owen 1903- *WhoMus 72*
Dowdy, Bill 1933- *BiDAmM*
Dowdy, Helen *DrBlPA*
Dowell, Anthony 1943- *CnOxB, DancEn 78*
Dowell, Horace Kirby 1904-1974 *AmSCAP 66, -80*
Dowell, Joe 1940- *RkOn*
Dowell, Ray *ConMuA 80B*
Dowell, Saxie 1904-1974 *BgBands 74, CmpEPM, WhoJazz 72*
Dower, Catherine A 1924- *IntWWM 77, -80*
Dowiakowska-Klimowiczowa, Bronislawa 1840-1910 *NewGrD 80*
Dowlan, William C *Film 1*
Dowland, John 1562-1626 *Baker 78, BnBkM 80, OxMus*
Dowland, John 1563-1626 *CmpBCM, DcCom 77, DcCom&M 79, GrComp, MusMk, NewGrD 80*
Dowland, Robert 1586?-1641 *OxMus*
Dowland, Robert 1591-1641 *Baker 78, NewGrD 80*
Dowling, Allan 1903- *AmSCAP 66*
Dowling, Constance 1920-1969 *ForYSC*
Dowling, Constance 1923-1969 *FilmgC, HalFC 80, WhoHol B*
Dowling, Denis Valentine *CmOp, WhoMus 72*
Dowling, Doris 1921- *FilmgC, HalFC 80, WhoHol A*
Dowling, Doris 1922- *ForYSC*
Dowling, Eddie d1976 *Film 2, WhoHol C*
Dowling, Eddie 1894- *What 2[port], WhoThe 72*
Dowling, Eddie 1894-1976 *BiE&WWA, EncMT, HalFC 80, NotNAT B, PlP&P[port], WhThe*
Dowling, Eddie 1895- *CmpEPM*
Dowling, Eddie 1895-1976 *AmSCAP 66*
Dowling, Eric 1907- *IntWWM 77*
Dowling, Joan 1928-1954 *NotNAT B, WhScrn 74, -77, WhThe, WhoHol B*
Dowling, Joan 1929-1954 *FilmgC, HalFC 80*
Dowling, Joseph J 1848-1928 *WhScrn 74, -77, WhoHol B*
Dowling, Joseph S 1850-1928 *Film 1, -2, TwYS*
Dowling, Robert W 1895-1973 *BiE&WWA, NotNAT B*
Dowlining, Constance 1920-1969 *WhScrn 74, -77*
Down, John *Film 2*
Down, Lesley-Ann 1954- *IntMPA 80*
Down, Lesley-Anne 1954- *FilmEn, HalFC 80*
Down Towners *BiDAmM*
Downbeats *BiDAmM*
Downer, Alan 1912- *BiE&WWA*
Downes, Derek William 1933- *WhoMus 72*
Downes, Edward 1926- *CmOp*
Downes, Edward Olin Davenport 1911- *Baker 78, IntWWM 77, -80, NewGrD 80*
Downes, Edward Olin Davenport 1924- *Baker 78, NewGrD 80*
Downes, Edward Olin Davenport 1926- *WhoOp 76*
Downes, Edwin Olin 1886-1955 *BiDAmM*
Downes, Gwladys Violet 1915- *CreCan 2*
Downes, John *OxThe*
Downes, Lewis Thomas 1824-1910 *BiDAmM*
Downes, Olin 1886-1955 *Baker 78, NewGrD 80, WhScrn 74, -77*
Downes, Ralph William 1904- *IntWWM 77, -80, NewGrD 80, WhoMus 72*
Downey, Fairfax Davis 1893- *AmSCAP 66, -80*
Downey, James Cecil 1931- *IntWWM 77, -80*
Downey, John Wilham 1927- *AmSCAP 80, Baker 78, ConAmC, IntWWM 77, -80*
Downey, Morton d1961 *AmPS B, WhoHol A*
Downey, Morton 1901-1961 *AmSCAP 66, -80, BiDAmM, CmpEPM*
Downey, Morton 1902-1961 *Film 2, ForYSC, What 2[port]*
Downey, Raymond J 1912- *AmSCAP 80*
Downey, Raymond Joseph 1914- *AmSCAP 66*
Downey, Robert 1936- *FilmEn*
Downey, Roger Bayard 1937- *ConAmTC*
Downey, Sean Morton, Jr. 1933- *AmSCAP 66, -80*
Downie, Andrew 1922- *WhoMus 72*
Downing *PupTheA*
Downing, David 1943- *DrBlPA*
Downing, Harry 1894-1972 *WhScrn 77, WhoHol B*
Downing, Henry Frances 1851- *BlkAmP*
Downing, Joseph 1903-1975 *WhScrn 77, WhoHol C*
Downing, Robert d1975 *WhoHol C*
Downing, Robert 1914-1975 *BiE&WWA, NotNAT, -B*
Downing, Robert 1915-1975 *WhScrn 77*
Downing, Robert L 1857-1944 *NotNAT B, WhoStg 1906, -1908*
Downing, Walter 1874-1937 *WhScrn 74, -77, WhoHol B*
Downs, Cathy 1924- *FilmgC, HalFC 80, MotPP*
Downs, Cathy 1926- *ForYSC*
Downs, Hugh 1921- *IntMPA 77, -75, -76, -78, -79, -80, NewYTET*
Downs, Jane *WhoThe 72, -77*
Downs, Johnny 1913- *CmpEPM, FilmEn, Film 2, FilmgC, ForYSC, HalFC 80, What 4[port], WhoHol A*
Downs, Lamont Wayne 1951- *ConAmC*
Downs, M Clifford, III 1953- *AmSCAP 80*
Downs, Thomas Nelson 1867-1938 *MagIlD*
Downs, William Andrew 1890- *AmSCAP 66*
Dowsey, Rose Walker *WhScrn 74, -77*
Dowson, Graham R 1923- *IntMPA 77, -75, -76, -78, -79, -80*
Dowton, Emily d1924 *NotNAT B*
Dowton, William 1764-1851 *NotNAT B, OxThe*
Doxat-Pratt, Bernard E 1896- *IlWWBF*
Doyague, Manuel Jose 1755-1842 *NewGrD 80*
Doyen, Albert 1882-1935 *Baker 78*
Doyen, Ginette 1921- *WhoMus 72*
Doyle, Sir Arthur Conan 1859-1930 *FilmgC, HalFC 80, NotNAT B, PlP&P, WhThe, WhoHrs 80*
Doyle, Bobby *Film 2*
Doyle, Buddy 1901-1939 *WhScrn 74, -77, WhoHol B*
Doyle, David 1925- *HalFC 80, WhoHol A*
Doyle, Desmond 1932- *CnOxB, DancEn 78*
Doyle, Frank 1911- *IntMPA 75, -76*
Doyle, Gene 1909- *BiE&WWA*
Doyle, James d1927 *NotNAT B*
Doyle, James S *Film 2*
Doyle, John T 1873-1935 *Film 2, NotNAT B, WhScrn 77, WhoHol B*
Doyle, Kevin 1933- *IntMPA 77, -75, -76, -78, -79, -80*
Doyle, Laird 1907-1936 *HalFC 80*
Doyle, Len 1893-1959 *NotNAT B, WhScrn 74, -77*
Doyle, Mariam d1962 *NotNAT B*
Doyle, Maxine 1915-1973 *WhScrn 77, WhoHol B*
Doyle, Mimi *WhoHol A*
Doyle, Patricia 1915-1975 *WhScrn 77, WhoHol C*
Doyle, Regina 1907-1931 *Film 2, TwYS, WhScrn 74, -77*
Doyle, Robert 1939- *CreCan 1*
Doyle, Robert Joseph 1925- *AmSCAP 80*
Doyle, Walter 1899-1945 *AmSCAP 66, -80*
D'Oyly Carte, Bridget *WhoMus 72*
D'Oyly Carte, Richard 1844-1901 *NotNAT B, OxThe, BnBkM 80*
D'Oyly Carte, Rupert 1876-1948 *NotNAT B, WhThe*
Dozier, William M 1908- *FilmgC, HalFC 80, IntMPA 75, -76, NewYTET*
Dozsa, Imre 1941- *CnOxB*
Dozza, Evangelista *NewGrD 80*
Dr. Buzzard's Original Savannah Band *RkOn 2[port]*
Dr. Feelgood *ConMuA 80A, IlEncR[port]*
Dr. Hook *ConMuA 80A*
Dr. Hook And The Medicine Show *IlEncR RkOn 2[port]*
Dr. John 1940- *RkOn 2[port]*
Dr. John 1941- *IlEncR*
Dr. John, The Night Tripper *BiDAmM*
Dr. Seuss *AmSCAP 80*
Drabble, Margaret *WomWMM*
Drabek, Kurt 1912- *IntWWM 77*
Drabkin, William Morris 1947- *IntWWM 77, -80*
Drach, Michel 1930- *FilmEn, HalFC 80*
Drache, Heinz *WhoHrs 80*
Drachman, Ted 1945- *AmSCAP 80*
Drachmann, Holger Henrik Herholdt 1846-1908 *NotNAT B, OxThe*
Draconi, Giovanni Andrea *NewGrD 80*
Draeger, Walter 1888- *IntWWM 77, -80*
Draeseke, Felix 1835-1913 *Baker 78, NewGrD 80*
Draga, George 1935- *Baker 78*
Dragatakis, Dimitri 1914- *NewGrD 80*
Dragatakis, Dimitris 1914- *DcCM*
Drager, Brian Michael 1943- *AmSCAP 80*
Drager, Hans-Heinz 1909-1968 *NewGrD 80*
Draghi, Antonio *OxMus*
Draghi, Antonio 1634?-1700 *NewGrD 80*
Draghi, Antonio 1635-1700 *Baker 78, MusMk*
Draghi, Bernardino d1592 *NewGrD 80*
Draghi, Bernardo d1592 *NewGrD 80*
Draghi, Giovanni Battista *Baker 78*
Draghi, Giovanni Battista 1640?-1708 *NewGrD 80*
Draghi, Giovanni Battista 1667-1706 *OxMus*
Drago, Bernardo *NewGrD 80*
Drago, Cathleen d1938 *NotNAT B*
Dragoi, Sabin V 1894-1968 *Baker 78, NewGrD 80*
Dragon, Carmen 1914- *AmSCAP 66, -80, Baker 78, WhoMus 72*
Dragonette, Jessica *CmpEPM, PlP&P[port], What 1[port], WhoMus 72*
Dragonetti, Domenico 1763-1846 *Baker 78, BnBkM 80, NewGrD 80[port]*
Dragoni, Giovanni Andrea 1540?-1598 *NewGrD 80*
Dragoti, Stan *HalFC 80*
Dragoumis, Marc 1934- *NewGrD 80*
Dragoumis, Markos Ph 1934- *IntWWM 77, -80*
Dragovic, Ljiljana Cvetko 1934- *WhoOp 76*
Dragun, Osvaldo 1929- *CroCD*
Drain, Emile *Film 2*
Drainie, John 1916-1966 *CreCan 2, WhScrn 74, -77, WhoHol B*
Drake, Alfred *AmPS B*
Drake, Alfred 1914- *BiE&WWA, CmpEPM, CnThe, EncMT, FamA&A[port], FilmgC, HalFC 80, NotNAT, WhoHol A, WhoThe 72, -77*
Drake, Archie Arthur 1925- *WhoOp 76*
Drake, Betsy 1923- *FilmEn, FilmgC, ForYSC, HalFC 80, MotPP, WhoHol A*
Drake, Bryan Ernest Hare 1925- *IntWWM 77, -80, WhoMus 72, WhoOp 76*
Drake, Charles 1914- *FilmEn, FilmgC, ForYSC, HalFC 80, IntMPA 77, -75, -76, -78, -79, -80, WhoHol A*
Drake, Charlie 1925- *FilmgC, HalFC 80, IlWWBF[port], IntMPA 77, -75, -76, -78, -79, -80, RkOn*
Drake, Dona 1920- *FilmEn, FilmgC, ForYSC, HalFC 80, IntMPA 77, -75, -76, -78, -79, -80, WhoHol A*
Drake, Donna *MotPP*
Drake, Dorothy *Film 1, WhoHol A*
Drake, Earl R 1865-1916 *Baker 78, NewGrD 80*
Drake, Edwin Dale 1944- *AmSCAP 80*
Drake, Erik 1788-1870 *NewGrD 80*
Drake, Ervin M 1919- *AmSCAP 66, -80, BiDAmM, NewCBMT, PopAmC SUP[port]*
Drake, Fabia 1904- *FilmgC, HalFC 80, WhThe, WhoHol A*
Drake, Florence *PupTheA*
Drake, Frances *ForYSC*

Drake, Frances 1908- *FilmEn, ThFT[port], WhoHol A*
Drake, Frances 1912- *HalFC 80*
Drake, Frances Ann Denny d1875 *NotNAT B*
Drake, Sir Francis 1540?-1596 *OxMus*
Drake, George Warren James 1939- *IntWWM 77, -80*
Drake, James G 1802-1852 *BiDAmM*
Drake, Jim 1935- *AmSCAP 66, -80*
Drake, Josephine Eleanor 1931- *AmSCAP 80*
Drake, Josephine S d1929 *Film 2, WhScrn 74, -77, WhoHol B*
Drake, Milton 1916- *AmSCAP 66, -80, CmpEPM*
Drake, Nick 1948-1974 *ConMuA 80A, IlEncR*
Drake, Pauline *WhoHol A*
Drake, Pete 1932- *EncFCWM 69, IlEncCM[port]*
Drake, Peter 1933- *BiDAmM*
Drake, Ronald 1928- *BiE&WWA*
Drake, Ronald B 1937- *AmSCAP 80*
Drake, Samuel, Sr. 1768-1854 *FamA&A[port]*
Drake, Steve 1923-1948 *WhScrn 74, -77*
Drake, Susan 1946- *IntWWM 77, -80, WhoMus 72*
Drake, Sylvie 1930- *ConAmTC*
Drake, Tom *IntMPA 77, -75, -76, -78, -79, -80, MotPP*
Drake, Tom 1918- *FilmEn, ForYSC, HalFC 80, MGM[port], WhoHol A*
Drake, Tom 1919- *FilmgC, MovMk, What 4[port]*
Drake, William A 1899-1965 *WhThe*
Drakeford, Richard Jeremy 1936- *IntWWM 77, WhoMus 72*
Drakoulalos, Bill *PupTheA*
Dramatics, The *RkOn 2[port]*
Drane, Sam Dade d1916 *WhScrn 77*
Dranem 1869-1935 *WhScrn 74, -77, WhoHol B*
Drange, Emily d1961 *NotNAT B*
Drangosch, Ernesto 1882-1925 *Baker 78*
Dranishnikov, Vladimir Alexandrovich 1893-1939 *Baker 78, NewGrD 80*
Dransite, Robert Stanley 1933- *IntWWM 77*
Drapal, Julia 1917- *CnOxB*
Draper, Anne 1938- *BiE&WWA, NotNAT*
Draper, Charles 1869-1952 *NewGrD 80*
Draper, George William 1911- *WhoMus 72*
Draper, Glenn Wright 1928- *IntWWM 80*
Draper, Haydn 1889-1934 *NewGrD 80*
Draper, Joseph d1962 *NotNAT B*
Draper, Old Colonel 1855?-1915 *WhScrn 77*
Draper, Paul 1909- *CnOxB, DancEn 78[port], WhoHol A*
Draper, Paul 1913- *BiE&WWA, NotNAT*
Draper, Peter 1925- *FilmgC, HalFC 80*
Draper, Raymond Allen 1940- *BiDAmM, EncJzS 70*
Draper, Rusty *AmPS A, -B, RkOn[port]*
Draper, Ruth 1884-1956 *EncWT, Ent[port], NotNAT A, -B, OxThe*
Draper, Ruth 1889-1956 *WhThe*
Draper, Stephen 1906- *BiE&WWA, NotNAT*
Draper, Tom *ConMuA 80B*
Drashin, Sidney *ConMuA 80B*
Drasnin, Irv *NewYTET*
Draud, Georg 1573-1635? *NewGrD 80*
Draudius, Georg 1573-1635? *NewGrD 80*
Draut, Georg 1573-1635? *NewGrD 80*
Drawbaugh, Jacob W, Jr. 1928- *AmSCAP 66, -80*
Draycott, Wilfred 1848- *WhThe*
Draylin, Paul d1970 *WhoHol B*
Drayson, Edith d1926 *NotNAT B*
Drayton, Alfred 1881-1949 *Film 2, FilmgC, HalFC 80, IlWWBF, NotNAT B, WhScrn 74, -77, WhThe, WhoHol B*
Drayton, Clarence R, Jr. 1947- *AmSCAP 80*
Drayton, Michael 1563-1631 *McGEWD, PlP&P*
Drayton, Ronald *BlkAmP*
Drazinic, Ivan 1942- *IntWWM 77, -80*
Drdla, Frantisek Alois 1869-1944 *NewGrD 80*
Drdla, Franz Alois 1868-1944 *Baker 78, OxMus*
Drdla, Franz Alois 1869-1944 *NewGrD 80*
Dream Weavers *AmPS A*
Dreamlovers, The *RkOn*
Dreamweavers, The *RkOn*
Dreaper *NewGrD 80*
Drechsel *NewGrD 80*
Drechsler *NewGrD 80*
Drechsler, Joseph 1782-1852 *Baker 78, NewGrD 80*
Dreer, Herman 1889- *BlkAmP*
Dreesen, Tom *JoeFr*
Dreger, Alvin Brice 1912- *IntWWM 77, -80*
Dregert, Alfred 1836-1893 *Baker 78*
Dreher, Theodore 1912- *AmSCAP 80*
Dreher, Walter Arthur d1962 *NotNAT B*
Dreibrodt, Irving D 1920- *AmSCAP 80*
Dreier, Alex 1916- *HalFC 80*
Dreier, Hans 1884-1966 *FilmgC, HalFC 80*
Dreier, Hans 1885-1966 *FilmEn, WorEFlm*
Dreier, John T 1913- *BiE&WWA*
Dreier, Per Erling 1929- *IntWWM 77, -80*
Dreifuss, Arthur 1908- *FilmEn, FilmgC, HalFC 80, IntMPA 77, -75, -76, -78, -79, -80*
Dreiser, Edward M d1958 *NotNAT B*
Dreiser, Paul *NewGrD 80*
Dreiser, Theodore 1871-1945 *CnMD, FilmgC, HalFC 80, ModWD, NotNAT B, WhThe*
Drejsl, Radim 1923-1953 *Baker 78*
Drelinger, Art 1916- *WhoJazz 72*
Drennan, Dorothy Carter 1929- *CpmDNM 74*
Drennan, Dorothy E 1929- *ConAmC*
Drenters, Yosef Gertrudis 1929- *CreCan 2*
Dresdel, Sonia 1909-1976 *FilmgC, HalFC 80, WhoHol A, -C, WhoThe 72, -77*
Dresden, Albert Curley *Film 2*
Dresden, Sem 1881-1957 *Baker 78, CompSN[port], NewGrD 80, OxMus*
Drese, Adam 1620?-1701 *NewGrD 80*
Drese, Claus Helmut 1922- *WhoOp 76*
Dresel, Otto 1826-1890 *Baker 78*
Dressel *NewGrD 80*
Dressel, Christoph d1686 *NewGrD 80*
Dressel, Erwin 1909-1972 *Baker 78, NewGrD 80*
Dressel, Johann Christian 1687- *NewGrD 80*
Dressel, Johann Tobias 1687-1758 *NewGrD 80*
Dressel, Tobias 1635-1717 *NewGrD 80*
Dresser, Lee M 1941- *AmSCAP 80*
Dresser, Louise d1965 *AmPS B, MotPP, WhoHol B*
Dresser, Louise 1878-1965 *FilmEn, ThFT*
Dresser, Louise 1879-1965 *Film 2, ForYSC, MovMk[port], TwYS*
Dresser, Louise 1881-1965 *FilmgC, HalFC 80*
Dresser, Louise 1882-1965 *WhScrn 74, -77, WhThe*
Dresser, Mark 1952- *EncJzS 70*
Dresser, Norman 1916- *ConAmTC*
Dresser, Paul 1857-1906 *AmPS, AmSCAP 66, -80, BiDAmM, CmpEPM, NewGrD 80, NotNAT B, PopAmC[port], Sw&Ld B*
Dresskell, O Nadine 1911- *IntWWM 77*
Dresskell, Oleka Nadine 1911- *IntWWM 80*
Dressler *NewGrD 80*
Dressler, Eric 1896- *BiE&WWA, NotNAT*
Dressler, Eric 1900- *WhThe*
Dressler, Ernst Christoph 1734-1779 *NewGrD 80*
Dressler, Gallus 1533-1589 *NewGrD 80*
Dressler, Gunter Albert 1927- *WhoOp 76*
Dressler, Marie d1934 *GrMovC[port], MotPP, WhoHol B, WhoStg 1906, -1908*
Dressler, Marie 1868-1934 *ThFT[port]*
Dressler, Marie 1869-1934 *BiDFilm, -81, CmpEPM, EncMT, FilmEn, Film 1, -2, FilmgC, Funs[port], HalFC 80, JoeFr[port], MGM[port], MovMk[port], NotNAT B, OxFilm, TwYS, WhScrn 74, -77, WhThe, WorEFlm*
Dressler, Marie 1870-1934 *ForYSC*
Dressler, Marie 1871-1934 *OxThe*
Dreszer, Anastazy Wilhelm 1845-1907 *NewGrD 80*
Dretke, Leora Nylce *ConAmC*
Dretke, Leora Nylee *AmSCAP 80*
Dretzel *NewGrD 80*
Dretzel, Cornelius Heinrich 1697-1775 *NewGrD 80*
Dretzel, Georg 1608?-1676? *NewGrD 80*
Dretzel, Valentin d1599 *NewGrD 80*
Dretzel, Valentin 1578-1658 *NewGrD 80*
Dretzl *NewGrD 80*
Dreux d1805 *NewGrD 80*
Dreux, Jacques-Philippe *NewGrD 80*
Dreux, Jean *NewGrD 80*
Drever, Constance d1948 *NotNAT B, WhThe*
Dreves, Guido Maria 1854-1909 *Baker 78, NewGrD 80*
Dreville, Jean 1906- *DcFM, FilmEn, FilmgC, HalFC 80*
Drew, Ann 1891-1974 *Film 2, WhScrn 77, WhoHol B*
Drew, David *WhoHol A*
Drew, David 1930- *IntWWM 77, -80, NewGrD 80, WhoMus 72*
Drew, David 1938- *CnOxB*
Drew, Ellen 1915- *FilmEn, FilmgC, ForYSC, HalFC 80[port], IntMPA 77, -75, -76, -78, -79, -80, MotPP, MovMk[port], ThFT[port], WhoHol A*
Drew, Gene *WhoHol A*
Drew, Georgiana Emma 1856-1892 *EncWT, PlP&P*
Drew, Gladys Rankin d1914 *WhScrn 77*
Drew, James 1929- *AmSCAP 80, Baker 78, CpmDNM 77, -78, -79, ConAmC, IntWWM 77, -80*
Drew, Jerry *Film 2*
Drew, John 1827-1862 *EncWT, FamA&A[port], NotNAT B, OxThe*
Drew, John 1853-1927 *CnThe, EncWT, Ent, FamA&A[port], Film 1, NotNAT A, -B, OxThe, PlP&P[port], WhThe, WhoStg 1906, -1908*
Drew, Mrs. John 1818-1897 *FamA&A[port]*
Drew, Mrs. John 1820-1897 *PlP&P*
Drew, Kenneth Sidney 1928- *BiDAmM, EncJzS 70*
Drew, Kenny 1928- *CmpEPM*
Drew, Kenny Sidney 1928- *AmSCAP 80*
Drew, Lillian *Film 1*
Drew, Louisa d1954 *NotNAT B*
Drew, Louisa Lane 1820-1897 *EncWT, Ent, NotNAT A, -B, OxThe*
Drew, Lowell *Film 2*
Drew, Lucille McVey d1925 *NotNAT B*
Drew, Michael *ConAmTC*
Drew, Paul *ConMuA 80B*
Drew, Philip Yale *Film 2*
Drew, Polly *WomWMM*
Drew, Robert J *WhoHol A*
Drew, Roderick 1940-1970 *CnOxB, DancEn 78*
Drew, Roland 1903- *Film 2, ForYSC, TwYS*
Drew, S Rankin 1892-1918 *Film 1, WhScrn 77*
Drew, Sidney 1864-1919 *TwYS, WhScrn 77, WhoHol B, WomWMM*
Drew, Sidney 1864-1920 *EncWT, Film 1, FilmgC, HalFC 80*
Drew, Sidney 1868-1919 *OxThe*
Drew, Mrs. Sidney 1868-1925 *FilmgC, HalFC 80*
Drew, Mrs. Sidney 1890-1925 *WhScrn 74, -77, WhoHol B*
Drew, Mrs. Sidney 1895-1925 *TwYS*
Drewanz, Hans 1929- *WhoOp 76*
Drewery, Isiah 1942- *AmSCAP 80*
Drewitt, Stanley 1878- *WhThe*
Drews, Steve 1945- *ConAmC*
Drexel, Johann Chrysostomus 1758-1801 *NewGrD 80*
Drexel, Johann Evangelist *NewGrD 80*
Drexel, Nancy 1910- *Film 2, TwYS*
Drexler, Elias J 1911- *IntMPA 77, -75, -76, -78, -79, -80*
Drexler, Rosalyn 1926- *ConDr 73, -77, NotNAT*
Drexler, Werner 1928- *IntWWM 77*
Dreyer, Bernd 1946- *CnOxB*
Dreyer, Carl Theodor 1889-1968 *BiDFilm, -81, ConLC 16, DcFM, FilmEn, FilmgC, HalFC 80, MovMk[port], OxFilm, WhoHrs 80, WorEFlm*
Dreyer, Dave 1894- *AmSCAP 66, -80, CmpEPM*
Dreyer, Giovanni Filippo Maria 1703?-1772 *NewGrD 80*
Dreyer, Johann Melchior 1747-1824 *Baker 78, NewGrD 80*
Dreyer, Max 1862-1946 *ModWD*
Dreyfus, Alfred 1859-1935 *FilmgC, HalFC 80, OxFilm*
Dreyfus, George 1928- *Baker 78, IntWWM 77, -80, NewGrD 80*

Dreyfus, Huguette 1928- *IntWWM 77, -80, NewGrD 80*
Dreyfuss, Henry 1904- *WhThe*
Dreyfuss, Jane 1924- *BiE&WWA*
Dreyfuss, Michael 1928-1960 *NotNAT B, WhScrn 74, -77, WhoHol B*
Dreyfuss, Richard 1948- *FilmEn*
Dreyfuss, Richard 1949- *HalFC 80, IntMPA 77, -75, -76, -78, -79, -80, WhoHol A, WhoHrs 80[port]*
Dreyschock, Alexander 1818-1869 *Baker 78, BnBkM 80, NewGrD 80*
Dreyschock, Felix 1860-1906 *Baker 78*
Dreyschock, Raimund 1824-1869 *Baker 78*
Drieberg, Friedrich Von 1780-1856 *Baker 78*
Driesch, Kurt 1904- *IntWWM 80*
Driessler, Johannes 1921- *Baker 78, DcCM, NewGrD 80*
Driffelde *NewGrD 80*
Drifters, The *AmPS A, -B, BiDAmM, ConMuA 80A, IlEncR, RkOn[port]*
Driftin' Slim *BluesWW*
Driftin' Smith *BluesWW*
Driftwood, Jimmie 1917- *IlEncCM*
Driftwood, Jimmy 1917- *BiDAmM, CounME 74, -74A, EncFCWM 69*
Driggers, Donald Clayton 1893-1972 *WhScrn 77, WhoHol B*
Driggs, Collins H 1911-1966 *AmSCAP 66, -80*
Drigo, Riccardo 1846-1930 *Baker 78, CnOxB, DancEn 78, NewGrD 80, OxMus*
Drilling, Joseph C 1922- *IntMPA 75, -76*
Drinkall, Roger Lee 1937- *WhoMus 72*
Drinker, Henry S, Jr. 1880-1965 *Baker 78, NewGrD 80*
Drinkwater, Albert Edwin d1923 *NotNAT B, WhThe*
Drinkwater, John 1882-1937 *CnMD, CnThe, EncWT, Ent, McGEWD[port], ModWD, NotNAT A, -B, OxMus, OxThe, PlP&P[port], WhThe*
Drischner, Max 1891-1971 *NewGrD 80*
Driscoll, Bobby 1936-1968 *FilmgC*
Driscoll, Bobby 1937-1968 *FilmEn, ForYSC, HalFC 80, HolP 40[port], WhScrn 74, -77, WhoHol B*
Driscoll, Charles Richard *IntWWM 77*
Driscoll, John 1947- *ConAmC*
Driscoll, Loren 1928- *NewGrD 80, WhoOp 76*
Driscoll, Patricia *WhoHol A*
Driscoll, Sam W 1868-1956 *WhScrn 74, -77*
Driscoll, Tex *Film 1*
Drislane, Jack *Sw&Ld B*
Drissen, Margit Else 1905- *IntWWM 77*
Drivas, Robert 1938- *BiE&WWA, ForYSC, HalFC 80, MotPP, NotNAT, PlP&P[port], WhoHol A, WhoThe 77*
Driver, Ann *WhoMus 72*
Driver, Donald 1952- *ConDr 73, -77D, WhoThe 77*
Driver, Robert Baylor 1942- *WhoOp 76*
Driver, Tom F 1925- *BiE&WWA, NotNAT*
Droardus Trecensis *NewGrD 80*
Drobacznski, Ryszard 1923- *IntWWM 80*
Drobisch, Moritz Wilhelm 1802-1896 *Baker 78*
Drobner, Mieczyslaw 1912- *IntWWM 77, -80*
Drocos, Jean *NewGrD 80*
Droeshout, Adrian 1897-1965 *WhScrn 77*
Drogheda, Earl Of 1910- *NewGrD 80*
Droghierina, La *NewGrD 80*
Drollet, David *Film 2*
Dromael, Jean 1600?-1650? *NewGrD 80*
Dromal, Jean 1600?-1650? *NewGrD 80*
Dromgold, George *Film 2*
Dromgoole, Nicholas 1927- *CnOxB*
Dromgoole, Patrick 1930- *WhoThe 72, -77*
Dromm, Andrea 1942- *ForYSC*
Drootin, Al 1916- *EncJzS 70*
Drootin, Albert M 1916- *EncJzS 70*
Drootin, Benjamin 1920- *EncJzS 70*
Drootin, Buzzy 1920- *EncJzS 70*
Drossin, Julius 1918- *CpmDNM 79, -80, ConAmC, IntWWM 80*
Droste, Doreen 1907- *ConAmC*
Droste-Hulshoff, Annette Von 1797-1848 *NewGrD 80*
Drottnerova, Marta 1941- *CnOxB*
Drouet, Louis Francois-Philippe 1792-1873 *Baker 78, NewGrD 80*
Drouet, Robert 1870-1914 *NotNAT B, WhScrn 77, WhThe, WhoStg 1906, -1908*
Drouin, Simone Routier *CreCan 1*
Droumael, Jean *NewGrD 80*
Droz, Henry *ConMuA 80B*
Drozdov, Anatol 1883-1950 *Baker 78*
Drozdov, Anatoly Nikolayevich 1883-1950 *NewGrD 80*
Drozdova, Margarita 1948- *CnOxB*
Drozdowski, Jan 1857-1918 *Baker 78, NewGrD 80*
Dru, Joanne 1923- *BiDFilm, -81, CmMov, FilmEn, FilmgC, ForYSC, HalFC 80, IntMPA 77, -75, -76, -78, -79, -80, MotPP, WhoHol A, WorEFlm*
Druce, Duncan 1939- *IntWWM 77, -80*
Druce, Herbert 1870-1931 *NotNAT B*
Druce, Hubert 1870-1931 *Film 2, WhScrn 77, WhThe*
Drucker, Arno Paul 1933- *IntWWM 77, -80*
Drucker, Stanley 1929- *BnBkM 80, NewGrD 80*
Druckman, Jacob 1928- *AmSCAP 80, Baker 78, BnBkM 80, CpmDNM 80, ConAmC, DcCM, NewGrD 80*
Druian, Joseph 1916- *IntWWM 77, -80*
Druilhe, Paule 1908- *IntWWM 77, -80*
Druks, Renate *WomWMM B*
Drulie, Sylvia 1928- *BiE&WWA, NotNAT*
Drumier, Jack *Film 2*
Drumier, Jack d1939 *WhoHol B*
Drumier, Jack 1869-1929 *WhScrn 74, -77*
Drumm, George 1874-1959 *AmSCAP 66, -80*
Drummond, Alexander M 1884-1956 *NotNAT B*
Drummond, Alice *WhoHol A*
Drummond, Dean *ConAmC A*
Drummond, Dean J 1949- *AmSCAP 80*
Drummond, Dolores 1834-1926 *NotNAT B, WhThe*
Drummond, John Richard Gray 1934- *IntWWM 80*
Drummond, Philip John 1951- *IntWWM 80*
Drummond, Pippa 1943- *IntWWM 80*
Drummond, Salome Blanche 1902- *IntWWM 77*
Drummond, Sophia Theresa Pemberton Deane *CreCan 1*
Drummond, William Henry 1854-1907 *CreCan 1*
Druriolanus, Augustus *OxThe*
Drury, Charles 1890- *AmSCAP 66, -80*
Drury, James *IntMPA 75, -76, -78, -79, -80*
Drury, James 1934- *FilmgC, HalFC 80, IntMPA 77, MotPP, WhoHol A*
Drury, James 1935- *ForYSC*
Drury, Weston, Jr. 1916- *IntMPA 77, -75, -76, -78, -79, -80*
Drury, William Price 1861-1949 *NotNAT B, WhThe*
Druschetzky, Georg 1745-1819 *NewGrD 80*
Drusina, Benedict De 1520?-1573? *NewGrD 80*
Druskin, Mikhail Semyonovich 1905- *NewGrD 80*
Drusky, Roy 1930- *CounME 74[port], IlEncCM[port]*
Drusky, Roy Frank 1930- *BiDAmM, CounME 74A, EncFCWM 69*
Druten, John Van *OxThe, PlP&P*
Drutman, Irving 1910-1978 *AmSCAP 66, -80*
Druxman, Michael B 1941- *IntMPA 77, -75, -76, -78, -79, -80*
Druzecky, Jiri *NewGrD 80*
Druzinsky, Edward 1924- *IntWWM 77, -80*
Dryden, John 1631-1700 *CnThe, DcPup, EncWT, Ent[port], McGEWD[port], NewEOp 71, NewGrD 80, NotNAT A, -B, OxMus, OxThe, PlP&P, REnWD[port]*
Dryden, Vaughan 1875- *WhThe*
Drye, John W, Jr. 1900- *BiE&WWA, NotNAT*
Dryffeld, Robert *NewGrD 80*
Dryhurst, Edward 1904- *FilmgC, HalFC 80, IlWWBF*
Drysdale, Grace *PupTheA*
Drysdale, Learmont 1866-1909 *Baker 78, NewGrD 80*
Drzecky, Jiri *NewGrD 80*
Drzewiecki, Conrad 1926- *CnOxB*
Drzewiecki, Zbigniew 1890-1971 *NewGrD 80*
Drzic, Marin 1508?-1567 *EncWT, Ent*
Du-Pond, Carlos Diaz 1911- *WhoOp 76*
Duals, The *RkOn*
Duane, Eddy *AmSCAP 80*
Duane, Frank 1926- *BiE&WWA*
Duane, Jack *Film 2, WhScrn 77*
Duane, L Ray 1897- *AmSCAP 66*
Duarte, Anselmo 1920- *DcFM, WorEFlm*
Duarte, Eva *FilmEn*
Duarte, John William 1919- *ConAmC A, IntWWM 77, -80*
Duarte, Maria Eva Evita 1919-1952 *WhScrn 77*
Dubbins, Don 1929- *FilmgC, HalFC 80, IntMPA 77, -75, -76, -78, -79, -80, WhoHol A*
Dube, Marcel 1930- *CnThe, CreCan 1, McGEWD, REnWD[port]*
Dube, Rodolphe 1905- *CreCan 1*
DuBellay, Joachim 1522-1560 *NewGrD 80*
Duben *NewGrD 80*
Duben, Anders 1597?-1662 *NewGrD 80*
Duben, Anders Von 1673-1738 *NewGrD 80*
Duben, Andreas 1597?-1662 *NewGrD 80*
Duben, Carl Gustaf 1700-1758 *NewGrD 80*
Duben, Carl Wilhelm Von 1724-1790 *NewGrD 80*
Duben, Gustaf 1628?-1690 *NewGrD 80*
Duben, Gustaf Von 1660-1726 *NewGrD 80*
Dubencourt, Jean *Film 2*
Dubenova, Dagmar 1940- *IntWWM 77, -80*
Dubens, Stanley 1920- *IntMPA 77, -75, -76, -78, -79, -80*
Dubensky, Arcady 1890-1966 *AmSCAP 66, -80, Baker 78, BiDAmM, ConAmC, OxMus*
Dubensky, Leo Arcady 1914- *AmSCAP 66, -80*
Duberman, Martin 1930- *ConDr 73, -77, CroCD, NatPD[port]*
Duberstein, Helen 1926- *NatPD[port]*
Dubey, Matt 1928- *AmSCAP 66, -80, BiE&WWA, NotNAT*
Dubillard, Roland 1923- *CnMD SUP, CroCD, Ent, ModWD, REnWD[port]*
DuBillon, Jhan *NewGrD 80*
Dubin, Al 1891-1945 *AmPS, AmSCAP 66, -80, BiDAmM, CmpEPM, NotNAT B, Sw&Ld C*
Dubin, Charles S *NewYTET*
Dubin, Joseph S *IntMPA 77, -75, -76, -78, -79, -80*
Dubinsky, Vladimir 1876-1938 *Baker 78*
Dublac, Emilio Antonio 1911- *IntWWM 80*
Duboff, Al 1909- *AmSCAP 66*
Dubois, Gene d1962 *NotNAT B*
DuBois, Gladys *Film 2*
DuBois, Helen *Film 2*
DuBois, Ja'net 1938- *DrBlPA*
DuBois, Jean 1888-1957 *WhScrn 74, -77*
DuBois, Leon 1859-1935 *Baker 78, NewGrD 80, OxMus*
Dubois, Marie 1937- *FilmAG WE[port], FilmEn*
Dubois, Philippe 1575?-1610 *NewGrD 80*
Dubois, Pierre-Max 1930- *Baker 78, NewGrD 80*
DuBois, Raoul Pene 1914- *WhoThe 72, -77*
DuBois, Rob Louis 1934- *DcCM, IntWWM 77, -80*
DuBois, Shirley Graham 1907-1977 *BlkAmP, MorBAP*
Dubois, Theodore 1837-1924 *Baker 78, BnBkM 80, NewGrD 80, OxMus*
DuBois, W E B 1868-1963 *MorBAP*
Dubois, William 1774?-1854? *BiDAmM*
DuBois, William Edward Burghardt 1868-1963 *BlkAmP*
Dubos, Jean-Baptiste 1670-1742 *NewGrD 80*
Dubosc, Gaston d1941 *NotNAT B*
DuBosc, Simon d1557? *NewGrD 80*
Dubose, Charles Benjamin 1949- *IntWWM 77, -80*
DuBoulay, Christine 1923- *DancEn 78*
Dubourg, A W d1910 *NotNAT B*
Dubourg, Evelyne 1929- *IntWWM 77, -80*
Dubourg, Matthew 1703-1767 *NewGrD 80, OxMus*
Dubov, Paul d1979 *WhoHrs 80*
Dubow, Marilyn 1942- *WhoMus 72*
DuBray, Claire 1893- *Film 2*
Dubreuil, Alain 1944- *CnOxB*

Dubreuil, Jean 1710?-1775 *NewGrD 80*
DuBrey, Clair 1893- *Film 2*
DuBrey, Claire 1893- *Film 1, TwYS*
DuBrey, Claire 1894- *ForYSC*
Dubrovay, Laszlo 1934- *IntWWM 80*
Dubrovay, Laszlo 1943- *Baker 78, IntWWM 77*
Dubrovska, Felia *CnOxB*
Dubs, The *RkOn[port]*
Dubuc *NewGrD 80, -80*
Dubuc, Alexander 1812-1898 *Baker 78*
DuBuisson *NewGrD 80*
DuBuisson d1688? *NewGrD 80*
DuBuisson d1710 *NewGrD 80*
DuBuisson, Gabriel *NewGrD 80*
DuBuisson, Jacques *NewGrD 80*
DuBuisson, Mathurin *NewGrD 80*
DuBuisson, Michel-Charles *NewGrD 80*
DuBuisson, R *NewGrD 80*
DuBuisson, Rene 1703- *NewGrD 80*
Dubuque, Alexander Ivanovich 1812-1898 *NewGrD 80*
DuBus, Gervais *NewGrD 80*
DuBus, Gerves *NewGrD 80*
DuBut *NewGrD 80*
Dubut, Louis *NewGrD 80*
Dubut, Nicolas 1638-1692? *NewGrD 80*
Dubut, Pierre *NewGrD 80*
Dubut, Toussaint *NewGrD 80*
DuBuysson *NewGrD 80*
Duc, Filippo 1550?-1586? *NewGrD 80*
Duc, Filippo De 1550?-1586? *NewGrD 80*
Duc, Philippe De 1550?-1586? *NewGrD 80*
DuCamp Guillebert, Pierre *NewGrD 80*
Ducander, Sten Carl 1923- *IntWWM 77, -80*
DuCange, Charles DuFresne, Sieur 1610-1688 *Baker 78, NewGrD 80*
Ducasse, Jean Roger *NewGrD 80*
Ducasse, Roger Jean Jules Aimable *BnBkM 80*
DuCaurroy, Eustache 1549-1609 *NewGrD 80*
DuCaurroy, Francois-Eustache, Sieur 1549-1609 *Baker 78*
DuCello, Countess *Film 1*
Duceppe, Jean 1924- *CreCan 1*
Ducey, Lillian *WomWMM*
Duch, Benedictus *NewGrD 80*
DuChambge, Pauline 1778?-1858 *NewGrD 80*
Duchamp, Jean-Francois 1949- *IntWWM 80*
Duchamp, Marcel *Film 2*
Duchamp, Marcel 1887-1968 *FilmEn*
Duchamps, Marcel 1887-1968 *WhScrn 77*
Duchaussoy, Michel 1938- *FilmAG WE[port]*
Duche DeVancy, Joseph-Francois 1668-1704 *NewGrD 80*
DuChemin, Nicolas 1515?-1576 *NewGrD 80*
Duchesne, Rafael 1900-1958 *AmSCAP 80*
Duchess Olga 1899-1953 *WhScrn 74, -77*
Duchin, Eddy d1951 *BgBands 74[port]*
Duchin, Eddy 1909-1951 *BiDAmM, WhScrn 74, -77, WhoHol B*
Duchin, Eddy 1910-1951 *CmpEPM*
Duchin, Peter 1937- *AmSCAP 80, WhoHol A*
Duchow, Marvin 1914- *IntWWM 77, -80*
Ducis, Benedictus 1490?-1544 *Baker 78, NewGrD 80*
Ducis, Jean-Francois 1733-1816 *NotNAT B, OxThe*
Ducke, Rudolf 1912- *WhoOp 76*
Duckles, Vincent Harris 1913- *Baker 78, NewGrD 80, OxMus*
Ducks Deluxe *ConMuA 80A*
Duckworth, Eleanor Ruth 1935- *IntWWM 77*
Duckworth, Guy 1924- *IntWWM 77*
Duckworth, Harry 1932- *WhoMus 72*
Duckworth, Manly 1906- *IntWWM 77, -80*
Duckworth, William 1943- *AmSCAP 80, CpmDNM 76, ConAmC*
Duckworth, Willie Lee 1924- *AmSCAP 66, -80*
Duclos 1668?-1748 *OxThe*
Duclos 1688?-1748 *NotNAT B*
DuClou, Adrienne Jeannette 1938- *IntWWM 77, -80*
Ducloux, Walter Ernest 1913- *AmSCAP 66, -80, Baker 78, IntWWM 77, -80*
Duclow, Geraldine 1946- *NotNAT*
Duconge, Albert 1895?- *NewOrJ*
Duconge, Oscar 1870?-1924? *NewOrJ*
Duconge, Pete 1900?- *NewOrJ*
DuConge, Peter 1903- *WhoJazz 72*
DuCousu, Antoine 1600?-1658 *NewGrD 80*
Ducrest DeSaint-Aubin, Stephanie-F *NewGrD 80*
Ducreux, Louis 1911- *WhoOp 76*
DuCroisy 1626-1695 *OxThe*
DuCroisy, Philibert Gassot 1626-1695 *NotNAT B*
Ducrow, Andrew 1793-1842 *Ent[port]*
DuCrow, Tate *Film 2*
Duczmal-Jaroszewska, Agnieszka 1946- *IntWWM 77, -80*
Dudarova, Veronica 1916- *Baker 78*
Duddy, John H 1904- *AmSCAP 66, -80, ConAmC A*
Duddy, Lyn *AmSCAP 66, -80*
Dudek, Gerd 1938- *EncJzS 70*
Dudek, Gerhard Rochus 1938- *EncJzS 70*
Dudek, Jaroslav 1932- *EncWT*
Dudek, Les *AmSCAP 80*
Dudek, Louis 1918- *CreCan 2*
Dudelson, Stanley E 1924- *IntMPA 77, -75, -76, -78, -79, -80*
Dudgeon, Elspeth 1871-1955 *WhScrn 77*
Dudgeon, Gus *ConMuA 80B*
Dudinskaya, Natalia Mikhailovna 1912- *CnOxB, DancEn 78[port]*
Dudlah, David 1892-1947 *WhScrn 74, -77*
Dudlay, Adeline d1934 *NotNAT B*
Dudley, Bernard *Film 2*
Dudley, Bide 1877-1944 *WhThe*
Dudley, Charles *Film 1, -2*
Dudley, Dave 1928- *CounME 74[port], -74A, EncFCWM 69, IlEncCM[port], RkOn[port]*
Dudley, David 1928- *BiDAmM*
Dudley, Doris *WhoHol A*
Dudley, Florence *Film 2*
Dudley, Jane 1912- *CmpGMD, CnOxB, DancEn 78*
Dudley, Jimmy 1903- *WhoJazz 72*
Dudley, John 1894-1966 *WhScrn 77*
Dudley, John Charles Eric 1938- *IntWWM 80*
Dudley, Jonathan 1940- *WhoOp 76*
Dudley, Margaret 1949- *BlkWAB[port]*
Dudley, Marjorie Eastwood *ConAmC A*
Dudley, Raymond Coleman 1931- *IntWWM 77, -80, WhoMus 72*
Dudley, Robert Y 1875-1955 *Film 2, WhScrn 74, -77, WhoHol B*
Dudley, S H *BlkAmP, BlksB&W C*
Dudley, Sherman H *BlksB&W*
Dudley, Walter Bronson 1877-1944 *AmSCAP 66, -80, NotNAT B*
Dudley, William 1947- *WhoOp 76, WhoThe 77*
Dudley-Ward, Penelope 1919- *HalFC 80, WhoHol A*
Dudman, Michael Philip 1938- *IntWWM 80*
Dudow, Slatan 1903-1963 *DcFM, FilmEn, OxFilm, WorEFlm*
Dudziak, Urszula 1943- *EncJzS 70*
Duehlmeier, Susan Hunter 1949- *IntWWM 80*
Duel, Pete 1940-1971 *FilmgC, HalFC 80*
Duel, Peter d1972 *WhoHol B*
Duel, Peter 1940-1971 *WhScrn 74, -77*
Duering, Carl *WhoHol A*
Duerkob, Dorothy *PupTheA*
Duerkob, Manfred *PupTheA*
Duerksen, George Louis 1934- *IntWWM 77, -80*
Duerr, Edwin 1906- *BiE&WWA, NotNAT*
Duerrenmatt, Friedrich 1921- *BiE&WWA, NotNAT*
Duese, Jacques *NewGrD 80*
Duesenberry, John 1950- *ConAmC*
Dueto, Antonio 1530?-1594? *NewGrD 80*
Duey, Philip Alexander 1901- *AmSCAP 66, -80*
Dufallo, Richard 1933- *Baker 78*
Dufau d1686? *NewGrD 80*
Dufau, Jenny 1878-1924 *Baker 78*
DuFault d1686? *NewGrD 80*
DuFaur DePibrac, Guy *NewGrD 80*
Dufaut d1686? *NewGrD 80*
Dufay, Guillaume 1400?-1474 *Baker 78, BnBkM 80, CmpBCM, GrComp, MusMk, NewGrD 80[port]*
Dufay, Guillermus 1400?-1474 *OxMus*
Dufay, Gulielmus 1400?-1474 *OxMus*
DuFeche, Willem *NewGrD 80*
Duff, Amanda *ForYSC*
Duff, Arleigh Elton 1924- *BiDAmM*
Duff, Gordon 1909- *IntMPA 75, -76*
Duff, Howard *MotPP, WhoHol A*
Duff, Howard 1913- *MovMk[port]*
Duff, Howard 1917- *FilmEn, FilmgC, ForYSC, HalFC 80, IntMPA 77, -75, -76, -78, -79, -80*
Duff, John 1787-1831 *NotNAT B*
Duff, Mary Ann 1794-1857 *NotNAT A, -B, OxThe*
Duff, Warren 1904-1973 *WhScrn 77*
Duffalo, Richard 1933- *NewGrD 80*
Duffell, Peter *IlWWBF*
Duffell, Peter 1924- *HalFC 80*
Duffell, Peter 1939?- *FilmgC*
Duffey, John *EncFCWM 69*
Duffield, George, Jr. 1818-1888 *BiDAmM*
Duffield, Harry *Film 2*
Duffield, Kenneth 1885- *WhThe*
Duffield, Samuel Augustus Willoughby 1843-1887 *BiDAmM*
Duffus, John Logie Lyall 1946- *IntWWM 80, WhoOp 76*
Duffy, Albert 1903- *IntMPA 77, -75, -76*
Duffy, Henry 1890-1961 *NotNAT B, WhScrn 74, -77*
Duffy, Herbert d1952 *NotNAT B*
Duffy, Jack 1879-1939 *Film 2, TwYS*
Duffy, Jack 1882-1939 *WhScrn 74, -77, WhoHol B*
Duffy, James *Film 2*
Duffy, James E *IntMPA 77, -75, -76, -78, -79, -80, NewYTET*
Duffy, James J, Jr. 1925- *AmSCAP 80*
Duffy, John *Film 1*
Duffy, John 1928- *AmSCAP 80, ConAmC, IntWWM 77, -80*
Duffy, John 1934- *BiDAmM*
Duffy, Maureen 1933- *ConDr 73, -77*
Duffy, Patrick *IntMPA 79, -80*
Duffy, Philip 1954- *IntWWM 80*
Duffy, Philip Edmund 1943- *IntWWM 77, -80*
Duffy, Terence 1940- *IntWWM 77, -80*
Duffy, Timothy E 1948- *AmSCAP 80*
Dufkin, Sam 1891-1952 *WhScrn 74*
Duflos, Huguette *Film 2*
Duflos, Raphael d1946 *NotNAT B, WhThe*
Dufly, Jacques *NewGrD 80*
Dufon, Jean 1574-1634 *NewGrD 80*
Dufort, Alphonse *Film 1*
Dufour, Yvon 1930- *CreCan 1*
Dufourcq, Norbert 1904- *Baker 78, IntWWM 77, -80, NewGrD 80, WhoMus 72*
Dufraine, Rosa 1901-1935 *WhScrn 74, -77*
Dufranne, Hector 1870-1951 *Baker 78*
Dufresne 1693-1767 *Ent, NotNAT B, OxThe*
Dufresne, Catherine-Marie-Jeanne Dupre d1759 *OxThe*
Dufresne, Charles 1611?-1684? *NotNAT B, OxThe*
Dufresny, Charles-Riviere 1648?-1724 *Ent[port]*
Dufresny, Charles-Riviere 1654-1724 *McGEWD, NotNAT B, OxThe*
Duga, Irene Verbitsky *WomWMM B*
Dugan, Delbert R 1935- *IntWWM 77*
Dugan, Dennis 1948- *HalFC 80*
Dugan, Franjo 1874-1948 *Baker 78*
Dugan, James *Film 2*
Dugan, Marie *WhScrn 74, -77*
Dugan, Mary *Film 2*
Dugan, Tom 1889-1955 *FilmgC, HalFC 80, Vers B[port], WhScrn 74, -77, WhoHol B*
Dugan, Tom 1889-1958 *Film 2, ForYSC, TwYS*
Dugan, Tommy 1889-1958 *Film 2*
Dugan, Walter *Film 2*
Dugan, William Francis *Film 2*
Dugas, Emma L N *AmSCAP 66, -80*
Dugas, Jean-Paul *CreCan 2*
Dugas, Marcel 1883-1947 *CreCan 1*
Dugay, Yvette 1932- *ForYSC*
Dugazon 1746-1809 *Ent*
Dugazon, Gustave 1782?-1826? *NewGrD 80*
Dugazon, Jean-Baptiste-Henri Gourgaud 1746-1809 *NotNAT B, OxThe*
Dugazon, Jean-Baptiste-Henry Gourgaud 1746-1809 *EncWT*
Dugazon, Louise-Rosalie 1755-1821 *Baker 78, NewGrD 80, NotNAT B*

Dugazon, Louise-Rose 1755-1821 *EncWT*
Dugazon, Marie-Marguerite Gourbaud 1742-1799 *NotNAT B*
Dugazon, Marie-Marguerite Gourgaud 1742-1799 *OxThe*
Dugdale, Sandra 1946- *WhoOp 76*
Duggan, Andrew 1923- *BiE&WWA, FilmgC, ForYSC, HalFC 80, MotPP, WhoHol A*
Duggan, Daniel Joseph 1949- *IntWWM 77, -80*
Duggan, Dorothy *PupTheA*
Duggan, Edmund d1938 *NotNAT B*
Duggan, Jan *ForYSC*
Duggan, Joseph Francis 1817-1900 *Baker 78*
Duggan, Maggie d1919 *NotNAT B*
Duggan, Pat 1910- *FilmgC, HalFC 80*
Duggan, Tom 1915-1969 *ForYSC, WhScrn 74, -77, WhoHol B*
Duggelin, Werner *WhoOp 76*
Dugger, Edwin 1940- *ConAmC*
Dugie, Red *NewOrJ*
DuGrain, Jean d1765? *NewGrD 80*
Dugren, Johann Jeremias d1765? *NewGrD 80*
Dugy, Hans *NewGrD 80*
Dugy, Johannes *NewGrD 80*
Duhamel, Antoine 1925- *Baker 78, NewGrD 80*
Duhamel, Georges 1884-1966 *ModWD*
Duhamel, Roger 1916- *CreCan 1*
Duhe, Lawrence 1887-1959 *NewOrJ[port]*
Duiffoprugcar *NewGrD 80*
Duiffoprugcar, Gaspar 1514-1571 *Baker 78*
Dujardin, Marbrianus *NewGrD 80*
Dujarric, Enrique DeMarchena-Dujarric *DcCM*
Dukakis, Olympia *NotNAT, WhoHol A*
Dukas, James *WhoHol A*
Dukas, Paul 1865-1935 *Baker 78, BnBkM 80, CmOp, CompSN[port], CnOxB, DancEn 78, DcCom&M 79, MusMk, NewEOp 71, NewGrD 80[port], OxMus*
Dukat, Josef Leopold Vaclav 1684-1717 *NewGrD 80*
Duke, Betty *AmSCAP 80*
Duke, Bill *BlkAmP*
Duke, Billy 1927- *AmSCAP 66*
Duke, Charles *AmSCAP 80*
Duke, Charlie 1913-1973 *NewOrJ[port]*
Duke, George Mac 1946- *AmSCAP 80, EncJzS 70*
Duke, Henry 1920- *WhoMus 72*
Duke, Ivy 1895- *Film 1, -2, FilmgC, HalFC 80*
Duke, Ivy 1896- *IlWWBF, WhThe*
Duke, John Woods 1899- *AmSCAP 66, -80, Baker 78, BiDAmM, CpmDNM 79, ConAmC, NewGrD 80, OxMus, WhoMus 72*
Duke, Keno 1927- *EncJzS 70*
Duke, Lewis Byron 1924- *ConAmC*
Duke, Patty *MotPP, WhoHol A*
Duke, Patty 1946- *BiE&WWA, FilmEn, FilmgC, ForYSC, HalFC 80, MovMk[port], NotNAT*
Duke, Patty 1947- *IntMPA 77, -75, -76, -78, -79, -80, RkOn 2[port]*
Duke, Richard *NewGrD 80*
Duke, Robert 1917- *BiE&WWA, NotNAT*
Duke, Vernon 1903- *AmPS, AmSCAP 66, -80, Baker 78, BiE&WWA, CnOxB, DcCM, OxMus*
Duke, Vernon 1903-1968 *NewCBMT*
Duke, Vernon 1903-1969 *BestMus, BiDAmM, CmpEPM, ConAmC, DancEn 78, EncMT, HalFC 80, NewGrD 80, NotNAT A, -B, PopAmC[port], PopAmC SUP, WhThe*
Duke Of Buckingham *PlP&P[port]*
Duke Of Earl *AmPS A*
Duke Of Paducah *CounME 74, EncFCWM 69*
Duke Of Paducah 1901- *IlEncCM[port]*
Dukelsky, Vladimir 1903-1969 *Baker 78, DcCM, MusMk, NewGrD 80, OxMus*
Dukelsy, Vladimir 1903-1969 *AmSCAP 80*
Dukes, Ashley 1885-1959 *CnThe, EncWT, NotNAT A, -B, OxThe, WhThe*
Dukes, John Willie 1942- *IntWWM 77*
Dukes, Laura 1907- *BlkWAB[port], BluesWW*
Dukes Of Dixieland *BiDAmM, CmpEPM*
Dukoff, Bobby *BgBands 74*
Dulac, Arthur 1910-1962 *NotNAT B, WhScrn 74, -77, WhoHol B*
Dulac, Germaine 1882-1942 *BiDFilm, -81, DcFM, FilmEn, FilmgC, HalFC 80, OxFilm, WomWMM, WorEFlm*
Dulack, Henrik 1913- *IntWWM 77, -80*
DuLany, Howard *CmpEPM*
Dulberger, Alan *ConMuA 80B*
Dulce, Maria 1936- *FilmAG WE*
Dulcken *NewGrD 80*
Dulcken, Anton d1763 *NewGrD 80*
Dulcken, Ferdinand Quentin 1837-1902 *BiDAmM*
Dulcken, Ferinand Quentin 1837-1901 *Baker 78*
Dulcken, Johan Daniel d1769? *NewGrD 80*
Dulcken, Johan Lodewijk 1736- *NewGrD 80*
Dulcken, Johan Lodewijk 1761- *NewGrD 80*
Dulcken, Luise 1811-1850 *Baker 78*
Duleba, Jozef 1842-1869 *NewGrD 80*
Dulemba, Jozef 1842-1869 *NewGrD 80*
Dulichius, Philipp 1562-1631 *NewGrD 80*
Dulichius, Philippus 1562-1631 *Baker 78*
Dulien, Tobe 1893-1969 *WhScrn 77*
Dulken, Sophie *NewGrD 80*
Dullea, Keir *IntMPA 75, -76, MotPP, WhoHol A*
Dullea, Keir 1936- *FilmEn, FilmgC, HalFC 80, IntMPA 77, -78, -79, -80, NotNAT, WhoHrs 80, WhoThe 77*
Dullea, Keir 1939- *ForYSC, MovMk[port]*
Dullin, Charles 1885-1949 *CnThe, EncWT, Ent, Film 2, NotNAT B, OxThe, WhScrn 77, WhThe, WhoHol B*
Dullot, Francois *NewGrD 80*
Dullzell, Paul 1879-1961 *NotNAT B, WhThe*
Dulmage, Will E 1883-1953 *AmSCAP 66*
DuLocle, Camille Theophile G DuCommun 1832-1903 *Baker 78, NewEOp 71*
Dulon, Friedrich Ludwig 1769-1826 *Baker 78, NewGrD 80*
Dulot, Francois *NewGrD 80*
Dulova, Vera Georgiyevna 1910- *NewGrD 80*
DuLuart, Yolanda *WomWMM B*
DuLuart, Yolande *WomWMM*
Dulzer, Marie Ann 1935- *ConAmTC*
Duma, Evelyn *Film 2*
Dumage, Pierre 1674-1751 *NewGrD 80*
Dumaine, Louis 1890?-1949? *NewOrJ[port]*
Dumanoir, Guillaume 1615-1697 *NewGrD 80*
Dumar, Luis *Film 2*
Dumas, Aaron *BlkAmP, MorBAP*
Dumas, Alexandre, Fils 1824-1895 *CnThe, DrBlPA, EncWT, Ent, FilmgC, HalFC 80, McGEWD[port], NewEOp 71, NotNAT A, -B, OxThe, REnWD[port]*
Dumas, Alexandre, Pere d1870 *PlP&P*
Dumas, Alexandre, Pere 1802-1870 *CnThe, DcPup, Ent, FilmgC, HalFC 80, McGEWD[port], NewEOp 71, NotNAT A, -B, REnWD[port]*
Dumas, Alexandre, Pere 1803-1870 *EncWT, OxThe*
Dumas, James Madison 1941- *BiDAmM*
Dumas, Jean *Film 2*
Dumas, Jean 1696-1770 *NewGrD 80*
DuMaurier, Daphne 1907- *BiE&WWA, EncWT, FilmgC, HalFC 80, NotNAT, OxThe, WhThe*
DuMaurier, George Louis Palmella Busson 1834-1896 *EncWT, NotNAT B, OxThe*
DuMaurier, Sir Gerald Hubert Edward 1873-1934 *CnThe, EncWT, Ent, Film 1, HalFC 80, NotNAT A, -B, OxThe, WhScrn 77, WhThe, WhoHol B*
DuMaurier, Guy 1865-1916 *EncWT, NotNAT B, OxThe*
DuMaurier, Muriel Beaumont 1881-1957 *OxThe*
Dumbar, Helen *Film 2*
D'Umberto, Angelo *AmSCAP 80*
Dumbrille, Dorothy 1897- *CreCan 2*
Dumbrille, Douglas 1888- *ForYSC*
Dumbrille, Douglas 1890-1974 *FilmEn, FilmgC, MovMk[port]*
Dumbrille, Douglass 1888-1974 *HolCA[port]*
Dumbrille, Douglass 1890-1974 *HalFC 80, Vers A[port], WhScrn 77, WhoHol B*
Dumeny, Camille d1920 *NotNAT B*
Dumercier, Jean *Film 1*
Dumesnil, Evangeline Lehman *ConAmC*
Dumesnil, Marie-Francoise 1713-1803 *EncWT, Ent, NotNAT B, OxThe*
Dumesnil, Maurice 1886-1974 *Baker 78*
Dumesnil, Rene 1879-1967 *Baker 78, NewGrD 80*
Dumicic, Petar 1901- *IntWWM 77, -80*
Dumilatre, Adele 1821-1909 *CnOxB*
Dumilieu *PupTheA*
Dumitrescu, Gheorghe 1914- *Baker 78, NewGrD 80*
Dumitrescu, Iancu Ioan 1944- *IntWWM 80*
Dumitrescu, Ion 1913- *Baker 78, NewGrD 80*
Dumke, Ralph 1900-1964 *FilmgC, ForYSC, HalFC 80, NotNAT B, WhScrn 74, -77, WhoHol B*
Dumler, Franz Anton *NewGrD 80*
Dumler, Martin G 1868-1958 *Baker 78*
Dumo, Evelyn *Film 2*
Dumonchau, Charles-Francois 1775-1820 *NewGrD 80*
DuMond, Joseph H 1898- *AmSCAP 66*
DuMont, Allen B d1965 *NewYTET*
Dumont, Gene *Film 2*
DuMont, Gordon 1894-1965 *WhoHol B*
DuMont, Gordon 1894-1966 *WhScrn 77*
Dumont, Henri 1610-1684 *Baker 78*
DuMont, Henry 1610-1684 *NewGrD 80*
Dumont, J M *Film 1, -2*
Dumont, Louise 1862-1932 *EncWT, NotNAT B*
Dumont, Margaret 1889-1965 *BiDFilm, -81, FilmEn, Film 2, HalFC 80, MotPP, OxFilm, ThFT[port], WhScrn 74, -77, WhoHol B, WorEFlm*
Dumont, Margaret 1890-1965 *FilmgC, ForYSC, MovMk[port], Vers A[port]*
Dumont, Montague *Film 1*
Dumont, Paul *WhoHol A*
Dumouchel, Albert 1916- *CreCan 1*
Dumoulin, David *CnOxB*
Dumoulin, Maxime 1893-1972 *NewGrD 80*
Dumstable, John *NewGrD 80*
Duna, Steffi 1913- *FilmEn, FilmgC, ForYSC, HalFC 80, ThFT[port], WhoHol A*
Dunas, William A 1947- *CmpGMD, CnOxB*
Dunaway, Faye *IntMPA 75, -76*
Dunaway, Faye 1940- *ForYSC*
Dunaway, Faye 1941- *BiDFilm, -81, FilmEn, FilmgC, HalFC 80, IntMPA 77, -78, -79, -80, MotPP, MovMk[port], OxFilm, WhoHol A, WhoThe 77, WorEFlm[port]*
Dunayevsky, Isaac 1900-1955 *DcFM*
Dunayevsky, Isaak Iosifovich 1900-1955 *Baker 78, NewGrD 80*
Dunbar, Alice *MorBAP*
Dunbar, Clark Dennis 1938- *WhoOp 76*
Dunbar, Dave *Film 2*
Dunbar, David 1893-1953 *WhScrn 74, -77, WhoHol B*
Dunbar, Dixie *ForYSC*
Dunbar, Dixie 1915- *HalFC 80*
Dunbar, Dixie 1919- *FilmEn, ThFT[port], WhoHol A*
Dunbar, Dorothy *BlksB&W C, Film 2*
Dunbar, Earl Theodore 1937- *EncJzS 70*
Dunbar, Erroll *WhoStg 1908*
Dunbar, Helen 1868-1933 *Film 1, -2, TwYS, WhScrn 74, -77, WhoHol B*
Dunbar, Paul Laurence 1872-1906 *BiDAmM, BlkAmP, MorBAP*
Dunbar, Robert Leon 1951- *AmSCAP 80*
Dunbar, Roslyn Frances Jessie 1937- *IntWWM 80*
Dunbar, Rudolph 1907- *Baker 78, ConAmC*
Dunbar, Rudolph 1917- *WhoMus 72*
Dunbar, Scott 1904- *BluesWW[port]*
Dunbar, Ted 1937- *EncJzS 70*
Dunbar-Nelson, Alice Moore 1875-1935 *BlkAmP*
Duncan, A E *Film 1*
Duncan, Albert Bud 1886-1961 *Film 2, TwYS*
Duncan, Alma *WomWMM*
Duncan, Andrew Christie 1929- *IntWWM 80, WhoHol A*
Duncan, Angus 1912- *BiE&WWA, NotNAT, WhoHol A, WhoThe 72, -77*
Duncan, Archie 1914- *FilmgC, HalFC 80, WhoHol A, WhoThe 72, -77*
Duncan, Augustin 1873-1954 *NotNAT B, WhThe*
Duncan, Beverly *WomWMM B*
Duncan, Bob 1904-1967 *WhScrn 74, -77, WhoHol B*
Duncan, Bud *FilmEn*

Duncan, Bud 1883-1960 *WhScrn 77, WhoHol B*
Duncan, C H Stuart *WhoMus 72*
Duncan, Charles F, Jr. 1940- *IntWWM 77*
Duncan, Charles F, Jr. 1941- *IntWWM 80*
Duncan, David 1913- *WhoHrs 80*
Duncan, Dell *Film 1*
Duncan, Edith Johnson *WhScrn 74, -77*
Duncan, Elizabeth 1874-1948 *CnOxB*
Duncan, Evelyn 1893-1972 *WhScrn 77, WhoHol B*
Duncan, F Martin *DcFM*
Duncan, Hank 1894-1968 *WhoJazz 72*
Duncan, Hank 1896-1968 *EncJzS 70, IlEncJ*
Duncan, Henry 1896-1968 *EncJzS 70*
Duncan, Irma 1897- *CnOxB, DancEn 78*
Duncan, Isadora *OxMus*
Duncan, Isadora 1877-1927 *NewGrD 80[port]*
Duncan, Isadora 1878-1927 *CmpGMD[port], CnOxB, DancEn 78[port], NotNAT B*
Duncan, Isadora 1880-1927 *WhThe*
Duncan, James L 1926- *ConAmC*
Duncan, Jeff 1930- *CmpGMD, CnOxB, DancEn 78*
Duncan, Jimmy 1935- *AmSCAP 66, -80*
Duncan, John 1907- *WhoMus 72*
Duncan, John 1913- *ConAmC*
Duncan, John, Jr. *MorBAP*
Duncan, Johnny 1925?- *WhoHrs 80*
Duncan, Johnny 1938- *CounME 74, -74A, IlEncCM[port]*
Duncan, Keene 1902-1972 *WhScrn 77*
Duncan, Kenne 1902-1972 *WhoHol B, WhoHrs 80[port]*
Duncan, Kent *ConMuA 80B*
Duncan, Larry Wayne 1945- *AmSCAP 80*
Duncan, Lesley *IlEncR*
Duncan, Malcolm 1878-1942 *NotNAT B, WhoStg 1908*
Duncan, Malcolm 1881-1942 *WhThe*
Duncan, Maria-Theresa *CnOxB*
Duncan, Mary 1903- *FilmEn, MotPP, ThFT[port], WhThe, WhoHol A*
Duncan, Mary 1905- *Film 2, ForYSC*
Duncan, Norman 1871-1916 *CreCan 2*
Duncan, Pamela 1932?- *WhoHrs 80[port]*
Duncan, Richard Lawrence 1945- *IntWWM 77, -80*
Duncan, Ronald 1914- *CnMD, CnThe, ConDr 73, -77, CroCD, EncWT, ModWD, WhoMus 72, WhoThe 72, -77*
Duncan, Rosetta d1959 *WhThe, WhoHol B*
Duncan, Rosetta 1900-1959 *AmSCAP 66, -80, JoeFr, WhScrn 74, -77*
Duncan, Rosetta 1902-1959 *NotNAT B*
Duncan, Sandy 1946- *EncMT, FilmEn, FilmgC, HalFC 80, IntMPA 77, -75, -76, -78, -79, -80, WhoHol A, WhoThe 77*
Duncan, Sara Jeannette *CreCan 1*
Duncan, Taylor *Film 2*
Duncan, Ted *Film 1, -2*
Duncan, Thelma *BlkAmP, MorBAP*
Duncan, Todd *AmPS B*
Duncan, Todd 1900- *EncMT, WhThe*
Duncan, Todd 1903- *BiDAmM, BiE&WWA, DrBlPA, NotNAT, PlP&P[port], WhoHol A*
Duncan, Tommy 1911-1967 *BiDAmM, IlEncCM*
Duncan, Trevor 1924- *WhoMus 72*
Duncan, Virginia Bauer 1929- *WomWMM B*
Duncan, Vivian *WhThe*
Duncan, Vivian 1899- *What 3[port], WhoHol A*
Duncan, Vivian 1902- *AmSCAP 66, -80, JoeFr*
Duncan, Wayne O 1949- *AmSCAP 80*
Duncan, William *PupTheA*
Duncan, William 1878-1961 *Film 1, -2*
Duncan, William 1880-1961 *FilmEn, ForYSC, MotPP, NotNAT B, TwYS, -A, WhScrn 74, -77, WhoHol B*
Duncan, William 1946- *IntWWM 77*
Duncan, William Cary 1874-1945 *AmSCAP 66, -80, CmpEPM, NotNAT B, WhScrn 74, -77, WhThe, WhoHol B*
Duncan, William Edmondstoune 1866-1920 *Baker 78*
Duncan-Shorrock, Sarah Esther Janina 1953- *IntWWM 80*
Duncan Sisters, The *CmpEPM, EncMT, Film 2, ForYSC, JoeFr, ThFT[port]*
Dundee, Calva *MorBAP*
Dundee, Jimmy 1901-1953 *WhScrn 74, -77, WhoHol B*
Dundreary *OxThe*
Dunfee, Jack 1901- *WhThe, WhoThe 72*
Dunford, Benjamin C 1917- *ConAmC*
Dungan, Olive 1903- *AmSCAP 66, -80, ConAmC*
Dunham, Bertha Mabel 1881- *CreCan 2*
Dunham, Corydon B, Jr. *NewYTET*
Dunham, Henry Morton 1853-1929 *Baker 78, BiDAmM*
Dunham, Joanna 1936- *WhoThe 77*
Dunham, Katherine *CmpGMD[port]*
Dunham, Katherine 1910- *AmSCAP 66, BiE&WWA, DrBlPA, NotNAT, -A, WhoHol A, WhoThe 72, -77*
Dunham, Katherine 1912- *CnOxB*
Dunham, Katherine 1914- *DancEn 78[port]*
Dunham, Kaye Lawrence 1933- *AmSCAP 80*
Dunham, Mabel 1881-1957 *CreCan 2*
Dunham, Meneve 1930- *IntWWM 80*
Dunham, Minnie Gertrude 1900- *IntWWM 77, WhoMus 72*
Dunham, Phil 1885-1972 *WhoHol B*
Dunham, Phillip 1885-1972 *Film 2, WhScrn 77*
Dunham, Sonny 1914- *BgBands 74[port], CmpEPM, WhoJazz 72*
Dunham, William D 1910- *AmSCAP 66, -80*
Dunhill, Thomas Frederick 1877-1946 *Baker 78, NewGrD 80, OxMus*
Duni, Antonio 1700?-1766? *NewGrD 80*
Duni, Egidio 1708-1775 *NewGrD 80[port]*
Duni, Egidio Romoaldo 1709-1775 *Baker 78, MusMk*
Dunicz, Jan Jozef 1910-1945 *NewGrD 80*
Duniecki, Stanislaw 1839-1870 *NewGrD 80*
Duning, George 1906- *AmSCAP 80*
Duning, George 1908- *AmSCAP 66, CmMov, ConAmC, FilmEn, FilmgC, HalFC 80, IntMPA 77, -75, -76, -78, -79, -80, WorEFlm*
Dunkels, Alfreds 1907- *IntWWM 77, -80*
Dunkels, Dorothy 1907- *WhThe*
Dunkels, Marjorie 1916- *WhThe*
Dunkerley, Patricia 1940- *IntWWM 77, -80*
Dunkinson, Harry *Film 1, -2*
Dunkley, Ferdinand Luis 1869-1956 *AmSCAP 66, Baker 78*
Dunkley, George Albert Charles 1938- *IntWWM 77*
Dunlap, Ethel Margaret d1968 *WhoHol B*
Dunlap, Florence *WhoHol A*
Dunlap, John Robert 1934- *WhoOp 76*
Dunlap, Louis M 1911- *AmSCAP 66*
Dunlap, Paul 1919- *AmSCAP 80, WhoHrs 80*
Dunlap, Richard D 1923- *IntMPA 77, -75, -76, -78, -79, -80*
Dunlap, Scott 1892- *TwYS A*
Dunlap, Scott R 1892-1970 *FilmEn*
Dunlap, William 1766-1839 *BiDAmM, CnThe, EncWT, Ent, McGEWD, NotNAT A, -B, OxThe, PlP&P[port], REnWD[port]*
Dunlevy, Brian *Film 2*
Dunlop, Francis 1928- *BiDAmM, EncJzS 70*
Dunlop, Frank 1927- *PlP&P A[port], WhoThe 72, -77*
Dunlop, Frankie 1928- *EncJzS 70*
Dunlop, Ian 1927- *OxFilm*
Dunlop, Isobel 1901-1975 *Baker 78, WhoMus 72*
Dunmar, David *Film 2*
Dunn, Arthur d1932 *NotNAT B*
Dunn, Bobby d1939 *Film 1, -2, WhoHol B*
Dunn, Bonnie 1920- *AmSCAP 66, -80*
Dunn, Craig Andrew 1947- *IntWWM 77*
Dunn, Crystal Lynn Kesler 1951- *IntWWM 77*
Dunn, Eddie *EncFCWM 69*
Dunn, Eddie 1896-1951 *Film 2, Vers B[port], WhoHol B*
Dunn, Edward F 1896-1951 *WhScrn 74, -77*
Dunn, Edward Thomas 1925- *AmSCAP 80*
Dunn, Edwin Wallace d1931 *NotNAT B*
Dunn, Emma 1875-1966 *FilmEn, Film 2, FilmgC, ForYSC, HalFC 80, HolCA[port], Vers A[port], WhScrn 74, -77, WhThe, WhoHol B*
Dunn, Gary 1950- *ConAmC*
Dunn, Geoffrey 1903- *NewGrD 80, WhoThe 72, -77*
Dunn, Gregg d1964 *NotNAT B*
Dunn, Harvey B 1894-1968 *WhScrn 77, WhoHol B*
Dunn, J E *Film 1*
Dunn, J Malcolm d1946 *NotNAT B, WhScrn 74, -77, WhoHol B*
Dunn, Jack 1917-1938 *WhScrn 74, -77*
Dunn, James d1967 *MotPP, WhoHol B*
Dunn, James 1901-1967 *HolP 30[port]*
Dunn, James 1905-1967 *FilmEn, FilmgC, ForYSC, HalFC 80, MovMk, WhScrn 74, -77*
Dunn, James 1906-1967 *BiE&WWA, NotNAT B*
Dunn, James Philip 1884-1936 *AmSCAP 66, -80, Baker 78, BiDAmM, ConAmC*
Dunn, John 1866-1940 *Baker 78*
Dunn, John J 1906-1938 *Film 1, WhScrn 74, -77*
Dunn, John P 1908- *NatPD[port]*
Dunn, John Petri 1878-1931 *Baker 78*
Dunn, Johnny 1897-1937 *CmpEPM, WhoJazz 72*
Dunn, Johnny 1900-1938 *BiDAmM*
Dunn, Johnny 1906-1938 *WhoHol B*
Dunn, Joseph Barrington d1920 *NotNAT B*
Dunn, Josephine 1906- *FilmEn, Film 2, ForYSC, MovMk, ThFT[port], TwYS, WhoHol A*
Dunn, Judith *CmpGMD*
Dunn, Lester Lay 1912- *IntWWM 77, -80*
Dunn, Louise M *PupTheA*
Dunn, Malcolm d1946 *Film 2*
Dunn, Marion *WomWMM*
Dunn, Michael d1973 *MotPP, WhoHol B*
Dunn, Michael 1918- *AmSCAP 66, -80*
Dunn, Michael 1934-1973 *BiE&WWA, FilmEn, ForYSC, NotNAT B, WhScrn 77, WhoHrs 80*
Dunn, Michael 1935-1973 *FilmgC, HalFC 80, MovMk*
Dunn, Michael Peter 1943- *IntWWM 77, -80*
Dunn, Mignon *WhoOp 76*
Dunn, Monte 1946- *AmSCAP 80*
Dunn, Pauline *WhoMus 72*
Dunn, Ralph 1900-1968 *BiE&WWA, NotNAT*
Dunn, Ralph 1902-1968 *Vers B[port], WhScrn 77, WhoHol A, -B*
Dunn, Rebecca Welty 1890- *AmSCAP 66, -80, ConAmC*
Dunn, Richard 1929- *IntWWM 77, -80*
Dunn, Robert 1891-1939 *WhScrn 74, -77*
Dunn, Robert H 1896-1960 *WhScrn 74, -77, WhoHol B*
Dunn, Robinson Porter 1825-1867 *BiDAmM*
Dunn, Roy Sidney 1922- *BluesWW[port]*
Dunn, Russell 1910- *AmSCAP 80*
Dunn, Stephen E 1894- *IntMPA 75, -76*
Dunn, Thomas 1925- *NewGrD 80*
Dunn, Violet *WhoHol A*
Dunn, William R *Film 1, -2*
Dunne, Charles d1951 *WhScrn 74, -77*
Dunne, Dominick *IntMPA 77, -75, -76, -78, -79, -80*
Dunne, Herbert Peyton 1909- *AmSCAP 80*
Dunne, Irene *IntMPA 77, -75, -76, -78, -79, -80, MotPP, WhoHol A, WomWMM*
Dunne, Irene 1898- *FilmEn*
Dunne, Irene 1901- *EncMT, FilmgC, HalFC 80, ThFT[port]*
Dunne, Irene 1904- *BiDFilm, -81, BiE&WWA, CmMov, CmpEPM, ForYSC[port], MovMk[port], OxFilm, What 1[port], WhThe, WorEFlm*
Dunne, J W *PlP&P*
Dunne, Philip 1908- *BiDFilm, DcFM, FilmEn, FilmgC, HalFC 80, IntMPA 77, -75, -76, -78, -79, -80, WorEFlm*
Dunne, Stephen 1918- *ForYSC*
Dunne, Steve *WhoHol A*
Dunnicliff, Frank Henry 1905- *WhoMus 72*
Dunning, Albert 1936- *NewGrD 80*
Dunning, George 1920- *DcFM, FilmEn, OxFilm, WorEFlm*
Dunning, John 1916- *IntMPA 77, -75, -76, -78, -79, -80*
Dunning, Philip Hart 1890-1968 *CnMD,*

ModWD, WhThe
Dunning, Philip Hart 1891-1957 *McGEWD*
Dunning, Philip Hart 1891-1968 *BiE&WWA, NotNAT, -B*
Dunning, Ruth 1911- *WhoHol A, WhoThe 72, -77*
Dunninger, Joseph 1892-1975 *MagIlD*
Dunnock, Mildred *BiE&WWA, CnThe, IntMPA 77, -75, -76, -78, -79, -80, MotPP, NotNAT, PlP&P[port], WhoHol A, WhoThe 72*
Dunnock, Mildred 1900- *Ent, ForYSC, HolCA[port], Vers A[port], WhoThe 77*
Dunnock, Mildred 1904- *FilmgC, HalFC 80*
Dunnock, Mildred 1906- *FilmEn, MovMk[port]*
Dunphie, Charles J d1908 *NotNAT B*
Dunrobin, Lionel Claude 1875-1950 *WhScrn 74, -77*
Dunsany, Lord 1878-1957 *EncWT, Ent*
Dunsany, Alfred, Lord 1878-1957 *NotNAT A, -B*
Dunsany, Lord Edward John M D Plunkett 1878-1957 *CnMD, CnThe, McGEWD, ModWD, OxThe, PlP&P, REnWD[port], WhThe*
Dunskus, Erich 1890-1967 *WhScrn 74, -77*
Dunsmuir, Alexander 1877-1938 *WhScrn 74, -77*
Dunstable, John d1453 *OxMus*
Dunstable, John 1370-1453 *CmpBCM, GrComp*
Dunstable, John 1380?-1453 *Baker 78*
Dunstable, John 1385?-1453 *BnBkM 80*
Dunstable, John 1390?-1453 *MusMk, NewGrD 80*
Dunstan, Ralph 1857-1933 *Baker 78*
Dunstapell, John 1390?-1453 *NewGrD 80*
Dunstaple, John 1390?-1453 *NewGrD 80*
Dunstedter, Eddie 1897-1974 *AmSCAP 66, -80, CmpEPM*
Dunster, Mark *BlkAmP*
Dunszt, Maria 1936- *WhoOp 76*
Dunton, Helen d1920 *WhScrn 74, -77*
Dunton, John *Film 2*
Dunville, T E 1870?-1924 *NotNAT B, OxThe*
Dunwell, Wilfrid 1902- *WhoMus 72*
Duny, Egide *NewGrD 80*
Duny, Egidio Romoaldo 1709-1775 *OxMus*
DuPage, Florence 1910- *AmSCAP 66, -80, ConAmC*
DuPage, Richard 1908- *AmSCAP 66, -80, ConAmC A*
DuParc 1630?-1664 *OxThe*
Duparc, Elisabeth d1778? *NewGrD 80[port]*
Duparc, Henri 1848-1933 *Baker 78, BnBkM 80, DcCom 77, GrComp[port], MusMk, NewGrD 80, OxMus*
DuParc, Marquise-Therese DeGorla 1633-1668 *Ent, NotNAT B, OxThe*
DuParc, Rene Berthelot d1664 *EncWT, NotNAT B*
DuParc, Therese DeGorla, Marquise 1633-1668 *EncWT*
DuPea, Tatzumbie 1849-1970 *WhScrn 77*
Duperey, Anny *WhoHol A*
Duperey, Anny 1947- *FilmEn*
Duphly, Jacques 1715-1789 *NewGrD 80*
Dupin, Paul 1865-1949 *Baker 78, OxMus*
Duplessis *NewGrD 80*
DuPlessis, Christian 1944- *IntWWM 77, -80, WhoOp 76*
DuPlessis, Hubert 1922- *IntWWM 77, -80, NewGrD 80*
Duplessis, Jean-Baptiste *NewGrD 80*
Duplessis, Joseph *NewGrD 80*
DuPlessis, Karl L 1932- *IntWWM 77, -80*
Duplessis, Lenoir 1754- *NewGrD 80*
Duponchel, Giacomo d1685 *NewGrD 80*
Duponchel, Jacques d1685 *NewGrD 80*
DuPont, Miss 1894-1973 *FilmEn, Film 2, TwYS, WhoHol B*
Dupont, Adley 1946- *IntMPA 77, -75, -76, -78, -79, -80*
Dupont, Auguste 1827-1890 *OxMus*
Dupont, Charles 1907- *NewOrJ*
Dupont, E A 1891-1956 *BiDFilm, -81, FilmEn, FilmgC, HalFC 80, IlWWBF*
Dupont, Ewald Andre 1891-1956 *DcFM, OxFilm, WorEFlm*
Dupont, G *NewGrD 80*
Dupont, Gabriel Edouard Xavier 1878-1914 *Baker 78, NewGrD 80, OxMus*
Dupont, Guillaume-Pierre 1718-1778? *NewGrD 80*
Dupont, Henri-Denis 1660-1727 *NewGrD 80*
Dupont, Jacques 1909- *CnOxB, NewGrD 80*
Dupont, Jean-Baptiste *NewGrD 80*
Dupont, Nicolas 1575?-1623 *NewGrD 80*
DuPont, Patricia 1894-1973 *WhScrn 77*
DuPont, Paul d1957 *NotNAT B*
Dupont, Pierre d1740 *NewGrD 80*
Dupont, Pierre 1821-1870 *Baker 78*
Dupont, Pierre-Guillaume 1718-1778? *NewGrD 80*
Duport *NewGrD 80*
Duport, Denise 1938- *IntWWM 80*
Duport, Jean-Louis 1749-1819 *Baker 78, BnBkM 80, NewGrD 80, OxMus*
Duport, Jean-Pierre 1741-1818 *NewGrD 80, OxMus*
Duport, Louis Antoine 1781?-1853 *CnOxB, DancEn 78*
Duport, Pierre Landrin 1762-1841 *BiDAmM*
Dupouy, Jean 1938- *WhoOp 76*
Duprat, Regis 1930- *NewGrD 80*
Duprat, Rogerio 1932- *DcCM, NewGrD 80*
Duprato, Jules-Laurent 1827-1892 *Baker 78*
Dupre *NewGrD 80*
Dupre, David 1930- *DancEn 78*
Dupre, Desmond John 1916-1974 *NewGrD 80, WhoMus 72*
Dupre, Elias *NewGrD 80*
Dupre, Heather 1949- *IntWWM 77, -80*
Dupre, Helias *NewGrD 80*
DuPre, Jacqueline 1945- *Baker 78, BnBkM 80, IntWWM 77, -80, NewGrD 80, WhoMus 72*
Dupre, Jimmy R 1906- *AmSCAP 66, -80*
Dupre, Laurent *NewGrD 80*
Dupre, Louis 1697-1774 *CnOxB, DancEn 78*
Dupre, Marcel 1886-1971 *Baker 78, BnBkM 80, DcCM, MusMk, MusSN[port], NewGrD 80, OxMus*
Dupre D'Angleterre *NewGrD 80*
Dupree, Harry 1911- *AmSCAP 66, -80*
Dupree, Minnie d1947 *WhoHol B, WhoStg 1908*
Dupree, Minnie 1873-1947 *Film 2, FilmgC, HalFC 80, NotNAT B, WhScrn 74, -77*
Dupree, Minnie 1875-1945 *ThFT[port]*
Dupree, Minnie 1875-1947 *WhThe*
Dupree, William Thomas 1910- *BluesWW[port]*
Duprees, The *RkOn[port]*
Duprez, Fred 1884-1938 *NotNAT B, WhScrn 77, WhThe, WhoHol B*
Duprez, Gilbert 1806-1896 *CmOp*
Duprez, Gilbert Louis 1806-1896 *BnBkM 80, NewEOp 71, NewGrD 80*
Duprez, June 1918- *FilmEn, FilmgC, ForYSC, HalFC 80, MotPP, WhThe, WhoHol A*
Duprez, Louis-Gilbert 1806-1896 *Baker 78*
Duprez, May Moore d1946 *NotNAT B*
Dupuis, Adolphe d1891 *NotNAT B*
Dupuis, Albert 1877-1967 *Baker 78, NewGrD 80*
DuPuis, Arthur 1901-1952 *WhScrn 77*
Dupuis, Paul 1916- *FilmgC, HalFC 80, WhoHol A*
Dupuis, Sylvain 1856-1931 *Baker 78, NewGrD 80*
Dupuis, Thomas Sanders 1733-1796 *NewGrD 80, OxMus*
Dupuits, Jean-Baptiste *NewGrD 80*
Dupuy, Dominique 1930- *CnOxB*
Dupuy, Francoise 1925- *CnOxB*
DuPuy, Henry *NewGrD 80*
Dupuy, J B E L C 1770-1822 *OxMus*
Dupuy, Jean Baptiste Edouard 1770?-1822 *NewGrD 80*
Dupuy, Rene 1920- *WhoMus 72*
Duquennois, Francis 1915- *IntWWM 77, -80*
Duques, Augustin 1899-1972 *BiDAmM*
Duquesne, Edmond 1855- *WhThe*
Duquesnoy, Charles 1759-1822 *NewGrD 80*
Duquette, Tony 1918- *BiE&WWA, NotNAT*
Duran, Domingo Marcos 1460?-1529 *NewGrD 80*
Duran, Elena 1949- *IntWWM 80*
Duran, Jose d1791? *NewGrD 80*
Duran, Father Narciso 1776-1846 *BiDAmM*
Duran, Val 1896-1937 *WhScrn 74, -77, WhoHol B*
Durand *NewGrD 80*
Durand, Charles 1912- *BiE&WWA, NotNAT*
Durand, David *Film 2*
Durand, Edouard 1871-1926 *NotNAT B, WhScrn 74, -77, WhoHol B*
Durand, Edward *Film 2*
Durand, Emile 1830-1903 *Baker 78*
Durand, Fernand Charles Olivier 1952- *IntWWM 77*
Durand, Jacques Massacrie 1865-1928 *NewGrD 80*
Durand, Jean 1882-1946 *DcFM, FilmEn, WhScrn 77*
Durand, Marc 1949- *IntWWM 77, -80*
Durand, Marie-Auguste 1830-1909 *Baker 78, NewGrD 80*
Durand, Maurice 1893-1961 *NewOrJ[port]*
Durand, Wade Hampton 1887-1964 *AmSCAP 66, -80*
Durand, Xavier *CreCan 1*
Durang, Charles 1796-1870 *NotNAT B*
Durang, Christopher 1949- *AmSCAP 80*
Durang, John 1768-1822 *BiDAmM, CnOxB, DancEn 78, NotNAT A*
Duranowski, August 1770?-1834 *NewGrD 80*
Durant, Edouard *Film 2*
Durant, Jack *JoeFr*
Durant, M *Film 2*
Durant, Ray 1910- *WhoJazz 72*
Durant, Thomas *Film 2*
Durante, Francesco 1684-1755 *Baker 78, BnBkM 80, GrComp, MusMk, NewEOp 71, NewGrD 80[port], OxMus*
Durante, Jimmy 1893-1980 *AmPS, -B, AmSCAP 66, -80, BiDAmM, BiE&WWA, CmpEPM, EncMT, Ent, FilmEn, Film 2, FilmgC, ForYSC, Funs[port], HalFC 80[port], IntMPA 77, -75, -76, -78, -79, -80, JoeFr[port], MGM[port], MotPP, MovMk[port], NewYTET, NotNAT, -A, WhThe, WhoHol A*
Durante, Ottavio *NewGrD 80*
Durante, Silvestro d1672? *NewGrD 80*
Duranty, Louis Emile *DcPup*
Duras, Marguerite 1914- *CnMD SUP, CnThe, CroCD, EncWT, Ent, FilmEn, FilmgC, HalFC 80, McGEWD[port], ModWD, OxFilm, REnWD[port], WhoThe 72, -77, WomWMM, WorEFlm*
Durastanti, Margherita *NewGrD 80[port]*
Durazzo, Count Giacomo 1717-1794 *NewGrD 80*
Durbin, Deanna *AmPS B*
Durbin, Deanna 1921- *CmMov, CmpEPM, FilmEn, FilmgC, HalFC 80, MotPP, MovMk[port], ThFT[port], WhoHol A, WorEFlm*
Durbin, Deanna 1922- *BiDAmM, BiDFilm, -81, ForYSC, OxFilm*
Durbin, Maud d1936 *NotNAT B*
Durbridge, Francis 1912- *IntMPA 77, -75, -76, -78, -79, -80*
Dure, Robert 1934- *ConAmC, WhoOp 76*
DuRell Twin Brothers *AmPS B*
DuReneau *NewGrD 80*
Duret, Marie d1881 *NotNAT B*
DuRetz, Jakub *NewGrD 80*
Durey, Louis 1888-1979 *Baker 78, BnBkM 80, DcCM, NewGrD 80, OxMus*
Durfee, Joyce Mary 1937- *IntWWM 77*
Durfee, Minta d1975 *MotPP, WhoHol C*
Durfee, Minta 1889-1975 *ForYSC, TwYS*
Durfee, Minta 1890-1975 *WhScrn 77*
Durfee, Minta 1897-1975 *FilmEn, Film 1, FilmgC, HalFC 80*
D'Urfey, Thomas 1653-1723 *NewGrD 80, NotNAT B, OxMus, OxThe*
Durgin, Cyrus W 1907-1962 *NotNAT B*
Durgin, Don 1924- *IntMPA 77, -75, -76, NewYTET*
Durham, Alice Marie *MorBAP*
Durham, Eddie 1906- *CmpEPM, EncJzS 70, IlEncJ, WhoJazz 72*
Durham, Eddie 1909- *AmSCAP 66, -80*
Durham, Edward Lee 1915- *BluesWW*
Durham, Judith *EncFCWM 69*
Durham, Lowell M 1917- *ConAmC*

Durham, Nancy Ruth 1947- IntWWM 77
Durham, Thomas J, Sr. 1924- AmSCAP 66
Duric-Klajn, Stana 1908- NewGrD 80
Durieux, Tilla 1880-1971 EncWT, Ent
Durieux, Tilla 1881-1971 Film 2, WhScrn 74, -77, WhoHol B
Durkin, Betsy AmSCAP 80
Durkin, Eleanor WhScrn 74, -77, WhoHol B
Durkin, James Peter 1879-1934 NotNAT B, WhScrn 74, -77, WhoHol B
Durkin, Junior 1915-1935 FilmEn, FilmgC, ForYSC, HalFC 80, WhScrn 74, -77, WhoHol B
Durko, Zsolt 1934- Baker 78, DcCM, NewGrD 80
Durland, Edward Film 2
Durme, Jef Van 1907-1965 Baker 78, NewGrD 80
Durme, Jozef Van 1907-1965 NewGrD 80
Durning, Bernard Film 1, -2
Durning, Bernard J 1893-1923 WhScrn 74, -77, WhoHol B
Durning, Charles IntMPA 80
Durning, Charles 1923- NotNAT, PIP&P A[port], WhoHol A
Durning, Charles 1933- FilmEn, HalFC 80
Durocher NewGrD 80
Durollet, Marie Francois Louis Gand L NewGrD 80
Duron, Diego 1658?-1731 NewGrD 80
Duron, Sebastian 1660-1716 NewGrD 80
Duronceray, Marie Justine Benoite NewGrD 80
Durov, Vladimir 1863?-1934 Ent
Durr, Alfred 1918- IntWWM 80, NewGrD 80
Durr, Clifford J d1975 NewYTET
Durr, Walther 1932- IntWWM 77, -80, NewGrD 80
Durrah, James W MorBAP
Durrah, Jim BlkAmP
Durrant, Frederick Thomas 1895- IntWWM 77, WhoMus 72
Durrant, Frederick W IIWWBF
Durrant, James 1929- IntWWM 77, -80, WhoMus 72
Durrant, John 1911- WhoMus 72
Durrell, Lawrence 1912- CnMD, ConDr 73, -77, ModWD
Durrenmatt, Friedrich 1921- CnMD, CnThe, CroCD, EncWT, Ent, McGEWD[port], ModWD, OxThe, PIP&P, REnWD[port], WhoThe 77
Durrner, Johann NewGrD 80
Durrner, Ruprecht Johannes Julius 1810-1859 Baker 78
Durrschmied, Carl NewGrD 80
Durso, Michael Alfred 1905-1975 AmSCAP 80
Durst, Edward 1917-1945 WhScrn 74, -77, WhoHol B
Durst, James Rodney 1945- AmSCAP 80
Durston, David E 1925- IntMPA 77, -75, -76, -78, -79, -80
Durston, Roger Andrew Cadle 1948- IntWWM 77, -80
Duru, Alfred d1889 NotNAT B
Durufle, Maurice 1902- Baker 78, BnBkM 80, DcCom&M 79, DcCM, IntWWM 77, -80, MusMk, NewGrD 80, OxMus
Durwood, Richard M 1929- IntMPA 78, -79, -80
Durwood, Stanley H 1920- IntMPA 77, -75, -76, -78, -79, -80
Dury, Ian ConMuA 80A
Duryea, Dan 1907-1968 BiDFilm, -81, CmMov, FilmEn, FilmgC, ForYSC, HalFC 80, HolP 40[port], MotPP, MovMk[port], NotNAT B, OxFilm, WhScrn 74, -77, WhoHol B, WorEFlm[port]
Duryea, George 1898-1963 FilmEn
Duryea, George 1904-1963 Film 2, ForYSC, TwYS, WhScrn 74, -77, WhoHol B
Duryea, Mary d1949 NotNAT B
Duryea, Peter 1939- ForYSC
DuRyer, Pierre 1606-1658 McGEWD
DuSablon, Antoine NewGrD 80
Dusbury, Elspeth 1912-1967 WhScrn 74
Duscheck, Frantisek Xaver 1731-1799 NewGrD 80
Duschek, Frantisek Xaver 1731-1799 NewGrD 80
Duschek, Josepha 1754-1824 NewGrD 80
Duschmalui, Joseph NewGrD 80
Duse, Carl Film 2
Duse, Eleanora 1858-1924 Film 2, NotNAT A, -B, WhScrn 74, -77, WhoHol B, WorEFlm
Duse, Eleanora 1859-1924 WhoStg 1908
Duse, Elenora 1859-1924 Film 1
Duse, Eleonora 1858-1924 EncWT, Ent, FamA&A[port], FilmEn, FilmgC, HalFC 80, OxFilm, OxThe, PIP&P[port]
Duse, Eleonora 1859-1924 CnThe, WhThe
Dusek, Frantisek 1780-1844 NewGrD 80
Dusek, Frantisek Xaver 1731-1799 NewGrD 80
Dusek, Josefa 1754-1824 NewGrD 80
Dusek, Milan 1931- IntWWM 77, -80
Dusen, Frank 1880?-1940 BiDAmM
Dushkin, Dorothy 1903- ConAmC
Dushkin, Samuel 1891-1976 Baker 78, NewGrD 80
DuShon, Jean Atwell 1936- BiDAmM
Dusiacki, Kazimierz Stanislaw Rudomina NewGrD 80
Dusik NewGrD 80
Dusik, Frantisek Josef 1766-1816? NewGrD 80
Dusikova, Katerina Veronika Anna 1769-1833 NewGrD 80
Dusikova, Veronika Elisabeta NewGrD 80
Dusinello, Giuseppe 1540?-1574? NewGrD 80
Dusk RkOn 2[port]
Duskova, Josefa NewGrD 80
Duson, Frank 1881-1936 NewOrJ[port]
DuSouchet, Henry A 1852-1922 NotNAT B, WhThe
Dussault, Nancy 1936- BiE&WWA, EncMT, WhoThe 72, -77
Dussault, Nancy 1938- NotNAT
Dussaut, Therese IntWWM 77, -80
D'Usseau, Arnaud 1916- BiE&WWA, NotNAT, WhThe
Dussek NewGrD 80
Dussek, Franz 1731-1799 Baker 78
Dussek, Franz Benedikt 1766-1816? NewGrD 80
Dussek, Franz Xaver NewGrD 80
Dussek, Jan 1738-1818 NewGrD 80
Dussek, Jan Ladislav 1760-1812 Baker 78, BnBkM 80, GrComp[port], MusMk, NewGrD 80[port], OxMus
Dussek, Johann Joseph 1738-1818 NewGrD 80
Dussek, Johann Ladislaus 1760-1812 NewGrD 80[port]
Dussek, Sophia 1775-1847 NewGrD 80
Dussek, Veronika Rosalia 1769-1833 NewGrD 80
Dussik NewGrD 80
Dussouil, Jacques 1933- IntWWM 80
Dustmann, Marie Luise 1831-1899 Baker 78
Dusty, Slim 1927- IlEncCM
DuTartre, Jean-Baptiste d1749 NewGrD 80
Dutch Swing College Band EncJzS 70
DuTerreaux, Louis Henry d1878 NotNAT B
Dutertre, Armand Film 2
DuTertre, Estienne NewGrD 80
Dutfield, Ray IntMPA 77, -75, -76, -78, -79, -80
Dutilleu, Pierre 1754-1798 NewGrD 80
DuTilleul, Pierre 1754-1798 NewGrD 80
Dutilleux, Henri 1916- Baker 78, CompSN[port], DcCM, IntWWM 77, -80, NewGrD 80
Dutillieu, Pierre 1754-1798 NewGrD 80
Dutkiewicz, Marek W 1948- IntWWM 77
Dutoit, Charles 1936- Baker 78, NewGrD 80
DuToit, Julius Ronald 1934- IntWWM 77, -80
DuToit, Nellie 1929- WhoOp 76
Dutourd, Jean 1920- McGEWD
Dutrey, Honore 1892-1937 BiDAmM
Dutrey, Honore 1894-1935 WhoJazz 72
Dutrey, Honore 1894-1937 NewOrJ
Dutrey, Sam, Jr. 1915?-1971 NewOrJ[port]
Dutrey, Sam, Sr. 1888-1941 NewOrJ
Dutsch, Georgy Ottonovich 1857-1891 NewGrD 80
Dutsch, Otto Johann Anton 1823?-1863 NewGrD 80
Dutton, Brenton Price 1950- CpmDNM 73
Dutton, Deodatus, Jr. 1808-1832 BiDAmM
Dutton, Derrick Banks 1923- WhoMus 72
Dutton, Frederic M 1928- ConAmC
Duval, Mademoiselle d1769? NewGrD 80
Duval, Denise 1921- CmOp, NewGrD 80
Duval, Francois 1672?-1728 NewGrD 80
Duval, Georges 1847-1919 NotNAT B, WhThe
Duval, Georgette Film 2
DuVal, Joe 1907-1966 WhScrn 77, WhoHol B
Duval, Juan d1954 WhScrn 77
Duval, Paulette Film 2
Duval, Pierre 1932- CreCan 2, WhoOp 76
Duvall, Robert 1931- BiDFilm 81, FilmEn, FilmgC, HalFC 80, IntMPA 77, -75, -76, -78, -79, -80, MovMk[port], WhoHol A
Duvall, Shelley 1949- HalFC 80, WhoHol A
Duvall, Shelley 1950- FilmEn
Duvalle, William Film 1
Duvalles 1895-1971 WhScrn 77
Duveen, Lorna Film 2
Duvernay, Pauline 1813-1894 CnOxB
Duvernois, Frederic Nicolas 1765-1838 NewGrD 80
Duvernois, Henri 1875-1937 McGEWD, NotNAT B
Duvernoy, Charles 1776-1845 Baker 78
Duvernoy, Frederic 1765-1839 OxMus
Duvernoy, Frederic Nicolas 1765-1838 NewGrD 80
Duvernoy, Henri-Louis-Charles 1820-1906 Baker 78
Duvernoy, Victor Alphonse 1842-1907 Baker 78, NewGrD 80
Duvivier, George B 1920- CmpEPM, EncJzS 70
Duvivier, Julien 1896-1967 BiDFilm, -81, DcFM, FilmEn, FilmgC, HalFC 80, MovMk[port], OxFilm, WorEFlm
Duvoisin, Yvette Film 1
Duvosel, Lieven 1877-1956 Baker 78, NewGrD 80
Dux, Benedictus NewGrD 80
Dux, Claire 1885-1967 Baker 78, BiDAmM, CmOp, NewGrD 80
Dux, Emilienne 1874- WhThe
Dux, Pierre 1908- EncWT, Ent
Duxbury, Elspeth 1909-1967 WhThe
Duxbury, Elspeth 1912-1967 WhScrn 77, WhoHol B
Duyse, Flor Van 1843-1910 NewGrD 80
Duyse, Florimond Van 1843-1910 NewGrD 80
Dvarionas, Balis 1904-1972 Baker 78
Dvarionas, Balys 1904-1972 NewGrD 80
Dvonch, Frederick 1914- BiE&WWA, NotNAT
Dvoracek, Jiri 1928- Baker 78, IntWWM 77, -80, NewGrD 80
Dvorak, Ann 1912- Film 2, FilmgC, ForYSC, HalFC 80, HolP 30[port], MotPP, MovMk, ThFT[port], What 2[port], WhoHol A
Dvorak, Ann 1912-1979 FilmEn
Dvorak, Antonin 1841-1904 Baker 78, BiDAmM, BnBkM 80[port], CmOp, CmpBCM, CnOxB, DcCom 77[port], DcCom&M 79, DcPup, GrComp[port], MusMk[port], NewEOp 71, NewGrD 80[port], OxMus
Dvorak, DeLyle Dennis 1941- IntWWM 77, -80
Dvorak, Robert ConAmC
Dvorakova, Ludmila 1923- CmOp[port], NewGrD 80, WhoOp 76
Dvorakova, Ludmilla IntWWM 77
Dvorine, Shura 1923- AmSCAP 80, ConAmC
Dvorkin, Judith 1930- ConAmC
Dvorsky, Michel NewGrD 80
Dwan, Alan 1885- MovMk[port]
Dwan, Allan 1885- AmFD, BiDFilm, -81, DcFM, FilmEn, FilmgC, HalFC 80, IntMPA 77, -75, -76, -78, -79, -80, OxFilm, TwYS A, WhoHrs 80, WorEFlm
Dwan, Dorothy Film 2, ForYSC, TwYS
Dwiggens, Jay d1919 Film 1
Dwiggins, Jay d1919 WhScrn 77
Dwiggins, W A DcPup, PupTheA
Dwight, John Sullivan 1813-1893 Baker 78, BiDAmM, NewGrD 80
Dwight, Timothy 1752-1817 BiDAmM
Dwire, Earl 1884-1940 ForYSC, WhScrn 77, WhoHol B
Dworak, Paul Edward 1951- CpmDNM 80, ConAmC
Dworkin, Susan NatPD[port]

Dworkind, Betty 1928- *IntWWM 77, -80*
Dwyer, Ada d1952 *NotNAT B, WhThe, WhoStg 1908*
Dwyer, Edward *ConMuA 80B*
Dwyer, Hilary 1935- *IlWWBF, WhoHol A*
Dwyer, John T 1877-1936 *Film 2, WhScrn 77*
Dwyer, Leslie 1906- *Film 2, FilmgC, HalFC 80, IntMPA 77, -75, -76, -78, -79, -80, WhThe, WhoHol A, WhoThe 72*
Dwyer, Ruth *Film 1, -2*
Dyagilev, Sergey Pavlovich 1872-1929 *NewGrD 80*
Dyal, Susan *WomWMM B*
Dyall, Franklin 1874-1950 *Film 2, FilmgC, HalFC 80, IlWWBF, NotNAT B, WhScrn 74, -77, WhThe, WhoHol B*
Dyall, Valentine 1908- *FilmgC, HalFC 80, WhoHol A, WhoHrs 80, WhoThe 72, -77*
Dyananda *Film 2*
Dybeck, Richard 1811-1877 *NewGrD 80*
Dybwad, Johanne 1867-1950 *Ent, OxThe*
Dyce, William 1806-1864 *NewGrD 80*
Dyck, Ernest Van *NewEOp 71*
Dyck, Ernest Van 1861-1923 *CmOp*
Dycke, Marjorie L 1916- *BiE&WWA, NotNAT*
D'Yd, Jean d1964 *Film 2, WhScrn 77*
Dydo, Stephen 1949- *ConAmC*
Dye, Carol Finch d1962 *NotNAT B*
Dye, Lyle, Jr. 1930- *BiE&WWA, NotNAT*
Dyer, Anson 1876- *FilmgC, HalFC 80*
Dyer, Bob 1900-1965 *WhScrn 74, -77*
Dyer, Charles 1928- *BiE&WWA, ConDr 73, -77, CroCD, EncWT, NotNAT, WhoHol A, WhoThe 72, -77*
Dyer, Janice Williams 1946- *AmSCAP 80*
Dyer, John E 1884-1951 *WhScrn 74, -77*
Dyer, Louise B M 1890-1962 *Baker 78, OxMus*
Dyer, Madge *Film 1*
Dyer, Michael George 1930- *IntWWM 77, -80*
Dyer, Samuel 1785-1835 *BiDAmM*
Dyer, William *Film 2*
Dyer, William Dewitt 1934- *AmSCAP 80*
Dyer, William J *Film 1*
Dyer-Bennet, Richard 1913- *Baker 78, BiDAmM, EncFCWM 69*
Dyers, Lien *Film 2*
Dyess, Tony R Q 1910- *AmSCAP 66, -80*
Dyett, Walter Fairman 1873- *WhoStg 1906, -1908*
Dygon, John *NewGrD 80*
Dyk, Peter Van 1929- *CnOxB*
Dyke, Dave Van *ConMuA 80B*
Dyke & The Blazers *RkOn 2[port]*
Dykema, Peter William 1873-1951 *Baker 78, BiDAmM, OxMus*
Dykes, John Bacchus 1823-1876 *Baker 78, NewGrD 80, OxMus*
Dykes Bower, Sir John 1905- *IntWWM 77, -80, NewGrD 80, WhoMus 72*
Dykstra, John *WhoHrs 80*
Dylan, Bob 1941- *AmSCAP 66, Baker 78, BiDAmM, ConMuA 80A[port], EncFCWM 69, IlEncR[port], NewGrD 80, PopAmC SUP[port], RkOn 2[port]*
Dylan, Robert 1941- *AmSCAP 66, -80*
Dylecki, Mikolaj *NewGrD 80*
Dymov, Ossip 1878-1959 *CnMD, ModWD, OxThe*
Dynalix, Paulette 1917- *CnOxB*
Dyne, Michael *NotNAT*
Dyneley, Peter 1921-1978 *FilmgC, HalFC 80, WhoHol A*
Dyonnet, Edmond 1859-1954 *CreCan 2*
Dyott, George M *Film 2*
Dyrenforth, James 1895- *WhThe, WhoMus 72*
Dyrese, Jacqueline *Film 2*
Dysart, Richard A 1929?- *NotNAT, PlP&P A[port], WhoHol A, WhoThe 77*
Dyson, Barbara Ruth 1917- *WhoMus 72*
Dyson, Dierdra *MorBAP*
Dyson, Sir George 1883-1964 *Baker 78, MusMk, NewGrD 80, OxMus*
Dyson, Hal 1884- *AmSCAP 66, -80*
Dyson, Laura d1950 *NotNAT B*
Dyson, Ronnie 1950- *DrBlPA, RkOn 2[port]*
Dyson, Ruth 1917- *IntWWM 77, -80*
Dyubyuk, Alexander Ivanovich *NewGrD 80*
Dyutsch, Otto Johann Anton *NewGrD 80*
Dyutsh, Georgy Ottonovich *NewGrD 80*
Dzegelenok, Alexander 1891-1969 *Baker 78*
Dzegelyonok, Alexander Mikhaylovich 1891-1969 *NewGrD 80*
Dzerzhinsky, Ivan Ivanovich 1909-1978 *Baker 78, IntWWM 77, -80, MusMk, NewEOp 71, NewGrD 80, OxMus*
Dzhudzhev, Stoyan 1902- *NewGrD 80*
Dziewulska, Maria Amelia 1909- *IntWWM 77, -80*
Dzigan, Yefim 1898- *DcFM, FilmEn*
Dzikowska-Kamasa, Barbara 1935- *IntWWM 80*

E

E R CreCan 1
Eacott, Kenneth Clifford 1923- IntWWM 80
Eade, Kenneth James 1913- IntWWM 77, WhoMus 72
Eades, Linnea Erma 1938- IntWWM 77
Eades, Wilfrid 1920- IntMPA 77, -75, -76, -78, -79, -80
Eadie, Barbara Jean 1947- IntWWM 77, -80
Eadie, Dennis 1869-1928 WhThe
Eadie, Dennis 1875-1928 NotNAT B
Eady, David 1924- FilmgC, HalFC 80, IlWWBF
Eady, Rosemary 1934- IntWWM 77, -80
Eady, W P R CreCan 2
Eagan, Evelyn 1908-1946 WhScrn 74, -77
Eagan, Jack Film 2
Eagels, Jeanne 1890-1929 FamA&A[port], ThFT[port]
Eagels, Jeanne 1894-1929 FilmEn, Film 2, FilmgC, HalFC 80, NotNAT A, -B, TwYS, WhScrn 74, -77, WhThe, WhoHol B
Eager, Allen 1927- CmpEPM, IlEncJ
Eager, Edward 1911-1964 AmSCAP 66, -80
Eager, Jimmy BluesWW
Eager, Johnney 1930-1963 WhScrn 74, -77
Eager, Johnny 1930-1963 WhoHol B
Eager, Mary Ann AmSCAP 66, -80
Eagle, Chief Black Film 1
Eagle, Dan Red Film 2
Eagle, David W 1929- IntWWM 80
Eagle, Frances Red Film 2
Eagle, James 1907-1959 Film 2, WhScrn 77
Eagle, S P FilmEn
Eagle Band BiDAmM
Eagle Eye Film 2
Eagle Eye, William Film 2
Eagle Wing, Chief Film 2
Eagles, The ConMuA 80A[port], IlEncCM[port], IlEncR[port], NewGrD 80, RkOn 2[port]
Eagles, Jeanne 1894-1929 Film 1
Eagles, Moneta M 1924- ConAmC, IntWWM 77, -80, WhoMus 72
Eagleshirt, William Film 1
Eaglin, Fird 1936- BluesWW[port]
Eagling, Wayne 1950- CnOxB
Eaken, John Reese 1949- IntWWM 77, -80
Eaker, Ira 1922- BiE&WWA, NotNAT
Eakin, Charles 1927- ConAmC
Eakin, Thomas ConAmC
Eakin, Vera 1900- AmSCAP 66
Eakin, Vera O 1890- ConAmC
Eames, Charles 1907- WorEFlm
Eames, Clare 1896-1930 Film 2, NotNAT B, WhScrn 74, -77, WhThe, WhoHol B
Eames, Emma 1865-1952 Baker 78, BiDAmM, BnBkM 80, CmOp, MusSN[port], NewEOp 71, NewGrD 80
Eames, Henry Purmont 1872-1950 BiDAmM
Eames, Henry Purmort 1872-1950 Baker 78
Eames, Juanita AmSCAP 66
Eames, Marian DancEn 78
Eames, Ray WorEFlm
Eames, Virginia d1971 WhoHol B
Eanes, Homer Robert, Jr. 1923- BiDAmM
Eardley, Jon 1928- BiDAmM
Earhart, Amelia 1898-1937 WomWMM
Earhart, Will 1871-1960 AmSCAP 66, -80, Baker 78, BiDAmM
Earl, Billy AmSCAP 80
Earl, Catherine V 1886-1946 WhScrn 74, -77
Earl, David Thomas Nelson 1951- IntWWM 77, -80
Earl, Don L 1917- IntWWM 77
Earl, Donn L 1917- IntWWM 80
Earl, Kathleen 1913-1954 WhScrn 74, -77
Earl, Mary AmSCAP 80
Earl, Virginia 1875-1937 WhoStg 1906, -1908
Earl Of Rochester PlP&P
Earland, Charles 1941- EncJzS 70
Earlcott, Gladys d1939 WhScrn 74, -77
Earle, Arthur Film 1, -2
Earle, Blanche 1883-1952 WhScrn 74, -77, WhoHol B
Earle, Dorothy d1958 Film 2, WhScrn 74, -77, WhoHol B
Earle, Edna Film 2, TwYS
Earle, Edward d1972 ForYSC, MotPP
Earle, Edward 1882-1972 WhScrn 77
Earle, Edward 1884-1972 FilmEn, Film 1, -2, TwYS
Earle, Jack 1906-1952 Film 2, WhScrn 77
Earle, John 1601?-1665 OxMus
Earle, Josephine 1892- Film 1, -2, IlWWBF
Earle, Lilias d1935 NotNAT B
Earle, Virginia 1875-1937 NotNAT B, WhThe
Earles, Harry Film 2
Earles, Harry 1900?- WhoHrs 80[port]
Earls, The RkOn[port]
Earls, Paul 1934- ConAmC, IntWWM 77, -80
Early, Delloreese Patricia 1931- AmSCAP 80
Early, Fergus 1946- CnOxB
Early, Margot 1915-1936 WhScrn 74, -77, WhoHol B
Early, Pearl M 1879-1960 WhScrn 74, -77, WhoHol B
Early, Robert Bruce 1940- AmSCAP 80
Early, Ruth WhoMus 72
Early, Tom 1880?-1958 NewOrJ
Earnfred, Thomas 1894- NotNAT
Earnfred, Thomas 1915- BiE&WWA
Earnhart, Myron L 1913- AmSCAP 66
Earnshaw, Hartley A PupTheA
Earp, Wyatt 1848-1928 HalFC 80
Earp, Wyatt 1848-1929 OxFilm
Earsden, John NewGrD 80
Earth Opera BiDAmM
Earth Wind & Fire ConMuA 80A[port], IlEncR, RkOn 2[port]
Easdale, Brian 1909- Baker 78, FilmgC, HalFC 80, NewGrD 80
Easmon, R Sarif ConDr 77
Easmon, Raymond Sarif 1925- ConDr 73
Eason, B Reeves 1886-1956 FilmEn, FilmgC, HalFC 80, OxFilm
Eason, Breezy 1913-1921 WhoHol B
Eason, Leon 1910- WhoJazz 72
Eason, Lorraine Film 2
Eason, Myles 1915- WhoThe 72, -77
Eason, Reeves 1866-1956 Film 2, TwYS
Eason, Reeves 1891-1956 TwYS A
Eason, Reeves B Breezy 1886-1956 WhScrn 77
Eason, Reeves Breezy, Jr. 1913-1921 WhScrn 77
East, Angela 1949- IntWWM 77, -80
East, Denis WhoMus 72
East, Ed 1894-1952 AmSCAP 66, -80
East, Ed 1896-1952 WhScrn 74, -77, WhoHol B
East, Graeme Douglas 1935- WhoMus 72
East, John M 1866-1924 IlWWBF A, NotNAT A, WhoHol B
East, John Michael 1929- WhoMus 72
East, Leslie 1949- IntWWM 80
East, Michael 1580?-1648 MusMk, NewGrD 80
East, Thomas d1608 NewGrD 80
East, Thomas 1535?-1609 Baker 78
East Side Kids JoeFr
Eastburn, James Wallace 1797-1819 BiDAmM
Easte, Michael NewGrD 80
Easte, Thomas NewGrD 80
Easterbrook, Harry PupTheA
Eastes, Helen M 1892- AmSCAP 66, -80
Eastham, J 1932- WhoMus 72
Eastham, Richard 1933- ForYSC, WhoHol A
Eastlake, Mary d1911 NotNAT B
Eastman, Andrea WomWMM
Eastman, Carole WomWMM
Eastman, Charles NatPD[port]
Eastman, Frederick 1859-1920 NotNAT B, WhThe
Eastman, George 1854-1932 Baker 78, DcFM, FilmEn, FilmgC, HalFC 80, OxFilm, OxMus, WorEFlm
Eastman, John ConMuA 80B
Eastman, Julius 1940- ConAmC
Eastman, Lee ConMuA 80B
Eastman, Luke 1790-1847 BiDAmM
Eastman, Peter WhoHol A
Easton, Amos 1905- BluesWW[port]
Easton, Florence 1884-1955 Baker 78, CmOp, MusSN[port], NewEOp 71, NewGrD 80
Easton, Jack 1918- AmSCAP 80
Easton, Jay Film 2
Easton, Joyce ForYSC, WhoHol A
Easton, Lorraine Film 2
Easton, Richard 1933- BiE&WWA, NotNAT, WhoThe 72, -77
Easton, Robert 1898- IntWWM 77, -80, WhoMus 72
Easton, Robert 1930- ForYSC, Vers A[port], WhoHol A
Easton, Sidney BlkAmP, BlksB&W C
Easton, Sidney 1886-1971 AmSCAP 80
Easton, Sidney 1891- BlksBF
Easton, Sidney 1896- AmSCAP 66
Easton, William E BlkAmP, MorBAP
Eastwood, Anthony Dexter 1939- IntWWM 77
Eastwood, Bill 1899-1960? NewOrJ
Eastwood, Charles Frederick WhoMus 72

Eastwood, Clint 1930- BiDFilm, -81, FilmEn, FilmgC, ForYSC, HalFC 80, IntMPA 77, -75, -76, -78, -79, -80, MotPP, MovMk[port], OxFilm, WhoHol A, WhoHrs 80, WorEFlm[port]
Eastwood, Janis Yvonne 1950- AmSCAP 80
Eastwood, Thomas Hugh 1922- IntWWM 77, -80, NewGrD 80, WhoMus 72
Easy Aces AmPS B, JoeFr
Easybeats, The ConMuA 80A, RkOn 2[port]
Eathorne, Wendy 1939- IntWWM 77, -80, WhoMus 72
Eaton, Charles Film 2
Eaton, Connie IlEncCM[port]
Eaton, Darryl 1940- IntWWM 80
Eaton, David Hugh James 1947- IntWWM 80
Eaton, Doris Film 2
Eaton, Elwin Film 1
Eaton, Evelyn 1924-1964 WhScrn 77
Eaton, Frances E PupTheA
Eaton, James 1934-1964 WhScrn 77
Eaton, Jay 1900-1970 Film 2, WhScrn 74, -77, WhoHol B
Eaton, Jimmy 1906- AmSCAP 66
Eaton, John C 1935- AmSCAP 66, Baker 78, ConAmC, IntWWM 77, -80, NewGrD 80
Eaton, Louis 1872-1927 Baker 78
Eaton, Mabel d1916 WhScrn 77
Eaton, Malcolm 1914- AmSCAP 66, -80
Eaton, Mary d1948 NotNAT B, WhThe, WhoHol B
Eaton, Mary 1901-1948 HalFC 80, WhScrn 74, -77
Eaton, Mary 1902-1946 CmpEPM, ForYSC
Eaton, Mary 1902-1948 EncMT, Film 2
Eaton, Roy Felix 1930- AmSCAP 80
Eaton, Shirley 1936- FilmgC, ForYSC, HalFC 80, MotPP, WhoHol A
Eaton, Shirley 1937- FilmAG WE, FilmEn, IlWWBF
Eaton, Wallas 1917- WhoThe 72, -77
Eaton, Walter Prichard 1878-1957 NotNAT B, PlP&P, WhThe
Eaubonne, Jean D' 1903-1971 DcFM, FilmEn
Eaves, Hilary 1914- WhThe
Ebadi, Ahmed 1904- IntWWM 77, -80
Ebb, Fred 1932- ConDr 77D, EncMT, NewCBMT, NotNAT
Ebb, Fred 1933- WhoThe 72, -77
Ebbage, David 1942- IntWWM 77, -80
Ebbelaar, Han 1943- CnOxB
Ebbins, Milton Keith 1914- AmSCAP 66, -80
Ebdon, Thomas 1738-1811 NewGrD 80, OxMus
Ebel, Arnold 1883-1963 Baker 78
Ebeling, Christoph Daniel 1741-1817 NewGrD 80
Ebeling, Johann Georg 1637-1676 NewGrD 80
Ebell, Heinrich Carl 1775-1824 NewGrD 80
Eben, Al WhoHol A
Eben, Petr 1929- Baker 78, DcCM, IntWWM 77, -80, NewGrD 80
Ebenhoh, Horst 1930- IntWWM 77, -80
Eberg, Victor 1925-1972 WhScrn 77
Eberhard Von Freising NewGrD 80
Eberhard, Dennis ConAmC
Eberhard, Ernst 1839-1913 BiDAmM
Eberhard, Johann August 1739-1809 NewGrD 80
Eberhardt, Goby 1852-1926 NewGrD 80
Eberhardt, Johann Jakob 1852-1926 NewGrD 80
Eberhardt, Mignon C 1899- HalFC 80
Eberhardt, Siegfried 1883-1960 Baker 78, NewGrD 80
Eberhart, Constance BiE&WWA
Eberhart, Nelle Richmond 1871-1944 AmSCAP 66, -80, BiDAmM
Eberhart, Richard 1904- BiE&WWA, NotNAT
Eberl, Anton Franz Josef 1765-1807 Baker 78, NewGrD 80
Eberle, Bob AmPS B, WhoHol A
Eberle, Bruce 1942- IntWWM 77
Eberle, Eugene A 1840-1917 NotNAT B, WhoStg 1906, -1908
Eberle, Ray 1919- BgBands 74[port], CmpEPM
Eberlin, Daniel 1647-1715? NewGrD 80
Eberlin, Johann Ernst 1702-1762 Baker 78, NewGrD 80
Eberly, Bob 1916- CmpEPM, What 4[port]
Eberly, John Wilgus 1913- IntWWM 77, -80
Ebers, Carl Friedrich 1770-1836 NewGrD 80
Ebers, John 1785?-1830? NewGrD 80
Eberson, Drew 1904- IntMPA 77, -75, -76, -78, -79, -80
Ebert, Bernie 1915-1969 WhScrn 74, -77
Ebert, Carl 1887- CmOp, EncWT, Film 1, -2, IntWWM 77, -80, NewEOp 71, NewGrD 80
Ebert, Charles 1887- NewGrD 80
Ebert, Joyce 1933- BiE&WWA, NotNAT, WhoThe 77
Ebert, Peter 1918- CreCan 2, WhoMus 72, WhoOp 76
Eberwein, Carl 1786-1868 Baker 78, NewGrD 80
Eberwein, Traugott Maximilian 1775-1831 Baker 78, NewGrD 80
Ebi, Earl 1903-1973 IntMPA 75, -76, WhScrn 77
Ebinger, Blandine Film 2
Ebio, Matthias 1591-1676 NewGrD 80
Ebner, Wolfgang 1612-1665 NewGrD 80
Ebram NewGrD 80
Ebran NewGrD 80
Ebreo, Guglielmo 1440?- CnOxB
Ebreo DaPesaro, Guglielmo NewGrD 80
Ebsen, Buddy 1906- ForYSC
Ebsen, Buddy 1908- AmSCAP 66, CmpEPM, EncMT, FilmEn, FilmgC, HalFC 80, IntMPA 77, -75, -76, -78, -79, -80, MotPP, MovMk, NewYTET, WhoHol A
Ebsen, Christian, Jr. 1908- AmSCAP 80
Ebsen, Vilma WhoHol A
Ebsworth, Eileen WhoMus 72
Ebsworth, Joseph d1868 NotNAT B
Ebsworth, Mary Emma d1881 NotNAT B
Ebsworth, Phyllis IntWWM 77, -80, WhoMus 72
Eburne, Maude 1875-1960 FilmgC, ForYSC, HalFC 80, HolCA[port], MotPP, MovMk, NotNAT B, ThFT[port], WhScrn 74, -77, WhoHol B
Eby, George W 1914- IntMPA 77, -75, -76, -78, -79, -80
Eby, Margarette Fink 1931- IntWWM 77, -80
Eby-Rock, Helen WhoHol A
Eccard, Johann 1553-1611 MusMk, OxMus
Eccard, Johannes 1553-1611 Baker 78, BnBkM 80, NewGrD 80
Ecchienus, Caspar NewGrD 80
Eccles NewGrD 80
Eccles, Aimee WhoHol A
Eccles, Donald 1908- WhoThe 72, -77
Eccles, Henry OxMus
Eccles, Henry 1640?-1711 NewGrD 80
Eccles, Henry 1652?-1742? OxMus
Eccles, Henry 1670?-1742? Baker 78
Eccles, Henry 1675?-1745? NewGrD 80
Eccles, Jane 1896-1966 WhScrn 74, -77, WhoHol B
Eccles, Janet 1895-1966 WhThe
Eccles, John 1650?-1735 BnBkM 80, OxMus
Eccles, John 1668?-1735 Baker 78, MusMk, NewGrD 80
Eccles, Solomon 1617?-1682 NewGrD 80
Eccles, Solomon 1640?-1710 NewGrD 80
Eccles, Solomon, I 1618-1683 OxMus
Eccles, Solomon, II OxMus
Eccles, Ted WhoHol A
Eccles, Thomas OxMus
Eccleston, William d1625? OxThe
Echaniz, Jose 1905-1969 Baker 78
Echarri, Isabel 1929- WhoOp 76
Echavaria NewGrD 80
Echegaray, Jose d1832 NotNAT B
Echegaray, Jose 1832-1916 CnMD, EncWT, McGEWD[port], ModWD, OxThe
Echegaray, Miguel WhThe
Echevarria NewGrD 80
Echevarria, Domingo De NewGrD 80
Echevarria, Jose De NewGrD 80
Echevarria, Jose De d1691? NewGrD 80
Echevarria, Jose De Eizaga Y NewGrD 80
Echevarria, Jose Marigomez De NewGrD 80
Echevarria, Juan Marigomez De d1805 NewGrD 80
Echevarria, Pedro De NewGrD 80
Echito, Martie 1951- AmSCAP 80
Echoes, The RkOn
Echols, Ann J BlkAmP
Eck NewGrD 80
Eck, Franz 1774-1804 NewGrD 80
Eck, Friedrich Johann 1767-1838 NewGrD 80
Eck, Georg NewGrD 80
Eck, Imre 1930- CnOxB
Eckard, Johann Gottfried 1735-1809 Baker 78, NewGrD 80
Eckardt, Hans 1905-1969 Baker 78, NewGrD 80
Eckardt, Johann Gottfried 1735-1809 NewGrD 80
Eckart, Jean 1921- BiE&WWA, NotNAT, PlP&P[port], WhoThe 72, -77
Eckart, Johann Gottfried 1735-1809 NewGrD 80
Eckart, William Joseph 1920- BiE&WWA, NotNAT, PlP&P, WhoThe 72, -77
Eckel, Matthias NewGrD 80
Eckelt, Johann Valentin 1673-1732 Baker 78, NewGrD 80
Eckenberg, Johann Carl 1685-1748 OxThe
Ecker, Heinz-Klaus 1942- WhoOp 76
Ecker, Judith K 1933- AmSCAP 66, -80
Ecker, Thomas R 1935- AmSCAP 66
Ecker, Tom 1935- AmSCAP 80
Eckerberg, Sixten 1909- Baker 78
Eckerlein, John E 1884-1926 WhScrn 74, -77, WhoHol B
Eckerson, Olive PupTheA
Eckert, George 1927- BiE&WWA, NotNAT
Eckert, Gertraud 1941- WhoOp 76
Eckert, Karl Anton Florian 1820-1879 Baker 78
Eckert, Thor, Jr. 1949- ConAmTC
Eckhard, Jacob 1757-1833 Baker 78
Eckhard, Jacob, Sr. 1757-1833 BiDAmM
Eckhardt, Andreas 1943- IntWWM 80
Eckhardt, Oliver J 1873-1952 Film 2, WhScrn 74, -77, WhoHol B
Eckhardt-Gramatte, S C 1902?- DcCM
Eckhardt-Gramatte, S-C 1902-1974 NewGrD 80
Eckhardt-Gramatte, Sonia CreCan 1
Eckhardt-Gramatte, Sonia 1902-1974 Baker 78
Eckhardt-Gramatte, Sophie Carmen CreCan 1, WhoMus 72
Eckhoff, Oivind 1916- IntWWM 77
Ecklebe, Alexander 1904- IntWWM 77, -80
Eckles, Lewis C 1888-1950 WhScrn 77
Eckles, Robert d1975 WhoHol C
Ecklund, Carol 1934-1939 WhScrn 74, -77
Eckoldt, Johann Valentin NewGrD 80
Eckstein, Billy AmPS B
Eckstein, George NewYTET
Eckstein, Maxwell 1905-1974 AmSCAP 66, -80
Eckstein, Pavel 1911- Baker 78, IntWWM 77, -80, NewGrD 80, WhoOp 76
Eckstein, William Clarence 1914- NewGrD 80
Eckstine, Billy 1914- AmPS A, Baker 78, BgBands 74[port], BiDAmM, BlksB&W C, CmpEPM, DrBlPA, EncJzS 70, IlEncJ, NewGrD 80, WhoHol A, WhoMus 72
Eckstine, William Clarence 1914- EncJzS 70
Ecorcheville, Jules 1872-1915 Baker 78, NewGrD 80
Ecstasy Passion & Pain RkOn 2[port]
Ecton, Robert Max 1915- AmSCAP 80
Eda-Pierre, Christiane IntWWM 80, WhoOp 76
Edander, Gunnar 1942- IntWWM 80
Eddie And The Hot Rods IlEncR
Eddinger, Lawrence Film 2
Eddinger, Wallace 1881-1929 NotNAT B, WhThe
Eddington, John P Film 2
Eddington, Paul 1927- WhoThe 72, -77
Eddison, Robert 1908- WhoThe 72, -77
Eddleman, David 1936- AmSCAP 80, ConAmC
Eddleman, G David 1936- IntWWM 77, -80
Eddleman, Jack 1933- WhoOp 76
Eddy, Albert CreCan 2
Eddy, Alethea Mary 1914- IntWWM 77
Eddy, Arthur W IntMPA 77, -75, -76, -78
Eddy, Augusta Rossner 1860-1925 WhScrn 74, -77
Eddy, Clarence 1851-1937 Baker 78,

NewGrD 80
Eddy, Daniel C 1823-1896 BiDAmM
Eddy, David Manton 1928- AmSCAP 66, -80
Eddy, Dorothy 1907-1959 WhScrn 74, -77, WhoHol B
Eddy, Duane 1938- AmPS A, ConMuA 80A, RkOn[port]
Eddy, Edward 1822-1875 NotNAT B, OxThe
Eddy, Helen Jerome 1897- Film 1, -2, ForYSC, HolCA[port], MotPP, ThFT[port], TwYS
Eddy, Hiram Clarence 1851-1937 BiDAmM
Eddy, Jenifer WhoMus 72
Eddy, Lorraine Film 2
Eddy, Mary 1821-1910 BiDAmM
Eddy, Nelson d1967 AmPS B
Eddy, Nelson 1901-1967 Baker 78, BiDAmM, CmMov, CmpEPM, FilmEn, FilmgC, HalFC 80, MGM[port], MotPP, MovMk[port], NotNAT B, OxFilm, WhScrn 74, -77, WhThe, WhoHol B
Eddy, Nelson 1902-1967 ForYSC
Eddy, Ted 1904- AmSCAP 66, -80
Eddy, Walter AmSCAP 80
Ede, Aegidius VanDen NewGrD 80
Ede, Gilles VanDen 1708?-1782 NewGrD 80
Edegran, Lars Ivar 1944- NewOrJ SUP[port]
Edel, Herman 1926- IntWWM 77
Edel, Yitzhak 1896-1973 NewGrD 80
Edelawer, Hermann NewGrD 80
Edele, Durand J IntMPA 77, -75, -76, -78, -79, -80
Edelheit, Harry 1891-1955 AmSCAP 66, -80
Edelheit, Martha WomWMM B
Edell, Nancy WomWMM B
Edelman, Herb 1930- FilmgC, WhoHol A
Edelman, Louis F 1901-1976 HalFC 80, NewYTET
Edelmann, Herb 1930- HalFC 80
Edelmann, Jean-Frederic 1749-1794 Baker 78, NewGrD 80
Edelmann, Johann Friedrich 1749-1794 NewGrD 80
Edelmann, Moritz d1680 NewGrD 80
Edelmann, Otto 1916- CmOp
Edelmann, Otto Karl 1917- IntWWM 77, -80, NewEOp 71, NewGrD 80, WhoMus 72, WhoOp 76
Edelmann, Toni 1945- IntWWM 77, -80
Edelson, Edward 1929- AmSCAP 66, -80
Edelstein, Walter 1903- AmSCAP 80
Eden, Aegidius VanDen NewGrD 80
Eden, Barbara 1934- FilmEn, FilmgC, ForYSC, HalFC 80, MovMk, WhoHol A
Eden, Bracha 1928- NewGrD 80
Eden, Conrad Eden WhoMus 72
Eden, Conrad William 1905- IntWWM 77, -80
Eden, Gilles VanDen 1708?-1782 NewGrD 80
Edens, Roger 1905- FilmEn
Edens, Roger 1905-1970 AmSCAP 66, -80, BestMus, CmMov, CmpEPM, FilmgC, HalFC 80, WorEFlm
Eder, Claudia 1948- WhoOp 76
Eder, Helmut 1916- Baker 78, DcCM, IntWWM 80, NewGrD 80
Eder, Joseph 1760-1835 NewGrD 80
Ederle, Gertrude 1907?- What 1[port], WhoHol A
Edes, Marjorie Beryl WhoMus 72
Edeson, Arthur 1891-1970 CmMov, DcFM, FilmEn, FilmgC, HalFC 80, WorEFlm
Edeson, Robert 1868-1930 MovMk[port]
Edeson, Robert 1868-1931 FilmEn, Film 1, -2, ForYSC, NotNAT B, OxThe, TwYS, WhScrn 74, -77, WhThe, WhoHol B, WhoStg 1906, -1908
Edgar, David 1948- ConDr 77
Edgar, Marriott 1880-1951 FilmgC, HalFC 80, NotNAT B, WhThe
Edgar, Mrs. Richard d1937 NotNAT B
Edgar, Tripp d1927 NotNAT B
Edgar Broughton Band IlEncR
Edgar-Bruce, Toni 1892-1966 WhScrn 74, -77, WhoHol B
Edgar-Bruce, Tonie WhThe
Edgcumbe, Richard 1764-1839 NewGrD 80
Edgett, Edwin Francis 1867-1946 NotNAT B, WhThe
Edgeworth, Jane 1922- WhoThe 72, -77
Edgington, Brian John 1928- IntWWM 77
Edginton, Mary Joyce 1908- WhoMus 72
Edginton, May d1957 WhThe
Edgren, Gustaf 1895-1954 FilmEn
Edinger, Christiane 1945- IntWWM 77, -80, WhoMus 72
Edington, John P Film 2
Edington, May d1957 NotNAT B
Edinoff, Ellen CnOxB
Edison, Harry 1915- AmSCAP 66, -80, BiDAmM, CmpEPM, EncJzS 70, IlEncJ
Edison, Sweets 1915- EncJzS 70, WhoJazz 72
Edison, Thomas Alva 1847-1931 DcFM, FilmEn, FilmgC, HalFC 80, MusMk[port], NewGrD 80[port], NotNAT B, OxFilm, OxMus, WorEFlm
Edison Lighthouse RkOn 2[port]
Ediss, Connie 1871-1934 NotNAT B, WhThe
Ediss, Connie 1877-1934 WhoStg 1908
Edlefsen, Blaine E 1930- IntWWM 77, -80
Edler, Charles 1877-1942 WhScrn 74, -77, WhoHol B
Edlerawer, Hermann NewGrD 80
Edlin, Tubby 1882- Film 2, WhThe
Edlund, Lars 1922- NewGrD 80
Edlund, Mikael 1950- IntWWM 80
Edman, Goesta 1887-1938 WhScrn 74
Edmonds, Daisy Mary WhoMus 72
Edmonds, Edith PupTheA
Edmonds, Henriette BlkAmP
Edmonds, Irene MorBAP
Edmonds, Michael 1927- WhoMus 72
Edmonds, Randolph 1900- BlkAmP, DrBlPA, MorBAP
Edmonds, Shepard N 1876-1957 AmSCAP 66, -80
Edmonds, Thomas James 1934- IntWWM 77, -80
Edmondson, Dian EncFCWM 69
Edmondson, John Baldwin 1933- AmSCAP 80, ConAmC, IntWWM 77, -80
Edmondson, Travis EncFCWM 69
Edmondson, William BlksB&W, -C
Edmund NewGrD 80
Edmund, Lada, Jr. WhoHol A
Edmunds, Christopher Montague 1899- Baker 78, IntWWM 77, -80, WhoMus 72
Edmunds, Dave 1944- ConMuA 80A, -80B, IlEncR, RkOn 2[port]
Edmunds, Floyd Elsie WhoMus 72
Edmunds, Janet Ward 1933- IntWWM 77, -80, WhoMus 72
Edmunds, John 1913- AmSCAP 66, Baker 78, ConAmC, NewGrD 80
Edmunds, John Francis 1928- AmSCAP 80
Edmundsen, Al 1896-1954 Film 2, WhScrn 77
Edmundson, Carolyn PupTheA
Edmundson, Garth 1895- BiDAmM, ConAmC
Edmundson, Garth 1900- AmSCAP 66, -80
Edmundson, Harry Film 1
Edney, Florence 1879-1950 NotNAT B, WhThe
Edouarde, Carl Film 2
Edouart, Alexander Farciot 1895?-1980 WhoHrs 80
Edouart, Farciot FilmgC, HalFC 80
Edouin, May d1944 NotNAT B
Edouin, Rose 1844-1925 NotNAT B, WhThe
Edouin, Willie 1846-1908 NotNAT B, OxThe
Edsels, The RkOn[port]
Edson, Bob ConMuA 80B
Edson, Lewis 1748-1820 Baker 78, BiDAmM, NewGrD 80
Edson, Lewis, Jr. 1771-1845 BiDAmM
Edstrom, Katherine 1901-1973 WhScrn 77
Edthofer, Anton Film 2
Eduardova, Eugenia Platonovna 1882-1960 CnOxB, DancEn 78
Edvina, Louise 1880?-1938 CmOp
Edvina, Louise 1880-1948 NewGrD 80
Edward IV 1442-1483 OxMus
Edward VI 1537-1553 OxMus
Edward VII 1841-1910 OxMus
Edward VIII 1894-1936 OxMus
Edward, Jimmy AmSCAP 80
Edward, Nils Film 2
Edward, Paul AmSCAP 80
Edward Bear RkOn 2[port]
Edwardes, Conway d1880 NotNAT B
Edwardes, Felix d1954 NotNAT B, WhThe
Edwardes, George 1852-1915 CnThe, EncWT, NotNAT A, -B, OxThe, PlP&P, WhThe, WhoStg 1906, -1908
Edwardes, George 1855-1915 EncMT
Edwardes, Olga 1917- WhThe
Edwardes, Paula WhThe, WhoStg 1906, -1908
Edwardes, Richard 1524-1566 NewGrD 80
Edwards NewGrD 80
Edwards, Miss NewGrD 80
Edwards, A C 1909- BiE&WWA, NotNAT
Edwards, Alan d1954 MotPP, NotNAT B, WhoHol B
Edwards, Alan 1893-1954 Film 2
Edwards, Alan 1900-1954 WhScrn 74, -77
Edwards, Andrew J C ConAmC
Edwards, Anne WhoOp 76
Edwards, Anne Hill 1924- IntWWM 77
Edwards, Bass 1898-1965 WhoJazz 72
Edwards, Ben 1916- BiE&WWA, NotNAT, WhoThe 72, -77
Edwards, Bernard ConMuA 80B
Edwards, Bill 1918- WhoHol A
Edwards, Blake 1922- BiDFilm, -81, CmMov, FilmEn, FilmgC, HalFC 80, IntMPA 77, -75, -76, -78, -79, -80, MovMk[port], NewYTET, OxFilm, WorEFlm
Edwards, Bobby RkOn
Edwards, Bruce d1927 NotNAT B
Edwards, Charles 1933- BluesWW[port]
Edwards, Cherry Ann Redden 1942- IntWWM 77
Edwards, Clara 1887-1974 AmSCAP 66, -80, Baker 78, ConAmC
Edwards, Cliff 1895-1971 AmPS B, CmpEPM, FilmEn, Film 2, FilmgC, ForYSC, HalFC 80, MotPP, MovMk, Vers B[port], What 3[port], WhScrn 74, -77, WhoHol B
Edwards, David 1915- BluesWW[port]
Edwards, Dorothy May WhoMus 72
Edwards, Douglas 1917- IntMPA 77, -75, -76, -78, -79, -80, NewYTET
Edwards, Eddie 1891-1963 CmpEPM, NewOrJ[port], WhoJazz 72
Edwards, Edith Film 2
Edwards, Edna Park 1895-1967 WhScrn 74, -77, WhoHol B
Edwards, Edwin Branford 1891-1963 AmSCAP 66, -80, BiDAmM
Edwards, Elaine ForYSC
Edwards, Eleanor 1883-1968 WhScrn 74, -77, WhoHol B
Edwards, Frank 1909- BluesWW[port]
Edwards, Fred 1860- WhoStg 1908
Edwards, Frederick George 1853-1909 NewGrD 80
Edwards, G Spencer d1916 WhThe
Edwards, George 1943- CpmDNM 79, ConAmC
Edwards, Gloria DrBlPA
Edwards, Glyn DcPup
Edwards, Gus d1945 Sw&Ld C, WhoHol B
Edwards, Gus 1879-1945 AmPS, AmSCAP 66, -80, BiDAmM, CmpEPM, Film 2, NotNAT B, PopAmC[port]
Edwards, Gus 1881-1945 WhScrn 74, -77
Edwards, Gwynne 1909- WhoMus 72
Edwards, H Neil 1931- ConAmC, IntWWM 77, -80
Edwards, H T V BlkAmP
Edwards, Harry Film 1, -2
Edwards, Harry 1888- FilmEn
Edwards, Henry 1882-1952 FilmEn, FilmgC, HalFC 80, IlWWBF[port], WhScrn 74, -77
Edwards, Henry 1883-1952 FilmAG WE, Film 1, -2, NotNAT B, WhThe
Edwards, Henry John 1854-1933 Baker 78
Edwards, Henry Sutherland 1829-1906 Baker 78
Edwards, Hilton 1903- OxThe, PlP&P[port], WhoThe 72, -77
Edwards, J Gordon 1867-1925 HalFC 80, TwYS A
Edwards, J Gordon 1885?-1925 FilmEn
Edwards, J Gordon, Jr. Film 2
Edwards, Jack Film 2
Edwards, Jack 1922- AmSCAP 66
Edwards, Jack 1924- AmSCAP 80
Edwards, James 1912-1970 WhScrn 74, -77
Edwards, James 1916-1970 DrBlPA
Edwards, James 1918-1970 ForYSC

Edwards, James 1922-1970 *FilmgC, HalFC 80, MovMk, WhoHol B*
Edwards, Jennifer *WhoHol A*
Edwards, Jessie B *ConAmC*
Edwards, Jimmy 1920- *AmSCAP 80, FilmgC, HalFC 80, IIWWBF[port], -A, WhoHol A*
Edwards, Joan 1919- *CmpEPM*
Edwards, Joan 1920- *AmSCAP 66, -80*
Edwards, Jodie d1967 *BlksBF*
Edwards, John Vivian 1945- *IntWWM 77, -80*
Edwards, Johnny 1922-1973 *NewOrJ SUP[port]*
Edwards, Jonathan 1946- *CounME 74, -74A, RkOn 2[port]*
Edwards, Julian 1855-1910 *Baker 78, BiDAmM, CmpEPM, NewGrD 80, NotNAT B, WhoStg 1906, -1908*
Edwards, Julie Andrews 1935- *AmSCAP 80*
Edwards, Junius *BlkAmP*
Edwards, Karen *WomWMM*
Edwards, Leo 1886-1978 *AmSCAP 66, -80*
Edwards, Leo 1937- *ConAmC*
Edwards, Leslie 1916- *CnOxB, DancEn 78*
Edwards, Mattie 1886-1944 *WhScrn 74, -77, WhoHol B*
Edwards, Meredith 1917- *FilmgC, HalFC 80, WhoHol A*
Edwards, Michael 1893-1962 *AmSCAP 66, -80*
Edwards, Morfen 1938- *IntWWM 77, -80*
Edwards, Nate 1902-1972 *WhScrn 77*
Edwards, Neely 1889-1965 *Film 1, TwYS, WhScrn 74, -77, WhoHol B*
Edwards, Neely 1889-1975 *Film 2*
Edwards, Nigel Rousseau 1952- *IntWWM 80*
Edwards, Olen 1923- *AmSCAP 80*
Edwards, Oliver Henry 1902- *WhoMus 72*
Edwards, Osman 1864-1936 *NotNAT B, WhThe*
Edwards, Owain Tudor 1940- *IntWWM 77, -80*
Edwards, Paul 1916- *NewOrJ*
Edwards, Penny 1919- *FilmgC, HalFC 80*
Edwards, Penny 1928- *ForYSC, WhoHol A*
Edwards, Ralph 1913- *NewYTET, What 3[port]*
Edwards, Richard d1566 *NotNAT B*
Edwards, Richard d1604 *NotNAT B*
Edwards, Richard 1522?-1566 *Baker 78*
Edwards, Richard 1523?-1566 *OxMus*
Edwards, Richard 1524-1566 *NewGrD 80*
Edwards, Robert *OxMus*
Edwards, Ross 1943- *Baker 78, DcCM, IntWWM 77, -80, NewGrD 80*
Edwards, Ryan *ConAmC*
Edwards, Sam *ForYSC, WhoHol A*
Edwards, Sarah 1883-1955 *Film 2, Vers B[port], WhoHol B*
Edwards, Sarah 1883-1965 *WhScrn 74, -77*
Edwards, Sherman 1919- *AmSCAP 66, -80, EncMT, WhoThe 72, -77*
Edwards, Snitz d1960 *Film 2, ForYSC, TwYS*
Edwards, Snitz 1862-1937 *WhScrn 74, -77, WhoHol B*
Edwards, Stoney *CounME 74[port], -74A*
Edwards, Susie d1963 *NotNAT B*
Edwards, Susie 1896-1963 *BluesWW[port]*
Edwards, Ted 1883-1945 *WhScrn 74, -77, WhoHol B*
Edwards, Teddy 1924- *EncJzS 70*
Edwards, Theodore Marcus 1924- *BiDAmM, EncJzS 70*
Edwards, Thomas Jay 1954- *AmSCAP 80*
Edwards, Thomas Morgan 1932- *AmSCAP 80*
Edwards, Thornton *Film 1*
Edwards, Tom 1880- *WhThe*
Edwards, Tom 1923- *RkOn[port]*
Edwards, Tommy 1922-1969 *AmPS A, DrBlPA, RkOn[port]*
Edwards, Vince 1926- *ForYSC*
Edwards, Vince 1928- *FilmEn, FilmgC, HalFC 80, IntMPA 77, -75, -76, -78, -79, -80, MotPP, MovMk[port], WhoHol A*
Edwards, Virginia d1964 *NotNAT B, WhScrn 74, -77, WhoHol B*
Edwards, Vivian *Film 1*
Edwards, Walter *TwYS A*
Edwards, Warwick Anthony 1944- *IntWWM 80*
Edwards, Webley Elgin 1902-1977 *AmSCAP 80*
Edwards, Wilbur S *IntMPA 75, -76*
Edwards, William 1918- *ForYSC*
Edwards, William J 1930- *ConAmTC*
Edwards, Willy *NewOrJ*
Edwin, Elizabeth Rebecca Richards 1771?-1854 *EncWT, OxThe*
Edwin, John 1749-1790 *EncWT, Ent, OxThe*
Edwin, John 1768-1803 *EncWT, OxThe*
Edwin, Robert *AmSCAP 80*
Edwin, T Emery d1951 *NotNAT B*
Edwinn, Edwin Frank 1922- *IntWWM 77, -80*
Eede, Gilles VanDen 1708?-1782 *NewGrD 80*
Eeden, Gilles VanDen 1708?-1782 *NewGrD 80*
Eeden, Jan VanDen 1842-1917 *NewGrD 80*
Eeden, Jean Baptiste VanDen 1842-1917 *Baker 78, NewGrD 80*
Eethe, Gilles VanDen 1708?-1782 *NewGrD 80*
Eff, Roy *AmSCAP 80*
Effendy, Basuki 192-?- *DcFM*
Effinger, Cecil Stanley 1914- *AmSCAP 66, -80, Baker 78, ConAmC, IntWWM 77, -80, NewGrD 80*
Effrat, John 1908-1965 *BiE&WWA, NotNAT B*
Effrem, Mutio 1555?-1626? *NewGrD 80*
Effrem, Muzio 1555?-1626? *NewGrD 80*
Effros, Bob 1899- *WhoJazz 72*
Effros, Robert 1900- *AmSCAP 66, -80*
Efimoff, Nicholas *CnOxB*
Efimov, Ivan Semionovich 1878-1959 *DcPup*
Efimova, Nina Simonovich 1877-1948 *DcPup*
Efrati, Moshe 1934- *CnOxB*
Efrein, Laurie *ConAmC*
Efrem, Mutio 1555?-1626? *NewGrD 80*
Efrem, Muzio 1555?-1626? *NewGrD 80*
Egan, Denis 1919- *WhoMus 72*
Egan, Eddie 1924- *HalFC 80*
Egan, Frank C d1927 *NotNAT B*
Egan, Gladys *Film 1*
Egan, Jack *Film 2, TwYS*
Egan, Jefferson *WhoStg 1908*
Egan, Jenny *NotNAT, PlP&P[port], WhoHol A*
Egan, John C 1892-1940 *AmSCAP 66, -80*
Egan, Michael 1895-1956 *NotNAT B, WhThe*
Egan, Mishka 1891-1964 *WhScrn 74, -77*
Egan, Mishska 1891-1964 *NotNAT B*
Egan, Peter 1945- *HalFC 80*
Egan, Pierce 1772-1849 *NotNAT A, -B, OxThe*
Egan, Raymond B 1890-1952 *AmPS, AmSCAP 66, -80, BiDAmM, CmpEPM*
Egan, Richard *MotPP*
Egan, Richard 1921- *FilmEn, FilmgC, ForYSC, HalFC 80, MovMk, WhoHol A*
Egan, Richard 1923- *IntMPA 77, -75, -76, -78, -79, -80*
Egan, Walter Lindsay 1948- *AmSCAP 80, ConMuA 80A*
Egardus *NewGrD 80*
Egbert, Brothers *WhThe*
Egbert, Albert *IIWWBF*
Egbert, Seth *IIWWBF*
Egberts, Sandrie 1929- *IntWWM 77, -80*
Egbuna, Obi 1938- *ConDr 73, -77*
Ege, Helena Gregg *PupTheA*
Ege, Julie 1947?- *FilmgC, HalFC 80, WhoHol A, WhoHrs 80*
Egedacher *NewGrD 80*
Egedacher, Johann Christoph 1664-1747 *NewGrD 80*
Egedacher, Johann Georg *NewGrD 80*
Egedacher, Johann Ignaz 1675-1744 *NewGrD 80*
Egedacher, Johann Rochus *NewGrD 80*
Egedacher, Joseph Christoph d1706 *NewGrD 80*
Egenolff, Christian 1502-1555 *Baker 78, NewGrD 80*
Eger, John *NewYTET*
Eger, Joseph 1925- *IntWWM 77, -80*
Eger VonKalkar, Heinrich 1328-1408 *NewGrD 80*
Egeria *NewGrD 80*
Egerton, George d1945 *NotNAT B, WhThe*
Egerton, Julian 1848-1945 *NewGrD 80*
Eggan, Carel Rowe *WomWMM B*
Eggar, Jack 1904- *WhThe*
Eggar, Samantha *MotPP, WhoHol A*
Eggar, Samantha 1938- *ForYSC*
Eggar, Samantha 1939- *FilmAG WE, FilmEn, FilmgC, HalFC 80, MovMk*
Eggar, Samantha 1940- *IIWWBF[port], IntMPA 77, -75, -76, -78, -79, -80*
Egge, Klaus 1903- *DcCM*
Egge, Klaus 1906- *Baker 78, CompSN[port], NewGrD 80*
Egge, Peter 1869-1959 *CnMD*
Egge, Ray *BluesWW*
Eggebrecht, Hans Heinrich 1919- *Baker 78, IntWWM 77, -80, NewGrD 80*
Eggebrecht, Jorg 1939- *IntWWM 77, -80*
Eggeling, Viking 1880-1925 *DcFM, FilmEn, OxFilm, WorEFlm*
Eggen, Arne 1881-1955 *Baker 78, NewGrD 80*
Eggen, Erik 1877-1957 *Baker 78, NewGrD 80*
Eggenton, Joseph 1870-1946 *WhScrn 74, -77, WhoHol B*
Eggers, Kevin *ConMuA 80B*
Eggers, Robert Wayne 1939- *AmSCAP 80*
Eggert, E W *Film 2*
Eggert, Joachim Nicolas 1779-1813 *NewGrD 80*
Eggerth, Marta *WhoHol A*
Eggerth, Marta 1912- *FilmAG WE, FilmEn*
Eggerth, Marta 1916- *WhThe*
Eggerth, Marta 1919- *BiE&WWA, ForYSC, NotNAT*
Eggerton, Beryl *Film 2*
Egghard, Julius 1834-1867 *Baker 78*
Eggington, John 1926- *IntWWM 77, -80*
Eggleston, Anne E 1934- *IntWWM 80*
Eghiazaryan, Grigor 1908- *NewGrD 80*
Egidi, Arthur 1859-1943 *Baker 78*
Egidius *NewGrD 80*
Egidius De Morino *NewGrD 80*
Egidius De Murino *NewGrD 80*
Egidius De Pusiex *NewGrD 80*
Egidius De Zamora *NewGrD 80*
Egilson, Gunnar 1927- *IntWWM 77, -80*
Egk, Werner 1901- *Baker 78, BnBkM 80, CmOp, CompSN[port], CpmDNM 80, CnOxB, DancEn 78, DcCM, IntWWM 77, -80, NewEOp 71, NewGrD 80, OxMus, WhoMus 72*
Eglevsky, Andre 1917- *CnOxB, DancEn 78[port], What 3[port]*
Eglevsky, Marina 1951- *CnOxB*
Egli, David Christian 1937- *AmSCAP 80*
Egli, Johann Heinrich 1742-1810 *Baker 78, NewGrD 80*
Egli, Joseph E 1900-1974 *WhScrn 77*
Eglington, J *WomWMM*
Eglinton, Earl Of 1739-1819 *NewGrD 80, OxMus*
Egmond, Max Rudolf Van 1936- *IntWWM 77, -80, NewGrD 80, WhoMus 72*
Egnatzik, Joseph 1920- *AmSCAP 66, -80*
Egner, Philip 1870-1956 *AmSCAP 66, -80*
Egner, Richard John 1924- *IntWWM 77, -80*
Egnot, Johnnye F 1943- *IntWWM 80*
Egorova, Lubov 1880-1972 *CnOxB, DancEn 78[port]*
Egressy, Beni 1814-1851 *NewGrD 80*
Egressy, Benjamin 1814-1851 *NewGrD 80*
Egressy, Gabor 1808-1866 *OxThe*
Egressy, Galambos 1814-1851 *NewGrD 80*
Egri, Lajos 1888-1967 *BiE&WWA, NotNAT B*
Egri, Susanna 1926- *CnOxB*
Egues, Manuel De 1657-1729 *NewGrD 80*
Egyud, Anna Judith 1927- *AmSCAP 80*
Ehe *NewGrD 80*
Ehe, Friedrich 1669-1743 *NewGrD 80*
Ehe, Georg 1595-1668 *NewGrD 80*
Ehe, Isaak 1586-1632 *NewGrD 80*
Ehe, Johann Leonhard 1638-1707 *NewGrD 80*
Ehe, Johann Leonhard 1664-1724 *NewGrD 80*
Ehe, Johann Leonhard 1700-1771 *NewGrD 80*
Ehe, Martin Friedrich 1714-1779 *NewGrD 80*
Ehe, Wolf Magnus 1690-1722 *NewGrD 80*
Ehe, Wolf Magnus 1726-1794 *NewGrD 80*
Ehfe, William 1887-1940 *WhScrn 77*
Ehle, Robert Cannon 1939- *AmSCAP 80, CpmDNM 74, -78, -80, ConAmC, IntWWM 77, -80*
Ehlers, Alice 1887- *NewGrD 80*
Ehlers, Alice 1890- *BiDAmM*
Ehlers, Christl *Film 2*
Ehlert, Louis 1825-1884 *Baker 78*
Ehmann, Wilhelm 1904- *Baker 78, BnBkM 80, NewGrD 80*

Ehrenberg, Carl Emil Theodor 1878-1962 *Baker 78, NewGrD 80*
Ehrenbote *NewGrD 80*
Ehrenhaus, German Hermann 1921- *IntWWM 77, -80*
Ehrenkreutz, Steve 1949- *ConAmC*
Ehrensperger, Carlos 1911- *IntWWM 77, -80*
Ehrensperger, Gisela 1943- *WhoOp 76*
Ehrensperger, Harold A 1897-1973 *BiE&WWA, NotNAT B*
Ehrenstein, Johann Jakob Stupan Von *NewGrD 80*
Ehret, Walter Charles 1918- *AmSCAP 66, -80*
Ehrhart, Barbara *WhoHol A*
Ehrie, Kurt *Film 2*
Ehrismann, Alfred 1926- *IntWWM 77, -80*
Ehrlich, Abel 1915- *Baker 78, DcCM, NewGrD 80*
Ehrlich, Arthur 1921- *IntMPA 75, -76*
Ehrlich, David 1949- *IntWWM 80*
Ehrlich, Gretal 1946- *WomWMM B*
Ehrlich, Heinrich 1822-1899 *Baker 78, NewGrD 80*
Ehrlich, Jesse 1920- *ConAmC*
Ehrlich, Sam 1872-1927 *AmSCAP 66, -80*
Ehrling, Sixten 1918- *Baker 78, BnBkM 80, IntWWM 77, -80, MusSN[port], NewGrD 80, WhoMus 72, WhoOp 76*
Ehrstrom, Edgar Edvin 1933- *IntWWM 77*
Ehry, Alfred F 1936- *AmSCAP 80*
Ehtemam, Mohammad 1948- *IntWWM 77, -80*
Eibenschutz, Ilona 1873-1967 *NewGrD 80*
Eibenschutz, Jose 1872-1952 *Baker 78*
Eibenschutz, Lia *Film 2*
Eichbaum, Heinrich Alexander 1914- *IntWWM 77, -80*
Eichberg, Julius 1824-1893 *Baker 78, BiDAmM, NewGrD 80*
Eichberg, Richard 1888-1952 *WhScrn 77*
Eichborn, Hermann 1847-1918 *Baker 78*
Eichelbaum, Samuel 1894-1967 *ModWD, OxThe*
Eichelbaum, Stanley 1926- *BiE&WWA, ConAmTC, NotNAT*
Eichelberger, Susan Elaine 1948- *WhoOp 76*
Eichendorff, Josef Frieherr Von 1788-1857 *EncWT*
Eichendorff, Baron Joseph Von 1788-1857 *McGEWD, NewGrD 80*
Eicher, Eugene Christian 1927- *IntWWM 77, -80*
Eichheim, Henry 1870-1942 *Baker 78, BiDAmM, ConAmC, NewGrD 80*
Eichheim, Meinhard *Baker 78*
Eichhorn, Bernhard Guenther 1904- *WhoMus 72*
Eichhorn, Hermene Warlick 1906- *AmSCAP 66, -80, ConAmC A*
Eichinger, Hans 1902- *IntWWM 77, -80*
Eichler, Julian 1910- *AmSCAP 66, -80*
Eichman, Mark 1949- *NatPD[port]*
Eichmann, Peter 1561-1623 *NewGrD 80*
Eichner, Adelheid 1760?-1787 *NewGrD 80*
Eichner, Ernst 1740-1777 *Baker 78, NewGrD 80*
Eichner, Saul 1930- *IntWWM 77, -80*
Eichnor, Edna *Film 2*
Eichorn, Johann 1524-1583 *NewGrD 80*
Eickstaedt, Karin 1942- *WhoOp 76*
Eidbo, Olav Elling 1918- *IntWWM 77*
Eidenbenz, Johann Christian Gottlob 1761-1799 *NewGrD 80*
Eiermann, Edward 1894?-1971 *NewOrJ*
Eiges, Sydney H 1909- *IntMPA 75, -76*
Eighth Day, The *RkOn 2[port], -2A*
Eigsti, Karl 1938- *WhoThe 77*
Eijcken, Simon Van *NewGrD 80*
Eijken, Jan Albert Van *Baker 78*
Eilemann, Gunter Gustav Willi 1923- *WhoMus 72*
Eilers, Albert 1830-1896 *Baker 78*
Eilers, Joyce Elaine 1934- *AmSCAP 80*
Eilers, Joyce Elaine 1941- *ConAmC*
Eilers, Sally 1908-1978 *FilmEn, Film 2, FilmgC, ForYSC, HalFC 80, HolP 30[port], MotPP, MovMk[port], ThFT[port], TwYS, What 4[port], WhoHol A*
Eilhardt, Carl 1843-1911 *NewGrD 80*
Eimert, Herbert 1897-1972 *Baker 78, DcCM, NewGrD 80*
Einecke, C Harold 1904- *BiDAmM*
Einem, Gottfried Von 1918- *Baker 78, CmOp, CompSN[port], CnOxB, DcCM, MusMk, NewEOp 71, NewGrD 80[port], OxMus*
Einfeldt, Dieter 1935- *IntWWM 77, -80*
Einstein, Alfred 1880-1952 *Baker 78, BiDAmM, NewGrD 80, OxMus*
Einstein, David *ConMuA 80B*
Einstein, Harry 1904-1958 *ForYSC, NotNAT B, WhScrn 74, -77*
Einwald, Carl Joseph 1679?-1753 *NewGrD 80*
Eisbrenner, Werner 1908- *WhoMus 72*
Eisele, Robert H 1948- *NatPD[port]*
Eisen, Max *BiE&WWA*
Eisenberg, Maurice 1900-1972 *Baker 78*
Eisenberg, Maurice 1902-1972 *NewGrD 80, WhoMus 72*
Eisenberg, Michael Allen 1956- *AmSCAP 80*
Eisenberg, Sylvia White *AmSCAP 80*
Eisenberger, Severin 1879-1945 *Baker 78*
Eisenbrandt, C H 1790-1861 *NewGrD 80*
Eisenbrandt, Henry 1790-1861 *NewGrD 80*
Eisenhauer, William G 1925- *AmSCAP 66, -80*
Eisenhuet, Thomas 1644-1702 *NewGrD 80*
Eisenhuet, Tobias 1644-1702 *NewGrD 80*
Eisenhut, Thomas 1644-1702 *NewGrD 80*
Eisenhut, Tobias 1644-1702 *NewGrD 80*
Eisenman, Herbert *ConMuA 80B*
Eisenmann, Will 1906- *IntWWM 77, -80*
Eisenstadt, Evelyn *AmSCAP 80*
Eisenstein, Alfred 1899- *AmSCAP 66, -80, ConAmC, IntWWM 80*
Eisenstein, Judith Kaplan *ConAmC*
Eisenstein, Sam A 1932- *NatPD[port]*
Eisenstein, Sergei 1898-1948 *BiDFilm, DcFM, FilmgC, HalFC 80, MovMk[port], OxFilm, WorEFlm*
Eisenstein, Sergei 1898-1949 *WomWMM*
Eisenstein, Sergei Mihailovich 1898-1948 *EncWT*
Eisenstein, Sergei Mikhailovich 1898-1948 *FilmEn*
Eisenstein, Sergei Mikhailovitch 1898-1948 *BiDFilm 81*
Eisenstein, Sergey 1898-1948 *NewGrD 80*
Eisenstein, Stella Price 1886-1969 *ConAmC*
Eisfeld, Theodor 1816-1882 *Baker 78*
Eisikovits, Max 1908- *IntWWM 77, -80*
Eisinger, Irene 1906- *WhThe*
Eisinger, Jo *FilmgC, HalFC 80*
Eisler, Edmund *NewGrD 80*
Eisler, Hanns 1898-1962 *Baker 78, DcCM, DcFM, EncWT, FilmEn, NewGrD 80[port], OxFilm, OxMus, WorEFlm*
Eisler, Hanns 1898-1963 *FilmgC, HalFC 80*
Eisler, Lawrence 1919- *AmSCAP 80*
Eisler, Paul 1875-1951 *Baker 78*
Eisley, Anthony *ForYSC, WhoHol A*
Eisley, Anthony 1925?- *WhoHrs 80[port]*
Eisma, Will 1929- *Baker 78, CpmDNM 76, DcCM, IntWWM 77, -80, NewGrD 80*
Eisma-Reeser, Wilhelmina Adriana 1930- *IntWWM 77*
Eisman, Mark 1948- *NatPD[port]*
Eisner, Lotte *OxFilm*
Eisner, Michael D 1942- *IntMPA 78, -79, -80, NewYTET*
Eist, Dietmar Von *NewGrD 80*
Eitler, Esteban 1913-1960 *Baker 78*
Eitler, Marta 1922- *WhoMus 72*
Eitner, Robert 1832-1905 *Baker 78, NewGrD 80, OxMus*
Eitz, Carl 1848-1924 *NewGrD 80*
Eitz, Karl Andreas 1848-1924 *Baker 78*
Ejvin Paltbo, Susanne 1942- *IntWWM 77, -80*
Ek, Anders 1916- *FilmEn*
Ek, Gunnar 1900- *Baker 78, NewGrD 80*
Ek, Jens Christian 1925- *WhoOp 76*
Ek, Niklas 1943- *CnOxB*
Ekberg, Anita *IntMPA 75, -76*
Ekberg, Anita 1931- *FilmEn, FilmgC, HalFC 80, IntMPA 77, -78, -79, -80, MotPP, MovMk[port], WhoHol A, WorEFlm*
Ekberg, Anita 1938- *ForYSC*
Ekborg, Lars 1926-1969 *WhScrn 77*
Ekerot, Bengt *WhoHrs 80*
Ekhof, Konrad 1720-1778 *CnThe, EncWT, Ent, NotNAT B, OxThe*
Ekholm, Stig Lennart 1934- *IntWWM 77*
Ekier, Jan 1913- *Baker 78*
Ekk, Nikolai 1896- *FilmEn*
Ekk, Nikolai 1898- *DcFM, WorEFlm*
Ekk, Nikolai 1902- *HalFC 80, OxFilm*
Ekkehard III 950?-1000? *NewGrD 80*
Ekkehard IV 980?-1060 *NewGrD 80*
Ekkehard V *NewGrD 80*
Ekkehard I Decanus 910?-973 *NewGrD 80*
Ekkehard Of St. Gall *NewGrD 80*
Ekkehard II Palatinus 940?-990 *NewGrD 80*
Ekland, Britt 1941- *ForYSC*
Ekland, Britt 1942- *FilmAG WE, FilmEn, FilmgC, HalFC 80, IntMPA 77, -75, -76, -78, -79, -80, WhoHol A, WhoHrs 80*
Eklund, Alice *WomWMM*
Eklund, Hans 1927- *Baker 78, NewGrD 80*
Ekmalyan, Makar Grigori 1856-1905 *NewGrD 80*
Ekman, Goesta 1887-1938 *WhScrn 77, WhoHol B*
Ekman, Gosta 1887-1937 *Film 2, FilmgC, HalFC 80*
Ekman, Gosta 1890- *FilmEn*
Ekman, Gosta 1890-1938 *EncWT, Ent, OxFilm*
Ekman, Hasse 1915- *FilmEn, OxFilm, WorEFlm*
Ekman, John 1880-1949 *Film 1, -2, WhScrn 77*
Ekman, Karl 1869-1947 *Baker 78*
Ekstrand, Ray 1917- *AmSCAP 66*
Ekstrom, Marta 1899-1952 *WhScrn 74, -77*
Ekulona, Ademola *BlkAmP*
Ekwueme, Lazarus Edward Nnanyelu 1936- *IntWWM 80*
El, Leatrice *BlkAmP*
El Atrash, Farid *NewGrD 80*
El Chicano *RkOn 2[port]*
El-Dabh, Halim 1921- *Baker 78, ConAmC, NewGrD 80*
El Maestro Capitan *NewGrD 80*
El Muhajir *MorBAP*
El Nahhas, Hashim *WomWMM*
El Shawwan, Aziz *NewGrD 80*
El Sheikh, Kamel 1918- *DcFM*
El-Tour, Anna 1886-1954 *Baker 78*
Elam, Jack *MotPP, WhoHol A*
Elam, Jack 1916- *FilmEn, FilmgC, ForYSC, HalFC 80, HolCA[port], MovMk*
Elam, Jack 1917- *CmMov*
Elam, Robert W 1938- *IntWWM 77*
Elba, Marta 1920-1954 *WhScrn 74, -77*
Elber, George A 1910- *IntMPA 75, -76*
Elbrown *BluesWW[port]*
Elcar, Dana 1927- *BiE&WWA, NotNAT, WhoHol A*
Elder, David George 1942- *IntWWM 77, -80*
Elder, Dottie 1929-1965 *WhScrn 74, -77*
Elder, Eldon 1924- *BiE&WWA, NotNAT, WhoThe 72, -77*
Elder, Eric Yale 1950- *AmSCAP 80*
Elder, J Harvey 1890- *IntMPA 75, -76*
Elder, Lonne, III *BlkAmP, MorBAP, NatPD[port], NewYTET, PlP&P A[port]*
Elder, Lonne, III 1931- *ConDr 73, -77, DcLB 7[port], WhoThe 77*
Elder, Lonne, III 1932?- *DrBlPA*
Elder, Lonne, III 1933- *NotNAT*
Elder, Mark Philip 1947- *IntWWM 80, NewGrD 80, WhoOp 76*
Elder, Richard 1911-1963 *WhScrn 74, -77*
Elder, Ruth *Film 2*
Elder, Sarah *WomWMM B*
Elders, Wilhelmus 1934- *NewGrD 80*
Elders, Willem 1934- *NewGrD 80*
ElDorados, The *RkOn*
Eldred, Arthur d1942 *NotNAT B, WhThe*
Eldredge, John 1904-1960 *MovMk*
Eldredge, John 1904-1961 *FilmgC, HalFC 80, WhoHol B*
Eldredge, John 1905-1961 *ForYSC, Vers A[port]*
Eldridge, Anna Mae 1894-1950 *WhScrn 74, -77*
Eldridge, Charles 1854-1922 *Film 1, -2, WhScrn 74, -77, WhoHol B*
Eldridge, David Roy 1911- *AmSCAP 80, BiDAmM, EncJzS 70*
Eldridge, Florence 1901- *BiE&WWA, CnThe,*

FilmEn, Film 2, FilmgC, ForYSC, HalFC 80, MotPP, MovMk, NotNAT, ThFT[port], WhThe, WhoHol A, WhoThe 72
Eldridge, Guy Henry 1904- WhoMus 72
Eldridge, Joe 1908-1952 WhoJazz 72
Eldridge, John 1904-1961 WhScrn 74, -77
Eldridge, John 1917- FilmgC, HalFC 80, IlWWBF
Eldridge, Little Jazz 1911- EncJzS 70, NewGrD 80
Eldridge, Louisa d1905 NotNAT B
Eldridge, Roy 1911- CmpEPM, DrBlPA, IlEncJ, MusMk, NewGrD 80
Eldridge, Roy David 1911- WhoJazz 72
Electric Flag BiDAmM, ConMuA 80A, IlEncR
Electric Indian RkOn 2A
Electric Light Orchestra ConMuA 80A, IlEncR, RkOn 2[port]
Electric Prunes, The BiDAmM, RkOn 2[port]
Eleftheriadis, Emilios NewGrD 80
Elegants, The AmPS A, RkOn[port]
Elek, Judit 1937- OxFilm, WomWMM
Element, Ernest 1909- WhoMus 72
Elen, Gus 1862-1940 NotNAT B, OxThe, PlP&P, WhThe, WhoStg 1908
Elephant's Memory, The BiDAmM, RkOn 2[port]
Eler, Andre-Frederic 1764-1821 NewGrD 80
Eler, Franciscus 1500?-1590 NewGrD 80
Eler, Franz 1500?-1590 NewGrD 80
Elert, Peter 1600?-1653 NewGrD 80
Elert, Pietro 1600?-1653 NewGrD 80
Elert, Piotr 1600?-1653 NewGrD 80
Elerus, Franciscus 1500?-1590 NewGrD 80
Elerus, Franz 1500?-1590 NewGrD 80
Eles, Sandor 1946- FilmgC, HalFC 80
Eleventh House, The IlEncJ
Elewijck, Xavier Victor Van 1825-1888 Baker 78, NewGrD 80
Elewyck, Xavier Van 1825-1888 NewGrD 80
Eley, Rose 1918- WhoMus 72
Elfand, Martin IntMPA 77, -78, -79, -80
Elford, Richard 1675?-1714 NewGrD 80
Elg, Taina 1930- FilmEn
Elg, Taina 1931- FilmgC, ForYSC, HalFC 80, IntMPA 77, -75, -76, -78, -79, -80, MotPP, WhoHol A
Elg-Lundberg, Otto Film 2
Elgar, Avril 1932- WhoThe 72, -77
Elgar, Charles 1879- NewOrJ[port]
Elgar, Charlie 1885- WhoJazz 72
Elgar, Sir Edward 1857-1934 Baker 78, BnBkM 80, CompSN[port], DcCom 77[port], DcCom&M 79, DcCM, DcTwCC, MusMk[port], NewGrD 80[port], OxMus
Elgart, Larry 1922- BiDAmM, CmpEPM
Elgart, Les 1918- BgBands 74, BiDAmM, CmpEPM
ElHabashi, Nagi Ibrahim Ahmed 1936- IntWWM 77, -80
Elias NewGrD 80
Elias Salomo NewGrD 80
Elias The Carmelite NewGrD 80
Elias, Albert Sahley 1929- AmSCAP 80
Elias, Alfonso De 1902- Baker 78
Elias, Hal IntMPA 77, -75, -76, -78, -79, -80
Elias, Hector WhoThe 77
Elias, Herman NewGrD 80
Elias, Jose NewGrD 80
Elias, Lorna WhoMus 72
Elias, Manuel Jorge De 1939- Baker 78
Elias, Michael 1918-1974 AmSCAP 66, -80
Elias, Miriam Film 2
Elias, Rosalind 1931- CmOp, IntWWM 77, -80, MusSN[port], NewEOp 71, NewGrD 80
Elias, Rosalind 1933- WhoOp 76
Elias, Salomon Baker 78
Eliasberg, Jay NewYTET
Eliasen, Johnny 1949- CnOxB
Eliason, Robert E 1933- IntWWM 80
Eliasson, Anders 1947- Baker 78, IntWWM 80
Eliasson, Sven Olof 1933- WhoOp 76
Elie, Justin 1883-1931 AmSCAP 66, -80
Elie, Robert 1915- CreCan 1
Elifritz, Eileen Denton 1918- AmSCAP 80
Elin, Hanns NewGrD 80
Eline, Marie Film 1
Elinor, Carli D 1890-1958 WhScrn 74, -77
Elinor, Peggy Film 2
Elinore, Kate d1924 NotNAT B
Eliot, Arthur d1936 NotNAT B
Eliot, John OxMus
Eliot, Margaret 1914- WhoMus 72
Eliot, Marge MorBAP
Eliot, Max d1911 NotNAT B
Eliot, T S 1888-1965 BiE&WWA, CnThe, CroCD, DcLB 7[port], HalFC 80, McGEWD[port], ModWD, NewGrD 80, NotNAT A, PlP&P[port], REnWD[port], WhThe
Eliot, Thomas Stearns 1888-1965 CnMD, EncWT, Ent[port], NotNAT B, OxThe
Eliran, Ron 1940- BiDAmM, EncFCWM 69
Eliscu, Edward 1902- AmPS, AmSCAP 66, -80, CmpEPM
Eliscu, Fernanda 1882-1968 WhScrn 77, WhThe
Elisha, Haim 1935- CpmDNM 76, -77
Elitch, Mary d1936 NotNAT A
Elizabeth BiDAmM
Elizabeth I 1533-1603 HalFC 80, NewGrD 80[port], OxMus
Elizaga, Jose Mariano 1786-1842 NewGrD 80
Elizalde, Federico 1907-1979 NewGrD 80
Elizalde, Federico 1908-1979 Baker 78
Elizalde, Fred 1907-1979 NewGrD 80
Elizalde, John Santiago 1925- AmSCAP 80
Elizaroff, E Film 2
Elizondo, Hector IntMPA 76, -78, -79, -80
Elizondo, Hector 1936- IntMPA 77, WhoHol A, WhoThe 77
Elizondo, Hector 1939?- HalFC 80
Elizondo, Joaquin 1896-1952 WhScrn 74, -77
Elkan, Henri 1897- Baker 78, NewGrD 80, WhoMus 72
Elkan, K NewGrD 80
Elkan-Vogel NewGrD 80
Elkas, Edward Film 2
Elkin, Michael 1949- ConAmTC
Elkin, Saul 1932- NotNAT
Elkins, Hillard 1929- NotNAT A, WhoThe 72, -77
Elkins, Margreta 1936- WhoMus 72, WhoOp 76
Elkins, Marie Louise d1961 NotNAT B
Elkins, Ronald Bernard 1915- WhoMus 72
Elkins, Saul 1907- IntMPA 77, -75, -76, -78, -79, -80
Elkus, Albert 1884-1946 AmSCAP 66
Elkus, Albert 1884-1962 AmSCAP 80, Baker 78, ConAmC
Elkus, Albert Israel 1884-1946 BiDAmM
Elkus, Albert Israel 1884-1962 NewGrD 80
Elkus, Edward Film 1
Elkus, Jonathan 1931- AmSCAP 66, -80, Baker 78, CpmDNM 79, ConAmC, IntWWM 77, -80
Ella, Istvan 1947- IntWWM 80
Ella, John 1802-1888 Baker 78, NewGrD 80, OxMus
Ellberg, Ernst Henrik 1868-1948 Baker 78, NewGrD 80
Elledge, Jimmy 1944- RkOn[port]
Ellefson, Art 1932- IntWWM 80
Ellegaard, France 1912- Baker 78
Ellenberg, David 1917- WhoMus 72
Ellenshaw, Harrison 1947?- WhoHrs 80
Ellenshaw, Peter 1913- WhoHrs 80
Ellenstein, Robert ForYSC, WhoHol A
Eller, Heino 1887-1970 NewGrD 80
Eller, Louis 1820-1862 Baker 78
Eller, Rudolf 1914- NewGrD 80
Ellerbe, Harry BiE&WWA, NotNAT, WhoHol A
Ellerbeck, Anna-Marie CreCan 1
Ellerbusch, Joe NewOrJ
Ellert, Laurence B 1878-1940 Baker 78
Ellerton, John Lodge 1801-1873 Baker 78, NewGrD 80
Elleviou, Jean 1769-1842 Baker 78, NewGrD 80
Ellicott, Rosalind Frances 1857-1924 Baker 78
Elliman, Yvonne 1953- IlEncR, RkOn 2[port], WhoHol A
Elling, Catharinus 1858-1942 NewGrD 80, OxMus
Elling, Catherinus 1858-1942 Baker 78
Ellinger, Desiree 1893-1951 NotNAT B, WhThe
Ellingford, William 1863-1936 Film 1, -2, WhScrn 74, -77, WhoHol B
Ellingson, Linda Jeanne 1947- IntWWM 77, -80
Ellington, Duke 1899-1974 AmPS, AmSCAP 66, BgBands 74[port], BiE&WWA, BlkAmP, CmpEPM, DrBlPA, EncJzS 70, FilmgC, HalFC 80, IlEncJ, MnPM[port], NewGrD 80, NotNAT A, -B, OxMus, PopAmC[port], PopAmC SUP, PopAmC SUPN, Sw&Ld C, WhScrn 77, WhoHol B, WhoJazz 72, WhoMus 72
Ellington, Edward, II 1944- EncJzS 70
Ellington, Edward Kennedy 1899-1974 AmSCAP 80, Baker 78, BiDAmM, BnBkM 80, ConAmC, EncJzS 70, MusMk[port], NewGrD 80
Ellington, Mercer Kennedy 1919- AmSCAP 66, -80, BiDAmM, CmpEPM, DrBlPA, EncJzS 70, IlEncJ
Ellington, Ray 1916- WhoMus 72
Ellington's Orchestra, Duke BiDAmM
Ellingwood, Helmert 1907-1971 WhScrn 77, WhoHol B
Ellinwood, Leonard Webster 1905- Baker 78, NewGrD 80
Elliot, Arthur d1936 NotNAT B
Elliot, Biff WhoHol A
Elliot, Cass 1943-1974 WhoHol B
Elliot, George 1899- WhThe
Elliot, Grace WomWMM
Elliot, John Harold 1900- WhoMus 72
Elliot, Laura 1929- FilmgC, HalFC 80
Elliot, Willard Somers 1926- CpmDNM 79, -80, ConAmC, IntWWM 77, -80
Elliot, William d1931 NotNAT B
Elliot, William F ConAmC
Elliot, Win 1915- IntMPA 75, -76
Elliott, Alonzo 1891-1964 AmSCAP 66, -80, BiDAmM, ConAmC A, NotNAT B
Elliott, Andrew Jackson 1899-1965 CreCan 1
Elliott, Bert 1929-1972 WhScrn 77
Elliott, Bill 1904-1965 ForYSC
Elliott, Bill 1934- DrBlPA
Elliott, Bob 1923- JoeFr
Elliott, Braxton AmSCAP 80
Elliott, Cass RkOn 2[port]
Elliott, Cassandra 1941-1974 WhScrn 77
Elliott, Clinton ConAmC
Elliott, David AmSCAP 80, WhoHol A
Elliott, Del Film 2
Elliott, Denholm 1922- BiE&WWA, CnThe, FilmAG WE, FilmEn, FilmgC, ForYSC, HalFC 80, IlWWBF, IntMPA 77, -75, -76, -78, -79, -80, NotNAT, WhoHol A, WhoThe 72, -77
Elliott, Dick 1886-1961 ForYSC, NotNAT B, Vers A[port], WhScrn 74, -77, WhoHol B
Elliott, Don 1926- BiDAmM, BiE&WWA, CmpEPM, EncJzS 70, NotNAT
Elliott, Douglas Ferguson 1916- IntWWM 77, -80
Elliott, Frank Film 2
Elliott, George Henry 1884-1962 NotNAT B, OxThe, WhThe
Elliott, Gertrude 1874-1950 Film 1, NotNAT B, WhScrn 74, -77, WhThe, WhoHol B, WhoStg 1908
Elliott, Gordon d1965 ForYSC
Elliott, Gordon 1904-1965 WhScrn 74, -77, WhoHol B
Elliott, Gordon William 1906-1965 Film 2
Elliott, Graham John 1944- IntWWM 77, -80
Elliott, Jack 1914- CmpEPM
Elliott, Jack 1931- BluesWW[port]
Elliott, Jane OxMus
Elliott, John B 1907- AmSCAP 66, -80
Elliott, John H 1876-1956 Film 2, WhScrn 77
Elliott, John M 1914-1972 AmSCAP 66, -80, BiDAmM
Elliott, John Tiffany d1963 NotNAT B
Elliott, Lang 1949- IntMPA 80
Elliott, Laura ForYSC
Elliott, Leonard WhoHol A
Elliott, Leslie 1893- WhoMus 72

Elliott, Lester 1888-1954 *WhScrn 74, -77*
Elliott, Lewis 1921- *AmSCAP 66*
Elliott, Lillian 1875-1959 *Film 2, WhScrn 74, -77, WhoHol B*
Elliott, Madge 1898-1955 *NotNAT B, WhThe*
Elliott, Marjorie Reeve 1890- *AmSCAP 80, ConAmC*
Elliott, Maxine 1868-1940 *EncWT, Ent, FamA&A[port], NotNAT A, -B, OxThe*
Elliott, Maxine 1871-1940 *Film 1, -2, TwYS, WhThe*
Elliott, Maxine 1873-1940 *WhScrn 74, -77, WhoHol B, WhoStg 1906, -1908*
Elliott, May Gertrude 1874-1950 *EncWT, Ent, OxThe*
Elliott, Michael 1931- *WhoThe 72, -77*
Elliott, Milton Skeets 1896-1920 *WhScrn 77*
Elliott, Patricia 1942- *NotNAT, WhoThe 77*
Elliott, Paul 1941- *WhoThe 77*
Elliott, Paul Murray Christopher 1950- *IntWWM 80*
Elliott, Paula Kelch 1938- *IntWWM 77, -80*
Elliott, Pauline 1917- *WhoMus 72*
Elliott, Peggy *WomWMM*
Elliott, Ramblin' Jack 1931- *BiDAmM, EncFCWM 69*
Elliott, Rambling Jack 1931- *IlEncCM[port]*
Elliott, Rena McQuary 1904- *IntWWM 77*
Elliott, Robert *CreCan 1, ForYSC*
Elliott, Robert d1963 *WhoHol B*
Elliott, Robert 1879-1951 *Film 1, -2, HolCA[port], TwYS, WhScrn 74, -77, WhoHol B*
Elliott, Robert Conyers *IntWWM 77, -80, WhoMus 72*
Elliott, Ronald Charles 1944- *AmSCAP 80*
Elliott, Ross *ForYSC, WhoHol A*
Elliott, Sam 1944- *HalFC 80, WhoHol A*
Elliott, Stephen 1945- *NotNAT, WhoHol A, WhoThe 77*
Elliott, Sticky 1898- *WhoJazz 72*
Elliott, Sue *WomWMM B*
Elliott, Sumner Locke 1917- *BiE&WWA, NotNAT*
Elliott, Susan *ConMuA 80B*
Elliott, Timothy Allen 1946- *ConAmC*
Elliott, Vernon Pelling 1912- *IntWWM 77, -80, WhoMus 72*
Elliott, Victoria 1922- *CmOp*
Elliott, Walter Ulric 1913- *AmSCAP 80*
Elliott, Wild Bill d1965 *ForYSC, MotPP, WhoHol B*
Elliott, Wild Bill 1903-1965 *HolP 40[port]*
Elliott, Wild Bill 1904-1965 *HalFC 80*
Elliott, Wild Bill 1906-1965 *CmMov, FilmgC*
Elliott, William *ForYSC, WhoHol A*
Elliott, William 1880-1932 *WhScrn 77*
Elliott, William 1885-1932 *Film 1, NotNAT B, WhThe, WhoHol B*
Elliott, William 1903-1965 *FilmEn*
Elliott, William Wild Bill 1904-1965 *WhScrn 74, -77*
Ellis, Alexander John 1814-1890 *Baker 78, NewGrD 80*
Ellis, Angela 1920- *CnOxB, DancEn 78*
Ellis, Anita 1926- *BiE&WWA, CmpEPM, NotNAT*
Ellis, Anthony L d1944 *NotNAT B, WhThe*
Ellis, Bobby *ForYSC*
Ellis, Brandon d1916 *NotNAT B*
Ellis, Brent E 1946- *WhoOp 76*
Ellis, Catherine J 1935- *NewGrD 80*
Ellis, David 1921- *CnOxB, DancEn 78*
Ellis, Diane 1909-1930 *Film 2, WhScrn 74, -77, WhoHol B*
Ellis, Don 1934-1978 *Baker 78, ConAmC, ConMuA 80B, EncJzS 70, IlEncJ, NewGrD 80*
Ellis, Donald Johnson 1934-1978 *BiDAmM, EncJzS 70*
Ellis, Edith d1960 *NotNAT B, WhThe*
Ellis, Edward 1871-1952 *Vers A[port], WhScrn 74, -77, WhoHol B*
Ellis, Edward 1872-1952 *FilmgC, ForYSC, HalFC 80, NotNAT B, WhThe*
Ellis, Elaine *Film 2*
Ellis, Evelyn 1894-1958 *DrBlPA, NotNAT B, WhScrn 74, -77, WhoHol B*
Ellis, Frank *Film 2*
Ellis, Frank B d1969 *WhScrn 77, WhoHol B*
Ellis, Gregory A 1955- *AmSCAP 80*
Ellis, Herb 1921- *CmpEPM, EncJzS 70*
Ellis, Jack 1908- *AmSCAP 66, -80*
Ellis, John Tilstone 1929- *WhoMus 72*
Ellis, Lillian *Film 2*
Ellis, Linus Marvin, III 1943- *IntWWM 77, -80*
Ellis, Lloyd 1920- *EncJzS 70*
Ellis, Martin John 1943- *IntWWM 77, -80*
Ellis, Mary *AmPS B, BiE&WWA, NotNAT*
Ellis, Mary 1899- *FilmEn, ThFT[port], WhoHol A*
Ellis, Mary 1900- *EncMT, FilmgC, HalFC 80, WhoThe 72, -77*
Ellis, Max d1964 *NotNAT B*
Ellis, Merrill 1916- *AmSCAP 80, CpmDNM 78, -79, ConAmC, IntWWM 77, -80*
Ellis, Michael 1917- *BiE&WWA, NotNAT*
Ellis, Miriam A *OxMus*
Ellis, Mitchell Herbert 1921- *BiDAmM, EncJzS 70*
Ellis, Osian 1928- *BnBkM 80, IntWWM 77, -80, NewGrD 80, WhoMus 72*
Ellis, Patricia 1916-1970 *FilmEn, FilmgC, ForYSC, HalFC 80, ThFT[port], WhScrn 74, -77, WhoHol B*
Ellis, Paul *Film 2*
Ellis, Raymond *Film 2*
Ellis, Richard 1918- *CnOxB, DancEn 78*
Ellis, Robert 1892-1935 *FilmEn, Film 1, -2, ForYSC, TwYS, WhScrn 74, -77, WhoHol B*
Ellis, Robert 1933-1973 *WhScrn 77, WhoHol B*
Ellis, Seger *BgBands 74*
Ellis, Seger 1904- *AmSCAP 66, -80, CmpEPM*
Ellis, Seger 1906- *WhoJazz 72*
Ellis, Shirley 1941- *RkOn[port]*
Ellis, T E *OxMus*
Ellis, Terry *ConMuA 80B*
Ellis, Vivian 1903- *NewGrD 80*
Ellis, Vivian 1904- *BestMus, EncMT, HalFC 80, WhoMus 72, WhoThe 72, -77*
Ellis, Walter 1874-1956 *NotNAT B, WhThe*
Ellis, Wilbert Thirkield 1914-1977 *BluesWW[port]*
Ellis, William *OxMus*
Ellis-Fermor, Una Mary 1894-1958 *NotNAT B*
Ellison, Ebenezer Blay 1943- *IntWWM 77, -80*
Ellison, James 1910- *FilmEn, FilmgC, ForYSC, HalFC 80, MovMk, WhoHol A*
Ellison, Margorie *Film 1*
Ellison, Maxine A 1952- *IntWWM 77, -80*
Ellison, Sidney 1917- *WhoMus 72*
Ellison, Sydney d1930 *NotNAT B*
Ellison, Thomas 1952- *IntWWM 77*
Elliston, Daisy 1894- *WhThe*
Elliston, Grace 1881-1950 *NotNAT B, WhThe, WhoStg 1906, -1908*
Elliston, Robert William 1774-1831 *EncWT, Ent, NotNAT A, -B, OxThe, PlP&P*
Elliston, Ronald Robert 1935- *ConAmC*
Ellman, Stephen A 1935- *IntMPA 77, -75, -76, -78, -79*
Ellmerich, Luis 1913- *IntWWM 77, -80*
Elloway, Julian Dominic 1950- *IntWWM 80*
Elloway, Kenneth Albert 1916- *IntWWM 80*
Ellrod, John G 1924- *NatPD[port]*
Ellsasser, Richard 1926- *AmSCAP 66, -80, ConAmC A*
Ellsler, Effie 1823-1918 *NotNAT B*
Ellsler, Effie 1855-1942 *Film 2, NotNAT B, WhScrn 74, -77, WhoHol B*
Ellsler, John Adam 1822-1900 *NotNAT A*
Ellstein, Abraham 1907-1963 *AmSCAP 66, -80, ConAmC, NotNAT B*
Ellsworth, Jack Herschel 1911-1949 *WhScrn 74, -77*
Ellsworth, James 1927- *IntMPA 77, -75, -76, -78, -79, -80*
Ellsworth, Robert *Film 2*
Ellsworth, Robert H 1895- *AmSCAP 66, -80*
Ellwood And Ripel *PupTheA*
Elman, Harry 1914-1968 *AmSCAP 66, -80, WhScrn 74, -77*
Elman, Irving 1922- *AmSCAP 66, -80*
Elman, Mischa 1891-1967 *AmSCAP 66, -80, Baker 78, BiDAmM, BnBkM 80, Film 2, MusSN[port], NewGrD 80*
Elman, Ziggy 1914-1968 *BiDAmM, CmpEPM, EncJzS 70, WhoHol B, WhoJazz 72*
Elmendorff, Karl 1891-1962 *NewEOp 71, NewGrD 80*
Elmenhorst, Heinrich E 1632-1704 *NewGrD 80*
Elmer, Billy 1870-1945 *Film 1, WhScrn 74, -77, WhoHol B*
Elmer, Cedric Nagel 1939- *AmSCAP 66, -80*
Elmer, Clarence Jay *Film 1, -2*
Elmer, Rita *WomWMM*
Elmer, William *Film 2*
Elmes, Guy 1920- *FilmgC, HalFC 80, IntMPA 77, -75, -76, -78, -79, -80*
Elmitt, Martin 1944- *WhoMus 72*
Elmitt, Mavis 1935- *WhoMus 72*
Elmo, Cloe 1910-1962 *CmOp, NewGrD 80*
Elmore, Bruce 1885-1940 *WhScrn 77*
Elmore, Cenieth Catherine 1930- *IntWWM 77*
Elmore, Pearl *Film 1*
Elmore, Robert Hall 1913- *AmSCAP 66, -80, Baker 78, ConAmC*
Elms, Lauris 1931- *WhoOp 76*
Elms, Roderick James Charles 1951- *IntWWM 77, -80*
Elmslie, Kenward G 1929- *AmSCAP 66, -80*
Elmsly, John Anthony 1952- *IntWWM 80*
Elnecave, Viviane *WomWMM*
Eloul, Rita Letendre *CreCan 2*
Elow, Lawrence 1927- *AmSCAP 66, -80*
Eloy D'Amerval *NewGrD 80*
Eloy, Jean-Claude 1938- *Baker 78, DcCM, NewGrD 80*
Elphistone, Emma d1888 *NotNAT B*
Elrod, Elizabeth Louella 1935- *IntWWM 77, -80*
Elsbeth, Thomas d1624? *NewGrD 80*
Elschek, Oskar 1931- *IntWWM 77, -80, NewGrD 80*
Elsenheimer, Nicholas J 1866-1935 *Baker 78*
Elser, Frank B d1935 *NotNAT B, PlP&P*
Elsie, Lily 1886-1962 *EncMT, NotNAT B, WhThe*
Elsmann, Heinrich *NewGrD 80*
Elsmo, Ralph Norman 1919- *AmSCAP 66, -80*
Elsmo, Sverre S 1910-1968 *AmSCAP 66, -80*
Elsner, Joseph 1769-1854 *Baker 78, OxMus*
Elsner, Joseph Anton Franciskus 1769-1854 *NewGrD 80*
Elsner, Joseph Xaver 1769-1854 *NewGrD 80*
Elsner, Jozef Antoni Franciszek 1769-1854 *NewGrD 80*
Elsner, Jozef Ksawery 1769-1854 *NewGrD 80*
Elsner, Jurgen 1932- *IntWWM 77, -80, NewGrD 80*
Elsom, Isobel 1893- *FilmEn, Film 1, -2, FilmgC, HalFC 80, HolCA[port], IlWWBF[port], MovMk, WhThe*
Elsom, Isobel 1894- *Vers A[port], WhoHol A*
Elsom, Isobel 1896- *BiE&WWA, NotNAT*
Elsom, Phyllis Lois 1908- *WhoMus 72*
Elson, Anita 1898- *WhThe*
Elson, Arthur B 1873-1940 *Baker 78, BiDAmM*
Elson, Bill *ConMuA 80B*
Elson, Charles 1909- *NotNAT*
Elson, Isobel 1894- *ForYSC*
Elson, L C 1848-1920 *OxMus*
Elson, Louis Charles 1848-1920 *Baker 78, BiDAmM, NewGrD 80*
Elson, Norman 1907- *IntMPA 77, -75, -76, -78, -79, -80*
Elssler *NewGrD 80*
Elssler, Fanny 1810-1884 *CnOxB, DancEn 78[port], NewGrD 80, NotNAT B, OxMus*
Elssler, Johann 1769-1843 *NewGrD 80*
Elssler, Joseph d1782 *NewGrD 80*
Elssler, Theresa 1808-1878 *DancEn 78*
Elssler, Therese 1808-1878 *OxMus*
Elst, Jan VanDer 1598-1670 *NewGrD 80*
Elst, Johannes VanDer 1598-1670 *NewGrD 80*
Elste, Rudolf Otto Martin 1952- *IntWWM 77, -80*
Elston, Arnold 1907-1971 *ConAmC, NewGrD 80*
Elston, Robert 1934- *BiE&WWA, NotNAT*
Elsworth, Cecilie Edna Woods 1934- *WhoMus 72*
Elter, Amielka *Film 2*

Eltinge, Julian 1882-1940 WhoHol B
Eltinge, Julian 1882-1941 Film 1, -2, FilmgC, HalFC 80
Eltinge, Julian 1883-1941 ForYSC, NotNAT B, OxThe, TwYS, WhScrn 74, -77, WhThe
Elton, Antony 1935- IntWWM 77, -80, WhoMus 72
Elton, Sir Arthur 1906-1973 FilmEn, FilmgC, HalFC 80, OxFilm, WorEFlm[port]
Elton, Christopher Douglas 1944- IntWWM 77, -80
Elton, Edmund Film 1
Elton, Edward William 1794-1843 NotNAT B, OxThe
Elton, Frank d1954 NotNAT B
Elton, Fred 1931-1960 AmSCAP 80
Elton, George 1875-1942 NotNAT B, WhThe
Elton, John M 1923- AmSCAP 80
Eltz, Theodore Von 1894-1964 FilmEn
Elvers, Rudolf 1924- NewGrD 80
Elvey, Sir George Job 1816-1893 Baker 78, NewGrD 80, OxMus
Elvey, Maurice 1887-1967 FilmEn, Film 1, FilmgC, HalFC 80, IlWWBF, OxFilm, WhThe, WorEFlm
Elvey, Stephen 1805-1860 Baker 78, NewGrD 80, OxMus
Elvidge, June 1893-1965 Film 1, -2, TwYS, WhScrn 74, -77, WhoHol B
Elvin, Joe 1862-1935 NotNAT B, OxThe, WhThe
Elvin, Rene 1896- IntWWM 77, -80, WhoMus 72
Elvin, Violetta 1924- DancEn 78[port]
Elvin, Violetta 1925- CnOxB, WhThe
Elvira, Pablo 1938- WhoOp 76
Elward, James NatPD[port]
Elwart, Amable 1808-1877 NewGrD 80
Elwart, Antoine-Aimable-Elie 1808-1877 Baker 78, NewGrD 80
Elwell, George 1896-1916 WhScrn 77
Elwell, Herbert 1898-1974 AmSCAP 66, -80, Baker 78, BiDAmM, ConAmC, NewGrD 80, OxMus
Elwes, Gervase 1866-1921 Baker 78, BiDAmM, NewGrD 80, OxMus
Ely, G A Film 1
Ely, Harry R 1883-1951 WhScrn 74, -77
Ely, Lyn BiE&WWA, NotNAT
Ely, Ron 1938- FilmEn, ForYSC, MotPP, WhoHol A, WhoHrs 80
Elyn, Mark Alvin 1932- IntWWM 77, -80
Elyot, Sir Thomas 1490?-1546 DcPup, OxMus
Elzer, Karl Film 2
Eman, Dawn WhoHol A
Eman, Tracey WhoHol A
Emanuel, David 1910- IntMPA 77, -75, -76, -78, -79, -80
Emblen, Ronald 1933- CnOxB, DancEn 78
Embree, Charles B, Jr. 1919- AmSCAP 66, -80
Emden, Henry d1930 NotNAT B
Emden, Margaret d1946 NotNAT B
Emer, Michel 1906- WhoMus 72
Emerald, Charles Film 2
Emerald, Connie d1959 NotNAT B, WhThe, WomWMM
Emerich, Paul 1895- WhoMus 72
Emerick, Besse 1875-1939 WhScrn 74, -77, WhoHol B
Emerick, Robert 1916-1973 WhScrn 77
Emerman, Mack ConMuA 80B
Emerson PupTheA
Emerson, Billy 1846-1902 AmPS B, BiDAmM
Emerson, Edward 1910-1975 WhScrn 77, WhoHol C
Emerson, Eric 1945-1975 WhScrn 77
Emerson, Faye 1917- BiE&WWA, FilmEn, FilmgC, ForYSC, HalFC 80, HolP 40[port], MotPP, MovMk[port], NewYTET, What 2[port], WhThe, WhoHol A, WhoThe 72
Emerson, Gordon C 1931- IntWWM 77, -80
Emerson, Harriett Anne AmSCAP 80
Emerson, Hope d1960 MotPP, NotNAT B, WhoHol B
Emerson, Hope 1897-1960 FilmEn, FilmgC, HalFC 80, HolCA[port], WhScrn 74, -77
Emerson, Hope 1898-1960 ForYSC, MovMk, Vers A[port]
Emerson, John 1874-1956 FilmEn, Film 1, NotNAT B, TwYS A, WhScrn 74, -77, WhThe, WhoHol B, WorEFlm
Emerson, John 1878-1946 DcFM
Emerson, June 1937- IntWWM 77, -80
Emerson, Ken ConMuA 80B
Emerson, Luther Orlando 1820-1915 Baker 78, BiDAmM
Emerson, Mary d1921 NotNAT B
Emerson, Ralph Film 2
Emerson, Ralph Waldo 1803-1882 BiDAmM
Emerson, Roy Kenneth 1940- IntWWM 77, -80
Emerson, William Robert 1929- BluesWW
Emerson Lake And Palmer ConMuA 80A IlEncR[port], RkOn 2[port]
Emerton, Roy 1892-1944 FilmgC, HalFC 80, NotNAT B, WhScrn 74, -77, WhThe, WhoHol B
Emeruwa, L W MorBAP
Emeruwa, Leatrice BlkAmP
Emery, Dick 1919- FilmgC, HalFC 80
Emery, Edward d1938 EncWT
Emery, Edward 1861-1938 NotNAT B, WhoStg 1906, -1908
Emery, Mrs. Edward WhScrn 74, -77
Emery, Edwin T d1951 NotNAT B
Emery, Ellen Chyann 1951- AmSCAP 80
Emery, Fernando 1904- DancEn 78
Emery, Frederick d1930 NotNAT B
Emery, Gilbert MotPP
Emery, Gilbert 1875-1945 FilmgC, HalFC 80, HolCA[port], NotNAT B, Vers B, WhScrn 74, -77, WhThe, WhoHol B
Emery, Gilbert 1882-1934 WhScrn 74, -77
Emery, Gilbert 1889-1945 Film 2, ForYSC, MovMk
Emery, Isabel Winifred 1862-1924 EncWT
Emery, John d1965 NotNAT B
Emery, John 1777-1822 EncWT, OxThe
Emery, John 1905-1964 BiE&WWA, EncWT, FilmEn, FilmgC, ForYSC, HalFC 80, MotPP, MovMk[port], Vers A[port], WhScrn 74, -77, WhThe, WhoHol B
Emery, Katherine 1908- BiE&WWA, NotNAT, PlP&P[port], WhThe
Emery, Louise d1943 NotNAT B
Emery, Pollie 1875-1958 NotNAT B, WhThe
Emery, Polly 1875-1958 WhoHol B
Emery, Rose d1934 NotNAT B
Emery, Samuel Anderson 1817-1881 EncWT, NotNAT B, OxThe
Emery, Stephen Albert 1841-1891 Baker 78, BiDAmM
Emery, Valerie 1916- IntWWM 80
Emery, Walter 1909-1974 Baker 78, NewGrD 80, WhoMus 72
Emery, Winifred 1862-1924 NotNAT B, OxThe, WhThe
Emhardt, Robert 1900?- FilmEn
Emhardt, Robert 1901?- BiE&WWA, FilmgC, ForYSC, HalFC 80, NotNAT, WhThe, WhoHol A
Emhardt, Robert 1916- HolCA[port]
Emig, Jack Wayne 1925- IntWWM 77
Emig, Lois Irene 1925- AmSCAP 80, IntWWM 77, -80
Emig, Lois Meyer 1925- ConAmC
Emil-Behnke, Kate d1957 NotNAT B
Emili, Romano 1937- WhoOp 76
Emilson, C Rudolph 1939- IntWWM 77, -80
Emilsson, Gudmundur 1951- IntWWM 80
Emlyn, Fairy Film 2
Emmanuel, Maurice 1862-1938 Baker 78, NewGrD 80, OxMus
Emmer, Luciano 1918- DcFM, FilmEn, FilmgC, HalFC 80, OxFilm, WorEFlm
Emmerich, Robert D 1904- AmSCAP 66, -80
Emmert, Johann Joseph 1732-1809 NewGrD 80
Emmes, David 1939- NotNAT
Emmet, Alfred 1908- WhoThe 72, -77
Emmet, Joseph K 1841-1891 BiDAmM
Emmet, Katherine d1960 NotNAT B, WhScrn 74, -77
Emmett, Catherine d1960 Film 2, WhoHol B
Emmett, Dan 1815-1904 AmPS, -B, NotNAT B, PopAmC[port]
Emmett, Daniel Decatur 1815-1904 Baker 78, BiDAmM, MusMk, NewGrD 80, OxMus, PlP&P, Sw&Ld A
Emmett, E V H 1902- FilmgC, HalFC 80
Emmett, Fern 1896-1946 WhScrn 74, -77, WhoHol B
Emmett, J K d1891 NotNAT B
Emmit, Daniel Decatur 1815-1904 NewGrD 80
Emmons, Buddy 1937- IlEncCM[port]
Emmons, Louise 1852-1935 WhScrn 74, -77, WhoHol B
Emmons, M Film 1
Emney, Fred 1865-1917 OxThe, WhThe
Emney, Fred 1900- FilmgC, HalFC 80, IlWWBF, -A, OxThe, WhoThe 72, -77
Emney, Joan Fred WhThe
Emny, Fred 1865-1917 NotNAT B
Emory, Gilbert Film 2
Emory, Maude Film 1, -2
Emory, May Film 1
Emory, Richard ForYSC
Emotions, The RkOn 2[port]
Empey, Arthur Guy 1883-1963 TwYS A
Empey, Arthur Guy 1884-1963 WhScrn 74, -77
Empey, Guy d1963 Film 1, WhoHol B
Empress, Marie Film 1
Empy, Guy d1963 NotNAT B
Emrys-Roberts, Kenton 1923- IntWWM 77, -80
Emsheimer, Ernst 1904- NewGrD 80
Emshwiller, Ed 1925- OxFilm
Emurian, Ernest Krikor 1912- AmSCAP 80
Emurian, Ernest Krikov 1912- AmSCAP 66
En Earl, William Allan 1946- AmSCAP 80
Ena, Rose Film 2
Enacovici, George 1891-1965 Baker 78
Enchantment RkOn 2[port]
Encina, Juan Del 1468-1529 Baker 78
Encina, Juan Del 1468-1530? NewGrD 80
Encina, Juan Del 1468?-1537? NotNAT B, OxThe
Encina, Juan Del 1469?-1529? EncWT, McGEWD
Enciso, Franz 1941- ConAmC
Enckhausen, Heinrich Friedrich 1799-1885 Baker 78
End, Jack 1918- ConAmC
Ende, Heinrich Vom 1858-1904 Baker 78
Ender, Edmund Sereno 1886- BiDAmM
Enderle, Wilhelm Gottfried 1722-1790 NewGrD 80
Enders, Harvey 1892-1947 AmSCAP 66, -80, ConAmC A
Enders, Karel Vilem 1778?-1841 NewGrD 80
Enders, Karl NewGrD 80
Enders, Robert IntMPA 77, -78, -79, -80
Endfield, C Raker 1914- WorEFlm[port]
Endfield, Cy 1914- BiDFilm, -81, FilmEn, FilmgC, HalFC 80, IlWWBF, WorEFlm
Endfield, Cyril 1914- WhoHrs 80
Endler, Johann Samuel 1694-1762 NewGrD 80
Endore, Guy 1900-1970 FilmEn
Endore, Guy 1901-1970 NotNAT B
Endoviensis, Christophe Van NewGrD 80
Endres, Caspar 1674- NewGrD 80
Endres, Karl NewGrD 80
Endres, Olive Philomene 1898- ConAmC
Endrey, Eugene NotNAT A
Endter NewGrD 80
Endter, Georg 1562-1630 NewGrD 80
Endter, Georg 1585-1629 NewGrD 80
Endter, Johann Andreas 1625-1670 NewGrD 80
Endter, Wolfgang 1593-1659 NewGrD 80
Endter, Wolfgang 1622-1655 NewGrD 80
Enei, Yevgeni 1890- DcFM
Enenbach, Fredric 1945- ConAmC
Enesco, Georges 1881-1955 Baker 78, BnBkM 80, CompSN[port], DcCom&M 79, MusMk, MusSN[port], NewGrD 80[port], OxMus
Enescu, George 1881-1955 DcCM, NewGrD 80[port]
Enevoldsen, Bob 1920- CmpEPM
Enevoldsen, Robert Martin 1920- BiDAmM
Enfield, Cy 1914- IntMPA 77, -75, -76, -78, -79, -80
Enfield, Cyril Raker 1914- DcFM
Enfield, Hugh WhScrn 74, -77
Enfield, Patrick Keen 1929- IntWWM 77, -80, WhoMus 72
Engardus NewGrD 80
Engblom, Verne A 1919- AmSCAP 66
Engblom, Verne A 1924- AmSCAP 80

Engel, A Lehman 1910- *BiDAmM*
Engel, Alexander 1902-1968 *WhScrn 74, -77, WhoHol B*
Engel, Billie *Film 2*
Engel, Carl 1818-1882 *Baker 78, NewGrD 80, OxMus*
Engel, Carl 1883-1944 *AmSCAP 66, -80, Baker 78, BiDAmM, ConAmC, NewGrD 80, OxMus*
Engel, David Hermann 1816-1877 *Baker 78*
Engel, Erich 1891-1966 *EncWT, Ent, FilmEn, OxFilm*
Engel, Francis Werner 1920- *IntWWM 80*
Engel, Fred 1930- *IntMPA 75, -76*
Engel, Gabriel 1892-1952 *Baker 78*
Engel, Gary Alan 1948- *AmSCAP 80*
Engel, Gustav Eduard 1823-1895 *Baker 78*
Engel, Hans 1894-1970 *Baker 78, NewGrD 80*
Engel, Joel 1868-1927 *Baker 78, NewGrD 80*
Engel, Johann Jakob 1741-1802 *Baker 78, NewGrD 80*
Engel, Karl Rudolf 1923- *IntWWM 77, -80*
Engel, Lehman 1910- *Baker 78, BiE&WWA, BlkAmP, ConAmC, DancEn 78, DcCM, IntWWM 77, -80, NewGrD 80, NotNAT, -A, WhoMus 72*
Engel, Marie d1971 *WhoHol B*
Engel, Morris 1918- *DcFM, FilmEn, FilmgC, HalFC 80, IntMPA 77, -75, -76, -78, -79, OxFilm, WomWMM, WorEFlm*
Engel, Olga *Film 2*
Engel, Paul 1920- *IntWWM 77, -80, WhoMus 72*
Engel, Roy *WhoHol A*
Engel, Samuel 1904- *FilmEn, FilmgC, HalFC 80*
Engel, Susan 1935- *WhoHol A, WhoThe 72, -77*
Engel, Yehuda 1924- *IntWWM 80*
Engelbert Of Admont d1331 *NewGrD 80*
Engelbrecht, Eileen 1945- *IntWWM 77, -80*
Engelhardt, Walther 1894- *IntWWM 77*
Engelke, Bernhard 1884-1950 *Baker 78*
Engelmann, Georg 1575?-1632 *NewGrD 80*
Engelmann, Georg 1601?-1663 *NewGrD 80*
Engelmann, Hans-Ulrich 1921- *Baker 78, IntWWM 77, -80, NewGrD 80*
Engels, Georg d1907 *NotNAT B*
Engen, Keith 1925- *WhoMus 72*
Engen, Kieth S 1925- *WhoOp 76*
Enger, Elling 1905- *IntWWM 77*
Enghaus, Christine 1817-1910 *EncWT*
England *NewGrD 80*
England, Barry 1934- *ConDr 77*
England, Barry 1935- *EncWT*
England, Daisy d1943 *NotNAT B*
England, George d1773 *NewGrD 80, OxMus*
England, George Pike 1765?-1816 *NewGrD 80, OxMus*
England, John *NewGrD 80*
England, Leslie *WhoMus 72*
England, Nicholas M 1923- *NewGrD 80*
England, Paul 1893-1968 *WhScrn 77, WhThe*
England, Sue *ForYSC, WhoHol A*
England Dan & John Ford Coley *RkOn 2[port]*
Englander, Lester 1911- *IntWWM 77, -80*
Englander, Ludwig d1914 *WhThe, WhoStg 1906, -1908*
Englander, Ludwig 1853-1914 *EncMT*
Englander, Ludwig 1859-1914 *BiDAmM, CmpEPM, NewCBMT, NotNAT B, PopAmC*
Englander, Richard 1889-1966 *NewGrD 80*
Englander, Roger *NewYTET*
Engle, Billy 1889-1966 *WhScrn 74, -77, WhoHol B*
Engle, Fannie Goldsmith *PupTheA*
Engle, Marie 1902-1971 *WhScrn 74, -77*
Englefield, Violet 1886-1946 *NotNAT B*
Engleman, Andrews *Film 2*
Englemann, Hans Ulrich 1921- *DcCM*
Engler *NewGrD 80*
Engler, Gottlieb Benjamin 1734-1793 *NewGrD 80*
Engler, Michael 1650?-1720? *NewGrD 80*
Engler, Michael 1688-1760 *NewGrD 80*
Engler, Ole 1940- *IntWWM 77, -80*
Engler, Richard *ConMuA 80B*
Englert, Anton 1674-1751 *NewGrD 80*
Englert, Eugene E 1931- *ConAmC*
Englert, Giuseppe Gigio 1927- *DcCM*
Englert, Giuseppe Giorgio 1927- *Baker 78, WhoMus 72*
Engles, George 1916- *AmSCAP 80*
Englisch, Lucie 1897-1956 *WhoHol B*
Englisch, Lucie 1897-1965 *WhScrn 74, -77*
English, Colonel *Film 2*
English, Deidre *WomWMM B*
English, Gerald 1925- *IntWWM 77, -80, NewGrD 80, WhoMus 72*
English, Granville 1895-1968 *Baker 78, ConAmC*
English, Granville 1900-1968 *AmSCAP 66, -80*
English, James *Film 2*
English, John 1903-1969 *FilmEn, WhoHrs 80*
English, Logan *EncFCWM 69*
English, Marla 1930?- *WhoHrs 80[port]*
English, Marla 1935- *ForYSC*
English, Michael 1931- *WhoMus 72*
English, Robert *Film 2*
English, Thomas Dunn 1819-1902 *BiDAmM*
English, Tina *AmSCAP 80*
English Aristophanes, The *OxThe*
Englitt *NewGrD 80*
Englund, Einar 1916- *Baker 78, DcCM, NewGrD 80*
Englund, George H 1926- *FilmEn, FilmgC, HalFC 80, IntMPA 77, -75, -76, -78, -79, -80*
Englund, Ken 1911- *FilmEn*
Englund, Ken 1914- *FilmgC, HalFC 80, IntMPA 77, -75, -76, -78, -79, -80*
Englund, Maude Beatrice Galbraith 1891-1962 *NotNAT B*
Englund, Patricia *WhoHol A*
Englund, Richard 1931- *CnOxB*
Englund, Sorella 1945- *CnOxB*
Engramelle, Marie Dominique Joseph 1727-1805 *NewGrD 80*
Engvall, Anna Elisabet 1907- *IntWWM 77, -80*
Engvall, John Alvar Ake 1902- *IntWWM 77, -80*
Eniccelius, Tobias 1635?-1680 *NewGrD 80*
Enkelmann, Siegfried 1905- *CnOxB, DancEn 78*
Enna, August 1859-1939 *NewGrD 80*
Enna, August 1860-1939 *Baker 78*
Ennelin, Sebastien 1660-1747 *NewGrD 80*
Ennery, Adolphe D' 1812-1899 *NotNAT B*
Ennicellius, Tobias *NewGrD 80*
Ennio, Aegidio *NewGrD 80*
Ennis, Charles 1917- *BiE&WWA*
Ennis, Ethel 1934- *BiDAmM*
Ennis, Patrick *Film 1*
Ennis, Skinnay d196-? *BgBands 74[port]*
Ennis, Skinnay 1907-1963 *HalFC 80, WhScrn 74, -77, WhoHol B*
Ennis, Skinnay 1909-1963 *CmpEPM, WhoJazz 72*
Ennis, Susan Lee 1950- *AmSCAP 80*
Ennius 239BC-169BC *Ent*
Ennius, Quintus 239BC-169BC *NotNAT B, OxThe*
Enno, Sebastian d1655 *NewGrD 80*
Enno, Sebastiano d1655 *NewGrD 80*
Enns, Harold R 1930- *WhoOp 76*
Eno, Brian 1948- *ConMuA 80A, -80B, IlEncR*
Enrichelli, Pasquale *NewGrD 80*
Enrico, Eugene Joseph 1944- *IntWWM 77, -80*
Enrico, Robert 1931- *FilmEn, FilmgC, HalFC 80, OxFilm, WhoHrs 80, WorEFlm*
Enright, Florence d1961 *WhScrn 74, -77, WhoHol B*
Enright, Josephine d1976 *WhoHol C*
Enright, Ray 1896-1965 *BiDFilm, -81, FilmEn, FilmgC, HalFC 80, TwYS A*
Enright, Raymond 1896-1965 *WorEFlm*
Enright, Sara 1888-1963 *NotNAT B*
Enrique *NewGrD 80*
Enriquez, Franco 1927- *WhoOp 76*
Enriquez, Manuel 1926- *Baker 78, CpmDNM 75, DcCM, IntWWM 77, -80, NewGrD 80*
Enriquez DeValderrabano, Enrique *Baker 78*
Enstedt, Howard *Film 2*
Enters, Angna 1907- *BiE&WWA, CmpGMD, CnOxB, DancEn 78[port], Ent[port], NotNAT, -A, OxThe*
Enters, Warren 1927- *BiE&WWA, NotNAT*
Enthoven, Emil 1903-1950 *Baker 78*
Enthoven, Emile 1903-1950 *NewGrD 80*
Enthoven, Gabrielle 1868-1950 *NotNAT B, OxThe, WhThe*
Entraigues *NewGrD 80*
Entratter, Jack 1913-1971 *WhScrn 77*
Entremont, Philippe 1934- *Baker 78, IntWWM 77, -80, MusSN[port], NewGrD 80*
Entremont, Phillippe 1934- *WhoMus 72*
Entrikin, Helen *PupTheA*
Entrikin, Paul *PupTheA*
Entwistle, Harold 1865-1944 *WhScrn 74, -77, WhoHol B*
Entwistle, John *ConMuA 80B, IlEncR*
Entwistle, Lillian Millicent d1932 *NotNAT B*
Entwistle, Peg 1908-1932 *WhScrn 74, -77, WhoHol B*
Enzina, Juan Del *NewGrD 80*
Eorsi, Istvan 1931- *CroCD*
Eosze, Laszlo 1923- *IntWWM 77, -80, NewGrD 80*
Eotvos, Peter 1944- *NewGrD 80*
Ephraem The Syrian 306?-373 *NewGrD 80*
Ephraim Syrus 306?-373 *NewGrD 80*
Ephraim, Lee 1877-1953 *WhThe*
Ephrem Moire d1100? *NewGrD 80*
Ephrem Syrus 306?-373 *NewGrD 80*
Ephriam, Lee 1877-1953 *NotNAT B*
Ephrikian, Angelo 1913- *NewGrD 80*
Ephron, Henry 1912- *BiE&WWA, FilmEn, FilmgC, HalFC 80, NotNAT, WomWMM*
Ephron, Phoebe 1914-1971 *FilmEn*
Ephron, Phoebe 1916-1971 *BiE&WWA, NotNAT B, WomWMM*
Ephros, Gershon 1890- *AmSCAP 66, -80, BiDAmM, ConAmC A*
Epicharmus 550?BC-460BC *NotNAT B, OxThe, PlP&P*
Epinal, Gautier D' *NewGrD 80*
Episcopius, Ludovicus 1520?-1595 *NewGrD 80*
Episcopius DeBisschop, Ludovicus 1520?-1595 *NewGrD 80*
Episcopus, Melchior *NewGrD 80*
Episkopoulos, Antonios *NewGrD 80*
Episkopoulos, Benediktos *NewGrD 80*
Eppel, John Valentine 1871-1931 *BiDAmM*
Eppelsheim, Jurgen 1930- *NewGrD 80*
Epperley, Glenn Barry 1944- *IntWWM 77*
Epperly, Glenn Barry 1944- *IntWWM 80*
Epperson, Don 1938-1973 *WhScrn 77*
Epperson, Gordon 1921- *IntWWM 77, -80*
Epperson, John William 1950- *CpmDNM 74, ConAmC*
Eppert, Carl 1882-1961 *AmSCAP 66, -80, Baker 78, BiDAmM, ConAmC*
Epps, David 1934- *WhoMus 72*
Epps, Marjorie Florence 1902- *WhoMus 72*
Epps, Preston *RkOn*
Eppstein, Hans 1911- *IntWWM 77, -80, NewGrD 80*
Epstein, Alvin 1925- *BiE&WWA, NotNAT, PlP&P[port], WhoThe 72, -77*
Epstein, Alvin L 1926- *ConAmC*
Epstein, Brian 1934- *IlEncR*
Epstein, David M 1930- *AmSCAP 66, -80, Baker 78, ConAmC, IntWWM 77, -80*
Epstein, Dena J 1916- *IntWWM 77, -80*
Epstein, Donald K 1933- *AmSCAP 66, -80*
Epstein, Eli K 1958- *IntWWM 77, -80*
Epstein, Jean 1897-1953 *BiDFilm, -81, DcFM, FilmEn, FilmgC, HalFC 80, OxFilm, WorEFlm*
Epstein, Julius 1832-1926 *Baker 78*
Epstein, Julius J 1909- *BiE&WWA, FilmEn, FilmgC, HalFC 80, NotNAT, WorEFlm*
Epstein, Marie *WomWMM*
Epstein, Mel 1910- *IntMPA 77, -75, -76, -78, -79, -80*
Epstein, Michael *ConMuA 80B*
Epstein, Paul 1938- *ConAmC*
Epstein, Peter 1901-1932 *Baker 78*
Epstein, Philip G 1909-1952 *FilmgC, HalFC 80, NotNAT B*
Epstein, Richard 1869-1919 *Baker 78*
Eques Auratus Romanus *NewGrD 80*
Era, Antonietta Dell' 1861- *CnOxB*
Erard *NewGrD 80*
Erard, Jean-Baptiste d1826 *NewGrD 80*

Erard, Sebastien 1752-1831 *Baker 78, NewGrD 80*
Erars, Jehan 1200?-1259? *NewGrD 80*
Erart, Jehan 1200?-1259? *NewGrD 80*
Erasmus Of Horitz *NewGrD 80*
Erasmus, Desiderius 1469-1536 *NewGrD 80*
Erastoff, Edith 1887-1945 *FilmEn, Film 1, WhScrn 77*
Eratosthenes 276?BC-194?BC *Baker 78*
Eratosthenes 284?BC-202?BC *NewGrD 80*
Erb, Donald 1927- *Baker 78, CpmDNM 72, -75, -77, -78, -79, ConAmC, DcCM, IntWWM 77, -80, NewGrD 80*
Erb, John Lawrence 1877-1950 *Baker 78, BiDAmM, ConAmC*
Erb, John Warren 1887-1948 *Baker 78, ConAmC*
Erb, Karl 1877-1958 *CmOp, NewGrD 80*
Erb, Marie Joseph 1858-1944 *Baker 78*
Erba, Dionigi *NewGrD 80*
Erba, Giuseppe 1916- *WhoOp 76*
Erbach, Christian 1568?-1635 *NewGrD 80*
Erbach, Christian 1570-1635 *Baker 78*
Erbach, Friedrich Karl, Count Of 1680-1731 *NewGrD 80*
Erbacher, Shirley *WomWMM B*
Erben, Balthasar 1626-1686 *NewGrD 80*
Erben, Henry 1800-1884 *NewGrD 80*
Erben, Peter 1769-1861 *BiDAmM*
Erber, James Edwin 1951- *IntWWM 80*
Erbse, Heimo 1924- *Baker 78, DcCM, IntWWM 77, -80, WhoMus 72*
Erby, John J 1902- *BluesWW[port]*
Erckmann, Emile 1822-1899 *NewEOp 71, NotNAT B*
Erckmann-Chatrian *NewEOp 71, OxThe, PlP&P*
Ercoleo, Marzio 1623-1706 *NewGrD 80*
Ercse, Margit 1942- *WhoOp 76*
Erculei, Marzio 1623-1706 *NewGrD 80*
Erculeo, Marzio 1623-1706 *NewGrD 80*
Erdeli, Xenia 1878-1971 *NewGrD 80*
Erdelyi, Miklos 1928- *IntWWM 77, -80, NewGrD 80*
Erdman, Dick 1925- *ForYSC*
Erdman, Ernie 1879-1946 *AmSCAP 66, -80*
Erdman, Jean *CmpGMD, CnOxB, DancEn 78[port], NotNAT*
Erdman, Nikolai Robertovich 1902-1970 *ModWD*
Erdman, Richard 1925- *FilmEn, FilmgC, HalFC 80, IntMPA 77, -75, -76, -78, -79, -80, MotPP, Vers B[port], WhoHol A*
Erdman, Theodore John 1930- *AmSCAP 66*
Erdman, Theodore John 1939- *AmSCAP 80*
Erdmann, Dietrich 1917- *IntWWM 80*
Erdmann, Eduard 1896-1958 *Baker 78*
Erdmann, Gunther 1939- *IntWWM 80*
Erdmann, Nikolai 1902-1936 *CnMD*
Erdmannsdorfer, Max Von 1848-1905 *Baker 78*
Erdnase, S W *MagIlD*
Erdody, Leo 1888-1949 *AmSCAP 66, -80, ConAmC A*
Erduran, Refik 1928- *REnWD[port]*
Erede, Alberto 1908- *Baker 78, IntWWM 77, -80, WhoOp 76*
Erede, Alberto 1909- *CmOp, NewEOp 71, NewGrD 80*
Erede, Alberto 1910- *WhoMus 72*
Eredi, Francesco 1575?-1629? *NewGrD 80*
Eredia, Pietro *NewGrD 80*
Eremeef, Ivan *OxMus*
Eremita, Giulio 1550?-1600? *NewGrD 80*
Erenberg, Elena *WomWMM B*
Erfordia, Johannes De *NewGrD 80*
Erhard, Laurentius 1598-1669 *NewGrD 80*
Erhardi, Laurentius 1598-1669 *NewGrD 80*
Erhardt, Ludwik Jerzy 1934- *IntWWM 77, -80*
Erhardt, Otto 1888-1971 *Baker 78, CmOp, NewEOp 71*
Erhardt, Thomas 1928- *BiE&WWA*
Eric, Fred 1874-1935 *NotNAT B, WhThe*
Ericchelli, Pasquale *NewGrD 80*
Erice, Victor *HalFC 80*
Erich, Daniel 1660?-1730? *NewGrD 80*
Erich, Nicolaus 1588-1631 *NewGrD 80*
Erichius, Nicolaus 1588-1631 *NewGrD 80*
Erichsen-Brown, Gwethalyn Graham *CreCan 1*
Erickson, Carl Fredrik Swerker 1920- *IntWWM 77*
Erickson, Chris 1945-1971 *WhScrn 77*
Erickson, Corydon 1944- *IntMPA 77, -75, -76, -78, -79, -80*
Erickson, Eddy G 1925- *IntMPA 77, -75, -76, -78, -79*
Erickson, Frank 1923- *AmSCAP 66, ConAmC, IntWWM 77, -80*
Erickson, Frank William 1923- *AmSCAP 80*
Erickson, Gordon McVey 1917- *IntWWM 77, -80*
Erickson, Helene *IntMPA 75*
Erickson, Jack 1898- *AmSCAP 66*
Erickson, Knute 1871-1946 *Film 2, WhScrn 74, -77, WhoHol B*
Erickson, Launcelot 1949- *IntMPA 77, -75, -76, -78, -79*
Erickson, Leif 1911- *BiE&WWA, FilmEn, FilmgC, ForYSC, HalFC 80, IntMPA 77, -75, -76, -78, -79, MotPP, MovMk[port], WhoHol A*
Erickson, Robert 1917- *Baker 78, ConAmC, DcCM, IntWWM 77, -80, NewGrD 80*
Ericson, Barbro 1930- *IntWWM 80, WhoOp 76*
Ericson, Eric Gustaf 1918- *IntWWM 77, -80*
Ericson, John *BiE&WWA, WhoHol A*
Ericson, John 1926- *FilmEn, IntMPA 77, -75, -76, -78, -79, -80, NotNAT*
Ericson, John 1927- *FilmgC, ForYSC, HalFC 80, MGM[port], WhoHrs 80*
Ericson, Leif 1911- *BiDAmM, PlP&P[port]*
Ericson, Rolf 1922- *CmpEPM*
Erier, Thomas *NewGrD 80*
Erigena, John Scotus *NewGrD 80*
Eriksen, Jostein 1926- *IntWWM 80*
Eriksen, Richard Dahl 1918- *IntWWM 77, -80*
Erikson, Launcelot 1949- *IntMPA 80*
Erikson, Leif 1911- *IntMPA 80*
Eriksson, Bjorn 1927- *IntWWM 77, -80*
Eriksson, Goran 1943- *IntWWM 77*
Eriksson, John M 1923- *IntWWM 77, -80*
Eriksson, Lillemor *IntWWM 77*
Eriksson, Walter Algot 1926- *AmSCAP 80*
Eriugena, Johannes *NewGrD 80*
Erk, Ludwig 1807-1883 *Baker 78, NewGrD 80*
Erkel *NewGrD 80*
Erkel, Elek 1843-1893 *NewGrD 80*
Erkel, Ferenc 1810-1893 *CmOp, MusMk, NewGrD 80[port], OxMus*
Erkel, Franz 1810-1893 *Baker 78, NewEOp 71*
Erkel, Gyula 1842-1909 *NewGrD 80*
Erkel, Laszlo 1844-1896 *NewGrD 80*
Erkel, Sandor 1846-1900 *NewGrD 80*
Erkin, Ulvi Cemal 1906-1972 *Baker 78, NewGrD 80*
Erlanger, Abraham L 1860-1930 *EncMT, NotNAT B, WhThe*
Erlanger, Camille 1863-1919 *Baker 78, NewEOp 71*
Erlanger, Baron Francois Rodolphe D' 1872-1932 *NewGrD 80*
Erlanger, Baron Frederic D' 1868-1943 *DancEn 78, NewGrD 80, OxMus*
Erlebach, Philipp Heinrich 1657-1714 *Baker 78, NewGrD 80*
Erlebach, Rupert 1894- *Baker 78*
Erler, Hermann *NewGrD 80*
Erler, Liselotte *WhoOp 76*
Erlih, Devy 1928- *WhoMus 72*
Erling, Ole 1938- *IntWWM 77, -80*
Erlo, Louis 1929- *NewGrD 80, WhoOp 76*
Ermatinger, Erhart 1900-1966 *Baker 78*
Ermelli, Claudio 1892-1964 *WhScrn 74, -77, WhoHol B*
Ermler, Friedrich 1898-1967 *DcFM, FilmEn, WorEFlm*
Ermler, Friedrich 1908-1967 *OxFilm*
Ermolenko, George 1925- *IntWWM 77, -80*
Ermolieff, Joseph N 1890-1962 *NotNAT B*
Ernani, Francesco 1937- *WhoOp 76*
Erne, Vincent 1884- *WhThe*
Ernesaks, Gustav 1908- *Baker 78, IntWWM 77, -80*
Ernesaks, Gustav Gustavovich 1918- *NewGrD 80*
Ernest, David John 1929- *ConAmC, IntWWM 77, -80*
Ernest, Sister M *ConAmC*
Ernie *RkOn 2A*
Ernoul Le Vielle De Gastinois *NewGrD 80*
Ernous Le Vielle De Gastinois *NewGrD 80*
Ernsberger, James E 1938- *AmSCAP 80*
Ernst Ludwig 1667-1739 *NewGrD 80*
Ernst, Alfred 1860-1898 *Baker 78, NewGrD 80*
Ernst, David 1945- *ConAmC*
Ernst, Earle 1911- *BiE&WWA, NotNAT*
Ernst, Heinrich Wilhelm 1814-1865 *Baker 78, BnBkM 80, NewGrD 80, OxMus*
Ernst, Otto 1862-1926 *ModWD*
Ernst, Paul 1866-1933 *CnMD, EncWT, McGEWD, ModWD, NotNAT B, OxThe*
Ernst, Robert 1900- *IntWWM 77, -80*
Erod, Ivan 1936- *IntWWM 77, -80*
Erokan, Dennis *ConMuA 80B*
Eros, Peter 1932- *Baker 78, IntWWM 77, -80, WhoMus 72*
Erpf, Hermann 1891-1969 *Baker 78, NewGrD 80*
Errani, Achille 1823-1897 *BiDAmM*
Errante, Belisario Anthony 1920- *AmSCAP 80*
Errante, F Gerard 1941- *CpmDNM 76, IntWWM 77, -80*
Errichelli, Pasquale 1730-1775? *NewGrD 80*
Errico, Gregory Vince 1948- *AmSCAP 80*
Errington, Charles Sydney 1905- *WhoMus 72*
Errisson, King 1941- *EncJzS 70*
Errol, John *BlkAmP, MorBAP*
Errol, Leon 1881-1951 *CmpEPM, EncMT, FilmEn, Film 2, FilmgC, ForYSC, Funs[port], HalFC 80, JoeFr, MotPP, MovMk, NotNAT B, PlP&P[port], WhScrn 74, -77, WhThe, WhoHol B*
Errol, Leon 1881-1952 *Vers B[port]*
Erseus, Torsten 1923- *IntWWM 77, -80*
Ersfeld, Ernest Joseph 1919- *IntWWM 77*
Erskin, Chester 1903- *WhThe*
Erskine, Chester 1905- *FilmEn, FilmgC, HalFC 80*
Erskine, Sir David d1837 *NotNAT B*
Erskine, Howard 1926- *BiE&WWA, NotNAT, WhoThe 72, -77*
Erskine, John 1879-1951 *Baker 78, BiDAmM, NotNAT B, OxMus*
Erskine, Marilyn *ForYSC, WhoHol A*
Erskine, Marilyn 1924- *FilmEn*
Erskine, Peter 1954- *EncJzS 70*
Erskine, Wallace *WhoStg 1908*
Erskine, Wallace 1862-1943 *NotNAT B, WhScrn 74, -77, WhoHol B*
Erskine, William Robin 1943- *IntWWM 77, -80*
Ertegun, Ahmet *ConMuA 80B*
Ertegun, Nesuhi *ConMuA 80B*
Ertel, Paul 1865-1933 *Baker 78*
Ertel, Sebastian 1550?-1618 *NewGrD 80*
Ertelius, Sebastian 1550?-1618 *NewGrD 80*
Erthel, Sebastian 1550?-1618 *NewGrD 80*
Ertl, Sebastian 1550?-1618 *NewGrD 80*
Ertmann, Dorothea Von 1781-1849 *NewGrD 80*
Ertugrul, Mushin 1888- *DcFM*
Ervin, Booker Telleferro, Jr. 1930-1970 *BiDAmM, EncJzS 70, IlEncJ*
Ervin, Thomas Ross 1942- *IntWWM 77*
Ervine, John St. John Greer 1883-1971 *EncWT, OxThe*
Ervine, St. John 1883-1971 *CnMD, CnThe, Ent, McGEWD, ModWD, NotNAT B, PlP&P, REnWD[port], WhThe*
Erwen, Keith 1942- *WhoOp 76*
Erwin, Barbara *WhoHol A*
Erwin, George 1913- *AmSCAP 66, -80, BiDAmM, EncJzS 70*
Erwin, June 1918-1965 *WhScrn 74, -77, WhoHol B*
Erwin, Lee Orville 1908- *AmSCAP 66, -80*
Erwin, Madge d1967 *WhoHol B*
Erwin, Margie *PupTheA*
Erwin, Pee Wee 1913- *CmpEPM, EncJzS 70, WhoJazz 72*
Erwin, Roy 1925-1958 *WhScrn 74, -77*
Erwin, Stu 1903-1967 *BiE&WWA, NotNAT B*
Erwin, Stuart d1967 *MotPP, WhoHol B*
Erwin, Stuart 1902-1967 *FilmEn, HolCA[port], WhScrn 74, -77*
Erwin, Stuart 1903-1967 *Film 2, FilmgC, HalFC 80, MovMk[port]*

Erwin, Stuart 1905-1967 *ForYSC*
Erythraus, Gotthart 1560?-1617 *NewGrD 80*
Esaulov, Andrey Petrovich 1800?-1850? *NewGrD 80*
Escalante, Eduardo Alberto 1937- *IntWWM 77, -80*
Escalas, Roman 1945- *IntWWM 77, -80*
Escande, Maurice 1893-1973 *WhScrn 77*
Escatefer *NewGrD 80*
Eschenbach, Chirstoph 1940- *IntWWM 77, -80*
Eschenbach, Christoph 1940- *BnBkM 80, MusSN[port], NewGrD 80, WhoMus 72*
Eschenburg, Johann Joachim 1743-1820 *NewGrD 80*
Escher, Rudolf 1912- *Baker 78, DcCM, NewGrD 80*
Eschig, Max 1872-1927 *Baker 78, NewGrD 80*
Eschmann, Johann Karl 1826-1882 *Baker 78*
Eschstruth, Hans Adolph Friedrich Von 1756-1792 *NewGrD 80*
Escobar, Andre De *NewGrD 80*
Escobar, Cristobal *NewGrD 80*
Escobar, Luis Antonio 1925- *Baker 78, DcCM, IntWWM 80, NewGrD 80*
Escobar, Maria Luisa 1910- *IntWWM 77, -80*
Escobar, Pedro De 1465?-1535? *NewGrD 80*
Escobar-Budge, Roberto 1926- *Baker 78*
Escobedo, Bartolome 1515?-1563 *Baker 78*
Escobedo, Bartolome De 1500?-1563 *NewGrD 80*
Escoffier, Marcel 1910- *DcFM, FilmEn, WhoOp 76*
Escoriguela, Isidro d1723 *NewGrD 80*
Escorihuela, Isidro d1723 *NewGrD 80*
Escosa, John Briscoe, Sr. 1928- *AmSCAP 80*
Escot, Pozzi 1933- *Baker 78, ConAmC, IntWWM 77, -80*
Escovado, Robin 1931- *ConAmC*
Escovar, Andres De *NewGrD 80*
Escribano, Juan 1478?-1557 *NewGrD 80*
Escudero, Bernardo DePeralta *NewGrD 80*
Escudero, Francisco 1913- *NewGrD 80*
Escudero, Ralph 1898-1970 *WhoJazz 72*
Escudero, Vicente 1882?- *DancEn 78*
Escudero, Vincente 1892- *CnOxB*
Escudier *NewGrD 80*
Escudier, Leon 1816-1881 *Baker 78*
Escudier, Leon 1821-1881 *NewGrD 80*
Escudier, Marie-Pierre-Yves 1819-1880 *NewGrD 80*
Escudier, Monique 1940- *IntWWM 80*
Escue, Joann Howard 1926- *IntWWM 77*
Escurel, Jehannot DeL' *NewGrD 80*
Esdale, Charles 1873-1937 *Film 2, WhScrn 77*
Eshelby, Mary *IntWWM 77*
Eshkol, Noa 1924- *CnOxB*
Eshpai, Andrei 1925- *Baker 78, DcCM*
Eshpai, Andrey Yakoulevitch 1925- *IntWWM 77, -80*
Eshpai, Yakov 1890-1963 *Baker 78*
Eshpay, Andrey Yakovlevich 1925- *NewGrD 80*
Esipova, Anna Nikolayevna 1851-1914 *NewGrD 80*
Esipova, Annette Nikolayevna 1851-1914 *NewGrD 80*
Eskdale, George 1897-1960 *NewGrD 80*
Eskilson, Richard E 1923- *AmSCAP 66*
Eskin, David *ConMuA 80B*
Eskovitz, Bruce Louis 1955- *AmSCAP 80*
Eslava *NewGrD 80*
Eslava, Fernan Gonzalez De *OxThe*
Eslava, Hilarion 1807-1878 *NewGrD 80*
Eslava, Miguel Hilarion 1807-1878 *OxMus*
Eslava Y Elizondo, Miguel Hilarion 1807-1878 *Baker 78*
Esler, Lemist 1888-1960 *NotNAT B*
Esling, Catherine Harbison 1812-1897 *BiDAmM*
Esmelton, Fred *Film 1*
Esmelton, Frederick *Film 2*
Esmond, Annie 1873-1945 *Film 2, NotNAT B, WhThe, WhoHol B*
Esmond, Carl 1905- *FilmEn, FilmgC, HalFC 80, WhThe*
Esmond, Carl 1906- *ForYSC, IntMPA 77, -75, -76, -78, -79, -80, Vers A[port], WhoHol A*
Esmond, Georgette *Film 2*
Esmond, Henry V 1869-1922 *NotNAT B, OxThe, WhThe, WhoStg 1908*
Esmond, Jill 1908- *FilmEn, FilmgC, ForYSC, HalFC 80, WhThe, WhoHol A*
Espagne, Franz 1828-1878 *Baker 78, NewGrD 80*
Espar, Sheri Gillette *WomWMM B*
Esparza, Elfego 1929- *IntWWM 77, -80*
Espelt, Francisco *NewGrD 80*
Esperanca, Pedro Da 1598?-1660 *NewGrD 80*
Espert, Nuria 1938- *Ent*
Espina, Noni 1923- *IntWWM 80*
Espinal, Carlos *PupTheA*
Espinal, Gautier D' *NewGrD 80*
Espinos Molto, Victor 1871-1948 *NewGrD 80*
Espinosa *CnOxB*
Espinosa, Bridget E 1928- *CnOxB*
Espinosa, Edouard 1872-1950 *NotNAT A, WhThe*
Espinosa, Edouard E 1871-1950 *CnOxB*
Espinosa, Edward Kelland- *CnOxB*
Espinosa, Felipe *ConAmC*
Espinosa, Geoffrey E *CnOxB*
Espinosa, Guillermo 1905- *Baker 78, NewGrD 80*
Espinosa, Juan De *NewGrD 80*
Espinosa, Julio Garcia 193-?- *DcFM*
Espinosa, Lea *CnOxB*
Espinosa, Leon E 1825-1904 *CnOxB*
Espla, Oscar 1886-1976 *Baker 78, DcCM, NewGrD 80, OxMus*
Espla Triay, Oscar 1886-1976 *IntWWM 77*
Esposito, Alex 1880?-1951? *NewOrJ[port]*
Esposito, Andree 1934- *WhoOp 76*
Esposito, Giancarlo *WhoHol A*
Esposito, Michele 1855-1929 *Baker 78, NewGrD 80, OxMus*
Esposito, Robert *NatPD[port]*
Esposito, Vincent *WhoHol A*
Espy, L' *EncWT, OxThe*
Espy, William Gray *WhoHol A*
Esquires *RkOn 2A*
Esquivel, Jorge 1950- *CnOxB*
Esquivel Barahona, Juan 1563?-1613? *NewGrD 80*
Esrom, D A *AmSCAP 80*
Esrum-Hellerup, Dag Henrik 1803-1891 *NewGrD 80*
Essah, Daniel Richard 1930- *IntWWM 77, -80*
Essen, Viola *WhoHol B*
Essenfeld, Barry 1936- *IntMPA 77, -75, -76, -78, -79, -80*
Essenga, Salvadore d1575 *NewGrD 80*
Essenga, Salvatore d1575 *NewGrD 80*
Essengha, Salvadore d1575 *NewGrD 80*
Essengha, Salvatore d1575 *NewGrD 80*
Esser, Carl 1935- *AmSCAP 80*
Esser, Heinrich 1818-1872 *Baker 78, NewGrD 80, OxMus*
Esser, Hermin 1928- *CmOp, WhoOp 76*
Esser, Michael, Ritter Von 1737-1795? *NewGrD 80*
Esser, Peter 1896-1970 *WhScrn 74, -77*
Essert, Gary 1938- *IntMPA 80*
Essex, The *RkOn[port]*
Essex, Clifford *OxMus*
Essex, David 1947- *HalFC 80, IlEncR, IntMPA 77, -75, -76, -78, -79, -80, RkOn 2[port], WhoHol A*
Essex, Francis 1929- *IntMPA 77, -75, -76, -78, -79, -80*
Essex, Harry 1910- *WhoHrs 80*
Essex, Harry J *IntMPA 75, -76, -78, -79, -80*
Essex, Harry J 1910- *FilmEn, FilmgC, HalFC 80, IntMPA 77*
Essex, Kenneth *WhoMus 72*
Essig, Hermann 1878-1918 *CnMD, ModWD*
Essipoff, Anna 1851-1914 *Baker 78*
Essipoff, Annette 1851-1914 *BnBkM 80*
Essipova, Anna Nikolayevna 1851-1914 *BnBkM 80*
Esslair, Ferdinand 1772-1840 *OxThe*
Essler, Fred 1896-1973 *WhScrn 77, WhoHol B*
Esslin, Martin 1918- *BiE&WWA, NotNAT, WhoThe 77*
Esslinger, Nell Daniel 1903- *IntWWM 80*
Esson, Louis 1879-1943 *ModWD*
Esswood, Paul Lawrence Vincent 1942- *IntWWM 77, -80, NewGrD 80, WhoMus 72*
Est, John *OxMus*
Est, Michael *NewGrD 80, OxMus*
Est, Thomas *OxMus*
Estabrook, Dean Monte 1940- *ConAmC*
Estabrook, Howard 1884-1978 *FilmEn, HalFC 80, TwYS A, WhThe*
Estabrook, Howard 1894-1978 *Film 1, FilmgC*
Estabrook, Lizzie S 1858-1913 *BiDAmM*
Estampio, Juan Sanchez-Valencia 1883-1957 *CnOxB*
Estcourt, Dick 1668-1712 *OxThe*
Estcourt, Richard 1668-1712 *NotNAT B*
Este *NewGrD 80*
Este, Isabella D' *NewGrD 80*
Este, Michael 1580?-1648? *NewGrD 80, OxMus*
Este, Thomas 1540?-1608? *NewGrD 80, OxMus*
Esteban, Julio 1906- *Baker 78, IntWWM 77, -80*
Estebe Y Grimau, Pablo *NewGrD 80*
Estee, Adelyn 1871-1941 *WhScrn 74, -77*
Estelita d1966 *ForYSC, WhoHol B*
Estella, Jose 1870-1943 *NewGrD 80*
Estelle, Vicki *AmSCAP 80*
Esten, Mrs. 1763-1865 *NotNAT B*
Esterhazy *NewGrD 80*
Esterhazy, Countess Agnes *Film 2*
Esterhazy, Anton 1738-1794 *NewGrD 80*
Esterhazy, Caroline 1805-1851 *NewGrD 80*
Esterhazy, Count Franz 1715-1785 *NewGrD 80*
Esterhazy, Count Johann 1754-1840 *NewGrD 80*
Esterhazy, Count Johann 1775-1834 *NewGrD 80*
Esterhazy, Joseph 1687-1721 *NewGrD 80*
Esterhazy, Princess Maria Octavia 1686?-1762 *NewGrD 80*
Esterhazy, Marie 1802-1837 *NewGrD 80*
Esterhazy, Michael 1671-1721 *NewGrD 80*
Esterhazy, Count Michael 1783-1874 *NewGrD 80*
Esterhazy, Nikolaus 1582?-1645 *NewGrD 80*
Esterhazy, Nikolaus 1714-1790 *NewGrD 80*
Esterhazy, Nikolaus 1765-1833 *NewGrD 80*
Esterhazy, Pal 1635-1713 *NewGrD 80*
Esterhazy, Paul 1635-1713 *NewGrD 80*
Esterhazy, Paul Anton 1711-1762 *NewGrD 80*
Esterhazy, Countess Rosine Festetics 1779-1854 *NewGrD 80*
Estes, Charles Byron 1946- *ConAmC*
Estes, Charles E 1882-1968 *Baker 78*
Estes, James Warner 1944- *IntWWM 77*
Estes, John 1904- *BiDAmM*
Estes, John Adams 1899-1977 *BluesWW[port]*
Estes, Richard *AmSCAP 80*
Estes, Simon 1938- *DrBlPA, NewGrD 80*
Estevan, Fernand *NewGrD 80*
Esteve, Pablo 1730?-1794 *Baker 78*
Esteve, Pierre 1720-1779? *NewGrD 80*
Esteve Y Grimau, Pablo d1794 *NewGrD 80*
Esteves, Joao Rodrigues 1700?-1751? *NewGrD 80*
Estevez, Antonio 1916- *Baker 78, NewGrD 80*
Estey, J Harry *NewGrD 80*
Estey, Jacob 1814-1890 *NewGrD 80*
Estey, Jacob Gray *NewGrD 80*
Estey, Julius 1845-1902 *NewGrD 80*
Estienne, Francois 1671-1755 *NewGrD 80*
Estill, Ann H M *IntWWM 77, -80*
Estocart, Paschal DeL' *NewGrD 80*
Estrada, Arthur *IntMPA 77, -75, -76*
Estrada, Carlos 1909-1970 *Baker 78, DcCM, NewGrD 80*
Estrada, Erik 1948- *HalFC 80*
Estrada, Garcia Juan Agustin 1895- *Baker 78*
Estrada, Jose *PupTheA*
Estrange, Roger *OxMus*
Estree, Jean D' d1576 *NewGrD 80*
Estreicher, Zygmunt 1917- *NewGrD 80*
Estrella, Arnaldo 1908- *IntWWM 77, -80*
Estrella, Joseph C 1908- *AmSCAP 66, -80*
Estridge, Robin 1920- *FilmgC, HalFC 80*
Estudillo, Leo B 1900-1957 *WhScrn 74, -77*
Estwick, Sampson 1656?-1739 *NewGrD 80*
Esty, Bob *ConMuA 80B*
Esty, Jacob 1814-1890 *BiDAmM*
Esztenyi, Szabolcs Laszlo 1939- *IntWWM 77, -80*
Etaix, Pierre 1928- *BiDFilm, -81, DcFM, FilmAG WE, FilmEn, FilmgC, HalFC 80, OxFilm, WorEFlm*

Etcheverry, Bertrand 1900-1960 *CmOp, NewGrD 80*
Etcheverry, Diego 1933- *WhoOp 76*
Etcheverry, Jesus *WhoOp 76*
Etchevery, Jean-Jacques 1916- *CnOxB, DancEn 78*
Eternals, The *RkOn*
Ethel, Agnes 1852-1903 *FamA&A[port]*
Ethel, Agnes 1853-1903 *NotNAT B*
Ethelred *NewGrD 80*
Etherden, Alan Bradley 1956- *IntWWM 80*
Etherege, Sir George 1634?-1691? *CnThe, EncWT, Ent, OxThe, REnWD[port]*
Etherege, Sir George 1635?-1691? *McGEWD, NotNAT A, -B, PlP&P[port]*
Etheria *NewGrD 80*
Etherington, James 1902-1948 *NotNAT B, WhThe*
Ethier, Alphonse 1875-1943 *Film 1, -2, ForYSC, WhScrn 74, -77, WhoHol B*
Ethier, Alphonz *TwYS*
Ethikos, Nikephoros *NewGrD 80*
Ethridge, Roxelyn Robbins Rhymer 1934- *IntWWM 77*
Ethuin, Paul 1924- *WhoOp 76*
Etienne Of Liege *NewGrD 80*
Etienne, Denis Germain 1781-1859 *BiDAmM*
Etkes, Nadine *WomWMM B*
Etkes, Raphael *IntMPA 80*
Etkin, Mariano 1943- *DcCM*
Etler, Alvin D 1913-1973 *Baker 78, ConAmC, DcCM, NewGrD 80*
Etlik, Milan 1927- *IntWWM 77, -80*
Etlinger, Dick *ConMuA 80B*
Eto, Toshiya 1927- *NewGrD 80*
Etrog, Sorel 1933- *CreCan 1*
Ett, Kaspar 1788-1847 *Baker 78*
Etti, Karl 1912- *IntWWM 77, -80, WhoMus 72*
Etting, Ruth d1978 *AmPS B*
Etting, Ruth 1896-1978 *BiDAmM, FilmEn*
Etting, Ruth 1897-1978 *HalFC 80, What 5[port], WhoHol A*
Etting, Ruth 1903?-1978 *CmpEPM*
Etting, Ruth 1907-1978 *EncMT, ForYSC, WhThe*
Ettinger, Edwin D 1921- *IntMPA 77, -75, -76, -78, -79, -80*
Ettinger, Max 1874-1951 *Baker 78, NewGrD 80*
Ettinger, Solomon 1800?-1856 *McGEWD*
Ettinghausen, Elizabeth S 1918- *IntWWM 77, -80*
Ettlinger, John A 1924- *IntMPA 77, -75, -76, -78, -79, -80*
Ettlinger, Karl *Film 2*
Ettlinger, Yona 1924- *IntWWM 80, WhoMus 72*
Ettore, Eugene 1921- *AmSCAP 66, -80, ConAmC A*
Etzkorn, Cleaon 1919- *IntWWM 77, -80*
Etzkorn, K Peter 1932- *IntWWM 77, -80*
Eubanks, Charles G 1942- *ConAmC*
Eubanks, Horace 1900- *WhoJazz 72*
Eubanks, Rachel Amelia *IntWWM 77, -80*
Euclid *Baker 78, NewGrD 80*
Eugene, Billy *Film 2*
Eugene, Homer 1914- *NewOrJ[port]*
Eugene, Wendell 1923- *NewOrJ*
Eugene, William *Film 2*
Eugenikos, Markos *NewGrD 80*
Eugster, Carl 1925- *AmSCAP 80*
Eukleides *NewGrD 80*
Eule, Carl Diedrich 1776-1827 *NewGrD 80*
Eulenberg, Herbert 1876-1949 *CnMD, ModWD, NotNAT B*
Eulenburg, Ernst 1847-1926 *Baker 78, NewGrD 80*
Eulenstein, Charles 1802-1890 *NewGrD 80, OxMus*
Euler, Josephine Mary *IntWWM 77, -80, WhoMus 72*
Euler, Leonhard 1707-1783 *NewGrD 80*
Euler, Leonhardt 1707-1783 *Baker 78*
Eulo, Ken 1939- *NatPD[port]*
Eumelos Of Corinth *NewGrD 80*
Eumelus Of Corinth *NewGrD 80*
Eunson, Dale 1904- *BiE&WWA, NotNAT*
Euphorion *OxThe*
Eupolis 446?BC-411?BC *OxThe*
Eureka, Leonard *ConAmTC*
Eureka Brass Band *BiDAmM*
Euresicchio, Antonio *NewGrD 80*
Euripedes 480BC-406BC *REnWD[port]*
Euripedes 484BC-406BC *CnThe*
Euripedes 485?BC-406?BC *McGEWD[port]*
Euripides 480BC-406BC *NewEOp 71*
Euripides 484?BC-406?BC *EncWT, Ent[port], OxThe*
Euripides 484BC-407BC *PlP&P[port]*
Euripides 485?BC-406?BC *NewGrD 80*
Euripides 486?BC-407BC *NotNAT A, -B*
Eurisechio, Antonio *NewGrD 80*
Europe, James Reese 1879-1919 *BlksBF*
Europe, James Reese 1881-1919 *BiDAmM, DrBlPA, WhoJazz 72*
Eury, Nicolas *NewGrD 80*
Eustace, Fred *Film 1*
Eustace, Jennie A 1865-1936 *NotNAT B, WhoStg 1908*
Eustache De Rains *NewGrD 80*
Eustache Le Peintre De Reims *NewGrD 80*
Eustache, Jean 1938- *FilmEn*
Eustachio Romano *NewGrD 80*
Eustachius Gallus *NewGrD 80*
Eustacius Leodiensis *NewGrD 80*
Eustrel, Anthony 1904- *HalFC 80*
Eustrel, Antony 1904- *WhThe*
Euthymius Of Iviron d1028 *NewGrD 80*
Euting, Ernst 1874-1925 *Baker 78*
Eva, Evi *Film 2*
Evald, Johanna *Film 2*
Evan, Blanche *DancEn 78*
Evan-Zohar, Simha 1915- *WhoOp 76*
Evangelatos, Antiochos 1904- *DcCM*
Evangelisti, Franco 1926- *Baker 78, DcCM, NewGrD 80*
Evangelisti, Victor *Film 2*
Evangelisti Dalla Pergola, Domenico *NewGrD 80*
Evanghelatos, Antiochos 1903- *NewGrD 80*
Evans, Albert *NatPD[port]*
Evans, Alison Ridley 1929- *BiE&WWA*
Evans, Anne Elizabeth 1942- *IntWWM 80, WhoOp 76*
Evans, Barry 1943- *IntMPA 77, -75, -76, -78, -79, -80*
Evans, Barry 1945- *FilmgC, HalFC 80*
Evans, Bergen 1904- *NewYTET*
Evans, Bill 1929- *EncJzS 70, IlEncJ, NewGrD 80*
Evans, Bill 1946- *CnOxB*
Evans, Billy G 1938- *ConAmC*
Evans, Bob 1904-1961 *WhScrn 77*
Evans, Brandon d1958 *WhoHol B*
Evans, Bruce *WhoHol A*
Evans, Caradoc d1945 *NotNAT B, WhThe*
Evans, Cecile *Film 2*
Evans, Cecilia 1902-1960 *WhScrn 74, -77, WhoHol B*
Evans, Charles 1875- *ForYSC*
Evans, Charles E 1856-1945 *NotNAT B, WhoStg 1906, -1908*
Evans, Charles E 1857-1945 *Film 2, WhScrn 74, -77, WhoHol B*
Evans, Clifford 1912- *FilmgC, HalFC 80, IlWWBF, IntMPA 77, -75, -76, -78, -79, -80, WhThe, WhoHol A*
Evans, Dale 1912- *AmSCAP 66, -80, BiDAmM, CmpEPM, CounME 74, -74A, EncFCWM 69, FilmEn, FilmgC, ForYSC, HalFC 80, HolP 40[port], IlEncCM[port], MotPP, MovMk, WhoHol A*
Evans, Damon 1950- *DrBlPA*
Evans, David 1874-1948 *OxMus*
Evans, David Emlyn 1843-1913 *Baker 78, NewGrD 80, OxMus*
Evans, David Gruffydd 1925- *IntWWM 77, -80*
Evans, David John 1948- *WhoMus 72*
Evans, Doc 1907- *CmpEPM, WhoJazz 72*
Evans, Don *BlkAmP, MorBAP, NatPD[port]*
Evans, Douglas 1904-1968 *WhScrn 74, -77, WhoHol B*
Evans, Edgar 1914- *IntWWM 77, -80, WhoMus 72*
Evans, Edith 1888- *IntMPA 76*
Evans, Edith 1888-1976 *CnThe, EncWT, Ent[port], FilmAG WE[port], FilmEn, Film 1, FilmgC, ForYSC, HalFC 80, IlWWBF[port], -A, IntMPA 77, -75, MotPP, MovMk[port], NotNAT A, OxFilm, OxThe, PlP&P[port], WhoHol A, WhoThe 72, -77, WorEFlm[port]*
Evans, Edith 1894-1962 *WhScrn 74, -77, WhoHol B*
Evans, Edward R 1913- *IntMPA 75, -76*
Evans, Edwin d1945 *NotNAT B*
Evans, Edwin 1871-1945 *NewGrD 80*
Evans, Edwin 1874-1945 *Baker 78, DancEn 78, OxMus*
Evans, Edwin, Sr. 1844-1923 *Baker 78*
Evans, Ernest 1941- *AmSCAP 80*
Evans, Estelle *DrBlPA*
Evans, Evan 1901-1954 *WhScrn 74, -77, WhoHol B*
Evans, Evan E 1875-1962 *NotNAT B*
Evans, Evans *WhoHol A*
Evans, Frank *Film 1, -2*
Evans, Fred 1889-1951 *FilmEn, Film 1, -2, IlWWBF*
Evans, Frederick Shailer 1863-1954 *BiDAmM*
Evans, Gene *WhoHol A*
Evans, Gene 1922- *FilmEn, FilmgC, ForYSC, HalFC 80*
Evans, Gene 1924- *IntMPA 77, -75, -76, -78, -79, -80*
Evans, George 1870-1915 *AmPS B, BiDAmM, CmpEPM*
Evans, Sir Geraint Llewellyn 1922- *Baker 78, BnBkM 80, CmOp, IntWWM 77, -80, MusMk, MusSN[port], NewEOp 71, NewGrD 80, WhoMus 72, WhoOp 76*
Evans, Gil 1912- *Baker 78, BiDAmM, CmpEPM, ConAmC, EncJzS 70, IlEncJ, NewGrD 80*
Evans, Graham Norman 1938- *IntWWM 80*
Evans, Harry Lindley 1895- *IntWWM 77*
Evans, Helena Phillips 1875-1955 *WhScrn 74, -77, WhoHol B*
Evans, Henry Ridgely 1861-1949 *MagIlD, PupTheA*
Evans, Herbert 1883-1952 *Vers B[port], WhScrn 74, -77, WhoHol B*
Evans, Herschel 1909-1939 *BiDAmM, CmpEPM, IlEncJ, WhoJazz 72*
Evans, Humphrey, III *ConAmC*
Evans, Ivor *WhoMus 72*
Evans, J C 1930- *IntMPA 75, -76*
Evans, Jack 1893-1950 *Film 2, WhScrn 74, -77, WhoHol B*
Evans, James Roderick 1930- *AmSCAP 80*
Evans, Jean Marie *AmSCAP 80*
Evans, Jerome M 1923- *IntMPA 77, -75, -76, -78, -79, -80*
Evans, Jessie 1918- *WhoThe 72, -77*
Evans, Joan 1934- *FilmEn, FilmgC, ForYSC, HalFC 80, MotPP, WhoHol A*
Evans, Joe 1891-1967 *Film 1, -2, IlWWBF*
Evans, Joe 1916-1973 *WhScrn 77*
Evans, John Glynne 1930- *WhoMus 72*
Evans, John Rhys 1930- *WhoMus 72*
Evans, Joy *WhoMus 72*
Evans, Julius *IntMPA 77, -75, -76, -78, -79, -80*
Evans, Karin *Film 2*
Evans, Lee 1933- *AmSCAP 80*
Evans, Leo L 1927- *AmSCAP 66*
Evans, Linda *WhoHol A*
Evans, Lindley 1895- *WhoMus 72*
Evans, Lloyd Ranney 1932- *WhoOp 76*
Evans, Lyle *PlP&P[port]*
Evans, Madge 1909- *BiE&WWA, FilmEn, Film 1, -2, FilmgC, ForYSC, HalFC 80, MGM[port], MotPP, MovMk[port], ThFT[port], TwYS, WhThe, WhoHol A*
Evans, Margaret 1920- *WhoMus 72*
Evans, Margie 1940- *BluesWW[port]*
Evans, Margie 1941- *EncJzS 70*
Evans, Marguerite *Film 2*
Evans, Marion 1926- *AmSCAP 66, -80*
Evans, Mark *IntWWM 80, WomWMM*
Evans, Mary Jane 1923- *BiE&WWA, NotNAT*
Evans, Maurice 1901- *BiE&WWA, CnThe, EncMT, EncWT, FamA&A[port], FilmEn, FilmgC, ForYSC, HalFC 80, IlWWBF, IntMPA 77, -75, -76, -78, -79, -80, MotPP, MovMk, NewYTET, NotNAT, OxThe, PlP&P, WhoHol A, WhoThe 72, -77*
Evans, Meriel 1934- *DancEn 78*

Evans, Michael *DrBlPA*
Evans, Michael 1922- *WhThe, WhoThe 72*
Evans, Michael 1926- *BiE&WWA, NotNAT*
Evans, Michael Aubrey 1932- *WhoMus 72*
Evans, Mike *MorBAP, WhoHol A*
Evans, Myddleton *Film 2*
Evans, Nancy d1963 *WhScrn 74, -77, WhoHol B*
Evans, Nancy 1915- *NewGrD 80, WhThe, WhoMus 72*
Evans, Norman 1901-1962 *HalFC 80, NotNAT B*
Evans, Pat *WomWMM B*
Evans, Patricia Margaret 1935- *WhoMus 72*
Evans, Paul 1925- *NewGrD 80*
Evans, Paul 1938- *AmSCAP 66, -80, RkOn[port]*
Evans, Pauline 1917-1952 *WhScrn 74, -77*
Evans, Peter Angus 1929- *NewGrD 80, WhoMus 72*
Evans, Ralph M 1905- *IntMPA 75, -76*
Evans, Ray 1915- *AmPS, BiE&WWA, CmpEPM, FilmEn, FilmgC, HalFC 80, IntMPA 77, -75, -76, -78, -79, -80, NotNAT, Sw&Ld C*
Evans, Ray And Jay Livingston *Sw&Ld C*
Evans, Raymond Bernard 1915- *AmSCAP 66, -80, BiDAmM*
Evans, Redd Louis 1912-1972 *AmSCAP 66, -80, BiDAmM*
Evans, Renee 1908-1971 *WhScrn 74, -77*
Evans, Rex 1903-1969 *FilmgC, HalFC 80, Vers A[port], WhScrn 74, -77, WhoHol B*
Evans, Rhys Sterling 1923- *AmSCAP 80*
Evans, Richard *AmSCAP 80, WhoHol A*
Evans, Robert 1930- *BiDFilm 81, FilmEn, FilmgC, ForYSC, HalFC 80, IntMPA 77, -75, -76, -78, -79, -80, MotPP, WhoHol A*
Evans, Rothbury d1944 *NotNAT B*
Evans, Roy 1890?-1943? *NewOrJ*
Evans, Sally Hazen *ConAmC*
Evans, Stomp 1900-1930 *BiDAmM*
Evans, Stump 1900-1930 *WhoJazz 72*
Evans, Sue 1951- *EncJzS 70*
Evans, Sy *IntMPA 77, -75, -76, -78, -79, -80*
Evans, Tenniel 1926- *WhoThe 72, -77*
Evans, Tudor 1912- *WhoMus 72*
Evans, Wilbur 1908- *BiE&WWA, ForYSC, NotNAT, WhoHol A*
Evans, Will 1873-1931 *NotNAT B, WhThe*
Evans, Will 1875-1931 *IlWWBF, OxThe*
Evans, William Edwin 1851-1915 *BiDAmM*
Evans, William John 1929- *BiDAmM, EncJzS 70, NewGrD 80*
Evans, William Robert, III 1940- *AmSCAP 80*
Evans, Winifred 1890- *WhThe*
Evans, Wynford 1946- *IntWWM 77, -80*
Evans, Zishaw *MorBAP*
Evans-Charles, Marti *DrBlPA*
Evanson, Edith *ForYSC, WhoHol A*
Evarts, William H d1940 *NotNAT B*
Evdokimova, Eva 1948- *CnOxB*
Eve, Alphonse D' 1662-1727 *OxMus*
Eve, Alphonse D' 1666-1727 *NewGrD 80*
Evein, Bernard 1929- *DcFM, FilmEn, FilmgC, HalFC 80, WorEFlm*
Eveleigh, Michael George William 1924- *WhoMus 72*
Eveling, Stanley 1925- *ConDr 73, -77, EncWT, WhoThe 72, -77*
Evelyn *What 4[port]*
Evelyn, Baby *Film 2*
Evelyn, Clara 1886- *WhThe*
Evelyn, John 1620-1706 *DcPup, NewGrD 80, OxMus*
Evelyn, Judith 1913-1967 *BiE&WWA, FilmgC, ForYSC, HalFC 80, MotPP, NotNAT B, WhScrn 74, -77, WhThe, WhoHol B*
Evelyn, Mildred *Film 2*
Evelynne, May 1856-1943 *WhScrn 74, -77*
Evennett, Wallace 1888- *WhThe*
Evens, Clifford Robert 1952- *AmSCAP 80*
Evens, Clifford Wallis 1921- *IntWWM 77, -80*
Everard, Walter d1924 *NotNAT B*
Everding, August 1928- *WhoOp 76*
Everding, August 1929- *EncWT*
Everest, Barbara d1968 *MotPP, WhoHol B*
Everest, Barbara 1890-1968 *NotNAT B, WhScrn 74, -77, WhThe*
Everest, Barbara 1891-1967 *HalFC 80*
Everest, Barbara 1891-1968 *FilmgC*
Everest, Charles William 1814-1877 *BiDAmM*
Everett, Asa Brooks 1828-1875 *BiDAmM, NewGrD 80*
Everett, Betty 1939- *RkOn 2[port]*
Everett, Chad *WhoHol A*
Everett, Chad 1936- *FilmEn, ForYSC, IntMPA 77, -75, -76, -78, -79, -80*
Everett, Chad 1937- *FilmgC, HalFC 80*
Everett, Chad 1939- *MovMk*
Everett, Ellen 1942- *CnOxB*
Everett, Francine 1920- *BlksB&W, -C*
Everett, Horace *AmSCAP 80*
Everett, L C 1818-1867 *BiDAmM*
Everett, Ron *BlkAmP*
Everett, Sophie d1963 *NotNAT B*
Everett, Thomas G 1944- *CpmDNM 73, ConAmC, IntWWM 77, -80*
Everett, Tim 1938- *NotNAT*
Everett, Timmy 1938- *BiE&WWA*
Everhart, Rex 1920- *BiE&WWA, NotNAT, WhoThe 72, -77*
Everitt, Richard M 1935- *AmSCAP 66, -80*
Everleigh, Kate d1926 *NotNAT B*
Everly, Don 1937- *CounME 74, IlEncCM[port]*
Everly, Donald 1937- *AmSCAP 80, BiDAmM*
Everly, Phil 1939- *CounME 74, IlEncCM[port]*
Everly, Philip 1939- *BiDAmM*
Everly Brothers *AmPS A, -B, ConMuA 80A, CounME 74[port], -74A, IlEncCM, IlEncR[port], RkOn[port]*
Evers, Ann *WhoHol A*
Evers, Arthur *Film 1*
Evers, Ernest P 1874-1945 *WhScrn 74, -77*
Evers, Jason *ForYSC, HalFC 80, WhoHol A*
Evers, King *Film 2*
Evershed-Martin, Leslie *PlP&P[port]*
Everson, Celeste Jean 1953- *IntWWM 77*
Everson, Lottie *BluesWW[port]*
Everson, Marian Christine Deever 1917- *IntWWM 77*
Everson, Ronald Gilmour 1903- *CreCan 1*
Everson, William K 1929- *IntMPA 77, -75, -76, -78, -79, -80*
Everth, Francis *Film 2*
Everton, Paul 1868-1948 *NotNAT B, WhoStg 1908*
Everton, Paul 1869-1948 *Film 1, -2, Vers A[port], WhScrn 74, -77, WhoHol B*
Evertz, Theodor *NewGrD 80*
Every Mother's Son *BiDAmM, RkOn 2[port]*
Evesham, Walter *NewGrD 80*
Evesham, Walter De *OxMus*
Evesson, Isabelle d1914 *NotNAT B*
Evesson, Isabelle 1870- *WhoStg 1906, -1908*
Evett, Robert 1874-1949 *NotNAT B, WhThe*
Evett, Robert 1922-1975 *Baker 78, ConAmC, DcCM*
Eville, William *Film 1, -2*
Evju, Helge 1942- *IntWWM 80*
Evlakhov, Orest Alexandrovich 1912-1973 *NewGrD 80*
Evreinoff *PlP&P*
Evreinov, Nikolai Nikolaivich 1879-1953 *CnMD, CnThe, OxThe*
Evseyev, Sergei 1893-1956 *Baker 78*
Evstatie Of Putna *NewGrD 80*
Evteyeva, Elena *CnOxB*
Ewald, Johannes 1743-1781 *CnThe, NotNAT B, OxThe, REnWD[port]*
Ewald, Victor 1860-1935 *Baker 78*
Ewaldt *NewGrD 80*
Ewart, John Graham 1949- *IntWWM 80*
Ewart, Stephen T 1869- *WhThe*
Ewell, Caroline d1909 *NotNAT B*
Ewell, Don 1916- *CmpEPM*
Ewell, Donald Tyson 1916- *AmSCAP 80*
Ewell, Tom *IntMPA 75, -76, -78, -79, -80*
Ewell, Tom 1909- *BiE&WWA, FilmEn, FilmgC, ForYSC, Funs[port], HalFC 80, IntMPA 77, MotPP, MovMk[port], NotNAT, WhoHol A, WhoThe 72, -77, WorEFlm[port]*
Ewen, David 1907- *Baker 78, BiE&WWA, NewGrD 80, WhoMus 72*
Ewen, Paterson 1925- *CreCan 2*
Ewer *NewGrD 80*
Ewer, John Jeremiah *NewGrD 80*
Ewing, Alexander 1830-1895 *NewGrD 80*
Ewing, Billy *BlksBF*
Ewing, Cecil Cameron 1925- *IntWWM 77*
Ewing, Louise *PupTheA*
Ewing, Maryhelen 1946- *IntWWM 77, -80*
Ewing, Roger *WhoHol A*
Ewing, Streamline John 1917- *WhoJazz 72*
Exaude, Andre-Joseph 1710?-1762 *NewGrD 80*
Exaudee, Andre-Joseph 1710?-1762 *NewGrD 80*
Exaudet, Andre-Joseph 1710?-1762 *NewGrD 80*
Excellents, The *RkOn*
Excestre, William 1390?-1410 *Baker 78*
Excetre, J *NewGrD 80*
Exciters, The *RkOn[port]*
Exerea *NewGrD 80*
Exereo *NewGrD 80*
Eximeno, Antonio 1729-1808 *Baker 78, NewGrD 80*
Exline, Jerry Michael 1942- *IntWWM 77*
Expert, Henry 1863-1952 *Baker 78, NewGrD 80, OxMus*
Expilly, Gabriel 1630?-1690? *NewGrD 80*
Exter, Aleksandra 1884-1949 *Ent*
Exter, Alexander *PlP&P*
Exter, Alexandra 1884-1949 *EncWT*
Exton, Clive 1930- *ConDr 73, -77C*
Eybler, Joseph Leopold 1765-1846 *Baker 78, NewGrD 80*
Eyck, Jacob Van 1589?-1657 *NewGrD 80*
Eyck, Peter Van *FilmAG WE*
Eyen, Tom 1940- *ConDr 73*
Eyen, Tom 1941- *ConDr 77, NatPD[port], WhoThe 72, -77*
Eyer, Richard *ForYSC*
Eyer, Richard 1946?- *WhoHrs 80[port]*
Eyermann, Albert Timothy 1946- *AmSCAP 80*
Eyk, Tonny 1940- *IntWWM 77, -80*
Eyken, Jan Albert Van 1823-1868 *Baker 78*
Eyken, Simon Van *NewGrD 80*
Eymann, Dale Weber 1916- *AmSCAP 80*
Eymieu, Henry 1860-1931 *Baker 78*
Eynstone, Mary June 1935- *WhoMus 72*
Eyramya, Carmen Stanley 1936- *IntWWM 77, -80*
Eyre, Gerald d1885 *NotNAT B*
Eyre, John Edmund d1816 *NotNAT B*
Eyre, Laurence 1881-1959 *NotNAT B, WhThe*
Eyre, Peter 1942- *WhoHol A, WhoThe 77*
Eyre, Richard 1943- *WhoThe 77*
Eyre, Ronald 1929- *EncWT, WhoThe 72, -77*
Eyser, Eberhard 1932- *Baker 78, IntWWM 77, -80*
Eysler, Edmund S 1874-1949 *Baker 78, NewGrD 80*
Eysoldt, Gertrud 1870-1950 *EncWT*
Eysoldt, Gertrud 1870-1955 *OxThe*
Eysoldt, Gertrud 1871-1955 *WhScrn 74, -77*
Eysselinck, Walter 1931- *WhoThe 72, -77*
Eyssell, Gustav S 1901- *IntMPA 75, -76*
Eythe, William 1918-1947 *FilmgC*
Eythe, William 1918-1957 *FilmEn, ForYSC, HalFC 80, HolP 40[port], MotPP, NotNAT B, WhScrn 74, -77, WhThe, WhoHol B*
Eytinge, Rose 1835-1911 *FamA&A[port], NotNAT A, -B, WhoStg 1906, -1908*
Eyton, Bessie 1890- *Film 1, -2, TwYS*
Eyton, Frank 1894- *WhThe*
Ezaki, Kenjiro 1926- *Baker 78, DcCM*
Ezekian, Harry *WhoHrs 80*
Ezell, Helen Ingle 1903- *AmSCAP 66, -80, CpmDNM 80, ConAmC*
Ezilie *BlkAmP*
Ezrahi, Yariv 1904- *IntWWM 77, -80*
Ezrin, Bob *ConMuA 80B*

F

Faa DiBruno, Giovanni Matteo *NewGrD 80*
Fabares, Shelley *AmPS A*
Fabares, Shelley 1942- *FilmgC, HalFC 80, WhoHol A*
Fabares, Shelley 1943- *ForYSC*
Fabares, Shelly 1944- *RkOn*
Fabbri, Diego 1911- *CnMD, CnThe, EncWT, Ent[port], McGEWD[port], ModWD, OxThe*
Fabbri, Flora *CnOxB, DancEn 78*
Fabbri, Franca 1935- *WhoOp 76*
Fabbri, Guerrina 1868-1946 *CmOp*
Fabbri, Jacques 1925- *EncWT*
Fabbri, Mario 1931- *NewGrD 80*
Fabbri, Stefano *NewGrD 80*
Fabbrichesi, Salvatore 1760-1827 *OxThe*
Fabbrini, Giuseppe d1708 *NewGrD 80*
Faber, Benedictus 1573-1634 *NewGrD 80*
Faber, Benedikt 1573-1634 *NewGrD 80*
Faber, Beryl d1912 *WhThe*
Faber, Erwin *Film 2*
Faber, Frederick William *OxMus*
Faber, Gregor 1520?-1554? *NewGrD 80*
Faber, Heinrich 1500?-1552 *Baker 78, NewGrD 80*
Faber, J A J *OxMus*
Faber, Joachim 1913- *IntWWM 80*
Faber, Johann Christoph *NewGrD 80*
Faber, Leslie 1879-1929 *NotNAT B, WhThe, WhoHol B*
Faber, Mrs. Leslie 1880- *WhThe*
Faber, Nicolaus *NewGrD 80*
Faber, Nicolaus 1490?-1554 *NewGrD 80*
Faber, Stephan 1580?-1632 *NewGrD 80*
Faber, William E 1902-1967 *AmSCAP 66, -80*
Faber Stapulensis, Jacobus 1455?-1537 *NewGrD 80*
Fabian 1940- *FilmEn*
Fabian 1942- *FilmgC, HalFC 80, MotPP, WhoHol A*
Fabian 1943- *BiDAmM, ForYSC, RkOn[port]*
Fabian, Francoise 1932- *FilmAG WE[port]*
Fabian, Francoise 1935- *FilmEn, WhoHol A*
Fabian, Imre 1930- *IntWWM 77, -80*
Fabian, Madge 1880- *WhThe*
Fabian, Marta 1946- *NewGrD 80*
Fabini, Eduardo 1882-1950 *Baker 78, DcCM, NewGrD 80*
Fabio, Sarah Webster 1928- *BlkAmP, MorBAP*
Fabray, Nanette *MotPP, NotNAT, WhoHol A*
Fabray, Nanette 1920- *BiDAmM, BiE&WWA, FilmEn, Film 2, FilmgC, ForYSC, HalFC 80, IntMPA 77, -75, -76, -78, -79, -80, WhoThe 72, -77*
Fabray, Nanette 1922- *CmpEPM, EncMT*
Fabre, Emile 1869-1955 *McGEWD, NotNAT B*
Fabre, Emile 1870-1955 *WhThe*
Fabre, Fernand *Film 2*
Fabre, Saturnin 1884-1961 *HalFC 80, WhScrn 74, -77, WhoHol B*
Fabre D'Eglantine, Philippe-Francois N 1755-1794 *OxThe*
Fabre D'Olivet, Antoine 1767-1825 *NewGrD 80*
Fabregas, Virginia 1870-1950 *WhScrn 74, -77*
Fabreti, Bartolomeo *NewGrD 80*
Fabri, Adam *NewGrD 80*
Fabri, Annibale Pio 1697-1760 *NewGrD 80[port]*
Fabri, Martinus *NewGrD 80*
Fabri, Petrus *NewGrD 80*
Fabri, Stefano d1609 *NewGrD 80*
Fabri, Stefano 1606?-1658 *NewGrD 80*
Fabri, Thomas *NewGrD 80*
Fabri, Tomas *NewGrD 80*
Fabri, Zoltan 1917- *DcFM, FilmEn, FilmgC, HalFC 80, OxFilm, WorEFlm*
Fabrianese, Tiberio *NewGrD 80*
Fabric, Bent 1927- *AmPS A, RkOn*
Fabricius, Albinus *NewGrD 80*
Fabricius, Bernhard *NewGrD 80*
Fabricius, Georg 1516-1571 *NewGrD 80*
Fabricius, Jacob 1949- *IntWWM 80*
Fabricius, Jakob 1840-1919 *NewGrD 80*
Fabricius, Johann Albert 1668-1736 *Baker 78*
Fabricius, Peter 1587-1651 *NewGrD 80*
Fabricius, Petrus 1587-1651 *NewGrD 80*
Fabricius, Werner 1633-1679 *Baker 78, NewGrD 80*
Fabrini, Giuseppe *NewGrD 80*
Fabritiis, Oliviero De *NewGrD 80*
Fabritius, Albinus d1635 *NewGrD 80*
Fabritius, Petrus *NewGrD 80*
Fabrizi, Aldo *IntMPA 75, -76, -78, -79, -80*
Fabrizi, Aldo 1905- *FilmEn, FilmgC, HalFC 80, IntMPA 77, MovMk[port], WhoHol A*
Fabrizi, Aldo 1906- *FilmAG WE*
Fabrizi, Franco 1926- *FilmEn*
Fabrizi, Mario 1925-1963 *NotNAT B, WhScrn 74, -77, WhoHol B*
Fabrizi, Vincenzo 1764-1812? *NewGrD 80*
Fabrizzi, Aldo 1905- *OxFilm*
Facchetti, Giovanni Battista *NewGrD 80*
Facchi, Agostino d1662 *NewGrD 80*
Facchinetti, Giovanni Battista *NewGrD 80*
Faccho, Agostino d1662 *NewGrD 80*
Faccini, Giovanni Battista *NewGrD 80*
Faccio, Franco 1840-1891 *Baker 78, CmOp, NewEOp 71, NewGrD 80*
Facco, Agostino *NewGrD 80*
Facco, Giacomo 1680?-1753 *NewGrD 80*
Facco, Jaime 1680?-1753 *NewGrD 80*
Facco, Jayme 1680?-1753 *NewGrD 80*
Facenda, Tommy 1939- *RkOn[port]*
Faces *BiDAmM, ConMuA 80A, IlEncR[port], RkOn 2[port]*
Facey, Hugh *NewGrD 80*
Fachetti, Giovanni Battista *NewGrD 80*
Fachiri, Adila 1886-1962 *Baker 78, NewGrD 80*
Facho, Agostino *NewGrD 80*
Facie, Hugh *NewGrD 80*
Facien, Jehan *NewGrD 80*
Facio, Anselmo Di *NewGrD 80*
Facio, Hugh *NewGrD 80*
Fack, Renate 1937- *WhoOp 76*
Facoli, Marco *NewGrD 80*
Factor, Alan Jay 1925- *IntMPA 77, -75, -76, -78, -79, -80*
Facy, Hugh *NewGrD 80*
Facye, Hugh *NewGrD 80*
Fadden, Genevieve d1959 *WhScrn 74, -77, WhoHol B*
Fadden, Tom 1895- *ForYSC, Vers A[port], WhoHol A*
Faddis, Jon 1953- *EncJzS 70*
Fadeyechev, Nicolai Borisovich 1933- *CnOxB, DancEn 78*
Fadiman, Clifton 1904- *IntMPA 77, -75, -76, -78, -79, What 3[port]*
Faelten, Carl 1846-1925 *Baker 78, BiDAmM*
Faelten, Reinhold 1856-1949 *Baker 78*
Faerber, Jorg 1929- *NewGrD 80*
Faesi, Robert 1883-1972 *CnMD*
Fagan, Barney 1850-1937 *NotNAT B*
Fagan, Eleanora *NewGrD 80*
Fagan, Gideon 1904-1980 *Baker 78, NewGrD 80*
Fagan, James Bernard 1873-1933 *CnThe, NotNAT B, OxThe, WhThe*
Fagan, Joan 1934- *BiE&WWA, NotNAT*
Fagan, Myron C *WhThe*
Fagan, Scott William 1945- *AmSCAP 80*
Fagan, Thomas O 1936- *AmSCAP 80*
Fagas, James Jimmie 1924- *AmSCAP 80*
Fagas, Jimmie 1924- *AmSCAP 66*
Fage, Jean DeLa *NewGrD 80*
Fagella, Anthony 1899- *AmSCAP 66*
Fagerlund, Soren Evert 1929- *IntWWM 77*
Fagerquist, Don 1927-1974 *CmpEPM, EncJzS 70*
Fagerquist, Donald A 1927-1974 *BiDAmM, EncJzS 70*
Faggioli, Michelangelo 1666-1733 *NewGrD 80*
Faggioni, Piero Antonio 1936- *WhoOp 76*
Fagius, Hans 1951- *IntWWM 77, -80*
Fagnola, Annibale 1865?-1939 *NewGrD 80*
Fago *NewGrD 80*
Fago, Lorenzo 1704-1793 *NewGrD 80*
Fago, Nicola 1677-1745 *Baker 78, MusMk, NewGrD 80*
Fago, Pasquale 1740?-1794? *NewGrD 80*
Fagus, Guillaume *NewGrD 80*
Fahey, Brian Michael 1919- *IntWWM 77, -80, WhoMus 72*
Fahey, John 1939- *ConMuA 80A, IlEncR*
Fahey, Myrna 1939-1973 *ForYSC, WhScrn 77, WhoHol B, WhoHrs 80*
Fahey, Patrick James 1933- *IntWWM 80*
Fahrbach, Philipp 1815-1885 *Baker 78, NewGrD 80*
Fahrney, Madcap Merry d1974 *WhoHol B*
Fahrney, Milton H 1871-1941 *WhScrn 74, -77, WhoHol B*
Faichney, James B *IntMPA 77, -75, -76, -78, -79, -80*
Faidit, Gaucelm 1150?-1220? *NewGrD 80*
Faier, Yuri Fedorovich 1890-1971 *CnOxB,*

DancEn 78
Faigel, Eva Maria *CnOxB*
Faignant, Noe 1540?-1595? *NewGrD 80*
Faignant, Noel *NewGrD 80*
Faignient, Noe *NewGrD 80*
Faignient, Noe 1540?-1595? *Baker 78*
Faignient, Noel *NewGrD 80*
Faiko, Alexei Mikhailovich 1893- *OxThe*
Failoni, Sergei 1890-1948 *CmOp*
Failoni, Sergio 1890-1948 *NewGrD 80*
Fain, John 1915-1970 *WhScrn 74, -77, WhoHol B*
Fain, Sammy 1902- *AmPS, AmSCAP 66, -80, Baker 78, BiDAmM, BiE&WWA, CmpEPM, EncMT, FilmEn, IntMPA 77, -75, -76, -78, -79, -80, NewCBMT, NewGrD 80, NotNAT, PopAmC[port], PopAmC SUP, Sw&Ld C*
Faine, Hy 1910- *BiE&WWA*
Faini, Philip James 1931- *IntWWM 77, -80*
Fair, Adrah 1897- *WhThe*
Fair, Charles B 1921- *AmSCAP 66, -80*
Fair, Elinor 1902-1957 *FilmEn, Film 1, -2, TwYS, WhoHol B*
Fair, Elinor 1903-1957 *WhScrn 77*
Fair, Florence *Film 2*
Fair, Melvin Anthony 1939- *AmSCAP 80*
Fair, Ronald L 1932- *BlkAmP*
Fair, Sue Braumiller 1936- *IntWWM 77*
Fair, William B 1851-1909 *OxThe*
Fairbanks, A C 1852-1896? *NewGrD 80*
Fairbanks, Douglas 1883-1939 *BiDFilm, -81, CmMov, FilmEn, Film 1, -2, FilmgC, HalFC 80[port], MotPP, MovMk[port], NotNAT B, OxFilm, WhScrn 74, -77, WhThe, WhoHol B, WorEFlm*
Fairbanks, Douglas 1884-1939 *TwYS*
Fairbanks, Douglas, Jr. *IlWWBF A, MotPP, WhoHol A*
Fairbanks, Douglas, Jr. 1907- *FilmgC*
Fairbanks, Douglas, Jr. 1908- *OxFilm*
Fairbanks, Douglas, Jr. 1909- *BiDFilm, -81, CmMov, FilmEn, Film 2, ForYSC, HalFC 80[port], IntMPA 77, -75, -76, -78, -79, -80, MovMk, TwYS, WhoThe 77, WorEFlm*
Fairbanks, Flobelle *Film 2*
Fairbanks, Gladys *Film 1*
Fairbanks, Jerry *IntMPA 77, -75, -76, -78, -79, -80*
Fairbanks, Lucille *ForYSC*
Fairbanks, Madeleine *Film 1*
Fairbanks, Marion *Film 1*
Fairbanks, William 1894-1945 *Film 2, TwYS, WhScrn 77*
Fairbanks Twins *Film 2*
Fairbrother, Sidney d1941 *WhoHol B*
Fairbrother, Sydney 1872-1941 *IlWWBF, NotNAT A, -B, OxThe, WhScrn 74, -77, WhThe*
Fairbrother, Sydney 1873-1941 *Film 1, -2, FilmgC, HalFC 80*
Fairbrother, Vera Guendolen 1909- *WhoMus 72*
Fairchild, Barbara 1950- *CounME 74[port], -74A, IlEncCM[port]*
Fairchild, Blair 1877-1933 *Baker 78, BiDAmM, ConAmC, NewGrD 80*
Fairchild, Craig E 1949- *AmSCAP 80*
Fairchild, Edgar 1898-1975 *AmSCAP 66, -80*
Fairchild, William 1918- *CmMov, FilmgC, HalFC 80, IlWWBF, IntMPA 77, -75, -76, -78, -79, -80*
Faircloth, Charlie Raiford 1927- *BiDAmM*
Fairclough, Eric John 1900- *WhoMus 72*
Fairclough, George Herbert 1869-1954 *Baker 78*
Fairclough, Thomas H 1905- *AmSCAP 66, -80*
Faire, Betty *Film 2*
Faire, Virginia Brown 1899-1948 *WhScrn 74, WhoHol B*
Faire, Virginia Brown 1904-1948 *Film 2, ForYSC, TwYS*
Fairfax, Bryan 1930- *NewGrD 80*
Fairfax, James d1962 *ForYSC*
Fairfax, James 1897-1961 *WhScrn 74, -77, WhoHol B*
Fairfax, Lance 1899- *WhThe*
Fairfax, Lettice 1876-1948 *NotNAT B, WhThe*
Fairfax, Marion 1879- *WhThe, WomWMM*
Fairfax, Robert *NewGrD 80*
Fairfax, Thurman *Film 2*
Fairhurst, Harold 1903- *IntWWM 80, WhoMus 72*
Fairhurst, Lyn 1920- *FilmgC, HalFC 80*
Fairhurst, Robin Angus 1941- *IntWWM 77, -80, WhoMus 72*
Fairlamb, James Remington 1838-1908 *Baker 78, BiDAmM*
Fairleigh, James Parkinson 1938- *IntWWM 77, -80*
Fairley, E Lee 1917- *IntWWM 77, -80*
Fairlie, Allan John 1909- *WhoMus 72*
Fairlie, Gerard *IlWWBF A[port]*
Fairlie, Kenneth Macleod 1938- *AmSCAP 80*
Fairlie, Margaret *ConAmC*
Fairman, Austin 1892-1964 *NotNAT B, WhScrn 74, -77, WhThe, WhoHol B*
Fairman, George 1881-1962 *AmSCAP 66, -80*
Fairport Convention *ConMuA 80A, IlEncR*
Fairweather, David Carnegy 1899- *WhoThe 72, -77*
Fairweather, Helen *Film 2*
Fairweather, Virginia 1922- *WhoThe 72, -77*
Fairweather-Low, Andy *ConMuA 80A, IlEncR*
Faisandat, Michel *NewGrD 80*
Faison, George 1945- *CmpGMD, DrBlPA, PlP&P A[port]*
Faison, Josephine Proffitt *AmSCAP 80*
Faisst, Immanuel Gottlob Friedrich 1823-1894 *Baker 78, NewGrD 80*
Fait, A *Film 2*
Faitello, Vigilio Blasio 1710-1768 *NewGrD 80*
Faith, Adam 1940- *ConMuA 80A, FilmgC, IlEncR, IlWWBF A*
Faith, Angela *IntWWM 77*
Faith, Percy 1908-1976 *AmPS A, AmSCAP 66, -80, Baker 78, BiDAmM, CmpEPM, CreCan 1, HalFC 80, RkOn[port]*
Faith, Richard Bruce 1926- *AmSCAP 80, ConAmC*
Faith, Russell H 1929- *AmSCAP 66, -80*
Faith Hope And Charity *RkOn 2[port]*
Faithful, Marianne *ConMuA 80A*
Faithfull, Geoffrey 1894- *FilmgC, HalFC 80, IntMPA 77, -75, -76, -78, -79, -80*
Faithfull, Marianne *IlEncR[port], WhoHol A*
Faithfull, Marianne 1946- *WhoThe 72, -77*
Faithfull, Marianne 1947- *FilmgC, HalFC 80*
Faithfull, Marianne 1948- *RkOn 2[port]*
Faizi, Djaudat Kharisovich 1910- *IntWWM 77, -80*
Fajardo, Raoul Jose 1919- *IntWWM 77, -80*
Fakaerli, George *NewGrD 80*
Fakaerti, George *NewGrD 80*
Fakhr Al-Din *NewGrD 80*
Fako, Nancy Jordan 1942- *IntWWM 77, -80*
Falabella, Roberto 1926-1958 *NewGrD 80*
Falabella Correa, Roberto 1926-1958 *Baker 78*
Falana, Lola 1944?- *AmSCAP 80, DrBlPA, WhoHol A*
Falaro, Anthony J 1938- *ConAmC*
Falchi, Stanislao 1851-1922 *Baker 78*
Falciglia, Patrick 1942- *AmSCAP 66*
Falck, Georg 1630?-1689 *NewGrD 80*
Falck, Jorma Antero 1939- *WhoOp 76*
Falck, Karin *WomWMM*
Falck, Lionel 1889-1971 *WhThe*
Falckenberg, Otto 1873-1947 *EncWT*
Falckenhagen, Adam 1697-1761 *NewGrD 80*
Falco, Anthony M 1923- *AmSCAP 66*
Falco, Louis 1942- *CmpGMD, CnOxB*
Falco, Michele 1688?-1732? *NewGrD 80*
Falco, Simone De *NewGrD 80*
Falcon, Cornelie 1814-1897 *NewGrD 80*
Falcon, Marie-Cornelie 1812-1897 *NewEOp 71*
Falcon, Marie-Cornelie 1814-1897 *Baker 78, CmOp*
Falcone, Achille 1570?-1600 *NewGrD 80*
Falconer, Edmund 1815-1879 *NotNAT B*
Falconetti 1901-1946 *FilmgC, HalFC 80, WhoHol B*
Falconetti, Maria 1902-1946 *Film 2*
Falconetti, Marie *MotPP*
Falconetti, Renee 1892-1946 *FilmEn*
Falconetti, Renee 1893-1946 *WorEFlm*
Falconetti, Renee 1901-1946 *FilmAG WE, OxFilm, WhScrn 74, -77*
Falconi, Signor *PupTheA*
Falconi, Armando *WhThe*
Falconi, Arturo d1934 *NotNAT B, WhoHol B*
Falconi, Placido *NewGrD 80*
Falconieri, Andrea 1585?-1656 *NewGrD 80*
Falconieri, Andrea 1586-1656 *Baker 78, MusMk*
Falconio, Placido *NewGrD 80*
Falcons, The *BiDAmM, RkOn[port]*
Falena, Ugo 1875-1931 *FilmEn*
Faleron, Jean *Film 2*
Fales, Victoria Nancy *NatPD[port]*
Falewicz, Magdalena 1946- *WhoOp 76*
Falguera, Jose 1778-1824? *NewGrD 80*
Falik, Jurii 1936- *DcCM*
Falik, Yury Alexandrovich 1936- *NewGrD 80*
Falk, Lee *NatPD[port]*
Falk, Per 1924- *DancEn 78*
Falk, Peter 1927- *BiE&WWA, FilmEn, FilmgC, ForYSC, HalFC 80, IntMPA 77, -75, -76, -78, -79, -80, MotPP, MovMk, NotNAT, WhoHol A*
Falk, Richard 1878-1949 *Baker 78*
Falk, Richard 1912- *BiE&WWA, NotNAT*
Falk, Rossella 1926- *EncWT, Ent[port]*
Falk, Sawyer 1898-1961 *NotNAT B*
Falkenberg, Jinx 1919- *ForYSC*
Falkenburg, Jinx 1919- *FilmgC, HalFC 80, WhoHol A*
Falkener, Robert *NewGrD 80*
Falkenhagen, Adam *NewGrD 80*
Falkenhain, Patricia 1926- *BiE&WWA, NotNAT*
Falkenstein, Julius *Film 1, -2*
Falkman, Carl Johan *IntWWM 80*
Falkner, Donald Keith 1900- *Baker 78*
Falkner, Dorothy Hazel Gladys 1898- *WhoMus 72*
Falkner, Sir Keith 1900- *IntWWM 77, -80, NewGrD 80, OxMus, WhoMus 72*
Fall, Fritz 1901-1974 *Baker 78*
Fall, Leo 1873-1925 *Baker 78, NewGrD 80, NotNAT B*
Fall, Leo 1878-1925 *OxMus*
Fall, Moritz 1848-1922 *NewGrD 80*
Fall, Richard 1882- *NewGrD 80*
Fall, Siegfried 1877- *NewGrD 80*
Falla, Dorothea 1921- *IntWWM 77*
Falla, Manuel De 1876-1946 *Baker 78, BnBkM 80, CmOp, CompSN[port], CnOxB, DcCom 77[port], DcCom&M 79, DcCM, DcPup, DcTwCC, MusMk, NewEOp 71, NewGrD 80[port], OxMus*
Fallamero, Gabriele *NewGrD 80*
Fallen Sparrows *BiDAmM*
Faller, Nikola 1862-1938 *Baker 78*
Fallis, Barbara 1924- *CnOxB, DancEn 78*
Fallon, Charles 1885-1936 *WhScrn 74, -77, WhoHol B*
Fallon, Richard 1923- *BiE&WWA, NotNAT*
Fallows, David 1945- *IntWWM 80*
Falls, Gregory A 1922- *BiE&WWA, NotNAT*
Falter, Joseph 1782-1846 *NewGrD 80*
Falter, Macarius 1762-1843 *NewGrD 80*
Faltin, F R 1835-1918 *OxMus*
Faltin, Friedrich Richard 1835-1918 *NewGrD 80*
Faltin, Peter 1939- *IntWWM 80*
Faltskog, Agnetha Ase 1950- *IntWWM 77*
Falusi, Michele Angelo *NewGrD 80*
Falvy, Zoltan 1928- *IntWWM 77, -80, NewGrD 80*
Falzone, Salvatore Joseph 1933- *EncJzS 70*
Falzone, Sam 1933- *EncJzS 70*
Fame, Georgie 1943- *EncJzS 70, IlEncR, RkOn 2[port]*
Family *ConMuA 80A, IlEncR[port]*
Famintsin, Alexander Sergeyevich 1841-1896 *NewGrD 80*
Famintsyn, Alexander 1841-1896 *Baker 78*
Fanatzeanu, Corneliu 1933- *WhoOp 76*
Fancelli, Giuseppe 1833-1888 *NewGrD 80*
Fanciulli, Francesco 1850-1915 *Baker 78*
Fanck, Arnold 1889-1974 *DcFM, FilmEn, OxFilm, WorEFlm*
Fanck, Arnold 1889-1975 *HalFC 80*
Fancourt, Darrell 1888-1953 *NotNAT B, WhThe*
Fancy *RkOn 2[port]*
Fane, Dorothy *Film 2*

Fane, John *NewGrD 80*
Fanelli, Ernest 1860-1917 *Baker 78, OxMus*
Fanelli, Frances 1942- *IntWWM 77, -80*
Fanfani, Giuseppe Maria 1723?-1757? *NewGrD 80*
Fang, Charles *Film 1, -2*
Fanidi, Theo *AmSCAP 80*
Faning, Eaton 1850-1927 *NewGrD 80*
Faning, Eaton 1853-1927 *Baker 78*
Fann, Al 1925- *BlkAmP, DrBlPA, MorBAP*
Fann, Ernie *BlkAmP, MorBAP*
Fanning, David John 1955- *IntWWM 80*
Fanning, Frank B 1880-1934 *WhScrn 74, -77, WhoHol B*
Fanning, Win 1918- *BiE&WWA*
Fanny *IlEncR*
Fano, Fabio 1908- *NewGrD 80*
Fano, Guido Alberto 1875-1961 *Baker 78, NewGrD 80*
Fano, Michel 1929- *NewGrD 80*
Fanselau, Rainer 1934- *IntWWM 77, -80*
Fanshawe, Colin Basil 1930- *WhoMus 72*
Fanshawe, David Arthur 1942- *IntWWM 77, -80*
Fant, Kenne 1923- *FilmEn*
Fantapie, Henri-Claude 1938- *IntWWM 77, -80*
Fantastic Johnny C *RkOn 2A*
Fantini, Girolamo 1600?- *NewGrD 80*
Fantoni, Sergio 1930- *FilmgC, HalFC 80, WhoHol A*
Fantozzi, Tony 1933- *IntMPA 77, -75, -76, -78, -79, -80*
Fapp, Daniel *FilmgC, HalFC 80, WorEFlm*
Fapp, Daniel L 1900?- *FilmEn*
Fara, Giulio 1880-1949 *Baker 78*
Faraday, Michael 1791-1867 *OxMus*
Faraday, Philip Michael 1875-1944 *NotNAT B, WhThe*
Farago, Marcel 1924- *AmSCAP 80, CpmDNM 80*
Faragoh, Francis Edward 1898- *FilmEn*
Farber, Bart 1927- *IntMPA 79, -80*
Farber, Burton A 1913- *AmSCAP 66*
Farber, Burton Albert 1913- *AmSCAP 80*
Farber, Nathaniel C 1918-1975 *AmSCAP 66, -80*
Farber, Otto Leopold Friedrich 1902- *IntWWM 77, -80*
Farber, Viola 1931- *CmpGMD, CnOxB*
Farberman, Harold 1929- *AmSCAP 80, ConAmC, NewGrD 80*
Farberman, Harold 1930- *AmSCAP 66, BiDAmM*
Farbers, Johannes *NewGrD 80*
Farcas, Florin 1937- *WhoOp 76*
Farco, Michele *NewGrD 80*
Farding, Thomas *NewGrD 80*
Fardon, Don *RkOn 2[port]*
Farebrother, Violet 1888-1969 *Film 2, WhScrn 77, WhThe, WhoHol B*
Farentino, James 1938- *FilmEn, FilmgC, ForYSC, HalFC 80, IntMPA 77, -75, -76, -78, -79, -80, MotPP, WhoHol A*
Farey, John 1766-1826 *NewGrD 80*
Farfan, Marian 1913-1965 *WhScrn 74, -77*
Farfariello 1881-1946 *WhScrn 74, -77*
Farfaro, Nicolo d1647 *NewGrD 80*
Fargas, Antonio 1947?- *DrBlPA*
Fargo, Donna 1949- *CounME 74[port], -74A, IlEncCM[port], RkOn 2[port]*
Fargo, Milford H 1928- *AmSCAP 80*
Faria, Luiz Calixto DaCosta E *NewGrD 80*
Farina *DrBlPA, Film 2*
Farina, Carlo 1600?-1640? *NewGrD 80, OxMus*
Farina, Francesco d1575 *NewGrD 80*
Farina, Mimi 1945- *AmSCAP 80, IlEncR*
Farina, Richard 1936-1966 *BiDAmM*
Farina, Richard 1937-1966 *IlEncR, WhScrn 77*
Farina, Richard & Mimi *ConMuA 80A*
Farinas, Carlos 1934- *NewGrD 80, WhoMus 72*
Farine, Jean *OxThe*
Farinel *NewGrD 80*
Farinel, Francois d1672 *NewGrD 80*
Farinel, Giovanni Battista 1655-1720? *NewGrD 80*
Farinel, Jean-Baptiste 1655-1720? *NewGrD 80*
Farinel, Michel 1649- *NewGrD 80*
Farinelli *NewGrD 80*
Farinelli 1705-1782 *Baker 78, BnBkM 80, CmOp, MusMk, NewEOp 71, NewGrD 80[port]*
Farinelli, Carlo Broschi 1705-1782 *OxMus*
Farinelli, Giuseppe 1769-1836 *Baker 78, NewGrD 80*
Farinelli, Jean Baptiste *OxMus*
Farinelli, Michel 1649- *OxMus*
Farinello 1705-1782 *NewGrD 80[port]*
Faris, Alexander 1921- *IntWWM 77, -80, WhoMus 72*
Farish, Margaret K 1918- *IntWWM 77, -80*
Farish, Stephen Thomas, Jr. 1936- *IntWWM 77, -80*
Farjeon, Annabel 1919- *DancEn 78*
Farjeon, Benjamin Leopold d1903 *NotNAT B*
Farjeon, Harry 1878-1948 *Baker 78, BiDAmM*
Farjeon, Herbert 1887-1945 *EncMT, NotNAT B, OxThe, WhThe*
Farjeon, Joseph Jefferson 1883-1955 *NotNAT B, WhThe*
Farkas, Edmund 1851-1912 *Baker 78*
Farkas, Ferenc 1905- *Baker 78, DcCM, IntWWM 77, -80, NewGrD 80, WhoMus 72*
Farkas, Odon 1851-1912 *NewGrD 80*
Farkas, Philip Francis 1914- *IntWWM 77, -80, NewGrD 80*
Farkoa, Maurice 1864- *WhoStg 1908*
Farkoa, Maurice 1867-1916 *WhThe*
Farlander, Arthur William 1898- *BiDAmM*
Farleigh, Lynn 1942- *WhoThe 72, -77*
Farleman *PupTheA*
Farley, Carole Ann 1946- *Baker 78, IntWWM 77, -80, WhoOp 76*
Farley, Charles d1859 *NotNAT B*
Farley, Dot 1881-1971 *WhScrn 77*
Farley, Dot 1894-1971 *Film 1, -2, ForYSC, MotPP, TwYS*
Farley, Eddie 1905- *CmpEPM, WhoJazz 72*
Farley, Edward J 1904- *AmSCAP 66, -80*
Farley, James 1882-1947 *Film 1, -2, ForYSC, TwYS, WhScrn 74, -77, WhoHol B*
Farley, Morgan 1898- *BiE&WWA, Film 2, NotNAT, WhoHol A*
Farley, Morgan 1901- *WhThe*
Farley, Roland 1892-1932 *AmSCAP 66, ConAmC A*
Farlow, Tal 1921- *CmpEPM, EncJzS 70*
Farlow, Talmadge Holt 1921- *BiDAmM, EncJzS 70*
Farlowe, Chris 1940- *IlEncR*
Farmaniantz, Georgi 1921- *DancEn 78*
Farmanyantz, Georgi Karapetovich 1921- *CnOxB*
Farmelo, Francis *NewGrD 80*
Farmer, Addison Gerald 1928-1963 *BiDAmM*
Farmer, Anthony Elgar 1919- *WhoOp 76*
Farmer, Art 1928- *CmpEPM, EncJzS 70, IlEncJ*
Farmer, Arthur Stewart 1928- *BiDAmM, EncJzS 70*
Farmer, Bess 1919- *BiDAmM*
Farmer, Frances d1970 *MotPP, PlP&P[port], WhoHol B*
Farmer, Frances 1913-1970 *FilmEn, ThFT[port]*
Farmer, Frances 1914-1970 *FilmgC, ForYSC, HalFC 80, HolP 30[port], NotNAT A, WhScrn 74, -77*
Farmer, Frances 1915-1970 *MovMk*
Farmer, Henry George 1882-1965 *Baker 78, NewGrD 80*
Farmer, Henry George 1882-1966 *OxMus*
Farmer, John 1570?- *Baker 78, NewGrD 80, OxMus*
Farmer, John 1836-1901 *Baker 78, NewGrD 80, OxMus*
Farmer, Mimsie *ForYSC*
Farmer, Mimsy 1945- *FilmgC, HalFC 80, WhoHol A*
Farmer, Peter 1941- *CnOxB, ConAmC*
Farmer, Thomas d1688 *NewGrD 80*
Farmer, Virginia 1922- *IntWWM 77, -80*
Farmer, Willie *BgBands 74*
Farnaby, Giles 1560?-1600? *DcCom&M 79*
Farnaby, Giles 1560?-1640 *OxMus*
Farnaby, Giles 1563?-1640 *NewGrD 80*
Farnaby, Giles 1565?-1640 *Baker 78, BnBkM 80, MusMk*
Farnaby, Richard 1594?- *NewGrD 80, OxMus*
Farnadi, Edith *IntWWM 77, -80, WhoMus 72*
Farnadi, Edith 1921-1973 *NewGrD 80*
Farnam, Lynnwood 1885-1930 *BnBkM 80*
Farnam, W Lynnwood 1885-1930 *Baker 78, NewGrD 80*
Farncombe, Charles 1919- *IntWWM 77, -80, NewGrD 80, WhoMus 72*
Farndell, Mary Cynthia *WhoMus 72*
Farney, Billy *Film 2*
Farney, Milton *Film 2*
Farnie, H B d1889 *NotNAT B*
Farnie, Henry Brougham d1889 *BiDAmM*
Farnol, Lynn d1963 *NotNAT B*
Farnon, Christine M *ConMuA 80B*
Farnon, Robert Joseph 1917- *BiDAmM, FilmgC, HalFC 80, IntWWM 77, -80, OxMus*
Farnsworth, Charles Hubert 1859-1947 *Baker 78*
Farnsworth, Philo T d1971 *NewYTET*
Farnum, Charles Edward 1951- *AmSCAP 80*
Farnum, Dorothy *WomWMM*
Farnum, Dustin d1929 *MotPP, WhoHol B*
Farnum, Dustin 1870-1929 *FilmgC, HalFC 80*
Farnum, Dustin 1874-1929 *FilmEn, Film 1, -2, NotNAT B, TwYS, WhScrn 74, -77, WhThe*
Farnum, Dustin 1876-1929 *WhoStg 1906, -1908*
Farnum, Franklyn d1961 *NotNAT B, WhoHol B*
Farnum, Franklyn 1876-1961 *FilmEn, Film 1, FilmgC, ForYSC, HalFC 80, WhScrn 74, -77*
Farnum, Franklyn 1883-1961 *Film 2, TwYS*
Farnum, G Dustin d1912 *NotNAT B*
Farnum, Helen *Film 2*
Farnum, W Lynnwood 1885-1930 *BiDAmM*
Farnum, William 1872-1953 *ForYSC, TwYS*
Farnum, William 1876-1953 *FilmEn, Film 1, -2, FilmgC, HalFC 80, MotPP, MovMk, NotNAT B, WhScrn 74, -77, WhThe, WhoHol B*
Farnworth, Don 1927- *CnOxB*
Farolfi, Raoul 1930- *WhoOp 76*
Farquhar, David Andross 1928- *IntWWM 77, -80, NewGrD 80, WhoMus 72*
Farquhar, George 1678-1707 *CnThe, EncWT, Ent, McGEWD[port], NotNAT B, OxThe, PlP&P[port], REnWD[port]*
Farquhar, Malcolm 1924- *WhoThe 72, -77*
Farquhar, Robroy 1916- *BiE&WWA, NotNAT*
Farquharson, Robert d1966 *WhoHol B*
Farquharson, Robert 1877-1966 *WhThe*
Farquharson, Robert 1878-1966 *WhScrn 74, -77*
Farr, Derek 1912- *FilmEn, FilmgC, HalFC 80, IlWWBF[port], IntMPA 77, -75, -76, -78, -79, -80, WhoHol A, WhoThe 72, -77*
Farr, Felicia 1932- *FilmEn, FilmgC, ForYSC, HalFC 80, IntMPA 77, -75, -76, -78, -79, -80, MotPP, WhoHol A*
Farr, Florence 1860-1917 *NotNAT B, OxThe, WhThe*
Farr, Frankie 1903-1953 *WhScrn 74, -77*
Farr, Jamie *WhoHol A*
Farr, Karl d1961 *WhScrn 77*
Farr, Patricia 1915-1948 *WhScrn 74, -77, WhoHol B*
Farrah, Abd' Elkader 1926- *WhoThe 72, -77*
Farrall, Gordon Roussell 1922- *WhoMus 72*
Farrally, Betty 1915- *CreCan 2, DancEn 78*
Farrand, Noel 1928- *ConAmC*
Farrant, Daniel d1661? *NewGrD 80*
Farrant, John *Baker 78, NewGrD 80, OxMus*
Farrant, John 1575-1618 *NewGrD 80*
Farrant, Richard 1525?-1580 *NewGrD 80*
Farrant, Richard 1530?-1580 *Baker 78*
Farrant, Richard 1530?-1581 *BnBkM 80*
Farrant, Richard 1580?- *OxMus*
Farrar, Carol Ann Reglin 1942- *IntWWM 77, -80*
Farrar, David 1908- *FilmAG WE, FilmEn, FilmgC, ForYSC, HalFC 80,*

IlWWBF[port], -A, IntMPA 77, -75, -76, -78, -79, -80, WhoHol A
Farrar, Ernest Bristow 1885-1918 Baker 78, NewGrD 80
Farrar, Geraldine 1882-1967 AmSCAP 66, -80, Baker 78, BiDAmM, BnBkM 80, CmOp, FilmEn, Film 1, -2, FilmgC, HalFC 80, MusSN[port], NewEOp 71, NewGrD 80, TwYS, WhScrn 74, -77, WhoHol B
Farrar, Gwen 1899-1944 WhThe, WhoHol B
Farrar, John ConMuA 80B
Farrar, Margaret 1901-1925 WhScrn 74, -77
Farrar, Ruth Price 1901- IntWWM 80
Farrar, Sidney Bob 1928- AmSCAP 80
Farrar, Stanley 1911-1974 WhScrn 77
Farrar, Walton T 1918-1976 AmSCAP 66, -80
Farrell, Anthony B 1899- BiE&WWA
Farrell, Bill 1926?- CmpEPM
Farrell, Catherine F d1964 NotNAT B
Farrell, Charles AmPS B, MotPP
Farrell, Charles 1901?- CmpEPM, FilmEn, Film 2, FilmgC, HalFC 80, IntMPA 77, -75, -76, -78, -79, -80, MovMk[port]
Farrell, Charles 1902- Film 2, ForYSC, TwYS, What 2[port], WhoHol A
Farrell, Charles 1906- IntMPA 77, -75, -76, -78, -79, -80, WhoThe 72, -77
Farrell, Charles 1919-1962 WhScrn 74, -77
Farrell, Eileen 1920- Baker 78, BiDAmM, BnBkM 80, CmOp, CmpEPM, IntWWM 77, -80, MusSN[port], NewEOp 71, NewGrD 80, WhoOp 76
Farrell, Frances F 1947- IntWWM 77, -80
Farrell, Front Page What 5[port]
Farrell, Glenda 1904-1971 AmPS B, BiE&WWA, FilmEn, Film 2, FilmgC, ForYSC, HalFC 80, HolP 30[port], MotPP, MovMk[port], NotNAT B, OxFilm, ThFT[port], WhScrn 74, -77, WhThe, WhoHol B, WhoThe 72
Farrell, Henry IntMPA 77, -75, -76, -78, -79, -80
Farrell, Joe 1937- EncJzS 70
Farrell, John J WhoStg 1908
Farrell, John W 1885-1953 WhScrn 74, -77, WhoHol B
Farrell, Kenneth L 1920- AmSCAP 80, ConAmC
Farrell, M J 1905- WhThe
Farrell, Marguerite d1951 NotNAT B
Farrell, Mary BiE&WWA, NotNAT
Farrell, Mike WhoHol A
Farrell, Paul 1893- WhThe
Farrell, Peter Snow 1924- IntWWM 77, -80
Farrell, Sharon ForYSC, WhoHol A
Farrell, Skip 1919-1962 WhoHol B
Farrell, Susan Caust 1944- IntWWM 77, -80
Farrell, Suzanne 1945- CnOxB, DancEn 78[port]
Farrell, Timothy Robert Warwick 1943- IntWWM 77, -80, WhoMus 72
Farrell, Tommy WhoHol A
Farrell, Vessie 1890-1935 WhScrn 74, -77, WhoHol B
Farren, Babs 1904- WhThe
Farren, Elizabeth 1759-1829 NotNAT A, -B, OxThe
Farren, Ellen 1848-1904 EncWT, OxThe
Farren, Fred d1956 NotNAT B, WhThe
Farren, Fred 1874-1956 DancEn 78
Farren, George Francis d1935 NotNAT B
Farren, George Percy d1861 NotNAT B
Farren, Henry 1826-1860 EncWT, NotNAT B, OxThe
Farren, Jack IntMPA 77, -75, -76, -78, -79, -80
Farren, Martin 1942- ConAmC
Farren, Nellie 1848-1904 NotNAT B
Farren, Percival 1784-1843 EncWT, NotNAT B, OxThe
Farren, Percival William 1853-1937 EncWT
Farren, William 1725-1795 EncWT, NotNAT B, OxThe
Farren, William 1786-1861 EncWT, NotNAT B, OxThe
Farren, William 1825-1908 EncWT, NotNAT B, OxThe
Farren, William Percival 1853-1937 NotNAT B, OxThe, WhThe
Farrenc NewGrD 80
Farrenc, Aristide 1794-1865 Baker 78, NewGrD 80
Farrenc, Louise 1804-1875 Baker 78, NewGrD 80
Farrenc, Victorine Louise 1826-1859 NewGrD 80
Farrer, Ann 1916- WhThe
Farrer, Carl Edvert 1926- AmSCAP 80
Farres, Aurelio Capmany I NewGrD 80
Farrier, Walter Halliday, Jr. 1932- IntWWM 77, -80
Farrington, Adele 1867-1936 Film 1, -2, WhScrn 74, -77, WhoHol B
Farrington, Betty d1968 Film 2, WhScrn 77
Farrington, Frank 1874-1924 Film 1, -2, WhScrn 74, -77, WhoHol B
Farrington, Harry Webb 1880-1931 BiDAmM
Farrington, Michael James 1935- IntWWM 77, -80
Farriss, Audrey DancEn 78
Farron, Julia 1922- CnOxB
Farron, Julia 1929- DancEn 78
Farrow, Ernest 1928- EncJzS 70
Farrow, John 1904-1963 BiDFilm, -81, CmMov, FilmEn, FilmgC, HalFC 80, MovMk[port], NotNAT B, WorEFlm
Farrow, Johnny 1912- AmSCAP 66, -80
Farrow, Mia IntMPA 77, -75, -76, -78, -79, -80, MotPP, WhoHol A
Farrow, Mia 1945- BiDFilm, -81, FilmEn, FilmgC, ForYSC, HalFC 80, OxFilm, WhoHrs 80, WorEFlm
Farrow, Mia 1946- MovMk[port], WhoThe 77
Farrow, Miles 1871-1953 BiDAmM
Farrow, Norman D 1916- Baker 78
Farrow, Olivia Ledbetter 1913- IntWWM 77
Farrow, Tisa WhoHol A
Farthing, Thomas d1520 NewGrD 80
Farunt, Daniel NewGrD 80
Farwell, Arthur 1872-1952 AmSCAP 66, -80, Baker 78, BiDAmM, ConAmC, OxMus
Farwell, Arthur 1877-1952 NewGrD 80
Fasang, Arpad 1912- IntWWM 77, -80
Fasano, Renato 1902- NewGrD 80
Fasch, Carl Friedrich Christian 1736-1800 NewGrD 80, OxMus
Fasch, Johann Friedrich 1688-1758 Baker 78, MusMk, NewGrD 80, OxMus
Fasch, Karl Friedrich Christian 1736-1800 Baker 78, MusMk, NewGrD 80
Fascilla, Roberto 1937- CnOxB, DancEn 78
Fascinato, Jack 1915- AmSCAP 66, -80
Fasman, Barry Alan 1946- AmSCAP 80
Fasoli, Fiorenzo De' NewGrD 80
Fasoli, Francesco d1712 NewGrD 80
Fasolo, Il NewGrD 80
Fasolo, Giovanni Battista 1600?-1659? NewGrD 80
Fass, Bernie 1932- AmSCAP 80
Fass, M Monroe 1901- IntMPA 77, -78, -79, -80
Fass, Monroe M 1901- IntMPA 76
Fassbaender, Brigitte 1939- IntWWM 77, -80, NewGrD 80, WhoOp 76
Fassbander, Zdenka 1880-1954 CmOp, NewEOp 71
Fassbender, Zdenka 1879-1954 NewGrD 80
Fassbinder, Rainer Werner 1946- BiDFilm, -81, Ent, FilmEn, HalFC 80, OxFilm
Fassett, Jay 1889- BiE&WWA, NotNAT, WhoHol A
Fassini, Alberto Maria 1938- WhoOp 76
Fassion NewGrD 80
Fast, Lawrence Roger 1951- AmSCAP 80
Fast, Willard S 1922- ConAmC
Faster, Otto NewGrD 80
Fates, Gil NewYTET
Father Of The Halls OxThe
Fatima 1880-1921 Film 1
Fatima, LaBelle 1880-1921 WhScrn 77
Fatius, Anselmus NewGrD 80
Fatool, Nicholas 1915- BiDAmM, EncJzS 70
Fatool, Nick 1915- CmpEPM, EncJzS 70, WhoJazz 72
Fator, Finis Ewing 1947- AmSCAP 80
Fattori, Massimiano NewGrD 80
Fattorin Da Reggio NewGrD 80
Fattorini, Gabriele Baker 78, NewGrD 80
Fauchald, Nora 1898-1971 BiDAmM
Fauche, Miriam Film 2
Faucher, Jean 1924- CreCan 2
Fauchet, Paul Robert 1881-1937 Baker 78
Fauchey, Paul 1858-1936 Baker 78
Fauchois, Rene 1882-1962 McGEWD[port], ModWD, WhThe
Faucit, Harriet 1789-1857 NotNAT B
Faucit, Helen 1817-1898 EncWT, NotNAT A, -B, OxThe
Faugues, Guillaume NewGrD 80
Faulcon, Clarence August 1928- IntWWM 77, -80
Faulcon, Jacqueline Frances Beach 1934- IntWWM 77, -80
Faulconer, James H 1945- ConAmC
Faulds, Andrew 1923- FilmgC, HalFC 80
Faulk, John Henry NewYTET, WhoHol A
Faulkes, John Sebastian 1904- WhoMus 72
Faulkes, William 1863-1933 Baker 78
Faulkner, Colin 1939- WhoMus 72
Faulkner, Doris 1920- IntWWM 77
Faulkner, Edward WhoHol A
Faulkner, Fred 1941- AmSCAP 66
Faulkner, Helen 1953- IntWWM 80
Faulkner, Jack 1918- AmSCAP 66, -80
Faulkner, James WhoHol A
Faulkner, Ralph 1891- WhoHol A
Faulkner, Rex PupTheA
Faulkner, Sandford C 1803-1874 BiDAmM
Faulkner, Seldon 1929- BiE&WWA, NotNAT
Faulkner, William 1897-1962 CnMD, CroCD, DcFM, FilmEn, FilmgC, HalFC 80, ModWD, NotNAT B, OxFilm, WorEFlm
Faunch, Paul 1933- IntWWM 77, -80, WhoMus 72
Faure, Antoine NewGrD 80
Faure, Dawn Sylvia 1938- WhoMus 72
Faure, Elie 1873-1937 OxFilm, WorEFlm
Faure, Gabriel 1845-1924 Baker 78, BnBkM 80, CmpBCM, CompSN[port], DcCom 77, DcCom&M 79, DcTwCC, -A, MusMk, NewEOp 71, NewGrD 80[port], OxMus
Faure, Jean-Baptiste 1830-1914 Baker 78, CmOp, NewEOp 71, NewGrD 80[port], OxMus
Faure, Jeanne 1863-1950 BiDAmM
Faussett, Hudson 1917- IntMPA 77, -75, -76, -78, -79
Faust, Edward Film 2
Faust, Georg 1480-1538 DcPup
Faust, George T 1937- ConAmC
Faust, Hazel Lee 1910-1973 WhScrn 77, WhoHol B
Faust, Irvin Conv 3
Faust, Johann 1488-1541 FilmgC, HalFC 80
Faust, Johnny PupTheA
Faust, Karl Richard Robert 1929- IntWWM 80
Faust, Lotta 1880-1910 WhoStg 1908
Faust, Lotta 1881-1910 CmpEPM, NotNAT B
Faust, Martin 1886-1943 Film 1, -2, WhScrn 74, -77, WhoHol B
Faust, Randall Edward 1947- AmSCAP 80, IntWWM 77, -80
Faustina NewGrD 80
Faustini, Giovanni 1619?-1651 NewGrD 80
Faustini, Marco d1675? NewGrD 80
Faustman, Erik 1919-1961 FilmEn
Faustman, Erik Hampe 1919-1961 WhScrn 77
Faustmann, Erik 1919-1961 DcFM
Fauzio PupTheA
Favaretto, Giorgio 1902- WhoMus 72
Favarger, Rene 1815-1868 Baker 78
Favart NewGrD 80
Favart, Madame 1727-1772 NotNAT B
Favart, Charles Nicolas Joseph Justin 1749-1806 NewGrD 80
Favart, Charles-Simon 1710-1792 Baker 78, Ent, NewEOp 71, NewGrD 80, NotNAT B, OxMus, OxThe
Favart, Edmee d1941 NotNAT B, WhThe
Favart, Maria 1833-1908 NotNAT B
Favart, Marie Justine Benoiste 1727-1772 OxThe
Favart, Marie Justine Benoite 1727-1772 NewGrD 80[port]
Favel, Andree NewGrD 80
Favereo, Janino NewGrD 80
Favereo, Joannin NewGrD 80
Faveretto, Bartolomeo d1616 NewGrD 80
Favero, Mafalda 1905- NewGrD 80
Faversham, Edith Campbell d1945 NotNAT B

Faversham, Julie Opp 1871-1921 *NotNAT B*
Faversham, Philip *WhoHol A*
Faversham, William 1868-1940 *FamA&A[port], Film 1, -2, NotNAT B, OxThe, PlP&P, TwYS, WhScrn 74, -77, WhThe, WhoHol B, WhoStg 1906, -1908*
Favieres, Henry *Film 2*
Favors, Malachi 1937- *EncJzS 70*
Favre, Antoine 1670?-1737? *NewGrD 80*
Favre, Georges 1905- *IntWWM 77, -80, NewGrD 80, WhoMus 72*
Favre, Gina *WhThe*
Favre, Max 1921- *IntWWM 77, -80*
Favreau, Marc 1929- *CreCan 1*
Favreau, Michele *WomWMM*
Favretto, Bartolomeo *NewGrD 80*
Fawaz, Florence *NewGrD 80*
Fawcett *NewGrD 80*
Fawcett, Charles S 1855-1922 *NotNAT B, WhThe*
Fawcett, Eric 1904- *WhThe*
Fawcett, Farrah *WhoHol A*
Fawcett, George 1860-1939 *FilmEn, Film 1, -2, MotPP, NotNAT B, TwYS, WhScrn 74, -77, WhThe, WhoHol B*
Fawcett, George 1861-1939 *MovMk*
Fawcett, George 1862-1939 *ForYSC*
Fawcett, Mrs. George d1945 *Film 2, WhoHol B*
Fawcett, James 1905-1942 *WhScrn 74, -77*
Fawcett, John *PlP&P*
Fawcett, John 1770?-1855 *NewGrD 80*
Fawcett, John 1789-1867 *NewGrD 80, OxMus*
Fawcett, John 1824?-1857 *NewGrD 80*
Fawcett, Joshua 1805?-1864 *NewGrD 80*
Fawcett, L'Estrange *WhThe*
Fawcett, Marion 1886-1957 *NotNAT B, WhThe*
Fawcett, Norman *WhoMus 72*
Fawcett, Owen 1839-1904 *NotNAT B*
Fawcett, Verdi 1869- *NewGrD 80*
Fawcett, William d1974 *ForYSC, WhScrn 77, WhoHol B*
Fawcett-Majors, Farrah 1946- *FilmEn*
Fawcett-Majors, Farrah 1947- *HalFC 80, IntMPA 78, -79, -80*
Fawkes, Isaac d1731 *MagIlD[port]*
Fawkes, Wally 1924- *BiDAmM*
Fawkyner *NewGrD 80*
Fawn, James 1850-1923 *WhThe*
Fax, Jesslyn d1975 *ForYSC, WhoHol C*
Fax, Mark 1911-1974 *ConAmC, MorBAP*
Fay, Amy 1844-1928 *Baker 78, BiDAmM*
Fay, Brendan 1921-1975 *WhScrn 77, WhoHol A, -C*
Fay, Dorothy *WhoHol A*
Fay, Eddy *WhoHol A*
Fay, Edward M d1964 *NotNAT B*
Fay, Frank 1870-1931 *EncWT, NotNAT B, OxThe*
Fay, Frank 1894-1961 *HalFC 80, WhScrn 74, -77*
Fay, Frank 1897-1961 *CmpEPM, EncMT, Film 2, JoeFr, NotNAT A, -B, WhThe, WhoHol B*
Fay, Frank 1898-1961 *ForYSC*
Fay, Gaby *FilmEn, WhScrn 77*
Fay, Hugh *Film 1, -2*
Fay, Jack 1903-1928 *WhScrn 74, -77*
Fay, Maud 1879-1964 *Baker 78*
Fay, Patrick J *IntMPA 77, -75, -76, -78, -79, -80*
Fay, Sinclair *AmSCAP 80*
Fay, Stephen 1870?- *BiDAmM*
Fay, Terry *BiE&WWA*
Fay, Vincent Michael 1952- *AmSCAP 80*
Fay, W G 1872-1947 *WhoHol B*
Fay, William George 1872-1947 *EncWT, Ent, NotNAT B, OxThe, WhScrn 74, -77*
Fay, William George 1872-1949 *WhThe*
Faya, Aurelio Della *NewGrD 80*
Faye, Alice *AmPS B, MotPP, WhoHol A*
Faye, Alice 1912- *BiDFilm, -81, CmMov, CmpEPM, FilmEn, FilmgC, HalFC 80, MovMk[port], ThFT[port], WorEFlm*
Faye, Alice 1915- *BiDAmM, ForYSC, OxFilm*
Faye, Herbie *WhoHol A*
Faye, Joey 1910- *BiE&WWA, JoeFr[port], NotNAT, WhoHol A, WhoThe 72, -77*
Faye, Julia d1966 *MotPP, WhoHol B*
Faye, Julia 1894-1966 *Film 1, -2, ForYSC, TwYS*
Faye, Julia 1896-1966 *FilmEn, WhScrn 74, -77*
Faye, Randall *IlWWBF*
Faye, Rita 1944- *BiDAmM*
Fayer, Yury Fyodorovich 1890- *NewGrD 80*
Faylauer, Adolph 1884-1961 *WhScrn 74, -77, WhoHol B*
Faylen, Frank *IntMPA 77, -75, -76, -78, -79, -80, MotPP*
Faylen, Frank 1907- *FilmEn, FilmgC, ForYSC, HalFC 80, MovMk[port], WhoHol A*
Faylen, Frank 1909- *HolCA[port], Vers A[port]*
Fayman, Lynn *WomWMM B*
Fayne, Greta *WhThe*
Fayolle, Berthe d1934 *NotNAT B*
Fayolle, Francois-Joseph-Marie 1774-1852 *Baker 78, NewGrD 80*
Fayre, Eleanor 1910- *WhThe*
Fayrefax, Robert 1464-1521 *NewGrD 80*
Fayrfax, Robert 1464-1521 *Baker 78, BnBkM 80, NewGrD 80, OxMus*
Fazal, Ruth 1952- *IntWWM 80*
Fazalbhoy, M A 1902- *IntMPA 77, -75, -76, -78, -79, -80*
Fazan, Adrienne *HalFC 80, WomWMM*
Fazan, Eleanor 1930- *WhoThe 72, -77*
Fazenda, Louis d1962 *NotNAT B*
Fazenda, Louise d1962 *MotPP, WhoHol B*
Fazenda, Louise 1889-1962 *WhScrn 74, -77*
Fazenda, Louise 1895-1962 *FilmEn, Film 1, -2, FilmgC, ForYSC, HalFC 80, MovMk[port], ThFT[port], TwYS, WorEFlm*
Fazer *NewGrD 80*
Fazer, Georg *NewGrD 80*
Fazer, K G *NewGrD 80*
Fazio, Anselmo Di *NewGrD 80*
Fazio, Suzanne M 1951- *AmSCAP 80*
Fazioli, Bernardo 1897-1942 *AmSCAP 66, -80*
Fazioli, Billy 1898-1924 *AmSCAP 66, -80*
Fazola, Irving 1912-1949 *BiDAmM, CmpEPM, IlEncJ, NewOrJ[port]*
Fazola, Irving Henry 1912-1949 *WhoJazz 72*
Fazzari, Hans 1932- *IntWWM 77, -80*
Fazzini, Giovanni Battista *NewGrD 80*
Fead, Bob *ConMuA 80B*
Fealy, Margaret *Film 2*
Fealy, Maude 1881-1971 *MotPP, WhScrn 74, -77, WhoHol B*
Fealy, Maude 1883-1971 *WhThe*
Fealy, Maude 1886-1971 *WhoStg 1906, -1908*
Fear, Margaret *IntWWM 77, -80*
Fearis, John S 1867-1932 *BiDAmM*
Fearnley, Jane *Film 1*
Fearnley, John 1914- *BiE&WWA, NotNAT*
Fearon, George Edward 1901- *WhThe, WhoThe 72*
Fears, Peggy 1906- *What 3[port], WhoHol A*
Feasel, Richard *ConAmC*
Feasey, Norman Edward 1903- *IntWWM 80, WhoMus 72*
Feather, Leonard Geoffrey 1914- *AmSCAP 66, -80, Baker 78, CmpEPM, IntWWM 77*
Feathers, Charlie 1932- *IlEncCM*
Featherston, Eddie *Film 2*
Featherston, Vane 1864-1948 *NotNAT B, WhThe*
Featherstone, John *Film 1*
Featherstonhaugh, Buddy 1909- *CmpEPM*
Febbraio, Salvatore Michael Turlizzo 1935- *IntWWM 77, -80*
Febvrier, Pierre *NewGrD 80*
Feche, Willem Du *NewGrD 80*
Fechner, Gustave Theodor 1801-1887 *Baker 78*
Fecht, Johanna-Lotte *IntWWM 80, WhoOp 76*
Fechter, Charles Albert 1824-1879 *EncWT, FamA&A[port], NotNAT A, -B, OxThe, PlP&P[port]*
Feczko, Elzbieta Maria 1922- *IntWWM 77, -80*
Fedderson, Don *NewYTET*
Fede, Innocenzo d1687? *NewGrD 80*
Fede, Johannes 1415?-1477? *NewGrD 80*
Fedele, John Anthony 1947- *IntWWM 77, -80*
Fedeli *NewGrD 80*
Fedeli, Carlo 1622?-1685 *NewGrD 80*
Fedeli, Giuseppe *NewGrD 80*
Fedeli, Ruggiero 1655?-1722 *NewGrD 80*
Fedeli, Vito 1866-1933 *Baker 78*
Feder, A H 1909- *WhoThe 77*
Feder, Abe 1909- *BiE&WWA, NotNAT*
Feder, Franz Georg 1927- *IntWWM 77, -80*
Feder, Georg 1927- *NewGrD 80*
Feder, I *Film 1*
Feder, Jean *NewGrD 80*
Federhofer, Hellmut 1911- *IntWWM 80, NewGrD 80*
Federhofer, Helmut 1911- *Baker 78*
Federhofer-Konigs, Renate 1930- *IntWWM 80*
Federici, Francesco *NewGrD 80*
Federici, Vincenzo 1764-1826 *Baker 78, NewGrD 80*
Federico, Frank 1908?- *NewOrJ*
Federl, Ekkehard Friedrich Thomas 1905- *IntWWM 77, -80*
Federlein, Gottfried H 1883-1952 *Baker 78*
Federlein, Gottfried Harrison 1883-1952 *AmSCAP 66, -80*
Federlein, Gottfried Heinrich 1883-1952 *BiDAmM*
Federlein, Gottlieb 1835-1922 *Baker 78*
Fedicheva, Kaleria Ivanovna 1936- *CnOxB*
Fedor, Tania *CreCan 1*
Fedor, Viliam 1913- *IntWWM 77, -80*
Fedorov, Vladimir 1901-1979 *Baker 78, IntWWM 77, NewGrD 80*
Fedorova, Alexandra 1884-1972 *CnOxB, DancEn 78*
Fedorova, Sophia Vasilievna 1879-1963 *CnOxB, DancEn 78*
Fedorovitch, Sophie 1893-1953 *CnOxB, DancEn 78, OxThe*
Fedoseyev, Andrei Aleksandrovich 1934- *WhoOp 76*
Fedotov, Pavel Andreyevich 1815-1852 *NewGrD 80*
Feducha, Bertha *Film 2*
Fee, Vickie 1947-1975 *WhScrn 77, WhoHol C*
Feelgood, Doctor *BluesWW*
Feely, Terence John 1928- *WhoThe 72, -77*
Feeney, Francis *Film 2*
Feese, Francis L 1926- *AmSCAP 80*
Feferman, Linda *WomWMM B*
Feghg, Willem De *NewGrD 80*
Fegte, Ernst 1900-1976 *FilmEn, FilmgC, HalFC 80*
Feher, Friedrich *Film 1*
Feher, Friedrich 1889-1945 *DcFM*
Feher, Friedrich 1895- *OxFilm*
Feher, Imre 1926- *OxFilm, WorEFlm*
Fehl, Fred 1906- *CnOxB*
Fehling, Jurgen 1885-1968 *EncWT, Ent*
Fehmiu, Bekim 1932- *FilmgC, HalFC 80, WhoHol A*
Fehmiu, Bekim 1936- *ForYSC*
Fehr, Joseph Anton 1761-1807? *NewGrD 80*
Fehr, Max 1887-1963 *Baker 78, NewGrD 80*
Fehr, Rudi 1911- *HalFC 80, IntMPA 77, -75, -76, -78, -79, -80*
Fehrman, Minny *NewGrD 80*
Fei *NewGrD 80*
Fei, Andrea d1658? *NewGrD 80*
Fei, Giacomo *NewGrD 80*
Fei, Michel'angelo *NewGrD 80*
Feibel, Frederick 1906- *AmSCAP 66, -80*
Feicht, Hieronim 1894-1967 *Baker 78, NewGrD 80*
Feidje, Asmund Ivar 1948- *IntWWM 80*
Feiersinger, K S Sebastian 1913- *WhoMus 72*
Feiffer, Judy *WomWMM*
Feiffer, Jules 1929- *CnThe, ConDr 73, -77, CroCD, DcLB 7[port], EncWT, Ent, FilmgC, HalFC 80, McGEWD, NotNAT, WhoThe 72, -77*
Feigay, Paul 1920- *BiE&WWA, NotNAT*
Feigin, Sara 1928- *IntWWM 80*
Feijoo Y Montenegro, Benito Jeronimo 1676-1764 *NewGrD 80*
Feil, Arnold 1925- *NewGrD 80*
Feiler, Herta 1916-1970 *WhScrn 74, -77, WhoHol B*
Feiler, Max Christian 1904- *CnMD*
Fein, David N 1953- *IntWWM 77, -80*
Fein, Irving A 1911- *IntMPA 77, -75, -76, -78,*

-79, *NewYTET*
Fein, Michael S 1951- *AmSCAP 80*
Fein, Pearl 1900- *AmSCAP 66, -80*
Feinberg, Abe I d1962 *NotNAT B*
Feinberg, Milton *IntMPA 77, -75, -76, -78, -79, -80*
Feinberg, Sammy *NewGrD 80*
Feinberg, Samuel 1890-1962 *Baker 78*
Feind, Barthold 1678-1721 *NewGrD 80*
Feingold, Michael 1945- *ConAmTC*
Feinhals, Fritz 1869-1940 *CmOp*
Feininger, Laurence Karl Johann 1909-1976 *NewGrD 80*
Feininger, Laurentius Karl Johann 1909-1976 *NewGrD 80*
Feininger, Lorenzo Karl Johann 1909-1976 *NewGrD 80*
Feinman, Sigmund d1909 *NotNAT B*
Feinsmith, Marvin Paul 1932- *AmSCAP 80, IntWWM 77, -80*
Feinstein, Harry 1906- *IntMPA 77, -75, -76, -78, -79, -80*
Feintuch, Gerald S 1942- *IntWWM 77, -80*
Feirstein, Frederick *NatPD[port]*
Feist, Felix E 1906-1965 *FilmEn, HalFC 80, WhoHrs 80*
Feist, Felix E 1910-1965 *FilmgC*
Feist, Gene 1930- *NotNAT, WhoThe 72, -77*
Feist, Leo 1870-1930 *BiDAmM*
Feist, Leonard 1910- *ConMuA 80B, IntWWM 77, -80*
Feitshans, Buzz *IntMPA 80*
Fejos, Paul 1893-1963 *FilmgC, HalFC 80*
Fejos, Paul 1897-1963 *FilmEn, WorEFlm*
Fejos, Paul 1898-1963 *DcFM*
Fekaris, Dino George 1945- *AmSCAP 80*
Fel, Antoine 1694-1771 *NewGrD 80*
Fel, Marie 1713-1794 *NewGrD 80*
Felbermayer, Anny *IntWWM 77, -80, WhoMus 72*
Felby, Celeta *AmSCAP 80*
Felch-Monokoski, Patricia 1947- *IntWWM 80*
Felciano, Richard 1930- *AmSCAP 80, Baker 78, CpmDNM 79, ConAmC*
Feld, Eliot 1943- *CnOxB*
Feld, Fritz 1900- *FilmEn, Film 2, FilmgC, ForYSC, HalFC 80, HolCA[port], IntMPA 77, -75, -76, -78, -79, -80, MovMk, TwYS, Vers A[port], WhoHol A*
Feld, Jindrich 1925- *Baker 78, CpmDNM 80, DcCM, IntWWM 77, -80, NewGrD 80*
Feld, Morey 1915-1971 *BiDAmM, CmpEPM, EncJzS 70, WhoJazz 72*
Feld, Norman *IntMPA 77, -75, -76, -78, -79*
Feldary, Eric 1920-1968 *WhScrn 74, -77, WhoHol B*
Feldbrill, Victor 1924- *CreCan 2, IntWWM 80, NewGrD 80*
Feldbusch, Eric 1922- *Baker 78, IntWWM 77, -80, NewGrD 80, WhoMus 72*
Felder, David C 1953- *AmSCAP 80*
Felder, Donald William 1947- *AmSCAP 80*
Felder, Michael Earl 1946- *AmSCAP 80*
Felder, Wilton Lewis 1940- *BiDAmM, EncJzS 70*
Felderhof, Jan 1907- *Baker 78, IntWWM 77, -80, NewGrD 80*
Feldhaus-Weber, Mary *NatPD[port], WomWMM B*
Feldhoff, Gerd 1931- *WhoOp 76*
Feldkamp, Elmer d1938 *CmpEPM*
Feldkamp, Fred 1914- *IntMPA 77, -75, -76, -78, -79, -80*
Feldman, Andrea d1972 *WhScrn 77, WhoHol B*
Feldman, Charles K 1904-1968 *FilmEn, FilmgC, HalFC 80, WorEFlm*
Feldman, Charles K 1905-1968 *NotNAT B*
Feldman, David Edward 1939- *ConAmTC*
Feldman, Edward H *NewYTET*
Feldman, Edward S 1929- *IntMPA 77, -75, -76, -78, -79, -80*
Feldman, Edythe A 1913-1971 *WhScrn 74, -77, WhoHol B*
Feldman, Elliott David 1950- *IntWWM 80*
Feldman, Gladys d1974 *Film 2, WhoHol B*
Feldman, Gladys 1892-1974 *WhScrn 77*
Feldman, Gladys 1899-1974 *BiE&WWA*
Feldman, Herbert Byron 1931- *ConAmC*
Feldman, Imogen Carpenter *AmSCAP 80*
Feldman, Joann E 1941- *ConAmC*
Feldman, Laurence 1926- *BiE&WWA*
Feldman, Ludovic 1893- *Baker 78, IntWWM 77, -80, NewGrD 80*
Feldman, Marty 1933- *FilmgC, HalFC 80, IntMPA 79, -80, WhoHol A, WhoHrs 80*
Feldman, Marty 1938- *FilmEn*
Feldman, Morton 1926- *Baker 78, BiDAmM, BnBkM 80, ConAmC, DcCom&M 79, DcCM, MusMk, NewGrD 80*
Feldman, Myrna Herzog 1951- *IntWWM 77, -80*
Feldman, Phil 1922- *IntMPA 77, -75, -76, -78, -79, -80*
Feldman, Vic 1934- *EncJzS 70*
Feldman, Victor Stanley 1934- *AmSCAP 80, BiDAmM, EncJzS 70*
Feldmann, Fritz 1905- *NewGrD 80*
Feldner, Roberta Emily 1939- *AmSCAP 80*
Feldon, Barbara 1939- *HalFC 80, WhoHol A*
Feldsher, Howard M 1936- *CpmDNM 78, IntWWM 77, -80*
Feldstein, Albert 1925- *WhoHrs 80*
Feldstein, Saul 1940- *AmSCAP 66, -80, ConAmC*
Feleky, Leslie 1912-1971 *BiDAmM*
Felgate, Peter 1919- *WhThe, WhoThe 72*
Felice, Ernie *CmpEPM*
Felice, John 1938- *ConAmC*
Felici, Alessandro 1742-1772 *NewGrD 80*
Felici, Bartolomeo 1695-1776 *NewGrD 80*
Feliciani, Andrea d1596 *NewGrD 80*
Feliciano, Jose 1945- *AmSCAP 80, BiDAmM, RkOn 2[port]*
Felicitas *DancEn 78*
Felipe, Alfredo 1931-1958 *WhScrn 74, -77*
Felis, Stefano 1550?-1603? *NewGrD 80*
Felix 1896?-1941 *CnOxB*
Felix, George 1866-1949 *Film 1, WhScrn 74, -77, WhoHol B*
Felix, Hugo 1866-1934 *Baker 78, BiDAmM, NotNAT B, WhThe*
Felix, Leonard 1920- *IntWWM 77, -80*
Felix, Margery Edith 1907- *WhoMus 72*
Felix, Maria *WhoHol A*
Felix, Maria 1915- *FilmEn, FilmgC, HalFC 80*
Felix, Maria 1916?- *OxFilm*
Felix, Sarah d1877 *NotNAT B*
Felix, Seymour 1892-1961 *CmMov, FilmEn, FilmgC, HalFC 80*
Felix, Vaclav 1928- *Baker 78, IntWWM 77, -80, NewGrD 80*
Felix, Werner 1927- *IntWWM 77, -80*
Felix-Miolan, Marie *NewGrD 80*
Fell, Arthur Marshall 1935- *AmSCAP 80*
Fell, Norman *ForYSC, HalFC 80, IntMPA 80, WhoHol A*
Fell, Tom *AmSCAP 80*
Fellegara, Vittorio 1927- *Baker 78, DcCM, NewGrD 80*
Fellegi, Adam 1941- *IntWWM 77, -80, NewGrD 80*
Feller *NewGrD 80*
Feller, Anton *NewGrD 80*
Feller, Carlos 1925- *WhoOp 76*
Feller, Franz *NewGrD 80*
Feller, Franz 1787-1843 *NewGrD 80*
Feller, Joachim 1628-1691 *NewGrD 80*
Feller, Josef *NewGrD 80*
Feller, Sherman 1918- *AmSCAP 66, -80*
Fellerer, Karl Gustav 1902- *Baker 78, IntWWM 77, -80, NewGrD 80*
Fellerman, Max 1899- *IntMPA 77, -75, -76, -78, -79, -80*
Fellinger, Imogen 1928- *IntWWM 77, -80, NewGrD 80*
Fellini, Federico 1920- *BiDFilm, -81, DcFM, FilmEn, FilmgC, HalFC 80, IntMPA 77, -75, -76, -78, -79, -80, MovMk[port], WomWMM, WorEFlm*
Fellini, Federico 1921- *ConLC 16, OxFilm*
Fellman, Daniel R 1943- *IntMPA 77, -75, -76, -78, -79, -80*
Fellman, Nat D 1910- *IntMPA 77, -75, -76, -78, -79, -80*
Fellner, Ferdinand 1847-1916 *EncWT*
Fellner, Hermann Helmer 1849-1919 *EncWT*
Fellner, Rudolph 1913- *WhoMus 72*
Fellowes, Amy *OxThe*
Fellowes, Edmund Horace 1870-1951 *Baker 78, NewGrD 80, OxMus*
Fellowes, Rockcliffe 1885-1950 *MotPP, NotNAT B*
Fellowes, Rockliffe 1885-1950 *Film 1, -2, FilmgC, HalFC 80, TwYS, WhScrn 74, -77, WhoHol B*
Fellowes-Robinson, Dora d1946 *NotNAT B, WhThe*
Fellows, Dexter William 1871-1937 *NotNAT A, -B*
Fellows, Edith 1923- *FilmEn, Film 2, FilmgC, ForYSC, HalFC 80, ThFT[port], What 5[port], WhoHol A*
Fellows, Floyd George 1907- *AmSCAP 80*
Fellows, Harold E d1960 *NewYTET*
Fellows, Robert 1903-1969 *FilmgC, HalFC 80*
Fellows, Rockliffe 1885-1950 *ForYSC*
Fells, George 1902-1960 *WhScrn 74, -77*
Felmy, Hansjoerg 1931- *HalFC 80*
Felmy, Hansjorg 1931- *FilmAG WE*
Fels, Elena 1907- *IntWWM 77*
Fels-Noth, Elena 1907- *IntWWM 80*
Felsenfeld, Herb 1940- *NotNAT*
Felsenstein, Walter 1901- *NewEOp 71, WhoOp 76*
Felsenstein, Walter 1901-1975 *Baker 78, CmOp, EncWT, NewGrD 80[port]*
Felsztyn, Sebastian Von 1490?-1543? *Baker 78*
Felsztyna, Sebastian Z *NewGrD 80*
Felt, Ruth Allison 1939- *WhoOp 76*
Felter, Susan *WomWMM B*
Feltkamp, Johannes 1896-1962 *NewGrD 80*
Felton, H S *MorBAP*
Felton, Haleemon Shaik *BlkAmP*
Felton, Happy 1908-1964 *BgBands 74, WhScrn 74, -77, WhoHol B*
Felton, Norman *NewYTET*
Felton, Verna 1890-1966 *FilmgC, HalFC 80, Vers B[port], WhScrn 74, -77, WhoHol B*
Felton, Verna 1890-1967 *ForYSC*
Felton, William 1715-1769 *NewGrD 80, OxMus*
Felts, Narvel 1939- *CounME 74, -74A, IlEncCM[port]*
Felumb, Mathilde *Film 2*
Felumb, Svend Christian 1898-1972 *Baker 78*
Felyne, Renee 1884-1910 *NotNAT B*
Femme DuPostillon *CreCan 1*
Fen-Taylor, Alan 1934- *WhoMus 72*
Fenady, Andrew J 1928- *AmSCAP 80, IntMPA 77, -75, -76, -78, -79, -80*
Fenaroli, Fedele 1730-1818 *Baker 78, NewGrD 80*
Fenby, Eric William 1906- *Baker 78, IntWWM 77, -80, NewGrD 80, WhoMus 72*
Fendall, Percy d1917 *NotNAT B*
Fendell, Muriel Roberts 1936- *AmSCAP 80*
Fender, Freddy 1937- *IlEncCM[port], RkOn 2[port]*
Fender, Leo 1907- *IlEncR*
Fendermen, The *RkOn*
Fenderson, Reginald *BlksB&W[port], -C*
Fendler, Edvard 1902- *AmSCAP 66, -80, Baker 78*
Fendt *NewGrD 80*
Fendt, Bernard 1756-1832 *NewGrD 80*
Fendt, Francis *NewGrD 80*
Fendt, Jacob 1815-1849 *NewGrD 80*
Fendt, Martin 1812-1850? *NewGrD 80*
Fendt, Simon 1800-1851 *NewGrD 80*
Fenemore, Hilda *WhoHol A*
Fenigstein, Victor 1924- *IntWWM 77, -80*
Fenimore, Ford d1941 *WhScrn 74, -77*
Feninger, Mario *ConAmC*
Fenis, Rudolf Von *NewGrD 80*
Fenlon, Iain Alexander 1949- *IntWWM 77, -80*
Fenn, Ezekiel 1620- *OxThe*
Fenn, Frederick 1868-1924 *NotNAT B, WhThe*
Fenn, George Manville 1831-1909 *NotNAT B*
Fenn, Hugh John Horace 1913- *WhoMus 72*
Fenn, Jean 1930- *WhoMus 72*
Fenn, Jean Dorothy *WhoOp 76*
Fenn, Peggy *BiE&WWA*
Fennell, Albert 1920- *HalFC 80*
Fennell, Frederick 1914- *Baker 78, WhoMus 72*

Fennell, James 1766-1816 *FamA&A[port], NotNAT A, -B, OxThe*
Fennelly, Brian 1937- *CpmDNM 75, -77, -78, -80, ConAmC, DcCM, IntWWM 77, -80, NewGrD 80*
Fennelly, Michael 1948- *IlEncR*
Fennelly, Parker *ForYSC, WhoHol A*
Fennelly, Vincent M 1920- *IntMPA 77, -75, -76, -78, -79, -80, NewYTET*
Fenneman, George *IntMPA 77, -75, -76, -78, -79, -80*
Fenner, Beatrice 1904- *AmSCAP 66, -80*
Fenner, Burt L 1929- *AmSCAP 80, CpmDNM 77, -78, ConAmC*
Fenner, Walter S 1882-1947 *WhScrn 77*
Fennimore, Joseph 1940- *AmSCAP 80, ConAmC, IntWWM 77, -80*
Fenno, Dick 1927- *AmSCAP 66, -80*
Fenonjois, Roger 1920- *CnOxB, DancEn 78*
Fenoux, Jacques d1930 *NotNAT B*
Fenske, David Edward 1943- *IntWWM 77, -80*
Fensted, E A 1870-1941 *BiDAmM*
Fenster, Boris Alexandrovich 1916-1960 *CnOxB, DancEn 78*
Fenster, Harry 1919- *AmSCAP 66, -80*
Fenstock, Belle *AmSCAP 66, -80*
Fention *BluesWW*
Fenton, Carl *CmpEPM*
Fenton, Frank 1906-1957 *FilmgC, HalFC 80, NotNAT B, PlP&P[port], Vers A[port], WhScrn 74, -77, WhoHol B*
Fenton, Howard *AmSCAP 66, -80*
Fenton, Lavinia 1708-1760 *NotNAT A, -B, OxThe*
Fenton, Leslie d1978 *MotPP*
Fenton, Leslie 1902-1978 *FilmEn, Film 2, FilmgC, HalFC 80, TwYS*
Fenton, Leslie 1903-1978 *ForYSC, MovMk*
Fenton, Lucile 1916?-1966 *WhoHol B*
Fenton, Lucille 1916?-1966 *WhScrn 74, -77*
Fenton, Mabel 1868-1931 *NotNAT B, WhScrn 74, -77, WhoHol B*
Fenton, Mabel 1872- *WhoStg 1908*
Fenton, Marc *Film 1, -2*
Fenton, Mark 1870-1925 *WhScrn 74, -77, WhoHol B*
Fenwick, Angela Mary 1940- *IntWWM 77, -80*
Fenwick, Edward John 1932- *CreCan 1*
Fenwick, Irene 1887-1936 *Film 1, NotNAT B, WhScrn 74, -77, WhThe, WhoHol B*
Fenwick, John 1932- *CreCan 1*
Fenwick, Roland 1932- *CreCan 1*
Fenwick, William Roland *CreCan 1*
Fenyves, Lorand 1918- *IntWWM 77*
Feo, Francesco 1691-1761 *Baker 78, NewGrD 80[port]*
Feo, Ser *NewGrD 80*
Feodoroff, Leo 1867-1949 *Film 2, WhScrn 74, -77, WhoHol B*
Feodorova, Eugenia *DancEn 78*
Feodorovna, Vera d1910 *NotNAT B*
Fer, Philibert Jambe De *NewGrD 80*
Feradini, Antonio *NewGrD 80*
Feragut, Beltrame 1385?-1450? *NewGrD 80*
Ferand, Ernest T 1887-1972 *NewGrD 80*
Ferand, Ernst Thomas 1887-1972 *Baker 78*
Ferandiere, Fernando *NewGrD 80*
Ferandini, Giovanni Battista *NewGrD 80*
Feraro, Sando 1916- *IntWWM 77*
Feraudy, Jacques De *Film 2, WhThe*
Feraudy, Maurice De 1859- *WhThe*
Ferber, Albert 1911- *IntWWM 80, NewGrD 80, WhoMus 72*
Ferber, Edna 1887-1968 *BiE&WWA, CnMD, CnThe, EncWT, FilmgC, HalFC 80, McGEWD[port], ModWD, NotNAT A, -B, OxThe, PlP&P, WhThe*
Ferber, Mel *NewYTET*
Ferbos, Lionel 1911- *NewOrJ SUP[port]*
Ferchault, Guy 1904- *Baker 78, NewGrD 80*
Ferchiou, Sofia *WomWMM*
Ferdin, Pamelyn *WhoHol A*
Ferdinand III 1608-1657 *NewGrD 80*
Ferdinand Of Aragon *NewGrD 80*
Ferdinand, Buddy *AmSCAP 80*
Ferdinand, Roger 1898-1967 *CnMD, EncWT, McGEWD*
Ferdinand, Val *BlkAmP, MorBAP*
Ferdyng, Thomas *NewGrD 80*
Fere, Vladimir 1902-1971 *Baker 78*
Feremans, Jan-Jozef Francisca Gaston 1907- *WhoMus 72*
Ferencsik, Janos 1907- *IntWWM 77, -80, NewGrD 80, WhoOp 76*
Ferenczy, Oto 1921- *Baker 78, NewGrD 80*
Feres, Maria Simone 1925- *WhoMus 72*
Fergusio, Giovanni Battista *NewGrD 80*
Ferguson, Al 1888-1971 *Film 2, TwYS, WhScrn 77*
Ferguson, Allyn M 1924- *AmSCAP 66, BiDAmM*
Ferguson, Barney d1924 *NotNAT B*
Ferguson, Betty June 1933- *WomWMM B*
Ferguson, Casson 1891-1929 *Film 1, -2, TwYS, WhoHol B*
Ferguson, Casson 1894-1929 *WhScrn 74, -77*
Ferguson, Catherine 1895- *WhThe*
Ferguson, Donald Nivison 1882- *Baker 78*
Ferguson, Edwin Earle 1910- *AmSCAP 80, ConAmC, IntWWM 77, -80*
Ferguson, Elsie d1961 *MotPP, WhoHol B*
Ferguson, Elsie 1883-1961 *FilmEn, Film 1, -2, FilmgC, HalFC 80, MovMk, NotNAT B, TwYS, WhScrn 74, -77*
Ferguson, Elsie 1885-1961 *WhThe*
Ferguson, Frank d1937 *NotNAT B*
Ferguson, Frank 1899-1979 *FilmgC, ForYSC, HalFC 80, MovMk, WhoHol A*
Ferguson, Freda Evelyn 1912- *WhoMus 72*
Ferguson, Gene 1940- *WhoOp 76*
Ferguson, George S 1884-1944 *WhScrn 74, -77, WhoHol B*
Ferguson, H W *PupTheA*
Ferguson, Helen 1901- *FilmEn, Film 1, -2, IntMPA 77, -75, -76, -78, -79, -80, MotPP, TwYS, WhoHol A*
Ferguson, Hilda 1903-1933 *WhScrn 74, -77, WhoHol B*
Ferguson, Howard 1908- *Baker 78, IntWWM 77, -80, NewGrD 80, OxMus, WhoMus 72*
Ferguson, James Mikel 1942- *AmSCAP 80*
Ferguson, Jay *ConMuA 80A*
Ferguson, Johnny 1937- *RkOn*
Ferguson, Leonard 1923- *NewOrJ[port]*
Ferguson, Mattie *Film 1*
Ferguson, Max 1924- *CreCan 1*
Ferguson, Maynard 1928- *BgBands 74, BiDAmM, CmpEPM, EncJzS 70, IlEncJ*
Ferguson, Myrtle *Film 2*
Ferguson, Ray Pylant 1932- *WhoMus 72*
Ferguson, Robert B 1927- *BiDAmM*
Ferguson, Robert S 1915- *IntMPA 77, -75, -76, -78, -79, -80*
Ferguson, Robert Stanley 1948- *IntWWM 77, -80*
Ferguson, Robert V *WhoStg 1908*
Ferguson, Roma 1894- *WhoMus 72*
Ferguson, Suzanne 1939- *IntWWM 77, -80*
Ferguson, W J 1845-1930 *WhoHol B*
Ferguson, William d1961 *NotNAT B*
Ferguson, William J 1845-1930 *Film 2, NotNAT B, WhScrn 74, -77, WhoStg 1908*
Fergusson, Francis 1904- *BiE&WWA, NotNAT*
Ferini, Battista *NewGrD 80*
Ferkauf, Betty *Film 2*
Ferland, Albert 1872-1943 *CreCan 2*
Ferlendis, Giuseppe 1755-1802 *NewGrD 80*
Ferlinghetti, Lawrence 1919- *ConDr 73, -77, CroCD*
Fermoselle, Juan De *NewGrD 80*
Fern, Fritzie 1901-1932 *WhScrn 74, -77, WhoHol B*
Fern, Sable 1876- *WhThe*
Fernald, Chester Bailey 1869-1938 *NotNAT B, WhThe*
Fernald, John Bailey 1905- *OxThe, WhoThe 72, -77*
Fernandel 1903-1971 *FilmAG WE[port], FilmEn, FilmgC, ForYSC, HalFC 80, JoeFr, MotPP, MovMk[port], OxFilm, WhScrn 74, -77, WhoHol B, WorEFlm*
Fernandes, Antonio 1595?-1680? *NewGrD 80*
Fernandes, Armando Jose 1906- *NewGrD 80*
Fernandes, Berta Luisa 1935-1954 *WhScrn 74, -77*
Fernandes, Gaspar 1570?-1629? *NewGrD 80*
Fernandes, Nascimento 1880?-1955? *WhScrn 74, -77*
Fernandes, Nascimento 1886-1955 *FilmAG WE*
Fernandez, Bijou 1877-1961 *Film 2, NotNAT B, WhScrn 74, -77, WhThe, WhoHol B, WhoStg 1906, -1908*
Fernandez, Diego *NewGrD 80*
Fernandez, E L *Film 1*
Fernandez, Emilio 1904- *DcFM, FilmEn, FilmgC, HalFC 80, OxFilm, WhoHol A, WorEFlm*
Fernandez, Esther *WhoHol A*
Fernandez, James 1835-1915 *WhThe*
Fernandez, Lucas 1474-1542 *McGEWD*
Fernandez, Maria Antonia Vallejo *NewGrD 80*
Fernandez, Mildred *BluesWW*
Fernandez, Oscar Lorenzo 1897-1948 *Baker 78, DcCM, NewGrD 80, OxMus*
Fernandez, Oscar Rubens 1939- *IntWWM 77, -80*
Fernandez, Pedro 1485?-1574 *NewGrD 80*
Fernandez, Peter *WhoHol A*
Fernandez, Puncho *PupTheA*
Fernandez, Ramon S 1922-1962 *WhScrn 74, -77*
Fernandez, Richard 1922- *IntWWM 77*
Fernandez, Royes 1929- *CnOxB, DancEn 78[port]*
Fernandez, Severo d1961 *WhScrn 77*
Fernandez Arbos, Enrique *Baker 78, NewGrD 80*
Fernandez Ardavin, Luis 1892- *McGEWD[port]*
Fernandez Bordas, Antonio 1870-1950 *Baker 78*
Fernandez Caballero, Manuel 1835-1906 *Baker 78, NewGrD 80*
Fernandez-Cid DeTemes, Antonio 1916- *NewGrD 80*
Fernandez DeHuete, Diego *NewGrD 80*
Fernandez DeMoratin, Leandro 1760-1828 *McGEWD, OxThe*
Fernandez DeMoratin, Nicolas 1737-1780 *McGEWD[port], OxThe*
Fernandez Hidalgo, Gutierre 1553-1620? *NewGrD 80*
Fernandez Palero, Francisco d1597 *NewGrD 80*
Fernandiere, Fernando *NewGrD 80*
Fernando, Joseph *PupTheA*
Fernando, Sarathchandra Vichremadithya 1937- *IntWWM 80*
Fernando, Sarathchandra Vickremadithya 1937- *IntWWM 77*
Fernback, Gerald A 1922- *IntMPA 75*
Fernett, Gene *IntMPA 77, -75, -76, -78, -79*
Ferneyhough, Brian 1943- *NewGrD 80*
Ferns, Martin Allen 1921- *IntWWM 77, -80*
Fernstrom, John 1897-1961 *Baker 78, NewGrD 80*
Fernstrom, Karl-Eric 1926- *IntWWM 80*
Fernyhough, G *WhoMus 72*
Feroci, Francesco 1673-1750 *NewGrD 80*
Ferrabosco *NewGrD 80*
Ferrabosco, Alfonso *OxMus*
Ferrabosco, Alfonso 1543-1588 *Baker 78, BnBkM 80, MusMk, NewGrD 80, OxMus*
Ferrabosco, Alfonso 1575?-1628 *Baker 78, MusMk, OxMus*
Ferrabosco, Alfonso 1578?-1628 *NewGrD 80*
Ferrabosco, Costantino *NewGrD 80*
Ferrabosco, Domenico Maria 1513-1574 *Baker 78, NewGrD 80*
Ferrabosco, Henry *OxMus*
Ferrabosco, John 1626-1682 *NewGrD 80, OxMus*
Ferrabosco, Matthia 1550-1616 *NewGrD 80*
Ferraday, Lisa *ForYSC, WhoHol A*
Ferradini, Antonio 1718?-1779 *NewGrD 80*
Ferran, Jose 1924- *CnOxB*
Ferrand, Emma 1948- *IntWWM 77, -80*
Ferrand, Eula Pearl d1970 *WhScrn 74, -77*
Ferrandiere, Fernando *NewGrD 80*
Ferrandini, Antonio 1718?-1779 *NewGrD 80*
Ferrandini, Giovanni Battista 1710?-1791 *NewGrD 80*
Ferrante, Arthur 1921- *AmSCAP 66, -80*
Ferrante, Dennis Christopher 1946- *AmSCAP 80*
Ferrante, John 1925- *WhoOp 76*
Ferrante And Teicher *AmPS A, RkOn*
Ferrar, Ada d1951 *NotNAT B*

Ferrar, Beatrice d1958 *NotNAT B, WhThe*
Ferrar, Gwen 1899-1944 *NotNAT B*
Ferrara, Franco 1911- *Baker 78*
Ferrara, Frank W 1909- *AmSCAP 80*
Ferrare, Cristina *WhoHol A*
Ferrarese DelBene, Adriana 1755?-1799? *NewGrD 80*
Ferraresi DelBene, Adriana 1755?-1799? *NewGrD 80*
Ferrari Dalla Tiorba 1603?-1681 *NewGrD 80*
Ferrari DellaTiorba 1603?-1681 *NewGrD 80*
Ferrari, Angelo *Film 2*
Ferrari, Antonio *NewGrD 80*
Ferrari, Beatriz 1922- *DancEn 78*
Ferrari, Benedetto 1597-1681 *Baker 78*
Ferrari, Benedetto 1603?-1681 *NewGrD 80*
Ferrari, Carlotta 1837-1907 *Baker 78*
Ferrari, Domenico 1722?-1780 *Baker 78, NewGrD 80*
Ferrari, Francesco *NewGrD 80*
Ferrari, Gabrielle 1851-1921 *Baker 78*
Ferrari, Giacomo Gotifredo 1763-1842 *Baker 78, NewGrD 80*
Ferrari, Giovanni *NewGrD 80*
Ferrari, Girolamo 1600?-1664? *NewGrD 80*
Ferrari, Gotifredo Jacopo 1763-1842 *NewGrD 80*
Ferrari, Gustave 1872-1948 *Baker 78*
Ferrari, Luc 1929- *DcCM, NewGrD 80*
Ferrari, Massimo *NewGrD 80*
Ferrari, Paolo 1822-1889 *McGEWD[port], NotNAT B, OxThe*
Ferrari, Victor 1923- *DancEn 78*
Ferrari, William d1962 *NotNAT B*
Ferrari-Barassi, Elena 1936- *IntWWM 77, -80*
Ferrari-Fontana, Edoardo 1878-1936 *Baker 78, BiDAmM*
Ferrari Trecate, Luigi 1884-1964 *Baker 78, NewGrD 80*
Ferrario, Carlo 1833-1907 *NewGrD 80*
Ferrario, Paolo Agostino *NewGrD 80*
Ferraris, Amalia 1830-1904 *CnOxB, DancEn 78*
Ferraris, Franco 1922- *WhoMus 72*
Ferraris, Richard 1922- *AmSCAP 66, -80*
Ferraro, Antonio 1595?- *NewGrD 80*
Ferraro, Giuseppe *NewGrD 80*
Ferraro, Joseph 1895- *AmSCAP 66*
Ferraro, Piermiranda 1924- *WhoOp 76*
Ferraro, Ralph Albert 1929- *AmSCAP 80*
Ferras, Christian 1933- *IntWWM 77, -80, NewGrD 80, WhoMus 72*
Ferrata, Giuseppe 1865-1928 *Baker 78*
Ferrati, Sarah 1906- *EncWT*
Ferravilla, Edoardo 1846-1915 *NotNAT B, OxThe*
Ferrazano, Anthony Joseph 1937- *AmSCAP 80, CpmDNM 72, -73, -77, -80, ConAmC*
Ferrazzi, Giovanni Battista *NewGrD 80*
Ferre, Clifford F 1920- *AmSCAP 66, -80*
Ferre, Leo 1916- *WhoMus 72*
Ferre, Susan Ingrid 1945- *IntWWM 80*
Ferree, M E *PupTheA*
Ferreira, Antonio *OxThe, REnWD[port]*
Ferreira, Arthur 1922- *DancEn 78*
Ferreira, Carel Pieter 1943- *IntWWM 80*
Ferreira, Djalma 1913- *AmSCAP 66, -80*
Ferreira, Manuel d1797 *NewGrD 80*
Ferreira, Procopio *OxThe*
Ferreira Veiga, Jose Augusto Da 1838-1903 *NewGrD 80*
Ferrell, Ben Payne 1953- *AmSCAP 80*
Ferreol, Marcel Auguste 1899-1974 *McGEWD*
Ferrer, Anselmo 1882- *NewGrD 80*
Ferrer, Edward Harry 1894- *NewOrJ*
Ferrer, Frank William 1896- *NewOrJ*
Ferrer, Guillermo *NewGrD 80*
Ferrer, Jose *MotPP, WhoHol A*
Ferrer, Jose 1909- *FilmgC, HalFC 80, WorEFlm*
Ferrer, Jose 1912- *BiDFilm, -81, BiE&WWA, CnThe, EncMT, EncWT, FilmEn, ForYSC, IntMPA 77, -75, -76, -78, -79, -80, MovMk[port], NotNAT, OxFilm, WhoThe 72, -77*
Ferrer, Mateo 1788-1864 *Baker 78, NewGrD 80*
Ferrer, Mel 1917- *BiDFilm, -81, BiE&WWA, FilmEn, FilmgC, ForYSC, HalFC 80, IntMPA 77, -75, -76, -78, -79, -80, MGM[port], MotPP, MovMk, NotNAT, OxFilm, WhoHol A, WorEFlm*
Ferrer, Pedro *NewGrD 80*
Ferrer, Rafael 1911- *Baker 78*
Ferrer, Santiago 1762-1824 *NewGrD 80*
Ferreri, Marco 1928- *BiDFilm, -81, DcFM, FilmEn, FilmgC, HalFC 80, WorEFlm*
Ferrero, Anna Maria 1931- *FilmEn*
Ferrero, Leo 1903-1933 *CnMD, McGEWD*
Ferrero, Willy 1906-1954 *Baker 78*
Ferrers, George d1579 *NotNAT B*
Ferrers, Helen d1943 *NotNAT B, WhThe*
Ferretti, Dom Paolo 1866-1938 *Baker 78*
Ferretti, Giacomo 1784-1852 *NewGrD 80*
Ferretti, Giacopo 1784-1852 *NewGrD 80*
Ferretti, Giovanni 1540?-1609? *NewGrD 80*
Ferretti, Jacopo 1784-1852 *NewGrD 80*
Ferretti, Paolo 1866-1938 *NewGrD 80*
Ferreyra, Jose A 1889-1943 *DcFM, FilmEn*
Ferri, Baldassare 1610-1680 *Baker 78, NewGrD 80*
Ferri, Baldassarre 1610-1680 *NewGrD 80*
Ferri, Lambert *NewGrD 80*
Ferri, Olga 1928- *CnOxB*
Ferri, Olga 1931- *DancEn 78*
Ferri, Roger *IntMPA 77, -75, -76, -78, -79, -80*
Ferrier, Garry 1936- *IntWWM 80*
Ferrier, Kathleen 1912-1953 *Baker 78, BnBkM 80, CmOp, MusMk, MusSN[port], NewEOp 71, NewGrD 80[port]*
Ferrier, Michel *NewGrD 80*
Ferrier, Paul 1843-1920 *NotNAT B*
Ferrin, Agostino 1928- *WhoOp 76*
Ferrini, Giovanni Battista *NewGrD 80*
Ferris, Audrey 1909- *Film 2, WhoHol A*
Ferris, Barbara *ForYSC, WhoHol A, WhoThe 72, -77*
Ferris, Barbara 1940- *FilmgC, HalFC 80*
Ferris, Barbara 1943- *NotNAT*
Ferris, Dillon J 1914-1951 *WhScrn 74, -77*
Ferris, Don A 1919- *AmSCAP 66, -80*
Ferris, Glenn Arthur 1950- *EncJzS 70*
Ferris, Harry *PupTheA*
Ferris, Joan *ConAmC*
Ferris, Theodore Parker 1908- *BiDAmM*
Ferris, Walter 1886- *FilmEn*
Ferris, William 1937- *Baker 78, ConAmC*
Ferritto, John E 1937- *ConAmC*
Ferro, Giulio d1594? *NewGrD 80*
Ferro, Marco Antonio d1662 *NewGrD 80*
Ferro, Vincenzo *NewGrD 80*
Ferron, Jacques 1921- *CreCan 1*
Ferron, Marcelle 1924- *CreCan 1*
Ferroni, Vincenzo Emidio Carmine 1858-1934 *Baker 78*
Ferroud, Pierre Octave 1900-1936 *Baker 78, NewGrD 80, OxMus*
Ferry, Bryan 1945- *ConMuA 80A, IlEncR*
Ferry, Felix d1953 *NotNAT B*
Ferry, Jean 1906- *DcFM*
Ferry, Minna *Film 2*
Ferry, Robert Bird 1912- *WhoMus 72*
Fersen, Alessandro 1911- *EncWT*
Ferte, Armand Emile Georges *WhoMus 72*
Fertek, Mack Benjamen 1917- *AmSCAP 80*
Ferzetti, Gabriele 1925- *FilmAG WE, FilmEn, FilmgC, HalFC 80, OxFilm, WorEFlm[port]*
Fesca, Alexander Ernst 1820-1849 *Baker 78, NewGrD 80*
Fesca, Friedrich Ernst 1789-1826 *Baker 78, NewGrD 80*
Fesch, Willem De 1687-1761 *Baker 78, NewGrD 80*
Fescourt, Henri 1880-1966 *FilmEn*
Fescourt, Herni 1880-1966 *DcFM*
Fessel, Erik Oskar 1933- *IntWWM 77, -80*
Festa, Costanzo 1480?-1545 *Baker 78*
Festa, Costanzo 1490?-1545 *MusMk, NewGrD 80, OxMus*
Festa, Sebastiano 1495?-1524 *NewGrD 80*
Festa Campanile, Pasquale 1927- *FilmEn, WorEFlm[port]*
Festing, John d1772 *OxMus*
Festing, Michael Christian d1752 *NewGrD 80*
Festing, Michael Christian 1680?-1752 *Baker 78, OxMus*
Fetchit, Stepin d1977 *ForYSC, MotPP*
Fetchit, Stepin 1892-1977 *DrBlPA, WhoHol A*
Fetchit, Stepin 1896-1977 *JoeFr*
Fetchit, Stepin 1898-1977 *FilmgC, HalFC 80*
Fetchit, Stepin 1902- *FilmEn*
Fetchit, Stepin 1902-1977 *Film 2, HolP 30[port], MovMk[port]*
Fetherston, Eddie d1965 *WhScrn 74, -77*
Fetherstone, Eddie d1965 *WhoHol B*
Fethy, Sir John *NewGrD 80*
Fetis *NewGrD 80*
Fetis, Adolphe Louis Eugene 1820-1873 *NewGrD 80*
Fetis, Edouard-Louis Francois 1812-1909 *Baker 78, NewGrD 80*
Fetis, Francois-Joseph 1784-1871 *Baker 78, NewGrD 80[port], OxMus*
Fetler, Paul 1920- *AmSCAP 80, ConAmC*
Fetras, Oscar 1854-1931 *NewGrD 80*
Fetsch, Wolfgaang 1923- *IntWWM 80*
Fetsch, Wolfgang 1923- *IntWWM 77*
Fetter, David 1938- *AmSCAP 80*
Fetter, Ted 1906- *AmSCAP 80*
Fetter, Ted 1910- *AmSCAP 66*
Fetterer, Harry *PupTheA*
Fettke, Tom *ConAmC*
Fetzer, Henrietta *PupTheA*
Fetzer, John E 1901- *IntMPA 77, -75, -76, -78, -79, -80*
Feuchtwanger, Lion 1884-1958 *CnMD, EncWT, Ent, McGEWD[port], ModWD*
Feuchtwanger, Lion 1884-1959 *NotNAT B*
Feuer, Cy 1911- *BiE&WWA, EncMT, NotNAT, WhoThe 72, -77*
Feuer, Donya 1934- *CnOxB*
Feuer, Maria 1932- *IntWWM 77, -80*
Feuermann, Emanuel 1902-1942 *Baker 78, BiDAmM, BnBkM 80, MusSN[port], NewGrD 80*
Feuerstein, Robert 1949- *IntWWM 80*
Feuillade, Louis 1873-1925 *BiDFilm, -81, DcFM, FilmEn, FilmgC, HalFC 80, OxFilm, WorEFlm[port]*
Feuillere, Edwige 1907- *CnThe, EncWT, Ent, FilmAG WE, FilmEn, FilmgC, HalFC 80, MovMk, OxFilm, OxThe, WhThe, WhoHol A, WorEFlm*
Feuillet, Octave 1821-1890 *NotNAT B*
Feuillet, Raoul-Ager d1710 *DancEn 78*
Feuillet, Raoul-Auger *OxMus*
Feuillet, Raoul-Auger 1659?-1710 *NewGrD 80*
Feuillet, Raoul-Auger 1675?-1710 *CnOxB*
Feusier, Norman 1885-1945 *WhScrn 74, -77, WhoHol B*
Feval, Paolo d1887 *NotNAT B*
Fever Tree, The *BiDAmM*
Fevin, Antoine De 1470?-1512? *NewGrD 80*
Fevin, Antoine De 1474-1512 *Baker 78*
Fevin, Robert De *Baker 78, NewGrD 80*
Fevre *NewGrD 80*
Fevrier, Henri 1875-1957 *Baker 78, NewEOp 71*
Fevrier, Henry 1875-1957 *NewGrD 80*
Fevrier, Jacques 1900- *NewGrD 80, WhoMus 72*
Fevrier, Pierre 1696-1779? *NewGrD 80*
Few, Margerie *WhoMus 72*
Fewkes, Jesse Walter 1850-1930 *NewGrD 80*
Fewster, Barbara *CnOxB*
Fey, Barry *ConMuA 80B*
Feydeau, Georges 1862-1921 *CnMD, CnThe, EncWT, Ent, FilmgC, HalFC 80, McGEWD[port], ModWD, NotNAT A, -B, OxThe, PlP&P, REnWD[port]*
Feyder, Jacques 1885-1948 *DcFM, FilmEn*
Feyder, Jacques 1887-1948 *BiDFilm, -81, OxFilm, WorEFlm*
Feyder, Jacques 1888-1948 *FilmgC, HalFC 80, MovMk[port]*
Feyder, Jacques 1894-1948 *TwYS A*
Feyerabend, Sigmund 1527?-1590 *NewGrD 80*
Feyne, Buddy 1912- *AmSCAP 66, -80*
Fezandat, Michel *NewGrD 80*
Ffolkes, David 1912- *WhThe*
Ffolliott, Gladys d1928 *NotNAT B, WhThe*
Ffrangcon-Davies, David Thomas 1855-1918 *Baker 78, OxMus*
Ffrangcon-Davies, Gwen 1896- *CnThe, PlP&P, WhoThe 72, -77*
Ffry, Walter *NewGrD 80*
Fiala, George Joseph 1922- *Baker 78,*

IntWWM 77, -80
Fiala, Jaromir 1892-1967 NewGrD 80
Fiala, Joseph 1748?-1816 NewGrD 80
Fialka, Ladislav 1931- CroCD, EncWT
Fiamengo, Arnoldo NewGrD 80
Fiamengo, Francesco NewGrD 80
Fiamengo, Mathias NewGrD 80
Fiammingo, Vincenzo Beltramo Fulgenzi NewGrD 80
Fiander, Lewis 1940?- HalFC 80
Fias, Gabor 1941- IntWWM 80
Fiasconaro, Gregorio 1915- IntWWM 80, NewGrD 80, WhoOp 76
Fibich, Zdenek 1850-1900 CmOp, GrComp, NewEOp 71, NewGrD 80[port], OxMus
Fibich, Zdenko 1850-1900 Baker 78, NewGrD 80[port]
Ficarelli, Mario 1937- IntWWM 77, -80
Fich NewGrD 80
Fichandler, William 1886- AmSCAP 66
Fichandler, Zelda 1924- BiE&WWA, NotNAT, PlP&P, WhoThe 72, -77
Ficher, Jacobo 1896- Baker 78, CpmDNM 75, DcCM, IntWWM 77, -80, NewGrD 80
Fichthorn, Claude L 1885-1972 AmSCAP 66, -80, ConAmC A
Ficino, Marsilio 1433-1499 NewGrD 80
Fickenscher, Arthur 1871-1954 Baker 78, BiDAmM, ConAmC
Ficker, Rudolf Von 1886-1954 Baker 78, NewGrD 80
Fickett, Mary BiE&WWA, ForYSC, NotNAT, WhoHol A
Ficklen, Bessie Alexander PupTheA
Fickler, Yehuda Julius 1931- IntWWM 77
Fickovskaya, Lena Film 2
Fiddaman, Michael Robert 1928- WhoMus 72
Fiddes, Josephine d1923 NotNAT B
Fiddian, Ian Paull 1909- IntWWM 77, -80, WhoMus 72
Fidelis, Lancilotto NewGrD 80
Fidler, Ben 1867-1932 WhScrn 74, -77
Fidler, Jack 1936- BiDAmM
Fidler, Jimmie 1900- WhoHol A
Fidler, Jimmy 1900- What 3[port]
Fido, John 1570?-1640? NewGrD 80
Fidoe, John 1570?-1640? NewGrD 80
Fidor, John 1570?-1640? NewGrD 80
Fidow, John 1570?-1640? NewGrD 80
Fiebig, Kurt 1908- IntWWM 77, -80
Fiedel, Barry ConMuA 80B
Fiedel, Brad 1951- AmSCAP 80
Fiedel, Ivan 1927- AmSCAP 80
Fiedel, Sam S 1916- AmSCAP 66, -80
Fiedler, Arthur 1894-1979 Baker 78, BiDAmM, BnBkM 80, IntWWM 77, MusSN[port], NewGrD 80
Fiedler, John 1925- BiE&WWA, FilmgC, HalFC 80, NotNAT, WhoHol A
Fiedler, Max 1859-1939 Baker 78, NewGrD 80
Fieger, Adeline Oppenheimer AmSCAP 80
Field, Al G 1852-1921 NotNAT A, -B
Field, Alexander 1892- WhThe
Field, Andrew 1922- IntWWM 80
Field, Barbara NatPD[port]
Field, Ben d1939 Film 2, NotNAT B, WhThe, WhoHol B
Field, Betty 1918-1973 BiE&WWA, FilmEn, FilmgC, ForYSC[port], HalFC 80, HolP 40[port], MotPP, MovMk[port], NotNAT B, PlP&P, ThFT[port], WhScrn 77, WhoHol B, WhoThe 72, -77
Field, Chester Film 2
Field, Christopher David Steadman 1938- IntWWM 77, -80, WhoMus 72
Field, Crystal NotNAT
Field, Edward Salisbury d1936 NotNAT B, WhThe
Field, Elinor Film 2
Field, Eugene 1850-1895 AmSCAP 66, -80, BiDAmM
Field, George 1878-1925 Film 1, -2, WhScrn 77
Field, Gladys d1920 Film 2, WhScrn 74, -77
Field, Grace Film 1
Field, Horace 1902- WhoMus 72
Field, John 1782-1837 Baker 78, BnBkM 80, DcCom 77, DcCom&M 79, GrComp[port], MusMk, NewGrD 80[port], OxMus
Field, John 1921- CnOxB, DancEn 78
Field, Jonathan 1912- WhThe
Field, Joseph M d1856 NotNAT B
Field, Kate d1896 NotNAT B
Field, Leonard S 1908- BiE&WWA, NotNAT
Field, Lila d1954 NotNAT B
Field, Lorraine F 1921- AmSCAP 80
Field, Madalynne Film 2
Field, Margaret WhoHol A
Field, Mary 1896-1968 FilmEn, FilmgC, ForYSC, HalFC 80, IlWWBF, WhoHol A, WomWMM
Field, Michael 1915-1971 BiDAmM
Field, Nat 1587-1620 PlP&P
Field, Nathan 1587-1620 CnThe, EncWT
Field, Nathan 1587-1620? Ent
Field, Nathan 1587-1620 NotNAT A, -B, OxThe, REnWD[port]
Field, Nathaniel d1633 NotNAT B
Field, Norman 1879-1956 WhScrn 74, -77, WhoHol B
Field, Percy Film 2
Field, Rachel 1894-1942 FilmgC, HalFC 80, NotNAT B
Field, Robert WhScrn 77
Field, Robin 1935- IntWWM 77, -80
Field, Ron WhoThe 77
Field, Ron 1932?- NotNAT
Field, Ron 1934- EncMT
Field, Sally 1946- FilmEn, FilmgC, HalFC 80, IntMPA 79, -80, WhoHol A
Field, Shirley Ann 1938- FilmEn, FilmgC, HalFC 80, MotPP, WhoHol A, WhoHrs 80
Field, Shirley Anne IntMPA 75, -76, -78, -79, -80
Field, Shirley Anne 1936- IlWWBF[port]
Field, Shirley Anne 1938- IntMPA 77
Field, Sid 1904-1950 FilmgC, HalFC 80, IlWWBF, -A[port], NotNAT A, -B, WhScrn 74, -77, WhThe, WhoHol B
Field, Sylvia Film 2, WhoHol A
Field, Sylvia 1901- BiE&WWA, NotNAT
Field, Sylvia 1902- WhThe
Field, Virginia 1917- FilmEn, FilmgC, ForYSC, HalFC 80, IntMPA 77, -75, -76, -78, -79, -80, MovMk, ThFT[port], What 5[port], WhThe, WhoHol A
Field, William H 1915-1971 BiDAmM
Field-Dodgson, Robert 1926- NewGrD 80
Field-Hyde, Margaret 1905- IntWWM 77, -80, NewGrD 80
Fielden, Thomas Perceval 1882- WhoMus 72
Fielder, Alvin 1935- EncJzS 70
Fielder, Charles N 1900- AmSCAP 66
Fielder, Denis Britton 1911- WhoMus 72
Fielder, Margaret WomWMM
Fieldhouse, Minnie Christine WhoMus 72
Fielding, Clarissa Film 2
Fielding, Claude Film 2
Fielding, Edward d1945 ForYSC
Fielding, Edward 1880-1945 NotNAT B, WhScrn 77, WhoHol B
Fielding, Edward 1885-1945 WhScrn 74
Fielding, Fenella WhoHol A
Fielding, Fenella 1930?- FilmgC, HalFC 80
Fielding, Fenella 1934- WhoThe 72, -77
Fielding, Gerald Film 2
Fielding, Harold EncMT, WhoThe 72, -77
Fielding, Henry 1707-1754 CnThe, DcPup, EncWT, Ent[port], HalFC 80, McGEWD[port], NotNAT B, OxThe, PlP&P, REnWD[port]
Fielding, Jerry HalFC 80, IntMPA 76, -78, -79, -80
Fielding, Jerry 1922-1980 AmSCAP 66, -80, CmpEPM, ConAmC, FilmEn, FilmgC, IntMPA 77
Fielding, Lee 1888-1963 AmSCAP 66, -80
Fielding, Margaret Film 2
Fielding, Marjorie 1892-1956 FilmgC, HalFC 80, NotNAT B, WhScrn 74, -77, WhThe, WhoHol B
Fielding, Michael AmSCAP 80
Fielding, Minnie 1871-1936 WhScrn 74, -77
Fielding, Romaine d1927 Film 1, TwYS A, WhoHol B
Fielding, Romaine 1877-1927 Film 2, TwYS
Fielding, Romaine 1882-1927 WhScrn 74, -77
Fielding, Timothy d1738 OxThe
Fields, Arthur 1888-1953 AmSCAP 66, -80, CmpEPM, NotNAT B
Fields, Arthur B 1889-1965 AmSCAP 80, NotNAT B
Fields, Benny 1894-1959 HalFC 80, NotNAT B, WhScrn 74, -77, WhoHol B
Fields, Buddy 1889-1965 AmSCAP 66
Fields, Carl Donnell 1915- BiDAmM, CmpEPM, WhoJazz 72
Fields, Charles William 1924- AmSCAP 80
Fields, Dorothy d1974 WhoHol B
Fields, Dorothy 1904-1974 EncMT, WhScrn 77
Fields, Dorothy 1905-1974 AmPS, AmSCAP 66, -80, BestMus, BiDAmM, BiE&WWA, CmpEPM, ConDr 73, EncWT, FilmEn, NewCBMT, NotNAT B, Sw&Ld C, WhThe, WhoThe 72
Fields, Eddie AmSCAP 80
Fields, Edward 1905-1959 WhoJazz 72
Fields, Ernie RkOn
Fields, Frank 1914- NewOrJ
Fields, Freddie 1923- IntMPA 77, -75, -76, -78, -79, -80
Fields, Gracie 1898-1979 BiDAmM, CmpEPM, Ent, FilmAG WE, FilmEn, FilmgC, ForYSC, HalFC 80, IlWWBF[port], -A, JoeFr, MotPP, MovMk, NotNAT A, OxFilm, OxThe, ThFT[port], WhThe, WhoHol A
Fields, Harry 1913- AmSCAP 80
Fields, Harry D d1961 NotNAT B
Fields, Herbert 1897-1958 BestMus, EncMT, FilmEn, NewCBMT, NotNAT B, WhThe
Fields, Herbert 1898-1958 EncWT
Fields, Herbert 1919-1958 BiDAmM, WhoJazz 72
Fields, Herbie 1919-1958 CmpEPM
Fields, Irving 1915- AmSCAP 66, -80, ConAmC A
Fields, James 1948- Baker 78
Fields, James Thomas 1820-1881 BiDAmM
Fields, John 1876-1938 WhScrn 74, -77
Fields, Joseph 1885- NewCBMT
Fields, Joseph 1895-1966 BiE&WWA, CnMD, EncMT, EncWT, FilmEn, McGEWD[port], ModWD, NotNAT B, WhThe
Fields, Julius 1903- WhoJazz 72
Fields, Kathy WhoHol A
Fields, Lew 1867-1941 CmpEPM, EncMT, EncWT, FamA&A[port], FilmEn, Film 1, -2, NotNAT A, -B, TwYS, WhScrn 74, -77, WhThe, WhoHol B, WhoStg 1908
Fields, Lewis Maurice 1867-1941 WhoStg 1906
Fields, Louisa May BlkAmP
Fields, Mercedes Garman d1967 NewOrJ
Fields, Oscar ConMuA 80B
Fields, Phyllis WomWMM B
Fields, Robert WhoHol A
Fields, Shep BgBands 74[port], WhoHol A
Fields, Shep 1910- BiDAmM, CmpEPM
Fields, Shep 1911- What 3[port]
Fields, Sid 1898-1975 WhScrn 77
Fields, Sidney 1898-1975 WhoHol C
Fields, Stanley 1880-1941 ForYSC, MovMk, WhScrn 74, -77, WhoHol B
Fields, Stanley 1883-1941 HolCA[port]
Fields, Stanley 1884-1941 FilmgC, HalFC 80
Fields, Sylvia Film 2
Fields, Totie 1931-1978 JoeFr[port]
Fields, Verna HalFC 80, WomWMM
Fields, W C GrMovC[port]
Fields, W C 1869-1946 FamA&A[port]
Fields, W C 1876-1946 ForYSC
Fields, W C 1879-1946 BiDFilm, -81, CmMov, EncMT, FilmEn, Film 1, -2, FilmgC, HalFC 80[port], MotPP, MovMk[port], NotNAT A, -B, OxFilm, PlP&P[port], TwYS, WhScrn 74, -77, WhThe, WhoHol B, WorEFlm
Fields, W C 1880-1946 Funs[port], JoeFr[port]
Fields, William d1961 NotNAT B
Fields, William Claude 1879-1946 OxThe
Fields, William Claude 1880-1946 Ent
Fielitz, Alexander Von 1860-1930 Baker 78, NewGrD 80
Fien, Lupin 1908- AmSCAP 66, -80
Fierdanck, Johann NewGrD 80
Fierro, Paul WhoHol A

Fierstein, Ronald K 1950- *AmSCAP 80*
Fierszewicz, Daniel d1707? *NewGrD 80*
Fies, Giulio 1519?-1586? *NewGrD 80*
Fiesco, Giulio 1519?-1586? *NewGrD 80*
Fiescus, Giulio 1519?-1586? *NewGrD 80*
Fiestas, The *RkOn*
Fifield, Anne *PupTheA*
Fifield, Christopher George 1945- *IntWWM 77, -80, WhoOp 76*
Fifield, Elaine 1930- *CnOxB, WhThe*
Fifield, Elaine 1931- *DancEn 78*
Fifth Dimension, The *BiDAmM, IlEncR, RkOn 2[port]*
Fifth Estate, The *BiDAmM, RkOn 2[port]*
Fig, Anton Michael 1952- *AmSCAP 80*
Figatner, Nancy 1957- *IntWWM 77, -80*
Figgs, Carrie Law Morgan *BlkAmP*
Figler, Byrnell Walter 1927- *IntWWM 77, -80*
Figman, Max d1952 *Film 1, -2, NotNAT B, WhoHol B*
Figman, Max 1867-1952 *WhScrn 77*
Figman, Max 1868-1952 *WhThe, WhoStg 1906, -1908*
Figman, Oscar Brimberton 1882-1930 *Film 2, NotNAT B, WhScrn 77, WhoHol B*
Figner, Medea 1859-1952 *NewGrD 80[port]*
Figner, Nicolay 1857-1919 *Baker 78*
Figner, Nikolay Nikolayevich 1857-1918 *NewGrD 80[port]*
Figner, Nikolay Nikolayevich 1857-1919 *CmOp*
Figueiredo, Guilherme 1915- *CnThe, REnWD[port]*
Figueredo, Carlos 1910- *Baker 78*
Figueroa, Gabriel 1907- *DcFM, FilmEn, FilmgC, HalFC 80, OxFilm, WorEFlm*
Figueroa, Jose 1905- *IntWWM 77, -80*
Figueroa, Ruben *WhoHol A*
Figulus, Wolfgang 1525?-1589 *Baker 78, NewGrD 80*
Figus, Viliam 1875-1937 *NewGrD 80*
Figus-Bystry, Viliam 1875-1937 *NewGrD 80*
Figus-Bystry, Villiam 1875-1937 *Baker 78*
Fikhtengol'ts, Mikhail Izrailevich 1920- *NewGrD 80*
Filago *NewGrD 80*
Filago, Carlo *NewGrD 80*
Filandre 1616-1691 *OxThe*
Filas, Thomas J 1908- *AmSCAP 66, -80, ConAmC*
Filatoff, Vera 1945- *CnOxB*
Filauri, Antonio 1889-1964 *WhScrn 77*
Fildes, Audrey 1922- *WhThe*
Filev, Ivan 1941- *Baker 78*
Filhe, George 1872-1954 *NewOrJ[port]*
Filiasi, Lorenzo 1878-1963 *Baker 78*
Filiatrault, Jean 1919- *CreCan 1*
Filiberi, Orazio *NewGrD 80*
Filibertus DeLaurentiis *NewGrD 80*
Filimon, Nicolae 1819-1865 *NewGrD 80*
Filion, Jean-Paul 1927- *CreCan 2*
Filip, Paul Francis 1917- *AmSCAP 80*
Filipoctus De Caserta *NewGrD 80*
Filipov, Alexander 1947- *CnOxB*
Filipova, Natalia Victorovna 1935- *CnOxB*
Filippi, Filippo 1830-1887 *Baker 78, NewGrD 80*
Filippi, Gaspare d1655 *NewGrD 80*
Filippi, Rosina 1866-1930 *NotNAT B, WhThe*
Filippini, Rocco 1943- *IntWWM 80*
Filippini, Stefano 1601?-1690 *NewGrD 80*
Filipucci, Agostino 1625?-1679? *NewGrD 80*
Filipuzzi, Agostino 1625?-1679? *NewGrD 80*
Filitrani, Antonello *NewGrD 80*
Filke, Max 1855-1911 *Baker 78*
Filkins, Grace d1962 *NotNAT B, WhThe, WhoStg 1906, -1908*
Fill, George William 1902- *WhoMus 72*
Fillago, Carlo 1586?-1644 *NewGrD 80*
Filleborn, Daniel 1841-1904 *NewGrD 80*
Filler, Harry 1908- *AmSCAP 66, -80*
Filler, Susan M 1947- *IntWWM 80*
Filleul, Henry 1877-1959 *Baker 78*
Fillmore, Clyde 1874-1946 *WhScrn 77*
Fillmore, Clyde 1876-1946 *Film 1, -2, ForYSC, TwYS, WhoHol B*
Fillmore, Henry 1881-1956 *AmSCAP 66, -80, Baker 78, ConAmC*
Fillmore, James H 1849-1941 *BiDAmM*
Fillmore, John Comfort 1843-1898 *Baker 78, BiDAmM, NewGrD 80*
Fillmore, Nellie 1864-1942 *WhScrn 74, -77*
Filmer, A E *WhThe*
Filmer, Edward 1589?-1650 *NewGrD 80*
Filoi *Film 2*
Fils, Anton 1733-1760 *NewGrD 80*
Fils, Baron *Film 2*
Filson, Al W *Film 1, -2*
Filson, Mrs. Al W *Film 1*
Filtsch, Karl 1830-1845 *NewGrD 80*
Filtsch, Karoly 1830-1845 *NewGrD 80*
Filtz, Anton 1730?-1760 *OxMus*
Filtz, Anton 1733-1760 *Baker 78, NewGrD 80*
Filz, Anton 1733-1760 *NewGrD 80*
Fimberg, Harold Alfred 1907- *AmSCAP 66*
Fina, Jack 1913- *BgBands 74*
Fina, Jack 1913-1968 *AmSCAP 66, WhScrn 77*
Fina, Jack 1913-1970 *AmSCAP 80, CmpEPM*
Finagin, Alexei 1890-1942 *Baker 78*
Finatti, Giovanni Pietro *NewGrD 80*
Finazzi, Filippo 1706?-1776 *NewGrD 80*
Finberg, Jack Gerald *IntMPA 77, -75, -76, -78, -79, -80*
Finch, Calvin *AmSCAP 80*
Finch, Dick 1898-1955 *AmSCAP 66, -80*
Finch, Edward 1664-1738 *NewGrD 80*
Finch, Flora 1869-1940 *FilmEn, Film 1, -2, FilmgC, HalFC 80, NotNAT B, TwYS, WhScrn 74, -77, WhoHol B*
Finch, John *ConDr 73, -77C*
Finch, John 1911- *NatPD[port]*
Finch, Jon 1941- *FilmEn, FilmgC, HalFC 80, IntMPA 80, WhoHol A, WhoHrs 80[port]*
Finch, Jon 1942- *FilmAG WE*
Finch, Kaye *WomWMM A, -B*
Finch, Peter 1916-1977 *BiDFilm, -81, CmMov, FilmAG WE, FilmEn, FilmgC, ForYSC, HalFC 80[port], IlWWBF[port], IntMPA 77, -75, -76, MotPP, MovMk[port], OxFilm, WhThe, WhoHol A, WhoThe 72, WorEFlm*
Finch, Robert Duer Claydon 1900- *CreCan 2*
Finch, Ruth Goddard 1906- *AmSCAP 66, -80*
Finck, H T 1854-1926 *OxMus*
Finck, Heinrich 1444?-1527 *NewGrD 80[port]*
Finck, Heinrich 1445-1527 *Baker 78, MusMk*
Finck, Henry Theophilus 1854-1926 *Baker 78, BiDAmM, NewGrD 80*
Finck, Herman 1872-1939 *NewGrD 80, WhThe*
Finck, Hermann 1527-1558 *Baker 78, MusMk, NewGrD 80*
Finck, Joan *WomWMM B*
Finckel, Edwin A 1917- *AmSCAP 66, -80*
Finckel, Michael Philip 1945- *ConAmC*
Finco, Giuseppe Francesco *NewGrD 80*
Findeisen, Nicolai 1868-1928 *Baker 78*
Findeisen, Nikolay Fyodorovich 1868-1928 *NewGrD 80*
Findeisen, Otto 1862-1947 *Baker 78*
Findeyzen, Nikolay Fyodorovich 1868-1928 *NewGrD 80*
Findlater, John *WhoHol A*
Findlay, Elsie 1902- *IntWWM 77, -80*
Findlay, James B 1904-1973 *MagIlD*
Findlay, Roberta *WomWMM*
Findlay, Ruth 1904-1949 *NotNAT B, WhScrn 74, -77, WhoHol B*
Findlay, Thomas Bruce 1874-1941 *Film 2, NotNAT B, WhoHol B*
Findley, Thomas Bruce 1874-1941 *WhScrn 74, -77*
Findon, B W 1859-1943 *NotNAT B, WhThe*
Fine, Aaron d1963 *NotNAT B*
Fine, Albert M 1932- *IntWWM 77*
Fine, Bud *Film 2*
Fine, Hank 1904- *IntMPA 75, -76*
Fine, Harry *IntMPA 77, -75, -76, -78, -79, -80*
Fine, Irving 1914-1962 *AmSCAP 66, -80, Baker 78, CompSN[port], ConAmC, DcCom&M 79, DcCM, NewGrD 80, OxMus*
Fine, Irving Gifford 1914-1962 *BiDAmM*
Fine, Jack Wolf 1922- *AmSCAP 66, -80*
Fine, Larry 1911-1975 *FilmEn, ForYSC, JoeFr, MotPP, WhScrn 77, WhoHol C*
Fine, Oronce 1494-1555 *NewGrD 80*
Fine, Sidney 1904- *AmSCAP 66*
Fine, Sylvia *AmSCAP 66, -80*
Fine, Vivian 1913- *AmSCAP 80, Baker 78, BiDAmM, CpmDNM 78, -79, -80, ConAmC, DcCM, IntWWM 77, -80, NewGrD 80*
Fine, Wendy Marion *CmOp, WhoOp 76*
Finegan, Bill 1917- *CmpEPM*
Finegan, William J 1917- *AmSCAP 66, -80, BiDAmM*
Finegold, Helen 1945- *IntWWM 77*
Finel, Paul Jean-Marie 1924- *WhoOp 76*
Fineshriber, William H, Jr. 1909- *IntMPA 77, -75, -76, -78, -79, -80*
Finetti, Giacomo *NewGrD 80*
Finfgeld, Carolyn Ayers 1937- *IntWWM 77*
Finger, Godfrey 1660?-1730 *NewGrD 80*
Finger, Gottfried 1660?- *MusMk*
Finger, Gottfried 1660?-1730 *NewGrD 80*
Fini, Leonor 1908- *CnOxB, DancEn 78*
Fink, Christian 1822-1911 *Baker 78*
Fink, Emma 1910-1966 *WhScrn 74, -77*
Fink, Gottfried Wilhelm 1783-1846 *Baker 78, NewGrD 80*
Fink, Henry 1893-1963 *AmSCAP 66, -80, Film 2*
Fink, John *WhoHol A*
Fink, Laure *IntWWM 77, -80*
Fink, Lorraine 1931- *IntWWM 77, -80*
Fink, Lucille *PupTheA*
Fink, Michael 1939- *AmSCAP 66, ConAmC*
Fink, Michael Armand 1939- *AmSCAP 80, IntWWM 77, -80*
Fink, Myron S 1932- *ConAmC*
Fink, Reginald H 1931- *IntWWM 77, -80*
Fink, Robert Russell 1933- *ConAmC, IntWWM 77, -80*
Finke, Fidelio Friedrich 1891-1968 *NewGrD 80*
Finke, Fidelio Fritz 1891-1968 *Baker 78*
Finke, John, Jr. 1898-1965 *AmSCAP 66, -80*
Finkel, Abem 1889-1948 *FilmEn*
Finkel, Bob *NewYTET*
Finkel, Shelly *ConMuA 80B*
Finkelstein, Herman 1903- *IntMPA 77, -75, -76, -78, -79, -80*
Finklehoffe, Fred F 1910-1977 *FilmEn*
Finklehoffe, Fred F 1911-1977 *BiE&WWA, FilmgC, HalFC 80, NotNAT*
Finlay, Bob d1929 *Film 1, WhoHol B*
Finlay, Frank *ForYSC, WhoThe 72*
Finlay, Frank 1926- *CnThe, FilmEn, FilmgC, HalFC 80, IlWWBF, PlP&P[port], WhoHol A, WhoThe 77*
Finlay, Ian Forbes 1924- *WhoMus 72*
Finlay, Redmon *Film 2*
Finlay, Robert 1888-1929 *WhScrn 74, -77*
Finlayson, Henderson 1887-1953 *WhScrn 74, -77*
Finlayson, James 1877-1953 *FilmgC, HalFC 80*
Finlayson, James 1887-1953 *FilmEn, Film 1, -2, WhoHol B*
Finlayson, Jimmy 1887-1953 *TwYS*
Finlayson, Jimmy 1887-1959 *ForYSC*
Finlayson, Walter Alan 1919- *AmSCAP 80*
Finley, Guy Larry 1949- *AmSCAP 80*
Finley, Lorraine Noel 1898-1972 *ConAmC*
Finley, Lorraine Noel 1899-1972 *AmSCAP 66, -80*
Finley, Ned d1920 *Film 1, WhScrn 77*
Finn, Arthur *IlWWBF, WhThe*
Finn, Henry James 1790?-1840 *NotNAT B, OxThe*
Finn, Konstantin Yakovlevich 1904- *OxThe*
Finn, Mickey *ForYSC*
Finn, Sam 1893-1958 *WhScrn 74, -77*
Finn, William Joseph 1881-1961 *AmSCAP 66, -80, BiDAmM, ConAmC*
Finnegan, Larry 1941- *RkOn[port]*
Finnegan, Tom *ConMuA 80B*
Finnegan, Walter 1873-1943 *WhScrn 74, -77*
Finnell, Carrie d1963 *NotNAT B*
Finnerty, Barry 1951- *EncJzS 70*
Finnerty, David Edmund 1950- *AmSCAP 80*
Finnerty, Louis 1883-1937 *WhScrn 74, -77, WhoHol B*
Finnerty, Walter d1974 *WhoHol B*
Finnerty, Warren 1934-1974 *WhScrn 77*
Finney, Albert *IntMPA 75, -76*
Finney, Albert 1936- *BiDFilm, -81, BiE&WWA, CnThe, EncWT, Ent, FilmAG WE[port], FilmEn, FilmgC,*

ForYSC, HalFC 80, IlWWBF[port], IntMPA 77, -78, -79, -80, MotPP, MovMk[port], NotNAT, PlP&P[port], WhoHol A, WhoThe 72, -77, WorEFlm
Finney, Albert 1937- *OxFilm*
Finney, Benjamin F, Jr. *Film 2*
Finney, David 1897- *WhoMus 72*
Finney, Edith *PupTheA*
Finney, Edward *IntMPA 77, -75, -76, -78, -79, -80*
Finney, Jameson Lee 1863- *WhoStg 1908*
Finney, Mary 1906-1973 *BiE&WWA, NotNAT B*
Finney, Ross Lee 1906- *AmSCAP 66, -80, Baker 78, BiDAmM, BnBkM 80, CompSN[port], CpmDNM 72, -79, -80, ConAmC, DcCM, IntWWM 77, -80, NewGrD 80, WhoMus 72*
Finney, Theodore Mitchell 1902- *Baker 78, NewGrD 80, WhoMus 72*
Finney, Truman 1944- *CnOxB*
Finnila, Birgit 1931- *IntWWM 77, -80, WhoMus 72, WhoOp 76*
Finnissy, Michael Peter 1946- *NewGrD 80, WhoMus 72*
Fino, Giocondo 1867-1950 *Baker 78*
Finola, George 1945- *NewOrJ SUP[port]*
Finot, Dominique *NewGrD 80*
Finotto, Dominique *NewGrD 80*
Finscher, Ludwig 1930- *IntWWM 77, -80, NewGrD 80*
Finsterbusch, Reinhold 1825-1902 *NewGrD 80*
Finston, Lewis Norman 1894-1974 *AmSCAP 80*
Finston, Nat W *AmSCAP 66, -80*
Finzi, Gerald 1901-1956 *Baker 78, DcCom&M 79, MusMk, NewGrD 80[port], OxMus*
Fio Rito, Ted 1900-1971 *CmpEPM, WhScrn 74, -77, WhoHol B*
Fiocco *NewGrD 80*
Fiocco, Gioseffo Hectore 1703-1741 *OxMus*
Fiocco, Jean-Joseph 1686-1746 *Baker 78, NewGrD 80*
Fiocco, Joseph-Hector 1703-1741 *Baker 78, MusMk, NewGrD 80*
Fiocco, Pierre Antoine 1650?-1714 *NewGrD 80*
Fiocco, Pietro Antonio 1650?-1714 *Baker 78, NewGrD 80, OxMus*
Fiocre, Eugenie 1845-1908 *CnOxB*
Fiorani, Cristoforo *NewGrD 80*
Fiorato, Hugo 1914- *DancEn 78*
Fioravanti, Valentino 1764-1837 *Baker 78, NewGrD 80*
Fioravanti, Vincenzo 1799-1877 *Baker 78, NewGrD 80*
Fiore, Andrea Stefano 1686-1732 *NewGrD 80*
Fiore, Angelo Maria 1660?-1723 *NewGrD 80*
Fiore, Joan *WomWMM*
Fiore, Maria 1935- *FilmAG WE*
Fiorentino, Imero *NewYTET*
Fiorentino, Perino *NewGrD 80*
Fiorenza, Alfredo 1868-1931 *WhScrn 74, -77*
Fiorenza, Nicola d1764 *NewGrD 80*
Fiorenzo De' Fasoli *NewGrD 80*
Fiorilli, Tiberio 1608-1694 *EncWT, Ent, NotNAT B*
Fiorillo, Beatrice F Vitellini d1654 *EncWT*
Fiorillo, Beatrice Vitelli *OxThe*
Fiorillo, Carlo 1590?-1616? *NewGrD 80*
Fiorillo, Dante 1905- *Baker 78, BiDAmM, ConAmC, OxMus*
Fiorillo, Federigo 1755-1823? *Baker 78, NewGrD 80*
Fiorillo, Federigo 1755-1823 *OxMus*
Fiorillo, Giovan Battista 1614?-1651 *EncWT, OxThe*
Fiorillo, Ignazio 1715-1787 *Baker 78, NewGrD 80*
Fiorillo, Silvio *DcPup*
Fiorillo, Silvio d1630 *EncWT*
Fiorillo, Silvio 1570?-1632? *Ent, OxThe*
Fiorillo, Tiberio 1608-1694 *OxThe*
Fiorillo, Tiborio 1608-1694 *PlP&P[port]*
Fiorini, Ippolito 1549?-1621 *NewGrD 80*
Fiorino, Gasparo *NewGrD 80*
Fiorino, Ippolito 1549?-1621 *NewGrD 80*
Fiorino, Vincent C 1899- *AmSCAP 66, -80*
Fiorito, Ernest 1907-1960 *AmSCAP 66, -80*
Fiorito, Ted 1900-1971 *AmPS, AmSCAP 66, -80, BgBands 74, BiDAmM, Sw&Ld C*
Fiorone, Giovanni Andrea 1704?-1778 *NewGrD 80*
Fioroni, Giovanni Andrea 1704?-1778 *NewGrD 80*
Fique, Karl 1867-1930 *Baker 78*
Firca, Gheorghe Bujor 1935- *IntWWM 77, -80*
Fireballs, The *RkOn*
Firefall *RkOn 2[port]*
Fireflies, The *RkOn*
Firehouse Five Plus Two *CmpEPM*
Firestone, Cinda *WomWMM A, -B*
Firestone, Eddie 1920- *BiE&WWA, ForYSC, WhoHol A*
Firestone, Elizabeth *WomWMM*
Firestone, Idabelle 1874-1954 *AmSCAP 66, -80, ConAmC*
Firfov, Zivko 1907- *IntWWM 77, -80*
Firkusny, Rudolf 1912- *Baker 78, BnBkM 80, IntWWM 77, -80, MusSN[port], NewGrD 80, WhoMus 72*
Firmin, Angela *CreCan 2*
Firpo, Luis Angel *Film 2*
First Choice, The *RkOn 2[port]*
First Class *RkOn 2[port]*
First Natural Hair Band *BiDAmM*
First Nighter, The *What 5[port]*
Firth, Anne 1918- *WhThe*
Firth, Elizabeth 1884- *WhThe*
Firth, Everett Joseph 1930- *AmSCAP 80, IntWWM 77, -80*
Firth, John 1789-1864 *NewGrD 80*
Firth, Mike *NatPD[port]*
Firth, Peter 1953- *FilmEn, HalFC 80, IntMPA 80, PlP&P A[port]*
Firth, Tazeena 1935- *WhoThe 77*
Firth, Thomas Preston 1883-1945 *WhScrn 77*
Firth Hall And Pond *NewGrD 80*
Fischbach, Elis Beck 1921- *IntWWM 77, -80*
Fischbach, Gerald Frederick 1942- *IntWWM 77, -80*
Fischbeck, Harry *HalFC 80*
Fischer, Adam 1949- *WhoOp 76*
Fischer, Alice 1869-1947 *NotNAT B, WhThe, WhoStg 1908*
Fischer, Annie 1914- *IntWWM 77, -80, NewGrD 80, WhoMus 72*
Fischer, Anton 1778-1808 *NewGrD 80*
Fischer, Carl 1849-1923 *Baker 78, NewGrD 80, OxMus*
Fischer, Carl Theodore 1912-1954 *AmSCAP 66, -80, CmpEPM*
Fischer, Christoph 1618-1701 *NewGrD 80*
Fischer, Clare 1928- *BiDAmM, EncJzS 70*
Fischer, Clifford C d1951 *NotNAT B*
Fischer, Edgar 1942- *IntWWM 77, -80*
Fischer, Edith Steinkraus 1922- *CpmDNM 76, -79, ConAmC*
Fischer, Edna *AmSCAP 66, -80*
Fischer, Eduard 1930- *IntWWM 77, -80*
Fischer, Edward Arnold 1950- *AmSCAP 80*
Fischer, Edwin 1886-1960 *Baker 78, BnBkM 80, MusSN[port], NewGrD 80*
Fischer, Emil 1838-1914 *Baker 78, CmOp, NewEOp 71*
Fischer, Erich 1887- *Baker 78*
Fischer, Ewald 1924- *IntWWM 80*
Fischer, Felix *Film 2*
Fischer, Frederick 1868-1931 *Baker 78*
Fischer, Georg 1935- *NewGrD 80, WhoOp 76*
Fischer, Gunnar 1910- *DcFM, FilmEn, OxFilm, WorEFlm[port]*
Fischer, Gunnar 1911- *FilmgC, HalFC 80*
Fischer, Irwin 1903- *ConAmC, NewGrD 80*
Fischer, J 1841-1901 *NewGrD 80*
Fischer, Jacobo 1896- *BiDAmM*
Fischer, Jan Frank 1921- *Baker 78, NewGrD 80*
Fischer, Johann 1665?-1746 *MusMk*
Fischer, Johann Caspar Ferdinand 1646-1717? *NewGrD 80*
Fischer, Johann Caspar Ferdinand 1665?-1746 *Baker 78*
Fischer, Johann Caspar Ferdinand 1670?-1746 *NewGrD 80*
Fischer, Johann Christian 1733-1800 *NewGrD 80[port]*
Fischer, Johann Kaspar Ferdinand 1670?-1746 *NewGrD 80*
Fischer, Johannes *NewGrD 80*
Fischer, John W 1947- *AmSCAP 80*
Fischer, Johnny *NewOrJ*
Fischer, Joseph *NewGrD 80*
Fischer, Joseph 1841-1901 *Baker 78*
Fischer, Joseph A *IntMPA 77, -75, -76, -78, -79, -80*
Fischer, Klaus Peter 1937- *IntWWM 77, -80*
Fischer, Kurt Von 1913- *NewGrD 80*
Fischer, Leck 1904-1956 *CnMD*
Fischer, Ludwig 1745-1825 *Baker 78, BnBkM 80, CmOp, NewEOp 71, NewGrD 80*
Fischer, Lynn Connor 1935- *WomWMM A, -B*
Fischer, Margarita 1886-1975 *WhScrn 77*
Fischer, Margarita 1893- *Film 1*
Fischer, Matthaus 1763-1840 *NewGrD 80*
Fischer, Matthias 1763-1840 *NewGrD 80*
Fischer, Max 1909-1974 *WhoHol A*
Fischer, Michael Gottard 1773-1829 *NewGrD 80*
Fischer, Michael Gotthard 1773-1829 *Baker 78*
Fischer, O W 1915- *FilmEn*
Fischer, O W 1915-1973 *FilmgC, HalFC 80*
Fischer, Otto Wilhelm 1915-1973 *FilmAG WE[port]*
Fischer, Raymond Rudolph 1928- *WhoMus 72*
Fischer, Res 1896-1974 *NewGrD 80*
Fischer, Robert *Film 2*
Fischer, Robert E 1923- *BiE&WWA*
Fischer, Robert Warren 1935- *AmSCAP 80*
Fischer, Ruth 1895- *BiE&WWA*
Fischer, Ruth 1919- *BiE&WWA*
Fischer, Theresia 1896-1974 *NewGrD 80*
Fischer, Wilhelm 1886-1962 *Baker 78, NewGrD 80*
Fischer, William Gustavus 1835-1912 *Baker 78, BiDAmM, NewGrD 80*
Fischer, William S 1935- *AmSCAP 80, BiDAmM, ConAmC, EncJzS 70, IntWWM 77, -80*
Fischer-Dieskau, Dietrich 1925- *Baker 78, BnBkM 80[port], CmOp, IntWWM 77, -80, MusMk[port], MusSN[port], NewEOp 71, NewGrD 80[port], WhoMus 72, WhoOp 76*
Fischer-Dieskau, Klaus 1921- *IntWWM 77, -80, WhoMus 72*
Fischer-Koppe, Hugo *Film 2*
Fischetti, Domenico 1725?-1810? *NewGrD 80*
Fischhof, Joseph 1804-1857 *Baker 78, NewGrD 80*
Fischietti, Domenico 1725?-1810? *NewGrD 80*
Fischinger, Oskar 1900-1967 *DcFM, FilmEn, HalFC 80, OxFilm, WorEFlm*
Fischman, David 1910-1958 *WhScrn 74, -77*
Fischoff, George Allan 1938- *AmSCAP 80*
Fiser, Lubos 1935- *Baker 78, DcCM, NewGrD 80*
Fish, Hamilton *What 1[port]*
Fishbach, Greg *ConMuA 80B*
Fishbein, Frieda 1895- *NotNAT*
Fishbein, Lawrence 1904- *BiE&WWA*
Fishbein, Robert Edward 1933- *IntWWM 77, -80*
Fishburn, Christopher *NewGrD 80*
Fisher, Al *IntMPA 77, -75, -76, -78, -79, -80*
Fisher, Alfred 1849-1933 *Film 2, WhScrn 74, -77, WhoHol B*
Fisher, Alfred 1942- *ConAmC*
Fisher, Anne *WomWMM B*
Fisher, Art *NewYTET*
Fisher, Brian 1939- *CreCan 2*
Fisher, Bruce C 1951- *AmSCAP 80*
Fisher, Carl 1909- *BiE&WWA*
Fisher, Carrie 1956- *FilmEn, WhoHrs 80*
Fisher, Carrie 1957- *HalFC 80, WhoHol A*
Fisher, Clara 1811-1898 *FamA&A[port], NotNAT A, -B, OxThe*
Fisher, Dan 1920- *AmSCAP 66, -80*
Fisher, Doris 1915- *AmSCAP 66, -80, CmpEPM, ConAmC*
Fisher, Eddie 1928- *AmPS A, -B, BiDAmM, CmpEPM, FilmEn, FilmgC, ForYSC, HalFC 80, IntMPA 77, -75, -76, -78, -79, -80, NewYTET, RkOn[port], WhoHol A*
Fisher, Edward A 1920- *ConAmTC*
Fisher, Esther Frances Eveleigh *IntWWM 77, -80, WhoMus 72*
Fisher, Eve 1934- *WhoMus 72*
Fisher, F E *NewGrD 80*
Fisher, Florence Mary 1901- *WhoMus 72*

Fisher, Frank H 1907- *IntMPA 77, -75, -76, -78, -79, -80*
Fisher, Fred 1875-1942 *AmPS, AmSCAP 66, -80, BiDAmM, CmpEPM, NotNAT B, PopAmC[port], Sw&Ld C*
Fisher, Fred 1930- *CpmDNM 73, ConAmC*
Fisher, Freda Ellen May 1919- *WhoMus 72*
Fisher, Freddie Schnickelfritz 1904-1967 *WhScrn 77*
Fisher, Freddie Schnicklefritz 1904-1967 *CmpEPM*
Fisher, Frederick Schnickelfritz 1904-1967 *WhoHol B*
Fisher, Gail 1935?- *DrBlPA*
Fisher, George 1894-1960 *Film 1, -2, WhScrn 74, -77, WhoHol B*
Fisher, Gerry 1926- *FilmEn, FilmgC, HalFC 80*
Fisher, Gladys W 1900- *ConAmC*
Fisher, Harry d1923 *NotNAT B, WhoHol B*
Fisher, Harry 1885-1917 *WhScrn 77*
Fisher, Holly *WomWMM B*
Fisher, Irving d1959 *NotNAT B*
Fisher, Jack Berry 1924- *IntWWM 77, -80*
Fisher, Jane d1869 *NotNAT B*
Fisher, Jeanne Elizabeth 1955- *IntWWM 77*
Fisher, Jessie Sevil Neusman 1909- *AmSCAP 80*
Fisher, Jessie Sevil Neussan 1909- *AmSCAP 66*
Fisher, John 1926- *BlkAmP*
Fisher, John Abraham 1744-1806 *NewGrD 80*
Fisher, John C d1921 *NotNAT B*
Fisher, John Henry 1944- *IntWWM 80*
Fisher, Judith Booth 1941- *IntWWM 77, -80*
Fisher, Jules 1937- *BiE&WWA, NotNAT, WhoThe 77*
Fisher, Larry *Film 2*
Fisher, Laurence *Film 2*
Fisher, Lawrence V 1923- *IntWWM 77, -80*
Fisher, Lewis T 1915- *BiE&WWA*
Fisher, Lois *WomWMM*
Fisher, Lola d1926 *BiE&WWA, NotNAT*
Fisher, Lola 1892-1926 *NotNAT B*
Fisher, Lola 1896-1926 *WhThe*
Fisher, Maggie 1854-1938 *WhScrn 74, -77*
Fisher, Maisie *Film 2*
Fisher, Margarita 1893- *Film 2, TwYS*
Fisher, Margarite *WhScrn 77*
Fisher, Marjorie Williams 1916- *AmSCAP 66, -80*
Fisher, Mark 1895-1948 *AmSCAP 66, -80*
Fisher, Marve A 1907-1957 *AmSCAP 66, -80*
Fisher, Marvin 1916- *AmSCAP 66, -80*
Fisher, Max 1909-1974 *WhScrn 77*
Fisher, Millicent *Film 2*
Fisher, Nancy Lou *AmSCAP 80*
Fisher, Nelle 1914- *BiE&WWA, NotNAT*
Fisher, Nicholas E 1894-1961 *AmSCAP 66, -80*
Fisher, Nicola *WomWMM*
Fisher, Norma 1940- *IntWWM 77, -80, WhoMus 72*
Fisher, Norman Z 1920- *ConAmC*
Fisher, Patty *AmSCAP 80*
Fisher, Paul G 1922- *IntWWM 77, -80*
Fisher, Reuben 1923- *AmSCAP 66, -80*
Fisher, Roger Anthony 1936- *IntWWM 77, -80*
Fisher, Rudolph 1897-1934 *BlkAmP, MorBAP*
Fisher, Sallie 1881-1950 *CmpEPM, NotNAT B, WhoHol B*
Fisher, Sally 1881-1950 *WhScrn 74, -77*
Fisher, Shug *WhoHol A*
Fisher, Shug 1907- *IlEncCM*
Fisher, Stephen D 1940- *CpmDNM 79, ConAmC*
Fisher, Sylvia Gwendoline Victoria 1910- *CmOp, IntWWM 80, NewGrD 80*
Fisher, Terence 1904- *BiDFilm, -81, CmMov, DcFM, FilmgC, HalFC 80, IlWWBF, IntMPA 77, -75, -76, -78, -79, -80, WorEFlm*
Fisher, Terence 1904-1980 *FilmEn, WhoHrs 80[port]*
Fisher, Toni *RkOn*
Fisher, Trevor *WhoMus 72*
Fisher, Truman Rex 1927- *ConAmC*
Fisher, William 1868-1933 *WhScrn 74, -77, WhoHol B*
Fisher, William Arms 1861-1948 *AmSCAP 66, -80, Baker 78, BiDAmM, NewGrD 80*
Fisher, William G 1883-1949 *WhScrn 74, -77*
Fisher, William H 1913-1972 *BiDAmM*
Fisher, Zeal Isay 1930- *IntWWM 77, -80*
Fishkin, Paul *ConMuA 80B*
Fishko, Sara *WomWMM B*
Fishman, Henry d1964 *NotNAT B*
Fishman, Jack *ConAmC*
Fishman, Jay David 1927- *AmSCAP 80*
Fishman, Marian 1941- *CpmDNM 74, ConAmC*
Fishman, Natan L'vovich 1909- *NewGrD 80*
Fishwick, John Charles 1951- *IntWWM 77, -80*
Fisk, Charles Brenton 1925- *NewGrD 80*
Fisk, James *PlP&P*
Fiske, Mrs. 1865-1932 *EncWT, Film 1*
Fiske, Harrison Grey 1861-1942 *NotNAT B, WhThe, WhoStg 1906, -1908*
Fiske, Homer 1914- *AmSCAP 66, -80*
Fiske, Isaac 1820-1894 *NewGrD 80*
Fiske, June 1941- *IntWWM 80, WhoOp 76*
Fiske, Minnie Maddern 1865-1932 *Ent, FamA&A[port], NotNAT A, -B, OxThe, PlP&P[port], WhScrn 77, WhThe, WhoHol B, WhoStg 1906, -1908*
Fiske, Minnie Maddern 1866-1922 *HalFC 80*
Fiske, Richard 1915-1944 *WhScrn 77*
Fiske, Robert L 1889-1944 *WhScrn 77*
Fiske, Roger Elwyn *WhoMus 72*
Fiske, Roger Elwyn 1910- *NewGrD 80*
Fiske, Stephen 1840-1916 *NotNAT B, WhThe*
Fison, Kathleen Mary *WhoMus 72*
Fissinger, Alfred J 1925- *ConAmC*
Fissinger, Edwin Russell 1920- *ConAmC, IntWWM 77, -80*
Fissore, Enrico 1939- *WhoOp 76*
Fissot, Alexis-Henri 1843-1896 *Baker 78*
Fistoulari, Anatole 1907- *Baker 78, IntWWM 77, -80, NewGrD 80, WhoMus 72*
Fisz, Benjamin 1922- *FilmgC, HalFC 80, IntMPA 77, -75, -76, -78, -79, -80*
Fitch, Charles Harold 1895- *WhoMus 72*
Fitch, Clyde 1865-1909 *BiDAmM, CnMD, CnThe, McGEWD[port], ModWD, NotNAT A, -B, PlP&P[port], REnWD[port]*
Fitch, Eleazer Thompson 1791-1871 *BiDAmM*
Fitch, Joseph 1921- *BiE&WWA, NotNAT*
Fitch, Theodore F 1900- *AmSCAP 66, ConAmC*
Fitch, Mrs. Theodore F *ConAmC*
Fitch, William Clyde 1865-1909 *DcLB 7[port], EncWT, Ent, OxThe, WhoStg 1906, -1908*
Fite, Isabella 1933- *WhoOp 76*
Fitelberg, Gregor 1879-1953 *Baker 78*
Fitelberg, Grzegorz 1879-1953 *NewGrD 80*
Fitelberg, Jerzy 1903-1951 *Baker 78, BiDAmM, ConAmC, DcCM, NewGrD 80*
Fitelson, H William 1905- *IntMPA 77, -75, -76, -78, -79, -80*
Fitt, Robert J 1945- *ConAmC*
Fitts, Dudley 1903-1968 *BiE&WWA, NotNAT B*
Fitz, Charles E d1920 *NotNAT B*
Fitz, Richard *ConAmC*
Fitz-Gerald, S J Adair 1859-1925 *WhThe*
Fitzball, Edward 1792-1873 *NotNAT B, OxThe*
Fitzenhagen, Wilhelm 1848-1890 *NewGrD 80*
Fitzer, James Robert 1930- *IntWWM 77*
Fitzgerald, Aubrey *Film 2*
Fitzgerald, Aubrey Whitestone 1876- *WhThe*
Fitzgerald, Barry 1881-1961 *ForYSC*
Fitzgerald, Barry 1888-1961 *BiDFilm, -81, FilmEn, FilmgC, HalFC 80[port], HolCA[port], HolP 40[port], MotPP, MovMk[port], NotNAT B, OxFilm, PlP&P, WhScrn 74, -77, WhThe, WhoHol B*
Fitzgerald, Cissy 1874-1941 *Film 2, ForYSC, NotNAT B, WhScrn 74, -77, WhoHol B*
Fitzgerald, Cissy 1894-1941 *Film 1, TwYS*
Fitzgerald, Dallas M *TwYS A*
Fitzgerald, Deborah *WomWMM B*
Fitzgerald, Edward 1876- *WhThe, WhoStg 1908*
Fitzgerald, Edward P 1883-1942 *WhScrn 74, -77, WhoHol B*
Fitzgerald, Ella *AmPS A, -B*
Fitzgerald, Ella 1918- *AmSCAP 66, -80, Baker 78, BiDAmM, CmpEPM, DrBlPA, EncJzS 70, HalFC 80, IlEncJ, IntWWM 77, -80, MusMk[port], WhoMus 72*
Fitzgerald, Ella 1920- *NewGrD 80*
Fitzgerald, F Scott 1896-1940 *CnMD, FilmgC, HalFC 80, NotNAT B, OxFilm*
Fitzgerald, Felicia *PupTheA*
Fitzgerald, Florence Irene 1890-1962 *NotNAT B, WhScrn 74, -77, WhoHol B*
Fitzgerald, Francis Scott Key 1896-1940 *WorEFlm*
Fitzgerald, Geraldine *MotPP, PlP&P A[port]*
Fitzgerald, Geraldine 1912- *FilmgC, HalFC 80*
Fitzgerald, Geraldine 1914- *BiE&WWA, FilmEn, ForYSC, HolP 40[port], IlWWBF, IntMPA 77, -75, -76, -78, -79, -80, MovMk, NotNAT, ThFT[port], WhoHol A, WhoThe 72, -77*
Fitzgerald, James M 1897-1919 *WhScrn 77*
Fitzgerald, Larry *ConMuA 80B*
Fitzgerald, Lilian d1947 *NotNAT B*
Fitzgerald, Lillian d1947 *WhScrn 77, WhoHol B*
Fitzgerald, Lionel LeMoine 1890-1956 *CreCan 1*
Fitzgerald, Neil 1898- *WhoHol A, WhoThe 77*
Fitzgerald, Pegeen *IntMPA 77, -75, -76, -78, -79, -80*
Fitzgerald, Percy Hetherington 1834-1925 *NotNAT B, WhThe*
Fitzgerald, R Bernard 1911- *ConAmC*
Fitzgerald, Robert 1925- *IntMPA 77, -75, -76, -78, -79, -80*
Fitzgerald, Robert Bernard 1911- *AmSCAP 80, IntWWM 77, -80*
Fitzgerald, S J Adair 1859-1925 *NotNAT B*
Fitzgerald, Walter 1896- *BiE&WWA, FilmgC, IntMPA 77, -75, -76, WhThe, WhoHol A, WhoThe 72*
Fitzgerald, Walter 1896-1976 *HalFC 80*
Fitzgibbon, Louis A d1961 *NotNAT B*
Fitzgibbons, Esme *Film 2*
Fitzhamon, Lewin 1869-1961 *IlWWBF[port]*
Fitzharris, Edward 1890-1974 *WhScrn 77, WhoHol B*
Fitzjames, Louise 1809- *CnOxB*
Fitzjames, Nathalie 1819- *CnOxB*
Fitzmaurice, George 1877-1963 *CnThe, McGEWD, ModWD, REnWD[port]*
Fitzmaurice, George 1885-1940 *CmMov, FilmgC, WhoHol B*
Fitzmaurice, George 1885-1941 *HalFC 80*
Fitzmaurice, George 1895-1940 *FilmEn, TwYS A, WhScrn 74, -77*
Fitzmaurice, Michael T 1908-1967 *WhScrn 74, -77, WhoHol B*
Fitzpatrick, Charlotte *Film 1*
Fitzpatrick, Horace Allgier 1934- *IntWWM 77, -80*
Fitzpatrick, James A 1902- *FilmgC, HalFC 80, IlWWBF, IntMPA 77, -75, -76, -78, -79, -80*
Fitzpatrick, Michael J 1863-1950 *AmSCAP 66*
Fitzpatrick, Noreen 1955- *IntWWM 80*
Fitzpatrick, Pat *WhoHol A*
Fitzpatrick, Sean Kevin 1941- *AmSCAP 80*
Fitzrandolph, Charles I 1921- *ConAmC*
Fitzroy, Emily 1861-1954 *Film 1, -2, ForYSC, TwYS, WhScrn 74, -77, WhoHol B*
Fitzroy, Louis *Film 1*
Fitzsimmons, Edith Dizon 1922- *IntWWM 80*
Fitzsimmons, Robert *Film 1*
Fitzthumb, Ignaz *NewGrD 80*
Fitzwilliam, Edward Francis 1824-1857 *NewGrD 80*
Fitzwilliam, Richard, Viscount 1745-1816 *Baker 78*
Fiume, Orazio 1908- *Baker 78*
Five, The *NewGrD 80*
Five Americans, The *RkOn 2[port]*
Five Blobs, The *RkOn*
Five Discs, The *RkOn[port]*
Five Du-Tones, The *RkOn*
Five Keys, The *RkOn[port]*
Five Man Electrical Band, The *RkOn 2[port]*
Five Pennies *BiDAmM*
Five Royales, The *RkOn[port]*

Five Satins, The *RkOn*
Five Stairsteps, The *RkOn 2[port]*
Fix, Paul 1901- *FilmEn, Film 2, TwYS*
Fix, Paul 1902- *FilmgC, ForYSC, HalFC 80, HolCA[port], IntMPA 77, -75, -76, -78, -79, -80, MovMk, Vers B[port], WhoHol A*
Fix, Ress 1893-1975 *WhScrn 77*
Fixman, Sydney 1933- *WhoMus 72*
Fizdale, Robert 1920- *Baker 78, NewGrD 80*
Fjelde, Rolf *NatPD[port]*
Fjeldstad, Oivin 1903- *IntWWM 77, -80, NewGrD 80, WhoMus 72*
Fjord, Olaf *Film 2*
Flaccomio, Giovanni Pietro 1565?-1617 *NewGrD 80*
Flack, Luise *WomWMM*
Flack, Michael John 1952- *AmSCAP 80*
Flack, Roberta 1939- *IlEncR*
Flack, Roberta 1940- *BiDAmM, DrBlPA, EncJzS 70, RkOn 2[port]*
Flackton, William 1709-1798 *Baker 78, NewGrD 80*
Flagello, Ezio 1931- *NewGrD 80*
Flagello, Ezio Domenico 1933- *WhoOp 76*
Flagello, Nicholas 1928- *AmSCAP 66, WhoMus 72*
Flagello, Nicolas 1928- *AmSCAP 80, Baker 78, CpmDNM 79, ConAmC, IntWWM 77, -80, NewGrD 80*
Flagg, Ann *BlkAmP*
Flagg, Fannie *WhoHol A*
Flagg, James Montgomery 1877-1960 *Film 1, WhScrn 77*
Flagg, Josiah 1737-1794 *BiDAmM*
Flagg, Josiah 1737-1795? *Baker 78, NewGrD 80*
Flagler, Isaac VanVleck 1842-1909 *BiDAmM*
Flagler, Isaac VanVleck 1844-1909 *Baker 78*
Flagler, Robert S 1890-1935 *AmSCAP 66*
Flagstad, Kirsten 1895-1962 *Baker 78, BiDAmM, BnBkM 80[port], CmOp, FilmgC, HalFC 80, MusMk, MusSN[port], NewEOp 71, NewGrD 80[port], WhScrn 74, -77, WhoHol B*
Flaherty, Pat J, Sr. 1903-1970 *ForYSC, WhScrn 74, -77, WhoHol B*
Flaherty, Patrick James 1954- *IntWWM 80*
Flaherty, Robert 1884-1951 *AmFD, BiDFilm, -81, DcFM, FilmgC, HalFC 80, IlWWBF A, MovMk[port], OxFilm, WomWMM, WorEFlm[port]*
Flaherty, Robert J 1884-1951 *FilmEn*
Flaiano, Ennio 1910- *OxFilm*
Flaiano, Ennio 1910-1972 *FilmEn*
Flaks, Stephen 1941- *IntMPA 80*
Flame, Ditra 1905- *What 5[port]*
Flament, Edouard 1880-1958 *Baker 78*
Flamin' Groovies, The *ConMuA 80A, IlEncR*
Flaming Ember, The *RkOn 2[port]*
Flamingos, The *RkOn[port]*
Flamm, Donald 1899- *BiE&WWA, NotNAT*
Flamma, Luca *Film 2*
Flammer, Harold 1889-1939 *Baker 78*
Flanagan, Bud *WhScrn 74, -77*
Flanagan, Bud 1896-1968 *EncMT, FilmEn, FilmgC, HalFC 80, IlWWBF, -A[port], NotNAT B, WhScrn 74, -77, WhThe, WhoHol B*
Flanagan, Edward J 1880-1925 *WhScrn 74, -77, WhoHol B*
Flanagan, Fionnuala *WhoHol A*
Flanagan, Hallie 1890-1969 *BiE&WWA, EncWT, Ent, NotNAT B, OxThe, PlP&P, WhThe*
Flanagan, Kellie *WhoHol A*
Flanagan, Ralph 1919- *AmSCAP 66, -80, BgBands 74[port], CmpEPM*
Flanagan, Rebecca 1876-1938 *WhScrn 74, -77*
Flanagan, Richard d1917 *NotNAT B, WhThe*
Flanagan, Thomas J, Jr. 1927- *ConAmC*
Flanagan, Tommy Lee 1930- *BiDAmM, CmpEPM, EncJzS 70*
Flanagan, William 1923-1969 *Baker 78, BiDAmM, ConAmC, NewGrD 80*
Flanagan, William 1926-1969 *DcCM*
Flanders, Ed 1934- *HalFC 80, NotNAT*
Flanders, Michael 1922-1975 *BiE&WWA, JoeFr, NotNAT B, OxThe, WhScrn 77, WhThe, WhoHol C, WhoMus 72, WhoThe 72*
Flanders, Michael And Donald Swann *JoeFr*
Flandrus, Arnoldus d1608? *NewGrD 80*
Flanigan, Laura Wilson 1926- *IntWWM 77, -80*
Flanigan, Robert Lee 1926- *AmSCAP 66, -80*
Flannery, Susan *HalFC 80, WhoHol A*
Flanz, Marta *WomWMM*
Flares, The *RkOn*
Flash Cadillac & The Continental Kids *RkOn 2[port]*
Flaster, Karl 1905-1965 *AmSCAP 66, -80*
Flateau, Georges 1882-1953 *NotNAT B, WhScrn 74, -77, WhoHol B*
Flato, Ludwig 1911- *AmSCAP 66, -80*
Flatow, Leon 1889-1944 *AmSCAP 66, -80*
Flatt, Ernest O 1918- *NewYTET, NotNAT*
Flatt, Lester Raymond 1914- *BiDAmM, CmpEPM, CounME 74[port], -74A, EncFCWM 69, IlEncCM[port]*
Flatt And Scruggs *CounME 74A, IlEncCM*
Flattery, Thomas L 1922- *IntMPA 77, -75, -76, -78, -79, -80*
Flaubert, Gustave 1821-1880 *EncWT, Ent, NewEOp 71*
Flaum, Harley 1945- *AmSCAP 80*
Flaum, Thea *WomWMM B*
Flavin, James 1906-1976 *FilmEn, FilmgC, ForYSC, HalFC 80, IntMPA 75, -76, MovMk, Vers B[port], WhoHol A*
Flavin, Martin 1883-1967 *BiE&WWA, CnMD, McGEWD, ModWD, NotNAT B, WhThe*
Flavio *OxThe*
Flax, Marty 1924-1972 *EncJzS 70*
Flaxland, Gustave-Alexandre 1821-1895 *Baker 78, NewGrD 80*
Flaxman, John P 1934- *IntMPA 77, -75, -76, -78, -79, -80*
Flay, Alfred Leonard 1905- *IntWWM 77, -80, WhoMus 72*
Fleagle, Brick 1906- *WhoJazz 72*
Fleagle, Jacob Roger 1906- *AmSCAP 80*
Fleay, Frederick Gard d1909 *NotNAT B*
Flecha, Mateo 1481-1553 *NewGrD 80*
Flecha, Mateo 1520?-1604 *OxMus*
Flecha, Mateo 1530?-1604 *Baker 78, NewGrD 80*
Flechtenmacher, Adolf 1823- *OxMus*
Flechtenmacher, Alexandru 1823-1898 *NewGrD 80*
Fleck, Charles S 1916- *AmSCAP 66, -80*
Fleck, Henry T 1863-1937 *Baker 78*
Fleck, Johann Friedrich Ferdinand 1757-1801 *EncWT, NotNAT B, OxThe*
Fleck, Sophie Louise 1777-1846 *EncWT*
Flecker, James Elroy 1884-1915 *CnThe, EncWT, McGEWD, NotNAT B, OxThe*
Fleckno, Richard d1678? *NewGrD 80*
Flecknoe, Richard d1678? *NewGrD 80*
Fleece, Marianne *IntWWM 77, -80*
Fleeson, Neville 1887-1945 *AmSCAP 66, -80*
Fleet, Edgar 1931- *WhoMus 72*
Fleet, Marlene 1942- *WhoMus 72*
Fleet, Thomas *OxMus*
Fleetcroft, J E 1920- *WhoMus 72*
Fleetwood, Charles d1745? *NotNAT B, OxThe, PlP&P*
Fleetwood, James 1935- *WhoOp 76*
Fleetwood, Susan 1944- *WhoThe 77*
Fleetwood Mac *ConMuA 80A[port], IlEncR[port], RkOn 2[port]*
Fleetwoods, The *AmPS A, RkOn[port]*
Flegg, Bruce *WhoMus 72*
Flegier, Ange 1846-1927 *Baker 78*
Fleigel, Gustaf *Film 2*
Fleischer, Anton 1891-1945 *Baker 78*
Fleischer, Dave 1894-1979 *AmSCAP 66, -80, FilmEn, HalFC 80, IntMPA 77, -75, -76, -78, -79, OxFilm, WorEFlm[port]*
Fleischer, David 1894-1979 *DcFM*
Fleischer, Friedrich Gottlob 1722-1806 *NewGrD 80*
Fleischer, Gerda 1920- *IntWWM 77, -80*
Fleischer, Leon 1928- *BiDAmM*
Fleischer, Max 1889- *DcFM, FilmEn, WorEFlm[port]*
Fleischer, Max 1889-1972 *OxFilm*
Fleischer, Max 1889-1973 *FilmgC, HalFC 80*
Fleischer, Oskar 1856-1933 *Baker 78, NewGrD 80, OxMus*
Fleischer, Richard 1916- *BiDFilm, -81, CmMov, DcFM, FilmEn, FilmgC, HalFC 80, IntMPA 77, -75, -76, -78, -79, -80, OxFilm, WhoHrs 80, WorEFlm[port]*
Fleischer, Robert 1902- *AmSCAP 80*
Fleischhacker, David 1933- *AmSCAP 66, -80*
Fleischhauer, Gunter 1928- *NewGrD 80*
Fleischman, David 1912- *AmSCAP 66, -80*
Fleischman, Harvey *IntMPA 75*
Fleischman, Maurice L d1963 *NotNAT B*
Fleischman, Stephen *NewYTET*
Fleischmann, Aloys Georg 1910- *IntWWM 77, -80, NewGrD 80, WhoMus 72*
Fleischmann, Ernest Martin 1924- *IntWWM 77, -80, WhoMus 72*
Fleischmann, Friedrich 1766-1798 *NewGrD 80*
Fleischmann, Harry 1899-1943 *WhScrn 74, -77, WhoHol B*
Fleischmann, Julius 1900-1968 *BiE&WWA, NotNAT B*
Fleischmann, Mort 1927- *IntMPA 75, -76*
Fleisher, Bud *NatPD[port]*
Fleisher, Edwin A 1877-1959 *Baker 78, NewGrD 80*
Fleisher, Leon 1928- *Baker 78, BnBkM 80, IntWWM 77, -80, MusSN[port], NewGrD 80*
Fleisher, Mark 1907- *AmSCAP 66*
Fleisher, Richard 1916- *MovMk[port]*
Fleisser, Marieluise 1901-1974 *CnMD, EncWT, Ent*
Fleitman, Alexander Oscar 1924- *AmSCAP 80*
Fleming, Alice 1882-1952 *NotNAT B, WhScrn 74, -77, WhoHol B*
Fleming, Amaryllis *IntWWM 77, -80, WhoMus 72*
Fleming, Sir Ambrose 1849-1945 *OxMus*
Fleming, Art *WhoHol A*
Fleming, Billy Conn 1941- *AmSCAP 80*
Fleming, Bob 1878-1933 *WhScrn 77*
Fleming, Brandon 1889- *WhThe*
Fleming, Bryant *FilmEn*
Fleming, Carroll *Film 2*
Fleming, Claude *Film 2*
Fleming, Conn 1941- *NatPD[port]*
Fleming, Eric d1966 *WhoHol B*
Fleming, Eric 1924-1966 *FilmgC, HalFC 80, WhoHrs 80[port]*
Fleming, Eric 1926-1966 *WhScrn 74, -77*
Fleming, Eric 1926-1967 *ForYSC*
Fleming, Erin *WhoHol A*
Fleming, George 1858-1938 *NotNAT B, WhThe*
Fleming, Ian 1888-1969 *FilmgC, HalFC 80, WhScrn 74, -77, WhThe, WhoHol B*
Fleming, Ian 1906-1964 *FilmgC, HalFC 80, WhoHrs 80*
Fleming, Louise *WomWMM B*
Fleming, Lucy 1947- *WhoThe 72, -77*
Fleming, Michael Paschal Marcon 1928- *IntWWM 77, WhoMus 72*
Fleming, Noel d1950 *NotNAT B*
Fleming, Paul 1609-1640 *NewGrD 80*
Fleming, Philip B *Film 2*
Fleming, Rhonda *IntMPA 77, -75, -76, -78, -79, -80, MotPP, WhoHol A*
Fleming, Rhonda 1922- *FilmgC, HalFC 80*
Fleming, Rhonda 1923- *BiDFilm, -81, FilmEn, ForYSC, MovMk[port], WorEFlm[port]*
Fleming, Robert *Film 1*
Fleming, Robert 1921-1976 *Baker 78, CreCan 1, DancEn 78, DcCM, NewGrD 80*
Fleming, Shari Beatrice *ConAmC*
Fleming, Shirley Moragne 1930- *IntWWM 77, -80*
Fleming, Susan 1909- *ThFT[port], WhoHol A*
Fleming, Tom 1927- *WhoThe 72, -77*
Fleming, Victor 1883-1949 *AmFD, BiDFilm, -81, DcFM, FilmEn, FilmgC, HalFC 80, MovMk[port], OxFilm, TwYS A, WhoHrs 80, WorEFlm*
Fleming, Victor Albert 1901- *IntWWM 77, -80, WhoMus 72*
Fleming, William d1921 *NotNAT B*
Flemming, Bill *NewYTET*
Flemming, Claude 1884-1952 *NotNAT B,*

WhThe
Flemming, Herb 1900- *WhoJazz 72*
Flemming, Jean Marilyn 1952- *IntWWM 77*
Flemming, Paul 1609-1640 *NewGrD 80*
Flemyng, Gordon 1934- *FilmgC, HalFC 80, IlWWBF, WhoHrs 80*
Flemyng, Robert 1912- *BiE&WWA, FilmEn, FilmgC, ForYSC, HalFC 80, IntMPA 77, -75, -76, -78, -79, -80, NotNAT, WhoHol A, WhoHrs 80, WhoThe 72, -77*
Flentrop, Dirk 1910- *NewGrD 80*
Flers, P L 1867-1932 *NotNAT B, WhThe*
Flers, Robert, Marquis De 1872-1927 *McGEWD, ModWD, NotNAT B, WhThe*
Flers, Robert De 1872-1927 *EncWT*
Flesch, Carl 1873-1944 *Baker 78, BnBkM 80, NewGrD 80*
Fleschelles *OxThe*
Fleta, Miguel 1893-1938 *Baker 78, CmOp, NewGrD 80, OxMus*
Fleta, Pierre 1925- *Baker 78, WhoOp 76*
Fletcher, Alice Cunningham 1838-1923 *Baker 78, BiDAmM, NewGrD 80, OxMus*
Fletcher, Allen 1922- *BiE&WWA, NotNAT, WhoThe 72, -77*
Fletcher, Archie 1890- *AmSCAP 66, -80*
Fletcher, Bramwell 1904- *FilmEn, Film 2, ForYSC, HalFC 80, WhoHol A, WhoHrs 80, WhoThe 72, -77*
Fletcher, Bramwell 1906- *BiE&WWA, NotNAT*
Fletcher, Branwell 1904- *FilmgC*
Fletcher, Cecil *Film 1*
Fletcher, Cyril 1913- *FilmgC, HalFC 80*
Fletcher, Delia 1940- *WhoMus 72*
Fletcher, Douglas 1884- *BiDAmM*
Fletcher, Dusty *BlksB&W C*
Fletcher, E Howard 1933- *WhoMus 72*
Fletcher, Eric 1933- *IntWWM 80*
Fletcher, Grant 1913- *AmSCAP 66, Baker 78, CpmDNM 72, -78, -79, -80, ConAmC*
Fletcher, H Grant 1913- *AmSCAP 80, CpmDNM 76, -77*
Fletcher, Jack *WhoHol A*
Fletcher, John *ConDr 77B*
Fletcher, John 1579-1625 *CnThe, EncWT, Ent, McGEWD[port], NotNAT A, -B, OxMus, OxThe, PlP&P[port], REnWD[port]*
Fletcher, John 1950- *CnOxB*
Fletcher, John Gould 1886-1950 *BiDAmM*
Fletcher, John Malcolm 1934- *WhoMus 72*
Fletcher, John Richard William 1941- *IntWWM 77, WhoMus 72*
Fletcher, Lawrence M 1902-1970 *WhScrn 74, -77, WhoHol B*
Fletcher, Lester *WhoHol A*
Fletcher, Louise 1934- *FilmEn*
Fletcher, Louise 1936- *HalFC 80, IntMPA 77, -78, -79, -80, WhoHol A*
Fletcher, Malcolm John 1955- *IntWWM 80*
Fletcher, Maria *NewGrD 80*
Fletcher, Percy 1879-1932 *Baker 78, NewGrD 80, NotNAT B, WhThe*
Fletcher, Peter G 1936- *IntWWM 80, WhoMus 72*
Fletcher, Robert 1923- *BiE&WWA, NotNAT, WhoOp 76, WhoThe 72, -77*
Fletcher, Shane 1951- *IntWWM 80*
Fletcher, Tex 1910- *AmSCAP 66, -80*
Fletcher, Tom 1873-1954 *NotNAT A*
Fletcher, Yvonne *WomWMM*
Fleu, Dorris Bell 1922-1955 *WhScrn 74, -77, WhoHol B*
Fleuret, Maurice 1932- *NewGrD 80*
Fleurie *NewGrD 80*
Fleury 1750-1822 *NotNAT A, -B, OxThe*
Fleury, Andre 1903- *Baker 78, NewGrD 80, WhoMus 72*
Fleury, Louis *OxMus*
Fleury, Louis 1878-1925 *Baker 78*
Fleury, Louis 1878-1926 *NewGrD 80*
Fleury, Nicolas 1630?-1678? *NewGrD 80*
Flexer, David 1909- *IntMPA 77, -75, -76, -78, -79, -80*
Flexmore, Richard 1824-1860 *CnOxB*
Flexner, Anne Crawford 1874-1955 *NotNAT B, WhThe*
Flick, Bob *EncFCWM 69*
Flick, Pat C 1899-1955 *WhScrn 74, -77, WhoHol B*
Flick-Flood, Dora *AmSCAP 66, ConAmC A, WhoMus 72*
Flickenschildt, Elisabeth 1905- *EncWT, Ent, FilmAG WE*
Flicker, Mike *ConMuA 80B*
Flicker, Theodore J 1929?- *FilmgC, HalFC 80*
Flicker, Theodore J 1930- *BiE&WWA, NewYTET, NotNAT, OxFilm, WorEFlm*
Fliegel, Mrs. Ernie d1966 *WhScrn 74, -77, WhoHol B*
Flier, Jaap 1934- *CnOxB, DancEn 78*
Flier, Jacob *NewGrD 80*
Flies, Bernhard *OxMus*
Flight, Benjamin 1767?-1847 *NewGrD 80*
Flight And Robson *OxMus*
Flimm, Florence *Film 1*
Flinch, Bob *PupTheA*
Flindell, Edwin Frederick 1926- *IntWWM 77, -80*
Flindt, Flemming 1936- *CnOxB, DancEn 78[port]*
Flindt, Vivi 1943- *CnOxB*
Flinn, Isobel 1939- *WhoMus 72*
Flinn, John C 1917- *IntMPA 77, -75, -76, -78, -79, -80*
Flint, Hazel 1893-1959 *WhScrn 74, -77, WhoHol B*
Flint, Helen 1898-1967 *WhScrn 74, -77, WhoHol B*
Flint, Joseph W 1893-1933 *WhScrn 74, -77*
Flint, Sam 1882- *ForYSC, Vers B[port]*
Flint, Shelby *RkOn*
Flint, Shirley H 1935- *IntWWM 77*
Flint-Shipman, Veronica 1931- *WhoThe 77*
Flintoft, Luke 1680?-1727 *NewGrD 80, OxMus*
Flippen, Jay C d1971 *MotPP, WhoHol B*
Flippen, Jay C 1898-1971 *CmpEPM, FilmgC, HalFC 80, HolCA[port], MovMk[port], Vers B[port], WhScrn 74, -77*
Flippen, Jay C 1899-1971 *CmMov, ForYSC*
Flippen, Jay C 1900-1971 *FilmEn*
Flipper d1971 *WhScrn 74, -77*
Flittner, Johannes 1618-1678 *NewGrD 80*
Fliyer, Yakov 1912-1977 *NewGrD 80*
Flo And Eddie *ConMuA 80A, IlEncR*
Floaters, The *RkOn 2[port]*
Flodin, Karl 1858-1925 *Baker 78, NewGrD 80*
Floersheim, Otto 1853-1917 *Baker 78*
Floersheimer, Albert, Jr. 1917- *IntMPA 77, -75, -76, -78, -79, -80*
Flohrs, Virginia *Film 2*
Flon, Suzanne 1923- *EncWT, FilmEn, WhoHol A*
Flood, Bernard 1907- *WhoJazz 72*
Flood, Grattan 1859-1928 *Baker 78*
Flood, James 1895-1953 *FilmEn, TwYS A*
Flood, John d1924 *NotNAT B*
Flood, Richard E 1932- *BiDAmM*
Flood, W H Grattan 1859-1928 *NewGrD 80*
Flood, William Henry Grattan 1859-1928 *OxMus*
Flood-Murphy, Pip 1933- *WhoOp 76*
Floquet, Etienne Joseph 1748-1785 *Baker 78, NewGrD 80*
Flor, Cesar Arrospide DeLa *NewGrD 80*
Flor, Christian 1626-1697 *NewGrD 80*
Flor, Samuel 1912- *IntWWM 77, -80*
Florath, Albert 1888-1957 *WhScrn 77*
Florath, Albert 1889-1957 *WhScrn 74*
Florczak, Kazimierz 1942- *IntWWM 77, -80*
Florea, John 1916- *IntMPA 77, -75, -76, -78, -79, -80*
Florei, Nicolae 1927- *WhoOp 76*
Florelle 1901-1974 *WhScrn 77*
Florelle, Odette *Film 2*
Floren, Myron 1919- *AmSCAP 66, -80*
Florence, Evangeline 1873-1928 *Baker 78*
Florence, Gordon Louis 1915- *AmSCAP 80*
Florence, Katherine *WhoStg 1908*
Florence, Robert C 1932- *BiDAmM*
Florence, William Jermyn 1831-1891 *FamA&A[port], NotNAT B, OxThe, PlP&P*
Florence, Mrs. William Jermyn 1831-1906 *NotNAT B, PlP&P*
Florentia, Franciscus De *NewGrD 80*
Florentius De Faxolis *NewGrD 80*
Flores, Alfonso *NewGrD 80*
Flores, Alonso *NewGrD 80*
Flores, Bernal 1937- *Baker 78*
Flores, Ignacio F 1934- *AmSCAP 66, -80*
Flores Dalcaraz, Alfonso *NewGrD 80*
Flores Dalcaraz, Alonso *NewGrD 80*
Flores Reyes, Rene Augusto 1924- *IntWWM 77, -80*
Floresco, Michel d1925 *WhScrn 77*
Floresta, Gabriele 1936- *WhoOp 76*
Florey, Robert 1900-1979 *BiDFilm, -81, CmMov, DcFM, FilmEn, Film 2, FilmgC, HalFC 80, MovMk[port], OxFilm, TwYS A, WhoHrs 80, WorEFlm*
Flori *NewGrD 80*
Flori, Francesco d1583 *NewGrD 80*
Flori, Francesco d1588 *NewGrD 80*
Flori, Franciscus d1583 *NewGrD 80*
Flori, Franciscus d1588 *NewGrD 80*
Flori, Franz d1583 *NewGrD 80*
Flori, Franz d1588 *NewGrD 80*
Flori, Georg 1558?-1594? *NewGrD 80*
Flori, Georgi 1558?-1594? *NewGrD 80*
Flori, Giorgio 1558?-1594? *NewGrD 80*
Flori, Giovanni *NewGrD 80*
Flori, Iohan *NewGrD 80*
Flori, Jacob *NewGrD 80*
Flori, Jacobus *NewGrD 80*
Flori, Jean *NewGrD 80*
Flori, Johann *NewGrD 80*
Flori, Johannes *NewGrD 80*
Florian, Ion 1929- *IntWWM 77, -80*
Florida Boys Quartet *BiDAmM*
Florida Playboys *BiDAmM*
Floridan *NewGrD 80*
Floridia, Pietro 1860-1932 *Baker 78, BiDAmM*
Florido De Silvestri *NewGrD 80*
Floridor 1608-1671 *EncWT, Ent*
Floridor 1608-1672 *OxThe*
Floridus De Sylvestris *NewGrD 80*
Florie, Martin *NewGrD 80*
Florii *NewGrD 80*
Florimi, Giovanni Andrea d1683 *NewGrD 80*
Florimo, Francesco 1800-1888 *Baker 78, NewGrD 80*
Florinda, La *NewGrD 80*
Florio *NewGrD 80*
Florio, Andrea Nicola 1927- *AmSCAP 80*
Florio, Caryl 1843-1920 *Baker 78, NewGrD 80*
Florio, Charles H d1820 *NewGrD 80*
Florio, Lawrence 1924- *WhoOp 76*
Florio, Pietro Grassi 1740?-1795 *NewGrD 80*
Florio, Zackie Cooper 1912- *AmSCAP 80*
Florius *NewGrD 80*
Floros, Constantin 1930- *IntWWM 77, -80, NewGrD 80*
Flory, Med 1926- *EncJzS 70*
Flory, Meredith 1926- *EncJzS 70*
Flory, Regine 1894-1926 *NotNAT B, WhThe*
Flosman, Oldrich 1925- *Baker 78, NewGrD 80*
Flosso, Al *PupTheA*
Flothuis, Marius Hendrikus 1914- *Baker 78, CpmDNM 76, -80, DcCM, IntWWM 77, -80, NewGrD 80*
Flotow, Friedrich, Freiherr Von 1812-1883 *DcCom&M 79, NewEOp 71, NewGrD 80*
Flotow, Friedrich Von 1812-1883 *Baker 78, BnBkM 80, CmOp, CmpBCM, DcCom 77, GrComp[port], MusMk, OxMus*
Flotzinger, Rudolf 1939- *NewGrD 80*
Flouker, Mack *Film 2*
Flour, Mireille Juiliette Antoinett 1906- *IntWWM 77, -80*
Flournoy, Roberta Jean 1927- *AmSCAP 80*
Flower, Alice *Film 2*
Flower, Sir Archibald d1950 *NotNAT B*
Flower, Eliza 1803-1846 *OxMus*
Flower, Sir Newman 1879-1964 *Baker 78, NewGrD 80*
Flowers, Bess 1900- *FilmEn, Film 2, ForYSC, HalFC 80, TwYS, WhoHol A*
Flowers, Dorothy 1909- *IntWWM 77*
Flowers, Mary *BluesWW*
Flowers, Tiger *BlksB&W C*
Flowerton, Consuelo 1900-1965 *WhScrn 74, -77, WhoHol B*
Flowler, Gene 1890-1960 *NotNAT B*
Floyd, Alfred Ernest 1877- *WhoMus 72*

Floyd, Alpha *WhoOp 76*
Floyd, Calvin James 1931- *AmSCAP 66, –80*
Floyd, Carlisle 1926- *AmSCAP 66, –80, Baker 78, BiDAmM, BnBkM 80, CompSN[port], CpmDNM 72, ConAmC, DcCM, NewEOp 71, NewGrD 80, OxMus*
Floyd, Eddie 1935- *BiDAmM, RkOn 2[port]*
Floyd, Frank 1908- *BluesWW[port]*
Floyd, Gwendolen d1950 *NotNAT B, WhThe*
Floyd, Henrietta *Film 2*
Floyd, John Morrison 1950- *IntWWM 77, –80, NewGrD 80*
Floyd, King 1945- *RkOn 2[port]*
Floyd, Max *ConMuA 80B*
Floyd, Monte Keene 1941- *CpmDNM 72*
Floyd, Samuel A, Jr. 1937- *IntWWM 77, –80*
Floyd, Stafford Marquette 1951- *AmSCAP 80*
Floyd, William J *AmSCAP 80*
Fluck, Alan Paul 1928- *IntWWM 77, –80*
Fludd, Robert 1574-1637 *NewGrD 80*
Flude, John *NewGrD 80*
Fluegel, Dale Edward 1931- *IntWWM 77*
Fluegel, Neal L 1937- *IntWWM 77, –80*
Fluellen, Joel *BlksB&W C, DrBlPA, WhoHol A*
Flugrath, Edna *Film 1*
Fluker, Mack *Film 2*
Flury, Richard 1896-1967 *Baker 78, NewGrD 80*
Flusser, Richard Stuart 1927- *WhoMus 72*
Fly, Fenton 1934- *IntWWM 77*
Fly, James Lawrence d1966 *NewYTET*
Flying Burrito Brothers *BiDAmM, ConMuA 80A, IlEncCM[port], IlEncR[port]*
Flying Machine, The *RkOn 2[port]*
Flynn, Allan 1894-1965 *AmSCAP 66, –80*
Flynn, Don *NatPD[port]*
Flynn, Edward F 1913- *AmSCAP 66*
Flynn, Edythe *Film 2*
Flynn, Elinor 1910-1938 *WhScrn 77*
Flynn, Emmett 1892-1937 *TwYS A*
Flynn, Emmett J 1892-1937 *FilmEn*
Flynn, Errol 1909-1959 *BiDFilm, –81, CmMov, FilmEn, FilmgC, ForYSC[port], HalFC 80[port], MotPP, MovMk[port], NotNAT B, OxFilm, WhScrn 74, –77, WhoHol B, WorEFlm*
Flynn, Frank 1900-1964 *AmSCAP 66, –80*
Flynn, George William 1937- *AmSCAP 80, ConAmC, IntWWM 77*
Flynn, Hazel E 1899-1964 *NotNAT B, WhScrn 74, –77, WhoHol B*
Flynn, Joe 1924-1974 *FilmEn, WhScrn 77, WhoHol B*
Flynn, Joe 1925-1974 *HalFC 80*
Flynn, Joe 1926- *ForYSC*
Flynn, John *FilmEn, HalFC 80, IntMPA 77, –75, –76, –78, –79, –80*
Flynn, M B Lefty *Film 2*
Flynn, Maurice 1876-1959 *Film 2, TwYS*
Flynn, Maurice B Lefty 1893-1959 *WhScrn 77*
Flynn, Maurice Lefty d1959 *WhoHol B*
Flynn, Rita *Film 2*
Flynn, Sean 1941-1970 *ForYSC, HalFC 80, MotPP*
Flynn, William George 1917- *IntWWM 77, –80*
Flynt, Henry Allen, III 1940- *ConAmC*
Fo, Dario 1926- *CroCD, EncWT, Ent[port]*
Foch, Dirk 1886-1973 *Baker 78, ConAmC*
Foch, Nina 1924- *BiE&WWA, FilmEn, FilmgC, ForYSC, HalFC 80, HolP 40[port], IntMPA 77, –75, –76, –78, –79, –80, MotPP, MovMk[port], NotNAT, WhoHol A, WhoHrs 80, WhoThe 72, –77*
Fock, Gerard VonBrucken *NewGrD 80*
Fockerod, Johann Arnold *NewGrD 80*
Focus *ConMuA 80A, IlEncR, RkOn 2[port]*
Fodi, John 1944- *Baker 78, IntWWM 80*
Fodor *NewGrD 80*
Fodor, Carolus Antonius 1768-1846 *NewGrD 80*
Fodor, Carolus Emanuel 1759- *NewGrD 80*
Fodor, Eugene 1950- *Baker 78*
Fodor, Josephine Mainvielle- 1789-1870 *NewGrD 80*
Fodor, Josephus Andreas 1751-1828 *NewGrD 80*
Fodor, Ladislaus 1898- *CnMD, WhThe*
Fodor-Mainvielle, Josephine 1789-1870 *CmOp, NewGrD 80*
Fody, Ilona 1920- *AmSCAP 66, –80*
Foeley, Cora Virginia *PupTheA*
Foerster, Adolph Martin 1854-1927 *Baker 78, BiDAmM*
Foerster, Christoph *NewGrD 80*
Foerster, Josef 1833-1907 *NewGrD 80*
Foerster, Josef Bohuslav 1859-1951 *Baker 78, MusMk, NewGrD 80[port], OxMus*
Foetisch, Charles 1838-1918 *NewGrD 80*
Fog, Dan 1919- *NewGrD 80*
Fogarty, Frank d1925 *NotNAT B*
Fogarty, J Paul 1893-1976 *AmSCAP 66, –80*
Fogarty, Jack V *IntMPA 77, –75, –76, –78, –79, –80*
Fogarty, Joseph R *NewYTET*
Fogazzaro, Antonio 1842-1911 *McGEWD*
Fogel, Johann Christoph *NewGrD 80*
Fogel, Maurice *MagIID*
Fogel, V P *Film 2*
Fogel, Vladimir *Film 2*
Fogelberg, Dan 1951- *IlEncR[port], RkOn 2[port]*
Fogelberg, Daniel Grayling 1951- *AmSCAP 80*
Fogell, Martin Maurice 1929- *IntWWM 77, –80, WhoMus 72*
Fogelman, Lou *ConMuA 80B*
Fogelson, Andrew 1942- *IntMPA 77, –75, –76, –78, –79, –80*
Fogelson, David 1903- *IntMPA 77, –75, –76, –78, –79, –80*
Fogerty, Elsie 1866-1945 *NotNAT A, –B, OxThe, WhThe*
Fogerty, John Cameron 1945- *AmSCAP 80, ConMuA 80A, IlEncR*
Fogg, Eric 1903-1939 *Baker 78, NewGrD 80, OxMus*
Foggia, Antonio 1650?-1707 *NewGrD 80*
Foggia, Enrico Radesca Di *NewGrD 80*
Foggia, Francesco 1604-1688 *Baker 78, NewGrD 80*
Foggin, Myers *WhoMus 72*
Foggy Mountain Boys *BiDAmM, EncFCWM 69*
Foghat *ConMuA 80A, IlEncR, RkOn 2[port]*
Fogle, George *PupTheA*
Foglesong, Jim *ConMuA 80B*
Fogliani, Jacopo 1468-1548 *NewGrD 80*
Fogliani, Lodovico d1539? *NewGrD 80*
Fogliani, Lodovico d1538 *Baker 78*
Fogliano Da Modena 1468-1548 *NewGrD 80*
Fogliano, Giacomo 1468-1548 *Baker 78, NewGrD 80*
Fogliano, Lodovico d1539? *NewGrD 80*
Fogwell, Reginald G *IlWWBF*
Foignet *NewGrD 80*
Foignet, Charles Gabriel 1750-1823 *NewGrD 80*
Foignet, Francois 1782-1845 *NewGrD 80*
Foignet, Jacques 1750-1823 *NewGrD 80*
Fokin, Mikhail 1880-1942 *NewGrD 80*
Fokina, Vera Petrovna 1886-1958 *CnOxB, DancEn 78*
Fokine, Michel 1880-1942 *DancEn 78[port], NotNAT B, WhThe*
Fokine, Mikhail Mikhailovich 1880-1942 *CnOxB, NewGrD 80*
Fokker, Adriaan Daniel 1887-1972 *NewGrD 80*
Fokkerod, Gottfried *NewGrD 80*
Fokkerod, Johann Arnold d1720? *NewGrD 80*
Folani, Femi *BlkAmP*
Folc De Marseille *NewGrD 80*
Foldes, Andor 1913- *Baker 78, IntWWM 77, –80, NewGrD 80, WhoMus 72*
Foldes, Imre 1934- *IntWWM 77, –80*
Foldi, Andrew Harry 1926- *WhoOp 76*
Folds, Charles Weston 1938- *EncJzS 70*
Folds, Chuck 1938- *EncJzS 70*
Foley, A J 1835-1899 *NewGrD 80*
Foley, Allan James 1835-1899 *Baker 78*
Foley, Betty 1933- *EncFCWM 69*
Foley, Clyde Julian 1910-1968 *BiDAmM*
Foley, Daniel 1952- *ConAmC*
Foley, David 1945- *ConAmC*
Foley, Elizabeth P *PupTheA*
Foley, George *Film 1, –2*
Foley, George F 1919- *IlWWBF[port], IntMPA 77, –75, –76, –78, –79, –80*
Foley, Joe d1955 *WhoHol B*
Foley, Joseph F 1910-1955 *WhScrn 74, –77*
Foley, Paul A 1902- *NotNAT*
Foley, Paul A 1905- *BiE&WWA*
Foley, Red 1910- *CounME 74A*
Foley, Red 1910-1968 *AmPS A, –B, CmpEPM, CounME 74, EncFCWM 69, IlEncCM[port], WhScrn 74, –77, WhoHol B*
Foley, Richard *EncFCWM 69*
Foley, Syd 1909- *AmSCAP 66, –80*
Folger, Henry Clay 1857-1930 *NotNAT B, OxThe*
Foli, A J 1835-1899 *NewGrD 80*
Folianus, Ludovicus *NewGrD 80*
Folianus, Ludovicus d1539? *NewGrD 80*
Foliot, Edme d1752? *NewGrD 80*
Folkenstein, Julius *Film 2*
Folkina, Vera d1958 *NotNAT B*
Follas, Ronald W 1946- *AmSCAP 80*
Follen, Eliza Lee Cabot 1787-1860 *BiDAmM*
Folley, Lawrence Aurelius 1929- *WhoOp 76*
Follis, Dorothy 1802-1923 *NotNAT B*
Follmer, Frank *PupTheA*
Follmer, Patricia *WomWMM B*
Folquet De Marseille 1150?-1231 *NewGrD 80*
Folsey, George *IntMPA 77, –75, –76, –78, –79, –80, WorEFlm*
Folsey, George J 1898- *FilmgC, HalFC 80*
Folsey, George J 1900- *CmMov, FilmEn*
Folsom, Frank M d1970 *NewYTET*
Folts, Martha Neary 1940- *IntWWM 77, –80*
Foltyn, Maria 1924- *IntWWM 77, –80*
Foltz, Willard *PupTheA*
Folville, Juliette Eugenie-Emilie 1870-1946 *Baker 78*
Folwell, Denis 1905-1971 *WhScrn 77, WhoHol B*
Folz, Hans 1440?-1513 *NewGrD 80, OxThe*
Fomeen, Basil 1902- *AmSCAP 66, –80*
Fomin, Evstignei 1761-1800 *Baker 78*
Fomin, Evstigney Ipatovich 1761-1800 *NewGrD 80*
Fomin, Evstigney Ivanovich 1761-1800 *MusMk*
Fomina, Nina Viktorovna 1937- *WhoOp 76*
Fominaya, Eloy 1925- *ConAmC*
Fominych, Lubov Nicolaevna 1952- *CnOxB*
Fonaroff, Nina 1914- *CmpGMD, CnOxB, DancEn 78*
Fonda, Henry 1905- *BiDFilm, –81, BiE&WWA, CmMov, Ent, FilmEn, FilmgC, ForYSC, HalFC 80, IntMPA 77, –75, –76, –78, –79, –80, MotPP, MovMk[port], NotNAT, OxFilm, PlP&P[port], WhoHol A, WhoThe 72, –77, WorEFlm[port]*
Fonda, Jane 1937- *BiDFilm, –81, BiE&WWA, FilmEn, FilmgC, ForYSC, HalFC 80, IntMPA 77, –75, –76, –78, –79, –80, MotPP, MovMk[port], NotNAT, –A, OxFilm, WhoHol A, WhoHrs 80[port], WhoThe 72, –77, WomWMM, WorEFlm*
Fonda, Jean-Pierre 1937- *IntWWM 77, –80, WhoMus 72*
Fonda, Peter *MotPP, WhoHol A*
Fonda, Peter 1939- *FilmEn, FilmgC, ForYSC, HalFC 80, IntMPA 77, –75, –76, –78, –79, –80, MovMk[port], OxFilm*
Fonda, Peter 1940- *BiDFilm, –81*
Fonda Family *NotNAT A*
Fong, Benson *ForYSC, WhoHol A*
Fong, Brian *WhoHol A*
Fong, Kam *WhoHol A*
Fongaard, Bjorn 1919- *Baker 78, IntWWM 77, –80*
Fongheto, Paolo 1572?-1630? *NewGrD 80*
Fonghetti, Paolo 1572?-1630? *NewGrD 80*
Fonghetto, Paolo 1572?-1630? *NewGrD 80*
Fons, DeLa *NewGrD 80*
Fonseca, Julio 1885-1950 *Baker 78, NewGrD 80*
Fonss, Olaf 1882-1949 *Film 1, WhScrn 74, –77*
Font, DeLa *NewGrD 80*
Font, Nydia E 1927- *IntWWM 77, –80*
Fontagnere, Guy Gaston 1924- *WhoOp 76*
Fontaine, Eddie *WhoHol A*
Fontaine, Frank *IntMPA 77, –75, –76, WhoHol A*
Fontaine, Jean DeLa *DcPup*

Fontaine, Joan 1917- *BiDFilm, -81, BiE&WWA, CmMov, FilmEn, FilmgC, ForYSC, HalFC 80, IntMPA 77, -75, -76, -78, -79, -80, MotPP, MovMk[port], OxFilm, ThFT[port], WhoHol A, WhoHrs 80, WomWMM, WorEFlm*
Fontaine, Lilian 1886-1975 *WhScrn 77, WhoHol C*
Fontaine, Pierre 1390?-1450? *NewGrD 80*
Fontaine, Tony 1927-1974 *WhScrn 77, WhoHol B*
Fontaine-Besson *NewGrD 80*
Fontan, Rodolfo 1932- *DancEn 78*
Fontana, Carl Charles 1928- *BiDAmM, EncJzS 70*
Fontana, Don Gifford 1931- *AmSCAP 80*
Fontana, Fabrizio 1620?-1695 *NewGrD 80*
Fontana, Giovanni Battista d1630? *NewGrD 80*
Fontana, Julian 1810-1865 *NewGrD 80*
Fontana, Vincenzo *NewGrD 80*
Fontana, Wayne & The Mindbenders *RkOn 2[port]*
Fontane, Theodor 1819-1898 *EncWT*
Fontane, Tony *AmSCAP 66*
Fontane Sisters *AmPS A, -B, RkOn*
Fontanelli, Alfonso 1557-1622 *Baker 78, MusMk, NewGrD 80*
Fontanne, Lynn *BiE&WWA, FilmEn, NotNAT, PlP&P[port], WhoHol A*
Fontanne, Lynn 1882- *ForYSC*
Fontanne, Lynn 1887- *CnThe, EncWT, Ent, FamA&A[port], Film 2, FilmgC, HalFC 80, NotNAT A, OxThe, ThFT[port]*
Fontanne, Lynn 1892- *WhoThe 72, -77*
Fonte, Nicolo d1647? *NewGrD 80*
Fontei, Nicolo d1647? *NewGrD 80*
Fonteijo, Giovanni *NewGrD 80*
Fonteio, Giovanni *NewGrD 80*
Fonteio, Nicolo d1647? *NewGrD 80*
Fontenay, Hugues De d1635? *NewGrD 80*
Fontenelle, Bernard LeBovier De 1657-1757 *OxThe*
Fontenla, Norma 1933-1971 *CnOxB, DancEn 78*
Fonteyn, Margot 1919- *CnOxB, DancEn 78[port], NewGrD 80, WhThe*
Fonteyns *NewGrD 80*
Fontijn, Jacqueline 1930- *NewGrD 80*
Fontrier, Gabriel 1918- *ConAmC*
Fontyn, Jacqueline 1930- *Baker 78, CpmDNM 75, IntWWM 77, -80*
Fonvizin, Denis 1745-1782 *CnThe, McGEWD, REnWD[port]*
Fonvizin, Denis 1745-1792 *Ent*
Fonvizin, Denis Ivanovich 1744-1792 *NotNAT B, OxThe*
Foo, Lee Tung d1966 *WhScrn 77*
Foo, Wing 1910-1953 *WhScrn 74, -77, WhoHol B*
Fook, Monte 1908-1933 *WhScrn 74, -77*
Foor, Morris Milton 1952- *IntWWM 77*
Foord, Stuart 1897- *WhoMus 72*
Foort, Reginald 1893- *NewGrD 80*
Foote, Arthur 1853-1937 *Baker 78, BiDAmM, BnBkM 80, CompSN[port], NewGrD 80, OxMus*
Foote, Courtenay d1925 *Film 1, -2, MotPP, TwYS*
Foote, Courteney d1925 *WhScrn 77*
Foote, George 1886-1956 *Baker 78, ConAmC*
Foote, Horton *BiE&WWA, ConDr 73, -77C, NotNAT, WhoThe 72, -77*
Foote, John Taintor d1950 *NotNAT B*
Foote, Lydia 1844-1892 *NotNAT B, OxThe*
Foote, Maria 1797?-1867 *OxThe*
Foote, Samuel 1720-1777 *EncWT, McGEWD, NotNAT A, -B, OxThe*
Foppa, Giuseppe 1760-1845 *NewGrD 80*
Foran, Arthur F 1912-1967 *WhScrn 74, -77*
Foran, Dick 1910-1979 *CmpEPM, FilmEn, FilmgC, ForYSC, HalFC 80, IlEncCM, IntMPA 77, -75, -76, -78, -79, WhoHol A, WhoHrs 80*
Foran, Richard 1910-1979 *MovMk*
Forberg, August Robert 1833-1880 *NewGrD 80*
Forbert, Samuel Stephen 1954- *AmSCAP 80*
Forbes, Athol d1917 *NotNAT B*
Forbes, Brenda 1909- *BiE&WWA, ForYSC, NotNAT, WhoHol A, WhoThe 72, -77*
Forbes, Bryan 1926- *BiDFilm, -81, CmMov, ConDr 73, -77A, FilmEn, FilmgC, ForYSC, HalFC 80, IlWWBF[port], -A, IntMPA 77, -75, -76, -78, -79, -80, MovMk[port], OxFilm, WhoHol A, WhoHrs 80, WorEFlm*
Forbes, Elliot 1917- *Baker 78, IntWWM 77, -80, NewGrD 80*
Forbes, Freddie 1895-1952 *WhThe*
Forbes, Gordon B *IntMPA 78, -79, -80*
Forbes, Henry 1804-1859 *Baker 78, NewGrD 80*
Forbes, James 1871-1938 *ModWD, NotNAT B, WhThe*
Forbes, Janet 1932- *IntWWM 77, -80, WhoMus 72*
Forbes, John *MorBAP*
Forbes, John d1675 *NewGrD 80, OxMus*
Forbes, John Douglas *PupTheA*
Forbes, Kenneth Keith 1892- *CreCan 2*
Forbes, Lou 1902- *AmSCAP 66, -80*
Forbes, Mary 1880-1974 *WhScrn 77, WhThe, WhoHol B*
Forbes, Mary 1882-1974 *HalFC 80*
Forbes, Mary 1883-1974 *FilmEn*
Forbes, Mary 1888-1964 *ForYSC*
Forbes, Mary Elizabeth 1880-1964 *Film 1, -2, FilmgC, MovMk, Vers A[port], WhScrn 74, -77, WhoHol B*
Forbes, Meriel 1913- *BiE&WWA, FilmgC, HalFC 80, NotNAT, WhoHol A, WhoThe 72, -77*
Forbes, Norman *Film 1*
Forbes, Norman 1858-1932 *WhThe*
Forbes, Patrick George Cran 1920- *WhoMus 72*
Forbes, Ralph d1951 *MotPP, WhoHol B*
Forbes, Ralph 1896-1951 *Film 2, ForYSC, TwYS, WhScrn 74, -77*
Forbes, Ralph 1902-1951 *FilmEn, FilmgC, HalFC 80, MovMk*
Forbes, Ralph 1905-1951 *NotNAT B, WhThe*
Forbes, Scott 1920- *ForYSC, HalFC 80, WhoHol A*
Forbes, Sebastian 1941- *IntWWM 77, -80, NewGrD 80, WhoMus 72*
Forbes, Watson 1909- *IntWWM 77, -80, WhoMus 72*
Forbes-Robertson, Beatrice 1883-1967 *WhThe*
Forbes-Robertson, Eric 1865-1935 *NotNAT B, OxThe*
Forbes-Robertson, Frank 1885-1947 *NotNAT B, WhThe*
Forbes-Robertson, Lady Gertrude *PlP&P*
Forbes-Robertson, Ian 1858-1936 *OxThe*
Forbes-Robertson, Jean 1905-1962 *EncWT, NotNAT B, OxThe, PlP&P, WhScrn 77, WhThe*
Forbes-Robertson, Sir Johnston 1853-1937 *CnThe, EncWT, Ent, FamA&A[port], Film 1, NotNAT A, -B, OxThe, PlP&P[port], WhScrn 74, -77, WhThe, WhoHol B, WhoStg 1906, -1908*
Forbes-Robertson, Norman 1858-1932 *NotNAT B*
Forbes-Robertson, Norman 1859-1932 *OxThe*
Forbush, Gladys *PupTheA*
Force, Floyd Charles 1876-1947 *WhScrn 74, -77, WhoHol B*
Forcer, Francis 1650?-1704? *NewGrD 80*
Forcheim, Johann Wilhelm *NewGrD 80*
Forchert, Arno 1925- *NewGrD 80*
Forchheim, Johann Wilhelm *NewGrD 80*
Forcroy LeNeveu *NewGrD 80*
Forcucci, Samuel L 1922- *ConAmC*
Ford, Aleksander 1908- *DcFM, FilmEn, OxFilm, WorEFlm*
Ford, Alexander 1908- *FilmgC, HalFC 80*
Ford, Anna Mae 1916- *IntWWM 77*
Ford, Anthony Dudley 1935- *IntWWM 80*
Ford, Arthur *Film 1*
Ford, Audrey *WhThe*
Ford, Barry *WhoHol A*
Ford, Benjamin Francis 1901- *BiDAmM*
Ford, Carl 1920- *AmSCAP 66, -80*
Ford, Cecil F 1911- *FilmgC, HalFC 80, IntMPA 77, -75, -76, -78, -79, -80*
Ford, Charles A 1908- *IntWWM 77, -80, OxFilm*
Ford, Clarence *Film 2*
Ford, Clebert *DrBlPA*
Ford, Clifford Robert 1947- *IntWWM 80*
Ford, Constance *BiE&WWA, FilmgC, ForYSC, MotPP, NotNAT, WhoHol A*
Ford, Constance 1929- *HalFC 80*
Ford, Daisy 1906-1959 *WhScrn 74, -77*
Ford, Delvin Allen 1948- *AmSCAP 80*
Ford, Denham Vincent 1921- *IntWWM 77, -80*
Ford, Derek 1932- *IlWWBF*
Ford, Dorothy 1923- *ForYSC, HalFC 80*
Ford, Ed E *WhThe*
Ford, Ernest 1858-1919 *Baker 78, NewGrD 80*
Ford, Ernest Bevil 1916- *AmSCAP 66, -80*
Ford, Ernest Jennings 1919- *AmSCAP 66, -80, BiDAmM*
Ford, Eugenie 1898-1940 *Film 1, -2*
Ford, Francis d1953 *MotPP, NotNAT B, WhoHol B, WomWMM*
Ford, Francis 1882-1953 *FilmEn, ForYSC, HolCA[port], TwYS, -A, Vers B[port], WhScrn 74, -77*
Ford, Francis 1883-1953 *Film 1, -2, FilmgC, HalFC 80*
Ford, Frank 1916- *BiE&WWA, NotNAT*
Ford, Frank B *NatPD[port]*
Ford, Frankie *RkOn*
Ford, Frederick W *NewYTET*
Ford, Geoffrey Thomas 1931- *WhoMus 72*
Ford, George 1879- *NotNAT*
Ford, Glenn 1916- *BiDFilm, -81, CmMov, FilmEn, FilmgC, ForYSC, HalFC 80, IntMPA 77, -75, -76, -78, -79, -80, MotPP, MovMk[port], OxFilm, WhoHol A, WorEFlm[port]*
Ford, Grace 1910?- *WhoHrs 80*
Ford, Harriet d1949 *NotNAT B, WhThe*
Ford, Harrison *HalFC 80, MotPP, WhoHol A*
Ford, Harrison 1884-1957 *NotNAT B, WhoHol B*
Ford, Harrison 1892-1957 *FilmEn*
Ford, Harrison 1892-1959 *Film 1, -2, TwYS*
Ford, Harrison 1894-1957 *WhScrn 74, -77*
Ford, Harrison 1942- *FilmEn*
Ford, Harry 1877- *WhThe*
Ford, Harry 1900-1971 *BiDAmM*
Ford, Helen *BiE&WWA, CmpEPM, EncMT, NotNAT, WhThe*
Ford, Henry 1878?-1919? *NewOrJ*
Ford, Herbert Eugene 1950- *AmSCAP 80*
Ford, Hugh *TwYS A*
Ford, James *Film 2*
Ford, Joan 1921- *AmSCAP 66, -80*
Ford, John *OxMus*
Ford, John d1963 *NotNAT B*
Ford, John 1586-1639? *CnThe, EncWT, Ent, McGEWD, NotNAT A, OxThe, PlP&P, REnWD[port]*
Ford, John 1586-1640? *NotNAT B*
Ford, John 1895-1973 *AmFD, BiDFilm, -81, CmMov, ConLC 16, DcFM, FilmEn, Film 1, -2, FilmgC, HalFC 80, MovMk[port], OxFilm, TwYS A, WhScrn 77, WorEFlm*
Ford, John Carter *PupTheA*
Ford, John Thomson 1829-1894 *NotNAT B, OxThe*
Ford, Mrs. L G *OxMus*
Ford, Lena Guilbert d1918 *BiDAmM*
Ford, Lori 1928- *AmSCAP 66, -80*
Ford, Marty 1900-1954 *WhScrn 74, -77*
Ford, Olive Elizabeth 1918- *AmSCAP 80*
Ford, Paul 1901-1976 *BiE&WWA, FilmEn, FilmgC, ForYSC, HalFC 80, MotPP, NotNAT, -B, WhoThe 72, -77*
Ford, Paul 1902- *MovMk[port]*
Ford, Peter Hilary 1931- *IntWWM 80*
Ford, Phil *Film 1*
Ford, Philip d1976 *Film 2, WhoHol C*
Ford, Powell I *AmSCAP 80*
Ford, Richard 1902- *IntWWM 77, -80, WhoMus 72*
Ford, Richard Allen 1954- *EncJzS 70*
Ford, Ricky 1954- *EncJzS 70*
Ford, Robben Lee 1951- *EncJzS 70*
Ford, Ross 1923- *ForYSC, WhoHol A*
Ford, Ruth 1920- *BiE&WWA, NotNAT, WhoHol A, WhoThe 72, -77*
Ford, Sherman, Jr. 1929- *AmSCAP 66, -80*
Ford, Tennessee Ernie 1919- *AmPS A, -B, AmSCAP 80, CmpEPM,*

CounME 74[port], -74A, EncFCWM 69, IlEncCM[port], IntMPA 77, -75, -76, -78, -79, -80, NewYTET, RkOn
Ford, Thomas 1580?-1648 *Baker 78, MusMk, NewGrD 80, OxMus*
Ford, Tom *AmSCAP 80*
Ford, Tony 1925- *IntMPA 77, -75, -76, -78, -79, -80*
Ford, Wallace d1966 *MotPP, WhoHol B*
Ford, Wallace 1897-1966 *FilmgC, HalFC 80, MovMk[port], WhoHrs 80*
Ford, Wallace 1898-1966 *BiE&WWA, FilmEn, HolCA[port], NotNAT B, WhThe*
Ford, Wallace 1899-1966 *ForYSC, Vers B[port], WhScrn 74, -77*
Ford, Whitey 1901- *CounME 74, EncFCWM 69*
Ford, Wyn Kelson 1927- *IntWWM 77, -80, WhoMus 72*
Forde, Eugene 1898- *FilmEn, Film 1, FilmgC, HalFC 80*
Forde, Eugenie 1898-1940 *Film 2, TwYS, WhScrn 77*
Forde, Florrie 1876-1940 *NotNAT B, OxThe, WhThe*
Forde, Hal d1955 *CmpEPM, Film 1, -2, NotNAT B, WhoHol B*
Forde, Joan Williams 1943- *IntWWM 77*
Forde, John *MorBAP*
Forde, Stanley H 1881-1929 *Film 2, WhScrn 77*
Forde, Stanley Hamilton 1878- *WhoStg 1908*
Forde, Victoria 1897-1964 *Film 1, WhScrn 77, WhoHol B*
Forde, Walter 1896- *FilmgC, HalFC 80*
Forde, Walter 1897- *FilmEn, Film 2, IlWWBF, -A*
Fordell, Erik Fritiof 1917- *Baker 78, IntWWM 80*
Fordin, Hugh G 1935- *BiE&WWA, NotNAT*
Fordred, Dorice 1902- *WhThe*
Foree, James Meldin 1917- *AmSCAP 80*
Foregger, Nicolai Mikhailovich 1892-1939 *CnOxB*
Foreigner *ConMuA 80A[port], IlEncR, RkOn 2[port]*
Foreman, Carl 1914- *BiDFilm, -81, CmMov, ConDr 73, -77A, DcFM, FilmEn, FilmgC, HalFC 80, IntMPA 77, -75, -76, -78, -79, -80, OxFilm, WorEFlm*
Foreman, Charles L 1949- *IntWWM 80*
Foreman, Edward Vaught 1937- *IntWWM 77*
Foreman, Jane *PupTheA*
Foreman, John *IntMPA 77, -75, -76, -78, -79, -80*
Foreman, Laura *CmpGMD*
Foreman, Milos 1932- *IntMPA 80*
Foreman, Richard 1937- *ConDr 73, -77*
Foreman, Thomas Elton 1918- *ConAmTC*
Forepaugh, Adam 1830-1890 *NotNAT B*
Forepaugh, John A d1895 *NotNAT B*
Forest *NewGrD 80*
Forest, Alan *Film 1*
Forest, Ann *Film 2*
Forest, Frank 1896-1976 *WhScrn 77*
Forest, Jean *Film 2*
Forest, Jean Kurt 1909-1975 *NewGrD 80*
Forest, Karl *Film 2*
Forest, Mark 1933- *FilmgC, ForYSC, HalFC 80, WhoHol A, WhoHrs 80*
Forest, Michael *WhoHol A*
Forest, Sally 1928- *ForYSC*
Forest City Joe *BluesWW[port]*
Forestelle, W H *Film 1*
Forester, C S 1899-1966 *FilmgC, HalFC 80*
Forestier, Mathurin *NewGrD 80*
Forestyn, Mathurin *NewGrD 80*
Foresythe, Reginald 1907-1958 *CmpEPM, NewGrD 80*
Forgach, Jozsef 1941- *CnOxB*
Forgay, Wenonnah *Film 2*
Forget, Florent 1918- *CreCan 1*
Fork, Gunter 1930- *IntWWM 77, -80*
Forkel, Johann Nicolaus 1749-1818 *NewGrD 80*
Forkel, Johann Nikolaus 1749-1818 *Baker 78, BnBkM 80, NewGrD 80, OxMus*
Forlong, Michael *IlWWBF*
Forman, David Jesse 1949- *AmSCAP 80*
Forman, Sir Denis 1917- *IntMPA 79, -80*
Forman, J Denis 1917- *IntMPA 77, -75, -76, -78*
Forman, Janet *WomWMM B*
Forman, Jeanne 1916- *IntWWM 77, -80*
Forman, Joanne 1934- *CpmDNM 76, -78, -79, ConAmC*
Forman, Joel *WhoHol A*
Forman, Justice Miles d1915 *NotNAT B*
Forman, Milos 1932- *BiDFilm, -81, DcFM, FilmEn, FilmgC, HalFC 80, IntMPA 77, -78, -79, MovMk[port], OxFilm, WorEFlm[port]*
Forman, Tom 1893-1926 *WhScrn 77*
Forman, Tom 1893-1938 *Film 1, -2, ForYSC, MotPP, TwYS, -A, WhoHol B*
Forman, William R 1913- *IntMPA 77, -75, -76, -78, -79, -80*
Formby, George *OxMus, WhThe*
Formby, George 1904-1961 *FilmAG WE, FilmEn, Film 1, IlWWBF[port], -A[port], OxFilm, WhScrn 74, -77, WhoHol B*
Formby, George 1905-1961 *FilmgC, HalFC 80, OxThe*
Forme, Nicolas 1567-1638 *NewGrD 80*
Formelis, Guilelmus 1541?-1582 *NewGrD 80*
Formelis, Wilhelmus 1541?-1582 *NewGrD 80*
Formellis, Guilelmus 1541?-1582 *NewGrD 80*
Formellis, Wilhelmus 1541?-1582 *NewGrD 80*
Formes, Carl, Jr. *Film 1*
Formes, Karl Johann 1815-1889 *Baker 78*
Formes, Karl Johann 1816-1889 *NewGrD 80*
Formes, Theodor 1826-1874 *Baker 78, NewGrD 80*
Formes DeVaraz, Carl 1810-1889 *BiDAmM*
Formica, Antonino 1575?-1638 *NewGrD 80*
Formica, Antonio 1575?-1638 *NewGrD 80*
Formschneider, Hieronymus d1556 *NewGrD 80*
Formschneider, Jeronimus d1556 *NewGrD 80*
Fornaci, Giacomo *NewGrD 80*
Fornarino, Il *NewGrD 80*
Fornaroli, Cia 1888-1954 *CnOxB, DancEn 78*
Fornella, Martha 1939- *WhoMus 72*
Forner, Christian 1610-1678 *NewGrD 80*
Fornerod, Aloys-Henri-Gerard 1890-1965 *Baker 78, NewGrD 80*
Fornes, Maria Irene 1930- *AmSCAP 80, ConDr 73, -77, DcLB 7, NotNAT*
Forni, Pietro Paolo *NewGrD 80*
Fornia, Rita d1922 *NotNAT B*
Fornia, Rita P Newman 1879-1922 *BiDAmM*
Fornia-Labey, Rita 1878-1922 *Baker 78*
Forns Y Cuadras, Jose 1898-1952 *NewGrD 80*
Fornuto, Donato Dominic 1931- *AmSCAP 80, ConAmC*
Foronda, Elena Isabel 1947- *IntWWM 77, -80*
Foroni, Jacopo 1825-1858 *Baker 78*
Forqueray *NewGrD 80*
Forqueray, Antoine 1671-1745 *Baker 78, NewGrD 80*
Forqueray, Jean-Baptiste 1699-1782 *NewGrD 80*
Forqueray, Michel 1681-1757 *NewGrD 80*
Forqueray, Nicolas-Gilles 1703-1761 *NewGrD 80*
Forquet, Philippe *WhoHol A*
Forrage, Stephen *OxMus*
Forrai, Katalin 1926- *IntWWM 77, -80*
Forrai, Miklos 1913- *IntWWM 77, -80*
Forrell, Gene 1915- *AmSCAP 80*
Forrest, Alan 1889-1941 *Film 1, -2, WhScrn 74, -77, WhoHol B*
Forrest, Allan 1889-1941 *MotPP, TwYS*
Forrest, Allen *Film 2*
Forrest, Ann 1897- *Film 1, -2, MotPP, TwYS*
Forrest, Anne 1897- *WhThe*
Forrest, Arthur 1859-1933 *Film 2, NewYTET, NotNAT B, WhoHol B*
Forrest, Belford 1878-1938 *WhScrn 74, -77, WhoHol B*
Forrest, Ben 1907- *AmSCAP 66*
Forrest, Chet *AmSCAP 80*
Forrest, Edwin 1806-1872 *CnThe, EncWT, Ent[port], FamA&A[port], NotNAT A, -B, OxThe, PlP&P[port]*
Forrest, Mrs. Edwin 1817-1891 *NotNAT B*
Forrest, Frederic *HalFC 80, IntMPA 77, -75, -76, -78, -79, -80*
Forrest, Fredric *WhoHol A*
Forrest, George 1915- *AmPS, AmSCAP 66, -80, BiE&WWA, CmpEPM, EncMT, NewCBMT, NotNAT, PopAmC SUP[port]*
Forrest, George And Wright, Robert *PopAmC SUP[port]*
Forrest, Hamilton 1901- *Baker 78, ConAmC*
Forrest, Helen 1918- *CmpEPM, WhoHol A*
Forrest, James Robert 1920- *EncJzS 70*
Forrest, Jimmy 1920- *CmpEPM, EncJzS 70*
Forrest, John R *AmSCAP 66*
Forrest, Sally 1928- *FilmEn, FilmgC, HalFC 80, MotPP, WhoHol A, WomWMM*
Forrest, Sam 1870-1944 *NotNAT A, -B, WhThe*
Forrest, Sidney 1918- *IntWWM 80*
Forrest, Stella B *PupTheA*
Forrest, Steve *IntMPA 75, -76, -78, -79, -80*
Forrest, Steve 1924- *FilmEn, FilmgC, HalFC 80, IntMPA 77, WhoHol A*
Forrest, Steve 1925- *ForYSC*
Forrest, Thomas *PlP&P*
Forrest, William *ForYSC, WhoHol A*
Forrestall, Thomas DeVany 1936- *CreCan 1*
Forrester, Frederick C d1952 *NotNAT B*
Forrester, Howard Wilson 1922- *BiDAmM*
Forrester, Hugh *AmSCAP 80*
Forrester, Jack d1963 *NotNAT B*
Forrester, Larry 1924- *IntMPA 77, -75, -76, -78, -79, -80*
Forrester, Leon *WhoMus 72*
Forrester, Maureen 1930- *Baker 78, BnBkM 80, IntWWM 77, -80, MusSN[port], NewGrD 80, WhoOp 76*
Forrester, Maureen 1931- *CreCan 2, WhoMus 72*
Forrester, Ross *PlP&P*
Fors, Nils Lennart 1932- *IntWWM 77*
Forsberg, Helen *ConAmTC*
Forsberg, Roland 1939- *IntWWM 77, -80*
Forsblom, Enzio 1920- *IntWWM 77, -80*
Forsell, Johan 1868-1941 *NewGrD 80*
Forsell, John 1868-1941 *Baker 78, NewEOp 71, NewGrD 80*
Forshay, Harold *Film 1*
Forsingdal, John 1930- *IntWWM 77*
Forsman, John Vaino 1924- *IntWWM 77, -80*
Forssell, Lars 1928- *CnMD, CroCD, McGEWD[port], REnWD[port]*
Forst, Judith Doris 1943- *WhoOp 76*
Forst, Rudolf 1900-1973 *AmSCAP 80, BiDAmM, ConAmC*
Forst, Willi 1903- *DcFM, FilmAG WE, Film 2, HalFC 80, OxFilm*
Forst, Willi 1903-1980 *FilmEn*
Forster *NewGrD 80*
Forster, Alban 1849-1916 *Baker 78*
Forster, August 1829-1897 *Baker 78*
Forster, Christoph 1693-1745 *NewGrD 80*
Forster, Dorothy 1884-1950 *AmSCAP 66*
Forster, Emanuel Aloys 1748-1823 *Baker 78, NewGrD 80*
Forster, Francis Michael 1907- *CreCan 2*
Forster, Friedrich 1895-1958 *CnMD, McGEWD*
Forster, Friedrich August 1829-1897 *NewGrD 80*
Forster, Georg 1510?-1568 *Baker 78, NewGrD 80*
Forster, Georg 1514-1568 *OxMus*
Forster, James Alderson 1818?-1886 *NewGrD 80*
Forster, John 1812-1876 *NotNAT B, OxThe*
Forster, John Charles Stirling 1915- *IntWWM 80, WhoMus 72*
Forster, John Marshall 1948- *AmSCAP 80*
Forster, John Wycliffe Lowes 1850-1938 *CreCan 1*
Forster, Josef *NewGrD 80*
Forster, Josef Bohuslav 1859-1951 *BnBkM 80, NewGrD 80*
Forster, Joseph 1833-1907 *Baker 78*
Forster, Kaspar 1616-1673 *NewGrD 80*
Forster, Laura Kathleen 1902- *IntWWM 77, -80, WhoMus 72*
Forster, Michael *CreCan 2*
Forster, Ralph *Film 1*
Forster, Robert *ForYSC, WhoHol A*
Forster, Robert 1941- *FilmEn, IntMPA 77, -75, -76, -78, -79, -80*
Forster, Robert 1942- *FilmgC, HalFC 80*

Forster, Rudolf 1884-1968 *FilmAG WE, NotNAT B, WhScrn 77, WhoHol B*
Forster, Rudolf 1885-1969 *Film 2*
Forster, Rudolph 1884-1968 *FilmgC, HalFC 80*
Forster, Sheila Mary Mathew 1918- *IntWWM 77*
Forster, Simon Andrew 1801-1870 *NewGrD 80*
Forster, Wilfred 1872-1924 *NotNAT B, WhThe*
Forster, Will *OxMus*
Forster, William 1739-1808 *NewGrD 80*
Forster, William 1764?-1824 *NewGrD 80*
Forster, William 1788-1824 *NewGrD 80*
Forster And Andrews *NewGrD 80*
Forster-Bovill, W B 1871- *WhThe*
Forsting, Jackie *ConMuA 80B*
Forsyne, Ida 1883- *BlksBF[port]*
Forsyth *NewGrD 80*
Forsyth, Algernon *NewGrD 80*
Forsyth, Bertram d1927 *NotNAT B*
Forsyth, Bruce 1921- *FilmgC*
Forsyth, Bruce 1927- *HalFC 80*
Forsyth, Bruce 1928- *WhoThe 72, -77*
Forsyth, Cecil 1870-1941 *AmSCAP 66, -80, Baker 78, ConAmC A, NewGrD 80, OxMus*
Forsyth, Henry d1885 *NewGrD 80*
Forsyth, James d1908 *NewGrD 80*
Forsyth, James 1913- *BiE&WWA, CnMD, ConDr 73, -77, ModWD, NotNAT*
Forsyth, James Alexander 1939- *IntWWM 80*
Forsyth, Josephine 1889-1940 *Baker 78*
Forsyth, Malcolm Denis 1936- *Baker 78, IntWWM 77, -80*
Forsyth, Matthew 1896-1954 *NotNAT B, WhThe*
Forsyth, Neil 1866-1915 *WhThe*
Forsyth, Rosemary 1943?- *ForYSC*
Forsyth, Rosemary 1944- *FilmEn, FilmgC, HalFC 80, WhoHol A*
Forsyth, W O 1863-1937 *NewGrD 80*
Forsythe, Blanche *IlWWBF*
Forsythe, Charles 1928- *BiE&WWA, NotNAT*
Forsythe, Henderson 1917- *BiE&WWA, NotNAT, WhoThe 72, -77*
Forsythe, John 1918- *BiE&WWA, FilmEn, FilmgC, ForYSC, HalFC 80, IntMPA 77, -75, -76, -78, -79, -80, MorBAP, MotPP, MovMk, NotNAT, WhoHol A, WhoThe 72, -77*
Forsythe, Mimi 1922-1952 *WhScrn 74, -77, WhoHol B*
Fort, Eleanor H 1914- *AmSCAP 66, -80*
Fort, Paul 1872-1960 *EncWT*
Fort, Syvilla 1917-1975 *DrBlPA*
Forte, Allen 1926- *NewGrD 80*
Forte, Chet *NewYTET*
Forte, Fabian 1940- *FilmEn, ForYSC, IntMPA 77, -75, -76, -78, -79, -80*
Forte, James 1936- *CpmDNM 75, -78, ConAmC*
Forte, Joe 1896-1967 *WhScrn 74, -77, WhoHol B*
Forte, Nicholas A 1938- *AmSCAP 80*
Forte, Rene *Film 2*
Forte, Wayne *ConMuA 80B*
Fortenberry, Martha Carolyn 1937- *IntWWM 77*
Fortepianov, Vasily *NewGrD 80*
Fortes, Paulo 1927- *WhoOp 76*
Fortescue, Miss 1862-1950 *WhThe*
Fortescue, John Henry 1923-1976 *BluesWW[port]*
Fortescue, Julia d1899 *NotNAT B*
Fortescue, Kenneth *MotPP*
Fortescue, May 1862-1950 *NotNAT B*
Fortescue, Viola d1953 *NotNAT B*
Fortescue, Virginia 1922- *WhoMus 72*
Fortgang, Jeffrey 1949- *AmSCAP 80*
Forti, Anton 1790-1859 *NewGrD 80*
Forti, Simone *CmpGMD*
Fortia DePiles, Alphonse, Comte De 1758-1826 *NewGrD 80*
Fortier, B *NewGrD 80*
Fortier, Herbert 1867-1949 *WhScrn 74, -77, WhoHol B*
Fortier, Monique *WomWMM*
Fortin, Marc-Aurele 1888-1970 *CreCan 2*
Fortini, James 1926- *AmSCAP 80*
Fortini, James Timothy Peter 1958- *AmSCAP 80*
Fortis, Johnny 1913- *AmSCAP 66, -80*
Fortlage, Karl 1806-1881 *Baker 78*
Fortner, Clarke 1904- *AmSCAP 80*
Fortner, Jack 1935- *CpmDNM 77, ConAmC*
Fortner, Wolfgang 1907- *Baker 78, CmOp, CompSN[port], CpmDNM 80, CnOxB, DancEn 78, DcCM, IntWWM 77, -80, NewEOp 71, NewGrD 80[port], OxMus, WhoMus 72*
Fortsch, Johann Philip 1652-1732 *OxMus*
Fortsch, Johann Philipp 1652-1732 *NewGrD 80*
Fortunate, Lou M 1938- *AmSCAP 80*
Fortunati, Gian Francesco 1746-1821 *NewGrD 80*
Fortunato, Andrew, III 1951- *IntWWM 77, -80*
Fortunatus, Venantius 530-609 *OxMus*
Fortunatus, Venantius 540?-600? *NewGrD 80*
Fortune, Edmund 1863-1939 *WhScrn 77*
Fortune, George *WhoOp 76*
Fortune, Joe *AmSCAP 80*
Fortune, Nigel 1924- *NewGrD 80*
Fortune, Sonny 1939- *EncJzS 70*
Fortune, Wallace 1884-1926 *WhScrn 74, -77*
Fortunes, The *RkOn 2[port]*
Fortuny, Mariano 1871-1949 *OxThe*
Forzano, Giovacchino 1883-1970 *CmOp*
Forzano, Giovacchino 1884-1970 *CnMD, ModWD*
Fosby, Anders Julius 1905- *IntWWM 80*
Foscarini, Giovanni Paolo *NewGrD 80*
Fosco, Piero *FilmEn, OxFilm*
Foscolo, Ugo 1778-1827 *McGEWD[port]*
Fosdick, Dudley 1902-1957 *CmpEPM, WhoJazz 72*
Fosdick, Harry Emerson 1878-1969 *BiDAmM*
Fosdick, William Whiteman 1825-1862 *BiDAmM*
Foshay, Harold A 1884-1953 *WhScrn 74, -77, WhoHol B*
Foss, Ardeen J 1916- *IntWWM 77*
Foss, Darrell *Film 1*
Foss, George R 1859-1938 *NotNAT B, WhThe*
Foss, Harlan S 1941- *WhoOp 76*
Foss, Hubert James 1899-1953 *Baker 78, NewGrD 80, OxMus*
Foss, Kenelm 1885-1963 *Film 1, -2, IlWWBF*
Foss, Lukas 1922- *AmSCAP 66, Baker 78, BiDAmM, BnBkM 80, CompSN[port], CpmDNM 80, ConAmC, DcCom&M 79, DcCM, IntWWM 77, -80, MusMk, NewEOp 71, NewGrD 80, OxMus, WhoMus 72*
Fossa, Johannes De 1540?-1603 *NewGrD 80*
Fossa, Pietro Da *NewGrD 80*
Fossato, Giovanni Battista *NewGrD 80*
Fosse, Bob *ConDr 77D, IntMPA 75, -76, WhoHol A*
Fosse, Bob 1925- *OxFilm, WorEFlm*
Fosse, Bob 1927- *BiDFilm, -81, BiE&WWA, CmMov, CnOxB, DancEn 78, EncMT, FilmEn, FilmgC, ForYSC, HalFC 80, IntMPA 77, -78, -79, -80, MovMk[port], NotNAT, WhoThe 72, -77*
Fosse, Bunty 1916- *Film 2*
Fosser, Per E 1939- *WhoOp 76*
Fossey, Brigitte 1945- *FilmgC, HalFC 80, WhoHol A*
Fossey, Brigitte 1946- *FilmEn*
Fossis, Pietro De d1527? *NewGrD 80*
Foster, Abbey 1900-1962 *NewOrJ[port]*
Foster, Al 1924- *AmSCAP 66, -80*
Foster, Alex 1953- *BlkAmP, EncJzS 70, MorBAP*
Foster, Allan K *Film 2*
Foster, Anne Katharine 1915- *WhoMus 72*
Foster, Anthony 1926- *IntWWM 77, -80, WhoMus 72*
Foster, Arnold 1896-1963 *NewGrD 80*
Foster, Arnold Wilfrid Allen 1898-1963 *OxMus*
Foster, Barry 1931- *FilmgC, HalFC 80, WhoHol A, WhoHrs 80, WhoThe 72, -77*
Foster, Basil S 1882-1959 *NotNAT B, WhThe*
Foster, Beryl 1944- *IntWWM 80*
Foster, Buddy *WhoHol A*
Foster, Charles W 1948- *AmSCAP 80*
Foster, Chuck 1912- *BgBands 74, CmpEPM*
Foster, Claiborne 1896- *WhThe*
Foster, Darby *Film 2*
Foster, David 1929- *ConMuA 80B, IntMPA 77, -76, -78, -79, -80, NewYTET*
Foster, Diane 1928- *ForYSC*
Foster, Dianne 1928- *FilmEn, FilmgC, HalFC 80, MotPP, WhoHol A*
Foster, Donald 1889-1969 *WhScrn 74, -77, WhoHol B*
Foster, Donald Herbert 1934- *IntWWM 77, -80*
Foster, Dorothy 1930- *ConAmC, IlWWBF*
Foster, Dude 1890?-1958? *NewOrJ*
Foster, Dudley 1925-1973 *WhScrn 77, WhoHol B*
Foster, Dudley 1935- *ConAmC, IntWWM 77, -80*
Foster, Earl 1902?- *NewOrJ*
Foster, Edna *Film 1*
Foster, Edward 1876-1927 *WhThe*
Foster, Elizabeth *OxMus*
Foster, Fay 1886-1960 *AmSCAP 66, Baker 78, BiDAmM, ConAmC*
Foster, Frances 1924- *DrBlPA, WhoHol A*
Foster, Frank Benjamin 1928- *AmSCAP 66, -80, BiDAmM, CmpEPM, EncJzS 70*
Foster, Fred *ConMuA 80B*
Foster, Gary 1936- *EncJzS 70*
Foster, George 1915- *WhoJazz 72*
Foster, George Murphy 1892-1969 *BiDAmM, EncJzS 70, NewOrJ[port]*
Foster, Geronimo Baqueiro *NewGrD 80*
Foster, Gloria 1936- *DrBlPA, NotNAT, WhoHol A, WhoThe 77*
Foster, Greg *MorBAP*
Foster, Helen 1907- *Film 2, ForYSC, TwYS, WhoHol A*
Foster, Ivor Reginald 1904- *WhoMus 72*
Foster, J Morris 1882-1966 *Film 1, WhScrn 77, WhoHol B*
Foster, Jerry Gaylon 1935- *AmSCAP 80*
Foster, Jim *BluesWW*
Foster, Jodie *WhoHol A*
Foster, Jodie 1962- *HalFC 80, IntMPA 77, -78, -79, -80, WhoHrs 80*
Foster, Jodie 1963- *FilmEn*
Foster, John d1677 *NewGrD 80*
Foster, Julia *WhoHol A*
Foster, Julia 1941- *FilmgC, HalFC 80*
Foster, Julia 1942- *IlWWBF[port], WhoThe 72, -77*
Foster, Julia 1944- *IntMPA 77, -75, -76, -78, -79, -80*
Foster, Kemp *IntMPA 78*
Foster, Lawrence 1941- *Baker 78, BiDAmM, IntWWM 77, -80, MusSN[port], NewGrD 80*
Foster, Lawrence Jerome 1909- *AmSCAP 66, -80*
Foster, Lawrence T 1941- *WhoOp 76*
Foster, Leroy 1923-1958 *BluesWW[port]*
Foster, Lewis 1898-1974 *AmSCAP 66*
Foster, Lewis 1899-1974 *HalFC 80*
Foster, Lewis 1900- *FilmgC*
Foster, Lewis R 1900-1974 *FilmEn*
Foster, Lillian d1949 *NotNAT B*
Foster, Linda *ForYSC*
Foster, Maurice David *IntMPA 77, -75, -76, -78, -79, -80*
Foster, May *Film 2*
Foster, Megan 1898- *WhoMus 72*
Foster, Muriel 1877-1937 *Baker 78, NewGrD 80*
Foster, Myles Birket 1851-1922 *Baker 78*
Foster, Norman 1900-1976 *BiDFilm, -81, FilmEn, Film 2, FilmgC, ForYSC, HalFC 80, IntMPA 75, -76, MovMk, NewYTET, WhThe, WhoHol A, WorEFlm*
Foster, Paul 1931- *ConDr 73, -77, NatPD[port], WhoThe 77*
Foster, Paul Alexander 1953- *EncJzS 70*
Foster, Paula Hartford 1944- *AmSCAP 80*
Foster, Phil 1913- *JoeFr[port], WhoHol A*
Foster, Phoebe 1896- *WhThe*
Foster, Pops 1892-1969 *CmpEPM, EncJzS 70, WhoJazz 72*
Foster, Preston d1970 *MotPP, WhoHol B*
Foster, Preston 1900-1970 *AmSCAP 66, -80, WhScrn 74, -77, WhoHrs 80*
Foster, Preston 1901-1970 *FilmgC,*

HalFC 80[port], HolP 30[port]
Foster, Preston 1902-1970 FilmEn, ForYSC, MovMk[port]
Foster, Robert Estill 1939- AmSCAP 80, ConAmC, IntWWM 77, -80
Foster, Robert Ivan 1918- IntWWM 77, -80, WhoMus 72
Foster, Ron WhoHol A
Foster, Rudolph 1884-1968 WhScrn 74
Foster, Sidney 1917-1977 Baker 78
Foster, Stephen Collins 1826-1864 AmPS, Baker 78, BiDAmM, DcCom 77, FilmgC, HalFC 80, MusMk[port], NewGrD 80, NotNAT B, OxMus, PlP&P, PopAmC[port], Sw&Ld A
Foster, Stuart 1918- CmpEPM
Foster, Susanna 1924- FilmEn, FilmgC, ForYSC, HalFC 80, HolP 40[port], MotPP, MovMk, What 3[port], WhoHol A
Foster, Thomas William, Jr. 1922- IntWWM 77, -80
Foster, Warren 1904- AmSCAP 66, -80
Foster, Will J 1890-1960 ConAmC
Foster, William Patrick 1919- IntWWM 77
Foster, Willie 1888- NewOrJ
Foster, Willie 1922- BluesWW
Foster, Willy 1922- BluesWW
Foster, Zena WomWMM B
Foster Kemp, Cecil R IntMPA 77, -75, -76, -79, -80
Fote, Richard Joseph 1932- AmSCAP 80
Fotek, Jan 1928- Baker 78, IntWWM 80, NewGrD 80
Foti, Jacques 1924- AmSCAP 66, -80
Fotin, Larry 1911- AmSCAP 66, -80
Fotinakis, Dorothy Owens 1912- AmSCAP 80
Fotinakis, Lawrence Constantine 1911- AmSCAP 80
Fotine, Dorothy AmSCAP 80
Fou, Sen DcFM
Fou, Ts'ong 1934- IntWWM 77, -80, NewGrD 80, WhoMus 72
Foucault, Henry NewGrD 80
Fouche, Earl 1903- NewOrJ
Foucquet NewGrD 80
Foucquet, Antoine d1708 NewGrD 80
Foucquet, Antoine d1740? NewGrD 80
Foucquet, Pierre d1735? NewGrD 80
Foucquet, Pierre-Claude 1694?-1772 NewGrD 80
Fougerat, Tony 1900- NewOrJ
Fougers, Pierre d1922 WhScrn 74, -77
Fougez, Anna 1895-1966 WhScrn 74, -77
Fougstedt, Nils-Eric 1910-1961 Baker 78, NewGrD 80
Fougt, Henric 1720-1782 NewGrD 80
Fougt, Henry 1720-1782 NewGrD 80
Foulds, John Herbert 1880-1939 Baker 78, NewGrD 80, OxMus
Foulger, Byron d1970 MotPP, WhoHol B
Foulger, Byron 1899-1970 Vers A[port]
Foulger, Byron 1900-1970 FilmgC, HalFC 80, HolCA[port], WhScrn 74, -77, WhoHrs 80[port]
Foulger, Byron 1902?- ForYSC
Foulger, Dorothy 1904- WhoMus 72
Foulis, David 1710-1773 NewGrD 80
Foulk, Robert ForYSC, WhoHol A
Foundas, George 1924- FilmEn
Foundations, The RkOn 2[port]
Fountain, Arthur WhoMus 72
Fountain, Pete 1930- CmpEPM, EncJzS 70, NewOrJ[port]
Fountain, Peter Dewey, Jr. 1930- BiDAmM, EncJzS 70
Fountaine, William Film 2
Fountaine, William E BlksB&W, -C
Fouque, Octave 1844-1883 NewGrD 80
Fouques Duparc, Henri NewGrD 80
Fouquet NewGrD 80
Four Aces, The AmPS A, -B, RkOn
Four Brothers BiDAmM
Four Coins, The RkOn[port]
Four Deuces, The RkOn
Four Esquires, The RkOn
Four Fellows, The RkOn
Four Freshmen, The CmpEPM, RkOn
Four Graduates BiDAmM
Four Guys BiDAmM
Four Jacks & A Jill RkOn 2[port]
Four Knights, The RkOn
Four Lads, The AmPS A, -B, RkOn[port]
Four Lovers, The RkOn
Four Preps, The AmPS A, RkOn
Four Seasons, The AmPS A, -B, BiDAmM, ConMuA 80A, IlEncR[port], RkOn[port], -2[port]
Four Sounds BiDAmM
Four Tops, The BiDAmM, ConMuA 80A, IlEncR, RkOn 2[port]
Four Tunes, The AmPS A, RkOn
Four Voices, The RkOn[port]
Fourdrain, Felix 1880-1923 Baker 78
Fourestier, Louis 1892-1976 Baker 78, NewGrD 80, WhoMus 72
Fouret, Maurice 1888-1962 Baker 78
Fourie, David Gerhardus 1944- IntWWM 80
Fourmy, Ruth 1922- WhoMus 72
Fourneaux, J B Napoleon 1808-1846 NewGrD 80
Fournet, Jean 1913- NewGrD 80, WhoMus 72, WhoOp 76
Fournier, Claude 1931- CreCan 1
Fournier, Emile-Eugene-Alix 1864-1897 Baker 78
Fournier, Jean 1911- IntWWM 77, -80, NewGrD 80, WhoMus 72
Fournier, Pierre 1906- Baker 78, BnBkM 80, IntWWM 77, -80, MusSN[port], NewGrD 80, WhoMus 72
Fournier, Pierre-Simon 1712-1768 Baker 78, NewGrD 80
Fournier, Vernal Anthony 1928- BiDAmM
Fouse, Sarah Baird 1935- IntWWM 77, -80
Fouts, Tom C 1918- AmSCAP 66, -80, BiDAmM
Fowke, Philip Francis 1950- IntWWM 77, -80
Fowler, Art 1902-1953 WhScrn 74, -77
Fowler, Brenda 1883-1942 WhScrn 74, -77, WhoHol B
Fowler, Bruce 1947- EncJzS 70
Fowler, Charles Bruner 1931- IntWWM 77, -80
Fowler, Francis Norman 1930- IntWWM 77, -80
Fowler, Gene HalFC 80
Fowler, Gene, Jr. HalFC 80, WhoHrs 80
Fowler, Gertrude d1935 NotNAT B
Fowler, Giles Merrill 1934- ConAmTC
Fowler, Harry 1926- FilmgC, ForYSC, HalFC 80, IlWWBF, IntMPA 77, -75, -76, -78, -79, -80, PupTheA, WhoHol A
Fowler, Hugh 1904?-1975 HalFC 80
Fowler, J Film 2
Fowler, Jennifer 1939- IntWWM 77, -80, NewGrD 80
Fowler, John NewGrD 80
Fowler, John C 1869-1952 WhScrn 77
Fowler, Keith 1939- NotNAT
Fowler, Marje 1917- ConAmC
Fowler, Marjorie WomWMM
Fowler, Rex March 1947- AmSCAP 80
Fowler, Richard d1643 OxThe
Fowler, Wally 1917- BiDAmM, IlEncCM
Fowler, William L 1917- BiDAmM, EncJzS 70
Fowler, William Randolph 1922- AmSCAP 66, -80
Fowles, Glenys Rae IntWWM 77, -80, WhoOp 76
Fowley, Douglas 1911- FilmEn, FilmgC, ForYSC, HalFC 80, HolCA[port], IntMPA 77, -75, -76, -78, -79, -80, MovMk, Vers A[port], WhoHol A
Fowley, Kim 1942- ConMuA 80B, IlEncR
Fowlie, Wallace 1908- BiE&WWA, NotNAT
Fowlkes, Charles Baker 1916- BiDAmM, EncJzS 70
Fowlkes, Charlie 1916- EncJzS 70
Fox, Alan Hugo 1934- IntWWM 77, -80
Fox, Alice PupTheA
Fox, Ancella M 1847-1920 BiDAmM
Fox, Arnim LeRoy 1910- IlEncCM
Fox, Barbara B WomWMM B
Fox, Barry ConMuA 80B
Fox, Baynard Layne 1932- AmSCAP 80
Fox, Bernard WhoHol A
Fox, Beryl 1931- CreCan 2, WomWMM
Fox, Carol 1926- NewGrD 80, WhoOp 76
Fox, Charles ForYSC, HalFC 80
Fox, Charles 1921- WhoMus 72
Fox, Charles 1940- ConAmC
Fox, Charles Kemble 1833-1875 OxThe
Fox, Charles Warren 1904- Baker 78, NewGrD 80
Fox, Charlotte 1860-1916 Baker 78
Fox, Curly And Texas Ruby IlEncCM
Fox, Della AmPS B
Fox, Della May 1870-1913 BiDAmM
Fox, Della May 1871-1913 NotNAT B, WhThe
Fox, Della May 1872-1913 WhoStg 1906, -1908
Fox, Dick ConMuA 80B
Fox, Don ConMuA 80B
Fox, Douglas Gerard Arthur 1893- WhoMus 72
Fox, Edward 1937- FilmEn, FilmgC, HalFC 80, IlWWBF, IntMPA 78, -79, -80, MovMk, WhoHol A
Fox, Felix 1876-1947 Baker 78, ConAmC
Fox, Frances PupTheA
Fox, Franklyn 1894-1967 WhScrn 74, -77, WhoHol B
Fox, Fred 1884-1949 WhScrn 77
Fox, Fred 1931- ConAmC
Fox, Frederick 1910- BiE&WWA, NotNAT, WhThe, WhoThe 72
Fox, Frederick Alfred 1931- AmSCAP 80, CpmDNM 76
Fox, George 1624-1691 OxMus
Fox, George Washington Lafayette 1825-1877 NotNAT B, OxThe
Fox, Glory M 1918- AmSCAP 66
Fox, Harry 1882-1959 AmPS B, CmpEPM, Film 1, NotNAT B, WhScrn 74, -77, WhoHol B
Fox, Inez 1942- RkOn
Fox, Irwin NewYTET
Fox, J Bertram 1881-1946 AmSCAP 66, -80
Fox, James 1939- FilmAG WE, FilmEn, FilmgC, ForYSC, HalFC 80, IlWWBF, IntMPA 77, -75, -76, -78, -79, -80, MovMk[port], WhoHol A
Fox, Janet WhoHol A
Fox, John, Jr. Film 2
Fox, John Richard 1927- CreCan 1
Fox, John Victor 1929- IntWWM 77, -80, WhoMus 72
Fox, Josephine 1877-1953 WhScrn 77
Fox, Jules Lee 1916- AmSCAP 80
Fox, Kenneth Thomas WhoMus 72
Fox, Leland Stanford 1931- IntWWM 77, -80
Fox, Lucy Film 2
Fox, Mary Film 2
Fox, Matthew d1964 NewYTET
Fox, Maxine 1943- NotNAT
Fox, Mrs. Milligan OxMus
Fox, Oscar J 1879-1961 AmSCAP 66, -80, ConAmC
Fox, Ray Errol AmSCAP 80, NatPD[port]
Fox, Reginald Film 2
Fox, Robert ConMuA 80B
Fox, Robin 1913-1971 WhThe
Fox, Rose 1899-1966 WhScrn 77, WhoHol B
Fox, Roy 1901- NewGrD 80
Fox, Roy 1902?- CmpEPM
Fox, Sam 1882-1971 BiDAmM, NewGrD 80
Fox, Sidney 1910-1942 HalFC 80, NotNAT B, ThFT[port], WhScrn 74, -77, WhThe, WhoHol B
Fox, Sidney 1911-1942 ForYSC
Fox, Stuart d1951 NotNAT B
Fox, Virgil 1912- Baker 78, BnBkM 80, MusSN[port], NewGrD 80, WhoMus 72
Fox, Virginia Film 2
Fox, Wallace 1895- TwYS A
Fox, Wallace 1895-1958 FilmEn, WhoHrs 80
Fox, Wallace 1898-1958 HalFC 80
Fox, Walter Kent 1947- AmSCAP 80
Fox, Wilbur Film 2
Fox, Will H 1858- WhThe
Fox, William 1879-1952 DcFM, FilmEn, FilmgC, HalFC 80, OxFilm, WorEFlm
Fox, William 1911- WhoThe 72, -77
Fox, William Price 1926- MorBAP
Fox Strangways, A H 1859-1948 NewGrD 80
Fox-Strangways, Arthur Henry 1859-1948 Baker 78, OxMus
Foxe, Earle MotPP
Foxe, Earle 1888- TwYS

Foxe, Earle 1889- *ForYSC*
Foxe, Earle 1891- *Film 1, -2*
Foxell, Maurice F *OxMus*
Foxley, Frederick Sydney Robert 1912- *IntWWM 77*
Foxwell, Ivan 1914- *FilmgC, HalFC 80, IntMPA 77, -75, -76, -78, -79, -80*
Foxworth, Robert *IntMPA 77, -78, -79, -80*
Foxx, Inez 1942- *DrBlPA*
Foxx, Red 1922- *IntMPA 77, -75, -76, -78, -79, -80*
Foxx, Redd 1922- *DrBlPA, HalFC 80, JoeFr[port], WhoHol A*
Foy, Bryan 1895-1977 *HalFC 80*
Foy, Bryan 1896-1977 *FilmEn*
Foy, Bryan 1900- *FilmgC, IntMPA 77, -75, -76*
Foy, Charles *WhoHol A*
Foy, Eddie *AmPS B*
Foy, Eddie 1854-1928 *CmpEPM, EncMT, Film 1, FilmgC, HalFC 80, JoeFr, WhScrn 74, -77, WhThe, WhoHol B, WhoStg 1906, -1908*
Foy, Eddie 1856-1928 *BiDAmM, NotNAT A, -B, OxThe*
Foy, Eddie, III *ForYSC, WhoHol A*
Foy, Eddie, Jr. 1905- *CmpEPM, EncMT, FilmEn, FilmgC, ForYSC, HalFC 80, WhoHol A, WhoThe 72, -77*
Foy, Eddie, Jr. 1910- *BiE&WWA, Film 2, NotNAT*
Foy, Mary *Film 2, WhoHol A*
Foy, Patricia 1929- *IntWWM 77*
Foy, Richard d1947 *NotNAT B*
Foyer, Eddie 1883-1934 *WhScrn 74, -77, WhoHol B*
Foys, Seven Little *Film 1*
Frabizio, William V 1929- *ConAmC*
Fracassi, Americo 1880-1936 *Baker 78*
Fracassi, Elmerico 1874-1930 *Baker 78*
Fracassini, Aloisio Lodovico 1733-1798 *NewGrD 80*
Fracci, Carla 1936- *CnOxB, DancEn 78[port]*
Frackenpohl, Arthur Roland 1924- *AmSCAP 66, -80, Baker 78, CpmDNM 74, -80, ConAmC*
Fradetal, Marcel 1908- *WorEFlm*
Fradkin, Fredric 1892-1963 *Baker 78*
Fradkin, Leslie Martin 1951- *AmSCAP 80*
Fradkin, Mark Grigoryevich 1914- *IntWWM 77, -80*
Fraemcke, August 1870-1933 *Baker 78*
Fraenkel, Wolfgang 1897- *Baker 78, ConAmC*
Fraganza, Trixie *Film 2*
Frager, Malcolm 1935- *Baker 78, BnBkM 80, IntWWM 77, -80, NewGrD 80, WhoMus 72*
Fragson, Harry 1869-1913 *OxThe*
Fraieli, Loreto 1910- *AmSCAP 80*
Frajt, Ludmila 1919- *IntWWM 77, -80*
Fraker, William A 1923- *FilmEn, FilmgC, HalFC 80, IntMPA 77, -76, -78, -79, -80, WorEFlm*
Fralick, Freddie 1888-1958 *WhScrn 74, -77, WhoHol B*
Frame, Floyd Earl 1929- *IntWWM 77*
Framer, Walt 1908- *IntMPA 77, -75, -76, -78, -79, -80, NewYTET*
Framer, Walter H 1908- *AmSCAP 66, -80*
Framery, Nicolas Etienne 1745-1810 *Baker 78, NewGrD 80*
Frampton, Peter 1950- *AmSCAP 80, ConMuA 80A[port], IlEncR[port], RkOn 2[port]*
Franc, Guillaume d1570 *OxMus*
Franc, Martin Le *NewGrD 80*
Franc, Tugomir 1935- *WhoOp 76*
Franca, Celia 1921- *CnOxB, CreCan 1, DancEn 78*
Franca, Eurico Nogueira 1913- *NewGrD 80*
Franca Junior, Joaquin Jose Da *OxThe*
Francais, Jacques Pierre 1923- *NewGrD 80*
Francaix, Jean 1912- *Baker 78, BnBkM 80, CompSN[port], CpmDNM 80, CnOxB, DancEn 78, IntWWM 77, -80, MusMk, NewEOp 71, NewGrD 80, OxMus*
France, Alexis 1906- *WhThe*
France, Anatole 1844-1924 *DcPup, NewEOp 71, PlP&P[port], WhThe*
France, C V 1868-1949 *FilmgC, HalFC 80, WhoHol B*
France, Charles Vernon 1868-1949 *NotNAT B, WhScrn 74, -77, WhThe*
France, Rachel 1936- *NotNAT*
France, Richard 1930- *BiE&WWA, NotNAT*
France, Richard 1938- *DcLB 7[port], NatPD[port]*
France-Ellys *WhThe*
Francen, Victor 1888-1977 *FilmAG WE, FilmEn, Film 2, FilmgC, ForYSC, HalFC 80, HolCA[port], IntMPA 77, -75, -76, -78, MovMk, Vers B[port], WhoHol A*
Frances, Esteban 1915- *CnOxB, DancEn 78*
Frances, Paula 1924- *AmSCAP 66, -80*
Frances Delribarren, Juan 1698-1767 *NewGrD 80*
Francescatti, Rene 1902- *NewGrD 80*
Francescatti, Zino 1902- *Baker 78, IntWWM 77, -80, MusSN[port], NewGrD 80, WhoMus 72*
Francescatti, Zino 1905- *BnBkM 80*
Franceschi *NewGrD 80*
Franceschi, Francesco d1599? *NewGrD 80*
Franceschi, Giovan Antonio De' *NewGrD 80*
Franceschi, M *Film 2*
Franceschini, Petronio 1650?-1680 *NewGrD 80*
Franceschini, Romulus 1929- *AmSCAP 80, ConAmC*
Francesci, Paul *Film 2*
Francesco Canova Da Milano 1497-1543 *NewGrD 80*
Francesco Da Barberino 1264-1348 *NewGrD 80*
Francesco Da Milano *NewGrD 80*
Francesco Da Parigi 1497-1543 *NewGrD 80*
Francesco Degli Organi *NewGrD 80*
Francesco Fiamengo *NewGrD 80*
Francesco Milanese *NewGrD 80*
Francesco Varoter *NewGrD 80*
Francesconi, Renato 1934- *WhoOp 76*
Francesina *NewGrD 80*
Franceur, Francois 1698-1787 *OxMus*
Francey, Bill *Film 2*
Franchere, Joseph Charles 1866-1921 *CreCan 2*
Franchetti, Alberto 1860-1942 *Baker 78, MusMk, NewGrD 80, OxMus*
Franchetti, Arnold 1906- *ConAmC*
Franchetti, Jean-Pierre 1944- *CnOxB*
Franchetti, Raymond 1921- *CnOxB*
Franchi, Franco 1922- *FilmAG WE*
Franchi, Giovanni Pietro d1731 *NewGrD 80*
Franchi, Sergio *WhoHol A*
Franchi-Verney, Giuseppe Ippolito 1848-1911 *Baker 78*
Franchina, Sandra *WomWMM*
Franchini, Anthony Joseph 1898- *AmSCAP 66, -80*
Franchini, Francesco d1757 *NewGrD 80*
Franchini, Franco d1757 *NewGrD 80*
Franchisena, Cesar Mario 1923- *IntWWM 77, -80*
Franchois LeBertoul *NewGrD 80*
Franchois, Johannes *NewGrD 80*
Franchomme, Auguste-Joseph 1808-1884 *Baker 78, NewGrD 80, OxMus*
Franci, Benvenuto 1891- *NewGrD 80*
Franci, Carlo 1927- *NewGrD 80, WhoOp 76*
Francine, Anne 1917- *BiE&WWA, NotNAT, WhoHol A*
Franciolini, Gianni 1910-1960 *DcFM*
Franciolini, Leopoldo 1844-1920 *NewGrD 80*
Franciosa, Anthony 1928- *BiE&WWA, FilmEn, FilmgC, HalFC 80, IntMPA 77, -75, -76, -78, -79, -80, MotPP, MovMk[port], NotNAT, WhoHol A*
Franciosa, Tony 1928- *ForYSC*
Francis *FilmgC*
Francis I *NewGrD 80*
Francis, Albert 1894- *NewOrJ*
Francis, Alec B d1934 *ForYSC*
Francis, Alec B 1857-1934 *Film 1, -2, TwYS, WhScrn 74, -77, WhoHol B*
Francis, Alec B 1864?-1934 *HalFC 80*
Francis, Alec B 1869-1934 *FilmEn*
Francis, Alfred 1909- *WhoThe 72, -77*
Francis, Alma *Film 2*
Francis, Alun 1943- *IntWWM 80*
Francis, Anne *IntMPA 77, -75, -76, -78, -79, -80, MotPP, WhoHol A*
Francis, Anne 1930- *FilmEn, ForYSC, HalFC 80, MGM[port], MovMk*
Francis, Anne 1932- *FilmgC, WhoHrs 80[port]*
Francis, Anne 1934- *WorEFlm*
Francis, Annette 1928- *AmSCAP 66, -80*
Francis, Arlene 1908- *BiE&WWA, FilmgC, ForYSC, HalFC 80, IntMPA 77, -75, -76, -78, -79, -80, NewYTET, NotNAT, WhoHol A, WhoThe 72, -77*
Francis, Arlene 1912- *FilmEn*
Francis, Art *AmSCAP 80*
Francis, Bennie *AmSCAP 80*
Francis, Coleman 1919-1973 *WhScrn 77*
Francis, Connie 1938- *AmPS A, -B, AmSCAP 66, -80, BiDAmM, FilmEn, FilmgC, ForYSC, HalFC 80, IntMPA 77, -75, -76, -78, -79, -80, MotPP, RkOn[port], WhoHol A*
Francis, David A 1918- *EncJzS 70*
Francis, Derek 1923- *DcPup, HalFC 80*
Francis, Doris 1903- *WhThe*
Francis, Edna *NewOrJ*
Francis, Eugene *WhoHol A*
Francis, Eva *Film 2*
Francis, Freddie 1917- *DcFM, FilmEn, FilmgC, HalFC 80, IlWWBF, IntMPA 77, -75, -76, -78, -79, -80, WhoHrs 80[port]*
Francis, Freddie 1918- *WorEFlm*
Francis, Hannah Mary 1945- *IntWWM 77, -80*
Francis, Harry 1908- *IntWWM 77, -80, WhoMus 72*
Francis, Ivor *WhoHol A*
Francis, J O d1956 *NotNAT B*
Francis, James *NewGrD 80*
Francis, John 1908- *WhoMus 72*
Francis, Kay d1968 *MotPP, WhoHol B*
Francis, Kay 1899-1968 *FilmgC, HalFC 80, OxFilm*
Francis, Kay 1903-1968 *CmMov, FilmEn, MovMk[port], ThFT[port], WhScrn 74, -77, WorEFlm*
Francis, Kay 1905-1968 *ForYSC, WhThe*
Francis, Kay 1906-1968 *BiDFilm, -81, Film 2*
Francis, Kenneth 1936- *WhoOp 76*
Francis, Kenneth 1938- *IntWWM 77, -80*
Francis, Kevin 1944- *IntMPA 77, -75, -76, -78, -79, -80*
Francis, Kevin 1948?- *WhoHrs 80*
Francis, Lee *AmSCAP 80*
Francis, M E d1930 *NotNAT B, WhThe*
Francis, Martha *Film 2*
Francis, Michael Frank 1950- *AmSCAP 80*
Francis, Noel *ThFT[port]*
Francis, Olin 1892-1952 *Film 2, WhScrn 74, -77*
Francis, Panama 1918- *DrBlPA, EncJzS 70, WhoJazz 72*
Francis, Paul P 1911- *AmSCAP 66, -80*
Francis, Peter J *WhoMus 72*
Francis, Robert 1930-1955 *FilmgC, ForYSC, HalFC 80, MotPP, NotNAT B, WhScrn 74, -77, WhoHol B*
Francis, Sarah Janet *IntWWM 77, -80, WhoMus 72*
Francis, Seseen 1937- *AmSCAP 66, -80*
Francis, William *NewGrD 80*
Francis, Wilma *WhoHol A*
Francis Day And Hunter *NewGrD 80*
Franciscello *NewGrD 80*
Francischello *NewGrD 80*
Francisci, Jan 1691-1758 *NewGrD 80*
Francisco DeNovo Portu *NewGrD 80*
Francisco, Betty 1900-1950 *Film 2, TwYS, WhScrn 74, -77, WhoHol B*
Francisco, Manuel *AmSCAP 80*
Francisco, Maurine Elise Moore 1929-1978 *BlkWAB[port]*
Franciscus Cecus Horghanista DeFlorentia *NewGrD 80*
Franciscus DeFlorentia *NewGrD 80*
Franciscus Venetus *NewGrD 80*
Franciscus, James 1934- *FilmEn, FilmgC, ForYSC, HalFC 80, IntMPA 77, -75, -76, -78, -79, -80, MotPP, WhoHol A, WhoHrs 80*
Franciscus, Magister *NewGrD 80*
Francisque, Anthoine 1575?-1605 *NewGrD 80*
Francisque, Antoine 1575?-1605 *NewGrD 80*
Franck, Cesar 1822-1890 *Baker 78,*

BnBkM 80[port], CmpBCM, CnOxB, DcCom 77[port], DcCom&M 79, GrComp[port], MusMk[port], NewEOp 71, NewGrD 80[port], OxMus
Franck, Eduard 1817-1893 Baker 78, NewGrD 80, OxMus
Franck, Georges 1926- IntWWM 80
Franck, Hans d1964 NotNAT B
Franck, Hans 1879-1963? ModWD
Franck, Johann 1618-1677 NewGrD 80
Franck, Johann Wolfgang 1644-1710? Baker 78, MusMk, NewGrD 80
Franck, Johannes NewGrD 80
Franck, Joseph 1820-1891 OxMus
Franck, Joseph 1825-1891 Baker 78
Franck, Melchior 1579-1639 Baker 78, NewGrD 80
Franck, Michael 1609-1677 NewGrD 80
Franck, Richard 1858-1938 Baker 78
Franck, Salomo 1659-1725 NewGrD 80
Franck, Salomon 1659-1725 NewGrD 80
Franck, Sebastian NewGrD 80
Francke, August Hermann 1663-1727 NewGrD 80
Francke, Donald Max 1929- IntWWM 77, -80, WhoMus 72
Francke, Salomo 1659-1725 NewGrD 80
Francke, Salomon 1659-1725 NewGrD 80
Franckenstein, Clemens Von 1875-1942 Baker 78
Francks, Don 1932- FilmgC, HalFC 80, WhoHol A
Franco Of Cologne Baker 78, NewGrD 80, OxMus
Franco Of Paris NewGrD 80
Franco, Clare J ConAmC
Franco, Debra WomWMM B
Franco, Enrique 1920- NewGrD 80
Franco, Fernando 1532-1585 NewGrD 80
Franco, Hernando 1532-1585 NewGrD 80
Franco, Jesus WhoHrs 80
Franco, Johan 1908- Baker 78, ConAmC, DcCM, IntWWM 77, -80, NewGrD 80, WhoMus 72
Franco, Marilia 1924?- DancEn 78
Franco, Rodolfo 1890-1954 DancEn 78
Franco Primus NewGrD 80
Francoeur NewGrD 80
Francoeur, Francois 1698-1787 Baker 78, MusMk, NewGrD 80
Francoeur, Joseph 1662?-1741? NewGrD 80
Francoeur, Louis 1692-1745 NewGrD 80
Francoeur, Louis-Joseph 1738-1804 Baker 78, NewGrD 80
Francois I 1494-1547 NewGrD 80
Francois DeValois 1494-1547 NewGrD 80
Francois, Andree Paulette 1938- WhoOp 76
Francois, Charles Film 2
Francois, Samson 1924-1970 Baker 78, NewGrD 80
Francoise Et Dominique CnOxB
Franconero, Constance AmSCAP 80
Franconi, Antoine 1738-1836 Ent
Francour, Charles Harvey 1947- AmSCAP 80
Francus De Insula NewGrD 80
Francy, Paul 1927- IntWWM 77, -80, WhoMus 72, WhoOp 76
Frandero CreCan 2
Frandsen, Edite 1914- CnOxB
Frandsen, Per Kynne 1932- IntWWM 77, -80
Franey, Agnes Film 2
Franey, Billy 1885-1940 WhoHol B
Franey, William 1885-1940 Film 1, -2, WhScrn 74, -77
Frangkiser, Carl 1894- AmSCAP 66, -80, ConAmC A
Franjo, H R G 1933- IntWWM 77, -80
Franju, George 1912- WorEFlm
Franju, Georges 1912- BiDFilm, -81, DcFM, FilmEn, FilmgC, HalFC 80, MovMk[port], OxFilm, WhoHrs 80
Frank NewGrD 80
Frank, Alan Clifford 1910- Baker 78, IntWWM 77, -80, NewGrD 80, OxMus
Frank, Alcide 1875-1942 NewOrJ
Frank, Andrew 1946- CpmDNM 78, -79, ConAmC
Frank, Arlyne 1930- BiE&WWA
Frank, Barry NewYTET
Frank, Bernice Film 2
Frank, Bruno 1887-1945 CnMD, EncWT, McGEWD, ModWD, NotNAT B, WhThe
Frank, Bruno 1887-1946 OxThe
Frank, Camilla Mays 1899- AmSCAP 66, -80
Frank, Carl 1909-1972 WhScrn 77, WhoHol B
Frank, Charles 1910- FilmgC, HalFC 80
Frank, Christian J 1890-1967 Film 2, WhScrn 77
Frank, Claude 1925- Baker 78, BnBkM 80, IntWWM 77, -80, NewGrD 80, WhoMus 72
Frank, David Michael 1948- AmSCAP 80
Frank, Erik 1915- IntWWM 77
Frank, Ernst 1847-1889 Baker 78, NewGrD 80
Frank, Evelyn Lucy 1945- IntWWM 77, -80
Frank, Fred ConMuA 80B
Frank, Frederic M 1911- IntMPA 75
Frank, Fredric M 1911- CmMov, HalFC 80, IntMPA 77, -76
Frank, George AmSCAP 80
Frank, Gilbert 1870?-1933 NewOrJ
Frank, Harriet FilmgC, HalFC 80, WomWMM
Frank, Harriet, Jr FilmEn
Frank, Herbert Film 1, -2
Frank, Horst 1929- FilmAG WE
Frank, J L 1900-1952 BiDAmM, EncFCWM 69, IlEncCM
Frank, Jacob Film 2
Frank, Jean Forward 1927- ConAmC
Frank, Johann NewGrD 80
Frank, Johnny BluesWW
Frank, Kathro PupTheA
Frank, Leonhard 1882-1961 CnMD, McGEWD[port], ModWD
Frank, Marcel Gustave 1906- AmSCAP 80
Frank, Marcel Gustave 1909- AmSCAP 66, CpmDNM 80, ConAmC
Frank, Mary K 1911- BiE&WWA, NotNAT
Frank, Melvin IntMPA 77, -75, -76, -78, -79, -80
Frank, Melvin 1913- FilmEn, WorEFlm
Frank, Melvin 1917- FilmgC, HalFC 80
Frank, Michael NewGrD 80
Frank, Rene 1910-1965 AmSCAP 66, -80, ConAmC A
Frank, Reuven NewYTET
Frank, Robert 1924- WorEFlm
Frank, Robert E 1943- ConAmC
Frank, Ruth Verd 1899-1977 AmSCAP 66, -80
Frank, Salomon NewGrD 80
Frank, Sandy NewYTET
Frank, T David 1944- NotNAT
Frank, Will 1880-1925 Film 2, WhoHol B
Frank, William 1880-1925 WhScrn 74, -77
Frankau, Ronald 1894-1951 FilmgC, HalFC 80, NotNAT B, WhScrn 74, -77, WhThe, WhoHol B
Franke, Johann NewGrD 80
Frankel, Benjamin 1906-1973 Baker 78, FilmgC, HalFC 80, NewGrD 80, OxFilm, OxMus, WhoMus 72
Frankel, Cyril 1921-1973 FilmgC, HalFC 80, IlWWBF
Frankel, Daniel 1903- IntMPA 77, -75, -76, -78, -79, -80
Frankel, Emily 1930?- CnOxB
Frankel, Franchon 1874-1937 WhScrn 74, -77, WhoHol B
Frankel, Gene 1923- NotNAT, WhoThe 72, -77
Frankel, Harry d1948 WhScrn 77
Franken, Cootje 1913- IntWWM 77, -80
Franken, Mannus 189-?-1953 DcFM
Franken, Rose 1895- WhThe
Franken, Rose 1898- BiE&WWA, CnMD, ModWD, NotNAT
Franken, Steve ForYSC, WhoHol A
Franken, Wim 1922- IntWWM 77, -80
Frankenberger, Yoshiko Takagi 1946- IntWWM 80
Frankenburger, Paul NewGrD 80
Frankenfield, Parke T 1929- AmSCAP 66, -80
Frankenheimer, John 1930- AmFD, BiDFilm, -81, DcFM, FilmEn, FilmgC, HalFC 80, IntMPA 77, -75, -76, -78, -79, -80, MovMk[port], NewYTET, OxFilm, WhoHrs 80, WorEFlm
Frankenstein, Alfred 1906- Baker 78, NewGrD 80, WhoMus 72
Frankeur, Paul 1905-1974 WhScrn 77, WhoHol B
Frankfeldt, Chester 1942- IntWWM 77, -80
Frankham, David WhoHol A
Frankie, Lou AmSCAP 80
Frankiss, Betty 1912- WhThe
Frankl, Greta 1910- IntWWM 77
Frankl, Peter 1935- IntWWM 77, -80, NewGrD 80, WhoMus 72
Frankle, Hubert Axel Donato 1930- IntWWM 77, -80
Franklin PupTheA
Franklin, Alberta d1976 WhoHol C
Franklin, Alfred John 1929- IntWWM 77, -80
Franklin, Aretha ConMuA 80A[port]
Franklin, Aretha 1942- Baker 78, BiDAmM, DrBlPA, EncJzS 70, IlEncR[port]
Franklin, Aretha 1943- RkOn[port]
Franklin, Benjamin 1706-1790 Baker 78, NewGrD 80, OxMus
Franklin, Bonnie WhoHol A
Franklin, Carl 1930?- DrBlPA
Franklin, Chester M 1890- TwYS A
Franklin, Chester M 1890-1948? FilmEn
Franklin, Clarence 1932- BlkAmP
Franklin, Dave 1895-1970 AmSCAP 66, -80, CmpEPM
Franklin, David 1908-1973 NewGrD 80
Franklin, Edward Lamonte 1928-1975 BluesWW[port]
Franklin, Elsa WomWMM
Franklin, Erma 1940- BiDAmM
Franklin, Frederic 1914- CnOxB, DancEn 78[port]
Franklin, Harold B 1890-1941 NotNAT B, WhThe
Franklin, Henry 1903-1969 NewOrJ[port]
Franklin, Henry Carl 1940- AmSCAP 80
Franklin, Hugh WhoHol A
Franklin, Irene d1941 CmpEPM, ForYSC, WhoHol B
Franklin, Irene 1876-1941 NotNAT B, WhThe
Franklin, Irene 1884?-1941 WhScrn 74, -77
Franklin, J E BlkAmP, DrBlPA, MorBAP, NatPD[port]
Franklin, Jeff ConMuA 80B
Franklin, Jimmie 1909- AmSCAP 66
Franklin, Joe NewYTET
Franklin, John 1937- AmSCAP 80
Franklin, Johnny 1930- DancEn 78
Franklin, Malvin Maurice 1889- AmSCAP 66, -80
Franklin, Marjorie WomWMM B
Franklin, Martha 1876-1929 Film 2, WhScrn 77
Franklin, Michael Harold 1923- IntMPA 78, -79, -80
Franklin, Pamela WhoHol A
Franklin, Pamela 1949- FilmAG WE[port], FilmgC, HalFC 80, WhoHrs 80
Franklin, Pamela 1950- FilmEn, ForYSC, IntMPA 77, -75, -76, -78, -79, -80
Franklin, Richard AmSCAP 80
Franklin, Roger WhoOp 76
Franklin, Rupert 1862-1939 WhScrn 74, -77, WhoHol B
Franklin, Shirley S 1931- IntWWM 77
Franklin, Sidney 1870-1931 Film 2, WhScrn 74, -77, WhoHol B
Franklin, Sidney 1893-1972 BiDFilm, -81, DcFM, FilmEn, FilmgC, HalFC 80, MovMk[port], TwYS A, WorEFlm[port]
Franklin, Staines CreCan 1
Franklin, Wendell Film 2
Franklin, Wendell James DrBlPA
Franklyn, Arthur R 1928- IntMPA 77, -75, -76, -78, -79, -80
Franklyn, Beth d1956 NotNAT B
Franklyn, Blanche 1895-1973 AmSCAP 66, -80
Franklyn, Irwin 1904-1966 WhScrn 77, WhoHol B
Franklyn, Leo 1897-1975 WhScrn 77, WhThe, WhoHol C, WhoThe 72
Franklyn, Milt J 1897-1962 AmSCAP 66, -80
Franklyn, Sidney 1893-1972 CmMov
Franklyn, William 1926- FilmgC, HalFC 80
Franklyn-Lynch, Grace WhoStg 1908

Frankman, Charles *Film 1*
Franko, Nahan 1861-1930 *Baker 78*
Franko, Nathan 1861-1930 *BiDAmM*
Franko, Sam 1857-1937 *Baker 78, BiDAmM*
Frankovich, M J 1910- *IntMPA 77, -75, -76, -78, -79, -80, WorEFlm*
Frankovich, Mike 1910- *FilmgC, ForYSC, HalFC 80, WhoHol A, WorEFlm*
Frankovich, Mike J 1910- *FilmEn*
Franks 1914- *NewOrJ*
Franks, Arthur Henry 1907-1963 *CnOxB, DancEn 78*
Franks, Celia *CreCan 1*
Franks, Chloe 1963- *WhoHrs 80*
Franks, Dennis 1902-1967 *WhScrn 74, -77*
Franks, Roderick 1956- *IntWWM 80*
Franks, Tillman B 1920- *AmSCAP 66*
Franks-Williams, Joan 1930- *NewGrD 80*
Fransman, Holger Alexander 1909- *IntWWM 77, -80*
Frantz, Dalies 1908-1965 *WhScrn 77, WhoHol B*
Frantz, Dorothy 1918- *AmSCAP 80*
Frantz, Ferdinand 1906-1959 *CmOp, NewGrD 80*
Frantz, Patrick 1943- *CnOxB*
Franz, Adele *BiE&WWA*
Franz, Arthur 1920- *FilmEn, FilmgC, ForYSC, HalFC 80, IntMPA 77, -75, -76, -78, -79, -80, Vers B[port], WhoHol A, WhoHrs 80[port]*
Franz, Carl 1738-1802 *NewGrD 80*
Franz, Eduard 1902- *FilmEn, ForYSC, HalFC 80, MotPP, WhoHol A, WhoThe 77*
Franz, Edward 1902- *FilmgC*
Franz, Ellen *OxThe*
Franz, J H *NewGrD 80*
Franz, Joseph J *Film 2*
Franz, Paul 1876-1950 *NewGrD 80*
Franz, Robert 1815-1892 *Baker 78, BnBkM 80, CmpBCM, GrComp[port], MusMk, NewGrD 80, OxMus*
Franz, Siegfried Walter 1913- *WhoMus 72*
Franz, William Frederic 1947- *AmSCAP 80*
Franzella, Sal 1915-1968 *CmpEPM, NewOrJ, WhoJazz 72*
Franzen, Hans 1935- *WhoOp 76*
Franzen, Olov Alfred 1946- *IntWWM 80*
Franzl *NewGrD 80*
Franzl, Ferdinand 1767-1833 *NewGrD 80*
Franzl, Ferdinand 1770-1833 *Baker 78*
Franzl, Ferdinand Rudolph 1710-1782 *NewGrD 80*
Franzl, Ignaz 1736-1811 *Baker 78, NewGrD 80*
Franzl, Willy 1898- *CnOxB*
Franzoni, Amante *NewGrD 80*
Fraschini, Gaetano 1816-1887 *NewGrD 80*
Fraser, Agnes *WhThe*
Fraser, Alec 1884- *WhThe*
Fraser, Barbara 1933- *IntWWM 77, -80*
Fraser, Bill *WhoHol A*
Fraser, Bill 1907- *FilmgC, HalFC 80*
Fraser, Bill 1908- *WhoThe 72, -77*
Fraser, Bryant *WhoHol A*
Fraser, Carol Lucille 1930- *CreCan 2*
Fraser, Claud Lovat 1890-1921 *NotNAT B*
Fraser, Claude Lovat 1890-1921 *EncWT, OxThe*
Fraser, Constance 1910-1973 *WhScrn 77, WhoHol B*
Fraser, Derek Peter 1929- *IntWWM 77, -80*
Fraser, Elizabeth *ForYSC, WhoHol A*
Fraser, Harry 1889-1974 *Film 1, WhScrn 77*
Fraser, Ian 1933- *AmSCAP 80*
Fraser, Janet *WhoMus 72*
Fraser, John 1931- *FilmEn, FilmgC, HalFC 80, IlWWBF, WhoHol A*
Fraser, Liz 1933- *FilmgC, HalFC 80*
Fraser, Lovat 1908- *WhThe*
Fraser, Marjory Kennedy *OxMus*
Fraser, Moyra 1923- *DancEn 78, FilmgC, HalFC 80, WhoHol A, WhoThe 72, -77*
Fraser, Norman George 1904- *Baker 78, IntWWM 77, -80, WhoMus 72*
Fraser, Phyllis *WhoHol A*
Fraser, Richard 1913-1971 *FilmEn, FilmgC, HalFC 80, WhoHol B*
Fraser, Robert 1891-1944 *Film 1, -2*
Fraser, Sir Robert 1904- *IntMPA 77, -75, -76, -78, -79, -80*
Fraser, Ronald 1930- *FilmEn, FilmgC, HalFC 80, IntMPA 77, -75, -76, -78, -79, -80, PlP&P, WhoHol A*
Fraser, Shelagh *WhoHol A, WhoThe 72, -77*
Fraser, Shena Eleanor 1910- *IntWWM 77, -80, WhoMus 72*
Fraser, Stanley *WhoHol A*
Fraser, Tony *Film 2*
Fraser, Winifred 1872- *WhThe*
Fraser-Simpson, Harold 1878-1944 *BestMus, NotNAT B*
Fraser-Simson, Harold 1872-1944 *NewGrD 80*
Fraser-Simson, Harold 1878-1944 *WhThe*
Frasi, Giulia *NewGrD 80*
Frasier, Jane Eleanor 1951- *CpmDNM 80*
Frasnau, Jehan *NewGrD 80*
Frasure, Jack 1935- *AmSCAP 80*
Fratti, Mario 1927- *ConAmTC, ConDr 73, -77, CroCD, ModWD, NatPD[port]*
Fratturo, Louis M 1928- *ConAmC*
Frauenholtz, Johann Christoph 1684-1754 *NewGrD 80*
Frauenholz, Johann Christoph 1684-1754 *NewGrD 80*
Frauenlob 125-?-1318 *NewGrD 80*
Frawley, James *ForYSC, IntMPA 80*
Frawley, Paul *AmPS B*
Frawley, T Daniel d1936 *NotNAT B*
Frawley, William *JoeFr*
Frawley, William 1887-1966 *FilmEn, Film 1, -2, FilmgC, HalFC 80, HolCA[port], MotPP, MovMk[port], Vers B[port], WhScrn 74, -77, WhoHol B*
Frawley, William 1893-1966 *ForYSC*
Frayn, Michael 1933- *ConDr 73, -77, Ent, WhoThe 77*
Frayne, John G 1894- *IntMPA 75, -76*
Frazee, Harry Herbert 1880-1929 *NotNAT B, WhThe*
Frazee, Jane *IntMPA 75*
Frazee, Jane 1918- *FilmEn, FilmgC, HalFC 80, What 5[port], WhoHol A*
Frazee, Jane 1919?- *CmpEPM, ForYSC*
Frazee, Jane 1936- *IntWWM 77, -80*
Frazer, Alex 1900-1958 *WhScrn 74, -77, WhoHol B*
Frazer, Austin *IntMPA 77, -75, -76, -78, -79, -80*
Frazer, Dan *WhoHol A*
Frazer, Robert 1891-1944 *FilmEn, Film 2, ForYSC, HolCA[port], TwYS, WhScrn 74, -77, WhoHol B*
Frazeur, Theodore C 1929- *ConAmC, IntWWM 77, -80*
Frazier, Brenda 1921- *What 2[port]*
Frazier, Calvin H 1915-1972 *BluesWW[port]*
Frazier, Cliff 1934- *DrBlPA, IntMPA 77, -75, -76, -78, -79, -80*
Frazier, Dallas 1939- *BiDAmM, CounME 74, EncFCWM 69, IlEncCM[port]*
Frazier, Eddie 1898-1972 *AmSCAP 80*
Frazier, H C 1894-1949 *WhScrn 74, -77*
Frazier, James, Jr. 1940- *DrBlPA*
Frazier, Josiah 1904- *NewOrJ[port]*
Frazier, Larry Richard 1947- *IntWWM 77, -80*
Frazier, Levi, Jr. *BlkAmP*
Frazier, Richard *Film 2*
Frazier, Robert *Film 2*
Frazier, Sheila E 1948- *DrBlPA, IntMPA 80, WhoHol A*
Frazier, Shelia E 1948- *IntMPA 77, -75, -76, -78, -79*
Frazin, Gladys 1901-1939 *Film 2, WhScrn 74, -77, WhoHol B*
Frazzi, Vito 1888-1975 *Baker 78, NewGrD 80*
Frazzini, Al 1890-1963 *AmSCAP 66, -80*
Frazzoni, Gigliola 1927- *WhoOp 76*
Frcek, Josef 1931- *IntWWM 77, -80*
Frear, Fred *WhoStg 1908*
Frears, Stephen 1931- *FilmgC, HalFC 80*
Freas, Elizabeth H 1943- *IntWWM 77, -80*
Freberg, Stan 1926- *AmSCAP 66, -80, JoeFr, RkOn, WhoHol A*
Freccia, Massimo 1906- *Baker 78, IntWWM 77, -80, WhoMus 72*
Frechette, Mark 1947-1975 *HalFC 80, WhScrn 77, WhoHol C*
Fred, John And His Playboy Band *BiDAmM, RkOn 2[port]*
Freda, Riccardo 1909- *BiDFilm, DcFM, FilmEn, FilmgC, HalFC 80, WhoHrs 80, WorEFlm[port]*
Freddi, Amadio *NewGrD 80*
Freddi, Amedeo *NewGrD 80*
Freddie & The Dreamers *RkOn 2[port]*
Freddie The Freeloader *JoeFr*
Frede, Richard 1934- *NatPD[port]*
Frederic, Marc 1916- *IntMPA 77, -75, -76, -78, -79, -80*
Frederic, William *Film 2*
Frederici, Blanche 1870-1933 *HalFC 80*
Frederici, Blanche 1878-1933 *Film 2, NotNAT B, TwYS, WhScrn 77, WhoHol B*
Frederick 1800-1876 *OxThe*
Frederick II 1712-1786 *Baker 78, NewGrD 80*
Frederick The Great 1712-1786 *BnBkM 80, NewGrD 80, OxMus*
Frederick, Cassandra 1741?- *NewGrD 80*
Frederick, Donald R 1917- *AmSCAP 80*
Frederick, Freddie Burke *Film 2*
Frederick, Hal *WhoHol A*
Frederick, John *PupTheA*
Frederick, Kurt 1907- *IntWWM 77, -80*
Frederick, Pauline d1938 *MotPP, NewYTET, WhoHol B*
Frederick, Pauline 1881-1938 *TwYS*
Frederick, Pauline 1883-1938 *FilmEn, Film 1, -2, FilmgC, ForYSC, HalFC 80, OxFilm, ThFT[port]*
Frederick, Pauline 1884-1938 *WhScrn 74, -77, WhoStg 1908*
Frederick, Pauline 1885-1938 *MovMk, NotNAT A, -B, WhThe*
Fredericks, Albert d1901 *NotNAT B*
Fredericks, Charles 1920-1970 *WhScrn 74, -77, WhoHol B*
Fredericks, Dean *ForYSC*
Fredericks, Ellsworth *FilmgC, HalFC 80*
Fredericks, Fred d1939 *NotNAT B*
Fredericks, Marc 1927- *AmSCAP 66, -80*
Fredericks, Sam d1922 *NotNAT B*
Fredericks, William A 1924- *AmSCAP 66*
Frederickson, H Gray, Jr. 1937- *IntMPA 77, -75, -76, -78, -79, -80*
Fredman, Alice d1950 *NotNAT B*
Fredman, Myer 1932- *NewGrD 80, WhoMus 72*
Fredrich, Gunter 1927- *NewGrD 80*
Fredrici, Gustaf *NewGrD 80*
Fredricks, Richard 1933- *IntWWM 77, -80, WhoOp 76*
Fredricks, William Arthur 1924- *AmSCAP 80*
Fredrickson, L Thomas 1928- *AmSCAP 80*
Fredrickson, Thomas 1928- *AmSCAP 66, ConAmC*
Fredrik, Burry 1925- *BiE&WWA*
Fredriksson, Karin 1922- *IntWWM 77*
Fredriksson, Risto Lennart 1941- *IntWWM 77, -80*
Fredro, Count Aleksander 1793-1876 *CnThe, McGEWD[port], OxThe, REnWD[port]*
Fredutii, Massimiliano *NewGrD 80*
Free *ConMuA 80A, IlEncR, RkOn 2[port]*
Free Movement, The *RkOn 2[port]*
Freear, Louie 1871-1939 *NotNAT B, WhThe*
Freeborn, Cassius d1954 *NotNAT B*
Freeborn, Stuart 1914- *WhoHrs 80*
Freed, Alan 1922-1965 *IlEncR, WhScrn 77*
Freed, Arnold 1926- *AmSCAP 80, ConAmC*
Freed, Arthur 1894-1973 *AmPS, AmSCAP 66, -80, BestMus, BiDAmM, BiDFilm, -81, CmMov, CmpEPM, DcFM, FilmEn, FilmgC, HalFC 80, OxFilm, Sw&Ld C, WorEFlm*
Freed, Bert *ForYSC, WhoHol A*
Freed, Dorothy Whitson 1919- *IntWWM 77, -80*
Freed, Fred d1974 *NewYTET*
Freed, Isadore 1900- *Baker 78*
Freed, Isadore 1900-1960 *AmSCAP 80, BiDAmM, ConAmC, DcCM, NewGrD 80*
Freed, Isadore 1900-1961 *AmSCAP 66*
Freed, Lazar *Film 2*
Freed, Ralph 1907-1973 *AmPS, AmSCAP 66, -80, CmpEPM*
Freed, Ruth *AmSCAP 66, -80*
Freed, Sam *PlP&P A[port]*

Freed, Walter 1903- *AmSCAP 66, -80, ConAmC A*
Freedley, George 1904-1967 *BiE&WWA, NotNAT B, OxThe, WhThe*
Freedley, Vinton 1891-1969 *BiE&WWA, EncMT, NotNAT B, PlP&P, WhThe*
Freedley, Vinton 1892-1969 *WhScrn 77*
Freedman, Bill 1929- *WhoThe 72, -77*
Freedman, Gerald 1927- *AmSCAP 66, -80, NotNAT, WhoOp 76, WhoThe 77*
Freedman, Guy L 1916- *AmSCAP 66*
Freedman, Harold *BiE&WWA*
Freedman, Harry 1922 *Baker 78, CreCan 2, DcCM, NewGrD 80*
Freedman, Herman W 1925- *IntMPA 77, -75, -76, -78, -79*
Freedman, Irwin B 1924- *IntMPA 77, -75, -76, -78, -79*
Freedman, Israel 1910- *ConAmC*
Freedman, Lenore d1964 *NotNAT B*
Freedman, Lewis *NewYTET*
Freedman, M Claire *AmSCAP 80*
Freedman, Mary Morrison *CreCan 2*
Freedman, Max C 1893-1962 *AmSCAP 66, -80*
Freedman, Melvin Howard 1920- *AmSCAP 80*
Freedman, Robert Morris 1934- *AmSCAP 66, -80, ConAmC*
Freegard, Michael J 1933- *IntWWM 77, -80*
Freel, Aleta d1935 *NotNAT B*
Freeland, Thornton 1898- *FilmEn, FilmgC, HalFC 80, IlWWBF*
Freeman, Al 1884-1956 *WhScrn 74, -77, WhoHol B*
Freeman, Al, Jr. *ForYSC*
Freeman, Al, Jr. 1934- *DrBlPA, HalFC 80, NotNAT, WhoHol A, WhoThe 77*
Freeman, Al, Jr. 1939- *FilmgC*
Freeman, Arnie *WhoHol A*
Freeman, Arny 1908- *WhoThe 77*
Freeman, Bee *BlksB&W C, DrBlPA*
Freeman, Berdella *AmSCAP 80*
Freeman, Bobby 1940- *RkOn[port]*
Freeman, Bud 1906- *CmpEPM, EncJzS 70, IlEncJ, NewGrD 80, WhoJazz 72*
Freeman, Bud 1915- *AmSCAP 66, -80*
Freeman, Carol S 1941- *BlkAmP*
Freeman, Charles J d1964 *NotNAT B*
Freeman, Charles K 1900- *BiE&WWA, ConAmTC, NotNAT*
Freeman, David 1945- *ConDr 73, -77, NatPD[port]*
Freeman, Earl Lavon 1922- *EncJzS 70*
Freeman, Edwin Armistead 1928- *ConAmC*
Freeman, Elizabeth 1951- *IntWWM 80*
Freeman, Enoch Weston 1798-1835 *BiDAmM*
Freeman, Ernest Aaron, Jr. 1922- *AmSCAP 66, -80*
Freeman, Ernie 1929- *RkOn*
Freeman, Everett 1911- *FilmEn, FilmgC, HalFC 80, IntMPA 77, -75, -76, -78, -79, -80*
Freeman, Frank 1892-1962 *WhThe*
Freeman, Frank Y 1890- *FilmgC, HalFC 80*
Freeman, George D 1937- *AmSCAP 66, -80*
Freeman, H A d1929 *NotNAT B*
Freeman, H Lawrence 1875- *BlkAmP*
Freeman, Harry *WhThe*
Freeman, Harry Lawrence 1869-1954 *Baker 78, NewGrD 80*
Freeman, Harry Lawrence 1875-1943 *BiDAmM*
Freeman, Howard 1899-1967 *BiE&WWA, FilmEn, FilmgC, HalFC 80, MotPP, Vers B[port], WhScrn 74, -77, WhoHol B*
Freeman, Howard 1902-1967 *ForYSC*
Freeman, Isadore 1912- *IntWWM 77, -80*
Freeman, James 1759-1835 *BiDAmM*
Freeman, Jayne Stewart 1933- *ConAmTC*
Freeman, Joan 1942- *ForYSC, WhoHol A*
Freeman, Joel 1922- *IntMPA 79, -80*
Freeman, John 1666-1736 *NewGrD 80*
Freeman, John Henry 1908- *WhoMus 72*
Freeman, Kathleen 1919?- *FilmgC, ForYSC, HalFC 80, HolCA[port], WhoHol A*
Freeman, Kenn *DrBlPA*
Freeman, L Sharon 1949- *BlkWAB[port]*
Freeman, Lawrence 1906- *AmSCAP 66, -80, BiDAmM, EncJzS 70, NewGrD 80*
Freeman, Leonard d1973 *NewYTET*
Freeman, Leonard 1921-1974 *HalFC 80*
Freeman, Maurice 1872-1953 *WhScrn 74, -77, WhoHol B*
Freeman, Max d1912 *NotNAT B, WhoStg 1906, -1908*
Freeman, Mona 1926- *FilmEn, FilmgC, ForYSC, HalFC 80, HolP 40[port], MotPP, MovMk, WhoHol A*
Freeman, Sir N Bernard 1896- *IntMPA 77, -75, -76, -78, -79, -80*
Freeman, Ned 1895- *AmSCAP 66, -80, ConAmC A*
Freeman, Pam *WhoHol A*
Freeman, Paul 1935- *BiDAmM*
Freeman, Raoul 1894-1971 *WhScrn 77*
Freeman, Robert 1935?- *FilmgC, HalFC 80, NewGrD 80*
Freeman, Robert Bruce 1952- *IntWWM 77, -80*
Freeman, Robert Norman 1939- *IntWWM 77, -80*
Freeman, Roderick *NewGrD 80*
Freeman, Roy Robert 1926- *AmSCAP 80*
Freeman, Russ 1926- *CmpEPM, EncJzS 70*
Freeman, Russell Donald 1926- *AmSCAP 66, -80, BiDAmM, EncJzS 70*
Freeman, Scott *AmSCAP 80*
Freeman, Stan 1920- *AmSCAP 66, -80, CmpEPM, NotNAT*
Freeman, Stella 1910-1936 *NotNAT B, WhThe*
Freeman, Ticker 1911- *AmSCAP 66, -80*
Freeman, Von 1922- *EncJzS 70*
Freeman, William B d1932 *WhScrn 77*
Freeman-Mitford, Rupert 1895-1939 *WhScrn 74, -77, WhoHol B*
Freemen, William *Film 1*
Freer, Eleanor Everest 1864-1942 *Baker 78, BiDAmM*
Frees, Paul 1920- *AmSCAP 66, ForYSC, WhoHol A*
Frees, Paul 1925?- *WhoHrs 80*
Freesoil, Mason *AmSCAP 80*
Freeze, George Richard 1948- *AmSCAP 80*
Freezer, Herbert J d1963 *NotNAT B*
Frege, Livia 1818-1891 *NewGrD 80*
Fregni, Mirella *NewGrD 80*
Fregoli, Leopold d1936 *NotNAT B*
Fregonese, Hugo 1908- *BiDFilm, -81, FilmEn, FilmgC, HalFC 80, IntMPA 77, -75, -76, -78, -79, -80, WorEFlm*
Frei, Hans *NewGrD 80*
Freil, Edward 1878-1938 *WhScrn 74, -77*
Freiman, Lillian 1908- *CreCan 1*
Freinsberg, Jean Adam Guillaume *NewGrD 80*
Freire, Nelson 1944- *NewGrD 80, WhoMus 72*
Freislich, Johann Balthasar Christian 1687-1764 *NewGrD 80*
Freislich, Maximilian Dietrich 1673-1731 *NewGrD 80*
Freisslich, Johann Balthasar Christian 1687-1764 *NewGrD 80*
Freisslich, Maximilian Dietrich 1673-1731 *NewGrD 80*
Freitag, Dorothea 1914- *AmSCAP 80, BiE&WWA, ConAmC, NotNAT*
Freitag, Erik 1940- *IntWWM 80*
Freitas, Branco, Luiz De 1890-1955 *Baker 78*
Freitas, Frederico De 1902- *DcCM, NewGrD 80, WhoMus 72*
Freitas, Richard 1915- *AmSCAP 66, -80*
Freitas Branco, Luis De 1890-1955 *NewGrD 80*
Freithoff, Johan Henrik 1713-1767 *NewGrD 80*
Freleng, Friz *WorEFlm*
Freleng, Friz 1900?- *FilmEn*
Freleng, Isadore 1906- *AmSCAP 80*
Fremart, Henri d1646? *NewGrD 80*
Fremault, Anita *FilmEn, Film 2*
Fremaux, Louis 1921- *IntWWM 77, -80, NewGrD 80, WhoMus 72*
Fremder, Alfred 1920- *ConAmC*
Fremont, Alfred *Film 1, -2*
Fremont, Frank *AmSCAP 80*
Fremstad, Olive 1871-1951 *Baker 78, BnBkM 80, CmOp, MusSN[port], NewEOp 71, NewGrD 80*
Fremstad, Olive 1872-1951 *BiDAmM*
French, Albert 1910- *NewOrJ[port]*
French, Arthur *DrBlPA, WhoHol A*
French, Behrman 1900- *NewOrJ*
French, Brandon *WomWMM B*
French, Carroll *PupTheA*
French, Charles J *ForYSC*
French, Charles K 1860-1952 *Film 1, -2, TwYS, WhScrn 74, -77, WhoHol B*
French, David 1939- *ConDr 77*
French, Dick *Film 2*
French, Don 1940- *RkOn*
French, Earl 1944- *AmSCAP 80*
French, Edmund *AmSCAP 80*
French, Edward 1761-1845 *BiDAmM*
French, Edwige 1948- *FilmAG WE*
French, Elizabeth *WhThe*
French, Elsie *WhThe*
French, Evelyn *Film 2*
French, George B 1883-1961 *Film 1, -2, TwYS, WhScrn 74, -77, WhoHol B*
French, Mrs. H E *PupTheA*
French, Harold 1897- *FilmEn, Film 2, FilmgC, HalFC 80, IlWWBF, -A*
French, Harold 1900- *IntMPA 77, -75, -76, -78, -79, -80, WhoThe 72, -77*
French, Helen 1863-1917 *WhScrn 77*
French, Herbert C d1924 *NotNAT B*
French, Hermene 1924- *WhThe*
French, Hugh 1910- *WhThe*
French, Jacob 1754-1817 *Baker 78, BiDAmM, NewGrD 80*
French, Leigh *WhoHol A*
French, Leslie *WhoHol A*
French, Leslie 1899- *FilmgC, HalFC 80*
French, Leslie 1904- *WhoThe 72, -77*
French, Maida Parlow 1901- *CreCan 1*
French, Mary Margaret *PupTheA*
French, Maurice 1890?- *NewOrJ*
French, Patsy Ruth 1936- *IntWWM 77, -80*
French, Pauline *Film 2, WhoStg 1906, -1908*
French, Percy 1854-1920 *NewGrD 80*
French, Ruth 1906- *CnOxB, DancEn 78*
French, Samuel d1898 *NotNAT B*
French, Stanley J 1908-1964 *NotNAT B, WhThe*
French, Susan *WhoHol A*
French, T Henry d1902 *NotNAT B*
French, Valerie *ForYSC, WhoHol A*
French, Valerie 1931- *FilmgC, HalFC 80*
French, Valerie 1932- *WhoThe 72, -77*
French, Victor *NewYTET, WhoHol A*
French, William 1885- *TwYS A*
Frend, Charles 1909-1977 *CmMov, DcFM, FilmEn, FilmgC, HalFC 80, IlWWBF, IntMPA 77, -75, -76, OxFilm, WorEFlm*
Freni, Mirella *IntWWM 77, -80, WhoMus 72*
Freni, Mirella 1935- *Baker 78, BnBkM 80, MusSN[port], NewGrD 80, WhoOp 76*
Freni, Mirella 1936- *CmOp, NewEOp 71*
Frenke, Eugene *IntMPA 77, -75, -76, -78, -79, -80*
Frenyear, Mabel *Film 1*
Frere, Rudolph Walter Howard 1863-1938 *Baker 78*
Frere, Walter Howard 1863-1938 *NewGrD 80, OxMus*
Frerichs, Doris Coulston 1911- *IntWWM 77, -80*
Frerks, Geraldine *WomWMM B*
Fersmillan, Carlos Adalberto 1938- *IntWWM 77, -80*
Freschi, Domenico 1630?-1710 *NewGrD 80*
Freschi, Giovanni Domenico 1625?-1710 *Baker 78*
Fresco, Robert M 1928- *IntMPA 77, -75, -76, -78, -79, -80*
Frescobaldi, Girolamo 1583-1643 *Baker 78, BnBkM 80, CmpBCM, DcCom 77[port], DcCom&M 79, GrComp[port], MusMk, NewGrD 80[port], OxMus*
Freshman, William A 1905- *Film 2, IlWWBF*
Fresnau, Jehan *NewGrD 80*
Fresnay, Pierre 1897- *BiE&WWA, CnThe, Film 2, FilmgC, WhThe, WorEFlm*
Fresnay, Pierre 1897-1973 *MovMk[port]*
Fresnay, Pierre 1897-1975 *EncWT, Ent, FilmAG WE, FilmEn, HalFC 80, OxFilm, WhScrn 77, WhoHol C*
Fresneau, Henry *NewGrD 80*
Fresneau, Jehan *NewGrD 80*
Fresnel, Baude d1398? *NewGrD 80*
Freso, Tibor 1918- *Baker 78, NewGrD 80*
Fresson, Bernard 1933- *FilmEn*
Fretwell, Elizabeth *WhoMus 72, WhoOp 76*

Fretwell, Elizabeth 1922- CmOp
Freud, Eli IntWWM 80
Freud, Sigmund 1856-1939 FilmgC, HalFC 80
Freudenberg, Wilhelm 1838-1928 Baker 78
Freudenthal, Josef 1903-1964 AmSCAP 66, -80, ConAmC A
Freudenthal, Otto 1934- IntWWM 77, -80
Freulich, Henry 1906- IntMPA 77, -75, -76, -78, -79, -80
Freund, Darral J 1919- AmSCAP 80
Freund, Don 1947- CpmDNM 79
Freund, Donald Wayne 1947- ConAmC
Freund, John Christian 1848-1924 Baker 78
Freund, Joki 1926- EncJzS 70
Freund, Karl 1890-1969 BiDFilm, -81, CmMov, DcFM, FilmEn, FilmgC, HalFC 80, OxFilm, WhoHrs 80, WorEFlm[port]
Freund, Marya 1876-1966 Baker 78, NewGrD 80
Freund, Walter Jakob 1926- EncJzS 70
Freundlich, Ralph B 1912- AmSCAP 80
Freundt NewGrD 80
Freundt, Cornelius 1535-1591 Baker 78, NewGrD 80
Freundt, Johann 1615?-1678 NewGrD 80
Freundt, Johann Georg 1590?-1667 NewGrD 80
Freundt, Leonhard 1640?-1727 NewGrD 80
Freundt, Leopold 1640?-1727 NewGrD 80
Freutiers, Jan NewGrD 80
Frewin, Leslie 1916- IntMPA 75
Frey, Adolf 1865-1938 Baker 78
Frey, Arno 1900-1961 WhScrn 77, WhoHol B
Frey, Emil 1889-1946 Baker 78, NewGrD 80
Frey, Fran CmpEPM
Frey, Frank 1947- CnOxB
Frey, Glenn L 1948- AmSCAP 80
Frey, Hugo 1873-1952 AmSCAP 66, -80
Frey, Jacques-Joseph 1781-1838 NewGrD 80
Frey, Leonard WhoHol A
Frey, Leonard 1938- HalFC 80, NotNAT
Frey, Leonard 1939- FilmgC
Frey, Lia 1949- IntWWM 80
Frey, Maurice AmSCAP 80
Frey, Nathaniel 1913-1970 WhScrn 74, -77, WhThe, WhoHol B, WhoThe 72
Frey, Nathaniel 1923-1970 BiE&WWA, NotNAT B
Frey, Sami 1937- FilmAG WE[port], FilmEn
Frey, Sidney 1920- AmSCAP 66, -80
Frey, Walter 1898- Baker 78, NewGrD 80, -80
Freyer, August 1803-1883 NewGrD 80
Freyer, Ellen WomWMM B
Freyhan, Michael 1940- IntWWM 77, -80, WhoMus 72
Freylinghausen, Johann Anastasius 1670-1739 NewGrD 80, OxMus
Freyman, Zachary CnOxB
Freytag, Gustav 1816-1895 EncWT, McGEWD[port], OxThe, REnWD[port]
Frezza, Giovanni NewGrD 80
Frezzolini, Erminia 1818-1884 CmOp
Friar, Ernest Richard 1939- IntWWM 80
Friar Of Bristol NewGrD 80
Friar's Society Orchestra BiDAmM
Fribec, Kresimir 1908- Baker 78, DcCM, IntWWM 77, -80, NewGrD 80
Friberg, Carl 1939- AmSCAP 80
Fribert, Joseph NewGrD 80
Friberth, Joseph NewGrD 80
Friberth, Karl NewGrD 80
Fric, Martin 1902-1968 DcFM, FilmEn, OxFilm, WorEFlm
Frichot, Louis Alexandre 1760-1825 NewGrD 80
Frick, Gottlob 1906- CmOp, IntWWM 77, -80, NewGrD 80
Frick, Marta Elisabet 1918- IntWWM 77
Frick, Philipp Joseph 1740-1798 NewGrD 80
Fricke, David ConMuA 80B
Fricker, Herbert Austin 1868-1943 Baker 78, NewGrD 80
Fricker, Peter Racine 1920- Baker 78, ConAmC, DcCom&M 79, DcCM, IntWWM 77, -80, MusMk, NewGrD 80[port], OxMus, WhoMus 72
Fricker, Sylvia 1940- BiDAmM
Fricsay, Ferenc 1914-1963 Baker 78, CmOp, NewEOp 71, NewGrD 80[port]
Fricz, Thomas NewGrD 80
Frid, Geza 1904- Baker 78, IntWWM 77, -80, NewGrD 80, OxMus, WhoMus 72
Frid, Jonathan WhoHol A, WhoHrs 80[port]
Friderici, Blanche d1933 Film 2, ForYSC
Friderici, Blanche 1878-1933 HolCA[port]
Friderici, Daniel 1584-1638 Baker 78, NewGrD 80
Friderici-Jakowicka, Teodozja NewGrD 80
Fridericia, Allan 1921- CnOxB
Fridman, Liber PupTheA
Fridman, Ruth 1921- IntWWM 77, -80
Fridman-Kochevskoy, Sonia De NewGrD 80
Fridolin OxThe
Fridrich Von Hausen NewGrD 80
Fridzeri, Alessandro Mario Antonio 1741-1825 NewGrD 80
Frie, Walter NewGrD 80
Friebert, Joseph 1724-1799 NewGrD 80
Frieberth, Carlo 1736-1816 NewGrD 80
Frieberth, Joseph 1724-1799 NewGrD 80
Frieberth, Karl 1736-1816 NewGrD 80
Friebus, Florida 1909- BiE&WWA, NotNAT
Friebus, Theodore 1879-1917 Film 1, WhScrn 77
Fried, Alexander 1902- WhoMus 72
Fried, Alexej 1922- Baker 78, EncJzS 70
Fried, Barbara Ruth 1924- AmSCAP 80
Fried, Floyd Frank 1947- IntWWM 77
Fried, Gerald 1926- HalFC 80
Fried, Gerald 1928- AmSCAP 66, -80
Fried, Martin AmSCAP 66, -80, NotNAT
Fried, Miriam 1946- IntWWM 77, -80, NewGrD 80
Fried, Oskar 1871-1941 Baker 78, NewGrD 80
Fried, Suellen 1932- AmSCAP 80
Fried, Walter 1910-1975 BiE&WWA, NotNAT B, PlP&P[port]
Friedberg, Carl 1872-1955 Baker 78
Friedberg, Mana Mollie 1901- IntWWM 77
Friedberg, Patricia Ann 1934- AmSCAP 80
Friedel, Sebastian Ludwig NewGrD 80
Friedell, Egon 1878-1938 EncWT
Friedell, Harold William 1905-1958 AmSCAP 80, ConAmC
Friedenberg, Richard C 1933- AmSCAP 80
Friederich, W J 1916- BiE&WWA, NotNAT
Friederici NewGrD 80
Friederici, Christian Ernst 1709-1780 NewGrD 80
Friederici, Christian Ernst Wilhelm 1782-1872 NewGrD 80
Friederici, Christian Gottfried 1714-1777 NewGrD 80
Friederici, Christian Gottlob 1750-1805 NewGrD 80
Friederici, Ernst Ludwig 1806-1883 NewGrD 80
Friedgen, John Raymond 1893-1966 WhScrn 77
Friedheim, Arthur 1859-1932 Baker 78, BiDAmM, NewGrD 80
Friedhofer, Hugo 1902- CmMov, CmpEPM, FilmEn, FilmgC, HalFC 80, NewGrD 80, WorEFlm
Friedkin, Joel 1885-1954 WhScrn 77
Friedkin, John IntMPA 80
Friedkin, William 1939- BiDFilm, -81, FilmEn, FilmgC, HalFC 80, IntMPA 77, -75, -76, -78, -79, -80, MovMk[port], WhoHrs 80
Friedl, Sebastian Ludwig 1768-1857? NewGrD 80
Friedlaender, Max 1852-1934 Baker 78, NewGrD 80
Friedland, Anatole 1881-1938 AmSCAP 66, -80, BiDAmM
Friedland, Anatole 1888-1938 NotNAT B, PopAmC
Friedland, Louis N NewYTET
Friedlander, Annekate Emma 1902- IntWWM 77, -80
Friedlander, Annekate Emma 1903- WhoMus 72
Friedlander, Ernst Peter 1906-1966 CreCan 1
Friedlander, Jane 1939- BiE&WWA
Friedlander, Louis FilmEn
Friedlander, Max 1852-1934 NewGrD 80
Friedlander, William Barr 1884-1968 AmSCAP 80
Friedlander, William Barr 1899-1968 AmSCAP 66, WhThe
Friedlein, Rudolf Fryderyk 1811-1873 NewGrD 80
Friedler, Egon 1932- IntWWM 80
Friedman, Arnold J 1928- IntMPA 75, -76, -79, -80
Friedman, Arthur 1935- ConAmTC
Friedman, Bonnie WomWMM A, -B
Friedman, Bruce Jay 1930- ConDr 73, -77, McGEWD, NatPD[port]
Friedman, Charles 1902- AmSCAP 66, -80, NatPD[port]
Friedman, David WhoHrs 80
Friedman, David A 1944- AmSCAP 80, EncJzS 70
Friedman, David F 1923- IntMPA 77, -75, -76, -78, -79, -80
Friedman, Don 1935- EncJzS 70
Friedman, Donald Ernest 1935- BiDAmM, EncJzS 70
Friedman, Erick 1939- WhoMus 72
Friedman, Fred 1924- IntMPA 77, -75, -76, -78, -79
Friedman, Henry 1897- AmSCAP 80
Friedman, Ignacy 1882-1948 NewGrD 80
Friedman, Ignaz 1882-1948 Baker 78, BnBkM 80
Friedman, Irving 1903- AmSCAP 66, -80
Friedman, Izzy 1903- CmpEPM, WhoJazz 72
Friedman, Jake 1867- WhThe
Friedman, James M 1927- AmSCAP 80
Friedman, Jerry 1938- AmSCAP 66
Friedman, Joseph IntMPA 77, -75, -76, -78, -79, -80
Friedman, Ken 1939- Baker 78, ConAmC, DcCM
Friedman, Kinky IlEncR
Friedman, Kinky 1944- CounME 74[port], -74A, IlEncCM[port]
Friedman, Leo 1869-1927 AmSCAP 66, -80, BiDAmM
Friedman, Leo B BiE&WWA
Friedman, Leonard 1930- WhoMus 72
Friedman, Leopold IntMPA 77, -75, -76, -78, -79
Friedman, Martin 1913- IntMPA 77, -75, -76, -78, -79, -80
Friedman, Maurice Herman 1905- AmSCAP 80
Friedman, Max d1964 NotNAT B
Friedman, Paul 1921- NewYTET
Friedman, Phil 1921- BiE&WWA, NotNAT
Friedman, Richard 1944- Baker 78, ConAmC
Friedman, Richard H 1924-1954 AmSCAP 66, -80
Friedman, Robert L 1930- IntMPA 79, -80
Friedman, Ron 1932- AmSCAP 80
Friedman, Samuel 1912- BiE&WWA, NotNAT
Friedman, Samuel B 1919- AmSCAP 66
Friedman, Seymour Mark 1917- FilmEn, IntMPA 77, -75, -76, -78, -79, -80
Friedman, Sidney PupTheA
Friedman, Sol 1920- AmSCAP 66, -80
Friedman, Sonia CreCan 1, NewGrD 80
Friedman, Stanleigh P 1884-1960 AmSCAP 80
Friedman, Stanleigh P 1884-1961 AmSCAP 66
Friedman, Stephen IntMPA 77, -75, -76, -78, -79, -80
Friedman, Theodore Leopold 1892-1971 AmSCAP 80
Friedman, Viktor 1938- IntWWM 80
Friedman, Yona WomWMM
Friedman-Gramatte, Sonia CreCan 1
Friedmann, Moshe 1947- IntWWM 77, -80
Friedmann, Shraga 1923-1970 WhScrn 74, -77, WhoHol B
Friedrich II Baker 78, NewGrD 80
Friedrich Von Hausen 1150?-1190 NewGrD 80
Friedrich Von Husen 1150?-1190 NewGrD 80
Friedrich Von Sonnenburg d1287? NewGrD 80
Friedrich Von Suneburg d1287? NewGrD 80
Friedrich Von Sunnenburc d1287? NewGrD 80
Friedrich Von Sunnenburg d1287? NewGrD 80
Friedrich, Gotz 1930- CmOp, NewGrD 80, WhoOp 76
Friedrichs NewGrD 80
Friedrichs, Gunter 1935- NewGrD 80
Friel, Brian 1929- CnThe, ConDr 73, -77, McGEWD, ModWD, NotNAT, REnWD[port], WhoThe 72, -77
Frieman, Gustaw 1842-1902 NewGrD 80
Frieman, Zbigniew 1927- IntWWM 77, -80
Friemann, Witold 1889- Baker 78,

IntWWM 77, –80, NewGrD 80
Friend, Cliff 1893-1974 *AmPS, AmSCAP 66, –80, BiDAmM, CmpEPM, Sw&Ld C*
Friend, Helene *Film 2*
Friend, Lionel 1945- *IntWWM 80, WhoOp 76*
Friend, Philip 1915- *FilmEn, FilmgC, ForYSC, HalFC 80, IlWWBF, IntMPA 77, –75, –76, –78, –79, –80, WhoHol A*
Friend, Rodney 1939- *WhoMus 72*
Friend & Lover *RkOn 2[port]*
Friendly, Ed *NewYTET*
Friendly, Fred W 1915- *IntMPA 75, –76, NewYTET*
Friendly, Ray *AmSCAP 80*
Friends Of Distinction, The *RkOn 2[port]*
Frierson, Andrew *DrBlPA*
Frierson, Monte L 1930- *BiE&WWA, NotNAT*
Fries, Charles W 1928- *IntMPA 77, –75, –76, –78, –79, –80, NewYTET*
Fries, Hans *NewGrD 80*
Fries, Otto *Film 2*
Fries, Wulf 1825-1902 *Baker 78*
Friese-Greene, William 1855-1921 *FilmEn, FilmgC, HalFC 80, IlWWBF A[port], OxFilm, WorEFlm*
Friesen, Gil *ConMuA 80B*
Frieser, Erika 1927- *IntWWM 80*
Friess, Inge *Film 2*
Friganza, Trixie 1870-1955 *CmpEPM, Film 2, TwYS, WhScrn 74, –77, WhThe, WhoHol B, WhoStg 1908*
Frigel, Pehr 1750-1842 *NewGrD 80*
Frigerio, Ezio 1930- *EncWT, WhoOp 76*
Frigimelica Roberti, Count Girolamo 1653-1732 *NewGrD 80*
Frigo, John Virgil 1916- *AmSCAP 80, BiDAmM*
Frigon, Chris D 1949- *ConAmC*
Frijid Pink *RkOn 2[port]*
Frijsh, Povla 1881-1960 *Baker 78, MusSN[port]*
Frike, Philipp Joseph *NewGrD 80*
Frikell, Wiljalba 1818-1903 *MagIlD*
Friley, Vern 1924- *CmpEPM*
Friml, Charles Rudolf 1881- *WhThe*
Friml, Rudolf 1879-1972 *AmPS, AmSCAP 66, –80, Baker 78, BestMus[port], BiDAmM, BnBkM 80, CmpEPM, ConAmC, EncMT, EncWT, FilmgC, HalFC 80, MusMk, NewCBMT, NewGrD 80, NotNAT B, PlP&P[port], PopAmC[port], PopAmC SUP, PopAmC SUPN, Sw&Ld C*
Friml, Rudolph 1879-1972 *BiE&WWA, What 3[port]*
Friml, William 1921- *AmSCAP 66*
Friml, William 1921-1973 *AmSCAP 80*
Frimmel, Theodor Von 1853-1928 *Baker 78, NewGrD 80*
Frings, Ketti 1915- *BiE&WWA, FilmEn, FilmgC, HalFC 80, McGEWD, NatPD[port], NotNAT*
Frink, Charles 1928- *NatPD[port]*
Frink, George M D 1931- *AmSCAP 80, ConAmC*
Frinton, Freddie 1912-1968 *WhScrn 74, –77, WhoHol B*
Fripp, Robert *ConMuA 80A*
Fripp, Thomas William 1864-1931 *CreCan 2*
Fris, Maria 1932-1961 *CnOxB, DancEn 78*
Frisby, Mildred d1939 *WhoHol B*
Frisby, Terence 1932- *ConDr 73, –77, WhoThe 72, –77*
Frisch, Albert T 1916-1976 *AmSCAP 66, –80*
Frisch, Billy 1882-1968 *AmSCAP 66, –80*
Frisch, Larry 1929- *IntMPA 77, –75, –76, –78, –79, –80*
Frisch, Lore 1925-1962 *WhScrn 74, –77*
Frisch, Max 1911- *BiE&WWA, CnMD, CnThe, CroCD, EncWT, Ent, McGEWD[port], ModWD, NotNAT, OxThe, REnWD[port], WhoThe 72, –77*
Frisch, Paula *Baker 78*
Frischenschlager, Friedrich 1885-1970 *Baker 78*
Frischknecht, Hans Eugen 1939- *IntWWM 77, –80*
Frischmuth, Johann Christian 1741-1790 *NewGrD 80*
Frisco, Albert *Film 2*
Frisco, Joe 1890-1958 *JoeFr[port], NotNAT B, WhScrn 74, –77, WhoHol B*
Frisco, Johnny 1895-1969 *NewOrJ*
Frisell, Sonja Bettie 1937- *WhoOp 76*
Frishberg, Dave 1933- *EncJzS 70*
Frishberg, David L 1933- *AmSCAP 80, BiDAmM, EncJzS 70*
Frisius, Johannes 1505-1565 *NewGrD 80*
Friskin, James 1886-1961 *BiDAmM*
Friskin, James 1886-1967 *Baker 78, ConAmC, NewGrD 80, OxMus*
Friskin, Rebecca Clarke *ConAmC*
Frisoli, John *ConMuA 80B*
Friss, Gabor 1926- *IntWWM 77, –80*
Fristorp, Karl Goran 1948- *IntWWM 80*
Frith, J Leslie 1889-1961 *WhThe*
Frith, John Leslie 1889-1961 *NotNAT B*
Frith, Leslie 1889-1961 *WhoHol B*
Frith, Thomas Preston 1883-1945 *WhScrn 74*
Frith, Tom d1945 *WhoHol B*
Frith, Walter d1941 *NotNAT B*
Fritsch, Balthasar 157-?-1608? *NewGrD 80*
Fritsch, Johannes 1941- *NewGrD 80*
Fritsch, Johannes G 1941- *DcCM*
Fritsch, Thomas 1563-1619 *NewGrD 80*
Fritsch, Willy 1899-1973 *FilmAG WE*
Fritsch, Willy 1901-1973 *FilmEn, Film 2, FilmgC, HalFC 80, WhScrn 77, WhoHol B*
Fritschel, James Erwin 1929- *AmSCAP 80*
Fritschius, Thomas 1563-1619 *NewGrD 80*
Fritso, Egil Gerhart 1941- *IntWWM 80*
Fritter, Genevieve Davisson 1915- *AmSCAP 80, IntWWM 77, –80*
Fritz, Barthold 1697-1766 *NewGrD 80*
Fritz, Chris *ConMuA 80B*
Fritz, Gaspard 1716-1783 *NewGrD 80*
Fritz, Joachimus Fridericus 1525?-1597? *NewGrD 80*
Fritz, Kaspar 1716-1783 *NewGrD 80*
Fritz, Ken *ConMuA 80B*
Fritz, Richard Ernest 1932- *AmSCAP 80*
Fritzeri, Alessandro Mario Antonio *NewGrD 80*
Fritzius, Joachimus Fridericus 1525?-1597? *NewGrD 80*
Fritzsch, Ernst Wilhelm 1840-1902 *Baker 78*
Fritzsche, Gottfried 1578-1638 *NewGrD 80*
Frixer DiFrizeri, Alessandro Mario A *NewGrD 80*
Frizeri, Alessandro Mario Antonio *NewGrD 80*
Frizsch, Thomas *NewGrD 80*
Frizzell, Lefty 1928- *IlEncCM[port]*
Frizzell, Lefty 1928-1975 *CounME 74[port], –74A, EncFCWM 69, RkOn 2[port]*
Frizzell, Lou *WhoHol A*
Frizzell, William Orville 1928- *BiDAmM*
Frobe, Gert 1912- *FilmAG WE, FilmEn, FilmgC, IntMPA 80, MotPP, MovMk, WhoHol A, WhoHrs 80*
Frobe, Gert 1913- *ForYSC, HalFC 80*
Frobenius *NewGrD 80*
Frobenius, Erik *NewGrD 80*
Frobenius, Theodor 1885-1972 *NewGrD 80*
Frobenius, Walther *NewGrD 80*
Frobenius, Wolf 1940- *IntWWM 80*
Froberger, Johann 1616-1667 *GrComp*
Froberger, Johann Jacob 1616-1667 *MusMk, NewGrD 80, OxMus*
Froberger, Johann Jakob 1616-1667 *Baker 78, BnBkM 80, NewGrD 80*
Frock, George A 1938- *AmSCAP 80, ConAmC*
Froeba, Frank 1907?- *CmpEPM, WhoJazz 72*
Froeba, Frank, Jr. 1904- *NewOrJ*
Froeber, Richard Reinhold 1929- *AmSCAP 66, –80*
Froehlich, Gustav *WhoHol A*
Froelich, Carl 1875-1953 *DcFM, FilmEn, OxFilm*
Froelich, Gustav *Film 2*
Froelich, William J d1963 *NotNAT B*
Froes, Walter J 1922-1958 *WhScrn 74, –77, WhoHol B*
Froeschel, George 1891-1979 *FilmEn*
Froeschner, Donna Anderson *WomWMM B*
Froese, Reinhard 1944- *IntWWM 77, –80*
Frogmen, The *RkOn*
Frohbeiter, Ann W 1942- *ConAmC*
Frohlich *NewGrD 80*
Frohlich, Anna 1793-1880 *NewGrD 80*
Frohlich, Barbara Franziska 1797-1879 *NewGrD 80*
Frohlich, Friedrich Theodor 1803-1836 *NewGrD 80*
Frohlich, Gustav 1902- *FilmEn, FilmgC, HalFC 80*
Frohlich, Johannes Frederik 1806-1860 *NewGrD 80*
Frohlich, Josefine 1803-1878 *NewGrD 80*
Frohlich, Joseph 1780-1862 *NewGrD 80*
Frohlich, Katharina 1800-1879 *NewGrD 80*
Frohlich, Willy 1894- *IntWWM 77, –80*
Frohmader, Jerold C 1938- *ConAmC*
Frohman, Charles 1860-1915 *CnThe, EncMT, EncWT, Ent, NotNAT A, –B, OxThe, PlP&P[port], WhThe, WhoStg 1906, –1908*
Frohman, Daniel 1851-1940 *EncWT, Ent, NotNAT A, –B, OxThe, PlP&P, WhThe*
Frohman, Daniel 1853-1940 *WhoStg 1906, –1908*
Frohman, Gustave 1855-1930 *NotNAT B, OxThe*
Frohne, Vincent Sauter 1936- *DcCM, IntWWM 77, –80*
Froidebise, Pierre 1914-1962 *Baker 78, NewGrD 80*
Fromageot, Henri Pierre-Marcel 1937- *IntWWM 77, –80*
Froman, Jane *AmPS A, –B*
Froman, Jane 1907- *CmpEPM, What 5[port], WhoHol A*
Froman, Jane 1911- *ForYSC*
Froman, Margarita Petrovna 1890-1970 *CnOxB, DancEn 78*
Frome, Milton *ForYSC, WhoHol A*
Froment, Louis De 1921- *Baker 78*
Fromentin, Philippe *NewGrD 80*
Fromholz, Steve 1945- *IlEncCM*
Fromholz, Steven John 1945- *AmSCAP 80*
Fromkess, Leon 1907- *IntMPA 77, –75, –76*
Fromm, Andreas 1621-1683 *Baker 78, NewGrD 80*
Fromm, Herbert 1905- *AmSCAP 66, –80, Baker 78, BiDAmM, ConAmC*
Fromm, Paul *NewGrD 80*
Fromme, Arnold 1925- *IntWWM 77, –80*
Frommel, Gerhard 1906- *IntWWM 77, –80, NewGrD 80*
Fronde, Louis *Film 2*
Frondi, Signor *Film 2*
Frondoni, Angelo 1808?-1891 *NewGrD 80*
Front, Theodore 1909- *IntWWM 77, –80*
Frontiere, Dominic 1931- *HalFC 80, IntMPA 77, –75, –76, –78, –79, –80*
Frontini, Francesco Paolo 1860-1939 *Baker 78*
Frosch, Aaron R 1924- *BiE&WWA, NotNAT*
Frosch, Johannes 1480?-1533 *NewGrD 80*
Froschauer, Johann *Baker 78*
Froschius, Johannes 1480?-1533 *NewGrD 80*
Froseth, James O 1936- *IntWWM 77, –80*
Froseth, Nancy Ellen Aurora Thompson 1936- *IntWWM 77, –80*
Frosini, Pietro 1885-1951 *AmSCAP 66, –80*
Frost, Bobby Jean 1932- *IntWWM 80*
Frost, Charles Joseph 1848-1918 *Baker 78*
Frost, David 1939- *HalFC 80, IntMPA 77, –75, –76, –78, –79, –80, NewYTET*
Frost, Frank Otis 1936- *BluesWW[port]*
Frost, Harold G 1893-1959 *AmSCAP 66, –80*
Frost, Henry Frederick 1848-1901 *Baker 78*
Frost, John Harvey 1924- *WhoMus 72*
Frost, Larry Stone 1934- *IntWWM 77, –80*
Frost, Leila *Film 2*
Frost, Ronald 1933- *IntWWM 77, –80, WhoMus 72*
Frost, Thomas 1821- *MagIlD*
Frost, Thomas 1925- *IntWWM 77, –80*
Frothingham, Octavius Brooks 1822-1895 *BiDAmM*
Frotscher, Gotthold 1897-1967 *Baker 78, NewGrD 80*
Frotzler, Carl 1873-1960 *Baker 78*
Frounberg, Ivar 1950- *IntWWM 80*
Frouvo, Joao Alvares 1608-1682 *NewGrD 80*
Frovo, Joao Alvares 1608-1682 *NewGrD 80*
Froyez, Maurice *WhThe*
Froytiers, Jan *NewGrD 80*

Frubert, Joseph *NewGrD 80*
Fruchtman, Milton A *IntMPA 77, -75, -76, -78, -79, -80, NewYTET*
Fruen, Patricia *Film 2*
Frugatta, Giuseppe 1860-1933 *Baker 78*
Frugoni, Carlo Innocenzio 1692-1768 *NewGrD 80*
Frugoni, Carlo Innocenzo 1692-1768 *NewGrD 80*
Frugoni, Orazio 1921- *IntWWM 77, -80, NewGrD 80, WhoMus 72*
Fruh, Armin Leberecht 1820-1894 *Baker 78*
Fruh, Huldreich Georg 1903-1945 *Baker 78, NewGrD 80*
Fruhbeck DeBurgos, Rafael 1933- *Baker 78, BnBkM 80, IntWWM 77, -80, MusSN[port], NewGrD 80*
Fruit Jar Drinkers *BiDAmM, EncFCWM 69*
Fruitier, Jan *NewGrD 80*
Frumerie, Gunnar De 1908- *Baker 78, NewGrD 80*
Frumker, Linda 1940- *ConAmC*
Fruscella, Tony 1927-1969 *EncJzS 70*
Frusciante, John Augustus 1945- *IntWWM 77, -80*
Frush, Sherry Lynn Penkert 1951- *IntWWM 77*
Frutolfus Of Michelsberg d1103 *NewGrD 80*
Fruytiers, Jan d1581? *NewGrD 80*
Fruytiers, Jean d1581? *NewGrD 80*
Fry, Bridget 1928- *WhoMus 72*
Fry, Charles 1845-1928 *NotNAT A, -B*
Fry, Christopher 1907- *BiE&WWA, CnMD, CnThe, ConDr 73, -77, CroCD, EncWT, Ent, McGEWD[port], ModWD, NotNAT, -A, OxThe, PlP&P[port], WhoThe 72, -77, WorEFlm*
Fry, Christopher Charles 1938- *IntWWM 77, -80, WhoMus 72*
Fry, Gary D 1955- *AmSCAP 80*
Fry, Henry S 1875-1946 *BiDAmM*
Fry, Lynette *CreCan 2*
Fry, Nellie E *PupTheA*
Fry, Stephen Michael 1941- *IntWWM 77, -80*
Fry, Tommy Joe 1933- *AmSCAP 80*
Fry, William Henry 1813-1864 *Baker 78, NewGrD 80, OxMus*
Fry, William Henry 1815?-1864 *BiDAmM, MusMk*
Fryatt, John *CmOp*
Fryberg, Mart 1890-1952 *AmSCAP 66, -80*
Frydenland, Per Karsten 1943- *IntWWM 80*
Frydlewicz, Miroslav 1934- *WhoOp 76*
Frye, Carl B 1907- *WhoJazz 72*
Frye, Clayton *Film 2*
Frye, David 1934- *JoeFr*
Frye, Don 1903- *WhoJazz 72*
Frye, Dwight 1899-1943 *FilmgC, ForYSC, HalFC 80, HolCA[port], WhScrn 74, -77, WhoHol B, WhoHrs 80[port]*
Frye, Gil *ForYSC*
Frye, Michael Robert 1949- *IntWWM 77*
Frye, Walter *Baker 78, NewGrD 80*
Frye, William *IntMPA 77, -76, -78, -79, -80*
Fryer, Dorothy Kathleen 1902- *WhoMus 72*
Fryer, George Herbert 1877-1957 *Baker 78*
Fryer, Jack 1929- *IntWWM 77, -80, WhoMus 72*
Fryer, Judith Anne 1935- *IntWWM 77, -80*
Fryer, Robert 1919?- *FilmgC*
Fryer, Robert 1920- *BiE&WWA, EncMT, HalFC 80, NotNAT, WhoThe 72, -77*
Fryklof, Harald Leonard 1882-1919 *Baker 78, NewGrD 80*
Fryklund, Daniel 1879-1965 *NewGrD 80*
Fryklund, Lars Axel Daniel 1879-1965 *Baker 78*
Fryland, Alphons *Film 2*
Frysinger, J Frank 1878-1954 *Baker 78, ConAmC*
Fryxell, Regina Holmen 1899- *ConAmC*
Fu Manchu 1904-1974 *MagIlD*
Fuchs, Albert 1858-1910 *Baker 78, NewGrD 80*
Fuchs, Alois 1799-1853 *NewGrD 80*
Fuchs, Aloys 1799-1853 *NewGrD 80*
Fuchs, Carl 1838-1922 *NewGrD 80*
Fuchs, Charles Emilio 1907- *AmSCAP 66, ConAmC*
Fuchs, Georg 1868-1949 *EncWT*
Fuchs, Georg-Friedrich 1752-1821 *NewGrD 80*
Fuchs, Ignacije *NewGrD 80*
Fuchs, Jacob 1923- *IntWWM 77, -80*
Fuchs, Johann Leopold 1785-1853 *NewGrD 80*
Fuchs, Johann Nepomuk 1842-1899 *Baker 78, NewGrD 80*
Fuchs, Joseph 1900- *Baker 78, NewGrD 80*
Fuchs, Karl Dorius Johann 1838-1922 *Baker 78*
Fuchs, Leo *AmSCAP 80*
Fuchs, Leo 1911- *BiE&WWA, NotNAT, WhoHol A*
Fuchs, Leo L 1929- *IntMPA 77, -75, -76, -78, -79, -80*
Fuchs, Lillian *ConAmC*
Fuchs, Lillian 1903- *NewGrD 80*
Fuchs, Lillian 1912- *WhoMus 72*
Fuchs, Lillian F *IntWWM 77, -80*
Fuchs, Lukas *Baker 78*
Fuchs, Marta 1898-1974 *CmOp, NewEOp 71, NewGrD 80*
Fuchs, Melchior *NewGrD 80*
Fuchs, Peter 1753-1831 *NewGrD 80*
Fuchs, Peter 1933- *IntWWM 77, -80*
Fuchs, Peter Paul 1916- *AmSCAP 80, ConAmC, IntWWM 77, -80*
Fuchs, Pietro 1753-1831 *NewGrD 80*
Fuchs, Robert 1847-1927 *Baker 78, NewGrD 80*
Fuchs, Theodore 1904- *BiE&WWA, NotNAT*
Fuchs, Viktor 1891-1966 *Baker 78*
Fuchsberger, Joachim 1927- *FilmAG WE[port]*
Fuchsova, Liza 1913- *IntWWM 77, -80, WhoMus 72*
Fuchswild, Johannes *NewGrD 80*
Fucik, Julius 1872-1916 *Baker 78, NewGrD 80*
Fuenllana, Miguel De d1568? *Baker 78, NewGrD 80*
Fuente, Luis 1946- *CnOxB*
Fuentealba, Victor *ConMuA 80B*
Fuentes, Fernando De 1895-1952 *FilmEn*
Fuentes, Fernando De 190-?- *DcFM*
Fuentes, Giorgio 1756-1821 *EncWT*
Fuentes, Juan Bautista 1869-1955 *Baker 78*
Fuentes, Martha Ayers *NatPD[port]*
Fuentes, Pascual 1722?-1768 *NewGrD 80*
Fuerburg, DeGarcia *Film 2*
Fuerstner, Carl 1912- *Baker 78, ConAmC, WhoMus 72*
Fuerstner, Fiona 1936- *CnOxB*
Fuest, Robert 1927- *FilmEn, FilmgC, HalFC 80, IlWWBF, IntMPA 77, -75, -76, -78, -79, -80, WhoHrs 80*
Fuetterer, Werner *Film 2*
Fuga, Sandro 1906- *NewGrD 80*
Fugard, Athol 1932- *CnThe, ConDr 73, -77, EncWT, Ent, NotNAT, PlP&P A[port], WhoThe 72, -77*
Fugate, Richard Dell 1954- *AmSCAP 80*
Fugelle, Jacquelyn 1952- *IntWWM 80*
Fuger, Caspar 1561-1617 *NewGrD 80*
Fugere, Jean-Paul 1921- *CreCan 2*
Fugere, Lucien 1848-1935 *Baker 78, NewGrD 80*
Fugger *NewGrD 80*
Fugger, Anton 1493-1560 *NewGrD 80*
Fugger, Christoph 1566-1615 *NewGrD 80*
Fugger, Georg 1453-1506 *NewGrD 80*
Fugger, Georg 1518-1569 *NewGrD 80*
Fugger, Jakob 1459-1525 *NewGrD 80*
Fugger, Jakob 1542-1598 *NewGrD 80*
Fugger, Jakob 1567-1626 *NewGrD 80*
Fugger, Johann 1531-1598 *NewGrD 80*
Fugger, Johann Jakob 1516-1575 *NewGrD 80*
Fugger, Marcus 1564-1614 *NewGrD 80*
Fugger, Octavian, II 1549-1600 *NewGrD 80*
Fugger, Raimund 1489-1535 *NewGrD 80*
Fugger, Raimund 1528-1569 *NewGrD 80*
Fugger, Ulrich 1441-1510 *NewGrD 80*
Fugitives, The *BiDAmM*
Fuglesang, Kare Halvard 1921- *IntWWM 77, -80*
Fugs, The *BiDAmM, ConMuA 80A, IlEncR*
Fuhrer, Robert 1807-1861 *Baker 78, NewGrD 80*
Fuhrmann, Georg Leopold *NewGrD 80*
Fuhrmann, Martin Heinrich 1669-1745 *NewGrD 80*
Fujikawa, Jerry *WhoHol A*
Fujikawa, Mayumi 1946- *IntWWM 77, -80*
Fujimoto, Sanezumi 1910- *IntMPA 77, -75, -76, -78, -79, -80*
Fujino, Hideo *Film 2*
Fujita, Toyo *Film 1, -2*
Fujiwara, Hamao 1947- *IntWWM 80*
Fuka, Vaclav 1933- *IntWWM 77, -80*
Fukagawa, Hideo 1949- *CnOxB*
Fukai, Shiro 1907- *Baker 78*
Fukuda, Jun *WhoHrs 80*
Fukuda, Tsuneari 1912- *CnMD, ModWD*
Fukui, Naohiro 1912- *IntWWM 77, -80*
Fukumura, Hiroshi 1949- *EncJzS 70*
Fukushima, Kazuo 1930- *Baker 78, NewGrD 80*
Fulbertus Episcopus Karnotensis 960?-1028 *NewGrD 80*
Fulbright, Dick 1901-1962 *WhoJazz 72*
Fulcher, Ellen Georgina *WhoMus 72*
Fulco Anfos *NewGrD 80*
Fuld, James J 1916- *IntWWM 77, -80, NewGrD 80*
Fuld, Leo 1913- *AmSCAP 66*
Fulda, Adam Von *NewGrD 80*
Fulda, Ludwig 1862-1939 *EncWT, ModWD, NotNAT B*
Fuleihan, Anis 1900-1970 *AmSCAP 66, -80, Baker 78, BiDAmM, ConAmC, DcCM, OxMus*
Fuleihan, Anis 1901-1970 *NewGrD 80*
Fuley, Elizabeth *Film 2*
Fulford, David 1925- *BiE&WWA, NotNAT*
Fulford, Tommy 1912-1956 *WhoJazz 72*
Fulgentio Fiammingo, Vincenzo Beltramo *NewGrD 80*
Fulgentius, Fabius Planciades *NewGrD 80*
Fulgenzi Fiammingo, Vincenzo Beltramo *NewGrD 80*
Fulgham, Mary H *PupTheA*
Fulin, Angelique Jeanne Amelie 1927- *IntWWM 77, -80*
Fulkerson, James 1945- *ConAmC*
Fulkerson, Tavi *WomWMM B*
Fullbrook, Charles 1950- *IntWWM 80*
Fuller, Albert 1926- *NewGrD 80, WhoMus 72*
Fuller, Barbara 1925- *ForYSC*
Fuller, Barbra *WhoHol A*
Fuller, Sir Benjamin John 1875- *WhThe*
Fuller, Blind Boy 1903-1940 *BiDAmM*
Fuller, Blind Boy 1908-1941 *BluesWW[port]*
Fuller, Blind Boy 1909?-1941 *NewGrD 80*
Fuller, Blind Boy, Number 2 *BluesWW*
Fuller, Bobby 1942-1966 *WhScrn 77*
Fuller, Bobby, Four *RkOn 2[port]*
Fuller, Buell R *PupTheA*
Fuller, Charles *Film 1*
Fuller, Charles 1939- *BlkAmP, DrBlPA, MorBAP, NatPD[port]*
Fuller, Charles Oliver 1916- *IntWWM 77, -80*
Fuller, Clem 1909-1961 *WhScrn 74, -77, WhoHol B*
Fuller, Curtis Dubois 1934- *BiDAmM, EncJzS 70*
Fuller, Dale 1897- *Film 1, -2, ForYSC, TwYS*
Fuller, Dean 1922- *AmSCAP 66, -80, BiE&WWA, NotNAT*
Fuller, Donald Sanborn 1919- *ConAmC*
Fuller, Esther Mary 1907- *AmSCAP 66*
Fuller, Frances 1907- *BiE&WWA, NotNAT, ThFT[port], WhoHol A*
Fuller, Frances 1908- *WhThe*
Fuller, Frederick 1908- *IntWWM 77, -80*
Fuller, Haidee *Film 1*
Fuller, Hoyt W 1928- *ConAmTC*
Fuller, Irene *WhScrn 74, -77*
Fuller, Irene 1898-1945 *WhScrn 74, -77, WhoHol B*
Fuller, Isaac 1606-1672 *OxThe*
Fuller, Jack Dubose 1921- *IntMPA 77, -75, -76, -78, -79, -80*
Fuller, Jeanne Weaver 1917- *ConAmC*
Fuller, Jerry *RkOn*
Fuller, Jesse 1896-1976 *BiDAmM, BluesWW[port], EncFCWM 69*
Fuller, Jesse 1897-1976 *EncJzS 70*
Fuller, John G 1913- *BiE&WWA, NotNAT*
Fuller, John W *PupTheA*
Fuller, Johnny 1929- *BluesWW[port]*
Fuller, Lance *ForYSC, WhoHol A*
Fuller, Leland F 1899-1962 *NotNAT B*
Fuller, Leslie 1889-1948 *FilmgC, HalFC 80,*

IlWWBF[port], WhScrn 74, –77, WhoHol B
Fuller, Little Boy BluesWW
Fuller, Loie d1928 CmpGMD[port], WhThe, WhoStg 1906, –1908
Fuller, Loie 1862-1928 CnOxB, DancEn 78, WomWMM
Fuller, Loie 1863-1928 NotNAT B
Fuller, Lorenzo Dow 1919- AmSCAP 80
Fuller, Margaret 1905-1952 WhScrn 74, –77, WhoHol B
Fuller, Mary 1893- Film 1, MotPP, TwYS
Fuller, Mollie 1865-1933 NotNAT B, WhoStg 1906
Fuller, Olive Gordon 1896- Film 1, –2, TwYS
Fuller, Oscar Anderson 1904- BiDAmM
Fuller, Playboy BluesWW
Fuller, Ramon C 1930- ConAmC
Fuller, Richard Lee BluesWW
Fuller, Robert 1934- FilmgC, ForYSC, HalFC 80, WhoHol A
Fuller, Robert Edward 1945- IntWWM 77
Fuller, Rocky BluesWW
Fuller, Rosalinde 1901- Film 2, OxThe, WhoThe 72, –77
Fuller, Samuel IntMPA 77, –75, –76, –78, –79, –80
Fuller, Samuel 1911- DcFM, FilmEn, FilmgC, OxFilm, WorEFlm
Fuller, Samuel 1912- BiDFilm, –81, HalFC 80
Fuller, Samuel 1916- CmMov
Fuller, Sarah Ann 1939- NewGrD 80
Fuller, Walter 1910- BiDAmM, CmpEPM, WhoJazz 72
Fuller, Walter Gilbert 1920- BiDAmM
Fuller Maitland, J A 1856-1936 NewGrD 80
Fuller-Maitland, John Alexander 1856-1936 Baker 78, OxMus
Fullerton, Fiona 1955- FilmgC, HalFC 80
Fullerton, Joan WhoMus 72
Fullmer, Charles Curtis 1926- WhoOp 76
Fullsach, Zacharias 1580?-1621? NewGrD 80
Fullsack, Zacharias 1580?-1621? NewGrD 80
Fulop, Viktor 1929- CnOxB
Fulsom, Lowell 1921- BiDAmM, BluesWW[port]
Fulson, Lowell 1921- BluesWW[port]
Fulton, Arnold 1896- WhoMus 72
Fulton, Charles J 1857-1938 NotNAT B, WhThe
Fulton, Dave ConMuA 80B
Fulton, Eileen BiE&WWA, WhoHol A
Fulton, Gaye 1939- CnOxB
Fulton, Jack 1903- AmSCAP 66, CmpEPM
Fulton, James F Film 2
Fulton, Joan FilmEn, WhoHol A
Fulton, John Collins 1903- AmSCAP 80
Fulton, John P 1902-1965 DcFM, FilmgC, HalFC 80, WhoHrs 80
Fulton, Maude 1881-1950 Film 2, NotNAT B, WhScrn 74, –77, WhThe, WhoHol B
Fulton, Norman 1909- NewGrD 80, WhoMus 72
Fulton, Reg 1924- AmSCAP 66, –80
Fulton, Rosswell Henry, Sr. 1929- AmSCAP 80
Fulton, Wilson PupTheA
Fumagalli NewGrD 80
Fumagalli, Adolfo 1828-1856 Baker 78, NewGrD 80, OxMus
Fumagalli, Disma 1826-1893 Baker 78, NewGrD 80
Fumagalli, Luca 1837-1908 Baker 78, NewGrD 80
Fumagalli, Polibio 1830-1891 Baker 78
Fumagalli, Polibio 1830-1900 NewGrD 80
Fumet, Dynam-Victor 1867-1949 Baker 78, NewGrD 80
Fumi, Vinceslao 1823-1880 Baker 78
Funccius, David 1630?-1690? NewGrD 80
Funck, David 1630?-1690? NewGrD 80
Funcke, Friedrich 1642-1699 NewGrD 80
Funes, Louis De 1914- FilmEn
Fung, Willie 1896-1945 Film 2, WhScrn 77
Fung, Willie 1900- ForYSC, Vers B[port]
Funghetto, Paolo NewGrD 80
Fungoni, Papebrochio NewGrD 80
Funicello, Annette 1942- BiDAmM, FilmgC, ForYSC, HalFC 80, MotPP, WhoHol A
Funk, Emmy 1919- WhoMus 72
Funk, Eric 1949- CpmDNM 72, –73, –74, ConAmC
Funk, Heinrich 1893- IntWWM 77, –80
Funk, Joseph 1778-1862 NewGrD 80
Funk, Larry BgBands 74
Funk, Nancy Melich 1942- ConAmTC
Funkadelic IlEncR, RkOn 2[port]
Funke, Lewis 1912- BiE&WWA, NotNAT
Funkhouser, Frederick A 1905- IntWWM 77, –80
Funster, Otto 1886-1958 NewGrD 80
Funt, Allen 1914- AmSCAP 66, FilmgC, HalFC 80, NewYTET
Fuoco, Joseph G 1954- AmSCAP 80
Fuoco, Sofia 1830-1916 CnOxB, DancEn 78
Fuqua, Charles 1911-1971 WhScrn 74, –77
Fuqua, Charlie 1911-1971 WhoHol B
Furay, Paul Richard AmSCAP 80
Furay, Richie ConMuA 80A
Furber, Douglas 1885-1961 EncMT, NotNAT B, WhThe
Furber, Percival E 1906- IntMPA 77, –75, –76, –78, –79, –80
Furbish, Ralph E 1914-1974 WhScrn 77
Furchheim, Johann Wilhelm 1635?-1682 NewGrD 80
Furci, Antoine NewGrD 80
Furedi, Judith Susan 1949- AmSCAP 80
Furey, Barney 1888-1938 WhScrn 77
Furie, Sidney J 1933- FilmEn, FilmgC, HalFC 80, IlWWBF, IntMPA 77, –75, –76, –78, –79, –80, MovMk[port], OxFilm, WhoHrs 80, WorEFlm
Furio, Pedro NewGrD 80
Furlan, Lamberto Olindo 1935- WhoOp 76
Furlanetto, Bonaventura 1738-1817 NewGrD 80
Furley, Shelagh d1951 NotNAT B
Furman, James 1937- ConAmC
Furman, Roger BlkAmP, DrBlPA, MorBAP
Furman, Sam H 1918- AmSCAP 66
Furman, Samuel Herbert 1918-1970 AmSCAP 80
Furmedge, Edith NewGrD 80
Furnberg, Louis 1909-1957 CnMD
Furneaux, Yvonne 1928- FilmgC, ForYSC, HalFC 80, IntMPA 77, –75, –76, –78, –79, –80, WhoHol A, WhoHrs 80
Furness, Alan 1949- IntWWM 77, –80
Furness, Betty 1916- FilmEn, ForYSC, NewYTET, ThFT[port], WhoHol A
Furness, Margaret Aimee Eileen 1925- WhoMus 72
Furness, William Henry 1802-1896 BiDAmM
Furney, James A Film 1
Furniss, Cathy AmSCAP 80
Furniss, Grace Livingston d1938 NotNAT B, WhThe
Furniss, Harry 1854-1925 WhScrn 77
Furnival, F J 1825-1910 NotNAT B
Furno, Giovanni 1748-1837 Baker 78, NewGrD 80
Furnstman, Georgia Film 1
Furrer, Ulrich 1942- WhoOp 76
Furrer, Urs 1934-1975 HalFC 80
Furrer, Walter 1902- IntWWM 77, –80
Fursch-Madi, Emma 1847-1894 Baker 78
Fursch-Madi, Emmy 1847-1894 BiDAmM
Furse, Jill d1944 NotNAT A
Furse, Judith 1912- FilmgC, HalFC 80, WhThe, WhoHol A
Furse, Margaret 1911-1974 HalFC 80
Furse, Roger 1903-1972 FilmgC, HalFC 80, NotNAT B, WhThe, WhoThe 72, WorEFlm
Furse, Rogr K 1903-1972 FilmEn
Furse, Russell L 1908- IntMPA 77, –75, –76, –78, –79, –80
Furst, Paul Walter 1926- NewGrD 80
Furst, William Wallace 1852-1917 BiDAmM, NotNAT B
Furstenau NewGrD 80
Furstenau, Anton Bernhard 1792-1852 NewGrD 80
Furstenau, Caspar 1772-1819 NewGrD 80
Furstenau, Moritz 1824-1889 Baker 78, NewGrD 80
Furstenberg, Dorothee 1942- WhoOp 76
Furstenberg, Ira ForYSC, WhoHol A
Furstner NewGrD 80
Furstner, Adolf 1833-1908 Baker 78
Furstner, Adolph 1833-1908 NewGrD 80
Furstner, Otto 1886-1958 Baker 78
Furstner, Ursula Baker 78
Fursy, Antoine NewGrD 80
Furtado, Teresa 1845-1877 NotNAT B
Furtado, Thomas A 1928- AmSCAP 66, –80
Furtenbach, Josef 1591-1667 OxThe
Furter, Georg 1560?-1612? NewGrD 80
Furth, George 1932- ConDr 73, –77D, ForYSC, NatPD[port], PlP&P A[port], WhoHol A, WhoThe 77
Furth, Jaro Film 2
Furthman, Jules 1888-1960 FilmEn, OxFilm
Furthman, Jules 1888-1966 DcFM, FilmgC, HalFC 80, WorEFlm
Furtner, Georg 1560?-1612? NewGrD 80
Furttenbach, Josef 1591-1667 EncWT
Furtter, Georg 1560?-1612? NewGrD 80
Furttner, Georg 1560?-1612? NewGrD 80
Furtwangler, Gise 1917- CnOxB
Furtwangler, Philipp NewGrD 80
Furtwangler, Wilhelm 1886-1954 Baker 78, BnBkM 80[port], CmOp, MusMk, MusSN[port], NewEOp 71, NewGrD 80[port]
Furuhjelm, Erik Gustaf 1883-1964 Baker 78
Fury, Barney Film 2
Fury, Billy 1941- HalFC 80
Fury, Ed ForYSC, WhoHol A
Fury, Loretta WhoHol A
Furze, Jessie 1903- IntWWM 77, –80, WhoMus 72
Fusco, Giovanni 1906- DcFM, FilmEn, FilmgC, HalFC 80, OxFilm, WorEFlm
Fuselier, Louis NewGrD 80
Fusellier, Louis NewGrD 80
Fusetti, Gian Paolo d1690 NewGrD 80
Fusetti, Giovanni Paolo d1690 NewGrD 80
Fusetto, Gian Paolo d1690 NewGrD 80
Fusetto, Giovanni Paolo d1690 NewGrD 80
Fusier-Gir, Jeanne d1974 WhoHol B
Fuss, Johann Evangelist NewGrD 80
Fuss, Kurt Film 2
Fussan, Werner 1912- Baker 78, NewGrD 80
Fussell, Charles C 1938- ConAmC
Fussell, John Michael 1933- IntWWM 77, –80
Fussl, Karl Heinz 1924- NewGrD 80
Fusz, Janos NewGrD 80
Fusz, Janos 1777-1819 NewGrD 80
Futch, Edward Garvin 1944- AmSCAP 80
Futor, Mildred PupTheA
Futter, Georg NewGrD 80
Futter, Jorg NewGrD 80
Futterer, Carl 1873-1927 Baker 78
Futterman, Enid Susan 1943- AmSCAP 80
Futterman, Lewis ConMuA 80B
Fux, Ivan Ivanovich NewGrD 80
Fux, Johann Joseph 1660-1741 Baker 78, BnBkM 80, MusMk, NewGrD 80[port], OxMus
Fux, Leopol'd Ivanovich NewGrD 80
Fux, Maria Anna NewGrD 80
Fux, Pietro NewGrD 80
Fuzelier, Louis 1672-1752 OxThe
Fuzelier, Louis 1674-1752 NewGrD 80
Fuzelier, Louis 1677-1752 CnOxB, DancEn 78
Fuzellier, Louis 1674-1752 NewGrD 80
Fyfe, H Hamilton 1869-1951 NotNAT B, WhThe
Fyffe, Will 1884-1947 FilmgC, HalFC 80, WhScrn 74, WhoHol B
Fyffe, Will 1885-1947 EncWT, Ent, FilmAG WE, IlWWBF, NotNAT B, OxThe
Fyffe, Will 1911-1947 WhScrn 77
Fyles, Franklin d1911 NotNAT B
Fyodorova, Elizaveta Semyonovna NewGrD 80
Fyson, Ruth 1919- WhoMus 72

G

G, Jane *ConMuA 80B*
G-Clefs, The *RkOn[port]*
Gaal, Charles J 1893- *AmSCAP 66, –80*
Gaal, Franceska 1904-1972 *FilmEn, ForYSC, HalFC 80*
Gaal, Franceska 1909- *FilmgC*
Gaal, Franciska 1904-1972 *FilmEn, ThFT[port], WhoHol B*
Gaal, Franziska 1904-1972 *FilmEn*
Gaal, Istvan 1933- *FilmEn, OxFilm*
Gaarenstroom, Harry 1918- *IntWWM 77, –80*
Gaarn-Larsen, Hanna 1951- *IntWWM 77, –80*
Gabb, Harry 1909- *IntWWM 77, –80, WhoMus 72*
Gabbalone, Michele *NewGrD 80*
Gabbelone, Gaspare *NewGrD 80*
Gabbrielli, Giovanni Baptista *NewGrD 80*
Gabel, Martin 1912- *BiE&WWA, FilmEn, FilmgC, ForYSC, HalFC 80, MovMk, NotNAT, WhoHol A, WhoThe 72, –77*
Gabel, Scilla 1937- *FilmgC, HalFC 80*
Gabella, Giovanni Battista *NewGrD 80*
Gabellone, Gaspare 1727-1796 *NewGrD 80*
Gabellone, Michele *NewGrD 80*
Gaber, George 1916- *IntWWM 77, –80*
Gaber, Harley 1943- *CpmDNM 78, ConAmC*
Gabichvadze, Revaz Kondrat'yevich 1913- *NewGrD 80*
Gabignet, Pierre *NewGrD 80*
Gabin, Jean 1904-1976 *BiDFilm, –81, FilmAG WE[port], FilmEn, FilmgC, ForYSC, HalFC 80, IntMPA 77, –75, –76, MotPP, MovMk[port], OxFilm, WhoHol A, WorEFlm[port]*
Gable, Christopher 1940- *CnOxB, DancEn 78, HalFC 80*
Gable, Clark 1901-1960 *BiDFilm, –81, CmMov, FilmEn, Film 2, FilmgC, ForYSC, HalFC 80[port], MGM[port], MotPP, MovMk[port], NotNAT B, OxFilm, WhScrn 74, –77, WhThe, WhoHol B, WorEFlm[port]*
Gable, June 1945- *NotNAT*
Gabler, Joseph 1700-1771 *NewGrD 80*
Gabler, Milton 1911- *AmSCAP 66, –80*
Gabold, Ingolf Georg August 1942- *Baker 78, IntWWM 77, –80*
Gabor, Constantin 1929- *WhoOp 76*
Gabor, Eva *MotPP, WhoHol A*
Gabor, Eva 1921- *FilmgC, HalFC 80*
Gabor, Eva 1924?- *FilmEn, MovMk[port]*
Gabor, Eva 1926- *BiE&WWA, ForYSC*
Gabor, Pal 1932- *OxFilm*
Gabor, Zsa Zsa *MotPP, WhoHol A*
Gabor, Zsa Zsa 1919- *FilmgC, HalFC 80, WhoHrs 80*
Gabor, Zsa Zsa 1920- *FilmEn*
Gabor, Zsa Zsa 1921- *ForYSC*
Gabor, Zsa Zsa 1923- *IntMPA 77, –75, –76, –78, –79, –80, MovMk[port]*
Gabos, Gabor 1930- *IntWWM 77, –80, NewGrD 80*
Gabovich, Mikhail Markovich 1905-1965 *CnOxB, DancEn 78*
Gabovich, Mikhail Mikhailovich 1948- *CnOxB*
Gabriel And The Angels *RkOn*
Gabriel DeTexerana *NewGrD 80*
Gabriel Hieromonachus *NewGrD 80*
Gabriel, Albert 1875- *NewOrJ*
Gabriel, Charles H, Jr. 1892-1934 *AmSCAP 66, –80*
Gabriel, Charles H, Sr. 1856-1932 *AmSCAP 80*
Gabriel, Charles Hutchinson 1856-1932 *AmSCAP 66*
Gabriel, Charles Hutchison 1856-1932 *NewGrD 80*
Gabriel, Clarence 1905-1973 *NewOrJ*
Gabriel, Gilbert W 1890-1952 *NotNAT B, WhThe*
Gabriel, John *WhoHol A*
Gabriel, Manny 1897- *NewOrJ*
Gabriel, Mary Ann Virginia 1825-1877 *Baker 78*
Gabriel, Peter 1950- *ConMuA 80A, IlEncR*
Gabrieli, Andrea 1510?-1586 *Baker 78, DcCom&M 79, NewGrD 80, OxMus*
Gabrieli, Andrea 1520?-1586 *BnBkM 80, DcCom 77, GrComp, MusMk*
Gabrieli, Domenico 1650?-1690 *Baker 78*
Gabrieli, Giovanni 1553?-1612 *NewGrD 80*
Gabrieli, Giovanni 1554?-1612 *Baker 78*
Gabrieli, Giovanni 1557-1612 *BnBkM 80, CmpBCM, DcCom 77, DcCom&M 79, GrComp, MusMk, OxMus*
Gabrielli, Adriana *NewGrD 80*
Gabrielli, Adriana 1755- *CmOp*
Gabrielli, Caterina 1730-1796 *Baker 78, CmOp, NewGrD 80*
Gabrielli, Domenico 1651-1690 *Baker 78, NewGrD 80*
Gabrielli, Francesca *NewGrD 80*
Gabrielli, Francesco d1654 *OxThe*
Gabrielli, Francesco 1588-1636 *EncWT, Ent*
Gabrielli, Giovanni d1603? *EncWT*
Gabrielli, Giovanni 1588?-1635? *OxThe*
Gabrielli, Girolamo *OxThe*
Gabrielli, Giulia *OxThe*
Gabrielli, Count Nicola 1814-1891 *NewGrD 80*
Gabrielli, Count Nicolo 1814-1891 *Baker 78, NewGrD 80*
Gabril, Mercdes *AmSCAP 80*
Gabrilovich, Ossip 1878-1936 *NewGrD 80*
Gabrilowitsch, Ossip 1878-1936 *Baker 78, BiDAmM, BnBkM 80, MusSN[port]*
Gabrio, Gabriel *Film 2*
Gabry, Gyorgy 1927- *NewGrD 80*
Gabrys, Ewa 1936- *IntWWM 77, –80*
Gabucci, Giulio Cesare *NewGrD 80*
Gabugah, O O 1945- *BlkAmP*
Gabuniya, Nodar Kalistratovich 1933- *NewGrD 80*
Gaburo, Kenneth 1926- *AmSCAP 66, –80, Baker 78, BiDAmM, ConAmC, DcCM, NewGrD 80*
Gabusi, Giulio Cesare 1555?-1611 *NewGrD 80*
Gabussi, Giulio Cesare 1555?-1611 *Baker 78, NewGrD 80*
Gabussi, Vincenzo 1800-1846 *NewGrD 80*
Gaby, Frank 1896-1945 *WhScrn 74, –77, WhoHol B*
Gace Brule 1160?-1213? *NewGrD 80*
Gachet, Alice d1960 *NotNAT B*
Gad, Peter Urban 1879-1947 *DcFM*
Gad, Urban 1879-1947 *FilmEn*
Gadbois, Charles E 1905- *ConAmC*
Gadd, Jack Norman 1931- *IntWWM 77, –80*
Gadd, Renee 1908- *IlWWBF, WhThe, WhoHol A*
Gadd, Ulf 1943- *CnOxB*
Gaddarn, William James 1924- *IntWWM 77, –80, WhoMus 72*
Gaddis, Jan-E Preece 1946- *IntWWM 77*
Gade, Axel Willy 1860-1921 *Baker 78*
Gade, Jacob 1879-1963 *Baker 78, NotNAT B*
Gade, Niels 1817-1890 *Baker 78, BnBkM 80, DcCom&M 79, GrComp[port], MusMk, NewGrD 80[port], OxMus*
Gade, Per 1944- *IntWWM 77, –80*
Gade, Sven 1877-1952 *DcFM, FilmEn*
Gade, Svend 1877-1952 *EncWT*
Gade, W *Film 2*
Gaden, Alexander *Film 1*
Gades, Antonio 1936- *CnOxB, DancEn 78[port]*
Gadifer D'Avion *NewGrD 80*
Gadjibekov, Ismail Ogly 1918- *IntWWM 77, –80*
Gadouas, Robert *CreCan 2*
Gadsby, Henry Robert 1842-1907 *Baker 78, NewGrD 80*
Gadski, Johanna 1872-1932 *Baker 78, MusSN[port], NewEOp 71, NewGrD 80*
Gadson, Jacqueline *Film 2*
Gadzhibekov, Sultan *NewGrD 80*
Gadzhibekov, Uzeir 1885-1948 *Baker 78, NewGrD 80*
Gadzhiyev, Akhmet *NewGrD 80*
Gaelle, Johannes 1752-1816 *NewGrD 80*
Gaelle, Meingosus 1752-1816 *NewGrD 80*
Gaetani, Jan De *NewGrD 80*
Gaetano d1792? *NewGrD 80*
Gafa, Alexander 1941- *EncJzS 70*
Gaffarello *NewGrD 80*
Gaffi, Tommaso Bernardo 1665?-1744 *NewGrD 80*
Gaffney, Floyd 1930- *NotNAT*
Gaffney, Liam 1911- *WhThe*
Gaffney, Marjorie *WomWMM*
Gaffney, Robert 1931- *IntMPA 77, –75, –76, –78, –79, –80*
Gafford, Charlotte *WomWMM A, –B*
Gaffurio, Franchino *Baker 78*
Gaffurius, Franchinus 1451-1522 *NewGrD 80[port]*
Gafori 1451-1522 *OxMus*
Gafori, Franchinus 1451-1522 *NewGrD 80[port]*
Gaforio 1451-1522 *OxMus*
Gaforio, Franchino 1451-1522 *Baker 78*
Gafurius, Franchinus 1451-1522 *NewGrD 80[port]*
Gage, Edwin 1915- *IntMPA 77, –75, –76, –78, –79, –80*

Gage, Erford 1913-1945 *WhScrn 77*
Gage, Richard N 1905- *BiE&WWA*
Gagen, Robert Ford 1847-1926 *CreCan 1*
Gagliano *NewGrD 80*
Gagliano, Alessandro *Baker 78, NewGrD 80, OxMus*
Gagliano, Carlo *NewGrD 80*
Gagliano, Ferdinando 1724?-1781 *Baker 78, NewGrD 80, OxMus*
Gagliano, Frank 1931- *ConDr 73, -77, NatPD[port], WhoThe 72, -77*
Gagliano, Gennaro 1700-1788 *Baker 78, NewGrD 80, OxMus*
Gagliano, Giovanbattista Da 1594-1651 *NewGrD 80*
Gagliano, Giovanni *NewGrD 80*
Gagliano, Giovanni Battista Da 1594-1651 *NewGrD 80*
Gagliano, Giuseppe *OxMus*
Gagliano, Januarius *NewGrD 80*
Gagliano, Joannes *NewGrD 80*
Gagliano, Marco Da 1575?-1642 *BnBkM 80, CmOp, MusMk, OxMus*
Gagliano, Marco Da 1582-1643 *Baker 78, NewGrD 80[port]*
Gagliano, Nicola 1695-1758 *Baker 78, NewGrD 80*
Gagliano, Nicolo *OxMus*
Gagliardi, George Anthony 1947- *AmSCAP 80*
Gagliardi, Nick 1921- *NewOrJ*
Gagnard, Frank Lewis 1929- *ConAmTC*
Gagnebin, Henri 1886-1977 *Baker 78, DcCM, NewGrD 80, OxMus, WhoMus 72*
Gagnebin, Ruth 1921- *IntWWM 77, -80*
Gagnier, Claire 1924- *CreCan 1*
Gagnier, Gerald Ray D'Iese 1926-1951? *CreCan 2*
Gagnier, Josephat Jean 1885-1949 *CreCan 2*
Gagnon, Charles 1934- *CreCan 2*
Gagnon, Clarence Alphonse 1881-1942 *CreCan 1*
Gagnon, Henri 1887-1961 *NewGrD 80*
Gagnon, Jean-Louis 1913- *CreCan 1*
Gagnon, Maurice 1912- *CreCan 2*
Gagnon, Paul-Andre 1947- *IntWWM 80*
Gahagan, Helen 1900- *BiE&WWA, HalFC 80, NotNAT, WhThe, WhoHol A*
Gahagan, Helen 1900-1980 *FilmEn*
Gahmlich, Wilfried 1939- *WhoOp 76*
Gai, Loris 1928- *CnOxB*
Gaiani, Giovanni Battista 1757-1819 *NewGrD 80*
Gaidaroff, E *Film 2*
Gaidarov, Vladimir *Film 2*
Gaidelis, Julius 1909- *ConAmC*
Gaidifer D'Avion *NewGrD 80*
Gaier, Johann Christoph *NewGrD 80*
Gaiettane, Fabrice Marin *NewGrD 80*
Gaiffre, Georges-Adam *NewGrD 80*
Gaige, Crosby 1882-1949 *NotNAT A, -B, WhThe*
Gaige, Russell d1974 *WhScrn 77, WhoHol B*
Gaige, Truman *BiE&WWA, NotNAT*
Gail, Jane *Film 1*
Gail, Sophie 1775-1819 *NewGrD 80*
Gail, Zoe *WhThe*
Gailhard, Andre 1885-1966 *NewGrD 80*
Gailhard, Pedro 1848-1918 *NewGrD 80*
Gailhard, Pierre 1848-1918 *Baker 78, NewEOp 71, NewGrD 80*
Gailing, Gretchen 1918-1961 *WhScrn 74, -77*
Gaillard, Bulee 1916- *AmSCAP 66, -80*
Gaillard, Marius-Francois 1900-1973 *Baker 78, NewGrD 80*
Gaillard, Paul-Andre 1922- *IntWWM 77, -80, NewGrD 80*
Gaillard, Robert *Film 1*
Gaillard, Slim 1916- *CmpEPM, DrBlPA, IlEncJ, WhoJazz 72*
Gain, Richard 1939- *CnOxB*
Gaines, Adrian Donna 1948- *AmSCAP 80*
Gaines, Charlie 1900- *WhoJazz 72*
Gaines, Earl *PupTheA*
Gaines, Ernestine *Film 2*
Gaines, J E *BlkAmP, MorBAP*
Gaines, James E 1928- *DrBlPA*
Gaines, James M 1911- *IntMPA 77, -75, -76, -78, -79, -80*
Gaines, Lee 1914- *AmSCAP 66, -80*
Gaines, Richard H 1904-1975 *WhScrn 77, WhoHol C*
Gaines, Samuel Richards 1869-1945 *AmSCAP 66, -80, Baker 78, BiDAmM*
Gaines, William *Film 2*
Gaines, William M 1922- *WhoHrs 80*
Gaines-Shelton, Ruth *BlkAmP*
Gainey, Celeste *WomWMM*
Gainsborough, Thomas 1727-1788 *OxMus*
Gaisbauer, Dieter 1944- *IntWWM 77, -80*
Gaisseau, Pierre-Dominique 1923- *DcFM*
Gaisser, Dom Ugo Atanasio 1853-1919 *Baker 78*
Gaisser, Hughes 1853-1919 *NewGrD 80*
Gaisser, Hugo 1853-1919 *NewGrD 80*
Gaisser, Ugo Atanasio 1853-1920 *OxMus*
Gaites, Joseph M d1940 *NotNAT B*
Gaither, Gant *IntMPA 77, -75, -76, -78, -79, -80*
Gaither, Gloria Lee 1942- *AmSCAP 80*
Gaither, William James 1936- *AmSCAP 80, NewGrD 80*
Gaito, Constantino 1878-1945 *Baker 78, NewGrD 80*
Gaius, Jo *NewGrD 80*
Gaiway, James 1939- *WhoMus 72*
Gajani, Giovanni Battista *NewGrD 80*
Gajard, Joseph 1885-1972 *NewGrD 80*
Gajdov, Stefan 1905- *IntWWM 77, -80*
Gajec, John Joseph 1918- *IntWWM 77*
Gajewski, Ferdinand John Vincent 1941- *IntWWM 77, -80*
Gal, Hans 1890- *Baker 78, DcCM, IntWWM 77, -80, NewGrD 80, OxMus, WhoMus 72*
Galajikian, Florence Grandland 1900- *BiDAmM, ConAmC*
Galambos, Beni *NewGrD 80*
Galamian, Ivan 1902- *Baker 78*
Galamian, Ivan 1903- *NewGrD 80*
Galan, Cristobal 1630?-1684 *NewGrD 80*
Galan, Natalio 1919- *WhoMus 72*
Galante, M Christina 1942- *IntMPA 77, -78, -79, -80*
Galao, Joaquim Cordeiro 1762?-1834? *NewGrD 80*
Galban, Ventura *NewGrD 80*
Galbinski, Liviu 1947- *IntWWM 80*
Galbraith, Barry 1919- *CmpEPM*
Galbraith, Gordon 1930- *AmSCAP 80*
Galbraith, Joseph Barry 1919- *BiDAmM, EncJzS 70*
Galbraith, Victoria Garrett 1948- *AmSCAP 80*
Galbreath, Frank 1913-1971 *WhoJazz 72*
Galdos *OxThe*
Galdos, Benito Perez 1845-1920 *NotNAT B*
Galdston, Philip Edward 1950- *AmSCAP 80*
Gale, Alice *Film 1*
Gale, Bob 1952- *IntMPA 79, -80*
Gale, David *WhoHol A*
Gale, Eddie *AmSCAP 80*
Gale, Eddra *WhoHol A*
Gale, Elizabeth *CmOp*
Gale, George *IntMPA 77, -75, -76, -78, -79, -80*
Gale, Jean *WhoHol A*
Gale, John 1929- *WhoThe 72, -77*
Gale, John Clifford 1932- *WhoMus 72*
Gale, June *ForYSC, WhoHol A*
Gale, Kira *WomWMM B*
Gale, Marc F 1956- *IntWWM 77*
Gale, Margaret *Film 1*
Gale, Marguerite H 1885-1948 *WhScrn 74, -77, WhoHol B*
Gale, Stephen *AmSCAP 80*
Gale, Theophilus 1628-1678 *DcPup*
Gale, William Keene 1940- *ConAmTC*
Gale, Zona 1874-1938 *CnMD, McGEWD, ModWD, NotNAT A, -B, WhThe*
Galeazzi, Francesco 1758-1819 *NewGrD 80*
Galeen, Henrik 1881-1949 *FilmgC, HalFC 80*
Galeen, Henrik 1882-1949 *BiDFilm, -81, DcFM, FilmEn, OxFilm, WhScrn 77, WorEFlm*
Galeffi, Carlo 1882-1961 *NewGrD 80*
Galeno, Giovanni Battista 1550?-1626? *NewGrD 80*
Galento, Tony 1910- *What 5[port], WhoHol A*
Galeotti, Cesare 1872-1929 *Baker 78*
Galeotti, Salvatore *NewGrD 80*
Galeotti, Stefano 1723?-1790? *NewGrD 80*
Galeotti, Vincenzo 1733-1816 *CnOxB, DancEn 78*
Galerati, Caterina *NewGrD 80*
Galerini, Pietro Antonio *NewGrD 80*
Galeron, Jean *Film 2*
Gales, Larry 1936- *EncJzS 70*
Gales, Lawrence Bernard 1936- *BiDAmM, EncJzS 70*
Gales, Weston 1877-1939 *Baker 78*
Galfas, Stephen *ConMuA 80B*
Galfridus De Anglia *NewGrD 80*
Galiani, Ferdinando 1728-1787 *McGEWD*
Galilei, Vincentio 152-?-1591 *NewGrD 80*
Galilei, Vincenzio 152-?-1591 *NewGrD 80*
Galilei, Vincenzo 152-?-1591 *Baker 78, MusMk, NewGrD 80*
Gallel, Vincenzo 1533?-1591 *OxMus*
Galimafre *OxThe*
Galimberti, Ferdinando *NewGrD 80*
Galimir, Felix 1910- *IntWWM 77, -80*
Galin, Pierre 1786-1821 *Baker 78, NewGrD 80, OxMus*
Galin-Perinic, Jasenka 1945- *WhoOp 76*
Galina, Anna 1936- *CnOxB, DancEn 78*
Galinberti, Ferdinando *NewGrD 80*
Galindo, Alejandro 1911- *DcFM*
Galindo, Blas 1910- *Baker 78, DcCM*
Galindo, Nacho d1973 *WhScrn 77, WhoHol B*
Galindo Dimas, Blas 1910- *NewGrD 80*
Galinin, German Germanovich 1922-1966 *NewGrD 80*
Galiot, Johannes *NewGrD 80*
Galipaux, Felix 1860-1931 *NotNAT B, WhThe*
Galipeau, Jacques 1924- *CreCan 1*
Galitzin, Nikolay Borisovich *NewGrD 80*
Galitzin, Yury Nikolayevich *NewGrD 80*
Galkin, Elliot W 1921- *NewGrD 80*
Galkin, Elliott 1921- *Baker 78*
Gall, Hugues Randolph 1940- *WhoOp 76*
Gall, Jan Karol 1856-1912 *NewGrD 80*
Galla-Rini, Anthony 1904- *AmSCAP 80, Baker 78, ConAmC*
Gallacher, Tom 1934- *ConDr 73, -77*
Gallagher, Bill *ConMuA 80B*
Gallagher, Christopher S 1940- *ConAmC*
Gallagher, Donald *Film 2*
Gallagher, Edward A 1928- *AmSCAP 66, -80*
Gallagher, Glen B 1909-1960 *WhScrn 74, -77*
Gallagher, Helen 1926- *BiE&WWA, EncMT, NotNAT, PlP&P, WhoHol A, WhoThe 72, -77*
Gallagher, Jack 1947- *CpmDNM 78, ConAmC, IntWWM 80*
Gallagher, James Richard 1943- *AmSCAP 66, -80*
Gallagher, John *ConMuA 80B*
Gallagher, Johnny *Film 2*
Gallagher, Ray 1889-1953 *Film 1, -2, IntMPA 75, TwYS*
Gallagher, Richard 1891-1955 *FilmEn*
Gallagher, Richard 1896-1955 *MovMk, NotNAT B*
Gallagher, Richard 1900-1955 *WhThe*
Gallagher, Richard Skeets 1891-1955 *Film 2, ForYSC, HolP 30[port], TwYS*
Gallagher, Rory *ConMuA 80A, IlEncR[port]*
Gallagher, Skeets 1891-1955 *FilmgC, HalFC 80, MotPP, WhScrn 74, -77, WhoHol B*
Gallagher And Lyle *ConMuA 80A, IlEncR*
Gallagher And Shean *AmPS B, CmpEPM, JoeFr*
Gallahads, The *RkOn*
Gallaher, Donald 1895- *Film 1, -2, WhThe*
Galland, Bertha 1876-1932 *NotNAT B, WhThe, WhoStg 1908*
Gallant, Ann d1973 *WhoHol B*
Gallant, Mavis DeTrafford 1922- *CreCan 2*
Gallardo, Luis Rojas d1957 *WhScrn 74, -77*
Gallasch, David Russel 1934- *IntWWM 77, -80*
Gallasch, Florel Anne 1918- *IntWWM 80*
Gallassi, Antonio *NewGrD 80*
Gallatin, Alberta d1948 *NotNAT B*
Gallaty, Bill, Jr. 1910- *NewOrJ*
Gallaty, Bill, Sr. 1880-1943 *NewOrJ[port]*
Gallaud, Louis 1897- *NewOrJ[port]*
Gallaudet, John 1903- *ForYSC, Vers A[port]*
Gallaudet, Thomas Hopkins 1787-1851 *BiDAmM*
Gallavotti, Signor *PupTheA*

Gallaway, Marian 1903- *BiE&WWA, NotNAT*
Gallay, Jacques Francois 1795-1864 *NewGrD 80*
Gallay, Jules 1822-1897 *Baker 78*
Galle, Jules 1903?- *NewOrJ*
Gallea, Christina 1940- *CnOxB*
Gallegos, Charles B *AmSCAP 66, -80*
Gallegos, Dora Marie *AmSCAP 66*
Gallenberg, Robert, Graf Von 1783-1839 *NewGrD 80*
Gallenberg, Wenzel Robert 1783-1839 *Baker 78*
Galleno, Giovanni Battista *NewGrD 80*
Gallerano, Leandro *NewGrD 80*
Gallery *RkOn 2[port]*
Gallery, Tom *Film 2, TwYS*
Galles, Jose 1761-1836 *Baker 78*
Gallet, Francois *NewGrD 80*
Gallet, Luciano 1893-1931 *NewGrD 80*
Gallet, Sebastien 1753-1807 *CnOxB*
Galletius, Franciscus *NewGrD 80*
Galley, Johann Michael 1650?-1696 *NewGrD 80*
Galli, Amintore 1845-1919 *Baker 78, NewGrD 80*
Galli, Antoine d1565 *NewGrD 80*
Galli, Antonius d1565 *NewGrD 80*
Galli, Caterina 1723?-1804 *NewGrD 80*
Galli, Domenico *NewGrD 80*
Galli, Filippo 1783-1853 *CmOp, NewGrD 80*
Galli, Giuseppe *NewGrD 80*
Galli, Rosina 1896-1940 *CnOxB, DancEn 78, NotNAT B, WhoHol B*
Galli-Bibbiena *OxThe*
Galli-Bibiena *NewGrD 80, OxThe*
Galli-Bibiena, Alessandro 1686-1748 *NewGrD 80*
Galli-Bibiena, Alessandro 1687-1769 *EncWT*
Galli-Bibiena, Antonio 1697?-1774 *NewGrD 80*
Galli-Bibiena, Antonio 1700-1774 *EncWT*
Galli-Bibiena, Carlo 1721?-1787 *NewGrD 80*
Galli-Bibiena, Carlo 1725-1787 *EncWT*
Galli-Bibiena, Ferdinando 1656-1743 *NewGrD 80*
Galli-Bibiena, Ferdinando 1657-1743 *EncWT, Ent*
Galli-Bibiena, Francesco 1659-1737 *NewGrD 80*
Galli-Bibiena, Francesco 1659-1739 *EncWT*
Galli-Bibiena, Giovanni Carlo Sicinio 1720?-1760 *NewGrD 80*
Galli-Bibiena, Giovanni Maria 1694-1777 *NewGrD 80*
Galli-Bibiena, Giovanni Maria 1704-1769 *EncWT*
Galli-Bibiena, Giovanni Maria Galli 1619-1665 *EncWT*
Galli-Bibiena, Giuseppe 1695-1757 *NewGrD 80*
Galli-Bibiena, Giuseppe 1696-1757 *EncWT, Ent*
Galli-Curci, Amelita 1882-1963 *Baker 78, BiDAmM, BnBkM 80[port], CmOp, MusSN[port], NewEOp 71, NewGrD 80[port]*
Galli DaBibbiena *OxThe*
Galli-Marie, Celestine 1840-1905 *Baker 78, CmOp, NewGrD 80*
Galli-Marie, Marie Celestine 1840-1905 *NewEOp 71*
Gallia, Maria *NewGrD 80*
Gallian, Ketti 1913-1959 *HalFC 80*
Gallian, Ketti 1913-1972 *ThFT[port], WhScrn 77, WhoHol B*
Galliard, Johann Ernst 1680?-1749 *Baker 78*
Galliard, Johann Ernst 1687?-1749 *NewGrD 80*
Galliard, John Ernest 1680?-1749 *MusMk*
Galliard, John Ernest 1687?-1749 *NewGrD 80, OxMus*
Galliari *NewGrD 80*
Galliari, Bernardino 1707-1794 *EncWT, Ent, NewGrD 80, NotNAT B*
Galliari, Fabrizio 1709-1790 *EncWT, NewGrD 80, NotNAT B*
Galliari, Gaspare 1761-1823 *NewGrD 80, NotNAT B*
Galliari, Giovanni 1672-1722 *NewGrD 80*
Galliari, Giovanni 1746-1818 *NotNAT B*
Galliari, Giovanni Antonio 1714-1783 *EncWT, NewGrD 80*
Galliari, Giovannino 1746-1818 *NewGrD 80*
Galliari, Giuseppino 1742-1817 *NewGrD 80*
Galliari, Giuseppino 1752-1817 *NotNAT B*
Galliari Family *OxThe*
Gallico, Al *ConMuA 80B*
Gallico, Claudio 1929- *IntWWM 77, -80, NewGrD 80*
Gallico, Grace Lane 1921- *AmSCAP 66*
Gallico, Grace Thorpe 1921- *AmSCAP 80*
Gallico, Paolo 1868-1955 *Baker 78, NewGrD 80*
Gallico, Paul 1897-1976 *FilmgC, HalFC 80*
Galliculus, Johannes *NewGrD 80*
Gallicus, Johannes *NewGrD 80*
Gallienne, Eva Le *OxThe*
Galliera, Alceo 1910- *NewGrD 80, WhoMus 72*
Gallignani, Giuseppe 1851-1923 *Baker 78, NewGrD 80*
Gallimberto, Ferdinando *NewGrD 80*
Gallimore, Catherine d1962 *NotNAT B*
Gallimore, Florrie 1867- *WhThe*
Gallina, Jill C 1946- *AmSCAP 80*
Gallini, Giovanni Andrea *DancEn 78*
Gallinius, Marcin d1562 *NewGrD 80*
Gallion, Robert H 1922- *BiDAmM*
Galliver, David *IntWWM 77, -80*
Galliver, David 1925- *NewGrD 80, WhoMus 72*
Gallmeyer, Josephine 1838-1884 *EncWT*
Gallo, Alberto d1964 *NotNAT B*
Gallo, Domenico *NewGrD 80*
Gallo, F Alberto 1932- *IntWWM 77, -80, NewGrD 80*
Gallo, Fortune 1878-1963 *Baker 78*
Gallo, Fortune 1878-1970 *NewEOp 71, NotNAT B*
Gallo, Giovanni Pietro *NewGrD 80*
Gallo, Giuseppe *NewGrD 80*
Gallo, Lillian *NewYTET*
Gallo, Mario 1878-1945 *DcFM, FilmEn*
Gallo, Pietrantonio 1695?-1777 *NewGrD 80*
Gallo, Pietro Antonio 1695?-1777 *NewGrD 80*
Gallo, R *NewGrD 80*
Gallo, Vincenzo 1560?-1624 *NewGrD 80*
Gallodoro, Al *CmpEPM*
Gallois, Henri 1944- *WhoOp 76*
Gallois-Montbrun, Raymond 1918- *NewGrD 80*
Gallon, Jean 1878-1959 *Baker 78, NewGrD 80*
Gallon, Nellie Tom d1938 *NotNAT B*
Gallon, Noel 1891-1966 *Baker 78, NewGrD 80*
Gallon, Tom d1914 *NotNAT B*
Gallone, Carmine 1886-1973 *DcFM, FilmEn, FilmgC, HalFC 80, IIWWBF, WorEFlm*
Gallop, Frank *RkOn*
Gallop, Rodney 1901-1948 *NewGrD 80*
Gallop, Sammy 1915-1971 *AmSCAP 66, -80, BiDAmM, CmpEPM*
Gallot *NewGrD 80*
Gallot, Antoine d1647 *NewGrD 80*
Gallot, Henry Francois d1684 *NewGrD 80*
Gallot, Jacques d1690? *NewGrD 80*
Gallot Le Jeune d1716? *NewGrD 80*
Galloway, Charles 1865?-1914 *BiDAmM*
Galloway, Charlie d1916? *NewOrJ*
Galloway, Don 1937- *HalFC 80, WhoHol A*
Galloway, George 1917- *IntWWM 77, WhoMus 72*
Galloway, Louise d1949 *NotNAT B*
Galloway, Michael 1946- *ConAmC*
Galloway, Morgan *WhoHol A*
Galloway, Tod B 1863-1935 *AmSCAP 66, -80*
Gallu, Samuel 1918- *FilmgC, HalFC 80*
Gallus, Antonius *NewGrD 80*
Gallus, Giuseppe *NewGrD 80*
Gallus, Jacobus 1550-1591 *Baker 78, BnBkM 80, NewGrD 80*
Gallus, Joannes *NewGrD 80*
Gallus, Johannes 1543?- *Baker 78*
Gallus, Udalricus *NewGrD 80*
Gallus-Mederitsch, Johann *NewGrD 80*
Galluzzo, Marino R, Jr. 1951- *IntWWM 80*
Galm, Tina d1962 *NotNAT B*
Galper, Avrahm 1921- *IntWWM 80*
Galper, Hal 1938- *EncJzS 70*
Galper, Harold 1938- *EncJzS 70*
Galpin, Ellen *PupTheA*
Galpin, Francis William 1858-1945 *Baker 78, NewGrD 80, OxMus*
Galston, Gottfried 1879-1950 *Baker 78, BiDAmM*
Galstyan, Vilen 1941- *CnOxB*
Galsworthy, John 1867-1933 *CnMD, CnThe, EncWT, Ent, FilmgC, HalFC 80, McGEWD[port], ModWD, NotNAT A, -B, OxThe, PlP&P[port], REnWD[port], WhThe*
Galt, John 1779-1839 *NotNAT B, OxMus*
Galton, Sir Francis 1822-1911 *OxMus*
Galton, Ray 1930- *FilmgC, HalFC 80*
Galun, Andrija 1945- *IntWWM 77, -80*
Galuppi, Baldassare 1706-1785 *Baker 78, BnBkM 80, CmOp, GrComp[port], MusMk, NewEOp 71, NewGrD 80[port], OxMus*
Galuten, Albhy *ConMuA 80B*
Galvan, Ventura *NewGrD 80*
Galvani, Dino 1890-1960 *Film 2, FilmgC, HalFC 80, NotNAT B, WhScrn 74, -77, WhThe, WhoHol B*
Galvany, Marisa 1936- *WhoOp 76*
Galvez, Gabriel 1510?-1578 *NewGrD 80*
Galvin, Kathy *WhoHol A*
Galvin, Robby *WhoHol A*
Galway, James 1939- *Baker 78, IntWWM 80, NewGrD 80*
Galy, Paul *PupTheA*
Gam, Rita *MotPP, PlP&P, WhoHol A*
Gam, Rita 1928- *BiE&WWA, FilmEn, FilmgC, ForYSC, HalFC 80, NotNAT*
Gam, Rita 1929- *MovMk[port]*
Gamba, Pierino 1936- *WhoMus 72*
Gamba, Pierino 1937- *NewGrD 80*
Gamba, Piero 1936- *Baker 78*
Gamba, Piero 1937- *NewGrD 80*
Gambalo, Francesco *NewGrD 80*
Gambarelli, Maria *DancEn 78[port], WhoHol A*
Gambarini, Elisabetta De 1731-1765 *NewGrD 80*
Gambell, Doris 1903- *WhoMus 72*
Gamberini, Leopoldo 1922- *IntWWM 80*
Gamberini, Michelangelo *NewGrD 80*
Gamberni, Leopoldo 1922- *IntWWM 77*
Gambino, James John 1919- *ConAmC*
Gamble, Fred d1939 *Film 1, -2, WhoHol B*
Gamble, Fred 1868-1939 *WhScrn 77*
Gamble, Fred 1869-1939 *WhScrn 74*
Gamble, Jerry *Film 2*
Gamble, John d1687 *NewGrD 80*
Gamble, Kenneth *ConMuA 80B*
Gamble, Ralph 1902-1966 *WhScrn 74, -77, WhoHol B*
Gamble, Theodore Roosevelt d1960 *NotNAT B*
Gamble, Tom 1898- *WhThe*
Gamble, Warburton d1945 *Film 1, -2, NotNAT B, WhoHol B*
Gamboa, Pero Da d1638 *NewGrD 80*
Gambold, Fred *Film 2*
Gambold, Geoffrey 1930- *IntWWM 80, WhoMus 72*
Gambon, Michael 1940- *WhoThe 77*
Gamby-Hale Ballet Girls *Film 2*
Gamer, Carlton *ConAmC*
Gamley, Ailsa *WhoMus 72*
Gamley, Douglas 1924- *WhoMus 72*
Gammeltoft-Hansen, Bendt 1932- *IntWWM 77, -80*
Gammon, Philip 1940- *WhoMus 72*
Gammon, William A 1905-1974 *NewOrJ[port]*
Gammond, Peter 1925- *WhoMus 72*
Gamsjager, Rudolf 1909- *WhoOp 76*
Gamson, Arnold 1926- *IntWWM 77, -80*
Gamucci, Baldassare 1822-1892 *Baker 78*
Gamut, David *Film 2*
Gan, Chester 1909-1959 *WhScrn 74, -77, WhoHol B*
Ganassa, Zan 1540?-1584? *EncWT, Ent, OxThe*
Ganassi, Giacomo *NewGrD 80*
Ganassi DalFontego, Sylvestro Di 1492- *NewGrD 80*
Gance, Abel 1889- *BiDFilm, -81, DcFM, FilmEn, FilmgC, HalFC 80, OxFilm, WorEFlm*
Gance, Marguerite *Film 2*
Ganche, Edouard 1880-1945 *Baker 78, NewGrD 80*
Gand *NewGrD 80*
Gand, Charles Adolphe 1812-1866 *NewGrD 80*
Gand, Charles Francois 1787-1845 *NewGrD 80*

Gand, Charles Nicolas Eugene 1825-1892 *NewGrD 80*
Gand, Guillaume Charles Louis 1792-1858 *NewGrD 80*
Gandee, Al 1900-1944 *WhoJazz 72*
Gandillot, Leon d1912 *NotNAT B*
Gandini, Gerardo 1936- *DcCM, NewGrD 80*
Gando *NewGrD 80*
Gando, Nicolas d1767 *NewGrD 80*
Gando, Pierre Francois 1733-1800 *NewGrD 80*
Gandolfi, Riccardo 1839-1920 *Baker 78*
Gandy, Carolyn Virginia 1941- *AmSCAP 80*
Gane, Nolan d1915 *WhScrn 77*
Ganer, Christopher *NewGrD 80*
Gangbar, Lynne Carol 1957- *IntWWM 80*
Gange, Fraser 1886-1962 *Baker 78*
Gange, Kenneth Edward 1939- *IntWWM 80*
Gangemi, Charles David 1928- *IntWWM 77, -80*
Gangflot, Soren 1921- *IntWWM 77, -80*
Gangware, Edgar B, Jr. 1921- *ConAmC*
Ganibalova, Vazira Mikhailovna 1948- *CnOxB*
Ganick, Peter 1946- *ConAmC*
Ganio, Denys 1950- *CnOxB*
Ganis, Sidney M 1940- *IntMPA 77, -75, -76, -78, -79, -80*
Ganne, Louis Gaston 1862-1923 *Baker 78, NewGrD 80*
Gannett, Kent 1887- *AmSCAP 66*
Gannett, William Channing 1840-1923 *BiDAmM*
Gannino, Ruth Lillian 1916- *AmSCAP 66*
Gannon, James Kimball 1900-1974 *AmSCAP 80*
Gannon, John 1903-1969 *WhScrn 74, -77*
Gannon, Kim 1900-1974 *AmSCAP 66, CmpEPM*
Gano, David Earl 1941- *WhoOp 76*
Gansbacher, Johann 1778-1844 *Baker 78, NewGrD 80*
Ganson, Lewis *MagIlD*
Ganson, Paul 1941- *IntWWM 77, -80*
Gansz, George Lewis 1924- *IntWWM 77, -80*
Gant, Cecil 1913-1951 *BluesWW*
Gant, Marjorie Vera 1906- *WhoMus 72*
Gant, William Campbell 1916- *IntWWM 77, -80*
Gant, Willie 1900- *WhoJazz 72*
Gantez, Annibal 1600?-1668? *NewGrD 80*
Ganthony, Richard d1924 *NotNAT B*
Ganthony, Robert d1931 *NotNAT A, -B*
Gantillon, Simon 1887-1961 *McGEWD*
Gantvoori, Carl *Film 2*
Gantvoort, Arnold Johann 1857-1937 *Baker 78*
Gantvoort, Herman L 1887-1937 *WhScrn 74, -77*
Gantvoort, Mary Gretchen Morris 1894-1971 *BiDAmM*
Ganz *NewGrD 80*
Ganz, Aaron *AmSCAP 80*
Ganz, Adolf 1796-1870 *NewGrD 80*
Ganz, Moritz 1806-1868 *NewGrD 80*
Ganz, P Felix 1922- *IntWWM 77, -80*
Ganz, Rudolph 1877-1972 *AmSCAP 66, -80, Baker 78, BiDAmM, BnBkM 80, ConAmC, MusSN[port]*
Ganz, Wilhelm 1833-1914 *Baker 78, NewGrD 80*
Ganzarolli, Wladimiro 1939- *WhoMus 72, WhoOp 76*
Ganzhern, Jack 1881-1956 *Film 2*
Ganzhorn, Jack 1881-1956 *WhoHol B*
Ganzhorn, John 1881-1956 *WhScrn 74, -77*
Gaon, Saadya *NewGrD 80*
Gaona, Ralph Raymond, Sr. 1922- *AmSCAP 80*
Gaona, Ralph Raymond, Sr. 1925- *AmSCAP 66*
Gara, Eugenio 1888- *NewGrD 80*
Garabedian, Edna 1939- *IntWWM 80, WhoOp 76*
Garagiola, Joe 1926- *NewYTET*
Garaguly, Carl 1900- *Baker 78*
Garant, Albert Antonio Serge *CreCan 2*
Garant, Serge 1929- *Baker 78, CreCan 2, DcCM, IntWWM 80, NewGrD 80*
Garas, Kaz *HalFC 80*
Garat, Monsieur *Film 2*
Garat, Henri 1902-1958 *FilmEn*
Garat, Henri 1902-1959 *MotPP, NotNAT B, WhScrn 74, -77*
Garat, Henry 1902-1959 *WhoHol B*
Garat, Pierre-Jean 1762-1823 *Baker 78, NewGrD 80*
Garau, Francisco *NewGrD 80*
Garaude, Alexis De 1779-1852 *Baker 78, NewGrD 80*
Garavaglia, Aida *PupTheA*
Garavaglia, Florencio *PupTheA*
Garaventa, Ottavio 1934- *WhoOp 76*
Garay, Luis De 1613-1673 *NewGrD 80*
Garay, Narciso 1876-1953 *NewGrD 80*
Garay, Narciso 1879-1953 *Baker 78*
Garazzi, Peyo 1937- *WhoOp 76*
Garbarek, Jan 1947- *EncJzS 70, NewGrD 80*
Garbelotto, Antonio 1906- *IntWWM 77, -80*
Garber, Herbert 1919- *IntWWM 77, -80*
Garber, Jan 1897- *BgBands 74[port], CmpEPM*
Garber, Lloyd Elmer 1940- *IntWWM 77, -80*
Garber, Matthew 1956- *FilmgC, HalFC 80, WhoHol A*
Garbig, Johann Anton *NewGrD 80*
Garbini, Aristide *Film 2*
Garbo, Greta *MotPP, WhoHol A*
Garbo, Greta 1905- *BiDFilm, -81, CmMov, FilmEn, Film 2, FilmgC, HalFC 80[port], MGM[port], MovMk[port], OxFilm, ThFT[port], WorEFlm*
Garbo, Greta 1906- *ForYSC, IntMPA 77, -75, -76, -78, -79, -80, TwYS*
Garborg, Arne 1851-1924 *CnMD*
Garbousova, Raya 1905- *Baker 78*
Garbousova, Raya 1906- *NewGrD 80*
Garbuzov, Nikolai 1880-1955 *Baker 78*
Garceau, Lucien Joseph 1936- *IntWWM 77*
Garceau, Raymond 1919- *CreCan 1*
Garcia *CmOp, NewGrD 80*
Garcia Estrada *Baker 78*
Garcia, Signor *PupTheA*
Garcia, Al Ernest *Film 1*
Garcia, Albert 1875-1946 *CmOp, OxMus*
Garcia, Albert Y 1938- *AmSCAP 66*
Garcia, Allan *Film 2*
Garcia, Allen 1887-1938 *WhScrn 77*
Garcia, Eugenie 1818-1880 *Baker 78*
Garcia, Felix 1906- *AmSCAP 66, -80*
Garcia, Fernando 1930- *DcCM*
Garcia, Francisco Javier 1731-1809 *Baker 78*
Garcia, Glenda *ConMuA 80B*
Garcia, Gustave 1837-1925 *CmOp, NewGrD 80, OxMus*
Garcia, Henry 1904-1970 *WhScrn 74, -77*
Garcia, Humberto Rodriguez 1915-1960 *WhScrn 74, -77*
Garcia, Jean 1936- *CnOxB*
Garcia, Jerome John 1942- *AmSCAP 80*
Garcia, Jerry 1941- *BiDAmM, ConMuA 80A*
Garcia, Jose Luis 1944- *WhoMus 72*
Garcia, Jose Mauricio Nunes 1767-1830 *NewGrD 80*
Garcia, King 1905- *WhoJazz 72*
Garcia, M *PupTheA*
Garcia, Manuel 1775-1832 *BnBkM 80, CmOp, NewGrD 80[port], OxMus*
Garcia, Manuel 1805-1906 *CmOp, NewGrD 80, OxMus*
Garcia, Manuel DelPopolo Vicente 1775-1832 *Baker 78, NewEOp 71*
Garcia, Manuel DelPopolo Vincente 1775-1832 *BiDAmM*
Garcia, Manuel Patricio Rodriguez 1805-1906 *Baker 78, NewEOp 71*
Garcia, Maria Felicia 1808-1836 *NewGrD 80, OxMus*
Garcia, Marta 1945?- *CnOxB*
Garcia, Pauline 1821-1910 *OxMus*
Garcia, Pauline Viardot- *Baker 78*
Garcia, Russ 1916- *CmpEPM*
Garcia, Russell 1916- *AmSCAP 66, -80, BiDAmM*
Garcia-Abril, Anton 1933- *DcCM*
Garcia-Asensio, Enrique 1937- *WhoMus 72*
Garcia-Caturla, Alejandro 1906-1940 *DcCM*
Garcia De Basurto, Juan 1477?-1547 *NewGrD 80*
Garcia DeLaHuerta, Vicente 1734-1787 *McGEWD[port], OxThe*
Garcia Fajer, Francisco Javier 1731-1809 *NewGrD 80*
Garcia Gutierrez, Antonio 1813-1884 *McGEWD[port], NotNAT B, OxThe*
Garcia Leoz, Jesus *NewGrD 80*
Garcia Lorca, Federico 1898-1936 *CnOxB, McGEWD[port], ModWD, NewGrD 80, OxThe, REnWD[port]*
Garcia Lorca, Federico 1899-1936 *NotNAT A, -B*
Garcia Mansilla, Eduardo 1870-1930 *Baker 78*
Garcia Matos, Manuel 1912-1974 *NewGrD 80*
Garcia Morillo, Roberto 1911- *NewGrD 80*
Garcia Navarro, Luis Antonio 1941- *IntWWM 77, -80*
Garcia Pacheco, Fabian 1725?-1808? *NewGrD 80*
Garcia Robles, Jose 1835-1910 *NewGrD 80*
Garcin, Henri 1929- *FilmAG WE[port]*
Garcin, Jules Auguste 1830-1896 *NewGrD 80*
Garcisanz, Isabel 1934- *WhoOp 76*
Gard, Alex d1948 *NotNAT B*
Gard, Alex 1900-1948 *DancEn 78*
Gard, Robert E 1910- *BiE&WWA, NotNAT*
Gard, Robert Joseph 1927- *WhoOp 76*
Gardane *NewGrD 80*
Gardane, Alessandro 1539?-1591? *NewGrD 80*
Gardane, Antoine 1509-1569 *NewGrD 80*
Gardane, Antonio 1509-1569 *NewGrD 80*
Gardano *NewGrD 80*
Gardano, Allesandro *AmSCAP 80*
Gardano, Angelo 1540-1611 *NewGrD 80*
Gardano, Antonio 1500?-1569 *Baker 78*
Garde, Betty 1905- *BiE&WWA, Film 2, ForYSC, NotNAT, WhoHol A, WhoThe 72, -77*
Garde, Pierre De *NewGrD 80*
Gardel *NewGrD 80*
Gardel, Carlos 1887?-1935 *WhScrn 74, -77*
Gardel, Claude d1774 *NewGrD 80*
Gardel, Maximilian *OxMus*
Gardel, Maximilien 1741-1787 *CnOxB, DancEn 78, NewGrD 80*
Gardel, Pierre Gabriel 1758-1840 *CnOxB, DancEn 78, NewGrD 80*
Gardella, Tess d1950 *NotNAT B*
Gardelli, Lamberto 1915- *NewGrD 80, WhoMus 72, WhoOp 76*
Garden, E W 1845-1939 *NotNAT B, WhThe*
Garden, Edward James Clarke 1930- *IntWWM 77, -80, NewGrD 80, WhoMus 72*
Garden, Faith *Film 2*
Garden, Mary 1874-1967 *Baker 78, CmOp, MusSN[port], NewGrD 80[port], WhScrn 74, -77*
Garden, Mary 1875-1967 *Film 1, TwYS, WhoHol B*
Garden, Mary 1877-1967 *BiDAmM, BnBkM 80[port], NewEOp 71*
Gardener, Buster *Film 2*
Gardenia, Vincent *PlP&P A[port], WhoHol A*
Gardenia, Vincent 1922- *FilmgC, HalFC 80, WhoThe 77*
Gardenia, Vincent 1923- *BiE&WWA, IntMPA 77, -75, -76, -78, -79, -80, NotNAT*
Gardes, Roger 1922- *Baker 78*
Gardi, Francesco 1760?-1810? *NewGrD 80*
Gardien, Jacques 1909- *IntWWM 77, -80, NewGrD 80*
Gardin, Vladimir 1877-1950 *FilmEn*
Gardin, Vladimir 1877-1965 *DcFM, OxFilm, WhScrn 77*
Gardin, W R *WomWMM*
Gardiner, Cyril 1897- *WhThe*
Gardiner, George R *PupTheA*
Gardiner, Henry Balfour 1877-1950 *Baker 78, NewGrD 80, OxMus*
Gardiner, John Eliot 1928- *IntWWM 77*
Gardiner, John Eliot 1943- *IntWWM 80, NewGrD 80*
Gardiner, John Ernest 1928- *IntWWM 80, WhoMus 72*
Gardiner, Lisa 1894-1956 *CnOxB, DancEn 78*
Gardiner, Patrick 1926-1970 *WhScrn 74, -77*
Gardiner, Peter *PupTheA*
Gardiner, Reece *Film 1*
Gardiner, Reginald 1903- *BiE&WWA, FilmgC, ForYSC, HalFC 80, IIWWBF, MotPP, MovMk[port], Vers A[port], What 4[port],*

WhThe, WhoHol A
Gardiner, Reginald 1903-1980 *FilmEn*
Gardiner, William 1770-1853 *Baker 78, NewGrD 80*
Gardini, Ubaldo Graziano 1924- *IntWWM 80*
Gardner, Adelaide *AmSCAP 80*
Gardner, Amelia *Film 1*
Gardner, Arthur *IntMPA 77, -75, -76, -78, -79, -80*
Gardner, Ava 1922- *BiDFilm, -81, FilmEn, FilmgC, ForYSC, HalFC 80, IntMPA 77, -75, -76, -78, -79, -80, MGM[port], MotPP, MovMk[port], OxFilm, WhoHol A, WorEFlm*
Gardner, Betty *Film 2*
Gardner, Charles A d1924 *NotNAT B*
Gardner, Charles Vaness 1935- *AmSCAP 80*
Gardner, Cyril 1898-1942 *WhScrn 74, -77*
Gardner, Dave *AmSCAP 80*
Gardner, David Emmett 1928- *CreCan 2*
Gardner, Don 1932-1958 *WhScrn 77*
Gardner, Don And Dee Dee Ford *RkOn*
Gardner, Donald Yetter 1912- *AmSCAP 66*
Gardner, Donald Yetter 1913- *AmSCAP 80*
Gardner, Ed 1901-1963 *HalFC 80, NotNAT B, WhScrn 74, -77, WhoHol B*
Gardner, Ed 1905- *JoeFr*
Gardner, Edith *PupTheA*
Gardner, Eric *ConMuA 80B*
Gardner, Erle Stanley 1889-1970 *FilmgC, HalFC 80*
Gardner, Freddy 1911?-1950 *CmpEPM*
Gardner, Gary David 1949- *IntWWM 80*
Gardner, George 1868-1929 *WhScrn 74, -77*
Gardner, Helen d1968 *Film 1, -2, MotPP, WhScrn 74, -77, WhoHol B*
Gardner, Helen 1885?-1968 *FilmEn*
Gardner, Herb 1934- *BiE&WWA, NotNAT*
Gardner, Hunter 1899-1952 *WhScrn 74, -77, WhoHol B*
Gardner, Jack d1950 *NotNAT B*
Gardner, Jack 1876-1929 *Film 1, -2, WhScrn 74, -77, WhoHol B*
Gardner, Jack 1903-1957 *WhoJazz 72*
Gardner, Jack 1915-1955 *WhScrn 74, -77, WhoHol B*
Gardner, James *Film 2, TwYS*
Gardner, Janet *WomWMM B*
Gardner, Joan 1914- *AmSCAP 80, FilmgC, HalFC 80, IlWWBF, WhoHol A*
Gardner, Joan A *WomWMM B*
Gardner, Johann Von 1898- *NewGrD 80*
Gardner, John Linton 1917- *Baker 78, CpmDNM 80, IntWWM 77, -80, MusMk, NewGrD 80, OxMus, WhoMus 72*
Gardner, Julie 1925- *BlkWAB[port]*
Gardner, Kenny *CmpEPM*
Gardner, Kossi 1941- *AmSCAP 80*
Gardner, Margaret *PupTheA*
Gardner, Maurice 1909- *AmSCAP 66, -80*
Gardner, Michael 1920- *AmSCAP 66*
Gardner, Mildred Alvine 1899- *ConAmC*
Gardner, Newport 1746- *BiDAmM*
Gardner, Peter 1898-1953 *WhScrn 74, -77*
Gardner, R H 1918- *ConAmTC*
Gardner, Randy Clyburn 1952- *IntWWM 77, -80*
Gardner, Richard d1972 *WhoHol B*
Gardner, Rita *BiE&WWA, NotNAT*
Gardner, Robert Alexander 1897- *BiDAmM*
Gardner, Robert N 1936- *IntWWM 77*
Gardner, Robert Neil 1922- *IntWWM 77, -80, WhoMus 72*
Gardner, Samuel 1891- *AmSCAP 66, -80, Baker 78, BiDAmM, ConAmC, IntWWM 77, -80, NewGrD 80, WhoMus 72*
Gardner, Shayle 1890-1945 *Film 2, NotNAT B, WhThe, WhoHol B*
Gardner, Will 1879- *WhThe*
Gardner, William Henry 1865-1932 *AmSCAP 66, -80*
Gardner And Brewer *PupTheA*
Gardonyi, Zoltan 1906- *NewGrD 80*
Garducci, Tommaso *NewGrD 80*
Gare, Lou 1939- *EncJzS 70*
Garellick, Jack L 1918-1975 *AmSCAP 80*
Gareth, Benedetto 1450?-1514 *NewGrD 80*
Garf, Gene 1918- *AmSCAP 80*
Garfein, Jack 1930- *BiE&WWA, FilmEn, FilmgC, HalFC 80, NotNAT, WorEFlm*
Garfield, Allen 1939- *FilmEn, HalFC 80, WhoHol A*
Garfield, Bernard H 1924- *CpmDNM 80, ConAmC*
Garfield, David Leneord 1956- *AmSCAP 80*
Garfield, John 1913-1952 *BiDFilm, -81, CmMov, FilmEn, FilmgC, ForYSC, HalFC 80, MotPP, MovMk[port], NotNAT A, -B, OxFilm, PlP&P[port], WhScrn 74, -77, WhThe, WhoHol B, WorEFlm[port]*
Garfield, John, Jr. 1943- *ForYSC*
Garfield, John David *WhoHol A*
Garfield, Julie 1946- *ForYSC, WhoHol A*
Garfield, Warren 1936- *IntMPA 77, -75, -76, -78, -79, -80*
Garfinkle, Louis 1928- *IntMPA 77, -75, -76, -78, -79, -80, NatPD[port]*
Garford, Colin 1936- *WhoMus 72*
Garforth, David 1942- *IntWWM 80*
Garfunkel, Art *ConMuA 80A[port]*
Garfunkel, Art 1941- *IlEncR*
Garfunkel, Art 1942- *BiDAmM, RkOn 2[port]*
Garfunkel, Arthur *IntMPA 77, -75, -76, -78, -79, -80*
Garfunkel, Arthur 1937- *FilmgC, HalFC 80*
Gargallo, Luis Vicente 162-?-1682 *NewGrD 80*
Gargan, Ed 1902-1964 *FilmgC, HalFC 80, HolCA[port]*
Gargan, Edward d1964 *NotNAT B, WhoHol B*
Gargan, Edward 1901-1964 *Vers A[port]*
Gargan, Edward 1902-1964 *ForYSC, MovMk[port], WhScrn 74, -77*
Gargan, William 1905-1979 *FilmEn, FilmgC, ForYSC, HalFC 80, HolP 30[port], IntMPA 77, -75, -76, -78, -79, MotPP, MovMk[port], What 5[port], WhThe, WhoHol A*
Gargano, Giovanni Battista *NewGrD 80*
Gargiulo, Terenzio 1905- *WhoMus 72*
Gari, Brian 1952- *AmSCAP 80*
Gari, Frank 1942- *RkOn*
Garibay, Emilio 1927-1965 *WhScrn 77*
Gariel, Edoardo 1860-1923 *Baker 78*
Garinus *NewGrD 80*
Garland, Beverly *MotPP, WhoHol A*
Garland, Beverly 1926- *FilmEn, FilmgC, ForYSC, HalFC 80, MovMk, WhoHrs 80[port]*
Garland, Beverly 1930- *IntMPA 77, -75, -76, -78, -79, -80*
Garland, Donald *AmSCAP 80*
Garland, Ed 1895- *BiDAmM, NewOrJ[port]*
Garland, Edward B 1885- *EncJzS 70*
Garland, Hamlin 1860-1940 *NotNAT B*
Garland, Joe 1903- *CmpEPM*
Garland, Joe 1907- *EncJzS 70, WhoJazz 72*
Garland, John *OxMus*
Garland, Joseph Copeland 1903- *AmSCAP 66, -80, BiDAmM*
Garland, Joseph Copeland 1907- *EncJzS 70*
Garland, Judy d1969 *AmPS A, -B*
Garland, Judy 1922-1969 *BiDAmM, BiDFilm, -81, CmMov, CmpEPM, FilmEn, FilmgC, HalFC 80, MGM[port], MotPP, MovMk[port], NewGrD 80, NewYTET, NotNAT A, OxFilm, ThFT[port], WhScrn 74, -77, WhoHol B, WhoHrs 80[port], WorEFlm*
Garland, Judy 1923-1969 *ForYSC*
Garland, Les *ConMuA 80B*
Garland, Montudi 1895- *WhoJazz 72*
Garland, Montudie 1885- *EncJzS 70*
Garland, P Harvey 1919- *IntMPA 77, -75, -76, -78, -79, -80*
Garland, Patrick *WhoThe 72, -77*
Garland, Red 1923- *EncJzS 70*
Garland, Richard d1969 *ForYSC, WhScrn 77, WhoHol B, WhoHrs 80[port]*
Garland, Robert 1895-1955 *NotNAT B, WhThe*
Garland, Roger Kimberley 1945- *IntWWM 77, -80*
Garland, William M 1923- *EncJzS 70*
Garlandia, Johannes De 1195?- *Baker 78, NewGrD 80*
Garlick, Antony 1927- *CpmDNM 76, -77, -79, -80, ConAmC, IntWWM 77, -80*
Garlick, Lew *ConMuA 80B*
Garlock, Thomas Martin 1929- *AmSCAP 66, -80*
Garlow, Clarence Joseph 1911- *BluesWW[port]*
Garly, Edward H d1938 *WhScrn 74, -77*
Garmes, Lee *IntMPA 77, -75, -76, -78*
Garmes, Lee 1897-1978 *FilmgC, HalFC 80*
Garmes, Lee 1898-1978 *CmMov, DcFM, FilmEn, OxFilm, WorEFlm*
Garmo, John Charles 1947- *AmSCAP 80*
Garneau, Hector DeSaint-Denys *CreCan 1*
Garneau, Henri DeSaint-Denys *CreCan 1*
Garneau, Joseph Rene Sylvain *CreCan 2*
Garneau, St.-Denys 1912-1943 *CreCan 1*
Garneau, Sylvain 1930-1953 *CreCan 2*
Garner, Adam 1898- *AmSCAP 66, -80*
Garner, Erroll 1921-1974 *BiDAmM, MusMk[port]*
Garner, Erroll 1921-1977 *Baker 78, ConAmC, NewGrD 80*
Garner, Erroll 1923-1977 *AmSCAP 66, -80, CmpEPM, DrBlPA, EncJzS 70, IlEncJ*
Garner, Hugh 1913- *CreCan 1*
Garner, James 1928- *CmMov, FilmEn, FilmgC, ForYSC, HalFC 80, IntMPA 77, -75, -76, -78, -79, -80, MotPP, MovMk[port], WhoHol A, WorEFlm*
Garner, Letitia Norris 1943- *WhoOp 76*
Garner, Linton S 1915- *AmSCAP 66, -80*
Garner, Peggy Ann *MotPP, WhoHol A*
Garner, Peggy Ann 1931- *FilmEn, FilmgC, HalFC 80, MovMk[port], What 3[port]*
Garner, Peggy Ann 1932- *ForYSC, HolP 40[port], IntMPA 77, -75, -76, -78, -79, -80*
Garnes, Sherman 1941- *BiDAmM*
Garnesey, John d1459? *NewGrD 80*
Garnett, Carlos 1938- *EncJzS 70*
Garnett, Edward 1868-1937 *NotNAT B, WhThe*
Garnett, Gale *RkOn 2[port]*
Garnett, Henry Fred 1892- *WhoMus 72*
Garnett, Tay *IntMPA 77, -75, -76, -78, NewYTET*
Garnett, Tay 1892-1977 *OxFilm*
Garnett, Tay 1894-1977 *FilmEn*
Garnett, Tay 1895-1977 *FilmgC, HalFC 80*
Garnett, Tay 1898-1977 *BiDFilm, -81, DcFM, MovMk[port]*
Garnett, Tay 1905- *WorEFlm*
Garnett, Tony 1936- *FilmgC, HalFC 80, OxFilm*
Garnier *NewGrD 80*
Garnier, Francois *NewGrD 80*
Garnier, Francois-Joseph 1755-1825? *NewGrD 80*
Garnier, Gabriel d1730? *NewGrD 80*
Garnier, Louis *NewGrD 80*
Garnier, Robert 1535?-1600? *OxThe*
Garnier, Robert 1544-1590 *McGEWD*
Garnier, Robert 1545?-1590 *CnThe, Ent, REnWD[port]*
Garofalo, Carlo Giorgio 1886-1962 *AmSCAP 80*
Garofalo, Robert Joseph 1939- *IntWWM 77, -80*
Garon, Norm 1934-1975 *WhScrn 77*
Garon, Norman 1934-1975 *WhoHol C*
Garon, Pauline 1901-1965 *FilmEn, Film 2, ForYSC, MotPP, TwYS, WhScrn 74, -77, WhoHol B*
Garon, Pauline 1901-1967 *Film 1*
Garovi, Angelo 1944- *IntWWM 80*
Garr, Eddie 1900-1956 *WhScrn 74, -77, WhoHol B*
Garr, Teri *WhoHol A*
Garr, Teri 1952- *HalFC 80*
Garralaga, Martin *ForYSC*
Garralagna, Martin *WhoHol A*
Garrana, Rifaat 1924- *NewGrD 80*
Garrard, Don 1931- *CmOp, IntWWM 77, -80, WhoMus 72, WhoOp 76*
Garratt, Alfred Charles 1896- *IntWWM 77, WhoMus 72*
Garratt, Percival 1877-1953 *Baker 78*
Garre, Edmee Sophie *NewGrD 80*
Garrel, S *Film 2*
Garreta, Julio 1875-1925 *Baker 78, NewGrD 80*
Garrett, Almeida 1799-1854 *CnThe,*

REnWD[port]
Garrett, Arthur 1869-1941 *WhThe*
Garrett, Betty *AmPS B, IntMPA 77, -75, -76, -78, -79, -80, MotPP*
Garrett, Betty 1919- *CmMov, CmpEPM, FilmEn, FilmgC, ForYSC, HalFC 80, MGM[port], MovMk, WhoHol A, WhoThe 72, -77*
Garrett, Betty 1920- *BiE&WWA, NotNAT*
Garrett, Eric *WhoMus 72*
Garrett, George Mursell 1834-1897 *Baker 78, NewGrD 80, OxMus*
Garrett, Glen 1948- *EncJzS 70*
Garrett, Hank *WhoHol A*
Garrett, Jarrell Jackson, Jr. 1955- *AmSCAP 80*
Garrett, Jimmy *BlkAmP, MorBAP*
Garrett, Joao Baptista DaS L DeAlmeida *OxThe*
Garrett, Jon *ConMuA 80B*
Garrett, Leif 1961- *RkOn 2[port]*
Garrett, Lloyd Fry 1886- *AmSCAP 66*
Garrett, Oliver H P 1897-1952 *FilmgC, HalFC 80, NotNAT B*
Garrett, Otis 1895?-1941 *HalFC 80*
Garrett, Pat 1850-1908 *HalFC 80*
Garrett, Patsy 1921- *AmSCAP 80*
Garrett, Vicky *AmSCAP 80*
Garrick, David 1717-1779 *CnThe, EncWT, Ent[port], FilmgC, HalFC 80, McGEWD[port], NewEOp 71, NewGrD 80, NotNAT A, -B, OxMus, OxThe, PlP&P[port]*
Garrick, Mrs. David 1724-1822 *NotNAT B*
Garrick, Gus *WhThe*
Garrick, Helen Collier d1954 *NotNAT B*
Garrick, John 1902- *Film 2, FilmgC, HalFC 80, IlWWBF, WhThe, WhoHol A*
Garrick, Michael 1933- *IntWWM 80*
Garrick, Richard T 1879-1962 *NotNAT B, WhScrn 74, -77, WhoHol B*
Garrido, Pablo 1905- *Baker 78, NewGrD 80*
Garrido-Lecca, Celso 1926- *Baker 78, DcCM, NewGrD 80*
Garriguenc, Pierre 1921- *ConAmC*
Garriguenc, Rene 1908- *ConAmC*
Garrison, Geraldine *PupTheA*
Garrison, Greg *NewYTET*
Garrison, Isabelle *Film 2*
Garrison, James Emory 1934-1976 *BiDAmM, EncJzS 70*
Garrison, Jerome 1951- *IntWWM 77*
Garrison, Jimmy 1934-1976 *EncJzS 70*
Garrison, Lucy McKim 1842-1877 *NewGrD 80*
Garrison, Mabel 1886-1963 *Baker 78*
Garrison, Mabel 1888-1963 *BiDAmM*
Garrison, Michael 1923-1966 *WhScrn 74, -77*
Garrison, Paul *IntMPA 77, -75, -76, -78, -79, -80*
Garrison, Robert *Film 2*
Garrison, Robert C 1934- *AmSCAP 80*
Garrison, Sean 1937- *FilmgC, HalFC 80, WhoHol A*
Garrison, Sean 1938- *ForYSC*
Garrison, William Allen Slickem *Film 2*
Garriss, Phyllis Weyer 1923- *IntWWM 77, -80*
Garro, Francisco 1556?-1623 *NewGrD 80*
Garrod, Maurice 1907- *WhoMus 72*
Garron, Kurt *Film 2*
Garrott, Alice 1948- *IntWWM 80*
Garrow, William 1893- *AmSCAP 80*
Garroway, Dave 1913- *IntMPA 77, -75, -76, -78, -79, -80, NewYTET*
Garry, Charles d1939 *NotNAT B*
Garry, Claude d1918 *NotNAT B, WhoHol B*
Garry, Sid 1901?-1973 *CmpEPM*
Garsi, Ascanio *NewGrD 80*
Garsi, Donino *NewGrD 80*
Garsi, Santino 1542-1604 *NewGrD 80*
Garsi DaParma, Santino 1542-1604 *NewGrD 80*
Garsia, Marston *Film 2*
Garside, John 1887-1958 *NotNAT B, WhThe*
Garside, Patricia Ann 1934- *IntWWM 77, -80*
Garson, Alfred 1924- *WhoMus 72*
Garson, Arline *WomWMM, -B*
Garson, Barbara 1941- *NatPD[port]*
Garson, Greer *IntMPA 77, -75, -76, -78, -79, -80, MotPP*
Garson, Greer 1906- *OxFilm, ThFT[port]*
Garson, Greer 1908- *CmMov, FilmEn, FilmgC, ForYSC, HalFC 80, MGM[port], MovMk[port], WhThe, WhoHol A, WorEFlm*
Garson, Greer 1914- *BiDFilm, -81*
Garson, Harry *TwYS A*
Garson, John *WhoHol A*
Garson, Mort 1924- *AmSCAP 66, -80*
Gart, John 1905- *AmSCAP 80*
Garten, H F 1904- *BiE&WWA, NotNAT*
Gartenlaub, Odette 1922- *IntWWM 80*
Garth, John 1722?-1810? *NewGrD 80, OxMus*
Garth, Lester Alan 1944- *AmSCAP 80*
Garth, Midi 1920- *CmpGMD, CnOxB, DancEn 78*
Garth, Otis 1901-1955 *WhScrn 74, -77, WhoHol B*
Gartin, Fay Sheaffer 1913- *IntWWM 77*
Gartlan, George H 1882-1963 *AmSCAP 66, -80*
Gartler, Robert 1933- *ConAmC*
Gartner *NewGrD 80*
Gartner, Anton 1721-1771? *NewGrD 80*
Gartner, Josef 1796-1863 *NewGrD 80*
Garton, Graham 1929- *WhoMus 72*
Gartrell, Carol Ann 1952- *IntWWM 80*
Gartside, Joyce *WhoMus 72*
Gartside, Trevor 1929- *WhoMus 72*
Garugli, Bernardo 1535-1565? *NewGrD 80*
Garulli, Bernardo 1535-1565? *NewGrD 80*
Garullus, Bernardo 1535-1565? *NewGrD 80*
Garutso, Stephen E d1964 *NotNAT B*
Garvelmann, Donald M 1927- *IntWWM 77, -80*
Garver, Kathy *WhoHol A*
Garvey, Amy Ashwood *BlkAmP*
Garvey, David *IntWWM 77, -80*
Garvey, Ed 1865-1939 *Film 2*
Garvie, Ed 1865-1939 *WhScrn 77*
Garvie, Edward 1865-1939 *NotNAT B*
Garvin, Amelia Beers Warnock *CreCan 1*
Garvin, Anita 1907- *Film 1, -2, TwYS*
Garvin, J L *OxMus*
Garvin, Larry *BlkAmP*
Garvin, Lawrence W 1945- *NotNAT*
Garwood, John *WhoHol A*
Garwood, Margaret 1927- *AmSCAP 80, ConAmC*
Garwood, William 1884-1950 *Film 1, WhScrn 77*
Gary, Carlotta 1940- *BlkWAB[port]*
Gary, Curt *ConMuA 80B*
Gary, Harold *WhoHol A*
Gary, John 1932- *AmSCAP 66, -80, BiDAmM, WhoHol A*
Gary, Lorraine *HalFC 80, WhoHol A*
Gary, Marianne 1903- *IntWWM 80*
Gary, Romain 1914- *WorEFlm*
Gary, Sid 1901-1973 *WhScrn 77*
Garyine, Anita *Film 2*
Garza, Edward *ConAmC*
Garza, Eva 1917-1966 *WhScrn 74, -77*
Gas, Jose d1713 *NewGrD 80*
Gasca, Louis Angel 1940- *EncJzS 70*
Gasca, Luis 1940- *EncJzS 70*
Gascogne, Mathieu *NewGrD 80*
Gascoigne, Bamber 1935- *WhoThe 72, -77*
Gascoigne, Brian Alvery 1943- *IntWWM 77, -80*
Gascoigne, George 1535?-1577 *Ent, McGEWD, OxThe*
Gascoigne, George 1542?-1577 *CnThe, REnWD[port]*
Gascon, Adam-Nicolas 1623-1668 *NewGrD 80*
Gascon, Jean 1921- *CreCan 1, WhoThe 72, -77*
Gascone, Mathieu *NewGrD 80*
Gascongne, Johannes *NewGrD 80*
Gascongne, Mathieu *NewGrD 80*
Gascongus, Mathieu *NewGrD 80*
Gascue Y Murga, Francisco 1848-1920 *NewGrD 80*
Gaskell, Jane *WomWMM*
Gaskell, Sonia 1904-1974 *CnOxB, DancEn 78*
Gaskill, Clarence 1892-1947 *AmSCAP 66, -80, CmpEPM*
Gaskill, William 1930- *EncWT, WhoThe 72, -77*
Gaskin, Michael Allan 1945- *AmSCAP 80, IntWWM 77*
Gaskin, Roderick Victor 1934- *BiDAmM, EncJzS 70*
Gaskin, Vic 1934- *EncJzS 70*
Gaskue Y Murga, Francisco 1848-1920 *NewGrD 80*
Gaslini, Giorgio 1929- *EncJzS 70, NewGrD 80*
Gasman, Ira 1942- *AmSCAP 80*
Gasnier, Louis d1963 *NotNAT B*
Gasnier, Louis 1880-1963 *TwYS A*
Gasnier, Louis 1882-1962 *OxFilm*
Gasnier, Louis J 1878-1963 *FilmEn*
Gasnier, Louis J 1882- *DcFM*
Gasnier, Louis J 1882-1963 *HalFC 80*
Gaspar De Padua *NewGrD 80*
Gaspar Van Weerbeke *NewGrD 80*
Gaspar, Margit 1908- *CroCD*
Gaspard, Ed 1877?- *NewOrJ*
Gaspard, Nelson Octave 1870- *NewOrJ*
Gaspard, Vic 1875-1957 *NewOrJ*
Gaspardini, Gasparo d1714? *NewGrD 80*
Gasparek, Tibor 1913- *NewGrD 80*
Gaspari, Gaetano 1807-1881 *Baker 78*
Gaspari, Gaetano 1808-1881 *NewGrD 80*
Gasparini, Domenico Maria Angiolo *NewGrD 80*
Gasparini, Francesco 1668-1727 *Baker 78, MusMk, NewGrD 80*
Gasparini, Quirino 1721-1778 *NewGrD 80*
Gasparo Da Salo 1540-1609 *NewGrD 80*
Gasparo DaSalo 1540-1609 *Baker 78*
Gasparre, Dick *BgBands 74*
Gasperini, Guido 1865-1942 *Baker 78, NewGrD 80*
Gassman, Florian Leopold 1729-1774 *Baker 78*
Gassman, Josephine d1962 *NotNAT B*
Gassman, Vittorio 1922- *BiDFilm, -81, EncWT, Ent[port], FilmAG WE[port], FilmEn, FilmgC, ForYSC, HalFC 80, IntMPA 77, -75, -76, -78, -79, -80, MotPP, MovMk[port], WhoHol A, WorEFlm[port]*
Gassmann, F L 1729-1774 *OxMus*
Gassmann, Florian Leopold 1729-1774 *MusMk, NewGrD 80*
Gassmann, Frank Silver 1939- *IntWWM 77, -80*
Gassmann, Maria Anna 1771-1852 *Baker 78*
Gassmann, Remi 1908- *ConAmC, DancEn 78*
Gassmann, Therese Maria 1774-1837 *Baker 78*
Gassmann, Vittorio 1912- *OxThe*
Gassner, Ferdinand Simon 1798-1851 *Baker 78, NewGrD 80*
Gassner, John 1903-1967 *BiE&WWA, NotNAT B, WhThe*
Gassner, John Waldhorn 1903-1969 *EncWT*
Gasso, Bernard 1926- *AmSCAP 66, -80*
Gast, Peter 1854-1918 *Baker 78, NewGrD 80, OxMus*
Gastaldon, Stanislas 1861-1939 *Baker 78*
Gastatz, Mathias *NewGrD 80*
Gaste, Louis 1908- *WhoMus 72*
Gastelle, Stella d1936 *NotNAT B*
Gaster, Adrian 1919- *IntWWM 77, -80*
Gastharts, Mathias *NewGrD 80*
Gastinel, Leon-Gustave-Cyprien 1823-1906 *Baker 78*
Gastoldi, Giovanni Giacomo 155-?-1622 *Baker 78*
Gastoldi, Giovanni Giacomo 155-?-1622? *NewGrD 80*
Gastoldi, Giovanni Giacomo 1555?-1622 *OxMus*
Gaston Febus 1331-1391 *NewGrD 80*
Gaston, George 1843-1937 *NotNAT B*
Gaston, Lyle R 1929- *AmSCAP 66, -80*
Gaston, Mae *Film 1*
Gastoni, Lisa 1935- *FilmAG WE, FilmgC, ForYSC, HalFC 80*
Gastorius, Severus 1646-1682 *NewGrD 80*
Gastoue, Amedee 1873-1943 *Baker 78, NewGrD 80, OxMus*
Gastritz, Mathias d1596 *NewGrD 80*
Gastritzsch, Mathias d1596 *NewGrD 80*
Gastrock, Phail *Film 1*
Gastyne, Serge De 1930- *CpmDNM 74, -77*
Gatayes *NewGrD 80*
Gatayes, Felix 1809-1860? *NewGrD 80*
Gatayes, Guillaume-Pierre-Antoine 1774-1846 *NewGrD 80*
Gatayes, Joseph-Leon 1805-1877 *NewGrD 80*
Gates, B Cecil 1877-1941 *AmSCAP 66, -80*
Gates, Bernard 1685?-1773 *NewGrD 80, OxMus*
Gates, Bert 1883-1952 *WhScrn 74, -77*
Gates, Crawford Marion 1921- *AmSCAP 66, -80, ConAmC, IntWWM 77, -80*

Gates, David 1940- *AmSCAP 80, IlEncR, RkOn 2[port]*
Gates, Eleanor 1875-1951 *NotNAT B, WhThe, WomWMM*
Gates, Ellen 1835-1920 *BiDAmM*
Gates, Everett *ConAmC*
Gates, George E 1920- *AmSCAP 80, ConAmC*
Gates, J Terry 1936- *IntWWM 77, -80*
Gates, Keith 1949- *ConAmC*
Gates, Larry 1915- *BiE&WWA, FilmgC, ForYSC, HalFC 80, NotNAT, WhoHol A, WhoThe 72, -77*
Gates, Maxine *WhoHol A*
Gates, Nancy 1926- *FilmEn, FilmgC, ForYSC, HalFC 80, MotPP, WhoHol A*
Gates, Ruth 1888-1966 *BiE&WWA, NotNAT B*
Gates, Tudor *WhoHrs 80*
Gates, Virgil William 1914- *AmSCAP 80*
Gateson, Marjorie 1891-1977 *BiE&WWA, FilmEn, ForYSC, HalFC 80, HolCA[port], NotNAT, ThFT[port], WhoHol A*
Gateson, Marjorie 1897- *WhThe*
Gateson, Marjorie 1900- *MovMk[port]*
Gateway Singers, The *BiDAmM, EncFCWM 69*
Gateway Trio *EncFCWM 69*
Gatewood, L A *BlkAmP*
Gath, Joseph *NatPD[port]*
Gati, Laszlo 1925- *IntWWM 77, -80*
Gatlin, Helen Stanley *ConAmC*
Gatlin, Larry 1949- *IlEncCM[port]*
Gatsby, Paco *AmSCAP 80*
Gatt, Martin 1936- *WhoMus 72*
Gattermeyer, Heinrich 1923- *IntWWM 77, -80*
Gatti, Armand 1924- *CnMD SUP, CnThe, CroCD, DcFM, EncWT, Ent, McGEWD, ModWD, REnWD[port], WorEFlm*
Gatti, Carlo 1876-1965 *NewGrD 80*
Gatti, Gabriella 1916- *NewGrD 80*
Gatti, Guido M 1892-1973 *WhoMus 72*
Gatti, Guido Maria 1892- *OxMus*
Gatti, Guido Maria 1892-1973 *Baker 78, NewGrD 80*
Gatti, Sir John M 1872-1929 *WhThe*
Gatti, Luigi 1740-1817 *NewGrD 80*
Gatti, Teobaldo Di 1650?-1727 *NewGrD 80*
Gatti, Theobalde Di 1650?-1727 *NewGrD 80*
Gatti, Theobaldo Di 1650?-1727 *NewGrD 80*
Gatti-Aldrovandi, Clelia 1901- *NewGrD 80*
Gatti-Casazza, Giulio 1868-1940 *Baker 78*
Gatti-Casazza, Giulio 1869-1940 *BiDAmM, NewEOp 71, NewGrD 80*
Gatti-Casazza, Guilio d1940 *NotNAT B*
Gattie, A W d1925 *NotNAT B*
Gatto, Armando 1928- *WhoOp 76*
Gatto, Simon 154-?-1595? *NewGrD 80*
Gatto, Simone 154-?-1595? *NewGrD 80*
Gatty, Nicholas Comyn 1874-1946 *Baker 78, OxMus*
Gatty, Scott *Film 2*
Gatwood, Robin Frederick 1916- *IntWWM 77, -80*
Gatz, Felix Maria 1892-1942 *Baker 78*
Gatzmann, Wolfgang *NewGrD 80*
Gaubert, Philippe 1879-1941 *Baker 78, NewEOp 71, OxMus*
Gaucher, Yves 1934- *CreCan 2*
Gaucquier, Alard Du 1534?-1582? *NewGrD 80*
Gaudard, Lucette *WomWMM*
Gaudentius *NewGrD 80*
Gaudimel, Claude *Baker 78*
Gaudio, Antonio Dal *NewGrD 80*
Gaudio, Cheryl *WomWMM B*
Gaudio, Jennie *IntWWM 80*
Gaudio, Tony 1885-1951 *DcFM, FilmEn, FilmgC, HalFC 80, WorEFlm*
Gaudlin, Robert 1931- *ConAmC*
Gaudry, Michel 1928- *EncJzS 70*
Gauge, Alexander 1914-1960 *FilmgC, HalFC 80, NotNAT B, WhScrn 74, -77, WhoHol B*
Gauger, Thomas 1935- *ConAmC*
Gauggel, George William 1912- *IntWWM 80*
Gauguin, Lorraine 1924-1974 *WhScrn 77*
Gauk, Alexander Vasil'yevich 1893-1963 *NewGrD 80*
Gaukstad, Oystein 1912- *NewGrD 80*
Gaul, Alfred Robert 1837-1913 *Baker 78, NewGrD 80, OxMus*
Gaul, George 1885-1939 *NotNAT B, PlP&P, WhThe*
Gaul, Harvey Bartlett 1881-1945 *AmSCAP 66, -80, Baker 78, BiDAmM, ConAmC*
Gault, Mildred 1905-1938 *WhScrn 74, -77*
Gault, Willis Manning 1908- *IntWWM 77, -80*
Gaulthier, Denis 1603-1672 *NewGrD 80*
Gaulthier, Ennemond 1575-1651 *NewGrD 80*
Gaultier DeMarseille *NewGrD 80*
Gaultier LeJeune 1597?-1672 *BnBkM 80*
Gaultier, Camille 1872-1943 *MagIlD*
Gaultier, Denis 1600?-1672 *Baker 78*
Gaultier, Denis 1603-1672 *NewGrD 80*
Gaultier, Denys 1597?-1672 *BnBkM 80*
Gaultier, Ennemond 1575-1651 *NewGrD 80*
Gaultier, Henry *Film 2*
Gaultier, Jacques *NewGrD 80*
Gaultier, Pierre *NewGrD 80*
Gaultier-Garguille 1573?-1633 *NotNAT B, OxThe*
Gaumont, Leon 1863-1946 *DcFM, FilmgC, HalFC 80, OxFilm, WomWMM, WorEFlm*
Gaumont, Leon 1864-1946 *FilmEn*
Gaunt, Percy 1852-1896 *AmPS, BiDAmM, NotNAT B, PopAmC*
Gaunt, Valerie 1933?- *WhoHrs 80[port]*
Gauntier, Gene d1966 *MotPP, WomWMM*
Gauntier, Gene 1880?-1966 *WhScrn 74, -77*
Gauntier, Gene 1891-1966 *Film 1, TwYS*
Gauntlett, H J 1805-1876 *OxMus*
Gauntlett, Henry John 1805-1876 *NewGrD 80*
Gaussin, Jeanne-Catherine 1711-1767 *OxThe*
Gauterius De Castello Rainardi *NewGrD 80*
Gauthier *PupTheA*
Gauthier, Eva 1885-1958 *Baker 78*
Gauthier, Eva 1886-1958 *BiDAmM*
Gauthier-Villars, Henri 1859-1931 *Baker 78*
Gautier De Chatillon *NewGrD 80*
Gautier De Coincy 1177?-1236 *NewGrD 80*
Gautier De Dargies 1165?-1236? *NewGrD 80*
Gautier De Lille *NewGrD 80*
Gautier D'Espinal 1220?-1272? *NewGrD 80*
Gautier, Denis *NewGrD 80*
Gautier, Dick *WhoHol A*
Gautier, Dick 1931- *AmSCAP 66, -80*
Gautier, Dick 1939- *FilmgC, HalFC 80*
Gautier, Ennemond *NewGrD 80*
Gautier, Eugene 1822-1878 *NewGrD 80*
Gautier, Francois *NewGrD 80*
Gautier, Gene d1966 *WhoHol B*
Gautier, Jacques d1660? *NewGrD 80[port]*
Gautier, Jean-Francois-Eugene 1822-1878 *Baker 78*
Gautier, Judith 1845-1917 *NewGrD 80*
Gautier, Pierre d1638? *NewGrD 80*
Gautier, Pierre 1642?-1696 *NewGrD 80*
Gautier, Theophile 1811-1872 *BnBkM 80, CnOxB, DancEn 78, DcPup, EncWT, NewEOp 71, NewGrD 80, NotNAT B*
Gauvreau, Claude 1925- *CreCan 2*
Gauzargues, Charles 1725?-1799 *NewGrD 80*
Gavalda, Jose 1818-1890 *NewGrD 80*
Gavalda, Miguel Querol *NewGrD 80*
Gavaldon, Roberto 1909- *FilmEn*
Gavall, John 1919- *WhoMus 72*
Gavault, Paul 1867- *WhThe*
Gavaux, Pierre *NewGrD 80*
Gavazzeni, Gianandrea 1909- *Baker 78, CmOp, NewGrD 80, OxMus, WhoOp 76*
Gavazzeni, Gianandrea 1919- *IntWWM 77, -80*
Gavazzi, Ernesto 1941- *WhoOp 76*
Gaveau *NewGrD 80*
Gaveau, Etienne 1872-1943 *NewGrD 80*
Gaveau, Joseph 1824-1903 *NewGrD 80*
Gaveau, Pierre 1760-1825 *NewGrD 80*
Gaveaux, Pierre 1760-1825 *NewGrD 80*
Gaveaux, Pierre 1761-1825 *MusMk*
Gavella, Branko 1885-1962 *EncWT*
Gaven, Jean 1922- *FilmEn*
Gaver, Jack *BiE&WWA, NotNAT*
Gavin, Bill *ConMuA 80B*
Gavin, John *IntMPA 77, -75, -76, -78, -79, -80, MotPP, WhoHol A*
Gavin, John 1928- *FilmEn, FilmgC, ForYSC, HalFC 80*
Gavin, John 1934- *MovMk[port]*
Gavine, Winifred *WhoMus 72*
Gavinies, Pierre 1728-1800 *Baker 78, NewGrD 80*
Gaviniez, Pierre 1728-1800 *NewGrD 80*
Gavoty, Bernard 1908- *Baker 78, NewGrD 80, WhoMus 72*
Gavrilin, Valery 1939- *Baker 78*
Gavrilov, Alexander 1892-1959 *CnOxB, DancEn 78*
Gawlik, Roland 1944- *CnOxB*
Gawriloff, Saschko 1929- *NewGrD 80*
Gawronski, Adalbert 1868-1910 *Baker 78*
Gawronski, Wojciech 1868-1910 *NewGrD 80*
Gawryluk, Jerzy 1909- *IntWWM 77, -80*
Gawthorne, Peter 1884-1962 *Film 2, FilmgC, HalFC 80, NotNAT B, WhScrn 74, -77, WhThe, WhoHol B*
Gaxton, William 1893-1963 *AmPS B, CmpEPM, EncMT, Film 2, FilmgC, HalFC 80, NotNAT B, PlP&P[port], WhScrn 74, -77, WhThe, WhoHol B*
Gay, Bram 1930- *IntWWM 80*
Gay, Byron 1886-1945 *AmSCAP 66, -80*
Gay, Cedric *MorBAP*
Gay, Dixie *Film 2*
Gay, Fred 1882-1955 *WhScrn 74, -77*
Gay, George Errol 1941- *IntWWM 77, -80*
Gay, Gregory *Film 2, WhoHol A*
Gay, Inez d1975 *WhoHol C*
Gay, Jesus Bal Y 1685-1732 *NewGrD 80*
Gay, John *BnBkM 80, HalFC 80*
Gay, John 1685-1732 *Baker 78, CnThe, DcPup, EncWT, Ent[port], McGEWD[port], MusMk, NewEOp 71, NewGrD 80, NotNAT A, -B, OxMus, OxThe, PlP&P[port], -A[port], REnWD[port]*
Gay, Maisie 1883-1945 *EncMT, NotNAT B, WhScrn 74, -77, WhThe*
Gay, Maria 1879-1943 *Baker 78, BiDAmM, NewGrD 80, NotNAT B*
Gay, Marjorie 1917- *Film 2*
Gay, Noel 1898-1954 *EncMT, NewGrD 80, NotNAT B, WhThe*
Gay, Paul 1936- *CpmDNM 75*
Gay, Ramon 1917-1960 *WhScrn 74, -77, WhoHrs 80*
Gay, Walter d1936 *NotNAT B*
Gay, Ynex d1975 *WhScrn 77*
Gaye, Albie d1965 *WhScrn 74, -77, WhoHol B*
Gaye, Derek 1919- *WhoMus 72*
Gaye, Freda 1907- *BiE&WWA, NotNAT, WhThe, WhoThe 72*
Gaye, Gregory 1900- *Film 2, HalFC 80, Vers B[port]*
Gaye, Howard *Film 1, -2, TwYS A*
Gaye, Irwin *MorBAP*
Gaye, Lisa *ForYSC, WhoHol A*
Gaye, Marvin 1939- *BiDAmM, ConMuA 80A, DrBlPA, IlEncR[port], RkOn[port]*
Gayer, Catherine 1939- *NewGrD 80, WhoMus 72, WhoOp 76*
Gayer, Echlin 1878-1926 *Film 2, NotNAT B, WhScrn 77, WhoHol B*
Gayer, Johann Christoph 1668?-1734 *NewGrD 80*
Gayer, Johann Joseph Georg 1746-1811 *NewGrD 80*
Gayfer, James McDonald 1916- *CreCan 1, IntWWM 77*
Gaylard, James W, III 1943- *IntMPA 77, -76, -78, -79, -80*
Gaylard, James W, Jr. 1915- *IntMPA 77, -75, -76, -78, -79, -80*
Gayle, Crystal *RkOn 2[port]*
Gayle, Crystal 1951- *IlEncCM[port]*
Gayle, Peter *IntMPA 80*
Gayle, Peter 1937- *IntMPA 76*
Gayle, Peter 1943- *IntMPA 75*
Gayle, Peter 1944- *IntMPA 77, -78, -79*
Gayle, Rozelle I, Jr. *AmSCAP 80*
Gayle, Walter *PupTheA*
Gayler, Charles 1820-1892 *NotNAT B*
Gayler, Wolfgang 1934- *IntWWM 80, WhoOp 76*
Gaylor, Ruth 1918-1972 *CmpEPM*
Gaylord, Monica 1948- *IntWWM 80*
Gaylords, The *RkOn*
Gaynes, George 1917- *BiE&WWA, NotNAT, WhoHol A, WhoThe 77*

Gayno, Creole *BluesWW[port]*
Gaynor, Charles 1909-1975 *AmSCAP 66, -80, BiE&WWA, EncMT, NotNAT B*
Gaynor, Gloria 1949- *RkOn 2[port]*
Gaynor, Gloria 1950?- *DrBlPA*
Gaynor, Janet *AmPS B*
Gaynor, Janet 1906- *BiDFilm, -81, FilmEn, Film 2, FilmgC, ForYSC, HalFC 80, MotPP, MovMk, OxFilm, ThFT[port], TwYS, What 2[port], WhoHol A, WorEFlm[port]*
Gaynor, Janet 1907- *CmMov, CmpEPM*
Gaynor, Jessie Lovel Smith 1863-1921 *Baker 78, BiDAmM*
Gaynor, Mitzi *IntMPA 75, -76, -78, -79, -80*
Gaynor, Mitzi 1930- *CmMov, CmpEPM, FilmEn, FilmgC, HalFC 80, IntMPA 77, MotPP, MovMk[port], OxFilm, WhoHol A, WorEFlm*
Gaynor, Mitzi 1931- *ForYSC*
Gaynor, Ruth d1919 *WhScrn 77*
Gayson, Eunice 1931- *FilmgC, HalFC 80*
Gaytan Y Arteaga, Manuel 1710?-1785 *NewGrD 80*
Gayten, Paul *RkOn*
Gaythorne, Pamela 1882- *WhThe*
Gaz, Jose *NewGrD 80*
Gazder, Adi Jamshed 1930- *IntWWM 77, -80*
Gaze Cooper, Walter Thomas 1895- *IntWWM 77, -80*
Gaziadis, Dimitrios 1897-1961 *DcFM*
Gazkue Y Murga, Francisco *NewGrD 80*
Gaztambide, Joaquin 1822-1870 *Baker 78, NewGrD 80*
Gazzaniga, Giuseppe 1743-1818 *Baker 78, NewEOp 71, NewGrD 80*
Gazzara, Ben 1930- *BiDFilm, -81, BiE&WWA, FilmEn, FilmgC, ForYSC, HalFC 80, IntMPA 77, -76, -78, -79, -80, MotPP, MovMk[port], NotNAT, OxFilm, PlP&P A, WhoHol A, WhoThe 72, -77*
Gazzelloni, Severino 1919- *NewGrD 80*
Gazzelloni, Severino 1920- *IntWWM 77, -80, WhoMus 72*
Gazzo, Michael V 1923- *BiE&WWA, McGEWD, NotNAT, PlP&P[port], WhoHol A*
Ge, George 1893-1962 *CnOxB*
Geallis, Paul James 1923- *AmSCAP 80*
Gear, Luella *Film 2, PlP&P[port], WhoHol A*
Gear, Luella 1897- *CmpEPM, EncMT*
Gear, Luella 1899- *BiE&WWA, NotNAT, WhThe, WhoThe 72*
Gearhart, Livingston 1916- *AmSCAP 66, -80, ConAmC A*
Gearhiser, LaVerne 1906- *AmSCAP 80*
Gearinger, Lemuel Cyrus 1894- *AmSCAP 80*
Geary, Barbara Ann 1935- *IntWWM 77, -80*
Geary, Bud 1899-1946 *WhScrn 74, -77, WhoHol B*
Geary, Maine *Film 2*
Geary, Thomas Augustine 1775-1801 *NewGrD 80*
Geary, Timothy 1775-1801 *NewGrD 80*
Gebauer *NewGrD 80*
Gebauer, Alexis 1815-1889 *NewGrD 80*
Gebauer, Constantin 1846-1920 *NewGrD 80*
Gebauer, Etienne Francois 1777-1823 *NewGrD 80*
Gebauer, Francois Rene 1773-1845 *NewGrD 80*
Gebauer, Franz Xaver 1784-1822 *NewGrD 80*
Gebauer, Johan Christian 1808-1884 *NewGrD 80*
Gebauer, Michel Joseph 1763-1812 *NewGrD 80*
Gebauer, Pierre Paul 1775- *NewGrD 80*
Gebauer, Victor Earl 1938- *IntWWM 80*
Gebel *NewGrD 80*
Gebel, Bruno *DcFM*
Gebel, Franz Xaver 1787-1843 *NewGrD 80*
Gebel, Georg 1685-1750? *NewGrD 80*
Gebel, Georg 1709-1753 *Baker 78*
Gebel, Georg 1709-1755 *NewGrD 80*
Gebel, Georg Siegmund 1715?-1775 *NewGrD 80*
Gebert, Ernst d1961 *NotNAT B*
Gebest, Charles J 1872-1937 *AmSCAP 66, -80*
Gebethner, Gustaw Adolf 1831-1901 *NewGrD 80*
Gebhard, Heinrich 1878-1963 *Baker 78, NewGrD 80*
Gebhardt, Frank *Film 1*
Gebhardt, Mrs. Frank *Film 1*
Gebhardt, Fred 1925- *IntMPA 77, -75, -76, -78, -79, -80*
Gebhardt, George M 1879-1919 *WhScrn 77*
Gebhardt, Rio 1907-1944 *NewGrD 80*
Gebuehr, Otto 1877-1954 *Film 2, WhScrn 74, -77*
Gebuhr, Ann K 1945- *ConAmC*
Gebuhr, Otto 1877-1954 *Film 2*
Geck, Martin 1936- *IntWWM 77, -80, NewGrD 80*
Geczy, Joseph 1944- *IntWWM 80*
Gedalge, Andre 1856-1926 *Baker 78, NewGrD 80*
Gedda, Giulio Cesare 1899-1970 *Baker 78*
Gedda, Nicolai 1925- *Baker 78, BiDAmM, BnBkM 80, CmOp, IntWWM 77, -80, MusMk, MusSN[port], NewEOp 71, NewGrD 80, WhoMus 72, WhoOp 76*
Geddes, Barbara Bel 1922- *MotPP, OxThe*
Geddes, David *RkOn 2[port]*
Geddes, Henry 1912- *IntMPA 77, -75, -76, -78, -79, -80*
Geddes, Norman Bel 1893-1958 *NotNAT A, -B, OxThe, PlP&P, WhThe*
Geddis, Ralph *PupTheA*
Gedge, David Patrick 1939- *IntWWM 77, -80, WhoMus 72*
Gedike, Alexander Fyodorovich 1877-1957 *NewGrD 80*
Gedzhadze, Irakly 1925- *Baker 78*
Gee, George 1895-1959 *NotNAT B, WhScrn 74, -77, WhThe, WhoHol B*
Gee, George D d1917 *WhScrn 77*
Gee, Harry Raglan 1924- *IntWWM 77, -80*
Gee, Lottie *BlksBF[port]*
Gee, Matthew, Jr. 1921-1979 *AmSCAP 80*
Gee, Maxine Nell Lowery 1924- *IntWWM 77*
Gee, Shirley *ConDr 77B*
Geehl, Henry Ernest 1881-1961 *Baker 78, NewGrD 80*
Geer, Ellen 1941- *BiE&WWA, NotNAT, WhoHol A*
Geer, Lennie *WhoHol A*
Geer, Will 1902-1978 *BiE&WWA, FilmEn, FilmgC, ForYSC, HalFC 80, IntMPA 77, -75, -76, -78, MovMk[port], NotNAT, WhoHol A, WhoThe 72, -77*
Geeres, John d1642 *NewGrD 80*
Geerhart *NewGrD 80*
Geerhart, Jan *NewGrD 80*
Geerheart, Jan *NewGrD 80*
Geering, Arnold Felix Christoph 1902- *IntWWM 77, -80, NewGrD 80*
Geersh, Eafim 1899- *AmSCAP 66*
Geertsom, Jan Van *NewGrD 80*
Geesin, Ron 1943- *IntWWM 77, -80*
Geesink, Joop 1913- *DcFM, FilmgC, HalFC 80*
Geeson, Judy 1948- *FilmAG WE, FilmEn, FilmgC, ForYSC, HalFC 80, IlWWBF, IntMPA 77, -75, -76, -78, -79, -80, MovMk, WhoHol A, WhoHrs 80*
Geeson, Sally 1950- *FilmgC, HalFC 80, IlWWBF*
Geffen, David 1944- *ConMuA 80B, IlEncR*
Gefors, Hans Gustaf 1952- *IntWWM 80*
Gegauff, Paul 1922- *FilmEn*
Gehlhaar, Rolf 1943- *NewGrD 80*
Gehling, Ronda 1921- *IntWWM 77, -80*
Gehman, Richard 1921- *BiE&WWA*
Gehot, Jean 1756-1820? *Baker 78, BiDAmM, OxMus*
Gehot, Joseph 1756-1820? *NewGrD 80*
Gehrenbeck, David Maulsby 1931- *ConAmC*
Gehrig, Lou 1903-1941 *WhScrn 77*
Gehring, Jacob 1888-1970 *NewGrD 80*
Gehring, Philip 1925- *ConAmC*
Gehring, Viktor *Film 2*
Gehringer, Charles 1904- *What 3[port]*
Gehris, Walter *PupTheA*
Gehrkens, Karl Wilson 1882-1975 *Baker 78, BiDAmM, WhoMus 72*
Gehrman, Carl *NewGrD 80*
Gehrman, Lucy d1954 *WhScrn 74, -77*
Geib *NewGrD 80*
Geib, Adam 1780-1849 *BiDAmM, NewGrD 80*
Geib, George 1782-1842 *BiDAmM*
Geib, John 1744-1818 *NewGrD 80*
Geib, John 1780-1821 *NewGrD 80*
Geib, William 1763-1860 *NewGrD 80*
Geibel, Adam 1855-1933 *AmSCAP 66, -80, BiDAmM*
Geiger, Carroll C 1910- *IntWWM 77, -80*
Geiger, Edith Lucile 1911- *IntWWM 77, -80*
Geiger, Emil 1908- *IntWWM 77, -80*
Geiger, George 1905- *AmSCAP 66, -80*
Geiger, Hans 1920- *IntWWM 77, -80, WhoMus 72*
Geiger, Hermann 1913-1966 *WhScrn 74, -77*
Geiger, Isy *WhoMus 72*
Geiger, Loren Dennis 1946- *IntWWM 77, -80*
Geiger, Ruth 1923- *IntWWM 77, -80, WhoMus 72*
Geiger-Torel, Herman B 1907- *CreCan 1, WhoOp 76*
Geijer, Erik Gustaf 1783-1847 *NewGrD 80*
Geils, J, Band *ConMuA 80A, RkOn 2[port]*
Gein, VanDen *NewGrD 80*
Geiringer, Jean d1962 *NotNAT B*
Geiringer, Karl 1899- *Baker 78, IntWWM 77, -80, NewGrD 80, OxMus*
Geisel, Theodor Seuss 1904- *AmSCAP 66, NewYTET*
Geisel, Theodore Seuss 1904- *AmSCAP 80*
Geisenhof, Hans 1570?-1615? *NewGrD 80*
Geisenhof, Johann 1570?-1615? *NewGrD 80*
Geisenhofer, Hans 1570?-1615? *NewGrD 80*
Geisenhofer, Johann 1570?-1615? *NewGrD 80*
Geiser, Brigitte 1941- *IntWWM 77, -80*
Geiser, Walther 1897- *Baker 78, CpmDNM 80, IntWWM 77, -80, NewGrD 80*
Geisler, Paul 1856-1919 *Baker 78, NewGrD 80*
Geissenhof, Franciscus 1754-1821 *NewGrD 80*
Geissler, Benedict *NewGrD 80*
Geissler, Fredrick Dietzmann 1946- *ConAmC*
Geissler, Fritz 1921- *NewGrD 80*
Geissler, Walter Fritz 1921- *IntWWM 77, -80*
Geist, Christian 1640?-1711 *NewGrD 80*
Geist, Gerhard 1932- *WhoOp 76*
Geistinger, Maria Charlotte Cacilia 1883-1903 *Baker 78*
Geitel, Klaus 1924- *CnOxB, DancEn 78*
Geitner, Leopold 1898- *IntWWM 77, -80*
Geizel, John *Film 2*
Gelabert, Fructuoso 1874-1955 *DcFM*
Gelb, Arthur 1924- *BiE&WWA, NotNAT*
Gelb, Barbara *NotNAT*
Gelb, James *BiE&WWA, NotNAT*
Gelbart, Larry *NewYTET*
Gelbart, Larry 1928- *AmSCAP 66, -80*
Gelbart, Larry S 1923- *BiE&WWA, NotNAT*
Gelber, Jack *MorBAP*
Gelber, Jack 1926- *CnMD*
Gelber, Jack 1932- *BiE&WWA, CnThe, ConDr 73, -77, CroCD, DcLB 7[port], McGEWD, ModWD, NotNAT, PlP&P, REnWD[port], WhoThe 72, -77*
Gelber, Stanley Jay 1936- *AmSCAP 66, -80*
Gelbloom, Gerald 1926- *IntWWM 77, -80*
Gelbrun, Artur 1913- *Baker 78, IntWWM 77, -80, NewGrD 80*
Gelckler, Robert *Film 2*
Geld, Gary 1935- *AmSCAP 66, -80*
Geldart, Clarence 1867-1935 *WhoHol B*
Geldart, Clarence 1867-1936 *Film 1*
Geldert, Clarence 1867-1935 *WhScrn 74, -77*
Geldert, Clarence 1867-1936 *Film 2, ForYSC, TwYS*
Gelenbevi, Baha 1902- *DcFM*
Gelin, Daniel 1921- *BiDFilm, -81, EncWT, FilmAG WE[port], FilmEn, FilmgC, HalFC 80, OxFilm, WhoHol A, WorEFlm*
Gelinas, Gratien 1909- *CreCan 2, McGEWD, REnWD[port]*
Gelinas, Gratien 1910- *CnThe*
Gelinas, Pierre 1925- *CreCan 2*
Gelineau, Joseph 1920- *Baker 78*
Gelineck, Josef 1758-1825 *NewGrD 80*
Gelinek, Josef 1758-1825 *NewGrD 80*
Gelinek, Joseph 1758-1825 *Baker 78*
Geliot, Michael 1933- *IntWWM 77, -80, WhoOp 76*
Gelker, Ellton Groth 1922- *IntWWM 77, -80*
Gelker, Vivi *CnOxB*

Geller, Arnie *ConMuA 80B*
Geller, Bernard 1948- *IntWWM 77, -80*
Geller, Bruce *IntMPA 75, -76, -78*
Geller, Bruce 1930- *AmSCAP 66, IntMPA 77, NewYTET*
Geller, Henry *NewYTET*
Geller, Herb 1928- *CmpEPM, EncJzS 70*
Geller, Herbert 1928- *BiDAmM, EncJzS 70*
Geller, Ian 1943- *ConAmC*
Geller, Joyce *WomWMM*
Geller, Uri *MagIlD*
Gellert, Christian Furchtegott 1715-1769 *NewGrD 80*
Gellert, Lawrence 1898- *AmSCAP 66, -80*
Gellhorn, Peter 1912- *IntWWM 77, -80, WhoMus 72*
Gellman, Steven 1948- *Baker 78*
Gellman, Steven D 1947- *IntWWM 80*
Gellner, Julius 1899- *WhoThe 72, -77*
Gellner, Julius 1900- *EncWT*
Gelman, Harold S 1912- *AmSCAP 66, -80*
Gelman, Larry *WhoHol A*
Gelmetti, Vittorio 1926- *IntWWM 77, -80*
Gelms, Bob *ConMuA 80B*
Gelotte, Lars Goran 1945- *IntWWM 77*
Gelpi, Rene 1904- *NewOrJ[port]*
Gelt, Andrew Lloyd 1951- *ConAmC*
Geltzer, Yekaterina Vassilyevna 1876-1962 *CnOxB, DancEn 78[port]*
Geltzmann, Wolfgang *NewGrD 80*
Gelzmann, Wolfgang *NewGrD 80*
Gemblaco, Johannes Franchois De *NewGrD 80*
Gemier, Firmin d1933 *Film 2, WhoHol B*
Gemier, Firmin 1865-1933 *NotNAT B, OxThe, WhThe*
Gemier, Firmin 1869-1933 *EncWT, Ent*
Gemier, Firmin 1886-1933 *WhScrn 77*
Geminiani, Francesco 1687-1762 *Baker 78, BnBkM 80, CmpBCM, GrComp[port], MusMk[port], NewGrD 80[port], OxMus*
Gemma, Giuliano 1938- *FilmAG WE[port]*
Gemma, Giuliano 1940- *HalFC 80*
Gemmell, Don 1903- *WhoThe 72, -77*
Gemora, Charles 1903-1961 *WhoHrs 80*
Gemora, Charlie 1903-1961 *HalFC 80, WhScrn 74, -77, WhoHol B*
Gemunder, August Martin Ludwig 1814-1895 *Baker 78, BiDAmM*
Gemunder, George 1816-1899 *BiDAmM*
Gena, Peter 1947- *ConAmC, IntWWM 77, -80*
Gencer, Leyla 1928?- *CmOp, NewGrD 80[port], WhoOp 76*
Gencsy, Eva Von *CreCan 2*
Gendre, Jean Le *NewGrD 80*
Gendron, Maurice 1920- *IntWWM 77, -80, NewGrD 80, WhoMus 72*
Gendron, Pierre 1896-1956 *Film 2, MotPP, NotNAT B, WhScrn 74, -77, WhoHol B*
Gendron, Pierre 1934- *CreCan 1*
Gene And Debbe *RkOn 2A*
Gene And Eunice *RkOn*
Gene And Glenn *CmpEPM*
Genee, Adeline 1878-1970 *CnOxB, DancEn 78, WhThe, WhoStg 1908*
Genee, Alexander d1938 *NotNAT B*
Genee, Richard 1823-1895 *Baker 78, NewGrD 80*
Genella, Julian 1907- *AmSCAP 66*
Generali, Pietro 1773-1832 *Baker 78, NewGrD 80*
Genesis *ConMuA 80A, IlEncR, RkOn 2[port]*
Genesius, Saint *EncWT*
Genest, Emile *CreCan 1*
Genest, John d1839 *NotNAT B*
Genet, Elzear *NewGrD 80*
Genet, Jean 1909- *CnThe, REnWD[port]*
Genet, Jean 1910- *BiE&WWA, CnMD, CroCD, EncWT, Ent, McGEWD[port], ModWD, NotNAT, -A, OxThe, PlP&P, -A[port], WhoThe 72, -77*
Genet, Marianne *ConAmC*
Genetz, Emil 1852-1930 *Baker 78*
Genevieve 1930- *BiE&WWA*
Gengenbach, Nikolaus 1590?-1636 *NewGrD 80*
Gengenbach, Pamphilus *OxThe*
Genger, Roger *AmSCAP 66, -80*
Geniat, Marcelle d1959 *NotNAT B, WhThe, WhoHol B*
Genies, The *RkOn*
Genin, Eugene 1903- *WhoMus 72*
Genina, Augusto 1892-1947 *FilmgC*
Genina, Augusto 1892-1957 *DcFM, FilmEn, HalFC 80, WorEFlm*
Genishta, Josif Josifovich 1795-1853 *NewGrD 80*
Genlis, Stephanie-Felicite, Countess Of 1746-1830 *NewGrD 80[port]*
Genn, Edward P d1947 *NotNAT B*
Genn, Leo 1905-1978 *BiE&WWA, FilmEn, FilmgC, ForYSC, HalFC 80, IlWWBF, IntMPA 77, -75, -76, -78, MotPP, MovMk[port], NotNAT, WhoHol A, WhoThe 72, -77*
Gennaro, Peter 1924- *BiE&WWA, CnOxB, DancEn 78, EncMT, NotNAT*
Gennrich, Friedrich 1883-1967 *Baker 78, NewGrD 80*
Genock, Ted 1907- *IntMPA 77, -75, -76, -78, -79, -80*
Genoves Y Lapetra, Tomas 1805-1861 *NewGrD 80*
Genovese, Gen 1917- *AmSCAP 66*
Genrich, Elizabeth *PupTheA*
Gensler, Irina Georgievna 1930- *CnOxB*
Gensler, Lewis E 1896-1978 *AmSCAP 66, -80, CmpEPM*
Gentele, Goeran 1917-1972 *Baker 78, NewEOp 71, WhoMus 72*
Gentele, Goran 1917-1972 *CmOp, NewGrD 80*
Gentemann, Sister Mary Elaine 1909- *ConAmC*
Gentiam *NewGrD 80*
Gentian *NewGrD 80*
Gentien *NewGrD 80*
Gentile, Ortensio *NewGrD 80*
Gentilesca, Franco 1943- *WhoOp 76*
Gentili, Giorgio 1669?-1731? *NewGrD 80*
Gentilucci, Armando 1939- *NewGrD 80*
Gentle, Alice 1889-1958 *WhScrn 74, -77, WhoHol B*
Gentle, Lili 1941- *ForYSC, WhoHol A*
Gentle Giant *ConMuA 80A, IlEncR*
Gentleman, Francis 1728-1784 *NotNAT B, OxThe*
Gentlemen, The *BiDAmM*
Gentry, Amelia d1963 *NotNAT B*
Gentry, Bob d1962 *NotNAT B, WhoHol B*
Gentry, Bobbie 1942- *BiDAmM, PopAmC SUP[port]*
Gentry, Bobbie 1944- *AmSCAP 80, CounME 74, -74A, EncFCWM 69, IlEncCM[port], RkOn 2[port]*
Gentry, Chuck 1911- *WhoJazz 72*
Gentry, Eve *DancEn 78[port]*
Gentry, Gerald Frank 1927- *IntWWM 77, -80*
Gentry, Jacques 1921- *IntWWM 80*
Gentry, Minnie 1915- *DrBlPA*
Gentry, Race 1934- *ForYSC*
Gentrys, The *RkOn 2[port]*
Genty, Jacques 1921- *IntWWM 77*
Genuino, Francesco 1580?-1633? *NewGrD 80*
Genus, Karl *NewYTET*
Genzmer, Harald 1909- *Baker 78, DcCM, IntWWM 77, -80, NewGrD 80*
Geoffroy, Jean-Baptiste 1601-1675 *NewGrD 80*
Geoffroy, Jean-Nicolas d1694 *NewGrD 80*
Geoffroy-Dechaume, Antoine 1905- *NewGrD 80*
Geoly, Andrew 1907- *BiE&WWA, NotNAT*
Geopffem, Georges-Adam 1727?-1809? *NewGrD 80*
Georg, Duke Of Saxe-Meiningen 1826-1914 *Ent*
Georg II, Duke Of Saxe-Meiningen 1826-1914 *EncWT*
Georg Rudolph 1595-1653 *NewGrD 80*
Georgantones, Jimmy P 1940- *AmSCAP 80*
George II 1683-1760 *OxMus*
George III 1738-1820 *OxMus*
George IV 1762-1830 *OxMus*
George V 1865-1936 *OxMus*
George, Mademoiselle 1787-1867 *EncWT, Ent, NotNAT B, OxThe*
George Mt'acmideli d1065 *NewGrD 80*
George II Of Saxe-Meiningen 1826-1914 *OxThe*
George, A E 1869-1920 *NotNAT B, WhThe*
George, Alan Norman 1949- *IntWWM 77, -80*
George, Anthony *ForYSC, WhoHol A*
George, Barbara 1942- *RkOn*
George, Cassietta *AmSCAP 80*
George, Chief Dan 1899- *HalFC 80*
George, Christopher 1929- *FilmEn, FilmgC, HalFC 80, WhoHol A*
George, Christopher 1934- *ForYSC*
George, Colin 1929- *WhoThe 72, -77*
George, Dan 1899- *FilmgC, WhoHol A*
George, Don 1909- *AmSCAP 66, -80*
George, Don R 1903-1978 *AmSCAP 66, -80*
George, Dona Lyn *AmSCAP 80*
George, Earl 1924- *AmSCAP 66, Baker 78, ConAmC*
George, Earl Robert 1924- *AmSCAP 80*
George, George Louis 1907- *IntMPA 77, -75, -76, -78, -79, -80*
George, George W 1920- *IntMPA 77, -75, -76, -78, -79, -80*
George, Gil *AmSCAP 80*
George, Gladys d1954 *MotPP, WhoHol B*
George, Gladys 1900-1954 *FilmEn, FilmgC, HalFC 80, HolCA[port], MovMk, WhScrn 74, -77*
George, Gladys 1902-1954 *Film 1, -2*
George, Gladys 1904-1954 *ForYSC, NotNAT B, ThFT[port], TwYS, Vers A[port], WhThe*
George, Grace 1879-1961 *FamA&A[port], HalFC 80, NotNAT B, OxThe, WhScrn 74, -77, WhThe, WhoHol B*
George, Grace 1880-1961 *WhoStg 1906, -1908*
George, Graham Elias 1912- *BiDAmM, CreCan 2, IntWWM 80*
George, Gwyneth *WhoMus 72*
George, Hal *WhoOp 76*
George, Heinrich 1893-1946 *EncWT, Ent, FilmAG WE, FilmEn, Film 2, HalFC 80, WhScrn 74, -77, WhoHol B*
George, Isabel *WhoHol A*
George, Jimmy *AmSCAP 80*
George, John *ConDr 73, -77B, ForYSC*
George, John 1898-1968 *Film 2, WhScrn 77*
George, Karl 1910?- *WhoJazz 72*
George, Katrina 1936- *WhoMus 72*
George, Lial-Gene Plowe 1918- *IntWWM 80*
George, Lila Gene Plowe Kennedy 1918- *ConAmC*
George, Lila-Gene Plowe Kennedy 1918- *IntWWM 77*
George, Linda Day *HalFC 80*
George, Louis 1935- *IntMPA 79, -80*
George, Lowell *ConMuA 80A*
George, Lynda Day *WhoHol A*
George, Marie 1879-1955 *NotNAT B, WhThe, WhoStg 1906, -1908*
George, Maud 1890- *Film 1, -2, TwYS*
George, Muriel 1883-1965 *FilmgC, HalFC 80, WhScrn 74, -77, WhThe, WhoHol B*
George, Nathan *DrBlPA*
George, Paul *Film 2*
George, Peggy *Film 1*
George, Phyllis *NewYTET*
George, Roger 1921- *CnOxB*
George, Ronald Alan 1955- *IntWWM 80*
George, Sue *ForYSC*
George, Susan 1950- *FilmAG WE[port], FilmEn, FilmgC, ForYSC, HalFC 80, IlWWBF[port], IntMPA 77, -75, -76, -78, -79, -80, MovMk[port], WhoHol A*
George, Thom Ritter 1942- *AmSCAP 80, CpmDNM 80, ConAmC, IntWWM 80*
George, Voya 1895-1951 *Film 2, WhScrn 74, -77, WhoHol B*
George, Warren Edwin 1936- *IntWWM 77, -80*
Georges, Alexandre 1850-1938 *Baker 78*
Georges, Katerine d1973 *WhScrn 77*
Georges-Picot, Olga 1944- *FilmAG WE*
Georgescu, Corneliu-Dan 1938- *Baker 78*
Georgescu, Dan Corneliu 1938- *IntWWM 80*
Georgescu, George 1887-1964 *NewGrD 80*
Georgescu, Georges 1887-1964 *Baker 78*
Georgescu, Remus 1932- *IntWWM 80*
Georgi, Katja *WomWMM*
Georgi, Yvonne 1903-1975 *CnOxB, DancEn 78*
Georgia Bill *BluesWW[port]*
Georgia Clodhoppers *BiDAmM*
Georgia Grinder *BluesWW[port]*
Georgia Minstrels *BiDAmM*
Georgia Pine *BluesWW[port]*
Georgia Pine Boy *BluesWW[port]*
Georgia Slim *BluesWW[port]*
Georgia Tom *BluesWW[port], NewGrD 80*

Georgia Wildcats *BiDAmM*
Georgiades, Thrasybulos G 1907-1977 *Baker 78, NewGrD 80*
Georgiadis, Georges 1912- *Baker 78*
Georgiadis, John Alexander 1939- *IntWWM 80, WhoMus 72*
Georgiadis, Nicholas 1925- *CnOxB, DancEn 78*
Georgiceo, Athanasius 1590?-1640? *NewGrD 80*
Georgiceus, Athanasius 1590?-1640? *NewGrD 80*
Georgievich, Athanasius 1590?-1640? *NewGrD 80*
Georgii, Walter 1887-1967 *Baker 78*
Georgius A Brugis *NewGrD 80*
Geppert, Carl *Film 2*
Gerachty, Carmelita 1901-1966 *Film 2*
Geraedts, Jaap 1924- *IntWWM 77, -80, NewGrD 80*
Geraert, Jan *NewGrD 80*
Geraghty, Carmelita 1901-1966 *ForYSC, MotPP, TwYS, WhScrn 74, -77, WhoHol B*
Geraghty, Maurice 1908- *IntMPA 77, -75, -76, -78, -79, -80*
Gerak, Berrie Lee 1942- *AmSCAP 80*
Gerald De Barri *NewGrD 80*
Gerald Of Wales *OxMus*
Gerald, Ara 1900-1957 *NotNAT B, WhThe, WhoHol B*
Gerald, Florence d1942 *NotNAT B*
Gerald, Frank 1855-1942 *NotNAT B*
Gerald, Helen *IntMPA 77, -76, -78, -79, -80*
Gerald, Jim 1889-1958 *Film 2, FilmgC, HalFC 80, WhScrn 74, -77, WhoHol B*
Gerald, Peter *Film 1*
Geraldo 1904-1974 *CmpEPM, NewGrD 80*
Geraldy, Paul 1885- *CnMD, McGEWD[port], ModWD, WhThe*
Gerard, Ambassador *Film 1*
Gerard, Bette *PupTheA*
Gerard, Bill *PupTheA*
Gerard, Carl *Film 1, -2*
Gerard, Charles *Film 1, -2*
Gerard, Henri-Philippe 1760-1848 *NewGrD 80*
Gerard, Jan *NewGrD 80*
Gerard, Jenny *WomWMM*
Gerard, Joseph *Film 2*
Gerard, Joseph Smith 1871-1949 *WhScrn 74, -77*
Gerard, Lillian *IntMPA 77, -75, -76, -78, -79, -80*
Gerard, Philip R 1913- *IntMPA 77, -75, -76, -78, -79, -80*
Gerard, Richard H 1876-1948 *AmSCAP 66, -80, BiDAmM*
Gerard, Rolf 1909- *WhoOp 76*
Gerard, Rolf 1910?- *NotNAT*
Gerard, Teddie d1942 *Film 2, WhoHol B*
Gerard, Teddie 1890-1942 *WhScrn 74, -77*
Gerard, Teddie 1892-1942 *WhThe*
Gerard, Will *AmSCAP 80*
Gerard, Yves Rene Jean 1932- *IntWWM 77, -80, NewGrD 80*
Gerarde, Derick *NewGrD 80*
Gerarde, Theodoricus *NewGrD 80*
Gerardi, Jess Louis, Jr. 1938- *AmSCAP 80*
Gerardi, Robert 1937- *AmSCAP 80*
Gerardis, Giovanni Battista Pinellus De *NewGrD 80*
Gerardo *NewGrD 80*
Gerardus *NewGrD 80*
Gerardus, Jan *NewGrD 80*
Gerardy, Jean 1877-1929 *Baker 78, NewGrD 80*
Gerasch, Alfred *Film 2*
Gerasimov, Anatole 1945- *EncJzS 70*
Gerasimov, Sergei 1906- *BiDFilm, -81, DcFM, Film 2, FilmgC, HalFC 80, OxFilm, WorEFlm[port]*
Gerasimov, Sergei 1906-1972 *FilmEn*
Geray, Steve 1904-1976 *FilmgC, HalFC 80, MovMk[port], WhThe*
Geray, Steven 1898-1973 *WhScrn 77*
Geray, Steven 1899-1974 *FilmEn*
Geray, Steven 1904-1973 *ForYSC, IntMPA 77, -75, -76, -78, -79, -80, Vers B[port], WhoHol B*
Gerber, Alex 1895-1969 *AmSCAP 66, -80*
Gerber, Christian 1660-1731 *NewGrD 80*
Gerber, Daisy *WomWMM B*
Gerber, David *IntMPA 77, -75, -76, -78, -79, -80, NewYTET*
Gerber, Ella 1916- *BiE&WWA, NotNAT*
Gerber, Ernst Ludwig 1746-1819 *Baker 78, NewGrD 80, OxMus*
Gerber, Heinrich Nikolaus 1702-1775 *NewGrD 80*
Gerber, Heinrich Nikolaus 1746-1819 *Baker 78*
Gerber, Judith 1946- *CnOxB*
Gerber, Michael H 1944- *IntMPA 77, -75, -76, -78, -79, -80*
Gerber, Miklos Teghze 1906-1969 *AmSCAP 80*
Gerber, Neva *Film 1, -2, TwYS*
Gerber, Rene 1908- *Baker 78, IntWWM 77, -80, NewGrD 80, WhoMus 72*
Gerber, Rudolf 1899-1957 *Baker 78, NewGrD 80*
Gerbert D'Aurillac 940?-1003 *NewGrD 80*
Gerbert, Martin 1720-1793 *Baker 78, NewGrD 80*
Gerbic, Fran 1840-1917 *NewGrD 80*
Gerbich, Johann Anton *NewGrD 80*
Gerbig, Johann Anton *NewGrD 80*
Gerbrandt, Carl J 1940- *IntWWM 77, -80*
Gerbrecht, Pinky 1901-1963 *NewOrJ*
Gerdes, Emily *Film 2*
Gerdes, Federico 1873-1953 *NewGrD 80*
Gerdt, Paul 1844-1917 *DancEn 78*
Gerdt, Pavel Andreyevich 1844-1917 *CnOxB*
Gerdt, Yelisaveta Pavlovna 1891-1975 *CnOxB*
Gerdt, Yelizaveta 1891-1975 *DancEn 78*
Gere, Richard 1949- *FilmEn, HalFC 80, IntMPA 79, -80*
Gerelli, Ennio 1907-1970 *Baker 78*
Gergely, Jean G 1911- *IntWWM 77, -80, NewGrD 80*
Gerhard *NewGrD 80*
Gerhard, Christian August 1745-1817 *NewGrD 80*
Gerhard, Johann Christian Adam 1780-1837 *NewGrD 80*
Gerhard, Johann Ernst Gottfried 1786-1823 *NewGrD 80*
Gerhard, Justinus Ehrenfried 1710?-1786 *NewGrD 80*
Gerhard, Karl d1964 *NotNAT B*
Gerhard, Livia *NewGrD 80*
Gerhard, Roberto 1896-1970 *Baker 78, BnBkM 80, CnOxB, DcCom&M 79, DcCM, MusMk, NewGrD 80[port], OxMus*
Gerhardt, Elena 1883-1961 *Baker 78, BnBkM 80, MusSN[port], NewGrD 80*
Gerhardt, Paul 1607-1676 *NewGrD 80*
Gerhardt, Paulus 1607-1676 *NewGrD 80*
Gerhardt, Reinhold *WhoMus 72*
Gerhardt, Walter 1912- *IntWWM 77, -80, WhoMus 72*
Gerhart, Martha *IntWWM 80*
Gerhon, John *ConMuA 80B*
Gerich, Valentine 1898- *AmSCAP 66, -80*
Gericke, Wilhelm 1845-1925 *Baker 78, BiDAmM, NewGrD 80*
Gerig *NewGrD 80*
Gerig, Hans 1910-1978 *NewGrD 80*
Gerig, Reginald Roth 1919- *IntWWM 77, -80*
Gerima, Haile *MorBAP*
Gering, Marion 1901-1977 *FilmEn, FilmgC, HalFC 80*
Gerke, Wellman E 1907- *AmSCAP 80*
Gerl *NewGrD 80*
Gerl, Barbara 1770-1806 *NewGrD 80*
Gerl, Franz Xaver 1764-1827 *NewGrD 80*
Gerl, Thaddaus 1774-1844 *NewGrD 80*
Gerl, Thaddeus 1766-1844 *CmOp*
Gerlach, Arthur Von 1877-1925 *DcFM*
Gerlach, Catharina d1591 *NewGrD 80*
Gerlach, Dietrich d1575 *NewGrD 80*
Gerlach, Fred 1925- *BiDAmM, EncFCWM 69*
Gerlach, Reinhard 1934- *NewGrD 80*
Gerlach, Sonja 1936- *IntWWM 77, -80*
Gerlach, Theodor d1575 *NewGrD 80*
Gerlach, Theodor 1861-1940 *Baker 78*
Gerlach-Jacobi *Film 2*
Gerlandus *NewGrD 80*
Gerlatz, Dietrich *NewGrD 80*
Gerle, Conrad d1521 *NewGrD 80*
Gerle, Georg d1589? *NewGrD 80*
Gerle, Hans 1500?-1570 *Baker 78, NewGrD 80*
Gerle, Melchior *NewGrD 80*
Gerle, Robert 1924- *IntWWM 80, WhoMus 72*
Gerlin, Ruggero 1899- *NewGrD 80, WhoMus 72*
Germain, John Norman 1930- *WhoOp 76*
Germain, Karl 1878-1959 *MagIlD*
Germaine, Auguste d1915 *NotNAT B*
Germaine, Mary 1933- *FilmgC, HalFC 80, WhoHol A*
German, Sir Edward 1862-1936 *Baker 78, DcCom&M 79, MusMk, NewGrD 80, OxMus, WhThe, WhoStg 1908*
German Reed, Thomas 1817-1888 *NewGrD 80*
Germani, Fernando 1906- *BnBkM 80, IntWWM 77, -80, NewGrD 80, WhoMus 72*
Germano, Eddy *ConMuA 80B*
Germanos Of Constantinople 634?-733 *NewGrD 80*
Germanos Of New Patrai d1700? *NewGrD 80*
Germanova, Maria Nikolaevna 1884-1940 *OxThe, PlP&P*
Germanus Of Constantinople 634?-733 *NewGrD 80*
Germeten, Gunnar, Jr. 1947- *IntWWM 80*
Germi, Pietro *IntMPA 75*
Germi, Pietro 1904-1974 *FilmgC, WhScrn 77*
Germi, Pietro 1914-1974 *DcFM, FilmEn, HalFC 80, MovMk[port], OxFilm, WhoHol B, WorEFlm*
Germinaro, Richard 1945- *AmSCAP 80*
Germino, Mark Raymond 1950- *AmSCAP 80*
Germon, Effie d1914 *NotNAT B, WhoStg 1908*
Germonprez, Valerie *Film 1*
Gernsheim, Friedrich 1839-1916 *Baker 78, NewGrD 80*
Gero, Giovan *NewGrD 80*
Gero, Ihan *NewGrD 80*
Gero, Jan *NewGrD 80*
Gero, Jehan *NewGrD 80*
Gero, Jhan *Baker 78, NewGrD 80*
Gerold, Arthur 1923- *BiE&WWA, NotNAT*
Gerold, Theodore 1866-1956 *Baker 78, NewGrD 80*
Geronimo *AmSCAP 80*
Geronimo 1829-1909 *HalFC 80*
Gerosa, Joe *NewOrJ*
Geroule, Henri d1934 *NotNAT B*
Gerow, Albert Patrick 1921- *IntWWM 77*
Gerrard, Charles 1887- *Film 1, -2, ForYSC, MotPP, TwYS*
Gerrard, Douglas 1885-1950 *TwYS A*
Gerrard, Douglas 1888-1950 *Film 1, -2, ForYSC, TwYS, WhScrn 77*
Gerrard, Gene 1892-1971 *FilmgC, HalFC 80, IlWWBF, WhScrn 74, -77, WhThe, WhoHol B*
Gerrard, Teddie 1892-1942 *NotNAT B*
Gerrard, William *AmSCAP 80*
Gerringer, Robert 1926- *BiE&WWA, NotNAT*
Gerrish, John O 1910- *ConAmC*
Gerrish, Laurence 1916- *WhoMus 72*
Gerritsen, Lisa *WhoHol A*
Gerritzen, Gunther 1935- *IntWWM 77*
Gerron, Kurt *Film 2*
Gerron, Kurt d1943 *WhoHol B*
Gerron, Kurt d1944 *WhScrn 77*
Gerry, Alex 1908- *Vers A[port], WhoHol A*
Gerry & The Pacemakers *RkOn 2[port]*
Gerschefski, Edwin 1909- *Baker 78, BiDAmM, ConAmC, DcCM, IntWWM 77, -80, NewGrD 80*
Gersem, Gery *NewGrD 80*
Gershenson, Joseph 1904- *AmSCAP 80, FilmEn, FilmgC, HalFC 80, IntMPA 77, -75, -76, -78, -79, -80, WhoHrs 80*
Gershfeld, David 1911- *Baker 78*
Gershkovich, Filip 1906- *NewGrD 80*
Gershkovitch, Jacques 1884-1953 *Baker 78*
Gershon, Fred *ConMuA 80B*
Gershvin, Jacob 1898-1937 *NewGrD 80[port]*
Gershwin, Arthur 1900- *AmSCAP 66, -80*
Gershwin, George 1898-1937 *AmPS, AmSCAP 66, -80, Baker 78, BestMus, BiDAmM, BnBkM 80, CmMov, CmOp,*

CmpEPM, CompSN[port], CnOxB, ConAmC, DcCom 77[port], DcCom&M 79, DcCM, EncMT, EncWT, FilmEn, HalFC 80, McGEWD, MnPM[port], MusMk[port], NewCBMT, NewEOp 71, NewGrD 80[port], NotNAT A, -B, OxFilm, OxMus, PIP&P[port], PopAmC[port], PopAmC SUP, Sw&Ld C, WhThe
Gershwin, George 1899-1937 *DcFM, FilmgC*
Gershwin, Henry *AmSCAP 80*
Gershwin, Ira 1896- *AmPS, AmSCAP 66, -80, Baker 78, BestMus, BiDAmM, BiE&WWA, CmpEPM, EncMT, EncWT, Ent, FilmEn, FilmgC, HalFC 80, IntMPA 77, -75, -76, -78, -79, -80, NewCBMT, NotNAT, -A, PIP&P, Sw&Ld C, WhThe, WhoMus 72*
Gershwins, The *PIP&P[port]*
Gerson, Betty Lou *ForYSC, WhoHol A*
Gerson, Charles *Film 2*
Gerson, Eva 1903-1959 *WhScrn 74, -77, WhoHol B*
Gerson, George 1790-1825 *NewGrD 80*
Gerson, Jean Charlier De 1363-1429 *NewGrD 80*
Gerson, Paul 1871-1957 *WhScrn 74, -77, WhoHol B*
Gerson-Kiwi, E Edith 1908- *IntWWM 77*
Gerson-Kiwi, Edith 1908- *IntWWM 80, NewGrD 80*
Gersonides *NewGrD 80*
Gerstad, John 1924- *BiE&WWA, NotNAT, WhoThe 72, -77*
Gerstad, Merritt B *CmMov*
Gerstberger, Karl 1892-1955 *Baker 78*
Gerstein, Cassandra *WomWMM B*
Gersten, Bernard 1923- *BiE&WWA, NotNAT, WhoThe 77*
Gersten, Berta 1894-1972 *WhScrn 77, WhoHol B*
Gerstenberg, Heinrich Wilhelm Von 1727-1823 *NewGrD 80*
Gerstenberg, Heinrich Wilhelm Von 1737-1823 *McGEWD*
Gerstenberg, Johann Daniel 1758-1841 *NewGrD 80*
Gerstenberg, Walter 1904- *NewGrD 80*
Gerstenbuttel, Joachim 1650?-1721 *NewGrD 80*
Gerster, Etelka 1855-1920 *Baker 78, CmOp, NewEOp 71, NewGrD 80*
Gerster, Joachim 1936- *CnOxB*
Gerster, Ottmar 1897-1969 *Baker 78, CmOp, NewGrD 80*
Gerster, Robert 1945- *ConAmC*
Gerstle, Frank *ForYSC*
Gerstle, Frank 1915-1970 *WhScrn 77*
Gerstle, Frank 1917-1970 *WhScrn 74, WhoHol B*
Gerstman, Blanche 1910- *Baker 78*
Gerstman, Felix G d1967 *BiE&WWA, NotNAT, -B*
Gert, Valeska 1900- *CnOxB, Film 2, OxFilm*
Gertler, Andre 1907- *Baker 78, IntWWM 77, -80, NewGrD 80, WhoMus 72*
Gertner, Richard *IntMPA 77, -75, -76, -78, -79, -80*
Gertsman, Maury 1910?- *FilmgC, HalFC 80*
Gertz, Irving 1915- *AmSCAP 80, ConAmC, IntMPA 77, -75, -76, -78, -79, -80*
Gerun, Tom *BgBands 74, CmpEPM*
Gerussi, Bruno *WhThe, WhoThe 72*
Gervais DeBus *NewGrD 80*
Gervais, Charles-Hubert 1671-1744 *NewGrD 80*
Gervais, Laurent *NewGrD 80*
Gervais, Lise 1933- *CreCan 1*
Gervais, Pierre-Noel 1746?-1805? *NewGrD 80*
Gervais-L'Heureux, Suzanne *WomWMM*
Gervaise, Claude *Baker 78, NewGrD 80*
Gervasius De Anglia *NewGrD 80*
Gervasoni, Carlo 1762-1819 *NewGrD 80*
Gervays *NewGrD 80*
Gervers, Hilda F 1909- *IntWWM 80*
Gerville-Reache, Jeanne 1882-1915 *Baker 78, BiDAmM, NewEOp 71*
Gese, Bartholomaus *NewGrD 80*
Gesek, Tadeusz 1925- *NotNAT*
Gesensway, Louis 1906-1976 *AmSCAP 66, -80, Baker 78, CpmDNM 74, ConAmC, WhoMus 72*
Gesius, Barthel 1555?-1613? *NewGrD 80*
Gesius, Bartholomaus 1555?-1613? *NewGrD 80, OxMus*
Gesner, Clark 1938- *AmSCAP 66, -80, EncMT, NatPD[port]*
Gesner, Conrad 1516-1565 *NewGrD 80*
Gesoff, Hilda I *AmSCAP 66*
Gesoff, Hilda Ida *AmSCAP 80*
Gessler, Caroline 1908- *ConAmC*
Gessner, Konrad 1516-1565 *NewGrD 80*
Gessner-Asten, Erika 1928- *IntWWM 77, -80*
Gest, Inna 1922-1965 *WhScrn 74, -77, WhoHol B*
Gest, Morris 1881-1942 *NotNAT B, WhThe*
Gestewitz, Friedrich Christoph 1753-1805 *NewGrD 80*
Gesualdo, Carlo 1560?-1613 *Baker 78, BnBkM 80, CmpBCM, GrComp[port], MusMk, OxMus*
Gesualdo, Carlo 1561?-1613 *NewGrD 80*
Geszler, Gyorgy 1913- *IntWWM 77, -80*
Geszty, Sylvia 1934- *NewGrD 80, WhoMus 72, WhoOp 76*
Getan, Jesus 1916- *IntWWM 77, -80*
Getchell, Charles Munro 1909-1963 *NotNAT B*
Getchell, Summer *Film 2*
Gettel, William D *ConAmC*
Gettinger, William d1966 *WhScrn 77, WhoHol B*
Gettman, Lorraine *WhoHol A*
Getty, J Ronald 1929- *IntMPA 77, -75, -76, -78, -79, -80*
Getz, Johnnie G d1964 *NotNAT B*
Getz, Stan 1927- *CmpEPM, EncJzS 70, IlEncJ, NewGrD 80*
Getz, Stan & Astrud Gilberto *RkOn 2A*
Getz, Stan And Charlie Byrd *RkOn*
Getz, Stanley 1927- *BiDAmM, EncJzS 70*
Getzmann, Wolfgang *NewGrD 80*
Getzov, Ramon M 1925- *AmSCAP 66, -80*
Geuck, Valentin 1570?-1596 *NewGrD 80*
Geurin-Catelain, Raymond *Film 2*
Geva, Tamara *AmPS B, ForYSC, WhoThe 72*
Geva, Tamara 1907- *BiE&WWA, EncMT, Film 2, NotNAT, WhThe, WhoHol A*
Geva, Tamara 1908- *CnOxB, DancEn 78*
Gevaert, Francois Auguste 1828-1908 *Baker 78*
Gevaert, Francois-Auguste 1828-1908 *NewGrD 80, OxMus*
Gevanche, Adam De *NewGrD 80*
Gevers, Frederick 1923- *IntWWM 77, -80*
Gevicensis, Andrea Chrysoponos *NewGrD 80*
Gevicenus, Andrea Chrysoponos *NewGrD 80*
Geyer, Johann Christoph *NewGrD 80*
Geyer, Stefi 1888-1956 *NewGrD 80*
Geymond, Vital *Film 2*
Geymuller, Marguerite-Camille-Louise De 1897- *IntWWM 80*
Geyra, Ellida *WomWMM*
Ghaffary, Farrokh 1922- *DcFM*
Ghandar, Ann 1943- *IntWWM 80*
Ghatak, Ritwik 1924- *DcFM*
Ghazarian, Sona 1945- *WhoOp 76*
Gheciu, Diamandi 1892- *IntWWM 80*
Ghedini, Giorgio Federico 1892-1965 *Baker 78, DcCM, NewEOp 71, NewGrD 80, OxMus*
Gheerken DeHondt *NewGrD 80*
Gheerkin *NewGrD 80*
Gheerkin DeHondt *NewGrD 80*
Gheine, VanDen *NewGrD 80*
Ghelderode, Michel De 1898-1962 *CnMD, CnThe, DcPup, EncWT, Ent, McGEWD[port], ModWD, NotNAT B, OxThe, REnWD[port]*
Gheluwe, Leo Van 1837-1914 *NewGrD 80*
Gheluwe, Leon Van 1837-1914 *Baker 78*
Ghent, Derek *Film 2*
Ghent, Emmanuel 1925- *AmSCAP 80, Baker 78, CpmDNM 78, ConAmC, DcCM, NewGrD 80*
Gheon, Henri 1875-1943 *OxThe*
Gheon, Henri 1875-1944 *CnMD, CnThe, EncWT, Ent, McGEWD[port], ModWD*
Gheorghiu, Valentin 1928- *Baker 78, NewGrD 80, WhoMus 72*
Gheraert DeHondt *NewGrD 80*
Gherardello Da Firenze 1320?-1363? *NewGrD 80*
Gherardeschi, Filippo Maria 1738-1808 *NewGrD 80*
Gherardi, Biagio *NewGrD 80*
Gherardi, Evaristo 1663-1700 *EncWT, Ent, NotNAT B, OxThe*
Gherardi, Gherardo 1890-1949 *CnMD*
Gherardi, Gherardo 1891-1949 *McGEWD*
Gherardi, Giovanni *NewGrD 80*
Gherardi, Giovanni d1683 *EncWT, OxThe*
Gherardi, Giovanni Battista Pinello Di *NewGrD 80*
Gherardi, Piero 1909-1971 *FilmEn, WorEFlm*
Gherardini, Arcangelo *NewGrD 80*
Gherdjikow, Pavel Iwanow 1938- *IntWWM 80*
Gherl, Johann Kaspar *NewGrD 80*
Ghero, Jhan *NewGrD 80*
Ghersem, Gery 1573?-1630 *NewGrD 80*
Ghertovici, Adia 1919- *IntWWM 77, -80*
Gheusi, Pierre B 1867- *WhThe*
Gheyn, Matthias VanDen 1721-1785 *Baker 78*
Gheyn, VanDen *NewGrD 80*
Ghezzi, Ippolito 1650?-1709? *NewGrD 80*
Ghezzo, Dinu Dumitru 1940- *AmSCAP 80*
Ghezzo, Dinu Dumitru 1941- *Baker 78, CpmDNM 76, -77, -79, -80, IntWWM 77, -80*
Ghezzo, Marta Elisabeth 1940- *IntWWM 77, -80*
Ghiaurov, Nicolai 1929- *Baker 78, MusSN[port], NewEOp 71, NewGrD 80, WhoOp 76*
Ghibel, Heliseo 1520?-1581? *NewGrD 80*
Ghibelli, Heliseo 1520?-1581? *NewGrD 80*
Ghibellini, Heliseo 1520?-1581? *NewGrD 80*
Ghiglia, Oscar 1938- *BnBkM 80, NewGrD 80, WhoMus 72*
Ghiglieri, Sylvia Marie 1933- *ConAmC, IntWWM 77, -80*
Ghignone, Giovanni Pietro *Baker 78, NewGrD 80*
Ghinste, Peter VanDer 1789-1861 *NewGrD 80*
Ghio, Nino 1887-1956 *WhScrn 74, -77*
Ghione, Emile *Film 2*
Ghione, Emilio 1879-1930 *DcFM, FilmAG WE, FilmEn, WorEFlm*
Ghione, Francesco 1886-1964 *NewEOp 71*
Ghione, Franco 1886-1964 *Baker 78, NotNAT B*
Ghirardellus De Florentia *NewGrD 80*
Ghirardi, Giovanni Battista Pinello Di *NewGrD 80*
Ghirardo *NewGrD 80*
Ghirardo, Jan *NewGrD 80*
Ghircoiasiu, Romeo 1919- *IntWWM 77, -80, NewGrD 80*
Ghis, Henri 1839-1908 *Baker 78*
Ghiselin Danckerts *NewGrD 80*
Ghiselin, Johannes *NewGrD 80*
Ghisi, Federico 1901-1975 *Baker 78, NewGrD 80*
Ghislanzoni, Antonio 1824-1893 *Baker 78, NewEOp 71, NewGrD 80*
Ghitalla, Armando 1925- *NewGrD 80*
Ghitti, Franco 1932- *WhoOp 76*
Ghiuselev, Nicola 1936- *WhoMus 72, WhoOp 76*
Ghivizzani, Alessandro 1572?-1632? *NewGrD 80*
Ghizeghem, Hayne Van *NewGrD 80*
Ghizzolo *NewGrD 80*
Ghizzolo, Giovanni d1625? *NewGrD 80*
Gholmieh, Walid 1938- *IntWWM 80*
Gholson, Julie *WhoHol A*
Ghosal, Mrs. 1857-1932 *NotNAT B*
Ghosh, Girish Chandra *REnWD[port]*
Ghosh, Nikhil Jyoti 1919- *IntWWM 77*
Ghosh, Nikhiljyoti 1919- *IntWWM 80*
Ghostley, Alice 1926- *BiE&WWA, ForYSC, HalFC 80, MotPP, NotNAT, WhoHol A, WhoThe 72, -77*
Ghro, Johann *NewGrD 80*
Ghyoros, Julien J C 1922- *IntWWM 77, -80*
Ghys, Joseph 1801-1848 *Baker 78*
Giaccio, Horatio 1590?-1660? *NewGrD 80*
Giaccio, Orazio 1590?-1660? *NewGrD 80*
Giachero, Roberto 1925- *DancEn 78*
Giachetti, Fosco 1904-1974 *FilmAG WE, WhScrn 77, WhoHol B*
Giacobbe, Juan Francisco 1907- *NewGrD 80*
Giacobbe, Nello 1940- *AmSCAP 80*

Giacobbi, Girolamo 1567-1629 *NewGrD 80*
Giacobetti, Pietro Amico *NewGrD 80*
Giacomelli, Geminiano 1692?-1740 *Baker 78, NewGrD 80*
Giacometti, Bortolomeo 1741-1809 *NewGrD 80*
Giacometti, Giovanni Battista 1550?-1603? *NewGrD 80*
Giacometti, Paolo 1816-1882 *McGEWD[port], NotNAT B, OxThe*
Giacomini, Bernardo 1532-1563? *NewGrD 80*
Giacomini, Giuseppe 1940- *WhoOp 76*
Giacomino 1884-1956 *WhScrn 74, -77*
Giacomo Da Chieti *NewGrD 80*
Giacomo, Salvatore Di *NewGrD 80*
Giacomotti, Alfredo 1933- *WhoOp 76*
Giacopone Da Todi *NewGrD 80*
Giacopone De' Benedetti *NewGrD 80*
Giacosa, Giuseppe 1847-1906 *BnBkM 80, CmOp, CnThe, EncWT, McGEWD[port], ModWD, NewGrD 80, NotNAT B, OxThe, REnWD[port]*
Giacosa, Guiseppe 1847-1906 *Ent*
Giai, Francesco Saverio *NewGrD 80*
Giai, Giovanni Antonio 1690?-1764 *NewGrD 80*
Giaii, Francesco Saverio *NewGrD 80*
Giaii, Giovanni Antonio 1690?-1764 *NewGrD 80*
Giaij, Francesco Saverio *NewGrD 80*
Giaij, Giovanni Antonio 1690?-1764 *NewGrD 80*
Giaiotti, Bonaldo 1932- *WhoOp 76*
Gialdini, Gialdino 1843-1919 *Baker 78*
Giallelis, Stathis 1939- *FilmgC, HalFC 80, WhoHol A*
Gialleris, Stathis 1943- *ForYSC*
Giamberti, Gioseppe 1600?-1664? *NewGrD 80*
Giamberti, Giuseppe 1600?-1664? *NewGrD 80*
Giami, Guiliano *WhoHol A*
Giammei, Lamberto 1910- *WhoOp 76*
Gian Toscan *NewGrD 80*
Gianacconi, Giuseppe *NewGrD 80*
Giancarli, Gigio Artemio *McGEWD*
Giancursio, Joseph 1921- *AmSCAP 80*
Giandomenico, Emilio 1939- *AmSCAP 66*
Gianella, Louis 1778?-1817 *NewGrD 80*
Gianelli, Francesco *NewGrD 80*
Gianelli, Pietro 1770?-1830 *NewGrD 80*
Gianeselli, Iginio 1938- *WhoOp 76*
Gianettini, Antonio 1648-1721 *Baker 78*
Giangreco, Thomas 1911- *AmSCAP 80*
Gianneo, Luis 1897-1968 *Baker 78, BiDAmM, NewGrD 80*
Giannetti, Giovanni 1869-1934 *Baker 78*
Giannettini, Antonio 1648-1721 *NewGrD 80*
Giannetto *NewGrD 80*
Giannini, Dusolina 1900- *NewGrD 80*
Giannini, Dusolina 1902- *Baker 78, BiDAmM, CmOp, MusSN[port], NewEOp 71*
Giannini, Giancarlo 1942- *FilmEn, HalFC 80, IntMPA 77, -78, -79, -80, WhoHol A*
Giannini, Olga *WhThe*
Giannini, Vittorio 1903-1966 *AmSCAP 66, -80, Baker 78, BiDAmM, BnBkM 80, CmOp, CompSN[port], ConAmC, DcCM, NewEOp 71, NewGrD 80, OxMus*
Giannini, Walter *ConAmC*
Giannotti, Donato 1492-1573 *McGEWD*
Giannotti, Giacomo *NewGrD 80*
Giannotti, Pierre d1765 *NewGrD 80*
Gianoli, Reine *WhoMus 72*
Gianotti, Giacomo *NewGrD 80*
Gianotti, Pietro d1765 *NewGrD 80*
Giansetti, Giovanni Battista *NewGrD 80*
Gianturco, Carolyn M 1934- *NewGrD 80*
Giaranzana *NewGrD 80*
Giarda, Luigi Stefano 1868-1953 *Baker 78*
Giardina, Ernest 1870?- *NewOrJ*
Giardina, Tony 1897-1956? *NewOrJ[port]*
Giardini, Felice De' 1716-1796 *Baker 78, BnBkM 80, MusMk, NewGrD 80, OxMus*
Giarratano, Tony 1907- *AmSCAP 66, -80*
Giasson, Paul Emile 1921- *AmSCAP 66, -80*
Giaurov, Nicolai 1929- *CmOp*
Giay, Francesco Saverio *NewGrD 80*
Giay, Giovanni Antonio 1690?-1764 *NewGrD 80*
Giazotto, Remo 1910- *Baker 78, NewGrD 80*
Gibaldi, Louis Milo 1951- *AmSCAP 80*
Gibb, Andy 1958- *ConMuA 80A, RkOn 2[port]*
Gibb, James *WhoMus 72*
Gibb, Robert W 1893-1964 *AmSCAP 66, -80, ConAmC*
Gibb, Stanley Garth 1940- *AmSCAP 80, ConAmC*
Gibb, Stephen M 1945- *AmSCAP 80*
Gibberson, William 1919- *BiE&WWA*
Gibbes, Joseph *PupTheA*
Gibbes, Richard *NewGrD 80*
Gibbins, Clarence Wingfield Mingay 1916- *IntWWM 80*
Gibbon, Edward 1737-1794 *OxMus*
Gibbon, John Murray 1875-1952 *CreCan 1*
Gibbon, Laurence 1932- *WhoMus 72*
Gibbons, Arthur 1871-1935 *NotNAT B, WhThe*
Gibbons, Barbara Janet 1926- *WhoMus 72*
Gibbons, Carroll 1903-1954 *NewGrD 80*
Gibbons, Cedric 1893-1956 *OxFilm*
Gibbons, Cedric 1893-1960 *DcFM, FilmEn, WorEFlm*
Gibbons, Cedric 1895-1960 *FilmgC, HalFC 80, NotNAT B, WhoHrs 80*
Gibbons, Christopher 1615-1676 *Baker 78, NewGrD 80[port], OxMus*
Gibbons, Edward *NewGrD 80*
Gibbons, Edward 1568-1650? *Baker 78*
Gibbons, Edward 1570?-1650? *OxMus*
Gibbons, Ellis 1573-1603 *Baker 78, NewGrD 80, OxMus*
Gibbons, Irene *BluesWW[port]*
Gibbons, Irene 1907-1962 *NotNAT B*
Gibbons, Orlando 1583-1625 *Baker 78, BnBkM 80, CmpBCM, DcCom 77, DcCom&M 79, GrComp[port], MusMk, NewGrD 80[port], OxMus*
Gibbons, Rose 1886-1964 *NotNAT B, WhScrn 74, -77, WhoHol B*
Gibbons, William *Baker 78*
Gibbs, Mrs. 1770-1844 *NotNAT B, OxThe*
Gibbs, Alan 1932- *IntWWM 77, -80*
Gibbs, Anthony 1925- *HalFC 80*
Gibbs, Arthur H 1895-1956 *AmSCAP 66, -80*
Gibbs, Cecil Armstrong 1889-1960 *Baker 78, NewGrD 80, OxMus*
Gibbs, Eddie Leroy 1908- *WhoJazz 72*
Gibbs, Geoffrey David 1940- *ConAmC, IntWWM 77, -80*
Gibbs, Georgia *AmPS A, -B*
Gibbs, Georgia 1920- *CmpEPM*
Gibbs, Georgia 1926- *RkOn*
Gibbs, Gerald 1910?- *FilmgC, HalFC 80*
Gibbs, Harold Becket 1868-1956 *BiDAmM*
Gibbs, John *OxMus*
Gibbs, John 1937- *WhoOp 76*
Gibbs, Joseph 1699-1788 *MusMk[port], NewGrD 80[port], OxMus*
Gibbs, Michael 1937- *ConAmC, EncJzS 70, IntWWM 77, NewGrD 80*
Gibbs, Mike 1937- *EncJzS 70*
Gibbs, Nancy d1956 *NotNAT B, WhThe*
Gibbs, Parker *CmpEPM*
Gibbs, Raton *Film 1*
Gibbs, Raymond Douglas *WhoOp 76*
Gibbs, Richard *NewGrD 80, OxMus*
Gibbs, Robert Paton d1940 *NotNAT B*
Gibbs, Ronald A 1945- *IntWWM 77, -80*
Gibbs, Sheila Shand *WhoHol A*
Gibbs, Terry 1924- *AmSCAP 66, -80, BiDAmM, CmpEPM, EncJzS 70, IlEncJ*
Gibbs, Vernon *ConMuA 80B*
Gibbs, Wolcott 1902-1958 *EncWT, NotNAT B, OxThe*
Gibel, Otto 1612-1682 *NewGrD 80*
Gibelius, Otto 1612-1682 *NewGrD 80*
Gibelli, Lorenzo 1719?-1812 *NewGrD 80*
Gibert, Paul-Cesar 1717-1787 *NewGrD 80*
Giblyn, Charles d1933 *Film 2, TwYS A*
Gibney, Frank 1924- *BiE&WWA*
Gibney, Sheridan 1903- *FilmEn*
Gibson, Alan 1938- *HalFC 80, WhoHrs 80*
Gibson, Albert Andrew 1913-1961 *AmSCAP 66, -80*
Gibson, Alexander 1926- *CmOp, IntWWM 77, -80, NewEOp 71, WhoMus 72, WhoOp 76*
Gibson, Sir Alexander 1926- *NewGrD 80*
Gibson, Alfred 1849-1924 *NewGrD 80*
Gibson, Andy Albert 1913-1961 *WhoJazz 72*
Gibson, Archer 1875-1952 *Baker 78, ConAmC*
Gibson, Arthur John 1923- *WhoMus 72*
Gibson, Bob 1931- *EncFCWM 69*
Gibson, Brenda 1870- *WhThe*
Gibson, Charles Dana 1867-1944 *WhScrn 77*
Gibson, Chloe 1899- *WhThe, WhoThe 72*
Gibson, Clifford 1901-1963 *BluesWW*
Gibson, David *PupTheA*
Gibson, David 1943- *CpmDNM 76, ConAmC*
Gibson, Dick 1925- *EncJzS 70*
Gibson, Don 1928- *CounME 74, -74A, EncFCWM 69, IlEncCM[port], RkOn[port]*
Gibson, Donald 1928- *BiDAmM*
Gibson, Edmund 1669-1748 *OxMus*
Gibson, Edward Hoot 1892-1962 *WhScrn 77*
Gibson, Ethlyn *Film 2*
Gibson, Florence *Film 2*
Gibson, Gertrude 1903- *WhoMus 72*
Gibson, Helen *ForYSC*
Gibson, Helen 1892- *FilmEn, Film 1, -2, FilmgC, HalFC 80, WhoHol A*
Gibson, Helen 1893- *TwYS*
Gibson, Henry *HalFC 80, WhoHol A*
Gibson, Hoot 1892-1962 *FilmEn, Film 1, -2, FilmgC, HalFC 80, MotPP, MovMk, NotNAT B, OxFilm, TwYS, WhScrn 74, WhoHol B*
Gibson, Hoot 1895-1962 *ForYSC*
Gibson, Ian Wallace 1919- *CreCan 1*
Gibson, James 1866-1938 *Film 2, WhScrn 74, -77, WhoHol B*
Gibson, James 1926- *WhoMus 72*
Gibson, Jim *NewOrJ*
Gibson, Jon C 1940- *ConAmC*
Gibson, Kenneth *Film 2*
Gibson, Madeline 1909- *WhThe*
Gibson, Margaret *Film 1, WhScrn 77*
Gibson, Maude Virginia Janie Phelps 1909- *IntWWM 77, -80*
Gibson, Michael P 1948- *ConAmC*
Gibson, Mimi *ForYSC*
Gibson, Orville H 1856-1918 *NewGrD 80*
Gibson, Powell Willard 1875- *BlkAmP*
Gibson, Preston d1937 *NotNAT B*
Gibson, Richard Derbin 1925- *EncJzS 70*
Gibson, Robert 1931- *BiDAmM*
Gibson, Robert Douglas 1894- *WhoMus 72*
Gibson, Robert L 1938- *IntWWM 77*
Gibson, Roxie E 1934- *AmSCAP 80*
Gibson, Virginia *ForYSC, WhoHol A*
Gibson, Vivian *Film 2*
Gibson, Walter B *MagIlD*
Gibson, William 1914- *BiE&WWA, CnMD, ConDr 73, -77, DcLB 7[port], EncWT, McGEWD, ModWD, NatPD[port], NotNAT, -A, PlP&P, WhoThe 72, -77*
Gibson, William McHargue 1916- *IntWWM 77, -80*
Gibson, Wynne *MotPP*
Gibson, Wynne 1899- *FilmgC, HalFC 80, MovMk*
Gibson, Wynne 1903- *HolP 30[port]*
Gibson, Wynne 1905- *BiE&WWA, FilmEn, ThFT[port], WhThe, WhoHol A*
Gibson, Wynne 1907- *Film 2, ForYSC*
Giddens, George 1845-1920 *NotNAT B, WhThe*
Giddens, George 1855-1920 *WhoStg 1906, -1908*
Gidding, Nelson 1915?- *FilmgC, HalFC 80*
Giddings, Jack *Film 2*
Gide, Andre 1869-1951 *CnMD, EncWT, Ent, ModWD, NotNAT B, OxThe, REnWD[port]*
Gideon, Johnny d1901 *NotNAT B*
Gideon, Mariam 1906- *CpmDNM 77, -80*
Gideon, Melville J 1884-1933 *NotNAT B, WhThe*
Gideon, Miriam 1906- *Baker 78, BiDAmM, CompSN[port], ConAmC, DcCM, IntWWM 77, -80, NewGrD 80, WhoMus 72*
Gidino Da Sommacampagna *NewGrD 80*
Giebel, Agnes 1921- *IntWWM 77, -80, NewGrD 80, WhoMus 72*
Giebler, Albert Cornelius 1921- *IntWWM 77, -80*
Gieburowski, Waclaw 1876-1943 *Baker 78*
Gieburowski, Waclaw 1878-1943 *NewGrD 80*

Giefer, Willy 1930- *NewGrD 80*
Giegling, Franz 1921- *Baker 78, NewGrD 80*
Giehse, Therese 1898-1975 *EncWT, Ent, FilmAG WE*
Giehse, Therese 1899-1975 *WhScrn 77, WhoHol C*
Gielen, Josef 1890-1968 *EncWT*
Gielen, Michael Andreas 1927- *Baker 78, DcCM, IntWWM 77, -80, NewGrD 80, WhoMus 72, WhoOp 76*
Gielgud, Sir John 1904- *BiDFilm, -81, BiE&WWA, CnThe, EncWT, Ent[port], FamA&A[port], FilmAG WE, FilmEn, Film 2, FilmgC, ForYSC, HalFC 80, IlWWBF[port], -A, IntMPA 77, -75, -76, -78, -79, -80, MotPP, MovMk[port], NotNAT, -A, OxFilm, OxThe, PlP&P[port], WhoHol A, WhoThe 72, -77, WorEFlm*
Gielgud, Maina 1945- *CnOxB*
Gielgud, Val 1900- *NotNAT A, WhThe*
Gierasch, Stefan 1926- *NotNAT, WhoHol A*
Giere, Helen *Film 2*
Gierlach, Chester Mitchell 1919- *AmSCAP 66, -80*
Giero, Jhan *NewGrD 80*
Gierow, Karl Ragnar Kunt 1904- *CnMD, ModWD*
Gierster, Hans 1925- *IntWWM 77, -80, WhoOp 76*
Gieseking, Walter 1895-1956 *Baker 78, BnBkM 80[port], MusMk, MusSN[port], NewGrD 80[port]*
Gieseler, Walter 1919- *NewGrD 80*
Giesler, Jerry d1962 *NotNAT B*
Gietz, Heinz 1924- *WhoMus 72*
Gietzen, Herbert Alfons 1947- *WhoOp 76*
Gievenci, Adam De *NewGrD 80*
Giffard, Henry 1694?-1772 *NotNAT B, OxThe*
Giffen, Robert Lawrence d1946 *NotNAT B*
Gifford, Alan *WhoHol A*
Gifford, Alan 1905- *FilmgC, HalFC 80*
Gifford, Alan 1911- *IntMPA 77, -75, -76, -78, -79, -80*
Gifford, Anthea 1949- *IntWWM 77, -80*
Gifford, Frances *MotPP*
Gifford, Frances 1920- *FilmEn, ForYSC, WhoHol A*
Gifford, Frances 1922- *FilmgC, HalFC 80, MGM[port]*
Gifford, Frank 1930- *NewYTET, WhoHol A*
Gifford, Gene 1908-1970 *CmpEPM, EncJzS 70*
Gifford, Gene Harold Eugene 1908-1970 *WhoJazz 72*
Gifford, Gerald Michael 1949- *IntWWM 77, -80*
Gifford, Gordon d1962 *NotNAT B*
Gifford, H Eugene 1908- *AmSCAP 66*
Gifford, H Eugene 1908-1970 *AmSCAP 80*
Gifford, Harold Eugene 1908-1970 *EncJzS 70*
Gifford, Helen Margaret 1935- *IntWWM 77, -80, NewGrD 80*
Gifford, Henry *PlP&P*
Gift, Don *ForYSC*
Giftos, Elaine *WhoHol A*
Gigandet, Joseph H 1915- *AmSCAP 66*
Gigault, Nicolas 1627?-1707 *NewGrD 80*
Gigler, Andre d1570 *NewGrD 80*
Gigler, Andreas d1570 *NewGrD 80*
Gigli *NewGrD 80*
Gigli, Beniamino d1958 *WhoHol B*
Gigli, Beniamino 1890-1957 *Baker 78, BiDAmM, BnBkM 80, CmOp, FilmgC, HalFC 80, MusMk, MusSN[port], NewEOp 71, NewGrD 80[port], WhScrn 74, -77*
Gigli, Giovanni Battista d1692? *NewGrD 80*
Giglio, A Gino *BiE&WWA, NotNAT*
Giglio, Tommaso *NewGrD 80*
Gignac, Marguerite 1928- *IntWWM 77, -80*
Gignoux, Hubert 1915- *EncWT*
Gignoux, Regis 1878- *WhThe*
Gigout, Eugene 1844-1925 *Baker 78, BnBkM 80, NewGrD 80, OxMus*
Giguere, Diane 1937- *CreCan 1*
Giguere, Roland 1929- *CreCan 2*
Gil, David 1930- *IntMPA 77, -75, -76, -78, -79, -80*
Gil, Robert Velazquez 1923- *AmSCAP 80*
Gil Garcia, Bonifacio 1898-1964 *NewGrD 80*
Gil-Marchex, Henri 1894-1970 *Baker 78*
Gil Y Zarate, Antonio 1793-1861 *McGEWD[port]*
Gil'ad, Nelly *WomWMM*
Gilardi, Gilardo 1889-1963 *Baker 78, NewGrD 80*
Gilardoni, Eugenio *Film 2*
Gilbert, Anne 1821-1904 *NotNAT A*
Gilbert, Anthony 1934- *DcCM, IntWWM 77, -80, NewGrD 80, WhoMus 72*
Gilbert, Arthur N 1920- *IntMPA 77, -75, -76, -78, -79, -80*
Gilbert, Benjamin A 1904- *BiE&WWA*
Gilbert, Billy *MotPP*
Gilbert, Billy 1891-1961 *WhScrn 74, -77*
Gilbert, Billy 1893-1971 *FilmgC, HalFC 80, WhoHol B*
Gilbert, Billy 1894-1971 *BiE&WWA, FilmEn, Film 1, -2, ForYSC, JoeFr[port], MovMk[port], NotNAT B, TwYS, What 2[port], WhScrn 74, -77*
Gilbert, Billy 1896-1971 *Vers A[port]*
Gilbert, Bob 1898-1973 *WhoHol B*
Gilbert, Bobby 1898-1973 *WhScrn 77*
Gilbert, Bruce *IntMPA 80*
Gilbert, David 1936- *BiDAmM, ConAmC*
Gilbert, Denis Alan 1930- *WhoMus 72*
Gilbert, Edwin J *Film 1*
Gilbert, Eugenia *TwYS*
Gilbert, Eugenie *Film 2*
Gilbert, Florence *Film 2*
Gilbert, Gabriel 1620?-1680? *OxThe*
Gilbert, Geoffrey 1914- *NewGrD 80, WhoMus 72*
Gilbert, Geoffrey Winzer 1914- *IntWWM 77*
Gilbert, Mrs. George H 1821-1904 *FamA&A[port], NotNAT B, OxThe, PlP&P*
Gilbert, George Henry d1866 *NotNAT B*
Gilbert, Goeffrey 1914- *IntWWM 80*
Gilbert, Harry M 1879- *ConAmC*
Gilbert, Henry Franklin Belknap 1868-1928 *Baker 78, BiDAmM, CompSN[port], NewGrD 80, OxMus*
Gilbert, Herbert 1926- *CreCan 2*
Gilbert, Herschel Burke 1918- *AmSCAP 80*
Gilbert, Jack *Film 1*
Gilbert, Jean *CmpEPM*
Gilbert, Jean 1879-1942 *Baker 78, NewGrD 80*
Gilbert, Jean 1879-1943 *NotNAT B, WhThe*
Gilbert, Joanne *ForYSC, WhoHol A*
Gilbert, Jody 1916- *ForYSC, WhoHol A*
Gilbert, Joe 1903-1959 *WhScrn 74, -77*
Gilbert, John d1936 *MotPP, WhoHol B*
Gilbert, John 1810-1889 *FamA&A[port], NotNAT B, OxThe, PlP&P*
Gilbert, John 1895-1936 *CmMov, FilmEn, Film 1, -2, FilmgC, ForYSC, HalFC 80, TwYS*
Gilbert, John 1897-1936 *BiDFilm, -81, MovMk[port], NotNAT B, OxFilm, WhScrn 74, -77, WorEFlm*
Gilbert, Kenneth 1931- *CreCan 2, IntWWM 77, -80, NewGrD 80, WhoMus 72*
Gilbert, Kittie Bruneau *CreCan 1*
Gilbert, L Wolfe 1886-1970 *AmPS, AmSCAP 66, -80, Baker 78, CmpEPM, Sw&Ld C*
Gilbert, Lauren *WhoHol A*
Gilbert, Leatrice Joy *WhoHol A*
Gilbert, Lela 1946- *AmSCAP 80*
Gilbert, Lewis 1920- *BiDFilm, -81, CmMov, FilmEn, Film 2, FilmgC, HalFC 80, IlWWBF, IntMPA 77, -75, -76, -78, -79, -80, MovMk, WhoHrs 80, WorEFlm[port]*
Gilbert, Lou 1909- *BiE&WWA, NotNAT, WhoHol A, WhoThe 72, -77*
Gilbert, Louis Wolfe 1886-1970 *BiDAmM, ConAmC*
Gilbert, Maude d1953 *WhScrn 74, -77*
Gilbert, Max *WhoMus 72*
Gilbert, Mercedes d1952 *BlkAmP, BlksB&W, -C, NotNAT B*
Gilbert, Nicole *WomWMM*
Gilbert, Oh Gran *WhScrn 74*
Gilbert, Olive *WhoThe 72, -77*
Gilbert, Paul 1917- *HalFC 80*
Gilbert, Paul 1924-1975 *FilmgC, WhoHol C*
Gilbert, Philip *WhoHol A*
Gilbert, Pia 1921- *ConAmC*
Gilbert, R Bloye Wanstall 1923- *IntWWM 77*
Gilbert, Ray 1912-1976 *AmSCAP 66, -80*
Gilbert, Richard E 1919- *AmSCAP 66, -80*
Gilbert, Ronnie *WhoHol A*
Gilbert, Ruth *WhoHol A*
Gilbert, Steven E 1943- *ConAmC*
Gilbert, Timothy *Baker 78*
Gilbert, Timothy Prout 1942- *AmSCAP 80*
Gilbert, Vernon *NewOrJ*
Gilbert, W S 1836-1911 *BnBkM 80, CmOp, HalFC 80*
Gilbert, Walter 1887-1947 *NotNAT B, WhScrn 77, WhoHol B*
Gilbert, Walter Bond 1829-1910 *BiDAmM*
Gilbert, William 1916- *AmSCAP 80*
Gilbert, William Herbert *CreCan 2*
Gilbert, Sir William Schwenck 1836-1911 *Baker 78, CnThe, FilmgC, McGEWD[port], ModWD, NotNAT A, -B, OxThe, REnWD[port], WhoStg 1908*
Gilbert, Sir William Schwenk 1836-1911 *DcPup, EncWT, Ent, OxMus*
Gilbert, Willie 1916- *BiE&WWA, NotNAT*
Gilbert And Sullivan *PlP&P[port]*
Gilberte, Hallett 1872-1946 *Baker 78, ConAmC*
Gilberto, Astrud 1940- *AmSCAP 80, BiDAmM*
Gilberto, Joao 1931- *BiDAmM*
Gilbertson, Virginia Mabry 1914- *AmSCAP 66, -80, ConAmC*
Gilboa, Jacob 1920- *Baker 78, NewGrD 80*
Gilboa, Yaakov 1920- *DcCM*
Gilbride, Claire 1919- *AmSCAP 66*
Gilchrist, Anne Geddes 1863-1954 *NewGrD 80, OxMus*
Gilchrist, Connie 1865-1946 *NotNAT B, OxThe*
Gilchrist, Connie 1901- *FilmEn, FilmgC, ForYSC, HalFC 80, HolCA[port], WhoHol A*
Gilchrist, Connie 1904- *MovMk*
Gilchrist, Connie 1906- *MGM[port], Vers A[port]*
Gilchrist, Rubina d1956 *NotNAT B*
Gilchrist, William Wallace 1846-1916 *Baker 78, BiDAmM, NewGrD 80*
Gildea, Agnes d1964 *NotNAT B*
Gildea, Mary d1957 *NotNAT B*
Gilder, Eric 1911- *WhoMus 72*
Gilder, Jeanette d1916 *NotNAT B*
Gilder, Nick *ConMuA 80A*
Gilder, Richard Watson 1844-1909 *BiDAmM*
Gilder, Rosamond *BiE&WWA, NotNAT, PlP&P[port], WhoThe 72*
Gilder, Rosamond 1891- *ConAmTC, WhoThe 77*
Gilder, Rosamond 1900- *OxThe*
Gilder, Rosamund 1900- *EncWT*
Gildon, Charles d1724 *NotNAT B*
Gilels, Emil 1916- *Baker 78, BnBkM 80, IntWWM 77, -80, MusSN[port], NewGrD 80*
Gilels, Emile 1916- *WhoMus 72*
Giler, David *HalFC 80*
Giles, Allan Leonard 1922- *WhoMus 72*
Giles, Allan Ronald 1945- *IntWWM 80*
Giles, Anna 1874-1973 *WhScrn 77, WhoHol B*
Giles, Charles 1783-1867 *BiDAmM*
Giles, Corliss *Film 2*
Giles, Johnny 1911- *AmSCAP 66, -80*
Giles, Nathaniel 1558?-1633 *Baker 78, OxMus*
Giles, Nathaniel 1558?-1634 *NewGrD 80*
Giles, Paul Kirk 1895- *BiE&WWA, NotNAT*
Giles, Paul W 1903- *IntWWM 77, -80*
Giles, Verna *PupTheA*
Gilespie, Haven 1888- *CmpEPM*
Gilfert, Charles H 1787-1829 *BiDAmM, NewGrD 80*
Gilfert, George 1764?-1814? *BiDAmM*
Gilfether, Daniel 1854-1919 *Film 1, WhScrn 77*
Gilfillan, Frank Allen 1921- *IntWWM 77, -80*
Gilfond, Henry *NatPD[port]*
Gilford, Jack *BiE&WWA, ForYSC, IntMPA 77, -75, -76, -78, -79, -80,*

NotNAT, PlP&P[port], WhoHol A, WhoThe 72, -77
Gilford, Jack 1907- *FilmEn, FilmgC, HalFC 80*
Gilford, Jack 1913- *EncMT*
Gilford, Jack 1919- *MovMk[port]*
Gilhooley, Jack *NatPD[port]*
Giliardi, Arnolfo *NewGrD 80*
Gilibert, Charles 1866-1910 *Baker 78, BiDAmM, CmOp*
Gilkey, Stanley 1900- *BiE&WWA, NotNAT*
Gilkinson, Donald Mitchel 1950- *AmSCAP 80*
Gilkison, Anthony 1913- *IntMPA 77, -75, -76, -78, -79, -80*
Gilkyson, Hamilton Henry 1919?- *BiDAmM*
Gilkyson, Terry 1919?- *EncFCWM 69*
Gilkyson, Terry 1928- *RkOn[port]*
Gill, Basil 1877-1955 *Film 1, -2, IlWWBF, NotNAT B, WhScrn 74, -77, WhThe, WhoHol B*
Gill, Brendan 1914- *BiE&WWA, ConAmTC, NotNAT, -A, WhoThe 72, -77*
Gill, Carolyn 1918- *AmSCAP 66, -80*
Gill, Charles-Ignace Adelard 1871-1918 *CreCan 1*
Gill, Dominic 1941- *IntWWM 80, WhoMus 72*
Gill, Elizabeth *WomWMM B*
Gill, Florence 1877-1965 *WhScrn 77*
Gill, Henry d1954 *NotNAT B*
Gill, Laurel *DancEn 78*
Gill, Maud *Film 2*
Gill, Michael *NewYTET*
Gill, Milton *ConAmC*
Gill, Paul d1934 *WhThe*
Gill, Paul d1953 *NotNAT B*
Gill, Peter 1939- *ConDr 73, -77, WhoThe 72, -77*
Gill, Ralph 1919- *AmSCAP 66, -80*
Gill, Richard Thomas 1927- *IntWWM 77, -80, WhoOp 76*
Gill, Robert S 1911- *CreCan 1*
Gill, Stuart John 1937- *WhoMus 72*
Gill, Tom 1916-1971 *WhoHol A, WhoThe 72, -77*
Gillam, David S 1915- *AmSCAP 66, -80*
Gillam, Russell C 1909- *ConAmC*
Gillard, David Owen 1947- *IntWWM 77, -80*
Gillaspy, Richard M 1927- *IntMPA 77, -75, -76, -78, -79, -80, NewYTET*
Gille Li Vinier 1190?-1252 *NewGrD 80*
Gille, Jacob Edvard 1814-1880 *NewGrD 80*
Gillebert De Berneville *NewGrD 80*
Gillebert, Gloria Caroline *NewGrD 80*
Gillen, Bill 1903- *NewOrJ*
Gillen, Ernest *Film 2*
Gillen, Gerard Thomas Mary 1942- *IntWWM 77, -80*
Giller, Walter 1927- *FilmAG WE[port]*
Gilleri, Fulvio 1920- *WhoOp 76*
Gilles, D B 1947- *NatPD[port]*
Gilles, Eloise 1929- *AmSCAP 66, -80*
Gilles, Genevieve 1946- *FilmgC, HalFC 80*
Gilles, Henri Noel 1778-1834 *BiDAmM*
Gilles, Jean 1668-1705 *NewGrD 80*
Gilles, Peter, Jr. 1776-1839 *BiDAmM*
Gillespie, A Arnold 1899- *IntMPA 77, -75, -76, -78*
Gillespie, A Arnold 1899-1978 *FilmEn*
Gillespie, Albert T *Film 1*
Gillespie, Arnold 1889-1978 *WhoHrs 80*
Gillespie, Dizzy 1917- *AmSCAP 66, BgBands 74[port], CmpEPM, Conv 2[port], DrBlPA, EncJzS 70, IlEncJ, NewGrD 80[port]*
Gillespie, Don C 1936- *IntWWM 80*
Gillespie, Donald 1942- *ConAmC*
Gillespie, George *ConMuA 80B*
Gillespie, Greg *ConMuA 80B*
Gillespie, Haven 1888- *BiDAmM*
Gillespie, Haven 1888-1975 *AmSCAP 66, -80*
Gillespie, James Ernest, Jr. 1940- *IntWWM 77, -80*
Gillespie, John Birks 1917- *AmSCAP 80, Baker 78, BiDAmM, EncJzS 70*
Gillespie, John Dizzy 1917- *MusMk*
Gillespie, Marian Evans 1889-1946 *AmSCAP 66, -80*
Gillespie, Rhondda Marie 1941- *IntWWM 77, -80, WhoMus 72*
Gillespie, Richard Henry 1878-1952 *NotNAT B, WhThe*
Gillespie, William 1894- *Film 1, -2, TwYS*
Gillet, Ernest 1856-1940 *Baker 78*
Gillet, Florence *Film 1*
Gillet, Georges 1854- *BnBkM 80*
Gillet & Johnston *OxMus*
Gillett, Charlie 1942- *ConMuA 80B, IlEncR*
Gillett, Elma 1874-1941 *WhScrn 74, -77*
Gillett, Eric 1893- *WhThe*
Gillette, A S 1904- *BiE&WWA, NotNAT*
Gillette, Abram Dunn 1807-1882 *BiDAmM*
Gillette, Anita 1936- *BiE&WWA, NotNAT, WhoThe 72, -77*
Gillette, James Robert 1886-1963 *Baker 78, ConAmC*
Gillette, John Carroll 1941- *IntWWM 77, -80*
Gillette, Leland James 1912- *AmSCAP 66, -80*
Gillette, Robert *Film 2*
Gillette, Ruth 1907- *BiE&WWA, NotNAT, WhoHol A*
Gillette, Viola *WhoStg 1908*
Gillette, William d1937 *NotNAT A*
Gillette, William 1853-1937 *TwYS, WhoStg 1906, -1908*
Gillette, William 1855-1937 *EncWT, Ent, FamA&A[port], Film 1, FilmgC, HalFC 80, McGEWD[port], ModWD, NotNAT B, OxThe, PlP&P, WhThe*
Gillette, William 1856-1937 *WhScrn 74, -77, WhoHol B*
Gilley, Mickey *IlEncCM[port]*
Gillham, Art 1895-1961 *CmpEPM*
Gilliam, Roger Wayne 1948- *ConAmC, IntWWM 77, -80*
Gilliam, Stu 1943- *DrBlPA, WhoHol A*
Gilliam, Ted *MorBAP*
Gilliat, Leslie 1917- *FilmgC, HalFC 80, IntMPA 77, -75, -76, -78, -79, -80*
Gilliat, Sidney 1908- *DcFM, FilmEn, FilmgC, HalFC 80, IlWWBF, IntMPA 77, -75, -76, -78, -79, -80, OxFilm, WorEFlm*
Gilliatt, Penelope *FilmgC, WomWMM*
Gilliatt, Penelope 1933- *HalFC 80*
Gillie, Jean 1915-1949 *FilmgC, HalFC 80, IlWWBF, NotNAT B, WhScrn 74, -77, WhThe, WhoHol B*
Gillier, Jean-Claude 1667-1737 *NewGrD 80*
Gillies, Anne Lorne 1944- *IntWWM 77, -80*
Gillies, Don 1926- *CreCan 1, DancEn 78*
Gilligan, Sonja Carl 1936- *WomWMM B*
Gilliland, Helen 1897-1942 *NotNAT B, WhThe*
Gilliland, Thomas d1816? *NotNAT B*
Gillin, Donald T 1914- *IntMPA 77, -75, -76, -78, -79, -80*
Gillin, Mike 1868?- *NewOrJ*
Gilling, John 1912- *FilmEn, FilmgC, HalFC 80, IlWWBF, IntMPA 77, -75, -76, -78, -79, -80, WhoHrs 80*
Gillingham, Diana 1932- *IntWWM 77, -80, WhoMus 72*
Gillingham, George 1770-1826 *BiDAmM*
Gillingwater, Claude 1870-1939 *FilmgC, ForYSC, HalFC 80, HolCA[port], WhScrn 74, -77, WhoHol B*
Gillingwater, Claude 1870-1940 *MovMk[port]*
Gillingwater, Claude 1879-1939 *Film 2, TwYS*
Gillis, Ann 1927- *FilmEn, FilmgC, ForYSC, HalFC 80, WhoHol A*
Gillis, Anne 1927- *IntMPA 77, -75, -76, -78, -79, -80*
Gillis, Don 1912-1978 *AmSCAP 66, -80, Baker 78, BiDAmM, ConAmC, DcCom&M 79, DcCM, NewGrD 80, WhoMus 72*
Gillis, Richard W 1938- *AmSCAP 80*
Gillis, Sylvester 1899- *AmSCAP 66, -80*
Gillis, Verna 1942- *IntWWM 77, -80*
Gillis, William S d1946 *WhScrn 74, -77, WhoHol B*
Gillman, Arita *Film 2*
Gillman, Carolyn Annette 1938- *AmSCAP 80*
Gillman, Mabelle 1880- *WhThe, WhoStg 1908*
Gillman, Robert Edward 1943- *IntWWM 80*
Gillmor, Alan Murray 1938- *IntWWM 77, -80*
Gillmore, Frank 1867-1943 *NotNAT B, WhThe, WhoStg 1906, -1908*
Gillmore, Margalo 1897- *BiE&WWA, FilmgC, HalFC 80, MotPP, NotNAT, -A, WhThe, WhoHol A*
Gillock, William L 1917- *Baker 78, CpmDNM 80*
Gillon, Baruch 1901- *IntWWM 80*
Gillot, Claude *DancEn 78*
Gillum, William McKinley 1904-1966 *BluesWW[port]*
Gilly, Dinh 1877-1940 *NewGrD 80*
Gilman, Ada d1921 *NotNAT B*
Gilman, Benjamin Ives 1852-1933 *NewGrD 80*
Gilman, Caroline Howard 1794-1888 *BiDAmM*
Gilman, Fred *Film 2*
Gilman, Hazel Inez 1904- *AmSCAP 80*
Gilman, Irvin Edward 1926- *IntWWM 77, -80*
Gilman, L *OxMus*
Gilman, Lawrence 1878-1939 *Baker 78, BiDAmM, NewGrD 80*
Gilman, Richard 1925- *ConAmTC*
Gilman, Sam *WhoHol A*
Gilman, Samuel 1790-1858 *BiDAmM*
Gilmer, Jim *AmPS B*
Gilmer, Jimmy And The Fireballs *AmPS A*
Gilmer, Jimmy And The Fireballs 1940- *RkOn[port]*
Gilmore, Barney *Film 2*
Gilmore, Barney 1867- *WhoStg 1906, -1908*
Gilmore, Bernard 1937- *CpmDNM 72, -74, ConAmC*
Gilmore, Boyd 1913?- *BluesWW*
Gilmore, Charlotte Politte 1935- *AmSCAP 80*
Gilmore, Douglas d1950 *Film 2, NotNAT B, WhoHol B*
Gilmore, Eddie 1897?- *NewOrJ*
Gilmore, Elizabeth McCabe 1874-1953 *AmSCAP 66*
Gilmore, Frank 1867-1943 *WhoHol B*
Gilmore, Helen 1900-1947 *Film 2, WhScrn 77*
Gilmore, J H *Film 2*
Gilmore, Janette 1905- *WhThe*
Gilmore, John 1931- *BiDAmM, EncJzS 70*
Gilmore, Joseph Henry 1834-1918 *BiDAmM*
Gilmore, Lillian *Film 2*
Gilmore, Lowell d1959 *ForYSC*
Gilmore, Lowell 1907-1960 *FilmgC, HalFC 80, WhScrn 74, -77, WhoHol B*
Gilmore, Margalo 1897- *ForYSC*
Gilmore, Patrick Sarsfield *BnBkM 80*
Gilmore, Patrick Sarsfield 1829-1892 *Baker 78, BiDAmM, NewGrD 80*
Gilmore, Peter 1931- *WhoHol A, WhoThe 72, -77*
Gilmore, Spence *PupTheA*
Gilmore, Stuart 1913-1971 *HalFC 80*
Gilmore, Virginia 1919- *BiE&WWA, FilmEn, FilmgC, ForYSC, HalFC 80, HolP 40[port], MotPP, MovMk[port], NotNAT, WhThe, WhoHol A*
Gilmore, W H *WhThe*
Gilmour, Brian 1894-1954 *NotNAT B, WhThe*
Gilmour, Edith 1896- *AmSCAP 66*
Gilmour, Glenn Harvey 1939- *CreCan 2*
Gilmour, Gordon d1962 *NotNAT B*
Gilmour, J H *WhoStg 1908*
Gilmour, John *Film 1*
Gilmour, John H d1922 *NotNAT B*
Gilmour, Sally 1921- *CnOxB, DancEn 78*
Gilpin, Charles S 1878-1930 *BlksBF, DrBlPA, FamA&A[port], NotNAT B, OxThe, WhThe, WhoHol B*
Gilpin, Charles S 1879-1930 *BlksB&W, -C, WhScrn 74, -77*
Gilpin, John 1930- *CnOxB, DancEn 78*
Gilroy, Frank D 1925- *ConDr 73, -77, CroCD, DcLB 7[port], McGEWD[port], ModWD, NotNAT, WhoThe 72, -77*
Gilroy, John 1872-1937 *AmSCAP 66, -80*
Gilse, Jan Van 1881-1944 *Baker 78, NewGrD 80*
Gilson, Charles *Film 2*
Gilson, Jef 1926- *EncJzS 70*
Gilson, Lottie d1912 *AmPS B, BiDAmM, NotNAT B*
Gilson, Paul 1865-1942 *Baker 78, CompSN[port], DcCM, MusMk, NewGrD 80, OxMus*
Gilson, Tom 1934-1962 *WhScrn 77, WhoHol B*
Giltay, Berend 1910-1975 *Baker 78, NewGrD 80*

Gim, H W 1908-1973 *WhScrn 77, WhoHol B*
Gimbel, Norman 1927- *BiE&WWA*
Gimbel, Roger *IntMPA 77, -78, -79, -80*
Gimble, Herman *ConMuA 80B*
Gimble, Johnny *IlEncCM[port]*
Gimenez, Eduardo Gracia 1940- *WhoOp 76*
Gimenez, Jeronimo 1854-1923 *Baker 78, NewGrD 80*
Gimenez Arnau Y Gran, Jose Antonio 1912- *McGEWD[port]*
Gimpel, Bronislav *WhoMus 72*
Gimpel, Bronislav 1911-1979 *NewGrD 80*
Gimpel, Bronislaw 1911- *Baker 78*
Gimpel, Jakob 1906- *WhoMus 72*
Gimson, Agnes Bessie *WhoMus 72*
Ginastera, Alberto *WhoMus 72*
Ginastera, Alberto 1916- *AmSCAP 80, Baker 78, BiDAmM, BnBkM 80, CompSN[port], DcCM, MusMk, NewEOp 71, NewGrD 80[port], OxMus*
Ginastero, Alberto E 1916- *IntWWM 77, -80*
Gindhart, Thomas J 1908- *AmSCAP 66*
Gindron, Francois 1491?-1560? *NewGrD 80*
Giner Y Vidal, Salvador 1832-1911 *NewGrD 80*
Gines Perez, Juan *NewGrD 80*
Ging, Jack 1931- *ForYSC, WhoHol A*
Gingold, Dan *IntMPA 77, -75, -76, -78, -79, -80*
Gingold, Baroness Helene d1926 *NotNAT B*
Gingold, Hermione *MotPP, PlP&P[port], WhoHol A*
Gingold, Hermione 1897- *BiE&WWA, EncMT, FilmEn, FilmgC, ForYSC, HalFC 80, IlWWBF, -A, MovMk, WhoThe 72, -77*
Gingold, Hermione 1899- *NotNAT*
Gingold, Josef 1909- *Baker 78, NewGrD 80, WhoMus 72*
Gingras, Andree *WhoOp 76*
Ginguene, Pierre Louis 1748-1816 *Baker 78, NewGrD 80*
Ginisty, Paul d1932 *NotNAT B*
Ginisty, Paul 1858- *WhThe*
Giniva, John Alaska Jack 1868-1936 *WhScrn 74, -77*
Ginn, Jim 1935- *CpmDNM 72, ConAmC*
Ginn, Sophie 1933- *IntWWM 77, -80*
Ginn, Wells Watson 1891-1959 *WhScrn 74, -77*
Ginna, Robert Emmett, Jr. 1925- *IntMPA 77, -75, -76, -78, -79, -80*
Ginner, Ruby 1886- *CnOxB, WhThe*
Ginnes, Abram S 1914- *BiE&WWA*
Ginsberg, Allen 1926- *PlP&P A[port]*
Ginsberg, Ernst 1904-1964 *EncWT*
Ginsberg, Harry *Film 2*
Ginsberg, Henry 1897- *IntMPA 77, -75, -76, -78, -79*
Ginsberg, Ruta *CreCan 2*
Ginsberg, Sidney 1920- *IntMPA 77, -75, -76, -78, -79, -80*
Ginsberg, Sol 1885-1963 *AmSCAP 66, -80*
Ginsburg, Gerald M 1932- *AmSCAP 80, ConAmC, IntWWM 77, -80*
Ginsburg, Lev 1907- *Baker 78*
Ginsburg, Lewis S 1914- *IntMPA 77, -75, -76, -78, -79, -80*
Ginsburg, Semion 1901- *Baker 78*
Ginsbury, Norman 1902- *BiE&WWA, NotNAT*
Ginsbury, Norman 1903- *WhoThe 72, -77*
Ginty, Elizabeth Beall d1949 *NotNAT B*
Gintzler, Simon 1500?-1547? *NewGrD 80*
Ginzburg, Dov 1906- *IntWWM 77, -80*
Ginzburg, Grigory 1904-1961 *NewGrD 80*
Ginzburg, Lev Solomonovich 1907- *NewGrD 80*
Ginzburg, Natalia 1916- *EncWT*
Ginzburg, Semyon L'vovich 1901- *NewGrD 80*
Gioe, Joseph Guiseppe 1890-1957 *AmSCAP 80*
Gioffre, Marissa *MorBAP*
Gioi, Vivi 1917-1975 *FilmAG WE, WhScrn 77, WhoHol C*
Gioia, Gaetano 1768-1826 *CnOxB*
Giono, Jean 1895- *CnMD, McGEWD[port]*
Giono, Jean 1895-1970 *ModWD*
Giono, Jean 1895-1971 *OxFilm*
Giordani, Carmine *OxMus*
Giordani, Carmine 1685?-1758 *NewGrD 80*
Giordani, Giuseppe 1743-1798 *Baker 78*
Giordani, Giuseppe 1753?-1798 *MusMk, NewGrD 80, OxMus*
Giordani, Tommaso 1730?-1806 *Baker 78, MusMk*
Giordani, Tommaso 1733?-1806 *NewGrD 80*
Giordani, Tommaso 1740?-1806 *OxMus*
Giordano, Antonia *Baker 78*
Giordano, Francesco *Baker 78*
Giordano, Gus 1930- *CnOxB*
Giordano, Marina *Baker 78*
Giordano, Nicolina *Baker 78*
Giordano, Umberto 1867-1948 *Baker 78, BnBkM 80, CmOp, CmpBCM, CompSN[port], DcCom 77, DcCom&M 79, NewEOp 71, NewGrD 80, OxMus*
Giorgetti, Ferdinando 1796-1867 *NewGrD 80*
Giorgi, Geltrude *NewGrD 80*
Giorgi, Giovanni d1762 *NewGrD 80*
Giorgi-Belloc, Teresa *NewGrD 80*
Giorni, Aurelio 1895-1938 *Baker 78, BiDAmM, ConAmC*
Giornovichi, Giovanni Mane 1735?-1804 *Baker 78, NewGrD 80*
Giornovichi, Ivan Mane 1735?-1804 *NewGrD 80*
Giorza, Paolo 1832-1914 *Baker 78, NewGrD 80*
Giorza, Paolo 1837-1914 *BiDAmM*
Giovan Maria DaCrema *NewGrD 80*
Giovanelli, Ruggiero 1560?-1625 *Baker 78, NewGrD 80*
Giovaninetti, Reynald Jean 1932- *WhoOp 76*
Giovaninetti, Silvio 1901-1959 *McGEWD[port]*
Giovannelli, Ruggiero 1560-1625 *Baker 78, NewGrD 80*
Giovanni Ambrosio *NewGrD 80*
Giovanni Da Cascia *NewGrD 80[port]*
Giovanni Da Foligno *NewGrD 80*
Giovanni Da Prato 1367-1445? *NewGrD 80*
Giovanni DaCascia *Baker 78*
Giovanni De Florentia *NewGrD 80*
Giovanni DelViolone *NewGrD 80*
Giovanni Di Niccolo Degli Organi *NewGrD 80*
Giovanni Gherardi *NewGrD 80*
Giovanni Leonardo Dell'Arpa *NewGrD 80*
Giovanni Maria DaCrema *NewGrD 80*
Giovanni Mazzuoli *NewGrD 80*
Giovanni, Edoardo Di *CreCan 2*
Giovanni, Jose 1923- *FilmEn, WorEFlm*
Giovannini d1782? *NewGrD 80*
Giovannini, Caesar 1925- *AmSCAP 66, -80, CpmDNM 80*
Giovannini, Simone 1550?-1621 *NewGrD 80*
Giovannino DaRoma *NewGrD 80*
Giovannino DelVioloncello *NewGrD 80*
Giovannone, Anthony J 1923- *AmSCAP 66*
Giovenardi, Bartolomeo *NewGrD 80*
Gippenbusch, Jacob 1612-1664 *NewGrD 80*
Gippius, Evgeny Vladimirovich 1903- *NewGrD 80*
Gipps, Bryan 1910- *IntWWM 80*
Gipps, Ruth 1921- *Baker 78, IntWWM 77, -80, NewGrD 80, WhoMus 72*
Giracci, May *Film 1, -2*
Giraci, Mary *Film 2*
Giradot, Etienne 1856-1939 *WhScrn 74, -77*
Giraldi, Georgis *AmSCAP 80*
Giraldi, Giambattista 1504-1573 *OxThe*
Giraldi, Giovanni Battista 1504-1573 *NotNAT B*
Giraldi Cinthio, Giambattista 1504-1573 *McGEWD[port]*
Giraldoni, Eugenio 1871-1924 *Baker 78*
Giraldus Cambrensis 1146?-1223? *NewGrD 80*
Giraldus De Barri *MusMk[port]*
Giramo, Pietro Antonio *NewGrD 80*
Girard *NewGrD 80*
Girard, Adele *AmSCAP 80*
Girard, Benoit 1932- *CreCan 2*
Girard, Bernard 1929?- *FilmgC, HalFC 80*
Girard, Bernard 1930?- *FilmEn*
Girard, Bernardo d1835 *NewGrD 80*
Girard, George 1930-1957 *NewOrJ[port]*
Girard, Giuseppe *NewGrD 80*
Girard, Henri *McGEWD[port]*
Girard, Jan *NewGrD 80*
Girard, Joe 1871-1949 *WhScrn 77*
Girard, Joseph 1871-1949 *Film 1, -2, ForYSC, TwYS, WhoHol B*
Girard, Kate d1885 *NotNAT B*
Girard, Pete *Film 1*
Girard, Philippe Jean 1949- *IntWWM 80*
Girardeau, Isabella *NewGrD 80*
Girardi, Alexander 1850-1918 *EncWT, Ent, NewGrD 80*
Girardin, Ray *WhoHol A*
Girardot, Annie 1931- *FilmAG WE, FilmEn, FilmgC, HalFC 80, IntMPA 77, -75, -76, -78, -79, -80, OxFilm, WhoHol A, WorEFlm[port]*
Girardot, Etienne 1856-1939 *Film 1, FilmgC, ForYSC, HalFC 80, HolCA[port], MovMk, NotNAT B, Vers B[port], WhoHol B, WhoStg 1906, -1908*
Girardot, Isabelle *WhoStg 1906, -1908*
Giraud, Claude 1923- *IntWWM 80*
Giraud, Francois-Joseph d1790? *NewGrD 80*
Giraud, Giovanni 1776-1834 *McGEWD[port], NotNAT B*
Giraud, Marthe *NewGrD 80*
Giraudeau, Jean 1916- *WhoMus 72*
Giraudet, Alfred-Auguste 1845-1911 *Baker 78*
Giraudoux, Jean 1882-1944 *CnMD, CnThe, EncWT, Ent, McGEWD[port], ModWD, NotNAT A, -B, OxThe, PlP&P, REnWD[port], WhThe*
Giraut De Borneill 1140?-1200? *NewGrD 80*
Giraut De Bornelh 1140?-1200? *NewGrD 80*
Girautz De Borneill 1140?-1200? *NewGrD 80*
Girautz De Bornelh 1140?-1200? *NewGrD 80*
Girdler, William 1947-1978 *WhoHrs 80*
Girdlestone, Cuthbert Morton 1895-1975 *Baker 78, NewGrD 80, WhoMus 72*
Girdlestone, Errol Nelson Richey 1945- *WhoMus 72*
Girelli, Antonia Maria *NewGrD 80*
Girelli, Santino *NewGrD 80*
Giritlian, Virginia *WomWMM B*
Girls Of The Golden West *BiDAmM, IlEncCM*
Girnatis, Walter 1894- *WhoMus 72*
Giro, Manuel 1848-1916 *NewGrD 80*
Girolamo DaUdine *NewGrD 80*
Girolamo, Pietro Antonio *NewGrD 80*
Giron, Arsenio 1932- *CpmDNM 74, -77, ConAmC*
Girotti, Mario 1939- *FilmAG WE[port], FilmEn*
Girotti, Massimo 1918- *FilmAG WE, FilmEn, FilmgC, HalFC 80, WhoHol A, WorEFlm*
Giroud, Francoise *WomWMM*
Giroust, Francois 1737-1799 *NewGrD 80*
Giroux, Andre 1916- *CreCan 1*
Giroux, Antoinette *CreCan 2*
Giroux, Colette Mary Elizabeth *CreCan 2*
Giroux, Germaine *CreCan 2*
Giroux, Lee 1911-1973 *WhScrn 77*
Giroux, Paul Henry 1916- *IntWWM 77, -80*
Giroveanu, Aurel 1916- *IntWWM 77*
Girvin, Sharon 1931- *AmSCAP 80*
Girvoeanu, Aurel 1916- *IntWWM 80*
Gisca, Nicolae 1942- *IntWWM 80*
Gischia, Leon 1903- *EncWT*
Gish, Clay *ConMuA 80B*
Gish, Dorothy 1898-1968 *BiE&WWA, FamA&A[port], FilmEn, Film 1, -2, FilmgC, ForYSC, HalFC 80[port], MotPP, MovMk[port], NotNAT A, -B, OxFilm, TwYS, WhScrn 74, -77, WhThe, WhoHol B, WomWMM, WorEFlm*
Gish, Lillian *MotPP, PlP&P[port], WomWMM*
Gish, Lillian 1893- *FamA&A[port], ThFT[port], WhoThe 72, -77*
Gish, Lillian 1896- *BiDFilm, -81, CmMov, FilmEn, Film 1, -2, FilmgC, ForYSC, HalFC 80, MovMk[port], NotNAT A, TwYS, WhoHol A, WorEFlm[port]*
Gish, Lillian 1899- *BiE&WWA, IntMPA 77, -75, -76, -78, -79, -80, NotNAT, OxFilm*
Gish, Mary *Film 1*
Gismondi, Celeste d1735 *NewGrD 80*
Gissey, Henri 1621-1673 *DancEn 78, OxThe*
Gist, Robert 1924- *FilmgC, HalFC 80*
Gistelinck, Elias 1935- *IntWWM 77, -80, NewGrD 80*
Gistou, Nicolas d1609 *NewGrD 80*
Gistow, Nicolas d1609 *NewGrD 80*
Gitana, Gertie 1887-1957 *Ent, NotNAT B, WhThe*
Gitana, Gertie 1889-1957 *EncWT, OxThe*
Gitfiddle Jim *BluesWW[port]*

Githens, W French 1906- *IntMPA 77, -75, -76, -78, -79, -80*
Gitlin, Irving d1967 *NewYTET*
Gitlin, Murray *ConMuA 80B*
Gitlis, Ivry 1922- *IntWWM 77, -80, NewGrD 80*
Gitlis, Ivry 1927- *WhoMus 72*
Gittings, John William 1940- *IntWWM 80*
Gittleson, Frank 1896- *BiDAmM*
Gittleson, Harry 1897- *IntMPA 76*
Giudice, Cesare Del *NewGrD 80*
Giudici, Augusto 1820-1886 *NewGrD 80*
Giuffre, James Peter 1921- *BiDAmM, ConAmC, EncJzS 70, NewGrD 80*
Giuffre, Jimmy 1921- *CmpEPM, EncJzS 70, IIEncJ, NewGrD 80*
Giuglini, Antonio 1827-1865 *NewGrD 80*
Giuleanu, Victor 1914- *IntWWM 77, -80*
Giuliani, Francesco *NewGrD 80*
Giuliani, Giovanni Francesco 1760?-1818? *NewGrD 80*
Giuliani, Mauro *OxMus*
Giuliani, Mauro 1781-1828 *BnBkM 80*
Giuliani, Mauro 1781-1829 *Baker 78, NewGrD 80*
Giuliano Bonaugurio DaTivoli *NewGrD 80*
Giuliano, Giuseppe 1934- *WhoOp 76*
Giuliano, Juan 1930- *CnOxB, DancEn 78*
Giulini, Carlo Maria *WhoMus 72*
Giulini, Carlo Maria 1914- *BnBkM 80, CmOp[port], IntWWM 77, -80, MusSN[port], NewEOp 71, NewGrD 80[port], WhoOp 76*
Giulini, Carlo Mario 1914- *Baker 78*
Giulini, Giorgio 1716-1780 *Baker 78*
Giulini, Johann Andreas Joseph 1723-1772 *NewGrD 80*
Giulio Romano *NewGrD 80*
Giunta *NewGrD 80*
Giunta, Bernardo DiFilippo DiBenedetto d1648 *NewGrD 80*
Giunta, Giovan Maria d1569 *NewGrD 80*
Giunta, Giovan Maria d1632? *NewGrD 80*
Giunta, Luc'Antonio d1602 *NewGrD 80*
Giunta, Luc'Antonio 1457-1538 *NewGrD 80*
Giunta, Tommaso d1618 *NewGrD 80*
Giunta, Tommaso 1494-1566 *NewGrD 80*
Giunti *NewGrD 80*
Giuranna, Barbara 1902- *NewGrD 80*
Giuranna, Bruno 1933- *IntWWM 77, -80, NewGrD 80, WhoMus 72*
Giuseppino *NewGrD 80*
Giusti, Vincenzo 1532-1619 *McGEWD[port]*
Giustini, Lodovico 1685-1743 *NewGrD 80*
Giustiniani, Leonardo 1387?-1446 *NewGrD 80*
Giustiniani, Vincenzo 1564-1637 *NewGrD 80*
Givenci, Adam De *NewGrD 80*
Givens, Jimmie d1964 *NotNAT B*
Givler, Mary Louise d1964 *NotNAT B*
Givney, Kathryn 1896-1978 *ForYSC, HalFC 80, WhoHol A*
Givot, George 1903- *FilmgC, ForYSC, HalFC 80, MovMk*
Gizzi, Domenico 1680?-1758 *NewGrD 80*
Gizziello *NewGrD 80*
Gjonnaess, Sunniva 1934- *IntWWM 77, -80*
Glachant, Antoine-Charles 1770-1851 *NewGrD 80*
Glachant, Jean-Pierre *NewGrD 80*
Glackin, William Charles 1917- *ConAmTC*
Gladden, Eddie 1937- *EncJzS 70*
Gladden, Edward 1937- *EncJzS 70*
Gladden, Frank A *BlkAmP*
Gladden, James *TwYS*
Gladden, Washington 1836-1918 *BiDAmM*
Glade, Sven *TwYS A*
Gladiolas, The *RkOn*
Gladkowska, Konstancja 1810-1889 *NewGrD 80*
Gladman, Annabelle 1899-1948 *WhScrn 74, -77*
Gladman, Florence d1956 *NotNAT B*
Gladmore, Johnny *PupTheA*
Gladstein, Robert 1943- *CnOxB*
Gladstone, Francis Edward 1845-1928 *Baker 78*
Gladstone, Gerald 1929- *CreCan 2*
Gladstone, Jerry 1923- *AmSCAP 80*
Gladwin, Thomas 1710?-1799? *NewGrD 80*
Glaeser, Franz *NewGrD 80*
Glagolin, Boris 1879-1948 *NotNAT A*
Glagolin, Boris S 1878-1948 *WhScrn 74, -77*
Glahe, Will *AmPS A*
Glahn, Henrik 1919- *NewGrD 80*
Glancova-Krupickova, Eva 1926- *IntWWM 80*
Glankova-Krupickova, Eva 1926- *IntWWM 77*
Glanner, Caspar d1577 *NewGrD 80*
Glantz, Leib 1898-1964 *NewGrD 80*
Glanville, Maxwell 1918- *DrBlPA, NatPD*
Glanville-Hicks, Peggy 1912- *Baker 78, BiDAmM, CompSN[port], ConAmC, DcCM, NewEOp 71, NewGrD 80, OxMus*
Glanz, Elemer 1924- *IntWWM 77, -80*
Glapion, Raymond 1895?- *NewOrJ*
Glarean, Heinrich 1488-1563 *NewGrD 80[port]*
Glareanus, Henricus 1488-1563 *Baker 78, NewGrD 80[port]*
Glarum, L Stanley 1908- *AmSCAP 66, ConAmC*
Glarum, L Stanley 1919-1976 *AmSCAP 80*
Glasel, John 1930- *AmSCAP 66*
Glasenapp, Carl Friedrich 1847-1915 *Baker 78, NewGrD 80*
Glaser, Charles 1936- *BiDAmM*
Glaser, Chuck *EncFCWM 69*
Glaser, Chuck 1933- *CounME 74[port]*
Glaser, Darel *WhoHol A*
Glaser, Donald Howard 1941- *AmSCAP 80*
Glaser, Ernst 1904- *IntWWM 77, -80*
Glaser, Franz 1798-1861 *NewGrD 80*
Glaser, Hy 1923- *AmSCAP 66, -80*
Glaser, James 1937- *BiDAmM*
Glaser, Jim *EncFCWM 69*
Glaser, Jim 1937- *CounME 74[port]*
Glaser, Lillian d1969 *WhoHol B*
Glaser, Lulu 1874-1958 *CmpEPM, NotNAT B, WhThe, WhoHol B, WhoStg 1906, -1908*
Glaser, Lynn 1934- *AmSCAP 80*
Glaser, Michael *WhoHol A*
Glaser, Paul Michael *IntMPA 78, -79, -80*
Glaser, Sam 1912- *AmSCAP 66, -80*
Glaser, Sidney 1912- *IntMPA 77, -75, -76, -78, -79, -80*
Glaser, Sioma 1919- *AmSCAP 66, -80*
Glaser, Tompall 1933- *BiDAmM, CounME 74[port], -74A, EncFCWM 69, IlEncCM*
Glaser, Vaughan 1872-1958 *WhScrn 74, -77*
Glaser, Vaughn 1872-1958 *WhoHol B*
Glaser, Victoria Merrylees 1918- *AmSCAP 66, -80, ConAmC*
Glaser, Werner Wolf 1910- *Baker 78, CpmDNM 78, IntWWM 77, -80, NewGrD 80*
Glaser Brothers, The *CounME 74[port], -74A*
Glasgow, Robert Ellison 1925- *WhoMus 72*
Glason, Billy 1904- *AmSCAP 66, -80*
Glasow, Glenn *ConAmC*
Glaspell, Susan 1882-1948 *CnMD, DcLB 7[port], McGEWD, ModWD, NotNAT B, OxThe, PlP&P, WhThe*
Glass, Booker T 1888- *NewOrJ[port]*
Glass, Dudley 1899- *WhThe*
Glass, Everett 1891-1966 *WhScrn 77, WhoHol B*
Glass, Gaston d1965 *MotPP, WhoHol B*
Glass, Gaston 1898-1965 *WhScrn 74, -77*
Glass, Gaston 1899-1965 *Film 1, -2, ForYSC, TwYS*
Glass, George 1910- *IntMPA 77, -75, -76, -78, -79, -80*
Glass, Jennifer 1944- *WhoMus 72*
Glass, Jerome 1920- *IntWWM 77, -80*
Glass, Joanna M *NatPD[port]*
Glass, Louis Christian August 1864-1936 *Baker 78, NewGrD 80*
Glass, Montague 1877-1934 *NotNAT B, WhThe*
Glass, Ned *ForYSC, WhoHol A*
Glass, Nowell 1927- *NewOrJ*
Glass, Paul 1910- *AmSCAP 80*
Glass, Paul Eugene 1934- *AmSCAP 66, -80, ConAmC*
Glass, Philip 1937- *AmSCAP 80, Baker 78, ConAmC, NewGrD 80*
Glass, Ron 1945?- *DrBlPA*
Glass, Seamon *WhoHol A*
Glass, Theodore T *PupTheA*
Glassberg, Irving *WorEFlm*
Glassco, John 1909- *CreCan 2*
Glasser, Albert 1916- *AmSCAP 66, -80, ConAmC, IntWWM 77, WhoHrs 80*
Glasser, Stanley 1926- *IntWWM 77, -80, NewGrD 80, WhoMus 72*
Glassford, David 1866-1935 *NotNAT B, WhThe*
Glassman, Barnett 1914- *IntMPA 75*
Glassman, Judith M 1946- *WomWMM B*
Glassman, Seth 1947- *NatPD[port]*
Glassman, William 1945- *CnOxB*
Glassmire, Augustin J Gus 1879-1946 *WhScrn 74, -77*
Glassmire, Gus 1879-1946 *WhoHol B*
Glassner, Erika *Film 2*
Glasstone, Richard 1935- *CnOxB*
Glauber, Lynn 1954- *CnOxB*
Glaucus Of Rhegium *NewGrD 80*
Glaukos Of Rhegium *NewGrD 80*
Glaum, Louise d1970 *MotPP, WhoHol B*
Glaum, Louise 1894-1970 *Film 1, -2, TwYS*
Glaum, Louise 1900-1970 *WhScrn 74, -77*
Glaz, Herta 1908- *Baker 78, MusSN[port]*
Glaz, Herta 1914- *NewEOp 71*
Glaze, Gary *WhoOp 76*
Glaze, Red Hot Willie *BluesWW[port]*
Glazebrook, Alan William 1925- *WhoMus 72*
Glazer, Benjamin 1887-1958 *FilmEn*
Glazer, David 1913- *IntWWM 80*
Glazer, Esther 1926- *WhoMus 72*
Glazer, Eve F 1903-1960 *WhScrn 74, -77*
Glazer, Frank 1915- *IntWWM 77, -80, WhoMus 72*
Glazer, Melvin Jacob 1931- *AmSCAP 66, -80*
Glazer, Thomas Zachariah 1914- *AmSCAP 80, BiDAmM*
Glazer, Tom 1914- *AmSCAP 66, EncFCWM 69*
Glazer, Tom And The Children's Chorus *RkOn*
Glazier, Sidney 1918- *IntMPA 77, -75, -76, -78, -79, -80*
Glazor, Stuart *ConAmC*
Glazounov, Alexander 1865-1936 *DancEn 78*
Glazunof Alexander 1865-1936 *OxMus*
Glazunov, Aleksandr 1865-1936 *BnBkM 80*
Glazunov, Alexander 1865-1936 *Baker 78, CmpBCM, CompSN[port], CnOxB, DcCom 77[port], DcCom&M 79, MusMk[port], NewGrD 80[port]*
Gleason, Ada *Film 1, -2*
Gleason, Dorothy *PupTheA*
Gleason, Fred 1854-1933 *WhScrn 74, -77*
Gleason, Frederick Grant 1848-1903 *Baker 78, BiDAmM, NewGrD 80*
Gleason, Harold 1892- *Baker 78, IntWWM 77, -80*
Gleason, Jackie 1916- *AmSCAP 66, -80, BiE&WWA, CmpEPM, EncMT, FilmEn, FilmgC, ForYSC, HalFC 80, IntMPA 77, -75, -76, -78, -79, -80, JoeFr[port], MovMk[port], NewYTET, WhoHol A*
Gleason, James 1886-1959 *FilmEn, Film 2, FilmgC, ForYSC, HalFC 80[port], HolCA[port], MotPP, MovMk[port], NotNAT B, TwYS, Vers A[port], WhScrn 74, -77, WhThe, WhoHol B*
Gleason, John 1941- *WhoThe 77*
Gleason, Keogh *IntMPA 77, -75, -76, -78, -79, -80*
Gleason, Lucile Webster d1947 *NotNAT B*
Gleason, Lucille 1886-1947 *Film 2, FilmgC, ForYSC, HalFC 80*
Gleason, Lucille 1888-1947 *WhScrn 74, -77, WhoHol B*
Gleason, Mary M 1931- *AmSCAP 66*
Gleason, Ralph J 1917-1975 *EncJzS 70*
Gleason, Russell d1945 *NotNAT B, WhoHol B*
Gleason, Russell 1906-1945 *ForYSC, MovMk*
Gleason, Russell 1908-1945 *Film 2, FilmgC, HalFC 80, WhScrn 74, -77*
Gleaves, Ian Beresford 1937- *IntWWM 77, -80, WhoMus 72*
Glebov, Anatoli Glebovich 1899- *ModWD*
Glebov, Igor *Baker 78, DancEn 78, NewGrD 80*
Gleckler, Gayle *WomWMM*
Gleckler, Robert P 1890-1939 *Film 2, WhScrn 74, -77, WhoHol B*
Gleich, Clemens Chr J Von 1930- *IntWWM 77, -80*
Gleich, Joseph Alois 1772-1841 *OxThe*

Gleim, Johann Wilhelm Ludwig 1719-1803 *NewGrD 80*
Glein, Erasmus De d1599 *NewGrD 80*
Gleisman, Carl Erik 1767-1804 *NewGrD 80*
Gleissner, Franz 1759-1818 *NewGrD 80*
Gleissner, Franz 1760-1820? *OxMus*
Gleizer, Judith *Film 2*
Glen *NewGrD 80*
Glen, Alexander 1801-1873 *NewGrD 80*
Glen, Alexander 1878-1951 *NewGrD 80*
Glen, David d1958 *NewGrD 80*
Glen, David 1850- *NewGrD 80*
Glen, Irma *AmSCAP 66, ConAmC*
Glen, John 1833-1904 *Baker 78, NewGrD 80*
Glen, Robert 1835-1911 *NewGrD 80*
Glen, Thomas Macbean 1804-1873 *NewGrD 80*
Glencoves, The *RkOn*
Glendenning, Ernest 1884-1936 *Film 2, TwYS*
Glendinning, Ernest 1884-1936 *NotNAT B, WhScrn 74, -77, WhThe, WhoHol B*
Glendinning, Ethel 1910- *WhThe*
Glendinning, John 1857-1916 *NotNAT B, WhThe, WhoStg 1906, -1908*
Glendon, Frank d1937 *WhoHol B*
Glendon, J Frank 1885-1937 *Film 1, -2, TwYS*
Glendon, Jonathan Frank 1887-1937 *WhScrn 74, -77*
Glenister, Frank 1860-1945 *WhThe*
Glenn, Bonita Lavada 1946- *WhoOp 76*
Glenn, Charles Owen 1938- *IntMPA 77, -75, -76, -78, -79, -80*
Glenn, Evans Tyree 1912-1974 *BiDAmM, EncJzS 70*
Glenn, Fareil 1949- *AmSCAP 80*
Glenn, Jack 1904- *IntMPA 75, -76*
Glenn, Lloyd 1909- *WhoJazz 72*
Glenn, Raymond *FilmEn*
Glenn, Raymond d1974 *Film 2, WhScrn 77, WhoHol B*
Glenn, Roy *ForYSC*
Glenn, Roy E, Sr. 1911-1971 *BlksB&W*
Glenn, Roy E, Sr. 1914?-1971 *DrBlPA*
Glenn, Roy E, Sr. 1915-1971 *HalFC 80, WhScrn 74, -77, WhoHol B*
Glenn, Tony *AmSCAP 80*
Glenn, Tyree 1912-1974 *AmSCAP 66, -80, CmpEPM, DrBlPA, IlEncJ, WhoJazz 72*
Glenne, Daphne 1900- *IlWWBF[port]*
Glennie, Brian 1912- *WhThe*
Glennon, Bert 1893-1967 *FilmgC, HalFC 80*
Glennon, Bert 1895-1967 *CmMov, FilmEn, WorEFlm*
Glenny, Albert 1870-1958 *NewOrJ[port]*
Glenny, Charles H 1857-1922 *NotNAT B, WhThe*
Glenville, Peter 1913- *BiE&WWA, CnThe, EncWT, FilmEn, FilmgC, HalFC 80, IlWWBF, NotNAT, WhoThe 72, -77, WorEFlm*
Glenville, Shaun 1884-1968 *NotNAT B, WhThe*
Gless, Eleanor Mattie 1908- *AmSCAP 66, -80*
Gletle, Johann Melchior 1626-1683 *NewGrD 80*
Glett, Charles Lionel 1902- *IntMPA 75, -76*
Glew, Dave *ConMuA 80B*
Glick, David Alan 1946- *IntWWM 77, -80*
Glick, Henrietta *ConAmC*
Glick, Hyman J 1904- *IntMPA 77, -75, -76, -78, -79, -80*
Glick, Irving 1934- *CreCan 1*
Glick, Jacob 1926- *IntWWM 77, -80*
Glick, Jesse G M 1874-1938 *AmSCAP 66, -80*
Glick, Srul Irving 1934- *Baker 78, CreCan 1*
Glickman, Eugene C *ConAmC*
Glickman, Fred 1903- *AmSCAP 66, -80*
Glickman, Joel 1930- *IntMPA 77, -75, -76, -78, -79, -80*
Glickman, Mort H 1898-1952 *AmSCAP 80*
Glickman, Susan Rae 1945- *AmSCAP 80*
Glickman, Sylvia 1932- *ConAmC*
Glickman, Will 1910- *BiE&WWA*
Glicksman, Frank *NewYTET*
Glier, J W *OxMus*
Glier, Reyngol'd Moritsevich 1875-1956 *NewGrD 80*
Gliere, Reinhold 1875-1956 *Baker 78, BnBkM 80, CompSN[port], DancEn 78, DcCom&M 79, DcCM, MusMk, NewGrD 80, OxMus*
Gliere, Reinhold Moritzovich 1876-1956 *CnOxB*
Gliese, Rochus 1891-1976 *EncWT*
Gligo, Niksa 1946- *IntWWM 77, -80*
Gligor, Jovan 1914- *WhoOp 76*
Glines, John 1933- *AmSCAP 80*
Glinka, Michael 1804-1857 *NewEOp 71, OxMus*
Glinka, Michail 1804-1857 *DcCom&M 79*
Glinka, Mikhail 1804-1857 *Baker 78, BnBkM 80, CmOp, CmpBCM, CnOxB, DcCom 77, GrComp[port], MusMk[port], NewGrD 80[port]*
Glinski, Mateusz 1892-1976 *Baker 78, IntWWM 77, NewGrD 80*
Glinski, Matteo 1892-1976 *NewGrD 80*
Glitter, Gary 1944- *ConMuA 80A, IlEncR, RkOn 2[port]*
Glixman, Jeff *ConMuA 80B*
Globokar, Vinko 1934- *DcCM, NewGrD 80*
Globokar, Vinko 1935- *Baker 78*
Globus, Diane *WomWMM B*
Glock, Sir William 1908- *Baker 78, IntWWM 77, -80, NewGrD 80, OxMus, WhoMus 72*
Glodeanu, Liviu 1938- *Baker 78, DcCM, IntWWM 77, -80*
Gloeckner-Kramer, Pepi 1874-1954 *WhScrn 74, -77*
Glogau, Jack 1886-1953 *AmSCAP 66, -80*
Gloor, Elisabeth 1915- *IntWWM 77, -80*
Glori, Enrico 1901-1966 *WhScrn 74, -77*
Glorieux, Francois 1932- *Baker 78, IntWWM 77, -80, NewGrD 80*
Glory, Mary *Film 2*
Glosch, Carl Wilhelm 1731?-1809 *NewGrD 80*
Glossop, David William 1951- *IntWWM 80*
Glossop, Joseph d1835 *NotNAT B*
Glossop, Mrs. Joseph d1853 *NotNAT B*
Glossop, Peter 1928- *CmOp, IntWWM 77, -80, NewGrD 80, WhoMus 72, WhoOp 76*
Glossop-Harris, Florence 1883-1931 *NotNAT B, WhThe*
Glosup, Edgar D 1907- *AmSCAP 80*
Glosup, Lorene St. Clare 1911- *AmSCAP 80*
Glover, Betty S 1923- *IntWWM 77, -80*
Glover, Bruce *WhoHol A*
Glover, Charles Joseph 1951- *AmSCAP 80*
Glover, Charles William d1863 *NotNAT B*
Glover, Cynthia *WhoMus 72*
Glover, David Carr, Jr. 1925- *AmSCAP 66, -80*
Glover, Dorothy H *PupTheA*
Glover, Edmund 1813-1860 *NotNAT B, OxThe*
Glover, Felix Kwadwo Mukeli 1946- *IntWWM 77, -80*
Glover, Halcott 1877-1949 *NotNAT B, WhThe*
Glover, James Mackey 1861- *WhThe*
Glover, Jane Alison 1949- *IntWWM 77, -80*
Glover, Joe 1903- *AmSCAP 66, -80*
Glover, John William 1815-1899 *Baker 78, NewGrD 80*
Glover, Julia 1779-1850 *OxThe*
Glover, Julia 1781-1850 *NotNAT B*
Glover, Julian 1935- *FilmgC, HalFC 80, WhoHol A, WhoThe 72, -77*
Glover, Lawrence 1931- *IntWWM 80, WhoMus 72*
Glover, Sarah Ann 1785-1867 *OxMus*
Glover, Sarah Ann 1786-1867 *Baker 78*
Glover, Sarah Anna 1786-1867 *NewGrD 80*
Glover, William 1911- *BiE&WWA, ConAmTC, NotNAT*
Glover, William Henry 1819-1875 *BiDAmM*
Glover, William Howard 1819-1875 *Baker 78, NewGrD 80*
Glovinsky, Ben 1942- *ConAmC*
Glowinski, Jan 1645?-1712? *NewGrD 80*
Gluck, Alma 1884-1938 *Baker 78, BiDAmM, CmOp, MusSN[port], NewEOp 71, NewGrD 80*
Gluck, Christoph Wilibald Ritter Von 1714-1787 *DancEn 78*
Gluck, Christoph Willibald Ritter Von 1714-1787 *Baker 78, BnBkM 80[port], CmOp, CmpBCM, CnOxB, DcCom 77[port], DcCom&M 79, GrComp[port], MusMk[port], NewEOp 71, NewGrD 80[port], OxMus*
Gluck, John R 1925- *AmSCAP 66, -80*
Gluck, Norman E 1914- *IntMPA 77, -75, -76, -78, -79, -80*
Gluck, Rena 1933- *CnOxB*
Gluckman, Bernard Louis 1909- *AmSCAP 66, -80*
Gluckman, Leon 1922- *WhoThe 77*
Glucksman, Ernest D *IntMPA 77, -75, -76, -78, -79, -80, NewYTET*
Gluskin, Lud 1901- *CmpEPM*
Gluszkovsky, Adam 1793-1870? *CnOxB*
Glut, Don 1943?- *WhoHrs 80*
Glyde, Henry George 1906- *CreCan 2*
Glyde, Judith Pamela 1944- *IntWWM 77, -80*
Glykes, Gregorios *NewGrD 80*
Glykys, Joannes *NewGrD 80*
Glyn, Elinor 1864-1943 *Film 2, FilmgC, HalFC 80, IlWWBF A, OxFilm, WomWMM*
Glyn, Margaret Henrietta 1865-1946 *Baker 78, NewGrD 80*
Glyn, Neva Carr d1975 *WhScrn 77, WhoHol C*
Glynn, Franklin 1885- *BiDAmM*
Glynne, Angela 1933- *WhThe*
Glynne, Derke *Film 2*
Glynne, Howell 1906-1969 *NewGrD 80*
Glynne, Howell 1907-1969 *CmOp*
Glynne, Marg 1898-1954 *Film 1, -2*
Glynne, Mary 1898-1954 *FilmgC, HalFC 80, IlWWBF, NotNAT B, WhScrn 74, -77, WhThe, WhoHol B*
Glynne-Jones, Marjorie Lilian 1936- *WhoMus 72*
Gnam, Adrian 1940- *IntWWM 77, -80*
Gnass, Friedrich 1892-1958 *WhScrn 77*
Gnatt, Poul 1923- *CnOxB, DancEn 78*
Gnattali, Radames 1906- *NewGrD 80*
Gnazzo, Anthony Joseph 1936- *AmSCAP 80, Baker 78, ConAmC*
Gnecchi, Vittorio 1876-1954 *Baker 78, NewGrD 80, OxMus*
Gnecco, Francesco 1769?-1811? *NewGrD 80*
Gnesin, Mikhail Fabianovich 1883-1957 *NewGrD 80*
Gnessin, Menahem 1882-1953 *OxThe*
Gnessin, Mikhail 1883-1957 *Baker 78*
Gneuss, Helmut Walter Georg 1927- *IntWWM 77, -80*
Gniessin, Michael 1883-1957 *OxMus*
Gniot, Walerian Jozef 1902- *NewGrD 80*
Gnocchi, Pietro 1677-1771 *NewGrD 80*
Goatman, Alan H 1918- *IntMPA 77, -75, -76, -78, -79, -80*
Gobatti, Stefano 1852-1913 *NewGrD 80*
Gobbaerts, Jean-Louis 1835-1886 *Baker 78*
Gobbato, Angelo 1943- *WhoOp 76*
Gobbi, Anna *WomWMM*
Gobbi, Tito 1913- *Baker 78*
Gobbi, Tito 1915- *CmOp[port], IntWWM 77, -80, MusMk[port], MusSN[port], NewEOp 71, NewGrD 80[port], WhoMus 72, WhoOp 76*
Gobble, Harry A Hank 1923-1961 *WhScrn 74, -77*
Gobbo DellaRegina, Il *NewGrD 80*
Gobeil, Charlotte *WomWMM*
Gobel, Franz Xaver *NewGrD 80*
Gobel, George 1919- *EncFCWM 69, FilmgC, ForYSC, HalFC 80, NewYTET, WhoHol A*
Gobel, George 1920- *JoeFr[port]*
Gobel, George Leslie 1919- *BiDAmM*
Gobelinus Person *NewGrD 80*
Goberman, Max d1962 *NotNAT B*
Gobert, Boy 1925- *EncWT*
Gobert, Thomas d1672 *NewGrD 80*
Gobetti, Francesco 1675-1723 *NewGrD 80*
Gobin De Reims *NewGrD 80*
Gobin De Reins *NewGrD 80*
Goble, Robert 1903- *NewGrD 80*
Gocciolo, Giovanni Battista *NewGrD 80*
Gockley, R David 1943- *WhoOp 76*
Godard, Benjamin 1849-1895 *Baker 78, DcCom&M 79, NewEOp 71, NewGrD 80, OxMus*
Godard, Jean-Luc 1930- *BiDFilm, -81, DcFM, FilmEn, FilmgC, HalFC 80, MovMk[port], OxFilm, WhoHrs 80, WomWMM, WorEFlm*
Godard, Robert *NewGrD 80*

Godard DeBeauchamps, Pierre-Francois *NewGrD 80*
Godart, Robert *NewGrD 80*
Godbid, William d1679 *NewGrD 80*
Godbold, Geoff 1935- *IntMPA 77, -75, -76, -78, -79, -80*
Godbout, Jacques 1933- *CreCan 1*
Godd, Barbara d1944 *NotNAT B*
Goddard, Alf 1897- *Film 2, IlWWBF*
Goddard, Arabella 1836-1922 *Baker 78, NewGrD 80, OxMus*
Goddard, Bob 1913- *ConAmTC*
Goddard, Charles W 1879-1951 *NotNAT B, WhThe*
Goddard, Frederick Albert George 1908- *WhoMus 72*
Goddard, Glendon Boyce 1899- *AmSCAP 66, -80*
Goddard, Leroy A 1915- *AmSCAP 80*
Goddard, Mark *ForYSC, WhoHol A*
Goddard, Paulette 1911- *BiDFilm, -81, CmMov, FilmEn, Film 2, FilmgC, ForYSC, HalFC 80[port], IntMPA 77, -75, -76, -78, -79, -80, MotPP, MovMk[port], OxFilm, ThFT[port], What 1[port], WhoHol A, WhoHrs 80, WorEFlm*
Goddard, Scott 1895-1965 *NewGrD 80*
Goddard, Willoughby 1926- *WhoThe 72, -77*
Goddard, Willoughby 1927- *FilmgC*
Goddard, Willoughby 1932- *HalFC 80*
Goddart, Robert *NewGrD 80*
Godden, Grace Esther Mary 1925- *WhoMus 72*
Godden, Jimmy 1879-1955 *NotNAT B, WhThe*
Godden, Peter David 1947- *IntWWM 77*
Godden, Reginald 1905- *CreCan 1*
Godden, Rumer 1907- *FilmgC, HalFC 80*
Godderis, Albert 1882-1971 *WhScrn 77*
Godeau, Antoine 1605-1672 *NewGrD 80*
Godebrye, Jacob d1529 *NewGrD 80*
Godecharle, Eugene 1742?-1798 *NewGrD 80*
Godecharle, Lambert-Francois 1753?-1819 *NewGrD 80*
Godecharles, Eugene 1742?-1798 *NewGrD 80*
Godecharles, Lambert-Francois 1753?-1819 *NewGrD 80*
Godefroid, Felix 1818-1897 *NewGrD 80*
Godefroy, Clair d1878? *NewGrD 80*
Goderis, Albert 1882-1971 *WhoHol B*
Godescalcus Lintpurgensis *NewGrD 80*
Godfrey *NewGrD 80*
Godfrey Of Strasbourg *OxMus*
Godfrey, Arthur 1868-1939 *NewGrD 80*
Godfrey, Arthur 1903- *AmPS A, -B, AmSCAP 66, -80, BiDAmM, CmpEPM, ForYSC, IntMPA 77, -75, -76, -78, -79, -80, NewYTET, WhoHol A*
Godfrey, Bob 1921- *FilmEn, FilmgC, HalFC 80*
Godfrey, Charles 1790-1863 *NewGrD 80*
Godfrey, Charles 1839-1919 *NewGrD 80*
Godfrey, Charles 1851-1900 *OxThe*
Godfrey, Charles 1866-1935 *NewGrD 80*
Godfrey, Dan 1831-1903 *NewGrD 80*
Godfrey, Dan 1893-1935 *NewGrD 80*
Godfrey, Sir Dan 1868-1939 *Baker 78, NewGrD 80*
Godfrey, Daniel, Sr. 1831-1903 *Baker 78*
Godfrey, Derek 1924- *WhoThe 72, -77*
Godfrey, Fred 1837-1882 *NewGrD 80*
Godfrey, G W d1897 *NotNAT B*
Godfrey, George *Baker 78, Film 2*
Godfrey, Isidore 1900- *IntWWM 77*
Godfrey, Keith d1976 *NewYTET*
Godfrey, Kenneth 1906- *AmSCAP 80*
Godfrey, Louis 1930- *CnOxB, DancEn 78*
Godfrey, Peter 1899-1970 *FilmEn, FilmgC, HalFC 80, WhScrn 74, -77, WhThe, WhoHol B*
Godfrey, Peter David Hensman 1922- *IntWWM 80, NewGrD 80, WhoMus 72*
Godfrey, Renee Haal 1920-1964 *NotNAT B, WhScrn 74, -77, WhoHol B*
Godfrey, Robert H 1904- *IntMPA 77, -75, -76, -78, -79*
Godfrey, Robert H 1905- *AmSCAP 66, -80*
Godfrey, Sam d1935 *WhoHol B*
Godfrey, Samuel T 1891-1935 *WhScrn 74, -77*
Godfrey, Thomas 1736-1763 *EncWT, Ent, NotNAT B, OxThe, PlP&P*
Godfrey, Victor John 1934- *WhoMus 72, WhoOp 76*
Godfrey Family *OxMus*
Godfrey-Turner, L *WhThe*
Godfroy, Clair *NewGrD 80*
Godimel, Claude *Baker 78, NewGrD 80*
Godin, Imrich Karol 1907- *IntWWM 77, -80*
Godin, Jacques 1930- *CreCan 2*
Godios, Joseph Thomas 1929- *AmSCAP 80*
Godmilow, Jill *WomWMM A, -B*
Godomar, Leonor *PupTheA*
Godounov, Alexander *CnOxB*
Godowsky, Dagmar 1897-1975 *FilmEn, Film 2, MotPP, TwYS, What 1[port], WhScrn 77, WhoHol C*
Godowsky, Leopold 1870-1938 *AmSCAP 66, -80, Baker 78, BiDAmM, BnBkM 80[port], ConAmC, MusMk, MusSN[port], NewGrD 80, OxMus*
Godreau, Miguel 1946- *CnOxB*
Godric 1069?-1170 *NewGrD 80*
Godron, Hugo 1900-1971 *Baker 78, NewGrD 80*
Godsall, Lesley Jill 1937- *WhoMus 72*
Godschalck, Eugene *NewGrD 80*
Godschalck, Lambert-Francois *NewGrD 80*
Godsell, Vanda 1919?- *FilmgC, HalFC 80, WhoHol A*
Godske, Poul 1929- *IntWWM 80*
Godson, Daphe *IntWWM 77*
Godson, Daphne 1932- *IntWWM 80, WhoMus 72*
Godunov, Boris Alexander 1949- *CnOxB*
Godwin, Edward William 1833-1886 *NotNAT B, OxThe*
Godwin, Edward William 1933- *CreCan 1*
Godwin, Frank *IntMPA 77, -75, -76, -78, -79, -80*
Godwin, Harry Easton 1906- *AmSCAP 66, -80*
Godwin, Joscelyn 1945- *ConAmC*
Godwin, Joscelyn Roland Jasber Chloestro 1945- *IntWWM 80*
Godwin, Joscelyn Roland Jasper Chloestro 1945- *IntWWM 77*
Godwin, Shelagh MacDonald 1948- *IntWWM 77*
Godwin, Ted 1933- *CreCan 1*
Godymel, Claude *NewGrD 80*
Godziszewski, Jerzy 1935- *IntWWM 80*
Godzyatsky, Vitaly Alexeyevich 1936- *NewGrD 80*
Goeb, Roger 1914- *Baker 78, ConAmC, NewGrD 80, WhoMus 72*
Goebels, Franzpeter 1920- *IntWWM 77, -80*
Goebert, Robert Jacob 1920- *AmSCAP 80*
Goedecke, David Stewart 1929- *IntWWM 77, -80*
Goedicke, Alexander 1877-1957 *Baker 78*
Goedicke, Kurt-Hans 1935- *IntWWM 77, -80, WhoMus 72*
Goehr, Alexander 1932- *Baker 78, CmOp, CpmDNM 80, DcCom&M 79, DcCM, IntWWM 77, -80, MusMk, NewGrD 80[port], OxMus, WhoMus 72*
Goehr, Rudolph *ConAmC*
Goehr, Walter 1903-1960 *Baker 78, NewGrD 80*
Goehring, George Andrew 1933- *AmSCAP 66, -80*
Goeke, Leo 1936- *WhoOp 76*
Goell, Kermit 1915- *AmSCAP 66, -80*
Goemanne, Noel 1926- *AmSCAP 80, ConAmC, IntWWM 77, -80*
Goemans, Pieter Willem 1925- *IntWWM 77, -80*
Goepfart, Christian H 1835-1890 *BiDAmM*
Goepfart, Karl Eduard 1859-1942 *Baker 78*
Goepfert, Georges-Adam 1727?-1809? *NewGrD 80*
Goepffer, Georges-Adam 1727?-1809? *NewGrD 80*
Goepp, Philip Henry 1864-1936 *Baker 78, BiDAmM*
Goeppfert, Georges-Adam 1727?-1809? *NewGrD 80*
Goering, Al 1898-1963 *AmSCAP 66, -80, CmpEPM*
Goering, Reinhard 1887-1936 *CnMD, EncWT, Ent, McGEWD, ModWD*
Goertz, Harald 1924- *IntWWM 77, -80*
Goes, Damian *NewGrD 80*
Goes, Derryl F 1929- *AmSCAP 80*
Goesen, Maistre *NewGrD 80*
Goessen, Maistre *NewGrD 80*
Goethals, Lucien 1931- *Baker 78, DcCM, IntWWM 77, -80, NewGrD 80*
Goethals, Stanley *Film 2*
Goethe 1749-1832 *OxMus*
Goethe, Johann Wolfgang Von 1749-1832 *CnThe, DcPup, EncWT, Ent[port], McGEWD[port], NewEOp 71, NewGrD 80, NotNAT B, OxThe, REnWD[port], WhoHrs 80*
Goethe, Wolfgang Von 1749-1832 *Baker 78*
Goetschius, Marjorie 1915- *AmSCAP 66, -80, ConAmC*
Goetschius, Percy 1853-1943 *Baker 78, BiDAmM, NewGrD 80, OxMus*
Goetz, Abraham 1916- *IntWWM 77*
Goetz, Augustus d1957 *NotNAT B*
Goetz, Ben 1891- *FilmgC, HalFC 80*
Goetz, Carl *Film 2*
Goetz, Curt 1888-1960 *CnMD, CroCD, EncWT, Ent, McGEWD[port]*
Goetz, E Ray 1886-1954 *AmSCAP 66, -80, BiDAmM, CmpEPM, EncMT, NewCBMT, NotNAT B*
Goetz, Harry M 1888- *IntMPA 77, -75, -76, -78, -79*
Goetz, Hermann 1840-1876 *Baker 78, NewEOp 71, NewGrD 80, OxMus*
Goetz, Joseph F 1908- *IntMPA 75*
Goetz, Ruth Goodman 1912- *BiE&WWA, NotNAT, WhoThe 72, -77*
Goetz, Valerie VonMartens *EncWT*
Goetz, William 1903-1968 *FilmgC, WorEFlm*
Goetz, William 1903-1969 *FilmEn, HalFC 80*
Goetz, Wolfgang 1885-1955 *CnMD, ModWD*
Goetze, Walter W 1883-1961 *Baker 78*
Goetzel, Charlotte *CreCan 2*
Goetzke, Bernard *Film 2*
Goetzke, Bernhard 1884-1964 *WhScrn 77*
Goetzl, Anselm 1878-1923 *Baker 78, NotNAT B*
Goetzl, Thomas Maxwell 1943- *AmSCAP 80*
Goeyvaerts, Karel 1923- *Baker 78, DcCM, NewGrD 80*
Goeyvaerts-Falk, Karel August 1923- *IntWWM 77, -80*
Goff, Ivan 1910- *FilmgC, HalFC 80, IntMPA 75, -76, WorEFlm*
Goff, Lewin 1919- *BiE&WWA, NotNAT*
Goff, Martin 1923- *IntWWM 77*
Goff, Martyn 1923- *IntWWM 80, WhoMus 72*
Goff, Norman *JoeFr*
Goff, Norris 1906- *WhoHol A*
Goff, Thomas 1898-1975 *NewGrD 80*
Goffin, Cora 1902- *WhThe*
Goffin, Peter 1906- *WhThe*
Goffriller, Matteo 1659?-1742 *NewGrD 80*
Goforth, Frances *BiE&WWA, NotNAT*
Gofriller, Matteo 1659?-1742 *NewGrD 80*
Gofton, E Story d1939 *NotNAT B*
Goga, Jack Alan 1944- *AmSCAP 80*
Gogava, Antonius Hermannus 1529-1569 *NewGrD 80*
Goggin, Dan 1934- *BiDAmM*
Goggin, Muriel *CreCan 1*
Gogh, Lucy Van *CreCan 1*
Gogler, L *PupTheA*
Gogoberidze, Lana *WomWMM*
Gogol, Nikolai 1809-1852 *NewEOp 71*
Gogol, Nikolai Vasilievich 1809-1852 *CnThe, OxThe, PlP&P, REnWD[port]*
Gogol, Nikolai Vasilyevich 1809-1852 *DcPup, EncWT*
Gogol, Nikolai Vasilyevitch 1809-1852 *Ent*
Gogol, Nikolai Vassilievitch 1809-1852 *NotNAT A, -B*
Gogol, Nikolay Vasilyevich 1809-1852 *McGEWD[port]*
Gogol, Nikolay Vasil'yevich 1809-1852 *NewGrD 80*
Gogorza, Emilio Edoardo De 1874-1949 *Baker 78*
Goh, Taijiro 1907-1970 *Baker 78*
Gohler, Georg 1874-1954 *Baker 78, NewGrD 80*

Gohman, Donald 1927- *AmSCAP 66, -80*
Gohringer, Francilla *NewGrD 80*
Goicoechea Errasti, Vicente 1854-1916 *NewGrD 80*
Goilav, Florenza 1933- *IntWWM 77, -80*
Goilav, Yoan 1933- *IntWWM 77, -80*
Goimbault, Odette *IlWWBF*
Going, Frederica 1895-1959 *WhScrn 77*
Goins, Paul Douglas 1944- *AmSCAP 80*
Gois, Damiao De 1502-1574 *NewGrD 80*
Goitein, George 1914- *AmSCAP 80*
Golabek, Jakub 1739-1789 *NewGrD 80*
Golabovski, Sotir 1937- *IntWWM 77, -80*
Golan, Gila 1940?- *FilmEn, FilmgC, ForYSC, HalFC 80, WhoHol A*
Golan, Menahem 1929- *FilmEn*
Golan, Menahem 1931- *FilmgC, HalFC 80*
Golan, Orit 1946- *IntWWM 77, -80*
Golan, Ron 1924- *IntWWM 77, -80*
Goland, Arnold 1928- *AmSCAP 80*
Golani-Erdesz, Rivka 1946- *IntWWM 80*
Gold, Andrew 1951- *IlEncR, RkOn 2[port]*
Gold, Anita 1932- *AmSCAP 66, -80*
Gold, Arthur 1917- *Baker 78*
Gold, Arthur 1919- *NewGrD 80*
Gold, Belle *WhoStg 1906, -1908*
Gold, Bert Joseph 1917- *AmSCAP 66, -80*
Gold, Cecil *IntWWM 77*
Gold, Edward Louis 1947- *NatPD[port]*
Gold, Ernest 1921- *AmSCAP 66, -80, Baker 78, CmpEPM, CpmDNM 75, ConAmC, FilmEn, FilmgC, HalFC 80, IntWWM 77, -80, OxFilm, PopAmC SUP[port], WorEFlm*
Gold, H Hy *IntMPA 75, -76*
Gold, Hal *AmSCAP 80*
Gold, Harry *WhoMus 72*
Gold, Jack 1930- *FilmEn, FilmgC, HalFC 80, IlWWBF*
Gold, Jacob 1921- *AmSCAP 66, -80*
Gold, Jimmy 1886-1967 *FilmgC, HalFC 80, IlWWBF, WhScrn 74, -77, WhoHol B*
Gold, Joe 1894- *AmSCAP 66, -80*
Gold, Joe D 1922- *AmSCAP 80*
Gold, Julius 1884-1969 *Baker 78*
Gold, Kathe 1907- *EncWT*
Gold, Lloyd *NatPD[port]*
Gold, Lou *CmpEPM*
Gold, Manny 1920- *AmSCAP 80*
Gold, Martin 1915- *AmSCAP 66*
Gold, Marty 1915- *AmSCAP 80*
Gold, Melvin 1909- *IntMPA 77, -75, -76, -78, -79, -80*
Gold, Michael 1894-1967 *CnMD, ModWD*
Gold, Morton 1933- *ConAmC, IntWWM 77, -80*
Gold, Steve *ConMuA 80B*
Gold, Sylviane 1948- *ConAmTC*
Gold, Wally 1928- *AmSCAP 66*
Gold, Walter 1928- *AmSCAP 80*
Goldar, Robert *NewGrD 80*
Goldbach, Stanislaw 1896- *Baker 78*
Goldbeck, Fred 1902- *Baker 78*
Goldbeck, Robert 1839-1908 *Baker 78, BiDAmM*
Goldbeck, Willis 1899-1979 *HalFC 80*
Goldbeck, Willis 1900- *FilmgC, WorEFlm*
Goldbeck, Willis 1900-1979 *FilmEn*
Goldberg, Albert 1898- *Baker 78*
Goldberg, Bernard 1932- *IntMPA 78, -79, -80*
Goldberg, Bernard Z 1923- *AmSCAP 80*
Goldberg, Danny *ConMuA 80B*
Goldberg, Dick 1947- *DcLB 7[port]*
Goldberg, Doris 1880-1928 *AmSCAP 80*
Goldberg, Eric 1890- *CreCan 2*
Goldberg, Fred 1921- *IntMPA 77, -75, -76, -78, -79, -80*
Goldberg, Harry 1910- *AmSCAP 80*
Goldberg, Harry 1912- *AmSCAP 66, -80*
Goldberg, Irwin Steven 1949- *IntWWM 77, -80*
Goldberg, Jenny *WomWMM B*
Goldberg, Johann Gottlieb 1727-1756 *Baker 78, NewGrD 80, OxMus*
Goldberg, Joseph 1825-1890 *NewGrD 80*
Goldberg, Leon 1900- *IntMPA 77, -75, -76, -78, -79, -80*
Goldberg, Leonard *IntMPA 77, -76, -78, -79, -80*
Goldberg, Louise 1937- *IntWWM 80*
Goldberg, Mark Leon 1927- *AmSCAP 66, -80*
Goldberg, Molly *JoeFr*
Goldberg, Nathan d1961 *NotNAT B*
Goldberg, Neil Brian 1943- *AmSCAP 80*
Goldberg, Reiner 1939- *WhoOp 76*
Goldberg, Reuben L 1883-1970 *AmSCAP 66, -80*
Goldberg, Richard 1928- *BiDAmM*
Goldberg, Rube 1883-1970 *JoeFr, WhScrn 77*
Goldberg, Sharon *WomWMM B*
Goldberg, Stephen Edward 1952- *ConAmC*
Goldberg, Szymon 1909- *Baker 78, BiDAmM, IntWWM 77, -80, NewGrD 80, WhoMus 72*
Goldberg, Theo 1921- *Baker 78*
Goldberg, Theophile *NewGrD 80*
Goldberg, William B 1917- *ConAmC*
Goldberger, David 1925- *IntWWM 77, -80*
Goldberger-Jacoby, Susan *WomWMM B*
Goldblatt, Harold M 1888- *AmSCAP 66*
Goldblatt, Rose 1913- *IntWWM 80*
Golde, Walter H 1887-1963 *AmSCAP 66, -80, Baker 78, ConAmC*
Goldemberg, Rose Leiman *NatPD[port]*
Golden, Bill d1959 *NewYTET*
Golden, Bob *WhoHol A*
Golden, Edward J, Jr. 1934- *BiE&WWA, NotNAT*
Golden, Ernie 1890- *AmSCAP 66*
Golden, Herbert L *IntMPA 77, -75, -76, -78, -79, -80*
Golden, Jerome B 1917- *IntMPA 77, -75, -76, -78, -79, -80*
Golden, John 1874-1955 *AmSCAP 66, -80, CmpEPM, NotNAT A, -B, WhThe*
Golden, Joseph 1928- *BiE&WWA, NotNAT*
Golden, Marta *Film 1*
Golden, Michael *WhoHol A*
Golden, Michael 1913- *HalFC 80, WhoThe 72, -77*
Golden, Nathan D 1895- *IntMPA 77, -75, -76, -78, -79, -80*
Golden, Olive *Film 1*
Golden, Olive Fuller *WhoHol A*
Golden, Richard 1854- *WhoStg 1906, -1908*
Golden, Sylvia *AmSCAP 66*
Golden, Sylvia 1904- *AmSCAP 80*
Golden Earring *IlEncR, RkOn 2[port]*
Golden West Cowboys *BiDAmM*
Goldenberg, Billy 1931?- *HalFC 80*
Goldenberg, Morris Oscar 1911-1969 *AmSCAP 66, -80*
Goldenberg, Sam d1945 *WhoHol B*
Goldenberg, Samuel 1886-1945 *WhScrn 74, -77*
Goldenberg, William Leon 1936- *AmSCAP 66, ConAmC*
Goldenson, Leonard H 1905- *IntMPA 77, -75, -76, -78, -79, -80, NewYTET*
Gol'denveyzer, Alexander 1875-1961 *NewGrD 80*
Goldenweiser, Alexander 1875-1961 *Baker 78, NewGrD 80*
Golder, Jennie d1928 *NotNAT B*
Golder, Lew d1962 *NotNAT B*
Golder, Robert 1510?-1563? *NewGrD 80*
Goldfaden, Abraham 1840-1908 *BiDAmM, CnThe, McGEWD, ModWD, NotNAT B, OxThe, REnWD[port]*
Goldfaden, Wolf *Film 2*
Goldfarb, Herb *ConMuA 80B*
Goldfarb, Irv *ConMuA 80B*
Goldhahn, Richard Thomas 1915- *AmSCAP 80*
Goldie, F Wyndham 1897-1957 *NotNAT B, WhThe*
Goldie, Hugh 1919- *WhoThe 72, -77*
Goldie, Wyndham 1897-1957 *WhoHol B*
Goldin, Horace 1873-1939 *MagIlD[port], WhThe*
Goldin, Pat 1902-1971 *WhScrn 77*
Goldina, Miriam 1898- *BiE&WWA, NotNAT, WhoHol A*
Golding, David 1913- *IntMPA 77, -75, -76, -78, -79, -80*
Golding, John *NewGrD 80*
Golding, Robin Mavesyn 1928- *IntWWM 77, -80, WhoMus 72*
Golding, William 1911- *ModWD*
Goldini, Carlo 1707-1793 *CnThe*
Goldkette, Jean 1899-1962 *BgBands 74[port], BiDAmM, CmpEPM, WhoJazz 72*
Goldman, A E O 1947- *NatPD[port]*
Goldman, Brenda Chasen *IntWWM 77*
Goldman, Edmund 1906- *IntMPA 77, -78, -79, -80*
Goldman, Edward Merrill 1917- *AmSCAP 80*
Goldman, Edwin Franko 1878-1956 *AmSCAP 66, -80, Baker 78, BiDAmM, ConAmC, NewGrD 80, NotNAT B, PopAmC[port]*
Goldman, Elliot *ConMuA 80B*
Goldman, Irving 1909- *BiE&WWA*
Goldman, James 1927- *BiE&WWA, ConDr 73, -77, FilmgC, HalFC 80, McGEWD, NotNAT*
Goldman, Les 1913- *IntMPA 77, -75, -76, -78, -79, -80*
Goldman, Marvin *IntMPA 78, -79, -80*
Goldman, Maurice 1910- *AmSCAP 66, -80*
Goldman, Michael F 1939- *IntMPA 77, -78, -79, -80*
Goldman, Michal *WomWMM B*
Goldman, Milton 1914- *BiE&WWA*
Goldman, Richard Franko 1910- *AmSCAP 66, Baker 78, ConAmC, IntWWM 77, -80*
Goldman, Robert 1932- *AmSCAP 66, -80*
Goldman, William 1931- *BiE&WWA, ConDr 73, -77A, FilmgC, HalFC 80, IntMPA 78, -79, -80, NotNAT*
Goldmann, Friedrich 1941- *NewGrD 80*
Goldmann, Helmut 1929- *IntWWM 77, -80*
Goldmann, Max *NewGrD 80*
Goldmark, Andrew G 1951- *AmSCAP 80*
Goldmark, Carl 1830-1915 *CmOp, DcCom 77, MusMk, NewGrD 80*
Goldmark, Karl 1830-1915 *Baker 78, BnBkM 80, CmpBCM, DcCom&M 79, GrComp[port], NewEOp 71, NewGrD 80, OxMus*
Goldmark, Karoly 1830-1915 *NewGrD 80*
Goldmark, Peter C *NewYTET*
Goldmark, Rubin 1872-1936 *Baker 78, BiDAmM, ConAmC, NewGrD 80, OxMus*
Goldner, Charles 1900-1955 *FilmgC, HalFC 80, NotNAT B, WhScrn 74, -77, WhThe, WhoHol B*
Goldner, Dorothy T *PupTheA*
Goldner, Nancy 1943- *CnOxB*
Goldner, Orville C *PupTheA*
Goldoni, Carlo 1707-1793 *DcPup, EncWT, Ent[port], McGEWD[port], NewEOp 71, NewGrD 80, NotNAT A, -B, OxThe, PlP&P[port], REnWD[port]*
Goldoni, Leila 1938?- *WhoHrs 80*
Goldoni, Lelia 1938?- *FilmgC, HalFC 80, WhoHol A*
Goldovsky, Boris 1908- *Baker 78, BiDAmM, IntWWM 77, -80, NewEOp 71, NewGrD 80, WhoMus 72*
Goldsand, Robert 1911- *Baker 78, NewGrD 80, WhoMus 72*
Goldsboro, Bobby 1942- *RkOn[port]*
Goldsbrough, Arnold 1892-1964 *NewGrD 80*
Goldsby, Robert 1926- *BiE&WWA, NotNAT*
Goldschmidt, Adalbert Von 1848-1906 *Baker 78, NewGrD 80*
Goldschmidt, Berthold 1903- *Baker 78, NewGrD 80, WhoMus 72*
Goldschmidt, Georg *NewGrD 80*
Goldschmidt, Gusta 1913- *WhoMus 72*
Goldschmidt, Harry 1910- *IntWWM 77, -80, NewGrD 80*
Goldschmidt, Hugo 1859-1920 *Baker 78, NewGrD 80*
Goldschmidt, Nicholas 1908- *WhoMus 72*
Goldschmidt, Otto 1829-1907 *Baker 78, NewGrD 80*
Goldschmidt, Walter 1917- *WhoOp 76*
Goldscholl, Mildred *WomWMM*
Goldscholl, Morton *WomWMM*
Goldsen, Michael H 1912- *AmSCAP 80*
Goldsholl, Millie *WomWMM B*
Goldsmith, Edward David Barnabas 1930- *WhoMus 72*
Goldsmith, Frank *Film 1*
Goldsmith, George *BiE&WWA*
Goldsmith, Jerry *ConAmC*
Goldsmith, Jerry 1929- *Baker 78, HalFC 80*
Goldsmith, Jerry 1930- *CmMov, FilmEn, FilmgC, IntMPA 77, -75, -76, -78, -79, -80, WorEFlm*

Goldsmith, Lee 1923- *AmSCAP 80, NatPD[port]*
Goldsmith, Lewis *PupTheA*
Goldsmith, Lynn *ConMuA 80B*
Goldsmith, Martin M 1913- *IntMPA 77, -75, -76, -78, -79, -80*
Goldsmith, Oliver 1728?-1774 *DcPup, McGEWD[port], NewEOp 71, NotNAT A, -B, OxMus*
Goldsmith, Oliver 1730?-1774 *CnThe, EncWT, Ent, OxThe, PlP&P[port], REnWD[port]*
Goldsmith, Owen L 1932- *ConAmC*
Goldsmith, Silvianna *WomWMM B*
Goldsmith, Ted 1909- *BiE&WWA*
Goldstein, Arnold H 1934- *AmSCAP 80*
Goldstein, Becky 1887-1971 *WhScrn 74, -77*
Goldstein, Benjamin 1944- *AmSCAP 80*
Goldstein, Bob *AmSCAP 80*
Goldstein, David M 1937- *IntMPA 77, -75, -76, -78, -79, -80*
Goldstein, Harvey 1944- *AmSCAP 80*
Goldstein, Jennie 1897-1960 *NotNAT B, WhoHol B*
Goldstein, Jerry *ConMuA 80B*
Goldstein, Kay *WomWMM B*
Goldstein, Malcolm 1936- *CpmDNM 77, -80, ConAmC, DcCM, IntWWM 77, -80*
Goldstein, Mark David 1947- *AmSCAP 80*
Goldstein, Marvin Allan 1950- *IntWWM 77*
Goldstein, Michael 1917- *IntWWM 77, -80, MusMk*
Goldstein, Mikhail 1917- *Baker 78*
Goldstein, Milton 1926- *IntMPA 77, -75, -76, -78, -79, -80*
Goldstein, Robert 1903-1974 *HalFC 80*
Goldstein, Robert Gary 1938- *AmSCAP 66*
Goldstein, William 1942- *ConAmC*
Goldstein, William S 1926- *AmSCAP 66, -80*
Goldstick, Robert J 1943- *AmSCAP 80*
Goldston, Christopher 1894-1968 *NewOrJ[port]*
Goldston, Will 1878-1948 *MagIID*
Goldstone, Anthony Keith 1944- *IntWWM 77, -80, WhoMus 72*
Goldstone, James 1931- *FilmEn, FilmgC, HalFC 80, IntMPA 77, -75, -76, -78, -79, -80*
Goldstone, Jules C 1900- *IntMPA 77, -75, -76, -78, -79, -80*
Goldstone, Richard 1912- *FilmgC, HalFC 80, IntMPA 77, -75, -76, -78, -79, -80*
Goldsworthy, William Arthur 1878- *AmSCAP 66, -80, BiDAmM, ConAmC A*
Goldthorp, Gordon Beverly 1943- *IntWWM 77*
Goldthorpe, Michael 1942- *IntWWM 77, -80*
Goldwin, John 1667?-1719 *NewGrD 80*
Goldwurm, Jean *IntMPA 77, -75, -76, -78, -79, -80*
Goldwyn, Beryl 1930- *CnOxB, DancEn 78*
Goldwyn, Sam 1884- *TwYS B*
Goldwyn, Samuel 1882-1974 *FilmEn, FilmgC, HalFC 80, OxFilm*
Goldwyn, Samuel 1884-1974 *BiDFilm, -81, DcFM, WorEFlm*
Goldwyn, Samuel, Jr. 1926- *FilmgC, HalFC 80, IntMPA 77, -75, -76, -78, -79, -80*
Golea, Antoine 1906- *NewGrD 80*
Goleizovsky, Kasian 1892-1970 *DancEn 78*
Goleizovsky, Kasyan Yaroslavovich 1892-1970 *CnOxB*
Goleminov, Marin 1908- *Baker 78, DcCM, NewGrD 80*
Golestan, Ebrahim 1923- *DcFM*
Golestan, Stan 1872-1956 *Baker 78, OxMus*
Golestan, Stan 1875-1956 *NewGrD 80*
Golikova, Tatyana Nikolaievna 1945- *CnOxB*
Golin, Guilielmo *NewGrD 80*
Golinelli, Giovanni d1884 *CnOxB*
Golinelli, Stefano 1818-1891 *NewGrD 80*
Golishev, Efim 1897-1970 *NewGrD 80*
Golishev, Jef 1897-1970 *NewGrD 80*
Golitsin, Prince Nikolay Borisovich 1794-1866 *NewGrD 80*
Golitsin, Prince Yury Nikolayevich 1823-1872 *NewGrD 80*
Golitzen, Alexander 1907- *HalFC 80, WorEFlm*
Golitzin, Nikolai 1794-1866 *Baker 78*
Golizin, Natalie *Film 2*
Goll, Gertrude *IntWWM 77, -80*
Goll, Ivan 1891-1950 *EncWT*
Goll, Yvan 1891-1950 *Ent, ModWD*
Gollahon, Gladys 1908- *AmSCAP 66, -80, ConAmC A*
Golland, John 1942- *IntWWM 77, -80*
Gollberg, Johann Gottlieb *NewGrD 80*
Gollberg, Theophile *NewGrD 80*
Gollerich, August 1859-1923 *Baker 78*
Gollings, Franklin *IntMPA 77, -75, -76, -78, -79, -80*
Gollmick, Adolf 1825-1883 *Baker 78*
Gollmick, Karl 1796-1866 *Baker 78*
Gollner, Marie-Louise 1932- *IntWWM 77, -80, NewGrD 80*
Gollner, Nana 1920- *CnOxB, DancEn 78[port]*
Gollner, Theodor 1929- *IntWWM 77, -80, NewGrD 80*
Golm, Ernest 1886-1962 *WhScrn 77*
Golm, Lisa d1964 *ForYSC, WhScrn 77*
Golonka, Arlene 1936- *BiE&WWA, NotNAT, WhoHol A*
Golos, Jerzy Stanislaw 1931- *IntWWM 80*
Golovanov, Nikolai 1891-1953 *Baker 78*
Golovanov, Nikolay Semyonovich 1891-1958 *NewGrD 80*
Golovin, Alexander Jacovlevich 1863-1930 *CnOxB*
Golovine, Alexander 1864-1930 *DancEn 78*
Golovine, Serge 1924- *CnOxB, DancEn 78*
Golovkina, Sophia Nikolaievna 1915- *CnOxB, DancEn 78*
Golovnya, Anatoli Dimitryevitch 1900- *FilmEn*
Golovnya, Anatoli N 1900- *DcFM*
Golschmann, Boris 1906-1943? *NewGrD 80*
Golschmann, Vladimir 1893-1972 *Baker 78, BiDAmM, BnBkM 80, MusSN[port], NewGrD 80*
Golson, Benny 1929- *AmSCAP 66, BiDAmM, EncJzS 70*
Golson, Florence 1891- *ConAmC*
Golstein, Marvin Allan 1950- *IntWWM 80*
Goltberg, Johann Gottlieb *NewGrD 80*
Goltberg, Theophile *NewGrD 80*
Goltermann, Georg 1824-1898 *Baker 78, NewGrD 80, OxMus*
Goltermann, Julius 1825-1876 *NewGrD 80*
Golther, Wolfgang 1863-1945 *Baker 78*
Goltz, Christel 1912- *CmOp, IntWWM 77, -80, NewGrD 80*
Golubeff, Gregory d1958 *WhScrn 74, -77, WhoHol B*
Golyscheff, Jefim 1897-1970 *Baker 78*
Golz, Rosemary 1880-1963 *WhScrn 77*
Gomarov, Mikhail *Film 2*
Gombau, Gerardo 1906- *DcCM*
Gombauld, Jean 1570-1666 *OxThe*
Gombell, Minna *ForYSC*
Gombell, Minna 1892-1973 *MovMk, WhScrn 77, WhoHol B*
Gombell, Minna 1893-1973 *FilmEn, HolCA[port], ThFT[port], WhThe*
Gombell, Minna 1900-1973 *Film 2, FilmgC, HalFC 80*
Gomberg, Harold 1916- *BnBkM 80, IntWWM 77, -80, NewGrD 80*
Gomberg, Ralph 1921- *NewGrD 80*
Gombert, Karl E 1933- *IntWWM 77, -80*
Gombert, Nicholas *OxMus*
Gombert, Nicolas 1490?-1556 *Baker 78, GrComp*
Gombert, Nicolas 1495?-1560? *NewGrD 80*
Gombert, Nicolas 1500?-1556? *BnBkM 80*
Gombosi, Otto Johannes 1902-1955 *Baker 78, NewGrD 80*
Gombrowicz, Witold 1904-1969 *CnMD, CroCD, Ent, McGEWD[port], ModWD*
Gombrowicz, Witold 1904-1970 *EncWT*
Gomes, Andre DaSilva 1752-1844 *NewGrD 80*
Gomes, Antonio Carlos 1836-1896 *Baker 78*
Gomes, Carlos 1836-1896 *NewEOp 71, NewGrD 80*
Gomes, Pietro *NewGrD 80*
Gomes Correia, Fernao *NewGrD 80*
Gomes DaRocha, Francisco *NewGrD 80*
Gomes DeAraujo, Joao 1846-1942 *Baker 78*
Gomez Calleja *Baker 78*
Gomez, Augustine Augie Whitecloud 1891-1966 *WhScrn 74, -77*
Gomez, Eddie 1944- *EncJzS 70*
Gomez, Edgar 1944- *BiDAmM, EncJzS 70*
Gomez, Inez *Film 2*
Gomez, Jill 1942- *CmOp, NewGrD 80*
Gomez, Julio 1886-1973 *Baker 78*
Gomez, Pietro *NewGrD 80*
Gomez, Ralph 1897-1954 *WhScrn 74, -77*
Gomez, Richard 1950- *AmSCAP 80*
Gomez, Thomas 1905-1971 *BiE&WWA, CmMov, FilmEn, FilmgC, ForYSC, HalFC 80, HolCA[port], MovMk, NotNAT B, Vers A[port], WhScrn 74, -77, WhoHol B*
Gomez, Tomas d1688 *NewGrD 80*
Gomez, Urbano 1926- *AmSCAP 80*
Gomez, Vicente 1911- *AmSCAP 66, -80, ConAmC A*
Gomez, Victor E 1930- *IntWWM 77, -80*
Gomez, William Arthur 1939- *IntWWM 77, -80, WhoMus 72*
Gomez Camargo, Miguel 1618-1690 *NewGrD 80*
Gomez Carrillo, Manuel 1883-1968 *NewGrD 80*
Gomez DeAvellaneda, Gertrudis 1814-1873 *CnThe, REnWD[port]*
Gomez DeHerrera, Martin *NewGrD 80*
Gomez Garcia, Domingo Julio 1886-1973 *NewGrD 80*
Gomez Martinez, Miguel Angel 1949- *IntWWM 80, WhoOp 76*
Gomez-Quinones, Ronda *WomWMM*
Gomezanda, Antonio 1894- *Baker 78*
Gomidas *NewGrD 80*
Gomis Y Colomer, Jose Melchor 1791-1836 *NewGrD 80*
Gomm, Elizabeth 1951- *IntWWM 77, -80*
Gomolka, Michal 1564-1609 *Baker 78*
Gomolka, Mikolaj 1535?-1609? *Baker 78, NewGrD 80*
Gomolka, Nicolas 1539?-1609 *OxMus*
Gomorov, G *Film 2*
Gomorov, Mikhail *Film 2*
Goncalez, Jose Bernal *NewGrD 80*
Goncharov, George 1904-1954 *CnOxB*
Goncharov, Vasili M d1915 *FilmEn*
Goncharova, Nathalia Sergeievna 1881-1962 *CnOxB*
Goncharova, Nathalie 1881-1962 *OxThe*
Goncourt, Edmond-Louis-Antoine Huot De 1822-1896 *EncWT, Ent, NotNAT B, OxThe*
Goncourt, Jules-Alfred Huot De 1830-1870 *EncWT, NotNAT B, OxThe*
Goncourt, Jules De 1830-1870 *Ent*
Gonda, Janos 1932- *IntWWM 77, -80*
Gonder, Bill *Film 2*
Gondi, Harry 1900-1968 *WhScrn 74, -77*
Gondimel, Claude *Baker 78*
Gone All-Stars, The *RkOn[port]*
Goneke, John F 1790?-1844? *BiDAmM*
Gonella, Giuseppe 1666-1745 *NewGrD 80*
Gonella, Nat 1908- *CmpEPM*
Gonelli, Giuseppe 1666-1745 *NewGrD 80*
Gonet, Tadeusz 1903- *IntWWM 77*
Gonet, Valerien d1613 *NewGrD 80*
Gong *ConMuA 80A, IlEncR*
Gonga, Dawillie *AmSCAP 80*
Gonima, Manuel 1712?-1793? *NewGrD 80*
Gonoty *PupTheA*
Gonsalves, John P 1925- *AmSCAP 66*
Gonsalves, Mex 1920-1974 *EncJzS 70*
Gonsalves, Paul 1920-1974 *BiDAmM, CmpEPM, EncJzS 70, IlEncJ*
Gonsky, Larry E 1949- *AmSCAP 80*
Gonsoulin, Tommy 1910- *NewOrJ*
Gonta, Leonid 1918- *DancEn 78*
Gontcharova, Nathalie 1881-1962 *DancEn 78*
Gontier De Soignies *NewGrD 80*
Gontijo, Flavio 1948- *IntWWM 77, -80*
Gonzaga *NewGrD 80*
Gonzaga, Ferdinando d1626 *NewGrD 80*
Gonzaga, Francesco 1590-1628 *NewGrD 80*
Gonzaga, Gianfrancesco d1444 *NewGrD 80*
Gonzaga, Guglielmo 1538-1587 *NewGrD 80*
Gonzales, Babs 1919- *EncJzS 70*
Gonzales, Gilberto d1954 *WhoHol B*
Gonzales, Guillermo Jose 1892-1971 *BiDAmM*
Gonzales, Jimmy d1971 *WhoHol B*
Gonzales, Mark *Film 2*
Gonzales, Myrtle *Film 1*
Gonzales, Ofelia 1953- *CnOxB*
Gonzales-Gonzales, Pedro 1926- *ForYSC*
Gonzalez *NewGrD 80*

Gonzalez, Aaron Ruben 1908- *AmSCAP 66, -80*
Gonzalez, Carmen Pagliaro 1939- *WhoOp 76*
Gonzalez, Dalmacio 1946- *IntWWM 80*
Gonzalez, Dominique *NewGrD 80*
Gonzalez, Gilberto 1906-1954 *WhScrn 74, -77*
Gonzalez, Gloria *NatPD[port]*
Gonzalez, Lily 1924- *AmSCAP 80*
Gonzalez, Luis Jorge 1936- *ConAmC*
Gonzalez, Manuel 1944- *WhoOp 76*
Gonzalez, Manuel B *ConAmC*
Gonzalez, Mario Tecero 1919-1957 *WhScrn 74, -77*
Gonzalez, Myrtle 1891-1918 *WhScrn 77*
Gonzalez, Nilda 1929- *BiE&WWA*
Gonzalez, Victor 1877-1956 *NewGrD 80*
Gonzalez Acilu, Agustin 1929- *NewGrD 80*
Gonzalez-Avila, Jorge 1925- *Baker 78*
Gonzalez Barron, Ramon 1897- *NewGrD 80*
Gonzalez Garcia, Pablo 1932- *IntWWM 80*
Gonzalez-Gonzales, Pedro 1926- *WhoHol A*
Gonzalez-Gonzalez, Pedro 1926- *IntMPA 77, -75, -76, -78, -79, -80*
Gonzalez-Zuleta, Fabio 1920- *Baker 78, IntWWM 77, -80, NewGrD 80*
Gonzalo, Gisela Hernandez *DcCM, NewGrD 80*
Gonzalo, Maria Eduarda 1929-1955 *WhScrn 74, -77*
Gooch, Silas N *CreCan 2*
Gooch, Steve 1945- *ConDr 77*
Goochison, Professor *PupTheA*
Good, Anny Ida 1920- *IntWWM 77, -80*
Good, Dolly 1915-1967 *BiDAmM*
Good, Florence Elizabeth *WhoMus 72*
Good, Jack *MorBAP*
Good, Kip 1919-1964 *NotNAT B, WhScrn 74, -77, WhoHol B*
Good, Margaret *WhoMus 72*
Good, Millie 1913- *BiDAmM*
Good, Ronald 1910- *IntWWM 77, -80, WhoMus 72*
Good, William Sidney 1935- *IntWWM 77*
Good Rockin' Charles *BluesWW[port]*
Good Rocking Sam *BluesWW[port]*
Goodale, Elois *Film 2*
Goodale, Ezekiel 1780- *BiDAmM*
Goodale, George P d1920 *NotNAT B*
Goodall, Charlotte d1830 *NotNAT B*
Goodall, Edyth 1886-1929 *NotNAT B, WhThe*
Goodall, Grace *Film 2*
Goodall, Reginald 1905- *Baker 78, CmOp, NewGrD 80, WhoMus 72, WhoOp 76*
Goodbody, Slim *AmSCAP 80*
Goodchild, Arthur 1899- *WhoMus 72*
Goode, Daniel 1936- *ConAmC, IntWWM 77, -80*
Goode, Jack 1908-1971 *BiDAmM, WhScrn 74, -77, WhoHol B*
Goode, Jack C 1921- *ConAmC*
Goode, Richard 1943- *NewGrD 80*
Goode, Richard L 1922- *IntMPA 77, -75, -76*
Goode, Russell Carlton 1926- *IntWWM 77*
Gooden, Rola Eddins 1908- *IntWWM 77*
Goodenough, Forrest 1918- *ConAmC*
Goodfried, Robert *IntMPA 77, -75, -76, -78, -79, -80*
Goodfriend, James 1932- *IntWWM 80*
Goodge, Arthur 1914- *WhoMus 72*
Goodgroome, John 1630?-1704 *NewGrD 80*
Goodhart, Al 1905-1955 *AmSCAP 66, -80, CmpEPM*
Goodhart, William *NotNAT*
Gooding, Cynthia 1924- *BiDAmM, EncFCWM 69*
Goodis, Jay 1931- *AmSCAP 66, -80*
Goodison, Benjamin 1736- *NewGrD 80*
Goodkind, Herbert Knowlton 1905- *IntWWM 77, -80*
Goodlett, Robert Vincent, II 1949- *IntWWM 77*
Goodliffe *MagIlD[port]*
Goodliffe, Michael 1914-1976 *FilmgC, HalFC 80, WhoHol C, WhoThe 72, -77*
Goodloe, Robert D 1936- *WhoOp 76*
Goodman, A Harold 1924- *IntWWM 77, -80*
Goodman, Abe I *IntMPA 77, -75, -76, -78, -79, -80*
Goodman, Ailene Sybil 1929- *AmSCAP 80*
Goodman, Al 1890-1972 *CmpEPM, ConAmC*
Goodman, Alfred 1890-1972 *BiDAmM*
Goodman, Alfred 1920- *Baker 78, ConAmC, NewGrD 80*
Goodman, Alfred Grant 1890-1972 *AmSCAP 66, -80, BiE&WWA*
Goodman, Alfred Grant 1920- *IntWWM 77, -80, WhoMus 72*
Goodman, Benjamin David 1909- *BiDAmM, EncJzS 70, NewGrD 80[port]*
Goodman, Benny 1909- *AmPS B, AmSCAP 66, -80, Baker 78, BgBands 74[port], BnBkM 80, CmpEPM, EncJzS 70, FilmgC, HalFC 80, IlEncJ, MnPM[port], MusMk[port], NewGrD 80[port], WhoHol A, WhoJazz 72*
Goodman, Bernard Maurice 1914- *IntWWM 77, -80*
Goodman, Cardell 1649?-1699 *OxThe*
Goodman, Cardell 1653-1713? *NotNAT A*
Goodman, Cardonnel 1649?-1699 *OxThe*
Goodman, David Zelag *HalFC 80*
Goodman, Dickie 1934- *RkOn*
Goodman, Dody *BiE&WWA, NotNAT, WhoHol A, WhoThe 72, -77*
Goodman, Edward d1962 *NotNAT B, PlP&P*
Goodman, Erika 1947- *CnOxB*
Goodman, Frank 1894-1958 *AmSCAP 66*
Goodman, Frank 1916- *BiE&WWA*
Goodman, Harry 1906?- *CmpEPM*
Goodman, Irving 1914- *CmpEPM*
Goodman, Isador 1909- *NewGrD 80*
Goodman, John *ConAmC*
Goodman, John B 1901- *CmMov, IntMPA 77, -75, -76, -78, -79, -80*
Goodman, Joseph Magnus 1918- *AmSCAP 80, CpmDNM 77, ConAmC*
Goodman, Jules Eckert 1876-1962 *McGEWD, NotNAT B, WhThe*
Goodman, Julian 1922- *IntMPA 77, -75, -76, -78, -79, -80, NewYTET*
Goodman, Lillian Rosedale 1887- *AmSCAP 66, -80*
Goodman, Mark D 1880- *AmSCAP 66*
Goodman, Mary Sheena 1923- *WhoMus 72*
Goodman, Maurice, Jr. 1921- *AmSCAP 66, -80*
Goodman, Mort 1910- *IntMPA 77, -75, -76, -78, -79, -80*
Goodman, Murray 1911- *IntMPA 77, -75, -76, -78, -79, -80*
Goodman, Paul 1911-1972 *ConDr 73*
Goodman, Pearlyn *WomWMM B*
Goodman, Peter 1921- *WhoMus 72*
Goodman, Philip d1940 *NotNAT B, WhThe*
Goodman, Randolph 1908- *BiE&WWA, NotNAT*
Goodman, Richard John 1944- *AmSCAP 80*
Goodman, Saul 1906- *AmSCAP 66, -80, CpmDNM 79, ConAmC*
Goodman, Steve 1948- *AmSCAP 80, ConMuA 80A, IlEncR*
Goodman, Wallace Richard 1942- *IntWWM 77, -80*
Goodman, Walter Terence 1916- *WhoMus 72*
Goodner, Carol 1904- *BiE&WWA, IlWWBF, NotNAT, WhThe, WhoHol A*
Goodrich, Alfred John 1847-1920 *BiDAmM*
Goodrich, Alfred John 1848-1920 *Baker 78*
Goodrich, Amy 1889-1939 *WhScrn 74, -77*
Goodrich, Arthur 1878-1941 *NotNAT B, WhThe*
Goodrich, Charles W 1861-1931 *WhScrn 74, -77*
Goodrich, Diane *WomWMM B*
Goodrich, Ebenezer 1780?-1841 *BiDAmM*
Goodrich, Edna 1883- *Film 1, WhThe, WhoStg 1906, -1908*
Goodrich, Edna 1883-1971 *WhScrn 77*
Goodrich, Edna 1883-1974 *WhoHol B*
Goodrich, Frances *BiE&WWA, NotNAT*
Goodrich, Frances 1891- *FilmEn, McGEWD, WomWMM, WorEFlm*
Goodrich, Frances 1896- *CmMov*
Goodrich, Frances 1901- *FilmgC, HalFC 80*
Goodrich, G W d1931 *WhoHol B*
Goodrich, Jack *Film 2*
Goodrich, John Wallace 1871-1952 *BiDAmM*
Goodrich, Katherine *Film 1*
Goodrich, Louis 1865-1945 *NotNAT B, WhScrn 74, -77, WhThe, WhoHol B*
Goodrich, Wallace 1871-1952 *Baker 78, ConAmC*
Goodrich, William Marcellus 1777-1833 *BiDAmM, NewGrD 80*
Goodsell, Alice *Film 2*
Goodsell, G Dean 1907- *BiE&WWA*
Goodsmith, Ruth B 1892- *ConAmC*
Goodson, Katharine 1872-1958 *Baker 78*
Goodson, Mark 1915- *IntMPA 77, -78, -79, -80*
Goodson, Richard 1655?-1718 *NewGrD 80*
Goodson, Sadie 1900?- *NewOrJ*
Goodwin, Aline *Film 2*
Goodwin, Andrew John 1947- *IntWWM 77, -80*
Goodwin, Bernard 1907- *IntMPA 77, -75, -76, -78, -79, -80*
Goodwin, Bill 1910-1958 *FilmEn, FilmgC, HalFC 80, MotPP, WhScrn 74, -77*
Goodwin, Bill 1910-1959 *ForYSC, WhoHol B*
Goodwin, Bill 1942- *EncJzS 70*
Goodwin, Charles Douglas 1929- *AmSCAP 66, -80*
Goodwin, Ewart 1907- *BiE&WWA*
Goodwin, Gordon 1941- *ConAmC*
Goodwin, Harold *WhoHol A*
Goodwin, Harold 1902- *Film 1, -2, ForYSC, TwYS, Vers B[port]*
Goodwin, Harold 1917- *FilmgC, HalFC 80*
Goodwin, Henry Clay 1907- *WhoJazz 72*
Goodwin, J Cheever 1850- *WhThe, WhoStg 1906, -1908*
Goodwin, J Cheever 1856-1912 *BiDAmM*
Goodwin, Jim *WhoHol A*
Goodwin, Joe 1889-1943 *AmSCAP 66, -80, CmpEPM*
Goodwin, John 1921- *WhoThe 72, -77*
Goodwin, Nat C 1857-1919 *NotNAT A, -B, OxThe, WhScrn 77, WhThe*
Goodwin, Nat C 1857-1920 *WhScrn 74, WhoHol B*
Goodwin, Nat C 1859-1919 *Film 1*
Goodwin, Nathaniel Carl, Jr. 1857-1919 *FamA&A[port], WhoStg 1906, -1908*
Goodwin, Noel 1927- *CnOxB, NewGrD 80, WhoMus 72*
Goodwin, Peter Anthony 1945- *IntWWM 80*
Goodwin, Reginald Brian 1924- *WhoMus 72*
Goodwin, Richard 1934- *IntMPA 80*
Goodwin, Robert L *DrBlPA*
Goodwin, Rom *Film 1*
Goodwin, Ron *CmMov, FilmEn, FilmgC, RkOn*
Goodwin, Ron 1930?- *HalFC 80*
Goodwin, Ronald *IntMPA 77, -75, -76, -78, -79, -80*
Goodwin, Ronald Alfred 1925- *WhoMus 72*
Goodwin, Ruby Berkley d1961 *WhScrn 74, -77, WhoHol B*
Goodwin, Tom *Film 2*
Goodwin, Walter 1889- *AmSCAP 66, -80*
Goodwin, William R 1942- *BiDAmM, EncJzS 70*
Goodwins, Ercell Woods *WhScrn 74, -77*
Goodwins, Fred *Film 1, -2*
Goodwins, Fred 1891- *IlWWBF*
Goodwins, Leslie 1899-1969 *FilmEn, FilmgC, HalFC 80, WhScrn 74, -77, WhoHol B*
Goodwyn, Zoe *WhoMus 72*
Googe, Barnabe 1540-1594 *OxMus*
Goold, Sam 1893-1931 *AmSCAP 66, -80*
Goolden, Richard 1891- *WhoThe 77*
Goolden, Richard 1895- *FilmgC, HalFC 80, WhoThe 72*
Goorhuis, Rob 1948- *IntWWM 77, -80*
Goosen, Frederic 1927- *ConAmC*
Goossen, Frederic 1927- *CpmDNM 75*
Goossen, Jacob Frederic 1927- *IntWWM 77, -80*
Goossens *CmOp, NewGrD 80*
Goossens, Adolphe d1916 *OxMus*
Goossens, Eugene 1845-1906 *CmOp, NewGrD 80, OxMus*
Goossens, Eugene 1867-1958 *CmOp, NewGrD 80, OxMus*
Goossens, Eugene 1893-1962 *OxMus*
Goossens, Sir Eugene 1892-1962 *CmOp*
Goossens, Sir Eugene 1893-1962 *Baker 78, BnBkM 80, DcCM, MusMk, MusSN[port], NewEOp 71, NewGrD 80[port], NotNAT B*

Goossens, Jehan d1581 NewGrD 80
Goossens, Leon OxMus
Goossens, Leon 1897- Baker 78, BnBkM 80, NewGrD 80[port], WhoMus 72
Goossens, Marie Henriette 1894- IntWWM 77, -80, NewGrD 80[port], OxMus, WhoMus 72
Goossens, Sidonie 1899- IntWWM 77, -80, NewGrD 80[port], OxMus, WhoMus 72
Goovaerts, Alphonse Jean Marie Andre 1847-1922 Baker 78, NewGrD 80
Gooyer, Rijk De FilmAG WE
Gopal, Ram 1917- WhThe
Gopal, Ram 1920- CnOxB, DancEn 78
Gopo, Ion Popescu DcFM
Goraczkiewicz, Wincenty 1789-1858 NewGrD 80
Goralski, Robert NewYTET
Goransson, Harald 1917- IntWWM 77, -80
Gorbig, Johann Anton 1684?-1737 NewGrD 80
Gorcey, Bernard 1888-1955 Film 2, FilmgC, ForYSC, HalFC 80, NotNAT B, Vers B[port], WhScrn 74, -77, WhoHol B, WhoHrs 80
Gorcey, David ForYSC
Gorcey, Leo 1915-1969 FilmEn, FilmgC, ForYSC, HalFC 80, MotPP, MovMk[port], WhScrn 74, -77, WhoHol B, WhoHrs 80[port]
Gorcey, Leo 1917-1969 JoeFr[port], What 2[port]
Gorchakov, Nicolai Mikhailovich 1899-1958 OxThe
Gorczycki, Gregor Gervasius 1664?-1734 Baker 78
Gorczycki, Grzegorz 1664?-1734 MusMk
Gorczycki, Grzegorz Gerwazy 1667?-1734 NewGrD 80
Gorczyn, Alexander OxMus
Gorczyn, Jan Aleksander 1618-1694? NewGrD 80
Gordeli, Otar 1928- Baker 78
Gordell, Evan ConAmC
Gordet, Allen 1905?-1954 NewOrJ
Gordeyev, Vatcheslav 1948- CnOxB
Gordigiani, Giovanni Battista 1795-1871 NewGrD 80
Gordigiani, Luigi 1806-1860 Baker 78
Gordin, Jacob 1853-1909 CnThe, McGEWD, ModWD, NotNAT B, OxThe, REnWD[port]
Gordon, A George 1882-1953 WhScrn 74, -77
Gordon, Adoniram Judson 1836-1895 BiDAmM
Gordon, Alen 1932- AmSCAP 66
Gordon, Alex 1922- IntMPA 77, -75, -76, -78, -79, -80
Gordon, Alex 1925?- WhoHrs 80
Gordon, Alexander 1692?-1755? NewGrD 80
Gordon, Arthur Arnold 1928- AmSCAP 80
Gordon, Barbara WomWMM B
Gordon, Barry RkOn
Gordon, Barry 1948- BiE&WWA
Gordon, Beatrice Mary June WhoMus 72
Gordon, Ben 1912- AmSCAP 80
Gordon, Bert 1898-1974 WhScrn 77, WhoHol B
Gordon, Bert 1900- JoeFr[port]
Gordon, Bert I 1922- FilmEn, FilmgC, HalFC 80, IntMPA 77, -75, -76, -78, -79, -80, WhoHrs 80
Gordon, Bette WomWMM B
Gordon, Betty Film 2
Gordon, Bob AmSCAP 80
Gordon, Bob 1928-1955 CmpEPM
Gordon, Bobby 1904-1973 WhScrn 77
Gordon, Bobby 1913- Film 2
Gordon, Bruce TwYS, WhoHol A
Gordon, Bruce 1916- BiE&WWA, ForYSC, NotNAT
Gordon, Bruce 1919- Film 2, FilmgC, HalFC 80
Gordon, C Henry d1940 MotPP, WhoHol B
Gordon, C Henry 1874-1940 MovMk[port]
Gordon, C Henry 1882-1940 HalFC 80
Gordon, C Henry 1883-1940 FilmEn, WhScrn 74, -77
Gordon, C Henry 1884-1940 FilmgC, ForYSC, Vers A[port]
Gordon, Carl 1932- DrBlPA
Gordon, Charles BlkAmP, Film 2
Gordon, Charles Kilbourn 1888- WhThe
Gordon, Charles William CreCan 1
Gordon, Clarke WhoHol A
Gordon, Colin 1911-1972 FilmgC, HalFC 80, WhScrn 77, WhThe, WhoHol B, WhoThe 72
Gordon, Constance Kitty 1888-1974 WhScrn 77
Gordon, Dane R 1925- AmSCAP 80
Gordon, Daniel WhoHol A
Gordon, David CmpGMD
Gordon, David Alex 1933- IntWWM 77, -80
Gordon, David Marvin 1908- AmSCAP 80
Gordon, Dexter 1923- BiDAmM, CmpEPM, EncJzS 70, IlEncJ
Gordon, Don WhoHol A
Gordon, Dorothy Film 2, WhoHol A
Gordon, Douglas WhoHol A
Gordon, Douglas 1871-1935 NotNAT B, WhThe
Gordon, Mrs. E S PupTheA
Gordon, Edward R 1886-1938 WhScrn 74, -77, WhoHol B
Gordon, Eva Film 2
Gordon, Frank John 1945- AmSCAP 80
Gordon, G Swayne 1880-1949 NotNAT B, WhScrn 74, -77
Gordon, Gale 1905- HalFC 80
Gordon, Gale 1906- FilmgC, ForYSC, IntMPA 77, -75, -76, -78, -79, -80, MovMk[port], WhoHol A
Gordon, Gavin 1901-1970 Baker 78, Film 2, FilmgC, ForYSC, HalFC 80, NotNAT B, WhScrn 74, -77, WhThe, WhoHol B
Gordon, George Angier 1853-1929 BiDAmM
Gordon, George Lash d1895 NotNAT B
Gordon, Gloria d1962 NotNAT B, WhScrn 74, -77, WhoHol B
Gordon, Grace Film 2
Gordon, Grant WhoHol A
Gordon, Gray BgBands 74, CmpEPM
Gordon, Hal 1894-1946 FilmgC, HalFC 80, WhoHol B
Gordon, Hal 1910- AmSCAP 66, -80
Gordon, Harold 1919-1959 WhScrn 74, -77, WhoHol B
Gordon, Harris 1887-1947 Film 2, WhScrn 74, -77, WhoHol B
Gordon, Hayes 1920- BiE&WWA, WhoThe 77
Gordon, Hortense 1887-1961 CreCan 2
Gordon, Huntley 1897-1956 Film 1, ForYSC, MotPP, MovMk, NotNAT B, TwYS, WhoHol B
Gordon, Huntly 1897-1956 Film 2, WhScrn 74, -77
Gordon, Ida 1905- WhoMus 72
Gordon, Irving 1915- AmSCAP 66, -80
Gordon, Jack 1929- IntMPA 80
Gordon, Jacques 1899-1948 Baker 78
Gordon, James 1881-1941 Film 2, WhScrn 74, -77, WhoHol B
Gordon, James Carel Gerhard 1791-1845? Baker 78
Gordon, James M d1944 NotNAT B
Gordon, Jerry Lee 1938- IntWWM 77, -80
Gordon, Joan Film 2
Gordon, John AmSCAP 80
Gordon, Joseph Henry 1928-1963 BiDAmM
Gordon, Julia Swayne 1879-1933 FilmEn, Film 1, -2, ForYSC, TwYS, WhScrn 74, -77, WhoHol B
Gordon, Kay Film 2
Gordon, Kelly L 1932- AmSCAP 80
Gordon, Ken BlkAmP
Gordon, Kitty 1870- Film 1, TwYS
Gordon, Kitty 1877?-1974 CmpEPM
Gordon, Kitty 1878-1974 WhThe, WhoHol B
Gordon, Leo 1922- FilmEn, FilmgC, ForYSC, HalFC 80, HolCA[port], WhoHol A, WhoHrs 80
Gordon, Leon 1884-1960 WhThe
Gordon, Leon 1895-1960 NotNAT B, WhoHol B
Gordon, Lois Jackson 1932- IntWWM 77
Gordon, Louis B ConAmC
Gordon, Mack 1904-1959 AmPS, AmSCAP 66, -80, BiDAmM, CmpEPM, NotNAT B, Sw&Ld C, WhoHol B
Gordon, Marjorie 1893- WhThe
Gordon, Mary d1963 MotPP, WhoHol B
Gordon, Mary 1881-1963 Film 2, ForYSC
Gordon, Mary 1882-1963 FilmEn, FilmgC, HalFC 80, HolCA[port], MovMk[port], ThFT[port], Vers B[port], WhScrn 74, -77, WhoHrs 80
Gordon, Maud Turner 1868-1940 WhScrn 77
Gordon, Maude Turner 1870- Film 1, -2, TwYS
Gordon, Max 1892- BiE&WWA, EncMT, NotNAT, -A, What 3[port], WhThe
Gordon, Michael 1909- BiDFilm, -81, BiE&WWA, FilmEn, FilmgC, HalFC 80, IntMPA 77, -75, -76, -78, -79, -80, MovMk[port], NotNAT, WorEFlm
Gordon, Michael James 1928- WhoMus 72
Gordon, Nathan IntWWM 77, -80
Gordon, Noele 1923- WhThe
Gordon, Nora 1894-1970 WhScrn 74, -77, WhoHol B
Gordon, Odetta Holmes Felious 1930- AmSCAP 80, BluesWW[port]
Gordon, Paul 1886-1929 NotNAT B, WhScrn 77
Gordon, Pete Film 2
Gordon, Peter 1888-1943 WhScrn 74, -77
Gordon, Peter Jon 1946- IntWWM 77, -80
Gordon, Peter Laurence 1951- ConAmC
Gordon, Philip 1894- AmSCAP 66, -80, CpmDNM 80, ConAmC
Gordon, Richard 1925- IntMPA 77, -75, -76, -78, -79, -80
Gordon, Richard H 1893-1956 WhScrn 74, -77, WhoHol B
Gordon, Robert NatPD[port], OxMus
Gordon, Robert 1895-1971 FilmEn, Film 1, -2, TwYS, WhScrn 74, -77, WhoHol B
Gordon, Robert Cameron 1941- AmSCAP 66, -80
Gordon, Robert J 1911- AmSCAP 66, -80
Gordon, Roy Turner Film 2
Gordon, Ruth 1896- BiDFilm 81, BiE&WWA, CnThe, EncWT, Ent, FilmEn, Film 1, FilmgC, ForYSC, HalFC 80, IntMPA 77, -75, -76, -78, -79, -80, MotPP, MovMk[port], NatPD[port], NotNAT, -A, OxFilm, PlP&P, WhoHol A, WhoHrs 80, WhoThe 72, -77, WomWMM, WorEFlm
Gordon, Ruth L 1913- AmSCAP 80
Gordon, Sadie Film 2
Gordon, Shep ConMuA 80B
Gordon, Slim BluesWW[port]
Gordon, Stewart Lynell 1930- IntWWM 77, -80
Gordon, Vera 1886-1948 FilmEn, Film 2, ForYSC, MovMk, NotNAT B, TwYS, WhScrn 74, -77, WhoHol B
Gordon, Walter d1892 NotNAT B
Gordon, William Marvin 1947- AmSCAP 80
Gordon-Lee, Kathleen WhThe
Gordon-Lennox, Cosmo 1869-1921 NotNAT B, WhThe
Gordon Woodhouse, Violet 1872-1948 NewGrD 80
Gordone, Charles MorBAP, PlP&P, WhoHol A
Gordone, Charles 1925- BlkAmP, ConDr 73, -77, DcLB 7[port], DrBlPA, McGEWD, NotNAT
Gordone, Charles Edward 1927- WhoThe 77
Gordoni, Arthur Film 2
Gordy, Berry, Jr. 1929- AmSCAP 80, DrBlPA, IntMPA 77, -78, -79, -80
Gordy, Berry Jr. 1929- ConMuA 80B
Gore, Altovise 1935- DrBlPA
Gore, Catherine d1861 NotNAT B
Gore, Charlie Mansfield 1930- BiDAmM
Gore, Lesley 1946- AmPS A, BiDAmM, ConMuA 80A, RkOn[port], WhoHol A
Gore, Richard Taylor 1908- ConAmC, IntWWM 77
Gore, Rosa 1867-1941 Film 2, WhScrn 74, -77, WhoHol B
Gore, Walter 1910- CnOxB, DancEn 78
Gore-Browne, Robert 1893- WhThe
Gorecki, Henryk Mikolaj 1933- Baker 78, NewGrD 80[port], OxMus
Gorelik, Mordecai 1899- BiE&WWA, EncWT, NotNAT, PlP&P, WhoThe 72, -77
Gorelli, Olga 1920- ConAmC
Goren, Eli Alexander 1923- IntWWM 77, -80,

NewGrD 80, WhoMus 72
Goretta, Claude 1929- *FilmEn*
Goretti, Antonio 1570?-1649 *NewGrD 80*
Gorgeous George 1915-1963 *NewYTET, WhScrn 74, -77, WhoHol B*
Gorgeous Weed *BluesWW[port]*
Gorger Saint Jorgen, Anna Maria Von *NewGrD 80*
Gorgey, Gabor 1929- *CroCD*
Gorham, Charles *Film 2*
Gorham, Kathleen 1932- *CnOxB, DancEn 78*
Gorham, William Walter 1946- *IntWWM 77*
Goria, Alexandre Edouard 1823-1860 *NewGrD 80*
Gorin, Igor 1908- *AmSCAP 66, -80, Baker 78, ConAmC*
Goring, Marius 1912- *CnThe, EncWT, FilmEn, FilmgC, ForYSC, HalFC 80, IlWWBF, IntMPA 77, -75, -76, -78, -79, -80, MotPP, MovMk, PlP&P, WhoHol A, WhoThe 72, -77*
Gorini, Gino 1914- *Baker 78, NewGrD 80*
Gorini, Luigino 1914- *NewGrD 80*
Goritz, Otto 1873-1929 *Baker 78*
Gorki, Maxim 1868-1936 *CnMD, NotNAT A, -B, PlP&P[port], -A[port]*
Gorky, Maxim 1868-1936 *CnThe, EncWT, Ent, FilmgC, HalFC 80, McGEWD[port], ModWD, NewEOp 71, OxFilm, OxThe, REnWD[port]*
Gorl *NewGrD 80*
Gorley, Edward *Film 2*
Gorlier, Simon *NewGrD 80*
Gorman, Bill *Film 2*
Gorman, Buddy *ForYSC*
Gorman, Charles *Film 2*
Gorman, Cliff 1936- *FilmEn, HalFC 80, NotNAT, WhoHol A, WhoThe 77*
Gorman, Eric 1886-1971 *WhScrn 74, -77, WhoHol B*
Gorman, Frederick C 1939- *AmSCAP 80*
Gorman, Israel 1895-1965 *NewOrJ[port]*
Gorman, Kenneth F *IntMPA 80*
Gorman, Patrick E 1892- *AmSCAP 66, -80*
Gorman, Robert Lee 1928- *AmSCAP 80*
Gorman, Ross 1890?-1953 *CmpEPM*
Gorman, Stephanie 1949-1965 *WhScrn 77*
Gorman, Tom 1908-1971 *WhScrn 74, -77, WhoHol B*
Gorme, Eydie 1931- *AmPS B, AmSCAP 80, BiDAmM, RkOn[port]*
Gorner, Hans-Georg 1908- *IntWWM 77, -80, NewGrD 80*
Gorner, Johann Gottlieb 1697-1778 *NewGrD 80*
Gorner, Johann Valentin 1702-1762 *NewGrD 80*
Gorney, Jay 1896- *AmPS, AmSCAP 66, -80, Baker 78, BiDAmM, BiE&WWA, CmpEPM, NewCBMT, NotNAT, PopAmC[port]*
Gorney, Karen *HalFC 80, WhoHol A*
Gorno, Albino 1859-1944 *BiDAmM*
Gorno, Albino 1859-1945 *Baker 78*
Gorno, Romeo 1870-1931 *Baker 78*
Gorodnitzki, Sascha 1905- *Baker 78*
Gorody, George 1914- *AmSCAP 66, -80*
Gorog, Laszlo 1903- *IntMPA 77, -75, -76, -78, -79, -80*
Gorovets, Emil 1926- *AmSCAP 80*
Gorr, Rita 1926- *CmOp, IntWWM 77, -80, NewGrD 80, WhoMus 72*
Gorrie, Alan E 1946- *AmSCAP 80*
Gorshin, Frank 1935- *FilmgC, ForYSC, HalFC 80, JoeFr[port], WhoHol A, WhoHrs 80[port]*
Gorski, Paul S 1941- *IntWWM 77, -80*
Gorski, Wladyslaw 1846-1915 *NewGrD 80*
Gorsky, Alexander Alexeievich 1871-1924 *CnOxB, DancEn 78, NewGrD 80*
Gorss, Saul M 1908-1966 *WhScrn 74, -77, WhoHol B*
Gorsse, Henry De 1868- *WhThe*
Gorter, Albert 1862-1936 *Baker 78*
Gortikov, Stan *ConMuA 80B*
Gortner, Marjoe 1941- *HalFC 80, IntMPA 80, WhoHol A*
Gorton, James Allen 1947- *IntWWM 80*
Gorton, Thomas Arthur 1910- *IntWWM 77, -80, WhoMus 72*
Gorton, William d1712 *NewGrD 80*
Gortva, Iren 1939- *IntWWM 80*
Gorvin, Carl 1912- *IntWWM 77, -80*
Gorvin, Joana Maria 1922- *EncWT*
Gorzanis, Giacomo 1520?-1579? *NewGrD 80*
Gorzanis, Jacomo 1520?-1579? *NewGrD 80*
Gorzycki, Grzegorz Gerwazy *NewGrD 80*
Gorzynski, Zdzislaw 1895- *IntWWM 77, -80*
Gorzzyski, Grzegorz Gerwazy *NewGrD 80*
Gosa, Maistre *NewGrD 80*
Goscalch *NewGrD 80*
Gosden, Freeman F 1896-1976 *NewYTET, WhoHol A*
Gosden, Freeman F 1899-1976 *JoeFr*
Gose, Bartholomaus *NewGrD 80*
Gosek, Stanley Leo 1949- *IntWWM 77*
Gosfield, Maurice 1913-1964 *WhScrn 74, -77, WhoHol B*
Gosford, Alice Peckham 1886-1919 *WhScrn 77*
Gosh, Bobby 1936- *AmSCAP 80*
Goshman, Al *MagIlD*
Gosho, Heinosuke 1901- *FilmgC, HalFC 80*
Gosho, Heinosuke 1902- *BiDFilm, -81, DcFM, FilmEn, OxFilm, WorEFlm*
Goshorn, Lawrence Jay 1947- *AmSCAP 80*
Goslar, Lotte *CnOxB, DancEn 78*
Goslenus *NewGrD 80*
Goslich, Siegfried 1911- *IntWWM 77, -80, NewGrD 80*
Gosling, Harold 1897- *WhThe*
Gosling, Nigel *CnOxB, DancEn 78*
Gosnell, Evelyn 1896-1947 *Film 2, WhScrn 77*
Gospel Minnie *BluesWW[port]*
Gospel Singing Caravan *BiDAmM*
Goss, Bartholomaus *NewGrD 80*
Goss, Clay 1946- *BlkAmP, DrBlPA, MorBAP*
Goss, Estyn L 1935- *IntWWM 77*
Goss, Helen *WhoHol A*
Goss, John 1894-1953 *Baker 78*
Goss, Sir John 1800-1880 *Baker 78, NewGrD 80, OxMus*
Goss, Peter 1946- *CnOxB*
Goss, Walter *Film 2*
Goss-Custard, Henry 1871-1964 *NewGrD 80*
Goss-Custard, Reginald 1877-1956 *NewGrD 80*
Gosschalk, Kathy 1941- *CnOxB*
Gosse, Sir Edmund William 1849-1928 *NotNAT B*
Gosse, Maistre *NewGrD 80*
Gossec, Francois-Joseph 1734-1829 *Baker 78, DcCom&M 79, GrComp, MusMk, NewEOp 71, NewGrD 80[port], OxMus*
Gosselin, Genevieve 1791-1818 *CnOxB*
Gosselin, Louis F 1800-1860 *CnOxB*
Gossen, Maistre *NewGrD 80, -80*
Gossett, Lou 1936- *DrBlPA, HalFC 80, WhoHol A*
Gossett, Louis 1936- *BiE&WWA, NotNAT*
Gossett, Philip 1941- *IntWWM 77, -80, NewGrD 80*
Gossman, Irving d1964 *NotNAT B*
Gosson, Stephen 1554-1642 *NotNAT B*
Gossvino, Antonius 1546?-1598? *NewGrD 80*
Gosswin, Antonius 1546?-1598? *NewGrD 80*
Gostelow, Sylvia Ruby *WhoMus 72*
Gostena, Giovanni Battista Della *NewGrD 80*
Gosting, Richard 1941- *AmSCAP 66*
Gostling, John 1650?-1733 *NewGrD 80*
Gostling, William 1696-1777 *NewGrD 80*
Gostomski, Henryk 1929- *IntWWM 77, -80*
Gostuski, Dragutin 1923- *Baker 78, NewGrD 80*
Got, Edmond-Francois-Jules 1822-1901 *NotNAT B, OxThe*
Gotfrid Von Strassburg *NewGrD 80*
Goth, Trudy 1913- *DancEn 78*
Gotham Quartette, The *Film 2*
Gothie, Robert *WhoHol A*
Gotkovsky, Ida Rose Esther 1933- *IntWWM 77, WhoMus 72*
Gotkovsky, Nell 1939- *IntWWM 77, -80, NewGrD 80, WhoMus 72*
Gotlieb, Phyllis Fay Bloom 1926- *CreCan 2*
Gotovac, Jakov 1895- *Baker 78, CmOp, DcCM, IntWWM 77, -80, NewGrD 80*
Gotshalks, Irene Apinee *CreCan 2*
Gotshalks, Juris 1924- *CreCan 1*
Gotshalks, Jury 1924- *CreCan 1*
Gotshalks, Yury 1924- *CreCan 1*
Gott, Barbara d1944 *Film 2, WhThe*
Gottel, Oscar *Film 2*
Gottel, Otto *Film 2*
Gotterher, Richard *ConMuA 80B*
Gottesfeld, Chone d1964 *NotNAT B*
Gottfredson, Vicki 1959- *IntWWM 77*
Gottfried Von Strassburg *NewGrD 80*
Gottfried, Jonas 1929- *AmSCAP 80*
Gottfried, Martin 1933- *BiE&WWA, ConAmTC, NotNAT*
Gottfried Von Strassburg *OxMus*
Gotthard, Johann Peter *NewGrD 80*
Gotthelf, Felix 1857-1930 *Baker 78*
Gotthoffer, Catherine Johnk 1923- *IntWWM 77, -80*
Gotti, Tito 1927- *IntWWM 80*
Gotting, Valentin *NewGrD 80*
Gottler, Archie 1896-1959 *AmSCAP 66, -80, CmpEPM, Film 2*
Gottler, Jerome Sheldon 1915- *AmSCAP 66, -80*
Gottlieb, Alex 1906- *AmSCAP 80, IntMPA 77, -75, -76, -78, -79, -80*
Gottlieb, Anna 1774-1856 *NewGrD 80*
Gottlieb, Arthur d1962 *NotNAT B*
Gottlieb, David d1962 *NotNAT B*
Gottlieb, Ira 1916- *IntMPA 77, -75, -76, -78, -79*
Gottlieb, Jack 1930- *AmSCAP 66, -80, Baker 78, CpmDNM 72, -80, ConAmC, DcCM*
Gottlieb, Jay Mitchell 1948- *ConAmC, IntWWM 77, -80*
Gottlieb, Linda *WomWMM, -B*
Gottlieb, Lou *EncFCWM 69*
Gottlieb, Louis E 1923- *AmSCAP 66, BiDAmM*
Gottlieb, Martin 1903- *IntMPA 79, -80*
Gottlieb, Morton 1921- *BiE&WWA, NotNAT, WhoThe 72, -77*
Gottlieb, Nanette 1774-1856 *NewGrD 80*
Gottlieb, Stan 1917- *IntMPA 77, -76, -78, -79, -80*
Gottlober, Abraham Dov Ber 1811-1899 *McGEWD[port]*
Gottlober, Sigmund 1888-1967 *NotNAT B*
Gottowt, John *Film 2*
Gottron, Adam 1889-1971 *NewGrD 80*
Gottschalg, Alexander Wilhelm 1827-1908 *Baker 78*
Gottschalk Von Limburg d1098 *NewGrD 80*
Gottschalk, Arthur William 1951- *CpmDNM 76, -77*
Gottschalk, Arthur William 1952- *IntWWM 77, -80*
Gottschalk, Christian *Film 2*
Gottschalk, Ferdinand 1858-1944 *MovMk, NotNAT B, WhThe*
Gottschalk, Ferdinand 1869-1944 *Film 2, HalFC 80, WhScrn 74, -77, WhoHol B*
Gottschalk, Ferdinand 1899-1944 *ForYSC*
Gottschalk, Joachim 1904-1941 *FilmAG WE, WhScrn 77*
Gottschalk, L Gaston 1847- *BiDAmM*
Gottschalk, Louis Moreau 1829-1869 *Baker 78, BiDAmM, BnBkM 80, MusMk, NewGrD 80[port], OxMus*
Gottschalk, Robert 1918- *IntMPA 77, -75, -76, -78, -79, -80*
Gottschall, Rudolf Von d1909 *NotNAT B*
Gottsched, Johann Christoph 1700-1766 *CnThe, EncWT, Ent[port], McGEWD[port], NewGrD 80, NotNAT B, OxThe, REnWD[port]*
Gottschovius, Nikolaus 1575?-1624? *NewGrD 80*
Gottuso, Tony 1916- *AmSCAP 66, -80*
Gottwald, Clytus 1925- *NewGrD 80*
Gotvrit Von Strasburg *NewGrD 80*
Gotwals, John W, III 1938- *AmSCAP 66*
Gotz, Carl *Film 2*
Gotz, Curt *Film 2*
Gotz, Franz 1755-1815 *NewGrD 80*
Gotz, Hermann 1840-1876 *BnBkM 80*
Gotz, Johann Michael 1735?-1810 *NewGrD 80*
Gotz, Karl 1906- *Film 2, IntWWM 77*
Gotz, Werner 1934- *WhoOp 76*
Gotze, Emil 1856-1901 *Baker 78*
Gotze, Johann Nikolaus Konrad 1791-1861 *Baker 78*
Gotze, Karl 1836-1887 *Baker 78*
Goubault, Christian 1938- *IntWWM 80*
Goube, Paul 1912- *CnOxB*

Gouch, John 1897- *Film 2*
Goudal, Jetta 1898- *FilmEn, Film 2, FilmgC, HalFC 80, MotPP, MovMk[port], TwYS, WhoHol A*
Goudeau, Lee, Jr. 1936- *AmSCAP 66*
Goudie, Big Boy Frank 1899-1964 *WhoJazz 72*
Goudie, Frank 1898-1964 *NewOrJ[port]*
Goudimel, Claude d1572 *OxMus*
Goudimel, Claude 1505-1572 *GrComp*
Goudimel, Claude 1510?-1572 *Baker 78, MusMk*
Goudimel, Claude 1514?-1572 *BnBkM 80, NewGrD 80*
Goudoever, Henri Daniel Van 1898-1977 *Baker 78*
Goudsmit, Lex 1913- *FilmAG WE*
Gougaloff, Peter Georgiev 1929- *WhoOp 76*
Gough, Alexander 1614- *OxThe*
Gough, Hugh 1916- *NewGrD 80*
Gough, John d1543 *NewGrD 80*
Gough, John 1897-1968 *TwYS, WhScrn 74, -77, WhoHol B*
Gough, Lloyd *ForYSC, WhoHol A*
Gough, Michael 1917- *FilmEn, FilmgC, ForYSC, HalFC 80, IlWWBF[port], MovMk, WhoHol A, WhoHrs 80[port], WhoThe 72, -77*
Gough, Robert d1625 *OxThe*
Gough, Wilfred Captain *Film 2*
Goughis, R A *MorBAP*
Gouin, Isabel 1904- *IntWWM 80*
Gouin, Pierre 1947- *IntWWM 77, -80*
Goulart, Simon 1543-1628 *NewGrD 80*
Gould, Baring S *OxMus*
Gould, Bernard d1945 *NotNAT B*
Gould, Billy 1869-1950 *Film 2, NotNAT B, WhScrn 77, WhoHol B*
Gould, Bryce 1925- *WhoMus 72*
Gould, Coral Lydia 1937- *IntWWM 80*
Gould, Danny 1921- *AmSCAP 66, -80*
Gould, David *IntMPA 75, -76*
Gould, Diana 1913- *CnOxB, DancEn 78, WhThe, WomWMM A, -B*
Gould, Dorothy *WhoHol A*
Gould, Edith Kingdon d1921 *NotNAT B*
Gould, Edward E 1911- *AmSCAP 66, -80*
Gould, Eleanor Diane *IntWWM 77, -80*
Gould, Elizabeth 1904- *AmSCAP 66, -80, ConAmC*
Gould, Elliott 1938- *BiE&WWA, EncMT, FilmEn, FilmgC, ForYSC, HalFC 80, IntMPA 77, -75, -76, -78, -79, -80, MovMk[port], WhoHol A, WhoThe 72, -77*
Gould, Fred d1917 *NotNAT B*
Gould, Glenn 1932- *Baker 78, BnBkM 80, CreCan 2, IntWWM 77, -80, MusMk, MusSN[port], NewGrD 80, WhoMus 72*
Gould, Hannah Flagg 1792-1865 *BiDAmM*
Gould, Harold d1952 *NotNAT B*
Gould, Harold 1923- *HalFC 80, WhoHol A*
Gould, Harry 1898- *BiE&WWA*
Gould, Howard d1938 *NotNAT B, WhoStg 1908*
Gould, Jack 1917- *AmSCAP 66, -80, NewYTET*
Gould, James F 1908- *IntMPA 77, -75, -76, -78, -79, -80*
Gould, James F 1917- *IntWWM 77, -80*
Gould, John Edgar 1822-1875 *BiDAmM*
Gould, John Leslie 1940- *IntWWM 77, -80, WhoThe 77*
Gould, Joseph 1915- *IntMPA 77, -75, -76, -78, -79, -80*
Gould, Julian 1915- *AmSCAP 66*
Gould, Morton 1913- *AmSCAP 66, -80, Baker 78, BiDAmM, BiE&WWA, BnBkM 80, CmpEPM, CompSN[port], CpmDNM 80, CnOxB, ConAmC, DancEn 78, DcCom&M 79, DcCM, IntWWM 77, -80, NewCBMT, NewGrD 80, NotNAT, OxMus, PopAmC[port], PopAmC SUP, WhoMus 72*
Gould, Morton 1913-1976 *MusMk*
Gould, Murray Joseph 1932- *IntWWM 77, -80*
Gould, Myrtle 1880-1941 *WhScrn 74, -77*
Gould, Nathaniel Duren 1781-1864 *BiDAmM*
Gould, Peter Philip William 1948- *IntWWM 77, -80*
Gould, Raymond 1922- *IntWWM 77, -80*
Gould, Ronald John 1911- *IntWWM 77, -80*
Gould, Sandra *WhoHol A*
Gould, Sid *WhoHol A*
Gould, Violet 1884-1962 *WhScrn 74, -77*
Gould, Walter 1875-1955 *BiDAmM*
Gould, William *Film 2*
Gould, William A 1915-1960 *WhScrn 77*
Goulding, Alf 1896-1972 *Film 2*
Goulding, Alfred 1896-1972 *FilmgC, HalFC 80, IlWWBF, TwYS A, WhScrn 77*
Goulding, Dorothy 1898- *CreCan 2*
Goulding, Edmund 1891-1951 *CmMov*
Goulding, Edmund 1891-1959 *AmSCAP 66, -80, BiDFilm, -81, DcFM, FilmEn, FilmgC, HalFC 80, MovMk[port], NotNAT B, OxFilm, TwYS A, WhScrn 77, WhThe, WorEFlm*
Goulding, George *NewGrD 80*
Goulding, Ivis *WhScrn 77*
Goulding, Ray 1922- *JoeFr*
Goulet, Robert 1933- *AmPS A, -B, BiDAmM, BiE&WWA, EncMT, FilmgC, ForYSC, HalFC 80, IntMPA 77, -75, -76, -78, -79, -80, NotNAT, RkOn[port], WhoHol A, WhoThe 77*
Gounod, Charles 1818-1893 *Baker 78, BnBkM 80, CmOp, CmpBCM, DcCom 77[port], DcCom&M 79, DcPup, GrComp[port], MusMk[port], NewEOp 71, NewGrD 80[port], NotNAT B, OxMus*
Goupillet, Nicolas 1650?-1713? *NewGrD 80*
Goupillier, Nicolas 1650?-1713? *NewGrD 80*
Gouriadec, Yvette Brind'Amour Le *CreCan 1*
Gourlay, Ian *IntWWM 77, -80, WhoMus 72*
Gourley, James Pasco, Jr. 1926- *BiDAmM, EncJzS 70*
Gourley, Jimmy 1926- *EncJzS 70*
Gouse-Renal, Christine *WomWMM*
Gousseau, Lelia 1909- *WhoMus 72*
Gouvy, Louis Theodore 1819-1898 *Baker 78, NewGrD 80*
Gouy, Jacques De d1650? *NewGrD 80*
Gover, Gerald 1914- *WhoMus 72*
Govi, Gilberto 1885-1966 *WhScrn 74, -77*
Govich, Bruce Michael 1930- *IntWWM 77, -80*
Goviloff, George 1932- *DancEn 78*
Goviloff, Georges 1932- *CnOxB*
Govrin, Gloria 1942- *CnOxB, DancEn 78[port]*
Govsky, John M 1921- *AmSCAP 66, -80*
Gow *NewGrD 80*
Gow, Andrew 1760?-1794 *NewGrD 80*
Gow, David Godfrey 1924- *WhoMus 72*
Gow, Donald *OxMus*
Gow, George Coleman 1860-1938 *Baker 78, BiDAmM*
Gow, James 1907-1952 *NotNAT B, WhThe*
Gow, John 1764?-1826 *NewGrD 80*
Gow, Joyce Mary 1920- *WhoMus 72*
Gow, Nathaniel 1763-1831 *Baker 78, OxMus*
Gow, Nathaniel 1766-1831 *NewGrD 80*
Gow, Neil 1727-1807 *NewGrD 80*
Gow, Neil, Jr. 1795-1823 *NewGrD 80*
Gow, Niel 1727-1807 *Baker 78, NewGrD 80, OxMus*
Gow, Niel 1795-1823 *OxMus*
Gow, Ronald 1897- *ConDr 73, -77, WhoThe 72, -77*
Gow, William 1751-1791 *OxMus*
Gow, William 1755?-1791 *NewGrD 80*
Gowan, Elsie Park Young 1905- *CreCan 1*
Gowans, Brad 1903-1954 *CmpEPM, WhoJazz 72*
Goward, Annie d1907 *NotNAT B*
Goward, Mary Ann 1806-1899 *NotNAT B*
Goward, Mary Anne 1805-1899 *NewGrD 80*
Gowdowsky, Dagmar 1897-1975 *Film 1*
Gowdy, Curt 1919- *IntMPA 77, -75, -76, -78, -79, -80, NewYTET*
Gower, Albert E, Jr. 1935- *AmSCAP 80, ConAmC*
Gower, Christopher Stainton 1939- *IntWWM 77, -80, WhoMus 72*
Gower, John Henry 1855-1922 *BiDAmM*
Gowers, Sulky d1970 *WhScrn 74, -77*
Gowing, Gene *Film 2*
Gowland, Gibson 1872-1951 *FilmEn, ForYSC, HalFC 80, WhScrn 74, -77, WhoHol B*
Gowland, Gibson 1882-1951 *Film 1, -2, FilmgC, TwYS*
Gowman, Milton J 1907-1952 *WhScrn 74, -77*
Goya, Carola *DancEn 78[port]*
Goya, Mona *WhoHol A*
Goya, Tito *PlP&P A[port]*
Goya And Matteo *DancEn 78[port]*
Goyer, Echlen *Film 2*
Goykovich, Dusko 1931- *EncJzS 70*
Gozzi, Carlo 1720-1806 *CnThe, DcPup, EncWT, Ent[port], McGEWD[port], NewEOp 71, NotNAT A, -B, OxMus, OxThe, REnWD[port]*
Gozzi, Patricia 1950- *FilmgC, HalFC 80*
Gozzo, Conrad Joseph 1922-1964 *BiDAmM, CmpEPM*
Graaf, Christian Ernst *NewGrD 80*
Graas, John 1924-1962 *BiDAmM, CmpEPM*
Grabbe, Christian Dietrich 1801-1836 *CnThe, EncWT, Ent, McGEWD[port], NotNAT B, OxThe, REnWD[port]*
Grabbe, Johann 1585-1655 *NewGrD 80*
Graben-Hoffmann, Gustav 1820-1900 *Baker 78, NewGrD 80*
Grabert, Martin 1868-1951 *Baker 78*
Grabie, Monica Helen 1950- *IntWWM 77, -80*
Grable, Betty 1913-1973 *ThFT[port]*
Grable, Betty 1916-1973 *BiDAmM, BiDFilm, -81, CmMov, CmpEPM, FilmEn, Film 2, FilmgC, ForYSC, HalFC 80[port], MotPP, MovMk[port], OxFilm, WhScrn 77, WhThe, WhoHol B, WhoThe 72, WorEFlm[port]*
Grabner, Eric Hans 1943- *WhoMus 72*
Grabner, Hermann 1886-1969 *Baker 78, NewGrD 80*
Grabovsky, Leonid 1935- *Baker 78, DcCM, NewGrD 80*
Grabowski, Ambrozy 1782-1868 *NewGrD 80*
Grabowski, Lenore *PupTheA*
Grabowski, Stanislaw 1791-1852 *NewGrD 80*
Grabs, Manfred 1938- *IntWWM 77, -80*
Grabu, Lewis *NewGrD 80*
Grabu, Louis *NewGrD 80*
Grabue, Louis *NewGrD 80*
Grabut, Louis *NewGrD 80*
Graca, Fernando Lopes *DcCM*
Graccia, Ugo *Film 2*
Grace, Amy d1945 *NotNAT B*
Grace, Bess Davis 1892- *AmSCAP 80*
Grace, Carol 1923- *BiE&WWA, NotNAT*
Grace, Charity 1879-1965 *WhScrn 74, -77*
Grace, Dick 1915-1965 *WhScrn 77*
Grace, Dinah d1963 *WhScrn 74, -77*
Grace, Frank Devaney 1891- *AmSCAP 66, -80*
Grace, Harvey 1874-1944 *Baker 78, NewGrD 80, OxMus*
Grace, Teddy *CmpEPM*
Gracie, Charlie 1936- *AmPS A, AmSCAP 66, RkOn[port]*
Gracie, Sally *BiE&WWA, NotNAT, WhoHol A*
Gracis, Ettore 1915- *NewGrD 80*
Gracq, Julien 1910- *CnMD*
Grad, Gabriel 1890-1950 *Baker 78*
Grade, Lord Lew 1906?- *IntMPA 78, -79, -80*
Grade, Francis *AmSCAP 80*
Grade, Lew *IntMPA 75, -76*
Grade, Lew 1906?- *HalFC 80*
Grade, Lord Lew *IntMPA 77, NewYTET*
Gradener, Carl 1812-1883 *NewGrD 80*
Gradener, Hermann 1844-1929 *Baker 78, NewGrD 80*
Gradener, Karl Georg Peter 1812-1883 *Baker 78*
Gradenigo, Paolo *NewGrD 80*
Gradenthaler, Hieronymus 1637-1700 *NewGrD 80*
Gradenthaller, Hieronymus 1637-1700 *NewGrD 80*
Gradenwitz, Peter 1910- *Baker 78, IntWWM 80, NewGrD 80, OxMus*
Gradstein, Alfred 1904-1954 *Baker 78, NewGrD 80*
Gradus, Ben *IntMPA 80*
Gradus, Ben 1918- *IntMPA 77, -75, -76, -78*
Grady, Billy d1973 *NotNAT A*
Grady, Billy, Jr. 1917- *IntMPA 77, -75, -76, -78, -79, -80*
Grady, Don *WhoHol A*
Grady, J W 1943- *ConAmC*
Grady's Commanders, Eddie *BiDAmM*

Graeffe, A Didier *ConAmC*
Graeme, Joyce 1918- *CnOxB, DancEn 78*
Graeme, Peter 1921- *IntWWM 77, -80, WhoMus 72*
Graener, Paul 1872-1944 *Baker 78, CmOp, NewEOp 71, NewGrD 80*
Graesch, David G 1947- *IntWWM 77*
Graeser, Wolfgang 1906-1928 *Baker 78*
Graetz, Joseph 1760-1826 *NewGrD 80*
Graetz, Paul 1890-1937 *Film 2, WhScrn 74, -77, WhoHol B*
Graetz, Paul 1899-1966 *FilmEn, WorEFlm*
Graetz, Paul 1901-1966 *FilmgC, HalFC 80*
Graetzer, Guillermo 1914- *Baker 78*
Graf *NewGrD 80*
Graf, Christian Ernst 1723-1804 *NewGrD 80*
Graf, Conrad 1782-1851 *NewGrD 80*
Graf, Erich Louis 1948- *IntWWM 77, -80*
Graf, Friedrich Hartmann 1727-1795 *NewGrD 80*
Graf, Herbert 1903-1973 *Baker 78, BiDAmM, WhoMus 72*
Graf, Herbert 1904- *NewEOp 71*
Graf, Herbert 1904-1973 *CmOp, NewGrD 80*
Graf, Johann 1684-1750 *NewGrD 80*
Graf, Max 1873-1958 *Baker 78, NewGrD 80*
Graf, Peter 1872-1951 *WhScrn 74, -77*
Graf, Peter-Lukas 1929- *IntWWM 77, -80, WhoMus 72*
Graf, Robert 1923-1966 *WhScrn 77*
Graf, Walter 1903- *IntWWM 77, -80, NewGrD 80*
Graf, William 1946- *ConAmC*
Grafe, Johann Friedrich 1711-1787 *NewGrD 80*
Graff, Charlotte Boheim *NewGrD 80*
Graff, E Jonny 1911- *AmSCAP 66*
Graff, George, Jr. 1886-1973 *AmPS, AmSCAP 66, -80, BiDAmM*
Graff, Johann *NewGrD 80*
Graff, Johann Michael 1714-1782 *BiDAmM*
Graff, Jonny Elias 1911- *AmSCAP 80*
Graff, Richard 1924- *IntMPA 77, -75, -76, -78, -79, -80*
Graff, Robert D 1919- *IntMPA 77, -75, -76, -78, -79, -80*
Graff, Sigmund 1898- *ModWD*
Graff, Wilton 1903-1969 *BiE&WWA, ForYSC, WhScrn 74, -77, WhoHol B*
Graffenried-Villars, Baron Emmanuel De d1964 *NotNAT B*
Graffigna, Achille 1816-1896 *Baker 78*
Graffman, Gary 1928- *Baker 78, BnBkM 80, IntWWM 77, -80, MusSN[port], NewGrD 80*
Grafing, Keith Gerhart 1942- *IntWWM 77*
Grafinger, Wolfgang *NewGrD 80*
Graflinger, Franz 1876-1962 *Baker 78*
Grafton, Garth *CreCan 1*
Grafton, Louise *Film 2*
Grafton, Richard *NewGrD 80*
Grafton, Sue *WomWMM*
Gragnani, Antonio *NewGrD 80*
Gragson, Wesley 1923- *ConAmC*
Graham, Alasdair 1934- *IntWWM 77, -80, WhoMus 72*
Graham, Arthur *BlkAmP, MorBAP*
Graham, Betty Jane *Film 2*
Graham, Bill 1931- *ConMuA 80B, IlEncR*
Graham, Breta *WhoMus 72*
Graham, Charles *Film 1, -2*
Graham, Charlie 1897-1943 *WhScrn 74, -77, WhoHol B*
Graham, Colin 1931- *CmOp, IntWWM 77, -80, NewGrD 80, WhoMus 72, WhoOp 76*
Graham, David Victor 1948- *ConAmTC*
Graham, Diane T *WomWMM B*
Graham, Eddie 1937- *EncJzS 70*
Graham, Edward B 1937- *EncJzS 70*
Graham, Ernest d1945 *NotNAT B*
Graham, Frank 1915-1950 *WhScrn 74, -77, WhoHol B*
Graham, Fred *WhoHol A*
Graham, Frederick H *Film 2*
Graham, George d1939 *NotNAT B*
Graham, Gwethalyn 1913-1965 *CreCan 1*
Graham, Harold Leroy 1897- *AmSCAP 66, -80*
Graham, Harry 1874-1936 *EncMT, NotNAT B, WhThe*
Graham, Irvin 1909- *AmSCAP 66, -80, BiE&WWA, NotNAT*
Graham, J F 1850-1932 *NotNAT B*
Graham, Joe F 1850-1933 *NotNAT A*
Graham, John *WhoHol A*
Graham, Johnny 1911-1978 *AmSCAP 66, -80*
Graham, Julia Ann 1915-1935 *WhScrn 74, -77, WhoHol B*
Graham, Katharine M 1917- *NewYTET*
Graham, Kenneth L 1915- *BiE&WWA, NotNAT*
Graham, Kenny 1924- *WhoMus 72*
Graham, L Lee 1945- *AmSCAP 80*
Graham, Lewis 1900- *AmSCAP 66*
Graham, Lucille *WhoMus 72*
Graham, Margaret 1937- *DancEn 78*
Graham, Martha *Film 2*
Graham, Martha 1893- *DancEn 78[port]*
Graham, Martha 1894- *CmpGMD[port], CnOxB, NotNAT A*
Graham, Martha 1900- *NewGrD 80*
Graham, Martha 1902- *BiE&WWA, WhThe*
Graham, Mildred *PupTheA*
Graham, Morland 1891-1949 *FilmgC, HalFC 80, NotNAT B, PlP&P, WhScrn 74, -77, WhThe, WhoHol B*
Graham, Ottie *BlkAmP*
Graham, Robert 1912- *AmSCAP 66, -80, ConAmC, IntWWM 77*
Graham, Robert Emmet 1858- *WhoStg 1906, -1908*
Graham, Roderick 1934- *IntMPA 80*
Graham, Roger 1885-1938 *AmSCAP 66, -80, BiDAmM*
Graham, Ronald 1912-1950 *NotNAT B, WhScrn 74, -77, WhoHol B*
Graham, Ronny 1919- *AmSCAP 66, -80, BiE&WWA, NotNAT, WhoHol A, WhoThe 72, -77*
Graham, Sheila 1908?- *FilmEn*
Graham, Sheilah 1912?- *HalFC 80*
Graham, Shirley *BlkAmP*
Graham, Steve *AmSCAP 80*
Graham, Susan Christine 1941- *WhoMus 72*
Graham, Thomas *OxMus*
Graham, Violet 1890-1967 *WhThe*
Graham, Virginia d1964 *NotNAT B*
Graham, William 1930?- *FilmgC, HalFC 80*
Graham, William Allen 1946- *IntWWM 77, -80*
Graham-Browne, W *WhThe*
Graham Central Station *IlEncR, RkOn 2[port]*
Graham-Jones, Ian 1937- *IntWWM 77, -80*
Grahame, Bert 1892-1971 *WhScrn 74, -77, WhoHol B*
Grahame, Gloria *MotPP*
Grahame, Gloria 1924- *FilmgC, HalFC 80*
Grahame, Gloria 1925- *BiDFilm, -81, FilmEn, ForYSC, MGM[port], MovMk[port], WhoHol A, WhoHrs 80[port], WorEFlm[port]*
Grahame, Gloria 1929- *IntMPA 77, -75, -76, -78, -79, -80*
Grahame, Margot 1911- *FilmEn, FilmgC, ForYSC, HalFC 80, IlWWBF[port], ThFT[port], WhThe, WhoHol A*
Grahame, Shirley 1936- *CnOxB, DancEn 78*
Grahm, Robert David 1954- *AmSCAP 80*
Grahm, Ruth Herscher 1924- *AmSCAP 80*
Grahm, Ruth Lillian 1924- *AmSCAP 66*
Grahn, Lucile 1819-1907 *CnOxB, DancEn 78[port], NewGrD 80*
Grahn, Mary 1901- *BiE&WWA, NotNAT*
Grahn, Ulf 1942- *Baker 78, ConAmC, IntWWM 77, -80*
Grainer, Ron *IntMPA 77, -75, -76, -78, -79, -80*
Grainer, Ron 1922- *WhoThe 72, -77*
Grainer, Ron 1925?- *FilmgC, HalFC 80*
Grainger, Edmund 1906- *FilmEn, FilmgC, HalFC 80*
Grainger, Gawn 1937- *WhoThe 77*
Grainger, James Edmund *IntMPA 77, -75, -76, -78, -79, -80*
Grainger, Jimmy, Jr. *Film 2*
Grainger, Percy 1882-1961 *AmSCAP 66, -80, Baker 78, BiDAmM, BnBkM 80, CompSN[port], ConAmC, DcCom&M 79, DcCM, MusMk, NewGrD 80[port], NotNAT B, OxMus*
Grainger, Porter *BlkAmP, DrBlPA*
Grainger, Stewart 1913- *IlWWBF[port]*
Grainger, William F 1854-1938 *WhScrn 74, -77*
Gralinski, Waldemar Jerzy 1946- *IntWWM 77, -80*
Gralla, Dina *Film 2*
Gram, Hans 1754-1804 *Baker 78, NewGrD 80*
Gram, Peder 1881-1956 *Baker 78, NewGrD 80*
Gramatges, Harold 1918- *Baker 78*
Gramatica, Emma d1965 *WhThe, WhoHol B*
Gramatica, Emma 1874-1965 *OxThe*
Gramatica, Emma 1875-1965 *EncWT, FilmEn, WhScrn 74, -77*
Gramatica, Irma 1870?-1962 *EncWT, Ent*
Gramatica, Irma 1873-1962 *OxThe, WhThe*
Gramatte, Sophie-Carmen Eckhardt- *CreCan 1*
Gramenz, Francis L 1944- *IntWWM 80*
Gramm, Donald John 1927- *Baker 78, MusSN[port], NewGrD 80*
Gramm, Donald John 1929- *WhoOp 76*
Grammann, Karl 1844-1897 *Baker 78*
Grammateus, Henricus 1492?-1526? *NewGrD 80*
Grammer, Billy 1925- *BiDAmM, CounME 74, -74A, EncFCWM 69, IlEncCM[port], RkOn*
Gran, Albert 1862-1932 *Film 1, -2, WhScrn 74, -77, WhoHol B*
Granach, Alexander 1879-1945 *NotNAT A, -B*
Granach, Alexander 1890-1945 *Film 2, FilmgC, HalFC 80, WhoHol B*
Granach, Alexander 1890-1949 *FilmEn*
Granach, Alexander 1891-1945 *WhScrn 74, -77*
Granade, John Alexander d1807 *BiDAmM*
Granado, Manuel *Film 2*
Granados, Eduardo 1894-1928 *Baker 78*
Granados, Edward 1894-1928 *OxMus*
Granados, Enrique 1867-1916 *Baker 78, BnBkM 80, CmOp, CompSN[port], DcCom 77[port], DcCM, MusMk, NewEOp 71, NewGrD 80[port], OxMus*
Granahan, Gerry *RkOn*
Granat, Arnie *ConMuA 80B*
Granat, Juan Wolfgang 1918- *IntWWM 77, -80*
Granata, Giovanni Battista d1684? *NewGrD 80*
Granata, Rocco *RkOn*
Granath, Herbert A *NewYTET*
Granberg, Mickey *ConMuA 80B*
Granby, Cornelius W d1886 *NotNAT B*
Granby, Joseph 1885-1965 *Film 1, WhScrn 74, -77, WhoHol B*
Grancini, Michel'Angelo 1605-1669 *NewGrD 80*
Grancino, Andrea *Baker 78*
Grancino, Francesco *Baker 78*
Grancino, Giovanni *Baker 78, NewGrD 80*
Grancino, Giovanni Battista *Baker 78*
Grancino, Michel'Angelo 1605-1669 *Baker 78, NewGrD 80*
Grancino, Paolo *Baker 78*
Grand, Georges d1921 *NotNAT B*
Grand, Murray 1919- *AmSCAP 66, -80*
Grand Funk *IlEncR[port], RkOn 2[port]*
Grand Funk Railroad *BiDAmM, ConMuA 80A*
Grandais, Susanne d1920 *WhScrn 74, -77*
Grandbois, Alain 1900- *CreCan 1*
Grande, Vincent 1902-1970 *AmSCAP 80*
Grandee, George *Film 2*
Granderson, John Lee 1913- *BluesWW[port]*
Grandert, Johnny 1939- *Baker 78*
Grandi, Alessandro d1630 *BnBkM 80*
Grandi, Alessandro 1575?-1630 *NewGrD 80*
Grandi, Alessandro 1577-1630 *Baker 78*
Grandi, Alessandro 1638-1697 *NewGrD 80*
Grandi, Hans 1904- *IntWWM 77, -80*
Grandi, Margherita 1894- *NewGrD 80*
Grandi, Margherita 1899- *CmOp, NewEOp 71*
Grandi, Ottavio Maria *NewGrD 80*
Grandin, Elmer d1933 *Film 1, NotNAT B*
Grandin, Ethel 1896- *Film 1, -2, MotPP, TwYS*
Grandin, Francis *Film 1*
Grandis, Renato De 1927- *NewGrD 80*
Grandis, Vincenzo De *NewGrD 80*
Grandjany, Marcel 1891-1975 *AmSCAP 66, -80, Baker 78, BnBkM 80, ConAmC, DcCom&M 79, NewGrD 80*
Grandjean, Axel Karl William 1847-1932 *Baker 78*

Grandjean, Louise d1934 *NotNAT B*
Grandon, Frank *Film 1, TwYS A*
Grand'Ry, Genevieve *WomWMM*
Grandstedt, Greta *Film 2, ForYSC*
Grandval, Charles-Francois Racot De 1711-1784 *NotNAT B*
Grandval, Charles-Francois Racot De 1714-1784 *OxThe*
Grandval, Marie Felicie C DeReiset 1830-1907 *Baker 78*
Grandval, Nicolas Racot De 1676-1753 *NewGrD 80*
Granelli, Gerald John 1940- *BiDAmM*
Graner, Gertrude *WhoHol A*
Granet, Bert 1910- *IntMPA 77, -76, -78, -79, -80*
Granet, Bert 1919- *IntMPA 75*
Graneti, Johannes *NewGrD 80*
Grange, Red 1903- *Film 2, What 1[port], WhoHol A*
Granger, Dorothy *Film 2, MotPP, WhoHol A*
Granger, Elsa G 1904-1955 *WhScrn 74, -77*
Granger, Farley 1925- *BiDFilm, -81, BiE&WWA, FilmEn, FilmgC, ForYSC, HalFC 80, HolP 40, IntMPA 77, -75, -76, -78, -79, -80, MotPP, MovMk, NotNAT, WhoHol A, WorEFlm*
Granger, Frederick 1795?-1830 *BiDAmM*
Granger, Lou *AmSCAP 80*
Granger, Stewart 1913- *BiDFilm, -81, CmMov, FilmAG WE, FilmEn, FilmgC, ForYSC, HalFC 80[port], IntMPA 77, -75, -76, -78, -79, -80, MGM[port], MotPP, MovMk, OxFilm, WhThe, WhoHol A, WorEFlm*
Granger, William F 1854-1938 *WhScrn 77, WhoHol B*
Grangier, Gilles 1911- *DcFM, FilmEn, FilmgC, HalFC 80, WorEFlm*
Grani, Alvise d1633 *NewGrD 80*
Granichstaedten, Bruno 1879-1944 *Baker 78*
Granick, Harry *NatPD[port]*
Granier, Francois 1717-1779 *NewGrD 80*
Granier, Jeanne d1939 *NotNAT B, WhThe*
Granier, Louis 1740-1800 *NewGrD 80*
Granier-Deferre, Pierre 1927- *FilmEn*
Granik, Theodore d1970 *NewYTET*
Granis, Aloysius De *NewGrD 80*
Granjon, Robert 1513-1589? *NewGrD 80*
Granlund, Nils Thor 1882-1957 *NotNAT A, -B*
Grannis, Sidney Martin 1827- *BiDAmM*
Grano, John Baptist 1692?-1748? *NewGrD 80*
Granom, Lewis Christian Austin 1725?-1791? *NewGrD 80*
Granouilhet, Jean *NewGrD 80*
Granovsky, Alexander 1890-1937 *EncWT, NotNAT B, OxFilm, OxThe*
Granstedt, Greta *TwYS*
Grant, Alexander 1925- *CnOxB, DancEn 78*
Grant, Alfred 1913- *BlksB&W, -C*
Grant, Alfred J 1914- *AmSCAP 66, -80*
Grant, Allan 1892- *AmSCAP 66, -80, ConAmC*
Grant, Amy Lee 1960- *AmSCAP 80*
Grant, Anne *WomWMM B*
Grant, Arthur 1915?-1972 *CmMov, FilmgC, HalFC 80*
Grant, B Donald *NewYTET*
Grant, Barney d1962 *NotNAT B*
Grant, Bert 1878-1951 *AmSCAP 66, -80*
Grant, Bob 1932- *WhoThe 72, -77*
Grant, Bruce *ConAmC*
Grant, Carol 1942- *CnOxB*
Grant, Cary 1904- *BiDFilm, -81, CmMov, EncMT, FilmEn, FilmgC, ForYSC, HalFC 80, IntMPA 77, -75, -76, -78, -79, -80, MotPP, MovMk[port], OxFilm, WhoHol A, WhoHrs 80, WorEFlm[port]*
Grant, Charles N 1887-1937 *AmSCAP 66, -80*
Grant, Claude D 1944- *BlkAmP*
Grant, Clifford Scantlebury 1930- *CmOp[port], IntWWM 77, -80, NewGrD 80, WhoOp 76*
Grant, Corrine *Film 1*
Grant, Darryl Clarence 1953- *ConAmTC*
Grant, Donald P 1932- *ConAmC*
Grant, Earl 1931-1970 *DrBlPA, RkOn, WhScrn 74, -77, WhoHol B*
Grant, Earl 1933- *BiDAmM*
Grant, Frances Miller *Film 2*
Grant, Frank K 1942- *AmSCAP 80*
Grant, Garry 1940- *CnOxB*
Grant, Gerald Frederick 1923- *AmSCAP 80*
Grant, Gogi 1936- *AmPS A, -B, RkOn[port]*
Grant, Harry 1922- *AmSCAP 66*
Grant, Harry Allen *Film 2*
Grant, Hilda Kay *CreCan 1*
Grant, James Edward 1902-1966 *CmMov, FilmEn, FilmgC, HalFC 80*
Grant, James Edward 1904-1966 *WorEFlm*
Grant, Janie 1945- *RkOn*
Grant, Jerry 1923- *AmSCAP 66*
Grant, Katherine *Film 2*
Grant, Kathryn 1933- *FilmEn, FilmgC, ForYSC, HalFC 80, MotPP, WhoHol A, WhoHrs 80*
Grant, Kay *CreCan 1*
Grant, Kirby 1911- *FilmEn, WhoHol A*
Grant, Kirby 1914- *FilmgC, ForYSC, HalFC 80*
Grant, Lawrence d1952 *ForYSC*
Grant, Lawrence 1869-1952 *HolCA[port]*
Grant, Lawrence 1870-1952 *HalFC 80, MovMk, WhScrn 74, -77, WhoHol B*
Grant, Lawrence 1898-1952 *Film 1, -2, TwYS*
Grant, Lee *IntMPA 75, -76, -78, -79, -80*
Grant, Lee 1926- *ForYSC*
Grant, Lee 1927- *FilmEn*
Grant, Lee 1929- *BiE&WWA, FilmgC, HalFC 80, IntMPA 77, MotPP, MovMk[port], NotNAT, WhoHol A*
Grant, Leola B 1893- *BluesWW[port]*
Grant, M Arnold 1908- *IntMPA 77, -75, -76, -78, -79, -80*
Grant, Marshall 1926- *AmSCAP 66, -80*
Grant, Marshall Garnett 1928- *BiDAmM*
Grant, Maxwell d1961 *NotNAT B*
Grant, Micki *BlkAmP, DrBlPA, MorBAP*
Grant, Neil 1882- *WhThe*
Grant, Pauline 1915- *CnOxB, DancEn 78, WhoThe 72, -77*
Grant, Peter *ConMuA 80B*
Grant, Richard *BlkAmP*
Grant, Rupert 1914-1961 *BiDAmM*
Grant, Shelby *WhoHol A*
Grant, Sydney 1873-1953 *Film 1, NotNAT B, WhScrn 74, -77, WhoHol B*
Grant, Valentine 1894-1948 *Film 1, TwYS, WhScrn 77*
Grant, W F d1923 *NotNAT B*
Grant, W Parks 1910- *CpmDNM 73, ConAmC*
Grant, William 1927- *WhoMus 72*
Grant, William Parks 1910- *BiDAmM, IntWWM 77, -80*
Grant, Willis 1907- *IntWWM 77, -80, WhoMus 72*
Grant-Schaefer, George Alfred 1872-1939 *Baker 78, ConAmC*
Grantham, Donald 1947- *ConAmC*
Grantham, Wilfrid 1898- *WhThe*
Grantley, Lord *IlWWBF A*
Grantzeva, Tatiana *CnOxB, DancEn 78*
Grantzova, Adele 1843-1877 *DancEn 78*
Grantzow, Adele 1845-1877 *CnOxB*
Granville, Audrey 1910-1972 *WhScrn 77, WhoHol B*
Granville, Bernard 1886-1936 *NotNAT B, WhThe*
Granville, Bonita 1923- *FilmEn, FilmgC, ForYSC, HalFC 80, HolP 30[port], MotPP, MovMk, ThFT[port], WhoHol A*
Granville, Charlotte 1863-1942 *WhScrn 77, WhThe*
Granville, Fred Leroy 1886- *IlWWBF*
Granville, George d1735 *NotNAT B*
Granville, Louise 1896-1969 *WhScrn 74, -77, WhoHol B*
Granville, Sydney d1959 *NotNAT B, WhThe*
Granville-Barker, Harley 1877-1946 *CnMD, EncWT, Ent, McGEWD[port], ModWD, NotNAT A, -B, OxThe, PlP&P[port], REnWD[port], WhThe*
Granville-Barker, Helen d1950 *NotNAT B, WhThe*
Granz, Norman 1918- *BiDAmM, ConMuA 80B, EncJzS 70, NewGrD 80*
Grapewin, Charles *MotPP*
Grapewin, Charles 1869-1956 *NotNAT B*
Grapewin, Charles 1875-1956 *MovMk[port], WhScrn 74, -77, WhoHol B*
Grapewin, Charles 1896-1956 *Vers A[port]*
Grapewin, Charley 1869-1956 *FilmgC, HalFC 80, HolCA[port]*
Grapewin, Charley 1875-1956 *FilmEn*
Grapewin, Charley 1890-1956 *ForYSC*
Grapewin, Charley 1896-1956 *Film 2*
Grapheus, Hieronymus *NewGrD 80*
Grappelli, Stephane 1908- *EncJzS 70, IlEncJ, IntWWM 80, NewGrD 80[port]*
Grappelly, Stephane 1908- *CmpEPM, NewGrD 80[port]*
Gras, Enrico 1919- *DcFM*
Grasbeck, Gottfrid 1927- *Baker 78, NewGrD 80*
Grasberger, Franz 1915- *NewGrD 80*
Graschinsky, Ernest Louis *NewGrD 80*
Grasgreen, Martin 1925- *IntMPA 77, -76, -78, -79, -80*
Grass, Cliff *CmpEPM*
Grass, Gunter 1927- *CnOxB, CroCD, EncWT, Ent, McGEWD[port], ModWD, REnWD[port]*
Grass, Gunter 1928- *CnMD*
Grass, Gunther 1927- *CnThe*
Grass Roots, The *RkOn 2[port]*
Grassby, Bertram 1880-1953 *Film 1, -2, TwYS, WhScrn 77*
Grassby, Mrs. Gerard A 1877-1962 *WhScrn 74, -77*
Grasse, Edwin 1884-1954 *Baker 78, BiDAmM, ConAmC*
Grasset, Jean-Jacques 1769?-1839 *NewGrD 80*
Grasshoff, Alex *IntMPA 77, -75, -76, -78, -79, -80*
Grassi, Cecilia 1740?-1782? *NewGrD 80*
Grassi, Eugene 1881-1941 *Baker 78*
Grassi, Franco Pio 1930- *AmSCAP 80*
Grassi, Paolo 1919- *EncWT, WhoOp 76*
Grassi, Paulo *IntWWM 77, -80*
Grassilli, Raoul 1924- *WhoOp 76*
Grassineau, James d1767 *NewGrD 80*
Grassini, Francesco Maria *NewGrD 80*
Grassini, Giuseppina 1773-1850 *NewGrD 80*
Grassini, Josephina 1773-1850 *Baker 78, NewEOp 71, NewGrD 80*
Grasso, Giovanni 1875-1930 *NotNAT B, OxThe, WhThe*
Grasso, Ralph 1934- *AmSCAP 66, -80*
Gratale, Franco 1933- *WhoOp 76*
Grateful Dead, The *BiDAmM, ConMuA 80A[port], IlEncR[port], RkOn 2[port]*
Grater, Adrian 1941- *CnOxB*
Gratiano, Tomaso *NewGrD 80*
Gratiosus De Padua *NewGrD 80*
Graton, Francoise 1930- *CreCan 1*
Grattan, H Plunkett d1889 *NotNAT B*
Grattan, Harry 1867-1951 *WhThe*
Grattan, Lawrence d1941 *NotNAT B*
Gratton, Fred 1894-1966 *WhThe*
Gratton, Harry 1867-1951 *NotNAT B*
Gratton, Stephen *Film 2*
Gratz, Joseph *NewGrD 80*
Gratz, Paul *Film 2*
Grau, Irene Rosenberg 1927- *IntWWM 77, -80*
Grau, Jacinto 1877-1958 *ModWD*
Grau, Jorge 1930- *WorEFlm*
Grau, Maurice 1849-1907 *Baker 78, BiDAmM, NewEOp 71*
Grau, Maurice 1851-1907 *NotNAT B*
Grau, Maurice 1857-1934 *NotNAT B*
Grau, Robert d1916 *NotNAT B*
Grau Delgado, Jacinto 1877-1958 *McGEWD*
Graubart, Michael 1930- *IntWWM 77, -80, WhoMus 72*
Graubins, Jekabs 1886-1961 *NewGrD 80*
Graubner, Gottlieb 1767-1836 *NewGrD 80*
Graubner, Johann Christian Gottlieb *NewGrD 80*
Graudan, Nicolai 1896-1964 *BiDAmM*
Graudan, Nikolai 1896-1964 *Baker 78, WhoMus 72*
Graudan, Nikolay 1896-1964 *NewGrD 80*
Grauer, Ben 1908- *Film 1, IntMPA 77, -75, -76*
Grauer, Bunny *Film 2*
Grauer, Victor A 1937- *ConAmC*
Grauman, Max 1871-1933 *BiDAmM*
Grauman, Sid 1879-1950 *HalFC 80,*

NotNAT B, WhoHol B
Grauman, Walter 1922- *FilmEn, FilmgC, HalFC 80*
Graumann, Karl *Film 2*
Graumann, Mathilde *NewGrD 80*
Graun *NewGrD 80*
Graun, August Friedrich 1698?-1765 *NewGrD 80*
Graun, August Friedrich 1699-1765 *Baker 78*
Graun, Carl Heinrich 1701-1759 *MusMk[port]*
Graun, Carl Heinrich 1703?-1759 *NewGrD 80[port]*
Graun, Carl Heinrich 1704-1759 *Baker 78*
Graun, Johann Gottlieb 1702?-1771 *NewGrD 80*
Graun, Johann Gottlieb 1703-1771 *Baker 78, BnBkM 80*
Graun, Karl Heinrich 1701-1759 *NewEOp 71*
Graun, Karl Heinrich 1704?-1759 *BnBkM 80, GrComp[port]*
Graunke, Kurt Karl Wilhelm 1915- *WhoMus 72*
Graupner, Catherine Hillier 1777?-1821 *BiDAmM*
Graupner, Christoph 1683-1760 *Baker 78, GrComp, NewEOp 71, NewGrD 80*
Graupner, Gottlieb 1767-1836 *NewGrD 80*
Graupner, Johann Christian Gottlieb 1767-1836 *Baker 78, BiDAmM*
Grauso, Joe 1897-1952 *WhoJazz 72*
Grautmann, Dorothea Von *NewGrD 80*
Gravenson, Anne W *WomWMM B*
Graves, Alfred Perceval 1846-1931 *OxMus*
Graves, Billy *RkOn*
Graves, C Mel 1946- *CpmDNM 76*
Graves, Clo d1932 *NotNAT B*
Graves, Clotilde Inez Mary 1863-1932 *WhThe*
Graves, Ernest *WhoHol A*
Graves, George 1876-1949 *IlWWBF, NotNAT A, -B, WhScrn 77, WhThe, WhoHol B*
Graves, John Woodcock *OxMus*
Graves, Laura d1925 *NotNAT B*
Graves, Mel 1946- *IntWWM 77, -80*
Graves, Michael George 1953- *IntWWM 77*
Graves, Milford 1941- *BiDAmM, EncJzS 70, IlEncJ, NewGrD 80*
Graves, Nancy *WomWMM B*
Graves, Peter *IntMPA 75, -76*
Graves, Peter 1911- *FilmgC, ForYSC, HalFC 80, IntMPA 77, -75, -76, -78, -79, -80, WhoHol A, WhoThe 72, -77*
Graves, Peter 1925- *FilmEn, FilmgC, ForYSC, HalFC 80, MotPP, MovMk, WhoHol A, WhoHrs 80[port]*
Graves, Peter 1936- *IntMPA 77, -78, -79, -80*
Graves, Lord Peter 1911- *IlWWBF*
Graves, Ralph 1900- *Film 1, -2, ForYSC, MotPP, MovMk, TwYS*
Graves, Ralph 1900-1977 *FilmEn*
Graves, Ralph 1901-1977 *HalFC 80*
Graves, Ralph Seaman, Jr. 1923- *AmSCAP 66, -80*
Graves, Richard 1715-1804 *OxMus*
Graves, Richard Harding 1926- *WhoMus 72*
Graves, Samuel 1794-1878 *NewGrD 80*
Graves, Taylor *Film 2*
Graves, Teresa *WhoHol A*
Graves, Teresa 1947?- *HalFC 80*
Graves, Teresa 1949?- *DrBlPA*
Graves, William 1916- *AmSCAP 66, -80*
Graves, William Lester, Jr. 1915- *ConAmC, IntWWM 77, -80*
Gravet, Fernand 1904-1970 *FilmgC, HalFC 80, MovMk[port], WhScrn 74, -77, WhoHol B*
Gravet, Fernand 1905- *ForYSC*
Graveure, Louis 1888-1965 *Baker 78, MusSN[port]*
Gravey, Fernand 1904-1970 *FilmEn*
Gravina, Caesare 1858- *Film 1, -2*
Gravina, Cesare 1858- *TwYS*
Gravitis, Olgerts 1926- *NewGrD 80*
Gray *PupTheA*
Gray, Alan 1855-1935 *Baker 78, NewGrD 80, OxMus*
Gray, Alexander *CmpEPM*
Gray, Alexander 1902-1975 *Film 2, MotPP, WhScrn 77*
Gray, Alexander 1929- *CreCan 1*
Gray, Alfred Rudolph, Jr. 1933- *BlkAmP*
Gray, Allan 1904- *OxFilm*
Gray, Amlin 1946- *NatPD[port]*
Gray, Arnold *Film 2*
Gray, Arthur D *PupTheA*
Gray, Arvella 1906- *BluesWW[port]*
Gray, Barry *IntMPA 77, -75, -76, -78, -79, -80, PupTheA*
Gray, Betty d1919 *Film 1, WhScrn 77*
Gray, Billy *WhoHol A*
Gray, Billy 1938- *ForYSC, What 4[port]*
Gray, Billy 1940?- *HalFC 80*
Gray, Billy Joe 1941-1966 *WhScrn 77*
Gray, C *MorBAP*
Gray, Carole 1940- *FilmgC, HalFC 80, WhoHrs 80*
Gray, Cecil 1895-1951 *Baker 78, NewGrD 80, OxMus*
Gray, Charles 1928- *ForYSC, HalFC 80, WhoHrs 80, WhoThe 72*
Gray, Charles D 1928- *BiE&WWA, FilmgC, NotNAT, WhoHol A, WhoThe 77*
Gray, Chauncey Eugene 1904- *AmSCAP 66, -80*
Gray, Claude 1932- *BiDAmM, CounME 74[port], -74A, EncFCWM 69, IlEncCM*
Gray, Clifford *Film 2*
Gray, Coleen 1922- *FilmEn, ForYSC, IntMPA 77, -75, -76, -78, -79, MotPP, WhoHol A, WhoHrs 80*
Gray, Colleen 1922- *FilmgC, HalFC 80, IntMPA 80*
Gray, D Vincent 1889-1950 *BiDAmM*
Gray, Dallas A 1898- *AmSCAP 66*
Gray, David 1932- *WhoMus 72*
Gray, Dennis *DancEn 78*
Gray, Dobie 1942- *IlEncR[port], RkOn 2[port]*
Gray, Dolores *MotPP, WhoHol A*
Gray, Dolores 1924- *CmpEPM, EncMT, FilmgC, ForYSC, HalFC 80, WhoThe 72, -77*
Gray, Dolores 1930- *BiE&WWA, NotNAT*
Gray, Don 1901-1966 *WhScrn 77*
Gray, Donald 1903-1969 *Baker 78*
Gray, Donald 1914-1978 *FilmgC, HalFC 80, WhoHol A*
Gray, Dulcie 1919- *FilmEn, FilmgC, HalFC 80, IlWWBF, -A, IntMPA 77, -75, -76, -78, -79, -80, WhoHol A, WhoThe 72, -77*
Gray, Eddie 1898-1969 *WhScrn 77, WhoHol B*
Gray, Eden *Film 2*
Gray, Elspet 1929- *WhoThe 72, -77*
Gray, Elwood *Film 2*
Gray, Eve 1904- *Film 2, IlWWBF, WhThe*
Gray, Farnum Moore 1940- *ConAmTC*
Gray, Felicity 1914- *DancEn 78*
Gray, Gary 1936- *FilmgC, HalFC 80*
Gray, Gene 1899-1950 *WhScrn 74, -77, WhoHol B*
Gray, George *WhThe*
Gray, George Arthur *Film 2*
Gray, George Branson 1945- *IntWWM 77, -80*
Gray, George Charles 1897- *IntWWM 77, -80, WhoMus 72*
Gray, George G 1894-1967 *WhScrn 74, -77, WhoHol B*
Gray, Gilda d1959 *AmPS B, MotPP, NotNAT B, WhoHol B*
Gray, Gilda 1898?-1959 *CmpEPM*
Gray, Gilda 1899-1959 *Film 1, -2, TwYS*
Gray, Gilda 1901-1959 *FilmEn, FilmgC, HalFC 80, WhScrn 74, -77*
Gray, Glen *AmPS B*
Gray, Glen 1900-1963 *WhScrn 74, -77, WhoHol B*
Gray, Glen 1906-1963 *BiDAmM, CmpEPM*
Gray, Glenn 1906-1963 *WhoJazz 72*
Gray, Gordon 1905- *IntMPA 77, -75, -76, -78, -79, -80*
Gray, H W *OxMus*
Gray, Harold 1903- *WhoMus 72*
Gray, Harry *Film 2*
Gray, Helen *PupTheA*
Gray, Henry 1925- *BluesWW[port]*
Gray, Ida M d1942 *NotNAT B*
Gray, Iris *Film 2*
Gray, Isabel 1898- *WhoMus 72*
Gray, Jack 1880-1956 *WhScrn 74, -77, WhoHol B*
Gray, Jack 1927- *ConDr 73, -77*
Gray, Jean 1902-1953 *WhScrn 74, -77*
Gray, Jennifer 1916-1962 *WhThe*
Gray, Jerry 1915-1976 *AmSCAP 66, -80, Baker 78, BgBands 74, CmpEPM*
Gray, Joan Mary *WhoMus 72*
Gray, Joe d1971 *WhScrn 77*
Gray, John 1927- *CreCan 1*
Gray, John Anthony 1932- *WhoMus 72*
Gray, John Baker *AmSCAP 80*
Gray, John W 1924- *BiDAmM*
Gray, Jonathan 1779-1837 *NewGrD 80*
Gray, Judith *ConAmC*
Gray, Lawrence 1898-1970 *FilmEn, Film 2, ForYSC, TwYS, WhScrn 74, -77, WhoHol B*
Gray, Leonard d1964 *NotNAT B*
Gray, Lilian *Film 2*
Gray, Linda 1910- *WhoThe 72, -77*
Gray, Linda 1913-1963 *WhScrn 74, -77, WhoHol B*
Gray, Madeline *Film 2*
Gray, Margery *BiE&WWA*
Gray, Nadia 1923- *FilmEn, Film 1, FilmgC, ForYSC, HalFC 80, WhoHol A*
Gray, Nicholas Stuart 1919- *WhoThe 72, -77*
Gray, Otto 1890- *CounME 74, IlEncCM*
Gray, Paul 1930- *BiE&WWA*
Gray, Peggy 1926- *WhoMus 72*
Gray, Richard 1896- *WhThe*
Gray, Robert S 1911- *BiE&WWA*
Gray, Sally 1916- *FilmAG WE, FilmEn, FilmgC, HalFC 80, WhThe, WhoHol A*
Gray, Sally 1918- *IlWWBF[port]*
Gray, Sam d1932 *BlksBF*
Gray, Simon 1936- *CnThe, ConDr 73, -77, CreCan 2, EncWT, Ent, NotNAT, PlP&P A[port], WhoThe 72, -77*
Gray, Stella *Film 1*
Gray, Stephen *Film 1*
Gray, Stephen 1923- *IntWWM 77, -80, WhoMus 72*
Gray, Terence 1895- *OxThe, WhThe*
Gray, Thomas 1716-1771 *NewGrD 80*
Gray, Thomas 1803-1849 *BiDAmM*
Gray, Thomas J 1888-1924 *AmSCAP 66, -80, NotNAT B*
Gray, Tick Thomas B 1905?- *WhoJazz 72*
Gray, Timothy *AmSCAP 66, BiE&WWA, NotNAT*
Gray, Vernon *IntMPA 77, -75, -76, -78, -79, -80, WhoHol A*
Gray, Wardell 1921-1955 *BiDAmM, CmpEPM, IlEncJ*
Gray, William d1943 *NotNAT B*
Gray, William B d1932 *BiDAmM*
Gray Bey, Michael Ashley 1947- *AmSCAP 80*
Graybill, Joseph 1887-1913 *Film 1, WhScrn 77, WhoHol B*
Graybill, Lucille P 1916- *IntWWM 77*
Graydon, J L 1844- *WhThe*
Graydon, Wiley Lee, III 1944- *IntWWM 77*
Graymen, The *BiDAmM, EncFCWM 69*
Grayson, Alan 1930- *AmSCAP 66, -80*
Grayson, Bette d1954 *NotNAT B*
Grayson, Ethel Vaughan Kirk 1890- *CreCan 1*
Grayson, Godfrey 1913- *IlWWBF*
Grayson, Jessie *DrBlPA*
Grayson, Kathryn *MotPP, WhoHol A*
Grayson, Kathryn 1921- *MovMk[port]*
Grayson, Kathryn 1922- *CmMov, CmpEPM, FilmEn, FilmgC, ForYSC[port], HalFC 80, MGM[port]*
Grayson, Kathryn 1923- *BiDAmM, IntMPA 77, -75, -76, -78, -79, -80*
Grayson, Paul *AmSCAP 80*
Grayson, Richard 1925- *BiE&WWA, NotNAT*
Grayson, Richard 1941- *ConAmC*
Graz, Joseph *NewGrD 80*
Grazer, Wanda *Film 2*
Graziani *NewGrD 80*
Graziani, Bonifazio 1604?-1664 *NewGrD 80*
Graziani, Bonifazio 1605-1664 *Baker 78*
Graziani, Carlo d1787 *NewGrD 80*
Graziani, Francesco 1828-1901 *NewGrD 80*
Graziani, Giuseppe 1819-1905 *NewGrD 80*
Graziani, Lodovico 1820-1885 *NewGrD 80*

Graziani, Tomaso 1550?-1634 *NewGrD 80*
Graziani, Vincenzo 1836-1906 *NewGrD 80*
Graziano, Ann 1928- *AmSCAP 66*
Graziano, Caesar Frankie 1904- *AmSCAP 66, -80*
Graziano, Rocky 1922- *WhoHol A*
Grazioli, Giovanni Battista 1746-1820? *NewGrD 80*
Grazioso Da Padova *NewGrD 80*
Grazzini, Anton Francesco 1503-1584 *McGEWD*
Grba, Nedeljko 1929- *IntWWM 77, -80*
Greager, Richard C 1946- *IntWWM 77, -80*
Grean, Charles Randolph 1913- *AmSCAP 80, RkOn 2A[port]*
Grean, Robin T 1950- *AmSCAP 80*
Greane, David *BlkAmP*
Greanias, George 1948- *NatPD[port]*
Greanin, Leon 1895-1948 *DancEn 78*
Grease Band *IlEncR*
Great Gildersleeve, The *What 5[port]*
Great Society *BiDAmM*
Greatheed, Bertie d1826 *NotNAT B*
Greatorex, Henry Wellington 1811-1858 *BiDAmM*
Greatorex, Henry Wellington 1813-1858 *NewGrD 80*
Greatorex, Richard 1919- *WhoMus 72*
Greatorex, Susan Marian 1948- *ConAmTC*
Greatorex, Thomas 1758-1831 *Baker 78, NewGrD 80*
Greatorex, Wilfred 1921- *ConDr 73, -77C*
Greaves, Donald 1943- *BlkAmP*
Greaves, Florence Marjorie *WhoMus 72*
Greaves, R B 1944- *RkOn 2[port]*
Greaves, Terence 1933- *IntWWM 77, -80*
Greaves, Thomas *NewGrD 80, OxMus*
Greaves, William 1926- *DrBlPA, MorBAP*
Greaza, Walter N 1897-1973 *BiE&WWA, NotNAT B, WhScrn 77, WhoHol B*
Greaza, Walter N 1900-1973 *WhThe*
Greban, Arnoul 1420?-1471? *NewGrD 80*
Grebanier, Bernard 1903- *BiE&WWA, NotNAT*
Grebe, Maria Ester 1928- *IntWWM 77, -80, NewGrD 80*
Greber, Jakob d1731 *NewGrD 80*
Grebus, Louis *NewGrD 80, -80*
Grech, Pawlu 1938- *IntWWM 77, -80*
Grechaninov, Aleksandr 1864-1956 *BnBkM 80*
Grechaninov, Alexander 1864-1956 *MusMk*
Grechaninov, Alexandr Tikhonovich 1864-1956 *NewGrD 80*
Greco, Achille *PupTheA*
Greco, Anthony Battista 1948- *AmSCAP 80*
Greco, Armando 1926- *AmSCAP 66, -80, BiDAmM*
Greco, Buddy 1926- *CmpEPM, RkOn[port]*
Greco, Cosetta 1930- *FilmAG WE*
Greco, Cyndi *RkOn 2A*
Greco, Gaetano *PupTheA*
Greco, Gaetano 1657?-1728? *NewGrD 80*
Greco, Jose 1918- *WhoHol A*
Greco, Jose 1919- *CnOxB, DancEn 78[port]*
Greco, Juliette 1926- *FilmEn*
Greco, Juliette 1927- *FilmgC, HalFC 80, WhoHol A*
Greco, Juliette 1931?- *ForYSC*
Grede, Kjell 1936- *OxFilm, WorEFlm*
Gredler, Ake Samuel 1929- *IntWWM 77, -80*
Gredley, John 1930- *WhoMus 72*
Gredy, Jean-Pierre 1920- *McGEWD*
Greear, Geraine *Film 2*
Greef, Arthur De 1862-1940 *Baker 78, NewGrD 80*
Greeley, Aurora 1905- *BlksBF*
Greeley, Evelyn *Film 1*
Greeley, George Henry 1917- *AmSCAP 80*
Greely, Evelyn *Film 2*
Green, Abel 1900-1973 *AmSCAP 66, -80, BiE&WWA, NotNAT B, WhScrn 77, WhThe, WhoThe 72*
Green, Adolph 1915- *AmPS, AmSCAP 66, -80, BiDAmM, BiE&WWA, CmMov, CmpEPM, ConDr 73, -77D, EncMT, FilmgC, HalFC 80, IntMPA 77, -75, -76, -78, -79, -80, NewCBMT, NotNAT, OxFilm, WhoThe 72, -77, WorEFlm[port]*
Green, Adolph 1918- *FilmEn*
Green, Al *ConMuA 80A*
Green, Al 1946- *DrBlPA, IlEncR[port], RkOn 2[port]*
Green, Alfred E 1889-1960 *FilmEn, FilmgC, HalFC 80, MovMk[port]*
Green, Alfred E 1890-1960 *TwYS A*
Green, Alfred Martin 1952- *AmSCAP 80*
Green, Anna *WhoOp 76*
Green, Bennie 1923- *BiDAmM, EncJzS 70*
Green, Benny 1923- *CmpEPM*
Green, Benny 1927- *EncJzS 70*
Green, Bernard 1908-1975 *AmSCAP 66, -80, ConAmC*
Green, Bernard 1927- *EncJzS 70*
Green, Bruce H 1943- *AmSCAP 80*
Green, Bud 1897- *AmSCAP 66, -80, BiDAmM, CmpEPM*
Green, Calvin E *AmSCAP 66*
Green, Carelton d1962 *NotNAT B*
Green, Carolyn *BiE&WWA, NotNAT*
Green, Charles *Film 2*
Green, Charlie 1900-1935 *BiDAmM*
Green, Charlie 1900-1936 *CmpEPM, WhoJazz 72*
Green, Clarence 1929- *BluesWW[port]*
Green, Cora *BlksBF*
Green, Cornelius 1928- *BluesWW[port]*
Green, Danny 1903- *FilmgC, HalFC 80, WhoHol A*
Green, David Lewis 1951- *AmSCAP 80*
Green, David Llewellyn 1935- *WhoMus 72*
Green, Denis 1905-1954 *WhScrn 74, -77, WhoHol B*
Green, Dennis 1905-1954 *NotNAT B*
Green, Dorothy *WhoHol A*
Green, Dorothy 1886-1961 *NotNAT B, WhThe*
Green, Dorothy 1892-1963 *Film 1, NotNAT B, WhScrn 74, -77, WhoHol B*
Green, Douglass Marshall 1926- *IntWWM 77, -80*
Green, Eddie 1901- *BlksB&W, -C, BlksBF, DrBlPA*
Green, Elizabeth *PupTheA*
Green, Ernest Gilmore *NewGrD 80*
Green, Eve *WomWMM*
Green, Frank T 1951- *AmSCAP 80*
Green, Fred E 1890-1940 *WhScrn 74, -77, WhoHol B*
Green, Freddie 1911- *CmpEPM, EncJzS 70, IlEncJ*
Green, Frederick William 1911- *BiDAmM, EncJzS 70, WhoJazz 72*
Green, Gary M 1954- *AmSCAP 80*
Green, George 1930- *ConAmC*
Green, Gilbert *WhoHol A*
Green, Gordon 1905- *IntWWM 77, -80, WhoMus 72*
Green, Grant 1931- *BiDAmM, EncJzS 70*
Green, Guy 1913- *BiDFilm, -81, FilmEn, FilmgC, HalFC 80, IlWWBF, IntMPA 77, -75, -76, -78, -79, -80, WorEFlm*
Green, H Leland 1907- *AmSCAP 66, -80*
Green, Harold 1912- *AmSCAP 66*
Green, Harold 1913- *AmSCAP 80*
Green, Harriette Patricia 1952- *BlkWAB[port]*
Green, Harry 1892-1958 *Film 2, FilmgC, HalFC 80, MotPP, WhScrn 74, -77, WhThe, WhoHol B*
Green, Helen *Film 1*
Green, Howard P, Sr. 1892- *AmSCAP 66*
Green, Hughie 1920- *FilmgC, HalFC 80, IlWWBF, WhoHol A*
Green, Ingeborg *WomWMM*
Green, Isadore d1963 *NotNAT B*
Green, James Burton d1922 *NotNAT B*
Green, Jane *PlP&P[port]*
Green, Janet 1914- *BiE&WWA, FilmEn, FilmgC, HalFC 80, IntMPA 77, -75, -76, -78, -79, -80, WhThe*
Green, Janie 1922- *IntWWM 77*
Green, John *NewGrD 80*
Green, John 1908- *AmPS, AmSCAP 66, -80, Baker 78, BestMus, BiDAmM, ConAmC, IntMPA 77, -75, -76, -78, -79, -80, OxThe, PopAmC SUP, WhoMus 72*
Green, John H 1915- *BiE&WWA, NotNAT*
Green, Johnny *BgBands 74*
Green, Johnny 1908- *BiE&WWA, CmMov, CmpEPM, FilmEn, FilmgC, HalFC 80, PopAmC[port]*
Green, Johnny L *BlkAmP*
Green, Jonathan D 1945- *IntWWM 80*
Green, Joseph 1905- *IntMPA 77, -75, -76, -78, -79, -80*
Green, Judd *Film 2*
Green, Julian 1900- *ModWD*
Green, Julien 1900- *CnMD, McGEWD[port], REnWD[port]*
Green, Kenneth 1908-1969 *WhScrn 74, -77, WhoHol B*
Green, L Dunton 1872-1933 *Baker 78*
Green, Lewis G 1909- *AmSCAP 66, -80*
Green, Lillian 1919-1954 *BluesWW[port]*
Green, Lillian Pearl 1951- *AmSCAP 80*
Green, Lloyd 1937- *IlEncCM[port]*
Green, Mabel 1890- *WhThe*
Green, Margaret Eleanor 1933- *WhoMus 72*
Green, Marion 1890-1956 *NotNAT B, WhThe*
Green, Martyn 1899-1975 *BiE&WWA, BnBkM 80, FilmgC, HalFC 80, NotNAT A, -B, WhScrn 77, WhoHol C, WhoThe 72, -77*
Green, Maxie *AmSCAP 80*
Green, Michael L *IntMPA 77, -75, -76, -78, -79, -80*
Green, Miriam Stewart 1915- *IntWWM 77*
Green, Mitzi *AmPS B*
Green, Mitzi 1920-1969 *FilmEn, Film 2, FilmgC, ForYSC, HalFC 80, HolP 30[port], MotPP, NotNAT B, ThFT[port], WhScrn 74, -77, WhThe, WhoHol B*
Green, Morris d1963 *NotNAT B*
Green, Morton Joseph 1919- *AmSCAP 66, -80*
Green, Nathalie Smith *PupTheA*
Green, Nathaniel Charles 1903- *IntMPA 77, -75, -76, -78, -79, -80*
Green, Nigel 1924-1972 *FilmEn, FilmgC, ForYSC, HalFC 80, WhScrn 77, WhoHol B, WhoHrs 80*
Green, Norma *AmSCAP 80*
Green, Norman G 1907-1975 *BluesWW[port]*
Green, Paul *MorBAP*
Green, Paul 1894- *AmSCAP 66, BiE&WWA, CnMD, CnThe, ConDr 77, DcLB 7[port], Ent, McGEWD, ModWD, NotNAT, -A, OxThe, PlP&P, REnWD[port], WhoThe 72, -77*
Green, Paul Eliot 1894- *AmSCAP 80, ConDr 73, EncWT*
Green, Peter *IlEncR*
Green, Philip 1917?- *FilmgC, HalFC 80, IntMPA 77, -75, -76, -78, -79, -80*
Green, Ray *PupTheA*
Green, Ray 1907- *ConAmC*
Green, Ray 1908- *BiDAmM*
Green, Ray 1909- *AmSCAP 66, Baker 78, DcCM*
Green, Richard d1914 *NotNAT B*
Green, Robert 1940-1965 *WhScrn 77*
Green, Robert Lee 1927- *ConAmC*
Green, Roger 1945- *IntWWM 77, -80, WhoMus 72*
Green, Rosa *BluesWW[port]*
Green, Ruth *BiE&WWA*
Green, Sadie *BluesWW[port]*
Green, Sally Shaw 1915- *IntWWM 77*
Green, Samuel 1740-1786 *OxMus*
Green, Samuel 1740-1796 *NewGrD 80*
Green, Sanford 1914- *AmSCAP 66, -80*
Green, Shecky *JoeFr[port]*
Green, Stanley 1923- *BiE&WWA, NotNAT*
Green, Sue 1902-1939 *WhScrn 74, -77, WhoHol B*
Green, Thurman Alexander 1940- *EncJzS 70*
Green, Urban Clifford 1926- *AmSCAP 66, -80, BiDAmM, EncJzS 70*
Green, Urbie 1926- *CmpEPM, EncJzS 70*
Green, Vernice, Jr. 1935- *BiDAmM*
Green, Violet *BluesWW[port]*
Green, Willard d1978 *WhoHrs 80*
Green, William 1913- *AmSCAP 66, -80*
Green, William 1926- *NotNAT*
Green, William Earnest 1925- *BiDAmM*
Green, William M *NatPD[port]*
Green And Lund *PupTheA*
Green Minstrels, Silas *BiDAmM*
Green Valley Boys *BiDAmM*
Greenawalt, Terrence Lee 1936- *IntWWM 77,*

–80
Greenbank, Henry H d1899 *NotNAT B*
Greenbank, Percy 1878-1968 *CmpEPM, EncMT, NotNAT B, WhThe*
Greenbaum, Hyam 1901-1942 *NewGrD 80*
Greenbaum, Hyam 1910- *WhThe*
Greenbaum, Kyla 1922- *NewGrD 80, WhoMus 72*
Greenberg, Abner 1889-1959 *AmSCAP 66, –80*
Greenberg, Berry 1912- *IntMPA 77, –75, –76, –78, –79, –80*
Greenberg, Edward M 1924- *NotNAT*
Greenberg, Florence *ConMuA 80B*
Greenberg, Gerald 1936- *HalFC 80*
Greenberg, Hank 1911- *What 2[port]*
Greenberg, Henry F 1912- *AmSCAP 66, –80*
Greenberg, Jerry *ConMuA 80B*
Greenberg, Marvin 1936- *IntWWM 77, –80*
Greenberg, Noah 1919-1966 *Baker 78, BnBkM 80, NewGrD 80*
Greenberg, Norman 1930- *AmSCAP 80*
Greenberg, Roger D 1944- *IntWWM 77, –80*
Greenberg, Stanley R *HalFC 80*
Greenberg, Susan M 1944- *AmSCAP 80*
Greenbriar Boys *BiDAmM, CounME 74, –74A, IlEncCM EncFCWM 69*
Greene, Alan 1921- *AmSCAP 80*
Greene, Allen Walker 1921- *IntWWM 77, –80*
Greene, Angela *ForYSC, WhoHol A*
Greene, Billy M 1897-1973 *WhScrn 77, WhoHol B*
Greene, Billy M 1927-1970 *WhoHol B*
Greene, Bob 1922- *EncJzS 70*
Greene, Burton 1937- *EncJzS 70*
Greene, Charles *ConMuA 80B*
Greene, Charles 1918?- *MorBAP*
Greene, Clarence 1918?- *FilmEn, FilmgC, HalFC 80, IntMPA 80*
Greene, Clay Meredith 1850-1933 *NotNAT B, WhThe, WhoStg 1908*
Greene, David 1924- *BiDFilm, –81, FilmEn, FilmgC, HalFC 80, IntMPA 77, –75, –76, –78, –79, –80*
Greene, Eric 1876-1917 *NotNAT B*
Greene, Evie 1876-1917 *WhThe, WhoStg 1906, –1908*
Greene, Genevieve 1924- *IntWWM 77*
Greene, Gordon K 1927- *IntWWM 77, –80*
Greene, Graham 1904- *BiE&WWA, CnMD, CnThe, ConDr 73, –77, CroCD, EncWT, Ent[port], FilmEn, FilmgC, HalFC 80, IlWWBF A, McGEWD, ModWD, NotNAT, –A, OxFilm, OxThe, PlP&P, WhoThe 72, –77, WorEFlm*
Greene, Harrison 1884-1945 *WhScrn 74, –77, WhoHol B*
Greene, Harry 1928- *AmSCAP 66*
Greene, Harry Plunket 1865-1936 *Baker 78, OxMus*
Greene, Harry Wellington 1928- *AmSCAP 80*
Greene, Herbert 1921- *BiE&WWA, NotNAT*
Greene, Herbert Wilbur 1851-1924 *BiDAmM*
Greene, Jack Henry 1930- *BiDAmM, CounME 74[port], –74A, EncFCWM 69, IlEncCM[port]*
Greene, Jerry 1910- *NewOrJ[port]*
Greene, Joe 1915- *AmSCAP 66*
Greene, John *NewGrD 80*
Greene, John L 1912- *AmSCAP 66, –80*
Greene, Joseph Perkins 1915- *AmSCAP 80*
Greene, Kempton 1890- *Film 1, –2, TwYS*
Greene, Leon *HalFC 80*
Greene, Loretta *DrBlPA*
Greene, Lorne 1915- *BiE&WWA, CreCan 2, FilmEn, FilmgC, ForYSC, HalFC 80, IntMPA 77, –75, –76, –78, –79, –80, MotPP, MovMk, RkOn 2[port], WhoHol A*
Greene, Martin M 1918- *IntWWM 77*
Greene, Maurice 1695-1755 *Baker 78, MusMk, OxMus*
Greene, Maurice 1696-1755 *NewGrD 80[port]*
Greene, Max 1896-1968 *FilmgC, HalFC 80*
Greene, Milton L *AmSCAP 66, –80, BiE&WWA, NotNAT*
Greene, Mort 1912- *AmSCAP 66, –80*
Greene, Nancy Ellen *WomWMM B*
Greene, Narada 1937- *EncJzS 70*
Greene, Norman d1945 *NotNAT B*
Greene, Norman 1930- *AmSCAP 66, –80*
Greene, Otis *BlkAmP*
Greene, Patterson 1899-1968 *BiE&WWA, NotNAT B*
Greene, Plunket 1865-1936 *NewGrD 80*
Greene, Reuben 1938- *DrBlPA, WhoHol A*
Greene, Richard *MotPP*
Greene, Richard 1914- *HalFC 80, HolP 30[port]*
Greene, Richard 1918- *FilmEn, FilmgC, ForYSC, IlWWBF, MovMk[port], WhoHol A*
Greene, Robert 1558-1592 *CnThe, EncWT, Ent, McGEWD, NotNAT B, PlP&P, REnWD[port]*
Greene, Robert 1560?-1592 *OxThe*
Greene, Robert A *PupTheA*
Greene, Robert Victor 1941- *AmSCAP 80*
Greene, Ry *NewGrD 80*
Greene, Schuyler 1880-1927 *AmSCAP 66, –80*
Greene, Shecky *WhoHol A*
Greene, Stanley 1911- *DrBlPA, WhoHol A*
Greene, Thomas Enoch 1935- *IntWWM 77, –80*
Greene, W Howard d1956 *HalFC 80*
Greene, Walter d1963 *NotNAT B*
Greene, Walter Wesley 1910- *AmSCAP 80*
Greene, Will 1923- *BiE&WWA*
Greene, William 1927-1970 *WhScrn 74, –77*
Greene, William Howard *FilmEn*
Greener, Dorothy 1917-1971 *BiE&WWA, NotNAT B, WhThe, WhoThe 72*
Greenfield, Amy *WomWMM A, –B*
Greenfield, Bruce Henry 1948- *IntWWM 77, –80*
Greenfield, Edward 1928- *Baker 78, WhoMus 72*
Greenfield, Elizabeth Taylor 1809-1876 *BiDAmM*
Greenfield, Irving H 1902- *IntMPA 77, –75, –76, –78, –79, –80*
Greenfield, Josh *MorBAP*
Greenfield, Leo 1916- *IntMPA 77, –75, –76, –78, –79, –80*
Greenfield, Lois *WomWMM B*
Greenhaw, Julia Helen 1912- *IntWWM 77*
Greenhill, Harold Walter 1902- *WhoMus 72*
Greenhill, Mitch 1944- *AmSCAP 66, –80*
Greenholz, Martin 1904- *AmSCAP 66*
Greenhouse, Bernard 1916- *NewGrD 80*
Greenhouse, Martha *WhoHol A*
Greening, Anthony John 1940- *IntWWM 80*
Greening, Richard George 1927- *IntWWM 77, –80*
Greenlaw, Walter 1900- *AmSCAP 66*
Greenleaf, Mace d1912 *WhScrn 77*
Greenleaf, Raymond 1892-1963 *FilmgC, HalFC 80, NotNAT B, WhScrn 74, –77, WhoHol B*
Greenleaf, Raymond 1892-1965 *ForYSC*
Greenlee, Rufus 1895?-1963 *BlksBF*
Greenlee, Sam *MorBAP*
Greenlee And Drayton *BlksBF*
Greenlund, Alys Gertrude 1902- *AmSCAP 66, –80*
Greenridge, Gertrude *MorBAP*
Greenslade *IlEncR*
Greensmith, John Brian 1929- *IntWWM 80, WhoMus 72*
Greenspan, Lou *IntMPA 77, –75, –76, –78, –79, –80*
Greenstreet, Sidney 1879-1954 *FilmgC, MovMk[port]*
Greenstreet, Sidney 1880-1954 *ForYSC*
Greenstreet, Sydney 1879-1954 *BiDFilm, –81, CmMov, FilmEn, HalFC 80, HolCA[port], HolP 40[port], MotPP, NotNAT B, OxFilm, Vers A[port], WhScrn 74, –77, WhThe, WhoHol B, WorEFlm*
Greenwald, Joel 1938- *AmSCAP 66, –80*
Greenwald, Joseph d1938 *NotNAT B, WhThe*
Greenwald, Robert *MorBAP*
Greenwalt, Mrs. M H *OxMus*
Greenway, Ann *Film 2*
Greenway, John *EncFCWM 69*
Greenway, Kenneth James 1926- *WhoMus 72*
Greenway, Lee *WhoHrs 80*
Greenway, Tom *ForYSC*
Greenwich, Ellie *ConMuA 80A*
Greenwich, Lorenzo Keith, Jr. 1936- *IntWWM 77*
Greenwich, Sonny 1936- *EncJzS 70*
Greenwood, Barrie Leck 1934- *IntWWM 77, –80*
Greenwood, Charlotte *AmPS B*
Greenwood, Charlotte d1978 *JoeFr[port]*
Greenwood, Charlotte 1890-1978 *Funs[port], HalFC 80*
Greenwood, Charlotte 1893- *BiE&WWA, CmpEPM, EncMT, Film 1, –2, FilmgC, ForYSC, IntMPA 77, –75, –76, –78, MotPP, MovMk[port], NotNAT, ThFT[port], Vers A[port], WhThe, WhoHol A*
Greenwood, Charlotte 1893-1978 *FilmEn*
Greenwood, Edwin 1895- *IlWWBF*
Greenwood, Ethel 1898-1970 *WhScrn 74, –77*
Greenwood, Frank J *BlkAmP, MorBAP*
Greenwood, Jack 1919- *FilmgC, HalFC 80, IntMPA 77, –75, –76, –78, –79, –80*
Greenwood, James *OxMus*
Greenwood, Jane 1934- *NotNAT, WhoOp 76, WhoThe 72, –77*
Greenwood, Joan 1921- *BiDFilm, –81, BiE&WWA, CnThe, FilmAG WE, FilmEn, FilmgC, HalFC 80, IlWWBF[port], IntMPA 77, –75, –76, –78, –79, –80, MotPP, MovMk, NotNAT, OxFilm, WhoHol A, WhoThe 72, –77, WorEFlm[port]*
Greenwood, John Danforth Herman 1889- *FilmgC, HalFC 80, WhoMus 72*
Greenwood, Michael Vernon 1951- *AmSCAP 80*
Greenwood, Walter 1903-1974 *ConDr 73, HalFC 80, WhThe, WhoThe 72*
Greenwood, Winifred 1892-1961 *Film 1, –2, TwYS, WhScrn 77*
Greenwood, Winnifred 1892-1961 *WhoHol B*
Greer, Bonnie *MorBAP*
Greer, Dabbs 1917- *ForYSC, WhoHol A*
Greer, Dabbs 1920?- *WhoHrs 80*
Greer, David Clive 1937- *IntWWM 80, WhoMus 72*
Greer, Edward G 1920- *NotNAT*
Greer, Jane 1924- *FilmEn, FilmgC, ForYSC, HalFC 80, IntMPA 77, –75, –76, –78, –79, –80, MotPP, MovMk[port], WhoHol A*
Greer, Jesse 1896- *AmSCAP 66, –80, CmpEPM*
Greer, Julian 1871-1928 *WhScrn 74, –77, WhoHol B*
Greer, LaVerne G 1916- *IntWWM 77*
Greer, Linda 1939- *IntWWM 77, –80*
Greer, Michael 1917- *WhoHol A*
Greer, Michael Barry 1938- *AmSCAP 80*
Greer, Sonny 1903- *CmpEPM, EncJzS 70, IlEncJ, WhoJazz 72*
Greer, Thomas Henry 1916- *IntWWM 77, –80*
Greer, William Alexander 1903- *BiDAmM, EncJzS 70*
Greet, Sir Ben 1857-1936 *EncWT, OxThe, PlP&P, WhoStg 1906, –1908*
Greet, Clare 1871-1939 *Film 2, NotNAT B, WhScrn 74, –77, WhThe, WhoHol B*
Greet, Maurice d1951 *NotNAT B*
Greet, Mildred C d1964 *NotNAT B*
Greet, Sir Philip 1857-1936 *NotNAT A, –B, WhThe*
Greeting, Thomas d1682 *NewGrD 80*
Greevy, Bernadette *WhoMus 72*
Grefe, William *IntMPA 77, –75, –76, –78, –79, –80, WhoHrs 80*
Greff Bakfark, Valentin *NewGrD 80*
Grefinger, Wolfgang 147-?-1515? *NewGrD 80*
Greger, Emmy 1944- *WhoOp 76*
Gregg, Arnold *Film 2*
Gregg, Bobby And His Friends *RkOn*
Gregg, Everley 1888?-1959 *HalFC 80*
Gregg, Everley 1903-1959 *NotNAT B, WhThe, WhoHol B*
Gregg, Everly d1959 *WhScrn 74, –77*
Gregg, Hubert *WhoHol A*
Gregg, Hubert 1914- *FilmgC, HalFC 80*
Gregg, Hubert 1916- *WhoThe 72, –77*
Gregg, Mary Louise 1921- *AmSCAP 66, –80*
Gregg, Virginia *ForYSC, WhoHol A*
Greggs, Herbert D 1931- *BlkAmP*
Greggs, William 1652?-1710 *NewGrD 80*
Gregh, Louis 1843-1915 *Baker 78*
Gregoir, Edouard 1822-1890 *Baker 78,*

NewGrD 80
Gregoir, Jacques 1817-1876 *NewGrD 80*
Gregoir, Joseph Jacques 1817-1876 *Baker 78*
Gregor, Bohumil 1911- *IntWWM 77*
Gregor, Bohumil 1926- *IntWWM 80, NewGrD 80, WhoMus 72, WhoOp 76*
Gregor, Cestmir 1926- *Baker 78, NewGrD 80*
Gregor, Christian Friedrich 1723-1801 *Baker 78, NewGrD 80*
Gregor, Josef 1940- *IntWWM 80*
Gregor, Joseph 1888-1960 *EncWT*
Gregor, Nora 1890?-1949 *HalFC 80, NotNAT B, OxFilm, WhScrn 74, -77, WhoHol B*
Gregor, Vladimir 1916- *IntWWM 77, -80*
Gregora, Frantisek 1819-1887 *NewGrD 80*
Gregorc, Jancz 1934- *IntWWM 80*
Gregorc, Joza 1914- *IntWWM 77, -80*
Gregoretti, Ugo 1930- *WorEFlm*
Gregori, Annibale d1633? *NewGrD 80*
Gregori, Giovanni Lorenzo 1663-1745 *NewGrD 80*
Gregori, Mercia 1901- *WhThe*
Gregorian, Henry 1924- *IntWWM 80*
Gregorian, Rouben 1915- *ConAmC, IntWWM 77, -80*
Gregory I 540-604 *Baker 78*
Gregory, Lady 1852-1932 *EncWT, Ent, ModWD, PlP&P[port]*
Gregory, Lady 1859-1932 *WhThe*
Gregory Of Handzta 759-861 *NewGrD 80*
Gregory Of Narek 950-1003 *NewGrD 80*
Gregory Of Tours 538-594 *NewGrD 80*
Gregory, Saint *OxMus*
Gregory The Great 540?-604 *NewGrD 80*
Gregory, Andre *NotNAT, WhoThe 77*
Gregory, Anne *WomWMM B*
Gregory, Lady Augusta 1852-1932 *CnThe, McGEWD[port], NotNAT A, -B, OxThe*
Gregory, Barbara Elizabeth 1921- *IntWWM 77, -80*
Gregory, Bobby 1900- *AmSCAP 80, BiDAmM*
Gregory, Bobby 1900-1971 *AmSCAP 66, WhScrn 74, -77*
Gregory, Catherine Elizebeth 1913- *AmSCAP 80*
Gregory, Cynthia 1946- *CnOxB*
Gregory, David *IntMPA 77, -75, -76, -78, -79, -80*
Gregory, David L 1944- *AmSCAP 80*
Gregory, Dick 1932- *DrBlPA, JoeFr[port], NotNAT A, WhoHol A*
Gregory, Dora 1872-1954 *NotNAT B, WhThe*
Gregory, Dora 1873-1954 *WhScrn 74, -77, WhoHol B*
Gregory, Edna 1905-1965 *Film 2, TwYS, WhScrn 74, -77*
Gregory, Ena *Film 2, TwYS, WhoHol A*
Gregory, Frank 1884- *WhThe*
Gregory, Lady Isabella Augusta 1852-1932 *REnWD[port]*
Gregory, James 1911- *BiE&WWA, FilmEn, FilmgC, ForYSC, HalFC 80, MotPP, MovMk, NotNAT, WhoHol A*
Gregory, Jill 1918- *CnOxB, DancEn 78*
Gregory, Johann Gottfried 1631-1675 *OxThe*
Gregory, John 1914- *CnOxB, DancEn 78*
Gregory, John 1924- *IntWWM 77*
Gregory, John R 1918- *IntMPA 77, -75, -76, -78, -79, -80*
Gregory, Linda O'Hara *AmSCAP 80*
Gregory, Mollie 1940- *WomWMM A, -B*
Gregory, Paul 1905?- *FilmgC, HalFC 80*
Gregory, Paul 1920- *BiE&WWA, NewYTET, NotNAT*
Gregory, Sara 1921- *WhThe*
Gregory, Thea *WhoHol A*
Gregory, W A 1923- *BiE&WWA*
Gregory, Will d1926 *Film 2, WhoHol B*
Gregory, William *NewGrD 80*
Gregory, William 1605?-1663 *NewGrD 80*
Gregory, William H d1926 *WhScrn 74, -77*
Gregson, Edward 1945- *IntWWM 77, -80, WhoMus 72*
Gregson, Harry 1885?-1963 *NewOrJ*
Gregson, James R 1889- *WhThe*
Gregson, John 1919-1975 *CmMov, FilmAG WE, FilmEn, FilmgC, ForYSC, HalFC 80, IlWWBF[port], IntMPA 75, WhScrn 77, WhoHol C*
Greicius, Betty-Jean *CreCan 2*
Greif, Andreas *McGEWD[port]*
Greig, Gavin 1856-1914 *NewGrD 80*
Greig, Robert 1880-1958 *FilmEn, FilmgC, HalFC 80, HolCA[port], MovMk[port], Vers B[port], WhScrn 74, -77, WhoHol B*
Greig, William Sydney 1910- *WhoMus 72*
Grein, J T 1862-1935 *WhThe*
Grein, Mrs. J T *WhThe*
Grein, Jack Thomas 1862-1935 *EncWT, OxThe, PlP&P[port]*
Grein, Jacob Thomas 1862-1935 *NotNAT A, -B*
Grein, Louis *Baker 78*
Greindl, Josef 1912- *CmOp, NewGrD 80, WhoOp 76*
Greindlks, Josef *WhoMus 72*
Greiner, Alvin G 1911- *AmSCAP 66, -80*
Greiner, Fritz *Film 2*
Greiner, Nancy *WomWMM B*
Greines, Edwin 1934- *AmSCAP 66*
Greiss, Yusef 1899-1961 *NewGrD 80*
Greissle, Felix 1899- *Baker 78*
Greiter, Mathis 1495?-1550 *NewGrD 80*
Greiter, Matthaeus 1490?-1550 *Baker 78*
Greiter, Matthias 1495?-1550 *NewGrD 80*
Greitter, Matthaeus 1495?-1550 *NewGrD 80*
Greitter, Matthias 1495?-1550 *NewGrD 80*
Greive, Thomas 1799-1882 *NotNAT B*
Greive, William 1800-1844 *NotNAT B*
Grell, Eduard August 1800-1886 *Baker 78, NewGrD 80*
Gremillon, Jean 1901-1959 *BiDFilm, -81, FilmEn, FilmgC, HalFC 80, OxFilm, WorEFlm*
Gremillon, Jean 1902-1959 *DcFM*
Gremo, Maryla *DancEn 78*
Grene, David 1913- *BiE&WWA*
Greneker, Claude P d1949 *NotNAT B*
Grenet, Eliseo 1893-1950 *AmSCAP 66, -80*
Grenet, Francois Lupien 1700?-1753 *NewGrD 80*
Grenet-Dancourt, E d1913 *NotNAT B*
Grenfell, Joyce 1910-1979 *BiE&WWA, EncMT, Ent, FilmEn, FilmgC, ForYSC, HalFC 80, IlWWBF[port], -A, MotPP, MovMk[port], NotNAT, OxThe, WhoHol A, WhoThe 72, -77*
Grenier *NewGrD 80*
Grenier, Francois *NewGrD 80*
Grenier, Louis *NewGrD 80*
Grennan, Laurie *WomWMM*
Grennard, Elliott 1907-1968 *AmSCAP 66, -80*
Grenon, Nicolas 1380?-1456 *NewGrD 80*
Grenouillet, Jean *NewGrD 80*
Grenser *NewGrD 80*
Grenser, Carl Augustin 1720-1807 *NewGrD 80*
Grenser, Carl Augustin 1756-1814 *NewGrD 80*
Grenser, Johann Heinrich Wilhelm 1764-1813 *NewGrD 80*
Grenville, Lillian 1888-1928 *BiDAmM*
Grequillon, Thomas *NewGrD 80*
Gresac, Fred *WhThe*
Gresak, Jozef 1907- *Baker 78*
Gresemund, Dietrich 1472-1512 *NewGrD 80*
Gresham, Ann *ConAmC*
Gresham, Edgar *PupTheA*
Gresham, Herbert d1921 *NotNAT B*
Gresham, Hubert E 1916- *AmSCAP 80*
Gresham, Sir Thomas 1519?-1579 *OxMus*
Gresham And Gresham *BlksBF*
Greshler, Abner J 1914- *IntMPA 77, -75, -76, -78, -79, -80*
Gresnich, Antoine-Frederic 1755-1799 *Baker 78, NewGrD 80*
Gresnick, Antoine-Frederic 1755-1799 *NewGrD 80*
Gresnick, Antoine Frederic 1755-1799 *OxMus*
Gresse, Jacob *NewGrD 80*
Gressel, Joel 1943- *ConAmC*
Gresset, Jean-Baptiste-Louis 1709-1777 *McGEWD[port], OxThe*
Gressieker, Hermann 1903- *CnMD*
Gretchaninof, Alexander 1864-1956 *OxMus*
Gretchaninoff, Alexander 1864-1956 *BiDAmM, CompSN[port]*
Gretchaninov, Alexander 1864-1956 *Baker 78, NewEOp 71*
Greth, Roma *NatPD[port]*
Gretillat *Film 1*
Gretillat, Jacques *Film 2*
Gretler, Heinrich 1897- *FilmAG WE, Film 2*
Gretry, Andre Ernest Modeste 1741-1813 *Baker 78, BnBkM 80, CmOp, DcCom 77[port], GrComp[port], MusMk, NewEOp 71, NewGrD 80[port], OxMus*
Gretry, Andre Ernest Modeste 1742-1813 *DcCom&M 79*
Greuter, Matthias *NewGrD 80*
Grevenius, Herbert 1901- *ModWD*
Grever, Maria 1894-1951 *AmSCAP 66, -80*
Greville, Edmond T 1905-1966 *IlWWBF*
Greville, Edmond T 1906-1966 *FilmEn, FilmgC, HalFC 80, WhScrn 77, WorEFlm*
Greville, Sir Fulke 1554-1628 *REnWD[port]*
Grevillius, Nils 1893-1970 *Baker 78, NewGrD 80*
Grevin, Jacques 1538?-1570? *OxThe*
Grew, Mary 1902-1971 *NotNAT B, WhThe, WhoThe 72*
Grey, Al 1925- *EncJzS 70*
Grey, Albert Thornton 1925- *BiDAmM, EncJzS 70*
Grey, Anne 1907- *Film 2, IlWWBF, WhThe*
Grey, Beryl 1927- *CnOxB, DancEn 78[port], WhThe*
Grey, Carolyn 1922- *CmpEPM*
Grey, Clifford 1887-1941 *AmPS, AmSCAP 66, -80, BiDAmM, CmpEPM, EncMT, NewCBMT, NotNAT B, WhThe*
Grey, Ethel *Film 2*
Grey, Eve *WhThe*
Grey, Frank H 1883-1951 *AmSCAP 66, -80, NotNAT B*
Grey, Gandalf T *AmSCAP 80*
Grey, Geoffrey David 1934- *WhoMus 72*
Grey, Ginger *AmSCAP 80*
Grey, Gloria 1909-1947 *Film 2, WhScrn 74, -77, WhoHol B*
Grey, Jack *Film 2*
Grey, Jane 1883-1944 *Film 1, NotNAT B, WhScrn 74, -77, WhThe, WhoHol B*
Grey, Jerry 1910-1954 *WhScrn 74, -77*
Grey, Joel *IntMPA 75, -76*
Grey, Joel 1931- *ForYSC*
Grey, Joel 1932- *EncMT, FilmEn, HalFC 80, IntMPA 77, -78, -79, -80, NotNAT, WhoHol A, WhoThe 72, -77*
Grey, Joseph W 1879-1956 *AmSCAP 66, -80*
Grey, Katherine 1873-1950 *NotNAT B, WhScrn 77, WhThe, WhoStg 1906, -1908*
Grey, Lanny 1909- *AmSCAP 66, -80*
Grey, Leonard d1918 *WhScrn 77*
Grey, Lewis *ConMuA 80B*
Grey, Lita *MotPP*
Grey, Lita 1908- *Film 2*
Grey, Lita 1909- *HalFC 80, WhoHol A*
Grey, Lynda 1913-1963 *WhScrn 77*
Grey, Lytton d1931 *NotNAT B*
Grey, Madeleine 1896- *Baker 78*
Grey, Madeleine 1897- *NewGrD 80*
Grey, Madeline 1887-1950 *WhScrn 74, -77, WhoHol B*
Grey, Marie De d1897 *NotNAT B*
Grey, Marion d1949 *NotNAT B*
Grey, Mary *WhThe*
Grey, Minna *Film 2*
Grey, Nan 1918- *FilmEn, FilmgC, ForYSC, HalFC 80, MovMk, ThFT[port], WhoHol A*
Grey, Olga 1897-1973 *Film 1, WhScrn 77*
Grey, Ray *Film 1, -2*
Grey, Sylvia d1958 *NotNAT B*
Grey, Virginia 1917- *FilmEn, Film 2, FilmgC, ForYSC, HalFC 80, MGM[port], ThFT[port], What 5[port], WhoHol A*
Grey, Virginia 1918- *MovMk[port]*
Grey, Virginia 1923- *IntMPA 77, -75, -76, -78, -79, -80*
Grey, Zane 1875-1939 *FilmgC, HalFC 80*
Grey Owl 1888-1938 *CreCan 1*
Greyter, Matthias *NewGrD 80*
Grgic, Marijan 1929- *IntWWM 77, -80*
Grgicevic, Athanasius *NewGrD 80*
Gribble, George Dunning 1882-1956 *WhThe*
Gribble, Harry Wagstaff 1896- *BiE&WWA, NotNAT, WhThe*
Gribbon, Eddie 1890-1965 *Vers A[port], WhoHol B*
Gribbon, Eddie 1892-1965 *Film 1, -2, TwYS*

Gribbon, Eddie 1893-1965 *ForYSC*
Gribbon, Edward T 1890-1965 *WhScrn 74, -77*
Gribbon, Harry 1886-1960 *ForYSC*
Gribbon, Harry 1886-1961 *NotNAT B, WhScrn 74, -77*
Gribbon, Harry 1888-1960 *Film 1, -2, TwYS, WhoHol B*
Gribenski, Jean Francois 1944- *IntWWM 77, -80*
Gribov, Alexander Ivanovich 1934- *CnOxB*
Gribov, Alexei Nikolaevich 1902- *WhThe*
Griboyedov, Aleksandr 1793-1829 *McGEWD[port]*
Griboyedov, Alexander 1793-1829 *CnThe, REnWD[port]*
Griboyedov, Alexander 1795-1829 *EncWT, Ent, NotNAT B, OxThe, PlP&P*
Gribunin, V F *PlP&P[port]*
Grice, Paul Russell 1943- *WhoMus 72*
Grice, Wayne *DrBlPA*
Grider, Rufus 1817- *Baker 78*
Gridin, Anatoli Vasilyevich 1929- *CnOxB*
Grieb, Herbert C 1898-1973 *AmSCAP 66, -80, ConAmC*
Griebling, Otto 1896-1972 *Ent*
Grieg, Edvard Hagerup 1843-1907 *Baker 78, BnBkM 80, CmpBCM, CnOxB, DcCom 77[port], DcCom&M 79, GrComp[port], MusMk, NewGrD 80[port], NotNAT B, OxMus*
Grieg, Edward 1843-1907 *DcPup*
Grieg, Nina Hagerup 1845-1935 *Baker 78, NewGrD 80[port]*
Grieg, Nordahl Brun 1902-1943 *CnMD, CnThe, EncWT, McGEWD[port], ModWD, NotNAT B, OxThe, REnWD[port]*
Griem, Helmut 1940- *FilmgC, HalFC 80, WhoHol A*
Griend, Koos VanDe 1905-1950 *Baker 78, NewGrD 80*
Griepenkerl, Friedrich Konrad 1782-1849 *Baker 78, NewGrD 80*
Griepenkerl, Wolfgang Robert 1810-1868 *Baker 78, NewGrD 80*
Grier, Christopher 1922- *WhoMus 72*
Grier, Sir Edmund Wyly *CreCan 2*
Grier, Eldon Brockwill 1917- *CreCan 2*
Grier, Francis John Roy 1955- *IntWWM 77*
Grier, Gene 1942- *AmSCAP 80*
Grier, George Edward 1934- *IntWWM 77*
Grier, Hugh Christopher 1922- *IntWWM 77, -80*
Grier, James W 1902-1959 *AmSCAP 66, -80*
Grier, Jimmie 1902-1959 *BgBands 74, CmpEPM*
Grier, Jimmy 1902-1959 *WhScrn 77*
Grier, Pam *FilmEn, WhoHol A*
Grier, Pam 1949- *HalFC 80*
Grier, Pam 1950?- *DrBlPA*
Grier, Roosevelt *HalFC 80*
Grier, Roosevelt 1932- *DrBlPA*
Grier, Rosey *WhoHol A*
Grier, Sir Wyly 1862-1957 *CreCan 2*
Grierson, David Allan 1950- *IntWWM 77*
Grierson, John 1898-1972 *BiDFilm, -81, DcFM, FilmEn, FilmgC, HalFC 80, IlWWBF, -A, OxFilm, WorEFlm[port]*
Grierson, John Alexander 1928- *WhoMus 72*
Gries, Thomas S 1922- *IntMPA 77, -75, -76*
Gries, Tom d1976 *NewYTET*
Gries, Tom 1922- *CmMov, FilmgC*
Gries, Tom 1922-1977 *FilmEn, HalFC 80*
Griesbach, John Henry 1798-1875 *Baker 78, NewGrD 80*
Griesbach, Karl-Rudi 1916- *NewGrD 80*
Griesbacher, Peter 1864-1933 *Baker 78*
Griesbaum, Leonard 1932- *AmSCAP 66*
Griese, Friedrich 1890-1975 *CnMD, ModWD*
Griesinger, Georg August 1769-1845 *NewGrD 80*
Grieve, Alexander John 1923- *IntWWM 80*
Grieve, John Henderson 1770-1845 *NotNAT B, OxThe*
Grieve, Thomas 1799-1882 *OxThe*
Grieve, Thomas Walford 1841-1882 *OxThe*
Grieve, William 1800-1844 *OxThe*
Grieviler, Jehan De *NewGrD 80*
Griff, John Ray 1942- *AmSCAP 80*
Griff, Ray 1940- *IlEncCM*
Griffel, Kay *IntWWM 77, -80, WhoOp 76*
Griffel, L Michael 1942- *IntWWM 77, -80*
Griffell, Jose Martinez 1905-1955 *WhScrn 74, -77*
Griffen, Benjamin d1740 *NotNAT B*
Griffes, Charles Tomlinson 1884-1920 *AmSCAP 66, -80, Baker 78, BiDAmM, BnBkM 80, CompSN[port], ConAmC, DcCom&M 79, DcCM, MusMk, NewGrD 80[port], OxMus*
Griffett, James Kenneth George 1939- *IntWWM 80*
Griffey, Dick *ConMuA 80B*
Griffey, Louise Pate 1922- *IntWWM 77*
Griffies, Ethel 1878-1975 *BiE&WWA, FilmgC, ForYSC, HalFC 80, MotPP, MovMk, NotNAT, WhScrn 77, WhThe, WhoHol C, WhoThe 72*
Griffin, Anne *IntWWM 77*
Griffin, Arthur d1953 *NotNAT B*
Griffin, Basil *Film 2*
Griffin, Carlton Elliott 1893-1940 *Film 2, WhScrn 74, -77, WhoHol B*
Griffin, Charles 1888-1956 *WhScrn 74, -77*
Griffin, Chris 1915- *CmpEPM*
Griffin, Claud N, Jr. 1940- *AmSCAP 80*
Griffin, Cris Gordon 1915- *WhoJazz 72*
Griffin, Dennis *CpmDNM 76*
Griffin, Elsie *WhThe*
Griffin, Frank 1861- *TwYS A*
Griffin, Frank L 1889-1953 *WhScrn 74, -77*
Griffin, Gerald d1840 *NotNAT B*
Griffin, Gerald d1962 *NotNAT B*
Griffin, Gerald 1854-1919 *Film 1, WhScrn 77*
Griffin, Gerald 1891-1962 *AmSCAP 66, -80*
Griffin, Gerald 1892-1962 *WhScrn 77*
Griffin, Harvi Alonzo 1936- *IntWWM 77, -80*
Griffin, Hayden 1930- *BiE&WWA*
Griffin, Hayden 1943- *WhoThe 77*
Griffin, Henry William 1935- *ConAmTC*
Griffin, John Arnold, III 1928- *BiDAmM, EncJzS 70*
Griffin, Johnny 1928- *EncJzS 70, IlEncJ*
Griffin, Josephine 1928- *FilmgC, HalFC 80, WhoHol A*
Griffin, Judson 1951- *IntWWM 80*
Griffin, Katharine Shelagh Marguerite 1920- *WhoMus 72*
Griffin, Ken *CmpEPM*
Griffin, Kenneth Wilson 1909-1956 *AmSCAP 80*
Griffin, Lawrence E 1925- *IntWWM 77*
Griffin, Lilah Anne *WhoMus 72*
Griffin, Margaret Fuller *WhScrn 74, -77*
Griffin, Meg *ConMuA 80B*
Griffin, Merv 1925- *CmpEPM, ForYSC, IntMPA 77, -75, -76, -78, -79, -80, NewYTET, WhoHol A*
Griffin, Norman 1887- *WhThe*
Griffin, Oscar *MorBAP*
Griffin, Rex 1912- *IlEncCM*
Griffin, Robert A, Jr. 1949- *AmSCAP 80*
Griffin, Rodney *CmpGMD*
Griffin, Russell Francis *Film 2*
Griffin, Susan 1943- *NatPD[port]*
Griffin, Wally *AmSCAP 66, -80*
Griffin, William *NatPD[port]*
Griffin, Z Wayne 1907- *IntMPA 77, -75, -76, -78, -79*
Griffin, Zaidee *PupTheA*
Griffini, Giacomo *NewGrD 80*
Griffis, Elliot 1893-1967 *AmSCAP 66, Baker 78, BiDAmM, ConAmC, NewGrD 80*
Griffith, Andy 1926- *BiE&WWA, FilmEn, FilmgC, ForYSC, HalFC 80, IntMPA 77, -75, -76, -78, -79, -80, MotPP, WhoHol A*
Griffith, Brenda 1917- *WhoMus 72*
Griffith, Carlton 1893-1940 *Film 2*
Griffith, Charles B *WhoHrs 80*
Griffith, Corinne *AmSCAP 66, MotPP*
Griffith, Corinne 1896?- *ThFT[port], What 2[port]*
Griffith, Corinne 1896-1979 *FilmEn*
Griffith, Corinne 1898- *Film 1, -2, FilmgC, HalFC 80, MovMk[port], TwYS*
Griffith, Corinne 1899?- *ForYSC, WhoHol A*
Griffith, D W d1948 *WhoHol B, WomWMM*
Griffith, D W 1874-1948 *FilmgC, HalFC 80, WhoHrs 80*
Griffith, D W 1875-1948 *AmFD, BiDFilm, -81, FilmEn*
Griffith, D W 1880-1948 *CmMov*
Griffith, David 1939- *WhoOp 76*
Griffith, David Wark 1875-1948 *DcFM, Film 1, MovMk[port], OxFilm, TwYS, -A, WhScrn 74, -77, WorEFlm[port]*
Griffith, David Wark 1880-1948 *WhThe*
Griffith, Dennis 1938- *DancEn 78*
Griffith, Edward H 1894- *FilmEn, FilmgC, HalFC 80, TwYS A*
Griffith, Eleanor *Film 2*
Griffith, Gordon 1907-1958 *Film 1, -2, WhScrn 74, -77, WhoHol B*
Griffith, Hubert 1896-1953 *NotNAT B, OxThe, WhThe*
Griffith, Hugh 1912- *BiE&WWA, FilmAG WE, FilmgC, ForYSC, HalFC 80, IntMPA 77, -75, -76, -78, -79, -80, MotPP, MovMk[port], NotNAT, WhoHol A, WhoThe 72, -77*
Griffith, Hugh 1912-1980 *FilmEn*
Griffith, James *ForYSC, WhoHol A*
Griffith, James 1919- *FilmgC, HalFC 80*
Griffith, James J 1916- *AmSCAP 66, -80, Vers A[port]*
Griffith, Katherine 1858-1934 *Film 1, -2, WhoHol B*
Griffith, Kenneth 1921- *FilmgC, HalFC 80, WhoHol A*
Griffith, Linda 1884-1949 *NotNAT B, WhScrn 74, -77*
Griffith, Lydia Eliza 1832-1897 *NotNAT B*
Griffith, Melanie *FilmEn, WhoHol A*
Griffith, Peter 1943- *ConAmC*
Griffith, R D 1877-1958 *NewGrD 80*
Griffith, Raymond d1957 *GrMovC[port], MotPP, NotNAT B, WhoHol B*
Griffith, Raymond 1890-1957 *FilmEn, TwYS, WhScrn 74, -77*
Griffith, Raymond 1894-1937 *FilmgC, HalFC 80*
Griffith, Raymond 1896-1957 *Film 1, -2, MovMk*
Griffith, Richard 1912-1969 *FilmEn, FilmgC, HalFC 80*
Griffith, Robert 1847-1911 *NewGrD 80*
Griffith, Robert 1907-1961 *EncMT, Film 2, NotNAT B, WhoHol B*
Griffith, Robert B 1914- *ConAmC*
Griffith, Shirley 1908-1974 *BluesWW*
Griffith, William M 1897-1960 *WhScrn 74, -77, WhoHol B*
Griffiths, Albert 1910- *WhoMus 72*
Griffiths, Ann *IntWWM 77, -80, WhoMus 72*
Griffiths, Chris M 1948- *IntWWM 80*
Griffiths, Christopher 1948- *IntWWM 77*
Griffiths, David John 1950- *IntWWM 77, -80*
Griffiths, David Maurice 1907- *IntWWM 77, -80*
Griffiths, Derek 1946- *WhoThe 77*
Griffiths, Dorothea Gladys 1917- *WhoMus 72*
Griffiths, Eric *WhoMus 72*
Griffiths, Frederic James *WhoMus 72*
Griffiths, Gwynedd Emily 1914- *WhoMus 72*
Griffiths, Gwyneth 1943- *IntWWM 77, -80*
Griffiths, Jane *WhoHol A*
Griffiths, Jane 1929-1975 *WhScrn 77*
Griffiths, Jane 1930- *FilmgC, HalFC 80, WhThe, WhoThe 72*
Griffiths, Keith Charles 1941- *WhoMus 72*
Griffiths, Leonard James 1925- *WhoMus 72*
Griffiths, Marion Kathleen 1932- *WhoMus 72*
Griffiths, Paul 1947- *IntWWM 77, -80*
Griffiths, Robert 1824-1903 *NewGrD 80*
Griffiths, Thomas Vernon 1894- *WhoMus 72*
Griffiths, Trevor 1935- *ConDr 73, -77, WhoThe 77*
Griffo *Film 1*
Griffoni, Matteo 1351-1426 *NewGrD 80*
Grigg, Ann *Film 2*
Griggs, Elfreda Marjorie *WhoMus 72*
Griggs, Frances *IntWWM 80*
Griggs, John 1909-1967 *WhScrn 74, -77, WhoHol B*
Griggs, Loyal 1904- *FilmgC, HalFC 80, WorEFlm*
Griggs, Loyal 1907?-1978 *FilmEn*
Griggs, Ruby Frances *WhoMus 72*
Grignani, Lodovico *NewGrD 80*
Grignon, Claude-Henri 1894- *CreCan 2*

Grignon, Germaine Guevremont *CreCan 1*
Grignon, Ricard Lamote De *Baker 78*
Grigny, Nicolas De 1671-1703 *OxMus*
Grigny, Nicolas De 1672-1703 *BnBkM 80, NewGrD 80*
Grigorescu, Elena 1943- *WhoOp 76*
Grigoriev, Serge Leonovich 1883-1968 *CnOxB, DancEn 78*
Grigorieva, Tamara 1918- *CnOxB, DancEn 78*
Grigoriu, Teodor 1926- *NewGrD 80*
Grigoriu, Theodor 1926- *Baker 78, IntWWM 77, -80*
Grigorova, Romayne 1926- *CnOxB*
Grigorovich, Yuri Nikolaievich 1927- *CnOxB, DancEn 78*
Grigsby, Beverly Pinsky 1928- *ConAmC*
Griller, Arnold 1937- *ConAmC*
Griller, Sidney Aaron 1911- *IntWWM 77, -80, WhoMus 72*
Grillet, Laurent 1851-1901 *NewGrD 80*
Grilli, Umberto 1934- *WhoOp 76*
Grillo, Basil F 1910- *IntMPA 77, -75, -76, -78, -79, -80*
Grillo, Frank R 1912- *AmSCAP 80*
Grillo, Giovanni Battista d1622 *NewGrD 80*
Grillo, Joann Danielle 1939- *IntWWM 80, WhoOp 76*
Grillo, John 1942- *ConDr 73, -77*
Grillparzer, Franz 1791-1872 *CnThe, EncWT, Ent, McGEWD[port], NewGrD 80, NotNAT B, OxThe, REnWD[port]*
Grimace *NewGrD 80*
Grimache *NewGrD 80*
Grimaldi *PupTheA*
Grimaldi, Alberto 1926- *FilmEn*
Grimaldi, Alberto 1927- *IntMPA 79, -80*
Grimaldi, George H d1951 *NotNAT B*
Grimaldi, Giorgio 1936- *WhoOp 76*
Grimaldi, Hugo *WhoHrs 80*
Grimaldi, Joseph 1778-1837 *CnThe, EncWT, Ent[port], OxThe, PlP&P[port]*
Grimaldi, Joseph 1779-1837 *DancEn 78, NotNAT A*
Grimaldi, Marion 1926- *WhoThe 72, -77*
Grimaldi, Nicola *NewEOp 71*
Grimaldi, Nicolo *NewGrD 80*
Grimani, Julia d1806 *NotNAT B*
Grimani, Maria Margherita *NewGrD 80*
Grimault, Paul 1905- *DcFM, FilmEn, HalFC 80, OxFilm, WorEFlm*
Grimes, Anne Laylin 1912- *BiDAmM, EncFCWM 69*
Grimes, Calvin Bernard 1939- *IntWWM 77*
Grimes, Doreen 1932- *ConAmC*
Grimes, Gary 1955- *FilmEn, HalFC 80, IntMPA 77, -75, -76, -78, -79, -80, WhoHol A*
Grimes, Henry Alonzo 1935- *BiDAmM*
Grimes, J Scott 1949- *IntWWM 80*
Grimes, Lloyd 1916- *AmSCAP 80*
Grimes, Lloyd 1917- *EncJzS 70*
Grimes, Tammy 1934- *BiDAmM, BiE&WWA, CnThe, EncMT, FilmEn, MotPP, NotNAT, WhoHol A, WhoThe 72, -77*
Grimes, Thomas 1887-1934 *WhScrn 77*
Grimes, Tiny 1916- *IlEncJ, WhoJazz 72*
Grimes, Tiny 1917- *CmpEPM, EncJzS 70*
Grimke, Angeline Weld 1880-1958 *BlkAmP, MorBAP*
Grimley, Irene 1913- *WhoMus 72*
Grimm, C *OxMus*
Grimm, Carl Hugo 1890- *Baker 78, ConAmC, WhoMus 72*
Grimm, Friedrich-Karl 1902- *WhoMus 72*
Grimm, Baron Friedrich Melchior Von 1723-1807 *Baker 78, NewEOp 71, NewGrD 80, OxMus, OxThe*
Grimm, Heinrich 1592?-1637 *NewGrD 80*
Grimm, Heinrich 1593?-1637 *Baker 78*
Grimm, Hetta Pamela 1923- *WhoMus 72*
Grimm, Jacob 1785-1863 *DcPup*
Grimm, Jakob 1785-1863 *FilmgC, HalFC 80, NewEOp 71*
Grimm, Julius Otto 1827-1903 *Baker 78*
Grimm, Karl 1794-1855 *NewGrD 80*
Grimm, Karl 1819-1888 *Baker 78*
Grimm, Karl Konstantin Ludwig 1820-1882 *Baker 78*
Grimm, Louis 1821-1882 *NewGrD 80*
Grimm, Oliver 1948- *HalFC 80*
Grimm, Wilhelm 1786-1859 *DcPup, FilmgC, HalFC 80*
Grimm Brothers, The *DcPup*
Grimoin-Sanson, Raoul 1860-1941 *DcFM, FilmEn, OxFilm*
Grims-Land, Ebbe Bertil Vilhelm 1915- *IntWWM 77, -80*
Grimston, Dorothy May *WhThe*
Grimwood, Herbert 1875-1929 *Film 1, -2, NotNAT B, WhThe, WhoHol B*
Grin *ConMuA 80A*
Grinberg, Faye Joyce 1941- *IntWWM 77*
Grinberg, Mariya 1908- *NewGrD 80*
Grinberg, Sherman 1927- *IntMPA 77, -75, -76, -78, -79, -80*
Grinblat, Romuald 1930- *Baker 78*
Grinde, Nicholas 1894- *TwYS A*
Grinde, Nick 1891- *FilmgC, HalFC 80*
Grinde, Nick 1893- *FilmEn, WhoHrs 80*
Grinde, Nils 1927- *IntWWM 77, -80*
Grindea, Carola *IntWWM 77, -80, WhoMus 72*
Grindea, Nadia-Myra 1943- *IntWWM 77, -80*
Griner, Barbara 1934- *BiE&WWA, NotNAT*
Gringoire, Pierre 1470?-1539? *McGEWD*
Gringore, Pierre *OxThe*
Gringore, Pierre 1480-1539 *NotNAT B*
Grinhauz, Berta C R 1940- *IntWWM 77, -80*
Grinhauz, Luis 1942- *IntWWM 77, -80*
Grinke, Frederick 1911- *IntWWM 77, -80, NewGrD 80, WhoMus 72*
Grinstead, Dorothy 1887- *WhoMus 72*
Grinwis, Paul *DancEn 78*
Griot *NewGrD 80*
Gripenberg, Thomas 1942- *WhoOp 76*
Gripp, Harry *Film 1, -2*
Grippe, Ragnar 1951- *IntWWM 80*
Grippo, Jan 1906- *IntMPA 77, -75, -76, -78, -79, -80, WhoHrs 80*
Grisar, Albert 1808-1869 *Baker 78, MusMk, NewGrD 80*
Grisart, Charles Jean Baptiste 1837-1904 *Baker 78*
Grischkat, Hans 1903-1977 *NewGrD 80*
Grisel, Louis R 1848-1928 *WhScrn 74, -77, WhoHol B*
Grisel, Louis Racine 1849-1928 *WhoStg 1906, -1908*
Griselle, Thomas 1891-1955 *AmSCAP 66, Baker 78, ConAmC*
Griselle, Thomas Elwood 1893-1955 *AmSCAP 80*
Grisi, Carlotta 1819-1899 *CnOxB, DancEn 78, NewGrD 80, NotNAT B, OxMus*
Grisi, Giuditta 1805-1840 *Baker 78, CmOp, NewGrD 80*
Grisi, Giulia 1811-1869 *Baker 78, BnBkM 80, CmOp, NewEOp 71, NewGrD 80[port]*
Grisier, Georges d1909 *NotNAT B*
Grisman, Sam H *WhThe*
Grismer, Joseph Rhode 1849-1922 *NotNAT B, WhThe, WhoStg 1906, -1908*
Grissom, Dan *CmpEPM*
Grist, Reri *CmOp, DrBlPA, IntWWM 77, -80, WhoMus 72, WhoOp 76*
Grist, Reri 1932?- *NewGrD 80*
Grist, Reri 1934?- *MusSN[port]*
Griswold, Alexander Viets 1766-1843 *BiDAmM*
Griswold, Grace d1927 *Film 2, NotNAT B, WhThe, WhoHol B*
Griswold, Herbert Spencer *Film 2*
Griswold, James *Film 1*
Griswold, Putnam 1875-1914 *Baker 78, BiDAmM*
Gritsch, Willy *Film 2*
Gritter, Matthias *NewGrD 80*
Gritton, Eric William 1889- *WhoMus 72*
Grizzard, George *WhoHol A*
Grizzard, George 1925- *HalFC 80*
Grizzard, George 1928- *BiE&WWA, CnThe, ForYSC, IntMPA 80, NotNAT, PlP&P, WhoThe 72, -77*
Grizzard, George 1929- *FilmgC*
Grjebina, Irina 1909- *CnOxB*
Gro, Johann *NewGrD 80*
Grob, Anita Jean 1927- *AmSCAP 80*
Grob-Prandl, Gertrud 1917- *CmOp*
Grob-Prandl, Gertrude *WhoMus 72*
Grobbelaar, Michal J 1927- *WhoOp 76*
Grobe, Charles 1817-1880 *NewGrD 80*
Grobe, Donald Roth 1929- *IntWWM 77, -80, NewGrD 80, WhoMus 72, WhoOp 76*
Grobstimme *NewGrD 80*
Groce, Larry Thomas 1948- *AmSCAP 80, RkOn 2A*
Grocheio, Johannes De *NewGrD 80*
Grocheo, Johannes De *Baker 78*
Grock 1880-1959 *EncWT, Ent[port], FilmgC, HalFC 80, NotNAT A, OxThe, WhScrn 77*
Grocock, Robert 1925- *IntWWM 77, -80*
Grodin, Charles 1935- *FilmEn, HalFC 80, IntMPA 78, -79, -80, NotNAT, WhoHol A, WhoThe 77*
Grodner, Murray 1922- *IntWWM 77, -80*
Groe, Johann *NewGrD 80*
Groen, Dora VanDer *FilmAG WE*
Groenemann, Johann Albert Heinrich *NewGrD 80*
Groeneveld, Ben 1899-1962 *WhScrn 77*
Groenveld, Ben d1962 *NotNAT B*
Groesse, Paul 1906- *IntMPA 77, -75, -76, -78, -79, -80*
Groetz, Carl *Film 2*
Grofe, Ferde 1892-1972 *AmSCAP 66, -80, Baker 78, CmpEPM, DcCom&M 79, MnPM[port], MusMk, OxMus, PopAmC[port], PopAmC SUP*
Grofe, Ferdinand Rudolf Von 1892-1972 *BiDAmM*
Grofe, Ferdinand Rudolph Von 1892-1972 *ConAmC*
Grogan, Phil 1909-1970 *AmSCAP 66, -80*
Grogan, Reb *Film 2*
Groh, B J *AmSCAP 80*
Groh, David *WhoHol A*
Groh, Johann 1575?-1627? *NewGrD 80*
Grohe, Johann 1575?-1627? *NewGrD 80*
Groland, Peter *NewGrD 80*
Grolnic, Sidney 1946- *ConAmC*
Gromon, Francis 1890- *AmSCAP 66*
Gron, C Ancher 1943- *IntWWM 77*
Gron, Chr Ancher 1943- *IntWWM 80*
Gronamann, Sybilla *NewGrD 80*
Gronau, Daniel Magnus 1700?-1747 *NewGrD 80*
Gronau, Ernst *Film 2*
Gronberg, Ake 1914-1969 *FilmEn, WhScrn 77*
Grondahl, Agathe 1847-1907 *NewGrD 80*
Grondahl, Launy 1886-1960 *Baker 78*
Groneman, Albertus 1710?-1778 *NewGrD 80*
Groningen, Stefan Van 1851-1926 *Baker 78*
Gronland, Peter 1761-1825 *NewGrD 80*
Gronow, Pekka 1943- *IntWWM 77*
Gronquist, Robert 1938- *ConAmC*
Gronroos, Georg *Film 1*
Groody, Louise 1897-1961 *AmPS B, CmpEPM, EncMT, NotNAT B, WhThe*
Groom, Dewey 1918- *EncFCWM 69*
Groom, Lester Herbert 1929- *ConAmC, IntWWM 77, -80*
Groom, Walter Cyril 1889- *WhoMus 72*
Grooms, Red *ConDr 73, -77E*
Grooney, Ernest G d1946 *WhScrn 74, -77*
Groot, Cor De 1914- *Baker 78*
Gropius, Walter 1883-1969 *DcPup, EncWT*
Groppenberger, Walter 1938- *IntWWM 77, -80*
Gropper, Milton Herbert 1896-1955 *NotNAT B, WhThe*
Gros, Charles *OxMus*
Gros, Jean *PupTheA*
Gros-Guillaume 1600-1634 *NotNAT B, OxThe*
Grosbard, Ulu 1929- *BiE&WWA, FilmEn, NotNAT, WhoThe 72, -77*
Grosbayne, Benjamin 1893-1976 *Baker 78*
Groschel, Ernst Ludwig, Sr. 1896- *IntWWM 77, -80*
Groschel, Werner 1940- *WhoOp 76*
Grosheim, Georg Christoph 1764-1841 *Baker 78, NewGrD 80*
Grosjean, Ernest 1944-1936 *Baker 78*
Grosjean, Jean Romary 1815-1888 *Baker 78*
Grosklos, Betsy *WomWMM B*
Gross, Anthony 1905- *WorEFlm*
Gross, Bethuel 1905- *AmSCAP 66, -80, ConAmC A*
Gross, Charles 1934- *AmSCAP 66, -80, ConAmC*
Gross, Emily L 1925- *IntWWM 77*
Gross, Eric 1926- *IntWWM 77, -80*

Gross, Henry 1950- *RkOn 2[port]*
Gross, Jerry *IntMPA 77, -75, -76, -78, -79, -80, WhoHrs 80*
Gross, Jesse 1929- *BiE&WWA, NotNAT*
Gross, Kenneth H *IntMPA 77, -75, -76, -78, -79, -80*
Gross, Leon T 1912-1973 *BluesWW*
Gross, Marcel 1924- *IntWWM 77, -80*
Gross, Marjorie P 1924- *ConAmTC*
Gross, Robert 1912- *IntMPA 77, -75, -76, -78, -79, -80*
Gross, Robert A 1914- *ConAmC, NewGrD 80*
Gross, Shelly 1921- *BiE&WWA, NotNAT, WhoThe 77*
Gross, Walter 1909-1967 *AmSCAP 66, -80, CmpEPM*
Gross, William J 1837-1924 *WhScrn 74, -77, WhoHol B*
Gross, Zygmunt 1903- *IntWWM 77, -80*
Grossberg, Jack 1927- *IntMPA 77, -75, -76, -78, -79, -80*
Grosse, Erwin G Friedrich 1904- *IntWWM 77, -80*
Grossel, Ira *AmSCAP 80*
Grosseteste, Robert 1168?-1253 *NewGrD 80*
Grossgebauer, Theophil 1627-1667 *NewGrD 80*
Grossi, Andrea *NewGrD 80*
Grossi, Carlo 1634?-1688 *NewGrD 80*
Grossi, Ed *ConMuA 80B*
Grossi, Giovanni Antonio d1684 *NewGrD 80*
Grossi, Giovanni Francesco 1653-1697 *NewGrD 80*
Grossi, Pasquale 1942- *WhoOp 76*
Grossi, Pietro 1917- *NewGrD 80*
Grossi DaViadana, Lodovico *NewGrD 80*
Grossim, Estienne *NewGrD 80*
Grossin, Estienne *NewGrD 80*
Grosskopf, Erhard 1934- *DcCM, NewGrD 80*
Grosskurth, Kurt 1909-1975 *WhScrn 77, WhoHol C*
Grossman, Albert 1926- *ConMuA 80B, IlEncR*
Grossman, Bernard 1885-1951 *AmSCAP 66, -80*
Grossman, Edward 1891- *AmSCAP 66*
Grossman, Ernie 1924- *IntMPA 77, -75, -76, -78, -79, -80*
Grossman, Jan 1925- *EncWT*
Grossman, Lawrence K *NewYTET*
Grossman, Ludwik 1835-1915 *NewGrD 80*
Grossman, Norman *ConAmC*
Grossman, Reda *WomWMM B*
Grossman, Steven 1951- *EncJzS 70*
Grossmann, Ferdinand 1887-1970 *Baker 78*
Grossmann, Gustav Friedrich Wilhelm 1743?-1796 *NewGrD 80*
Grossmith, Ena 1896-1944 *NotNAT B, WhThe*
Grossmith, George 1847-1912 *EncWT, NotNAT B, OxThe*
Grossmith, George 1874-1935 *EncMT, EncWT, HalFC 80, IlWWBF, -A, NotNAT A, -B, OxThe, WhThe, WhoHol B*
Grossmith, George 1875-1935 *WhScrn 74, -77*
Grossmith, George, Jr. *WhoStg 1906, -1908*
Grossmith, Lawrence 1877-1944 *EncWT, NotNAT B, OxThe, WhScrn 74, -77, WhThe, WhoHol B, WhoStg 1906, -1908*
Grossmith, Walter Weedon 1852-1919 *NotNAT A, -B, OxThe*
Grossmith, Weedon 1852-1919 *EncWT, Ent, WhThe, WhoStg 1906, -1908*
Grossvogel, David 1925- *BiE&WWA, NotNAT*
Grosvenor, Ralph L 1893- *AmSCAP 66, -80, Baker 78, ConAmC*
Grosz, George 1893-1959 *EncWT*
Grosz, Paul 1911- *IntMPA 77, -75, -76, -78, -79, -80*
Grosz, Wilhelm 1894-1939 *AmSCAP 80, Baker 78, BiDAmM, NewGrD 80*
Grot, Anton 1884-1974 *FilmgC, HalFC 80*
Grothe, Anders 1944- *IntWWM 80*
Grothe, Franz 1908- *NewGrD 80*
Grothoff, Curtis Eugene, II 1938- *AmSCAP 80*
Groto, Luigi 1541-1585 *McGEWD, OxThe*
Grotowski, Jerzy 1933- *EncWT, Ent, NotNAT A*
Grotte, Nicolas DeLa *NewGrD 80*
Groulx, Georges 1922- *CreCan 1*
Groulx, Gilles 1931- *CreCan 2, WorEFlm*
Groundhogs *ConMuA 80A, IlEncR*
Grousil, Nicolas *NewGrD 80*
Groussy, Nicolas *NewGrD 80*
Grout, Donald Jay 1902- *Baker 78, IntWWM 77, -80, NewGrD 80*
Grout, James 1927- *WhoThe 72, -77*
Grout, Philip 1930- *WhoThe 72, -77*
Grouya, Theodor J 1910- *AmSCAP 66*
Grouya, Theodore J 1910- *AmSCAP 80*
Grouzy, Nicolas d1568 *NewGrD 80*
Grov, Magne 1938- *IntWWM 77, -80*
Grove, Dick 1927- *EncJzS 70*
Grove, F C d1902 *NotNAT B*
Grove, Fred 1851-1927 *NotNAT B, WhThe*
Grove, Frederick Philip 1871?-1948 *CreCan 1*
Grove, Sir George 1820-1900 *Baker 78, BnBkM 80, NewGrD 80[port], OxMus*
Grove, Gerald *Film 2*
Grove, Richard Dean 1927- *AmSCAP 66, -80, BiDAmM, EncJzS 70*
Grove, Stefans 1922- *Baker 78, IntWWM 80, NewGrD 80*
Grove, Stephanus 1922- *NewGrD 80*
Grove, Sybil 1891- *Film 2, TwYS*
Groven, Eivind 1901- *Baker 78, DcCM, NewGrD 80*
Groven, Sigmund 1946- *IntWWM 80*
Grover, Arthur 1918- *AmSCAP 66, -80*
Grover, Betty Oliphant *CreCan 1*
Grover, Cyril Russell 1941- *IntWWM 77, -80*
Grover, Leonard d1926 *NotNAT B*
Grover, Paul Barton 1908- *IntWWM 77, -80*
Grover, Stanley 1926- *BiE&WWA, NotNAT*
Groves, Charles d1909 *NotNAT B*
Groves, Charles 1875-1955 *NotNAT B, WhThe*
Groves, Charles Barnard 1915- *IntWWM 77, -80, NewGrD 80, WhoMus 72*
Groves, Edgar Stephens 1935- *IntWWM 77*
Groves, Fred 1880-1955 *Film 2, IlWWBF, NotNAT B, WhThe*
Groves, John Phillip 1949- *IntWWM 77, -80*
Groves, Lorine Schumann Votaw 1903- *IntWWM 77*
Groves, Olive 1900- *WhoMus 72*
Grovlez, Gabriel 1879-1944 *Baker 78, NewGrD 80, OxMus*
Grower, Russell Gordon d1958 *WhScrn 74, -77*
Growiec, Michalina Izabela 1933- *IntWWM 77, -80*
Grua *NewGrD 80*
Grua, Carlo Luigi Pietro 1665?- *Baker 78, NewGrD 80*
Grua, Carlo Pietro 1695?-1773 *Baker 78*
Grua, Carlo Pietro 1700?-1773 *NewGrD 80*
Grua, Francesco DePaula 1753-1833 *Baker 78*
Grua, Franz Paul 1753-1833 *NewGrD 80*
Grua, Gasparo Pietragrua d1651? *NewGrD 80*
Grubbs, Carl Gordon 1944- *EncJzS 70*
Grubbs, Earl Delci 1942- *EncJzS 70*
Grubcheva, Ivanka *WomWMM*
Grube, Max d1934 *NotNAT B*
Gruber, Albion 1931- *ConAmC*
Gruber, Edmund L 1879-1941 *BiDAmM*
Gruber, Erasmus d1684 *NewGrD 80*
Gruber, Ferry 1926- *WhoOp 76*
Gruber, Frank 1904-1969 *FilmEn, FilmgC, HalFC 80*
Gruber, Franz Xaver 1787-1863 *Baker 78, NewGrD 80*
Gruber, Georg 1904- *Baker 78*
Gruber, Georg Wilhelm 1729-1796 *NewGrD 80*
Gruber, Gernot 1939- *IntWWM 77, -80*
Gruber, H K 1943- *NewGrD 80*
Gruber, Johann Sigmund 1759-1805 *NewGrD 80*
Gruber, Josef 1855-1933 *NewGrD 80*
Gruber, Kathryn Cline *IntWWM 77*
Gruber, Lilo 1915- *CnOxB*
Gruber, Ludwig *McGEWD[port]*
Gruber, Roman Il'ich 1895-1962 *NewGrD 80*
Gruberova, Edita 1946- *WhoOp 76*
Grubich, Joachim Antoni 1935- *IntWWM 77, -80, NewGrD 80*
Grubler, Ekkehard Karl Bernhard 1928- *WhoOp 76*
Grubman, Alan *ConMuA 80B*
Gruca, Witold 1928- *CnOxB*
Grueber, Arthur 1910- *WhoOp 76*
Grueber, Georg Wilhelm *NewGrD 80*
Gruel, Henri 1923- *DcFM, FilmEn, WorEFlm*
Gruelle, Johnny 1880-1938 *AmSCAP 66, -80*
Gruen, John 1927- *ConAmC*
Gruen, Robert 1913- *IntMPA 77, -75, -76, -78, -79, -80*
Gruenberg, Axel 1902- *IntMPA 77, -75, -76, -78, -79, -80*
Gruenberg, Erich 1924- *NewGrD 80, WhoMus 72*
Gruenberg, Eugene 1854-1928 *Baker 78*
Gruenberg, Jerry 1927- *IntMPA 77, -75, -76, -78, -79, -80*
Gruenberg, Leonard S 1913- *IntMPA 77, -75, -76, -78, -79, -80*
Gruenberg, Louis 1883-1964 *BiDAmM, ConAmC*
Gruenberg, Louis 1884-1964 *AmSCAP 66, -80, Baker 78, CompSN[port], DcCM, NewEOp 71, NewGrD 80, NotNAT B, OxMus*
Gruendgens, Gustaf 1900-1963 *WhScrn 74, -77*
Gruendgens, Gustav 1899-1963 *FilmEn, HalFC 80*
Gruener, Allan *WhoHol A*
Gruenwald, Alfred 1886-1951 *AmSCAP 66, -80*
Gruhn, Nora 1905- *IntWWM 77, -80, WhoMus 72*
Gruhn, Nora 1908- *Baker 78*
Gruise, Thomas S *Film 2*
Grumiaux, Arthur 1921- *Baker 78, BnBkM 80, IntWWM 77, -80, MusSN[port], NewGrD 80[port], WhoMus 72*
Grumlikova, Nora 1930- *WhoMus 72*
Grummelgut, Johannes *NewGrD 80*
Grummer, Elisabeth 1911- *CmOp, NewGrD 80*
Grummer, Elisabeth 1921- *IntWWM 77, -80, WhoMus 72*
Grummer, Paul 1879-1965 *Baker 78, NewGrD 80*
Grummitt, Margaret Halliday 1905- *IntWWM 77, -80, WhoMus 72*
Grun, Bernard 1901- *WhThe*
Grun, Jakob 1837-1916 *Baker 78*
Grunberg, Jacques *AmSCAP 66*
Grunberg, Karl 1891- *CnMD*
Grunberg, Max *Film 2*
Grund, Friedrich Wilhelm 1791-1874 *Baker 78*
Grundgens, Gustaf 1899-1963 *CroCD, Ent, FilmAG WE, FilmEn, NotNAT B, OxThe*
Grundgens, Gustav 1899-1963 *CnThe, EncWT*
Grundheber, Franz 1937- *WhoOp 76*
Grundig, Johann Zacharias 1669-1720 *NewGrD 80*
Grundman, Clare Ewing 1913- *AmSCAP 66, -80, BiE&WWA, CpmDNM 72, -73, -74, -79, ConAmC, NotNAT*
Grundstad, Aage 1923- *IntWWM 80*
Grundtvig, Svend 1824-1883 *NewGrD 80*
Grundy, James 1861?-1914 *BlksBF*
Grundy, Lily *WhThe*
Grundy, Owen 1921- *WhoMus 72*
Grundy, Sydney 1848-1914 *McGEWD, NotNAT B, OxThe, WhThe, WhoStg 1906, -1908*
Grune, Karl 1885-1962 *OxFilm*
Grune, Karl 1890-1962 *DcFM, FilmEn, HalFC 80*
Grunebaum, Hermann 1872-1954 *NewGrD 80*
Grunenwald, Jean-Jacques 1911- *Baker 78, FilmEn, IntWWM 80, NewGrD 80*
Gruner, Nathanael Gottfried 1732-1792 *NewGrD 80*
Gruner, Walther Karl 1905- *IntWWM 77, WhoMus 72*
Gruner-Hegge, Odd 1899- *WhoMus 72*
Grunewald, Gottfried 1675-1739 *NewGrD 80*
Grunewald, Jean-Jacques 1911- *IntWWM 77, WhoMus 72*
Grunewald, William P 1907- *IntWWM 77, -80*
Grunfarb, Josef Mendel 1920- *IntWWM 77, -80*
Grunfeld, Alfred 1852-1924 *Baker 78*
Grunfeld, Heinrich 1855-1931 *Baker 78*
Gruning, Ilka *Film 2*
Grunn, Homer 1880-1944 *AmSCAP 66, -80*
Grunn, John Homer 1880-1944 *Baker 78, ConAmC*

Grunner-Hegge, Odd 1899-1973 *Baker 78*
Grunsky, Karl 1871-1943 *Baker 78*
Grunth, Lars 1938- *IntWWM 77, -80*
Gruntz, George 1932- *EncJzS 70*
Grunwald, Alfred d1951 *NotNAT B*
Grunwald, Harry *Film 2*
Grunwald, Hugo 1869-1956 *Baker 78*
Grupp, Martin 1925- *AmSCAP 80*
Gruppe, Paulo Mesdag 1891- *Baker 78, IntWWM 77, -80*
Gruselle, Christiane 1935- *WhoOp 76*
Grusin, Dave 1934- *BiDAmM, EncJzS 70, HalFC 80*
Grusin, David *IntMPA 79, -80*
Gruson, Sheila 1951- *IntWWM 77, -80*
Gruszczynski, Ryszard 1916- *IntWWM 77, -80*
Grutzmacher, Friedrich 1832-1903 *Baker 78, NewGrD 80*
Gruver, Elbert A d1962 *NotNAT B*
Gruys, Hans 1903- *IntWWM 77, -80*
Gruzinsky, D *Film 2*
Gryphius, Andreas 1616-1664 *CnThe, EncWT, Ent[port], McGEWD[port], OxThe, REnWD[port]*
Gryphon *IlEncR[port]*
Grzanna, Donald E 1931- *AmSCAP 66, -80*
Grzinic, Vyekoslav 1932- *IntWWM 77*
Gschwenter, Herbert Carl 1894- *WhoMus 72*
Gsovska, Tatiana 1902- *DancEn 78*
Gsovsky, Tatjana 1901- *CnOxB*
Gsovsky, Victor 1902-1974 *CnOxB, DancEn 78*
Guaccero, Domenico 1927- *NewGrD 80*
Guadagni, Gaetano 1725?-1792 *Baker 78, CmOp, NewEOp 71, NewGrD 80*
Guadagnini *NewGrD 80*
Guadagnini, Ernest Richard 1945- *IntWWM 77, -80*
Guadagnini, Gaetano 1745-1817 *Baker 78*
Guadagnini, Giovanni Baptista 1711-1786 *NewGrD 80*
Guadagnini, Giovanni Battista 1711-1786 *Baker 78*
Guadagnini, Giuseppe 1736-1805 *Baker 78, NewGrD 80*
Guadagnini, J B 1711?-1786 *NewGrD 80*
Guadagnini, Lorenzo 1690?-1748 *NewGrD 80*
Guadagnini, Lorenzo 1695-1745 *Baker 78*
Guadagnini, Paolo d1942 *Baker 78*
Guadagno, Anton 1925- *IntWWM 77, -80, NewGrD 80, WhoMus 72, WhoOp 76*
Guaitoli, Francesco Maria 1563-1628 *NewGrD 80*
Gual, Adria 1872-1943 *OxThe*
Gualandi, Antonio *NewGrD 80*
Gualdo, Giovanni d1771 *Baker 78*
Gualillo, Nicholas D 1903- *ConAmC, IntWWM 77, -80*
Gualterus Ab Insula *NewGrD 80*
Gualtieri, Alessandro d1655 *NewGrD 80*
Gualtieri, Antonio d1650? *NewGrD 80*
Guami *NewGrD 80*
Guami, Domenico 1580?-1631 *NewGrD 80*
Guami, Francesco 1544?-1602 *Baker 78, NewGrD 80*
Guami, Gioseffo 1540?-1611 *NewGrD 80*
Guami, Gioseffo 1540?-1612 *Baker 78*
Guami, Giuseppe 1540?-1611 *NewGrD 80*
Guami, Valerio 1587-1649 *NewGrD 80*
Guami, Vincenzo d1615 *NewGrD 80*
Guaraldi, Vince 1928-1976 *EncJzS 70, RkOn*
Guaraldi, Vincent Anthony 1928-1976 *BiDAmM, EncJzS 70*
Guard, Dave 1934- *BiDAmM*
Guard, Kit 1894-1961 *Film 2, ForYSC, NotNAT B, TwYS, WhScrn 74, -77, WhoHol B*
Guard, Sully d1916 *WhScrn 77*
Guard, William J d1932 *NotNAT B*
Guardasoni, Domenico 1731?-1806 *NewGrD 80*
Guardino, Harry 1925- *BiE&WWA, FilmEn, FilmgC, ForYSC, HalFC 80, IntMPA 77, -75, -76, -78, -79, -80, MovMk, WhoHol A*
Guardino, Louis Joseph 1923-1968 *AmSCAP 80*
Guarducci, Tommaso 1720?-1770? *NewGrD 80*
Guare, John 1930- *EncWT*
Guare, John 1938- *AmSCAP 80, ConDr 73, -77, DcLB 7[port], Ent, NatPD[port], NotNAT, PlP&P A[port], WhoThe 77*
Guarente, Frank 1893-1942 *WhoJazz 72*
Guareschi, Giovanni 1908-1968 *FilmgC, HalFC 80*
Guarini, Alfredo 1901- *IntMPA 77, -75, -76, -78, -79, -80*
Guarini, Battista 1538-1612 *EncWT, Ent[port], NewGrD 80*
Guarini, Gian Battista 1538-1612 *McGEWD*
Guarini, Giovan Battista 1538-1612 *REnWD[port]*
Guarini, Giovanni Battista 1537-1612 *OxThe*
Guarino, Carmine 1893-1965 *Baker 78*
Guarino, Felix 1898?- *NewOrJ*
Guarino, Piero 1919- *IntWWM 77, -80*
Guarnera, Guido 1929- *WhoOp 76*
Guarneri *BnBkM 80, NewGrD 80*
Guarneri, Andrea 1625?-1698 *Baker 78*
Guarneri, Andrea 1626?-1698 *BnBkM 80, MusMk, NewGrD 80*
Guarneri, Giuseppe 1666-1739? *BnBkM 80*
Guarneri, Giuseppe 1666-1740? *Baker 78, NewGrD 80*
Guarneri, Giuseppe 1698-1744 *Baker 78, BnBkM 80, NewGrD 80*
Guarneri, Pietro 1695-1762 *Baker 78, BnBkM 80, NewGrD 80*
Guarneri, Pietro Giovanni 1655-1720 *Baker 78, BnBkM 80, NewGrD 80*
Guarneri String Quartet *BiDAmM*
Guarnier *NewGrD 80*
Guarnieri, Antonio 1880-1952 *NewGrD 80*
Guarnieri, Camargo 1907- *BiDAmM, CompSN[port], DcCM, NewGrD 80, OxMus*
Guarnieri, Camargo Mozart 1907- *Baker 78*
Guarnieri, John Albert 1917- *AmSCAP 66, -80, BiDAmM, EncJzS 70*
Guarnieri, Johnny 1917- *CmpEPM, EncJzS 70, IlEncJ, WhoJazz 72*
Guarrera, Frank 1923- *NewEOp 71*
Guarrera, Frank 1924- *WhoOp 76*
Guascogna, Johannes *NewGrD 80*
Guascogna, Mathieu *NewGrD 80*
Guastamacchia, Nichy Nicola 1934- *WhoOp 76*
Guastavino, Carlos 1912- *Baker 78*
Guayrinet *NewGrD 80*
Guazzi, Eleuterio 1597-1622 *NewGrD 80*
Guazzoni, Enrico 1876-1949 *DcFM, FilmEn, WorEFlm*
Guba, Vladimir 1938- *Baker 78*
Gubaidulina, Sofia 1931- *DcCM*
Gubaydulina, Sofiya Asgatovna 1931- *NewGrD 80*
Gubby, Roy 1911- *IntWWM 77, -80, WhoMus 72*
Gubenko, Julius 1924- *AmSCAP 80*
Guber, Lee 1920- *BiE&WWA, ConMuA 80B, NotNAT, WhoThe 77*
Guber, Peter *IntMPA 78, -79, -80*
Gubert, Nikolay Al'bertovich 1840-1888 *NewGrD 80*
Gubin, S *Film 2*
Gubisch, Barbara 1938- *WhoOp 76*
Guckenheimer, Fritz *AmSCAP 80*
Gudauskas, Giedra 1923- *ConAmC*
Gudbrandsen, Hakon Roald 1931- *IntWWM 80*
Gude, John *NewYTET*
Gudegast, Hans *ForYSC, WhoHol A*
Gudehus, Donald H 1939- *ConAmC*
Gudehus, Heinrich 1845-1909 *Baker 78, NewGrD 80*
Gudel, Joachim 1927- *IntWWM 77, -80*
Guden, Hilde 1917- *CmOp*
Gudenian, Haig 1886- *ConAmC*
Gudewill, Kurt 1911- *NewGrD 80*
Gudgeon, Bertrand C d1948 *WhScrn 74, -77, WhoHol B*
Gudger, William Dillard 1947- *IntWWM 80*
Gudmel, Claude *Baker 78*
Gudmundsen-Holmgreen, Pelle 1932- *Baker 78, DcCM, IntWWM 77, -80, NewGrD 80*
Gudrun, Ann *WhoHol A*
Gue, George 1893-1962 *DancEn 78*
Gueden, Hilde 1917- *Baker 78, IntWWM 77, -80, MusSN[port], NewEOp 71, NewGrD 80, WhoMus 72*
Guedon DePresles d1754? *NewGrD 80*
Guedon DePresles, Honore-Claude d1730? *NewGrD 80*
Guedron, Pierre 1565-1620 *OxMus*
Guedron, Pierre 1565-1621 *Baker 78*
Guedron, Pierre 1570?-1620? *NewGrD 80*
Gueinz, Christian 1592-1650 *NewGrD 80*
Guelfi, Antonio *NewGrD 80*
Guelfi, Giangiacomo *WhoOp 76*
Guelstorff, Max 1882-1947 *Film 2, WhScrn 77*
Guenin, Alexandre 1744-1835 *Baker 78*
Guenin, Marie-Alexandre 1744-1835 *NewGrD 80*
Guensteq, F F 1862-1936 *WhScrn 74, -77*
Guenther, Eileen Morris 1948- *IntWWM 77, -80*
Guenther, Felix 1886-1951 *Baker 78*
Guenther, Johannes Von 1866- *McGEWD*
Guenther, Ralph R 1914- *CpmDNM 80, ConAmC*
Guenther, Ruth 1910-1974 *WhScrn 77, WhoHol B*
Gueranger, Prosper Louis Pascal 1805-1875 *Baker 78*
Guerard, Roland 1905- *DancEn 78*
Guerard, Yoland 1923- *CreCan 1*
Guerau, Francisco *NewGrD 80*
Guercio, James William 1945- *ConMuA 80B, IlEncR*
Guerin, Bruce *Film 2*
Guerin, Emile 1911- *NewOrJ[port]*
Guerin, John Payne 1939- *AmSCAP 80, EncJzS 70*
Guerin, Roger 1926- *EncJzS 70*
Guerin D'Etriche, Isaac Francois 1636?-1728 *OxThe*
Guerini, Francesco *NewGrD 80*
Guernsey, Otis Love, Jr. 1918- *ConAmTC, NatPD[port]*
Gueroult, Guillaume d1565? *NewGrD 80*
Guerra, Antonio 1810-1846 *CnOxB, DancEn 78*
Guerra, Armand *Film 2*
Guerra, Nicola 1862-1942 *DancEn 78*
Guerra, Nicola 1865-1942 *CnOxB*
Guerra, Ruy 1931- *WorEFlm*
Guerra, Santiago 1902- *WhoOp 76*
Guerra-Peixe, Cesar 1914- *Baker 78, DcCM, NewGrD 80*
Guerra Vicente, Jose 1907- *IntWWM 77, -80*
Guerrant, Mary Thorington 1925- *IntWWM 77, -80*
Guerrero 1868-1928 *WhThe*
Guerrero, Antonio 1700?-1776 *NewGrD 80*
Guerrero, Francisco 1527-1599 *BnBkM 80, OxMus*
Guerrero, Francisco 1528-1599 *Baker 78, NewGrD 80[port]*
Guerrero, Jacinto 1895-1951 *NewGrD 80*
Guerrero, Joseph *NewGrD 80*
Guerrero, Maria 1868-1928 *NotNAT B*
Guerrero, Maria 1951- *CnOxB*
Guerrero, Pedro 1520?- *NewGrD 80, OxMus*
Guerrero Brothers *PupTheA*
Guerrero Diaz, Felix 1917- *NewGrD 80*
Guerrieri, Agostino *NewGrD 80*
Guerrini, Guido 1890-1965 *Baker 78, NewGrD 80*
Guerrini, Paolo 1880-1960 *Baker 78, NewGrD 80*
Guertin, Robert Harvey 1921-1974 *AmSCAP 80*
Guertzman, Paul *Film 2*
Guesdron, Pierre *NewGrD 80*
Guesnon, George 1907-1968 *BluesWW[port], NewOrJ[port]*
Guess Who, The *BiDAmM, IlEncR, RkOn 2[port]*
Guest, Alison Anne 1946- *IntWWM 80*
Guest, Charlie *Film 2*
Guest, Christopher Haden 1948- *AmSCAP 80*
Guest, Douglas 1916- *IntWWM 77, -80, NewGrD 80*
Guest, Douglas Albert 1916- *WhoMus 72*
Guest, George 1771-1831 *NewGrD 80*
Guest, George Howell 1924- *IntWWM 77, -80, NewGrD 80, WhoMus 72*
Guest, Ivor 1920- *CnOxB, DancEn 78*
Guest, Jane Mary 1765?-1814? *NewGrD 80*
Guest, Jean H 1921- *BiE&WWA, NotNAT*
Guest, Peggy Maureen 1936- *WhoMus 72*
Guest, Val 1911- *FilmEn, FilmgC, HalFC 80, IntMPA 77, -75, -76, -78, -79, -80, WhoHrs 80*
Guest, Val 1921- *IlWWBF*
Guetary, Georges *WhoHol A*

Guetary, Georges 1915- *FilmgC, HalFC 80*
Guetary, Georges 1917- *WhThe, WhoThe 72*
Guetfreund, Peter 1570?-1625 *NewGrD 80*
Guette, Toto *Film 2*
Guettel, Henry 1928- *BiE&WWA, NotNAT*
Guettel, Mary Rodgers 1931- *AmSCAP 80*
Guettler, Knut Arne 1943- *IntWWM 77, -80*
Guevara, Pedro DeLoyola *NewGrD 80*
Guevara, Ruben 1942- *AmSCAP 80*
Guevremont, Germaine 1896-1968 *CreCan 1*
Guezec, Jean-Pierre 1934-1971 *Baker 78, DcCM, NewGrD 80*
Guffey, Burnett 1905- *CmMov, DcFM, FilmEn, FilmgC, HalFC 80, IntMPA 77, -75, -76, -78, -79, -80, WorEFlm*
Guffey, Cary 1973- *WhoHrs 80*
Gugl, Matthaus 1683?-1721 *NewGrD 80*
Guglielmi *NewGrD 80*
Guglielmi, Bernadine 1907- *AmSCAP 66*
Guglielmi, Danny 1909- *AmSCAP 66*
Guglielmi, Giacomo 1782-1820? *NewGrD 80*
Guglielmi, Jacopo d1731? *NewGrD 80*
Guglielmi, Margherita 1938- *WhoOp 76*
Guglielmi, Pier 1728-1804 *NewGrD 80*
Guglielmi, Piero 1728-1804 *NewGrD 80*
Guglielmi, Pietro Alessandro 1728-1804 *Baker 78, NewGrD 80*
Guglielmi, Pietro Carlo 1763?-1817 *Baker 78, NewGrD 80*
Guglielmini, Pietro Carlo *NewGrD 80*
Guglielmo Ebreo *CnOxB, DancEn 78*
Guglielmo Ebreo Da Pesaro 1425?-1480? *NewGrD 80*
Guglielmo Roffredi d1190 *NewGrD 80*
Guhl, George d1943 *WhScrn 74, -77, WhoHol B*
Guhr, Karl 1787-1848 *NewGrD 80*
Gui D'Uisel 1170?-1225? *NewGrD 80*
Gui D'Uissel 1170?-1225? *NewGrD 80*
Gui D'Ussel 1170?-1225? *NewGrD 80*
Gui, Vittorio 1885-1975 *Baker 78, CmOp, IntWWM 77, -80, MusSN[port], NewEOp 71, NewGrD 80, OxMus, WhoMus 72*
Guibbory, Yenoin Ephraim 1946- *IntWWM 77*
Guibert Kaukesel *NewGrD 80*
Guichard, Francois, Abbe 1745-1807 *NewGrD 80*
Guichard, Henry, Sieur D'Herapine *NewGrD 80*
Guichard, Leon 1899- *IntWWM 77, -80, NewGrD 80*
Guichard, Louis-Joseph 1752-1829 *NewGrD 80*
Guiches, Gustave 1860- *WhThe*
Guide, Paul *Film 2*
Guide, Richard De 1909-1962 *NewGrD 80*
Guidetti, Giovanni Domenico 1530-1592 *Baker 78, NewGrD 80*
Guidi, Giovanni Gualberto 1817-1883 *NewGrD 80*
Guidi-Drei, Claudio Cafiero 1927- *IntWWM 77, -80*
Guido *NewGrD 80*
Guido Augensis *NewGrD 80*
Guido D'Arezzo 995?-1050? *OxMus*
Guido D'Arezzo 997?-1050? *Baker 78, MusMk*
Guido De Cariloco *NewGrD 80*
Guido De Caroli-loco *NewGrD 80*
Guido Frater *NewGrD 80*
Guido Of Aretinus 991?-1033? *NewGrD 80[port]*
Guido Of Arezzo 990?-1050 *BnBkM 80*
Guido Of Arezzo 991?-1033? *NewGrD 80[port]*
Guido, Giovanni Antonio d1728? *NewGrD 80*
Guiffre, Joe *NewOrJ*
Guiffre, John *NewOrJ*
Guiglielmo Di Santo Spirito *NewGrD 80*
Guignard, Eric 1913- *IntWWM 77, -80*
Guignon, Jean-Pierre 1702-1774 *Baker 78, NewGrD 80*
Guilain *NewGrD 80*
Guilaroff, Sydney 1910- *HalFC 80*
Guilbault, George J 1935- *IntWWM 77*
Guilbeau, Phillip 1926- *BiDAmM*
Guilbert, Andre Louis Eugene 1780?-1835? *BiDAmM*
Guilbert, Yvette d1944 *Film 2, WhoHol B, WhoStg 1906, -1908*
Guilbert, Yvette 1865-1944 *NewGrD 80, NotNAT A, -B*
Guilbert, Yvette 1867-1944 *Baker 78, EncWT, Ent*
Guilbert, Yvette 1868-1944 *WhScrn 77, WhThe*
Guilbert, Yvette 1869-1944 *OxThe*
Guild, Nancy *MotPP*
Guild, Nancy 1925- *FilmEn, ForYSC, HalFC 80, WhoHol A*
Guild, Nancy 1926- *FilmgC*
Guiler, William *Film 2*
Guilet, Daniel Luc 1899- *WhoMus 72*
Guilford, Lord *OxMus*
Guilfoyle, James 1892-1964 *Film 2, WhScrn 77*
Guilfoyle, Paul 1902-1960 *ForYSC*
Guilfoyle, Paul 1902-1961 *FilmgC, HalFC 80, HolCA[port], MotPP, MovMk[port], NotNAT B, Vers A[port], WhScrn 74, -77, WhoHol B*
Guilhene, Jacques *Film 1*
Guilielmus De Francia *NewGrD 80[port]*
Guillard, Nicolas Francois 1752-1814 *NewGrD 80*
Guillaume De Dijon d1031 *NewGrD 80*
Guillaume De Machaut *BnBkM 80, NewGrD 80*
Guillaume IX, Duke Of Aquitaine 1071-1127 *NewGrD 80*
Guillaume X, Duke Of Aquitaine 1099-1137 *NewGrD 80*
Guillaume Le Grain *NewGrD 80*
Guillaume Li Vinier 1190?-1245 *NewGrD 80*
Guillaume Veau *NewGrD 80*
Guillaume, Bob *BlkAmP*
Guillaume, Edith 1943- *IntWWM 77, -80, WhoOp 76*
Guillaume, Robert 1927- *DrBlPA*
Guillaume D'Amiens, Paignour *NewGrD 80*
Guillebert De Berneville *NewGrD 80*
Guillelmus Monachus *NewGrD 80*
Guillemain, Gabriel 1705-1770 *Baker 78, OxMus*
Guillemain, Louis-Gabriel 1705-1770 *NewGrD 80*
Guillemant, Benoit *NewGrD 80*
Guillemaud, Marcel 1867- *WhThe*
Guillemot, Agnes *WomWMM*
Guillermin, John 1923- *BiDFilm, -81*
Guillermin, John 1925- *CmMov, FilmEn, FilmgC, HalFC 80, IlWWBF, IntMPA 77, -75, -76, -78, -79, -80, WorEFlm*
Guillet, Charles d1654 *NewGrD 80*
Guillet, Karel d1654 *NewGrD 80*
Guilliaud, Maximilian 1522-1597 *NewGrD 80*
Guillon *NewGrD 80*
Guillon, Henri-Charles *NewGrD 80*
Guillon, Madelaine *WomWMM*
Guillot-Gorju 1600-1648 *OxThe*
Guillou, Jean 1930- *Baker 78, NewGrD 80, WhoMus 72*
Guillou, Victor 1790?-1843? *BiDAmM*
Guilmant, Alexandre 1837-1911 *Baker 78, BnBkM 80, NewGrD 80*
Guilmant, Felix Alexandre 1837-1911 *OxMus*
Guilmant, Jean-Baptiste 1793-1890 *Baker 78*
Guilmartin, Kenneth Kells 1946- *AmSCAP 80*
Guimard, La 1743-1816 *NotNAT B*
Guimard, Madeleine 1743-1816 *DancEn 78, NewGrD 80*
Guimard, Marie-Madeleine d1816 *CnOxB*
Guimera, Angel d1924 *WhThe*
Guimera, Angel 1845-1924 *NotNAT B*
Guimera, Angel 1847-1924 *McGEWD[port], OxThe*
Guimond, Olivier 1915- *CreCan 1*
Guin, Francois 1938- *EncJzS 70*
Guin, Frick 1938- *EncJzS 70*
Guinaldo, Norberto 1937- *ConAmC*
Guinan, Texas d1934 *HalFC 80, WhoHol B*
Guinan, Texas 1888?-1933 *CmpEPM*
Guinan, Texas 1891-1933 *Film 1, -2, NotNAT B, TwYS, WhScrn 74, -77*
Guindon, Arthur 1864-1923 *CreCan 1*
Guindon, Pierre Adolphe Arthur 1864-1923 *CreCan 1*
Guinjoan, Juan 1931- *NewGrD 80*
Guinn, Nedra 1914- *AmSCAP 80*
Guinness, Sir Alec 1914- *BiDFilm, -81, BiE&WWA, CmMov, CnThe, EncWT, Ent, FamA&A[port], FilmAG WE, FilmEn, FilmgC, ForYSC, HalFC 80, IlWWBF[port], -A, IntMPA 77, -75, -76, -78, -79, -80, MotPP, MovMk[port], NotNAT, -A, OxFilm, OxThe, PlP&P, WhoHol A, WhoHrs 80, WhoThe 72, -77, WorEFlm[port]*
Guinon, Albert 1863- *WhThe*
Guiol, Fred 1898-1964 *FilmgC, HalFC 80, NotNAT B*
Guion, David W 1892-1972 *AmSCAP 66, Baker 78, PopAmC[port]*
Guion, David Wendel Fentress 1895-1972 *OxMus*
Guion, David Wendell 1892-1972 *AmSCAP 80, ConAmC*
Guion, David Wendell DeFentresse 1892-1972 *BiDAmM*
Guion, Jean *NewGrD 80*
Guiot De Dijon *NewGrD 80*
Guiot De Provins d1208? *NewGrD 80*
Guiot, Andrea 1928- *WhoOp 76*
Guiraud, Ernest 1837-1892 *Baker 78, BiDAmM, NewEOp 71, NewGrD 80, OxMus*
Guiraut De Bornelh *NewGrD 80*
Guiraut D'Espanha De Toloza *NewGrD 80*
Guiraut Riquier *NewGrD 80*
Guise, Thomas *Film 1, -2*
Guise, Wyndham *Film 2*
Guisinger, Earl C 1904- *AmSCAP 80*
Guitar, Bonnie *RkOn*
Guitar, Willie 1894?-1945? *NewOrJ*
Guitar Eddy *BluesWW[port]*
Guitar Junior *BluesWW[port]*
Guitar Nubbitt *BluesWW[port]*
Guitar Pete *BluesWW[port]*
Guitar Red *BluesWW[port]*
Guitar Shorty *BluesWW[port]*
Guitar Slim *BluesWW[port]*
Guiterman, Arthur 1871-1943 *BiDAmM*
Guiterrez Heras, Joaquin 1927- *Baker 78*
Guiton, Helen 1894- *CreCan 2*
Guitry, Jean d1920 *NotNAT B*
Guitry, Lucien-Germain 1860-1925 *EncWT, NotNAT B, OxThe, WhThe*
Guitry, Sacha 1885-1957 *BiDFilm, -81, CnMD, CnThe, DcFM, EncWT, Ent, FilmAG WE, FilmEn, FilmgC, HalFC 80, McGEWD[port], ModWD, MovMk, NotNAT A, -B, OxFilm, OxThe, PlP&P, WhScrn 74, -77, WhThe, WhoHol B, WorEFlm*
Guitry, Yvonne Printemps 1895- *OxThe*
Guitty, Madeleine 1871-1936 *Film 2, WhScrn 74, -77, WhoHol B*
Guiu, Jose Melis 1920- *AmSCAP 80*
Guivizzani, Alessandro *NewGrD 80*
Guizar, Tito 1912- *CmpEPM, ForYSC, WhoHol A*
Guizerix, Jean 1945- *CnOxB*
Guizzardo, Cristoforo *NewGrD 80*
Gulager, Clu 1929?- *HalFC 80*
Gulager, Clu 1934- *ForYSC*
Gulager, Clu 1935- *FilmgC, WhoHol A*
Gulak-Artemovsky, Semyon Stepanovich 1813-1873 *Baker 78, NewGrD 80*
Gulbins, Max 1862-1932 *Baker 78*
Gulbranson, Ellen 1863-1947 *Baker 78, NewGrD 80*
Gulbranson, Ellen 1963-1947 *OxMus*
Gulda, Friedrich 1930- *Baker 78, IntWWM 77, -80, NewGrD 80, WhoMus 72*
Gulesian, Grace Warner *AmSCAP 66, ConAmC*
Guliaiev, Vadim Nicolaievich 1947- *CnOxB*
Gulin, Angeles 1939- *WhoMus 72, WhoOp 76*
Gulke, Peter 1934- *IntWWM 77, NewGrD 80*
Gullan, Campbell d1939 *Film 2, NotNAT B, WhThe, WhoHol B*
Gulley, John 1934- *IntWWM 77, -80*
Gulli, Franco 1926- *IntWWM 77, -80, NewGrD 80*
Gulli, Luigi 1859-1918 *NewGrD 80*
Gullicksen, Richard Conrad 1931- *WhoOp 76*
Gullickson, Grant Orvis 1944- *AmSCAP 80*
Gulliksen, Kenneth 1945- *AmSCAP 80*
Gullin, Lars 1928-1976 *CmpEPM, NewGrD 80*

Gullin, Lars Gunnar Victor 1928-1976 *EncJzS 70*
Gullin, Lars Gunnar Viktor 1928- *IntWWM 77*
Gullino, Walter 1933- *WhoOp 76*
Gulliver, Andrew *AmSCAP 80*
Gulliver, Charles 1882-1961 *WhThe*
Gulliver, Dorothy 1910?- *FilmEn*
Gulliver, Dorothy 1913- *Film 2, ForYSC, TwYS, WhoHol A*
Gully Jumpers, The *IlEncCM[port]*
Gulsdorff, Max *Film 2*
Gulyas, Gyorgy 1916- *IntWWM 77, -80*
Guma, Paul 1919- *NewOrJ*
Gumbert, Ferdinand 1818-1896 *Baker 78*
Gumbert, Friedrich Adolf 1841-1906 *NewGrD 80*
Gumble, Albert 1883-1946 *AmSCAP 66, -80*
Gumbs, Onaje Allan 1949- *EncJzS 70*
Gumina, Thomas Joseph 1931- *BiDAmM, EncJzS 70*
Gumina, Tommy 1931- *EncJzS 70*
Gumm, Albert *NewGrD 80*
Gumm, Harold *NewGrD 80*
Gumm, Suzanne d1964 *NotNAT B*
Gummesson, Thord Erik 1930- *IntWWM 77, -80*
Gump, Richard 1906- *AmSCAP 66, -80, ConAmC A*
Gumpel, Karl-Werner 1930- *IntWWM 77, -80*
Gumpeltzhaimer, Adam 1559?-1625 *Baker 78, NewGrD 80[port]*
Gumpelzhaimer, Adam 1559-1625 *NewGrD 80[port]*
Gumpert, Friedrich Adolf 1841-1906 *Baker 78*
Gumprecht, Armand J 1861-1943 *Baker 78*
Gumprecht, Otto 1823-1900 *Baker 78*
Gundersheimer, Muriel Blumberg 1924- *IntWWM 77, -80*
Gundisalvi, Domingo *NewGrD 80*
Gundissalinus, Domenicus *NewGrD 80*
Gundrey, V Gareth *IlWWBF*
Gundry, Inglis 1905- *Baker 78, IntWWM 77, -80, NewGrD 80, OxMus, WhoMus 72*
Gungl, Janos 1828-1883 *NewGrD 80*
Gungl, Johann 1828-1883 *NewGrD 80*
Gungl, Joseph 1810-1889 *Baker 78, MusMk, NewGrD 80, OxMus*
Gungl, Jozsef 1810-1889 *NewGrD 80*
Gunn, Abb Lynn 1939- *IntWWM 77*
Gunn, Barnabas d1753 *NewGrD 80*
Gunn, Bill 1934- *BlkAmP, DrBlPA, MorBAP*
Gunn, Charles E 1883-1918 *Film 1, WhScrn 77*
Gunn, Earl 1902-1963 *WhScrn 77*
Gunn, Franzi *Film 2*
Gunn, Gilbert 1912?- *FilmgC, HalFC 80, IlWWBF*
Gunn, Glenn Dillard 1874-1963 *Baker 78, BiDAmM*
Gunn, Haidee 1882-1961 *WhThe*
Gunn, Hartford N, Jr. *NewYTET*
Gunn, John 1765?-1824? *Baker 78, NewGrD 80*
Gunn, Judy 1914- *WhThe*
Gunn, Mildred Helen 1920- *IntWWM 77*
Gunn, Moses 1929- *DrBlPA, FilmEn, HalFC 80, IntMPA 77, -75, -76, -78, -79, -80, WhoHol A, WhoThe 72, -77*
Gunn, Sherman 1940- *IntWWM 77*
Gunnarsson, Bengt-Ove 1940- *IntWWM 77, -80*
Gunnarsson, Jon Hrolfur 1952- *IntWWM 77*
Gunnell, John 1911- *BiE&WWA*
Gunnell, Richard d1634 *OxThe*
Gunner, Marjorie Janet 1922- *ConAmTC*
Gunnerfeldt, Louise Ulla 1917- *IntWWM 77, -80*
Gunning, Louise 1878?-1960 *CmpEPM*
Gunning, Louise 1879-1960 *NotNAT B, WhThe*
Gunning, Sarah 1910- *EncFCWM 69*
Gunovsky, Vilem 1912- *IntWWM 77, -80*
Gunsberg, Sheldon 1920- *IntMPA 77, -75, -76, -78, -79, -80*
Gunsbourg, Raoul 1859-1955 *Baker 78, NewGrD 80*
Gunsky, Maurice J 1888-1945 *AmSCAP 66, -80*
Guntekin, Resat Nuri 1889-1956 *EncWT, REnWD[port]*
Gunter, A C d1907 *NotNAT B*
Gunter, Arthur Neal 1926-1976 *BluesWW[port]*
Gunter, Edward Charles 1917- *AmSCAP 66, -80*
Gunter, Jane Hutton 1938- *IntWWM 77*
Gunter, Patricia *WomWMM B*
Gunter, Sidney Louie, Jr. 1925- *BiDAmM*
Gunter-McCoy, Jane Hutton 1938- *IntWWM 80*
Gunther, Dorothee 1896-1975 *CnOxB*
Gunther, Paul *Film 2*
Gunther, Robert 1929- *NewGrD 80*
Gunther, Ulrich 1923- *IntWWM 77, -80*
Gunther, Ursula 1927- *NewGrD 80*
Gunther, William 1924- *AmSCAP 66, -80*
Gunther Sprecher, William 1924- *ConAmC*
Gunzburg, M L *IntMPA 77, -75, -76, -78, -79, -80*
Gupta, Shyamal 1922- *IntWWM 77, -80*
Gura, Eugen 1842-1906 *Baker 78, NewEOp 71, NewGrD 80*
Gura, Hermann 1870-1944 *NewGrD 80*
Gurd, Alec 1907- *WhoMus 72*
Gurecky, Josef Antonin 1709-1769 *NewGrD 80*
Gurecky, Vaclav Matyas 1705-1743 *NewGrD 80*
Gurian, Paul R 1946- *IntMPA 79, -80*
Guridi, Jesus 1886-1961 *Baker 78, NewGrD 80, OxMus*
Gurie, Sigrid 1911-1969 *FilmEn, FilmgC, HalFC 80, ThFT[port], WhScrn 74, -77, WhoHol B*
Gurie, Sigrid 1915-1969 *ForYSC*
Gurievitch, Grania *WomWMM B*
Gurilyov, Alexander L'vovich 1803-1858 *NewGrD 80*
Gurilyov, Lev Stepanovich 1770-1844 *NewGrD 80*
Gurin, Ellen 1948-1972 *WhScrn 77, WhoHol B*
Gurit, Anna *WomWMM*
Gurlitt, Cornelius 1820-1901 *Baker 78, OxMus*
Gurlitt, Manfred 1890-1972 *Baker 78*
Gurlitt, Manfred 1890-1973 *NewGrD 80*
Gurlitt, Wilibald 1889-1963 *Baker 78, NewGrD 80, OxMus*
Gurnee, Hal *NewYTET*
Gurney, A R, Jr. 1930- *ConDr 77, NatPD[port]*
Gurney, Claud 1897-1946 *NotNAT B, WhThe*
Gurney, Dennis 1897- *BiE&WWA, NotNAT*
Gurney, Edmund 1847-1888 *NewGrD 80*
Gurney, Edmund 1852-1925 *Film 2, NotNAT B, WhScrn 74, -77, WhoHol B*
Gurney, Henry B 1873-1956 *BiDAmM*
Gurney, Ivor 1890-1937 *Baker 78, NewGrD 80, OxMus*
Gurney, Rachel *WhoThe 72, -77*
Gurnyak, K *Film 2*
Gurowetz, Adalbert *NewGrD 80*
Gursching, Albrecht 1934- *Baker 78*
Gurtler, Arnold B, Jr. *BiE&WWA*
Gurtler, Friedrich 1933- *IntWWM 77, -80*
Gurtner, Heinrich 1924- *IntWWM 80*
Gurvin, Olav 1893-1974 *NewGrD 80*
Guryan, Margo 1937- *AmSCAP 80*
Guschlbauer, Theodor 1939- *IntWWM 77, -80, WhoMus 72, WhoOp 76*
Gusella, Mario 1913- *WhoOp 76*
Gusenoff, Steven Ira 1946- *AmSCAP 80*
Gusev, Pyotr 1905- *DancEn 78*
Gusev, Pyotr Andreievich 1904- *CnOxB*
Gush, Jacqueline 1936- *IntWWM 77, -80*
Gushee, Lawrence 1931- *NewGrD 80*
Gusikof, Michael Joseph 1806-1837 *OxMus*
Gusikoff, Michel 1895- *AmSCAP 66, Baker 78, ConAmC*
Gusman, Meyer 1894-1960 *AmSCAP 66, -80*
Gusmeroli, Giovanni 1937- *WhoOp 76*
Guss, Jack Raphael 1919- *NatPD[port]*
Guss, Louis 1918- *BiE&WWA, NotNAT*
Gussago, Cesario *NewGrD 80*
Gusset, Monique L 1928- *IntWWM 77, -80*
Gussin, David 1899- *AmSCAP 66, -80*
Gussow, Mel *ConAmTC*
Gustaf, Prince 1827-1852 *NewGrD 80*
Gustafson, Carol 1925- *BiE&WWA, NotNAT*
Gustafson, Dwight Leonard 1930- *ConAmC, IntWWM 77, -80*
Gustafson, Howard Joseph 1915- *AmSCAP 80*
Gustafson, Ralph Barker 1909- *CreCan 2*
Gustafson, Vera 1918- *AmSCAP 66*
Gustafsson, Kaj-Erik 1942- *IntWWM 77, -80*
Gustav III 1746-1792 *OxThe*
Gustavson, Corliss Ann 1951- *IntWWM 80*
Gustin, Lyell 1895- *IntWWM 77, -80, WhoMus 72*
Gustine, Paul 1893-1974 *WhScrn 77*
Gusyev, Victor Mikhailovich 1908-1944 *NotNAT B, OxThe*
Gutche, Gene 1907- *Baker 78, CpmDNM 78, ConAmC, DcCM, WhoMus 72*
Gutcheon, Jeffrey 1941- *AmSCAP 80*
Guterson, Vladimar d1964 *NotNAT B*
Gutheil *NewGrD 80*
Gutheil, Alexander Bogdanovich 1818-1883 *NewGrD 80*
Gutheil-Schoder, Marie 1874-1935 *Baker 78, CmOp, NewEOp 71*
Guthrie, A B, Jr. *CmMov*
Guthrie, Arlo 1947- *AmSCAP 80, BiDAmM, ConMuA 80A, EncFCWM 69, IlEncR[port], RkOn 2[port], WhoHol A*
Guthrie, Charles W 1871-1939 *WhScrn 74, -77*
Guthrie, Frederick 1924- *WhoOp 76*
Guthrie, Gary *ConMuA 80B*
Guthrie, Isobel Miller Graham 1912- *WhoMus 72*
Guthrie, Jack 1915- *IlEncCM*
Guthrie, John 1912- *IntWWM 77, -80, WhoMus 72*
Guthrie, Tyrone 1900-1971 *CmOp*
Guthrie, Sir Tyrone 1900-1971 *BiE&WWA, CnThe, CreCan 1, EncWT, Ent, NotNAT A, -B, OxThe, PlP&P[port], WhThe, WhoHol B, WhoThe 72*
Guthrie, William Tyrone 1900-1971 *CreCan 1*
Guthrie, Woodrow Wilson 1912-1967 *BiDAmM, BluesWW[port], NewGrD 80*
Guthrie, Woody 1912-1967 *Baker 78, CmpEPM, ConMuA 80A, CounME 74, -74A, EncFCWM 69, IlEncCM, IlEncR, MusMk[port], NewGrD 80*
Gutierrez, Alicia 1928-1967 *WhScrn 77*
Gutierrez, Gonzalo 1540?-1605 *Baker 78*
Gutierrez, Horacio 1948- *BnBkM 80, IntWWM 77, -80*
Gutierrez, Manuel B *PupTheA*
Gutierrez, Sal 1905-1974 *NewOrJ SUP[port]*
Gutierrez DePadilla, Juan *NewGrD 80*
Gutierrez Espinosa, Felipe 1825-1899 *NewGrD 80*
Gutierrez-Heras, Joaquin 1927- *DcCM*
Gutkelch, Walter 1901- *CnMD*
Gutman, D *Film 2*
Gutman, Karl *Film 2*
Gutman, Robert W 1925- *Baker 78*
Gutmann, Adolf 1819-1882 *OxMus*
Gutmann, Adolph 1819-1882 *Baker 78*
Gutowski, Eugene 1925- *IntMPA 77, -75, -76, -78, -79, -80*
Gutowski, Gene 1925- *FilmEn, FilmgC, HalFC 80*
Gutsche, Romeo E *Baker 78*
Gutstein, Ernst 1924- *WhoOp 76*
Guttman, Irving Allen 1928- *CreCan 1, WhoOp 76*
Guttoveggio, Giuseppe *NewGrD 80*
Guttuso, Renato 1912- *CnOxB*
Gutzkow, Karl Ferdinand 1811-1878 *EncWT, McGEWD[port], NotNAT B, OxThe*
Guy De Chalis *NewGrD 80*
Guy De Cherlieu d1158 *NewGrD 80*
Guy De Saint-Denis *NewGrD 80*
Guy D'Eu *NewGrD 80*
Guy, Alice *Film 1*
Guy, Alice 1873-1968 *FilmEn*
Guy, Athol *EncFCWM 69*
Guy, Barry John 1947- *IntWWM 77, -80, NewGrD 80*
Guy, Buddy 1936- *BiDAmM, ConMuA 80A*
Guy, Elizabeth Benson 1928- *CreCan 2*
Guy, Eula d1960 *WhScrn 77*
Guy, Fred 1899-1971 *EncJzS 70, WhoJazz 72*
Guy, George 1936- *BluesWW[port]*
Guy, Harry P 1870-1950 *BiDAmM*
Guy, Helen *NewGrD 80*
Guy, Joseph Luke 1920- *BiDAmM*
Guy, Maureen *WhoMus 72*
Guy, Nicholas d1629? *NewGrD 80*
Guy, Rosa *BlkAmP*

Guy, Rose Marie 1925- *AmSCAP 80*
Guy-Blache, Alice 1873-1965 *DcFM, FilmgC, HalFC 80, MovMk[port], OxFilm*
Guy-Blache, Alice 1873-1968 *FilmEn*
Guy-Ropartz *Baker 78*
Guy-Ropartz, Joseph *NewGrD 80*
Guyer, Lawrence McIlroy 1907- *AmSCAP 80*
Guyer, Percy *NewGrD 80*
Guyett, Harold P 1920- *IntMPA 77, -75, -76, -78, -79, -80*
Guymont *NewGrD 80*
Guynes, Charlsa Anne 1933- *AmSCAP 66*
Guyon, Jean 1514?-1574? *NewGrD 80*
Guyonnet, Jacques 1933- *Baker 78, DcCM, IntWWM 77, -80, NewGrD 80*
Guyot, Jean 1512-1588 *Baker 78, NewGrD 80*
Guyse, Sheila *BlksB&W[port], -C, DrBlPA*
Guzikov, Michal Jozef 1806-1837 *Baker 78*
Guzikow, Michal Jozef 1806-1837 *NewGrD 80*
Guzmab, Robert E *Film 2*
Guzman, Jorge De *NewGrD 80*
Guzman, Luis De d1528 *NewGrD 80*
Gwaltier, James *NewGrD 80*
Gwaltney, Thomas O 1921- *BiDAmM*
Gwenn, Edmond d1959 *PlP&P*
Gwenn, Edmund 1875-1959 *FilmAG WE, FilmEn, Film 1, -2, FilmgC, ForYSC, HalFC 80, HolCA[port], IlWWBF, MotPP, MovMk[port], NotNAT B, OxFilm, WhScrn 74, -77, WhThe, WhoHol B, WhoHrs 80[port]*
Gwenn, Edmund 1876-1959 *Vers A[port]*
Gwenn, Edmund 1877-1959 *BiDFilm, -81*
Gwilt, David 1932- *WhoMus 72*
Gwilt, George 1927- *IntWWM 77, -80*
Gwilt, John 1930- *WhoMus 72*
Gwilym, Mike 1949- *WhoThe 77*
Gwineth *OxMus*
Gwinner, Volker 1912- *NewGrD 80*
Gwinnett, Richard d1717 *NotNAT B*
Gwirtz, Irvin R 1903-1957 *AmSCAP 66, -80*
Gwyn, Nell 1650-1687 *NotNAT A, -B*
Gwynn, Michael 1916-1976 *FilmgC, HalFC 80, WhoHol A, WhoThe 72, -77*
Gwynn, Nell 1650-1687 *CnThe, EncWT, Ent[port], OxThe*
Gwynne, Anne 1918- *FilmEn, FilmgC, ForYSC, HalFC 80, IntMPA 77, -75, -76, -78, -79, -80, MotPP, WhoHol A, WhoHrs 80*
Gwynne, Fred *WhoHol A*
Gwynne, Fred 1924?- *FilmgC, HalFC 80*
Gwynne, Fred 1926- *NotNAT, WhoThe 77*
Gwynne, Julia d1934 *NotNAT B*
Gwynne, Michael 1916-1976 *WhoHrs 80*
Gwynne, Michael C *WhoHol A*
Gwynne, Nell 1650-1687 *PlP&P*
Gwynneth, John 1495?-1562? *NewGrD 80*
Gwyther, Geoffrey Matheson 1890-1944 *NotNAT B, WhThe*
Gyarfas, Ibolyka 1904- *IntWWM 77, -80*
Gyarfas, Laszlo *Film 2*
Gyarfas, Miklos 1915- *CroCD*
Gyarto, Stefan 1940- *IntWWM 80*
Gye, Frederick 1809-1878 *NewGrD 80*
Gye, Marie-Louise Emma Cecile Lajeunesse *CreCan 2*
Gyimesi, Kalman 1933- *IntWWM 80*
Gyles, Nathaniel *NewGrD 80*
Gyllenborg, Carl 1679-1746 *OxThe*
Gynt, Greta 1916- *FilmAG WE, FilmEn, FilmgC, ForYSC, HalFC 80, IlWWBF, WhThe, WhoHol A*
Gyongy, Pal 1902- *IntWWM 77*
Gyongy, Paul 1902- *IntWWM 80*
Gypsy Gould *WhScrn 74, -77*
Gyrmathy, Livia *WomWMM*
Gyrowetz, Adalbert 1763-1850 *Baker 78, CnOxB, MusMk, NewGrD 80, OxMus*
Gyrowez, Adalbert 1763-1850 *NewGrD 80*
Gys, Leda 1892-1957 *FilmAG WE*
Gyselynck, Franklin Benjamin 1950- *IntWWM 80*
Gysi, Fritz 1888-1967 *Baker 78*
Gyulai-Gaal, Janos 1924- *IntWWM 77, -80*
Gyurkovics, Maria 1915-1973 *NewGrD 80*
Gyuzelev, Nikola 1936- *NewGrD 80*

H

H P Lovecraft *ConMuA 80A*
Ha, Jae Eun 1937- *CpmDNM 76, -77, ConAmC, IntWWM 77, -80*
Ha Ha, Minnie *Film 1*
Haack, Bruce C 1932- *AmSCAP 66, -80, ConAmC A*
Haack, Charles 1751-1819 *NewGrD 80*
Haack, Friedrich Wilhelm 1760-1827 *NewGrD 80*
Haack, Helmut Bernhard 1931- *IntWWM 77, -80*
Haack, Kaethe *Film 2*
Haack, Karl 1751-1819 *NewGrD 80*
Haack, Kathe 1892- *FilmAG WE*
Haacke, Friedrich Wilhelm 1760-1827 *NewGrD 80*
Haacke, Karl 1751-1819 *NewGrD 80*
Haade, William 1903-1966 *ForYSC, WhScrn 77, WhoHol B*
Haag, Jan *WomWMM B*
Haaga, Agnes 1916- *BiE&WWA*
Haagen, Al H 1871-1953 *WhScrn 74, -77*
Haager, Max Ludwig Michael 1905- *WhoMus 72*
Haager, Maximilian Ludwig Michael 1905- *IntWWM 77, -80*
Haahti, Marjatta 1938- *IntWWM 77, -80*
Haak, Friedrich Wilhelm 1760-1827 *NewGrD 80*
Haak, Karl 1751-1819 *NewGrD 80*
Haake, Friedrich Wilhelm 1760-1827 *NewGrD 80*
Haake, Karl 1751-1819 *NewGrD 80*
Haakon, Paul 1914- *CnOxB, DancEn 78*
Haal, Renee d1964 *WhScrn 74, -77, WhoHol B*
Haan, Willem De 1849-1930 *Baker 78*
Haanstra, Bert 1916- *DcFM, FilmEn, FilmgC, HalFC 80, OxFilm, WorEFlm*
Haapanen, Toivo 1889-1950 *Baker 78, NewGrD 80*
Haar, James 1929- *NewGrD 80*
Haarklou, Johannes 1847-1925 *Baker 78, NewGrD 80*
Haas *NewGrD 80*
Haas, Charles F 1913- *FilmEn, FilmgC, HalFC 80, WorEFlm*
Haas, Christoph Leonhard 1949- *WhoOp 76*
Haas, Dolly 1910- *BiE&WWA, HalFC 80, NotNAT, WhoHol A*
Haas, Dolly 1911- *FilmgC*
Haas, Ernst Johann Conrad 1723-1792 *NewGrD 80*
Haas, Friedrich 1811-1886 *NewGrD 80*
Haas, Hugh d1968 *WhoHol B*
Haas, Hugo d1968 *MotPP*
Haas, Hugo 1901-1968 *FilmEn, FilmgC, HalFC 80*
Haas, Hugo 1902-1968 *ForYSC, HolCA[port], NotNAT B, WhScrn 74, -77*
Haas, Ildephons 1735-1791 *NewGrD 80*
Haas, Johann Adam 1769-1817 *NewGrD 80*
Haas, Johann Georg 1735-1791 *NewGrD 80*
Haas, Johann Wilhelm 1649-1723 *NewGrD 80*
Haas, Joseph 1879-1960 *Baker 78, DcCM, NewGrD 80*
Haas, Julien Emile 1930- *WhoMus 72, WhoOp 76*
Haas, Karl 1900-1970 *NewGrD 80*
Haas, Monique 1906- *Baker 78*
Haas, Monique 1909- *NewGrD 80, WhoMus 72*
Haas, Olga De 1944- *CnOxB*
Haas, Otto 1874-1955 *NewGrD 80*
Haas, Pavel 1899-1944 *Baker 78, NewGrD 80*
Haas, Peter 1929- *AmSCAP 80*
Haas, Robert M *FilmEn*
Haas, Robert M d1962 *NotNAT B*
Haas, Robert Maria 1886-1960 *Baker 78, NewGrD 80*
Haas, Walter 1900- *IntMPA 77, -75, -76*
Haas, Wolf Wilhelm 1681-1760 *NewGrD 80*
Haase, Friedrich 1825-1911 *EncWT, NotNAT B*
Haase, Hans 1929- *Baker 78, IntWWM 77, -80*
Haase, Wolfgang *NewGrD 80*
Haasnoot, Leendert 1917- *IntWWM 77, -80*
Haass, Georg *NewGrD 80*
Haavikko, Paavo 1931- *CroCD*
Haayen, Fred *ConMuA 80B*
Haba, Alois 1893- *IntWWM 77, -80, NewEOp 71, OxMus, WhoMus 72*
Haba, Alois 1893-1972 *DcCM*
Haba, Alois 1893-1973 *Baker 78, NewGrD 80[port]*
Haba, Karel 1898-1972 *Baker 78, DcCM, NewGrD 80, OxMus*
Haban, Sister M Teresine 1914- *ConAmC*
Habash, John 1926- *AmSCAP 66*
Habay, Andree *Film 2*
Habeck, Ted *ConMuA 80B*
Habeeb, Tony 1927- *IntMPA 77, -75, -76, -78, -79*
Habeebullah, Shyama *WomWMM*
Habelhauer, Josef Franz *NewGrD 80*
Habeneck, Francois-Antoine 1781-1849 *Baker 78, BnBkM 80, NewGrD 80[port], OxMus*
Haber, Joyce 1932- *IntMPA 77, -75, -76, -78, -79, -80*
Haber, Julius 1905- *IntMPA 75*
Haber, Louis 1915- *ConAmC*
Haberbier, Ernst 1813-1869 *Baker 78*
Haberfield, Graham 1941-1975 *WhScrn 77, WhoHol C*
Haberhauer, Josef Franz 1746-1799 *NewGrD 80*
Haberhauer, Maurus 1746-1799 *NewGrD 80*
Haberl, Ferdinand 1906- *IntWWM 77, -80*
Haberl, Franz Xaver 1840-1910 *Baker 78, NewGrD 80, OxMus*
Habermann, Franciscus 1706-1783 *NewGrD 80*
Habermann, Frantisek Vaclav 1706-1783 *NewGrD 80*
Habermann, Franz 1706-1783 *NewGrD 80*
Habermann, Philipp *NewGrD 80*
Habert, Jan Evangelista 1833-1896 *NewGrD 80*
Habert, Johann Evangelista 1833-1896 *NewGrD 80*
Habert, Johannes Evangelista 1833-1896 *Baker 78, NewGrD 80*
Habib, Don 1935- *EncJzS 70*
Habib, Donald 1935- *EncJzS 70*
Habich, Eduard 1880-1960 *NewGrD 80*
Habif, Sheron Lee Kessler 1942- *IntWWM 77*
Habig, Dorothy Kathryn 1945- *IntWWM 77, -80*
Habington, William d1654 *NotNAT B*
Habsburg *NewGrD 80*
Habunek, Vlado 1906- *WhoOp 76*
Habyngton, Henry *OxMus*
Haccart, Carel *NewGrD 80*
Haccart, Carolus *NewGrD 80*
Hache, Reginald W J 1932- *IntWWM 77, -80*
Hachimura, Yoshio 1938- *DcCM*
Hack, Herman 1899-1967 *WhScrn 74, -77*
Hack, Signe 1899-1973 *WhScrn 77, WhoHol B*
Hackady, Hal *NatPD[port]*
Hackathorne, George 1886-1940 *ForYSC*
Hackathorne, George 1895-1940 *HalFC 80*
Hackathorne, George 1896-1940 *Film 1, -2, MotPP, TwYS, WhScrn 74, -77, WhoHol B*
Hackbarth, Glen Allen 1949- *CpmDNM 80*
Hackberry Ramblers, The *IlEncCM*
Hackely, E Azalia d1923 *BiDAmM*
Hacker, Alan Ray 1938- *IntWWM 77, -80, NewGrD 80, WhoMus 72*
Hacker, Charles R *IntMPA 77, -75, -76, -78, -79, -80*
Hacker, Maria 1904-1963 *NotNAT B, WhScrn 74, -77*
Hacker, Samuel 1903- *IntMPA 77, -75, -76, -78*
Hackerman, Nancy *WomWMM B*
Hacket, Harley *MorBAP*
Hackett, Albert 1900- *BiE&WWA, CmMov, FilmEn, Film 1, -2, FilmgC, HalFC 80, ModWD, NotNAT, TwYS, WorEFlm*
Hackett, Alfred *Film 2*
Hackett, Arthur 1884- *BiDAmM*
Hackett, Bobby 1915-1976 *BgBands 74, CmpEPM, EncJzS 70, IlEncJ, WhoJazz 72*
Hackett, Buddy 1924- *AmSCAP 66, -80, BiE&WWA, FilmEn, FilmgC, ForYSC, HalFC 80, IntMPA 77, -75, -76, -78, -79, -80, JoeFr[port], MotPP, MovMk, WhoHol A*
Hackett, Catharine Lee Sugg 1797-1845 *OxThe*
Hackett, Charles 1889-1942 *Baker 78, BiDAmM, ConAmC, NotNAT B*
Hackett, Dolly *AmPS B*
Hackett, Florence 1882-1954 *Film 1, MotPP, NotNAT B, WhScrn 74, -77, WhoHol B*
Hackett, Hal 1923-1967 *WhScrn 74, -77, WhoHol B*
Hackett, Mrs. J H d1909 *NotNAT B*
Hackett, Mrs. J H 1797-1845 *NotNAT B*
Hackett, James Henry 1800-1871 *Ent,*

FamA&A[port], NotNAT B, OxThe, PlP&P
Hackett, James K 1869-1926 *FamA&A[port], Film 1, NotNAT B, OxThe, PlP&P, WhScrn 74, -77, WhThe, WhoHol B, WhoStg 1906, -1908*
Hackett, James Keteltas 1869-1926 *EncWT*
Hackett, Jeanette *Film 1*
Hackett, Joan *BiE&WWA, MotPP, NotNAT, WhoHol A*
Hackett, Joan 1933- *MovMk[port]*
Hackett, Joan 1934- *FilmgC, HalFC 80*
Hackett, Joan 1942- *FilmEn, IntMPA 77, -76, -78, -79, -80*
Hackett, Karl 1893-1948 *ForYSC, WhScrn 74, -77, WhoHol B*
Hackett, Karleton Spaulding 1867-1935 *BiDAmM*
Hackett, Lillian 1899-1973 *Film 2, WhScrn 77, WhoHol B*
Hackett, Maria 1783-1874 *OxMus*
Hackett, Norman Honore 1874- *WhThe*
Hackett, Raymond d1958 *MotPP, WhoHol B*
Hackett, Raymond 1902-1958 *FilmEn, FilmgC, ForYSC, HalFC 80, NotNAT B, WhScrn 74, -77, WhThe*
Hackett, Raymond 1903-1958 *Film 1, -2*
Hackett, Robert Leo 1915- *BiDAmM, EncJzS 70*
Hackett, Steve *ConMuA 80A*
Hackett, Walter 1876-1944 *NotNAT B, WhThe*
Hackforth, Norman 1908- *WhoMus 72*
Hackh, Otto Christoph 1852-1917 *Baker 78, BiDAmM*
Hackman, Gene *WhoHol A*
Hackman, Gene 1930- *BiDFilm, -81, CmMov, FilmgC, HalFC 80, IntMPA 77, -75, -76, -78, -79, -80*
Hackman, Gene 1931- *FilmEn, ForYSC, MovMk[port], OxFilm*
Hackney, Alan 1924- *FilmgC, HalFC 80*
Hackney, Mabel d1914 *NotNAT B, WhThe*
Hacks, Peter 1928- *CnMD, CroCD, EncWT, Ent, McGEWD, ModWD*
Hacomblen, Robert 1455?-1528 *NewGrD 80*
Hacomplaynt, Robert 1455?-1528 *NewGrD 80*
Hacquart, Carel 1640?-1701? *NewGrD 80*
Hacquart, Carolus 1640?-1701? *NewGrD 80*
Hacumblen, Robert 1455?-1528 *NewGrD 80*
Hadamowsky, Franz *DcPup*
Hadari, Omri 1941- *IntWWM 80*
Hadassah *DancEn 78[port]*
Hadda, David Gerhart 1923- *WhoMus 72*
Haddad, Don 1935- *ConAmC*
Haddad, Donald Wayne 1935- *AmSCAP 80, CpmDNM 76*
Hadden, Frances Roots 1910- *AmSCAP 66, -80, ConAmC*
Hadden, J Cuthbert 1861-1914 *NewGrD 80*
Hadden, James Cuthbert 1861-1914 *Baker 78*
Hadden, Richard Moulton 1910- *AmSCAP 66, -80*
Haddon, Archibald 1871-1942 *NotNAT B, WhThe*
Haddon, Peggy Ann 1931- *IntWWM 77, -80*
Haddon, Peter 1898-1962 *Film 2, FilmgC, HalFC 80, NotNAT B, WhScrn 74, -77, WhThe, WhoHol B*
Haddrick, Ron 1929- *WhoThe 72, -77*
Haddrill, Philip Heileman 1917- *AmSCAP 80*
Hadelich DeFerreira, Valeska 1943- *IntWWM 80*
Haden, Charles Edward 1937- *BiDAmM, EncJzS 70*
Haden, Charlie 1937- *EncJzS 70, IlEncJ*
Haden, Sara 1897-1973 *FilmEn, HalFC 80, HolCA[port], MGM[port], MovMk, WhoHol A*
Haden, Sara 1899- *FilmgC, Vers A[port]*
Haden, Sarah 1903- *ForYSC*
Hadfield, Harry *Film 1*
Hadges, Tommy *ConMuA 80B*
Hadidian, Eileen 1948- *IntWWM 80*
Hading, Jane d1941 *NotNAT B*
Hading, Jane 1859-1933 *NotNAT B, WhThe*
Hadjidakis, Manos 1925- *FilmEn, HalFC 80, NewGrD 80, OxFilm, WorEFlm*
Hadjiev, Parashkev 1912- *NewGrD 80*
Hadjinikos, George 1927- *IntWWM 77, -80, WhoMus 72*
Hadl, Vitezslav 1945- *IntWWM 77, -80*
Hadley, Bert *Film 2*
Hadley, Henry 1871-1937 *AmSCAP 66, -80, Baker 78, BiDAmM, BnBkM 80, ConAmC, NewEOp 71, NewGrD 80, OxMus*
Hadley, James F 1922- *BiDAmM*
Hadley, Patrick Arthur Sheldon 1899-1973 *Baker 78, NewGrD 80, OxMus, WhoMus 72*
Hadley, R W, Jr. *IntMPA 77, -75, -76, -78, -79*
Hadley, Reed 1911-1974 *FilmEn, FilmgC, ForYSC, HalFC 80, Vers B[port], WhScrn 77, WhoHol B*
Hadlock, Channing M *IntMPA 77, -75, -76, -78, -79, -80*
Hadow, Sir Henry 1859-1937 *NewGrD 80*
Hadow, W H 1859-1937 *NewGrD 80*
Hadow, Sir William Henry 1859-1937 *Baker 78, OxMus*
Hadraba, Josef 1903- *IntWWM 80*
Hadrian I, Pope *NewGrD 80*
Hadrianius, Emmanuel *NewGrD 80*
Hadrianus, Emmanuel *NewGrD 80*
Hadrys, Stefan 1929- *IntWWM 77, -80*
Hadzhiev, Parashken 1912- *Baker 78*
Hadzidakis, Manos 1925- *Baker 78*
Haebler, Ingrid 1929- *IntWWM 77, -80, NewGrD 80, WhoMus 72*
Haecker, Hans Joachim 1910- *CnMD*
Haefeli, Charles Jockey 1889-1955 *WhScrn 74, -77, WhoHol B*
Haeffliger, Ernest *WhoMus 72*
Haeffner, Johann Christian Friedrich 1759-1833 *Baker 78, NewGrD 80*
Haefliger, Ernst 1919- *NewGrD 80, WhoOp 76*
Haefliger, Ernst 1921- *IntWWM 77, -80*
Haeger, Bengt 1916- *DancEn 78*
Haemel, Sigmund *NewGrD 80*
Haenchen, Hartmut 1943- *IntWWM 80*
Haenckels, Paul *Film 2*
Haendel, Ida 1924- *IntWWM 77, -80, NewGrD 80*
Haendel, Ida 1928- *WhoMus 72*
Haenflein, Robert Henriques 1924- *IntWWM 77, -80*
Haenschen, Gus *CmpEPM*
Haenschen, Gustave *AmSCAP 66, -80*
Haentjes, Werner 1923- *IntWWM 77, -80, NewGrD 80*
Haesaerts, Paul 1901- *FilmEn*
Haesche, William Edwin 1867-1929 *Baker 78*
Haeser, August Ferdinand 1779-1844 *NewGrD 80*
Haeussler, Paul 1895- *AmSCAP 66, ConAmC A*
Hafer, John Richard 1927- *BiDAmM*
Hafez, Abdel-Halim 1929- *NewGrD 80*
Hafez, Bahija *WomWMM*
Haffkine, Ron *ConMuA 80B*
Haffner, Jacobus 1615?-1671 *NewGrD 80*
Haffner, Johann Ulrich 1711-1767 *NewGrD 80*
Hafford, Mary Gale 1902- *IntWWM 77, -80*
Hafliger, Ernst 1919- *CmOp*
Hafner, Philipp 1735-1764 *OxThe*
Hafner, Robert John 1932- *AmSCAP 80*
Hafter, Robert 1897-1955 *WhScrn 77*
Haga, Herman Jan 1920- *IntWWM 77*
Hagan, Cass 1904- *CmpEPM*
Hagan, Helen Eugenia 1893-1964 *BiDAmM*
Hagan, James B d1947 *NotNAT B*
Hagan, Paul Wandel 1930- *IntWWM 77, -80*
Hagar, Sammy *ConMuA 80A*
Hagart, Dorothy *Film 1*
Hage, Louis 1938- *IntWWM 77, -80*
Hagegaard, Erland Boerje 1944- *IntWWM 77, -80*
Hagegard, Erland Borje 1944- *WhoOp 76*
Hagegard, Hakan 1945- *WhoOp 76*
Hagel, Richard 1872-1941 *Baker 78*
Hagel, Robert K 1940- *IntMPA 77, -75, -76, -78, -79, -80*
Hageman, Maurits Leonard 1829-1906 *Baker 78*
Hageman, Richard 1882-1966 *AmSCAP 66, -80, Baker 78, CmMov, ConAmC, FilmEn, HalFC 80, NewEOp 71, NewGrD 80, WhScrn 77*
Hagemann, Christian Franz Severin 1724?-1812 *NewGrD 80*
Hagemann, Phillip *ConAmC*
Hagen, Betty-Jean 1930- *CreCan 2*
Hagen, Charles F 1872-1958 *WhScrn 74, -77, WhoHol B*
Hagen, Chet *NewYTET*
Hagen, Edna *Film 2*
Hagen, Francis Florentine 1815-1907 *Baker 78, NewGrD 80*
Hagen, Friedrich Heinrich VonDer 1780-1856 *Baker 78*
Hagen, Jean *IntMPA 77, -75, -76, MotPP, WhoHol A*
Hagen, Jean 1923-1977 *FilmEn*
Hagen, Jean 1924-1977 *FilmgC, HalFC 80, MGM[port]*
Hagen, Jean 1925- *ForYSC, MovMk, What 5[port]*
Hagen, Johann *NewGrD 80*
Hagen, John Milton 1902- *AmSCAP 66, -80*
Hagen, Kevin *WhoHol A*
Hagen, Konrad Von *NewGrD 80*
Hagen, Margarethe 1890-1966 *WhScrn 74, -77*
Hagen, P A Von 1779?-1837 *NewGrD 80*
Hagen, Peter Albrecht Van, Jr. *BiDAmM*
Hagen, Peter Albrecht Van, Sr. *BiDAmM*
Hagen, Peter Van *OxMus*
Hagen, Ross *WhoHol A*
Hagen, Theodor 1823-1871 *Baker 78*
Hagen, Uta 1919- *BiE&WWA, CnThe, Ent, NotNAT, PlP&P[port], WhoHol A, WhoThe 72, -77*
Hagen-William, Louis 1938- *WhoOp 76*
Hagenau, Reinmar Von *NewGrD 80*
Hagenbeck, Carl 1844-1913 *Ent*
Hager, Bengt 1916- *CnOxB*
Hager, Carl 1911- *ConAmC*
Hager, Clyde d1944 *WhoHol B*
Hager, Clyde 1886-1944 *AmSCAP 66, -80*
Hager, Clyde 1887-1944 *WhScrn 74, -77*
Hager, Georg 1552-1634 *NewGrD 80[port]*
Hager, Ghita F 1929- *WhoOp 76*
Hager, Jim *CounME 74[port]*
Hager, John *CounME 74[port]*
Hager, Leopold 1935- *WhoOp 76*
Hager, Paul 1925- *WhoOp 76*
Hager-Zimmermann, Hilde 1907- *IntWWM 77, -80*
Hagers, The *CounME 74[port], -74A*
Hagerthy, Ron 1932- *ForYSC, WhoHol A*
Hagerty, James C *NewYTET*
Hagerup Bull, Edvard 1922- *Baker 78, IntWWM 77, -80*
Hagg, Gustaf Wilhelm 1867-1925 *Baker 78*
Hagg, Jacob Adolf 1850-1928 *Baker 78, NewGrD 80*
Haggar, George A 1897- *AmSCAP 66*
Haggar, William 1851-1924 *FilmgC, HalFC 80, IlWWBF*
Haggard, Sir H Rider 1856-1925 *FilmgC, HalFC 80*
Haggard, Merle 1937- *Baker 78, BiDAmM, CounME 74[port], -74A, EncFCWM 69, IlEncCM[port], RkOn 2[port], WhoHol A*
Haggard, Piers 1939- *FilmgC, HalFC 80*
Haggard, Stephen d1943 *WhoHol B*
Haggard, Stephen 1911-1943 *NotNAT A, -B, WhThe*
Haggard, Stephen 1912-1943 *WhScrn 74, -77*
Haggart, Bob 1914- *CmpEPM, EncJzS 70, WhoJazz 72*
Haggart, Margaret *IntWWM 77, -80, WhoOp 76*
Haggart, Robert Sherwood 1914- *AmSCAP 66, -80, BiDAmM, EncJzS 70*
Haggbom, Nils Ake 1942- *CnOxB*
Hagger, Roger Watson 1925- *IntWWM 77, -80, WhoMus 72*
Haggerty, Charles *Film 1*
Haggerty, Don *ForYSC, WhoHol A*
Haggerty, H B *WhoHol A*
Haggh, Raymond Herbert 1920- *ConAmC, IntWWM 77, -80*
Haggin, Bernard H 1900- *Baker 78*
Haggin, James Ben Ali 1882-1951 *NotNAT B*
Haggott, John Cecil d1964 *NotNAT B*
Hagius, Conrad 1550-1616 *NewGrD 80*
Hagius, Conradus 1550-1616 *NewGrD 80*
Hagius, Johann 1530?-1575? *NewGrD 80*

Hagius, Konrad 1550-1616 NewGrD 80
Hagman, Larry 1930- FilmgC, HalFC 80, WhoHol A
Hagman, Larry 1935- ForYSC
Hagman, Larry 1939- FilmEn
Hagman, Marie Margaret 1911- AmSCAP 80
Hagmann, Stuart 1939- FilmgC, HalFC 80
Hagney, Frank 1884-1973 Film 2, ForYSC, TwYS, WhScrn 77, WhoHol B
Hagon, Kenneth Hurlow 1928- WhoMus 72
Hague, Albert 1920- AmPS, AmSCAP 66, -80, BiDAmM, BiE&WWA, EncMT, NewCBMT, NotNAT, PopAmC[port], WhoThe 72, -77
Hague, Albert 1926- PopAmC SUP
Hague, Charles 1769-1821 NewGrD 80
Hague, Elsie Victoria 1897- WhoMus 72
Hague, William 1808-1887 BiDAmM
Hahn, Carl 1874-1929 AmSCAP 66, -80, Baker 78
Hahn, Carl 1879-1929 ConAmC
Hahn, Elizabeth Wyn Wood CreCan 1
Hahn, Emanuel Otto 1881-1957 CreCan 1
Hahn, Emilie 1891-1971 BiDAmM
Hahn, Georg Joachim Joseph 1690?-1769? NewGrD 80
Hahn, Gunnar A 1908- IntWWM 77, -80
Hahn, Gustav 1866-1962 CreCan 1
Hahn, Herbert R 1924- IntMPA 77, -75, -76, -78, -79, -80
Hahn, Jacob H 1847-1902 BiDAmM
Hahn, Jerry Donald 1940- BiDAmM, EncJzS 70, IntWWM 77
Hahn, Jess WhoHol A
Hahn, Paul WhoHol A
Hahn, Reynaldo 1874-1947 Baker 78
Hahn, Reynaldo 1875-1947 BnBkM 80, MusMk, NewEOp 71, NewGrD 80, OxMus
Hahn, Sally 1908-1933 WhScrn 74, -77
Hahn, Sandra Lea 1940- CpmDNM 80, ConAmC
Hahn, Ulrich d1478? Baker 78, NewGrD 80
Hahnel, Jacob NewGrD 80
Hahnel, Johannes NewGrD 80
Haibel, Jacob 1762-1826 NewGrD 80
Haibel, Jakob 1762-1826 NewGrD 80
Haibel, Petrus Jakob 1762-1826 Baker 78
Haibel, Sophie NewGrD 80
Haid, Grit WhScrn 77
Haid, Liane Film 2
Haid, Liane 1895- FilmAG WE
Haid, William 1901-1973 AmSCAP 66, -80
Haiden NewGrD 80
Haiden, David 1580-1660 NewGrD 80
Haiden, Hans 1536-1613 NewGrD 80
Haiden, Hans Christoph 1572-1617 NewGrD 80
Haider, Larry 1935- CreCan 1
Haider, Laurence Joseph 1935- CreCan 1
Haider, Lawrence 1935- CreCan 1
Haieff, Alexei 1914- AmSCAP 66, -80, Baker 78, BiDAmM, CompSN[port], CnOxB, ConAmC, DancEn 78, DcCM, NewGrD 80, OxMus, WhoMus 72
Haien, Jeannette IntWWM 77, -80
Haig, Al 1923- CmpEPM
Haig, Al 1924- EncJzS 70, IlEncJ, NewGrD 80
Haig, Alan W 1923- BiDAmM
Haig, Allan 1925- IntWWM 77
Haig, Allan W 1924- EncJzS 70
Haig, Bernard AmSCAP 80
Haig, Douglas Film 2
Haig, Emma 1898-1939 NotNAT B, WhThe
Haig, Raymond V 1917-1963 WhScrn 74, -77
Haig, Robin 1937- CnOxB
Haig, S Colson- CreCan 2
Haig, Sid WhoHol A
Haig-Brown, Roderick Langmere Haig 1908- CreCan 1
Haigh, Kenneth 1929- BiE&WWA, CnThe, FilmgC, HalFC 80, NotNAT, PlP&P[port], WhoHol A, WhoThe 72, -77
Haigh, Morris 1932- ConAmC
Haigh, Thomas 1769-1808 NewGrD 80
Haight, George 1905- BiE&WWA, WhThe
Haight, John Lewis 1902- AmSCAP 80
Hail NewGrD 80
Haile, Eugen 1873-1933 Baker 78
Hailey, Arthur 1920- CreCan 2
Hailey, Edward Nebraska 1946- AmSCAP 80
Hailey, Marian NotNAT
Hailey, Oliver 1932- ConDr 73, -77, NatPD[port], NotNAT, WhoThe 72, -77
Hailland, Petrus d1571 NewGrD 80
Hailparn, Lydia Rosen 1938- IntWWM 77, -80
Hailstork, Adolphus C, III 1941- AmSCAP 80, ConAmC
Haim, Harry Film 2
Haim, Nicola Francesco NewGrD 80
Haimo, Ethan T 1950- ConAmC
Haimsohn, Naomi Carroll 1894- IntWWM 77
Hain, Nadine WomWMM
Haindl, Franz Sebastian 1727-1812 NewGrD 80
Haine Van Ghizeghem NewGrD 80
Haine, Horace J 1868-1940 WhScrn 74, -77, WhoHol B
Haines, Connie 1922- CmpEPM, WhoHol A
Haines, Donald d1942? Film 2, WhScrn 77
Haines, Edmund 1914-1974 AmSCAP 66, -80, ConAmC
Haines, Edward Benjamin ConAmC
Haines, Elizabeth PupTheA
Haines, Ella Film 1
Haines, Frederick Stanley 1879-1960 CreCan 2
Haines, Herbert E 1880-1923 NotNAT B, WhThe
Haines, Horace J Film 1
Haines, J Talbot d1843 NotNAT B
Haines, James A 1925- AmSCAP 66, -80
Haines, Joseph d1701 OxThe, PlP&P
Haines, Louis Film 2
Haines, Napoleon J 1824-1900 BiDAmM
Haines, Rea TwYS
Haines, Rhea 1895-1964 Film 2, NotNAT B, WhScrn 74, -77, WhoHol B
Haines, Robert Terrel 1870-1943 Film 1, -2, NotNAT B, TwYS, WhScrn 74, -77, WhThe, WhoStg 1906, -1908
Haines, Ronald 1901- IlWWBF
Haines, William 1900-1973 FilmEn, Film 2, FilmgC, ForYSC, Funs[port], HalFC 80, MotPP, MovMk, TwYS, What 4[port], WhScrn 77, WhoHol B
Haines, William Wister 1908- BiE&WWA, ModWD, NotNAT
Hainl, Francois 1807-1873 Baker 78, NewGrD 80
Hainl, George 1807-1873 NewGrD 80
Hainl, Georges 1807-1873 NewGrD 80
Hainla NewGrD 80
Hainlein NewGrD 80
Hainlein, Hans 1598-1671 NewGrD 80
Hainlein, Paul 1626-1686 NewGrD 80[port]
Hainlein, Paulus 1626-1686 NewGrD 80[port]
Hainlein, Sebastian d1631 NewGrD 80
Hainlein, Sebastian 1594-1655 NewGrD 80
Haipus, Eino 1910- IntWWM 77, -80
Hair, Graham Barry 1943- IntWWM 80
Hair, Harriet Inez 1935- IntWWM 77, -80
Hair, Norman J 1931- ConAmC
Haire, Wilson John 1932- ConDr 77
Hairston, Jester 1901- AmSCAP 66, -80, ConAmC, DrBlPA, WhoHol A
Hairston, William BlkAmP, DrBlPA, MorBAP, NatPD[port]
Haisman, Irene Film 2
Haitink, Bernard 1929- Baker 78, BnBkM 80, IntWWM 77, -80, MusMk[port], MusSN[port], NewGrD 80[port], WhoMus 72
Haitzinger, Anton 1796-1869 Baker 78, NewGrD 80
Haizinger, Anton 1796-1869 NewGrD 80
Haizlip, Ellis 1932- DrBlPA
Hajdu, Andre 1932- Baker 78, NewGrD 80
Hajdu, Julia 1925- IntWWM 77, -80
Hajdu, Lorant 1937- Baker 78, IntWWM 80
Hajdu, Mihaly 1909- Baker 78, IntWWM 77, -80, NewGrD 80
Hajek, Ales 1937- IntWWM 77, -80
Hajibeyov, Sultan 1919-1974 NewGrD 80
Hajibeyov, Uzeir 1885-1948 NewGrD 80
Hajiyev, Akhmet 1917- NewGrD 80
Hajman, L Film 2
Hajn, Bronislaw 1934- IntWWM 77
Hajos, Karl 1889-1950 AmSCAP 66, -80, ConAmC A
Hajos, Mitzi 1891- CmpEPM, WhThe
Haka, Richard 1645?-1709 NewGrD 80
Hakanson, Knut 1887-1929 NewGrD 80
Hakansson, Julia Mathilda 1853- WhThe
Hakansson, Knut Algot 1887-1929 Baker 78
Hakart, Carel NewGrD 80
Hakart, Carolus NewGrD 80
Hake, John NewGrD 80
Hakenberger, Andreas 1574?-1627 NewGrD 80
Hakim, Andre 1915- FilmEn, FilmgC, HalFC 80
Hakim, Raymond 1909- FilmgC, HalFC 80, OxFilm
Hakim, Raymond 1909-1980 FilmEn
Hakim, Robert 1907- FilmEn, FilmgC, HalFC 80, OxFilm
Hakim, Sadik 1922- BiDAmM, EncJzS 70
Hakim, Talib Rasul 1940- Baker 78, BlkCS[port], ConAmC
Hala, Vlastimil 1924- IntWWM 77, -80
Halacz, Bogna 1934- IntWWM 77, -80
Halaczinsky, Rudolf 1920- NewGrD 80
Halahan, Guy Frederick Crosby 1917- IntWWM 77, -80, WhoMus 72
Halary NewGrD 80
Halas, John 1912- DcFM, FilmEn, FilmgC, HalFC 80, IntMPA 77, -75, -76, -78, -79, -80, OxFilm, WorEFlm
Halas, Joy Batchelor 1914- FilmgC
Halas, Susan WomWMM B
Halasz, Laszlo 1905- Baker 78, CmOp, NewEOp 71, WhoOp 76
Halasz, Michael 1938- IntWWM 77, -80, WhoOp 76
Halbe, Max 1865-1944 CnMD, EncWT, McGEWD, ModWD, NotNAT B
Halby, Flemming 1940- CnOxB
Halcrow, Leonard John Digby 1922- WhoMus 72
Haldane, Bert IlWWBF
Haldane, Don 1914- CreCan 1
Haldeman, Lynn E 1935- ConAmC
Haldeman, Oakley 1909- AmSCAP 66, -80
Haldemann-Gerster, Rita 1925- IntWWM 77, -80
Hale, Adam DeLa Baker 78, NewGrD 80, OxMus
Hale, Alan 1892-1950 CmMov, FilmEn, Film 1, -2, FilmgC, ForYSC, HalFC 80, HolCA[port], MotPP, MovMk[port], NotNAT B, TwYS, Vers A[port], WhScrn 74, -77, WhoHol B
Hale, Alan, Jr. 1918- FilmgC, ForYSC, HalFC 80, IntMPA 77, -75, -76, -78, -79, -80, WhoHol A
Hale, Barbara 1921- FilmEn
Hale, Barbara 1922- FilmgC, ForYSC, HalFC 80, IntMPA 77, -75, -76, -78, -79, -80, MotPP, MovMk, WhoHol A
Hale, Barnaby 1927-1964 WhScrn 74, -77, WhoHol B
Hale, Binnie 1899- EncMT, FilmgC, HalFC 80, WhThe, WhoHol A
Hale, Chanin WhoHol A
Hale, Chester 1897- DancEn 78, What 4[port]
Hale, Creighton 1882-1965 FilmEn, Film 1, -2, FilmgC, ForYSC, HalFC 80, MotPP, MovMk[port], TwYS, WhScrn 74, -77, WhoHol B
Hale, Dorothy 1905-1938 NotNAT B, WhScrn 77, WhoHol B
Hale, Edward Everett 1822-1909 BiDAmM
Hale, Edward Everett, III d1953 NotNAT B
Hale, Eugenia AmSCAP 80
Hale, Florence Film 2
Hale, George d1956 NotNAT B
Hale, Georgia MotPP, WhoHol A
Hale, Georgia 1903- HalFC 80
Hale, Georgia 1905?- MovMk
Hale, Georgia 1906- FilmEn, Film 2, TwYS
Hale, Helen WhoStg 1908
Hale, J Robert 1874-1940 NotNAT B, WhThe
Hale, James Lee 1944- AmSCAP 80
Hale, Jean WhoHol A
Hale, John d1947 NotNAT B, WhoHol B
Hale, John 1926- ConDr 73, -77
Hale, Jonathan d1966 MotPP, WhoHol B
Hale, Jonathan 1891-1966 FilmEn, ForYSC, HolCA[port], WhScrn 74, -77
Hale, Jonathan 1892-1966 FilmgC, HalFC 80, MovMk, Vers B[port]

Hale, Katherine 1878-1956 *CreCan 1*
Hale, Leroy Franklin 1923- *AmSCAP 80*
Hale, Lewis David 1930- *ConAmTC*
Hale, Lionel 1909- *WhoThe 72, -77*
Hale, Louise Closser 1872-1933 *FilmEn, Film 2, HalFC 80, MotPP, MovMk[port], NotNAT B, OxThe, ThFT[port], WhScrn 74, -77, WhThe, WhoHol B*
Hale, Louise Closser 1873-1933 *ForYSC*
Hale, Mark *AmSCAP 80*
Hale, Mary *AmSCAP 80*
Hale, Mary Whitwell 1810-1862 *BiDAmM*
Hale, Monte 1919- *HalFC 80, IntMPA 77, -75, -76, -78, -79, -80*
Hale, Monte 1921- *FilmEn, ForYSC, IlEncCM, WhoHol A*
Hale, Noel 1907- *WhoMus 72*
Hale, Philip 1854-1934 *Baker 78, BiDAmM, NewGrD 80, NotNAT B, OxMus*
Hale, Ralph G 1923- *IntWWM 80*
Hale, Reginald *AmSCAP 80*
Hale, Richard *HalFC 80, WhoHol A*
Hale, Robert 1874-1940 *WhScrn 74, -77, WhoHol B*
Hale, Robert 1933- *IntWWM 77, -80*
Hale, Robert 1937- *WhoOp 76*
Hale, Robertson 1891-1967 *WhScrn 74, -77*
Hale, Ruth d1934 *NotNAT B*
Hale, S T 1899- *WhThe*
Hale, Sarah Josepha Buell 1788-1879 *BiDAmM*
Hale, Sonnie 1902-1959 *EncMT, Film 2, FilmgC, HalFC 80, IlWWBF, NotNAT B, WhScrn 74, -77, WhThe, WhoHol B*
Hale, Theron 1883-1954 *IlEncCM*
Hale, Theron And Daughters *IlEncCM*
Hale, William 1928- *FilmgC, HalFC 80*
Haleff, Maxine *WomWMM B*
Halek, Vaclav 1937- *IntWWM 77, -80*
Halen, Walter J 1930- *ConAmC, IntWWM 77, -80*
Hales, Barbara 1930- *WhoMus 72*
Hales, Hubert 1902-1965 *Baker 78*
Hales, Jonathan 1937- *WhoThe 77*
Hales, Robert d1616? *NewGrD 80*
Hales, Thomas 1740?-1780 *NotNAT B*
Hales, William 1747-1831 *NewGrD 80*
Halevy, Fromental 1799-1862 *BnBkM 80, CmOp, MusMk, NewGrD 80[port]*
Halevy, Fromentin 1799-1862 *NewGrD 80[port]*
Halevy, Jacques 1799-1862 *CmpBCM, DancEn 78, GrComp[port]*
Halevy, Jacques-Francois-Fromental-Elie 1799-1862 *Baker 78, OxMus*
Halevy, Jacques Fromental 1799-1862 *NewEOp 71*
Halevy, Leon d1883 *NotNAT B*
Halevy, Ludovic 1834-1908 *CmOp, McGEWD[port], ModWD, NotNAT B, PlP&P*
Haley, Alex *MorBAP*
Haley, Arthur George *IntWWM 77*
Haley, Bill *AmPS A, -B, ConMuA 80A*
Haley, Bill 1925- *AmSCAP 66, -80, BiDAmM, IlEncCM, NewGrD 80*
Haley, Bill 1927- *IlEncR[port], MusMk[port]*
Haley, Bill And The Comets *RkOn[port]*
Haley, Elizabeth 1952- *IntWWM 80*
Haley, Jack *AmPS B, WhoHol A*
Haley, Jack 1899-1979 *FilmEn, FilmgC, HalFC 80[port], MovMk[port], WhoHrs 80[port]*
Haley, Jack 1901- *BiE&WWA, CmpEPM, ForYSC*
Haley, Jack 1902- *EncMT, JoeFr[port], What 3[port], WhThe*
Haley, Jack, Jr. 1934- *HalFC 80, IntMPA 77, -75, -76, -78, -79, -80, NewYTET*
Haley, Johnetta A Randolph 1923- *IntWWM 77, -80*
Haley, William D'Arcy 1828-1890 *BiDAmM*
Haley-Jarvis, Emilie 1909- *IntWWM 77*
Halffter *NewGrD 80*
Halffter, Cristobal 1930- *Baker 78, DcCM, IntWWM 80, NewGrD 80*
Halffter, Ernesto 1905- *Baker 78, DcCM, MusMk, NewGrD 80*
Halffter, Escriche Ernesto 1905- *OxMus*
Halffter, Rodolfo 1900- *Baker 78, DcCM, NewGrD 80, OxMus*
Halford, Margery 1927- *IntWWM 77, -80*
Halfpenny, Eric 1906-1979 *NewGrD 80*
Halfpenny, Tony 1913- *WhThe*
Haliassas, James Nicolas 1921- *CpmDNM 78, -79*
Halikopoulos, Nicolaos *NewGrD 80*
Halir, Carl 1859-1909 *Baker 78*
Halir, Karel 1859-1909 *NewGrD 80*
Halir, Karl 1859-1909 *NewGrD 80*
Hall, Adelaide *AmPS B*
Hall, Adelaide 1895- *EncMT*
Hall, Adelaide 1909- *BiDAmM, CmpEPM, EncJzS 70, WhoJazz 72*
Hall, Adelaide 1910- *BiE&WWA, DrBlPA, NotNAT*
Hall, Adrian 1928- *BiE&WWA, NotNAT*
Hall, Al 1915- *CmpEPM, WhoJazz 72*
Hall, Alan Geoffrey 1925- *WhoMus 72*
Hall, Albert 1937- *DrBlPA*
Hall, Albert Wesley 1915- *BiDAmM*
Hall, Alexander 1894-1968 *FilmEn, FilmgC, HalFC 80, MovMk[port], NotNAT B, WhScrn 74, -77, WhoHol B*
Hall, Alexander Ernest 1890- *WhoMus 72*
Hall, Alfred 1895-1946 *BiDAmM*
Hall, Alfred Henry 1880-1943 *WhScrn 74, -77*
Hall, Alice 1924- *AmSCAP 66*
Hall, Amariah 1785-1827 *BiDAmM*
Hall, Andrew 1944- *NewOrJ SUP[port]*
Hall, Anmer 1863-1953 *NotNAT B, WhThe*
Hall, Anne 1916- *AmSCAP 80*
Hall, Arthur Edwin 1901-1978 *AmSCAP 80, ConAmC*
Hall, Ben *Film 2*
Hall, Bettina 1906- *AmPS B, EncMT, WhThe*
Hall, Betty 1914- *Film 2*
Hall, Bob 1907- *BiE&WWA*
Hall, Carol 1936- *AmSCAP 80*
Hall, Carol Ann 1937- *CpmDNM 80*
Hall, Charles 1890?-1959 *FilmEn*
Hall, Charles D 1899- *FilmEn*
Hall, Charles D 1899-1959 *DcFM, Film 2, FilmgC, HalFC 80, -80, WhScrn 74, -77*
Hall, Charles John 1925- *AmSCAP 80, CpmDNM 75, ConAmC*
Hall, Charles King 1845-1895 *Baker 78*
Hall, Charlie d1959 *ForYSC, TwYS, WhoHol B*
Hall, Clarence 1900?- *NewOrJ*
Hall, Claude *ConMuA 80B*
Hall, Cliff d1972 *WhoHol B*
Hall, Connie 1929- *BiDAmM, CounME 74, EncFCWM 69*
Hall, Conrad 1926- *FilmEn, FilmgC, HalFC 80, IntMPA 80, OxFilm, WorEFlm*
Hall, Conrad 1927- *CmMov, IntMPA 77, -75, -76, -78, -79*
Hall, D C 1822-1900 *NewGrD 80*
Hall, Dannie Belle 1938- *AmSCAP 80*
Hall, Daryl & John Oates *IlEncR*
Hall, David 1929- *WhThe, WhoThe 72*
Hall, Donald 1878-1948 *Film 1, -2, WhScrn 77*
Hall, Dorothy 1906-1953 *Film 2, NotNAT B, WhScrn 74, -77, WhThe, WhoHol B*
Hall, Drake *ConMuA 80B*
Hall, Dudley d1960 *WhoHol B*
Hall, Ed 1901-1967 *CmpEPM*
Hall, Ed 1931- *DrBlPA*
Hall, Edmond 1901-1967 *AmSCAP 66, -80, BiDAmM, EncJzS 70, IlEncJ, NewOrJ[port], WhoJazz 72*
Hall, Edward 1875?- *NewOrJ*
Hall, Ella 1896- *Film 1, -2, TwYS, WhoHol A*
Hall, Elsie 1877-1976 *NewGrD 80*
Hall, Ernest 1890- *NewGrD 80*
Hall, Ethel May d1967 *WhoHol B*
Hall, Evelyn Walsh *Film 2, TwYS*
Hall, Fernau 1915- *CnOxB, DancEn 78*
Hall, Frances *ConAmC*
Hall, Fred 1895-1946 *NewOrJ*
Hall, Fred 1898-1964 *AmSCAP 66, CmpEPM*
Hall, Frederick Douglass 1898-1964 *BiDAmM*
Hall, Gabrielle d1967 *WhScrn 74, -77*
Hall, George *BgBands 74[port], CmpEPM*
Hall, George Lawrence *OxMus*
Hall, George M 1890-1930 *Film 1, WhScrn 74, -77, WhoHol B*
Hall, Geraldine 1905-1970 *WhScrn 74, -77, WhoHol B*
Hall, Gertrude 1912- *AmSCAP 66, -80*
Hall, Graeme Edison 1937- *IntWWM 77, -80*
Hall, Grayson *MotPP, NotNAT, WhoHol A, WhoThe 77*
Hall, H *MorBAP*
Hall, Hallene d1966 *WhoHol B*
Hall, Helen d1977 *AmSCAP 66, -80*
Hall, Henry *IlWWBF A*
Hall, Henry 1656?-1707 *NewGrD 80*
Hall, Henry 1898- *NewGrD 80, WhoMus 72*
Hall, Henry 1899- *HalFC 80*
Hall, Henry Leonard d1954 *Film 2, WhScrn 74, -77, WhoHol B*
Hall, Herb 1904?- *NewOrJ*
Hall, Herb 1907- *EncJzS 70, WhoJazz 72*
Hall, Herbert L 1907- *EncJzS 70*
Hall, Huntz 1920- *FilmEn, FilmgC, ForYSC, HalFC 80, IntMPA 77, -76, -78, -79, -80, JoeFr, MovMk, WhoHol A, WhoHrs 80*
Hall, Ian Gosford Desmond 1940- *IntWWM 77*
Hall, J A *Film 1*
Hall, J Robinson *Film 1*
Hall, J W *WhThe*
Hall, James 1897-1940 *Film 2, TwYS*
Hall, James 1900-1940 *FilmEn, FilmgC, ForYSC, HalFC 80, MovMk, NotNAT B, WhScrn 74, -77, WhoHol B*
Hall, James Stanley 1930- *BiDAmM, ConAmC, EncJzS 70*
Hall, Jane 1880-1975 *WhScrn 77*
Hall, Jenni *WomWMM*
Hall, Jim 1930- *EncJzS 70, IlEncJ*
Hall, Jim 1940- *AmSCAP 80*
Hall, Joe 1952- *EncJzS 70*
Hall, John *ConMuA 80A, PupTheA*
Hall, John 1529?-1565? *Baker 78*
Hall, John 1529?-1566 *NewGrD 80*
Hall, John 1878-1936 *WhScrn 74, -77, WhoHol B*
Hall, John C, Jr. 1929- *BiE&WWA*
Hall, John Gerald 1905- *WhoMus 72*
Hall, John Joseph Michael 1943- *IntWWM 77, -80*
Hall, Jon 1913- *CmMov, FilmgC, ForYSC, HalFC 80, IntMPA 77, -75, -76, -78, -79, -80, MovMk[port], What 3[port], WhoHol A*
Hall, Jon 1913-1979 *FilmEn, WhoHrs 80*
Hall, Josephine d1920 *Film 2, NotNAT B*
Hall, Juanita d1968 *BiE&WWA, MotPP, WhoHol B*
Hall, Juanita 1901-1968 *EncMT, FilmgC, HalFC 80, NotNAT B*
Hall, Juanita 1902-1968 *DrBlPA, WhScrn 74, -77*
Hall, Juanita 1907-1968 *CmpEPM, ForYSC*
Hall, Kate C *PupTheA*
Hall, Kathryn *WhScrn 74*
Hall, Ken G 1901- *IntMPA 77, -75, -76, -78, -79, -80*
Hall, Kristina Scholder 1951- *IntWWM 77, -80*
Hall, Larry 1941- *RkOn*
Hall, Laura Nelson 1876- *WhThe*
Hall, Lillian *Film 1, -2*
Hall, Lois *WhoHol A*
Hall, Marie 1884-1956 *Baker 78, NewGrD 80*
Hall, Mark *WhoHol A*
Hall, Martin Vincent 1933- *WhoMus 72*
Hall, Minor 1897-1959 *BiDAmM*
Hall, Minor 1897-1963 *NewOrJ[port]*
Hall, Monty 1923- *NewYTET*
Hall, Morris Eugene 1913- *IntWWM 77*
Hall, Morton *ConMuA 80B*
Hall, Natalie 1904- *AmPS B, EncMT, WhThe*
Hall, Nelson L 1881-1944 *WhScrn 74, -77*
Hall, Newton *Film 2*
Hall, Owen 1853-1906 *WhoStg 1906, -1908*
Hall, Owen 1853-1907 *EncMT, NotNAT B*
Hall, Pauline d1974 *WhoHol B*
Hall, Pauline 1860-1919 *NotNAT B, WhThe, WhoStg 1906, -1908*
Hall, Pauline 1890-1969 *Baker 78, DcCM, NewGrD 80*
Hall, Peter 1930- *BiE&WWA, CmOp, CnThe, CroCD, EncWT, Ent, FilmgC, HalFC 80,*

IlWWBF, IntWWM 77, –80, NewGrD 80, NotNAT, OxFilm, OxThe, PlP&P, WhoOp 76, WhoThe 72, –77, WorEFlm
Hall, Sir Peter 1930- *FilmEn*
Hall, Peter John 1926- *WhoOp 76*
Hall, Peter John 1940- *WhoMus 72*
Hall, Porter d1953 *MotPP, WhoHol B*
Hall, Porter 1883-1963 *MovMk*
Hall, Porter 1888-1953 *FilmEn, FilmgC, ForYSC, HalFC 80, HolCA[port], NotNAT B, Vers B[port], WhScrn 74, –77*
Hall, Ram 1897-1959 *WhoJazz 72*
Hall, Reginald 1926- *ConAmC*
Hall, Rene 1905- *NewOrJ*
Hall, Richard 1903- *ConAmC, NewGrD 80, WhoMus 72*
Hall, Robert 1912- *NewOrJ*
Hall, Ruth 1912- *ForYSC, WhoHol A*
Hall, Mrs. S C d1881 *NotNAT B*
Hall, Sam 1904?-1934? *NewOrJ[port]*
Hall, Sharon *WomWMM B*
Hall, Skip 1909- *WhoJazz 72*
Hall, Sleepy *CmpEPM*
Hall, Stephen Charles 1936- *WhoOp 76*
Hall, Thomas Munroe 1943- *IntWWM 77, –80*
Hall, Thurston d1958 *MotPP, WhoHol B*
Hall, Thurston 1882-1958 *HolCA[port], NotNAT B, WhThe, WhoStg 1906, –1908*
Hall, Thurston 1883-1958 *FilmEn, FilmgC, HalFC 80, MovMk[port], Vers A[port], WhScrn 74, –77*
Hall, Thurston 1883-1959 *Film 1, –2, ForYSC, TwYS*
Hall, Tom T 1936- *CounME 74[port], –74A, IlEncCM[port], RkOn 2[port]*
Hall, Trevor H *MagIlD*
Hall, Tubby 1895-1946 *WhoJazz 72*
Hall, Vera 1905-1964 *BiDAmM, EncFCWM 69*
Hall, Vera 1906?-1964 *BluesWW[port]*
Hall, Vicki Eileen 1943- *WhoOp 76*
Hall, Walter Henry 1862-1935 *Baker 78, BiDAmM*
Hall, Wendell 1896-1969 *IlEncCM*
Hall, Wendell Woods 1896-1969 *AmPS B, AmSCAP 66, –80, BiDAmM, CmpEPM*
Hall, Willard Lee *Film 2*
Hall, William d1700 *NewGrD 80*
Hall, William 1796-1866 *BiDAmM*
Hall, Willis 1929- *CnMD, CnThe, ConDr 73, –77, CroCD, EncWT, Ent, FilmgC, HalFC 80, ModWD, PlP&P, WhoThe 72, –77*
Hall, Winter 1878-1947 *Film 1, –2, ForYSC, TwYS, WhScrn 77*
Hall, Zooey *WhoHol A*
Hall And Oates *ConMuA 80A[port], RkOn 2[port]*
Hall-Caine, Lily d1914 *NotNAT B*
Hall-Davies, Lillian 1901-1933 *WhoHol B*
Hall-Davis, Lilian 1901-1933 *Film 1, –2, IlWWBF, WhScrn 74, –77*
Hallagan, Robert H 1926- *AmSCAP 66*
Hallam, Miss *PlP&P[port]*
Hallam, Adam d1738 *NotNAT B, PlP&P*
Hallam, Ann d1740 *NotNAT B*
Hallam, Basil 1889-1916 *NotNAT B, WhThe*
Hallam, Harry *Film 2*
Hallam, Henry *Film 1*
Hallam, Isabella 1746-1826 *OxThe*
Hallam, John *WhoHol A*
Hallam, Lewis d1755 *BiDAmM*
Hallam, Lewis 1714-1756 *EncWT, Ent, NotNAT B, OxThe, PlP&P*
Hallam, Mrs. Lewis d1773 *NotNAT B, PlP&P[port]*
Hallam, Lewis, Jr. 1740?-1808 *EncWT, Ent, FamA&A[port], NotNAT B, OxThe, PlP&P[port]*
Hallam, Lewis, Jr. 1741?-1808 *BiDAmM*
Hallam, Nancy 1759-1761 *NotNAT B*
Hallam, Sarah *NotNAT B*
Hallam, Thomas d1735 *NotNAT B*
Hallam, William d1758 *NotNAT B, PlP&P*
Hallanger, Isabel *PupTheA*
Hallard, C M 1866-1942 *WhScrn 74, –77, WhoHol B*
Hallard, Charles Maitland 1865-1942 *NotNAT B, WhThe*
Hallatt, Henry 1888-1952 *NotNAT B, WhThe, WhoHol B*
Hallatt, Mary *WhoHol A*
Hallatt, May 1882- *FilmgC, HalFC 80*
Hallatt, W H d1927 *NotNAT B*
Hallberg, Bengt 1932- *CmpEPM, EncJzS 70, NewGrD 80*
Hallberg, Bjorn Wilho 1938- *Baker 78*
Halldoff, Jan 1940- *WorEFlm*
Halldorsson, Skuli 1914- *NewGrD 80*
Halle, Adam DeLa *Baker 78, NewGrD 80*
Halle, Sir Charles 1819-1895 *Baker 78, BnBkM 80, MusMk, NewGrD 80[port], OxMus*
Halleck, Deedee *WomWMM A, –B*
Hallelujah Joe *BluesWW[port]*
Hallen, A 1846-1925 *OxMus*
Hallen, Andreas 1846-1925 *Baker 78, NewGrD 80*
Haller, Daniel *CmMov*
Haller, Daniel 1926- *FilmEn*
Haller, Daniel 1928- *FilmgC, HalFC 80, WhoHrs 80*
Haller, Daniel 1929- *WorEFlm*
Haller, Ernest 1896-1970 *CmMov, DcFM, FilmEn, FilmgC, HalFC 80, OxFilm, WhoHrs 80, WorEFlm*
Haller, Hans Peter 1929- *NewGrD 80*
Haller, Hermann 1914- *IntWWM 77, –80, NewGrD 80*
Haller, Jan 1467?-1525 *NewGrD 80*
Haller, Michael 1840-1915 *Baker 78*
Haller, Ray *Film 2*
Halleran, Edith *Film 1*
Hallet, Agnes 1880-1954 *WhScrn 74, –77*
Hallet, Judith *WomWMM B*
Hallett, Albert 1870-1935 *WhScrn 74, –77, WhoHol B*
Hallett, Alfred 1921- *WhoMus 72*
Hallett, Edward Merrihew, Jr. 1906- *AmSCAP 80*
Hallett, Jim *Film 2*
Hallett, John C *AmSCAP 66, –80*
Hallett, Mal 1893?-1952 *BgBands 74, CmpEPM*
Hallgrimsson, Haflidhi 1941- *NewGrD 80*
Hallgrimsson, Haflidi Magnus 1941- *Baker 78*
Hallhuber, Heino 1927- *CnOxB, DancEn 78*
Halliday, Andrew d1877 *NotNAT B*
Halliday, Bryant *WhoHrs 80*
Halliday, Gardner 1910-1966 *WhScrn 74, –77*
Halliday, John 1880-1947 *FilmEn, Film 2, FilmgC, ForYSC, HalFC 80[port], HolCA[port], MovMk[port], NotNAT B, WhScrn 74, –77, WhThe, WhoHol B*
Halliday, Joseph *OxMus*
Halliday, Lena d1937 *NotNAT B, WhThe*
Halliday, Richard 1905-1973 *BiE&WWA, NotNAT B*
Halliday, Robert 1893- *AmPS B, CmpEPM, EncMT, WhThe*
Halligan, Lillian *Film 2*
Halligan, William 1884-1957 *WhScrn 74, –77, WhoHol B*
Hallin, Margareta *IntWWM 80*
Hallin, Margareta 1931- *NewGrD 80*
Hallin, Margareta 1939- *WhoOp 76*
Hallin, Margreta 1931- *WhoMus 72*
Halling, Peter 1928- *WhoMus 72*
Hallis, Adolph 1896- *NewGrD 80*
Halliwell, Bruce 1946- *WhoOp 76*
Halliwell, David 1936- *ConDr 73, –77, WhoThe 72, –77*
Halliwell, David 1937- *CroCD, EncWT*
Halliwell-Phillips, James Orchard d1888 *NotNAT B*
Hallman, Ludlow B, III 1941- *IntWWM 77, –80*
Hallmann, Paul 1600-1650 *NewGrD 80*
Hallnas, Eyvind Johan 1937- *IntWWM 77, –80*
Hallnas, Hilding 1903- *Baker 78, IntWWM 77, –80, NewGrD 80*
Hallock, Peter R 1924- *ConAmC*
Hallor, Edith 1896-1971 *WhScrn 74, –77, WhoHol B*
Hallor, Ray 1900-1944 *Film 1, –2, TwYS, WhScrn 74, –77, WhoHol B*
Halloran, Don 1933- *ConAmC*
Halloran, Donald C 1933- *CpmDNM 80*
Halloran, Edward G 1909- *AmSCAP 66*
Hallowell, Russell F 1897-1965 *AmSCAP 66*
Halls, Ethel May 1882-1967 *WhScrn 74, –77, WhoHol B*
Hallstein, Ingeborg 1939- *WhoMus 72, WhoOp 76*
Hallstrom, Henry 1906- *BiDAmM, ConAmC*
Hallstrom, Ivar 1826-1901 *Baker 78, NewEOp 71, NewGrD 80, OxMus*
Hallstrom, Per 1866-1960 *ModWD, OxThe, WhThe*
Hallum, Rosemary Nora *AmSCAP 80*
Hallward, M *Film 1*
Halm, August Otto 1869-1929 *Baker 78, NewGrD 80*
Halm, Friedrich 1806-1871 *OxThe*
Halm, Hans 1898-1965 *NewGrD 80*
Halm, Harry *Film 2*
Halmen, Pet 1942- *WhoOp 76*
Halmos, Istvan 1929- *NewGrD 80*
Halop, Billy 1920-1976 *FilmEn, FilmgC, ForYSC, HalFC 80, IntMPA 77, –75, –76*
Halop, Billy 1921- *What 3[port]*
Halop, Billy 1922- *WhoHol A*
Halop, Florence *WhoHol A*
Halos, The *RkOn[port]*
Halpain, Sue Richards 1940- *IntWWM 77*
Halperin, Nan d1963 *AmPS B, NotNAT B*
Halperin, Victor 1895- *FilmEn, FilmgC, HalFC 80, WhoHrs 80*
Halpern, Adelaide Gardner 1904-1976 *AmSCAP 80*
Halpern, Leivick *McGEWD[port], REnWD[port]*
Halpern, Leon 1908- *AmSCAP 66, ConAmC A*
Halpern, Martin 1929- *NotNAT*
Halpern, Morty *BiE&WWA*
Halpern, Nathan L 1914- *IntMPA 77, –75, –76, –78, –79, –80*
Halpern, Stella 1923- *ConAmC*
Halpin, Luke *ForYSC, WhoHol A*
Halpin, Patricia 1935- *IntWWM 77, –80*
Halprin, Ann 1920- *CmpGMD, CnOxB, ConDr 73, –77E*
Halprin, Daria *WhoHol A*
Hals *NewGrD 80*
Hals, Karl 1822-1898 *NewGrD 80*
Hals, Petter 1823-1871 *NewGrD 80*
Halsey, Betty *Film 2*
Halsey, Brett *ForYSC, MotPP, WhoHol A*
Halsey, Brett 1935?- *WhoHrs 80*
Halsey, Jim *ConMuA 80B*
Halsey, Louis 1922- *NewGrD 80*
Halsey, Louis Arthur Owen 1929- *IntWWM 77, –80, WhoMus 72*
Halsey, Richard Kenneth Bitton 1944- *IntWWM 77*
Halsey, William *BlkAmP*
Halski, Czeslaw Raymund 1908- *WhoMus 72*
Halsman, David *AmSCAP 80*
Halstan, Margaret 1879- *WhThe*
Halstead, Anthony 1945- *WhoMus 72*
Halstead, William P 1906- *BiE&WWA, NotNAT*
Halston, Howard *Film 2*
Halt, James *Film 2*
Haltenberger, Bernhard 1748-1780 *NewGrD 80*
Haltiner, Fred 1936-1973 *WhScrn 77*
Halton, Charles 1876-1959 *FilmEn, FilmgC, ForYSC, HalFC 80, HolCA[port], MotPP, MovMk, Vers A[port], WhScrn 74, –77, WhoHol B*
Halton, Florence Margaret 1901- *WhoMus 72*
Halvorsen, Johan 1864-1935 *Baker 78, MusMk, NewGrD 80, OxMus*
Halvorsen, Leif 1887-1959 *Baker 78*
Ham, Al *IntWWM 77*
Ham, Albert 1858-1940 *Baker 78*
Ham, Albert William 1925- *AmSCAP 80*
Ham, Bill *ConMuA 80B*
Ham, Harry 1891-1943 *Film 1, –2, TwYS, WhScrn 77*
Ham Gravy *BluesWW[port]*
Hama, Mie 1945?- *WhoHrs 80*
Hamal *NewGrD 80*
Hamal, Henri 1744-1820 *NewGrD 80*
Hamal, Henri-Guillaume 1685-1752 *Baker 78, NewGrD 80*
Hamal, J N 1709-1778 *OxMus*
Hamal, Jean-Noel 1709-1778 *NewGrD 80*

Hamar, Clifford E 1914- *BiE&WWA, NotNAT*
Hamari, Julia 1942- *WhoOp 76*
Hambacher, Josefa *NewGrD 80*
Hambe, Alf Gunnar 1931- *IntWWM 77*
Hamblen, Bernard 1877-1962 *AmSCAP 66, -80*
Hamblen, Carl Stuart 1908- *BiDAmM*
Hamblen, Stuart 1908- *AmSCAP 80, CmpEPM, CounME 74, -74A, EncFCWM 69, IlEncCM*
Hamblen, Suzy *AmSCAP 66, -80*
Hambleton, Anne B C d1962 *NotNAT B*
Hambleton, Jack *CreCan 2*
Hambleton, John 1901-1961 *CreCan 2*
Hambleton, Ronald 1917- *CreCan 2*
Hambleton, T Edward 1911- *BiE&WWA, NotNAT, PlP&P, WhoThe 72, -77*
Hamblin, Frank C 1918- *AmSCAP 80*
Hamblin, Mrs. T S d1849 *NotNAT B*
Hamblin, Mrs. T S d1873 *NotNAT B*
Hamblin, Thomas Sowerby 1800-1853 *NotNAT B, OxThe*
Hambling, Arthur 1888- *WhThe*
Hambourg *NewGrD 80*
Hambourg, Boris 1884-1954 *BiDAmM, CreCan 2, NewGrD 80*
Hambourg, Boris 1885-1954 *Baker 78*
Hambourg, Jan 1882-1947 *Baker 78, NewGrD 80*
Hambourg, Mark 1879-1960 *Baker 78, MusSN[port], NewGrD 80*
Hambourg, Michael 1855-1916 *NewGrD 80*
Hambourg, Michael 1856-1916 *Baker 78*
Hambourg, Mikhail 1855-1916 *NewGrD 80*
Hamboys, John *Baker 78, NewGrD 80*
Hambraeus, Bengt 1928- *Baker 78, DcCM, IntWWM 77, -80, NewGrD 80*
Hamburg, Otto 1924- *IntWWM 80*
Hamburger, Klara 1934- *IntWWM 77, -80*
Hamburger, Paul 1920- *IntWWM 77, -80, WhoMus 72*
Hamburger, Povl 1901-1972 *NewGrD 80*
Hamel, Fred 1903-1957 *Baker 78, NewGrD 80*
Hamel, Margarete *NewGrD 80*
Hamel, Marie-Pierre 1786-1879 *Baker 78, NewGrD 80*
Hamel, Martine Van 1945- *CnOxB, CreCan 2*
Hamel, Peter-Michael 1947- *EncJzS 70*
Hamel, Suzanne Paradis *CreCan 1*
Hamelin, Clement d1957 *NotNAT B*
Hamelle, Jacques d1917 *Baker 78*
Hamer, Fred B 1873-1953 *WhScrn 74, -77*
Hamer, George Frederick 1862-1945 *BiDAmM*
Hamer, Gerald 1886-1972 *WhScrn 77, WhoHol B*
Hamer, Gerald 1886-1973 *FilmgC, HalFC 80*
Hamer, Gladys *Film 2*
Hamer, Joseph 1925- *IntWWM 80*
Hamer, Robert 1911-1963 *BiDFilm, -81, CmMov, DcFM, FilmEn, FilmgC, HalFC 80, IlWWBF, MovMk[port], NotNAT B, OxFilm, WorEFlm*
Hamer, Rusty *WhoHol A*
Hamerik *NewGrD 80*
Hamerik, Angul 1848-1931 *OxMus*
Hamerik, Asger 1843-1923 *Baker 78, NewGrD 80, OxMus*
Hamerik, Ebbe 1898-1951 *Baker 78, NewGrD 80, OxMus*
Hamerstein, Oscar *Film 2*
Hames, Richard David 1945- *IntWWM 77, -80, WhoMus 72*
Hamfoot Ham *BluesWW[port]*
Hamid, Sweeney 1898?-1968 *WhScrn 74, -77*
Hamil, Lucille *Film 1*
Hamill, Charlotte *Film 2*
Hamill, Claire 1955- *IlEncR[port]*
Hamill, Mark *IntMPA 79, -80*
Hamill, Mark 1952- *FilmEn, HalFC 80*
Hamill, Paul Robert 1930- *AmSCAP 80, ConAmC, IntWWM 77, -80*
Hamill, Pete 1935- *IntMPA 77, -75, -76, -78, -79, -80, WomWMM*
Hamilton, Arthur *AmSCAP 66, -80*
Hamilton, Bernie *DrBlPA, WhoHol A*
Hamilton, Big John *WhoHol A*
Hamilton, Bill *NewOrJ*
Hamilton, Bob *ConMuA 80B*
Hamilton, Bob 1899- *AmSCAP 66, -80*
Hamilton, Bugs 1911-1947 *WhoJazz 72*
Hamilton, Lady Catherine 1738?-1782 *NewGrD 80*
Hamilton, Charles *Film 2*
Hamilton, Charles 1941- *WhoOp 76*
Hamilton, Charlie 1904- *NewOrJ*
Hamilton, Chico 1921- *CmpEPM, DrBlPA, EncJzS 70, IlEncJ*
Hamilton, Christina Dee 1935- *IntWWM 77, -80*
Hamilton, Cicely 1872-1952 *NotNAT B, WhThe*
Hamilton, Clarence Grant 1865-1934 *OxMus*
Hamilton, Clarence Grant 1865-1935 *Baker 78, BiDAmM*
Hamilton, Clayton 1881-1946 *NotNAT B, WhThe*
Hamilton, Cosmo 1879-1942 *NotNAT B, WhThe*
Hamilton, David 1935- *IntWWM 77, -80, NewGrD 80*
Hamilton, David John Loudon 1937- *IntWWM 77, -80*
Hamilton, Diana 1898-1951 *NotNAT B, WhThe*
Hamilton, Dorothy 1897- *WhThe*
Hamilton, Dran *WhoHol A*
Hamilton, Edward Leslie 1937- *AmSCAP 80*
Hamilton, Foreststorn 1921- *AmSCAP 66, BiDAmM, EncJzS 70*
Hamilton, Frances *Film 2*
Hamilton, Frank S 1934- *AmSCAP 80*
Hamilton, Frederick J 1895- *AmSCAP 66*
Hamilton, George *BluesWW[port], IntMPA 75, -76, MotPP, WhoHol A*
Hamilton, George 1888- *NewOrJ*
Hamilton, George 1939- *FilmEn, FilmgC, ForYSC, HalFC 80, IntMPA 77, -78, -79, -80*
Hamilton, George 1940- *MovMk[port]*
Hamilton, George, IV 1937- *AmPS B, BiDAmM, CounME 74[port], -74A, EncFCWM 69, IlEncCM[port], RkOn[port]*
Hamilton, George W 1901-1957 *AmSCAP 66, -80, CmpEPM, WhScrn 74, -77*
Hamilton, Gladys *Film 2*
Hamilton, Gladys Dildarian 1922- *IntWWM 77*
Hamilton, Gordon 1918-1959 *CnOxB, DancEn 78*
Hamilton, Gordon George d1939 *WhScrn 74, -77, WhoHol B*
Hamilton, Guy 1922- *BiDFilm, -81, CmMov, FilmEn, FilmgC, HalFC 80, IlWWBF, IntMPA 77, -75, -76, -78, -79, -80, WhoHrs 80, WorEFlm*
Hamilton, Hale 1880-1942 *ForYSC, MotPP, MovMk, NotNAT B, TwYS, WhScrn 74, -77, WhThe, WhoHol B*
Hamilton, Hale 1883-1942 *Film 1, -2*
Hamilton, Henry d1918 *NotNAT B, WhThe*
Hamilton, Henry Speirs 1921- *IntWWM 80*
Hamilton, Iain 1922- *Baker 78, CmOp, CpmDNM 72, -76, -77, -78, ConAmC, DcCM, IntWWM 77, -80, NewGrD 80, OxMus, WhoMus 72*
Hamilton, Ian 1922- *DcCom&M 79*
Hamilton, Jack Shorty 1879?-1925 *Film 1, -2, WhScrn 77*
Hamilton, James 1917- *BiDAmM*
Hamilton, James Alexander 1785-1845 *Baker 78*
Hamilton, Jerald 1927- *IntWWM 77, -80, WhoMus 72*
Hamilton, Jimmy 1917- *CmpEPM, EncJzS 70, IlEncJ, WhoJazz 72*
Hamilton, Joe *NewYTET*
Hamilton, Joe Frank & Reynolds *RkOn 2[port]*
Hamilton, John 1886-1958 *HalFC 80*
Hamilton, John 1887-1958 *Vers B[port], WhScrn 74, -77, WhoHol B*
Hamilton, John F 1893-1967 *BiE&WWA, NotNAT B*
Hamilton, John F 1894-1967 *WhScrn 74, -77*
Hamilton, John Shorty d1967 *WhoHol B*
Hamilton, John T *Film 2*
Hamilton, Joseph H 1898-1965 *WhScrn 77*
Hamilton, Karen Sue 1946-1969 *WhScrn 74, -77*
Hamilton, Kelly *NatPD[port]*
Hamilton, Kilu Anthony *BlkAmP*
Hamilton, Kim *DrBlPA, ForYSC, WhoHol A*
Hamilton, Kipp *ForYSC, WhoHol A*
Hamilton, L Hill 1917- *AmSCAP 66, -80*
Hamilton, Lance *BiE&WWA*
Hamilton, Laurel L d1955 *WhScrn 74, -77, WhoHol B*
Hamilton, Lindisfarne 1910- *WhThe*
Hamilton, Lloyd *HalFC 80*
Hamilton, Lloyd 1891-1935 *FilmEn, Film 1, -2, ForYSC, TwYS, WhScrn 74, -77, WhoHol B*
Hamilton, Lloyd 1892-1935 *TwYS A*
Hamilton, Lumas 1912- *NewOrJ*
Hamilton, Lynn *DrBlPA*
Hamilton, Mahlon d1960 *MotPP, NotNAT B, WhoHol B*
Hamilton, Mahlon 1883-1960 *WhScrn 77*
Hamilton, Mahlon 1885-1960 *Film 1, -2, ForYSC, TwYS*
Hamilton, Margaret 1902- *BiE&WWA, FilmEn, FilmgC, ForYSC, HalFC 80, HolCA[port], IntMPA 77, -75, -76, -78, -79, -80, MovMk[port], NotNAT, ThFT[port], Vers A[port], WhoHol A, WhoHrs 80[port], WhoThe 72, -77*
Hamilton, Mark *Film 2*
Hamilton, Murray *BiE&WWA, NotNAT, WhoHol A*
Hamilton, Murray 1923- *FilmgC, HalFC 80*
Hamilton, Murray 1925?- *ForYSC, MovMk*
Hamilton, Nancy 1908- *AmSCAP 66, -80, BiE&WWA, CmpEPM, EncMT, NotNAT*
Hamilton, Neil 1899- *BiE&WWA, FilmEn, Film 2, FilmgC, ForYSC, HalFC 80, MovMk, NotNAT, TwYS, What 5[port], WhThe, WhoHol A*
Hamilton, Newburgh *NewGrD 80*
Hamilton, Patrick 1904-1962 *CnMD, EncWT, Ent, HalFC 80, ModWD, NotNAT B, WhThe*
Hamilton, Roland *BlkAmP*
Hamilton, Rose 1874- *WhThe*
Hamilton, Rosemary Deveson *CreCan 2*
Hamilton, Roy 1929-1969 *BiDAmM, DrBlPA, RkOn[port]*
Hamilton, Russ *AmPS A*
Hamilton, Theodore 1837- *WhoStg 1908*
Hamilton, Tom 1946- *ConAmC*
Hamilton, Wallace *NatPD[port], PlP&P*
Hamler, John E 1891-1969 *WhScrn 74, -77*
Hamlett, Dilys 1928- *WhoThe 72, -77*
Hamley-Clifford, Molly d1956 *NotNAT B*
Hamlin, Anna 1902- *BiDAmM*
Hamlin, George 1868-1923 *Baker 78, BiDAmM*
Hamlin, George 1920-1964 *BiE&WWA, NotNAT B*
Hamlin, Mary Frances 1901- *WhoMus 72*
Hamlin, William H 1885-1951 *WhScrn 74, -77*
Hamlisch, Marvin *IntMPA 78, -79, -80*
Hamlisch, Marvin 1944- *AmSCAP 66, -80, Baker 78*
Hamlisch, Marvin 1945- *FilmEn, RkOn 2[port]*
Hamlisch, Marvin 1946- *HalFC 80*
Hamlish, Joseph *Film 1*
Hamlyn, Brenda 1925- *CnOxB*
Hamm, Adolf 1882-1938 *Baker 78*
Hamm, Mrs. C S *PupTheA*
Hamm, Charles 1925- *ConAmC, DcCM, NewGrD 80*
Hamm, Michael Edward 1934- *IntWWM 77, -80, WhoMus 72*
Hammack, Bobby 1922- *AmSCAP 66, -80*
Hamman, Joe 1885- *FilmEn*
Hammel, Claus 1932- *CroCD*
Hammel, William Carl, Jr. 1944- *AmSCAP 80*
Hammer, Alvin *WhoHol A*
Hammer, Barbara *WomWMM B*
Hammer, Ben *WhoHol A*
Hammer, Erik 1945- *IntWWM 77, -80*
Hammer, George *NatPD[port]*
Hammer, Heinrich Albert Eduard 1862-1954 *Baker 78*
Hammer, Howard Robert 1930- *BiDAmM*
Hammer, Hubert Pater Gabriel 1934- *IntWWM 77*
Hammer, Jack *AmSCAP 80*
Hammer, Jan 1948- *AmSCAP 80,*

ConMuA 80A, EncJzS 70
Hammer, Jane Amelia Ross 1916- *IntWWM 77, -80*
Hammer, Robert 1930- *AmSCAP 66, -80*
Hammer, Tac *ConMuA 80B*
Hammer, Will 1887-1957 *FilmgC, HalFC 80, NotNAT B*
Hammeren, Torsten *Film 2*
Hammerich, Angul 1848-1931 *Baker 78, NewGrD 80, -80*
Hammerich, Asger *NewGrD 80*
Hammerich, Dick *ConAmTC*
Hammerman, Herman 1912- *AmSCAP 66, -80*
Hammerschlag, Janos 1885-1954 *Baker 78, NewGrD 80*
Hammerschmid, Andreas 1611?-1675 *NewGrD 80[port]*
Hammerschmid, Hans 1930- *WhoMus 72*
Hammerschmidt, Andreas 1611?-1675 *NewGrD 80[port], OxMus*
Hammerschmidt, Andreas 1612-1675 *Baker 78, BnBkM 80, GrComp, MusMk*
Hammerschmied, Andreas 1611?-1675 *NewGrD 80[port]*
Hammerstein, Alice 1921- *AmSCAP 66*
Hammerstein, Arthur d1955 *AmSCAP 80*
Hammerstein, Arthur 1872-1955 *EncMT, EncWT, PlP&P*
Hammerstein, Arthur 1873-1955 *NotNAT B*
Hammerstein, Arthur 1876-1955 *WhThe*
Hammerstein, Elaine 1897-1948 *FilmEn, Film 1, -2, MotPP, TwYS, WhScrn 74, -77, WhoHol B*
Hammerstein, Elaine 1898-1948 *NotNAT B*
Hammerstein, James 1931- *BiE&WWA, NotNAT, WhoThe 77*
Hammerstein, Oscar 1846-1919 *Baker 78, NewEOp 71, OxMus*
Hammerstein, Oscar 1847-1919 *BiDAmM, EncMT, EncWT, NotNAT A, -B, WhThe, WhoStg 1906, -1908*
Hammerstein, Oscar, II 1895-1960 *AmPS, AmSCAP 66, -80, Baker 78, BestMus, BiDAmM, BnBkM 80, CmpEPM, EncMT, Ent, FilmEn, FilmgC, HalFC 80, McGEWD, ModWD, NewCBMT, NewGrD 80, NotNAT A, -B, OxThe, PlP&P[port], Sw&Ld C, WhScrn 77, WhThe*
Hammerstein, Oscar, II 1895-1961 *EncWT*
Hammerstein, Reinhold 1915- *NewGrD 80*
Hammerstein, William 1874-1914 *EncWT*
Hammerton, Stephen *OxThe*
Hammett, Dashiell 1891-1961 *DcFM*
Hammett, Dashiell 1894-1961 *CmMov, FilmEn, FilmgC, HalFC 80, OxFilm, WorEFlm*
Hammett, Paul Dean 1915- *AmSCAP 80*
Hammid, Alexander 1910?- *FilmgC, HalFC 80, WomWMM*
Hammie *BluesWW[port]*
Hammill, Mark 1952- *WhoHrs 80*
Hammitt, Orlin 1916- *AmSCAP 66, -80*
Hammon, William *Film 1*
Hammond, Albert 1942- *RkOn 2[port]*
Hammond, Arthur 1904- *IntWWM 77, -80, WhoMus 72*
Hammond, Aubrey 1893-1940 *NotNAT B, WhThe*
Hammond, Bert E 1880- *WhThe*
Hammond, C Norman *Film 2*
Hammond, Charles *Film 2*
Hammond, Christopher *McGEWD[port]*
Hammond, Cleon E 1908- *AmSCAP 66, -80*
Hammond, Don 1917- *ConAmC*
Hammond, Dorothy d1950 *NotNAT B, WhScrn 77, WhThe*
Hammond, Earl R 1886- *AmSCAP 66*
Hammond, Edward Payson 1831-1910 *BiDAmM*
Hammond, Gilmore *Film 1*
Hammond, Gladys 1902- *WhoMus 72*
Hammond, Harriet *Film 2*
Hammond, J H *OxMus*
Hammond, Joan 1912- *CmOp, IntWWM 77, -80, NewGrD 80, WhoMus 72*
Hammond, John 1910- *IlEncR*
Hammond, John, Jr. 1943- *BiDAmM, ConMuA 80A, -80B, EncFCWM 69*
Hammond, John Hays, Jr. 1888-1965 *Baker 78*
Hammond, John Henry 1910- *EncJzS 70*
Hammond, John James 1910- *WhoMus 72*
Hammond, John Paul 1942- *BiDAmM, BluesWW[port]*
Hammond, Johnny 1933- *EncJzS 70*
Hammond, Kay 1909- *CnThe, Film 2, FilmgC, HalFC 80, IlWWBF[port], WhThe, WhoHol A*
Hammond, Kay 1909-1980 *FilmEn*
Hammond, Laurens 1895-1973 *Baker 78, WhoMus 72*
Hammond, Michael *ConAmC*
Hammond, Percy 1873-1936 *NotNAT A, -B, OxThe, WhThe*
Hammond, Percy 1873-1956 *EncWT*
Hammond, Peter 1923- *FilmgC, HalFC 80, IntMPA 77, -75, -76, -78, -79, -80, WhThe*
Hammond, Richard 1896- *BiDAmM, ConAmC, NewGrD 80*
Hammond, Sam *ConAmC*
Hammond, Samuel Leroy d1864 *BiDAmM*
Hammond, Terrence *ConAmC*
Hammond, Tom *WhoMus 72*
Hammond, Vernon 1910- *WhoMus 72*
Hammond, Virginia 1894-1972 *BiE&WWA, Film 1, -2, ForYSC, NotNAT B, TwYS, WhScrn 77, WhoHol B*
Hammond, W C 1890- *IlWWBF*
Hammond, William Churchill 1860-1949 *BiDAmM*
Hammond, William G 1874-1945 *AmSCAP 66, -80, ConAmC*
Hammond, Zey *PupTheA*
Hammond-Stroud, Derek 1929- *CmOp, IntWWM 77, -80, NewGrD 80, WhoMus 72, WhoOp 76*
Hamner, Earl *NewYTET*
Hamp *NewGrD 80*
Hamp, Johnny *BgBands 74, CmpEPM*
Hampden, Walter 1879-1955 *EncWT, FamA&A[port], FilmEn, Film 1, FilmgC, ForYSC, HalFC 80, HolCA[port], MotPP, MovMk[port], NotNAT B, Vers B[port], WhScrn 74, -77, WhThe, WhoHol B, WhoStg 1908*
Hampden, Walter 1879-1956 *OxThe*
Hampe, Christiane 1948- *WhoOp 76*
Hampe, Michael 1935- *IntWWM 80, WhoOp 76*
Hampel, Anton Joseph 1710?-1771 *NewGrD 80, OxMus*
Hampel, Gunter 1937- *EncJzS 70*
Hampel, Hans 1822-1884 *NewGrD 80*
Hamper, Genevieve 1889-1971 *Film 1, -2, WhScrn 74, -77, WhoHol B*
Hampl, Anton Joseph 1710?-1771 *NewGrD 80*
Hampla, Anton Joseph 1710?-1771 *NewGrD 80*
Hample, Stuart 1926- *AmSCAP 66*
Hampshire, Richard 1465?-1515? *NewGrD 80*
Hampshire, Susan *IntMPA 75, -76, WhoHol A, WhoThe 72*
Hampshire, Susan 1938- *FilmEn, FilmgC, HalFC 80*
Hampshire, Susan 1941- *FilmAG WE, ForYSC, IntMPA 77, -78, -79, -80*
Hampshire, Susan 1942- *IlWWBF[port], WhoThe 77*
Hampton, Cherrie Roberts 1946- *IntWWM 77*
Hampton, Christopher 1946- *CnThe, ConDr 73, -77, WhoThe 72, -77*
Hampton, Christopher 1948- *CroCD*
Hampton, Eric 1946- *CnOxB*
Hampton, Faith 1909-1949 *WhScrn 74, -77, WhoHol B*
Hampton, George Calvin 1938- *ConAmC*
Hampton, Gladys *Film 2*
Hampton, Gladys Riddle 1914?-1971 *BlkWAB*
Hampton, Grayce 1876-1963 *WhScrn 77*
Hampton, Hope 1899- *HalFC 80*
Hampton, Hope 1901- *Film 2, MotPP, TwYS, WhoHol A*
Hampton, Ian 1935- *IntWWM 77, -80*
Hampton, James *WhoHol A*
Hampton, John 1455?-1521? *NewGrD 80*
Hampton, Lionel *BgBands 74[port]*
Hampton, Lionel 1909- *Baker 78, CmpEPM, WhoJazz 72*
Hampton, Lionel 1913- *BiDAmM, DrBlPA, EncJzS 70, IlEncJ, MusMk[port], NewGrD 80, WhoHol A*
Hampton, Locksley Wellington 1932- *BiDAmM, EncJzS 70*
Hampton, Louise 1881-1954 *HalFC 80, NotNAT B, WhScrn 74, -77, WhThe, WhoHol B*
Hampton, Margaret *Film 2*
Hampton, Mary d1931 *NotNAT B*
Hampton, Myra 1901-1945 *Film 2, NotNAT B, WhScrn 77, WhoHol B*
Hampton, Paul 1940- *AmSCAP 80, WhoHol A*
Hampton, Raphiel *WhoHol A*
Hampton, Slide 1932- *EncJzS 70*
Hamrick, Burwell F 1906-1970 *WhScrn 77, WhoHol B*
Hamshere, Richard *NewGrD 80*
Hamsun, Knut 1859-1952 *CnMD, EncWT, NotNAT B, REnWD[port]*
Hamund, St. John d1929 *NotNAT B*
Hamvas, Lewis 1919- *ConAmC, IntWWM 77, -80*
Han, Tong-Il 1941- *WhoMus 72*
Han, Ulrich 1425?-1478? *Baker 78, NewGrD 80*
Han-Gorski, Adam 1941- *IntWWM 80, WhoMus 72*
Hanaford, Phoebe A 1829-1921 *BiDAmM*
Hanak, Dorit 1938- *WhoOp 76*
Hanako, Ohta 1882- *WhThe*
Hanalis, Blanche *WomWMM*
Hanani, Yehuda 1943- *WhoMus 72*
Hanard, Martin *NewGrD 80*
Hanart, Martin *NewGrD 80*
Hanauer, Walter W 1915- *AmSCAP 66*
Hanaway, Frank *Film 1*
Hanboys, John *Baker 78, NewGrD 80*
Hanbury, Lily d1908 *NotNAT B*
Hanbury, Maie *Film 2*
Hanbury, Victor 1897-1954 *FilmEn*
Hanbury, W Victor 1897-1954 *IlWWBF*
Hanby, Benjamin R 1833-1867 *BiDAmM*
Hanby, William 1808-1880 *BiDAmM*
Hanchett, Henry Granger 1853-1918 *Baker 78, BiDAmM*
Hancke, Karl *NewGrD 80*
Hancke, Martin *NewGrD 80*
Hancock, Christopher 1928- *WhoThe 72, -77*
Hancock, Eleanor *Film 2*
Hancock, Eugene Wilson 1929- *ConAmC*
Hancock, Gerre 1934- *ConAmC, IntWWM 77, -80, WhoMus 72*
Hancock, Herbert Jeffrey 1940- *BiDAmM, BlkCS[port], EncJzS 70*
Hancock, Herbie 1940- *ConMuA 80A, DrBlPA, EncJzS 70, IlEncJ, IlEncR*
Hancock, John *PlP&P*
Hancock, John 1938- *MovMk[port]*
Hancock, John 1939- *FilmEn, HalFC 80, IntMPA 77, -75, -76, -78, -79, -80*
Hancock, Leonard Harry 1921- *WhoMus 72*
Hancock, Matthew *PupTheA*
Hancock, Reba *WomWMM*
Hancock, Sheila 1933- *FilmgC, HalFC 80, WhoThe 72, -77*
Hancock, Tony 1924-1968 *FilmgC, HalFC 80, IlWWBF, -A[port], NotNAT B, WhScrn 74, -77, WhoHol B*
Hancox, Daisy 1898- *WhThe*
Hand, Bethlyn J *IntMPA 77, -78, -79, -80*
Hand, Colin 1929- *IntWWM 77, -80, WhoMus 72*
Hand, David 1900- *FilmEn, FilmgC, HalFC 80*
Hand, Frederic W 1947- *IntWWM 77, -80*
Handa, Frank *Film 2*
Handel, Darrell Dale 1933- *AmSCAP 80, IntWWM 77, -80*
Handel, Georg Friederich 1685-1759 *NewGrD 80*
Handel, George Frederic 1685-1759 *DancEn 78*
Handel, George Frederick 1685-1759 *DcCom&M 79*
Handel, George Frideric 1685-1759 *Baker 78, BnBkM 80[port], CmOp, CmpBCM, CnOxB, DcCom 77[port], GrComp[port], MusMk[port], NewEOp 71, NewGrD 80, OxMus*
Handel, Leo A 1941- *IntMPA 77, -75, -76, -78, -79, -80*
Handford, George 1582?-1647 *NewGrD 80*
Handford, Maurice 1929- *IntWWM 77, -80, WhoMus 72*

Handforth, Ruth Film 1
Handke, Moric NewGrD 80
Handke, Peter 1942- CroCD, EncWT, Ent, McGEWD[port], PlP&P A[port]
Handl, Irene WhoHol A
Handl, Irene 1901- FilmEn, IlWWBF, WhoThe 72, -77
Handl, Irene 1902- FilmgC, HalFC 80
Handl, Jacob 1550-1591 Baker 78, MusMk, NewGrD 80[port], OxMus
Handl, Jakob 1550-1591 BnBkM 80, NewGrD 80[port]
Handleman, David ConMuA 80B
Handley, Tommy 1894-1949 FilmgC, HalFC 80
Handley, Tommy 1902-1949 IlWWBF, -A, WhScrn 74, -77, WhoHol B
Handley, Vernon George 1930- IntWWM 77, -80, NewGrD 80, WhoMus 72
Handley, William A 1906- IntMPA 75, -76
Handley-Taylor, Geoffrey 1920- WhoMus 72
Handlo, Robert De NewGrD 80
Handman, Lou 1894-1956 AmSCAP 66, -80, CmpEPM
Handman, Wynn 1922- BiE&WWA, NotNAT, WhoThe 72, -77
Handrock, Julius 1830-1894 Baker 78
Hands, Terry 1941- EncWT, Ent, WhoThe 72, -77
Handschin, Jacques 1886-1955 Baker 78, NewGrD 80
Handt, Herbert 1926- NewGrD 80
Handworth, Harry d1916 WhScrn 77
Handworth, Octavia Film 1, MotPP
Handy, Captain 1900-1971 WhoJazz 72
Handy, George 1920- BiDAmM, CmpEPM, ConAmC A
Handy, John 1890-1971 BiDAmM
Handy, John 1900-1971 EncJzS 70, NewOrJ
Handy, John Richard, III 1933- BiDAmM, EncJzS 70
Handy, Sylvester 1900-1972 NewOrJ
Handy, W C 1873-1958 Baker 78, BnBkM 80, CmpEPM, DrBlPA, IlEncJ, MnPM[port], MorBAP, MusMk[port], PopAmC[port], PopAmC SUP
Handy, Will Baker 78
Handy, William Christopher 1873-1958 AmPS, AmSCAP 66, -80, BiDAmM, ConAmC, NewGrD 80, NotNAT B, OxMus, WhoJazz 72
Handyside, Clarence d1931 Film 1, NotNAT B
Handysides, Clarence d1931 WhoHol B
Handzel, Leon 1921- IntWWM 77, -80
Handzta, Gregory Of 759-861 NewGrD 80
Hanell, Robert 1925- DcCM
Hanet, Jean-Baptiste NewGrD 80
Haney, Carol AmPS B
Haney, Carol 1924-1964 EncMT, NotNAT B, WhoHol B
Haney, Carol 1925-1964 CnOxB, DancEn 78
Haney, Carol 1928-1964 FilmgC, HalFC 80
Haney, Carol 1934-1964 WhScrn 74, -77
Haney, J Francis d1964 NotNAT B
Haney, Joe Tom 1927- AmSCAP 80
Haney, Ray 1921- AmSCAP 66, -80
Hanff, Johann Nicolaus 1665-1712? NewGrD 80
Hanff, Johann Nikolaus 1665-1711 Baker 78
Hanford, Charles B 1859-1926 NotNAT B, WhScrn 77
Hanford, Roy Film 1
Hanfstangel, Marie 1846-1917 Baker 78
Hangen, Welles NewYTET
Hani, Susumi WomWMM B
Hani, Susumu 1926- FilmEn
Hani, Susumu 1929- WorEFlm
Hanigan, Carol Hovey AmSCAP 80
Hanighen, Bernard D AmSCAP 66, -80
Hanighen, Bernie 1908- CmpEPM
Hanin, Roger 1925- FilmAG WE[port], FilmEn, WhoHol A
Hanington PupTheA
Hanisch, Eduard 1908- IntWWM 77, -80
Hanisch, Joseph 1812-1892 Baker 78
Hanka, Erika 1905-1958 CnOxB, DancEn 78
Hanke, Friedemann 1941- WhoOp 76
Hanke, Karl 1750?-1803 Baker 78, NewGrD 80
Hanke, Martin 1574?-1617? NewGrD 80
Hanke, Susanne 1948- CnOxB
Hankerson, Alvin 1923- BluesWW
Hankin, Edward Charles St. John 1869-1909 NotNAT B, OxThe
Hankin, George 1912- WhoMus 72
Hankin, Jeffrey D 1949- ConAmC
Hankin, Marion 1920- WhoMus 72
Hankin, St. John 1860-1909 CnThe, REnWD[port]
Hankin, St. John 1869-1909 CnMD, McGEWD, ModWD
Hankinson, Michael Neville 1946- IntWWM 77, -80
Hanks, Thompson Willis, Jr. 1941- IntWWM 77, -80
Hanley, Ethel PupTheA
Hanley, James 1901- CnMD SUP, ConDr 73, -77
Hanley, James Frederick 1892-1942 AmSCAP 66, -80, CmpEPM, EncMT
Hanley, Jimmy 1918-1970 FilmEn, FilmgC, HalFC 80, IlWWBF, WhScrn 74, -77, WhoHol B
Hanley, Leo Film 2
Hanley, Linda WomWMM B
Hanley, Michael E 1858-1942 WhScrn 74, -77
Hanley, William 1931- BiE&WWA, CnMD SUP, ConDr 73, -77, CroCD, ModWD, MorBAP, NotNAT, WhoThe 72, -77
Hanley, William B, Jr. 1900-1959 WhScrn 74, -77, WhoHol B
Hanlon, Alma Film 1
Hanlon, Bert d1973 AmSCAP 80
Hanlon, Bert 1890-1972 BiDAmM
Hanlon, Bert 1895-1972 AmSCAP 66, WhScrn 77, WhoHol B
Hanlon, Jack Film 2
Hanlon, Kenneth M 1941- ConAmC
Hanlon, Richard Brendan 1936- AmSCAP 80
Hanlon, Tom 1907-1970 WhScrn 77
Hanlon-Lees OxThe
Hanly, Brian Vaughan 1940- IntWWM 77, -80
Hanmer, Ronald Charles Douglas 1917- WhoMus 72
Hann, George 1897-1950 CmOp
Hann, Walter 1838-1922 NotNAT B, WhThe
Hanna, Betty Joy 1934- IntWWM 77, -80
Hanna, Franklyn Film 1, -2
Hanna, Jake 1931- BiDAmM, EncJzS 70
Hanna, James B 1922- ConAmC
Hanna, James R 1922- IntWWM 77, -80
Hanna, John 1931- EncJzS 70
Hanna, John Bastick PupTheA
Hanna, Lee IntMPA 77, -75, -76, -78, -79, -80, NewYTET
Hanna, Mark WhoHrs 80
Hanna, Nabil Iskandar 1934- IntWWM 77, -80
Hanna, R Philip 1910-1957 AmSCAP 66, -80
Hanna, Sir Roland P 1932- BiDAmM, EncJzS 70
Hanna, William IntMPA 79, -80
Hanna, William 1910- FilmEn
Hanna, William 1911- HalFC 80
Hanna, William 1920- FilmgC, OxFilm, WorEFlm
Hannahs, Roger C ConAmC
Hannam, Ken HalFC 80
Hannan, Michael Francis 1949- IntWWM 80
Hannan, Patricia Film 1
Hannay, Roger Durham 1930- AmSCAP 80, Baker 78, CpmDNM 78, ConAmC, NewGrD 80
Hanne, Pat Film 2
Hanneford, Edwin Poodles 1892-1967 WhScrn 74, -77
Hanneford, Poodles 1892-1967 Film 2, WhoHol B
Hannemann, Walter A IntMPA 77, -75, -76, -78, -79, -80
Hannemann, Yvonne WomWMM B
Hannen, Hermione 1913- WhThe
Hannen, Nicholas 1881-1972 PlP&P, WhScrn 77, WhThe
Hanner, Barry Neil 1936- IntWWM 80, WhoOp 76
Hanner, David N 1949- AmSCAP 80
Hannesson, Hannes Jon 1948- IntWWM 77
Hannesson, Thorsteinn 1917- IntWWM 80
Hannikainen NewGrD 80
Hannikainen, Arvo 1897-1942 NewGrD 80
Hannikainen, Ilmari 1892-1955 Baker 78, NewGrD 80
Hannikainen, Pekka 1854-1924 Baker 78, NewGrD 80
Hannikainen, Pietari 1854-1924 NewGrD 80
Hannikainen, Tauno 1896-1968 Baker 78, MusSN[port], NewGrD 80
Hannikainen, Vaino 1900-1960 Baker 78, NewGrD 80
Hannington PupTheA
Hannon, Bob CmpEPM
Hannreither, Erasmus NewGrD 80
Hannum, Lewis d1884 BiDAmM
Hanofer, Frank 1897-1955 WhScrn 74, -77
Hanon, Charles-Louis 1819-1900 Baker 78
Hanot, Francois 1697-1770 NewGrD 80
Hanoun, Marcel 1929- WorEFlm
Hanousek, Vladimir 1907- IntWWM 77, -80
Hanray, Laurence 1874-1947 WhoHol B
Hanray, Lawrence 1874-1947 HalFC 80, NotNAT B, WhThe
Hans Jacob VonMailandt NewGrD 80
Hans VonBasel NewGrD 80
Hans VonBronsart NewGrD 80
Hans VonConstanz NewGrD 80
Hans VonWurms NewGrD 80
Hans Stockfisch OxThe
Hansberry, Lorraine 1930-1965 BiE&WWA, BlkAmP, CnMD SUP, ConDr 77F, CroCD, DcLB 7[port], DrBlPA, EncWT, Ent, McGEWD[port], ModWD, MorBAP, NotNAT B, PlP&P, -A[port]
Hansel, Peter 1770-1831 NewGrD 80
Hansell, Kathleen Amy Kuzmick 1941- IntWWM 77, -80
Hansell, Sven Hostrup 1934- IntWWM 77, -80
Hanselt, Adolf NewGrD 80
Hanselt, Adolph NewGrD 80
Hansen NewGrD 80
Hansen, Aksel H 1919- AmSCAP 66, -80
Hansen, Al ConDr 73, -77E
Hansen, Alfred W 1854-1922 Baker 78
Hansen, Alfred Wilhelm 1854-1923 NewGrD 80
Hansen, Asger 1889- Baker 78
Hansen, Charles F 1867-1947 BiDAmM
Hansen, Chet ConMuA 80B
Hansen, Christiern d1545? OxThe
Hansen, Edward Duane 1937- AmSCAP 80
Hansen, Einar d1927 TwYS, WhoHol B
Hansen, Emil 1843-1927 CnOxB
Hansen, Emile 1843-1927 DancEn 78
Hansen, Gunnar WhoHrs 80
Hansen, Hanne Wilhelm 1927- IntWWM 80
Hansen, Hans 1886-1962 NotNAT B, WhScrn 74, -77, WhoHol B
Hansen, Harold I 1914- BiE&WWA, NotNAT
Hansen, Janis WhoHol A
Hansen, Jens Wilhelm NewGrD 80
Hansen, Jonas Wilhelm 1850-1919 Baker 78, NewGrD 80
Hansen, Joseph 1842-1907 CnOxB
Hansen, Juanita 1895-1961 HalFC 80
Hansen, Juanita 1897-1961 Film 1, -2, MotPP, NotNAT B, TwYS, WhScrn 74, -77, WhoHol B
Hansen, Karen Film 2
Hansen, Laura d1914 NotNAT B
Hansen, Lawrence William 1905-1968 AmSCAP 66, -80
Hansen, Linda ConAmTC
Hansen, Max Film 2
Hansen, Myrna 1934- ForYSC
Hansen, Ove Verner 1932- IntWWM 77, -80
Hansen, Peter WhoHol A
Hansen, Peter 1917- IntWWM 77, -80
Hansen, Peter 1924?- ForYSC
Hansen, Poul Erik 1945- IntWWM 77, -80
Hansen, Richard Kent 1951- IntWWM 77
Hansen, Robert 1860-1926 Baker 78
Hansen, Roberta Ann 1936- AmSCAP 80
Hansen, Svend 1890- Baker 78
Hansen, Theodore Carl 1935- AmSCAP 80, ConAmC
Hansen, Wilhelm 1821-1904 Baker 78
Hansen, William 1911-1975 WhScrn 77, WhoHol C
Hansen, Willy Blok 1916- CreCan 1

Hansen-Eide, Kaja Andrea Karoline *NewGrD 80*
Hanser, Wilhelm 1738-1789? *NewGrD 80*
Hanshaw, Annette 1910- *CmpEPM*
Hanshumaker, James Richard 1931- *IntWWM 77, -80*
Hansler, George E 1921- *IntWWM 77, -80*
Hansley *PupTheA*
Hansli, Asbjorn 1944- *IntWWM 77, -80*
Hanslick, Eduard 1825-1904 *Baker 78, NewEOp 71, NewGrD 80, OxMus*
Hanslick, Edward *BnBkM 80*
Hanslip, Ann *WhoHol A*
Hanson, Alfred E 1923- *AmSCAP 80*
Hanson, Daryl L 1924- *AmSCAP 80*
Hanson, Einar 1899-1927 *Film 2*
Hanson, Einer 1899-1927 *WhScrn 74, -77*
Hanson, Erling *Film 2*
Hanson, Ethwell Idair 1893- *AmSCAP 66, -80*
Hanson, Geoffrey 1939- *WhoMus 72*
Hanson, Gladys 1884-1973 *WhScrn 77, WhoHol B*
Hanson, Gladys 1887- *Film 1, WhThe*
Hanson, Gwendoline May *WhoMus 72*
Hanson, Harry 1895- *WhThe*
Hanson, Howard 1896- *AmSCAP 66, -80, Baker 78, BiDAmM, BnBkM 80, CompSN[port], ConAmC, DcCom&M 79, DcCM, IntWWM 77, -80, NewEOp 71, NewGrD 80, OxMus, WhoMus 72*
Hanson, Jo *AmSCAP 80*
Hanson, John *IntMPA 77, -78, -79, -80*
Hanson, John 1922- *WhoThe 72, -77*
Hanson, John R 1936- *IntWWM 77, -80*
Hanson, Julius *PupTheA*
Hanson, Kitty d1947 *NotNAT B*
Hanson, Lars d1965 *MotPP, WhoHol B*
Hanson, Lars 1886-1965 *FilmEn, OxFilm*
Hanson, Lars 1887-1965 *Film 1, -2, FilmgC, HalFC 80, TwYS, WhScrn 74, -77*
Hanson, Lloyd Theodore 1926- *AmSCAP 80*
Hanson, Peter *IntMPA 77, -75, -76, -78, -79, -80*
Hanson, Raymond Charles 1913- *IntWWM 77*
Hanson, Spook *Film 1*
Hanson, Willy Blok 1916- *CreCan 1*
Hanssens *NewGrD 80*
Hanssens, Charles-Louis 1802-1871 *Baker 78, NewGrD 80*
Hanssens, Charles-Louis-Joseph 1777-1852 *NewGrD 80*
Hanssens, Joseph-Jean 1770?-1816 *NewGrD 80*
Hanssler *NewGrD 80*
Hanssler, Friedrich *NewGrD 80*
Hansson, Peter 1922- *HalFC 80*
Hansson, Sigrid Valborg 1874- *WhThe*
Hantak, Frantisek 1910- *NewGrD 80*
Hantke, Moric 1723?-1804 *NewGrD 80*
Hantzsch, Andreas d1611? *NewGrD 80*
Hantzsch, Georg 1520?-1583 *NewGrD 80*
Hanus, Jan 1915- *Baker 78, NewGrD 80*
Hanus, Karel 1929- *WhoOp 76*
Hapgood, Elizabeth Reynolds 1894- *BiE&WWA, NotNAT*
Hapgood, Norman 1868-1937 *NotNAT B*
Happenings, The *BiDAmM, RkOn 2[port]*
Happiness Boys, The *JoeFr*
Haprose, Johannes Symonis *NewGrD 80*
Hapsburg *NewGrD 80*
Haquinius, Johan Algot 1886-1966 *NewGrD 80*
Hara, Nobuo 1926- *EncJzS 70*
Harada, Higo 1927- *ConAmC*
Harada, Wayne *ConAmTC*
Haradon, Virginia 1913- *AmSCAP 66, -80*
Harangozo, Gyula 1908-1974 *CnOxB*
Harant Z Polzic A Bezdruzic, Krystof 1564-1621 *NewGrD 80*
Harapat, Jindrich 1895- *IntWWM 77, -80*
Harapes, Vlastimil 1946- *CnOxB*
Harareet, Haya 1931- *FilmEn*
Harareet, Haya 1934?- *FilmgC, ForYSC, HalFC 80, MotPP*
Harareet, Peter 1922- *HalFC 80*
Harari, Robert *IntMPA 77, -75, -76, -78, -79, -80*
Harasiewicz, Adam 1932- *Baker 78*
Harasowski, Adam 1904- *Baker 78*
Harasta, Milan 1919-1946 *NewGrD 80*
Harasteanu, Pompei 1935- *WhoOp 76*
Haraszti, Emil 1885-1958 *NewGrD 80*
Haraszti, Emile 1885-1958 *Baker 78*
Harbach, Otto 1873-1963 *AmPS, AmSCAP 66, -80, BestMus, BiDAmM, CmpEPM, EncMT, NewCBMT, NotNAT B, Sw&Ld C, WhThe*
Harbach, William O 1919- *IntMPA 77, -75, -76, -78, -79, -80*
Harbacher, Karl *Film 2*
Harbage, Alfred 1901- *BiE&WWA, NotNAT*
Harbaugh, Carl 1886-1960 *Film 1, -2, WhScrn 74, -77, WhoHol B*
Harbaugh, Henry 1817-1867 *BiDAmM*
Harben, Hubert 1878-1941 *Film 2, NotNAT B, WhScrn 74, -77, WhThe, WhoHol B*
Harben, Joan 1909-1953 *NotNAT B, WhThe, WhoHol B*
Harbers, Dalton R F 1935- *IntWWM 77*
Harbert, James K 1930- *AmSCAP 66, -80*
Harbin, Robert 1910-1978 *MagIlD[port]*
Harbison, John 1938- *Baker 78, BnBkM 80, ConAmC, DcCM*
Harbo, Erik 1937- *IntWWM 77, -80*
Harbord, Carl *Film 2, WhThe*
Harbord, Gordon 1901- *WhThe*
Harborough, William 1899-1924 *WhScrn 74, -77*
Harbou, Thea Von 1888-1954 *DcFM, FilmEn, OxFilm*
Harburg, E Y 1896- *AmSCAP 80*
Harburg, E Y 1898- *AmPS, AmSCAP 66, BestMus, BiE&WWA, CmpEPM, ConDr 73, -77D, EncMT, FilmEn, NewCBMT, NotNAT, Sw&Ld C, WhoHrs 80*
Harburg, Edgar Yipsel 1898- *BiDAmM, Ent, WhoThe 72, -77*
Harburgh, Bert *Film 2*
Harbury, Charles d1928 *NotNAT B*
Harby, Isaac 1788-1828 *NotNAT B*
Harcourt, Cyril d1924 *NotNAT B, WhThe*
Harcourt, Eugene D' 1859-1918 *Baker 78*
Harcourt, James 1873-1951 *NotNAT B, WhThe, WhoHol B*
Harcourt, Leslie 1890- *WhThe*
Harcourt, Marguerite D' 1884-1964 *Baker 78*
Harcourt, Peggie d1916 *WhScrn 77*
Hard, Johann Daniel *NewGrD 80*
Hardacre, John Pitt 1855-1933 *NotNAT B, WhThe*
Hardee, John 1919- *EncJzS 70*
Hardee, Lewis J, Jr. 1937- *AmSCAP 80*
Hardeen, Theo 1876-1944 *MagIlD*
Hardegg, Grad 1834-1867 *Baker 78*
Hardel *NewGrD 80*
Hardel, Francois 1642- *NewGrD 80*
Hardel, Gilles *NewGrD 80*
Hardel, Guillaume d1676? *NewGrD 80*
Hardel, Jacques *NewGrD 80*
Hardelot, Guy D' 1858-1936 *Baker 78, NewGrD 80, OxMus*
Harden, Arleen 1945- *BiDAmM, CounME 74, EncFCWM 69, IlEncCM*
Harden, Bobby *CounME 74*
Harden, Bobby L *AmSCAP 80, EncFCWM 69*
Harden, Maximilian 1861-1927 *EncWT*
Harden, Robbie *CounME 74, EncFCWM 69*
Harden Trio *BiDAmM, CounME 74, -74A, EncFCWM 69*
Harder, August 1775-1813 *NewGrD 80*
Harder, Emil, Jr. *Film 2*
Harder, Glenn John 1943- *WhoOp 76*
Harder, Paul Oscar 1923- *AmSCAP 80, ConAmC*
Hardie, A C d1939 *NotNAT B*
Hardie, Andrew 1909- *CnOxB*
Hardie, Gary 1948- *ConAmC*
Hardie, Russell 1904-1973 *BiE&WWA, ForYSC, MovMk, NotNAT B, WhScrn 77, WhoHol B*
Hardie, Russell 1906-1973 *WhThe*
Hardigan, Patrick *Film 2*
Hardiman, James W 1926- *IntMPA 79, -80*
Hardiman, Terrence 1937- *WhoThe 72, -77*
Hardin, Burton Ervin 1936- *CpmDNM 76, ConAmC, IntWWM 77, -80*
Hardin, Henry 1905?-1955? *NewOrJ*
Hardin, Lil *WhoJazz 72*
Hardin, Lilian 1898-1971 *BiDAmM*
Hardin, Louis Thomas 1916- *AmSCAP 80, ConAmC*
Hardin, Neil *Film 1*
Hardin, Tim 1940- *ConMuA 80A, IlEncR[port]*
Hardin, Ty 1930- *FilmEn, FilmgC, ForYSC, HalFC 80, MotPP, WhoHol A*
Harding, A A 1880-1958 *Baker 78*
Harding, Alfred d1945 *NotNAT B*
Harding, Ann *MotPP*
Harding, Ann 1901- *FilmEn, ThFT[port]*
Harding, Ann 1902- *BiE&WWA, Film 2, FilmgC, ForYSC, HalFC 80, MovMk[port], NotNAT, OxFilm, WhThe, WhoHol A, WhoThe 72*
Harding, Ann 1904- *IntMPA 77, -75, -76, -78, -79, -80*
Harding, Ben *Film 1*
Harding, Blanche *PupTheA*
Harding, Buster 1917-1965 *CmpEPM, WhoJazz 72*
Harding, D Lyn 1867-1952 *WhThe*
Harding, Gilbert 1907-1960 *HalFC 80, WhScrn 74, -77, WhoHol B*
Harding, J Rudge d1932 *NotNAT B*
Harding, James d1626 *NewGrD 80*
Harding, John 1948- *ConDr 77, PlP&P, WhoHol A, WhoThe 77*
Harding, John Phillips 1950- *IntWWM 77, -80*
Harding, June *WhoHol A*
Harding, Kathleen 1885-1958 *DancEn 78*
Harding, Lavere 1917-1965 *BiDAmM*
Harding, Lyn 1867-1952 *Film 2, FilmgC, ForYSC, HalFC 80, IlWWBF, NotNAT B, WhScrn 74, -77, WhoHol B*
Harding, Roland *PupTheA*
Harding, Rosamond E M 1898- *NewGrD 80*
Harding, Rudge *WhThe*
Harding, William H 1945- *IntMPA 77, -75, -76, -78, -79*
Hardinge, H C M *WhThe*
Hardison, Clifton James 1958- *IntWWM 77, -80*
Hardman, Bill 1933- *EncJzS 70*
Hardman, William Franklin, Jr. 1933- *EncJzS 70*
Hardmuth, Paul 1889-1962 *NotNAT B*
Hardouin, Henri 1727-1808 *NewGrD 80*
Hardouin, Pierre Jean 1914- *IntWWM 77, -80, NewGrD 80*
Hards, Ira 1872-1938 *NotNAT B, WhThe*
Hardt, Eloise *WhoHol A*
Hardt, Ernst 1876-1947 *McGEWD, ModWD*
Hardt, Johann Daniel 1696-1755? *NewGrD 80*
Hardt, Richard *AmSCAP 80*
Hardt, Victor H 1919- *AmSCAP 80*
Hardtmuth, Paul 1889-1962 *WhScrn 74, -77, WhoHol B*
Hardwick, Archer F 1918- *AmSCAP 66, -80*
Hardwick, Otto Toby 1904-1970 *CmpEPM*
Hardwick, Paul 1918- *WhoThe 72, -77*
Hardwick, Toby 1904-1970 *WhoJazz 72*
Hardwicke, Sir Cedric 1883-1964 *FilmEn*
Hardwicke, Sir Cedric 1893-1964 *BiE&WWA, CnThe, EncWT, Film 1, -2, FilmgC, ForYSC, HalFC 80, HolCA[port], IlWWBF, -A, MotPP, MovMk[port], NotNAT A, -B, OxFilm, OxThe, PlP&P[port], WhScrn 74, -77, WhThe, WhoHol B, WhoHrs 80*
Hardwicke, Sir Cedric 1896-1964 *BiDFilm, -81*
Hardwicke, Clarice 1900- *WhThe*
Hardwicke, Edward 1932- *WhoThe 72, -77*
Hardwicke, Otto 1904-1970 *BiDAmM, EncJzS 70*
Hardwicke, Toby 1904-1970 *EncJzS 70, IlEncJ*
Hardy, Alexandre 1570?-1632 *McGEWD*
Hardy, Alexandre 1572?-1631 *NotNAT B*
Hardy, Alexandre 1572?-1632? *Ent*
Hardy, Alexandre 1575?-1631? *OxThe*
Hardy, Arthur *Film 2*
Hardy, Arthur F 1870- *WhThe*
Hardy, Ashton R *NewYTET*
Hardy, Betty 1904- *WhThe*
Hardy, Charles J 1895-1966 *NewOrJ SUP[port]*
Hardy, Cherry d1963 *NotNAT B*
Hardy, Emmett Louis 1903-1925 *NewOrJ, WhoJazz 72*
Hardy, Francoise *WhoHol A*

Hardy, Hagood 1937- BiDAmM
Hardy, Joseph WhoHol A
Hardy, Joseph 1918- NotNAT
Hardy, Joseph 1929- WhoThe 72, -77
Hardy, June 1921- WhoMus 72
Hardy, Martin 1938- WhoMus 72
Hardy, Oliver 1892-1957 CmMov, FilmEn, Film 1, -2, FilmgC, ForYSC, Funs[port], HalFC 80, JoeFr[port], MGM[port], MotPP, MovMk[port], NotNAT B, OxFilm, TwYS, WhScrn 74, -77, WhoHol B, WhoHrs 80[port], WorEFlm[port]
Hardy, Robert 1925- CnThe, FilmgC, HalFC 80, WhoHol A, WhoThe 72, -77
Hardy, Sam 1883-1935 Film 1, -2, ForYSC, NotNAT B, TwYS, WhScrn 74, -77, WhoHol B, WhoStg 1908
Hardy, Sam 1905-1958 WhScrn 77
Hardy, Shirley MorBAP
Hardy, Thomas 1840-1928 FilmgC, HalFC 80, ModWD, NewEOp 71, OxMus
Hardy, Weston Vernon, III 1951- AmSCAP 80
Hardy, William Film 2
Hardy, William D 1913- AmSCAP 66
Hardy, William George 1895- CreCan 1
Hare NewGrD 80
Hare, Betty 1900- WhThe, WhoThe 72
Hare, David 1947- CnThe, ConDr 73, -77, EncWT, Ent, WhoThe 77
Hare, Doris 1905- WhoHol A, WhoThe 72, -77
Hare, Elizabeth d1741 NewGrD 80
Hare, Ernest 1881-1939 JoeFr
Hare, Ernest Dudley 1900- WhoThe 72, -77
Hare, F Lumsden 1874-1964 WhScrn 74, -77
Hare, Gilbert 1869-1951 NotNAT B, WhThe
Hare, J Robertson 1891- IlWWBF[port], WhoThe 72, -77
Hare, John d1725? NewGrD 80
Hare, Sir John 1844-1921 EncWT, NotNAT B, OxThe, PlP&P, WhScrn 77, WhThe, WhoStg 1908
Hare, Joseph d1733 NewGrD 80
Hare, Kate d1957 NotNAT B
Hare, Lumsden d1964 NotNAT B, WhoHol B
Hare, Lumsden 1874-1964 TwYS
Hare, Lumsden 1875-1964 BiE&WWA, Film 1, -2, FilmgC, ForYSC, HalFC 80, HolCA[port]
Hare, Lumsden 1895-1964 MovMk
Hare, Marilyn ForYSC
Hare, Robert Yates 1921- IntWWM 77, -80
Hare, Robertson 1891-1979 CnThe, FilmAG WE, FilmgC, HalFC 80, IlWWBF A[port], IntMPA 75, WhoHol A
Hare, Will 1919- WhoThe 77
Hare, Winifred 1875- WhThe
Harel-Lisztman, Colette WomWMM
Harelbecanus, Sigerus Paul NewGrD 80
Harell, Marte 1909- FilmAG WE
Harens, Dean 1921- WhoHol A
Harewood, Earl Of 1923- IntWWM 77, -80, NewGrD 80, OxMus
Harewood, Alphonse 1923- BiDAmM
Harewood, Dorian 1950?- DrBlPA
Harewood, George H H Lascelles, Earl Of 1923- Baker 78, WhoMus 72, WhoOp 76
Harewood, Countess Marion 1926- WhoMus 72
Harford, W WhThe
Hargan, Alison Douglas 1943- IntWWM 77, -80, WhoMus 72
Hargis, Reginald J 1951- AmSCAP 80
Hargitay, Mickey 1926- ForYSC, WhoHol A
Hargrave, Anna PupTheA
Hargrave, Martha PupTheA
Hargrave, Roy 1908- WhThe
Hargraves, William Film 2
Hargreaves, John IntMPA 77, -75, -76, -78, -79, -80
Hargreaves, John 1914- CmOp
Hargreaves, Walter Barrow 1907- IntWWM 77, -80
Hargrove, Dean NewYTET
Hargrove, Linda 1951- IlEncCM[port]
Hari, Eugene DancEn 78
Harian, Kenneth Film 2
Harich-Schneider, Eta 1897- IntWWM 77, -80, NewGrD 80
Harien, Macey Film 2
Haring, Bob 1896- CmpEPM
Haring, Robert 1896-1975 AmSCAP 66, -80
Harington, Henry 1727-1816 NewGrD 80
Harington, Joy 1914- IntMPA 77, -75, -76, -78, -79, -80
Haritun, Rosalie Ann 1938- IntWWM 77, -80
Harju, Gary Andrew 1948- AmSCAP 80
Harkarvy, Benjamin 1930- CnOxB, DancEn 78
Harker, Arthur Clifford WhoMus 72
Harker, Clifford IntWWM 77, -80
Harker, F Flaxington 1876-1936 Baker 78
Harker, Frederick d1941 NotNAT B
Harker, Gordon 1885-1967 FilmAG WE, FilmEn, Film 2, FilmgC, HalFC 80, IlWWBF[port], WhScrn 74, -77, WhThe, WhoHol B
Harker, Joseph 1892- WhThe
Harker, Joseph C 1855-1927 NotNAT A, -B, WhThe
Harkin, Edward Brandon, Jr. 1948- AmSCAP 80
Harkins, Dixie 1906-1963 WhScrn 74, -77, WhoHol B
Harkins, Marion d1962 NotNAT B
Harkins, William S d1945 NotNAT B
Harkness, Carter B Film 1
Harkness, Rebekah 1915- AmSCAP 66, -80, CnOxB, ConAmC, DancEn 78
Harlam, Macey d1923 Film 1, -2, WhoHol B
Harlan, Byron G CmpEPM
Harlan, Charles Leroy 1920-1972 ConAmC
Harlan, Cris Film 2
Harlan, Kenneth 1895-1967 FilmEn, Film 1, -2, FilmgC, ForYSC, HalFC 80, MotPP, MovMk, TwYS, WhScrn 74, -77, WhoHol B
Harlan, Macey d1923 WhScrn 74, -77
Harlan, Marion Film 2
Harlan, Otis 1865-1940 FilmEn, Film 1, -2, FilmgC, ForYSC, HalFC 80, MotPP, NotNAT B, TwYS, WhScrn 74, -77, WhThe, WhoHol B, WhoStg 1906, -1908
Harlan, Richard Film 2
Harlan, Russell 1903-1974 CmMov, FilmEn, FilmgC, HalFC 80, WhScrn 77, WorEFlm
Harlan, Veidt 1899-1964 FilmEn, WorEFlm
Harlan, Veit 1899-1964 BiDFilm, -81, DcFM, FilmgC, HalFC 80, OxFilm, WhScrn 77
Harlan, Viet 1899-1964 WhoHol B
Harlein, Lillian d1971 WhoHol B
Harlem Chorale BiDAmM
Harlem Dictators BiDAmM
Harleville, Collin D' 1755-1806 OxThe
Harley, Alexander Medard 1894- IntWWM 80
Harley, Ed Film 1
Harley, Frances Marjorie 1914- IntWWM 80
Harley, Helen 1924- WhoMus 72
Harley, Margot 1935- NotNAT
Harley, Rufus 1936- EncJzS 70
Harley, Steve And Cockney Rebel ConMuA 80A
Harley, William G NewYTET
Harline, Leigh 1907-1969 AmSCAP 66, -80, Baker 78, ConAmC, FilmEn, FilmgC, HalFC 80, OxFilm, WorEFlm
Harling, Jean M 1923- IntWWM 80
Harling, W Franke 1887-1958 AmSCAP 66, -80
Harling, William Franke 1887-1958 Baker 78, BiDAmM, ConAmC
Harlos, Steven ConAmC
Harlow, Gertrude d1947 NotNAT B
Harlow, Jean 1911-1937 BiDFilm, -81, FilmEn, Film 2, FilmgC, ForYSC, HalFC 80, MGM[port], MotPP, MovMk[port], NotNAT B, OxFilm, ThFT[port], TwYS, WhScrn 74, -77, WhoHol B, WorEFlm[port]
Harlow, John 1896- FilmgC, HalFC 80, IlWWBF
Harlow, Robert G 1923- CreCan 2
Harlow, Samuel Ralph 1885-1972 BiDAmM
Harman, Alec 1917- NewGrD 80
Harman, Alexander 1917- NewGrD 80
Harman, Audrey CnOxB
Harman, Barry Michael 1950- AmSCAP 80
Harman, Bernard Albert 1919- IntWWM 77, -80, WhoMus 72
Harman, Carter 1918- Baker 78, ConAmC, DcCM, NewGrD 80
Harman, Dave Rex 1948- IntWWM 80
Harman, Hugh 1903- DcFM
Harman, Hugh 1908- FilmEn
Harman, Richard Alexander 1917- IntWWM 77, -80, WhoMus 72
Harmat, Arthur 1885-1962 NewGrD 80
Harmat, Artur 1885-1962 Baker 78
Harmati, Sandor 1892-1936 AmSCAP 66, -80, Baker 78, BiDAmM
Harmer, Daniel Jevon 1911- CreCan 1
Harmer, Jack P 1884-1962 AmSCAP 66, -80
Harmer, Lillian 1886-1946 WhScrn 74, -77, WhoHol B
Harmer, Shirley 1930- CreCan 2
Harmeyer, Michael Richard 1951- AmSCAP 80
Harmon, Charlotte BiE&WWA, NotNAT
Harmon, Henry Film 1
Harmon, Joel, Jr. 1773-1833 BiDAmM
Harmon, John Vers B[port], WhoHol A
Harmon, John C 1935- ConAmC
Harmon, John Henry 1952- AmSCAP 80
Harmon, Lewis 1911- BiE&WWA, NotNAT
Harmon, Pat 1888-1958 WhScrn 74, -77, WhoHol B
Harmon, Pat 1890- Film 1, -2, TwYS
Harmon, Robert ConAmC
Harmon, Thomas F 1939- IntWWM 77, -80
Harmon, Tom 1919- IntMPA 77, -75, -76, -78, -79, -80, WhoHol A
Harmon Four Quartette Film 2
Harmonic, Phil 1949- ConAmC
Harmonica Frank BluesWW[port]
Harmonica Harry BluesWW[port]
Harmonica King BluesWW[port]
Harmonica Slim BluesWW[port]
Harmonicats, The AmPS A, CmpEPM
Harmony Emperor's Quartet Film 2
Harms, Benjamin William 1942- IntWWM 77, -80
Harms, Donald PupTheA
Harms, Johann Oswald 1643-1708 EncWT, Ent, NewGrD 80
Harms, Molly 1913- IntWWM 77, -80
Harms, Valerie 1940- WomWMM B
Harmsworth, Evelyn Grace 1914- WhoMus 72
Harnack, Curtis NatPD[port]
Harned, Virginia 1868-1946 NotNAT B, WhoStg 1906, -1908
Harned, Virginia 1872-1946 WhThe
Harnell, Joe RkOn
Harnell, Joseph 1924- AmSCAP 66, -80
Harner, Dolly d1956 NotNAT B
Harner, Martin W 1920- IntWWM 77, -80
Harness, William Edward 1940- IntWWM 77, -80, WhoOp 76
Harnett, Sunny WhoHol A
Harney, Ben AmPS B
Harney, Ben 1872-1938 PopAmC
Harney, Benjamin Robertson 1871-1938 BiDAmM
Harney, Benjamin Robertson 1872-1938 AmPS, NotNAT B
Harnick, Jay 1928- BiE&WWA, NotNAT
Harnick, Sheldon 1924- AmPS, BiDAmM, BiE&WWA, ConAmC, EncMT, NewCBMT, NotNAT, PlP&P
Harnisch, Otto Siegfried 1568?-1623 NewGrD 80
Harnoncourt, Nikolaus 1929- BnBkM 80, IntWWM 77, -80, NewGrD 80
Harolde, Ralf 1899-1974 FilmgC, HalFC 80, WhScrn 77, WhoHol B
Haroon, El-Hajj Daoud Abdurahman 1934- IntWWM 77
Harout, Yeghishe d1974 WhScrn 77
Harp, Nola Jay AmSCAP 80
Harper NewGrD 80, PlP&P[port]
Harper, Arthur Lee 1951- AmSCAP 80
Harper, Billy R 1943- AmSCAP 80, EncJzS 70
Harper, C Paul 1927- AmSCAP 80
Harper, Charles Abraham 1819-1893 NewGrD 80
Harper, Don 1921- IntWWM 80
Harper, Earl Enyeart 1895-1967 BiDAmM

Harper, Edmund 1821?-1869 *NewGrD 80*
Harper, Edward James 1941- *IntWWM 77, -80, NewGrD 80, WhoMus 72*
Harper, Fred d1963 *NotNAT B*
Harper, Gerald 1929- *HalFC 80, WhoThe 72, -77*
Harper, Heather 1930- *Baker 78, BnBkM 80, CmOp[port], IntWWM 77, -80, NewGrD 80, WhoMus 72, WhoOp 76*
Harper, Ian 1939- *WhoMus 72*
Harper, James *WhScrn 77*
Harper, James Cunningham, Sr. 1893- *IntWWM 77, -80*
Harper, Jessica 1953?- *HalFC 80*
Harper, Joe 1941- *IntMPA 77, -75, -76, -78, -79, -80*
Harper, John D, Jr. 1943- *IntMPA 77, -75, -76, -78, -79*
Harper, Ken 1939?- *DrBlPA, MorBAP*
Harper, Kenneth *IntMPA 77, -75, -76, -78, -79, -80*
Harper, Leonard 1899-1943 *BlksBF*
Harper, M C 1903- *BiDAmM*
Harper, Margaret Pease 1911- *IntWWM 77, -80*
Harper, Marjorie 1895- *AmSCAP 66, -80, ConAmC A, WhoMus 72*
Harper, Mark Anthony 1952- *AmSCAP 80*
Harper, Maurice Coe 1903- *AmSCAP 80*
Harper, Redd 1903- *AmSCAP 66*
Harper, Richard A *IntMPA 79, -80*
Harper, Richard A 1918- *IntMPA 77, -75, -76, -78*
Harper, Roy 1941- *ConMuA 80A, IlEncR[port]*
Harper, Thomas d1656 *NewGrD 80*
Harper, Thomas 1786-1853 *NewGrD 80*
Harper, Thomas 1816-1898 *NewGrD 80*
Harper, Valerie 1940- *FilmEn, HalFC 80, IntMPA 77, -76, -78, -79, -80, WhoHol A*
Harper, Wally 1941- *AmSCAP 80*
Harper, William A 1915- *IntMPA 77, -75, -76, -78, -79, -80*
Harper, William Donald 1921- *IntWWM 77, WhoMus 72*
Harper's Bizarre *BiDAmM, RkOn 2[port]*
Harpham, James Stanley Medcalf 1940- *IntWWM 77, -80*
Harpo, Slim *BluesWW[port], RkOn*
Harptones, The *RkOn[port]*
Harraden, Samuel 1821-1897 *Baker 78*
Harran, Don 1936- *IntWWM 77, -80, NewGrD 80*
Harreld, Kemper 1885- *BiDAmM*
Harrell, Gordon Lowry 1940- *AmSCAP 80*
Harrell, Kelly 1899-1942 *IlEncCM*
Harrell, Lynn 1944- *BnBkM 80, IntWWM 77, -80, NewGrD 80*
Harrell, Mack 1909-1960 *Baker 78, BiDAmM, NewEOp 71*
Harrer, Gottlob 1703-1755 *NewGrD 80*
Harrer, James P 1946- *ConAmC*
Harrex, Patrick 1946- *IntWWM 77, -80*
Harrhy, Eiddwen 1949- *NewGrD 80*
Harrhy, John Douglas 1919- *IntWWM 77, -80, WhoMus 72*
Harries, David 1933- *NewGrD 80, WhoMus 72*
Harries, Kenneth Clive 1951- *IntWWM 77, -80*
Harrigan, Edward 1843-1911 *NotNAT A, WhoStg 1906, -1908*
Harrigan, Edward 1844-1911 *EncMT*
Harrigan, Edward 1845-1911 *AmPS, BiDAmM, CnThe, EncWT, Ent, FamA&A[port], McGEWD[port], ModWD, NotNAT B, OxThe, PlP&P, REnWD[port], Sw&Ld B*
Harrigan, Nedda 1900- *ForYSC*
Harrigan, Nedda 1902- *BiE&WWA, Film 2, WhThe, WhoHol A*
Harrigan, William 1886-1966 *NotNAT B*
Harrigan, William 1887-1966 *Film 2*
Harrigan, William 1894-1966 *BiE&WWA, FilmgC, HalFC 80, WhScrn 74, -77, WhThe, WhoHol B*
Harring, Hildegard *Film 2*
Harrington, Countess Of *OxThe*
Harrington, Alice d1954 *NotNAT B*
Harrington, Amber Roobenian 1905- *AmSCAP 80, ConAmC*
Harrington, Buck d1971 *WhScrn 77*
Harrington, Calvin S 1826-1886 *BiDAmM*
Harrington, Curtis 1928- *FilmEn, FilmgC, HalFC 80, IntMPA 77, -75, -76, -78, -79, -80, WhoHrs 80*
Harrington, Donal 1905- *BiE&WWA, NotNAT*
Harrington, Florence d1942 *NotNAT B*
Harrington, Grace 1927- *IntWWM 77, -80*
Harrington, Hamtree *BlksB&W C*
Harrington, Helmi Hanni Strahl 1945- *IntWWM 77, -80*
Harrington, Henry *NewGrD 80*
Harrington, J P 1865- *WhThe*
Harrington, Joe *Film 2*
Harrington, John *Film 2*
Harrington, John B, Jr. d1973 *NewYTET*
Harrington, John David 1910- *WhoJazz 72*
Harrington, Joy 1914- *WomWMM*
Harrington, Karl Pomeroy 1861-1953 *BiDAmM*
Harrington, Kate *WhoHol A*
Harrington, Pat, Jr. *IntMPA 77, -75, -76, -78, -79, -80, WhoHol A*
Harrington, Pat, Sr. 1900-1965 *BiE&WWA, NotNAT B, WhoHol B*
Harrington, Robert Maxon 1912- *AmSCAP 80*
Harrington, Vicki 1911-1971 *AmSCAP 80*
Harrington, Victor B 1915- *AmSCAP 66, -80*
Harrington, W Clark 1905- *AmSCAP 66, ConAmC*
Harrington, William Clark 1905- *AmSCAP 80*
Harrington, William O 1918- *AmSCAP 66, -80*
Harriott, Arthurlin 1928-1973 *BiDAmM, EncJzS 70*
Harriott, Joe 1928-1972 *IlEncJ*
Harriott, Joe 1928-1973 *EncJzS 70*
Harris *NewGrD 80*
Harris, Alan 1934- *WhoMus 72*
Harris, Albert 1916- *AmSCAP 80, ConAmC*
Harris, Alice Eaton 1924- *IntWWM 77, -80*
Harris, Andrew B 1944- *NatPD[port]*
Harris, Arthur 1927- *ConAmC*
Harris, Arville S 1904-1954 *WhoJazz 72*
Harris, Asa Ace 1910-1964 *NotNAT B, WhScrn 77*
Harris, Audrey Sophia 1901-1966 *NotNAT B, WhThe*
Harris, Sir Augustus 1851-1896 *CnThe*
Harris, Sir Augustus 1852-1896 *Baker 78, NewEOp 71, NewGrD 80, NotNAT B, OxThe*
Harris, Augustus Glossop 1825-1873 *NotNAT B, OxThe*
Harris, Averell d1966 *WhScrn 74, -77, WhoHol B*
Harris, Barbara *BiE&WWA, IntMPA 77, -75, -76, -78, -79, -80, MotPP, NotNAT, WhoHol A, WhoThe 72*
Harris, Barbara 1935- *BiDAmM*
Harris, Barbara 1936- *HalFC 80*
Harris, Barbara 1937- *EncMT, FilmEn, WhoThe 77*
Harris, Barbara 1940- *FilmgC*
Harris, Barry Doyle 1929- *BiDAmM, EncJzS 70*
Harris, Beaver 1936- *EncJzS 70*
Harris, Belle 1926- *AmSCAP 66*
Harris, Benjamin 1919-1975 *BiDAmM, EncJzS 70*
Harris, Benny 1919-1975 *EncJzS 70*
Harris, Bill 1916- *BlkAmP, MorBAP, WhoJazz 72*
Harris, Bill 1916-1973 *CmpEPM, EncJzS 70*
Harris, Bill 1916-1974 *IlEncJ*
Harris, Bill 1925- *EncJzS 70*
Harris, Blanche *CreCan 1*
Harris, Brad *ForYSC, WhoHol A*
Harris, Buddy *Film 2*
Harris, Carl Gordon, Jr. 1935- *IntWWM 77, -80*
Harris, Caroline *Film 1*
Harris, Catharine Elizabeth 1949- *IntWWM 77, -80*
Harris, Charles A d1962 *NotNAT B*
Harris, Charles Kassell d1930 *Sw&Ld B*
Harris, Charles Kassell 1865-1930 *AmSCAP 66, Baker 78, Film 2, WhoStg 1908*
Harris, Charles Kassell 1867-1930 *AmPS, AmSCAP 80, BiDAmM, NotNAT B, PopAmC[port]*
Harris, Clare d1949 *NotNAT B, WhThe*
Harris, Clarence *MorBAP*
Harris, Clement 1871-1897 *NewGrD 80*
Harris, Cornelia Clark *PupTheA*
Harris, D G T *OxMus*
Harris, Dave 1889- *AmSCAP 66, CmpEPM*
Harris, Dennis *NewOrJ[port]*
Harris, Don 1938- *BluesWW[port], EncJzS 70*
Harris, Donald 1931- *AmSCAP 80, Baker 78, ConAmC, IntWWM 77, -80*
Harris, Eddie *RkOn[port]*
Harris, Eddie 1934- *BiDAmM, DrBlPA*
Harris, Eddie 1936- *EncJzS 70*
Harris, Edna Mae 1914- *BlksB&W, -C, DrBlPA*
Harris, Edward C 1899- *AmSCAP 66, -80, ConAmC A*
Harris, Edward M 1916- *IntMPA 77, -75, -76, -78, -79, -80*
Harris, Edward P 1923-1953 *BluesWW*
Harris, Ellen Muriel May 1906- *WhoMus 72*
Harris, Ellen T 1945- *IntWWM 80*
Harris, Elmer Blaney 1878-1966 *BiE&WWA, Film 2, NotNAT B, WhThe*
Harris, Elsie 1892-1953 *WhScrn 74, -77*
Harris, Emmylou 1947- *ConMuA 80A, IlEncR*
Harris, Emmylou 1949- *IlEncCM[port]*
Harris, Ethel Ramos 1908- *AmSCAP 66, -80, ConAmC*
Harris, Eugene 1933- *EncJzS 70*
Harris, Florence Glossop- 1883-1931 *WhThe*
Harris, Floyd Olin 1913- *ConAmC, IntWWM 77, -80*
Harris, Frank 1856-1931 *CnMD, NotNAT B*
Harris, Fred Orin 1901- *BiE&WWA, NotNAT*
Harris, Gale S *AmSCAP 80*
Harris, Gene 1933- *BiDAmM, EncJzS 70*
Harris, Genevieve H *PupTheA*
Harris, George *Film 2*
Harris, George W d1929 *NotNAT B*
Harris, Harry 1901- *AmSCAP 66, -80, NewYTET*
Harris, Helen *Film 2*
Harris, Helen Webb *BlkAmP, MorBAP*
Harris, Henry 1634?-1704 *OxThe, PlP&P*
Harris, Henry B 1866-1912 *NotNAT B, WhThe, WhoStg 1908*
Harris, Herbert H 1896?-1949 *NotNAT B*
Harris, Hi Tide 1946- *BluesWW[port]*
Harris, Homer 1916- *BluesWW*
Harris, Howard C, Jr. 1940- *AmSCAP 80, ConAmC*
Harris, Ivy *Film 2*
Harris, J Robert 1925- *AmSCAP 80*
Harris, Jack 1905-1971 *HalFC 80*
Harris, Jack H 1929?- *WhoHrs 80*
Harris, James 1709-1780 *NewGrD 80*
Harris, James B 1924- *FilmgC, HalFC 80*
Harris, James B 1928- *FilmEn, IntMPA 77, -75, -76, -78, -79, -80*
Harris, James D 1921- *BluesWW[port]*
Harris, Jay Morton 1928- *AmSCAP 66, -80*
Harris, Jed 1900- *BiE&WWA, NotNAT, -A, WhThe*
Harris, Jeff Steve 1935- *AmSCAP 80*
Harris, Jeffery 1936- *WhoMus 72*
Harris, Jenks *Film 2*
Harris, Jerry Weseley 1933- *AmSCAP 66, -80, ConAmC A, IntWWM 77*
Harris, Jessica B 1948- *ConAmTC*
Harris, Joan 1920- *CnOxB, DancEn 78*
Harris, Joe *NewOrJ, PupTheA*
Harris, Joe 1908-1952 *CmpEPM, WhoJazz 72*
Harris, Joe 1926- *EncJzS 70*
Harris, Joe Chandler 1848-1908 *DcPup*
Harris, John 1677?-1743 *NewGrD 80*
Harris, John H 1898- *IntMPA 77, -75, -76, -78, -79, -80*
Harris, Jonathan 1919?- *FilmgC, HalFC 80, WhoHol A*
Harris, Joseph *BiE&WWA*
Harris, Joseph 1661-1699 *NotNAT B*
Harris, Joseph 1745?-1814 *NewGrD 80*
Harris, Joseph 1870-1953 *Film 1, WhScrn 74, -77, WhoHol B*
Harris, Joseph Allison 1926- *EncJzS 70*
Harris, Joseph B *AmSCAP 80*
Harris, Judy *WhoHol A*
Harris, Julie 1925- *BiDFilm, -81, BiE&WWA,*

CnThe, EncWT, Ent[port], FilmEn, FilmgC, ForYSC, HalFC 80, –80, IntMPA 77, –75, –75, –76, –76, –78, –78, –79, –79, –80, –80, MovMk[port], NotNAT, OxFilm, PlP&P A[port], WhoHrs 80, WhoThe 72, –77
Harris, Julius 1924?- DrBlPA, HalFC 80, WhoHol A
Harris, Kay d1972 WhoHol B
Harris, Kay 1920-1971 WhScrn 77
Harris, Kenneth L 1936- AmSCAP 80
Harris, Kid 1906?-1951? NewOrJ
Harris, Landrey IntWWM 77
Harris, Larry ConMuA 80B
Harris, Lawren Phillips 1910- CreCan 1
Harris, Lawren Stewart 1885-1970 CreCan 2
Harris, Leland B 1912- BiE&WWA
Harris, Lenore 1879-1953 Film 1, WhoHol B
Harris, Leon A, Jr. 1926- AmSCAP 66, –80
Harris, Leonore 1879-1953 NotNAT B, WhScrn 77
Harris, LeRoy W, Jr. 1916- WhoJazz 72
Harris, Lorraine 1955- IntWWM 77
Harris, Louis 1906- IntMPA 77, –75, –76, –78, –79
Harris, Mae BluesWW[port]
Harris, Major RkOn 2[port]
Harris, Mamie BluesWW[port]
Harris, Marcia Film 1, –2
Harris, Margaret F 1904- WhoThe 72, –77
Harris, Margaret R 1943- BlkWAB
Harris, Maria Film 2
Harris, Marilyn 1923?- WhoHrs 80[port]
Harris, Marion Film 2
Harris, Marion 1896-1944 CmpEPM
Harris, Mildred 1901-1944 FilmEn, ForYSC, NotNAT B, TwYS, WhScrn 74, –77, WhoHol B
Harris, Mildred 1905-1944 Film 1, –2
Harris, Mitchell 1883-1948 NotNAT B, WhScrn 77, WhoHol B
Harris, Morris O d1974 WhoHol B
Harris, Myron 1922- AmSCAP 66, –80
Harris, Neil 1936- BlkAmP, MorBAP, NatPD[port]
Harris, Pearl BluesWW[port]
Harris, Peppermint 1925?- BluesWW[port]
Harris, Phil AmPS A, –B, BgBands 74, JoeFr, MotPP, WhoHol A
Harris, Phil 1901- MovMk
Harris, Phil 1904- CmpEPM
Harris, Phil 1906- BiDAmM, FilmEn, FilmgC, ForYSC, HalFC 80, IntMPA 77, –75, –76, –78, –79, –80
Harris, Randy David 1953- AmSCAP 80
Harris, Remus Anthony 1916- AmSCAP 66, –80
Harris, Renatus 1652?-1724 NewGrD 80, OxMus
Harris, Rene 1652?-1724 NewGrD 80
Harris, Rex 1904- IntWWM 77, –80, WhoMus 72
Harris, Richard MotPP, WhoHol A
Harris, Richard 1921- FilmAG WE
Harris, Richard 1929- BiDAmM
Harris, Richard 1930- ForYSC, IntMPA 77, –75, –76, –78, –79, –80
Harris, Richard 1932- FilmEn, FilmgC, HalFC 80, OxFilm
Harris, Richard 1933- BiDFilm, –81, MovMk[port], RkOn 2[port], WhThe, WhoThe 72, WorEFlm
Harris, Richard 1937- IlWWBF[port]
Harris, Rick ConMuA 80B
Harris, Robert 1849-1919 CreCan 1
Harris, Robert 1900- FilmgC, HalFC 80, WhoHol A, WhoThe 72, –77
Harris, Robert A 1928- IntWWM 77, –80
Harris, Robert A 1938- ConAmC
Harris, Robert H 1909?- FilmgC, HalFC 80, WhoHol A, WhoHrs 80[port]
Harris, Roger W 1940- ConAmC
Harris, Rolf 1930- IntWWM 77, RkOn
Harris, Rona 1936- AmSCAP 80
Harris, Ronald Norman 1940- WhoMus 72
Harris, Ronald S 1941- AmSCAP 80
Harris, Rosemary 1930- BiE&WWA, CnThe, FilmgC, HalFC 80, IntMPA 77, –75, –76, –78, –79, –80, MotPP, NotNAT, WhoHol A, WhoThe 72, –77
Harris, Roy 1898-1979 Baker 78, BiDAmM, BnBkM 80, CompSN[port], ConAmC, DcCom&M 79, DcCM, MusMk, NewGrD 80[port], OxMus
Harris, Russell G 1914- ConAmC, IntWWM 80
Harris, Sadie 1888- WhoStg 1908
Harris, Sam H 1872-1941 EncMT, NotNAT B, WhThe, WhoStg 1906, –1908
Harris, Simon John Minshaw 1935- WhoMus 72
Harris, Stacy B 1918-1973 ForYSC, WhScrn 77, WhoHol B
Harris, Stan NewYTET
Harris, Stanley James Philip 1909- IntWWM 77, –80
Harris, Sugarcane BluesWW[port]
Harris, Susan K WomWMM B
Harris, Sydney J ConAmTC
Harris, Sylvia 1906-1966 NotNAT B
Harris, Tasso 1918- BiDAmM
Harris, Theodore 1912- AmSCAP 66, –80
Harris, Theresa DrBlPA
Harris, Thomas d1685? NewGrD 80
Harris, Thoro 1874- BiDAmM
Harris, Thurston RkOn
Harris, Tim 1882?- NewOrJ
Harris, Tom BlkAmP, NewOrJ
Harris, Vernon 1910?- FilmgC, HalFC 80
Harris, Victor 1869-1943 AmSCAP 66, –80, Baker 78
Harris, Victor Francis 1911- AmSCAP 80
Harris, Viola WhoHol A
Harris, Wadsworth 1865-1942 Film 2, WhScrn 74, –77, WhoHol B
Harris, Will J 1900-1967 AmSCAP 66, –80, BiDAmM, NotNAT B
Harris, Willard Palmer 1916-1973 BiDAmM, EncJzS 70
Harris, William d1916 NotNAT B
Harris, William, Jr. 1884-1946 NotNAT B, WhThe
Harris, William Godvin 1936- EncJzS 70
Harris, Sir William Henry 1883-1973 NewGrD 80, OxMus, WhoMus 72
Harris, William Lewarne Capes 1929- IntWWM 77, –80
Harris, William Victor 1869-1943 BiDAmM
Harris, Willie 1925- BiDAmM, EncJzS 70
Harris, Winifred Film 1, –2
Harris, Woody 1911- AmSCAP 66, –80
Harris, Wynonie 1915-1969 BluesWW[port]
Harrison, Arthur 1902- AmSCAP 66
Harrison, Austin 1873-1928 NotNAT B, WhThe
Harrison, Beatrice 1892-1965 Baker 78, NewGrD 80
Harrison, Bob 1915- AmSCAP 66
Harrison, Carey 1890-1957 Film 2, WhScrn 74, –77, WhoHol B
Harrison, Cass 1922- AmSCAP 66, –80
Harrison, Charles F 1883-1955 AmSCAP 66
Harrison, Charles Scott 1950- ConAmC
Harrison, Derek Birch 1947- IntWWM 77, –80
Harrison, Doane d1968 HalFC 80
Harrison, Duncan d1934 NotNAT B
Harrison, E Earnest 1918- IntWWM 77, –80
Harrison, Eugene Donald 1949- AmSCAP 80
Harrison, Fanny d1909 NotNAT B
Harrison, Francis Llewelyn 1905- IntWWM 77, –80, NewGrD 80
Harrison, Frank 1905- NewGrD 80
Harrison, Frederick d1926 NotNAT B, WhThe
Harrison, G Donald 1889-1956 NewGrD 80
Harrison, Gabriel d1902 NotNAT B
Harrison, George 1943- Baker 78, ConMuA 80A, FilmEn, ForYSC, IlEncR[port], IntWWM 77, MotPP, NewGrD 80, RkOn 2[port], WhoHol A
Harrison, Guy Fraser 1894- Baker 78
Harrison, Hazel 1881- BiDAmM
Harrison, Irma Film 2
Harrison, James Henry 1900-1931 BiDAmM
Harrison, Jay Smolens 1927-1974 Baker 78, IntWWM 77, –80, WhoMus 72
Harrison, Jeanne WomWMM B
Harrison, Jimmy Film 1, –2, TwYS
Harrison, Jimmy 1900-1931 CmpEPM, IlEncJ, WhoJazz 72
Harrison, Joan 1911- FilmEn, FilmgC, HalFC 80, IntMPA 77, –75, –76, –78, –79, –80, WomWMM
Harrison, John ConDr 73, –77B
Harrison, John 1922- IntMPA 77, –75, –76, –78, –79, –80
Harrison, John 1924- WhoThe 77
Harrison, John Charles 1913- WhoMus 72
Harrison, Julius 1885-1963 Baker 78, NewGrD 80, OxMus
Harrison, June 1926-1974 WhScrn 77, WhoHol B
Harrison, Kathleen 1898- FilmgC, HalFC 80, IlWWBF, IntMPA 77, –75, –76, –78, –79, –80, OxFilm, WhoHol A, WhoThe 72, –77
Harrison, Kenneth Richard 1952- AmSCAP 80
Harrison, Larry Benton 1947- IntWWM 77
Harrison, Lee d1916 NotNAT B
Harrison, Linda 1945- HalFC 80, WhoHol A
Harrison, Lou 1917- Baker 78, BiDAmM, BnBkM 80, CpmDNM 73, –75, –80, ConAmC, DcCM, MusMk, NewGrD 80, OxMus, WhoMus 72
Harrison, Louis d1936 NotNAT B
Harrison, Maud WhoStg 1906, –1908
Harrison, May 1891-1959 Baker 78, NewGrD 80
Harrison, Michael FilmEn, WhoHol A
Harrison, Mona d1957 NotNAT B, WhThe
Harrison, Noel 1933- BiDAmM, ForYSC, RkOn 2A, WhoHol A
Harrison, Pamela 1915- IntWWM 77, –80, NewGrD 80, WhoMus 72
Harrison, Paul Carter 1936- BlkAmP, DrBlPA, MorBAP
Harrison, Rex 1908- BiDFilm, –81, BiE&WWA, CnThe, EncMT, EncWT, Ent, FamA&A[port], FilmAG WE, FilmEn, Film 2, FilmgC, ForYSC, HalFC 80, IlWWBF[port], –A, IntMPA 77, –75, –76, –78, –79, –80, MotPP, MovMk[port], NotNAT, –A, OxFilm, PlP&P[port], WhoHol A, WhoThe 72, –77, WorEFlm[port]
Harrison, Richard Berry 1864-1935 DrBlPA, ForYSC, HalFC 80, NotNAT B, OxThe, PlP&P
Harrison, Robert d1953 NotNAT B
Harrison, Robin 1932- WhoMus 72
Harrison, Ronald Derwyn 1932- IntWWM 80
Harrison, Samuel 1760-1812 NewGrD 80
Harrison, Sandra 1938?- WhoHrs 80
Harrison, Shirley Patricia 1931- IntWWM 77
Harrison, Sidney 1903- IntWWM 77, –80, NewGrD 80, WhoMus 72
Harrison, Thomas James 1908- AmSCAP 80
Harrison, Vernon 1925- BluesWW[port]
Harrison, Wilbert 1929- AmPS A, RkOn
Harrison, William 1813-1868 NewGrD 80
Harriss, Charles Albert Edwin 1862-1929 Baker 78, NewGrD 80
Harriss, Donald Steven 1948- IntWWM 80
Harriss, Elaine Atkins 1945- IntWWM 80
Harriss, Robert Preston 1902- ConAmTC
Harriton, Maria WomWMM A, –B
Harrity, Richard 1907-1973 BiE&WWA, NotNAT A, –B
Harrod, Sheila Georgina 1944- IntWWM 77, –80
Harrold, Orville 1878-1933 AmPS B, BiDAmM, NotNAT B
Harrold, Robert 1923- CnOxB, DancEn 78
Harron, Mrs. Film 1
Harron, Bobby 1894-1920 WhScrn 74, –77
Harron, Don 1924- ConDr 73
Harron, Donald 1924- BiE&WWA, NotNAT, WhoHol A
Harron, Jessie Film 1
Harron, John 1903-1939 FilmEn, ForYSC, TwYS, WhScrn 74, –77, WhoHol B
Harron, Johnny 1903-1939 Film 1, –2
Harron, LeRoy Peter 1908- IntWWM 77, –80
Harron, Mary Film 1
Harron, Robert 1894-1920 FilmEn, Film 1, –2, FilmgC, HalFC 80, MotPP, NotNAT B, TwYS, WhoHol B
Harron, Tessie d1920 WhScrn 74, WhoHol B
Harron, Tessie 1896-1918 WhScrn 77
Harrop, Sarah NewGrD 80

Harry, Blind *OxMus*
Harryhausen, Ray 1920?- *CmMov, FilmgC, HalFC 80, IntMPA 77, -75, -76, -78, -79, -80, WhoHrs 80*
Harsa *OxThe*
Harsanyi, Tibor 1898-1954 *Baker 78, NewGrD 80*
Harsdorfer, Georg Philipp 1607-1658 *NewGrD 80*
Harsdorffer, Georg Philipp 1607-1658 *NewGrD 80*
Harsha, Sri 590?-647 *CnThe, REnWD[port]*
Harshaw, Margaret 1912- *Baker 78, CmOp, NewEOp 71, NewGrD 80, WhoMus 72*
Harst, Coelestin 1698-1776 *NewGrD 80*
Harston, Gillian Diane 1949- *IntWWM 77*
Hart *NewGrD 80*
Hart, Albert 1874-1940 *Film 2, WhScrn 74, -77, WhoHol B*
Hart, Alex *Film 2*
Hart, Andro d1621 *NewGrD 80, OxMus*
Hart, Annie d1947 *NotNAT B*
Hart, Bernard 1911-1964 *BiE&WWA, NotNAT B, WhThe*
Hart, Billy 1864-1942 *WhScrn 74, -77*
Hart, Billy 1940- *EncJzS 70*
Hart, Bob *AmSCAP 80, Film 2*
Hart, Bruce 1938- *AmSCAP 66, -80*
Hart, Charles d1683 *EncWT, Ent, OxThe, PIP&P*
Hart, Charles 1873-1917 *BlksBF*
Hart, Clyde 1910-1945 *CmpEPM, WhoJazz 72*
Hart, Cynthia Mary Kathleen *AmSCAP 80*
Hart, Diane 1926- *WhoHol A, WhoThe 72, -77*
Hart, Dolores *MotPP*
Hart, Dolores 1930- *ForYSC*
Hart, Dolores 1938- *FilmEn, FilmgC, HalFC 80, WhoHol A*
Hart, Dolores 1939- *MovMk[port]*
Hart, Dorothy 1923- *ForYSC, HalFC 80, WhoHol A*
Hart, Dunstan 1903- *IntWWM 77, -80, WhoMus 72*
Hart, Elizabeth Jane Smith 1913- *IntWWM 77*
Hart, Ferdinand *WhoHrs 80*
Hart, Florence *Film 2*
Hart, Frances *AmSCAP 80*
Hart, Freddie 1930- *CounME 74[port], -74A*
Hart, Freddie 1933- *BiDAmM, IlEncCM[port]*
Hart, Frederic Patton 1894- *Baker 78*
Hart, Frederic Patton 1898- *BiDAmM, ConAmC*
Hart, Fritz 1874-1949 *Baker 78, NewGrD 80*
Hart, George *Baker 78*
Hart, George 1839-1891 *Baker 78*
Hart, Gypsy *Film 1*
Hart, Harvey 1928- *FilmEn, FilmgC, HalFC 80, IntMPA 77, -75, -76, -78, -79, -80*
Hart, Helen *Film 1*
Hart, Henry Clay, III *AmSCAP 80*
Hart, Herbert *Baker 78*
Hart, Indian Jack 1872-1974 *WhoHol B*
Hart, Isabella *Film 1*
Hart, Jack 1872-1974 *WhScrn 77*
Hart, James 1647-1718 *Baker 78, NewGrD 80*
Hart, James T 1868-1926 *WhScrn 74, -77*
Hart, Johann Daniel *NewGrD 80*
Hart, John *Baker 78, WhoHol A*
Hart, John d1937 *NotNAT B*
Hart, John 1921- *CnOxB, DancEn 78*
Hart, John Thomas 1805-1874 *Baker 78*
Hart, Joseph 1858-1921 *NotNAT B, WhoStg 1906, -1908*
Hart, Joseph 1945- *NatPD[port]*
Hart, Ken Woodrow 1917- *AmSCAP 66, -80*
Hart, Kenneth Stuart 1913- *IntWWM 77*
Hart, Larry 1895-1943 *NewGrD 80*
Hart, Leen't 1920- *IntWWM 77, -80*
Hart, Lisa *AmSCAP 80*
Hart, Lorenz 1895-1943 *AmPS, AmSCAP 66, -80, Baker 78, BestMus, BiDAmM, CmpEPM, EncMT, EncWT, Ent, McGEWD[port], MnPM, NewCBMT, NewGrD 80, NotNAT B, OxFilm, PlP&P[port], Sw&Ld C, WhThe*
Hart, Lucille 1917- *AmSCAP 80*
Hart, M Blair 1907- *BiE&WWA, NotNAT*
Hart, Mabel 1886-1960 *WhScrn 77*
Hart, Mary *FilmEn, WhoHol A*
Hart, Mary Conaleeta 1950- *IntWWM 77*
Hart, Maurice 1909- *AmSCAP 66, -80*
Hart, Moss 1904-1961 *BestMus, BiDAmM, CnMD, CnThe, DcLB 7[port], EncMT, EncWT, Ent, FilmEn, FilmgC, HalFC 80, McGEWD[port], ModWD, NewCBMT, NotNAT A, -B, OxThe, PlP&P, REnWD[port], WhThe, WorEFlm*
Hart, Neal 1879-1949 *Film 1, -2, TwYS, WhScrn 74, -77, WhoHol B*
Hart, Oliver 1723-1795 *BiDAmM*
Hart, Perry 1928- *IntWWM 77, -80, WhoMus 72*
Hart, Philip 1674?-1749 *Baker 78, NewGrD 80*
Hart, Richard 1915-1951 *FilmgC, HalFC 80, MGM[port], NotNAT B*
Hart, Richard 1916-1951 *WhScrn 74, -77, WhoHol B*
Hart, Ruth *Film 1*
Hart, Samuel C 1905- *IntMPA 75, -76*
Hart, Sunshine 1886- *Film 2, TwYS*
Hart, Susan 1935?- *WhoHrs 80*
Hart, Susan 1941- *ForYSC, WhoHol A*
Hart, Teddy 1897-1971 *BiE&WWA, ForYSC, NotNAT B, WhScrn 74, -77, WhThe, WhoHol B*
Hart, Thomas George 1949- *ConAmTC*
Hart, Tony 1855-1891 *EncMT, FamA&A[port], NotNAT A, -B, OxThe*
Hart, Vivian *WhThe*
Hart, Walter Cunliffe 1911- *WhoMus 72*
Hart, Weldon 1911-1957 *AmSCAP 80, Baker 78, ConAmC*
Hart, William S 1862-1946 *WhScrn 74, -77*
Hart, William S 1864-1946 *MotPP, WhoHol B*
Hart, William S 1870-1946 *BiDFilm, -81, CmMov, FilmEn, Film 1, -2, FilmgC, HalFC 80[port], MovMk[port], NotNAT B, OxFilm, TwYS, WhThe, WorEFlm[port]*
Hart, William Sebastian 1920- *ConAmC, IntWWM 77, WhoMus 72*
Hart, William Sebastion 1920- *IntWWM 80*
Hart, William V Pop 1867-1925 *WhScrn 74, -77*
Hart, William W 1940- *EncJzS 70*
Hart & Sons *Baker 78*
Hartau, Ludwig *Film 2*
Harte, Betty 1883-1965 *Film 1, WhScrn 74, -77, WhoHol B*
Harte, Francis Bret 1836-1902 *NotNAT B*
Harte, Roy 1924- *BiDAmM*
Harte, Ruth Alison *WhoMus 72*
Hartel *NewGrD 80*
Hartel, Renate 1927- *WhoOp 76*
Harteveld, Wilhelm 1859-1927 *NewGrD 80*
Hartford, Chapin *AmSCAP 80*
Hartford, David 1876-1932 *Film 1, TwYS A, WhScrn 74, -77, WhoHol B*
Hartford, Dee 1927- *WhoHol A*
Hartford, Eden *ForYSC, WhoHol A*
Hartford, Huntington 1911- *BiE&WWA*
Hartford, John 1937- *BiDAmM, EncFCWM 69, IlEncCM*
Hartford, K 1922- *IntMPA 77, -75, -76, -78, -79, -80*
Hartford-Davis, Robert 1923-1977 *FilmgC, HalFC 80, IlWWBF, IntMPA 77, -75, -76*
Harth, Sidney 1929- *Baker 78, NewGrD 80*
Harth, Sidney 1930- *WhoMus 72*
Harth, Teresa Testa *Baker 78*
Harthan, Hans 1855-1936 *Baker 78*
Hartig, Franz Christian 1750-1819 *NewGrD 80*
Hartig, Heinz 1907-1969 *Baker 78, DcCM*
Hartig, Herbert 1930- *AmSCAP 66, -80*
Hartig, Michael Frank 1936- *BiE&WWA, NotNAT*
Hartigan, Pat 1881- *Film 2, TwYS, -A*
Hartinger, Albert F 1946- *IntWWM 80*
Hartke, Gilbert 1907- *BiE&WWA, NotNAT*
Hartke, Stephen Paul 1952- *CpmDNM 80, ConAmC*
Hartknoch *NewGrD 80*
Hartknoch, Johann Friedrich 1740-1789 *NewGrD 80*
Hartknoch, Johann Friedrich 1768-1819 *NewGrD 80*
Hartknoch, Karl Eduard 1796-1834 *NewGrD 80*
Hartl, Karl 1899- *HalFC 80, WhoHrs 80*
Hartleb, Hans 1910- *WhoOp 76*
Hartleben, Otto Erich 1864-1905 *ModWD, NotNAT B*
Hartley, Charles 1852-1930 *WhScrn 74, -77, WhoHol B*
Hartley, Clifford 1906- *WhoMus 72*
Hartley, Elda *WomWMM A, -B*
Hartley, Elizabeth 1751-1824 *NotNAT B, OxThe*
Hartley, Fred 1905- *WhoMus 72*
Hartley, Fred A 1902- *What 1[port]*
Hartley, Frederick James 1945- *AmSCAP 80*
Hartley, Gerald 1921- *ConAmC*
Hartley, Harold Hay 1934- *IntWWM 77*
Hartley, Irving *Film 2*
Hartley, John *ForYSC*
Hartley, Keef 1944- *IlEncR*
Hartley, Keith 1947- *IntWWM 80*
Hartley, Mariette *WhoHol A*
Hartley, Mariette 1940- *HalFC 80*
Hartley, Mariette 1941- *ForYSC*
Hartley, Mark *ConMuA 80B*
Hartley, Neil 1919- *BiE&WWA, NotNAT*
Hartley, Pete *Film 2*
Hartley, Raymond Oswald 1929- *AmSCAP 66, -80*
Hartley, Ted *ForYSC, WhoHol A*
Hartley, Walter Sinclair 1927- *AmSCAP 66, -80, ConAmC, DcCM, IntWWM 77, -80*
Hartley-Milburn, Julie 1904-1949 *Film 2, WhThe*
Hartman, Agnes A 1860-1932 *WhScrn 74, -77*
Hartman, Anton 1918- *NewGrD 80*
Hartman, David 1940?- *ForYSC, HalFC 80, IntMPA 77, -76, -78, -79, -80, NewYTET, WhoHol A*
Hartman, Diane *AmSCAP 80*
Hartman, Don 1900-1958 *AmSCAP 66, -80, FilmEn*
Hartman, Don 1901-1958 *FilmgC, HalFC 80, NotNAT B*
Hartman, Elizabeth *MotPP, WhoHol A*
Hartman, Elizabeth 1941- *FilmEn, FilmgC, ForYSC, HalFC 80*
Hartman, Elizabeth 1943- *IntMPA 77, -75, -76, -78, -79, -80, MovMk[port]*
Hartman, Ena *DrBlPA*
Hartman, George 1910-1966 *NewOrJ[port]*
Hartman, Grace 1907-1955 *NotNAT B, WhScrn 74, -77, WhoHol B*
Hartman, Gretchen 1897- *Film 1, -2, MotPP, TwYS*
Hartman, John Maurice 1923- *EncJzS 70*
Hartman, Johnny 1923- *DrBlPA, EncJzS 70*
Hartman, Jonathan William Pop 1872-1965 *WhScrn 74, -77*
Hartman, Margot *WhoHol A*
Hartman, Paul 1904-1973 *Film 2, MovMk[port], NotNAT B, WhScrn 77, WhoHol B*
Hartman, Paul 1910- *BiE&WWA, ForYSC, IntMPA 77, -75, -76, -78, -79, -80*
Hartman, Vernon 1952- *IntWWM 80*
Hartmann *NewGrD 80*
Hartmann Von Aue 1160?-1210? *NewGrD 80*
Hartmann Von Ouwe 1160?-1210? *NewGrD 80*
Hartmann, Arthur Martinus 1881-1956 *AmSCAP 66, Baker 78, BiDAmM, ConAmC*
Hartmann, August Wilhelm 1775-1850 *Baker 78*
Hartmann, C V *OxMus*
Hartmann, Carl 1895-1969 *Baker 78*
Hartmann, Charles 1898- *NewOrJ[port]*
Hartmann, Christian Karl 1750-1804 *NewGrD 80*
Hartmann, Edmund L 1911- *FilmEn*
Hartmann, Eduard Von 1842-1906 *Baker 78*
Hartmann, Emil 1836-1898 *Baker 78, NewGrD 80, OxMus*
Hartmann, Georges d1900 *NewGrD 80*
Hartmann, Heinrich 1580?-1616 *NewGrD 80*
Hartmann, J P E 1805-1900 *OxMus*
Hartmann, Johan Peder Emilius 1805-1900 *Baker 78*

Hartmann, Johan Peter Emilius 1805-1900 *NewGrD 80*
Hartmann, Johann Ernst 1726-1793 *Baker 78, NewGrD 80*
Hartmann, Johann Peter 1805-1900 *MusMk*
Hartmann, Joseph 1726-1793 *NewGrD 80*
Hartmann, Karl Amadeus 1905-1963 *Baker 78, DcCM, MusMk, NewGrD 80[port], OxMus*
Hartmann, Pater 1863-1914 *Baker 78*
Hartmann, Rudolf 1900- *CmOp, NewEOp 71, NewGrD 80, WhoOp 76*
Hartmann, Rudolf A 1937- *WhoOp 76*
Hartmann, Sadakichi 1864?-1944 *Film 2, WhScrn 77*
Hartmann, Thomas De 1885-1956 *Baker 78, NewGrD 80*
Hartmann, Wilhelm Emilius Zinn 1836-1898 *NewGrD 80*
Hartmeyer, John *ConAmC*
Hartnell, Billy 1908-1975 *IlWWBF*
Hartnell, William 1908-1975 *FilmEn, FilmgC, HalFC 80, IntMPA 75, -76, WhScrn 77, WhThe, WhoHol C, WhoThe 72*
Hartnoll, Phyllis 1906- *BiE&WWA, NotNAT*
Harto, James *PupTheA*
Hartog, Edouard De 1829-1909 *Baker 78*
Hartog, Eduard De 1829-1909 *NewGrD 80*
Hartog, Howard 1913- *WhoMus 72*
Hartog, Jacques 1837-1917 *Baker 78*
Hartog, Jan De 1914- *EncWT*
Hartong, Corrie 1906- *DancEn 78*
Hartsough, Lewis 1828-1919 *BiDAmM*
Hartung, Gustav 1887-1946 *EncWT*
Hartung, Hans 1493?-1554 *NewGrD 80*
Hartung, Johannes 1493?-1554 *NewGrD 80*
Hartung, Michael *NewGrD 80*
Hartway, James John 1944- *ConAmC*
Hartweg, Jerry 1939- *ConAmC*
Hartwell, Hugh Kenneth 1945- *IntWWM 80*
Hartwell, Jimmy 1900?- *WhoJazz 72*
Hartwig, Dieter 1934- *IntWWM 77, -80, NewGrD 80*
Hartwig, Walter d1941 *NotNAT B*
Harty, Sir Hamilton 1879-1941 *Baker 78, BnBkM 80, MusSN[port], NewGrD 80*
Harty, Herbert Hamilton 1879-1941 *OxMus*
Hartz, Jim 1940- *IntMPA 77, -78, -79, -80, NewYTET*
Hartz, Joseph Michael 1836-1903 *MagIlD*
Hartzell, Lawrence William 1942- *ConAmC*
Hartzell, Marjorie 1938- *IntWWM 77, -80*
Hartzenbusch, Juan Eugenio 1806-1880 *NotNAT B, OxThe*
Hartzenbusch Y Martinez, Juan Eugenio 1806-1880 *McGEWD[port]*
Hartzer, Balthasar *NewGrD 80*
Hartzog, Tom 1937- *NotNAT*
Harutiunian, Aleksander Grigor *DcCM*
Harutunian, John Martin 1948- *IntWWM 77, -80*
Harutunyan, Alexander Grigori 1920- *NewGrD 80*
Harve, M *Film 1*
Harvel *PupTheA*
Harverson, Alan *IntWWM 77, -80, WhoMus 72*
Harvey, Alex 1935- *ConMuA 80A*
Harvey, Alex 1945- *IlEncCM[port]*
Harvey, Anthony 1931- *FilmEn, FilmgC, HalFC 80, IntMPA 77, -75, -76, -78, -79, -80*
Harvey, Anthony Keith 1938- *IntWWM 77, -80, WhoMus 72*
Harvey, Arthur Wallace 1939- *IntWWM 77, -80*
Harvey, Bobby 1935- *IntWWM 80*
Harvey, Charles 1885?- *NewOrJ*
Harvey, Don C d1963 *NotNAT B, WhoHol B*
Harvey, Don C 1911-1963 *WhScrn 77*
Harvey, Don C 1912-1963 *WhScrn 74*
Harvey, Dorothy Fay 1935- *IntWWM 77, -80*
Harvey, Edward 1893-1975 *WhScrn 77, WhoHol C*
Harvey, Fletcher *Film 1*
Harvey, Forrester 1880-1945 *WhScrn 74, -77*
Harvey, Forrester 1890-1945 *Film 2, FilmgC, HalFC 80, HolCA[port], IlWWBF, NotNAT B, WhoHol B*
Harvey, Frank d1903 *NotNAT B*
Harvey, Frank 1885-1965 *WhThe*
Harvey, Frank 1912- *FilmgC, HalFC 80, WhoThe 72, -77*
Harvey, George Y *Film 2*
Harvey, Georgette d1952 *NotNAT B, WhoHol B*
Harvey, Georgia d1960 *NotNAT B*
Harvey, Hank d1929 *WhScrn 74, -77*
Harvey, Harry *TwYS A*
Harvey, Harry, Sr. 1901- *Vers B[port], WhoHol A*
Harvey, Helen 1916- *BiE&WWA, NotNAT*
Harvey, Herk *WhoHrs 80*
Harvey, Jack 1881-1954 *Film 1, WhoHol B*
Harvey, Jean 1900-1966 *WhScrn 77, WhoHol B*
Harvey, Jean 1932- *IntWWM 80, WhoMus 72*
Harvey, Jean-Charles 1891-1967 *CreCan 2*
Harvey, John 1881-1954 *WhScrn 74, -77*
Harvey, John 1917-1970 *BiE&WWA, WhScrn 77, WhoHol B*
Harvey, John Augustus 1908- *WhoMus 72*
Harvey, John Henry 1911- *ConAmTC*
Harvey, Sir John Martin- 1863-1944 *Film 2, NotNAT B, OxThe, WhThe*
Harvey, Jonathan Dean 1939- *IntWWM 77, -80, NewGrD 80, WhoMus 72*
Harvey, Laurence d1973 *MotPP, WhoHol B*
Harvey, Laurence 1927-1973 *OxFilm*
Harvey, Laurence 1928-1973 *BiDFilm, -81, BiE&WWA, FilmAG WE[port], FilmEn, FilmgC, ForYSC, HalFC 80, IlWWBF[port], -A, MovMk[port], NotNAT A, -B, WhScrn 77, WhThe, WhoThe 72, WorEFlm*
Harvey, Lew *Film 2*
Harvey, Lilian d1968 *WhoHol B*
Harvey, Lilian 1906-1968 *FilmAG WE, FilmEn, FilmgC, HalFC 80, ThFT[port]*
Harvey, Lilian 1907-1968 *Film 2, ForYSC, MovMk, NotNAT B, OxFilm, TwYS, WhScrn 74, -77*
Harvey, Lillian d1968 *MotPP*
Harvey, Lillian 1907-1968 *WorEFlm*
Harvey, Lottie 1890-1948 *WhScrn 74, -77*
Harvey, Lucy Quinn 1932- *AmSCAP 80*
Harvey, Marilyn 1929-1973 *WhScrn 77*
Harvey, Marion Bradley 1916- *IntWWM 77, -80*
Harvey, Mary 1629-1704 *NewGrD 80*
Harvey, May d1930 *NotNAT B*
Harvey, Michael Martin *Film 2*
Harvey, Morris 1877-1944 *NotNAT B, WhThe, WhoHol B*
Harvey, Nicholas 1901- *AmSCAP 80*
Harvey, Paul 1883-1953 *HolCA[port]*
Harvey, Paul 1884-1955 *Film 2, FilmgC, ForYSC, HalFC 80, MovMk, NotNAT B, Vers B[port], WhScrn 74, -77, WhoHol B*
Harvey, Paul 1918- *NewYTET*
Harvey, Paul Milton 1935- *IntWWM 77, -80, WhoMus 72*
Harvey, Paul Ragle 1940- *WhoMus 72*
Harvey, Peter 1933- *WhoThe 72, -77*
Harvey, Rupert 1887-1954 *NotNAT B, WhThe*
Harvey, Russell *ConAmC*
Harvey, Stephanie *WomWMM B*
Harvey, Trevor 1911- *IntWWM 77, -80, NewGrD 80, WhoMus 72*
Harvey, Violet Mabel 1909- *IntWWM 77, -80, WhoMus 72*
Harvey, Walter F W 1903- *IntMPA 77, -75, -76, -78, -79, -80*
Harvey, William *Film 2*
Harvis, Sidney *Film 2*
Harwell, William Earnest 1918- *AmSCAP 80*
Harwood, Basil 1859-1949 *Baker 78, NewGrD 80, OxMus*
Harwood, Benjamin 1946- *AmSCAP 80*
Harwood, Bobbie *Film 2*
Harwood, Edward 1707-1787 *OxMus*
Harwood, Elizabeth 1938- *Baker 78, CmOp[port], IntWWM 80, NewGrD 80, WhoMus 72, WhoOp 76*
Harwood, Harold Marsh 1874-1959 *NotNAT B, OxThe, WhThe*
Harwood, Harry d1926 *NotNAT B*
Harwood, Ian 1931- *NewGrD 80*
Harwood, John 1876-1944 *NotNAT B, WhThe*
Harwood, John Edmund 1771-1809 *NotNAT B, OxThe*
Harwood, Raven *WomWMM B*
Harwood, Ronald 1934- *IntMPA 77, -75, -76, -78, -79, -80*
Harwood, Vanessa 1947- *CnOxB*
Haryton, George *Film 2*
Harzebsky, Adam *NewGrD 80*
Has, Stanislaw 1914- *IntWWM 77, -80*
Has, Wojciech 1925- *BiDFilm, -81, FilmEn, OxFilm, WorEFlm*
Hasa, Jaroslav 1908- *IntWWM 77, -80*
Hasaan Ibn Ali 1931- *BiDAmM*
Hasbrouck, Olive 1902- *Film 2*
Hasbrouck, Olive 1907- *TwYS*
Hasbrouck, Vera *Film 2*
Hascall, Lon d1932 *NotNAT B*
Hasche, William Edwin 1867-1929 *BiDAmM*
Hase, Georg *NewGrD 80*
Hase, Wolfgang 1611-1673 *NewGrD 80*
Hasegawa, Kazuo 1908- *FilmEn, OxFilm*
Hasegawa, Yoshio 1907- *NewGrD 80*
Hasek, Jaroslav 1883-1923 *EncWT*
Hasek, Josef Vaclav 1903- *IntWWM 77, -80*
Haselauer, Elisabeth 1939- *IntWWM 80*
Haselbach, Josef 1936- *IntWWM 77, -80*
Haselbock, Hans 1928- *NewGrD 80*
Hasenclever, Walter 1890-1940 *CnMD, EncWT, Ent, McGEWD[port], ModWD*
Hasenhut, Anton 1766-1841 *OxThe*
Hasenknopf, Sebastian 1545?-1597? *NewGrD 80*
Hasenmueller, Robert Duane 1931- *IntWWM 77*
Hasenoehrl, Franz 1885- *WhoMus 72*
Haser, August Ferdinand 1779-1844 *Baker 78*
Hash, Burl *PlP&P A[port]*
Hashagen, Klaus 1924- *DcCM, NewGrD 80*
Hashashian, Arousiak *WhScrn 77*
Hashewell, Thomas *NewGrD 80*
Hashim, Edmund 1932-1974 *WhScrn 77, WhoHol B*
Hashimoto, Eiji 1931- *IntWWM 77, -80*
Hashr, Agha *REnWD[port]*
Haskel, Leonhard *Film 2*
Haskell, Al d1969 *WhScrn 77, WhoHol B*
Haskell, Arnold Lionel 1903- *CnOxB, DancEn 78[port]*
Haskell, Burt *AmSCAP 80*
Haskell, Jack *CmpEPM*
Haskell, Jean *Film 2*
Haskell, Jimmie *AmSCAP 80*
Haskell, Molly *WomWMM*
Haskell, Peter *WhoHol A*
Haskil, Clara 1895-1960 *Baker 78, BnBkM 80, NewGrD 80[port]*
Haskin, Abby *AmSCAP 80*
Haskin, Byron 1899- *BiDFilm, -81, CmMov, FilmEn, FilmgC, HalFC 80, IntMPA 77, -75, -76, -78, -79, -80, MovMk[port], WhoHrs 80, WorEFlm*
Haskin, Charles W 1868-1927 *WhScrn 74, -77*
Haskins, Douglas 1928-1973 *WhScrn 77*
Haskins, Inez Clare *PupTheA*
Haskins, Robert James 1937- *ConAmC*
Haslam, David P 1940- *IntWWM 80*
Haslam, Herbert 1928- *AmSCAP 66, -80, ConAmC*
Haslanger, Martha *WomWMM B*
Haslet, Jessie *Film 2*
Haslin, Velma R 1928- *IntWWM 77*
Haslinger *NewGrD 80*
Haslinger, Tobias 1787-1842 *Baker 78, NewGrD 80*
Haslmayr, Adam 1550?-1617? *NewGrD 80*
Haslum, Bengt Sirgurd 1923- *IntWWM 77, -80*
Hasprois Jehan Simon *NewGrD 80*
Hasprois Johannes Symonis *NewGrD 80*
Hass *NewGrD 80*
Hass, Dietrich Christopher 1731- *NewGrD 80*
Hass, Georg *NewGrD 80*
Hass, Hieronymus Albrecht 1689-1761? *NewGrD 80*
Hass, Johann Adolph d1776? *NewGrD 80*
Hass, Peter *NewGrD 80*
Hassall, Christopher 1912-1963 *EncMT, NotNAT B, WhThe*
Hassanein, Salah M *IntMPA 77, -75, -76, -78, -79, -80*

Hassard, J R G *OxMus*
Hassard, John Rose Green 1836-1888 *Baker 78*
Hassard, John Rose Greene 1836-1888 *BiDAmM*
Hasse *NewGrD 80*
Hasse, Andreas *NewGrD 80*
Hasse, Faustina 1700?-1781 *Baker 78, NewGrD 80*
Hasse, Friedrich *NewGrD 80*
Hasse, Johann Adolf 1699-1783 *NewGrD 80[port]*
Hasse, Johann Adolph 1699-1783 *Baker 78, BnBkM 80, GrComp[port], MusMk[port], NewEOp 71, OxMus*
Hasse, Johann Ludwig *NewGrD 80*
Hasse, Karl 1883-1960 *Baker 78, NewGrD 80*
Hasse, Max 1859-1935 *Baker 78*
Hasse, Nicolaus 1617?-1672 *NewGrD 80*
Hasse, Nikolaus 1617?-1672 *NewGrD 80*
Hasse, O E 1903-1978 *EncWT, FilmEn, HalFC 80*
Hasse, Otto Eduard 1903- *FilmAG WE*
Hasse, Peter 1585?-1640 *NewGrD 80*
Hasse, Peter 1659-1708 *NewGrD 80*
Hasse, Petrus 1585?-1640 *NewGrD 80*
Hasselbeck, Rosa *NewGrD 80*
Hasselgard, Stan 1922-1948 *CmpEPM*
Hassell, George 1881-1937 *Film 1, -2, NotNAT B, WhScrn 74, -77, WhoHol B*
Hassell, Jon 1937- *AmSCAP 80, Baker 78, ConAmC*
Hassell, Michael Richard 1951- *ConAmC*
Hasselmann, Ronald Henry 1933- *IntWWM 77, -80*
Hasselmans *NewGrD 80*
Hasselmans, Alphonse 1845-1912 *NewGrD 80*
Hasselmans, Josef H 1814-1902 *NewGrD 80*
Hasselmans, Louis 1878-1947 *NewEOp 71*
Hasselmans, Louis 1878-1957 *Baker 78, BiDAmM, NewGrD 80*
Hasselquist, Jenny 1894- *CnOxB, Film 2, WhThe*
Hasselqvist, Jenny 1894- *FilmEn, OxFilm*
Hassen *NewGrD 80*
Hassen, Jamiel *Film 2*
Hassen, Umar Ben *MorBAP*
Hassett, Marilyn *WhoHol A*
Hassilev, Alex 1932- *BiDAmM, EncFCWM 69*
Hassler *NewGrD 80*
Hassler, Caspar 1562-1618 *Baker 78*
Hassler, Hans Leo 1562-1612 *NewGrD 80[port]*
Hassler, Hans Leo 1564-1612 *Baker 78, BnBkM 80, GrComp[port], MusMk, OxMus*
Hassler, Isaak 1530?-1591 *NewGrD 80*
Hassler, Jakob 1569-1622 *Baker 78, NewGrD 80*
Hassler, Johann 1562-1612 *NewGrD 80[port]*
Hassler, Johann Wilhelm 1747-1822 *Baker 78, NewGrD 80, OxMus*
Hassler, Kaspar 1562-1618 *NewGrD 80*
Hassler, Mark 1834-1906 *BiDAmM*
Hassler, Simon 1832-1900? *BiDAmM*
Hasso, Signe *MotPP, WhoHol A*
Hasso, Signe 1910- *FilmgC, HalFC 80*
Hasso, Signe 1915- *FilmEn, MovMk[port]*
Hasso, Signe 1918- *BiE&WWA, ForYSC, HolP 40[port], NotNAT, WhoThe 72, -77*
Hassreiter, Joseph 1845-1940 *CnOxB*
Hast, Louis H 1830?-1890 *BiDAmM*
Hasti, Robert *WhThe*
Hastie Family *OxMus*
Hastings, Baird 1919- *IntWWM 77, -80*
Hastings, Basil Macdonald 1881-1928 *NotNAT B, WhThe*
Hastings, Bob *ForYSC, WhoHol A*
Hastings, Carey L *Film 1*
Hastings, Don 1934- *IntMPA 77, -75, -76, -78, -79, -80*
Hastings, Francis H 1834-1916 *BiDAmM*
Hastings, Fred *WhThe*
Hastings, Harold 1916- *AmSCAP 66, -80, BiE&WWA*
Hastings, Hugh 1917- *WhoThe 72, -77*
Hastings, Michael 1938- *ConDr 73, -77*
Hastings, Sir Patrick 1880-1952 *NotNAT B, WhThe*
Hastings, Ross 1915- *AmSCAP 66, -80, ConAmC*
Hastings, Seymour *Film 1*
Hastings, Sue *PupTheA, PupTheA SUP*
Hastings, Thomas 1784-1872 *Baker 78, BiDAmM, NewGrD 80*
Hastings, Thomas 1787-1872 *OxMus*
Hastings, Victoria d1934 *WhScrn 74, -77*
Haston, Hugh *NewGrD 80*
Hastreiter, Helene 1858-1922 *Baker 78*
Haswell, Percy 1871-1945 *NotNAT B, WhScrn 74, -77, WhThe, WhoHol B, WhoStg 1906, -1908*
Hasz, Georg 1560?-1623? *NewGrD 80*
Hatas *NewGrD 80*
Hatas, Dismas 1724-1777 *NewGrD 80*
Hatas, Heinrich Christoph 1756- *NewGrD 80*
Hatasova, Anna Franziska 1728-1781 *NewGrD 80*
Hatch, Arthur J 1910- *IntMPA 75, -76*
Hatch, Donald J 1919- *IntWWM 77, -80*
Hatch, Elizabeth A 1897- *ConAmTC*
Hatch, Frank d1938 *NotNAT B*
Hatch, Ike d1961 *NotNAT B, WhoHol B*
Hatch, James V 1928- *BiE&WWA, BlkAmP, MorBAP, NotNAT*
Hatch, Provine, Jr. 1921- *BluesWW*
Hatch, Riley 1865-1925 *WhScrn 77*
Hatch, Tony 1939- *IntWWM 77*
Hatch, William Riley *Film 1, -2*
Hatcher, Althea *PupTheA*
Hatcher, Paula Braniff 1947- *IntWWM 80*
Hatfield, Bobby 1940- *IntMPA 77, -75, -76, -78, -79, -80*
Hatfield, Edwin Francis 1807-1883 *BiDAmM*
Hatfield, Hurd *IntMPA 77, -75, -76, -78, -79, -80, MotPP*
Hatfield, Hurd 1918- *BiDFilm, -81, FilmEn, FilmgC, ForYSC, HalFC 80, MovMk, WhoHol A, WhoHrs 80*
Hatfield, Hurd 1920- *BiE&WWA, NotNAT*
Hatfield, Lenore Sherman 1935- *IntWWM 77, -80*
Hatfield, Leslie William Quye 1915- *WhoMus 72*
Hatfield, Michael 1936- *IntWWM 77, -80*
Hatfield, Ted 1936- *IntMPA 77, -78, -79, -80*
Hathaway, Charles 1904-1966 *AmSCAP 66, -80*
Hathaway, Donny 1945- *RkOn 2[port]*
Hathaway, Henry 1898- *AmFD, BiDFilm, -81, CmMov, DcFM, FilmEn, FilmgC, HalFC 80, IntMPA 77, -75, -76, -78, -79, -80, MovMk[port], OxFilm, WorEFlm*
Hathaway, Jean 1876-1938 *Film 1, WhScrn 74, -77, WhoHol B*
Hathaway, Lilian 1876-1954 *WhScrn 74, -77*
Hathaway, Lillian *Film 1*
Hathaway, Peggy *Film 2*
Hathaway, Red *Film 2*
Hathaway, Rhody 1869-1944 *WhScrn 74, -77*
Hathaway, Rod d1944 *WhoHol B*
Hatherton, Arthur d1924 *NotNAT B, WhThe*
Hatlen, Theodore 1911- *BiE&WWA*
Hatley, Jearld Jaye 1937- *AmSCAP 80*
Hatley, T Marvin 1905- *AmSCAP 66*
Hatley, Thomas Marvin 1905- *AmSCAP 80*
Hatrak, Edward D 1920- *AmSCAP 66*
Hatrik, Juraj 1941- *Baker 78, NewGrD 80*
Hatswell, Donald *Film 2*
Hatten, Charles *Film 2*
Hatten, Rondo 1894-1946 *WhoHrs 80[port]*
Hattey, Philip 1911- *WhoMus 72*
Hattoepiscopus Trecensis *NewGrD 80*
Hatton, Adele Bradford d1957 *NotNAT B*
Hatton, Alma W 1917- *AmSCAP 66, -80*
Hatton, Ann Julia Curtis 1757?- *BiDAmM*
Hatton, Bradford 1906-1969 *WhScrn 77*
Hatton, Dick d1931 *WhoHol B*
Hatton, Fanny d1939 *NotNAT B, WhThe*
Hatton, Frances 1888-1971 *Film 2, WhScrn 74, -77, WhoHol B*
Hatton, Frederick 1879-1946 *NotNAT B, WhThe*
Hatton, Gaylen 1928- *ConAmC*
Hatton, John Liptrot 1808-1886 *NewGrD 80*
Hatton, John Liptrot 1809-1886 *Baker 78, OxMus*
Hatton, Joseph d1907 *NotNAT B*
Hatton, Mercy *Film 2*
Hatton, Rachel Lenora 1933- *IntWWM 77, -80*
Hatton, Raymond 1887-1971 *FilmEn, FilmgC, HalFC 80, HolCA[port], MotPP, WhoHol B*
Hatton, Raymond 1890- *ForYSC*
Hatton, Raymond 1892-1971 *Film 1, -2, MovMk[port], TwYS, Vers B[port], WhScrn 74, -77*
Hatton, Richard 1891-1931 *WhScrn 74, -77*
Hatton, Rondo 1894-1946 *FilmgC, HalFC 80, WhScrn 77, WhoHol B*
Hatton, Rondo 1895-1946 *WhScrn 74*
Hatton, Rondo 1904?-1946 *ForYSC*
Hattori, Kozo 1924- *NewGrD 80*
Hattstaedt, John James 1851-1931 *Baker 78, BiDAmM*
Hatze, Josip 1879-1959 *Baker 78*
Hatzinassios, George 1945- *IntWWM 77, -80*
Haubenstock-Ramati, Roman 1919- *Baker 78, DcCM, MusMk, NewGrD 80, WhoMus 72*
Hauber, Billy *Film 1, -2*
Hauber, Robert 1931- *IntWWM 77*
Haubiel, Charles 1892- *AmSCAP 66, Baker 78, BiDAmM, DcCM*
Haubiel, Charles Throwbridge 1892- *WhoMus 72*
Haubiel, Charles Trowbridge 1892- *ConAmC, IntWWM 77*
Haubold, Ingrid *WhoOp 76*
Hauch, Johannes Carsten 1790-1872 *NotNAT B, OxThe*
Hauck, Justus d1618 *NewGrD 80*
Haucourt, Johannes *NewGrD 80*
Haudebert, Lucien 1877-1963 *Baker 78*
Haueisen, Wilhelm 1740-1804 *NewGrD 80*
Haueisen, Wolfgang Nicolaus 1740-1804 *NewGrD 80*
Hauer, Josef Matthias 1883-1959 *Baker 78, DcCM, NewGrD 80, OxMus*
Hauf, Carlous VonDer *NewGrD 80*
Haufler, August Otto 1944- *IntWWM 77, -80*
Haufler, Max 1910-1965 *FilmAG WE*
Haufrecht, Herbert 1909- *BiDAmM, CpmDNM 76, ConAmC, IntWWM 77*
Haug, Gustav 1871-1956 *Baker 78*
Haug, Halvor 1952- *IntWWM 80*
Haug, Hans 1900-1967 *Baker 78, NewEOp 71, NewGrD 80*
Haug, Leonard H 1910- *IntWWM 77, -80*
Haugan, Kristine Judith 1940- *WhoOp 76*
Haugan, Paul 1945- *IntWWM 80*
Haugen, Bonnie Gail 1943- *IntWWM 77*
Haugen, Ruben Glenn 1922- *IntWWM 77*
Hauger, George 1921- *BiE&WWA*
Haughton, Chauncey 1909- *WhoJazz 72*
Haughton, John Alan 1880-1951 *AmSCAP 66, -80*
Haughton, Peter John 1933- *WhoMus 72*
Haugk, Dietrich 1925- *WhoOp 76*
Haugk, Virgilius 1490?-1555? *NewGrD 80*
Haugland, A Oscar 1922- *ConAmC*
Haugland, Aage 1944- *WhoOp 76*
Hauk, Gunther 1932- *NewGrD 80*
Hauk, Minnie 1851-1929 *Baker 78, CmOp, NewEOp 71, NewGrD 80*
Hauk, Minnie 1852-1929 *BiDAmM*
Haukane And Lonya *PupTheA*
Hauke, Adolph Covel 1920- *WhoMus 72*
Hauksson, Thorsteinn 1949- *IntWWM 77, -80*
Haulteterre, Elisabeth De *NewGrD 80*
Haultin, Jerome *NewGrD 80*
Haultin, Pierre d1589? *NewGrD 80*
Haun, Harry *ConAmTC*
Haunreuther, Erasmus *NewGrD 80*
Haupt, Albrecht Otto Thorolf 1929- *IntWWM 80*
Haupt, Charles Victor 1939- *WhoMus 72*
Haupt, Karl August 1810-1891 *Baker 78*
Haupt, Ullrich 1887-1931 *WhScrn 74, -77*
Haupt, Ulrich 1887-1931 *Film 2, ForYSC, TwYS, WhoHol B*
Haupt, Walter 1935- *IntWWM 77, -80*
Haupt-Nolen, Paulette 1944- *WhoOp 76*
Hauptmann, Carl 1858-1921 *CnMD, EncWT, McGEWD, ModWD, NotNAT B*
Hauptmann, Gerhart 1862-1946 *CnMD, CnThe, EncWT, Ent, McGEWD[port], ModWD, NewEOp 71, NotNAT A, -B, OxThe, PlP&P, REnWD[port], WhThe*
Hauptmann, Moritz 1792-1868 *Baker 78, NewGrD 80, OxMus*

Hauricq, Damianus *NewGrD 80*
Haurkus, Damianus *NewGrD 80*
Hauschild, Richard Curtis 1949- *AmSCAP 80*
Hauschka, Vincenz 1766-1840 *Baker 78*
Hause, James B 1929- *IntWWM 77, -80*
Hause, Newton *Film 2*
Hausegger, Friedrich Von 1837-1899 *Baker 78, OxMus*
Hausegger, Siegmund Von 1872-1948 *Baker 78, OxMus*
Hauser, Frank 1922- *CnThe, WhoThe 72, -77*
Hauser, Frantisek 1794-1870 *NewGrD 80*
Hauser, Franz 1794-1870 *NewGrD 80*
Hauser, Gustave M *NewYTET*
Hauser, Harald 1912- *CnMD, CroCD*
Hauser, Johann Ernst 1803-1874? *NewGrD 80*
Hauser, Miska 1822-1887 *Baker 78*
Hauser, William 1812-1880 *BiDAmM, NewGrD 80*
Hausler, Josef 1926- *NewGrD 80*
Hausman, Howard L 1914- *BiE&WWA, NotNAT*
Hausmann, Manfred 1898- *CnMD*
Hausmann, Robert 1852-1909 *Baker 78, NewGrD 80*
Hausmann, Valentin *NewGrD 80*
Hausner, Henry H 1901- *IntWWM 80*
Hausner, Jerry *WhoHol A*
Haussermann, John 1909- *ConAmC*
Haussermann, Reinhold *Film 2*
Hausskeller, Simon *NewGrD 80*
Haussler, Gustaw Adolf Pawel 1850-1940 *NewGrD 80*
Haussmann, Cecily Margaret *WhoMus 72*
Haussmann, Valentin 1484- *Baker 78*
Haussmann, Valentin 1565?-1614? *NewGrD 80*
Haussmann, Valentin, II *Baker 78*
Haussmann, Valentin, III *Baker 78*
Haussmann, Valentin, IV 1647?- *Baker 78*
Haussmann, Valentin Bartholomaus, V 1678- *Baker 78*
Hausswald, Gunter 1908-1974 *Baker 78, NewGrD 80*
Hautcousteaux, Arthur *NewGrD 80*
Haute, Sir William 1430?-1497 *NewGrD 80*
Hauteroche 1617?-1707 *Ent*
Hauteroche, Noel-Jacques LeBreton De 1616?-1707 *OxThe*
Hauterre *NewGrD 80*
Hauterre, Elizabeth De *NewGrD 80*
Hauteterre *NewGrD 80*
Hauteterre, Elizabeth De *NewGrD 80*
Hautman, Nicholas *NewGrD 80*
Hautvast, Willy 1932- *IntWWM 80*
Hautzig, Walter 1921- *IntWWM 77, -80*
Hauville, Antoine De *NewGrD 80*
Hauxvell, John 1925- *IntWWM 77, -80*
Havard, William d1778 *NotNAT B*
Havas, Ferenc 1935- *CnOxB*
Havas, Kato 1920- *IntWWM 77, -80, WhoMus 72*
Havel, Joe 1869-1932 *WhScrn 74, -77, WhoHol B*
Havel, Vaclav 1936- *CnThe, CroCD, EncWT, Ent, ModWD, REnWD[port]*
Havelaar, Charles Eduard 1908- *IntWWM 77, -80*
Havelka, Svatopluk 1925- *Baker 78, DcCM, NewGrD 80*
Havelock-Allan, Anthony 1905- *FilmEn*
Havelock-Allan, Sir Anthony 1905- *FilmgC, HalFC 80, IntMPA 75, -76*
Havelock-Allen, Sir Anthony *IntMPA 77, -78, -79*
Havelock-Allen, Sir Anthony 1905- *IntMPA 80*
Havemann, Gustav 1882-1960 *Baker 78*
Havemann, William G 1923- *AmSCAP 66, -80*
Haven, Charna 1925-1971 *WhScrn 77, WhoHol B*
Havens, Bob 1930- *EncJzS 70*
Havens, John F 1912- *BiE&WWA*
Havens, Richard Pierce 1941- *BiDAmM, BluesWW[port]*
Havens, Richie *ConMuA 80A, IlEncR*
Havens, Richie 1941- *DrBlPA, RkOn 2[port]*
Havens, Robert L 1930- *BiDAmM, EncJzS 70*
Haver, June 1926- *BiDAmM, CmMov, CmpEPM, FilmEn, -, FilmgC, ForYSC, HalFC 80, MotPP, MovMk[port], What 3[port], WhoHol A*
Haver, Phyllis 1899-1960 *FilmEn, Film 1, -2, FilmgC, ForYSC, HalFC 80, MotPP, MovMk, NotNAT B, WhScrn 74, -77*
Haver, Phyllis 1899-1961 *TwYS, WhoHol B*
Havergal, Giles 1938- *WhoThe 72, -77*
Havergal, Henry MacLeod 1902- *IntWWM 77, -80, WhoMus 72*
Havergal, William Henry 1793-1870 *NewGrD 80*
Haverhoek, Hendrik 1947- *EncJzS 70*
Haverhoek, Henk 1947- *EncJzS 70*
Haverick, Damianus *NewGrD 80*
Haverick, Damien *NewGrD 80*
Havericq, Damianus *NewGrD 80*
Havericq, Damien *NewGrD 80*
Haverly, Charles Ernest *AmPS B*
Havez, Jean 1874-1925 *AmSCAP 66, -80*
Havez, Jean C *Film 2*
Havier, Alex J d1945 *WhoHol B*
Havier, Jose Alex 1909-1945 *WhScrn 74, -77*
Haviland, Augusta d1925 *NotNAT B*
Haviland, Rena 1878-1954 *WhScrn 74, -77*
Haviland, William 1860-1917 *NotNAT B, WhThe*
Havingha, Gerhardus 1696-1753 *Baker 78, NewGrD 80*
Havlicek, Franz Frantisek 1921- *IntWWM 77, -80*
Havlick, Gene 1895?-1959 *HalFC 80*
Havlikova, Klara 1931- *IntWWM 77, -80*
Havlin, John H d1924 *NotNAT B*
Havlu, Ivo T 1923- *IntWWM 77, -80*
Havoc, June 1916- *BiE&WWA, CmpEPM, FilmEn, FilmgC, ForYSC, HalFC 80, HolP 40[port], IntMPA 77, -75, -76, -78, -79, -80, MotPP, MovMk[port], NotNAT, -A, WhoHol A, WhoThe 72, -77*
Haward *NewGrD 80*
Hawdon, Matthias d1787 *NewGrD 80*
Haweis, Hugh Reginald 1838-1901 *OxMus*
Hawel, Jan Wincenty 1936- *Baker 78, IntWWM 77, -80, NewGrD 80*
Hawes, Baldwin 1919- *BiDAmM*
Hawes, Bess Lomax 1921- *BiDAmM, EncFCWM 69*
Hawes, Butch 1919- *EncFCWM 69*
Hawes, David S 1910- *NotNAT*
Hawes, David S 1919- *BiE&WWA*
Hawes, Hampton 1928-1977 *BiDAmM, CmpEPM, EncJzS 70, IlEncJ*
Hawes, Jack Richards 1916- *IntWWM 77, -80, WhoMus 72*
Hawes, Maria *NewGrD 80*
Hawes, Mary *Film 2*
Hawes, William 1785-1846 *Baker 78, NewGrD 80, OxMus*
Hawil, Adriano *NewGrD 80*
Hawk, Eddie *AmSCAP 80*
Hawk, Jeremy 1918- *WhoHol A, WhoThe 72, -77*
Hawke, Rohn Olin 1924-1967 *WhScrn 74, -77*
Hawker, Peter 1786-1853 *NewGrD 80*
Hawkes, Jaquetta *PlP&P*
Hawkes, John 1925- *ConDr 73, -77, CroCD, DcLB 7[port]*
Hawkesworth, Walter d1606 *NotNAT B*
Hawkey, William Richard 1932- *IntWWM 77, -80*
Hawkins, Anthony Hope d1933 *NotNAT B*
Hawkins, Brian 1936- *IntWWM 77, -80*
Hawkins, Cecil Gordon 1911- *IntWWM 77*
Hawkins, Charlotte *AmSCAP 66, -80*
Hawkins, Coleman 1904-1969 *Baker 78, BiDAmM, CmpEPM, DrBlPA, EncJzS 70, IlEncJ, MusMk[port], NewGrD 80[port], WhScrn 77, WhoJazz 72*
Hawkins, Dale 1938- *ConMuA 80A, RkOn[port]*
Hawkins, Dolores *CmpEPM*
Hawkins, Duffy Thomas 1921- *IntWWM 77*
Hawkins, Edward Randolph 1930- *AmSCAP 80*
Hawkins, Edwin, Singers *RkOn 2[port]*
Hawkins, Erick 1909- *CmpGMD[port], CnOxB, DancEn 78[port]*
Hawkins, Erskine 1914- *AmSCAP 66, -80, BgBands 74[port], BiDAmM, CmpEPM, DrBlPA, EncJzS 70, WhoJazz 72*
Hawkins, Etta d1945 *NotNAT B*
Hawkins, Floyd Wesley 1904- *AmSCAP 66, -80*
Hawkins, Harold F 1921-1963 *BiDAmM, EncFCWM 69*
Hawkins, Hawkshaw 1921- *CounME 74A*
Hawkins, Hawkshaw 1921-1963 *CounME 74[port], IlEncCM[port]*
Hawkins, Iris 1893- *WhThe*
Hawkins, Isaac *OxMus*
Hawkins, Jack 1910-1973 *BiDFilm, -81, CmMov, FilmAG WE[port], FilmEn, FilmgC, ForYSC, HalFC 80, IlWWBF[port], -A, MotPP, MovMk[port], NotNAT B, OxFilm, PlP&P, WhScrn 77, WhThe, WhoHol B, WhoHrs 80, WorEFlm*
Hawkins, Jalacy J 1929- *BluesWW[port]*
Hawkins, James 1662?-1729 *NewGrD 80*
Hawkins, Jason *AmSCAP 80*
Hawkins, John 1944- *Baker 78*
Hawkins, Sir John 1719-1789 *Baker 78, BnBkM 80, NewGrD 80[port], OxMus*
Hawkins, John Isaac 1772-1855 *BiDAmM, NewGrD 80*
Hawkins, Joyce Patricia 1933- *WhoMus 72*
Hawkins, Margarete 1906- *WhoMus 72*
Hawkins, Martin *WhoMus 72*
Hawkins, Micah 1777-1825 *BiDAmM*
Hawkins, Osie 1913- *NewEOp 71*
Hawkins, Puny d1947 *WhScrn 74, -77*
Hawkins, Roger *ConMuA 80B*
Hawkins, Ronnie 1935- *ConMuA 80A, IlEncR, RkOn*
Hawkins, Screamin Jay 1929- *RkOn[port]*
Hawkins, Stockwell 1874-1927 *NotNAT B, WhThe*
Hawkins, William Brian *WhoMus 72*
Hawkridge, Douglas Leighton 1907- *IntWWM 80, WhoMus 72*
Hawks, Annie 1835-1918 *BiDAmM*
Hawks, Charles Monroe 1874-1951 *WhScrn 74, -77*
Hawks, Howard 1896-1977 *AmFD, BiDFilm, -81, CmMov, DcFM, FilmEn, FilmgC, HalFC 80, IntMPA 77, -75, -76, -78, MovMk[port], OxFilm, TwYS A, WhoHrs 80, WorEFlm*
Hawks, Wells d1941 *NotNAT B*
Hawkwind *ConMuA 80A, IlEncR*
Hawley, Allen Burton 1895-1925 *WhScrn 74, -77, WhoHol B*
Hawley, Charles Beach 1858-1915 *AmSCAP 66, -80, Baker 78, BiDAmM*
Hawley, Dean *RkOn*
Hawley, Dudley 1879-1941 *Film 1, NotNAT B, WhScrn 74, -77*
Hawley, Esther 1906-1968 *NotNAT B*
Hawley, H Dudley 1879-1941 *WhoHol B*
Hawley, H Stanley 1867-1916 *OxMus*
Hawley, Helen *Film 2*
Hawley, Ida *WhoStg 1908*
Hawley, Michael James 1953- *ConAmTC*
Hawley, Monte *BlksB&W C*
Hawley, Ormi 1890-1942 *Film 1, MotPP, TwYS, WhScrn 77*
Hawley, Portia *PupTheA*
Hawley, Wanda 1897- *FilmEn, Film 1, -2, MotPP, TwYS*
Hawley, William Palmer 1950- *AmSCAP 80*
Hawn, Goldie 1945- *BiDFilm 81, FilmEn, FilmgC, HalFC 80, IntMPA 77, -75, -76, -78, -79, -80, JoeFr[port], MotPP, MovMk[port], WhoHol A*
Hawn, John Happy Jack 1883-1964 *WhScrn 77*
Haworth, Bobs Cogill 1904- *CreCan 1*
Haworth, C E 1860-1929 *BiDAmM*
Haworth, Don *ConDr 73, -77B*
Haworth, Jill 1945- *FilmEn, FilmgC, ForYSC, HalFC 80, MotPP, WhoHol A*
Haworth, Joseph 1855-1903 *NotNAT B*
Haworth, Martha d1966 *WhoHol B*
Haworth, Mary 1918- *IntWWM 77*
Haworth, Peter 1889- *CreCan 2*
Haworth, Roger A 1939- *AmSCAP 80*
Haworth, Zema Barbara Cogill 1904- *CreCan 1*
Hawrylo, Frank Zygmunt 1936- *AmSCAP 66, -80*
Hawryluk, Brian Douglas 1955- *IntWWM 80*
Haws, Terry Leonard 1938- *IntWWM 77*
Hawte, William *NewGrD 80*

Hawthorn, Maggie 1929- *ConAmTC*
Hawthorne, Alice *NewGrD 80*
Hawthorne, David d1942 *Film 2, IlWWBF, NotNAT B, WhThe, WhoHol B*
Hawthorne, Grace d1922 *NotNAT B*
Hawthorne, Grace 1939- *AmSCAP 80*
Hawthorne, Lil *WhThe*
Hawthorne, Nathaniel 1804-1864 *DcPup, FilmgC, HalFC 80, NewEOp 71*
Hawthorne, Nigel 1929- *WhoThe 72, -77*
Hawthorne-Baker, Allan *WhoMus 72*
Hawthorne-Baker, Allan 1909-1954 *IntWWM 77, -80*
Hawtrey, Anthony 1909-1954 *WhScrn 74, -77, WhThe, WhoHol B*
Hawtrey, Charles 1855- *WhoStg 1906, -1908*
Hawtrey, Charles 1914- *FilmgC, HalFC 80, IlWWBF[port], WhThe, WhoHol A*
Hawtrey, Sir Charles Henry 1858-1923 *CnThe, NotNAT A, -B, OxThe, WhScrn 77, WhThe*
Hawtrey, George P d1910 *NotNAT B*
Hawtrey, Marjory 1900- *WhThe*
Hawtrey, William P d1914 *NotNAT B*
Hawtry, Anthony 1909-1954 *NotNAT B*
Haxby, Thomas 1729-1796 *NewGrD 80*
Haxthausen, August 1792-1866 *NewGrD 80*
Hay, Alex *CmpGMD*
Hay, Alexandra 1944?- *FilmgC, HalFC 80, WhoHol A*
Hay, Alexandra 1945?- *ForYSC*
Hay, Austin *WhoHol A*
Hay, Charles *Film 2*
Hay, Deborah 1941- *CmpGMD, CnOxB*
Hay, Edward Norman 1889-1943 *Baker 78*
Hay, Frederick Charles 1888-1945 *Baker 78*
Hay, George Dewey 1895-1968 *BiDAmM, EncFCWM 69, IlEncCM[port], WhoHol B*
Hay, George Gray 1946- *WhoMus 72*
Hay, Gyula 1900- *CroCD, ModWD*
Hay, Ian 1876-1952 *NotNAT B, OxThe, WhThe*
Hay, Joan 1894- *WhThe*
Hay, John 1838-1905 *BiDAmM*
Hay, Julius 1900-1975 *CnMD, EncWT*
Hay, Mary 1901-1957 *Film 1, -2, NotNAT B, WhScrn 74, -77, WhThe, WhoHol B*
Hay, Patricia 1944- *WhoOp 76*
Hay, Sara Henderson 1906- *AmSCAP 66*
Hay, Valerie 1910- *WhThe*
Hay, Will 1888-1949 *CmMov, FilmAG WE, FilmEn, FilmgC, HalFC 80, IlWWBF[port], -A, OxFilm, WhoHol B, WorEFlm*
Hay, William 1888-1949 *WhScrn 74, -77*
Hayakawa, Sessue 1889-1973 *FilmEn, Film 1, -2, FilmgC, ForYSC, HalFC 80, MotPP, OxFilm, TwYS, WhScrn 77, WhoHol B*
Hayakawa, Sessue 1890-1973 *MovMk*
Hayasaka, Fumio 1914-1955 *Baker 78, NewGrD 80*
Hayashi, Hikaru 1931- *NewGrD 80*
Hayashi, Kenzo 1899-1976 *NewGrD 80*
Hayashi, Nakako 1932- *IntWWM 77, -80*
Hayashi, Tetsuya 1946- *IntWWM 80*
Hayashi, Yasuko 1948- *WhoOp 76*
Haydee, Marcia 1939- *CnOxB, DancEn 78*
Haydel, Dorothy *Film 1*
Haydel, Richard 1927-1949 *WhScrn 77*
Hayden, George 1722- *NewGrD 80*
Hayden, Harry 1882-1955 *WhScrn 74, -77*
Hayden, Harry 1884-1955 *HolCA[port], Vers B[port], WhoHol B*
Hayden, Jeffrey *NewYTET*
Hayden, Joy Lavonne 1941- *AmSCAP 80*
Hayden, Linda 1951- *FilmEn, FilmgC, HalFC 80, WhoHol A*
Hayden, Linda 1954- *WhoHrs 80*
Hayden, Margaret *WhScrn 74, -77*
Hayden, Mary *WhoHol A*
Hayden, Melissa 1923- *CnOxB, DancEn 78[port], WhoHol A*
Hayden, Nora *Film 2, WhoHol A*
Hayden, Robert 1913- *BlkAmP, MorBAP*
Hayden, Russell 1912- *FilmEn, FilmgC, ForYSC, HalFC 80, IntMPA 77, -75, -76, -78, -79, -80, What 5[port], WhoHol A*
Hayden, Russell Michael 1910- *AmSCAP 80*
Hayden, Scott 1882-1915 *BiDAmM*
Hayden, Sterling *IntMPA 77, -75, -76, -78, -79, -80, MotPP*
Hayden, Sterling 1916- *BiDFilm, -81, FilmEn, FilmgC, ForYSC, HalFC 80, HolP 40[port], WhoHol A, WorEFlm[port]*
Hayden, Sterling 1917- *MovMk[port], OxFilm*
Hayden, Terese 1921- *BiE&WWA, NotNAT, WhoThe 72, -77*
Hayden-Clarendon, J 1878- *WhoStg 1906, -1908*
Hayden-Coffin, Adeline *Film 2*
Haydn, Franz Joseph 1732-1809 *CmpBCM, CnOxB, DcPup, NewEOp 71*
Haydn, Johann Michael 1737-1806 *OxMus*
Haydn, Joseph 1732-1809 *Baker 78, BnBkM 80[port], CmOp, DcCom 77[port], DcCom&M 79, GrComp[port], MusMk[port], NewGrD 80, OxMus*
Haydn, Michael 1737-1806 *Baker 78, DcCom 77, MusMk, NewGrD 80[port]*
Haydn, Richard *IntMPA 77, -75, -76, -78, -79, -80*
Haydn, Richard 1905- *FilmEn, FilmgC, ForYSC, HalFC 80, MovMk, WhoHol A, WorEFlm*
Haydn, Richard 1907- *Vers B[port]*
Haydock, John d1918 *WhScrn 77*
Haydon, Benjamin Robert 1786-1846 *DcPup*
Haydon, Ethel 1878-1954 *WhThe*
Haydon, Florence d1918 *NotNAT B, WhThe*
Haydon, Glen 1896-1966 *Baker 78, ConAmC, NewGrD 80*
Haydon, John S d1907 *NotNAT B*
Haydon, Julie 1910- *BiE&WWA, FilmEn, ForYSC, NotNAT, PlP&P[port], ThFT[port], WhThe, WhoHol A*
Haydon, Marian Rosemary 1925- *WhoMus 72*
Haye, Helen 1874-1957 *Film 2, FilmgC, HalFC 80, NotNAT B, OxThe, WhScrn 74, -77, WhThe, WhoHol B*
Hayer, Nicholas 1898- *WorEFlm*
Hayer, Nicolas 1898- *FilmEn*
Hayer, Nicolas 1902- *DcFM*
Hayers, Sidney 1921- *FilmgC, HalFC 80, IlWWBF*
Hayes *NewGrD 80*
Hayes, Ada d1962 *NotNAT B*
Hayes, Alice *Film 1*
Hayes, Allison 1930-1977 *FilmgC, ForYSC, HalFC 80, WhoHol A, WhoHrs 80[port]*
Hayes, Bill *AmPS A, -B*
Hayes, Bill 1925- *BiE&WWA, ForYSC, NotNAT, WhoHol A*
Hayes, Bill 1926- *RkOn*
Hayes, Billie *WhoHol A*
Hayes, Billy 1906- *AmSCAP 66, -80*
Hayes, Bonny-Adele 1953- *AmSCAP 80*
Hayes, Carrie 1878-1954 *WhScrn 74, -77*
Hayes, Catherine 1825-1861 *NewGrD 80*
Hayes, Catherine 1886-1941 *WhScrn 74, -77, WhoHol B*
Hayes, Charles R 1914- *AmSCAP 66*
Hayes, Clancy 1908-1972 *CmpEPM, EncJzS 70*
Hayes, Clarence Leonard 1908-1972 *BiDAmM, EncJzS 70*
Hayes, Dana *AmSCAP 80*
Hayes, Daniel L *Film 2*
Hayes, Danny *Film 2*
Hayes, Deborah 1939- *IntWWM 77, -80*
Hayes, Edgar *BgBands 74*
Hayes, Edgar Junius 1904- *CmpEPM, WhoJazz 72*
Hayes, Edgar Junius 1905- *AmSCAP 66, -80*
Hayes, Edward Brian 1935-1973 *EncJzS 70*
Hayes, Ernest W 1929- *AmSCAP 80*
Hayes, F W d1918 *NotNAT B*
Hayes, Frank d1924 *Film 1, -2*
Hayes, Frank 1875-1923 *WhScrn 74, -77, WhoHol B*
Hayes, Gabby 1885-1969 *OxFilm*
Hayes, George 1885-1969 *CmMov, FilmEn, Film 2, FilmgC, ForYSC[port], HalFC 80, HolCA[port], MotPP, MovMk[port], Vers B[port], WhScrn 74, -77, WhoHol B*
Hayes, George 1888-1967 *BiE&WWA, PlP&P[port], WhScrn 77, WhThe, WhoHol B*
Hayes, Gerald Ravenscourt 1889-1955 *Baker 78*
Hayes, Gloria *AmSCAP 80*
Hayes, Harry *CmpEPM*
Hayes, Hazel *WhoHol A*
Hayes, Helen *MotPP, WhoHol A*
Hayes, Helen 1900- *BiE&WWA, CnThe, EncWT, Ent[port], FamA&A[port], FilmEn, Film 1, -2, FilmgC, ForYSC, HalFC 80, MGM[port], MovMk[port], NotNAT, -A, OxFilm, OxThe, PlP&P[port], ThFT[port], WhoThe 72, -77, WorEFlm[port]*
Hayes, Helen 1901- *IntMPA 77, -75, -76, -78, -79, -80*
Hayes, Hubert d1964 *NotNAT B*
Hayes, Isaac *ConMuA 80A*
Hayes, Isaac 1942- *BiDAmM, ConAmC, DrBlPA, EncJzS 70, RkOn 2[port], WhoHol A*
Hayes, Issac 1943- *IlEncR[port]*
Hayes, J Milton 1884-1940 *WhThe*
Hayes, Jack Joseph 1919- *AmSCAP 80*
Hayes, James J *PupTheA*
Hayes, Jimmy *WhoHol A*
Hayes, John Francis 1904- *CreCan 1*
Hayes, John Michael 1919- *FilmEn, FilmgC, HalFC 80, IntMPA 77, -75, -76, -78, -79, -80, WorEFlm*
Hayes, John S 1910- *IntMPA 77, -75, -76, -78, -79*
Hayes, Joseph 1918- *BiE&WWA, NotNAT*
Hayes, Joseph 1920- *ConAmC*
Hayes, Larry Ray 1940- *AmSCAP 66, -80*
Hayes, Laurence C 1903-1974 *WhScrn 77, WhoHol B*
Hayes, Linda Joyce 1947- *AmSCAP 80*
Hayes, Louis Sedell 1937- *BiDAmM, EncJzS 70*
Hayes, Maggie 1924- *BiE&WWA, ForYSC*
Hayes, Margaret 1915-1977 *HalFC 80*
Hayes, Margaret 1924- *WhoHol A*
Hayes, Margaret 1924-1977 *FilmEn*
Hayes, Margaret 1925- *IntMPA 77, -75, -76*
Hayes, Melvyn 1935- *HalFC 80*
Hayes, Milton 1884-1940 *NotNAT B*
Hayes, Patricia 1909- *WhThe*
Hayes, Paul Ignatius 1951- *IntWWM 77, -80*
Hayes, Peter Lind 1915- *AmSCAP 66, -80, BiE&WWA, ForYSC, IntMPA 77, -75, -76, -78, -79, -80, NotNAT, WhoHol A*
Hayes, Philip 1738-1797 *Baker 78, NewGrD 80, OxMus*
Hayes, Rea *AmSCAP 66, -80*
Hayes, Reginald d1953 *NotNAT B*
Hayes, Richard *IntMPA 77, -75, -76, -78, -79, -80*
Hayes, Richard 1930- *AmSCAP 66*
Hayes, Roland 1887- *BiDAmM, OxMus*
Hayes, Roland 1887-1976 *BnBkM 80, DrBlPA, NewGrD 80*
Hayes, Roland 1887-1977 *Baker 78, MusSN[port]*
Hayes, Ron *WhoHol A*
Hayes, Sam 1905-1958 *WhScrn 77*
Hayes, Sidney 1865-1940 *WhScrn 74, -77*
Hayes, Theodore, Jr. 1951- *AmSCAP 80*
Hayes, Tubby 1935-1973 *EncJzS 70, IlEncJ*
Hayes, William *ConAmC*
Hayes, William 1705-1777 *OxMus*
Hayes, William 1707-1777 *Baker 78*
Hayes, William 1708-1777 *NewGrD 80[port]*
Hayes, William 1741-1790 *NewGrD 80*
Hayes, William 1887-1937 *Film 2, WhScrn 74, -77*
Hayes Trio *BiDAmM*
Hayl *NewGrD 80*
Hayland, Petrus *NewGrD 80*
Hayle, Grace 1889-1963 *WhScrn 74, -77, WhoHol B*
Hayles, Brian 1930-1978 *HalFC 80*
Haym, Hans 1860-1921 *NewGrD 80*
Haym, Nicola Francesco 1678-1729 *NewGrD 80*
Hayman, Al d1917 *NotNAT B, WhThe*
Hayman, Alf 1865-1921 *NotNAT B*
Hayman, Joe 1903- *WhoJazz 72*
Hayman, Leonard d1962 *NotNAT B*
Hayman, Lillian 1922- *DrBlPA, WhoHol A, WhoThe 77*
Hayman, Richard 1920- *AmSCAP 66,*

CmpEPM, RkOn[port]
Hayman, Richard Perry 1951- *Baker 78, ConAmC, IntWWM 77, -80*
Hayman, Richard Warren Joseph 1920- *AmSCAP 80*
Hayman, Terence Raymond 1942- *IntWWM 80*
Haymer, Herbie 1915-1949 *CmpEPM, WhoJazz 72*
Haymes, Bob 1922?- *CmpEPM*
Haymes, Dick *AmPS A, -B, IntMPA 75, -76, -78, -79, -80*
Haymes, Dick 1916- *CmpEPM, FilmgC, ForYSC, HalFC 80, HolP 40[port], IntMPA 77, MotPP, WhoHol A*
Haymes, Dick 1916-1980 *FilmEn*
Haymes, Dick 1918- *BiDAmM, What 2[port]*
Haymes, Joe 1908- *BgBands 74, CmpEPM, WhoJazz 72*
Hayn, Gabriel *NewGrD 80*
Hayne VanGhizeghem 1445?-1497? *NewGrD 80*
Hayne, Gilles 1590-1650 *NewGrD 80*
Haynen, Irma *PupTheA*
Haynes, Alfred W d1924 *NotNAT B*
Haynes, Antony Paul 1941- *IntWWM 77, WhoMus 72*
Haynes, Arthur 1914-1966 *WhScrn 74, -77, WhoHol B*
Haynes, Cyril 1915?- *WhoJazz 72*
Haynes, Daniel L 1894-1954 *DrBlPA, Film 2, WhScrn 74, -77, WhoHol B*
Haynes, Elizabeth Sterling d1957 *CreCan 2*
Haynes, Eugene 1929- *IntWWM 77, -80*
Haynes, Frank 1931-1965 *BiDAmM*
Haynes, Henry D 1917- *IlEncCM*
Haynes, Henry D 1920-1971 *BiDAmM, EncFCWM 69*
Haynes, Hilda 1912- *DrBlPA, WhoHol A*
Haynes, John C 1829-1907 *Baker 78*
Haynes, John C 1830-1907 *BiDAmM*
Haynes, Kenneth D 1942- *AmSCAP 80*
Haynes, Lincoln Murray 1924- *AmSCAP 80*
Haynes, Lloyd 1934- *DrBlPA, WhoHol A*
Haynes, Roberta 1927- *ForYSC, WhoHol A*
Haynes, Roy Owen 1926- *BiDAmM, CmpEPM, EncJzS 70*
Haynes, T P d1915 *NotNAT B*
Haynes, Tiger 1907- *DrBlPA, PlP&P A[port]*
Haynes, Walter Battison 1859-1900 *Baker 78*
Haynes, William S 1864-1939 *NewGrD 80*
Haynie, William S 1918- *AmSCAP 66, -80*
Hays, Bill 1938- *WhoThe 72, -77*
Hays, Billy Silas 1898- *AmSCAP 66, -80*
Hays, Blind Charlie 1885?-1949 *NewOrJ*
Hays, David 1930- *BiE&WWA, CnOxB, DancEn 78, NotNAT, WhoThe 72, -77*
Hays, Doris 1941- *AmSCAP 80, Baker 78, CpmDNM 76, -77, -80, ConAmC, IntWWM 77, -80*
Hays, Guerney *Film 2*
Hays, Kathryn *ForYSC, WhoHol A*
Hays, Lee 1914- *BiDAmM, EncFCWM 69*
Hays, Robert D 1923- *ConAmC*
Hays, Will d1937 *WhoHol B*
Hays, Will H 1879-1954 *DcFM, FilmEn, FilmgC, HalFC 80, OxFilm, TwYS B, WorEFlm*
Hays, Will S 1837-1907 *PopAmC*
Hays, William Paul 1929- *IntWWM 77, -80*
Hays, William Shakespeare 1837-1907 *AmPS, Baker 78, BiDAmM, NotNAT B, Sw&Ld A*
Hayse, Emil *Film 2*
Hayter, James 1907- *FilmEn, FilmgC, ForYSC, HalFC 80, IlWWBF, IntMPA 77, -75, -76, -78, -79, -80, WhoHol A, WhoThe 72, -77*
Haythorne, Harry 1926- *CnOxB, DancEn 78*
Haythorne, Joan 1915- *FilmgC, HalFC 80, WhoHol A, WhoThe 72, -77*
Hayton, Lennie *CmMov*
Hayton, Lennie d1970 *BgBands 74*
Hayton, Lennie 1908-1971 *CmpEPM, EncJzS 70, WhoJazz 72*
Hayton, Leonard George 1908-1971 *AmSCAP 66, -80, Baker 78, BiDAmM, ConAmC, EncJzS 70*
Hayward, Christopher Robert 1925- *AmSCAP 66, -80*
Hayward, Helen *Film 2*
Hayward, J *WhoMus 72*
Hayward, Leland 1902-1971 *BiE&WWA, EncMT, FilmEn, FilmgC, HalFC 80, NewYTET, NotNAT B, WhThe, WhoThe 72*
Hayward, Lillie *WomWMM*
Hayward, Lillie 1892-1978 *FilmEn*
Hayward, Lou *ConAmC*
Hayward, Louis 1909- *CmMov, FilmEn, FilmgC, ForYSC, HalFC 80, IntMPA 77, -75, -76, -78, -79, -80, MotPP, MovMk[port], What 5[port], WhoHol A, WhoHrs 80, WorEFlm*
Hayward, Mae Shepard *ConAmC*
Hayward, Marie *IntWWM 77, -80, WhoMus 72*
Hayward, Roger *PupTheA*
Hayward, Susan 1918- *FilmgC, MotPP, OxFilm, ThFT[port], WorEFlm[port]*
Hayward, Susan 1918-1974 *CmMov*
Hayward, Susan 1918-1975 *BiDFilm, -81, FilmEn, HalFC 80, WhScrn 77*
Hayward, Susan 1919-1975 *ForYSC, IntMPA 75, MovMk[port], WhoHol C*
Hayward, Tom *PupTheA*
Hayward, W T *WhoMus 72*
Hayward, William John 1945- *WhoMus 72*
Haywell, Frederick d1889 *NotNAT B*
Haywood, Cedric 1914-1969 *EncJzS 70, WhoJazz 72*
Haywood, Charles 1904- *IntWWM 77, -80, NewGrD 80*
Haywood, Charles 1905- *Baker 78*
Haywood, Doris *Film 1*
Haywood, Eliza d1756 *NotNAT B*
Haywood, Lorna 1939- *NewGrD 80*
Haywood, Lorna Marie 1942- *WhoOp 76*
Haywood, William Alan 1925- *WhoMus 72*
Hayworth, Rita *AmPS B, MotPP, WhoHol A, WomWMM*
Hayworth, Rita 1918- *BiDFilm, -81, CmMov, FilmEn, FilmgC, ForYSC, HalFC 80[port], MovMk[port], OxFilm, ThFT[port], WorEFlm*
Hayworth, Rita 1919- *IntMPA 77, -75, -76, -78, -79, -80*
Hayworth, Terry 1926- *CnOxB*
Hayworth, Vinton J 1906-1970 *WhScrn 74, -77, WhoHol B*
Hazam, Lou *NewYTET*
Hazard, Richard P 1921- *BiDAmM*
Haze, Jonathan 1935?- *WhoHrs 80[port]*
Haze, Joseph H 1898- *IntMPA 75*
Hazel, Arthur 1903-1968 *EncJzS 70, NewOrJ[port]*
Hazel, Hy 1920-1970 *WhScrn 77*
Hazel, Monk 1903-1968 *CmpEPM, EncJzS 70, WhoJazz 72*
Hazell, Hy 1920-1970 *FilmgC, HalFC 80, WhScrn 74, WhoHol B*
Hazell, Hy 1922-1970 *EncMT, IlWWBF[port], WhThe*
Hazelman, Herbert R 1913- *ConAmC*
Hazeltin, George Cochrane, Jr. *WhoStg 1908*
Hazeltine, William 1866- *WhoStg 1908*
Hazelton, Joseph 1853-1936 *WhScrn 74, -77*
Hazeltone, Miss *Film 1*
Hazelwood, E Clayton 1903- *AmSCAP 80*
Hazelwood, Lee 1929- *BiDAmM*
Hazen, Joseph H 1898- *IntMPA 77, -76, -78, -79, -80*
Hazen, Sara 1935- *ConAmC*
Hazlehurst, Marjorie *WhoMus 72*
Hazleton, George C d1921 *NotNAT B*
Hazleton, Joseph H *Film 2*
Hazlett, William *WhScrn 77*
Hazlewood, C H d1875 *NotNAT B*
Hazlewood, Lee 1929- *AmSCAP 66, -80*
Hazlitt, William 1778-1830 *DcPup, EncWT, NotNAT A, -B, OxThe*
Hazy, Erzsebet *WhoOp 76*
Hazzard, Alvira *BlkAmP*
Hazzard, Claire Hatsue Sakai 1951- *IntWWM 80*
Hazzard, John E 1888-1935 *CmpEPM*
Hazzard, John Edward 1881-1935 *AmSCAP 66, NotNAT B, WhThe*
Hazzard, Peter Peabody 1949- *AmSCAP 80, ConAmC, IntWWM 77, -80*
H'Doubler, Margaret N 1889- *DancEn 78*
Heaburn, Ferdinando *NewGrD 80*
Head, Brian David 1936- *WhoMus 72*
Head, Bruce 1931- *CreCan 1*
Head, Cedric *PupTheA*
Head, Edith 1907- *FilmEn, FilmgC, HalFC 80, IntMPA 77, -75, -76, -78, -79, -80*
Head, George Bruce 1931- *CreCan 1*
Head, Leslie George Walter *WhoMus 72*
Head, Mabel *PupTheA*
Head, Michael 1900-1976 *Baker 78, NewGrD 80, OxMus*
Head, Michael Dewar *IntWWM 77, WhoMus 72*
Head, Murray *HalFC 80, WhoHol A*
Head, Roy 1941- *RkOn 2[port]*
Headington, Christopher 1930- *Baker 78, IntWWM 77, -80, NewGrD 80, WhoMus 72*
Headrick, Richard 1917- *Film 1, -2, TwYS*
Heagney, William H 1882-1955 *AmSCAP 66, -80*
Heal, Joan 1922- *WhoHol A, WhoThe 72, -77*
Heald-Smith, Geoffrey 1930- *IntWWM 77, -80, WhoMus 72*
Healey, Derek Edward 1936- *Baker 78, IntWWM 77, -80, WhoMus 72*
Healey, John Proctor 1913- *WhoMus 72*
Healey, Myron 1922- *ForYSC, HolCA[port], IntMPA 77, -75, -76, -78, -79, -80, WhoHol A*
Healy, Dan 1889-1969 *CmpEPM, Film 2, WhScrn 74, -77, WhoHol B*
Healy, Gerald d1963 *NotNAT B*
Healy, John T *IntMPA 77, -75, -76, -78, -79, -80*
Healy, Mary 1918- *BiE&WWA, ForYSC, NotNAT, WhoHol A*
Healy, Ted *JoeFr*
Healy, Ted 1886-1937 *FilmgC, HalFC 80*
Healy, Ted 1896-1937 *ForYSC, WhScrn 74, -77, WhoHol B*
Heap, Charles Swinnerton 1847-1900 *Baker 78, NewGrD 80*
Heap, James Arthur 1922- *BiDAmM*
Heard, Alan 1942- *IntWWM 80*
Heard, Gordon *IntWWM 77, -80, WhoMus 72*
Heard, J C 1917- *CmpEPM, EncJzS 70, WhoJazz 72*
Heard, James Charles 1917- *BiDAmM, EncJzS 70*
Heard, Paul F 1913- *IntMPA 77, -75, -76, -78, -79, -80*
Heard, Richard Martin 1936- *AmSCAP 66, -80*
Heard, Thomas 1952- *IntWWM 77, -80*
Hearn, Edward 1888-1963 *Film 1, -2, ForYSC, WhScrn 77, WhoHol B*
Hearn, Fred *Film 1*
Hearn, George *Film 2*
Hearn, James d1913 *NotNAT B*
Hearn, Lew 1882- *Film 2, WhThe*
Hearn, Mary *Film 2*
Hearn, Norman Lewins 1918- *WhoMus 72*
Hearn, Sam 1889-1964 *WhScrn 74, -77, WhoHol B*
Hearne, Edward 1888- *TwYS*
Hearne, James A *Film 2*
Hearne, John Michael 1937- *WhoMus 72*
Hearne, Richard *WhoHol A*
Hearne, Richard 1908-1979 *FilmgC, HalFC 80*
Hearne, Richard 1909- *IlWWBF, IntMPA 75, -76, WhThe, WhoThe 72*
Hearst, William Randolph 1863-1950 *HalFC 80, OxFilm*
Hearst, William Randolph 1863-1951 *DcFM, FilmEn, FilmgC, WorEFlm*
Heart *ConMuA 80A, IlEncR, RkOn 2[port]*
Heartbeats, The *RkOn[port]*
Heartfield, John 1891-1968 *EncWT*
Hearts, The *RkOn*
Heartsman, Johnny *RkOn*
Heartz, Daniel 1928- *Baker 78, NewGrD 80*
Heath, Albert 1935- *BiDAmM, EncJzS 70*
Heath, Arch B 1890- *TwYS A*
Heath, Bobby 1889-1952 *AmSCAP 66, -80*
Heath, Caroline d1887 *NotNAT B*
Heath, Dody *WhoHol A*

Heath, Edward 1900-1969 *EncJzS 70, NewGrD 80*
Heath, Edward R G 1916- *IntWWM 77, -80*
Heath, Eira 1940- *WhoThe 72, -77*
Heath, George *WhoStg 1908*
Heath, Gordon 1918- *BiE&WWA, DrBlPA, NotNAT*
Heath, Ida d1950 *NotNAT B*
Heath, James Edward 1926- *BiDAmM, ConAmC, EncJzS 70*
Heath, Jimmy 1926- *EncJzS 70*
Heath, John *NewGrD 80*
Heath, Kenneth Rippiner 1919- *WhoMus 72*
Heath, Laurence *NewYTET*
Heath, Leslie *PupTheA*
Heath, Lyman 1804-1870 *BiDAmM*
Heath, Percy 1923- *BiDAmM, CmpEPM, EncJzS 70*
Heath, Rosalie *Film 2*
Heath, Ted *BgBands 74*
Heath, Ted 1900-1969 *CmpEPM, EncJzS 70, NewGrD 80*
Heath, Ted 1902-1969 *WhScrn 74, -77, WhoHol B*
Heath, Tootie 1935- *EncJzS 70*
Heath, Walter Henry 1890-1965 *AmSCAP 66, -80*
Heath, Wilbur F 1843-1915 *BiDAmM*
Heath-Davies, Valerie *IntWWM 77, -80*
Heath-Gracie, George Handel *IntWWM 80*
Heathcote, A M d1934 *NotNAT B*
Heathcote, Thomas *WhoHol A*
Heather, William 1584?-1627 *NewGrD 80, OxMus*
Heatherley, Clifford 1888-1937 *WhScrn 74, -77, WhThe, WhoHol B*
Heatherly, Clifford 1888-1937 *Film 2, NotNAT B*
Heatherton, Joey 1944- *BiDAmM, FilmEn, FilmgC, ForYSC, HalFC 80, MotPP, RkOn 2A, WhoHol A*
Heatherton, Ray 1909?- *CmpEPM*
Heatherton, Ray 1910- *BiE&WWA, NotNAT*
Heaton, Anne 1930- *CnOxB, DancEn 78*
Heaton, Eloise 1909- *IntWWM 80*
Heaton, Wallace 1914- *AmSCAP 66, -80, ConAmC A*
Heatter, Gabriel 1890-1972 *What 1[port], WhScrn 77*
Heatwave *RkOn 2[port]*
Heavener, David B 1953- *AmSCAP 80*
Hebb, Bobby 1939- *RkOn 2[port]*
Hebbel, Christian Friedrich 1813-1863 *NotNAT A, -B*
Hebbel, Friedrich 1813-1863 *CnThe, EncWT, Ent, McGEWD[port], NewEOp 71, OxThe, REnWD[port]*
Hebble, Robert Christian 1934- *ConAmC, WhoMus 72*
Hebden, John *NewGrD 80*
Hebenstreit, Michael 1812?-1850? *NewGrD 80*
Hebenstreit, Pantaleon 1667-1750 *Baker 78, NewGrD 80*
Hebenstreit, Pantaleon 1669-1750 *OxMus*
Heberle, Therese 1806-1840 *CnOxB*
Hebert, Adrien 1890- *CreCan 2*
Hebert, Anne 1916- *CreCan 1*
Hebert, Bliss 1930- *WhoOp 76*
Hebert, Fred 1911-1972 *BiE&WWA, NotNAT B*
Hebert, Henri 1884-1950 *CreCan 2*
Hebert, Joseph Gilbert, Jr. 1940- *AmSCAP 80*
Hebert, Louis Phillippe 1850-1917 *CreCan 1*
Hebert, Marjolaine *CreCan 2*
Hebert, Pamela Elizabeth 1946- *WhoOp 76*
Hebert, Paul 1924- *CreCan 2*
Hebert, Pierre 1944- *CreCan 2, WorEFlm*
Hebert, Ronald A 1946- *IntWWM 77, -80*
Hebestreitt, Pantaleon 1667-1750 *NewGrD 80*
Hebran *NewGrD 80*
Hecht, Ben 1893-1964 *CnMD, CnThe, FilmEn*
Hecht, Ben 1894-1964 *BiDFilm, -81, CmMov, DcFM, DcLB 7[port], EncWT, Ent, FilmgC, HalFC 80, McGEWD[port], ModWD, NotNAT A, -B, OxFilm, WhScrn 77, WhThe, WorEFlm*
Hecht, Edward 1832-1887 *NewGrD 80*
Hecht, Ethel *PupTheA*
Hecht, Harold 1907- *FilmEn, FilmgC, HalFC 80, IntMPA 77, -75, -76, -78, -79, -80, WorEFlm*
Hecht, Jack *ConMuA 80B*
Hecht, Jenny 1943-1971 *WhScrn 77, WhoHol B*
Hecht, Joshua *WhoOp 76*
Hecht, Ken 1914- *AmSCAP 66, -80*
Hecht, Paul 1941- *NotNAT*
Hecht, Philip 1909- *WhoMus 72*
Hecht, Ruth 1929- *IntWWM 77, -80*
Hecht, Ted 1908-1969 *WhScrn 74, -77, WhoHol B*
Hechy, Alice *Film 2*
Heck, J C *OxMus*
Heck, John Casper 1740?-1791 *NewGrD 80*
Heck, Stanton *Film 2*
Heck, Thomas F 1943- *IntWWM 77, -80*
Heckart, Eileen 1919- *BiE&WWA, FilmEn, FilmgC, ForYSC, HalFC 80, IntMPA 77, -75, -76, -78, -79, -80, MotPP, MovMk[port], NotNAT, PlP&P, WhoHol A, WhoThe 72, -77*
Heckel *NewGrD 80*
Heckel, Auguste 1880-1914 *NewGrD 80*
Heckel, Emil 1831-1908 *Baker 78*
Heckel, Friedrich Alwin 1845- *NewGrD 80*
Heckel, Johann Adam 1812-1877 *Baker 78, NewGrD 80*
Heckel, Karl 1808-1866 *NewGrD 80*
Heckel, Theodor 1885- *NewGrD 80*
Heckel, Wilhelm 1856-1909 *NewGrD 80, OxMus*
Heckel, Wilhelm Hermann 1879-1952 *NewGrD 80*
Heckel, Wolf 1515?-1562? *Baker 78, NewGrD 80*
Heckel, Wolff 1515?-1562? *NewGrD 80*
Heckman, Don 1935- *EncJzS 70*
Heckman, Donald J 1932- *BiDAmM*
Heckman, Donald J 1935- *EncJzS 70*
Heckman, Harald 1924- *NewGrD 80*
Heckmann, Harald 1924- *IntWWM 77, -80*
Heckroth, Hein *DancEn 78*
Heckroth, Hein 1897- *OxFilm*
Heckroth, Hein 1897-1970 *FilmEn*
Heckroth, Hein 1901-1970 *CnOxB, EncWT, FilmgC, HalFC 80*
Heckscher, August 1913- *BiE&WWA*
Heckscher, Celeste DeLongpre 1860-1928 *Baker 78*
Hecksher, Ernie *CmpEPM*
Hecl, Jan 1929- *IntWWM 77, -80*
Hector, A B *OxMus*
Hecyrus, Christoph 1520-1593 *NewGrD 80*
Hedberg, Tor 1862-1931 *CnMD, OxThe*
Hedburg, Franz 1828-1908 *NotNAT B*
Hedburg, Tor 1862-1931 *NotNAT B*
Heddle, Muriel *PupTheA*
Hedeby, Kerstin 1926- *DancEn 78*
Hedge, Frederick Henry 1805-1890 *BiDAmM*
Hedges, Anthony John 1931- *IntWWM 77, -80, NewGrD 80, WhoMus 72*
Hedges, Arthur Edward 1909- *WhoMus 72*
Hedges, Doris Ryde 1900- *CreCan 1*
Hedges, Hazelle *PupTheA*
Hedin, June *WhoHol A*
Hedison, David 1926- *HalFC 80*
Hedison, David 1928- *FilmgC, MotPP, WhoHol A, WhoHrs 80*
Hedison, David 1929- *ForYSC*
Hedley, Arthur 1905-1969 *Baker 78, NewGrD 80*
Hedley, H B d1931 *NotNAT B, WhThe*
Hedley, Jack 1930- *FilmgC, HalFC 80*
Hedlund, Guy 1884-1964 *Film 1, WhScrn 77*
Hedlund, Ronald 1937- *WhoOp 76*
Hedman, Martha 1888- *WhThe*
Hedmann, Trine *WomWMM*
Hedmondt, Charles 1857-1940 *NewGrD 80*
Hedmont, Charles 1857-1940 *CmOp, NewGrD 80*
Hedmont, Emmanuel Christian 1857-1940 *NewGrD 80*
Hedore, Win *CreCan 2*
Hedouin, Pierre 1789-1868 *Baker 78*
Hedquist, Ivan *Film 2*
Hedqvist, Ivan 1880-1935 *FilmEn*
Hedren, Tippi 1935- *BiDFilm, -81, FilmEn, FilmgC, ForYSC, HalFC 80, MotPP, WhoHol A*
Hedrick, A Earl 1896- *IntMPA 77, -75, -76, -78, -79, -80*
Hedrick, Clarence d1969 *WhoHol B*
Hedstrom, Ruth Elaine 1925- *IntWWM 77, -80*
Hedwall, Lennart 1932- *Baker 78, IntWWM 77, -80*
Hedwall, Paul D 1939- *ConAmC*
Hedwig, Gordon W 1913- *IntMPA 77, -75, -76, -78, -79, -80*
Heefner, David Kerry 1945- *NatPD[port]*
Heeley, Desmond 1931- *CreCan 1, WhoOp 76, WhoThe 72, -77*
Heenan, Ashley David Joseph 1925- *IntWWM 77, -80, NewGrD 80*
Heenan, James *Film 2*
Heer, Johannes 1489?-1553 *NewGrD 80*
Heeringen, Ernest Von *BiDAmM*
Heerkens, Adrianus Ludovicus Cornelis D 1913- *IntWWM 77, -80*
Heerman, Victor 1892- *HalFC 80*
Heerman, Victor 1893- *FilmEn, TwYS A*
Heermann, Hugo 1844-1935 *Baker 78, NewGrD 80*
Heermann, Johann 1585-1647 *NewGrD 80*
Heerup, Gunnar 1903- *NewGrD 80*
Heeschen, Barbara Ann Stuhlmacher 1931- *IntWWM 77, -80*
Heestand, Diane *WomWMM B*
Heffernan, John 1934- *BiE&WWA, NotNAT, WhoHol A, WhoThe 72, -77*
Heffley, Wayne *WhoHol A*
Heffner, Hubert 1901- *BiE&WWA, NotNAT*
Heffner, Richard D 1925- *IntMPA 77, -75, -76, -78, -79, -80*
Heffron, Richard T *HalFC 80, IntMPA 77, -78, -79, -80*
Heffron, Thomas N 1872- *TwYS A*
Heflin, Frances *WhoHol A*
Heflin, Frances 1922- *BiE&WWA, NotNAT*
Heflin, Frances 1924- *WhThe*
Heflin, Kate *WhoHol A*
Heflin, Nora *WhoHol A*
Heflin, Van 1909-1971 *WhThe*
Heflin, Van 1910-1971 *BiDFilm, -81, BiE&WWA, CmMov, FilmEn, FilmgC, ForYSC, HalFC 80, MGM[port], MotPP, MovMk[port], NotNAT B, OxFilm, PlP&P, WhScrn 74, -77, WhoHol B, WorEFlm[port]*
Hefner, Keith 1929- *AmSCAP 66, -80*
Hefner, Sharon Ann 1952- *IntWWM 77, -80*
Heft, David Yule Marchbank 1943- *IntWWM 80*
Hefti, Neal 1922- *AmSCAP 66, -80, BgBands 74, BiDAmM, CmpEPM, ConAmC, EncJzS 70, RkOn 2A*
Hegamin, Lucille 1894-1970 *BluesWW[port], CmpEPM*
Hegamin, Lucille 1897-1970 *WhoJazz 72*
Hegar, Friedrich 1841-1927 *Baker 78, NewGrD 80*
Hegdal, Magne Gunnar 1944- *IntWWM 77, -80*
Hegedus, Arpad *ConAmC*
Hegedus, Ferencz 1881-1944 *Baker 78*
Hegedus, Margit Franciska 1922- *IntWWM 77, -80, WhoMus 72*
Hegedus, Olga 1920- *IntWWM 77, -80, WhoMus 72*
Hegeman, Alice *Film 2*
Hegenbart, Alex F 1922- *ConAmC*
Heger, Jiri 1947- *IntWWM 77, -80*
Heger, Robert 1886-1978 *Baker 78, CmOp, NewEOp 71, NewGrD 80*
Heger, Robert 1888- *WhoMus 72*
Heger, Theodore Ernest 1907- *IntWWM 77, -80*
Hegewald *Film 2*
Heggen, Almar Gunvald 1933- *WhoOp 76*
Heggen, Thomas O 1919-1949 *McGEWD, NotNAT B*
Heggie, O P 1879-1936 *Film 2, FilmgC, ForYSC, HalFC 80, HolCA[port], MovMk, NotNAT B, TwYS, WhScrn 74, -77, WhThe, WhoHol B, WhoHrs 80[port]*
Hegierski, Kathleen 1947- *IntWWM 77, -80*
Hegira, Anne d1971? *WhScrn 77, WhoHol A*
Hegner, Anton 1861-1915 *Baker 78, BiDAmM*
Hegner, Otto 1876-1907 *Baker 78*
Hegyesi, Louis 1853-1894 *Baker 78*

Hegyi, Barnabas *DcFM*
Hegyi, Erzsebet *NewGrD 80*
Heibel, Jacob *NewGrD 80*
Heiberg, Gunnar 1857-1929 *CnMD, CnThe, McGEWD, ModWD, NotNAT B, OxThe, REnWD[port]*
Heiberg, Harold 1922- *IntWWM 77, -80*
Heiberg, Johan Ludvig 1791-1860 *McGEWD[port], NotNAT B, OxThe, REnWD[port]*
Heiberg, Johanne Luise Patges 1812-1890 *OxThe*
Heiberg, Peder Andreas 1758-1841 *OxThe*
Heichelmann, Palle 1935- *IntWWM 77, -80*
Heick, Susan *WomWMM B*
Heicking, Wolfram 1927- *IntWWM 77, -80*
Heidegger, Johann Jakob 1666-1749 *NewGrD 80*
Heidemann, Paul 1886-1968 *Film 2, WhScrn 74, -77*
Heiden *NewGrD 80*
Heiden, Bernhard 1910- *Baker 78, BiDAmM, ConAmC, DcCM, NewGrD 80*
Heiden, Heino 1923- *CnOxB, CreCan 2*
Heider, Frederick 1917- *AmSCAP 80, IntMPA 77, -75, -76, -78, -79, -80*
Heider, Max-Hermann 1922- *WhoMus 72*
Heider, Wally *ConMuA 80B*
Heider, Werner 1930- *Baker 78, DcCM, NewGrD 80*
Heidingsfeld, Ludwig 1854-1920 *Baker 78*
Heidsieck, Eric 1936- *WhoMus 72*
Heidt, Horace 1901- *AmPS A, -B, BgBands 74[port], CmpEPM, What 2[port], WhoHol A*
Heidt, Joseph d1962 *NotNAT B*
Heifetz, Daniel 1948- *IntWWM 80*
Heifetz, Harold *NatPD[port]*
Heifetz, Jascha 1901- *AmSCAP 66, -80, Baker 78, BiDAmM, BnBkM 80[port], IntWWM 77, -80, MusMk, MusSN[port], NewGrD 80, WhoHol A, WhoMus 72*
Heifetz, Vladimir 1893- *AmSCAP 66, -80, ConAmC*
Heifits, Joseph 1904- *FilmgC, HalFC 80*
Heifits, Josif 1906- *OxFilm*
Heifitz, Josef 1905- *FilmEn*
Heifitz, Joseph 1905- *WorEFlm*
Heifitz, Josif 1905- *DcFM*
Heigh, Helene *WhoHol A*
Heighington, Musgrave 1679-1764 *NewGrD 80*
Height, Jean d1967 *WhoHol B*
Heije, Jan Pieter 1809-1876 *NewGrD 80*
Heijermans, Herman 1864-1924 *CnMD, CnThe, EncWT, McGEWD[port], ModWD, OxThe, REnWD[port], WhThe*
Heijermans, Hermann 1864-1924 *NotNAT B*
Heikkila, Hannu Tapani 1922- *WhoOp 76*
Heilbron, Annette Marian *IntWWM 77, -80*
Heilbron, Fritz *CmpEPM*
Heilbronn, William 1879- *WhThe*
Heilicher, Ira *ConMuA 80B*
Heiller, Anton 1923-1979 *Baker 78, BnBkM 80, DcCM, IntWWM 77, NewGrD 80, WhoMus 72*
Heilman, William Clifford 1877-1946 *Baker 78, ConAmC*
Heilmann, Harald Arthur 1924- *IntWWM 77, -80, NewGrD 80*
Heilmann, Ingeborg 1903- *IntWWM 77, -80*
Heilner, Irwin 1908- *BiDAmM, ConAmC, IntWWM 77, -80*
Heilweil, Samantha Lee *WomWMM B*
Heim, Elsbeth 1917- *IntWWM 77, -80*
Heim, Emery 1906-1946 *AmSCAP 66, -80*
Heim, Emmy 1885-1954 *CreCan 2*
Heim, Leo Edward 1913- *IntWWM 77, -80*
Heim, Norman Michael 1929- *CpmDNM 78, -79, -80, ConAmC, IntWWM 80*
Heim, Werner 1909- *IntWWM 77, -80*
Heimall, Linda Jeanne 1941- *WhoOp 76*
Heiman, Tom *ConMuA 80B*
Heims, Jo *IntMPA 77, -75, -76, -78*
Hein, Albert d1949 *NotNAT B*
Hein, Beverly J 1920- *AmSCAP 66, -80*
Hein, Birgit *WomWMM*
Hein, Carl 1864-1945 *Baker 78*
Hein, Silvio 1879-1928 *AmSCAP 66, -80, BiDAmM, CmpEPM, NotNAT B, WhThe*
Hein, Wilhelm *WomWMM*
Heina, Francois-Joseph 1729-1790 *NewGrD 80*
Heindl, Franz Sebastian *NewGrD 80*
Heindorf, Ray *IntMPA 75, -76, -78, -79, -80*
Heindorf, Ray 1908- *AmSCAP 66, -80, CmpEPM*
Heindorf, Ray 1908-1980 *FilmEn*
Heindorf, Ray 1910- *CmMov, FilmgC, HalFC 80, IntMPA 77*
Heine, Friedrich 1764-1821 *NewGrD 80*
Heine, Harry 1797-1856 *NewGrD 80*
Heine, Heinrich 1797-1856 *CnOxB, NewEOp 71, NewGrD 80, OxMus*
Heinecke, Ruth C *IntMPA 77, -75, -76, -78, -79, -80*
Heinefetter *NewGrD 80*
Heinefetter, Clara 1813-1857 *NewGrD 80*
Heinefetter, Eva *Baker 78*
Heinefetter, Fatima *Baker 78*
Heinefetter, Kathinka 1819-1858 *NewGrD 80*
Heinefetter, Katinka 1820-1858 *Baker 78*
Heinefetter, Maria 1816-1857 *Baker 78*
Heinefetter, Nanette *Baker 78*
Heinefetter, Sabina 1809-1872 *Baker 78*
Heinefetter, Sabine 1809-1872 *NewGrD 80*
Heineken, Mary Francesca 1922- *IntWWM 77, -80*
Heinel, Anna Friedrike 1753-1808 *CnOxB*
Heinel, Anne Friedrike 1753-1808 *DancEn 78*
Heineman, John *ConAmC*
Heinemann, Alfred 1908- *Baker 78*
Heinemann, Eda 1880- *BiE&WWA, NotNAT*
Heinemann, George *NewYTET*
Heinemeyer, Ernst Wilhelm 1827-1869 *Baker 78*
Heiner, Brita 1915- *IntWWM 77, -80*
Heinichen, Johann David 1683-1729 *Baker 78, NewGrD 80*
Heininen, Paavo 1938- *Baker 78, DcCM, IntWWM 77, -80, NewGrD 80*
Heininger, Robert M *PupTheA*
Heinio, Mikko Kyosti 1948- *Baker 78, IntWWM 77, -80*
Heinisch, Joseph 1800?-1840 *NewGrD 80*
Heinisch, Jozsef 1800?-1840 *NewGrD 80*
Heinitz, Thomas 1921- *IntWWM 77, -80, WhoMus 72*
Heinitz, Wilhelm 1883-1963 *Baker 78, NewGrD 80*
Heink, Schuman *Film 2*
Heinke, James 1945- *ConAmC*
Heinlein *NewGrD 80*
Heinlein, Federico A 1912- *IntWWM 77, -80*
Heinlein, Mary Virginia d1961 *NotNAT B*
Heinlein, Paul *NewGrD 80*
Heinlein, Robert 1907- *WhoHrs 80*
Heinmets, Robert 1906- *IntWWM 77*
Heinrich Julius, Duke Of Brunswick 1564-1613 *EncWT, OxThe*
Heinrich XXIV, Prince 1855-1910 *OxMus*
Heinrich Von Augsburg *NewGrD 80*
Heinrich Von Meissen *NewGrD 80*
Heinrich Von Morungen d1222 *NewGrD 80*
Heinrich Von Ofterdingen 1200?- *NewGrD 80*
Heinrich Von Veldeke *NewGrD 80*
Heinrich Zur Meise *NewGrD 80*
Heinrich, Adel 1926- *ConAmC*
Heinrich, Annemarie 1912- *DancEn 78*
Heinrich, Anthony Philip 1781-1861 *Baker 78, BiDAmM, NewGrD 80*
Heinrich, Anton Philipp 1781-1861 *NewGrD 80*
Heinrich, George *Film 2*
Heinrich, Helga 1933- *CnOxB, DancEn 78*
Heinrich, Max 1853-1916 *Baker 78, BiDAmM*
Heinrich, Nikolaus *NewGrD 80*
Heinrich, Peter 1942- *WhoOp 76*
Heinrich, Rudolf 1926- *WhoOp 76*
Heinrich, Siegfried 1935- *IntWWM 77, -80*
Heinrichshofen *NewGrD 80*
Heinrichshofen, Adalbert 1859-1932 *NewGrD 80*
Heinrichshofen, Theodor 1805-1901 *NewGrD 80*
Heinrichshofen, Wilhelm Von 1760-1881 *NewGrD 80*
Heinricus De Libero Castro *NewGrD 80*
Heinroth, Charles 1874-1963 *Baker 78*
Heinroth, Johann August Gunther 1780-1846 *Baker 78, NewGrD 80*
Heins, Francis Donaldson 1878- *BiDAmM*
Heins, Marjorie *WomWMM B*
Heinse, Wilhelm 1746-1803 *NewGrD 80*
Heinsheimer, Hans 1900- *Baker 78*
Heinsius, Peter d1590 *NewGrD 80*
Heintz, Wolff 1490?-1552 *NewGrD 80*
Heintz, Wolfgang 1490?-1552 *NewGrD 80*
Heintze, Gustaf Hjalmar 1879-1946 *Baker 78, NewGrD 80*
Heintze, Hans 1911- *NewGrD 80*
Heintze, Wilhelm *NewGrD 80*
Heiny, Margaret Harris 1911- *IntWWM 77, -80*
Heinz, Gerard 1903-1972 *FilmgC, HalFC 80, WhoHol B*
Heinz, Gerard 1904- *WhThe, WhoThe 72*
Heinz, Jerome *NewGrD 80*
Heinz, John F 1926- *AmSCAP 66, -80*
Heinz, Wolfgang 1900- *EncWT*
Heinze, Sir Bernard Thomas 1894- *Baker 78, IntWWM 77, -80, NewGrD 80*
Heinze, Gustav Adolf 1820-1904 *NewGrD 80*
Heinze, Gustav Adolph 1820-1904 *Baker 78*
Heiremans, Luis Alberto 1928-1964 *CroCD*
Heise, Michael 1940- *IntWWM 80, WhoOp 76*
Heise, Peter Arnold 1830-1879 *Baker 78, NewGrD 80, OxMus*
Heiseler, Bernt Von 1907- *CnMD, ModWD*
Heiseler, Henry Von 1875-1928 *ModWD*
Heisinger, Brent *ConAmC*
Heisler, Stuart 1894-1979 *BiDFilm, -81, FilmEn, FilmgC, HalFC 80, IntMPA 77, -75, -76, -78, -79, MovMk[port], WorEFlm*
Heiss, Carol 1940- *FilmgC, HalFC 80*
Heiss, Hermann 1897-1966 *NewGrD 80*
Heiss, John Carter 1938- *AmSCAP 80, CpmDNM 79, ConAmC, IntWWM 77, -80*
Heisto, Karin 1954- *IntWWM 80*
Heisto Strand, Rigmor 1951- *IntWWM 80*
Heitmann, Fritz 1891-1953 *NewGrD 80*
Heitor, Luiz *NewGrD 80*
Heitz, Klaus 1941- *IntWWM 77, -80*
Hekking, Andre 1866-1925 *Baker 78*
Hekking, Anton 1856-1935 *Baker 78*
Hekking, Gerard 1879-1942 *Baker 78*
Hekking, Robert Gerard 1820-1875 *Baker 78*
Hekster, Walter 1937- *Baker 78, CpmDNM 80*
Helander, Gunvor Hedda Kristina 1941- *IntWWM 80*
Helbert, Jack *Film 2*
Helbig, Otto H 1914- *AmSCAP 66, -80, ConAmC*
Helburn, Theresa 1887-1959 *EncMT, NotNAT A, -B, PlP&P, WhThe*
Held, Anna *AmPS B*
Held, Anna 1865-1918 *BiDAmM, FamA&A[port]*
Held, Anna 1873-1918 *CmpEPM, EncMT, Film 1, HalFC 80, NotNAT B, WhScrn 77, WhThe, WhoHol B, WhoStg 1906, -1908*
Held, Helga 1935- *DancEn 78*
Held, Martin 1908- *EncWT, Ent, FilmAG WE, HalFC 80*
Held, Peter 1937- *IntWWM 77*
Held, Wilbur C 1914- *ConAmC*
Heldabrand, John *WhoHol A*
Helder, Bartholomaus 1585?-1635 *Baker 78, NewGrD 80*
Helderus, Bartholomaus 1585?-1635 *NewGrD 80*
Heldt, Gerhard Alfred 1943- *IntWWM 77, -80*
Heldy, Fanny 1888-1973 *CmOp, NewGrD 80*
Hele, George DeLa 1547-1586 *NewGrD 80*
Helen Trent *What 3[port]*
Helena, Edith 1876- *WhoStg 1908*
Helena, Vera *DancEn 78*
Helfer, Charles D' d1664? *NewGrD 80*
Helfer, Walter 1896-1959 *AmSCAP 66, -80, Baker 78, BiDAmM, ConAmC*
Helfert, Vladimir 1886-1945 *Baker 78, NewGrD 80*
Helferting VanWewen, Franz *NewGrD 80*
Helffer, Claude 1922- *IntWWM 77, -80, NewGrD 80, WhoMus 72*
Helffer, Mireille 1928- *IntWWM 80*
Helfferting VanWewen, Franz *NewGrD 80*
Helfgot, Daniel 1946- *WhoOp 76*

Helfman, Max 1901-1963 *AmSCAP 66, –80, Baker 78, ConAmC*
Helfritz, Hans 1902- *Baker 78, DcCM*
Helgason, Hallgrimur 1914- *NewGrD 80*
Helgason, Johann 1949- *IntWWM 77*
Helger, Lutz 1913- *IntWWM 77, –80*
Heliotis, Michael 1929- *WhoOp 76*
Hell, Theodor *NewGrD 80*
Hellden, Daniel 1917- *IntWWM 77, –80*
Hellendaal, Peter 1721-1799 *NewGrD 80[port], OxMus*
Hellendaal, Peter, Jr. *OxMus*
Hellendaal, Petrus 1721-1799 *NewGrD 80[port]*
Hellendaal, Pieter 1721-1799 *Baker 78, MusMk, NewGrD 80[port]*
Hellendaal, Pietro 1721-1799 *NewGrD 80[port]*
Heller, Alfred E 1931- *AmSCAP 80, ConAmC*
Heller, Claire 1929- *BiE&WWA, NotNAT*
Heller, Frank *Film 2*
Heller, Franklin *IntMPA 77, –75, –76, –78, –79, –80*
Heller, Fred *ConMuA 80B*
Heller, Gloria *Film 2*
Heller, Hans Ewald 1894-1966 *Baker 78, ConAmC*
Heller, Hugh *IntMPA 77, –75, –76, –78, –79, –80*
Heller, Istvan 1813-1888 *NewGrD 80*
Heller, Jack Joseph 1932- *IntWWM 77, –80*
Heller, James Gutheim 1892-1971 *Baker 78, BiDAmM, ConAmC*
Heller, Jeanne d1908 *NotNAT B*
Heller, Joachim 1518?-1590? *NewGrD 80*
Heller, Joel Harrison 1931- *AmSCAP 80*
Heller, Johann Kilian 1633?-1674 *NewGrD 80*
Heller, John 1928- *AmSCAP 66*
Heller, John Henry, Jr. 1945- *ConAmC, IntWWM 77, –80*
Heller, Joseph 1923- *ConDr 73, –77, NotNAT*
Heller, Larry *ConMuA 80B*
Heller, Little Jackie 1908- *CmpEPM*
Heller, Lukas 1930- *FilmEn, FilmgC, HalFC 80*
Heller, Otto 1896-1970 *FilmEn, FilmgC, HalFC 80, OxFilm, WorEFlm*
Heller, Paul M 1927- *IntMPA 77, –75, –76, –78, –79, –80*
Heller, Ray *Film 2*
Heller, Richard 1919- *IntWWM 77, –80*
Heller, Richard 1954- *IntWWM 80*
Heller, Robert 1830?-1878 *Ent, MagIlD, PupTheA*
Heller, Roberta *AmSCAP 80*
Heller, Rosilyn *WomWMM*
Heller, Stephen 1813-1888 *Baker 78, NewGrD 80, OxMus*
Heller, Stephen 1814-1888 *MusMk*
Heller, William Clarke 1951- *AmSCAP 80*
Heller, Wilson B 1893- *IntMPA 77, –75, –76, –78, –79, –80*
Hellerman, Fred 1927- *AmSCAP 66, –80, BiDAmM, EncFCWM 69*
Hellermann, William David 1939- *CpmDNM 80, ConAmC, DcCM*
Hellerus Leucopetraeus *NewGrD 80*
Hellesnes-Hukvari, Astrid 1937- *IntWWM 77, –80*
Hellewell, David Walter 1932- *IntWWM 77, –80*
Hellier, Harry Clifford *IntWWM 77, –80, WhoMus 72*
Helliger, Richard 1901- *WhoMus 72*
Hellinck, Lupus 1496?-1541 *MusMk, NewGrD 80*
Hellinck, Wulfaert 1496?-1541 *NewGrD 80*
Hellinger, Mark 1903-1947 *BiDFilm, –81, CmMov, DcFM, FilmEn, FilmgC, HalFC 80, NotNAT A, –B, OxFilm, WhScrn 77, WorEFlm*
Helliwell, Clifton 1907- *IntWWM 77, –80, WhoMus 72*
Hellman, Jerome *IntMPA 77, –76, –78, –79, –80*
Hellman, Lillian *IntMPA 77, –75, –76, –78, –79, –80, WomWMM*
Hellman, Lillian 1905- *CnMD, CnThe, CroCD, DcFM, EncWT, Ent, FilmEn, FilmgC, HalFC 80, McGEWD[port], ModWD, OxFilm, OxThe, PlP&P[port], REnWD[port], WhoThe 72, –77, WorEFlm*
Hellman, Lillian 1906- *DcLB 7[port]*
Hellman, Lillian 1907- *BiE&WWA, ConDr 73, –77, NatPD[port], NotNAT, –A*
Hellman, Marcel 1898- *FilmgC, HalFC 80, IntMPA 77, –75, –76, –78, –79, –80*
Hellman, Miriam *Film 2*
Hellman, Monte 1931- *FilmgC, HalFC 80*
Hellman, Monte 1932- *BiDFilm, –81, FilmEn*
Hellmann, Maximilian Joseph 1703?-1763 *NewGrD 80*
Hellmer, Kurt 1909- *BiE&WWA, NotNAT*
Hellmesberger *NewGrD 80*
Hellmesberger, Ferdinand 1863-1940 *NewGrD 80*
Hellmesberger, Georg 1800-1873 *Baker 78, BnBkM 80, NewGrD 80*
Hellmesberger, Georg 1830-1852 *Baker 78, NewGrD 80*
Hellmesberger, George 1800-1873 *OxMus*
Hellmesberger, George 1830-1852 *OxMus*
Hellmesberger, Josef 1828-1893 *OxMus*
Hellmesberger, Josef 1855-1907 *CnOxB, OxMus*
Hellmesberger, Joseph 1828-1893 *Baker 78, NewGrD 80*
Hellmesberger, Joseph 1855-1907 *Baker 78, NewGrD 80*
Hellmesberger, Pepi 1855-1907 *NewGrD 80*
Hellmich, Wolfgang 1935- *WhoOp 76*
Hellouin, Frederic 1864-1924 *Baker 78*
Hellum, Barney *Film 2*
Hellwig, Karl Friedrich Ludwig 1773-1838 *Baker 78, NewGrD 80*
Hellyer, Roger 1942- *WhoMus 72*
Helm, Anne *ForYSC, WhoHol A*
Helm, Brigette 1908- *Film 2*
Helm, Brigitta 1906- *OxFilm*
Helm, Brigitte 1906- *FilmAG WE, FilmEn, FilmgC, HalFC 80, WhoHol A, WhoHrs 80[port]*
Helm, Brigitte 1907- *MovMk, WorEFlm[port]*
Helm, Eugene 1928- *NewGrD 80*
Helm, Everett 1913- *Baker 78, ConAmC, DcCM, NewGrD 80*
Helm, Fay 1910?- *FilmgC, ForYSC, HalFC 80*
Helm, Frances *BiE&WWA, NotNAT, WhoHol A*
Helm, Franz 1748-1826 *NewGrD 80*
Helm, Hans 1934- *WhoOp 76*
Helm, Karl 1938- *WhoOp 76*
Helm, Rupert 1748-1826 *NewGrD 80*
Helm, Theodor Otto 1843-1920 *Baker 78, NewGrD 80*
Helman, Zofia 1937- *IntWWM 77, –80*
Helmbold, Ludwig 1532-1598 *NewGrD 80*
Helmer, Axel 1925- *NewGrD 80*
Helmer, Erik Axel 1925- *IntWWM 77, –80*
Helmer, Hermann *EncWT*
Helmholtz, Hermann Von 1821-1894 *Baker 78, NewGrD 80, OxMus*
Helmick, Carl N, Jr. 1937- *IntWWM 77, –80*
Helmond, Katherine 1929?- *HalFC 80*
Helmont, Adrien-Joseph Van 1747-1830 *NewGrD 80*
Helmont, Charles-Joseph Van 1715-1790 *NewGrD 80*
Helmore, Arthur 1858-1941 *NotNAT B*
Helmore, Arthur 1859-1941 *WhThe*
Helmore, Thomas 1811-1890 *NewGrD 80*
Helmore, Tom 1916- *BiE&WWA, ForYSC, NotNAT, WhoHol A*
Helms, Bobby 1933- *AmPS A, BiDAmM, CounME 74, –74A, EncFCWM 69, RkOn[port]*
Helms, Bobby 1935- *IlEncCM[port]*
Helms, Hans G 1932- *Baker 78, NewGrD 80*
Helms, James Herman 1933- *AmSCAP 80*
Helms, Norma Hale *AmSCAP 80*
Helms, Ruth *Film 2*
Helms, Ruth d1960 *WhScrn 77*
Helms, Ruth d1961 *WhoHol B*
Helmsley, Charles Thomas Hunt- 1865-1940 *NotNAT B, WhThe*
Helpman, Sir Robert 1909- *FilmEn*
Helpmann, Barbara Chilcott Davis *CreCan 1*
Helpmann, Sir Robert 1909- *BiE&WWA, CnThe, CnOxB, DancEn 78[port], Ent[port], FilmgC, ForYSC, HalFC 80, IntMPA 77, –75, –76, –78, –79, –80, MovMk, NotNAT, –A, OxThe, PlP&P, WhoHol A, WhoThe 72, –77*
Helprin, Morris 1904- *IntMPA 77, –75, –76, –78, –79, –80*
Helps, D I *WhoMus 72*
Helps, Robert 1928- *Baker 78, CpmDNM 78, ConAmC, DcCM, NewGrD 80*
Helsted, Gustaf 1857-1924 *Baker 78*
Heltai, Jeno 1871-1957 *OxThe*
Heltay, Laszlo 1930- *IntWWM 80, NewGrD 80, WhoMus 72*
Helton, Alf d1937 *NotNAT B*
Helton, Peggy *MotPP*
Helton, Percy 1894-1971 *Film 2, FilmgC, ForYSC, HalFC 80, Vers A[port], WhScrn 74, –77, WhoHol B, WhoHrs 80*
Helweg, Per 1924- *IntWWM 77, –80*
Helwerding VanWewen, Franz *NewGrD 80*
Hely, Benjamin *NewGrD 80*
Hely, Cuthbert *NewGrD 80*
Hely-Hutchinson, Victor 1901-1947 *NewGrD 80, OxMus*
Hemberg, Eskil 1938- *Baker 78, IntWWM 77, –80, NewGrD 80*
Hemel, Oscar Van 1892- *Baker 78, NewGrD 80*
Hemel, Sigmund *NewGrD 80*
Hemen *NewGrD 80*
Heming, Arthur Henry Howard 1870-1940 *CreCan 2*
Heming, John 1556-1630 *PlP&P*
Heming, Percy 1883-1956 *CmOp, NewGrD 80*
Heming, Percy 1885- *WhThe*
Heming, Violet 1893- *Film 1, TwYS*
Heming, Violet 1895- *BiE&WWA, NotNAT, WhThe, WhoHol A*
Heminge, John 1556?-1630 *EncWT, Ent, NotNAT B, OxThe*
Hemingway, Ernest 1898-1961 *OxFilm*
Hemingway, Ernest 1899-1961 *CnMD, FilmgC, HalFC 80, ModWD, NotNAT B, WorEFlm*
Hemingway, Margaux *HalFC 80, WhoHol A*
Hemingway, Marie 1893-1939 *NotNAT B, WhThe, WhoHol B*
Hemingway, Richard C *WhScrn 77*
Hemion, Dwight *NewYTET*
Hemion, Mac *NewYTET*
Hemke, Frederick 1935- *Baker 78*
Hemmel, Sigmund d1564 *NewGrD 80*
Hemment, Marguerite Esther 1908- *AmSCAP 66, –80*
Hemmenway, James 1800-1849 *BiDAmM*
Hemmer, Eugene 1929- *AmSCAP 66, –80, Baker 78, ConAmC*
Hemmerde, Edward George 1871-1948 *NotNAT B, WhThe*
Hemmerlein *NewGrD 80*
Hemmerlein, Anton 1730-1811 *NewGrD 80*
Hemmerlein, Ignaz Carl 1773-1840 *NewGrD 80*
Hemmerlein, Johann Nikolaus *NewGrD 80*
Hemmerlein, Joseph 1799- *NewGrD 80*
Hemmerlein, Marquard Joseph 1766-1838 *NewGrD 80*
Hemming, Alfred d1942 *NotNAT B*
Hemming, Alicia Lisle 1914- *IntWWM 77*
Hemming, Violet 1893- *Film 2*
Hemmings, David 1941- *ConMuA 80B, FilmAG WE[port], FilmEn, FilmgC, ForYSC, HalFC 80, IlWWBF[port], IntMPA 77, –75, –76, –78, –79, –80, MotPP, MovMk[port], WhoHol A, WorEFlm*
Hemmings, Douglas Cyril 1898- *WhoMus 72*
Hemmings, Peter William 1934- *IntWWM 77, –80, WhoMus 72, WhoOp 76*
Hemon, Sedje *IntWWM 77, –80*
Hemony *NewGrD 80*
Hemony, Francois 1609?-1667 *NewGrD 80*
Hemony, Pieter 1619-1680 *NewGrD 80*
Hempel, Charles William 1777-1855 *NewGrD 80*
Hempel, Frieda 1885-1955 *Baker 78, CmOp, MusSN[port], NewEOp 71, NewGrD 80*
Hempfling, Volker Wolfgang 1944- *IntWWM 77, –80*
Hemphill, F L *Film 1*
Hemphill, Jessie Mae 1932- *BlkWAB[port]*
Hemphill, Julius 1940- *EncJzS 70*
Hemphill, Scad 1906-1959 *WhoJazz 72*

Hemphill, Shelton 1906- *BiDAmM*
Hempson, Celeste *NewGrD 80*
Hempson, Denis 1695-1807 *NewGrD 80*
Hempson, Dennis A 1695-1807 *OxMus*
Hemsi, Alberto 1896-1975 *Baker 78, NewGrD 80*
Hemsley, Estelle 1887-1968 *DrBlPA, WhScrn 74, -77, WhoHol B*
Hemsley, Estelle 1892-1968 *BiE&WWA, NotNAT B*
Hemsley, Gilbert Vaughn, Jr. 1936- *WhoOp 76*
Hemsley, Harry May 1877-1951 *NotNAT B, WhThe*
Hemsley, Sherman 1938- *DrBlPA*
Hemsley, Thomas Jeffrey 1927- *CmOp, IntWWM 77, -80, NewGrD 80, WhoMus 72*
Hemsley, W T 1850-1918 *NotNAT B, WhThe*
Hemsley, Winston Dewitt *DrBlPA*
Hen, Ferdinand Joseph De *NewGrD 80*
Henaberry, Joseph 1888-1976 *Film 1*
Henabery, Joseph 1886-1976 *HalFC 80*
Henabery, Joseph 1888-1976 *FilmEn, TwYS A, WhoHol C*
Henahan, Donal J 1921- *IntWWM 77, -80*
Henault, Gilles 1920- *CreCan 2*
Hencke, Johann 1697-1766 *NewGrD 80*
Henckels, Paul 1885-1967 *Film 2*
Henckles, Paul 1885-1967 *WhScrn 77*
Hendee, Harold F 1879-1966 *WhScrn 74, -77*
Hendel, Henriette 1772-1849 *CnOxB*
Hendel, Penelope 1943- *IntWWM 77*
Henders, Harriet 1904-1972 *BiDAmM*
Henderson *PupTheA*
Henderson, Alex F 1866-1933 *NotNAT B, WhThe*
Henderson, Alva *ConAmC*
Henderson, Alva 1940- *Baker 78*
Henderson, Bert *Film 2*
Henderson, Bill 1930- *EncJzS 70*
Henderson, Bobby 1910-1969 *EncJzS 70, WhoJazz 72*
Henderson, Carlesta Elliott 1925- *IntWWM 77, -80*
Henderson, Catherine *BluesWW[port]*
Henderson, Cedric 1918- *WhoMus 72*
Henderson, Charles A 1907- *IntMPA 77, -75, -76, -78, -79, -80*
Henderson, Charles E 1907-1970 *AmSCAP 66, -80*
Henderson, David 1853-1908 *NotNAT B, WhoStg 1906, -1908*
Henderson, Del 1877-1956 *Film 1, -2, NotNAT B*
Henderson, Del 1883-1946 *TwYS A*
Henderson, Del 1883-1956 *FilmEn, ForYSC, TwYS, WhScrn 74, -77, WhoHol B*
Henderson, Dickie 1922- *IntMPA 77, -75, -76, -78, -79, -80, WhoThe 72, -77*
Henderson, Donald A 1903- *IntMPA 77, -75, -76, -78, -79, -80*
Henderson, Douglas *ForYSC, WhoHol A*
Henderson, Eddie 1940- *EncJzS 70*
Henderson, Edward Jackson 1940- *EncJzS 70*
Henderson, Elvira 1903- *WhThe*
Henderson, Fletcher d1952 *BgBands 74[port]*
Henderson, Fletcher 1897-1952 *AmSCAP 66, -80*
Henderson, Fletcher 1898-1952 *CmpEPM, DrBlPA, IlEncJ, MusMk, NewGrD 80*
Henderson, Florence 1934- *BiE&WWA, EncMT, HalFC 80, NotNAT, WhoHol A, WhoThe 72, -77*
Henderson, George *CreCan 2*
Henderson, George 1900- *NewOrJ*
Henderson, George A d1923 *WhScrn 74, -77, WhoHol B*
Henderson, Grace 1860-1944 *Film 1, NotNAT B, WhScrn 77, WhoHol B*
Henderson, Gwen 1908- *AmSCAP 66*
Henderson, Harry *BlksB&W C*
Henderson, Hazel Juanita 1929- *AmSCAP 80*
Henderson, Henrietta I *IntWWM 77*
Henderson, Horace 1904- *BiDAmM, CmpEPM, IlEncJ, WhoJazz 72*
Henderson, Horace W 1914- *AmSCAP 80*
Henderson, Ian H 1925- *IntWWM 77, -80*
Henderson, Ivo d1968 *WhScrn 77, WhoHol B*
Henderson, J Raymond 1929- *AmSCAP 66*
Henderson, Jack *Film 1*
Henderson, Jack d1957 *NotNAT B*
Henderson, Jack Douglas 1922- *WhoMus 72*
Henderson, James 1871-1951 *CreCan 2*
Henderson, James Fletcher 1897-1952 *BiDAmM*
Henderson, Joe 1937- *EncJzS 70, IlEncJ, RkOn*
Henderson, John 1747-1785 *EncWT, Ent, OxThe*
Henderson, John Raymond d1937 *NotNAT B*
Henderson, Joseph *Film 2*
Henderson, Joseph A 1937- *BiDAmM, EncJzS 70*
Henderson, Joseph Raymond 1929- *AmSCAP 80*
Henderson, Katherine 1909- *BluesWW[port]*
Henderson, Kenneth 1928- *ConAmC*
Henderson, Laura d1944 *NotNAT B*
Henderson, Leora Meoux 1890?-1958? *BlkWAB[port]*
Henderson, Lucius 1848-1947 *Film 2, NotNAT B, WhScrn 74, -77, WhoHol B*
Henderson, Luther 1919- *AmSCAP 66, -80, BiE&WWA, CmpEPM, DrBlPA, NotNAT*
Henderson, Lyle Cedric 1918- *BiDAmM*
Henderson, Marcia 1930- *HalFC 80*
Henderson, Marcia 1932- *FilmEn, ForYSC*
Henderson, Marcia 1934- *IntMPA 77, -75, -76, -78, -79, -80*
Henderson, Marcia 1950- *FilmgC*
Henderson, Marie d1902 *NotNAT B*
Henderson, May 1884- *WhThe*
Henderson, Michael 1951- *EncJzS 70*
Henderson, Nancy *NatPD[port]*
Henderson, Patrick 1949- *AmSCAP 80*
Henderson, Ray 1896- *AmPS*
Henderson, Ray 1896-1970 *AmSCAP 66, -80, Baker 78, BiE&WWA, CmpEPM, ConAmC, EncMT, HalFC 80, NewCBMT, NewGrD 80, NotNAT B, PopAmC[port], PopAmC SUP, Sw&Ld C, WhThe*
Henderson, Ray 1896-1971 *BiDAmM*
Henderson, Robert 1904- *WhoThe 72, -77*
Henderson, Robert Bolden 1910-1969 *EncJzS 70*
Henderson, Robert Morton 1926- *NotNAT*
Henderson, Rosa 1896-1968 *BluesWW[port], CmpEPM, WhoJazz 72*
Henderson, Rosamon 1894- *ConAmC*
Henderson, Roy Galbraith 1899- *CmOp, IntWWM 77, -80, NewGrD 80, WhoMus 72*
Henderson, Skitch 1918- *AmSCAP 66, -80, BgBands 74, CmpEPM, IntMPA 77, -75, -76, -78, -79, -80, IntWWM 77*
Henderson, Smack 1897-1952 *WhoJazz 72*
Henderson, Steffi d1967 *WhScrn 77*
Henderson, Talbot V 1879-1946 *WhScrn 74, -77, WhoHol B*
Henderson, Ted d1962 *WhoHol B*
Henderson, Tommy 1905?- *NewOrJ*
Henderson, Ty *DrBlPA*
Henderson, Wayne Maurice 1939- *BiDAmM, EncJzS 70*
Henderson, Wight 1913- *WhoMus 72*
Henderson, William James 1855-1937 *Baker 78, BiDAmM, NewGrD 80, OxMus*
Henderson, William Randall 1930- *BiDAmM, EncJzS 70*
Henderson, William Verdun 1917- *WhoMus 72*
Henderson-Bland, Robert d1941 *WhScrn 74, -77, WhoHol B*
Henderson-DeSylva-Brown *CmpEPM*
Hendl, Walter 1917- *Baker 78, BnBkM 80, ConAmC, IntWWM 80, NewGrD 80*
Hendler, Herb 1918- *AmSCAP 66, -80*
Hendrick, B Susan 1954- *IntWWM 77*
Hendrick, Richard *Film 2*
Hendricks, Barbara 1948- *BnBkM 80, WhoOp 76*
Hendricks, Ben *Film 1*
Hendricks, Ben, Jr. 1893-1938 *Film 2, WhScrn 74, -77, WhoHol B*
Hendricks, Ben, Sr. 1862-1930 *NotNAT B, WhScrn 74, -77, WhoHol B*
Hendricks, Bill L *IntMPA 77, -75, -76, -78, -79, -80*
Hendricks, Bobby 1938- *RkOn*
Hendricks, Cathy *WomWMM B*
Hendricks, Frederick Wilmoth 1901-1973 *AmSCAP 66, -80*
Hendricks, John Carl 1921- *BiDAmM, EncJzS 70*
Hendricks, Jon Carl 1921- *AmSCAP 66, -80, EncJzS 70, MorBAP*
Hendricks, Louis d1923 *Film 2, WhScrn 74, -77, WhoHol B*
Hendricks, Steve *PupTheA*
Hendricks, William L 1904- *AmSCAP 80*
Hendrickson, Al 1920- *CmpEPM*
Hendrickson, Alton Reynolds 1920- *BiDAmM*
Hendrickson, Paul Gunnar 1931- *CpmDNM 80*
Hendrie, Ernest 1859-1929 *NotNAT B, WhThe*
Hendrie, Gerald Mills 1935- *IntWWM 77, -80*
Hendrik Van Veldeke 1140?-1210? *NewGrD 80*
Hendrik Van Veldeken 1140?-1210? *NewGrD 80*
Hendriks, Francis Milton 1881-1969 *AmSCAP 80*
Hendriks, Francis Milton 1883- *AmSCAP 66, ConAmC*
Hendrikson, Anders 1896-1965 *WhScrn 77*
Hendrikx, Lode 1927- *WhoOp 76*
Hendrix, James Marshall 1942-1970 *BiDAmM, BluesWW[port]*
Hendrix, Jimi d1971 *ConMuA 80A[port]*
Hendrix, Jimi 1942-1970 *Baker 78, DrBlPA, IlEncR[port]*
Hendrix, Jimi 1947-1970 *WhScrn 77, WhoHol B*
Hendrix, Jimi, Experience *BiDAmM, RkOn 2[port]*
Hendrix, N E Shorty d1973 *WhScrn 77*
Hendrix, Richard 1958- *IntWWM 80*
Hendrix, Wanda 1928- *FilmEn, FilmgC, ForYSC, HalFC 80, HolP 40[port], IntMPA 77, -75, -76, -78, -79, -80, MotPP, MovMk[port], WhoHol A*
Hendry, Anita *Film 1*
Hendry, Gloria 1949- *DrBlPA, WhoHol A*
Hendry, Ian 1931- *FilmgC, HalFC 80, IlWWBF, IntMPA 77, -75, -76, -78, -79, -80, WhoHol A*
Hendry, Thomas 1929- *ConDr 73, -77, CreCan 2*
Heneker, David 1906- *EncMT, IntWWM 77, WhoThe 72, -77*
Heneker, David William 1906- *WhoMus 72*
Henestrosa, Luis Venegas De *NewGrD 80*
Hengeveld, Gerard 1910- *Baker 78*
Henie, Sonja d1969 *MotPP, WhoHol B*
Henie, Sonja 1910-1969 *FilmgC, HalFC 80, ThFT[port]*
Henie, Sonja 1912-1969 *CmpEPM, FilmEn, Film 2, OxFilm, WhScrn 74, -77*
Henie, Sonja 1913-1969 *CmMov, ForYSC, MovMk, What 1[port]*
Henigbaum, John 1922- *IntWWM 77*
Henigbaum, Nancy 1952- *AmSCAP 80*
Henignbaum, John 1922- *IntWWM 80*
Heninger, Robert E 1924- *ConAmC*
Henius, Carla 1919- *NewGrD 80*
Henke, Johann *NewGrD 80*
Henke, Mel 1915- *CmpEPM, WhoJazz 72*
Henkel *NewGrD 80*
Henkel, Georg Andreas 1805-1871 *NewGrD 80*
Henkel, George A 1903- *AmSCAP 66*
Henkel, Heinrich 1822-1899 *Baker 78, NewGrD 80*
Henkel, Michael 1780-1851 *Baker 78, NewGrD 80*
Henkemans, Hans 1913- *Baker 78, NewGrD 80, WhoMus 72*
Henken, Tabitha Jane 1928- *IntWWM 77*
Henkin, Daniel J *IntWWM 77, -80*
Henkin, Howard H 1926- *IntMPA 77, -75, -76, -78, -79, -80*
Henle *NewGrD 80*
Henle, Gunter 1899-1979 *IntWWM 77, NewGrD 80*
Henley, E J d1898 *NotNAT B*
Henley, Herbert James 1882-1937 *NotNAT B, WhThe*
Henley, Hobart 1886-1964 *TwYS A*
Henley, Hobart 1891-1964 *Film 1, WhScrn 74, -77, WhoHol B*
Henley, Joan 1904- *WhThe, WhoThe 72*
Henley, John Lee 1919- *BluesWW*

Henley, Rosina *Film 1*
Henley, William Ernest 1849-1903 *NotNAT B*
Henley James, R 1911- *WhoMus 72*
Henn, Randahl Woodruff 1953- *CpmDNM 80*
Henn, Richard A 1946- *AmSCAP 80, ConAmC*
Hennagin, Michael 1936- *AmSCAP 80, ConAmC*
Henneberg, Albert 1901- *Baker 78, NewGrD 80*
Henneberg, Fritz 1932- *IntWWM 77*
Henneberg, Johann Baptist 1768-1822 *Baker 78, NewGrD 80*
Henneberg, Richard 1853-1925 *Baker 78*
Henneberger, Barbara-Marie 1941-1964 *WhScrn 77*
Hennecke, Clarence R 1894-1969 *WhScrn 74, -77, WhoHol B*
Hennenberg, Fritz 1932- *IntWWM 80, NewGrD 80*
Hennequin, Alfred d1887 *NotNAT B*
Hennequin, Maurice d1926 *NotNAT B, WhThe*
Hennerberg, Carl Fredrik 1871-1932 *Baker 78*
Hennes, Aloys 1827-1889 *Baker 78*
Hennessey, David 1852-1926 *WhScrn 74, -77*
Hennessey, Frank Charles 1894-1941 *CreCan 1*
Hennessey, Johnny *Film 2*
Hennessey, Sharon *WomWMM B*
Hennessy, Christine 1936- *CnOxB, DancEn 78*
Hennessy, Roland Burke 1870-1939 *NotNAT B, WhThe*
Hennessy, Swan 1866-1929 *Baker 78*
Hennesey, Dale *WhoHrs 80*
Hennig, Carl 1819-1873 *Baker 78*
Hennig, Carl Rafael 1845-1914 *Baker 78*
Hennig, Dennis John 1951- *IntWWM 80*
Hennig, Rudolph 1850-1904 *BiDAmM*
Henniger, Rolf 1925- *WhThe*
Henning, Carl Wilhelm 1784-1867 *NewGrD 80*
Henning, Cosmo Grenville 1932- *IntWWM 77, -80*
Henning, Douglas *MagIlD*
Henning, Ervin Arthur 1910- *Baker 78, ConAmC*
Henning, Eva 1920- *FilmEn*
Henning, Frances *PupTheA*
Henning, Linda Kay 1944- *IntMPA 75, -76, -78, -79, -80*
Henning, Linda Kaye 1944- *IntMPA 77, WhoHol A*
Henning, Pat 1911-1973 *WhScrn 77, WhoHol B*
Henning, Paul 1911- *IntMPA 77, -75, -76, -78, -79, -80, NewYTET*
Henning, Roslyn Brogue 1919- *ConAmC, IntWWM 77, -80*
Henning, Uno *Film 2*
Henning-Jensen, Astrid 1914- *DcFM, FilmEn, HalFC 80, WomWMM, WorEFlm*
Henning-Jensen, Bjarne 1908- *DcFM, FilmEn, WorEFlm*
Henninger, George R 1895-1953 *AmSCAP 66, -80*
Henninger, Jacqueline Pates 1946- *IntWWM 80*
Hennings, Betty 1850-1939 *NotNAT B, WhThe*
Hennings, John d1933 *WhScrn 74, -77, WhoHol B*
Hennio, Aegidio *NewGrD 80*
Hennius, Aegidius *NewGrD 80*
Hennock, Frieda B d1960 *NewYTET*
Henny, Jeanne Katherine 1952- *IntWWM 80*
Henreid, Monika *WhoHol A*
Henreid, Paul *IntMPA 75, -76, MotPP*
Henreid, Paul 1907- *CmMov, FilmgC, HalFC 80*
Henreid, Paul 1908- *BiDFilm, -81, FilmEn, ForYSC, IntMPA 77, -78, -79, -80, MovMk[port], OxFilm, WhoHol A, WorEFlm*
Henrey, Bobby 1939- *FilmgC, HalFC 80, IlWWBF A, WhoHol A*
Henri III, Duke Of Brabant 1231-1261 *NewGrD 80*
Henri, Louie d1947 *NotNAT B*
Henrici, Christian Friedrich 1700-1764 *NewGrD 80*
Henrickson, Richard 1948- *NatPD[port]*
Henricus *NewGrD 80*
Henricus De Zeelandia *NewGrD 80*
Henricus Helayne *NewGrD 80*
Henricus Helene *NewGrD 80*
Henricus Hessman De Argentorato *NewGrD 80*
Henricus Of Augsburg 1000?-1083 *NewGrD 80*
Henricus Organista *NewGrD 80*
Henricus, Nikolaus 1575?-1654 *NewGrD 80*
Henriksen, Elvi 1916- *IntWWM 80*
Henrikson, Anders 1896-1965 *FilmEn*
Henrion, Paul 1819-1901 *NewGrD 80*
Henriot, Nicole 1925- *Baker 78*
Henriques, Fini Valdemar 1867-1940 *Baker 78, NewGrD 80*
Henriques, Madeline d1929 *NotNAT B*
Henriques, Robert 1858-1914 *Baker 78*
Henritze, Bette *NotNAT, WhoHol A, WhoThe 77*
Henrotte, Gayle Allen 1935- *IntWWM 77, -80*
Henry *PupTheA*
Henry I 1068-1135 *OxMus*
Henry III 1207-1272 *OxMus*
Henry IV *OxMus*
Henry V 1387-1422 *Baker 78*
Henry V 1388-1422 *OxMus*
Henry VI 1421-1471 *Baker 78, OxMus*
Henry VII 1456-1509 *OxMus*
Henry VIII 1491-1547 *Baker 78, MusMk[port], NewGrD 80[port], OxMus*
Henry Of Meissen *OxMus*
Henry, Alexander Victor 1943- *WhThe*
Henry, Ben 1902- *IntMPA 75*
Henry, Bill *WhoHol A*
Henry, Bob *NewYTET*
Henry, Buck 1930- *ConDr 73, -77A, FilmEn, FilmgC, HalFC 80, IntMPA 77, -75, -76, -78, -79, -80, WhoHol A*
Henry, Carol M 1928- *AmSCAP 80*
Henry, Charles 1885-1960 *NewOrJ[port]*
Henry, Charles 1890-1968 *NotNAT B, WhThe*
Henry, Charlotte 1913- *ForYSC, WhoHol A*
Henry, Charlotte 1913-1980 *FilmEn*
Henry, Charlotte 1914- *ThFT[port]*
Henry, Charlotte 1916- *FilmgC, HalFC 80*
Henry, Charlotte 1916-1980 *WhoHrs 80[port]*
Henry, Chevon C 1953- *AmSCAP 80*
Henry, Clarence Frogman 1937- *RkOn*
Henry, Creagh d1946 *NotNAT B*
Henry, E William *NewYTET*
Henry, Ernie 1926-1958 *IlEncJ*
Henry, Francis 1905-1953 *AmSCAP 66, -80*
Henry, Frank Thomas Patrick 1894-1963 *WhScrn 74, -77*
Henry, Fred *IntMPA 77, -75, -76, -78, -79, -80*
Henry, Gale 1893- *Film 1, -2, TwYS, WomWMM*
Henry, George H 1903- *BiE&WWA, NotNAT*
Henry, Gloria 1923- *ForYSC, WhoHol A*
Henry, Hank *WhoHol A*
Henry, Harold 1884-1956 *Baker 78, ConAmC*
Henry, Haywood 1909- *WhoJazz 72*
Henry, Hugh Thomas 1862-1946 *Baker 78*
Henry, James Donald 1933- *IntWWM 77, -80*
Henry, Jay 1910-1951 *WhScrn 74, -77, WhoHol B*
Henry, Jean-Claude 1934- *IntWWM 80*
Henry, Jeff 1922- *CreCan 2*
Henry, Jehan 1560-1635 *NewGrD 80*
Henry, John 1738-1794 *NotNAT B, OxThe, PlP&P*
Henry, John 1882-1958 *WhScrn 74, -77, WhoHol B*
Henry, John, Jr. d1974 *Film 2, WhScrn 77*
Henry, Joseph 1823-1870 *NewGrD 80*
Henry, Joseph 1930- *ConAmC*
Henry, Leigh Vaughan 1889-1958 *Baker 78*
Henry, Leonard *IlWWBF A*
Henry, Louis-Xavier-Stanislas 1784-1836 *CnOxB*
Henry, Louise *ForYSC*
Henry, Maria *PlP&P*
Henry, Martha 1938- *NotNAT*
Henry, Martha 1939- *CreCan 1*
Henry, Martin 1872-1942 *NotNAT B, WhThe*
Henry, Michael Earl 1942- *AmSCAP 80*
Henry, Michel 1555- *Baker 78, NewGrD 80*
Henry, Mike 1936- *ForYSC*
Henry, Mike 1937- *WhoHrs 80*
Henry, Mike 1939- *FilmgC, HalFC 80, WhoHol A*
Henry, O 1862-1910 *FilmgC, HalFC 80*
Henry, Oscar 1888- *NewOrJ[port]*
Henry, Otto W 1933- *ConAmC*
Henry, Patrick, II 1935- *BiE&WWA*
Henry, Pierre 1927- *Baker 78, CnOxB, DcCM, NewGrD 80*
Henry, Robert Buzz 1931-1971 *WhScrn 77, WhoHol B*
Henry, S R *AmSCAP 80*
Henry, Son *NewOrJ[port]*
Henry, Tal *CmpEPM*
Henry, Thomas B *WhoHrs 80[port]*
Henry, Tom Brown *ForYSC*
Henry, Trigger Sam 1875?- *NewOrJ*
Henry, Victor 1943- *WhoThe 72*
Henry, Will *AmSCAP 80*
Henry, William 1918- *FilmEn, Film 2, FilmgC, ForYSC, HalFC 80, Vers A[port]*
Henry Aldrich *What 3[port]*
Henry Cow *IlEncR*
Hens, Charles Ferdinand 1898- *WhoMus 72*
Hensby, Geoffrey Christopher 1910- *WhoMus 72*
Henschel, Georg 1850-1934 *NewGrD 80*
Henschel, Sir George 1850-1934 *Baker 78, BnBkM 80, NewGrD 80, OxMus*
Henschel, Lilian *NewGrD 80*
Henschel, Lillian Bailey 1860-1901 *BiDAmM*
Henschel, Lillian June 1860-1901 *Baker 78*
Henschen, Dorothy Adele Dregalla 1921- *IntWWM 77, -80*
Hense, Marie 1937- *BlkWAB*
Hensel, Fanny Cacilia 1805-1847 *Baker 78, NewGrD 80*
Hensel, Heinrich 1874-1935 *Baker 78, NewGrD 80*
Hensel, Octavia 1837-1897 *Baker 78*
Hensel, Richard 1926- *ConAmC*
Hensel, Sophie Friederike 1738-1789 *NotNAT B, OxThe*
Hensel, Walther 1887-1956 *Baker 78*
Henselt, Adolf Von 1814-1889 *BnBkM 80, MusMk, NewGrD 80, OxMus*
Henselt, Adolph Von 1814-1889 *Baker 78, NewGrD 80*
Hensen, Herwig 1917- *CnMD, ModWD*
Henshaw, James Ene 1924- *ConDr 73, -77, MorBAP, REnWD[port]*
Hensler, Elsie 1836-1929 *BiDAmM*
Hensley, Harold Glenn 1922- *AmSCAP 80, BiDAmM*
Hensley, William Paden 1909- *BluesWW[port]*
Henslowe, Philip 1550?-1616 *CnThe, EncWT, Ent, NotNAT A, -B, OxThe, PlP&P*
Henson, Gladys 1897- *FilmgC, HalFC 80, WhoHol A, WhoThe 72, -77*
Henson, Herbert Lester 1925- *BiDAmM*
Henson, James Maury 1936- *AmSCAP 80*
Henson, Jim 1936- *IntMPA 80, NewYTET*
Henson, Joan *WomWMM*
Henson, Leslie 1891-1957 *EncMT, FilmgC, HalFC 80, IlWWBF, -A, NotNAT B, OxThe, WhScrn 74, -77, WhThe, WhoHol B*
Henson, Leslie 1891-1958 *Film 1, -2*
Henson, Nicky 1945- *HalFC 80, WhoThe 72, -77*
Henson, Norris Christy 1918- *AmSCAP 66, -80*
Henson, Robert 1934- *AmSCAP 66*
Henstridge, Daniel 1646?-1736 *NewGrD 80*
Hentke-Mueller, Paula *WhoMus 72*
Hentschel, Carl d1930 *NotNAT B*
Hentschel, Ernst Julius 1804-1875 *Baker 78*
Hentschel, Franz 1814-1889 *Baker 78*
Hentschel, Irene 1891- *WhThe*
Hentschel, Theodor 1830-1892 *Baker 78*
Henville, Sandra Lee *WhoHol A*
Henze, Hans Werner 1925- *WhoOp 76*
Henze, Hans Werner 1926- *Baker 78, BnBkM 80, CmOp, CompSN[port], CnOxB, DancEn 78, DcCom 77, DcCom&M 79, DcCM, IntWWM 77, -80, MusMk[port], NewEOp 71, NewGrD 80[port], OxMus, WhoMus 72*
Henze, Russell Smith 1939- *IntWWM 77*
Hepburn, Audrey 1929- *BiDFilm, -81, BiE&WWA, FilmEn, FilmgC, ForYSC, HalFC 80, IntMPA 77, -75, -76, -78, -79,*

-80, *MotPP, MovMk[port], NotNAT, OxFilm, WhoHol A, WorEFlm*
Hepburn, Barton 1906-1955 *Film 2, WhScrn 74, -77, WhoHol B*
Hepburn, David 1924- *DrBlPA*
Hepburn, Katharine *MotPP, PlP&P[port], WomWMM*
Hepburn, Katharine 1907- *FilmEn, FilmgC, HalFC 80, MGM[port], ThFT[port], WhoHol A*
Hepburn, Katharine 1909- *BiDFilm, -81, BiE&WWA, CmMov, EncMT, EncWT, Ent, FamA&A[port], ForYSC, IntMPA 77, -75, -76, -78, -79, -80, MovMk[port], NotNAT, -A, OxFilm, WhoThe 72, -77*
Hepburn, Katherine 1909- *CnThe, WorEFlm*
Hepburn, Philip 1941?- *DrBlPA*
Heppener, Robert 1925- *Baker 78, NewGrD 80*
Hepple, Jeanne 1936- *WhoThe 72, -77*
Hepple, Peter 1927- *WhoThe 77*
Heppner, Rosa *WhoThe 72, -77*
Heppner, Sam 1913- *WhoMus 72*
Heptinstall, John *NewGrD 80*
Hepworth, Alfred *WhoMus 72*
Hepworth, Baby *Film 1*
Hepworth, Cecil 1874-1953 *FilmEn*
Hepworth, Mrs. Cecil *Film 1*
Hepworth, Cecil Milton 1874-1953 *DcFM, Film 1, FilmgC, HalFC 80, IlWWBF, -A, OxFilm, WhScrn 77, WorEFlm*
Herald, Douglas *Film 2*
Herald, Heinz d1964 *NotNAT B*
Herald, John *EncFCWM 69*
Herald, Peter 1920- *IntMPA 77, -75, -76, -78, -79, -80*
Heraud, John A 1799-1887 *NotNAT A, -B*
Herbage, Julian 1904-1976 *NewGrD 80, WhoMus 72*
Herbain, Chevalier D' 1730?-1769 *NewGrD 80*
Herbart, Johann Friedrich 1776-1841 *Baker 78, NewGrD 80*
Herbe, Michele 1940- *WhoOp 76*
Herbeck, Johann Von 1831-1877 *Baker 78, NewGrD 80*
Herbeck, Ray 1915?- *BgBands 74, CmpEPM*
Herberigs, Robert 1886-1974 *Baker 78, NewGrD 80, WhoMus 72*
Herbert, A J *Film 2*
Herbert, A P 1870-1971 *EncMT*
Herbert, Sir Alan Patrick 1890-1971 *Ent, WhThe, WhoThe 72*
Herbert, Arthur 1907- *WhoJazz 72*
Herbert, Diana *WhoHol A*
Herbert, Don *BiE&WWA, NewYTET, NotNAT*
Herbert, Doris 1938- *WhoOp 76*
Herbert, Edward 1583-1648 *NewGrD 80*
Herbert, Evelyn 1898- *AmPS B, CmpEPM, EncMT, WhThe*
Herbert, F Hugh 1897-1957 *FilmgC, HalFC 80*
Herbert, F Hugh 1897-1958 *FilmEn, McGEWD, NotNAT B, WhThe*
Herbert, Frederick 1909-1966 *AmSCAP 80*
Herbert, George 1593-1633 *NewGrD 80*
Herbert, Gregory Delano 1947- *EncJzS 70*
Herbert, Gwynne *Film 1, -2*
Herbert, Hans 1875-1957 *WhScrn 74, -77, WhoHol B*
Herbert, Helen 1873-1946 *WhScrn 74, -77*
Herbert, Henry 1879-1947 *NotNAT B, WhThe, WhoHol B*
Herbert, Sir Henry 1596-1673 *NotNAT B, OxThe*
Herbert, Henry J 1879-1942 *Film 1, -2*
Herbert, Henry J 1879-1947 *WhScrn 74, -77*
Herbert, Herbie *AmSCAP 80*
Herbert, Heyes *MotPP*
Herbert, Holmes 1882-1953 *WhoHrs 80*
Herbert, Holmes 1882-1956 *Film 1, -2, FilmgC, ForYSC, HalFC 80, HolCA[port], IntMPA 77, -75, -76, -78, -79, -80, MotPP, MovMk, NotNAT B, TwYS, WhScrn 74, -77, WhoHol B*
Herbert, Holmes 1883-1956 *FilmEn*
Herbert, Hugh 1887-1951 *Film 2, MovMk[port]*
Herbert, Hugh 1887-1952 *FilmEn, FilmgC, ForYSC, HalFC 80, HolCA[port], MotPP, NotNAT B, Vers A[port], WhScrn 74, -77, WhoHol B, WhoHrs 80*
Herbert, Ian 1930- *WhoMus 72*
Herbert, Jack *Film 1, -2*
Herbert, James Wesley 1939- *IntWWM 80*
Herbert, Jean 1905- *AmSCAP 66, -80*
Herbert, Jocelyn 1917- *EncWT, WhoThe 72, -77*
Herbert, Jocelyn 1927- *NotNAT*
Herbert, Joe *Film 2*
Herbert, John 1926- *ConDr 73, -77*
Herbert, Joseph d1923 *NotNAT B*
Herbert, Lew 1903-1968 *WhScrn 74, -77, WhoHol B*
Herbert, Louisa d1921 *NotNAT B*
Herbert, Nuala 1935- *IntWWM 77, -80*
Herbert, Percy 1925- *FilmgC, HalFC 80, WhoHol A*
Herbert, Pitt *WhoHol A*
Herbert, Ralph 1909- *WhoOp 76*
Herbert, Sidney *Film 2*
Herbert, Thomas F 1888-1946 *WhScrn 74, -77*
Herbert, Tom d1946 *WhoHol B*
Herbert, Victor 1859-1924 *AmPS, AmSCAP 66, -80, Baker 78, BestMus, BiDAmM, BnBkM 80, CmOp, CmpEPM, EncMT, HalFC 80, McGEWD, MusMk, NewCBMT, NewEOp 71, NewGrD 80, NotNAT B, OxMus, PlP&P[port], PopAmC[port], Sw&Ld B, WhThe, WhoStg 1906, -1908*
Herbert, Walter 1902- *WhoOp 76*
Herbert, Zbigniew 1924- *ModWD*
Herbert-Caesari, Edgar Felix 1884- *WhoMus 72*
Herbert-Smith, Cynthia Mostyn 1904- *WhoMus 72*
Herbertt, Stanley 1919- *CnOxB, DancEn 78, PupTheA*
Herbig, Gunther 1931- *IntWWM 77, -80, NewGrD 80*
Herbig, Luce 1938- *WhoMus 72*
Herbing, August Bernhard Valentin 1735-1766 *NewGrD 80*
Herbolzheimer, Peter Alexander 1935- *IntWWM 77*
Herbsleb, Catherine 1941- *AmSCAP 80*
Herbst, Haring *Film 2*
Herbst, Johann Andreas 1588-1666 *NewGrD 80[port]*
Herbst, Johannes 1734-1812 *BiDAmM*
Herbst, Johannes 1735-1812 *Baker 78, NewGrD 80*
Herbstritt, Larry W 1950- *AmSCAP 80*
Herbuveaux, Jules 1897- *IntMPA 77, -75, -76, -78, -79, -80, NewYTET*
Hercenstein, Matteo *NewGrD 80*
Hercigonja, Nikola 1911- *Baker 78, NewGrD 80*
Herczeg, Ferenc 1863-1950 *NotNAT B*
Herczeg, Ferenc 1863-1954 *OxThe*
Herczeg, Geza d1954 *NotNAT B*
Herczog, Istvan 1943- *CnOxB*
Herd, The *BiDAmM*
Herd, Dick *WhoHol A*
Herder, Johann Gottfried 1744-1803 *NewGrD 80*
Herder, Ronald 1930- *ConAmC*
Herder, W Ed 1931- *IntMPA 79, -80*
Herdman, John *Film 2*
Heredi, Francesco *NewGrD 80*
Heredia, Pedro d1648 *NewGrD 80*
Heredia, Rene Cortes 1939- *AmSCAP 80*
Heredia, Sebastian Aguilera De *NewGrD 80*
Hereford-Lambert, Johnny *AmSCAP 66*
Heremans, Jean *CmMov*
Heremita, Giulio *NewGrD 80*
Herendeen, Fred 1893-1962 *NotNAT B*
Herendeen, Frederick 1893-1962 *AmSCAP 66*
Herfel, Chris 1927- *IntMPA 77, -75, -76, -78, -79, -80*
Herford, Beatrice d1952 *NotNAT B*
Herfurt, Skeets 1911- *CmpEPM, WhoJazz 72*
Herfurth, C Paul 1893- *ConAmC*
Herger *NewGrD 80*
Herget, Bob 1924- *BiE&WWA, NotNAT*
Hergot, Hans d1527 *NewGrD 80*
Hergot, Kunegunde d1547 *NewGrD 80*
Hergotin, Kunegunde d1547 *NewGrD 80*
Heriat, Philippe 1898-1971 *Film 2, WhScrn 77*
Heriban, Josef 1922- *WhoOp 76*
Heribell, Renee *Film 2*
Herier, Thomas *NewGrD 80*
Heriger *NewGrD 80*
Herigerus d1007 *NewGrD 80*
Herincx, Raimund 1927- *NewGrD 80, WhoMus 72*
Herincx, Raymond 1927- *CmOp, NewGrD 80*
Hering, Doris 1920- *BiE&WWA, CnOxB, DancEn 78, NotNAT*
Hering, Gerhard 1908- *EncWT*
Hering, Karl 1819-1889 *Baker 78*
Hering, Karl Gottlieb 1765-1853 *Baker 78*
Hering, Karl-Josef *WhoOp 76*
Herissant, Jean *NewGrD 80*
Herissant, Jehan *NewGrD 80*
Heritage, Richard Abraham 1852-1929 *BiDAmM*
Heritte-Viardot, Louise-Pauline-Marie 1841-1918 *Baker 78*
Herlea, Nicolae 1927- *NewGrD 80, WhoOp 76*
Herlein, Lillian 1895?-1971 *WhScrn 74, -77, WhoHol B*
Herlicius, Elias *NewGrD 80*
Herlie, Eileen *WhoHol A*
Herlie, Eileen 1919- *FilmgC, ForYSC, HalFC 80, MovMk*
Herlie, Eileen 1920- *Ent, FilmEn, NotNAT, WhoThe 72, -77*
Herlie, Eileen 1922- *BiE&WWA*
Herlihy, Ed *IntMPA 77, -75, -76*
Herlihy, James Leo 1927- *BiE&WWA, ConDr 73, -77, NotNAT*
Herlinger, Carl *Film 2*
Herlinger, Jan *ConAmC*
Herlischka, Bohumil 1919- *WhoOp 76*
Herlth, Robert 1893-1962 *DcFM, FilmEn*
Herman Elias *NewGrD 80*
Herman The Monk Of Salzburg *NewGrD 80*
Herman, Al 1886-1967 *WhScrn 77, WhoHol B*
Herman, George *ConAmTC*
Herman, Gerald 1933- *NewGrD 80*
Herman, Helena *Film 2*
Herman, Henry d1894 *NotNAT B*
Herman, Jerry *AmSCAP 66, NotNAT, PlP&P*
Herman, Jerry 1932- *AmPS, EncMT, HalFC 80*
Herman, Jerry 1933- *AmSCAP 80, Baker 78, BestMus, BiDAmM, BiE&WWA, ConAmC, NewCBMT, NewGrD 80, PopAmC SUP[port], WhoThe 77*
Herman, Jill Kraft 1931-1970 *WhScrn 74, -77*
Herman, John *BiE&WWA*
Herman, Leonard Wood 1913- *IntMPA 77, -75, -76, -78, -79, -80*
Herman, Lewis 1905- *BiE&WWA*
Herman, Marguerite S 1914- *BiE&WWA*
Herman, Milton C 1896-1951 *WhScrn 74, -77*
Herman, Nicolaus 1500-1561 *NewGrD 80*
Herman, Niklas 1500-1561 *NewGrD 80*
Herman, Norman *IntMPA 77, -75, -76, -78, -79, -80*
Herman, Patricia Elizabeth 1927- *WhoMus 72*
Herman, Pinky 1905- *AmSCAP 66, -80, IntMPA 77, -75, -76, -78, -79, -80*
Herman, Reinhold 1849-1920? *Baker 78*
Herman, Robert 1925- *WhoOp 76*
Herman, Samuel 1891- *AmSCAP 66*
Herman, Selma *WhoStg 1908*
Herman, Thomas 1947- *ConAmC*
Herman, Tom 1909-1972 *WhScrn 77*
Herman, Tommy d1972 *WhoHol B*
Herman, Vasile 1929- *Baker 78, IntWWM 80, NewGrD 80*
Herman, Wanda *WomWMM B*
Herman, Witold Walenty 1932- *IntWWM 77, -80*
Herman, Woodrow Charles 1913- *BiDAmM, EncJzS 70, NewGrD 80*
Herman, Woodrow Wilson 1913- *AmSCAP 66, -80*
Herman, Woody 1913- *AmPS A, -B, Baker 78, BgBands 74[port], CmpEPM, EncJzS 70, IlEncJ, IntWWM 77, MusMk[port], NewGrD 80, WhoHol A, WhoJazz 72, WhoMus 72*

Hermann Der Lahme 1013-1054 *NewGrD 80*
Hermann Von Reichenau 1013-1054 *NewGrD 80*
Hermann, David 1876-1930 *NotNAT B, OxThe*
Hermann, Eduard 1850-1937 *Baker 78*
Hermann, Evelyn L 1923- *IntWWM 77*
Hermann, Hans 1870-1931 *Baker 78*
Hermann, Ralph J 1914- *AmSCAP 66, -80*
Hermann, Robert 1869-1912 *Baker 78*
Hermann, Roland 1936- *WhoOp 76*
Hermanns, Alfred 1919- *IntWWM 80*
Hermannus Contractus 1013-1054 *Baker 78, MusMk, NewGrD 80*
Hermannus De Atrio *NewGrD 80*
Hermans, Guglielmo 1601-1683 *NewGrD 80*
Hermans, Nico 1919- *IntWWM 77, -80*
Hermans, Willem 1601-1683 *NewGrD 80*
Herman's Hermits *ConMuA 80A, RkOn 2[port]*
Hermanson, Ake 1923- *Baker 78, IntWWM 77, -80, NewGrD 80*
Hermant, Abel 1862-1950 *NotNAT B, WhThe*
Hermelink, Siegfried 1914-1975 *NewGrD 80*
Hermes, Alice *BiE&WWA*
Hermesdorff, Michael 1833-1885 *Baker 78*
Hermine, Hilda d1975 *WhScrn 77, WhoHol C*
Hermitte, Alfredo *PupTheA*
Hermstedt, Johann Simon 1778-1846 *Baker 78*
Hermstedt, Simon 1778-1846 *NewGrD 80*
Hern, Pepe *WhoHol A*
Hernadi, Lajos 1906- *IntWWM 77, -80*
Hernandez, Albert 1899-1948 *WhScrn 74, -77*
Hernandez, Alejandro Rene 1916- *AmSCAP 66*
Hernandez, Amalia *CnOxB, DancEn 78*
Hernandez, Anna 1867-1945 *Film 2, WhScrn 77*
Hernandez, Antonio Acevedo Y *OxThe*
Hernandez, George F 1863-1922 *Film 1, -2, WhScrn 77*
Hernandez, Hermilio 1931- *Baker 78*
Hernandez, Juan De 1881-1945 *NewGrD 80*
Hernandez, Juan G Juano 1896-1970 *WhScrn 74, -77*
Hernandez, Juano d1970 *MotPP, WhoHol B*
Hernandez, Juano 1896-1970 *BlksB&W, -C, DrBlPA, FilmEn*
Hernandez, Juano 1898?- *ForYSC*
Hernandez, Juano 1898-1970 *Vers A[port]*
Hernandez, Juano 1900-1968 *HalFC 80*
Hernandez, Juano 1900-1970 *FilmgC, MovMk*
Hernandez, Jusepe *PupTheA*
Hernandez, Pablo 1834-1910 *Baker 78*
Hernandez Gonzalo, Gisela 1912-1971 *DcCM, NewGrD 80*
Hernandez-Lopez, Rhazes 1918- *Baker 78*
Hernandez Moncada, Eduardo 1899- *Baker 78, NewGrD 80*
Hernandez Salces, Pablo 1834-1910 *NewGrD 80*
Hernando, Rafael Jose Maria 1822-1888 *Baker 78, NewGrD 80*
Herndon, Agnes d1920 *NotNAT B*
Herndon, Anita *Film 1*
Herndon, Richard Gilbert d1958 *NotNAT B, WhThe*
Herndon, Thomas 1937- *WhoOp 76*
Herndon, Venable 1927- *NatPD[port]*
Herne, Chrystal 1883-1950 *NotNAT B, WhThe, WhoStg 1906, -1908*
Herne, Huxley *CreCan 1*
Herne, James A 1839-1901 *CnThe, FamA&A[port], McGEWD[port], ModWD, NotNAT B, OxThe, PlP&P, REnWD[port]*
Herne, Julie 1881-1955 *NotNAT B, WhoStg 1908*
Herne, Katherine Corcoran 1857-1943 *NotNAT B, PlP&P*
Hernon, Nan *WomWMM*
Hernried, Robert 1883-1951 *Baker 78, ConAmC, NewGrD 80*
Hero Of Alexandria *NewGrD 80*
Herod, Henry Newton 1915- *IntWWM 77*
Herodas 300?BC-250BC *OxThe*
Herold, Douglas *Film 2*
Herold, Ferdinand 1791-1833 *CmOp, GrComp[port], MusMk, NewGrD 80[port]*
Herold, Helmuth 1928- *IntWWM 77*
Herold, Johannes 1550?-1603 *NewGrD 80*
Herold, Louis Joseph Ferdinand 1791-1833 *Baker 78, BnBkM 80, CnOxB, NewEOp 71, OxMus*
Herold, Vilhelm Kristoffer 1865-1937 *NewGrD 80*
Heroldt, Johannes 1550?-1603 *NewGrD 80*
Heron, Agnes Henrietta 1918- *IntWWM 77*
Heron, Bijou d1937 *NotNAT B*
Heron, Dalziel d1911 *NotNAT B*
Heron, Joyce 1916- *WhoHol A, WhoThe 72, -77*
Heron, Matilda Agnes 1830-1877 *EncWT, Ent, FamA&A[port], NotNAT B, OxThe*
Heron-Allen, Edward 1861-1943 *Baker 78, OxMus*
Heros, Eugene *WhThe*
Heroux, Franz 1760-1814? *NewGrD 80*
Herpol, Homer 1520?-1574? *NewGrD 80*
Herpol, Homerus 1520?-1574? *NewGrD 80*
Herpolitanus, Homer 1520?-1574? *NewGrD 80*
Herpoll, Homer 1520?-1574? *NewGrD 80*
Herr, Joyce Elaine Dissinger 1933- *IntWWM 77, -80*
Herr, Melvin 1916- *BiE&WWA, NotNAT*
Herrand, Marcel 1897-1953 *EncWT*
Herrando, Jose 1700?-1765? *NewGrD 80*
Herrando, Joseph 1700?-1765? *NewGrD 80*
Herraud, Marcel d1953 *NotNAT B*
Herren, Eric Albert Richard 1916- *IntMPA 75, -76*
Herren, Lloyd K 1922- *IntWWM 77, -80*
Herren, Roger *WhoHol A*
Herrer, Michael 1550?-1609? *NewGrD 80*
Herrera, Ernesto 1886-1917 *ModWD*
Herrera, Ernesto 1887-1917 *OxThe*
Herrera, Humberto Angel 1900- *AmSCAP 66, -80*
Herrera, Juan De 1665?-1738? *NewGrD 80*
Herrera, Martin Gomez De *NewGrD 80*
Herrera, Rufo 1933- *IntWWM 77, -80*
Herrera, Tomas De *NewGrD 80*
Herrera DeLaFuente, Luis 1916- *Baker 78*
Herrerius, Michael *NewGrD 80*
Herrgott, Hans *NewGrD 80*
Herrgott, Kunegunde d1547 *NewGrD 80*
Herrick, Abbie *WomWMM B*
Herrick, Christopher 1942- *IntWWM 77, -80*
Herrick, Jack *Film 2*
Herrick, Joe *Film 2*
Herrick, Joseph d1807 *BiDAmM*
Herrick, Lynn 1936- *AmSCAP 80*
Herrick, Margaret *IntMPA 77, -75, -76, -78*
Herrick, Paul Young 1910-1958 *AmSCAP 66, -80*
Herrick, Robert 1591-1674 *OxMus*
Herridge, Frances *BiE&WWA, ConAmTC, NotNAT*
Herring, Aggie d1938 *Film 1, -2, ForYSC, TwYS, WhoHol B*
Herring, Fanny d1906 *NotNAT B*
Herring, Jess *Film 2*
Herring, John *AmSCAP 66, -80*
Herring, Sandra Kay 1951- *IntWWM 77*
Herrington, Henry *OxMus*
Herriot, Edouard 1872-1957 *Baker 78*
Herrman, Bernard 1911- *FilmgC*
Herrman, Daniel W, Jr. 1910- *AmSCAP 66, -80*
Herrmann, Alexander 1843-1896 *Ent, MagIlD[port]*
Herrmann, Bernard 1911-1975 *Baker 78, BiDAmM, CmMov, CmpEPM, ConAmC, DcFM, FilmEn, HalFC 80, IntMPA 75, -76, IntWWM 77, MusMk[port], NewGrD 80, OxFilm, OxMus, WhoHrs 80, WhoMus 72, WorEFlm*
Herrmann, Gottfried 1808-1878 *NewGrD 80*
Herrmann, Hugo 1896-1967 *Baker 78, DcCM, NewGrD 80*
Herrmann, Jakob Zeugheer *NewGrD 80*
Herrmann, Klaus 1903- *CnMD*
Herrmann, Ronald Lee 1947- *AmSCAP 80*
Herrnfeld, Anton 1865-1929 *WhScrn 74, -77*
Herron, Joel 1916- *AmSCAP 66, -80*
Herrschaft, William *PupTheA, PupTheA SUP*
Herschel, Caroline *OxMus*
Herschel, Frederick William 1738-1822 *OxMus*
Herschel, Friedrich Wilhelm 1738-1822 *Baker 78, NewGrD 80[port]*
Herschel, Jacob *OxMus*
Herschel, Sir William 1738-1822 *MusMk[port], NewGrD 80[port]*
Herschensohn, Bruce 1932- *IntMPA 77, -75, -76, -78, -79*
Herscher, Lou 1894-1974 *AmSCAP 80*
Herscher, Louis 1894- *AmSCAP 66*
Herscher, Sylvia 1913- *BiE&WWA, NotNAT*
Herschmann, Heinz 1924- *IntWWM 77, -80, WhoMus 72*
Herscovici, Philipp *NewGrD 80*
Hersee, Rose 1845-1924 *NewGrD 80*
Herseth, Adolph 1921- *NewGrD 80*
Hersey, David 1939- *WhoThe 77*
Hersey, Elizabeth Kelton Smith 1901- *IntWWM 77*
Hersh, Arthur B 1900- *AmSCAP 66, -80*
Hersh, Evelyn S 1911- *AmSCAP 66, -80*
Hershey, Barbara *HalFC 80, IntMPA 75, -76, -78, -79, -80*
Hershey, Barbara 1947- *ForYSC*
Hershey, Barbara 1948- *FilmEn, FilmgC, IntMPA 77, WhoHol A*
Hershey, Burnet 1896-1971 *BiE&WWA, NotNAT B*
Hershfield, Harry 1885-1974 *Film 2, WhScrn 77*
Hershfield, Harry 1886-1974 *JoeFr*
Hersholt, Jean 1886-1956 *FilmEn, Film 1, -2, FilmgC, HalFC 80[port], HolCA[port], MGM[port], MotPP, MovMk[port], NotNAT B, TwYS, WhScrn 74, -77, WhoHol B, WorEFlm*
Hersholt, Jean 1887-1956 *ForYSC*
Hersin, Andre-Philippe 1934- *CnOxB*
Hersko, Janos 1926- *FilmEn, OxFilm*
Herskovitz, Arthur M 1920- *IntMPA 77, -75, -76, -78, -79, -80*
Hersom, Frank E 1894-1941 *AmSCAP 66, -80*
Herst, Jerome P 1909- *AmSCAP 80*
Herst, Jerry 1909- *AmSCAP 66*
Herstein, Peter *ConAmC*
Hert *NewGrD 80*
Hertel *NewGrD 80*
Hertel, Adolph R 1878-1958 *WhScrn 74, -77*
Hertel, Francois *CreCan 1*
Hertel, Hanns 1896- *IntWWM 80*
Hertel, Jakob Christian *NewGrD 80*
Hertel, Johann Christian 1699-1754 *NewGrD 80*
Hertel, Johann Wilhelm 1727-1789 *NewGrD 80*
Hertel, Peter Ludwig 1817-1899 *CnOxB, DancEn 78*
Herter, Francis *Film 2*
Herth, Milt d1969 *CmpEPM*
Hertman, Camille *NewGrD 80*
Hertog, Ary Den 1889-1958 *CnMD*
Hertog, Johannes Den 1904- *Baker 78*
Hertz, Aleksander 1879-1928 *DcFM, FilmEn*
Hertz, Alfred 1872-1942 *Baker 78, BiDAmM, MusSN[port], NewEOp 71, NewGrD 80*
Hertz, Carl 1859-1924 *MagIlD, WhThe*
Hertz, Fred 1933- *AmSCAP 66, -80*
Hertz, Heinrich Rudolph 1857-1894 *OxMus*
Hertz, Henrik 1798-1870 *McGEWD[port], NotNAT B, OxThe*
Hertz, Michal 1844-1918 *NewGrD 80*
Hertz, Talmon 1933- *IntWWM 80*
Hertz, William *IntMPA 75, -76, -78, -79, -80*
Hertzell, Eric *CreCan 1*
Hertzka, Emil 1869-1932 *Baker 78*
Hertzmann, Erich 1902-1963 *Baker 78, NewGrD 80*
Herve 1825-1892 *Baker 78, NewGrD 80*
Hervelois, Louis DeCaix D' *NewGrD 80*
Hervey, Arthur 1855-1922 *Baker 78, NewGrD 80*
Hervey, Grizelda 1901- *WhThe, WhoHol A*
Hervey, Irene *WhoHol A*
Hervey, Irene 1910- *FilmEn, ThFT[port]*
Hervey, Irene 1916- *FilmgC, ForYSC, HalFC 80, MovMk*
Hervieu, Paul 1857-1915 *McGEWD[port], ModWD, NotNAT B, OxThe, WhThe*
Hervig, Richard B 1917- *Baker 78, ConAmC*
Herwart, Johann Heinrich 1520-1583 *NewGrD 80*
Herwich, Madame *Film 2*
Herz, Gerhard W 1911- *IntWWM 77, -80*
Herz, Heinrich 1803-1888 *NewGrD 80, OxMus*

Herz, Henri 1803-1888 *Baker 78, BnBkM 80, NewGrD 80*
Herz, Joachim 1924- *WhoOp 76*
Herz, Ralph C 1878-1921 *CmpEPM, NotNAT B, WhThe, WhoStg 1908*
Herz, Talmon 1933- *IntWWM 77, WhoMus 72*
Herzberg, Abel J 1898- *CnMD*
Herzberg, Tana *DancEn 78*
Herzbrun, Bernard d1964 *NotNAT B*
Herzig, James Martin 1944- *AmSCAP 80*
Herzinger, Charles *Film 2*
Herzmansky, Bernhard *NewGrD 80*
Herzog, Benedictus *NewGrD 80*
Herzog, Eduard 1916- *NewGrD 80*
Herzog, Emilie 1859-1923 *Baker 78*
Herzog, Fred *Film 2*
Herzog, Frieda I 1932- *AmSCAP 66*
Herzog, George 1901- *Baker 78, NewGrD 80*
Herzog, Johann Georg 1822-1909 *Baker 78, NewGrD 80*
Herzog, Sigmund 1868-1932 *Baker 78*
Herzog, Werner 1942- *BiDFilm, -81, ConLC 16, FilmEn, HalFC 80, OxFilm*
Herzogenberg, Heinrich Von 1843-1900 *Baker 78, NewGrD 80, OxMus*
Hes, Vilem 1860-1908 *NewGrD 80*
Hesbert, Rene-Jean 1899- *IntWWM 77, -80, NewGrD 80*
Hesch, Wilhelm *NewGrD 80*
Heschke, Richard J 1939- *IntWWM 77, -80*
Hesdin, Nicolle DesCelliers De d1538 *NewGrD 80*
Heseltine, James 1692?-1763 *NewGrD 80, OxMus*
Heseltine, Philip 1894-1930 *Baker 78, NewGrD 80, OxMus*
Hesford, Michael Bryan 1930- *IntWWM 77, -80, WhoMus 72*
Hesiod *NewGrD 80*
Heskes, Irene 1928- *IntWWM 77, -80*
Heslewood, Tom 1868-1959 *NotNAT B, WhThe*
Heslop, Charles 1883-1966 *WhScrn 74, -77, WhThe*
Heslop, Charles 1884-1966 *FilmgC, HalFC 80, WhoHol B*
Hesperia 1885- *FilmEn*
Hesperia, Alda *Film 2*
Hespos, Hans-Joachim 1938- *IntWWM 77, NewGrD 80*
Hess, Andrea *IntWWM 80*
Hess, Cliff 1894-1959 *AmSCAP 66, -80*
Hess, Constance *PupTheA*
Hess, David 1936- *AmSCAP 66, -80, BiDAmM*
Hess, Ernst 1912-1968 *NewGrD 80*
Hess, Frederick 1863-1941 *BiDAmM*
Hess, Joachim 1732-1819 *NewGrD 80*
Hess, Joachim 1925- *WhoOp 76*
Hess, Jurgen 1923- *IntWWM 80, WhoMus 72*
Hess, Ludwig 1877-1944 *Baker 78*
Hess, Myra 1890-1965 *Baker 78, BnBkM 80[port], MusMk, MusSN[port], NewGrD 80[port]*
Hess, Rodger 1938- *BiE&WWA*
Hess, Willy 1859-1939 *Baker 78, NewGrD 80*
Hess, Willy 1906- *Baker 78, NewGrD 80*
Hesse *NewGrD 80*
Hesse, Baron Von d1936 *WhoHol B*
Hesse, Adolf Friedrich 1809-1863 *NewGrD 80, OxMus*
Hesse, Adolph 1808-1863 *Baker 78*
Hesse, Alice *Film 2*
Hesse, Axel Ernst 1935- *IntWWM 77, -80*
Hesse, Ernst Christian 1676-1762 *Baker 78, NewGrD 80*
Hesse, Isa *WomWMM*
Hesse, Jean-Baptiste Francois De *CnOxB*
Hesse, Johann Heinrich 1712?-1778 *NewGrD 80*
Hesse, Julia *Film 2*
Hesse, Julius 1823-1881 *Baker 78*
Hesse, Ludwig Christian 1716-1772 *NewGrD 80*
Hesse, Marjorie Anne 1911- *IntWWM 77, -80*
Hesse, Max 1858-1907 *Baker 78*
Hesse, Ruth Margot *WhoOp 76*
Hesse, Baron William 1885-1936 *WhScrn 74, -77*
Hesse-Bukowska, Barbara 1930- *IntWWM 77, -80*
Hesselberg, Edouard Gregory 1870-1935 *Baker 78*
Hesselius, Mons Gustoff 1682-1755 *BiDAmM*
Hesseltine, Stark 1929- *BiE&WWA, NotNAT*
Hesselwood, Tom *Film 2*
Hessemer, Al 1909- *NewOrJ*
Hessen, Alexander F, Landgraf Von 1863-1945 *Baker 78*
Hessenberg, Kurt 1908- *Baker 78, IntWWM 77, -80, NewGrD 80*
Hessler, Gordon *IntMPA 75, -76, -78, -79, -80*
Hessler, Gordon 1925- *IlWWBF*
Hessler, Gordon 1930- *FilmgC, HalFC 80, IntMPA 77, WhoHrs 80*
Hessling, Catherine *Film 2, OxFilm*
Hessling, Catherine 1900- *FilmEn*
Hessman De Argentoratus, Henricus *NewGrD 80*
Hest, Jeffrey 1943- *AmSCAP 80*
Hester, Carolyn 1937?- *AmSCAP 80, BiDAmM, EncFCWM 69*
Hester, Harvey d1967 *WhScrn 77, WhoHol B*
Hester, Wesley Hester 1933- *AmSCAP 80*
Hesterberg, Trude 1897-1967 *Film 2, WhScrn 77*
Heston, Charlton *MotPP, WhoHol A*
Heston, Charlton 1922- *WhoThe 72, -77*
Heston, Charlton 1923- *BiE&WWA, FilmEn, MovMk[port]*
Heston, Charlton 1924- *BiDFilm, -81, CmMov, FilmgC, ForYSC, HalFC 80, IntMPA 77, -75, -76, -78, -79, -80, OxFilm, WhoHrs 80[port], WorEFlm*
Hestor, George 1877-1925 *NotNAT B, WhThe*
Hestwood, Harold *PupTheA*
Hestwood, Robert *PupTheA*
Hetes, Jan *NewGrD 80*
Hetsch, Louis 1806-1872 *NewGrD 80*
Hetsch, Ludwig Friedrich 1806-1872 *Baker 78, NewGrD 80*
Hettema, Gerhardus Johannes 1941- *IntWWM 77, -80*
Hettisch, Johann *NewGrD 80*
Hettrick, William Eugene 1939- *IntWWM 77, -80*
Hetu, Jacques 1938- *Baker 78, CreCan 1*
Hetzel, Ralph D 1912- *IntMPA 77, -75, -76, -78, -79, -80*
Heuberger, Richard 1850-1914 *Baker 78, NewGrD 80*
Heubi, Peter 1943?- *CnOxB*
Heubner, Konrad 1860-1905 *Baker 78*
Heudeline, Louis *NewGrD 80*
Heudelinne, Louis *NewGrD 80*
Heugel *NewGrD 80*
Heugel, Francois Henri 1922- *NewGrD 80*
Heugel, Henri Georges 1844-1916 *NewGrD 80*
Heugel, Henry 1789-1841 *Baker 78*
Heugel, Jacques-Leopold 1811-1883 *Baker 78*
Heugel, Jacques Leopold 1815-1883 *NewGrD 80*
Heugel, Johannes 1500?-1585? *NewGrD 80*
Heugel, Paul 1890-1979 *NewGrD 80*
Heugel, Philippe Gerard Andre 1924- *NewGrD 80*
Heulyn, Meinir 1948- *IntWWM 77, -80*
Heurteur, Guillaume *NewGrD 80*
Heuschkel, Johann Peter 1773-1853 *NewGrD 80*
Heuss, Alfred Valentin 1877-1934 *Baker 78, NewGrD 80*
Heussenstamm, George 1926- *AmSCAP 80, CpmDNM 72, -73, -74, -76, -77, -78, -79, -80, ConAmC, IntWWM 77, -80*
Heussner, Horst 1926- *IntWWM 77, -80*
Heuston, Alfred *WhScrn 77*
Heuze, Andre 1880-1942 *DcFM, Film 2*
Heuzenroeder, Moritz 1849-1897 *NewGrD 80*
Hevar, Hedy d1975 *AmSCAP 66, -80*
Heve, Alphonse D' *NewGrD 80*
Hevesi, Sandor 1873-1939 *OxThe*
Heward, Efa Prudence 1896-1947 *CreCan 1*
Heward, Leslie 1897-1943 *Baker 78, NewGrD 80*
Heward, Prudence 1896-1947 *CreCan 1*
Hewes, Harry E, Jr. 1910- *AmSCAP 66, -80*
Hewes, Henry 1917- *BiE&WWA, ConAmTC, NotNAT, OxThe, WhoThe 72, -77*
Hewett, Christopher *BiE&WWA, NotNAT, WhoThe 72, -77*
Hewett, Dorothy 1923- *ConDr 77*
Hewett, Russell Charles 1954- *AmSCAP 80*
Hewitt, Agnes d1924 *NotNAT B, WhThe*
Hewitt, Alan 1915- *BiE&WWA, NotNAT, WhoHol A*
Hewitt, Barnard Wolcott 1906- *BiE&WWA, NotNAT*
Hewitt, Daniel C *OxMus*
Hewitt, Don *NewYTET*
Hewitt, Gordon C 1913- *IntMPA 77, -75, -76, -78, -79*
Hewitt, Harry Donald 1921- *AmSCAP 80, ConAmC*
Hewitt, Helen 1900-1977 *Baker 78, NewGrD 80*
Hewitt, Henry 1885-1968 *NotNAT B, WhScrn 77, WhThe*
Hewitt, Horatio Dawes d1894 *BiDAmM*
Hewitt, James 1770-1827 *Baker 78, BiDAmM, NewGrD 80, OxMus*
Hewitt, James Lang 1807-1853 *Baker 78, BiDAmM*
Hewitt, John Hill 1801-1890 *Baker 78, BiDAmM, NewGrD 80, NotNAT B, PopAmC[port]*
Hewitt, Joseph F 1886-1957 *AmSCAP 66, -80*
Hewitt, Maurice 1884-1971 *Baker 78*
Hewitt, Russell *Film 1*
Hewitt, Zoe Adeline 1907- *AmSCAP 80*
Hewitt-Jones, Tony 1926- *IntWWM 77, -80, WhoMus 72*
Hewland, Philip *Film 2*
Hewlett, James *DrBlPA*
Hewlett, Maurice 1861-1923 *NotNAT B, WhThe*
Hews, George 1806-1873 *BiDAmM*
Hewson, David Graham 1953- *IntWWM 80*
Hewson, George Henry Phillips 1881- *OxMus*
Hewson, J James d1923 *NotNAT B*
Hewson, Richard 1938- *WhoMus 72*
Hewston, Alfred H 1880-1947 *WhScrn 77*
Hewton, Randolph Stanley 1888-1960 *CreCan 1*
Hey, Betty *CreCan 2*
Hey, Julius 1832-1909 *Baker 78, NewGrD 80*
Hey, Richard 1926- *CnMD, CroCD*
Heybourne, Ferdinando *NewGrD 80*
Heyburn, Weldom 1904- *ForYSC*
Heyburn, Weldon 1904-1951 *NotNAT B, WhScrn 74, -77, WhoHol B*
Heyde, Norma 1927- *IntWWM 77, -80*
Heyden *NewGrD 80*
Heyden, Hans 1536-1613 *Baker 78*
Heyden, Sebald 1499-1561 *Baker 78, NewGrD 80*
Heydt, Louis Jean d1961 *WhoHol B*
Heydt, Louis Jean 1905-1960 *FilmEn, FilmgC, HalFC 80, MotPP, MovMk, NotNAT B, Vers A[port], WhScrn 74, -77, WhThe*
Heydt, Louis Jean 1906-1960 *ForYSC*
Heyduck, Peter 1924- *WhoOp 76*
Heyer, John 1916- *FilmgC, HalFC 80, IntMPA 77, -75, -76, -78, -79, -80*
Heyer, Wilhelm 1849-1913 *Baker 78, NewGrD 80*
Heyes, Douglas 1923- *FilmgC, HalFC 80*
Heyes, Herbert 1889-1958 *Film 1, -2, NotNAT B, TwYS, Vers A[port], WhScrn 74, -77, WhoHol B*
Heyes, Herbert 1890-1962 *ForYSC*
Heyl *NewGrD 80*
Heylanus, Petrus *NewGrD 80*
Heyman, Alan Charles 1931- *IntWWM 77, -80*
Heyman, Barton *WhoHol A*
Heyman, Ed 1907- *CmpEPM*
Heyman, Edward 1907- *AmPS, AmSCAP 66, -80, BiDAmM, Sw&Ld C*
Heyman, Henrik *McGEWD[port]*
Heyman, John 1933- *FilmgC, HalFC 80*
Heyman, Katherine Ruth Willoughby 1877-1944 *Baker 78, BiDAmM*
Heymann, Werner Richard 1896-1961 *Baker 78, ConAmC, FilmEn*
Heyme, Hansguenther 1935- *WhoOp 76*
Heyne VanGhizeghem *NewGrD 80*
Heyne, Gilles *NewGrD 80*
Heynicke, Kurt 1891- *ModWD*
Heynis, Aafje 1924- *NewGrD 80,*

WhoMus 72
Heynrijck VonVeldeke *NewGrD 80*
Heyns, Cornelius *NewGrD 80*
Heyse, Hans-Joachim 1929- *WhoOp 76*
Heyse, Paul d1914 *NotNAT B*
Heyther, William 1563?-1627 *NewGrD 80*
Heyther, William 1584?-1627 *OxMus*
Heyward, Dorothy 1890-1961 *DcLB 7[port], ModWD, NotNAT B, PlP&P, WhThe*
Heyward, DuBose 1885-1940 *AmSCAP 66, -80, BnBkM 80, CnMD, DcLB 7[port], McGEWD[port], ModWD, NotNAT A, -B, PlP&P[port], WhThe*
Heyward, Leland 1902-1971 *BiDAmM*
Heyward, Louis M 1920- *IntMPA 77, -75, -76, -78, -79, -80*
Heyward, Samuel Edwin, Jr. 1904- *AmSCAP 66, -80, ConAmC A*
Heywood, Anne *IntMPA 75, -76, -78, -79, -80*
Heywood, Anne 1931- *FilmgC, HalFC 80, IntMPA 77, WhoHol A*
Heywood, Anne 1932- *FilmAG WE, FilmEn, IlWWBF[port]*
Heywood, Anne 1933?- *ForYSC*
Heywood, Donald d1967 *AmSCAP 66, -80, BlkAmP*
Heywood, Eddie 1926- *RkOn[port]*
Heywood, Eddie, Jr. 1915- *BiDAmM, CmpEPM, EncJzS 70, IlEncJ, WhoJazz 72*
Heywood, Herbert 1881-1964 *WhScrn 77*
Heywood, John 1497-1579? *NewGrD 80*
Heywood, John 1497?-1580 *CnThe, EncWT, Ent[port], NotNAT B, OxThe, REnWD[port]*
Heywood, John 1497?-1589? *McGEWD[port]*
Heywood, Pat 1927- *FilmgC, HalFC 80*
Heywood, Percival Meredith 1912- *WhoMus 72*
Heywood, Thomas 1570?-1641 *NotNAT B, OxThe*
Heywood, Thomas 1573?-1641 *EncWT*
Heywood, Thomas 1574?-1641 *CnThe, Ent, McGEWD[port], REnWD[port]*
Heyworth, Peter Lawrence Frederick 1921- *IntWWM 77, -80, NewGrD 80, WhoMus 72*
Hi-Fi's *BiDAmM*
Hi-Hat Hattie *BluesWW[port]*
Hiarne, Urban 1641-1724 *OxThe*
Hiatt, Ruth 1908- *Film 2, ForYSC, TwYS, WhoHol A*
Hibbard, Bruce Alan 1953- *AmSCAP 80*
Hibbard, Edna 1895-1942 *NotNAT B, WhScrn 74, -77, WhThe, WhoHol B*
Hibbard, William 1939- *ConAmC, DcCM*
Hibbeler, Ray Oscar 1892- *AmSCAP 80*
Hibberd, Jack 1940- *ConDr 77*
Hibberd, Lloyd *OxMus*
Hibbert, Geoffrey 1922-1969 *FilmgC, HalFC 80, WhScrn 74, -77, WhoHol B*
Hibbert, Henry George 1862-1924 *NotNAT B, WhThe*
Hibbler, Al 1915- *BiDAmM, CmpEPM, DrBlPA, RkOn[port]*
Hibbs, Jesse 1906- *FilmEn, FilmgC, HalFC 80*
Hibler, Al *AmPS B*
Hibler, Winston 1910- *AmSCAP 66, -80, IntMPA 75, -76*
Hibler, Winston 1911-1976 *HalFC 80*
Hicart, Bernhard *NewGrD 80*
Hice, Daniel D 1942- *AmSCAP 80*
Hice, Ruby F *AmSCAP 80*
Hichens, Robert Smythe 1864-1950 *NotNAT B, WhThe*
Hick, Susan Elizabeth 1949- *IntWWM 80*
Hicken, Kenneth Lambert 1934- *IntWWM 77, -80*
Hickey, Ersel *RkOn[port]*
Hickey, Howard L 1897-1942 *WhScrn 74, -77*
Hickey, William 1928?- *BiE&WWA, NotNAT, WhoHol A*
Hicklin, Margery 1904- *WhThe*
Hicklin, Terry L 1949- *WhoOp 76*
Hickman, Alfred 1873-1931 *Film 1, -2, NotNAT B, WhScrn 74, -77, WhoHol B*
Hickman, Art 1886-1930 *AmSCAP 66, -80, BgBands 74, CmpEPM*
Hickman, Charles 1905- *EncMT, WhoThe 72, -77*
Hickman, Darryl 1930- *What 5[port]*
Hickman, Darryl 1931- *BiE&WWA, FilmEn, FilmgC, ForYSC, HalFC 80, MovMk[port], WhoHol A*
Hickman, Darryl 1933- *IntMPA 77, -75, -76, -78, -79, -80*
Hickman, Dwayne 1934- *FilmEn, FilmgC, ForYSC, HalFC 80, MotPP, MovMk, WhoHol A*
Hickman, Howard 1880-1940 *HalFC 80*
Hickman, Howard 1880-1949 *Film 1, -2, ForYSC, NotNAT B, TwYS, WhScrn 74, -77, WhoHol B*
Hickman, J Hampton 1937- *BiE&WWA*
Hickman, Roger M 1888-1968 *AmSCAP 66, -80*
Hickmann, Carl *WhoMus 72*
Hickmann, Ellen 1934- *IntWWM 77, -80*
Hickmann, Hans Robert Hermann 1908-1968 *Baker 78, NewGrD 80*
Hickock, James Butler 1837-1876 *OxFilm*
Hickok, Rodney 1892-1942 *WhScrn 74, -77, WhoHol B*
Hickok, Wild Bill 1837-1876 *HalFC 80*
Hickox, Douglas 1929- *FilmgC, HalFC 80, IlWWBF*
Hickox, Harry *ForYSC, WhoHol A*
Hickox, Richard Sidney 1948- *IntWWM 77, -80*
Hickox, Sid *HalFC 80*
Hickox, Sidney 1895- *FilmEn, WorEFlm*
Hicks, Bert 1920-1965 *WhScrn 74, -77*
Hicks, Betty Seymour 1905- *WhThe*
Hicks, Brenda *WomWMM B*
Hicks, Charlie 1900-1963 *BluesWW*
Hicks, Dan *ConMuA 80A*
Hicks, Dan And His Hot Licks *IlEncR*
Hicks, David 1937- *IntWWM 80, WhoOp 76*
Hicks, Edna 1895-1925 *BluesWW*
Hicks, Sir Edward Seymour 1871-1949 *NotNAT A, -B, WhThe, WhoStg 1908*
Hicks, Edwin 1914- *IntMPA 77, -75, -76, -78, -79, -80*
Hicks, Henry 1904?-1950? *WhoJazz 72*
Hicks, Hilly 1950- *DrBlPA, WhoHol A*
Hicks, John B, Sr. 1934- *AmSCAP 80*
Hicks, Julian 1858-1941 *WhThe*
Hicks, Laurence Henry 1912- *WhoMus 72*
Hicks, Leonard M 1918-1971 *WhScrn 77*
Hicks, Maxine Elliott *Film 2, WhoHol A*
Hicks, Newton Treen d1873 *NotNAT B*
Hicks, Otis V 1913-1974 *BluesWW[port]*
Hicks, Peggy Glanville *DcCM, OxMus*
Hicks, Robert 1902-1931 *BluesWW[port]*
Hicks, Russell 1895-1957 *FilmEn, FilmgC, ForYSC, HalFC 80, HolCA[port], MotPP, MovMk, NotNAT B, Vers A[port], WhScrn 74, -77, WhoHol B*
Hicks, Sir Seymour 1871-1949 *CnThe, EncMT, FilmEn, Film 1, -2, FilmgC, HalFC 80, IlWWBF, -A, OxThe, WhScrn 74, -77, WhoHol B*
Hicks, Stephen 1949- *WhoMus 72*
Hicks, Val J 1933- *AmSCAP 80*
Hicks, William Alan 1908- *WhoMus 72*
Hickson, Joan 1906- *FilmgC, HalFC 80, WhoHol A, WhoThe 72, -77*
Hickson, William Edward 1803-1870 *NewGrD 80*
Hidalgo, Elvira De 1882- *CmOp*
Hidalgo, Elvira De 1892-1980 *NewEOp 71, NewGrD 80*
Hidalgo, Gutierre Fernandez *NewGrD 80*
Hidalgo, Juan 1600?-1685 *Baker 78*
Hidalgo, Juan 1612?-1685 *NewGrD 80*
Hidas, Frigyes 1928- *Baker 78, NewGrD 80*
Hider, Robert T 1937- *AmSCAP 66*
Hider, Ruth Marie *WhoOp 76*
Hidey, Hal Smith *AmSCAP 80*
Hiebert, John William 1947- *IntWWM 77*
Hiebert, Paul Gerhardt 1892- *CreCan 2*
Hier, Ethel Glenn 1889-1971 *Baker 78, ConAmC*
Hieromonachus, Gabriel *NewGrD 80*
Hieronimus DeZentis Viterbiensis *NewGrD 80*
Hieronymus Bononiensis *NewGrD 80*
Hieronymus De Moravia *NewGrD 80*
Hieronymus Of Moravia *OxMus*
Hieronymus, Clara Booth Wiggins 1913- *ConAmTC*
Hierosolymites, Andrew *NewGrD 80*
Hiers, Walter 1893-1933 *Film 1, -2, ForYSC, TwYS, WhScrn 74, -77, WhoHol B*
Hiester, Mary Augusta *CreCan 2*
Hift, Fred 1924- *IntMPA 77, -75, -76, -78, -79, -80*
Higbee, Dale 1925- *IntWWM 77, -80*
Higby, Wilbur 1866-1934 *Film 1, -2, WhScrn 74, -77, WhoHol B*
Higgie, T H d1893 *NotNAT B*
Higgin, Howard 1893- *FilmEn*
Higginbotham, Irene Evelyn 1918- *AmSCAP 66, -80*
Higginbotham, J C 1906-1973 *CmpEPM, EncJzS 70, IlEncJ, WhoJazz 72*
Higginbotham, Jack 1906-1973 *BiDAmM, EncJzS 70*
Higgins, Billy 1888- *BlksBF*
Higgins, Billy 1936- *BiDAmM, EncJzS 70*
Higgins, Cathy Eisenberg 1948- *IntWWM 77, -80*
Higgins, Colin *IntMPA 79, -80*
Higgins, David 1858-1936 *Film 2, NotNAT B, WhScrn 77, WhoHol B*
Higgins, Dick *ConDr 73, -77E*
Higgins, Edward 1475?-1538 *NewGrD 80*
Higgins, Elliot Lloyd 1941- *IntWWM 77, -80*
Higgins, Esther S 1903- *AmSCAP 80*
Higgins, Francis Edward 1915- *IntWWM 77, -80*
Higgins, Frank 1915- *WhoMus 72*
Higgins, Frank L *PupTheA*
Higgins, Haydn 1932- *BiDAmM*
Higgins, Joe *WhoHol A*
Higgins, John Michael 1948- *AmSCAP 80*
Higgins, Ken 1919- *HalFC 80*
Higgins, Michael 1922- *BiE&WWA, NotNAT, WhoHol A*
Higgins, Norman 1898- *WhThe, WhoThe 72*
Higgins, Richard Carter 1938- *Baker 78, ConAmC*
Higginsen, Vy *DrBlPA*
Higginson, Gary Michael 1952- *IntWWM 77*
Higginson, Henry Lee 1834-1919 *Baker 78*
Higginson, Joseph Vincent 1896- *AmSCAP 66, -80, ConAmC A*
Higginson, Thomas Wentworth 1823-1911 *BiDAmM*
Higgons, Edward 1475?-1538 *NewGrD 80*
Higgs, Timothy John 1951- *IntWWM 77, -80*
High, Freeman 1897- *AmSCAP 66, -80*
High, Miles *AmSCAP 80*
Higham, John 1940- *IntWWM 77, -80, WhoMus 72*
Highland, George A d1954 *NotNAT B*
Highley, Reginald 1884- *WhThe*
Highsmith, Patricia 1921- *HalFC 80*
Hight, Harold Edward *WhoMus 72*
Hightower, Charles *BlkAmP*
Hightower, Gail 1946- *BlkWAB[port]*
Hightower, Harold *Film 2*
Hightower, Marilyn 1923- *WhThe*
Hightower, Robert *MorBAP*
Hightower, Rosella 1920- *CnOxB, DancEn 78[port]*
Hightower, Willie 1889-1959 *NewOrJ, WhoJazz 72*
Highwater, Jamake 1942- *NatPD[port]*
Highwaymen, The *RkOn*
Higley, Brewster M 1823-1911 *BiDAmM*
Hignard, Aristide 1822-1898 *Baker 78*
Hignell, Rose 1896- *WhThe*
Hignett, H R 1870-1959 *NotNAT B, WhThe, WhoHol B*
Higons, Richard *NewGrD 80*
Higuet, Nestor Gustave Ghislain 1903- *IntWWM 77, -80*
Hijman, Julius 1901-1969 *Baker 78, ConAmC*
Hiken, Gerald 1927- *BiE&WWA, NotNAT, WhoHol A, WhoThe 72, -77*
Hiken, Nat 1914-1968 *AmSCAP 66, -80, BiE&WWA, NewYTET, NotNAT B*
Hikmet, Nazim 1902-1963 *CnMD*
Hikmet Ran, Nazim 1901-1963 *EncWT*
Hilaire Daleo *NewGrD 80*
Hilaire Penet *NewGrD 80*
Hilaire Turleron *NewGrD 80*
Hilaire, Andrew H 1900?-1936? *WhoJazz 72*
Hilarides, Marianna 1933- *CnOxB, DancEn 78*

Hilarius *NewGrD 80*
Hilarius Pictavensis *NewGrD 80*
Hilary, Bishop *OxMus*
Hilary Of Poitiers 315?-367? *NewGrD 80*
Hilary, Jennifer 1942- *WhoHol A, WhoThe 72, -77*
Hilber, Johann Baptist 1891- *NewGrD 80*
Hilbert, Egon 1899-1968 *NewEOp 71*
Hilbert, Georg *Film 2*
Hilburn, Robert *ConMuA 80B*
Hildach, Eugen 1849-1924 *Baker 78*
Hildebrand *NewGrD 80, PupTheA*
Hildebrand, Arthur Anthony 1946- *IntWWM 77*
Hildebrand, Christian 1570?-1649 *NewGrD 80*
Hildebrand, Johann 1614-1684 *NewGrD 80*
Hildebrand, Johann Heinrich *NewGrD 80*
Hildebrand, John G 1942- *IntWWM 77, -80*
Hildebrand, Lo 1894-1936 *WhoHol B*
Hildebrand, Rodney 1893-1962 *Film 2, WhScrn 77, WhoHol B*
Hildebrand, Warren *ConMuA 80B*
Hildebrandt *NewGrD 80*
Hildebrandt, Johann *NewGrD 80*
Hildebrandt, Johann Gottfried 1724?-1775 *NewGrD 80*
Hildebrandt, Zacharias 1688-1757 *NewGrD 80*
Hildegard Of Bingen 1098-1179 *NewGrD 80*
Hildegard, Saint 1098-1179 *MusMk*
Hildegarde 1906?- *AmPS B, CmpEPM*
Hilderbrand, Diane *AmSCAP 80*
Hilderbrand, Lo 1894-1936 *WhScrn 74, -77*
Hildesheimer, Wolfgang 1916- *CnMD, CroCD, EncWT, Ent, McGEWD, ModWD*
Hildreth, Kathryn *Film 2*
Hildyard, Jack 1908- *HalFC 80*
Hildyard, Jack 1915- *FilmEn, FilmgC, WorEFlm*
Hiler, Charlotte Ailene 1910-1958 *AmSCAP 66*
Hiles, Henry 1826-1904 *Baker 78, NewGrD 80*
Hiley, David 1947- *IntWWM 80*
Hilferdin VanWewen, Franz *NewGrD 80*
Hilferding *CnOxB*
Hilford, Lawrence B *IntMPA 80*
Hilforde, Mary 1853-1927 *WhScrn 74, -77*
Hilfred, Borge 1918- *IntWWM 77, -80*
Hill *NewGrD 80*
Hill, Aaron 1685-1750 *NotNAT B, OxThe*
Hill, Abram 1911- *BlkAmP, DrBlPA, MorBAP*
Hill, Al *AmSCAP 80, Film 2*
Hill, Alex 1906-1937 *WhoJazz 72*
Hill, Alex 1907-1937 *BiDAmM*
Hill, Alfred 1870-1960 *Baker 78, NewGrD 80*
Hill, Alfred Ebsworth 1862-1940 *Baker 78*
Hill, Andrew 1936- *IlEncJ*
Hill, Andrew 1937- *BiDAmM, EncJzS 70*
Hill, Andrew 1942- *Baker 78*
Hill, Ann 1921- *BiE&WWA, NotNAT*
Hill, Annie d1943 *NotNAT B*
Hill, Anthony Nicholas Finch 1936- *IntWWM 80*
Hill, Armenter *MorBAP*
Hill, Arthur 1875-1932 *WhScrn 74, -77*
Hill, Arthur 1922- *BiE&WWA, FilmEn, FilmgC, ForYSC, HalFC 80, IntMPA 77, -75, -76, -78, -79, -80, MotPP, NotNAT, PlP&P[port], WhoHol A, WhoThe 72, -77*
Hill, Arthur Frederick 1860-1939 *Baker 78*
Hill, Arthur George 1857-1923 *NewGrD 80*
Hill, Bass 1900-1964 *WhoJazz 72*
Hill, Ben A 1894-1969 *WhScrn 74, -77, WhoHol B*
Hill, Benjamin 1925- *IntMPA 77, -75, -76, -78, -79, -80*
Hill, Benny 1925- *FilmgC, HalFC 80, IlWWBF, WhoHol A*
Hill, Benson Earle d1845 *NotNAT A, -B*
Hill, Bertha 1905-1950 *BiDAmM, BluesWW[port]*
Hill, Bertha Chippie 1900?-1950 *CmpEPM*
Hill, Beverly Jean 1938- *BluesWW[port]*
Hill, Billie *WhThe*
Hill, Billy 1899-1940 *AmPS, CmpEPM, NotNAT B, PopAmC*
Hill, Bonnie *Film 1*
Hill, Carole 1945- *CnOxB*
Hill, Catharine Charlotte Benita 1951- *IntWWM 80*
Hill, Cecil 1936- *IntWWM 77, -80*
Hill, Cecilia Mary *WhoMus 72*
Hill, Charles Bud 1929- *IntWWM 80*
Hill, Charles Lee 1910- *AmSCAP 66, -80*
Hill, Chippie 1900?-1950 *WhoJazz 72*
Hill, Dan 1954- *RkOn 2[port]*
Hill, David 1952- *AmSCAP 80, Baker 78*
Hill, Dedette Lee 1900-1950 *AmSCAP 66, -80*
Hill, Doris *Film 2, ForYSC, TwYS, WhoHol A*
Hill, Doris 1905?- *FilmEn*
Hill, Dudley S 1881-1960 *WhScrn 74, -77*
Hill, Edward Burlingame 1872-1960 *AmSCAP 66, -80, Baker 78, BiDAmM, ConAmC, DcCM, NewGrD 80, OxMus*
Hill, Emma *WomWMM*
Hill, Eric James 1942- *IntWWM 77, -80*
Hill, Eric Jason 1910- *WhoMus 72*
Hill, Errol 1921- *BlkAmP, ConDr 73, -77, DrBlPA, MorBAP, NotNAT*
Hill, F *MorBAP*
Hill, Frances Patricia 1933- *WhoMus 72*
Hill, Frederic Stanhope d1851 *NotNAT B*
Hill, Frederick Roosevelt 1932- *BiDAmM*
Hill, George 1872-1945 *WhScrn 74, -77*
Hill, George 1888-1934 *HalFC 80, WhoHol B*
Hill, George 1888-1939 *FilmgC*
Hill, George Byron 1953- *AmSCAP 80*
Hill, George Handel 1809-1849 *FamA&A[port], NotNAT A, -B*
Hill, George Roy *IntMPA 77, -75, -76, -78, -79, -80*
Hill, George Roy 1922- *BiDFilm, -81, FilmEn, FilmgC, HalFC 80, OxFilm, WhoThe 72, -77, WorEFlm*
Hill, George Roy 1923- *BiE&WWA, NotNAT*
Hill, George Roy 1926- *MovMk[port]*
Hill, George William 1861-1934 *CreCan 2*
Hill, George William 1895-1934 *DcFM, FilmEn, TwYS A*
Hill, Gladys *WomWMM*
Hill, Goldie 1933- *BiDAmM, CounME 74, -74A, EncFCWM 69, IlEncCM[port]*
Hill, Granville 1878-1953 *Baker 78*
Hill, Hallene 1876-1966 *WhScrn 77*
Hill, Henry 1781-1839 *NewGrD 80*
Hill, Henry 1907- *AmSCAP 80*
Hill, Henry Lockey 1774-1835 *NewGrD 80*
Hill, Howard 1899-1975 *WhScrn 77, WhoHol C*
Hill, Jack *WhScrn 77, WhoHrs 80*
Hill, Jackson 1941- *AmSCAP 80, ConAmC, IntWWM 77*
Hill, James 1916- *FilmEn, FilmgC, HalFC 80*
Hill, James 1919- *FilmEn, FilmgC, HalFC 80, IlWWBF, MovMk[port]*
Hill, James Lawrence 1928- *AmSCAP 80*
Hill, James Vaughn 1930- *BiDAmM*
Hill, Jennie 1851-1896 *NotNAT B*
Hill, Jenny 1851-1896 *OxThe, PlP&P*
Hill, Jenny 1944- *IntWWM 77, -80*
Hill, Jessie *RkOn*
Hill, John-Edward 1947- *NotNAT*
Hill, John J d1962 *NotNAT B*
Hill, John Leubrie 1873-1916 *BiDAmM*
Hill, John M 1942- *AmSCAP 80*
Hill, John Walter 1942- *IntWWM 77, -80*
Hill, Joseph 1715-1784 *Baker 78, NewGrD 80*
Hill, Josephine *Film 2*
Hill, Junius Welch 1840-1916 *Baker 78*
Hill, Kathryn *Film 2, WhScrn 77*
Hill, King Solomon *BluesWW[port]*
Hill, Lawrence 1912- *BiE&WWA*
Hill, Lee *Film 1, -2*
Hill, Leslie Pinkey 1880-1960 *BlkAmP*
Hill, Leubrie 1873-1916 *BlkAmP*
Hill, Lucienne *BiE&WWA, NotNAT, WhoThe 72, -77*
Hill, Mabel Wood 1891-1954 *BiDAmM*
Hill, Malcolm John 1944- *IntWWM 80*
Hill, Margaret 1924- *DancEn 78*
Hill, Margaret 1929-1975 *CnOxB*
Hill, Margaret Shirley 1930- *IntWWM 77, -80*
Hill, Marianna *WhoHol A*
Hill, Mars 1927- *BlkAmP, MorBAP, NatPD[port]*
Hill, Martha *BiE&WWA, CnOxB, DancEn 78, NotNAT*
Hill, Martyn Geoffrey 1944- *IntWWM 77, -80*
Hill, Mary *WomWMM B*
Hill, Maud *Film 1*
Hill, Maude *Film 2*
Hill, May 1888- *AmSCAP 66*
Hill, Mildred J 1859-1916 *AmSCAP 66, -80, BiDAmM*
Hill, Pamela *WomWMM B*
Hill, Pat *PupTheA*
Hill, Peter Murray 1908- *WhThe*
Hill, Phyllis *WhoHol A*
Hill, Ralph 1900-1950 *Baker 78, NewGrD 80*
Hill, Raymond 1891-1941 *WhScrn 74, -77*
Hill, Richard S 1901-1961 *Baker 78, NewGrD 80, OxMus*
Hill, Robert F 1886- *FilmEn, TwYS A*
Hill, Robert Leslie 1945- *IntWWM 77, -80*
Hill, Roger d1674 *NewGrD 80*
Hill, Ronnie 1911- *WhoThe 72, -77*
Hill, Rosa Lee 1910-1968 *BluesWW*
Hill, Rose 1914- *WhoThe 72, -77*
Hill, Rowland *OxMus*
Hill, Ruby 1922- *BlksB&W, DrBlPA*
Hill, Ruth *PupTheA*
Hill, Scott 1947- *NewOrJ SUP[port]*
Hill, Sinclair 1894-1945 *FilmEn, FilmgC, HalFC 80*
Hill, Sinclair 1896-1945 *IlWWBF, NotNAT B, WhThe*
Hill, Stephen Jackson 1941- *IntWWM 80*
Hill, Stephen P 1806-1884 *BiDAmM*
Hill, Steven 1924- *FilmgC, HalFC 80, MotPP, WhoHol A*
Hill, Susan *ConDr 73, -77B*
Hill, Teddy *BgBands 74*
Hill, Teddy 1906- *CmpEPM*
Hill, Teddy 1909- *BiDAmM, WhoJazz 72*
Hill, Terence 1941- *FilmAG WE, FilmEn, HalFC 80, IntMPA 77, -75, -76, -78, -79, -80, WhoHol A*
Hill, Terry S 1946- *IntWWM 77, -80*
Hill, Thelma 1906-1938 *Film 2, WhScrn 74, -77, WhoHol B*
Hill, Thomas d1893 *NewGrD 80*
Hill, Thomas 1818-1891 *BiDAmM*
Hill, Tiny *BgBands 74*
Hill, Tiny d1971 *WhoHol B*
Hill, Tiny 1906-1972 *CmpEPM*
Hill, Ureli Corelli Uriah 1802-1875 *Baker 78, BiDAmM, NewGrD 80*
Hill, Ureli K 1780-1844 *NewGrD 80*
Hill, Uri K 1780-1844 *BiDAmM, NewGrD 80*
Hill, Violette *PupTheA*
Hill, Virginia 1917-1966 *WhScrn 77, WhoHol B*
Hill, W Alexander 1906-1936 *AmSCAP 66, -80*
Hill, Walter 1942- *FilmEn, HalFC 80, IntMPA 77, -75, -76, -78, -79, -80*
Hill, Walter Osborn d1963 *NotNAT B*
Hill, Wesley d1930 *NotNAT B*
Hill, Wilhelm 1838-1902 *Baker 78*
Hill, William 1745-1790 *NewGrD 80*
Hill, William 1789-1870 *NewGrD 80*
Hill, William Ebsworth 1817-1895 *Baker 78, NewGrD 80*
Hill, William Henry 1857-1927 *Baker 78*
Hill, William Herbert 1930- *CpmDNM 77*
Hill, William Joseph 1899-1940 *AmSCAP 66, -80, BiDAmM*
Hill, Willie L, Jr. 1946- *IntWWM 77*
Hillage, Steve *ConMuA 80A, IlEncR*
Hillaire, Marcel *WhoHol A*
Hillanis, Johannes 1460?-1518? *NewGrD 80*
Hillary, Ann 1931- *BiE&WWA, NotNAT*
Hillberg, Gosta *Film 2*
Hillbilly Cat, The *EncFCWM 69*
Hillburn, Betty *Film 2*
Hillburn, Raymond 1940- *AmSCAP 80*
Hille, Eduard 1822-1891 *Baker 78*
Hille, Johann Georg d1744 *NewGrD 80*
Hille, Waldemar 1908- *ConAmC*
Hillebrand, Fred 1893-1963 *AmSCAP 66, -80, ConAmC A*
Hillebrand, Peter William 1941- *IntWWM 77*
Hillebrecht, Hildegard 1927- *NewGrD 80, WhoOp 76*
Hillel-Erlanger, Irene *WomWMM*
Hillemacher, Lucien Joseph Edouard 1860-1909 *Baker 78, NewGrD 80, OxMus*
Hillemacher, Paul 1852-1933 *Baker 78*

Hillemacher, Paul Joseph Guillaume 1852-1933 *NewGrD 80*
Hillemacher, Paul Joseph William 1852-1893 *OxMus*
Hillemacher, Paul-Lucien *NewGrD 80*
Hillen, Kees 1946- *IntWWM 80*
Hiller, Arthur 1923- *BiDFilm, -81, FilmEn, HalFC 80, IntMPA 77, -75, -76, -78, -79, -80*
Hiller, Arthur 1924- *FilmgC, MovMk[port]*
Hiller, Ferdinand 1811-1885 *Baker 78, MusMk, NewGrD 80, OxMus*
Hiller, Friedrich Adam 1767?-1812 *NewGrD 80*
Hiller, Friedrich Adam 1768-1812 *Baker 78*
Hiller, Johann Adam 1728-1804 *Baker 78, BnBkM 80, GrComp, NewEOp 71, NewGrD 80[port], OxMus*
Hiller, Kurt *Film 2*
Hiller, Lejaren 1924- *AmSCAP 66, -80, Baker 78, BiDAmM, BnBkM 80, ConAmC, DcCM, IntWWM 77, -80, NewGrD 80*
Hiller, Max *Film 2*
Hiller, Phyllis 1927- *AmSCAP 66, -80*
Hiller, Roger Lewis 1933- *IntWWM 77, -80*
Hiller, Wendy 1912- *BiE&WWA, CnThe, Ent, FilmAG WE, FilmEn, FilmgC, ForYSC, HalFC 80, IlWWBF, IntMPA 77, -75, -76, -78, -79, -80, MotPP, MovMk[port], NotNAT, OxFilm, ThFT[port], WhoHol A, WhoThe 72, -77*
Hillerman, John 1931?- *HalFC 80, WhoHol A*
Hillert, Richard Walter 1923- *CpmDNM 72, -77, -79, -80, ConAmC*
Hillery, Mable 1929-1976 *BluesWW[port]*
Hillhouse, Augustus Lucas 1792-1859 *BiDAmM*
Hilliard, Bob 1918-1971 *AmPS, AmSCAP 66, -80, BiDAmM, BiE&WWA, CmpEPM, NotNAT B, Sw&Ld C*
Hilliard, Donald L 1932- *IntWWM 77*
Hilliard, Ernest 1886-1946 *Film 2, TwYS*
Hilliard, Ernest 1890-1946 *ForYSC*
Hilliard, Ernest 1890-1947 *WhScrn 74, -77, WhoHol B*
Hilliard, Harriet *MotPP, WhoHol A*
Hilliard, Harriet 1911- *ThFT[port]*
Hilliard, Harriet 1912?- *CmpEPM*
Hilliard, Harriet 1914- *FilmEn, FilmgC, ForYSC, HalFC 80*
Hilliard, Harry d1966 *Film 1, -2, TwYS, WhScrn 74, -77, WhoHol B*
Hilliard, Hazel d1971 *WhoHol B*
Hilliard, J N *MagIID*
Hilliard, Jacqueline Dalya 1918- *AmSCAP 80*
Hilliard, Jan *CreCan 1*
Hilliard, Kathlyn 1896-1933 *NotNAT B, WhThe*
Hilliard, Mrs. Mack 1886-1963 *WhScrn 74, -77, WhoHol B*
Hilliard, Patricia 1916- *WhThe*
Hilliard, Robert Cochran 1857-1927 *NotNAT B, WhThe, WhoStg 1906, -1908*
Hilliard, Thomas Lee 1930- *IntWWM 77, -80*
Hillias, Margaret Peg d1960 *WhScrn 74, -77*
Hillias, Peg d1961 *WhoHol B*
Hillie, Verna *ForYSC*
Hillier, Erwin 1911- *FilmEn, FilmgC, HalFC 80, IntMPA 77, -75, -76, -78, -79, -80*
Hillier, Helen 1937- *IntWWM 77, -80*
Hillier, Marion Lucy 1932- *IntWWM 77, -80*
Hilligardt, Frederick Phillip 1947- *AmSCAP 80*
Hillis, Margaret 1921- *Baker 78, BnBkM 80, NewGrD 80, WhoMus 72, WomCom[port]*
Hillman, Chris *ConMuA 80A*
Hillman, David 1934- *WhoMus 72*
Hillman, George 1906- *DrBlPA*
Hillman, Joseph 1833-1890 *BiDAmM*
Hillman, Marcia 1932- *AmSCAP 80*
Hillman, Michael 1902-1941 *NotNAT B, WhThe*
Hillman, Richard 1914- *AmSCAP 66*
Hillman, Richard Paul 1917- *AmSCAP 80*
Hillman, Roc 1910- *AmSCAP 66*
Hillman, Roscoe Vanos 1910- *AmSCAP 80*
Hillmer, Leann 1942- *IntWWM 80*
Hillmon, Betty Jean 1945- *IntWWM 77, -80*
Hills, Beverly *ForYSC*
Hills, Charles Walter 1922- *IntWWM 77, -80*
Hills, William H 1859-1930 *BiDAmM*
Hillside Singers *RkOn 2A*
Hilltoppers, The *AmPS A, -B, BiDAmM, RkOn*
Hillyer, Lambert 1889- *DcFM, FilmEn, FilmgC, HalFC 80, WhoHrs 80*
Hillyer, Lambert 1893- *TwYS A*
Hillyer, Lonnie 1940- *BiDAmM, EncJzS 70*
Hilmar, Frantisek Matej 1803-1881 *NewGrD 80*
Hilo Hattie *WhoHol A*
Hilpert, Heinz 1890-1967 *EncWT, Ent*
Hils, Clifford A 1918- *AmSCAP 66, -80*
Hilsberg, Alexander 1897-1961 *Baker 78*
Hilsberg, Ignace 1894-1973 *Baker 78, BiDAmM*
Hilse, Walter 1941- *ConAmC*
Hilton, Arthur 1897- *IntMPA 77, -75, -76*
Hilton, Daisy 1908-1969 *WhScrn 77*
Hilton, Hermine *AmSCAP 80*
Hilton, James 1900-1953 *FilmgC*
Hilton, James 1900-1954 *FilmEn, HalFC 80, NotNAT B*
Hilton, Janet Lesley 1945- *IntWWM 77, -80*
Hilton, John 1560?-1608 *Baker 78, NewGrD 80, OxMus*
Hilton, John 1599-1657 *Baker 78, NewGrD 80, OxMus*
Hilton, Les 1907- *AmSCAP 66*
Hilton, Lewis Booth 1920- *AmSCAP 80, IntWWM 77, -80*
Hilton, Mars 1951- *IntMPA 77, -75, -76, -78, -79, -80*
Hilton, Minna *WomWMM B*
Hilton, Ruth B 1926- *IntWWM 80*
Hilton, Violet 1908-1969 *WhScrn 77*
Hilton, Wayne Edward 1947- *AmSCAP 80*
Hilty, Everett Jay 1910- *ConAmC, IntWWM 77, -80*
Hilverding, Franz Anton Christoph d1768 *CnOxB*
Hilverding, Franz VanWewen 1710-1768 *DancEn 78*
Hilverding VanWewen, Franz 1710-1768 *NewGrD 80*
Hilyard, Maud d1926 *NotNAT B*
Himber, Richard 1907-1966 *AmSCAP 66, -80, BgBands 74, CmpEPM*
Hime *NewGrD 80*
Hime, Humphrey *NewGrD 80*
Hime, Morris d1828 *NewGrD 80*
Himel, Otto 1904?- *NewOrJ*
Himes, Chester 1909- *BlkAmP*
Himmel, Friedrich Heinrich 1765-1814 *Baker 78, MusMk, NewGrD 80, OxMus*
Hinchcliff, Colin W *WhoMus 72*
Hinckley, Alfred *WhoHol A*
Hinckley, Allen Carter 1877-1954 *Baker 78, BiDAmM*
Hinckley, William L 1894-1918 *Film 1, WhScrn 77*
Hind, Earl *Film 2*
Hind, John Norman 1916- *WhoMus 72*
Hind O'Malley, Pamela 1923- *IntWWM 77, -80, WhoMus 72*
Hindar, Johannes 1917- *IntWWM 77, -80*
Hinde, Arnold 1907- *WhoMus 72*
Hindemith, Paul 1895-1963 *Baker 78, BiDAmM, BnBkM 80[port], CmOp, CompSN[port], CnOxB, ConAmC, DancEn 78, DcCom 77[port], DcCom&M 79, DcCM, DcTwCC, -A, MusMk[port], NewEOp 71, NewGrD 80[port], NotNAT B, OxMus*
Hinden, Jonathan 1938- *IntWWM 80*
Hinderas, Natalie 1927- *DrBlPA, NewGrD 80*
Hinderer, Everett Roland 1914- *AmSCAP 66, -80*
Hindermann, Walter F 1931- *IntWWM 77, -80*
Hindin, Philip 1916- *IntMPA 77, -75, -76, -78, -79, -80*
Hindle, Alan James 1937- *IntWWM 80*
Hindle, John 1761-1796 *Baker 78*
Hindmarch, Alan Wilson 1916- *WhoMus 72*
Hinds, Anthony 1922- *FilmgC, HalFC 80, WhoHrs 80*
Hinds, Esther C 1943- *WhoOp 76*
Hinds, Samuel S 1875-1948 *FilmEn, Film 2, FilmgC, ForYSC, HalFC 80, HolCA[port], MotPP, MovMk, Vers A[port], WhScrn 74, -77, WhoHol B*
Hinds, Werner 1911- *IntWWM 77*
Hindsley, Mark Hubert 1905- *IntWWM 77, -80*
Hine, Daryl 1936- *CreCan 2*
Hine, Hubert d1950 *NotNAT B*
Hine, William 1687-1730 *Baker 78, NewGrD 80, OxMus*
Hine, William Daryl 1936- *CreCan 2*
Hines, Adrian R 1903-1946 *WhScrn 74, -77*
Hines, Albert *PupTheA*
Hines, Dixie d1928 *NotNAT B*
Hines, Earl *BgBands 74*
Hines, Earl 1905- *AmSCAP 66, -80, Baker 78, BiDAmM, CmpEPM, DrBlPA, EncJzS 70, IlEncJ, MusMk[port], NewGrD 80*
Hines, Elizabeth 1894?-1971 *CmpEPM, EncMT*
Hines, Elizabeth 1899-1971 *WhThe*
Hines, Fatha 1903- *WhoJazz 72*
Hines, Fatha 1905- *EncJzS 70*
Hines, George Thomas 1916- *AmSCAP 66, -80*
Hines, Harry 1889-1967 *ForYSC, WhScrn 74, -77, WhoHol B*
Hines, Jerome 1921- *AmSCAP 80, Baker 78, BiDAmM, CmOp, IntWWM 80, MusSN[port], NewEOp 71, NewGrD 80, WhoMus 72, WhoOp 76*
Hines, John *MorBAP*
Hines, Johnny d1970 *MotPP, WhoHol B*
Hines, Johnny 1895-1970 *Film 1, -2, FilmgC, HalFC 80, TwYS*
Hines, Johnny 1897-1970 *WhScrn 74, -77*
Hines, Mimi 1933- *BiDAmM*
Hines, Patrick 1930- *BiE&WWA, NotNAT, WhoThe 77*
Hines, Robert S 1926- *IntWWM 77, -80*
Hines, Samuel E 1881-1939 *WhScrn 74, -77, WhoHol B*
Hingeston, John d1688 *NewGrD 80[port]*
Hingle, Pat *MotPP, PlP&P[port], -A[port], WhoHol A*
Hingle, Pat 1923- *FilmEn, FilmgC, HalFC 80, IntMPA 77, -75, -76, -78, -79, -80, WhoThe 72, -77*
Hingle, Pat 1924- *BiE&WWA, ForYSC, MovMk[port], NotNAT*
Hingley, Herbert Barrie 1938- *IntWWM 80*
Hingston, John d1683 *Baker 78, OxMus*
Hingston, John d1688 *NewGrD 80[port]*
Hinkel, Cecil E 1913- *BiE&WWA, NotNAT*
Hinkle, Ellen Clair Fuqua *IntWWM 77, -80*
Hinkle, Robert 1930- *IntMPA 77, -75, -76, -78, -79, -80*
Hinkson, Mary 1930- *BiE&WWA, CnOxB, DancEn 78[port]*
Hinlopen, Francina 1908- *IntWWM 77, -80*
Hinnant, Bill 1935- *NotNAT*
Hinner, Philipp Joseph 1754-1805? *NewGrD 80*
Hino, Motohiko 1946- *EncJzS 70*
Hino, Terumasa 1942- *EncJzS 70*
Hinreiner, Ernst 1920- *IntWWM 80*
Hinrichs, Gustav 1850-1942 *Baker 78, BiDAmM, NewEOp 71*
Hinrichsen, Heinrich 1868-1942 *Baker 78*
Hinrichsen, Max 1901-1965 *Baker 78*
Hinrichsen, Walter 1907-1969 *Baker 78*
Hinshaw, William Wade 1867-1947 *Baker 78, BiDAmM, NotNAT B*
Hinterhofer, Grete 1899- *IntWWM 80, WhoMus 72*
Hinterhoffer, Grete 1899- *IntWWM 77*
Hinton, Arthur 1869-1941 *Baker 78*
Hinton, Dallas Edward 1946- *IntWWM 77, -80*
Hinton, Ed 1928-1958 *WhScrn 74, -77, WhoHol B*
Hinton, Joe *RkOn*
Hinton, Judge 1910- *EncJzS 70*
Hinton, Mary 1896- *WhThe*
Hinton, Milt 1910- *CmpEPM, EncJzS 70, IlEncJ*
Hinton, Milton John 1910- *AmSCAP 80, BiDAmM, EncJzS 70, WhoJazz 72*
Hinton, Paula 1924- *CnOxB, DancEn 78*
Hinton, Sam 1917- *BiDAmM, EncFCWM 69*
Hinton-Braaten, Kathleen 1941- *IntWWM 80*
Hintz, Ewaldt d1666? *NewGrD 80*
Hintze, Jacob 1622-1702 *NewGrD 80*
Hinwood, Peter *WhoHol A*

Hinze-Reinhold, Bruno 1877-1964 *Baker 78*
Hiob, Hanne 1923- *EncWT*
Hiolski, Andrzej 1922- *NewGrD 80*
Hipkins, Alfred James 1826-1903 *Baker 78, NewGrD 80, OxMus*
Hippe, Lew 1880-1952 *WhScrn 74, -77*
Hippisley, John d1748 *NotNAT B*
Hippisley, John d1767 *NotNAT B*
Hirao, Kishio 1907-1953 *Baker 78, NewGrD 80*
Hirata, Kyoko *WhoOp 76*
Hirayoshi, Takekuni 1936- *Baker 78*
Hirche, Peter 1923- *CnMD, CroCD*
Hird, Thora *WhoHol A*
Hird, Thora 1914- *FilmgC, HalFC 80, IntMPA 77, -75, -76, -78, -79, -80, OxFilm*
Hird, Thora 1916- *WhoThe 72, -77*
Hired Hands *BiDAmM*
Hirose, George 1899-1974 *WhScrn 77*
Hirose, Ryohei 1930- *NewGrD 80*
Hirsau, William Of *NewGrD 80*
Hirsch, Charles Henry 1870- *WhThe*
Hirsch, Elroy 1924- *ForYSC, WhoHol A*
Hirsch, Georges *DancEn 78*
Hirsch, Godfrey M 1907- *BiDAmM*
Hirsch, Harry *ConMuA 80B*
Hirsch, John Stephan 1930- *NotNAT, WhoThe 72, -77*
Hirsch, John Stephen 1930- *CreCan 2*
Hirsch, Judd *IntMPA 78, -79, -80*
Hirsch, Leonard 1902- *IntWWM 77, -80, NewGrD 80*
Hirsch, Leonard 1909- *WhoMus 72*
Hirsch, Louis Achille d1924 *Sw&Ld B*
Hirsch, Louis Achille 1881-1924 *WhThe*
Hirsch, Louis Achille 1887-1924 *AmPS, AmSCAP 66, -80, BiDAmM, CmpEPM, EncMT, NewCBMT, NotNAT B, PopAmC[port]*
Hirsch, Max d1925 *NotNAT B*
Hirsch, Paul Adolf 1881-1951 *Baker 78, NewGrD 80, OxMus*
Hirsch, Robert 1924- *FilmEn*
Hirsch, Robert 1926- *EncWT*
Hirsch, Robert 1929- *FilmgC, HalFC 80*
Hirsch, Samuel 1917- *BiE&WWA, ConAmTC*
Hirsch, Walter 1891- *AmSCAP 66, -80, CmpEPM*
Hirschbein, Peretz 1880-1948 *McGEWD[port]*
Hirschbein, Peretz 1880-1949 *NotNAT B, OxThe*
Hirschfeld, Al 1903- *BiE&WWA, NotNAT*
Hirschfeld, Georg 1873-1942 *McGEWD, ModWD*
Hirschfeld, Gerald *FilmgC, HalFC 80*
Hirschfeld, Kurt 1902-1964 *EncWT*
Hirschfeld, Robert 1857-1914 *Baker 78*
Hirschfield, Alan J *IntMPA 77, -75, -76, -78, -79, -80*
Hirschman, Herbert *IntMPA 77, -75, -76, -78, -79, -80, NewYTET*
Hirschmann, Henri 1872- *WhThe*
Hirsemenzel, Lebrecht *NewGrD 80*
Hirsh, Albert 1915- *IntWWM 77, -80*
Hirshan, Leonard 1927- *IntMPA 77, -75, -76, -78, -79, -80*
Hirshbein, Peretz 1880-1948 *CnThe, ModWD, REnWD[port]*
Hirshberg, Jack 1917- *IntMPA 77, -75, -76, -78, -79, -80*
Hirshhorn, Naomi Caryl *AmSCAP 66, -80*
Hirshhorn, Philipp 1946- *IntWWM 77, -80*
Hirson, Roger O *NotNAT*
Hirst, Alan 1931-1937 *WhScrn 74, -77*
Hirst, Grayson 1939- *WhoOp 76*
Hirt, Al 1922- *CmpEPM, IntMPA 77, -75, -76, -78, -79, -80, NewOrJ[port], RkOn 2[port]*
Hirt, Alois Maxwell 1922- *BiDAmM*
Hirt, Charles Carleton 1911- *AmSCAP 80*
Hirt, Franz Josef 1899- *Baker 78, IntWWM 77, -80*
Hirt, Franz Joseph 1899- *NewGrD 80*
Hirt, Fritz 1888-1970 *Baker 78*
Hirt, Gerald P *NewOrJ*
Hirt, Gerald P 1924- *BiDAmM*
Hirte, Klaus 1937- *IntWWM 80, WhoOp 76*
Hirtzel, Robert Lewis 1913- *IntWWM 77, -80*
Hiscott, James Michael 1948- *IntWWM 80*
Hiscott, Leslie 1894-1968 *FilmgC, HalFC 80, IlWWBF*
Hiscott, Leslie Stephenson 1894-1968 *FilmEn*
Hisle, Betsy Ann *Film 2*
Hislop, Joseph *WhoMus 72*
Hislop, Joseph 1884-1977 *NewGrD 80*
Hislop, Joseph 1887- *WhThe*
Hislop, Joseph Dewar 1884- *IntWWM 77, -80*
Hislop, Robert Alexander 1954- *IntWWM 77*
Hisnauius, Christoph *NewGrD 80*
Hisnauius, Johann *NewGrD 80*
Hiss, Alger 1904- *What 1[port]*
Hita, Arcipreste De *NewGrD 80*
Hita, Antonio Rodriguez De *NewGrD 80*
Hitchcock *NewGrD 80*
Hitchcock, Alfred 1899-1980 *AmFD, BiDFilm, -81, CmMov, ConLC 16, DcFM, FilmEn, Film 2, FilmgC, HalFC 80, IlWWBF[port], -A[port], IntMPA 77, -75, -76, -78, -79, -80, MovMk[port], NewYTET, OxFilm, WhoHrs 80[port], WorEFlm[port]*
Hitchcock, Charles *Film 1*
Hitchcock, H Wiley 1923- *Baker 78, IntWWM 77, -80, NewGrD 80*
Hitchcock, John d1774 *NewGrD 80*
Hitchcock, Keith d1966 *WhScrn 77, WhoHol B*
Hitchcock, Pat *WhoHol A*
Hitchcock, Raymond d1929 *AmPS B, MotPP, WhoHol B, WhoStg 1906*
Hitchcock, Raymond 1865-1929 *CmpEPM, EncMT, Film 1, -2, NotNAT B, TwYS, WhThe*
Hitchcock, Raymond 1870-1929 *WhScrn 74, -77*
Hitchcock, Raymond 1871-1929 *WhoStg 1908*
Hitchcock, Rex d1950 *WhoHol B*
Hitchcock, Robert d1809 *NotNAT B*
Hitchcock, Thomas d1700? *NewGrD 80*
Hitchcock, Thomas 1685?-1733? *NewGrD 80*
Hitchcock, Walter d1917 *WhScrn 77*
Hitchins, Aubrey 1906-1969 *CnOxB, DancEn 78*
Hite, Catharine L *WhoOp 76*
Hite, David Leroy 1923- *IntWWM 77, -80*
Hite, Les 1903-1962 *AmSCAP 66, -80, BgBands 74, BiDAmM, CmpEPM, WhoJazz 72*
Hite, Mabel 1885-1912 *NotNAT B, WhoStg 1906, -1908*
Hite, Matie 1890?-1935? *BluesWW*
Hite, Mattie 1890?-1935? *BluesWW*
Hite, Nellie *BluesWW[port]*
Hitler, Adolf 1889-1945 *HalFC 80*
Hitt, J T 1922- *IntMPA 77, -75, -76, -78, -79, -80*
Hitzenauer, Christoph *NewGrD 80*
Hitzenauer, Johann *NewGrD 80*
Hitzler, Daniel 1576-1635 *NewGrD 80*
Hively, Jack 1907?- *FilmgC, HalFC 80*
Hively, Wells 1902-1969 *ConAmC*
Hivnor, Robert 1916- *ConDr 73, -77, CroCD*
Hix, Al 1918- *IntMPA 77, -75, -76, -78, -79, -80*
Hix, Don d1964 *WhScrn 74, -77, WhoHol B*
Hixon, Donald L 1942- *IntWWM 77, -80*
Hjelde, Hakon *Film 2*
Hjelmborg, Bjorn 1911- *IntWWM 77, -80*
Hjorleifsson, Siguringi 1902- *NewGrD 80*
Hjort Albertsen, Per 1919- *Baker 78*
Hladnik, Bostjan 1929- *OxFilm*
Hlavac, Miroslav 1923- *IntWWM 77, -80*
Hlawiczka, Karol 1894- *IntWWM 77, -80*
Hlobil, Emil 1901- *Baker 78, IntWWM 77, -80, NewGrD 80*
Hlohovsky, Jiri *NewGrD 80*
Hmelev, Hmelyov *OxThe*
Hnilicka, Alois 1858-1939 *NewGrD 80*
Ho, Chew *Film 2*
Ho, Don *RkOn 2A*
Ho, Edward Sze-Nang 1939- *IntWWM 80, WhoMus 72*
Ho, Laura *WomWMM B*
Ho-Chang, King *Film 2*
Hoadley, Bishop *PIP&P*
Hoadley, Benjamin d1757 *NotNAT B*
Hoadley, John d1776 *NotNAT B*
Hoadly, Benjamin 1706-1757 *OxThe*
Hoag, Charles K *CpmDNM 80, ConAmC*
Hoag, Mitzi *WhoHol A*
Hoagey, Catherine Yeakel 1908- *AmSCAP 66, -80*
Hoagland, Everett *BgBands 74*
Hoagland, Harland 1896-1971 *WhScrn 74, -77*
Hoare, Douglas 1875- *WhThe*
Hoare, Frank Alan 1894- *IntMPA 77, -75, -76, -78*
Hoare, George William 1911- *WhoMus 72*
Hoare, Prince d1834 *NotNAT B*
Hoare, Victor J *IntMPA 77, -75, -76, -78, -79, -80*
Hoare, William Acton 1928- *IntWWM 77, -80*
Hoban, Agnes E d1962 *NotNAT B*
Hoban, John 1926- *NewGrD 80*
Hoban, Tana *WomWMM B*
Hobart, Doty d1958 *NotNAT B*
Hobart, George V 1867-1926 *AmSCAP 66, -80, CmpEPM, NotNAT B, WhThe, WhoStg 1908*
Hobart, Rose 1906- *BiE&WWA, FilmEn, FilmgC, ForYSC, HalFC 80, MovMk, NotNAT, ThFT[port], WhThe, WhoHol A*
Hobbes, Halliwell 1877-1962 *FilmEn, Film 2, FilmgC, HalFC 80, HolCA[port], IntMPA 77, -75, -76, -78, -79, -80, MotPP, MovMk, NotNAT B, Vers A[port], WhScrn 74, -77, WhoHol B*
Hobbes, Halliwell 1878-1962 *ForYSC*
Hobbes, Herbert Halliwell 1877-1962 *WhThe*
Hobbes, John Oliver d1906 *NotNAT B*
Hobbes, Nancy Marsland d1968 *WhoHol B*
Hobbs, Allen 1937- *IntWWM 80*
Hobbs, Carleton 1898- *WhThe*
Hobbs, Cecelia Ann 1959- *BlkWAB*
Hobbs, Christopher 1950- *DcCM*
Hobbs, Frederick 1880-1942 *NotNAT B, WhThe*
Hobbs, Hayford *Film 2*
Hobbs, J Kline 1938- *NatPD[port]*
Hobbs, Jack 1893-1968 *Film 1, -2, FilmgC, HalFC 80, IlWWBF, NotNAT B, WhScrn 77, WhThe*
Hobbs, Jerry David 1941- *AmSCAP 80*
Hobbs, Oliver P 1907- *IntWWM 77, -80*
Hobbs, Peter *WhoHol A*
Hobbs, William 1939- *WhoThe 72, -77*
Hobcroft, Rex Kelvin 1925- *IntWWM 77, -80*
Hobden, Andree Maillet *CreCan 2*
Hoberecht, John Lewis *NewGrD 80*
Hobgood, Burnet 1922- *BiE&WWA, NotNAT*
Hobi, Frank 1923- *DancEn 78*
Hobi, Frank 1923-1967 *CnOxB*
Hobin, Bill 1923- *IntMPA 77, -75, -76, -78, -79, -80, NewYTET*
Hobley, McDonald *IntMPA 77, -75, -76, -78, -79, -80*
Hoboken, Anthony Van 1887- *Baker 78, NewGrD 80*
Hobrecht, Jacob *NewGrD 80*
Hobson, Ann Stephens 1943- *IntWWM 80*
Hobson, Ann Stevens 1943- *BlkWAB[port]*
Hobson, Bruce 1943- *IntWWM 77, -80*
Hobson, Harold 1904- *BiE&WWA, CroCD, EncWT, NotNAT, WhoThe 72, -77*
Hobson, Maud d1913 *NotNAT B*
Hobson, May 1889- *WhThe*
Hobson, Richard H 1944- *AmSCAP 80*
Hobson, Robert Bruce 1943- *CpmDNM 80*
Hobson, Valerie 1913- *ForYSC*
Hobson, Valerie 1917- *FilmEn, FilmgC, HalFC 80, IlWWBF[port], MovMk, OxFilm, ThFT[port], WhoHol A, WhoHrs 80*
Hoch, Emil H 1866-1944 *Film 2, WhScrn 77*
Hoch, Francesco 1943- *IntWWM 77, -80*
Hoch, Winton C *IntMPA 77, -75, -76, -78, -79*
Hoch, Winton C 1905-1979 *HalFC 80*
Hoch, Winton C 1908?- *CmMov, FilmgC, WorEFlm*
Hoch, Winton C 1910- *FilmEn*
Hochberg, Count Bolko Von 1843-1926 *Baker 78*
Hochberg, Hans Heinrich, Bolko Graf Von 1843-1926 *NewGrD 80*
Hochberg, Victoria *WomWMM B*
Hochbrucker *NewGrD 80*
Hochbrucker, Christian 1733-1792? *NewGrD 80*
Hochbrucker, Coelestin 1727-1809 *NewGrD 80*

Hochbrucker, Jakob 1673?- *NewGrD 80*
Hochbrucker, Simon 1699-1750? *NewGrD 80*
Hocher, William 1943- *AmSCAP 80*
Hochfeder, Kasper *NewGrD 80*
Hochhauser, Victor 1923- *WhoMus 72*
Hochheimer, Laura 1933- *IntWWM 77, -80*
Hochhuth, Rolf 1931- *CnMD, CnThe, CroCD, EncWT, Ent, McGEWD[port], ModWD, NotNAT, REnWD[port], WhoThe 72, -77*
Hochman, Sandra *WomWMM B*
Hochprugger *NewGrD 80*
Hochreiter, Emil 1871-1938 *Baker 78*
Hochreiter, Joseph Balthasar 1668?-1731 *NewGrD 80*
Hochstetter, Armin Caspar 1899- *WhoMus 72*
Hochuli, Paul d1964 *NotNAT B*
Hochwalder, Fritz 1911- *CnMD, CnThe, CroCD, EncWT, Ent, McGEWD[port], ModWD, OxThe, REnWD[port]*
Hock, Mort 1929- *IntMPA 77, -75, -76, -78, -79, -80*
Hock, Richard 1933-1961 *WhScrn 74, -77*
Hockensmith, Hadley 1949- *AmSCAP 80*
Hocker, David 1911- *BiE&WWA, NotNAT*
Hockh, Carl 1707-1773 *NewGrD 80*
Hockland, Robert *NewGrD 80*
Hockley, Herbert Joseph 1900- *WhoMus 72*
Hockridge, Edmund 1919- *WhThe, WhoThe 72*
Hoctor, Harriet 1907- *BiE&WWA, CnOxB, DancEn 78, NotNAT, WhThe*
Hodas, Dorothy Gertrude 1912- *AmSCAP 66, -80*
Hodatyev, Nikolai *DcFM*
Hodd, Joseph B, Sr. 1896-1965 *WhScrn 74, -77*
Hodder-Williams, Christopher 1927- *IntMPA 77, -75, -76, -78, -79, -80*
Hoddinot, Alun 1929- *MusMk*
Hoddinott, Alun 1929- *Baker 78, CpmDNM 80, DcCom&M 79, IntWWM 77, -80, NewGrD 80, OxMus, WhoMus 72*
Hodeir, Andre 1921- *Baker 78, EncJzS 70, NewGrD 80*
Hodell, Ake 1919- *IntWWM 77, -80*
Hodemont, Leonard De 1575?-1636 *NewGrD 80*
Hodenfield, Jan *ConAmTC*
Hodes, Art 1904- *CmpEPM, EncJzS 70, IlEncJ, WhoJazz 72*
Hodes, Arthur W 1904- *AmSCAP 66, BiDAmM, EncJzS 70*
Hodes, Linda *CnOxB, DancEn 78*
Hodes, Roberta *WomWMM A, -B*
Hodes, Sophie *AmSCAP 80*
Hodes, Stuart 1924- *CmpGMD, CnOxB, DancEn 78[port]*
Hodgdon, Samuel K d1922 *NotNAT B*
Hodge, Francis Richard 1915- *BiE&WWA, NotNAT*
Hodge, Merton 1904-1958 *NotNAT B, WhThe*
Hodge, Runa *Film 1*
Hodge, William Thomas 1874-1932 *NotNAT B, OxThe, WhThe*
Hodgeman, Thomas 1875-1931 *WhScrn 74, -77*
Hodges *NewGrD 80*
Hodges, Anthony Thomas 1934- *IntWWM 80*
Hodges, Charles Edward, Sr. 1947- *AmSCAP 80*
Hodges, Clifford Cecil 1905- *WhoMus 72*
Hodges, Eddie 1947- *BiE&WWA, ForYSC, MotPP, RkOn[port], WhoHol A*
Hodges, Edward 1796-1867 *Baker 78, NewGrD 80, OxMus*
Hodges, Edward 1796-1876 *BiDAmM*
Hodges, Faustina Hasse 1823-1895 *NewGrD 80*
Hodges, Horace 1865-1951 *NotNAT B, WhThe, WhoHol B*
Hodges, J Sebastian B 1830-1915 *NewGrD 80*
Hodges, James S 1885- *AmSCAP 66, -80*
Hodges, John Cornelius 1906-1970 *BiDAmM, EncJzS 70*
Hodges, John G 1915-1971 *BiDAmM*
Hodges, John Sebastian Bach 1830-1915 *BiDAmM*
Hodges, Johnny 1906-1970 *Baker 78, CmpEPM, EncJzS 70, IlEncJ, MusMk, NewGrD 80, WhoJazz 72*
Hodges, Johnny 1907-1970 *AmSCAP 66, -80, DrBlPA*
Hodges, Joy 1916- *CmpEPM, ForYSC, WhoHol A*
Hodges, Ken 1922- *FilmgC, HalFC 80*
Hodges, Kenneth 1929- *IntWWM 77*
Hodges, Leigh Mitchell 1876-1954 *BiDAmM*
Hodges, Mike 1932- *FilmgC, HalFC 80*
Hodges, Rabbit 1906-1970 *EncJzS 70, WhoJazz 72*
Hodges, Russ d1971 *WhoHol B*
Hodges, William Cullen 1876-1961 *WhScrn 74, -77, WhoHol B*
Hodges, William Kennedy 1951- *IntWWM 77, -80*
Hodgins, Earl 1899-1964 *ForYSC, WhScrn 74, -77, WhoHol B*
Hodgins, Earle 1899-1964 *NotNAT B, Vers B[port]*
Hodgins, Leslie 1885-1927 *WhScrn 74, -77*
Hodgkinson, John 1765?-1805 *NotNAT B*
Hodgkinson, John 1767-1805 *BiDAmM, FamA&A[port], OxThe, PlP&P[port]*
Hodgkinson, Mrs. John 1770?-1803 *BiDAmM, NotNAT B, PlP&P*
Hodgson, Alfreda *IntWWM 77, -80*
Hodgson, Brian 1938- *CnOxB*
Hodgson, Frederic *WhoMus 72*
Hodgson, Leland d1949 *WhScrn 77*
Hodgson, Leyland 1893-1949 *Vers A[port], WhoHol B*
Hodgson, Mary Muir 1918- *WhoMus 72*
Hodgson, May *WhoMus 72*
Hodgson, Thomas Sherlock 1924- *CreCan 2*
Hodiak, John 1914-1955 *CmMov, FilmEn, FilmgC, ForYSC, HalFC 80, HolP 40[port], MGM[port], MotPP, MovMk[port], NotNAT B, WhScrn 74, -77, WhoHol B*
Hodinarova, Elvira 1927- *IntWWM 77, -80*
Hodkinson, Sydney Phillip 1934- *Baker 78, CpmDNM 77, -78, -79, -80, ConAmC, DcCM, IntWWM 77, -80*
Hodkinson, W W 1881-1971 *FilmEn*
Hodowud, Edward Fred 1924- *AmSCAP 66, -80*
Hodsdon, Alec 1900- *NewGrD 80*
Hodsdon, Margaret 1898- *WhoMus 72*
Hodson, Henrietta 1841-1910 *NotNAT B, OxThe*
Hodson, James Landsdale d1956 *NotNAT B*
Hodson, Kate d1917 *NotNAT B*
Hodson, Nellie d1940 *NotNAT B*
Hodson, Sylvia d1893 *NotNAT B*
Hodston, Leland d1949 *WhScrn 74*
Hoeberechts, John Lewis 1760?-1820? *NewGrD 80*
Hoeberg, Georg 1872-1950 *Baker 78*
Hoecke, Micha Van 1945- *CnOxB*
Hoeckele, Andrew L 1942- *IntWWM 77, -80*
Hoedemont, Leonard De *NewGrD 80*
Hoeflich, Lucie 1883-1956 *WhScrn 74, -77*
Hoeg, Carsten 1896-1961 *NewGrD 80*
Hoeg, Michael Erling 1948- *IntWWM 77, -80*
Hoekman, Guus 1913- *NewGrD 80, WhoMus 72*
Hoelcl, Gisela *WomWMM B*
Hoellering, George 1900- *FilmgC, HalFC 80, OxFilm*
Hoelscher, Jean *WomWMM A, -B*
Hoeltzel, Michael 1936- *IntWWM 77, -80*
Hoene, Barbara 1944- *WhoOp 76*
Hoengen, Elisabeth *IntWWM 77, -80*
Hoengen, Elisabeth 1906- *CmOp*
Hoenich, Richard S 1955- *IntWWM 77, -80*
Hoenig, Lawrence Martin 1942- *IntWWM 77, -80*
Hoepner, Stephan 1580?-1628 *NewGrD 80*
Hoerbiger, Paul 1894- *FilmAG WE*
Hoerburger, Felix 1916- *NewGrD 80*
Hoeree, Arthur 1897- *Baker 78, NewGrD 80*
Hoesick, Ferdinand 1867-1941 *Baker 78*
Hoesslin, Franz Von 1885-1946 *Baker 78, NewEOp 71*
Hoeven, Carl VanDer 1580-1661 *NewGrD 80*
Hoey, Dennis d1961 *WhoHol B*
Hoey, Dennis 1893-1960 *FilmEn, FilmgC, HalFC 80, NotNAT B, WhScrn 74, -77, WhThe, WhoHrs 80*
Hoey, Dennis 1895-1960 *ForYSC*
Hoey, George J 1885-1955 *WhScrn 74, -77*
Hoey, Iris 1885- *WhThe*
Hoey, Juliet Therese 1937- *IntWWM 80*
Hoey, William d1897 *NotNAT B*
Hof, Nickel Von *NewGrD 80*
Hofacker, Andreas *NewGrD 80*
Hofen, Carolus VonDer *NewGrD 80*
Hofer, Andreas 1629-1684 *NewGrD 80*
Hofer, Chris 1920-1964 *NotNAT B, WhScrn 74, -77*
Hofer, Josepha *NewGrD 80*
Hofer, Walter *ConMuA 80B*
Hoff, Brynjar 1940- *IntWWM 77, -80*
Hoff, Carl 1905?- *BgBands 74, CmpEPM*
Hoff, J Robert 1909- *IntMPA 77, -75, -76, -78, -79, -80*
Hoff, Louise 1921- *BiE&WWA*
Hoff, Vivian Beaumont 1911- *AmSCAP 66, -80*
Hoffa, Portland *JoeFr*
Hoffding, Finn 1899- *Baker 78, DcCM, NewGrD 80, OxMus*
Hoffe, Barbara *WhThe*
Hoffe, Monckton 1880-1951 *NotNAT B, WhScrn 74, -77, WhThe, WhoHol B*
Hoffelt, Robert O 1920- *CpmDNM 74, ConAmC A*
Hoffen, Carl VanDer *NewGrD 80*
Hoffenstein, Samuel 1889-1947 *FilmEn*
Hoffenstein, Samuel 1890-1947 *HalFC 80*
Hoffer, Andreas *NewGrD 80*
Hoffer, Bernard 1934- *AmSCAP 80*
Hoffer, Emil *Film 2*
Hoffer, Jay *AmSCAP 80*
Hoffer, Johann Berthold Von 1667-1718 *NewGrD 80*
Hoffer, Paul 1895-1949 *Baker 78, NewGrD 80*
Hoffer-V Winterfield, Linde 1919- *IntWWM 77, -80*
Hoffert, Paul 1943- *IntWWM 80*
Hoffgen, Marga 1921- *NewGrD 80*
Hoffhaimer, Paul *NewGrD 80*
Hoffler, Konrad 1647-1705? *NewGrD 80*
Hoffman, Aaron 1880-1924 *NotNAT B, WhThe*
Hoffman, Al 1902-1960 *AmSCAP 66, -80, BiDAmM, CmpEPM, Sw&Ld C*
Hoffman, Alfred 1929- *IntWWM 77, -80*
Hoffman, Allen 1942- *AmSCAP 80, CpmDNM 79, ConAmC*
Hoffman, Bern *WhoHol A*
Hoffman, Bill d1962 *NotNAT B*
Hoffman, Brad *ConMuA 80B*
Hoffman, Cary 1940- *AmSCAP 80*
Hoffman, Charles 1911-1972 *FilmEn*
Hoffman, Charles Fenno 1806-1884 *BiDAmM*
Hoffman, Dave A 1890-1958 *AmSCAP 66*
Hoffman, David 1904-1961 *WhScrn 77*
Hoffman, Donald Stuart 1931- *WhoMus 72*
Hoffman, Dustin 1937- *BiDFilm 81, Ent, FilmEn, FilmgC, ForYSC, HalFC 80, IntMPA 77, -75, -76, -78, -79, -80, MotPP, MovMk[port], OxFilm, WhoHol A, WhoThe 72, -77*
Hoffman, Eberhard 1883-1957 *WhScrn 74, -77, WhoHol B*
Hoffman, Edith Ritter 1914- *AmSCAP 80*
Hoffman, Elisha Albright 1839-1929 *NewGrD 80*
Hoffman, Elliot *ConMuA 80B*
Hoffman, Ferdi *WhoHol A*
Hoffman, Francois-Benoit 1760-1828 *NewGrD 80, OxThe*
Hoffman, Gertrude 1898-1955 *NotNAT B, WhScrn 74, -77*
Hoffman, Gertrude W 1871-1959 *ForYSC*
Hoffman, Gertrude W 1871-1966 *WhScrn 74, -77, WhoHol B*
Hoffman, Goldie 1925- *NewGrD 80*
Hoffman, Grace 1925- *CmOp, IntWWM 77, -80, NewGrD 80, WhoOp 76*
Hoffman, Gustav *NewGrD 80*
Hoffman, Guy *CreCan 1*
Hoffman, H F *Film 1*
Hoffman, Harold M 1908- *BiE&WWA*
Hoffman, Herman *IntMPA 77, -75, -76, -78, -79, -80*
Hoffman, Hermine H 1921-1971 *WhScrn 74, -77*
Hoffman, Howard R 1893-1969 *WhScrn 74, -77, WhoHol B*
Hoffman, Irwin 1924- *CreCan 1,*

IntWWM 77, -80, WhoMus 72
Hoffman, Jack 1917- *AmSCAP 66, -80*
Hoffman, James Senate 1922- *AmSCAP 80*
Hoffman, Jan 1814-1849 *NewGrD 80*
Hoffman, Jan 1906- *IntWWM 77, -80*
Hoffman, Jane *BiE&WWA, NotNAT, WhoHol A, WhoThe 72, -77*
Hoffman, Jaromir 1847-1918 *NewGrD 80*
Hoffman, Jerzy 1932- *FilmEn*
Hoffman, Joel Harvey 1953- *AmSCAP 80*
Hoffman, Joseph *IntMPA 77, -75, -76, -78, -79, -80*
Hoffman, Lola B *PupTheA*
Hoffman, Ludwig 1925- *IntWWM 77, -80*
Hoffman, Mark 1904- *WhoMus 72*
Hoffman, Maud *WhThe, WhoStg 1908*
Hoffman, Max 1873-1963 *CmpEPM, NotNAT B*
Hoffman, Max, Jr. 1902-1945 *NotNAT B, WhScrn 74, -77, WhoHol B*
Hoffman, Olivia Watson *AmSCAP 66, -80*
Hoffman, Otto 1879-1944 *Film 1, -2, ForYSC, TwYS, WhScrn 77*
Hoffman, Renaud 1900- *TwYS A*
Hoffman, Richard *AmSCAP 80*
Hoffman, Richard 1831-1909 *Baker 78, NewGrD 80*
Hoffman, Robert 1939- *FilmAG WE*
Hoffman, Roni *WomWMM B*
Hoffman, Ruby *Film 1, -2*
Hoffman, Stan *WhoHol A*
Hoffman, Stanley 1929- *IntWWM 77, -80*
Hoffman, Stanley David *AmSCAP 80*
Hoffman, Stanley David 1926- *AmSCAP 66*
Hoffman, Theodore 1922- *BiE&WWA, NotNAT*
Hoffman, Theodore 1925- *IntWWM 77, -80*
Hoffman, Theodore B 1925- *ConAmC*
Hoffman, William Lea 1943- *ConAmTC*
Hoffman, William M 1939- *AmSCAP 80, ConDr 73, -77, NotNAT*
Hoffman-Uddgren, Anna *WomWMM*
Hoffmann *NewGrD 80*
Hoffmann, A H *OxMus*
Hoffmann, Adolf G 1890-1968 *AmSCAP 66, -80, ConAmC A*
Hoffmann, Agnes *PupTheA*
Hoffmann, Bruno 1913- *IntWWM 77, -80, NewGrD 80*
Hoffmann, Carl 1881-1947 *FilmEn*
Hoffmann, E T A 1776-1822 *BnBkM 80, CmOp, NewGrD 80[port], OxMus*
Hoffmann, Ede *NewGrD 80*
Hoffmann, Eduard *NewGrD 80*
Hoffmann, Emilie 1816-1882 *NewGrD 80*
Hoffmann, Ernst Theodor Amadeus 1776-1822 *Baker 78, CnOxB, NewEOp 71*
Hoffmann, Eucharius d1588 *NewGrD 80*
Hoffmann, Gerhard 1690-1756? *NewGrD 80*
Hoffmann, Hans 1902-1949 *Baker 78*
Hoffmann, Heinrich August 1798-1874 *Baker 78*
Hoffmann, Horst 1935- *WhoOp 76*
Hoffmann, James A 1929- *ConAmC*
Hoffmann, Johann 1660?-1725 *NewGrD 80*
Hoffmann, Johann Wilhelm *NewGrD 80*
Hoffmann, Kurt 1912- *HalFC 80*
Hoffmann, Louis 1839-1919 *MagIlD*
Hoffmann, Ludwig 1925- *WhoMus 72*
Hoffmann, Max 1873-1963 *AmSCAP 66, -80*
Hoffmann, Melchior 1685?-1715 *NewGrD 80*
Hoffmann, Newton 1921- *ConAmC*
Hoffmann, Paul 1902- *EncWT*
Hoffmann, Peggy 1910- *ConAmC*
Hoffmann, Richard 1831-1909 *BiDAmM*
Hoffmann, Richard 1925- *Baker 78, CpmDNM 79, -80, ConAmC, DcCM, IntWWM 77, -80*
Hoffmann-Erbrecht, Lothar 1925- *IntWWM 77, -80, NewGrD 80*
Hoffmann VonFallersleben, August H 1798-1874 *NewGrD 80*
Hoffmeister, Franz Anton 1754-1812 *Baker 78, NewGrD 80*
Hoffmeister, Karel 1868-1952 *NewGrD 80*
Hoffnung, Gerard 1925-1959 *NewGrD 80*
Hoffrichter, Bertha Chaitkin 1915- *ConAmC*
Hoffstetter, Johann Urban Alois 1742-1808? *NewGrD 80*
Hoffstetter, Roman 1742-1815 *NewGrD 80*
Hofgen, Lothar 1936- *CnOxB, DancEn 78*
Hofhaimer, Paul 1459-1537 *Baker 78, MusMk, NewGrD 80*
Hofhaymer, Paul 1459-1537 *NewGrD 80*
Hoflich, Lucie 1883-1956 *EncWT, Ent, NotNAT B, WhoHol B*
Hofman, Shlomo 1909- *Baker 78, IntWWM 77, -80*
Hofman, Srdjan 1944- *IntWWM 77, -80*
Hofmann, Casimir 1842-1911 *Baker 78, NewGrD 80*
Hofmann, Eucharius *NewGrD 80*
Hofmann, Heinrich 1842-1902 *Baker 78, NewGrD 80*
Hofmann, Hermann Wolfgang *IntWWM 77, -80*
Hofmann, Hubert *WhoOp 76*
Hofmann, Josef 1876-1957 *Baker 78, BnBkM 80[port], MusSN[port], NewGrD 80, OxMus*
Hofmann, Joseph 1876-1957 *ConAmC*
Hofmann, Kazimierz 1842-1911 *NewGrD 80*
Hofmann, Leopold 1738-1793 *Baker 78, NewGrD 80*
Hofmann, Ludwig 1895-1963 *CmOp*
Hofmann, Richard 1844-1918 *Baker 78*
Hofmannsthal, Hugo Von 1874-1929 *BnBkM 80, CmOp, CnMD, CnThe, DcPup, EncWT, Ent, McGEWD[port], ModWD, NewEOp 71, NewGrD 80, NotNAT B, OxMus, OxThe, REnWD[port]*
Hofmans, Mathijs *NewGrD 80*
Hofmeister, Friedrich 1782-1864 *Baker 78, NewGrD 80*
Hofner, Adolph *IlEncCM*
Hofstetter, Georg *NewGrD 80*
Hofstetter, Igo 1926- *IntWWM 77, -80*
Hofstetter, Romanus 1742-1815 *Baker 78*
Hofzinser, Johann 1806-1875 *MagIlD*
Hogan, Earl Hap d1944 *Film 2, WhScrn 77*
Hogan, Ernest 1859?-1909 *BlksBF[port]*
Hogan, Ernest 1865- *BiDAmM*
Hogan, Francis T 1916- *AmSCAP 66*
Hogan, Frank *NatPD[port]*
Hogan, J P *Film 2*
Hogan, Jack *WhoHol A*
Hogan, James P 1891-1943 *FilmEn, FilmgC, HalFC 80, TwYS A*
Hogan, Michael 1898- *WhThe*
Hogan, Michael 1899- *IntMPA 77, -75, -76*
Hogan, Michael 1929- *DancEn 78*
Hogan, Pat 1931-1966 *WhScrn 74, -77, WhoHol B*
Hogan, Robert *WhoHol A*
Hogan, Silas 1911- *BluesWW[port]*
Hogan, Society Kid 1899-1962 *WhScrn 74, -77, WhoHol B*
Hogan, William *ConAmTC*
Hogarth, Ann *DcPup*
Hogarth, George 1783-1870 *Baker 78, NewGrD 80, OxMus*
Hogarth, John M 1931- *IntMPA 77, -75, -76, -78, -79, -80*
Hogarth, Lionel 1874-1946 *NotNAT B*
Hogarth, William 1697-1764 *DcPup, OxMus, PlP&P[port]*
Hogenson, Robert Charles 1936- *ConAmC*
Hoger De Laon *NewGrD 80*
Hogg, Andrew 1914-1960 *BluesWW[port]*
Hogg, Curly 1917-1974 *WhoHol B*
Hogg, Ian 1937- *WhoHol A, WhoThe 72, -77*
Hogg, Jack 1917-1974 *WhScrn 77*
Hogg, John 1912- *BluesWW[port]*
Hogg, Merle E 1922- *ConAmC, IntWWM 77, -80*
Hogg, Noela Lesley 1942- *IntWWM 77*
Hogg, Willie Anderson 1908- *BluesWW*
Hogler, Fritz 1901- *WhoMus 72*
Hoguet, Michael-Francois 1793-1871 *CnOxB*
Hogwood, Christopher Jarvis 1941- *IntWWM 80, NewGrD 80*
Hohengarten, Carl 1902- *AmSCAP 66*
Hohensee, Wolfgang Johann August 1927- *IntWWM 80*
Hohenstine, Joann *PupTheA*
Hohl, Arthur 1889-1964 *FilmgC, ForYSC, HalFC 80, HolCA[port], IntMPA 77, -75, -76, -78, -79, -80, Vers B[port], WhScrn 77*
Hohman, George C 1912- *AmSCAP 80*
Hohmann, Christian Heinrich 1811-1861 *NewGrD 80*
Hohmann, Walter H 1892-1971 *ConAmC*
Hohner, M *NewGrD 80*
Hoiby, Lee 1926- *AmSCAP 66, -80, Baker 78, BiDAmM, CpmDNM 79, ConAmC, DcCM, NewGrD 80*
Hoier, Esther W *Film 1*
Hoier, John Charles 1949- *AmSCAP 80*
Hoier, Thomas P d1951 *NotNAT B*
Hoijer, Bjorn-Erik 1907- *CnMD*
Hoijer, Johan Leonard 1815-1884 *NewGrD 80*
Hoing, Clifford Alfred 1903- *IntWWM 77, -80, WhoMus 72*
Hoiseth, Kolbjorn 1932- *NewGrD 80, WhoMus 72, WhoOp 76*
Hokanson, Dorothy Cadzow 1916- *ConAmC*
Hokanson, Margrethe 1893- *AmSCAP 66, -80, ConAmC*
Hoke, Hans Gunter 1928- *IntWWM 77, -80*
Hol, Dirk 1907- *IntWWM 77, -80*
Hol, Richard 1825-1904 *Baker 78, NewGrD 80, OxMus*
Hol, Rijk 1825-1904 *NewGrD 80*
Holan Rovensky, Vaclav Karel 1644-1718 *NewGrD 80*
Holasek, Ladislav 1929- *IntWWM 77, -80*
Holbach, Baron Paul Heinrich Dietrich D' 1723-1789 *OxMus*
Holbeck, Severin 1647?-1700 *NewGrD 80*
Holben, Lawrence Robert 1945- *AmSCAP 80*
Holberg, Ludvig 1684-1754 *CnThe, EncWT, Ent[port], McGEWD[port], NewEOp 71, OxThe, REnWD[port]*
Holberg, Ludwig 1684-1754 *NotNAT B*
Holberg, Waltraud 1914- *IntWWM 77*
Holborne, Anthony d1602 *BnBkM 80, OxMus*
Holborne, Antony d1602 *NewGrD 80*
Holborne, William *NewGrD 80, OxMus*
Holborne, William 1575- *BnBkM 80*
Holbrook, Ann Catherine d1837 *NotNAT B*
Holbrook, Gerald W 1946- *ConAmC*
Holbrook, Hal 1925- *BiE&WWA, FilmEn, FilmgC, HalFC 80, IntMPA 77, -75, -76, -78, -79, -80, MotPP, NotNAT, WhoHol A, WhoThe 72, -77*
Holbrook, Joseph Perry 1822-1888 *BiDAmM*
Holbrook, Louise *WhThe*
Holbrooke, Josef 1878-1958 *Baker 78, NewEOp 71, NewGrD 80*
Holbrooke, Joseph Charles 1878-1958 *NewGrD 80, OxMus*
Holcomb, Bruce Ring 1926- *IntWWM 80*
Holcomb, Helen *Film 2*
Holcomb, Roscoe 1913- *BiDAmM, EncFCWM 69*
Holcombe, Harry *ForYSC, WhoHol A*
Holcombe, Henry 1693?-1750 *NewGrD 80*
Holcombe, Ray Edward 1898- *BiE&WWA*
Holcombe, Wilford Lawshe, Jr. 1924- *AmSCAP 80*
Holcroft, Thomas 1744-1809 *EncWT, NotNAT B, OxThe*
Holcroft, Thomas 1745-1809 *Ent*
Hold, Trevor James 1939- *IntWWM 80, WhoMus 72*
Holde, Artur 1885-1962 *Baker 78*
Holden, Albert Junos 1841-1916 *BiDAmM*
Holden, Anne Stratton 1887- *AmSCAP 66*
Holden, David Justin 1911- *ConAmC*
Holden, Elisabeth 1934- *WhoMus 72*
Holden, Fay d1973 *MotPP, WhoHol B*
Holden, Fay 1893-1973 *HolCA[port], Vers A[port]*
Holden, Fay 1894-1973 *FilmgC, HalFC 80*
Holden, Fay 1895-1973 *FilmEn, ForYSC, MGM[port], MovMk, ThFT[port], WhScrn 77*
Holden, Gloria 1908- *FilmEn, FilmgC, HalFC 80, HolCA[port]*
Holden, Gloria 1909- *WhoHrs 80*
Holden, Gloria 1911- *ForYSC, IntMPA 77, -75, -76, -78, -79, -80*
Holden, Harry Moore 1868-1944 *Film 1, -2, WhScrn 74, -77, WhoHol B*
Holden, Jan 1931- *WhoHol A, WhoThe 72, -77*
Holden, John d1771? *NewGrD 80*
Holden, Joyce *ForYSC, WhoHol A*
Holden, Libby 1923- *AmSCAP 66*

Holden, Mary *Film 2*
Holden, Oliver 1765-1844 *Baker 78, BiDAmM, NewGrD 80*
Holden, Paul 1940- *AmSCAP 80*
Holden, Poppy 1948- *IntWWM 77, -80*
Holden, Randall LeConte 1943- *IntWWM 77, -80*
Holden, Ron 1939- *RkOn*
Holden, Scott *WhoHol A*
Holden, Sidney 1900-1947 *AmSCAP 66, -80*
Holden, Smollet d1813 *NewGrD 80*
Holden, Stanley 1928- *CnOxB, DancEn 78*
Holden, Steve *ConMuA 80B*
Holden, Thomas Lee 1926- *IntWWM 77, -80*
Holden, Viola d1967 *WhScrn 74, -77, WhoHol B*
Holden, William 1872-1932 *Film 2, HalFC 80[port], WhScrn 74, -77, WhoHol B*
Holden, William 1918- *BiDFilm, -81, CmMov, FilmEn, FilmgC, ForYSC, HalFC 80, IntMPA 77, -75, -76, -78, -79, -80, MotPP, MovMk[port], OxFilm, WhoHol A, WorEFlm[port]*
Holder, Alison Joyce 1917- *IntWWM 77, -80*
Holder, Christian 1949- *CnOxB*
Holder, Dawn 1938- *WhoMus 72*
Holder, Geoffrey 1930- *BiE&WWA, CnOxB, DancEn 78, DrBlPA, NotNAT, PlP&P A[port], WhoHol A, WhoThe 77*
Holder, Henry Richard 1924- *IntWWM 77, -80*
Holder, John Wesley 1939?- *BluesWW[port]*
Holder, Lawrence *BlkAmP*
Holder, Owen 1921- *WhoThe 72, -77*
Holder, Ram John 1940?- *DrBlPA*
Holder, Ray 1925- *IntWWM 77*
Holder, Roy Upton 1930- *IntWWM 77*
Holder, Stanley Donald 1929- *IntWWM 77*
Holder, Terrence 1898?- *WhoJazz 72*
Holder, William 1616-1696 *NewGrD 80*
Holderlin, Friedrich 1770-1843 *EncWT, McGEWD[port]*
Holderness, Fay *Film 1, -2*
Holdich, Margaret Cowen *WhoMus 72*
Holding, Thomas 1880-1929 *Film 1, -2, TwYS, WhScrn 77*
Holdorf, Udo Karl 1946- *WhoOp 76*
Holdren, Judd 1915-1974 *WhScrn 77, WhoHol B, WhoHrs 80*
Holdridge, Barbara 1929- *BiE&WWA*
Holdridge, Lee Elwood 1944- *AmSCAP 80, ConAmC*
Holdsworth, Frank 1930- *IntWWM 77, -80*
Holdsworth, Gerard 1904- *IntMPA 77, -75, -76, -78, -79, -80*
Hole, Harry Alfred 1900- *WhoMus 72*
Hole, Jonathan *WhoHol A*
Hole, William *NewGrD 80*
Hole, William J, Jr. *WhoHrs 80*
Holecek, Alfred 1907- *NewGrD 80*
Holecek, Josef 1939- *IntWWM 77, -80*
Holewa, Hans 1905- *Baker 78, NewGrD 80*
Holgate, Edwin Headley 1892- *CreCan 1*
Holger-Madsen 1878-1943 *DcFM*
Holger-Madsen, Forest 1878-1943 *FilmEn*
Holguin, Guillermo 1915-1959 *Baker 78*
Holiday, Billie 1915-1959 *AmPS B, Baker 78, BiDAmM, CmpEPM, DrBlPA, HalFC 80, IlEncJ, MusMk, NewGrD 80, NotNAT B, WhoHol B, WhoJazz 72*
Holiday, Hope *ForYSC, WhoHol A*
Holiday, Jimmy Edward 1934- *AmSCAP 80*
Holiday, Judy 1922-1965 *JoeFr[port]*
Holiday, Leila *WhoHol A*
Holiday, Marva Jean 1948- *AmSCAP 80*
Holien, Danny Leroy 1949- *AmSCAP 80*
Holifield, Harold *BlkAmP, MorBAP*
Holiner, Mann 1897-1958 *AmSCAP 66, -80*
Holinshed, Raphael d1580? *NotNAT B*
Holl, John William 1928- *IntWWM 77, -80*
Hollaender, Alexis 1840-1924 *Baker 78*
Hollaender, Frederick 1896- *WorEFlm*
Hollaender, Friedrich *NewGrD 80*
Hollaender, Gustav 1855-1915 *Baker 78, NewGrD 80*
Hollaender, Victor 1866-1940 *NewGrD 80*
Hollaender, Viktor 1866-1940 *Baker 78*
Holland, A K 1892-1980 *NewGrD 80*
Holland, Anthony 1912- *WhoThe 72, -77*
Holland, Anthony 1933- *BiE&WWA, NotNAT, WhoHol A*
Holland, Betty Lou 1931- *BiE&WWA, NotNAT, WhoHol A*
Holland, C Maurice d1974 *WhScrn 77*
Holland, Cecil *Film 2*
Holland, Charles d1796 *NotNAT B*
Holland, Charles d1849 *NotNAT B*
Holland, Clifford *Film 2*
Holland, David 1946- *EncJzS 70*
Holland, Denis 1913- *IntMPA 75, -76*
Holland, Dulcie Sybil 1913- *IntWWM 77, -80, WhoMus 72*
Holland, Eddie 1941- *RkOn*
Holland, Edmund Milton 1848-1913 *NotNAT B, OxThe, WhThe, WhoStg 1906, -1908*
Holland, Edna *WhoHol A*
Holland, Edward *Film 1*
Holland, Edwin *Film 2*
Holland, Fanny d1931 *NotNAT B*
Holland, George d1910 *NotNAT B*
Holland, George 1791-1870 *FamA&A[port], NotNAT A, -B, OxThe*
Holland, Gladys *WhoHol A*
Holland, Jacynth *IntWWM 77, -80*
Holland, James 1933- *IntWWM 77, -80, WhoMus 72*
Holland, Jan Dawid 1746-1827 *NewGrD 80*
Holland, Joe *Film 2*
Holland, Johann David 1746-1827 *NewGrD 80*
Holland, John *Film 2, WhoHol A*
Holland, John 1900- *ForYSC*
Holland, Jon Burnett 1949- *IntWWM 80*
Holland, Joseph Jefferson 1860-1926 *NotNAT B, OxThe*
Holland, Josiah Gilbert 1819-1881 *BiDAmM*
Holland, Justin 1819-1886 *BiDAmM, NewGrD 80*
Holland, Mildred 1869-1944 *NotNAT B, WhScrn 77, WhThe*
Holland, Miriam 1917-1948 *WhScrn 74, -77*
Holland, Peanuts 1910- *CmpEPM, WhoJazz 72*
Holland, R V 1916- *BiE&WWA, NotNAT*
Holland, Ralph 1888-1939 *WhScrn 74, -77*
Holland, Theodore 1878-1947 *Baker 78, NewGrD 80*
Holland, Wilfrid Marshall 1920- *IntWWM 77, -80*
Hollanda, Chico Buarque De 1942- *BiDAmM*
Hollande, Jean De *NewGrD 80*
Hollander, Alexis 1840-1924 *NewGrD 80*
Hollander, Alice *WhThe*
Hollander, Christian 1510?-1569? *NewGrD 80*
Hollander, Fred 1896- *CmpEPM*
Hollander, Frederick 1892-1976 *FilmgC, HalFC 80*
Hollander, Frederick 1896-1976 *AmPS, FilmEn, NewGrD 80, OxFilm*
Hollander, Gustav *NewGrD 80*
Hollander, Lorin 1944- *Baker 78, ConAmC*
Hollander, Ralph 1916- *AmSCAP 66, -80, ConAmC A*
Hollander, Sebastian *NewGrD 80*
Hollander, Victor *NewGrD 80*
Hollar, Lloyd *DrBlPA*
Holle, Hugo 1890-1942 *Baker 78*
Hollenbeck, Don d1954 *NewYTET*
Hollender, Alfred L *IntMPA 77, -75, -76, -78, -79, -80*
Holler, Augustin 1744-1814 *NewGrD 80*
Holler, John 1904- *AmSCAP 66, -80, ConAmC A*
Holler, Karl 1907- *Baker 78, NewGrD 80*
Holler, York 1944- *NewGrD 80*
Holles, Antony 1901-1950 *FilmgC, HalFC 80, NotNAT B, WhScrn 74, -77, WhThe, WhoHol B*
Holles, Robert *ConDr 73, -77C*
Holles, William 1867-1947 *WhThe*
Holley, Doyle *EncFCWM 69*
Holley, Major Quincy, Jr. 1924- *BiDAmM, EncJzS 70*
Holley, Ruth *Film 2*
Holley, William 1930- *WhoOp 76*
Holli, Andreas Franz *NewGrD 80*
Holliday, Billie 1915-1959 *WhScrn 77*
Holliday, Derek Michael 1947- *AmSCAP 80*
Holliday, Doc 1849-1885 *HalFC 80*
Holliday, Frank, Jr. 1913-1948 *WhScrn 74, -77*
Holliday, Fred *WhoHol A*
Holliday, John H 1850-1885 *OxFilm*
Holliday, Judy d1965 *BiE&WWA, MotPP, WhoHol B*
Holliday, Judy 1921-1965 *BiDFilm, -81, EncMT, WorEFlm[port]*
Holliday, Judy 1922-1965 *Ent, FilmEn, FilmgC, Funs[port], HalFC 80, MovMk[port], NotNAT B*
Holliday, Judy 1923-1965 *CmMov, OxFilm, WhScrn 74, -77, WhThe*
Holliday, Judy 1924-1965 *ForYSC*
Holliday, Kent Alfred 1940- *ConAmC*
Holliday, Margaret May 1921- *WhoMus 72*
Holliday, Marjorie 1920-1969 *WhScrn 74, -77, WhoHol B*
Hollier, Donald Russell 1934- *DcCM, IntWWM 80, NewGrD 80*
Hollier, John *NewGrD 80*
Hollies, The *ConMuA 80A, IlEncR, RkOn 2[port]*
Holliger, Hans 1939- *IntWWM 77, -80*
Holliger, Heinz 1939- *Baker 78, BnBkM 80, DcCM, NewGrD 80[port], WhoMus 72*
Holliman, Earl *IntMPA 77, -75, -76, -78, -79, -80, MotPP, WhoHol A*
Holliman, Earl 1928- *FilmEn, FilmgC, HalFC 80*
Holliman, Earl 1931- *ForYSC*
Holliman, Jamesetta 1938- *IntWWM 77, -80*
Hollinger, Hy *IntMPA 77, -75, -76, -78, -79, -80*
Hollingshead, Gordon 1892-1952 *WhScrn 74, -77*
Hollingshead, John 1827-1904 *NotNAT A, -B, OxThe*
Hollingshead-Love, Kermit *PupTheA*
Hollingsworth, Alfred 1874-1926 *Film 1, WhScrn 74, -77, WhoHol B*
Hollingsworth, Alfred 1875-1926 *NotNAT B*
Hollingsworth, Harry 1888-1947 *WhScrn 74, -77, WhoHol B*
Hollingsworth, John 1916-1963 *Baker 78*
Hollingsworth, Layne Ruskin 1918- *AmSCAP 80*
Hollingsworth, Samuel H, Jr. 1922- *IntWWM 80*
Hollingsworth, Stanley 1924- *Baker 78, ConAmC*
Hollingsworth, Thelka *AmSCAP 66, -80*
Hollinrake, Roger Barker 1929- *IntWWM 77, -80*
Hollins, Alfred 1865-1942 *Baker 78, OxMus*
Hollins, Mabel 1887- *WhoStg 1906, -1908*
Hollins, Tony 1900?-1959? *BluesWW*
Hollis, Alan *Film 2*
Hollis, Hylda *Film 1*
Hollis, Murray Cobb, III 1940- *AmSCAP 80*
Hollis, R W *PupTheA*
Hollis, William 1867-1947 *NotNAT B*
Hollister *NewGrD 80*
Hollister, Alice *MotPP*
Hollister, Alice 1886-1973 *WhScrn 77*
Hollister, Alice 1890- *Film 1, -2, TwYS*
Hollister, David M 1929- *CpmDNM 80, ConAmC*
Hollister, Frederick 1761- *NewGrD 80*
Hollister, Jane Love 1952- *IntWWM 77, -80*
Hollister, Philip d1760 *NewGrD 80*
Hollister, Robert *NewGrD 80*
Hollister, Thomas *NewGrD 80*
Hollister, William Castels d1802 *NewGrD 80*
Hollmann, Joseph 1852-1927 *Baker 78*
Hollodan, Damaskas *AmSCAP 80*
Hollombe, Daniel Ephraim 1957- *AmSCAP 80*
Holloway, Anthony 1922- *ConAmTC*
Holloway, Baliol 1883-1967 *PlP&P, WhThe*
Holloway, Brenda 1946- *RkOn 2[port]*
Holloway, Carol *Film 1, -2, TwYS*
Holloway, Clyde 1936- *IntWWM 77, -80*
Holloway, David 1942- *IntWWM 77, -80, WhoOp 76*
Holloway, Helen Joyce 1900- *AmSCAP 80*
Holloway, James L 1927- *BiDAmM, EncJzS 70*
Holloway, Kildee d1953 *NewOrJ*
Holloway, Red 1927- *EncJzS 70*
Holloway, Robert Charles 1927- *AmSCAP 80, IntWWM 77*
Holloway, Robin 1943- *Baker 78, NewGrD 80*
Holloway, Stanley 1890- *AmPS B,*

BiE&WWA, EncMT, EncWT, Ent, FilmAG WE, FilmEn, Film 2, FilmgC, ForYSC, HalFC 80, IlWWBF, -A[port], IntMPA 77, -75, -76, -78, -79, -80, MovMk[port], NotNAT, -A, WhoHol A, WhoThe 72, -77
Holloway, Sterling 1905- BiE&WWA, FilmEn, Film 2, FilmgC, ForYSC, HalFC 80, HolCA[port], IntMPA 77, -75, -76, -78, -79, -80, JoeFr, MotPP, MovMk[port], NotNAT, PlP&P, Vers B[port], What 3[port], WhoHol A
Holloway, W J d1913 NotNAT B
Holloway, William Edwyn 1885-1952 NotNAT B, WhThe
Hollreiser, Heinrich 1913- NewGrD 80, WhoOp 76
Hollweg, Ilse 1922- WhoMus 72
Hollweg, Werner Friedrich 1936- IntWWM 77, -80, WhoOp 76
Holly, Andreas Franz NewGrD 80
Holly, Buddy 1936-1959 AmPS A, ConMuA 80A[port], IlEncCM[port], IlEncR[port], RkOn[port]
Holly, Charles Hardin d1959 BiDAmM
Holly, Doyle 1936- CounME 74[port], -74A, IlEncCM
Holly, Ellen 1931- BiE&WWA, DrBlPA, NotNAT, WhoHol A
Hollywood, Daniel 1914- BiE&WWA, NotNAT
Hollywood, Edwin L TwYS A
Hollywood, Jimmy d1955 WhScrn 77
Hollywood Argyles, The AmPS A, RkOn[port]
Hollywood Flames, The RkOn[port]
Holm, Astrid 1919- Film 2
Holm, Celeste 1919- BiDAmM, BiE&WWA, CmpEPM, EncMT, FilmEn, FilmgC, ForYSC, HalFC 80, HolP 40[port], IntMPA 77, -75, -76, -78, -79, -80, MotPP, MovMk[port], NotNAT, OxFilm, WhoHol A, WhoThe 72, -77
Holm, Christian Blache 1943- IntWWM 77
Holm, Darry Film 2
Holm, Eleanor 1914- What 2[port], WhoHol A
Holm, Eske 1940- CnOxB, DancEn 78
Holm, Hanya CmpGMD, DancEn 78[port], WhoThe 72
Holm, Hanya 1893- BiE&WWA, EncMT, NotNAT, -A, WhoThe 77
Holm, Hanya 1898- CnOxB
Holm, Ian WhoHol A
Holm, Ian 1931- FilmEn, IlWWBF, WhoThe 72, -77
Holm, Ian 1932- FilmgC, HalFC 80
Holm, John Cecil WhoHol A
Holm, John Cecil 1904- AmSCAP 80, BiE&WWA, ModWD, NotNAT, WhoThe 72, -77
Holm, John Cecil 1906- CnMD
Holm, Klaus 1920- BiE&WWA, NotNAT
Holm, Magda Film 2
Holm, Mogens Winkel 1936- Baker 78, CpmDNM 80
Holm, Peder 1926- IntWWM 77, -80, NewGrD 80
Holm, Renate 1931- WhoOp 76
Holm, Richard WhoMus 72
Holm, Richard 1912- CmOp, NewGrD 80
Holm, Richard 1921- WhoOp 76
Holm, Sonia 1922-1974 WhScrn 77, WhoHol A
Holman, Bill 1927- EncJzS 70
Holman, Derek 1931- WhoMus 72
Holman, Eddie 1946- RkOn 2[port]
Holman, Harry 1874-1947 WhScrn 74, -77, WhoHol B
Holman, Joseph G d1817 NotNAT B
Holman, Libby 1906-1971 AmPS B, BiDAmM, BiE&WWA, CmpEPM, EncMT, NotNAT B, PlP&P, What 1[port], WhScrn 77, WhThe, WhoHol B
Holman, M Carl 1919- BlkAmP
Holman, Peter Kenneth 1946- IntWWM 77, -80
Holman, Russell IntMPA 77, -75, -76, -78, -79, -80
Holman, Willis 1927- BiDAmM, ConAmC, EncJzS 70
Holmboe, Vagn 1909- Baker 78, CpmDNM 80, DcCM, IntWWM 77, -80, MusMk, NewGrD 80[port], OxMus, WhoMus 72
Holme, Myra d1919 NotNAT B
Holme, Stanford 1904- WhThe
Holme, Thea 1907- WhoThe 72, -77
Holmes, Alfred 1837-1876 Baker 78, NewGrD 80
Holmes, Ann Hitchcock 1922- ConAmTC
Holmes, Anna-Marie PupTheA
Holmes, Anna-Marie 1943- CnOxB, CreCan 1
Holmes, Augusta 1847-1903 Baker 78, MusMk, NewGrD 80, OxMus
Holmes, Ben 1890-1943 Film 2, WhScrn 74, -77, WhoHol B
Holmes, Berenice CnOxB, DancEn 78
Holmes, Bobby d1968 WhoJazz 72
Holmes, Burton 1870-1958 WhScrn 74, -77, WhoHol B
Holmes, Cecil ConMuA 80B
Holmes, Charlie 1910- BiDAmM, CmpEPM, WhoJazz 72
Holmes, Clint 1946- RkOn 2[port]
Holmes, David 1928- CnOxB
Holmes, David Leonard 1936- CreCan 2
Holmes, Doloris WomWMM B
Holmes, Donald Bert 1931- AmSCAP 80
Holmes, Edward 1797-1850 BiDAmM
Holmes, Edward 1797-1859 Baker 78, NewGrD 80, OxMus
Holmes, Eugene 1934- WhoOp 76
Holmes, G E 1873-1945 AmSCAP 66, -80, ConAmC A
Holmes, George d1721 NewGrD 80
Holmes, Gerda Film 1
Holmes, Groove 1931- EncJzS 70
Holmes, Helen 1892-1950 FilmEn, Film 1, -2, MotPP, NotNAT B, TwYS, WhScrn 74, -77, WhThe, WhoHol B
Holmes, Henry 1839-1905 BiDAmM, NewGrD 80
Holmes, Herbert Film 2
Holmes, Ione Film 2
Holmes, J Merrill 1889-1950 WhScrn 77
Holmes, Jack 1932- BiE&WWA
Holmes, Jacqueline 1938- WhoMus 72
Holmes, Joe 1897-1949 BluesWW
Holmes, John OxMus
Holmes, John d1629 NewGrD 80
Holmes, John 1923- WhoMus 72
Holmes, John Grier 1939- AmSCAP 80
Holmes, John Haynes 1879-1964 BiDAmM
Holmes, Kathleen PupTheA
Holmes, Leon Film 2
Holmes, Leroy AmPS A
Holmes, Leroy 1913- AmSCAP 66, -80, CmpEPM, RkOn
Holmes, Lois Film 1
Holmes, Marian WhoHol A
Holmes, Markwood 1899- ConAmC
Holmes, Marty 1925- AmSCAP 66, -80
Holmes, Milton Film 2
Holmes, Oliver Wendell 1809-1894 BiDAmM
Holmes, Paul 1923- ConAmC
Holmes, Phillips d1942 MotPP, WhoHol B
Holmes, Phillips 1907-1942 Film 2, HalFC 80, HolP 30[port], MovMk, NotNAT B
Holmes, Phillips 1909-1942 FilmEn, FilmgC, ForYSC, WhScrn 74, -77
Holmes, Ralph 1889-1945 NotNAT B, WhScrn 74, -77, WhoHol B
Holmes, Ralph 1937- IntWWM 80, NewGrD 80, WhoMus 72
Holmes, Rapley 1868-1928 WhScrn 77
Holmes, Raymond CreCan 1
Holmes, Reed Film 2
Holmes, Richard RkOn 2A
Holmes, Richard Arnold 1931- BiDAmM, EncJzS 70
Holmes, Richard G WhoHol A
Holmes, Robert 1862-1930 CreCan 2
Holmes, Robert 1899-1945 Film 2, NotNAT B, WhThe, WhoHol B
Holmes, Rupert 1947- AmSCAP 80
Holmes, Stuart 1887-1971 FilmEn, Film 1, -2, ForYSC, TwYS, WhScrn 74, -77, WhoHol B
Holmes, Taylor d1959 MotPP, WhoHol B
Holmes, Taylor 1872-1959 Film 1, -2, FilmgC, ForYSC, HalFC 80, MovMk, TwYS, WhScrn 74, -77
Holmes, Taylor 1878-1959 NotNAT B, Vers A[port], WhThe
Holmes, Thomas 1580?-1638 NewGrD 80, OxMus
Holmes, Wendell 1915-1962 NotNAT B, WhScrn 74, -77, WhoHol B
Holmes, William Henry 1812-1885 NewGrD 80
Holmes, William J 1877-1946 WhScrn 74, -77, WhoHol B
Holmes, Wright 1905- BluesWW
Holmes-Gore, Dorothy 1896-1915 WhThe
Holmgren, Bjorn 1920- CnOxB, DancEn 78
Holmquist, Nils-Gustaf 1906- IntWWM 77, -80
Holmquist, Sigrid Film 2
Holmstrand, Jean Marie 1932- AmSCAP 66
Holnthaner, Eduard 1944- IntWWM 77, -80
Holofcener, Lawrence 1926- AmSCAP 66, -80
Holoman, Dallas Kern 1947- IntWWM 77, -80
Holoubek, Ladislav 1913- Baker 78, NewGrD 80
Holroyd, John Dudley 1933- IntWWM 77, -80
Holschneider, Andreas Georg 1931- IntWWM 77, -80, NewGrD 80
Holst, Edvard 1843-1899 Baker 78
Holst, Gustav 1874-1934 Baker 78, BnBkM 80, CmOp, CompSN[port], DcCom 77[port], DcCom&M 79, DcCM, DcTwCC, MusMk[port], NewEOp 71, NewGrD 80[port], OxMus
Holst, Henry 1899- Baker 78, IntWWM 77, -80, NewGrD 80, WhoMus 72
Holst, Imogen 1907- Baker 78, IntWWM 77, -80, NewGrD 80, OxMus
Holstein, Franz Von 1826-1878 Baker 78, NewGrD 80
Holstein, Jean-Paul 1939- IntWWM 80
Holster, Rusty Reid 1952- AmSCAP 80
Holt, Anthony Edward 1940- IntWWM 80
Holt, Benjamin 1774-1861 BiDAmM
Holt, Carol Rosemary Smedley 1939- IntWWM 80
Holt, Charlene 1938- ForYSC
Holt, Charlene 1939- FilmgC, HalFC 80, WhoHol A
Holt, Clarence d1903 NotNAT B
Holt, Clarence d1920 NotNAT B
Holt, David Jack 1927- AmSCAP 66, -80
Holt, Denis IntMPA 77, -78, -79, -80
Holt, Edwart Film 1
Holt, Edwin Film 1
Holt, George Film 1, -2, MotPP, TwYS A
Holt, Gloria Film 2
Holt, Hans 1909- CnMD
Holt, Harold d1953 NotNAT B
Holt, Henry PupTheA
Holt, Henry 1934- WhoOp 76
Holt, Isaac 1932- BiDAmM
Holt, Jack 1888-1951 FilmEn, Film 1, -2, FilmgC, ForYSC, HalFC 80, MotPP, MovMk, NotNAT B, TwYS, WhScrn 74, -77, WhoHol B
Holt, Jennifer 1920- FilmEn, ForYSC, HalFC 80, WhoHol A
Holt, Morris 1937- BluesWW[port]
Holt, Nancy WomWMM B
Holt, Nat 1892-1971 FilmgC, HalFC 80
Holt, Nat 1894-1971 FilmEn
Holt, Nora 1895?-1974 DrBlPA
Holt, Patrick 1912- FilmgC, HalFC 80, IlWWBF, IntMPA 77, -75, -76, -78, -79, -80, WhoHol A
Holt, Seth 1923-1971 BiDFilm, -81, DcFM, FilmEn, FilmgC, HalFC 80, IlWWBF, OxFilm, WhoHrs 80, WorEFlm
Holt, Simeon Ten 1923- Baker 78, NewGrD 80
Holt, Stella BiE&WWA
Holt, Steven MorBAP
Holt, Tim d1973 MotPP, WhoHol B
Holt, Tim 1918-1973 FilmEn, FilmgC, ForYSC, HolP 40[port], MovMk, What 2[port]
Holt, Tim 1919-1973 HalFC 80, WhScrn 77
Holt, Will 1929- AmSCAP 66, -80, MorBAP, PlP&P A[port]
Holtei, Karl Von 1798-1880 EncWT
Holten, Bo 1948- IntWWM 80

Holtenau, Rudolf Heinrich *WhoOp 76*
Holter, Iver 1850-1941 *Baker 78, NewGrD 80*
Holthusius, Johannes *NewGrD 80*
Holton, Robert W 1922- *AmSCAP 66, -80*
Holts, Roosevelt 1905- *BluesWW[port]*
Holtsclaw, Bennie Charles 1936- *AmSCAP 80*
Holtz, Josef 1930- *IntWWM 77, -80*
Holtz, Lou 1898- *BiE&WWA, EncMT, JoeFr, NotNAT, WhThe*
Holtz, Tenen *Film 2*
Holtz, Tubea *Film 2*
Holtzendorff, Virginia Sheffield 1914- *IntWWM 77, -80*
Holtzman, David M 1908-1965 *NotNAT B*
Holtzman, Jonathan Craig 1953- *AmSCAP 80*
Holtzman, Julie 1945- *IntWWM 77, -80*
Holtzmann, David Marshall 1908-1965 *BiE&WWA*
Holtzner, Anton d1635 *Baker 78*
Holtzwart, Fritz 1892- *IntWWM 77, -80*
Holubar, Alan *Film 1*
Holubar, Allan 1889-1925? *TwYS A*
Holubar, Allen 1889-1925 *WhScrn 77*
Holy, Alfred 1866-1948 *Baker 78, NewGrD 80*
Holy, Ondrej Frantisek 1747?-1783 *NewGrD 80*
Holy, Walter 1921- *NewGrD 80*
Holy Modal Rounders *BiDAmM*
Holynborne *NewGrD 80*
Holyoke, Samuel 1762-1820 *Baker 78, BiDAmM, NewGrD 80*
Holz, Arno 1863-1929 *CnMD, EncWT, Ent, ModWD, OxThe*
Holz, Karl 1798-1858 *NewGrD 80*
Holz, Rudolf 1938- *DancEn 78*
Holzbauer, Ignaz 1711-1783 *Baker 78, NewGrD 80*
Holzbogen, Johann Georg 1727-1775 *NewGrD 80*
Holzbogen, Joseph Georg 1727-1775 *NewGrD 80*
Holzer, Adela *WhoThe 77*
Holzer, Gerhard 1932- *IntWWM 77, -80*
Holzer, Hans 1920- *AmSCAP 66, -80*
Holzer, Lou 1913- *AmSCAP 66*
Holzhay, Johann Nepomuk 1741-1809 *NewGrD 80*
Holzknecht, Vaclav 1904- *IntWWM 77, -80, NewGrD 80*
Holzman, Benjamin F d1963 *NotNAT B*
Holzmann, Abraham 1874-1939 *AmSCAP 66, -80*
Holzmann, Rodolfo 1910- *NewGrD 80*
Holzmann, Rudolf 1910- *NewGrD 80*
Holzmeister, Clemens 1886- *EncWT*
Holzner, Anton 1599?-1635 *NewGrD 80*
Holzworth, Fred d1970 *WhScrn 74, -77*
Homan, David 1907- *WhThe*
Homan, Gertrude d1951 *NotNAT B*
Homans, Peter 1951- *ConAmC*
Homans, Robert E 1874-1947 *HolCA[port]*
Homans, Robert E 1875-1947 *Film 2, TwYS, Vers B[port], WhScrn 74, -77, WhoHol B*
Homberg, Hans 1903- *CnMD*
Homberger, Paul 1560?-1634 *NewGrD 80*
Hombres *RkOn 2[port]*
Homburg, Al 1937- *BiDAmM, IntWWM 77*
Home, John 1722-1808 *NotNAT B, OxThe*
Home, William Douglas 1912- *BiE&WWA, CnMD, CnThe, ConDr 73, -77, CroCD, EncWT, Ent, ModWD, NotNAT, PlP&P, WhoThe 72, -77*
Homeier, Skip 1929- *FilmgC, HalFC 80*
Homeier, Skip 1930- *FilmEn, ForYSC, IntMPA 77, -75, -76, -78, -79, -80, WhoHol A*
Homer *NewEOp 71, NewGrD 80, PlP&P[port]*
Homer 1918- *CounME 74[port]*
Homer, Ben 1917- *CmpEPM*
Homer, Benjamin 1917-1975 *AmSCAP 66, -80*
Homer, Louise 1871-1947 *Baker 78, BiDAmM, BnBkM 80, CmOp, MusSN[port], NewEOp 71, NewGrD 80*
Homer, Raymond R *IntMPA 78, -79, -80*
Homer, Sidney 1864-1953 *AmSCAP 66, -80, Baker 78, BiDAmM, NewGrD 80, OxMus*
Homer And Jethro *BiDAmM, CounME 74[port], -74A, IlEncCM*
Homer The Great *BluesWW[port]*
Homes, Geoffrey *FilmEn*
Homesick James *BluesWW[port]*
Homet, Louis 1691-1777 *NewGrD 80*
Hometowners *BiDAmM*
Homfrey, Gladys d1932 *NotNAT B, WhThe*
Homilius, Gottfried August 1714-1785 *Baker 78, NewGrD 80*
Hommann, Charles *NewGrD 80*
Hommel, Friedrich Ferdinand 1929- *NewGrD 80*
Homoki Nagy, Istvan 1914- *DcFM, FilmgC, HalFC 80*
Homoky Nagy, Istvan 1914- *OxFilm*
Homolka, Oscar *MotPP*
Homolka, Oscar 1898- *WhThe, WhoHol A*
Homolka, Oscar 1898-1978 *FilmEn, HolCA[port]*
Homolka, Oscar 1899- *FilmgC, HalFC 80, Vers A[port]*
Homolka, Oscar 1899-1978 *WhoHrs 80*
Homolka, Oscar 1900?- *MovMk[port]*
Homolka, Oscar 1901- *BiDFilm, Film 2, OxFilm*
Homolka, Oscar 1901-1938 *Ent*
Homolka, Oscar 1901-1976 *EncWT*
Homolka, Oscar 1901-1979 *BiDFilm 81*
Homolka, Oscar 1903- *BiE&WWA, ForYSC, NotNAT*
Homs, Joaquim 1906- *DcCM, NewGrD 80*
Homs, Joaquin 1906- *Baker 78*
Homs Oller, Joaquin 1906- *IntWWM 77, -80*
Honauer, Leontzi 1730?-1790? *NewGrD 80*
Honda, Frank 1884-1924 *WhScrn 74, -77, WhoHol B*
Honda, Inoshiro *WhoHrs 80*
Honda, Takashi 1945- *EncJzS 70*
Honda, Takehiro 1945- *EncJzS 70*
Hondells, The *RkOn 2[port]*
Hondt, Cornelius De *NewGrD 80*
Hondt, Gheerkin De *NewGrD 80*
Hondt, Gheraert De *NewGrD 80*
Hone, Mary 1904- *WhThe*
Hone, William 1780-1842 *DcPup*
Honegger, Arthur 1892-1955 *Baker 78, BnBkM 80, CmOp, CompSN[port], CnOxB, DancEn 78, DcCom 77[port], DcCom&M 79, DcCM, DcFM, DcTwCC, FilmEn, FilmgC, HalFC 80, MusMk[port], NewEOp 71, NewGrD 80[port], NotNAT B, OxFilm, OxMus, WorEFlm*
Honegger, Henri Charles 1904- *Baker 78, IntWWM 80*
Honegger, Marc 1926- *Baker 78, IntWWM 77, -80, NewGrD 80*
Honer, Mary 1914-1965 *CnOxB, DancEn 78, WhThe*
Hones, Julia Anne 1944- *IntWWM 77, -80*
Honey, Albert Edward 1919- *IntWWM 77, -80, WhoMus 72*
Honey, George Alfred 1823-1880 *NotNAT B*
Honey, Gordon *WhoMus 72*
Honey Cone *RkOn 2[port]*
Honey Eddie *BluesWW*
Honeyboy *BluesWW*
Honeycombs, The *RkOn 2[port]*
Honeycones, The *RkOn*
Honeydripper, The *BluesWW*
Honeyman, John *WhoMus 72*
Hong, James *WhoHol A*
Hong, Wilson S 1934- *IntMPA 77, -75, -76, -78, -79, -80*
Hong, Yat-Lam 1940- *IntWWM 77, -80*
Hongen, Elisabeth 1906- *NewGrD 80, WhoMus 72*
Honig, Edwin 1919- *BiE&WWA, NotNAT*
Honingh, P 1935- *IntWWM 80*
Honkanen, Antero Terho 1941- *IntWWM 77, -80*
Honn, Eldon 1890-1927 *WhScrn 74, -77*
Honner, Derek 1921- *WhoMus 72*
Honner, Robert d1852 *NotNAT B*
Honnett, Mickie *Film 2*
Honningen, Mette 1944- *CnOxB*
Honold, Rolf 1919- *CnMD*
Honore, Gideon J 1904- *WhoJazz 72*
Honore, Hal 1905- *IntMPA 77, -75, -76, -78, -79*
Honorio, Romualdo *NewGrD 80*
Honri, Baynham *IntMPA 77, -75, -76, -78, -79, -80*
Honri, Percy 1874-1953 *NotNAT B, WhThe*
Honterus, Johannes 1498-1549 *NewGrD 80*
Honyman, John 1613-1636 *OxThe*
Honyman, Richard 1618- *OxThe*
Hood, Alan 1924- *AmSCAP 66*
Hood, Alan 1924- *AmSCAP 80*
Hood, Alex 1930- *WhoMus 72*
Hood, Alexander 1930- *IntWWM 77, -80*
Hood, Ann 1940- *WhoOp 76*
Hood, Ann Neville 1940- *IntWWM 77, -80*
Hood, Basil 1864-1917 *EncMT, NotNAT B, WhThe*
Hood, Bill 1924- *EncJzS 70*
Hood, Burrel Samuel, III 1943- *IntWWM 77, -80*
Hood, Darla 1931- *What 2[port]*
Hood, Darla 1931-1979 *FilmEn*
Hood, Darla 1933- *WhoHol A*
Hood, David *ConMuA 80B*
Hood, Ernie 1923- *EncJzS 70*
Hood, George 1807-1882 *BiDAmM*
Hood, Helen 1863-1949 *Baker 78*
Hood, Hugh John Blagdon 1928- *CreCan 1*
Hood, Mantle 1918- *Baker 78, NewGrD 80*
Hood, Marguerite Vivian *IntWWM 77, -80*
Hood, Robert Allison 1880-1958 *CreCan 2*
Hood, Tom 1919-1950 *WhScrn 74, -77*
Hood, Walton Donnie, III 1933- *IntWWM 77, -80*
Hood, William H 1924- *BiDAmM, EncJzS 70*
Hoof, Jef Van 1886-1959 *Baker 78, NewGrD 80*
Hoogenakker, Virginia Ruth 1921- *IntWWM 77, -80*
Hoogerwerf, Frank W 1946- *IntWWM 80*
Hoogstraten, Willem Van 1884-1965 *Baker 78*
Hook, Elias 1805-1881 *BiDAmM*
Hook, George G 1807-1880 *BiDAmM*
Hook, James 1746-1827 *Baker 78, BnBkM 80, MusMk, NewGrD 80[port], OxMus*
Hook, Theodore d1842 *NotNAT B*
Hook, Theodore 1788-1841 *Ent*
Hook, Walter E 1941- *WhoOp 76*
Hook, William George 1913- *WhoMus 72*
Hooke, Emelie *WhoMus 72*
Hooke, Robert 1635-1702 *NewGrD 80*
Hooke, Wayne Raymond 1941- *IntWWM 77, -80*
Hooker, Brian 1880-1946 *AmSCAP 66, -80, BiDAmM, CmpEPM, EncMT, NewEOp 71, NotNAT B*
Hooker, Earl Zebedee 1930-1970 *BluesWW[port]*
Hooker, George 1882- *NewOrJ*
Hooker, Ian Anthony 1948- *IntWWM 80*
Hooker, John Lee *ConMuA 80A*
Hooker, John Lee 1915- *RkOn*
Hooker, John Lee 1917- *BiDAmM, BluesWW[port], EncFCWM 69, IlEncJ, NewGrD 80*
Hooker, Walter Melville 1907- *WhoMus 72*
Hooker Joe *BluesWW*
Hooks, Benjamin L *NewYTET*
Hooks, David 1920- *BiE&WWA, NotNAT, WhoHol A*
Hooks, Jerry 1911- *AmSCAP 80*
Hooks, Kevin 1958- *DrBlPA, WhoHol A*
Hooks, Robert 1937- *DrBlPA, FilmEn, FilmgC, HalFC 80, NotNAT, PlP&P A[port], WhoHol A, WhoThe 77*
Hool, Roger Van *FilmAG WE*
Hoole, John d1803 *NotNAT B*
Hoope, Aaf Bouber-Ten d1974 *WhScrn 77*
Hooper, Buddy 1933- *AmSCAP 80*
Hooper, Edmund 1553?-1621 *NewGrD 80*
Hooper, Edward d1865 *NotNAT B*
Hooper, Edwin *MagIlD*
Hooper, Ewan 1935- *WhoThe 72, -77*
Hooper, Frank *Film 2*
Hooper, Joyce *WomWMM*
Hooper, Lou 1894- *EncJzS 70*
Hooper, Louis Stanley 1894- *EncJzS 70*
Hooper, Nesbert 1938- *BiDAmM, EncJzS 70*
Hooper, Stix 1938- *EncJzS 70*
Hooper, Tobe 1946- *WhoHrs 80*
Hooper, William Loyd 1931- *ConAmC, IntWWM 77, -80*

Hoopes, Isabella *WhoHol A*
Hoopii, Sol 1905-1953 *WhScrn 74, -77*
Hoops, Arthur 1870-1916 *Film 1, WhScrn 77*
Hoorn, Carol Lucille *CreCan 2*
Hoornik, Ed 1910-1970 *CnMD*
Hooser, William S *Film 2*
Hoosier Hot Shots *CmpEPM, IlEncCM, JoeFr*
Hoosman, Al 1918-1968 *WhScrn 77*
Hooton, Florence *WhoMus 72*
Hooven, Joseph D *AmSCAP 66, -80*
Hooven, Marilyn 1924- *AmSCAP 66, -80*
Hoover, J Edgar 1895-1972 *WhScrn 77*
Hoover, Katherine 1937- *AmSCAP 80*
Hoover, Willis David 1945- *AmSCAP 80*
Hopcraft, Arthur *ConDr 73, -77C*
Hope, Adele Blood d1936 *NotNAT B*
Hope, Anthony 1863-1933 *FilmgC, HalFC 80, NotNAT B, WhThe*
Hope, Bob *AmPS B, GrMovC[port], MotPP, NewYTET, WhoHol A*
Hope, Bob 1903- *BiE&WWA, CmpEPM, EncMT, FilmEn, FilmgC, ForYSC, Funs[port], HalFC 80, IntMPA 77, -75, -76, -78, -79, -80, JoeFr[port], MovMk[port], OxFilm, WhThe, WhoHrs 80, WorEFlm[port]*
Hope, Bob 1904- *BiDFilm, -81, CmMov*
Hope, Diana 1872-1942 *WhScrn 74, -77, WhoHol B*
Hope, Elmo 1923-1967 *EncJzS 70, IlEncJ*
Hope, Eric *IntWWM 77, -80, WhoMus 72*
Hope, Evelyn d1966 *WhThe*
Hope, Gloria 1901- *Film 1, -2, MotPP, TwYS*
Hope, Harry *IntMPA 77, -75, -76, -78, -79, -80*
Hope, Mabel Ellams d1937 *NotNAT B*
Hope, Maidie 1881-1937 *NotNAT B, WhScrn 77, WhThe, WhoHol B*
Hope, St. Elmo Sylvester 1923-1967 *EncJzS 70*
Hope, Vida 1918-1962 *FilmgC, HalFC 80, WhoHol B*
Hope, Vida 1918-1963 *NotNAT B, WhScrn 74, -77, WhThe*
Hope, Wyn Swanson 1909- *AmSCAP 80*
Hope-Jones, Robert 1859-1914 *Baker 78, NewGrD 80, OxMus*
Hope-Wallace, Philip A 1911- *WhoMus 72, WhoThe 72, -77*
Hopekirk, Helen 1856-1945 *Baker 78*
Hopf, Hans 1916- *CmOp, NewEOp 71, NewGrD 80, WhoMus 72*
Hopf, Hans 1920- *WhoOp 76*
Hopfmueller, Martin Christian 1929- *IntWWM 77*
Hopfmuller, Martin Christian 1929- *IntWWM 80*
Hopfner, Hedi *CnOxB*
Hopfner, Margot *CnOxB*
Hopfner Sisters *CnOxB*
Hopken, Arvid Niclas, Freiherr Von 1710-1778 *NewGrD 80*
Hopkin, Mary 1950- *RkOn 2[port]*
Hopkins, Anthony *PlP&P[port], -A[port], WhoHol A*
Hopkins, Anthony 1937- *CnThe, FilmEn, WhoThe 72, -77*
Hopkins, Anthony 1941- *FilmgC, HalFC 80, IntMPA 78, -79, -80*
Hopkins, Antony 1921- *IntWWM 77, -80, NewGrD 80, OxMus, WhoMus 72*
Hopkins, Arthur *PlP&P*
Hopkins, Arthur 1878-1950 *NotNAT A, -B, WhThe*
Hopkins, Arthur 1879-1950 *EncWT*
Hopkins, Asa 1779-1838 *NewGrD 80*
Hopkins, Bill 1943- *DcCM, NewGrD 80, WhoMus 72*
Hopkins, Bo *FilmEn, HalFC 80, IntMPA 77, -76, -78, -79, -80, WhoHol A*
Hopkins, Bob 1918-1962 *NotNAT B, WhScrn 74, -77, WhoHol B*
Hopkins, Charles 1884-1953 *NotNAT B, WhThe*
Hopkins, Charles Jerome 1836-1898 *Baker 78*
Hopkins, Claude *BgBands 74[port]*
Hopkins, Claude 1903- *BiDAmM, CmpEPM, EncJzS 70, IlEncJ, WhoJazz 72*
Hopkins, Claude D 1906- *AmSCAP 66, -80*
Hopkins, Clyde *Film 1*
Hopkins, Doc 1899- *IlEncCM*
Hopkins, Douglas Edward 1902- *WhoMus 72*
Hopkins, Edward 1818-1901 *NewGrD 80*
Hopkins, Edward Jerome 1836-1898 *BiDAmM, OxMus*
Hopkins, Edward John 1818-1901 *Baker 78, OxMus*
Hopkins, G W 1943- *NewGrD 80*
Hopkins, Harry Patterson 1873-1954 *BiDAmM, ConAmC*
Hopkins, Ida Maude *WhoMus 72*
Hopkins, J H *OxMus*
Hopkins, James Frederick 1939- *ConAmC*
Hopkins, James Fredrick 1939- *AmSCAP 80*
Hopkins, Jerome 1836-1898 *NewGrD 80*
Hopkins, Joan 1915- *WhThe*
Hopkins, Joel 1904-1975 *BluesWW*
Hopkins, John d1570 *OxMus*
Hopkins, John 1927- *NewGrD 80, WhoMus 72*
Hopkins, John 1931- *ConDr 73, -77, EncWT, FilmgC, HalFC 80, NotNAT*
Hopkins, John Henry 1820-1891 *Baker 78, BiDAmM*
Hopkins, John Henry 1861-1945 *BiDAmM*
Hopkins, John Henry 1901- *BluesWW*
Hopkins, John Larkin 1819-1873 *OxMus*
Hopkins, John Raymond 1927- *IntWWM 80*
Hopkins, Josiah 1786-1862 *BiDAmM*
Hopkins, Kenyon *WorEFlm*
Hopkins, Lightnin' 1912- *EncFCWM 69, NewGrD 80*
Hopkins, Linda 1925- *BiDAmM, BlkAmP, DrBlPA, EncJzS 70, MorBAP, WhoHol A*
Hopkins, Mae *Film 1*
Hopkins, Maurice 1914- *Film 2*
Hopkins, Miriam 1902- *ForYSC*
Hopkins, Miriam 1902-1972 *BiDFilm, -81, BiE&WWA, FilmEn, HalFC 80, MotPP, MovMk[port], NotNAT B, OxFilm, ThFT[port], WhScrn 77, WhThe, WhoHol B, WorEFlm*
Hopkins, Miriam 1902-1973 *FilmgC*
Hopkins, Nancy L D S *IntWWM 77*
Hopkins, Nicky 1944- *ConMuA 80A, IlEncR*
Hopkins, Pauline Elizabeth 1859-1930 *BlkAmP, MorBAP*
Hopkins, Sam *ConMuA 80A*
Hopkins, Sam 1912- *BiDAmM, BluesWW[port], IlEncJ, NewGrD 80*
Hopkins, Shirley Knight *HalFC 80*
Hopkins, Smith Anderson 1920- *AmSCAP 80*
Hopkins, Zuilmah Bland 1925- *IntWWM 80*
Hopkinson *NewGrD 80*
Hopkinson, Cecil 1898-1977 *NewGrD 80*
Hopkinson, Francis 1737-1791 *Baker 78, BiDAmM, NewGrD 80, OxMus*
Hopkinson, John 1811-1886 *NewGrD 80*
Hopkinson, Joseph 1770-1843 *BiDAmM, OxMus*
Hopkinson, Peter *IlWWBF A*
Hopkirk, Gordon *Film 2*
Hopkirk, James 1908- *BiDAmM*
Hopner, Stephan *NewGrD 80*
Hopp, Julius 1819-1885 *NewGrD 80*
Hoppe, Marianne 1911- *FilmAG WE*
Hopper, Charles H d1916 *NotNAT B*
Hopper, Dale F 1941- *IntWWM 77*
Hopper, Dennis *MotPP, WhoHol A*
Hopper, Dennis 1935- *FilmgC, HalFC 80*
Hopper, Dennis 1936- *FilmEn, ForYSC, IntMPA 77, -75, -76, -78, -79, -80, MovMk[port]*
Hopper, DeWolf 1858-1935 *CmpEPM, EncMT, FamA&A[port], JoeFr, NotNAT A, -B, OxThe, TwYS, WhScrn 74, -77, WhThe, WhoHol B*
Hopper, DeWolfe 1858-1935 *Film 1*
Hopper, DeWolfe, Jr. *Film 1*
Hopper, E Mason 1885-1966 *FilmEn, TwYS A*
Hopper, Edna Wallace d1959 *CmpEPM, WhoStg 1906, -1908*
Hopper, Edna Wallace 1864-1959 *NotNAT B, WhThe*
Hopper, Edna Wallace 1874-1959 *WhScrn 74, -77*
Hopper, Edward 1816-1888 *BiDAmM*
Hopper, Frank *Film 2*
Hopper, Hal 1912-1970 *WhScrn 77*
Hopper, Harold S 1912-1970 *AmSCAP 66, -80*
Hopper, Hedda 1885-1966 *ThFT[port]*
Hopper, Hedda 1890-1966 *FilmEn, FilmgC, HalFC 80, MovMk, NotNAT B, OxFilm, WhScrn 74, -77, WorEFlm*
Hopper, Hedda 1891-1966 *Film 1, -2, ForYSC, TwYS, WhoHol B*
Hopper, Jerry 1907- *FilmEn, FilmgC, HalFC 80, IntMPA 77, -75, -76, -78, -79, -80*
Hopper, Rika d1963 *NotNAT B*
Hopper, Victoria 1909- *FilmEn, FilmgC, HalFC 80, IlWWBF, WhThe*
Hopper, William 1915-1969 *FilmgC, HalFC 80*
Hopper, William 1915-1970 *WhScrn 74, -77, WhoHol B, WhoHrs 80*
Hopper, William DeWolf 1858-1935 *BiDAmM, WhoStg 1906, -1908*
Hopper, William DeWolfe 1915- *ForYSC*
Hoppin, Richard Hallowell 1913- *Baker 78, IntWWM 77, -80, NewGrD 80*
Hopping, Robert Daniel 1949- *IntWWM 77*
Hopps, Stuart Gary 1942- *CnOxB*
Hopson, Hal 1933- *AmSCAP 80, ConAmC*
Hopson, Violet *Film 1, -2, IlWWBF[port]*
Hopton, Russell 1900-1945 *WhScrn 74, -77, WhoHol B*
Hopton, Russell 1900-1946 *ForYSC*
Hopwood, Avery 1882-1928 *McGEWD[port], ModWD, NotNAT B, WhThe*
Hopwood, Barbara Helen 1951- *IntWWM 80*
Hopwood, Dorothy Ena 1909- *WhoMus 72*
Hor, Clemens 1515?-1572 *NewGrD 80*
Hora, Jan 1936- *IntWWM 77, -80*
Horace 065BC-008BC *DcPup, NewGrD 80*
Horacek, Jaroslav 1926- *WhoMus 72, WhoOp 76*
Horacek, Leo *ConAmC*
Horak, Adolph 1850-1921 *Baker 78*
Horak, Antonin 1875-1910 *Baker 78*
Horak, Eduard 1838-1892 *Baker 78*
Horak, Jaroslav 1914- *IntWWM 77, -80*
Horak, Josef 1931- *Baker 78, IntWWM 77, -80, NewGrD 80*
Horak, Vaclav 1800-1871 *NewGrD 80*
Horak, Wenzel Emanuel 1800-1871 *Baker 78, NewGrD 80*
Horan, Albert Henry 1932- *IntWWM 77, -80*
Horan, Catherine Anne 1948- *IntWWM 77*
Horan, Charles *TwYS A*
Horan, Edward 1898- *WhThe*
Horan, James 1908-1967 *WhScrn 74, -77*
Horbiger, Attila 1896- *EncWT*
Horbiger, Paul 1894- *EncWT, Film 2*
Horbowski, Mieczyslaw Apolinary 1849-1937 *NewGrD 80*
Hordern, Michael 1911- *CnThe, FilmAG WE, FilmEn, FilmgC, ForYSC, HalFC 80, IlWWBF, IntMPA 77, -75, -76, -78, -79, -80, MovMk[port], WhoHol A, WhoThe 72, -77*
Hordisch, Lucas 1503?-1538? *NewGrD 80*
Horecki, Feliks 1796-1870 *NewGrD 80*
Horein, Kathleen Marie 1952- *IntWWM 80*
Horenstein, Jascha 1898-1973 *Baker 78, BiDAmM*
Horenstein, Jascha 1899-1973 *NewGrD 80[port], WhoMus 72*
Horgan, Patrick *WhoHol A*
Horghanista DeFlorentia *NewGrD 80*
Horheim, Bernger Von *NewGrD 80*
Hori, Kyusaku 1900- *IntMPA 75*
Horicius, Erasmus 1465?- *NewGrD 80*
Horine, Charles 1912- *NatPD[port]*
Horitz, Joseph F d1961 *NotNAT B*
Horitz, Karel 1913- *WhoMus 72*
Horkheimer, Herbert M d1962 *NotNAT B*
Horky, Karel 1909- *Baker 78, NewGrD 80*
Horlick, Harry *CmpEPM*
Hormann, Johann Heinrich *NewGrD 80*
Hormel, George *ConMuA 80B*
Horn, August 1825-1893 *Baker 78*
Horn, Bob 1949- *AmSCAP 80*
Horn, Camilla 1906- *FilmEn, Film 2, FilmgC, HalFC 80, TwYS, WhoHol A*
Horn, Camillo 1860-1941 *Baker 78, OxMus*
Horn, Charles Edward 1786-1840 *OxMus*
Horn, Charles Edward 1786-1849 *Baker 78,*

BiDAmM, NewGrD 80
Horn, Jack IntMPA 75, -76
Horn, Johann Caspar 1630?-1685? NewGrD 80
Horn, Karl Friedrich 1762-1830 Baker 78, NewGrD 80, OxMus
Horn, Leonard 1926-1975 FilmgC, HalFC 80, IntMPA 75
Horn, Lois Burley 1928- IntWWM 77, -80
Horn, Mary 1916- WhThe
Horn, Paul 1930- AmSCAP 66, BiDAmM, ConAmC, EncJzS 70
Horn, Shirley 1934- BiDAmM
Horn Quintet BiDAmM
Hornbeck, William W 1901- FilmEn, HalFC 80, IntMPA 77, -75, -76, -78, -79, -80
Hornberger, Mary Lou 1935- AmSCAP 80
Hornblow, Arthur d1942 NotNAT B
Hornblow, Arthur, Jr. 1893-1976 FilmEn, FilmgC, HalFC 80, IntMPA 75, -76
Hornbostel, Erich Moritz Von 1877-1935 Baker 78, NewGrD 80
Hornbrook, Charles Gus 1874-1937 WhScrn 74, -77
Hornby, Anne WhoMus 72
Horne PlP&P[port]
Horne, A P WhThe
Horne, Cleeve 1912- CreCan 1
Horne, David 1898-1970 FilmgC, HalFC 80, IntMPA 77, -75, -76, -78, -79, -80, WhScrn 74, -77, WhThe, WhoHol B
Horne, Geoffrey 1926?- HalFC 80
Horne, Geoffrey 1933- BiE&WWA, ForYSC, MotPP, NotNAT, WhoHol A
Horne, James V 1880-1942 CmMov, FilmgC, HalFC 80
Horne, James W 1880-1942 FilmEn, TwYS A
Horne, James W 1881-1942 WhScrn 77
Horne, Kenneth 1900- WhThe, WhoThe 72
Horne, Lena AmPS B, IntMPA 75, -76, -78, -79, -80
Horne, Lena 1912- BlksB&W[port], -C
Horne, Lena 1917- Baker 78, BiDAmM, BiE&WWA, CmpEPM, DrBlPA, EncMT, Ent, FilmEn, FilmgC, ForYSC, HalFC 80, IntMPA 77, MGM[port], MotPP, MovMk[port], NotNAT, WhoHol A
Horne, Marilyn WhoMus 72
Horne, Marilyn 1929- NewGrD 80
Horne, Marilyn 1934- Baker 78, BiDAmM, BnBkM 80, CmOp, IntWWM 77, -80, MusSN[port], NewEOp 71, WhoOp 76
Horne, Michael Jeffrey WhoHol A
Horne, Richard Sherman 1930- IntWWM 77, -80
Horne, Victoria 1920?- FilmgC, ForYSC, HalFC 80, WhoHol A
Horne, W Film 1
Horneman, Christian Frederik Emil 1840-1906 Baker 78, NewGrD 80
Horneman, Johan Ole 1809-1870 Baker 78
Horneman And Erslev NewGrD 80
Horner, Anton 1877-1971 BiDAmM, BnBkM 80
Horner, Gladys Irene 1911- WhoMus 72
Horner, Harry 1910- FilmEn, FilmgC, HalFC 80, IntMPA 77, -75, -76, -78, -79, -80, WorEFlm
Horner, Harry 1912- BiE&WWA, NotNAT
Horner, Jed 1922- BiE&WWA, NotNAT
Horner, Lottie d1964 NotNAT B
Horner, Peter P 1910- IntMPA 77, -75, -76, -78, -79
Horner, Ralph Joseph 1848-1926 Baker 78
Horner, Richard 1920- BiE&WWA, NotNAT, WhoThe 77
Horner, Thomas 1525?-1605? NewGrD 80
Horner, Violet Film 1
Horner, William George 1786-1837 FilmEn
Horney, Brigitte 1921- FilmAG WE, WhoHol A
Horngacher, Maximilian 1926- NewGrD 80
Horniman, Annie Elizabeth Fredericka 1860-1937 CnThe, EncWT, NotNAT A, -B, OxThe, WhThe
Horniman, Roy 1872-1930 NotNAT B, WhThe
Hornisher, Christina WomWMM B
Hornsby, Joseph Leith 1907- AmSCAP 80
Hornsby, Nancy 1910-1958 NotNAT B, WhThe
Hornstein, Robert Von 1833-1890 Baker 78
Hornung, Karin Helena 1939- IntWWM 77
Horologius, Alexander NewGrD 80
Horoszkiewicz, Andrzej 1775-1838 NewGrD 80
Horovitz, Israel 1939- ConDr 73, -77, CroCD, DcLB 7[port], EncWT, NatPD[port], NotNAT, PlP&P, WhoThe 72, -77
Horovitz, Joseph 1920- CpmDNM 80
Horovitz, Joseph 1926- IntWWM 77, -80, NewGrD 80, WhoMus 72
Horowitz, Anthony 1945- AmSCAP 80
Horowitz, Caroline 1909- AmSCAP 80
Horowitz, David J 1942- AmSCAP 80, EncJzS 70
Horowitz, Norman 1932- IntWWM 77, -80, WhoMus 72
Horowitz, Vladimir 1904- Baker 78, BiDAmM, BnBkM 80[port], IntWWM 77, -80, MusMk[port], MusSN[port], NewGrD 80[port], WhoMus 72
Horres, Kurt 1932- WhoOp 76
Horrod, Norman 1936- IntWWM 77, -80
Horsbrugh, Walter WhoHol A
Horschelt, Friedrich 1793-1876 CnOxB
Horschitzky, Franz NewGrD 80
Horschky, Franz NewGrD 80
Horsfall, Bernard 1930- HalFC 80
Horsfall, Jean Mary 1923- WhoMus 72
Horsitzky, Franz NewGrD 80
Horsley, Charles Edward 1822-1876 Baker 78, BiDAmM, NewGrD 80
Horsley, Colin 1920- IntWWM 77, -80, NewGrD 80, WhoMus 72
Horsley, Imogene 1919- NewGrD 80
Horsley, John HalFC 80, WhoHol A
Horsley, William 1774-1858 Baker 78, NewGrD 80, OxMus
Horslips ConMuA 80A, IlEncR
Horsman, Charles d1886 NotNAT B
Horsnell, Horace 1883-1949 NotNAT B, WhThe
Horst, Anthon VanDer 1899-1965 Baker 78, NewGrD 80
Horst, Louis 1884-1964 CnOxB, DancEn 78[port], DcCM
Horstman-Person, Lu Ann 1939- AmSCAP 80
Horszowski, Mieczyslaw 1892- Baker 78, MusSN[port], NewGrD 80
Hortense 1783-1837 NewGrD 80
Hortense, Queen OxMus
Hortin, Christopher 1934- IntWWM 80
Horton, Austin Asadata Dafora 1890-1965 Baker 78
Horton, Benjamin 1872-1952 WhScrn 74, -77
Horton, Clara MotPP
Horton, Clara 1904- Film 1, -2, TwYS
Horton, Edward Everett d1970 MotPP, WhoHol B
Horton, Edward Everett 1866-1970 TwYS
Horton, Edward Everett 1886-1970 BiE&WWA, FilmEn, Film 2, FilmgC, ForYSC, Funs[port], HalFC 80, JoeFr[port], OxFilm, WhScrn 74, -77, WhThe, WhoHrs 80
Horton, Edward Everett 1887-1970 MovMk[port]
Horton, Edward Everett 1888-1970 Vers A[port]
Horton, Edward Everett 1888-1971 WorEFlm
Horton, Elizabeth 1902- AmSCAP 66, -80
Horton, George Vaughn 1911- AmSCAP 80
Horton, Howard Leavitt, Sr. 1904- IntWWM 77
Horton, Joanne Barbara 1932- BluesWW[port]
Horton, John Warner DrBlPA
Horton, John William 1905- IntWWM 77, -80, NewGrD 80, WhoMus 72
Horton, Johnny d1960 AmPS A, -B, IlEncCM[port]
Horton, Johnny 1927-1960 RkOn[port]
Horton, Johnny 1929- CounME 74A
Horton, Johnny 1929-1960 BiDAmM, CounME 74, EncFCWM 69
Horton, Kenneth John 1950- ConAmC
Horton, Kenneth Reginald 1912- WhoMus 72
Horton, Lester 1906-1953 CmpGMD, CnOxB, DancEn 78[port]
Horton, Lewis Henry 1898- AmSCAP 66, -80, ConAmC
Horton, Louise WhoHol A
Horton, Philip 1912- AmSCAP 66, -80
Horton, Robert 1870- WhThe
Horton, Robert 1924- FilmgC, ForYSC, HalFC 80, IntMPA 77, -75, -76, -78, -79, -80, MotPP, WhoHol A
Horton, Robert H 1899- WhoJazz 72
Horton, Vaughn 1911- AmSCAP 66, BiDAmM, EncFCWM 69
Horton, Walter Film 2
Horton, Walter 1917- BluesWW[port]
Horton, William Lamar 1935- IntWWM 77, -80
Horusitzky, Zoltan 1903- IntWWM 77, -80
Horvat, Milan 1919- NewGrD 80
Horvat, Stanko 1930- Baker 78, NewGrD 80
Horvath, Bela Imre 1950- AmSCAP 80
Horvath, Cecile Ayres De 1889- BiDAmM
Horvath, Charles ForYSC, WhoHol A
Horvath, Ian 1945- CnOxB
Horvath, Janet 1952- IntWWM 80
Horvath, Janos Karoly 1949- IntWWM 77
Horvath, Jeno 1914- IntWWM 77, -80
Horvath, Joan WomWMM A
Horvath, Josef Maria 1931- Baker 78, DcCM, IntWWM 77, -80
Horvath, Odon Von 1901-1938 CnMD, CnThe, EncWT, Ent, McGEWD[port], ModWD, REnWD[port]
Horvath, Zoltan De 1886- BiDAmM
Horvit, Michael 1932- CpmDNM 80
Horvit, Michael Miller 1932- AmSCAP 80, CpmDNM 75, -78, ConAmC, IntWWM 77, -80
Horwart, Johann Heinrich NewGrD 80
Horwich, Frances R IntMPA 77, -75, -76, -78, -79, -80
Horwin, C Jerome d1954 NotNAT B
Horwits, Al 1905- IntMPA 77, -75, -76, -78, -79
Horwitt, Arnold B 1918- AmSCAP 66, BiE&WWA, EncMT, NotNAT
Horwitz, Howie d1976 NewYTET
Horwitz, Joseph 1858-1922 WhScrn 74, -77
Horwitz, Karl 1884-1925 Baker 78
Horwitz, Kurt 1897-1974 EncWT
Horwitz, Lewis M 1931- IntMPA 77, -75, -76, -78, -79, -80
Horwitz, Murray Lee 1949- AmSCAP 80
Horwood, Blanche Frances 1903- WhoMus 72
Horwood, Michael S 1947- ConAmC
Horwood, William d1484? NewGrD 80
Horysa, Inghild 1944- WhoOp 76
Horzizky, Franciscus 1756?-1805 NewGrD 80
Horzizky, Franz 1756?-1805 NewGrD 80
Horzizky, Franziskus 1756?-1805 NewGrD 80
Hosalla, Hans-Dieter 1919- NewGrD 80
Hosch, Inez Marie Johnson 1911- IntWWM 77
Hoschke, Frederick Albert OxMus
Hoschna, Karl 1877-1911 AmPS, AmSCAP 66, -80, BiDAmM, CmpEPM, EncMT, NewCBMT, NotNAT B, PopAmC[port]
Hoschna, Karl L 1877-1911 NewGrD 80
Hoschner, Karl L 1877-1911 NewGrD 80
Hose, Anthony 1944- IntWWM 77, -80, WhoOp 76
Hosea, Barbara E 1949- IntWWM 77
Hosey, Athena 1929- AmSCAP 66, -80
Hosford, Maud Film 1
Hoshi, Akira 1931- IntWWM 77, -80
Hoshino, Hiroshi 1932- IntWWM 77, -80
Hosier, John 1928- IntWWM 80
Hosier, Richard NewGrD 80
Hoskin, Mai WomWMM
Hoskins, Allan Clayton Farina 1920- Film 2
Hoskins, Allen Clayton 1920- DrBlPA, WhoHol A
Hoskins, Bob 1942- WhoHol A, WhoThe 77
Hoskins, Jannie Film 2
Hoskins, William Barnes 1917- ConAmC
Hoskwith, Arnold K 1917- BiE&WWA, NotNAT
Hosmer, Elmer Samuel 1862-1945 Baker 78
Hosmer, Frederick Lucian 1840-1929 BiDAmM
Hosmer, Herbert, Jr. PupTheA
Hosmer, James B 1911- ConAmC
Hosmer, Lucius 1870-1935 AmSCAP 66, -80, Baker 78, ConAmC
Hossack, Donna 1931- IntWWM 77, -80

Hossein, Robert 1927- FilmAG WE, FilmEn, FilmgC, ForYSC, HalFC 80, OxFilm, WhoHol A, WorEFlm[port]
Hoste DaReggio NewGrD 80
Hoste, Catherine M L AmSCAP 80
Hostetler, Fred St. John 1945- AmSCAP 80
Hostetler, Paul 1921- NotNAT
Hostetter, Roy 1885-1951 WhScrn 74, -77
Hostikka, Pertti Antero 1936- IntWWM 77, -80
Hostinsky, O 1847-1910 OxMus
Hostinsky, Otakar 1847-1910 Baker 78, NewGrD 80
Hostrup, Jens Christian 1818-1892 OxThe
Hot RkOn 2[port]
Hot, Pierre Film 2
Hot Butter RkOn 2A
Hot Chocolate ConMuA 80A, IlEncR[port], RkOn 2[port]
Hot Five And Seven BiDAmM
Hot Shot Willie BluesWW
Hot-Toddys, The RkOn
Hot Tuna ConMuA 80A[port], IlEncR
Hotaling, Arthur D 1872-1938 WhScrn 74, -77, WhoHol B
Hotchkis, Joan WhoHol A
Hotchkis, John 1916- IntWWM 80, WhoMus 72
Hoteley, Mae MotPP
Hotely, Mae 1872-1954 Film 1, WhScrn 77
Hoterre NewGrD 80
Hoteterre Family NewGrD 80, OxMus
Hothby, John d1487 OxMus
Hothby, John 1410?-1487 NewGrD 80
Hothby, John 1415?-1487 Baker 78
Hothersall, Edith WhoMus 72
Hotinet, Jean NewGrD 80
Hotman, Nicholas d1663 NewGrD 80
Hotmann, Nicholas d1663 NewGrD 80
Hotter, Hans 1909- Baker 78, BnBkM 80, CmOp, IntWWM 77, -80, MusMk, NewEOp 71, NewGrD 80[port], WhoMus 72
Hotteterre NewGrD 80
Hotteterre, Colin 1653-1727 NewGrD 80
Hotteterre, Elizabeth De NewGrD 80
Hotteterre, Jacques 1674-1763 NewGrD 80
Hotteterre, Jacques 1684?-1761? BnBkM 80
Hotteterre, Jacques 1684?-1762 Baker 78
Hotteterre, Jean d1720 NewGrD 80
Hotteterre, Jean 1605?-1692? NewGrD 80
Hotteterre, Jean 1648?-1732 NewGrD 80
Hotteterre, Louis d1719 Baker 78
Hotteterre, Louis 1645?-1716 NewGrD 80
Hotteterre, Martin 1640?-1712 Baker 78, NewGrD 80
Hotteterre, Nicolas 1637-1694 Baker 78, NewGrD 80
Hotteterre, Nicolas 1653?-1727 Baker 78, NewGrD 80
Hottmann, Nicholas NewGrD 80
Hotton, Lucille Film 2
Hotvedt, Phyllis Shaw d1964 NotNAT B
Houbfeldt, Bernhard NewGrD 80
Houck, Joy N, Jr. WhoHrs 80
Houck, Leo Film 2
Houdard, Georges Louis 1860-1913 Baker 78, NewGrD 80
Houdin, Robert PupTheA
Houdini, Harry d1926 PupTheA
Houdini, Harry 1873-1926 FilmgC, HalFC 80, TwYS, WhThe
Houdini, Harry 1874-1926 DcPup, FilmEn, Film 1, -2, MagIlD[port], OxFilm, WhScrn 74, -77, WhoHol B, WhoHrs 80
Houdini, Harry 1876-1928 Ent[port]
Houdini, Wilmouth AmSCAP 80
Houdoy, Jules Francois Aristide 1818-1883 Baker 78
Houen, Carl VanDer NewGrD 80
Hough, Charles Wayne 1933- IntWWM 77, -80
Hough, Harold IlWWBF
Hough, Jan 1941- WhoHrs 80
Hough, John 1941- FilmEn, HalFC 80, IntMPA 77, -75, -76, -78, -79, -80
Hough, Will 1882-1962 AmSCAP 66, -80, BiDAmM, CmpEPM, NotNAT B
Houghmaster, John PupTheA
Houghton, Alice 1888-1944 WhScrn 74, -77
Houghton, Belle d1964 NotNAT B
Houghton, John 1906- IntWWM 77
Houghton, Katharine 1945- FilmgC, HalFC 80, WhoHol A
Houghton, Norris 1909- BiE&WWA, NotNAT, WhoThe 72, -77
Houghton, Stanley 1881-1913 CnMD, EncWT, Ent, McGEWD, ModWD, NotNAT B, OxThe
Houldsworth, Molly WhoMus 72
Houlihan, Mildred PupTheA
Houluskas, Anton PupTheA
Hounsell, Ronald William 1945- IntWWM 77
Houpfeld, Bernhard NewGrD 80
House, Billy 1890-1961 ForYSC, NotNAT B, Vers A[port], WhScrn 74, -77, WhoHol B
House, Eddie James, Jr. 1902- BiDAmM, BluesWW[port]
House, Eric WhoThe 72, -77
House, Jack 1887-1963 WhScrn 74, -77, WhoHol B
House, Marguerite Film 1
House, Newton Film 2
House, Robert William 1920- IntWWM 77, -80
House, Son 1902- EncFCWM 69
Houseley, Henry 1851-1925 BiDAmM
Houseley, Henry 1852-1925 Baker 78
Houseman, Arthur 1890-1942 WhScrn 74, -77
Houseman, John NewYTET, WhoHol A
Houseman, John 1902- BiDFilm, -81, BiE&WWA, CnThe, FilmEn, FilmgC, HalFC 80, IntMPA 77, -75, -76, -78, -79, -80, NotNAT, -A, PlP&P, WhoOp 76, WhoThe 72, -77
Houseman, John 1903?- WorEFlm
Houseman, Laurence 1865-1959 CnThe
Houser, Mervin Joseph IntMPA 75, -76
Houser, Roy 1920- IntWWM 77, -80
Houser, Thomas J NewYTET
Housewright, Wiley Lee 1913- IntWWM 77, -80
Housman, A E 1859-1936 NewGrD 80
Housman, Arthur 1883-1937 ForYSC
Housman, Arthur 1888-1942 FilmgC, HalFC 80, WhoHol B
Housman, Arthur 1890-1937 Film 1, -2, TwYS
Housman, Laurence 1865-1959 CnMD, McGEWD, ModWD, NotNAT A, -B, OxThe, WhThe
Housman, Rosalie 1888-1949 Baker 78, ConAmC
Housser, Muriel Yvonne McKague CreCan 2
Housser, Yvonne McKague 1898- CreCan 2
Housset, Pierre NewGrD 80
Houston, Cisco 1918-1961 EncFCWM 69
Houston, Cisco 1919-1961 WhScrn 74, -77, WhoHol B
Houston, Clint 1946- EncJzS 70
Houston, Clinton Joseph 1946- EncJzS 70
Houston, David 1938- BiDAmM, CounME 74[port], -74A, EncFCWM 69, IlEncCM[port], RkOn 2A
Houston, Donald 1923- FilmEn, FilmgC, HalFC 80, IlWWBF, WhoHol A, WhoThe 72, -77
Houston, Edward Wilson 1938- BluesWW[port]
Houston, George d1945 WhoHol B
Houston, George 1898-1944 FilmEn
Houston, George 1900-1944 ForYSC, NotNAT B, WhScrn 74, -77
Houston, Gilbert Vandine 1918-1961 BiDAmM
Houston, Glyn 1926- FilmgC, HalFC 80, WhoHol A
Houston, Jane WhThe
Houston, Jean d1965 WhScrn 77
Houston, John Charles 1933- BiDAmM
Houston, Josephine 1911- Film 2, WhThe
Houston, Matthew 1910- NewOrJ[port]
Houston, Patricia Alice 1942- IntWWM 77, -80
Houston, Renee 1902- FilmgC, HalFC 80, IlWWBF, -A, WhoHol A, WhoThe 72, -77
Houston, Roxane Mary IntWWM 77, -80, WhoMus 72
Houston, Sam 1793-1863 HalFC 80
Houston, Thelma DrBlPA, RkOn 2[port]
Houtmann, Jacques 1935- IntWWM 77, -80
Houven, Carl VanDer NewGrD 80
Hovde, Ellen Giffard WomWMM B
Hovdesven, E A 1893- AmSCAP 66, ConAmC A
Hovdesven, Elmer Archibald 1893- AmSCAP 80
Hove, Joachim VanDen 1567-1620 NewGrD 80
Hove, Michael Ostergard 1950- IntWWM 80
Hove, Peter VanDen NewGrD 80
Hoven, Carl VanDer NewGrD 80
Hoven, J NewGrD 80
Hover, Larry Robert 1951- AmSCAP 80
Hovey, Ann WhoHol A
Hovey, Carol AmSCAP 80
Hovey, Richard 1864-1900 BiDAmM
Hovey, Serge 1920- AmSCAP 80, ConAmC
Hovey, Tim 1945- FilmgC, ForYSC, IntMPA 77, -75, -76, -78, -79, -80
Hovhaness, Alan 1911- Baker 78, BiDAmM, BnBkM 80, CompSN[port], CpmDNM 72, -73, -74, -76, -79, -80, CnOxB, DancEn 78, DcCM, IntWWM 77, -80, MusMk, NewGrD 80, OxMus
Hovhanesyan, Edgar Sergeyi 1930- NewGrD 80
Hovhannes Mandakuni NewGrD 80
Hovhannes, Alan 1911- ConAmC
Hovick, Louise 1914-1970 FilmEn, ThFT[port], WhoHol B
Hovick, Rose Louise WhScrn 74, -77
Hoving, Lucas CmpGMD, CnOxB, DancEn 78[port]
Hovington, Franklin 1919- BluesWW
Hovland, Egil 1924- Baker 78, DcCM, NewGrD 80
Hovmand, Annelise WomWMM
How, Martin John Richard 1931- WhoMus 72
Howald, Fred 1946- CnOxB
Howard, Alan DancEn 78
Howard, Alan 1930- CnOxB
Howard, Alan 1937- WhoHol A, WhoThe 72, -77
Howard, Andree 1910-1968 CnOxB, DancEn 78, NotNAT B, WhThe
Howard, Ann 1936- CmOp, IntWWM 77, -80, WhoMus 72, WhoOp 76
Howard, Anna G 1893- AmSCAP 80
Howard, Art 1892-1963 NotNAT B, WhScrn 74, -77
Howard, Arthur 1910- Film 1, FilmgC, HalFC 80, WhoHol A
Howard, Avery 1908-1966 BiDAmM, NewOrJ[port]
Howard, Bart 1915- AmSCAP 66, -80, BiE&WWA, NotNAT
Howard, Beatrice Thomas 1905- AmSCAP 66, -80
Howard, Bert 1873-1958 WhScrn 74, -77
Howard, Bertrand E 1937- ConAmC
Howard, Bob 1906- BlksB&W, -C, CmpEPM, WhoJazz 72
Howard, Booth 1889-1936 WhScrn 74, -77
Howard, Boothe 1889-1936 WhoHol B
Howard, Bronson 1842-1908 CnThe, EncWT, McGEWD[port], ModWD, NotNAT A, -B, OxThe, PlP&P[port], REnWD[port], WhoStg 1906, -1908
Howard, Carolyne AmSCAP 80
Howard, Cecil d1895 NotNAT B
Howard, Charles 1882-1947 WhScrn 77
Howard, Clint WhoHol A
Howard, Constance Film 2
Howard, Cordelia 1848-1941 NotNAT B
Howard, Curly FilmEn
Howard, Curly 1906-1952 ForYSC, MotPP, WhoHol B
Howard, Cy 1915- FilmEn, FilmgC, HalFC 80, IntMPA 77, -75, -76, -78, -79, -80
Howard, Cyril IntMPA 77, -75, -76, -78, -79, -80
Howard, Darnell d1966 IlEncJ
Howard, Darnell 1892-1966 BiDAmM, EncJzS 70
Howard, Darnell 1895?-1966 CmpEPM, WhoJazz 72
Howard, David H 1860-1944 WhScrn 74, -77
Howard, Dean Clinton 1918- ConAmC, IntWWM 77, -80
Howard, Dick AmSCAP 80
Howard, Earle 1904- WhoJazz 72
Howard, Eddie AmPS B

Howard, Eddy d1963 *AmPS A, BgBands 74[port]*
Howard, Eddy 1909-1963 *WhScrn 74, -77, WhoHol B*
Howard, Eddy 1914-1963 *AmSCAP 66, -80, CmpEPM*
Howard, Edwin 1924- *ConAmTC*
Howard, Ernest 1875-1940 *WhScrn 74, -77*
Howard, Esther 1893-1965 *FilmgC, HalFC 80, WhScrn 74, -77, WhoHol B*
Howard, Eugene d1965 *CmpEPM, JoeFr*
Howard, Eugene 1880-1965 *WhThe*
Howard, Eugene 1881-1965 *BiE&WWA, Film 2, NotNAT B, WhScrn 74, -77, WhoHol B*
Howard, Fannie 1885- *BiDAmM*
Howard, Florence 1879- *WhoStg 1908*
Howard, Florence 1888-1954 *WhScrn 74, -77*
Howard, Florence Gladys Louise *WhoMus 72*
Howard, Frances *Film 2*
Howard, Frank 1823- *BiDAmM*
Howard, Frank 1833-1900? *BiDAmM*
Howard, Frankie 1921- *FilmgC*
Howard, Fred 1896- *AmSCAP 66, -80*
Howard, Frederick *Film 2*
Howard, Gaynor Margaret 1932- *IntWWM 80*
Howard, George d1921 *NotNAT B*
Howard, George Bronson d1922 *NotNAT B*
Howard, George Sallade 1903- *AmSCAP 66, -80, ConAmC, IntWWM 77, -80*
Howard, George W *Film 2*
Howard, Gertrude 1892-1934 *DrBlPA, Film 2, WhScrn 74, -77, WhoHol B*
Howard, Harlan 1929- *BiDAmM, EncFCWM 69, IlEncCM[port]*
Howard, Harold 1875- *WhoStg 1908*
Howard, Helen 1899-1975 *Film 1, -2, WhScrn 77*
Howard, J B d1895 *NotNAT B*
Howard, J Bannister 1867-1946 *NotNAT A, -B, WhThe*
Howard, Jack *Film 2*
Howard, Jan 1932- *BiDAmM, CounME 74[port], -74A, EncFCWM 69, IlEncCM[port]*
Howard, Jason *WhoHol A*
Howard, Jean *WhoHol A*
Howard, Jerome Curly 1906-1952 *WhScrn 74, -77*
Howard, Jerry 1911-1952 *JoeFr[port]*
Howard, Joe 1870-1946 *NewOrJ*
Howard, Joe 1878-1961 *CmpEPM*
Howard, Joe 1919- *CmpEPM*
Howard, John 1913- *FilmEn, FilmgC, ForYSC, HalFC 80, MotPP, MovMk, WhoHol A*
Howard, John Alvin 1944- *AmSCAP 80*
Howard, John Tasker 1890-1964 *AmSCAP 66, -80, Baker 78, BiDAmM, ConAmC, NewGrD 80, NotNAT B, OxMus*
Howard, Joseph 1912- *IntWWM 77, -80*
Howard, Joseph A 1928- *AmSCAP 66, -80, IntWWM 80*
Howard, Joseph E 1867-1961 *AmPS, NotNAT B, PopAmC[port]*
Howard, Joseph E 1878-1961 *BiDAmM*
Howard, Joseph Edgar 1867- *AmPS B*
Howard, Joseph Edgar 1878-1961 *AmSCAP 66, -80*
Howard, Joyce 1922- *FilmgC, HalFC 80, IlWWBF, WhoHol A, WhoMus 72*
Howard, Kathleen 1879-1956 *FilmEn, FilmgC, ForYSC, HalFC 80, WhScrn 74, -77, WhoHol B*
Howard, Kathleen 1884-1956 *Baker 78*
Howard, Keble 1875-1928 *NotNAT B, WhThe*
Howard, Ken 1944- *FilmEn, HalFC 80, NotNAT, WhoHol A, WhoThe 72, -77*
Howard, Kid 1908-1966 *WhoJazz 72*
Howard, Leslie d1943 *MotPP, PlP&P[port], WhoHol B*
Howard, Leslie 1890-1943 *FilmgC, HalFC 80*
Howard, Leslie 1893-1943 *BiDFilm, -81, CmMov, EncWT, FamA&A[port], FilmEn, Film 1, -2, ForYSC, IlWWBF[port], -A, MovMk[port], NotNAT A, -B, OxFilm, WhScrn 74, -77, WhThe, WorEFlm*
Howard, Leslie John 1948- *IntWWM 77, -80*
Howard, Lewis d1956 *WhoHol B*
Howard, Lewis 1919-1951 *WhScrn 77*
Howard, Lionelle *IlWWBF[port]*
Howard, Lisa K 1930-1963 *WhScrn 77*
Howard, Lisa K 1930-1965 *WhoHol B*
Howard, Mabel 1884- *WhoStg 1908*
Howard, Marjorie *WhoHol A*
Howard, Mary *ForYSC, WhoHol A*
Howard, May 1870-1935 *WhScrn 74, -77*
Howard, Mel 1912- *AmSCAP 66, -80*
Howard, Michael 1922- *IntWWM 80, NewGrD 80, WhoHol A*
Howard, Moe *FilmEn*
Howard, Moe 1897-1975 *ForYSC, MotPP, WhScrn 77, WhoHol C*
Howard, Moe 1905-1975 *JoeFr[port]*
Howard, Noah 1943- *EncJzS 70, IlEncJ*
Howard, Norah 1901-1968 *NotNAT B, WhThe*
Howard, Norman D 1945- *IntWWM 77*
Howard, Patricia 1937- *IntWWM 77, -80*
Howard, Paul Jack 1908- *BiDAmM, IlEncCM[port]*
Howard, Paul Leroy 1895- *WhoJazz 72*
Howard, Paul Mason 1909-1975 *AmSCAP 66, -80*
Howard, Penelope 1933- *WhoMus 72*
Howard, Peter 1878-1969 *WhScrn 74, -77*
Howard, Peter 1908-1965 *WhScrn 77*
Howard, Peter 1927- *BiE&WWA, NotNAT*
Howard, Peter 1934-1968 *WhScrn 77, WhoHol B*
Howard, Rance *WhoHol A*
Howard, Randall Lamar 1950- *AmSCAP 80*
Howard, Ray *AmSCAP 80, Film 2*
Howard, Ray Reid 1948- *IntWWM 80*
Howard, Richard 1890- *AmSCAP 66, -80, Film 2*
Howard, Sir Robert d1698 *NotNAT B, PlP&P*
Howard, Robert T *IntMPA 77, -76, -78, -79, -80, NewYTET*
Howard, Robin 1924- *CnOxB*
Howard, Roger 1938- *ConDr 73, -77*
Howard, Rollin 1840-1879 *BiDAmM*
Howard, Ron *HalFC 80, WhoHol A*
Howard, Ron 1954- *FilmEn, IntMPA 77, -75, -76, -78, -79, -80*
Howard, Ronald 1918- *FilmEn, FilmgC, ForYSC, HalFC 80, IlWWBF, IntMPA 77, -75, -76, -78, -79, -80, WhoHol A*
Howard, Ronnie 1953- *ForYSC*
Howard, Ronny 1953- *FilmgC, HalFC 80*
Howard, Rosetta 1914?-1974 *BluesWW[port], WhoJazz 72*
Howard, Ruth 1894-1944 *WhScrn 74, -77, WhoHol B*
Howard, Ruth 1907- *IntWWM 77, -80*
Howard, Sallie *BlkAmP*
Howard, Sam d1964 *NotNAT B*
Howard, Samuel 1710-1782 *NewGrD 80*
Howard, Samuel 1900-1955 *WhScrn 74, -77*
Howard, Samuel 1901-1955 *JoeFr[port]*
Howard, Samuel Eugene 1937- *IntWWM 77, -80*
Howard, Sandy 1927- *IntMPA 77, -75, -76, -78, -79, -80*
Howard, Shemp d1955 *FilmEn, MotPP, WhoHol B*
Howard, Shemp 1890-1955 *ForYSC*
Howard, Shemp 1901-1955 *FilmgC, HalFC 80*
Howard, Shemp And Moe Howard *ForYSC*
Howard, Shingzie *BlksB&W, -C*
Howard, Sidney Coe 1891-1939 *CnMD, CnThe, DcLB 7[port], EncWT, Ent, FilmEn, FilmgC, HalFC 80, McGEWD[port], ModWD, NotNAT B, OxThe, PlP&P, REnWD[port], WhThe*
Howard, Sydney 1884-1946 *Film 2, FilmgC, HalFC 80, WhoHol B*
Howard, Sydney 1885-1946 *EncMT, IlWWBF, NotNAT B, WhScrn 74, -77, WhThe*
Howard, T E *DcPup*
Howard, Tom 1886-1955 *WhScrn 74, -77, WhoHol B*
Howard, Trevor 1915- *ForYSC*
Howard, Trevor 1916- *BiDFilm, -81, CmMov, FilmAG WE, FilmEn, FilmgC, HalFC 80, IlWWBF[port], IntMPA 77, -75, -76, -78, -79, -80, MotPP, MovMk, OxFilm, PlP&P, WhoHol A, WhoThe 72, -77, WorEFlm[port]*
Howard, Vilma *MorBAP*
Howard, Vince *WhoHol A*
Howard, Vincente *Film 1*
Howard, Walter 1866-1922 *NotNAT B, WhThe*
Howard, Wanda *Film 1*
Howard, Wayne 1942- *IntWWM 80*
Howard, Wendy 1925-1972 *WhScrn 77, WhoHol B*
Howard, William 1884-1944 *WhScrn 74, -77, WhoHol B*
Howard, William J 1899-1954 *TwYS A*
Howard, William K 1899-1954 *BiDFilm, -81, FilmEn, FilmgC, HalFC 80, MovMk[port], OxFilm, WorEFlm*
Howard, William W d1963 *NotNAT B*
Howard, Willie d1949 *Film 2, WhoHol B*
Howard, Willie 1883-1949 *WhThe*
Howard, Willie 1886-1949 *CmpEPM, EncMT, JoeFr, NotNAT B*
Howard, Willie 1887-1949 *WhScrn 74, -77*
Howard, Willie And Eugene *AmPS B*
Howard DeWalden, Lord *OxMus*
Howard-Jones, Evlyn 1877-1951 *NewGrD 80*
Howarth, Donald 1931- *ConDr 73, -77, WhoThe 72, -77*
Howarth, Elgar 1935- *IntWWM 80, NewGrD 80, WhoMus 72*
Howarth, Lees 1914- *WhoMus 72*
Howat, Audrey Miner 1903- *IntWWM 80*
Howat, Clark *WhoHol A*
Howatt, William *Film 2*
Howchyn, Nicholas *NewGrD 80*
Howdy, Clyde 1920-1969 *WhScrn 77*
Howe *NewGrD 80, PupTheA*
Howe, Betty *Film 1*
Howe, Elias 1820-1895 *BiDAmM, NewGrD 80*
Howe, Gary Wayne 1945- *IntWWM 77*
Howe, George 1900- *BiE&WWA, WhoThe 72, -77*
Howe, George Warren 1909- *AmSCAP 66, -80*
Howe, Henry 1812-1896 *NotNAT B, OxThe*
Howe, Hubert S, Jr. 1942- *CpmDNM 75, ConAmC, IntWWM 80*
Howe, J B d1908 *NotNAT A, -B*
Howe, James Hakin 1917- *IntWWM 77, -80*
Howe, James Wong 1889-1976 *DcFM*
Howe, James Wong 1899-1976 *FilmEn, FilmgC, HalFC 80, IntMPA 75, -76, OxFilm, WorEFlm*
Howe, John d1519 *NewGrD 80*
Howe, John d1571 *NewGrD 80*
Howe, Julia Ward 1819-1910 *BiDAmM, NotNAT B*
Howe, Mary 1882-1964 *AmSCAP 66, -80, Baker 78, BiDAmM, ConAmC*
Howe, Maude Johnson 1887- *AmSCAP 66, -80*
Howe, Quincy 1900- *IntMPA 77, -75, -76*
Howe, Solomon 1750-1835 *BiDAmM*
Howe, Sylvia *WomWMM B*
Howe, Wallace *Film 2*
Howe, Willard 1898- *WhoStg 1908*
Howell, Alice 1892- *Film 1, -2, TwYS*
Howell, Almonte Charles, Jr. 1925- *IntWWM 77, -80*
Howell, Chauncey *ConAmTC*
Howell, Clarissa 1955- *BlkWAB*
Howell, Dorothy 1898- *Baker 78, OxMus, WhoMus 72*
Howell, Gene Mac *AmSCAP 80*
Howell, Glynne *CmOp*
Howell, Gwynne Richard 1938- *NewGrD 80, WhoOp 76*
Howell, Henry William 1936- *IntWWM 80*
Howell, Hudson Davis 1919- *ConAmC*
Howell, Jane *WhoThe 72, -77*
Howell, John 1670?-1708 *NewGrD 80*
Howell, John 1888-1928 *NotNAT B, WhThe*
Howell, John Daggett 1911- *BiE&WWA*
Howell, Joshua Barnes 1888-1966 *BluesWW[port]*
Howell, Michael 1943- *EncJzS 70*
Howell, Miriam *BiE&WWA*
Howell, Robert B 1944- *AmSCAP 66, -80*
Howell, Ronald Thomas 1942- *IntWWM 80*
Howell, Thomas B 1921- *AmSCAP 66*
Howell, Yvonne *Film 2*
Howells, Anne Elizabeth 1941- *CmOp, IntWWM 77, -80, NewGrD 80,*

WhoMus 72, WhoOp 76
Howells, Herbert 1892- *Baker 78, DcCM, IntWWM 77, -80, MusMk, NewGrD 80, OxMus, WhoMus 72*
Howells, Ursula 1922- *FilmgC, HalFC 80, IntMPA 77, -75, -76, -78, -79, -80, WhoHol A, WhoThe 72, -77*
Howells, William Dean 1837-1920 *McGEWD, ModWD, NotNAT B, PlP&P[port]*
Howen, Carl VanDer *NewGrD 80*
Howerd, Frankie *IntMPA 75, -76, -78, -79, -80*
Howerd, Frankie 1921- *FilmEn, HalFC 80, IntMPA 77, WhoHol A, WhoThe 72, -77*
Howerd, Frankie 1927- *IlWWBF, -A*
Howerton, Clarence Major Mite 1913-1975 *WhoHol C*
Howerton, Clarency Major Mite 1913-1975 *WhScrn 77*
Howerton, George 1905- *WhoMus 72*
Howery, Robert Ray 1932- *WhoOp 76*
Howes, Basil 1901- *WhThe*
Howes, Bobby *FilmEn*
Howes, Bobby 1895- *WhoThe 72*
Howes, Bobby 1895-1972 *EncMT, Film 2, FilmgC, HalFC 80, IlWWBF, WhScrn 77, WhThe, WhoHol B*
Howes, Dulcie 1910- *CnOxB, DancEn 78*
Howes, Frank Stewart 1891-1974 *Baker 78, NewGrD 80, OxMus, WhoMus 72*
Howes, Reed 1900-1964 *FilmEn, Film 2, ForYSC, TwYS, WhScrn 77, WhoHol B*
Howes, Robert Frederick 1947- *IntWWM 77, -80, WhoMus 72*
Howes, Sally Ann *WhoThe 72*
Howes, Sally Ann 1930- *BiE&WWA, EncMT, FilmEn, FilmgC, HalFC 80, IlWWBF[port], MotPP, MovMk, NotNAT, WhoHol A, WhoThe 77*
Howes, Sally Ann 1934- *ForYSC*
Howes, William d1676 *NewGrD 80*
Howet, Gregorio *NewGrD 80*
Howett, Gregorio *NewGrD 80*
Howgill, Pauline Jane 1932- *WhoMus 72*
Howie, Mary Frances 1930- *IntWWM 77*
Howland, Alan d1946 *NotNAT B*
Howland, Horace *OxMus*
Howland, Jobyna d1936 *ForYSC, PlP&P[port], WhoHol B*
Howland, Jobyna 1880-1936 *CmpEPM, Film 1, -2, NotNAT B, ThFT[port], TwYS, WhThe*
Howland, Jobyna 1881-1936 *WhScrn 74, -77*
Howland, Olin 1896-1959 *Film 1, -2, MovMk, NotNAT B, WhoHol B*
Howland, Olin 1896-1960 *ForYSC*
Howland, William Legrand 1873-1915 *Baker 78, ConAmC*
Howle, Margaret May 1937- *WhoMus 72*
Howlett, Neil 1934- *IntWWM 80, WhoOp 76*
Howlett, Noel 1901- *FilmgC, HalFC 80, WhoThe 72, -77*
Howlin, Olin 1896-1959 *FilmgC, HalFC 80, Vers B[port], WhScrn 74, -77, WhoHrs 80[port]*
Howlin' Wolf *BiDAmM, BluesWW*
Howson, Frank A d1945 *NotNAT B*
Howson, John d1887 *NotNAT B*
Hoxie, Hart *TwYS*
Hoxie, Jack 1885-1965 *FilmEn, Film 1, ForYSC, TwYS*
Hoxie, Jack 1885-1975 *Film 2*
Hoxie, Jack 1890-1965 *WhScrn 74, -77, WhoHol B*
Hoy, Bonnee 1936- *ConAmC*
Hoy, Bonnee L 1936- *IntWWM 77, -80*
Hoy, Danny 1916- *Film 2*
Hoyem, Nell Marie 1906- *IntWWM 80*
Hoyem, Robert 1930- *WhoOp 76*
Hoyer, Dore 1911-1967 *CnOxB, DancEn 78*
Hoyer, Karl 1891-1936 *Baker 78*
Hoyeux, Balduin 1547?-1594 *NewGrD 80*
Hoyle, John *NewGrD 80*
Hoyle, Ted 1942- *IntWWM 77, -80*
Hoyningen-Huene, George d1968 *WorEFlm*
Hoyol, Balduin 1547?-1594 *NewGrD 80*
Hoyos, Rodolfo *ForYSC, WhoHol A*
Hoyou, Balduin 1547?-1594 *NewGrD 80*
Hoyoul, Balduin 1547?-1594 *NewGrD 80*
Hoyt, Arthur *Film 1, -2, ForYSC, TwYS*
Hoyt, Arthur 1873-1953 *HolCA[port]*
Hoyt, Arthur 1874-1953 *WhScrn 74, -77, WhoHol B*
Hoyt, Arthur 1876-1955 *MovMk[port]*
Hoyt, Caroline Miskel d1898 *NotNAT B*
Hoyt, Mrs. Charles H d1893 *NotNAT B*
Hoyt, Charles Hale 1860-1900 *BiDAmM, CnThe, EncMT, ModWD, NotNAT A, -B, OxThe, PlP&P, REnWD[port]*
Hoyt, Clegg 1911-1967 *WhScrn 74, -77, WhoHol B*
Hoyt, Edward N 1859- *WhoStg 1908*
Hoyt, G W *PupTheA*
Hoyt, Harry O 1880-1961 *TwYS A*
Hoyt, Harry O 1891-1961 *FilmEn*
Hoyt, Hazel *PupTheA*
Hoyt, Howard 1913- *BiE&WWA*
Hoyt, John 1905- *FilmgC, ForYSC, HalFC 80, MovMk, Vers A[port], WhoHol A, WhoHrs 80[port]*
Hoyt, Julia 1897-1955 *Film 2, NotNAT B, WhScrn 74, -77, WhoHol B*
Hoyt, Richard *PupTheA*
Hoyu, Balduin 1547?-1594 *NewGrD 80*
Hoyul, Balduin 1547?-1594 *NewGrD 80*
Hoz Y Mota, Juan Claudio DeLa 1622?-1714? *McGEWD*
Hrabanus Maurus 780?-856 *NewGrD 80*
Hradecky, Emil 1913-1974 *NewGrD 80*
Hrastnik, Franz 1904- *CnMD*
Hrazdira, Cyril Metodej 1868-1926 *NewGrD 80*
Hrimala, Marie 1839-1921 *NewGrD 80*
Hrimaly *NewGrD 80*
Hrimaly, Adalbert 1842-1908 *Baker 78*
Hrimaly, Bohuslav 1848-1894 *NewGrD 80*
Hrimaly, Jan 1844-1915 *NewGrD 80*
Hrimaly, Jaromir 1845-1905 *NewGrD 80*
Hrimaly, Johann 1844-1915 *Baker 78*
Hrimaly, Otakar 1883-1945 *Baker 78, NewGrD 80*
Hrimaly, Vojtech 1809-1880 *NewGrD 80*
Hrimaly, Vojtech 1842-1908 *NewGrD 80*
Hrisandie, Alexandre Demeter 1936- *IntWWM 77*
Hrisanide, Alexandru 1936- *DcCM, NewGrD 80*
Hrisanidis, Alexandre Demetre 1936- *Baker 78, IntWWM 77, -80*
Hristic, Stevan 1885-1958 *Baker 78, NewGrD 80*
Hristic, Zoran 1938- *IntWWM 80*
Hrostwitha 930?-1000 *DcPup*
Hrosvitha *REnWD[port]*
Hrosvitha 930?-1000 *DcPup*
Hroswitha *OxThe*
Hroswitha VonGandersheim 935?-975? *EncWT*
Hrotsvitha 930?-1000 *DcPup*
Hrotsvitha 935?-1001? *CnThe, REnWD[port]*
Hrotsvitha Of Gandersheim 935?-973? *NotNAT B*
Hrotswitha 935?- *NewGrD 80*
Hrovatin, Radoslav 1908- *IntWWM 77, -80*
Hruba, Vera *FilmEn*
Hruby, Dolores Marie 1923- *AmSCAP 80*
Hruby, Frank M 1918- *IntWWM 77, -80*
Hruby, Norbert J 1918- *BiE&WWA, NotNAT*
Hruby, Stanislav 1932- *IntWWM 77, -80*
Hruby, Viktor 1894- *WhoMus 72*
Hruschka, Wilhelm 1912- *WhoOp 76*
Hrusovsky, Ivan 1927- *Baker 78, NewGrD 80*
Hruza, Lubos 1933- *WhoOp 76*
Hsia, Kuei-Ying *WomWMM*
Hsien, Hsing-Hai 1905-1945 *NewGrD 80*
Hsiung, Shih I 1902- *BiE&WWA, WhThe*
Hsu, Dolores Menstell 1930- *IntWWM 77, -80*
Hsu, John 1931- *WhoMus 72*
Hsu, John Tseng-Hsin 1931- *IntWWM 77, -80*
Hsu, Tsang-Houei 1929- *NewGrD 80*
Hsu, Wen-Ying 1909- *ConAmC, IntWWM 77, -80*
Hsueh, Nancy *WhoHol A*
Huang, Al 1937- *CnOxB*
Huang, Cham-Ber 1925- *NewGrD 80*
Hubad, Samo 1917- *IntWWM 77, -80*
Hubalek, Claus 1926- *CnMD, ModWD*
Huban, Eileen 1895-1935 *NotNAT B, WhThe*
Hubay, Eugen 1858-1937 *NewGrD 80*
Hubay, Jeno 1858-1937 *Baker 78, BnBkM 80, NewEOp 71, NewGrD 80, OxMus*
Hubbard, Anthony *OxMus*
Hubbard, Arthur Stanley 1929- *IntWWM 77*
Hubbard, Frank 1920-1976 *NewGrD 80*
Hubbard, Freddie 1938- *DrBlPA, EncJzS 70, IlEncJ*
Hubbard, Frederick Dewayne 1938- *BiDAmM, EncJzS 70*
Hubbard, Gordon 1921- *IntMPA 77, -75, -76, -78, -79, -80*
Hubbard, Jack *PupTheA*
Hubbard, John 1759-1810 *BiDAmM*
Hubbard, John 1914- *FilmgC, ForYSC, HalFC 80, WhoHol A*
Hubbard, Lorna 1910- *WhThe*
Hubbard, Lucien 1888-1971 *FilmgC, HalFC 80*
Hubbard, O B *PupTheA*
Hubbard, Tom d1974 *WhScrn 77*
Hubbel, Raymond 1879-1954 *NotNAT B*
Hubbell, Carl 1903- *What 1[port]*
Hubbell, Edwin *Film 2*
Hubbell, Frank Allen 1907- *AmSCAP 66, -80, Baker 78, ConAmC*
Hubbell, Raymond 1870-1954 *ConAmC*
Hubbell, Raymond 1879-1954 *AmSCAP 66, -80, BiDAmM, CmpEPM, EncMT, NewCBMT, PopAmC[port], WhThe*
Hubble, Ed 1928- *EncJzS 70*
Hubble, John Edgar 1928- *BiDAmM, EncJzS 70*
Hubble, Malcolm James 1930- *IntWWM 77*
Hubble, Martie 1922- *AmSCAP 66, -80*
Hubeau, Jean 1917- *Baker 78, WhoMus 72*
Huber, Anna Gertrud 1894-1971 *NewGrD 80*
Huber, Calvin Raymond 1925- *AmSCAP 80, ConAmC*
Huber, Chad *Film 2*
Huber, Christian d1697 *NewGrD 80*
Huber, Ferdinand 1791-1863 *NewGrD 80*
Huber, Gusti 1914- *BiE&WWA, NotNAT, WhThe, WhoHol A*
Huber, Hans 1852-1921 *Baker 78, NewGrD 80, OxMus*
Huber, Harold 1904-1959 *FilmgC, HalFC 80*
Huber, Harold 1910-1959 *HolCA[port], NotNAT B, Vers A[port], WhScrn 74, -77, WhoHol B*
Huber, Horst 1933- *IntWWM 77, -80*
Huber, Jeno *NewGrD 80*
Huber, John Elwyn 1940- *IntWWM 77, -80*
Huber, Juanita Billie 1905-1965 *WhScrn 74, -77*
Huber, Klaus 1924- *Baker 78, DcCM, IntWWM 77, -80, NewGrD 80*
Huber, Kurt 1893-1943 *Baker 78, NewGrD 80*
Huber, Nicolaus A 1939- *DcCM, NewGrD 80*
Huber, Paul 1918- *IntWWM 77, -80*
Huber, Walter Simon 1898- *IntWWM 77, -80*
Huberdeau, Gustave 1878-1945 *BiDAmM*
Huberman, Barbara *CreCan 1*
Huberman, Bronislaw 1882-1947 *Baker 78, MusSN[port], NewGrD 80[port]*
Hubert, Andre 1634?-1700 *OxThe*
Hubert, Christian Gottlob 1714-1793 *NewGrD 80*
Hubert, Dick *NewYTET*
Hubert, George 1881-1963 *NotNAT B, WhScrn 74, -77, WhoHol B*
Hubert, Jo Ellen Stevens 1949- *IntWWM 77*
Hubert, Marcel 1906- *IntWWM 77, -80*
Hubert, Nicolai 1840-1888 *Baker 78*
Hubert, Nikolay Al'bertovich *NewGrD 80*
Hubert, Paul *Film 2*
Hubert, Roger 1903-1964 *DcFM, FilmEn*
Huberti, Antoine 1722?-1791 *NewGrD 80*
Huberti, Gustave-Leon 1843-1910 *Baker 78, NewGrD 80*
Huberty De Salinis *NewGrD 80*
Huberty, Albert 1879-1955 *Baker 78*
Huberty, Anton 1722?-1791 *NewGrD 80*
Hubicki, Margaret Olive *WhoMus 72*
Hubin, Frank B *PupTheA*
Hublay, Miklos 1918- *CroCD*
Hubley, Faith *WomWMM, WorEFlm*
Hubley, John 1914-1977 *DcFM, FilmEn, FilmgC, HalFC 80, OxFilm, WomWMM, WorEFlm*
Hubley, John And Hubley, Faith *NewYTET*
Hubley, Season *HalFC 80, WhoHol A*
Hubschmid, Paul 1917- *FilmAG WE, FilmEn, FilmgC, ForYSC, HalFC 80, WhoHol A*

Huby, Roberta *WhThe*
Hucbald 840?-930 *Baker 78, BnBkM 80, NewGrD 80*
Hucbald 849-930 *OxMus*
Huchel, Peter 1903- *CnMD*
Hucher, Antonio *NewGrD 80*
Hucher, Yves 1914- *NewGrD 80*
Huchons, Richard *NewGrD 80*
Huchyn, Nicholas *NewGrD 80*
Hucke, Helmut 1927- *NewGrD 80*
Hucko, Michael Andrew 1918- *AmSCAP 80, BiDAmM, EncJzS 70*
Hucko, Peanuts 1918- *CmpEPM, EncJzS 70, WhoJazz 72*
Huckridge, Edward John 1904- *WhoMus 72*
Hucks, William Richard, Jr. 1922- *AmSCAP 80*
Hudadoff, Igor 1926- *IntWWM 77*
Hudak, Andrew, Jr. 1918- *AmSCAP 66, –80*
Hudd, Walter 1898-1963 *FilmgC, HalFC 80, NotNAT B, WhScrn 74, –77, WhThe, WhoHol B*
Huddleston, David *WhoHol A*
Huddleston, Floyd Houston 1919- *AmSCAP 66, –80*
Hudec, Konstantin 1901-1952 *NewGrD 80*
Hudec, Vladimir 1929- *NewGrD 80*
Hudecek, Vaclav 1952- *IntWWM 77, –80*
Hudes, Eric Aubrey 1920- *IntWWM 77, –80*
Hudez, Karl 1904- *IntWWM 77, –80, WhoMus 72*
Hudgebut, John *NewGrD 80*
Hudgins, Torrence B *IntMPA 77, –75, –76, –78, –79, –80*
Hudis, Norman *IntMPA 77, –75, –76, –78, –79, –80*
Hudman, Wes d1964 *WhoHol B*
Hudman, Wesley 1916-1964 *NotNAT B, WhScrn 74, –77*
Hudson, Barton 1936- *IntWWM 77, –80*
Hudson, Charles d1897 *NotNAT B*
Hudson, Dean 1906?- *BgBands 74, CmpEPM*
Hudson, Derek Colbourne 1934- *IntWWM 77, –80, WhoMus 72*
Hudson, Eli 1877-1919 *NewGrD 80*
Hudson, Fred *MorBAP*
Hudson, Frederick 1913- *Baker 78, IntWWM 77, –80, NewGrD 80, WhoMus 72*
Hudson, George *OxMus*
Hudson, George 1615?-1672 *NewGrD 80*
Hudson, Helen Louise 1953- *AmSCAP 80*
Hudson, John 1922- *ForYSC, WhoHol A*
Hudson, Joseph A 1952- *ConAmC*
Hudson, Larry 1920-1961 *WhScrn 74, –77, WhoHol B*
Hudson, Laurence Whitmarsh 1906- *WhoMus 72*
Hudson, Linda Constance 1910- *WhoMus 72*
Hudson, Paul 1945- *IntWWM 77, –80, WhoMus 72, WhoOp 76*
Hudson, Richard 1617?-1668 *NewGrD 80*
Hudson, Richard Albert 1924- *CpmDNM 80, ConAmC, IntWWM 77, –80*
Hudson, Robert 1732-1815 *NewGrD 80*
Hudson, Rochelle 1914- *ForYSC*
Hudson, Rochelle 1914-1971 *FilmgC*
Hudson, Rochelle 1914-1972 *FilmEn, HalFC 80, MotPP, MovMk, ThFT[port], WhScrn 77, WhoHol B*
Hudson, Rochelle 1915- *What 3[port]*
Hudson, Rock *MotPP, WhoHol A*
Hudson, Rock 1924- *BiDFilm, –81*
Hudson, Rock 1925- *CmMov, FilmEn, FilmgC, ForYSC[port], HalFC 80, IntMPA 77, –75, –76, –78, –79, –80, MovMk[port], OxFilm, WorEFlm[port]*
Hudson, Roy *ConAmTC*
Hudson, Wade *MorBAP*
Hudson, Walter *AmSCAP 80*
Hudson, Will 1908- *AmSCAP 66, –80, BiDAmM, CmpEPM, WhoJazz 72*
Hudson, William 1922- *ForYSC*
Hudson, William 1925-1974 *WhScrn 77, WhoHol B*
Hudson & Landry *RkOn 2A*
Hudson Brothers, The *RkOn 2[port]*
Hudson-DeLange *BgBands 74[port]*
Hudson Dusters *BiDAmM*
Hudson-Ford *IlEncR*
Hudspeth, Alfred Douglas 1914- *WhoMus 72*
Hudspeth, William G *AmSCAP 80*
Hudy, Wolfgang 1928- *IntWWM 77, –80*
Hue De La Ferte *NewGrD 80*
Hue, Georges-Adolphe 1858-1948 *Baker 78, NewGrD 80, OxMus*
Hueber, Kurt Anton 1928- *IntWWM 77, –80*
Huebing, Craig *WhoHol A*
Huebner, Ilse 1898- *AmSCAP 66*
Hueffer, Francis 1843-1889 *Baker 78, NewGrD 80*
Huehn, Julius M 1904-1971 *Baker 78*
Huehn, Julius M 1910-1971 *BiDAmM*
Huene, Friedrich Alexander VonHoyningen 1929- *IntWWM 77, NewGrD 80*
Huerter, Charles 1885- *AmSCAP 66, BiDAmM*
Hues Corporation, The *RkOn 2[port]*
Huestis, Russell 1894-1964 *WhScrn 74, –77*
Hueston, Billy 1896-1957 *AmSCAP 66, –80*
Huet, Gregorio 1550?-1616? *NewGrD 80*
Huete, Diego Fernandez De *NewGrD 80*
Huff, Forrest 1876-1947 *WhScrn 74, –77, WhoHol B*
Huff, Jack *WhScrn 77*
Huff, Jackie *Film 2*
Huff, Jay A 1926- *ConAmC*
Huff, Leon *ConMuA 80B*
Huff, Louise 1896-1973 *Film 1, –2, MotPP, TwYS, WhScrn 77, WhoHol B*
Huff, Luther Henry 1910-1973 *BluesWW[port]*
Huffaker, Clair 1927- *CmMov, FilmgC, HalFC 80, WorEFlm*
Huffam, Pelenton Lemuel 1940- *AmSCAP 80*
Huffer, Franz *NewGrD 80*
Huffman, Eugene H *MorBAP*
Huffman, Jessie C d1935 *NotNAT B*
Huffman, W Spencer *ConAmC*
Hufschmidt, Wolfgang 1934- *NewGrD 80*
Hug *NewGrD 80*
Hug, Armand 1910- *AmSCAP 66, CmpEPM, WhoJazz 72*
Hug, Armand 1910-1977 *NewOrJ[port]*
Hug, Jakob Christoph 1776-1855 *NewGrD 80*
Hug, Theo 1906- *IntWWM 80*
Hugard, Jean 1872-1959 *MagIlD*
Hugel-Stouthandel, Constance Elisabeth 1928- *IntWWM 77*
Huggins, Roy 1914- *FilmEn, FilmgC, HalFC 80, IntMPA 77, –75, –76, –78, –79, –80, NewYTET*
Huggler, John Stillman 1928- *ConAmC, IntWWM 77, –80*
Hugh Of St. Victor 1078?-1141 *NewGrD 80*
Hugh Primas Of Orleans 1095?-1160 *NewGrD 80*
Hugh, Robert Ap *NewGrD 80*
Hugh-Jones, Elaine *IntWWM 77, –80, WhoMus 72*
Hughes, Adelaide d1937 *NotNAT B*
Hughes, Adelaide d1960 *NotNAT B*
Hughes, Alfred Rea 1925- *AmSCAP 80*
Hughes, Allen 1921- *DancEn 78*
Hughes, Allison *MorBAP*
Hughes, Andrew 1937- *IntWWM 77, –80, NewGrD 80*
Hughes, Anna May 1918- *BiE&WWA, NotNAT*
Hughes, Annie 1869-1954 *NotNAT B, WhThe, WhoStg 1906, –1908*
Hughes, Anselm 1889-1974 *NewGrD 80, OxMus*
Hughes, Anthony George 1928- *IntWWM 77, –80*
Hughes, Archie d1860 *NotNAT B*
Hughes, Arthur *WhoHol A*
Hughes, Arwel 1909- *NewGrD 80, WhoMus 72*
Hughes, Babette *BlkAmP*
Hughes, Barnard 1915- *HalFC 80, NotNAT, WhoHol A, WhoThe 77*
Hughes, Carol 1915- *ForYSC, WhoHol A*
Hughes, Catharine Rachel 1935- *ConAmTC*
Hughes, Ceiriog *OxMus*
Hughes, Charissa d1963 *WhScrn 74, –77*
Hughes, Charles *OxMus*
Hughes, Charles William 1900- *IntWWM 77, –80*
Hughes, David *WhoMus 72*
Hughes, David 1924-1945 *WhScrn 77*
Hughes, David Edmund *OxMus*
Hughes, David G 1926- *NewGrD 80*
Hughes, David Hillary d1974 *WhScrn 77, WhoHol B*
Hughes, Del *BiE&WWA, NotNAT*
Hughes, Dickson *AmSCAP 80*
Hughes, Dom Anselm 1889-1974 *Baker 78, WhoMus 72*
Hughes, Donald Jefferson 1913- *WhoMus 72*
Hughes, Dorothy *Film 2, WhoMus 72*
Hughes, E Kent *ConAmC*
Hughes, Edward John 1913- *CreCan 1*
Hughes, Edwin 1884-1965 *Baker 78, BiDAmM*
Hughes, Elinor 1906- *BiE&WWA, NotNAT*
Hughes, Ernest d1962 *NotNAT B*
Hughes, Ernest 1915- *AmSCAP 66, –80*
Hughes, Fanny d1888 *NotNAT B*
Hughes, Floyd Keith 1958- *AmSCAP 80*
Hughes, Francis 1666?-1744 *NewGrD 80*
Hughes, Frank C *ConAmC*
Hughes, Gareth 1894-1965 *FilmEn, Film 1, –2, MotPP, TwYS, WhScrn 74, –77, WhoHol B*
Hughes, Gertrude 1913- *BlkWAB*
Hughes, Gervase 1905- *NewGrD 80*
Hughes, Glenn 1894-1964 *BiE&WWA, NotNAT B*
Hughes, Glenn Vernon 1927- *AmSCAP 80*
Hughes, Harry *IlWWBF*
Hughes, Hatcher 1881-1945 *CnMD, ModWD*
Hughes, Hatcher 1883-1945 *NotNAT B, WhThe*
Hughes, Hazel 1913- *WhThe, WhoHol A, WhoThe 72*
Hughes, Henry d1872 *NotNAT B*
Hughes, Herbert 1882-1937 *Baker 78, OxMus*
Hughes, Howard 1904-1976 *TwYS B*
Hughes, Howard 1905-1976 *BiDFilm, –81, DcFM, FilmEn, FilmgC, HalFC 80, IntMPA 75, –76, OxFilm, WorEFlm*
Hughes, Howard Leo 1930- *AmSCAP 80, ConAmC*
Hughes, Isabelle Grace Bragg 1912- *CreCan 1*
Hughes, J Anthony 1904-1970 *WhoHol B*
Hughes, James *BiE&WWA*
Hughes, Jann *WomWMM B*
Hughes, Jimmy *RkOn 2[port]*
Hughes, John d1720 *NotNAT B*
Hughes, Joseph Anthony 1904-1970 *WhScrn 77*
Hughes, Kathleen *WhoHol A*
Hughes, Kathleen 1928- *ForYSC, IntMPA 77, –75, –76, –78, –79, –80*
Hughes, Kathleen 1929- *FilmgC, HalFC 80*
Hughes, Ken 1922- *BiDFilm, –81, FilmEn, FilmgC, HalFC 80, IlWWBF, IntMPA 77, –75, –76, –78, –79, –80, WorEFlm*
Hughes, Langston 1902-1967 *AmSCAP 66, –80, BiDAmM, BiE&WWA, BlkAmP, CnMD, CroCD, DcLB 7[port], DrBlPA, EncJzS 70, EncWT, Ent, McGEWD, ModWD, MorBAP, NotNAT A, –B*
Hughes, LaVaughn Rachel 1919- *AmSCAP 66, –80*
Hughes, Lloyd 1896-1958 *HalFC 80*
Hughes, Lloyd 1897-1958 *FilmgC, MotPP, MovMk, NotNAT B, WhScrn 74, –77, WhoHol B*
Hughes, Lloyd 1897-1960 *Film 1, –2, ForYSC, TwYS*
Hughes, Margaret 1643-1719 *NotNAT B, PIP&P[port]*
Hughes, Marjorie *CmpEPM*
Hughes, Mark *ConAmC*
Hughes, Martin Glyn 1950- *IntWWM 80*
Hughes, Martin John 1951- *IntWWM 80*
Hughes, Sister Martina 1902- *ConAmC*
Hughes, Mary Beth 1919- *FilmEn, FilmgC, ForYSC, HalFC 80, MovMk, WhoHol A*
Hughes, Morris *Film 2*
Hughes, Patrick Cairns 1908- *WhoMus 72*
Hughes, Richard Samuel 1855-1893 *NewGrD 80*
Hughes, Robert *ConAmC*
Hughes, Robert E 1934- *AmSCAP 80*
Hughes, Robert James 1916- *AmSCAP 66, –80*
Hughes, Robert Watson 1912- *Baker 78, NewGrD 80, WhoMus 72*
Hughes, Roddy 1891- *FilmgC, HalFC 80, WhThe, WhoHol A*

Hughes, Rosemary 1911- *NewGrD 80*
Hughes, Rupert 1872-1956 *AmSCAP 66, -80, Baker 78, NotNAT B, TwYS A, WhScrn 77, WhThe, WhoStg 1908*
Hughes, Rush 1910-1958 *Film 2, WhScrn 77*
Hughes, Sherrie *AmSCAP 80*
Hughes, Spike 1908- *CmpEPM, NewGrD 80*
Hughes, Stacy 1930- *IntWWM 77, -80*
Hughes, Thomas *REnWD[port]*
Hughes, Thomas Arthur 1887-1953 *WhScrn 74, -77, WhoHol B*
Hughes, Tom 1932- *BiE&WWA, NotNAT*
Hughes, Tom E *WhThe*
Hughes, Trevor John 1953- *IntWWM 80*
Hughes, William Henry 1930- *BiDAmM*
Hughes, Yvonne Evelyn 1900-1950 *Film 2, WhScrn 77*
Hughes-Hughes, Augustus 1857-1942 *NewGrD 80*
Hughly, Young *BlkAmP*
Huglo, Michel 1921- *IntWWM 77, -80, NewGrD 80*
Hugo And Luigi *RkOn[port]*
Hugo De Lantins *NewGrD 80*
Hugo Of Reutlingen *NewGrD 80*
Hugo Von Montfort 1357-1423 *NewGrD 80*
Hugo, John Adam 1873-1945 *Baker 78, ConAmC*
Hugo, Laurence 1917- *BiE&WWA, IntMPA 77, -75, -76, -78, -79, -80, NotNAT, WhoHol A*
Hugo, Mauritz 1909-1974 *WhScrn 77, WhoHol B*
Hugo, Richard *NewGrD 80*
Hugo, Victor Marie 1802-1885 *CnThe, DcPup, EncWT, Ent, McGEWD[port], NewEOp 71, NewGrD 80, NotNAT A, -B, OxMus, OxThe, REnWD[port], WhoHrs 80*
Hugon, Georges 1904- *Baker 78*
Hugot, Antoine 1761-1803 *NewGrD 80*
Huguenet, Felix 1858-1926 *NotNAT B, WhThe*
Huguenet, Jacques-Christophe 1680-1729 *NewGrD 80*
Hugueny, Sharon *ForYSC, WhoHol A*
Hugues De Berze 1150?-1220 *NewGrD 80*
Hugues De Bregi 1150?-1220 *NewGrD 80*
Huhn, Bruno 1871-1950 *AmSCAP 66, -80, Baker 78, BiDAmM, ConAmC*
Huigens, Constantijn *NewGrD 80*
Huighens, Constantijn *NewGrD 80*
Huiol, Balduin *NewGrD 80*
Huisman, Maurice 1912- *WhoOp 76*
Huizar, Candelario 1883-1970 *Baker 78*
Huizar, Candelario 1888-1970 *NewGrD 80*
Hujsak, Joy Detenbeck 1924- *IntWWM 77, -80*
Hujus, Balduin *NewGrD 80*
Huke, Bob 1937- *IntMPA 77, -75, -76, -78, -79, -80*
Hukvari, Eugene 1908- *AmSCAP 80*
Hukvary, Eugene 1908- *IntWWM 77, -80*
Hula, Zdenek 1901- *IntWWM 77, -80*
Hulak-Artemovsky, Semen 1813-1873 *OxMus*
Hulbert, Claude 1900-1963 *Film 2, FilmgC, HalFC 80*
Hulbert, Claude 1900-1964 *IlWWBF, NotNAT B, WhScrn 74, -77, WhThe, WhoHol B*
Hulbert, Hugh Reginald 1884- *WhoMus 72*
Hulbert, Jack *FilmEn*
Hulbert, Jack 1892-1978 *EncMT, FilmgC, HalFC 80, IlWWBF[port], -A, WhoHol A, WhoThe 72, -77*
Hulbert, Tony 1944- *CnOxB*
Hulburd, H L d1973 *WhScrn 77*
Hulburt, John W 1907- *BiE&WWA*
Huldt-Nystrom, Hampus 1917- *NewGrD 80*
Hulett, William C d1785 *BiDAmM*
Hulette, Gladys *Film 1, -2, MotPP, TwYS*
Huley, Pete 1893-1973 *WhScrn 77, WhoHol B*
Hulick, Budd *JoeFr*
Hulin, Sylvia *WomWMM*
Huling, Lorraine *Film 1*
Hull, Anne 1888- *Baker 78, ConAmC*
Hull, Arthur Eaglefield 1876-1928 *Baker 78, NewGrD 80*
Hull, Arthur S *Film 2*
Hull, Dianne *WhoHol A*
Hull, Dorothy Spafard 1924- *AmSCAP 80*
Hull, Henry 1890- *Vers A[port], WhThe, WhoHol A*
Hull, Henry 1890-1977 *BiE&WWA, FilmEn, Film 1, -2, FilmgC, ForYSC, HalFC 80, HolCA[port], IntMPA 77, -75, -76, MotPP, MovMk[port], NotNAT, PlP&P, TwYS, WhoHrs 80[port]*
Hull, Jerry D 1933- *IntWWM 77*
Hull, Josephine d1957 *MotPP, PlP&P, WhoHol B*
Hull, Josephine 1884-1957 *FilmEn, FilmgC, HalFC 80, MovMk[port], ThFT[port], WhScrn 74, -77*
Hull, Josephine 1886-1957 *ForYSC, NotNAT A, -B, Vers B[port], WhThe*
Hull, Loraine *NotNAT*
Hull, Sir Percy 1878-1968 *NewGrD 80*
Hull, Shelly d1919 *NotNAT B, WhScrn 77*
Hull, Thomas d1808 *NotNAT B*
Hull, Thomas William James 1912- *WhoMus 72*
Hull, Warren 1903-1974 *FilmEn, FilmgC, ForYSC, HalFC 80, NewYTET, WhScrn 77, WhoHol B*
Hullah, John Pyke 1812-1884 *Baker 78, NewGrD 80, OxMus*
Huller, Johann Adam *Baker 78*
Hullet, Daniele *WomWMM*
Hullmandel, James Nicolas 1756-1823 *NewGrD 80*
Hullmandel, Jean Nicolas 1756-1823 *NewGrD 80*
Hullmandel, Nicolas-Joseph 1756-1823 *Baker 78, NewGrD 80*
Hulphers, Abraham Abrahamsson 1734-1798 *NewGrD 80*
Hulsteyn, Joai'n C Van *BiDAmM*
Hulswit, Martin *WhoHol A*
Hult, Eve *AmSCAP 80*
Hult, Ruby *BlkAmP, MorBAP*
Hultberg, Warren Earle 1921- *IntWWM 77, -80*
Hulten, George P 1891- *AmSCAP 66, -80*
Hultin, Jill *WomWMM A, -B*
Hultz, A C *NewGrD 80*
Humair, Daniel 1938- *EncJzS 70*
Human, William *Film 1*
Human Beinz *RkOn 2A*
Humberstone, Bruce 1903- *CmMov*
Humberstone, H Bruce 1903- *FilmEn, FilmgC, HalFC 80, MovMk[port], WhoHrs 80*
Humbert, George *Film 2*
Humbert, Georges 1870-1936 *Baker 78*
Humble, Keith 1927- *Baker 78, NewGrD 80, WhoMus 72*
Humble Pie *ConMuA 80A, IlEncR[port], RkOn 2[port]*
Hume, Alan 1924- *HalFC 80*
Hume, Benita 1906-1967 *FilmEn, Film 2, FilmgC, ForYSC, HalFC 80, IlWWBF[port], MotPP, MovMk, NotNAT B, ThFT[port], WhScrn 74, -77, WhoHol B*
Hume, Benita 1906-1968 *WhThe*
Hume, Cyril *WhoHrs 80*
Hume, Douglas *WhoHol A*
Hume, Fergus d1932 *NotNAT B*
Hume, Kenneth 1926-1967 *FilmgC, HalFC 80*
Hume, Margaret *Film 2*
Hume, Marjorie 1900- *Film 2, IlWWBF*
Hume, Paul 1915- *Baker 78*
Hume, Paul 1916- *BiDAmM*
Hume, Sam *PlP&P*
Hume, Tobias 1569?-1645 *NewGrD 80, OxMus*
Humel, Gerald 1931- *CnOxB, ConAmC, DcCM*
Humes, Fred *Film 2*
Humes, Helen 1913- *AmSCAP 80, BiDAmM, BluesWW[port], CmpEPM, EncJzS 70, WhoJazz 72*
Humfraus *NewGrD 80*
Humfress, Gordon Stanley Thomas 1918- *WhoMus 72*
Humfrey, Jane 1937- *IntWWM 77*
Humfrey, Pelham 1647-1674 *Baker 78, BnBkM 80, MusMk, NewGrD 80, OxMus*
Humieres, Robert D' *NotNAT B*
Humiston, William Henry 1869-1923 *Baker 78, BiDAmM*
Hummel *NewGrD 80*
Hummel, Burchard 1731-1797 *NewGrD 80*
Hummel, Burghard 1731-1797 *NewGrD 80*
Hummel, Elisabeth Christina 1751-1818 *NewGrD 80*
Hummel, Ferdinand B 1855-1928 *Baker 78, NewGrD 80*
Hummel, Johann Bernhard 1760-1805? *NewGrD 80*
Hummel, Johann Julius 1728-1798 *NewGrD 80*
Hummel, Johann Nepomuk 1778-1837 *Baker 78, BnBkM 80, MusMk, NewGrD 80[port], OxMus*
Hummel, Johann Nepomux 1778-1837 *GrComp[port]*
Hummel, Johannes *Baker 78*
Hummel-Rockl, Elisabeth 1793-1883 *Baker 78*
Hummell, Mary Rockwell 1889-1946 *WhScrn 74, -77*
Hummell, Wilson *Film 2*
Humperdinck, Engelbert 1854-1921 *Baker 78, BnBkM 80, CmOp, CmpBCM, DcCom 77, DcCom&M 79, DcPup, GrComp[port], MusMk, NewEOp 71, NewGrD 80, NotNAT B, OxMus*
Humperdinck, Engelbert 1936- *Baker 78, BiDAmM, RkOn 2[port]*
Humpert, Hans 1901-1943 *Baker 78*
Humpert, Hans Ulrich 1940- *NewGrD 80*
Humpherson, William Allen 1932- *WhoMus 72*
Humpherys, Sydney 1926- *WhoMus 72*
Humphrey, Barbara Ann 1950- *BlkWAB, EncJzS 70*
Humphrey, Bessie d1933 *WhScrn 74, -77*
Humphrey, Bobbi 1950- *DrBlPA, EncJzS 70*
Humphrey, Cavada *BiE&WWA, NotNAT, WhoHol A, WhoThe 72, -77*
Humphrey, Doris d1958 *NotNAT B*
Humphrey, Doris 1895-1958 *CmpGMD[port], CnOxB, DancEn 78[port]*
Humphrey, Earl 1902-1971 *NewOrJ*
Humphrey, Edith Alice 1906- *WhoMus 72*
Humphrey, Griffith *Film 2*
Humphrey, Jack Weldon 1901-1967 *CreCan 2*
Humphrey, Jim 1861?-1937 *NewOrJ[port]*
Humphrey, Jim 1870?- *BiDAmM*
Humphrey, Ola *Film 1*
Humphrey, Orral *Film 1, -2*
Humphrey, Paul 1935- *EncJzS 70*
Humphrey, Paul Nelson 1935- *BiDAmM*
Humphrey, Pelham *NewGrD 80*
Humphrey, Percy G 1905- *BiDAmM, NewOrJ[port]*
Humphrey, Ralph S 1944- *EncJzS 70*
Humphrey, Raymond George 1916- *WhoMus 72*
Humphrey, William 1874-1942 *FilmEn, Film 1, -2, WhScrn 77*
Humphrey, William J, Jr. 1901- *BiDAmM*
Humphrey, Willie Eli 1880-1964 *NewOrJ*
Humphrey, Willie James 1900- *NewOrJ[port], WhoJazz 72*
Humphreys, Alfred Wendell 1915- *IntWWM 77*
Humphreys, Carey 1922- *IntWWM 77, -80, WhoMus 72*
Humphreys, Cecil 1883-1947 *Film 2, NotNAT B, WhScrn 74, -77, WhThe, WhoHol B*
Humphreys, Cecil 1886-1947 *IlWWBF*
Humphreys, Garry Paul 1946- *IntWWM 80*
Humphreys, Henry S 1909- *ConAmC*
Humphreys, John 1945- *WhoMus 72*
Humphreys, M R *WhoMus 72*
Humphreys, Samuel 1698?-1738 *NewGrD 80*
Humphries, Barry 1934- *Ent*
Humphries, Bill 1927- *NewOrJ*
Humphries, Charles 1892-1978 *NewGrD 80*
Humphries, J S 1707?-1740? *NewGrD 80*
Humphries, Joe *Film 2*
Humphries, John d1927 *NotNAT B, WhThe*
Humphries, John 1707-1730? *OxMus*
Humphries, John 1707?-1740? *NewGrD 80*
Humphries, Roger 1944- *BiDAmM*
Humphris, Gordon 1921- *WhThe*
Humphris, Ian William 1927- *IntWWM 77, WhoMus 72*
Hun, Hadi 1900-1969 *WhScrn 74, -77*
Hunchback Of Arras *OxMus*

Hundley, Craig L 1953- *AmSCAP 80, EncJzS 70*
Hundley, Richard 1931- *AmSCAP 66, -80, ConAmC*
Hundoegger, Agnes *OxMus*
Hundziak, Andrzej 1927- *IntWWM 77, -80*
Hunebelle, Andre 1896- *FilmEn*
Hunefeld, Andreas 1581-1666 *NewGrD 80*
Huneker, James Gibbons 1857-1921 *Baker 78, NewGrD 80*
Huneker, James Gibbons 1859-1921 *NotNAT B*
Huneker, James Gibbons 1860-1921 *BiDAmM, EncWT, OxMus, OxThe*
Hung, Shen 1893-1955 *REnWD[port]*
Hungate, Dick *ConMuA 80B*
Hungate, William Leonard 1922- *AmSCAP 80*
Hungerford, Bruce 1922- *IntWWM 77, -80, WhoMus 72*
Hungerford, Bruce 1922-1977 *Baker 78*
Huni-Mihacsek, Felice 1891-1976 *CmOp*
Huni-Mihaczek, Felice 1891-1976 *NewGrD 80*
Hunkins, Arthur B 1937- *ConAmC*
Hunkins, Eusebia Simpson 1902- *AmSCAP 66, -80, ConAmC*
Hunkins, Leecynth 1930- *BlkAmP*
Hunnicut, Arthur 1911-1979 *FilmEn*
Hunnicut, Gayle 1943- *FilmEn, IntMPA 77, -75, -76, -78, -79, -80, WhoHrs 80*
Hunnicutt, Arthur 1911- *CmMov, FilmgC, ForYSC, HalFC 80, IntMPA 77, -75, -76, -78, -79, -80, MovMk[port], Vers A[port], WhoHol A*
Hunnicutt, Gayle 1941- *ForYSC*
Hunnicutt, Gayle 1942- *FilmgC, HalFC 80, WhoHol A*
Hunnies, William d1597 *NewGrD 80*
Hunnis, William d1597 *NewGrD 80*
Hunnys, William d1597 *NewGrD 80*
Hunold, Christian Friedrich 1681-1721 *NewGrD 80*
Hunsberger, Donald 1932- *AmSCAP 80, IntWWM 77, -80*
Hunsecker, Ralph Blane 1914- *AmSCAP 80*
Hunt, Al d1964 *NotNAT B*
Hunt, Alexandra *IntWWM 77, -80, WhoOp 76*
Hunt, Alice May 1901- *WhoMus 72*
Hunt, Arabella 1645?-1705 *NewGrD 80, OxMus*
Hunt, Betty Lee 1920- *BiE&WWA*
Hunt, Billy H 1926- *IntMPA 77, -75, -76, -78, -79, -80*
Hunt, Brian William 1950- *IntWWM 80*
Hunt, Charles J *TwYS A*
Hunt, Christopher Ben MacMichael 1938- *WhoMus 72*
Hunt, Donald Frederick 1930- *IntWWM 77, -80, WhoMus 72*
Hunt, Dora DePedery- *CreCan 1*
Hunt, Edgar Hubert 1909- *IntWWM 77, -80, WhoMus 72*
Hunt, Enid Clara 1911- *IntWWM 80, WhoMus 72*
Hunt, F V *NatPD[port]*
Hunt, G Carleton 1908- *IntMPA 77, -75, -76, -78, -79, -80*
Hunt, G W 1854-1940 *BiDAmM*
Hunt, Gale *PupTheA*
Hunt, George 1906?-1946? *WhoJazz 72*
Hunt, Gordon 1950- *IntWWM 80*
Hunt, Helen *Film 2*
Hunt, Hugh 1911- *BiE&WWA, CnThe, NotNAT, PlP&P, WhoThe 72, -77*
Hunt, Irene *Film 2*
Hunt, J Leland 1947- *IntWWM 77*
Hunt, Jacqueline May 1942- *IntWWM 77*
Hunt, James Henry Leigh 1784-1859 *OxMus*
Hunt, Jay 1857-1932 *Film 2, WhScrn 74, -77, WhoHol B*
Hunt, Jerry E 1943- *Baker 78, ConAmC*
Hunt, Jimmy *MotPP*
Hunt, Jno Leland 1947- *IntWWM 80*
Hunt, John 1905- *WhoMus 72*
Hunt, Leigh 1784-1859 *NotNAT B, OxThe*
Hunt, Leslie *Film 2*
Hunt, Madge 1875-1935 *Film 2, WhScrn 77*
Hunt, Marsha 1917- *BiE&WWA, FilmEn, FilmgC, ForYSC, HalFC 80, IntMPA 77, -75, -76, -78, -79, -80, MGM[port], MotPP, MovMk[port], NotNAT, ThFT[port], WhThe, WhoHol A*
Hunt, Marsha 1920- *What 4[port]*
Hunt, Martita 1900-1969 *BiE&WWA, FilmAG WE, FilmEn, FilmgC, ForYSC, HalFC 80, IlWWBF, MotPP, MovMk[port], NotNAT B, Vers A[port], WhScrn 74, -77, WhThe, WhoHol B*
Hunt, Michael Francis 1945- *AmSCAP 80, ConAmC*
Hunt, Pee Wee 1907- *AmPS A, CmpEPM, WhoJazz 72*
Hunt, Peter 1928- *CmMov, FilmEn, FilmgC, HalFC 80, IntMPA 77, -76, -78, -79, -80, WhoHrs 80*
Hunt, Peter H 1938- *FilmEn, IntMPA 77, -75, 76, -78, -79, -80, WhoThe 72, -77*
Hunt, Phil 1868- *WhoStg 1906, -1908*
Hunt, Rea M 1893-1961 *WhScrn 77, WhoHol B*
Hunt, Reginald Heber 1891- *IntWWM 77, -80, WhoMus 72*
Hunt, Richard d1683 *NewGrD 80*
Hunt, Sophie Anne *NewGrD 80*
Hunt, Thomas *NewGrD 80, OxMus*
Hunt, Thomas W 1929- *ConAmC*
Hunt, Vanzula Carter 1909- *BlkWAB*
Hunt, W P 1859-1934 *WhScrn 77*
Hunt, William E 1923- *BiE&WWA, NotNAT*
Hunt, Willie 1941- *IntMPA 80*
Hunte, Otto 1881- *FilmEn*
Hunten, Franz 1793-1878 *Baker 78, NewGrD 80*
Hunter, Alberta 1895- *BluesWW[port]*
Hunter, Alberta 1897- *AmSCAP 66, -80, CmpEPM, WhoJazz 72*
Hunter, B J *AmSCAP 80*
Hunter, Charles H 1878-1906 *BiDAmM*
Hunter, Eddie 1888- *BlkAmP, DrBlPA, MorBAP*
Hunter, Edna *Film 1*
Hunter, Evan 1926- *AmSCAP 66, -80, FilmgC, HalFC 80, WorEFlm[port]*
Hunter, Francis John 1946- *IntWWM 77, -80*
Hunter, Frank *ConAmTC*
Hunter, Frederic *NatPD[port]*
Hunter, Frederick J 1916- *BiE&WWA, NotNAT*
Hunter, George *Film 1*
Hunter, George W 1851- *WhThe*
Hunter, Glen 1897-1945 *PlP&P*
Hunter, Glenn d1945 *MotPP, WhoHol B*
Hunter, Glenn 1893-1945 *Film 2, NotNAT B*
Hunter, Glenn 1896-1945 *TwYS, WhThe*
Hunter, Glenn 1897-1945 *FilmgC, HalFC 80, WhScrn 74, -77*
Hunter, Harrison d1923 *NotNAT B*
Hunter, Hilda 1919- *IntWWM 80, WhoMus 72*
Hunter, Ian 1900-1975 *ConMuA 80A, FilmEn, Film 2, FilmgC, ForYSC, HolP 30[port], IlWWBF[port], IntMPA 75, MotPP, MovMk[port], WhScrn 77, WhThe, WhoHol A*
Hunter, Ian 1900-1976 *HalFC 80*
Hunter, Ian 1946- *IlEncR[port]*
Hunter, Ian Bruce Hope 1919- *WhoMus 72*
Hunter, Ian Timothy 1942- *IntWWM 80*
Hunter, Isla Herald 1922- *WhoMus 72*
Hunter, Ivory Joe d1974 *RkOn[port]*
Hunter, Ivory Joe 1911- *BiDAmM*
Hunter, Ivory Joe 1912-1974 *EncJzS 70*
Hunter, Jackie 1901-1951 *NotNAT B, WhScrn 74, -77*
Hunter, Jeff *MotPP*
Hunter, Jeffrey d1969 *WhoHol B*
Hunter, Jeffrey 1925-1969 *FilmEn, FilmgC, HalFC 80*
Hunter, Jeffrey 1926-1969 *WhScrn 74, -77*
Hunter, Jeffrey 1927-1969 *BiDFilm, ForYSC, MovMk[port], WorEFlm*
Hunter, Kenneth 1882- *WhThe*
Hunter, Kermit 1910- *BiE&WWA, ModWD, NotNAT*
Hunter, Kevin 1939- *AmSCAP 80*
Hunter, Kim 1922- *BiE&WWA, FilmEn, FilmgC, ForYSC, HalFC 80, IntMPA 77, -75, -76, -78, -79, -80, MotPP, MovMk[port], NotNAT, WhoHol A, WhoThe 72, -77*
Hunter, Marian *WomWMM A, -B*
Hunter, Meyer Michael *IntMPA 78*
Hunter, Nancy Victoria 1946- *IntWWM 77*
Hunter, Norman Charles 1908-1971 *CnMD, ConDr 77F, CroCD, EncWT, WhThe, WhoThe 72*
Hunter, Patsy *BluesWW*
Hunter, Paul *NatPD[port]*
Hunter, Ralph *ConAmC*
Hunter, Rebecca Lee 1945- *WomWMM B*
Hunter, Richard 1875-1962 *NotNAT B, WhScrn 74, -77, WhoHol B*
Hunter, Richard Sydney 1904- *WhoMus 72*
Hunter, Rita 1933- *CmOp, IntWWM 77, -80, NewGrD 80, WhoMus 72, WhoOp 76*
Hunter, Robert Christie 1941- *AmSCAP 80, IntWWM 77*
Hunter, Ross *IntMPA 77, -75, -76, -78, -79, -80, MotPP*
Hunter, Ross 1916- *CmMov, FilmEn, ForYSC, WhoHol A*
Hunter, Ross 1921- *FilmgC, HalFC 80, WorEFlm*
Hunter, Ruth *NotNAT A*
Hunter, Slim *BluesWW*
Hunter, T Hayes d1944 *IlWWBF*
Hunter, T Hayes 1881-1944 *FilmgC, HalFC 80*
Hunter, T Hayes 1896-1944 *FilmEn, TwYS A*
Hunter, Tab 1931- *AmPS A, FilmEn, FilmgC, ForYSC, HalFC 80, IntMPA 77, -75, -76, -78, -79, -80, MotPP, MovMk, RkOn, WhoHol A*
Hunter, Victor William 1910- *WhoThe 72, -77*
Hunter, Virginia 1924- *IntWWM 77, -80*
Hunter, W C *PlP&P*
Hunter, William 1811-1877 *BiDAmM*
Huntington, Billy 1937- *NewOrJ*
Huntington, Catharine 1889- *BiE&WWA, NotNAT*
Huntington, DeWitt Clinton 1830-1912 *BiDAmM*
Huntington, Frederick Dan 1819-1904 *BiDAmM*
Huntington, Joan *WomWMM*
Huntington, Jonathan 1771-1838 *BiDAmM*
Huntington, Lawrence 1900-1968 *FilmEn, FilmgC, HalFC 80, IlWWBF*
Huntley, Chet 1912-1974 *NewYTET, WhScrn 77, WhoHol B*
Huntley, Elizabeth Maddox *BlkAmP*
Huntley, Fred 1861-1931 *Film 1, -2, WhoHol B*
Huntley, Fred 1862-1931 *WhScrn 74, -77*
Huntley, G P 1904- *WhThe*
Huntley, George Patrick 1868-1927 *NotNAT B, WhThe*
Huntley, Grace d1896 *NotNAT B*
Huntley, Hugh *Film 2*
Huntley, Jobe 1918- *AmSCAP 66, -80, MorBAP*
Huntley, Luray *Film 1*
Huntley, Raymond 1904- *FilmAG WE, FilmgC, HalFC 80, IlWWBF, IntMPA 77, -75, -76, -78, -79, -80, WhoHol A, WhoThe 72, -77*
Huntley, Tim 1904- *WhThe*
Huntley-Wright, Betty 1911- *WhThe, WhoThe 72*
Huntley-Wright, Jose 1918- *WhThe*
Huntoon, Helen *Film 2*
Huntzinger, John H *PupTheA*
Hunys, William *NewGrD 80*
Hunziker, Dominique 1944- *IntWWM 77, -80*
Huot, Charles Edouard Masson 1855-1930 *CreCan 1*
Huot, Guy Eugene 1943- *IntWWM 80*
Huot, Juliette *CreCan 1*
Hupfeld, Bernhard 1717-1796 *NewGrD 80*
Hupfeld, Charles Frederick 1788-1864 *BiDAmM*
Hupfeld, Herman 1894-1951 *AmPS, AmSCAP 66, -80, BiDAmM, NotNAT B*
Hupfield, Charles d1819 *BiDAmM*
Hupfield, Herman 1894-1951 *CmpEPM*
Hupp, Deborah Kay 1948- *AmSCAP 80*
Huppert, Isabelle 1955- *FilmEn*
Hupperts, Paul 1919- *NewGrD 80*
Huray, Peter Le *NewGrD 80*
Hurd, Barry T 1949- *AmSCAP 80*
Hurd, Daniel George 1918- *AmSCAP 66, -80*
Hurd, Earl d1940 *FilmEn*
Hurd, George N *PupTheA*
Hurd, Ingraham 1952- *ConAmC*

Hurd, James L Peterson 1945- *IntWWM 77*
Hurd, Michael John 1928- *IntWWM 77, -80, NewGrD 80, WhoMus 72*
Hurde, Patrick 1936- *DancEn 78*
Hure, Jean 1877-1930 *Baker 78, NewGrD 80, OxMus*
Hurel, Charles *NewGrD 80*
Hurford, Peter John 1930- *IntWWM 77, -80, NewGrD 80, WhoMus 72*
Hurgon, Austen A d1942 *NotNAT B, WhThe*
Hurka, Franciscus Wencsslaus 1762-1805 *NewGrD 80*
Hurka, Friedrich Franz 1762-1805 *NewGrD 80*
Hurka, Hans *Film 2*
Hurlburt, Glen 1909-1961 *AmSCAP 66, -80*
Hurlburt, William Henry 1827-1895 *BiDAmM*
Hurlbut, Gladys *ForYSC, NotNAT A*
Hurlbut, W J 1883- *WhThe*
Hurlebusch, Conrad Friedrich 1696?-1765 *NewGrD 80*
Hurley, Alec 1871-1913 *OxThe, WhoStg 1908*
Hurley, Clyde L 1916- *CmpEPM, WhoJazz 72*
Hurley, Julia 1847-1927 *Film 1, -2, WhScrn 77*
Hurley, Kathy 1947- *NatPD[port]*
Hurley, Laurel 1927- *Baker 78*
Hurlock, Madeleine *Film 2*
Hurlock, Madeleine 1905?- *FilmEn*
Hurlock, Madeline *MotPP, TwYS, WhoHol A*
Hurlock, Roger W 1912- *IntMPA 77, -75, -76, -78, -79, -80*
Hurlstone, William Yeates 1876-1906 *Baker 78, NewGrD 80, OxMus*
Hurn, Douglas 1925-1974 *WhScrn 77*
Hurndall, Richard 1910- *FilmgC, HalFC 80, WhoThe 72, -77*
Hurney, Kate 1941- *IntWWM 77, -80*
Hurnik, Ilja 1922- *Baker 78, DcCM, IntWWM 77, -80, NewGrD 80*
Hurok, Sol 1888-1974 *Baker 78, BiE&WWA, NewGrD 80, NotNAT B, WhThe, WhoThe 72*
Hurok, Sol 1889-1974 *HalFC 80*
Hurok, Solomon 1888-1974 *DancEn 78*
Hurok, Solomon Isaievich 1888- *BiDAmM*
Hurok, Solomon Israelevich 1888-1974 *CnOxB*
Hurran, Dick 1911- *WhoThe 72, -77*
Hurrell, Clarence E 1912-1975 *AmSCAP 66, -80*
Hurrell, John D 1924- *BiE&WWA, NotNAT*
Hurry, Leslie 1909- *CnThe, CnOxB, CreCan 2, DancEn 78, OxThe, WhoThe 72, -77*
Hursey, John Richard 1944- *IntWWM 80*
Hurst, Brandon 1866-1947 *Film 1, -2, ForYSC, HolCA[port], NotNAT B, TwYS, WhScrn 74, -77, WhoHol B*
Hurst, Brian Desmond 1900- *FilmEn, FilmgC, HalFC 80, IlWWBF, IntMPA 75, MovMk[port]*
Hurst, David *WhoHol A*
Hurst, David 1925- *FilmgC, HalFC 80*
Hurst, David 1926- *BiE&WWA, NotNAT*
Hurst, Fannie 1889-1968 *FilmgC, HalFC 80, NotNAT B, WhThe*
Hurst, George 1926- *ConAmC, IntWWM 77, -80, NewGrD 80, WhoMus 72*
Hurst, Paul d1953 *MotPP, WhoHol B*
Hurst, Paul 1886-1953 *TwYS A*
Hurst, Paul 1888-1953 *HolCA[port], Vers A[port], WhScrn 74, -77*
Hurst, Paul 1889-1953 *Film 1, -2, FilmgC, ForYSC, HalFC 80, MovMk, TwYS*
Hurst, Roy 1906- *WhoMus 72*
Hurst, Veronica 1931- *FilmgC, HalFC 80, IlWWBF[port], WhoHol A*
Hurston, Zora Neale 1903-1960 *BlkAmP, DrBlPA, MorBAP*
Hurt, John 1940- *FilmAG WE, FilmEn, FilmgC, HalFC 80, WhoHol A, WhoThe 72, -77*
Hurt, John Smith 1893-1966 *BluesWW[port]*
Hurt, Mary Kathryn 1940- *AmSCAP 80*
Hurt, Mississippi John 1892-1966 *BiDAmM, DrBlPA, EncFCWM 69*
Hurt, Mississippi John 1894-1966 *NewGrD 80*
Hurt, R N 1902- *IntMPA 77, -75, -76, -78, -79, -80*
Hurtado De Xeres *NewGrD 80*
Hurte, Leroy Edward 1915- *AmSCAP 80*
Hurteau, Jean-Pierre 1924- *WhoOp 76*
Hurteur, Guillaume Le *NewGrD 80*
Hurth, Harold *Film 2*
Hurtig, Louis d1924 *NotNAT B*
Hurton, Clarence *Film 2*
Hurtubise, Jacques 1939- *CreCan 2*
Hurum, Alf 1882-1972 *Baker 78, NewGrD 80*
Hurwicz, Angelika 1922- *EncWT*
Hurwitch, Moses 1844-1910 *NotNAT B*
Hurwitz, Emanuel 1919- *IntWWM 77, -80, NewGrD 80, WhoMus 72*
Hurwitz, Leo 1909- *FilmEn, OxFilm, WorEFlm*
Hurwitz, Moshe 1844-1910 *ModWD*
Hurwitz, Robert Irving 1939- *IntWWM 80*
Hus, Eugene 1758-1823 *CnOxB*
Hus, Jan 1371?-1415 *NewGrD 80*
Hus, Jean-Baptiste 1733-1805 *CnOxB*
Hus, Jerome *CnOxB*
Hus, Pietro *CnOxB*
Hus-Desforges, Pierre Louis 1773-1838 *Baker 78*
Hus-Desforges, Pierre-Louis 1773-1838 *NewGrD 80*
Hus Family *CnOxB*
Husa, Karel 1921- *Baker 78, CpmDNM 72, -73, -74, -76, -77, -78, -79, -80, ConAmC, DcCM, IntWWM 77, -80, MusMk, NewGrD 80, WhoMus 72*
Husband, John Jenkins 1760-1825 *BiDAmM*
Husch, Gerhard 1901- *NewEOp 71, NewGrD 80, WhoMus 72*
Husch, Richard J d1948 *NotNAT B*
Huschen, Heinrich 1915- *IntWWM 77, -80, NewGrD 80*
Huseby, Gerardo Victor 1943- *IntWWM 77, -80*
Huselton, Marion Jackson 1950- *IntWWM 77, -80*
Husen, Elly *PupTheA*
Hush, Lisabeth *WhoHol A*
Hush, Lisbeth *WomWMM B*
Husing, Ted 1901-1962 *WhScrn 77, WhoHol B*
Husk, William Henry 1814-1887 *NewGrD 80, OxMus*
Husky, Ferlin 1927- *BiDAmM, CounME 74[port], -74A, EncFCWM 69, IlEncCM[port], RkOn*
Husmann, Heinrich 1908- *IntWWM 77, -80, NewGrD 80*
Husmann, Ron 1937- *BiE&WWA, NotNAT, WhoHol A, WhoThe 77*
Husmann, Valentin *NewGrD 80*
Husni, Kameran *DcFM*
Huss, Henry Holden 1862-1953 *Baker 78, BiDAmM, NewGrD 80*
Huss, John 1373-1415 *OxMus*
Hussein, Waris 1938- *FilmgC, HalFC 80, IntMPA 77, -78, -79, -80*
Hussels, Helga 1930- *IntWWM 77, -80*
Hussey, Dyneley 1893-1972 *NewGrD 80, OxMus, WhoMus 72*
Hussey, Jimmy 1891-1930 *NotNAT B, WhThe, WhoHol B*
Hussey, Olivia 1950- *ForYSC*
Hussey, Olivia 1951- *FilmEn, FilmgC, HalFC 80, MotPP, WhoHol A*
Hussey, Ruth *BiE&WWA, MotPP, NotNAT*
Hussey, Ruth 1913- *ThFT[port]*
Hussey, Ruth 1914- *FilmEn, FilmgC, ForYSC, HalFC 80, MGM[port], MovMk[port], What 4[port], WhThe, WhoHol A*
Hussie, Barbara *WomWMM B*
Hussler, Johann *NewGrD 80*
Husson, Albert 1912- *BiE&WWA, McGEWD*
Hussy, Jimmy 1891-1930 *WhScrn 74, -77*
Hustad, Donald Paul 1918- *AmSCAP 80, IntWWM 77*
Husted, Benjamin *ConAmC*
Husted, Beverly d1975 *WhoHol C*
Husten, Bruce H 1948- *ConAmTC*
Husting, Lucille 1900?-1972 *WhScrn 77*
Hustis, James Humphrey, III 1924- *IntWWM 77, -80*
Huston, Anjelica 1952- *FilmgC, HalFC 80, WhoHol A*
Huston, Carla A 1944- *AmSCAP 80*
Huston, Frank C 1871-1959 *AmSCAP 66, -80*
Huston, John *ConAmC, IntMPA 75, -76*
Huston, John 1905- *ForYSC*
Huston, John 1906- *AmFD, BiDFilm, -81, CmMov, ConDr 73, -77A, DcFM, FilmEn, FilmgC, HalFC 80, IntMPA 77, -78, -79, -80, MovMk[port], OxFilm, WhoHol A, WorEFlm[port]*
Huston, Patricia *WhoHol A*
Huston, Philip 1908- *BiE&WWA, NotNAT, WhoHol A*
Huston, Scott 1916- *Baker 78, ConAmC, NewGrD 80*
Huston, Steven Charles 1949- *AmSCAP 80*
Huston, Thomas Scott, Jr. 1916- *IntWWM 77, -80*
Huston, Tony *WhoHol A*
Huston, Virginia 1925- *IntMPA 77, -75, -76, -78, -79, -80*
Huston, Walter 1884-1950 *AmPS B, BiDFilm, -81, EncMT, EncWT, Ent, FamA&A[port], FilmEn, Film 2, FilmgC, ForYSC, HalFC 80, MotPP, MovMk[port], NotNAT B, OxFilm, PlP&P, WhScrn 74, -77, WhThe, WhoHol B, WorEFlm*
Huston, William Dale 1918- *AmSCAP 66, -80*
Huszar-Puffy, Karl *Film 2*
Huszka, Jeno 1875-1960 *NewGrD 80*
Huszti, Joseph Bela 1936- *IntWWM 77, -80*
Hutchenrider, Clarence Behrens 1908- *BiDAmM, CmpEPM, EncJzS 70, WhoJazz 72*
Hutchens, Frank 1892-1965 *Baker 78, NewGrD 80*
Hutcherson, Bobby 1941- *EncJzS 70, IlEncJ*
Hutcherson, Levern *NotNAT*
Hutcherson, Robert 1941- *BiDAmM, EncJzS 70*
Hutcheson, David 1905- *FilmgC, HalFC 80, WhoHol A, WhoThe 72, -77*
Hutcheson, Ernest 1871-1951 *Baker 78, BiDAmM, ConAmC, NewGrD 80*
Hutcheson, Francis *NewGrD 80*
Hutcheson, Jere Trent 1938- *CpmDNM 76, -78, -79, -80, ConAmC, IntWWM 77, -80*
Hutcheson, LaVerne *BiE&WWA*
Hutcheson, Ronita Marlene 1945- *AmSCAP 80*
Hutcheson, Thomas 1942- *ConAmC*
Hutchings, Arthur James Bramwell 1905- *IntWWM 80*
Hutchings, Arthur James Bramwell 1906- *NewGrD 80, OxMus, WhoMus 72*
Hutchings, Chiquita *PupTheA*
Hutchings, George Sherburn 1835-1913 *NewGrD 80*
Hutchings, John 1911- *WhoMus 72*
Hutchins, Bobby Wheezer *Film 2*
Hutchins, Daryl 1920-1971 *AmSCAP 66, -80*
Hutchins, Farley Kennan 1921- *ConAmC*
Hutchins, Fred B 1911- *BiE&WWA*
Hutchins, Guy Starr 1905- *ConAmC*
Hutchins, Kathryn Lynn 1953- *IntWWM 77*
Hutchins, Linda *ForYSC*
Hutchins, Will 1932- *FilmgC, ForYSC, HalFC 80, WhoHol A*
Hutchinson *NewGrD 80*
Hutchinson, Abby 1829-1892 *NewGrD 80*
Hutchinson, Abigail Jemima 1829-1892 *BiDAmM*
Hutchinson, Ann 1918- *CnOxB, DancEn 78*
Hutchinson, Asa 1823-1884 *BiDAmM, NewGrD 80*
Hutchinson, Canon Charles 1887-1969 *WhScrn 74, -77*
Hutchinson, Charles *Film 1, -2, TwYS, -A*
Hutchinson, Dorothy d1962 *NotNAT B*
Hutchinson, Emma d1817 *NotNAT B*
Hutchinson, George *WhoMus 72*
Hutchinson, Godfrey Michel Langley 1936- *WhoMus 72*
Hutchinson, Harry 1892- *WhoHol A, WhoThe 72, -77*
Hutchinson, Jesse *NewGrD 80*
Hutchinson, John 1616- *NewGrD 80*
Hutchinson, John Wallace 1821-1908 *BiDAmM, NewGrD 80*
Hutchinson, Josephine *BiE&WWA, NotNAT*
Hutchinson, Josephine 1898- *HalFC 80, HolP 30*

Hutchinson, Josephine 1904- *FilmEn, FilmgC, ForYSC, ThFT[port], WhThe, WhoHol A*
Hutchinson, Josephine 1909- *MovMk[port]*
Hutchinson, Judson 1817-1859 *NewGrD 80*
Hutchinson, Kathryn *WhoStg 1908*
Hutchinson, Lucie M 1918- *IntWWM 80*
Hutchinson, Lucie M 1919- *IntWWM 77*
Hutchinson, Muriel 1915-1975 *WhScrn 77*
Hutchinson, Paul *ConMuA 80B*
Hutchinson, Richard d1646 *NewGrD 80*
Hutchinson, Victor Hely *OxMus*
Hutchinson, William 1869-1918 *WhScrn 77*
Hutchinson Family *AmPS B, BiDAmM*
Hutchinson Scott, Jay 1924- *WhThe*
Hutchison, Bruce 1901- *CreCan 1*
Hutchison, Emma d1965 *WhThe*
Hutchison, Margaret *CreCan 2*
Hutchison, Muriel 1915-1975 *WhThe, WhoHol C*
Hutchison, Percy 1875-1945 *NotNAT B, WhThe*
Hutchison, Warner 1930- *AmSCAP 80, CpmDNM 72, -73, -75, -78, -79, ConAmC, IntWWM 77, -80*
Hutchison, William Bruce 1901- *CreCan 1*
Huth, Harold 1892-1967 *FilmEn, Film 2, FilmgC, HalFC 80, IlWWBF, WhScrn 74, -77, WhThe, WhoHol B*
Hutner, Herbert L *AmSCAP 80*
Hutner, Meyer Michael *IntMPA 77, -75, -76, -79, -80*
Hutschenruyter *NewGrD 80*
Hutschenruyter, Willem 1863-1950 *NewGrD 80*
Hutschenruyter, Willem Jacob 1828-1889 *NewGrD 80*
Hutschenruyter, Wouter 1796-1878 *Baker 78, NewGrD 80, OxMus*
Hutschenruyter, Wouter 1859-1943 *Baker 78, NewGrD 80, OxMus*
Hutson, David Laurence 1938- *EncJzS 70*
Hutt, William 1920- *CreCan 1, WhoThe 72, -77*
Huttel, Josef 1893-1951 *NewGrD 80*
Huttel, Walter Oskar 1920- *IntWWM 77, -80, NewGrD 80*
Huttenbrenner, Anselm 1794-1868 *Baker 78, NewGrD 80, OxMus*
Huttenrauch, Karl August 1794-1848 *NewGrD 80*
Hutter, Josef 1894-1959 *NewGrD 80*
Hutto, Jack 1928- *BiE&WWA, NotNAT*
Hutto, Joseph Benjamin 1926- *BluesWW[port]*
Hutton, Betty 1921- *BiDAmM, BiE&WWA, CmMov, CmpEPM, FilmEn, FilmgC, ForYSC, HalFC 80[port], IntMPA 77, -75, -76, -78, -79, -80, MotPP, MovMk[port], OxFilm, WhoHol A*
Hutton, Brian G 1935- *FilmEn, FilmgC, HalFC 80, IntMPA 77, -75, -76, -78, -79, -80*
Hutton, Ina Ray *BgBands 74[port]*
Hutton, Ina Ray 1914?- *CmpEPM*
Hutton, Ina Ray 1916- *WhoJazz 72*
Hutton, Ina Ray 1917- *What 4[port]*
Hutton, Ina Ray 1918- *BiDAmM*
Hutton, Jim d1979 *MotPP, WhoHol A*
Hutton, Jim 1933-1979 *FilmEn*
Hutton, Jim 1934-1979 *HalFC 80*
Hutton, Jim 1935?-1979 *MovMk*
Hutton, Jim 1938-1979 *FilmgC, IntMPA 77, -78, -79*
Hutton, Jim 1940?-1979 *ForYSC*
Hutton, Joseph 1787-1828 *NotNAT B*
Hutton, June 1918?-1973 *CmpEPM, WhoHol B*
Hutton, Lauren 1943- *FilmEn, HalFC 80, WhoHol A*
Hutton, Laurence d1904 *NotNAT B*
Hutton, Leona 1892-1949 *WhScrn 74, -77*
Hutton, Linda *WhoHol A*
Hutton, Lucille *Film 1, -2*
Hutton, Marion 1919- *CmpEPM*
Hutton, Marion 1920- *FilmgC, HalFC 80, WhoHol A*
Hutton, Raymond *Film 2*
Hutton, Robert 1920- *FilmEn, FilmgC, ForYSC, HalFC 80, HolP 40[port], IntMPA 77, -75, -76, -78, -79, -80, MotPP, WhoHol A, WhoHrs 80*
Huw, Robert Ap *NewGrD 80*
Huwet, Gregorio *NewGrD 80*
Huxford, John Calvitt 1931- *IntWWM 77*
Huxford, John Clifford 1955- *IntWWM 77*
Huxham, Kendrick 1892-1967 *WhScrn 77*
Huxhan, Kendrick 1892-1967 *WhScrn 74, WhoHol B*
Huxley, Aldous 1894-1963 *CnMD, FilmEn, HalFC 80, ModWD, NotNAT B*
Huxley, Sir Julian 1887-1975 *OxFilm*
Huybers, Bernard M 1922- *IntWWM 77, -80*
Huybrechts, Albert 1899-1938 *Baker 78, NewGrD 80*
Huybrechts, Francois 1946- *NewGrD 80*
Huyck, Willard *WomWMM*
Huygens, Christiaan 1629-1695 *NewGrD 80*
Huygens, Sir Constantijn 1596-1687 *NewGrD 80*
Huyghens, Sir Constantijn 1596-1687 *NewGrD 80*
Huyn, Jacques 1613-1652 *NewGrD 80*
Huys, Bernard 1934- *IntWWM 77, -80*
Huys, Johan 1942- *IntWWM 77, -80*
Huzaya, Joseph *NewGrD 80*
Hvorov, Ioan 1928- *WhoOp 76*
Hyames, John *Film 2*
Hyams, Barry 1911- *BiE&WWA, NotNAT*
Hyams, Jerome 1915- *IntMPA 77, -75, -76, -78, -79, -80*
Hyams, John 1877-1940 *WhScrn 74, -77, WhoHol B*
Hyams, Joseph 1927- *IntMPA 77, -75, -76, -78, -79, -80*
Hyams, Leila 1905-1977 *FilmEn, Film 2, FilmgC, ForYSC, HalFC 80, MovMk, ThFT[port], TwYS, WhoHol A, WhoHrs 80[port]*
Hyams, Marge 1923- *CmpEPM*
Hyams, Nessa *WomWMM*
Hyams, Peter 1943- *FilmEn, HalFC 80, IntMPA 77, -75, -76, -78, -79, -80*
Hyatt, Clayton d1932 *WhScrn 74, -77*
Hyatt, Gordon *NewYTET*
Hyatt, Herman 1906-1968 *WhScrn 74, -77*
Hyatt, John W 1837-1920 *FilmEn*
Hyatt, Willard Clark 1907- *AmSCAP 80*
Hycart, Bernar *NewGrD 80*
Hyde, Abby Bradley 1799-1872 *BiDAmM*
Hyde, Alexander 1898-1956 *AmSCAP 66, -80*
Hyde, Douglas 1860-1949 *ModWD*
Hyde, George *ConAmC*
Hyde, Harry *Film 1*
Hyde, Lewis 1899- *WhoMus 72*
Hyde, Madeline 1907- *AmSCAP 66, -80*
Hyde, Miriam Beatrice 1913- *IntWWM 80, WhoMus 72*
Hyde, Rosel H *NewYTET*
Hyde, Tommy 1916- *IntMPA 77, -75, -76, -78, -79, -80*
Hyde, Walter 1875-1951 *Baker 78, CmOp, NewGrD 80*
Hyde, William DeWitt 1858-1917 *BiDAmM*
Hyde-Smith, Christopher 1935- *IntWWM 77, -80, WhoMus 72*
Hyde-White, Wilfrid 1903- *BiE&WWA, FilmAG WE, FilmEn, FilmgC, ForYSC, HalFC 80, MovMk, NotNAT, OxFilm, WhoHol A, WhoThe 72, -77*
Hyem, Constance Ethel d1928 *NotNAT B, WhThe*
Hyer, Martha *MotPP*
Hyer, Martha 1924- *FilmEn, ForYSC, WhoHol A*
Hyer, Martha 1929- *FilmgC, HalFC 80, MovMk[port], WhoHrs 80[port]*
Hyer, Martha 1930- *IntMPA 77, -75, -76, -78, -79, -80*
Hyer Sisters Colored Minstrels *BiDAmM*
Hyers, Anna Madah 1854-1924? *BiDAmM*
Hyers, Emma Louise 1853-1916? *BiDAmM*
Hyggyns, Edward *NewGrD 80*
Hygons, Richard 1435?-1509? *NewGrD 80*
Hykes, Adelaide *PupTheA*
Hyla, Leon 1952- *ConAmC*
Hylaire Daleo *NewGrD 80*
Hylan, Donald 1899-1968 *WhScrn 74, -77*
Hylan, William H 1915- *IntMPA 77, -75, -76, -78, -79*
Hyland, Augustin Allen 1905-1963 *NotNAT B, WhScrn 74, -77*
Hyland, Brian 1943- *AmPS A, RkOn[port]*
Hyland, Diana 1936-1977 *BiE&WWA, ForYSC, HalFC 80, WhoHol A*
Hyland, Dick Irving 1906- *IntMPA 77, -75, -76, -78, -79, -80*
Hyland, Frances 1927- *CreCan 2, WhoThe 72, -77*
Hyland, Peggy *Film 1, -2, IlWWBF[port], MotPP, TwYS*
Hyland, William H *NewYTET*
Hylin, Birgitta Charlotta Kristina 1915- *IntWWM 77, -80*
Hyllary, Thomas *NewGrD 80*
Hyllested, August 1856-1946 *Baker 78, BiDAmM*
Hylton, Brent Eugene 1948- *IntWWM 77, -80*
Hylton, Jack 1892-1965 *BgBands 74, CmpEPM, EncMT, NewGrD 80, NotNAT B, WhThe*
Hylton, Jane d1979 *WhoHol A*
Hylton, Jane 1926-1979 *FilmgC, ForYSC, HalFC 80*
Hylton, Jane 1927-1979 *IlWWBF[port], IntMPA 77, -75, -76, -78, -79*
Hylton, Millie 1868-1920 *NotNAT B, WhThe*
Hylton, Richard d1962 *NotNAT B, WhoHol B*
Hylton, Richard 1920-1962 *WhThe*
Hylton, Richard 1921-1962 *FilmgC, ForYSC, HalFC 80, WhScrn 74, -77*
Hymack, Mister *WhScrn 74, -77*
Hyman, Bynunsky *Film 2*
Hyman, Dick 1927- *AmPS A, BiDAmM, CmpEPM, EncJzS 70, RkOn*
Hyman, Earle 1926- *BiE&WWA, DrBlPA, NotNAT, WhoHol A, WhoThe 72, -77*
Hyman, Eliot 1904- *IntMPA 75, -76*
Hyman, Jackie D 1949- *AmSCAP 80*
Hyman, John Wigginton 1899- *NewOrJ*
Hyman, Joseph M 1901- *BiE&WWA, WhThe*
Hyman, Kenneth 1928- *FilmgC, HalFC 80, IntMPA 75, -76*
Hyman, Louis *Film 2*
Hyman, Pete *ConMuA 80B*
Hyman, Prudence *WhThe*
Hyman, Richard R 1927- *AmSCAP 66, -80*
Hyman, Richard Roven 1927- *EncJzS 70*
Hyman, Spaff *PupTheA*
Hymaturgus, Johann *NewGrD 80*
Hymbert De Salinis *NewGrD 80*
Hymer, John B d1953 *NotNAT B, WhThe*
Hymer, Warren 1906-1948 *Film 2, FilmgC, ForYSC, HalFC 80, HolCA[port], NotNAT B, Vers A[port], WhScrn 74, -77, WhoHol B*
Hynd, Ronald 1931- *CnOxB, DancEn 78*
Hynes, Elizabeth 1947- *IntWWM 77, -80*
Hynes, John E 1853-1931 *WhScrn 74, -77*
Hynninen, Jorma Kalervo 1941- *WhoOp 76*
Hyrst, Eric 1927- *CreCan 1, DancEn 78*
Hyson, Dorothy 1915- *FilmgC, HalFC 80, IlWWBF[port], WhThe*
Hyson, Winifred P 1925- *IntWWM 80*
Hytinkoski, Antero Juhani 1914- *CpmDNM 76, IntWWM 77, -80*
Hytrek, Sister Theophane 1915- *ConAmC*
Hytten, Olaf 1888-1955 *Film 2, FilmgC, HalFC 80, WhScrn 74, -77, WhoHol B*
Hytten, Olaf 1899-1955 *IlWWBF*
Hywel, John *WhoMus 72*
Hywell, Suzanne 1944- *CnOxB*

I

Iacobus DeOudenaerde *NewGrD 80*
Iacobus Leodiensis *NewGrD 80*
Iacopone Da Todi *McGEWD*
Iacovelli, Mercurio *NewGrD 80*
Ian And Sylvia *CounME 74, -74A, EncFCWM 69*
Ian, Janis 1951- *AmSCAP 80, BiDAmM, ConMuA 80A, IlEncR[port], RkOn 2[port]*
Ianculescu, Magda 1929- *IntWWM 80, WhoOp 76*
Iannaccone, Anthony 1943- *AmSCAP 80, CpmDNM 76, IntWWM 77, -80*
Iannaccone, Anthony J 1943- *ConAmC*
Iannelli, Theresa Rose 1936- *AmSCAP 66, -80*
Iannucci, Salvatore J 1927- *IntMPA 77, -75, -76, -78, -79, -80*
Iannuzzi, Ralph J 1914- *IntMPA 77, -75, -76, -78, -79, -80*
Ianus, Martin *NewGrD 80*
Iasilli, Gerardo 1880- *AmSCAP 66*
Iatauro, Michael Anthony 1943- *AmSCAP 80*
Ibach *NewGrD 80*
Ibach, Carl Rudolph 1804-1863 *NewGrD 80*
Ibach, Johannes Adolf 1766-1848 *Baker 78*
Ibach, Johannes Adolph 1766-1848 *NewGrD 80*
Ibach, P A Rudolf 1843-1892 *NewGrD 80*
Ibach, Richard 1813-1889 *NewGrD 80*
Ibanez, Bonaventura *Film 2*
Ibanez, Ramon *Film 2*
Ibberson, H *Film 2*
Ibberson, Mary 1892- *OxMus, WhoMus 72*
Ibbetson, Arthur 1921- *FilmEn, FilmgC*
Ibbetson, Arthur 1922- *HalFC 80*
Ibbott, Daphne 1918- *IntWWM 77, -80, WhoMus 72*
Ibert, Jacques 1890- *WhoMus 72*
Ibert, Jacques 1890-1960 *CnOxB*
Ibert, Jacques 1890-1961 *DcFM*
Ibert, Jacques 1890-1962 *Baker 78, BnBkM 80, CmOp, CompSN[port], DancEn 78, DcCom&M 79, DcCM, FilmEn, HalFC 80, MusMk, NewEOp 71, NewGrD 80, NotNAT B, OxFilm, OxMus, WorEFlm*
Ibler, Eric Fairbairn 1954- *IntWWM 77*
Ibn Abd Rabbihi 860-940 *NewGrD 80*
Ibn Al-Khatib 1313-1374 *NewGrD 80*
Ibn Al-Nadim 930?-990 *NewGrD 80*
Ibn Bajja 1090?-1138 *NewGrD 80*
Ibn Ghaybi Al-Hafiz Al-Maraghi *NewGrD 80*
Ibn Jurjis Al-Lubnani Mikha'il Mushaqa *NewGrD 80*
Ibn Rushd 1126-1198 *NewGrD 80*
Ibn Sina 980-1037 *NewGrD 80*
Ibn Zayla d1048 *NewGrD 80*
Ibrahim Al-Mawsili 742-804 *NewGrD 80*
Ibrahim Al-Nadim 742-804 *NewGrD 80*
Ibrahim Ibn Al-Mahdi 779-839 *NewGrD 80*
Ibrahim-Khan, Mitza *DcFM*
Ibsen, Henrik 1828-1906 *CnMD, CnThe, DcPup, EncWT, Ent[port], McGEWD[port], ModWD, NewEOp 71, NotNAT A, -B, OxMus, OxThe, PlP&P[port], REnWD[port]*
Ibycus *NewGrD 80*
Icart, Bernar *NewGrD 80*
Ice, Bob 1914?- *NewOrJ*
Ice, Bob 1931- *NewOrJ*
Iceberg Slim *BlkAmP*
Ichac, Marcel 1906- *DcFM, FilmEn, WorEFlm*
Ichikawa, Kon 1915- *BiDFilm, -81, DcFM, FilmEn, FilmgC, HalFC 80, MovMk[port], OxFilm, WorEFlm*
Ichikawa, Sadanje d1940 *NotNAT B*
Ichiyanagi, Toshi 1933- *NewGrD 80*
Ichyanagi, Toshi *ConAmC*
Ide, Geneva Evelyn 1922- *IntWWM 77, -80*
Ide, George Barton 1806-1872 *BiDAmM*
Ide, Harold 1917- *AmSCAP 66, -80*
Ide, Patrick 1916- *WhoThe 72, -77*
Idelsohn, Abraham Zevi 1882-1938 *Baker 78, OxMus*
Idelsohn, Abraham Zvi 1882-1938 *NewGrD 80*
Idemitsu, Mako *WomWMM B*
Iden, Rosalind 1911- *CnThe, WhThe*
Ides Of March, The *RkOn 2[port]*
Idriss, Ramez 1911-1971 *AmSCAP 66, -80*
Idzikowski, Stanislas 1894- *DancEn 78, WhThe*
Idzikowsky, Stanislas 1894- *CnOxB*
Idzior, Wladyslaw Piotr 1932- *IntWWM 77, -80*
Ienner, Jimmy *ConMuA 80B*
Ieuan Gwyllt *NewGrD 80*
If *IlEncR*
Iffland, August Wilhelm 1759-1814 *CnThe, EncWT, Ent, McGEWD[port], NotNAT B, OxThe, REnWD[port]*
Ifield, Frank 1936- *FilmgC, HalFC 80*
Ifield, Frank 1937- *RkOn*
Ifukube, Akira 1914- *Baker 78, NewGrD 80, WhoHrs 80*
Igdalsky, Zviah *WhoHol A*
Igesz, Bodo 1935- *WhoOp 76*
Iglehart, James *DrBlPA*
Iglesias, Eugene *ForYSC, WhoHol A*
Iglesias, Roberto 1927?- *CnOxB, DancEn 78*
Iglesias Alvarez, Antonio 1918- *NewGrD 80*
Iglesias Villoud, Hector 1913- *NewGrD 80*
Igloi, Thomas George 1947- *IntWWM 77*
Ignanimus, Angelus d1543 *NewGrD 80*
Ignannino, Angelo d1543 *NewGrD 80*
Ignatius, Anja 1911- *IntWWM 80*
Ignatowicz, Ewa 1941- *IntWWM 77, -80*
Igumnov, Konstantin 1873-1948 *Baker 78, NewGrD 80*
Ihloff, Jutta-Renate 1944- *WhoOp 76*
Ihnat, Steve d1972 *ForYSC, WhoHol B*
Ihnat, Steve 1934-1972 *FilmgC, HalFC 80*
Ihnat, Steve 1935-1972 *WhScrn 77*
Ihnen, Wiard 1897- *FilmEn*
Ihrke, Walter R 1908- *ConAmC*
Iimori, Taijiro 1940- *WhoOp 76*
Ijames, Mary Tunstall 1894-1963 *AmSCAP 80*
Ike And Tina *BiDAmM*
Ikebe, Shin-Ichiro 1943- *Baker 78*
Ikebe, Shinichiro 1943- *DcCM*
Ikenouchi, Tomojiro 1906- *Baker 78, NewGrD 80*
Ikettes, The *BiDAmM, RkOn[port]*
Ikonen, Lauri 1888-1966 *Baker 78*
Ikonomov, Boyan Georgiev 1900-1973 *Baker 78, NewGrD 80*
Il Cinthio *PlP&P[port]*
Il Verso, Antonio 1560?-1621 *NewGrD 80*
Ilberman, Mel *ConMuA 80B*
Ileborgh, Adam *NewGrD 80, OxMus*
Ilenkov, Vasili Pavlovich 1897- *ModWD*
Ilerici, Kemal 1910- *Baker 78*
Iles, Edna *IntWWM 77, -80*
Iles, John Henry 1872-1951 *OxMus*
Ilial, Leo *CreCan 2*
Iliev, Constantin 1924- *DcCM*
Iliev, Konstantin 1924- *Baker 78, NewGrD 80*
Iliff, James Frederick 1923- *IntWWM 77, -80, WhoMus 72*
Iliffe, Barrie John 1925- *IntWWM 77, -80, WhoMus 72*
Iliffe, Frederick 1847-1928 *Baker 78*
Ilinski, Count Jan Stanislaw 1795-1860 *NewGrD 80*
Ilinski, Count Janusz Stanislaw 1795-1860 *NewGrD 80*
Ilitsch, Daniza 1914-1965 *Baker 78*
Iliu, Victor 1912-1968 *DcFM*
Illek, Karel 1936- *IntWWM 77, -80*
Illery, Pola *Film 2*
Illes, Endre 1902- *CroCD*
Illes, Eva *WhoOp 76*
Illica, Luigi 1857-1919 *Baker 78, BnBkM 80, NewEOp 71, NewGrD 80, OxThe*
Illing, Peter 1899-1966 *FilmgC, ForYSC, HalFC 80, WhScrn 74, -77*
Illing, Peter 1905-1966 *WhThe, WhoHol B*
Illing, Robert Henry 1917- *IntWWM 77, -80*
Illing, Rosamund Elizabeth Anne 1953- *IntWWM 80*
Illington, Margaret 1879-1934 *OxThe*
Illington, Margaret 1881-1934 *Film 1, NotNAT B, WhScrn 74, -77, WhThe, WhoHol B, WhoStg 1906, -1908*
Illington, Marie d1927 *NotNAT B, WhThe*
Illingworth, Ruth 1905- *WhoMus 72*
Illius, Tim *ConMuA 80B*
Illouz, Betsy *NewGrD 80*
Illyes, Gyula 1902- *CnMD, CroCD, McGEWD*
Ilmer, Irving 1919- *IntWWM 77, WhoMus 72*
Ilosfalvy, Robert 1927- *NewGrD 80, WhoOp 76*
Ilott, Pamela *NewYTET*
Ilson, Saul And Ernest Chambers *NewYTET*
Ilvess, Charles K 1905- *AmSCAP 66*
Ilyenkov, Vassily 1897- *CnMD*
Il'yinsky, Alexander Alexandrovich 1859-1920 *Baker 78, NewGrD 80*
Ilyinsky, Igor Vladimirovich 1901- *EncWT, OxThe*
Imadashvilli, A *Film 2*
Image, Jean 1911- *FilmgC, HalFC 80*

Imai, Tadashi 1912- *DcFM, FilmEn, WorEFlm*
Imalska, Aleksandra 1933- *WhoOp 76*
Imamura, Shohei 1926- *FilmEn, WorEFlm*
Iman, Kasisi Yusef *BlkAmP, MorBAP*
Imbault, Jean-Jerome 1753-1832 *NewGrD 80*
Imber, Naphtali Herz 1856-1909 *BiDAmM*
Imbert, Hugues 1842-1905 *Baker 78, NewGrD 80*
Imboden, David 1887-1974 *Film 2, WhScrn 77, WhoHol B*
Imboden, Hazel d1956 *WhScrn 74, -77, WhoHol B*
Imbrie, Andrew Welsh 1921- *Baker 78, BiDAmM, BnBkM 80, ConAmC, DcCM, NewGrD 80, OxMus*
Imbrie, McCrea 1918- *NatPD[port]*
Imdahl, Heinz 1924- *WhoOp 76*
Imer, Teresa *NewGrD 80*
Imeson, A B *Film 2*
Imhof, Roger 1875-1958 *NotNAT B, Vers B[port], WhScrn 74, -77, WhoHol B*
Imholz, Joseph *Film 2*
Imig, Warner 1913- *AmSCAP 66, -80*
Imlay, Timothy John 1951- *ConAmC*
Immelman, Niel 1944- *IntWWM 77, -80*
Immerman, William J 1937- *IntMPA 77, -78, -79, -80*
Immerman, William J 1938- *IntMPA 76*
Immermann, Karl Leberecht 1796-1840 *EncWT, McGEWD[port], OxThe*
Immyns, John d1764 *NewGrD 80*
Impalas, The *AmPS A, RkOn[port]*
Impekoven, Niddy 1904- *CnOxB*
Imperials *BiDAmM*
Imperio, Pastora 1894-1961 *CnOxB*
Impolito, John 1887-1962 *WhScrn 77*
Impressions, The *BiDAmM, ConMuA 80A, IlEncR[port], RkOn*
Imre, Zoltan 1943- *CnOxB*
Imrie, Kathy *WhoHol A*
Inagaki, Hiroshi 1905- *DcFM, FilmEn*
Inbal, Eliahu 1936- *IntWWM 77, -80, NewGrD 80, WhoMus 72, WhoOp 76*
Ince, Alexander 1892- *BiE&WWA*
Ince, Ethel *WhScrn 74, -77*
Ince, John d1947 *MotPP, WhoHol B*
Ince, John 1877-1947 *WhScrn 74, -77*
Ince, John 1879-1947 *FilmEn, ForYSC, TwYS A*
Ince, John Edwards *Film 1*
Ince, Ralph 1882-1937 *HolCA[port]*
Ince, Ralph 1887-1937 *IlWWBF*
Ince, Ralph Waldo 1887-1935 *NotNAT B*
Ince, Ralph Waldo 1887-1937 *FilmEn, Film 1, -2, FilmgC, ForYSC, HalFC 80, MovMk[port], TwYS, -A, WhScrn 74, -77, WhoHol B*
Ince, Thomas H 1882-1924 *FilmEn*
Ince, Thomas Harper 1880-1924 *AmFD*
Ince, Thomas Harper 1882-1924 *BiDFilm, -81, CmMov, DcFM, Film 1, FilmgC, HalFC 80, MovMk[port], OxFilm, TwYS A, WhScrn 74, -77, WhoHol B, WorEFlm*
Incerti, Bruno 1910- *IntWWM 77, -80*
Inch, Herbert Reynolds 1904- *Baker 78, BiDAmM, ConAmC, WhoMus 72*
Inchbald, Elizabeth 1753-1821 *NotNAT A, -B, OxThe*
Inchbald, Joseph d1779 *NotNAT B*
Inclan, Miguel 1900-1956 *WhScrn 74, -77, WhoHol B*
Incledon, Benjamin 1763-1826 *NewGrD 80*
Incledon, Charles 1763-1826 *NewGrD 80*
Incledon, Charles Benjamin 1763-1826 *NotNAT B, OxMus*
Incredible String Band, The *BiDAmM, ConMuA 80A, IlEncR*
Ind, Peter Vincent 1928- *EncJzS 70, IntWWM 77, -80*
Indelli, William 1924- *AmSCAP 66, -80*
India, Sigismondo D' 1580?-1629? *Baker 78*
India, Sigismondo D' 1582?-1629? *NewGrD 80*
Indiana Five *BiDAmM*
Indrani *DancEn 78[port]*
Indrani, Rehman *CnOxB*
Indrisano, John 1906-1968 *ForYSC, WhScrn 74, -77, WhoHol B*
Indursky, Arthur *ConMuA 80B*
Indy, Vincent D' 1851-1931 *Baker 78, BnBkM 80, CompSN[port], DcCom 77, DcCom&M 79, NewEOp 71, NewGrD 80[port]*
Inescort, Elaine d1964 *WhThe*
Inescort, Frieda 1900-1976 *HolCA[port]*
Inescort, Frieda 1901-1976 *FilmEn, FilmgC, ForYSC, HalFC 80, MotPP, MovMk[port], ThFT[port], What 4[port], WhThe, WhoHol C, WhoHrs 80*
Inescourt, Elaine d1964 *NotNAT B*
Ineson, E W *WhoMus 72*
Infantas, Fernando DeLas 1534-1610? *Baker 78, NewGrD 80*
Infante, Manuel 1883-1958 *Baker 78*
Infante, Pedro 1918-1957 *WhScrn 74, -77*
Influence *BiDAmM*
Ingall, Susan Marjory 1953- *IntWWM 80*
Ingalls, Albert M *ConAmC*
Ingalls, Don *IntMPA 77, -75, -76, -78, -79, -80*
Ingalls, Jeremiah 1764-1828 *BiDAmM*
Ingalls, Jeremiah 1764-1838 *NewGrD 80*
Inge, Clinton Owen 1909- *AmSCAP 66, -80*
Inge, Edward Frederick 1906- *WhoJazz 72*
Inge, Joseph Darrell 1941- *AmSCAP 80*
Inge, William 1913-1973 *BiE&WWA, CnMD, CnThe, ConDr 73, -77F, CroCD, DcLB 7[port], EncWT, Ent, FilmEn, FilmgC, HalFC 80, McGEWD[port], ModWD, NotNAT A, -B, OxThe, PlP&P[port], REnWD[port], WhScrn 77, WhThe, WhoThe 72, WorEFlm[port]*
Ingebretsen, Kjell 1943- *WhoOp 76*
Ingebrigtsen, Stein 1945- *IntWWM 80*
Ingegneri, Angelo 1550?-1613? *OxThe*
Ingegneri, Marc'Antonio 1547?-1592 *NewGrD 80*
Ingegneri, Marco Antonio 1545?-1592 *Baker 78, OxMus*
Ingegnieri, Marc'Antonio 1547?-1592 *NewGrD 80*
Ingels, Marty 1936- *FilmEn, FilmgC, ForYSC, HalFC 80, IntMPA 77, -75, -76, -78, -79, -80, WhoHol A*
Ingemann, Bernhard Severin 1789-1862 *OxThe*
Ingenhoven, Jan 1876-1951 *Baker 78, NewGrD 80*
Ingersoll, William 1860-1936 *Film 2, NotNAT B, WhScrn 74, -77, WhoHol B*
Ingerson, Richard Wayne 1952- *AmSCAP 80*
Ingham, Barrie 1934- *FilmgC, HalFC 80, WhoThe 77*
Ingham, Barrie 1942- *WhoThe 72*
Ingham, Nelson 1893- *AmSCAP 66*
Inghelbrecht, D-E 1880-1965 *NewGrD 80*
Inghelbrecht, Desire Emile 1880-1965 *Baker 78, NewEOp 71, OxMus*
Inghilleri, Giovanni 1894-1959 *CmOp*
Ingibergsson, Haukur 1947- *IntWWM 77*
Ingignero, Marc'Antonio *NewGrD 80*
Ingignieri, Marc'Antonio *NewGrD 80*
Ingis, Robert L 1935- *IntMPA 77, -75, -76, -78, -79, -80*
Ingle, Charles d1940 *NotNAT B*
Ingle, Red 1907-1965 *CmpEPM, WhScrn 77*
Ingle, William Earl 1934- *WhoOp 76*
Ingleby, Muriel G *WhoMus 72*
Ingleby, William Stevens 1923- *WhoMus 72*
Inglesby, Mona 1918- *CnOxB, DancEn 78, WhThe*
Ingleton, George *Film 2*
Inglis, William H 1937- *NotNAT*
Inglott, William 1554-1621 *NewGrD 80*
Ingmann, Jorgen 1932- *RkOn[port]*
Ingpen, Joan 1916- *WhoOp 76*
Ingraham, Herbert Irving 1883-1910 *AmSCAP 66, -80*
Ingraham, Lloyd 1885?-1956 *FilmEn*
Ingraham, Lloyd 1893-1956 *Film 1, -2, ForYSC, TwYS A, WhScrn 74, -77, WhoHol B*
Ingraham, Roy 1895- *AmSCAP 66, -80*
Ingram, Allyn Cheryl 1951- *AmSCAP 80*
Ingram, Amo *Film 2*
Ingram, Clifford *Film 2*
Ingram, Frances 1888- *BiDAmM*
Ingram, Harold *WhoMus 72*
Ingram, Jack 1903-1969 *ForYSC, WhScrn 74, -77, WhoHol B*
Ingram, James M 1951- *IntWWM 77*
Ingram, Luther *RkOn 2[port]*
Ingram, Marvin 1938- *AmSCAP 66*
Ingram, Reginald William 1930- *IntWWM 80*
Ingram, Rex d1969 *BlksB&W, -C*
Ingram, Rex 1892-1950 *CmMov, DcFM, FilmEn, Film 1, HalFC 80, TwYS A, WhScrn 74, WhoHol B, WorEFlm*
Ingram, Rex 1892-1969 *AmFD*
Ingram, Rex 1893-1950 *BiDFilm, -81, FilmgC, OxFilm, WhScrn 77, WomWMM*
Ingram, Rex 1894-1969 *MovMk[port]*
Ingram, Rex 1895-1969 *BiE&WWA, DrBlPA, FilmEn, FilmgC, ForYSC, HalFC 80, HolCA[port], NotNAT B, OxFilm, Vers A[port], WhScrn 74, -77, WhThe, WhoHol B, WhoHrs 80[port]*
Ingram, Rex 1896-1969 *Film 2*
Ingram, Robert James 1937- *IntWWM 80*
Ingram, William D 1857-1926 *WhScrn 74, -77*
Ingrassia, Ciccio 1923- *FilmAG WE*
Ingris, Eduard 1905- *AmSCAP 80*
Ingster, Boris *IntMPA 75, -78*
Ingster, Boris 1913?- *FilmgC, HalFC 80, IntMPA 77, -76, -79, -80*
Ink Spots *AmPS A, -B, CmpEPM*
Inkizhinov, Valerji *Film 2*
Inman, Daniel 1921- *WhoMus 72*
Inman, Robert Autrey 1929- *BiDAmM*
Innaurato, Albert 1948- *NatPD[port]*
Inneo, Anthony *NatPD[port]*
Innes, Audrey Muriel 1936- *IntWWM 77, -80, WhoMus 72*
Innes, Betty K 1941- *AmSCAP 80*
Innes, George *WhoHol A*
Innes, Jean *WhoHol A*
Innes, John 1863-1941 *CreCan 1*
Innes, Robert Burns 1941- *AmSCAP 80*
Inness, Jean *ForYSC*
Inness-Brown, Virginia Royall 1901- *BiE&WWA, NotNAT*
Innis, Mary Emma Quayle 1899- *CreCan 1*
Inniss, Josephine Consola *IntWWM 77, -80*
Innocence, The *RkOn 2[port]*
Innocente DalCornetto *NewGrD 80*
Innocents, The *RkOn*
Inomata, Takeshi 1936- *EncJzS 70*
Inoue, Michi 1946- *IntWWM 80*
Inouye, Masso *Film 2*
Insanguine, Giacomo 1728-1795 *Baker 78, NewGrD 80*
Insetta, Paul Peter 1915- *AmSCAP 66*
Inskip, Rosalie Earle 1916- *IntWWM 77, WhoMus 72*
Inslee, Charles *Film 1*
Instone, Anna *WhoMus 72*
Inten, Ferdinand 1848-1918 *Baker 78*
Interlenghi, Franco 1930- *OxFilm*
Interlenghi, Franco 1931- *FilmEn*
Intropodi, Ethel d1946 *NotNAT B*
Intropodi, Josie d1941 *NotNAT B*
Intruders, The *RkOn, -2[port]*
Inverarity, R Bruce *DcPup, PupTheA*
Invernici, Ottavio *NewGrD 80*
Invernizzi, Ottavio *NewGrD 80*
Inwood, Mary Ruth 1928- *CpmDNM 76, -79, IntWWM 77, -80*
Inzalaco, Anthony 1938- *EncJzS 70*
Inzalaco, Tony 1938- *EncJzS 70*
Inzegneri, Marc'Antonio *NewGrD 80*
Inzenga, Jose 1828-1891 *Baker 78, NewGrD 80*
Ioanne A Cruce Clodiensis *NewGrD 80*
Ioannidis, Yannis 1930- *Baker 78, DcCM, NewGrD 80*
Ion *OxThe*
Ion Of Chios 490?BC-422?BC *NewGrD 80*
Iona, Andy 1902- *AmSCAP 66*
Ionel, Dumitru 1915- *IntWWM 77, -80*
Ionesco, Eugene 1912- *BiE&WWA, CnMD, CnThe, CroCD, EncWT, Ent, McGEWD[port], ModWD, NotNAT, -A, OxThe, PlP&P, REnWD[port], WhoThe 72, -77*
Ionescu, George 1934- *WhoOp 76*
Ionescu, Liviu 1928- *IntWWM 77, -80*
Iordachescu, Dan 1934- *IntWWM 77, -80*
Iorga, Nicolae 1871-1940 *CnMD*
Iovenardi, Bartolome *NewGrD 80*
Iovine, Jimmy *ConMuA 80B*

Iparraguirre Y Balerdi, Jose Maria De 1820-1881 *Baker 78*
Ipavec, Benjamin 1829-1909 *Baker 78, NewGrD 80*
Ipleer, Joseph *NewGrD 80*
Ippolitof-Ivanof, Michael 1859-1935 *OxMus*
Ippolitov-Ivanov, Mikhail 1859-1935 *Baker 78, BnBkM 80, DcCom&M 79, MusMk, NewGrD 80*
Ipsen, Bodil Louise Jensen 1889-1964 *DcFM, OxThe*
Ipuche-Riva, Pedro 1924- *Baker 78*
Iradier, Sebastian 1809-1865 *NewGrD 80*
Irani, Ardeshir M 1885- *DcFM*
Iranyi, Gabriel 1946- *IntWWM 80*
Iranzo Y Herrero, Agustin 1748-1804 *NewGrD 80*
Irbe, Marie-Louise *Film 2*
Irby, Fred, III 1948- *IntWWM 77*
Ireland, Anthony 1902-1957 *NotNAT B, WhScrn 74, -77, WhThe, WhoHol B*
Ireland, Charles T, Jr. d1972 *NewYTET*
Ireland, Frances *MagIlD*
Ireland, Francis 1721-1780 *NewGrD 80*
Ireland, George Thomas 1865-1963 *BiDAmM*
Ireland, Jill 1936- *FilmEn, FilmgC, HalFC 80, IlWWBF[port], IntMPA 77, -78, -79, -80, WhoHol A*
Ireland, John *MotPP, WhoHol A*
Ireland, John 1879-1962 *Baker 78, BnBkM 80, CompSN[port], DcCom 77, DcCom&M 79, DcCM, MusMk, NewGrD 80[port], OxMus*
Ireland, John 1914- *CmMov, FilmEn, FilmgC, ForYSC, HalFC 80*
Ireland, John 1915- *IntMPA 77, -75, -76, -78, -79, -80, MovMk[port], OxFilm*
Ireland, John 1916- *BiE&WWA, NotNAT*
Ireland, Joseph Norton d1898 *NotNAT B*
Ireland, Kenneth 1920- *WhoThe 72, -77*
Ireland, Patrick 1923- *IntWWM 77, -80*
Ireland, William Henry 1775-1835 *NotNAT B, OxThe*
Ireland, William Patrick 1923- *WhoMus 72*
Irene 1901-1962 *FilmEn, FilmgC, HalFC 80*
Ireson, John Balfour 1937- *AmSCAP 80*
Ireton, Glenn F 1906- *IntMPA 77, -75, -76, -78, -79, -80*
Ireton, Kikuko Monica 1929- *IntMPA 77, -75, -76, -78, -79, -80*
Irgat, Cahit 1916-1971 *WhScrn 74, -77*
Irgens Jensen, Ludwig 1894-1969 *Baker 78*
Iriarte, Tomas De 1750-1791 *NewGrD 80*
Iribe, Marie-Louise *WomWMM*
Irick, John 1923- *AmSCAP 80*
Irino, Yoshiro 1921- *Baker 78, DcCM, NewGrD 80*
Irish, Annie 1862- *WhoStg 1908*
Irish, Annie 1865-1947 *NotNAT B, WhThe*
Irish, George 1910-1959 *WhoJazz 72*
Irish Rovers *RkOn 2A*
Irman, Vladimir 1919- *DancEn 78*
Irmen, Hans-Josef 1938- *IntWWM 77, -80*
Iron Butterfly *BiDAmM, ConMuA 80A, IlEncR, RkOn 2[port]*
Irons, Arthur 1901- *WhoMus 72*
Irons, Earl D 1891- *AmSCAP 66, -80*
Irons, Edward D, Jr. 1954- *AmSCAP 80*
Irons, Jack 1937- *IntWWM 77, -80*
Irosch, Mirjana 1939- *WhoOp 76*
Irrgang, Heinrich Bernhard 1869-1916 *Baker 78*
Irts, Lily *Film 2*
Iruarrizaga, Luis 1891-1928 *NewGrD 80*
Irvin, Leslie 1895-1966 *WhScrn 77*
Irvine, Daryl 1932- *IntWWM 77, -80*
Irvine, Demar Buel 1908- *IntWWM 77, -80*
Irvine, Harry d1951 *NotNAT B*
Irvine, Jessie S 1836-1887 *BiDAmM*
Irvine, Louva Elizabeth 1939- *WomWMM A, -B*
Irvine, Richard 1910- *IntMPA 75, -76*
Irvine, Robin 1901-1933 *Film 2, IlWWBF, NotNAT B, WhThe, WhoHol B*
Irvine, Weldon *MorBAP*
Irving, Amy 1954- *WhoHrs 80*
Irving, Ann *WomWMM B*
Irving, Ben 1919-1968 *BiE&WWA, NotNAT B*
Irving, Charles *WhoHol A*
Irving, Daisy d1938 *NotNAT B, WhThe*
Irving, Dorothea Baird 1875-1933 *OxThe*
Irving, Elizabeth 1904- *WhThe*
Irving, Ellis 1902- *WhoThe 72, -77*
Irving, Ernest 1878-1953 *NewGrD 80*
Irving, Ethel 1869-1963 *NotNAT B, WhThe*
Irving, George *WhoStg 1908*
Irving, George 1874-1961 *FilmEn, Film 2, ForYSC, MovMk, TwYS, -A, Vers A[port], WhScrn 74, -77, WhoHol B*
Irving, George H 1858-1936 *PupTheA*
Irving, George S 1922- *BiE&WWA, NotNAT, WhoHol A, WhoThe 72, -77*
Irving, Gordon 1918- *IntMPA 77, -75, -76, -78, -79, -80*
Irving, H B 1870-1919 *WhScrn 77, WhThe*
Irving, Harry James 1908- *AmSCAP 66*
Irving, Sir Henry 1838-1905 *CnThe, EncWT, Ent[port], FamA&A[port], NotNAT A, -B, OxThe, PlP&P[port]*
Irving, Henry Brodribb 1870-1919 *EncWT, NotNAT B, OxThe, WhoStg 1906, -1908*
Irving, Henry Forster 1897- *EncWT*
Irving, Isabel 1871-1944 *NotNAT B, WhThe, WhoStg 1906, -1908*
Irving, Mrs. Joseph d1925 *NotNAT B*
Irving, Joseph Henry d1870 *NotNAT B*
Irving, Jules 1925- *BiE&WWA, Ent, NotNAT, PlP&P[port], -A[port], WhoThe 72, -77*
Irving, K Ernest 1878-1953 *NotNAT B, WhThe*
Irving, Laurence Henry Forster 1897-1914 *OxThe, WhThe*
Irving, Laurence Sidney 1871-1914 *EncWT, OxThe, WhThe*
Irving, Lawrence Sidney 1871-1914 *NotNAT B*
Irving, Margaret 1900?- *MovMk[port], PlP&P[port]*
Irving, Mary Jane *Film 1, -2*
Irving, Paul 1877-1959 *WhScrn 74, -77, WhoHol B*
Irving, Robert 1913- *CnOxB, DancEn 78, NewGrD 80, WhoMus 72*
Irving, W J *Film 1*
Irving, Washington 1783-1859 *DcPup, NewEOp 71, NotNAT B, OxThe, PlP&P*
Irving, William J 1893-1943 *Film 2, WhScrn 74, -77, WhoHol B*
Irvis, Charlie 1899?-1939? *BiDAmM, WhoJazz 72*
Irwin, Boyd 1880-1957 *WhScrn 74, -77, WhoHol B*
Irwin, Boyd 1880-1963 *Film 2, ForYSC, TwYS*
Irwin, Caroline *Film 2*
Irwin, Cecil 1902-1935 *WhoJazz 72*
Irwin, Charles W 1888-1969 *WhScrn 74, -77, WhoHol B*
Irwin, Edward 1867-1937 *NotNAT B, WhThe*
Irwin, Felix d1950 *NotNAT B*
Irwin, Flo d1930 *NotNAT B*
Irwin, Gene 1916-1966 *AmSCAP 66, -80*
Irwin, Grace Lilian 1907- *CreCan 2*
Irwin, Jack H 1925- *IntWWM 80*
Irwin, John *Film 2*
Irwin, Lois 1926- *AmSCAP 66, -80*
Irwin, May *AmPS B, MotPP*
Irwin, May 1862- *TwYS, WhoStg 1906, -1908*
Irwin, May 1862-1938 *BiDAmM, FamA&A[port], FilmEn, Film 1, NotNAT B, WhThe*
Irwin, May 1862-1958 *WhScrn 74, -77, WhoHol B*
Irwin, May 1863-1958 *HalFC 80*
Irwin, P K *CreCan 1*
Irwin, Phyllis Ann 1929- *IntWWM 77, -80*
Irwin, Wallace 1875-1959 *WhScrn 77*
Irwin, Will 1874-1948 *WhScrn 77*
Irwin, Will 1907- *BiE&WWA, NotNAT*
Irwin, William 1923- *AmSCAP 66, -80*
Irwin, William C K 1907- *AmSCAP 66, -80*
Irwin, Wynn *WhoHol A*
Irwin-Hunt, William 1884- *WhoMus 72*
Isaac D'Orleans, Sieur *DancEn 78*
Isaac, B *NewGrD 80*
Isaac, Cecil 1930- *IntWWM 77, -80*
Isaac, Heinrich 1450?-1517 *Baker 78, BnBkM 80, NewGrD 80, OxMus*
Isaac, Henricus 1450?-1517 *NewGrD 80*
Isaac, Merle John 1898- *AmSCAP 66, -80, IntWWM 77*
Isaack, B d1703 *NewGrD 80*
Isaacs, Alvin Kalanikauikealaneo 1904- *AmSCAP 66, -80*
Isaacs, Barbara *WomWMM A, -B*
Isaacs, Charles E 1923- *EncJzS 70*
Isaacs, Claude Reese 1901-1953 *AmSCAP 80*
Isaacs, Edith Juliet 1878-1956 *NotNAT B, OxThe, WhThe*
Isaacs, Edward 1881-1953 *NewGrD 80*
Isaacs, Gregory *ConAmC*
Isaacs, Harry 1902- *WhoMus 72*
Isaacs, Ike 1923- *EncJzS 70*
Isaacs, Isaac 1919- *IntWWM 77*
Isaacs, Isadore Ike 1901-1957 *WhScrn 74, -77*
Isaacs, John Kenneth 1936- *IntWWM 77, -80, WhoMus 72*
Isaacs, Kelly 1922- *IntWWM 77, -80, WhoMus 72*
Isaacs, Leonard 1909- *WhoMus 72*
Isaacs, Phil 1922- *IntMPA 77, -75, -76, -78, -79, -80*
Isaacson, Carl L 1920- *BiE&WWA, NotNAT*
Isaacson, Michael Neil 1946- *ConAmC*
Isaak, Heinrich *NewGrD 80*
Isaak, Hendryk 1450?-1517 *BnBkM 80*
Isaak, Henricus *NewGrD 80*
Isabella Leonarda 1620-1700? *NewGrD 80*
Isabella Of Castile *NewGrD 80*
Isacson, Einar 1942- *IntWWM 77, -80*
Isador, Michael 1939- *IntWWM 77, -80*
Isaiah The Serb *NewGrD 80*
Isaksen, Lone 1941- *CnOxB, DancEn 78*
Isamitt, Carlos 1887-1974 *Baker 78, DcCM, NewGrD 80*
Isasi, Andres 1890?-1940 *NewGrD 80*
Isbert, Jose 1884-1966 *WhScrn 74, -77*
Iseler, Elmer Walter 1927- *CreCan 1, NewGrD 80*
Iselin, John Jay *NewYTET*
Iselin, Ludwig 1559-1612 *NewGrD 80*
Isenbergh, Max 1913- *IntWWM 77, -80*
Isepp, Martin *WhoMus 72*
Isepp, Martin Johannes Sebastian 1930- *IntWWM 77, -80*
Isgro, Robert M 1932- *IntWWM 77*
Isham, Frederic S d1922 *NotNAT B*
Isham, Sir Gyles 1903-1976 *WhThe, WhoHol C*
Isham, John 1680?-1726 *NewGrD 80*
Isham, John W *MorBAP*
Isham's Oriental America Company *BiDAmM*
Ishaq Al-Mawsili 767-850 *NewGrD 80*
Ishee, Jean Bowers 1919- *IntWWM 77*
Isherwood, Cherry Joan Mary *IntWWM 77, -80, WhoMus 72*
Isherwood, Christopher 1904- *CnMD, ConDr 73, -77, EncWT, HalFC 80, McGEWD, ModWD, PlP&P, WhThe*
Ishii, Kan 1901-1972 *WhScrn 77*
Ishii, Kan 1921- *Baker 78, DcCM, NewGrD 80*
Ishii, Maki 1936- *Baker 78, NewGrD 80*
Ishiketa, Mareo 1916- *NewGrD 80*
Ishkabibble *BiDAmM*
Isidore Of Seville 559?-636 *NewGrD 80*
Isidore Of Seville 560?-636 *Baker 78*
Ising, Rudolph *DcFM*
Isla, Cristobal De 1586-1651? *NewGrD 80*
Isler, Ernst 1879-1944 *Baker 78, NewGrD 80*
Isler, Helen J *AmSCAP 66, -80*
Isler, Justus F *AmSCAP 66, -80*
Isley, Ernest *AmSCAP 80*
Isley, Keith *ConMuA 80B*
Isley, Marvin *AmSCAP 80*
Isley, O Kelly 1937- *AmSCAP 80*
Isley, Phyllis *FilmEn, ForYSC*
Isley, Ronald 1941- *AmSCAP 80*
Isley, Rudolph 1939- *AmSCAP 80*
Isley Brothers, The *BiDAmM, IlEncR, RkOn[port]*
Islofsson, Pall 1893- *IntWWM 77, -80*
Ismagilov, Zagir Garipovich 1917- *IntWWM 77, -80*
Ismai, Osman *DcFM*
Ismail, Aly 1924-1974 *NewGrD 80*
Ismailov, Serge 1912- *DancEn 78*
Ismailova, Galya Bayasetovna 1925- *CnOxB*
Isnard *NewGrD 80*

Isnard, Jean-Baptiste 1726-1800 *NewGrD 80*
Isnard, Jean-Esprit 1707-1781 *NewGrD 80*
Isnardi, Paolo 1536-1596 *NewGrD 80*
Iso, Pierre *NewGrD 80*
Isoiar, Nicolo *NewGrD 80*
Isoir, Andre Jean Mark 1935- *IntWWM 77, -80*
Isola, Emile d1945 *NotNAT B*
Isola, Vincent d1947 *NotNAT B*
Isolfsson, Pall 1893- *DcCM*
Isolfsson, Pall 1893-1974 *Baker 78, NewGrD 80*
Isore, Guillaume *NewGrD 80*
Isorelli, Duritio *NewGrD 80*
Isouard, Nicolas 1775-1818 *NewGrD 80*
Isouard, Nicolo 1775-1818 *Baker 78, NewGrD 80, OxMus*
Isoz, Eticnnc 1905- *IntWWM 80*
Isoz, Kalman 1878-1956 *NewGrD 80*
Israel, Brian 1951- *CpmDNM 79, -80*
Israel, Brian M 1951- *ConAmC*
Israel, Charles Edward 1920- *CreCan 1*
Israel, Larry H *NewYTET*
Israel, McKellar 1931- *ConAmC*
Israel, Robert 1939- *WhoOp 76*
Israelievitch, Jacques 1948- *IntWWM 77, -80*
Israels, Charles Henry 1936- *BiDAmM, ConAmC, EncJzS 70*
Israels, Chuck 1936- *EncJzS 70*
Issandon, Jean *NewGrD 80*
Issell, Robert 1938- *IntWWM 77, -80*
Isserlis, Julius 1888-1968 *Baker 78*
Istel, Edgar 1880-1948 *Baker 78, NewGrD 80*
Istomin, Eugene 1925- *Baker 78, BiDAmM, BnBkM 80, MusSN[port], NewGrD 80, WhoMus 72*
Istomina, Anna 1925- *DancEn 78*
Istomina, Avdotia Ilyinitshna 1799-1848 *CnOxB, DancEn 78*
Istrate, Mircea 1929- *Baker 78, IntWWM 80*
Istvan, Miloslav 1928- *Baker 78, DcCM, NewGrD 80*
Isum, John *NewGrD 80*
Itallie, Jean-Claude Van 1936- *EncWT*
Itelman, Ana 1932- *CnOxB, DancEn 78*
Itibere, Brazilio 1896-1967 *NewGrD 80*
Itier, Bernardus 1163-1225 *NewGrD 80*
Itkin, Bella 1920- *BiE&WWA, NotNAT*
Ito, Daisuke 1898- *DcFM, FilmEn*
Ito, Kyoko 1927- *WhoOp 76*
Ito, Michio 1894-1961 *DancEn 78*
Ito, Robert *WhoHol A*
Ito, Ryuto 1922- *Baker 78*
Ito, Yoshio 1904- *IntWWM 77, -80*
It's A Beautiful Day *ConMuA 80A, IlEncR*
Iturbi, Amparo 1899-1969 *WhScrn 77, WhoHol B*
Iturbi, Jose 1895- *Baker 78, BiDAmM, BnBkM 80, FilmgC, ForYSC, HalFC 80, IntWWM 77, -80, MGM[port], MovMk, MusSN[port], NewGrD 80, What 5[port], WhoHol A, WhoMus 72*
Iturbi, Jose 1895-1980 *FilmEn*
Iturriaga, Enrique 1918- *NewGrD 80*
Iturriberry, Juan Jose 1936- *Baker 78*
Iuqui, Leda *DancEn 78*
Ivaldi, Christian 1938- *IntWWM 80*
Ivan *RkOn*
Ivan The Terrible *BnBkM 80*
Ivan, Rosalind 1884-1959 *FilmEn, FilmgC, ForYSC, HalFC 80, MovMk, NotNAT B, WhScrn 74, -77, WhoHol B*
Ivan, Rosiland *MotPP*
Ivano, Paul 1900- *FilmgC, HalFC 80, IntMPA 77, -75, -76, -78, -79, -80*
Ivanoff, Nicola 1810-1880 *NewGrD 80*
Ivanoff, Nikolay 1810-1880 *NewGrD 80*
Ivanoff, Rose 1908- *AmSCAP 66, -80*
Ivanov, Alexander *FilmEn*
Ivanov, Georgi 1924- *Baker 78*
Ivanov, I *Film 2*
Ivanov, Lev Ivanovich *NewGrD 80*
Ivanov, Lev Ivanovich 1834-1901 *CnOxB, DancEn 78[port]*
Ivanov, Mikhail Mikhaylovich 1849-1927 *Baker 78, NewGrD 80*
Ivanov, Nicola 1810-1880 *NewGrD 80*
Ivanov, Nikolay 1810-1880 *NewGrD 80*
Ivanov, Semion 1906- *FilmEn*
Ivanov, Vsevolod Vyacheslavovich 1895-1963 *CnMD, McGEWD, ModWD, OxThe, PlP&P*
Ivanov, Vsevolod Vycheslavovich 1895-1963 *EncWT*
Ivanov-Barlov, Yevgeni 1892- *FilmEn*
Ivanov-Boretsky, Mikhail Vladimirovich 1874-1936 *NewGrD 80*
Ivanov-Boretzky, Mikhail 1874-1936 *Baker 78*
Ivanov-Radkevitch, Nicolai 1904-1962 *Baker 78*
Ivanov-Vano, Ivan 1900- *FilmEn*
Ivanovich, Cristoforo 1628-1689 *NewGrD 80*
Ivanovici, Ion 1845-1902 *Baker 78*
Ivanovici, Iosif 1845?-1902 *NewGrD 80*
Ivanovs, Janis 1906- *NewGrD 80*
Ivanovsky, Alexander *FilmEn*
Ivanovsky, Nicolai Pavlovich 1893-1961 *CnOxB, DancEn 78*
Ivanschiz, Amandus *NewGrD 80*
Ivantschiz, Amandus *NewGrD 80*
Ivashov, Vladimir *WhoHol A*
Ivashov, Vladimir 1939- *FilmEn*
Ive, Simon 1600-1662 *NewGrD 80*
Ive, Simon 1626?-1662? *NewGrD 80*
Ivens, Joris 1898- *BiDFilm, -81, DcFM, FilmEn, FilmgC, HalFC 80, MovMk, OxFilm, WorEFlm[port]*
Ivens, Josephine Franciscus 1927- *IntWWM 77*
Ivermee, Phyllis Ada 1908- *WhoMus 72*
Ivernel, Daniel 1920- *EncWT*
Ivers, James D d1964 *NotNAT B*
Ivers, Julia Crawford *WomWMM*
Ivers, Peter 1946- *ConAmC*
Ivers, Robert *ForYSC*
Iversen, Carl Morten 1948- *IntWWM 80*
Iversen, Einar 1930- *IntWWM 80*
Iversen, Henri *NewGrD 80*
Ives, Anne 1892?- *NotNAT*
Ives, Benoni I 1822-1912 *BiDAmM*
Ives, Burl 1909- *AmSCAP 66, -80, Baker 78, BiDAmM, BiE&WWA, CmMov, CmpEPM, CounME 74[port], -74A, EncFCWM 69, FilmEn, FilmgC, ForYSC, HalFC 80[port], IntMPA 77, -75, -76, -78, -79, -80, MotPP, MovMk[port], NotNAT, PlP&P[port], RkOn[port], WhoHol A, WhoMus 72, WhoThe 72, -77, WorEFlm*
Ives, Charles 1874-1954 *BnBkM 80[port], CompSN[port], DcCom 77, DcCM, DcTwCC, MusMk[port], OxMus*
Ives, Charles Edward 1874-1954 *Baker 78, BiDAmM, ConAmC, DcCom&M 79, NewGrD 80[port]*
Ives, Charlotte *Film 1*
Ives, Douglas d1969 *WhScrn 74, -77, WhoHol B*
Ives, Elam, Jr. 1802-1864 *BiDAmM*
Ives, George *Baker 78, WhoHol A*
Ives, Simon 1600-1662 *Baker 78, MusMk, NewGrD 80, OxMus*
Ives, Simon 1626?-1662? *NewGrD 80*
Iveson, John Christopher 1944- *WhoMus 72*
Ivey, Jean Eichelberger 1923- *AmSCAP 80, CpmDNM 74, -75, -78, ConAmC, IntWWM 77, -80, NewGrD 80, WomCom[port]*
Ivimey, Irene *WhoMus 72*
Ivings, Jacqueline Margaret 1935- *CreCan 1*
Ivins, Perry 1895-1963 *WhScrn 77*
Ivins, Sidna Beth *Film 2*
Ivo De Vento *NewGrD 80*
Ivo, Barry *NewGrD 80*
Ivo, Tommy *ForYSC*
Ivogun, Maria 1891- *Baker 78, CmOp, NewEOp 71, NewGrD 80*
Ivor, Frances *WhThe*
Ivory, James 1928- *FilmEn, FilmgC, HalFC 80, OxFilm*
Ivory, James 1930- *BiDFilm, -81, WorEFlm*
Ivory Lee *BluesWW*
Ivry, Richard D' 1829-1903 *Baker 78*
Ivy, Simon *NewGrD 80*
Ivy, Simon 1600-1662 *NewGrD 80*
Ivy, Simon 1626?-1662? *NewGrD 80*
Ivy Three, The *RkOn*
Iwaki, Hiroyuki 1932- *IntWWM 77, -80, WhoMus 72*
Iwamoto, Marito 1926- *Baker 78*
Iwanejko, Maria Wanda 1921- *IntWWM 77, -80*
Iwanow, Wladimir 1957- *IntWWM 80*
Iwashita, Shima 1941- *FilmEn*
Iwaszkiewicz, Jaroslaw 1894- *CnMD, ModWD*
Iwerks, Ub 1900-1971 *FilmgC, HalFC 80, WhoHrs 80*
Iwerks, Ub 1901-1971 *DcFM, FilmEn, OxFilm, WorEFlm*
Iyaun, Ifa *MorBAP*
Izard, Winifred *Film 2*
Izay, Victor *WhoHol A*
Izenour, George 1912- *BiE&WWA, NotNAT*
Izenzon, David 1932- *BiDAmM, EncJzS 70*
Izmailova, Galia 1923- *DancEn 78*
Izmailova, Galya Bayazetovna *CnOxB*
Izquierdo, Juan Pablo 1935- *IntWWM 80*
Izumo, Takeda 1691-1756 *CnThe, EncWT, REnWD[port]*
Izvitzkaya, Isolda 1933-1971 *WhScrn 77*
Izzo, Christopher Anthony 1924- *IntWWM 77*

J

J, Trebla Seno 1939- *AmSCAP 80*
J B *BluesWW*
J Geils Band *IlEncR*
Jaani, Kulwant Singh 1932- *IntWWM 77*
Jabez *CreCan 2*
Jablonow, Scott 1950- *IntMPA 80*
Jablonski, Marek 1939- *NewGrD 80*
Jablonsky, Stephen 1941- *ConAmC*
Jabusch, Willard Francis 1930- *AmSCAP 80*
Jacaway, Taffy Marie 1928- *ConAmTC*
Jaccard, Jacques 1885- *TwYS A*
Jacchia, Agide 1875-1932 *Baker 78*
Jacchini, Giuseppe Maria 1663?-1727 *NewGrD 80*
Jaccottet, Christiane 1937- *IntWWM 77, –80*
Jacey, Frank *AmSCAP 80*
Jaches DeWert *NewGrD 80*
Jachet Of Mantua 1495?-1559 *Baker 78*
Jachimecki, Zdzislaw 1882-1953 *Baker 78, NewGrD 80*
Jachino, Carlo 1887-1971 *Baker 78, IntWWM 77, –80, NewGrD 80, WhoMus 72*
Jachmann-Wagner, Johanna *NewGrD 80*
Jachobus De Bononia, Magister *NewGrD 80*
Jacinto, Frei *NewGrD 80*
Jack And Evelyn *WhThe*
Jack, Donald Lamont 1924- *CreCan 1*
Jack, Sam *MorBAP*
Jack, T C 1882-1954 *WhScrn 74, –77, WhoHol B*
Jacker, Corinne *NatPD[port]*
Jacker, Corrine *NewYTET*
Jackie, Bill d1954 *WhoHol B*
Jackie, William 1890-1954 *WhScrn 74, –77*
Jackley, George d1950 *NotNAT B*
Jackley, Janice *PupTheA*
Jackman, Fred 1881- *TwYS A*
Jackman, Isaac *NotNAT B*
Jackman, James L 1927- *IntWWM 77*
Jackman, Jerry R 1948- *CpmDNM 80*
Jackman, Marvin *MorBAP*
Jackman, Robert Kenneth 1915- *AmSCAP 80*
Jacks, The *RkOn*
Jacks, Robert L 1922- *FilmgC, HalFC 80, IntMPA 77, –75, –76, –78, –79, –80*
Jacks, Terry *RkOn 2[port]*
Jackson, Al, Jr. *BiDAmM*
Jackson, Albert 1898- *NewOrJ*
Jackson, Alexander Young 1882- *CreCan 2*
Jackson, Andrew, IV 1887-1953 *WhScrn 74, –77*
Jackson, Anne *MotPP, WhoHol A*
Jackson, Anne 1924- *MovMk[port]*
Jackson, Anne 1925- *FilmgC, HalFC 80*
Jackson, Anne 1926- *BiE&WWA, FilmEn, ForYSC, NotNAT, WhoThe 72, –77*
Jackson, Arthur 1911-1977? *BluesWW[port]*
Jackson, Aunt Mollie 1880-1960 *IlEncCM*
Jackson, Aunt Molly 1880-1960 *EncFCWM 69*
Jackson, Babs *WomWMM B*
Jackson, Bags *NewGrD 80*
Jackson, Bags 1923- *EncJzS 70*
Jackson, Barbara Ann Garvey Seagrave 1929- *IntWWM 77, –80*
Jackson, Barbara May 1926- *WhoMus 72*
Jackson, Barry *WhoHol A*
Jackson, Sir Barry Vincent 1878-1961 *CnThe, PlP&P[port]*
Jackson, Sir Barry Vincent 1879-1961 *EncWT, Ent, NotNAT A, –B, OxThe, WhThe*
Jackson, Bee *Film 2*
Jackson, Benjamin Clarence 1919- *BluesWW[port]*
Jackson, Bessie *BluesWW*
Jackson, Bill 1906- *BluesWW*
Jackson, Brian 1931- *IntMPA 77, –75, –76, –78, –79, –80*
Jackson, Brian Henry 1926- *CreCan 1*
Jackson, Brian Robert 1952- *EncJzS 70*
Jackson, Bud *Film 2*
Jackson, Bullmoose *RkOn[port]*
Jackson, Butter 1909-1976 *EncJzS 70, WhoJazz 72*
Jackson, C Bernard 1909-1976 *MorBAP*
Jackson, C D 1902- *BiE&WWA*
Jackson, C Gernard *BlkAmP*
Jackson, Calvin 1919- *BiDAmM*
Jackson, Carl 1953- *IlEncCM[port]*
Jackson, Charles *Film 1*
Jackson, Charles 1903-1968 *NotNAT B*
Jackson, Charles Melvin 1950- *EncJzS 70*
Jackson, Charlie d1938 *BluesWW[port]*
Jackson, Charlotte *Film 2*
Jackson, Chip 1950- *EncJzS 70*
Jackson, Chubby 1918- *CmpEPM, EncJzS 70, WhoJazz 72*
Jackson, Chuck 1937- *ConMuA 80B, RkOn[port]*
Jackson, Cliff 1902-1970 *CmpEPM, EncJzS 70, WhoJazz 72*
Jackson, Clifton Luther 1902-1970 *BiDAmM, EncJzS 70*
Jackson, Colette d1969 *WhoHol B*
Jackson, Collette d1969 *WhScrn 77*
Jackson, David *ConMuA 80B*
Jackson, David 1935- *WhoOp 76*
Jackson, David L 1944- *ConAmC*
Jackson, Deon 1945- *RkOn 2[port]*
Jackson, Dewey 1900- *WhoJazz 72*
Jackson, Duff Clark 1953- *EncJzS 70*
Jackson, Duffy 1953- *EncJzS 70*
Jackson, Duke W, Jr. 1946- *ConAmC*
Jackson, Eddie 1867?-1938 *NewOrJ*
Jackson, Eddie 1896?- *WhoHol A*
Jackson, Elaine *BlkAmP, MorBAP*
Jackson, Ernestine *DrBlPA, NotNAT, PlP&P A[port]*
Jackson, Ethel *WhScrn 74, –77*
Jackson, Ethel 1877-1957 *NotNAT B, WhThe*
Jackson, Ethel Shannon *WhScrn 74, –77*
Jackson, Eugene *Film 2, WhoHol A*
Jackson, Eugenia Lutcher *BlkAmP*
Jackson, Francis Alan 1917- *IntWWM 77, –80, NewGrD 80, WhoMus 72*
Jackson, Frank 1866?-1912? *NewOrJ*
Jackson, Franz 1912- *AmSCAP 66, BiDAmM, CmpEPM, WhoJazz 72*
Jackson, Fred 1921- *WhoMus 72*
Jackson, Freda 1909- *FilmEn, FilmgC, HalFC 80, IntMPA 77, –75, –76, –78, –79, –80, PlP&P, WhoHol A, WhoHrs 80, WhoThe 72, –77*
Jackson, Frederic 1886-1953 *WhThe*
Jackson, Frederic Marsh 1905- *WhoMus 72*
Jackson, Gator 1932- *EncJzS 70*
Jackson, Geoffrey William 1939- *IntWWM 77, –80, WhoMus 72*
Jackson, George 1931- *CnOxB*
Jackson, George K 1745-1822 *Baker 78*
Jackson, George K 1745-1823 *BiDAmM*
Jackson, George K 1757-1822 *NewGrD 80*
Jackson, George Pullen 1874-1953 *Baker 78, NewGrD 80, OxMus*
Jackson, Gerald E 1900- *WhoMus 72*
Jackson, Glenda *IntMPA 75, –76, WhoHol A*
Jackson, Glenda 1936- *Ent[port], FilmEn, IlWWBF[port], OxFilm, WhoThe 72, –77*
Jackson, Glenda 1937- *BiDFilm 81, FilmAG WE, FilmgC, HalFC 80*
Jackson, Glenda 1938- *IntMPA 77, –78, –79, –80, MovMk[port]*
Jackson, Glenna *WomWMM B*
Jackson, Gordon 1923- *FilmAG WE, FilmEn, FilmgC, ForYSC, HalFC 80, IlWWBF, IntMPA 77, –75, –76, –78, –79, –80, WhoHol A, WhoThe 72, –77*
Jackson, Gregory A *CpmDNM 80*
Jackson, Greig Stewart 1918- *AmSCAP 66, –80, BiDAmM, EncJzS 70*
Jackson, Hal 1922- *DrBlPA*
Jackson, Hanley 1939- *AmSCAP 80, CpmDNM 76, ConAmC, IntWWM 77, –80*
Jackson, Harold *IntWWM 77, –80, WhoMus 72*
Jackson, Harry Conrad 1927-1974 *AmSCAP 80*
Jackson, Harry J 1931- *IntWWM 77*
Jackson, Henry 1909- *IntWWM 80*
Jackson, Henry 1927-1973 *WhScrn 77*
Jackson, Howard Manucy 1900- *AmSCAP 66, –80*
Jackson, J J *RkOn 2A*
Jackson, James A 1879- *BlksBF*
Jackson, James Thomas *MorBAP*
Jackson, Jay *IntMPA 77, –75, –76, –78, –79, –80*
Jackson, Jennie d1976 *WhoHol C*
Jackson, Jesse *BlkAmP*
Jackson, Jill 1913- *AmSCAP 66, –80*
Jackson, Jim 1890?-1937? *BluesWW[port]*
Jackson, Jo *BlkAmP*
Jackson, Joe *ConMuA 80A*
Jackson, Joe d1942 *WhoHol B*
Jackson, Joe 1875-1942 *Film 1, NotNAT B*
Jackson, John d1688 *NewGrD 80*
Jackson, John d1806 *NotNAT B*
Jackson, John Calvin 1919- *AmSCAP 80*
Jackson, John H 1924- *BluesWW[port]*
Jackson, John Henry 1916- *IntMPA 77, –75, –76, –78, –79, –80*

Jackson, Josephine *MorBAP*
Jackson, Judge 1883-1958 *NewGrD 80*
Jackson, Kate 1950?- *HalFC 80, IntMPA 78, -79, -80, WhoHol A*
Jackson, Keith *NewYTET*
Jackson, Lee 1907- *BluesWW[port]*
Jackson, Leonard 1928- *DrBlPA, WhoHol A*
Jackson, Lewis James 1936- *AmSCAP 80*
Jackson, Lisa *WomWMM B*
Jackson, Mahalia 1911-1972 *Baker 78, BiDAmM, CmpEPM, DrBlPA, EncJzS 70, NewGrD 80, WhScrn 77, WhoHol B*
Jackson, Marilyn *AmSCAP 80*
Jackson, Mary *WhoHol A*
Jackson, Mary Ann 1923- *Film 2, TwYS*
Jackson, Melvin 1915-1976 *BluesWW[port]*
Jackson, Mike 1888-1945 *AmSCAP 66, -80, BiDAmM*
Jackson, Millie 1944- *DrBlPA, RkOn 2[port]*
Jackson, Milt 1923- *CmpEPM, DrBlPA, EncJzS 70, IlEncJ, NewGrD 80*
Jackson, Milton 1923- *BiDAmM, EncJzS 70*
Jackson, Milton 1932- *ConAmC*
Jackson, Nagle 1936- *NotNAT*
Jackson, Nelson 1870- *WhThe*
Jackson, Nicholas Fane Saint George 1934- *WhoMus 72*
Jackson, Oliver, Jr. 1934- *BiDAmM, EncJzS 70*
Jackson, Pat 1916- *FilmEn, FilmgC, HalFC 80, IlWWBF, WorEFlm*
Jackson, Paul Joseph 1927- *IntWWM 77, -80*
Jackson, Peaches *Film 1, -2, TwYS*
Jackson, Pickles d1972 *NewOrJ*
Jackson, Preston 1903- *BiDAmM, NewOrJ[port]*
Jackson, Preston 1904- *EncJzS 70, WhoJazz 72*
Jackson, Quentin Leonard 1909-1976 *BiDAmM, CmpEPM, EncJzS 70, IlEncJ*
Jackson, R Eugene 1941- *NatPD[port]*
Jackson, Raymond T 1933- *IntWWM 77, -80*
Jackson, Richard 1936- *IntWWM 80*
Jackson, Richard 1949- *IntWWM 80*
Jackson, Mrs. Robert Lacy 1913- *WhoMus 72*
Jackson, Roland 1925- *NewGrD 80*
Jackson, Rowena 1926- *CnOxB, DancEn 78*
Jackson, Roy William 1907- *AmSCAP 66*
Jackson, Rudy 1901- *WhoJazz 72*
Jackson, Sammy *ForYSC, WhoHol A*
Jackson, Samuel P 1818-1885 *Baker 78, BiDAmM*
Jackson, Selmer 1888-1971 *Film 2, ForYSC, HolCA[port], Vers B[port], WhScrn 77, WhoHol B*
Jackson, Sherry 1942- *ForYSC, WhoHol A*
Jackson, Skeeter *NewOrJ*
Jackson, Spencer *BlkAmP, MorBAP*
Jackson, Stonewall 1932- *AmPS A, BiDAmM, CounME 74[port], -74A, EncFCWM 69, IlEncCM[port], RkOn[port]*
Jackson, Thomas E 1886-1967 *FilmEn, HalFC 80, MovMk, WhScrn 74, -77*
Jackson, Thomas E 1895-1967 *Film 2, Vers A[port], WhoHol B*
Jackson, Tony 1876-1921 *BiDAmM, NewOrJ[port], WhoJazz 72*
Jackson, Walker d1798 *NewGrD 80*
Jackson, Wanda 1937- *BiDAmM, CounME 74, -74A, EncFCWM 69, IlEncCM[port], RkOn*
Jackson, Warren 1893-1950 *WhScrn 74, -77, WhoHol B*
Jackson, William *BlkAmP*
Jackson, William 1730-1803 *Baker 78, BnBkM 80, NewGrD 80, OxMus*
Jackson, William 1815-1866 *Baker 78, NewGrD 80, OxMus*
Jackson, William E 1938- *AmSCAP 80*
Jackson, Willie 1895?- *NewOrJ*
Jackson, Willis 1932- *EncJzS 70*
Jackson Five, The *BiDAmM, RkOn 2[port]*
Jacksons, The *ConMuA 80A[port], IlEncR*
Jackter, Norman 1922- *IntMPA 77, -75, -76, -78, -79, -80*
Jackter, Rube 1900- *IntMPA 77, -75, -76, -78, -79, -80*
Jacob De Brouck *NewGrD 80*
Jacob De Senleches *NewGrD 80*
Jacob DeReys *OxMus*
Jacob LePolonais *OxMus*
Jacob Polak *OxMus*
Jacob, Benjamin 1778-1829 *Baker 78, NewGrD 80, OxMus*
Jacob, Clement 1906-1977 *NewGrD 80*
Jacob, Georg 1862-1937 *DcPup*
Jacob, Gordon Percival Septimus 1895- *Baker 78, CpmDNM 74, -75, -76, -79, DcCom&M 79, IntWWM 77, -80, NewGrD 80, OxMus, WhoMus 72*
Jacob, Gunther 1685-1734 *NewGrD 80*
Jacob, Helen *AmSCAP 80*
Jacob, Kurt 1922- *CnOxB, DancEn 78*
Jacob, Martin *Film 2*
Jacob, Max 1888-1967 *DcPup*
Jacob, Maxime 1906-1977 *Baker 78, DcCM, NewGrD 80*
Jacob, Naomi 1889-1964 *NotNAT A, -B, WhThe*
Jacob, Patti *AmSCAP 80*
Jacob, William Jacob 1929-1970 *AmSCAP 80*
Jacobacci, Vincenzo *NewGrD 80*
Jacobelus Bianchy *NewGrD 80*
Jacobi, Christian August 1688-1725 *NewGrD 80*
Jacobi, Derek 1938- *Ent, PlP&P[port], WhoHol A, WhoThe 72, -77*
Jacobi, Derek 1939- *HalFC 80*
Jacobi, Erwin R 1909-1978 *Baker 78, IntWWM 77, -80, NewGrD 80*
Jacobi, Frederick 1891-1952 *AmSCAP 66, -80, Baker 78, BiDAmM, ConAmC, DcCM, NewGrD 80, OxMus*
Jacobi, Georg 1840-1906 *NewGrD 80*
Jacobi, George 1840-1906 *Baker 78, OxMus*
Jacobi, Georges 1840-1906 *CnOxB*
Jacobi, Lou 1913- *BiE&WWA, FilmEn, HalFC 80, NotNAT, WhoHol A, WhoThe 72, -77*
Jacobi, Maurice d1939 *NotNAT B*
Jacobi, Michael 1618-1663 *NewGrD 80*
Jacobi, Peter Paul 1930- *ConAmTC*
Jacobi, Roger Edgar 1924- *IntWWM 77, -80*
Jacobi, Samuel 1652-1721 *NewGrD 80*
Jacobi, Victor 1883-1921 *BiDAmM, NotNAT B, PopAmC*
Jacobi, Viktor 1883-1921 *NewGrD 80*
Jacobini, Maria 1890-1944 *FilmAG WE, FilmEn*
Jacobs, Al 1903- *AmSCAP 66, -80, CmpEPM*
Jacobs, Angela 1893-1951 *WhScrn 74, -77, WhoHol B*
Jacobs, Arthur David 1922- *Baker 78, IntWWM 77, -80, NewGrD 80, WhoMus 72*
Jacobs, Arthur P 1918-1973 *FilmgC, HalFC 80*
Jacobs, Arthur P 1922-1973 *FilmEn*
Jacobs, Barry 1924- *IntMPA 77, -75, -76, -78, -79, -80*
Jacobs, Benjamin 1778-1829 *NewGrD 80*
Jacobs, Billy *Film 1*
Jacobs, Carl Frederick 1910- *IntWWM 77*
Jacobs, Charles Gilbert 1934- *IntWWM 77, -80*
Jacobs, Dick 1918- *AmSCAP 66, -80, RkOn*
Jacobs, Dorothy *WomWMM B*
Jacobs, Elaine *WomWMM B*
Jacobs, Harry M 1917- *IntWWM 77, -80*
Jacobs, Helen Hull 1908- *What 1[port]*
Jacobs, Hendrik 1629?-1699 *NewGrD 80*
Jacobs, Jacob 1889-1977 *AmSCAP 80*
Jacobs, James Harold 1942- *AmSCAP 80*
Jacobs, James Leslie 1906- *WhoMus 72*
Jacobs, Jay *ConMuA 80B*
Jacobs, Jerome Joseph 1921- *IntWWM 77*
Jacobs, Jim 1942- *ConDr 77D, NatPD[port]*
Jacobs, Lawrence-Hilton 1953- *DrBlPA*
Jacobs, Lewis 1906- *OxFilm*
Jacobs, Marion Walter 1930-1968 *BluesWW[port]*
Jacobs, Matthew 1929?- *BluesWW[port]*
Jacobs, Morris 1906- *BiE&WWA, NotNAT*
Jacobs, Morton P 1917- *AmSCAP 66*
Jacobs, Naomi *Film 2*
Jacobs, Newton P 1900- *IntMPA 77, -75, -76, -78, -79, -80*
Jacobs, Paul *Film 1*
Jacobs, Paul 1930- *BnBkM 80, NewGrD 80*
Jacobs, Pete ' Edward 1899-1952? *WhoJazz 72*
Jacobs, Rene 1946- *IntWWM 80*
Jacobs, Robert Louis 1904- *IntWWM 77, -80, WhoMus 72*
Jacobs, Sally 1932- *WhoThe 72, -77*
Jacobs, Sylvia 1933- *WhoMus 72*
Jacobs, Thomas 1954- *IntWWM 77, -80*
Jacobs, W W 1863-1943 *HalFC 80*
Jacobs, Walter *BluesWW, NewGrD 80*
Jacobs, Wesley D 1946- *IntWWM 77, -80*
Jacobs, William Wymark 1863-1943 *NotNAT B, WhThe*
Jacobs-Bond, Carrie *Baker 78*
Jacobsen, Erwin 1926- *IntWWM 77, -80*
Jacobsen, Eunice *AmSCAP 80*
Jacobsen, L H d1941 *NotNAT B*
Jacobsen, Palle 1940- *CnOxB*
Jacobsohn, Siegfried 1881-1926 *EncWT*
Jacobsohn, Simon E 1839-1902 *BiDAmM*
Jacobson, Bud 1906-1960 *WhoJazz 72*
Jacobson, Denise *WomWMM B*
Jacobson, Elaine Rathbun 1924- *IntWWM 77*
Jacobson, H J *Film 2*
Jacobson, Harvey 1936- *IntWWM 77, -80*
Jacobson, Irving 1905- *BiE&WWA, NotNAT*
Jacobson, Kenneth *AmSCAP 80*
Jacobson, Leonid Benjaminovich 1904-1975 *CnOxB*
Jacobson, Lilly *Film 2*
Jacobson, Maurice 1896-1976 *Baker 78, NewGrD 80, OxMus, WhoMus 72*
Jacobson, Sam d1964 *NotNAT B*
Jacobson, Sidney 1929- *AmSCAP 66, -80*
Jacobson, Sol 1912- *BiE&WWA, NotNAT*
Jacobsson, John-Eric 1931- *WhoOp 76*
Jacobsson, Ulla 1929- *FilmEn, FilmgC, HalFC 80, WhoHol A, WorEFlm*
Jacobsthal, Gustav 1845-1912 *Baker 78, NewGrD 80*
Jacobus Corbus De Padua *NewGrD 80*
Jacobus De Benedictus *NewGrD 80*
Jacobus De Bononia *NewGrD 80*
Jacobus De Brouck *NewGrD 80*
Jacobus De Navernia *NewGrD 80*
Jacobus De Regio *NewGrD 80*
Jacobus Theatinus *NewGrD 80*
Jacoby, Elliott 1902- *AmSCAP 66*
Jacoby, Frank David 1925- *IntMPA 77, -75, -76, -78, -79, -80*
Jacoby, Hanoch 1909- *Baker 78, IntWWM 77, -80, NewGrD 80*
Jacoby, Heinrich 1889-1964 *NewGrD 80*
Jacoby, Heinrich 1909- *NewGrD 80*
Jacoby, Hugh William 1935- *ConAmC*
Jacoby, Joseph 1942- *IntMPA 77, -75, -76, -78, -79, -80*
Jacoby, Richard 1940- *IntWWM 77, -80*
Jacoby, Robert John 1940- *IntWWM 77, -80, WhoMus 72*
Jacoby, Scott 1956- *HalFC 80, WhoHol A*
Jacomelli, Geminiano *NewGrD 80*
Jacomelli, Giovanni Battista *NewGrD 80*
Jacomet, Johann Georg 1946- *IntWWM 77, -80*
Jacomi De Santluch *NewGrD 80*
Jacon, Bernard *IntMPA 77, -75, -76, -78, -79, -80*
Jacopetti, Gualtiero 1919- *FilmEn*
Jacopetti, Gualtiero 1922- *WorEFlm*
Jacopo Da Bologna *Baker 78, NewGrD 80*
Jacopone Da Todi 1228?-1306 *NewGrD 80*
Jacopone Da Todi 1230?-1306 *McGEWD, REnWD[port]*
Jacopus De Tuderto *NewGrD 80*
Jacotin 1445?-1529 *Baker 78, NewGrD 80*
Jacoupy, Jacqueline *WomWMM B*
Jacovacci, Vincenzo 1811-1881 *NewGrD 80*
Jacovelli, Mercurio *NewGrD 80*
Jacoves, Felix 1907- *FilmgC, HalFC 80*
Jacquard, Leon *NewGrD 80*
Jacquelin *CreCan 2*
Jacquemart Le Cuvelier *NewGrD 80*
Jacquemin, Andre 1952- *IntWWM 77*
Jacquemis De Sanleches *NewGrD 80*
Jacques De Cysoing *NewGrD 80*
Jacques De Liege 1260?-1330? *Baker 78, NewGrD 80*
Jacques Le Polonais *NewGrD 80*

Jacques, Hattie 1924- *FilmgC, HalFC 80, WhoHol A, WhoThe 72, -77*
Jacques, Janet Elizabeth 1943- *IntWWM 77, -80*
Jacques, John Michael 1944- *WhoMus 72*
Jacques, Reginald 1894-1969 *NewGrD 80*
Jacques, Robert C 1919- *IntMPA 77, -75, -76, -78, -79, -80*
Jacquet *NewGrD 80*
Jacquet De Berchem *NewGrD 80*
Jacquet Of Mantua 1483-1559 *NewGrD 80*
Jacquet, Claude *NewGrD 80*
Jacquet, Claude d1702 *NewGrD 80*
Jacquet, Claude 1605-1675? *NewGrD 80*
Jacquet, Gaston *Film 2*
Jacquet, Illinois 1922- *CmpEPM, DrBlPA, IlEncJ*
Jacquet, Jean d1686? *NewGrD 80*
Jacquet, Jean Baptiste 1922- *BiDAmM, EncJzS 70*
Jacquet, Jehan d1658? *NewGrD 80*
Jacquet, Nicolas *NewGrD 80*
Jacquet, Pierre 1666?-1729 *NewGrD 80*
Jacquet, Robert Russell 1917- *BiDAmM*
Jacquet DeLaGuerre, Elisabeth-Claude 1666?-1729 *NewGrD 80*
Jacquillat, Jean-Pierre 1935- *WhoOp 76*
Jacquot, Jean 1909- *IntWWM 80, NewGrD 80*
Jadassohn, Salomon 1831-1902 *Baker 78, NewGrD 80, OxMus*
Jadin *NewGrD 80*
Jadin, Hyacinthe 1769-1802 *NewGrD 80*
Jadin, Jean B d1789? *NewGrD 80*
Jadin, Louis Emmanuel 1768-1853 *Baker 78, NewGrD 80*
Jadlowker, Hermann 1877-1953 *Baker 78, NewGrD 80*
Jadlowker, Hermann 1879-1953 *NewEOp 71*
Jadot, Jacquemin *OxThe*
Jaeckel, Richard 1926- *FilmEn, FilmgC, ForYSC, HalFC 80, IntMPA 77, -75, -76, -78, -79, -80, MotPP, MovMk, Vers A[port], WhoHol A*
Jaeger, Albert 1910- *IntMPA 77, -75, -76, -78, -79*
Jaeger, Alfred 1869-1953 *NewOrJ*
Jaeger, Andrew P 1917- *IntMPA 77, -75, -76, -78, -79, -80*
Jaeger, August 1860-1909 *NewGrD 80*
Jaeger, Ina Claire Burlingham 1929- *IntWWM 77, -80*
Jaeger, Patricia Paul 1930- *IntWWM 77, -80*
Jaell, Alfred 1832-1882 *Baker 78, NewGrD 80, OxMus*
Jaell, Marie 1846-1925 *NewGrD 80*
Jaell-Trautmann, Marie 1846-1925 *Baker 78*
Jaenzon, Julius 1885-1961 *DcFM, FilmEn*
Jaffa, Max 1912- *WhoMus 72*
Jaffe, Allan 1935- *NewOrJ*
Jaffe, Ben 1902- *AmSCAP 66, -80*
Jaffe, Carl 1902-1974 *FilmgC, HalFC 80, WhScrn 77, WhoHol B*
Jaffe, Gerald G 1925- *CpmDNM 78*
Jaffe, Gerard G 1925- *CpmDNM 75, ConAmC*
Jaffe, Henry *NewYTET*
Jaffe, Herb *BiE&WWA, IntMPA 77, -75, -76, -78, -79, -80*
Jaffe, Joel 1943- *AmSCAP 80*
Jaffe, Leo 1909- *IntMPA 77, -75, -76, -78, -79, -80*
Jaffe, Moe 1901-1972 *AmSCAP 66, -80*
Jaffe, Monte *WhoOp 76*
Jaffe, Nat 1918-1945 *CmpEPM, WhoJazz 72*
Jaffe, Pat *WomWMM B*
Jaffe, Patricia Lewis *WomWMM*
Jaffe, Phil *PupTheA*
Jaffe, Sam *MotPP, WhoHol A*
Jaffe, Sam 1891- *FilmEn*
Jaffe, Sam 1893- *BiE&WWA, ForYSC, HolCA[port], NotNAT, WhoThe 72, -77*
Jaffe, Sam 1896- *IntMPA 77, -75, -76, -78, -79, -80, MovMk[port]*
Jaffe, Sam 1897- *FilmgC, HalFC 80, WhoHrs 80*
Jaffe, Sam 1901- *IntMPA 77, -75, -76, -78, -79, -80*
Jaffe, Stanley R 1940- *IntMPA 77, -75, -76, -78, -79, -80*
Jaffe, Stephen Abram 1954- *CpmDNM 80*
Jaffe, William B 1904- *IntMPA 77, -75, -76, -78, -79, -80*
Jaffey, Herbert *IntMPA 77, -75, -76, -78, -79, -80*
Jagamas, Janos 1913- *NewGrD 80*
Jagd-Hautbois *NewGrD 80*
Jagel, Frederick 1897- *Baker 78, BiDAmM, IntWWM 77, -80, NewEOp 71*
Jager, Robert Edward 1939- *AmSCAP 80, CpmDNM 78, -80, ConAmC, IntWWM 77, -80*
Jaggard, William 1568-1623 *NotNAT B*
Jagger, Dean *MotPP, WhoHol A*
Jagger, Dean 1903- *FilmEn, Film 2, FilmgC, ForYSC, HalFC 80, HolCA[port], IntMPA 77, -75, -76, -78, -79, -80, MovMk, WhoHrs 80*
Jagger, Dean 1904- *WhThe*
Jagger, Mack *ConMuA 80B*
Jagger, Mick *ConMuA 80A*
Jagger, Mick 1939- *FilmgC, HalFC 80, WhoHol A*
Jagger, Mick 1944- *FilmAG WE*
Jaggerz, The *RkOn 2[port]*
Jago, Mary 1946- *CnOxB*
Jagoda, Barry *NewYTET*
Jagodynski, Stanislaw Serafin 1590?-1644? *NewGrD 80*
Jahn, Gertrude 1940- *WhoOp 76*
Jahn, Hans Henny 1894-1959 *CroCD*
Jahn, Martin 1620?-1682? *NewGrD 80*
Jahn, Otto 1813-1869 *Baker 78, NewGrD 80, OxMus*
Jahn, Theodore L 1939- *IntWWM 80*
Jahn, Wilfried 1943- *CnOxB*
Jahn, Wilhelm 1834-1900 *Baker 78*
Jahncke, Ernest Lee, Jr. 1912- *IntMPA 77, -75, -76, -78, -79, -80*
Jahnn, Hans Henny 1894-1959 *CnMD, EncWT, Ent, McGEWD, ModWD, NewGrD 80, OxMus*
Jahns, Friedrich Wilhelm 1809-1888 *Baker 78, NewGrD 80*
Jahns-Gaehtgens, Renate Ursula Theophile 1927- *IntWWM 77, -80*
Jahr, Adolf 1894-1964 *NotNAT B, WhScrn 74, -77*
Jaia, Gianni 1930- *WhoOp 76*
Jairazbhoy, Nazir A 1927- *NewGrD 80*
Jaisun, Jef 1946- *AmSCAP 80*
Jakey, Lauren Ray 1937- *IntWWM 77, -80*
Jakob, Friedrich 1932- *IntWWM 80, NewGrD 80*
Jakob, Friedrich 1932- *IntWWM 77*
Jakobsen, Erik 1921- *IntWWM 77*
Jakoby, Richard Matthias 1929- *IntWWM 77, -80*
Jakowicka-Friderici, Teodozja 1836-1889 *NewGrD 80*
Jakubenas, Vladas 1904- *ConAmC*
Jakubowska, Wanda 1907- *DcFM, FilmEn, HalFC 80, OxFilm, WomWMM, WorEFlm*
Jakubowska, Wanda 1930- *IntWWM 77, -80*
Jalas, Armas Veikko 1908- *WhoOp 76*
Jalas, Jussi 1908- *Baker 78*
Jalland, Henry 1861-1928 *NotNAT B, WhThe*
Jallaud, Sylvia *WomWMM*
Jam, The *IlEncR*
Jamal, Ahmad 1930- *BiDAmM, DrBlPA, EncJzS 70*
Jamal, Khan 1946- *EncJzS 70*
Jambe DeFer, Philibert 1515?-1566? *NewGrD 80*
Jambor, Agi 1909- *ConAmC, IntWWM 77, -80*
Jamerson, Thomas H 1942- *IntWWM 80, WhoOp 76*
James *NewGrD 80*
James Of Edessa d708 *NewGrD 80*
James II, Of England 1633-1701 *OxMus*
James I, Of Scotland 1394-1437 *MusMk[port], OxMus*
James III, Of Scotland 1451-1488 *OxMus*
James IV, Of Scotland 1473-1513 *OxMus*
James V, Of Scotland 1512-1542 *OxMus*
James VI, Of Scotland 1560-1625 *OxMus*
James, Alan *AmSCAP 80*
James, Alf P 1865-1946 *WhScrn 74, -77*
James, Alfred P 1865-1946 *WhoHol B*
James, Allen *AmSCAP 80*
James, Art d1972 *WhoHol B*
James, Ben 1921-1966 *WhScrn 77*
James, Benjamin Phillip 1940- *IntWWM 77, -80*
James, Billy *BluesWW*
James, Billy 1895-1965 *AmSCAP 66, -80*
James, Bob 1939- *ConMuA 80B, EncJzS 70*
James, Cairns d1946 *NotNAT B*
James, Carolyne 1945- *IntWWM 80, WhoOp 76*
James, Cecil 1913- *NewGrD 80*
James, Charles James d1888 *NotNAT B*
James, Claire *WhoHol A*
James, Clifton *WhoHol A*
James, Clifton 1898-1963 *NotNAT B, WhScrn 74, WhoHol B*
James, Clifton 1921- *BiE&WWA, HalFC 80, NotNAT*
James, Clifton 1922- *IntMPA 77, -76, -78, -79, -80*
James, Cornelius 1927- *BiDAmM*
James, Daisy *WhThe*
James, David *Film 2*
James, David 1839-1893 *NotNAT B, OxThe*
James, David, Jr. d1917 *NotNAT B*
James, Dennis 1917- *IntMPA 77, -75, -76, -78, -79, -80, NewYTET*
James, Dick *ConMuA 80B*
James, Donald William 1935- *IntWWM 77, -80, WhoMus 72*
James, Dorothy 1901- *Baker 78, BiDAmM, ConAmC, NewGrD 80*
James, Eddie 1880-1944 *Film 2, WhScrn 74, -77, WhoHol B*
James, Edwin F 1861-1921 *NewGrD 80*
James, Elmer 1910-1954 *BiDAmM, BluesWW, WhoJazz 72*
James, Elmore 1918-1963 *BluesWW[port]*
James, Elmore 1920?-1963 *BiDAmM*
James, Elmore, Jr. *BluesWW*
James, Emrys 1930- *WhoHol A, WhoThe 72, -77*
James, Etta 1938- *RkOn*
James, Evan 1833-1902 *OxMus*
James, Forrest *Film 2*
James, Frances 1903- *CreCan 1*
James, Francis 1907- *WhThe*
James, Freeman Kelly, Jr. 1927- *AmSCAP 66, -80*
James, Gardner *Film 2, ForYSC*
James, George 1906- *WhoJazz 72*
James, Gerald d1964 *NotNAT B*
James, Gerald 1917- *WhoThe 72, -77*
James, Gladden 1892-1948 *Film 1, -2, ForYSC, WhScrn 74, -77, WhoHol B*
James, Gordon *Film 2*
James, Harry 1916- *AmPS A, -B, AmSCAP 66, -80, BgBands 74[port], BiDAmM, CmpEPM, EncJzS 70, FilmEn, FilmgC, ForYSC, HalFC 80, HolP 40[port], IlEncJ, IntMPA 77, -75, -76, -78, -79, -80, MovMk[port], WhoHol A, WhoJazz 72*
James, Henry 1843-1916 *CnMD, CnThe, DcPup, EncWT, HalFC 80, McGEWD[port], ModWD, NewEOp 71, NotNAT B, OxThe, REnWD[port]*
James, Homesick *BluesWW*
James, Horace D 1853-1925 *Film 2, NotNAT B, WhScrn 74, -77, WhoHol B*
James, Ifor 1931- *IntWWM 77, -80, WhoMus 72*
James, Inez Eleanor 1919- *AmSCAP 66, -80*
James, Ivor 1882-1963 *NewGrD 80*
James, J Wharton *Film 2*
James, Jack d1745? *NewGrD 80*
James, Jean Eileen 1934- *AmSCAP 66, -80*
James, Jesse 1847-1882 *HalFC 80, OxFilm*
James, Jimmy *BluesWW*
James, Joe 1901-1964 *NewOrJ*
James, John d1745? *NewGrD 80*
James, John d1960 *WhScrn 74, -77, WhoHol B*
James, Joni 1930- *AmPS A, CmpEPM, RkOn*
James, Julia 1890-1964 *NotNAT A, -B, WhThe*
James, Kate d1913 *NotNAT B*

James, Kid 1907- *NewOrJ*
James, Lance Colan 1951- *AmSCAP 80*
James, Laura 1933- *IntMPA 77, -75, -76, -78, -79, -80*
James, Lee *AmSCAP 80*
James, Len *PupTheA*
James, Leonard William 1930- *WhoMus 72*
James, Lewis *CmpEPM*
James, Louis 1842-1910 *NotNAT B, OxThe, WhoStg 1908*
James, Louis 1890-1967 *NewOrJ[port]*
James, M R 1862-1936 *HalFC 80*
James, Marion 1913- *AmSCAP 66, -80*
James, Millie 1876- *WhoStg 1908*
James, Monique *WomWMM*
James, Myron *AmSCAP 80*
James, Natalie 1909- *WhoMus 72*
James, Nehemiah 1902-1969 *BiDAmM, BluesWW[port], EncJzS 70*
James, Olga *DrBlPA, WhoHol A*
James, Percy Edward, Jr. 1929- *BiDAmM*
James, Pete *AmSCAP 80*
James, Peter Haydn 1940- *IntWWM 77, -80, WhoThe 77*
James, Philip 1890-1975 *AmSCAP 66, -80, Baker 78, BiDAmM, ConAmC, NewGrD 80, OxMus*
James, Polly 1941- *IntMPA 77, -75, -76, -78, -79, -80, WhoThe 77*
James, Rian d1953 *NotNAT B*
James, Richard 1592-1638 *OxMus*
James, Richard H 1931- *NotNAT*
James, Richard Ifor 1931- *WhoMus 72*
James, Robert McElhiney 1939- *AmSCAP 80, EncJzS 70*
James, Ruth d1970 *WhScrn 77, WhoHol B*
James, Seymour 1899-1926 *BlksBF*
James, Shaylor L 1942- *IntWWM 77*
James, Sheila *WhoHol A*
James, Sid 1913-1976 *FilmgC, HalFC 80*
James, Sidney 1913- *IntMPA 75, -76*
James, Sidney 1913-1976 *FilmAG WE, IlWWBF, WhoHol A*
James, Skip 1902-1969 *EncFCWM 69, EncJzS 70*
James, Sonny 1929- *AmPS A, BiDAmM, CounME 74[port], -74A, EncFCWM 69, IlEncCM[port], RkOn[port], -*
James, Stafford Louis 1946- *EncJzS 70*
James, Thomas *ConAmC*
James, Tommy & The Shondells *ConMuA 80A, RkOn 2[port]*
James, Vincent 1932- *IntWWM 77, -80*
James, Walter 1886-1946 *Film 2, WhScrn 74, -77, WhoHol B*
James, Warren E 1922- *IntWWM 77, -80*
James, Wilfred 1872-1941 *NewGrD 80*
James, Will 1896- *AmSCAP 66, -80*
James, William *Film 2*
James, William 1936- *BiDAmM*
James, William Garnet 1892- *IntWWM 77, -80*
James, Willis Laurence 1909- *BiDAmM*
James, Wilson 1872- *WhThe*
James, Woodrow Cecil 1936- *ConAmC, IntWWM 77*
James Gang, The *IlEncR, RkOn 2[port]*
Jameson, Amable *Film 2*
Jameson, D D *OxMus*
Jameson, House 1902-1971 *BiE&WWA, NotNAT B*
Jameson, House 1903-1971 *PlP&P, WhScrn 74, -77, WhoHol B*
Jameson, Jerry *HalFC 80*
Jameson, Joyce 1932- *BiE&WWA, ForYSC, NotNAT, WhoHol A*
Jameson, Nick *ConMuA 80B*
Jameson, Pauline 1920- *WhoHol A, WhoThe 72, -77*
Jameson, R Philip 1941- *IntWWM 77, -80*
Jameson, Robert 1947- *AmSCAP 80*
Jamet, Marie-Claire 1933- *NewGrD 80*
Jamet, Pierre 1893- *NewGrD 80*
Jameyson, H E 1894- *IntMPA 77, -75, -76, -78, -79*
Jamgochian, Robert *AmSCAP 80*
Jamiaque, Yves 1922- *CnMD*
Jamies, The *RkOn[port]*
Jamieson, Edna Jaques 1910- *CreCan 2, WhoMus 72*
Jamieson, Nannie Hamilton *IntWWM 77, -80, WhoMus 72*
Jamieson, W H 1907- *IntMPA 77, -75, -76, -78, -79, -80*
Jamin, Georges 1907-1971 *WhScrn 74, -77*
Jamison, Anne 1910-1961 *WhScrn 77, WhoHol B*
Jamison, Bud 1894-1943 *ForYSC, WhoHol B*
Jamison, Bud 1894-1944 *FilmgC, HalFC 80*
Jamison, Judith 1943- *DrBlPA*
Jamison, Judith 1944- *CnOxB*
Jamison, Marshall 1918- *BiE&WWA*
Jamison, Roger Alan 1950- *IntWWM 77*
Jamison, Samuel W 1855-1930 *BiDAmM*
Jamison, William Bud 1894-1943 *Film 1, -2, TwYS*
Jamison, William Bud 1894-1944 *WhScrn 74, -77*
Jammers, Ewald 1897- *NewGrD 80*
Jammin' Jim *BluesWW*
Jamois, Marguerite 1901-1964 *WhScrn 77*
Jampolis, Neil Peter 1943- *NotNAT, WhoOp 76*
Jamroz, Krystyna 1928- *WhoOp 76*
Jan *NewGrD 80*
Jan And Arnie *RkOn*
Jan And Dean *AmPS A, BiDAmM, ConMuA 80A, IlEncR, RkOn[port]*
Jan Polak *NewGrD 80*
Jan Z Glogowa 1445?-1507 *NewGrD 80*
Jan Z Lublina *NewGrD 80*
Jan, Karl Von 1836-1899 *Baker 78*
Jan, Kurt Von 1836-1899 *NewGrD 80*
Jan, Martin *NewGrD 80*
Jana, La *Film 2*
Janacconi, Giuseppe *NewGrD 80*
Janacek, Bedrich 1920- *IntWWM 77, -80*
Janacek, Leo Eugen 1854-1928 *NewGrD 80[port]*
Janacek, Leos 1854-1928 *Baker 78, BnBkM 80, CmOp, CompSN[port], CnOxB, DcCom 77[port], DcCom&M 79, DcCM, DcTwCC, -A, MusMk, NewEOp 71, NewGrD 80[port], OxMus*
Janauschek, Fanny 1830-1904 *FamA&A[port]*
Janauschek, Francesca Romana Maddalena 1830-1904 *OxThe*
Janauschek, Francesca Romana Magdalena 1830-1904 *NotNAT B*
Jancourt, Eugene 1815-1901 *NewGrD 80*
Jancso, Miklos 1921- *BiDFilm, -81, DcFM, FilmEn, FilmgC, HalFC 80, OxFilm, WorEFlm*
Janda, Petr 1942- *IntWWM 77*
Jander, Owen 1930- *NewGrD 80*
Janecek, Karel 1903-1974 *Baker 78, NewGrD 80*
Janequin, Clement 1485?-1558 *BnBkM 80, NewGrD 80*
Janequin, Clement 1485?-1560? *Baker 78*
Janes, Kenneth H *BiE&WWA, NotNAT*
Janes, Robert 1806-1866 *OxMus*
Janet, Pierre-Honore *NewGrD 80*
Janetton, La *NewGrD 80*
Jang, Amir *Film 2*
Janiak, Bronislaus 1916- *IntWWM 77, -80*
Janiec, Henry 1929- *IntWWM 77, -80*
Janiewicz, Feliks 1762-1848 *NewGrD 80*
Janiewicz, Felix 1762-1848 *OxMus*
Janigro, Antonio 1918- *Baker 78, BnBkM 80, IntWWM 77, -80, NewGrD 80*
Janin, Jules-Gabriel 1804-1874 *CnOxB, NotNAT B, OxThe*
Janis, Beverly *AmSCAP 80*
Janis, Byron 1928- *Baker 78, BnBkM 80, IntWWM 77, -80, MusSN[port], NewGrD 80, WhoMus 72*
Janis, Conrad *MotPP*
Janis, Conrad 1926- *FilmgC, HalFC 80*
Janis, Conrad 1928- *BiDAmM, BiE&WWA, CmpEPM, NotNAT, WhoHol A, WhoThe 72, -77*
Janis, Dorothy 1910- *Film 2, TwYS*
Janis, Elsie 1889-1956 *AmSCAP 66, -80, CmpEPM, EncMT, FamA&A[port], Film 1, -2, FilmgC, HalFC 80, NotNAT A, -B, TwYS, WhScrn 74, -77, WhThe, WhoHol B, WhoStg 1906, -1908*
Janis, Harold E 1906- *IntMPA 77, -75, -76, -78, -79, -80*
Janis, Joan Gardner 1926- *AmSCAP 66, -80*
Janis, Stephen 1907- *AmSCAP 66*
Janitsch, Johann Gottlieb 1708-1763? *Baker 78, NewGrD 80*
Janitsh, Johann Gottlieb 1708-1763? *NewGrD 80*
Janitzch, Johann Gottlieb 1708-1763? *NewGrD 80*
Jankelevitch, Vladimir 1903- *Baker 78, NewGrD 80*
Janko, Paul Von 1856-1919 *Baker 78, NewGrD 80*
Jankovic 1894-1974 *NewGrD 80*
Jankovic, Danica S 1898-1960 *NewGrD 80*
Jankovic, Ljubica S 1894-1974 *NewGrD 80*
Jankowski, Horst *RkOn 2A*
Jankowski, Loretta Patricia 1950- *IntWWM 77, -80*
Janku, Hanna *WhoOp 76*
Jannaconi, Giuseppe 1741-1816 *Baker 78, NewGrD 80*
Jannequin, Clement *NewGrD 80*
Jannequin, Clement 1472-1560 *OxMus*
Jannequin, Clement 1475?-1560? *MusMk*
Jannequin, Clement 1485-1560 *GrComp*
Jannery, Arthur A 1932- *CpmDNM 77, -78, ConAmC*
Janney, Ben 1927- *BiE&WWA, NotNAT*
Janney, Leon 1917- *BiE&WWA, Film 2, ForYSC, NotNAT, WhoHol A*
Janney, Russell 1884-1963 *WhThe*
Janney, William 1908-1938 *Film 2, ForYSC, WhScrn 77*
Janni, Joseph 1916- *FilmEn, FilmgC, HalFC 80, IntMPA 77, -75, -76, -78, -79, -80*
Jannings, Emil d1950 *MotPP, WhoHol B*
Jannings, Emil 1882-1950 *HalFC 80*
Jannings, Emil 1884-1950 *BiDFilm, -81, EncWT, FilmAG WE, FilmEn, FilmgC, TwYS, WhoHrs 80, WorEFlm[port]*
Jannings, Emil 1886-1950 *Film 1, -2, MovMk[port], NotNAT B, OxFilm, WhScrn 74, -77*
Janns, Rose *AmSCAP 80*
Jannson, Jean-Baptiste-Aime Joseph *NewGrD 80*
Jannson, Louis-Auguste-Joseph *NewGrD 80*
Jannuzi, Gail *PupTheA*
Janotha, Natalia 1856-1932 *NewGrD 80*
Janotta, Monique 1945- *CnOxB*
Janous, Josef 1927- *WhoOp 76*
Janovicky, Karel 1930- *IntWWM 77, -80, WhoMus 72*
Janovka, Tomas Baltazar 1669-1741 *NewGrD 80*
Janowitz, Gundala 1937- *CmOp*
Janowitz, Gundula 1937- *IntWWM 77, -80, MusSN[port], WhoMus 72, WhoOp 76*
Janowitz, Gundula 1939- *NewGrD 80*
Janowka, Thomas Balthasar 1660- *Baker 78*
Janowka, Thomas Balthasar 1669-1741 *NewGrD 80*
Janowski, Marek 1939- *WhoOp 76*
Jans, Alaric 1949- *AmSCAP 80*
Jans, Harry 1900-1962 *NotNAT B, WhScrn 74, -77, WhoHol B*
Jansa, Leopold 1795-1875 *Baker 78, NewGrD 80*
Jansch, Bert 1943- *IlEncR*
Janse, Donald L 1929- *AmSCAP 80*
Jansen, Alexander C B 1936- *IntWWM 77, -80*
Jansen, Dorothy Kathleen Emily *WhoMus 72*
Jansen, Guy Elwyn 1935- *IntWWM 80*
Jansen, Harry A *WhScrn 74, -77*
Jansen, Jojannes Felix Johanna Maria 1923- *IntWWM 77, -80*
Jansen, Marie 1857-1914 *NotNAT B, WhoStg 1906, -1908*
Jansen, Rudolf 1940- *IntWWM 77, -80*
Jansen, Simon C 1911- *NewGrD 80*
Janson, Alfred 1937- *Baker 78, DcCM*
Janson, Hugh Michael 1936- *AmSCAP 80*
Janson, Jean-Baptiste-Aime Joseph 1742?-1803 *NewGrD 80*
Janson, Louis-Auguste-Joseph *NewGrD 80*
Janson, Victor 1885-1960 *Film 2, WhScrn 74, -77, WhoHol B*
Jansons, Andrejs 1938- *IntWWM 77, -80*
Jansons, Arvid 1914- *NewGrD 80*
Jansons, Arvids 1914- *NewGrD 80*

Janssen, David *AmSCAP 80, MotPP, WhoHol A*
Janssen, David 1930- *FilmgC, ForYSC, HalFC 80, MovMk[port]*
Janssen, David 1930-1980 *FilmEn*
Janssen, David 1931- *IntMPA 77, -75, -76, -78, -79, -80*
Janssen, Eileen 1937- *ForYSC, HalFC 80*
Janssen, Herbert 1892-1965 *NewGrD 80*
Janssen, Herbert 1895-1965 *Baker 78, CmOp, NewEOp 71*
Janssen, Walter *Film 2*
Janssen, Werner 1899- *AmSCAP 80, Baker 78, ConAmC, NewGrD 80*
Janssen, Werner 1900- *AmSCAP 66, BiDAmM, CmpEPM, DcCM*
Janssens, Charles 1906- *FilmAG WE*
Janssens, Charles Romain 1932- *WhoOp 76*
Janssens, Jean-Francois-Joseph 1801-1835 *Baker 78*
Janssens, Robert 1939- *IntWWM 80*
Jansson, Henrik Daniel Johannes 1916- *IntWWM 77, -80*
Janszoon, Peter *NewGrD 80*
Jantarski, George 1905- *IntWWM 77, -80*
Janua, Johannes De *NewGrD 80*
January, Herb *AmSCAP 80*
January, Lois 1913- *ForYSC, WhoHol A*
January, Rona *AmSCAP 80*
Janue, Antonius *NewGrD 80*
Janulako, Wassili 1933- *WhoOp 76*
Janus, Dianne Rock *WomWMM B*
Janus Chorale, The *BiDAmM*
Januschowsky, Georgine Von *BiDAmM*
Januszowski, Jan Lazarzowicz *NewGrD 80*
Janvier, Emma d1924 *NotNAT B*
Janzer, Georges 1914- *IntWWM 77, -80*
Japart, Jean *NewGrD 80*
Japarte, Jean *NewGrD 80*
Japhet, Clifton, Sr. 1909- *AmSCAP 80*
Jappart, Jean *NewGrD 80*
Jaque De Cambrai *NewGrD 80*
Jaque De Cisoing *NewGrD 80*
Jaque De Cysoing *NewGrD 80*
Jaque De Dampierre *NewGrD 80*
Jaques Le Vinier *NewGrD 80*
Jaques, Edna 1891- *CreCan 2*
Jaques-Dalcroze, Emile 1865-1950 *Baker 78, BnBkM 80, CnOxB, DancEn 78, DcCM, NewGrD 80, OxMus*
Jaquet Of Mantua *NewGrD 80*
Jaquet, Frank 1885-1958 *WhScrn 77*
Jara, Maurice *ForYSC*
Jaray, Hans *Film 2*
Jarbeau, Vernona d1914 *NotNAT B*
Jarboro, Caterina 1903- *BiDAmM, DrBlPA*
Jarda, Tudor 1922- *NewGrD 80*
Jardanyi, Pal 1920-1966 *Baker 78, NewGrD 80*
Jardiel Poncela, Enrique 1901-1952 *CnMD, CroCD, McGEWD[port], ModWD*
Jardine, Betty d1945 *NotNAT B, WhThe*
Jardine, George 1801-1883 *NewGrD 80*
Jardon, Dorothy 1889- *AmSCAP 66*
Jardon, Edward *Film 2*
Jarecki, Henryk 1846-1918 *Baker 78, NewGrD 80*
Jarecki, Tadeusz 1888-1955 *Baker 78, ConAmC*
Jarecki, Tadeusz 1889-1955 *NewGrD 80*
Jarl, Birger Charles 1923- *IntWWM 77, -80*
Jarman, Christopher John Bailey 1945- *IntWWM 80*
Jarman, Claude, Jr. 1933- *ForYSC*
Jarman, Claude, Jr. 1934- *FilmEn, FilmgC, HalFC 80, IntMPA 77, -75, -76, -78, -79, -80, MGM[port], MotPP, MovMk, What 4[port], WhoHol A*
Jarman, Herbert 1871-1919 *NotNAT B, WhThe*
Jarman, Joseph 1937- *EncJzS 70, IlEncJ*
Jarman, Thomas 1788?-1862 *OxMus*
Jarmels, The *RkOn*
Jarmin, Jill *WhoHol A*
Jarmusiewicz, Jan 1781-1844 *NewGrD 80*
Jarmyn, Jill *ForYSC*
Jarnach, Philipp 1892- *Baker 78, NewGrD 80, OxMus*
Jarnefelt, Armas 1869-1958 *Baker 78, MusMk, NewGrD 80, OxMus*
Jarnefelt, Maikki 1871-1929 *Baker 78*
Jarno, Georg 1868-1920 *Baker 78*
Jarno, Josef 1866-1932 *EncWT*
Jarnovic, Ivan Mane *NewGrD 80*
Jarnovicki, Ivan Mane *NewGrD 80*
Jarnowick, Giovanni *Baker 78*
Jarnowick, Ivan Mane *NewGrD 80*
Jarnowick, Pierre Louis Hus-Desforges *Baker 78*
Jarnowick, Pierre-Louis Hus-Desforges *NewGrD 80*
Jaroch, Jiri 1920- *Baker 78, NewGrD 80*
Jaronski, Feliks 1823-1895 *NewGrD 80*
Jaroslawzeff, W *Film 2*
Jaroslow, Ruth *WhoHol A*
Jaroszewski, Andrzej 1938- *IntWWM 77*
Jarov, Sergei 1896- *Baker 78*
Jarratt, Alfred *IntMPA 77, -75, -76, -78, -79, -80*
Jarratt, Howard Marrug 1912- *IntWWM 77, -80*
Jarre, Maurice 1924- *Baker 78, CmMov, DcFM, FilmEn, FilmgC, HalFC 80, IntMPA 77, -75, -76, -78, -79, -80, MusMk, NewGrD 80, OxFilm, WorEFlm*
Jarreau, Al *ConMuA 80A*
Jarred, Mary 1899- *NewGrD 80*
Jarrel, Stig 1910- *FilmEn*
Jarrett, Art 1909- *BgBands 74, CmpEPM*
Jarrett, Arthur L 1888-1960 *WhScrn 74, -77, WhoHol B*
Jarrett, Dan 1894-1938 *WhScrn 74, -77, WhoHol B*
Jarrett, Henry C d1886 *NotNAT B*
Jarrett, Henry C d1903 *NotNAT B*
Jarrett, Jack Marius 1934- *ConAmC*
Jarrett, James Leon 1942- *IntWWM 77*
Jarrett, Keith 1945- *BiDAmM, ConAmC, EncJzS 70, IlEncJ*
Jarrico, Paul 1915- *IntMPA 77, -75, -76, -78, -79, -80*
Jarriel, Tom *NewYTET*
Jarrott, Charles 1927- *FilmEn, FilmgC, HalFC 80, IlWWBF, IntMPA 77, -75, -76, -78, -79, -80*
Jarry, Alfred 1873-1907 *CnMD, CnThe, DcPup, EncWT, Ent, McGEWD, ModWD, NotNAT B, OxThe, REnWD[port]*
Jarva, Risto 1934- *WorEFlm[port]*
Jarvis, Al d1970 *CmpEPM*
Jarvis, Al 1909-1970 *AmSCAP 66, -80*
Jarvis, Al 1910-1970 *WhScrn 74, -77, WhoHol B*
Jarvis, Barbara A *WomWMM B*
Jarvis, Brian Taylor 1953- *AmSCAP 80*
Jarvis, Caleb Edward *WhoMus 72*
Jarvis, Charles *OxMus*
Jarvis, Charles H 1837-1895 *BiDAmM*
Jarvis, Charles W 1809?-1871 *BiDAmM*
Jarvis, Clifford 1941- *EncJzS 70*
Jarvis, Donald 1923- *CreCan 1*
Jarvis, Edward Keith 1939- *IntWWM 77, -80*
Jarvis, Gerald 1930- *WhoMus 72*
Jarvis, Jane *AmSCAP 80*
Jarvis, Jean 1903-1933 *WhScrn 74, -77, WhoHol B*
Jarvis, Laura E 1866-1933 *WhScrn 74, -77*
Jarvis, Lilian 1931- *CreCan 2, DancEn 78*
Jarvis, Lucy *NewYTET*
Jarvis, Robert C 1892-1971 *WhScrn 74, -77, WhoHol B*
Jarvis, Roger Stanley 1943- *IntWWM 77, -80*
Jarvis, Sidney *Film 2*
Jarvis, Sydney 1881-1939 *WhScrn 74, -77, WhoHol B*
Jarzebski, Adam d1649? *NewGrD 80*
Jarzebski, Pawel 1948- *EncJzS 70*
Jashenko, Elena *WomWMM*
Jasinski, Roman 1912- *CnOxB, DancEn 78*
Jasmin, Andre 1922- *CreCan 2*
Jasmin, Claude 1930- *CreCan 2*
Jasmina, Arthur *Film 2*
Jasmyn, Joan 1898-1955 *AmSCAP 66[port]*
Jasny, Vojtech 1925- *DcFM, FilmEn, WorEFlm[port]*
Jason, Alfred P 1914- *AmSCAP 66, -80*
Jason, Daniel *AmSCAP 80*
Jason, David 1940- *HalFC 80*
Jason, Leigh 1904-1979 *FilmEn, FilmgC, HalFC 80, IntMPA 77, -75, -76, -78, -79*
Jason, Mitchell *WhoHol A*
Jason, Rick *MotPP, WhoHol A*
Jason, Rick 1926- *ForYSC, IntMPA 77, -75, -76, -78, -79, -80*
Jason, Rick 1929- *FilmgC, HalFC 80*
Jason, Sybil 1929- *FilmEn, FilmgC, ForYSC, HalFC 80, ThFT[port], WhoHol A*
Jason, Will 1899-1970 *FilmgC, HalFC 80*
Jason, Will 1910- *AmSCAP 66, -80, CmpEPM, FilmEn*
Jaspar, Bobby 1926-1963 *CmpEPM*
Jaspar, Robert B 1926-1963 *BiDAmM*
Jasper, Bella 1933- *WhoOp 76*
Jasper, Suzanne 1945- *WomWMM B*
Jasper, Thena *Film 2*
Jasset, Victorin 1862-1913 *DcFM, FilmEn, WorEFlm*
Jassim, Linda *WomWMM A, -B*
Jasspe, Arthur *NatPD[port]*
Jaubert, Maurice 1900-1940 *Baker 78, DcFM, FilmEn, FilmgC, HalFC 80, NewGrD 80, OxFilm, WorEFlm*
Jaudenes, Jose Alvares Lepe 1891-1967 *WhScrn 74, -77*
Jaufre Rudel *NewGrD 80*
Jauhianen, Lauri Kustaa 1925- *IntWWM 77*
Jausions, Dom Paul 1834-1870 *Baker 78*
Javits, Joan *AmSCAP 80*
Javits, Joan 1928- *AmSCAP 66*
Javor, Pal 1902-1959 *WhScrn 74, -77*
Javor, Paul d1959 *WhoHol B*
Jaworek, Jozef 1756-1840 *NewGrD 80*
Jawurek, Jozef 1756-1840 *NewGrD 80*
Jaxon, Frankie 1895- *BluesWW[port], CmpEPM*
Jaxon, Half Pint 1895- *WhoJazz 72*
Jay, Arnold *AmSCAP 80*
Jay, Dorothy 1897- *WhThe*
Jay, Ernest d1957 *WhoHol B*
Jay, Ernest 1893-1957 *NotNAT B, WhScrn 77, WhThe*
Jay, Ernest 1894-1957 *FilmgC, HalFC 80, WhScrn 74*
Jay, Griffin *WhoHrs 80*
Jay, Harriet 1863-1932 *NotNAT B*
Jay, Harriett 1863-1932 *WhThe*
Jay, Isabel 1879-1927 *NotNAT B, WhThe*
Jay, Jean *Film 2*
Jay, John Herbert 1871-1942 *NotNAT B, WhThe*
Jay, Morty 1924- *IntMPA 77, -75, -76, -78, -79, -80*
Jay, Penny 1930- *BiDAmM*
Jay And The Americans *BiDAmM, ConMuA 80A, RkOn[port]*
Jay And The Techniques *RkOn 2[port]*
Jay And The Techniques *BiDAmM*
Jaye, Henry *NewGrD 80*
Jaye, Jerry *AmSCAP 80, RkOn 2[port]*
Jayhawks, The *RkOn*
Jayne, Jennifer 1935?- *WhoHrs 80*
Jayne, Mitch 1930- *BiDAmM, EncFCWM 69*
Jayne, Susan *WhoHol A*
Jaynetts, The *RkOn*
Jayston, Michael 1936- *FilmgC, HalFC 80, WhoHol A, WhoThe 72, -77*
Jazz Composers Orchestra *BiDAmM*
Jazz Corp, The *BiDAmM*
Jazz Crusaders *BiDAmM*
Jazz Ensemble *BiDAmM*
Jazz Messengers *BiDAmM, IlEncJ*
Jcoa *EncJzS 70*
Jeakins, Dorothy 1914- *BiE&WWA, NotNAT*
Jean *Film 1*
Jean De Chartreux *NewGrD 80*
Jean De Hollande *NewGrD 80*
Jean De Namur *NewGrD 80*
Jean De Noyers *NewGrD 80*
Jean, Madame *Film 2*
Jean Paul 1763-1825 *NewGrD 80*
Jean, Claude Petit *NewGrD 80*
Jean, Elsie 1907-1953 *AmSCAP 66, -80*
Jean, Gloria *MotPP*
Jean, Gloria 1926- *FilmEn, What 4[port]*
Jean, Gloria 1927- *ThFT[port]*
Jean, Gloria 1928- *CmpEPM, FilmgC, ForYSC, HalFC 80, MovMk[port], WhoHol A*
Jean, Nelson 1902- *NewOrJ*

Jean, Norma 1938- *BiDAmM, CounME 74[port], -74A, EncFCWM 69*
Jean, Ulysses 1905?- *NewOrJ*
Jean-Aubry, Georges 1882-1949 *Baker 78, NewGrD 80*
Jeanette, Gertrude 1918- *BlkAmP, DrBlPA*
Jeanette, Joe *BlksB&W C*
Jeanmaire *WhoHol A*
Jeanmaire, Renee 1924- *CnOxB*
Jeanmaire, Renee 1925- *DancEn 78[port]*
Jeanmaire, Zizi 1924- *BiE&WWA, FilmEn, FilmgC, HalFC 80*
Jeanmarie, Renee *MotPP*
Jeanneret, Albert 1886- *Baker 78*
Jeannette, Gertrude *MorBAP*
Jeannin, Jules Cecilien 1866-1933 *Baker 78, NewGrD 80*
Jeans, Isabel 1891- *FilmAG WE, FilmEn, Film 1, -2, FilmgC, ForYSC, HalFC 80, IlWWBF, Vers B[port], WhoHol A, WhoThe 72, -77*
Jeans, Ronald 1887- *WhThe*
Jeans, Susi 1911- *IntWWM 77, -80, NewGrD 80, WhoMus 72*
Jeans, Ursula 1906-1973 *FilmEn, Film 2, FilmgC, ForYSC, HalFC 80, IlWWBF, NotNAT B, PlP&P, WhScrn 77, WhThe, WhoHol B, WhoThe 72*
Jeanson, Bo Gunnar 1898-1939 *Baker 78*
Jeanson, Henri 1900- *HalFC 80*
Jeanson, Henri 1900-1970 *DcFM, FilmEn, FilmgC, WorEFlm*
Jeapes, Constance *WhoMus 72*
Jeayes, Allan 1885-1963 *Film 2, FilmgC, HalFC 80, NotNAT B, WhScrn 74, -77, WhThe, WhoHol B*
Jebb, John 1805-1885 *OxMus*
Jebb, John 1805-1886 *NewGrD 80*
Jebe, Halfdan 1868?-1937 *NewGrD 80*
Jebson, Peter Frederick 1950- *IntWWM 77, -80*
Jecks, Clara d1951 *NotNAT B, WhThe*
Jedd, Gerry 1924-1962 *NotNAT B*
Jedlicka, Dalibor 1929- *WhoOp 76*
Jedliczka, Ernst 1855-1904 *Baker 78*
Jedlizka, Marie *NewGrD 80*
Jedrzykiewicz, Zofia 1923- *IntWWM 77, -80*
Jedynak, Eddie Stanley 1922- *AmSCAP 80*
Jedynak, Edward S 1922- *AmSCAP 66*
Jeep, Johann 1581?-1644 *NewGrD 80*
Jeep, Johannes 1581?-1644 *Baker 78, NewGrD 80*
Jeffee, Saul 1918- *IntMPA 77, -75, -76, -78, -79, -80*
Jefferies, Douglas 1884-1959 *NotNAT B, WhThe, WhoHol B*
Jefferies, James J *Film 2*
Jefferies, Stephen 1951- *CnOxB*
Jeffers, John 1860-1939 *BiDAmM*
Jeffers, John S 1874-1939 *WhScrn 74, -77*
Jeffers, Robinson 1887-1962 *CnMD, EncWT, McGEWD, ModWD, NotNAT A, -B*
Jeffers, Ronald H 1943- *CpmDNM 74, -75, ConAmC*
Jeffers, Russell Lee 1946- *AmSCAP 80*
Jeffers, William L 1898-1959 *WhScrn 74, -77, WhoHol B*
Jefferson *RkOn 2A*
Jefferson, Andrew 1912- *NewOrJ[port]*
Jefferson, Anetta G *MorBAP*
Jefferson, Ben *PlP&P A[port]*
Jefferson, Blind Lemon 1889?-1930 *CmpEPM*
Jefferson, Blind Lemon 1897-1930 *BiDAmM, DrBlPA, IlEncJ, NewGrD 80*
Jefferson, Bonnie 1919- *BluesWW*
Jefferson, Charles Burke 1851-1908 *NotNAT B, OxThe*
Jefferson, Cornelia Frances Thomas 1796-1849 *NotNAT B, OxThe*
Jefferson, Daisy 1889-1967 *WhScrn 77, WhoHol B*
Jefferson, Eddie 1918- *EncJzS 70*
Jefferson, Edgar 1918- *EncJzS 70*
Jefferson, Herbert, Jr. 1946- *DrBlPA*
Jefferson, Herbert Farjeon 1887-1945 *OxThe*
Jefferson, Hilton 1903-1968 *BiDAmM, CmpEPM, EncJzS 70, IlEncJ, WhoJazz 72*
Jefferson, Hilton W 1902-1968 *WhScrn 74, -77, WhoHol B*
Jefferson, Joseph 1774-1832 *BiDAmM, EncWT, FamA&A[port], NotNAT B, OxThe, PlP&P[port]*
Jefferson, Joseph 1804-1842 *NotNAT B, OxThe*
Jefferson, Joseph 1829-1905 *EncWT, Ent, FamA&A, Film 1, NotNAT A, -B, OxThe, PlP&P[port], REnWD[port], WhScrn 77, WhoHol B*
Jefferson, Joseph Warren d1919 *NotNAT B*
Jefferson, Lemon Blind 1897-1929? *BluesWW[port]*
Jefferson, Maceo B 1900?- *WhoJazz 72*
Jefferson, Meriel Kathleen *IntWWM 77, -80, WhoMus 72*
Jefferson, Michael Graham 1927- *ConAmC*
Jefferson, Thomas 1732-1797 *EncWT, NotNAT B*
Jefferson, Thomas 1732-1807 *OxThe*
Jefferson, Thomas 1859-1923 *Film 1, -2*
Jefferson, Thomas 1859-1932 *FilmEn, NotNAT B, TwYS, WhScrn 74, -77, WhoHol B*
Jefferson, Thomas 1923- *NewOrJ*
Jefferson, William *Film 1*
Jefferson, William Winter d1946 *NotNAT B, WhScrn 77*
Jefferson Airplane *BiDAmM, ConMuA 80A[port], IlEncR[port], RkOn 2[port]*
Jefferson Starship *ConMuA 80A[port], RkOn 2[port]*
Jeffery, Robert Ernest Lee 1915-1976 *BluesWW[port]*
Jeffery, William 1949- *AmSCAP 80*
Jefferys, Charles *NewGrD 80*
Jefferys, Charles William 1869-1951 *CreCan 2*
Jefford, Barbara *ForYSC, WhoHol A*
Jefford, Barbara 1930- *BiE&WWA, CnThe, NotNAT, WhoThe 72, -77*
Jefford, Barbara 1931- *FilmgC, HalFC 80*
Jefford, Frances *AmSCAP 80*
Jeffrey, Herb 1916- *DrBlPA*
Jeffrey, Herbert *BlksB&W C*
Jeffrey, Joe, Group *RkOn 2A[port]*
Jeffrey, John Albert 1855-1929 *BiDAmM*
Jeffrey, Michael 1895-1960 *WhScrn 74, -77, WhoHol B*
Jeffrey, Nat *AmSCAP 80*
Jeffrey, Paul H 1933- *EncJzS 70*
Jeffrey, Peter 1929- *FilmgC, HalFC 80, WhoHol A, WhoThe 77*
Jeffrey, Walter Roy 1921- *IntWWM 80*
Jeffreys, Anne *IntMPA 77, -75, -76, -78, -79, -80, MotPP*
Jeffreys, Anne 1923- *FilmEn, FilmgC, ForYSC, HalFC 80, MovMk, WhoHol A, WhoThe 72, -77*
Jeffreys, Anne 1928- *BiE&WWA, NotNAT*
Jeffreys, Celia 1948- *WhoOp 76*
Jeffreys, Ellis d1943 *WhoHol B*
Jeffreys, Ellis 1868-1943 *WhoStg 1906, -1908*
Jeffreys, Ellis 1872-1943 *NotNAT B, WhThe*
Jeffreys, Ellis 1877-1943 *WhScrn 74, -77*
Jeffreys, George d1685 *NewGrD 80*
Jeffreys-Goodfriend, Ida d1926 *NotNAT B*
Jeffries, Fran *ForYSC, WhoHol A*
Jeffries, George d1685 *Baker 78, OxMus*
Jeffries, Herb *AmSCAP 66*
Jeffries, Herb 1912?- *CmpEPM*
Jeffries, Herb 1916- *DrBlPA*
Jeffries, James J 1875-1953 *Film 1, -2, WhScrn 77*
Jeffries, Jay *AmSCAP 80*
Jeffries, Lang *ForYSC, WhoHol A*
Jeffries, Lionel 1926- *FilmEn, FilmgC, ForYSC, HalFC 80, IlWWBF[port], IntMPA 77, -75, -76, -78, -79, -80, MovMk, WhoHol A, WhoHrs 80[port]*
Jeffries, Matthew *NewGrD 80*
Jeffries, Maud 1869-1946 *NotNAT B, WhThe*
Jeffries, Maud 1870- *WhoStg 1906, -1908*
Jeffrys, George d1755 *NotNAT B*
Jehan *NewGrD 80*
Jehan Bretel *NewGrD 80*
Jehan De Braine 1200?-1240 *NewGrD 80*
Jehan De Grieviler *NewGrD 80*
Jehan De Lescurel *NewGrD 80*
Jehan De Nuevile 1200?-1250? *NewGrD 80*
Jehan De Trie 1225?-1302? *NewGrD 80*
Jehan De Villeroye *NewGrD 80*
Jehan Des Murs 1300?-1350? *NewGrD 80*
Jehan I, Le Roux, Comte De Bretagne 1217-1250 *NewGrD 80*
Jehan Lebeuf D'Abbeville En Pontieu *NewGrD 80*
Jehan L'Orgeneur *NewGrD 80*
Jehan, Claude Petit *NewGrD 80*
Jehan, Marie-Therese 1944- *IntWWM 77, -80*
Jehanne, Edith *Film 2*
Jehannot De L'Escurel d1304 *NewGrD 80*
Jehin, Francois 1839-1899 *Baker 78*
Jehin-Prume, Francois 1839-1899 *NewGrD 80*
Jehin-Prume, Frantz 1839-1899 *NewGrD 80*
Jehlinger, Charles 1866-1952 *NotNAT B*
Jelesnik, Eugene 1914- *AmSCAP 66*
Jelic, Vincenz 1596-1636? *NewGrD 80*
Jelic, Vincenzo 1596-1636? *NewGrD 80*
Jelic, Vinko 1596-1636? *NewGrD 80*
Jelich, Vincenz 1596-1636? *Baker 78, NewGrD 80*
Jelicich, Vincenz 1596-1636? *NewGrD 80*
Jelinek, Hanns 1901-1969 *Baker 78, NewGrD 80, OxMus*
Jelinek, Jerone 1931- *IntWWM 77, -80*
Jelinek, Josef *NewGrD 80*
Jelinek, Milena *WomWMM B*
Jelinek, Stanislav 1945- *IntWWM 77, -80*
Jelinkova-Kurkova, Danuse 1931- *IntWWM 77, -80*
Jellen, Alan 1927- *WhoMus 72*
Jellen, Joyce Linda 1925- *WhoMus 72*
Jellicoe, Ann 1927- *CnThe, ConDr 73, -77, CroCD, EncWT, McGEWD, ModWD, NotNAT, REnWD[port], WhoThe 72, -77*
Jelliffe, Rowena Woodham 1892- *BiE&WWA, NotNAT*
Jellinek, George 1919- *AmSCAP 80*
Jellinek, Irene 1910- *CreCan 1*
Jelly Beans *RkOn 2A*
Jelmoli, Hans 1877-1936 *Baker 78, NewGrD 80*
Jelonek, Leon 1916- *IntWWM 77, -80*
Jelski, Michal 1831-1904 *NewGrD 80*
Jelyotte, Pierre De 1713-1797 *NewGrD 80*
Jemnitz, Alexander 1890-1963 *NewGrD 80*
Jemnitz, Sandor 1890-1963 *Baker 78, DcCM, NewGrD 80*
Jencks, Richard W *NewYTET*
Jeney, Zoltan 1915- *IntWWM 77*
Jeney, Zoltan 1943- *Baker 78, DcCM, IntWWM 80, NewGrD 80*
Jenkins *BluesWW*
Jenkins, Allen d1974 *MotPP, WhoHol B*
Jenkins, Allen 1890?-1974 *WhScrn 77*
Jenkins, Allen 1900-1974 *FilmEn, FilmgC, ForYSC, HalFC 80, HolCA[port], IntMPA 77, -75, -76, -78, -79, -80, MovMk[port], Vers A[port], What 4[port]*
Jenkins, Arthur E, Jr. 1936- *AmSCAP 80*
Jenkins, Butch *MotPP*
Jenkins, Carol 1944- *DrBlPA*
Jenkins, Charles 1941- *IntMPA 77, -75, -76, -78, -79, -80*
Jenkins, Charles Francis 1867-1934 *FilmEn, OxMus*
Jenkins, Charles Francis 1868-1934 *DcFM, NewYTET*
Jenkins, Clarence C 1942- *AmSCAP 80*
Jenkins, Dan 1916- *IntMPA 77, -75, -76, -78, -79, -80*
Jenkins, David *NotNAT*
Jenkins, David 1848-1915 *Baker 78, NewGrD 80, OxMus*
Jenkins, David Ian 1949- *AmSCAP 80*
Jenkins, Edward Walker *ConAmC*
Jenkins, Elizabeth 1879-1965 *WhScrn 74, -77, WhoHol B*
Jenkins, Ella L 1924- *AmSCAP 66, -80*
Jenkins, Freddie Frederic Douglass 1906- *WhoJazz 72*
Jenkins, Freddy 1906- *BiDAmM*
Jenkins, George *BiE&WWA, IntMPA 77, -75, -76, -78, -79, -80, NotNAT, WhoThe 72, -77*
Jenkins, George 1915?- *FilmEn*
Jenkins, George 1917-1967 *WhoJazz 72*
Jenkins, Gordon *AmPS B*
Jenkins, Gordon 1910- *AmSCAP 66, -80,*

BiDAmM, CmpEPM
Jenkins, Gordon And Weavers *AmPS A*
Jenkins, Gus 1931- *BluesWW[port]*
Jenkins, Harry *NatPD[port]*
Jenkins, J W *Film 2*
Jenkins, Jackie 1937- *FilmEn, HalFC 80, MGM[port], MovMk, What 3[port]*
Jenkins, Jackie 1938- *FilmgC, ForYSC, WhoHol A*
Jenkins, John 1592-1678 *Baker 78, MusMk, NewGrD 80, OxMus*
Jenkins, John 1942- *IntWWM 80*
Jenkins, John Philip 1940- *WhoMus 72*
Jenkins, John Pickens 1916- *BluesWW[port]*
Jenkins, John Wesley 1859-1930 *BlksBF*
Jenkins, Joseph Willcox 1928- *AmSCAP 66, -80, ConAmC*
Jenkins, Joyce *WomWMM B*
Jenkins, Laurence L 1939- *IntWWM 80*
Jenkins, Leroy 1932- *EncJzS 70, IlEncJ*
Jenkins, Louis 1947- *AmSCAP 80*
Jenkins, Marvin Lee 1932- *BiDAmM*
Jenkins, Megan Mary 1934- *WhoMus 72*
Jenkins, Megs 1917- *FilmgC, HalFC 80, WhoHol A, WhoThe 72, -77*
Jenkins, Merril 1945- *IntWWM 77, -80*
Jenkins, Neil 1945- *IntWWM 77, -80*
Jenkins, Newell 1915- *IntWWM 77, -80, NewGrD 80*
Jenkins, Pat Sidney 1914- *WhoJazz 72*
Jenkins, Patricia Anne *CreCan 1*
Jenkins, Posey Frederic Douglass 1906- *WhoJazz 72*
Jenkins, R Claud 1878-1967 *WhThe*
Jenkins, Rae *WhoMus 72*
Jenkins, Ray H *What 1[port]*
Jenkins, Terry 1941- *IntWWM 77, -80*
Jenkins, Warren *WhoThe 72, -77*
Jenko, Davorin 1835-1914 *Baker 78, NewGrD 80*
Jenks, Abraham S 1820-1895 *BiDAmM*
Jenks, Alden Ferriss 1940- *Baker 78, CpmDNM 80, ConAmC*
Jenks, Frank d1962 *MotPP, NotNAT B, WhoHol B*
Jenks, Frank 1902-1962 *FilmEn, FilmgC, HalFC 80, WhScrn 74, -77*
Jenks, Frank 1903-1962 *ForYSC, Vers A[port]*
Jenks, Lulu Burns 1870-1939 *WhScrn 74, -77*
Jenks, Si 1876-1970 *Vers B[port], WhScrn 77, WhoHol B*
Jenks, Stephen 1772-1856 *BiDAmM, NewGrD 80*
Jenks, William Elliott 1946- *IntWWM 80*
Jenkyns, Peter Thomas Hewitt 1921- *IntWWM 77, -80*
Jennens, Charles 1700-1773 *NewGrD 80*
Jenner, Ann 1944- *CnOxB*
Jenner, Caryl 1917- *WhThe, WhoThe 72*
Jenner, George Harris 1943- *IntWWM 77*
Jenner, Gustav 1865-1920 *Baker 78*
Jenner, Robert William 1937- *IntWWM 77, -80, WhoMus 72*
Jenney, Jack 1910-1945 *BgBands 74[port], CmpEPM, WhoJazz 72*
Jenni, Donald *ConAmC*
Jennings, Al 1864-1961 *FilmEn, HalFC 80, WhScrn 74, -77, WhoHol B*
Jennings, Al 1864-1962 *Film 1, -2*
Jennings, Anna *Film 2*
Jennings, Claudia *WhoHol A*
Jennings, DeWitt 1879-1937 *Film 1, -2, ForYSC, HolCA[port], NotNAT B, TwYS, WhScrn 74, -77, WhoHol B*
Jennings, Dorothy L *PupTheA*
Jennings, Gertrude E d1958 *NotNAT B, WhThe*
Jennings, Gladys 1902- *Film 1, -2*
Jennings, Gladys 1903- *IlWWBF*
Jennings, Gordon 1900?-1953 *WhoHrs 80*
Jennings, Hilde *Film 2*
Jennings, Humphrey 1907-1950 *BiDFilm, -81, DcFM, FilmEn, FilmgC, HalFC 80, OxFilm, WorEFlm*
Jennings, Humphrey 1917-1950 *IlWWBF, -A*
Jennings, Jane *Film 2*
Jennings, Jerry 1936- *WhoOp 76*
Jennings, John 1933- *AmSCAP 66, -80*
Jennings, John Michael 1944- *IntWWM 77, -80*
Jennings, Patricia Prattis 1941- *BlkWAB[port]*
Jennings, Robert Leslie 1936- *WhoMus 72*
Jennings, Robert Maurice 1924- *ConAmTC*
Jennings, S E *Film 1*
Jennings, Talbot 1905?- *CmMov, FilmEn, IntMPA 77, -75, -76, -78, -79, -80*
Jennings, Waylon 1937- *BiDAmM, ConMuA 80A[port], CounME 74[port], -74A, EncFCWM 69, IlEncCM[port], IlEncR, RkOn 2[port], WhoHol A*
Jennings, William Stewart 1942- *AmSCAP 66, -80*
Jenny, Markus 1924- *IntWWM 77, -80, NewGrD 80*
Jenoure, Aida *WhThe*
Jens, Eleonore Henriette 1925- *IntWWM 77, -80*
Jens, Salome 1935- *BiE&WWA, FilmEn, FilmgC, ForYSC, HalFC 80, MotPP, NotNAT, WhoHol A, WhoThe 72, -77*
Jensch, Lothar 1916- *NewGrD 80*
Jensen, Adolf 1837-1879 *Baker 78, NewGrD 80, OxMus*
Jensen, Arthur 1925- *IntWWM 77*
Jensen, Authur 1925- *IntWWM 80*
Jensen, Eric Christian 1943- *ConAmC*
Jensen, Eugen *Film 2*
Jensen, Eulalie *Film 1, -2, TwYS*
Jensen, Frederick *Film 2*
Jensen, Gail Patricia 1949- *AmSCAP 80*
Jensen, Gordon 1951- *AmSCAP 80*
Jensen, Gustav 1843-1895 *Baker 78, OxMus*
Jensen, Henning Borge 1929- *IntWWM 77*
Jensen, Herluf 1919- *IntWWM 77, -80*
Jensen, James A 1944- *ConAmC*
Jensen, Karen *WhoHol A*
Jensen, Kris 1942- *RkOn*
Jensen, Lars 1943- *IntWWM 77*
Jensen, Ludvig Irgens 1894-1969 *Baker 78, NewGrD 80, OxMus*
Jensen, Niels Martin 1937- *NewGrD 80*
Jensen, Niels Peter 1802-1846 *Baker 78*
Jensen, Owen 1907- *WhoMus 72*
Jensen, Ronald Scott 1951- *AmSCAP 80*
Jensen, Sterling *WhoHol A*
Jensen, Svend Erik 1913- *CnOxB, DancEn 78*
Jensen, Wilma Hoyle 1929- *WhoMus 72*
Jenson, Arthur Clifford 1931- *IntWWM 77*
Jenson, Roy *ForYSC, WhoHol A*
Jentes, Harry 1897-1958 *AmSCAP 66, -80*
Jentsch, Walter 1900- *IntWWM 77, -80*
Jentzsch, Wilfried 1941- *NewGrD 80*
Jephcott, Samuel C 1944- *IntMPA 77, -76, -78, -79, -80*
Jephson, Robert d1803 *NotNAT B*
Jepp, Johannes *NewGrD 80*
Jeppesen, Knud 1892-1974 *Baker 78, DcCM, NewGrD 80, OxMus, WhoMus 72*
Jepson, Beryl 1920- *IntWWM 80*
Jepson, Harry Benjamin 1870-1952 *Baker 78, BiDAmM, ConAmC*
Jepson, Helen 1905- *Baker 78, WhoHol A*
Jepson, Helen 1906- *NewEOp 71*
Jepson, Helen 1907- *BiDAmM*
Jepson, Warner 1930- *ConAmC*
Jeremiah, Abram *OxMus*
Jeremias *NewGrD 80*
Jeremias, Bohuslav 1859-1918 *Baker 78, NewGrD 80*
Jeremias, Jaroslav 1889-1919 *Baker 78, NewGrD 80*
Jeremias, Josef Alois 1808-1883 *NewGrD 80*
Jeremias, Otakar 1892-1962 *Baker 78, NewGrD 80*
Jeremy, John *MorBAP*
Jeremy And The Satyrs *BiDAmM*
Jergens, Adele 1917- *FilmEn, What 5[port]*
Jergens, Adele 1922- *FilmgC, ForYSC, HalFC 80, IntMPA 77, -75, -76, -78, -79, -80, MotPP, WhoHol A*
Jergens, Diane *ForYSC, MotPP, WhoHol A*
Jergenson, Dale *ConAmC*
Jerger, Alfred 1889-1976 *CmOp, NewEOp 71, NewGrD 80*
Jerger, Wilhelm 1902-1978 *NewGrD 80*
Jeritza, Maria 1887- *Baker 78, CmOp, IntWWM 77, -80, MusSN[port], NewEOp 71, NewGrD 80, What 2[port]*
Jeritza, Mizzi 1887- *NewGrD 80*
Jermingham, Edward d1812 *NotNAT B*
Jerndorff, Klaus 1932- *IntWWM 77, -80*
Jernek, Karel 1910- *WhoOp 76*
Jernigan, Malcolm Lathon 1937- *IntWWM 77, -80*
Jerome 345?-420? *NewGrD 80*
Jerome Of Bologna *NewGrD 80*
Jerome Of Moravia *NewGrD 80, OxMus*
Jerome, Saint *OxMus*
Jerome, Ben M d1938 *NotNAT B*
Jerome, Daisy 1881- *WhThe*
Jerome, Edwin 1884-1959 *NotNAT B, WhScrn 74, -77, WhoHol B*
Jerome, Elmer 1872-1947 *WhScrn 77*
Jerome, Helen 1883- *WhThe*
Jerome, Henry *PupTheA*
Jerome, Henry 1917- *AmSCAP 66, -80, BgBands 74, CmpEPM*
Jerome, Jerome 1906-1964 *AmSCAP 66, -80*
Jerome, Jerome Klapka 1859-1927 *EncWT, HalFC 80, McGEWD[port], ModWD, NotNAT A, -B, OxThe, WhThe, WhoStg 1908*
Jerome, Jerry 1912- *CmpEPM, EncJzS 70, WhoJazz 72*
Jerome, M K 1893- *AmSCAP 66, -80, CmpEPM, Film 2*
Jerome, Maude Nugent 1877-1958 *AmSCAP 66, -80*
Jerome, Peter 1893-1967 *WhScrn 74, -77*
Jerome, Rowena 1890- *WhThe*
Jerome, Sadie 1876-1950 *NotNAT B, WhThe*
Jerome, William 1865-1932 *AmPS, AmSCAP 66, -80, BiDAmM, CmpEPM, NotNAT B, Sw&Ld B*
Jeronelle *PupTheA*
Jerrett, Jean 1924- *AmSCAP 66, -80*
Jerrold, Douglas William 1803-1857 *McGEWD[port], NotNAT B, OxThe*
Jerrold, Mary 1877-1955 *FilmgC, HalFC 80, NotNAT B, WhScrn 74, -77, WhThe, WhoHol B*
Jerrold, William Blanchard 1826-1884 *NotNAT B, OxThe*
Jersey, Lady 1785-1867 *OxMus*
Jersey, Gwen *WomWMM B*
Jersild, Jorgen 1913- *Baker 78, NewGrD 80*
Jerusalem, Ignacio 1710?-1769 *NewGrD 80*
Jervis-Read, Harold Vincent 1883-1945 *Baker 78*
Jesinghaus, Walter 1902-1966 *Baker 78*
Jeske, George 1891-1951 *WhScrn 74, -77, WhoHol B*
Jeske-Choinska-Mikorska, Ludmila 1849-1898 *NewGrD 80*
Jesse, Fryniwyd Tennyson d1958 *NotNAT B, WhThe*
Jesse, Stella 1897- *WhThe*
Jessel, George 1898- *AmPS B, AmSCAP 66, -80, BiE&WWA, CmMov, CmpEPM, EncMT, FilmEn, Film 1, -2, FilmgC, ForYSC, HalFC 80, IntMPA 77, -75, -76, -78, -79, -80, JoeFr[port], MovMk, NotNAT, -A, TwYS, WhoHol A, WhoThe 72, -77*
Jessel, Ian 1939- *IntMPA 77, -78, -79, -80*
Jessel, Leon 1871-1942 *Baker 78, NewGrD 80*
Jessel, Patricia 1920-1968 *BiE&WWA, NotNAT B, WhScrn 74, -77, WhThe, WhoHol B*
Jessel, Patricia 1921-1968 *FilmgC, HalFC 80, WhoHrs 80[port]*
Jessen, John Pagaard 1909- *IntWWM 77*
Jessett, Michael 1932- *WhoMus 72*
Jessett, Michael Peter 1931- *IntWWM 77, -80*
Jessner, Irene 1901- *IntWWM 77, -80*
Jessner, Irene 1909- *NewEOp 71*
Jessner, Irene 1910- *CreCan 1*
Jessner, Leopold 1878-1945 *CnThe, EncWT, Ent, NotNAT B, OxThe*
Jesson, Roy 1926- *WhoMus 72*
Jessop, George H d1915 *NotNAT B*
Jessua, Alain 1923- *WorEFlm*
Jessua, Alain 1932- *FilmEn, FilmgC, HalFC 80, OxFilm*
Jessup, Stanley 1878-1945 *NotNAT B, WhScrn 77*
Jessye, Eva 1895- *AmSCAP 66, -80, BiDAmM, ConAmC, DrBlPA*
Jester, G W *PupTheA*
Jesters, The *RkOn*

Jeter, Leonard 1881-1970 *BiDAmM*
Jethro Tull *ConMuA 80A, IlEncR, RkOn 2[port]*
Jett, Sheldon 1901-1960 *WhScrn 74, -77, WhoHol B*
Jeune, Claude Le *NewGrD 80*
Jeunehomme, Mademoiselle *OxMus*
Jeurissen, Herman G A 1952- *IntWWM 80*
Jevicsky, Ondrej *NewGrD 80*
Jevon, Thomas d1688 *NotNAT B, OxThe*
Jew Baby *WhScrn 77*
Jew Of Pesaro *DancEn 78*
Jewel, Betty *Film 2*
Jewel, Ian Douglas 1944- *IntWWM 77, -80, WhoMus 72*
Jewel, Isabel 1913- *Vers A[port]*
Jewel, Izetta 1883- *WhoStg 1908*
Jewel, John 1522-1571 *OxMus*
Jewell, Austin *Film 2*
Jewell, Isabel d1972 *ForYSC*
Jewell, Isabel 1909-1972 *FilmEn, ThFT[port]*
Jewell, Isabel 1910-1972 *MovMk[port], WhScrn 77, WhoHol B*
Jewell, Isabel 1913-1972 *FilmgC, HalFC 80*
Jewell, Izetta 1883- *WhThe*
Jewell, James *PupTheA*
Jewell, James 1929- *BiE&WWA, NotNAT*
Jewell, Lucina 1874- *BiDAmM*
Jewell, William A 1932- *AmSCAP 80*
Jewels, The *RkOn*
Jewett, Ethel *Film 1*
Jewett, Henry d1930 *NotNAT B, WhoStg 1906, -1908*
Jewett, Randolph 1603?-1675 *NewGrD 80*
Jewison, Norman 1926- *BiDFilm, -81, FilmEn, FilmgC, HalFC 80, NewYTET, OxFilm, WorEFlm*
Jewison, Norman 1927- *MovMk[port]*
Jewison, Norman P *IntMPA 77, -75, -76, -78, -79, -80*
Jewson, Frederick Bowen 1823-1891 *NewGrD 80*
Jez, Jakob 1928- *IntWWM 77, -80, NewGrD 80*
Jezek, Jaroslav 1906-1942 *Baker 78, NewGrD 80*
Jezewski, Zbigniew 1921- *IntWWM 77, -80*
Jezierski, Kazimierz *NewGrD 80*
Jeziorska, Wanda Maria 1929- *WhoMus 72*
Jhan *NewGrD 80*
Jhering, Herbert 1888-1977 *EncWT*
Jhung, Finis 1937- *CnOxB*
Jick *BluesWW*
Jiggs d1932 *WhScrn 77*
Jigsaw *RkOn 2[port]*
Jilek, Frantisek 1913- *IntWWM 77, -80, NewGrD 80, WhoOp 76*
Jiler, John 1946- *NatPD[port]*
Jiles, Albert 1905-1964 *NewOrJ*
Jiles, Albert, Sr. 1878?-1922? *NewOrJ*
Jiles, Clay 1880?-1927 *NewOrJ*
Jillana 1936- *DancEn 78*
Jim And Jesse *BiDAmM, CounME 74[port] -74A, IlEncCM*
Jim Crow *OxThe*
Jimenez, Jeronimo *NewGrD 80*
Jimenez, Jose *NewGrD 80*
Jimenez, Jose 1924- *RkOn*
Jimenez-Mabarak, Carlos 1916- *Baker 78*
Jiminez, Soledad 1874-1966 *WhScrn 74, -77, WhoHol B*
Jiminez, Soledad 1874-1967 *ForYSC*
Jiminez, Solidad 1874-1967 *Film 2*
Jindrak, Jindrich 1931- *IntWWM 77, -80, WhoOp 76*
Jindrich, Jindrich 1876-1967 *NewGrD 80*
Jingu, Miyoshi 1894-1969 *WhScrn 77, WhoHol B*
Jinkins, Gus *BluesWW*
Jinman, Cyril 1902- *WhoMus 72*
Jira, Milan 1935- *IntWWM 77, -80*
Jirak, K B 1891-1972 *NewGrD 80*
Jirak, Karel Boleslav 1891-1972 *Baker 78, ConAmC, MusMk, OxMus*
Jiranek, Jaroslav 1922- *NewGrD 80*
Jiranek, Josef 1855-1940 *Baker 78*
Jirasek, Ivo 1920- *Baker 78, IntWWM 77, -80*
Jirko, Ivan 1926-1978 *Baker 78, NewGrD 80*
Jiro, Manuel *NewGrD 80*
Jirous, Jiri 1923- *WhoOp 76*
Jirousek, Miroslav Vaclav 1903- *IntWWM 80*
Jirousek, Moroslav Vaclav 1903- *IntWWM 77*
Jirovec, Vojtech Matyas *NewGrD 80*
Jive Bombers, The *RkOn*
Jive Five, The *RkOn*
Jo Debillon *NewGrD 80*
Jo Jo Gunne *IlEncR, RkOn 2[port]*
Joachim, Amalie 1839-1899 *Baker 78*
Joachim, Heinrich 1910- *IntWWM 77, -80*
Joachim, Joseph 1831-1907 *Baker 78, BnBkM 80[port], MusMk[port], NewGrD 80[port], OxMus*
Joachim, Otto 1910- *Baker 78, CreCan 1, DcCM, IntWWM 80, NewGrD 80*
Joachim, Walter 1912- *CreCan 2*
Joad *PupTheA*
Joan Maria DaCrema *NewGrD 80*
Joan Of Arc *NewEOp 71*
Joannes Laskaris *NewGrD 80*
Joannon, Leo 1904-1969 *FilmEn, WorEFlm*
Joannoti, Camillo *NewGrD 80*
Joao IV 1604-1656 *Baker 78, NewGrD 80*
Joao De Badajos *NewGrD 80*
Joaquim, Manuel 1894- *NewGrD 80*
Job, Thomas 1900-1947 *NotNAT B, WhThe*
Jobe, Ben Anderson 1945- *AmSCAP 80*
Jobennardi, Bartolome *NewGrD 80*
Jobert *NewGrD 80*
Jobert, Jean 1883-1957 *Baker 78, NewGrD 80*
Jobert, Marlene 1943- *FilmAG WE[port], FilmgC, HalFC 80, WhoHol A*
Jobes, Ruth Elinor 1933- *IntWWM 77*
Jobim, Antonio Carlos 1927- *BiDAmM, EncJzS 70*
Jobin, Bernard d1594? *NewGrD 80*
Jobin, Bernhard d1594? *NewGrD 80*
Jobin, Bernhart d1594? *NewGrD 80*
Jobin, Louis 1845-1928 *CreCan 2*
Jobin, Raoul 1906-1974 *CmOp, CreCan 1, NewEOp 71, NewGrD 80*
Jobson, Edward *Film 2*
Joby, Hans 1884-1943 *WhScrn 74, -77, WhoHol B*
Jocelin De Dijon *NewGrD 80*
Jocelyn, Simeon 1746-1823 *BiDAmM, NewGrD 80*
Jochim, Anthony *ForYSC*
Jochsberger, Tzipora H 1920- *AmSCAP 80, ConAmC*
Jochum *NewGrD 80*
Jochum, Eugen 1902- *Baker 78, BnBkM 80, IntWWM 77, -80, NewEOp 71, NewGrD 80[port], WhoMus 72, WhoOp 76*
Jochum, Eugene 1902- *CmOp*
Jochum, Georg Ludwig 1909-1970 *Baker 78, NewGrD 80*
Jochum, George Ludwig 1909- *WhoMus 72*
Jochum, Otto 1898-1969 *Baker 78, NewGrD 80*
Jochum, Veronica *IntWWM 80*
Jodal, Gabor 1913- *Baker 78, NewGrD 80*
Joddrell, Richard Paul d1831 *NotNAT B*
Jode, Fritz 1887-1970 *Baker 78, NewGrD 80*
Jodelet 1600?-1660 *EncWT, Ent, OxThe*
Jodelle, Etienne 1532-1573 *EncWT, Ent, McGEWD, OxThe*
Jodimars, The *RkOn*
Jodimel, Claude *NewGrD 80*
Jodocus Pratensis *NewGrD 80*
Jodorowsky, Alexandro 1930- *WhoHrs 80*
Joel, Billy 1949- *ConMuA 80A, RkOn 2[port]*
Joel, Clara 1890- *WhThe*
Joel, Elizabeth *ConMuA 80B*
Joel, Lydia *BiE&WWA, DancEn 78*
Joel, William Martin 1949- *AmSCAP 80*
Joels, Merrill E *IntMPA 77, -75, -76, -78, -79, -80*
Joelson, Elliott W 1905- *IntWWM 77, -80*
Joerns, Helge O L 1941- *IntWWM 80*
Joffe, Alex 1918- *FilmEn*
Joffe, Charles H *IntMPA 77, -76, -78, -79, -80*
Joffe, Edward *IntMPA 77, -75, -76, -78, -79, -80*
Joffe, Shlomo 1909- *NewGrD 80*
Joffre, Madame *Film 2*
Joffre, Monsieur *Film 2*
Joffrey, Robert 1930- *CnOxB, DancEn 78[port]*
Johann Ernst, Prince Of Weimar 1696-1715 *NewGrD 80*
Johann, Hans *NewGrD 80*
Johann, Zita 1904- *FilmEn, ForYSC, HalFC 80, ThFT[port], What 4[port], WhThe, WhoHol A, WhoHrs 80*
Johannes Affligemensis *NewGrD 80*
Johannes Bacus Correcarius De Bononia *NewGrD 80*
Johannes Bosquet *NewGrD 80*
Johannes Chrysorrhoas, Saint 700?-754 *Baker 78*
Johannes Cuvellarius *NewGrD 80*
Johannes De Bosco *NewGrD 80*
Johannes De Burgundia *NewGrD 80*
Johannes De Erfordia *NewGrD 80*
Johannes De Florentia *NewGrD 80*
Johannes De Garlandia *NewGrD 80*
Johannes De Grocheo *NewGrD 80*
Johannes De Janua *NewGrD 80*
Johannes De Lymburgia *NewGrD 80*
Johannes De Meruco *NewGrD 80*
Johannes De Muris *NewGrD 80*
Johannes De Olomons *NewGrD 80*
Johannes De Quadris *NewGrD 80*
Johannes De Quatris *NewGrD 80*
Johannes De Sacro Buscho *NewGrD 80*
Johannes De Sacrobosco *NewGrD 80*
Johannes De Sarto *NewGrD 80*
Johannes Eriugena *NewGrD 80*
Johannes Filius Dei *NewGrD 80*
Johannes Fulginatis *NewGrD 80*
Johannes Gallicus *NewGrD 80*
Johannes Kepler *NewEOp 71*
Johannes Le Fauconer *NewGrD 80*
Johannes Le Petit *NewGrD 80*
Johannes Legalis *NewGrD 80*
Johannes Primarius *NewGrD 80*
Johannesen, Grant 1921- *Baker 78, ConAmC, IntWWM 77, -80, NewGrD 80, WhoMus 72*
Johannsen, Cary 1939-1966 *WhScrn 74, -77*
Johannsson, Anna 1860-1917 *CnOxB*
Johannsson, Bengt 1914- *DcCM*
Johannsson, Magnus Blondal 1925- *Baker 78, DcCM, IntWWM 77, -80*
Johanos, Donald 1928- *Baker 78, NewGrD 80*
Johansen, Aud 1930- *WhThe*
Johansen, David *ConMuA 80A*
Johansen, David Monrad 1888-1974 *Baker 78, NewGrD 80*
Johansen, Egil 1934- *EncJzS 70*
Johansen, Gunnar 1906- *Baker 78, IntWWM 80*
Johansen, Gunnar 1907- *ConAmC*
Johansen, Johan *NewGrD 80*
Johansen, Per 1939- *IntWWM 77, -80*
Johanson, Bryan 1951- *CpmDNM 78*
Johanson, Ernest Robert 1928- *AmSCAP 80*
Johanson, Sven-Eric 1919- *Baker 78, NewGrD 80*
Johansson, Anna 1860-1917 *DancEn 78*
Johansson, Bengt 1914- *Baker 78, IntWWM 77, -80, NewGrD 80*
Johansson, Bjorn Emanuel 1913- *IntWWM 77, -80*
Johansson, Christian 1817-1903 *CnOxB, DancEn 78*
Johansson, Gunde 1922- *IntWWM 80*
Johansson, Hans 1944- *WhoOp 76*
Johansson, Ingemar 1932- *What 4[port], WhoHol A*
Johansson, Jan 1931-1968 *NewGrD 80*
Johansson, Magnus Blondal 1925- *NewGrD 80*
Johansson, Rolf Ingemar 1939- *IntWWM 77*
Johansson, Ronny 1891- *DancEn 78*
John I 1350-1395 *NewGrD 80*
John IV 1604-1656 *NewGrD 80*
John XXII 1245?-1334 *OxMus*
John XXII 1245?-1334 *NewGrD 80*
John Chrysorrhoas 675?-749? *NewGrD 80*
John Chrysostom *NewGrD 80*
John Damascene 675?-749? *NewGrD 80*
John Of Damascus, Saint *NewGrD 80, OxMus*
John Of Fornsete d1238? *NewGrD 80, OxMus*
John Of Garland *NewGrD 80*
John Of Lublin *NewGrD 80*
John Of Salisbury 1115?-1180 *NewGrD 80*

John XIX, Pope *OxMus*
John Scotus Erigena 810?-877? *NewGrD 80*
John The Scot *NewGrD 80*
John Wright *DcPup*
John, Alex *WhoMus 72*
John, Alice d1956 *NotNAT B, WhoHol B*
John, Barbara *WomWMM*
John, Bertram *Film 2*
John, Elton 1947- *Baker 78, ConMuA 80A[port], HalFC 80, IlEncR[port], RkOn 2[port], WhoHol A*
John, Errol 1925?- *CnMD, ConDr 73, -77, DrBlPA, ModWD, MorBAP*
John, Evan 1901-1953 *NotNAT B, WhThe*
John, Evan B 1923- *WhoMus 72*
John, Georg *Film 2*
John, Geraint Llewellyn 1931- *WhoMus 72*
John, Graham 1887- *WhThe*
John, Little Willie d1968 *BiDAmM*
John, Patricia Spaulding 1916- *IntWWM 77, -80*
John, Robert *RkOn 2[port]*
John, Mrs. Robert *PupTheA*
John, Rosamund 1913- *FilmAG WE, FilmEn, FilmgC, HalFC 80, IlWWBF, WhThe, WhoHol A*
John Peel *OxMus*
Johner, Dominicus 1874-1955 *Baker 78, NewGrD 80*
Johnnie And Jack *EncFCWM 69*
Johnnie And Joe *RkOn[port]*
Johnny *AmSCAP 80, What 1[port]*
Johnny And Jack *IlEncCM[port]*
Johnny And Jack *BiDAmM*
Johnny And The Hurricanes *RkOn*
Johnova, Miroslava *NewGrD 80*
Johns, Al 1878-1928 *AmSCAP 66, -80*
Johns, Bertram *Film 2*
Johns, Brooke *Film 2*
Johns, Clayton 1857-1932 *Baker 78, BiDAmM*
Johns, Donald 1926- *ConAmC*
Johns, Emile d1842 *BiDAmM*
Johns, Emile 1800-1860 *Baker 78*
Johns, Eric 1907- *WhThe, WhoThe 72*
Johns, Erik 1927- *AmSCAP 80*
Johns, Florence *Film 2*
Johns, Glyn *ConMuA 80B*
Johns, Glynis 1923- *BiE&WWA, FilmAG WE, FilmEn, FilmgC, ForYSC, HalFC 80, IlWWBF[port], IntMPA 77, -75, -76, -78, -79, -80, MotPP, MovMk[port], NotNAT, OxFilm, WhoHol A, WhoHrs 80[port], WhoThe 72, -77*
Johns, Harriette 1921- *WhoHol A, WhoThe 72, -77*
Johns, Jasper 1930- *CnOxB*
Johns, Louis Edgar 1886- *ConAmC*
Johns, Malcolm Maclean 1915- *IntWWM 77*
Johns, Mark 1919- *IntMPA 77, -75, -76, -78*
Johns, Mervyn 1899- *FilmEn, FilmgC, HalFC 80, IlWWBF, IntMPA 77, -75, -76, -78, -79, -80, WhoHol A, WhoThe 72, -77*
Johns, Rosalinda Jill 1950- *AmSCAP 80*
Johns, Sammy 1946- *RkOn 2[port]*
Johnsen, Hallvard Olav 1916- *Baker 78, IntWWM 80, NewGrD 80*
Johnsen, Henrik Philip 1717-1779 *NewGrD 80*
Johnsen, Hinrich Philip 1717-1779 *NewGrD 80*
Johnsen, Stanley Allen 1955- *AmSCAP 80*
Johnson, A Emory 1894-1960 *WhScrn 74, -77*
Johnson, Agnes *WomWMM*
Johnson, Albert 1910-1967 *BiE&WWA, NotNAT B*
Johnson, Albert E 1912- *BiE&WWA, NotNAT*
Johnson, Albert J 1910- *BiDAmM, EncJzS 70*
Johnson, Albertus Wayne 1942- *AmSCAP 80*
Johnson, Alfred *ConAmC*
Johnson, Alma *PupTheA*
Johnson, Alonzo 1889-1970 *BluesWW[port]*
Johnson, Alphonse 1900?- *NewOrJ*
Johnson, Alvin H 1914- *NewGrD 80*
Johnson, Ann *Film 2*
Johnson, Ann M 1921- *AmSCAP 80*
Johnson, Anne Spear 1916- *AmSCAP 80*
Johnson, Arch 1923- *ForYSC, WhoHol A*
Johnson, Arnold *DrBlPA*
Johnson, Arnold 1893-1975 *AmSCAP 66, -80, CmpEPM*
Johnson, Arte *HalFC 80, WhoHol A*
Johnson, Artemas Nixon 1817- *BiDAmM*
Johnson, Arthur V 1876-1916 *FilmEn, Film 1, TwYS, -A, WhScrn 77, WhoHol B*
Johnson, Ben *IntMPA 77, -75, -76, -78, -79, -80*
Johnson, Ben 1919- *CmMov, FilmgC, HalFC 80, HolCA[port], MovMk[port], WhoHol A*
Johnson, Ben 1920- *FilmEn, ForYSC*
Johnson, Bengt Emil 1936- *Baker 78, IntWWM 77, -80, NewGrD 80*
Johnson, Betty 1932- *RkOn*
Johnson, Big Bill *BluesWW*
Johnson, Bill 1872- *BiDAmM*
Johnson, Bill 1918-1957 *EncMT, WhScrn 77, WhThe, WhoHol B*
Johnson, Bill William 1912-1962? *WhoJazz 72*
Johnson, Bill William K 1905?-1955 *WhoJazz 72*
Johnson, Bill William Manuel 1872- *WhoJazz 72*
Johnson, Billy 1858-1916 *BlksBF*
Johnson, Blind Boy *BluesWW*
Johnson, Blind Willie 1902-1949 *BiDAmM*
Johnson, Blind Willie 1902?-1950? *NewGrD 80*
Johnson, Blues *BluesWW*
Johnson, Bruce Christopher 1953- *IntWWM 80*
Johnson, Bubber *RkOn*
Johnson, Budd 1910- *CmpEPM, EncJzS 70, IlEncJ, WhoJazz 72*
Johnson, Buddy 1870?-1927 *NewOrJ[port]*
Johnson, Buddy 1912- *RkOn*
Johnson, Buddy 1915- *AmSCAP 66, CmpEPM, WhoJazz 72*
Johnson, Bunk 1879-1949 *Baker 78, CmpEPM, IlEncJ, NewGrD 80, WhoJazz 72*
Johnson, Burges 1878-1963 *WhScrn 77*
Johnson, Calvert 1949- *IntWWM 80*
Johnson, Cammilla *Film 2*
Johnson, Carmencita *Film 2*
Johnson, Celeste Jean Everson 1953- *IntWWM 80*
Johnson, Celia 1908- *BiDFilm, -81, CnThe, FilmAG WE, FilmEn, FilmgC, ForYSC, HalFC 80, IlWWBF[port], IntMPA 77, -75, -76, -78, -79, -80, MotPP, MovMk, OxFilm, PlP&P, WhoHol A, WhoThe 72, -77*
Johnson, Charles *BlksBF*
Johnson, Charles d1748 *NotNAT B*
Johnson, Charles 1928- *AmSCAP 66, -80*
Johnson, Charles L 1876-1950 *AmSCAP 66, -80, BiDAmM*
Johnson, Charles Lavere 1910- *AmSCAP 80*
Johnson, Charlie 1891-1959 *CmpEPM, WhoJazz 72*
Johnson, Chic 1891-1962 *FilmEn, FilmgC, HalFC 80, JoeFr, MovMk[port], WhScrn 74, -77, WhThe, WhoHol B*
Johnson, Chick 1891-1962 *EncMT, ForYSC, NewOrJ[port]*
Johnson, Christopher *ConAmC*
Johnson, Chubby 1903-1974 *ForYSC, WhScrn 77, WhoHol B*
Johnson, Clint d1975 *WhoHol C*
Johnson, Clyde E 1930- *ConAmC*
Johnson, Dave Ernest 1890?-1932? *NewOrJ*
Johnson, David 1940- *DcCM*
Johnson, David Charles 1942- *IntWWM 80*
Johnson, David Earle 1938- *AmSCAP 80*
Johnson, David Ernst 1937- *IntWWM 77*
Johnson, David N 1922- *ConAmC*
Johnson, Delilah Deckert Foster 1908- *IntWWM 77*
Johnson, Dick Winslow *Film 2*
Johnson, Dink 1892-1954 *BluesWW, NewOrJ[port], WhoJazz 72*
Johnson, Dolores *Film 2*
Johnson, Don *WhoHol A*
Johnson, Donna Lee *WomWMM B*
Johnson, Dora Dean d1949 *BlksBF*
Johnson, Dotts 1913- *DrBlPA, WhoHol A*
Johnson, Duck 1888?-1931? *NewOrJ*
Johnson, Easy Papa *BluesWW*
Johnson, Edith 1895-1969 *FilmEn, Film 1, -2, MotPP, TwYS, WhScrn 74, -77*
Johnson, Edith North 1905?- *BluesWW*
Johnson, Edward *NewGrD 80, OxMus, PupTheA*
Johnson, Edward 1862-1925 *WhScrn 74, -77, WhoHol B*
Johnson, Edward 1878-1959 *Baker 78, BiDAmM, CmOp, MusSN[port], NewGrD 80*
Johnson, Edward 1881-1959 *NewEOp 71*
Johnson, Edward 1910-1961 *AmSCAP 66, -80*
Johnson, Elizabeth 1790-1810 *NotNAT B, OxThe*
Johnson, Elizabeth Clark *PupTheA*
Johnson, Ella 1923- *BluesWW[port]*
Johnson, Emanuel 1952- *AmSCAP 80*
Johnson, Emma Corella Piner 1935- *IntWWM 77*
Johnson, Emory d1960 *Film 1, -2, NotNAT B, WhoHol B*
Johnson, Erastus 1826-1909 *BiDAmM*
Johnson, Ernest W *Film 2*
Johnson, Ethel May d1964 *NotNAT B*
Johnson, Eugene *BlkAmP*
Johnson, Fannie *BluesWW*
Johnson, Felton *MorBAP*
Johnson, Florence 1902- *BiE&WWA, NotNAT*
Johnson, Francis 1792-1844 *BiDAmM*
Johnson, Frank 1792-1844 *NewGrD 80*
Johnson, Fred *WhoHol A*
Johnson, Freddy 1904-1961 *WhoJazz 72*
Johnson, Frederic H 1908-1967 *EncJzS 70*
Johnson, G Griffith 1912- *IntMPA 77, -75, -76, -78, -79, -80*
Johnson, Gene Eugene McClane 1902-1958 *WhoJazz 72*
Johnson, George 1876-1962 *MagIID*
Johnson, George 1910?- *WhoJazz 72*
Johnson, George Perry 1887- *DrBlPA*
Johnson, George W 1839-1917 *BiDAmM*
Johnson, Georgia Douglas 1886-1966 *BlkAmP, MorBAP*
Johnson, Gladys *BluesWW*
Johnson, Gloria *ConMuA 80B*
Johnson, Gordon A 1924- *CpmDNM 73, ConAmC*
Johnson, Grace Gray 1924- *IntWWM 77, -80*
Johnson, Graham Rhodes 1950- *IntWWM 80*
Johnson, Greer 1920-1974 *BiE&WWA, NotNAT B*
Johnson, Gus 1913- *BiDAmM, CmpEPM, EncJzS 70, IlEncJ, WhoJazz 72*
Johnson, Guy 1933- *IntWWM 77, -80*
Johnson, Hall 1887-1970 *Baker 78*
Johnson, Hall 1888-1970 *AmSCAP 66, -80, BiDAmM, BlkAmP, ConAmC, DrBlPA, MorBAP, NewGrD 80, NotNAT B, WhScrn 77, WhoHol B*
Johnson, Hall 1888-1971 *BlksBF[port]*
Johnson, Harold 1918- *EncJzS 70*
Johnson, Harold Ogden 1891-1962 *NotNAT B*
Johnson, Harold Victor 1918- *AmSCAP 66, -80, ConAmC*
Johnson, Harriett *ConAmC*
Johnson, Helen *WhoHol A*
Johnson, Henry *ConAmC*
Johnson, Henry 1908-1974 *BluesWW[port]*
Johnson, Herbert 1857-1904 *BiDAmM*
Johnson, Herman *BlkAmP, MorBAP*
Johnson, Horace 1893-1964 *AmSCAP 66, Baker 78, BiDAmM, ConAmC, WhoMus 72*
Johnson, Howard 1887-1941 *AmPS, AmSCAP 66, -80, BiDAmM, CmpEPM*
Johnson, Howard Lewis 1941- *EncJzS 70*
Johnson, Hunter 1906- *AmSCAP 66, -80, Baker 78, BiDAmM, ConAmC, DancEn 78, DcCM, NewGrD 80*
Johnson, Isa d1941 *NotNAT B*
Johnson, J Bond 1926- *IntMPA 77, -75, -76, -78, -79, -80*
Johnson, J C 1896- *AmSCAP 66, -80, CmpEPM*
Johnson, J George 1913- *AmSCAP 66, -80*
Johnson, J J 1924- *CmpEPM, DrBlPA, EncJzS 70, IlEncJ, NewGrD 80*
Johnson, J Rosamond *BlkAmP, MorBAP*
Johnson, J Rosamond 1873-1954 *AmSCAP 66, Baker 78, CmpEPM, NewGrD 80, NotNAT B*
Johnson, Jack 1878-1946 *BlksB&W C, WhScrn 77*

Johnson, James 1750?-1811 *NewGrD 80*
Johnson, James 1888?- *BluesWW*
Johnson, James 1905?-1972? *BluesWW*
Johnson, James 1946- *WhoOp 76*
Johnson, James A 1917-1976 *AmSCAP 66, -80*
Johnson, James Louis 1924- *BiDAmM, ConAmC, EncJzS 70, NewGrD 80*
Johnson, James Osie 1923- *BiDAmM*
Johnson, James P 1891-1955 *AmSCAP 66, -80, BiDAmM, CmpEPM, ConAmC A, IlEncJ, MusMk, NewGrD 80, WhoJazz 72*
Johnson, James Weldon 1871-1938 *AmSCAP 66, -80, Baker 78, BiDAmM, DrBlPA*
Johnson, Janet 1915- *WhThe*
Johnson, Jay 1928-1954 *WhScrn 74, -77, WhoHol B*
Johnson, Jay W 1903- *AmSCAP 66, -80*
Johnson, Jean *Film 2*
Johnson, Jimmy *ConMuA 80B*
Johnson, Jimmy 1876?-1937? *NewOrJ*
Johnson, Joe 1890?-1928 *NewOrJ*
Johnson, Joe 1942- *BluesWW*
Johnson, John *AmSCAP 80, NewGrD 80*
Johnson, John 1759-1819 *BiDAmM*
Johnson, John 1938- *DrBlPA*
Johnson, John Bird 1934- *IntWWM 77, -80*
Johnson, John Lester *BlksB&W C*
Johnson, John Rosamond 1873-1954 *BiDAmM, ConAmC, DrBlPA*
Johnson, Johnny *PlP&P A[port]*
Johnson, Johnny 1902?- *CmpEPM*
Johnson, Joseph Alan 1948- *IntWWM 77, -80*
Johnson, Karen *WomWMM A, -B*
Johnson, Katie 1878-1957 *FilmgC, HalFC 80, MotPP, NotNAT B, WhScrn 74, -77, WhoHol B*
Johnson, Kay 1904-1975 *FilmEn, Film 2, FilmgC, ForYSC, HalFC 80, HolP 30[port], MotPP, ThFT[port], WhThe, WhoHol C*
Johnson, Kay 1905?- *MovMk*
Johnson, Keg 1908-1967 *CmpEPM, EncJzS 70, WhoJazz 72*
Johnson, Kenneth, II 1912-1974 *WhoHol B*
Johnson, Kyle *DrBlPA*
Johnson, Lamont *IntMPA 77, -75, -76, -78, -79, -80, WhoHol A*
Johnson, Lamont 1920- *FilmEn, FilmgC, HalFC 80*
Johnson, Lamont 1922- *BiE&WWA, ForYSC, NotNAT*
Johnson, Lamont 1941- *AmSCAP 80*
Johnson, Laraine *WhoHol A*
Johnson, Larry 1938- *BluesWW[port]*
Johnson, LaRue 1908- *IntWWM 77, -80*
Johnson, Laurie *IntWWM 77*
Johnson, Laurie 1927- *IntMPA 77, -75, -76, -78, -79, -80*
Johnson, Lawrence *Film 2*
Johnson, Lemuel Charles 1909- *BluesWW[port], WhoJazz 72*
Johnson, Leslie 1933- *BluesWW[port]*
Johnson, Lloyd *PupTheA*
Johnson, Lockrem 1924-1977 *Baker 78, ConAmC, IntWWM 77, -80*
Johnson, Lonnie 1889-1970 *BiDAmM, BluesWW, CmpEPM, EncJzS 70, IlEncJ, NewOrJ, WhoJazz 72*
Johnson, Lorimer George 1859-1941 *Film 2, WhScrn 74, -77, WhoHol B*
Johnson, Louis *DancEn 78*
Johnson, Louis 1930- *CnOxB, NotNAT*
Johnson, Louis 1933- *DrBlPA*
Johnson, Lucile 1907- *AmSCAP 66, -80*
Johnson, Luther 1934-1976 *BluesWW[port]*
Johnson, Luther, Jr. 1939- *BluesWW[port]*
Johnson, Manzie Isham 1906-1971 *BiDAmM, EncJzS 70, WhoJazz 72*
Johnson, Margaret *BluesWW[port]*
Johnson, Margaret 1923-1967 *AmSCAP 80*
Johnson, Marion Pollock *WhoStg 1906, -1908*
Johnson, Marjorie Priscilla *PupTheA*
Johnson, Mark *AmSCAP 80*
Johnson, Martha *BluesWW*
Johnson, Martha Caroline *PupTheA*
Johnson, Martin 1884-1937 *DcFM, FilmEn, Film 1, -2, HalFC 80, TwYS, -A, -B, WhScrn 77*
Johnson, Marv 1938- *RkOn[port]*
Johnson, Mary *Film 2*
Johnson, Mary 1896- *FilmEn*
Johnson, Mary 1900?- *BluesWW[port]*
Johnson, Mary P *PupTheA*
Johnson, Meathead *BluesWW*
Johnson, Melodie *WhoHol A*
Johnson, Merritt 1902- *ConAmC*
Johnson, Michael F 1915- *IntMPA 77, -78, -79, -80*
Johnson, Moffat 1886-1935 *WhScrn 77*
Johnson, Molly 1903- *WhThe*
Johnson, Money 1918- *EncJzS 70, WhoJazz 72*
Johnson, Nancy 1934- *DancEn 78[port]*
Johnson, Nicholas 1934- *NewYTET*
Johnson, Nicholas 1947- *CnOxB*
Johnson, Noble 1897- *Film 1, -2, FilmgC, ForYSC, HalFC 80, TwYS, WhoHrs 80*
Johnson, Noble M 1881-1957? *BlksB&W[port], -C, DrBlPA*
Johnson, Noon 1903-1969 *NewOrJ[port]*
Johnson, Norris *Film 2*
Johnson, Nunnally 1897-1977 *BiDFilm, -81, CmMov, DcFM, FilmEn, FilmgC, HalFC 80, IntMPA 77, -75, -76, OxFilm, WorEFlm*
Johnson, Oliver 1892-1954 *BluesWW*
Johnson, Ollie 1892-1954 *BiDAmM*
Johnson, Orrin 1865-1943 *WhScrn 77, WhThe*
Johnson, Osa 1894-1953 *WhScrn 77, WomWMM*
Johnson, Osie 1923-1966 *CmpEPM*
Johnson, Otis 1910- *WhoJazz 72*
Johnson, Owen 1878- *WhoStg 1908*
Johnson, Page *WhoHol A*
Johnson, Pamela *WomWMM B*
Johnson, Patricia *WhoMus 72*
Johnson, Patricia Marion *WhoOp 76*
Johnson, Paul Alan 1946- *AmSCAP 80*
Johnson, Paul Harlen 1917- *AmSCAP 80*
Johnson, Pauline *Film 2*
Johnson, Pauline 1862?-1913 *CreCan 2*
Johnson, Pauline 1900- *IlWWBF*
Johnson, Penelope 1916-1979 *BlkWAB*
Johnson, Per-Olof 1928- *WhoMus 72*
Johnson, Pete 1904-1967 *AmSCAP 66, -80, BiDAmM, CmpEPM, EncJzS 70, IlEncJ, WhoJazz 72*
Johnson, Philip 1900- *WhThe*
Johnson, Plas John, Jr. 1931- *BiDAmM, EncJzS 70*
Johnson, Rafer 1935- *DrBlPA, FilmEn, FilmgC, ForYSC, HalFC 80, WhoHol A*
Johnson, Regena Fix 1911- *IntWWM 77, -80*
Johnson, Reginald Volney 1940- *BiDAmM*
Johnson, Richard 1927- *BiE&WWA, FilmAG WE[port], FilmEn, FilmgC, HalFC 80, IlWWBF[port], IntMPA 77, -75, -76, -78, -79, -80, MovMk, WhoHol A, WhoThe 72, -77*
Johnson, Richard 1929- *ForYSC*
Johnson, Richard Howie 1952- *AmSCAP 80*
Johnson, Rita d1965 *MotPP, WhoHol B*
Johnson, Rita 1912-1965 *FilmEn, FilmgC, HalFC 80, MGM[port], MovMk, ThFT[port]*
Johnson, Rita 1913-1965 *ForYSC, WhScrn 74, -77*
Johnson, Robert *OxMus*
Johnson, Robert 1490?-1560? *MusMk*
Johnson, Robert 1500?-1560? *NewGrD 80*
Johnson, Robert 1583?-1633 *MusMk, NewGrD 80*
Johnson, Robert 1583?-1634? *OxMus*
Johnson, Robert 1910?-1938 *ConMuA 80A*
Johnson, Robert 1911- *BlksB&W*
Johnson, Robert 1912?-1938 *BluesWW, NewGrD 80*
Johnson, Robert 1913-1937 *BiDAmM, IlEncJ*
Johnson, Robert C 1935- *IntWWM 77*
Johnson, Robert D 1940- *WhoOp 76*
Johnson, Robert Sherlaw 1932- *Baker 78, DcCM, IntWWM 77, -80, NewGrD 80, WhoMus 72*
Johnson, Rock *AmSCAP 80*
Johnson, Roger 1941- *AmSCAP 80, CpmDNM 75, ConAmC*
Johnson, Roy *MagIID*
Johnson, Roy Andrew 1936- *IntWWM 77*
Johnson, Roy Henry 1933- *ConAmC*
Johnson, Russell *IntMPA 77, -75, -76, -78, -79, -80, WhoHol A*
Johnson, Russell 1920?- *WhoHrs 80*
Johnson, Russell 1924- *ForYSC*
Johnson, Ruth *IntMPA 79*
Johnson, S Kenneth, II 1912-1974 *WhScrn 77*
Johnson, Samuel 1698?-1773? *NewGrD 80*
Johnson, Samuel 1709-1784 *DcPup, Ent[port], NotNAT B, OxMus, OxThe, PlP&P*
Johnson, Samuel 1822-1882 *BiDAmM*
Johnson, Sara *BluesWW*
Johnson, Searcy Lee 1908- *AmSCAP 66*
Johnson, Sessel Ann *Film 2*
Johnson, Sivert Bertil 1930- *EncJzS 70*
Johnson, Steve 1865?- *NewOrJ*
Johnson, Stuart 1936- *IntWWM 80*
Johnson, Stump *BluesWW*
Johnson, Susan 1927- *BiE&WWA, NotNAT*
Johnson, Swan 1908- *WhoJazz 72*
Johnson, Sy 1930- *EncJzS 70*
Johnson, Syl 1937- *BluesWW*
Johnson, Tefft 1887-1956 *Film 1, -2, TwYS A, WhScrn 77*
Johnson, Theodore Oliver, Jr. 1929- *IntWWM 77, -80*
Johnson, Thomas Arnold 1908- *IntWWM 77, -80, WhoMus 72*
Johnson, Thor 1913-1975 *Baker 78, BiDAmM, NewGrD 80*
Johnson, Tom 1939- *Baker 78, CpmDNM 78, -80, ConAmC*
Johnson, Tommy 1896?-1956 *BluesWW[port]*
Johnson, Tor 1903-1971 *WhScrn 77, WhoHol B, WhoHrs 80[port]*
Johnson, Van 1916- *BiDFilm, -81, BiE&WWA, CmMov, CmpEPM, FilmEn, FilmgC, ForYSC, HalFC 80, IntMPA 77, -75, -76, -78, -79, -80, MGM[port], MotPP, MovMk[port], OxFilm, WhoHol A, WhoThe 77, WorEFlm*
Johnson, Vel *MorBAP*
Johnson, Virginia D 1926- *AmSCAP 80*
Johnson, W Gerald d1963 *NotNAT B*
Johnson, Walter 1904- *BiDAmM, WhoJazz 72*
Johnson, Wayne Eaton 1930- *ConAmTC*
Johnson, William 1912-1960 *AmSCAP 66, -80*
Johnson, William 1916-1957 *NotNAT B, WhScrn 74, -77*
Johnson, William Alexander 1931?- *AmSCAP 66*
Johnson, William Allen 1816-1901 *NewGrD 80*
Johnson, William Bunk 1879-1949 *MusMk[port]*
Johnson, William Geary *NewGrD 80*
Johnson, William Manuel 1872-1975 *NewOrJ*
Johnson, Willie *NewGrD 80*
Johnson, Willie Geary 1879-1949 *BiDAmM, NewOrJ[port]*
Johnson, Willie Lee 1923- *BluesWW[port]*
Johnson, Woodrow Wilson 1915- *AmSCAP 80*
Johnson, Yank 1878?-1938 *NewOrJ*
Johnson Family Singers *BiDAmM*
Johnson-Hamilton, Joyce 1938- *IntWWM 80*
Johnsrud, Harold d1939 *NotNAT B*
Johnsson, Bengt 1921- *IntWWM 80, NewGrD 80*
Johnstad, Ellen Anna Elisa 1902- *IntWWM 77*
Johnston, Albert Chandler, Jr. 1925- *AmSCAP 66, -80*
Johnston, Albert Richard 1917- *IntWWM 80*
Johnston, Alison Aileen Annie 1916- *IntWWM 77, -80*
Johnston, Andrew *Film 2*
Johnston, Arthur James 1898-1954 *AmPS, AmSCAP 66, -80, CmpEPM, NotNAT B*
Johnston, Ben 1926- *CpmDNM 76, -77, ConAmC, DcCM, NewGrD 80*
Johnston, Benjamin Burwell, Jr. 1926- *AmSCAP 80, Baker 78, IntWWM 77, -80*
Johnston, Bob 1932- *AmSCAP 80, ConMuA 80B*
Johnston, David *IntWWM 77, -80*
Johnston, David Francis 1935- *WhoMus 72*
Johnston, Denis 1901- *BiE&WWA, CnMD, CnThe, ConDr 73, -77, EncWT, McGEWD[port], ModWD, NotNAT, OxThe, PlP&P, REnWD[port], WhThe*
Johnston, Donald O 1929- *AmSCAP 80, ConAmC*
Johnston, Edith 1895-1969 *WhoHol B*
Johnston, Eric A 1895-1963 *DcFM, FilmgC,*

HalFC 80
Johnston, Eric A 1896-1962 *FilmEn*
Johnston, Ernestine *WhoHol A*
Johnston, Francis Hans 1888-1949 *CreCan 1*
Johnston, Frank H 1888-1949 *CreCan 1*
Johnston, Frank Roderick 1931- *AmSCAP 80*
Johnston, Franz 1888-1949 *CreCan 1*
Johnston, Gene 1900-1966 *AmSCAP 80*
Johnston, Gene 1908- *AmSCAP 66*
Johnston, George Benson 1913- *CreCan 1*
Johnston, Gladys *Film 2*
Johnston, Henry Erskine 1777-1845 *OxThe*
Johnston, J L *Film 2*
Johnston, J W 1876-1946 *Film 1, -2, WhoHol B*
Johnston, Jack *ConAmC*
Johnston, James 1900?- *CmOp, NewGrD 80*
Johnston, James 1915- *CreCan 2*
Johnston, John W 1876-1946 *WhScrn 74, -77*
Johnston, Johnnie 1914- *CmpEPM*
Johnston, Johnny *WhoHol A*
Johnston, Johnny 1869-1931 *WhScrn 74, -77*
Johnston, Johnny 1915- *FilmEn*
Johnston, Johnny 1916- *ForYSC*
Johnston, Joy A 1937- *AmSCAP 80*
Johnston, Julanne 1906- *FilmEn, Film 1, -2, TwYS, WhoHol A*
Johnston, Julianne 1906- *ForYSC*
Johnston, Justine *BiE&WWA, NotNAT*
Johnston, Lora *PupTheA*
Johnston, Lorimer *Film 2*
Johnston, Margaret *IntMPA 77, -75, -76, -78, -79, -80, WhoHol A*
Johnston, Margaret 1917- *FilmgC, HalFC 80*
Johnston, Margaret 1918- *FilmEn, IlWWBF[port], WhoThe 72, -77*
Johnston, Mary *AmSCAP 80*
Johnston, Mary 1925- *AmSCAP 66*
Johnston, Moffat 1886-1935 *NotNAT B, WhThe*
Johnston, Oliver 1888-1966 *HalFC 80, WhScrn 74, -77, WhoHol B*
Johnston, Patricia 1922-1953 *AmSCAP 66, -80*
Johnston, Percy *BlkAmP*
Johnston, Renita *Film 2*
Johnston, Roger 1918-1958 *NewOrJ[port]*
Johnston, Suzanne *WomWMM A*
Johnston, Thomas 1708?-1767 *BiDAmM, NewGrD 80*
Johnston, Thomas Hamilton 1928- *IntWWM 77, -80*
Johnstone, Anna Hill 1913- *BiE&WWA, NotNAT*
Johnstone, Arthur Edward 1860-1944 *Baker 78*
Johnstone, Beryl d1969 *WhoHol B*
Johnstone, Clarence d1953 *NotNAT B*
Johnstone, David 1926- *IntMPA 80*
Johnstone, Elizabeth Leese *CreCan 2*
Johnstone, George Graham 1920- *WhoMus 72*
Johnstone, Gordon 1876-1926 *AmSCAP 66, -80*
Johnstone, Harry Diack 1935- *IntWWM 77, -80*
Johnstone, J B d1891 *NotNAT B*
Johnstone, John Alfred 1861-1941 *Baker 78*
Johnstone, Justine 1899- *Film 2, TwYS, WhThe*
Johnstone, Keith *ConDr 73, -77*
Johnstone, Lamar 1886-1919 *Film 1, WhScrn 77*
Johnstone, Madge d1913 *NotNAT B*
Johnstone, Maurice 1900-1976 *IntWWM 77, -80, NewGrD 80, WhoMus 72*
Johnstone, Ralph *PupTheA*
Johnstone, Thomas A 1888- *AmSCAP 66, -80*
Johnstone, Wesley 1912- *WhoMus 72*
Johnstone, William *WhoHol A*
Johnstone-Smith, George d1963 *NotNAT B*
Johst, Hanns 1890- *CnMD, EncWT, ModWD*
Joice, Celia Annie 1923- *WhoMus 72*
Joiner, Barbara d1961 *NotNAT B*
Joiner, Thomas Witherington 1954- *IntWWM 80*
Joiner Arkansas Junior High School Band *RkOn*
Joio, Norman Dello 1913- *MusMk*
Jokel, Lana Tse Ping *WomWMM B*
Jokinen, Erikki 1941- *Baker 78*
Jokinen, Erkki 1941- *NewGrD 80*
Jokinen, Urpo Oskari 1920- *IntWWM 77, -80*
Jokl, Georg 1896-1954 *Baker 78, ConAmC*
Jokl, Otto 1891-1963 *Baker 78, ConAmC*
Jolas, Belsy *CpmDNM 78*
Jolas, Betsy 1926- *Baker 78, BnBkM 80, DcCM, NewGrD 80, WomCom[port]*
Jolas, Elizabeth 1926- *NewGrD 80*
Jolivet, Andre 1905-1974 *Baker 78, BnBkM 80, CompSN[port], CnOxB, DcCM, NewGrD 80[port], OxMus, WhoMus 72*
Jolivet, Rita 1894- *Film 1, -2, TwYS, WhThe*
Jollage, Charles-Alexandre d1761 *NewGrD 80*
Jolley, Florence Werner 1917- *AmSCAP 66, -80, ConAmC*
Jolley, I Stanford *ForYSC, Vers A[port], WhoHol A*
Jolley, Stan 1926- *IntMPA 77, -75, -76, -78, -79, -80*
Jolly, Albert Rivers 1914- *WhoMus 72*
Jolly, Cynthia *WhoMus 72*
Jolly, George 1640-1673 *NotNAT B, OxThe*
Jolly, Pete 1932- *AmSCAP 66, BiDAmM, EncJzS 70*
Jolly, Peter 1932- *AmSCAP 80*
Jolson, Al d1950 *AmPS A, -B, MotPP, WhoHol B*
Jolson, Al 1882-1950 *CmMov*
Jolson, Al 1883?-1950 *EncWT, OxFilm*
Jolson, Al 1885-1950 *ForYSC*
Jolson, Al 1886-1950 *AmPS, AmSCAP 66, -80, BiDAmM, BiDFilm, -81, CmpEPM, EncMT, Ent[port], FamA&A[port], FilmEn, FilmgC, HalFC 80[port], MovMk[port], NewGrD 80, NotNAT A, -B, WhScrn 74, -77, WhThe, WorEFlm*
Jolson, Al 1888-1950 *Film 2, PlP&P[port]*
Jolson, Harry d1953 *NotNAT B*
Joltin, Jan *WomWMM B*
Joly, Simon 1524-1559? *NewGrD 80*
Joly, Simon 1952- *IntWWM 80*
Joly, Yves *DcPup*
Joly Braga Santos, Jose Manuel 1924- *IntWWM 80*
Jomelli, Niccolo 1714-1774 *NewGrD 80[port]*
Jomelli, Nicolo 1714-1774 *NewGrD 80[port]*
Jommelli, Niccolo 1714-1774 *Baker 78, BnBkM 80, GrComp[port], MusMk, NewEOp 71, NewGrD 80[port], OxMus*
Jommelli, Nicolo 1714-1774 *NewGrD 80[port]*
Jonak, Zdenek 1917- *Baker 78, IntWWM 77, -80*
Jonas, Alberto 1868-1943 *Baker 78, BiDAmM*
Jonas, Emile 1827-1905 *Baker 78, NewGrD 80*
Jonas, Joan *WomWMM B*
Jonas, Justus 1493-1555 *NewGrD 80*
Jonas, Maryla 1911-1959 *Baker 78*
Jonas, Nita *AmSCAP 66*
Jonas, Oswald 1897-1978 *Baker 78, NewGrD 80*
Jonasova, Jana 1943- *WhoOp 76*
Jonasson, Frank *Film 1, -2*
Joncheva, Galia Mitova 1946- *WhoOp 76*
Joncieres, Victorin De 1839-1903 *Baker 78, NewGrD 80*
Jonckers, Goessen *NewGrD 80*
Jones, Ada *CmpEPM*
Jones, Agnes *AmSCAP 80*
Jones, Al 1909- *BiE&WWA, NotNAT*
Jones, Alan 1907- *BiDAmM*
Jones, Alan Wynne 1942- *IntWWM 77, -80*
Jones, Albert *AmSCAP 80*
Jones, Allan *AmPS A, -B, MotPP, WhoHol A*
Jones, Allan 1907- *FilmgC, HalFC 80, HolP 30[port]*
Jones, Allan 1908- *CmpEPM, FilmEn, ForYSC, MovMk, OxFilm, What 5[port]*
Jones, Alton 1899-1971 *Baker 78, BiDAmM*
Jones, Andrew Vernon 1947- *IntWWM 77, -80*
Jones, Anissa 1958- *WhoHol A*
Jones, Arnold *MorBAP*
Jones, Arnold 1906- *WhoMus 72*
Jones, Arthur 1909- *AmSCAP 66, -80*
Jones, Arthur Hefin 1931- *WhoMus 72*
Jones, Arthur Morris 1889- *NewGrD 80*
Jones, Arthur Morris 1899- *IntWWM 77, -80*
Jones, Arthur Tabor *OxMus*
Jones, Augusta *BluesWW*
Jones, B B *BluesWW*
Jones, Barbara Ann 1948- *AmSCAP 66*
Jones, Barry 1893- *BiE&WWA, FilmgC, ForYSC, HalFC 80, IlWWBF, IntMPA 77, -75, -76, -78, -79, -80, MovMk, NotNAT, PlP&P, WhThe, WhoHol A*
Jones, Basil 1915- *WhoMus 72*
Jones, Bertram Llywelyn 1897- *IntWWM 80*
Jones, Betty *WhoOp 76*
Jones, Betty 1926- *CnOxB, DancEn 78*
Jones, Betty Hall 1911- *AmSCAP 80*
Jones, Biff 1930- *AmSCAP 66, -80*
Jones, Bill 1889-1940 *JoeFr*
Jones, Billy 1889-1940 *Film 2*
Jones, Birmingham 1937- *BluesWW[port]*
Jones, Bobby 1902- *What 1[port]*
Jones, Bobby 1928- *EncJzS 70*
Jones, Booker T 1944- *BiDAmM*
Jones, Brian 1943-1969 *ConMuA 80A, WhScrn 77*
Jones, Bris 1926- *NewOrJ[port]*
Jones, Bronwen Dilys 1927- *IntWWM 77, -80, WhoMus 72*
Jones, Brooks 1934- *BiE&WWA, NotNAT*
Jones, Bruce *ConAmTC*
Jones, Buck 1889-1942 *FilmEn, Film 1, -2, FilmgC, ForYSC, HalFC 80, MotPP, MovMk, NotNAT B, TwYS, WhScrn 74, -77, WhoHol B*
Jones, Buck 1891-1942 *CmMov, OxFilm*
Jones, Carmell 1936- *BiDAmM, EncJzS 70*
Jones, Carolyn *MotPP, WhoHol A*
Jones, Carolyn 1929- *FilmEn, FilmgC, ForYSC, HalFC 80, WhoHrs 80*
Jones, Carolyn 1933- *IntMPA 77, -75, -76, -78, -79, -80, MovMk[port]*
Jones, Charles *WhScrn 74*
Jones, Charles 1910- *AmSCAP 66, -80, Baker 78, BiDAmM, ConAmC, DcCM, NewGrD 80*
Jones, Charles 1931- *ConAmC*
Jones, Charles Martin 1912- *AmSCAP 80*
Jones, Charlotte *WhoHol A*
Jones, Chester d1975 *WhScrn 77, WhoHol C*
Jones, Chester 1913- *NewOrJ*
Jones, Christopher 1940- *ForYSC*
Jones, Christopher 1941- *FilmgC, HalFC 80, MotPP, WhoHol A*
Jones, Chuck *NewYTET*
Jones, Chuck 1912- *DcFM, FilmEn, IntMPA 77, -75, -76, -78, -79, -80, WorEFlm*
Jones, Chuck 1915- *FilmgC, HalFC 80*
Jones, Chuck 1942- *IntMPA 80*
Jones, Clarence M 1889-1949 *AmSCAP 66, -80*
Jones, Clark R 1920- *IntMPA 77, -75, -76, -78, -79, -80*
Jones, Claude 1901-1962 *BiDAmM, CmpEPM, WhoJazz 72*
Jones, Clifford 1900?-1947 *NewOrJ*
Jones, Collier *ConAmC*
Jones, Curtis 1906-1971 *BiDAmM, BluesWW[port]*
Jones, Curtis Ashy 1873-1956 *WhScrn 74, -77*
Jones, Daniel 1881- *OxMus*
Jones, Daniel Jenkyn 1912- *Baker 78, IntWWM 77, -80, NewGrD 80, OxMus, WhoMus 72*
Jones, Darby *WhoHrs 80*
Jones, Darius Eliot 1815-1881 *BiDAmM*
Jones, David *IntMPA 78*
Jones, David 1888?-1953 *NewOrJ*
Jones, David 1913- *IntMPA 77, -75, -76, -79, -80*
Jones, David 1934- *EncWT, WhoThe 72, -77*
Jones, David Henry, Jr. 1949- *AmSCAP 80*
Jones, David Hugh 1900- *AmSCAP 66, -80, ConAmC A*
Jones, David Hugh 1932- *IntWWM 77, -80, WhoMus 72*
Jones, Dean *MotPP, WhoHol A*
Jones, Dean 1933- *FilmgC, HalFC 80, WhoHrs 80*
Jones, Dean 1935- *BiE&WWA, FilmEn, ForYSC*
Jones, Dean 1936- *IntMPA 77, -75, -76, -78, -79, -80*
Jones, Deborah Anne Penkert 1954- *IntWWM 77*
Jones, Delia M 1931- *IntWWM 77*
Jones, Della 1946- *IntWWM 77, -80*
Jones, Dennis 1932- *CreCan 1*

Jones, Dick 1927- *FilmEn, ForYSC, WhoHol A*
Jones, Dill 1923- *EncJzS 70*
Jones, Dillwyn Owen 1923- *EncJzS 70*
Jones, Disley 1926- *WhoThe 72, -77*
Jones, Donald R 1922- *ConAmC*
Jones, Doris Goodrich *PupTheA*
Jones, Douglas Gordon 1929- *CreCan 1*
Jones, Douglas P, Jr. d1964 *NotNAT B*
Jones, Duane 1940?- *DrBlPA, WhoHrs 80[port]*
Jones, Dudley 1914- *WhoThe 72, -77*
Jones, E H 1925- *BlkAmP*
Jones, Eddie *Film 2*
Jones, Eddie 1926-1959 *BluesWW[port]*
Jones, Edgar *Film 1*
Jones, Edward *NewGrD 80*
Jones, Edward d1917 *NotNAT B, WhThe*
Jones, Edward 1752-1824 *Baker 78, NewGrD 80, OxMus*
Jones, Edward German *NewGrD 80*
Jones, Elayne 1929?- *BlkWAB[port]*
Jones, Elias Walter 1921- *WhoMus 72*
Jones, Elinor *WomWMM B*
Jones, Elizabeth Tiny d1952 *WhScrn 74, -77, WhoHol B*
Jones, Elvin Lee 1939- *AmSCAP 80*
Jones, Elvin Ray 1927- *BiDAmM, EncJzS 70, IlEncJ, NewGrD 80*
Jones, Emrys 1915-1972 *FilmgC, HalFC 80, WhScrn 77, WhThe, WhoHol B, WhoThe 72*
Jones, Eric 1948- *IntWWM 80*
Jones, Eric Jeffrey 1936- *WhoMus 72*
Jones, Ernestine *BlksB&W, -C*
Jones, Esther Young *NewGrD 80*
Jones, Etta 1928- *EncJzS 70*
Jones, Evlyn Howard *NewGrD 80*
Jones, F Richard 1890?- *FilmEn*
Jones, Floyd 1917- *BiDAmM, BluesWW[port]*
Jones, Fred *Film 1, -2*
Jones, Freddie 1927- *FilmgC, HalFC 80, WhoHol A, WhoHrs 80*
Jones, Fuzzy Q *WhScrn 74, -77*
Jones, Gayle *MorBAP*
Jones, Gemma 1942- *WhoHol A, WhoThe 72, -77*
Jones, Gene-Olivar *BlkAmP*
Jones, George 1931- *BiDAmM, CounME 74[port], -74A, EncFCWM 69, IlEncCM*
Jones, George Morton 1929- *IntWWM 77, -80*
Jones, George Sykes *ConAmC*
Jones, George Thaddeus 1917- *AmSCAP 66, -80, ConAmC, IntWWM 77, -80*
Jones, Geraint Iwan 1917- *IntWWM 77, -80, NewGrD 80, WhoMus 72*
Jones, Gethin 1924- *WhoMus 72*
Jones, Gloria R *AmSCAP 80*
Jones, Gordon 1911-1963 *ForYSC, Vers A[port], WhScrn 74, -77, WhoHol B*
Jones, Gordon G *AmSCAP 80*
Jones, Grace *ConMuA 80A*
Jones, Grandpa 1913- *CounME 74, -74A, EncFCWM 69, IlEncCM[port]*
Jones, Griffith 1910- *FilmgC, HalFC 80, IlWWBF, IntMPA 77, -75, -78, -79, -80, WhoHol A, WhoThe 72, -77*
Jones, Gwendolyn K 1948- *IntWWM 77, -80*
Jones, Gwyneth 1936- *CmOp, IntWWM 77, -80, MusSN[port], WhoMus 72, WhoOp 76*
Jones, Gwyneth 1937- *NewGrD 80*
Jones, Hank 1918- *CmpEPM, EncJzS 70, IlEncJ*
Jones, Hannah *Film 2*
Jones, Harmon 1911-1972 *FilmEn, FilmgC, HalFC 80*
Jones, Harold 1936- *WhoMus 72*
Jones, Harold Charles 1918- *WhoMus 72*
Jones, Harold Ian 1942- *IntWWM 80*
Jones, Harold J 1940- *EncJzS 70*
Jones, Harry *Film 2*
Jones, Hazel d1974 *WhoHol B*
Jones, Hazel 1895-1974 *WhScrn 77*
Jones, Hazel 1896-1974 *WhThe*
Jones, Henry 1912- *BiE&WWA, FilmEn, FilmgC, ForYSC, HalFC 80, NotNAT, WhoHol A*
Jones, Henry 1918- *BiDAmM, EncJzS 70*
Jones, Henry Arthur 1851-1929 *CnThe, EncWT, Ent, McGEWD[port], ModWD, NotNAT A, -B, OxThe, PlP&P, REnWD[port], WhThe, WhoStg 1906, -1908*
Jones, Henry Festing d1928 *OxMus*
Jones, Henry Z, Jr. 1940- *AmSCAP 66, -80*
Jones, Herbert Ingham 1943- *IntWWM 77*
Jones, Herbert Kelsey 1922- *CreCan 1*
Jones, Herbert Robert 1923- *BiDAmM*
Jones, Hester *NewGrD 80*
Jones, Heywood S 1891-1959 *AmSCAP 66, -80*
Jones, Howell Thomas, Jr. 1933- *IntWWM 77*
Jones, Sister Ida 1898- *ConAmC*
Jones, Inigo 1573-1652 *CnThe, EncWT, Ent, NewGrD 80, NotNAT A, -B, OxMus, OxThe, PlP&P*
Jones, Inigo 1575-1652 *DancEn 78*
Jones, Iona *WhoMus 72*
Jones, Isaiah, Jr. 1940- *AmSCAP 80*
Jones, Isham 1894-1956 *AmPS, -B, AmSCAP 66, -80, BgBands 74[port], BiDAmM, CmpEPM, NotNAT B, PopAmC[port], WhoJazz 72*
Jones, Isham Russell, II 1932- *EncJzS 70*
Jones, Ivor Harold 1934- *WhoMus 72*
Jones, J Earl 1939- *IntWWM 77, -80*
Jones, J Matheson d1931 *NotNAT B*
Jones, J Parke *Film 1*
Jones, J W *Film 1*
Jones, J Wilton d1897 *NotNAT B*
Jones, Jack 1938- *AmPS A, -B, BiDAmM, RkOn[port], WhoHol A*
Jones, Jacqueline *WomWMM B*
Jones, James Earl 1931- *BiE&WWA, DrBlPA, Ent, FilmEn, HalFC 80, NotNAT, PlP&P[port], -A[port], WhoHol A, WhoThe 72, -77*
Jones, James Edward 1921- *BiDAmM*
Jones, James Henry 1918- *BiDAmM, EncJzS 70*
Jones, Jeanne Nannette 1948- *IntWWM 77, -80*
Jones, Jeffrey 1944- *ConAmC*
Jones, Jennifer 1919- *BiDFilm, -81, BiE&WWA, CmMov, FilmEn, FilmgC, ForYSC, HalFC 80[port], IntMPA 77, -75, -76, -78, -79, -80, MotPP, MovMk[port], OxFilm, WhoHol A, WhoHrs 80[port], WorEFlm*
Jones, Jimmy 1918- *CmpEPM, EncJzS 70*
Jones, Jimmy 1937- *RkOn[port]*
Jones, Jo 1911- *CmpEPM, EncJzS 70, IlEncJ, NewGrD 80, WhoJazz 72*
Jones, Joan Granville d1974 *WhScrn 77, WhoHol B*
Jones, Joe 1926- *RkOn*
Jones, John 1728-1796 *NewGrD 80*
Jones, John 1917- *BiE&WWA, NotNAT*
Jones, John 1924-1964 *BluesWW[port]*
Jones, John 1937- *CnOxB*
Jones, John Bush 1940- *ConAmTC*
Jones, John L 1910- *NewOrJ SUP[port]*
Jones, John Owen 1876-1962 *NewGrD 80*
Jones, John Price d1961 *NotNAT B*
Jones, Johnny 1908-1962 *Film 1, -2, TwYS, WhScrn 74, -77, WhoHol B*
Jones, Jonah 1908- *EncJzS 70, WhoJazz 72*
Jones, Jonah 1909- *CmpEPM, DrBlPA, IlEncJ*
Jones, Jonathan 1911- *AmSCAP 66, -80, BiDAmM, EncJzS 70, NewGrD 80*
Jones, Jonathan Barrie 1946- *IntWWM 77, -80*
Jones, Jonathan James Hellyer 1951- *IntWWM 77, -80*
Jones, Joseph Rudolph 1923- *BiDAmM, EncJzS 70*
Jones, Joseph Steven 1809-1877 *NotNAT B, OxThe*
Jones, Joyce Gilstrap 1933- *IntWWM 77, -80, WhoMus 72*
Jones, Julia *ConDr 77C*
Jones, Julia 1923- *ConDr 73*
Jones, July *BlksB&W C*
Jones, Kathleen *WhoMus 72*
Jones, Kelsey 1922- *Baker 78, CreCan 1, IntWWM 77, -80, NewGrD 80*
Jones, Kenneth Baden 1915- *WhoMus 72*
Jones, Kenneth Eugene 1942- *AmSCAP 80*
Jones, Kenneth V 1925?- *HalFC 80*
Jones, Kenneth Victor 1924- *IntWWM 77, -80, WhoMus 72*
Jones, Keva 1948- *DrBlPA*
Jones, L Q 1936- *FilmgC, ForYSC, HalFC 80, WhoHol A, WhoHrs 80*
Jones, Lauren 1942- *DrBlPA*
Jones, Lee 1908- *AmSCAP 80*
Jones, Lee 1909- *AmSCAP 66*
Jones, LeRoi 1934- *ConDr 73, -77, CroCD, DrBlPA, EncWT, Ent, McGEWD[port], ModWD, MorBAP, NotNAT, PlP&P A[port]*
Jones, Leslie 1905- *WhoMus 72*
Jones, Leslie Julian 1910- *WhThe*
Jones, Lewis Ernest Beddoe 1933- *WhoMus 72*
Jones, Linda 1945-1975 *RkOn 2[port]*
Jones, Lindley A 1911-1964 *BiDAmM*
Jones, Lindley A 1911-1965 *AmSCAP 80*
Jones, Llewellyn Bruce 1905- *WhoMus 72*
Jones, Lorenzo *What 5[port]*
Jones, Louis Marshall 1913- *BiDAmM*
Jones, Louis Vaughn 1893- *BiDAmM*
Jones, Lynn Berta Springbett *CreCan 2*
Jones, Maggie 1900?- *BluesWW[port]*
Jones, Mamie *BluesWW*
Jones, Marcia Mae 1924- *FilmEn, FilmgC, ForYSC, HalFC 80, What 4[port], WhoHol A*
Jones, Marcia May 1924- *ThFT[port]*
Jones, Margo 1913-1953 *EncWT*
Jones, Margo 1913-1955 *NotNAT B, OxThe, WhThe*
Jones, Maria B d1873 *NotNAT B*
Jones, Marilyn 1940- *CnOxB, DancEn 78*
Jones, Marjorie *AmSCAP 80*
Jones, Mark 1890-1965 *WhScrn 77*
Jones, Martin Edwin Mervyn 1940- *IntWWM 77, -80, WhoMus 72*
Jones, Mary 1915- *WhoHol A, WhoThe 72, -77*
Jones, Mary Olwen 1937- *IntWWM 77, -80*
Jones, Maude *BluesWW*
Jones, Merle S d1976 *NewYTET*
Jones, Morgan 1879-1951 *WhScrn 74, -77, WhoHol B*
Jones, Muriel Ada 1922- *IntWWM 77*
Jones, Natalie R *WomWMM*
Jones, Norman *WhoMus 72*
Jones, Norman 1928-1963 *WhScrn 74, -77*
Jones, Norman Holford 1910- *WhoMus 72*
Jones, Ola Verine 1949- *BlkWAB*
Jones, Oliver 1925- *AmSCAP 80*
Jones, Park *Film 1, -2*
Jones, Parry 1891-1963 *Baker 78, NewGrD 80*
Jones, Patricia Collins 1943- *IntWWM 77, -80*
Jones, Paul *WhoHol A*
Jones, Paul 1901-1968 *FilmEn, FilmgC, HalFC 80*
Jones, Paul 1942- *HalFC 80, WhoThe 72, -77*
Jones, Paul 1943- *FilmgC*
Jones, Paul Meredith 1897-1966 *WhScrn 74, -77*
Jones, Percy 1914- *WhoMus 72*
Jones, Peter 1920- *FilmgC, HalFC 80, WhoHol A, WhoThe 72, -77*
Jones, Philip 1928- *IntWWM 77, -80, NewGrD 80, WhoMus 72*
Jones, Philip 1933- *IntWWM 77, -80, WhoMus 72*
Jones, Philly Joe 1923- *CmpEPM, EncJzS 70*
Jones, Phyllis Ann d1962 *NotNAT B*
Jones, Preacher Wardell 1905?- *WhoJazz 72*
Jones, Preston 1936-1979 *DcLB 7[port]*
Jones, Quincy *BgBands 74, ConMuA 80B*
Jones, Quincy 1933- *AmSCAP 66, -80, Baker 78, BiDAmM, ConAmC, DrBlPA, EncJzS 70, MusMk[port]*
Jones, Quincy 1935- *FilmgC, HalFC 80, IntMPA 77, -75, -76, -78, -79, -80*
Jones, R D d1925 *WhScrn 74, -77*
Jones, Ralph 1951- *ConAmC, IntWWM 80*
Jones, Raymond R *PupTheA*
Jones, Reunald, Sr. 1910- *BiDAmM, WhoJazz 72*
Jones, Richard *OxThe, TwYS A*
Jones, Richard d1744 *NewGrD 80, OxMus*
Jones, Richard d1851 *NotNAT B*
Jones, Richard C 1906- *AmSCAP 66, -80*
Jones, Richard Elfyn 1944- *IntWWM 80*
Jones, Richard M 1892-1945 *AmSCAP 66, -80*

Jones, Richard Myknee 1889-1945 *BiDAmM, CmpEPM, NewOrJ[port], WhoJazz 72*
Jones, Robert *BlkAmP, BnBkM 80, NewGrD 80, OxMus*
Jones, Robert 1485?-1536? *Baker 78*
Jones, Robert, II *Baker 78*
Jones, Robert Carroll 1931- *AmSCAP 80*
Jones, Robert Earl *WhoHol A*
Jones, Robert Earl 1900- *DrBlPA*
Jones, Robert Edmond 1887-1954 *DancEn 78, EncWT, NotNAT A, -B, OxThe, PlP&P, WhThe*
Jones, Robert Edmund 1887-1954 *CnThe*
Jones, Robert Elliott 1908- *EncJzS 70*
Jones, Robert Elliott 1909- *BiDAmM*
Jones, Robert G 1936- *DrBlPA*
Jones, Robert Hope *OxMus*
Jones, Robert Milton 1944- *IntWWM 80*
Jones, Robert William 1932- *AmSCAP 80, ConAmC*
Jones, Robin C 1933- *AmSCAP 80*
Jones, Roderick 1910- *WhoMus 72*
Jones, Roger Parks 1944- *ConAmC*
Jones, Roland Leo 1932- *IntWWM 77, -80*
Jones, Rowland *WhoMus 72*
Jones, Rozene K 1890-1964 *NotNAT B, WhScrn 74, -77*
Jones, Rufus 1936- *BiDAmM*
Jones, Rupel Johnson 1895-1964 *BiE&WWA, NotNAT B*
Jones, Rusty 1932- *EncJzS 70*
Jones, Sadie *BluesWW*
Jones, Salena 1930- *EncJzS 70*
Jones, Sam 1924- *EncJzS 70*
Jones, Samantha *WhoHol A*
Jones, Samuel 1924- *BiDAmM, EncJzS 70*
Jones, Samuel 1935- *AmSCAP 80, ConAmC*
Jones, Samuel Major d1952 *NotNAT B, WhThe*
Jones, Samuel Turner 1909- *AmSCAP 80*
Jones, Shirley 1934- *BiDAmM, BiDFilm, -81, BiE&WWA, CmMov, FilmEn, FilmgC, ForYSC, HalFC 80, IntMPA 77, -75, -76, -78, -79, -80, MotPP, MovMk[port], WhoHol A, WorEFlm*
Jones, Sidney 1861-1946 *Baker 78, NewGrD 80, OxMus*
Jones, Sidney 1869-1946 *EncMT, NotNAT B, WhThe*
Jones, Silas 1940- *MorBAP, NatPD[port]*
Jones, Sisseretta 1869-1933 *DrBlPA*
Jones, Sissieretta 1868-1933 *Baker 78, BiDAmM*
Jones, Sissieretta 1870-1933 *BlksBF[port]*
Jones, Slick 1907-1969 *EncJzS 70, WhoJazz 72*
Jones, Snags Clifford 1900?-1947 *WhoJazz 72*
Jones, Spike *AmPS B, BgBands 74*
Jones, Spike 1911-1964 *AmSCAP 66, CmpEPM, JoeFr[port]*
Jones, Spike 1911-1965 *Baker 78, FilmgC, HalFC 80, NewGrD 80, WhScrn 74, -77, WhoHol B*
Jones, Spike 1912-1965 *ForYSC*
Jones, Spike And City Slickers *AmPS A*
Jones, Stan 1914-1963 *AmSCAP 66, -80, WhoHol B*
Jones, Stanley 1914-1963 *NotNAT B, WhScrn 74, -77*
Jones, Stephen d1827 *NotNAT B*
Jones, Stephen Oscar 1880-1967 *AmSCAP 66, -80, ConAmC A*
Jones, Mrs. Sutton 1927- *AmSCAP 66*
Jones, T A 1932- *NewGrD 80*
Jones, T C 1920-1971 *BiE&WWA, NotNAT B*
Jones, T C 1921-1971 *WhScrn 74, -77, WhoHol B*
Jones, Thad 1923- *CmpEPM, DrBlPA, EncJzS 70, IlEncJ*
Jones, Thaddeus Joseph 1923- *AmSCAP 80, BiDAmM, EncJzS 70*
Jones, Thomas Gwynn 1921- *IntWWM 77, -80*
Jones, Thomas John *WhoMus 72*
Jones, Timothy Russell Hellyer 1956- *IntWWM 80*
Jones, Tiny d1952 *Film 2, WhoHol B*
Jones, Tom 1928- *AmSCAP 66, -80, BiE&WWA, ConDr 73, -77D, EncMT, NewCBMT, NotNAT*
Jones, Tom 1940- *Baker 78, BiDAmM, RkOn 2[port]*
Jones, Tommy Lee 1946- *HalFC 80*
Jones, Trefor 1902-1965 *WhThe*
Jones, Trevor Alan 1932- *IntWWM 77, -80*
Jones, Victor Charles *PupTheA*
Jones, W W *Film 2*
Jones, Wallace 1883-1936 *WhScrn 74, -77, WhoHol B*
Jones, Wallace Leon 1906- *WhoJazz 72*
Jones, Walter *BlkAmP, MorBAP*
Jones, Walter 1872- *WhoStg 1906, -1908*
Jones, Welton H, Jr. 1936- *ConAmTC*
Jones, Wendal S 1932- *ConAmC*
Jones, Wendy Vickers 1949- *AmSCAP 80*
Jones, Whitworth 1873- *WhThe*
Jones, Willa Saunders 1904- *BlkAmP*
Jones, Willard Wood, Jr. 1919- *AmSCAP 80*
Jones, William 1726-1800 *Baker 78, NewGrD 80*
Jones, Sir William 1746-1794 *Baker 78, NewGrD 80*
Jones, William John 1926- *IntWWM 77, -80*
Jones, Wilmore Slick 1907-1969 *CmpEPM, EncJzS 70*
Jones, Wynford Lyn 1948- *IntWWM 77, -80*
Jones And Hare *CmpEPM*
Jones Boys, The *EncFCWM 69*
Jones-Moreland, Betsy *WhoHrs 80*
Joneses, The *RkOn 2[port]*
Jong, Bettie De *CnOxB*
Jong, Erica *WomWMM*
Jong, Marinus De 1891- *Baker 78, NewGrD 80*
Jongen, Joseph 1873-1953 *Baker 78, BnBkM 80, CompSN[port], DcCom&M 79, DcCM, NewGrD 80, OxMus*
Jongen, Leon 1884-1969 *Baker 78, NewGrD 80, OxMus*
Jongeneelen, Margaretha Augustina 1930- *AmSCAP 80*
Jongers, Alphonse 1872-1945 *CreCan 1*
Jonic, Bettina 1935- *WhoMus 72*
Jonson, Ben 1572-1637 *CnThe, DcPup, EncWT, Ent[port], McGEWD[port], NewGrD 80, PlP&P[port], REnWD[port]*
Jonson, Ben 1573?-1637 *DancEn 78, NewEOp 71, NotNAT A, -B, OxMus*
Jonson, Benjamin 1572-1637 *OxThe*
Jonson, Guy *IntWWM 77, -80, WhoMus 72*
Jonsson, Busk Margit 1929- *WhoOp 76*
Jonsson, Josef Petrus 1887-1969 *Baker 78*
Jonsson, Thorarinn 1900-1974 *NewGrD 80*
Jood *PupTheA*
Jooss, Kurt 1901- *CnOxB, DancEn 78[port], NewGrD 80, OxMus, WhThe*
Jope-Slade, Christine d1942 *NotNAT B*
Joplin, Janis 1943-1970 *AmSCAP 80, Baker 78, BiDAmM, BluesWW[port], ConMuA 80A, IlEncR, RkOn 2[port], WhScrn 77, WhoHol B*
Joplin, Scott *MorBAP*
Joplin, Scott 1868-1917 *Baker 78, BlkAmP, BnBkM 80, CmpEPM, CnOxB, DrBlPA, IlEncJ, MusMk[port], NewGrD 80, WhoJazz 72*
Joplin, Scott 1868-1919 *AmSCAP 66, -80, BiDAmM, NotNAT B, PopAmC*
Jora, Michel 1891- *OxMus*
Jora, Mihail 1891-1971 *Baker 78, DcCM, NewGrD 80*
Joran, Jiri 1920- *WhoOp 76*
Jorda, Enrique 1911- *Baker 78, IntWWM 77, -80, NewGrD 80, WhoMus 72*
Jordahl, Robert A 1926- *ConAmC*
Jordan *NewGrD 80*
Jordan, Abraham *OxMus*
Jordan, Abraham d1716? *NewGrD 80*
Jordan, Abraham -1756? *NewGrD 80*
Jordan, Alice 1916- *AmSCAP 80, ConAmC, IntWWM 77*
Jordan, Archie Paul 1951- *AmSCAP 80*
Jordan, Armin 1932- *IntWWM 80*
Jordan, Bernard d1962 *NotNAT B*
Jordan, Bobby 1923-1965 *ForYSC, HalFC 80, JoeFr, WhoHol B, WhoHrs 80*
Jordan, Charles 1890?-1954 *BluesWW[port]*
Jordan, Clifford Laconia 1931- *BiDAmM, EncJzS 70*
Jordan, Cyril H G 1948- *AmSCAP 80*
Jordan, David 1930- *IntWWM 77, -80, WhoMus 72*
Jordan, Dorothea 1762-1816 *OxMus*
Jordan, Dorothy *FilmgC, MotPP*
Jordan, Dorothy 1761-1816 *NotNAT A, OxThe*
Jordan, Dorothy 1762?-1816 *NotNAT B*
Jordan, Dorothy 1908- *FilmEn, Film 2, ForYSC, ThFT[port], WhThe, WhoHol A*
Jordan, Dorothy 1910- *MovMk*
Jordan, Duke 1922- *CmpEPM, EncJzS 70*
Jordan, Egon V *Film 2*
Jordan, Glenn S *NewYTET*
Jordan, Henrietta *IntMPA 77, -75, -76, -78, -79, -80*
Jordan, Irene 1919- *Baker 78, WhoMus 72*
Jordan, Irving Sidney 1922- *BiDAmM, EncJzS 70*
Jordan, Jack *Film 2*
Jordan, Jack 1929- *DrBlPA*
Jordan, James Taft 1915- *BiDAmM, EncJzS 70*
Jordan, Jan *NewGrD 80*
Jordan, Jim 1896- *WhoHol A*
Jordan, Jim 1897- *JoeFr*
Jordan, Jimmy *BluesWW*
Jordan, Joe 1882-1971 *AmSCAP 66, -80, BiDAmM*
Jordan, John William 1941- *IntWWM 77, -80*
Jordan, Jules 1850-1927 *Baker 78, BiDAmM*
Jordan, Kevin 1951- *EncJzS 70*
Jordan, Leroy *AmSCAP 80*
Jordan, Louis 1908-1975 *BgBands 74[port], BiDAmM, BlksB&W, -C, BluesWW[port], CmpEPM, DrBlPA, EncJzS 70, IlEncJ, WhoHol C, WhoJazz 72*
Jordan, Margaret *PupTheA*
Jordan, Marian 1897-1961 *WhScrn 74, -77, WhoHol B*
Jordan, Marian 1898-1961 *NotNAT B*
Jordan, Marion F *IntMPA 77, -75, -76, -78, -79, -80*
Jordan, Mary 1879-1961 *Baker 78*
Jordan, Miriam 1908- *FilmEn, ForYSC, ThFT[port]*
Jordan, Olga Genrichova 1907-1971 *CnOxB*
Jordan, Patrick *WhoHol A*
Jordan, Paul 1939- *ConAmC*
Jordan, Rhoda d1962 *WhScrn 77*
Jordan, Richard 1938- *HalFC 80, WhoHol A*
Jordan, Ricky *WhScrn 77*
Jordan, Robert 1923-1965 *WhScrn 74, -77*
Jordan, Robert 1944- *IntWWM 77, -80*
Jordan, Roland 1938- *ConAmC*
Jordan, Roy 1916- *AmSCAP 66, -80*
Jordan, Royland 1915- *WhoMus 72*
Jordan, Sheila 1929- *EncJzS 70*
Jordan, Shelia 1929- *BiDAmM*
Jordan, Sid *Film 1, -2*
Jordan, Steve 1919- *CmpEPM, WhoJazz 72*
Jordan, Sverre 1889-1972 *Baker 78, NewGrD 80*
Jordan, Taft 1915- *CmpEPM, WhoJazz 72*
Jordan, Tom *BluesWW*
Jordan, Victor Howard 1938- *AmSCAP 80*
Jordan, Walter C d1951 *NotNAT B*
Jordan, Willie *BluesWW*
Jordanaires *BiDAmM, CounME 74, -74A, EncFCWM 69, IlEncCM[port]*
Jordans, Hein Jacobus Maria 1914- *IntWWM 77, -80*
Jordans, Wieke Maria Hubert 1922- *IntWWM 77, -80*
Jordon, Charley *BluesWW*
Jordon, Domaine *Film 2*
Jordon, Norman 1938- *BlkAmP*
Jorge, Armando 1938- *CreCan 1*
Jorge, Paul *Film 2*
Jorge, Paul d1939 *WhoHol B*
Jorge, Paul 1849-1929 *WhScrn 74, -77*
Jorgens, Alice *Film 1*
Jorgensen, Christine 1926- *What 1[port]*
Jorgensen, Erik 1912- *Baker 78, NewGrD 80*
Jorgensen, Jesper 1946- *IntWWM 80*
Jorgensen, Paul 1934- *WhoOp 76*
Jorgensen, Poul 1934- *IntWWM 77, -80*
Jorgensen, Robert 1903- *WhThe*
Jorgenson, M Pauline Lillian 1900- *IntWWM 77*

Joris Van Langhveld *NewGrD 80*
Joris Van Lankveld *NewGrD 80*
Joris, Hans Herbert 1925- *WhoOp 76*
Jorn, Karl 1876-1947 *Baker 78*
Jory, Jon V 1938- *NotNAT*
Jory, Victor *MotPP, WhoHol A*
Jory, Victor 1901- *Vers A[port]*
Jory, Victor 1902- *FilmEn, FilmgC, ForYSC, HalFC 80, HolP 30[port], IntMPA 77, –75, –76, –78, –79, –80, MovMk, WhoHrs 80[port], WhoThe 72, –77*
Jory, Victor 1903- *BiE&WWA, NotNAT*
Jorysz, Walter 1919- *IntWWM 80, WhoMus 72*
Josane, Lola *Film 2*
Josayne *Film 2*
Jose Mauricio *NewGrD 80*
Jose, Dick 1873-1941 *AmPS B, BiDAmM*
Jose, Edward 1880?- *FilmEn, Film 1, TwYS A*
Jose-Periera, Fernando Antonio *AmSCAP 80*
Josef, Ladislav 1907- *IntWWM 77, –80*
Joseffy, Rafael 1852-1915 *Baker 78, BiDAmM, BnBkM 80, MusSN[port], NewGrD 80*
Josefovits, Teri 1909-1958 *AmSCAP 66, –80*
Joseloff, Stanley 1907- *AmSCAP 66*
Joselovitz, Ernest A *NatPD[port]*
Joseph I 1678-1711 *NewGrD 80*
Joseph Huzaya *NewGrD 80*
Joseph Ibn-Aknin *NewGrD 80*
Joseph, Don Verne 1926- *ConAmC, IntWWM 77*
Joseph, Edgar 1906-1977 *NewOrJ*
Joseph, Georg *NewGrD 80*
Joseph, Harold *IntWWM 77, –80*
Joseph, Harry d1962 *NotNAT B*
Joseph, Helen Haiman *DcPup, PupTheA*
Joseph, Irving 1925- *AmSCAP 80*
Joseph, Jackie *WhoHol A*
Joseph, James 1934- *WhoMus 72*
Joseph, John 1877-1965 *NewOrJ[port]*
Joseph, Kenneth 1922- *IntMPA 77, –75, –76, –78, –79, –80*
Joseph, Larry 1911-1974 *WhScrn 77*
Joseph, Ota 1937- *IntWWM 80*
Joseph, Pleasant 1907- *BluesWW[port], NewOrJ*
Joseph, Ray *AmSCAP 80*
Joseph, Robert 1913-1969 *HalFC 80*
Joseph, Robert Farras 1935- *NatPD[port]*
Joseph, Robert L 1924- *BiE&WWA, NotNAT*
Joseph, Ronald A Peter 1954- *IntWWM 77, –80*
Joseph, Sal *AmSCAP 80*
Joseph, Samuel 1937- *IntWWM 77, –80*
Joseph, Stephen 1921-1966 *OxThe*
Joseph, Vivian 1917- *WhoMus 72*
Joseph, Waldren 1918- *NewOrJ*
Joseph, Warren 1924- *ConAmC*
Joseph, William *ConMuA 80B*
Joseph, William Span 1919- *IntWWM 77*
Joseph, Willie 1892?-1951 *NewOrJ[port]*
Josephs, George M 1908- *IntMPA 77, –75, –76, –78, –79*
Josephs, Norman Arthur 1943- *IntWWM 80*
Josephs, Susan *ConMuA 80B*
Josephs, Wilfred 1927- *ConAmC, IntWWM 77, –80, NewGrD 80, WhoMus 72*
Josephson, David 1942- *IntWWM 77, –80*
Josephson, Jacob Axel 1818-1880 *Baker 78, NewGrD 80*
Josephson, Kenneth George 1926- *IntWWM 77, –80*
Josephson, Marvin *ConMuA 80B, NewYTET*
Josephson, Ragnar 1891-1966 *CnMD, ModWD*
Joshi, Dhruva Tara 1915- *IntWWM 77, –80*
Josif, Enrico 1924- *NewGrD 80*
Josif, Enriko 1924- *Baker 78, DcCM*
Josipovici, Gabriel *ConDr 77B*
Joslin, Howard 1908-1975 *WhScrn 77, WhoHol C*
Joslin, Margaret *Film 1*
Joslyn, Allyn 1901- *FilmEn, What 5[port]*
Joslyn, Allyn 1905- *FilmgC, ForYSC, HalFC 80, IntMPA 77, –75, –76, –78, –79, –80, MovMk[port], Vers A[port], WhThe, WhoHol A*
Joslyn, Jay Thomas 1923- *ConAmTC*
Josquin Des Pres 1440?-1521 *BnBkM 80[port], OxMus*
Josquin Des Pres 1450-1521 *CmpBCM, GrComp[port], MusMk[port]*
Josquin Des Prez 1440?-1521 *DcCom 77[port], NewGrD 80[port]*
Josquinus, Antonius *NewGrD 80*
Josse *NewGrD 80*
Jost, Paul J 1952- *AmSCAP 80*
Josten, Werner 1885-1963 *AmSCAP 66, –80, Baker 78, BiDAmM, ConAmC, DcCM, NewGrD 80, OxMus*
Jostyn, Jay *WhoHol A*
Josz, Marcel 1899- *FilmAG WE*
Joteyko, Tadeusz 1872-1932 *Baker 78, NewGrD 80*
Jothen, Michael Jon 1944- *AmSCAP 80*
Jotuni, Maria 1880-1943 *CroCD*
Jouard, Paul E 1928- *AmSCAP 66, –80, ConAmC A*
Joube, M *Film 1*
Joube, Romauld *Film 2*
Joubert, Celestin 1861-1934 *NewGrD 80*
Joubert, Duxie Anna Maria 1919- *IntWWM 77, –80*
Joubert, Hendrik Johannes 1926- *IntWWM 77, –80*
Joubert, John 1927- *Baker 78, IntWWM 80, NewGrD 80, OxMus, WhoMus 72*
Joubert, Molly 1925- *IntWWM 77, –80*
Joudry, Patricia 1921- *CreCan 2*
Joule, Benjamin St. John Baptist 1817-1895 *NewGrD 80*
Jourdan, Louis *MotPP, WhoHol A*
Jourdan, Louis 1919- *FilmEn, FilmgC, HalFC 80, MovMk[port]*
Jourdan, Louis 1920- *BiE&WWA, ForYSC, NotNAT*
Jourdan, Louis 1921- *IntMPA 77, –75, –76, –78, –79, –80*
Jouret, Leon 1828-1905 *Baker 78*
Journee, Leon *Film 2*
Journet, Marcel 1867-1933 *Baker 78, CmOp, MusSN[port], NewEOp 71, NewGrD 80*
Journey *ConMuA 80A, IlEncR*
Journeymen, The *BiDAmM, EncFCWM 69*
Jousse, Jean 1760-1837 *Baker 78*
Jouvet, Louis 1887-1951 *BiDFilm, –81, CnThe, EncWT, Ent, FilmAG WE, FilmEn, FilmgC, HalFC 80, MovMk, NotNAT B, OxFilm, OxThe, WhThe, WhoHol B, WorEFlm*
Jouvet, Louis 1888-1951 *WhScrn 74, –77*
Jouvet, Louis 1891-1951 *NotNAT A*
Jouy, Victor Joseph Etienne De 1764-1846 *NewEOp 71*
Jovannes De Cascia *NewGrD 80*
Jovannes De Florentia 1360?-1426 *NewGrD 80*
Jovanovic, Vladimir 1937- *IntWWM 80*
Jovernardi, Bartolome 1600?-1668 *NewGrD 80*
Jovernardi, Bartolomeo 1600?-1668 *NewGrD 80*
Jowers, Lucie Giles *PupTheA*
Jowitt, Anthony *Film 2*
Jowitt, Deborah 1934- *CnOxB*
Joy, Beatrice *Film 2*
Joy, Ernest *Film 1, –2*
Joy, Genevieve 1919- *Baker 78*
Joy, Genvieve *WhoMus 72*
Joy, Gloria *Film 2*
Joy, Jimmy *BgBands 74, CmpEPM*
Joy, K E *PupTheA*
Joy, Leatrice *MotPP, What 1[port]*
Joy, Leatrice 1896- *FilmEn, ThFT[port]*
Joy, Leatrice 1897- *ForYSC, MovMk, TwYS*
Joy, Leatrice 1899- *Film 1, –2, FilmgC, HalFC 80, WhoHol A*
Joy, Leonard W 1894-1961 *AmSCAP 66, –80, NotNAT B*
Joy, Nicholas *ForYSC*
Joy, Nicholas d1964 *MotPP, WhoHol B*
Joy, Nicholas 1883-1964 *NotNAT B*
Joy, Nicholas 1884-1964 *PlP&P[port], WhScrn 74, –77*
Joy, Nicholas 1889-1964 *WhThe*
Joy, Nicholas 1894-1964 *HalFC 80*
Joy Of Cooking *IlEncR*
Joyal, Raoul 1914- *IntWWM 77*
Joyce, Adrian *WomWMM*
Joyce, Alice d1955 *MotPP, WhoHol B*
Joyce, Alice 1889-1955 *Film 1, –2, FilmgC, HalFC 80, MovMk[port]*
Joyce, Alice 1890-1955 *FilmEn, ForYSC, NotNAT B, TwYS, WhScrn 74, –77*
Joyce, Archibald 1873-1963 *NewGrD 80, NotNAT B*
Joyce, Beatrice 1900- *AmSCAP 66*
Joyce, Brenda *MotPP*
Joyce, Brenda 1915- *FilmEn*
Joyce, Brenda 1916- *ThFT[port]*
Joyce, Brenda 1918- *CmMov, FilmgC, ForYSC, HalFC 80, MovMk[port], WhoHol A*
Joyce, Dorothea *AmSCAP 80*
Joyce, Eileen 1912- *IntWWM 77, –80, MusMk[port], NewGrD 80*
Joyce, Elaine *WhoHol A*
Joyce, Fonda M 1946- *AmSCAP 80*
Joyce, Jack *Film 2*
Joyce, James *OxMus, WhoHol A*
Joyce, James 1882-1941 *CnMD, EncWT, McGEWD[port], ModWD, NewGrD 80, NotNAT B*
Joyce, John 1939- *NewOrJ*
Joyce, Kathleen *WhoMus 72*
Joyce, Martin 1915-1937 *WhScrn 74, –77*
Joyce, Mary Southwell *WhoMus 72*
Joyce, Natalie *Film 2, WhoHol A*
Joyce, Patrick Weston 1827-1914 *OxMus*
Joyce, Peggy Hopkins 1893-1957 *Film 2, MotPP, NotNAT B, WhScrn 74, –77, WhoHol B*
Joyce, Robert Henry 1927- *IntWWM 77, –80, WhoMus 72*
Joyce, Roger 1943- *AmSCAP 80*
Joyce, Stephen 1931- *WhoThe 72, –77*
Joyce, Stephen 1933- *NotNAT*
Joyce, Virginia *Film 2*
Joyce, Walter d1916 *NotNAT B*
Joyce, Yootha 1927- *FilmgC, HalFC 80, WhoHol A*
Joye, Gilles 1424?-1483 *NewGrD 80[port]*
Joyeux, Odette 1917- *FilmEn*
Joyner, Francis *Film 1, –2, TwYS*
Joys Of Cooking *BiDAmM*
Joyzelle *Film 2, TwYS*
Jozzi, Giuseppe 1710?-1770? *NewGrD 80*
JPJ Quartet *EncJzS 70*
Jua, Chakula Cha *BlkAmP*
Juan I *NewGrD 80*
Juana 1926- *DancEn 78*
Juanas, Antonio d1819? *NewGrD 80*
Juano *WhScrn 74, –77*
Juarez, Alonso *NewGrD 80*
Juarez, Manuel 1937- *IntWWM 77, –80*
Juarez, Saveria Irma 1930- *AmSCAP 80*
Juch, Emma d1939 *NotNAT B*
Juch, Emma 1863-1939 *Baker 78, NewEOp 71, NewGrD 80*
Juch, Emma 1865-1939 *BiDAmM*
Juchelka, Miroslav 1922- *Baker 78*
Judd, Edward *WhoHol A*
Judd, Edward 1932- *FilmEn, FilmgC, ForYSC, HalFC 80, IlWWBF, WhoHrs 80*
Judd, Edward 1934- *IntMPA 77, –75, –76, –78, –79, –80*
Judd, James 1949- *IntWWM 80*
Judd, Margaret Evelyn *IntWWM 77, –80, WhoMus 72*
Jude, Charles 1953- *CnOxB*
Judel, Charles 1882-1969 *WhScrn 77*
Judels, Charles *Film 1, –2*
Judelson, David N *IntMPA 77, –75, –76, –78, –79, –80*
Judenkunig, Hans 1450?-1526 *NewGrD 80*
Judeu 1705-1739 *OxThe*
Judge, Arlene 1912-1974 *WhScrn 77*
Judge, Arline 1912-1974 *FilmEn, FilmgC, ForYSC, HalFC 80, HolP 30[port], MotPP, MovMk, ThFT[port], WhoHol B*
Judge, Brian Richard 1934- *WhoMus 72*
Judge, Jack 1878-1938 *Baker 78, OxMus*
Judge, Timmy *ConMuA 80B*
Judice, Brunilde 1902- *FilmAG WE*
Judice, Caesar De *NewGrD 80*
Judice, Patricia *WomWMM B*
Judith, Madame 1827-1912 *NotNAT A, –B*
Judson, Adoniram 1788-1850 *BiDAmM*
Judson, Arthur 1881-1975 *Baker 78, BiDAmM, NewYTET*

Judson, Sarah Hull Boardman 1803-1845 *BiDAmM*
Judson, Stanley *DancEn 78*
Juen, Joseph P 1902- *AmSCAP 66, -80*
Juet, Randall *NewGrD 80*
Jug Stompers *BiDAmM*
Juglott *NewGrD 80*
Jugo, Jenny 1905- *FilmAG WE, Film 2*
Juhan, Alexander 1765-1845 *Baker 78*
Juhan, James *Baker 78, OxMus*
Juhasz, Elod 1938- *IntWWM 77, -80*
Juhl, Jerry R *AmSCAP 80*
Juhos, Joseph Frank 1935- *IntWWM 77, -80*
Juhrke, Werner 1932- *WhoOp 76*
Juillard, Robert 1906- *DcFM, FilmEn, HalFC 80*
Juilliard, Augustus D 1836-1919 *Baker 78, BnBkM 80*
Juilliard String Quartet, The *BiDAmM*
Julia, Raul 1940- *WhoHol A, WhoThe 77*
Julian, Alexander 1893-1945 *WhScrn 74, -77*
Julian, Don And The Meadowlarks *RkOn*
Julian, Edward Joseph 1918- *AmSCAP 80*
Julian, Hubert F 1897- *What 1[port]*
Julian, John 1839-1913 *OxMus*
Julian, Joseph *NatPD[port]*
Julian, Joseph 1948- *CpmDNM 76, ConAmC, IntWWM 77, -80*
Julian, Max *BlkAmP*
Julian, Rupert 1886-1943 *Film 1, -2, FilmgC, HalFC 80*
Julian, Rupert 1889-1943 *BiDFilm, DcFM, FilmEn, TwYS, -A, WhScrn 74, -77, WhoHol B, WorEFlm*
Julian, Russell A 1911- *IntWWM 77*
Juliano, Anthony Raymond, Jr. 1947- *AmSCAP 80*
Julie, Lady *Film 2*
Julien, Jay 1919- *BiE&WWA, NotNAT*
Julien, Max *DrBlPA, MorBAP, WhoHol A*
Julien, Octave-Henri 1852-1908 *CreCan 2*
Juliet, Miss d1962 *NotNAT B*
Juliette 1927- *CreCan 2*
Julio, El Doctor *PupTheA*
Julius, Herr *PupTheA*
Julius, Heinrich, Duke 1564-1613 *Ent*
Julius, J *DcFM*
Juliusson, Guom Runar 1945- *IntWWM 77*
Jullet, Herbert d1545 *NewGrD 80*
Jullien, Adolphe 1845-1932 *NewGrD 80*
Jullien, Gilles 1650?-1703 *Baker 78, NewGrD 80*
Jullien, Jean 1854-1919 *ModWD, NotNAT B, WhThe*
Jullien, Jean-Lucien-Adolphe 1845-1932 *Baker 78*
Jullien, Louis Antoine 1812-1860 *Baker 78, BnBkM 80, CmOp, MusMk, NewGrD 80, OxMus*
Jullien, Marcel-Bernard 1798-1881 *Baker 78*
Jullien, Sandra 1950- *FilmAG WE*
Jumentier, Bernard 1749-1829 *NewGrD 80*
Jumilhac, Pierre-Benoit De 1611-1682 *Baker 78, NewGrD 80*
Junck, Benedetto 1852-1903 *Baker 78, NewGrD 80*
Junckers, Gosse *NewGrD 80*
Juncta *NewGrD 80*
June *IlWWBF A*
June 1901- *EncMT, WhThe*
June, Ava *CmOp*
June, Ava 1931- *NewGrD 80*
June, Ava 1934- *WhoOp 76*
June, Mildred 1906-1940 *Film 2, WhScrn 74, -77, WhoHol B*
June, Ray 1898-1958 *FilmEn, WorEFlm*
June, Ray 1908-1958 *CmMov, FilmgC, HalFC 80*
Jung, Allen *WhoHol A*
Jung, Doris *WhoOp 76*
Jung, Rudolph *Film 2*
Jungbauer, Coelestin 1747-1823 *NewGrD 80*
Junge, Alfred 1886-1964 *FilmEn, FilmgC, HalFC 80, OxFilm*
Junge, Winfried 1936- *HalFC 80*
Junge, Winifred *WomWMM*
Junger, Ervin 1931- *NewGrD 80*
Junghans, Carl 1897- *DcFM*
Jungk, Klaus 1916- *IntWWM 77, -80, WhoMus 72*
Jungst, Hugo 1853-1923 *Baker 78*
Jungwirth, Manfred 1919- *NewGrD 80, WhoOp 76*
Junior, John *Film 1*
Junk, Victor 1875- *DancEn 78*
Junker, Carl Ludwig 1748-1797 *NewGrD 80*
Junkerman, Hans *Film 2*
Junkermann, Hans 1872?-1943 *WhScrn 77*
Junkin, Harry *IntMPA 77, -75, -76, -78*
Junkin, Raymond 1918- *IntMPA 77, -75, -76, -78, -79, -80*
Junta *NewGrD 80*
Juon, Paul 1872-1940 *Baker 78, CompSN[port], NewGrD 80*
Jupenlaz, Matilda D *PupTheA*
Jupin, Charles-Francois 1805-1839 *Baker 78*
Jupither, Rolf 1932- *WhoOp 76*
Jurado, Elena *Film 2*
Jurado, Katy 1927- *FilmEn, FilmgC, ForYSC, HalFC 80, IntMPA 77, -75, -76, -78, -79, -80, MovMk, OxFilm, WhoHol A*
Juraitis, Algis 1928- *IntWWM 80*
Juran, Nathan 1907- *FilmEn, FilmgC, HalFC 80, WhoHrs 80*
Jurgens, Curd 1912- *BiDFilm, -81, OxFilm, WorEFlm*
Jurgens, Curt 1912- *BiDFilm, -81, FilmAG WE, FilmEn, FilmgC, HalFC 80, MotPP, MovMk[port], OxFilm, WhoHol A, WhoHrs 80*
Jurgens, Curt 1915- *IntMPA 78, -79, -80*
Jurgens, Curt 1916- *ForYSC*
Jurgens, Dick *BgBands 74[port]*
Jurgens, Dick 1910- *AmSCAP 80, CmpEPM*
Jurgens, Dick 1911- *AmSCAP 66*
Jurgens, Fritz 1888-1915 *Baker 78*
Jurgens, Hellmut 1902- *DancEn 78*
Jurgens, Jurgen 1925- *IntWWM 80, NewGrD 80*
Jurgenson, Pyotr Ivanovich 1836-1904 *Baker 78, NewGrD 80*
Juri, Constantino Gabriel 1923- *WhoOp 76*
Jurinac, Sena 1921- *Baker 78, CmOp, IntWWM 77, -80, MusSN[port], NewEOp 71, NewGrD 80[port], WhoMus 72, WhoOp 76*
Jurinac, Srebrenka 1921- *NewGrD 80[port]*
Jurisalu, Heino 1930- *NewGrD 80*
Jurjans, Andrejs 1856-1922 *Baker 78, NewGrD 80*
Jurkovic, Milos 1937- *IntWWM 77*
Jurmann, Walter 1903-1971 *AmSCAP 66, -80, CmpEPM*
Jurovsky, Simon 1912-1963 *Baker 78, NewGrD 80*
Jurow, Martin 1914- *FilmgC, HalFC 80, IntMPA 77, -75, -76, -78, -79, -80*
Jurrens, James William 1926- *CpmDNM 80*
Jurres, Andre Georges 1912- *IntWWM 77, -80, NewGrD 80*
Jurriens, Henny 1949- *CnOxB*
Juschino *NewGrD 80*
Jussonius, Antonius *NewGrD 80*
Jusswein, Antonius *NewGrD 80*
Just, Helen 1903- *IntWWM 77, -80, NewGrD 80*
Just, Johann August 1750?-1791 *NewGrD 80*
Just Plain Bill *What 3[port]*
Justice, James Robertson *FilmEn*
Justice, James Robertson 1905-1975 *FilmgC, ForYSC, HalFC 80, IlWWBF, MovMk[port], WhScrn 77, WhoHol C*
Justice, James Robertson 1906-1975 *FilmAG WE*
Justice, Katherine *WhoHol A*
Justin, John 1917- *FilmEn, FilmgC, ForYSC, HalFC 80, IlWWBF, IntMPA 77, -75, -76, -78, -79, -80, WhoHol A, WhoThe 72, -77*
Justin, Morgan 1927-1974 *WhScrn 77, WhoHol B*
Justinus A Desponsatione d1723 *NewGrD 80*
Justis, Bill 1926- *RkOn*
Justus, William 1936- *IntWWM 77, -80, WhoOp 76*
Jutila, Unto Vaino 1944- *IntWWM 77, -80*
Jutra, Claude 1930- *CreCan 1, DcFM, FilmEn, OxFilm, WorEFlm*
Jutzi, Phil 1894- *DcFM, FilmEn*
Jutzi, Piel 1894- *WorEFlm*
Juul, Ralph 1888-1955 *WhScrn 74, -77*
Juvara, Filippo 1676-1736 *NewGrD 80*
Juvarra, Filippo 1676-1736 *NewGrD 80, NotNAT B, OxThe*
Juzeliunas, Julius 1916- *Baker 78, NewGrD 80*
Jyrkiainen, Reijo 1934- *Baker 78, DcCM, NewGrD 80*

K

K C & The Sunshine Band *IlEncR, RkOn 2[port]*
K-Doe, Ernie *RkOn[port]*
Kaa, Franz Ignaz 1739-1818 *NewGrD 80*
Kaaihue, Johnny 1901-1971 *BiDAmM*
Kaan, Jindrich Z Albestu 1852-1926 *NewGrD 80*
Kaan-Albest, Heinrich 1852-1926 *Baker 78*
Kaapuni, Sam 1915- *AmSCAP 66*
Kaapuni, Samuel Keanini 1915-1968 *AmSCAP 80*
Kaaren, Suzanne *WhoHol A*
Kaarresalo-Kasara, Elia *WomWMM B*
Kaarresalo-Kasari, Eila *WomWMM*
Kaart, Hans 1924-1963 *NotNAT B, WhScrn 74, -77*
Kabaivanska, Raina 1934- *CmOp, NewGrD 80, WhoOp 76*
Kabak, Milton 1926- *AmSCAP 66, -80*
Kabaka, Lawrence *MorBAP*
Kabakov, Joel *ConAmC*
Kabalevsky, Dimitri Borisovich 1904- *DcCom&M 79, IntWWM 77, -80*
Kabalevsky, Dmitri 1904- *Baker 78, CmOp, CompSN[port], DcCM, MusMk, NewEOp 71, OxMus*
Kabalevsky, Dmitry 1904- *BnBkM 80, NewGrD 80, WhoMus 72*
Kabalewski, Wladyslaw 1919- *IntWWM 77, -80*
Kabasta, Oswald 1896-1946 *Baker 78*
Kabelac, Miloslav 1908-1979 *Baker 78, DcCM, IntWWM 77, -80, NewGrD 80, WhoMus 72*
Kabibble, Abe *JoeFr*
Kabibble, Ish 1908- *CmpEPM, ForYSC, JoeFr, What 4[port], WhoHol A*
Kabos, Ilona 1893-1973 *NewGrD 80*
Kabos, Ilona 1902- *WhoMus 72*
Kachalov, Vasili Ivanovich 1875-1948 *NotNAT B, OxThe*
Kachalov, Vassili Ivanovich 1875-1948 *EncWT*
Kachalov, Vassilli Ivanovich d1948 *WhoHol B*
Kacher, Del 1937- *AmSCAP 80*
Kacher, Delton 1937- *IntWWM 80*
Kachloff, Vassily *PlP&P*
Kachulev, Ivan 1905- *NewGrD 80*
Kachyna, Karel 1924- *FilmEn*
Kacinkas, Jeronimas 1907- *Baker 78*
Kacinskas, Jeronimas 1907- *ConAmC*
Kacsoh, Pongrac 1873-1923 *NewGrD 80*
Kaczkowski, Joachim 1789-1829 *NewGrD 80*
Kaczynski, Adam 1933- *IntWWM 77, -80, NewGrD 80*
Kaczynski, Tadeusz 1932- *IntWWM 77, -80*
Kada-Abd-El-Kader *Film 2*
Kadar, Jan 1918-1979 *DcFM, FilmEn, FilmgC, HalFC 80, IntMPA 77, -78, -79, MovMk[port], OxFilm*
Kade, Otto 1819-1900 *Baker 78, NewGrD 80*
Kadelburg, Gustav 1851-1925 *EncWT*
Kader-Ben-Ali, Abdel *Film 2*
Kaderavek, Milan 1924- *ConAmC*
Kadiddlehopper, Clem *JoeFr*
Kadison, Philip 1919- *AmSCAP 66, -80*
Kadlubiski, Jan Konrad 1931- *IntWWM 77, -80*
Kadner, Johann *NewGrD 80*
Kadosa, Pal 1903- *Baker 78, DcCM, IntWWM 77, -80, NewGrD 80*
Kaeck, Alexander Paki 1926-1971 *AmSCAP 66, -80*
Kaegi, Werner 1926- *IntWWM 77, -80*
Kaeired, Katharine *Film 2*
Kael, Pauline 1919- *IntMPA 77, -76, -78, -79, -80, OxFilm, WomWMM*
Kael, Pauline 1920- *IntMPA 75*
Kaelin, Pierre 1913- *IntWWM 77, -80*
Kaelred, Katharine 1882- *Film 1, WhThe*
Kaemper, Dietrich 1936- *IntWWM 77, -80*
Kaempfert, Bert *AmPS A, -B, RkOn*
Kaempfert, Max 1871-1941 *Baker 78*
Kaesen, Robert 1931- *CnOxB, DancEn 78*
Kafenda, Frico 1883-1963 *NewGrD 80*
Kafenda, Fridrich 1883-1963 *NewGrD 80*
Kafer, Johann Philipp 1672-1730 *NewGrD 80*
Kaffel, Ralph *ConMuA 80B*
Kaffka, Johann Christoph 1754-1815 *Baker 78*
Kaffka, Johann Christoph 1759-1803? *NewGrD 80*
Kafka, Franz 1883-1924 *CnMD, EncWT, NewEOp 71*
Kafka, Johann Nepomuk 1819-1886 *Baker 78, NewGrD 80*
Kagan, Diane *NatPD[port]*
Kagan, Jeremy Paul *HalFC 80*
Kage, Jonas 1950- *CnOxB*
Kagel, Mauricio 1931- *Baker 78, NewGrD 80[port], WhoMus 72*
Kagel, Mauricio 1932- *DcCM*
Kagel, Maurizio 1931- *NewGrD 80[port]*
Kagen, Sergius 1909-1964 *Baker 78, ConAmC, NotNAT B*
Kagno, Marcia *Film 2*
Kahal, Irving 1903-1942 *AmPS, AmSCAP 66, -80, BiDAmM, CmpEPM, NewCBMT*
Kahana, Michael 1948- *WhoOp 76*
Kahanamoka, Duke P 1890-1968 *Film 2*
Kahanamoku, Duke P 1890-1968 *WhScrn 74, -77, WhoHol B*
Kahane, Anne 1924- *CreCan 1*
Kahl, Elsa *DancEn 78*
Kahl, Willi 1893-1962 *Baker 78, NewGrD 80*
Kahle, Dennis E 1944- *ConAmC*
Kahler, Willibald 1866-1938 *Baker 78*
Kahlert, August Karl Timotheus 1807-1864 *Baker 78*
Kahman, Chesley *ConAmC*
Kahmann, Sieglinde 1937- *WhoOp 76*
Kahn, Art *CmpEPM, Film 2*
Kahn, Bernard Maurice 1930- *AmSCAP 66, -80, NatPD[port]*
Kahn, Dave 1910- *AmSCAP 66, -80*
Kahn, David E 1932- *IntWWM 77, -80*
Kahn, Donald Gustave 1918- *AmSCAP 66, -80*
Kahn, Erich Itor 1905-1956 *Baker 78, BiDAmM, ConAmC*
Kahn, Florence d1951 *WhoHol B, WhoStg 1908*
Kahn, Florence 1877-1951 *OxThe*
Kahn, Florence 1878-1951 *NotNAT B, WhThe*
Kahn, Grace Leboy 1890- *AmSCAP 80*
Kahn, Grace LeBoy 1891- *AmSCAP 66*
Kahn, Gus 1886-1941 *AmPS, AmSCAP 66, -80, BestMus, BiDAmM, CmpEPM, EncMT, FilmEn, HalFC 80, NotNAT B, Sw&Ld C*
Kahn, Irving B 1917- *IntMPA 77, -75, -76, -78, -79, NewYTET*
Kahn, Josslyn *WhoMus 72*
Kahn, L Stanley d1964 *NotNAT B*
Kahn, Madeleine 1942- *HalFC 80*
Kahn, Madeline *IntMPA 75, -76, -78, -79, -80*
Kahn, Madeline 1942- *FilmEn*
Kahn, Madeline 1943- *IntMPA 77, MovMk, PlP&P A[port], WhoHol A*
Kahn, Marcus 1890?-1946? *NewOrJ*
Kahn, Marvin Irving 1915- *AmSCAP 66, -80*
Kahn, Michael *NotNAT, WhoThe 72, -77*
Kahn, Milt 1934- *IntMPA 78*
Kahn, Milton Bernard 1934- *IntMPA 77, -75, -76, -79, -80*
Kahn, Otto Hermann 1867-1934 *Baker 78, NewEOp 71, NotNAT B*
Kahn, Richard 1929- *IntMPA 77, -75, -76, -78, -79, -80*
Kahn, Richard C 1897-1960 *WhScrn 74, -77, WhoHol B*
Kahn, Robert 1865-1951 *Baker 78, NewGrD 80*
Kahn, Roger Wolfe 1907-1962 *AmSCAP 66, -80, BgBands 74, CmpEPM, WhoJazz 72*
Kahn, Sherman 1934- *AmSCAP 66, -80*
Kahn, Si 1944- *AmSCAP 80*
Kahn, Sy M 1924- *NotNAT*
Kahn, Tiny 1924-1953 *CmpEPM*
Kahn, Walter B 1948- *AmSCAP 80*
Kahn, William Smitty 1882-1959 *WhScrn 74, -77, WhoHol B*
Kahnt, Christian Friedrich 1823-1897 *Baker 78, NewGrD 80*
Kahowez, Gunter 1940- *Baker 78*
Kahrer, Laura *NewGrD 80*
Kahry, Gerhard 1941- *WhoOp 76*
Kai, Una 1928- *CnOxB*
Kaim, Franz 1856-1935 *Baker 78*
Kain, Eddie *AmSCAP 80*
Kain, Gylan *BlkAmP*
Kain, Karen 1951- *CnOxB*
Kains, Maurice *Film 2*
Kainz, Josef 1858-1910 *EncWT, NotNAT B, OxThe*
Kainz, Joseph 1858-1910 *Ent*
Kainz, Walter 1907- *IntWWM 77, -80*
Kaioni, Ioan *NewGrD 80*
Kaioni, Joan *NewGrD 80*
Kaioni, Joannes *NewGrD 80*
Kaioni, Johannes *NewGrD 80*
Kaiser, Albert E 1920- *WhoOp 76*
Kaiser, Alfred 1872-1917 *Baker 78*
Kaiser, Alois 1840-1908 *BiDAmM*
Kaiser, Carl William 1933- *WhoOp 76*

Kaiser, Georg 1878-1945 CnMD, CnThe, EncWT, Ent, McGEWD[port], ModWD, NewEOp 71, NotNAT B, OxThe, PlP&P, REnWD[port], WhThe
Kaiser, Helen Film 2
Kaiser, James Edward 1944- AmSCAP 80
Kaiser, Joachim 1928- NewGrD 80
Kaiser, Kurt 1933- AmSCAP 80
Kaiser-Tietz, Erich Film 2
Kaiserman, David Norman 1937- IntWWM 77, -80
Kaja, Katrina Film 2
Kajanus, Robert 1856-1933 Baker 78, NewGrD 80
Kajoni, Ioan NewGrD 80
Kajoni, Joan NewGrD 80
Kajoni, Joannes NewGrD 80
Kajoni, Johannes NewGrD 80
Kakala, Sofele 1916- IntWWM 80
Kakoma, George Wilberforce 1922- WhoMus 72
Kalabis, Viktor 1923- Baker 78, DcCM, IntWWM 77, -80, NewGrD 80
Kalachnikov, Nicolay NewGrD 80
Kalafati, Vasily Pavovlich 1869-1942 NewGrD 80
Kalafati, Vassili 1869-1942 Baker 78
Kalajian, Berge 1924- AmSCAP 80
Kalamuniak, Helen Maria 1951- IntWWM 77, -80
Kalanag 1893-1963 MagIlD
Kalanzi, Benny 1938- AmSCAP 80
Kalapana, John AmSCAP 80
Kalas, Julius 1902-1967 NewGrD 80
Kalashnikov, Nikolay NewGrD 80
Kalatazov, Mikhail 1903-1973 DcFM
Kalatozov, Mikhail 1903-1973 FilmEn, HalFC 80, OxFilm, WorEFlm
Kalb, Dorothy B PupTheA
Kalb, Marie d1930 NotNAT B
Kalb, Marvin IntMPA 77, -75, -76, -78, -79, -80
Kalbeck, Max 1850-1921 Baker 78, NewGrD 80
Kalcheim, Lee 1938- ConDr 73, -77, NatPD[port]
Kalcher, Johann Nepomuk 1764-1827 NewGrD 80
Kalchner, Johann Nepomuk 1764-1827 NewGrD 80
Kaldenbach, Christoph 1613-1698 NewGrD 80
Kalef, Breda Avram 1936- WhoOp 76
Kaleidoscope, The BiDAmM, ConMuA 80A
Kalem, Theodore Eustace 1919- BiE&WWA, ConAmTC, NotNAT
Kaleolani, Alvin AmSCAP 80
Kaler, Doris WomWMM B
Kaleti, Marton 1905- DcFM
Kaletsky, J 1911- IntWWM 77, -80
Kaletzky, Jacob 1911- WhoMus 72
Kalf, Karl Walter 1946- IntWWM 77, -80
Kalfin, Robert 1933- NotNAT, PlP&P A[port]
Kalhauge, Sophus Viggo Harald 1840-1905 Baker 78
Kalich, Bertha 1874-1939 FamA&A[port], Film 1, NotNAT B, WhThe, WhoHol B
Kalich, Bertha 1875-1939 WhScrn 74, -77
Kalich, Jacob d1975 WhoHol C
Kalich, Jacob 1891-1975 BiE&WWA, NotNAT
Kalich, Jacob 1892-1975 WhScrn 77
Kalichstein, Joseph 1946- IntWWM 77, -80, WhoMus 72
Kalidasa 375?-415? CnThe, EncWT, NewEOp 71, REnWD[port]
Kalik, Vaclav 1891-1951 Baker 78, NewGrD 80
Kalikow, Leonard ConMuA 80B
Kalin Twins, The AmPS A, RkOn[port]
Kalina Z Choteriny, Matous NewGrD 80
Kalinich, Stephen John 1942- AmSCAP 80
Kalinnik Of Vassily 1866-1901 OxMus
Kalinnikov, Vasily Sergeyevich 1866-1901 NewGrD 80
Kalinnikov, Vassili 1866-1901 Baker 78, GrComp
Kalionzes, Janet 1922-1961 WhScrn 74, -77, WhoHol B
Kalioujny, Alexandre 1923- CnOxB
Kalioujny, Alexandre 1926?- DancEn 78
Kalisch, Alfred 1863-1933 NewGrD 80
Kalisch, Bertram 1902- IntMPA 77, -75, -76, -78, -79, -80
Kalisch, Paul 1855-1946 Baker 78, NewEOp 71, NewGrD 80
Kalischer, Alfred 1842-1909 Baker 78
Kalivoda, Jan Krtitel Vaclav NewGrD 80
Kaliz, Armand 1892-1941 Film 1, ForYSC, NotNAT B, TwYS, WhScrn 74, -77, WhoHol B
Kalkbrenner, Christian 1755-1806 Baker 78
Kalkbrenner, Frederic 1785-1849 NewGrD 80[port]
Kalkbrenner, Friedrich Wilhelm Michael 1785-1849 Baker 78, BnBkM 80, OxMus
Kalkhurst, Eric 1902-1957 WhScrn 74, -77, WhoHol B
Kallen, Kitty AmPS A, WhoHol A
Kallen, Kitty 1922- CmpEPM
Kallen, Kitty 1926- RkOn[port]
Kallen, Lucille WomWMM
Kallenberg, Siegfried Garibaldi 1867-1944 Baker 78, NewGrD 80
Kallianiotes, Helena WhoHol A
Kallir, Lilian IntWWM 77, -80, WhoMus 72
Kalliwoda, Johann Wenzel 1801-1866 Baker 78, NewGrD 80
Kalliwoda, Johannes Wenceslaus 1801-1866 OxMus
Kalliwoda, Wilhelm 1827-1893 Baker 78
Kallman, Chester Simon 1921-1975 AmSCAP 80, NewEOp 71, NewGrD 80
Kallman, Dick 1934- AmSCAP 66, BiE&WWA, ForYSC, WhoHol A
Kallman, Herbert E 1912- AmSCAP 66, -80
Kallmann, Helmut 1922- Baker 78, CreCan 2, IntWWM 80, NewGrD 80
Kallstenius, Edvin 1881-1967 Baker 78, DcCM, NewGrD 80
Kalman, Charles Emmerich 1929- IntWWM 77, -80
Kalman, Emmerich 1882-1953 AmSCAP 66, -80, Baker 78, CmpEPM, NewGrD 80, NotNAT B, WhThe
Kalman, Imre 1882-1953 NewGrD 80
Kalman, Oszkar 1887-1971 NewGrD 80
Kalmanoff, Martin 1920- AmSCAP 66, -80, ConAmC, IntWWM 77, -80
Kalmar, Bert 1884-1947 AmPS, AmSCAP 66, -80, BestMus, BiDAmM, CmpEPM, EncMT, HalFC 80, NewCBMT, NotNAT B, Sw&Ld C, WhThe
Kalmar, Laszlo 1931- Baker 78, NewGrD 80
Kalmar And Ruby BestMus
Kalmus, Alfred August Ulrich 1889-1972 NewGrD 80, WhoMus 72
Kalmus, Edwin F 1893- NewGrD 80
Kalmus, Herbert Thomas 1881-1963 DcFM, FilmEn, FilmgC, HalFC 80, WorEFlm
Kalnins, Aldonis 1928- NewGrD 80
Kalnins, Alfreds 1879-1951 Baker 78, NewGrD 80
Kalnins, Imants 1941- NewGrD 80
Kalnins, Janis 1904- Baker 78, IntWWM 77, -80, NewGrD 80
Kalomiris, Manolis 1883-1962 Baker 78, DcCM, NewGrD 80
Kalous, Vaclav 1715-1786 NewGrD 80
Kalser, Erwin 1883-1958 Film 2, WhScrn 74, -77, WhoHol B
Kalser, Konstantin 1920- IntMPA 77, -75, -76, -78, -79, -80
Kalsons, Romualds 1936- NewGrD 80
Kaltenbach, Paul PupTheA
Kalter, Sabine 1890-1957 NewGrD 80
Kalthoum, Um 1898-1975 WhScrn 77
Kalthum, Ibrahim Um 1908-1975 NewGrD 80
Kaltz, Armand 1892-1941 Film 2
Kalwitz, Seth NewGrD 80
Kam, Dennis 1942- ConAmC
Kamadjojo, Indra 1906- DancEn 78
Kamae, Edward L 1927- AmSCAP 80
Kamae, Myrna 1942- AmSCAP 80
Kamakahi, Dennis David 1953- AmSCAP 80
Kamano, John Nakula 1904- AmSCAP 66, -80
Kamasa, Stefan 1930- IntWWM 77, -80
Kamber, Bernard M IntMPA 77, -75, -76, -78, -79, -80
Kambisis, Joannes 1872-1902 NotNAT B
Kamburov, Ivan 1883-1955 Baker 78, NewGrD 80
Kamei, Fumio 1908- DcFM, FilmEn
Kamel, Antonin NewGrD 80
Kamel Morsi, Ahmad 1900?- DcFM
Kamen, Milt WhoHol A
Kamen, Milt 1922-1977 JoeFr
Kamen, Stanley A 1928- IntMPA 77, -75, -76, -78, -79, -80
Kamenikova, Valentina 1930- IntWWM 77, -80
Kamenka, Alexandre 1888-1969 DcFM
Kamenka, Alexandre 1888-1970 OxFilm
Kamensky, Alexander 1900-1952 Baker 78
Kamenzky, Eliezer 1889-1957 WhScrn 74, -77
Kamerko Balalaika Orchestra Film 2
Kames, Bob AmSCAP 80
Kamey, Paul 1912- IntMPA 77, -75, -76, -78, -79, -80
Kamien, Anna 1912- ConAmC
Kamienski, Lucian 1885-1964 Baker 78
Kamienski, Maciej 1734-1821 NewGrD 80
Kamienski, Mathias 1734-1821 Baker 78
Kamienski, Matthew 1734-1821 MusMk, OxMus
Kamilarov, Emil 1928- IntWWM 80
Kamin, Franz Tom 1931- CpmDNM 73, ConAmC
Kamins, Bernie 1915- IntMPA 77, -75, -76, -78, -79, -80
Kaminska, Ida 1899-1980 EncWT, Ent, FilmEn, FilmgC, HalFC 80, NotNAT A, WhoThe 72, -77
Kaminska, Ida 1900?- WhoHol A
Kaminski, Heinrich 1886-1946 Baker 78, NewGrD 80, OxMus
Kaminski, Joseph 1903-1972 Baker 78, NewGrD 80
Kaminski, Marcin 1913- IntWWM 77
Kaminsky, Lucian J 1924- AmSCAP 66
Kaminsky, Lucian John 1926- AmSCAP 80
Kaminsky, Max 1908- BiDAmM, CmpEPM, EncJzS 70, IlEncJ, WhoJazz 72
Kamiyama, Sojim Film 2
Kamiyama, Sojin 1884-1954 WhScrn 74, -77
Kammel, Antonin 1730-1787 NewGrD 80
Kammell, Antonin 1730-1787 NewGrD 80
Kammer, Klaus 1929-1964 NotNAT B, WhScrn 74, -77
Kammeren, Torsten Film 2
Kammerer, David Eames PupTheA
Kamml, Antonin NewGrD 80
Kamp, Theo VanDe 1941- IntWWM 77
Kampa, Johannes De NewGrD 80
Kampanus, Jan NewGrD 80
Kamper, Dietrich 1936- NewGrD 80
Kampers, Fritz 1891-1950 Film 2, WhScrn 77
Kampf, Karl 1874-1950 Baker 78
Kamphuysen, Dirk Rafaelszoon NewGrD 80
Kampka, Bernd 1919- WhoMus 72
Kamsler, Ben 1905- BiE&WWA
Kamu, Okko 1946- Baker 78, IntWWM 77, -80, NewGrD 80, WhoMus 72, WhoOp 76
Kamuca, Richard 1930- BiDAmM, EncJzS 70
Kamuca, Richie 1930- EncJzS 70
Kanagaraj, Alfred 1934- IntWWM 77
Kanawa, Kiri Te NewGrD 80
Kanazawa, Masakata 1934- IntWWM 77, -80, NewGrD 80
Kancheli, Giya Alexandrovich 1935- NewGrD 80
Kander, John 1927- BestMus, BiE&WWA, EncMT, HalFC 80, NewCBMT, NotNAT, PopAmC SUP[port], WhoThe 72, -77
Kander And Ebb BestMus
Kanders, Agnes NewGrD 80
Kandinsky, Vassily 1866-1944 EncWT
Kandler, Franz Sales 1792-1831 Baker 78, NewGrD 80
Kane, Bernie 1906- AmSCAP 66, -80
Kane, Beverly Jean 1957- BlkWAB[port]
Kane, Blanche 1889-1937 WhScrn 74, -77
Kane, Byron WhoHol A
Kane, Carol 1952- FilmEn, HalFC 80, WhoHol A
Kane, Dennis NewYTET
Kane, Diana Film 2
Kane, Eddie d1969 Film 2, WhoHol B
Kane, Eddie 1888-1969 WhScrn 74

Kane, Eddie 1889-1969 *WhScrn 77*
Kane, Gail d1966 *Film 1, MotPP, WhoHol B*
Kane, Gail 1885-1966 *WhScrn 74, -77*
Kane, Gail 1887-1966 *WhThe*
Kane, Gail 1892-1966 *Film 2, TwYS*
Kane, Helen *AmPS B*
Kane, Helen d1966 *WhoHol B*
Kane, Helen 1903-1966 *FilmEn, ThFT[port]*
Kane, Helen 1904-1966 *CmpEPM, EncMT, Film 2, ForYSC, HalFC 80, JoeFr[port]*
Kane, Helen 1910-1966 *BiDAmM*
Kane, Helen Babe 1908-1966 *WhScrn 74, -77*
Kane, Irving *ConAmC*
Kane, Jack *Film 2*
Kane, John J d1969 *WhScrn 74, -77, WhoHol B*
Kane, Joseph 1894-1975 *HalFC 80, IntMPA 77, -75, -76*
Kane, Joseph 1897- *FilmEn*
Kane, Joseph 1897-1975 *FilmgC*
Kane, Joseph 1904- *CmMov*
Kane, Lida d1955 *WhScrn 74, -77, WhoHol B*
Kane, Margie *Film 2*
Kane, Michael *WhoHol A*
Kane, Peter T 1942- *AmSCAP 80*
Kane, Richard 1938- *WhoThe 77*
Kane, Robert *Film 2*
Kane, Ruth *Film 2*
Kane, Sherwin A 1903- *IntMPA 75, -76*
Kane, Sid *WhoHol A*
Kane, Stanley D 1907- *IntMPA 77, -75, -76, -78, -79, -80*
Kane, Violet *Film 2*
Kane, Whitford 1881-1956 *NotNAT B, WhScrn 74, -77, WhThe, WhoHol B*
Kane, Whitford 1882-1956 *NotNAT A*
Kaner, Ruth d1964 *NotNAT B*
K'ang, Chin-Chih *REnWD[port]*
Kangaroo *BiDAmM*
Kani, John *PlP&P A[port]*
Kania, Emanuel 1827-1887 *NewGrD 80*
Kaniewska, Maria *WomWMM*
Kaniewski, Jan 1931- *IntWWM 77, -80*
Kanin, Fay *BiE&WWA, IntMPA 77, -75, -76, -78, -79, -80, NotNAT, WomWMM*
Kanin, Garson 1912- *AmSCAP 66, BiDFilm, -81, BiE&WWA, CmMov, CnMD, CnThe, ConDr 73, -77, DcFM, DcLB 7[port], EncWT, Ent, FilmEn, FilmgC, HalFC 80, IntMPA 77, -75, -76, -78, -79, -80, ModWD, MovMk[port], NatPD[port], NotNAT, -A, OxFilm, WhoThe 72, -77, WorEFlm*
Kanin, Michael 1910- *BiE&WWA, FilmEn, FilmgC, HalFC 80, IntMPA 77, -75, -76, -78, -79, -80, NotNAT*
Kanitz, Eernest 1894-1978 *IntWWM 77, -80*
Kanitz, Ernest 1894-1978 *AmSCAP 66, CpmDNM 72, ConAmC, NewGrD 80, WhoMus 72*
Kanitz, Ernst 1894-1978 *Baker 78, NewGrD 80*
Kanka, Jan Nepomuk 1772-1863 *NewGrD 80*
Kanka, Johann Nepomuk 1772-1863 *NewGrD 80*
Kann, Hans 1927- *Baker 78, IntWWM 77, -80*
Kann, Lilly *WhThe, WhoHol A*
Kann, Lily 1898?- *FilmgC, HalFC 80*
Kann, Sylvia *WhoHol A*
Kanne, Friedrich August 1778-1833 *NewGrD 80*
Kanner, Alexis 1942- *FilmgC, HalFC 80, WhoHol A, WhoThe 72, -77*
Kanner, Jerome Herbert 1903- *AmSCAP 66, -80, Baker 78, ConAmC*
Kanner-Rosenthal, Hedwig 1882-1959 *Baker 78*
Kanngiesser, Claus Dietmar 1945- *IntWWM 77, -80, WhoMus 72*
Kannon, Jackie 1919-1974 *WhScrn 77, WhoHol B*
Kansas *IlEncR, RkOn 2[port]*
Kansas City Band *BiDAmM*
Kansas Joe *BluesWW[port]*
Kansas Klodhoppers, Doc McCaully's *BiDAmM*
Kanski, Jozef Celestyn 1928- *IntWWM 77, -80*
Kanter, Hal 1918- *FilmEn, FilmgC, HalFC 80, IntMPA 77, -75, -76, -78, -79, -80, NewYTET, WorEFlm*
Kanter, Jay 1927- *IntMPA 77, -76, -78, -79, -80*
Kanter, Nancy Reed 1928- *AmSCAP 80*
Kantor, Eva Ida *IntWWM 77, -80*
Kantor, Joseph 1930- *AmSCAP 80, CpmDNM 77, -78, -79, ConAmC*
Kantor, Mackinlay 1904-1977 *FilmgC, HalFC 80*
Kantor, Tadeusz 1915- *EncWT*
Kantorow, Jean-Jacques Alain 1945- *IntWWM 77, -80, WhoMus 72*
Kantrovitch, U *WhoMus 72*
Kantrovitch, Vera *WhoMus 72*
Kanwischer, Alfred Oswald 1932- *ConAmC*
Kao, Tse-Ch'eng *REnWD[port]*
Kaonohi, David *AmSCAP 80*
Kapell, William 1922-1951 *BiDAmM*
Kapell, William 1922-1953 *Baker 78, BnBkM 80, NewGrD 80*
Kaper, Bronislau 1902- *AmPS, FilmgC, HalFC 80, IntMPA 77, -75, -76, -78, -80, WorEFlm[port]*
Kaper, Bronislaw 1902- *AmSCAP 66, -80, CmpEPM, ConAmC, FilmEn, IntMPA 79, NewGrD 80*
Kapf, Elinor *WomWMM*
Kaplan, Abraham 1931- *AmSCAP 80, NewGrD 80*
Kaplan, Althea E 1935- *IntWWM 77, -80*
Kaplan, Arthur William 1935- *AmSCAP 80*
Kaplan, Barbara *WomWMM B*
Kaplan, Barbara Connally 1923- *IntWWM 77, -80*
Kaplan, Benjamin 1929- *IntWWM 77, -80, WhoMus 72*
Kaplan, Boris 1897- *IntMPA 77, -75, -76, -78, -79, -80*
Kaplan, Bruce *ConMuA 80B*
Kaplan, Eddie Nuts d1964 *NotNAT B*
Kaplan, Elliot 1931- *AmSCAP 80, ConAmC*
Kaplan, Gabe 1946- *JoeFr[port]*
Kaplan, Gabriel *IntMPA 79, -80*
Kaplan, Harriet 1917- *BiE&WWA*
Kaplan, Helene G *WomWMM B*
Kaplan, Jack A 1947- *NatPD[port]*
Kaplan, John *ConMuA 80B*
Kaplan, Jonathan 1947- *FilmEn*
Kaplan, Leigh Wright 1937- *IntWWM 77*
Kaplan, Lois Jay 1932- *IntWWM 80*
Kaplan, Marvin *ForYSC, WhoHol A*
Kaplan, Marvin 1924- *FilmgC, HalFC 80*
Kaplan, Marvin 1927- *MovMk, Vers A[port]*
Kaplan, Mike 1918- *IntMPA 77, -75, -76, -78, -79, -80*
Kaplan, Murray M *IntMPA 77, -78, -79, -80*
Kaplan, Nelly *WomWMM*
Kaplan, Nelly 1931- *FilmEn*
Kaplan, Nelly 1934- *HalFC 80*
Kaplan, Robert Barnett 1924- *CpmDNM 78, -79, -80, ConAmC*
Kaplan, Saul 1898- *BiE&WWA*
Kaplan, Sharon Lynne 1941- *AmSCAP 80*
Kaplan, Sheldon Zachary 1911- *AmSCAP 66, -80*
Kaplan, Sol *HalFC 80*
Kaplan, Sol 1919- *BiE&WWA, NotNAT*
Kaplane, Darcy Anne 1954- *AmSCAP 80*
Kapler, Alexei 1904- *DcFM*
Kapoor, Prithvi Raj 1906-1972 *WhScrn 77*
Kapoor, Raj 1924- *DcFM, FilmEn*
Kapp *NewGrD 80*
Kapp, Arthur 1875-1952 *Baker 78*
Kapp, Artur 1878-1952 *NewGrD 80*
Kapp, Bruce *ConMuA 80B*
Kapp, David 1904- *AmSCAP 66*
Kapp, David 1904-1976 *AmSCAP 80*
Kapp, Dorothy Louise 1910- *IntWWM 77, -80*
Kapp, Eugen Arturovich 1908- *Baker 78, IntWWM 77, -80, NewGrD 80*
Kapp, Julius 1883-1962 *Baker 78, NewGrD 80*
Kapp, Paul 1907- *AmSCAP 66, -80*
Kapp, Villem 1913-1964 *Baker 78, NewGrD 80*
Kappel, Gertrude 1884-1971 *Baker 78, CmOp, MusSN[port], NewEOp 71, NewGrD 80*
Kappel, Ulla 1936- *IntWWM 77, -80*
Kappel, Vagn 1908- *IntWWM 77, WhoMus 72*
Kappeler, Alfred d1945 *NotNAT B*
Kapplmuller, Herbert 1941- *WhoOp 76*
Kapr, Jan 1914- *Baker 78, DcCM, IntWWM 77, -80, NewGrD 80*
Kapral, Vaclav 1889-1947 *Baker 78, NewGrD 80*
Kapralova, Vitezslava 1915-1940 *Baker 78, NewGrD 80*
Kaproff, Dana 1954- *AmSCAP 80*
Kaprow, Allan 1927- *ConDr 73, -77E*
Kaprow, Vaughan Rachel *WomWMM B*
Kaps, Fred *MagIlD*
Kapsberger, Johann Hieronymus 1580?-1651 *NewGrD 80*
Kapsberger, Johann Hieronymus Von 1575-1661 *Baker 78*
Kapusta, Jan 1932- *IntWWM 77*
Kapuste, Falco 1943- *CnOxB*
Karabasz, Kasimierz 1930- *DcFM*
Karai, Jozsef 1927- *IntWWM 77, -80*
Karajan, Herbert Von 1908- *Baker 78, BnBkM 80[port], CmOp, IntWWM 77, -80, MusMk, MusSN[port], NewEOp 71, NewGrD 80[port]*
Karajan, Theodor Georg Von 1810-1873 *Baker 78*
Karalli, Vera Alexeyevna 1888-1972 *DancEn 78*
Karalli, Vera Alexeyevna 1889-1972 *CnOxB*
Karamanuk, Sirvart 1916- *IntWWM 80*
Karant, Zoey Bryna *AmSCAP 80*
Karas, Simon 1905- *NewGrD 80*
Karasek, Bohumil 1926-1969 *NewGrD 80*
Karasek, Jiri 1925- *IntWWM 77, -80*
Karashville, Kokhta *Film 2*
Karasick, Simon 1910- *WhoMus 72*
Karasik, Gita 1949- *IntWWM 77, -80*
Karasowski, Maurycy 1823-1892 *NewGrD 80*
Karasowski, Moritz 1823-1892 *Baker 78*
Karastoyanov, Assen 1893-1976 *Baker 78, NewGrD 80*
Karatigin, Vyacheslav Gavrilovich 1875-1925 *NewGrD 80*
Karatygin, Vasily Andreyevich 1802-1853 *OxThe*
Karatygin, Vyacheslav 1875-1925 *Baker 78*
Karayev, Kara Abulfas Ogly 1918- *IntWWM 77, -80, NewGrD 80*
Karayn, Jim *NewYTET*
Karbowska, Helena 1906- *IntWWM 77, -80*
Karbusicky, Vladimir 1925- *IntWWM 77, -80, NewGrD 80*
Karchin, Louis S 1951- *ConAmC*
Karchmer, Andrea *NatPD[port]*
Kardar, Aaejay *DcFM*
Kardonne, Rick 1947- *IntWWM 80*
Kardos, Dezider 1914- *Baker 78, DcCM, IntWWM 77, -80, NewGrD 80, WhoMus 72*
Kardos, Gene *BgBands 74, CmpEPM*
Kardos, Istvan 1891-1975 *Baker 78, NewGrD 80*
Kareda, Urjo 1944- *ConAmTC*
Karel, Rudolf 1880-1945 *Baker 78, NewGrD 80*
Karels, Harvey d1975 *Film 2, WhScrn 77*
Karelskaya, Rimma Klavdiyevna 1927- *CnOxB*
Karen, Anna *WhoHol A*
Karenne, Diana *Film 2*
Karetnikov, Nicolai Nicolayevich 1930- *CnOxB*
Karetnikov, Nikolai Nicolayevich 1930- *DcCM*
Karetnikov, Nikolay Nikolayevich 1930- *NewGrD 80*
Karg, Sigfrid 1877-1933 *NewGrD 80*
Karg-Elert, Sigfrid 1877-1933 *Baker 78, BnBkM 80, NewGrD 80, OxMus*
Karg-Elert, Sigfried 1877-1933 *MusMk*
Kargel, Sixt 1540?-1594? *NewGrD 80*
Kargel, Sixtus 1540?-1594? *NewGrD 80*
Karges, Wilhelm 1613?-1699 *NewGrD 80*
Kargl, Sixt *NewGrD 80*
Karin, Rita *WhoHol A*
Karina, Anna *WhoHol A*
Karina, Anna 1940- *BiDFilm, -81, FilmAG WE[port], FilmEn, FilmgC, HalFC 80, MovMk[port]*
Karina, Anna 1941- *ForYSC, WorEFlm*
Karina, Anna 1942- *OxFilm*
Karina, Lilian 1910- *CnOxB, DancEn 78*
Karina, Tania 1930- *DancEn 78*
Karinska *BiE&WWA*
Karinska, Barbara 1886- *CnOxB, DancEn 78, NotNAT*

Karinthy, Ferenc 1921- *CroCD*
Karizs, Bela 1931- *WhoOp 76*
Karjalainen, Ahti 1907- *Baker 78*
Karki, Toivo Pietari Johannes 1915- *IntWWM 77*
Karkkoschka, Erhard 1923- *IntWWM 77*
Karkoff, Maurice Ingvar 1927- *Baker 78, DcCM, IntWWM 77, -80, NewGrD 80*
Karkoschka, Erhard 1923- *Baker 78, DcCM, IntWWM 80, NewGrD 80*
Karkowsky, Nancy *WomWMM B*
Karl And Harty *IlEncCM*
Karl, Kashen *CreCan 1*
Karl, Roger *Film 2*
Karl, Theodore O H 1912- *BiE&WWA, NotNAT*
Karl, Thomas 1846-1916 *BiDAmM*
Karl, Tom 1846-1916 *Baker 78*
Karlan, Richard *WhoHol A*
Karle, Arthur D 1905?-1967 *WhoJazz 72*
Karlin, Bo-Peep d1969 *Film 2, WhScrn 74, -77, WhoHol B*
Karlin, Elisabeth J *WomWMM B*
Karlin, Fred *HalFC 80, IntMPA 77, -78, -79, -80*
Karlin, Frederick James 1936- *AmSCAP 66, -80, ConAmC*
Karlin, Miriam 1925- *FilmgC, HalFC 80, WhoHol A, WhoThe 72, -77*
Karlin, Myron D 1918- *IntMPA 77, -75, -76, -78, -79, -80*
Karlins, M William 1932- *Baker 78, ConAmC*
Karlins, Martin William 1932- *CpmDNM 74, -76*
Karloff, Boris 1887-1969 *BiDFilm, -81, BiE&WWA, CmMov, FilmEn, Film 1, -2, FilmgC, ForYSC, HalFC 80[port], MotPP, MovMk[port], NotNAT A, -B, OxFilm, TwYS, WhScrn 74, -77, WhThe, WhoHol B, WhoHrs 80[port], WorEFlm[port]*
Karlowicz, Jan 1836-1903 *Baker 78, NewGrD 80*
Karlowicz, Mieczyslaw 1876-1909 *Baker 78, NewGrD 80*
Karlsen, Rolf Kare 1911- *IntWWM 80*
Karlskov, Poul 1927- *IntWWM 77, -80*
Karlson, Phil 1908- *BiDFilm, -81, FilmEn, FilmgC, HalFC 80, IntMPA 77, -75, -76, -78, -79, -80, MovMk[port], WhoHrs 80, WorEFlm*
Karlsrud, Edmond 1927- *WhoOp 76*
Karlsruhe Anonymous *NewGrD 80*
Karlstadt, Liesl 1893-1960 *WhScrn 74, -77, WhoHol B*
Karlweis, Oscar 1895-1956 *NotNAT B, WhThe, WhoHol B*
Karlweiss, Oscar *ForYSC*
Karlweiss, Oscar 1895-1956 *WhScrn 77*
Karmen, Roman Lasarevich 1906-1978 *DcFM, FilmEn, OxFilm, WorEFlm*
Karmen, Steve D 1937- *AmSCAP 80*
Karmon, Robert 1939- *NatPD[port]*
Karnelly, Leila *Film 2*
Karnes, Roscoe 1893-1970 *Film 1*
Karnilova, Maria 1920- *BiE&WWA, CnOxB, DancEn 78, EncMT, NotNAT, WhoHol A, WhoThe 72, -77*
Karno, Fred 1866-1941 *HalFC 80, IlWWBF A, NotNAT A, OxFilm, OxThe, WhThe*
Karns, Maurice *Film 2*
Karns, Roscoe 1893-1970 *FilmEn, Film 2, FilmgC, ForYSC, HalFC 80, MotPP, MovMk, TwYS, WhScrn 74, -77, WhoHol B*
Karns, Roscoe 1897-1970 *Vers B[port]*
Karolak, Marek 1954- *IntWWM 77, -80*
Karolak, Wojciech Krzyszlof 1939- *EncJzS 70*
Karolak, Wojciech Krzysztof 1939- *IntWWM 77*
Karolyi, Pal 1934- *IntWWM 77, -80, NewGrD 80*
Karow, Karl 1790-1863 *Baker 78*
Karp, Howard 1929- *WhoMus 72*
Karp, Michael 1952- *AmSCAP 80*
Karp, Natalia *WhoMus 72*
Karp, Natalla 1915- *IntWWM 77, -80*
Karp, Richard 1904- *BiDAmM*
Karp, Richard 1907- *WhoOp 76*
Karp, Russell H *NewYTET*
Karp, Sharon *WomWMM B*
Karp, Theodore C 1926- *NewGrD 80*
Karpath, Ludwig 1866-1936 *Baker 78*
Karpati, Janos 1932- *IntWWM 80, NewGrD 80*
Karpeles, Maud *OxMus*
Karpeles, Maud 1885-1976 *Baker 78, IntWWM 77, NewGrD 80*
Karr, Darwin 1875-1945 *Film 1, WhScrn 77*
Karr, Elizabeth R 1925- *AmSCAP 66, -80*
Karr, Gary Michael 1941- *Baker 78, BnBkM 80, IntWWM 77, -80, NewGrD 80*
Karr, Harold 1921-1968 *AmSCAP 66, -80, BiE&WWA, NotNAT*
Karr, Patti 1932- *BiE&WWA, NotNAT*
Karras, Alex *WhoHol A*
Karrer, Paul 1829-1896 *NewGrD 80*
Karreres, Paulos 1829-1896 *NewGrD 80*
Karrick, Cecil 1919- *ConAmC*
Karrington, Frank 1858-1936 *WhScrn 74, -77*
Kars, Jean-Rodolphe 1947- *NewGrD 80*
Karsavina, Tamara Platonovna 1885- *CnOxB, DancEn 78[port], WhThe*
Karson, Burton Lewis 1934- *IntWWM 80*
Karson, Kit d1940 *NotNAT B*
Karson, Nat d1954 *NotNAT B*
Karstadt, Georg 1903- *NewGrD 80*
Karstens, Gerda 1903- *CnOxB*
Kartalian, Buck *WhoHol A*
Kartousch, Louise d1964 *NotNAT B*
Kartzev, Alexander 1883-1953 *Baker 78*
Karvas, Peter 1920- *CnThe, CroCD, REnWD[port]*
Karvonen, Paul E 1917- *ConAmC*
Karyotakis, Theodore 1903-1978 *Baker 78, DcCM, NewGrD 80*
Kasatkina, Natalia Dmitrievna 1934- *CnOxB*
Kaschendorff, Stephan 1425?-1499? *NewGrD 80*
Kaschmann, Giuseppe 1847-1925 *NewGrD 80*
Kase, C Robert 1905- *BiE&WWA, NotNAT*
Kase, Julie Ann 1961- *IntWWM 77*
Kasem, Casey *WhoHol A*
Kasemets, Udo 1919- *Baker 78, CreCan 1, DcCM, NewGrD 80*
Kasenetz-Katz Singing Orchestral Circus *BiDAmM, RkOn 2[port]*
Kash, Eugene 1912- *CreCan 2*
Kash, Maureen Kathleen Stewart Forrester *CreCan 2*
Kasha, Al 1937- *AmSCAP 80*
Kasha, Lawrence N 1933- *BiE&WWA, NotNAT, WhoThe 72, -77*
Kasha, Phyllis L *AmSCAP 80*
Kashanski, Richard Paul 1947- *AmSCAP 80, CpmDNM 78*
Kashey, Abe 1903-1965 *WhScrn 77*
Kashfi, Anna 1935- *FilmEn, ForYSC, MotPP, WhoHol A*
Kashin, Daniil Nikitich 1769-1841 *Baker 78, NewGrD 80*
Kashkin, Nikolai 1839-1920 *Baker 78*
Kashkin, Nikolay Dmitriyevich 1839-1920 *NewGrD 80*
Kashner, Bruno *Film 2*
Kashner, David *Film 2*
Kashperov, Vladimir Nikitich 1826-1894 *Baker 78, NewGrD 80*
Kasich, Joan *WomWMM B*
Kasilag, Lucrecia Roces 1918- *IntWWM 77, -80, NewGrD 80*
Kaskel, Karl Von 1866-1943 *Baker 78*
Kasket, Harold 1916?- *FilmgC, HalFC 80, WhoHol A*
Kaslik, Vaclav 1917- *DcCM, IntWWM 77, -80, NewGrD 80, WhoMus 72, WhoOp 76*
Kaslow, David Martin 1943- *IntWWM 77, -80*
Kasman, Giuseppe *NewGrD 80*
Kasmire, Robert D *NewYTET*
Kasprowicz, Jan 1860-1926 *ModWD*
Kasrashsvili, Makvala Filimonovna 1942- *WhoOp 76*
Kass, Art *ConMuA 80B*
Kass, Gerald H 1943- *AmSCAP 80*
Kass, Herman 1923- *IntMPA 77, -75, -76, -78, -79, -80*
Kass, Jerome *NatPD[port], NewYTET*
Kassal, Luis *NewGrD 80*
Kassel, Art 1896-1965 *AmSCAP 66, -80, BgBands 74[port], CmpEPM*
Kassern, Tadeusz 1904-1957 *DcCM*
Kassern, Tadeusz Zygfrid 1904-1957 *Baker 78*
Kassern, Tadeusz Zygfryd 1904-1957 *NewGrD 80*
Kassern, Tadeuz Zygfried 1904-1957 *ConAmC*
Kassewitz, Helene *Film 2*
Kassila, Matti 1924- *DcFM*
Kassin, Arthur Robert 1917- *AmSCAP 66, -80*
Kassler, Jamie Croy *IntWWM 80*
Kassler, Michael 1941- *ConAmC*
Kassmayer, Moritz 1831-1884 *Baker 78*
Kast, Pierre 1920- *DcFM, FilmEn, OxFilm, WorEFlm*
Kastalsky, Alexander 1856-1926 *Baker 78, OxMus*
Kastal'sky, Alexandr Dmitriyevich 1856-1926 *NewGrD 80*
Kastberg, Dale Martin 1943- *IntWWM 77*
Kastendieck, Miles Merwin 1905- *Baker 78, WhoMus 72*
Kastendorffer, Stephan *NewGrD 80*
Kaster, Barbara *WomWMM B*
Kastl, Sonia 1929- *DancEn 78*
Kastl, Sonja 1929- *CnOxB*
Kastle, Leonard 1929- *AmSCAP 66, -80, Baker 78, ConAmC*
Kastner, Alfred 1870-1948 *Baker 78, NewGrD 80*
Kastner, Bruno d1958 *Film 2, WhScrn 77*
Kastner, Elliott 1930- *FilmEn, FilmgC, HalFC 80, IntMPA 77, -76, -78, -79, -80*
Kastner, Emerich 1847-1916 *NewGrD 80*
Kastner, Emmerich 1847-1916 *Baker 78*
Kastner, Erich 1899-1974 *CnMD, EncWT, HalFC 80, ModWD*
Kastner, Georg Friedrich 1852-1882 *Baker 78*
Kastner, Georges Frederic Eugene *NewGrD 80*
Kastner, Jean-Georges 1810-1867 *Baker 78, MusMk, NewGrD 80*
Kastner, Jean Georges 1810-1867 *OxMus*
Kastner, Johann Georg 1810-1867 *NewGrD 80*
Kastner, Johann Georg 1852-1882 *Baker 78*
Kastner, Macario Santiago 1908- *IntWWM 77, -80, NewGrD 80*
Kastner, Peter 1944- *FilmgC, HalFC 80, WhoHol A*
Kastner, Santiago 1908- *Baker 78*
Kastu, Matti *IntWWM 80*
Kasznar, Kurt 1913- *WhoThe 72*
Kasznar, Kurt 1913-1979 *BiE&WWA, FilmEn, FilmgC, ForYSC, HalFC 80, IntMPA 77, -75, -76, -78, -79, MotPP, MovMk[port], NotNAT, Vers B[port], WhoHol A, WhoThe 77*
Kataev, Valentin Petrovich 1897- *CnMD, ModWD*
Katahn, Enid 1932- *IntWWM 77, -80*
Katainen, Elina *WomWMM*
Kataja, Lassi Pellervo 1940- *IntWWM 77, -80*
Katanyan, Aram 1926- *IntWWM 77, -80*
Katayev, Valentin Petrovich 1897- *EncWT, McGEWD[port], OxThe*
Katch, Kurt 1896-1958 *FilmEn, FilmgC, HalFC 80, Vers A[port], WhScrn 74, -77, WhoHol B*
Katch, Kurt 1896-1959 *ForYSC*
Katchalof, V L *Film 2*
Katchalov, Vassily *PlP&P[port]*
Katcharov, Michel 1913- *DancEn 78*
Katchen, Julius 1926-1969 *Baker 78, NewGrD 80*
Katcher, Aram *WhoHol A*
Kate, Andre Ten 1796-1858 *Baker 78*
Kateb, Yacine 1929- *REnWD[port]*
Kates, Stephen 1943- *Baker 78*
Kates, Stephen Edward 1943- *IntWWM 80*
Katims, Milton *IntWWM 77, -80, WhoMus 72*
Katims, Milton 1909- *Baker 78, BiDAmM, NewGrD 80*
Katin, Peter Roy 1930- *IntWWM 77, -80, NewGrD 80, WhoMus 72*
Katleman, Harris L 1928- *IntMPA 77, -78, -79, -80*
Katlewicz, Jerzy 1927- *IntWWM 77, -80*
Katona, Bela *WhoMus 72*
Katona, Jozsef 1791-1830 *McGEWD[port],*

OxThe
Katona, Sandor Tibor 1915- *WhoOp 76*
Katonik, Carol *WomWMM B*
Katsarova, Rayna 1901- *NewGrD 80*
Katsas, John *PupTheA*
Katscher, Robert 1894-1942 *AmSCAP 66*
Katselas, Milton *IntMPA 75, -76, -78, -79, -80*
Katselas, Milton 1933- *IntMPA 77, WhoThe 72, -77*
Katski *NewGrD 80*
Katski, Antoni 1817-1899 *NewGrD 80*
Katski, Apolinary 1825-1879 *NewGrD 80*
Katski, Karol 1815-1867 *NewGrD 80*
Katski, Maria Eugenia 1816- *NewGrD 80*
Katski, Stanislaw 1820- *NewGrD 80*
Katt, William 1950?- *FilmEn, HalFC 80, IntMPA 79, -80*
Katterjohn, Arthur David 1929- *IntWWM 77, -80*
Kattnigg, Rudolf 1895-1955 *NewGrD 80*
Katuar, Georgy *NewGrD 80*
Katul'skaya, Elena Kliment'yevna 1888-1966 *NewGrD 80*
Katunda, Eunice DoMonte Lima 1915- *IntWWM 77, -80*
Katwijk, Paul Van 1885- *ConAmC*
Katwijk, Paul Van 1885-1974 *Baker 78*
Katz, Al *BgBands 74*
Katz, Alfred 1911- *IntMPA 75, -76*
Katz, Benjamin 1915- *AmSCAP 80*
Katz, Dick 1924- *EncJzS 70*
Katz, Dorothy 1924- *IntWWM 77, -80*
Katz, Eberhard 1928- *WhoOp 76*
Katz, Erich 1900-1973 *ConAmC, NewGrD 80*
Katz, Fred 1919- *AmSCAP 66, -80, WhoHrs 80*
Katz, Frederick 1919- *BiDAmM, ConAmC*
Katz, Gary *ConMuA 80B*
Katz, Gloria *WomWMM*
Katz, Israel J 1930- *Baker 78, IntWWM 77, -80, NewGrD 80*
Katz, Martha Strongin 1943- *IntWWM 77, -80*
Katz, Marty 1947- *IntMPA 80*
Katz, Mindru 1925-1978 *IntWWM 77, NewGrD 80, WhoMus 72*
Katz, Morton 1925- *AmSCAP 80*
Katz, Norman B 1919- *IntMPA 77, -75, -76, -78, -79, -80*
Katz, Oscar *NewYTET*
Katz, Paul 1907- *IntWWM 77, -80*
Katz, Paul 1941- *IntWWM 77, -80*
Katz, Raymond *BiE&WWA*
Katz, Reuben 1916- *AmSCAP 80*
Katz, Richard Aaron 1924- *BiDAmM, EncJzS 70*
Katz, William 1922- *AmSCAP 66*
Katz, William 1926- *AmSCAP 80*
Katzbock, Rudolf 1936- *WhoOp 76*
Katzenellenbogen, Elisabeth 1904- *IntWWM 77, -80*
Katzenelson, Isaac 1886-1941? *NotNAT B*
Katzer, Georg 1935- *NewGrD 80*
Katzin, Lee H *FilmEn, FilmgC, HalFC 80*
Katzman, Sam 1901-1973 *FilmEn, FilmgC, HalFC 80, WhoHrs 80, WorEFlm*
Kauder, Hugo 1888-1972 *Baker 78, ConAmC*
Kauer, Ferdinand 1751-1831 *Baker 78, NewGrD 80*
Kauer, Guenther Max 1921- *AmSCAP 80*
Kauer, Gunther *ConAmC*
Kauff, Peter *ConMuA 80B*
Kauffman, Helen Reed *AmSCAP 66*
Kauffman, Robert Allen 1929- *IntWWM 77, -80*
Kauffmann, Emil 1836-1909 *Baker 78*
Kauffmann, Ernst Friedrich 1803-1856 *Baker 78*
Kauffmann, Fritz 1855-1934 *Baker 78*
Kauffmann, Georg Friedrich 1679-1735 *NewGrD 80*
Kauffmann, Leo Justinus 1901-1944 *Baker 78, NewGrD 80*
Kauffmann, Paul 1568-1632 *NewGrD 80*
Kauffmann, Stanley Jules 1916- *ConAmTC*
Kaufman, Al *Film 2*
Kaufman, Alvin S *AmSCAP 66, -80*
Kaufman, Bill Myron 1930- *AmSCAP 66, -80*
Kaufman, Boris 1906- *WorEFlm*
Kaufman, Boris 1906-1980 *DcFM, FilmEn, FilmgC, HalFC 80, IntMPA 77, -75, -76, -78, -79, -80, OxFilm*
Kaufman, Curt 1930- *IntMPA 77, -75, -76, -78, -79*
Kaufman, Elkan 1923- *IntMPA 77, -75, -76*
Kaufman, George S 1889-1961 *BestMus, BiDAmM, CnMD, CnThe, DcLB 7[port], EncMT, EncWT, Ent, FilmEn, FilmgC, HalFC 80, McGEWD[port], ModWD, NewCBMT, NotNAT A, -B, OxThe, PlP&P, REnWD[port], WhThe, WorEFlm*
Kaufman, Hal 1924- *IntMPA 77, -75, -76, -78, -79, -80*
Kaufman, Harry 1894-1961 *Baker 78*
Kaufman, Harry A d1944 *NotNAT B*
Kaufman, Irving *CmpEPM*
Kaufman, J L *IntMPA 77, -75, -76, -78, -79, -80*
Kaufman, Jack M *PupTheA*
Kaufman, Joseph 1882-1918 *WhScrn 77*
Kaufman, Leonard 1913- *IntMPA 77, -75, -76, -78, -79, -80*
Kaufman, Leonard B *IntMPA 77, -75, -78, -79, -80*
Kaufman, Louis 1905- *Baker 78, WhoMus 72*
Kaufman, Martin Ellis 1899- *AmSCAP 66, -80*
Kaufman, Matthew *ConMuA 80B*
Kaufman, Mel B 1879-1932 *AmSCAP 66, -80*
Kaufman, Mikhail Abramovich 1897- *DcFM, FilmEn, OxFilm*
Kaufman, Millard *FilmEn, FilmgC, HalFC 80*
Kaufman, Morris 1911- *AmSCAP 80*
Kaufman, Nikolai 1925- *NewGrD 80*
Kaufman, Paul 1936- *AmSCAP 80*
Kaufman, Phil 1936- *FilmEn*
Kaufman, Philip 1936- *HalFC 80, IntMPA 77, -75, -76, -78, -79, -80*
Kaufman, Rita d1968 *WhoHol B*
Kaufman, S Jay 1886-1957 *NotNAT B*
Kaufman, Sidney 1910- *IntMPA 77, -75, -76, -78, -79, -80*
Kaufman, William d1967 *WhScrn 77*
Kaufman, Willy d1967 *WhoHol B*
Kaufmann, Armin 1902- *Baker 78, IntWWM 80, NewGrD 80, WhoMus 72*
Kaufmann, Christine *MotPP, WhoHol A*
Kaufmann, Christine 1944- *FilmgC, HalFC 80*
Kaufmann, Christine 1945- *FilmAG WE, FilmEn, ForYSC, IntMPA 77, -75, -76, -78, -79, -80*
Kaufmann, Dieter 1941- *IntWWM 77, -80*
Kaufmann, F K *OxMus*
Kaufmann, Friedrich 1785-1866 *Baker 78*
Kaufmann, Harald 1927-1970 *NewGrD 80*
Kaufmann, Helen Loeb 1887- *Baker 78, IntWWM 77, -80, WhoMus 72*
Kaufmann, Henry W 1913- *NewGrD 80*
Kaufmann, J G *OxMus*
Kaufmann, Ludwig 1907- *WhoMus 72*
Kaufmann, Maurice 1928- *FilmgC, HalFC 80, WhoHol A*
Kaufmann, Paul *NewGrD 80*
Kaufmann, Reinhard Hermann 1936- *WhoOp 76*
Kaufmann, Walter 1907- *Baker 78, ConAmC, NewGrD 80*
Kauke, Helen Lucas 1926- *AmSCAP 80*
Kaukesel, Guibert *NewGrD 80*
Kaul, Oskar 1885-1968 *Baker 78, NewGrD 80*
Kaulili, Alvina Nye 1918- *IntWWM 77, -80*
Kaun, Hugo 1863-1932 *Baker 78, NewGrD 80*
Kauser, Alice d1945 *NotNAT B*
Kaushik, Jagphool 1924- *IntWWM 77, -80*
Kautner, Helmut 1908-1980 *BiDFilm, -81, DcFM, FilmEn, FilmgC, HalFC 80, WorEFlm[port]*
Kavafian, Ani 1948- *IntWWM 77, -80*
Kavalauskas, Maryte *WomWMM*
Kavalier, Catarina *NewGrD 80*
Kavanagh, Denis 1906- *IIWWBF*
Kavanagh, Patrick d1967 *NotNAT B*
Kavanaugh, Patrick T *ConAmC*
Kavanaugh, Patrick T 1954- *CpmDNM 78*
Kavasch, Deborah 1949- *ConAmC*
Kavelin, Al *BgBands 74, CmpEPM*
Kavik 1897?- *CreCan 1*
Kawachi, Shozo 1926- *WhoOp 76*
Kawahara, Yoko *WhoOp 76*
Kawakami, Genichi 1912- *IntWWM 80*
Kawakita, Nagamasa 1903- *IntMPA 77, -75, -76, -78, -79, -80*
Kawalerowicz, Jerzy 1922- *DcFM, FilmEn, FilmgC, HalFC 80, OxFilm, WorEFlm*
Kawasaki, Masaru 1924- *IntWWM 77, -80*
Kawasaki, Ryo 1947- *EncJzS 70*
Kawka, Johann Christoph *NewGrD 80*
Kay, Armin *NewOrJ[port]*
Kay, Arthur *Film 2*
Kay, Authur *BiE&WWA*
Kay, Barry 1932- *CnOxB*
Kay, Beatrice *CmpEPM, What 5[port], WhoHol A*
Kay, Bernard *WhoHol A*
Kay, Billy *AmSCAP 80*
Kay, Charles 1930- *WhoHol A, WhoThe 72, -77*
Kay, Connie 1927- *BiDAmM, EncJzS 70*
Kay, Dean *AmSCAP 80*
Kay, Don 1933- *IntWWM 77, -80*
Kay, Edward J 1898-1973 *AmSCAP 66, -80, IntMPA 77, -75, -76, -78, -79, -80*
Kay, Elizabeth C *WomWMM B*
Kay, Gilbert Lee *IntMPA 77, -76, -78, -79, -80*
Kay, Gordon 1916- *IntMPA 77, -75, -76, -78, -79, -80*
Kay, Henry 1911-1968 *WhScrn 74, -77*
Kay, Herbie 1904?-1944 *CmpEPM*
Kay, Hershy 1919- *AmSCAP 66, -80, Baker 78, BiDAmM, BiE&WWA, CnOxB, ConAmC, DancEn 78, NewGrD 80, NotNAT*
Kay, Julian 1910-1975 *AmSCAP 66, -80*
Kay, Lisan 1910- *CnOxB, DancEn 78*
Kay, Mack H 1917- *AmSCAP 66, -80*
Kay, Marjorie *Film 1*
Kay, Monte *ConMuA 80B, NewYTET*
Kay, Richard 1937- *WhoHol A, WhoThe 72, -77*
Kay, Rick *ConMuA 80B*
Kay, Ronald 1929- *IntWWM 77*
Kay, Ulysees Simpson 1917- *DrBlPA*
Kay, Ulysses Simpson 1917- *Baker 78, BiDAmM, BlkCS[port], BnBkM 80, ConAmC, DcCM, IntWWM 77, -80, MorBAP, NewGrD 80, OxMus, WhoMus 72*
Kayama, Yuzo 1937- *IntMPA 77, -75, -76, -78, -79, -80*
Kayan, Orrin 1935- *CnOxB*
Kayatta, George N 1944- *AmSCAP 80*
Kayden, Mildred *AmSCAP 66, -80, ConAmC, MorBAP*
Kaye, Albert Patrick 1878-1946 *NotNAT B, WhThe*
Kaye, Barry L 1946- *AmSCAP 80*
Kaye, Benjamin M 1883-1970 *AmSCAP 66, -80*
Kaye, Benny *AmSCAP 80*
Kaye, Benny 1915- *AmSCAP 66*
Kaye, Bernard Louis 1927- *IntWWM 77, -80*
Kaye, Buddy *IntWWM 77, -80*
Kaye, Buddy 1918- *AmSCAP 66, -80, CmpEPM*
Kaye, Carmen d1962 *NotNAT B*
Kaye, Carol 1935- *EncJzS 70*
Kaye, Celia *WhoHol A*
Kaye, Chuck *ConMuA 80B*
Kaye, Danny *AmPS B, GrMovC[port]*
Kaye, Danny 1913- *BiDAmM, BiDFilm, -81, BiE&WWA, CmMov, CmpEPM, EncMT, FilmEn, FilmgC, ForYSC, Funs[port], HalFC 80, IntMPA 77, -75, -76, -78, -79, -80, JoeFr[port], MotPP, MovMk[port], NewYTET, NotNAT, OxFilm, OxThe, WhoHol A, WhoThe 72, -77, WorEFlm*
Kaye, Danny 1918- *NotNAT A*
Kaye, Florence *AmSCAP 80*
Kaye, Frederick *WhThe*
Kaye, Gerry *AmSCAP 80*
Kaye, Herbie *BgBands 74*
Kaye, James R 1929-1969 *AmSCAP 66, -80*
Kaye, Joseph *BiE&WWA, ConAmTC, NotNAT*
Kaye, Leonard Jay 1946- *AmSCAP 80*
Kaye, Michael 1925- *IntWWM 77, -80*
Kaye, Milton Jay *AmSCAP 80*
Kaye, Nora 1920- *CnOxB, DancEn 78[port]*
Kaye, Norman 1922- *AmSCAP 66, -80*
Kaye, Peter 1918- *AmSCAP 66, BiDAmM*
Kaye, Phil 1912-1959 *WhScrn 74, -77,*

WhoHol B
Kaye, Ronnie 1954- *AmSCAP 80*
Kaye, Sammy 1910- *AmSCAP 66, -80, BgBands 74[port], BiDAmM, CmpEPM, WhoHol A*
Kaye, Sparky 1906-1971 *WhScrn 74, -77, WhoHol B*
Kaye, Stanley 1901- *WhoMus 72*
Kaye, Stubby 1918- *AmPS B, BiE&WWA, FilmEn, FilmgC, ForYSC, HalFC 80, MotPP, NotNAT, PlP&P[port], WhoHol A, WhoThe 77*
Kaye, William 1917- *AmSCAP 66, -80*
Kaye-Perry, Leonard 1905- *WhoMus 72*
Kayli, Bob *RkOn*
Kaylin, Samuel 1890?- *ConAmC*
Kaylin, Samuel 1892- *AmSCAP 80*
Kayn, Roland 1933- *DcCM, NewGrD 80*
Kayser, Audun 1946- *IntWWM 77, -80*
Kayser, Hans 1891-1964 *NewGrD 80*
Kayser, Heinrich Ernst 1815-1888 *Baker 78*
Kayser, Isfrid 1712-1771 *NewGrD 80*
Kayser, Jan Henrik 1933- *WhoMus 72*
Kayser, Johann 1688?-1766? *NewGrD 80*
Kayser, Johann Melchior *NewGrD 80*
Kayser, Kathryn E 1896- *BiE&WWA, NotNAT*
Kayser, Leif 1919- *Baker 78, IntWWM 77, -80, NewGrD 80*
Kayser, Philipp Christoph 1755-1823 *Baker 78, NewGrD 80*
Kayssler, Christian 1898-1944 *WhScrn 77*
Kayssler, Friedrich 1874-1945 *EncWT, Film 2, WhScrn 77*
Kaz, Eric Justin 1946- *AmSCAP 80*
Kaz, John Peter 1928- *AmSCAP 80*
Kazachenko, Grigori 1858-1938 *Baker 78*
Kazan, Elia 1909- *AmFD, BiDFilm, -81, BiE&WWA, CnThe, ConLC 16, DcFM, EncWT, Ent, FilmEn, FilmgC, HalFC 80, IntMPA 77, -75, -76, -78, -79, -80, MovMk[port], NotNAT, -A, OxFilm, OxThe, PlP&P[port], WhThe, WhoHol A, WhoThe 72, WorEFlm*
Kazan, Lainie 1940- *WhoHol A*
Kazan, Molly 1906-1963 *BiE&WWA, NotNAT B*
Kazandjiev, Vasil 1934- *Baker 78*
Kazandzhiev, Vasil 1934- *NewGrD 80*
Kazanli, Nikolay Ivanovich 1869-1916 *NewGrD 80*
Kazanly, Nikolai 1869-1916 *Baker 78*
Kazantzakis, Nikos 1883-1957 *CnMD, NotNAT B*
Kazebier, Nate 1912-1969 *CmpEPM, WhoJazz 72*
Kazee, Buell Hilton 1900- *BiDAmM, CounME 74, -74A, EncFCWM 69, IlEncCM*
Kazhlayev, Murad 1931- *NewGrD 80*
Kaznar, Kurt *PlP&P[port]*
Kazuro, Stanislaw 1881-1961 *Baker 78, NewGrD 80*
Kazynski, Wiktor 1812-1867 *Baker 78, NewGrD 80*
Kazze, Louis 1896- *ConAmC*
Kchessinska, Mathilda 1872- *CnOxB, DancEn 78[port]*
Keach, Benjamin 1640-1704 *OxMus*
Keach, Elias *OxMus*
Keach, Stacey 1941- *BiDFilm*
Keach, Stacy 1941- *CnThe, FilmEn, FilmgC, HalFC 80, MovMk, NotNAT, WhoHol A, WhoThe 72, -77*
Keach, Stacy 1942- *IntMPA 77, -75, -76, -78, -79, -80*
Keach, Stacy, Sr. 1914- *IntMPA 77, -75, -76, -78, -79, -80*
Kealy, Thomas J 1874-1949 *WhThe*
Kealy, Tom 1874-1949 *NotNAT B*
Kean, Betty 1920- *BiE&WWA, NotNAT, WhoHol A*
Kean, Mrs. Charles 1806-1880 *NotNAT B*
Kean, Charles John 1811-1868 *EncWT, FamA&A[port], NotNAT A, -B, OxThe, PlP&P[port]*
Kean, Edmund 1787-1833 *CnThe, EncWT, Ent[port], FamA&A[port], NotNAT A, -B, OxThe, PlP&P[port]*
Kean, Edward George 1924- *AmSCAP 66, -80*
Kean, Ellen Tree 1806-1880 *OxThe*
Kean, Jane 1928- *BiE&WWA, NotNAT*
Kean, Marie 1922- *WhoHol A, WhoThe 72, -77*
Kean, Norman 1934- *BiE&WWA, NotNAT, WhoThe 77*
Kean, Richard 1892-1959 *WhScrn 74, -77, WhoHol B*
Kean, Thomas *OxThe, PlP&P[port]*
Keane, Constance *FilmEn, WhScrn 77*
Keane, David R 1943- *IntWWM 77, -80*
Keane, Doris 1881-1945 *NotNAT B, WhThe*
Keane, Doris 1885-1945 *Film 2, WhScrn 74, -77, WhoHol B*
Keane, Edward 1884-1959 *ForYSC, WhScrn 77*
Keane, Ellsworth McGranahan 1927- *BiDAmM*
Keane, James *Film 2*
Keane, John B 1928- *ConDr 77*
Keane, Raymond 1907-1973 *Film 2, MotPP, TwYS*
Keane, Robert Emmett 1883- *FilmgC, ForYSC, HalFC 80, Vers B[port], WhThe, WhoHol B*
Keane, Robert Emmett 1893- *MovMk*
Keaney, Jack 1940- *WhoMus 72*
Keanrey, John L 1871-1945 *WhScrn 77*
Kearney, Carolyn *WhoHol A*
Kearney, Don L 1918- *IntMPA 77, -75, -76, -78, -79*
Kearney, John *Film 2*
Kearney, Kate d1926 *NotNAT B*
Kearney, Michael *WhoHol A*
Kearney, Patrick d1933 *NotNAT B*
Kearns, Allen d1956 *AmPS B, Film 2, WhoHol B*
Kearns, Allen 1893-1956 *EncMT, NotNAT B, WhThe*
Kearns, Allen B 1895-1956 *WhScrn 74, -77*
Kearns, Joseph 1907-1962 *ForYSC, NotNAT B, WhScrn 74, -77, WhoHol B*
Kearns, William Henry 1794-1846 *NewGrD 80*
Kearns, William Kay 1928- *IntWWM 77, -80*
Kearton, Cherry 1871-1940 *FilmgC, HalFC 80*
Keatan, A Harry 1896-1966 *WhScrn 74, -77*
Keate, Gwen *Film 2*
Keathley, George 1925- *BiE&WWA, NotNAT*
Keating, Anna-Lena *WomWMM A, -B*
Keating, Charles 1941- *WhoThe 77*
Keating, Fred 1902-1961 *ForYSC, NotNAT B, WhScrn 74, -77, WhoHol B*
Keating, John G 1919-1968 *NotNAT B*
Keating, John Henry 1870-1963 *AmSCAP 66, -80*
Keating, Katherine *WhScrn 77*
Keating, Larry 1896-1963 *FilmEn, NotNAT B, Vers A[port], WhScrn 74, -77, WhoHol B*
Keating, Larry 1897-1963 *FilmgC, HalFC 80*
Keating, Larry 1899-1963 *ForYSC*
Keating, Roderic Maurice 1941- *WhoOp 76*
Keaton, Buster d1966 *GrMovC[port], MotPP, WhoHol B*
Keaton, Buster 1895-1966 *AmFD, BiDFilm, -81, CmMov, DcFM, FilmEn, Film 1, -2, FilmgC, Funs[port], HalFC 80[port], MovMk[port], OxFilm, WhScrn 74, -77, WorEFlm[port]*
Keaton, Buster 1896-1966 *ForYSC, JoeFr[port], TwYS, -A*
Keaton, Diane *IntMPA 77, -76, -78, -79, -80, WhoHol A*
Keaton, Diane 1946- *BiDFilm 81, MovMk[port]*
Keaton, Diane 1949- *FilmgC, HalFC 80*
Keaton, Harry d1966 *WhoHol B*
Keaton, Joe d1946 *Film 2, WhoHol B*
Keaton, Joseph 1878-1946 *HalFC 80*
Keaton, Joseph, Sr. 1867-1946 *WhScrn 74, -77*
Keaton, Myra d1955 *WhScrn 74, -77, WhoHol B*
Keats, Donald H 1929- *AmSCAP 66, -80, Baker 78, CpmDNM 74, ConAmC, IntWWM 77, -80, NewGrD 80*
Keats, John *OxMus*
Keats, John 1795-1821 *DcPup, NewGrD 80*
Keats, Steven 1945- *HalFC 80, WhoHol A*
Keats, Viola 1911- *WhoHol A, WhoThe 72, -77*
Kebede, Ashenafi 1938- *IntWWM 77, -80*
Kechley, David Stevenson 1947- *AmSCAP 80, ConAmC*
Kechley, Gerald 1919- *AmSCAP 66, -80, ConAmC*
Keck, Johannes 1400?-1450 *NewGrD 80*
Keckius 1400-1450 *NewGrD 80*
Keckley, Jane *Film 2*
Kecskemeti, Istvan 1920- *IntWWM 77, -80, NewGrD 80*
Keden, Joe 1898- *AmSCAP 66, -80*
Kedra, Wladyslaw 1918-1968 *NewGrD 80*
Kedrov, Mikhail Nikolayevich 1893-1972 *OxThe*
Kedrov, Mikhail Nikolayevich 1894-1972 *WhScrn 77*
Kedrova, Lila 1918- *FilmEn, FilmgC, ForYSC, HalFC 80, MotPP, MovMk[port], WhoHol A*
Kedzierzwska, Jadwiga *WomWMM B*
Kee, Cor 1900- *Baker 78, NewGrD 80*
Kee, Piet 1927- *Baker 78, IntWWM 77, -80, NewGrD 80, WhoMus 72*
Kee, Pieter 1927- *NewGrD 80*
Keeble, John 1711?-1786 *NewGrD 80*
Keech, Diana 1945- *IntWWM 77, -80*
Keedwell, Norval *Film 2*
Keefe, Cornelius 1900-1972 *WhScrn 77*
Keefe, Cornelius 1902-1972 *Film 2, TwYS*
Keefe, Zeena 1896- *Film 2, TwYS, WhoHol A*
Keefe, Zena 1896- *Film 1*
Keefer, Anne-Elise 1954- *IntWWM 80*
Keefer, Don *WhoHol A*
Keeffe, Bernard 1925- *IntWWM 77, -80, WhoMus 72*
Keegan, Arthur J 1895- *AmSCAP 66*
Keegan, James Magner, Jr. 1950- *AmSCAP 80*
Keehn, Neal 1909- *IntMPA 77, -75, -76, -78, -79*
Keel, Howard *IntMPA 75, -76, MotPP*
Keel, Howard 1917- *FilmEn, FilmgC, HalFC 80, IntMPA 77, -78, -79, -80*
Keel, Howard 1918?- *WhoHol A*
Keel, Howard 1919- *BiE&WWA, CmMov, CmpEPM, EncMT, ForYSC, MGM[port], MovMk, NotNAT, WhoThe 72, -77, WorEFlm*
Keel, Mary G *WhoMus 72*
Keeler, Christine 1942- *What 3[port]*
Keeler, Elisha C *WhoHol A*
Keeler, Ellis 1907- *WhoMus 72*
Keeler, Ruby *AmPS B, MotPP, PlP&P[port], What 1[port]*
Keeler, Ruby 1909- *BiDFilm, -81, CmMov, EncMT, FilmEn, FilmgC, ForYSC, HalFC 80, MovMk[port], ThFT[port], WhoHol A, WhoThe 72, -77*
Keeler, Ruby 1910- *BiDAmM, BiE&WWA, CmpEPM, CnOxB, NotNAT, OxFilm*
Keeler, Willie Sugar *Film 2*
Keeley, Louise 1833-1877 *OxThe*
Keeley, Lydia Alice Legge 1844-1892 *OxThe*
Keeley, Mary Ann Goward 1806-1899 *OxThe*
Keeley, Mary Anne *NewGrD 80*
Keeley, Robert 1793-1869 *NotNAT B, OxThe*
Keelin, Frank *NewOrJ[port]*
Keeling, Robert Lee *Film 1, -2*
Keely, Henry J 1839-1926 *BiDAmM*
Keen, Diane *WhoHol A*
Keen, Elizabeth *CmpGMD[port], CnOxB*
Keen, Geoffrey *WhoHol A*
Keen, Geoffrey 1916- *WhoThe 77*
Keen, Geoffrey 1918- *BiE&WWA, FilmgC, HalFC 80, MovMk, NotNAT, WhoThe 72*
Keen, Jane *PupTheA*
Keen, Malcolm 1887-1970 *BiE&WWA, Film 2, IlWWBF, NotNAT B, PlP&P, WhScrn 77, WhThe, WhoHol B*
Keen, Malcolm 1888-1970 *HalFC 80*
Keen, Noah *WhoHol A*
Keen, Richard *Film 2*
Keenan, Frances 1886-1950 *WhScrn 74, -77, WhoHol B*
Keenan, Frank d1929 *MotPP, WhoHol B*
Keenan, Frank 1858-1929 *Film 1, -2, NotNAT B, WhThe*
Keenan, Frank 1859-1929 *WhScrn 74, -77*
Keenan, Frank 1868-1929 *TwYS*
Keenan, Larry William 1941- *IntWWM 77, -80*
Keenan, Tom *ConMuA 80B*
Keene, Arthur F 1798?- *BiDAmM*

Keene, Bob 1922- *BiDAmM*
Keene, Christopher 1946- *Baker 78, ConAmC*
Keene, Christopher 1947- *BiDAmM*
Keene, Christopher Anthony 1946- *WhoOp 76*
Keene, Day d1969 *WhoHol B*
Keene, Donald 1922- *BiE&WWA, NotNAT*
Keene, Elsie d1973 *WhScrn 77*
Keene, Hamilton *Film 2*
Keene, James Allen 1932- *IntWWM 77, -80*
Keene, Kahn 1909- *AmSCAP 66, -80*
Keene, Laura d1873 *OxThe*
Keene, Laura 1820-1873 *FamA&A[port], NotNAT A, -B*
Keene, Laura 1826?-1873 *EncWT, PlP&P[port]*
Keene, Lela *AmSCAP 80*
Keene, Linda 1917- *CmpEPM*
Keene, Odette 1897- *AmSCAP 80*
Keene, Ralph 1902-1963 *FilmgC, HalFC 80*
Keene, Richard 1890-1971 *Film 2, WhScrn 77, WhoHol B*
Keene, Thomas Wallace 1840-1898 *NotNAT B, OxThe*
Keene, Tom d1963 *FilmEn, MotPP, NotNAT B, WhoHol B*
Keene, Tom 1896-1963 *FilmgC, HalFC 80*
Keene, Tom 1898-1963 *ForYSC, WhScrn 74, -77*
Keene, Tom 1904-1963 *Film 2*
Keener, Hazel *Film 2, WhoHol A*
Keeney, C H 1899- *NatPD[port]*
Keeney, Claire Handsaker 1899- *AmSCAP 80*
Keeney, Melvin L 1924- *IntWWM 77*
Keenlyside, Raymond 1928- *IntWWM 77, -80, WhoMus 72*
Keenon, Edgar Allen *WhoOp 76*
Keepfer, Margarete *Film 2*
Keepnews, Orrin 1923- *ConMuA 80B, EncJzS 70*
Keese, Ken 1914- *ConAmC*
Keeshan, Bob 1927- *IntMPA 77, -75, -76, -78, -79, -80, NewYTET*
Keezer, Ronald 1940- *ConAmC*
Kefauver, Estes 1903-1963 *WhScrn 77*
Kefer, Paul 1875-1941 *Baker 78, BiDAmM*
Kegg, George *PupTheA*
Kegley, Kermit 1918-1974 *BiE&WWA, NotNAT B*
Kehl, Johann Balthasar 1725-1778 *NewGrD 80*
Kehl, Sigrid 1932- *WhoOp 76*
Kehler, George Bela 1919- *IntWWM 77, -80*
Kehler, Linda Doreen 1947- *IntWWM 77, -80*
Kehler, Sonja *IntWWM 77, -80*
Kehlet, Niels 1938- *CnOxB, DancEn 78[port]*
Kehner, Clarence Way 1926- *AmSCAP 66, -80*
Kehoe, Isobel *WomWMM*
Kehrer, Ewald Willy 1902- *IntWWM 80*
Keiffer, Fred *PupTheA*
Keiffer, Grace *PupTheA*
Keifferer, Christian 1570?-1636 *NewGrD 80*
Keighley, William 1889- *CmMov, DcFM, FilmEn, FilmgC, HalFC 80, MovMk[port]*
Keighley, William 1893- *BiDFilm, -81, WorEFlm*
Keightley, Cyril 1875-1929 *NotNAT B, WhThe*
Keijzer, Arie Johannes 1932- *IntWWM 77, -80*
Keil, Alfredo 1850-1907 *Baker 78, NewGrD 80*
Keil, Birgit 1944- *CnOxB*
Keilberth, Joseph 1908-1968 *Baker 78, CmOp, NewEOp 71, NewGrD 80*
Keiling, Robert Lee *Film 2*
Keillor, Elaine 1939- *IntWWM 77, -80*
Keilstrup, Margaret 1945- *NatPD[port]*
Keim, Adelaide 1880- *WhThe*
Keim, Adelaide 1885- *WhoStg 1908*
Keim, Betty Lou 1938- *BiE&WWA, ForYSC, NotNAT, WhoHol A*
Keim, Buster C 1906-1974 *WhScrn 77*
Kein, Arnold *NewGrD 80*
Keiner, Fern Sybil *AmSCAP 80*
Keinspeck, Michael 1470?- *NewGrD 80*
Keipfer, Georges-Adam *NewGrD 80*
Keir, Andrew 1926- *FilmgC, HalFC 80, WhoHol A, WhoHrs 80*
Keirleber, Johann Georg *NewGrD 80*
Keiser, Lauren Keith 1945- *ConAmC*
Keiser, Marilyn Jean 1941- *IntWWM 77*
Keiser, Reinhard 1674-1739 *Baker 78, BnBkM 80, GrComp, MusMk, NewEOp 71, NewGrD 80, OxMus*
Keiser, Robert *AmSCAP 80*
Keiser, Ronald Lynn 1942- *IntWWM 77*
Keitel, Harvey *FilmEn, IntMPA 78, -79, -80*
Keitel, Harvey 1939- *IntMPA 77, MovMk, WhoHol A*
Keitel, Harvey 1947- *HalFC 80*
Keith 1949- *RkOn 2[port]*
Keith, Benjamin Franklin 1846-1914 *NotNAT B, OxThe, WhoStg 1906, -1908*
Keith, Brian *MotPP, WhoHol A*
Keith, Brian 1921- *FilmEn, FilmgC, ForYSC, HalFC 80, IntMPA 77, -75, -76, -78, -79, -80, WorEFlm*
Keith, Brian 1922- *MovMk[port]*
Keith, Donald 1905- *Film 2, ForYSC, TwYS*
Keith, Eugene *Film 2*
Keith, Ian 1899-1960 *FilmEn, Film 2, FilmgC, ForYSC, HalFC 80, MotPP, MovMk, NotNAT B, TwYS, WhScrn 74, -77, WhThe, WhoHol B*
Keith, Ian L 1911- *AmSCAP 66*
Keith, Isabel *Film 2*
Keith, James 1902-1970 *WhScrn 74, -77*
Keith, Janice Gail 1951- *IntWWM 80*
Keith, Jens 1898-1958 *CnOxB*
Keith, Jimmy 1915-1969 *WhoJazz 72*
Keith, Marian 1874-1961 *CreCan 1*
Keith, Marilyn *AmSCAP 80*
Keith, Penelope *WhoThe 77*
Keith, Ricky 1950- *What 5[port]*
Keith, Robert 1896-1966 *FilmgC, HalFC 80, MovMk*
Keith, Robert 1898-1966 *BiE&WWA, FilmEn, ForYSC, NotNAT, Vers A[port], WhScrn 74, -77, WhThe, WhoHol B*
Keith, Sherwood 1912-1972 *WhScrn 77*
Keith-Johnston, Colin 1896- *BiE&WWA, Film 2, NotNAT, WhThe*
Keithley, E Clinton 1880-1955 *AmSCAP 66, -80*
Kekesi, Maria 1941- *CnOxB*
Kelbe, Theodore 1862-1922 *Baker 78*
Kelber, Michel 1908- *DcFM, FilmEn, WorEFlm*
Kelberine, Alexander 1903-1940 *Baker 78, BiDAmM*
Kelcey, Herbert d1917 *WhoHol B*
Kelcey, Herbert 1855-1917 *NotNAT B, WhoStg 1906, -1908*
Kelcey, Herbert 1856-1917 *WhScrn 77, WhThe*
Kelcey, Herbert 1857-1917 *Film 1*
Keldermans, Raymond Albert 1911- *ConAmC*
Keldish, Yury 1907- *NewGrD 80*
Keldorfer, Robert 1901- *Baker 78, IntWWM 80*
Keldorfer, Viktor 1873-1959 *Baker 78, NewGrD 80*
Kelemen, Milko 1924- *Baker 78, DcCM, NewGrD 80*
Kelemen, Zoltan 1933-1979 *NewGrD 80, WhoOp 76*
Keler, Adalbert Paul Von 1820-1882 *NewGrD 80*
Keler, Bela 1820-1882 *NewGrD 80*
Keler-Bela 1820-1882 *Baker 78, OxMus*
Kelham, Avice 1892- *WhThe*
Kell, Reginald 1906- *Baker 78, NewGrD 80*
Kell, Reginald George 1918- *WhoMus 72*
Kell, Sally *IntWWM 77, -80*
Kelland-Espinosa, Edward 1906- *DancEn 78*
Kellar, Allan Dean 1934- *IntWWM 77, -80*
Kellar, Gertrude *Film 1*
Kellar, Harry 1849-1922 *MagIlD*
Kellar, Leon *Film 2*
Kellard, Ralph d1955 *Film 1, -2, WhoHol B*
Kellard, Ralph 1882-1955 *WhScrn 77*
Kellard, Ralph 1884-1955 *NotNAT B, WhoStg 1908*
Kellaway, Cecil 1891-1973 *FilmgC, HalFC 80[port], WhoHol B*
Kellaway, Cecil 1893-1973 *FilmEn, ForYSC, MovMk[port], WhScrn 77*
Kellaway, Cecil 1895-1973 *Vers A[port]*
Kellaway, Leon *CnOxB, DancEn 78*
Kellaway, Roger 1939- *AmSCAP 80, BiDAmM, EncJzS 70*
Kellberg, Marjorie *PupTheA*
Kelleher, Frank 1937- *IntWWM 80*
Kellem, Craig C 1943- *AmSCAP 66*
Kellem, Milton 1911- *AmSCAP 66, -80*
Keller, Alfred 1907- *IntWWM 77, -80*
Keller, Allen 1925- *AmSCAP 66*
Keller, Connie *AmSCAP 80*
Keller, E *Film 1*
Keller, Frank *Film 2*
Keller, Gertrude 1881-1951 *WhScrn 74, -77*
Keller, Godfrey d1704 *NewGrD 80*
Keller, Godfrido d1704 *NewGrD 80*
Keller, Gottfried d1704 *Baker 78, NewGrD 80*
Keller, Gottfried 1819-1890 *NewEOp 71*
Keller, Greta 1901- *BiDAmM*
Keller, Hans 1919- *Baker 78, IntWWM 77, -80, NewGrD 80, WhoMus 72*
Keller, Harrison 1888- *Baker 78*
Keller, Harry 1913- *FilmEn, FilmgC, HalFC 80, IntMPA 77, -75, -76, -78, -79, -80, WorEFlm*
Keller, Heinrich 1940- *IntWWM 77, -80*
Keller, Helen 1881-1968 *HalFC 80, WhoHol B*
Keller, Hermann 1885-1967 *Baker 78, NewGrD 80*
Keller, Hiram *WhoHol A*
Keller, Homer 1915- *ConAmC*
Keller, James Walter 1936- *AmSCAP 80*
Keller, Jerry Paul 1937- *AmSCAP 66, -80, IntWWM 77, RkOn*
Keller, Johann Peter *NewGrD 80*
Keller, Karl 1784-1855 *Baker 78*
Keller, Kate Adams *Film 1*
Keller, Marjorie Murray 1904- *IntWWM 77, -80*
Keller, Martha Rock *WomWMM B*
Keller, Marthe 1945- *FilmAG WE, FilmEn, HalFC 80, IntMPA 79, -80, WhoHol A*
Keller, Matthias 1813-1875 *Baker 78*
Keller, Matthias 1813-1883 *BiDAmM*
Keller, Max 1770-1855 *Baker 78*
Keller, Nan d1975 *WhScrn 77*
Keller, Nell Clark 1876-1965 *WhScrn 74, -77, WhoHol B*
Keller, Otto 1861-1928 *Baker 78*
Keller, Peter 1944- *IntWWM 77, -80*
Keller, Phillip Brooks *Film 1*
Keller, Sheldon B 1923- *AmSCAP 66, -80*
Keller, Walter 1873-1940 *Baker 78, ConAmC*
Kellerd, E John 1863- *WhoStg 1908*
Kellerd, John E 1863-1929 *NotNAT B, WhoStg 1906*
Kelleri, Fortunato *NewGrD 80*
Kellerman, Anette 1888-1975 *Film 1*
Kellerman, Annette d1975 *WhoHol C*
Kellerman, Annette 1887-1975 *FilmEn, TwYS, WhScrn 77*
Kellerman, Annette 1888-1975 *Film 2, FilmgC, HalFC 80, What 2[port]*
Kellerman, Sally *IntMPA 75, -76, WhoHol A*
Kellerman, Sally 1936- *IntMPA 77, -78, -79, -80*
Kellerman, Sally 1938- *FilmEn, MovMk[port]*
Kellerman, Sally 1941- *FilmgC, HalFC 80*
Kellerman, Wolfgang 1925- *IntWWM 77, -80*
Kellermann, Annette d1975 *WhThe*
Kellermann, Christian 1815-1866 *Baker 78*
Kellers, Frederic 1929- *IntMPA 77, -75, -76, -78, -79, -80*
Kellett, Bob 1927- *FilmgC, HalFC 80, IlWWBF*
Kelley, Arthur 1924- *BluesWW[port]*
Kelley, Barry 1908- *FilmgC, HalFC 80, IntMPA 77, -75, -76, -78, Vers B[port]*
Kelley, Birtie Mae 1898- *AmSCAP 80*
Kelley, Bob 1917-1966 *WhScrn 77*
Kelley, DeForest 1920- *ForYSC, MotPP, WhoHol A*
Kelley, DeForrest 1920- *FilmgC, HalFC 80*
Kelley, Edgar Stillman 1857-1944 *AmSCAP 66, -80, Baker 78, BiDAmM, NewGrD 80*
Kelley, Jessie Stillman 1866-1949 *Baker 78*
Kelley, Norman D 1917- *WhoOp 76*
Kelley, Pat *Film 1*
Kelley, Patrick *IntMPA 77, -76, -78, -79, -80*
Kelley, Peck 1900?- *CmpEPM, WhoJazz 72*
Kellie, Edward *OxMus*
Kellie, Lawrence 1862-1932 *Baker 78*

Kellie, Thomas A Erskine, Earl Of *NewGrD 80*
Kellin, Mike 1922- *AmSCAP 80, BiE&WWA, ForYSC, HalFC 80, NotNAT, WhoHol A*
Kellin, Orange 1944- *NewOrJ SUP[port]*
Kelling, Hajo 1907- *IntWWM 77, -80*
Kellino, Pamela 1916- *FilmgC, HalFC 80, WhoHol A*
Kellino, Roy 1912-1956 *FilmgC, HalFC 80, IlWWBF*
Kellino, W P 1873-1958 *IlWWBF*
Kellino, Will P 1873-1958 *FilmgC, HalFC 80*
Kellis, Leo Alan 1927- *AmSCAP 80, ConAmC*
Kelljan, Bob *WhoHrs 80*
Kellner, Andreas d1591 *NewGrD 80*
Kellner, David 1670?-1748 *NewGrD 80*
Kellner, Ernst August 1792-1839 *Baker 78*
Kellner, Johann Christoph 1736-1803 *NewGrD 80*
Kellner, Johann Peter 1705-1772 *NewGrD 80*
Kellogg, Charles W 1905- *AmSCAP 80*
Kellogg, Clara Louise 1842-1916 *Baker 78, BiDAmM, NewEOp 71, NewGrD 80*
Kellogg, Conelia 1877-1934 *WhScrn 74, -77*
Kellogg, Cornelia d1934 *WhoHol B*
Kellogg, John 1916- *Vers A[port], WhoHol A*
Kellogg, Kay 1901- *AmSCAP 66*
Kellogg, Lynn 1943- *AmSCAP 80*
Kellogg, Marjorie *WomWMM*
Kellogg, Philip M 1912- *IntMPA 77, -75, -76, -78, -79, -80*
Kellogg, Ray *WhoHrs 80*
Kellogg, Shirley 1888- *WhThe*
Kellogg, Virginia *WomWMM*
Kellogg, Wayne Alfred 1930- *IntWWM 77*
Kells, Iris 1927- *WhoMus 72*
Kelly, Earl Of 1732-1781 *MusMk, OxMus*
Kelly, Al d1966 *JoeFr[port], WhoHol B*
Kelly, Alexander 1929- *WhoMus 72*
Kelly, Ann d1852 *NotNAT B*
Kelly, Anthony Paul d1932 *NotNAT B*
Kelly, Barbara *WhoHol A*
Kelly, Bob *ConMuA 80B*
Kelly, Bob 1923- *BiE&WWA, NotNAT*
Kelly, Brian *ForYSC, WhoHol A*
Kelly, Bryan 1934- *NewGrD 80, WhoMus 72*
Kelly, Casey *AmSCAP 80*
Kelly, Chris 1891-1929 *NewOrJ*
Kelly, Claire *MotPP*
Kelly, Daniel Crosby 1898- *WhoMus 72*
Kelly, Daniel E 1843-1905 *BiDAmM*
Kelly, Danis 1946- *IntWWM 77, -80*
Kelly, Denise Maria Ann 1954- *IntWWM 77, -80*
Kelly, Desmond 1942- *CnOxB*
Kelly, Don *ConMuA 80B*
Kelly, Don 1924-1966 *WhScrn 77*
Kelly, Dorothy 1894-1966 *Film 1, MotPP, WhScrn 77, WhoHol B*
Kelly, Dorothy 1918- *WhoMus 72*
Kelly, Dorothy Helen 1918-1969 *WhScrn 74, -77, WhoHol B*
Kelly, Duke 1936- *IntMPA 77, -78, -79, -80*
Kelly, E H *WhThe*
Kelly, Elizabeth *WomWMM B*
Kelly, Emmett 1895-1979 *FilmgC, HalFC 80, WhoHol A*
Kelly, Emmett 1898-1979 *Ent[port], JoeFr*
Kelly, Ernest 1886?-1927? *NewOrJ*
Kelly, Eva 1880-1948 *NotNAT B, WhThe*
Kelly, Fannie 1876-1925 *WhScrn 74, -77, WhoHol B*
Kelly, Fanny d1882 *NotNAT B*
Kelly, Frances Maria 1790-1882 *NotNAT A, -B, OxThe*
Kelly, Francis T 1907- *IntMPA 75, -76*
Kelly, Frederick Septimus 1881-1916 *NewGrD 80*
Kelly, Gene 1912- *AmPS B, BiDAmM, BiDFilm, -81, BiE&WWA, CmMov, CmpEPM, CnOxB, DancEn 78[port], EncMT, Ent, FilmEn, FilmgC, ForYSC, HalFC 80, IntMPA 77, -75, -76, -78, -79, -80, MGM[port], MotPP, MovMk[port], NotNAT, -A, OxFilm, PlP&P, WhThe, WhoHol A, WorEFlm[port]*
Kelly, George 1887-1974 *BiE&WWA, CnMD, DcLB 7[port], EncWT, Ent, McGEWD[port], ModWD, OxThe, WomWMM*
Kelly, George 1890- *WhThe*
Kelly, George 1915- *WhoJazz 72*
Kelly, George Edward 1887-1974? *ConDr 73*
Kelly, Grace *AmPS B, IntMPA 77, -75, -76, -78, -79, -80, MotPP, WhoHol A*
Kelly, Grace 1928- *BiDFilm, -81, CmMov, FilmEn, FilmgC, HalFC 80, OxFilm*
Kelly, Grace 1929- *BiE&WWA, ForYSC, MovMk[port], NotNAT, WorEFlm[port]*
Kelly, Gregory 1891-1927 *Film 2, NotNAT B, WhScrn 74, -77, WhoHol B*
Kelly, Guy 1900-1930 *BiDAmM*
Kelly, Guy 1906-1940 *NewOrJ[port], WhoJazz 72*
Kelly, Harry *WhoStg 1906, -1908*
Kelly, Hugh 1739-1777 *NotNAT B, OxThe*
Kelly, J Arthur 1922- *IntMPA 77, -75, -76, -78, -79, -80*
Kelly, Jack 1927- *FilmEn, FilmgC, ForYSC, HalFC 80, WhoHol A*
Kelly, James 1915-1964 *NotNAT B, WhScrn 74, -77*
Kelly, James 1931-1978 *HalFC 80*
Kelly, James A 1891- *AmSCAP 66*
Kelly, James T *Film 1*
Kelly, Jennifer 1936- *DancEn 78*
Kelly, Jim *DrBlPA, IntMPA 77, -75, -76, -78, -79, -80, WhoHol A*
Kelly, Jo-Ann 1944- *BluesWW[port]*
Kelly, Jo-Ann 1949- *BlkAmP*
Kelly, Joe d1959 *WhScrn 77*
Kelly, John d1751 *NotNAT B*
Kelly, John 1901-1947 *Film 2, WhScrn 77*
Kelly, John Allen 1951- *AmSCAP 80*
Kelly, John T 1852-1922 *WhScrn 74, -77*
Kelly, John T 1855- *WhoStg 1906, -1908*
Kelly, Judy 1913- *FilmgC, HalFC 80, IlWWBF, WhThe, WhoHol A*
Kelly, Kevin 1930- *BiE&WWA*
Kelly, Kevin 1934- *ConAmTC, NotNAT*
Kelly, Kitty 1902-1968 *Film 2, WhScrn 74, -77, WhoHol B*
Kelly, Lew 1879-1944 *NotNAT B, WhScrn 74, -77, WhoHol B*
Kelly, Mary Bubbles 1895-1941 *WhScrn 74, -77, WhoHol B*
Kelly, Mary Elizabeth 1915- *IntWWM 77, -80*
Kelly, Mary Pat *WomWMM A, -B*
Kelly, Mary Russell Williams 1915- *IntWWM 77*
Kelly, Maurice 1928-1974 *WhScrn 77, WhoHol B*
Kelly, Michael d1826 *NotNAT A, -B*
Kelly, Michael 1762-1826 *Baker 78, CmOp, MusMk, NewEOp 71, NewGrD 80, OxMus*
Kelly, Montgomery Jerome 1910-1971 *AmSCAP 80*
Kelly, Monty 1919- *RkOn*
Kelly, Nancy 1921- *BiE&WWA, FilmEn, Film 2, FilmgC, ForYSC, HalFC 80, IntMPA 77, -75, -76, -78, -79, -80, MotPP, MovMk[port], NotNAT, ThFT[port], WhoHol A, WhoThe 72, -77*
Kelly, Nell 1910-1939 *WhScrn 74, -77*
Kelly, Pat 1891-1938 *WhScrn 77*
Kelly, Patsy 1910- *EncMT, FilmEn, FilmgC, ForYSC, Funs[port], HalFC 80, JoeFr, MotPP, MovMk, PlP&P, ThFT[port], What 1[port], WhoHol A, WhoThe 77*
Kelly, Paul 1899-1956 *FilmEn, Film 1, -2, FilmgC, ForYSC, HalFC 80, HolP 30[port], MotPP, MovMk, NotNAT B, TwYS, WhScrn 74, -77, WhThe, WhoHol B*
Kelly, Paula *CmpEPM, WhoHol A*
Kelly, Paula 1939- *HalFC 80*
Kelly, Paula 1944?- *DrBlPA*
Kelly, Peggy *Film 2*
Kelly, Renee 1888-1965 *WhThe*
Kelly, Robert d1949 *NotNAT B*
Kelly, Robert 1916- *Baker 78, ConAmC, DcCM, IntWWM 77, -80, PlP&P[port]*
Kelly, Ron 1929- *CreCan 2*
Kelly, Scotch *Film 2*
Kelly, Sherman 1943- *AmSCAP 80*
Kelly, Thomas Alexander Erskine, Earl Of 1732-1781 *NewGrD 80*
Kelly, Thomas Raymond 1927- *BiDAmM*
Kelly, Tim 1937- *NatPD[port]*
Kelly, Tommy 1925- *ForYSC, MotPP, WhoHol A*
Kelly, Tommy 1928- *HalFC 80*
Kelly, W W 1853-1933 *NotNAT B, WhThe*
Kelly, Walt 1913-1973 *AmSCAP 66*
Kelly, Walter C 1873-1939 *JoeFr, NotNAT A, -B, WhScrn 74, -77, WhThe, WhoHol B*
Kelly, Wells 1949- *AmSCAP 80*
Kelly, William J 1875?-1949 *NotNAT B, WhScrn 74, -77, WhoHol B*
Kelly, Willie *BluesWW[port]*
Kelly, Wynton 1931-1971 *BiDAmM, CmpEPM, EncJzS 70*
Kellyk, Hugh *NewGrD 80*
Kelman, Charles 1930- *AmSCAP 80*
Kelner, Johann Peter *NewGrD 80*
Kelpius, Johannes 1673-1708 *BiDAmM, NewGrD 80*
Kelsall, Moultrie 1901?- *FilmgC, HalFC 80, WhoHol A*
Kelsey, Fred 1884-1961 *Film 1, -2, ForYSC, HalFC 80, TwYS, Vers B[port], WhScrn 74, -77, WhoHol B*
Kelsey, Xenophon 1949- *IntWWM 77, -80*
Kelso, Bobby *Film 2*
Kelso, Mayme 1867-1946 *Film 1, -2, TwYS, WhScrn 77*
Kelso, Vernon 1893- *WhThe*
Kelson, George *Film 1*
Kelt, John d1935 *NotNAT B, WhoHol B*
Kelterborn, Louis 1891-1933 *BiDAmM*
Kelterborn, Rudolf 1931- *Baker 78, CpmDNM 78, -80, IntWWM 77, -80, NewGrD 80*
Kelterborn, Rudolph 1931- *DcCM*
Keltner, Jim 1942- *EncJzS 70*
Keltner, Jimmie Lee 1942- *EncJzS 70*
Kelton, Pert d1968 *BiE&WWA, WhoHol B*
Kelton, Pert 1907-1968 *FilmEn, Film 2, FilmgC, ForYSC, HalFC 80, MovMk, ThFT[port], WhScrn 74, -77*
Kelton, Pert 1909-1968 *NotNAT B*
Kelvin, Thelda *Film 2*
Kelway, Joseph 1702?-1782? *NewGrD 80, OxMus*
Kelway, Thomas d1744 *OxMus*
Kelway, Thomas 1695?-1749 *NewGrD 80*
Kelynack, Hilary Clifton 1915- *IntWWM 77, -80, WhoMus 72*
Kelz, Matthias *NewGrD 80*
Kelz, Matthias 1635?-1695 *NewGrD 80*
Kemble, Adelaide 1814-1879 *CmOp, NewGrD 80, NotNAT B*
Kemble, Charles 1775-1854 *EncWT, FamA&A[port], NotNAT A, -B, OxThe, PlP&P[port]*
Kemble, Mrs. Charles 1773?-1838 *NotNAT B*
Kemble, Elizabeth d1836 *NotNAT B*
Kemble, Fanny 1809-1893 *EncWT, Ent, NotNAT A, -B*
Kemble, Frances d1822 *NotNAT B*
Kemble, Frances Anne 1809-1893 *FamA&A[port], OxThe*
Kemble, Harry d1836 *NotNAT B*
Kemble, Henry 1848-1907 *NotNAT B, OxThe*
Kemble, Mrs. J P 1755-1845 *NotNAT B*
Kemble, John Mitchell d1857 *NotNAT B*
Kemble, John Philip 1757-1823 *CnThe, EncWT, Ent, NotNAT A, -B, OxThe, PlP&P[port]*
Kemble, Kenneth *DcPup*
Kemble, Roger 1721-1802 *EncWT, NotNAT B*
Kemble, Roger 1722-1802 *OxThe, PlP&P*
Kemble, Mrs. Roger d1807 *NotNAT B*
Kemble, Sarah Siddons *EncWT*
Kemble, Stephen 1758-1822 *EncWT, NotNAT B, OxThe, PlP&P[port]*
Kemble, Mrs. Stephen d1841 *NotNAT B*
Kemble, Theresa DeCamp 1773-1838 *OxThe*
Kemble-Cooper, Violet 1886-1961 *WhScrn 74, -77, WhoHol B*
Kemeny, John *IntMPA 77, -78, -79, -80*
Kemmer, Ed *ForYSC, WhoHol A, WhoHrs 80*
Kemmer, George W 1890- *AmSCAP 66, -80, ConAmC*
Kemner, Gerald Eugene 1932- *AmSCAP 80, ConAmC*
Kemp, Andrew *NewGrD 80*
Kemp, Anthony Eric 1934- *IntWWM 80*

Kemp, Arnold *BlkAmP*
Kemp, Barbara 1881-1959 *Baker 78, CmOp, NewGrD 80*
Kemp, Bobby 1867-1921 *BlksBF*
Kemp, Dorothy Elizabeth Walter 1926- *IntWWM 77, -80*
Kemp, Everett 1874-1958 *WhScrn 74, -77, WhoHol B*
Kemp, Hal *BgBands 74[port]*
Kemp, Hal 1904-1940 *WhScrn 74, -77, WhoHol B*
Kemp, Hal 1905-1940 *CmpEPM, WhoJazz 72*
Kemp, Hal 1911?-1940 *BiDAmM*
Kemp, Jeremy *WhoHol A*
Kemp, Jeremy 1934- *FilmgC, HalFC 80*
Kemp, Jeremy 1935- *FilmEn, ForYSC, IntMPA 77, -75, -76, -78, -79, -80, WhoThe 72, -77*
Kemp, Joseph 1778-1824 *Baker 78, NewGrD 80*
Kemp, Lindsay 1940?- *CnOxB*
Kemp, Malcolm David 1948- *IntWWM 77, -80*
Kemp, Margaret *Film 2*
Kemp, Matty 1907- *Film 2, IntMPA 78, -79, -80, TwYS*
Kemp, Paul 1899-1953 *WhScrn 74, -77, WhoHol B*
Kemp, Robert 1885-1959 *NotNAT B, OxThe*
Kemp, Robert C 1820-1897 *Baker 78, BiDAmM*
Kemp, Sally 1933- *BiE&WWA*
Kemp, Shirley Margaret 1931- *IntWWM 77, WhoMus 72*
Kemp, Thomas Charles 1891-1955 *NotNAT B, OxThe, WhThe*
Kemp, Walter Herbert 1938- *IntWWM 77, -80*
Kemp, Wayne 1941- *IlEncCM*
Kemp, William 1580-1603 *CnOxB, DancEn 78, NotNAT B, OxMus, PlP&P[port]*
Kemp-Potter, Joan *WhoMus 72*
Kemp-Welch, Joan *IntMPA 75, -76, -78, -79*
Kemp-Welch, Joan 1906- *FilmgC, HalFC 80, IntMPA 77, -80, WhoHol A, WhoThe 72, -77*
Kempa, Johannes De *NewGrD 80*
Kempe, Karin *WomWMM B*
Kempe, Rudolf 1910-1976 *Baker 78, BnBkM 80, CmOp, MusSN[port], NewEOp 71, NewGrD 80[port], WhoMus 72, WhoOp 76*
Kempe, William d1603 *EncWT, Ent, OxThe*
Kempen, Paul Van 1893-1955 *NewGrD 80*
Kemper *NewGrD 80*
Kemper, Adolf 1811-1880 *NewGrD 80*
Kemper, Charles 1901-1950 *ForYSC, WhScrn 74, -77, WhoHol B*
Kemper, Collin 1870-1955 *NotNAT B, WhThe, WhoStg 1908*
Kemper, Emanuel 1844-1933 *NewGrD 80*
Kemper, Emanuel Magnus 1906- *NewGrD 80*
Kemper, Emanuel Reinhold 1947- *NewGrD 80*
Kemper, Karl Reinhold 1880-1957 *NewGrD 80*
Kemper, Peter 1734-1820 *NewGrD 80*
Kemper, Ronnie 1912- *AmSCAP 66, CmpEPM*
Kemper, Ronold Vivian 1912- *AmSCAP 80*
Kemper, Victor J *HalFC 80*
Kempff, Wilhelm 1895- *Baker 78, BnBkM 80, IntWWM 77, -80, MusMk, MusSN[port], NewGrD 80[port], WhoMus 72*
Kempinski, Leo A 1891-1958 *AmSCAP 66, -80, ConAmC A*
Kempis *NewGrD 80*
Kemplen, Ralph 1912- *HalFC 80*
Kempson, Rachel 1910- *CnThe, FilmgC, HalFC 80, WhoHol A, WhoThe 72, -77*
Kempster, Katharine Helen 1905- *WhoMus 72*
Kempter, Karl 1819-1871 *Baker 78*
Kemter, Johannes Richard 1918- *WhoOp 76*
Ken, Bishop 1637-1711 *OxMus*
Kenan, Amos 1927- *CnMD SUP*
Kenbrovin, Jaan *AmSCAP 80*
Kendal, Mrs. 1849-1935 *WhoStg 1906*
Kendal, Doris *WhThe*
Kendal, Ezra 1861- *WhoStg 1906, -1908*
Kendal, Felicity 1946- *WhoThe 72, -77*
Kendal, Leo *Film 1*
Kendal, Madge *EncWT*
Kendal, Madge 1848-1935 *NotNAT A, OxThe, WhThe*
Kendal, Madge 1849-1935 *FamA&A[port], NotNAT B, WhoStg 1908*
Kendal, William Hunter 1843-1917 *EncWT, NotNAT A, -B, OxThe, WhThe, WhoStg 1906, -1908*
Kendale, Richard d1431 *NewGrD 80*
Kendall, Cy 1898-1953 *Vers A[port], WhScrn 74, -77, WhoHol B*
Kendall, Cyrus Q 1898-1953 *FilmgC, HalFC 80*
Kendall, Cyrus W *ForYSC*
Kendall, Gary *ConAmC*
Kendall, Henry 1897-1962 *FilmgC, HalFC 80, IlWWBF, -A, NotNAT A, -B, WhThe, WhoHol B*
Kendall, Henry 1898-1962 *Film 2, WhScrn 74, -77*
Kendall, John 1869- *WhThe*
Kendall, Kay d1959 *MotPP, WhoHol B*
Kendall, Kay 1926-1959 *FilmEn, FilmgC, ForYSC, HalFC 80, MovMk[port], NotNAT B, WhScrn 74, -77*
Kendall, Kay 1927-1959 *BiDFilm, -81, CmMov, FilmAG WE, IlWWBF[port], WorEFlm*
Kendall, Madge *PlP&P*
Kendall, Marie d1964 *NotNAT B*
Kendall, Nancy *WomWMM A, -B*
Kendall, Ross C 1886- *AmSCAP 66*
Kendall, Susy *ForYSC*
Kendall, Suzy *IntMPA 75, -76, -78, -79, -80*
Kendall, Suzy 1943?- *FilmgC, HalFC 80, IntMPA 77, WhoHol A*
Kendall, Suzy 1944- *FilmEn, IlWWBF[port]*
Kendall, William 1903- *PlP&P, WhoHol A, WhoThe 72, -77*
Kendell, Iain 1931- *IntWWM 77, -80, WhoMus 72*
Kenderdine, Augustus Frederick Lafosse 1870-1947 *CreCan 2*
Kendis, James 1883-1946 *AmSCAP 66, -80, BiDAmM*
Kendrick, Alfred 1869- *WhThe*
Kendrick, Brian 1930-1970 *WhScrn 74, -77*
Kendrick, James Michael 1952- *IntWWM 77, -80*
Kendrick, Ruby *Film 1*
Kendrick, Virginia 1910- *ConAmC, IntWWM 77, -80*
Kendricks, Eddie 1940- *DrBlPA, RkOn 2[port]*
Keneman, Feodor 1873-1937 *Baker 78*
Kenessey, Jeno 1905-1976 *NewGrD 80*
Kenessey, Jeno 1906-1976 *Baker 78*
Kenig, Jozef 1821-1900 *NewGrD 80*
Kenin, Herman 1901?-1970 *CmpEPM*
Kenins, Talivaldis 1919- *Baker 78, DcCM, IntWWM 77, -80, NewGrD 80*
Kenley, John 1907- *BiE&WWA, NotNAT*
Kenna, Mr. And Mrs. *PlP&P*
Kenna, Peter 1930- *ConDr 77*
Kennan, Kent Wheeler 1913- *AmSCAP 66, -80, Baker 78, BiDAmM, ConAmC, DcCM, NewGrD 80, WhoMus 72*
Kennard, Jane d1938 *NotNAT B*
Kennard, Victor *Film 1*
Kennaway, James 1928-1968 *FilmgC, HalFC 80, NotNAT B*
Kennaway, Lamont *WhoMus 72*
Kenneally, Philip *WhoHol A*
Kennedy, Adam *WhoHol A*
Kennedy, Adrienne 1931- *BlkAmP, ConDr 73, -77, CroCD, DrBlPA, EncWT, MorBAP, NotNAT*
Kennedy, Arthur 1914- *BiDFilm, -81, BiE&WWA, CmMov, FilmEn, FilmgC, ForYSC, HalFC 80, HolP 40[port], IntMPA 77, -75, -76, -78, -79, -80, MotPP, MovMk[port], NotNAT, PlP&P[port], WhoHol A, WhoThe 72, -77, WorEFlm[port]*
Kennedy, Beulah d1964 *NotNAT B*
Kennedy, Burt 1923- *BiDFilm, -81, CmMov, DcFM, FilmEn, FilmgC, HalFC 80, IntMPA 77, -75, -76, -78, -79, -80, WorEFlm*
Kennedy, Charles E 1867- *WhoStg 1908*
Kennedy, Charles Lamb d1881 *NotNAT B*
Kennedy, Charles Rann 1871-1950 *Film 2, NotNAT B, WhScrn 74, -77, WhThe, WhoHol B*
Kennedy, Cheryl 1947- *WhoHol A, WhoThe 72, -77*
Kennedy, David 1825-1886 *NewGrD 80*
Kennedy, Douglas 1915-1973 *FilmEn, FilmgC, ForYSC, HalFC 80, IntMPA 77, -75, -76, -78, -79, -80, Vers B[port], WhScrn 77, WhoHol B*
Kennedy, Edgar 1890-1948 *FilmEn, Film 1, -2, FilmgC, ForYSC, HalFC 80, MotPP, MovMk, NotNAT B, TwYS, Vers A[port], WhScrn 74, -77, WhoHol B*
Kennedy, Edmund 1873- *WhThe*
Kennedy, Edward *Film 2*
Kennedy, Elisabeth 1918- *DancEn 78*
Kennedy, Ethyl *WomWMM*
Kennedy, Fred d1958 *WhoHol B*
Kennedy, Frederick O 1910-1958 *WhScrn 74, -77*
Kennedy, George *MotPP, WhoHol A*
Kennedy, George 1925- *FilmEn, FilmgC, ForYSC, HalFC 80, MovMk[port], WorEFlm[port]*
Kennedy, George 1927- *CmMov, IntMPA 77, -75, -76, -78, -79, -80*
Kennedy, Gilbert Young 1916- *IntWWM 77, -80, WhoMus 72*
Kennedy, H A d1905 *NotNAT B*
Kennedy, Harold J *NotNAT, WhoThe 77*
Kennedy, Hazel *Film 2*
Kennedy, Helen d1973 *WhScrn 77*
Kennedy, Jack d1964 *Film 2, WhoHol B*
Kennedy, James *CnOxB*
Kennedy, James 1902- *WhoMus 72*
Kennedy, James Michael 1947- *AmSCAP 80*
Kennedy, Jay Richard 1904- *AmSCAP 66*
Kennedy, Jimmy *CmpEPM*
Kennedy, Joe 1923- *EncJzS 70*
Kennedy, John *BiE&WWA, NotNAT*
Kennedy, John Brodbin 1934- *ConAmC*
Kennedy, John F d1960 *WhScrn 74, -77, WhoHol B*
Kennedy, John Leo 1907- *CreCan 1*
Kennedy, Joseph C 1890-1949 *WhScrn 74, -77*
Kennedy, Joseph J, Jr. 1923- *BiDAmM, EncJzS 70*
Kennedy, Joseph P 1888-1969 *FilmEn, OxFilm, WorEFlm*
Kennedy, Josepha 1928- *IntWWM 77, -80*
Kennedy, Joyce 1898-1943 *NotNAT B, WhScrn 74, -77, WhThe, WhoHol B*
Kennedy, King 1904-1974 *WhScrn 77, WhoHol B*
Kennedy, Laura Nancy Hasenpflug 1932- *IntWWM 77*
Kennedy, Lauri 1896- *NewGrD 80*
Kennedy, Leo 1907- *CreCan 1*
Kennedy, Lila 1903- *BiE&WWA*
Kennedy, Madge 1892- *FilmEn, Film 1, -2, ForYSC, MotPP, TwYS, WhThe, WhoHol A*
Kennedy, Margaret 1896-1967 *HalFC 80, McGEWD, ModWD, WhThe*
Kennedy, Margaret Fairlie *WomWMM B*
Kennedy, Mary 1908- *Film 2, WhThe*
Kennedy, Maurice d1962 *NotNAT B*
Kennedy, Merna d1944 *NotNAT B, WhoHol B*
Kennedy, Merna 1908-1944 *FilmEn, Film 2, ForYSC, HalFC 80, TwYS, WhScrn 74, -77*
Kennedy, Merna 1909-1944 *MovMk*
Kennedy, Michael 1926- *IntWWM 77, -80, NewGrD 80, WhoMus 72*
Kennedy, Myrna *FilmgC*
Kennedy, Patricia 1917- *WhoThe 77*
Kennedy, Scott 1927- *DrBlPA*
Kennedy, Tom *HalFC 80*
Kennedy, Tom 1884-1965 *FilmEn, WhScrn 74, -77*
Kennedy, Tom 1885-1965 *Film 1, -2, ForYSC, TwYS, WhoHol B*
Kennedy, Tom 1887-1965 *Vers A[port]*
Kennedy-Fraser, Marjorie 1857-1930 *NewGrD 80*
Kennedy-Fraser, Marjory 1857-1930 *Baker 78, OxMus*
Kennedy-Koch, Valentine Charles 1913- *IntWWM 77, -80*
Kennedy Scott, Charles 1876- *OxMus, WhoMus 72*

Kennell, Richard Paul 1949- *ConAmC*
Kennelly, Norman *NatPD[port]*
Kenner, Chris *RkOn*
Kenner, Hugh 1923- *BiE&WWA*
Kenner, William Hugh 1923- *NotNAT*
Kennersley, Robert *NewGrD 80*
Kenneson, Claude 1935- *IntWWM 77, -80*
Kenneth, Harry D 1854-1929 *WhScrn 74, -77*
Kenneth, Keith 1887-1966 *WhScrn 77, WhoHol B*
Kenney, H Wesley *IntMPA 77, -75, -76, -78, -79, -80*
Kenney, Jack 1888-1964 *NotNAT B, WhScrn 74, -77*
Kenney, James d1849 *NotNAT B*
Kenney, James 1930- *FilmgC, HalFC 80, WhoHol A, WhoThe 72, -77*
Kenney, June 1938?- *WhoHrs 80*
Kenney, Sylvia W 1922-1968 *NewGrD 80*
Kenningham, Charles d1925 *NotNAT B*
Kennis, Guillaume Gommaire 1717-1789 *NewGrD 80*
Kennis, Guillaume Jacques Joseph 1768-1845 *NewGrD 80*
Kenny, Bill *DrBlPA*
Kenny, Charles Francis 1898- *AmSCAP 66, -80, CmpEPM*
Kenny, Colin d1968 *Film 1, -2, WhScrn 77*
Kenny, Courtney 1933- *WhoMus 72*
Kenny, George *AmSCAP 80*
Kenny, Leola 1892-1956 *WhScrn 74, -77, WhoHol B*
Kenny, Nick 1895-1975 *AmSCAP 66, CmpEPM, What 4[port], WhScrn 77*
Kenny, Nick A 1895-1975 *AmSCAP 80*
Kenny, Sean 1932-1973 *BiE&WWA, CnThe, EncWT, Ent, WhThe, WhoThe 72*
Kenny, Yvonne Denise 1950- *IntWWM 77, -80*
Kenojuak *CreCan 1*
Kensinger, Donald Carey 1937- *IntWWM 77, -80*
Kensington Market *BiDAmM*
Kenswil, Atma 1892- *IntWWM 77, -80*
Kent *AmSCAP 80*
Kent, Mrs. *Film 2*
Kent, Allegra 1938- *CnOxB, DancEn 78[port]*
Kent, Angela Virginia Sarie 1933- *WhoMus 72*
Kent, Arnold 1899-1928 *Film 2, WhScrn 74, -77, WhoHol B*
Kent, Arthur 1920- *AmSCAP 66, -80*
Kent, Barbara 1906- *FilmEn, Film 2, ThFT[port], TwYS, WhoHol A*
Kent, Barbara 1908- *ForYSC*
Kent, Barry 1932- *WhoThe 72, -77*
Kent, Benen 1917- *IntWWM 80*
Kent, Sister Benen 1917- *IntWWM 77*
Kent, Charles 1852-1923 *FilmEn, Film 1, -2, NotNAT B, TwYS, WhScrn 77, WhoHol B*
Kent, Charles Stanton 1914- *ConAmC*
Kent, Charlotte 1907- *AmSCAP 66*
Kent, Christopher *FilmEn, WhoHol A*
Kent, Christopher John 1949- *IntWWM 77, -80*
Kent, Crauford d1952 *WhoHol B*
Kent, Crauford 1881-1953 *Film 2, ForYSC, WhScrn 74, -77*
Kent, Mrs. Crauford *Film 2*
Kent, Crawford 1881-1953 *Film 1, NotNAT B, TwYS*
Kent, Dorothea 1917- *ThFT[port]*
Kent, Douglas *WhScrn 77*
Kent, Douglass *WhScrn 74*
Kent, Edgar *PlP&P*
Kent, Elinor d1957 *WhScrn 74, -77*
Kent, Ethel 1884-1952 *WhScrn 74, -77, WhoHol B*
Kent, Flora *IntWWM 80*
Kent, Flora 1911- *IntWWM 77, WhoMus 72*
Kent, Gary *AmSCAP 80*
Kent, Gerald d1944 *WhScrn 74, -77, WhoHol B*
Kent, James 1700-1776 *Baker 78, NewGrD 80, OxMus*
Kent, Jean 1921- *FilmAG WE, FilmEn, FilmgC, HalFC 80, IlWWBF[port], IntMPA 77, -75, -76, -78, -79, -80, WhoHol A, WhoThe 72, -77*
Kent, John B 1939- *IntMPA 77, -75, -76, -78, -79, -80*
Kent, Kate 1864-1934 *WhScrn 77*
Kent, Keneth 1882-1963 *HalFC 80*
Kent, Keneth 1892-1963 *WhScrn 74, -77, WhThe*
Kent, Kenneth d1963 *PlP&P, WhoHol B*
Kent, Larry *Film 2, ForYSC, TwYS*
Kent, Larry 1937- *CreCan 1*
Kent, Lawrence L 1937- *CreCan 1*
Kent, Leon *Film 1*
Kent, Marsha 1919-1971 *WhScrn 74, -77, WhoHol B*
Kent, Marshall *WhoHol A*
Kent, Patricia Elizabeth 1930- *WhoMus 72*
Kent, Ray 1886-1948 *WhScrn 77*
Kent, Richard Layton 1916- *AmSCAP 80, ConAmC, IntWWM 80*
Kent, Robert *ForYSC*
Kent, Robert d1954 *WhoHol B*
Kent, Robert 1908-1955 *WhScrn 77*
Kent, Robert 1912?-1954 *FilmEn*
Kent, Rockwell 1882- *What 1[port]*
Kent, S Miller d1948 *NotNAT B*
Kent, Sandra 1927- *AmSCAP 66, -80*
Kent, Walter 1911- *AmSCAP 66, -80, CmpEPM*
Kent, Willard 1883-1968 *WhScrn 77*
Kent, William T 1886-1945 *Film 2, NotNAT B, WhScrn 74, -77, WhThe, WhoHol B*
Kente, Gibson N 1932- *NewGrD 80*
Kentish, Agatha 1897- *WhThe*
Kentish, John *IntWWM 77, -80, WhoMus 72*
Kentner, Lajos 1905- *NewGrD 80*
Kentner, Louis Philip 1905- *Baker 78, IntWWM 77, -80, NewGrD 80, WhoMus 72*
Kenton, Earle C 1896-1980 *WhoHrs 80*
Kenton, Egon F 1891- *Baker 78, NewGrD 80*
Kenton, Erle C 1896-1980 *CmMov, FilmEn, FilmgC, HalFC 80, TwYS A*
Kenton, Godfrey 1902- *WhoThe 72, -77*
Kenton, Stan 1912-1979 *Baker 78, BgBands 74[port], CmpEPM, EncJzS 70, IlEncJ, IntWWM 77, -80, NewGrD 80*
Kenton, Stanley Newcomb 1912-1979 *AmSCAP 66, -80, BiDAmM, ConAmC, EncJzS 70*
Kentuckians *BiDAmM*
Kentucky Jubilee Singers *Film 2*
Kentucky Pardners *BiDAmM*
Kentucky Ramblers *BiDAmM*
Kenwith, Herbert *NewYTET*
Kenwood, Marty *AmSCAP 80*
Kenworthy, Ruth Dewolfe 1889-1971 *BiDAmM*
Kenyatta, Damon *BlkAmP*
Kenyon, Charles 1878-1961 *NotNAT B, WhThe*
Kenyon, Curtis *IntMPA 77, -75, -76, -78, -79, -80*
Kenyon, Doris 1897- *FilmEn, Film 1, -2, FilmgC, ForYSC, HalFC 80, MotPP, MovMk, ThFT[port], TwYS, What 4[port], WhThe, WhoHol A*
Kenyon, Nancye *Film 2*
Kenyon, Neil d1946 *WhThe*
Kenyon, Nicholas Roger 1951- *IntWWM 80*
Keogh, Dave *PupTheA*
Keogh, J A d1942 *NotNAT B*
Keogh, James Edward 1948- *ConAmTC*
Keogh, Violet *PupTheA*
Keogh, William T d1947 *NotNAT B*
Keonch, Boldizsar 1938- *IntWWM 80*
Keown, Eric 1904-1963 *NotNAT B, WhThe*
Kepitis, Janis 1908- *NewGrD 80*
Kepler, Edward *Film 2*
Kepler, Johannes 1571-1630 *Baker 78, NewEOp 71, NewGrD 80*
Keplinger, Lorraine Joyce 1931- *IntWWM 77, -80*
Kepner, Charles Fred 1921- *AmSCAP 80*
Kepner, Fred 1921- *AmSCAP 66, ConAmC*
Keppard, Freddie 1889-1933 *CmpEPM, NewGrD 80, NewOrJ[port], WhoJazz 72*
Keppard, Freddy 1889-1933 *BiDAmM*
Keppard, Louis 1888- *NewOrJ[port]*
Keppel, Lady Caroline *OxMus*
Keppens, Emile d1926 *WhScrn 74, -77*
Keppler, Johannes 1571-1630 *NewGrD 80*
Ker, Ann Steele 1937- *IntWWM 77*
Kerans, Barbara Kay *WomWMM B*
Kerasotes, George G 1911- *IntMPA 77, -75, -76, -78, -79, -80*
Kerby, Loretta Sue 1946- *IntWWM 77*
Kerby, Marion *Film 1*
Kerby, Marion d1956 *NotNAT B*
Kerby, Paul 1903- *AmSCAP 66, -80*
Kerchoven, Abraham VanDen 1618?-1701 *NewGrD 80*
Kerckhove, Abraham VanDen 1618?-1701 *NewGrD 80*
Kerckhoven, Abraham VanDen 1618?-1701 *NewGrD 80*
Kerek, Ferenc 1948- *IntWWM 80*
Keren, Zvi 1917- *IntWWM 77, -80*
Kerensky, Alexander 1881- *What 1[port]*
Kerensky, Oleg 1930- *CnOxB, WhoMus 72*
Kerenyi, Gyorgy 1902- *NewGrD 80*
Kerenyi, Nicholas George 1913- *IntWWM 77, -80*
Kerer, Rudol'f 1923- *NewGrD 80*
Keres, Imre 1930- *CnOxB*
Kerestan, Richard Michael 1945- *IntWWM 77*
Kerger, Ann J 1894- *AmSCAP 66, -80*
Kergommeaux, Duncan Robert De *CreCan 1*
Kergy, Albert *Film 2*
Kerima 1925- *FilmEn, FilmgC, HalFC 80*
Kerin, Nora 1883- *WhThe*
Kerker, Gustav 1857-1923 *CmpEPM*
Kerker, Gustave Adolph 1857-1923 *AmSCAP 66, -80, BiDAmM, EncMT, NewCBMT, NewGrD 80, NotNAT B, PopAmC[port], WhThe, WhoStg 1906, -1908*
Kerkorian, Kirk 1917- *IntMPA 80*
Kerl, Johann Caspar *NewGrD 80*
Kerl, Johann Kaspar *NewGrD 80*
Kerle, Jacobus De 1531?-1591 *Baker 78, NewGrD 80*
Kerle, Jacobus Van 1531?-1591 *OxMus*
Kerll, Johann 1627-1693 *MusMk[port]*
Kerll, Johann Caspar 1627-1693 *NewGrD 80[port], OxMus*
Kerll, Johann Kaspar 1627-1693 *Baker 78, NewGrD 80[port]*
Kerly, L *Film 2*
Kerman, David *WhoHol A*
Kerman, Joseph 1924- *Baker 78, IntWWM 77, -80, NewGrD 80, OxMus*
Kerman, Sheppard 1928- *NatPD[port]*
Kermoyan, Michael 1925- *BiE&WWA, NotNAT, WhoHol A*
Kern, Adele 1901- *CmOp, NewGrD 80*
Kern, James V 1909-1966 *AmSCAP 66, -80, FilmEn, FilmgC, HalFC 80, WhScrn 74, -77*
Kern, Jerome *BnBkM 80*
Kern, Jerome 1885-1943 *AmPS*
Kern, Jerome 1885-1945 *AmSCAP 66, -80, Baker 78, BestMus, BiDAmM, CmMov, CmpEPM, ConAmC, EncMT, EncWT, FilmEn, FilmgC, HalFC 80, McGEWD, MnPM[port], MusMk, NewCBMT, NewGrD 80[port], NotNAT A, -B, OxFilm, OxMus, PlP&P[port], PopAmC[port], PopAmC SUP, Sw&Ld C, WhThe*
Kern, Patricia 1927- *CmOp, NewGrD 80, WhoMus 72*
Kernan, David 1939- *WhoHol A, WhoThe 72, -77*
Kernan, Joseph Lewis d1964 *NotNAT B*
Kernberg, Johann Philipp *NewGrD 80*
Kerndl, Rainer 1928- *CroCD*
Kernell, William B 1891-1963 *AmSCAP 66, -80*
Kerner, Deborah M 1951- *AmSCAP 80*
Kernochan, Marshall Rutgers 1880-1955 *AmSCAP 66, -80, BiDAmM, ConAmC*
Kernochan, Sarah Marshall 1947- *AmSCAP 80, WomWMM*
Kernodle, George R 1907- *BiE&WWA, NotNAT*
Kerns, Eddie *Film 2*
Kerns, Gladys Hubbar 1896- *IntWWM 77*
Kerns, Robert Douglas 1933?- *CmOp, NewGrD 80, WhoOp 76*
Kernstock, Ottokar *OxMus*
Kerolenko, Agnes *Film 2*
Kerouac, Jack d1969 *WhoHol B*
Keroul, Henri 1857-1921 *NotNAT B*
Kerpely, Jeno *NewGrD 80*

Kerpen, Hugo Franz Karl Alexander Von 1749-1802 *NewGrD 80*
Kerr, Alfred 1867-1948 *EncWT, NotNAT B*
Kerr, Andrew Rogerson 1944- *WhoMus 72*
Kerr, Anita 1927- *AmSCAP 80, BiDAmM, EncFCWM 69, IlEncCM, WomWMM*
Kerr, Bill *WhoHol A, WhoThe 77*
Kerr, Bob *Film 2*
Kerr, Brooks 1951- *EncJzS 70*
Kerr, Chester Brooks, Jr. 1951- *EncJzS 70*
Kerr, Deborah 1921- *BiDFilm, -81, BiE&WWA, FilmAG WE[port], FilmEn, FilmgC, ForYSC, HalFC 80, IlWWBF[port], -A, IntMPA 77, -75, -76, -78, -79, -80, MGM[port], MotPP, MovMk[port], NotNAT, OxFilm, PlP&P A[port], WhoHol A, WhoHrs 80, WhoThe 77, WorEFlm*
Kerr, Fraser 1931- *IntMPA 77, -75, -76, -78, -79, -80*
Kerr, Frederick 1858-1933 *FilmgC, HalFC 80, NotNAT B, WhScrn 74, -77, WhThe, WhoHol B*
Kerr, Frederick 1858-1934 *Film 2*
Kerr, Geoffrey 1895- *BiE&WWA, Film 2, NotNAT, WhThe, WhoHol A*
Kerr, Harrison 1897- *Baker 78, ConAmC, DcCM, IntWWM 77, -80, NewGrD 80, WhoMus 72*
Kerr, Harrison 1899- *BiDAmM*
Kerr, Harry D 1880-1957 *AmSCAP 66, -80*
Kerr, Illingworth Holey 1905- *CreCan 1*
Kerr, James E *AmSCAP 80*
Kerr, Jane d1954 *WhScrn 74, -77, WhoHol B*
Kerr, Jean 1923- *AmSCAP 66, -80, BiE&WWA, NotNAT, WhoThe 72, -77*
Kerr, John 1931- *BiE&WWA, FilmEn, FilmgC, ForYSC, HalFC 80, IntMPA 77, -75, -76, -78, -79, -80, MotPP, NotNAT, WhoHol A*
Kerr, Lorence Larry d1968 *WhScrn 77*
Kerr, Marge *BiE&WWA*
Kerr, Molly 1904- *WhThe*
Kerr, Phil 1906-1960 *AmSCAP 66, -80*
Kerr, Russell 1930- *CnOxB, DancEn 78*
Kerr, Sophie 1880-1965 *NotNAT B*
Kerr, Thomas H, Jr. *ConAmC*
Kerr, Walter 1913- *AmSCAP 66, -80, BiE&WWA, ConAmTC, NotNAT, WhoThe 72, -77*
Kerr, William J 1890- *AmSCAP 66, -80*
Kerr-Sokal, Charlotte *WomWMM*
Kerrick, Thomas d1927 *WhScrn 74, -77, WhoHol B*
Kerridge, Mary 1914- *WhoHol A, WhoThe 72, -77*
Kerrigan, J M 1885-1964 *FilmgC, HalFC 80, WhThe*
Kerrigan, J M 1885-1965 *MovMk*
Kerrigan, J M 1887-1964 *FilmEn, Film 2, WhoHol B*
Kerrigan, J Warren 1880-1947 *Film 1, -2, FilmgC, HalFC 80, NotNAT B*
Kerrigan, J Warren 1889-1947 *FilmEn, MotPP, TwYS, WhScrn 74, -77, WhoHol B*
Kerrigan, Joseph M 1887-1964 *ForYSC, NotNAT B, Vers B[port], WhScrn 74, -77*
Kerrigan, Kathleen 1869-1957 *Film 2, WhScrn 77, WhoHol B*
Kerry, Lucyann Snyder 1949- *WomWMM B*
Kerry, Margaret *MotPP*
Kerry, Norman 1889-1956 *FilmEn, Film 1, -2, FilmgC, HalFC 80, MotPP, MovMk[port], NotNAT B, TwYS, WhScrn 74, -77, WhoHol B*
Kerry, Norman 1890-1956 *ForYSC*
Kersands, Billy 1840?-1915? *BiDAmM*
Kersands, Billy 1842-1915 *BlksBF[port]*
Kersenbaum, Sylvia Haydee 1944- *IntWWM 77, -80*
Kersey, Eda 1904-1944 *NewGrD 80*
Kersey, Ken 1916- *CmpEPM*
Kersey, Kenny 1916- *BiDAmM, WhoJazz 72*
Kersh, Kathy *WhoHol A*
Kershaw, Doug 1936- *ConMuA 80A, CounME 74[port], -74A, IlEncCM[port], IlEncR*
Kershaw, Douglas James 1936- *BiDAmM*
Kershaw, Mary Alexa Harriet 1947- *IntWWM 77*
Kershaw, Stewart 1941- *CnOxB*
Kershaw, Willette d1960 *Film 1, -2, WhoHol B*
Kershaw, Willette 1882-1960 *WhScrn 77*
Kershaw, Willette 1890-1960 *NotNAT B, WhThe*
Kershenbaum, David *ConMuA 80B*
Kershner, Irvin 1923- *BiDFilm, -81, FilmEn, FilmgC, HalFC 80, IntMPA 77, -75, -76, -78, -79, -80, MovMk[port], OxFilm, WorEFlm[port]*
Kersjes, Anton 1923- *NewGrD 80*
Kerslake, Barbara 1913- *IntWWM 77, -80*
Kersley, Leo 1920- *CnOxB, DancEn 78*
Kersten, Albert E *Film 2*
Kersters, Willem 1929- *Baker 78, NewGrD 80*
Kerstukos, Carolyn Irene Lewis 1947- *IntWWM 77*
Kert, Larry *PlP&P A[port], WhoHol A*
Kert, Larry 1930- *EncMT, WhoThe 72, -77*
Kert, Larry 1934- *BiE&WWA, NotNAT*
Kertesz, Istvan 1929-1973 *Baker 78, BnBkM 80, MusSN[port], NewEOp 71, NewGrD 80, WhoMus 72*
Kertesz, Michael *FilmEn*
Kertesz, Mihaly *DcFM*
Kertesz-Gabry, Edith 1927- *WhoOp 76*
Kertz, Peter 1934- *WhoOp 76*
Kerwood, Dick d1924 *WhScrn 77*
Kerz, Leo 1912- *BiE&WWA, NotNAT*
Kes, Willem 1856-1934 *Baker 78, NewGrD 80, OxMus*
Kesdekian, Mesrop 1920- *NotNAT*
Keshen, Amy *WomWMM B*
Keshner, Joyce Grove 1927- *IntWWM 77, -80*
Kesler, Henry S 1907- *IntMPA 75, -76*
Kesler, Lew *AmSCAP 80*
Kesler, Lew 1915- *AmSCAP 66*
Kesnar, Maurits 1900-1957 *AmSCAP 66, -80, ConAmC*
Kessel, Barney 1923- *AmSCAP 66, -80, BiDAmM, CmpEPM, EncJzS 70, IlEncJ*
Kessel, Johann *NewGrD 80*
Kesselheim, Silvia 1942- *CnOxB*
Kesselring, Joseph O 1902-1967 *BiE&WWA, McGEWD, ModWD, NotNAT B, WhThe*
Kessler, Dagmar 1946- *CnOxB*
Kessler, David d1920 *NotNAT B*
Kessler, Dietrich M 1929- *NewGrD 80*
Kessler, Edith *Film 2*
Kessler, Ferdinand 1793-1856 *Baker 78*
Kessler, Jascha Frederick 1929- *AmSCAP 66, -80*
Kessler, Jerome 1942- *IntWWM 77, -80*
Kessler, Joseph d1933 *NotNAT B*
Kessler, Joseph Christoph 1800-1872 *Baker 78*
Kessler, Leonard Irwin 1942- *ConAmTC*
Kessler, Martha 1930- *IntWWM 80*
Kessler, Minuetta *ConAmC, IntWWM 77, -80*
Kessler, Ralph 1919- *AmSCAP 66*
Kessler, Ralph 1929- *AmSCAP 80*
Kessler, Thomas 1937- *Baker 78, NewGrD 80*
Kessler, Wendelin *NewGrD 80*
Kessner, Daniel Aaron 1946- *ConAmC, IntWWM 77, -80*
Kestelman, Sara 1944- *WhoHol A, WhoThe 77*
Kesten, Hermann 1900- *ModWD*
Kesten, Paul W d1956 *NewYTET*
Kestenberg, Leo 1882-1962 *Baker 78, NewGrD 80*
Kester, Paul 1870-1933 *NotNAT B, OxThe, WhThe*
Kestner, John Nelson 1935- *AmSCAP 80*
Keszei, Janos 1936- *IntWWM 80, WhoMus 72*
Keszkowski, Henryk 1927- *IntWWM 77, -80*
Ketcham, Charles 1942- *IntWWM 77, -80*
Ketchum, David *WhoHol A*
Ketchum, Robyna Neilson d1972 *WhScrn 77*
Ketelaars, Leo Anton 1913- *IntWWM 77, -80*
Ketelbey, Albert W 1875-1959 *Baker 78, MusMk, NewGrD 80, OxMus*
Kethe, William d1608? *OxMus*
Ketola, Jouko Michael 1939- *IntWWM 77, -80*
Ketron, Larry 1947- *NatPD[port]*
Kettelhut, Erich 1893- *FilmEn*
Ketten, Henri 1848-1883 *Baker 78*
Kettenus, Aloys 1823-1896 *Baker 78*
Ketter, Paul Stephen 1932- *AmSCAP 80*
Ketterer, Eugene 1831-1870 *Baker 78*
Kettering, Eunice Lea 1906- *ConAmC*
Ketting, Otto 1935- *Baker 78, DcCM, NewGrD 80*
Ketting, Piet 1904- *Baker 78*
Ketting, Piet 1905- *NewGrD 80*
Kettle, Rupert 1940- *AmSCAP 80*
Kettles, The *HalFC 80*
Keuchenthal, Johannes 1522?-1583 *NewGrD 80*
Keuris, Tristan 1946- *Baker 78, NewGrD 80*
Keurvels, Edward H J 1853-1916 *Baker 78, NewGrD 80*
Keussler, Gerhard Von 1874-1949 *Baker 78, NewGrD 80*
Keuten, Serge 1947- *CnOxB*
Keuter, Cliff 1940- *CmpGMD, CnOxB*
Kevan, G Alex 1908- *ConAmC*
Kevan, Jack *WhoHrs 80*
Kevehazi, Gabor 1953- *CnOxB*
Keveson, Peter 1919- *AmSCAP 66, -80*
Kevess, Arthur S 1916-1973 *AmSCAP 66, -80*
Kewitsch, Theodor 1834-1903 *Baker 78*
Key, Francis Scott 1779-1843 *Baker 78, BiDAmM, OxMus*
Key, James R 1925- *AmSCAP 80*
Key, Kathleen d1954 *MotPP, NotNAT B, WhoHol B*
Key, Kathleen 1897-1954 *Film 2, TwYS*
Key, Kathleen 1906-1954 *WhScrn 74, -77*
Key, Pat Ann d1962 *NotNAT B*
Key, Pierre VanRensselaer 1872-1945 *Baker 78*
Keyawa, Stanley J 1920- *AmSCAP 66, -80*
Keyes, Baron 1898-1976 *AmSCAP 66, -80*
Keyes, Daniel F *WhoHol A*
Keyes, Donald C *AmSCAP 66*
Keyes, Evelyn *IntMPA 75, -76, -78, -79, -80*
Keyes, Evelyn 1917- *What 2[port]*
Keyes, Evelyn 1919- *FilmEn, FilmgC, ForYSC, HalFC 80, HolP 40[port], IntMPA 77, MotPP, MovMk[port], WhoHol A*
Keyes, Joe 1907?-1950 *WhoJazz 72*
Keyes, John 1892-1966 *WhScrn 77*
Keyes, Johnny *DrBlPA*
Keyes, Laurence 1914- *AmSCAP 66, -80*
Keyes, Nelson 1928- *AmSCAP 80, ConAmC*
Keyes, Paul W *NewYTET*
Keynes, Lord 1882-1946 *DancEn 78*
Keyrieber, Johann Georg 1639-1691? *NewGrD 80*
Keys, Anthony Nelson 1913?- *HalFC 80*
Keys, Calvin 1942- *EncJzS 70*
Keys, Ivor Christopher Banfield 1919- *IntWWM 77, -80, NewGrD 80, OxMus, WhoMus 72*
Keys, Nelson d1939 *Film 2, WhoHol B*
Keys, Nelson 1886-1939 *EncMT, IlWWBF, -A, NotNAT A, -B, WhThe*
Keys, Nelson 1887-1939 *HalFC 80, WhScrn 74, -77*
Keys, Robert 1914- *IntWWM 77, -80*
Keyser-Heyl, Willy *Film 2*
Keysor, Catherine Ryan *IntWWM 77*
Keystone Kids, The *Film 1*
Keystone Pets, The *Film 1*
Keyte, Christopher Charles 1935- *IntWWM 77, -80, WhoMus 72*
KGB *IlEncR*
Khachatur Of Taron 1100-1184 *NewGrD 80*
Khachaturian, Aram 1903- *DancEn 78*
Khachaturian, Aram 1903-1978 *Baker 78, BnBkM 80, CnOxB, DcCom 77, DcCom&M 79, DcCM, MusMk[port], NewGrD 80*
Khachaturian, Aram 1904-1978 *DcFM*
Khachaturian, Karen 1920- *Baker 78, NewGrD 80*
Khachaturian, Margaret Miles 1929- *IntWWM 77, -80*
Khachaturyan, Aram Ilych 1903- *WhoMus 72*
Khachaturyan, Karen Surenovich 1920- *IntWWM 77, -80*
Khadem-Missagh, Bijan 1948- *IntWWM 77, -80*
Khadjiev, Parashkev 1912- *Baker 78*
Khaikin, Boris 1904-1978 *NewGrD 80*

Khairat, Abu-Bakr 1910-1963 *NewGrD 80*
Khale, Shrinivas Vinayak 1926- *IntWWM 77, -80*
Khambatta, Persis *WhoHol A*
Khaml, Antonin *NewGrD 80*
Khan, Ali Akbar 1922- *BnBkM 80, ConAmC, NewGrD 80*
Khan, Chaka *ConMuA 80A[port]*
Khan, Hidayat I 1917- *IntWWM 77, -80*
Khan, Mazhar d1950 *WhScrn 77*
Khan, Ramjakhan Mehboob *DcFM*
Khan, Vilayat 1924- *NewGrD 80*
Khandoshkin, Ivan 1747-1804 *Baker 78, NewGrD 80, OxMus*
Khanzadian, Vahan 1942- *WhoOp 76*
Khatchaturian, Aram 1903- *CompSN[port], IntWWM 77, OxMus*
Khaykin, Boris *NewGrD 80*
Khessin, Alexander Borisovich 1869-1955 *NewGrD 80*
Khierzinger *NewGrD 80*
Khmelev, Nikolai Pavlovich 1901-1945 *OxThe*
Khmelof, N P *WhScrn 77*
Khmelyov, Nikolai Pavlovich 1901-1945 *NotNAT B, WhScrn 77*
Khnes, Jurij *NewGrD 80*
Khness, Jurij *NewGrD 80*
Khnies, Jurij *NewGrD 80*
Khodatayeva, O *WomWMM*
Khodateyev, Nikolai 1892- *DcFM*
Khodzha-Einatov, Leon 1904-1954 *Baker 78*
Khokhlov, Boris Ivanovich 1932- *CnOxB, DancEn 78*
Khokhlov, Pavel 1854-1919 *NewGrD 80*
Kholbio, Simon *NewGrD 80*
Kholfin, Nicolai Sergeyevich 1903- *CnOxB*
Kholminov, Alexander Nikolayevich 1925- *NewGrD 80*
Khorram, Homayoon 1930- *IntWWM 77, -80*
Khoury, Edith Leslie d1973 *WhScrn 77*
Khoury, Edward A 1916- *AmSCAP 66, -80*
Khrennikof, Tikhon Nikolayevich 1913- *OxMus*
Khrennikov, Tikhon Nikolayevich 1913- *Baker 78, DcCM, IntWWM 77, -80, MusMk, NewEOp 71, NewGrD 80*
Khristov, Dimiter 1933- *NewGrD 80*
Khristov, Dobri 1875-1941 *NewGrD 80*
Khu, Emilios *NewGrD 80*
Khubov, Georgy Nikitich 1902- *NewGrD 80*
Khuen, Johannes 1606-1675 *NewGrD 80*
Khues, Jurij *NewGrD 80*
Khuess, Jurij *NewGrD 80*
Khym, Carl 1770?-1819? *NewGrD 80*
Kiamos, Eleni *WhoHol A*
Kibbe, Michael Glenn 1945- *ConAmC, IntWWM 77*
Kibbee, Guy 1882-1956 *FilmEn, FilmgC, ForYSC, HalFC 80, HolCA[port], NotNAT B*
Kibbee, Guy 1886-1956 *MotPP, MovMk[port], Vers A[port], WhScrn 74, -77, WhoHol B*
Kibbee, Milton d1970 *Vers B[port], WhScrn 77*
Kibbee, Roland 1914- *FilmgC, HalFC 80, IntMPA 77, -75, -76, -78, -79, -80, NewYTET*
Kibkalo, Evgeny 1932- *NewGrD 80*
Kichler, Johann *NewGrD 80*
Kicklighter, Hampton 1940- *IntWWM 77, -80*
Kid, Mary *Film 2*
Kid Thomas *BluesWW[port]*
Kidd, Jim 1846-1916 *WhScrn 77*
Kidd, Johnny 1939- *IlEncR*
Kidd, Jonathan *WhoHol A*
Kidd, Kathleen 1899-1961 *NotNAT B, WhScrn 74, -77, WhoHol B*
Kidd, Kenneth 1935?- *BluesWW*
Kidd, Michael 1919- *BiE&WWA, CmMov, CnOxB, DancEn 78, EncMT, FilmEn, FilmgC, ForYSC, HalFC 80, NotNAT, WhoHol A, WhoThe 72, -77, WorEFlm*
Kidd, Robert 1943- *WhoThe 72, -77*
Kiddell, Sidney George 1908- *IntWWM 77, -80*
Kidder, Hugh 1880-1952 *WhScrn 74, -77, WhoHol B*
Kidder, Kathryn 1867-1939 *NotNAT B, WhThe, WhoStg 1906, -1908*
Kidder, Margot 1948- *FilmEn, HalFC 80, WhoHol A, WhoHrs 80*
Kidger, Wilfred Charles 1893- *WhoMus 72*
Kido, Shiro 1894- *IntMPA 77, -75, -76*
Kidson, Frank 1855-1926 *Baker 78, NewGrD 80, OxMus*
Kiefer, Bruno 1923- *IntWWM 77, -80, NewGrD 80*
Kiefer, J *AmSCAP 80*
Kiefer, Richard 1939- *BiDAmM*
Kieffer, Aldine S 1840-1904 *NewGrD 80*
Kiegel, Leonard 1929- *WorEFlm*
Kieken, Johannes *NewGrD 80*
Kiel, Edith *WomWMM*
Kiel, Friedrich 1821-1885 *Baker 78*
Kiel, Piet, Jr. 1937- *IntWWM 77*
Kiel, Richard 1939- *FilmEn, ForYSC, HalFC 80, WhoHol A, WhoHrs 80[port]*
Kieling, Wolfgang 1924- *HalFC 80*
Kielland, Olav 1901- *Baker 78, IntWWM 77, -80*
Kiener, Hazel *Film 2*
Kienitz, Marianne 1947- *IntWWM 77, -80*
Kienle, Ambrosius 1852-1905 *Baker 78*
Kienlen, Johann Christoph 1783-1829 *NewGrD 80*
Kienzl, Wilhelm 1857-1941 *Baker 78, NewEOp 71, NewGrD 80, OxMus*
Kiepura, Jan d1966 *OxMus, WhoHol B*
Kiepura, Jan 1902-1966 *Baker 78, CmOp, FilmAG WE, FilmEn, FilmgC, HalFC 80, MovMk, MusSN[port], NewEOp 71, NewGrD 80, NotNAT B, OxFilm, WhScrn 74, -77, WhThe*
Kiepura, Jan 1904-1966 *ForYSC*
Kiepura, Jan 1909- *BiE&WWA*
Kier, Udo 1944- *WhoHrs 80[port]*
Kieran, John F 1892- *What 3[port]*
Kierland, Joseph Scott 1932- *AmSCAP 80, NatPD[port]*
Kiernan, Baby Marie *Film 1*
Kiernan, James 1939-1975 *WhScrn 77*
Kies, Christopher *ConAmC*
Kies, Jeanine Marie 1940- *IntWWM 77*
Kieser, Karen Ann 1948- *IntWWM 80*
Kiesewetter, Raphael Georg 1773-1850 *Baker 78, NewGrD 80*
Kiesewetter, Tomasz 1911- *Baker 78*
Kiesler, Frederick J 1896- *BiE&WWA*
Kiesler, Frederick John 1890-1965 *NotNAT B*
Kiessling, Heinz 1926- *NewGrD 80*
Kievman, Louis 1910- *AmSCAP 80*
Kihlken, Henry 1939- *ConAmC*
Kihn, Albert d1974 *NewYTET*
Kiilerich, Jens Ole 1946- *IntWWM 80*
Kijima, Kiyohiko 1917- *Baker 78*
Kikaleishvili, Zurab Malakievy 1924- *CnOxB*
Kiker, Douglas *NewYTET*
Kikkawa, Eishi 1909- *IntWWM 77, -80, NewGrD 80*
Kikuchi, Hiroshi 1888-1948 *ModWD*
Kikuchi, Masabumi 1939- *EncJzS 70*
Kikume, Al 1894-1972 *WhScrn 77*
Kiladze, Grigory 1902-1962 *Baker 78*
Kilar, Wojciech 1932- *Baker 78, DcCM, NewGrD 80*
Kilbride, Percy 1888-1964 *FilmEn, FilmgC, ForYSC, HalFC 80, MotPP, MovMk[port], NotNAT B, Vers A[port], WhScrn 74, -77, WhoHol B*
Kilbride, Richard D 1919-1967 *WhScrn 74, -77, WhoHol B*
Kilburn, Nicholas 1843-1923 *Baker 78*
Kilburn, Paul 1936- *IntWWM 80*
Kilburn, Terry 1926- *FilmEn, FilmgC, HalFC 80, MotPP, WhoHol A*
Kilburn, Terry 1928- *ForYSC*
Kilduff, Helen 1888-1959 *WhScrn 74, -77, WhoHol B*
Kilduff, Michal C *WomWMM B*
Kilenyi, Edward, Jr. 1911- *Baker 78*
Kilenyi, Edward, Sr. 1884-1968 *AmSCAP 66, -80, Baker 78, ConAmC*
Kilenyi, Edward A 1911- *WhoMus 72*
Kiley, Richard 1922- *AmPS B, BiE&WWA, EncMT, FilmEn, FilmgC, ForYSC, HalFC 80, IntMPA 77, -75, -76, -78, -79, -80, NotNAT, WhoHol A, WhoThe 72, -77*
Kilfoil, Thomas F 1922- *BiE&WWA, NotNAT*
Kilgallen, Dorothy 1913-1965 *NotNAT B, WhScrn 74, -77, WhoHol B*
Kilgallen, Rob *WhoHol A*
Kilgen, Charles Christian 1859-1932 *NewGrD 80*
Kilgen, George d1902 *NewGrD 80*
Kilgore, Merle 1934- *CounME 74[port], -74A, EncFCWM 69, IlEncCM*
Kilgore, Wyatt Merle 1934- *BiDAmM*
Kilgour, Joseph 1863-1933 *Film 1, -2, NotNAT B*
Kilgour, Joseph 1864-1933 *TwYS, WhScrn 77, WhoHol B*
Kilham, Gene 1919- *AmSCAP 66, -80*
Kilhan, Eric Arthur 1904- *WhoMus 72*
Kilian, Hans 1515?-1595 *NewGrD 80*
Kilian, Ivan Edward George 1934- *IntWWM 77, -80*
Kilian, Johann 1515?-1595 *NewGrD 80*
Kilian, Victor 1891-1979 *BiE&WWA, FilmEn, Film 2, FilmgC, ForYSC, HolCA[port], NotNAT, Vers A[port], WhoHol A*
Kilian, Victor 1897-1979 *HalFC 80*
Kilian, Victor 1898-1979 *IntMPA 77, -75, -76, -78, -79, MovMk*
Killar, Ashley 1944- *CnOxB*
Killebrew, Gwendolyn *IntWWM 80, WhoOp 76*
Killeen, Joseph L 1893- *AmSCAP 66*
Killens, John Oliver 1916- *BlkAmP, DrBlPA, MorBAP*
Killgo, Keith Wesley 1954- *AmSCAP 80, EncJzS 70*
Killgrove, William Taliaferro 1895- *IntWWM 77, -80*
Killiam, Paul 1916- *FilmgC, HalFC 80, IntMPA 77, -75, -76, -78, -79, -80*
Killian, Al 1916-1950 *CmpEPM, IlEncJ, WhoJazz 72*
Killian, James R *NewYTET*
Killick, C Egerton 1891-1967 *WhThe*
Killigrew, Charles 1665-1725 *EncWT, NotNAT B, OxThe, PlP&P*
Killigrew, Thomas 1612-1683 *CnThe, EncWT, Ent, NotNAT A, -B, OxThe, PlP&P[port], REnWD[port]*
Killigrew, Thomas 1657-1719 *NotNAT B, OxThe*
Killigrew, Sir William 1606-1695 *NotNAT B, OxThe*
Killion, John *ConMuA 80B*
Killmayer, Wilhelm 1927- *Baker 78, CpmDNM 80, DcCM, NewGrD 80*
Killoran, John *PupTheA*
Killy, Jean-Claude 1943- *WhoHol A*
Kilmer, Joyce 1886-1918 *AmSCAP 66, -80*
Kilmorey, Earl Of d1915 *NotNAT B*
Kilpack, Bennett 1883-1962 *NotNAT B, WhScrn 74, -77, WhoHol B*
Kilpatrick, Jack Frederick 1915- *BiE&WWA, ConAmC*
Kilpatrick, Lincoln *BlkAmP, DrBlPA, HalFC 80, MorBAP, WhoHol A*
Kilpatrick, Thomas 1902- *BiE&WWA*
Kilpinen, Yrio 1892-1959 *OxMus*
Kilpinen, Yrjo 1892-1959 *Baker 78*
Kilpinen, Yryo 1892-1959 *NewGrD 80*
Kilty, Jerome 1922- *BiE&WWA, NotNAT, PlP&P, WhoThe 72, -77*
Kiltz, Rita 1895- *AmSCAP 66*
Kim, Andy *RkOn 2[port]*
Kim, Byong-Kon 1929- *CpmDNM 78, ConAmC, IntWWM 77, -80*
Kim, Dong Jin 1913- *IntWWM 80*
Kim, Earl 1920- *Baker 78, CpmDNM 80, ConAmC, NewGrD 80*
Kim, Eul 1920- *NewGrD 80*
Kim, Willa *NotNAT*
Kimball, Andrew 1880?-1929? *NewOrJ*
Kimball, Edward M 1859-1938 *Film 1, -2, WhScrn 74, -77, WhoHol B*
Kimball, Grace 1870- *WhThe, WhoStg 1908*
Kimball, Henry 1878-1931 *NewOrJ*
Kimball, Jacob, Jr. 1761-1826 *Baker 78, BiDAmM, NewGrD 80*
Kimball, Jeanette Salvant 1908- *BlkWAB[port]*
Kimball, Jeannette Salvant 1908- *NewOrJ[port]*
Kimball, Louis 1889-1936 *NotNAT B, WhThe*
Kimball, Margaret 1896?- *NewOrJ*
Kimball, Narvin Henry 1909- *AmSCAP 80, NewOrJ[port]*
Kimball, Pauline 1860-1919 *WhScrn 77*

Kimbell, David Rodney Bertram 1939- *IntWWM 80*
Kimbell, Michael Alexander 1946- *ConAmC, IntWWM 77, -80*
Kimberley, Cecil Charles Kenneth 1920- *WhoMus 72*
Kimberley, Mrs. F G d1939 *NotNAT B*
Kimberly, Adrian *RkOn*
Kimbley, Dennis *IntMPA 78, -79, -80*
Kimbrell, Walter Carroll 1929- *AmSCAP 80*
Kimbrough, Clint *WhoHol A*
Kimbrough, Clinton 1936- *BiE&WWA, NotNAT*
Kimbrough, Lena *BluesWW[port]*
Kimbrough, Lottie *BluesWW[port]*
Kimbrough, Steven 1936- *IntWWM 77, -80*
Kimes, Kenneth F 1920- *AmSCAP 66, -80*
Kimm, George 1910- *WhoMus 72*
Kimmel, Edwin Howard 1926- *AmSCAP 66, -80*
Kimmel, Walter S 1941- *ConAmC*
Kimmel, William Breyfogel 1908- *IntWWM 77, -80*
Kimmerling, Robert 1737-1799 *NewGrD 80*
Kimmins, Anthony 1901- *IntMPA 77, -75, -76, -78, -79, -80*
Kimmins, Anthony 1901-1963 *FilmEn, FilmgC, HalFC 80*
Kimmins, Anthony 1901-1964 *IlWWBF, NotNAT B, WhThe*
Kimmins, Arthur d1963 *WhoHol B*
Kimura, Massa Kichi 1890-1918 *WhScrn 77*
Kinasz-Mikolajczak, Bozena Anna 1927- *IntWWM 80*
Kincaid, Aron 1943- *ForYSC, WhoHol A*
Kincaid, Bradley 1894- *CounME 74[port], -74A*
Kincaid, Bradley 1895- *BiDAmM, CmpEPM, EncFCWM 69, IlEncCM[port]*
Kincaid, William 1895-1967 *BnBkM 80, NewGrD 80*
Kincaide, Dean 1911- *WhoJazz 72*
Kincaide, Deane 1911- *BiDAmM, CmpEPM*
Kincaide, Robert Deane 1911- *AmSCAP 80*
Kinch, Myra *CmpGMD, CnOxB, DancEn 78[port]*
Kinck, Hans 1865-1926 *OxThe*
Kind, Johann Friedrich 1768-1843 *NewGrD 80*
Kinder, Ralph 1876-1952 *Baker 78, BiDAmM, ConAmC A*
Kinderman, Wieslaw 1934- *WhoOp 76*
Kindermann, August 1817-1891 *CmOp*
Kindermann, Hedwig Reicher- *NewGrD 80*
Kindermann, Johann Erasmus 1616-1655 *Baker 78, NewGrD 80[port]*
Kindermann, Juergen 1931- *IntWWM 77, -80*
Kindersley, Robert d1634? *NewGrD 80*
Kindig, Wallace *PupTheA*
Kindler, Hans 1892-1949 *Baker 78, MusSN[port]*
Kindler, Hans 1893-1949 *BiDAmM*
Kindley, Jeffrey 1945- *NatPD[port]*
Kindschy, Robert *PupTheA*
Kinel, Mario 1921- *IntWWM 77*
King, Ada d1940 *NotNAT B, WhThe*
King, Al 1904- *AmSCAP 66, -80, IntWWM 77*
King, Al 1926- *BluesWW[port]*
King, Alan *ForYSC, IntMPA 77, -75, -76, -78, -79, -80, WhoHol A*
King, Alan 1924- *FilmgC, HalFC 80*
King, Alan 1927- *FilmEn, JoeFr[port]*
King, Albert 1923- *BluesWW[port], ConMuA 80A, IlEncR*
King, Aldine *DrBlPA*
King, Alec Hyatt 1911- *NewGrD 80*
King, Alexander Hyatt 1911- *IntWWM 77, -80, NewGrD 80, OxMus, WhoMus 72*
King, Allan 1930- *CreCan 2, FilmEn, WorEFlm[port]*
King, Allan 1933- *FilmgC, HalFC 80*
King, Allyn 1901-1930 *Film 2, WhScrn 77*
King, Alvin 1917- *ConAmC*
King, Andrea *IntMPA 77, -75, -76, -78, -79, -80, MotPP*
King, Andrea 1915- *FilmEn, FilmgC, HalFC 80*
King, Andrea 1916- *ForYSC*
King, Andrea 1918- *WhoHol A*
King, Anita 1880-1963 *TwYS*
King, Anita 1889-1963 *Film 1, FilmgC, HalFC 80, MotPP, WhScrn 74, -77, WhoHol B*
King, Archer *BiE&WWA*
King, B B 1925- *BluesWW[port], ConMuA 80A, DrBlPA, EncJzS 70, IlEncJ, IlEncR, MusMk, NewGrD 80, RkOn[port]*
King, Ben E 1938- *ConMuA 80A, DrBlPA, RkOn[port]*
King, Bertie 1912- *BiDAmM*
King, Betty Jackson 1928- *IntWWM 77*
King, Bonnie B *AmSCAP 80*
King, Bradley *MotPP*
King, Bruce 1925- *CnOxB*
King, Burton 1887- *TwYS A*
King, Cammie *WhoHol A*
King, Carlotta *Film 2*
King, Carlton W, III 1947- *IntWWM 77, -80*
King, Carole *ConMuA 80A[port]*
King, Carole 1941- *RkOn[port]*
King, Carole 1942- *IlEncR*
King, Carole 1944- *BiDAmM*
King, Catherine Mary 1952- *IntWWM 80*
King, Cecil d1958 *NotNAT B, WhThe*
King, Charles 1687-1748 *AmPS B, NewGrD 80, OxMus*
King, Charles 1889-1944 *EncMT, FilmgC, HalFC 80, NotNAT B, WhScrn 77, WhThe*
King, Charles 1894-1944 *CmpEPM, FilmEn, ForYSC, WhScrn 74, WhoHol B*
King, Charles 1895-1957 *FilmEn*
King, Charles 1898-1944 *Film 2, TwYS*
King, Charles, Jr. *ForYSC*
King, Charles E 1874-1950 *AmSCAP 66, -80*
King, Charles L, Sr. 1899-1957 *FilmgC, HalFC 80, Vers B[port], WhScrn 74, -77, WhoHol B*
King, Claude *AmPS A*
King, Claude 1876-1941 *NotNAT B, WhThe*
King, Claude 1879-1941 *Film 2, ForYSC, TwYS, WhScrn 74, -77, WhoHol B*
King, Claude 1933- *BiDAmM, CounME 74, -74A, EncFCWM 69, IlEncCM, RkOn[port]*
King, Constance Audrey *IntWWM 77, -80, WhoMus 72*
King, Dave 1929- *FilmgC, HalFC 80, IntMPA 75*
King, David *WhoHol A*
King, Dennis 1897- *AmPS B, ForYSC*
King, Dennis 1897-1971 *BiDAmM, BiE&WWA, CmpEPM, CnThe, EncMT, FilmEn, HalFC 80, NotNAT B, WhScrn 74, -77, WhThe, WhoHol B, WhoThe 72*
King, Dennis 1897-1972 *FilmgC*
King, Dennis, Jr. *WhoHol A*
King, E J d1844 *BiDAmM, NewGrD 80*
King, Edith 1896- *WhThe, WhoHol A, WhoThe 72*
King, Edith 1897-1963 *BiE&WWA, NotNAT, -B*
King, Edward C 1949- *AmSCAP 80*
King, Eleanor 1906- *CmpGMD, DancEn 78*
King, Emmett 1892-1953 *Film 1, -2, NotNAT B, TwYS, WhoHol B*
King, Emmett C 1866-1953 *WhScrn 74, -77*
King, Eugene W d1950 *WhScrn 74, -77, WhoHol B*
King, Fay *Film 2*
King, Frank 1914- *BiDAmM*
King, Freddie d1976 *ConMuA 80A*
King, Freddie 1917- *NewOrJ*
King, Freddie 1934- *BiDAmM, EncJzS 70, IlEncR*
King, Freddie 1934-1976 *BluesWW[port]*
King, Freddy *RkOn[port]*
King, George 1899-1966 *FilmEn, IlWWBF*
King, George 1900-1966 *FilmgC, HalFC 80*
King, Gerald *Film 2*
King, Harold Charles 1895- *Baker 78*
King, Henry *BgBands 74, CmpEPM*
King, Henry 1888- *AmFD, BiDFilm, -81, FilmEn, HalFC 80*
King, Henry 1892- *Film 1, FilmgC, MovMk[port], OxFilm, TwYS A, WorEFlm*
King, Henry 1896- *BiDAmM, CmMov, DcFM, IntMPA 77, -75, -76, -78, -79, -80*
King, Herman *IntMPA 77, -75, -76, -78, -79, -80*
King, Jack 1883-1943 *WhScrn 74, -77, WhoHol B*
King, Jack 1903-1943 *AmSCAP 66, -80*
King, James 1925- *CmOp, IntWWM 77, -80, MusSN[port], NewEOp 71, NewGrD 80, WhoMus 72, WhoOp 76*
King, Jeffrey 1942- *ConAmC*
King, Joe 1883-1951 *Film 1, -2, WhScrn 77*
King, John 1909- *FilmEn*
King, John 1911- *ForYSC*
King, John Dusty 1909- *WhoHol A*
King, John Lyndon 1953- *CpmDNM 79*
King, John-Michael 1929- *BiE&WWA*
King, John Reymes 1910- *IntWWM 77, -80*
King, John Wesley, Jr. 1921- *IntWWM 77*
King, Jonathan *ConMuA 80A*
King, Jonathan 1944- *RkOn 2[port]*
King, Jonathan 1948- *IlEncR*
King, Joseph *Film 2, ForYSC*
King, Judy *Film 2*
King, K K 1907- *IntMPA 75*
King, Karl 1890-1971 *BiDAmM*
King, Karl-Heinz 1931- *CnOxB*
King, Karl L 1891-1971 *Baker 78, ConAmC*
King, Kenneth *CmpGMD*
King, Kip *WhoHol A*
King, L H *Film 2*
King, Leslie 1876-1947 *Film 1, -2, WhScrn 77*
King, Liz 1951- *WhoOp 76*
King, Louis 1898-1962 *FilmEn, Film 2, FilmgC, HalFC 80, TwYS A*
King, Luther *BluesWW[port]*
King, Mabel *DrBlPA*
King, Malcolm 1943- *IntWWM 77, -80*
King, Margie *Film 2*
King, Marie *Film 2*
King, Matthew Peter 1773-1823 *Baker 78, NewGrD 80*
King, Maureen 1933- *WhoMus 72*
King, Maurice *IntMPA 77, -75, -76*
King, Mildred *AmSCAP 66*
King, Mollie 1898- *Film 1, MotPP*
King, Molly 1898- *Film 2, TwYS*
King, Monsier L d1887 *PupTheA*
King, Morgana *WhoHol A*
King, Morgana 1930- *BiDAmM, EncJzS 70*
King, Murray J 1914- *IntMPA 77, -75, -76, -78, -79, -80*
King, Nosmo d1949 *NotNAT B*
King, Oliver A 1855-1923 *Baker 78*
King, Pee Wee 1914- *AmPS A, CmpEPM, CounME 74, -74A, EncFCWM 69, IlEncCM[port]*
King, Peggy 1931- *IntMPA 77, -75, -76, -78, -79, -80, WhoHol A*
King, Perry 1948- *FilmEn, HalFC 80, IntMPA 77, -76, -78, -79, -80, WhoHol A*
King, Pete 1914- *AmSCAP 66, -80*
King, Peter 1928- *IntMPA 77, -75, -76, -78, -79, -80*
King, Philip 1904- *CnThe, WhoThe 72, -77*
King, Priscilla Tien-Tak 1948- *IntWWM 77, -80*
King, Riley B 1925- *BiDAmM, BluesWW[port], EncJzS 70, NewGrD 80*
King, Robert *NewGrD 80, OxMus*
King, Robert A 1862-1932 *AmPS, AmSCAP 66, -80, BiDAmM, NotNAT B, PopAmC*
King, Robert Davis 1913- *ConAmC*
King, Ruth *Film 2*
King, Stan 1900-1949 *WhoJazz 72*
King, Stanford 1912- *AmSCAP 80*
King, Stanley 1930- *IntWWM 80*
King, Stephen 1947- *WhoHrs 80*
King, Stoddard 1889-1933 *AmSCAP 66, -80, BiDAmM*
King, T S *AmSCAP 80*
King, Teddi 1929- *CmpEPM*
King, Tempo 1915?-1939 *CmpEPM*
King, Thea 1925- *IntWWM 77, -80, NewGrD 80, WhoMus 72*
King, Tom 1730-1804 *NotNAT B, OxThe*
King, Tony *DrBlPA, WhoHol A*
King, Vance 1910- *IntMPA 75*
King, Victor d1964 *NotNAT B*

King, Walter *AmSCAP 80*
King, Walter Riley 1951- *AmSCAP 80*
King, Walter Woolf 1899- *FilmgC, ForYSC, HalFC 80, WhThe, WhoHol A*
King, Wayne 1901- *AmPS B, AmSCAP 66, -80, BgBands 74[port], BiDAmM, CmpEPM*
King, Webb *BlksB&W C*
King, Wiley 1885?- *NewOrJ*
King, Will d1953 *WhoHol B*
King, Will 1886-1958 *WhScrn 74, -77*
King, William d1796 *BiDAmM*
King, William 1624-1680 *NewGrD 80, OxMus*
King, William 1663-1712 *OxMus*
King, William Atwell, Jr. 1949- *AmSCAP 80*
King, Woodie, Jr. 1937- *BlkAmP, DrBlPA, MorBAP*
King, Wright *WhoHol A*
King, Zalman *WhoHol A*
King Crimson *ConMuA 80A, IlEncR[port]*
King-Hall, Sir Stephen 1893-1966 *WhThe*
King Harvest *RkOn 2[port]*
King Ivory Lee *BluesWW[port]*
King Sisters *BiDAmM, CmpEPM, WhoHol A*
King-Wood, David *WhoHol A*
Kingdon, Dorothy 1894-1939 *WhScrn 74, -77, WhoHol B*
Kingdon, Frank d1937 *NotNAT B, WhoHol B*
Kingdon, John M d1876 *NotNAT B*
Kingdon-Gould, Edith Maughan d1921 *NotNAT B*
Kingery, Lionel Bruce 1921- *AmSCAP 80*
Kingfish, The *JoeFr*
Kinghorn, John Ritchie 1921- *WhoMus 72*
Kingma, Stanley George 1937- *IntWWM 77, -80*
Kingman, Daniel C 1924- *ConAmC*
Kingman, Dong 1911- *IntMPA 77, -75, -76, -78, -79, -80*
Kings Of Dixieland *BiDAmM*
Kings Of Rhythm *BiDAmM*
Kingsford, Alison 1899-1950 *WhScrn 74, -77*
Kingsford, Charles 1907- *AmSCAP 66, -80, ConAmC, IntWWM 77, -80, WhoMus 72*
Kingsford, Walter 1881-1958 *HolCA[port]*
Kingsford, Walter 1882-1958 *FilmEn, FilmgC, HalFC 80, WhScrn 74, -77*
Kingsford, Walter 1884-1956 *ForYSC*
Kingsford, Walter 1884-1958 *NotNAT B, Vers A[port], WhoHol B*
Kingsley, Albert *Film 2*
Kingsley, Arthur *Film 2*
Kingsley, Charles 1819-1875 *DcPup*
Kingsley, Colin 1925- *IntWWM 77, -80, WhoMus 72*
Kingsley, Dorothy *IntMPA 77, -75, -76, -78, -79, -80, WomWMM*
Kingsley, Dorothy 1908- *CmMov*
Kingsley, Dorothy 1909- *FilmEn, FilmgC, HalFC 80*
Kingsley, Dorothy Alexandra 1919- *IntWWM 77, WhoMus 72*
Kingsley, Emily Perl 1940- *AmSCAP 80*
Kingsley, Florida 1879- *Film 1, -2, TwYS*
Kingsley, Frank *Film 2*
Kingsley, George 1811-1884 *BiDAmM*
Kingsley, Gershon 1928- *ConAmC, IntWWM 77*
Kingsley, Gershon Gary 1925- *AmSCAP 80*
Kingsley, Grace d1962 *NotNAT B*
Kingsley, Margaret 1929- *IntWWM 77*
Kingsley, Margaret 1939- *IntWWM 80, WhoOp 76*
Kingsley, Mary d1936 *NotNAT B*
Kingsley, Paul 1926- *WhoMus 72*
Kingsley, Polly Arnold 1906- *AmSCAP 66*
Kingsley, Sidney 1906- *BiE&WWA, CnMD, CnThe, ConDr 73, -77, CroCD, DcLB 7[port], EncWT, Ent, FilmgC, HalFC 80, McGEWD[port], ModWD, NotNAT, OxThe, PlP&P[port], REnWD[port], WhoThe 72, -77*
Kingsley, Walter d1929 *NotNAT B*
Kingsley, Walter 1923- *IntMPA 77, -75, -76, -78, -79, -80*
Kingsmen, The *ConMuA 80A, RkOn[port]*
Kingston, Gertrude 1866-1937 *NotNAT B, OxThe, WhThe*
Kingston, Kiwi *WhoHrs 80*
Kingston, Muriel *Film 2, TwYS*
Kingston, Natalie 1905?- *FilmEn, Film 2, ForYSC, TwYS, WhoHol A*
Kingston, Sam F d1929 *NotNAT B*
Kingston, Thomas 1902-1959 *WhScrn 74, -77*
Kingston, Winifred 1895-1967 *FilmEn, Film 1, -2, MotPP, TwYS, WhScrn 74, -77, WhoHol B*
Kingston Trio *AmPS A, -B, BiDAmM, ConMuA 80A, RkOn[port]*
Kingswood, Peter John 1934- *IntWWM 77, -80*
Kinkaid, Frank Eugene 1922- *ConAmTC*
Kinkel, Johanna 1810-1858 *Baker 78*
Kinkeldey, Otto 1878-1966 *Baker 78, BiDAmM, NewGrD 80, OxMus*
Kinks, The *ConMuA 80A[port], IlEncR[port], RkOn 2[port]*
Kinley, David D *NewYTET*
Kinloch, William *NewGrD 80*
Kinlock, William *OxMus*
Kinnear, George *WhoMus 72*
Kinnear, Ken *ConMuA 80B*
Kinnear, Roy 1934- *FilmgC, HalFC 80, WhoHol A, WhoThe 72, -77*
Kinnell, Murray 1889-1954 *NotNAT B, WhScrn 74, -77, WhoHol B*
Kinner VonScherffenstein, Martin 1534-1597 *NewGrD 80*
Kinney, Elizabeth Clementine Stedman 1810-1889 *BiDAmM*
Kinney, Gordon J 1905- *ConAmC*
Kinney, Ray 1900-1972 *BiDAmM*
Kinney, Troy 1872-1938 *DancEn 78*
Kinnison, John 1924- *IntWWM 77*
Kinnoch, Ronald 1911?- *FilmgC, HalFC 80*
Kino, Goro *Film 2*
Kinoshita, Junji 1914- *CnMD, ModWD*
Kinoshita, Keisuke 1912- *DcFM, FilmEn, IntMPA 77, -75, -76, -78, -79, -80, OxFilm, WorEFlm[port]*
Kinoy, Ernest *IntMPA 77, -78, -79, -80, MorBAP, NewYTET, NotNAT*
Kinscella, Hazel Gertrude 1893-1960 *NewGrD 80*
Kinscella, Hazel Gertrude 1895-1960 *AmSCAP 66, ConAmC*
Kinsella, Kathleen 1878-1961 *NotNAT B, WhScrn 74, -77, WhoHol B*
Kinsella, Walter A 1900-1975 *IntMPA 75, -76, WhScrn 77, WhoHol C*
Kinsey, Lemuel 1896- *IntWWM 77*
Kinsey, Tony 1930- *IntWWM 77, -80*
Kinskey, Leonid 1903- *FilmEn, FilmgC, HalFC 80, IntMPA 77, -75, -76, -78, -79, Vers A[port], WhoHol A*
Kinski, Klaus 1926- *FilmAG WE, FilmEn, HalFC 80*
Kinsky, Georg Ludwig 1882-1951 *Baker 78, NewGrD 80*
Kinsky, Leonid 1903- *ForYSC*
Kinsolving, Lee 1938-1974 *ForYSC, HalFC 80, WhScrn 77, WhoHol B*
Kintner, Robert E *NewYTET*
Kinton, Leslie Wayne 1951- *IntWWM 80*
Kinugasa, Teinosuke Kukame 1896- *BiDFilm, -81, DcFM FilmEn, FilmgC, HalFC 80, OxFilm, WorEFlm[port]*
Kinyon, John 1918- *AmSCAP 66, ConAmC*
Kinyon, John L 1918- *AmSCAP 80*
Kinz, Franciska *Film 2*
Kinzl, Franz 1895- *IntWWM 77, -80*
Kio, Emil 1900-1965 *MagIlD*
Kionig, Carl Jorgen 1949- *IntWWM 80*
Kiorpes, George Anthony 1931- *IntWWM 77, -80*
Kipling, Edward *Film 2*
Kipling, Rudyard 1865-1936 *DcPup, FilmgC, HalFC 80, OxMus*
Kipness, Joseph *BiE&WWA, NotNAT, WhoThe 77*
Kipnis, Alexander 1891-1978 *Baker 78, BiDAmM, BnBkM 80, CmOp, IntWWM 77, MusMk, MusSN[port], NewEOp 71, NewGrD 80, WhoMus 72*
Kipnis, Igor 1930- *AmSCAP 80, Baker 78, BnBkM 80, IntWWM 77, -80, MusSN[port], NewGrD 80, WhoMus 72*
Kippen, Manart d1947 *WhScrn 74, -77, WhoHol B*
Kipper, Hermann 1826-1910 *Baker 78*
Kipphardt, Heinar 1922- *CnMD, CnThe, CroCD, EncWT, McGEWD[port], ModWD, REnWD[port], WhoThe 72, -77*
Kipps, Charles *ConMuA 80B*
Kipps, Lucy Helen Magdalen *WhoMus 72*
Kiralfy, Bolossy d1932 *NotNAT B*
Kiralfy, Imre d1919 *NotNAT B*
Kiraly, Erno 1919- *NewGrD 80*
Kiraly, Istvan Jozsef 1939- *IntWWM 80*
Kirby, Beecher Pete *IlEncCM*
Kirby, Charles D, II 1930- *AmSCAP 80*
Kirby, David D 1880-1954 *Film 2, WhScrn 74, -77, WhoHol B*
Kirby, F E 1928- *IntWWM 77, -80, NewGrD 80*
Kirby, George 1924- *DrBlPA*
Kirby, Hudson d1848 *NotNAT B*
Kirby, John *BgBands 74[port]*
Kirby, John d1930 *NotNAT B*
Kirby, John 1894- *WhThe*
Kirby, John 1908-1952 *BiDAmM, CmpEPM, IlEncJ, WhoJazz 72*
Kirby, John 1932-1973 *WhScrn 77, WhoHol B*
Kirby, Michael *NotNAT*
Kirby, Percival Robson 1887-1970 *NewGrD 80 OxMus*
Kirby, William 1817-1906 *CreCan 2*
Kirby, William Warner 1876-1914 *WhScrn 77*
Kirby Stone Four, The *RkOn[port]*
Kirbye, George d1634 *NewGrD 80, OxMus*
Kirchbauer, Alphons *NewGrD 80*
Kircher, Athanasius 1601-1680 *Baker 78, DcFM, NewGrD 80*
Kircher, Athanasius 1602-1680 *OxMus*
Kirchgassner, Maria Anna 1769-1808 *NewGrD 80*
Kirchgassner, Mariane 1769-1808 *NewGrD 80*
Kirchgassner, Marianne 1769-1808 *NewGrD 80*
Kirchgessner, Marianne 1769-1808 *NewGrD 80*
Kirchhoff, Gottfried 1685-1746 *NewGrD 80*
Kirchmann *NewGrD 80*
Kirchmayer, Thomas 1511-1563 *OxThe*
Kirchmeyer, Helmut Franz Maria 1930- *IntWWM 77, -80*
Kirchner, Billy *PupTheA*
Kirchner, Fritz 1840-1907 *Baker 78*
Kirchner, Klaus 1927- *WhoOp 76*
Kirchner, Leon 1919- *Baker 78, BiDAmM, BnBkM 80, CompSN[port], CpmDNM 72, ConAmC, DcCM, IntWWM 77, -80, NewGrD 80, OxMus*
Kirchner, Theodor Furchtegott 1823-1903 *Baker 78, NewGrD 80, OxMus*
Kirckman *NewGrD 80*
Kirckman, Abraham 1737-1794 *NewGrD 80[port]*
Kirckman, Jacob 1710-1792 *NewGrD 80*
Kirckman, Joseph *NewGrD 80*
Kirckman, Joseph 1790?-1877 *NewGrD 80*
Kirculescu, Nicola 1910- *IntWWM 77, -80*
Kireilis, Ramon John 1940- *IntWWM 77, -80*
Kirgo, George *WhoHol A*
Kiriac-Georgescu, Dumitru 1866-1928 *Baker 78, NewGrD 80*
Kirienko, Zinaida *WhoHol A*
Kirigin, Ivo 1914-1964 *Baker 78*
Kirk, Andrew D 1898- *AmSCAP 66, -80, BiDAmM*
Kirk, Andy 1898- *BgBands 74[port], CmpEPM, DrBlPA, IlEncJ, NewGrD 80, WhoJazz 72*
Kirk, Colleen Jean 1918- *IntWWM 77, -80*
Kirk, Eddie 1919- *BiDAmM, BluesWW[port], EncFCWM 69, IlEncCM*
Kirk, Elise Kuhl 1932- *IntWWM 80*
Kirk, Evans *Film 2*
Kirk, Fay B 1894-1954 *WhScrn 74, -77*
Kirk, Jack Pappy 1895-1948 *WhScrn 77*
Kirk, James D 1933- *IntWWM 77*
Kirk, Joe d1975 *WhoHol C*
Kirk, John d1948 *NotNAT B*
Kirk, John W 1932- *NatPD[port]*
Kirk, Lisa *CmpEPM, EncMT, MotPP*
Kirk, Lisa 1925- *WhoThe 77*

Kirk, Lisa 1926- *NotNAT*
Kirk, Phyllis *IntMPA 77, -75, -76, -78, -79, -80, MotPP*
Kirk, Phyllis 1926- *FilmgC, HalFC 80*
Kirk, Phyllis 1929- *FilmEn, ForYSC, WhoHol A*
Kirk, Phyllis 1930- *MovMk*
Kirk, Rahsaan Roland 1936-1977 *EncJzS 70, IlEncJ*
Kirk, Rahsaan Roland 1937- *DrBlPA*
Kirk, Roland 1936-1977 *Baker 78*
Kirk, Ronald T 1936- *BiDAmM*
Kirk, Theron Wilford 1919- *AmSCAP 66, -80, CpmDNM 80, ConAmC*
Kirk, Tommy 1941- *FilmEn, FilmgC, ForYSC, HalFC 80, WhoHol A, WhoHrs 80*
Kirk, Wilbert 1906?- *WhoJazz 72*
Kirkby, Ollie *Film 1*
Kirkby-Lunn, Louise 1873-1930 *Baker 78*
Kirkby-Mason, Barbara 1910- *IntWWM 77, -80, WhoMus 72*
Kirkconnell, Watson 1895- *CreCan 2*
Kirke, Donald 1902-1971 *WhScrn 77, WhoHol B*
Kirke, John 1638-1643 *NotNAT B, OxThe*
Kirkeby, Wallace Theodore 1891- *AmSCAP 66, WhoJazz 72*
Kirkendale, Ursula 1932- *NewGrD 80*
Kirkendale, Warren 1932- *IntWWM 77, -80, NewGrD 80*
Kirkham, Correan *Film 2*
Kirkham, Harold Gibson *WhoMus 72*
Kirkham, Kathleen 1895- *Film 1, -2, TwYS*
Kirkhuff, John *WhScrn 77*
Kirkland, Alexander 1908- *BiE&WWA, FilmEn, ForYSC, WhThe, WhoHol A*
Kirkland, David 1878-1964 *WhScrn 77*
Kirkland, Eddie 1928- *BluesWW[port]*
Kirkland, Gelsey 1953- *CnOxB*
Kirkland, Hardee 1864?-1929 *Film 1, -2, WhScrn 74, -77, WhoHol B*
Kirkland, Jack d1969 *PlP&P*
Kirkland, Jack 1901-1969 *CnMD, McGEWD[port]*
Kirkland, Jack 1902-1969 *BiE&WWA, EncWT, ModWD, NotNAT B, WhThe*
Kirkland, Michael *EncFCWM 69*
Kirkland, Mike James 1946- *AmSCAP 80*
Kirkland, Muriel 1903-1971 *BiE&WWA, FilmgC, ForYSC, HalFC 80, NotNAT B, WhScrn 74, -77, WhThe, WhoHol B, WhoThe 72*
Kirkland, Patricia 1925- *WhThe*
Kirkland, Sally 1944- *PlP&P[port], WhoHol A, WhoThe 77*
Kirkland, William Homer *AmSCAP 80*
Kirkman *NewGrD 80*
Kirkman, Abraham 1737-1794 *Baker 78*
Kirkman, Francis d1674 *NotNAT B*
Kirkman, Jakob 1710-1792 *Baker 78*
Kirkman, Kathleen *Film 2*
Kirkmeyer, Ted 1908- *IntMPA 75, -76*
Kirkop, Oreste 1926- *FilmgC, HalFC 80*
Kirkpatrick, Don 1905-1956 *WhoJazz 72*
Kirkpatrick, Donald A 1928- *AmSCAP 66, -80*
Kirkpatrick, Gary 1941- *IntWWM 77, -80*
Kirkpatrick, John 1905- *Baker 78, NewGrD 80*
Kirkpatrick, Ralph 1911- *Baker 78, BnBkM 80, IntWWM 77, -80, MusSN[port], NewGrD 80, WhoMus 72*
Kirkpatrick, William James 1838-1921 *BiDAmM, NewGrD 80*
Kirksey, Van *BlkAmP*
Kirkwall, Earl Of *OxMus*
Kirkwood, Antoinette 1930- *WhoMus 72*
Kirkwood, Gertrude Robinson d1962 *NotNAT B, WhScrn 74, -77, WhoHol B*
Kirkwood, Jack 1894-1964 *NotNAT B*
Kirkwood, Jack 1895-1964 *WhScrn 74, -77, WhoHol B*
Kirkwood, James 1883-1963 *FilmEn, Film 1, -2, ForYSC, HalFC 80, WhScrn 74, -77, WhoHol B*
Kirkwood, James 1883-1966 *TwYS*
Kirkwood, James 1930- *NatPD[port]*
Kirkwood, Joe *ForYSC*
Kirkwood, Joe, Jr. *WhoHol A*
Kirkwood, Pat 1921- *FilmgC, HalFC 80, IlWWBF[port], WhoHol A, WhoThe 72, -77*
Kirkwood-Hackett, Eva 1877-1968 *WhScrn 74, -77*
Kirkwood-Hackett, Eve d1968 *WhoHol B*
Kirnbauer, Susanne 1942- *CnOxB*
Kirnberger, Johann Philipp 1721-1783 *Baker 78, MusMk, NewGrD 80[port], OxMus*
Kirner, Michael 1944- *IntMPA 79, -80*
Kirova, Vera Lazarevna 1940- *CnOxB*
Kirsanoff, Dimitri 1899-1957 *DcFM, FilmEn*
Kirsanoff, Dmitri 1899-1957 *OxFilm*
Kirsanov, Dimitri 1889-1957 *WorEFlm*
Kirsanov, Dmitri 1899-1957 *FilmgC, HalFC 80*
Kirsch, Charlie *NewOrJ*
Kirsch, Martin 1889?- *NewOrJ*
Kirsch, Winfried 1931- *IntWWM 77, -80, NewGrD 80*
Kirschbaum, Bernard 1910- *IntWWM 77, -80*
Kirschstein, Leonora 1933- *WhoMus 72*
Kirschstein, Leonore 1936- *WhoOp 76*
Kirsh, Estelle *WomWMM B*
Kirshbaum, Ralph 1946- *NewGrD 80*
Kirshbaum, Thomas M 1928- *IntWWM 80*
Kirshbaum, Thomas M 1938- *IntWWM 77*
Kirshner, Don *ConMuA 80B[port], IlEncR, NewYTET*
Kirshon, Vladimir Mikhailovich 1902-1938 *CnMD, ModWD, OxThe*
Kirsova, Helene 1911?-1962 *CnOxB, DancEn 78*
Kirstein, Lincoln Edward 1907- *CnOxB, DancEn 78[port], WhoMus 72*
Kirsten, Dorothy 1917- *Baker 78, CmOp, MusSN[port], NewEOp 71, NewGrD 80, WhoHol A, WhoMus 72, WhoOp 76*
Kirsten, Dorothy 1919- *BiDAmM*
Kirtland, Clifford M, Jr. *NewYTET*
Kirtland, Harden *Film 2*
Kirtland, Louise 1905- *WhoThe 72, -77*
Kirtland, Louise 1910- *BiE&WWA, NotNAT*
Kirtley, Virginia *Film 1*
Kirwan, Anne Lindsey 1938- *IntWWM 77, -80*
Kirwan, Patrick d1929 *NotNAT B, WhThe*
Kirzinger *NewGrD 80*
Kis, Imre *Film 2*
Kis, Istvan 1920- *IntWWM 77, -80*
Kisch, Royalton 1919- *WhoMus 72*
Kisco, Charles William 1896- *AmSCAP 66, -80*
Kiser, Stephen Andrew 1951- *IntWWM 80*
Kiser, Wieslaw Maria 1937- *IntWWM 80*
Kisfaludy, Karoly 1788-1830 *McGEWD[port], NotNAT B, OxThe*
Kish, Anne *WomWMM B*
Kishibe, Shigeo 1912- *IntWWM 77, -80, NewGrD 80*
Kishida, Kyoko 1930- *FilmEn*
Kishon, Ephraim 1924- *REnWD[port]*
Kisielewski, Stefan 1911- *Baker 78, IntWWM 77, -80, NewGrD 80*
Kiss *ConMuA 80A[port], IlEncR[port], RkOn 2[port]*
Kiss, Gyula 1944- *IntWWM 80*
Kiss, Janos *IntWWM 77, -80*
Kiss, Janos 1920- *ConAmC*
Kiss, Janos 1921- *AmSCAP 80*
Kiss, Lajos 1900- *NewGrD 80*
Kiss, Nora 1908- *CnOxB, DancEn 78*
Kissaun, Maryann *IntWWM 77, -80, WhoMus 72*
Kissel, Howard William 1942- *ConAmTC*
Kisselgoff, Anna 1938- *CnOxB*
Kissoon, Mac & Katie Kisson *RkOn 2[port]*
Kist, Florentius Cornelis 1796-1863 *Baker 78, NewGrD 80*
Kistemaechers, Henry 1872-1938 *NotNAT B*
Kistemaeckers, Henry 1872-1938 *WhThe*
Kistler, Cyrill 1848-1907 *Baker 78, NewGrD 80*
Kistner, Carl Friedrich 1797-1844 *NewGrD 80*
Kistner, Julius 1805-1868 *NewGrD 80*
Kistner, Karl Friedrich 1797-1844 *Baker 78*
Kistner, Muriel Isabella *WhoMus 72*
Kitahara, Hideteru 1940- *CnOxB*
Kitamura, Eiji 1929- *EncJzS 70*
Kitch, Kenneth *PlP&P*
Kitchell, Iva 1912- *DancEn 78*
Kitchen, Dorothy Ellen Johnson 1937- *IntWWM 77, -80*
Kitchen, Fred d1951 *NotNAT B*
Kitchen, Otis D 1931- *IntWWM 77*
Kitchin, Alfred *WhoMus 72*
Kitchin, Laurence 1913- *WhoThe 77*
Kitchin, Margaret 1914- *WhoMus 72*
Kitchiner, John 1933- *IntWWM 77, -80, WhoOp 76*
Kitching, Colin 1941- *IntWWM 77, -80*
Kite, Christopher James 1947- *IntWWM 77, -80*
Kite-Powell, Jeffery Thomas 1941- *IntWWM 80*
Kithnou, Mademoiselle 1904- *Film 2*
Kithou 1904- *TwYS*
Kitsis, Bob 1917- *CmpEPM*
Kitson, Charles Herbert 1874-1944 *Baker 78, NewGrD 80, OxMus*
Kitsopoulos, Antonia *WhoOp 76*
Kitt, Eartha *AmPS B, IntMPA 77, -75, -76, -78, -79, -80, WhoHol A*
Kitt, Eartha 1928- *Baker 78, BiDAmM, DrBlPA, FilmEn, FilmgC, HalFC 80, MovMk, RkOn*
Kitt, Eartha 1930- *BiE&WWA, ForYSC, NotNAT, WhoThe 72, -77*
Kittel *NewGrD 80*
Kittel, Bruno 1870-1948 *Baker 78*
Kittel, Caspar 1603-1639 *NewGrD 80*
Kittel, Christoph *NewGrD 80*
Kittel, Johann Christian 1732-1809 *Baker 78, NewGrD 80*
Kittel, Johann Heinrich 1652-1682 *NewGrD 80*
Kittl, Jan Bedrich 1806-1868 *NewGrD 80*
Kittl, Johann Friedrich 1806-1868 *Baker 78*
Kitto, Ann *IntWWM 77, -80, WhoMus 72*
Kittredge, George Lyman 1860-1941 *BiDAmM, NotNAT B*
Kittredge, Walter 1834-1905 *BiDAmM*
Kittrell, Jean 1927- *BluesWW[port]*
Kitzinger, Fritz 1904-1947 *Baker 78*
Kitzler, Otto 1834-1915 *Baker 78*
Kitzmiller, John 1913-1965 *DrBlPA, FilmEn, FilmgC, HalFC 80, WhScrn 74, -77, WhoHol B*
Kiurkchiysky, Krasimir 1936- *Baker 78*
Kives, Philip *ConMuA 80B*
Kivi, Aleksis 1834-1872 *REnWD[port]*
Kivitt, Ted 1942- *CnOxB*
Kiyooka, Harry Mitsuo 1928- *CreCan 2*
Kiyooka, Roy Kenzie 1926- *CreCan 1*
Kiyose, Yasuji 1900- *Baker 78, DcCM, NewGrD 80*
Kiyotsuga, Kwanami *REnWD[port]*
Kjaer, Nils 1870-1924 *OxThe*
Kjaerulff-Schmidt, Palle 1931- *WorEFlm*
Kjeldaas, Arnljot 1916- *IntWWM 77*
Kjellin, Alf 1920- *FilmEn, FilmgC, ForYSC, HalFC 80, WhoHol A, WorEFlm*
Kjellin, John J 1904- *AmSCAP 66*
Kjellsby, Erling 1901-1976 *Baker 78*
Kjellstrom, Sven 1875-1950 *Baker 78*
Kjerulf, Halfdan Charles 1815-1868 *Baker 78, MusMk, NewGrD 80[port], OxMus*
Klaatu *ConMuA 80A*
Klabon, Krzysztof 1550?-1616? *NewGrD 80*
Klaboni, Krzysztof 1550?-1616? *NewGrD 80*
Klabund 1890-1928 *CnMD, EncWT, ModWD*
Klackenberg, Ivanka Teodossieva 1942- *IntWWM 80*
Klada, Joannes *NewGrD 80*
Klafsky, Anton Maria 1877-1965 *Baker 78*
Klafsky, Katalin 1855-1896 *NewGrD 80*
Klafsky, Katharina 1855-1896 *Baker 78, NewEOp 71, NewGrD 80*
Klages, Raymond W 1888-1947 *AmSCAP 66, -80, CmpEPM*
Klages, Theodore 1911- *AmSCAP 66, -80*
Klaiber, Joachim 1908- *WhoOp 76*
Klain, Jane 1947- *ConAmTC*
Klais, Hans Gerd 1930- *NewGrD 80*
Klais, Johannes 1852-1925 *NewGrD 80*
Klais, Johannes Caspar Wilhelm Maria 1890-1965 *NewGrD 80*
Klami, Uuno 1900-1961 *Baker 78, NewGrD 80*
Klampfer, John Walker 1945- *CreCan 2*
Klamt, Jutta 1890-1970 *CnOxB*
Klaric, Mirka 1934- *WhoOp 76*
Klassen, Ruth *WomWMM B*
Klatka, Anthony J 1946- *EncJzS 70*
Klatka, Tony 1946- *EncJzS 70*

Klatte, Wilhelm 1870-1930 *Baker 78*
Klatzkin, Leon 1914- *AmSCAP 66*
Klatzkin, Leon S 1924- *AmSCAP 80*
Klatzow, Peter James Leonard 1945- *IntWWM 80, NewGrD 80*
Klauber, Adolph 1879-1933 *NotNAT B, WhThe*
Klauber, Edward d1954 *NewYTET*
Klauber, Marcy 1896-1960 *AmSCAP 66, -80*
Klaudt Indian Family *BiDAmM*
Klaus, Francois 1947- *CnOxB*
Klaus, Henry *Film 2*
Klaus, Kenneth Blanchard 1923- *ConAmC, IntWWM 77, -80*
Klauser, Julius 1854-1907 *Baker 78, BiDAmM*
Klauser, Karl 1823-1905 *Baker 78, BiDAmM*
Klausmeyer, Peter Ballard 1942- *ConAmC*
Klausner, Margot *WomWMM*
Klauss, Kenneth *ConAmC*
Klauss, Noah 1901-1977 *AmSCAP 66, -80, ConAmC*
Klauwell, Adolf 1818-1879 *Baker 78*
Klauwell, Otto 1851-1917 *Baker 78, NewGrD 80*
Klavsen, Verner 1931- *CnOxB, DancEn 78*
Klavun, Walter 1906- *BiE&WWA, NotNAT, WhoHol A*
Klaw, Marc 1858-1936 *NotNAT B, WhThe, WhoStg 1908*
Klebe, Giselher 1925- *Baker 78, CnOxB, DancEn 78, DcCM, IntWWM 77, -80, MusMk, NewEOp 71, NewGrD 80*
Kleber, Leonhard 1490?-1556 *Baker 78*
Kleber, Leonhard 1495?-1556 *NewGrD 80*
Klecki, Paul 1900- *Baker 78, IntWWM 77, -80*
Klecki, Pawel *NewGrD 80*
Kleckner, Susan *WomWMM B*
Kleczkowska-Pospiech, Danuta 1939- *IntWWM 80*
Kleczynski, Jan 1837-1895 *NewGrD 80*
Klee, Bernhard 1936- *WhoOp 76*
Klee, Eugen 1869-1929 *Baker 78*
Klee, Ludwig 1846-1920 *Baker 78*
Klee, Mel 1893-1935 *JoeFr*
Klee, Paul 1879-1940 *DcPup*
Kleeb, Helen 1907- *ForYSC, WhoHol A*
Kleefeld, Wilhelm 1868-1933 *Baker 78*
Kleen, Johan Christoph *NewGrD 80*
Kleen, Leslie 1942- *ConAmC*
Klees, Robert E 1927- *IntMPA 80*
Kleffel, Arno 1840-1913 *Baker 78*
Klega, Miroslav 1926- *NewGrD 80*
Klega, Miroslav 1929- *Baker 78*
Kleiber, Carlos 1930- *Baker 78, BnBkM 80, NewGrD 80, WhoOp 76*
Kleiber, Erich 1890-1956 *Baker 78, BnBkM 80, CmOp, MusSN[port], NewEOp 71, NewGrD 80[port]*
Kleiman, Harlan Philip 1940- *NotNAT*
Kleiman, Stephen Robert 1943- *ConAmC*
Kleimert, Dorrit 1938- *WhoOp 76*
Klein, Abraham Moses 1909- *CreCan 1*
Klein, Adelaide 1904- *BiE&WWA, NotNAT, WhoHol A*
Klein, Adolf *Film 2*
Klein, Adrian Bernard *OxMus*
Klein, Al 1885-1951 *WhScrn 74, -77, WhoHol B*
Klein, Allen *ConMuA 80B, IlEncR*
Klein, Allen 1931- *IntMPA 77, -75, -76, -78, -79, -80*
Klein, Allen Charles 1940- *WhoOp 76*
Klein, Allen Edward 1938- *WhoOp 76*
Klein, Bernhard 1793-1832 *Baker 78, NewGrD 80*
Klein, Bonnie Sherr *WomWMM B*
Klein, Bonny *WomWMM*
Klein, Bruno Oscar 1856-1911 *BiDAmM*
Klein, Bruno Oscar 1858-1911 *Baker 78*
Klein, Buster 1895?-1946? *NewOrJ*
Klein, Charles 1867-1915 *NotNAT B, OxThe, WhThe, WhoStg 1906, -1908*
Klein, Charles 1898- *TwYS A*
Klein, Deanne Arkus 1934-1975 *AmSCAP 66, -80*
Klein, Earl 1915- *IntMPA 77, -75, -76, -78, -79*
Klein, Edward Arthur 1940- *IntWWM 77, -80*
Klein, Elisabeth 1911- *IntWWM 77, -80*
Klein, Eugene V 1921- *IntMPA 77, -75, -76, -78, -79, -80*
Klein, Frieder 1943- *WhoOp 76*
Klein, Fritz Heinrich 1892-1977 *Baker 78*
Klein, Gary *ConMuA 80B*
Klein, Gerald Louis 1926- *ConAmTC*
Klein, Gordon Leslie 1946- *IntWWM 77*
Klein, Hal 1914- *IntMPA 77, -75, -76, -78, -79, -80*
Klein, Harold J *IntMPA 77, -75, -76, -78, -79, -80*
Klein, Henrik 1756-1832 *NewGrD 80*
Klein, Herbert G *NewYTET*
Klein, Herman 1856-1934 *Baker 78, OxMus*
Klein, Ivy Frances 1895- *Baker 78*
Klein, Jacques 1930- *WhoMus 72*
Klein, Johann Joseph 1740-1823 *NewGrD 80*
Klein, John M 1915- *AmSCAP 66, -80, Baker 78, ConAmC*
Klein, Josef *Film 2*
Klein, Josef 1802-1862 *NewGrD 80*
Klein, Judith *WomWMM*
Klein, Julius *Film 2*
Klein, Kenneth 1939- *Baker 78, IntWWM 77, -80*
Klein, Leonard 1929- *ConAmC*
Klein, Lothar 1932- *AmSCAP 66, Baker 78, ConAmC, IntWWM 80*
Klein, Lothar 1935- *AmSCAP 80*
Klein, Lou 1888-1945 *AmSCAP 66, -80*
Klein, Malcolm C 1927- *IntMPA 77, -75, -76, -78, -79, -80*
Klein, Manny 1908- *CmpEPM, WhoJazz 72*
Klein, Manuel 1876-1919 *AmSCAP 66, -80, Baker 78, BiDAmM, CmpEPM, NewCBMT, NotNAT B, PopAmC[port]*
Klein, Miriam 1937- *EncJzS 70*
Klein, Mitchell Sardou 1947- *IntWWM 77, -80*
Klein, Oscar 1930- *EncJzS 70*
Klein, Paul L *IntMPA 80, NewYTET*
Klein, Paul L d1964 *NotNAT B*
Klein, Peter 1907- *CmOp, NewGrD 80, WhoMus 72*
Klein, Peter 1930- *IntWWM 77, -80*
Klein, Philip G *ConAmC*
Klein, Robert *Film 2*
Klein, Robert 1942- *JoeFr*
Klein, Robert Arnold 1928- *AmSCAP 80*
Klein, Rudolf 1920- *NewGrD 80*
Klein, Stewart Roy 1933- *ConAmTC*
Klein, William 1926- *FilmEn, OxFilm, WorEFlm*
Klein, William 1929- *FilmgC, HalFC 80*
Klein-Rogge, Rudolf 1888-1955 *FilmAG WE, FilmEn*
Klein-Rogge, Rudolf 1889-1955 *FilmgC, HalFC 80, WhScrn 74, -77, WhoHol B, WhoHrs 80*
Klein-Rogge, Rudolph 1889-1955 *Film 2*
Kleinau, Willy A d1957 *WhScrn 74, -77, WhoHol B*
Kleinecke, August 1881-1944 *AmSCAP 66*
Kleineidam, Horst 1932- *CroCD*
Kleiner, Harry 1916- *FilmEn, FilmgC, HalFC 80, IntMPA 77, -75, -76, -78, -79, -80*
Kleiner, Richard 1921- *AmSCAP 66, -80*
Kleinerman, Isaac *NewYTET*
Kleinert, Robert *Film 2*
Kleinheinz, Franz Xaver 1765-1832 *Baker 78*
Kleinknecht *NewGrD 80*
Kleinknecht, Christian Ludwig 1765-1794 *NewGrD 80*
Kleinknecht, Jakob Friedrich 1722-1794 *Baker 78, NewGrD 80*
Kleinknecht, Johann Stephan 1731-1791? *NewGrD 80*
Kleinknecht, Johann Wolfgang 1715-1786 *NewGrD 80*
Kleinknecht, Johannes 1676-1751 *NewGrD 80*
Kleinknecht, Martin 1665-1730 *NewGrD 80*
Kleinman, Isador I 1913- *AmSCAP 66, -80, ConAmC A*
Kleinman, Louis 1912- *ConAmTC*
Kleinmichel, Richard 1846-1901 *Baker 78, NewGrD 80*
Kleinsasser, Jerome Stewart 1939- *IntWWM 80*
Kleinsinger, George 1914- *AmSCAP 66, -80, Baker 78, BiDAmM, ConAmC*
Kleiser, Randal *HalFC 80*
Kleist, Heinrich Von 1777-1811 *CnThe, DcPup, EncWT, Ent, McGEWD[port], NewGrD 80, NotNAT A, -B, OxThe, REnWD[port]*
Kleist, Heinrich Wilhelm Von 1777-1811 *NewEOp 71*
Klekovic, Patricia 1935?- *CnOxB*
Klemczynski, Julian 1810-1851? *NewGrD 80*
Klement, Jerome 1922- *ConAmC*
Klemetti, Heikki 1876-1953 *Baker 78*
Klemisch, Dietlinde 1938- *CnOxB, DancEn 78*
Klemm, Eberhardt 1929- *NewGrD 80*
Klemm, Frederick August 1795?-1876 *NewGrD 80*
Klemm, Gustav 1897-1947 *AmSCAP 66, -80, ConAmC*
Klemm, Johann 1595?-1651? *NewGrD 80*
Klemm, Johann Gottlob 1690-1762 *Baker 78, BiDAmM, NewGrD 80*
Klemm, John G 1795- *NewGrD 80*
Klemm, John G 1797?-1867? *BiDAmM*
Klemm, Roberta Kohnhorst 1884-1975 *AmSCAP 80*
Klemme, Johann 1595?-1651? *NewGrD 80*
Klemmer, John 1946- *EncJzS 70*
Klemmio, Johann 1595?-1651? *NewGrD 80*
Klemmius, Johann 1595?-1651? *NewGrD 80*
Klemperer, Otto 1885-1973 *Baker 78, BiDAmM, BnBkM 80[port], CmOp, IntWWM 77, MusMk[port], MusSN[port], NewEOp 71, NewGrD 80[port], WhoMus 72*
Klemperer, Regina Mushabac 1949- *IntWWM 77, -80*
Klemperer, Werner *ForYSC, MotPP, WhoHol A*
Klemperer, Werner 1919- *FilmgC, HalFC 80*
Klemperer, Werner 1920- *FilmEn*
Klemperer, Werner 1930- *MovMk*
Klenau, Paul Von 1883-1946 *Baker 78, NewEOp 71, NewGrD 80, OxMus*
Klencke, Helmina *NewGrD 80*
Klencke, Wilhelmine Christiane Von *NewGrD 80*
Klenfner, Michael *ConMuA 80B*
Klengel, August Alexander 1783-1852 *Baker 78, NewGrD 80, OxMus*
Klengel, Julius 1859-1933 *Baker 78, NewGrD 80, OxMus*
Klengel, Paul 1854-1935 *Baker 78, NewGrD 80, OxMus*
Klenner, John 1890-1955 *ConAmC*
Klenner, John 1899-1955 *AmSCAP 66, -80*
Klenovsky, Nikolai 1853-1915 *Baker 78*
Klenovsky, Nikolai Semenovitch 1857-1915 *OxMus*
Klenovsky, Nikolay Semyonovich 1857-1915 *NewGrD 80*
Klenovsky, Paul *Baker 78, OxMus*
Klenz, William *ConAmC A*
Klepper, Michael M 1934- *AmSCAP 66*
Klepper, Walter Mihai 1929- *IntWWM 80*
Kleppinger, Bill 1897- *NewOrJ[port]*
Klercker, Georg A F 1877-1951 *WhScrn 77*
Klerk, Albert De 1917- *Baker 78, NewGrD 80*
Kletzki, Paul 1900-1973 *Baker 78, NewGrD 80, OxMus, WhoMus 72*
Kletzsch, Charles 1926- *ConAmC*
Kleve, Endre 1949- *IntWWM 80*
Kleven, Arvid 1899-1929 *Baker 78*
Klewer, Leonore N 1912- *BiE&WWA*
Klicka, Josef 1855-1937 *Baker 78*
Klicka, Vaclav 1882-1953 *NewGrD 80*
Klickmann, F Henri 1885- *AmSCAP 66, -80*
Klicpera, Vaclav Kliment 1792-1859 *CnThe, REnWD[port]*
Kliegl, Herbert 1904- *BiE&WWA*
Klien, Walter 1928- *IntWWM 77, -80, NewGrD 80, WhoMus 72*
Kliewer, Warren *NatPD[port]*
Klima, Stanislav Vaclav 1927- *IntWWM 77, -80*
Klimek, Zdzislaw 1930- *WhoOp 76*
Klimes, Robert 1926- *AmSCAP 66*
Klimisch, Mary Jane 1920- *IntWWM 77, -80*
Klimisch, Sister Mary Jane 1920- *ConAmC*
Klimko, Ronald James 1936- *ConAmC*
Klimo, Stefan 1919- *IntWWM 77, -80*

Klimov, Mikhail Georgiyevich 1881-1937 *Baker 78, NewGrD 80*
Klimov, Valery Alexandrovich 1931- *NewGrD 80*
Klimovsky, Leon *WhoHrs 80*
Klinda, Ferdinand 1929- *IntWWM 80*
Klinder, Lotte *Film 2*
Klindworth, Karl 1830-1916 *Baker 78, NewGrD 80, OxMus*
Kline, Dick *ConMuA 80B*
Kline, Edith L B *PupTheA*
Kline, Fred W 1918- *IntMPA 77, -75, -76, -78, -79, -80*
Kline, Herbert 1909- *DcFM, FilmEn, FilmgC, HalFC 80, OxFilm*
Kline, Joseph Leo 1930- *IntWWM 77*
Kline, Norman 1935- *NatPD[port]*
Kline, Olive *CmpEPM*
Kline, Richard 1926- *FilmEn, FilmgC, HalFC 80*
Kling, Henri 1842-1918 *NewGrD 80*
Kling, Heywood Woody 1925- *AmSCAP 80*
Kling, Paul 1929- *IntWWM 77, -80*
Kling, Taka Shimazaki 1936- *IntWWM 77, -80*
Klingemann, Ernst August 1777-1831 *EncWT*
Klingenberg, Friedrich Wilhelm 1809-1888 *Baker 78*
Klingenstein, Bernhard 1545?-1614 *NewGrD 80*
Klinger, Friedrich Maximilian 1752-1831 *EncWT, Ent*
Klinger, Friedrich Von 1752-1831 *McGEWD[port]*
Klinger, Henry 1908- *IntMPA 77, -75, -76, -78, -79, -80*
Klinger, Kurt 1928- *CnMD, CroCD*
Klinger, Michael 1920- *IntMPA 77, -75, -76, -78, -79, -80*
Klinger, Michael 1921- *HalFC 80*
Klingman, L Deborah *WomWMM*
Klingman, Lynzee *WomWMM B*
Klingsor *NewGrD 80*
Klink, Al 1915- *BiDAmM, CmpEPM*
Klinker, Effie *JoeFr*
Klinko, Albert 1924- *IntWWM 77, -80*
Klinkon, Ervin O 1933- *IntWWM 77, -80*
Klintbert, Walter *Film 1*
Klippstatter, Kurt 1934- *IntWWM 77, -80, WhoOp 76*
Klipstein, Abner D 1912- *BiE&WWA*
Klitzsch, Karl Emanuel 1812-1886 *Baker 78*
Klobaskova, Libuse *NewGrD 80*
Klobucar, Andelko 1931- *IntWWM 77, -80*
Klobucar, Berislav 1924- *WhoOp 76*
Klode, Christian *NewGrD 80*
Kloepfer, Eugen 1886-1950 *Film 2, WhScrn 77*
Kloffler, Johann Friedrich 1725-1790 *NewGrD 80*
Klohr, John N 1869-1956 *AmSCAP 66, -80*
Klondike, Pete *WhScrn 77*
Klook *NewGrD 80*
Kloos, Diet 1929- *IntWWM 77, -80*
Klop, Hendrik Teunis 1946- *IntWWM 77, -80*
Klopfenstein, Rene 1927- *IntWWM 77, -80*
Klopstock, Friedrich Gottlieb 1724-1803 *McGEWD[port], NewGrD 80*
Klos, Dieter 1931- *CnOxB*
Klos, Elmar 1910- *DcFM, FilmEn, FilmgC, HalFC 80, OxFilm*
Klos, Vladimir 1946- *CnOxB*
Klose, Friedrich 1862-1942 *Baker 78, NewGrD 80*
Klose, Hyacinth Eleanore 1808-1880 *OxMus*
Klose, Hyacinthe-Eleonore 1808-1880 *Baker 78, NewGrD 80*
Klose, Margarete 1902-1965 *CmOp*
Klose, Margarete 1902-1968 *Baker 78, NewGrD 80*
Klose, Margarete 1905-1968 *NewEOp 71*
Klosky, Linda *WomWMM B*
Kloss, Eric 1949- *AmSCAP 80, Conv 2[port], EncJzS 70*
Kloss, Erich 1863-1910 *Baker 78*
Kloten, Edgar Lawrence 1912- *ConAmTC*
Kloth, Timothy Tom 1954- *CpmDNM 80*
Klotman, Robert Howard 1918- *AmSCAP 66, -80, IntWWM 77, -80*
Klotz *NewGrD 80*
Klotz, Aegidius 1733-1805 *NewGrD 80*
Klotz, Florence *NotNAT, WhoThe 72, -77*
Klotz, Georg 1687-1737 *NewGrD 80*
Klotz, Hans 1900- *IntWWM 77, -80, NewGrD 80*
Klotz, Johann Carl 1709-1770? *NewGrD 80*
Klotz, Joseph 1743- *NewGrD 80*
Klotz, Leora 1928- *AmSCAP 66, -80, ConAmC*
Klotz, Mathias 1653-1743 *NewGrD 80*
Klotz, Matthias 1653-1743 *Baker 78, MusMk*
Klotz, Sebastian 1696-1760? *NewGrD 80*
Klotz, Sebastian 1696-1775 *Baker 78*
Klotzman, Dick *ConMuA 80B*
Klove, Jane *WomWMM*
Kloz *NewGrD 80*
Klucevsek, Guy 1947- *ConAmC*
Kluczko, John 1912-1977 *AmSCAP 80*
Klug, Geraldine Dolores 1915- *AmSCAP 80*
Klug, Heinrich 1935- *IntWWM 77, -80*
Kluge, Alexander 1932- *BiDFilm, -81, FilmEn, HalFC 80, OxFilm, WorEFlm*
Kluge, John W 1914- *NewYTET*
Klughardt, August 1847-1902 *Baker 78, NewGrD 80*
Klugman, Jack *BiE&WWA, IntMPA 77, -75, -76, -78, -79, -80, MotPP, NotNAT, WhoHol A*
Klugman, Jack 1922- *FilmEn, FilmgC, ForYSC, HalFC 80, WhoThe 72, -77*
Klugman, Jack 1924- *MovMk[port]*
Klukowski, Franciszek 1770-1830 *NewGrD 80*
Klukvin, I *Film 2*
Klund, Richard 1930- *AmSCAP 80*
Klune, Raymond A 1904- *IntMPA 75, -76*
Klupak, Jaroslav 1920- *IntWWM 77, -80*
Klusak, Jan 1934- *Baker 78, DcCM, IntWWM 77, -80, NewGrD 80*
Klusen, Ernst 1909- *NewGrD 80*
Klussmann, Ernst Gernot 1901- *NewGrD 80*
Klymshyn, Eugene John 1945- *IntWWM 77, -80*
Klynn, Herbert David 1917- *IntMPA 77, -75, -76, -78, -79, -80*
Klyuzner, Boris Lazarevich 1909- *NewGrD 80*
Kmen, Henry 1915- *NewOrJ*
Kmentt, Waldemar 1929- *IntWWM 77, -80, NewGrD 80, WhoOp 76*
Kmoch, Frantisek 1848-1912 *NewGrD 80*
Knab, Armin 1881-1951 *Baker 78, NewGrD 80*
Knabb, Harry G 1891-1955 *WhScrn 74, -77*
Knabe *NewGrD 80*
Knabe, Ernest 1827-1894 *Baker 78, NewGrD 80*
Knabe, Ernest 1837-1894 *BiDAmM*
Knabe, Ernest J *Baker 78*
Knabe, Valentine Wilhelm Ludwig 1797-1864 *BiDAmM*
Knabe, William 1803-1864 *Baker 78, NewGrD 80*
Knabe, William 1841-1889 *Baker 78, BiDAmM, NewGrD 80*
Knabe, William 1872-1939 *Baker 78*
Knafelius, Johann *NewGrD 80*
Knaggs, Skelton 1911-1955 *WhScrn 77, WhoHrs 80*
Knaggs, Skelton 1913-1955 *WhScrn 74, WhoHol B*
Knap, Rolf 1937- *Baker 78, CpmDNM 76*
Knape, Gerald Bearndt 1912- *AmSCAP 80*
Knape, Walter 1906- *Baker 78, NewGrD 80*
Knapp, Alexander Victor 1945- *IntWWM 77, -80*
Knapp, Budd 1915- *CreCan 2*
Knapp, David *WhoHol A*
Knapp, Evalyn 1908- *FilmEn, ForYSC, HalFC 80, ThFT[port], WhoHol A*
Knapp, Fred L d1962 *NotNAT B*
Knapp, J Merrill 1914- *NewGrD 80*
Knapp, Janet 1922- *NewGrD 80*
Knapp, Orville 1908?-1936 *BgBands 74[port], CmpEPM*
Knapp, Otto *Film 2*
Knapp, Peter 1947- *IntWWM 80*
Knapp, Phoebe Palmer 1839-1908 *Baker 78, BiDAmM*
Knapp, Robert *ForYSC*
Knapp, Wilfrid Arthur *CreCan 2*
Knapp, William 1698?-1768 *NewGrD 80*
Knappertsbusch, Hans 1888-1965 *Baker 78, CmOp, MusSN[port], NewEOp 71, NewGrD 80*
Knapton, Frederick William 1931- *IntWWM 77, -80*
Knapton, Philip 1788-1833 *NewGrD 80*
Knaub, Richard K 1928- *BiE&WWA, NotNAT*
Knaus, Hans Herwig 1929- *IntWWM 77, -80*
Knaus, William Barron 1925- *IntWWM 77*
Knauss, Van Devon 1938- *IntWWM 77*
Knauth, Joachim 1931- *CnMD*
Knauth, Robert *NewGrD 80*
Kneale, Nigel 1922- *CmMov, ConDr 73, -77C, FilmgC, HalFC 80, WhoHrs 80*
Kneale, Patricia 1925- *WhoThe 72, -77*
Knecht, Henry 1898-1968 *NewOrJ*
Knecht, Justin Heinrich 1752-1817 *Baker 78, NewGrD 80, OxMus*
Knechtel, Baird 1937- *IntWWM 80*
Knee, Bernie 1924- *AmSCAP 80*
Kneeland, Abner 1774-1844 *BiDAmM*
Kneeland, Levi 1803-1834 *BiDAmM*
Knees, Jurij *NewGrD 80*
Knef, Hildegard 1925- *FilmAG WE[port], FilmEn, HalFC 80, OxFilm*
Knef, Hildegarde 1925- *FilmgC, MovMk*
Knefel, Johann *NewGrD 80*
Kneif, Tibor 1932- *NewGrD 80*
Kneisel, Franz 1865-1926 *Baker 78, BiDAmM*
Kneisel, Marianne 1897-1972 *BiDAmM*
Kneller, Andreas 1649-1724 *NewGrD 80*
Kneller, Godfrey F *WhoMus 72*
Knepler, Georg 1906- *IntWWM 77, -80, NewGrD 80*
Knepp, Mary d1677 *NotNAT B, OxThe*
Knepper, James M 1927- *BiDAmM, EncJzS 70*
Knepper, Jimmy 1927- *EncJzS 70*
Knepper, Noah Allen 1921- *IntWWM 77, -80*
Kness, Jurij *NewGrD 80*
Kness, Richard M 1937- *IntWWM 77, -80, WhoOp 76*
Knez, Georg *NewGrD 80*
Knez, Jurij *NewGrD 80*
Knfusslin, Fritz 1917- *IntWWM 77, -80*
Kniaseff, Boris 1900-1975 *CnOxB*
Kniaseff, Boris 1905- *DancEn 78*
Knickerbocker, Paine 1912- *BiE&WWA, IntMPA 75, NotNAT*
Knickerbockers, The *RkOn 2[port]*
Knie, Roberta Joy 1938- *WhoOp 76*
Kniebusch, Carol Lee 1938- *IntWWM 80*
Kniese, Julius 1848-1905 *Baker 78*
Knieste, Adam 1917- *AmSCAP 66*
Knieter, Gerard L 1931- *IntWWM 77, -80*
Knight, Alfred Reynolds 1914- *WhoMus 72*
Knight, Arthur 1916- *IntMPA 77, -75, -76, -78, -79, -80, OxFilm*
Knight, Beatrice 1925- *AmSCAP 66*
Knight, Bill *Film 2*
Knight, Brenda Mary 1926- *IntWWM 77, -80, WhoMus 72*
Knight, Bryne *IntWWM 77, WhoMus 72*
Knight, Castleton 1894-1972 *FilmgC, HalFC 80, IlWWBF*
Knight, Christopher *WhoHol A*
Knight, Cyril Herbert 1908- *WhoMus 72*
Knight, David *WhoHol A*
Knight, David 1927- *FilmgC, HalFC 80, WhoThe 72, -77*
Knight, David 1928- *FilmEn, IntMPA 77, -75, -76, -78, -79, -80*
Knight, Dennis 1926- *WhoMus 72*
Knight, Don *WhoHol A*
Knight, Edward, Jr. 1795?-1833 *BiDAmM*
Knight, Eric W 1932- *AmSCAP 80*
Knight, Esmond 1906- *BiE&WWA, FilmEn, FilmgC, HalFC 80, IlWWBF, -A, IntMPA 77, -75, -76, -78, -79, -80, WhoHol A, WhoThe 72, -77*
Knight, Evelyn *AmPS A*
Knight, Felix 1913- *ForYSC*
Knight, Fuzzy 1901-1976 *FilmEn, FilmgC, ForYSC, HalFC 80, Vers A[port], WhoHol C*
Knight, G H H *OxMus*
Knight, G Wilson 1897- *BiE&WWA*
Knight, Gary *AmSCAP 80*
Knight, George Litch 1925- *WhoMus 72*
Knight, Gerald Hocken 1908-1979 *IntWWM 77, -80, NewGrD 80, WhoMus 72*

Knight, Gillian Rosemary *WhoOp 76*
Knight, Gladys 1944- *AmSCAP 80, BiDAmM, DrBlPA, RkOn[port]*
Knight, Gladys And The Pips *BiDAmM, ConMuA 80A, IlEncR[port], RkOn[port]*
Knight, Harlan E *Film 2*
Knight, Jack *WhoHol A*
Knight, James 1891- *Film 1, -2, IlWWBF*
Knight, James B 1929- *AmSCAP 66, -80*
Knight, Janice Mary 1947- *IntWWM 77, -80*
Knight, Jean *RkOn 2[port]*
Knight, John d1964 *NotNAT B*
Knight, John Forrest 1901-1976 *MovMk*
Knight, Joseph 1829-1907 *NotNAT B, OxThe*
Knight, Joseph Philip 1812-1887 *Baker 78*
Knight, Julius 1863-1941 *NotNAT B, WhThe*
Knight, June 1911- *EncMT, WhThe*
Knight, June 1913- *ForYSC*
Knight, Mark 1916- *IntWWM 77, -80*
Knight, Mark Anthony 1941- *IntWWM 80, WhoMus 72*
Knight, Morris 1933- *AmSCAP 80, ConAmC*
Knight, Norman James Clode 1931- *IntWWM 77, -80, WhoMus 72*
Knight, Patricia *WhoHol A*
Knight, Paul William 1954- *IntWWM 80*
Knight, Percival 1873?-1923 *NotNAT B, WhScrn 74, -77, WhoHol B*
Knight, Percy *Film 2*
Knight, Robert 1945- *RkOn 2[port]*
Knight, Rosalind *WhoHol A*
Knight, Sally Mary 1942- *IntWWM 77*
Knight, Sandra 1938?- *WhoHol A, WhoHrs 80[port]*
Knight, Shirley *MotPP*
Knight, Shirley 1936- *NotNAT*
Knight, Shirley 1937- *BiDFilm, -81, FilmEn, FilmgC, ForYSC, HalFC 80, IntMPA 77, -75, -76, -78, -79, -80, MovMk, WhoHol A, WhoThe 77*
Knight, Sonny *RkOn*
Knight, Ted *WhoHol A*
Knight, Terry 1943- *BiDAmM*
Knight, Terry & The Pack *RkOn 2[port]*
Knight, Thomas d1820 *NotNAT B*
Knight, Vick Ralph, Jr. 1928- *AmSCAP 80*
Knight, Vick Ralph, Sr. 1908- *AmSCAP 66, -80*
Knight, W R *Film 2*
Knighton, Percy 1898- *TwYS A*
Knill, C Edwin *BiE&WWA, NotNAT*
Knill, Hans 1941- *CnOxB*
Kniller, Anton *NewGrD 80*
Kniplova, Nadezda 1932- *NewGrD 80, WhoOp 76*
Knipp, Mary *OxThe*
Knipper, Lev 1898-1974 *Baker 78, NewGrD 80, OxMus*
Knipper, Olga 1870-1959 *EncWT, Ent[port]*
Knipper-Chekhova, Olga 1870-1959 *NotNAT B, OxThe, PlP&P[port]*
Knipper-Tschech, O *Film 2*
Knispel, Donald LeRoy 1936- *IntWWM 77*
Kniss, Richard Lawrence 1937- *AmSCAP 80*
Knister, Raymond 1899?-1932 *CreCan 1*
Knittl, Karel 1853-1907 *NewGrD 80*
Knittl, Karl 1853-1907 *Baker 78*
Knize, Frantisek Max 1784-1840 *NewGrD 80*
Knobel, Johann 1525?-1617? *NewGrD 80*
Knoblich, Hans Georg 1933- *WhoOp 76*
Knoblock, Edward 1874-1945 *EncWT, HalFC 80, ModWD, NotNAT B, OxThe, PlP&P, WhThe*
Knoch, Ernst 1875-1959 *Baker 78*
Knockouts, The *RkOn*
Knoechel, Robert F *IntMPA 79, -80*
Knofel, Johann 1525?-1617? *NewGrD 80*
Knoller, Andreas *NewGrD 80*
Knop, Luder d1665 *NewGrD 80*
Knopf *NewGrD 80*
Knopf, August 1865-1947 *NewGrD 80*
Knopf, Edgar 1928- *NewGrD 80*
Knopf, Edwin H 1899- *AmSCAP 66, -80, FilmEn, FilmgC, HalFC 80, IntMPA 77, -75, -76, -78, -79, -80*
Knopf, Herbert 1894-1969 *NewGrD 80*
Knopf, Johannes 1929- *NewGrD 80*
Knopf, Kurt 1900-1945 *NewGrD 80*
Knopf, Paul 1927- *AmSCAP 80*
Knopflin, Johann *NewGrD 80*
Knorr, Ernst-Lothar Von 1896-1973 *Baker 78, NewGrD 80*
Knorr, Iwan 1853-1916 *Baker 78, NewGrD 80, OxMus*
Knorr, Julius 1807-1861 *Baker 78*
Knorr VonRosenroth, Christian 1636-1689 *NewGrD 80*
Knote, Heinrich 1870-1953 *Baker 78, CmOp, NewEOp 71, NewGrD 80*
Knott, Adelbert 1859-1933 *Film 2, WhScrn 77*
Knott, Amanda 1945- *CnOxB*
Knott, Clara 1882-1926 *Film 2, WhScrn 74, -77, WhoHol B*
Knott, Else 1912-1975 *WhScrn 77, WhoHol C*
Knott, Frederick *BiE&WWA, NotNAT*
Knott, George Marion *Film 2*
Knott, Lydia 1866-1955 *WhScrn 77*
Knott, Lydia 1873- *Film 1, -2, TwYS*
Knott, Roselle 1870-1948 *NotNAT B, WhThe, WhoStg 1906, -1908*
Knotts, Don 1924- *FilmEn, FilmgC, ForYSC, HalFC 80, JoeFr, MotPP, MovMk[port], WhoHol A, WhoHrs 80*
Knowland, Alice 1879- *Film 1, -2, TwYS*
Knowland, William F 1908- *What 1[port]*
Knowlden, Marilyn 1925- *ThFT[port]*
Knowles, Alec 1850-1917 *NotNAT B*
Knowles, Alex 1850-1917 *WhThe*
Knowles, Bernard 1900- *CmMov, FilmEn, FilmgC, HalFC 80, IlWWBF, IntMPA 75*
Knowles, Dorothy *WomWMM B*
Knowles, Elsie Judith 1936- *IntWWM 77*
Knowles, Frances Goddard *WhoMus 72*
Knowles, James Davis 1798-1838 *BiDAmM*
Knowles, James Sheridan 1784-1862 *McGEWD, NotNAT B, OxThe*
Knowles, John Harris 1832-1908 *BiDAmM*
Knowles, Norman George 1938- *AmSCAP 80*
Knowles, Patric 1911- *FilmEn, FilmgC, ForYSC, HalFC 80, IntMPA 77, -75, -76, -78, -79, -80, MovMk[port], WhoHol A, WhoHrs 80*
Knowles, Richard George 1858-1919 *NotNAT B, OxThe*
Knowling, Ransom 1910-1967 *WhoJazz 72*
Knowlton, Maude *WhoStg 1908*
Knox, Alexander 1907- *BiE&WWA, FilmEn, FilmgC, ForYSC, HalFC 80, IlWWBF, IntMPA 77, -75, -76, -78, -79, -80, MotPP, MovMk[port], NotNAT, WhoHol A, WhoThe 72, -77*
Knox, Buddy 1933- *AmPS A, RkOn[port]*
Knox, Charles 1929- *AmSCAP 80, ConAmC*
Knox, Elyse 1917- *FilmEn, ForYSC, HalFC 80, WhoHol A*
Knox, Emile 1902-1976 *NewOrJ*
Knox, Foster *Film 1*
Knox, Gordon 1909- *IntMPA 77, -75, -76, -78, -79, -80*
Knox, Helen Boardman 1870-1947 *AmSCAP 66, -80*
Knox, Hugh d1926 *WhScrn 74, -77*
Knox, John 1505-1572 *OxMus*
Knox, Teddy 1896-1974 *Film 2, FilmgC, HalFC 80, IlWWBF*
Knox, W D C *Film 2*
Knudsen, David *Film 2*
Knudsen, Ebbe 1925- *IntWWM 80*
Knudsen, Gunnar 1907- *IntWWM 80*
Knudsen, K *BlkAmP*
Knudsen, Lennart Nordlof 1913- *IntWWM 80*
Knudsen, Mette *WomWMM*
Knudsen, Peggy 1923- *ForYSC, WhoHol A*
Knudsen, Peggy 1925- *HalFC 80*
Knudson, Paul *ConAmC*
Knudson, Peggy *MotPP*
Knudtson, Frederic L 1900?-1964 *HalFC 80*
Knull, Chuck 1947- *NatPD[port]*
Knuller, Andreas *NewGrD 80*
Knupfer, Paul 1866-1920 *NewGrD 80*
Knupfer, Sebastian 1633-1676 *NewGrD 80*
Knushevitsky, Svyatoslav Nikolayevich 1908-1963 *NewGrD 80*
Knussen, Oliver 1952- *Baker 78, IntWWM 77, -80, NewGrD 80*
Knussen, Stuart Oliver *WhoMus 72*
Knust, Albrecht 1896- *CnOxB*
Knutson, Wayne S 1926- *BiE&WWA, NotNAT*
Knyf *NewGrD 80*
Knyff *NewGrD 80*
Knyght, Thomas *NewGrD 80*
Knyvett, Charles, Jr. 1773-1859 *Baker 78*
Knyvett, Charles, Sr. 1752-1822 *Baker 78, NewGrD 80*
Knyvett, William 1779-1856 *Baker 78, NewGrD 80*
Kobald, Karl 1876-1957 *Baker 78*
Kobart, Ruth 1924- *BiE&WWA, NotNAT, WhoHol A, WhoThe 72, -77*
Kobayashi, Ichizo 1873-1960? *DcFM, FilmEn*
Kobayashi, Masaki 1915- *BiDFilm, -81, WorEFlm*
Kobayashi, Masaki 1916- *DcFM, FilmEn, FilmgC, HalFC 80, IntMPA 77, -75, -76, -78, -79, -80, OxFilm*
Kobayashi, Setsuo 1920- *FilmEn, OxFilm*
Kobbe, Gustav 1857-1918 *Baker 78, BiDAmM, NewEOp 71*
Kobe, Arturo *Film 2*
Kobe, Gail *WhoHol A*
Kobeleff, Konstantin 1885-1966 *DancEn 78*
Kobelius, Johann Augustin 1674-1731 *NewGrD 80*
Kobelt, Johannes 1945- *IntWWM 77, -80*
Kober, Arthur 1900-1975 *BiE&WWA, IntMPA 75, -76, ModWD, NotNAT B*
Kobey, Claudia *WomWMM B*
Kobierkiewicz, Jozef *NewGrD 80*
Kobierkowicz, Jozef *NewGrD 80*
Kobler Family *CnOxB*
Koblitz, David 1948- *ConAmC*
Kobrick, Leonard 1912- *AmSCAP 66, -80*
Kobs, Alfred 1881-1929 *WhScrn 74, -77*
Kobylanska, Krystyna 1925- *IntWWM 77, -80*
Koch *NewGrD 80*
Koch, Carl 1892-1963 *OxFilm*
Koch, Caspar Petrus 1872-1970 *Baker 78*
Koch, Eduard Emil 1809-1871 *Baker 78*
Koch, Erland Von 1910- *Baker 78, NewGrD 80*
Koch, Franjo Zaver *NewGrD 80*
Koch, Franz Paul 1761- *OxMus*
Koch, Fred, Jr. 1911- *BiE&WWA, NotNAT*
Koch, Frederick 1923- *AmSCAP 66, -80, IntWWM 77, -80*
Koch, Frederick 1924- *CpmDNM 73, -76, -78, -79, ConAmC*
Koch, Frederick Henry 1877-1944 *NotNAT B, OxThe*
Koch, Friedrich E 1862-1927 *Baker 78, NewGrD 80*
Koch, Georg *NewGrD 80*
Koch, Georg August *Film 2*
Koch, Gottfried Heinrich 1703-1775 *EncWT*
Koch, Heinrich Christoph 1749-1816 *Baker 78, NewGrD 80*
Koch, Heinrich Gottfried 1703-1775 *NotNAT B, OxThe*
Koch, Helmut 1908-1975 *Baker 78, NewGrD 80*
Koch, Herbie 1903- *AmSCAP 66, -80*
Koch, Howard 1902- *ConDr 73, -77A, FilmEn, FilmgC, HalFC 80, IntMPA 77, -75, -76, -78, -79, -80, WorEFlm*
Koch, Howard W 1916- *FilmEn, FilmgC, HalFC 80, IntMPA 77, -75, -76, -78, -79, -80, NewYTET, WorEFlm*
Koch, Hugo B *Film 1*
Koch, Jodocus *NewGrD 80*
Koch, John 1928- *ConAmC*
Koch, John James, Jr. 1920- *AmSCAP 66, -80*
Koch, Judith *AmSCAP 80*
Koch, Karl 1887-1971 *Baker 78*
Koch, Kenneth 1925- *ConDr 73, -77*
Koch, Ludwig 1881- *OxMus, WhoMus 72*
Koch, Marianne 1930- *FilmAG WE*
Koch, Marie 1912- *AmSCAP 66*
Koch, Paul d1546 *NewGrD 80*
Koch, Paul d1580 *NewGrD 80*
Koch, Peter Maria 1925- *IntWWM 80*
Koch, Rainer 1933- *IntWWM 77, -80*
Koch, Siegfried Gotthelf 1754-1831 *OxThe*
Koch, Sigurd Von 1879-1919 *Baker 78, NewGrD 80*
Koch, Stephan d1590 *NewGrD 80*
Koch, Wilfried 1937- *WhoOp 76*
Kochan, Gunter 1930- *Baker 78, DcCM, IntWWM 80, NewGrD 80*

Kochan, Gunther 1930- *IntWWM 77*
Kochanska, Prakseda Marcelina *NewGrD 80*
Kochanski, Paul 1887-1934 *Baker 78, BiDAmM*
Kochanski, Pawel 1887-1934 *NewGrD 80*
Kochel, Ludwig Von 1800-1877 *Baker 78, NewGrD 80, OxMus*
Kochem, Martin Von *NewGrD 80*
Kocher, Conrad 1786-1872 *Baker 78*
Kochermann, Rainer 1930- *CnOxB, DancEn 78*
Kocheverova, Nadezhda *WomWMM*
Kochitz, Nina *Film 2*
Kochno, Boris 1903- *DancEn 78*
Kochno, Boris 1904- *CnOxB*
Koci, Akil 1936- *IntWWM 77, -80*
Koci, Premysl 1917- *IntWWM 77, -80, WhoOp 76*
Kocian, Jaroslav 1883-1950 *Baker 78, NewGrD 80*
Kock, Virginia Downman 1935- *IntWWM 77, -80*
Kocsar, Miklos 1933- *Baker 78, NewGrD 80*
Kocsis, Zoltan 1952- *IntWWM 77, -80, NewGrD 80, WhoMus 72*
Koczalski, Raoul 1884-1948 *Baker 78, NewGrD 80*
Koczalski, Raul 1884-1948 *NewGrD 80*
Koczian, Johanna Von 1933- *FilmAG WE*
Koczirz, Adolf 1870-1941 *Baker 78, NewGrD 80*
Koczwara, Frantisek 1750?-1791 *NewGrD 80*
Kodalli, Nevit 1924- *Baker 78, NewGrD 80*
Kodaly, Zoltan 1882-1967 *Baker 78, BnBkM 80, CmOp, CompSN[port], CnOxB, DcCom 77[port], DcCom&M 79, DcCM, DcTwCC, -A, MusMk, NewEOp 71, NewGrD 80[port], OxMus*
Kodolanyi, Janos 1899- *OxThe*
Koeberg, Frits Ehrhardt Adriaan 1876-1961 *Baker 78*
Koebner, Richard 1910- *AmSCAP 66, -80*
Koechlin, Charles 1867-1950 *Baker 78, BnBkM 80, DcCM, MusMk, NewGrD 80[port], OxMus*
Koeckert, Rudolf 1913- *NewGrD 80*
Koegler, Horst 1927- *CnOxB, DancEn 78*
Koehler, George A 1921- *IntMPA 77, -75, -76, -78, -79*
Koehler, Ted 1894-1973 *AmPS, AmSCAP 66, -80, BiDAmM, CmpEPM, Sw&Ld C*
Koehler, Trevor Curtis 1936- *EncJzS 70*
Koehne, Graeme John 1956- *IntWWM 80*
Koelling, Eloise 1908- *ConAmC*
Koellner, Alfredo 1933- *CnOxB, DancEn 78*
Koellreutter, Hans Joachim 1915- *Baker 78, DcCM, IntWWM 77, -80, NewGrD 80*
Koelz, Ernst 1929- *IntWWM 77, -80*
Koemmenich, Louis 1866-1922 *Baker 78, BiDAmM*
Koenan, Frank *Film 2*
Koene, Rogers *Film 2*
Koenekamp, Fred *HalFC 80*
Koenemann, Theodore *Baker 78*
Koenen, Friedrich 1829-1887 *Baker 78*
Koenen, Tilly 1873-1941 *Baker 78*
Koenig *NewGrD 80*
Koenig, Fernand 1922- *IntWWM 80*
Koenig, Gottfried Michael 1926- *Baker 78, DcCM, NewGrD 80*
Koenig, John 1910-1963 *NotNAT B*
Koenig, Joseph 1846-1926 *NewGrD 80*
Koenig, Laird *BlkAmP*
Koenig, Paul-Marie 1887- *NewGrD 80*
Koenig, Rudolf 1832-1901 *NewGrD 80*
Koenig, Rudolph *OxMus*
Koenig, Wolf 1927- *CreCan 2, WorEFlm*
Koenigsberg, Robert Morris 1951- *AmSCAP 80*
Koenigsmark, Josef 1916- *IntWWM 77*
Koenkamp, Fred *FilmEn*
Koerber, Hilde 1906-1969 *WhScrn 74, -77, WhoHol B*
Koering, Rene 1940- *Baker 78, NewGrD 80*
Koerner, Howard B 1927- *IntMPA 75, -76*
Koerner, John 1938- *BluesWW[port]*
Koerner, John Michael Anthony *CreCan 2*
Koerppen, Alfred 1926- *NewGrD 80*
Koesberg, Nicolai *Film 2*
Koessler, Hans 1853-1926 *Baker 78, NewGrD 80, OxMus*
Koesun, Ruth Ann 1928- *CnOxB, DancEn 78*
Koetsier, Jan 1911- *Baker 78, IntWWM 80, NewGrD 80*
Koff, Charles 1909- *AmSCAP 66, -80*
Koffler, Josef 1896-1943 *Baker 78*
Koffler, Jozef 1896-1944? *NewGrD 80*
Koffman, Moe 1928- *EncJzS 70*
Koffman, Moe 1948- *RkOn*
Kofler, Leo 1837-1908 *Baker 78, BiDAmM*
Kofsky, Nathaniel Myer 1908- *IntWWM 77, -80, WhoMus 72*
Kogan, Leonid 1924- *Baker 78, BnBkM 80, IntWWM 77, -80, MusSN[port], NewGrD 80, WhoMus 72*
Kogan, Milt *WhoHol A*
Kogan, Nathan 1906- *IntWWM 77, -80*
Kogan, Peter Henry 1945- *IntWWM 77, -80*
Kogel, Gustav Friedrich 1849-1921 *Baker 78*
Kogel, Richard 1927- *WhoOp 76*
Kogen, Harry 1895- *AmSCAP 66, -80*
Kogoj, Marij 1895-1956 *NewGrD 80*
Kohanim, Shokrollah Shokie 1920- *AmSCAP 80*
Kohault, Josef 1738-1793? *NewGrD 80*
Kohaut, Josef 1738-1793? *NewGrD 80*
Kohaut, Karl 1726-1784 *NewGrD 80*
Kohl, Richard McClure 1940- *IntWWM 77, -80*
Kohlase, Max *Film 2*
Kohler *NewGrD 80*
Kohler, Donna Jeane 1937- *AmSCAP 66*
Kohler, Ernesto 1849-1907 *Baker 78*
Kohler, Ernst 1799-1847 *Baker 78*
Kohler, Estelle 1940- *WhoThe 72, -77*
Kohler, Franz 1877-1918 *Baker 78*
Kohler, Fred, Jr. 1905-1969 *ForYSC, IntMPA 77, -75, -76, -78, -79, -80*
Kohler, Fred, Sr. 1888-1938 *HalFC 80, HolCA[port]*
Kohler, Fred, Sr. 1889-1938 *FilmEn, Film 1, -2, ForYSC, TwYS, WhScrn 74, -77, WhoHol B*
Kohler, Hans 1735?-1805? *NewGrD 80*
Kohler, Irene 1912- *IntWWM 77, -80, NewGrD 80, WhoMus 72*
Kohler, Johannes 1735?-1805? *NewGrD 80*
Kohler, Johannes-Ernst 1910- *IntWWM 80, NewGrD 80*
Kohler, John 1735?-1805? *NewGrD 80*
Kohler, John 1770?-1870? *NewGrD 80*
Kohler, John Augustus 1810?-1878 *NewGrD 80*
Kohler, Karl-Heinz Helmut 1928- *IntWWM 77, -80, NewGrD 80*
Kohler, Louis 1820-1886 *Baker 78, OxMus*
Kohler, Marga *Film 2*
Kohler, Siegfried H 1927- *IntWWM 77, -80, NewGrD 80, WhoOp 76*
Kohler, Volkmar 1930- *IntWWM 77, -80*
Kohler-Richter, Emmy 1918- *CnOxB*
Kohlman, Churchill 1906- *AmSCAP 66, -80*
Kohlman, Freddie 1915- *NewOrJ*
Kohlmann, Clarence 1891-1944 *AmSCAP 66, -80*
Kohlmar, Fred 1905-1969 *FilmgC, HalFC 80, WorEFlm*
Kohlmar, Fred, Jr. 1905-1969 *FilmEn*
Kohlmar, Lee 1878-1946 *Film 2, NotNAT B, WhScrn 74, -77, WhoHol B*
Kohlrusch, Aram Clemens Ohannes 1922- *IntWWM 77, -80*
Kohn, Howard E, II *IntMPA 77, -75, -76, -78, -79, -80*
Kohn, Karl 1926- *AmSCAP 80, Baker 78, CpmDNM 74, -75, -76, -78, ConAmC, DcCM, NewGrD 80*
Kohn, Karl-Christian 1928- *WhoOp 76*
Kohn, Ronald Thomas 1948- *AmSCAP 80*
Kohner, Frederick 1905- *IntMPA 77, -75, -76, -78, -79, -80*
Kohner, Susan 1936- *BiE&WWA, FilmEn, FilmgC, ForYSC, HalFC 80, IntMPA 77, -75, -76, -78, -79, -80, MotPP, NotNAT, WhoHol A*
Kohout, Antonin 1919- *IntWWM 77, -80*
Kohout, Josef *NewGrD 80*
Kohout, Pavel 1928- *EncWT*
Kohoutek, Ctirad 1929- *Baker 78, DcCM, IntWWM 77, -80, NewGrD 80*
Kohs, Ellis B 1916- *Baker 78, CpmDNM 77, -79, ConAmC, DcCM, NewGrD 80, WhoMus 72*
Kohut, Adolf 1847-1917 *Baker 78*
Kohut, Daniel L 1935- *IntWWM 77, -80*
Koivistoinen, Eero 1946- *EncJzS 70, IntWWM 77*
Koizumi, Fumio 1927- *IntWWM 77, -80, NewGrD 80*
Koizumi, Isao 1907- *IntWWM 80*
Koizumi, Kazuhiro 1949- *IntWWM 80*
Kojian, Miran 1942- *IntWWM 80*
Kok, Felix 1924- *WhoMus 72*
Kok, George Christiaan 1945- *WhoOp 76*
Kok, Jan 1921- *ConAmC*
Kok, Ronald 1944- *IntWWM 77, -80*
Kokai, Rezso 1906-1962 *Baker 78, NewGrD 80*
Kokas, Klara 1929- *IntWWM 77, -80*
Kokat, Janis Russell 1937- *IntWWM 77*
Koken, Lee 1908- *IntMPA 75, -76*
Koker, Daniel N 1933- *AmSCAP 80*
Kokeritz, Helge d1964 *NotNAT B*
Kokinacis, Alexander 1917- *AmSCAP 80*
Kokkonen, Joonas 1921- *Baker 78, DcCM, IntWWM 77, -80, NewGrD 80*
Kokkonen, Lauri 1918- *CroCD*
Koko 1940-1968 *WhScrn 77*
Kokomo *IlEncR, RkOn[port]*
Kokorniak, Dobromila 1944- *IntWWM 77, -80*
Kokoschka, Oskar 1886-1980 *CnMD, EncWT, Ent[port], McGEWD, ModWD, REnWD[port]*
Kolafa, Jiri 1930- *IntWWM 77, -80*
Kolar, Henry 1923- *IntWWM 77, -80*
Kolar, Phil *Film 2*
Kolar, Slavko 1891-1963 *CnMD*
Kolar, Victor 1888-1941 *BiDAmM*
Kolar, Victor 1888-1957 *Baker 78, ConAmC*
Kolar, Walter William 1922- *IntWWM 77, -80*
Kolasinski, Jerzy 1906- *IntWWM 77, -80*
Kolassi, Irma 1925- *WhoMus 72*
Kolb, Barbara 1939- *CpmDNM 74, -80, ConAmC, DcCM, WomCom[port]*
Kolb, Carlmann 1703-1765 *NewGrD 80*
Kolb, Clarence 1874-1964 *ForYSC, HalFC 80, MotPP, Vers A[port], WhoHol B*
Kolb, Clarence 1875-1964 *FilmEn, FilmgC, MovMk[port], WhScrn 74, -77*
Kolb, John *Film 2*
Kolb, Simon 1556?-1614 *NewGrD 80*
Kolb, Therese 1856-1935 *Film 2, NotNAT B, WhScrn 77, WhThe*
Kolb, Wallace *Film 2*
Kolb And Dill *Film 1*
Kolbanus, Simon 1556?-1614 *NewGrD 80*
Kolbe, Grethe 1910- *IntWWM 77, -80*
Kolbe, Oskar 1836-1878 *Baker 78*
Kolbe-Dobrowolny, Elfriede Else Johanna 1902- *IntWWM 77, -80*
Kolbenhayer, Guido d1962 *NotNAT B*
Kolbenheyer, Erwin Guido 1878-1962 *ModWD*
Kolberer, Cajetan 1668-1732 *NewGrD 80*
Kolberg, Oskar 1814-1890 *Baker 78, NewGrD 80*
Kolchinskaya, Camilla 1940- *Baker 78*
Koldamova, Krassimira 1938- *CnOxB*
Koldenhoven, Darlene Joan 1950- *AmSCAP 80*
Koldofsky, Adolph 1905-1951 *NewGrD 80*
Kole, Robert *AmSCAP 80*
Koler, David 1532?-1565 *NewGrD 80*
Koler, Martin 1620?-1704? *NewGrD 80*
Kolesovsky, Zikmund 1817-1868 *NewGrD 80*
Kolessa, Filaret 1871-1947 *Baker 78, NewGrD 80*
Kolet, Ezra 1914- *IntWWM 77, -80*
Kolff, J VanSanten 1848-1896 *Baker 78*
Kolin, Nikolai *Film 2*
Kolin Z Choteriny, Matous *NewGrD 80*
Kolinski, Mieczyslaw 1901- *IntWWM 77, -80, NewGrD 80*
Kolisch, Rudolf 1896-1978 *Baker 78, NewGrD 80*
Kolisek, Alois 1868-1931 *NewGrD 80*
Koljonen, John Albert 1943- *IntWWM 77, -80, WhoMus 72*
Kolk, Scott *Film 2*
Kolk, Stanley 1935- *WhoOp 76*
Kolker, Henry 1874-1947 *Film 1, -2, FilmgC, ForYSC, HalFC 80, HolCA[port], NotNAT B, TwYS, Vers B[port], WhScrn 74, -77, WhThe, WhoHol B*

Koller, Hans 1921- *CmpEPM, EncJzS 70*
Kolling, Rudolf 1904-1970 *CnOxB*
Kollmann *NewGrD 80*
Kollmann, A F C *OxMus*
Kollmann, August Friedrich Christoph 1756-1829 *Baker 78*
Kollmann, Augustus Frederic Christopher 1756-1829 *NewGrD 80*
Kollmann, George Augustus 1789-1845 *NewGrD 80*
Kollmann, Joanna S 1786-1849 *NewGrD 80*
Kollmar, Richard 1910-1971 *BiE&WWA, NotNAT B, WhScrn 77, WhThe, WhoHol B*
Kollo, Rene 1937- *CmOp, IntWWM 77, -80, NewGrD 80, WhoOp 76*
Kollo, Walter 1878-1940 *Baker 78, NewGrD 80*
Kollodzieyski, Walter 1878-1940 *NewGrD 80*
Kolman, Peter 1937- *NewGrD 80*
Kolman, Petr 1937- *Baker 78*
Kolmar, Lee 1878-1946 *ForYSC*
Kolmar, Leo 1878-1946 *TwYS*
Kolmer, Leo 1878-1946 *Film 2*
Kolneder, Walter 1910- *Baker 78, IntWWM 77, NewGrD 80*
Kolodin, Irving 1908- *Baker 78, WhoMus 72*
Kolodin, Robert 1932- *AmSCAP 66, -80*
Kolosova, Eugenia 1780-1869 *CnOxB*
Kolossy, Erika d1963 *WhScrn 74, -77*
Kolpakova, Irina Alexandrovna 1933- *CnOxB, DancEn 78[port]*
Koltai, Ralph 1924- *WhoMus 72, WhoThe 72, -77*
Kolz, Matthias *NewGrD 80*
Komack, James *NewYTET*
Komack, Jimmie *WhoHol A*
Komai, Tetsu 1893- *Film 2, ForYSC, TwYS*
Komai, Tetsu 1894-1970 *WhScrn 77, WhoHrs 80*
Komaiko, William 1947- *ConAmC*
Komarov, Sergei *FilmEn*
Komeda *AmSCAP 80*
Komeda, K T 1932-1969 *WorEFlm*
Komeda, Krzysztof 1931-1969 *EncJzS 70, NewGrD 80*
Komeda, Krzysztof 1932-1969 *FilmEn*
Komensky, Jan Amos 1592-1670 *NewGrD 80*
Komiazyk, Magdalena 1945- *IntWWM 80*
Komisarjevskaya, Vera Fedorovna 1864-1910 *EncWT, NotNAT B, OxThe, PlP&P[port]*
Komisarjevsky, Theodore 1882-1954 *CnThe, EncWT, Ent, NotNAT A, -B, OxThe, PlP&P, WhThe*
Komissarov, Aleksandr 1904-1975 *WhScrn 77*
Komitas *NewGrD 80*
Komleva, Gabriella Trofimova 1938- *CnOxB*
Komlos, Katalin 1945- *IntWWM 77, -80*
Komlossy, Erzsebet 1933- *NewGrD 80, WhoOp 76*
Komma, Karl Michael 1913- *NewGrD 80*
Kommerell, Max 1902-1944 *CnMD*
Komorous, Rudolf 1931- *Baker 78, DcCM, NewGrD 80*
Komorowski, Ignacy Marceli 1824-1857 *NewGrD 80*
Komorzynski, Egon 1878-1963 *Baker 78, NewGrD 80*
Kompanek, Rudolph W 1943- *AmSCAP 80*
Komzak, Karel 1823-1893 *NewGrD 80*
Komzak, Karel 1850-1905 *NewGrD 80*
Konalski, Tadeusz *WomWMM*
Kondek, Patricia Lee 1939- *IntWWM 77, -80*
Kondor, R W 1937- *BiE&WWA*
Kondorossy, K Elizabeth Davis 1910- *IntWWM 77, -80*
Kondorossy, Leslie 1915- *AmSCAP 80, Baker 78, ConAmC, IntWWM 77, -80, WhoMus 72*
Kondouros, Nikos *DcFM*
Kondracki, Michael 1902- *IntWWM 77, -80*
Kondracki, Michal 1902- *Baker 78, DcCM, NewGrD 80*
Kondracki, Michel 1902- *ConAmC*
Kondrashin, Kiril 1914- *BnBkM 80, WhoMus 72, WhoOp 76*
Kondrashin, Kirill Petrovich 1914- *IntWWM 77, -80, NewGrD 80[port]*
Kondratieva, Marina Victorovna 1934- *CnOxB*
Kondratov, Yuri Grigorievich 1921-1967 *CnOxB, DancEn 78*
Kondratyeva, Marina 1933- *DancEn 78*
Konen, Valentina Dzhozefovna 1909- *NewGrD 80*
Koner, Pauline 1912- *CmpGMD, CnOxB, DancEn 78[port]*
Konetzni, Anni 1902-1968 *NewEOp 71*
Konetzni, Anny 1902-1968 *CmOp, NewGrD 80*
Konetzni, Hilde 1905-1980 *CmOp, NewEOp 71, NewGrD 80, WhoMus 72*
Kongshaug, Jan Erik 1944- *IntWWM 80*
Konicek, Zdenek 1918- *IntWWM 77, -80*
Konig *NewGrD 80*
Konig, Balthasar 1685?-1760? *NewGrD 80*
Konig, Balthasar Franz Joseph 1744-1766 *NewGrD 80*
Konig, Carl Philipp Joseph 1750-1795 *NewGrD 80*
Konig, Christian Ludwig 1717-1789 *NewGrD 80*
Konig, Johann Balthasar 1691-1758 *NewGrD 80*
Konig, Johann Kaspar Joseph 1726-1763 *NewGrD 80*
Konig, Johann Mattheus *NewGrD 80*
Konig, Johann Nicolaus 1729-1775 *NewGrD 80*
Konig, Johann Ulrich Von 1688-1744 *NewGrD 80*
Konigslow, Johann Wilhelm Cornelius Von 1745-1833 *Baker 78, NewGrD 80*
Konigslow, Otto Friedrich Von 1824-1898 *Baker 78*
Konigsperger, Marianus 1708-1769 *NewGrD 80*
Koninck, Servaas De d1718? *NewGrD 80*
Koning, David 1820-1876 *Baker 78*
Koning, Hans 1924- *AmSCAP 80*
Koning, Joachim 1939- *DancEn 78*
Konink, Servaas De d1718? *NewGrD 80*
Konitz, Lee 1927- *BiDAmM, CmpEPM, EncJzS 70, IlEncJ, NewGrD 80*
Konitzky, Sally White 1928- *IntWWM 77, -80*
Konius, Georgy *Baker 78*
Konjovic, Petar 1882-1970 *Baker 78*
Konjovic, Petar 1883-1970 *NewGrD 80*
Konjovic, Peter 1883- *IntWWM 77, -80*
Kono, Kristo 1907- *Baker 78*
Kono, Toshihiko 1930- *IntWWM 77, -80*
Konold, Wulf 1946- *IntWWM 80*
Konopasek, Jan 1931- *EncJzS 70*
Konowitz, Bert 1931- *IntWWM 77, -80*
Konowitz, Bertram D 1931- *ConAmC*
Konoye, Hidemaro 1898-1973 *Baker 78, WhoMus 72*
Konrad Von Wurzburc 122-?-1287 *NewGrD 80*
Konrad Von Wurzburg 122-?-1287 *NewGrD 80*
Konrad, Dorothy *WhoHol A*
Konrad, William 1869-1942 *BiDAmM*
Konstam, Anna 1914- *WhThe*
Konstam, Phyllis 1907-1976 *HalFC 80, IntMPA 77, -75, -76, WhThe*
Konstan, Michael Allan 1946- *AmSCAP 80*
Konstantin *NewGrD 80*
Konstantin, Leopoldine 1890?- *WhScrn 77*
Kont, Paul 1920- *Baker 78, IntWWM 77, -80, NewGrD 80*
Kontarsky, Alfons 1932- *Baker 78, NewGrD 80*
Kontarsky, Aloys 1931- *Baker 78, IntWWM 77, -80, NewGrD 80, WhoMus 72*
Kontarsky, Bernhard 1937- *Baker 78*
Konte, Frank Earl 1947- *AmSCAP 80*
Kontopetres, Georgios *NewGrD 80*
Kontopetris, Georgios *NewGrD 80*
Kontos, Spero L 1922- *IntMPA 77, -75, -76, -78, -79, -80*
Kontski, De *NewGrD 80*
Kontski, Antoine De 1817-1889 *Baker 78*
Kontski, Antoine De 1817-1899 *OxMus*
Kontski, Apollinaire De 1825-1879 *Baker 78*
Kontski, Charles De 1815-1867 *Baker 78*
Konwicki, Tadeusz 1926- *DcFM, FilmEn, OxFilm*
Konwitschny, Franz 1901-1962 *CmOp, NewEOp 71, NewGrD 80*
Konya, Sandor 1923- *CmOp, MusSN[port], NewEOp 71, NewGrD 80, WhoOp 76*
Konyus, Georgy Eduardovich 1862-1933 *NewGrD 80*
Kooiman, Elly 1945- *IntWWM 77, -80*
Kook, Edward 1903- *BiE&WWA, NotNAT*
Kooke, Simon Petrus Johannus 1915- *IntWWM 77, -80*
Kool & The Gang *RkOn 2[port]*
Koole, Arend 1908- *Baker 78, NewGrD 80*
Koonen, Alice 1899-1974 *EncWT, OxThe*
Koonin, Brian 1953- *IntWWM 77*
Kooninck, Servaas De *NewGrD 80*
Koonse, Johnny *AmSCAP 80*
Koonts, Cortlandt Morper 1927- *IntWWM 77, -80*
Koop, Theodore F *NewYTET*
Kooper, Al 1944- *IlEncR*
Koopman, Ton 1944- *IntWWM 77, -80*
Koos, Joseph 1936- *IntWWM 80*
Kootz, Gunter 1919- *IntWWM 80*
Kooy, Pete d1963 *NotNAT B, WhScrn 74, -77, WhoHol B*
Kopacki, Tadeusz 1930- *WhoOp 76*
Kopalin, Ilya Petrovich 1900- *DcFM*
Kopecky, Matej 1775-1847 *DcPup*
Kopecny, Frantisek 1915- *IntWWM 77, -80*
Kopelent, Marek 1932- *Baker 78, DcCM, NewGrD 80*
Kopell, Bernie *WhoHol A*
Kopelman, Jean R 1927- *IntMPA 77, -75, -76, -78, -79, -80*
Kopfer, Georges-Adam *NewGrD 80*
Kopilov, Alexander Alexandrovich 1854-1911 *NewGrD 80*
Kopit, Arthur 1937- *BiE&WWA, ConDr 73, -77, CroCD, DcLB 7[port], EncWT, Ent, McGEWD, NatPD[port], NotNAT, WhoThe 72, -77*
Kopit, Arthur 1938- *CnMD, ModWD*
Kopita, Murray 1903- *AmSCAP 66, -80*
Koplan, Harry 1918- *IntMPA 75, -76*
Kopleff, Florence 1924- *IntWWM 77, -80*
Koplik, Jim *ConMuA 80B*
Koplow, Donald H 1935- *AmSCAP 66, -80*
Kopp, Charles Michael 1951- *ConAmC*
Kopp, Erwin *Film 2*
Kopp, Frederick Edward 1914- *AmSCAP 66, -80, CpmDNM 76, ConAmC, IntWWM 77, -80*
Kopp, Georg d1666 *NewGrD 80*
Kopp, Leo Laszlo 1906- *WhoOp 76*
Kopp, Matthaeus Adam *NewGrD 80*
Kopp, Mila 1905-1973 *WhScrn 77*
Kopp, Rudolph George 1887-1971 *AmSCAP 80, CmMov*
Koppel, Herman David 1908- *Baker 78, CpmDNM 80, DcCM, IntWWM 77, -80, NewGrD 80*
Koppel, Julius 1910- *IntWWM 77, -80*
Koppel, Thomas Herman 1944- *Baker 78*
Koppell, Alfred Baldwin 1898-1963 *AmSCAP 66, -80*
Koppelman, Charles *ConMuA 80B*
Koppenhofer, Marie 1901-1948 *EncWT*
Koppens, Emile *WhScrn 74, -77*
Koppers, Maria 1939- *CnOxB*
Kopple, Barbara *WomWMM A, -B*
Kopriva *NewGrD 80*
Kopriva, Jan Jachym 1754-1792 *NewGrD 80*
Kopriva, Karel Blazej 1756-1785 *NewGrD 80*
Kopriva, Vaclav Jan 1708-1789 *NewGrD 80*
Koprowski, Peter Paul 1947- *IntWWM 80*
Kops, Bernard 1926- *BiE&WWA, CnMD, ConDr 73, -77, EncWT, ModWD, NotNAT, -A, WhoThe 72, -77*
Kops, Bernard 1928- *CroCD*
Kopstein, David Mark 1946- *IntWWM 77, -80*
Koptagel, Yuksel 1931- *IntWWM 77, -80*
Kopylov, Alexander 1854-1911 *Baker 78*
Kopytman, Mark 1929- *IntWWM 77, -80, NewGrD 80*
Koral, Can 1945- *WhoOp 76*
Koran, Al 1916-1972 *MagIlD*
Korayim, Mohamed 1898-1972 *WhScrn 77*
Korb, Arthur 1909- *AmSCAP 66, -80*
Korban, Bernard 1923- *IntMPA 77, -75, -76, -78, -79, -80*
Korbay, Francis Alexander 1846-1913 *Baker 78, OxMus*
Korber, Georg 1570?-1613? *NewGrD 80*
Korber, Gunter 1922- *NewGrD 80*

Korber, Hilde 1906-1969 *FilmAG WE*
Korbler, Ivo 1926- *IntWWM 77*
Korcak, Friedrich 1926- *IntWWM 77, -80*
Korchinska, Maria 1895-1979 *IntWWM 77, -80, NewGrD 80, WhoMus 72*
Korchmarev, Klimenty 1899-1958 *Baker 78*
Korchmaryov, Klimenty Arkad'yevich 1899-1958 *NewGrD 80*
Kord, Kazimierz *WhoOp 76*
Korda, Sir Alexander 1893-1956 *BiDFilm, -81, DcFM, FilmEn, FilmgC, HalFC 80, IlWWBF, -A[port], MovMk[port], NotNAT B, OxFilm, WorEFlm*
Korda, Janos 1929- *WhoOp 76*
Korda, Maria *Film 2, ForYSC, WhoHol A*
Korda, Vincent 1896-1979 *DcFM, FilmgC, HalFC 80*
Korda, Vincent 1897-1979 *FilmEn, OxFilm, WorEFlm*
Korda, Zoltan 1895-1961 *BiDFilm, -81, CmMov, DcFM, FilmEn, FilmgC, HalFC 80, IlWWBF, MovMk[port], NotNAT B, OxFilm, WorEFlm[port]*
Korecka-Soszkowska, Maria-Jadwiga 1943- *IntWWM 77, -80*
Koreh, Endre 1906-1960 *NewGrD 80*
Koren, Serge Gavrilovich 1907-1969 *CnOxB*
Koren, Sergei 1907-1969 *DancEn 78*
Korenchendler, Hersz Dawid 1948- *IntWWM 77*
Koreshchenko, Arseny 1870-1921 *Baker 78*
Korev, Yury Semyonovich 1928- *NewGrD 80*
Korff, Arnold 1870-1944 *NotNAT B*
Korff, Arnold 1871-1944 *Film 2, WhScrn 74, -77, WhoHol B*
Korff-Kawecka, Helena 1907- *IntWWM 80*
Korganov, Genari 1858-1890 *Baker 78*
Korinek, Miroslav 1925- *Baker 78*
Korjus, Miliza d1980 *ForYSC, What 5[port], WhoMus 72*
Korjus, Miliza 1900-1980 *FilmEn, ThFT[port]*
Korjus, Miliza 1902-1980 *FilmgC, WhoHol A*
Korjus, Miliza 1908-1980 *HalFC 80*
Korling, August 1842-1919 *NewGrD 80*
Korling, Felix 1864-1937 *NewGrD 80*
Korloff, Olga *Film 2*
Korman, Gerald 1936- *AmSCAP 66, -80*
Korman, Harvey *ConMuA 80B*
Korman, Harvey 1927- *FilmEn, HalFC 80, IntMPA 77, -75, -76, -78, -79, -80, WhoHol A*
Korman, Mary 1917-1973 *Film 2*
Korn, Clara Anna 1866-1940 *Baker 78*
Korn, Johann Daniel *NewGrD 80*
Korn, Mitchell 1950- *AmSCAP 80*
Korn, Peter Jona 1922- *AmSCAP 66, -80, Baker 78, ConAmC, DcCM, IntWWM 77, -80, NewGrD 80*
Korn, Richard 1908- *IntWWM 77, -80, WhoMus 72*
Kornaros, Vincenzo *REnWD[port]*
Kornauth, Egon 1891-1959 *Baker 78, NewGrD 80*
Kornblum, Isidore Benjamin 1895- *AmSCAP 66, -80*
Korneichuk, Aleksandr Evdokomovich 1905-1972 *CroCD*
Korneichuk, Aleksandr Yevdokimovich 1905-1972 *ModWD*
Korneichuk, Alexander Evdokimovich 1905-1972 *CnMD, OxThe*
Korneichuk, Alexander Yevdokimovich 1905-1972 *EncWT*
Kornelia, Irma *Film 2*
Korner, Alexis 1928- *ConMuA 80A, IlEncR[port]*
Korner, Christian Gottfried 1756-1831 *Baker 78*
Korner, Gotthilf Wilhelm 1809-1865 *Baker 78*
Korner, Hermine 1878-1960 *EncWT, Film 2*
Korner, John 1913- *CreCan 2*
Korner, Karl Theodor 1791-1831 *NewEOp 71*
Korner, Theodor 1791-1813 *NewGrD 80*
Kornerup, Thorwald Otto 1864-1938 *Baker 78*
Kornfeld, Paul 1889-1942 *CnMD, EncWT, McGEWD, ModWD*
Kornfeld, Peter *NewGrD 80*
Kornfeld, Robert *NatPD[port]*
Korngold, Erich Wolfgang 1897-1957 *AmSCAP 66, -80, Baker 78, BiDAmM, BnBkM 80, CmMov, CmOp, CmpEPM, ConAmC, DcCom&M 79, FilmEn, FilmgC, HalFC 80, MusMk, NewEOp 71, NewGrD 80, OxFilm, OxMus, WorEFlm*
Korngold, Julius 1860-1945 *Baker 78, BiDAmM*
Kornhauser, Bronia 1950- *IntWWM 80*
Korniychuk, Alexander 1905-1972 *Ent*
Kornman, Mary 1917-1973 *TwYS, WhScrn 77, WhoHol B*
Kornmuller, Utto 1824-1907 *Baker 78*
Kornyei, Bela 1875-1925 *NewGrD 80*
Kornzweig, Ben *BiE&WWA*
Korodi, Andras 1922- *NewGrD 80*
Korol, Taras *CreCan 2*
Korol, Ted *CreCan 2*
Korolyov, Denis Aleksandrovich 1938- *WhoOp 76*
Korolyova, Glafira Serafimovna 1936- *WhoOp 76*
Koromilas, Demetrios *REnWD[port]*
Korovine, Constantine 1861-1939 *DancEn 78*
Korpar, Zdravko 1934- *IntWWM 77*
Korris, Harry 1888-1971 *FilmgC, HalFC 80*
Korsten, Gerard 1930- *WhoOp 76*
Kortchmar, Danny *ConMuA 80A*
Korte, Karl 1928- *AmSCAP 66, -80, CpmDNM 76, -78, ConAmC, DcCom&M 79, IntWWM 77, -80, NewGrD 80*
Korte, Oldrich Frantisek 1926- *Baker 78, IntWWM 77, -80, NewGrD 80*
Korte, Werner 1906- *Baker 78, NewGrD 80*
Kortkamp, Jakob 1620?-1660? *NewGrD 80*
Kortkamp, Johann 1643-1721 *NewGrD 80*
Kortlander, Max 1890-1961 *AmSCAP 66, -80*
Kortman, Robert F 1887-1967 *Film 1, -2, WhScrn 77*
Kortner, Fritz 1892-1970 *CroCD, EncWT, Ent, FilmAG WE, FilmEn, Film 2, FilmgC, HalFC 80, MovMk, WhScrn 74, -77, WhoHol B*
Korton, Robert *Film 2*
Kortschak, Hugo 1884-1957 *Baker 78*
Kortsen, Bjarne 1930- *Baker 78*
Kortvelyes, Geza 1926- *CnOxB*
Korty, John 1936- *FilmEn, IntMPA 77, -75, -76, -78, -79, -80, NewYTET, OxFilm*
Korty, John 1941- *HalFC 80*
Korty, Sonia 1892-1955 *CnOxB*
Korvin, Charles *IntMPA 77, -75, -76, -78, -79, -80, MotPP*
Korvin, Charles 1907- *FilmEn, FilmgC, HalFC 80, MovMk, WhoHol A*
Korvin, Charles 1912- *BiE&WWA, ForYSC, NotNAT*
Kory, Agnes 1944- *IntWWM 77, -80*
Kos, Koraljka 1934- *IntWWM 77, -80*
Kos-Anatolskyi, Anatol Ossypovych 1909- *IntWWM 77, -80*
Kosa, Ferenc 1937- *OxFilm*
Kosa, Gyorgy 1897- *Baker 78, DcCM, NewGrD 80, WhoMus 72*
Kosak, Igor 1947- *CnOxB*
Kosakoff, Gabriel 1926- *IntWWM 77, -80*
Kosakoff, Reuven 1898- *AmSCAP 66, -80, Baker 78, BiDAmM, ConAmC*
Kosakowski, Wenceslaus Walter 1911- *AmSCAP 80*
Kosarin, Oscar 1918- *BiE&WWA, NotNAT*
Kosch, Franz 1894- *IntWWM 77, -80, WhoMus 72*
Koschat, Thomas 1845-1914 *Baker 78*
Koscheluch, Johann *NewGrD 80*
Koschmieder, Erwin 1895- *IntWWM 77, -80*
Koschovitz, Joseph *NewGrD 80*
Koscina, Sylva 1933- *FilmAG WE, FilmEn*
Koscina, Sylva 1935- *FilmgC, ForYSC, HalFC 80, WhoHol A*
Koselitz, Heinrich 1854-1918 *Baker 78, OxMus*
Koselitz, Johann Heinrich *NewGrD 80*
Koser, H *Film 2*
Kosersky, Rena *WomWMM A, -B*
Koseticky, Jiri Evermond 1639-1700 *NewGrD 80*
Kosev, Atanas Nedialkov 1934- *IntWWM 80*
Kosewski, Mieczyslaw 1908- *IntWWM 80*
Kosh, John *ConMuA 80B*
Koshelev, Vladimir Arkadievich 1935- *CnOxB*
Koshetz, Nina 1892-1965 *WhScrn 74, -77, WhoHol B*
Koshetz, Nina 1894-1965 *Baker 78*
Kosiner, Harry *IntMPA 77, -75, -76, -78, -79, -80*
Kosins, Martin Scot 1947- *CpmDNM 79, -80*
Koski, Joan *WomWMM B*
Kosleck, Julius 1825-1904 *Baker 78, BnBkM 80*
Kosleck, Julius 1825-1905 *NewGrD 80*
Kosleck, Julius 1835-1905 *OxMus*
Kosleck, Martin 1907- *FilmEn, FilmgC, ForYSC, HalFC 80, HolCA[port], IntMPA 77, -75, -76, -78, -79, -80, MotPP, MovMk, Vers B[port], WhoHol A, WhoHrs 80*
Kosler, Miroslav 1931- *IntWWM 77, -80*
Kosler, Zdenek 1928- *IntWWM 77, -80, NewGrD 80*
Kosloff, Lou 1904- *AmSCAP 66, -80*
Kosloff, Theodore 1882-1956 *FilmEn, Film 1, -2, NotNAT B, TwYS, WhScrn 74, -77, WhoHol B*
Koslov, Alexis 1887- *DancEn 78*
Koslov, Theodore 1881-1956 *DancEn 78*
Koslovski, Albert 1902- *CnOxB*
Kosma, Joseph 1905-1969 *Baker 78, DcFM, FilmEn, FilmgC, HalFC 80, NewGrD 80, OxFilm, WorEFlm*
Kosmala, Jerzy S 1931- *IntWWM 77, -80*
Kosmas Hagiopolites *NewGrD 80*
Kosmas Hierosolymites *NewGrD 80*
Kosmas Of Jerusalem *NewGrD 80*
Kosmas Of Maiuma *NewGrD 80*
Kosmas The Melode *NewGrD 80*
Kosmas The Monk *NewGrD 80*
Kosor, Josip 1879-1961 *CnMD*
Kosowicz, Francis John 1946- *IntWWM 80*
Kospoth, Otto Carl Erdmann, Freiherr Von 1753-1817 *NewGrD 80*
Kossler, Hans *Baker 78, NewGrD 80*
Kossmaly, Carl 1812-1893 *Baker 78*
Kossoff, David 1919- *FilmEn, FilmgC, HalFC 80, WhoHol A, WhoThe 72, -77*
Kossoff, Paul 1950- *IlEncR[port]*
Kossovits, Jozsef 1750?-1819? *NewGrD 80*
Kossow, Goldie Falk 1938- *AmSCAP 80*
Kossowski, Edmund 1920- *WhoOp 76*
Kosta, Tessa 1893- *CmpEPM, WhThe*
Kostal, Irwin 1915- *CmMov, FilmEn, FilmgC, HalFC 80*
Kostal, Irwin James 1911- *AmSCAP 80*
Kosteck, George *CpmDNM 75*
Kosteck, Gregory William-Paul 1937- *AmSCAP 80, CpmDNM 79, -80, ConAmC*
Kostelanetz, Andre 1901-1980 *Baker 78, BiDAmM, CmpEPM, IntWWM 77, MusSN[port], NewGrD 80, OxMus, WhoMus 72*
Koster, Dijck 1923- *IntWWM 77, -80*
Koster, Ernst 1904- *IntWWM 77, -80*
Koster, Henry 1905- *BiDFilm, -81, CmMov, DcFM, FilmEn, FilmgC, HalFC 80, IntMPA 77, -75, -76, -78, -79, -80, MovMk[port], WorEFlm*
Koster, Liselotte 1911- *CnOxB*
Kostic, Dusan 1925- *Baker 78, IntWWM 80*
Kostic, Dusan 1926- *NewGrD 80*
Kostic, Vojislav 1931- *Baker 78, IntWWM 80*
Kostlin, Heinrich Adolf 1846-1907 *Baker 78, NewGrD 80*
Kostlin, Karl Reinhold 1819-1894 *Baker 78*
Kostohryz, Milan 1911- *IntWWM 77, -80*
Kostov, Georgi 1941- *Baker 78*
Koswick, Michael *NewGrD 80*
Koszewski, Andrzej 1922- *IntWWM 77, -80, NewGrD 80*
Koszut, Urszula Lucia 1940- *IntWWM 80, WhoOp 76*
Koszut-Okruta, Urszula 1940- *WhoMus 72*
Kota, Lu *AmSCAP 80*
Kotcheff, Ted 1931- *FilmEn, FilmgC, HalFC 80*
Kotcheff, William Theodore 1931- *IntMPA 77, -75, -76, -78, -79, -80*
Kotcher, Jay H 1946- *WhoOp 76*
Kotchetovsky, Alexander 1889-1952 *DancEn 78*
Kotek, Georg 1889- *WhoMus 72*
Kotek, Joseph 1855-1885 *Baker 78, NewGrD 80*

Kotek, Yosif 1855-1885 *NewGrD 80*
Koth, Erika *IntWWM 77, -80*
Koth, Erika 1925- *WhoOp 76*
Koth, Erika 1927- *CmOp, NewEOp 71, NewGrD 80, WhoMus 72*
Kothe, Aloys 1828-1868 *Baker 78*
Kothe, Bernhard 1821-1897 *Baker 78*
Kothe, Robert 1869-1944 *Baker 78*
Kothe, Wilhelm 1831-1897 *Baker 78*
Kothen *NewGrD 80*
Kothen, Karl Axel 1871-1927 *Baker 78*
Kotik, Petr 1942- *Baker 78, ConAmC*
Kotilainen, Otto 1868-1936 *Baker 78*
Kotkin, Edward *WhoHol A*
Kotler, Marcie Susan Laitman 1941- *IntWWM 77, -80*
Kotlic, Milan 1924- *IntWWM 77*
Kotlowitz, Robert *NewYTET*
Kotonski, Wlodzimierz 1925- *Baker 78, DcCM, NewGrD 80, OxMus*
Kotsarenko, Anna *IntWWM 77, -80*
Kotsonaros, George d1933 *Film 2, WhScrn 77*
Kott, Jan 1914- *EncWT, PlP&P*
Kotter, Hans 1480?-1541 *Baker 78*
Kotter, Hans 1485?-1541 *NewGrD 80*
Kotter, Johannes 1485?-1541 *NewGrD 80*
Kotterer, Hans 1485?-1541 *NewGrD 80*
Kotther, Hans 1485?-1541 *NewGrD 80*
Kottick, Edward Leon 1930- *IntWWM 77, -80*
Kottke, Leo *AmSCAP 80, ConMuA 80A, IlEncR*
Kottlitz, Adolf 1820-1860 *Baker 78*
Kotto, Yaphet 1937- *DrBlPA, FilmEn, ForYSC, HalFC 80, IntMPA 77, -76, -78, -79, -80, WhoHol A*
Kotzebue, August Friedrich Ferdinand Von 1761-1819 *CnThe, EncWT, Ent[port], McGEWD[port], NewEOp 71[port], NewGrD 80[port], NotNAT A, -B, OxThe, REnWD[port]*
Kotzeluch, J A 1738-1814 *OxMus*
Kotzeluch, Leopold Anton *Baker 78, NewGrD 80*
Kotzolt, Heinrich 1814-1881 *Baker 78*
Kotzschmar, Hermann 1829-1909 *Baker 78, BiDAmM*
Kotzwara, Francis *NewGrD 80*
Kotzwara, Franz 1730-1791 *Baker 78, MusMk, OxMus*
Kouba, Jan 1931- *NewGrD 80*
Kouba, Maria *WhoOp 76*
Koubitzky, Alexandre *Film 2*
Koudelka, George John 1945- *IntWWM 77, -80*
Kougell, Arkadie 1897- *ConAmC*
Kougoucheff, Prince N *Film 2*
Kouguell, Arkadie 1897- *AmSCAP 66, -80, BiDAmM*
Kouguell, Arkadie 1898- *Baker 78*
Koukouzeles, Joannes 1280?-1375? *NewGrD 80*
Koukouzeles, John *OxMus*
Koulsoum, Ibrahim Oum *NewGrD 80*
Koun, Karolos 1908- *WhThe*
Kounadis, Arghyris 1924- *Baker 78, DcCM, NewGrD 80*
Koundouros, Nikos 1926- *DcFM*
Koundouros, Nikos 1929- *WorEFlm*
Kounduros, Nikos 1926- *FilmEn*
Kountz, Richard 1896-1950 *AmSCAP 66, -80, Baker 78, ConAmC*
Koury, Rex 1911- *AmSCAP 80*
Koussevitsky, Serge 1874-1951 *CmOp*
Koussevitzky, Serge 1874-1951 *Baker 78, BiDAmM, BnBkM 80[port], ConAmC, MusMk, MusSN[port]*
Koussevitzky, Sergei 1874-1951 *OxMus*
Koussevitzky, Sergey 1874-1951 *NewGrD 80[port]*
Kout, Jiri 1937- *WhoOp 76*
Koutoukas, H M *ConDr 73, -77*
Koutzen, Boris 1901-1966 *AmSCAP 66, -80, Baker 78, BiDAmM, ConAmC, DcCM*
Koutzen, Nadia 1930- *WhoMus 72*
Kovac, Roland 1927- *WhoMus 72*
Kovacevic, Kresimir 1913- *IntWWM 77, -80, NewGrD 80*
Kovach, Andor Andras 1915- *IntWWM 77, -80, NewGrD 80*
Kovach, George Daniel 1951- *AmSCAP 80*
Kovach, Nora 1931- *CnOxB*
Kovach, Nora 1932- *DancEn 78*
Kovach And Rabovsky *DancEn 78*
Kovacic, Boris 1934- *IntWWM 77*
Kovack, Nancy 1935- *FilmgC, ForYSC, HalFC 80, WhoHol A, WhoHrs 80*
Kovacs, Andras 1925- *OxFilm*
Kovacs, Bela 1937- *NewGrD 80*
Kovacs, Denes 1930- *IntWWM 77, -80, NewGrD 80*
Kovacs, Ernie 1919-1962 *AmSCAP 66, -80, FilmEn, FilmgC, Funs[port], HalFC 80, JoeFr[port], MotPP, MovMk[port], NewYTET, NotNAT B, WhScrn 74, -77, WhoHol B*
Kovacs, Ernie 1920-1962 *ForYSC*
Kovacs, Eszter 1939- *WhoOp 76*
Kovacs, Joseph 1912- *AmSCAP 66*
Kovacs, Laszlo 1932- *FilmEn, FilmgC, HalFC 80*
Kovacs, Rosalia 1945- *CnOxB*
Kovacs, Sandor 1886-1918 *NewGrD 80*
Kovaks, Laszlo *IntMPA 77, -75, -76, -78, -79, -80*
Koval, Marian Viktorovich 1907-1971 *Baker 78, NewGrD 80*
Koval, Rene d1936 *NotNAT B*
Koval-Samborsky, Ivan *Film 2*
Kovalenko, Oleg Ivanovitch 1936- *IntWWM 77, -80*
Kovalev, Pavel 1890-1951 *Baker 78*
Kovanko, Nathalie *Film 2*
Kovari, George *MagIlD*
Kovaricek, Frantisek 1924- *Baker 78, IntWWM 77, -80, NewGrD 80*
Kovarik, Chris *ConMuA 80B*
Kovarnova, Emma 1930- *IntWWM 77, -80*
Kovarovic, Karel 1862-1920 *Baker 78, MusMk, NewGrD 80*
Kovats, Barna 1920- *IntWWM 77, -80*
Kovats, Kolos 1948- *WhoOp 76*
Kove, Kenneth 1893- *IlWWBF, WhThe*
Kove, Martin *WhoHol A*
Koven, Reginald De 1859-1920 *Baker 78, MusMk*
Koverhult, Tommy 1945- *EncJzS 70*
Kovtun, Valeri 1945- *CnOxB*
Kowal, Mitchell 1916-1971 *WhScrn 74, -77, WhoHol B*
Kowalowski, Zenon Eugenieusz 1939- *IntWWM 77, -80*
Kowalski, Bernard L 1931- *FilmgC, HalFC 80, NewYTET, WhoHrs 80*
Kowalski, Henri 1841-1916 *Baker 78, NewGrD 80*
Kowalski, Julius 1912- *Baker 78, NewGrD 80*
Kowalski, Max 1882-1956 *Baker 78, NewGrD 80*
Kowell, Mitchell *ForYSC*
Kox, Hans 1930- *Baker 78, NewGrD 80*
Koy, Paul 1909-1964 *AmSCAP 80*
Koyama, Kiyoshige 1914- *Baker 78*
Kozak, Edward John 1925- *ConAmC, IntWWM 77*
Kozak, Yitka Reomira 1942- *WomWMM B*
Kozderkova, Jarmila 1934- *IntWWM 77, -80*
Kozelka, Paul 1909- *BiE&WWA, NotNAT*
Kozeluch, Jan Antonin 1747-1818 *NewGrD 80[port]*
Kozeluch, Johann Anton 1738-1814 *Baker 78, OxMus*
Kozeluch, Johann Antonin 1738-1814 *NewGrD 80*
Kozeluch, Leopold 1738-1814 *NewGrD 80[port]*
Kozeluch, Leopold Anton 1747-1818 *Baker 78*
Kozeluch, Leopold Anton 1752-1818 *CnOxB, OxMus*
Kozeluh, Leopold 1747-1818 *NewGrD 80[port]*
Kozeluh, Zdenek Petr 1936- *CnOxB*
Kozhukhova, Maria 1897-1959 *DancEn 78*
Koziel, Yola 1934- *IntWWM 77, -80*
Kozina, Marjan 1907-1966 *Baker 78, NewGrD 80*
Kozinski, David B 1917- *AmSCAP 66, -80, ConAmC*
Kozintsev, Grigori 1905-1973 *BiDFilm, -81, DcFM, FilmEn, FilmgC, HalFC 80, MovMk[port], OxFilm, WorEFlm*
Kozintsev, Grigory 1905-1973 *WhScrn 77*
Kozlenko, William *IntMPA 77, -75, -76, -78, -79*
Kozlovsky, Albert 1902- *DancEn 78*
Kozlovsky, Alexey 1905-1977 *NewGrD 80*
Kozlovsky, Ivan Semyonovich 1900- *NewGrD 80, WhoMus 72*
Kozlovsky, Nina 1908- *DancEn 78*
Kozlovsky, Sergei 1885-1962 *FilmEn*
Kozlowski, Joseph 1757-1831 *OxMus*
Kozlowski, Jozef 1757-1831 *NewGrD 80*
Kozma, Geza *Baker 78*
Kozma, Matei 1929- *Baker 78*
Kozolupov, Semyon Matveyevich 1884-1961 *NewGrD 80*
Kozubec, Lidia 1927- *IntWWM 80*
Kraak, Meinard 1938- *WhoOp 76*
Kraber, Karl 1935- *IntWWM 77, -80*
Kracauer, Siegfried 1889-1966 *FilmEn, OxFilm*
Kracher, Joseph Matthias 1752-1830? *NewGrD 80*
Krachmalnick, Samuel 1928- *WhoOp 76*
Kradenthaler, Hieronymus *NewGrD 80*
Krader, Barbara Lattimer 1922- *IntWWM 80, NewGrD 80*
Kraehenbuehl, David 1932- *ConAmC*
Kraemer, Hans 1906- *WhoOp 76*
Kraemer, Richard O 1919- *AmSCAP 80*
Kraf, Michael 1590?-1662 *NewGrD 80*
Krafft *NewGrD 80*
Krafft, Francois 1733-1783? *NewGrD 80*
Krafft, Francois-Joseph 1721-1795 *NewGrD 80*
Krafft, Georg Andreas *NewGrD 80*
Krafft, Jean-Laurent 1694-1768 *NewGrD 80*
Kraft *NewGrD 80*
Kraft, Adelaide *PupTheA*
Kraft, Anton 1749-1820 *Baker 78, NewGrD 80*
Kraft, Anton 1752-1820 *MusMk, OxMus*
Kraft, Friedrich Anton 1807-1874 *NewGrD 80*
Kraft, Georg Andreas 1660?-1726 *NewGrD 80*
Kraft, Gil 1926- *BiE&WWA*
Kraft, Gunther 1907-1977 *NewGrD 80*
Kraft, Hy 1899-1975 *BiE&WWA, NotNAT, -A, -B*
Kraft, Jean Marie *WhoOp 76*
Kraft, Jill 1930- *BiE&WWA, NotNAT*
Kraft, Leo 1922- *AmSCAP 66, -80, Baker 78, CpmDNM 75, -80, ConAmC, DcCM, IntWWM 77, -80, NewGrD 80*
Kraft, Leonard 1932- *BiE&WWA*
Kraft, Ludwicus *NewGrD 80*
Kraft, Nicolaus 1778-1853 *Baker 78, OxMus*
Kraft, Nikolaus 1778-1853 *NewGrD 80*
Kraft, Walter 1905- *NewGrD 80*
Kraft, William 1923- *AmSCAP 66, -80, Baker 78, CpmDNM 73, -77, ConAmC, DcCM*
Kraftschenko, Valerie *Film 2*
Kraftwerk *ConMuA 80A, IlEncR*
Kragerup, Peder Emil 1948- *IntWWM 80*
Kragh-Jacobsen, Svend 1909- *CnOxB, DancEn 78*
Krah, Earl Edward 1921- *AmSCAP 66, -80*
Krah, Marc 1906-1973 *WhScrn 77, WhoHol B*
Krahl, Hilde 1915- *FilmAG WE*
Krahl, Hilde 1917- *EncWT*
Krahly, Hanns 1885-1950 *DcFM, WhScrn 77*
Krainik, Ardis 1929- *WhoOp 76*
Krainis, Bernard 1924- *BnBkM 80*
Kral, Earl 1929- *CnOxB*
Kral, Irene 1932- *BiDAmM, EncJzS 70*
Kral, Ivan *AmSCAP 80*
Kral, Roy Joseph 1921- *BiDAmM, CmpEPM, EncJzS 70*
Kraly, Hans 1885-1950 *FilmEn*
Kram, David Ian 1948- *WhoOp 76*
Kramar, Frantisek Vicenc *NewGrD 80*
Kramer, A Walter 1890-1969 *AmSCAP 66, -80, Baker 78, ConAmC, NewGrD 80, OxMus*
Kramer, Aaron 1921- *AmSCAP 80*
Kramer, Adele 1900- *WhoMus 72*
Kramer, Albert H *NewYTET*
Kramer, Alex Charles 1903- *AmSCAP 66, -80, CmpEPM*
Kramer, Alexander Milton 1893-1955 *AmSCAP 66, -80*
Kramer, Arthur Walter 1890-1969 *BiDAmM*
Kramer, Barry *ConMuA 80B*
Kramer, Billy J & The Dakotas *RkOn 2[port]*
Kramer, Clorinda P DeGudino *PupTheA*
Kramer, David 1932- *IntMPA 75, -76*
Kramer, Eddie *ConMuA 80B*
Kramer, Edith *Film 2*

Kramer, Gregory Paul 1952- *ConAmC*
Kramer, Ida 1878-1930 *Film 2, WhScrn 77*
Kramer, Ivan 1942- *CnOxB*
Kramer, Jerome 1945- *IntMPA 77, -78, -79, -80*
Kramer, Jonathan D 1942- *ConAmC, IntWWM 77, -80*
Kramer, Larry 1935- *FilmgC, HalFC 80, IntMPA 77, -75, -76, -78, -79, -80*
Kramer, Leonie 1941- *DancEn 78*
Kramer, Leopold *Film 2*
Kramer, Louis Herman 1926- *CpmDNM 72*
Kramer, Michael *NewGrD 80*
Kramer, Phil 1900-1972 *WhScrn 77*
Kramer, Sidney *IntMPA 77, -75, -76, -78, -79, -80*
Kramer, Stan *PupTheA*
Kramer, Stanley 1913- *AmFD, BiDFilm, -81, DcFM, FilmEn, FilmgC, HalFC 80, IntMPA 77, -75, -76, -78, -79, -80, MovMk[port], OxFilm, WhoHrs 80, WorEFlm*
Kramer, Wright 1870-1941 *NotNAT B, WhScrn 74, -77, WhoHol B*
Kramer, Zoe Parenteau 1914- *AmSCAP 80*
Kramm, Joseph 1907- *BiE&WWA, CnMD, ModWD, NotNAT, WhoThe 72, -77*
Krampen, Elke 1948- *WhoOp 76*
Kramperova, Jindra 1940- *IntWWM 77, -80*
Krampf, Gunter 1899-195-? *FilmgC, HalFC 80*
Krampf, Gunther 1899- *FilmEn, WorEFlm*
Krams, Arthur 1912- *IntMPA 77, -75, -76, -78, -79, -80*
Krance, John P, Jr. 1935- *AmSCAP 66, ConAmC A*
Krance, John Paul, Jr. 1934- *AmSCAP 80*
Krane, Charles 1898- *AmSCAP 66*
Krane, David Marc 1953- *AmSCAP 80*
Krane, Sherman M 1927- *AmSCAP 66, -80, ConAmC A*
Kraner, Johannes Gunther 1930- *IntWWM 80*
Kranert, Veda Proctor *IntWWM 80*
Kranich, Frederick *Baker 78*
Kranich, Helmuth d1956 *Baker 78*
Kranich, Helmuth 1833-1902 *Baker 78*
Kranich, Victor *Baker 78*
Kraning, Suzan Pitt *WomWMM B*
Krantz, Eugen 1844-1898 *Baker 78*
Krantz, Milton 1912- *BiE&WWA*
Krantz, Steve 1923- *IntMPA 77, -75, -76, -78, -79, -80*
Kranz, Johann Friedrich 1752-1810 *NewGrD 80*
Krapf, Gerhard 1924- *Baker 78, CpmDNM 79, ConAmC, IntWWM 77, -80*
Krarup, Gunnar 1943- *IntWWM 77, -80*
Krarup, Vibeke 1944- *IntWWM 77, -80*
Krasa, Hans 1899-1944 *Baker 78, NewGrD 80*
Krasilovsky, Alexis Rafael *WomWMM, -B*
Krasinski, Zygmunt 1812-1857 *OxThe*
Krasinski, Zygmunt 1812-1858 *McGEWD[port]*
Krasinski, Zygmunt 1812-1859 *CnThe, EncWT, REnWD[port]*
Krasinsky, Ernest Louis *NewGrD 80*
Krasker, Robert 1913- *CmMov, DcFM, FilmEn, FilmgC, HalFC 80, OxFilm, WorEFlm*
Krasna, Norman 1909- *BiDFilm, -81, BiE&WWA, CmMov, EncWT, FilmEn, FilmgC, HalFC 80, IntMPA 77, -75, -76, -78, -79, -80, McGEWD, NotNAT, OxFilm, WhoThe 72, -77, WorEFlm*
Krasne, Philip N 1905- *IntMPA 75, -76*
Krasner, Louis 1903- *Baker 78, NewGrD 80, WhoMus 72*
Krasner, Milton 1898- *CmMov, FilmgC, HalFC 80, WorEFlm*
Krasner, Milton 1901- *FilmEn*
Krasnor, David 1921- *AmSCAP 66, -80*
Krasnow, Hermann 1910- *AmSCAP 66, -80*
Krasova, Marta 1901-1970 *Baker 78, NewGrD 80*
Krasowski *NewGrD 80*
Krasselt *NewGrD 80*
Krasselt, Alfred 1872-1908 *NewGrD 80*
Krasselt, Gustav 1846-1910? *NewGrD 80*
Krasselt, Rudolf 1879-1954 *NewGrD 80*
Krassovska, Nathalie 1918- *CnOxB*
Krassovska, Nathalie 1921- *DancEn 78[port]*
Krassovskaya, Vera Mikhailovna 1915- *CnOxB, DancEn 78*
Krassowski *NewGrD 80*
Krastev, Venelin 1919- *NewGrD 80*
Kratina, Valeria 1892- *CnOxB*
Kratish, Jack *ConMuA 80B*
Kratke, Grita 1907- *CnOxB*
Kratochvil, Jiri 1924- *IntWWM 77*
Kratochwil, Heinrich 1933- *IntWWM 80*
Kratochwil, Heinz 1933- *IntWWM 77*
Kratzenstein, Christian Gottlieb 1723- *OxMus*
Kratzer *NewGrD 80*
Kratzer, Franciszek Ksawery 1731-1818 *NewGrD 80*
Kratzer, Kazimierz Augustyn 1778-1860 *NewGrD 80*
Kratzer, Kazimierz Julian 1844-1890 *NewGrD 80*
Kratzer, Walenty Karol 1780-1855 *NewGrD 80*
Kraul, Earl Riedar 1929- *CreCan 1, DancEn 78*
Kraus, Alessandro 1820-1904 *Baker 78*
Kraus, Alfredo 1927- *CmOp, NewGrD 80, WhoMus 72, WhoOp 76*
Kraus, Detlef 1919- *IntWWM 77, -80*
Kraus, Egon 1912- *NewGrD 80*
Kraus, Ernst 1863-1941 *Baker 78, CmOp, NewEOp 71, NewGrD 80*
Kraus, Evelyn *PupTheA*
Kraus, Felix Von 1870-1937 *Baker 78, NewEOp 71*
Kraus, George 1912- *WhoMus 72*
Kraus, Gertrud 1903- *CnOxB*
Kraus, Greta 1907- *CreCan 2*
Kraus, John Fredrich 1931- *AmSCAP 80*
Kraus, Joseph Martin 1756-1792 *Baker 78, NewGrD 80*
Kraus, Karl 1874-1936 *CnMD, EncWT, McGEWD, ModWD*
Kraus, Lili *IntWWM 77, -80*
Kraus, Lili 1905- *Baker 78, BnBkM 80, MusSN[port], NewGrD 80*
Kraus, Lili 1908- *WhoMus 72*
Kraus, Otakar 1909- *CmOp, IntWWM 77, -80, NewGrD 80, WhoMus 72*
Kraus, Philip Charles 1918- *AmSCAP 66, -80*
Kraus, Richard 1902-1978 *NewGrD 80, WhoMus 72*
Kraus, Robert A 1926- *IntMPA 77, -75, -76, -78, -79*
Kraus, Ted M 1923- *BiE&WWA, ConAmTC, NotNAT*
Kraus, Werner 1884-1959 *NotNAT B*
Kraus, Werner 1885-1962 *ForYSC*
Krause, Adelheid 1950- *IntWWM 77*
Krause, Anton 1834-1907 *Baker 78*
Krause, Christian Gottfried 1719-1770 *NewGrD 80*
Krause, Eduard 1837-1892 *Baker 78*
Krause, Emil 1840-1916 *Baker 78*
Krause, Ernst 1911- *NewGrD 80*
Krause, Karl Christian Friedrich 1781-1832 *Baker 78*
Krause, Kenneth Charles 1929- *AmSCAP 80*
Krause, Lloyd Thomas 1920- *IntWWM 77, -80*
Krause, Martin 1853-1918 *Baker 78*
Krause, Robert James 1943- *ConAmC, IntWWM 77, -80*
Krause, Sharon 1955- *IntWWM 80*
Krause, Theodor 1833-1910 *Baker 78*
Krause, Tom 1934- *NewGrD 80, WhoOp 76*
Krause-Graumnitz, Heinz 1911- *IntWWM 77, -80*
Krausenecker, Adele 1899- *CnOxB*
Kraushaar, Keith Conrad Francis 1928- *IntWWM 77, -80*
Kraushaar, Otto 1812-1866 *Baker 78*
Kraushaar, Otto Jacob 1895- *IntWWM 77*
Kraushaar, Raoul 1908- *AmSCAP 80, HalFC 80*
Krauss, Charles d1926 *WhScrn 74, -77*
Krauss, Clemens 1893-1954 *Baker 78, CmOp, MusSN[port], NewEOp 71, NewGrD 80[port]*
Krauss, Felix Von 1870-1937 *CmOp*
Krauss, Gabrielle 1842-1906 *Baker 78, CmOp, NewEOp 71, NewGrD 80*
Krauss, Henri *Film 1*
Krauss, Henry *Film 2*
Krauss, Jacques 1900-1957 *FilmEn*
Krauss, Oscar *IntMPA 77, -75, -76, -78, -79, -80*
Krauss, Ruth 1911- *ConDr 73, -77*
Krauss, Werner 1884-1959 *BiDFilm, -81, EncWT, Ent, FilmAG WE, FilmEn, Film 1, -2, FilmgC, HalFC 80, MotPP, OxFilm, OxThe, WhScrn 74, -77, WhThe, WhoHol B, WhoHrs 80[port], WorEFlm*
Kraussneck, Arthur *Film 2*
Kraut, Johann *NewGrD 80*
Krautwurst, Franz 1923- *IntWWM 77, -80*
Krauze, Zygmunt 1938- *Baker 78, NewGrD 80*
Kravitz, Ellen King 1929- *IntWWM 77, -80*
Krawcowna DeBarbaro, Ludmila 1939- *IntWWM 77, -80*
Krawicz, Mecislas *WomWMM*
Krawitz, Seymour 1923- *BiE&WWA, NotNAT*
Krayk, Stefan 1914- *IntWWM 77, -80*
Kraynev, Vladimir 1944- *NewGrD 80*
Kremery-Vrtelova, Jela 1924- *IntWWM 77, -80*
Kreal, Ernest 1891- *WhoMus 72*
Krebbers, Herman Albertus 1923- *IntWWM 77, -80, NewGrD 80, WhoMus 72*
Krebs *NewGrD 80*
Krebs, Carl 1857-1937 *Baker 78*
Krebs, Carl August 1804-1880 *Baker 78*
Krebs, David *ConMuA 80B*
Krebs, Helmut 1913- *IntWWM 77, -80, WhoMus 72*
Krebs, Johann Gottfried 1741-1814 *NewGrD 80*
Krebs, Johann Ludwig 1713-1780 *Baker 78, BnBkM 80, MusMk, NewGrD 80, OxMus*
Krebs, Johann Tobias 1690-1762 *NewGrD 80*
Krebs, Karl August 1804-1880 *NewGrD 80*
Krebs, Lottie *IntWWM 77, -80, WhoMus 72*
Krech, Warren W *FilmEn, Film 2*
Krechmer, William Frederich 1909- *AmSCAP 66, -80*
Kredba, Oldrich 1904- *IntWWM 77, -80*
Kredel, Fritz *PupTheA*
Kreger, James 1947- *Baker 78*
Krehbiel, Henry Edward 1854-1923 *Baker 78, BiDAmM, NewGrD 80, OxMus*
Krehl, Stephan 1864-1924 *Baker 78, NewGrD 80*
Krehm, Ida *WhoMus 72*
Kreiger, Arthur V 1945- *ConAmC*
Kreiman, Robert T 1924- *IntMPA 77, -75, -76, -78, -79, -80*
Krein, Alexander 1883-1951 *Baker 78, OxMus*
Krein, Grigory 1879-1955 *Baker 78, OxMus*
Krein, Julian 1913- *Baker 78*
Krein, Julian 1914- *OxMus*
Kreiner, Marc *ConMuA 80B*
Kreisel, Henry 1922- *CreCan 1*
Kreisler, Alexander Von 1894-1969 *ConAmC*
Kreisler, Fritz 1875-1962 *AmSCAP 66, -80, Baker 78, BiDAmM, BnBkM 80[port], CmpEPM, ConAmC, MusMk, MusSN[port], NewGrD 80[port], NotNAT B, OxMus*
Kreiss, Hulda E 1924- *ConAmC*
Kreissle VonHellborn, Heinrich 1822-1869 *Baker 78*
Krejca, Otomar 1921- *EncWT*
Krejci, Isa 1904-1968 *Baker 78, DcCM, NewGrD 80*
Krejci, Josef 1821-1881 *Baker 78*
Krejci, Miroslav 1891-1964 *Baker 78, NewGrD 80*
Krek, Uros 1922- *Baker 78, IntWWM 77, -80, NewGrD 80*
Krelja, Petar 1903- *IntWWM 77*
Krellberg, Sherman S *IntMPA 77, -75, -76, -78, -79*
Krellmann, Hanspeter 1935- *NewGrD 80*
Kremberg, Jakob 1650?-1718? *NewGrD 80*
Kremberg, James 1650?-1718? *NewGrD 80*
Krembergh, Jakob 1650?-1718? *NewGrD 80*
Krembergh, James 1650?-1718? *NewGrD 80*
Krembs, Felix *Film 2*
Kremenliev, Boris 1911- *AmSCAP 80, Baker 78, CpmDNM 80, ConAmC, NewGrD 80*
Kremer, Gidon 1947- *BnBkM 80*
Kremer, Gloria Hayes 1924- *AmSCAP 80*
Kremer, Isa 1885-1956 *Baker 78*
Kremer, Theodore 1873- *WhThe*

Kremin, Ingrid 1944- *WhoOp 76*
Kremlev, Yuly 1908-1971 *Baker 78*
Kremlyov, Yuly Anatol'yevich 1908-1971 *NewGrD 80*
Kremmer, Rudolph *ConAmC*
Krempelsetzer, Georg 1827-1871 *Baker 78*
Kremser, Eduard 1838-1914 *Baker 78*
Krenek, Ernest 1900- *NewEOp 71*
Krenek, Ernst 1900- *Baker 78, BiDAmM, BnBkM 80, CmOp, CompSN[port], CpmDNM 76, -79, -80, ConAmC, DcCom 77[port], DcCM, IntWWM 77, -80, MusMk, NewGrD 80[port], OxMus, WhoMus 72*
Krenek, Mrs. Ernst *ConAmC*
Krengel, Gregor 155-?-1594? *NewGrD 80*
Krengel, Joseph Philip 1915- *AmSCAP 66, -80*
Krenn, Franz 1816-1897 *Baker 78*
Krenn, Werner 1943- *NewGrD 80, WhoMus 72*
Krentzlin, Richard 1864-1956 *Baker 78*
Krenz, Jan 1926- *Baker 78, NewGrD 80, OxMus, WhoMus 72*
Krenz, William F 1899- *AmSCAP 66*
Kreps, Bonnie *WomWMM B*
Kresa, Helmy 1904- *AmSCAP 66, -80*
Kresanek, Jozef 1913- *Baker 78, NewGrD 80*
Kreski, Connie *WhoHol A*
Kreskin *MagIlD[port]*
Kresky, Danny *ConMuA 80B*
Kresky, Jeffrey Jay 1948- *AmSCAP 80, ConAmC*
Kresnik, Hans 1939- *CnOxB*
Kress, Carl 1907-1965 *AmSCAP 80, BiDAmM, CmpEPM, WhoJazz 72*
Kress, Georg Philipp 1719-1779 *NewGrD 80*
Kress, Harold F 1913- *FilmEn, HalFC 80, IntMPA 77, -75, -76, -78, -79, -80*
Kress, Johann Albrecht 1644-1684 *NewGrD 80*
Kress, Johann Jakob 1685?-1728 *NewGrD 80*
Kreter, Leo 1933- *ConAmC*
Kretschmer, Edmund 1830-1908 *Baker 78*
Kretzmer, Herbert 1925- *WhoThe 72, -77*
Kretzschmar, August Ferdinand Hermann 1848-1924 *Baker 78*
Kretzschmar, Hermann 1848-1924 *NewGrD 80*
Kretzschmar, Wolfgang 1920- *WhoMus 72*
Kreube, Charles Frederic 1777-1846 *Baker 78*
Kreuder, Peter Paul 1905- *NewGrD 80*
Kreuger, Kurt 1916- *FilmEn, What 5[port]*
Kreuger, Kurt 1917- *FilmgC, ForYSC, HalFC 80, IntMPA 77, -75, -76, -78, -79, -80, MotPP, WhoHol A*
Kreusser, Georg Anton 1746-1810 *NewGrD 80*
Kreutz, Arthur 1906- *AmSCAP 66, Baker 78, BiDAmM, ConAmC, IntWWM 77, -80*
Kreutz, Robert Edward 1922- *ConAmC*
Kreutzbach *NewGrD 80*
Kreutzbach, Emil Bernhard Hermann 1843- *NewGrD 80*
Kreutzbach, Julius Urban 1845-1913 *NewGrD 80*
Kreutzbach, Richard 1839-1903 *NewGrD 80*
Kreutzbach, Urban 1796-1868 *NewGrD 80*
Kreutzberg, Harald 1902-1968 *CnOxB, DancEn 78[port]*
Kreutzer *NewGrD 80*
Kreutzer, Auguste 1778-1832 *Baker 78*
Kreutzer, Conrad 1780-1849 *NewGrD 80*
Kreutzer, Conradin 1780-1849 *NewEOp 71, NewGrD 80*
Kreutzer, Jean Nicolas Auguste 1778-1832 *NewGrD 80*
Kreutzer, Konradin 1780-1849 *Baker 78, MusMk*
Kreutzer, Leon Charles Francois 1817-1868 *Baker 78, NewGrD 80*
Kreutzer, Leonid 1884-1953 *Baker 78*
Kreutzer, Rodolphe 1766-1831 *Baker 78, BnBkM 80, MusMk, NewEOp 71, NewGrD 80, OxMus*
Kreuzer, Barton 1909- *IntMPA 75, -76*
Kreuzer, Conradin *NewGrD 80*
Kreymborg, Alfred 1883-1966 *AmSCAP 66, -80, DcPup, NotNAT A, -B, PupTheA*
Kreymborg, Dorothy *PupTheA*
Kreyn, Yulian Grigor'yevich 1913- *NewGrD 80*
Krich, Herman 1914- *AmSCAP 80*
Kricka, Jaroslav 1882-1969 *Baker 78, NewGrD 80*
Krieg, Richard Charles 1919- *AmSCAP 80*
Kriegck, Johann Jacob *NewGrD 80*
Kriegel, Harriet *WomWMM B*
Krieger, Adam 1634-1666 *Baker 78, NewGrD 80*
Krieger, Armando 1940- *Baker 78, NewGrD 80*
Krieger, Edino 1928- *Baker 78, DcCM, NewGrD 80*
Krieger, Henry 1945- *AmSCAP 80*
Krieger, Johann 1651-1735 *Baker 78*
Krieger, Johann 1652-1735 *NewGrD 80*
Krieger, Johann Philipp 1649-1725 *Baker 78, BnBkM 80, NewGrD 80*
Krieger, Lee 1919-1967 *WhScrn 74, -77, WhoHol B*
Krieger, Robert *ConAmTC*
Krieger, Victorina 1896- *DancEn 78*
Krieger, Victorina Vladimirovna 1893- *CnOxB*
Kriegher, Giovanni *NewGrD 80*
Kriegher, Giovanni Filippo *NewGrD 80*
Kriegk, Johann Jacob 1750-1814 *NewGrD 80*
Kriegstein, Melchior 1500?-1573? *NewGrD 80*
Kriens, Christiaan B 1881-1934 *BiDAmM, ConAmC*
Kriens, Christian 1881-1934 *Baker 78*
Krier, John N *IntMPA 77, -75, -76, -78, -79, -80*
Kriesberg, Matthias 1953- *ConAmC*
Kriesstein, Melchior 1500?-1573? *NewGrD 80*
Krigar, Hermann 1819-1880 *Baker 78*
Krigbaum, Charles Russell 1929- *IntWWM 77, -80*
Kriger, Johann Philipp *NewGrD 80*
Krilovici, Marina 1942- *WhoOp 76*
Krim, Arthur B 1910- *IntMPA 77, -75, -76, -78, -79, -80*
Krimer, Harry *Film 2*
Krimsky, John 1906- *BiE&WWA, NotNAT*
Kriner, Dora 1920- *DancEn 78*
Krinks, Elsie Madeleine Margharita 1912- *WhoMus 72*
Krips, Henry Joseph 1912- *IntWWM 77, -80, NewGrD 80, WhoMus 72*
Krips, Josef 1902-1974 *Baker 78, BnBkM 80, CmOp, IntWWM 77, MusSN[port], NewEOp 71, NewGrD 80, WhoMus 72*
Krips, Joseph 1902- *BiDAmM*
Krisanizh, Georgius *NewGrD 80*
Krisch, Winfried 1936- *DancEn 78*
Krisel, Gary *ConMuA 80B*
Krish, John 1923- *FilmgC, HalFC 80, IlWWBF*
Krish, Tanya Moiseiwitsch *CreCan 2*
Krishan, Rajinder 1919- *IntWWM 77*
Krismann, Franz Xaver *NewGrD 80*
Krist, Joachim Oswald Paulus 1948- *IntWWM 77, -80*
Kristel, Sylvia *WhoHol A*
Kristel, Sylvia 1948?- *HalFC 80*
Kristel, Sylvia 1952- *FilmAG WE, FilmEn*
Kristen, Marta *WhoHol A*
Krister, Dorothy *Film 2*
Kristina, Anita 1940- *CnOxB*
Kristinsson, Sigursveinn 1911- *NewGrD 80*
Kristjansson, Arni 1906- *NewGrD 80, WhoMus 72*
Kristjansson, Olafur 1927- *IntWWM 77*
Kristofferson, Kris *ConMuA 80A[port]*
Kristofferson, Kris 1936- *CounME 74[port], -74A, FilmEn, HalFC 80, IlEncCM[port], IlEncR[port], MovMk[port], RkOn 2[port], WhoHol A*
Kristofferson, Kris 1937- *IntMPA 78, -79, -80*
Kritschil, Bertha K *PupTheA*
Kritzman, Serge 1914- *IntMPA 80*
Kriukov, Nikolai 1908-1961 *Baker 78*
Kriukov, Vladimir 1902-1960 *Baker 78*
Krivinka, Gustav 1928- *Baker 78, IntWWM 77, -80, NewGrD 80*
Kriza, John 1919-1975 *CnOxB, DancEn 78*
Krizanic, Juraj 1617-1683 *NewGrD 80*
Krizek, Jiri 1942- *IntWWM 77, -80*
Krizkovsky, Karel 1820-1885 *Baker 78*
Krizkovsky, Paul 1820-1885 *OxMus*
Krizkovsky, Pavel 1820-1885 *NewGrD 80*
Krizman, Francisek Ksaver *NewGrD 80*
Krizman, Serge 1914- *IntMPA 77, -75, -76, -78, -79*
Krleza, Miroslav 1893- *CnMD, EncWT, ModWD*
Krob, Josef Theodor *NewGrD 80*
Kroeber, Alan Matthew 1948- *AmSCAP 80*
Kroeger, Berry 1912- *ForYSC, WhoHol A*
Kroeger, Ernest Richard 1862-1934 *Baker 78, BiDAmM*
Kroeger, Karl 1932- *AmSCAP 80, Baker 78, ConAmC, DcCM*
Kroell, Adrienne 1892-1949 *WhScrn 77*
Kroemer, Hugo Alfred 1888- *WhoMus 72*
Kroepfl, Francisco 1931- *NewGrD 80*
Kroes, Henk 1916- *IntWWM 77, -80*
Kroff, Josef Theodor *NewGrD 80*
Krofft, Sid 1929- *AmSCAP 80, PupTheA*
Krofft, Sid And Marty Krofft *NewYTET*
Krog, Erling 1938- *IntWWM 80*
Krog, Helge 1889-1962 *CnMD, McGEWD, ModWD, OxThe, REnWD[port]*
Krog, Karin 1937- *EncJzS 70, IntWWM 80*
Krogh, Grethe 1928- *IntWWM 77, -80*
Krogh, Torben 1895-1970 *NewGrD 80*
Krogh, Yngvar Ronald 1934- *WhoOp 76*
Krogulski, Jozef Wladyslaw 1815-1842 *NewGrD 80*
Krohn, Ernst C 1888-1975 *Baker 78, NewGrD 80*
Krohn, Felix 1898-1963 *Baker 78*
Krohn, I H R 1867-1960 *OxMus*
Krohn, Ilmari 1867-1960 *Baker 78, NewGrD 80*
Krohner, Sarah 1883-1959 *WhScrn 74, -77*
Kroitor, Roman 1927- *WorEFlm*
Kroitor, Roman Bogdan 1926- *CreCan 1*
Krol, Bernhard 1920- *NewGrD 80*
Krolick, Edward John 1923- *IntWWM 77, -80*
Krolik, Mary Stuart *AmSCAP 80*
Kroll, Erwin 1886-1976 *Baker 78, NewGrD 80*
Kroll, Franz 1820-1877 *Baker 78*
Kroll, Georg 1934- *NewGrD 80*
Kroll, Lucy *BiE&WWA, NotNAT*
Kroll, William 1901-1980 *AmSCAP 66, -80, Baker 78, ConAmC, NewGrD 80*
Kroller, Heinrich 1880-1930 *CnOxB, DancEn 78*
Kroman, Ann *Film 1*
Krombholc, Jaroslav 1918- *CmOp, IntWWM 77, -80, NewGrD 80, WhoMus 72, WhoOp 76*
Krombholc, Karlo 1905- *Baker 78*
Kromer, Helen *NatPD[port]*
Kromer, Marcin 1512-1589 *NewGrD 80*
Krommer, Franz 1759-1831 *Baker 78, NewGrD 80, OxMus*
Kromolicki, Joseph 1882-1961 *Baker 78*
Krondes, James John 1925- *AmSCAP 80*
Krondes, Jimmy 1925- *AmSCAP 66*
Krone, Gerald 1933- *BiE&WWA, NotNAT, PlP&P A[port]*
Kronenberger, Louis 1904- *BiE&WWA, NotNAT, WhoThe 72, -77*
Kronert, Max *Film 2*
Krones, Therese 1801-1830 *EncWT, OxThe*
Kronfeld, Eric *ConMuA 80B*
Kronick, William *IntMPA 77, -75, -76, -78, -79, -80*
Kroninger, Barry 1952- *IntWWM 77*
Kronish, Amy *WomWMM*
Kronke, Emil 1865-1938 *Baker 78*
Kronold, Hans 1872-1922 *Baker 78*
Kronold, Selma 1861-1920 *Baker 78*
Kronold, Selma 1866-1920 *BiDAmM, NewEOp 71*
Kronsberg, Jeremy *IntMPA 79, -80*
Kronstam, Henning 1934- *CnOxB, DancEn 78[port]*
Kroo, Gyorgy 1926- *NewGrD 80*
Kropfinger, Klaus 1930- *IntWWM 77, -80*
Kropfreiter, Augustinus Franz 1936- *NewGrD 80*
Kropstein, Nikolaus 1492?-1562 *NewGrD 80*
Krosnick, Joel 1941- *NewGrD 80*
Kross, Siegfried 1930- *IntWWM 77, -80, NewGrD 80*
Krost, Barry *ConMuA 80B*
Krouse, H Sylvester 1853-1940 *AmSCAP 66*
Krov, Josef Theodor 1797-1859 *NewGrD 80*
Krow, Josef Theodor 1797-1859 *Baker 78, NewGrD 80*
Kroyer, Theodor 1873-1945 *Baker 78, NewGrD 80*

Krpan, Vladimir 1938- IntWWM 77, -80
Krstic, Petar 1877-1957 Baker 78
Kru Film 2
Kruckl, Franz 1841-1899 Baker 78
Kruczkowski, Leon 1900-1962 CnMD, CroCD, EncWT, ModWD
Krueger, Benjamen 1899-1967 AmSCAP 80
Krueger, Benny 1899-1967 CmpEPM, WhoJazz 72
Krueger, Bum 1906-1971 WhScrn 74, -77, WhoHol B
Krueger, Carl 1908- IntMPA 77, -75, -76, -78, -79, -80
Krueger, Felix Emil 1874-1948 Baker 78, NewGrD 80
Krueger, George F 1907- IntWWM 77, -80
Krueger, Harold E 1928- IntWWM 77
Krueger, Karl 1894- Baker 78, BiDAmM
Krueger, Lorraine WhoHol A
Krueger, Sol Richard 1945- AmSCAP 80
Krug, Arnold 1849-1904 NewGrD 80
Krug, Diederich 1821-1880 NewGrD 80
Krug, Dietrich 1821-1880 Baker 78
Krug, Friedrich 1812-1892 Baker 78
Krug, Joseph 1858-1915 Baker 78
Krugel, Terrance D 1943- IntWWM 77
Kruger, Alma d1960 NotNAT B, WhThe, WhoHol B
Kruger, Alma 1868-1960 FilmEn, ForYSC, WhScrn 74, -77
Kruger, Alma 1871-1960 ThFT[port]
Kruger, Alma 1872-1960 FilmgC, HalFC 80, MovMk[port]
Kruger, Eduard 1807-1885 Baker 78, NewGrD 80
Kruger, Fred H 1913-1961 NotNAT B, WhScrn 74, -77, WhoHol B
Kruger, Hardy 1928- FilmAG WE, FilmEn, FilmgC, ForYSC, HalFC 80, IntMPA 77, -75, -76, -78, -79, -80, WhoHol A
Kruger, Harold Stubby 1897-1965 WhScrn 74, -77
Kruger, Jeffrey S 1931- IntMPA 77, -75, -76, -78, -79, -80, WhoMus 72
Kruger, Johann Philipp NewGrD 80
Kruger, Jules 1891- DcFM, FilmEn
Kruger, Lilly Canfield 1892-1969 AmSCAP 66, -80, ConAmC
Kruger, Natalie Wyatt 1934- IntWWM 77, -80
Kruger, Otto 1885-1974 BiE&WWA, FilmEn, Film 2, FilmgC, ForYSC, HalFC 80, HolCA[port], MotPP, MovMk[port], NotNAT B, PlP&P, Vers A[port], What 3[port], WhScrn 77, WhThe, WhoHol B, WhoHrs 80[port]
Kruger, Paul 1895- Film 2, TwYS
Kruger, Rudolf IntWWM 77, -80, WhoOp 76
Kruger, Stubby 1897-1965 WhoHol B
Kruger, Walther 1902- IntWWM 77, -80
Kruger, Wilhelm 1820-1883 Baker 78
Krugl, Johann Philipp NewGrD 80
Krugman, Lillian D 1911- AmSCAP 66, -80
Krugman, Lou WhoHol A
Krugman, Murray ConMuA 80B
Kruijsen, Bernard NewGrD 80
Kruis, M H Van't 1861-1919 Baker 78
Krul, Eli 1926- Baker 78, ConAmC
Krumbachova, Ester 1923- OxFilm, WomWMM
Krumbein, Maurice AmSCAP 80
Krumbholz, Martin NewGrD 80
Krumins, Diana WomWMM B
Krummel, D W 1929- NewGrD 80
Krumpholtz NewGrD 80
Krumpholtz, Anne-Marie 1755?-1824? NewGrD 80
Krumpholtz, Jan Krtitel 1742-1790 NewGrD 80
Krumpholtz, Jean-Baptiste 1742-1790 NewGrD 80
Krumpholtz, Johann Baptist 1742-1790 Baker 78, NewGrD 80
Krumpholtz, Vaclav 1750?-1817 NewGrD 80
Krumpholtz, Wenzel 1750-1817 Baker 78, NewGrD 80
Krumpholz NewGrD 80
Krumpholz, Johann Baptist 1745-1790 BnBkM 80, OxMus
Krumschmidt, Eberhard 1905-1956 WhScrn 74, -77, WhoHol B
Krunnfusz, Gordon 1931- AmSCAP 80
Krupa, Gene 1909-1973 Baker 78, BgBands 74[port], BiDAmM, CmpEPM, EncJzS 70, IlEncJ, MusMk, NewGrD 80, WhScrn 77, WhoHol B, WhoJazz 72, WhoMus 72
Krupp, Vera 1910-1967 WhScrn 74, -77
Krupska, Dania 1923- BiE&WWA, CnOxB, DancEn 78, NotNAT, WhoThe 72, -77
Krusceniski, Salomea 1872-1952 NewGrD 80
Krusceniski, Salomea 1872-1953 CmOp
Kruschen, Jack 1922- BiE&WWA, FilmEn, FilmgC, ForYSC, NotNAT, WhoHol A
Kruse, Bjorn Howard 1946- IntWWM 80
Kruse, Georg Richard 1856-1944 Baker 78
Kruse, Harald 1923- IntWWM 77, -80
Kruse, Johann Secundus 1859-1927 NewGrD 80
Kruse, Philip Antony 1949- IntWWM 77, -80
Kruseman, Jacob Philip 1887-1955 Baker 78
Krushchen, Jack 1922- HalFC 80
Kruspe NewGrD 80
Kruss, Johann NewGrD 80
Kruszelnicka, Salomea NewGrD 80
Krutch, Joseph Wood 1893-1970 BiE&WWA, EncWT, NotNAT B, OxThe, WhThe
Krutzfeldt, Werner J M 1928- IntWWM 77, -80
Kruuse, Marianne 1942- CnOxB
Kruyf, Ton De 1937- Baker 78, NewGrD 80
Kruysen, Bernard 1933- NewGrD 80
Krygell, Johan Adam 1835-1915 Baker 78
Krylov, Ivan Andrejevich 1768-1844 DcPup
Krylov, Pavel 1885-1935 Baker 78
Krystal, Hilly ConMuA 80B
Kryukov, Vladimir Nikolayevich 1902-1960 NewGrD 80
Kryzhanovsky, Ivan 1867-1924 Baker 78
Krzeminski, Franciszek 1925- IntWWM 77, -80
Krzesichleb, Piotr NewGrD 80
Krzyszkowska, Maria 1927- CnOxB
Krzywicki, Jan 1948- IntWWM 77, -80
Krzywicki, Zdzislaw 1938- WhoOp 76
Krzyzanowski, Ignacy 1826-1905 NewGrD 80
Krzyzanowski, Stanislaw Andrzej 1836-1922 NewGrD 80
Kschessinska, Mathilda Maria-Felixovna 1872-1971 CnOxB
Ktenaveas, Takis 1934- IntWWM 77, -80
Kuan, Han-Ch'ing CnThe, REnWD[port]
Kuba 1914-1967 CroCD
Kuba, Kurth Barthel 1914-1967 CnMD
Kuba, Ludvik 1863-1956 NewGrD 80
Kuban, Bob & The In-Men RkOn 2A
Kubelik, Jan 1880-1940 Baker 78, BnBkM 80, MusSN[port], NewGrD 80[port], OxMus
Kubelik, Rafael 1914- Baker 78, BiDAmM, BnBkM 80, CmOp, IntWWM 77, -80, MusMk, MusSN[port], NewEOp 71, NewGrD 80[port], WhoMus 72, WhoOp 76
Kubey, Arthur 1918- IntWWM 77, -80
Kubiak, Teresa 1937- CmOp, NewGrD 80, WhoOp 76
Kubiak-Wojtaszek, Teresa Janina 1937- IntWWM 80
Kubik, Gail 1914- AmSCAP 66, -80, Baker 78, BiDAmM, CpmDNM 75, ConAmC, DcCM, NewGrD 80, WhoMus 72
Kubik, Gerhard 1934- IntWWM 77, -80
Kubin, Rudolf 1909-1973 Baker 78, NewGrD 80
Kubin-Valic, Valeria 1938- IntWWM 80
Kubizek, Augustin 1918- IntWWM 77, -80
Kubizek, Karl Maria 1925- IntWWM 77, -80
Kubrick, Stanley 1928- AmFD, BiDFilm, -81, ConDr 73, -77A, ConLC 16, DcFM, FilmEn, FilmgC, HalFC 80, IntMPA 77, -75, -76, -78, -79, -80, MovMk[port], OxFilm, WhoHrs 80, WomWMM, WorEFlm
Kuby, Bernard F 1923- AmSCAP 66, -80
Kucera, Vaclav 1929- Baker 78, IntWWM 77, -80, NewGrD 80
Kuchar, Jan Krtitel 1751-1829 NewGrD 80
Kucharsch, Jan Krtitel 1751-1829 NewGrD 80
Kucharsky, Andrej 1932- WhoOp 76
Kucharz, Jan Krtitel 1751-1829 NewGrD 80
Kucharz, Johann Baptist 1751-1829 Baker 78
Kucheler, Johann 1738-1790 NewGrD 80
Kuchenthal, Johannes NewGrD 80
Kuchler, Johann 1738-1790 NewGrD 80
Kuchler, Kenneth Grant 1922- IntWWM 77, -80
Kuchta, Gladys 1923- WhoOp 76
Kucinski, Leo 1904- IntWWM 77, -80
Kucken, Friedrich Wilhelm 1810-1882 Baker 78, NewGrD 80, OxMus
Kuckertz, Josef 1930- IntWWM 80, NewGrD 80
Kuczinski, Paul 1846-1897 Baker 78
Kuczynski, Paul 1846-1897 NewGrD 80
Kudalkar, Laxmikant Shantaram 1937- IntWWM 77
Kudelski, Karl Matthias 1805-1877 Baker 78
Kudera, Lottie A 1920- AmSCAP 80
Kudo, E Takeo 1942- ConAmC
Kudyk, Jan 1942- IntWWM 77, -80
Kudykowski, Miroslaw 1948- EncJzS 70
Kuebler, David Kenneth 1947- IntWWM 80, WhoOp 76
Kueck, Rudolf Hermann 1931- IntWWM 77, -80
Kuehl, Joan WomWMM B
Kuehn, Bernard R 1916- AmSCAP 80
Kuehn, David Laurance 1940- IntWWM 77, -80
Kuen, Johannes NewGrD 80
Kuen, Otto Ludwig 1910- IntWWM 77, -80
Kuerti, Anton 1934- BiDAmM
Kuerti, Anton Emil 1938- IntWWM 77, -80, NewGrD 80
Kuertz, Charles H, Sr. 1923- IntMPA 77, -75, -76, -78, -79, -80
Kueteman, John-Anne 1918- IntWWM 77, -80
Kuf-Linx, The RkOn
Kufferath NewGrD 80
Kufferath, Antonia 1857-1939 NewGrD 80
Kufferath, Hubert-Ferdinand 1818-1896 Baker 78, NewGrD 80
Kufferath, Johann Hermann 1797-1864 Baker 78, NewGrD 80
Kufferath, Louis 1811-1882 Baker 78, NewGrD 80
Kufferath, Maurice 1852-1919 Baker 78, NewGrD 80
Kuffner, Joseph 1776-1856 Baker 78
Kugelmann, Barthel NewGrD 80
Kugelmann, Christoph NewGrD 80
Kugelmann, Hans 1495?-1542 NewGrD 80
Kugelmann, Johann 1495?-1542 NewGrD 80
Kugelmann, Melchior NewGrD 80
Kugelmann, Paul d1580 NewGrD 80
Kuh, Tobias NewGrD 80
Kuhac, Franjo Zaver 1834-1911 NewGrD 80
Kuhac, Frank Xaver 1834-1911 OxMus
Kuhac, Franz Xaver 1834-1911 Baker 78
Kuhe, Wilhelm 1823-1912 Baker 78, NewGrD 80
Kuhe, William 1823-1912 OxMus
Kuhl, Charlie 1897?-1947? NewOrJ
Kuhl, Ole DeFine 1950- IntWWM 77
Kuhlau, Frederik 1786-1832 NewGrD 80
Kuhlau, Friedrich 1786-1832 Baker 78, GrComp[port], MusMk, NewGrD 80, OxMus
Kuhmstedt, Friedrich Karl 1809-1858 Baker 78, NewGrD 80
Kuhn, Alfred 1938- WhoOp 76
Kuhn, Carl Theodor d1925 NewGrD 80
Kuhn, Franz NewGrD 80
Kuhn, Fritz 1919- CnMD
Kuhn, Gustav Friedrich 1946- WhoOp 76
Kuhn, Hellmut 1939- NewGrD 80
Kuhn, Joachim Kurt 1944- EncJzS 70
Kuhn, Johann NewGrD 80
Kuhn, Johann Nepomuk 1827-1888 NewGrD 80
Kuhn, Lee 1912-1955 AmSCAP 66, -80
Kuhn, Richard S 1907-1973 AmSCAP 66, -80
Kuhn, Rolf 1929- NewGrD 80
Kuhn, Sarah Sappington 1935- WomWMM B
Kuhn, Stephen Lewis 1938- BiDAmM, EncJzS 70
Kuhn, Steve 1938- EncJzS 70
Kuhn, Thomas G 1935- IntMPA 77, -75, -76, -78, -79, -80
Kuhn, Tobias 1565?-1615? NewGrD 80
Kuhnau, Johann 1660-1722 Baker 78, CmpBCM, GrComp[port], MusMk, NewGrD 80[port], OxMus

Kuhnau, Johann Christoph 1735-1805 *NewGrD 80*
Kuhne, Friedrich *Film 2*
Kuhne, Rolf 1932- *WhoOp 76*
Kuhnel, August 1645-1700? *NewGrD 80*
Kuhnel, Dietmar 1942- *WhoOp 76*
Kuhnelt, Hans Friedrich 1918- *CnMD, CroCD*
Kuhner, Basil 1840-1911 *Baker 78*
Kuhner, Konrad 1851-1909 *Baker 78*
Kuhnhausen, Johann Georg d1714 *NewGrD 80*
Kuhnle, Wesley 1898-1962 *NewGrD 80*
Kuhse, Hanne-Lore 1925- *NewGrD 80, WhoOp 76*
Kuijken *NewGrD 80*
Kuijken, Barthold 1949- *NewGrD 80*
Kuijken, Sigiswald 1944- *NewGrD 80*
Kuijken, Wieland 1938- *NewGrD 80*
Kujala, Walfrid Eugene 1925- *IntWWM 77, -80*
Kujawa, Robert Valentine 1925- *AmSCAP 80*
Kukoff, Benjamin 1933- *AmSCAP 80*
Kukuzeles *NewGrD 80*
Kulenkampff, Georg 1898-1948 *NewGrD 80*
Kulenkampff, Gustav 1849-1921 *Baker 78*
Kuleshov, Lev 1899-1970 *BiDFilm, -81, DcFM, FilmEn, OxFilm, WorEFlm*
Kulganek, W *Film 2*
Kulidjanov, Lev 1924- *DcFM*
Kulijanov, Lev 1924- *FilmEn*
Kulik, Buzz *NewYTET*
Kulik, Buzz 1922- *WorEFlm*
Kulik, Buzz 1923?- *FilmEn, FilmgC, HalFC 80*
Kulik, Seymour *IntMPA 77, -75, -76, -78, -79, -80*
Kulka, Henry d1965 *WhoHol B*
Kulka, Janos 1929- *WhoMus 72, WhoOp 76*
Kulka, Konstanty 1947- *WhoMus 72*
Kulkavich, Bomber *WhScrn 74, -77*
Kulky, Henry 1911-1965 *WhScrn 74, -77, WhoHrs 80[port]*
Kulky, Henry 1912-1965 *ForYSC*
Kullak *NewGrD 80*
Kullak, Adolf 1823-1862 *Baker 78*
Kullak, Adolph 1823-1862 *NewGrD 80*
Kullak, Ernst 1855-1914 *NewGrD 80*
Kullak, Franz 1844-1913 *Baker 78, NewGrD 80*
Kullak, Theodor 1818-1882 *Baker 78, NewGrD 80, OxMus*
Kulle, Jarl 1927- *FilmEn, WorEFlm*
Kullenbo, Lars Bertil 1942- *WhoOp 76*
Kuller, Sid C 1910- *AmSCAP 66, -80*
Kullman, Charles 1903- *Baker 78, CmOp, IntWWM 77, -80, MusSN[port], NewEOp 71, NewGrD 80*
Kullmann, Charles 1903- *BiDAmM*
Kullnes, Ake Arik Salomon 1910- *IntWWM 77*
Kulp, Nancy 1919?- *ForYSC, HalFC 80, WhoHol A*
Kulthum, Ibrahim Umm *NewGrD 80*
Kulukundis, Eddie 1932- *WhoThe 72, -77*
Kuluva, Will *WhoHol A*
Kuma, Profulla *Film 2*
Kumari, Meena 1932-1972 *WhScrn 77*
Kumchachi, Madame 1843- *WhThe*
Kumel, Harry 1940- *BiDFilm, -81*
Kumer, Zmaga 1924- *NewGrD 80*
Kummel, Werner Friedrich 1936- *IntWWM 77, -80*
Kummer, Clare 1888-1958 *AmSCAP 66, -80, NotNAT B, WhThe*
Kummer, Frederic Arnold 1873-1943 *NotNAT B, WhThe*
Kummer, Friedrich August 1797-1879 *Baker 78, NewGrD 80*
Kummer, Kaspar 1795-1870 *Baker 78*
Kummerfeld, Karoline 1745-1814 *EncWT*
Kummerfeld, Karoline 1745-1815 *OxThe*
Kummerle, Salomon 1832-1896 *NewGrD 80*
Kummerle, Salomon 1838-1896 *Baker 78*
Kumpan, Jan *NewGrD 80*
Kumudini 1930- *CnOxB*
Kun, Magda 1911-1945 *WhScrn 74, -77, WhoHol B*
Kun, Magda 1912-1945 *NotNAT B, WhThe*
Kun, Tobias *NewGrD 80*
Kun, Zsuzsa 1934- *CnOxB*
Kunad, Rainer 1936- *Baker 78, IntWWM 77, -80, NewGrD 80*
Kunakova, Lubov 1951- *CnOxB*
Kunc, Bozidar 1903-1964 *Baker 78, ConAmC, NewGrD 80*
Kunc, Jan 1883-1976 *Baker 78, NewGrD 80*
Kunde, Al 1888-1952 *WhScrn 74, -77*
Kunde, Anna d1960 *WhoHol B*
Kunde, Anne 1896-1960 *WhScrn 74, -77*
Kundera, Ludvik 1891-1971 *NewGrD 80*
Kunert, Kurt 1911- *IntWWM 77, -80*
Kunhenn, Paul *WomWMM*
Kuninska-Opacka, Maria 1918- *IntWWM 80*
Kunits, Luigi Von 1870-1931 *Baker 78, BiDAmM*
Kunitz, Richard E 1919- *AmSCAP 66, -80*
Kunkel, Charles 1840-1923 *Baker 78*
Kunkel, Franz Joseph 1808-1880 *Baker 78*
Kunkel, George 1867-1937 *WhScrn 74, -77, WhoHol B*
Kunkel, Jacob 1846-1882 *Baker 78*
Kunkle, George *Film 2*
Kunneke, Eduard 1885-1953 *Baker 78, NewGrD 80, WhThe*
Kuno, Motoji *IntMPA 77, -75, -76, -78, -79, -80*
Kunsemuller, Ernst 1885-1918 *Baker 78*
Kunsman, Roman 1941- *EncJzS 70*
Kunspeck, Michael *NewGrD 80*
Kunst, Jaap 1891-1960 *NewGrD 80*
Kunst, Jakob 1891-1960 *NewGrD 80*
Kunst, Jos 1936- *Baker 78, NewGrD 80*
Kuntaric, Ljubo 1925- *IntWWM 77*
Kuntner, Rudolf *WhoOp 76*
Kuntz, John B 1938- *AmSCAP 80*
Kuntze, Karl 1817-1883 *Baker 78*
Kuntzen *NewGrD 80*
Kuntzen, Friedrich 1761-1817 *MusMk*
Kunwald, Ernst 1868-1939 *Baker 78*
Kunz, Alfred 1929- *Baker 78*
Kunz, Erich 1909- *CmOp, IntWWM 77, -80, MusSN[port], NewEOp 71, NewGrD 80, WhoOp 76*
Kunz, Ernst 1891- *Baker 78, NewGrD 80*
Kunz, Fred Charly 1906- *IntWWM 77*
Kunz, Harald 1928- *NewGrD 80*
Kunz, Konrad Max 1812-1875 *Baker 78*
Kunz, Ludvik 1914- *IntWWM 77, -80*
Kunz, Mary Lou 1935- *IntWWM 77*
Kunz, Thomas Anton 1756-1830? *NewGrD 80*
Kunze, Caroline *PupTheA SUP*
Kunze, Otto *PupTheA, PupTheA SUP*
Kunze, Stefan 1933- *NewGrD 80*
Kunzen *NewGrD 80*
Kunzen, Adolf Carl 1720-1781 *Baker 78*
Kunzen, Adolph Carl 1720-1781 *NewGrD 80*
Kunzen, F L A 1761-1817 *OxMus*
Kunzen, Friedrich Ludwig Aemilius 1761-1817 *Baker 78, NewGrD 80*
Kunzen, Johann Paul 1696-1757 *NewGrD 80*
Kunzen, Louise Friederica Ulrica 1765-1839 *NewGrD 80*
Kunzova-Misikova, Viera 1942- *IntWWM 77, -80*
Kuo, Chang-Yang 1934- *IntWWM 77, -80*
Kuosma, Kauko Einari 1926- *IntWWM 77, -80*
Kuosmanen, Kari 1946- *Baker 78*
Kupcinet, Karen d1963 *WhoHol B*
Kupcinet, Karyn 1941-1963 *WhScrn 74, -77*
Kupele, David M 1921- *AmSCAP 66, -80*
Kupfer, Harry 1935- *WhoOp 76*
Kupfer, Margarete *Film 2*
Kupferman, Meyer 1926- *AmSCAP 66, -80, BiDAmM, ConAmC, DcCM, NewGrD 80*
Kupfermann, Meyer 1926- *Baker 78*
Kupka, Karel 1927- *NewGrD 80*
Kupka, Stephen Mackenzie 1946- *AmSCAP 80*
Kupkovic, Ladislav 1936- *Baker 78, DcCM, NewGrD 80*
Kupper, Annelies 1906- *CmOp, NewGrD 80*
Kupper, Annelies 1909- *WhoMus 72*
Kupper, W J 1896- *IntMPA 77, -75, -76, -78, -79, -80*
Kuppers, Johannes Theodorus *NewGrD 80*
Kura, Miroslav 1924- *CnOxB*
Kuralt, Charles *NewYTET*
Kurath, Gertrude Prokosch 1903- *NewGrD 80*
Kurau, Warren Peter 1952- *IntWWM 77, -80*
Kurc, Adolf 1913- *AmSCAP 80*
Kurek, Marcin *NewGrD 80*
Kurelek, William 1927- *CreCan 1*
Kurenko, Maria 1897- *WhoMus 72*
Kuretzky, Josef Antonin *NewGrD 80*
Kuretzky, Vaclav Matyas *NewGrD 80*
Kurgapkina, Ninel Alexandrovna 1929- *CnOxB, DancEn 78*
Kuri, Emile 1907- *IntMPA 77, -75, -76, -78, -79, -80*
Kuri, Yoji 1928- *FilmEn, WorEFlm*
Kuri-Aldana, Mario 1931- *Baker 78, DcCM, NewGrD 80*
Kuribayashi, Yoshinobu 1933- *WhoOp 76*
Kurka, Robert 1921-1957 *AmSCAP 80, Baker 78, ConAmC, NewGrD 80*
Kurkiewicz, Ludwik 1906- *IntWWM 80*
Kurmis, Guna Astrid 1926- *IntWWM 77, -80*
Kurnit, Phil *ConMuA 80B*
Kurnitz, Harry 1907-1968 *FilmgC, HalFC 80*
Kurnitz, Harry 1908-1968 *BiE&WWA, NotNAT B, WorEFlm*
Kurnitz, Harry 1909-1968 *FilmEn*
Kuroda, Toyoji 1920- *IntMPA 77, -75, -76, -78, -79, -80*
Kurosawa, Akira 1910- *BiDFilm, -81, ConLC 16, DcFM, FilmEn, FilmgC, HalFC 80, IntMPA 77, -75, -76, -78, -79, -80, MovMk[port], OxFilm, WorEFlm*
Kurpinski, Charles 1785-1857 *OxMus*
Kurpinski, Karol Kazimierz 1785-1857 *Baker 78, NewGrD 80*
Kursaal Flyers *IlEncR*
Kursteiner, Jean Paul 1864-1943 *Baker 78*
Kursunlu, Nazim 1911- *REnWD[port]*
Kurt, Melanie 1880-1941 *Baker 78, BiDAmM, CmOp, NewEOp 71, NewGrD 80*
Kurtag, Gyorgy 1926- *Baker 78, DcCM, NewGrD 80*
Kurth, Ernst 1886-1946 *Baker 78, NewGrD 80*
Kurth, Ernst 1886-1948 *OxMus*
Kurton, Peggy *WhThe*
Kurty, Hella d1954 *NotNAT B, WhThe*
Kurtz, Arthur Digby 1929- *ConAmC*
Kurtz, Edmund 1908- *WhoMus 72*
Kurtz, Edward Frampton 1881-1965 *Baker 78, BiDAmM, ConAmC*
Kurtz, Efrem 1900- *Baker 78, DancEn 78, IntWWM 77, -80, NewGrD 80, WhoMus 72*
Kurtz, Emanuel 1911- *AmSCAP 80*
Kurtz, Eugene Allen 1923- *ConAmC*
Kurtz, Gary 1941- *IntMPA 77, -75, -76, -78, -79, -80*
Kurtz, Joseph Felix Von 1717-1784 *NewGrD 80*
Kurtz, Judith *WomWMM B*
Kurtz, Marjorie 1942- *AmSCAP 66, -80*
Kurtz, S James 1934- *ConAmC, IntWWM 77, -80*
Kurtz, Swoosie *WhoHol A*
Kurtzinger *NewGrD 80, -80*
Kurylewicz, Andrzej Roman 1932- *IntWWM 77, -80*
Kurz, Emile *Film 2*
Kurz, Johann Felix Von 1717-1784 *EncWT*
Kurz, Joseph Felix Von 1715-1784 *NotNAT B, OxThe*
Kurz, Joseph Felix Von 1717-1784 *NewGrD 80*
Kurz, Selma 1874-1933 *Baker 78, CmOp, NewGrD 80*
Kurz, Selma 1875-1933 *MusSN[port], NewEOp 71*
Kurz, Siegfried 1930- *Baker 78, NewGrD 80, WhoOp 76*
Kurz, Vilem 1872-1945 *NewGrD 80*
Kurz-Bernardon, Joseph Felix Von 1717-1784 *NewGrD 80*
Kurzbach, Paul Johannes 1902- *IntWWM 77, -80, NewGrD 80*
Kurzinger *NewGrD 80*
Kurzinger, Fortunatus 1743-1805 *NewGrD 80*
Kurzinger, Ignaz Franz Xaver 1724-1797 *NewGrD 80*
Kurzinger, Johann *NewGrD 80*
Kurzinger, Paul Ignaz 1750-1820? *NewGrD 80*
Kusche, Benno 1916- *CmOp, NewGrD 80, WhoOp 76*
Kusevitsky, Moshe 1899-1966 *Baker 78*
Kusevitsky, Sergey *NewGrD 80*
Kushan, Esmail *DcFM*
Kushner, Cedric *ConMuA 80B*
Kushner, David Zakeri 1935- *IntWWM 77, -80*
Kusmider, Lauren C *WomWMM B*
Kusnetsov, Sviatoslav Petrovich 1930- *CnOxB*

Kusser, Johann Sigismund 1660-1727 *Baker 78, NewGrD 80*
Kussevitsky, Serge *Baker 78*
Kuster, Hermann 1817-1878 *Baker 78*
Kutaka, Geraldine Natsue 1951- *WomWMM B*
Kutb Al-Din *NewGrD 80*
Kutch, Eugene B 1926- *AmSCAP 66*
Kuter, Kay E *ForYSC, WhoHol A*
Kutev, Filip 1903- *Baker 78*
Kutev, Philipp 1903- *NewGrD 80*
Kuthen, Hans-Werner 1938- *IntWWM 80*
Kutscher, Artur 1878-1960 *EncWT*
Kutschera, Elsa 1867-1945 *Baker 78*
Kuttner, Fritz A 1903- *IntWWM 77, -80*
Kutusow, N *Film 2*
Kutz, James Fulton 1880-1976 *AmSCAP 66, -80*
Kutz, Kazimierz 1929- *FilmEn*
Kutzschbach, Hermann Ludwig 1875-1938 *Baker 78*
Kuula, Toivo 1883-1918 *Baker 78, NewGrD 80*
Kuusik, Tiyt 1911- *NewGrD 80*
Kuusisto, Ilkka Taneli 1933- *Baker 78, DcCM, IntWWM 77, -80*
Kuusisto, Taneli 1905- *Baker 78, NewGrD 80*
Kuusoja, Maiju 1925- *WhoOp 76*
Kuwa, George K 1885-1931 *Film 1, -2, WhScrn 77*
Kuyper, Elisabeth 1877-1953 *Baker 78*
Kuypers, Johannes Theodorus *NewGrD 80*
Kuzdo, Victor 1859-1966 *Baker 78*
Kuzell, Christopher 1927- *IntWWM 77, -80*
Kuzmanovic, Milorad 1932- *IntWWM 77, -80*
Kuzmina, Yelena *Film 2*
Kuznetsov, Konstantin Alexeyevich 1883-1953 *NewGrD 80*
Kuznetsova, Maria Nikolayevna 1880-1966 *CmOp, NewGrD 80*
Kuznetzoff, Adia 1890-1954 *WhScrn 74, -77, WhoHol B*
Kuznetzov, Konstantin 1883-1953 *Baker 78*
Kvam, Oddvar S 1927- *IntWWM 80*
Kvandal, Johan 1919- *Baker 78, IntWWM 77, -80, NewGrD 80*
Kvanine, K *Film 2*
Kvapil, Jaroslav 1892-1958 *Baker 78*
Kvapil, Jaroslav 1892-1959 *NewGrD 80*
Kvapil, Radoslav 1934- *IntWWM 77, -80, NewGrD 80*
Kvech, Otomar 1950- *IntWWM 77, -80*
Kvernadze, Alexander 1928- *Baker 78*
Kvernadze, Bidzina Alexander 1928- *NewGrD 80*
Kvernadze, Bidzina Alexandrovich 1928- *NewGrD 80*
Kvet, Jan Miroslav 1887-1961 *NewGrD 80*
Kveton, Jiri 1947- *IntWWM 80*
Kvitka, Klyment 1880-1953 *NewGrD 80*
Kwalwasser, Helen 1927- *Baker 78*
Kwalwasser, Jacob 1894-1927 *Baker 78, OxMus*
Kwan, Nancy 1938- *FilmgC, ForYSC, HalFC 80, MotPP, MovMk, WhoHol A*
Kwan, Nancy 1939- *FilmEn*
Kwanami, Kiyotsugo *REnWD[port]*
Kwartin, Zavel 1874-1953 *BiDAmM*
Kwas, Tone 1934- *AmSCAP 80*
Kwasnicka, Ursula 1943- *IntWWM 77, -80*
Kwast, James 1852-1927 *Baker 78*
Kweder, Charles J 1928- *AmSCAP 66, -80*
Kweskin, Jim *ConMuA 80A, EncFCWM 69, IlEncR*
Kweskin, Jim Jug Band *BiDAmM*
Kwiatkowski, Ryszard 1931- *IntWWM 77, -80, NewGrD 80*
Kwit, Nathaniel Troy, Jr. 1941- *IntMPA 77, -75, -76, -78, -79, -80*
Kwouk, Burt 1930- *HalFC 80*
Kya-Hill, Robert 1930- *DrBlPA*
Kyasht, Lydia *Film 2*
Kyasht, Lydia 1886- *WhThe*
Kyasht, Lydia Georgievna 1885-1959 *CnOxB, DancEn 78*
Kyd, Thomas 1558-1594 *CnThe, EncWT, Ent, McGEWD, NotNAT A, -B, OxThe, PlP&P, REnWD[port]*
Kydd, Sam 1917- *FilmgC, HalFC 80, WhoHol A*
Kyhm, Carl *NewGrD 80*
Kyle, Alex *Film 1*
Kyle, Austin C 1893-1916 *WhScrn 77*
Kyle, Billy 1914-1966 *CmpEPM, IlEncJ, WhoJazz 72*
Kyle, Howard d1950 *NotNAT B*
Kyle, William Osborne 1914-1966 *BiDAmM*
Kylian, Jiri 1947- *CnOxB*
Kymlicka, Milan 1936- *IntWWM 80*
Kynard, Charles E 1933- *BiDAmM, EncJzS 70*
Kynaston, Edward 1640?-1706 *Ent, NotNAT B, OxThe, PlP&P*
Kynaston, Nicolas 1941- *IntWWM 80, NewGrD 80*
Kynaston, Trent P 1946- *ConAmC*
Kyo, Machiko 1924- *FilmEn, FilmgC, HalFC 80, IntMPA 77, -75, -76, -78, -79, -80, MotPP, OxFilm, WhoHol A, WorEFlm*
Kyr, Robert Harry 1952- *ConAmC*
Kyriaki, Margarita *WhoOp 76*
Kyriakou, Rena 1918- *NewGrD 80*
Kyrle, Judith d1922 *NotNAT B*
Kyrou, Ado 1923- *OxFilm*
Kyrton *NewGrD 80*
Kyrzinger *NewGrD 80*
Kysar, Michael 1943- *IntWWM 77*
Kyser, Kay *AmPS A, -B, BgBands 74[port]*
Kyser, Kay 1897- *FilmEn, FilmgC, HalFC 80*
Kyser, Kay 1905- *BiDAmM, ForYSC, WhoHol A*
Kyser, Kay 1906- *CmpEPM, What 4[port]*
Kytson, Sir Thomas *OxMus*
Kyui, Tsezar Antonovich *NewGrD 80*
Kyung-Wha, Chung 1948- *Baker 78*
Kyurkchiiski, Krasimir 1936- *NewGrD 80*
Kyzlink, Jan 1930- *IntWWM 77, -80*

L

L T D *RkOn 2[port]*
La Beausse *NewGrD 80*
Laade, Wolfgang Karl 1925- *IntWWM 77, -80*
Laage, Barbara 1925- *FilmEn, FilmgC, HalFC 80, WhoHol A*
Laakmann, Willem *WhoOp 76*
Labach, Parker 1918- *ConAmC*
LaBadie, Florence 1893-1917 *FilmEn, Film 1, MotPP, NotNAT B, TwYS, WhScrn 77, WhoHol B*
Laban, Rudolf Von 1879-1958 *CnOxB, DancEn 78, NewGrD 80, OxMus*
Labar, Daniel 1944- *ConAmC*
LaBar, Tom 1938- *NatPD[port]*
LaBarbara, Joan 1947- *AmSCAP 80, Baker 78*
LaBarbera, Joe 1948- *EncJzS 70*
LaBarbera, John 1945- *EncJzS 70*
LaBarbera, Joseph James 1948- *EncJzS 70*
LaBarbera, Pascel 1944- *EncJzS 70*
LaBarbera, Pat 1944- *EncJzS 70*
LaBarre *NewGrD 80*
LaBarre, Anne De 1628-1688? *NewGrD 80*
LaBarre, Joseph De 1633-1678? *NewGrD 80*
LaBarre, Kenneth Archer 1915- *IntWWM 77, -80*
LaBarre, Michel De 1675?-1744? *NewGrD 80[port]*
LaBarre, Pierre d1600 *NewGrD 80*
LaBarre, Pierre De 1592-1656 *NewGrD 80*
LaBarre, Pierre De 1634-1710? *NewGrD 80*
Labarre, Theodore 1805-1870 *Baker 78, NewGrD 80*
LaBassee, Adam De d1286 *Baker 78, NewGrD 80*
Labatt, Leonard 1838-1897 *Baker 78*
Labaun *NewGrD 80*
Labaun, Jiri *NewGrD 80*
Labaun, Jiri Ondrej *NewGrD 80*
L'abbe *NewGrD 80*
L'abbe, Joseph-Barnabe Saint-Sevin 1727-1803 *Baker 78, NewGrD 80*
L'abbe, Pierre-Philippe Saint-Sevin 1700?-1768 *NewGrD 80*
L'abbe, Pierre Saint-Sevin 1710?-1777 *NewGrD 80*
Labbette, Dora 1898- *NewGrD 80*
LaBelle *ConMuA 80A[port], IlEncR[port], RkOn 2[port]*
Labelle, Nicole 1946- *IntWWM 80*
LaBelle, Patti *BiDAmM*
LaBelle, Patti And The Blue Belles *RkOn*
Laberius, Decimus *OxThe*
Labey, Marcel 1875-1968 *Baker 78, NewGrD 80*
Labhart, Walter 1944- *IntWWM 80*
Labia, Fausta 1870-1935 *Baker 78*
Labia, Maria 1880-1953 *Baker 78, NewGrD 80*
Labiche, Eugene 1815-1888 *CnThe, EncWT, Ent, McGEWD[port], NotNAT B, OxThe, REnWD[port]*
Labis, Attilio 1936- *CnOxB, DancEn 78*
LaBissoniere, Erin *Film 2*
Labitzky *NewGrD 80*
Labitzky, August 1832-1903 *Baker 78, NewGrD 80*
Labitzky, Joseph 1802-1881 *Baker 78, NewGrD 80*
Labitzky, Wilhelm 1829-1871 *NewGrD 80*
Lablache, Luibi d1914 *WhThe*
Lablache, Luigi 1794-1858 *Baker 78, BnBkM 80, CmOp[port], NewEOp 71, NewGrD 80[port], OxMus*
Labo, Flaviano Mario 1927- *WhoOp 76*
Labor, Josef 1842-1924 *Baker 78, NewGrD 80*
LaBorde, Jean-Baptiste De 1730-1777 *NewGrD 80*
Laborde, Jean-Benjamin De 1734-1794 *Baker 78*
LaBorde, Jean-Benjamin De 1734-1794 *NewGrD 80*
Labouchere, Henry d1912 *NotNAT B*
Labouchere, Mrs. Henry *OxThe*
Laboun *NewGrD 80*
Labounsky, Ann 1939- *IntWWM 77, -80*
Labounty, Edwin Murray 1927- *ConAmC*
LaBrake, Harrison 1891-1936 *WhScrn 77*
Labreche, Gaetan 1931- *CreCan 1*
Labro, Philippe 1936- *FilmEn*
Labroca, Mario 1896-1973 *Baker 78, NewGrD 80*
Labrunie, Gerard *NewGrD 80*
Labunski, Feliks Roderyk 1892- *NewGrD 80*
Labunski, Felix 1892- *AmSCAP 66, Baker 78, ConAmC, DcCM*
Labunski, Wiktor 1895-1974 *Baker 78, ConAmC, IntWWM 77, -80, NewGrD 80, WhoMus 72*
LaCalprenede, Gautier DeCostes De 1614-1663 *OxThe*
Lacarse, Esther M *PupTheA*
LaCasiniere, Yves De 1897-1971 *NewGrD 80*
Lacassagne, Joseph 1720?-1780? *NewGrD 80*
LaCava, Gregory 1892-1949 *BiDFilm, -81, DcFM, MovMk[port], OxFilm*
LaCava, Gregory 1892-1952 *AmFD, FilmEn, FilmgC, HalFC 80, TwYS A, WorEFlm*
Lacaze, Peter 1893- *NewOrJ*
Laccetti, Guido 1879-1943 *Baker 78*
LaCentra, Peg 1917?- *CmpEPM*
Lacepede, Bernard G E Medard, Count Of 1756-1825 *NewGrD 80*
Lacerda, Francisco De 1869-1934 *Baker 78, NewGrD 80*
Lacerda, Osvaldo 1927- *DcCM, IntWWM 77, -80, NewGrD 80*
Lacerna, Estacio De *NewGrD 80*
Lacey, Catherine 1904-1979 *FilmgC, HalFC 80, WhoHol A, WhoThe 72, -77*
Lacey, Franklin 1917- *BiE&WWA*
Lacey, Jack 1911-1965 *CmpEPM, WhoJazz 72*
Lacey, Li'l Mack *NewOrJ*
Lacey, Marion d1915 *NotNAT B*
Lacey, Mary 1909-1978 *AmSCAP 66, -80*
Lach, Robert 1874-1958 *Baker 78, NewGrD 80*
Lachapelle, Andree *CreCan 1*
LaChapelle, Jacques De *NewGrD 80*
LaChapelle, Jean De 1655-1723 *OxThe*
LaChaussee, Pierre-Claude Nivelle De 1692-1754 *EncWT, Ent, McGEWD, OxThe*
Lachenet, Didier *NewGrD 80*
Lachenmann, Helmut Friedrich 1935- *Baker 78, DcCM, NewGrD 80*
Lachert, Hanna Katarzyna 1944- *IntWWM 77, -80*
LaChevardiere, Louis Balthazard De 1730-1812 *NewGrD 80*
Lachlan, Jean *PupTheA*
Lachman, Hans 1906- *NewGrD 80*
Lachman, Harry 1886-1975 *FilmEn, FilmgC, HalFC 80, IlWWBF, WhoHrs 80*
Lachman, Heinz 1906- *NewGrD 80*
Lachman, Mort *NewYTET*
Lachmann, Robert 1892-1939 *Baker 78, NewGrD 80, OxMus*
Lachmund, Carl Valentine 1857-1928 *Baker 78, BiDAmM*
Lachner *NewGrD 80*
Lachner, Christiane *OxMus*
Lachner, Franz 1803-1890 *Baker 78, CmOp, NewGrD 80, OxMus*
Lachner, Ignaz 1807-1895 *Baker 78, NewGrD 80, OxMus*
Lachner, Thekla *OxMus*
Lachner, Theodor 1788-1877 *NewGrD 80, OxMus*
Lachner, Vincenz 1811-1893 *Baker 78, NewGrD 80, OxMus*
Lachner, Vinzenz 1811-1893 *NewGrD 80*
Lachnith, Louis-Wenceslas 1746-1820 *NewGrD 80*
Lachnith, Ludwig Wenzel 1746-1820 *Baker 78, NewGrD 80*
Lachnitt, Louis-Wenceslas 1746-1820 *NewGrD 80*
Lachnitt, Ludwig Wenzel 1746-1820 *NewGrD 80*
Lachoff, Sol 1911- *AmSCAP 66, -80*
Lachout, Karel 1929- *IntWWM 77, -80*
Lachow, Stan 1931- *NatPD[port]*
Laciar, Samuel Line 1874-1943 *BiDAmM*
Lack, Edwin Arthur 1934- *IntWWM 77, -80*
Lack, Simon 1917- *WhoHol A, WhoThe 72, -77*
Lack, Theodore 1846-1921 *Baker 78*
Lackaye, James 1867-1919 *Film 1, WhScrn 77*
Lackaye, Wilton 1862-1932 *Film 1, -2, NotNAT B, OxThe, WhScrn 74, -77, WhThe, WhoHol B, WhoStg 1906, -1908*
Lackey, Douglas M 1932- *AmSCAP 66, -80, ConAmC A*
Lackey, Kenneth d1976 *NotNAT B*
Lackovic, Olga Gavro 1937- *WhoOp 76*
Lackteen, Frank 1894-1968 *Film 1, -2, ForYSC, HolCA[port], TwYS, Vers B[port], WhScrn 74, -77, WhoHol B, WhoHrs 80*
Lacombe, Georges 1902- *DcFM, FilmEn*
Lacombe, Louis 1818-1884 *Baker 78, NewGrD 80, OxMus*

Lacombe, Paul 1837-1927 *Baker 78, NewGrD 80, OxMus*
Lacome, Paul 1838-1920 *Baker 78, NewGrD 80*
Lacome D'Estalenx, Paul 1838-1920 *NewGrD 80*
Lacorcia, Scipione 1585?-1620? *NewGrD 80*
LaCosta *IlEncCM[port]*
Lacoste, Louis De 1675?-175-? *NewGrD 80*
Lacoste, M *Film 2*
Lacotte, Pierre 1932- *CnOxB, DancEn 78*
Lacoume, Emile 1885-1946 *NewOrJ[port]*
Lacour, Jose Andre 1919- *CnMD*
LaCour, Niels 1944- *IntWWM 80*
LaCourt, Antoine *NewGrD 80*
LaCourt, Henri *NewGrD 80*
Lacroix, Antoine 1756-1806 *NewGrD 80*
LaCroix, Francois De 1683-1759 *NewGrD 80*
Lacroix, Richard 1939- *CreCan 1*
LaCrotte, Nicolas De *NewGrD 80*
Lacy, Frank 1867-1937 *NotNAT B, WhThe*
Lacy, George 1904- *WhThe*
Lacy, James d1774 *NotNAT B*
Lacy, Jerry *WhoHol A*
Lacy, John d1681 *NotNAT B, OxThe, PIP&P*
Lacy, John d1865? *NewGrD 80*
Lacy, Michael Rophino 1795-1867 *NewGrD 80*
Lacy, Robin T 1920- *BiE&WWA*
Lacy, Roger De d1212 *OxMus*
Lacy, Rophino d1867 *NotNAT B*
Lacy, Rubin 1901-1972? *BluesWW[port]*
Lacy, Steve 1934- *BiDAmM, EncJzS 70, IlEncJ*
Lacy, Thomas Hailes d1873 *NotNAT B*
Lacy, Walter d1898 *NotNAT B*
Lada, Anton 1890-1944 *AmSCAP 66, -80*
Lada, Anton 1893- *NewOrJ*
Lada, Kazimierz 1824-1871 *NewGrD 80*
Ladah *Film 2*
Ladd, Alan 1913-1964 *BiDFilm, -81, CmMov, FilmEn, FilmgC, ForYSC, HalFC 80[port], MotPP, MovMk[port], NotNAT B, OxFilm, WhScrn 74, -77, WhoHol B, WhoHrs 80, WorEFlm*
Ladd, Alan, Jr. 1937- *IntMPA 77, -78, -79, -80*
Ladd, Alan, Jr. 1938- *FilmEn, IntMPA 76*
Ladd, Alana 1943- *ForYSC, WhoHol A*
Ladd, Cheryl 1951- *HalFC 80*
Ladd, David 1947- *FilmEn, ForYSC, MotPP, WhoHol A*
Ladd, Diane 1932- *FilmEn, HalFC 80, WhoHol A*
Ladd, Helena Solberg *WomWMM B*
Lade, John 1916- *WhoMus 72*
Ladegast, Friedrich 1818-1905 *NewGrD 80*
Laderman, Ezra 1924- *AmSCAP 66, -80, Baker 78, CpmDNM 78, -80, ConAmC, DcCM, NewGrD 80*
Ladewski, Kazimierz *NewGrD 80*
Ladigin, Donald R 1939- *ConAmC*
Ladmiral, Nicole 1931-1958 *WhScrn 74, -77, WhoHol B*
Ladmirault, Paul-Emile 1877-1944 *Baker 78, NewGrD 80*
Ladnier, Tommy 1900-1939 *BiDAmM, CmpEPM, IlEncJ, MusMk, NewOrJ[port], WhoJazz 72*
LaDouardiere, Henri De *NewGrD 80*
Ladowski, Kazimierz *NewGrD 80*
Ladre, Marian *DancEn 78*
Ladunka, Naum 1730-1782 *Baker 78*
Ladurner, Ignace Antoine 1766-1839 *NewGrD 80*
Ladurner, Ignaz Anton Franz Xaver 1766-1839 *Baker 78*
Ladurner, Josef Alois 1769-1851 *NewGrD 80*
Lady *Film 2*
Lady Day *NewGrD 80*
Lady Gregory *PIP&P[port]*
Ladysz, Bernard 1922- *NewGrD 80*
Laemmele, Beth *Film 2*
Laemmle, Carl, Jr. 1908- *FilmgC, HalFC 80, TwYS B*
Laemmle, Carl, Jr. 1908-1979 *FilmEn*
Laemmle, Carl, Sr. 1867-1939 *BiDFilm 81, DcFM, FilmEn, FilmgC, HalFC 80, OxFilm, TwYS B, WhScrn 74, -77, WorEFlm*
Laemmle, Edward 1887- *TwYS A*
Laemmle, Ernst 1900- *TwYS A*
Laerkesen, Anna 1942- *CnOxB, DancEn 78[port]*
Laet, Jan De 1525?-1567? *NewGrD 80*
Laet, Jean De 1525?-1567? *NewGrD 80*
Laetrius, Petit Jean *NewGrD 80*
LaFage, Adrien De 1805-1862 *NewGrD 80*
LaFage, Jean De *NewGrD 80*
LaFage, Juste-Adrien-Lenoir De 1801-1862 *Baker 78*
Lafarge, Guy Pierre-Marie 1904- *WhoMus 72*
LaFarge, P De *NewGrD 80*
LaFarge, Peter 1931-1965 *BiDAmM, EncFCWM 69*
LaFaro, Scott 1936-1961 *BiDAmM*
LaFaya, Aurelio *NewGrD 80*
Lafaye, Georges *DcPup*
Lafaye, Ogden 1896- *NewOrJ*
Lafayette 1872-1911 *MagIlD*
Lafayette, Andree *Film 2*
Lafayette, Ruby 1844-1935 *Film 1, -2, TwYS, WhoHol B*
Lafayette, Ruby 1845-1935 *WhScrn 74, -77*
Lafayettes, The *RkOn*
LaFeillee, Francois De d1780? *NewGrD 80*
LaFerla, Sandro 1941- *WhoOp 76*
Laferriere, Adolphe d1877 *NotNAT B*
Laffan, Kevin Barry 1922- *ConDr 73, -77, EncWT, WhoThe 72, -77*
Laffan, Patricia 1919- *FilmgC, HalFC 80, WhThe, WhoHol A, WhoThe 72*
Lafferty, Donald 1942- *ConAmC*
Lafferty, Karen 1948- *AmSCAP 80*
Lafferty, Perry *IntMPA 75, -76, NewYTET*
Lafferty, Wilson d1962 *NotNAT B*
Laffey, James *Film 1*
L'Affilard, Michel 1656?-1708 *Baker 78, NewGrD 80*
L'Affillard, Michel 1656?-1708 *NewGrD 80*
Laffitte, Frank 1901- *IntWWM 77, -80, WhoMus 72*
Lafford, Lindsay Arthur James 1912- *IntWWM 77*
Lafitte, Jose White *NewGrD 80*
LaFleche, Marie Marguerite L Gisele *CreCan 2*
LaFleur *OxThe*
LaFleur, Francois Juvenon *OxThe*
LaFleur, Joy 1914-1957 *WhScrn 74, -77, WhoHol B*
LaFollette, Fola 1882-1970 *BiE&WWA, NotNAT B*
Lafon, Madeleine 1924-1967 *CnOxB, DancEn 78*
LaFonde, Virginia *Film 2*
Lafont, Bernadette 1938- *FilmAG WE, FilmEn*
Lafont, Charles-Philippe 1781-1839 *Baker 78, NewGrD 80*
Lafont, Pierre d1873 *NotNAT B*
Lafontaine, Mademoiselle De 1655?-1738? *CnOxB*
Lafontaine, Mademoiselle De 1665?-1738? *DancEn 78*
LaFontaine, Jean De 1621-1695 *DcPup, NewEOp 71, NewGrD 80*
LaForge, Frank 1877-1953 *BiDAmM, ConAmC*
LaForge, Frank 1879-1953 *AmSCAP 66, -80, Baker 78*
LaForge, Jack 1924-1966 *AmSCAP 66, -80*
LaFosse, Antoine D'Aubigny De 1653-1708 *McGEWD, OxThe*
LaFosse, Leopold 1928- *IntWWM 77, -80*
LaFrance *OxThe*
LaFrenais, Ian 1938?- *HalFC 80*
LaFreniere, Charles F 1914- *AmSCAP 66, -80*
LaFreniere, Emma P 1881-1961 *AmSCAP 66, -80*
Laga, Dolores 1933- *CnOxB*
Lagace, Bernard 1930- *CreCan 1, IntWWM 77, -80, NewGrD 80*
Lagace, Mireille Begin 1935- *CreCan 1*
LaGarde, Henri *Film 2*
Lagarde, Jocelyne *WhoHol A*
Lagarde, John *NewGrD 80*
LaGarde, Pierre De 1717-1792? *NewGrD 80*
LaGarsa *NewGrD 80*
Lagarto, Pedro De *NewGrD 80*
LaGassey, Homer *ConAmC*
Lageard, Guido Nello Eric 1933- *IntWWM 77*
Lagerborg, Anne-Marie 1919- *CnOxB, DancEn 78*
Lagerkvist, Par 1891-1974 *CnMD, CnThe, EncWT, Ent, McGEWD[port], ModWD, OxThe, REnWD[port]*
Lagerlof, Selma 1858-1940 *NewEOp 71, OxFilm*
Lagesen, Ruth 1914- *IntWWM 77, -80*
Lagger, Peter 1930- *IntWWM 77, -80, WhoOp 76*
Laghezza, Rosa 1939- *WhoOp 76*
Lagidze, Revaz Il'yich 1921- *NewGrD 80*
Lagkhner, Daniel 1550?-1607? *NewGrD 80*
Lago, Giovanni Del *NewGrD 80*
Lago, Roberto *DcPup, PupTheA*
Lagoanere, Oscar De 1853-1918 *Baker 78*
LaGrange 1639-1692 *EncWT*
LaGrange, Achille 1636-1709 *OxThe*
LaGrange, Charles Varlet 1639-1692 *Ent, NotNAT B, OxThe*
Lagrange, Felix d1901 *NotNAT B*
Lagrange, Joseph-Louis 1736-1813 *NewGrD 80*
Lagrange, Louise *Film 2*
LaGrange, Marie 1639-1737 *NotNAT B, OxThe*
LaGrange-Chancel, Joseph De 1677-1758 *NotNAT B, OxThe*
LaGrotte, Nicolas De 1530-1600? *NewGrD 80*
Lagudio, Paolo *NewGrD 80*
LaGuere, George *Film 2*
LaGuerre, Elisabeth-Claude Jacquet De 1659-1729 *Baker 78, MusMk, NewGrD 80*
Laguerre, John 1700?-1748 *NewGrD 80*
Laguerre, Marie-Josephine 1755-1783 *NewGrD 80*
LaGuerre, Michel De 1605?-1679 *Baker 78, NewGrD 80*
LaHache, Theodor Von *BiDAmM*
LaHalle, Adam De *NewGrD 80*
LaHarpe, Jean-Francois De 1739-1802 *OxThe*
LaHarpe, Jean Francois De 1739-1803 *NewGrD 80*
Lahee, Henry 1826-1912 *Baker 78*
Lahee, Henry Charles 1856-1953 *Baker 78, OxMus*
LaHele, George De 1547-1587 *Baker 78, NewGrD 80*
LaHire, Philippe De 1640-1718 *NewGrD 80*
Lahire, Philippe De 1640-1719 *Baker 78*
Lahm, David Fields 1940- *AmSCAP 80*
Lahmer, Reuel 1912- *AmSCAP 66, ConAmC, NewGrD 80*
LaHoussaye, Pierre 1735-1818 *Baker 78, NewGrD 80*
Lahr, Bert *AmPS B*
Lahr, Bert 1895-1967 *BiE&WWA, CmpEPM, CnThe, EncMT, Ent[port], FamA&A[port], FilmEn, ForYSC, Funs[port], JoeFr[port], MotPP, MovMk[port], NotNAT A, -B, PIP&P[port], WhScrn 74, -77, WhThe, WhoHol B*
Lahr, Bert 1895-1968 *FilmgC, HalFC 80, WhoHrs 80[port]*
Lahr, John 1941- *ConAmTC, NotNAT, WhoThe 77*
Lahtinen, Warner H Duke 1910-1968 *WhScrn 74, -77*
Lai, Francis 1932- *FilmEn*
Lai, Francis 1933?- *FilmgC, HalFC 80, OxFilm*
Lai, Francois *NewGrD 80*
Laidlaw, Anna Robena 1819-1901 *Baker 78*
Laidlaw, Ethan 1899-1963 *WhScrn 74, -77, WhoHol B*
Laidlaw, Ethan 1900-1963 *Film 2*
Laidlaw, Roy *Film 1, -2, TwYS*
Laidler, Francis 1870-1955 *NotNAT B, WhThe*
Laidley, Alice *Film 2*
Laidlow, Ethan 1900-1963 *ForYSC*
Laiglesia, Juan Antonio De 1917- *McGEWD*
Laiglesia Gonzalez Labarga, Alvaro De 1921- *McGEWD*
Laiman, Leah *WomWMM B*
Lainati, Carlo Ambrogio *NewGrD 80*
Laine, Alfred 1895-1957 *NewOrJ*
Laine, Cleo 1927- *DrBlPA, EncJzS 70, IlEncJ, IntWWM 80, NewGrD 80, WhoMus 72*

Laine, Denny *ConMuA 80A*
Laine, Doris 1931- *CnOxB, DancEn 78[port]*
Laine, Edwin 1905- *DcFM*
Laine, Flora Spraker 1924- *AmSCAP 66, -80*
Laine, Frankie 1913- *AmPS A, -B, AmSCAP 66, -80, BiDAmM, CmpEPM, FilmEn, FilmgC, ForYSC, HalFC 80, RkOn, WhoHol A*
Laine, George Vitelle 1873-1966 *BiDAmM, EncJzS 70*
Laine, Julian 1907-1957 *NewOrJ[port], WhoJazz 72*
Laine, Papa Jack 1873-1966 *EncJzS 70, NewOrJ[port], WhoJazz 72*
Laing, Alan 1944- *IntWWM 80*
Laing, David William 1940- *WhoMus 72*
Laing, Hugh 1911- *CnOxB, DancEn 78*
Laing, Peggie 1899- *WhThe*
Laing, Tony *Film 2*
Lair, Grace d1955 *WhScrn 74, -77*
Lair, John Lee 1894- *BiDAmM, IlEncCM*
Lairce, Margaret *Film 1*
Laird, Bruce *ConAmC*
Laird, Jack *NewYTET*
Laird, Jenny 1917- *FilmgC, HalFC 80, WhoHol A, WhoThe 72, -77*
Laird, Richard Quentin 1941- *EncJzS 70*
Laird, Rick 1941- *EncJzS 70*
Laire, Judson *WhoHol A*
Laires, Fernando 1925- *WhoMus 72*
Laires, Janet Lockhart 1938- *IntWWM 80*
Lais, Johan Dominico *NewGrD 80*
Laistner, Max 1853-1917 *Baker 78*
Lait, Jack 1883-1954 *NotNAT B, WhScrn 77*
LaJana 1905-1940 *WhScrn 77*
Lajarte, Theodore-Edouard Dufaure De 1826-1890 *Baker 78, NewGrD 80*
Lajeunesse, Emma *NewGrD 80*
Lajeunesse, Marie Louise Cecilia Emma *Baker 78*
Lajeunesse, Marie-Louise Emma Cecile *CreCan 2*
Lajos, Lajos Dohanyi *CreCan 1*
Lajovic, Anton 1878-1960 *NewGrD 80*
Lajtha, Laszlo 1892-1963 *Baker 78, DcCM, NewGrD 80*
Lakatos, Gabriella 1927- *CnOxB*
Lakatos, Istvan 1895- *NewGrD 80, WhoMus 72*
Lakatos, Stefan Istvan 1895- *IntWWM 77, -80, NewGrD 80*
Lake, Alice 1896-1967 *FilmEn, Film 1, -2, ForYSC, MotPP, TwYS, WhScrn 74, -77, WhoHol B*
Lake, Arthur 1905- *FilmEn, Film 1, -2, FilmgC, ForYSC, Funs[port], HalFC 80, IntMPA 77, -75, -76, -78, -79, -80, MotPP, MovMk, TwYS, What 2[port], WhoHol A*
Lake, Bonnie 1920- *AmSCAP 66, -80*
Lake, Candace *WomWMM B*
Lake, Florence *Film 2, WhoHol A*
Lake, Frank 1849-1936 *WhScrn 74, -77, WhoHol B*
Lake, George Ernest 1854-1893 *Baker 78*
Lake, Gregg *ConMuA 80B*
Lake, Harriet *FilmEn*
Lake, Harriette *Film 2*
Lake, Harry 1885-1947 *WhScrn 74, -77*
Lake, Ian Thomson 1935- *IntWWM 77, -80, WhoMus 72*
Lake, Janet *WhoHol A*
Lake, John 1904-1960 *WhScrn 74, -77*
Lake, Larry Ellsworth 1943- *IntWWM 80*
Lake, Leslie John Frederick 1944- *IntWWM 77, -80*
Lake, Lew d1939 *NotNAT B, WhThe*
Lake, Mary 1913- *WhoMus 72*
Lake, Meyhew Lester 1879-1955 *AmSCAP 66, -80*
Lake, Molly 1900- *CnOxB*
Lake, Molly 1909- *DancEn 78*
Lake, Oliver 1944?- *EncJzS 70*
Lake, Oliver Eugene 1942- *AmSCAP 80*
Lake, Sol 1932- *AmSCAP 80*
Lake, Veronica d1973 *MotPP, WhoHol B*
Lake, Veronica 1919-1973 *BiDFilm, -81, FilmEn, FilmgC, ForYSC, HalFC 80[port], MovMk[port], OxFilm, What 1[port], WhoHrs 80, WomWMM, WorEFlm*
Lake, Veronica 1921-1973 *WhScrn 77*
Lake, Wesley *Film 2*
Lakhdar Amina, Mohamed 1934- *DcFM*
Lakner, Yehoshua 1924- *Baker 78, DcCM, NewGrD 80*
Laks, Simon 1901- *Baker 78*
Laks, Szymon 1901- *NewGrD 80*
Lakso, Edward Joseph 1932- *AmSCAP 80*
Lal, Chatur 1925-1965 *NewGrD 80*
Lala, Joe *NewOrJ*
Lala, John 1893- *NewOrJ*
Lala, Mike 1908-1976 *NewOrJ[port]*
Lalande, Desire Alfred 1866-1904 *NewGrD 80*
Lalande, Maria 1913-1968 *FilmAG WE[port]*
Lalande, Michel Richard De *Baker 78*
Lalande, Michel Richard De 1657-1726 *BnBkM 80, MusMk, NewGrD 80[port], OxMus*
Lalandi, Lina *IntWWM 77, -80, WhoMus 72*
LaLanne, Jack *NewYTET*
LaLaurencie, Lionel De 1861-1933 *Baker 78, NewGrD 80*
Lalewicz, Georg 1875-1951 *Baker 78*
Laliberte, Alfred 1878-1953 *CreCan 2*
Laliberte, Alfred 1882-1952 *Baker 78*
Lalli, Domenico 1679-1741 *NewGrD 80*
Lallouette, Jean Francois 1651-1728 *NewGrD 80*
Lally, Gwen d1963 *WhThe*
Lally, William *WhoHol A*
Lalo, Charles 1877-1953 *Baker 78, NewGrD 80*
Lalo, Edouard 1823-1892 *Baker 78, CmOp, CmpBCM, DcCom 77, DcCom&M 79, GrComp[port], MusMk, NewEOp 71, NewGrD 80[port], OxMus*
Lalo, Edouard 1832-1892 *BnBkM 80*
Lalo, Pierre 1866-1943 *Baker 78, NewGrD 80*
Lalor, Frank 1869-1932 *Film 2, NotNAT B, WhScrn 77, WhThe, WhoHol B*
Lalouette, Jean Francois 1651-1728 *MusMk, NewGrD 80*
Laloy, Louis 1874-1944 *Baker 78, NewGrD 80*
Lam, Basil 1914- *WhoMus 72*
Lama, Lina 1932- *IntWWM 77, -80, WhoMus 72*
Lamac, Karel 1897-1952 *FilmEn*
Lamalle, Pierre 1648?-1722 *NewGrD 80*
Lamanno, Joe *EncFCWM 69*
Lamar, Slim 1900?- *NewOrJ*
LaMara *Baker 78*
Lamarche, Gerard 1918- *WhoOp 76*
LaMarchina, Robert A 1928- *Baker 78, IntWWM 77, -80, WhoOp 76*
Lamare, Hilton 1910- *AmSCAP 66, -80, BiDAmM, EncJzS 70*
Lamare, Hilton Napoleon 1907- *NewOrJ[port]*
Lamare, Nappy 1907- *CmpEPM, WhoJazz 72*
Lamare, Nappy 1910- *EncJzS 70*
LaMarge, Jimmie 1905-1971 *AmSCAP 66*
Lamarge, Jimmie 1905-1971 *AmSCAP 80*
LaMariana, Angelo 1914- *IntWWM 77, -80*
Lamarque, Libertad 1908- *FilmEn*
LaMarr, Barbara *MotPP*
LaMarr, Barbara 1896-1925 *WhScrn 74, WhoHol B*
LaMarr, Barbara 1896-1926 *FilmEn, FilmgC, HalFC 80, MovMk[port], NotNAT B, WhScrn 77*
LaMarr, Barbara 1897-1926 *Film 2, TwYS*
LaMarr, Frank 1904- *AmSCAP 66, -80*
Lamarr, Hedy *IntMPA 77, -75, -76, -78, -79, -80, MotPP*
Lamarr, Hedy 1913- *FilmAG WE, FilmEn, FilmgC, HalFC 80, MovMk[port], ThFT[port], What 4[port]*
Lamarr, Hedy 1914- *BiDFilm, -81, OxFilm*
Lamarr, Hedy 1915- *Film 2, ForYSC, MGM[port], WhoHol A, WorEFlm*
LaMarr, Margaret *Film 2*
LaMarr, Richard d1975 *WhScrn 77, WhoHol C*
LaMarre, De 1630?-1666? *NewGrD 80*
LaMarre, Jacques-Michel-Hurel De 1772-1823 *Baker 78*
LaMarre, Rene T 1907- *AmSCAP 66, -80*
LaMarre, Richard Duane 1912- *AmSCAP 80*
LaMarre, Robert Henri 1917- *AmSCAP 80*
Lamartine 1790-1869 *OxMus*
Lamartine, Alphonse De 1790-1869 *NewEOp 71, NewGrD 80*
LaMartoretta, Giandominico *NewGrD 80*
Lamas, Dulce Martins 1919- *IntWWM 80*
Lamas, Fernando *MotPP*
Lamas, Fernando 1915- *FilmEn, FilmgC, ForYSC, HalFC 80, MGM[port], MovMk, WhoHol A*
Lamas, Fernando 1923- *BiE&WWA*
Lamas, Fernando 1925- *IntMPA 77, -78, -79, -80*
Lamas, Fernando 1926- *IntMPA 75, -76*
Lamas, Jose Angel 1775-1814 *NewGrD 80*
Lamb, A C *MorBAP*
Lamb, Anthony Stuart 1947- *IntWWM 77, -80*
Lamb, Arthur Clifton 1909- *BlkAmP*
Lamb, Arthur J 1870-1928 *AmPS, AmSCAP 66, -80, BiDAmM, Sw&Ld B*
Lamb, Beatrice 1866- *WhThe*
Lamb, Benjamin *NewGrD 80*
Lamb, Charles *WhoHol A*
Lamb, Charles 1775-1834 *NotNAT B, OxMus, OxThe*
Lamb, Florence 1884-1966 *WhScrn 77*
Lamb, Gil 1906- *FilmgC, ForYSC, HalFC 80, IntMPA 77, -75, -76, -78, -79, -80, WhoHol A*
Lamb, Gordon Howard 1934- *IntWWM 77, -80*
Lamb, Hubert Weldon 1900- *ConAmC*
Lamb, John David 1935- *ConAmC*
Lamb, John Lee 1933- *BiDAmM*
Lamb, Joseph F 1887-1960 *AmSCAP 66, -80, BiDAmM, NewGrD 80*
Lamb, Kathleen Norah *WhoMus 72*
Lamb, Marvin Lee 1946- *AmSCAP 80, ConAmC*
Lamb, Molly *CreCan 2*
Lamb, Murray Alexander 1926- *IntWWM 77*
Lamb, Myrna *MorBAP, NatPD[port]*
Lamb, Natalie 1940?- *BluesWW[port]*
Lamb, Walter *PupTheA*
Lambardi, Camillo 1560?-1634 *Baker 78, NewGrD 80*
Lambardi, Francesco 1587-1642 *Baker 78, NewGrD 80*
Lambardi, Girolamo *NewGrD 80*
Lambardo, Girolamo *NewGrD 80*
Lambart, Ernest d1945 *NotNAT B*
Lambart, Evelyn *WomWMM, -B*
Lambart, Richard d1924 *NotNAT B*
Lambdin, John O d1923 *NotNAT B*
Lambe *NewGrD 80*
Lambe, Walter 1450?-1499? *NewGrD 80*
Lambelet, George 1875-1945 *Baker 78*
Lambelet, Napoleon 1864-1932 *NotNAT B, WhThe*
Lambert Ferri *NewGrD 80*
Lambert, Adam 1886?- *NewOrJ*
Lambert, Albert *Film 1*
Lambert, Alexander 1862-1929 *Baker 78, BiDAmM*
Lambert, Barbara Jane 1911- *WhoMus 72*
Lambert, Bertram Buddy 1931- *AmSCAP 80*
Lambert, Billy 1893?-1969 *NewOrJ[port]*
Lambert, Cecily *ConAmC*
Lambert, Clara d1921 *WhScrn 74, -77*
Lambert, Constant 1905-1951 *Baker 78, BnBkM 80, CnOxB, DancEn 78, DcCom&M 79, MusMk[port], NewGrD 80[port], OxMus, WhThe*
Lambert, Dave 1917-1966 *AmSCAP 66, -80, CmpEPM, EncJzS 70*
Lambert, David Alden 1917-1966 *BiDAmM, EncJzS 70*
Lambert, Dennis *ConMuA 80B*
Lambert, Don 1904-1962 *WhoJazz 72*
Lambert, Donald 1904-1962 *BiDAmM*
Lambert, Edward J 1897-1951 *AmSCAP 66, -80*
Lambert, Eugene *DcPup*
Lambert, Gavin 1924- *FilmgC, HalFC 80, WorEFlm*
Lambert, Herbert 1881-1936 *Baker 78, NewGrD 80*
Lambert, Hugh *BiE&WWA, NotNAT*
Lambert, Irene *Film 2*
Lambert, Isabel *DancEn 78*
Lambert, J W 1917- *WhoThe 72, -77*
Lambert, Jack 1899- *FilmgC, HalFC 80,*

WhoHol A, WhoThe 72, –77
Lambert, Jack 1920- FilmEn, FilmgC, ForYSC, HalFC 80, Vers A[port]
Lambert, Jerry AmSCAP 80
Lambert, Johann Heinrich 1728-1777 Baker 78, NewGrD 80
Lambert, John Arthur Neill 1926- NewGrD 80, WhoMus 72
Lambert, Juan Bautista 1884-1945 Baker 78, NewGrD 80
Lambert, Lanny Bruce 1947- AmSCAP 80
Lambert, Lawson 1870-1944 NotNAT B, WhThe
Lambert, Louis 1835-1910 BiDAmM
Lambert, Lucien 1828- BiDAmM
Lambert, Lucien 1858-1945 Baker 78
Lambert, Marcel Amedee 1934- IntWWM 80
Lambert, Margery 1939- CreCan 2
Lambert, Maude AmPS B
Lambert, Michel 1610-1696 Baker 78, NewGrD 80, OxMus
Lambert, Murray 1891- WhoMus 72
Lambert, Patricia 1945- IntWWM 77, –80
Lambert, Paul WhoHol A
Lambert, Pierre-Jean NewGrD 80
Lambert, Scrappy 1901- CmpEPM
Lambert, Sydney 1823- BiDAmM
Lambert, Victor 1917- IntWWM 77, –80
Lambert, Virginia VanHouten 1938- ConAmTC
Lamberti, Professor d1950 NotNAT B, WhScrn 74, –77, WhoHol B
Lambertini NewGrD 80
Lambertini, Ermete NewGrD 80
Lambertini, Evaristo NewGrD 80
Lambertini, Gioacchino 1790-1864 NewGrD 80
Lambertini, Giovan Tomaso NewGrD 80
Lambertini, Michel Angelo NewGrD 80
Lambertus, Magister NewGrD 80
Lambeth, Henry Albert 1822-1895 Baker 78
Lambetti, Ellie 1930- OxFilm
Lambillotte, Louis 1796-1855 Baker 78
Lamble, Lloyd 1914- FilmgC, HalFC 80, WhoHol A
Lambord, Benjamin 1879-1915 Baker 78, ConAmC
Lambrache, George 1937- WhoOp 76
Lambranzi, Gregorio CnOxB, DancEn 78, NewGrD 80[port]
Lambrinos, Vassili 1927?- DancEn 78, WhoHol A
Lambro, Phillip 1935- AmSCAP 66, –80, ConAmC, IntWWM 77, –80
Lambuleti, Johannes NewGrD 80
Lambusta, Joe ConMuA 80B
LaMeri 1898- CnOxB, DancEn 78[port]
Lamhut, Phyllis 1933- CmpGMD, CnOxB
Lami, Eugene Louis 1800-1890 NotNAT B
Lamigeon, Louise 1915- IntWWM 77, –80
LaMilo WhThe
Lamkin, Michael Deane 1945- IntWWM 77, –80
Lamm, Pavel Alexandrovich 1882-1951 Baker 78, NewGrD 80
Lamm, Robert Carson 1922- ConAmC, IntWWM 77, –80
Lamm, Robert William 1944- AmSCAP 80
Lammel, Inge 1924- IntWWM 80
Lammers, Gerda 1915- CmOp, NewGrD 80
Lammers, Julius 1829-1888 Baker 78
Lammers, Paul 1921-1968 NotNAT B
Lamming, Frank Film 2
LaMoeulle, Guillaume De 1485?-1556 NewGrD 80
LaMole, Guillaume De 1485?-1556 NewGrD 80
Lamon, Isabel Film 1
LaMonaca, Riccardo NewGrD 80
Lamond, Don 1920- CmpEPM
Lamond, Felix 1864-1940 BiDAmM
Lamond, Frederic Archibald 1868-1948 Baker 78, NewGrD 80
Lamond, Joyce PupTheA
Lamond, Robert PupTheA
Lamoninary, Jacques-Philippe 1707-1802 NewGrD 80
Lamont, Barbara 1939- DrBlPA
Lamont, Charles 1895- IntMPA 77, –75, –76, –78, –79, –80
Lamont, Charles 1898- FilmEn, FilmgC, HalFC 80, TwYS A, WhoHrs 80
Lamont, Denis 1932- DancEn 78
Lamont, Duncan 1918- FilmgC, HalFC 80, IntMPA 77, –75, –76, –78, –79, –80, WhoHol A
Lamont, Forrest 1885-1937 BiDAmM
LaMont, Frank Film 2
Lamont, George Film 2
LaMont, Harry 1887-1957 Film 2, WhScrn 74, –77, WhoHol B
Lamont, Jack 1893-1956 WhScrn 74, –77, WhoHol B
Lamont, Molly 1910- IlWWBF
Lamont, Victor AmSCAP 80
LaMontaine, John 1920- AmSCAP 66, –80, Baker 78, CpmDNM 76, ConAmC, DcCM, IntWWM 77, –80, NewGrD 80
Lamore, Isabel Film 2
Lamorisse, Albert 1922-1970 DcFM, FilmEn, HalFC 80, OxFilm, WorEFlm
Lamorisse, Albert 1922-1971 FilmgC
Lamote DeGrignon, Juan 1872-1949 Baker 78, NewGrD 80
Lamote DeGrignon, Ricard 1899-1962 Baker 78
Lamothe, Arthur 1928- CreCan 2, WorEFlm
Lamothe, Donat Romeo 1935- IntWWM 77, –80
Lamothe, Georges 1837-1894 Baker 78
Lamott, Jean Film 2
LaMotta, Bill 1922- AmSCAP 66
LaMotta, Frank Joseph 1904- AmSCAP 80
LaMotta, Wilbur L 1919- AmSCAP 80
Lamotte, Antoine Houdar De 1672-1731 NewGrD 80
LaMotte, Antoine Houdard De 1672-1731 OxThe
Lamotte, Franz 1751?-1781? NewGrD 80
Lamotte, Houdard De 1672-1731 NewGrD 80
Lamotte, Houdart De 1672-1731 NewGrD 80
LaMoulaz, Guillaume De NewGrD 80
Lamour, Dorothy 1914- AmPS B, BiDFilm, –81, CmMov, CmpEPM, FilmEn, FilmgC, ForYSC, HalFC 80[port], IntMPA 77, –75, –76, –78, –79, –80, MotPP, MovMk[port], OxFilm, ThFT[port], WhoHol A, WorEFlm
Lamouret, Robert d1959 WhScrn 77
Lamoureux, Charles 1834-1899 Baker 78, BnBkM 80, NewEOp 71, NewGrD 80[port], OxMus
Lamoureux, Edgar Claude 1912- IntMPA 75, –76
Lamoureux, Robert 1920- FilmEn
Lamoutte, Sylvia Maria 1935- IntWWM 80
Lamp Of Childhood BiDAmM
Lampadarios, Joannes NewGrD 80
Lampadius, Auctor 1500?-1559 NewGrD 80
Lampe, Charles John Frederick 1739?-1769? NewGrD 80, OxMus
Lampe, Del CmpEPM
Lampe, Frederick Adolf 1683-1729 OxMus
Lampe, Isabella NewGrD 80
Lampe, J Bodewalt 1869-1929 AmSCAP 66, –80
Lampe, Johann Friedrich 1744- NewGrD 80
Lampe, John Frederick 1703?-1751 MusMk, NewGrD 80, OxMus
Lampe, Walther 1872-1964 Baker 78
Lampel, Peter Martin 1894-1962 CnMD
Lampell, Millard 1919- BiE&WWA, EncFCWM 69, NotNAT, PlP&P
Lampens NewGrD 80
Lampert, Diane Charlotte 1924- AmSCAP 80, NatPD
Lampert, Zohra MotPP, WhoHol A
Lampert, Zohra 1936- BiE&WWA, FilmEn, ForYSC, HalFC 80
Lampert, Zohra 1937- NotNAT
Lamperti, Francesco 1811-1892 Baker 78
Lamperti, Francesco 1813-1892 NewEOp 71, NewGrD 80
Lamperti, Giovanni Battista 1839-1910 Baker 78
Lampin, Georges 1895-1979 FilmEn
Lampkin, Charles WhoHol A
Lampl, Carl G 1898-1962 AmSCAP 66, –80
Lamplugh, Henry Rawstorne 1885- WhoMus 72
Lamprecht, Christian Engelbertus 1927- IntWWM 77, –80
Lamprecht, Gerhard 1897- DcFM, FilmEn, OxFilm
Lamprey, Audrey Hardy 1945- IntWWM 77, –80
Lampropulos, Athena WhoOp 76
Lampton, Dee 1898-1919 Film 1, WhScrn 77
Lampugnani, Giovanni Battista 1706-1786? Baker 78, NewGrD 80, –80
Lamson, Ernest WhoStg 1906, –1908
LaMule, Guillaume De NewGrD 80
Lamy, Alfred Joseph 1850-1919 NewGrD 80
Lamy, Bernard 1640?-1715 NewGrD 80
Lamy, Charles Film 2
Lamy, Douglas N WhScrn 74, –77
Lamy, Fernand 1881-1966 NewGrD 80
Lan, David 1952- ConDr 77
Lan-Fang, Mei 1894-1943 NotNAT B
Lanari, Alessandro 1790-1862 NewGrD 80
Lancaster, Ann 1920-1970 WhScrn 74, –77, WhoHol B
Lancaster, Burt 1913- BiDFilm, –81, CmMov, FilmEn, FilmgC, ForYSC, HalFC 80, IntMPA 77, –75, –76, –78, –79, –80, MotPP, MovMk[port], OxFilm, WhoHol A, WhoHrs 80, WorEFlm[port]
Lancaster, Fred Film 2
Lancaster, John 1857-1935 Film 1, WhScrn 77
Lancaster, Lucie WhoHol A
Lancaster, Nora 1882- WhThe
Lancaster, Sir Osbert 1908- CnOxB, DancEn 78
Lancaster, Stuart WhoHol A
Lancaster, Thunderbird 1942- EncJzS 70
Lancaster, William Byard 1942- EncJzS 70
Lancaster, William Kinzea 1957- AmSCAP 80
Lancaster-Wallis, Ellen 1856-1940 NotNAT B
Lance, Albert 1925- WhoOp 76
Lance, Evelyn B 1934- WhoMus 72
Lance, Major 1941- RkOn[port]
Lance, Peter 1914- AmSCAP 66, –80
Lance, Victor Lewis 1939- AmSCAP 80
Lancelot DrBlPA
Lancelot, James Bennett 1952- IntWWM 77, –80
Lancelot, Sir WhoHrs 80
Lancen, Jean-Serge 1922- IntWWM 77, –80
Lancen, Serge Jean Mathieu 1922- Baker 78, CpmDNM 80
Lanchbery, John 1923- CnOxB, DancEn 78, IntWWM 77, –80, NewGrD 80, WhoMus 72
Lanchester, Elsa 1902- BiE&WWA, FilmAG WE, FilmEn, Film 2, FilmgC, ForYSC, HalFC 80, HolCA[port], IlWWBF, IntMPA 77, –75, –76, –78, –79, –80, MotPP, MovMk[port], NotNAT, OxFilm, PlP&P, ThFT[port], Vers A[port], WhThe, WhoHol A, WhoHrs 80[port]
Lanchester, Waldo S DcPup
Lanciani, Flavio Carlo 1655?-1724 NewGrD 80
Lancing, Carole 1940- AmSCAP 66
Lanclos, Henri De NewGrD 80
Lancret, Charles CreCan 1
Lanctin, Charles Francois Honore NewGrD 80
Land, Boukje 1923- IntWWM 77, –80
Land, Harold C, Jr. 1950- EncJzS 70
Land, Harold DeVance 1928- BiDAmM, EncJzS 70, IlEncJ
Land, Jan Pieter Nicholaas 1834-1897 Baker 78
Land, Jane Moody 1923- IntWWM 77
Land, Mary Film 2
Land, Robert PlP&P[port]
Landa, Anita 1929- CnOxB, DancEn 78
Landaeta, Juan Jose 1780-1814 NewGrD 80
Landau, Anneliese 1903- IntWWM 80
Landau, David 1878-1935 HolCA[port], NotNAT B, WhScrn 74, –77, WhThe, WhoHol B
Landau, Mrs. David Film 2
Landau, Ely A 1920- FilmEn, FilmgC, HalFC 80, IntMPA 77, –75, –76, –78, –79, –80, NewYTET, WorEFlm
Landau, Frances Film 2
Landau, Jack 1925-1967 BiE&WWA, NotNAT B
Landau, Jon ConMuA 80B
Landau, Lucy WhoHol A
Landau, Martin MotPP, WhoHol A
Landau, Martin 1925?- ForYSC
Landau, Martin 1931- FilmEn
Landau, Martin 1933- FilmgC, HalFC 80, MovMk

Landau, Martin 1934- *IntMPA 77, -75, -76, -78, -79, -80*
Landau, Richard H 1914- *IntMPA 77, -75, -76, -78, -79, -80*
Landau, Siegfried 1921- *AmSCAP 66, -80, Baker 78, ConAmC, IntWWM 77, -80*
Landau, Victor 1916- *ConAmC, IntWWM 77, -80*
Landauer, Erich *NewGrD 80*
Lande, Jean-Baptiste 1748- *CnOxB*
Landeau, Cecil 1906- *WhThe*
Landeck, Ben 1864-1928 *NotNAT B, WhThe*
Landen, Dinsdale 1932- *WhoHol A, WhoThe 72, -77*
Lander, Charles Oram d1934 *NotNAT B*
Lander, Harald 1905-1971 *CnOxB, DancEn 78[port]*
Lander, Jean Margaret Davenport 1829-1903 *FamA&A[port], NotNAT B, OxThe*
Lander, Margot 1910-1961 *CnOxB, DancEn 78[port]*
Lander, Petr 1931- *IntWWM 77*
Lander, Toni 1931- *CnOxB, DancEn 78[port]*
Landeros, Pepe 1910- *AmSCAP 66, -80*
Landers, Albert R 1920- *IntMPA 77, -75, -76, -78, -79, -80*
Landers, Harry *WhoHol A*
Landers, Lew 1901-1962 *FilmEn, FilmgC, HalFC 80, WhoHrs 80*
Landers, Muriel *WhoHol A*
Landesberg, Steve *AmSCAP 80, JoeFr[port]*
Landesman, Fran 1927- *AmSCAP 80*
Landesman, Frances 1927- *AmSCAP 66*
Landesman, Jay 1919- *BiE&WWA*
Landgard, Janet *WhoHol A*
Landi, Elissa 1904-1948 *FilmEn, Film 2, FilmgC, HalFC 80, HolP 30[port], IlWWBF, MotPP, MovMk[port], NotNAT B, ThFT[port], WhScrn 74, -77, WhThe, WhoHol B*
Landi, Elissa 1905-1948 *ForYSC*
Landi, Giuseppe *NewGrD 80*
Landi, Marla 1937?- *FilmgC, HalFC 80, WhoHol A*
Landi, Stefano 1586?-1639 *NewGrD 80*
Landi, Stefano 1590?-1639 *Baker 78*
Landi, Stefano 1590?-1655? *MusMk*
Landick, Olin 1895-1972 *WhScrn 77*
Landicutt, Philip *Film 1*
Landin, Hope 1893-1973 *WhScrn 77, WhoHol B*
Landini, Benedetto 1858-1938 *Baker 78*
Landini, Francesco 1325-1397 *Baker 78, MusMk, NewGrD 80[port]*
Landini, Francesco 1335?-1397 *BnBkM 80*
Landino, Francesco 1325-1397 *OxMus*
Landino, Francesco 1335?-1397 *BnBkM 80*
Landino, Franciscus 1325?-1397 *NewGrD 80[port]*
Landis, Carole 1919-1948 *FilmEn, FilmgC, ForYSC, HalFC 80, MotPP, MovMk, NotNAT B, WhScrn 74, -77, WhoHol B*
Landis, Clericus De *NewGrD 80[port]*
Landis, Cullen d1975 *MotPP, WhoHol C*
Landis, Cullen 1895-1975 *FilmEn, Film 1, -2, TwYS*
Landis, Cullen 1896-1975 *HalFC 80*
Landis, Cullen 1898-1975 *WhScrn 77*
Landis, Jessie Royce d1972 *WhoThe 72*
Landis, Jessie Royce 1900-1972 *HolCA[port]*
Landis, Jessie Royce 1904-1972 *FilmEn, FilmgC, ForYSC, HalFC 80, MovMk[port], NotNAT A, Vers B[port], WhScrn 77, WhoHol B*
Landis, Jessie Royce 1906-1972 *BiE&WWA, NotNAT B, WhThe*
Landis, John 1950- *HalFC 80*
Landis, John 1951?- *WhoHrs 80*
Landis, Margaret *Film 2*
Landis, William 1921- *BiE&WWA, NotNAT*
Landis, Winifred *Film 2*
Landley, Noel *IntMPA 80*
Landman, Elisheva *WhoMus 72*
Lando, Stefano 1530?-1571 *NewGrD 80*
Landolfi, Carlo Ferdinando *NewGrD 80*
Landolfi, Tony *WhoHol A*
Landon, Alfred M *What 1[port]*
Landon, Allan 1950- *AmSCAP 80*
Landon, Avice 1908- *WhoThe 77*
Landon, Avice 1910- *WhoThe 72*
Landon, Buddy *AmSCAP 80*
Landon, Charles W 1856-1918 *BiDAmM*
Landon, Christa 1921-1977 *NewGrD 80*
Landon, Eleanor Mary 1933- *IntWWM 80*
Landon, H C Robbins 1926- *Baker 78, IntWWM 77, NewGrD 80*
Landon, Howard Chandler Robbins 1926- *IntWWM 80*
Landon, Jane 1947- *CnOxB*
Landon, Margaret 1903- *PlP&P*
Landon, Michael *IntMPA 77, -76, -78, -79, -80*
Landon, Michael 1935- *ForYSC*
Landon, Michael 1937- *FilmgC, HalFC 80, MotPP, NewYTET, WhoHol A, WhoHrs 80*
Landon, Stewart *AmSCAP 80*
Landone, Avice 1910-1976 *FilmgC, HalFC 80, WhoHol A*
Landori, Edith 1940- *CreCan 1*
Landormy, Paul 1869-1943 *Baker 78, NewGrD 80*
Landory, Veronique 1940- *CreCan 1, DancEn 78*
Landowska, Wanda 1877-1959 *Baker 78, MusSN[port], OxMus*
Landowska, Wanda 1879-1959 *BnBkM 80[port], MusMk, NewGrD 80[port], WomCom[port]*
Landowska, Yona *Film 1*
Landowski, Marcel 1915- *Baker 78, DcCM, IntWWM 77, -80, NewGrD 80*
Landowski, W L, Madame 1899-1959 *Baker 78*
Landre, Guillaume 1874-1948 *NewGrD 80*
Landre, Guillaume 1905-1968 *Baker 78, DcCM, IntWWM 77, -80, MusMk, NewGrD 80*
Landre, Willem 1874-1948 *Baker 78, NewGrD 80*
Landres, Paul 1912- *FilmEn, FilmgC, HalFC 80, IntMPA 77, -75, -76, -78, -79, -80, WhoHrs 80*
Landreth, Gertrude Griffith 1897-1969 *WhScrn 74, -77, WhoHol B*
Landriani, Paolo 1770-1838 *OxThe*
Landron, J *MorBAP*
Landrum, Richie Pablo 1939- *EncJzS 70*
Landry, Alcide 1880?-1949 *NewOrJ*
Landry, John F 1952- *IntWWM 77, -80*
Landry, Richard Miles 1938- *ConAmC, IntWWM 77*
Landry, Ronald L 1934- *AmSCAP 80*
Landry, Tom 1870?- *NewOrJ*
Landsberg, Ludwig 1807-1858 *NewGrD 80*
Landsberg, Max 1845-1928 *BiDAmM*
Landsberg, Phyllis G 1927- *AmSCAP 66*
Landsburg, Alan 1933- *IntMPA 77, -75, -76, -78, -79, -80, NewYTET*
Landshoff, Ludwig 1874-1941 *Baker 78, BiDAmM, NewGrD 80*
Landshoff, Ruth *Film 2*
Landshoff, Werner 1905- *IntWWM 77, -80*
Landsley, Patrick Alfred 1926- *CreCan 2*
Landstone, Charles 1891- *WhThe, WhoThe 72*
Landweber, Ellen *WomWMM B*
Landy, H Leigh 1951- *ConAmC*
Landy, Tonny 1937- *IntWWM 80, WhoOp 76*
Lane, Abbe 1932- *ForYSC, WhoHol A*
Lane, Adele *Film 1, MotPP*
Lane, Allan d1973 *MotPP, WhScrn 77, WhoHol B*
Lane, Allan 1900-1973 *Film 2*
Lane, Allan 1901-1973 *ForYSC, HalFC 80*
Lane, Allan 1904-1973 *FilmEn, FilmgC*
Lane, Andrew Robert 1955- *IntWWM 80*
Lane, Barbara *WhoMus 72*
Lane, Ben *WhoHrs 80*
Lane, Brenda *Film 2*
Lane, Brian *ConMuA 80B*
Lane, Brian Martin 1928- *WhoMus 72*
Lane, Burton 1912- *AmPS, AmSCAP 66, -80, BestMus, BiDAmM, BiE&WWA, CmpEPM, EncMT, FilmEn, HalFC 80, NewCBMT, NewGrD 80, NotNAT, PlP&P, PopAmC[port], PopAmC SUP, Sw&Ld C, WhoThe 72, -77*
Lane, Charles 1869-1945 *WhScrn 77*
Lane, Charles 1899- *Film 1, -2, FilmgC, ForYSC, HalFC 80, MotPP, MovMk, TwYS, Vers A[port], WhoHol A*
Lane, Clara *WhoStg 1906, -1908*
Lane, Clarence 1910- *AmSCAP 66*
Lane, Dorothy 1890- *WhThe*
Lane, Dorothy 1905-1923 *WhScrn 74, -77*
Lane, Eastwood 1879-1951 *AmSCAP 66, Baker 78, ConAmC*
Lane, Eastwood 1897-1951 *AmSCAP 80*
Lane, Eddie *BgBands 74*
Lane, Edward 1915-1959 *AmSCAP 66, -80*
Lane, George Bertram 1943- *IntWWM 77, -80*
Lane, Gloria 1930- *WhoMus 72, WhoOp 76*
Lane, Grace 1876-1956 *NotNAT B, WhThe*
Lane, Harry 1910-1960 *WhScrn 74, -77, WhoHol B*
Lane, Horace 1880- *WhThe*
Lane, Ivan 1914- *AmSCAP 66, -80*
Lane, Jackie *MotPP*
Lane, James W *AmSCAP 66, -80*
Lane, Jocelyn *ForYSC, WhoHol A*
Lane, Katheryn *Film 2*
Lane, Kathleen *CmpEPM*
Lane, Kent *WhoHol A*
Lane, Kermit 1912- *AmSCAP 66, -80*
Lane, Laura 1927- *AmSCAP 66*
Lane, Leela *Film 2*
Lane, Lenita *WhoHol A*
Lane, Leone *Film 2*
Lane, Leota d1963 *WhoHol B*
Lane, Leslie 1915- *WhoMus 72*
Lane, Lewis 1903- *ConAmC*
Lane, Lola *MotPP*
Lane, Lola 1906- *WhoHol A*
Lane, Lola 1909- *FilmEn, Film 2, ForYSC, HalFC 80, ThFT[port], What 4[port]*
Lane, Louis 1923- *Baker 78*
Lane, Lupino 1892-1957 *Film 1, -2, ForYSC, TwYS*
Lane, Lupino 1892-1959 *EncMT, FilmEn, FilmgC, HalFC 80, IlWWBF[port], -A[port], JoeFr, NotNAT A, -B, OxThe, WhScrn 74, -77, WhThe, WhoHol B*
Lane, Magda *Film 2*
Lane, Maryon *WhoHol A*
Lane, Maryon 1931- *CnOxB, DancEn 78*
Lane, Mike *WhoHol A*
Lane, Nora *Film 2, ForYSC, TwYS*
Lane, Norman James 1921- *IntWWM 77*
Lane, Pat 1900-1953 *WhScrn 74, -77*
Lane, Philip Thomas 1950- *IntWWM 77, -80*
Lane, Priscilla 1917- *CmpEPM, FilmEn, ForYSC, HalFC 80, MotPP, MovMk, ThFT[port], WhoHol A*
Lane, Red *CounME 74, -74A, IlEncCM[port]*
Lane, Richard 1900- *FilmgC, ForYSC, HalFC 80, Vers A[port], WhoHol A*
Lane, Richard Bamford 1933- *AmSCAP 66, -80, ConAmC, IntWWM 77, -80*
Lane, Richard Joseph 1938- *AmSCAP 80*
Lane, Ronnie *ConMuA 80A*
Lane, Ronnie Slim Chance *IlEncR*
Lane, Rosemary d1974 *MotPP, WhoHol B*
Lane, Rosemary 1913-1974 *HalFC 80*
Lane, Rosemary 1914-1974 *FilmEn, ThFT[port], WhScrn 77*
Lane, Rosemary 1916-1974 *CmpEPM, ForYSC, MovMk[port]*
Lane, Sara *WhoHol A*
Lane, Sara 1823-1899 *OxThe*
Lane, Spencer 1843-1903 *BiDAmM*
Lane, Vicky *WhoHrs 80*
Lane, Wallace d1961 *WhScrn 74, -77, WhoHol B*
Lane, Walter *AmSCAP 80*
Lane Sisters, The *FilmgC, HalFC 80*
Laneare *NewGrD 80*
Laneer *NewGrD 80*
Laneri, Roberto 1945- *ConAmC, IntWWM 77, -80*
Laneuville, Eric 1952- *DrBlPA*
LaNeuville, Martin Joseph *NewGrD 80*
Laney, Luther King 1916- *AmSCAP 66, -80*
Lanfield, Sidney 1898-1972 *FilmEn*
Lanfield, Sidney 1900-1972 *FilmgC, HalFC 80*
Lanfranco, Giovanni Maria 1490?-1545 *NewGrD 80*
Lang, Alexander Matheson 1879-1948 *EncWT*
Lang, Andre 1893- *McGEWD*
Lang, Andrew 1844-1912 *DcPup*
Lang, Barbara *WhoHol A*
Lang, Benjamin Johnson 1837-1909 *Baker 78,*

BiDAmM, NewGrD 80
Lang, Charles *ForYSC*
Lang, Charles 1902- *CmMov, DcFM, FilmEn, FilmgC, HalFC 80, IntMPA 77, -75, -76, -78, -79, -80, OxFilm, WorEFlm*
Lang, Charles 1915- *FilmgC, HalFC 80*
Lang, Craig Sellar 1891- *WhoMus 72*
Lang, David 1913- *IntMPA 77, -75, -76, -78, -79, -80*
Lang, Doreen *WhoHol A*
Lang, Eddie 1902-1933 *AmSCAP 66, -80, BiDAmM, CmpEPM, NewGrD 80, WhoJazz 72*
Lang, Eddie 1904-1933 *IlEncJ*
Lang, Edith *ConAmC, WhoMus 72*
Lang, Eva Clara d1933 *NotNAT B*
Lang, Frederick David *WhoMus 72*
Lang, Fritz 1890-1976 *AmFD, BiDFilm, -81, CmMov, DcFM, FilmEn, FilmgC, HalFC 80, IntMPA 75, -76, MovMk[port], OxFilm, TwYS A, WhoHrs 80, WomWMM, WorEFlm*
Lang, Gertrude d1941 *NotNAT B*
Lang, Gertrude d1942 *NotNAT B*
Lang, Hans 1908- *Baker 78, WhoMus 72*
Lang, Harold 1923- *BiE&WWA, EncMT, WhoThe 72, -77*
Lang, Harold 1923-1970 *HalFC 80, WhScrn 74, -77*
Lang, Harold 1923-1971 *FilmgC, WhoHol B*
Lang, Harold 1924?- *CnOxB, DancEn 78*
Lang, Harold 1931-1975 *NotNAT B*
Lang, Harry 1895-1953 *NotNAT B, WhScrn 74, -77, WhoHol B*
Lang, Henry Albert 1854-1930 *Baker 78, BiDAmM*
Lang, Hermann *WhoMus 72*
Lang, Howard 1876-1941 *Film 2, NotNAT B, WhScrn 74, -77, WhThe, WhoHol B*
Lang, Hutin Britton 1876-1965 *OxThe*
Lang, Istvan 1933- *Baker 78, IntWWM 77, -80, NewGrD 80*
Lang, Jennings 1915- *FilmEn, HalFC 80, IntMPA 77, -75, -76, -78, -79, -80*
Lang, Johann Georg 1722-1798 *NewGrD 80*
Lang, Josephine *WhoMus 72*
Lang, Josephine 1815-1880 *Baker 78, NewGrD 80*
Lang, June 1915- *FilmEn, FilmgC, ForYSC, HalFC 80, ThFT[port], What 5[port], WhoHol A*
Lang, Ludwig d1932 *NotNAT B*
Lang, Margaret Ruthven 1867-1972 *Baker 78*
Lang, Maria 1948- *CnOxB*
Lang, Mary Jane 1941- *IntWWM 77*
Lang, Matheson 1879-1948 *CnThe, FilmEn, Film 1, -2, FilmgC, HalFC 80, IlWWBF[port], -A, NotNAT A, -B, OxThe, PlP&P, WhScrn 74, -77, WhThe, WhoHol B*
Lang, Matthaus 1468-1540 *NewGrD 80*
Lang, Michael 1954- *CpmDNM 80*
Lang, Michael Anthony 1941- *BiDAmM, EncJzS 70*
Lang, Mike 1941- *EncJzS 70*
Lang, Otto *IntMPA 77, -75, -76, -78, -79, -80*
Lang, Pal 1901- *NewGrD 80*
Lang, Paul Henry 1901- *Baker 78, IntWWM 77, -80, NewGrD 80, OxMus, WhoMus 72*
Lang, Pearl 1922- *BiE&WWA, CmpGMD, CnOxB, DancEn 78[port]*
Lang, Peter 1867-1932 *Film 1, -2, NotNAT B, WhScrn 74, -77, WhoHol B*
Lang, Philip J 1911- *AmSCAP 80, BiE&WWA, NotNAT*
Lang, Phillip 1911- *AmSCAP 66*
Lang, Robert 1934- *HalFC 80, WhoHol A, WhoThe 72, -77*
Lang, Ronnie 1927- *CmpEPM*
Lang, Rosemary Rita 1920- *IntWWM 77, -80*
Lang, Siegfried 1919- *IntWWM 77, -80*
Lang, Walter 1896-1966 *Baker 78, NewGrD 80*
Lang, Walter 1896-1972 *CmMov, FilmgC, HalFC 80*
Lang, Walter 1898-1972 *BiDFilm, -81, FilmEn, TwYS A, WhScrn 77, WorEFlm*
Lang, Walter 1936- *MovMk[port]*
Lang-Beck, Ivana 1912- *IntWWM 80*
Lang-Kostlin, Josephine 1815-1880 *Baker 78*
Langa, Francisco Soto De *NewGrD 80*
Langan, Glenn 1917- *FilmEn, FilmgC, ForYSC, HalFC 80, IntMPA 77, -75, -76, -78, -79, -80, MovMk, WhoHol A, WhoHrs 80[port]*
Langan, John 1902- *TwYS A*
Langan, Marius *Film 2*
Langbaine, Gerard d1692 *NotNAT B*
Langbecker, Emanuel Christian Gottlieb 1792-1843 *Baker 78*
Langbein, Brenton James 1928- *IntWWM 77, -80*
Langberg, Peter 1945- *IntWWM 77, -80*
Langdale-Brown, Christine Hilda 1889- *WhoMus 72*
Langden, John *Film 2*
Langdon, Chauncey 1763-1830 *BiDAmM*
Langdon, Dory 1929- *AmPS*
Langdon, Harry d1944 *GrMovC[port], MotPP, WhoHol B*
Langdon, Harry 1884-1944 *BiDFilm, -81, CmMov, DcFM, FilmEn, FilmgC, HalFC 80, JoeFr[port], MovMk[port], OxFilm, TwYS A, WhScrn 74, -77, WorEFlm[port]*
Langdon, Harry 1884-1945 *Funs[port]*
Langdon, Harry 1884-1946 *Film 2, ForYSC, TwYS*
Langdon, Harry 1885-1944 *NotNAT B*
Langdon, John David 1943- *IntWWM 77, -80, WhoMus 72*
Langdon, Lillian d1943 *Film 1, -2, TwYS, WhScrn 74, -77, WhoHol B*
Langdon, Michael 1920- *IntWWM 77, -80, NewGrD 80, WhoOp 76*
Langdon, Michael 1921- *CmOp, WhoMus 72*
Langdon, Richard 1729?-1803 *Baker 78, NewGrD 80*
Langdon, Rose *Film 2*
Langdon, Sue Ann 1940- *FilmgC, ForYSC, WhoHol A*
Langdon, Sue Anne 1940- *HalFC 80*
Langdon, Verne Loring 1941- *AmSCAP 80*
Lange, De *NewGrD 80*
Lange, Aloysia *NewGrD 80*
Lange, Arthur 1889-1956 *AmSCAP 66, -80, ConAmC A*
Lange, Barbara Pearson 1910- *BiE&WWA, NotNAT*
Lange, Daniel De 1841-1918 *Baker 78, NewGrD 80*
Lange, Dave *ConMuA 80B*
Lange, Francisco Curt 1903- *Baker 78, NewGrD 80*
Lange, Franz Kurt 1903- *NewGrD 80*
Lange, Gregor 1540?-1587 *NewGrD 80*
Lange, Gustav 1830-1889 *Baker 78*
Lange, Hans 1884-1960 *Baker 78*
Lange, Hartmut 1937- *CroCD, EncWT, Ent*
Lange, Helmut Karl Heinz 1928- *IntWWM 77, -80*
Lange, Henry W 1895- *AmSCAP 66, -80*
Lange, Hope *IntMPA 77, -75, -76, -78, -79, -80, MotPP, WhoHol A*
Lange, Hope 1931- *FilmEn, FilmgC, HalFC 80*
Lange, Hope 1933- *ForYSC, MovMk[port]*
Lange, Jessica 1950- *FilmEn, WhoHol A*
Lange, Johann Caspar *NewGrD 80*
Lange, Johnny 1909- *AmSCAP 66, -80*
Lange, Konrad Von 1855-1921 *Baker 78*
Lange, Mary 1913-1973 *WhScrn 77*
Lange, Robert John *ConMuA 80B*
Lange, Samuel De 1811-1884 *NewGrD 80*
Lange, Samuel De 1840-1911 *Baker 78, NewGrD 80*
Lange, Sven d1930 *NotNAT B*
Lange, Ted 1947?- *BlkAmP, DrBlPA*
Lange-Muller, Peter Erasmus 1850-1926 *Baker 78, NewGrD 80, OxMus*
Langella, Frank *WhoHol A*
Langella, Frank 1940- *Ent, HalFC 80, NotNAT, PlP&P A[port], WhoThe 77*
Langella, Frank 1944- *FilmgC*
Langenbeck, Curt 1906-1953 *CnMD*
Langendoen, Jacobus C 1890- *AmSCAP 66, ConAmC A*
Langendorff, Frieda 1868-1947 *Baker 78*
Langenfeld, Friedrich Spee Von *NewGrD 80*
Langenus, Gustave 1883-1957 *AmSCAP 66, -80, Baker 78, ConAmC A*
Langer, Eduard 1835-1905 *Baker 78*
Langer, Ferdinand 1839-1905 *Baker 78*
Langer, Frantisek 1888-1965 *CnMD, EncWT, Ent, ModWD, REnWD[port]*
Langer, Hans-Klaus 1903- *IntWWM 77, -80*
Langer, Hermann 1819-1889 *Baker 78*
Langer, Susanne K 1895- *NewGrD 80*
Langer, Victor 1842-1902 *Baker 78*
Langert, Johann August Adolf 1836-1920 *Baker 78*
Langert, Jules 1932- *ConAmC*
Langevin, Andre 1927- *CreCan 2*
Langey, Otto 1851-1922 *Baker 78*
Langford, Abraham d1774 *NotNAT B*
Langford, Anthony 1942- *IntWWM 77, -80*
Langford, Audrey 1912- *IntWWM 77, -80, WhoMus 72*
Langford, Colin Edward 1934- *WhoMus 72*
Langford, Frances *AmPS B, IntMPA 75, -76, -78, -79, -80*
Langford, Frances 1913- *BiDAmM, CmpEPM, ForYSC*
Langford, Frances 1914- *FilmEn, FilmgC, HalFC 80, IntMPA 77, MotPP, ThFT[port], What 2[port], WhoHol A*
Langford, Martha d1935 *WhScrn 74, -77*
Langford, Sam *BlksB&W C*
Langford, Samuel 1863-1927 *NewGrD 80*
Langford, William 1920-1955 *NotNAT B, WhScrn 74, -77, WhoHol B*
Langford-Reed, Joan *Film 2*
Langgaard, Rued 1893-1952 *Baker 78*
Langgaard, Siegfried 1852-1914 *Baker 78*
Langgard, Rud 1893-1952 *NewGrD 80*
Langgard, Rued 1893-1952 *NewGrD 80*
Langham, Jennifer 1948- *IntWWM 77, -80*
Langham, Michael 1919- *BiE&WWA, CreCan 1, NotNAT, WhoThe 72, -77*
Langham, Monica Elaine 1905- *WhoMus 72*
Langhans, Edward A 1923- *BiE&WWA, NotNAT*
Langhans, Friedrich Wilhelm 1832-1892 *Baker 78*
Langhans, Wilhelm 1832-1892 *NewGrD 80*
Langhedul *NewGrD 80*
Langhedul, Guillames *NewGrD 80*
Langhedul, Jan d1592 *NewGrD 80*
Langhedul, Mateo d1636? *NewGrD 80*
Langhedul, Mattheus d1636? *NewGrD 80*
Langhedul, Matthieu d1636? *NewGrD 80*
Langhedul, Matthijs d1636? *NewGrD 80*
Langhedul, Michiel *NewGrD 80*
Langhedul, Victor d1513? *NewGrD 80*
Langheld, Gretchen *WomWMM B*
Langhoff, Wolfgang 1901-1966 *EncWT*
Langhveldt, Joris Van *NewGrD 80*
Langius, Hieronymus Gregorius *NewGrD 80*
Langlais, Jean 1907- *Baker 78, BnBkM 80, DcCM, IntWWM 77, -80, NewGrD 80, WhoMus 72*
Langle, Honore Francois Marie 1741-1807 *Baker 78, NewGrD 80*
Langlen, Paula *Film 2*
Langley, Allan Lincoln 1892-1949 *Baker 78*
Langley, Bernard Peter Francis 1929- *IntWWM 77, WhoMus 72*
Langley, Cordes Jeffrey 1951- *AmSCAP 80*
Langley, Enid Maude *WhoMus 72*
Langley, Faith 1929-1972 *WhScrn 77*
Langley, Herbert 1888-1967 *Film 2, WhScrn 74, -77, WhoHol B*
Langley, James 1927- *IntWWM 80, WhoMus 72*
Langley, Kenneth John 1948- *IntWWM 77, -80*
Langley, Leanne 1953- *AmSCAP 80*
Langley, Noel 1911- *BiE&WWA, FilmEn, FilmgC, HalFC 80, IntMPA 77, -75, -76, -78, -79, NotNAT, WhThe, WhoThe 72*
Langley, Robin Patrick 1944- *IntWWM 77, -80*
Langley, Stuart d1970 *WhoHol B*
Langlois, Henri 1914-1977 *FilmEn, HalFC 80, OxFilm, WorEFlm*
Langlois, Isidore 1910?- *NewOrJ*
Langlotz, Karl A 1834-1915 *Baker 78*
Langmaid, Alan Gordon Richard 1908- *WhoMus 72*
Langner, Ilse 1899- *CnMD*
Langner, Lawrence 1890-1962 *EncMT, EncWT,*

ModWD, NotNAT A, -B, OxThe, PlP&P, WhThe
Langner, Philip 1926- BiE&WWA, IntMPA 79, -80, NotNAT, WhoThe 77
Langner-Saks, Gitle AmSCAP 80
Langoe-Conradsen, Christian 1895- IntMPA 75, -76
Langone, Frank C 1907- WhoJazz 72
Langpaap, Frances K PupTheA
Langreder, Martin d1602? NewGrD 80
Langridge, Philip Gordon 1939- IntWWM 77, -80, NewGrD 80, WhoMus 72
Langridge, Roy 1920- WhoMus 72
Langrish, Vivian WhoMus 72
Langstadt, Anne Kahane CreCan 1
Langstaff, John Meredith 1926- WhoMus 72
Langston, Ruth Film 2
Langston, Sidney WhoMus 72
Langstroth, Ivan Shed 1887-1971 AmSCAP 66, -80, Baker 78, BiDAmM, ConAmC, WhoMus 72
Langton, Basil C 1912-1929 WhThe
Langton, Paul 1913- ForYSC, IntMPA 77, -75, -76, -78, -79, -80, WhoHol A
Langton, Stephen d1228 OxMus
Langtry, Lillie 1852-1929 FamA&A[port], WhThe
Langtry, Lillie 1853-1929 EncWT, Ent[port], HalFC 80, OxThe, WhScrn 74, -77
Langtry, Lillie 1877- WhThe
Langtry, Lily 1852-1929 NotNAT A, -B, WhoStg 1906, -1908
Langtry, Lily 1853-1929 PlP&P, WhoHol B
Langtry, Lily 1856-1929 Film 1
Languepin, Jean-Jacques 1924- DcFM
Languirand, Jacques 1931- CreCan 1
Langveld, Joris Van NewGrD 80
Langwill, Lyndesay Graham 1897- NewGrD 80, WhoMus 72
Lani, Maria 1906-1954 WhScrn 74, -77
Lania, Leon d1961 NotNAT B
Lanier NewGrD 80
Lanier, Alfonso d1613 NewGrD 80
Lanier, Andrea d1660 NewGrD 80
Lanier, Clement d1661 NewGrD 80
Lanier, Gary ConAmC
Lanier, Henry d1633 NewGrD 80
Lanier, Innocent d1625 NewGrD 80
Lanier, Jerome d1657 NewGrD 80
Lanier, John d1572 NewGrD 80
Lanier, John d1616 NewGrD 80
Lanier, John d1650 NewGrD 80
Lanier, Nicholas d1612 NewGrD 80[port]
Lanier, Nicholas 1588-1666 Baker 78, BnBkM 80, MusMk, NewGrD 80
Lanier, Sidney 1842-1881 Baker 78, BiDAmM, NewGrD 80
Lanier, Thomas 1633-1686? NewGrD 80
Lanier, Verdell 1957- AmSCAP 80
Lanier, William 1618-1660? NewGrD 80
Laniere NewGrD 80
Lanigan, Jim 1902- WhoJazz 72
Lanigan, John 1921- CmOp, WhoMus 72
Lanin, Lester BgBands 74, CmpEPM
Lanin, Sam CmpEPM
Lank, Philip Joseph 1924- WhoMus 72
Lankester, Eric Film 2
Lankester, Michael John 1944- IntWWM 77, -80
Lankow, Anna 1850-1908 Baker 78
Lankston, John 1939- IntWWM 80
Lankveld, Joris Van NewGrD 80
Lanner, August 1834-1855 Baker 78
Lanner, Jorg 1939- CnOxB
Lanner, Josef 1801-1843 DcCom 77, MusMk
Lanner, Joseph 1801-1843 Baker 78, NewGrD 80, OxMus
Lanner, Katti 1829-1908 CnOxB, NotNAT B
Lanner, Katti 1831-1908 DancEn 78
Lannerholm, Torleif E T 1923- IntWWM 77, -80
Lanning, Frank Film 1, -2
Lannis, Johannes De NewGrD 80
Lannoy, Eduard 1787-1853 Baker 78
Lano, Alberto 1810?-1895? PupTheA
Lano, David 1874- NotNAT A, PupTheA, PupTheA SUP
Lano, Oliver 1832-1902 PupTheA
Lanoe, Jacques Film 2
Lanoix, August 1902- NewOrJ
Lanoue, Conrad 1908-1972 AmSCAP 66, -80, WhoJazz 72
LaNoue, Jean Sauve De 1701-1761 OxThe
Lanoy, Andre Film 2
Lanphier, Fay d1959 WhoHol B
Lanphier, Faye 1906-1959 WhScrn 74, -77
Lanphier, Florence Film 2
Lanphier, James F 1921-1969 WhScrn 77, WhoHol B
Lans, Michael J A 1845-1908 Baker 78
Lansburgh, Larry IntMPA 75, -76
Lansbury, Angela 1925- BiDFilm, -81, BiE&WWA, EncMT, FilmEn, FilmgC, ForYSC, HalFC 80, IntMPA 77, -75, -76, -78, -79, -80, MGM[port], MotPP, MovMk[port], NotNAT, OxFilm, WhoHol A, WhoThe 72, -77
Lansbury, Bruce 1930- IntMPA 77, -75, -76, -78, -79, -80
Lansbury, Edgar 1930- BiE&WWA, NotNAT, WhoThe 72, -77
Lanshe, Richard James 1930- IntWWM 77
Lansing, Joi d1972 ForYSC, MotPP, WhoHol B
Lansing, Joi 1928-1972 HolCA[port]
Lansing, Joi 1930-1972 WhScrn 77, WhoHrs 80
Lansing, Joi 1936-1972 FilmgC, HalFC 80
Lansing, Mary Film 2
Lansing, Robert 1929- BiE&WWA, FilmEn, FilmgC, ForYSC, HalFC 80, MotPP, NotNAT, WhoHol A
Lansing, Ruth Douglas 1881-1931 WhScrn 74, -77
Lansing, Sherry 1944- IntMPA 78, -79, -80
Lansky, Paul 1944- AmSCAP 80, ConAmC, DcCM
Lanson, Snooky 1914- CmpEPM, RkOn, What 4[port]
Lanteau, William WhoHol A
Lantelme, Mademoiselle d1911 NotNAT B
Lantieri, Marta 1924- WhoOp 76
Lantieri, Rita 1940- WhoOp 76
Lantins, De NewGrD 80
Lantins, Arnold De 1400?-1427 Baker 78, NewGrD 80
Lantins, Arnoldo De NewGrD 80
Lantins, Arnoldus De NewGrD 80
Lantins, Hugho De NewGrD 80
Lantins, Hugo De 1400?- Baker 78, NewGrD 80
Lantins, Raymond De NewGrD 80
Lantins, Ugho De NewGrD 80
Lantins, Ugo De NewGrD 80
Lantins De Bolsee, Berthold De NewGrD 80
Lantner, Martha Ruth 1905- IntWWM 77
Lantos NewGrD 80
Lantz, Robert 1914- BiE&WWA, IntMPA 75, -76, NotNAT
Lantz, Walter 1900- FilmEn, FilmgC, HalFC 80, IntMPA 77, -75, -76, -78, -79, -80, WorEFlm
Lany, Jean-Barthelemy 1718-1786 CnOxB, DancEn 78
Lany, Louise-Madeleine 1733-1777 CnOxB, DancEn 78
Lanyer NewGrD 80
Lanyon, Joyce Cecile 1911- WhoMus 72
Lanza NewGrD 80
Lanza, Alcides 1929- AmSCAP 80, DcCM, NewGrD 80
Lanza, Andrea 1947- IntWWM 77, -80
Lanza, Francesco 1783-1862 NewGrD 80
Lanza, Francesco Giuseppe 1750?-1812? NewGrD 80
Lanza, Gesualdo 1779-1859 NewGrD 80
Lanza, Giuseppe NewGrD 80
Lanza, Mario 1921-1959 AmPS A, -B, Baker 78, BiDAmM, CmMov, CmpEPM, FilmEn, FilmgC, ForYSC, HalFC 80, MGM[port], MotPP, MovMk[port], NotNAT B, OxFilm, OxMus, RkOn, WhScrn 74, -77, WhoHol B, WorEFlm
Lanza Tomasi, Gioacchino 1934- WhoOp 76
Lanzarone, Benjamin Anthony 1938- AmSCAP 80
Lanzetti, Domenico NewGrD 80
Lanzetti, Salvatore 1710?-1780? Baker 78, NewGrD 80
Lanzi, Francesco NewGrD 80
Lanzillotti, Leonore Agatha WhoOp 76
Lanzky-Otto, Ib 1940- IntWWM 77, -80
Lanzky-Otto, Wilhelm 1909- IntWWM 77, -80
LaPalm, Dick ConMuA 80B
Laparcerie, Cora WhThe
Laparra, Raoul 1876-1943 Baker 78, NewEOp 71, NewGrD 80, OxMus
LaPatelliere, Denys De 1921- DcFM
Lapauri, Aleksandr 1926-1975 WhScrn 77
Lapauri, Alexander Alexandrovich 1926-1975 CnOxB, DancEn 78
Lapell, Dorothy AmSCAP 80
LaPera, Sam WhoHol A
Lapetina, F M 1858-1943 BiDAmM
Lapham, Claude 1890-1957 BiDAmM
Lapicida, Erasmus 1440?-1547 NewGrD 80
Lapid, Jess d1968 WhScrn 77
Lapido, Duro MorBAP
Lapidos, Joseph 1914- AmSCAP 66
Lapierre, Eugene 1899- CreCan 2
Lapierre, Joseph Eugene CreCan 2
LaPierre, Louis-Maurice De 1697-1753 NewGrD 80
LaPierre, Paul De 1612-1690? NewGrD 80
Lapin, Geoffrey Scott 1949- IntWWM 77, -80
Lapin, Lawrence 1935- ConAmC
Lapine, Andre 1868-1952 CreCan 1
Lapine, Andreas Christian Gottfried 1868-1952 CreCan 1
Lapis, Santo NewGrD 80
LaPlanche, Rosemary 1923- ForYSC, HalFC 80, WhoHol A
LaPlante, Beatrice Film 2
Laplante, Charles AmSCAP 80
LaPlante, Laura 1904- FilmEn, Film 2, FilmgC, ForYSC, HalFC 80, ThFT[port], TwYS, What 2[port], WhThe, WhoHol A, WhoHrs 80
LaPlante, Violet Film 2
Lapo, Cecil Elwyn 1910- AmSCAP 66, -80
Lapointe, Gatien 1931- CreCan 2
Lapointe, Paul-Marie 1929- CreCan 2
LaPopeliniere, Alexandre-Jean-Joseph De NewGrD 80
Laport, Nelly DancEn 78
LaPorta, John Daniel 1920- AmSCAP 66, -80, BiDAmM, CmpEPM, ConAmC, EncJzS 70
LaPorta, Louis F 1944- CpmDNM 73, ConAmC
Laporte 1584?-1621? OxThe
Laporte, Andre 1931- Baker 78, NewGrD 80
Laporte, John NewOrJ
Laporte, Joseph De 1713-1779 Baker 78, NewGrD 80
Laporte, Pierre Francois d1841 NotNAT B
Lapotaire, Jane 1944- WhoThe 77
LaPoupliniere, Alexandre-Jean-Joseph De 1693-1762 Baker 78, NewGrD 80
Lapp, Arthur Edward 1952- IntWWM 77, -80
Lapp, Horace 1904- CreCan 1
Lappalainen, Martti Iimari 1941- IntWWM 77
Lappe, Gemze De 1921- CnOxB
Lappi, Pietro 1575?-1630 NewGrD 80
LaPrade, Ernest 1889-1969 Baker 78, ConAmC
LaPrelle, Gertrude Porter PupTheA
LaPresle, Jacques De 1888-1969 Baker 78
Lapsley, Jimmie Film 2
Lapson, Dvora 1907- DancEn 78
Lapzeson, Noemi 1940- CnOxB
Laquai, Reinhold 1894-1957 Baker 78
Lara, Madame 1876- WhThe
Lara, Agustin 1900-1969 NewGrD 80
Lara, Agustin 1900-1970 Baker 78
Lara, Isidore De Baker 78
Lara, Manuel Manrique De NewGrD 80
Lara-Bareiro, Carlos 1914- Baker 78
Larabee, Louise WhoHol A
LaRae, Grace d1956 NotNAT B
Laramore, Vivian Yeiser 1895- AmSCAP 66
Larch, John ForYSC, WhoHol A
Larchet, John F 1884-1967 NewGrD 80
Larchier, Federicus NewGrD 80
Larchier, Jean NewGrD 80
Larcom, Lucy 1826-1893 BiDAmM
Larde, Christian Pierre 1930- IntWWM 80
Lardenois, Antoine d1672? NewGrD 80
Lardner, Ring W 1885-1933 AmSCAP 66, -80, EncWT, Ent, NotNAT B

Lardner, Ring W, Jr. 1915- *FilmEn, IntMPA 77, -75, -76, -78, -79, -80, OxFilm*
Lardrot, Andre 1932- *IntWWM 77, -80*
Laredo, Jaime 1941- *Baker 78, IntWWM 77, -80, NewGrD 80*
Laredo, Ruth 1937- *WhoMus 72*
LaReno, Dick d1945 *WhoHol B*
LaReno, Richard 1873-1945 *Film 1, -2, WhScrn 74, -77*
Largay, Raymond J 1886-1974 *WhScrn 77, WhoHol B*
Large, Donald E 1909- *AmSCAP 66, -80*
Large, William Roy 1940- *IntWWM 77*
Largent, Edward J, Jr. 1936- *ConAmC*
Larimer, Robert Walker 1929- *AmSCAP 80*
Larimore, Earle 1899-1947 *NotNAT B, WhScrn 74, -77, WhThe, WhoHol B*
Larionov, Michael 1881-1964 *EncWT*
Larionov, Michel 1881-1964 *DancEn 78*
Larionov, Mikhail Fedorovich 1881-1969 *CnOxB*
Larive, Leon *Film 2*
Larivey, Pierre De 1540?-1612? *OxThe*
Larivey, Pierre De 1540?-1619 *Ent, McGEWD*
Larkin, Deirdre 1931- *WhoMus 72*
Larkin, George 1888-1946 *WhScrn 77*
Larkin, George 1889- *Film 1, -2, TwYS*
Larkin, James J 1925- *IntMPA 77, -75, -76, -78, -79, -80*
Larkin, John 1874-1936 *WhScrn 74, -77, WhoHol B*
Larkin, John 1902- *ForYSC*
Larkin, John 1912-1965 *ForYSC, WhScrn 74, -77, WhoHol B*
Larkin, John 1927- *ConAmC*
Larkin, Mary 1944- *AmSCAP 80*
Larkin, Moscelyne 1925- *CnOxB, DancEn 78*
Larkin, Oliver *PupTheA*
Larkin, Peter 1926- *BiE&WWA, NotNAT, WhoThe 72, -77*
Larkin, Tippy Milton 1910- *WhoJazz 72*
Larkina, Moussia *DancEn 78*
Larkins, Ellis 1923- *CmpEPM, DrBlPA, EncJzS 70*
Larks, The *RkOn[port]*
Larned, Mel d1955 *NotNAT B*
Larner, Gerald 1936- *IntWWM 77, -80, WhoMus 72*
Larner, Justina Helen 1950- *IntWWM 80*
Laro, Johannes Petrus 1927- *IntWWM 77, -80*
LaRoca, Peter Sims 1938- *BiDAmM*
LaRocca, Dominic James 1889-1961 *BiDAmM*
LaRocca, Dominick James 1889-1961 *AmSCAP 66, -80, NewOrJ[port]*
LaRocca, Nick 1889-1961 *Baker 78, CmpEPM, WhoJazz 72*
LaRoche, Edward *Film 2*
LaRoche, Francois De d1676 *NewGrD 80*
Laroche, Herman 1845-1904 *NewGrD 80*
Laroche, Hermann 1845-1904 *Baker 78*
Laroche, Johann 1745-1806 *EncWT, OxThe*
LaRoche, Karl Von 1794-1884 *EncWT*
LaRoche, Mary *WhoHol A*
Laroche, Pierre 1902-1962 *DcFM*
Laroche, Roland 1927- *CreCan 2*
LaRock, Marcia Bascom 1950- *IntWWM 77*
LaRocque, Rod 1896-1969 *FilmEn, FilmgC, ForYSC, HalFC 80, MovMk[port], TwYS*
LaRocque, Rod 1898-1969 *Film 1, -2, MotPP, WhScrn 74, -77, WhoHol B*
Laroque 1595?-1676 *OxThe*
Laroque, Philip 1780?-1838? *BiDAmM*
LaRosa, Carmen *ConMuA 80B*
LaRosa, Julius 1930- *AmPS A, -B, BiDAmM, NewYTET, RkOn[port]*
LaRosa, Michael Joseph 1948- *CpmDNM 74, -76, -78, -79*
Larose, Ludger 1868-1915 *CreCan 2*
Larosh, German Avgustovich 1845-1904 *NewGrD 80*
LaRotella, Pasquale 1880-1963 *Baker 78*
LaRoy, Rita 1907- *Film 2, ForYSC, MotPP, WhoHol A*
Larquey, Pierre 1884-1962 *NotNAT B, WhScrn 74, -77, WhoHol B*
Larra, Mariano *WhThe*
Larra, Mariano Jose De 1809-1837 *NotNAT B, OxThe*
Larra Y Sanchez DeCastro, Mariano J De 1809-1837 *McGEWD[port]*
Larrain, Michael *WhoHol A*
Larrauri, Anton 1932- *NewGrD 80*
Larrimore, Earle 1899-1947 *PlP&P*
Larrimore, Francine 1898-1975 *BiE&WWA, Film 1, NotNAT B, TwYS, WhScrn 77, WhThe, WhoHol C*
Larrin, Jay *AmSCAP 80*
Larrinaga, Forster *Film 2*
Larrivee, Henri 1737-1802 *NewGrD 80*
Larrocha, Alicia De 1923- *Baker 78, BnBkM 80, MusSN[port], NewGrD 80*
L'Arronge, Adolf 1838-1908 *Baker 78, OxThe*
Larsen, Bjarne 1922- *IntWWM 80*
Larsen, Carl 1934- *NatPD[port]*
Larsen, Elizabeth B 1950- *AmSCAP 80*
Larsen, George *PupTheA*
Larsen, Gerd 1921- *CnOxB, DancEn 78*
Larsen, Hans Juhl 1943- *IntWWM 77, -80*
Larsen, Jens Peter 1902- *Baker 78, IntWWM 77, -80, NewGrD 80, WhoMus 72*
Larsen, Keith 1925- *FilmgC, ForYSC, HalFC 80, IntMPA 77, -75, -76, -78, -79, -80, WhoHol A*
Larsen, Libby 1950- *ConAmC*
Larsen, Naomi Ruth 1909- *IntWWM 77, -80*
Larsen, Neil Robert 1948- *AmSCAP 80*
Larsen, Niels 1926- *IntMPA 75, -76*
Larsen, Niels Bjorn 1913- *CnOxB, DancEn 78*
Larsen, Nils 1888-1937 *Baker 78*
Larsen, Paul J 1917- *IntMPA 77, -75, -76, -78, -79*
Larsen, Peter Harry 1927- *IntWWM 77, -80*
Larsen, Robert L 1934- *IntWWM 77, -80*
Larsen, Seth Beegle *IntMPA 75, -76*
Larsen, Vigo 1880-1957 *FilmEn*
Larsen, Wayne Erik 1946- *IntWWM 77, -80*
Larsen, William *NotNAT*
Larsen, William 1951- *ConAmC*
Larsen-Todsen, Nanny 1884- *Baker 78, CmOp, NewEOp 71, NewGrD 80*
Larson, Bird d1927 *DancEn 78*
Larson, Christine *ForYSC, WhoHol A*
Larson, David Dynes 1926- *IntWWM 77, -80*
Larson, G Bennett *IntMPA 77, -75, -76, -78, -79, -80*
Larson, Glen A *NewYTET*
Larson, Jack *NatPD[port]*
Larson, Jack Edward 1933- *AmSCAP 80*
Larson, Larry *ConMuA 80B*
Larson, Leroy 1939- *AmSCAP 80*
Larson, Lorlee 1935-1954 *WhScrn 74, -77*
Larson, Nicolette 1952- *AmSCAP 80, ConMuA 80A*
Larson, Paul *WhoHol A*
Larson, William S 1899- *WhoMus 72*
Larsson, Helmer *Film 2*
Larsson, Kurt Vilhelm 1909- *IntWWM 77*
Larsson, Lars-Erik 1908- *Baker 78, DcCM, IntWWM 77, -80, NewGrD 80, OxMus, WhoMus 72*
Larsson, William *Film 1*
LaRubia, Marga *Film 2*
LaRue, Al 1917- *FilmEn*
LaRue, Al 1921- *ForYSC*
Larue, D C *AmSCAP 80*
LaRue, Danny 1928- *FilmgC, HalFC 80*
LaRue, Fontaine *Film 1, -2, TwYS*
LaRue, Frank H 1878-1960 *ForYSC, WhScrn 74, -77, WhoHol B*
LaRue, Grace d1956 *AmPS B, Film 1, WhoHol B*
LaRue, Grace 1881-1956 *WhScrn 74, -77*
LaRue, Grace 1882-1956 *CmpEPM, NotNAT B, WhThe*
LaRue, Jack *MotPP*
LaRue, Jack 1900- *ForYSC, HolCA[port], WhoHol A*
LaRue, Jack 1902- *FilmEn, What 5[port]*
LaRue, Jack 1903- *FilmgC, HalFC 80, MovMk*
LaRue, Jan 1918- *Baker 78, NewGrD 80*
LaRue, Jean 1901-1956 *WhScrn 74, -77, WhoHol B*
LaRue, Lash 1921- *WhoHol A*
LaRue, Petri De 1460?-1518 *BnBkM 80*
LaRue, Pierchon 1460?-1518 *BnBkM 80*
LaRue, Pierre De 1455?-1518 *Baker 78*
LaRue, Pierre De 1460?-1518 *BnBkM 80, NewGrD 80*
Laruette, Jean-Louis 1731-1792 *NewGrD 80*
LaRusso, Louis, II 1935- *NatPD[port]*
Larway, J H *NewGrD 80*
LaSalette, Joubert De 1743-1833 *Baker 78*
Lasalle, Jean-Louis *Baker 78*
LaSalle, Richard W 1918- *AmSCAP 66*
Lasansky, Mauricio *PupTheA*
Lascarini, Francesco Maria *NewGrD 80*
Lascelles, George Henry Hubert *NewGrD 80*
Lasceux, Guillaume 1740-1831? *NewGrD 80*
Laschi, Luisa 176-?-1790? *NewGrD 80*
Lascoe, Henry 1914-1964 *NotNAT B, WhScrn 74, -77, WhoHol B*
Lasdun, Gary *MorBAP*
Laserna, Blas De 1751-1816 *Baker 78, NewGrD 80*
Laserna, Estacio De *NewGrD 80*
Laseroms, Wim 1944- *IntWWM 77, -80*
Lash, Andre Duane 1947- *IntWWM 77, -80*
Lasha, William B 1929- *BiDAmM*
Lashchilin, Lev Alexandrovich 1888-1955 *CnOxB*
LaShelle, Joseph 1903- *CmMov, FilmgC, HalFC 80*
LaShelle, Joseph 1905- *FilmEn, WorEFlm*
LaShelle, Kirke 1863-1905 *NotNAT B*
Lashinsky, Phil *ConMuA 80B*
Lashley, Donald *Film 2*
Lashof, Sheryl Beth 1955- *IntWWM 77, -80*
Lashwood, George d1942 *NotNAT B, WhThe*
LasInfantas, Fernando De *Baker 78*
Laska, Edward 1894-1959 *AmSCAP 66*
Laska, Gustav 1847-1928 *Baker 78*
Laskaris Pigonitis *NewGrD 80*
Laskaris, Joannes *NewGrD 80*
Lasker, Henry 1908- *AmSCAP 66*
Lasker, Jay *ConMuA 80B*
Lasker-Schuler, Else 1869-1945 *EncWT*
Lasker-Schuler, Else 1876-1945 *CnMD*
Laskiewicz, Eugene 1950- *IntWWM 80*
Laskine, Lily 1893- *NewGrD 80*
Laskos, Orestis 1908- *DcFM*
Laskovsky, Ivan Fyodorovich 1799-1855 *NewGrD 80*
Laskowich, Gloria *WomWMM B*
Lasky, Evan *ConMuA 80B*
Lasky, Jesse, Jr. 1908- *FilmEn*
Lasky, Jesse, Jr. 1910- *CmMov, DcFM, FilmgC, HalFC 80, IntMPA 77, -75, -76, -78, -79, -80*
Lasky, Jesse L 1880-1958 *BiDFilm, -81, DcFM, FilmEn, FilmgC, HalFC 80, NotNAT B, OxFilm, WorEFlm*
Lasky, Jesse L 1881-1958 *TwYS B*
Lasky, Paul S 1924- *AmSCAP 80*
Lasley, David Eldon 1947- *AmSCAP 80*
Lasner, Ignaz 1815-1883 *Baker 78*
Lasnier, Rina 1915- *CreCan 1*
Lasos Of Hermione *NewGrD 80, -80*
Lassale, Jean 1847-1909 *NewEOp 71*
Lassalle, Jean-Louis 1847-1909 *Baker 78, CmOp*
Lassally, Walter 1926- *DcFM, FilmEn, FilmgC, HalFC 80, OxFilm, WorEFlm*
Lassander, Dagmar *FilmAG WE*
Lassen, Eduard 1830-1904 *Baker 78, NewGrD 80, OxMus*
Lasser, Johann Baptist 1751-1805 *NewGrD 80*
Lasser, Louise 1935?- *MovMk, NewYTET, WhoHol A*
Lasser, Louise 1940?- *HalFC 80*
Lasser, Louise 1941- *FilmEn*
Lassie *Film 2, FilmgC, HalFC 80, OxFilm*
Lassie 1940?- *ForYSC*
Lassie 1941-1959 *WhScrn 77*
Lassnig, Maria *WomWMM B*
Lasso *NewGrD 80*
Lasso, Orlando De 1532-1594 *CmpBCM*
Lasso, Orlando Di 1532-1594 *BnBkM 80, GrComp[port], NewGrD 80[port]*
Lasson, Mathieu d1595 *NewGrD 80*
Lassus *NewGrD 80*
Lassus, Ferdinand De d1609 *Baker 78*
Lassus, Ferdinand De d1635? *Baker 78*
Lassus, Ferdinand De 1560?-1609 *NewGrD 80*
Lassus, Orlande De 1532-1594 *NewGrD 80[port]*
Lassus, Orlando Di 1532-1594 *MusMk[port]*

Lassus, Orlandus 1532?-1594 BnBkM 80, OxMus
Lassus, Roland De 1532-1594 Baker 78, NewGrD 80[port]
Lassus, Rudolph De 1563?-1625 Baker 78, NewGrD 80
Lasswell, Mary AmSCAP 80
Last, Brenda 1938- CnOxB, DancEn 78
Last, Gert 1921- IntWWM 77, -80
Last, Joan 1908- IntWWM 77, -80, WhoMus 72
LaStarza, Roland WhoHol A
Lastfogel, Abe 1898- BiE&WWA, HalFC 80, IntMPA 77, -75, -76, -78, -79, -80, NotNAT
LaStrange, Dick Film 1
Lasus Of Hermione NewGrD 80
Laszlo, Alexander 1895- AmSCAP 80, Baker 78, ConAmC, OxMus
Laszlo, Andrew 1926- FilmEn, HalFC 80
Laszlo, Andy 1934- FilmgC
Laszlo, Ernest 1905- FilmgC, HalFC 80
Laszlo, Ernest 1906- FilmEn, WorEFlm
Laszlo, Ferenc 1937- NewGrD 80
Laszlo, Goran Beer 1939- IntWWM 77
Laszlo, Magda 1919- CmOp, NewEOp 71, NewGrD 80
LaTaille, Jean De 1533?-1607? McGEWD[port]
Latarche, Pauline Winifred 1937- IntWWM 80
Latchem, Malcolm 1931- IntWWM 80
Lateef, Yusef 1920- ConAmC, DrBlPA
Lateef, Yusef 1921- BiDAmM, EncJzS 70, IlEncJ
Lateiner, Isidor 1930- IntWWM 80
Lateiner, Jacob 1928- NewGrD 80, WhoMus 72
Lateiner, Joseph 1853-1935 ModWD, NotNAT B, OxThe
Latell, Lyle 1905-1967 WhScrn 74, -77, WhoHol B
Latere, Petit Jean De NewGrD 80
Lates, Charles d1810? OxMus
Lates, James 1740?-1777 NewGrD 80
Lates, John James d1777 OxMus
Latham, Christopher Paul 1935- IntWWM 77, -80
Latham, Dwight B 1903- AmSCAP 66, -80
Latham, Fred G d1943 NotNAT B
Latham, Frederick G d1943 WhThe
Latham, Hope d1951 NotNAT B
Latham, Lorran 1916- IntWWM 77, -80
Latham, Louise WhoHol A
Latham, Peter 1894-1970 NewGrD 80
Latham, Richard Oskatel 1906- IntWWM 77, -80, WhoMus 72
Latham, Walter John Gordon 1916- WhoMus 72
Latham, William Peters 1917- AmSCAP 66, -80, Baker 78, ConAmC, IntWWM 77, -80
Latham, Woodville 1838-1911 FilmEn
Lathan, Stan 1944?- DrBlPA
Lathbury, Mary Artemisia 1841-1913 BiDAmM
Lathbury, Stanley 1873- WhThe
Lathom, Earl Of WhThe
LaThorilliere, Anne-Maurice 1697?-1759 OxThe
LaThorilliere, Francois Lenoir De 1626-1680 OxThe
LaThorilliere, Pierre 1659-1731 OxThe
Lathrop, Donald 1888-1940 WhScrn 74, -77, WhoHol B
Lathrop, Gayle Posselt 1942- ConAmC
Lathrop, Philip H 1916- FilmEn, FilmgC, HalFC 80, WorEFlm[port]
Latilla, Gaetano 1711-1788 Baker 78, NewGrD 80
Latimer, Billy Film 2
Latimer, Edyth WhThe
Latimer, Florence Film 2
Latimer, Henry d1963 NotNAT B
Latimer, Hugh 1913- WhoHol A, WhoThe 72, -77
Latimer, James H 1934- AmSCAP 66, -80, ConAmC
Latimer, Jonathan FilmgC, HalFC 80, IntMPA 77, -75, -76, -78, -79, -80
Latimer, Len ConMuA 80B
Latimer, Robert 1921- IntWWM 77
Latimer, Sally 1910- WhThe
Latimore, Frank 1925- FilmEn, FilmgC, ForYSC, HalFC 80, WhoHol A
Latio, Giovanni NewGrD 80
Latiolais, Jayne 1928- ConAmC
Latius, Joannes NewGrD 80
LaTombelle, Fernand De 1854-1928 Baker 78, NewGrD 80
Latona, Jen 1881- WhThe
LaToree, Charles 1900- IntMPA 80
LaTorraca, Gerard 1935- AmSCAP 80
LaTorre, Charles WhoHol A
LaTorre, Charles 1900- IntMPA 77, -75, -76, -78, -79
LaTorre, Charles A 1895- Film 2, Vers A[port]
Latorre, Geronimo NewGrD 80
Latoszewski, Zygmunt 1902- IntWWM 80
Latouche, John 1917-1956 AmPS, AmSCAP 66, -80, BestMus, BiDAmM, CmpEPM, EncMT, McGEWD, NewCBMT, NotNAT B
Latoudie, John PlP&P
Latour, Francis Tatton NewGrD 80
LaToure PupTheA
LaTourneaux, Robert WhoHol A
Latre, Petit Jean De NewGrD 80
LaTrobe, Charles 1879-1967 WhThe
Latrobe, Christian Ignatius 1758-1836 NewGrD 80
Latshaw, George DcPup, PupTheA, PupTheA SUP
Latsis, Peter C 1919- IntMPA 77, -75, -76, -78, -79, -80
Latta, C J IntMPA 75
Lattanzi, Joseph W 1950- AmSCAP 80
Lattanzi, Peppino William 1926- AmSCAP 80
Lattimer, Peter Arthur 1938- WhoMus 72
Lattimore, Harlan 1908- CmpEPM, WhoJazz 72
Lattimore, Richmond 1906- BiE&WWA, NotNAT
Latto, Evelyn PupTheA
Lattuada, Alberto 1914- BiDFilm, -81, DcFM, FilmEn, FilmgC, HalFC 80, IntMPA 77, -75, -76, -78, -79, -80, OxFilm, WorEFlm
Lattuada, Felice 1882-1962 Baker 78, NewEOp 71, NewGrD 80
LaTuillerie, Jean-Francois Juvenon 1650-1688 OxThe
LaTuillerie, Louise Catherine 1657?-1706 OxThe
Latzsch, Herbert 1917- NewGrD 80
Lau, Heinz 1925-1975 NewGrD 80
Laub, Ferdinand 1832-1875 Baker 78, NewGrD 80
Laub, T L 1852-1927 OxMus
Laub, Thomas 1852-1927 NewGrD 80
Laube, Anton 1718-1784 NewGrD 80
Laube, Heinrich 1806-1884 EncWT, OxThe
Laubenthal, Horst R 1939- NewGrD 80, WhoOp 76
Laubenthal, Rudolf 1886-1971 NewEOp 71, NewGrD 80
Lauber, John H 1939- IntWWM 77
Lauber, Joseph 1864-1952 Baker 78, OxMus
Lauber, Terry Donald 1949- AmSCAP 80
Laubin, Gladys CnOxB, DancEn 78
Laubin, Reginald CnOxB, DancEn 78
Laubscher, Philippe 1936- IntWWM 77, -80
Lauchery, Albert 1779-1853 CnOxB
Lauchery, Etienne 1732-1820 CnOxB, NewGrD 80
Lauchlan, Agnes 1905- WhoThe 72, -77
Lauck, Chester 1902- JoeFr, WhoHol A
Lauckner, Rolf 1887-1954 CnMD, ModWD
Lauclos, Henri De NewGrD 80
Laud, William 1573-1645 OxMus
Laudeman, Pete 1908-1963 NewOrJ
Lauder, Sir Harry 1870-1950 CmpEPM, Ent[port], Film 2, FilmgC, HalFC 80, IlWWBF, JoeFr, NewGrD 80, NotNAT A, -B, OxThe, WhScrn 74, -77, WhThe, WhoHol B
Lauderdale, John Frederick 1935- IntWWM 80
Laudi, Victorino NewGrD 80
Laudis, Francesco d1600 NewGrD 80
Laudivio OxThe
Laufenberg, Heinrich 1390?-1460 NewGrD 80
Laufer, Beatrice 1923- AmSCAP 66, -80, ConAmC
Laufer, Calvin Weiss 1874-1938 BiDAmM
Laufer, Murray Bernard 1929- CreCan 1, WhoOp 76
Laufer, Wolfgang 1946- IntWWM 80
Lauffensteiner, Wolff Jacob 1676-1754 NewGrD 80
Laughing Charley BluesWW[port]
Laughlan, Agnes PlP&P
Laughlin, Anna 1885-1937 Film 1, NotNAT B, WhoHol B, WhoStg 1906, -1908
Laughlin, Billy 1932-1948 WhScrn 77
Laughlin, Kathleen WomWMM B
Laughlin, Sharon NotNAT
Laughlin, Tom IntMPA 77, -76, -78, -79, -80, WhoHol A, WomWMM
Laughlin, Tom 1931- MovMk[port]
Laughlin, Tom 1938- FilmEn, FilmgC, HalFC 80
Laughton, Charles 1899-1962 BiDFilm, -81, CmMov, CnThe, EncWT, FamA&A[port], FilmAG WE, FilmEn, Film 2, FilmgC, ForYSC, HalFC 80, IlWWBF[port], -A, MotPP, MovMk[port], NotNAT A, -B, OxFilm, PlP&P, WhScrn 74, -77, WhThe, WhoHol B, WhoHrs 80[port], WorEFlm[port]
Laughton, Eddie d1952 WhoHol B
Laughton, Edward 1903-1952 WhScrn 74, -77
Laugier, Marc-Antoine 1713-1769 NewGrD 80
Lauher, Bob 1931-1973 WhScrn 77
Laumer, Denise 1930- DancEn 78
Launay, Denise 1906- NewGrD 80
Launder, Frank 1907- FilmEn, FilmgC, HalFC 80, IlWWBF, -A, IntMPA 77, -75, -76, -78, -79, -80, OxFilm, WorEFlm
Launders, Perc 1905-1952 WhScrn 74, -77, WhoHol B
Launis, Armas Emanuel 1884-1959 Baker 78, NewGrD 80
Laurel, Bobby AmSCAP 80
Laurel, Kay 1890-1927 WhScrn 77
Laurel, Stan 1890-1965 BiDFilm 81, CmMov, FilmEn, Film 1, -2, FilmgC, Funs[port], HalFC 80[port], JoeFr[port], MGM[port], MotPP, MovMk[port], OxFilm, TwYS, WhScrn 74, -77, WhoHol B, WhoHrs 80[port], WorEFlm[port]
Laurel, Stan 1891-1965 ForYSC
Laurel, Stan And Oliver Hardy ForYSC
Laurel And Hardy BiDFilm, FilmEn, Funs[port], GrMovC[port], JoeFr[port], MotPP, OxFilm
Laurell, Kay Film 1
Lauren, Rod ForYSC
Lauren, Rod 1940- RkOn
Laurence, Anya IntWWM 80
Laurence, Bob ConMuA 80B
Laurence, Douglas 1922- IntMPA 77, -75, -76, -78, -79, -80
Laurence, Frederick 1884- Baker 78
Laurence, Gilbert PupTheA
Laurence, Jean Margaret Wemyss 1926- CreCan 1
Laurence, Margaret 1926- CreCan 1
Laurence, Michael 1928- AmSCAP 66, -80
Laurence, Paula 1916- BiE&WWA, NotNAT, WhoThe 72, -77
Laurence, Victor AmSCAP 80
Laurencie, Lionel DeLa Baker 78, NewGrD 80
Laurencin, Ferdinand Peter 1819-1890 Baker 78
Laurencin, Marie 1885-1956 CnOxB, DancEn 78
Laurencinus Romanus NewGrD 80
Laurendeau, Andre 1912-1968 CreCan 2
Laurens, Edmond 1852-1925 Baker 78
Laurenson, James 1935- HalFC 80
Laurent, Jeanne Marie Film 2
Laurenti NewGrD 80
Laurenti, Angelo Maria NewGrD 80
Laurenti, Antonia Maria Novelli NewGrD 80
Laurenti, Bartolomeo Girolamo 1644?-1726 Baker 78, NewGrD 80
Laurenti, Filiberto 1619?-1651? NewGrD 80
Laurenti, Franco Mattia 1928- WhoOp 76
Laurenti, Girolamo Nicolo d1751 NewGrD 80
Laurenti, Lodovico Filippo NewGrD 80
Laurenti, Pietro Paolo 1675?-1719 NewGrD 80
Laurentius De Florentia NewGrD 80
Laurentius Von Schnifis 1633-1702 NewGrD 80

Laurentius Von Schnuffis 1633-1702 *NewGrD 80*
Laurentius Von Schnufis 1633-1702 *NewGrD 80*
Laurents, Arthur *IntMPA 77, -75, -76, -78, -79, -80*
Laurents, Arthur 1918- *BestMus, BiE&WWA, ConDr 73, -77, EncMT, Ent, FilmEn, FilmgC, HalFC 80, McGEWD[port], NewCBMT, NotNAT, PlP&P, WhoThe 72, -77*
Laurents, Arthur 1920- *CnMD, EncWT, ModWD*
Laurenz, John 1909-1958 *WhScrn 74, -77*
Laurenze, John d1958 *WhoHol B*
Laurenzi, Filiberto 1619?-1651? *NewGrD 80*
Laurenzini *NewGrD 80*
Lauri, Edward d1919 *NotNAT B*
Lauri-Volpi, Giacomo 1892- *MusSN[port]*
Lauri-Volpi, Giacomo 1892-1979 *Baker 78, CmOp, NewGrD 80*
Lauri-Volpi, Giacomo 1894- *NewEOp 71*
Lauricella, Remo 1912- *WhoMus 72*
Lauricella, Remo 1918- *IntWWM 77, -80*
Lauridsen, Morten Johannes 1943- *AmSCAP 80, ConAmC*
Lauridsen, Morton 1943- *CpmDNM 74*
Laurie, Alison Margaret 1935- *IntWWM 80*
Laurie, Annie *RkOn*
Laurie, Cynthia 1924- *IntWWM 77, -80*
Laurie, Joe, Jr. 1892-1954 *JoeFr, NotNAT B*
Laurie, John 1897-1980 *FilmEn, FilmgC, HalFC 80, IntMPA 77, -75, -76, -78, -79, -80, MovMk, PlP&P, WhoHol A, WhoThe 72, -77*
Laurie, Linda *AmSCAP 80*
Laurie, Piper 1932- *CmMov, FilmEn, FilmgC, ForYSC, HalFC 80, IntMPA 77, -75, -76, -78, -79, -80, MotPP, MovMk, WhoHol A, WhoHrs 80, WorEFlm*
Laurie, Vere *WhoMus 72*
Laurier, Jay 1879-1969 *WhScrn 74, -77, WhThe, WhoHol B*
Laurillard, Edward 1870-1936 *WhThe*
Laurischkus, Max 1876-1929 *Baker 78*
Lauriston, Michael Owen 1951- *IntWWM 77, -80*
Lauritzen, Lau 1878-1938 *DcFM, FilmEn*
Lauritzen, Lau, Jr. 1910- *DcFM, FilmEn*
Lauro, Antonio 1917- *Baker 78*
Lauro, Domenico 1540-1607? *NewGrD 80*
Lauro, Hieronymo Del *NewGrD 80*
Laurus, Dominicus 1540-1607? *NewGrD 80*
Lausch, Laurenz *NewGrD 80*
Lauschmann, Richard Otto 1889- *IntWWM 77, -80*
Lauska, Franz 1764-1825 *Baker 78*
Lauste, Eugene 1856-1935 *DcFM, FilmEn*
Lauter, Ed 1936- *HalFC 80*
Lauter, Harry *ForYSC*
Lauter, Harry 1920- *FilmgC, HalFC 80, WhoHol A*
Lauter, Harry 1925- *HolCA[port], WhoHrs 80*
Lauterbach, Johann Christoph 1832-1918 *Baker 78, NewGrD 80*
Lauterer, Arch 1905-1957 *DancEn 78*
Lautner, Georges 1926- *FilmEn, WorEFlm*
Lauverjat, Pierre d1625? *NewGrD 80*
Laux, Karl 1896-1978 *NewGrD 80*
Lauxmin, Zygmunt 1596?-1670 *NewGrD 80*
Lava, William 1911-1971 *AmSCAP 66, -80*
Lavagne, Andre 1913- *Baker 78*
Lavagnino, Angelo Francesco 1909- *Baker 78*
Lavalette, Bernard 1926- *WhoMus 72*
Lavallade, Carmen De 1931- *CnOxB*
Lavalle, Paul 1908- *AmSCAP 66, -80, CmpEPM, IntMPA 75*
Lavalle-Garcia, Armando 1924- *Baker 78*
Lavallee, Calixa 1842-1891 *Baker 78, BiDAmM, NewGrD 80, OxMus*
Lavallee, Nicole *WomWMM*
LaValley, Doug Louis 1934- *BiDAmM*
Lavalliere, Eve 1866-1929 *NotNAT A, -B, WhThe*
Lavani, Carmen 1942- *WhoOp 76*
Lavarne, Laura *Film 1, -2*
LaVarre, Myrtland *Film 2*
Lavaux, Nicolas *NewGrD 80*
Lavedan, Henri 1859-1940 *CnMD, McGEWD[port], ModWD, NotNAT B, OxThe, WhThe*
Laveglia, Demetrio 1948- *IntWWM 77*
LaVelle, Barbara *Film 2*
LaVelle, Kay 1889-1965 *WhScrn 77*
Laven, Arnold 1922- *FilmEn, FilmgC, HalFC 80, IntMPA 77, -75, -76, -78, -79, -80*
Lavender *Film 2*
Lavenu *NewGrD 80*
Lavenu, Elizabeth *NewGrD 80*
Lavenu, Lewis d1818 *NewGrD 80*
Lavenu, Louis Henry 1818-1859 *NewGrD 80*
Laver, James 1899- *BiE&WWA, NotNAT A, OxThe, WhThe*
LaVere, Charles 1910- *AmSCAP 66*
Lavere, Charles 1910- *AmSCAP 80*
LaVere, Charles 1910- *WhoJazz 72*
LaVere, Earl d1962 *NotNAT B*
LaVere, Frank 1917-1976 *AmSCAP 80*
Lavergne, Antoine-Barthelemy 1670?-1726 *NewGrD 80*
Laverick, Beryl 1919- *WhThe*
Laverick, June 1932- *FilmgC, HalFC 80*
Laverne, Andrew Mark 1947- *AmSCAP 80*
LaVerne, Jane *Film 2*
LaVerne, Lucille 1869-1945 *ForYSC, TwYS*
LaVerne, Lucille 1872-1945 *Film 1, -2, HolCA[port], NotNAT B, WhScrn 74, -77, WhThe, WhoHol B*
Laverne, Pattie d1916 *NotNAT B*
LaVernie, Laura 1853-1939 *WhScrn 74, -77, WhoHol B*
Lavers, Marjorie 1916- *WhoMus 72*
Laverty, Jean *Film 2*
Lavery, Emmet *HalFC 80*
Lavery, Emmet 1902- *BiE&WWA, CnMD, ModWD, NotNAT*
Lavery, Emmet G, Jr. 1927- *HalFC 80, IntMPA 77, -75, -76, -78, -79, -80*
Lavery, Frank 1922- *WhoMus 72*
Lavi, Daliah 1940- *FilmEn, FilmgC, ForYSC, HalFC 80, MotPP, WhoHol A*
LaVieville, Jean Laurent LeCerf De *NewGrD 80*
Lavigna, Vincenzo 1776-1836 *Baker 78, NewGrD 80*
Lavignac, Albert 1846-1916 *Baker 78, NewGrD 80*
LaVigne, Andrieu De d1515? *McGEWD*
Lavigne, Antoine-Joseph 1816-1886 *Baker 78*
Lavin, Carlos 1883-1962 *NewGrD 80*
Lavin, Linda *IntMPA 79, -80, WhoHol A*
Lavin, Linda 1937- *WhoThe 72, -77*
Lavin, Linda 1939- *NotNAT*
Lavine, Jack *Film 2*
Lavinia *OxThe*
Laviola, Marisa Anne 1954- *IntWWM 80*
LaViolette, Juliette *Film 2*
LaViolette, Wesley 1894- *AmSCAP 66, Baker 78, BiDAmM, ConAmC, WhoMus 72*
Lavirgen, Pedro 1930- *NewGrD 80, WhoOp 76*
Lavista, Mario 1943- *Baker 78*
Lavoie, Elizabeth *AmSCAP 80*
Lavoie, Roland Kent 1943- *AmSCAP 80*
Lavoix, Henri-Marie-Francois 1846-1897 *Baker 78, OxMus*
Lavotha, Elemer Odon 1952- *IntWWM 77, -80*
Lavotta, Janos 1764-1820 *NewGrD 80*
LaVoye-Mignot, De d1684 *NewGrD 80*
Lavrangas, Denis 1864-1941 *Baker 78*
Lavrangas, Dionyssios 1860?-1941 *NewGrD 80*
Lavrenev, Boris Andreevich 1892-1959 *CnMD, ModWD*
Lavreniuk, Alexander Alexandrovich 1939- *CnOxB*
Lavrovskaya, Elizaveta Andreyevna 1845-1919 *NewGrD 80*
Lavrovsky, Leonid Mikhailovich 1905-1957 *DancEn 78, NewGrD 80*
Lavrovsky, Leonid Mikhailovich 1905-1967 *CnOxB*
Lavrovsky, Mikhail Leonidovich 1941- *CnOxB*
Lavry, Marc 1903-1967 *Baker 78, NewGrD 80*
Lavsky, Phyllis 1948- *AmSCAP 80*
Lavsky, Richard Harry 1940- *AmSCAP 80*
Law, Alex W 1909- *AmSCAP 66, -80*
Law, Andrew 1748-1821 *BiDAmM*
Law, Andrew 1749-1821 *Baker 78, NewGrD 80, OxMus*
Law, Arthur 1844-1913 *NotNAT B, WhThe*
Law, Burton 1880-1963 *Film 2, WhScrn 77*
Law, Daniel Ping-Leung 1946- *IntWWM 80*
Law, Don *ConMuA 80B*
Law, Don Fats 1920-1959 *WhoHol B*
Law, Donald 1920-1959 *WhScrn 74, -77*
Law, Jenny Lou d1961 *NotNAT B*
Law, John Philip 1936- *WhoHrs 80*
Law, John Philip 1937- *FilmgC, IntMPA 77, -75, -76, -78, -79, -80*
Law, John Phillip 1937- *FilmEn, ForYSC, HalFC 80, MotPP, WhoHol A*
Law, Mary 1891- *WhThe*
Law, Mouzon 1922- *BiE&WWA, NotNAT*
Law, Nellie Winifred 1901- *IntWWM 77, -80, WhoMus 72*
Law, Rodman 1885-1919 *WhScrn 77*
Law, Walter 1876-1940 *Film 1, -2, WhScrn 74, -77, WhoHol B*
Law, Winnie *Film 2*
Lawatsch, Anna Maria Demuth 1712-1759 *BiDAmM*
Lawergren, Bo 1937- *CpmDNM 80, ConAmC*
Lawes, Henry 1596-1662 *Baker 78, BnBkM 80, MusMk, NewGrD 80[port], OxMus*
Lawes, Lewis E 1884-1947 *WhScrn 74, -77*
Lawes, William 1602-1645 *Baker 78, BnBkM 80, NewGrD 80[port], OxMus*
Lawford, Betty 1910-1960 *Film 2, NotNAT B, WhScrn 74, -77, WhThe, WhoHol B*
Lawford, Ernest *Film 2*
Lawford, Ernest d1940 *NotNAT B, WhThe*
Lawford, Peter 1923- *FilmAG WE, FilmEn, FilmgC, ForYSC[port], HalFC 80, IntMPA 77, -75, -76, -78, -79, -80, MGM[port], MotPP, MovMk[port], OxFilm, WhoHol A, WorEFlm*
Lawford, Sir Sydney 1866-1953 *WhScrn 74, -77*
Lawlars, Ernest 1900-1961 *BluesWW*
Lawler, Anderson *Film 2*
Lawler, Jerome *Film 1*
Lawler, Ray 1921- *BiE&WWA, ConDr 77, EncWT, Ent, ModWD, NotNAT, OxThe*
Lawler, Ray 1922- *CnMD, CnThe, McGEWD, REnWD[port]*
Lawler, Raymond Evenor 1921?- *ConDr 73*
Lawley, John William Graham 1944- *IntWWM 80*
Lawlor, Charles B 1852-1925 *AmSCAP 66, -80, BiDAmM, NotNAT B*
Lawlor, Mary *WhThe, WhoHol A*
Lawlor, Robert *Film 1*
Lawlor, Thomas 1938- *IntWWM 77, -80*
Lawner, Morris 1910- *ConAmC*
Lawnhurst, Vee 1905- *AmSCAP 66, -80, CmpEPM*
Lawrance, Brian *CmpEPM*
Lawrance, Jody 1920- *ForYSC*
Lawrance, Jody 1930- *FilmEn, FilmgC, HalFC 80*
Lawrence, Adrian d1953 *NotNAT B*
Lawrence, Anne Dorothy 1922- *IntWWM 77, -80, WhoMus 72*
Lawrence, Arnie 1938- *EncJzS 70*
Lawrence, Arthur Peter 1937- *IntWWM 77, -80*
Lawrence, Ashley 1934- *CnOxB, NewGrD 80*
Lawrence, Azar 1953- *EncJzS 70*
Lawrence, Barbara *MotPP*
Lawrence, Barbara 1928- *FilmEn, FilmgC, ForYSC, HalFC 80*
Lawrence, Barbara 1930- *IntMPA 77, -75, -76, -78, -79, -80*
Lawrence, Bill d1972 *NewYTET*
Lawrence, Boyle 1869-1951 *NotNAT B, WhThe*
Lawrence, Bryan 1936- *CnOxB, DancEn 78*
Lawrence, C E d1940 *NotNAT B*
Lawrence, Carol *AmPS B, BiE&WWA, MotPP, WhoHol A*
Lawrence, Carol 1932- *EncMT*
Lawrence, Carol 1935- *ForYSC, WhoThe 77*
Lawrence, Charles 1896- *WhThe*
Lawrence, Charlie *WhScrn 77*
Lawrence, Charlie 1905- *WhoJazz 72*
Lawrence, Cornelius C 1902- *AmSCAP 66, -80*
Lawrence, D H 1885-1930 *CnThe, FilmgC, HalFC 80, ModWD, WhThe*

Lawrence, D H 1885-1940 *NotNAT B*
Lawrence, Dakota 1902- *Film 1, TwYS*
Lawrence, David Herbert 1885-1930 *CnMD*
Lawrence, David Herbert 1885-1931 *EncWT*
Lawrence, David John 1955- *IntWWM 80*
Lawrence, Delphi 1927?- *FilmgC, HalFC 80, WhoHol A*
Lawrence, Douglas Howard 1942- *IntWWM 77, -80, WhoOp 76*
Lawrence, E W *Film 1*
Lawrence, Eddie *AmSCAP 80, NatPD[port], RkOn*
Lawrence, Eddy d1931 *WhScrn 74, -77*
Lawrence, Edward d1931 *Film 2, WhoHol B*
Lawrence, Elizabeth *WhoHol A*
Lawrence, Elliot *BgBands 74[port]*
Lawrence, Elliot 1925- *AmSCAP 66, -80, CmpEPM, NotNAT*
Lawrence, Elliot 1926- *BiE&WWA*
Lawrence, Elliott 1925- *BiDAmM*
Lawrence, Florence 1886-1938 *FilmEn, FilmgC, HalFC 80*
Lawrence, Florence 1888-1938 *Film 1, -2, MotPP, NotNAT B, OxFilm, TwYS, WhScrn 74, -77, WhoHol B*
Lawrence, Georgia d1923 *NotNAT B*
Lawrence, Gerald 1873-1957 *Film 2, IlWWBF, NotNAT B, OxThe, WhThe, WhoHol B, WhoStg 1906, -1908*
Lawrence, Gertrude 1898-1952 *AmPS B, CmpEPM, CnThe, EncMT, EncWT, Ent[port], FamA&A[port], FilmEn, Film 2, FilmgC, ForYSC, HalFC 80, IlWWBF, -A, NotNAT A, -B, OxFilm, OxThe, PlP&P, ThFT[port], WhScrn 74, -77, WhThe, WhoHol B, WorEFlm*
Lawrence, Gregory 1916- *AmSCAP 66*
Lawrence, Harold 1906- *AmSCAP 66, -80*
Lawrence, Jack 1912- *AmSCAP 66, -80, BiE&WWA, CmpEPM*
Lawrence, Jerome 1915- *AmSCAP 66, -80, BiE&WWA, ConDr 73, -77, EncMT, ModWD, NotNAT, WhoThe 72, -77*
Lawrence, Jody 1930- *FilmEn, IntMPA 77, -75, -76, -78, -79, -80*
Lawrence, John 1910-1974 *WhScrn 77, WhoHol B*
Lawrence, Lawrence Shubert 1894-1965 *BiE&WWA, NotNAT B*
Lawrence, Lawrence Shubert, Jr. 1916- *BiE&WWA, NotNAT*
Lawrence, Leslie 1934- *CreCan 2*
Lawrence, Lillian 1870-1926 *Film 1, -2, WhScrn 74, -77, WhoHol B, WhoStg 1906, -1908*
Lawrence, Lou 1913-1978 *AmSCAP 80*
Lawrence, Lucile *IntWWM 80*
Lawrence, Marc *IntMPA 77, -75, -76, -78, -79, -80, WhoHol A*
Lawrence, Marc 1909- *Vers A[port]*
Lawrence, Marc 1910- *CmMov, FilmEn, FilmgC, ForYSC, HalFC 80, HolCA[port], MovMk, WhoHrs 80*
Lawrence, Margaret 1889-1929 *NotNAT B, WhThe*
Lawrence, Marjorie 1902-1979 *HalFC 80*
Lawrence, Marjorie 1907-1979 *Baker 78*
Lawrence, Marjorie 1909-1979 *CmOp, MusSN[port], NewEOp 71, NewGrD 80*
Lawrence, Marjorie Florence *WhoMus 72*
Lawrence, Marjory *Film 1*
Lawrence, Mark 1921- *AmSCAP 66, -80*
Lawrence, Martin 1909- *IntWWM 77, -80*
Lawrence, Mary *WhoHol A*
Lawrence, Michael Stephen 1945- *AmSCAP 80*
Lawrence, Morris Joseph, Jr. 1940- *AmSCAP 80*
Lawrence, Pamela *AmSCAP 80*
Lawrence, Pauline 1900-1971 *CnOxB, DancEn 78*
Lawrence, Quentin 1923?- *FilmgC, HalFC 80, IlWWBF*
Lawrence, Raymond *Film 2*
Lawrence, Reginald 1900-1967 *BiE&WWA, NotNAT B*
Lawrence, Robert 1912- *IntWWM 77, -80, NewEOp 71*
Lawrence, Robert L 1919- *IntMPA 77, -75, -76, -78, -79*
Lawrence, Russell Lee 1942- *NatPD[port]*
Lawrence, Sheila 1945- *IntWWM 77, -80*
Lawrence, Shirley 1932- *AmSCAP 66*
Lawrence, Sidney Jason 1909- *AmSCAP 80, IntWWM 77, -80*
Lawrence, Slingsby *OxThe*
Lawrence, Stan *BiE&WWA*
Lawrence, Stephen 1939- *AmSCAP 80*
Lawrence, Steve 1935- *AmPS A, AmSCAP 66, -80, BiDAmM, BiE&WWA, EncMT, NotNAT, RkOn[port], WhoHol A*
Lawrence, T E 1888-1935 *HalFC 80, PlP&P*
Lawrence, Vera Brodsky 1909- *Baker 78*
Lawrence, Vicki 1949- *RkOn 2[port], WhoHol A*
Lawrence, Vincent 1896- *WhThe*
Lawrence, Vincent S 1890-1946 *NotNAT B, WhThe*
Lawrence, Viola 1894-1973 *HalFC 80, WomWMM*
Lawrence, W E *Film 1*
Lawrence, Walter N d1920 *NotNAT B*
Lawrence, William d1921 *NotNAT B*
Lawrence, William E 1896-1947 *Film 2, WhScrn 74, -77, WhoHol B*
Lawrence, William John 1862-1940 *NotNAT B*
Lawrence, William John 1862-1941 *WhThe*
Lawrence-Archer, E A 1943- *IntWWM 77, -80*
Lawrenson, John 1932- *WhoMus 72*
Lawrowka, Elizaveta Andreyevna *NewGrD 80*
Lawry, Eleanor McChesney 1908- *IntWWM 77, -80*
Laws, Hubert 1939- *BiDAmM, DrBlPA, EncJzS 70*
Laws, Maury 1923- *AmSCAP 80*
Laws, Ronald Wayne 1950- *AmSCAP 80, EncJzS 70*
Laws, Sam *DrBlPA, WhoHol A*
Lawshe, Wilford *AmSCAP 80*
Lawson, Big Jim Harry 1904- *WhoJazz 72*
Lawson, Eleanor 1875-1966 *Film 2, WhScrn 77*
Lawson, Elsie *Film 1, -2*
Lawson, Ernest 1873-1939 *CreCan 2*
Lawson, Gordon Balfour Grant 1931- *WhoMus 72*
Lawson, Helen Mitchell Morosco *WhScrn 74, -77*
Lawson, James Kerr *CreCan 1*
Lawson, Mrs. James Sharp *CreCan 1*
Lawson, Joan 1907- *CnOxB*
Lawson, Joan 1908- *DancEn 78*
Lawson, John 1865-1920 *NotNAT B, WhThe*
Lawson, John 1911- *EncJzS 70*
Lawson, John Howard *PlP&P*
Lawson, John Howard 1886-1977 *DcFM, FilmgC, HalFC 80*
Lawson, John Howard 1894-1977 *BiE&WWA, ConDr 73, -77, FilmEn, IntMPA 77, -75, -76, -78, -79, -80, McGEWD, NotNAT, WorEFlm*
Lawson, John Howard 1895- *CnMD, CnThe, EncWT, ModWD, OxFilm, WhThe*
Lawson, John R 1911- *BiDAmM*
Lawson, Kate 1894- *BiE&WWA, NotNAT*
Lawson, Leigh 1944- *HalFC 80*
Lawson, Linda *WhoHol A*
Lawson, Mary 1910-1941 *NotNAT B, WhThe, WhoHol B*
Lawson, Peter 1950- *IntWWM 77, -80*
Lawson, Richard *DrBlPA*
Lawson, Richard Hugh Jerome 1935- *EncJzS 70*
Lawson, Robb d1947 *NotNAT B*
Lawson, Sarah 1928- *HalFC 80, IntMPA 77, -75, -76, -78, -79, -80, WhoHol A*
Lawson, Tedd *AmSCAP 80*
Lawson, Warner 1903- *BiDAmM*
Lawson, Wilfred 1900-1966 *CnThe*
Lawson, Wilfrid 1900-1966 *FilmAG WE, FilmEn, FilmgC, HalFC 80, IlWWBF[port], NotNAT B, WhScrn 74, -77, WhThe, WhoHol B*
Lawson, Winifred 1894-1961 *NotNAT B, WhThe*
Lawson, Yank 1911- *CmpEPM, EncJzS 70, IlEncJ, WhoJazz 72*
Lawton, Alma *WhoHol A*
Lawton, Charles, Jr. 1904-1965 *CmMov, FilmEn, HalFC 80, WorEFlm*
Lawton, Dorothy 1874-1960 *Baker 78, NewGrD 80*
Lawton, Frank d1914 *NotNAT B*
Lawton, Frank 1904-1969 *FilmAG WE, FilmEn, Film 2, FilmgC, ForYSC, HalFC 80, IlWWBF[port], WhScrn 74, -77, WhThe, WhoHol B*
Lawton, Jack *Film 1*
Lawton, Jimmy *AmSCAP 80*
Lawton, Mitzi *WhoMus 72*
Lawton, Robert H 1930- *IntWWM 77*
Lawton, Sidney Maurice 1924- *IntWWM 77, -80, WhoMus 72*
Lawton, Thais 1881-1956 *NotNAT B, WhScrn 74, -77, WhThe, WhoHol B*
Lawyer, M H 1909- *IntMPA 77, -75, -76, -78, -79, -80*
Lax, Frances 1895-1975 *WhScrn 77, WhoHol C*
Lay, Beirne, Jr. 1909- *CmMov, HalFC 80, IntMPA 77, -75, -76, -78, -79, -80*
Lay, Francois *NewGrD 80*
Lay, Irving T d1932 *WhScrn 74, -77*
Lay, Kenneth John 1953- *IntWWM 80*
Laycock, Ada *Film 2*
Laycock, Florence Hilda 1902- *WhoMus 72*
Laycock, Geoffrey Newton Stephen 1927- *IntWWM 77, -80, WhoMus 72*
Laycock, Jolyon 1946- *IntWWM 80*
Laycock, Ralph G *CpmDNM 80*
Laydu, Claude 1927- *FilmEn, FilmgC, HalFC 80*
Laye, Dilys 1934- *WhoHol A, WhoThe 72, -77*
Laye, Evelyn 1900- *BiE&WWA, EncMT, Film 2, FilmgC, ForYSC, HalFC 80, IlWWBF, -A, IntMPA 77, -75, -76, -78, -79, -80, NotNAT, -A, ThFT[port], WhoHol A, WhoThe 72, -77*
Layer, Friedemann 1941- *WhoOp 76*
Laylan, Rollo 1910?- *WhoJazz 72*
Layne, Ruth *AmSCAP 80*
Layolle, Alamanne De 1521?-1590 *NewGrD 80*
Layolle, Francesco De 1492-1540? *NewGrD 80*
Layritz, Friedrich 1808-1859 *NewGrD 80*
Layriz, Friedrich 1808-1859 *NewGrD 80*
Lays, Francois 1758-1831 *NewGrD 80*
Layton, Barbara Soehner 1945- *AmSCAP 80*
Layton, Billy Jim 1924- *AmSCAP 66, -80, Baker 78, ConAmC, DcCM, IntWWM 77, -80, NewGrD 80*
Layton, Dorothy *WhoHol A*
Layton, Edward *AmSCAP 80*
Layton, Irving Peter 1912- *CreCan 2*
Layton, J Turner *BlkAmP*
Layton, Joe 1931- *BiE&WWA, CnOxB, DancEn 78, EncMT, NotNAT, WhoThe 72, -77*
Layton, John Turner 1849-1916 *BiDAmM*
Layton, Robert 1930- *IntWWM 80, NewGrD 80, WhoMus 72*
Layton, Turner 1894- *BiDAmM, CmpEPM*
Layzer, Arthur 1927- *ConAmC*
Lazar, Filip 1894-1936 *Baker 78, NewGrD 80*
Lazar, Irving 1907- *BiE&WWA*
Lazar, Joel 1941- *IntWWM 77, -80*
Lazare, Martin 1829-1897 *Baker 78*
Lazarev, Alexander *WhoOp 76*
Lazari, Alberto *NewGrD 80*
Lazari, Ferdinando Antonio *NewGrD 80*
Lazaridis, Stefanos 1942- *WhoOp 76*
Lazarini, Scipione *NewGrD 80*
Lazaro, Francisco 1932- *WhoOp 76*
Lazarof, Henri 1932- *Baker 78, CpmDNM 77, -78, -79, ConAmC, DcCM, NewGrD 80*
Lazarref, Hal *ConMuA 80B*
Lazarus, Daniel 1898-1964 *Baker 78, NewGrD 80*
Lazarus, Emma 1849-1894 *BiDAmM*
Lazarus, Erna *IntMPA 77, -75, -76, -78, -79, -80*
Lazarus, Gustav 1861-1920 *Baker 78*
Lazarus, Henry 1815-1895 *NewGrD 80*
Lazarus, Margaret *WomWMM B*
Lazarus, Paul N 1913- *IntMPA 77, -75, -76, -78, -79, -80*
Lazarus, Paul N, III *IntMPA 77, -75, -76, -78, -79, -80*
Lazarus, Roy 1930- *WhoOp 76*
Lazarus, Theodore R 1919- *IntMPA 77, -75,*

-76, -78, -79, -80
Lazarus, Thomas L 1942- *IntMPA 77, -75, -76, -78, -79, -80*
Lazarz, Andrysowicz d1577 *NewGrD 80*
Lazenby, George 1939- *FilmgC, HalFC 80, MovMk, WhoHol A, WhoHrs 80*
Lazer, Peter 1946- *BiE&WWA*
Lazlo, Alexander 1895- *AmSCAP 66*
Lazowski, Yurek 1917- *CnOxB, DancEn 78[port]*
Lazy Lester *BluesWW[port]*
Lazy Slim Jim *BluesWW[port]*
Lazzari, Agostino Orlando 1919- *WhoOp 76*
Lazzari, Ferdinando Antonio 1678-1754 *NewGrD 80*
Lazzari, Sylvio 1857-1944 *Baker 78*
Lazzari, Virgilio 1887-1953 *CmOp, NewEOp 71, NewGrD 80*
Lazzarini, Scipione 1620?-1675? *NewGrD 80*
Lazzeri, Tony *Film 2*
Lazzini, Joseph 1927- *CnOxB, DancEn 78*
Le Strange *NewGrD 80*
Lea, Marion d1944 *NotNAT B*
Lea-Cox, Peter 1945- *IntWWM 80*
Leach, Andrew James Barnett 1937- *IntWWM 77, -80*
Leach, J M *WhoMus 72*
Leach, James 1762-1798 *NewGrD 80*
Leach, John 1931- *IntWWM 77, -80, WhoMus 72*
Leach, Rowland 1885- *BiDAmM, ConAmC*
Leach, Wilford 1929- *BiE&WWA, NotNAT*
Leachman, Cloris *IntMPA 75, -76, WhoHol A*
Leachman, Cloris 1926- *FilmEn, HalFC 80, MovMk[port]*
Leachman, Cloris 1927- *ForYSC*
Leachman, Cloris 1930- *IntMPA 77, -78, -79, -80*
Leachman, Cloris 1933- *FilmgC*
Leacock, Philip 1917- *BiDFilm, DcFM, FilmEn, FilmgC, HalFC 80, IlWWBF, NewYTET, WorEFlm*
Leacock, Richard 1921- *BiDFilm, -81, DcFM, FilmEn, FilmgC, HalFC 80, OxFilm, WomWMM, WorEFlm*
Leacock, Stephen 1869-1944 *CreCan 2*
Lead Belly *BluesWW[port]*
Leadbelly 1885-1949 *BiDAmM, BluesWW[port], ConMuA 80A, DrBlPA, EncFCWM 69, NewGrD 80*
Leader, Anton Morris *IntMPA 77, -75, -76, -78, -79, -80*
Leader, Harry *IntWWM 77, -80, WhoMus 72*
Leadlay, Edward O d1951 *WhThe*
Leaf, Ann *AmSCAP 66, -80*
Leaf, Caroline *WomWMM B*
Leaf, Paul *MorBAP*
League, Janet *DrBlPA*
League, Raymond *BlkAmP*
Leah, Philip John 1948- *IntWWM 77, -80*
Leahy, Eugene 1883-1967 *WhScrn 77, WhThe*
Leahy, Joseph J 1916-1974 *AmSCAP 80*
Leahy, Margaret d1967 *Film 2, WhScrn 77, WhoHol B*
Leahy, Mary Weldon 1926- *ConAmC*
Leake, James d1791 *NotNAT B*
Leakey, Phil *WhoHrs 80*
Leaks, Sylvester 1927- *BlkAmP, DrBlPA*
Leal, Eleuterio Franco 1758?-1840? *NewGrD 80*
Leal, John 1904- *AmSCAP 66*
Leal, Milagros 1902-1975 *WhScrn 77, WhoHol C*
Lealand, Princess *Film 2*
Leamar, Alice d1950 *NotNAT B*
Leamont, Robert 1760?-1810? *BiDAmM*
Leamore, Tom 1865-1939 *NotNAT B, WhThe*
Lean, Cecil 1878-1935 *CmpEPM, WhThe*
Lean, David 1908- *BiDFilm, -81, DcFM, FilmEn, FilmgC, HalFC 80, IlWWBF, -A, IntMPA 77, -75, -76, -78, -79, -80, MovMk[port], OxFilm, WorEFlm*
Leander, Zarah 1900- *FilmAG WE, FilmEn*
Leaper, Molly *IntWWM 77, WhoMus 72*
Lear, Evelyn *CmOp, IntWWM 77, -80, WhoMus 72*
Lear, Evelyn 1927- *Baker 78, MusSN[port]*
Lear, Evelyn 1928- *NewGrD 80*
Lear, Evelyn 1929- *BiDAmM*
Lear, Evelyn 1930- *NewEOp 71, WhoOp 76*
Lear, Norman *IntMPA 77, -78, -79, -80*
Lear, Norman 1922- *FilmEn*
Lear, Norman 1926- *FilmgC, HalFC 80, NewYTET*
Lear, Walter 1894- *WhoMus 72*
Leardini, Alessandro *NewGrD 80*
Learn, Bessie *Film 1, MotPP*
Leary, Ford 1908-1949 *CmpEPM, WhoJazz 72*
Leary, Gilda d1927 *NotNAT B*
Leary, Nolan *WhoHol A*
Lease, Anthony F 1925- *AmSCAP 66, -80*
Lease, Rex 1901-1966 *FilmEn, Film 2, ForYSC, TwYS, WhScrn 74, -77, WhoHol B*
Leask, Margaret Louise 1929- *IntWWM 77, -80*
Leat, Harry 1874-1949 *MagIlD*
Leathem, Barclay 1900- *BiE&WWA, NotNAT*
Leatherbee, Mary *BiE&WWA*
Leaud, Jean-Pierre 1944- *BiDFilm, -81, FilmAG WE, FilmEn, HalFC 80, MovMk, OxFilm, WhoHol A, WorEFlm*
Leaver, Philip 1904- *WhThe*
Leaver, Phillip *WhoHol A*
Leaves, The *RkOn 2[port]*
Leavins, Arthur 1917- *IntWWM 77, -80, WhoMus 72*
Leavitt, Donald Lee 1929- *IntWWM 80*
Leavitt, Douglas Abe 1883-1960 *WhScrn 74, -77, WhoHol B*
Leavitt, Joseph *IntWWM 77, -80*
Leavitt, Joshua 1794-1873 *BiDAmM*
Leavitt, Michael Bennett 1843-1935 *NotNAT A, -B*
Leavitt, Norman *WhoHol A*
Leavitt, Rafael Angel 1948- *AmSCAP 80*
Leavitt, Sam 1917- *FilmEn, FilmgC, HalFC 80, WorEFlm*
Leavitt, William G 1926- *AmSCAP 66*
Leb, Edith *CreCan 1*
LeBailly, Henry d1637 *NewGrD 80*
Lebano, Felice 1867-1916 *NewGrD 80*
LeBargy, Charles Gustave Auguste 1858-1936 *NotNAT B, WhThe, WhoHol B*
LeBaron, Louise *WhoStg 1908*
LeBaron, William 1883-1958 *AmSCAP 66, -80, CmpEPM, FilmEn, NotNAT B, WhThe*
LeBau, Blanche 1905- *AmSCAP 66*
LeBe, Guillaume 1525-1598 *Baker 78, NewGrD 80*
LeBeau, Madeline *WhoHol A*
LeBeau, Stephanie d1967 *WhScrn 74, -77*
Lebedeff, Ivan d1953 *MotPP, NotNAT B, WhoHol B*
Lebedeff, Ivan 1894-1953 *MovMk*
Lebedeff, Ivan 1895-1953 *FilmEn, Film 2, ForYSC, TwYS*
Lebedeff, Ivan 1899-1953 *FilmgC, HalFC 80, WhScrn 74, -77*
Lebedev, Yevgeni Alexeyevich 1917- *EncWT*
Lebedeva, Nelya Aleksandrovna 1939- *WhoOp 76*
Lebedeva, Nina Aleksandrovna 1939- *WhoOp 76*
Lebegue, Nicolas-Antoine 1631?-1702 *Baker 78, NewGrD 80*
LeBel, Barthelemy 1483?-1553 *NewGrD 80*
Lebel, Firmin d1573 *NewGrD 80*
Leber, Steve *ConMuA 80B*
Leberg, John Raoul 1938- *WhoOp 76*
Lebermann, Walter 1919- *NewGrD 80*
Lebermann, Walter K H 1910- *IntWWM 77, -80*
Lebert, Siegmund 1821-1884 *Baker 78*
Lebertoul, Franchois *NewGrD 80*
Lebeuf, Abbe Jean 1687-1760 *Baker 78*
Lebeuf, France *PupTheA*
Lebeuf, Jean 1687-1760 *NewGrD 80*
Lebeuf D'Abbeville En Pontieu, Jehan *NewGrD 80*
Lebherz, Richard 1921- *ConAmTC*
Lebic, Lojze 1934- *IntWWM 77, -80, NewGrD 80*
LeBienvenu, Fleurant *NewGrD 80*
Lebl, Vladimir 1928- *NewGrD 80*
LeBlan, Pierre-Joseph 1711-1765 *NewGrD 80*
Leblanc 1750?-1827 *NewGrD 80*
LeBlanc, Charles J 1898- *AmSCAP 66*
Leblanc, Dan 1902-1962 *NewOrJ*
LeBlanc, Didier *NewGrD 80*
LeBlanc, Georgette 1876-1941 *NotNAT A, -B, WhThe, WhoHol B*
LeBlanc, Hubert *NewGrD 80*
LeBlanc, Roger J 1945- *AmSCAP 80*
LeBlanc, Whitney J 1931- *BlkAmP*
LeBlanc & Carr *RkOn 2[port]*
Leblanc DuRoullet, Marie Francois L Gand *NewGrD 80*
LeBorg, Reginald 1902- *FilmEn, FilmgC, HalFC 80, IntMPA 77, -75, -76, -78, -79, -80, WhoHrs 80*
LeBorgy *Film 2*
Leborne, Aime-Ambroise-Simon 1797-1866 *Baker 78, NewGrD 80*
Leborne, Fernand 1862-1929 *Baker 78*
LeBoscu D'Arras, Adan *NewGrD 80*
Lebouc, Charles-Joseph 1822-1893 *Baker 78*
LeBouteiller, Jean *NewGrD 80*
Lebow, Leonard Stanley 1929- *AmSCAP 66, -80, ConAmC*
Lebowsky, Stanley 1926- *AmSCAP 66, -80, BiE&WWA, NotNAT*
LeBozoky, Barbara 1892-1937 *WhScrn 74*
LeBrandt, Gertrude N 1863-1955 *Film 2, WhScrn 74, -77, WhoHol B*
LeBret *NewGrD 80*
LeBreton *NewGrD 80*
LeBreton, Auguste 1915- *FilmgC, HalFC 80*
LeBreton, Flora 1898- *Film 2, IlWWBF, WhThe*
Lebrun *NewGrD 80*
Lebrun, Francesca 1756-1791 *NewGrD 80*
Lebrun, Franziska 1756-1791 *Baker 78, NewGrD 80*
Lebrun, Jean 1759-1809? *Baker 78, NewGrD 80*
Lebrun, Louis-Sebastien 1764-1829 *Baker 78, NewGrD 80*
Lebrun, Louise 1940- *WhoMus 72, WhoOp 76*
Lebrun, Ludwig August 1752-1790 *Baker 78, NewGrD 80*
LeBrun, Minon 1881-1941 *WhoHol B*
LeBrun, Minon 1888-1941 *WhScrn 74, -77*
Lebrun, Paul Henri Joseph 1863-1920 *Baker 78*
Lebrun, Rosine 1783-1855 *NewGrD 80*
Lebrun, Sophie 1781-1815? *NewGrD 80*
LeBrung, Jean *NewGrD 80*
Leca, Armando 1893- *Baker 78*
Lecail, Clovis *OxMus*
LeCaine, Hugh 1914- *Baker 78, DcCM, NewGrD 80*
LeCamus, Sebastien 1610?-1677 *NewGrD 80*
LeCarpentier, Adolphe-Clair 1809-1869 *Baker 78*
LeCarre, John 1931- *HalFC 80*
LeCerf DeLaVieville, Jean Laurent 1674-1707 *NewGrD 80*
LeChanois, Jean-Paul 1909- *DcFM, FilmEn, FilmgC, HalFC 80, OxFilm, WorEFlm*
Lechantre, Mademoiselle *OxMus*
LeChevalier, Amedee 1650?-1720 *NewGrD 80*
Lechler, Benedikt 1594-1659 *NewGrD 80*
Lechler, Johannes 1594-1659 *NewGrD 80*
Lechner, Konrad 1911- *NewGrD 80*
Lechner, Leonhard 1550?-1606 *Baker 78, OxMus*
Lechner, Leonhard 1553?-1606 *NewGrD 80*
Lechnerus, Leonardus Athesinus 1553?-1606 *NewGrD 80*
Lechthaler, Josef 1891-1948 *Baker 78*
Leckrone, Michael 1936- *AmSCAP 80*
Lecky, Eleazer 1903- *BiE&WWA, NotNAT*
Leclair *NewGrD 80*
Leclair, Andre 1930- *CnOxB*
LeClair, Blanche *Film 2*
Leclair, Jean-Benoit 1714-1759? *NewGrD 80*
Leclair, Jean-Marie 1697-1764 *Baker 78, BnBkM 80, DcCom&M 79, GrComp[port], MusMk, NewGrD 80[port], OxMus*
Leclair, Jean-Marie 1703-1777 *Baker 78, NewGrD 80*
Leclair, Pierre 1709-1784 *NewGrD 80*
Leclaire, Dennis James 1950- *IntWWM 77*
LeClerc, Charles-Nicolas 1697-1774 *NewGrD 80*

Leclerc, Felix 1914- *CreCan 1, NewGrD 80*
Leclerc, Ginette 1912- *FilmEn, FilmgC, HalFC 80, WhoHol A*
LeClerc, Jacques d1679 *NewGrD 80*
LeClerc, Jean-Pantaleon 1697?-1760? *NewGrD 80*
Leclercq, Jacques d1679 *NewGrD 80*
Leclercq, Pierre d1932 *NotNAT B*
LeClercq, Tanaquil 1929- *DancEn 78[port]*
LeClercy, Regina d1973 *WhScrn 77*
Leclere, Irwin 1893?- *NewOrJ[port]*
LeClerq, Florence d1960 *NotNAT B*
LeClerq, Tanaquil 1929- *CnOxB*
Lecocq, Alexandre Charles 1832-1918 *DancEn 78, NotNAT B*
Lecocq, Charles 1832-1918 *Baker 78, BnBkM 80, CmOp, MusMk, NewGrD 80, OxMus*
Lecocq, Jean *NewGrD 80*
Lecocq, Jehan *NewGrD 80*
LeCoincte, Louis *NewGrD 80*
Leconte, Marie *WhThe*
LeConte, Pierre-Michel 1921- *NewGrD 80*
LeCordeur, Muriel Coventry 1905- *IntWWM 77*
LeCornu, Florence Ivy 1925- *WhoMus 72*
LeCouppey, Felix 1811-1887 *Baker 78*
Lecouvreur, Adrienne 1692-1730 *CnThe, EncWT, Ent[port], NotNAT A, -B, OxThe*
Lecuna, Juan 1894-1954 *Baker 78*
Lecuna, Juan Vicente 1899-1954 *NewGrD 80*
Lecuona, Ernesto 1896-1963 *Baker 78, CmpEPM, NewGrD 80, NotNAT B*
Led Zeppelin *BiDAmM, ConMuA 80A[port], IlEncR, RkOn 2[port]*
Ledang, Ola Kai 1940- *NewGrD 80*
Ledbetter, David John 1943- *IntWWM 80*
Ledbetter, Huddie *EncFCWM 69*
Ledbetter, Huddie 1885-1949 *Baker 78, IlEncJ, NewGrD 80*
Ledbetter, Huddie 1888-1949 *MusMk*
Ledbetter, Huddie 1889-1949 *BluesWW[port], CmpEPM*
Ledebur, Carl 1806-1872 *Baker 78*
Ledebur, Friedrich *ForYSC, HalFC 80*
Ledeen, Raymond *AmSCAP 80*
Ledent, Felix-Etienne 1816-1886 *Baker 78*
Ledent, Robert 1911- *WhoMus 72*
Ledenyov, Roman 1930- *NewGrD 80*
Leder, Herbert Jay 1922- *IntMPA 77, -75, -76, -78, -79, -80*
Lederberg, Dov *WomWMM*
Lederer, Anton 1733-1796 *NewGrD 80*
Lederer, Charles 1906?- *FilmgC*
Lederer, Charles 1910-1976 *AmSCAP 80, FilmEn*
Lederer, Charles 1911-1976 *AmSCAP 66, BiE&WWA, HalFC 80, WorEFlm*
Lederer, Felix 1877-1957 *Baker 78*
Lederer, Francis *MotPP*
Lederer, Francis 1902- *WhoHol A*
Lederer, Francis 1906- *BiE&WWA, FilmEn, Film 2, FilmgC, ForYSC, HalFC 80, HolP 30[port], MovMk, NotNAT, What 4[port], WhThe, WhoHrs 80[port]*
Lederer, Franz Joseph 1936- *IntWWM 77, -80*
Lederer, George W 1861-1938 *EncMT, NotNAT B, WhThe*
Lederer, George W, Jr. d1924 *NotNAT B*
Lederer, Gretchen 1891-1955 *Film 1, MotPP, NotNAT B, TwYS, WhScrn 74, -77, WhoHol B*
Lederer, Joseph 1733-1796 *NewGrD 80*
Lederer, Otto 1886-1965 *Film 1, -2, TwYS, WhScrn 77*
Lederer, Pepi *Film 2*
Lederer, Richard 1916- *IntMPA 77, -75, -76, -78, -79, -80*
Lederhouse, Bruce *ConAmC*
Lederman, D Ross 1895-1972 *FilmEn, FilmgC, HalFC 80, WhScrn 77*
Lederman, Minna *DancEn 78*
Lederman, Sidney *IntWWM 80*
Ledesma, Damaso 1868-1928 *NewGrD 80*
Ledesma, Mariano Rodriguez De *NewGrD 80*
Ledesma, Nicolas 1791-1883 *NewGrD 80*
Ledger, Edward d1921 *NotNAT B*
Ledger, Frederick d1874 *NotNAT B*
Ledger, Philip Stevens 1937- *IntWWM 77, -80, NewGrD 80, WhoMus 72*
Lediakh, Gennadi 1928- *CnOxB*
Lediakh, Gennady 1928- *DancEn 78*
Ledlova-Kopecky, Dagmar 1935- *IntWWM 77, -80*
Ledner, David 1900-1957 *WhScrn 74, -77*
Ledoux, Chris Lee 1948- *AmSCAP 80*
Ledoux, Fernand 1897- *EncWT, FilmEn*
Leduc *NewGrD 80, PupTheA*
Leduc, Alphonse 1804-1868 *Baker 78, NewGrD 80*
Leduc, Alphonse 1844-1892 *NewGrD 80*
Leduc, Auguste 1779-1823 *NewGrD 80*
Leduc, Claude Alphonse 1910- *IntWWM 77, -80, NewGrD 80*
Leduc, Claudine d1969 *WhScrn 74, -77, WhoHol B*
Leduc, Emile-Alphonse 1878-1951 *NewGrD 80*
Leduc, Emma *NewGrD 80*
Leduc, Fernand 1916- *CreCan 2*
Leduc, Gilbert-Alphonse *NewGrD 80*
Leduc, Jacques 1932- *Baker 78, NewGrD 80*
Leduc, Jean 1910- *CreCan 1*
Leduc, Ozias 1864-1955 *CreCan 1*
LeDuc, Philippe *NewGrD 80*
LeDuc, Pierre *NewGrD 80*
Leduc, Pierre 1755-1816 *NewGrD 80*
Leduc, Roland 1907- *CreCan 2*
LeDuc, Simon 1745?-1777 *Baker 78*
Leduc, Simon 1748?-1777 *NewGrD 80*
Ledward, James Henry 1954- *IntWWM 80*
Lee, Alberta *Film 1*
Lee, Allen 1875-1951 *WhScrn 74, -77*
Lee, Alvin *ConMuA 80A*
Lee, Ann *WhoHol A*
Lee, Anna *IntMPA 75, -76, -78, -79, -80*
Lee, Anna 1913- *FilmEn, IlWWBF*
Lee, Anna 1914- *FilmgC, ForYSC, HalFC 80, IntMPA 77, MotPP, MovMk[port], WhoHol A*
Lee, Anna Virginia 1909- *IntWWM 77*
Lee, Auriol 1880-1941 *NotNAT B, WhScrn 74, -77, WhThe, WhoHol B*
Lee, Avalon *WhoHol A*
Lee, Barbara McCormick 1939- *AmSCAP 80*
Lee, Belinda 1935-1961 *FilmEn, FilmgC, ForYSC, HalFC 80, IlWWBF[port], NotNAT B, WhScrn 74, -77, WhoHol B*
Lee, Bernard 1908- *CmMov, FilmEn, FilmgC, HalFC 80, IlWWBF[port], IntMPA 77, -75, -76, -78, -79, -80, WhoHol A, WhoThe 72, -77*
Lee, Bernard 1909- *WhoHrs 80*
Lee, Bert 1880-1946 *NotNAT B, WhThe*
Lee, Bessie *BluesWW[port]*
Lee, Bessie 1904-1931 *WhScrn 74, -77*
Lee, Bessie 1906-1972 *WhScrn 77*
Lee, Betsy *Film 2*
Lee, Bill 1926- *NewOrJ*
Lee, Bill 1928- *EncJzS 70*
Lee, Bill 1929- *EncJzS 70*
Lee, Billy 1930- *HalFC 80*
Lee, Billy 1942- *BlkAmP*
Lee, Brenda 1942- *IlEncCM[port]*
Lee, Brenda 1944- *AmPS A, -B, BiDAmM, ConMuA 80A, CounME 74[port], -74A, RkOn[port]*
Lee, Bruce 1940-1973 *HalFC 80, MovMk, WhScrn 77, WhoHol B*
Lee, Bruce 1941-1973 *FilmEn*
Lee, Bryarly 1934- *BiE&WWA, NotNAT*
Lee, Byong Won 1941- *IntWWM 80*
Lee, C Y *NatPD[port]*
Lee, Canada 1907-1952 *BlksB&W C, DrBlPA, Ent[port], FilmgC, HalFC 80, MotPP, MovMk, NotNAT B, Vers A[port], WhScrn 74, -77, WhThe, WhoHol B*
Lee, Carey *Film 1*
Lee, Carl 1933- *DrBlPA*
Lee, Caroline *BluesWW[port]*
Lee, Carolyn 1935- *MotPP, WhoHol A*
Lee, Celeste *Film 2*
Lee, Charles d1947 *NotNAT B*
Lee, Charles T 1882-1927 *WhScrn 74, -77*
Lee, Christopher 1922- *CmMov, FilmAG WE, FilmEn, FilmgC, ForYSC, HalFC 80, IlWWBF[port], -A, IntMPA 77, -75, -76, -78, -79, -80, MotPP, MovMk, OxFilm, WhoHol A, WhoHrs 80[port]*
Lee, Chung 1942- *IntWWM 80*
Lee, Craig *AmSCAP 80*
Lee, Curtis 1941- *RkOn*
Lee, Dai-Keong 1915- *AmSCAP 66, -80, Baker 78, BiDAmM, CpmDNM 72, ConAmC*
Lee, Dave *PupTheA*
Lee, Davey 1925- *Film 2, HalFC 80*
Lee, David 1936- *AmSCAP 66, -80*
Lee, David, Jr. 1941- *EncJzS 70*
Lee, Deborah *CmpGMD*
Lee, Dennis Ean Hool 1946- *IntWWM 77, -80*
Lee, Dick *Film 2*
Lee, Dickey *CounME 74[port], -74A*
Lee, Dickey 1940- *RkOn[port]*
Lee, Dickey 1941- *IlEncCM[port]*
Lee, Dixie 1911-1952 *Film 1, -2, ForYSC, HalFC 80, TwYS, WhScrn 74, -77, WhoHol B*
Lee, Dorothy 1911- *Film 2, FilmgC, HalFC 80, ThFT[port], WhoHol A*
Lee, Douglas Allen 1932- *IntWWM 77, -80*
Lee, Duke R 1881-1959 *Film 2, WhScrn 74, -77, WhoHol B*
Lee, Earl 1886-1955 *WhScrn 74, -77, WhoHol B*
Lee, Edith Marjorie 1912- *WhoMus 72*
Lee, Ernest Markham 1874-1956 *Baker 78*
Lee, Ernie *IlEncCM[port]*
Lee, Etta 1906-1956 *Film 2, WhScrn 74, -77, WhoHol B*
Lee, Eu-Gene 1942- *CpmDNM 79, ConAmC*
Lee, Eugene *NotNAT*
Lee, Everett *DrBlPA*
Lee, Fletcher *AmSCAP 80*
Lee, Florence 1886-1962 *WhoHol B*
Lee, Florence 1888-1962 *NotNAT B, WhScrn 74, -77*
Lee, Ford Washington *BlksBF*
Lee, Ford Washington And John W Sublett *BlksB&W*
Lee, Fran *WhoHol A*
Lee, Frances 1908- *Film 2, TwYS, WhoHol A*
Lee, Francis *Film 2*
Lee, Frankie 1912- *Film 1, -2, MotPP, TwYS*
Lee, Franne *NotNAT*
Lee, Gary Thomas 1946- *IntWWM 77, -80*
Lee, George Alexander 1802-1851 *NewGrD 80*
Lee, George E 1896-1959 *WhoJazz 72*
Lee, Gwen 1904-1961 *Film 2, ForYSC, ThFT[port], TwYS, WhScrn 77, WhoHol B*
Lee, Gypsy Rose d1970 *MotPP, WhoHol B*
Lee, Gypsy Rose 1913-1970 *FilmgC, HalFC 80, WhThe*
Lee, Gypsy Rose 1914-1970 *BiE&WWA, EncMT, Ent[port], FilmEn, ForYSC, MovMk[port], NotNAT A, -B, WhScrn 74, -77, WorEFlm[port]*
Lee, H Rex *NewYTET*
Lee, Harry 1872-1932 *Film 2, WhScrn 74, -77, WhoHol B*
Lee, Harry A d1919 *NotNAT B*
Lee, Helen Morris *PupTheA*
Lee, Henry d1910 *NotNAT B, WhoHol B*
Lee, Henry 1765-1836 *NotNAT A, -B*
Lee, Hye-Ku 1909- *IntWWM 77, -80*
Lee, Jack 1913- *DcFM, FilmEn, FilmgC, HalFC 80, IlWWBF, IntMPA 77, -75, -76, WorEFlm*
Lee, Jackie *RkOn, -2A*
Lee, James *AmSCAP 80*
Lee, James 1919- *AmSCAP 66*
Lee, James 1923- *BiE&WWA, NotNAT*
Lee, Jane 1912-1957 *Film 1, MotPP, NotNAT B, TwYS, WhScrn 77, WhoHol B*
Lee, Janet *Film 1*
Lee, Jean d1963 *NotNAT B*
Lee, Jeanne 1939- *BiDAmM*
Lee, Jennie d1930 *NotNAT B, WhThe*
Lee, Jennie 1850-1925 *Film 1, NotNAT B, WhScrn 74, -77, WhoHol B*
Lee, Jim *MorBAP*
Lee, Jimmy *BluesWW[port]*
Lee, Joanna *NewYTET, WomWMM*
Lee, Joanna Downs 1907- *IntWWM 77*
Lee, Jocelyn *Film 2*
Lee, Joe *Film 1*
Lee, John *BlksB&W C, BluesWW[port]*

Lee, John 1908- *ConAmC*
Lee, John 1928- *IntMPA 77, -75, -76, -78, -79, -80*
Lee, John Arthur 1915- *BluesWW[port]*
Lee, John Arthur Landon 1921- *WhoMus 72*
Lee, John Barrow 1948- *AmSCAP 80*
Lee, John D 1898-1965 *WhScrn 74, WhoHol B*
Lee, Johnny *BluesWW[port]*
Lee, Johnny 1898-1965 *WhScrn 77*
Lee, Jonathan Butler 1947- *AmSCAP 80*
Lee, Julia 1902-1958 *BlkWAB, CmpEPM, WhoJazz 72*
Lee, Julia 1903-1958 *BluesWW[port]*
Lee, Julian 1923- *BiDAmM*
Lee, Katharine *Film 1*
Lee, Katherine *Film 2, TwYS*
Lee, Kathryn 1926- *DancEn 78*
Lee, Katie L 1919- *AmSCAP 66, -80*
Lee, King Ivory *BluesWW[port]*
Lee, Lance 1942- *NatPD[port]*
Lee, Laura *WhoHol A*
Lee, Leapy *RkOn 2A*
Lee, Leona d1975 *WhScrn 77, WhoHol C*
Lee, Leslie *BlkAmP, MorBAP*
Lee, Leslie 1935?- *DrBlPA*
Lee, Lester 1905-1956 *AmSCAP 66, -80*
Lee, Lila d1973 *MotPP, WhoHol B*
Lee, Lila 1901-1973 *FilmEn, ThFT[port], What 1[port]*
Lee, Lila 1902-1973 *FilmgC, HalFC 80, TwYS, WhScrn 77*
Lee, Lila 1905-1973 *Film 1, -2, ForYSC, MovMk*
Lee, Lila Dean 1890-1959 *WhScrn 74, -77*
Lee, Lilian Gwendoline 1902- *WhoMus 72*
Lee, Lillie d1941 *NotNAT B*
Lee, Lois *Film 2*
Lee, Lonesome *BluesWW[port]*
Lee, Lora *AmSCAP 80*
Lee, Loretta 1914- *CmpEPM*
Lee, Louis 1819-1896 *Baker 78, NewGrD 80*
Lee, Loye *AmSCAP 80*
Lee, Mabel 1898- *WhoMus 72*
Lee, Madeline *WhoHol A*
Lee, Margaret 1943- *FilmAG WE, Film 2*
Lee, Margo d1951 *WhScrn 74, -77, WhoHol B*
Lee, Marjorie Lederer 1921- *AmSCAP 66, -80*
Lee, Marvin 1880-1949 *AmSCAP 66, -80*
Lee, Mary A *BlkAmP*
Lee, Mary Ann 1823-1899 *CnOxB, DancEn 78*
Lee, Maurice *NewGrD 80*
Lee, Maurice 1821-1895 *Baker 78*
Lee, Michele *FilmEn, RkOn 2A*
Lee, Michele 1942- *BiE&WWA, FilmgC, HalFC 80, NotNAT, WhoHol A*
Lee, Michele 1944- *ForYSC*
Lee, Miles *PupTheA*
Lee, Ming Cho 1930- *BiE&WWA, NotNAT, WhoOp 76, WhoThe 72, -77*
Lee, Nammi *WomWMM B*
Lee, Nathaniel 1649?-1692 *EncWT*
Lee, Nathaniel 1653?-1692 *CnThe, Ent, McGEWD[port], NotNAT B, OxThe, PlP&P, REnWD[port]*
Lee, Nelson d1872 *NotNAT B*
Lee, Noel 1924- *ConAmC*
Lee, Norah 1898-1941 *AmSCAP 66*
Lee, Norman 1895- *CpmDNM 75, -76, ConAmC*
Lee, Norman H 1898- *IlWWBF, -A*
Lee, Olga 1899- *BiE&WWA*
Lee, Palmer 1942- *FilmEn, ForYSC, WhoHol A*
Lee, Patricia *WomWMM B*
Lee, Peggy *AmPS A, -B, AmSCAP 80*
Lee, Peggy 1920- *AmSCAP 66, CmpEPM, EncJzS 70, FilmEn, FilmgC, ForYSC, HalFC 80, IntMPA 77, -75, -76, -78, -79, -80, NewGrD 80, OxFilm, RkOn, WhoHol A*
Lee, Peggy 1922- *BiDAmM, IlEncJ*
Lee, Pinky 1916- *IntMPA 77, -75, -76, -78, -79, -80, JoeFr[port], NewYTET, What 2[port], WhoHol A*
Lee, R A 1917- *IntMPA 75*
Lee, Raymond 1910-1974 *Film 1, -2, WhScrn 77, WhoHol B*
Lee, Richard L 1872- *WhoStg 1908*
Lee, Robert *Film 2*
Lee, Robert Charles 1927- *AmSCAP 66, -80, IntWWM 80*
Lee, Robert Edwin 1918- *AmSCAP 66, -80, BiE&WWA, ConDr 73, -77, EncMT, ModWD, NewYTET, NotNAT, WhoThe 72, -77*
Lee, Roberta *Film 1*
Lee, Rohama *WomWMM B*
Lee, Ronald *Film 2*
Lee, Ronny 1927- *AmSCAP 66, -80*
Lee, Rose *WhScrn 74, -77*
Lee, Rose 1922- *BiDAmM*
Lee, Rowland V 1891-1975 *FilmEn, FilmgC, HalFC 80, IntMPA 75, -76, MovMk[port], TwYS A, WhScrn 77, WhoHrs 80*
Lee, Ruta 1935- *ForYSC, WhoHol A*
Lee, Ruth 1896-1975 *WhScrn 77, WhoHol C*
Lee, Sammy 1890-1968 *EncMT, NotNAT B, WhScrn 74, -77, WhoHol B*
Lee, Samuel d1776 *NewGrD 80*
Lee, Samuel James, II 1942- *AmSCAP 80*
Lee, Scotty *AmSCAP 80*
Lee, Sebastian 1805-1887 *Baker 78, NewGrD 80*
Lee, Sondra 1930- *BiE&WWA, NotNAT*
Lee, Sonny 1904- *CmpEPM, WhoJazz 72*
Lee, Sophia d1824 *NotNAT B*
Lee, Sung-Sook *IntWWM 77, -80*
Lee, Sylvan d1962 *Film 2, WhoHol B*
Lee, T Charles 1914- *ConAmC*
Lee, Tommy *WhoHol A*
Lee, Vanessa 1920- *WhoThe 72, -77*
Lee, Vernon *AmSCAP 80*
Lee, Virginia *Film 2*
Lee, Warren *BluesWW[port]*
Lee, Wendie 1923-1968 *WhScrn 77*
Lee, Will 1908- *BiE&WWA, NotNAT, WhoHol A*
Lee, William Franklin, III 1929- *AmSCAP 80, ConAmC, EncJzS 70*
Lee, William James Edwards 1928- *EncJzS 70*
Lee, Yvonne R *PupTheA*
Lee Sugg, Catharine 1797-1845 *OxThe*
Lee-Thompson, J 1914- *FilmEn, FilmgC, HalFC 80, IlWWBF, IntMPA 77, -75, -76, -78, -79, -80, MovMk[port]*
Lee Thompson, John 1914- *DcFM*
Leech, Alan Bruce 1944- *IntWWM 77, -80*
Leech, Bryan Jeffery 1931- *AmSCAP 80*
Leech, Karen Davidson 1945- *IntWWM 77, -80*
Leech, Lida Shivers 1873-1962 *AmSCAP 66, -80*
Leech, Richard 1922- *FilmgC, HalFC 80, WhoHol A, WhoThe 72, -77*
Leeder, Sigurd 1902- *CnOxB, DancEn 78*
Leeds, Andrea 1914- *FilmEn, FilmgC, ForYSC, HalFC 80, MovMk, ThFT[port], WhoHol A*
Leeds, Corinne 1909- *AmSCAP 66, -80*
Leeds, Dixie 1934- *ConAmTC*
Leeds, Herbert I 1900?-1954 *FilmEn, FilmgC, HalFC 80*
Leeds, Martin N 1916- *IntMPA 77, -75, -76, -78, -79, -80*
Leeds, Milton 1909- *AmSCAP 66, -80*
Leeds, Nancy Brecker 1924- *AmSCAP 66, -80*
Leeds, Percival Morrice 1908- *WhoMus 72*
Leeds, Peter *ForYSC, WhoHol A*
Leeds, Phil *BiE&WWA, NotNAT, WhoHol A*
Leeds, Steve *ConMuA 80B*
Leedy, Douglas 1938- *Baker 78*
Leedy, Douglas H 1938- *ConAmC*
Leedy, G Frank 1931- *AmSCAP 80*
Leeman, Cliff 1913- *CmpEPM, EncJzS 70, WhoJazz 72*
Leeman, Clifford 1913- *BiDAmM, EncJzS 70*
Leeman, Dicky 1911- *IntMPA 75, -76*
Leeman, Percy T 1908- *AmSCAP 66*
Leemans, Aybert Philippe Adrien d1771 *NewGrD 80*
Leemans, Hebert Philippe Adrien d1771 *NewGrD 80*
Leeming, Peter 1933- *WhoMus 72*
Leenhardt, Roger 1903- *BiDFilm, -81, DcFM, FilmEn, OxFilm, WorEFlm*
Leenhardt, Yvonne *WomWMM*
Leenhouts, Lewis Grant *IntMPA 77, -75, -76, -78, -79, -80*
Lees, Benjamin 1924- *AmSCAP 66, -80, Baker 78, BiDAmM, CompSN[port], CpmDNM 80, ConAmC, DcCM, NewGrD 80, WhoMus 72*
Lees, C Lowell 1904- *BiE&WWA*
Lees, Christine Brown 1943- *IntWWM 77, WhoMus 72*
Lees, Elsie *WhoMus 72*
Lees, Michelle 1947- *CnOxB*
Leese, Elizabeth d1962 *CreCan 2, DancEn 78*
Leeson, Cecil 1902- *ConAmC*
Leess, Stan 1926- *AmSCAP 66, -80*
Leeuw, Cornelis Janszoon 1613?-1662? *NewGrD 80*
Leeuw, Reinbert De 1938- *Baker 78*
Leeuw, Ton De 1926- *Baker 78, CpmDNM 79, NewGrD 80*
Leeuwen Boomkamp, Carel Van 1906- *NewGrD 80*
Leeves, William 1748-1828 *OxMus*
Leewood, Jack *IntMPA 77, -75, -76, -78, -79, -80*
LeFanu, J Sheridan 1814-1873 *HalFC 80*
LeFanu, Nicola Frances 1947- *Baker 78, IntWWM 77, -80, NewGrD 80*
Lefaur, Andre 1879-1952 *NotNAT B, WhScrn 74, -77*
Lefco, Seymour 1915- *AmSCAP 66, -80*
Lefeaux, Charles 1909- *WhThe, WhoThe 72*
Lefebre, Jorge *CnOxB*
Lefebure *NewGrD 80*
Lefebure, Andre *NewGrD 80*
Lefebure, Louis Antoine *NewGrD 80*
Lefebure, Louis-Francois Henri 1754-1840 *Baker 78*
Lefebure, Yvonne 1900- *NewGrD 80*
Lefebure, Yvonne 1904- *WhoMus 72*
Lefebure-Wely, Louis James Alfred 1817-1869 *Baker 78, OxMus*
Lefebvre *NewGrD 80*
Lefebvre, Andre d1763 *NewGrD 80*
Lefebvre, Channing 1895-1967 *BiDAmM*
Lefebvre, Charles Edouard 1843-1917 *Baker 78, NewGrD 80, OxMus*
Lefebvre, Denis *NewGrD 80*
Lefebvre, Gilles 1922- *IntWWM 77, -80*
LeFebvre, Jacques *NewGrD 80*
Lefebvre, Jacques *NewGrD 80*
Lefebvre, Jean-Pierre 1941- *CreCan 1, WorEFlm*
Lefebvre, Joseph 1761-1822? *NewGrD 80*
Lefebvre, Louis Antoine d1763 *NewGrD 80*
Lefebvre, Louise-Rosalie *NewGrD 80*
Lefebvre, Philippe Andre 1949- *IntWWM 77, -80*
LeFebvre, Robert 1907- *DcFM, FilmEn*
Lefebvre, Xavier *NewGrD 80*
Lefeld, Jerzy Albert 1898- *IntWWM 77, -80*
Lefeure *NewGrD 80*
LeFeuvre, Guy 1883-1950 *NotNAT B, WhThe*
LeFeuvre, Philip 1871-1939 *WhScrn 74, -77*
Lefever, Maxine Lane 1931- *ConAmC*
Lefevere, Kamiel 1888- *AmSCAP 66, ConAmC A*
Lefevre *NewGrD 80*
Lefevre, Andre *NewGrD 80*
Lefevre, Antoine 1524-1551 *NewGrD 80*
Lefevre, Charles *NewGrD 80*
Lefevre, Charles 1670-1737 *NewGrD 80*
Lefevre, Claude 1667- *NewGrD 80*
Lefevre, Clement 1630?-1709 *NewGrD 80*
LeFevre, Francois *NewGrD 80*
Lefevre, Germain 1656-1694 *NewGrD 80*
Lefevre, Guillaume *NewGrD 80*
LeFevre, Jacques *NewGrD 80*
Lefevre, Jacques Lievin 1621-1665? *NewGrD 80*
Lefevre, Jean *NewGrD 80*
Lefevre, Jean-Baptiste Nicolas 1705-1784 *NewGrD 80*
Lefevre, Jean Xavier 1763-1829 *Baker 78*
Lefevre, Leonard d1659? *NewGrD 80*
Lefevre, Louis 1708-1754 *NewGrD 80*
Lefevre, Louis Antoine *NewGrD 80*
Lefevre, Maurice *WhThe*
LeFevre, Ned 1912-1966 *WhScrn 77*
Lefevre, Nicolas *NewGrD 80*
Lefevre, Paul *McGEWD[port]*
LeFevre, Pierce Avon 1936- *BiDAmM*
Lefevre, Pierre 1670?-1737 *NewGrD 80*

Lefevre, Rene 1898- *FilmEn, OxFilm*
LeFevre, Urias 1910- *BiDAmM*
Lefevre, Xavier 1763-1829 *NewGrD 80*
Leff, Phyllis *WomWMM B*
Lefferts, George *IntMPA 77, -75, -76, -78, -79, -80, NewYTET*
Lefferty, Jean *Film 2*
Leffler, Anne Charlotte 1849-1892 *OxThe*
Leffler, Ed *ConMuA 80B*
Leffler, George d1951 *NotNAT B*
Leffler-Burckard, Martha 1865-1954 *Baker 78*
Leffloth, Johann Matthias 1705-1731 *NewGrD 80*
Lefko, Morris E 1907- *IntMPA 77, -75, -76, -78, -79, -80*
Lefkowitch, Stanley L 1917- *AmSCAP 66*
Lefkowitz, Murray 1924- *NewGrD 80*
Lefkowitz, Nat 1905- *BiE&WWA, IntMPA 77, -75, -76, -78, -79, -80*
LeFlem, Paul 1881- *Baker 78, NewGrD 80*
LeFleming, Antony 1941- *WhoMus 72*
LeFleming, Christopher Kaye 1908- *Baker 78, IntWWM 77, -80, WhoMus 72*
LeFleming, Naomi 1944- *IntWWM 80*
Lefleur, Leo 1902- *AmSCAP 66, -80*
LeFranc, Martin *NewGrD 80*
Lefrancois, Andre 1906- *IntWWM 80*
LeFre, Albert 1870- *WhThe*
LeFroid DeMereaux *NewGrD 80*
Left Banke, The *BiDAmM, ConMuA 80A, RkOn 2[port]*
Leftwich, Alexander 1884-1947 *EncMT, NotNAT B, WhScrn 77, WhThe*
Leftwich, Vernon 1881-1977 *AmSCAP 66, -80, ConAmC, WhoMus 72*
Lega, Luigi Maurizio 1940- *WhoOp 76*
Legal, Ernest 1881-1955 *WhScrn 74, -77*
Legal, Ernst *Film 2*
Legal, Ernst 1881-1955 *EncWT*
LeGalienne, Eva 1899- *FilmgC, HalFC 80*
LeGallienne, Dorian 1915-1963 *Baker 78, NewGrD 80*
LeGallienne, Eva 1899- *BiE&WWA, CnThe, EncWT, Ent[port], FamA&A[port], FilmEn, NotNAT, -A, OxThe, PlP&P, WhoHol A, WhoThe 72, -77*
Legany, Dezso 1916- *NewGrD 80*
Legar, John *NewGrD 80*
Legard, John *NewGrD 80*
Legarde, Millie *WhThe*
Legare, John *NewGrD 80*
Legat, Nadine Nicolaeva 1895- *DancEn 78*
Legat, Nicholas 1869-1937 *DancEn 78, NotNAT B*
Legat, Nicolai Gustavovich 1869-1937 *CnOxB*
Legat, Serge 1875-1905 *DancEn 78*
Legat, Sergei Gustavovich 1875-1905 *CnOxB*
Legat DeFurcy, Antoine 1740?-1790? *NewGrD 80*
LeGendre, Jean *NewGrD 80*
Leger, Fernand 1881-1955 *CnOxB, DcFM, EncWT, FilmEn, OxFilm, PlP&P, WorEFlm*
Legerton, Henry 1917- *CnOxB, DancEn 78*
Legeti, Gyorgy 1923- *IntWWM 77, -80*
Legg, Stuart 1910- *FilmEn, FilmgC, HalFC 80, IntMPA 77, -75, -76, -78, -79, -80, OxFilm*
Leggat, Donald Albert 1914- *WhoMus 72*
Leggate, Robin 1946- *IntWWM 80*
Leggatt, Alison 1904- *FilmgC, HalFC 80, WhoHol A, WhoThe 72, -77*
Legge, Harry 1914- *IntWWM 77, -80, WhoMus 72*
Legge, Wade 1934-1963 *BiDAmM*
Legge, Walter 1906-1979 *NewGrD 80, WhoMus 72*
Leginska, Ethel 1886-1970 *Baker 78, BiDAmM, ConAmC*
LeGlaire, Sonny 1915- *AmSCAP 66*
Leglaire, Sophia 1915- *AmSCAP 80*
Legley, Vic 1915- *NewGrD 80*
Legley, Victor 1915- *Baker 78, DcCM, WhoMus 72*
Leglise, Vic 1900?- *NewOrJ*
Legnani, Luigi 1790-1877 *NewGrD 80*
Legnani, Pierina 1863-1923 *CnOxB, DancEn 78*
Legneur, Charles 1892-1956 *WhScrn 74, -77*
Legnon, Albert 1898?- *NewOrJ*
Legnon, Roscoe 1895?-1963? *NewOrJ[port]*
LeGon, Jeni 1916- *BlksB&W, -C*
Legoshin, Vladimir 1904-1955 *DcFM, FilmEn*
Legouix, Edouard 1834-1916 *NewGrD 80*
LeGouriadec, Yvette Brind'Amour *CreCan 1*
Legouve, Ernest-Gabriel-Jean-Baptiste 1807-1903 *NotNAT B, OxThe*
Legrady, Thomas Theodore 1920- *IntWWM 77, -80*
Legrand *NewGrD 80*
Legrand, Etienne *NewGrD 80*
Legrand, Jean-Pierre 1734-1809 *NewGrD 80*
Legrand, Louis *NewGrD 80*
Legrand, Louis-Alexandre d1773 *NewGrD 80*
Legrand, Marc-Antoine 1673-1728 *EncWT, Ent, NotNAT B, OxThe*
Legrand, Mathieu *NewGrD 80*
Legrand, Michel *RkOn 2A*
Legrand, Michel 1932- *Baker 78, EncJzS 70, FilmEn, NewGrD 80, OxFilm, WorEFlm*
Legrand, Michel Jean 1931- *DcFM, FilmgC, HalFC 80, IntMPA 77, -75, -76, -78, -79, -80*
LeGrand, Phyllis *WhThe*
Legrand-Schwakopf, Krystyna 1925- *IntWWM 77, -80*
Legrant, Guillaume *NewGrD 80*
Legrant, Johannes *NewGrD 80*
Legrense, Johannes 1415?-1473 *NewGrD 80*
Legrenzi, Giovanni 1626-1690 *Baker 78, GrComp[port], NewGrD 80[port]*
Legros, Joseph 1730-1793 *CmOp*
Legros, Joseph 1739-1793 *NewGrD 80*
Leguar, John *NewGrD 80*
LeGuere, George 1871-1947 *Film 1, NotNAT B, WhScrn 77, WhoHol B*
Leguerney, Jacques 1906- *NewGrD 80*
Leguerre, John *NewGrD 80*
Leguizamon, Martinian 1858-1935 *OxThe*
Lehac, Ned 1899- *AmSCAP 66, -80*
Lehane, Maureen *IntWWM 77, -80, WhoMus 72*
Lehar, Ferencz 1870-1948 *NewGrD 80[port]*
Lehar, Franz 1870-1948 *Baker 78, BnBkM 80, CmOp, CmpEPM, DcCom 77[port], DcCom&M 79, MusMk, NewGrD 80[port], NotNAT B, OxMus, PlP&P, WhThe, WhoStg 1908*
LeHay, Daisy 1883- *WhThe*
Lehay, Eugene *Film 2*
LeHay, John 1854-1926 *NotNAT B, WhThe*
Lehel, Gyorgy 1926- *IntWWM 77, -80, NewGrD 80*
LeHeman *NewGrD 80*
LeHeurteur, Guillaume *NewGrD 80*
Lehman, Ernest *IntMPA 77, -75, -76, -78, -79, -80*
Lehman, Ernest 1915- *CmMov*
Lehman, Ernest 1920- *FilmEn, FilmgC, HalFC 80, WorEFlm*
Lehman, Gladys *IntMPA 77, -75, -76, -78, -79, -80, WomWMM*
Lehman, Jon Leonard 1940- *ConAmTC*
Lehman, Lillian *DrBlPA*
Lehman, Paul Robert 1931- *IntWWM 77, -80*
Lehman, Trent *WhoHol A*
Lehmann, Arnold O 1914- *IntWWM 77, -80*
Lehmann, Beatrix 1898-1979 *FilmgC, HalFC 80, WhoHol A*
Lehmann, Beatrix 1903- *WhoThe 72, -77*
Lehmann, Carla 1917- *FilmgC, HalFC 80, IlWWBF, WhThe, WhoHol A*
Lehmann, Dieter 1929- *IntWWM 77*
Lehmann, Elizabeth Nina Mary Frederika 1862-1918 *NewGrD 80, OxMus*
Lehmann, Else 1866-1940 *EncWT*
Lehmann, Friedrich J 1866-1950 *Baker 78*
Lehmann, George 1865-1941 *Baker 78*
Lehmann, Hans Peter *WhoOp 76*
Lehmann, Hans Ulrich 1937- *Baker 78, CpmDNM 80, DcCM, IntWWM 77, -80, NewGrD 80*
Lehmann, Lilli 1848-1921 *CmOp*
Lehmann, Lilli 1848-1929 *Baker 78, BiDAmM, BnBkM 80, MusSN[port], NewEOp 71, NewGrD 80*
Lehmann, Liza 1862-1918 *Baker 78, NewGrD 80*
Lehmann, Lotte 1886- *BiDAmM*
Lehmann, Lotte 1888-1976 *Baker 78, BnBkM 80, CmOp, IntWWM 77, MusMk, MusSN[port], NewEOp 71, NewGrD 80[port], What 2[port], WhoMus 72*
Lehmann, Marie 1851-1931 *Baker 78*
Lehmann, Markus Hugo 1919- *IntWWM 77, -80*
Lehmann, Maurice 1895- *DancEn 78*
Lehmann, Otto 1906-1971 *BiDAmM*
Lehmann, Robert 1841-1912 *Baker 78*
Lehmeyer, John Jay 1940- *WhoOp 76*
Lehms, Georg Christian 1684-1717 *NewGrD 80*
Lehner, Franz Xaver 1904- *IntWWM 77, -80*
Lehner, Leo 1900- *WhoMus 72*
Lehnerts, Frances *IntWWM 77, -80*
Lehnoff, Nikolaus 1939- *WhoOp 76*
Lehotka, Gabor 1938- *NewGrD 80*
Lehr, Anna *Film 1, -2, TwYS*
Lehr, Lew 1895-1950 *WhScrn 74, -77, WhoHol B*
Lehr, Mangham David 1928- *ConAmC*
Lehr, Milton H 1918- *IntMPA 77, -75, -76, -78, -79, -80*
Lehr, Wilson 1913- *BiE&WWA*
Lehrberger, Thomas Heinrich 1934- *WhoOp 76*
Lehrer, George J 1889-1966 *WhScrn 74, -77*
Lehrer, James C *NewYTET*
Lehrer, Thomas Andrew 1928- *AmSCAP 80, BiDAmM, IntWWM 77, -80*
Lehrer, Tom 1928- *AmSCAP 66, EncFCWM 69, JoeFr*
Lehrfield, Robert 1925- *IntWWM 77, -80*
Lehrman, Henry 1886-1946 *DcFM, FilmEn, Film 1, TwYS A, WhScrn 74, -77, WhoHol B*
Lehrman, Leonard Jordan 1949- *AmSCAP 80*
Lehrman, Leonard Jordon 1949- *ConAmC*
Lehrman, Theodore Howard 1929- *AmSCAP 66, -80*
Lehtinen, Rauno V 1932- *IntWWM 77*
LeHuray, Peter Geoffrey 1930- *IntWWM 77, -80, NewGrD 80, WhoMus 72*
Leib, Gunther 1927- *WhoOp 76*
Leiber, Fritz d1949 *WhoHol B*
Leiber, Fritz 1882-1949 *FilmEn, ForYSC, TwYS, Vers A[port], WhScrn 74, -77*
Leiber, Fritz 1883-1949 *Film 1, -2, FilmgC, HalFC 80, MovMk, NotNAT B, WhThe*
Leiber, Fritz 1883-1966 *HolCA[port]*
Leiber, Jerry *AmSCAP 80, ConMuA 80B*
Leiber, Jerry & Mike Stoller *IlEncR*
Leibert, Michael W 1940- *NotNAT*
Leibert, Richard William 1903-1976 *AmSCAP 66, -80*
Leibig, Bruce 1946- *ConAmC*
Leibman, Ron *IntMPA 75*
Leibman, Ron 1937- *FilmEn, HalFC 80, IntMPA 77, -76, -78, -79, -80, NotNAT, WhoHol A, WhoThe 72, -77*
Leibniz, Gottfried Wilhelm 1646-1716 *NewGrD 80*
Leibowitz, Rene 1913-1972 *Baker 78, DcCM, NewGrD 80, OxMus, WhoMus 72*
Leibowitz, Sam 1913- *IntMPA 77, -78, -79, -80*
Leibrock, Joseph Adolf 1808-1886 *Baker 78*
Leibrook, Min Wilford F 1903-1943 *WhoJazz 72*
Leicester, Ernest 1866-1939 *NotNAT B, WhThe*
Leicester, George F d1916 *NotNAT B*
Leicester, William 1915-1969 *WhScrn 77*
Leich, Roland 1911- *ConAmC*
Leichnamschneider *NewGrD 80*
Leichnamschneider, Franz *NewGrD 80*
Leichnamschneider, Johann *NewGrD 80*
Leichnamschneider, Johannes 1679-1725? *NewGrD 80*
Leichnamschneider, Michael 1676-1746? *NewGrD 80*
Leichner, Eckhardt *NewGrD 80*
Leicht, Helen *ConMuA 80B*
Leichtentritt, Hugo 1874-1951 *Baker 78, BiDAmM, ConAmC, NewGrD 80*
Leichtling, Alan Robert 1947- *CpmDNM 76, ConAmC, IntWWM 77, -80*
Leichty, David H 1946- *IntWWM 77*
Leider, Frida 1888-1975 *Baker 78, BnBkM 80, CmOp, MusSN[port], NewEOp 71, NewGrD 80[port]*

Leider, Gerald J 1931- *IntMPA 77, -75, -76, -78, -79, -80*
Leidesdorf, Marcus *NewGrD 80*
Leiding, Georg Dietrich 1664-1710 *NewGrD 80*
Leidtke, Harry *Film 2*
Leidy, Russel *PupTheA*
Leidzen, Erik 1894-1962 *AmSCAP 66, -80, ConAmC*
Leifs, Jon 1899-1968 *Baker 78, DcCM, NewGrD 80*
Leigh, Adele 1928- *CmOp, WhoMus 72*
Leigh, Andrew George 1887-1957 *NotNAT B, PlP&P, WhThe*
Leigh, Angela 1927- *CreCan 2*
Leigh, Anthony d1692 *OxThe*
Leigh, Barbara *WhoHol A*
Leigh, Carol Ann 1937?- *BluesWW[port]*
Leigh, Carolyn 1926- *AmPS, AmSCAP 66, -80, BiE&WWA, EncMT, NewCBMT, NotNAT*
Leigh, Charlotte 1907- *WhThe*
Leigh, Dorma 1893- *WhThe*
Leigh, Frank d1948 *Film 1, -2, TwYS, WhScrn 74, -77, WhoHol B*
Leigh, George d1957 *WhoHol B*
Leigh, Gerri J 1957- *AmSCAP 80*
Leigh, Gilbert *WhoHol A*
Leigh, Gracie d1950 *NotNAT B, WhThe*
Leigh, Henry S d1883 *NotNAT B*
Leigh, J H d1934 *NotNAT B*
Leigh, Jack *IlWWBF*
Leigh, Janet 1927- *BiDFilm, -81, FilmEn, FilmgC, ForYSC, HalFC 80, IntMPA 77, -75, -76, -78, -79, -80, MGM[port], MotPP, MovMk[port], OxFilm, WhoHol A, WhoHrs 80[port], WorEFlm*
Leigh, Jennifer *WhoHol A*
Leigh, Leslie *Film 1*
Leigh, Mary 1904-1943 *NotNAT B, WhThe*
Leigh, Mitch 1928- *AmSCAP 66, -80, EncMT, NewCBMT, NewGrD 80, NotNAT, PopAmC SUP[port]*
Leigh, Nelson 1914-1967 *ForYSC, WhoHol B*
Leigh, Philip d1935 *NotNAT B*
Leigh, Richard C *AmSCAP 80*
Leigh, Rowland 1902-1963 *WhThe*
Leigh, Suzanna 1945- *FilmEn, FilmgC, HalFC 80, IlWWBF, IntMPA 77, -75, -76, -78, -79, -80, WhoHol A*
Leigh, Vivien 1913-1967 *BiDFilm, -81, BiE&WWA, CnThe, EncMT, EncWT, Ent[port], FamA&A[port], FilmAG WE[port], FilmEn, FilmgC, ForYSC, HalFC 80, IlWWBF[port], -A, MotPP, MovMk[port], NotNAT A, -B, OxFilm, OxThe, PlP&P, ThFT[port], WhScrn 74, -77, WhThe, WhoHol B, WorEFlm*
Leigh, Walter 1905-1942 *Baker 78, NewGrD 80, OxMus, WhThe*
Leigh Hunt *OxThe*
Leigh-Hunt, Barbara *WhoHol A*
Leigh-Hunt, Barbara 1935- *NotNAT*
Leigh-Hunt, Barbara 1941- *FilmgC, HalFC 80*
Leigh-Hunt, Ronald 1916?- *FilmgC, HalFC 80, WhoHol A*
Leigheb, Claudio 1848- *WhThe*
Leighton, A C 1901-1965 *CreCan 2*
Leighton, Alexes d1926 *NotNAT B*
Leighton, Bernie 1921- *CmpEPM*
Leighton, Bert 1877-1964 *AmSCAP 66, -80, NotNAT B*
Leighton, Daniel 1880-1917 *WhScrn 77*
Leighton, Frank 1908-1962 *WhThe*
Leighton, Harry d1926 *NotNAT B*
Leighton, Herb *AmSCAP 80*
Leighton, James Albert 1877-1964 *BiDAmM*
Leighton, Kenneth 1929- *Baker 78, DcCM, IntWWM 80, NewGrD 80, WhoMus 72*
Leighton, Lillian 1874-1956 *Film 1, -2, TwYS, WhScrn 74, -77, WhoHol B*
Leighton, Margaret 1922-1976 *BiE&WWA, CnThe, EncWT, Ent, FilmAG WE, FilmEn, FilmgC, ForYSC, HalFC 80, IlWWBF, IntMPA 75, -76, MotPP, MovMk[port], OxThe, PlP&P, WhoHol C, WhoThe 72, -77*
Leighton, Queenie 1872-1943 *NotNAT B, WhThe*
Leighton, Sir William 1560?- *Baker 78*
Leighton, Sir William 1565?-1622 *NewGrD 80*
Leighton Brothers *AmPS B*
Leikin, Molly-Ann 1948- *AmSCAP 80*
Leimer, Kurt 1920-1974 *Baker 78*
Leinati, Giovanni Ambrogio *NewGrD 80*
Leinbach, Edward William 1823-1901 *NewGrD 80*
Leiner, Randy Dale 1953- *AmSCAP 80*
Leininger, Robert 1916- *IntWWM 77, -80*
Leinsdorf, Erich 1912- *Baker 78, BiDAmM, BnBkM 80, CmOp, IntWWM 77, -80, MusMk, MusSN[port], NewEOp 71, NewGrD 80[port], WhoMus 72, WhoOp 76*
Leiper, Joseph *NewGrD 80*
Leipp, Emile 1913- *NewGrD 80*
Leipzig, Nate 1873-1939 *MagIlD*
Leisen, J Mitchell 1898-1972 *MovMk[port], WhScrn 77*
Leisen, Mitchell 1897-1972 *BiDFilm, -81*
Leisen, Mitchell 1898-1972 *CmMov, FilmEn, FilmgC, HalFC 80, WhoHol B, WorEFlm*
Leisentrit, Johann 1527-1586 *NewGrD 80*
Leisentrit, Johannes 1527-1586 *NewGrD 80*
Leiser, Eric 1929- *AmSCAP 66, -80*
Leiser, Ernest *NewYTET*
Leiser, Erwin 1923- *DcFM, FilmEn, FilmgC, HalFC 80, WorEFlm*
Leiser, Henri 1903- *IntMPA 77, -75, -76, -78, -79, -80*
Leisewitz, Johann Anton 1752-1806 *EncWT, McGEWD*
Leish, Kenneth William 1936- *BiE&WWA*
Leisinger, Elisabeth 1864-1933 *Baker 78*
Leisner, Dorothy Mary Gostwick Roberts *CreCan 1*
Leisring, Volckmar 1588-1637 *NewGrD 80*
Leisringus, Volckmar 1588-1637 *NewGrD 80*
Leissringk, Volckmar 1588-1637 *NewGrD 80*
Leister, Frederick 1885-1970 *FilmgC, HalFC 80, WhThe, WhoHol B*
Leistikow, Gertrud 1885- *CnOxB*
Leistner, Wolfgang 1933- *DancEn 78*
Leisy, James Franklin 1927- *AmSCAP 80*
Leitao DeAvilez, Manuel *NewGrD 80*
Leite, Antonio DaSilva 1759-1833 *Baker 78, NewGrD 80*
Leite, Carlos 1914- *DancEn 78*
Leite, Clarisse 1917- *IntWWM 77, -80*
Leitermeyer, Fritz 1925- *IntWWM 77, -80*
Leitert, Johann Georg 1852-1901 *Baker 78*
Leitgeb, Ignaz *NewGrD 80*
Leitgeb, Joseph *NewGrD 80*
Leitgeb, Willey *Film 2*
Leith, Virginia 1932- *HalFC 80, WhoHol A*
Leitner, Ferdinand 1912- *CmOp, IntWWM 77, -80, NewGrD 80, WhoMus 72, WhoOp 76*
Leitzel, Lillian 1893-1931 *Ent*
Leitzmann, Albert 1867-1950 *Baker 78*
Leivick, H 1888-1962 *CnThe, McGEWD, ModWD, REnWD[port]*
Leiviska, Helvi 1902- *Baker 78, IntWWM 77, -80*
Lejet, Edith 1941- *IntWWM 80*
Lejeune, Andre 1934- *IntWWM 77*
LeJeune, Caroline 1897-1973 *IlWWBF A, OxFilm*
LeJeune, Claude 1528-1600 *Baker 78, MusMk, NewGrD 80[port]*
LeJeune, Claude 1530?-1600 *BnBkM 80*
LeJeune, Claudin 1528?-1600 *NewGrD 80[port]*
LeJeune, George Fitz Curwood 1841-1904 *BiDAmM*
Lekain 1729-1778 *EncWT, Ent*
Lekain, Henri-Louis 1729-1778 *NotNAT B, OxThe*
Lekberg, Sven 1899- *ConAmC*
Lekeu, Guillaume 1870-1894 *Baker 78, BnBkM 80, CmpBCM, GrComp[port], MusMk, NewGrD 80, OxMus*
Lekfeldt, Jorgen 1948- *IntWWM 80*
Lekprevick, Robert *OxMus*
Leland, James Miner 1940- *IntWWM 77, -80*
Leland, John 1754-1841 *BiDAmM*
Leland, Sara 1941- *CnOxB, DancEn 78*
Lelarge, Jacques-George 1713-1793? *NewGrD 80*
Lelei, Georg Simon *NewGrD 80*
Leleu, Jeanne 1898- *NewGrD 80*
Leleu, Jehan *NewGrD 80*
Leleu, Jennot *NewGrD 80*
Lelio *OxThe*
Lelouch, Claude 1937- *BiDFilm, -81, DcFM, FilmEn, FilmgC, HalFC 80, IntMPA 77, -75, -76, -78, -79, -80, MovMk[port], OxFilm, WorEFlm*
Lely, Durward d1944 *NotNAT B*
Lely, Madeleine *WhThe*
Lemacher, Heinrich 1891-1966 *Baker 78, NewGrD 80*
Lemacherier, Guillaume *NewGrD 80*
LeMaire, Charles *IntMPA 77, -75, -76, -78, -79, -80*
LeMaire, George 1884-1930 *WhScrn 74, -77, WhoHol B*
Lemaire, Jean 1473?-1514? *NewGrD 80*
Lemaire, Jean 1581?-1650? *Baker 78*
LeMaire, Jean 1581?-1650? *NewGrD 80*
Lemaire, Jean Eugene Gaston 1854-1928 *Baker 78*
Lemaire, Louis 1693?-1750? *NewGrD 80*
LeMaire, William 1892-1933 *WhScrn 74, -77, WhoHol B*
LeMaistre, Matthaeus 1505?-1577? *NewGrD 80*
LeMaistre, Mattheus 1505?-1577 *Baker 78*
Lemaitre *OxThe*
Lemaitre, Antoine-Louis-Prosper 1800-1876 *EncWT*
LeMaitre, Frederic 1800-1876 *NotNAT A, -B*
Lemaitre, Frederick 1800-1876 *CnThe, Ent*
Lemaitre, Gerard 1936- *CnOxB*
Lemaitre, Jules 1853-1914 *McGEWD[port], ModWD, NotNAT B, WhThe*
Lemaitre, Jules-Francois-Elie 1854-1914 *OxThe*
Leman, J William F 1880-1953 *BiDAmM*
Leman, Walter 1810- *NotNAT A*
Lemanis, Osvald 1903-1965 *CnOxB, DancEn 78*
LeMans, Marcel 1897-1946 *WhScrn 74, -77*
Lemare, Edwin Henry 1865-1934 *Baker 78, BiDAmM, OxMus*
Lemare, Iris Margaret Elsie *IntWWM 77, -80, WhoMus 72*
LeMassena, William H 1916- *BiE&WWA, NotNAT, WhoHol A, WhoThe 72, -77*
LeMat, Paul *WhoHol A*
LeMay, Alan 1899-1964 *CmMov, FilmEn, FilmgC, HalFC 80, NotNAT B*
LeMay, Alton T M B 1923- *IntWWM 77*
Lemay, Harding *NatPD[port]*
Lemay, Joseph *PupTheA*
Lembeck, Harvey *IntMPA 75, -76*
Lembeck, Harvey 1923- *BiE&WWA, ForYSC, WhoHol A*
Lembeck, Harvey 1925- *HalFC 80*
Lemblin, Lorenz *NewGrD 80*
Lemelin, Roger 1919- *CreCan 2*
LeMenu *NewGrD 80*
LeMenu DeSaint Philbert, Christoph 1720?-1780 *NewGrD 80*
Lemercier, Nepomucene 1771-1840 *NotNAT B, OxThe*
Lemeshev, Sergey 1902-1977 *NewGrD 80*
LeMessurier, Billy *PupTheA*
LeMesurier, John 1912- *FilmgC, HalFC 80, WhoHol A*
Lemiere DeCorvey, Jean Frederic Auguste 1770-1832 *NewGrD 80*
Lemierre DeCorvey, Jean Frederic Auguste 1770-1832 *NewGrD 80*
Lemieux, Jean-Paul 1904- *CreCan 1*
Lemieux, Paul *ConMuA 80B*
Leming, Warren Ewing 1941- *AmSCAP 80*
Lemit, William 1908-1966 *Baker 78*
Lemkes, Bouwe 1924- *IntWWM 77, -80*
Lemlein, Lorenz 1495?-1549? *NewGrD 80*
Lemlin, Lorenz 1495?-1549? *NewGrD 80*
Lemmens, Jaak Nikolaas 1823-1881 *NewGrD 80*
Lemmens, Jacques Nicolas 1823-1881 *NewGrD 80*
Lemmens, Nicolas Jacques 1823-1881 *Baker 78, BnBkM 80, OxMus*
Lemmens-Sherrington, Helen 1834-1906 *NewGrD 80*
Lemmon, Alfred E 1949- *IntWWM 80*

Lemmon, Christopher Boyd 1954- *AmSCAP 80*
Lemmon, Jack *IntMPA 75, -76, -78, -79, -80*
Lemmon, Jack 1923- *BiDFilm, -81*
Lemmon, Jack 1925- *BiE&WWA, CmMov, FilmEn, FilmgC, ForYSC, Funs[port], HalFC 80, IntMPA 77, MotPP, MovMk[port], OxFilm, WhoHol A, WorEFlm[port]*
Lemnitz, Tiana 1897- *CmOp, NewEOp 71, NewGrD 80*
Lemoine *NewGrD 80*
Lemoine, Achille-Philibert 1813-1895 *NewGrD 80*
Lemoine, Andre 1907- *NewGrD 80*
Lemoine, Antoine Henry 1786-1854 *NewGrD 80*
Lemoine, Antoine-Marcel 1753-1816 *Baker 78*
Lemoine, Antoine Marcel 1753-1817 *NewGrD 80*
Lemoine, Francois d1840 *NewGrD 80*
Lemoine, Gaston 1851?- *NewGrD 80*
Lemoine, Henry 1786-1854 *Baker 78*
Lemoine, Henry-Felicien 1848-1924 *NewGrD 80*
Lemoine, Henry Jean 1890-1970 *NewGrD 80*
Lemoine, Jean-Bernard 1920- *CnOxB*
Lemoine, Leon 1855-1916 *NewGrD 80*
Lemon, Mark 1809-1870 *NotNAT B, OxThe*
Lemon Pipers, The *RkOn 2[port]*
LeMonier, Joseph *PupTheA*
Lemonier, Tom 1870-1945 *AmSCAP 66, -80*
Lemont, Cedric Wilmont 1879-1954 *Baker 78*
Lemont, Cedric Wilmot 1879-1954 *AmSCAP 66, -80, ConAmC*
Lemont, John *IlWWBF, IntMPA 77, -75, -76, -78, -79, -80*
Lemontier, Jules *Film 1*
LeMoyne, Charles 1880-1956 *Film 2, WhScrn 74, -77, WhoHol B*
Lemoyne, Gabriel *NewGrD 80*
Lemoyne, Jean-Baptiste 1751-1796 *Baker 78, NewEOp 71, NewGrD 80*
LeMoyne, Sarah Cowell 1859-1915 *NotNAT B, WhThe, WhoStg 1906, -1908*
LeMoyne, W J 1831-1905 *NotNAT B*
Lempfert, Majorie O E 1921- *IntWWM 80*
Lempfert, Marjorie O E 1921- *IntWWM 77*
Lemshev, Sergey 1902- *CmOp*
Lemuels, William E 1891-1953 *WhScrn 74, -77, WhoHol B*
LeMunerat, Jean *NewGrD 80*
Lena, Lily 1879- *WhThe*
Lenaerts, Constant 1852-1931 *Baker 78*
Lenaerts, Rene Bernard 1902- *NewGrD 80, WhoMus 72*
Lenard, Grace *WhoHol A*
Lenard, Mark 1927- *BiE&WWA, NotNAT, WhoHol A*
Lenard, Melvyn 1936- *AmSCAP 66*
Lenares, Zeb 1885?-1928? *NewOrJ*
L'Enclos, Henri De 1592?-1649 *NewGrD 80*
L'Enclos, Ninon De *NewGrD 80*
Lencses, Lajos 1943- *IntWWM 77, -80*
Lender, Marcelle d1926 *NotNAT B, WhThe*
Lendvai, Erno 1925- *NewGrD 80*
Lendvai, Erwin 1882-1949 *Baker 78*
Lendvay, Kamillo 1928- *Baker 78, IntWWM 77, -80, NewGrD 80*
Lenear *NewGrD 80*
Lenel, Ludwig 1914- *ConAmC*
Lenepveu, Charles 1840-1910 *Baker 78, NewGrD 80*
Lener, Jeno 1871-1948 *BiDAmM*
Lener, Jeno 1894-1948 *Baker 78, NewGrD 80*
Leng, Alfonso 1884-1974 *Baker 78*
Leng, Alfonso 1894-1974 *DcCM, NewGrD 80*
Lengel, William Charles 1888-1965 *NotNAT B*
Lenglen, Suzanne 1899-1938 *WhScrn 74, -77, WhoHol B*
Lengnick *NewGrD 80*
Lengnick, Alfred d1904 *NewGrD 80*
Lengsfelder, Hans Jan 1903-1979 *AmSCAP 66, -80*
Lengyel, Melchior 1880- *CnMD*
Lengyel, Menyhert 1880- *ModWD*
Lenhart, Renate *WhoOp 76*
Lenher, Mrs. Samuel *PupTheA*
Leni, Paul 1885-1929 *BiDFilm, -81, CmMov, DcFM, FilmEn, FilmgC, HalFC 80, OxFilm, TwYS A, WhScrn 74, -77, WhoHrs 80, WorEFlm*
Lenica, Jan 1928- *DcFM, FilmEn, FilmgC, HalFC 80, OxFilm, WorEFlm[port]*
Lenihan, Deidre *WhoHol A*
Lenihan, Winifred d1964 *NotNAT B, WhoHol B*
Lenihan, Winifred 1898-1964 *WhThe*
Lenihan, Winifred 1899-1964 *WhScrn 74, -77*
Lenin 1870-1924 *HalFC 80, OxFilm*
Lenja, Lotte *NewGrD 80*
Lenk, Harry *AmSCAP 80*
Lenk, Marjorie *WomWMM B*
Lenke, Walter 1907- *AmSCAP 66*
Lenkeffy, Isa *Film 2*
Lenkovitch, Bernhard 1927- *OxMus*
Lennard, Arthur 1867-1954 *NotNAT B, WhThe*
Lennard, Horace d1920 *NotNAT B*
Lennart, Isabel 1915-1971 *FilmgC*
Lennart, Isobel 1914- *CmMov, WomWMM*
Lennart, Isobel 1915-1971 *FilmEn, HalFC 80*
Lenneberg, Hans H 1924- *IntWWM 77, -80*
Lennol, Roy *Film 2*
Lennon, John 1940- *Baker 78, ConMuA 80A, FilmEn, ForYSC, IlEncR[port], MotPP, MusMk[port], NewGrD 80, RkOn 2[port], WhoHol A*
Lennon, Nestor Forbes Richardson 1863- *WhoStg 1906, -1908*
Lennon Sisters, The *BiDAmM, RkOn*
Lennox, David 1928- *IntWWM 80, WhoMus 72*
Lennox, Lottie d1947 *NotNAT B*
Lennox, Vera 1904- *Film 2, WhThe*
Lenny, Jack *BiE&WWA*
Leno, Antonio De *NewGrD 80*
Leno, Antonius De *NewGrD 80*
Leno, Dan 1860-1904 *EncWT, Ent[port], IlWWBF, NotNAT A, OxThe, PlP&P*
Leno, Dan, Jr. d1962 *NotNAT B*
Leno, Sydney Paul Galvin 1892-1962 *OxThe*
Lenoble, Eustache 1643-1711 *OxThe*
Lenoidov, Leonid Mironovich 1873-1941 *WhoHol B*
LeNoir, Blanche *AmSCAP 66*
Lenoir, Charles *OxThe*
Lenoir, Claudine *WomWMM*
Lenoir, J B 1929-1967 *BluesWW[port]*
Lenoir, Pass 1874-1946 *WhScrn 74, -77*
Lenoir, Yves Roger Desire 1950- *IntWWM 77, -80*
LeNoire, Rosetta 1911- *BiE&WWA, DrBlPA, MorBAP, NotNAT, WhoHol A, WhoThe 72, -77*
Lenor, Jacque *Film 1*
Lenore, J B *BluesWW[port]*
Lenormand, Henri-Rene 1882-1951 *CnMD, EncWT, Ent, McGEWD, ModWD, NotNAT B, REnWD[port], WhThe*
Lenormand, Rene 1846-1932 *Baker 78*
Lenot, Jaques 1945- *IntWWM 77, -80*
Lenox, Fred *Film 1*
Lenox, John Thomas 1946- *AmSCAP 80*
Lenoy, Andre *Film 2*
Lenrow, Bernard 1903-1963 *WhScrn 74, -77, WhoHol B*
Lensky, Alexander Pavlovich 1847-1908 *NotNAT B, OxThe, PlP&P*
Lensky, Fedor 1913- *DancEn 78*
Lensky, Leib *WhoHol A*
Lensky, Margaret *WhoMus 72*
Lent, Ernest 1856-1922 *Baker 78*
Lenthall, Franklyn 1919- *BiE&WWA, NotNAT*
Lenti, Anna 1912-1975 *AmSCAP 80*
Lenton, John d1718? *NewGrD 80*
Lentz, Daniel 1942- *Baker 78, ConAmC*
Lentz, Donald Anthony 1908- *IntWWM 77, -80*
Lenya, Lotte 1898- *NewGrD 80[port]*
Lenya, Lotte 1899- *HalFC 80*
Lenya, Lotte 1900- *BiE&WWA, EncMT, EncWT, FilmEn, FilmgC, ForYSC, MotPP, NotNAT, OxFilm, WhoHol A, WhoThe 72, -77, WorEFlm*
Lenya, Lotte 1901- *CnThe*
Lenz, Jakob Michael Reinhold 1751-1792 *EncWT, McGEWD[port]*
Lenz, Kay 1953- *HalFC 80, WhoHol A*
Lenz, Rick 1939- *HalFC 80, WhoHol A*
Lenz, Siegfried 1926- *CnMD SUP, CroCD*
Lenz, Wilhelm Von 1809-1883 *Baker 78, NewGrD 80*
Leo *Film 1, NewGrD 80*
Leo DaModena 1571?-1648? *NewGrD 80*
Leo Hebraeus 1288?-1344 *NewGrD 80*
Leo Of Modena *OxMus*
Leo X, Pope *NewGrD 80*
Leo, Frank 1874- *WhThe*
Leo, John L *IntMPA 76*
Leo, Kid *ConMuA 80B*
Leo, Leonardo 1694-1744 *Baker 78, BnBkM 80, GrComp, MusMk, NewEOp 71, NewGrD 80, OxMus*
Leo, Lionardo 1694-1744 *NewGrD 80*
Leogrande, Ernest *ConAmTC*
Leon, Anne 1925- *WhThe*
Leon, Argeliers 1918- *NewGrD 80*
Leon, Bayani Mendoza De 1942- *NewGrD 80*
Leon, Bobby *AmSCAP 80*
Leon, Connie 1880-1955 *WhScrn 74, -77, WhoHol B*
Leon, Felipe Padilla De 1912- *NewGrD 80*
Leon, Garby 1947- *ConAmC*
Leon, Joseph *WhoHol A*
Leon, Max M 1904- *WhoOp 76*
Leon, Pauline Lightstone *CreCan 1*
Leon, Pierre Camille 1924- *WhoOp 76*
Leon, Sol 1913- *IntMPA 77, -76, -78, -79, -80*
Leon, Tania Justina 1944- *AmSCAP 80, BlkWAB[port]*
Leon, Valeriano 1892-1955? *WhScrn 74, -77*
Leon, Victor d1940 *NotNAT B*
Leon, W D d1964 *NotNAT B*
Leon DeBagnols, Magister *NewGrD 80*
Leonard, Anita 1922- *AmSCAP 66, -80*
Leonard, Archie 1917-1959 *WhScrn 74, -77, WhoHol B*
Leonard, Barbara *Film 2*
Leonard, Benny *Film 2*
Leonard, Bert *NewYTET*
Leonard, Bill *NewYTET*
Leonard, Billy 1892- *WhThe*
Leonard, Charles A 1907- *IntMPA 75, -76*
Leonard, Clair 1901- *BiDAmM*
Leonard, Claudie *DancEn 78*
Leonard, David A 1892-1967 *WhScrn 77, WhoHol B*
Leonard, Eddie *AmPS B*
Leonard, Eddie 1870-1941 *Film 2, NotNAT B, WhScrn 74, -77, WhoHol B*
Leonard, Eddie 1875-1941 *AmSCAP 66, -80, BiDAmM, CmpEPM, NotNAT A*
Leonard, Frank Lawrence *WhoMus 72*
Leonard, Grace 1909- *ConAmC*
Leonard, Gus 1856-1939 *Film 2, WhScrn 74, -77, WhoHol B*
Leonard, Harlan 1904- *BgBands 74, CmpEPM*
Leonard, Herbert B 1922- *HalFC 80, IntMPA 77, -75, -76, -78, -79, -80*
Leonard, Hubert 1819-1890 *Baker 78, NewGrD 80*
Leonard, Hugh 1926- *ConDr 73, -77, CroCD, WhoThe 72, -77*
Leonard, Jack *CmpEPM*
Leonard, Jack E 1911-1973 *NotNAT B, WhScrn 77, WhoHol B*
Leonard, Jack E 1911-1975 *JoeFr[port]*
Leonard, James 1868-1930 *Film 2, WhScrn 74, -77, WhoHol B*
Leonard, Julie 1923- *BiE&WWA*
Leonard, LaVerne *Film 2*
Leonard, Lawrence 1923- *IntWWM 77, -80*
Leonard, Marion d1956 *MotPP, NotNAT B, WhoHol B*
Leonard, Marion 1880-1956 *WhScrn 77*
Leonard, Marion 1881-1956 *Film 1, TwYS*
Leonard, Mary *Film 1*
Leonard, Melanie Elizabeth *PupTheA*
Leonard, Michael 1931- *AmSCAP 66*
Leonard, Mike Harlan Quentin 1905- *WhoJazz 72*
Leonard, Murray 1898-1970 *HalFC 80, WhScrn 74, -77, WhoHol B*
Leonard, Nels, Jr. 1931- *IntWWM 77, -80*
Leonard, Patricia 1916- *WhThe*
Leonard, Queenie *ForYSC, WhoHol A*
Leonard, Robert d1948 *NotNAT B, WhThe*
Leonard, Robert Duke 1901-1961 *AmSCAP 66, -80*

Leonard, Robert Z 1889-1968 *BiDFilm, -81, CmMov, DcFM, FilmEn, FilmgC, HalFC 80, MovMk[port], NotNAT B, WhScrn 74, -77, WorEFlm*
Leonard, Robert Z 1898-1970 *Film 1, TwYS A, WhoHol B*
Leonard, Roy 1931- *ConAmTC*
Leonard, Sheldon 1907- *FilmEn, FilmgC, ForYSC, HalFC 80, HolCA[port], IntMPA 77, -75, -76, -78, -79, -80, MotPP, MovMk, NewYTET, Vers A[port], WhoHol A*
Leonard, Stanley Sprenger 1931- *AmSCAP 80, IntWWM 77, -80*
Leonard-Boyne, Eva 1885-1960 *NotNAT B, WhThe*
Leonarda, Isabella *NewGrD 80*
Leonardi, Leonid 1901- *AmSCAP 66, ConAmC A*
Leonardo Da Vinci 1452-1519 *EncWT, NewGrD 80*
Leonardo, Harry 1903-1964 *WhScrn 74, -77*
Leonardo-Gelber, Bruno *WhoMus 72*
Leonardos, Urylee *DrBlPA*
Leonardus Athesinus *NewGrD 80*
Leonardus Nervius *NewGrD 80*
Leonati, Carlo Ambrogio *NewGrD 80*
Leoncavallo, Ruggero 1857-1919 *Baker 78, BnBkM 80, NewGrD 80[port]*
Leoncavallo, Ruggero 1858-1919 *DcCom&M 79, NotNAT B*
Leoncavallo, Ruggiero 1858-1919 *CmOp, CmpBCM, DcCom 77, GrComp[port], MusMk, NewEOp 71, OxMus*
Leone Da Modena *NewGrD 80*
Leone, Alfred 1926- *IntMPA 78, -79, -80*
Leone, Dave *ConMuA 80B*
Leone, Gennaro Cyprian, Jr. 1952- *AmSCAP 80*
Leone, Henri *Film 1*
Leone, Henry d1922 *NotNAT B, WhScrn 77, WhoHol B*
Leone, Leonard 1914- *BiE&WWA, NotNAT*
Leone, Mae Grace *IntWWM 77, -80*
Leone, Maude d1930 *NotNAT B*
Leone, Raphael 1948- *IntWWM 77, -80*
Leone, Sergio 1921- *BiDFilm 81, FilmEn, FilmgC, HalFC 80, OxFilm*
Leonel *NewGrD 80*
Leonelle *NewGrD 80*
Leonellus *NewGrD 80*
Leonetti, Giovanni Battista *NewGrD 80*
Leonetti, Tommy 1929- *AmSCAP 66*
Leong, James *Film 2*
Leonhard, Julius Emil 1810-1883 *Baker 78*
Leonhardt, Gustav 1928- *Baker 78, BnBkM 80, IntWWM 77, -80, NewGrD 80*
Leonhardt, Hans-Gunter 1937- *IntWWM 77*
Leonhart, James C 1940- *EncJzS 70*
Leonhart, Jay 1940- *EncJzS 70*
Leoni, Franco 1864-1949 *Baker 78, NewEOp 71, NewGrD 80, NotNAT B*
Leoni, Giovanni Antonio d1652? *NewGrD 80*
Leoni, Leo 1560?-1627 *NewGrD 80*
Leoni, Leone 1560?-1627? *Baker 78, NewGrD 80*
Leoni, Michael 1755?-1797 *NewGrD 80*
Leonidoff, Leon 1895- *Film 2, IntMPA 75, -76*
Leonidov, Leon *Film 2*
Leonidov, Leonid Mironovich 1873-1941 *EncWT, NotNAT B, OxThe*
Leonin *Baker 78, MusMk, NewGrD 80*
Leonov, Leonid Maksimovich 1899- *CnMD, McGEWD, ModWD*
Leonov, Leonid Maximovich 1899- *OxThe*
Leonova, Dar'ya Mikhaylovna 1829-1896 *Baker 78, NewGrD 80*
Leonova, Marina Konstantinovna 1949- *CnOxB*
Leontis, Christos 1940- *IntWWM 77, -80*
Leontovich, Eugenie 1894- *FilmgC, ForYSC, HalFC 80, WhoHol A*
Leontovich, Eugenie 1900- *BiE&WWA, FamA&A[port], NotNAT, WhoThe 72, -77*
Leontovych, Mykola Dmytrovich 1877-1921 *NewGrD 80*
Leopardi, Venanzio d1658? *NewGrD 80*
Leopold I 1640-1705 *Baker 78, NewGrD 80*
Leopold, Archduke Of Austria *Film 2*
Leopold Of Anhalt-Cothen *OxMus*
Leopold, J Walter 1890-1956 *AmSCAP 66, -80*
Leopold, Nathan *What 2[port]*
Leopolita, Marcin d1589 *NewGrD 80*
Leopolitanus, Martinus d1589 *NewGrD 80*
Leotard, Jules 1830-1870 *CnOxB, Ent, OxThe*
Leotsakos, George S 1935- *DcCM, NewGrD 80*
Leoz, Jesus Garcia 1904-1953 *NewGrD 80*
Lepage, Jane Weiner 1931- *IntWWM 80*
Lepage, Monique *CreCan 1*
LePage, Wilson John 1946- *WhoMus 72*
Lepak, Elizabeth R 1943- *IntWWM 77, -80*
LePan, Douglas Valentine 1914- *CreCan 1*
Lepanto, Victoria *Film 1*
LePaul, Paul 1901-1958 *WhScrn 74, -77, WhoHol B*
LePearl, Harry 1885-1946 *WhScrn 77*
Lepeshinskaya, Olga Vasilievna 1916- *CnOxB, DancEn 78*
LePetit, Johannes *NewGrD 80*
LePetomane 1857-1945 *Ent*
Lepeuve, Monique *WomWMM*
Lepiankiewicz, Julius Kazimierz 1910- *WhoMus 72*
LePicard *NewGrD 80*
LePicard, Antoine *NewGrD 80*
LePicard, Jean-Baptiste 1706-1760? *NewGrD 80*
LePicard, Joseph *NewGrD 80*
LePicard, Philippe d1702 *NewGrD 80*
LePicard, Philippe d1730? *NewGrD 80*
LePicq, Charles 1744-1806 *CnOxB*
LePicq, Charles 1749-1806 *DancEn 78*
L'Epine *NewGrD 80*
L'Epine, Adrian *NewGrD 80*
Lepine, David Foster 1928- *WhoMus 72*
L'Epine, Jean-Francois 1682?-1762 *NewGrD 80*
L'Epine, Jean-Francois 1732-1817 *NewGrD 80*
L'Epine, Margherita De 1683?-1746 *NewGrD 80*
L'Epine-Smith, Eric *IntMPA 77, -75, -76, -78, -79, -80*
Leplin, Emanuel 1917-1972 *Baker 78, ConAmC*
Lepore, Angelo J 1913- *AmSCAP 66*
Lepore, Louis Philippe 1955- *AmSCAP 80*
Leppard, Raymond John 1927- *Baker 78, BnBkM 80, IntWWM 77, -80, NewGrD 80, WhoMus 72, WhoOp 76*
Leps, Wassili 1870-1943 *Baker 78, ConAmC*
Lepsoe, Albert 1926- *IntWWM 77, -80*
Lequien, Colette 1920- *IntWWM 80*
LeQuoint, Louis 1652-1717 *NewGrD 80*
LeQuointe, Louis 1652-1717 *NewGrD 80*
LeQuoynte, Louis 1652-1717 *NewGrD 80*
Lerand, M d1920 *NotNAT B*
LeRat *NewGrD 80*
Lerberghe, Charles Van 1861-1907 *ModWD*
Lerch, Louis *Film 2*
Lerch, Richard 1913- *IntWWM 77, -80*
Lerchenfels, Johann Sixt Von *NewGrD 80*
Lerchenfelsu, Jan Sixt Z *NewGrD 80*
Lerdahl, Fred 1943- *ConAmC*
Lerethier, Isaac *NewGrD 80*
LeRiche, Antonius *NewGrD 80*
Lerman, Joseph W 1865-1935 *BiDAmM*
Lerman, Leo *ConAmTC*
Lerman, Omar K 1927- *BiE&WWA, NotNAT*
Lermontov, Mikhail Yurevich 1814-1841 *NewGrD 80, NotNAT B, OxThe*
Lermontov, Mikhail Yurievich 1814-1841 *EncWT*
Lermontov, Mikhail Yuryevich 1814-1841 *McGEWD*
Lerner, Al 1919- *AmSCAP 66, -80*
Lerner, Alan Jay 1918- *AmPS, AmSCAP 66, BestMus, BiDAmM, BiE&WWA, CmMov, CmpEPM, ConDr 73, -77D, EncMT, EncWT, Ent, FilmEn, FilmgC, HalFC 80, IntMPA 77, -75, -76, -78, -79, -80, ModWD, NewCBMT, NewGrD 80, NotNAT, OxFilm, PlP&P, WhoThe 72, -77, WorEFlm*
Lerner, Carl 1905?-1975 *HalFC 80*
Lerner, Edward R 1920- *NewGrD 80*
Lerner, Edwin H *MorBAP*
Lerner, Howard Marshall 1927- *AmSCAP 66, -80*
Lerner, Irma *Film 2*
Lerner, Irving 1909- *BiDFilm, FilmgC, IntMPA 77, -75, -76, WorEFlm*
Lerner, Irving 1909-1976 *BiDFilm 81, FilmEn*
Lerner, Irving 1909-1977 *HalFC 80*
Lerner, Jacques *Film 2*
Lerner, Joseph *IntMPA 77, -75, -76, -78, -79, -80*
Lerner, Joseph Yehuda 1849?-1907 *NotNAT B, OxThe*
Lerner, Robert 1921- *BiE&WWA, NotNAT*
Lerner, Samuel Manuel 1903- *AmSCAP 66, -80*
Lernet-Holenia, Alexander 1897-1976 *CnMD, CroCD, EncWT, McGEWD[port], ModWD, OxThe*
LeRochois, Marthe 1658?-1728 *NewGrD 80*
Lerolle, Jacques *NewGrD 80*
LeRouge, Guillaume *NewGrD 80*
LeRoux, Gaspard 1660?-1707? *MusMk, NewGrD 80*
LeRoux, Hugues 1860- *WhThe*
LeRoux, Jean-Louis 1927- *IntWWM 77, -80*
LeRoux, Maurice 1923- *Baker 78, NewGrD 80, WhoMus 72*
Leroux, Pauline 1809-1891 *CnOxB*
Leroux, Xavier 1863-1919 *Baker 78, NewEOp 71, NewGrD 80*
Leroy *BluesWW[port]*
LeRoy, Acme 1854- *FilmEn*
LeRoy, Adrian 1520?-1598 *NewGrD 80*
LeRoy, Baby 1931- *FilmgC, HalFC 80*
LeRoy, Baby 1932- *FilmEn*
Leroy, Baby 1932- *ForYSC*
LeRoy, Baby 1932- *MovMk[port]*
Leroy, Baby Face *BluesWW[port]*
LeRoy, Bartolomeo *NewGrD 80*
LeRoy, Gloria *WhoHol A*
LeRoy, Hal 1912- *CmpEPM*
LeRoy, Hal 1913- *EncMT, What 3[port], WhoHol A*
Leroy, Jehan *NewGrD 80*
LeRoy, Ken 1927- *BiE&WWA, NotNAT, WhoHol A*
LeRoy, Leslie Hurley *BlkAmP*
LeRoy, Mervyn 1900- *AmFD, BiDFilm, -81, CmMov, DcFM, FilmEn, Film 2, FilmgC, HalFC 80, IntMPA 77, -75, -76, -78, -79, -80, MovMk[port], OxFilm, TwYS A, WorEFlm*
LeRoy, Rene 1898- *Baker 78*
LeRoy, Rita *Film 2*
LeRoy, Servais 1865-1953 *MagIlD, WhThe*
LeRoy, Warner 1935- *BiE&WWA, NotNAT*
Leroy Brothers *PupTheA*
Lert, Ernst 1883-1955 *NewEOp 71*
Lert, Ernst Josef Maria 1883-1955 *Baker 78*
Lert, Ernst Joseph Maria 1883-1955 *BiDAmM*
Lert, Richard Johannes 1885- *Baker 78, BiDAmM*
Lertzman, Carl Myron 1908- *AmSCAP 66, -80*
Les Jazz Modes *BiDAmM*
LeSage, Alain Rene 1668-1747 *CnThe, DcPup, EncWT, Ent[port], McGEWD[port], NewEOp 71, NotNAT B, OxThe, REnWD[port]*
LeSage, Francois-Antoine 1700- *OxThe*
LeSage, Rene-Andre 1695-1743 *EncWT, OxThe*
LeSage, Sally 1937- *IntWWM 77, -80, WhoMus 72*
LeSage, Stanley 1880-1932 *WhThe*
LeSage DeRichee, Philipp Franz *NewGrD 80*
LeSaint, Edward 1870- *TwYS A*
LeSaint, Edward J 1871-1940 *WhScrn 74, -77, WhoHol B*
LeSaint, Stella R 1881-1948 *WhScrn 74, -77, WhoHol B*
Lesberg, Jack 1920- *BiDAmM, CmpEPM*
Lesbio, Antonio Marques 1639-1709 *NewGrD 80*
Lesch, Albrecht 1420?-1479? *NewGrD 80*
Leschenet, Didier d1603? *NewGrD 80*
Leschetizky, Theodor 1830-1915 *Baker 78, BnBkM 80[port], NewGrD 80[port], OxMus*
Lescot, C Francois 1720?-1801? *NewGrD 80*
Lescoulie, Jack 1917- *IntMPA 75, -76, NewYTET, WhoHol A*
L'Escurel, Jehannot De *NewGrD 80*

Lesczynski, Wladyslaw *NewGrD 80*
Lesemann, Frederick 1936- *AmSCAP 80, CpmDNM 73, ConAmC*
Leshay, Jerome 1926- *AmSCAP 66, -80*
Lesieur-Desaulniers, Gonzalve *CreCan 2*
Lesinsky, Adam Peter 1893- *IntWWM 77, -80*
Lesjak, Borut 1931- *IntWWM 77, -80*
Leske, Clemens Theodor 1923- *IntWWM 80*
Leskinen, Lauri 1918- *CroCD*
Leskova, Tatiana 1922- *CnOxB, DancEn 78*
Lesley, Carole 1935-1974 *FilmgC, HalFC 80, WhScrn 77, WhoHol B*
Leslie, Aleen 1908- *IntMPA 77, -75, -76, -78, -79, -80*
Leslie, Amy 1860-1939 *NotNAT B*
Leslie, Arthur 1902-1970 *WhScrn 77*
Leslie, Bethel 1929- *ForYSC*
Leslie, Bethel 1930- *FilmgC, HalFC 80, WhoHol A*
Leslie, Cy *ConMuA 80B*
Leslie, Edgar 1885-1976 *AmPS, AmSCAP 66, -80, BiDAmM, CmpEPM, Sw&Ld C*
Leslie, Edith d1973 *WhScrn 77, WhoHol B*
Leslie, Elsie 1881- *WhoStg 1908*
Leslie, Enid 1888- *WhThe*
Leslie, Fanny d1935 *NotNAT B*
Leslie, Fred 1855-1892 *NotNAT A, -B*
Leslie, Fred 1881- *WhThe*
Leslie, Fred 1884-1945 *WhScrn 77*
Leslie, Gene 1904-1953 *WhScrn 74, -77, WhoHol B*
Leslie, Gladys 1899- *Film 1, -2, MotPP, TwYS*
Leslie, Helen *Film 1*
Leslie, Henry d1881 *NotNAT B*
Leslie, Henry David 1822-1896 *Baker 78, NewGrD 80, OxMus*
Leslie, Joan 1925- *CmpEPM, FilmEn, FilmgC, ForYSC, HalFC 80, HolP 40[port], IntMPA 77, -75, -76, -78, -79, -80, MotPP, MovMk, What 1[port], WhoHol A*
Leslie, Kenneth 1892- *CreCan 2*
Leslie, Lawrence *Film 2*
Leslie, Lew 1886-1963 *EncMT, NotNAT B, WhThe*
Leslie, Lila *Film 2*
Leslie, Lilie *Film 1, MotPP*
Leslie, Lya *Film 2*
Leslie, Madge Flora 1896- *WhoMus 72*
Leslie, Marguerite 1884-1958 *WhThe*
Leslie, Nan 1926- *ForYSC, WhoHol A*
Leslie, Nathalie *CnOxB*
Leslie, Noel 1889-1974 *WhScrn 77, WhoHol B*
Leslie, Rolf *Film 2*
Leslie, Sylvia 1900- *WhThe*
Leslie, Tom d1964 *NotNAT B*
Leslie, Walter 1929- *AmSCAP 66, -80*
Leslie-Stuart, May *WhThe*
Lesnevitch, Gus 1915-1964 *WhScrn 77*
Lesniak, Lech Janusz 1941- *IntWWM 77, -80*
LeSourd, Jacques J O 1950- *ConAmTC*
Lespine *NewGrD 80*
Lessac, Arthur 1910- *BiE&WWA, NotNAT*
Lessard, John Ayres 1920- *ConAmC, DcCM, NewGrD 80, WhoMus 72*
Lessel, Franciszek 1780?-1838 *NewGrD 80*
Lessel, Franz 1780?-1838 *Baker 78*
Lessel, Wincenty Ferdynand 1750?-1825? *NewGrD 80*
Lessells, Sheila 1930- *WhoMus 72*
Lesser, Jeffrey David 1947- *AmSCAP 80*
Lesser, Julian *IntMPA 75, -76*
Lesser, Laura *WomWMM*
Lesser, Laurence 1938- *IntWWM 77, -80*
Lesser, Len *WhoHol A*
Lesser, Seymour H 1929- *IntMPA 77, -75, -76, -78, -79, -80*
Lesser, Sol 1890-1980 *CmMov, FilmEn, FilmgC, HalFC 80, IntMPA 77, -75, -76, -78, -79, -80, OxFilm, WhoHrs 80, WorEFlm*
Lesser, Wolfgang 1923- *NewGrD 80*
Lesserman, Carl 1901- *IntMPA 75, -76*
Lessey, Bob 1910- *WhoJazz 72*
Lessey, George A d1947 *Film 2, WhScrn 77*
Lessing, Doris 1919- *CnMD, ConDr 73, -77, CroCD, EncWT, ModWD*
Lessing, Gotthold Ephraim 1729-1781 *CnThe, EncWT, Ent, McGEWD[port], NotNAT A, -B, OxThe, REnWD[port]*
Lessing, Madge *WhThe, WhoStg 1908*
Lessman, Harry *WhoHol A*
Lessmann, Otto 1844-1918 *Baker 78*
Lessnau, Robert Gerald 1938- *AmSCAP 80*
Lessner, George 1904- *AmSCAP 66, -80, ConAmC*
Lessoth, Troilus A *NewGrD 80*
Lessy, Ben *ForYSC, WhoHol A*
L'Estelle, Eleanor Scott 1880-1962 *WhScrn 74, -77*
Lester, Albert Buddy 1917- *AmSCAP 80*
Lester, Alfred 1874-1925 *NotNAT B, WhThe*
Lester, Bruce 1912- *FilmgC, HalFC 80*
Lester, Buddy *ForYSC, WhoHol A*
Lester, Daphne F 1931- *IntWWM 80*
Lester, Dick 1932- *FilmgC, HalFC 80, IlWWBF*
Lester, Edward Lee 1946- *AmSCAP 80*
Lester, Edwin 1895- *BiE&WWA, NotNAT*
Lester, Elenore *ConAmTC*
Lester, Eugene 1921- *IntWWM 77, -80*
Lester, Harold 1931- *WhoMus 72*
Lester, Jack *WhoHol A*
Lester, James T 1933- *ConAmC*
Lester, Jerry 1911- *JoeFr[port], NewYTET, WhoHol A*
Lester, Jerry And Dagmar *JoeFr[port]*
Lester, Kate d1924 *Film 1, -2, TwYS, WhScrn 77, WhoStg 1906, -1908*
Lester, Keith 1904- *CnOxB, DancEn 78*
Lester, Ketty *AmPS A, RkOn[port]*
Lester, Ketty 1934- *BiDAmM*
Lester, Ketty 1938- *DrBlPA*
Lester, Louise 1867-1952 *Film 1, WhScrn 74, -77, WhoHol B*
Lester, Mark *IlWWBF A*
Lester, Mark 1876- *WhThe*
Lester, Mark 1957- *FilmgC*
Lester, Mark 1958- *FilmAG WE[port], FilmEn, ForYSC, HalFC 80, IntMPA 77, -75, -76, -78, -79, -80, WhoHol A, WhoHrs 80*
Lester, Richard 1932- *BiDFilm, -81, DcFM, FilmEn, IntMPA 77, -75, -76, -78, -79, -80, MovMk[port], OxFilm, WorEFlm*
Lester, Susan *WomWMM B*
Lester, Thomas William 1889-1956 *Baker 78, ConAmC*
Lester, Tom *WhoHol A*
Lester, Vicki *ForYSC*
Lestina, Adolphe *Film 1, -2*
L'Estocart, Paschal De 1539?-1584? *NewGrD 80*
Lestocq, George d1924 *NotNAT B*
Lestocq, Humphrey *WhoHol A*
Lestocq, William d1920 *NotNAT B, WhThe*
L'Estrange *NewGrD 80*
L'Estrange, Dick 1889-1963 *Film 2, WhScrn 74, -77, WhoHol B*
L'Estrange, Sir Hamon 1583-1654 *NewGrD 80*
L'Estrange, Julian 1878-1918 *Film 1, NotNAT B, WhThe, WhoHol B*
L'Estrange, Julian 1880-1918 *WhScrn 77*
L'Estrange, Sir Nicholas 1603-1655 *NewGrD 80*
L'Estrange, Sir Roger 1616-1704 *NewGrD 80, OxMus*
LeSueur, Hal 1904-1963 *NotNAT B, WhScrn 74, -77, WhoHol B*
LeSueur, Jean-Francois 1760-1837 *Baker 78, BnBkM 80, GrComp[port], MusMk, NewEOp 71, NewGrD 80[port], OxMus*
LeSueur, Lucille *Film 2*
Lesur, Daniel *NewGrD 80*
Lesur, Daniel 1908- *Baker 78, DcCM, OxMus*
Lesure, Francois 1923- *Baker 78, NewGrD 80*
Leszczynski, Aleksander 1616-1680 *NewGrD 80*
Leszczynski, Wladyslaw 1616-1680 *NewGrD 80*
Leszetycki, Teodor *NewGrD 80*
LeTansur, William *NewGrD 80*
Letelier, Alfonso 1912- *Baker 78, DcCM, NewGrD 80*
Letelier-Valdes, Miguel 1939- *DcCM*
Letendre, Rita 1929- *CreCan 2*
Leterrier, Francois 1929- *FilmEn, HalFC 80, OxFilm*
Lethbridge, J W *WhThe*
Lethbridge, Lionel *WhoMus 72*
Lethco, Amanda Vick Robbins 1921- *IntWWM 77, -80*
LeThiere, Roma Guillon d1903 *NotNAT B*
Letman, John Bernard 1917- *BiDAmM, IntWWM 77, WhoJazz 72*
Letondal, Henri 1902-1955 *WhScrn 74, -77, WhoHol B*
Letorey, Omer 1873-1938 *Baker 78*
Letourneau, Jacques *CreCan 2*
Letson, Roger L 1941- *IntWWM 77*
Letter, Louis N 1937- *IntMPA 77, -75, -76, -78, -79, -80*
Lettermen, The *RkOn*
Lettieri, Al d1975 *WhoHol C*
Lettieri, Al 1927-1975 *HalFC 80*
Lettieri, Alfredo 1928-1975 *WhScrn 77*
Lettinger *Film 2*
Letton, Francis 1912- *BiE&WWA, NotNAT*
Letts, Pauline 1917- *WhoHol A, WhoThe 72, -77*
Lettvin, Theodore 1926- *WhoMus 72*
Letz, George *FilmEn, WhoHol A*
Letz, Hans 1887-1969 *Baker 78*
Leuba, Christopher 1929- *IntWWM 77, -80*
Leubas, Louis *Film 1*
Leuchtmann, Horst 1927- *IntWWM 80*
Leuckart *NewGrD 80*
Leuckart, F Ernst Christoph 1748-1817 *Baker 78*
Leuckart, Franz Ernst Christoph 1748-1817 *NewGrD 80*
Leukauf, Robert 1902- *IntWWM 77, -80, WhoMus 72*
Leupold, Wayne Harvey 1943- *IntWWM 80*
Leutgeb, Ignaz 1745?-1811 *NewGrD 80*
Leutgeb, Joseph 1745?-1811 *NewGrD 80*
Leuthon, Karl *NewGrD 80*
Leuttner, Georg Christoph 1644-1703 *NewGrD 80*
Leuwerik, Ruth 1926- *FilmAG WE*
Leux, Lori *Film 2*
Leuzinger, Rudolf 1911- *IntWWM 77, -80*
Lev, Ray 1912-1968 *Baker 78*
Leva, Enrico De 1867-1955 *Baker 78*
Levade, Charles 1869-1948 *Baker 78*
Levan, Harry d1963 *NotNAT B*
Levan, Louis 1906- *AmSCAP 66, ConAmC A*
Levance, Cal d1951 *WhScrn 74, -77*
Levans, Daniel 1944- *CnOxB*
Levant, Lila 1933- *AmSCAP 80, NatPD[port]*
Levant, Oscar 1906-1972 *AmSCAP 66, -80, Baker 78, BiDAmM, CmMov, CmpEPM, ConAmC, FilmEn, FilmgC, ForYSC, HalFC 80, HolP 40[port], JoeFr, MotPP, MovMk, NewGrD 80, NewYTET, WhScrn 77, WhoHol B*
Levant, Oscar 1907-1972 *Film 2*
Levante, Les 1892-1978 *MagIlD*
Levarie, Siegmund 1914- *Baker 78, IntWWM 77, -80, NewGrD 80, WhoMus 72*
Levary, Tibor 1914- *IntWWM 77, -80*
Levashev, Vladimir Alexandrovich 1923- *CnOxB, DancEn 78*
Levashova, Ol'ga Evgen'yevna 1912- *NewGrD 80*
Levasseur, Andre 1927- *CnOxB*
Levasseur, Jean Henri 1764-1826? *NewGrD 80*
Levasseur, Jean-Henri 1765?-1823 *Baker 78*
Levasseur, Nicholas 1791-1871 *NewGrD 80*
Levasseur, Nicolas-Prosper 1791-1871 *Baker 78, NewEOp 71*
Levasseur, Rosalie 1749-1826 *Baker 78, CmOp, NewEOp 71, NewGrD 80*
Levasseur DeRebollo, Yvonne 1922- *IntWWM 77*
Levathes, Peter G 1911- *IntMPA 75, -76, NewYTET*
Leveaux, Montagu V 1875- *WhThe*
Levee, Michael *IntMPA 80*
Levee Joe *BluesWW[port]*
Leveen, Raymond 1893- *AmSCAP 80*
Leveen, Raymond 1899- *AmSCAP 66*
Leveillee, Claude 1932- *CreCan 1*
Levelle, Estelle 1896-1960 *WhScrn 74, -77*
Leven, Boris 1900?- *FilmEn, FilmgC, HalFC 80, IntMPA 77, -75, -76, -78, -79,*

-80
Leven, Melville Abner 1914- *AmSCAP 80*
Levene, Sam *IntMPA 75, -76*
Levene, Sam 1905- *BiE&WWA, EncMT, FilmgC, ForYSC, HalFC 80, IntMPA 77, -78, -79, -80, MotPP, MovMk, NotNAT, PlP&P[port], WhoHol A*
Levene, Sam 1906- *Vers B[port]*
Levene, Sam 1907- *FilmEn*
Levene, Samuel 1905- *Ent, WhoThe 72, -77*
Levenhagen, Marie 1903- *IntMPA 75, -76*
Levens, Charles 1689-1764 *Baker 78*
Levenson, Boris 1884-1947 *AmSCAP 66, -80, Baker 78, ConAmC*
Levenson, Robert 1897-1961 *AmSCAP 80*
Levenson, Sam 1911- *IntMPA 77, -75, -76, -78, -79, -80, JoeFr[port]*
Leventhal, Herbert 1914- *AmSCAP 66, -80*
Leventhal, Joseph Jules 1889-1949 *NotNAT B*
Leventhal, Ronald 1927- *AmSCAP 80*
Lever, Beatrice Rae 1897- *AmSCAP 66, -80*
Leveridge, Richard 1670?-1758 *Baker 78, NewGrD 80, OxMus*
Levering, Jack *Film 1*
Levers, Carrie 1902- *WhoMus 72*
Leverse, Loretta *BlkAmP, MorBAP*
Leversee, Loretta *WhoHol A*
Levesley, Neil 1936- *WhoMus 72*
Levesque, Elizabeth DeHauteterre *NewGrD 80*
Levesque, Marcel *Film 1*
Levesque, Raymond 1928- *CreCan 1*
Levett, David Maurice 1844-1914 *BiDAmM*
Levett, Harold *Film 2*
Levett, James Alfred 1909- *IntWWM 77, -80, WhoMus 72*
Leveugle, Daniel 1924- *WhoOp 76*
Levey *NewGrD 80*
Levey, Adele *WhThe*
Levey, Arthur 1903- *IntMPA 77, -75, -76, -78, -79, -80*
Levey, Carlotta *WhThe*
Levey, Ethel *AmPS B*
Levey, Ethel 1880-1955 *NotNAT B, WhoStg 1906, -1908*
Levey, Ethel 1881-1955 *EncMT, WhThe*
Levey, Harold A 1898- *AmSCAP 66, -80*
Levey, Joseph A 1925- *ConAmC*
Levey, Jules *IntMPA 75*
Levey, Lauren 1947- *ConAmC*
Levey, Richard C 1833-1904? *NewGrD 80*
Levey, Richard Michael 1811-1899 *Baker 78, NewGrD 80*
Levey, Stan 1925- *BiDAmM, CmpEPM, EncJzS 70*
Levey, William Charles 1837-1894 *Baker 78, NewGrD 80*
Levi, Giuseppe *NewGrD 80*
Levi, Hermann 1839-1900 *Baker 78, BnBkM 80, NewEOp 71, NewGrD 80, OxMus*
Levi, Jul 1930- *NewGrD 80*
Levi, Paolo 1919- *CnMD, EncWT*
Levi BenGershom, R *NewGrD 80*
Levi-Tanai, Sara 1911- *CnOxB, DancEn 78*
Levick, Gus d1909 *NotNAT B*
Levick, Halper 1888-1962 *OxThe*
Levidis, Dimitri *OxMus*
Levidis, Dimitri 1886-1951 *Baker 78*
Levidis, Dimitrios 1885?-1951 *NewGrD 80*
Levie, Francoise *WomWMM*
LeVien, Jack 1918- *FilmEn, FilmgC, HalFC 80, IntMPA 77, -75, -76, -78, -79, -80*
Levien, Sonya *WomWMM*
Levien, Sonya 1886-1960 *CmMov*
Levien, Sonya 1888-1960 *FilmgC, HalFC 80*
Levien, Sonya 1895-1960 *FilmEn*
Leviev, Milcho 1937- *EncJzS 70*
Levin, Barbara 1935- *IntWWM 77*
Levin, Bernard *BiE&WWA*
Levin, Charles d1962 *NotNAT B*
Levin, Edward Emanuel 1952- *AmSCAP 80*
Levin, Gerald M *NewYTET*
Levin, Gregory John 1943- *ConAmC, IntWWM 77, -80*
Levin, Henry 1909-1980 *BiDFilm, -81, DcFM, FilmEn, FilmgC, HalFC 80, IntMPA 77, -75, -76, -78, -79, -80, MovMk[port], WhoHrs 80, WorEFlm*
Levin, Herman 1907- *BiE&WWA, EncMT, NotNAT, WhoThe 72, -77*
Levin, Ira 1929- *AmSCAP 66, -80, BiE&WWA, HalFC 80, NotNAT, WhoHrs 80*
Levin, Irving H 1921- *IntMPA 77, -75, -76, -78, -79, -80*
Levin, Irving M 1916- *IntMPA 75, -76, -78, -79, -80*
Levin, Jack H *IntMPA 77, -75, -76, -78, -79, -80*
Levin, Joseph A 1917- *AmSCAP 66*
Levin, Louis 1952- *AmSCAP 80*
Levin, Lucy 1907-1939 *WhScrn 74, -77*
Levin, Marc Leonard 1942- *EncJzS 70*
Levin, Meyer 1905- *BiE&WWA, CnMD, NotNAT, PupTheA*
Levin, Morris Albert 1900- *AmSCAP 80*
Levin, Philip Arthur 1945- *IntWWM 77, -80*
Levin, Rami Yona 1954- *IntWWM 80*
Levin, Robert Jacob 1912- *IntWWM 77, -80*
Levina, Zara 1906-1976 *Baker 78*
Levine, Abe 1915- *AmSCAP 66, -80*
Levine, Albert Norman 1924- *CreCan 1*
Levine, Amy Miller 1939- *IntWWM 80*
Levine, Amy Miller 1940- *CpmDNM 76*
Levine, Bruce 1950- *CpmDNM 75, -76, -77, -78, ConAmC*
Levine, David *WhoMus 72*
Levine, David Eliot 1933- *NotNAT*
Levine, David Myer *AmSCAP 80*
Levine, Helen *Film 2*
Levine, Henry 1892-1976 *AmSCAP 66, -80, IntWWM 77*
Levine, Henry 1907- *CmpEPM, WhoJazz 72*
Levine, Howard A *IntMPA 80*
Levine, Irving R *NewYTET*
Levine, Jack *Film 2*
Levine, James 1943- *Baker 78, BiDAmM, BnBkM 80, CmOp, MusSN[port], NewGrD 80, WhoOp 76*
Levine, Jeffrey Leon 1942- *AmSCAP 80, ConAmC, IntWWM 77, -80*
Levine, Jerry K *IntMPA 75*
Levine, Joseph d1964 *NotNAT B*
Levine, Joseph 1912- *AmSCAP 80, WhoOp 76*
Levine, Joseph E 1905- *BiE&WWA, FilmEn, FilmgC, HalFC 80, IntMPA 77, -75, -76, -78, -79, -80, OxFilm, WorEFlm[port]*
Levine, Joseph I 1926- *BiE&WWA, NotNAT*
Levine, Les 1936- *CreCan 2*
Levine, Lucy Simon 1940- *AmSCAP 80*
Levine, Marks 1890-1971 *AmSCAP 66, -80, BiDAmM*
Levine, Martin 1909- *IntMPA 77, -75, -76, -78, -79, -80*
Levine, Naomi *WomWMM B*
Levine, Norman 1924- *CreCan 1*
Levine, Philip *WhoMus 72*
Levine, Rhoda Jane 1932- *WhoOp 76*
Levine, Stanley Mark 1947- *AmSCAP 80*
LeViness, Carl 1885-1964 *WhScrn 74, -77, WhoHol B*
Levinger, Henry W 1901- *WhoMus 72*
Levinger, Lowell Vincent 1944- *AmSCAP 80*
Levinnes, Carl *Film 2*
Levinsky, Ronald Frederick 1951- *AmSCAP 80*
Levinsky, Walter 1929- *AmSCAP 80*
Levinsohn, Lawrence Jay 1949- *AmSCAP 80*
Levinson, Andre Jacovlevich 1887-1933 *CnOxB, DancEn 78*
Levinson, Barry 1932- *BiE&WWA, IntMPA 77, -78, -79, -80*
Levinson, David *NewYTET*
Levinson, Gerald 1951- *CpmDNM 74, -77, -79, ConAmC*
Levinson, Jerry *CmpEPM*
Levinson, John M *AmSCAP 80*
Levinson, Norm 1925- *IntMPA 77, -76, -78, -79, -80*
Levinson, Paul 1947- *AmSCAP 80*
Levinson, Robert Wells *AmSCAP 80*
Levinson, Ruth Pologe *IntMPA 77, -75, -76, -78, -79, -80*
Levinson-Link *NewYTET*
Levit, Allen Bernard 1934- *AmSCAP 80*
Levitan, Fanny 1928- *IntWWM 80*
Levitan, Paul d1976 *NewYTET*
Levitan, Samuel 1919- *CreCan 1*
Levitch, Leon 1927- *AmSCAP 80, CpmDNM 72, -80, ConAmC*
Leviton, Stewart 1939- *WhoThe 77*
Levitov, Alexander 1892-1958 *DancEn 78*
Levitski, Mischa 1898-1941 *BiDAmM*
Levitt, Alan 1932- *EncJzS 70*
Levitt, Estelle 1941- *AmSCAP 66, -80*
Levitt, Helen *WomWMM A, -B*
Levitt, John *PlP&P[port]*
Levitt, Paul 1926-1968 *BiE&WWA, NotNAT B*
Levitt, Rodney Charles 1929- *BiDAmM, ConAmC*
Levitt, Ruby Rebecca 1907- *IntMPA 77, -75, -76, -78, -79, -80*
Levitt, Saul 1913- *BiE&WWA, NotNAT*
Levitz, Linda *WomWMM B*
Levitzki, Mischa 1898-1941 *AmSCAP 66, -80, Baker 78, ConAmC, MusSN[port]*
Levko, Valentina Nikolaevna 1926- *WhoOp 76*
Levoe, Marjorie *Film 2*
LeVoe, Spivy 1906-1971 *BiDAmM*
Levshin, A *Film 2*
Levy, Aaron *ConMuA 80B*
Levy, Alexandre 1864-1892 *Baker 78, NewGrD 80*
Levy, Benn Wolfe 1900-1973 *BiE&WWA, CnMD, ConDr 73, McGEWD[port], ModWD, NotNAT B, WhThe, WhoThe 72*
Levy, Bernard *IntMPA 77, -75, -76, -78, -79, -80*
Levy, Bud 1928- *IntMPA 77, -75, -76, -78, -79, -80*
Levy, Burt 1936- *Baker 78, CpmDNM 77, -78, ConAmC*
Levy, Carl D 1911- *IntMPA 75, -76*
Levy, Charles L 1911- *IntMPA 75, -76*
Levy, David 1913- *AmSCAP 80, IntMPA 77, -75, -76, -78, -79, -80, NewYTET*
Levy, Don 1932- *OxFilm*
Levy, Donald Benjamin 1949- *AmSCAP 80*
Levy, Edward I 1929- *ConAmC, DcCM*
Levy, Edwin L 1917- *BiE&WWA*
Levy, Ellis 1887- *ConAmC*
Levy, Emile *NewGrD 80*
Levy, Ernst 1895- *Baker 78, BiDAmM, ConAmC, DcCM, NewGrD 80*
Levy, Frank 1930- *AmSCAP 80, Baker 78, CpmDNM 74, ConAmC, IntWWM 77, -80*
Levy, Gerardo 1924- *IntWWM 77, -80*
Levy, Hal 1916-1970 *AmSCAP 66, -80*
Levy, Hank 1927- *EncJzS 70*
Levy, Helen Marsh d1962 *NotNAT B*
Levy, Heniot 1879-1946 *Baker 78, ConAmC*
Levy, Henry J 1927- *EncJzS 70*
Levy, Herman M 1904- *IntMPA 77, -75, -76, -78, -79, -80*
Levy, Isaac d1975 *NewYTET*
Levy, J Langley d1945 *NotNAT B*
Levy, Jacques 1935- *WhoThe 72, -77*
Levy, Jonathan *NatPD[port]*
Levy, Jonathan F 1935- *AmSCAP 80*
Levy, Jose G 1884-1936 *NotNAT B, WhThe*
Levy, Jules *NewGrD 80*
Levy, Jules 1930- *Baker 78*
Levy, Jules V 1923- *IntMPA 77, -75, -76, -78, -79, -80*
Levy, Kenneth J 1927- *NewGrD 80*
Levy, Lazare 1882-1964 *Baker 78*
Levy, Leeds *ConMuA 80B*
Levy, Leon *NewYTET*
Levy, Lou 1928- *CmpEPM, ConMuA 80B, EncJzS 70*
Levy, Louis 1893- *FilmgC, HalFC 80, IlWWBF A*
Levy, Louis 1928- *BiDAmM, EncJzS 70*
Levy, M A 1890- *IntMPA 75, -76*
Levy, Marvin David 1932- *AmSCAP 66, -80, Baker 78, ConAmC, NewGrD 80*
Levy, Mervin *PupTheA*
Levy, Michael Sigmund 1945- *IntWWM 77, -80*
Levy, Michel-Maurice 1883-1965 *Baker 78*
Levy, Morris *ConMuA 80B*
Levy, Morten 1939- *IntWWM 77, -80*
Levy, Norman 1935- *IntMPA 78, -79, -80*
Levy, Parke 1908- *AmSCAP 66, -80*
Levy, Ralph 1919- *FilmgC, HalFC 80, NewYTET*

Levy, Randy *ConMuA 80B*
Levy, Raoul 1922-1966 *DcFM, FilmEn*
Levy, Raoul 1922-1967 *FilmgC, HalFC 80*
Levy, Robert B 1943- *IntWWM 77*
Levy, Robert S 1932- *IntMPA 77, -75, -76, -78, -79, -80*
Levy, Roland Alexis Manuel *NewGrD 80*
Levy, Sara 1761-1854 *NewGrD 80*
Levy, Sol Paul 1881-1920 *AmSCAP 66, -80*
Levy, Sylvan 1906-1962 *NotNAT B, WhScrn 74, -77*
Levy, Trude 1908- *IntWWM 77*
Lewallen, James C 1926- *AmSCAP 80*
Lewando, Ralph 1898- *IntWWM 77, -80*
Lewandowski, Leon Leopold 1831-1896 *NewGrD 80*
Lewandowski, Louis 1821-1894 *Baker 78*
Lewenstein, Oscar 1917- *WhoThe 72, -77*
Lewenthal, Raymond 1926- *Baker 78, IntWWM 77, -80, NewGrD 80, WhoMus 72*
Lewes, Charles Lee 1740-1803 *NotNAT A, -B, OxThe*
Lewes, George Henry 1817-1878 *EncWT, NotNAT B, OxThe*
Lewes, Miriam *WhThe*
Lewin, Albert 1894-1968 *BiDFilm, -81, FilmEn, WorEFlm*
Lewin, Albert 1895-1968 *FilmgC, HalFC 80, MovMk[port], OxFilm*
Lewin, Albert 1902-1968 *DcFM*
Lewin, David *ConAmC*
Lewin, Frank 1925- *ConAmC, IntWWM 77, -80*
Lewin-Richter, Andres 1937- *IntWWM 77, -80*
Lewine, Richard 1910- *AmSCAP 66, -80, BiE&WWA, EncMT, NotNAT, WhoMus 72*
Lewine, Robert F 1913- *IntMPA 77, -75, -76, -78, -79, -80, NewYTET*
Lewinger, Max 1870-1908 *Baker 78*
Lewinsky, Josef d1907 *NotNAT B*
LeWinter, David 1908-1976 *AmSCAP 66, -80*
Lewis, Abby 1910- *BiE&WWA, NotNAT, WhoHol A*
Lewis, Ada 1875-1925 *CmpEPM, NotNAT B, WhThe, WhoStg 1908*
Lewis, Aden G 1924- *AmSCAP 66, -80*
Lewis, Al *IntMPA 77, -75, -76, -78, WhoHol A*
Lewis, Al 1901- *AmSCAP 66, BiDAmM, CmpEPM*
Lewis, Al 1901-1967 *AmSCAP 80*
Lewis, Al 1924- *AmSCAP 80*
Lewis, Albert E 1884-1978 *HalFC 80*
Lewis, Allan 1908- *BiE&WWA, ConAmTC, NotNAT, WhoHol A*
Lewis, Allie May 1859-1930 *BiDAmM*
Lewis, Andrew Coffman 1954- *IntWWM 77*
Lewis, Angelo 1839-1919 *MagIlD*
Lewis, Ann *WomWMM B*
Lewis, Anthony 1915- *IntWWM 77, -80, NewGrD 80, OxMus, WhoMus 72*
Lewis, Anthony David Stanley 1949- *IntWWM 77, -80*
Lewis, Arthur *IntMPA 80*
Lewis, Arthur 1846-1930 *NotNAT B, WhThe*
Lewis, Arthur 1916- *WhoThe 72, -77*
Lewis, Arthur 1935- *IntWWM 77, -80*
Lewis, Artie *WhoHol A*
Lewis, Barbara 1944- *RkOn*
Lewis, Bernard 1912- *IntMPA 77, -75, -76, -78, -79, -80*
Lewis, Bernie Kaai 1921- *AmSCAP 66, -80*
Lewis, Bertha 1887-1931 *NotNAT B, WhThe*
Lewis, Bill *AmSCAP 80*
Lewis, Bob *AmSCAP 80*
Lewis, Bobby *IlEncCM[port]*
Lewis, Bobby 1933- *AmPS A, RkOn[port]*
Lewis, Bobo *WhoHol A*
Lewis, Brenda 1921- *BiE&WWA*
Lewis, C Harold 1892-1955 *AmSCAP 66, -80*
Lewis, Catherine d1942 *NotNAT B*
Lewis, Cathy 1918-1968 *ForYSC, WhScrn 74, -77, WhoHol B*
Lewis, Claude P, Jr. 1926- *IntMPA 77, -75, -76, -78, -79, -80*
Lewis, Clifford Herbert 1902- *WhoMus 72*
Lewis, Curigwen *WhThe*
Lewis, Dandy 1888?-1932? *NewOrJ*
Lewis, Daniel J *IntMPA 75, -76*
Lewis, David *IntMPA 77, -75, -76, -78, -79, -80, WhoHol A*
Lewis, David 1906- *FilmEn*
Lewis, David 1939- *BlkAmP*
Lewis, Diana 1915- *ForYSC, HalFC 80, MotPP, WhoHol A*
Lewis, Donnell Joy 1961- *AmSCAP 80*
Lewis, Dora *Film 2*
Lewis, Dorothy W 1871-1952 *WhScrn 74, -77*
Lewis, Ed 1909- *WhoJazz 72*
Lewis, Ed Strangler 1890-1966 *WhScrn 77*
Lewis, Edgar 1872-1938 *TwYS A, WhScrn 77*
Lewis, Edgar P *Film 1*
Lewis, Edna *AmSCAP 66, -80*
Lewis, Edward *IntMPA 77, -75, -76, -78, -79, -80*
Lewis, Edward d1922 *NotNAT B*
Lewis, Edward A 1909- *AmSCAP 80*
Lewis, Elliott *WhScrn 74, -77, WhoHol A*
Lewis, Elliott 1917- *ForYSC*
Lewis, Elliott 1948- *AmSCAP 66*
Lewis, Emory 1919- *BiE&WWA, NotNAT*
Lewis, Enid 1894- *WhoMus 72*
Lewis, Eric 1855-1935 *NotNAT B, WhThe*
Lewis, Eric Michael 1946- *IntWWM 77, -80*
Lewis, Father Al 1903- *NewOrJ SUP[port]*
Lewis, Fiona 1946- *FilmEn, FilmgC, HalFC 80, WhoHol A*
Lewis, Foster *NewOrJ*
Lewis, Frank 1868?-1924 *BiDAmM*
Lewis, Frank 1870?-1924 *NewOrJ[port]*
Lewis, Frank A d1963 *NotNAT B*
Lewis, Fred *ConMuA 80B*
Lewis, Fred 1860-1927 *Film 2, NotNAT B, WhThe, WhoHol B*
Lewis, Frederick G 1873-1946 *NotNAT B, WhThe, WhoHol B, WhoStg 1906, -1908*
Lewis, Frederick G 1874-1947 *WhScrn 77*
Lewis, Freeman 1780-1859 *BiDAmM*
Lewis, Furry *BluesWW[port]*
Lewis, Gary 1945- *BiDAmM, ConMuA 80A*
Lewis, Gary & The Playboys *RkOn 2[port]*
Lewis, Gena 1888-1979 *HalFC 80*
Lewis, Geoffrey *WhoHol A*
Lewis, George 1900-1968 *BiDAmM, CmpEPM, EncJzS 70, IlEncJ, NewGrD 80, NewOrJ[port], WhoJazz 72*
Lewis, George 1904- *Film 2, ForYSC, TwYS*
Lewis, Gordon d1933 *WhScrn 74, -77*
Lewis, H Merrills 1908- *BiDAmM, ConAmC*
Lewis, Harry 1886-1950 *ForYSC, WhScrn 74, -77, WhoHol B*
Lewis, Haydn Francis 1910- *WhoMus 72*
Lewis, Henry *WhoOp 76*
Lewis, Henry 1932- *Baker 78, DrBlPA, IntWWM 77, -80, MusSN[port], NewGrD 80*
Lewis, Henry 1933- *BiDAmM*
Lewis, Henry B *Film 2*
Lewis, Herschell 1926- *HalFC 80, WhoHrs 80*
Lewis, Hugh X 1932- *BiDAmM*
Lewis, Ida 1871-1935 *Film 1, -2, NotNAT B, TwYS, WhScrn 74, -77, WhoHol B*
Lewis, Jack B 1924-1964 *AmSCAP 66, -80*
Lewis, James *PlP&P*
Lewis, James d1896 *NotNAT B*
Lewis, James 1938- *CpmDNM 75, -76, -77, -79, ConAmC*
Lewis, James H Daddy d1928 *WhScrn 74, -77, WhoHol B*
Lewis, Janet 1899- *AmSCAP 66, -80*
Lewis, Jarma *ForYSC*
Lewis, Jay 1914-1969 *FilmEn, Film 1, FilmgC, HalFC 80, IlWWBF*
Lewis, Jeffrey 1942- *IntWWM 77, -80, WhoMus 72*
Lewis, Mrs. Jeffrey *Film 1*
Lewis, Jeffreys d1926 *NotNAT B*
Lewis, Jeffrys *Film 2*
Lewis, Jera *Film 2*
Lewis, Jerry 1926- *AmPS A, BiDFilm, -81, CmMov, CmpEPM, FilmEn, FilmgC, ForYSC, Funs[port], GrMovC[port], HalFC 80, IntMPA 77, -75, -76, -78, -79, -80, JoeFr[port], MotPP, MovMk[port], OxFilm, RkOn, WhoHol A, WhoHrs 80[port], WorEFlm[port]*
Lewis, Jerry Lee 1935- *AmPS A, BiDAmM, ConMuA 80A[port], CounME 74[port], -74A, EncFCWM 69, IlEncCM[port], IlEncR, MusMk[port], RkOn[port], WhoHol A*
Lewis, Jessica 1890-1971 *BiDAmM*
Lewis, Joe 1898-1938 *WhScrn 74, -77, WhoHol B*
Lewis, Joe E *AmPS B*
Lewis, Joe E d1971 *NotNAT A, WhoHol B*
Lewis, Joe E 1901-1971 *FilmgC, HalFC 80*
Lewis, Joe E 1902-1971 *JoeFr[port], WhScrn 77*
Lewis, John Aaron 1920- *Baker 78, BiDAmM, CmpEPM, ConAmC, DrBlPA, EncJzS 70, IlEncJ, MusMk, NewGrD 80*
Lewis, John L 1880- *What 1[port]*
Lewis, John Leo 1911- *AmSCAP 66, -80, ConAmC*
Lewis, Johnie 1910?- *BluesWW[port]*
Lewis, Johnny *BluesWW[port]*
Lewis, Joseph H 1900- *BiDFilm, -81, FilmEn, FilmgC, HalFC 80, IntMPA 77, -75, -76, -78, -79, -80, WhoHrs 80, WorEFlm*
Lewis, Joseph Perley 1928- *CpmDNM 72*
Lewis, Joy *Film 1*
Lewis, Judy 1936- *IntMPA 77, -75, -76, -78, -79, -80*
Lewis, Julia 1878?-1908 *BlkWAB*
Lewis, Kate *BluesWW[port]*
Lewis, Katherine *Film 2*
Lewis, Kerry G 1948- *ConAmC*
Lewis, L Rhodes 1919- *IntWWM 77, -80*
Lewis, Laurie *WomWMM B*
Lewis, Leo Rich 1865-1945 *Baker 78*
Lewis, Leon 1890-1961 *AmSCAP 66, -80, ConAmC*
Lewis, Leopold d1890 *NotNAT B, PlP&P*
Lewis, Lester 1912- *IntMPA 77, -75, -76, -78, -79, -80*
Lewis, Lillian 1939- *AmSCAP 80*
Lewis, Linda *IlEncR*
Lewis, Lloyd Downs 1891-1949 *NotNAT B*
Lewis, Lorna Jane 1937- *IntWWM 77, -80*
Lewis, Lucy S 1904- *AmSCAP 66*
Lewis, Mabel Terry *WhThe*
Lewis, Malcolm 1925- *ConAmC*
Lewis, Marcia Ann 1941- *IntWWM 77, -80*
Lewis, Margaret Esther *PupTheA*
Lewis, Martin 1888-1970 *WhScrn 77, WhThe*
Lewis, Mary 1900-1941 *BiDAmM, WhScrn 74, -77, WhoHol B*
Lewis, Mary Rio *DrBlPA, WhoHol A*
Lewis, Matthew Gregory 1775-1818 *Ent, NotNAT B, OxThe*
Lewis, Meade Lux d1964 *WhoHol B*
Lewis, Meade Lux 1905-1964 *AmSCAP 66, -80, BiDAmM, CmpEPM, IlEncJ, MnPM[port], NewGrD 80, WhoJazz 72*
Lewis, Meade Lux 1906-1964 *WhScrn 74, -77*
Lewis, Mel 1929- *BiDAmM, CmpEPM, EncJzS 70*
Lewis, Merlin Charles 1904- *IntMPA 75*
Lewis, Michael 1931-1975 *WhScrn 77*
Lewis, Michael Henry 1932- *WhoMus 72*
Lewis, Michael J 1939- *HalFC 80, IntMPA 77, -75, -76, -78, -79, -80*
Lewis, Mitchell J 1880-1956 *Film 1, -2, ForYSC, MotPP, NotNAT B, TwYS, Vers A[port], WhScrn 74, -77, WhoHol B*
Lewis, Monica 1925- *CmpEPM, ForYSC, IntMPA 77, -75, -76, -78, -79, -80, WhoHol A*
Lewis, Morgan, Jr. 1906-1968 *AmSCAP 66, -80, CmpEPM, EncMT*
Lewis, Noah 1895-1961 *BluesWW[port]*
Lewis, Olive Winifred *WhoMus 72*
Lewis, Olwen Patricia 1952- *IntWWM 77*
Lewis, Ovid Barton 1905- *AmSCAP 80*
Lewis, Peter Tod 1932- *ConAmC*
Lewis, Philip d1931 *NotNAT B*
Lewis, Ralph 1872-1937 *Film 1, -2, ForYSC, MotPP, TwYS, WhScrn 74, -77, WhoHol B*
Lewis, Ramsey 1935- *DrBlPA, IlEncJ*
Lewis, Ramsey, Trio *RkOn 2[port]*
Lewis, Ramsey E, Jr. 1935- *BiDAmM*
Lewis, Raymond 1947- *IntWWM 80*
Lewis, Richard 1869-1935 *WhScrn 74, -77, WhoHol B*
Lewis, Richard 1914- *Baker 78, CmOp,*

IntWWM 80, NewGrD 80, WhoMus 72, WhoOp 76
Lewis, Robert 1900-1965 NewOrJ[port]
Lewis, Robert 1909- BiE&WWA, EncMT, NotNAT, PIP&P[port], WhoHol A, WhoThe 72, -77
Lewis, Robert Alan 1936- AmSCAP 80
Lewis, Robert Hall 1926- AmSCAP 80, CpmDNM 78, -80, ConAmC, DcCM, NewGrD 80
Lewis, Robert Q NewYTET, WhoHol A
Lewis, Robert Q 1921- ForYSC
Lewis, Robert Q 1924- JoeFr
Lewis, Roger 1885-1948 AmSCAP 66, -80
Lewis, Roger H 1918- IntMPA 77, -75, -76, -78, -79, -80
Lewis, Ronald 1928- FilmgC, HalFC 80, IlWWBF, WhoHol A
Lewis, Russell 1908- BiE&WWA
Lewis, Russell Roosevelt 1941- AmSCAP 80
Lewis, Sabby 1914- WhoJazz 72
Lewis, Sam d1964 NotNAT B
Lewis, Sam 1878-1963 WhScrn 74, -77
Lewis, Sam M 1885-1959 AmPS, CmpEPM
Lewis, Samella S WomWMM B
Lewis, Samuel M 1885-1959 AmSCAP 66, -80, BiDAmM, Sw&Ld C
Lewis, Shari DcPup
Lewis, Sheldon d1958 MotPP, NotNAT B, WhoHol B
Lewis, Sheldon 1868-1958 Film 1, -2, FilmgC, HalFC 80
Lewis, Sheldon 1869-1958 ForYSC, TwYS, WhScrn 74, -77, WhoHrs 80
Lewis, Sinclair 1885-1951 CnMD, FilmgC, HalFC 80, ModWD, NotNAT B
Lewis, Smiley 1920-1966 BluesWW[port], RkOn
Lewis, Steve 1896-1939 NewOrJ[port]
Lewis, Steve 1896-1941? WhoJazz 72
Lewis, Susan WomWMM B
Lewis, Sybil BlksB&W C
Lewis, Sylvester 1908- WhoJazz 72
Lewis, Ted AmPS B, AmSCAP 80
Lewis, Ted d1971 BgBands 74[port], WhoHol B
Lewis, Ted 1889-1971 FilmgC, HalFC 80
Lewis, Ted 1891-1971 BiDAmM, Film 2, ForYSC, NotNAT B, What 2[port], WhScrn 74, -77
Lewis, Ted 1892-1971 AmSCAP 66, CmpEPM, EncJzS 70, WhoJazz 72
Lewis, Thomas Christopher NewGrD 80
Lewis, Tom IntMPA 75, -76, -78, -79, -80
Lewis, Tom 1864-1927 Film 2, IntMPA 77, WhScrn 74, -77, WhoHol B
Lewis, Tommy BluesWW[port]
Lewis, Vera d1956 WhScrn 74, -77, WhoHol B
Lewis, Vera d1958 Film 1, -2, ForYSC, TwYS
Lewis, Vic 1919- CmpEPM
Lewis, Victor Joseph 1919- IntWWM 77, -80, WhoMus 72
Lewis, Vivian Anthony 1926- WhoMus 72
Lewis, Walter 1893- BluesWW[port]
Lewis, Walter 1918- NewOrJ SUP[port]
Lewis, Walter P 1871-1932 Film 1, -2, TwYS, WhScrn 77
Lewis, Wayne I 1957- AmSCAP 80
Lewis, Webster Samuel 1943- IntWWM 77
Lewis, Willard Film 2
Lewis, William 1935- WhoOp 76
Lewis, William Christopher 1953- AmSCAP 80
Lewis, William Thomas 1749-1811 NotNAT B, OxThe
Lewis, Willie 1905-1971 WhoJazz 72
Lewis, Windsor 1918-1972 BiE&WWA, NotNAT B
Lewis, Wyndham 1910- IntMPA 77, -75, -76, -78, -79, -80
Lewisohn, Adolph 1849-1938 Baker 78
Lewisohn, Alice d1972 BiE&WWA, NotNAT B, OxThe
Lewisohn, Arthur AmSCAP 80
Lewisohn, Irene d1944 NotNAT B, OxThe
Lewisohn, Victor Max 1897-1934 NotNAT B, WhThe
Lewiston, David 1929- IntWWM 77, -80
Lewitzky, Bella 1915- CmpGMD, CnOxB
Lewkovitch, Bernhard 1927- DcCM, NewGrD 80
Lewkowitch, Bernhard 1927- Baker 78
Lewton, Val 1904-1951 BiDFilm, -81, CmMov, DcFM, FilmEn, FilmgC, HalFC 80, OxFilm, WhoHrs 80, WorEFlm
Lewy, Leonard 1921- AmSCAP 66
Lexa, Jake d1973 WhScrn 77
Lexy, Edward 1897- FilmgC, HalFC 80, WhThe
Ley, Grita Film 2
Ley, Henry George 1887-1962 Baker 78, NewGrD 80, OxMus
Ley, Olga 1912- DancEn 78
Ley, Salvador 1907- Baker 78, DcCM, NewGrD 80
Ley-Piscator, Maria BiE&WWA
Leybach, Ignace Xavier Joseph 1817-1891 Baker 78, NewGrD 80
Leybourne, George 1842-1884 NotNAT B, OxThe, PIP&P
Leyda, Jay 1910- OxFilm
Leyden, James A 1921- AmSCAP 80
Leyden, John 1775-1811 NewGrD 80
Leyding, Georg Dietrich NewGrD 80
Leyel, Carl F 1875-1925 NotNAT B, WhThe
Leyer, Rhoda WomWMM
Leygraf, Hans 1920- Baker 78, WhoMus 72
Leyrac, Monique 1930?- NewGrD 80
Leyrac, Monique 1932?- CreCan 2
Leyssac, Paul d1946 NotNAT B, WhScrn 74, -77, WhoHol B
Leytens, Luc M E L 1936- IntWWM 77, -80
Leyton, George 1864-1948 NotNAT B, WhThe
Leyton, John ForYSC
Leyton, John 1939- FilmgC, HalFC 80, WhoHol A
L'Herbier, Marcel 1880-1979 OxFilm
L'Herbier, Marcel 1890-1979 BiDFilm, -81, DcFM, FilmEn, FilmgC, HalFC 80, MovMk[port], WorEFlm
Lheretier, Jean 1480?-1552? NewGrD 80
Lheritier, Antoine NewGrD 80
Lheritier, Isaac NewGrD 80
Lheritier, Jean 1480?-1552? NewGrD 80
L'Heureux, David Charles 1948- AmSCAP 80
Lhevinne, Josef 1874-1944 Baker 78, BiDAmM, BnBkM 80, MusSN[port], NewGrD 80[port]
Lhevinne, Rosina 1880-1976 Baker 78, BnBkM 80
Lhiretier, Jean 1480?-1552? NewGrD 80
Lhomme, Pierre 1930- FilmEn
L'Hoste DaReggio NewGrD 80
Lhotka, Fran 1883-1962 Baker 78, NewGrD 80
Lhotka, Nenad 1922- DancEn 78
Lhotka-Kalinski, Ivo 1913- Baker 78, IntWWM 77, -80, NewGrD 80
L'Huillier NewGrD 80
L'Hulier, John B 1780?-1848 BiDAmM
L'Huyllier NewGrD 80
Li, Judith Anderson 1938- IntWWM 77, -80
Li-Paz, Michael 1938- WhoOp 76
Liadof, Anatol 1855-1914 OxMus
Liadov, Anatol 1855-1914 BnBkM 80, CompSN[port], DcCom&M 79, MusMk[port]
Liadov, Anatol Konstantinovich NewGrD 80
Liadov, Anatoly 1855-1914 Baker 78
Liadov, Anatoly Konstantinovich NewGrD 80
Liadov, Konstantin 1820-1868 Baker 78
Liagre, Alfred De, Jr. 1904- WhThe
Liang, Ming-Yueh 1941- IntWWM 77, -80
Lianides, Thomas William 1920- AmSCAP 66
Liapunof, Serge 1859-1924 OxMus
Liapunov, Serge 1859-1924 MusMk
Liapunov, Sergei 1859-1924 Baker 78
Liardet, Jean-Paul 1939- IntWWM 77, -80
Liatoshinsky, Boris 1895-1968 Baker 78
Libaek, Sven Erik 1938- IntWWM 77, -80
Liban, Jerzy 1464-1546? NewGrD 80
Libbach, Roland Anton Bruno Friedrich 1914- IntWWM 80
Libbert, Jurgen 1941- IntWWM 77, -80
Libbey, Dee AmSCAP 66
Libbey, Delores R AmSCAP 80
Libbey, J Aldrich 1872-1925 WhScrn 77, WhoHol B
Libbey, James Aldrich 1872-1925 NotNAT B
Libby, Patrick Charles 1942- IntWWM 77, -80
Libby J Aldrich AmPS B
Libeau, Gustave 1877-1957 FilmAG WE
Liber, Joseph Anton 1732-1809 NewGrD 80
Liberace 1919- AmSCAP 66, FilmEn, FilmgC, HalFC 80, IntWWM 77, NewYTET, WhoHol A
Liberace 1920- IntMPA 77, -75, -76, -78, -79, -80
Liberace, George J 1911- AmSCAP 66, -80, What 3[port]
Liberace, V 1919- ForYSC
Liberace, Walter Valentino 1919- AmSCAP 80, Baker 78, BiDAmM, MusMk
Liberati, Antimo 1617-1692 NewGrD 80
Liberman, Frank P 1917- IntMPA 77, -75, -76, -78, -79, -80
Libero Castro, Heinricus De NewGrD 80
Libert, David ConMuA 80B
Libert, Gualterius NewGrD 80
Libert, Henri 1869-1937 Baker 78
Libert, Reginaldus NewGrD 80
Liberti, Gualtero NewGrD 80, -80
Liberti, Hendrik 1600?-1661? NewGrD 80
Liberti, Vincenzo NewGrD 80
Liberto, Roy 1928- NewOrJ
Libidins, David d1958 DancEn 78
Libin, Paul 1930- BiE&WWA, NotNAT, WhoThe 77
Liblick, Marvin 1929- AmSCAP 66, -80
Libon, Felipe 1775-1838 NewGrD 80
Libon, Philippe 1775-1838 Baker 78, NewGrD 80
Libott, Robert Y BiE&WWA
Licalzi, Lawrence Film 2
Licata, Sal ConMuA 80B
Liccardi, Vincent G IntMPA 77, -75, -76, -78, -79, -80
Liccioni, Georges WhoOp 76
Licette, Miriam 1892-1969 NewGrD 80
Lichard, Milan 1853-1935 Baker 78
Lichenstein, Charles M NewYTET
Lichey, Reinhold 1879-1957 Baker 78
Lichfild, Henry NewGrD 80, OxMus
Lichine, David 1909-1972 WhThe
Lichine, David 1910-1972 CnOxB, DancEn 78[port], WhScrn 77
Lichnowsky NewGrD 80
Lichnowsky, Prince Carl 1761-1814 Baker 78
Lichnowsky, Carl Von 1761-1814 NewGrD 80
Lichnowsky, Felix Von 1814-1848 NewGrD 80
Lichnowsky, Henriette Von 1769-1829? NewGrD 80
Lichnowsky, Karl Von 1761-1814 NewGrD 80
Lichnowsky, Moritz Von 1771-1837 NewGrD 80
Licho, Adolf Edgar Film 2
Licho, Edgar Adolph 1876-1944 WhScrn 74, -77, WhoHol B
Lichtegg, Max WhoMus 72
Lichtenauer, Paul Ignaz NewGrD 80
Lichtenberg, Leopold 1861-1935 Baker 78, BiDAmM
Lichtenberger, Henri 1864-1941 Baker 78
Lichtenegger, Mathilde NewGrD 80
Lichtenfeld, Monika 1938- NewGrD 80
Lichtenfels, Hainrich NewGrD 80
Lichtenhahn, Ernst 1934- NewGrD 80
Lichtenstein, Alfred 1901- IntWWM 77, -80
Lichtenstein, Karl August Von 1767-1845 Baker 78, NewGrD 80
Lichtenstein, Ulrich Von NewGrD 80
Lichtenthal, Peter 1780-1853 Baker 78, NewGrD 80
Lichtenthal, Pietro 1780-1853 NewGrD 80
Lichtenwanger, William 1915- Baker 78, BiDAmM, NewGrD 80
Lichter, Charles 1910- AmSCAP 66, -80, ConAmC
Lichtmann, Margaret Stevens 1945- IntWWM 80
Lichtmann, Theodor David 1938- IntWWM 77, -80
Lichtveld, Lou 1903- Baker 78
Licino, Agostino NewGrD 80
Lickl NewGrD 80
Lickl, Aegidius Karl 1803-1864 NewGrD 80
Lickl, Ferdinand 1803-1864 NewGrD 80
Lickl, Johann Georg 1769-1843 Baker 78,

NewGrD 80
Lickl, Karl Georg 1801-1877 *NewGrD 80*
Licudi, Gabriella 1943- *FilmgC, HalFC 80*
Lidarti, Christian Joseph 1730-1793? *NewGrD 80*
Lidarti, Cristiano Giuseppe 1730-1793? *NewGrD 80*
Liddell, Matthew 1902- *WhoMus 72*
Liddell, Nona Patricia 1927- *IntWWM 77, -80, WhoMus 72*
Liddicoat, Philip William 1920- *WhoMus 72*
Lidel, Andreas *NewGrD 80*
Lidell, Alvar 1908- *IntWWM 77, -80*
Lidell, Tord Alvar Quan 1908- *WhoMus 72*
Liden, Helge Joel 1923- *IntWWM 77*
Lider, Edward W 1922- *IntMPA 77, -75, -76, -78, -79, -80*
Lidgett, Scott d1953 *NotNAT B*
Lidholm, Ingvar 1921- *Baker 78, DancEn 78, DcCM, IntWWM 80, NewGrD 80*
Lidka, Maria *IntWWM 77, -80, WhoMus 72*
Lidl *NewGrD 80*
Lidl, Andreas d1789? *NewGrD 80*
Lidl, Joseph 1864-1946 *NewGrD 80*
Lidl, Vaclav 1894- *NewGrD 80*
Lidl, Vaclav 1922- *Baker 78, IntWWM 77, -80*
Lido, Serge 1906- *CnOxB, DancEn 78*
Lidon, Jose 1746-1827 *NewGrD 80*
Lidon, Jose 1748-1827 *Baker 78*
Lidova, Irene 1907- *CnOxB, DancEn 78*
Lidral, Frank Wayne 1920- *IntWWM 77, -80*
Lidstrom, Howard LeRoy 1910- *IntWWM 77*
Lidstrom, Kerstin 1946- *CnOxB*
Lie, Erika 1845-1903 *Baker 78*
Lie, Harald 1902-1942 *Baker 78*
Lie, Sigurd 1871-1904 *Baker 78, NewGrD 80, OxMus*
Lie-Hansen, Bjorn 1937- *WhoOp 76*
Lieb, Herman 1873-1966 *WhScrn 74, -77*
Lieb, Robert P *WhoHol A*
Lieb, Ziskind R 1930- *AmSCAP 66, -80, IntWWM 77*
Liebe, Christian 1654-1708 *NewGrD 80*
Liebe, Eduard Ludwig 1819-1900 *Baker 78*
Lieben, Christian 1654-1708 *NewGrD 80*
Liebeneiner, Wolfgang 1905- *DcFM*
Lieber, Christian 1654-1708 *NewGrD 80*
Lieber, Doodles *AmSCAP 80*
Lieber, Perry W 1905- *IntMPA 77, -75, -76, -78, -79, -80*
Lieberfarb, Warren *IntMPA 80*
Lieberman, David *ConMuA 80B*
Lieberman, Ernest Sheldon 1930- *AmSCAP 80*
Lieberman, Fredric 1940- *AmSCAP 80, ConAmC, IntWWM 80*
Lieberman, Glenn 1947- *CpmDNM 78, -80, ConAmC*
Lieberman, Jacob 1879-1956 *WhScrn 74, -77*
Lieberman, Peter 1954- *AmSCAP 80*
Liebermann, Rolf 1910- *Baker 78, CmOp, CompSN[port], DcCM, IntWWM 77, -80, NewEOp 71, NewGrD 80, OxMus, WhoMus 72, WhoOp 76*
Lieberson, Goddard 1911-1977 *AmSCAP 66, -80, Baker 78, ConAmC, WhoMus 72*
Lieberson, Peter Goddard 1946- *ConAmC, IntWWM 80*
Lieberson, Sandy 1936- *IntMPA 80*
Lieberstein, Marcus Edward 1933- *AmSCAP 80*
Liebert *NewGrD 80*
Liebert, William Edward 1925- *AmSCAP 80*
Liebeskind, Joseph 1866-1916 *Baker 78*
Liebhold *NewGrD 80*
Liebholdt *NewGrD 80*
Liebich, Ernst 1830-1884 *Baker 78*
Liebig, Karl 1808-1872 *Baker 78*
Liebler, Theodore A d1941 *NotNAT B*
Liebling, Emil 1851-1914 *Baker 78, BiDAmM*
Liebling, Estelle 1880-1970 *Baker 78, BiDAmM*
Liebling, Estelle 1884-1970 *AmSCAP 66, -80, NewEOp 71*
Liebling, Georg 1865-1945 *BiDAmM*
Liebling, Georg 1865-1946 *Baker 78*
Liebling, Howard 1928- *AmSCAP 66, -80, IntMPA 77, -78, -79, -80*
Liebling, Leonard 1874-1945 *Baker 78, ConAmC, NotNAT B*
Liebling, Leonard 1880-1945 *BiDAmM*
Liebling, William 1895- *BiE&WWA*
Liebman, Dave 1946- *EncJzS 70*
Liebman, David 1946- *EncJzS 70, IntWWM 77*
Liebman, Joseph H 1911- *AmSCAP 66, -80*
Liebman, Marcia 1947- *WhoOp 76*
Liebman, Marvin 1923- *WhoThe 72, -77*
Liebman, Max 1902- *AmSCAP 66, -80, BiE&WWA, IntMPA 77, -75, -76, -78, -79, -80, NewYTET, NotNAT*
Liebmann, Hans H 1895-1960 *WhScrn 74, -77, WhoHol B*
Liebner, Janos 1923- *WhoMus 72*
Lieburg, Max d1962 *NotNAT B*
Liedtke, Harry 1881-1945 *Film 2, WhScrn 77, WhoHol B*
Lief, Max 1899-1969 *AmSCAP 66, -80*
Lief, Nathaniel 1896-1944 *AmSCAP 66, -80*
Liefs, Jon *OxMus*
Liehtenstein, Ulrich Von *NewGrD 80*
Lienas, Juan De *NewGrD 80*
Lienau *NewGrD 80*
Lienau, Emil Robert 1838-1920 *NewGrD 80*
Lienau, Friedrich Wilhelm 1876-1973 *NewGrD 80*
Lienau, Robert *NewGrD 80*
Lienau, Robert 1838-1920 *Baker 78*
Lienau, Robert Heinrich 1866-1949 *NewGrD 80*
Lienau, Rosemarie *NewGrD 80*
Lienike *NewGrD 80*
Liepa, Maris 1930- *DancEn 78*
Liepa, Maris-Rudolph Eduardovich 1936- *CnOxB*
Liepe, Emil 1860-1940 *Baker 78*
Liepmannssohn, Leo 1840-1915 *NewGrD 80*
Liepolt, Werner 1944- *NatPD[port]*
Lier, Bertus Van 1906-1972 *Baker 78, NewGrD 80*
Lier, Jacques Van *Baker 78*
Lierhammer, Theodor 1866-1937 *Baker 78*
Liese, Johannes 1908- *IntWWM 80*
Liess, Andreas 1903- *IntWWM 77, -80, NewGrD 80, WhoMus 72*
Lieto, Bartolomeo *NewGrD 80*
Lietzau, Hans 1913- *EncWT*
Lieurance, Thurlow 1878-1963 *AmSCAP 66, -80, Baker 78, BiDAmM, ConAmC, NewGrD 80*
Lieven, Albert 1904-1971 *FilmAG WE*
Lieven, Albert 1906-1971 *FilmEn, FilmgC, HalFC 80, WhScrn 74, -77, WhThe, WhoHol B*
Lieven, Tatiana 1910- *WhThe*
Lifanoff, B *Film 2*
Lifar, Serge 1905- *CnOxB, DancEn 78[port], NewGrD 80, OxMus, WhThe*
Lifchitz, Max 1948- *ConAmC, IntWWM 80*
Liff, Samuel 1919- *BiE&WWA, NotNAT*
Lifschitz, Alexander *CnOxB*
Lifson, David *NatPD[port]*
Ligabue, Ilva Palmina 1932- *CmOp, WhoOp 76*
Ligendza, Catarina 1937- *NewGrD 80*
Ligendza, Caterina 1937- *CmOp, WhoOp 76*
Ligero, Miguel 1898-1968 *WhScrn 74, -77*
Ligeti, Gyorgy 1923- *Baker 78, BnBkM 80, CnOxB, DcCom&M 79, DcCM, MusMk, NewGrD 80[port], WhoMus 72*
Ligety, Louis 1881-1928 *WhScrn 74, -77*
Liggett, Louis *Film 2*
Liggett, Rosalie Smith 1912- *IntWWM 77*
Liggins, Joe *AmPS A*
Liggins, Joe 1915- *CmpEPM*
Liggins, Joseph Christopher 1916- *AmSCAP 80*
Liggon, Grover *Film 2*
Light, Alan 1916- *WhoOp 76*
Light, Ben 1893-1965 *BiDAmM*
Light, Ben 1894-1965 *AmSCAP 66, -80*
Light, Edward *OxMus*
Light, Edward 1747?-1832? *NewGrD 80*
Light, Enoch 1907-1978 *AmSCAP 66, -80, BgBands 74[port], CmpEPM*
Light, James d1964 *NotNAT B*
Light Crust Doughboys, The *EncFCWM 69, IlEncCM*
Lightfoot, Alexander 1924-1971 *BluesWW[port]*
Lightfoot, Gordon *ConMuA 80A*
Lightfoot, Gordon 1938- *AmSCAP 66, RkOn 2[port]*
Lightfoot, Gordon 1939- *CreCan 2, IlEncR[port]*
Lighthall, William Douw 1857-1954 *CreCan 2*
Lighthouse *RkOn 2[port]*
Lightman, M A, Jr. 1915- *IntMPA 77, -75, -76, -78, -79, -80*
Lightner, Winnie *AmPS B*
Lightner, Winnie 1899-1971 *FilmEn, ThFT[port]*
Lightner, Winnie 1901-1971 *CmpEPM, EncMT, Film 2, FilmgC, ForYSC, HalFC 80[port], MotPP, WhScrn 74, -77, WhThe, WhoHol B*
Lightnin' Junior *BluesWW[port]*
Lightnin' Slim *BluesWW[port]*
Lightoller, Elisabeth Susan 1945- *IntWWM 77, -80, WhoMus 72*
Lights, Frederick *MorBAP*
Lightstone, Gordon *IntMPA 77, -75, -76, -78, -79*
Lightstone, Leonard 1916- *IntMPA 75, -76*
Lightstone, Pauline *CreCan 1, NewGrD 80*
Lightwood, James Thomas 1856-1944 *OxMus*
Ligi, Josella 1948- *WhoOp 76*
Ligne, Charles-Joseph De 1735-1814 *NewGrD 80*
Lignell, Kathleen Ellen 1942- *IntWWM 77*
Ligniville, Eugene, Marquis Of 1730-1788 *NewGrD 80*
Ligon, Grover G 1885-1965 *Film 1, WhScrn 74, -77, WhoHol B*
Ligon, Tom *WhoHol A*
Ligotti, Albert F 1927- *IntWWM 77, -80*
Liikala, Isabelle *WomWMM B*
Likes, Don *Film 1*
Lilar, Suzanne 1901- *ModWD*
Lilavati, Devi 1926?- *CnOxB, DancEn 78*
Lilburn, Douglas Gordon 1915- *Baker 78, DcCM, IntWWM 77, -80, MusMk, NewGrD 80, WhoMus 72*
Lile, Professor *PupTheA*
Lilien, Ignace 1897-1964 *NewGrD 80*
Liliencron, Rochus Von 1820-1912 *Baker 78, NewGrD 80*
Lilienfeld, Richard *WhoMus 72*
Lilienstein, Saul E 1932- *IntWWM 77*
Lilienthal, Abraham W 1859-1928 *Baker 78*
Lilina, Maria Petrovna 1866-1954 *NotNAT B*
Liliuokalani, Queen Of Hawaii 1838-1917 *BiDAmM*
Lilius *NewGrD 80*
Lilius, Franciscus d1657 *NewGrD 80*
Lilius, Franciszek d1657 *NewGrD 80*
Lilius, Simon d1652? *NewGrD 80*
Lilius, Szymon d1652? *NewGrD 80*
Lilius, Vincentius d1640? *NewGrD 80*
Lilius, Wincenty d1640? *NewGrD 80*
Liliusz, Simon d1652? *NewGrD 80*
Liliusz, Szymon d1652? *NewGrD 80*
Liljeblad, Ingeborg 1887-1942 *Baker 78*
Liljedahl, Marie 1952?- *WhoHrs 80*
Liljefors, Ingemar 1906- *Baker 78, NewGrD 80*
Liljefors, Ruben 1871-1936 *Baker 78, NewGrD 80*
Lill, John Richard 1944- *IntWWM 77, -80, NewGrD 80, WhoMus 72*
Lillard, Charlotte 1844-1946 *WhScrn 74, -77, WhoHol B*
Lille, Professor *PupTheA*
Lille, Rainer Martin Max 1930- *WhoMus 72*
Lillenas, Bertha Mae 1889-1945 *AmSCAP 66, -80*
Lillenas, Haldor 1885-1959 *AmSCAP 66, -80*
Lilley, Edward 1896-1974 *FilmEn*
Lilley, John Mark 1939- *IntWWM 77, -80*
Lilley, Joseph J 1914- *AmSCAP 66, -80*
Lillie, Bea *MotPP*
Lillie, Beatrice 1894- *EncMT, FilmEn*
Lillie, Beatrice 1898- *CmpEPM, CnThe, EncWT, Ent, FamA&A[port], FilmgC, ForYSC, HalFC 80, JoeFr[port], MovMk[port], NotNAT A, ThFT[port], WhoHol A, WhoThe 72, -77*
Lillie, Beatrice 1903- *BiE&WWA, Film 2, NotNAT*
Lillie, Jessie 1890-1976 *AmSCAP 66, -80*
Lillies, Leonard 1860-1923 *NotNAT B, WhThe*
Lilliman, Keith 1932- *IntWWM 77*

Lillmore, Clyde Film 2
Lillo, George 1693-1739 EncWT, Ent, McGEWD[port], NotNAT B, OxThe, PlP&P, REnWD[port]
Lillo, Giuseppe 1814-1863 Baker 78, NewGrD 80
Lilly, John d1678 NewGrD 80
Lilo AmPS B
Lilova, Margarita Slateva 1935- WhoOp 76
Liltved, Oystein 1934- WhoOp 76
Lim, Kek-Tjiang 1928- IntWWM 77, -80
Lima, Arthur Moreira 1940- IntWWM 77, -80, WhoMus 72
Lima, Braz Francisco De 1752-1813 NewGrD 80
Lima, Candido DeOliveira 1939- IntWWM 77, -80, NewGrD 80
Lima, Jeronymo Francisco De 1743-1822 NewGrD 80
Lima, Luis 1948- IntWWM 80
Lima, Ruth DancEn 78
Lima Sequeiros, Juan De NewGrD 80
Limantour, Jose Yves 1919- Baker 78
Limbert, Frank 1866-1938 Baker 78
Limbert, Roy 1893-1954 NotNAT B, WhThe
Limburg, Olga Film 2
Lime, Yvonne ForYSC, WhoHol A
Limelighters, The RkOn[port]
Limeliters, The BiDAmM, EncFCWM 69
Limenius NewGrD 80
Limerick, Mona WhThe
Limnander DeNieuwenhove, Armand M G 1814-1892 Baker 78
Limoli, Michael David 1948- IntWWM 77, -80
Limon, Jose 1908-1972 CmpGMD[port], CnOxB, DancEn 78[port]
Limondjian, Hambardzum 1768-1839 NewGrD 80
Limpic, Gerald Richard 1951- AmSCAP 80
Limpus, Alban Brownlow 1878-1941 WhThe
Lin, Cho-Liang 1960- IntWWM 80
Linahan, Mona Elizabeth 1909- WhoMus 72
Linaker, Kay ForYSC
Linard, Sidney Lee 1936- AmSCAP 80
Linares-Rivas, Manuel WhThe
Linares Rivas Y Astray, Manuel 1867-1938 McGEWD[port]
Linceo NewGrD 80
Linck, Johannes 1561-1603 NewGrD 80
Lincke, Joseph 1783-1837 Baker 78, NewGrD 80
Lincke, Paul 1866-1946 Baker 78, MusMk, NewGrD 80, NotNAT B
Lincoln, Abbey 1930- BiDAmM, BlkAmP, DrBlPA, EncJzS 70, HalFC 80, WhoHol A
Lincoln, Abe 1907- CmpEPM, WhoJazz 72
Lincoln, Abraham 1809-1865 HalFC 80, OxFilm
Lincoln, Anya 1908- WhoMus 72
Lincoln, Brian William 1933- WhoMus 72
Lincoln, Caryl Film 2, WhoHol A
Lincoln, Charley BluesWW[port]
Lincoln, Charlie BluesWW[port]
Lincoln, E K d1958 Film 1, TwYS, WhScrn 77
Lincoln, Elmo 1889-1952 CmMov, Film 1, -2, FilmgC, HalFC 80, MovMk, NotNAT B, TwYS, WhScrn 74, -77, WhoHol B, WhoHrs 80
Lincoln, Elmo 1899-1952 FilmEn
Lincoln, Harry B 1922- NewGrD 80
Lincoln, Robert Dix 1924- Baker 78, ConAmC
Lincoln, Rosa Lee BlksB&W C
Lincoln, Steve WhoHol A
Lincoln, Tad PupTheA
Lincolniensis NewGrD 80
Lind, Bob 1944- RkOn 2[port]
Lind, Della WhoHol A
Lind, Gillian 1904- WhoHol A, WhoThe 72, -77
Lind, Jenny 1820-1887 Baker 78, BiDAmM, BnBkM 80[port], CmOp, Film 1, MusMk, NewEOp 71, NewGrD 80[port], OxMus
Lind, Johanna Maria 1820-1887 BnBkM 80[port], NewGrD 80[port]
Lind, Letty 1862-1923 NotNAT B, WhThe
Lind, Myrtle Film 1
Lind, Richard A 1949- IntWWM 77
Lind, Sarah Film 1
Lind, William Reinhold 1911- IntWWM 80
Lind-Goldschmidt, Jenny 1820-1887 NewGrD 80[port]
Lind-Goldschmidt, Johanna Maria 1820-1887 NewGrD 80[port]
Lind-Oquendo, Abraham 1933- WhoOp 76
Linda And The Stone Poneys BiDAmM
Lindars, Gladys WhoMus 72
Lindars, Herman 1899- IntWWM 77
Lindau, Paul 1839-1919 EncWT
Lindberg, Armas NewGrD 80
Lindberg, August 1846-1916 EncWT, Ent, OxThe, WhThe
Lindberg, Nils 1933- EncJzS 70, IntWWM 77, -80
Lindberg, O 1887-1955 OxMus
Lindberg, Oskar Fredrik 1887-1955 Baker 78, NewGrD 80
Lindberg, Per 1890-1944 EncWT, FilmEn
Lindberg, Yuco 1906-1948 DancEn 78
Lindbergh, Charles A 1902- What 1[port]
Lindblad, Adolf Fredrik 1801-1878 Baker 78, NewGrD 80
Lindblad, Otto Jonas 1809-1864 Baker 78, MusMk, NewGrD 80
Lindblom, Gunnel 1931- FilmEn, HalFC 80, IntMPA 79, -80, OxFilm, WorEFlm[port]
Lindblom, Gunnel 1939- FilmgC
Linde, Bo 1933-1970 Baker 78, NewGrD 80
Linde, Dennis 1943- IlEncCM[port]
Linde, Hans-Martin 1930- BnBkM 80, IntWWM 77, -80, NewGrD 80
Linde, Nancy WomWMM B
Lindeborg, Britt 1928- IntWWM 77
Lindegren, Johan 1842-1908 Baker 78, NewGrD 80
Lindelheim, Joanna Maria NewGrD 80
Lindeman NewGrD 80
Lindeman, Dora 1918- WhoMus 72
Lindeman, Edith 1898- AmSCAP 66, -80
Lindeman, L M 1812-1887 OxMus
Lindeman, Lucas P M 1926- IntWWM 77, -80
Lindeman, Ludvig Mathias 1812-1887 Baker 78, NewGrD 80
Lindeman, Ole Andreas 1769-1857 NewGrD 80
Lindeman, Osmo 1929- Baker 78, IntWWM 77, -80, NewGrD 80
Lindeman, Peter Brynie 1858-1930 NewGrD 80
Lindeman, Trygve Henrik 1896- NewGrD 80
Lindemanis, Haralds 1921- AmSCAP 80
Lindemann, Carl, Jr. NewYTET
Lindemann, Johannes 1550?-1634? NewGrD 80
Lindemann, Thomas 1940- IntWWM 77, -80
Lindemuth, William I 1915- AmSCAP 66, -80
Linden, Albert Vander 1913-1977 NewGrD 80
Linden, Anya 1933- CnOxB, DancEn 78
Linden, Einar Film 1
Linden, Eric 1909- FilmEn, FilmgC, ForYSC, HalFC 80, HolP 30[port], MotPP, WhThe, WhoHol A
Linden, Hal IntMPA 79, -80
Linden, Hal 1931- BiE&WWA, EncMT, NotNAT, WhoThe 72, -77
Linden, Hal 1932- HalFC 80
Linden, Jennie 1939- FilmgC, HalFC 80, WhoHol A
Linden, Kathy RkOn
Linden, Marie 1862- WhThe
Linden, Peggy Film 2
Linden, Robert 1912- BiE&WWA, NotNAT
Lindenburn, Henry 1874-1952 WhScrn 74, -77
Lindenfeld, Harris 1945- CpmDNM 72, -79, ConAmC
Lindenstrand, Sylvia 1942- WhoOp 76
Linder, Albert 1937- IntWWM 77, -80
Linder, Alfred d1957 WhScrn 74, -77, WhoHol B
Linder, Cec HalFC 80
Linder, Hans 1917- IntWWM 77, -80
Linder, Jack 1896- BiE&WWA
Linder, Judith Anna Ingegerd 1930- IntWWM 77, -80
Linder, Max 1882-1925 JoeFr, TwYS
Linder, Max 1883-1925 BiDFilm, -81, DcFM, FilmEn, Film 1, -2, FilmgC, HalFC 80, MotPP, NotNAT B, OxFilm, WhScrn 74, -77, WhoHol B, WorEFlm
Linder, Robert J 1937- IntWWM 77
Linder, Ursula 1922- IntWWM 77, -80
Lindergreen, Harold F PupTheA
Lindfors, Viveca 1920- BiDFilm, -81, BiE&WWA, FilmEn, FilmgC, ForYSC, HalFC 80, IntMPA 77, -75, -76, -78, -79, -80, MotPP, MovMk[port], NotNAT, WhoHol A, WhoThe 72, -77, WorEFlm
Lindgren, Adolf 1846-1905 NewGrD 80
Lindgren, Aron Film 1
Lindgren, Ernest 1910-1973 OxFilm
Lindgren, Floice Rhodes 1938- IntWWM 77, -80
Lindgren, Kurt 1937- IntWWM 77, -80
Lindgren, Lars-Magnus 1922- FilmgC, HalFC 80, WorEFlm
Lindgren, Robert 1923- CnOxB, DancEn 78
Lindh, Jody Wayne 1944- ConAmC
Lindhjem, Thorbjorn 1933- WhoOp 76
Lindholm, Berit Maria 1934- IntWWM 80, NewGrD 80, WhoMus 72, WhoOp 76
Lindholm, Cedric M PupTheA
Lindholm, Eric Film 1
Lindholm, Teppo Untamo 1920- IntWWM 77, -80
Lindisfarne ConMuA 80A, IlEncR
Lindlar, Heinrich 1912- NewGrD 80
Lindley, Audra 1918- WhThe, WhoHol A
Lindley, Bert Film 2
Lindley, Robert 1776-1855 Baker 78, NewGrD 80
Lindley, Simon Geoffrey 1948- IntWWM 77, -80
Lindley, William 1802-1869 NewGrD 80
Lindner, August 1820-1878 Baker 78
Lindner, Ernest 1897- CreCan 1
Lindner, Ernst Otto Timotheus 1820-1867 Baker 78
Lindner, Friedrich 1542?-1597 NewGrD 80
Lindner, Terrell M 1915- IntMPA 77, -75, -76, -78, -79, -80
Lindo, Frank d1933 NotNAT B
Lindo, Olga d1968 WhoHol B
Lindo, Olga 1898-1968 FilmgC, HalFC 80, WhThe
Lindo, Olga 1899-1968 WhScrn 74, -77
Lindon, Lionel 1905-1971 FilmEn, FilmgC, HalFC 80, WorEFlm
Lindon, Millie 1878- WhThe
Lindpaintner, Peter Josef Von 1791-1856 NewGrD 80
Lindpaintner, Peter Joseph Von 1791-1856 Baker 78
Lindrith, Nellie Film 1
Lindroos, Paul Bertel 1910- IntWWM 77, -80
Lindroos, Paul Peter Christer 1944- WhoOp 76
Lindroth, Helen Film 2
Lindsay, Alex 1919-1974 NewGrD 80
Lindsay, Lady Anne 1750-1825 OxMus
Lindsay, Antony 1934- WhoMus 72
Lindsay, Bryan Eugene 1931- AmSCAP 66, -80
Lindsay, Sir David 1490?-1555? CnThe, EncWT, Ent
Lindsay, Fred Film 2
Lindsay, Henry Francis Selwood WhoMus 72
Lindsay, Herb 1888?- NewOrJ
Lindsay, Howard 1888-1968 EncMT
Lindsay, Howard 1889-1968 BestMus, BiE&WWA, CnThe, EncWT, Film 2, FilmgC, HalFC 80, McGEWD[port], ModWD, NewCBMT, NotNAT B, OxThe, WhScrn 74, -77, WhThe, WhoHol B
Lindsay, Howard 1899-1968 BiDAmM
Lindsay, Howard And Russel Crouse CnMD
Lindsay, Hugh PupTheA
Lindsay, James 1869-1928 Film 2, NotNAT B, WhThe
Lindsay, James 1871-1928 IlWWBF
Lindsay, Jennie AmPS B
Lindsay, John 1894-1950 CmpEPM, NewOrJ[port]
Lindsay, John V 1921- BiE&WWA, WhoHol A
Lindsay, Johnny 1894-1950 BiDAmM
Lindsay, Kevin 1924-1975 WhScrn 77, WhoHol C
Lindsay, LaWanda 1953- CounME 74A
Lindsay, Lex 1901-1971 WhScrn 74, -77, WhoHol B
Lindsay, Margaret 1910- FilmEn, FilmgC, ForYSC, HalFC 80, HolP 30[port], MotPP, MovMk[port], ThFT[port],

WhoHol A
Lindsay, Mark 1944- *RkOn 2[port]*
Lindsay, Marquerita 1883-1955 *WhScrn 77*
Lindsay, Mary *WhoHol A*
Lindsay, Mort 1923- *IntWWM 80*
Lindsay, Powell *BlkAmP*
Lindsay, Rosemary 1927- *DancEn 78*
Lindsay, Sylvia 1925- *IntWWM 77, -80*
Lindsay, Vera 1911- *WhThe*
Lindsay And Crouse *BestMus*
Lindsay-Douglas, Carole 1946- *IntWWM 77, -80*
Lindsay-Hogg, Michael 1940- *FilmEn*
Lindsey, Ben *Film 2*
Lindsey, Claudia *WhoOp 76*
Lindsey, Emily 1887-1944 *WhScrn 74, -77*
Lindsey, George *WhoHol A*
Lindsey, John 1894-1950 *WhoJazz 72*
Lindsey, Joseph 1899- *NewOrJ*
Lindsey, LaWanda 1953- *CounME 74, IlEncCM*
Lindsey, Mort 1923- *AmSCAP 66, -80, IntWWM 77*
Lindsley, Guy d1923 *NotNAT B*
Lindstrom, Anders 1947- *IntWWM 80*
Lindstrom, Pia 1938- *ConAmTC, WhoHol A*
Lindstrom, Rune 1916- *WorEFlm*
Lindstrom, Solweig 1945- *WhoOp 76*
Lindtberg, Leopold 1902- *DcFM, EncWT, FilmEn, FilmgC, HalFC 80*
Linecke *NewGrD 80*
Lineff, Eugenie *NewGrD 80*
Linehan, George 1913- *WhoMus 72*
Linehan, Tommy 1911- *CmpEPM*
Lineva, Eugenie *NewGrD 80*
Lineva, Evgenia 1854-1919 *Baker 78*
Ling, Eugene 1915- *IntMPA 75, -76*
Ling, Jans Nils 1934- *NewGrD 80*
Ling, Richie d1937 *NotNAT B*
Lingard, Horace d1927 *NotNAT B*
Linge, Morrell Kennedy 1918- *IntWWM 80*
Linge, Ruth 1927- *IntWWM 77, -80, WhoOp 76*
Lingen, Theo 1903- *EncWT*
Linger, Carl 1810-1862 *NewGrD 80*
Lingham, Thomas J 1874-1950 *Film 1, -2, WhScrn 74, -77, WhoHol B*
Lingke, Georg Friedrich 1697-1777 *NewGrD 80*
Lingle, Paul 1902-1962 *BiDAmM, WhoJazz 72*
Lingman, Sven-Erik Anshelm 1928- *IntWWM 77*
Lingwood, Tom 1927- *WhoOp 76*
Linicke *NewGrD 80*
Linigke *NewGrD 80*
Linike *NewGrD 80*
Linike, Christian Bernhard 1673-1751 *NewGrD 80*
Linike, Ephraim 1665-1726 *NewGrD 80*
Linike, Johann Georg 1680?-1737? *NewGrD 80*
Linius *NewGrD 80*
Linjama, Jouko 1934- *Baker 78, NewGrD 80*
Link, Adolf d1933 *NotNAT B*
Link, Dorothy 1900- *AmSCAP 80*
Link, Harry 1896-1956 *AmSCAP 66*
Link, Harry 1896-1957 *AmSCAP 80*
Link, Joachim-Dietrich 1925- *IntWWM 77, -80*
Link, Peter 1944- *AmSCAP 80, WhoThe 77*
Link, William 1867-1937 *WhScrn 74, -77*
Link, William E 1897-1949 *WhScrn 74, -77*
Linke, Fritz 1923- *WhoOp 76*
Linke, Norbert 1933- *DcCM, IntWWM 77, -80, NewGrD 80*
Linke, Richard O *NewYTET*
Linker, Robert White 1905- *IntWWM 77, -80*
Linkevitch, Barbara *WomWMM B*
Linklater, Eric 1899-1974 *CnMD, EncWT, ModWD*
Linkletter, Art 1912- *IntMPA 77, -75, -76, -78, -79, -80, NewYTET, RkOn 2A, WhoHol A*
Linko, Ernst 1889-1960 *Baker 78*
Linley *NewGrD 80*
Linley, Doctor *PlP&P*
Linley, Betty 1890-1951 *NotNAT B, WhScrn 74, -77, WhThe, WhoHol B*
Linley, Elizabeth Ann 1754-1792 *NewGrD 80[port], PlP&P*
Linley, Francis 1770?-1800 *NewGrD 80*
Linley, Francis 1771-1800 *BiDAmM*
Linley, George 1798-1865 *Baker 78, NewGrD 80, NotNAT B, OxMus*
Linley, Mary 1758-1787 *NewGrD 80[port]*
Linley, Ozias Thurston 1765-1831 *NewGrD 80*
Linley, Thomas 1732-1795 *OxMus*
Linley, Thomas 1733-1795 *Baker 78, BnBkM 80, MusMk, NewGrD 80[port]*
Linley, Thomas, Jr. 1756-1778 *Baker 78, NewGrD 80[port], OxMus*
Linley, William 1771-1835 *NewGrD 80, NotNAT B, OxMus*
Linn, Bambi 1926- *BiE&WWA, CnOxB, DancEn 78, NotNAT, WhThe, WhoHol A, WhoThe 72*
Linn, Bud 1909-1968 *WhScrn 77, WhoHol B*
Linn, Gertrude 1905- *AmSCAP 66*
Linn, Margaret 1934-1973 *WhScrn 77, WhoHol B*
Linn, Ray Lawrence, Jr. 1914- *AmSCAP 80*
Linn, Ray S 1920- *AmSCAP 80, CmpEPM, EncJzS 70*
Linn, Raymond Sayre 1920- *EncJzS 70*
Linn, Robert 1925- *AmSCAP 66, -80, CpmDNM 72, -73, ConAmC, DcCM*
Linn County Blues Band *BiDAmM*
Linnala, Eino 1896-1973 *Baker 78, NewGrD 80*
Linnartz, Hans 1936- *IntWWM 77, -80*
Linnecare, Vera *WomWMM B*
Linney, Daniel A 1930- *BiE&WWA*
Linney, Romulus *NatPD[port], NotNAT*
Linnit, Sidney E d1956 *NotNAT B, WhThe*
Linow, Ivan *Film 2, ForYSC, TwYS*
Linscome, Sanford Abel 1931- *IntWWM 77, -80*
Linsky, Jeffrey James 1952- *AmSCAP 80*
Linstead, George Frederick 1908- *Baker 78, WhoMus 72*
Lintermans, Francois-Joseph 1808-1895 *Baker 78*
Linthicum, David H 1941- *ConAmC, IntWWM 77, -80*
Linton, Kent Randall 1947- *AmSCAP 80*
Linus *NewGrD 80*
Linville, Albert *WhoHol A*
Linville, Joanne *WhoHol A*
Linville, Larry *WhoHol A*
Linyova, Evgeniya 1854-1919 *NewGrD 80*
Lion, John 1944- *NotNAT*
Lion, Leon M 1879-1947 *IlWWBF, -A, NotNAT A, -B, WhScrn 77, WhThe, WhoHol B*
Lioncourt, Guy De 1885-1961 *Baker 78, NewGrD 80*
Lionel *NewGrD 80*
Lipatti, Constantin 1917-1950 *NewGrD 80*
Lipatti, Dinu 1917-1950 *Baker 78, BnBkM 80, MusMk, NewGrD 80*
Lipavsky, Josef 1772-1810 *NewGrD 80*
Lipawsky, Josef 1769-1810 *Baker 78*
Lipawsky, Joseph 1772-1810 *NewGrD 80*
Lipinski, Karol Jozef 1790-1861 *NewGrD 80*
Lipinsky, Carl 1790-1861 *Baker 78*
Lipkin, Malcolm Leyland 1932- *Baker 78, IntWWM 77, -80, NewGrD 80, WhoMus 72*
Lipkin, Seymour 1927- *WhoMus 72*
Lipkin, Stephen Barry 1941- *AmSCAP 80*
Lipkovska, Lydia 1884-1955 *Baker 78*
Lipkovskaya, Lydia 1882-1958 *NewGrD 80*
Lipkowska, Lydia 1882-1958 *NewGrD 80*
Lipman, Clara 1869-1952 *NotNAT B, WhThe, WhoStg 1906, -1908*
Lipman, Daniel *NatPD[port]*
Lipman, Harry *Film 2*
Lipman, Jerzy 1922- *DcFM, FilmEn, FilmgC, HalFC 80*
Lipovetsky, Leonidas *WhoMus 72*
Lipovsek, Marijan 1910- *NewGrD 80*
Lipowsky, Felix Joseph 1764-1842 *Baker 78, NewGrD 80*
Lipowsky, Thad Ferdinand 1738-1767 *Baker 78*
Lipowsky, Thaddaus Ferdinand 1738-1767 *NewGrD 80*
Lipp, Wilma 1925- *CmOp, NewGrD 80, WhoMus 72, WhoOp 76*
Lippard, John B 1919- *BiE&WWA*
Lipparini, Guglielmo *NewGrD 80*
Lipparino, Guglielmo *NewGrD 80*
Lippert, Marion Anna-Maria 1936- *WhoOp 76*
Lippert, Robert J, Jr. 1928- *IntMPA 77, -76, -78, -79, -80*
Lippert, Robert L 1909- *FilmgC, HalFC 80, IntMPA 77, -75, -76, WhoHrs 80*
Lippert, Robert L, Jr. 1928- *IntMPA 75*
Lipphardt, Walther 1906- *NewGrD 80*
Lippincott, David M 1925- *AmSCAP 66*
Lippincott, Gertrude 1913- *CnOxB, DancEn 78*
Lippius, Johannes 1585-1612 *NewGrD 80*
Lippman, Edward A 1920- *NewGrD 80*
Lippman, Joe 1915- *CmpEPM*
Lippman, Monroe 1905- *BiE&WWA, NotNAT*
Lippman, Sidney 1914- *AmSCAP 66, -80, CmpEPM*
Lippman, Susannah *WomWMM B*
Lippmann, Friedrich 1932- *IntWWM 77, -80, NewGrD 80*
Lippmann, Zilla *BiE&WWA, NotNAT*
Lippold, Klaus Eberhard 1938- *IntWWM 77, -80*
Lipps, Theodor 1851-1914 *Baker 78*
Liprott, Peggy *WomWMM*
Lipscomb, G D *BlkAmP*
Lipscomb, Helen 1921-1974 *AmSCAP 66, ConAmC*
Lipscomb, Mance 1895-1976 *BluesWW[port], NewGrD 80*
Lipscomb, W P 1887-1958 *FilmEn, HalFC 80*
Lipscomb, William Nunn, Jr. 1919- *IntWWM 77, -80*
Lipscomb, William Percy 1887-1958 *FilmgC, NotNAT B, WhThe*
Lipsett, Arthur *CreCan 2*
Lipsitz, Hilary J 1933- *AmSCAP 80*
Lipsius, Marie 1837-1927 *Baker 78, NewGrD 80*
Lipsky, Alexander *ConAmC*
Lipsky, David 1907- *BiE&WWA, NotNAT*
Lipsky, Oldrich 1924- *FilmEn*
Lipson, Melba 1901-1953 *WhScrn 74, -77*
Lipstein, Harold *WorEFlm*
Lipstone, Howard H *IntMPA 77, -75, -76, -78, -79, -80*
Liptak, David 1949- *CpmDNM 78, -79, -80*
Lipton, Celia 1923- *WhThe*
Lipton, David A 1906- *IntMPA 77, -75, -76, -78, -79, -80*
Lipton, George d1962 *NotNAT B*
Lipton, Harold Arlen 1911- *IntMPA 77, -75, -76, -78*
Lipton, James 1926- *AmSCAP 66, -80*
Lipton, Lawrence 1898-1975 *WhScrn 77*
Lipton, Lenny 1940- *AmSCAP 80*
Lipton, Martha 1915- *NewEOp 71*
Lipton, Peggy 1947- *BiDAmM, WhoHol A*
Lipton, Robert *WhoHol A*
Lipton, Sydney 1906- *WhoMus 72*
Lira Espejo, Eduardo 1912- *NewGrD 80*
Lirithier, Johannes *NewGrD 80*
Lirou, Jean Francois Espic, Chevalier De 1740-1806 *Baker 78*
Lisbon, Kenneth *AmSCAP 80*
Lisbona, Edward 1915- *AmSCAP 66, -80*
Liscano, Juan 1915- *NewGrD 80*
Lischka, Rainer 1942- *IntWWM 77, -80*
Lisenko, Nikolay Vital'yevich *NewGrD 80*
Lishin, Grigory 1854-1888 *Baker 78*
Lishner, Leon 1913- *WhoOp 76*
Lisi, Albert 1929- *AmSCAP 80*
Lisi, Verna *WhoHol A*
Lisi, Virna 1937- *FilmAG WE[port], FilmEn, FilmgC, ForYSC, HalFC 80, MotPP, MovMk*
Lisinski, Vatroslav 1819-1854 *Baker 78, NewGrD 80*
Lisitsyan, Pavel 1911- *CmOp, NewGrD 80*
Lisitzky, Ephram E d1962 *NotNAT B*
Lisk, Edward Stanley 1934- *IntWWM 77*
Liska, Zdenek 1922- *Baker 78*
L'isle, Alain De *NewGrD 80*
Lisle, Claude-Joseph Rouget De *NewGrD 80*
Lisle, Lucille *WhThe*
Lisley, John *OxMus*
Lismer, Arthur 1885-1969 *CreCan 2*
Lisowska, Hanna 1939- *WhoOp 76*
Lissa, Zofia 1908- *Baker 78, IntWWM 77, -80, NewGrD 80*

Lissauer, Fredric David 1945- *ConAmC*
Lissauer, Robert 1917- *AmSCAP 66, -80, ConAmC*
Lissenko, Nathalie *Film 2*
Lissenko, Nikolai 1842-1912 *Baker 78*
List, Emanuel 1886-1967 *NewGrD 80*
List, Emanuel 1891-1967 *Baker 78, MusSN[port], NewEOp 71*
List, Eugene 1918- *Baker 78, NewGrD 80*
List, Eugene 1921- *WhoMus 72*
List, Garrett *ConAmC*
List, Kurt 1913-1970 *Baker 78, BiDAmM*
Listemann, Bernard Friedrich Wilhelm 1841-1917 *BiDAmM*
Listemann, Bernhard 1841-1917 *Baker 78*
Listemann, Franz 1873-1930 *Baker 78, BiDAmM*
Listemann, Fritz 1839-1909 *Baker 78, BiDAmM*
Listemann, Paul 1871-1950 *Baker 78, BiDAmM*
Listenius, Nicolaus 1510?- *OxMus*
Listenius, Nikolaus 1510?- *NewGrD 80*
Lister, Craig L George 1950- *IntWWM 80*
Lister, Eve 1918- *WhThe*
Lister, Francis 1899-1951 *Film 2, FilmgC, HalFC 80, NotNAT B, WhScrn 74, -77, WhThe, WhoHol B*
Lister, Frank 1868-1917 *WhThe*
Lister, Lance 1901- *WhThe*
Lister, Laurier 1907- *WhoThe 72, -77*
Lister, Moira 1923- *FilmAG WE, FilmEn, FilmgC, HalFC 80, IlWWBF, IntMPA 77, -75, -76, -78, -79, -80, NotNAT A, WhoHol A, WhoThe 72, -77*
Lister, Rodney 1951- *ConAmC*
Liston, John 1776-1846 *NotNAT B, OxThe*
Liston, Melba Doretta 1926- *BiDAmM, BlkWAB[port], EncJzS 70*
Liston, Sonny 1932-1971 *WhScrn 77*
Liston, Victor 1838-1913 *NotNAT B, OxThe*
Liston, Virginia 1890?-1932? *BluesWW[port]*
Listov, Konstantin 1900- *Baker 78*
Liszcz, Kazimierz 1937- *IntWWM 77, -80*
Liszt, Ferenc 1811-1886 *CnOxB, NewGrD 80[port]*
Liszt, Ferencz 1811-1886 *BnBkM 80[port], OxMus*
Liszt, Franz 1811-1886 *Baker 78, BnBkM 80[port], CmpBCM, DancEn 78, DcCom 77[port], DcCom&M 79, GrComp[port], MusMk[port], NewEOp 71, NewGrD 80[port]*
Litaize, Gaston 1909- *Baker 78, BnBkM 80, NewGrD 80*
Litel, John 1892-1964 *ForYSC, MovMk*
Litel, John 1892-1972 *HolCA[port]*
Litel, John 1894-1972 *FilmEn, Vers A[port], WhScrn 77*
Litel, John 1895-1972 *Film 2, FilmgC, HalFC 80, WhoHol B*
Literes, Antonio 1673-1747 *NewGrD 80*
Literes Carrion, Antonio 1670?-1747 *Baker 78*
Litherland, Mildred 1916- *WhoMus 72*
Lithgow, Arthur W 1915- *BiE&WWA, NotNAT*
Lithgow, John 1945- *NotNAT*
Litinsky, Genrik 1901- *Baker 78*
Litkei, Andrea Fodor 1932- *AmSCAP 66, -80*
Litkei, Ervin 1921- *AmSCAP 66, -80*
Litle, Alev *WomWMM B*
Litman, Norman L 1917- *AmSCAP 80*
Litman, Steve *ConMuA 80B*
Litolff, Henry Charles 1818-1891 *Baker 78, MusMk, NewGrD 80, OxMus*
Litt, Jacob d1905 *NotNAT B*
Litta, Giulio 1822-1891 *Baker 78*
Litta, Marie VonElsner 1856-1883 *BiDAmM*
Littaur, David Allan 1925- *WhoMus 72*
Littee, Ramon 1905- *AmSCAP 80*
Littell, Robert 1896-1963 *NotNAT B, WhThe*
Litterell, Bob D 1949- *IntWWM 77*
Littkeman, Paul *NewGrD 80*
Little, Ann 1891- *Film 1, -2, TwYS*
Little, Billy 1895-1967 *WhScrn 74, -77, WhoHol B*
Little, Booker, Jr. 1938-1961 *BiDAmM, IlEncJ*
Little, C P d1914 *NotNAT B*
Little, Cleavon 1939- *DrBlPA, HalFC 80, MovMk, NotNAT, PlP&P A[port], WhoHol A, WhoThe 77*
Little, Don *AmSCAP 80*
Little, Dudley 1930- *AmSCAP 66, -80, BiDAmM*
Little, Florence Elizabeth 1911- *IntWWM 80*
Little, Francis E 1936- *IntWWM 77, -80*
Little, Frank 1936- *WhoOp 76*
Little, George 1920- *NewGrD 80*
Little, George A 1890-1946 *AmSCAP 66, -80*
Little, Gordon W Pawnee Bill 1860-1942 *WhScrn 77*
Little, Guy S, Jr. 1935- *BiE&WWA, NotNAT*
Little, Gwenlynn Lois 1937- *WhoMus 72, WhoOp 76*
Little, Jack 1900-1956 *AmSCAP 80*
Little, James F 1907-1969 *WhScrn 74, -77, WhoHol B*
Little, Jim *NewOrJ[port]*
Little, Little Jack d1956 *BgBands 74, WhoHol B*
Little, Little Jack 1900-1956 *AmSCAP 66, CmpEPM*
Little, Little Jack 1901-1956 *WhScrn 74, -77*
Little, Major Gordon W Pawnee Bill 1860-1942 *WhScrn 77*
Little, Pauline Mary 1942- *IntWWM 77, -80*
Little, Rich 1938- *JoeFr[port]*
Little, Richard Anthony 1948- *AmSCAP 80*
Little, Stuart W 1921- *BiE&WWA, NotNAT*
Little, Terence 1920- *BiE&WWA*
Little, Thomas F 1911- *IntMPA 75, -76*
Little, Vera Pearl *WhoOp 76*
Little, Weston Wilbur 1928- *EncJzS 70*
Little, William *NewGrD 80*
Little, William A 1929- *IntWWM 77, -80*
Little Anthony 1940- *DrBlPA*
Little Anthony And The Imperials *AmPS A, RkOn[port]*
Little Boy Blue *BluesWW[port]*
Little Bozo 1907-1952 *WhScrn 74, -77, WhoHol B*
Little Brother *BluesWW[port]*
Little Caesar And The Romans *RkOn*
Little Dippers, The *RkOn*
Little Esther *BluesWW[port]*
Little Esther Phillips 1935- *RkOn[port]*
Little Eva 1944- *AmPS A, RkOn*
Little Feat *ConMuA 80A, IlEncR[port]*
Little Henry *BluesWW[port]*
Little Hudson *BluesWW[port]*
Little Jack Little *AmPS B*
Little Jazz *NewGrD 80*
Little Joe *BluesWW[port]*
Little Joe And The Thrillers *RkOn*
Little Joey And The Flips *RkOn*
Little Johnny *BluesWW[port]*
Little Junior *BluesWW[port]*
Little Junior Parker *RkOn*
Little Laura *BluesWW[port]*
Little Lovin' Henry *BluesWW[port]*
Little Luther *BluesWW[port]*
Little Mack *BluesWW[port]*
Little Man *BluesWW[port]*
Little Milton 1934- *BluesWW[port], RkOn 2[port]*
Little Otis *BluesWW[port]*
Little Papa Joe *BluesWW[port]*
Little Papa Walter *BluesWW[port]*
Little Peggy March 1948- *RkOn[port]*
Little Ray *BluesWW[port]*
Little Richard *AmPS A, BluesWW[port], ConMuA 80A[port]*
Little Richard 1932- *RkOn[port]*
Little Richard 1935- *BiDAmM, DrBlPA*
Little River Band *RkOn 2[port]*
Little Sam *BluesWW[port]*
Little Sister *BluesWW[port], RkOn 2[port]*
Little Son *BluesWW[port]*
Little Son Joe *BluesWW[port]*
Little Sonny *BluesWW[port]*
Little Stevie Wonder *AmPS A*
Little T-Bone *BluesWW[port]*
Little Temple *BluesWW[port]*
Little Tich 1868-1928 *EncWT, NotNAT B, OxThe*
Little Walter *BluesWW[port]*
Little Walter 1930-1968 *NewGrD 80*
Little Walter 1930-1969 *BiDAmM*
Little Walter J *BluesWW[port]*
Little Walter Junior *BluesWW[port]*
Little Willie John 1937-1968 *RkOn[port]*
Little Wolf *BluesWW[port]*
Littledale, Richard d1951 *NotNAT B*
Littlefeather, Sacheen *WhoHol A*
Littlefied, Catherine 1905-1951 *CnOxB*
Littlefield, Catherine 1904-1951 *NotNAT B, WhThe*
Littlefield, Catherine 1908-1951 *DancEn 78*
Littlefield, Dorothie 1916-1952 *DancEn 78*
Littlefield, Emma 1883-1934 *NotNAT B, WhoStg 1908*
Littlefield, Lucian 1895-1959 *Film 2*
Littlefield, Lucien *MotPP*
Littlefield, Lucien 1895-1959 *Film 1, MovMk*
Littlefield, Lucien 1895-1960 *FilmEn, ForYSC, HalFC 80, HolCA[port], NotNAT B, TwYS, Vers A[port], WhScrn 74, -77, WhoHol B*
Littlefield, Lucien 1895-1966 *FilmgC*
Littlefield, Milton Smith 1864-1934 *BiDAmM*
Littlefield, Nancy *WomWMM, -B*
Littlefield, Willie 1931- *BluesWW[port]*
Littlejohn, David 1937- *ConAmTC*
Littlejohn, Dorothy *WomWMM B*
Littlejohn, Joan Anne 1937- *IntWWM 80*
Littlejohn, John 1931- *BiDAmM, BluesWW[port]*
Littlejohns, Frank 1914- *IntMPA 77, -75, -76*
Littler, Blanche 1899- *WhThe*
Littler, Sir Emile 1903- *EncMT, WhoThe 72, -77*
Littler, F R d1940 *NotNAT B*
Littler, Prince 1901-1973 *EncMT, WhThe*
Littleton *NewGrD 80*
Littleton, Betty Naomi 1938- *IntWWM 77*
Littleton, Billy Joe 1935- *AmSCAP 80*
Littlewood, Joan *BiE&WWA, CnThe, CroCD, WhoThe 72, -77, WomWMM*
Littlewood, Joan 1914- *EncWT, Ent, HalFC 80, OxThe*
Littlewood, Joan 1916- *FilmgC, OxFilm, PlP&P[port]*
Littlewood, Samuel Robinson 1875-1963 *WhThe*
Littman, Lynne *WomWMM A, -B*
Littman, Max 1862-1931 *EncWT*
Littman, Robert 1938- *IntMPA 77, -75, -76, -78*
Litto, George 1930- *IntMPA 77, -75, -76, -78, -79, -80*
Litton, James H 1934- *IntWWM 77, -80*
Litvak, Anatole 1902-1974 *AmFD, BiDFilm, -81, CmMov, DcFM, FilmEn, FilmgC, HalFC 80, MovMk[port], OxFilm, WhScrn 77, WorEFlm*
Litvak, Michael Anatole 1902- *IntMPA 75*
Litvinenko-Wohlgemut, Mariya 1895-1966 *NewGrD 80*
Litvinne, Felia 1860-1936 *CmOp, NewEOp 71*
Litvinne, Felia 1861-1936 *Baker 78, NewGrD 80*
Litz, Katherine 1918- *CmpGMD, CnOxB, DancEn 78*
Litzau, Johannes Barend 1822-1893 *Baker 78*
Litzmann, Berthold 1857-1926 *Baker 78*
Liu, Pan 190-?- *DcFM*
Liukko-Vaara, Eini Inkeri 1930- *WhoOp 76*
Liuzzi, Ferdinando 1884-1940 *NewGrD 80*
Liuzzi, Fernando 1884-1940 *Baker 78, NewGrD 80*
Livanov, Boris 1904-1972 *WhScrn 77*
Livanova, Tamara Nikolayevna 1909- *NewGrD 80*
LiVecche, George V 1914- *AmSCAP 66*
Liverati, Giovanni 1772-1846 *Baker 78, NewGrD 80*
Liveright, Horace Brisbin 1886-1933 *NotNAT B, OxThe, WhThe*
Livermore, Abiel Abbot 1811-1892 *BiDAmM*
Livermore, Sarah White 1789-1874 *BiDAmM*
Livesay, Dorothy 1909- *CreCan 2*
Livesay, Florence Randal 1874-1953 *CreCan 1*
Livesay, Meade A *AmSCAP 66*
Livesey, Barrie 1904- *WhThe*
Livesey, E Carter *WhThe*
Livesey, Jack 1901-1961 *FilmgC, HalFC 80, NotNAT B, WhScrn 74, -77, WhThe, WhoHol B*
Livesey, Roger 1906-1976 *FilmAG WE, FilmEn, Film 2, FilmgC, ForYSC, HalFC 80, IlWWBF[port], IntMPA 75,*

–76, *MovMk, PlP&P, WhoHol C, WhoThe 72, –77*
Livesey, Sam 1873-1936 *Film 2, FilmgC, HalFC 80, NotNAT B, WhScrn 74, –77, WhThe, WhoHol B*
Liviabella, Lino 1902-1964 *Baker 78*
Liviero, Antonio 1939- *WhoOp 76*
Livings, George 1945- *WhoOp 76*
Livings, Henry 1929- *CnMD SUP, CnThe, ConDr 73, –77, CroCD, EncWT, Ent, McGEWD, ModWD, REnWD[port], WhoThe 72, –77*
Livingston, Alan Wendell 1917- *AmSCAP 66, –80, ConMuA 80B*
Livingston, Barry *WhoHol A*
Livingston, Blanche *IntMPA 77, –75, –76, –78, –79, –80*
Livingston, Bob 1908- *Film 2, ForYSC*
Livingston, David 1925- *ConAmC*
Livingston, Deacon d1963 *NotNAT B*
Livingston, Fud 1906-1957 *CmpEPM, NewGrD 80, WhoJazz 72*
Livingston, Helen 1900- *AmSCAP 66, –80*
Livingston, Hugh Samuel, Jr. 1945- *AmSCAP 80*
Livingston, Jack *Film 1*
Livingston, Jay 1915- *AmPS, AmSCAP 66, –80, BiDAmM, BiE&WWA, CmpEPM, FilmEn, FilmgC, HalFC 80, IntMPA 77, –75, –76, –78, –79, –80, IntWWM 77, –80, NotNAT, PopAmC[port], PopAmC SUP, Sw&Ld C*
Livingston, Jefferson *IntMPA 77, –75, –76, –78, –79, –80*
Livingston, Jerry 1909- *AmPS, AmSCAP 66, –80, BiDAmM, CmpEPM, PopAmC SUP[port], Sw&Ld C*
Livingston, Joseph A 1906-1957 *AmSCAP 66, –80, NewGrD 80*
Livingston, Lillian 1935- *IntWWM 77*
Livingston, Margaret *MotPP*
Livingston, Margaret 1900- *FilmEn, ThFT[port], WhoHol A*
Livingston, Margaret 1902- *Film 1, –2, ForYSC, MovMk, TwYS*
Livingston, Mary *JoeFr*
Livingston, Myrtle A Smith 1901- *BlkAmP*
Livingston, Neil 1844-1886 *OxMus*
Livingston, Robert 1908- *FilmEn, WhoHol A*
Livingston, Robert H 1934- *NotNAT*
Livingston, Stanley 1950- *WhoHol A*
Livingston, Stephen Scott 1950- *AmSCAP 80*
Livingston, Ulysses 1912- *WhoJazz 72*
Livingston, William 1911- *AmSCAP 66, –80*
Livingstone, Belle *NotNAT A*
Livingstone, Ernest Felix 1915- *IntWWM 77, –80*
Livingstone, Jay 1915- *BestMus*
Livingstone, Laureen 1946- *IntWWM 80*
Livingstone, Mabel *AmSCAP 66*
Livingstone, Mary 1908- *What 5[port], WhoHol A*
Livingstone, Percy 1913- *IntMPA 77, –75, –76, –78, –79, –80*
Livingstone And Evans *BestMus*
Livio, Antoine 1937- *CnOxB*
Livius Andronicus 284?BC-204BC *Ent, OxThe, PlP&P[port]*
Livius Andronicus, Lucius *NewGrD 80*
Livry, Emma 1842-1862 *DancEn 78*
Livry, Emma 1842-1863 *CnOxB*
Livschitz, Alexander Grigorievich 1932- *CnOxB*
Livy 284?BC-204BC *EncWT*
Liza, Mona *Film 2*
Lizana, Florin J 1895-1967 *NewOrJ*
Lizardi, Joseph 1941- *NatPD[port]*
Lizzani, Carlo 1917- *FilmEn, OxFilm, WorEFlm*
Lizzani, Carlo 1922- *DcFM, FilmgC, HalFC 80*
Ljung, Viveka 1935- *CnOxB, DancEn 78*
Ljungberg, Gota 1893-1955 *Baker 78, MusSN[port], NewEOp 71, NewGrD 80*
Ljungdahl, Olle 1911- *IntWWM 77, –80*
Ljungh, Elizabeth Viola Lockerbie *CreCan 1*
Ljungh, Esse W 1904- *CreCan 1*
Llambias, Joe *NewOrJ*
Lland, Michael 1925?- *CnOxB*
Llanover, Lady *OxMus*
Lleo, Vicente 1870-1922 *NewGrD 80*
Llewellyn, Ernest Victor 1915- *WhoMus 72*
Llewellyn, Eve *Film 2*
Llewellyn, Fewlass 1866-1941 *Film 2, NotNAT B, WhThe, WhoHol B*
Llewellyn, Thomas Redvers 1901- *WhoMus 72*
Llewellyn, William Benjamin James 1925- *IntWWM 77, 80, WhoMus 72*
Llewelyn, Alfred H d1964 *NotNAT B*
Llissa, Francisco *NewGrD 80*
Llobet, Miguel 1875-1938 *Baker 78*
Llobet, Miguel 1878-1938 *NewGrD 80*
Llongueras Y Badia, Juan 1880-1953 *Baker 78*
Llords, Daniel *PupTheA SUP*
Llorens, Jose-Maria 1923- *IntWWM 77, –80*
Llorens, Julio 1904- *IntWWM 77*
Llorens Cistero, Jose Maria 1923- *NewGrD 80*
Lloveras, Juan *WhoOp 76*
Lloyd, A L 1908- *NewGrD 80*
Lloyd, Al 1884-1964 *NotNAT B, WhScrn 74, –77*
Lloyd, Alan 1943- *ConAmC*
Lloyd, Albert Lancaster 1908- *IntWWM 77, –80, WhoMus 72*
Lloyd, Albert S *Film 2*
Lloyd, Alice 1873-1949 *NotNAT B, WhScrn 77, WhThe*
Lloyd, Alison *Film 2*
Lloyd, Ashton *AmSCAP 80*
Lloyd, Caroline Parkhurst 1924- *ConAmC*
Lloyd, Charles *IlEncJ*
Lloyd, Charles 1938- *BiDAmM, EncJzS 70*
Lloyd, Charles Harford 1849-1919 *Baker 78, NewGrD 80, OxMus*
Lloyd, Charles M 1870-1948 *WhScrn 74, –77*
Lloyd, David Bellamy 1937- *IntWWM 77, –80, WhoMus 72*
Lloyd, David De 1883-1948 *NewGrD 80*
Lloyd, Doris d1968 *MotPP, WhThe, WhoHol B*
Lloyd, Doris 1896-1968 *HolCA[port]*
Lloyd, Doris 1899-1968 *FilmgC, HalFC 80, MovMk*
Lloyd, Doris 1900-1968 *FilmEn, Film 2, ForYSC, ThFT[port], TwYS, WhScrn 74, –77*
Lloyd, Edward 1845-1927 *NewGrD 80*
Lloyd, Ethel *Film 1*
Lloyd, Euan 1923- *FilmgC, HalFC 80, IntMPA 77, –75, –76, –78, –79, –80*
Lloyd, Florence 1876- *WhThe*
Lloyd, Frank 1887-1960 *FilmgC, HalFC 80*
Lloyd, Frank 1888-1960 *FilmEn, MovMk*
Lloyd, Frank 1889-1960 *AmFD, BiDFilm, –81, CmMov, DcFM, Film 1, NewYTET, OxFilm, TwYS A, WhScrn 74, –77, WhoHol B, WorEFlm*
Lloyd, Frederick William 1880-1949 *NotNAT B, WhScrn 74, –77, WhThe, WhoHol B*
Lloyd, Gabriel Frederic Garnons 1918- *IntWWM 77, –80, WhoMus 72*
Lloyd, Gaylord *Film 2*
Lloyd, George 1897- *Vers B[port]*
Lloyd, George 1913- *Baker 78, IntWWM 77, –80, NewGrD 80, OxMus*
Lloyd, Gerald Joseph 1938- *AmSCAP 80, ConAmC*
Lloyd, Gladys 1896-1971 *WhScrn 74, –77, WhoHol B*
Lloyd, Grace d1961 *NotNAT B*
Lloyd, Gweneth 1901- *CnOxB, CreCan 1, DancEn 78*
Lloyd, Harold d1971 *GrMovC[port]*
Lloyd, Harold 1893-1971 *BiDFilm, –81, CmMov, DcFM, FilmEn, Film 1, –2, FilmgC, ForYSC, Funs[port], HalFC 80[port], JoeFr[port], MotPP, MovMk[port], OxFilm, TwYS, WhScrn 74, –77, WhoHol B*
Lloyd, Harold 1894-1971 *What 2[port], WorEFlm[port]*
Lloyd, Harold, Jr. 1931-1971 *ForYSC, WhScrn 74, –77, WhoHol B*
Lloyd, Jack 1922-1976 *AmSCAP 66, –80*
Lloyd, John d1944 *NotNAT B, WhoHol B*
Lloyd, John 1475?-1523 *NewGrD 80*
Lloyd, John Ambrose 1815-1874 *OxMus*
Lloyd, John Morgan 1880-1960 *OxMus*
Lloyd, John Robert 1920- *BiE&WWA, NotNAT*
Lloyd, Llewellyn S 1876-1956 *NewGrD 80*
Lloyd, Llewelyn Southworth 1876-1956 *OxMus*
Lloyd, Margaret 1887-1960 *CnOxB, DancEn 78*
Lloyd, Marie 1870-1922 *EncWT, Ent, NotNAT A, –B, OxThe, PlP&P, WhThe*
Lloyd, Maude 1908- *CnOxB, DancEn 78*
Lloyd, Michael J 1948- *AmSCAP 66, –80, ConMuA 80B*
Lloyd, Norman 1909- *AmSCAP 66, –80, ConAmC, DancEn 78, DcCM*
Lloyd, Norman 1914- *BiE&WWA, FilmEn, FilmgC, HalFC 80, IntMPA 77, –75, –76, –78, –79, –80, NewYTET, NotNAT, Vers A[port], WhoHol A*
Lloyd, Patricia d1969 *WhoHol B*
Lloyd, Peter *WhoMus 72*
Lloyd, Powell 1900- *WhoMus 72*
Lloyd, Robert Andrew 1940- *IntWWM 77, –80, WhoOp 76*
Lloyd, Robin *WomWMM B*
Lloyd, Rollo 1883-1938 *WhScrn 74, –77, WhoHol B*
Lloyd, Rosie 1897-1944 *NotNAT B, WhThe*
Lloyd, Russell 1915- *HalFC 80*
Lloyd, Sherman *WhoHol A*
Lloyd, Sue 1939- *FilmgC, HalFC 80, IlWWBF, WhoHol A*
Lloyd, Violet 1879- *WhThe*
Lloyd, William *Film 1*
Lloyd-Jones, David 1934- *IntWWM 77, –80, NewGrD 80, WhoMus 72*
Lloyd-Pack, Charles 1905- *FilmgC, HalFC 80*
Lloyd Webber, Andrew 1948- *NewGrD 80, WhoThe 77*
Lloyd Webber, Jean Hermione 1922- *WhoMus 72*
Lloyd Webber, Julian 1951- *IntWWM 77, –80*
Lloyd Webber, William Southcombe 1914- *IntWWM 80, WhoMus 72*
Llull, Ramon *NewGrD 80*
Llussa, Francisco *NewGrD 80*
Loach, Ken 1936- *FilmgC, HalFC 80, IlWWBF, OxFilm*
Loader, A McLeod 1869- *WhThe*
Loader, Rosa *WhThe*
Loback, Marvin 1896-1938 *WhScrn 74, WhoHol B*
Loback, Marvin 1898-1938 *WhScrn 77*
Lobaczewska, Stefania 1888-1963 *NewGrD 80*
Loban, Maurice *WhoMus 72*
Lobarsky, Anat *WomWMM*
Lobaugh, Harold Bruce 1930- *IntWWM 77, –80*
Lobe, Friedrich *Film 2*
Lobe, Johann Christian 1797-1881 *Baker 78, NewGrD 80*
Loberg, Per 1942- *IntWWM 80*
LoBianco, Tony *HalFC 80, IntMPA 79, –80, WhoHol A*
Lobingier, Christopher Crumay 1944- *ConAmC*
Lobkovic *NewGrD 80*
Lobkowicz *NewGrD 80*
Lobkowitz *NewGrD 80*
Lobkowitz, Ferdinand Filipp Josef 1724-1784 *NewGrD 80*
Lobkowitz, Ferdinand Josef Jan 1797-1868 *NewGrD 80*
Lobkowitz, Ferdinand Joseph Johann 1797-1868 *NewGrD 80*
Lobkowitz, Ferdinand Philipp Joseph 1724-1784 *NewGrD 80*
Lobkowitz, Filipp Hyacint 1680-1734 *NewGrD 80*
Lobkowitz, Prince Franz Joseph Von 1772-1816 *Baker 78*
Lobkowitz, Josef Frantisek Maximilian 1772-1816 *NewGrD 80*
Lobkowitz, Joseph Franz Maximilian 1772-1816 *NewGrD 80*
Lobkowitz, Juan Caramuel Y *NewGrD 80*
Lobkowitz, Philipp Hyacinth 1680-1734 *NewGrD 80*
Lobo 1943- *RkOn 2[port]*
Lobo, Alonso 1555?-1617 *NewGrD 80*
Lobo, Duarte 1565?-1646 *Baker 78, NewGrD 80*
Lobo, Elias Alvares 1834-1901 *NewGrD 80*
Lobo DeBorja, Alonso 1555?-1617 *NewGrD 80*
Loboda, Samuel R 1916-1977 *AmSCAP 66, –80,*

ConAmC A
LoBuono, John A 1929- *AmSCAP 66*
Lobuono, John Anthony 1930- *AmSCAP 80*
Lobwasser, Ambrosius 1515-1585 *NewGrD 80*
Lobwasser, Ambrosius 1515-1587 *OxMus*
Locante, Sam *WhoHol A*
Locascio, Michael *PlP&P*
LoCascio, Salvatore *PupTheA*
Locatelli, Basileo d1650 *OxThe*
Locatelli, Domenico 1613-1671 *OxThe*
Locatelli, Giovanni Battista 1713-1790? *NewGrD 80*
Locatelli, Joseph J 1934- *BiDAmM*
Locatelli, Luisa Gabrielli *OxThe*
Locatelli, Pietro 1695-1764 *Baker 78, BnBkM 80, GrComp[port], MusMk, NewGrD 80[port], OxMus*
Locatello, Gasparo *NewGrD 80*
Locatello, Giovanni Battista *NewGrD 80*
Loccatello, Giovanni Battista *NewGrD 80*
L'Occhialino *NewGrD 80*
Lochemburgho, Johannes *NewGrD 80*
Locher, Felix 1882-1969 *WhScrn 74, -77, WhoHol B*
Lochhead, Douglas Grant 1922- *CreCan 2*
Lochhead, Kenneth Campbell 1926- *CreCan 1*
Lochon, Charles 1760?-1817? *NewGrD 80*
Lochon, Jacques-Francois 1660?- *NewGrD 80*
Lock, Matthew 1621?-1677 *NewGrD 80*
Lock, William Rowland 1932- *IntWWM 77, -80*
Locke, Eddie 1930- *EncJzS 70*
Locke, Edward 1869-1945 *NotNAT B, WhThe*
Locke, Edward 1930- *EncJzS 70*
Locke, Harry *WhoHol A*
Locke, Jeannine *WomWMM*
Locke, John *OxMus*
Locke, Katharine *WhoHol A*
Locke, Matthew 1621?-1677 *NewGrD 80*
Locke, Matthew 1630-1677 *Baker 78, BnBkM 80, GrComp[port], MusMk, OxMus*
Locke, Ralph 1949- *IntWWM 80*
Locke, Robinson 1856-1920 *NotNAT B*
Locke, Sam 1917- *BiE&WWA, NotNAT*
Locke, Sondra *WhoHol A*
Locke, Sondra 1946- *ForYSC*
Locke, Sondra 1947- *HalFC 80*
Locke, Terrence *WhoHol A*
Locke, Vivia 1917- *BiE&WWA*
Locke, Will H d1950 *NotNAT B*
Locke, William J *Film 2*
Locke, William John 1863-1930 *NotNAT B, WhThe*
Lockenburg, Jhanj d1591? *NewGrD 80*
Lockenburg, Johannes d1591? *NewGrD 80*
Locker, Alfred 1922- *IntWWM 77*
Lockerbee, Beth 1915-1968 *WhoHol B*
Lockerbie, Beth 1915-1968 *CreCan 1*
Lockerbie, Elizabeth Viola 1915-1968 *CreCan 1*
Lockett, David Robert 1951- *IntWWM 77, -80*
Lockett, Louis d1964 *NotNAT B*
Lockhart, Anna *Film 2*
Lockhart, Anne *WhoHol A*
Lockhart, Calvin 1934- *DrBlPA, FilmgC, HalFC 80, WhoHol A*
Lockhart, Eugene 1891-1957 *AmSCAP 66, -80*
Lockhart, Gene 1891-1957 *FilmEn, Film 2, FilmgC, ForYSC, HalFC 80, HolCA[port], MotPP, MovMk[port], NotNAT B, WhScrn 74, -77, WhThe, WhoHol B*
Lockhart, Gene 1891-1959 *Vers A[port]*
Lockhart, James Lawrence 1930- *IntWWM 77, -80, NewGrD 80, WhoMus 72, WhoOp 76*
Lockhart, John *Film 2*
Lockhart, June 1925- *BiE&WWA, FilmEn, FilmgC, ForYSC, HalFC 80, IntMPA 77, -75, -76, -78, -79, -80, MotPP, MovMk, NotNAT, WhoHol A*
Lockhart, Kathleen 1893-1978 *HalFC 80, WhoHol A*
Lockhart, Kathleen 1925-1978 *ForYSC*
Lockhart, Ronald Stuart 1946- *AmSCAP 80*
Lockhart, Tim 1930-1963 *WhScrn 74, -77*
Locklair, Dan Steven 1949- *AmSCAP 80, CpmDNM 79, -80, ConAmC, IntWWM 77, -80*
Locklear, Lieutenant 1891-1920 *WhoHol B*
Locklear, Omar 1891-1920 *WhScrn 74, -77*
Locklin, Hank 1918- *CounME 74[port], -74A, EncFCWM 69, IlEncCM[port], RkOn*
Locklin, Henry 1918- *BiDAmM*
Lockney, John P *Film 1, -2*
Lockridge, Richard 1898- *WhThe*
Lockshin, Florence Levin 1910- *ConAmC*
Lockspeiser, Edward 1905-1973 *Baker 78, NewGrD 80, WhoMus 72*
Lockton, Joan 1901- *WhThe*
Lockton, Joan 1903- *IlWWBF*
Lockwood, Alexander *WhoHol A*
Lockwood, Anna Ferguson 1939- *Baker 78, WhoMus 72*
Lockwood, Annea Ferguson 1939- *CpmDNM 79*
Lockwood, Arthur H 1900- *IntMPA 77, -75, -76, -78, -79*
Lockwood, Carolyn 1932- *BiE&WWA*
Lockwood, Gary 1937- *FilmEn, FilmgC, ForYSC, HalFC 80, IntMPA 77, -75, -76, -78, -79, -80, MotPP, WhoHol A, WhoHrs 80*
Lockwood, Harold 1887-1918 *FilmEn, NotNAT B, WhScrn 77, WhoHol B*
Lockwood, Harold 1887-1919 *Film 1, MotPP, TwYS*
Lockwood, Julia 1941- *FilmgC, HalFC 80, IntMPA 77, -75, -76, -78, -79, -80, WhoHol A*
Lockwood, King 1898-1971 *WhScrn 74, -77, WhoHol B*
Lockwood, Larry Paul 1943- *AmSCAP 80, CpmDNM 75, -76, -77, -78, -79, -80, ConAmC*
Lockwood, Lewis 1930- *NewGrD 80*
Lockwood, Margaret 1911- *IlWWBF[port], -A[port]*
Lockwood, Margaret 1916- *CmMov, FilmAG WE, FilmEn, FilmgC, ForYSC, HalFC 80[port], IntMPA 77, -75, -76, -78, -79, -80, MotPP, MovMk[port], OxFilm, ThFT[port], WhoHol A, WhoThe 72, -77, WorEFlm*
Lockwood, Normand 1906- *Baker 78, BiDAmM, ConAmC, DcCM, IntWWM 77, -80, NewGrD 80, WhoMus 72*
Lockwood, Ralph Gregory 1942- *IntWWM 77, -80*
Lockwood, Robert, Jr. 1915- *BiDAmM, BluesWW[port]*
Lockwood, Roger 1936- *IntMPA 77, -76, -78, -79, -80*
Lockyer, Malcolm N *WhoMus 72*
LoConti, Hank *ConMuA 80B*
Loconto, Francis Xavier 1931- *AmSCAP 66*
Loden, Barbara 1936- *BiDFilm, -81, BiE&WWA, HalFC 80, IntMPA 77, -75, -76, -78, -79, -80, NotNAT, OxFilm, WhoHol A, WomWMM*
Lodeon, Andre Maria Marcel 1928- *IntWWM 80*
Lodeon, Andre Marie Marcel 1928- *IntWWM 77*
Loder *NewGrD 80*
Loder, Basil 1885- *WhThe*
Loder, Edward James 1813-1865 *NewGrD 80, OxMus*
Loder, George 1816-1868 *NewGrD 80, NotNAT B*
Loder, John 1898- *FilmEn, Film 2, FilmgC, ForYSC, HalFC 80, IlWWBF[port], -A, MotPP, MovMk, What 4[port], WhoHol A*
Loder, John David 1788-1846 *NewGrD 80*
Loder, Kate 1825-1904 *NewGrD 80*
Loder, Ted *Film 2*
Lodge, David 1922?- *FilmgC, HalFC 80, WhoHol A*
Lodge, Jean *WhoHol A*
Lodge, John Davis 1903- *BiE&WWA, FilmEn, FilmgC, ForYSC, HalFC 80, WhoHol A*
Lodge, John Ellerton *NewGrD 80*
Lodge, Sir Oliver Joseph 1851-1940 *OxMus*
Lodge, Ruth 1914- *WhThe*
Lodge, Thomas 1558?-1625 *CnThe, Ent, PlP&P*
Lodi, Pietro Da *NewGrD 80*
Lodi, Theodore *Film 2*
Lodice, Don 1919- *AmSCAP 66, -80*
Lodijensky, General *Film 2*
Lodizhensky, Nikolay Nikolayevich 1843-1916 *NewGrD 80*
Lods, Jean 1903- *DcFM, WorEFlm*
Lodwick *NewGrD 80*
Lodzia Z Kepy, Jan 1300?-1346 *NewGrD 80*
Loeb, Arthur L 1923- *IntWWM 77, -80*
Loeb, David J 1939- *AmSCAP 80, ConAmC*
Loeb, Janice *WomWMM B*
Loeb, John Jacob 1910-1970 *AmSCAP 66, -80, Baker 78, CmpEPM*
Loeb, Philip 1894-1955 *HalFC 80, NotNAT B, WhScrn 74, -77, WhThe, WhoHol B*
Loeb, Steven M 1951- *AmSCAP 80*
Loedel, Adi 1937-1955 *WhScrn 74, -77*
Loeffelholz VonColberg, Christoph 1572-1619 *NewGrD 80*
Loeffler, Arthur 1894- *BiDAmM*
Loeffler, Charles Martin 1861-1935 *Baker 78, BiDAmM, BnBkM 80, CompSN[port], DcCom&M 79, NewGrD 80, OxMus*
Loeffler, Louis *IntMPA 77, -75, -76, -78, -79, -80*
Loehner-Beda, Doctor d1939 *NotNAT B*
Loehner-Beda, Fritz 1883-1942 *AmSCAP 66, -80*
Loeillet *NewGrD 80*
Loeillet, Etienne Joseph 1715-1797 *NewGrD 80*
Loeillet, Jacob 1685-1748 *NewGrD 80*
Loeillet, Jacques 1685-1746 *Baker 78*
Loeillet, Jacques 1685-1748 *NewGrD 80, OxMus*
Loeillet, Jean-Baptiste 1680-1730 *Baker 78, GrComp, NewGrD 80*
Loeillet, Jean Baptiste 1688-1720? *NewGrD 80, OxMus*
Loeillet, John 1680-1730 *Baker 78, OxMus*
Loeillet, Pierre 1674-1743 *NewGrD 80*
Loeillet, Pierre Noel 1651-1735 *NewGrD 80*
Loeillet, Pieter 1651-1735 *NewGrD 80*
Loer, Adam *NewGrD 80*
Loes, Harry Dixon 1892-1965 *AmSCAP 66, -80*
Loeschhorn, Albert *Baker 78*
Loeschhorn, Carl Albert 1819-1905 *NewGrD 80*
Loesser, Arthur 1894-1969 *Baker 78*
Loesser, Frank 1910-1969 *AmPS, AmSCAP 66, -80, Baker 78, BestMus, BiDAmM, BiE&WWA, CmpEPM, ConAmC, EncMT, EncWT, Ent, FilmEn, FilmgC, HalFC 80, MusMk, NewCBMT, NewGrD 80, NotNAT B, PlP&P, PopAmC[port], PopAmC SUP, Sw&Ld C, WhScrn 74, -77, WhThe, WhoHol B*
Loesser, Lynn *BiE&WWA, NotNAT*
Loetti, Gemignano *NewGrD 80*
Loevendie, Johannes Theodorus 1930- *IntWWM 77*
Loevendie, Theo 1930- *Baker 78, IntWWM 80*
Loevensohn, Marix 1880-1943 *Baker 78*
Loevinger, Lee *NewYTET*
Loew, Arthur M 1897- *IntMPA 77, -75, -76*
Loew, Marcus 1870-1927 *DcFM, FilmEn, FilmgC, HalFC 80, MGM A[port], NotNAT B, OxFilm, WorEFlm*
Loewe, Carl 1796-1869 *Baker 78, DcCom 77, MusMk, NewGrD 80[port], OxMus*
Loewe, Ferdinand *Baker 78*
Loewe, Frederick *FilmEn, NewCBMT*
Loewe, Frederick 1901- *AmSCAP 80, BiE&WWA, FilmgC, HalFC 80, WhoThe 77*
Loewe, Frederick 1904- *AmPS, AmSCAP 66, Baker 78, BestMus, BiDAmM, CmpEPM, ConAmC, EncMT, EncWT, IntMPA 77, -76, -78, -79, -80, MusMk, NewCBMT, NewGrD 80, PlP&P, PopAmC[port], PopAmC SUP*
Loewe, Karl 1796-1869 *CmpBCM, GrComp[port]*
Loewe, Myra 1929- *WhoMus 72*
Loewenberg, Alfred 1902-1949 *NewGrD 80, OxMus*
Loewenberg, Alfred 1902-1950 *Baker 78*
Loewengard, Max Julius 1860-1915 *Baker 78*
Loewenguth, Alfred 1911- *NewGrD 80, WhoMus 72*
Loewenstein, Herbert *NewGrD 80*
Loewy, Benjamin Wilfred 1915- *AmSCAP 80*

Loff, Jeanette 1906-1942 *Film 2, ForYSC, MotPP, TwYS, WhScrn 74, -77, WhoHol B*
Loffeloth, Johann Matthaus *NewGrD 80*
Loffler, Peter 1926- *WhoOp 76*
Lofgren, Marianne 1910-1957 *WhScrn 77*
Lofgren, Nils *AmSCAP 80, ConMuA 80A, IlEncR[port]*
Loforese, Angelo 1920- *WhoOp 76*
Loft, Abram 1922- *IntWWM 77, -80*
Loft, Arthur 1895?- *HalFC 80*
Loft, Arthur 1897-1947 *WhScrn 77*
Lofthouse, Charles Thornton 1895-1974 *NewGrD 80, WhoMus 72*
Lofting, Hugh 1886-1947 *DcPup*
Lofton, Clarence 1887-1957 *BluesWW[port]*
Lofton, Clarence 1896-1956 *BiDAmM*
Lofton, Cripple Clarence 1896-1957 *WhoJazz 72*
Lofton, Lawrence Ellis 1930- *BiDAmM, EncJzS 70*
Lofton, Tricky 1930- *EncJzS 70*
Loftus, Cecilia 1876-1943 *Film 1, FilmgC, HalFC 80, WhScrn 74, -77, WhoHol B, WhoStg 1906, -1908*
Loftus, Celia 1876-1943 *ForYSC*
Loftus, Cissie 1876-1943 *NotNAT A, OxThe*
Loftus, John 1901- *AmSCAP 66*
Loftus, Kitty 1867-1927 *NotNAT B, WhThe*
Loftus, Marie 1857-1940 *NotNAT B, WhThe*
Loftus, Marie Cecilia 1876-1943 *NotNAT B, WhThe*
Loftus, William C 1862-1931 *WhScrn 74, -77*
Logan, Campbell 1910- *IntMPA 77, -75, -76, -78, -79, -80*
Logan, Cornelius A 1806-1853 *NotNAT B*
Logan, Ella d1969 *AmPS B*
Logan, Ella 1910-1969 *WhThe*
Logan, Ella 1913-1969 *BiE&WWA, CmpEPM, EncMT, ForYSC, MotPP, NotNAT B, What 1[port], WhScrn 74, -77, WhoHol B*
Logan, Frederick Knight 1871-1928 *AmSCAP 66, -80, Baker 78, BiDAmM, ConAmC*
Logan, Giuseppi 1935- *BiDAmM*
Logan, Gwendolyn *Film 2*
Logan, Horace *EncFCWM 69*
Logan, Jacqueline 1900- *Film 2, ForYSC, TwYS*
Logan, Jacqueline 1901- *FilmEn, ThFT[port]*
Logan, Jacqueline 1903?- *MovMk*
Logan, Jacqueline 1904- *What 2[port], WhoHol A*
Logan, James *WhoHol A*
Logan, Janet 1919-1965 *WhScrn 77*
Logan, Jimmy 1928- *IntMPA 77, -75, -76, -78, -79, -80*
Logan, John 1924-1972 *WhScrn 77*
Logan, Joshua 1908- *BestMus, BiDAmM, BiDFilm, -81, BiE&WWA, CmMov, ConDr 73, -77D, DcFM, EncMT, EncWT, Ent, FilmEn, FilmgC, HalFC 80, IntMPA 77, -75, -76, -78, -79, -80, ModWD, MovMk[port], NewCBMT, NotNAT, OxFilm, WhoThe 72, -77, WorEFlm*
Logan, May d1969 *WhoHol B*
Logan, Nedda Harrigan 1900?- *BiE&WWA, NotNAT*
Logan, Olive 1839-1909 *NotNAT A, -B*
Logan, Robert 1926- *ConAmC*
Logan, Stanley 1885-1953 *NotNAT B, WhScrn 74, -77, WhThe, WhoHol B*
Logan, Virginia Knight 1850-1940 *AmSCAP 66, -80*
Logan, Wendell Morris 1940- *BiDAmM, ConAmC*
Logar, Mihovil 1902- *Baker 78, NewGrD 80*
Loggenburg, Dudley Von 1945- *CnOxB*
Loggia, Robert 1930- *FilmgC, ForYSC, HalFC 80, WhoHol A*
Loggins, Dave 1947- *RkOn 2[port]*
Loggins, David A 1947- *AmSCAP 80*
Loggins, Kenneth Clarke 1947- *AmSCAP 80*
Loggins And Messina *ConMuA 80A[port], IlEncR, RkOn 2[port]*
Logie-Smith, George 1914- *WhoMus 72*
Logier, Johann Bernard 1777-1846 *OxMus*
Logier, Johann Bernhard 1777-1846 *Baker 78, NewGrD 80*
Logothetis, Anestis 1921- *Baker 78, DcCM, IntWWM 77, -80, NewGrD 80*
Logrenia, Professor *PupTheA*
Logroscino, Nicola 1698- *Baker 78*
Logroscino, Nicola 1698-1765? *NewEOp 71*
Logroscino, Nicola Bonifacio 1698-1767? *NewGrD 80*
Logue, Christopher 1926- *CnMD, ModWD*
Logue, Joan Anne 1936- *IntWWM 80*
Lohelius, Joannes *NewGrD 80*
Lohenstein, Daniel Caspar Von 1635-1683 *OxThe*
Lohet, Simon 1550?-1611 *NewGrD 80*
Lohlein, Georg Simon 1725-1781 *Baker 78, NewGrD 80*
Lohman, Alwina Valleria *NewGrD 80*
Lohman, Bob *PupTheA*
Lohman, Zalla 1906-1967 *WhScrn 74, -77, WhoHol B*
Lohmann, Heinz Friedhelm 1934- *IntWWM 77, -80*
Lohmann, Peter 1833-1907 *Baker 78*
Lohner, Johann 1645-1705 *NewGrD 80*
Lohoefer, Evelyn 1921- *AmSCAP 66, ConAmC A*
Lohr, Hermann 1871-1943 *NewGrD 80*
Lohr, Lenox Riley d1968 *NewYTET*
Lohr, Marie 1890-1975 *FilmgC, HalFC 80, IntMPA 75, PlP&P, WhScrn 77, WhThe, WhoHol C, WhoThe 72*
Lohr, Michael 1591-1654 *NewGrD 80*
Lohse, Fred 1908- *IntWWM 77, -80, NewGrD 80*
Lohse, Otto 1858-1925 *Baker 78, NewGrD 80*
Lohse, Otto 1859-1925 *NewEOp 71*
Loigu, Valdeko 1911- *AmSCAP 66*
Loiselle, Helene 1928- *CreCan 2*
Loizeaux, Christine *WomWMM B*
Lojewski, Harry Victor 1917- *AmSCAP 66, ConAmC*
Loke, Mele *AmSCAP 80*
Lola And Armida *Film 2*
Lolita *RkOn[port]*
Lolli, Antonio 1725?-1802 *NewGrD 80[port]*
Lolli, Antonio 1730?-1802 *Baker 78*
Lollobrigida, Gina *MotPP*
Lollobrigida, Gina 1927- *BiDFilm, -81, FilmAG WE[port], FilmEn, FilmgC, HalFC 80, OxFilm, WhoHol A, WorEFlm[port]*
Lollobrigida, Gina 1928- *ForYSC, IntMPA 77, -75, -76, -78, -79, -80, MovMk[port]*
Lom, Herbert 1917- *CmMov, FilmAG WE, FilmEn, FilmgC, ForYSC, HalFC 80, IlWWBF[port], IntMPA 77, -75, -76, -78, -79, -80, MotPP, MovMk, WhThe, WhoHol A, WhoHrs 80[port]*
Lomakin, Gavriil Yakimovich 1812-1885 *Baker 78, NewGrD 80*
Loman, Judy 1936- *CreCan 1*
Loman, Jules 1910-1957 *AmSCAP 66, -80*
Lomani, Borys Grzegorz 1893- *IntWWM 77*
Lomas, Herbert 1887-1961 *FilmgC, HalFC 80, PlP&P, WhScrn 74, -77, WhThe, WhoHol B*
Lomas, Jack M 1911-1959 *WhScrn 74, -77, WhoHol B*
Lomax, Alan 1915- *Baker 78, BiDAmM, EncFCWM 69, NewGrD 80*
Lomax, Jackie *ConMuA 80A*
Lomax, John Avery *OxMus*
Lomax, John Avery 1867-1948 *Baker 78*
Lomax, John Avery 1875-1948 *BiDAmM, EncFCWM 69*
Lomax, Louis 1922-1970 *WhScrn 77*
Lomax, Pearl Cleage 1948- *BlkAmP*
Lomazzo, Filippo *NewGrD 80*
Lombard, Alain 1940- *IntWWM 77, -80, NewEOp 71, NewGrD 80, WhoOp 76*
Lombard, Carole d1942 *MotPP, WhoHol B*
Lombard, Carole 1908-1942 *BiDFilm, -81, FilmEn, FilmgC, HalFC 80[port], MovMk[port], OxFilm, ThFT[port], WorEFlm[port]*
Lombard, Carole 1909-1942 *Film 2, ForYSC, NotNAT B, TwYS, WhScrn 74, -77*
Lombard, Harry d1963 *NotNAT B*
Lombardi, Dillo *Film 2*
Lombardi, Nilson 1926- *IntWWM 77, -80*
Lombardini, Antonio *NewGrD 80*
Lombardini, Maddalena Laura *NewGrD 80*
Lombardo, Adele J 1934- *AmSCAP 80*
Lombardo, Anthony M 1905- *AmSCAP 66, -80*
Lombardo, Bartolomeo *NewGrD 80*
Lombardo, Carmen d1971 *WhoHol B*
Lombardo, Carmen 1903-1971 *AmSCAP 66, -80, Baker 78, BiDAmM, CmpEPM*
Lombardo, Carmen 1904-1971 *WhScrn 74, -77*
Lombardo, Gaetano Albert 1902- *CreCan 1*
Lombardo, Goffredo 1920- *IntMPA 77, -75, -76, -78, -79, -80*
Lombardo, Guy 1902-1977 *AmPS A, -B, Baker 78, BgBands 74[port], BiDAmM, BiE&WWA, CmpEPM, CreCan 1, NotNAT*
Lombardo, Mario 1931- *AmSCAP 66, -80, ConAmC*
Lombardo, Robert 1932- *ConAmC, DcCM, IntWWM 77, -80*
Lombardo, Sandra B 1936- *IntWWM 77*
Lomita, Sol 1937- *IntMPA 77, -78, -79, -80*
Lommel, Daniel 1943- *CnOxB*
Lommi, Enrique 1924- *CnOxB, DancEn 78*
Lomnicki, Jan 1929- *DcFM*
Lomnicki, Jan 1930- *FilmEn*
Lomnicki, Tadeusz 1925- *FilmEn*
Lomon, Ruth 1930- *CpmDNM 80, IntWWM 80*
Lonati, Carlo Ambrogio 1645?-1715? *NewGrD 80*
Loncar, Beba *WhoHol A*
Lonchampt, Jacques 1925- *NewGrD 80*
Loncin, Jean De 1575?-1593 *NewGrD 80*
Londariti, Francesco *NewGrD 80*
Londeix, Jean-Marie 1932- *IntWWM 77, -80*
London, Bishops Of *OxMus*
London, Babe 1901- *Film 2, TwYS, WhoHol A*
London, Barbara *WhoHol A*
London, Edwin 1929- *AmSCAP 80, ConAmC, DcCM, IntWWM 77, -80*
London, Ernest A d1964 *NotNAT B*
London, George 1919?- *Baker 78, BnBkM 80*
London, George 1920- *BiDAmM, CmOp, CreCan 1, IntWWM 77, -80, MusSN[port], NewGrD 80, WhoMus 72, WhoOp 76*
London, George 1921- *NewEOp 71*
London, Jack 1876-1916 *FilmgC, HalFC 80, NotNAT B*
London, Jack 1905-1966 *WhScrn 74, -77*
London, Joe *AmSCAP 80*
London, Julie 1926- *AmPS A, -B, AmSCAP 66, -80, BiDAmM, CmpEPM, FilmEn, FilmgC, ForYSC, HalFC 80, IntMPA 77, -75, -76, -78, -79, -80, MotPP, MovMk, RkOn[port], WhoHol A*
London, Laurie *RkOn*
London, Milton H 1916- *IntMPA 77, -75, -76, -78, -79, -80*
London, Roy *NatPD[port]*
London, S J 1917- *IntWWM 77, -80*
London, Steve *WhoHol A*
London, Tom d1963 *NotNAT B, WhoHol B*
London, Tom 1882-1963 *Film 2, ForYSC, TwYS*
London, Tom 1883-1963 *Vers A[port]*
London, Tom 1893-1963 *WhScrn 74, -77*
Lone Pine Mountaineers *BiDAmM*
Lonergan, Arthur 1906- *IntMPA 77, -75, -76, -78, -79, -80*
Lonergan, Lenore *PlP&P*
Lonergan, Lester 1869-1931 *Film 2, NotNAT B, WhScrn 74, -77, WhoHol B*
Lonergan, Lester, Jr. 1894-1959 *NotNAT B, WhScrn 74, -77, WhoHol B*
Lonero, Emilio 1924- *IntMPA 77, -75, -76, -78, -79*
Lonesome Lee *BluesWW[port]*
Lonesome Sundown *BluesWW[port]*
Loney, Glenn Meredith 1928- *ConAmTC, NotNAT*
Loney, June Ellen 1930- *IntWWM 80*
Long, Audrey 1924- *FilmEn, FilmgC, ForYSC, HalFC 80*
Long, Avon 1910- *BiE&WWA, DrBlPA, NotNAT, WhoHol A, WhoThe 77*
Long, Candace Lowe 1945- *AmSCAP 80*
Long, Carole Wilson 1937- *IntWWM 77, -80*

Long, Frederic 1857-1941 *WhScrn 74, -77, WhoHol B*
Long, Frederick 1857-1941 *Film 2*
Long, Glynn Lea 1895-1945 *NewOrJ*
Long, Hubert 1923- *EncFCWM 69*
Long, Huey P 1893-1935 *OxFilm*
Long, Jack d1938 *WhScrn 74, -77*
Long, Jack Edward 1911- *IntWWM 77, -80, WhoMus 72*
Long, John *ConMuA 80B*
Long, John Luther 1861-1927 *ModWD, NotNAT B, OxThe, PlP&P, WhThe, WhoStg 1908*
Long, John M 1925- *IntWWM 77*
Long, Johnny 1916?-1972 *AmPS A, BgBands 74[port], CmpEPM, WhoHol B*
Long, Kathleen 1896-1968 *NewGrD 80*
Long, Luray 1890-1919 *WhScrn 77*
Long, Margaret *WhoMus 72*
Long, Marguerite 1874-1966 *Baker 78, NewGrD 80*
Long, Mary Elitch d1936 *NotNAT B*
Long, Melvyn Harry 1895-1940 *WhScrn 74, -77*
Long, Mervyn Harry d1940 *WhoHol B*
Long, Newell Hillis 1905- *AmSCAP 80, ConAmC, IntWWM 80*
Long, Nick *Film 2*
Long, Nick, Jr. 1906-1949 *Film 2, NotNAT B, WhScrn 77, WhoHol B*
Long, Page Carroll 1933- *ConAmC, IntWWM 77, -80*
Long, Richard 1927-1974 *BlkAmP, FilmEn, FilmgC, ForYSC, HalFC 80, IntMPA 75, MotPP, MovMk[port], WhScrn 77, WhoHol B, WhoHrs 80*
Long, Ronald *WhoHol A*
Long, Sally *Film 2, WhoHol A*
Long, Shorty 1940-1969 *RkOn 2[port]*
Long, Slats 1910?- *WhoJazz 72*
Long, Sumner Arthur 1921- *BiE&WWA, NotNAT*
Long, Walter d1952 *BlksB&W C, MotPP, WhoHol B*
Long, Walter 1879-1952 *HalFC 80, WhScrn 74, -77*
Long, Walter 1882-1952 *Film 1, -2*
Long, Walter 1884-1952 *FilmgC, ForYSC, TwYS*
Longacre, Lindsay Bartholomew 1870-1952 *BiDAmM*
Longaker, Jon Dasu 1920- *ConAmTC*
L'Ongaretto *NewGrD 80*
Longas, Federico 1893-1968 *Baker 78*
Longas, Federico 1895-1968 *ConAmC*
Longaval, Antoine De *NewGrD 80*
Longden, John 1900-1971 *FilmEn, Film 2, FilmgC, HalFC 80, IlWWBF, WhThe, WhoHol A*
Longden, Terence 1922- *FilmgC, HalFC 80*
Longdon, Joan *WomWMM B*
Longdon, Terence 1922- *WhoHol A, WhoThe 72, -77*
Longepierre, Hilaire-Bernard De R 1659-1731 *OxThe*
Longet, Claudine *WhoHol A*
Longfellow, Henry Wadsworth 1807-1882 *BiDAmM, NewEOp 71*
Longfellow, Malvina *Film 1, -2, IlWWBF[port]*
Longfellow, Samuel 1819-1892 *BiDAmM*
Longfellow, Stephanie *Film 1, WhoStg 1908*
Longfield, Robert *PupTheA*
Longford, Edward A H Pakenham, Earl Of 1902-1961 *McGEWD, NotNAT B, OxThe, WhThe*
Longheval, Antoine De *NewGrD 80*
Longhurst, John Thomas 1940- *IntWWM 77, -80*
Longhurst, William Henry 1819-1904 *Baker 78, OxMus*
Longman, Harry Bernard 1907- *WhoMus 72*
Longmire, John Basil Hugh 1902- *IntWWM 77, WhoMus 72*
Longo, Achille 1900-1954 *Baker 78, NewGrD 80*
Longo, Alessandro 1864-1945 *Baker 78, NewGrD 80, OxMus*
Longo, Alfred 1896- *AmSCAP 66, -80*
Longo, Marie Cecile 1906- *IntWWM 77*
Longo, Michael Joseph 1939- *EncJzS 70*
Longo, Mike 1939- *EncJzS 70*
Longstaff, Grace *PupTheA*
Longstreet, Stephen 1907- *BiE&WWA, ConDr 73, -77D, FilmgC, HalFC 80, IntMPA 77, -75, -76, -78, -79, -80, NotNAT*
Longstreth, Marian 1906- *BiE&WWA*
Longthorne, Brian 1926- *IntWWM 77, WhoMus 72*
Longueval, Antoine De *NewGrD 80*
Longworth, Josephine *Film 1*
Longy, Georges 1868-1930 *Baker 78*
Longyear, Rey Morgan 1930- *IntWWM 77, -80, NewGrD 80*
Lonn, Anders 1943- *IntWWM 77, -80*
Lonnen, Jessie 1886- *WhThe*
Lonnen, Nellie 1887- *WhThe*
Lonnon, Alice 1872- *WhThe, WhoStg 1908*
Lonnrot, Elias 1802-1884 *OxMus*
Lonque, Georges 1900-1967 *Baker 78, NewGrD 80*
Lonquich, Heinz Martin 1937- *NewGrD 80*
Lonsdale, Christopher 1795?-1877 *NewGrD 80*
Lonsdale, Frederick 1881-1954 *CnMD, CnThe, EncWT, Ent, McGEWD, ModWD, NotNAT A, -B, OxThe, PlP&P, WhThe*
Lonsdale, H G d1923 *NotNAT B, WhoHol B*
Lonsdale, Harry G d1923 *Film 1, -2, WhScrn 77*
Lonsdale, Mary Martha 1928- *AmSCAP 80*
Lonsdale, Michel 1931- *FilmAG WE[port], FilmEn, WhoHol A*
Lonsdale, Pamela *IntMPA 79, -80*
Lonsdale, Thomas J d1928 *NotNAT B*
Lonstein, Eugene M 1936- *IntWWM 77*
Lontoc, Leon 1909-1974 *WhScrn 77, WhoHol B*
Lonzo And Oscar *BiDAmM, CounME 74[port], -74A, EncFCWM 69, IlEncCM[port]*
Loo, Bessie *WhoHol A*
Loo, Richard 1903- *FilmgC, ForYSC, HalFC 80, HolCA[port], MotPP, MovMk[port], Vers A[port], WhoHol A*
Loofbourrow, John G d1964 *NotNAT B*
Looking Glass *RkOn 2[port]*
Loomis, Clarence 1888-1965 *AmSCAP 66, -80, ConAmC*
Loomis, Clarence 1889-1965 *Baker 78*
Loomis, George *PupTheA*
Loomis, Harvey Worthington 1865-1930 *Baker 78, NewGrD 80*
Loomis, Harvey Worthington 1865-1931 *BiDAmM*
Loomis, Henry W *NewYTET*
Loomis, James Phillip 1929- *IntWWM 77, -80*
Loomis, Margaret *Film 1, -2, TwYS*
Loomis, Nancy 1955?- *WhoHrs 80*
Loomis, Virginia *Film 2*
Loong, Lee Siu *WhScrn 77*
Loop, Phil d1975 *WhScrn 77*
Looram, Mary Harden *IntMPA 77, -75, -76, -78, -79, -80*
Loos, Anita 1893- *BiE&WWA, Conv 3[port], FilmEn, FilmgC, HalFC 80, IntMPA 77, -75, -76, -78, -79, -80, NotNAT, -A, OxFilm, WhoThe 72, -77, WomWMM, WorEFlm[port]*
Loos, Armin 1904-1971 *ConAmC*
Loos, Mary 1914- *IntMPA 77, -75, -76, -78, -79, -80*
Loos, Theodor 1883-1954 *Film 2, WhScrn 74, -77, WhoHol B*
Loosemore, George d1682 *NewGrD 80*
Loosemore, Henry d1670 *NewGrD 80*
Loosemore, John 1613?-1681 *NewGrD 80*
Looser, Rolf 1920- *Baker 78*
Loosli, Arthur 1926- *IntWWM 80*
Loots, Joyce Mary Ann 1907- *IntWWM 77, -80, WhoMus 72*
Lopatnikof, Nicolai 1903- *OxMus*
Lopatnikoff, Nikolai 1903- *AmSCAP 66, BiDAmM, CompSN[port], ConAmC, DcCM, WhoMus 72*
Lopatnikoff, Nikolai 1903-1976 *AmSCAP 80, Baker 78, NewGrD 80*
Lopatnikoff, Nikolay 1903-1976 *NewGrD 80*
Lopatnikov, Nikolai 1903-1976 *MusMk, NewGrD 80*
Lopatnikov, Nikolay 1903-1976 *NewGrD 80*
Lope De Baena *NewGrD 80*
Lope DeRueda 1505?-1565 *Ent*
Lope DeRueda 1510?-1565 *EncWT*
Lope DeVega *OxThe*
Lope DeVega 1562-1635 *EncWT*
Lope DeVega Carpio 1562-1635 *Ent*
Loper, Don 1906-1972 *WhScrn 77, WhoHol B*
Loper, James L *NewYTET*
Lopes-Graca, Fernando 1906- *Baker 78, DcCM, IntWWM 77, -80, NewGrD 80*
Lopes Morago, Estevao *NewGrD 80*
Lopez, Augustina *Film 2*
Lopez, Carlos 1887-1942 *WhScrn 74, -77*
Lopez, Felix Maximo 1742-1821 *NewGrD 80*
Lopez, Francis 1916- *NewGrD 80*
Lopez, Jeffrey 1955- *AmSCAP 80*
Lopez, Miguel 1669-1723 *NewGrD 80*
Lopez, Miquel 1669-1723 *NewGrD 80*
Lopez, Perry 1931- *ForYSC, IntMPA 75, -76, MotPP, WhoHol A*
Lopez, Pilar 1912- *CnOxB, DancEn 78*
Lopez, Ray 1889-1976 *NewOrJ[port]*
Lopez, Raymond *Film 2*
Lopez, Raymond V 1921- *IntWWM 77, -80*
Lopez, Sabatino 1867-1951 *McGEWD[port], NotNAT B*
Lopez, Sylvia *WomWMM B*
Lopez, Tony 1902-1949 *WhScrn 74, -77*
Lopez, Trini 1933?- *HalFC 80*
Lopez, Trini 1937- *BiDAmM, ForYSC, RkOn[port], WhoHol A*
Lopez, Vincent d1975 *AmPS B, BgBands 74[port]*
Lopez, Vincent 1894-1975 *Baker 78*
Lopez, Vincent 1895-1975 *BiDAmM*
Lopez, Vincent 1898-1975 *AmSCAP 66, -80, CmpEPM, WhScrn 77*
Lopez-Buchardo, Carlos 1881-1948 *Baker 78, NewGrD 80*
Lopez-Calo, Jose 1922- *IntWWM 77, -80, NewGrD 80*
Lopez Capillas, Francisco 1615?-1673 *NewGrD 80*
Lopez-Chavarri Y Marco, Eduardo 1871-1970 *NewGrD 80*
Lopez Cobos, Jesus 1940- *IntWWM 77, -80, WhoOp 76*
Lopez DeAyala, Adelardo 1829-1879 *OxThe*
Lopez DeAyala Y Herrera, Adelardo 1828-1879 *McGEWD*
Lopez DeVelasco, Sebastian d1650? *NewGrD 80*
Lopez Jimenez, Melchor 1760-1822 *NewGrD 80*
Lopez Rubio, Jose 1903- *CroCD, McGEWD[port], ModWD*
Lopez-Soba, Elias 1927- *IntWWM 80*
Lopez Y Capillas, Francisco 1615?-1673 *NewGrD 80*
Lopokov, Andrei Vasilievich 1898-1947 *CnOxB*
Lopokov, Fyodor Vasilievich 1886-1973 *CnOxB*
Lopokova, Lydia *DancEn 78*
Lopokova, Lydia 1892- *WhThe*
Lopokova, Lydia Vasilievna 1891- *CnOxB*
Loposer, Avery 1898?- *NewOrJ*
Lopoukhova, Lydia 1891- *DancEn 78[port]*
Loppert, Max Jeremy 1946- *IntWWM 77*
LoPresti, Ronald 1933- *AmSCAP 80, Baker 78, CpmDNM 80, ConAmC*
Lopukhov, Andrei 1898-1947 *DancEn 78*
Lopukhov, Fedor 1886- *DancEn 78*
Loquasto, Santo *NotNAT, PlP&P A[port], WhoThe 77*
Loqueville, Richard d1418 *NewGrD 80*
Lora, Antonio 1899-1965 *ConAmC*
Loraine, Henry d1899 *NotNAT B*
Loraine, Keith Edward 1942- *IntWWM 77, -80*
Loraine, Robert 1876-1935 *EncWT, NotNAT A, -B, OxThe, WhThe, WhoStg 1908*
Loraine, Violet 1886-1956 *WhThe*
Lorand, Colette *WhoOp 76*
Lorand, Istvan 1933- *IntWWM 77, -80*
Lorand, Thomas 1923- *IntWWM 77, -80*
Lorano, Filippo De *NewGrD 80*
Lorbenthalu, Jan Petr Svosovsky Z *NewGrD 80*
Lorber, Johann Christoph 1645-1722 *NewGrD 80*
Lorca, Federico Garcia *CnOxB, NewGrD 80*
Lorca, Federico Garcia 1898-1936 *EncWT, Ent*
Lorca, Federico Garcia 1899-1936 *CnMD,*

CnThe, DcPup, McGEWD[port], OxThe, REnWD[port]
Lorch, Louis *Film 2*
Lorch, Theodore A 1873-1947 *Film 2, WhScrn 74, -77, WhoHol B*
Lorcia, Suzanne 1902- *CnOxB*
Lorcini, Marie Iosch 1930- *IntWWM 77, -80*
Lord, Arthur Edwin 1920- *IntWWM 77*
Lord, Barbara 1937- *BiE&WWA, NotNAT*
Lord, Basil 1913- *WhoThe 72, -77*
Lord, Bobby 1934- *BiDAmM, CounME 74, -74A, EncFCWM 69, IlEncCM*
Lord, David Malcolm 1944- *IntWWM 77, -80, WhoMus 72*
Lord, DeForest Dodge *PupTheA*
Lord, Del 1895-1970 *FilmgC, HalFC 80, TwYS A*
Lord, Eric Meredith 1923- *NatPD[port]*
Lord, Grace *Film 2*
Lord, Howard Blaine 1926- *ConAmTC*
Lord, Iris *MorBAP*
Lord, Jack *MotPP, WhoHol A*
Lord, Jack 1922- *FilmgC, HalFC 80*
Lord, Jack 1928- *FilmEn*
Lord, Jack 1930- *ForYSC, IntMPA 77, -75, -76, -78, -79, -80, MovMk*
Lord, Jimmy 1905?-1936 *WhoJazz 72*
Lord, John Malcolm Shaw 1932- *IntWWM 77, -80*
Lord, Marion 1883-1942 *Film 2, WhScrn 74, -77, WhoHol B*
Lord, Marjorie 1921- *ForYSC, MovMk, WhoHol A*
Lord, Marjorie 1922- *FilmEn, FilmgC, HalFC 80*
Lord, Pauline 1890-1950 *FamA&A[port], FilmgC, ForYSC, HalFC 80, NotNAT B, ThFT[port], WhScrn 74, -77, WhThe, WhoHol B*
Lord, Philip *Film 2*
Lord, Philip F 1879-1968 *WhScrn 77*
Lord, Phillip *ForYSC*
Lord, Phillips H 1902-1975 *WhScrn 77, WhoHol C*
Lord, Robert 1900-1976 *HalFC 80*
Lord, Robert 1902-1976 *FilmEn, IntMPA 75, -76*
Lord, Robert 1931- *IntWWM 77*
Lord, Robert 1945- *ConDr 77, NatPD[port]*
Lord, Roger *WhoMus 72*
Lord, Rosemary *IntMPA 79, -80*
Lord, Stephen *AmSCAP 80*
Lord, Walter 1917- *AmSCAP 66, -80*
Lord, William E *NewYTET*
Lord, William Umbach *WhoOp 76*
Lord Chamberlain *EncWT*
Lord Observer 1937- *DrBlPA*
Lord-Wood, June 1922- *IntWWM 77, -80*
Lorde, Andre De 1871- *WhThe*
Lorde, Athena 1915-1973 *WhScrn 77, WhoHol B*
Loredo, Linda *Film 2*
Loren, Bernice *NotNAT*
Loren, Bernie 1925- *AmSCAP 66*
Loren, Donna *WhoHol A*
Loren, Randy *AmSCAP 80*
Loren, Sophia 1932- *FilmAG WE[port]*
Loren, Sophia 1934- *BiDFilm, -81, CmMov, FilmEn, FilmgC, ForYSC, HalFC 80[port], IntMPA 77, -75, -76, -78, -79, -80, MotPP, MovMk[port], OxFilm, WhoHol A, WorEFlm*
Lorenc, Antoni 1909- *IntWWM 77, -80*
Lorenco De Firence *NewGrD 80*
Lorengar, Pilar 1928- *CmOp, IntWWM 77, -80, NewGrD 80, WhoOp 76*
Lorente, Andres 1624-1703 *NewGrD 80*
Lorento, Professor *PupTheA*
Lorentz, Alfred 1872-1931 *Baker 78*
Lorentz, Johan 1580?-1650 *NewGrD 80*
Lorentz, Johan 1610?-1689 *NewGrD 80*
Lorentz, Johann 1580?-1650 *NewGrD 80*
Lorentz, Johann 1610?-1689 *NewGrD 80*
Lorentz, Pare 1905- *AmFD, DcFM, HalFC 80, OxFilm, WorEFlm*
Lorentz, Pare 1905-1972 *FilmEn*
Lorentzen, Bent 1935- *IntWWM 77, -80, NewGrD 80*
Lorentzon, Vendla *AmSCAP 80*
Lorenz, Alfred Ottokar 1868-1939 *Baker 78, NewGrD 80*
Lorenz, Andrew Bela 1951- *IntWWM 77, -80*
Lorenz, Dolly *Film 2*
Lorenz, Edmund Simon 1854-1942 *AmSCAP 66, -80*
Lorenz, Ellen Jane 1907- *AmSCAP 66, -80, CpmDNM 79, ConAmC, IntWWM 77, -80, WhoMus 72*
Lorenz, Franz 1805-1883 *Baker 78*
Lorenz, Julius 1862-1924 *Baker 78*
Lorenz, Karl Adolf 1837-1923 *Baker 78*
Lorenz, Max 1901-1975 *Baker 78, CmOp, NewEOp 71, NewGrD 80, WhoMus 72*
Lorenz, Pare 1905-1972 *FilmgC*
Lorenz, Wendy Joy 1950- *IntWWM 77, -80*
Lorenzani, Paolo 1640-1713 *Baker 78, NewGrD 80*
Lorenzi, Filiberto *NewGrD 80*
Lorenzi, Giorgio 1846-1922 *NewGrD 80*
Lorenzi, Giovanni Battista 1721-1807 *OxThe*
Lorenzi, Sergio 1914-1974 *NewGrD 80*
Lorenzi, Stellio 1921- *DcFM*
Lorenzi-Fabris, Ausonio De 1861-1935 *Baker 78*
Lorenzini *NewGrD 80*
Lorenzini Del Liuto *NewGrD 80*
Lorenzini, Raimondo d1806 *NewGrD 80*
Lorenziti, Bernard 1764?-1813? *NewGrD 80*
Lorenzo Da Firenze d1373? *NewGrD 80*
Lorenzo, Ange 1894-1971 *AmSCAP 66, -80, BiDAmM*
Lorenzo, Leonardo De 1875-1962 *Baker 78*
Lorenzo, Tina Di 1872-1930 *WhThe*
Lorenzo Fernandez, Oscar 1897-1948 *NewGrD 80*
Lorenzon, Livio 1926-1971 *WhScrn 77*
Loretto, Alfred *Film 2*
Loretts, The *PupTheA*
Lorey, Forrest Patrick *WhoOp 76*
Lori, Arcangelo d1679 *NewGrD 80*
Lorimer, Jack 1883- *WhThe*
Lorimer, Louise *WhoHol A*
Lorimer, Michael 1946- *BiDAmM, IntWWM 80*
Lorimer, Wright 1874-1911 *NotNAT B, WhoStg 1908*
Lorin, Andre *DancEn 78*
Loring, Ann *WhoHol A*
Loring, Eugene 1914- *BiE&WWA, CnOxB, DancEn 78, WhoHol A*
Loring, Eva *Film 1*
Loring, Frances Norma 1887-1968 *CreCan 2*
Loring, Francis *WhoMus 72*
Loring, Lynn *WhoHol A*
Loring, Norman 1888-1967 *WhThe*
Loring, Richard 1925- *AmSCAP 66*
Loring, Richard Edwin 1927- *AmSCAP 80*
Loriod, Yvonne 1924- *Baker 78, IntWWM 77, -80, NewGrD 80, WhoMus 72*
Loris, Heinrich 1488-1563 *OxMus*
Loriti, Henricus *NewGrD 80*
Lorme, Joyce *Film 2*
Lormer, Jon *ForYSC, WhoHol A*
Lormi, Giorgio 1941- *WhoOp 76*
Lorne, Constance 1914-1969 *WhScrn 77, WhoHol A, WhoThe 72, -77*
Lorne, Marion d1968 *MotPP, WhoHol B*
Lorne, Marion 1886-1968 *FilmgC, HalFC 80*
Lorne, Marion 1888-1968 *BiE&WWA, ForYSC, NotNAT B, WhScrn 74, -77, WhThe*
LoRoy *NewGrD 80*
Lorraine, Duke Of *OxMus*
Lorraine, Betty 1908-1944 *WhScrn 77*
Lorraine, Emily d1944 *NotNAT B*
Lorraine, Guido *WhoHol A*
Lorraine, Harry 1886- *Film 2, IlWWBF[port]*
Lorraine, Irma 1885- *WhThe*
Lorraine, Jean *Film 2*
Lorraine, Leota 1893-1975 *Film 2, WhScrn 77, WhoHol C*
Lorraine, Lilian 1892-1955 *WhThe*
Lorraine, Lillian 1892-1955 *AmPS B, CmpEPM, EncMT, Film 1, -2, NotNAT B, TwYS, WhoHol B*
Lorraine, Louise 1901- *Film 1, -2, TwYS, WhoHol A*
Lorraine, Oscar 1878-1955 *WhScrn 74, -77*
Lorrayne, Vyvyan 1939- *CnOxB, DancEn 78*
Lorre, Peter 1904-1964 *BiDFilm, -81, CmMov, EncWT, FilmAG WE, FilmEn, FilmgC, HalFC 80, MotPP, MovMk[port], NotNAT B, OxFilm, Vers A[port], WhScrn 74, -77, WhoHol B, WhoHrs 80[port], WorEFlm[port]*
Lorre, Peter 1905-1964 *ForYSC*
Lorre, Peter, Jr. *WhoHol A*
Lorring, Joan *MotPP, NotNAT*
Lorring, Joan 1926- *FilmgC, HalFC 80, MovMk*
Lorring, Joan 1931- *BiE&WWA, ForYSC, WhoHol A*
Lorring, Lotte *Film 2*
Lortat-Jacob, Bernard 1941- *IntWWM 80*
Lortel, Lucille *BiE&WWA, NotNAT, WhoThe 72, -77*
Lortz, Robert *NatPD[port]*
Lortzing, Albert 1801-1851 *Baker 78, CmOp, DcCom 77, GrComp[port], MusMk, NewGrD 80[port]*
Lortzing, Gustav Albert 1801-1851 *NewEOp 71, OxMus*
Lorys, Denise *Film 2*
Los Bravos *RkOn 2[port]*
Los Indios Tabajaras *RkOn[port]*
Losack, Evelyn Curtis 1929- *IntWWM 77*
LosAngeles, Victoria De 1923- *CmOp, NewEOp 71, NewGrD 80[port]*
LosAngeles Neophonic Orchestra *BiDAmM*
Losch, Tilly d1975 *BiE&WWA, WhoHol C*
Losch, Tilly 1901-1975 *HalFC 80*
Losch, Tilly 1902-1975 *EncMT, ForYSC, WhScrn 77*
Losch, Tilly 1904?-1975 *CnOxB*
Losch, Tilly 1907-1975 *DancEn 78, NotNAT B, WhThe*
Losch, Tilly 1911?- *FilmgC*
Loschenkohl, Hieronymus 1753?-1807 *NewGrD 80*
Loschhorn, Albert 1819-1905 *Baker 78*
Loschhorn, Carl Albert *NewGrD 80*
Losee, Frank 1856-1937 *Film 1, -2, NotNAT B, TwYS, WhScrn 74, -77, WhoHol B*
Losel, Johann Georg Ernst Cajetan 1699?-1750 *NewGrD 80*
Losey, Joseph 1909- *BiDFilm, -81, DcFM, FilmEn, FilmgC, HalFC 80, IlWWBF, -A, IntMPA 77, -75, -76, -78, -79, -80, MovMk[port], OxFilm, WorEFlm*
Losey, Mary *WomWMM B*
Losonczy, Andor 1932- *IntWWM 80*
LosRios, Alvaro De *NewGrD 80*
Loss, Joe 1910- *NewGrD 80, WhoMus 72*
Lossen, Lena *Film 2*
Lossius, Lucas 1508-1582 *NewGrD 80*
Losy, Jan Antonin, Count Of Losinthal 1650?-1721 *NewGrD 80*
Lot *NewGrD 80*
Lotar, Eli 1905- *DcFM, OxFilm*
Lotar, Petr 1910- *OxThe*
Loth, L Leslie 1888- *AmSCAP 66*
Loth, Louis Leslie 1888- *ConAmC*
Loth, Urban d1637 *NewGrD 80*
Lothar, Eva *WomWMM B*
Lothar, Hanns d1967 *WhScrn 74, -77*
Lothar, Hans d1967 *WhoHol B*
Lothar, Mark 1902- *NewGrD 80*
Lothar And The Hand People *BiDAmM*
Loti, Pierre 1850-1923 *NewEOp 71*
Lotinga, Ernest 1876-1951 *WhScrn 77, WhThe, WhoHol B*
Lotinga, Ernest 1895-1951 *WhScrn 74*
Lotinga, Ernie 1876-1951 *Film 2, FilmgC, HalFC 80, IlWWBF, NotNAT B*
Lotinis, Johannes De *NewGrD 80*
Lotis, Dennis *WhoHol A*
Lotito, Louis A 1900- *BiE&WWA, NotNAT*
Lott, Jack Frederick 1800?-1871 *NewGrD 80*
Lott, John Frederick 1800?-1871 *NewGrD 80*
Lott, Mona *WomWMM*
Lotta 1847-1924 *OxThe, WhThe, WhoStg 1908*
Lotta, Charlotte 1847-1924 *NotNAT B*
Lotter *NewGrD 80*
Lotter, Esaias Daniel 1759-1820 *NewGrD 80*
Lotter, Johann Jakob 1683?-1738 *NewGrD 80*
Lotter, Johann Jakob 1726-1804 *NewGrD 80*
Lottermoser, Werner 1909- *NewGrD 80*
Lotti, Antonio 1667?-1740 *Baker 78, MusMk, NewGrD 80, OxMus*

Lottini, Antonio *NewGrD 80*
Lotto, Albert 1947- *BiDAmM*
Lotto, Izydor 1840?-1936 *NewGrD 80*
Lotufo, Aldo 1926- *DancEn 78*
Lotze, Lucas *NewGrD 80*
Lotze, Patricia Black 1912- *IntWWM 77*
Lotze, Rudolf Hermann 1817-1881 *Baker 78*
Lotzenhiser, George William 1923- *AmSCAP 80, IntWWM 77, -80*
Lou, Bonnie *RkOn*
Lou-Tellegen 1881-1934 *WhThe*
Loucheur, Raymond 1899-1979 *NewGrD 80*
Louchheim, Stuart F 1892-1971 *AmSCAP 66, -80*
Loud, Thomas d1833 *NewGrD 80*
Loud, Thomas, Jr. 1792?-1866? *BiDAmM*
Loud, Thomas, Sr. 1770?-1833 *BiDAmM*
Louden, Thomas 1874-1948 *WhScrn 74, -77, WhoHol B*
Loudermilk, John D 1934- *BiDAmM, CounME 74, -74A, EncFCWM 69, IlEncCM[port], PopAmC SUP[port], RkOn[port]*
Loudon, Dorothy 1933- *NotNAT, WhoThe 72, -77*
Loudova, Ivana 1941- *Baker 78, IntWWM 77, -80, NewGrD 80*
Louel, Jean 1914- *Baker 78, NewGrD 80*
Loufenburg, Heinrich *NewGrD 80*
Loughborough, William *ConAmC*
Loughery, Jackie 1930- *ForYSC, WhoHol A*
Loughnane, Lee David 1946- *AmSCAP 80*
Loughran, James 1931- *IntWWM 77, -80, NewGrD 80, WhoMus 72*
Loughran, Lewis 1950-1975 *WhScrn 77*
Louie, Alexina Diane 1949- *IntWWM 77*
Louis XIII 1601-1643 *Baker 78, NewGrD 80, OxMus*
Louis XIV 1638-1715 *DancEn 78, NewGrD 80[port], OxMus*
Louis Ferdinand, Prince Of Prussia 1772-1806 *Baker 78, NewGrD 80*
Louis, Gene 1950- *AmSCAP 80*
Louis, Jean 1907- *IntMPA 77, -75, -76, -78, -79, -80*
Louis, Joe *BlksB&W C*
Louis, Joe Hill 1921-1957 *BluesWW[port]*
Louis, Leslie Bertram 1948- *IntWWM 80*
Louis, Murray 1926- *CmpGMD[port], CnOxB, DancEn 78[port]*
Louis, Rudolf 1870-1914 *Baker 78, NewGrD 80*
Louis, Tobi *NatPD[port]*
Louis, Tommy *BluesWW*
Louis, Viola *Film 2*
Louis, Willard 1886-1926 *Film 1, -2, TwYS, WhScrn 74, -77, WhoHol B*
Louise, Anita 1915-1970 *FilmEn, FilmgC, ForYSC, HalFC 80, HolP 30[port], MotPP, MovMk[port], ThFT[port], WhScrn 74, -77, WhoHol B*
Louise, Anita 1917-1970 *Film 2*
Louise, Edouard 1941- *EncJzS 70*
Louise, Tina *IntMPA 77, -75, -76, -78, -79, -80, MotPP, WhoHol A*
Louise, Tina 1934- *FilmEn, FilmgC, HalFC 80*
Louise, Tina 1935- *ForYSC*
Louise, Tina 1937- *BiE&WWA*
Louise, Viola *Film 2*
Louisiana Hayriders *BiDAmM*
Louisiana Red 1936- *BluesWW, EncJzS 70*
Louiss, Eddy 1941- *EncJzS 70*
Loulie, Etienne *OxMus*
Loulie, Etienne d1702 *Baker 78*
Loulie, Etienne 1655?-1707? *NewGrD 80*
Loulie, L A 1775?- *OxMus*
Lourdault *NewGrD 80*
Lourie, Arthur Vincent 1892-1966 *Baker 78, ConAmC, DcCM, NewGrD 80, OxMus*
Lourie, Eugene 1905?- *FilmEn, FilmgC, HalFC 80, WhoHrs 80, WorEFlm*
Lourie, Miles *ConMuA 80B*
Louther, William 1942- *CnOxB*
Loutherbourg, Philip James De 1740-1812 *OxThe*
Loutherbourg, Philippe De 1740-1812 *Ent*
Louttit, Mark Edgar 1948- *IntWWM 80*
Louvier, Alain 1945- *CpmDNM 77, IntWWM 77, -80, NewGrD 80*
Louvier, Nicole 1933- *WhoMus 72*
Louvin, Charlie 1927- *BiDAmM, CounME 74[port], -74A, EncFCWM 69, IlEncCM*
Louvin, Ira 1924-1965 *BiDAmM, CounME 74[port], EncFCWM 69, IlEncCM*
Louvin Brothers *CounME 74[port], -74A, IlEncCM[port]*
Louwenaar, Karyl June 1940- *IntWWM 77, -80*
Louys, Jean 1530?-1563 *NewGrD 80*
Louys, Pierre 1870-1925 *NewEOp 71*
Lovanio *NewGrD 80*
Lovat, Nancie 1900-1946 *NotNAT B, WhThe*
Love *BiDAmM, ConMuA 80A, IlEncR*
Love, Bessie *MotPP, WhoThe 72, -77*
Love, Bessie 1891- *BiE&WWA, ForYSC, TwYS*
Love, Bessie 1898- *FilmEn, Film 1, -2, FilmgC, HalFC 80, IlWWBF, -A, IntMPA 77, -75, -76, -78, -79, -80, MovMk, NotNAT, OxFilm, ThFT[port], WhoHol A*
Love, Charlie 1885-1963 *NewOrJ[port]*
Love, Clayton 1927- *BluesWW*
Love, Darlene *RkOn*
Love, Dorothea *Film 2*
Love, James A 1918- *IntMPA 77, -75, -76, -78, -79, -80*
Love, Jerry *ConMuA 80B*
Love, Laura *WhScrn 74, -77*
Love, Loretta *ConAmC*
Love, Luther Halsey 1904- *AmSCAP 80*
Love, Mabel 1874-1953 *NotNAT B, WhThe*
Love, Montagu d1943 *MotPP, WhoHol B*
Love, Montagu 1877-1943 *FilmEn, Film 1, FilmgC, HalFC 80, HolCA[port], MovMk[port], NotNAT B, WhScrn 74, -77, WhThe*
Love, Montagu 1881-1943 *Vers A[port]*
Love, Montagu 1887-1943 *TwYS*
Love, Montague 1877-1943 *ForYSC*
Love, Montague 1887-1943 *Film 2*
Love, Phyllis 1925- *BiE&WWA, ForYSC, NotNAT, WhoHol A*
Love, Randolph Deyo 1950- *AmSCAP 80*
Love, Robert 1914-1948 *WhScrn 74, -77, WhoHol B*
Love, Shirley 1940- *WhoOp 76*
Love, Willie 1906-1953 *BluesWW[port]*
Love Sculpture *ConMuA 80A*
Love Unlimited *RkOn 2[port]*
Loveberg, Aase 1923- *Baker 78*
Lovec, Vladimir 1922- *IntWWM 77, -80*
Lovecraft, H P *BiDAmM*
Lovecraft, Howard Phillips 1890-1937 *WhoHrs 80*
Loveday, Alan Raymond 1928- *IntWWM 77, NewGrD 80, WhoMus 72*
Loveday, Carroll 1898-1955 *AmSCAP 66, -80*
Lovegrove, Arthur *WhoHol A*
Lovejoy, Addison Ray 1916- *AmSCAP 80*
Lovejoy, Alec 1893?-1946 *BlksB&W, -C*
Lovejoy, Frank d1962 *MotPP, WhoHol B*
Lovejoy, Frank 1912-1962 *FilmgC, HalFC 80*
Lovejoy, Frank 1914-1962 *FilmEn, ForYSC, MovMk, NotNAT B, WhScrn 74, -77*
Lovejoy, Michael Saunders 1941- *IntWWM 80*
Lovejoy, Robin 1923- *WhoThe 77*
Lovelace, Austin Cole 1919- *AmSCAP 80, CpmDNM 80, ConAmC*
Lovelace, Linda 1952- *HalFC 80, WhoHol A*
Loveland, Kenneth 1915- *IntWWM 77, -80, WhoMus 72*
Loveless, Wendell Phillips 1892- *NewGrD 80*
Lovell, Mrs. d1877 *NotNAT B*
Lovell, Edna Ruth *WhoMus 72*
Lovell, Eileen *WhoMus 72*
Lovell, George William d1878 *NotNAT B*
Lovell, Joan Isabel *WhoMus 72*
Lovell, Patricia Mary 1923- *IntWWM 77, -80*
Lovell, Percy Albert 1919- *IntWWM 77, -80, WhoMus 72*
Lovell, Raymond 1900-1953 *FilmgC, HalFC 80, IlWWBF, NotNAT B, WhScrn 74, -77, WhThe, WhoHol B*
Lovell, W T 1884- *WhThe*
Lovell, William James 1939- *ConAmC*
Lovello, Tony *AmSCAP 80*
Lovelock, John David 1911- *WhoMus 72*
Lovelock, William 1899- *WhoMus 72*
Lovely, Louise 1896- *Film 1, -2, TwYS*
Lovenskjold, Herman Severin 1815-1870 *Baker 78, CnOxB*
Lover, Samuel 1797-1868 *Baker 78, NewGrD 80, NotNAT A, -B, OxMus*
Loveridge, Iris *WhoMus 72*
Loveridge, Margaret *Film 1*
Loveridge, Marguerite 1892-1925 *WhScrn 77, WhoHol B*
Lovering, Mabel 1910- *WhoMus 72*
Loveroff, Frederic Nicholas 1894- *CreCan 2*
LoVerso, Antonio *NewGrD 80*
Lovett, Baby 1900?- *NewOrJ*
Lovett, Colleen 1936- *AmSCAP 66*
Lovett, Colleen 1946- *AmSCAP 80*
Lovett, George 1932- *AmSCAP 80, ConAmC*
Lovett, Josephine *WomWMM*
Lovett, Leon 1935- *WhoMus 72*
Lovett, Martin 1927- *WhoMus 72*
Lovett, Terence George 1922- *IntWWM 77, -80, WhoMus 72*
Lovetti, Gemignano *NewGrD 80*
Loveys, Pamela Mary 1938- *IntWWM 77*
Lovin' Spoonful *BiDAmM, IlEncR, RkOn 2[port]*
Lovin' Spoonfull *ConMuA 80A*
Lovinescu, Horia 1917- *CnMD, McGEWD[port]*
Lovingood, Penman, Sr. 1895- *AmSCAP 66, -80*
Lovingwood, Pennman, Sr. 1895- *ConAmC A*
Lovitts, Jerome *PupTheA*
Lovsky, Celia *ForYSC, WhoHol A*
Lovullo, Anthony 1932- *AmSCAP 80*
Lovy, Alex *IntMPA 77, -75, -76, -78, -79, -80*
Low, Betty *CreCan 1*
Low, Carl 1916- *BiE&WWA, NotNAT, WhoHol A*
Low, Colin 1926- *CreCan 2, DcFM, FilmEn, WorEFlm*
Low, Jack 1898-1958 *WhScrn 74, -77, WhoHol B*
Low, Joseph 1834-1886 *Baker 78*
Low, Warren 1905- *HalFC 80*
Low VonEisenach, Johann Jacob *NewGrD 80*
Lowdell, John 1935- *IntWWM 80, WhoMus 72*
Lowden, Robert William 1920- *AmSCAP 80*
Lowden, Ronald Douglas, Jr. 1928- *AmSCAP 80*
Lowe, Arthur *WhoHol A*
Lowe, Arthur 1904- *FilmgC*
Lowe, Arthur 1914- *HalFC 80*
Lowe, Arthur 1915- *IlWWBF, WhoThe 72, -77*
Lowe, Bernard 1917- *AmSCAP 80*
Lowe, Bernie 1917- *AmSCAP 66*
Lowe, Claude Egerton 1860-1947 *OxMus*
Lowe, David d1965 *NewYTET*
Lowe, Douglas 1882- *WhThe*
Lowe, Edmund d1971 *MotPP, WhoHol B*
Lowe, Edmund 1890-1971 *FilmgC, HalFC 80*
Lowe, Edmund 1892-1971 *FilmEn, Film 1, -2, ForYSC, MovMk, TwYS, WhScrn 74, -77, WhThe*
Lowe, Edward 1610?-1682 *NewGrD 80, OxMus*
Lowe, Enid 1908- *WhThe, WhoThe 72*
Lowe, Ferdinand 1865-1925 *Baker 78, NewGrD 80*
Lowe, Florence *PupTheA*
Lowe, Frank 1943- *EncJzS 70, IlEncJ*
Lowe, Gerda Sylvia 1900- *WhoMus 72*
Lowe, Irma *Film 2*
Lowe, Jack W 1917- *WhoMus 72*
Lowe, James B 1880-1963 *DrBlPA, Film 2, WhScrn 74, -77, WhoHol B*
Lowe, Jim 1927- *AmPS B, RkOn*
Lowe, John Stanley 1906- *IntWWM 77, -80, WhoMus 72*
Lowe, Joshua d1945 *NotNAT B*
Lowe, K Elmo d1971 *WhoHol B*
Lowe, K Elmo 1899-1971 *BiE&WWA, NotNAT B*
Lowe, K Elmo 1900-1971 *WhScrn 77*
Lowe, Karl *Baker 78*
Lowe, Margaret 1930- *WhoMus 72*
Lowe, Maude *Film 1*

Lowe, Michael Graeme 1947- *IntWWM 77*
Lowe, Mundell 1922- *AmSCAP 66, -80, BiDAmM, CmpEPM, EncJzS 70*
Lowe, Nick *ConMuA 80A, -80B*
Lowe, Philip L 1917- *IntMPA 77, -75, -76, -78, -79, -80*
Lowe, Philip M 1944- *IntMPA 79, -80*
Lowe, Rachel 1876- *WhThe*
Lowe, Robert d1939 *NotNAT B*
Lowe, Ruth 1914- *AmSCAP 66, -80*
Lowe, Samuel Milton 1918- *WhoJazz 72*
Lowe, Thomas d1783 *NewGrD 80*
Lowe, Timothy Malcolm 1953- *IntWWM 77, -80*
Lowe VonEisenach, Johann Jakob 1629-1703 *NewGrD 80*
Lowell, Dorothy 1916-1944 *WhScrn 74, -77*
Lowell, Eugene 1907- *AmSCAP 80*
Lowell, Helen 1866-1937 *Film 2, NotNAT B, WhScrn 74, -77, WhThe, WhoHol B*
Lowell, Jack 1924- *AmSCAP 80*
Lowell, James Russell 1819-1891 *BiDAmM*
Lowell, Joan 1900-1967 *WhScrn 74, -77, WhoHol B*
Lowell, John d1937 *WhScrn 74, -77, WhoHol B*
Lowell, Mollie *WhThe*
Lowell, Robert 1917- *CnThe, ConDr 73, -77, CroCD, EncWT, ModWD, NotNAT*
Lowen, Johann Friedrich 1729-1771 *EncWT*
Lowenbach, Jan 1880-1972 *NewGrD 80*
Lowenberg, Kenneth *ConAmC*
Lowenfield, Henry d1931 *NotNAT B*
Lowens, Curt *WhoHol A*
Lowens, Irving 1916- *Baker 78, ConAmC, IntWWM 80, NewGrD 80*
Lowenstein, Gunilla Marika 1929- *IntWWM 77*
Lowenstein, Larry 1919- *IntMPA 77, -75, -76, -78, -79*
Lowenstein, Norman *IntMPA 75, -76*
Lowenstern, Matthaus Apelles Von 1594-1648 *NewGrD 80*
Lower, Elmer W *IntMPA 77, -75, -76, -78, -79, -80, NewYTET*
Lowery, Bert *PupTheA*
Lowery, Bill *ConMuA 80B*
Lowery, Fred *CmpEPM*
Lowery, Harry 1896-1967 *OxMus*
Lowery, Robert d1971 *MotPP, WhoHol B*
Lowery, Robert 1914-1971 *FilmEn, WhScrn 74, -77, WhoHrs 80*
Lowery, Robert 1916-1971 *FilmgC, ForYSC, HalFC 80, MovMk[port]*
Lowery, Robert 1932- *BluesWW[port]*
Lowery, W E *Film 1*
Lowery, William *Film 2*
Lowin, John 1576-1653 *NotNAT B, OxThe*
Lowinsky, Edward E 1908- *Baker 78, NewGrD 80*
Lowlein, Hans 1909- *WhoOp 76*
Lowman, Kenneth E W 1916- *ConAmC*
Lown, Bert 1903-1962 *AmPS B, AmSCAP 66, -80, BgBands 74, CmpEPM*
Lowne, Charles Macready d1941 *NotNAT B, WhThe*
Lownes, Humfrey *NewGrD 80*
Lownes, Matthew *NewGrD 80*
Lowney, Raymond *Film 2*
Lowrey, Norman Eugene 1944- *AmSCAP 80*
Lowrie, Jeanette *WhoStg 1908*
Lowry, Clarence Malcolm 1909-1957 *CreCan 1*
Lowry, Elizabeth Alaire Howard 1943- *IntWWM 77, -80*
Lowry, John d1962 *NotNAT B*
Lowry, Judith *WhoHol A*
Lowry, Karen Lynnette 1955- *IntWWM 80*
Lowry, L *Film 1*
Lowry, Malcolm Boden 1909-1957 *CreCan 1*
Lowry, Morton 1908?- *HalFC 80*
Lowry, Robert 1826-1899 *Baker 78, BiDAmM, CpmDNM 79, NewGrD 80*
Lowry, Rudd 1892-1965 *WhScrn 74, -77*
Lowry, W McNeil 1913- *BiE&WWA, NotNAT*
Lowski, Woytec 1939- *CnOxB*
Lowther, Thomas Henry 1941- *IntWWM 77*
Lowtzky, Hermann 1871-1957 *Baker 78*
Lowy, Heinrich *NewGrD 80*
Lowys, Jean *NewGrD 80*
Loxam, Arnold 1916- *IntWWM 77*
Loxhay, Simon *NewGrD 80*
Loxley, Violet 1914- *WhThe*
Loxton, David *NewYTET*
Loy, D Gareth 1945- *ConAmC*
Loy, Matthias 1828-1915 *BiDAmM*
Loy, Max 1913- *Baker 78*
Loy, Myrna 1902- *OxFilm*
Loy, Myrna 1905- *BiDFilm, -81, CmMov, FilmEn, Film 2, FilmgC, ForYSC, HalFC 80, IntMPA 77, -75, -76, -78, -79, -80, MGM[port], MotPP, MovMk[port], ThFT[port], TwYS, WhoHol A, WorEFlm[port]*
Loy, Nanni 1925- *DcFM, FilmEn, FilmgC, HalFC 80, OxFilm, WorEFlm*
Loy, Robert H 1918- *ConAmTC*
Loy, S J *AmSCAP 80*
Loy, Sonny *Film 2*
Loyacano, Arnold 1889-1962 *NewOrJ[port]*
Loyacano, Freddie 1905?- *NewOrJ*
Loyacano, Joe 1893-1967 *NewOrJ[port]*
Loyacano, Joe 1906-1969 *NewOrJ*
Loyacano, John 1879-1960 *NewOrJ[port]*
Loyacano, Stephen Jacob 1926- *AmSCAP 80*
Loyacano, Steve 1903- *NewOrJ*
Loyal, Dash *Film 2*
Loyd, Alison d1935 *WhoHol B*
Loyer, Georges *Film 1*
Loynd, Roy *ConAmTC*
Loyola Guevara, Pedro De *NewGrD 80*
Loyonnet, Paul Louis 1889- *IntWWM 77, -80*
Loys *NewGrD 80*
Loys, Jean *NewGrD 80*
Loyset *NewGrD 80*
Lozano, Amalia 1926- *CnOxB, DancEn 78*
Lu, Sonny *Film 2*
Lu, Yen 1930- *ConAmC*
Lualdi, Adriano 1885-1971 *Baker 78, NewGrD 80*
Lualdi, Adriano 1887- *NewEOp 71*
Lualdi, Antonella 1931- *FilmEn, HalFC 80*
Luandrew, Albert 1907- *BluesWW[port]*
Luard-Selby, Bertram 1853-1918 *NewGrD 80*
Luban, Francia 1914- *AmSCAP 66, -80*
Lubbock, Mark Hugh 1898- *WhoMus 72*
Lubcke, Harry R 1905- *IntMPA 77, -75, -76, -78, -79, -80*
Lubeck, Ernst 1829-1876 *Baker 78*
Lubeck, Johann Heinrich 1799-1865 *Baker 78*
Lubeck, Louis 1838-1904 *Baker 78*
Lubeck, Vincent *NewGrD 80*
Lubeck, Vincent 1654-1740 *NewGrD 80*
Lubeck, Vincentius 1654-1740 *Baker 78*
Luben, Jack *Film 2*
Lubimoff, A *Film 2*
Lubin, Allene Berne 1949- *AmSCAP 80*
Lubin, Arthur 1901- *FilmEn, Film 2, FilmgC, HalFC 80, IntMPA 77, -75, -76, -78, -79, -80, MovMk[port], WhoHrs 80*
Lubin, Ernest Viviani 1916- *AmSCAP 66, -80, ConAmC, IntWWM 77, -80*
Lubin, Fred *PupTheA*
Lubin, Germaine 1890-1979 *CmOp, NewEOp 71, NewGrD 80[port]*
Lubin, Jerome *PupTheA*
Lubin, Sigmund 1850?-1923 *OxFilm*
Lubin, Sigmund 1851-1923 *FilmEn*
Lubin, Steven 1942- *IntWWM 77, -80*
Lubin, Tibi *Film 2*
Lubitsch, Ernst 1892-1947 *AmFD, BiDFilm, -81, CmMov, DcFM, FilmEn, Film 2, FilmgC, HalFC 80, MovMk[port], NotNAT B, OxFilm, TwYS A, WhScrn 74, -77, WhoHol B, WorEFlm*
Lubitz, Monika 1943- *CnOxB*
Lublow, Lenard B 1891- *AmSCAP 66*
Luboff, Norman 1917- *AmSCAP 66, -80, ConAmC*
Lubois, Marilyn *WomWMM B*
Luboshutz, Lea 1885-1965 *Baker 78*
Luboshutz, Lea 1887-1965 *BiDAmM*
Luboshutz, Pierre 1891-1971 *Baker 78*
Luboshutz, Pierre 1894-1971 *AmSCAP 66, -80, BiDAmM*
Lubotsky, Mark Davidovich 1931- *IntWWM 80, NewGrD 80*
Lubovitch, Lar 1943- *CmpGMD, CnOxB*
Lubrich, Fritz, Jr. 1888-1971 *Baker 78*
Lubrich, Fritz, Sr. 1862-1952 *Baker 78*
Luby, Edna 1884- *WhoStg 1906, -1908*
Luca, Alexander C 1805-1872 *BiDAmM*
Luca, D *NewGrD 80*
Luca, Dia 1912-1975 *CnOxB*
Luca, Giuseppe De *MusSN[port], NewEOp 71, NewGrD 80*
Luca, Saverio Di *NewGrD 80*
Luca, Sergiu 1943- *NewGrD 80*
Luca, Severo Di *NewGrD 80*
Luca DeTena, Juan Ignacio 1897- *McGEWD[port]*
Lucacich, Ivan *NewGrD 80*
Lucacih, Ivan *NewGrD 80*
Lucaciu, Teodora *WhoOp 76*
Lucan, Arthur 1887-1954 *FilmgC, HalFC 80, IlWWBF[port], NotNAT B, WhScrn 74, -77, WhoHol B, WhoHrs 80*
Lucantoni, Giovanni 1825-1902 *Baker 78*
Lucario, Giovanni Giacomo *NewGrD 80*
Lucas, Al 1916- *WhoJazz 72*
Lucas, Brenda *WhoMus 72*
Lucas, Carroll W 1909-1979 *AmSCAP 66, -80*
Lucas, Charles *BlksB&W C*
Lucas, Charles 1808-1869 *NewGrD 80*
Lucas, Christopher Norman 1912-1970 *AmSCAP 66, -80*
Lucas, Clarence 1866-1947 *BiDAmM, NewGrD 80*
Lucas, Clyde 1901- *BgBands 74, CmpEPM*
Lucas, Dave *ConMuA 80B*
Lucas, David John 1942- *IntWWM 77, -80*
Lucas, Gene 1886- *AmSCAP 66, -80*
Lucas, George 1944- *BiDFilm 81, ConLC 16*
Lucas, George 1945- *FilmEn, HalFC 80, IntMPA 77, -75, -76, -78, -79, -80, MovMk[port], WhoHrs 80*
Lucas, James 1927- *WhoMus 72*
Lucas, James 1933- *WhoOp 76*
Lucas, James 1942- *CpmDNM 72*
Lucas, Jane *BluesWW*
Lucas, Jimmy 1888-1949 *WhScrn 74, -77, WhoHol B*
Lucas, Jonathan 1922- *BiE&WWA*
Lucas, Jonathan 1928- *NotNAT*
Lucas, Leighton 1903- *Baker 78, FilmgC, HalFC 80, NewGrD 80, WhoMus 72*
Lucas, Marcia *WomWMM*
Lucas, Marie d1947 *BlkWAB[port]*
Lucas, Mary Anderson 1882-1952 *Baker 78*
Lucas, Nick 1897- *CmpEPM, Film 2, What 4[port], WhoHol A*
Lucas, Paul *Film 2*
Lucas, Roger 1940- *CnOxB*
Lucas, Rupert d1953 *NotNAT B*
Lucas, Sam 1840-1916 *BiDAmM, DrBlPA*
Lucas, Sam 1841-1916 *Film 1, WhScrn 77*
Lucas, Sam 1848-1916 *BlksBF[port]*
Lucas, Sharalee 1949- *AmSCAP 80*
Lucas, Slim *Film 1*
Lucas, Theodore D 1941- *ConAmC*
Lucas, Tony 1850- *BlksBF*
Lucas, Wilfred 1871-1940 *FilmEn, Film 1, -2, HalFC 80, HolCA[port], MotPP, TwYS, -A, WhScrn 74, -77, WhoHol B*
Lucas, Wilfrid d1940 *ForYSC*
Lucas, William 1918- *BluesWW[port]*
Lucas, William 1926- *FilmgC, HalFC 80, WhoHol A*
Lucas, William Roy 1932- *IntWWM 77, -80*
Lucatelli, Giovanni Battista *NewGrD 80*
Lucatello, Giovanni Battista *NewGrD 80*
Lucca, Francesco 1802-1872 *NewGrD 80*
Lucca, Pauline 1841-1908 *Baker 78, CmOp, NewEOp 71, NewGrD 80*
Luccacich, Ivan *NewGrD 80*
Luccardi, Giancarlo 1939- *WhoOp 76*
Lucchesi, Andrea 1741-1801 *NewGrD 80*
Lucchesi, Margaret Ann Cunningham 1928- *IntWWM 77, -80*
Lucchesina, La *NewGrD 80*
Lucchetti, Virginia *Film 2*
Lucchi, Francesca *NewGrD 80*
Lucci, Susan *WhoHol A*
Luccio, Francesco *NewGrD 80*
Lucciola, John 1926- *AmSCAP 66, -80*
Luce, Alexis B *Film 2*
Luce, Claire *BiE&WWA, NotNAT, PlP&P[port], WhoHol A, WhoThe 72, -77*
Luce, Claire 1903- *EncMT*
Luce, Claire Boothe 1903- *BiE&WWA*
Luce, Clare Booth 1903- *WomWMM*

Luce, Clare Boothe 1903- *McGEWD, NotNAT, -A*
Luce, Johnnie *AmSCAP 80*
Luce, Polly 1905- *WhThe*
Luce, William Aubert 1931- *AmSCAP 66, -80*
Luchaire, Corinne 1921-1950 *FilmgC, HalFC 80, WhScrn 74, -77, WhoHol B*
Luchesi, Andrea *NewGrD 80*
Luchetti, Veriano 1939- *NewGrD 80, WhoOp 76*
Luchini, Paolo 1535?-1598 *NewGrD 80*
Lucia, Fernando De *NewGrD 80*
Luciani, Sebastiano Arturo 1884-1950 *Baker 78, NewGrD 80*
Lucie, Larry 1914- *EncJzS 70*
Lucie, Lawrence 1907- *WhoJazz 72*
Lucie, Lawrence 1914- *EncJzS 70, IntWWM 77, -80*
Lucien, Jon 1942- *DrBlPA, EncJzS 70*
Lucier, Alvin 1931- *Baker 78, ConAmC, DcCM*
Lucier, Raymond J 1900- *AmSCAP 66*
Lucino, Francesco d1617 *NewGrD 80*
Lucio, Francesco 1628?-1658 *NewGrD 80*
Luciotti, Bonita L 1943- *AmSCAP 80*
Luciuk, Juliusz Mieczyslaw 1927- *Baker 78, IntWWM 77, -80, NewGrD 80*
Luck, Booth P d1962 *NotNAT B*
Luck, Rudolf 1927- *NewGrD 80*
Lucke, Hans 1927- *CnMD*
Lucke, Katharine E 1875-1962 *ConAmC*
Luckett, Keith d1973 *WhoHol B*
Luckett, Richard 1945- *IntWWM 77, -80*
Luckham, Cyril 1907- *WhoHol A, WhoThe 72, -77*
Luckinbill, Laurence 1938?- *HalFC 80*
Luckinbill, Laurence George 1934- *WhoHol A, WhoThe 77*
Luckman, Phyllis 1927- *ConAmC*
Luckstone, Isidore 1861-1941 *BiDAmM*
Lucky, Stepan 1919- *Baker 78, IntWWM 77, -80, NewGrD 80, WhoMus 72*
Lucocque, Horace Lisle *IlWWBF*
Luconto, Frank X 1931- *AmSCAP 80*
Lucraft, Howard 1916- *EncJzS 70*
Lucy, Arnold 1865-1945 *Film 2, NotNAT B, WhScrn 77, WhoHol B*
Ludden, Allen *NewYTET*
Ludden, William 1823-1912 *BiDAmM*
Luddy, Barbara *Film 2, WhoHol A*
Ludecus, Matthaus 1527-1606 *NewGrD 80*
Ludeke, Matthaus 1527-1606 *NewGrD 80*
Ludeke, Rainer 1927- *WhoOp 76*
Luden, Jack 1902- *Film 2, ForYSC, TwYS*
Luders, Adam 1950- *CnOxB*
Luders, Gustav 1865-1913 *AmPS, BiDAmM, EncMT, NewCBMT, NewGrD 80, NotNAT B, PopAmC[port], WhThe*
Luders, Gustav 1866-1913 *CmpEPM*
Ludewig, Wolfgang 1926- *NewGrD 80*
Ludewig-Verdehr, Elsa 1936- *IntWWM 77, -80*
Ludford, Nicholas 1485?-1557? *Baker 78, BnBkM 80, NewGrD 80, OxMus*
Ludgate, Jane Stearns *PupTheA*
Ludgin, Chester Hall 1925- *IntWWM 77, -80, WhoOp 76*
Ludikar, Pavel 1882-1970 *Baker 78, CmOp, NewEOp 71*
Ludin, Fritz 1934?- *CnOxB*
Ludington, Charles William 1921- *IntWWM 77*
Ludkewycz, Stanislaus 1879- *Baker 78*
Ludlam, Charles 1943- *ConDr 73, -77, NotNAT, WhoThe 77*
Ludlam, Helen *WhoHol A*
Ludlow, Benjamin, Jr. 1910- *AmSCAP 66, -80*
Ludlow, Conrad 1935- *CnOxB, DancEn 78*
Ludlow, Noah Miller 1795-1886 *NotNAT A, -B, OxThe, PlP&P*
Ludlow, Patrick 1903- *WhoHol A, WhoThe 72, -77*
Ludlum, Robert 1927- *BiE&WWA, NotNAT*
Ludlum, Stuart D 1907- *AmSCAP 66, -80*
Ludmilla, Anna *Film 2*
Ludovico Milanese 1480?-1537? *NewGrD 80*
Ludtke, Matthaus *NewGrD 80*
Ludvicus DeArimino *NewGrD 80*
Ludwig II, King 1845-1883 *Baker 78*
Ludwig, Arthur *Film 2*
Ludwig, August 1865-1946 *Baker 78*
Ludwig, Christa *IntWWM 77, -80, WhoMus 72, WhoOp 76*
Ludwig, Christa 1924- *NewEOp 71, NewGrD 80[port]*
Ludwig, Christa 1928- *Baker 78, CmOp, MusSN[port]*
Ludwig, Edward 1895- *FilmgC, HalFC 80*
Ludwig, Edward 1899- *FilmEn*
Ludwig, Emil 1881-1948 *NotNAT B*
Ludwig, Franz 1889-1955 *Baker 78*
Ludwig, Friedrich 1872-1930 *Baker 78, NewGrD 80*
Ludwig, Ilse 1929- *WhoOp 76*
Ludwig, Irving H 1910- *IntMPA 77, -75, -76, -78, -79, -80*
Ludwig, Joachim Carl Martin 1934- *WhoMus 72*
Ludwig, Johann Adam Jakob 1730-1782 *NewGrD 80*
Ludwig, John McKay 1935- *WhoOp 76*
Ludwig, Josef 1844-1924 *NewGrD 80*
Ludwig, Joseph 1844-1924 *NewGrD 80*
Ludwig, Leopold 1908-1979 *Baker 78, CmOp, MusSN[port], NewEOp 71, NewGrD 80, WhoOp 76*
Ludwig, Max 1882-1945 *NewGrD 80*
Ludwig, Norbert 1902-1960 *AmSCAP 66, -80*
Ludwig, Otto 1813-1865 *CnThe, EncWT, McGEWD[port], NotNAT B, OxThe, REnWD[port]*
Ludwig, Otto 1874-1922 *NewGrD 80*
Ludwig, Ralph *Film 2*
Ludwig, Robert L 1935- *IntWWM 77*
Ludwig, Salem 1915- *WhoHol A, WhoThe 72, -77*
Ludwig, Walther 1902- *WhoMus 72*
Ludwig, William 1912- *FilmEn, FilmgC, HalFC 80*
Ludwig, Wolf-Dieter 1928- *WhoOp 76*
Ludwin, Rick 1948- *AmSCAP 80*
Luebbert, Lynn *WomWMM B*
Luedders, Jerry Duane 1943- *IntWWM 77*
Luedeke, Raymond 1944- *CpmDNM 76, ConAmC*
Lueders, Guenther 1905-1975 *WhScrn 77, WhoHol C*
Lueders, Mary Cross 1942- *WhoOp 76*
Lueloff, Jorie *ConAmTC*
Luening, Otto 1900- *Baker 78, BiDAmM, BnBkM 80, CpmDNM 78, -79, -80, ConAmC, DcCM, IntWWM 77, -80, NewGrD 80, OxMus*
Luetkeman, Paul 1555?-1611? *NewGrD 80*
Luetti, Gemignano *NewGrD 80*
Luez, Laurette *ForYSC*
Luff, William *Film 2*
Lufkin, Dan W *IntMPA 79, -80*
Lufkin, Sam 1892-1952 *Film 2, WhScrn 77*
Luft, Herbert G *IntMPA 77, -75, -76, -78, -79, -80*
Luft, James *PupTheA*
Luft, John *PupTheA*
Luft, Ludmilla Gorny-Otzoup *CreCan 1*
Luft, Uriel 1933- *CreCan 1*
Lugert, Josef 1841-1936 *Baker 78*
Lugg, Alfred 1889- *WhThe*
Lugg, George 1898-1946 *WhoJazz 72*
Lugg, William 1852-1940 *WhThe*
Lugge, John 1587?-1647? *NewGrD 80*
Lugge, Robert *NewGrD 80*
Lugne-Poe, A F 1870-1940 *WhThe*
Lugne-Poe, Aurelien-Francois-Marie 1869-1940 *EncWT, Ent, OxThe*
Lugne-Poe, Aurelien-Marie 1869-1940 *CnThe, NotNAT A, -B*
Lugosi, Bela d1956 *MotPP, WhoHol B*
Lugosi, Bela 1882-1956 *CmMov, FilmEn, Film 1, -2, FilmgC, ForYSC, HalFC 80, MovMk[port], WhScrn 74, -77, WhoHrs 80[port], WorEFlm*
Lugosi, Bela 1883-1956 *TwYS*
Lugosi, Bela 1884-1956 *NotNAT B*
Lugosi, Bela 1888-1956 *BiDFilm, -81, OxFilm, WhThe*
Luguet, Andre 1892- *WhThe*
Luigi 1925- *CnOxB*
Luigini, Alexandre Clement Leon Joseph 1850-1906 *Baker 78, NewGrD 80, OxMus*
Luiken, Carol 1945- *WhoOp 76*
Luillier *NewGrD 80*
Luipart, Marcel 1912- *CnOxB*
Luipart, Marcel 1915- *DancEn 78*
Luisi, Francesco 1943- *IntWWM 77, -80*
Luisi, James *WhoHol A*
Luisillo 1928- *CnOxB, DancEn 78*
Luitjens, Helen *PupTheA*
Luiton, Carl *NewGrD 80*
Lukacic, Ioannes 1587-1648 *NewGrD 80*
Lukacic, Ivan 1587-1648 *Baker 78, NewGrD 80*
Lukacs, Ervin 1928- *WhoOp 76*
Lukacs, Miklos 1905- *WhoOp 76*
Lukacs, Pal 1919- *NewGrD 80*
Lukas, Karl *WhoHol A*
Lukas, Paul d1971 *MotPP, WhoHol B*
Lukas, Paul 1887-1971 *HalFC 80[port]*
Lukas, Paul 1891-1971 *FilmgC, TwYS*
Lukas, Paul 1894-1971 *BiE&WWA, FilmEn, ForYSC, HolP 30[port], NotNAT B*
Lukas, Paul 1895-1971 *BiDFilm, -81, Film 1, -2, MovMk[port], OxFilm, WhScrn 74, -77, WhThe, WorEFlm*
Lukas, Peter A 1917- *AmSCAP 66*
Lukas, Richard Anthony 1944- *IntWWM 77*
Lukas, Viktor 1931- *NewGrD 80*
Lukas, Zdenek 1928- *Baker 78, NewGrD 80*
Lukaszczyk, Jacek 1934- *IntWWM 77, -80*
Lukaszewicz, Maciej d1685 *NewGrD 80*
Lukaszewski, Wojciech 1936- *IntWWM 77*
Luke *Film 1*
Luke, Key 1911- *ForYSC*
Luke, Keye *IntMPA 76*
Luke, Keye 1904- *FilmEn, HalFC 80, HolCA[port], IntMPA 77, -78, -79, -80, MGM[port], MovMk, Vers A[port], WhoHol A*
Luke, Keye 1909- *FilmgC*
Luke, Peter 1919- *ConDr 73, -77, IntMPA 77, -76, -78, -79, -80, NotNAT*
Luke, Ray E 1928- *AmSCAP 80, ConAmC, IntWWM 77, -80*
Luke, Robin 1942- *RkOn*
Luke The Drifter *IlEncCM*
Lukin, Mrs. Cecil E Schultz *WhScrn 74, -77*
Lukom, Yelena Mikhailovna 1891-1968 *CnOxB, DancEn 78*
Lukomska, Halina 1929- *NewGrD 80, WhoMus 72*
Lukov, Leonid 1909-1963 *DcFM, FilmEn*
Lukowicz, Jerzy 1936- *IntWWM 77, -80*
Lukyanov, Sergei Vladimirovich 1910- *WhThe*
Lulier, Giovanni Lorenzo 1650?- *NewGrD 80*
Lulinus Venetus, Johannes *NewGrD 80*
Lull, Antonio d1582 *NewGrD 80*
Lull, Ramon 1232?-1315 *NewGrD 80*
Lull, Raymond 1232?-1315 *NewGrD 80*
Lulli, Folco 1912-1970 *FilmEn, FilmgC, HalFC 80, WhScrn 74, -77, WhoHol B*
Lulli, Giovanni Battista 1632-1687 *BnBkM 80[port], NewGrD 80[port]*
Lully *NewGrD 80*
Lully, Jean 1632-1687 *DcCom&M 79*
Lully, Jean-Baptise 1632-1687 *CmOp*
Lully, Jean-Baptiste 1632-1687 *Baker 78, BnBkM 80[port], CmpBCM*
Lully, Jean Baptiste 1632-1687 *CnOxB*
Lully, Jean-Baptiste 1632-1687 *DancEn 78, DcCom 77, GrComp[port], MusMk[port], NewEOp 71, NewGrD 80[port]*
Lully, Jean Baptiste 1632-1687 *OxMus*
Lully, Jean-Baptiste 1665-1743 *NewGrD 80*
Lully, Jean-Louis 1667-1688 *NewGrD 80*
Lully, Louis 1664-1734 *NewGrD 80*
Lulu 1948- *FilmgC, HalFC 80, RkOn 2[port], WhoHol A*
Lulu 1949- *ConMuA 80A*
Lulu Belle 1913- *BiDAmM, EncFCWM 69*
Lulu Belle And Scotty *IlEncCM[port]*
Lulubelle 1913- *CounME 74*
Lulubelle And Scotty *CounME 74, -74A*
Lum And Abner *HalFC 80, JoeFr, What 1[port]*
Luman, Bob 1937- *CounME 74[port], -74A, EncFCWM 69, IlEncCM[port]*
Luman, Bob 1938- *RkOn*
Luman, Bobby Glynn 1937- *BiDAmM*
Lumb, Geoffrey 1905- *BiE&WWA*
Lumb, Harold 1919- *IntWWM 77, -80, WhoMus 72*
Lumby, Herbert Horace 1906- *IntWWM 77, -80, WhoMus 72*

Lumby, Ilah R 1911- *BiE&WWA*
Lumbye *NewGrD 80*
Lumbye, Carl 1841-1911 *NewGrD 80*
Lumbye, Georg 1843-1922 *NewGrD 80*
Lumbye, Hans Christian 1810-1874 *Baker 78, CnOxB, NewGrD 80*
Lumet, Baruch 1898- *BiE&WWA, WhoHol A*
Lumet, Sidney 1924- *AmFD, BiDFilm, -81, BiE&WWA, DcFM, FilmEn, FilmgC, HalFC 80, IntMPA 77, -75, -76, -78, -79, -80, MovMk[port], NewYTET, NotNAT, OxFilm, WhoHol A, WorEFlm*
Lumiere, Antoine 1840-190-? *DcFM*
Lumiere, August L 1862-1954 *TwYS A*
Lumiere, Auguste 1862-1954 *BiDFilm, -81, DcFM, Film 1, NotNAT B, OxFilm, WorEFlm*
Lumiere, Louis 1864-1948 *BiDFilm, -81, DcFM, FilmEn, FilmgC, HalFC 80, NotNAT B, OxFilm, TwYS A, WorEFlm*
Lumiere Brothers *WomWMM*
Lumkin, A W *IntMPA 77, -75, -76, -78, -79, -80*
Lumley, Benjamin 1811-1874 *DancEn 78*
Lumley, Joanna 1946- *HalFC 80*
Lumley, Ralph R d1900 *NotNAT B*
Lumley, Rex Arthur Liulph 1918- *WhoMus 72*
Lummis, Dayton 1903- *ForYSC, Vers A[port], WhoHol A*
Lump Lump, Willie *JoeFr*
Lumsdaine, David Newton 1931- *Baker 78, IntWWM 80, NewGrD 80, WhoMus 72*
Lumsden, David James 1928- *IntWWM 77, -80, NewGrD 80, WhoMus 72*
Lumsden, Norman 1906- *IntWWM 77, -80, WhoMus 72*
Lumsden, Ronald 1938- *IntWWM 77, -80, WhoMus 72*
Lun *NewGrD 80, PlP&P*
Luna, Barbara *ForYSC*
Luna, Barbara 1937- *FilmgC, HalFC 80, WhoHol A*
Luna, Barbara 1939- *FilmEn*
Luna, Donyale *WhoHol A*
Luna, Pablo 1880-1942 *NewGrD 80*
Lunacharski, Anatoli 1875-1933 *CnMD*
Lunacharsky, Anatoli Vasilevich 1875-1933 *CnThe, ModWD, NotNAT B, OxThe*
Lunacharsky, Anatoli Vasilyevich 1875-1933 *EncWT*
Lunati, Carlo Ambrogio *NewGrD 80*
Lunceford, James Melvin 1902-1947 *AmSCAP 66, -80, NewGrD 80*
Lunceford, Jimmie d1947 *BgBands 74[port]*
Lunceford, Jimmie 1902- *IlEncJ*
Lunceford, Jimmie 1902-1947 *BiDAmM, CmpEPM, DrBlPA, NewGrD 80, WhoJazz 72*
Lunceford, Jimmy 1902-1947 *AmPS B, NewGrD 80, WhScrn 77*
Lund, Adrianne *PupTheA*
Lund, Alan *CreCan 2*
Lund, Alan Keith 1948- *AmSCAP 80*
Lund, Art *AmPS A*
Lund, Art 1915- *CmpEPM*
Lund, Art 1920- *BiE&WWA, NotNAT, WhoHol A, WhoThe 72, -77*
Lund, Blanche Harris *CreCan 1*
Lund, Deanna *WhoHol A*
Lund, Eddie 1909-1973 *AmSCAP 66, -80*
Lund, Gus A 1896-1951 *WhScrn 74, -77*
Lund, John 1913- *FilmEn, FilmgC, ForYSC, HalFC 80, HolP 40[port], MotPP, MovMk, WhoHol A*
Lund, John-Peter 1948- *ConAmC*
Lund, Jorgen *Film 2*
Lund, Lilleba 1940- *IntWWM 77, -80*
Lund, Lucille *WhoHol A*
Lund, O A C *Film 1*
Lund, Richard 1885-1960 *Film 1, -2, WhScrn 77*
Lund, Signe 1868-1950 *Baker 78*
Lund Christiansen, Anne 1928- *IntWWM 77, -80*
Lundberg, Kjell 1922- *IntWWM 77, -80*
Lundberg, Victor *RkOn 2A*
Lundborg, Charles Erik 1948- *ConAmC*
Lundborg, Erik 1948- *CpmDNM 80*
Lunde, Ivar, Jr. 1944- *CpmDNM 78, -79, -80, ConAmC, IntWWM 77, -80*
Lunde, Lawson 1935- *AmSCAP 80, ConAmC*
Lunde, Nanette Gomory 1943- *IntWWM 77, -80*
Lundel, Kert Fritjof 1936- *WhoThe 77*
Lundequist, Gerda 1871-1959 *OxThe*
Lundequist-Dahlstrom, Gerda *Film 2*
Lundgren, Olav 1941- *IntWWM 80*
Lundgren, P A 1911- *FilmEn*
Lundholm, Jan Lennart 1938- *IntWWM 77*
Lundholm, Lisa *Film 2*
Lundigan, William 1914-1975 *FilmEn, FilmgC, ForYSC, HalFC 80, IntMPA 75, -76, MotPP, MovMk, What 5[port], WhScrn 77, WhoHol C*
Lundin, Nils O 1921- *AmSCAP 80*
Lundquist, Christie *ConAmC*
Lundquist, H E 1910- *AmSCAP 66*
Lundquist, Matthew Nathanael 1886-1964 *AmSCAP 66, -80*
Lundquist, Torbjorn Iwan 1920- *Baker 78, IntWWM 77, -80*
Lundqvist, Alf-Roger 1957- *IntWWM 80*
Lundsdorffer, Albrecht Martin *NewGrD 80*
Lundsten, Ralph 1936- *Baker 78, IntWWM 77, -80*
Lundstrom, Haakan Sven Ingemar 1946- *IntWWM 77*
Lundvall, Bruce *ConMuA 80B*
Lunelli, Renato 1895-1967 *NewGrD 80*
Lunetta, Stanley George 1937- *Baker 78, ConAmC, IntWWM 77*
Lung, Charles d1974 *WhScrn 77, WhoHol B*
Lung, Clarence *WhoHol A*
Lunicke *NewGrD 80*
Lunin, Hanno 1934- *WhoOp 76*
Lunn, Charles 1838-1906 *Baker 78*
Lunn, Joseph d1863 *NotNAT B*
Lunn, Louise Kirkby 1873-1930 *CmOp, NewGrD 80*
Lunn, Robert 1912- *IlEncCM[port]*
Lunn, Roger Francis 1938- *IntWWM 77, -80*
Lunnon, Robert *DancEn 78*
Lunsford, Bascom Lamar 1882- *BiDAmM, EncFCWM 69*
Lunsford, Beverly *WhoHol A*
Lunsford, James Camille 1927-1978 *AmSCAP 80*
Lunssens, Martin 1871-1944 *Baker 78, NewGrD 80*
Lunt, Alfred 1892-1977 *BiE&WWA, CnThe, FilmEn, FilmgC, HalFC 80, NotNAT, OxThe, PlP&P[port], WhoHol A, WhoThe 72, -77*
Lunt, Alfred 1893- *EncWT, FamA&A[port], Film 2, NotNAT A, TwYS*
Lunt, Alfred 1893-1977 *Ent*
Lunt, John Reinhold 1859-1925 *BiDAmM*
Lunt, Lynn Fontanne 1887- *OxThe*
Lunt, William Parsons 1805-1857 *BiDAmM*
Lunt, Winifred May *WhoMus 72*
Lunts, The *PlP&P[port]*
Lupacchino, Bernardino d1555? *NewGrD 80*
Lupato, Pietro *NewGrD 80*
Lupberger, Pauline 1931- *AmSCAP 66, -80*
Luper, Albert T 1914- *IntWWM 80*
Lupescu, Magda 1896- *What 1[port]*
Lupi, Didier *NewGrD 80*
Lupi, Ignazio *Film 1*
Lupi, Johannes 1506?-1539 *NewGrD 80*
Lupi, Father Mariantonio 1695-1737 *DcPup*
Lupi, Roberto 1908-1971 *Baker 78, NewGrD 80*
Lupi, Roldano 1909- *FilmAG WE*
Lupi Second, Didier *NewGrD 80*
Lupino, Barry 1882-1962 *OxThe, WhThe*
Lupino, Barry 1884-1962 *Ent, NotNAT B*
Lupino, Francesco 1500?- *NewGrD 80*
Lupino, George 1853-1932 *NotNAT B*
Lupino, Henry George 1892-1959 *OxThe*
Lupino, Ida *IlWWBF A, MotPP, WhoHol A, WomWMM, -B*
Lupino, Ida 1914- *FilmgC, HalFC 80[port], WhoHrs 80*
Lupino, Ida 1916- *ForYSC, ThFT[port]*
Lupino, Ida 1918- *BiDFilm, -81, FilmEn, IntMPA 77, -75, -76, -78, -79, -80, MovMk[port], OxFilm, WorEFlm[port]*
Lupino, Mark 1894-1930 *NotNAT B, WhScrn 77*
Lupino, Stanley d1942 *WhoHol B*
Lupino, Stanley 1893-1942 *FilmgC, HalFC 80, OxThe, WhScrn 77*
Lupino, Stanley 1894-1942 *EncMT, NotNAT A, -B, WhThe*
Lupino, Stanley 1895-1942 *IlWWBF[port], WhScrn 74*
Lupino, Stanley 1895-1945 *IlWWBF A*
Lupino, Wallace d1961 *WhoHol B*
Lupino, Wallace 1897-1961 *Film 1, -2, WhThe*
Lupino, Wallace 1898-1961 *WhScrn 74, -77*
Lupino, Walter *Film 2*
Lupo *NewGrD 80*
Lupo, Alberto *WhoHrs 80[port]*
Lupo, Ambrose d1591 *NewGrD 80*
Lupo, Ambrosio d1591 *NewGrD 80*
Lupo, George G 1924-1973 *WhScrn 77*
Lupo, Gioseffo d1616 *NewGrD 80*
Lupo, Joseph d1616 *NewGrD 80*
Lupo, Josepho d1616 *NewGrD 80*
Lupo, Peter *NewGrD 80*
Lupo, Theophilus *NewGrD 80*
Lupo, Thomas *NewGrD 80*
Lupo, Thomas d1628 *NewGrD 80*
Luporini, Gaetano 1865-1948 *Baker 78*
Lupot, Nicolas 1758-1824 *MusMk, NewGrD 80*
Luppachino, Bernardino *NewGrD 80*
Luppagnino, Bernardino *NewGrD 80*
Luprano, Filippo De *NewGrD 80*
Lupton, John *ForYSC, WhoHol A*
Lupton-Smith, Lilian Ruth Gladys 1896- *IntWWM 80*
Lupu, Radu 1945- *IntWWM 77, -80, NewGrD 80, WhoMus 72*
Lupu-Pick 1886-1931 *DcFM, FilmEn, WorEFlm*
Lupus *NewGrD 80*
Lupus Hellinck *NewGrD 80*
Lupus, Eduardus *Baker 78, NewGrD 80*
Lupus, Manfred Barbarini *NewGrD 80*
Lupus, Martin *NewGrD 80*
Lupus, Michael 1500?-1567 *Baker 78*
Lupus, Peter 1937- *ForYSC, WhoHol A*
Lupus Italus *NewGrD 80*
Lurano, Filippo De 1475?-1520? *NewGrD 80*
Luraschi, Luigi G 1906- *IntMPA 77, -75, -76, -78, -79, -80*
Luray, Doris *Film 2*
Lurie, Jane *WomWMM B*
Lurie, Samuel *BiE&WWA*
Lurville, Armand *Film 2*
Luscinius, Othmar 1478?-1537 *NewGrD 80*
Luscombe, George 1926- *CreCan 2*
Luse, Robert *ConAmC*
Lush, Ernest 1908- *NewGrD 80, WhoMus 72*
Lusher *NewGrD 80*
Lushier *NewGrD 80*
Lushka, Mike *ConMuA 80B*
Lusitano, Manuel Leitao DeAvilez *NewGrD 80*
Lusitano, Vicente *NewGrD 80*
Lusk, Freeman 1906-1970 *ForYSC, WhScrn 77*
Lussan, Zelie De 1862-1949 *Baker 78*
Lusse, De 1720?-1774? *NewGrD 80*
Lusse, Christophe De *NewGrD 80*
Lusse, Jacques *NewGrD 80*
Lussi, Marie 1892-1968 *AmSCAP 66, -80*
Lussy, Mathis 1828-1910 *Baker 78, NewGrD 80*
Lustberg, Arthur 1925- *AmSCAP 80*
Lustberg, Jack 1903- *IntMPA 75, -76*
Lustberg, Jean Anne 1927- *AmSCAP 80*
Lustgarten, Edgar 1907-1979 *HalFC 80*
Lustig, Jacob Wilhelm 1706-1796 *NewGrD 80*
Lustig, Jan 1901-1978 *HalFC 80*
Lustig, Jan 1902- *IntMPA 75, -76*
Lusty, Archibald Henry 1895- *WhoMus 72*
Lutcher, Nellie 1915- *BlkWAB, CmpEPM, DrBlPA*
Lutcher, Nellie Rose 1915- *AmSCAP 80*
Lutge, Elizabeth Marie 1928- *IntWWM 77, -80*
Lutgendorff, Willibald Leo 1856-1937 *Baker 78*
Luther, Ann 1893-1960 *WhScrn 77*
Luther, Ann 1894-1960 *Film 2*
Luther, Anna 1894-1960 *Film 1, NotNAT B, TwYS, WhoHol B*
Luther, Frank 1905- *CmpEPM, IlEncCM*
Luther, Johnny 1909-1960 *WhScrn 74, -77, WhoHol B*

Luther, Lester 1888-1962 *NotNAT B, WhScrn 74, -77, WhoHol B*
Luther, Martin 1483-1546 *Baker 78, MusMk[port], NewGrD 80, OxMus*
Luther, Warren Phillips 1939- *ConAmC*
Luther, Wilhelm Martin 1912-1962 *NewGrD 80*
Luthon, Carl *NewGrD 80*
Luti, Vincent F *ConAmC*
Lutkemann, Paul *NewGrD 80*
Lutkin, Peter Christian 1858-1931 *Baker 78, BiDAmM, NewGrD 80, OxMus*
Lutolf, Max 1934- *IntWWM 77, -80, NewGrD 80*
Lutoslawski, Witold 1913- *Baker 78, BiDAmM, BnBkM 80, CompSN[port], CpmDNM 80, DcCom&M 79, DcCM, IntWWM 77, -80, MusMk[port], NewGrD 80[port], OxMus, WhoMus 72*
Lutrell, Helen *Film 1*
Lutry, Michel De 1924- *CnOxB*
Lutschg, Andrej 1926- *IntWWM 77, -80*
Lutschg, Karl 1839-1899 *Baker 78*
Lutter, Alfred *WhoHol A*
Luttringer, Alfonse 1879-1953 *WhScrn 74, -77*
Lutyens, Elisabeth 1906- *Baker 78, BnBkM 80, DcCom&M 79, DcCM, IntWWM 77, -80, MusMk[port], NewGrD 80[port], OxFilm, OxMus, WhoMus 72*
Lutyens, Sally Speare 1927- *ConAmC*
Lutz, Abbot 1917- *AmSCAP 66, -80*
Lutz, Caroline *PupTheA*
Lutz, E O 1919- *BiE&WWA, NotNAT*
Lutz, H B *BiE&WWA*
Lutz, Marjorie *WomWMM B*
Lutz, Meyer 1822?-1903 *NewGrD 80*
Lutz, Michael George 1949- *AmSCAP 80*
Lutz, Verena 1941- *WhoMus 72*
Lutz, Wilhelm Meyer 1822-1903 *Baker 78*
Lutzen, B Ludolf 1939- *IntWWM 77, -80*
Lutzkendorf, Felix 1906- *CnMD*
Luvisi, Lee 1937- *WhoMus 72*
Lux, Friedrich 1820-1895 *Baker 78*
Lux, Lillian Sylvia 1918- *AmSCAP 80*
Luxford, Nola *Film 2, WhoHol A*
Luxon, Benjamin 1937- *CmOp, IntWWM 77, -80, NewGrD 80, WhoMus 72, WhoOp 76*
Luxon, Charles Frederick 1913- *WhoMus 72*
Luxton, Lesley Vivienne 1955- *IntWWM 80*
Luypaerts, Guy Philippe 1931- *IntWWM 80*
Luyr, Adam *NewGrD 80*
Luython, Carl 1557?-1620 *NewGrD 80*
Luython, Carolus 1557?-1620 *NewGrD 80*
Luython, Charles 1556?-1620 *Baker 78*
Luython, Charles 1557?-1620 *NewGrD 80*
Luython, Karel 1557?-1620 *NewGrD 80*
Luzan, Ignacio 1702-1754 *OxThe*
Luzhsky, V V *PlP&P[port]*
Luzzaschi, Luzzasco 1545-1607 *Baker 78, NewGrD 80*
Luzzati, Emanuele 1921- *WhoOp 76*
Luzzatto, Livio 1897- *WhoOp 76*
Luzzi, Luigi 1828-1876 *Baker 78*
Luzzo, Francesco *NewGrD 80*
Lvof, Alexis 1798-1870 *OxMus*
L'vov *NewGrD 80*
Lvov, Alexei 1798-1870 *Baker 78*
L'vov, Alexey Fyodorovich 1798-1870 *NewGrD 80*
Lvov, Alexis 1798-1870 *MusMk*
L'vov, Fyodor Petrovich 1766-1836 *NewGrD 80*
L'vov, Nikolay Alexandrovich 1751-1803 *NewGrD 80*
Lvova, Ludmilla *CreCan 1*
Lwowa, Ludmila *CreCan 1*
Lwowa, Marcin Z *NewGrD 80*
Lwowczyk, Marcin Z *NewGrD 80*
Ly-Dells, The *RkOn*
Lyadov, Anatol Konstantinovich 1855-1914 *NewGrD 80*
Lyadov, Anatoly Konstantinovich 1855-1914 *NewGrD 80*
Lyall, Deecie Campbell *WhoMus 72*
Lyall, Laura Adeline Muntz *CreCan 1*
Lyall, Laura Muntz 1860-1930 *CreCan 1*
Lyall, Max Dail 1939- *AmSCAP 80, IntWWM 77, -80*
Lyapunov, Sergey Mikhaylovich 1859-1924 *NewGrD 80*
Lyatoshyns'ky, Boris Mykolayovich 1895-1968 *NewGrD 80*
Lyatoshyns'ky, Nikolayevich 1895-1968 *NewGrD 80*
Lybbert, Donald 1923- *Baker 78, CpmDNM 79, ConAmC, DcCM, NewGrD 80*
Lycophron 324?BC- *OxThe*
Lyddon, Paul W 1931- *IntWWM 77, -80*
Lyde, Cecil Orlando 1948- *AmSCAP 80*
Lydecker, Howard 1911-1969 *WhoHrs 80*
Lydecker, Theodore 1908- *WhoHrs 80*
Lydgate, John *OxMus*
Lydiate, Frederick *IntWWM 77, -80*
Lydon, James 1923- *FilmgC, HalFC 80, IntMPA 77, -75, -76, -78, -79, -80, MovMk*
Lydon, Jimmy 1923- *FilmEn, ForYSC, What 4[port], WhoHol A*
Lydzinski, Kazimierz Alexander 1917- *IntWWM 77, -80*
Lye, Len 1901- *DcFM, FilmgC, HalFC 80, OxFilm, WorEFlm[port]*
Lye, Len 1901-1980 *FilmEn*
Lyel, Viola 1900-1972 *FilmgC, HalFC 80, WhThe, WhoHol B, WhoThe 72*
Lyford, Ralph 1882-1927 *Baker 78*
Lygo, Mary d1927 *WhScrn 74, -77*
Lykkebo, Finn 1937- *IntWWM 77, -80*
Lyle, Bessie *Film 2*
Lyle, Cecil 1892-1955 *MagIID*
Lyle, Edythe *Film 1*
Lyle, K Curtis 1944- *BlkAmP, MorBAP*
Lyle, Lyston d1920 *NotNAT B, WhThe*
Lyles, A C 1918- *CmMov, FilmgC, HalFC 80, IntMPA 77, -75, -76, -78, -79, -80*
Lyles, Aubrey *MorBAP*
Lyles, Aubrey d1933 *JoeFr*
Lyles, Aubrey L 1884?-1932 *DrBlPA*
Lyly, John 1554?-1606 *CnThe, EncWT, Ent, McGEWD, NotNAT B, OxThe, PlP&P, REnWD[port]*
Lyman, Abe 1897-1957 *AmSCAP 66, -80, BgBands 74, CmpEPM, NotNAT B, WhScrn 74, -77, WhoHol B*
Lyman, Arthur *RkOn*
Lyman, Edward Parsons, Jr. 1932- *AmSCAP 80*
Lyman, Howard Wilder 1879- *Baker 78*
Lyman, John 1886-1967 *CreCan 2*
Lyman, Percy *PupTheA*
Lyman, Mrs. Percy *PupTheA*
Lyman, Tommy *AmPS B*
Lyman, Tommy d1964 *NotNAT B*
Lymburgia, Johannes De *NewGrD 80*
Lymon, Frankie *ConMuA 80A*
Lymon, Frankie 1942-1968 *DrBlPA, WhScrn 77*
Lymon, Frankie 1943-1968 *BiDAmM*
Lymon, Frankie And The Teenagers *AmPS A, RkOn[port]*
Lympany, Moura 1916- *IntWWM 77, -80, NewGrD 80, WhoMus 72*
Lyn, Dawn 1963- *WhoHol A*
Lyn, Jacquie *WhoHol A*
Lynas, Jeff *WhoHol A*
Lyncaster, Rhodea 1927- *IntWWM 77*
Lyncaster, Rhodes 1927- *IntWWM 80*
Lynch, Alfred 1933- *FilmgC, HalFC 80, PlP&P, WhoHol A*
Lynch, Allen Malcolm 1947- *IntWWM 77*
Lynch, Brid 1913-1968 *WhScrn 77*
Lynch, Edie *WomWMM B*
Lynch, Frank J d1932 *WhScrn 74, -77*
Lynch, Frank T 1869-1933 *WhScrn 74, -77*
Lynch, Helen 1904-1965 *Film 2, TwYS, WhScrn 77, WhoHol B*
Lynch, Jim d1916 *WhScrn 77*
Lynch, John *Film 2*
Lynch, Ken *ForYSC, WhoHol A*
Lynch, Ruth Sproule *WhScrn 77*
Lynch, T Murray 1920- *IntMPA 77, -75, -76, -78, -79, -80*
Lynch, Walter *Film 1*
Lynd, Gene *AmSCAP 80*
Lynd, Rosa 1884-1922 *NotNAT B, WhThe*
Lynde, Paul 1926- *BiE&WWA, EncMT, FilmEn, FilmgC, ForYSC, HalFC 80, IntMPA 77, -75, -76, -78, -79, -80, JoeFr[port], MotPP, MovMk[port], NotNAT, WhoHol A*
Lyndon, Alice 1874-1949 *WhScrn 74, -77, WhoHol B*
Lyndon, Barre 1896-1972 *FilmEn, FilmgC, HalFC 80, WhThe, WhoHrs 80*
Lyndon, Clarence *Film 1*
Lyndon, Larry *Film 1*
Lyndon, Victor *IntMPA 77, -75, -76, -78, -79, -80*
Lyndsay, Sir David 1490?-1555? *McGEWD, REnWD[port]*
Lyne, Felice 1887-1935 *Baker 78*
Lyne, Peter Howard 1946- *IntWWM 80*
Lynen, Robert 1921-1944 *FilmEn, HalFC 80*
Lynes, Frank 1858-1913 *Baker 78*
Lynes, Gary S 1934- *AmSCAP 66*
Lynex, Penelope Norah 1936- *IntWWM 77, -80*
Lynham, Deryck 1913-1951 *CnOxB, DancEn 78*
Lynley, Carol 1942- *FilmEn, FilmgC, ForYSC, HalFC 80[port], MotPP, MovMk[port], WhoHol A, WorEFlm*
Lynn, Ann *IntMPA 78, -79, -80*
Lynn, Ann 1934?- *HalFC 80*
Lynn, Ann 1939?- *FilmgC, IlWWBF, IntMPA 77, WhoHol A*
Lynn, Barbara 1942- *RkOn*
Lynn, Betty *ForYSC, WhoHol A*
Lynn, Cynthia *WhoHol A*
Lynn, Diana 1926-1971 *BiE&WWA, FilmEn, FilmgC, ForYSC, HalFC 80, MotPP, MovMk[port], NotNAT B, WhScrn 74, -77, WhoHol B*
Lynn, Eddie 1905-1975 *WhScrn 77*
Lynn, Eleanor *PlP&P[port]*
Lynn, Emmett 1897-1958 *ForYSC, Vers B[port], WhScrn 74, -77, WhoHol B*
Lynn, Emmy *Film 2*
Lynn, George 1906- *ForYSC*
Lynn, George 1915- *AmSCAP 66, -80, Baker 78, ConAmC*
Lynn, George M d1967 *WhScrn 77, WhoHol B*
Lynn, H S 1836-1899 *MagIID*
Lynn, Hastings 1879-1932 *WhScrn 74, -77*
Lynn, Homer *Film 2*
Lynn, Jeffrey 1909- *BiE&WWA, FilmEn, FilmgC, ForYSC, HalFC 80, IntMPA 77, -75, -76, -78, -79, -80, MotPP, MovMk, NotNAT, What 5[port], WhoHol A*
Lynn, Jill *Film 2*
Lynn, Johnny *AmSCAP 80*
Lynn, Joseph R, Jr. 1947- *IntWWM 77*
Lynn, Judith *WhoOp 76*
Lynn, Judy 1936- *BiDAmM, CounME 74[port], -74A, EncFCWM 69, IlEncCM*
Lynn, Kane W 1919- *IntMPA 77, -75, -76, -78, -79*
Lynn, Leni 1925- *FilmgC, HalFC 80, WhoHol A*
Lynn, Loretta 1935- *BiDAmM, CounME 74[port], -74A, EncFCWM 69, IlEncCM[port]*
Lynn, Mara 1929- *BiE&WWA, NotNAT, WhoHol A*
Lynn, Natalie d1964 *WhScrn 74, -77*
Lynn, Ralph d1962 *Film 2, WhoHol B*
Lynn, Ralph 1881-1962 *WhScrn 74, -77*
Lynn, Ralph 1882-1962 *IlWWBF[port], OxThe, WhThe*
Lynn, Ralph 1882-1964 *CnThe, FilmgC, HalFC 80*
Lynn, Robert *IntMPA 75, -76, -78, -79, -80*
Lynn, Robert 1897-1969 *WhScrn 74, -77, WhoHol B*
Lynn, Robert 1918- *FilmgC, HalFC 80, IlWWBF, IntMPA 77*
Lynn, Sharon d1963 *MotPP, WhoHol B*
Lynn, Sharon 1904-1963 *WhScrn 74, -77*
Lynn, Sharon 1907-1963 *ThFT[port]*
Lynn, Sharon 1908-1963 *Film 2, TwYS*
Lynn, Sharon 1910-1963 *ForYSC, HalFC 80*
Lynn, Sydney *Film 2*
Lynn, Vera *RkOn*
Lynn, Vera 1917- *CmpEPM*
Lynn, Vera 1921- *HalFC 80*
Lynn, William H 1889-1952 *NotNAT B, WhScrn 74, -77, WhoHol B*

Lynne, Carole 1918- *WhThe*
Lynne, Gillian *WhoThe 77*
Lynne, Gillian 1926- *CnOxB, DancEn 78*
Lynne, Gloria *RkOn*
Lynne, James Broom 1920- *ConDr 73*
Lynton, Mayme *Film 1*
Lynton, Mayne 1885- *WhThe*
Lynyrd Skynyrd *ConMuA 80A, IlEncR, RkOn 2[port]*
Lyon, Annabelle *CnOxB, DancEn 78*
Lyon, Barbara *WhoHol A*
Lyon, Ben 1901-1979 *FilmEn, Film 1, -2, FilmgC, ForYSC, HalFC 80, IlWWBF, -A, MotPP, MovMk, OxFilm, TwYS, What 4[port], WhThe, WhoHol A*
Lyon, David Norman 1938- *Baker 78, IntWWM 77, -80, WhoMus 72*
Lyon, Earle 1923- *IntMPA 77, -75, -76, -78, -79, -80*
Lyon, Francis D *IntMPA 75, -76, -78, -79*
Lyon, Francis D 1905- *FilmEn, FilmgC, HalFC 80, IntMPA 77, -80, WhoHrs 80*
Lyon, Frank 1901-1961 *WhScrn 74, -77, WhoHol B*
Lyon, Frank A *Film 2*
Lyon, George Washburn 1820- *Baker 78, NewGrD 80*
Lyon, George Washington 1825-1894 *BiDAmM*
Lyon, James 1735- *OxMus*
Lyon, James 1735-1794 *Baker 78, BiDAmM, NewGrD 80*
Lyon, James 1954- *IntWWM 80*
Lyon, John Henry Hobart d1961 *NotNAT B*
Lyon, John Thomas, Jr. 1930- *IntWWM 77, -80*
Lyon, Katherine Edelman 1915- *AmSCAP 80*
Lyon, Myer *NewGrD 80*
Lyon, Peter 1943- *WhoMus 72*
Lyon, Raymond Michel 1908- *IntWWM 80*
Lyon, Richard *WhoHol A*
Lyon, Sue 1946- *FilmEn, FilmgC, ForYSC, HalFC 80, IntMPA 77, -75, -76, -78, -79, -80, MotPP, WhoHol A*
Lyon, T E d1869 *NotNAT B*
Lyon, Therese d1975 *WhScrn 77, WhoHol C*
Lyon, Wanda 1897- *Film 2, WhThe*
Lyon & Healy *Baker 78*
Lyon-Shaw, W 1913- *IntMPA 75, -76*
Lyonel *NewGrD 80*
Lyonnet, Henry d1933 *NotNAT B*
Lyonnois, Marie *DancEn 78*
Lyons, A Neil 1880-1940 *WhThe*
Lyons, Bob 1868?-1949? *NewOrJ[port]*
Lyons, Candy 1945-1966 *WhScrn 74, -77, WhoHol B*
Lyons, Cliff Tex 1902-1974 *WhScrn 77, WhoHol B*
Lyons, Dan D *AmSCAP 80*
Lyons, Eddie 1886-1926 *FilmEn, TwYS, WhScrn 77*
Lyons, Edmund D d1906 *NotNAT B*
Lyons, Edward 1886- *Film 1, -2*
Lyons, Frances *Film 2*
Lyons, Frankie d1937 *WhScrn 77*
Lyons, Freckles 1909-1960 *WhScrn 74, -77*
Lyons, Fred d1921 *WhScrn 74, -77*
Lyons, Gene 1921-1974 *WhScrn 77, WhoHol B*
Lyons, Gretchen *WhoStg 1906, -1908*
Lyons, Harry Agar 1878-1919 *Film 2, IlWWBF*
Lyons, Harry M 1879-1919 *WhScrn 77*
Lyons, Jack 1942- *IntMPA 75*
Lyons, James 1925-1973 *Baker 78*
Lyons, James 1932- *BiDAmM, EncJzS 70*
Lyons, James 1954- *IntWWM 80*
Lyons, James Vincent 1935- *AmSCAP 66*
Lyons, Jean Elderkin *IntWWM 77, -80*
Lyons, Jimmy 1916- *EncJzS 70*
Lyons, Jimmy 1932- *EncJzS 70*
Lyons, Joseph Callaway 1930- *AmSCAP 80*
Lyons, Margaret Verity 1942- *IntWWM 77*
Lyons, Milton P *PupTheA*
Lyons, Richard E 1921- *IntMPA 77, -75, -76, -78, -79, -80*
Lyons, Robert F *WhoHol A*
Lyons, Ruth *AmSCAP 66, -80*
Lyons, Stuart 1928- *IntMPA 77, -75, -76, -78, -79, -80*
Lyons, Vicky *IntWWM 80*
Lyra, Justus Wilhelm 1822-1882 *Baker 78*
Lyric, Dora d1962 *NotNAT B*
Lys, F De *NewGrD 80*
Lysberg, Charles Samuel *Baker 78, NewGrD 80*
Lysenko, Mykola Vytal'yevych 1842-1912 *NewGrD 80*
Lystedt, Lars 1925- *EncJzS 70*
Lysy, Alberto 1935- *IntWWM 80, WhoMus 72*
Lytell, Bert d1954 *MotPP, WhoHol B*
Lytell, Bert 1885-1954 *FilmEn, MovMk, NotNAT B, WhScrn 74, -77, WhThe*
Lytell, Bert 1887-1954 *TwYS*
Lytell, Bert 1888-1954 *Film 1, -2, FilmgC, ForYSC, HalFC 80*
Lytell, Jimmy 1904- *AmSCAP 80, WhoJazz 72*
Lytell, Jimmy 1904-1972 *AmSCAP 66, CmpEPM, EncJzS 70, WhoHol B*
Lytell, Jimmy 1906-1973 *BiDAmM*
Lytell, Wilfred 1892-1954 *Film 1, -2, MotPP, NotNAT B, TwYS, WhScrn 74, -77, WhoHol B*
Lythgoe, Clive *WhoMus 72*
Lythgoe, Norman 1927- *WhoMus 72*
Lytle, John Dillard 1932- *BiDAmM, EncJzS 70*
Lytle, Johnny 1932- *EncJzS 70*
Lytle, Moe *ConMuA 80B*
Lyton, Robert *Film 1*
Lyttelton, Edith d1948 *NotNAT B, WhThe*
Lyttelton, Humphrey 1921- *CmpEPM, EncJzS 70, IlEncJ, NewGrD 80, WhoMus 72*
Lyttich, Johann 1581?-1611 *NewGrD 80*
Lytton *NewEOp 71*
Lytton, Baron 1803-1873 *McGEWD[port]*
Lytton, Lord 1803-1873 *NotNAT B*
Lytton, Doris 1893-1953 *NotNAT B, WhThe*
Lytton, Lord Edward G E L Bulwer-Lytton 1803-1873 *OxThe*
Lytton, Henry, Jr. 1904-1965 *WhThe*
Lytton, Henry A 1865-1936 *BnBkM 80*
Lytton, Sir Henry Alfred 1867-1936 *NotNAT A, -B, WhThe*
Lytton, L Rogers 1867-1924 *Film 1, -2, MotPP, WhScrn 77*
Lytton, Ruth *WhThe*
Lyudkevych, Stanislav Pylypovych 1879-1979 *NewGrD 80*
Lyveden, Lord d1926 *NotNAT B*
Lyvers, Helen *PupTheA*

M

Ma, Chih-Yuan 1260?-1321 *REnWD[port]*
Ma, Hiao-Tsiun 1911- *IntWWM 77, -80*
Ma, Si-Hon 1925- *IntWWM 77, -80*
Ma, Ssu-Ts'ung 1913- *NewGrD 80*
Ma Perkins *What 3[port]*
Maag, Peter 1919- *Baker 78, IntWWM 77, -80, NewGrD 80, WhoMus 72, WhoOp 76*
Maar, Lisl 1942- *CnOxB*
Maas, Audrey *WomWMM*
Maas, Chris 1922- *NewGrD 80*
Maas, Joseph 1847-1886 *NewGrD 80*
Maas, Louis 1852-1889 *Baker 78, BiDAmM*
Maas, Walter A F *NewGrD 80*
Maas, Walter Alfred Friedrich 1909- *IntWWM 77*
Maas, Willard *WomWMM*
Maasalo, Armas 1885-1960 *Baker 78, NewGrD 80*
Maasalo, Kai 1922- *NewGrD 80*
Maass, Arlene Fournier 1940- *AmSCAP 80*
Maass, Margaret Hartmann *AmSCAP 80*
Maass, Nikolaus d1615 *NewGrD 80*
Maassen, Jacques Johannes Josephus Maria 1947- *IntWWM 77, -80*
Maasz, Gerhard 1906- *IntWWM 77, -80, WhoMus 72*
Maayani, Ami 1936- *Baker 78, DcCM, NewGrD 80*
Maazel, Lorin 1930- *Baker 78, BiDAmM, BnBkM 80, CmOp, IntWWM 77, -80, MusMk, MusSN[port], NewEOp 71, NewGrD 80[port], WhoMus 72, WhoOp 76*
Mabaouj, Najet *WomWMM*
Mabellini, Teodulo 1817-1897 *Baker 78, NewGrD 80*
Mabern, Harold, Jr. 1936- *BiDAmM, EncJzS 70*
Mabery, Mary *Film 2*
Mabley, Edward H 1906- *AmSCAP 66, -80, BiE&WWA, NotNAT*
Mabley, Jackie Moms 1897-1975 *BlksB&W C, DrBlPA, WhScrn 77, WhoHol C*
Mabley, Moms 1897-1975 *JoeFr[port], RkOn 2[port]*
Mabley, Ted *PupTheA*
Mabon, Willie 1925- *BluesWW[port]*
Mabrook, Hossein *DcFM*
Mabry, Iris *CmpGMD, DancEn 78*
Mabry, John 1926- *ConAmC*
Mabuchi, Takeo 1905- *IntMPA 77, -75, -76, -78, -79, -80*
Mac And Bob *IlEncCM*
Mac, Baby *Film 2*
Mac, Nila *Film 1*
Macak, Ivan 1935- *NewGrD 80*
Macal, Zdenek 1936- *IntWWM 80, NewGrD 80, WhoMus 72*
Macaluso, Lenny 1947- *AmSCAP 80*
MacAndrews, John *Film 2*
Macanespie, Harry 1905- *WhoMus 72*
MacArdle, Donald Wales 1897-1964 *Baker 78, Film 2, NewGrD 80*
Macari, Giacomo 1700?-1744? *NewGrD 80*
Macarini Carmignani, Gherardo 1916- *NewGrD 80*
MacArthur, Charles 1895-1956 *DcFM, DcLB 7[port], EncWT, FilmEn, FilmgC, HalFC 80, McGEWD, ModWD, NotNAT A, -B, OxFilm, WhScrn 74, -77, WhThe, WhoHol B, WorEFlm[port]*
MacArthur, Colan William Porter 1920- *IntMPA 75*
Macarthur, Dana Beth Hayes 1948- *AmSCAP 80*
MacArthur, James 1937- *BiE&WWA, FilmEn, FilmgC, ForYSC, HalFC 80, IntMPA 77, -75, -76, -78, -79, -80, MotPP, WhoHol A*
MacArthur, Margaret Crowl 1928- *BiDAmM, EncFCWM 69*
MacArthur, Mary 1930-1949 *NotNAT B*
Macarthy, Harry 1834-1888 *BiDAmM*
Macarty, Eugene Victor 1821- *BiDAmM*
Macatsoris, Christofer 1936- *IntWWM 77, -80*
Macaulay, Joseph d1967 *WhThe, WhoHol B*
Macaulay, Thomas Babington 1800-1859 *DcPup*
Macauley, Richard *HalFC 80*
MacBean, L C *IlWWBF*
Macbeth, Allan 1856-1910 *Baker 78*
Macbeth, Florence 1891-1966 *Baker 78, BiDAmM*
Macbeth, Helen *WhThe*
Macbeth, Robert *BlkAmP, MorBAP*
MacBoyle, Darl 1880-1942 *AmSCAP 66, -80*
MacBride, David Huston 1951- *AmSCAP 80, CpmDNM 76, -78, -79, ConAmC*
MacBride, Donald d1957 *MotPP, NotNAT B, WhScrn 74, -77*
MacBride, Donald 1894-1957 *Film 1, Vers A[port], WhoHol B*
MacBride, Lux *Film 2*
MacCaffrey, George 1870-1939 *NotNAT B, WhThe*
Maccari, Giacomo 1700?-1744? *NewGrD 80*
MacCarthy, Sir Desmond 1877-1952 *EncWT, NotNAT B, OxThe, WhThe*
MacCarthy, Hector 1888- *AmSCAP 66, -80*
MacCarthy, Maud 1882- *OxMus*
Macchetti, Teofilo 1632-1714 *NewGrD 80*
Macchi, Egisto 1928- *NewGrD 80*
Macchi, Mario 1912- *WhoMus 72*
Macchia, John 1932-1967 *WhScrn 74, -77, WhoHol B*
Maccianti, Anna 1930- *WhoOp 76*
Maccioni, Giambattista d1678? *NewGrD 80*
Maccioni, Giovanni Battista d1678? *NewGrD 80*
MacClintock, Carol 1910- *NewGrD 80*
MacColl, Ewan 1915- *EncFCWM 69, NewGrD 80*
MacColl, Hugh Frederick 1885-1953 *BiDAmM, ConAmC*
MacColl, James A 1912-1956 *NotNAT B, WhScrn 74, -77, WhoHol B*
MacCorkindale, Simon 1952- *HalFC 80*
MacCormack, Frank d1941 *WhoHol B*
MacCormack, Franklyn 1908-1971 *WhScrn 77, WhoHol B*
MacCullough, Nancy *WomWMM B*
MacCunn, Hamish 1868-1916 *Baker 78, MusMk, NewGrD 80, OxMus*
MacCurdy, James Kyrle *WhoStg 1908*
MacDermid, James G 1875-1960 *AmSCAP 66, -80, Baker 78, ConAmC*
MacDermid, Sibyl Sammis 1876-1940 *Baker 78*
MacDermot, Galt 1928- *BiDAmM, EncMT, NotNAT, PlP&P, -A[port], WhoThe 77*
MacDermot, Robert 1910-1964 *WhThe*
Macdermott, The Great 1845-1901 *OxThe*
MacDermott, G H 1845-1901 *NotNAT B*
MacDermott, Galt 1928- *ConAmC*
MacDermott, John W Jack 1892-1946 *WhScrn 74, -77*
Macdermott, K H *OxMus*
MacDermott, Marc 1880-1929 *Film 2, MotPP, TwYS, WhScrn 77, WhoHol B*
Macdermott, Norman 1889- *WhThe*
Macdermott, Norman 1890- *OxThe*
Macdona, Charles d1946 *NotNAT B, WhThe*
MacDonagh, Donagh 1912-1968 *McGEWD, NotNAT B*
MacDonagh, J A Terence 1908- *IntWWM 80*
MacDonagh, Terence *WhoMus 72*
MacDonald, Abel *PupTheA*
Macdonald, Andrew d1790 *NotNAT B*
MacDonald, Ballard 1882-1935 *AmPS, AmSCAP 66, -80, BiDAmM, CmpEPM, NotNAT B*
Macdonald, Brian 1928- *CnOxB, CreCan 2, DancEn 78*
MacDonald, Catherine 1940- *ConAmC*
MacDonald, Charles *Film 2*
MacDonald, Christie 1875-1962 *CmpEPM, EncMT, NotNAT B, WhoStg 1906, -1908*
MacDonald, David 1904- *FilmEn, FilmgC, HalFC 80, IlWWBF, IntMPA 75*
MacDonald, Donald 1898-1959 *Film 1, -2, NotNAT B, WhScrn 74, -77, WhThe, WhoHol B*
MacDonald, Edmund 1911-1951 *WhScrn 74, -77, WhoHol B*
Macdonald, Grant Kenneth 1909- *CreCan 1*
MacDonald, Hugh John 1940- *IntWWM 77, -80, NewGrD 80, WhoMus 72*
MacDonald, J Farrell 1875-1951 *ForYSC, TwYS*
MacDonald, J Farrell 1875-1952 *FilmEn, Film 1, -2, FilmgC, HalFC 80, HolCA[port], MovMk, Vers B[port], WhScrn 74, -77, WhoHol B*
MacDonald, Mrs. J Farrell *Film 1*
MacDonald, Jack F *Film 2*
Macdonald, James Alexander Stirling 1921- *CreCan 1*
MacDonald, James Edward Hervey 1873-1932 *CreCan 2*
MacDonald, James F *ConAmC*
MacDonald, James Lee 1921- *AmSCAP 66, -80*
Macdonald, James V 1945- *IntWWM 80*

MacDonald, James Weatherby 1899-1962 NotNAT B, WhScrn 74, –77
Macdonald, James Williamson Galloway 1897-1960 CreCan 2
MacDonald, Jeanette d1965 AmPS A, –B, BiE&WWA, MotPP, NotNAT B, ThFT[port], WhoHol B
MacDonald, Jeanette 1901-1965 CmMov, CmpEPM, EncMT, FilmEn, MGM[port]
MacDonald, Jeanette 1902-1965 FilmgC, HalFC 80, OxFilm
MacDonald, Jeanette 1903-1965 BiDFilm, –81
MacDonald, Jeanette 1906-1965 Film 2, ForYSC, WhScrn 74, –77
MacDonald, Jeanette 1907-1965 BiDAmM, MovMk[port], WhThe, WorEFlm
Macdonald, Jock 1897-1960 CreCan 2
MacDonald, Joe 1906-1968 CmMov
MacDonald, John Alexander 1929- IntWWM 77, –80
MacDonald, John D 1916- HalFC 80
Macdonald, John Roy 1948- IntWWM 80
MacDonald, Joseph 1906-1968 FilmEn, FilmgC, HalFC 80, IntMPA 77, –75, –76, WorEFlm
MacDonald, Katherine 1891-1956 Film 1
MacDonald, Katherine 1894-1956 Film 2, MotPP, NotNAT B, TwYS, WhScrn 74, –77, WhoHol B
Macdonald, Keith Norman OxMus
MacDonald, Kenneth Film 2, ForYSC
MacDonald, Kenneth d1972 WhoHol B
Macdonald, Lucy Maud Montgomery CreCan 2
MacDonald, Malcolm 1916- IntWWM 77, –80, WhoMus 72
MacDonald, Malcolm 1948- IntWWM 77, –80
MacDonald, Manly Edward 1889- CreCan 2
Macdonald, Murray 1899- WhoThe 72, –77
Macdonald, Patrick OxMus
MacDonald, Philip 1896- HalFC 80, IntMPA 77, –75, –76, –78, –79, –80
MacDonald, Ray MotPP, WhScrn 74, –77
Macdonald, Richard 1920- DcFM, WorEFlm
MacDonald, Robert James 1927- IntWWM 77, –80
MacDonald, Ross 1915- HalFC 80
Macdonald, Ruby AmSCAP 66, –80
MacDonald, Sally WomWMM
MacDonald, Skeets 1915-1968 IlEncCM
MacDonald, Thoreau 1901- CreCan 1
Macdonald, Torbert H d1976 NewYTET
MacDonald, Wallace 1891- Film 1, –2, TwYS, WhoHol A
MacDonald, Wallace 1896- ForYSC
MacDonald, Wilson Puglsey 1880-1967 CreCan 1
MacDonell, Kathlene 1890- WhThe
Macdonnell, Leslie A 1903- WhThe, WhoThe 72
MacDonough, Glen 1870-1924 AmPS, AmSCAP 66, –80, BiDAmM, CmpEPM, EncMT, NewCBMT, NotNAT B, WhThe
MacDonough, Harry CmpEPM
MacDougall, Allan Ross 1894-1956 WhScrn 74, –77, WhoHol B
MacDougall, Elspeth WomWMM B
MacDougall, Judith WomWMM A, –B
MacDougall, Ranald 1915-1973 FilmEn, FilmgC, HalFC 80, WorEFlm
MacDougall, Robert ConAmC
MacDougall, Robert Bruce 1931- IntWWM 77, –80
MacDougall, Robin Film 1
MacDougall, Roger 1910- BiE&WWA, ConDr 77, FilmgC, HalFC 80, NotNAT, WhoThe 72, –77
MacDowell, Edward Alexander 1860-1908 Baker 78, BnBkM 80, NewGrD 80[port]
MacDowell, Edward Alexander 1861-1908 AmSCAP 66, –80, BiDAmM, CmpBCM, DcCom&M 79, GrComp[port], MusMk, OxMus
MacDowell, Melbourne 1857-1941 WhScrn 74, –77, WhoHol B, WhoStg 1906, –1908
MacDowell, William Melbourne 1857-1941 NotNAT B
MacDuff, Grace Gibson PupTheA
Mace, Borden 1920- IntMPA 75, –76
Mace, Denis 1600?-1664? NewGrD 80
Mace, Fred 1872-1917 FilmEn
Mace, Fred 1879-1917 Film 1, TwYS, WhScrn 77, WhoHol B
Mace, Raymond Arthur 1913- AmSCAP 80
Mace, Thomas 1612?-1706? NewGrD 80
Mace, Thomas 1620?-1710? OxMus
Mace, Wynn Film 2
Maceda, Corazon S 1911- IntWWM 77, –80
Maceda, Jose 1917- DcCM, IntWWM 77, –80, NewGrD 80
Macedo, Nelson De 1931- IntWWM 77, –80
Macedonio DiMutio, Giovanni Vincenzo 1560?-1606? NewGrD 80
Macell, Jerry 1899- AmSCAP 66, –80
Macenauer, Bedrich 1929- IntWWM 77, –80
Macer, Aubrey William John 1924- IntWWM 77, –80
Macero, Teo 1925- ConAmC, DcCM
Macerollo, Joseph 1944- IntWWM 77, –80
Macewan, Desiree WhoMus 72
MacEwan, Sydney 1908- WhoMus 72
MacEwen, Gwendolyn 1941- CreCan 1
MacEwen, Walter 1906- IntMPA 75, –76
Macey, Henry Charles 1946- IntWWM 77
MacFadden, Bernarr 1868-1955 WhScrn 77
MacFadden, Gertrude Mickey 1900-1967 WhScrn 74, –77
MacFadden, Hamilton 1901- FilmEn
MacFarland, Pamela Dashiell 1947- WhoOp 76
MacFarland, Spanky 1928- MotPP
MacFarlane, Bruce 1910-1967 WhScrn 74, –77, WhThe, WhoHol B
Macfarlane, Elsa 1899- WhThe
MacFarlane, George 1877-1932 WhScrn 74, –77, WhoHol B
Macfarlane, Will C 1870-1945 AmSCAP 66, –80
Macfarlane, William Charles OxMus
Macfarlane, William Charles 1870-1945 Baker 78
MacFarlane, William Charles 1870-1945 ConAmC
MacFarren, Sir George Alexander d1843 NotNAT B
Macfarren, Sir George Alexander 1813-1887 Baker 78, NewEOp 71, NewGrD 80, OxMus
Macfarren, Natalia OxMus
Macfarren, Natalie 1826-1916 Baker 78
Macfarren, Walter Cecil 1826-1905 Baker 78, NewGrD 80, OxMus
Macfayden, Alexander 1879-1936 AmSCAP 66, –80, ConAmC A
MacFeeley, P ConAmC
Macfoy, Emmanuel Kayasi 1948- AmSCAP 80
MacGeachey, Charles d1921 NotNAT B
MacGibbon, Harriet WhoHol A
MacGill, Moyna 1895-1975 ForYSC, WhScrn 77, WhThe, WhoHol C
MacGimsey, Robert AmSCAP 66
MacGimsey, Robert d1979 AmSCAP 80
MacGinnis, Niall 1913- FilmgC, ForYSC, HalFC 80, IlWWBF, IntMPA 77, –75, –76, –78, –79, –80, WhThe, WhoHol A
MacGowan, Kenneth 1888-1963 EncWT, FilmEn, FilmgC, HalFC 80, NotNAT B, OxFilm, OxThe, PlP&P, WhThe, WorEFlm
MacGowran, Jack d1973 WhoHol B
MacGowran, Jack 1916-1973 FilmgC, ForYSC, HalFC 80
MacGowran, Jack 1918-1973 WhScrn 77, WhThe, WhoThe 72
MacGrath, Leueen WhoHol A
MacGrath, Leueen 1914- NotNAT, WhoThe 72, –77
MacGrath, Leueen 1919- BiE&WWA
MacGraw, Ali MotPP, WhoHol A
MacGraw, Ali 1938- FilmEn, FilmgC, HalFC 80, IntMPA 77, –75, –76, –78, –79, –80
MacGraw, Ali 1939- MovMk[port]
MacGregor, Byron RkOn 2[port]
MacGregor, Edgar 1879-1957 EncMT
MacGregor, Franklyn NatPD[port]
MacGregor, Harman 1878-1948 WhScrn 74, –77
MacGregor, Irvine Thomas 1915- AmSCAP 66, –80
MacGregor, J Chalmers 1903- AmSCAP 66, –80
MacGregor, Lee d1961 WhoHol B
MacGregor, Lee d1964 WhScrn 77
MacGregor, Malcolm WhScrn 74, –77
MacGregor, Mary A 1948- AmSCAP 80, RkOn 2[port]
MacGregor, Mary Esther Miller CreCan 1
MacGregor, Robert M 1911-1974 BiE&WWA, NotNAT B
MacGruder, Anna Film 2
Mach, Ernst 1838-1916 Baker 78
Macha, Otmar 1922- Baker 78, DcCM, NewGrD 80
Machabey, Armand 1886-1966 Baker 78, NewGrD 80
Machado, Antonio 1875-1939 McGEWD[port]
Machado, Augusto 1845-1924 Baker 78, NewGrD 80
Machado, David 1938- WhoOp 76
Machado, Diogo Barbosa NewGrD 80
Machado, Lena 1907-1974 AmSCAP 66, –80
Machado, Manuel 1590?-1646 NewGrD 80
Machado, Manuel 1874-1947 McGEWD[port]
Machado Santos, Maria DeGraca 1933- IntWWM 77, –80
Machan, Benjamin A 1894-1966 AmSCAP 66, –80, ConAmC A
Macharen, Mary Film 1
Machat, Marty ConMuA 80B
Machatius, Franz-Jochen 1910- IntWWM 77, –80
Machaty, Gustav 1898-1963 FilmgC, HalFC 80, MovMk[port]
Machaty, Gustav 1901-1963 DcFM, FilmEn, OxFilm, WorEFlm
Machau, Guillaume De 1300?-1377 NewGrD 80
Machaud, Guillaume De 1300?-1377 NewGrD 80
Machault, Guillaume De 1300?-1377 NewGrD 80
Machaut, Guillaume De 1300?-1377 Baker 78, BnBkM 80, CmpBCM, GrComp, MusMk, NewGrD 80, OxMus
Machavariani, Alexei Davidovich 1913- Baker 78, IntWWM 77, –80
Machavariani, Alexey Davidovich 1913- NewGrD 80
Mache, Francois-Bernard 1935- NewGrD 80
Machek NewGrD 80
Machette, Catherine Cecilia 1916- IntWWM 77
Machiavelli, Niccolo DiBernardo Dei 1469-1527 CnThe, EncWT, Ent, McGEWD[port], NewEOp 71, NotNAT B, OxThe, PlP&P, REnWD[port]
Machida, Yoshiaki 1888- NewGrD 80
Machin, Alfred 1877-1929 DcFM, FilmEn
Machin, Alfred 1877-1930 WorEFlm
Machin, Richard NewGrD 80
Machin, Will Film 1
Machito AmSCAP 80
Machiz, Herbert 1923-1976 BiE&WWA, NotNAT, WhoThe 72, –77
Machl, Tadeusz 1922- Baker 78, IntWWM 77, –80
Machlis, Joseph 1906- Baker 78
Machold, Johann d1595? NewGrD 80
Machotkova, Marcela 1931- WhoOp 76
Machov, Sasa 1903-1951 CnOxB
Macht, Stephen HalFC 80
Machu, Stephan NewGrD 80
MacHugh, Augustin WhThe
Machula, Tibor De 1912- NewGrD 80
Machy, Sieur De NewGrD 80
Maciejewski, Roman 1910- NewGrD 80
Maciejewski, Tadeusz 1936- IntWWM 77, –80
Macigni, Giovanni NewGrD 80
MacIlwham, George 1926- WhoMus 72
Macingni, Giovanni NewGrD 80
MacInnes, Margo 1930- WomWMM B
MacInnis, Donald 1923- AmSCAP 80, ConAmC
Macintosh, Kenneth PlP&P[port]
MacIntosh, Louise 1865-1933 WhScrn 74, –77, WhoHol B
Macintyre, Donald 1934- CmOp
Maciste 1878-1947 FilmAG WE, Film 1, WorEFlm
Mack, Al 1912- AmSCAP 66, –80
Mack, Andrew 1863-1931 AmPS B, BiDAmM,

Film 2, NotNAT B, WhScrn 74, -77, WhThe, WhoHol B, WhoStg 1906, -1908
Mack, Annie d1935 *NotNAT B*
Mack, Arthur 1877-1942 *Film 2, WhScrn 74, -77, WhoHol B*
Mack, Baby *Film 2*
Mack, Bill d1961 *WhScrn 74, -77*
Mack, Billy d1961 *WhoHol B*
Mack, Bobby *Film 1, -2*
Mack, Brice 1917- *IntMPA 75, -76*
Mack, C K *NatPD[port]*
Mack, Cactus d1962 *WhoHol B*
Mack, Cecil 1883-1944 *AmPS, AmSCAP 66, BiDAmM, BlksBF, CmpEPM*
Mack, Charles *PupTheA*
Mack, Charles 1878-1956 *WhScrn 74, -77, WhoHol B*
Mack, Charles E 1887-1934 *Film 2, WhScrn 74, -77, WhoHol B*
Mack, Charles Emmett 1900-1927 *Film 2, TwYS, WhScrn 74, -77, WhoHol B*
Mack, Charles J d1976 *NewYTET*
Mack, Dick 1854-1920 *WhScrn 74, -77*
Mack, E J *Film 2*
Mack, Ethel *BlkAmP*
Mack, Frances 1907-1967 *WhScrn 74, -77*
Mack, George E d1948 *NotNAT B, WhoHol B*
Mack, Gertrude d1967 *WhoHol B*
Mack, Hayward *Film 1*
Mack, Helen 1913- *FilmEn, Film 2, FilmgC, ForYSC, HalFC 80, MotPP, ThFT[port], WhoHol A*
Mack, Hughie 1884-1927 *WhScrn 74, -77, WhoHol B*
Mack, Hughie 1887-1952 *Film 1, -2, TwYS*
Mack, Irving 1895- *IntMPA 77, -75, -76, -78, -79, -80*
Mack, James Buck d1959 *WhScrn 74, -77*
Mack, James T 1871-1948 *Film 2, WhScrn 74, -77, WhoHol B*
Mack, Joe 1878-1946 *Film 2, WhoHol B*
Mack, Joseph P 1878-1946 *WhScrn 74, -77*
Mack, Lester 1906-1972 *WhScrn 77, WhoHol B*
Mack, Lonnie 1941- *IlEncR, RkOn*
Mack, Marion 1905- *Film 2, TwYS*
Mack, Max 1885-1973 *WhScrn 77*
Mack, Nila d1953 *NotNAT B*
Mack, Noreen *AmSCAP 80*
Mack, Richard A d1963 *NewYTET*
Mack, Richard R 1900- *AmSCAP 66, -80*
Mack, Robert 1877-1949 *Film 2, WhScrn 77*
Mack, Ron *BlkAmP*
Mack, Rose 1866-1927 *WhScrn 74, -77*
Mack, Russell 1892-1972 *FilmEn, FilmgC, HalFC 80*
Mack, Ted 1904-1976 *BiDAmM, NewYTET*
Mack, Tom H 1914- *AmSCAP 66, -80*
Mack, Warner 1938- *BiDAmM, EncFCWM 69, IlEncCM[port]*
Mack, Wilbur 1873-1964 *Film 2, ForYSC, NotNAT B, WhScrn 74, -77, WhoHol B*
Mack, Willard 1873-1934 *Film 1, -2, TwYS, WhScrn 74, -77, WhoHol B*
Mack, Willard 1878-1934 *NotNAT B, WhThe*
Mack, William B 1872-1955 *Film 2, WhScrn 74, -77, WhoHol B*
Mackail, Dorothy 1905- *Film 2*
Mackaill, Dorothy *MotPP*
Mackaill, Dorothy 1903- *FilmEn, FilmgC, ForYSC, HalFC 80, ThFT[port], TwYS*
Mackaill, Dorothy 1904- *MovMk*
Mackaill, Dorothy 1906- *WhoHol A*
Mackathorne, George *Film 2*
Mackay, Barbara Edith 1944- *ConAmTC*
Mackay, Barry 1906- *FilmgC, HalFC 80, WhThe, WhoHol A*
Mackay, Charles 1785?-1857 *OxThe*
Mackay, Charles 1814-1889 *BiDAmM*
MacKay, Charles 1867-1935 *Film 2, WhScrn 74, -77, WhoHol B*
Mackay, Dave 1932- *EncJzS 70*
Mackay, David Owen 1932- *EncJzS 70*
Mackay, Edward J 1874-1948 *WhScrn 74, -77*
Mackay, Elsie 1894- *WhThe*
Mackay, Fenton d1929 *NotNAT B*
Mackay, Frank Finley d1923 *NotNAT B*
Mackay, Fulton 1922- *WhoThe 72, -77*
MacKay, Gilbert S *PupTheA*
MacKay, Harper *AmSCAP 66, ConAmC*
Mackay, Harper 1921- *AmSCAP 80*
MacKay, Hugh 1907- *AmSCAP 66, -80*
Mackay, J L 1867- *WhThe*
Mackay, Leonard d1929 *NotNAT B*
MacKay, Louis Alexander 1901- *CreCan 2*
Mackay, Patricia 1945- *NotNAT*
Mackay, Penelope 1943- *IntWWM 77, -80*
Mackay, Ronald Raymond 1928- *IntWWM 77*
Mackay, Ruth *WhThe*
Mackay, W Gayer d1920 *NotNAT B*
Mackaye, Dorothy 1898-1940 *WhScrn 77, WhoHol B*
MacKaye, James Morrison Steele 1842-1894 *McGEWD*
MacKaye, James Morrison Steele 1844-1894 *OxThe*
MacKaye, Norman 1906-1968 *WhScrn 74, -77, WhoHol B*
MacKaye, Percy Wallace 1875-1956 *CnMD, CnThe, EncWT, McGEWD[port], ModWD, NotNAT B, OxThe, PlP&P[port], WhThe, WhoStg 1908*
MacKaye, Steele 1842-1894 *EncWT, NotNAT A, -B, PlP&P*
Mackeben, Theo 1897-1953 *NewGrD 80*
Mackel, Billy 1912- *WhoJazz 72*
MacKellar, Helen 1891- *BiE&WWA, NotNAT*
Mackellar, Helen 1895- *WhThe*
Mackeller, Thomas 1812-1899 *BiDAmM*
Macken, Jane Virginia 1912- *AmSCAP 66*
Macken, Walter 1915-1967 *CnMD, NotNAT B, WhScrn 77, WhoHol B*
Mackend, Harvie 1926- *IntWWM 77*
Mackendrick, Alexander 1912- *BiDFilm, -81, CmMov, DcFM, FilmEn, FilmgC, HalFC 80, IlWWBF, IntMPA 77, -75, -76, MovMk[port], OxFilm, WorEFlm*
MacKenna, Kate d1957 *WhoHol B*
MacKenna, Kate 1877-1957 *WhScrn 77*
MacKenna, Kate 1878-1957 *WhScrn 74*
MacKenna, Kenneth 1899-1962 *FilmEn, Film 2, ForYSC, HalFC 80, NotNAT B, TwYS A, WhScrn 74, -77, WhThe, WhoHol B*
MacKenzie, Alex 1886-1966 *WhoHol B*
MacKenzie, Alexander 1886-1966 *WhScrn 77*
Mackenzie, Sir Alexander Campbell 1847-1935 *Baker 78, BnBkM 80, NewEOp 71, NewGrD 80, OxMus*
Mackenzie, Arthur 1928- *IntWWM 77*
Mackenzie, Sir Compton 1883-1972 *HalFC 80, OxMus*
MacKenzie, Donald 1880-1972 *Film 1, -2, WhScrn 77*
MacKenzie, George 1901-1975 *WhScrn 77, WhoHol C*
MacKenzie, Gisele 1927- *AmSCAP 66, CmpEPM, CreCan 2, RkOn[port]*
MacKenzie, Giselle 1927- *BiDAmM*
MacKenzie, John 1932- *FilmgC, HalFC 80*
MacKenzie, Joyce *ForYSC, WhoHol A*
Mackenzie, Leonard C, Jr. 1915- *AmSCAP 66, -80*
Mackenzie, Mary 1922-1966 *WhScrn 74, -77, WhThe, WhoHol B*
MacKenzie, Melissa Taylor 1925- *IntWWM 80*
MacKenzie, Midge *WomWMM B*
MacKenzie, Ronald d1932 *NotNAT B*
MacKenzie, Shelagh *WomWMM*
Mackeprang, Grete 1937- *IntWWM 77, -80*
Mackerness, Eric David 1920- *IntWWM 77, -80*
Mackerras, Alan Charles 1925- *DancEn 78, IntWWM 77, -80*
Mackerras, Charles 1925- *Baker 78, BnBkM 80, CmOp, CnOxB, IntMPA 77, -75, -76, -78, -79, -80, MusMk, NewGrD 80, WhoMus 72, WhoOp 76*
Mackerras, Joan C 1934- *IntWWM 77, -80*
Mackey, Mary Lourdes 1905- *IntWWM 77, -80*
Mackey, Warren B *PupTheA*
Mackey, Mrs. Warren B *PupTheA*
Mackey, William Wellington *BlkAmP, DrBlPA, MorBAP*
Mackie, Bert 1893-1967 *WhScrn 74, -77*
Mackie, David 1943- *IntWWM 80*
Mackie, Frank 1904-1969 *NewOrJ[port]*
Mackie, James Darwin 1928- *IntWWM 77*
Mackie, Jean 1920- *WhoMus 72*
Mackie, Melbon 1945- *WhoMus 72*
Mackie, Neil 1946- *IntWWM 77, -80*
Mackie, Philip *ConDr 73, -77C*
Mackie, Richard H 1906- *NewOrJ*
Mackie, Shirley M 1929- *IntWWM 77, -80*
Mackin, William 1883-1928 *WhScrn 74, -77*
Mackinder, Lionel d1915 *WhThe*
Mackinlay, Jean Sterling 1882-1958 *OxThe, WhThe*
MacKinlay, Jean Stirling 1882-1958 *NotNAT B*
Mackinlay, Malcolm Sterling 1876-1952 *Baker 78*
Mackinnon, Hugh A 1891- *BiDAmM*
Mackinnon, Kaye *CnOxB, DancEn 78[port]*
MacKinnon, Sheila 1937- *CreCan 2*
Mackintoch, Louise *Film 2*
Mackintosh, Jack *WhoMus 72*
Mackintosh, Robert 1745-1807 *NewGrD 80, OxMus*
Mackintosh, Robert 1925- *BiE&WWA, NotNAT*
Mackintosh, William 1855-1929 *NotNAT B, WhThe*
Macklean, Charles *OxMus*
Mackley, Mrs. Arthur *Film 1*
Macklin, Charles 1690?-1797 *EncWT*
Macklin, Charles 1699-1797 *NotNAT A, -B*
Macklin, Charles 1700?-1797 *CnThe, Ent[port], OxThe, PlP&P[port]*
Macklin, F H d1903 *NotNAT B*
Macklin, Mrs. F H d1904 *NotNAT B*
Mackney, E W 1835-1909 *OxThe*
Mackris, Orestes 1900-1975 *WhScrn 77*
Macks, Helen *Film 2*
MacLachlan, Janet *DrBlPA, WhoHol A*
Maclagan, Mary Drummond Hay 1905- *WhoMus 72*
MacLaine, Shirley 1934- *BiDFilm, -81, FilmEn, FilmgC, ForYSC, HalFC 80, IntMPA 77, -75, -76, -78, -79, -80, MotPP, MovMk[port], OxFilm, WhoHol A, WomWMM, WorEFlm[port]*
MacLane, Armand Ralph 1936- *WhoOp 76*
MacLane, Barton d1969 *MotPP, WhoHol B*
MacLane, Barton 1900-1969 *Film 2, FilmgC, HalFC 80, WhScrn 74, -77*
MacLane, Barton 1902-1969 *FilmEn, ForYSC, HolCA[port], MovMk, Vers A[port]*
MacLane, Kerry *WhoHol A*
MacLane, Mary d1929 *WhScrn 77*
MacLaren, Archibald d1826 *NotNAT B*
Maclaren, Ian 1879- *Film 2, WhThe*
MacLaren, Ian 1886- *ForYSC*
MacLaren, Ivor 1904-1962 *NotNAT B, WhScrn 74, -77, WhoHol B*
MacLaren, Mary 1896- *Film 1, -2, ForYSC, MotPP, TwYS, WhoHol A*
MacLarnie, Thomas d1931 *NotNAT B*
Maclean, Alexander Morvaren 1872-1936 *Baker 78, OxMus*
Maclean, Alick 1872-1936 *NewGrD 80*
MacLean, Alistair 1922- *FilmgC, HalFC 80*
Maclean, Charles Donald 1843-1916 *Baker 78, OxMus*
Maclean, Donald Hugh 1926- *WhoMus 72*
MacLean, Douglas 1890-1967 *FilmEn, Film 1, -2, FilmgC, HalFC 80, MotPP, MovMk, WhScrn 74, -77, WhoHol B*
MacLean, Douglas 1894-1967 *ForYSC, TwYS*
Maclean, Hector R *NewGrD 80*
MacLean, Ian 1894- *IntMPA 77, -75, -76, -78, -79, -80*
MacLean, J Arthur *PupTheA*
MacLean, John T 1933- *ConAmC*
Maclean, Quentin Stuart Morvaren 1896-1962 *Baker 78, CreCan 2, NewGrD 80, OxMus*
MacLean, R D 1859-1948 *NotNAT B, WhScrn 77, WhThe, WhoHol B*
MacLean, Rezin D 1859-1948 *WhScrn 74*
MacLean, Robert *Film 2*
MacLean, Ross 1904- *AmSCAP 66*
Maclean, T Ross 1904- *AmSCAP 80*
MacLeary, Donald 1937- *CnOxB, DancEn 78*
MacLeish, Archibald 1892- *AmSCAP 66, -80, BiDAmM, BiE&WWA, CnMD, CnThe, ConDr 73, -77, CroCD, DancEn 78, DcLB 7[port], EncWT, Ent, McGEWD,*

ModWD, NotNAT, OxThe, PlP&P, WhoThe 72, -77
MacLeish, Rod *NewYTET*
Maclennan, Francis 1870-1935 *BiDAmM*
Maclennan, Francis 1879-1935 *Baker 78*
MacLennan, Hugh 1907- *CreCan 2*
MacLennan, John Hugh *CreCan 2*
MacLennon, Andy *Film 2*
MacLeod, Angus 1874-1962 *NotNAT B*
Macleod, Annie *OxMus*
MacLeod, Beatrice 1910- *ConAmTC*
Macleod, Bobby 1925- *IntWWM 77, -80*
MacLeod, E E, Jr. *Film 2*
MacLeod, Elsie *Film 1*
MacLeod, Gavin *WhoHol A*
MacLeod, Janet *Film 2*
MacLeod, Kenneth 1895-1963 *WhScrn 74, -77*
MacLeod, Margaret Kathleen Nichol 1904-1949 *CreCan 1*
Macleod, Norman Macdonald 1908- *WhoMus 72*
MacLeod, Pegi Nicol 1904-1949 *CreCan 1*
Macleod, W Angus 1874-1962 *WhThe*
MacLiammoir, Micheal 1899-1978 *BiE&WWA, CnThe, EncWT, Ent, McGEWD, ModWD, NotNAT, -A, OxThe, PlP&P, WhoThe 72, -77*
MacLiammoir, Micheal 1901-1978 *FilmgC, HalFC 80*
Macloughlin, F *OxMus*
MacLow, Jackson 1922- *ConDr 73, -77*
MacMahon, Aline 1899- *BiE&WWA, FilmEn, FilmgC, ForYSC, HalFC 80, HolCA[port], IntMPA 77, -75, -76, -78, -79, -80, MotPP, MovMk, NotNAT, ThFT[port], Vers A[port], WhoHol A, WhoThe 72, -77*
MacMahon, Horace 1907-1971 *FilmgC, HalFC 80, Vers B[port]*
MacManus, Clive d1953 *NotNAT B, WhThe*
MacMaster, Anew 1895-1952 *CnThe*
MacMillan, Andrew 1914-1967 *CreCan 2*
MacMillan, Sir Ernest Campbell 1893-1973 *Baker 78, BiDAmM, BnBkM 80, CreCan 1, IntWWM 77, NewGrD 80[port], OxMus, WhoMus 72*
MacMillan, Keith Campbell 1920- *CreCan 1, WhoMus 72*
MacMillan, Kenneth 1929- *CnOxB*
MacMillan, Kenneth 1930- *DancEn 78*
MacMillan, Mary Lynn Prough 1944- *IntWWM 77, -80*
MacMillan, Violet 1887-1953 *Film 1, NotNAT B*
Macmillen, Francis 1885-1973 *Baker 78*
MacMillian, Violet 1887-1953 *WhScrn 74, -77, WhoHol B*
Macmullan, Charles Walden Kirkpatrick *McGEWD*
MacMurray, Fred 1907- *FilmgC, HalFC 80[port], WhoHrs 80*
MacMurray, Fred 1908- *BiDFilm, -81, CmpEPM, FilmEn, Film 2, ForYSC[port], IntMPA 77, -75, -76, -78, -79, -80, MotPP, MovMk[port], OxFilm, WhoHol A, WorEFlm*
MacMurray, John 1878?-1920? *NewOrJ*
Macnaghten, Anne Catherine 1908- *IntWWM 77, -80, NewGrD 80, WhoMus 72*
Macnair, Dorothy Kathleen Livesay *CreCan 2*
MacNally, Leonard d1820 *NotNAT B*
Macnamara, Brinsley d1963 *NotNAT B*
Macnamara, Brinsley 1890-1963 *CnMD, McGEWD, ModWD*
Macnamara, Brinsley 1891-1963 *OxThe*
Macnamara, Jim *ConMuA 80B*
MacNamara, Paul 1907- *IntMPA 75, -76*
MacNaughtan, Alan 1920- *WhoThe 72, -77*
MacNeal, F A 1867-1918 *WhScrn 77*
Macnee, Patrick 1922- *FilmgC, HalFC 80, MotPP, WhoHol A*
MacNeice, Louis 1907-1963 *CnMD, NotNAT B*
MacNeil, Cornell Hill 1922- *Baker 78, IntWWM 77, -80, MusSN[port], NewGrD 80, WhoOp 76*
MacNeil, James 1870?-1945 *NewOrJ*
MacNeil, Robert *NewYTET*
MacNeil, Wendell 1872?- *NewOrJ*
Macollum, Barry 1889?-1971 *WhScrn 77*
Macollum, Barry 1899?-1971 *Film 2*
Macon, John Wesley 1923-1973 *BluesWW[port]*
Macon, Uncle Dave 1870-1952 *BiDAmM, CmpEPM, CounME 74[port], -74A, EncFCWM 69, IlEncCM[port]*
Maconaghie, Ronald Dereck 1931- *WhoOp 76*
Maconchy, Elizabeth 1907- *Baker 78, IntWWM 77, -80, MusMk, NewGrD 80, OxMus, WhoMus 72*
Maconie, Robin 1942- *NewGrD 80*
Macowan, Michael 1906- *OxThe, WhoThe 72, -77*
Macowan, Norman 1877-1961 *FilmgC, HalFC 80, NotNAT B, WhScrn 74, -77, WhThe, WhoHol B*
MacPhail, Douglas 1910-1944 *HalFC 80*
MacPhail, William C *NewYTET*
Macpherson, Charles 1870-1927 *Baker 78, OxMus*
MacPherson, Douglas *Film 2*
MacPherson, George 1928- *WhoMus 72*
Macpherson, Gordon Clarke 1924- *IntWWM 77, -80*
MacPherson, Harry *AmSCAP 66, -80*
Macpherson, James 1736-1796 *NewEOp 71*
Macpherson, Jay 1931- *CreCan 1*
Macpherson, Jean Jay 1931- *CreCan 1*
MacPherson, Jeanie d1946 *CmMov*
MacPherson, Jeanie 1878?-1946 *HalFC 80, TwYS A, WhScrn 74, -77, WhoHol B*
MacPherson, Jeannie d1946 *Film 1*
MacPherson, Jeannie 1884-1946 *FilmEn*
MacPherson, Quinton d1940 *NotNAT B, WhoHol B*
Macpherson, Stewart 1865-1941 *Baker 78, NewGrD 80, OxMus*
MacQuarrie, Albert *Film 1, -2*
MacQuarrie, Frank *Film 1*
MacQuarrie, George *Film 1, -2*
MacQuarrie, Murdoch 1878-1942 *Film 1*
MacQuarrie, Murdock 1878-1942 *Film 2, TwYS A, WhScrn 74, -77, WhoHol B*
Macque, Giovanni De 1548?-1614 *NewGrD 80*
Macque, Giovanni De 1550?-1614 *Baker 78*
MacQueen, W J 1888-1960 *NotNAT B*
Macqueen-Pope, Walter James 1888-1960 *OxThe, WhThe*
Macquitty, William 1905- *FilmgC, HalFC 80, IntMPA 77, -75, -76, -78, -79, -80*
MacQuoid, Percy 1852-1925 *NotNAT B, WhThe*
MacRae, Arthur 1908-1962 *NotNAT B, WhThe*
Macrae, Duncan 1905-1967 *FilmgC, HalFC 80, WhScrn 74, -77, WhThe, WhoHol B*
MacRae, Elizabeth *WhoHol A*
MacRae, Fred Aylor 1929- *AmSCAP 80*
MacRae, Gordon 1921- *BiDAmM, CmMov, CmpEPM, FilmEn, Film 2, FilmgC, ForYSC*
Macrae, Gordon 1921- *HalFC 80*
MacRae, Gordon 1921- *IntMPA 77, -75, -76, -78, -79, -80, MotPP, MovMk, WhoHol A*
MacRae, Gordon 1931- *RkOn*
MacRae, Heather 1940- *CnOxB*
MacRae, Jean Dent 1930- *IntMPA 80*
MacRae, Meredith *WhoHol A*
Macready, George d1973 *MotPP, WhoHol B*
Macready, George 1908-1973 *HolCA[port], Vers A[port]*
Macready, George 1909-1973 *FilmEn, FilmgC, ForYSC, HalFC 80, MovMk, WhScrn 77, WhoHrs 80[port]*
Macready, George 1912-1973 *CmMov*
MacReady, William d1829 *NotNAT B*
Macready, William Charles 1793-1873 *CnThe, EncWT, Ent[port], FamA&A[port], NotNAT A, -B, OxThe, PlP&P[port]*
Macri, Paolo *NewGrD 80*
Macrobius, Ambrosius Theodosius *NewGrD 80*
Macropedius, Georgius 1475?-1558 *NewGrD 80*
Macrorie, Alma *WomWMM*
MacSarin, Kenneth 1912-1967 *WhScrn 74, -77*
Macsweeney, John *Film 2*
Macswiney, Owen *OxThe*
MacTaggart, James 1928-1974 *WhScrn 77*
Macudzinska, Sylvia 1906- *IntWWM 77, -80*
Macudzinski, Rudolf 1907- *IntWWM 77, -80*
Macurdy, John 1929- *IntWWM 77, -80, NewGrD 80, WhoOp 76*
MacVicar, Martha *FilmEn*
MacWatters, Virginia Abee *WhoMus 72*
MacWherter, Rod 1936- *WhoOp 76*
MacWilliams, Glen 1898- *HalFC 80*
Macy, Ann Sullivan *Film 1*
Macy, Bill 1922- *HalFC 80, WhoHol A*
Macy, Carleton 1861-1946 *Film 2, NotNAT B, WhScrn 74, -77, WhoHol B*
Macy, Carleton 1944- *ConAmC*
Macy, Carlton *Film 1*
Macy, Cora *Film 2*
Macy, Gertrude 1904- *BiE&WWA, NotNAT*
Macy, Jack 1886-1956 *WhScrn 74, -77, WhoHol B*
Macy, John W, Jr. *NewYTET*
Mad River, The *BiDAmM*
Mad Russian, The 1900- *JoeFr, What 3[port]*
Madach, Imre 1823-1864 *McGEWD[port], OxThe*
Madame Sul Te Wan *DrBlPA*
Madame Vestris *PlP&P*
Madame Violante *PlP&P*
Madan, Martin 1725?-1790 *NewGrD 80*
Madanes, Cecilio 1923- *WhoOp 76*
Madarova, Herta 1925- *IntWWM 77*
Madatov, Grigori 1898-1968 *Baker 78*
Madau Diaz, Antonello 1931- *WhoOp 76*
Madd, Pierette *Film 2*
Madden, Bill 1915- *IntMPA 75, -76, -79, -80*
Madden, Cecil Charles 1902- *DcPup, WhThe*
Madden, Ciaran 1945- *WhoThe 72, -77*
Madden, Donald 1933- *BiE&WWA, NotNAT, WhoThe 72, -77*
Madden, Doreen *Film 2*
Madden, Edward d1952 *Sw&Ld B*
Madden, Edward 1877-1952 *AmSCAP 80*
Madden, Edward 1878-1952 *AmPS, AmSCAP 66, BiDAmM, CmpEPM*
Madden, Edward Douglas 1906- *IntMPA 75, -76*
Madden, Edward J *ConAmC*
Madden, Frank 1900-1964 *AmSCAP 66, -80*
Madden, Golda 1894- *Film 1, -2, TwYS*
Madden, Henri *NewGrD 80*
Madden, Jerry *Film 2*
Madden, Peter 1910?- *FilmgC, HalFC 80, WhoHol A*
Madden, Richard d1951 *NotNAT B*
Madden, Tom *Film 2*
Madden, Will Anthony *MorBAP*
Maddern, Victor 1926- *FilmgC, HalFC 80, WhoHol A, WhoHrs 80*
Maddie, Ginette *Film 2*
Maddow, Ben *DcFM, FilmEn, HalFC 80, WorEFlm*
Maddox, Fannie Bell 1922- *AmSCAP 80*
Maddox, Gloria Demby *BlkAmP, MorBAP*
Maddox, Johnny 1929- *AmPS A, RkOn*
Maddox, Martha *Film 2*
Maddox, Robert Lee 1935- *IntWWM 77, -80*
Maddox, Rose 1926- *BiDAmM, CounME 74, -74A, EncFCWM 69, IlEncCM[port]*
Maddox, Walter Allen 1935- *IntWWM 80*
Maddy, Joe 1891-1966 *NewGrD 80*
Maddy, Joseph Edgar 1891-1966 *AmSCAP 66, -80, Baker 78, BiDAmM, NewGrD 80*
Madeira, Francis 1917- *Baker 78*
Madeira, Humberto 1921-1971 *WhScrn 74, -77, WhoHol B*
Madeira, Jean 1918-1972 *Baker 78, BiDAmM, NewGrD 80*
Madeira, Jean 1924-1972 *MusSN[port], NewEOp 71, WhoMus 72*
Madeira, Paul *AmSCAP 80*
Madelka, Simon Bar Jona d1599? *NewGrD 80*
Mader, Clarence 1904-1971 *ConAmC*
Maderna, Bruno 1920-1973 *Baker 78, BnBkM 80, DcCM, MusMk, NewGrD 80, OxMus*
Maderna, Bruno 1925-1973 *WhoMus 72*
Madetoja, Leevi 1887-1947 *Baker 78, NewGrD 80*
Madey, Boguslaw 1932- *Baker 78, IntWWM 77, -80, WhoOp 76*
Madhusudan, Michael *REnWD[port]*
Madi, Kalil 1926- *BiDAmM*

Madiera, Jean 1924-1972 *CmOp*
Madin, Henri 1698-1748 *NewGrD 80*
Madison, Bingie 1902- *WhoJazz 72*
Madison, C J d1975 *WhScrn 77, WhoHol C*
Madison, Cleo 1882-1964 *Film 1, -2, MotPP, NotNAT B, TwYS, WhoHol B, WomWMM*
Madison, Cleo 1883-1964 *WhScrn 74, -77*
Madison, Ethel *Film 1*
Madison, Guy 1922- *FilmEn, FilmgC, ForYSC, HalFC 80, IntMPA 77, -75, -76, -78, -79, -80, MotPP, MovMk, What 5[port], WhoHol A*
Madison, Harry 1877-1936 *WhScrn 74, -77, WhoHol B*
Madison, Kid Shots 1899-1948 *WhoJazz 72*
Madison, Louis 1899-1948 *NewOrJ[port]*
Madison, Martha *Film 2*
Madison, Nathaniel Joseph 1896-1968 *AmSCAP 66, -80*
Madison, Noel 1898-1975 *HalFC 80*
Madison, Noel N d1975 *HolCA[port]*
Madison, Noel N 1898-1975 *FilmEn*
Madison, Noel N 1905?-1975 *FilmgC, ForYSC, Vers B[port], WhScrn 77, WhoHol C*
Madison, Virginia *Film 2*
Madjera, Gottfried 1905- *WhoMus 72*
Madlseder, Nonnosus 1730-1797 *NewGrD 80*
Madonis, Luigi 1690?-1770? *NewGrD 80*
Madre DeDeus, Filipe Da 1630?-1688? *NewGrD 80*
Madrid, Juan Fernandez De *NewGrD 80*
Madrigal Singers *BiDAmM*
Madriguera, Enric d1973 *BgBands 74, WhoHol B*
Madriguera, Enric 1902-1973 *WhScrn 77*
Madriguera, Enric 1904-1973 *AmSCAP 66, -80, CmpEPM*
Madriguera, Enrique 1904-1973 *Baker 78*
Madriska, Lorraine A 1904- *IntWWM 77*
Madsen, Clifford K 1937- *IntWWM 77, -80*
Madsen, Cornelia May Bates 1939- *IntWWM 77, -80*
Madsen, Egon 1942- *CnOxB*
Madsen, Florence J *ConAmC*
Madsen, Forrest Holger 1878-1943 *WorEFlm*
Madsen, Harald 1890-1949 *FilmEn*
Madsen, Harold *Film 2*
Madsen, John Damgaard 1941- *IntWWM 77*
Madsen, Jorn 1939- *DancEn 78*
Madsen, Norma Lee 1927- *IntWWM 77, -80*
Madsen, Trygve 1940- *IntWWM 77, -80*
Madsen And Schenstrom *FilmEn*
Madureira, Antonio Jose 1949- *IntWWM 77, -80*
Maduri, Carl *ConMuA 80B*
Maduro, Charles 1883-1947 *AmSCAP 66, -80*
Mae, Jimsey 1894-1968 *WhScrn 74, -77, WhoHol B*
Maedel, Rolf 1917- *IntWWM 77, -80*
Maeder, Clara Fisher 1811-1898 *NotNAT A*
Maeder, Frederick George d1891 *NotNAT B*
Maeder, Mrs. James *OxThe*
Maegaard, Jan 1926- *Baker 78, DcCM, IntWWM 80, NewGrD 80*
Maekelberghe, August R 1909- *AmSCAP 66, ConAmC*
Maekelberghe, August R 1909-1975 *AmSCAP 80*
Mael, Russell *AmSCAP 80*
Maelzel *PupTheA*
Maelzel, Johann Nepomuk 1772-1838 *MusMk, NewGrD 80, OxMus*
Maelzel, Johannes Nepomuk 1772-1838 *Baker 78*
Maendler, Karl 1872-1958 *NewGrD 80*
Maercker, Matthias *NewGrD 80*
Maertens, Willy 1893-1967 *WhScrn 74, -77*
Maes, Ernest Paul 1939- *IntWWM 77, -80*
Maes, Jef 1905- *Baker 78, NewGrD 80*
Maes, Joseph M 1905- *WhoMus 72*
Maesch, LaVahn K 1904- *AmSCAP 80, ConAmC*
Maessens, Pieter 1505?-1563 *NewGrD 80*
Maessins, Pieter 1505?-1563 *NewGrD 80*
Maestri, Charles J 1907- *IntMPA 77, -75, -76, -78, -79, -80*
Maestri, Katz 1906- *NewOrJ*
Maestrini, Carlo 1920- *WhoOp 76*
Maestro Capitan, El *NewGrD 80*
Maeterlinck, Maurice 1862-1949 *BnBkM 80, CnMD, CnThe, DcPup, EncWT, Ent, McGEWD[port], ModWD, NewEOp 71, NewGrD 80, NotNAT A, -B, OxThe, PIP&P, REnWD[port], WhThe*
Maetzig, Kurt 1911- *DcFM, FilmEn*
Maffei, Andrea 1798-1885 *OxThe*
Maffei, Giovanni Camillo *NewGrD 80*
Maffei, Scipione 1675-1755 *EncWT, Ent, McGEWD[port], OxThe*
Maffeo, Gianni 1936- *WhoOp 76*
Maffon, Giovanni Francesco *NewGrD 80*
Maflin, Alfred W 1840- *WhoStg 1908*
Magalhaes, Domingo Jose Goncalves De 1811-1882 *OxThe*
Magalhaes, Filipe De 1571?-1652 *NewGrD 80*
Magallanes, Nicholas 1922- *CnOxB, DancEn 78[port]*
Magaloff, Nikita 1912- *Baker 78, IntWWM 77, -80, NewGrD 80, WhoMus 72*
Maganini, Quinto 1897-1974 *AmSCAP 66, -80, Baker 78, BiDAmM, ConAmC, NewGrD 80*
Magarill, Sophie *Film 2*
Magarshack, David 1899- *BiE&WWA, NotNAT*
Magdalaine, Robinet DeLa *NewGrD 80*
Magdaleno, Maurico 1906- *DcFM*
Magdeburg, Joachim 1525?-1587? *NewGrD 80*
Magdic, Josip 1937- *IntWWM 77, -80*
Mageau, Mary Jane 1934- *AmSCAP 80*
Mageau, Sister Mary Magdalen 1934- *ConAmC*
Magee, Bryan 1930- *IntWWM 77, -80, WhoMus 72*
Magee, Gordon *Film 2*
Magee, Harriett 1878-1954 *WhScrn 74, -77, WhoHol B*
Magee, Patrick 1924- *FilmgC, HalFC 80, NotNAT, WhoHol A, WhoHrs 80[port], WhoThe 72, -77*
Magee, Ray 1897- *AmSCAP 66, -80*
Magee, Virginia *Film 2*
Magelis, Charles *Film 2*
Mager, Jorg 1880-1939 *Baker 78, OxMus*
Magg, Fritz 1914- *IntWWM 77, -80*
Maggard, Cledus & The Citizen's Band *RkOn 2A*
Maggi, Carlo Maria 1630-1699 *NewGrD 80*
Maggi, Francesco *NewGrD 80*
Maggi, Luigi 1867-1946 *DcFM, FilmEn*
Maggiello, Dominico *NewGrD 80*
Maggini, Gio Paolo 1581?-1632? *NewGrD 80*
Maggini, Giovanni Paolo 1579-1630? *Baker 78*
Maggio, Francesco Di *NewGrD 80*
Maggioni, Aurelio Antonio 1908- *Baker 78*
Maggiorani, Lamberto *WhoHol A*
Maggiore, Francesco 1715?-1782? *NewGrD 80*
Maggs, Philip Charles 1934- *WhoMus 72*
Maghett, Magic Sam 1937-1969 *BiDAmM*
Maghett, Samuel 1937-1969 *BluesWW[port]*
Magic Lanterns, The *RkOn 2[port]*
Magic Sam *BluesWW*
Magic Singing Sam *BluesWW*
Magic Slim *BluesWW*
Magid, Larry *ConMuA 80B*
Magid, Lee 1926- *AmSCAP 80*
Magidson, Herb 1906- *AmPS, CmpEPM, Sw&Ld C*
Magidson, Herbert 1906- *AmSCAP 66, -80, BiDAmM*
Magiello, Dominico *NewGrD 80*
Magill, Mort 1907- *IntMPA 77, -75, -76, -78, -79, -80*
Magine, Frank 1892- *AmSCAP 66*
Maginn, Bonnie *WhoStg 1908*
Maginn, William d1942 *NotNAT B*
Maginnis *PupTheA*
Maginnis, William Richard 1938- *ConAmC*
Maginty, E A *OxMus*
Magma *IlEncR*
Magnani, Anna d1973 *MotPP, PIP&P, WhoHol B*
Magnani, Anna 1907-1973 *FilmgC, HalFC 80*
Magnani, Anna 1908-1973 *BiDFilm, -81, EncWT, FilmAG WE, FilmEn, ForYSC, MovMk[port], WorEFlm[port]*
Magnani, Anna 1909-1973 *OxFilm, WhScrn 77*
Magnani, Luigi 1906- *NewGrD 80*
Magnano, Anthony Salvatore 1929- *AmSCAP 80*
Magnante, Charles 1905- *AmSCAP 66, -80*
Magnard, Alberic 1865-1914 *Baker 78, MusMk, NewGrD 80, OxMus*
Magne, Michel 1930- *Baker 78, NewGrD 80*
Magnes *OxThe*
Magness, Annabelle *Film 2*
Magni *NewGrD 80*
Magni, Benedetto *NewGrD 80*
Magni, Paolo 1650?-1737 *NewGrD 80*
Magnier, Pierre 1869- *Film 2, WhThe*
Magnificents, The *RkOn*
Magnin, Charles 1793-1862 *DcPup*
Magno, Benedetto *NewGrD 80*
Magno, Susan 1946- *CnOxB*
Magnolia Band *BiDAmM*
Magnon, Jean 1620-1662 *OxThe*
Magnus, Albertus *NewGrD 80*
Magnus, Annabelle *Film 2*
Magnusson, Charles 1878-1948 *FilmEn, OxFilm*
Magnusson, Jakob Freeman 1953- *IntWWM 77*
Magomayev, Muslim 1885-1937 *Baker 78*
Magon, Jero *PupTheA, PupTheA SUP*
Magoon, Eaton, Jr. 1922- *AmSCAP 66, -80, NatPD[port]*
Magrane, Thais d1957 *NotNAT B*
Magrath, George 1857-1938 *BiDAmM*
Magraw, Donald Keith 1935- *IntWWM 77, -80*
Magri, Gennaro *CnOxB, NewGrD 80*
Magri, Paolo *NewGrD 80*
Magri, Count Primo 1849-1920 *WhScrn 77*
Magriel, Paul 1906- *DancEn 78*
Magrill, George 1900-1952 *Film 2, WhScrn 74, -77, WhoHol B*
Magruder, John Decker Boyd 1925- *EncJzS 70*
Magub, Roshan 1941- *IntWWM 80*
Maguier, Virginia *WomWMM B*
Maguire, Charles J 1882-1939 *WhScrn 74, -77*
Maguire, Edward 1867-1925 *WhScrn 77*
Maguire, Hugh 1927- *IntWWM 80, NewGrD 80, WhoMus 72*
Maguire, John 1921- *WhoHrs 80*
Maguire, Kathleen *BiE&WWA, NotNAT, WhoHol A*
Maguire, Tom 1869-1934 *WhScrn 74, -77, WhoHol B*
Magyar, Gabriel 1914- *IntWWM 77, -80*
Magyar, Thomas 1913- *IntWWM 77, -80, WhoMus 72*
Magyari, Imre 1894-1940 *WhScrn 74, -77*
Mahaim, Ivan 1897-1965 *Baker 78*
Mahal, Taj *DrBlPA*
Mahal, Taj 1940- *BluesWW[port]*
Mahal, Taj 1942- *BiDAmM, ConMuA 80A, IlEncR[port]*
Mahalalel *McGEWD[port]*
Mahan, Billy 1933- *WhoHol A*
Mahan, Jack Harold 1911- *IntWWM 77, -80*
Mahan, Katherine Hines 1928- *IntWWM 77, -80*
Mahan, Marilyn McAdams 1928- *AmSCAP 80*
Mahan, Vivian L 1902-1933 *WhScrn 74, -77*
Mahar, Ted *ConAmTC*
Maharam, Joseph 1898- *BiE&WWA, NotNAT*
Mahara's Minstrels *BiDAmM*
Maharis, George *MotPP, PIP&P[port], WhoHol A*
Maharis, George 1928- *FilmgC, HalFC 80*
Maharis, George 1933- *BiE&WWA*
Maharis, George 1938- *FilmEn, ForYSC, MovMk[port]*
Maharoni, George *Film 1*
Mahault, Antoine 1720?-1785? *NewGrD 80*
Mahaut, Antoine 1720?-1785? *NewGrD 80*
Mahavishnu *EncJzS 70*
Mahavishnu Orchestra *BiDAmM, IlEncJ, IlEncR*
Mahdi, Salah 1925- *IntWWM 77, -80*
Mahelot, Laurent 1634- *NotNAT B*
Maher, Wally 1908-1951 *WhoHol B*
Maher, Walter 1908-1951 *WhScrn 74, -77*
Maher, William Michael 1947- *AmSCAP 80*
M'ahesa, Sent d1970 *CnOxB*
Mahier, Louis 1902?- *NewOrJ*
Mahieu De Gant *NewGrD 80*
Mahieu Le Juif *NewGrD 80*
Mahillon *NewGrD 80*

Mahillon, Charles 1813-1887 *NewGrD 80*
Mahillon, Fernand 1866-1948 *NewGrD 80*
Mahillon, Fernand-Charles d1922 *NewGrD 80*
Mahillon, Fernand-Victor d1922 *NewGrD 80*
Mahillon, Victor-Charles 1841-1924 *Baker 78, BnBkM 80, NewGrD 80*
Mahin, John Lee *CmMov, IntMPA 77, -75, -76, -78, -79, -80*
Mahin, John Lee 1902- *FilmEn, WorEFlm*
Mahin, John Lee 1907- *FilmgC, HalFC 80*
Mahle, Ernst 1929- *IntWWM 77, -80*
Mahler, David Charles 1944- *IntWWM 77, -80*
Mahler, Fritz 1901-1973 *Baker 78, BiDAmM, IntWWM 77, -80, WhoMus 72*
Mahler, Gustav 1860-1911 *AmSCAP 66, -80, Baker 78, BiDAmM, BnBkM 80[port], CmOp, CmpBCM, CnOxB, DancEn 78, DcCom 77[port], DcCom&M 79, DcCM, DcTwCC, -A, GrComp[port], MusMk, MusSN[port], NewEOp 71, NewGrD 80[port], OxMus*
Mahler, Roni 1942- *CnOxB, DancEn 78*
Mahler-Kalkstein, Menehem *NewGrD 80*
Mahling, Christoph-Hellmut 1932- *NewGrD 80*
Mahlke, Knut 1943- *WhoOp 76*
Mahlmann, Lewis *PupTheA SUP*
Mahlstedt, Fred J *IntMPA 75*
Mahogany Rush *ConMuA 80A*
Mahomayev, Muslim 1885-1937 *NewGrD 80*
Mahon *NewGrD 80, PupTheA*
Mahon, Barry 1921- *IntMPA 77, -75, -76, -78, -79*
Mahon, John 1749?-1834 *NewGrD 80*
Mahon, William 1751?-1816 *NewGrD 80*
Mahone, John 1749?-1834 *NewGrD 80*
Mahones, Gildo 1929- *EncJzS 70*
Mahoney, Arthur *DancEn 78*
Mahoney, Jack Francis 1882-1945 *AmSCAP 66, -80, BiDAmM*
Mahoney, Jock 1919- *FilmEn, FilmgC, ForYSC, HalFC 80, IntMPA 77, -75, -76, -78, -79, -80, MotPP, WhoHol A, WhoHrs 80*
Mahoney, Will d1967 *Film 2, WhoHol B*
Mahoney, Will 1894-1966? *WhScrn 77*
Mahoney, Will 1896-1967 *WhThe*
Mahoon, John 1749?-1834 *NewGrD 80*
Mahoon, Joseph *NewGrD 80*
Mahoti, Antoine *NewGrD 80*
Mahout, Antoine *NewGrD 80*
Mahr, Emil 1851-1914 *BiDAmM*
Mahr, Herman Carl 1901-1964 *AmSCAP 66, -80, NotNAT B*
Mahrenholz, Christhard 1900- *Baker 78, IntWWM 77, -80, NewGrD 80*
Mahrenholz, Christian Reinhard 1900- *NewGrD 80*
Mahrer, Walte 1912- *IntWWM 77, -80*
Mahu, Stephan 1480?-1541? *NewGrD 80*
Mai, Peter Bernhard 1935- *IntWWM 77, -80*
Mai, Wolfgang Christoph 1942- *WhoOp 76*
Maia, Leonor 1921- *FilmAG WE*
Maia, Marise *Film 2*
Maiatian, Barbara *Film 2*
Maibaum, Richard 1909- *CmMov, FilmEn, FilmgC, HalFC 80, IntMPA 77, -75, -76, -78, -79, -80, WhoHrs 80, WorEFlm*
Maiben, William 1953- *CpmDNM 73, -74, -75, -76, -77, -78, -79, -80, ConAmC*
Maiboroda, Georgi Illarionovich 1913- *IntWWM 77, -80*
Maichelbeck, Franz Anton 1702-1750 *Baker 78, NewGrD 80*
Maichelbek, Franciscum Antonium 1702-1750 *NewGrD 80*
Maiden, Sidney 1923- *BluesWW*
Maiden, Tony 1949- *AmSCAP 80*
Maiden, William Ralph 1928-1976 *EncJzS 70*
Maiden, Willie 1928-1976 *EncJzS 70*
Maidman, Irving 1897- *BiE&WWA*
Maidment, George Joseph *IntMPA 77, -75, -76, -78, -79, -80*
Maier, Betty *AmSCAP 80*
Maier, Guy 1892-1956 *Baker 78, BiDAmM*
Maier, Hanns 1924- *WhoOp 76*
Maier, Julius Joseph 1821-1889 *Baker 78*
Maier, Michael 1568-1622 *NewGrD 80*
Maietta, Angelo Leonard 1905- *AmSCAP 66, -80*
Maigne, Charles 1881- *TwYS A*
Maigne, Charles M 1879-1929 *WhScrn 74, -77, WhoHol B*
Maigret, Adam *NewGrD 80*
Maigret, Robert *NewGrD 80*
Maiguashca, Mesias 1938- *NewGrD 80*
Maile, Stanley *DcPup*
Mailer, Norman *WhoHol A*
Mailer, Norman 1923- *FilmEn, FilmgC, HalFC 80, OxFilm*
Mailer, Norman 1925- *WorEFlm*
Mailes, Charles Hill 1870-1937 *Film 1, -2, ForYSC, TwYS, WhScrn 74, -77, WhoHol B*
Maillard, Monsieur *Film 2*
Maillard, Henry *Film 2*
Maillard, Jean *NewGrD 80*
Maillard, Jean Henri O 1926- *IntWWM 77, -80, NewGrD 80*
Maillard, Nellie *CreCan 2*
Maillard-Back, Andree 1945- *IntWWM 77, -80*
Maillart, Aime 1817-1871 *NewGrD 80*
Maillart, Louis 1817-1871 *Baker 78, OxMus*
Maillart, Pierre 1550-1622 *NewGrD 80*
Maillart, Pierre 1551-1622 *Baker 78*
Maille *NewGrD 80*
Maillet, Andree *CreCan 2*
Mailly, Alphonse-Jean-Ernest 1833-1918 *Baker 78*
Mailly, Fernand *Film 2*
Mailman, Martin 1932- *AmSCAP 66, -80, Baker 78, CpmDNM 72, ConAmC, IntWWM 77, -80*
Maimonides 1135-1204 *NewGrD 80*
Main, David 1929- *IntMPA 77, -76, -78, -79, -80*
Main, Edgar *CreCan 1*
Main, Hubert Platt 1839-1925 *BiDAmM*
Main, Laurie *WhoHol A*
Main, Marjorie 1890-1975 *FilmEn, FilmgC, ForYSC, Funs[port], HalFC 80, HolCA[port], IntMPA 75, MGM[port], MotPP, MovMk[port], ThFT[port], Vers A[port], What 2[port], WhScrn 77, WhoHol C*
Main Ingredient, The *RkOn 2[port]*
Mainardi, Enrico 1897-1976 *Baker 78, NewGrD 80, WhoMus 72*
Mainbocher 1890- *BiE&WWA, NotNAT*
Maindron, Ernest 1838-1907 *DcPup*
Maine, Basil 1894-1972 *Baker 78, NewGrD 80, WhoMus 72*
Maine, Bruno 1896-1962 *NotNAT B*
Mainente, Anton Eugene 1889-1963 *AmSCAP 66, -80, ConAmC A*
Mainer, J E 1898-1971 *CmpEPM, CounME 74, -74A, EncFCWM 69, IlEncCM[port]*
Mainer, Joseph E 1898-1971 *BiDAmM*
Mainer, Wade 1907- *IlEncCM[port]*
Mainerio, Giorgio 1535?-1582 *NewGrD 80*
Maines, Don 1869-1934 *WhScrn 74, -77, WhoHol B*
Mainhall, Harry *Film 1*
Mainieri, Michael, Jr. 1938- *BiDAmM, EncJzS 70*
Maintenon, Madame De 1635-1719 *OxThe*
Mainvielle-Fodor, Josephine *NewGrD 80*
Mainwaring, Bernard 1897- *IlWWBF*
Mainwaring, Daniel 1902- *FilmEn, WhoHrs 80, WorEFlm[port]*
Mainwaring, Ernest 1876-1941 *NotNAT B, WhThe*
Mainwaring, John 1724?-1807 *NewGrD 80*
Mainwaring, John 1735-1807 *Baker 78*
Mainwaring, William *NewGrD 80*
Mainzer, Friedrich *NewGrD 80*
Mainzer, Joseph 1801-1851 *Baker 78, NewGrD 80, OxMus*
Maio, Giovan Tomaso Di 1500?-1563 *NewGrD 80*
Maio, Giuseppe Di *NewGrD 80*
Maiocchi, Gilda 1925- *DancEn 78*
Maiocchi, Gilda 1928- *CnOxB*
Maione, John Guy 1953- *AmSCAP 80*
Maiorana, Victor E 1897-1964 *AmSCAP 66, -80, ConAmC A*
Maiorano, Robert 1947?- *CnOxB*
Maiorca, Alfonse Anthony 1927- *IntWWM 77, -80*
Maiorescu, Dorella Teodora 1948- *IntWWM 77, -80*
Maiorov, Genrik Alexandrovich 1936- *CnOxB*
Mair, Franz 1821-1893 *Baker 78*
Mair, George Herbert 1887-1926 *NotNAT B, WhThe*
Mairants, Ivor 1908- *IntWWM 77, -80, WhoMus 72*
Maire, Nicolas 1800-1878 *NewGrD 80*
Mairet, Jean 1604-1686 *CnThe, Ent, McGEWD, NotNAT B, OxThe, REnWD[port]*
Mais, Chester L 1936- *ConAmC*
Mais, Stuart Petre Brodie 1885- *WhThe*
Maisch, Ludwig 1776?-1816 *NewGrD 80*
Maisky, Mischa 1948- *IntWWM 77, -80*
Maison, Edna 1893-1946 *Film 1, MotPP, WhScrn 74, -77, WhoHol B*
Maison, Rene 1895-1962 *Baker 78, MusSN[port], NewEOp 71*
Maister, Al 1903- *AmSCAP 66*
Maister, Alexander 1903- *AmSCAP 80*
Maistre, Johann Friedrich *NewGrD 80*
Maistre, Matthaeus Le *NewGrD 80*
Maistre Jan 1485?-1545? *NewGrD 80*
Maistre Jehan 1485?-1545? *NewGrD 80*
Maistre Jhan 1485?-1545? *NewGrD 80*
Maitland, Anna Harriet 1911- *IntWWM 77*
Maitland, David Caldwell Bickerstaff 1925- *WhoMus 72*
Maitland, J A Fuller *NewGrD 80, OxMus*
Maitland, John Alexander Fuller *Baker 78*
Maitland, Lauderdale d1929 *NotNAT B, WhThe*
Maitland, Lauerdale d1929 *Film 2*
Maitland, Marne 1920- *FilmgC, HalFC 80, WhoHol A*
Maitland, Mike *ConMuA 80B*
Maitland, Richard *Film 2*
Maitland, Rollo Francis 1884-1953 *BiDAmM, ConAmC, Baker 78*
Maitland, Ruth 1880-1961 *WhThe, WhoHol A*
Maja, Zelma *Film 2*
Majd Al-Din Al-Ghazali d1126 *NewGrD 80*
Majer, Joseph Friedrich Bernhard Caspar 1689-1768 *NewGrD 80*
Majer, Kajetan *NewGrD 80*
Majeroni, Mario 1870-1931 *Film 2, NotNAT B, WhScrn 74, -77, WhoHol B*
Majeske, Daniel 1932- *Baker 78*
Majewski, Andrezej 1936- *WhoOp 76*
Majilton, Charles d1931 *NotNAT B*
Majo, Gian Francesco 1732-1770 *Baker 78, NewGrD 80*
Majo, Giovan Tomaso Di *NewGrD 80*
Majo, Giuseppe De 1697-1771 *Baker 78, NewGrD 80*
Majone, Ascanio *Baker 78*
Major, Bessie *WhThe*
Major, Blyth *IntWWM 77, -80*
Major, Charles d1913 *NotNAT B*
Major, Clare Tree d1954 *NotNAT B*
Major, Ervin 1901-1967 *Baker 78, NewGrD 80*
Major, Frank A 1925- *BiE&WWA, NotNAT*
Major, Gyula 1858-1925 *NewGrD 80*
Major, Jakab Gyula 1858-1925 *Baker 78*
Major, Julius 1858-1925 *NewGrD 80*
Major, Leon 1933- *CreCan 2*
Major, Malvina 1943- *NewGrD 80*
Major, Margaret *IntWWM 77, -80, WhoMus 72*
Major, Sam Collier d1955 *WhScrn 74, -77*
Major, Tony 1939- *DrBlPA*
Majorano, Gaetano *NewEOp 71, NewGrD 80*
Majors, The *RkOn*
Majors, Lee 1940- *FilmgC, HalFC 80, IntMPA 78, -79, -80, WhoHol A*
Majors, Lee 1942- *FilmEn*
Makai, Peter 1932- *WhoOp 76*
Makarenko, Daniel *Film 2*
Makaroff, V *Film 2*
Makarov, Askold Anatolevich 1925- *CnOxB, DancEn 78*
Makarova, Maria 1885- *DancEn 78*
Makarova, Natalia Romanovna 1940- *CnOxB, DancEn 78*
Makarova, Nina 1908-1976 *Baker 78*
Makavajev, Dusan 1932- *OxFilm*

Makavejev, Dusan 1932- *BiDFilm, -81, FilmEn, WorEFlm*
Makeba, Miriam *RkOn 2A*
Makeba, Miriam 1932- *Baker 78, EncFCWM 69*
Makeba, Miriam 1934- *DrBlPA*
Makeba, Miriam Zenzi *AmSCAP 66, -80*
Makeblite *NewGrD 80*
Makedonski, Kiril 1925- *Baker 78*
Makeham, Eliot 1882-1956 *FilmgC, HalFC 80, NotNAT B, WhScrn 74, -77, WhThe, WhoHol B*
Makem, Tommy 1932- *EncFCWM 69*
Makinen, Timo Juhani 1919- *IntWWM 77, -80, NewGrD 80*
Makino, Yutaka 1930- *NewGrD 80*
Makk, Karoly 1925- *DcFM, FilmEn, MovMk[port], OxFilm*
Maklakiewicz, Jan Adam 1899-1954 *Baker 78, NewGrD 80*
Maklakiewicz, Tadeusz Wojciech 1922- *IntWWM 77, -80*
Mako 1932- *ForYSC, HalFC 80, NotNAT, WhoHol A*
Makower, Mary *IntWWM 77, -80, WhoMus 72*
Makowicz, Adam 1940- *EncJzS 70*
Makowska, Helen *Film 2*
Makris, Andreas 1930- *AmSCAP 80, IntWWM 77, -80*
Maksimovic, Rajko 1935- *Baker 78*
Maksymiuk, Jerzy 1936- *NewGrD 80*
Mala 1906-1952 *FilmEn, HalFC 80, WhScrn 74, -77, WhoHol B*
Malachi, John 1919- *EncJzS 70*
Malagaray, Juan DeCastro Y *NewGrD 80*
Malagu, Stefania 1933- *WhoOp 76*
Malamed, Seymour H *IntMPA 75, -76*
Malan, Jacob Daniel 1919- *IntWWM 77, -80*
Malan, William 1868-1941 *Film 2, WhScrn 74, -77, WhoHol B*
Malaparte, Curzio 1898-1957 *CnMD, FilmEn*
Malas, Spiro 1933- *WhoOp 76*
Malas, Spiro 1935- *IntWWM 77, -80*
Malashkin, Leonid 1842-1902 *Baker 78*
Malaspina, Massimiliano 1925- *WhoOp 76*
Malaspina, Rita Orlandi 1937- *WhoOp 76*
Malat, Jan 1843-1915 *NewGrD 80*
Malatesta, David 1943- *AmSCAP 66*
Malatesta, Fred M 1889-1952 *Film 1, -2, TwYS, WhScrn 74, -77, WhoHol B*
Malatesta, John Paul 1944- *AmSCAP 66, -80*
Malaval, Julio 1939- *WhoOp 76*
Malawski, Artur 1904-1957 *Baker 78, NewGrD 80*
Malbecque, Guillaume 1400?-1465 *NewGrD 80*
Malbeke, Guillaume 1400?-1465 *NewGrD 80*
Malchair, Johann Baptist 1730-1812 *NewGrD 80*
Malchair, John 1730-1812 *NewGrD 80*
Malchenko, Vladimir Afanasievich 1945- *WhoOp 76*
Malcior De Wormatia *NewGrD 80*
Malcolm, Alexander 1685-1763 *NewGrD 80*
Malcolm, Alexander 1687-1763 *OxMus*
Malcolm, George 1917- *BnBkM 80, IntWWM 77, -80, NewGrD 80, WhoMus 72*
Malcolm, Marion P d1964 *NotNAT B*
Malcolm, Reginald 1884-1966 *WhScrn 74, -77*
Malcolmson, Kenneth Forbes 1911- *IntWWM 77, -80, WhoMus 72*
Malcuzynski, Witold 1914-1977 *Baker 78, IntWWM 77, -80, MusSN[port], NewGrD 80, WhoMus 72*
Maldeghem, Robert Julien Van 1806-1893 *Baker 78*
Maldeghem, Robert Julien Van 1810-1893 *NewGrD 80*
Malden, Herbert John 1882-1966 *WhThe*
Malden, Karl *MotPP, PlP&P, WhoHol A*
Malden, Karl 1913- *FilmgC, HalFC 80, NotNAT*
Malden, Karl 1914- *BiDFilm, -81, BiE&WWA, CmMov, FilmEn, ForYSC, IntMPA 77, -75, -76, -78, -79, -80, MovMk[port], OxFilm, WorEFlm*
Malder, Pierre Van 1724-1768 *OxMus*
Maldere, Pierre Van 1724-1768 *MusMk*
Maldere, Pierre Van 1729-1768 *Baker 78, NewGrD 80*
Maldoom, Royston 1943- *CnOxB*
Maldoror, Sarah *WomWMM*
Maldybayev, Abdylas 1906- *IntWWM 77, -80*
Maleady, Antoinette Kirkpatrick 1918- *IntWWM 77, -80*
Malec, Ivo 1925- *NewGrD 80*
Maleingreau, Paul De 1887-1956 *Baker 78*
Malenfant, Lloyd *CreCan 1*
Malengreau, Paul 1887-1959 *NewGrD 80*
Maler *NewGrD 80*
Maler, Laux d1552 *NewGrD 80*
Maler, Luca d1552 *NewGrD 80*
Maler, Lucas d1552 *NewGrD 80*
Maler, Sigismond d1552? *NewGrD 80*
Maler, Wilhelm 1902-1976 *Baker 78, DcCM, NewGrD 80*
Malerba, Michele *NewGrD 80*
Malery *NewGrD 80*
Maleski, Alice V K 1951- *IntWWM 80*
Malet, Kathleen Mary 1934- *IntWWM 77, -80*
Maletic, Vera *DancEn 78*
Maletty, Jean De d1583? *NewGrD 80*
Maletty, Jehan De d1583? *NewGrD 80*
Maletty, Jehen De d1583? *NewGrD 80*
Malewicz-Madey, Anna 1937- *WhoOp 76*
Maley, Florence Turner 1871-1962 *AmSCAP 66*
Malfitano, Catherine 1948- *MusSN[port], WhoOp 76*
Malfitano, Joseph John 1920- *IntWWM 77, -80*
Malgoire, Jean-Claude 1940- *IntWWM 80, NewGrD 80*
Mal'Herba, Michele *NewGrD 80*
Malherbe, Charles-Theodore 1853-1911 *Baker 78, NewGrD 80*
Malherbe, Edmond Paul Henri 1870-1963 *Baker 78*
Malibran, Maria Felicita 1808-1836 *Baker 78, BnBkM 80, CmOp[port], NewEOp 71, NewGrD 80[port]*
Malick, Terence 1945- *FilmEn, IntMPA 77, -75, -76, -78, -79, -80*
Malick, Terrence 1944- *MovMk[port]*
Malick, Terrence 1945- *HalFC 80*
Malick, Terrence 1950- *BiDFilm 81*
Malige, Alfred 1895- *IntWWM 77, -80*
Malijewski, Peter Martin 1946- *AmSCAP 80*
Malik, Jan *DcPup*
Malikoff, H *Film 2*
Malikoff, Nikolai *Film 2*
Malikowski, Helen C *PupTheA*
Malin, Donald Franklin 1896- *AmSCAP 66, -80*
Malin, Nicolas 1926- *NewGrD 80*
Malina, Judith *EncWT*
Malina, Judith 1926- *BiE&WWA, NotNAT, -A, PlP&P[port], WhoHol A, WhoThe 72, -77*
Maline, Guillaume 1793-1850? *NewGrD 80*
Malini, Max 1873-1942 *MagIlD*
Malinin, Dorothy Rearick 1935- *IntWWM 77, -80*
Malinin, Evgeny 1930- *NewGrD 80*
Malinofsky, Max d1963 *NotNAT B*
Malinovskya, V S *Film 2*
Malinowski, Jan Tadeusz 1915- *IntWWM 77, -80*
Malins, Geoffrey H 1887- *IlWWBF, -A*
Malipiero, Francesco 1824-1887 *Baker 78*
Malipiero, Francesco 1882-1973 *OxMus*
Malipiero, Gian Francesco 1882-1973 *Baker 78, BnBkM 80, CmOp, CompSN[port], DcCom 77, DcCom&M 79, DcCM, MusMk, NewEOp 71, NewGrD 80[port], WhoMus 72*
Malipiero, Luigi 1901-1975 *WhScrn 77*
Malipiero, Riccardo 1914- *Baker 78, DcCM, NewGrD 80, WhoMus 72*
Maliponte, Adriana 1942- *MusSN[port], NewGrD 80, WhoOp 76*
Maliszewski, Witold 1873-1939 *Baker 78, NewGrD 80*
Malkin, Jacques 1875-1964 *Baker 78*
Malkin, Joseph 1879-1969 *Baker 78, ConAmC*
Malkin, Manfred 1884-1966 *Baker 78*
Malkin, Norman 1918- *AmSCAP 66*
Malko, Nikolai 1883-1961 *Baker 78*
Malko, Nikolay 1883-1961 *NewGrD 80*
Malko, Nikolay Andreyevich 1883-1961 *ConAmC*
Mallaband, Ronald Thomas 1922- *WhoMus 72*
Mallagaray, Juan De *NewGrD 80*
Mallah, Hossein-Ali 1921- *IntWWM 77, -80*
Mallalieu, Aubrey 1873-1948 *NotNAT B, WhThe, WhoHol B*
Mallalieu, William d1927 *NotNAT B*
Mallandaine, Jean Patricia *IntWWM 77, -80*
Mallapert, Robin *NewGrD 80*
Mallard *IlEncR*
Mallard, Donna Suzanne Staton 1948- *IntWWM 80*
Mallarme, Stephane 1842-1898 *NewGrD 80, OxMus*
Malle, Louis 1932- *BiDFilm, -81, DcFM, FilmEn, FilmgC, HalFC 80, IntMPA 77, -76, -78, -79, -80, MovMk[port], OxFilm, WorEFlm*
Mallek, Peter 1948- *CnOxB*
Maller *NewGrD 80*
Mallers, Anthony 1933- *IntMPA 79, -80*
Mallery *NewGrD 80*
Malleson, Miles 1888-1969 *FilmEn, FilmgC, ForYSC, HalFC 80, IlWWBF, NotNAT B, OxThe, PlP&P, WhScrn 74, -77, WhThe, WhoHol B, WhoHrs 80*
Malleson, Miles 1889-1969 *MovMk*
Mallet, David 1705?-1765 *OxMus*
Mallet, Francis 1750-1834 *BiDAmM*
Mallett, Jane Keenleyside *CreCan 1*
Mallett, Lawrence Roger 1947- *IntWWM 77, -80*
Mallik, Provash 1918- *IntMPA 77, -78, -79*
Mallik, Umesh 1916- *IntMPA 77, -75, -76, -78, -79*
Mallin, Tom *ConDr 73, -77B*
Malling, Jorgen 1836-1905 *Baker 78, OxMus*
Malling, Otto 1848-1915 *Baker 78, NewGrD 80, OxMus*
Mallinger, Mathilde 1847-1920 *Baker 78, CmOp, NewEOp 71, NewGrD 80*
Mallinson, Albert 1870-1946 *Baker 78*
Mallinson, Rory *ForYSC*
Mallinson, William John 1900- *WhoMus 72*
Malloch, David *OxMus*
Mallon, Bobby *Film 2*
Mallorie *NewGrD 80*
Mallory, Boots 1913-1958 *FilmEn, ForYSC, HalFC 80, NotNAT B, ThFT[port], WhoHol B*
Mallory, Burton d1962 *NotNAT B*
Mallory, Drue *WhoHol A*
Mallory, Eddie 1905?-1961 *WhoJazz 72*
Mallory, Edward *WhoHol A*
Mallory, John *WhoHol A*
Mallory, Mary Lu *PupTheA*
Mallory, Mason 1916- *AmSCAP 66, -80*
Mallory, Patricia Boots 1913-1958 *MotPP, WhScrn 74, -77*
Mallory, Rene d1931 *NotNAT B*
Mallory, Robert 1920- *AmSCAP 66, -80*
Mallory, Victoria *NotNAT*
Mallory, William B 1912- *IntMPA 75, -76*
Malloy, John J 1898-1968 *WhScrn 74, -77, WhoHol B*
Malm, Linda *WomWMM B*
Malm, Sibyl *PupTheA*
Malm, William Paul 1928- *IntWWM 77, -80, NewGrD 80*
Malmerfelt, Sixten *Film 2*
Malmlof-Forssling, Carin G 1916- *IntWWM 80*
Malmsten, Birger 1920- *FilmEn*
Malmste'n, Georg 1902- *IntWWM 77, -80*
Malneck, Matty *BgBands 74*
Malneck, Matty 1903- *AmSCAP 80*
Malneck, Matty 1904- *AmSCAP 66, CmpEPM*
Malo *BiDAmM, RkOn 2[port]*
Malo, Gina 1909-1963 *FilmEn, FilmgC, HalFC 80, IlWWBF, WhScrn 74, -77, WhThe, WhoHol B*
Malone, Mr. *PlP&P[port]*
Malone, Andrew E d1939 *NotNAT B*
Malone, Carol *IntWWM 77, -80, WhoOp 76*
Malone, Dorothy *MotPP*
Malone, Dorothy 1925- *BiDFilm, -81, FilmEn, FilmgC, ForYSC, HalFC 80, HolP 40[port], MovMk, WhoHol A, WorEFlm[port]*

Malone, Dorothy 1930- *IntMPA 77, -75, -76, -78, -79, -80*
Malone, Dudley Field 1882-1950 *WhScrn 74, -77, WhoHol B*
Malone, Dudley Field 1931- *BiE&WWA, NotNAT*
Malone, Edmond 1741-1812 *OxThe*
Malone, Edmund 1741-1812 *NotNAT B*
Malone, Eileen *IntWWM 77, -80*
Malone, Elizabeth d1955 *NotNAT B*
Malone, Florence d1956 *Film 1, WhScrn 74, -77, WhoHol B*
Malone, J A E d1929 *NotNAT B, WhThe*
Malone, Mike *MorBAP*
Malone, Molly 1895-1952 *FilmEn, Film 1, -2, TwYS, WhScrn 74, -77, WhoHol B*
Malone, Nancy *WhoHol A, WomWMM B*
Malone, Pat d1963 *WhScrn 74, -77*
Malone, Patricia 1899- *WhThe*
Malone, Pick d1962 *NotNAT B, WhScrn 77*
Malone, Ray d1970 *WhScrn 77*
Malone, Thomas Hugh 1947- *EncJzS 70*
Malone, Tom 1947- *EncJzS 70*
Maloney, Clarence J *BlkAmP*
Maloney, Leo D 1888-1929 *Film 1, -2, TwYS, -A, WhScrn 74, -77, WhoHol B*
Maloof, William Joseph 1933- *AmSCAP 80, ConAmC*
Malorie *NewGrD 80*
Malory *NewGrD 80*
Malotte, Albert Hay 1895-1964 *AmSCAP 66, -80, Baker 78, BiDAmM, ConAmC*
Malovec, Jozef 1933- *Baker 78, DcCM, NewGrD 80*
Malraux, Andre 1901-1976 *CnMD, DcFM, EncWT, HalFC 80, OxFilm, WorEFlm*
Malsch, William 1855-1924 *NewGrD 80*
Malscher, John *NewGrD 80*
Malta, Alexander 1942- *IntWWM 80, WhoOp 76*
Maltby, Alfred d1901 *NotNAT B*
Maltby, H F 1880-1963 *FilmgC, HalFC 80, IlWWBF, -A, WhoHol B*
Maltby, Henry Francis 1880-1963 *WhScrn 74, -77, WhThe*
Maltby, Richard E *BgBands 74*
Maltby, Richard E 1914- *AmSCAP 66, -80, CmpEPM, ConAmC, RkOn*
Maltby, Richard E, Jr. 1937- *AmSCAP 66*
Malten, Therese 1855-1930 *Baker 78, CmOp, NewGrD 80*
Malther, Lars 1943- *IntWWM 77, -80*
Maltin, Bernard 1907-1952 *AmSCAP 66, -80*
Malton, Felicitas *Film 2*
Maltox, Martha *Film 2*
Maltz, Albert 1908- *BiE&WWA, CnMD, ConDr 73, -77, DcFM, FilmEn, FilmgC, HalFC 80, IntMPA 77, -75, -76, -78, -79, -80, ModWD, NotNAT*
Maltzath *NewGrD 80*
Maltzel, Jiri *NewGrD 80*
Malvezzi, Alberigo 1550?-1615 *NewGrD 80*
Malvezzi, Cristofano 1547-1599 *NewGrD 80*
Malvezzi, Cristoforo 1547-1599 *NewGrD 80*
Malvin, Arthur 1922- *AmSCAP 80*
Malycke, Steven 1920- *IntWWM 77, -80*
Malyon, Eily *ForYSC*
Malyon, Eily 1879-1961 *HalFC 80, WhScrn 77, WhoHol B*
Malzard *NewGrD 80*
Malzat *NewGrD 80*
Malzat, Ignaz 1757-1804 *NewGrD 80*
Malzat, Johann Michael 1749-1787 *NewGrD 80*
Malzat, Josef *NewGrD 80*
Mama Can Can *BluesWW*
Mamakos, Peter *WhoHol A*
Mamalick, Gordon 1931- *IntWWM 77*
Mamangakis, Nicos 1929- *NewGrD 80*
Mamangakis, Nikos 1929- *Baker 78*
Mamas And The Papas, The *BiDAmM, ConMuA 80A, IlEncR[port], RkOn 2[port]*
Mamedova, Shevket 1897- *NewGrD 80*
Mames, Leon 1933- *IntWWM 77, -80*
Mamet, David 1947- *DcLB 7[port], Ent, NatPD[port]*
Mamis, Toby *ConMuA 80B*
Mamiya, Michio 1929- *Baker 78, NewGrD 80*
Mamlok, Ursula 1928- *CpmDNM 79, ConAmC, IntWWM 77, -80*
Mammen, Joy 1937- *WhoMus 72*
Mamo, John *WhoHol A*
Mamoulian, Rouben 1896- *WorEFlm*
Mamoulian, Rouben 1897- *AmFD, BiE&WWA, CmMov, EncWT, FilmgC, HalFC 80, IntMPA 77, -75, -76, -78, -79, -80, NotNAT, WhoHrs 80*
Mamoulian, Rouben 1898- *BiDFilm, -81, ConLC 16, DcFM, EncMT, FilmEn, MovMk[port], OxFilm, WhThe*
Mamporia, I *Film 2*
Mamrick, Burwell *Film 1*
Mamula, Nicholas 1908- *IntMPA 75, -76*
Man *ConMuA 80A, IlEncR*
Man, Christopher *WhoHol A*
Man, David 1938- *AmSCAP 80*
Man, Ray 1890- *WorEFlm*
Man O' War 1917-1947 *Film 2*
Mana-Zucca 1887- *Baker 78, ConAmC*
Mana-Zucca 1894- *AmSCAP 80, BiDAmM, IntWWM 77, -80, NewGrD 80, WhoMus 72*
Mana-Zucca, Mademoiselle 1894- *AmSCAP 66*
Manaday, Buddy *NewOrJ*
Manalt, Francisco 1710?-1759 *NewGrD 80*
Manaois, Joe 1903- *AmSCAP 66*
Manara, Francesco *NewGrD 80*
Manari, Francesco *NewGrD 80*
Manassas *IlEncR[port]*
Manasse, George 1938- *IntMPA 77, -75, -76, -78, -79, -80*
Manby, C R 1920- *IntMPA 77, -75, -76, -78, -79, -80*
Mance, Gina *Film 2*
Mance, Julian C 1928- *BiDAmM, EncJzS 70*
Mance, Junior 1928- *CmpEPM, EncJzS 70*
Manchester, Joe 1932- *NatPD[port]*
Manchester, Melissa 1951- *ConMuA 80A[port], IlEncR[port], RkOn 2[port]*
Manchester, P W *DancEn 78*
Manchester, Phyllis Winifred 1910?- *CnOxB*
Manchester, Susan 1942- *AmSCAP 80*
Manchet, Eliane 1937- *WhoOp 76*
Manchicourt, Pierre De 1510?-1564 *NewGrD 80*
Mancia, Luigi 1660?-1708? *NewGrD 80*
Mancicourt, Pierre De *NewGrD 80*
Mancinelli, Domenico d1802 *NewGrD 80*
Mancinelli, Luigi 1848-1921 *Baker 78, CmOp, NewEOp 71, NewGrD 80*
Mancini, Albert 1899- *AmSCAP 66, -80*
Mancini, Curzio 1550?-1608? *NewGrD 80*
Mancini, Felice 1952- *AmSCAP 80*
Mancini, Francesco 1672-1737 *Baker 78, NewGrD 80*
Mancini, Francesco 1679-1739 *MusMk*
Mancini, Giambattista 1714-1800 *NewGrD 80*
Mancini, Girolamo *NewGrD 80*
Mancini, Henry 1922- *CmMov, IntMPA 77, -75, -76, -78, -79, -80, OxFilm*
Mancini, Henry 1924- *AmPS, AmSCAP 66, -80, Baker 78, BiDAmM, CmpEPM, ConAmC, FilmEn, FilmgC, HalFC 80, MusMk, NewGrD 80, PopAmC SUP[port], RkOn[port], WorEFlm*
Mancini, Henry Nicole 1924- *IntWWM 77, -80*
Mancini, Joseph *ConAmTC*
Mancini, Ric *WhoHol A*
Mancinus, Thomas 1550-1612? *NewGrD 80*
Mancuso, Fabio *NewGrD 80*
Mancuso, Frank G 1933- *IntMPA 78, -79, -80*
Mancuso, Gus 1933- *EncJzS 70*
Mancuso, Ronald Bernard 1933- *BiDAmM, EncJzS 70*
Mandac, Evelyn 1945- *IntWWM 77, -80, NewGrD 80, WhoOp 76*
Mandakuni, Hovhannes *NewGrD 80*
Mandala *BiDAmM*
Mandel, Alan Roger 1935- *IntWWM 77, -80*
Mandel, Eli 1922- *CreCan 2*
Mandel, Frances Wakefield 1891-1943 *WhScrn 74, -77, WhoHol B*
Mandel, Frank 1884-1958 *EncMT, NotNAT B, WhThe*
Mandel, Harry *IntMPA 77, -75, -76, -78, -79, -80*
Mandel, Harvey 1945- *EncJzS 70, IlEncR*
Mandel, John Alfred 1925- *AmSCAP 66, BiDAmM, ConAmC, EncJzS 70*
Mandel, Johnny 1925- *CmpEPM, EncJzS 70*
Mandel, Johnny 1926- *HalFC 80*
Mandel, Johnny Alfred 1925- *AmSCAP 80*
Mandel, Julie 1927- *AmSCAP 80*
Mandel, Loring 1928- *BiE&WWA, NewYTET, NotNAT*
Mandel, Mike d1963 *NotNAT B*
Mandel, Nancy Anne Siegmeister 1943- *IntWWM 77, -80*
Mandelbaum, Joel 1932- *ConAmC*
Mandelkern, Rivka Iventosch 1916- *IntWWM 77, -80*
Mandell, Abe *IntMPA 77, -75, -76, -78, -79, -80*
Mandell, David 1895- *HalFC 80*
Mandell, Harry L 1912- *IntMPA 75, -76*
Mandell, Herman 1920- *WhoMus 72*
Mandell, Israel d1962 *NotNAT B*
Mander, Francesco 1915- *WhoMus 72*
Mander, Miles 1888-1946 *FilmEn, Film 1, -2, FilmgC, ForYSC, HalFC 80, HolCA[port], IlWWBF, Vers A[port], WhScrn 74, -77, WhoHol B, WhoHrs 80*
Mander, Miles 1889-1946 *MovMk*
Mander, Noel Percy 1912- *IntWWM 77, -80, NewGrD 80, WhoMus 72*
Mander, Theodore *Film 2*
Mandic, Josip 1883-1959 *Baker 78*
Mandicevshi, Eusebie *NewGrD 80*
Mandikian, Arda 1924- *WhoMus 72*
Mandini *NewGrD 80*
Mandini, Maria *NewGrD 80*
Mandini, Paolo 1757-1842 *NewGrD 80*
Mandini, Stefano 1750-1810? *NewGrD 80*
Mandl, Richard 1859-1918 *Baker 78*
Mandrell, Barbara 1948- *CounME 74[port], -74A, IlEncCM[port]*
Mandrill *RkOn 2A*
Manduell, John 1928- *IntWWM 80, NewGrD 80, WhoMus 72*
Mandville, William C 1867-1917 *WhScrn 77*
Mandy, Jerry 1893-1945 *Film 2, WhScrn 74, -77, WhoHol B*
Mandyczewski, Eusebius 1857-1929 *Baker 78, NewGrD 80*
Manella, Margaret 1913- *WhoMus 72*
Manelli, Francesco 1594-1667 *NewGrD 80*
Manelli, Francesco 1595-1667 *Baker 78*
Manelli, Maddalena *NewGrD 80*
Manen, Hans Van 1932- *CnOxB*
Manen, Joan De 1883- *Baker 78, OxMus*
Manen, Juan 1883-1971 *NewGrD 80*
Manenti, Giampiero d1597 *NewGrD 80*
Manenti, Giovampierol d1597 *NewGrD 80*
Manenti, Giovanni Piero d1597 *NewGrD 80*
Maneri, Joseph Gabriel 1927- *AmSCAP 80, ConAmC*
Manes, Gina 1895- *FilmEn, Film 2*
Manes, Stephen Gabriel 1940- *IntWWM 77, -80, WhoMus 72*
Manetta, Fess 1889-1969 *WhoJazz 72*
Manetta, Manuel 1889-1969 *NewOrJ[port]*
Manetti, Lido *Film 2*
Maney, Richard 1891-1968 *NotNAT B*
Maney, Richard 1892-1968 *NotNAT A*
Manford, Barbara Ann 1929- *IntWWM 77, -80*
Manfred Mann *IlEncR*
Manfred Mann's Earth Band *IlEncR*
Manfredi, Lodovico *NewGrD 80*
Manfredi, Muzio 1535-1607 *McGEWD*
Manfredi, Nino 1921- *FilmEn, WhoHol A, WorEFlm*
Manfredini, Francesco 1680?-1748 *Baker 78*
Manfredini, Francesco 1688-1748 *OxMus*
Manfredini, Francesco Onofrio 1684-1762 *NewGrD 80*
Manfredini, Vincenzo 1737-1799 *Baker 78, NewGrD 80*
Mangahas, Ruby Kelley 1916- *IntWWM 80*
Mangano, Silvana *IntMPA 75, -76, -78, -79, -80*
Mangano, Silvana 1925- *ForYSC*
Mangano, Silvana 1930- *BiDFilm, -81, FilmAG WE, FilmEn, FilmgC, HalFC 80, IntMPA 77, MotPP, OxFilm, WorEFlm*
Mangano, Silvano *WhoHol A*
Mangean, Etienne 1710?-1756? *NewGrD 80*
Mangeant, Jacques d1633? *NewGrD 80*
Mangel, Carlos A *AmSCAP 80*

Mangelsdorff, Albert 1928- *EncJzS 70, NewGrD 80*
Mangeot, Andre 1883-1970 *NewGrD 80, OxMus*
Mangeot, Auguste *OxMus*
Mangeot, Edward Joseph 1834-1898 *OxMus*
Manger, Shelia *WomWMM B*
Manges, Kenny 1913- *AmSCAP 66, -80*
Mangeshkar, Hridaynath 1937- *IntWWM 77, -80*
Manggrum, Loretta C Cessor 1896- *IntWWM 77*
Mangiapane, Sherwood 1912- *NewOrJ[port]*
Mangin, Noel Victor 1932- *WhoMus 72*
Mangini, Cecilia *WomWMM*
Mangini, Marino Anthony 1950- *CpmDNM 80, ConAmC*
Mangione, Charles Frank 1940- *BiDAmM, EncJzS 70*
Mangione, Chuck 1940- *EncJzS 70*
Mangione, Gap 1938- *EncJzS 70*
Mangione, Gaspare Charles 1938- *EncJzS 70*
Mangold *NewGrD 80*
Mangold, Arland Alza 1937- *IntWWM 77, -80*
Mangold, Carl Amand 1813-1889 *NewGrD 80*
Mangold, Elva 1919- *ConAmTC*
Mangold, Johann Wilhelm 1735-1806 *NewGrD 80*
Mangold, Karl 1813-1889 *Baker 78*
Mangold, Wilhelm 1796-1875 *Baker 78, NewGrD 80*
Mangolt, Burk *NewGrD 80*
Mangolte, Babette *WomWMM B*
Mangon, Johannes 1525?-1578 *NewGrD 80*
Mangual, Jose Luis, Jr. 1948- *AmSCAP 80*
Manhattan Brothers, The *RkOn*
Manhattan Transfer *IlEncR, RkOn 2[port]*
Manhattans, The *RkOn 2[port]*
Manheim, Mannie *IntMPA 77, -75, -76, -78, -79, -80*
Maniates, Maria Rika 1937- *IntWWM 77, -80, NewGrD 80*
Manicke, Dietrich 1923- *IntWWM 77, -80, NewGrD 80*
Manikhao, Narong 1930- *IntWWM 77, -80*
Manilius, Gislain d1573 *NewGrD 80*
Manilow, Barry 1946- *ConMuA 80A, IlEncR, RkOn 2[port]*
Manina, Maria *NewGrD 80*
Manings, Allan *NewYTET*
Manini, Joseph, Jr. 1930-1964 *BiDAmM*
Manion, Mary Endres 1907- *AmSCAP 66, -80*
Manitas DePlata 1921- *IntWWM 77, -80*
Manjean, Teddy 1901-1964 *WhScrn 74, -77*
Mank, Charles 1902- *AmSCAP 80*
Mank, Chaw 1902- *AmSCAP 66*
Mankell *NewGrD 80*
Mankell, Gustaf Adolf 1812-1880 *NewGrD 80*
Mankell, Henning 1868-1930 *Baker 78, NewGrD 80*
Mankell, Johan Hermann 1796-1835 *NewGrD 80*
Mankiewicz, Don M 1922- *FilmgC, HalFC 80, IntMPA 77, -75, -76, -78, -79, -80*
Mankiewicz, Herman J 1897-1953 *DcFM, FilmEn, FilmgC, HalFC 80, NotNAT B, WorEFlm*
Mankiewicz, Herman J 1898-1953 *OxFilm*
Mankiewicz, Joseph L 1909- *AmFD, BiDFilm, -81, CmMov, ConDr 73, -77A, DcFM, FilmEn, FilmgC, HalFC 80, IntMPA 77, -75, -76, -78, -79, -80, MovMk[port], OxFilm, WorEFlm*
Mankiewitz, Tom *IntMPA 78, -79, -80*
Mankowitz, Wolf 1924- *ConDr 73, -77, FilmEn, FilmgC, HalFC 80, IntMPA 77, -75, -76, -78, -79, -80, NotNAT, WhoThe 72, -77*
Manley, Charles Daddy 1830-1916 *WhScrn 77*
Manley, Dave 1883-1943 *WhScrn 74, -77, WhoHol B*
Manley, Louis *PupTheA*
Manley, Marie *Film 1*
Manley, Mary d1724 *NotNAT B*
Manley And Brewer *PupTheA*
Manly, Ann 1949- *IntWWM 80*
Manly, Charles Macdonald 1855-1924 *CreCan 2*
Manly, Eva Mae Coffman 1920- *IntWWM 77*
Mann, Aaron 1899- *AmSCAP 66, -80*
Mann, Abby 1927- *FilmEn, FilmgC, HalFC 80, IntMPA 77, -75, -76, -78, -79, -80, NewYTET*
Mann, Alan 1914- *IntWWM 77, -80*
Mann, Alfred 1917- *Baker 78, NewGrD 80*
Mann, Alice *Film 1, -2*
Mann, Anthony 1906-1967 *BiDFilm, -81, CmMov, DcFM, FilmEn, FilmgC, HalFC 80, OxFilm, WorEFlm*
Mann, Anthony 1907-1967 *CmMov*
Mann, Arthur Henry 1850-1929 *Baker 78, NewGrD 80, OxMus*
Mann, Barry 1942- *ConMuA 80A, RkOn*
Mann, Billy d1974 *WhScrn 77*
Mann, Charles *MorBAP*
Mann, Charles Maynard 1949- *AmSCAP 80*
Mann, Charlton 1876-1958 *NotNAT B, WhThe*
Mann, Christopher 1903- *WhThe*
Mann, Daniel 1912- *BiDFilm, -81, BiE&WWA, DcFM, FilmEn, FilmgC, HalFC 80, IntMPA 77, -75, -76, -78, -79, -80, MovMk[port], NotNAT, OxFilm, WorEFlm*
Mann, David 1916- *AmSCAP 66, -80, BiDAmM, CmpEPM*
Mann, Delbert 1920- *BiDFilm, -81, DcFM, FilmEn, Film 2, FilmgC, HalFC 80, IntMPA 77, -75, -76, -78, -79, -80, MovMk[port], NewYTET, NotNAT, OxFilm, WorEFlm*
Mann, Edward 1924- *NotNAT*
Mann, Elias 1750-1825 *BiDAmM, NewGrD 80*
Mann, Erika 1905-1969 *EncWT*
Mann, Frances *Film 2*
Mann, Frankie *Film 1, -2*
Mann, Gloria *RkOn*
Mann, Hank 1887-1971 *FilmgC, HalFC 80, WhScrn 74, -77, WhoHol B*
Mann, Hank 1888- *ForYSC*
Mann, Hank 1888-1971 *FilmEn, Film 1, -2, TwYS*
Mann, Harry *Film 1, -2*
Mann, Heinrich 1871-1950 *EncWT, ModWD*
Mann, Helen *Film 2*
Mann, Herbert Jay 1930- *AmSCAP 80*
Mann, Herbie 1930- *AmSCAP 66, BiDAmM, EncJzS 70, RkOn 2[port]*
Mann, Herman 1771-1833 *BiDAmM*
Mann, Howard *WhoHol A*
Mann, James 1942- *ConAmC*
Mann, Jerome 1910- *AmSCAP 66, -80*
Mann, Johann *NewGrD 80*
Mann, Johann Christoph *NewGrD 80, OxMus*
Mann, John Russell 1928- *AmSCAP 66, -80*
Mann, Kal 1917- *AmSCAP 66, -80*
Mann, Klaus 1906-1949 *EncWT*
Mann, Larry D *WhoHol A*
Mann, Laurence 1931- *IntWWM 77, -80*
Mann, Leslie 1923- *Baker 78*
Mann, Lionel Frederic 1927- *WhoMus 72*
Mann, Lloyd *PupTheA*
Mann, Louis 1865-1931 *Film 2, NotNAT B, WhScrn 74, -77, WhThe, WhoHol B, WhoStg 1906, -1908*
Mann, Lynn *AmSCAP 80*
Mann, Manfred *ConMuA 80A, RkOn 2[port]*
Mann, Manfred, Earth Band *RkOn 2[port]*
Mann, Margaret 1868-1941 *Film 1, -2, TwYS, WhScrn 77*
Mann, Marion 1914- *CmpEPM*
Mann, Matthias Georg *NewGrD 80*
Mann, Ned H 1893-1967 *FilmEn, FilmgC, HalFC 80, WhScrn 74, -77*
Mann, Newton M 1836-1926 *BiDAmM*
Mann, Paul 1910- *AmSCAP 66, -80*
Mann, Paul 1915- *BiE&WWA, NotNAT, WhoHol A*
Mann, Peggy *AmSCAP 66, CmpEPM*
Mann, Ralph 1922- *BiE&WWA*
Mann, Robert *ConAmC*
Mann, Robert 1920- *Baker 78*
Mann, Robert 1925- *DcCM*
Mann, Robert E 1902-1978 *AmSCAP 66, -80*
Mann, Stanley 1884-1953 *WhScrn 74, -77, WhoHol B*
Mann, Stephen Follett 1945- *AmSCAP 80*
Mann, Steve *AmSCAP 80*
Mann, Sy 1920- *AmSCAP 66, -80*
Mann, Sydney Malcolm 1939- *WhoMus 72*
Mann, Ted *IntMPA 77, -78, -79, -80, PlP&P*
Mann, Theodore 1924- *BiE&WWA, NotNAT, WhoThe 72, -77*
Mann, Thomas 1875-1955 *EncWT, NewEOp 71, NewGrD 80, OxMus*
Mann, William Somervell 1924- *IntWWM 77, -80, NewGrD 80, WhoMus 72*
Manna *NewGrD 80*
Manna, Cristoforo 1704- *NewGrD 80*
Manna, Gaetano 1751-1804 *NewGrD 80*
Manna, Gennaro 1715-1779 *NewGrD 80*
Mannan, Laila *MorBAP*
Manne, S Anthony 1940- *IntMPA 80*
Manne, Sheldon 1920- *BiDAmM, EncJzS 70*
Manne, Shelly 1920- *AmSCAP 66, -80, CmpEPM, EncJzS 70, WhoHol A*
Manneke, Daan 1939- *Baker 78*
Manneke, Daniel 1939- *CpmDNM 76, IntWWM 77, -80, NewGrD 80*
Mannel, Olga *Film 2*
Mannelli, Carlo 1640-1697 *NewGrD 80*
Mannelli, Francesco *NewGrD 80*
Manner, Eeva-Liisa 1921- *CroCD*
Mannering, Dore Lewin 1879-1932 *NotNAT B, WhThe*
Mannering, Lewin 1879-1932 *Film 2, WhScrn 74, -77*
Mannering, Mary 1876-1953 *FamA&A[port], NotNAT B, WhThe, WhoStg 1906, -1908*
Mannering, Moya 1888- *WhThe*
Manners, Charles 1857-1935 *Baker 78, NewEOp 71, NewGrD 80*
Manners, Charles 1857-1955 *CmOp*
Manners, David *MotPP*
Manners, David 1900- *Film 2, ForYSC, WhoHol A*
Manners, David 1901- *FilmEn, FilmgC, HalFC 80, MovMk, What 1[port], WhoHrs 80*
Manners, David 1902- *HolP 30[port]*
Manners, David 1905- *WhThe*
Manners, Lady Diana *Film 1, -2*
Manners, Dudley 1894- *AmSCAP 66*
Manners, Fanny *NewGrD 80*
Manners, Jayne *BiE&WWA*
Manners, John *Film 2*
Manners, John Hartley 1870-1928 *ModWD, NotNAT B, OxThe, WhThe*
Manners, Laurette Taylor 1884-1946 *OxThe*
Manners, Maxine 1920- *AmSCAP 80*
Manners, Sheila *WhoHol A*
Manners, Zeke 1911- *AmSCAP 66, -80, IlEncCM*
Mannes, Clara Damrosch 1869-1948 *Baker 78*
Mannes, David 1866-1959 *Baker 78, BiDAmM, NewGrD 80*
Mannes, Florence V 1896-1964 *WhScrn 74, -77*
Mannes, Leo *AmSCAP 80*
Mannes, Leopold Damrosch 1899-1964 *Baker 78, BiDAmM, ConAmC, NotNAT B*
Manney, Charles Fonteyn 1872-1951 *AmSCAP 66, -80, Baker 78, BiDAmM, ConAmC*
Mannheim, Lucie 1895-1976 *HalFC 80*
Mannheim, Lucie 1899-1976 *EncWT, FilmAG WE*
Mannheim, Lucie 1905- *Film 2, FilmgC, WhThe, WhoHol A*
Mannheimer, Albert, Jr. *IntMPA 77, -75, -76*
Manni, Ettore 1927-1979 *FilmEn*
Manni, Marcello *OxMus*
Manning, Aileen *Film 2*
Manning, Aileen d1945 *WhoHol B*
Manning, Aileen 1886-1946 *WhScrn 74, -77*
Manning, Ambrose d1940 *Film 2, NotNAT B, WhThe*
Manning, Dick 1912- *AmSCAP 66, -80, CmpEPM*
Manning, Gordon *NewYTET*
Manning, Hallie *Film 2*
Manning, Hope *WhoHol A*
Manning, Hugh Gardner 1920- *WhoThe 72, -77*
Manning, Irene *MotPP*
Manning, Irene 1916- *FilmEn, ForYSC, WhoHol A*
Manning, Irene 1917- *FilmgC, HalFC 80, WhThe*

Manning, Irene 1918- *BiE&WWA, NotNAT*
Manning, Jack 1916- *BiE&WWA, Film 2, NotNAT, WhoHol A*
Manning, Jane Marian 1938- *IntWWM 77, -80, NewGrD 80, WhoMus 72*
Manning, Joseph d1946 *Film 1, WhScrn 74, -77, WhoHol B*
Manning, Kathleen Lockhart 1890-1951 *AmSCAP 66, -80, Baker 78, ConAmC*
Manning, Knox *ForYSC*
Manning, Laura 1926- *AmSCAP 66*
Manning, Laura 1936- *AmSCAP 80*
Manning, Mary *PlP&P*
Manning, Mary Lee d1937 *WhScrn 74, -77*
Manning, Mildred *Film 1, -2, MotPP*
Manning, Otis d1963 *NotNAT B*
Manning, Peter David 1948- *IntWWM 77, -80*
Manning, Phillipp *Film 2*
Manning, Richard 1914-1954 *AmSCAP 66, -80*
Manning, Tom 1880-1936 *WhScrn 74, -77, WhoHol B*
Mannini, Elena 1937- *WhoOp 76*
Mannino, Franco 1924- *Baker 78, NewGrD 80, WhoMus 72*
Mannion, Moira d1964 *NotNAT B*
Manno, Robert 1944- *ConAmC*
Manno, Tony 1912- *AmSCAP 66, -80*
Mannock, Patrick L 1887- *WhThe*
Mannone, Joseph 1900- *NewOrJ[port]*
Mannoni, Raymond 1921- *IntWWM 77, -80*
Manns, Angela M 1942- *IntWWM 80*
Manns, August *OxMus*
Manns, Sir August 1825-1907 *Baker 78, NewGrD 80*
Mannstadt, Franz 1852-1932 *Baker 78*
Manny, Charles d1962 *NotNAT B*
Manojlovic, Kosta 1890-1949 *Baker 78*
Manola, Marion d1914 *NotNAT B*
Manolesi, Carlo *NewGrD 80*
Manoli Blessi *NewGrD 80*
Manolov, Emanuil 1860-1902 *NewGrD 80*
Manon, Marcia *Film 1, -2*
Manone, Joe 1900- *AmSCAP 80*
Manone, Joseph 1900- *AmSCAP 66*
Manone, Joseph 1904- *BiDAmM, EncJzS 70*
Manone, Wingy 1904- *CmpEPM, EncJzS 70, IlEncJ*
Manone, Wingy Joseph 1904- *WhoJazz 72*
Manoogian, Betzi *WomWMM*
Manor, Chris *WhoHol A*
Manowarda, Josef Von 1890-1942 *CmOp*
Manrique DeLara, Manuel 1863-1929 *Baker 78, NewGrD 80*
Mansarova, Aida *WomWMM*
Manschinger, Kurt 1902-1968 *Baker 78*
Manser, Philip Simon Andrew 1951- *IntWWM 80*
Mansfeldt, Edgar *OxMus*
Mansfield, Alfred F d1938 *NotNAT B*
Mansfield, Alice d1938 *NotNAT B, WhThe*
Mansfield, Beatrice Cameron 1868-1940 *OxThe*
Mansfield, Duncan *Film 2*
Mansfield, Irving *NewYTET*
Mansfield, Jayne d1967 *MotPP, WhoHol B*
Mansfield, Jayne 1930-1967 *ForYSC*
Mansfield, Jayne 1932-1967 *FilmgC, HalFC 80, OxFilm, WhScrn 74, -77*
Mansfield, Jayne 1933-1967 *FilmEn, MovMk[port]*
Mansfield, Jayne 1934-1967 *BiDFilm, -81, WorEFlm[port]*
Mansfield, John 1919-1956 *WhScrn 74, -77, WhoHol B*
Mansfield, Kenneth Zoellin, Jr. 1932- *ConAmC*
Mansfield, Marie Moss *AmSCAP 66, -80*
Mansfield, Martha d1923 *MotPP, WhoHol B*
Mansfield, Martha 1899-1923 *Film 1, -2, TwYS*
Mansfield, Martha 1900-1923 *WhScrn 74, -77*
Mansfield, Orlando Augustine 1863-1936 *Baker 78*
Mansfield, Portia 1887- *BiE&WWA, DancEn 78, NotNAT*
Mansfield, Purcell James 1889-1968 *Baker 78*
Mansfield, Rankin d1969 *WhScrn 77*
Mansfield, Richard 1854-1907 *EncWT, FamA&A[port], NotNAT B, OxThe, PlP&P*
Mansfield, Richard 1857-1907 *CnThe, NotNAT A, WhoStg 1906, -1908*
Mansfield, Saxie 1910- *CmpEPM*
Mansfield, Scott Joel 1949- *AmSCAP 80*
Mansfield, Veronica *WhoMus 72*
Manshardt, Thomas 1927- *IntWWM 77, -80*
Mansingrova, Jarmila 1934- *CnOxB*
Mansion, Henry 1898?-1968 *NewOrJ*
Manski, Dorothee 1895-1967 *Baker 78, BiDAmM*
Manskopf, Nicholas 1869-1928 *Baker 78*
Manso, Carlos 1928- *IntWWM 77, -80*
Manso, Juanita 1873-1957 *WhScrn 74, -77*
Manson, Alan *WhoHol A*
Manson, Arthur 1928- *IntMPA 77, -75, -76, -78, -79, -80*
Manson, Eddy Lawrence 1919- *AmSCAP 66, ConAmC, IntWWM 77, -80*
Manson, Eddy Lawrence 1922- *AmSCAP 80*
Manson, Isabel Merson 1884-1952 *WhScrn 74, -77*
Manson, Maurice *WhoHol A*
Mansouri, Lotfi 1929- *WhoOp 76*
Manstadt, Margit *Film 2*
Mansur Zalzal Al-Darib *NewGrD 80*
Mansuryan, Tigran Yegiayi 1939- *NewGrD 80*
Mant, S G *WhoMus 72*
Mantee, Paul 1930?- *ForYSC, HalFC 80, WhoHol A, WhoHrs 80*
Mantegazza *NewGrD 80*
Mantegazza, Pietro Giovanni *NewGrD 80*
Mantel, Gerhard Friedrich 1930- *IntWWM 77, -80*
Mantell *PupTheA*
Mantell, Bruce d1933 *NotNAT B*
Mantell, Joe *ForYSC, WhoHol A*
Mantell, Marianne 1929- *BiE&WWA*
Mantell, Robert Bruce 1854-1928 *FamA&A[port], Film 1, -2, NotNAT A, -B, OxThe, WhScrn 74, -77, WhThe, WhoHol B, WhoStg 1906, -1908*
Manteo, Agrippino *PupTheA*
Manthey-Kotzur, Sonia 1922- *IntWWM 80*
Mantia, Aldo 1903- *IntWWM 77, -80, WhoMus 72*
Mantia, Joe 1914- *AmSCAP 66, -80*
Mantle, Burns 1873-1948 *WhThe*
Mantle, Robert Burns 1873-1948 *EncWT, NotNAT B, OxThe*
Mantler, Michael 1943- *EncJzS 70*
Mantler, Mike 1943- *BiDAmM, IlEncJ*
Mantley, John *NewYTET*
Manton, Franz 1921- *WhoMus 72*
Manton, Lily 1926- *WhoMus 72*
Manton, Robert William 1894-1967 *ConAmC*
Mantor, Marjorie *PupTheA*
Mantovani *AmPS A, -B, RkOn[port]*
Mantovani 1905-1980 *NewGrD 80*
Mantovani 1908- *CmpEPM*
Mantovani, A *WhoMus 72*
Mantovani, Annunzio Paolo 1905- *Baker 78, IntWWM 77, -80*
Mantovani, Tancredi 1863-1932 *Baker 78*
Mantovano, Alessandro *NewGrD 80*
Mantovano, Gian Pietro *NewGrD 80*
Mantovano, Publio Filippo *McGEWD*
Mantovano, Rossino *NewGrD 80*
Mantua, Jacquet De *NewGrD 80*
Mantuani, Josef 1860-1933 *Baker 78, NewGrD 80*
Mantuanus, Johannes *NewGrD 80*
Mantz, Paul 1903-1965 *HalFC 80*
Mantz, Paul 1904-1965 *WhScrn 74, -77, WhoHol B*
Mantzaros, Nicolaos 1795-1872 *NewGrD 80*
Mantzius, Karl d1921 *NotNAT B*
Manuel, Handel 1918- *IntWWM 77, -80*
Manuel, Niklas 1484-1530 *OxThe*
Manuel, Roland *Baker 78*
Manuguerra, Matteo 1924- *WhoOp 76*
Manuguerra, Matteo 1925?- *NewGrD 80*
Manulis, Martin 1915- *IntMPA 77, -75, -76, -78, -79, -80, NewYTET*
Manuppelli, Antonio 1892-1972 *AmSCAP 66, -80*
Manurita, Giovanni 1895- *WhoMus 72*
Manus, Fay Whitman 1926- *AmSCAP 80*
Manus, Jack 1909- *AmSCAP 66, -80*
Manusardi, Guido 1935- *EncJzS 70*
Manuti, Alfred Joseph 1909- *BiE&WWA*
Manvell, Roger 1909- *FilmgC, HalFC 80, IntMPA 77, -75, -78, -79, -80, OxFilm*
Manvers *PupTheA*
Manville, Margaret Roebling 1896- *IntWWM 77*
Manwaring, William d1763 *NewGrD 80*
Manx, Kate 1930-1964 *HalFC 80, WhScrn 74, -77, WhoHol B*
Manz, Andre 1942- *IntWWM 77, -80*
Manz, Paul 1919- *CpmDNM 79, -80, ConAmC*
Manza, Luigi *NewGrD 80*
Manza, Ralph *WhoHol A*
Manzanera, Phil *ConMuA 80A*
Manzarek, Raymond Daniel 1939- *AmSCAP 80*
Manzarraga, Tomas De 1908- *NewGrD 80*
Manziarly, Marcelle De 1899- *NewGrD 80*
Manzine, Italia Almirante *Film 1*
Manzini, Giovanni *OxThe*
Manzolo, Domenico *NewGrD 80*
Manzoni, Alessandro 1785-1873 *EncWT, McGEWD[port], NewEOp 71, NotNAT B, OxThe*
Manzoni, Giacomo 1932- *Baker 78, DcCM, NewGrD 80*
Manzotti, Luigi 1835-1905 *CnOxB, NotNAT B*
Manzuoli, Giovanni 1720?-1782 *NewGrD 80*
Mapes, Victor 1870-1943 *NotNAT B, WhThe, WhoStg 1906, -1908*
Maphis, Joe 1921- *CounME 74, -74A*
Maphis, Joe And Rose Lee *EncFCWM 69, IlEncCM*
Maphis, Otis W 1921- *BiDAmM*
Maphis, Rose Lee 1922- *CounME 74, -74A*
Maphon, Franciszek *NewGrD 80*
Maple, Audrey 1899-1971 *WhScrn 74, -77, WhoHol B*
Maple City Four *BiDAmM*
Mapleson, James Henry 1830-1901 *Baker 78, NewEOp 71, NewGrD 80*
Mapp, Jim E *DrBlPA*
Mar, Fien DeLa 1898-1965 *FilmAG WE*
Mar, Jeffrey Kenneth 1953- *AmSCAP 80*
Mar-Keys, The *RkOn*
Mara 1749-1833 *BnBkM 80*
Mara, La *NewGrD 80*
Mara, Adele 1923- *FilmEn, FilmgC, ForYSC, HalFC 80, IntMPA 77, -75, -76, -78, -79, MotPP, WhoHol A*
Mara, Adelle *IntMPA 80*
Mara, Gertrud Elisabeth 1749-1833 *Baker 78, NewGrD 80[port]*
Mara, Kya *Film 2*
Mara, Thalia *CnOxB, DancEn 78*
Marable, Fate 1890-1947 *BiDAmM, CmpEPM, WhoJazz 72*
Marable Band, Fate *BiDAmM*
Maracci, Carmalita 1911- *DancEn 78*
Maracci, Carmelita 1911- *CnOxB*
Maracineanu, Micaela 1942- *WhoOp 76*
Maraffi, Lewis Frederick *AmSCAP 80*
Maragno, Virtu 1928- *Baker 78*
Marais, Jean 1913- *BiDFilm, -81, EncWT, Ent, FilmAG WE[port], FilmEn, FilmgC, ForYSC, HalFC 80, IntMPA 77, -75, -76, -78, -79, -80, MotPP, MovMk[port], OxFilm, WhoHol A, WhoHrs 80, WorEFlm*
Marais, Josef 1905-1978 *AmSCAP 66, -80, Baker 78, ConAmC A, EncFCWM 69*
Marais, Marin 1656-1728 *Baker 78, BnBkM 80, MusMk, NewGrD 80[port], OxMus*
Marais, Miranda 1912- *BiDAmM, EncFCWM 69*
Marais, Roland *NewGrD 80*
Maraldo, William 1938- *ConAmC*
Maran, George Alfred 1926- *WhoMus 72*
Maranatha *BiDAmM*
Marangoni, Bruno Luigi 1935- *WhoOp 76*
Marano, Charles d1964 *NotNAT B*
Marasco, Robert 1936- *WhoThe 72, -77*
Marasco, Robert 1937- *NotNAT*
Marastone, Antonio d1628 *NewGrD 8*
Marastoni, Antonio d1628 *NewGrD 80*
Marathons, The *RkOn*
Maratini, Rosita *Film 2*
Maravan, Lila d1950 *NotNAT B, WhThe*
Marazzi, Silvio *NewGrD 80*
Marazzoli, Marco 1602?-1662 *Baker 78,*

NewGrD 80
Marba, Fred *Film 2*
Marba, Joseph *Film 1, -2*
Marbe, Myriam Lucia 1931- *Baker 78, IntWWM 80*
Marbeck, John *NewGrD 80*
Marbeck, John 1505?-1585? *BnBkM 80*
Marbeck, John 1510?-1585? *Baker 78*
Marbecke, John 1505?-1585? *BnBkM 80*
Marberg, Lili d1962 *NotNAT B*
Marble, Dan 1810-1849 *FamA&A[port]*
Marble, Danforth 1810-1849 *NotNAT A, -B, OxThe*
Marble, Emma d1930 *NotNAT B*
Marble, John 1844-1919 *WhScrn 77*
Marble, Mary 1876- *WhoStg 1908*
Marburgh, Bertram 1875-1956 *Film 1, -2, WhScrn 77*
Marbury, Elisabeth 1856-1933 *NotNAT A, -B*
Marbury, Elizabeth 1856-1933 *OxThe*
Marc, Ronald *AmSCAP 80*
Marc, Thomas *NewGrD 80*
Marc-Michel 1812-1868 *NotNAT B*
Marcabru 1100?- *NewGrD 80*
Marcabrun 1100?- *NewGrD 80*
Marcantonio Romano *NewGrD 80*
Marceau, Emilie *Film 1*
Marceau, Felicien 1913- *BiE&WWA, CnMD, EncWT, Ent, McGEWD[port], ModWD, NotNAT*
Marceau, Marcel *DcPup, WhoHrs 80*
Marceau, Marcel 1922- *JoeFr*
Marceau, Marcel 1923- *BiE&WWA, CnOxB, EncWT, Ent, NotNAT, OxThe, WhoHol A, WorEFlm[port]*
Marcel, Gabriel Honore 1889-1964 *CnMD, McGEWD[port], ModWD*
Marcel, Gabriel Honore 1889-1973 *EncWT, Ent*
Marcel, Luc-Andre 1919- *NewGrD 80*
Marcel, Lucille 1885-1921 *Baker 78*
Marcel-Dubois, Claudie 1913- *NewGrD 80*
Marcella, Marco d1962 *NotNAT B*
Marcelle, Dancer *Film 2*
Marcelle, Pauline 1911- *IntWWM 77, -80*
Marcelle-Maurette 1903- *BiE&WWA*
Marcelli, Nino 1890-1967 *Baker 78, ConAmC*
Marcelli, Nino 1892- *AmSCAP 66*
Marcelli, Nino 1892-1967 *AmSCAP 80*
Marcellino, Muzzy *CmpEPM*
Marcello DaCapua *NewGrD 80*
Marcello, Alessandro 1669-1747 *Baker 78*
Marcello, Alessandro 1684-1750 *NewGrD 80*
Marcello, Benedetto 1686-1739 *Baker 78, BnBkM 80, GrComp[port], MusMk, NewGrD 80, OxMus*
Marcellus, George W d1921 *NotNAT B*
Marcellus, John Robert, III 1939- *IntWWM 77, -80*
Marcels, The *AmPS A, RkOn*
March, Alex 1920- *IntMPA 77, -75, -76, -78, -79, -80, NewYTET*
March, Benjamin *PupTheA*
March, Daniel 1816-1909 *BiDAmM*
March, Elspeth *WhoHol A, WhoThe 72, -77*
March, Eve d1974 *WhScrn 77, WhoHol B*
March, Frederic 1897-1975 *CnThe, EncWT, Film 2, PlP&P*
March, Fredric 1897-1975 *BiDFilm, -81, BiE&WWA, Ent, FamA&A[port], FilmEn, FilmgC, ForYSC[port], HalFC 80, IntMPA 75, MotPP, MovMk[port], NotNAT B, OxFilm, WhScrn 77, WhThe, WhoHol C, WhoHrs 80[port], WhoThe 72, WorEFlm*
March, Hal 1920-1970 *BiE&WWA, ForYSC, HalFC 80, MotPP, NotNAT B, WhScrn 74, -77, WhoHol B*
March, Iris d1966 *WhScrn 77*
March, John Quarles 1949- *IntWWM 80*
March, Lori *WhoHol A*
March, Myrna Fox 1935- *AmSCAP 66, -80*
March, Nadine 1898-1944 *NotNAT B, WhThe, WhoHol B*
Marchal, Andre 1894- *BnBkM 80, IntWWM 77, -80, NewGrD 80, WhoMus 72*
Marchal, Arlette 1903- *FilmEn, Film 2*
Marchal, Georges 1920- *FilmEn*
Marchan, Bobby 1930- *RkOn[port]*
Marchand *NewGrD 80*
Marchand, Clement 1912- *CreCan 1*
Marchand, Colette 1925- *CnOxB, DancEn 78[port], WhoHol A*
Marchand, Corinne *FilmgC, WhoHol A*
Marchand, Corinne 1928- *HalFC 80*
Marchand, Corinne 1937- *FilmEn*
Marchand, Daniel *NewGrD 80*
Marchand, Guillaume 1694-1738 *NewGrD 80*
Marchand, Heinrich 1769-1812? *NewGrD 80*
Marchand, Henri 1898-1959 *FilmgC, HalFC 80*
Marchand, Jean 1636-1691 *NewGrD 80*
Marchand, Jean-Baptiste 1670-1751 *NewGrD 80*
Marchand, Jean-Noel 1666-1710 *NewGrD 80*
Marchand, Jean-Noel 1689-1757? *NewGrD 80*
Marchand, Leopold 1891-1952 *McGEWD, NotNAT B*
Marchand, Louis 1669-1732 *Baker 78, NewGrD 80, OxMus*
Marchand, Luc 1709-1799 *NewGrD 80*
Marchand, Margarethe *NewGrD 80*
Marchand, Nancy 1928- *BiE&WWA, NotNAT, WhoHol A, WhoThe 72, -77*
Marchand, Olivier 1928- *CreCan 1*
Marchand, Roger L 1938- *IntWWM 77*
Marchand, Theobald Hilarius 1741-1800 *NewGrD 80*
Marchant *NewGrD 80*
Marchant, Frank d1878 *NotNAT B*
Marchant, Hugh 1916- *IntWWM 77, WhoMus 72*
Marchant, Jay *TwYS A*
Marchant, Sir Stanley 1883-1949 *Baker 78, NewGrD 80, OxMus*
Marchant, William 1923- *BiE&WWA*
Marchat, Jean 1902-1966 *WhScrn 74, -77, WhoHol B*
Marchena-Dujarric, Enrique De *DcCM*
Marchese, Andrew L 1922- *AmSCAP 66, -80*
Marchese, Hector D 1901- *AmSCAP 66, -80*
Marchesi *CmOp, NewGrD 80*
Marchesi, Blanche 1863-1940 *Baker 78, CmOp, NewGrD 80*
Marchesi, Giulio *NewGrD 80*
Marchesi, Luigi 1754-1829 *Baker 78*
Marchesi, Luigi 1755-1829 *NewGrD 80*
Marchesi, Mathilde 1821-1913 *BnBkM 80, NewEOp 71, NewGrD 80*
Marchesi, Salvatore 1822-1908 *CmOp, NewEOp 71, NewGrD 80*
Marchesi, Tommaso 1773-1852 *NewGrD 80*
Marchesi DeCastrone, Mathilde 1821-1913 *Baker 78*
Marchesi DeCastrone, Salvatore 1822-1908 *Baker 78*
Marchesini, Luigi 1755-1829 *NewGrD 80*
Marchesini, Maria Antonia *NewGrD 80*
Marchetti, Filippo 1831-1902 *Baker 78, NewGrD 80*
Marchetti, Tomaso *NewGrD 80*
Marchettis, Joannes *NewGrD 80*
Marchetto Da Padova 1274?- *NewGrD 80*
Marchetto Da Padua 1274?- *Baker 78*
Marchettus De Padua 1274?- *NewGrD 80*
Marchfield, Rudy 1907- *AmSCAP 66, -80*
Marchi, Giovanni Maria d1740 *NewGrD 80*
Marchiolli, Sonja 1945- *CnOxB*
Marchisio *NewGrD 80*
Marchisio, Barbara 1833-1919 *NewGrD 80*
Marchisio, Carlo Victor 1904- *WhoMus 72*
Marchisio, Carlotta 1835-1872 *NewGrD 80*
Marchowsky, Marie *DancEn 78*
Marchwinski, Jerzy 1935- *IntWWM 77, -80*
Marchwinski, Wladyslaw 1945- *IntWWM 77, -80*
Marciani, Giovanni 1605?-1663? *NewGrD 80*
Marciano, Rocky 1923-1969 *WhScrn 77*
Marcil, Monique 1934- *IntWWM 77, -80*
Marcin, Max 1879-1948 *NotNAT B, WhThe*
Marciniak, Stanislaw 1939- *IntWWM 77, -80*
Marciniak-Gowarzewska, Stanislawa 1937- *IntWWM 77, -80*
Marckhl, Erich 1902- *WhoMus 72*
Marco Antonio Da Bologna *NewGrD 80*
Marco Dell'Arpa *NewGrD 80*
Marco, Eduardo Lopez-Chavarri Y *NewGrD 80*
Marco, Guy Anthony 1927- *IntWWM 77, -80*
Marco, Sano 1898-1970 *AmSCAP 66, -80*
Marco, Tomas 1942- *Baker 78, DcCM, NewGrD 80*
Marcone, Stephen F 1945- *AmSCAP 80*
Marcopoulos, Mata 1940- *WhoOp 76*
Marcori, Adamo 1763-1808 *NewGrD 80*
Marcos Y Navas, Francisco *NewGrD 80*
Marcour, Mickey d1961 *NewOrJ[port]*
Marcour, Oscar 1895-1956 *NewOrJ[port]*
Marcoux, Jean Emile Diogene *NewGrD 80*
Marcoux, Vanni *Film 2, NewGrD 80*
Marcoux, Vanni 1877-1962 *Baker 78, CmOp, MusSN[port], NewEOp 71*
Marcovicci, Andrea *AmSCAP 80*
Marcovici, Silvia 1952- *IntWWM 80*
Marcucci, Ferdinand 1800-1871 *NewGrD 80*
Marcucci, Robert 1930- *AmSCAP 66, -80*
Marcuori, Adamo *NewGrD 80*
Marcus *NewGrD 80*
Marcus, Ada Belle 1929- *AmSCAP 80*
Marcus, Adabelle Gross 1928- *IntWWM 77, -80*
Marcus, Adabelle Gross 1929- *ConAmC*
Marcus, Ben D 1911- *IntMPA 77, -75, -76, -78, -79, -80*
Marcus, Frank 1928- *BlkAmP, CnThe, ConDr 73, -77, CroCD, EncWT, McGEWD[port], WhoThe 72, -77*
Marcus, Howard 1950?- *CreCan 1*
Marcus, James A 1868-1937 *Film 1, -2, WhScrn 74, -77, WhoHol B*
Marcus, Joyce B 1921- *AmSCAP 66*
Marcus, Leonard Marshall 1930- *ConMuA 80B, IntWWM 77*
Marcus, Louis 1936- *IntMPA 77, -76, -78, -79, -80*
Marcus, Sol 1912-1976 *AmSCAP 66, -80*
Marcus, Stephen 1939- *EncJzS 70*
Marcus, Steve 1939- *EncJzS 70*
Marcus, Wade *ConAmC*
Marcuse, Theodore 1920-1967 *FilmgC, HalFC 80, WhScrn 74, -77, WhoHol B*
Marcussen *NewGrD 80*
Marcussen, Birgit 1934- *IntWWM 77*
Marcussen, Jurgen 1781-1860 *NewGrD 80*
Marczakowi, Marta *WomWMM*
Marczewska-Studzinska, Wiktoria *NewGrD 80*
Marczewski, Lucjan 1879-1935 *NewGrD 80*
Marczyk, Stefan 1924- *IntWWM 80*
Marczynski, Zdzislaw 1916- *IntWWM 80*
Marden, Adrienne *WhoHol A*
Marden, Michael *IntMPA 77, -78, -79, -80*
Mardijanian, Aurora *Film 1*
Mardin, Arif *ConMuA 80B*
Mardin, Jean I *PupTheA*
Mardoyan, Alfred 1930- *IntWWM 77*
Mare, Rolf De 1898-1964 *CnOxB*
Mare Island Navy Band *Film 2*
Marechal, Henri-Charles 1842-1924 *Baker 78, NewGrD 80*
Marechal, Judith Rutherford 1937- *BiE&WWA, NotNAT*
Marechal, Maurice 1892-1964 *Baker 78*
Marek Z Plocka *NewGrD 80*
Marek, Czeslaw Jozef 1891- *Baker 78, IntWWM 77, -80, NewGrD 80*
Marek, Jaroslav 1939- *IntWWM 77, -80*
Marek, Robert *ConAmC*
Marelli, Marco Arturo 1949- *WhoOp 76*
Marena, Emma *Film 2*
Marenco, Carlo 1800-1846 *McGEWD*
Marenco, Romualdo 1841-1907 *Baker 78, NewGrD 80*
Marenic, Vladimir Ivan 1921- *WhoOp 76*
Marenstein, Harold 1916- *IntMPA 77, -75, -76, -78, -79, -80*
Marenzio, Luca 1553-1599 *Baker 78, BnBkM 80, CmpBCM, GrComp[port], MusMk, NewGrD 80[port], OxMus*
Mares, Jan Antonin 1719-1794 *NewGrD 80*
Mares, Joseph P 1908- *NewOrJ SUP[port]*
Mares, Paul 1900-1949 *AmSCAP 66, -80, BiDAmM, CmpEPM, NewOrJ[port], WhoJazz 72*
Mares, Rolf 1930- *WhoOp 76*
Maresca, Benito 1940- *WhoOp 76*
Maresca, Ernest 1938- *AmSCAP 66*
Maresca, Ernie 1939- *RkOn*
Marescalchi, Luigi 1745-1805? *NewGrD 80*
Marescallus, Samuel 1554-1640 *NewGrD 80*

Maresch, J A *OxMus*
Maresch, Jan Antonin *NewGrD 80*
Maresch, Johann Anton 1719-1794 *Baker 78*
Mareschall, Samuel 1554-1640 *Baker 78, NewGrD 80*
Marescotti, Andre-Francois 1902- *Baker 78, DcCM, NewGrD 80*
Marescotti, Giorgio *NewGrD 80*
Maretini, Rosita *Film 2*
Maretskaya, Vera 1906- *FilmEn*
Maretzek, Max 1821-1897 *Baker 78, BiDAmM, NewEOp 71*
Marey, Etienne-Jules 1830-1904 *DcFM, FilmEn, OxFilm, WorEFlm*
Marez Oyens, Tera De 1932- *Baker 78, CpmDNM 76, NewGrD 80*
Marfield, Dwight *WhoHol A*
Margalit, Israela 1944- *WhoMus 72*
Margaraje *PupTheA*
Margaret Of Austria *NewGrD 80*
Margaretta D'Arcy *CnThe*
Margaretten, William J 1930- *AmSCAP 66, -80*
Margarill, Dofie *Film 2*
Margaritis, Harry 1947- *IntWWM 80*
Margaritis, Loris 1895-1953 *Baker 78*
Margaritov, Atanas 1912- *WhoMus 72*
Margaritov, Athanas 1912- *NewGrD 80*
Margaro, Polli *WhoHol A*
Margelis, Charles *Film 2*
Margerum, Michael Brad 1951- *AmSCAP 80*
Margetson, Arthur 1897-1951 *EncMT, FilmgC, HalFC 80, NotNAT B, WhScrn 74, -77, WhThe, WhoHol B*
Marggraf, Wolfgang 1935- *IntWWM 80*
Margheriti, Antonio *WhoHrs 80*
Margie, Baby *Film 2*
Margiotta, Sal 1896?-1970 *NewOrJ*
Margo *MotPP, PupTheA, WhThe*
Margo 1917- *FilmEn, ThFT[port]*
Margo 1918- *FilmgC, ForYSC, HalFC 80, IntMPA 77, -76, -78, -79, -80, MovMk[port], What 5[port], WhoHol A*
Margo 1920- *BiE&WWA, NotNAT*
Margo, George *WhoHol A*
Margola, Franco 1908- *Baker 78, NewGrD 80*
Margolies, Linda *DancEn 78*
Margolin, Janet 1943- *FilmEn, FilmgC, ForYSC, HalFC 80, IntMPA 80, MotPP, WhoHol A*
Margolin, Stuart 1940?- *HalFC 80, WhoHol A*
Margolis, Charles 1874-1926 *WhScrn 74, -77, WhoHol B*
Margolis, Henry 1909- *BiE&WWA, NotNAT*
Margolis, Jerome N 1941- *CpmDNM 74, ConAmC*
Margoni, Alain 1934- *IntWWM 80*
Margoshes, Steven *ConAmC*
Margouleff, Robert J 1940- *AmSCAP 80*
Margraf, Gustav B 1915- *IntMPA 77, -75, -76, -78, -79, -80*
Margueritte, Victor 1866-1942 *NotNAT B, WhThe*
Margulies, David 1937- *NotNAT*
Margulies, Irwin 1907- *IntMPA 77, -75, -76, -78, -79, -80*
Margulies, Stan 1920- *IntMPA 77, -75, -76, -78, -79, -80*
Margulies, Virginia M 1916-1969 *WhScrn 74, -77, WhoHol B*
Margulies Trio *BiDAmM*
Margulis, Charles 1903-1967 *AmSCAP 80, WhScrn 74, -77, WhoJazz 72*
Mari, Elvira *NewGrD 80*
Mari, Febo 1884-1939 *FilmEn*
Mari, Joseph *Film 2*
Maria Antonia Walpurgis 1724-1780 *Baker 78, NewGrD 80*
Maria, Warren De 1945- *CnOxB*
Marian, Ferdiand 1902-1946 *FilmAG WE*
Marian, Ferdinand 1902-1946 *WhScrn 77*
Mariana, Father *OxMus*
Mariana, Juan De 1536-1623 *NewGrD 80*
Mariani, Angelo 1821-1873 *Baker 78, NewGrD 80*
Mariani, Dacia *WomWMM*
Mariani, Enrico *NewGrD 80*
Mariani, Fiorella 1933- *WhoOp 76*
Mariani-Zampieri, Teresina 1871- *WhThe*
Mariano *PupTheA*
Mariano, Charles Hugo 1923- *AmSCAP 66, BiDAmM, EncJzS 70*
Mariano, Charlie 1923- *CmpEPM, EncJzS 70*
Mariano, Luis 1920-1970 *FilmEn, WhScrn 77, WhoHol B*
Mariassy, Felix 1919-1975 *DcFM, FilmEn, OxFilm*
Maric, Ljubica 1909- *Baker 78, DcCM, IntWWM 77, -80, NewGrD 80*
Maricle, Leona 1905- *BiE&WWA, NotNAT, WhoHol A*
Maricle, Marijane *WhoHol A*
Mariconda, Valeria 1939- *WhoOp 76*
Marie Anthony, Sister *PupTheA*
Marie DeLaSagesse, Soeur *CreCan 1*
Marie Jeanne 1920- *CnOxB, DancEn 78*
Marie, Gabriel 1852-1928 *Baker 78*
Marie, Jean-Etienne 1917- *DcCM, NewGrD 80*
Marie DeL'Isle, Celestine *NewGrD 80*
Marielle, Jean-Pierre *WhoHol A*
Mariemma *DancEn 78*
Mariemma 1920- *CnOxB*
Marien, Ambrosio d1584? *NewGrD 80*
Marietan, Pierre 1935- *DcCM, IntWWM 77, -80, NewGrD 80*
Marievsky, Josef *Film 2*
Marigo, Francisco 1916- *IntWWM 77, -80*
Marihugh, Tammy *ForYSC, WhoHol A*
Marillier, Jacques *WhoOp 76*
Marin, Constantin 1925- *NewGrD 80*
Marin, Edwin L 1899-1951 *FilmEn*
Marin, Edwin L 1901-1951 *FilmgC, HalFC 80*
Marin, Jacques 1919- *HalFC 80, WhoHol A*
Marin, Jose 1618?-1699? *NewGrD 80*
Marin, Joseph 1618?-1699? *NewGrD 80*
Marin, Marie-Martin Marcel, Vicomte De 1769-1861? *NewGrD 80*
Marin, Paul *WhoHol A*
Marin, Richard Anthony 1946- *AmSCAP 80*
Marinacci, Gloria 1938- *WhoOp 76*
Marinaccio, Gene 1931- *CnOxB*
Marinan, Terrence Richard 1945- *AmSCAP 80*
Marinelli, Carlo 1926- *IntWWM 77, -80*
Marinelli, Gaetano 1754-1820? *NewGrD 80*
Marinelli, H B 1864-1924 *NotNAT B*
Marinelli, Karl Von 1744-1803 *OxThe*
Marinelli, Karl Von 1745-1803 *EncWT*
Mariner, Francisco *NewGrD 80*
Marinetti, Filippo Tommaso 1876-1944 *CnMD, EncWT, McGEWD[port], ModWD*
Marini, Biagio 1587?-1663 *NewGrD 80*
Marini, Biagio 1596?-1665 *MusMk*
Marini, Biagio 1597-1665 *Baker 78, OxMus*
Marini, Carlo Antonio *NewGrD 80*
Marini, Francesco Maria *NewGrD 80*
Marini, Gioseffo *NewGrD 80*
Marini, Giovanni De *NewGrD 80*
Marini, Giuseppe *NewGrD 80*
Marini, Peer *AmSCAP 80*
Marinis, Giovanni De *NewGrD 80*
Marinkovic, Josif 1851-1931 *NewGrD 80*
Marino, Albert Ralph 1911- *AmSCAP 66, -80*
Marino, Alessandro d1605? *NewGrD 80*
Marino, Carlo Antonio 1670?-1717? *NewGrD 80*
Marino, Frank *ConMuA 80B*
Marino, Gioseffo *NewGrD 80*
Marino, Giuseppe *NewGrD 80*
Marino, Sev F 1915- *AmSCAP 66, -80*
Marinoff, Fania 1890-1971 *BiE&WWA, Film 1, NotNAT B, WhScrn 77, WhThe, WhoHol B*
Marinoff, Faria 1890-1971 *WhScrn 74*
Marinoni *NewGrD 80*
Marinoni, Giovanni Battista d1647 *NewGrD 80*
Marinoni, Giovanni Battista d1652? *NewGrD 80*
Marinoni, Girolamo *NewGrD 80*
Marinov, Ivan 1928- *Baker 78, NewGrD 80*
Marins, Jose Mojica *WhoHrs 80*
Marinski, Sophie 1917- *AmSCAP 66*
Marinuzzi, Gino 1882-1945 *NewEOp 71, NewGrD 80, OxMus*
Marinuzzi, Gino 1920- *Baker 78, NewGrD 80*
Marinuzzi, Giuseppe 1882-1945 *Baker 78*
Mario 1810-1883 *BnBkM 80, NewEOp 71*
Mario, Emilio *WhThe*
Mario, Giovanni Matteo 1810-1883 *Baker 78, CmOp, NewGrD 80[port]*
Mario, Queena 1896-1951 *Baker 78, BiDAmM, NewEOp 71*
Marion, Dave d1934 *NotNAT B*
Marion, Don 1917- *Film 2*
Marion, Edna 1908-1957 *Film 2, TwYS, WhScrn 74, -77, WhoHol B*
Marion, F *Film 1*
Marion, Frances 1887-1973 *FilmEn, Film 2*
Marion, Frances 1888-1973 *DcFM, Film 1, FilmgC, HalFC 80, TwYS A, WhScrn 77, WomWMM*
Marion, Frank *Film 2*
Marion, George, Jr. 1899- *CmpEPM*
Marion, George F 1860-1945 *Film 1, -2, ForYSC, NotNAT B, TwYS, WhScrn 74, -77, WhoHol B*
Marion, George F, Jr. 1899-1968 *AmSCAP 66, -80, BiE&WWA, NotNAT B, WhThe*
Marion, Joan 1908-1945 *WhThe*
Marion, Karl *AmSCAP 80*
Marion, Oscar *Film 2*
Marion, Paul *WhoHol A*
Marion, Sid 1900-1965 *WhScrn 74, -77, WhoHol B*
Marion, William 1878-1957 *Film 2, WhScrn 77*
Marion-Crawford, Howard 1914-1969 *FilmgC, HalFC 80, WhScrn 77, WhoHol B*
Marioneaux, James Elliot 1949- *IntWWM 77*
Mariotini, Cayetano d1817 *BiDAmM*
Mariotte, Antoine 1875-1944 *Baker 78, NewGrD 80*
Mariotti, Frederick *Film 2*
Maris, Livia *Film 2*
Maris, Mona 1903- *FilmEn, Film 2, FilmgC, ForYSC, HalFC 80, MotPP, MovMk, WhoHol A*
Maris, Roger *WhoHol A*
Marischka, Ernst 1893- *DcFM*
Mariscotti, Giorgio *NewGrD 80, -80*
Maritza, Sari 1910- *FilmEn, ForYSC, HalFC 80, IlWWBF, ThFT[port]*
Marius, Jean *NewGrD 80, OxMus*
Marivaux, Pierre Carlet DeChamblain De 1688-1763 *CnThe, EncWT, Ent[port], McGEWD[port], NotNAT B, OxThe, PlP&P, REnWD[port]*
Mariz, Vasco 1921- *Baker 78, NewGrD 80*
Mark, Andrew Peery 1950- *AmSCAP 80*
Mark, Michael 1889-1975 *WhScrn 77, WhoHol C, WhoHrs 80*
Mark, Ottalie *AmSCAP 66*
Mark, Ottalie 1940-1979 *AmSCAP 80*
Mark, Peter 1940- *IntWWM 80*
Mark, Peter 1940-1979 *IntWWM 77*
Mark, Phyllis *WomWMM B*
Mark IV, The *RkOn*
Markaitis, Bruno 1922- *ConAmC*
Markay, Barbara *AmSCAP 80*
Markby, Robert Brenner d1908 *NotNAT B*
Markell, Robert *NewYTET*
Marken, Jane 1895- *FilmgC, HalFC 80, WhoHol A*
Marker, Chris 1921- *BiDFilm, -81, DcFM, FilmEn, FilmgC, HalFC 80, OxFilm, WhoHrs 80, WorEFlm*
Markert, Russell Eldridge 1899- *CnOxB, DancEn 78*
Markes, Larry 1921- *AmSCAP 66, -80*
Marketta, Lisa *WhoMus 72*
Marketts, The *RkOn[port]*
Markevich, Igor 1912- *NewGrD 80[port], OxMus*
Markevitch, Dimitry 1923- *WhoMus 72*
Markevitch, Igor 1912- *Baker 78, BnBkM 80, IntWWM 77, -80, MusSN[port], WhoMus 72*
Markewich, Maurice 1936- *EncJzS 70*
Markewich, Reese Elish 1936- *EncJzS 70, IntWWM 77*
Markey, Enid *BiE&WWA, MotPP, WhoThe 72, -77*
Markey, Enid 1895- *Film 1, TwYS*
Markey, Enid 1896- *ForYSC, WhoHol A*
Markey, Enid 1902?- *NotNAT*
Markey, Gene 1895-1980 *FilmEn*
Markey, George Boone 1925- *WhoMus 72*
Markey, Melinda *ForYSC, WhoHol A*
Markham, David 1913- *WhoThe 72, -77*

Markham, Dewey 1906- *BlksB&W, -C, BlksBF, DrBlPA*
Markham, G *WhoMus 72*
Markham, Monte 1935- *FilmgC, ForYSC, HalFC 80, IntMPA 77, -75, -76, -78, -79, -80, WhoHol A*
Markham, Pauline d1919 *NotNAT B*
Markham, Ricardus *NewGrD 80*
Markham, Richard 1952- *IntWWM 80*
Marki, Josef 1928- *IntWWM 80*
Markiewicz, Leon 1928- *IntWWM 77, -80*
Markish, Peretz 1895-1955 *OxThe*
Markl, Jaroslav 1931- *NewGrD 80*
Markl, Josef 1928- *IntWWM 77*
Markle, Fletcher 1921- *CreCan 1, FilmgC, HalFC 80, IntMPA 77, -75, -76, -78, -79, -80, NewYTET*
Markle, Gil *ConMuA 80B*
Markle, Robert 1936- *CreCan 1*
Marko, Ivan 1947- *CnOxB*
Markoe, Gerald Jay 1941- *AmSCAP 80*
Markoe, Jerry 1941- *IntMPA 79, -80*
Markoff, Hildy 1929- *ConAmTC*
Markopoulos, Gregory J 1928- *OxFilm, WorEFlm[port]*
Markopoulos, Yannis 1939- *IntWWM 77, -80*
Markos, Albert 1914- *NewGrD 80*
Markov, Petr 1945- *IntWWM 77*
Markova, Alicia 1910- *CnOxB, DancEn 78[port], NewGrD 80, WhThe*
Markovic, Vera 1931- *DancEn 78*
Markovic, Zvonimir 1925- *IntWWM 77*
Markovich, Mitchell K 1944- *IntWWM 77*
Markovsky, John Ivanovich 1944- *CnOxB*
Markowitz, Philip L 1952- *AmSCAP 80*
Markowitz, Richard Allen 1926- *AmSCAP 66, -80*
Markowitz, Robert *IntMPA 80*
Markowski, Andrzej 1924- *DcCM, NewGrD 80*
Markowski, Victoria 1935- *WhoMus 72*
Marks, Alan 1949- *Baker 78, IntWWM 77, -80*
Marks, Albert A, Jr. *NewYTET*
Marks, Alfred *IntMPA 75, -76, -78, -79, -80*
Marks, Alfred 1921- *FilmgC, HalFC 80, IntMPA 77, WhoHol A, WhoThe 72, -77*
Marks, Arnold 1912- *ConAmTC, IntMPA 75, -76*
Marks, Arthur 1927- *IntMPA 77, -75, -76, -78, -79, -80*
Marks, Bruce 1937- *CnOxB, DancEn 78*
Marks, Charles B 1890- *AmSCAP 66*
Marks, Charles Barend 1888-1971 *JoeFr*
Marks, Charles Barend 1890- *AmSCAP 80*
Marks, Edward B *NewGrD 80*
Marks, Elias J 1880-1960 *AmSCAP 80*
Marks, Emmaretta *PlP&P[port]*
Marks, Franklyn 1911- *AmSCAP 66, ConAmC*
Marks, Franklyn 1911-1976 *AmSCAP 80*
Marks, George Harrison *IlWWBF A*
Marks, Gerald 1900- *AmSCAP 66, -80, CmpEPM*
Marks, Guy *WhoHol A*
Marks, Herbert E 1902- *BiE&WWA, NotNAT*
Marks, J David 1934- *IntMPA 75, -76*
Marks, James *ConAmC*
Marks, Jeanne Marie 1919- *AmSCAP 80*
Marks, Joe E 1891-1973 *WhScrn 77, WhoHol B*
Marks, John D 1909- *AmSCAP 66, BiDAmM*
Marks, Johnny 1909- *AmSCAP 80, CmpEPM*
Marks, Josephine Preston Peabody d1922 *NotNAT B*
Marks, Kilbourn *PupTheA*
Marks, Lilian Alicia 1910- *NewGrD 80*
Marks, Paul Frederick 1933- *ConMuA 80B, IntWWM 77, -80*
Marks, Sidney d1974 *WhoHol B*
Marks, Tim 1915- *IntMPA 75, -76*
Marks, Virginia Pancoast 1940- *IntWWM 77, -80*
Marks, Walter 1934- *AmSCAP 66, -80*
Marks, Willis *Film 1, -2*
Markson, Ben *IntMPA 77, -75, -76, -78, -79, -80*
Markson, Richard Charles 1949- *IntWWM 80, WhoMus 72*
Markstein, Mrs. *Film 2*
Markull, Friedrich Wilhelm 1816-1887 *Baker 78, NewGrD 80*
Markun, Martin 1942- *WhoOp 76*
Markward, Edward 1944- *IntWWM 77, -80*
Markwort, Johann Christian 1778-1886 *Baker 78*
Marlatt, Earl Bowman 1892- *BiDAmM*
Marlborough, Helen *Film 1*
Marlborough, Leah d1954 *NotNAT B*
Marle, Arnold 1888-1970 *WhScrn 74, -77, WhoHol B*
Marle, Nicolas De *NewGrD 80*
Marleau, Louise *CreCan 1*
Marlette, Bob *PupTheA*
Marley, Bob 1945- *Baker 78, ConMuA 80A, IlEncR[port]*
Marley, Bob & The Wailers *RkOn 2[port]*
Marley, J Peverell 1899-1964 *FilmgC, HalFC 80*
Marley, J Peverell 1901-1964 *CmMov, FilmEn, IntMPA 77, -75, -76, -78, -79, -80, WorEFlm*
Marley, John 1916- *FilmgC, HalFC 80, WhoHol A*
Marley, Robert Nesta 1945- *AmSCAP 80*
Marliani, Count Marco Aurelio 1805-1849 *Baker 78, NewGrD 80*
Marliave, Joseph De 1873-1914 *Baker 78*
Marliere, Andree 1934- *CnOxB*
Marlin, Max *BiE&WWA*
Marlin, Morris Wayne 1915- *BiDAmM*
Marlo, Mary 1898-1960 *WhScrn 74, -77, WhoHol B*
Marlor, Clark S 1922- *NotNAT*
Marlow, Bruce A 1946- *IntMPA 78, -79, -80*
Marlow, Eric 1925- *AmSCAP 80*
Marlow, George d1939 *NotNAT B*
Marlow, Harry d1957 *NotNAT B*
Marlow, Lucy 1932- *ForYSC, IntMPA 77, -75, -76, -78, -79, -80, MotPP*
Marlow, Ric 1925- *AmSCAP 66*
Marlow, Richard Kenneth 1939- *IntWWM 77, -80, WhoMus 72*
Marlow, Tony *Film 2*
Marlowe, Alan 1935-1975 *WhScrn 77*
Marlowe, Alona *Film 2*
Marlowe, Anthony 1910-1962 *WhScrn 74, -77, WhoHol A, -B*
Marlowe, Anthony 1913- *WhoThe 72, -77*
Marlowe, Charles *AmSCAP 80, WhThe*
Marlowe, Christopher 1564-1593 *CnThe, EncWT, Ent[port], McGEWD[port], NewEOp 71, NotNAT A, -B, OxThe, PlP&P[port], REnWD[port]*
Marlowe, Don Porky *WhoHol A*
Marlowe, Frank 1904-1964 *NotNAT B, WhScrn 74, -77, WhoHol B*
Marlowe, Hugh *IntMPA 77, -75, -76, -78, -79, -80*
Marlowe, Hugh 1911- *BiE&WWA, FilmEn, ForYSC, NotNAT, WhoHol A, WhoThe 72, -77*
Marlowe, Hugh 1914- *FilmgC, HalFC 80, MovMk, WhoHrs 80[port]*
Marlowe, James *Film 2*
Marlowe, Jeffry R 1939- *AmSCAP 80*
Marlowe, Jerry 1913- *AmSCAP 66*
Marlowe, Jo Ann *ForYSC*
Marlowe, Joan 1920- *BiE&WWA, NotNAT*
Marlowe, Julia 1865-1950 *NotNAT A, WhoStg 1906, -1908*
Marlowe, Julia 1866-1950 *FamA&A[port], NotNAT B, OxThe, WhThe*
Marlowe, Julia 1866-1953 *PlP&P[port]*
Marlowe, June 1903- *FilmEn, WhoHol A*
Marlowe, June 1907- *Film 2, ForYSC, TwYS*
Marlowe, Linda R 1936- *AmSCAP 80*
Marlowe, Louis J *IntMPA 77, -75, -76, -78, -79, -80*
Marlowe, Marilyn 1927-1975 *WhScrn 77, WhoHol C*
Marlowe, Marion 1929- *What 5[port]*
Marlowe, Marion 1930- *BiE&WWA*
Marlowe, Nora *WhoHol A*
Marlowe, Ronald M 1939- *AmSCAP 80*
Marlowe, Scott *ForYSC, HalFC 80, WhoHol A*
Marlowe, Sylvia 1908- *IntWWM 77, -80, NewGrD 80*
Marly, Florence *IntMPA 75, -76, -78, -79, -80*
Marly, Florence 1915?-1978 *ForYSC*
Marly, Florence 1918- *IntMPA 77*
Marly, Florence 1918-1978 *FilmEn, FilmgC, HalFC 80, WhoHol A, WhoHrs 80[port]*
Marmaduke, Sam *ConMuA 80B*
Marmalade *RkOn 2[port]*
Marmarosa, Dodo 1925- *CmpEPM*
Marmarosa, Dodo 1926- *IlEncJ*
Marmelstein, Linda *WomWMM B*
Marmelzat, Jeffrey Alan 1948- *AmSCAP 80*
Marmer, Lea 1918-1974 *WhScrn 77*
Marmier, Jules 1874-1975 *Baker 78*
Marmion, Shackerley d1639 *NotNAT B*
Marmont, Patricia *WhoHol A*
Marmont, Percy 1883-1977 *FilmEn, Film 1, -2, FilmgC, ForYSC, HalFC 80, IlWWBF, MovMk[port], TwYS, WhThe, WhoHol A*
Marmontel, Antoine Francois 1816-1898 *Baker 78, NewGrD 80*
Marmontel, Antonin Emile Louis 1850-1907 *Baker 78*
Marmontel, Jean Francois 1723-1799 *NewEOp 71, NewGrD 80, OxThe*
Marner, Carole Satrina *WomWMM A, -B*
Marney, Jacques *Film 2*
Marnitz, Fred 1907- *WhoMus 72*
Maro, Publius Vergilius *NewGrD 80*
Marokoff, M *Film 2*
Maronek, James 1931- *WhoOp 76*
Maros, Miklos 1943- *Baker 78, IntWWM 80*
Maros, Rudolf 1917- *Baker 78, CpmDNM 75, DcCM, NewGrD 80*
Maross, Joe *WhoHol A*
Marot, Clement 1496?-1544 *NewGrD 80, OxMus*
Marot, Gaston d1916 *NotNAT B, WhThe*
Marot, Leon Charles *PupTheA*
Marot DeCaserta, Antonellus *NewGrD 80*
Marothi, Gyorgy 1715-1744 *NewGrD 80*
Marothy, Janos 1925- *IntWWM 77, -80, NewGrD 80*
Marotta, Erasmo 1578-1641 *NewGrD 80*
Marotus DeCaserta, Antonellus *NewGrD 80*
Maroufi, Javad 1912- *IntWWM 77, -80*
Marova, Libuse 1943- *WhoOp 76*
Marowitz, Charles 1934- *WhoThe 72, -77*
Marpurg, Friedrich 1825-1884 *Baker 78*
Marpurg, Friedrich Wilhelm 1718-1795 *Baker 78, BnBkM 80, NewGrD 80, OxMus*
Marquand, Christian 1927- *FilmEn, FilmgC, ForYSC, HalFC 80, WhoHol A, WorEFlm[port]*
Marquand, John P 1893-1960 *FilmgC, HalFC 80*
Marquand, Timothy F 1941- *BiDAmM*
Marquand, Tina 1946- *ForYSC, WhoHol A*
Marques, Jose *NewGrD 80*
Marques, Maria Elena *WhoHol A*
Marques, Regina *WomWMM B*
Marques, Rene 1919- *CnThe, CroCD, ModWD, REnWD[port]*
Marques, Zaccaria 1937- *WhoOp 76*
Marques Lesbio, Antonio *NewGrD 80*
Marques Y Garcia, Pedro Miguel 1843-1918 *Baker 78*
Marques Y Garcia, Pedro Miguel 1843-1925 *NewGrD 80*
Marquet, Mary 1895- *WhThe*
Marquette, Hal *PupTheA*
Marquette, Renee *PupTheA*
Marquina, Eduardo 1879-1946 *McGEWD[port]*
Marquis, Don 1878-1937 *NotNAT A, WhThe*
Marquis, Donald Robert Perry 1878-1937 *NotNAT B*
Marquis, Marjorie Vonnegut d1936 *NotNAT B*
Marr, Beatrix Enid 1912- *WhoMus 72*
Marr, Denton *ConMuA 80B*
Marr, Edie *WhoMus 72*
Marr, Edward *WhoHol A*
Marr, Henry *Film 2*
Marr, Paula *WhThe*
Marr, Sally *WhoHol A*
Marr, William 1897-1960 *WhScrn 74, -77, WhoHol B*
Marraco Y Ferrer, Jose 1835-1913 *NewGrD 80*
Marranca, Bonnie 1947- *ConAmTC*
Marre, Albert 1925- *BiE&WWA, EncMT,*

NotNAT, WhoThe 72, -77
Marrero, Billy 1874?- *NewOrJ*
Marrero, Eddie 1902- *NewOrJ*
Marrero, John 1895?-1945? *NewOrJ*
Marrero, Laurence 1900-1959 *WhoJazz 72*
Marrero, Lawrence 1900-1959 *NewOrJ[port]*
Marrero, Simon 1897?- *NewOrJ*
Marri, Ascanio d1575 *NewGrD 80*
Marriner, Guy Vincent Rice 1898- *WhoMus 72*
Marriner, Neville 1924- *Baker 78, BnBkM 80, IntWWM 77, -80, NewGrD 80, WhoMus 72*
Marrion, Paul 1948- *WhoMus 72*
Marriott, Alice d1900 *NotNAT B*
Marriott, Anne 1913- *CreCan 1*
Marriott, Charles 1859-1917 *WhScrn 77*
Marriott, G M d1940 *NotNAT B*
Marriott, John 1893-1977 *DrBlPA, WhoHol A*
Marriott, Moore 1885-1949 *Film 2, FilmgC, HalFC 80, IlWWBF, NotNAT B, WhScrn 74, -77, WhoHol B*
Marriott, Peter 1921- *IntMPA 77, -75, -76, -78, -79, -80*
Marriott, Raymond Bowler 1911- *WhoThe 77*
Marriott, Sandee 1899-1962 *WhScrn 77*
Marriott, Sandee 1902-1962 *WhScrn 74, WhoHol B*
Marriott, Steve 1947- *IlEncR*
Marriott-Watson, Nan 1899- *WhThe*
Marrocco, W Thomas 1909- *NewGrD 80*
Marrocco, William Thomas 1909- *Baker 78, IntWWM 77, -80*
Marroney, Peter R 1913- *BiE&WWA, NotNAT*
Marrs, Stella 1932- *DrBlPA, EncJzS 70*
Marryat, Florence 1837-1899 *NotNAT B*
Marryat, Florence 1838-1899 *PlP&P*
Marryott, Ralph E 1908- *AmSCAP 66, -80, ConAmC A*
Mars, Mademoiselle 1779-1847 *EncWT, Ent[port], NotNAT B, OxThe*
Mars, Anne Francoise Hippolyte 1779-1847 *CnThe*
Mars, Antony 1861-1915 *NotNAT B*
Mars, Jean Odo De *NewGrD 80*
Mars, John 1942- *BluesWW[port]*
Mars, Kenneth 1936- *HalFC 80, WhoHol A*
Mars, Leo *WhoStg 1906, -1908*
Mars, Marjorie 1903- *WhThe*
Mars, Severin d1921 *Film 2, NotNAT B*
Mars, Sylvia 1933?- *BluesWW[port]*
Marsac, Maurice *ForYSC, WhoHol A*
Marsala, Adele Girard 1913- *AmSCAP 80*
Marsala, Joe 1907-1978 *AmSCAP 66, -80, CmpEPM, IlEncJ, WhoJazz 72*
Marsala, Joseph 1907- *BiDAmM*
Marsala, Marty 1909- *CmpEPM, WhoJazz 72*
Marsala, Marty 1909-1975 *EncJzS 70*
Marsand, Anselmo 1769-1841 *NewGrD 80*
Marschalk, Max 1863-1940 *Baker 78*
Marschausen, Theodore 1773-1843 *BiDAmM*
Marschilok, Edward Stephen 1952- *IntWWM 77*
Marschner, Franz 1855-1932 *Baker 78*
Marschner, Heinrich August 1795-1861 *Baker 78, BnBkM 80, CmOp, NewEOp 71, NewGrD 80[port], OxMus*
Marschner, Lydia *NewGrD 80*
Marschner, Wolfgang 1926- *WhoMus 72*
Marsden, Betty 1919- *WhoHol A, WhoThe 72, -77*
Marsden, David *ConMuA 80B*
Marsden, Joan 1933- *IntWWM 80*
Marsden, Mary *WhScrn 74, -77*
Marsden, Newton *OxMus*
Marsee, Susanne 1941- *IntWWM 80*
Marsee, Susanne 1944- *WhoOp 76*
Marseille, Daddy *PupTheA*
Marsh, Alexander d1947 *NotNAT B*
Marsh, Alfonso d1692 *NewGrD 80*
Marsh, Alfonso 1627-1681 *NewGrD 80*
Marsh, Betty *Film 1*
Marsh, Calvin W 1921- *WhoMus 72*
Marsh, Carol 1926- *FilmgC, HalFC 80, WhoHol A*
Marsh, Carol 1929- *IlWWBF[port]*
Marsh, Charles Howard 1885-1956 *AmSCAP 66, -80, ConAmC*
Marsh, Charles L d1953 *WhScrn 74, -77, WhoHol B*
Marsh, Dave *ConMuA 80B*
Marsh, Della d1973 *WhScrn 77*
Marsh, Donald T 1943- *AmSCAP 80*
Marsh, Fred Dana *PupTheA*
Marsh, Garry 1902- *FilmgC, HalFC 80, IlWWBF, WhThe, WhoHol A, WhoThe 72*
Marsh, Gene *Film 1*
Marsh, George W 1900?-1962 *WhoJazz 72*
Marsh, Gwendolen 1908- *IntWWM 77, -80*
Marsh, Hal S *PupTheA*
Marsh, Howard d1969 *EncMT*
Marsh, Jane 1942- *WhoMus 72*
Marsh, Jane 1944- *AmSCAP 80*
Marsh, Jane 1945- *WhoOp 76*
Marsh, Jean *WhoHol A*
Marsh, Joan 1913- *FilmEn, MovMk, ThFT[port], WhoHol A*
Marsh, Joan 1915- *ForYSC*
Marsh, John 1752-1828 *NewGrD 80*
Marsh, Leo A d1936 *NotNAT B*
Marsh, Linda *WhoHol A*
Marsh, Mae 1893-1968 *TwYS*
Marsh, Mae 1895-1968 *BiDFilm, -81, FilmEn, Film 1, -2, FilmgC, ForYSC, HalFC 80, MotPP, MovMk[port], OxFilm, ThFT[port], WhScrn 74, -77, WhoHol B, WorEFlm*
Marsh, Margaret *Film 1*
Marsh, Marguerite 1892-1925 *Film 1, -2, TwYS, WhScrn 74, -77, WhoHol B*
Marsh, Marian 1913- *FilmEn, MovMk, ThFT[port], WhoHol A*
Marsh, Marion 1913- *FilmgC, ForYSC, HalFC 80*
Marsh, Mary *WomWMM*
Marsh, Mildred *Film 2*
Marsh, Milton R W 1945- *ConAmC, IntWWM 77, -80*
Marsh, Myra 1894-1964 *WhScrn 77*
Marsh, Oliver H T 1893-1941 *HalFC 80*
Marsh, Paul *IntMPA 75, -76*
Marsh, Risley Halsey 1927-1965 *WhScrn 74, -77*
Marsh, Robert Charles 1924- *Baker 78*
Marsh, Rudy *AmSCAP 80*
Marsh, Simeon Bulkley 1798-1875 *BiDAmM*
Marsh, Stephan Hale Alonzo 1805-1888 *NewGrD 80*
Marsh, Warne Marion 1927- *BiDAmM, EncJzS 70, IlEncJ*
Marsh-Edwards, Michael Richard 1928- *IntWWM 77, -80, WhoMus 72*
Marshak, Samuel Yakovlevich 1887-1964 *NotNAT B*
Marshak, Samuil Yakovlevich 1887-1964 *ModWD*
Marshal, Alan 1909-1961 *FilmEn, FilmgC, ForYSC, HalFC 80, MotPP, WhScrn 74, -77, WhoHol B*
Marshall, Adelaide 1906- *IntWWM 77, -80*
Marshall, Alan 1909-1961 *NotNAT B*
Marshall, Armina 1900- *BiE&WWA, NotNAT, WhoThe 77*
Marshall, Arthur 1881-1956 *BiDAmM*
Marshall, Boyd 1885-1950 *Film 1, WhScrn 74, -77, WhoHol B*
Marshall, Brenda 1915- *FilmEn, FilmgC, ForYSC, HalFC 80, MotPP, MovMk, WhoHol A*
Marshall, Charles 1887-1951 *BiDAmM*
Marshall, Charles E Red 1899-1975 *WhScrn 77*
Marshall, Charles Red d1974 *WhoHol B*
Marshall, Chet 1932-1974 *WhScrn 77*
Marshall, Clark *Film 2*
Marshall, Connie 1938- *HalFC 80*
Marshall, Cyril Montague 1909- *WhoMus 72*
Marshall, Dodie *WhoHol A*
Marshall, Don *DrBlPA, WhoHol A*
Marshall, E G 1910- *BiE&WWA, FilmEn, FilmgC, ForYSC, HalFC 80, HolCA[port], IntMPA 77, -75, -76, -78, -79, -80, MotPP, MovMk[port], NotNAT, PlP&P[port], WhoHol A, WhoThe 77*
Marshall, Edward d1904 *NotNAT B*
Marshall, Edward Harry 1932- *AmSCAP 80*
Marshall, Elizabeth 1937- *IntWWM 77, -80*
Marshall, Everett 1901- *AmPS B, CmpEPM, ForYSC, WhThe*
Marshall, Frances *MagIlD*
Marshall, Frank d1889 *NotNAT B*
Marshall, Frank d1939 *NotNAT B*
Marshall, Garry *NewYTET*
Marshall, George 1891-1975 *BiDFilm, -81, CmMov, FilmEn, FilmgC, HalFC 80, IntMPA 75, MovMk[port], OxFilm, TwYS A, WhScrn 77, WhoHol C, WorEFlm*
Marshall, Henry I 1883-1958 *AmSCAP 66, -80*
Marshall, Herbert 1890-1966 *BiDFilm, -81, BiE&WWA, FilmEn, Film 2, FilmgC, HalFC 80, IlWWBF, MotPP, MovMk[port], NotNAT B, OxFilm, WhScrn 74, -77, WhThe, WhoHol B, WhoHrs 80, WorEFlm*
Marshall, Herbert 1890-1969 *FilmAG WE*
Marshall, Herbert 1891-1966 *ForYSC*
Marshall, Herbert 1900- *FilmgC, HalFC 80*
Marshall, Herbert 1906- *IntMPA 77, -75, -76, -78, -79, -80*
Marshall, Ingram Douglass 1942- *ConAmC, IntWWM 77, -80*
Marshall, J Richard 1929- *IntWWM 77, -80*
Marshall, Jack *Film 1*
Marshall, Jack Wilton 1921- *BiDAmM*
Marshall, Jack Wilton 1921-1973 *ConAmC, EncJzS 70*
Marshall, James 1941- *ConAmC, IntWWM 77, -80*
Marshall, Jane M 1924- *ConAmC*
Marshall, Jay *MagIlD*
Marshall, John Patton 1877-1941 *Baker 78, BiDAmM, ConAmC*
Marshall, Joyce 1913- *CreCan 2*
Marshall, Kaiser 1902-1948 *BiDAmM, CmpEPM, WhoJazz 72*
Marshall, Larry *IntMPA 77, -75, -76, -78, -79, -80*
Marshall, Lisa *WomWMM B*
Marshall, Lois 1924- *CreCan 2, IntWWM 77, -80*
Marshall, Lois 1925- *NewGrD 80*
Marshall, Madeleine *Film 2*
Marshall, Marilyn Young *CreCan 2*
Marshall, Marion *ForYSC, WhoHol A*
Marshall, Mort 1918- *BiE&WWA, NotNAT, WhoHol A*
Marshall, Nancy *WomWMM B*
Marshall, Nicholas 1942- *IntWWM 77, -80, WhoMus 72*
Marshall, Norman 1901- *CnThe, WhoThe 72, -77*
Marshall, Oswald 1875-1954 *WhScrn 74, -77*
Marshall, Pat *WhoHol A*
Marshall, Paul *AmSCAP 80, ConMuA 80B*
Marshall, Peggy 1916- *AmSCAP 66, -80*
Marshall, Penny 1942- *FilmEn, IntMPA 78, -79, -80, WhoHol A*
Marshall, Percy F d1927 *NotNAT B*
Marshall, Perle *Film 2*
Marshall, Peter *IntMPA 78, -79, -80, WhoHol A*
Marshall, Robert d1910 *NotNAT B*
Marshall, Robert Lewis 1939- *IntWWM 77, -80, NewGrD 80*
Marshall, Sandra *WomWMM B*
Marshall, Sarah 1933- *BiE&WWA, NotNAT, WhoHol A*
Marshall, Terry *Film 2*
Marshall, Trudy 1922- *FilmEn, FilmgC, ForYSC, HalFC 80, IntMPA 77, -75, -76, -78, -79, -80, WhoHol A*
Marshall, Tully 1864-1943 *FilmEn, Film 1, -2, FilmgC, HalFC 80, HolCA[port], MotPP, MovMk, NotNAT B, TwYS, WhScrn 74, -77, WhThe, WhoHol B*
Marshall, Tully 1865-1943 *ForYSC*
Marshall, Virginia *Film 2*
Marshall, Virginia 1947- *IntWWM 77*
Marshall, Wendell 1920- *BiDAmM*
Marshall, William *WhoHol A*
Marshall, William 1748-1833 *NewGrD 80, OxMus*
Marshall, William 1915?- *FilmgC, HalFC 80*
Marshall, William 1917- *FilmEn, IntMPA 77, -75, -76, -78, -79, -80, WhoHol A*
Marshall, William 1924- *BiE&WWA, DrBlPA, FilmEn, NotNAT, WhoHrs 80*
Marshall, Yale *ConAmC*
Marshall, Zena *IntMPA 75, -76, -78, -79, -80*

Marshall, Zena 1926- *FilmgC, HalFC 80, IntMPA 77, WhoHol A*
Marshall, Zena 1927- *IlWWBF*
Marshall-Hall, George W L 1862-1915 *NewGrD 80*
Marshall Tucker Band, The *ConMuA 80A, IlEncR, RkOn 2[port]*
Marshalov, Boris 1902-1967 *WhScrn 74, -77*
Marsicano, Merle *CmpGMD, CnOxB, DancEn 78[port]*
Marsick, Armand 1877-1959 *Baker 78, NewGrD 80, OxMus*
Marsick, Martin-Pierre-Joseph 1848-1924 *Baker 78, NewGrD 80, OxMus*
Marsili, Carlo 1828-1878 *NewGrD 80*
Marsoli, Pietro Maria 1580?-1615? *NewGrD 80*
Marsolo, Pietro Maria 1580?-1615? *NewGrD 80*
Marson, Aileen d1939 *NotNAT B, WhoHol B*
Marson, Aileen 1912-1939 *WhThe*
Marson, Aileen 1913-1939 *WhScrn 74, -77*
Marson, George 1570?-1632 *OxMus*
Marson, George 1573?-1632 *NewGrD 80*
Marson, Laurel Rose 1952- *CpmDNM 76*
Marsop, Paul 1856-1925 *Baker 78*
Marsters, Ann 1918- *AmSCAP 66, -80*
Marsters, Nancy L 1937- *AmSCAP 80*
Marstini, Marie *Film 2*
Marstini, Rosita 1894-1948 *Film 1, -2, WhScrn 74, -77, WhoHol B*
Marston, Ann 1939-1971 *WhScrn 74, -77, WhoHol B*
Marston, George W 1840-1901 *Baker 78, BiDAmM*
Marston, Henry d1883 *NotNAT B*
Marston, Mrs. Henry d1887 *NotNAT B*
Marston, Joel 1922- *ForYSC, WhoHol A*
Marston, John 1575?-1634 *McGEWD, NotNAT B, OxThe, PlP&P[port]*
Marston, John 1576-1634 *CnThe, EncWT, Ent, REnWD*
Marston, John 1890-1962 *NotNAT B, WhScrn 74, -77, WhoHol B*
Marston, John Westland 1819-1890 *NotNAT B, OxThe*
Marston, Rosemary Valmia 1938- *WhoMus 72*
Marszalek, Henry 1922- *AmSCAP 66, -80*
Marta, Jack 1905- *IntMPA 77, -75, -76, -78, -79, -80*
Martan, Manilla *Film 2*
Martan, Nita *Film 2*
Marteau, Henri 1874-1934 *Baker 78, NewGrD 80, OxMus*
Martel, Fernand 1919- *IntWWM 77, -80*
Martel, Flora *BiE&WWA, NotNAT*
Martel, Gene 1916- *IntMPA 77, -75, -76, -78, -79, -80*
Martel, Thomas Oliver 1949- *AmSCAP 80*
Martel, Tom *ConAmC*
Martel, William *WhoHol A*
Martelius, Elias *NewGrD 80*
Martell, Alphonse *Film 2*
Martell, Donna *WhoHol A*
Martell, Gillian 1936- *WhoThe 72, -77*
Martell, Gregg *ForYSC*
Martell, Helen Heron *AmSCAP 66, -80*
Martell, Linda *IlEncCM*
Martell, Paul 1905- *AmSCAP 66, -80*
Martell, Philip *WhoMus 72*
Martell, Ralph 1934- *AmSCAP 80*
Martell, Tony *ConMuA 80B*
Martellato, Ioanne *NewGrD 80*
Martelli, Carlo 1935- *WhoMus 72*
Martelli, Edith 1937- *WhoOp 76*
Martelli, Henri Ernest 1895- *Baker 78, IntWWM 77, -80, NewGrD 80*
Martelli, Lodovico 1503-1531 *McGEWD*
Martelli, Otello 1902- *WorEFlm*
Martelli, Otello 1903- *DcFM, FilmEn, FilmgC, HalFC 80*
Martello, Jacopo 1665-1727 *CnOxB*
Martello, Pier Jacopo 1665-1727 *NewGrD 80*
Marten, Helen *Film 1, MotPP*
Martenot, Ginette 1902- *IntWWM 77, -80, WhoMus 72*
Martenot, Maurice 1898- *Baker 78, NewGrD 80, OxMus*
Martens, Adolphe-Adhemar-Louis-Michel *McGEWD[port]*
Martens, Betsy *WomWMM B*
Martens, Frederick Herman 1874-1932 *AmSCAP 66, -80, Baker 78*
Martens, Gaston 1883-1967 *ModWD*
Martenson, Lasse 1934- *IntWWM 77*
Martenson, Mona *Film 2*
Marteny, Fred 1931- *CnOxB*
Marterie, Ralph 1914- *AmSCAP 66, CmpEPM, RkOn*
Marth, Frank *WhoHol A*
Marth, Helen Jun 1903- *AmSCAP 66, -80, ConAmC*
Martha And The Vandellas *BiDAmM, ConMuA 80A, RkOn[port]*
Marthold, Jules De 1842-1927 *NotNAT B, WhThe*
Marti, Bernabe *WhoOp 76*
Marti, Heinz 1934- *NewGrD 80*
Marti, Samuel 1906-1975 *NewGrD 80*
Martial, Michael *AmSCAP 80*
Martianus Mineus Felix Capella *NewGrD 80*
Martianus Minneus Felix Capella *NewGrD 80*
Martienssen, Carl Adolf 1881-1955 *Baker 78, NewGrD 80*
Martikke, Sigrid 1936- *WhoOp 76*
Martin Codax *NewGrD 80*
Martin Codaz *NewGrD 80*
Martin Le Franc 1410?-1461 *NewGrD 80*
Martin Peu D'Argent *NewGrD 80*
Martin, Professor *PupTheA*
Martin VonCochem 1634-1712 *NewGrD 80*
Martin VonKochem 1634-1712 *NewGrD 80*
Martin, Abraham *NewOrJ*
Martin, Al *IntMPA 77, -75, -76, -78, -79, -80*
Martin, Albert *NewOrJ*
Martin, Andra *ForYSC, WhoHol A*
Martin, Barbara Anne 1943- *AmSCAP 80*
Martin, Billy 1908- *AmSCAP 66, -80*
Martin, Bobbi *RkOn 2A*
Martin, Bobby 1902?- *WhoJazz 72*
Martin, Boyd d1963 *NotNAT B*
Martin, Bruce 1941- *WhoMus 72*
Martin, Buddy *Film 2*
Martin, C F 1796-1873 *NewGrD 80*
Martin, Carl 1906- *BluesWW[port]*
Martin, Carolann Frances 1935- *IntWWM 77, -80*
Martin, Charles E 1930- *AmSCAP 80, IntMPA 77, -75, -76, -78, -79, -80, WhoHol A*
Martin, Charlotte 1923- *IntWWM 77, -80*
Martin, Chink 1886- *NewOrJ, WhoJazz 72*
Martin, Chris-Pin 1893-1953 *FilmEn, HolCA[port]*
Martin, Chris-Pin 1894-1953 *Film 1, FilmgC, HalFC 80, MotPP, Vers A[port], WhScrn 74, -77, WhoHol B*
Martin, Christopher *Film 2*
Martin, Christopher 1942- *NotNAT*
Martin, Chuck *ConMuA 80B*
Martin, Cimbro *WhoMus 72*
Martin, Claude *NewGrD 80*
Martin, Claudia *WhoHol A*
Martin, Colin 1912- *WhoMus 72*
Martin, Constant *OxMus*
Martin, Coochie 1887?-1928? *NewOrJ*
Martin, Cris-Pin 1894-1953 *ForYSC*
Martin, Cye 1914-1972 *WhScrn 77*
Martin, David *MorBAP*
Martin, David 1907-1975 *AmSCAP 66, -80*
Martin, David 1911- *WhoMus 72*
Martin, David Glyn 1936- *IntWWM 77*
Martin, David L 1926- *ConAmC*
Martin, Dean 1917- *AmPS A, -B, BiDAmM, BiDFilm, -81, CmMov, CmpEPM, FilmEn, FilmgC, ForYSC, Funs[port], HalFC 80[port], IntMPA 77, -75, -76, -78, -79, -80, MotPP, MovMk[port], OxFilm, RkOn, WhoHol A, WhoHrs 80, WorEFlm*
Martin, Deana *WhoHol A*
Martin, Desire *NewGrD 80*
Martin, Dewey 1923- *FilmgC, ForYSC, HalFC 80, IntMPA 77, -75, -76, -78, -79, -80, MotPP, WhoHol A*
Martin, Dick *ForYSC*
Martin, Dick 1922- *FilmgC, WhoHol A*
Martin, Dick 1923- *HalFC 80*
Martin, Dick 1928- *JoeFr[port]*
Martin, Dino, Jr. 1951- *ForYSC, WhoHol A*
Martin, Don 1911- *IntMPA 77, -75, -76, -78, -79, -80*
Martin, Duke *Film 2*
Martin, D'Urville 1939- *DrBlPA*
Martin, Easthope 1882-1925 *NewGrD 80*
Martin, Edgardo 1915- *Baker 78, DcCM, IntWWM 77, -80, NewGrD 80*
Martin, Edie 1880-1964 *FilmgC, HalFC 80, NotNAT B, WhScrn 74, -77, WhThe, WhoHol B*
Martin, Edwin Dennis 1920- *IntMPA 77, -75, -76, -78, -79, -80*
Martin, Elliot 1924- *BiE&WWA, NotNAT, WhoThe 77*
Martin, Elsa 1898- *WhoMus 72*
Martin, Enoch, II 1921- *AmSCAP 66, -80*
Martin, Ernest H 1919- *BiE&WWA, EncMT, NotNAT, WhoThe 72, -77*
Martin, Fats 1900?- *NewOrJ*
Martin, Florence *Film 1*
Martin, Francois *NewGrD 80*
Martin, Francois 1727-1757 *NewGrD 80*
Martin, Frank 1890-1974 *Baker 78, BnBkM 80, CmOp, CompSN[port], CnOxB, DcCom&M 79, DcCM, MusMk, NewEOp 71, NewGrD 80[port], OxMus, WhoMus 72*
Martin, Frank D 1932- *WhoMus 72*
Martin, Frank Wells 1880-1941 *WhScrn 74, -77*
Martin, Freddy *AmPS A, -B, BgBands 74[port]*
Martin, Freddy 1906- *BiDAmM, CmpEPM*
Martin, Freddy 1907- *WhoHol A*
Martin, Gary William 1947- *AmSCAP 80*
Martin, Geoffrey G *IntMPA 75*
Martin, George *BluesWW*
Martin, George 1926- *ConMuA 80B, IlEncR, RkOn 2[port]*
Martin, Sir George 1844-1916 *Baker 78, NewGrD 80, OxMus*
Martin, George Andre *PupTheA*
Martin, George William 1825-1881 *NewGrD 80*
Martin, Gertrude Eloise 1910-1945 *BlkWAB[port]*
Martin, Gilbert M 1941- *AmSCAP 80, ConAmC*
Martin, Glenn *Film 1*
Martin, Gorman O 1934- *AmSCAP 66, -80*
Martin, Grady 1929- *BiDAmM*
Martin, Gyorgy 1932- *NewGrD 80*
Martin, Helen *BiE&WWA, DrBlPA, NotNAT*
Martin, Henry 1895?-1932? *NewOrJ*
Martin, Henry H 1912- *IntMPA 77, -75, -76, -78, -79, -80*
Martin, Herbert E 1926- *AmSCAP 66*
Martin, Herbert Woodward 1933- *BlkAmP*
Martin, Hiram *Film 2*
Martin, Hugh 1914- *AmPS, AmSCAP 66, -80, BestMus, BiDAmM, BiE&WWA, CmpEPM, ConAmC, EncMT, HalFC 80, NewCBMT, NotNAT, PopAmC[port], PopAmC SUP*
Martin, Hugh E 1929-1976 *AmSCAP 80*
Martin, J *NewGrD 80*
Martin, Jacques *OxMus*
Martin, Mrs. Jacques 1863-1936 *NotNAT B*
Martin, James Gautier 1931- *IntWWM 77*
Martin, James Henry 1927- *BiDAmM*
Martin, Janis 1939- *WhoOp 76*
Martin, Jared *WhoHol A*
Martin, Jean-Blaise 1768-1837 *Baker 78, NewGrD 80*
Martin, Jean Leonard 1931- *AmSCAP 80*
Martin, Jimmy 1927- *IlEncCM[port]*
Martin, Joe 1900-1975 *BluesWW[port], CmpEPM, Film 2*
Martin, Johannes *NewGrD 80*
Martin, John 1882- *MagIlD*
Martin, John 1893- *CnOxB, DancEn 78[port]*
Martin, John E 1770-1807 *NotNAT B*
Martin, John E 1865-1933 *WhScrn 74, -77*
Martin, John Horwood 1927- *IntWWM 80, WhoMus 72*
Martin, Jonathan 1705?-1737 *NewGrD 80*
Martin, Judy 1914- *AmSCAP 66*
Martin, Karl Heinz 1888-1948 *EncWT*
Martin, Keith 1943- *CnOxB*
Martin, Kiel *WhoHol A*
Martin, Larry 1933- *AmSCAP 66, -80*
Martin, Leila 1936- *BiE&WWA, NotNAT*

Martin, Lennie 1916-1963 AmSCAP 66
Martin, Lewis H d1969 WhScrn 74, -77, WhoHol B
Martin, Lock d1959? WhScrn 77
Martin, Lock d1969 WhoHrs 80
Martin, Mabel Justina 1909- WhoMus 72
Martin, Marcella WhoHol A
Martin, Marian 1916- IntMPA 77, -75, -76, -78, -79, -80
Martin, Marion 1916- FilmgC, ForYSC, HalFC 80, MovMk, WhoHol A
Martin, Marvin Film 1
Martin, Mary AmPS B
Martin, Mary 1913- BiDAmM, BiE&WWA, CmpEPM, CnThe, EncMT, EncWT, FamA&A[port], FilmEn, Film 1, FilmgC, ForYSC, HalFC 80, MotPP, MovMk, NewYTET, NotNAT, OxFilm, PlP&P[port], WhoHol A, WhoThe 72, -77
Martin, Mary 1914- IntMPA 77, -75, -76, -78, -79, -80, WhoMus 72
Martin, Mildred Palmer d1962 NotNAT B
Martin, Millicent 1934- EncMT, FilmEn, FilmgC, ForYSC, HalFC 80, IlWWBF, IntMPA 77, -75, -76, -78, -79, -80, WhoHol A, WhoThe 72, -77
Martin, Milton 1896-1977 NewOrJ
Martin, Nan BiE&WWA, NotNAT, PlP&P, WhoHol A
Martin, Nicolas 1498-1566 NewGrD 80
Martin, Olin E 1904- AmSCAP 80
Martin, Owen 1889-1960 NotNAT B, WhScrn 74, -77, WhoHol B
Martin, P J OxMus
Martin, Pamela WhoHol A
Martin, Paul A 1939- ConAmC
Martin, Pepper WhoHol A
Martin, Pete 1899-1973 WhScrn 77
Martin, Pete 1901- BiE&WWA
Martin, Peter AmSCAP 80
Martin, Peter 1921- IntWWM 77
Martin, Peter 1939- IntWWM 77, -80
Martin, Philip ConDr 77B
Martin, Quinn NewYTET
Martin, R E 1917- IntMPA 77, -75, -76, -78, -79, -80
Martin, Ralph Eugene 1934- AmSCAP 80
Martin, Ricardo 1881-1952 BiDAmM
Martin, Riccardo 1874-1952 Baker 78, NewEOp 71
Martin, Richard 1938- IntMPA 77, -76, -78, -79, -80, JoeFr
Martin, Rick AmSCAP 80
Martin, Robert Edward 1952- ConAmC
Martin, Robert Wesley NatPD[port]
Martin, Ross 1920- FilmEn, FilmgC, ForYSC, HalFC 80, IntMPA 77, -75, -76, -78, -79, -80, MotPP, WhoHol A, WhoHrs 80
Martin, Roy E, Jr. 1917- IntMPA 77, -75, -76, -78, -79, -80
Martin, Ruth Kelley 1914- AmSCAP 66, -80
Martin, Sam 1908- AmSCAP 66, -80
Martin, Sara 1884-1955 BluesWW[port]
Martin, Sara 1904?- CmpEPM
Martin, Sharon Stockard 1948- BlkAmP, NatPD[port]
Martin, Skip 1916- CmpEPM
Martin, Sobey 1909- IntMPA 77, -75, -76, -78, -79
Martin, Steve 1945- ConMuA 80A[port], JoeFr[port]
Martin, Strother 1919-1980 FilmEn
Martin, Strother 1920-1980 CmMov, FilmgC, ForYSC, HalFC 80, IntMPA 77, -75, -76, -78, -79, -80, WhoHol A, WhoHrs 80
Martin, Susan WomWMM, -B
Martin, T AmSCAP 80
Martin, Thomas M 1940- IntWWM 80
Martin, Thomas Mower 1838-1934 CreCan 2
Martin, Thomas Philipp 1909- AmSCAP 66, -80
Martin, Todd WhoHol A
Martin, Tom d1962 NotNAT B
Martin, Tony AmPS A, -B, MotPP, WhoHol A
Martin, Tony d1932 WhScrn 74, -77
Martin, Tony 1912- CmpEPM, FilmEn, FilmgC, HalFC 80
Martin, Tony 1913- ForYSC, IntMPA 77, -75, -76, -78, -79, -80, RkOn
Martin, Tony 1914- AmSCAP 66, BiDAmM
Martin, Townsend d1951 Film 2, NotNAT B
Martin, Troy L 1911- EncFCWM 69
Martin, Vernon 1929- AmSCAP 66, -80, CpmDNM 76, ConAmC
Martin, Vince And The Tarriers RkOn
Martin, Virginia BiE&WWA, NotNAT
Martin, Virginia d1971 WhoHol B
Martin, Virilene Kay 1937- IntWWM 77
Martin, Vivian 1893- Film 1, -2, MotPP, TwYS, WhThe
Martin, Vivian 1942- IntWWM 77, -80
Martin, Vivienne 1936- WhoHol A, WhoThe 72, -77
Martin, Walter Callahan, Jr. 1930- IntWWM 77, -80
Martin And Lewis Funs[port], MotPP, NewYTET
Martin Brothers PupTheA
Martin DuGard, Roger 1881-1958 McGEWD
Martin-Duncan, F DcFM
Martin-Harvey, Sir John 1863-1944 CnThe
Martin Harvey, Sir John 1863-1944 HalFC 80
Martin-Harvey, Sir John 1863-1944 NotNAT A, -B, OxThe, WhThe
Martin-Harvey, Muriel 1891- WhThe
Martin-Viscount, Bill 1940- CnOxB, CreCan 2
Martin-Viscount, William CreCan 2
Martin Y Coll, Antonio d1734? NewGrD 80
Martin Y Soler, Vicente 1754-1806 Baker 78, MusMk, NewEOp 71, NewGrD 80
Martin Y Soler, Vincent 1754-1806 OxMus
Martincek, Dusan 1936- Baker 78
Martindale, Wink 1934- RkOn
Martindel, Edward 1876-1955 Film 1, -2, ForYSC, MotPP, NotNAT B, TwYS, WhScrn 74, -77, WhoHol B
Martine, Stella d1961 NotNAT B
Martinek, H Oceano IlWWBF
Martinek, Ivy IlWWBF[port]
Martinelli, Alfredo Film 2
Martinelli, Angelica Alberigi OxThe
Martinelli, Caterina 1589?-1608 NewGrD 80
Martinelli, Drusiano d1606? OxThe
Martinelli, Drusiano d1608? EncWT
Martinelli, Elsa MotPP
Martinelli, Elsa 1932- FilmEn, MovMk
Martinelli, Elsa 1933- FilmgC, ForYSC, HalFC 80, WhoHol A
Martinelli, Elsa 1935- FilmAG WE, WorEFlm
Martinelli, Giovanni 1885-1969 Baker 78, BiDAmM, CmOp, Film 2, MusSN[port], NewEOp 71, NewGrD 80[port], What 2[port]
Martinelli, Tristano 1556?-1630 EncWT
Martinelli, Tristano 1557?-1630 OxThe
Martinenghi, Antonio Francesco NewGrD 80
Martinengo, Gabriele d1584 NewGrD 80
Martinengo, Giulio Cesare 1561?-1613 NewGrD 80
Martinet, Jean-Louis 1912- Baker 78, DcCM, NewGrD 80
Martinetti, Paul 1851- WhThe
Martinez, Anna Katharina Von NewGrD 80
Martinez, Arthur ConMuA 80B
Martinez, Conchita 1912-1960 WhScrn 74, -77
Martinez, Eduardo L 1900-1968 WhScrn 74, -77
Martinez, Enrique 1926- CnOxB, DancEn 78
Martinez, Joaquin WhoHol A
Martinez, Juan NewGrD 80
Martinez, Lorenzo P 1944- AmSCAP 80
Martinez, Luis 1930- EncJzS 70
Martinez, Marianne Di 1744-1812 Baker 78, NewGrD 80
Martinez, Menia 1938- CnOxB
Martinez, Odaline DeLa 1949- IntWWM 80
Martinez, Sabu 1930- EncJzS 70
Martinez, Samuel NewGrD 80
Martinez, Vicente NewGrD 80
Martinez DeBizcargui, Gonzalo d1538? NewGrD 80
Martinez DeLaRoca, Joaquin 1676?-1756? NewGrD 80
Martinez DeLaRosa, Francisco 1787-1862 McGEWD[port], NotNAT B, OxThe
Martinez DeOxinaga, Joaquin NewGrD 80
Martinez Sierra, Gregorio 1881-1947 CnMD, CnThe, Ent, McGEWD, ModWD, NotNAT B, OxThe
Martinez Verdugo, Sebastian 1575?-1654 NewGrD 80
Martini Il Tedesco 1741-1816 MusMk
Martini, Padre 1706-1784 BnBkM 80
Martini, Allen V 1919- IntMPA 75, -76, -78, -79, -80
Martini, Bennie 1910- AmSCAP 66, -80
Martini, Catherine AmSCAP 80
Martini, Fausto Maria 1886-1931 ModWD
Martini, Francesco 1560?-1626? NewGrD 80
Martini, Giambattista 1706-1784 MusMk, OxMus
Martini, Giovanni Battista 1706-1784 Baker 78, BnBkM 80, NewGrD 80[port]
Martini, Giovanni Marco 1650?-1730 NewGrD 80
Martini, Giuseppe NewGrD 80
Martini, Ignaz NewGrD 80
Martini, Jean Paul Egide 1741-1816 Baker 78, NewGrD 80
Martini, Johann Paul Aegidius 1741-1816 NewGrD 80
Martini, Johannes 1440?-1498? NewGrD 80
Martini, Martini Il Tedesco 1741-1816 OxMus
Martini, Nino d1976 AmPS B
Martini, Nino 1902-1976 Baker 78
Martini, Nino 1904-1976 FilmEn, FilmgC, ForYSC, HalFC 80
Martini, Padre 1706-1784 GrComp[port]
Martini, Vincenzo NewGrD 80
Martinikova, Marcela 1940- CnOxB
Martinn, Jacob-Joseph-Balthasar 1775-1836 NewGrD 80
Martino, Al 1927- AmPS A, -B, RkOn
Martino, Donald 1931- Baker 78, BiDAmM, CpmDNM 79, -80, ConAmC, DcCM, IntWWM 77, -80, NewGrD 80
Martino, Giovanni Battista NewGrD 80
Martino, Giuseppe NewGrD 80
Martino, Pat 1944- EncJzS 70
Martino, Ralph John 1945- AmSCAP 80
Martino, Russ Norman 1932- AmSCAP 80
Martino, Thomas James 1948- IntWWM 77, -80
Martinoiu, Vasile Constantin 1934- WhoOp 76
Martinon, Jean 1910-1976 Baker 78, BnBkM 80, CompSN[port], DcCM, MusSN[port], NewGrD 80, OxMus, WhoMus 72
Martinot, Sadie 1861-1923 NotNAT B, WhThe
Martinot, Sadie 1862-1923 WhoStg 1906, -1908
Martinotti, Sergio 1931- NewGrD 80
Martinov, Ivan Ivanovich 1908- NewGrD 80
Martinov, Nikolay Avksentevich 1938- NewGrD 80
Martins, Francisco 1620?-1680 NewGrD 80
Martins, Jay 1935- AmSCAP 66, -80
Martins, Maria DeLourdes 1926- NewGrD 80
Martins, Orlando IntMPA 75, -76, -78, -79, -80
Martins, Orlando 1899- FilmgC, HalFC 80, IntMPA 77, WhoHol A
Martins, Orlando 1900- DrBlPA
Martins, Peter 1946- CnOxB
Martins, Roberto 1943- IntWWM 77, -80
Martinson, Joseph B 1911- BiE&WWA
Martinson, Leslie H FilmEn, FilmgC, HalFC 80
Martinu, Bohuslav 1890-1959 Baker 78, BiDAmM, BnBkM 80, CmOp, CompSN[port], CnOxB, ConAmC, DcCom 77, DcCom&M 79, DcCM, DcTwCC, MusMk, NewEOp 71, NewGrD 80[port], OxMus
Martinucci, Nicola 1941- WhoOp 76
Martirano, Salvatore 1927- Baker 78, BiDAmM, ConAmC, DcCM, NewGrD 80
Martlew, Gillian 1934- DancEn 78
Martlew, Gillian 1935?- CnOxB
Martlew, Mary 1919- WhThe
Martoglio, Nino 1870-1920 DcFM
Martoglio, Nino 1870-1921 FilmEn, WorEFlm
Marton, Andrew 1904- CmMov, FilmEn, FilmgC, HalFC 80, IntMPA 77, -75, -76, -78, -79, -80, MovMk[port], WhoHrs 80, WorEFlm
Marton, Eva 1943- WhoOp 76
Marton, Pierre FilmEn

Martone, Don 1902- *AmSCAP 66, -80*
Martone, Prudence 1933- *AmSCAP 66*
Martoretta, Giandominico *NewGrD 80*
Marttinen, Tauno 1912- *Baker 78, DcCM, NewGrD 80*
Martucci, Giuseppe 1845-1909 *Baker 78*
Martucci, Giuseppe 1856-1909 *NewGrD 80, OxMus*
Martucci, Paolo 1883- *Baker 78*
Martufi, Pearl Gertrude 1897-1977 *AmSCAP 80*
Marty, Eugene Georges 1860-1908 *OxMus*
Marty, Georges-Eugene 1860-1908 *Baker 78*
Martyn *NewGrD 80*
Martyn, Barry 1941- *EncJzS 70*
Martyn, Bendall 1710?-1761? *NewGrD 80*
Martyn, Edward 1472?-1545 *NewGrD 80*
Martyn, Edward 1859-1923 *CnMD, CnThe, McGEWD, ModWD, REnWD[port]*
Martyn, Edward 1859-1924 *NotNAT A, OxThe*
Martyn, Eliza d1846 *NotNAT B*
Martyn, John 1948- *ConMuA 80A, IlEncR*
Martyn, Kid 1941- *EncJzS 70*
Martyn, Laurel 1916- *CnOxB, DancEn 78*
Martyn, Marty d1964 *WhScrn 77*
Martyn, May d1948 *NotNAT B*
Martyn, Peter 1928-1955 *WhScrn 74, -77, WhoHol B*
Martz, Jasun Allan 1953- *AmSCAP 80*
Martzy, Johanna 1924- *NewGrD 80*
Martzy, Johanna 1925- *WhoMus 72*
Marum, Marilyn Harvey 1929-1973 *WhScrn 77, WhoHol B*
Marus, Gina *Film 2*
Maruson *Film 2*
Marvelettes, The *BiDAmM, RkOn[port]*
Marvelows, The *RkOn 2[port]*
Marvenga, Ilse *WhThe*
Marvin And Johnny *RkOn*
Marvin, Frankie 1905- *IlEncCM[port]*
Marvin, Frederick 1923- *Baker 78, IntWWM 77, -80*
Marvin, Grace *Film 2*
Marvin, Jack d1956 *WhScrn 77*
Marvin, Johnny 1897-1944 *AmSCAP 66, -80, CmpEPM*
Marvin, Johnny 1898-1945 *IlEncCM*
Marvin, Ken 1924- *BiDAmM, EncFCWM 69*
Marvin, Lee 1924- *BiDFilm, -81, CmMov, FilmEn, FilmgC, ForYSC, HalFC 80, IntMPA 77, -75, -76, -78, -79, -80, MotPP, MovMk[port], OxFilm, WhoHol A, WorEFlm[port]*
Marvin, Mel Williams 1941- *AmSCAP 80*
Marvin, Tony 1912- *IntMPA 77, -75, -76, -78, -79, -80*
Marvin X *MorBAP*
Marx, Adolf Bernhard 1795-1866 *Baker 78, NewGrD 80*
Marx, Adolph Bernard 1795-1866 *OxMus*
Marx, Albert A 1892-1960 *WhScrn 74, -77*
Marx, Burle 1902- *Baker 78*
Marx, Chico 1886-1961 *FilmEn, HalFC 80*
Marx, Chico 1887-1961 *BiDFilm 81, Funs[port]*
Marx, Chico 1891-1961 *DcFM, EncMT, FamA&A[port], Film 2, ForYSC, JoeFr[port], MGM[port], MotPP, MovMk[port], NotNAT B, OxFilm, WhScrn 74, -77, WhoHol B*
Marx, Groucho d1977 *AmPS B*
Marx, Groucho 1880-1977 *FilmEn*
Marx, Groucho 1890-1977 *BiDFilm 81, Ent, ForYSC, Funs[port], HalFC 80*
Marx, Groucho 1895-1977 *BiE&WWA, DcFM, EncMT, FamA&A[port], Film 2, IntMPA 77, -75, -76, JoeFr[port], MGM[port], MotPP, MovMk[port], NewYTET, OxFilm, WhoHol A*
Marx, Gummo 1893-1977 *FilmEn, HalFC 80*
Marx, Gummo 1894-1977 *BiE&WWA, ForYSC*
Marx, Gummo 1897-1977 *Funs[port], JoeFr[port]*
Marx, Hans Joachim 1935- *NewGrD 80*
Marx, Harpo 1888-1964 *BiDFilm 81, FilmEn, Funs[port], HalFC 80*
Marx, Harpo 1893-1964 *AmSCAP 66, -80, BiE&WWA, DcFM, EncMT, FamA&A[port], Film 2, ForYSC, JoeFr[port], MGM[port], MotPP, NotNAT B, OxFilm, WhScrn 74, -77, WhoHol B*
Marx, Harpo 1894-1964 *MovMk[port]*
Marx, Joseph 1882-1964 *Baker 78, BnBkM 80, NewGrD 80, OxMus*
Marx, Karl 1897- *Baker 78, DcCM, IntWWM 77, -80, NewGrD 80*
Marx, Marvin 1925-1975 *NewYTET, WhScrn 77*
Marx, Max d1925 *WhScrn 74, -77, WhoHol B*
Marx, Michelle *WomWMM B*
Marx, Patricia *WomWMM B*
Marx, Peter Helmut 1936- *WhoOp 76*
Marx, Samuel *IntMPA 77, -75, -76, -78, -79, -80*
Marx, Walter Burle *NewGrD 80*
Marx, William Woollcott 1937- *BiDAmM*
Marx, Zeppo 1900-1979 *BiDFilm 81, OxFilm*
Marx, Zeppo 1901-1979 *BiE&WWA, EncMT, FamA&A[port], FilmEn, Film 2, ForYSC, Funs[port], HalFC 80, JoeFr[port], MGM[port], MovMk[port], What 4[port], WhoHol A*
Marx Brothers, The *BiDFilm, CmMov, CmpEPM, DcFM, EncMT, FamA&A[port], FilmEn, FilmgC, ForYSC, Funs[port], GrMovC[port], HalFC 80, IntMPA 75, JoeFr[port], MGM[port], MotPP, MovMk[port], NotNAT A, OxFilm, WorEFlm*
Marxsen, Eduard 1806-1887 *Baker 78, NewGrD 80*
Mary Angelita, Sister 1912- *BiE&WWA, NotNAT*
Mary Claude, Sister *PupTheA*
Mary Immaculate, Sister *BiE&WWA*
Mary I, Of England 1516-1558 *OxMus*
Mary, Queen Of Scots 1542-1587 *OxMus*
Mary, Jules 1851-1922 *NotNAT B, WhThe*
Maryan, Charles 1934- *NotNAT*
Marynowski, Jan 1924- *IntWWM 77, -80*
Maryon, Edward 1867-1954 *Baker 78, OxMus*
Marzendorfer, Ernst 1921- *WhoOp 76*
Marzo, Eduardo 1852-1929 *Baker 78, BiDAmM*
Marzolff, Serge 1940- *WhoOp 76*
Marzot, Vera 1931- *WhoOp 76*
Masalin, Armas *NewGrD 80*
Masanetz, Guido Bruno 1914- *IntWWM 80, NewGrD 80*
Masarie, Jack F 1942- *IntWWM 77, -80*
Mascagni, Pietro 1863-1945 *Baker 78, BnBkM 80, CmOp, CmpBCM, CompSN[port], DcCom 77[port], DcCom&M 79, MusMk[port], NewEOp 71, NewGrD 80, OxMus*
Mascardi *NewGrD 80*
Mascardi, Giacomo *NewGrD 80*
Mascardi, Giovanni *NewGrD 80*
Mascardi, Vitale *NewGrD 80*
Mascari, Joseph Rocco 1922- *AmSCAP 66, -80*
Maschdrakova, Rumiana 1941- *WhoOp 76*
Maschek *NewGrD 80, -80*
Maschek, Adrian Mathew 1918- *AmSCAP 66, -80*
Maschera, Fiorenzo *Baker 78*
Maschera, Florentio 1540?-1584? *NewGrD 80*
Maschera, Florenzo 1540?-1584? *NewGrD 80*
Mascheroni, Angelo *NewGrD 80*
Mascheroni, Edoardo 1852-1941 *Baker 78, CmOp*
Mascheroni, Edoardo 1859-1941 *NewGrD 80*
Mascheroni, Vittorio 1895- *WhoMus 72*
Maschwitz, Eric 1901- *WhoMus 72*
Maschwitz, Eric 1901-1969 *EncMT, IlWWBF A, WhThe*
Mascia, Madeline T 1928- *AmSCAP 66*
Mascia, Madeline Therese 1928- *AmSCAP 80*
Mascitti, Michel 1663?-1760 *NewGrD 80*
Mascitti, Michele 1663?-1760 *NewGrD 80*
Mascitti, Miquel 1663?-1760 *NewGrD 80*
Mascolino, Dolores Abigail 1916- *AmSCAP 80*
Mase, Marino *WhoHol A*
Masefield, John 1878-1967 *CnMD, McGEWD[port], ModWD, NotNAT B, OxThe, PlP&P, WhThe*
Masefield, Joseph R 1933- *IntMPA 77, -75, -76, -78, -79, -80*
Masek *NewGrD 80*
Masek, Albin 1804-1878 *NewGrD 80*
Masek, Kaspar 1794-1873 *NewGrD 80*
Masek, Pavel Lambert 1761-1826 *NewGrD 80*
Masek, Vincenc 1755-1831 *NewGrD 80*
Masek, Vincenz 1755-1831 *Baker 78*
Masekela, Hugh 1939- *DrBlPA, RkOn 2[port]*
Maselli, Francesco 1930- *DcFM, FilmEn, WorEFlm*
Masen, Mark *NewGrD 80*
Masenelli, Paolo *NewGrD 80*
Maser, Elery 1904-1972 *NewOrJ[port]*
Masetti, Enzo 1893-1961 *Baker 78*
Mashoko, Simon 1918- *IntWWM 77, -80*
Masi, Francesco 1786?-1853 *BiDAmM*
Masii, Laurentius *NewGrD 80*
Masin, Ronald 1937- *IntWWM 77, -80*
Masina, Giulietta *MotPP, WhoHol A*
Masina, Giulietta 1920- *FilmAG WE[port], FilmEn, OxFilm, WorEFlm*
Masina, Giulietta 1921- *FilmgC, HalFC 80, MovMk*
Masini, Angelo 1844-1926 *CmOp, NewGrD 80*
Masini, Antonio 1639-1678 *NewGrD 80*
Masini, Gianfranco 1937- *WhoOp 76*
Masini, Laurentius *NewGrD 80*
Masinter, Louis 1908- *NewOrJ*
Masked Marvel, The *BluesWW*
Maskel, Magdalene *IntMPA 77, -75, -76, -78, -79*
Maskell, Fanny d1919 *NotNAT B*
Maskell, Virginia 1936-1968 *FilmgC, HalFC 80, IlWWBF, MotPP, WhScrn 74, -77, WhoHol B*
Maskelyne, Jasper 1902-1973 *MagIlD*
Maskelyne, John Nevil 1839-1917 *Ent, MagIlD[port], WhThe*
Maskelyne, Nevil 1863-1924 *MagIlD*
Maskelyne and Cooke *MagIlD*
Maskelyne and Devant *MagIlD*
Maskelyne Family *OxMus*
Maslanka, David Henry 1943- *ConAmC*
Maslansky, Paul *IntMPA 80*
Maslennikov, Alexei *WhoOp 76*
Maslin, Harry *ConMuA 80B*
Maslow, Sophie *CmpGMD, CnOxB, DancEn 78[port]*
Maslow, Walter *WhoHol A*
Maslowski, Leon *NewGrD 80*
Masnelli, Paolo *NewGrD 80*
Masokha, Pyotr *Film 2*
Mason *NewGrD 80*
Mason, A E W 1865-1948 *HalFC 80*
Mason, Alfred Edward Woodley 1865-1948 *McGEWD, NotNAT B, WhThe*
Mason, Ann 1889-1948 *Film 1, NotNAT B, WhScrn 77*
Mason, Anne C 1936- *IntWWM 77, -80*
Mason, Archibald J 1889- *IntMPA 77, -75, -76, -78*
Mason, Barbara 1947- *RkOn 2[port]*
Mason, Beryl 1921- *WhoHol A, WhoThe 72, -77*
Mason, Billy 1888-1941 *Film 1, WhoHol B*
Mason, Brewster 1922- *WhoHol A, WhoThe 72, -77*
Mason, Bruce 1921- *ConDr 73, -77*
Mason, Buddy 1903-1975 *Film 2, WhScrn 77, WhoHol C*
Mason, Charles *Film 1, MorBAP*
Mason, Clifford 1932- *BlkAmP, DrBlPA, MorBAP*
Mason, Colin 1924-1971 *Baker 78, NewGrD 80*
Mason, Dan 1853-1929 *Film 1, -2, WhScrn 74, -77, WhoHol B*
Mason, Daniel Gregory 1820-1869 *BiDAmM, NewGrD 80*
Mason, Daniel Gregory 1873-1953 *AmSCAP 66, -80, Baker 78, BiDAmM, BnBkM 80, ConAmC, NewGrD 80, OxMus*
Mason, Dave 1946- *ConMuA 80A, IlEncR, RkOn 2[port]*
Mason, David 1926- *WhoMus 72*
Mason, David Frederick 1926- *IntWWM 77, -80*
Mason, Don P 1927- *AmSCAP 66*
Mason, Edith Barnes 1893-1973 *BiDAmM, CmOp, NewGrD 80*

Mason, Edna *Film 1*
Mason, Edward C 1929-1965 *CnOxB*
Mason, Edward Douglas Gaylor 1903- *WhoMus 72*
Mason, Elliot C d1949 *NotNAT B, WhThe*
Mason, Elliott 1897-1949 *FilmgC, HalFC 80, WhScrn 74, -77, WhoHol B*
Mason, Eric Morris 1925- *IntWWM 77, -80, WhoMus 72*
Mason, Evelyn M 1892-1926 *WhScrn 74, -77, WhoHol B*
Mason, F Stuart 1883-1929 *ConAmC*
Mason, Frances Gillian 1939- *IntWWM 77, -80, WhoMus 72*
Mason, Frank *PupTheA*
Mason, Frank Stuart 1883-1929 *BiDAmM*
Mason, George *NewGrD 80*
Mason, Gladys 1886- *WhThe*
Mason, Gregory 1889-1968 *WhScrn 77*
Mason, Gwendolen Alice Eilian *WhoMus 72*
Mason, Haddon 1898- *Film 2, IlWWBF*
Mason, Hal 1911- *IntMPA 75, -76*
Mason, Harold E 1932- *AmSCAP 80*
Mason, Harry Silvernale 1881- *BiDAmM*
Mason, Harvey, Jr. 1947- *EncJzS 70*
Mason, Harvey W 1947- *AmSCAP 80*
Mason, Henry *Baker 78*
Mason, Henry 1831-1890 *BiDAmM, NewGrD 80*
Mason, Herbert 1891-1960 *FilmgC, HalFC 80, IlWWBF, WhThe*
Mason, Homer B d1959 *NotNAT B*
Mason, Jack 1906-1965 *AmSCAP 66, -80*
Mason, Jackie 1930- *JoeFr*
Mason, James 1890-1959 *Film 1, -2, ForYSC, TwYS, WhScrn 74, -77, WhoHol B*
Mason, James 1909- *BiDFilm, -81, CmMov, FilmAG WE[port], FilmEn, FilmgC, HalFC 80, IlWWBF[port], -A[port], IntMPA 77, -75, -76, -78, -79, -80, MotPP, MovMk[port], OxFilm, WhThe, WhoHol A, WhoHrs 80, WorEFlm*
Mason, James Howard 1942- *AmSCAP 80*
Mason, James Robert 1930- *IntWWM 80*
Mason, Jean *PupTheA*
Mason, John *BlksBF*
Mason, John d1548 *NewGrD 80*
Mason, John B d1919 *Film 1, WhoHol B, WhoStg 1908*
Mason, John B 1857-1919 *NotNAT B, WhThe, WhoStg 1906*
Mason, John B 1859-1919 *WhScrn 77*
Mason, Judi Ann *MorBAP*
Mason, Kenneth 1917- *IntMPA 78, -79, -80*
Mason, Kenneth Jay 1955- *AmSCAP 80*
Mason, Kitty 1882- *WhThe*
Mason, Lawrence d1939 *NotNAT B*
Mason, LeRoy 1901-1947 *TwYS*
Mason, LeRoy 1903-1947 *Film 1, -2, ForYSC, NotNAT B, Vers A[port], WhScrn 74, -77, WhoHol B*
Mason, Lesley d1964 *NotNAT B*
Mason, Louis 1888-1959 *WhScrn 74, -77, WhoHol B*
Mason, Lowell 1792-1872 *Baker 78, BiDAmM, BnBkM 80, NewGrD 80, OxMus*
Mason, Lowell 1823-1885 *Baker 78, BiDAmM, NewGrD 80*
Mason, Lucas 1931- *ConAmC*
Mason, Luther Whiting 1828-1896 *Baker 78, BiDAmM*
Mason, Marilyn 1925- *NewGrD 80*
Mason, Marjorie d1968 *WhScrn 77, WhoHol B*
Mason, Marlyn *WhoHol A*
Mason, Marsha 1942- *FilmEn, HalFC 80, IntMPA 77, -75, -76, -78, -79, -80, MovMk, NotNAT, WhoHol A*
Mason, Marshall W 1940- *NotNAT*
Mason, Mary *WhoHol A*
Mason, Mathias *NewGrD 80*
Mason, Monica 1941- *CnOxB, DancEn 78*
Mason, Morgan *WhoHol A*
Mason, Myrna *Film 2*
Mason, Noel *FilmEn*
Mason, Norman 1895-1971 *WhoJazz 72*
Mason, Pamela 1918- *ForYSC, IntMPA 77, -75, -76, -78, -79, -80, WhoHol A*
Mason, Portland *WhoHol A*
Mason, Ralph 1938- *IntWWM 77, -80*
Mason, Reginald 1882-1962 *Film 2, NotNAT B, WhScrn 74, -77, WhThe, WhoHol B*
Mason, Robert Paul 1946- *AmSCAP 80*
Mason, Sandy *AmSCAP 80*
Mason, Sarah Y *FilmEn, WomWMM*
Mason, Shirley 1900- *Film 1, -2, FilmgC, HalFC 80, MotPP, WhoHol A*
Mason, Shirley 1901-1979 *FilmEn, TwYS*
Mason, Sidney *Film 1*
Mason, Sully P 1906-1970 *WhScrn 74, -77, WhoHol B*
Mason, Sydney L *WhoHol A*
Mason, Thom David 1941- *ConAmC*
Mason, Timothy George Stewart 1948- *IntWWM 77, -80*
Mason, Vito Edward 1928- *IntWWM 77, -80*
Mason, William 1724-1797 *OxMus*
Mason, William 1725-1797 *NewGrD 80*
Mason, William 1829-1908 *Baker 78, BiDAmM, NewGrD 80, OxMus*
Mason, William 1888-1941 *Film 1, WhScrn 74, -77, WhoHol B*
Mason And Hamlin *OxMus*
Mason And Hamlin *NewGrD 80*
Mason And Titus *PupTheA*
Masone, Patrick T 1928- *AmSCAP 66, -80*
Masoner, E L 1927- *ConAmC*
Masotti, Giulio *NewGrD 80*
Mass, Joseph R 1943- *IntMPA 77, -75, -76, -78, -79*
Massa, Juan Bautista 1885-1938 *Baker 78*
Massa, Nicolo 1854-1894 *Baker 78*
Massad, William 1932- *WhoOp 76*
Massaini, Tiburtio 1550?-1609? *NewGrD 80*
Massaini, Tiburzio 1550?-1609? *NewGrD 80*
Massaino, Tiburtio 1550?-1609? *NewGrD 80*
Massaino, Tiburzio 1550?-1609? *NewGrD 80*
Massana, Antonio 1890-1966 *NewGrD 80*
Massarani, Renzo 1898-1975 *Baker 78, NewGrD 80*
Massard, Robert 1925- *NewGrD 80*
Massarengo, Giovanni Battista 1569-1596? *NewGrD 80*
Massari, Lea *FilmgC, WhoHol A*
Massari, Lea 1933- *FilmEn, HalFC 80*
Massaro, Salvatore *AmSCAP 80, NewGrD 80*
Massarsky, Steve *ConMuA 80B*
Massart, Lambert-Joseph 1811-1892 *Baker 78, NewGrD 80*
Massart, Mary *Film 2*
Massart, Nestor-Henri-Joseph 1849-1899 *Baker 78*
Massary, Fritzi 1882-1969 *WhThe*
Masse, Denis *NewGrD 80*
Masse, Laurel Anne 1951- *AmSCAP 80*
Masse, Victor 1822-1884 *Baker 78, NewEOp 71, NewGrD 80, OxMus*
Masselos, William 1920- *Baker 78, NewGrD 80*
Massen, Louis F d1925 *NotNAT B*
Massen, Osa 1915- *FilmgC, HalFC 80, WhoHrs 80*
Massen, Osa 1916- *FilmEn, ForYSC, IntMPA 77, -75, -76, -78, -79, -80*
Massenet, Jules 1842-1912 *Baker 78, BnBkM 80, CmOp, CmpBCM, DcCom 77[port], DcCom&M 79, GrComp[port], MusMk[port], NewEOp 71, NewGrD 80[port], OxMus*
Massenkeil, Gunther 1926- *NewGrD 80*
Massenkeil, Gunther 1928- *IntWWM 77, -80*
Massenus Moderatus, Petrus *NewGrD 80*
Massenzio, Domenico d1650 *NewGrD 80*
Masser, Michael 1941- *AmSCAP 80*
Massera, Giuseppe 1912- *IntWWM 80*
Masseus, Jan 1913- *Baker 78, IntWWM 77, -80, NewGrD 80*
Massey, Andrew John 1946- *IntWWM 80*
Massey, Anna 1937- *BiE&WWA, FilmgC, HalFC 80, WhoHol A, WhoHrs 80, WhoThe 72, -77*
Massey, Blanche d1929 *NotNAT B*
Massey, Cal 1928-1972 *EncJzS 70*
Massey, Charles d1625 *OxThe*
Massey, Curt 1910- *CmpEPM*
Massey, D Curtis 1910- *AmSCAP 66, -80*
Massey, Daniel 1933- *BiE&WWA, FilmEn, FilmgC, ForYSC, HalFC 80, IntMPA 77, -75, -76, -78, -79, -80, NotNAT, WhoHol A, WhoThe 72, -77*
Massey, Gwendoline Winifred 1892- *IntWWM 77, WhoMus 72*
Massey, Ilona 1910-1974 *FilmEn, ForYSC, MotPP, MovMk, ThFT[port], WhScrn 77, WhoHol B*
Massey, Ilona 1912-1974 *CmpEPM, FilmgC, HalFC 80, What 1[port], WhoHrs 80*
Massey, Louise *CmpEPM, IlEncCM*
Massey, Maria *AmSCAP 80*
Massey, Pamela Grace 1948- *IntWWM 77, -80*
Massey, Raymond 1896- *BiDFilm, -81, BiE&WWA, CmMov, CnThe, FamA&A[port], FilmAG WE, FilmEn, FilmgC, ForYSC, HalFC 80, IlWWBF, IntMPA 77, -75, -76, -78, -79, -80, MotPP, MovMk[port], NotNAT, OxFilm, PlP&P, WhoHol A, WhoHrs 80, WhoThe 72, -77*
Massey, Roy Cyril 1934- *IntWWM 80, WhoMus 72*
Massi, Bernice *BiE&WWA, NotNAT, WhoThe 72, -77*
Massi, Luigi *NewGrD 80*
Massicot, Percy 1910- *NewOrJ SUP[port]*
Massie, Paul 1932- *FilmgC, ForYSC, HalFC 80, IntMPA 77, -75, -76, -78, -79, -80, WhoHol A, WhoHrs 80*
Massimer, Howard *Film 1*
Massin, Brigitte 1927- *NewGrD 80*
Massin, Leonid 1896-1979 *NewGrD 80*
Massine, Leonid 1895-1979 *HalFC 80*
Massine, Leonid 1896-1979 *NewGrD 80, WhoHol A*
Massine, Leonide 1896- *DancEn 78[port]*
Massine, Leonide 1896-1979 *Film 2, WhThe*
Massine, Leonide Fedorovich 1895- *CnOxB*
Massine, Lorca 1944- *CnOxB*
Massinger, Philip 1583-1640 *CnThe, EncWT, Ent[port], McGEWD[port], NotNAT A, -B, OxMus, OxThe, PlP&P, REnWD[port]*
Massingham, Dorothy 1889-1933 *NotNAT B, WhThe*
Massingham, Richard 1898-1953 *FilmEn, FilmgC, HalFC 80, IlWWBF, -A, OxFilm, WhScrn 74, -77*
Massini, Angelo Oliviero De *NewGrD 80*
Massip, Catherine 1946- *IntWWM 80*
Masso, George 1926- *EncJzS 70*
Massol, Eugene Etienne Auguste 1802-1887 *NewGrD 80*
Masson, Andre 1896- *EncWT*
Masson, Carol Foster *CpmDNM 79*
Masson, Charles *NewGrD 80*
Masson, Diego 1935- *NewGrD 80*
Masson, Elizabeth 1806-1865 *NewGrD 80*
Masson, Gerard 1936- *Baker 78, DcCM, NewGrD 80*
Masson, Henri Leopold 1907- *CreCan 2*
Masson, Jean-Pierre *CreCan 1*
Masson, Paul-Marie 1882-1954 *Baker 78, NewGrD 80*
Masson, Tom 1866-1934 *WhScrn 77*
Massonneau, Louis 1766-1848 *NewGrD 80*
Massot, Louis Bernard 1930- *IntWWM 77*
Massoudieh, Mohammad Taghi 1927- *IntWWM 77, -80*
Massucci, Teodoro *NewGrD 80*
Mastalir, Jaroslav 1906- *WhoMus 72*
Masteroff, Joe 1919- *BiE&WWA, ConDr 73, -77D, NotNAT*
Masters, Archie *AmSCAP 80*
Masters, Darryl 1913-1961 *WhoHol B*
Masters, Daryl 1913-1961 *WhScrn 74, -77*
Masters, David *AmSCAP 80*
Masters, Dennis Joseph 1923- *IntWWM 77, -80*
Masters, Frankie 1904- *AmSCAP 66, -80, BgBands 74, CmpEPM*
Masters, Harry 1885-1974 *WhScrn 77*
Masters, Les *ConAmTC*
Masters, Mary *Film 1*
Masters, Quentin 1946- *HalFC 80*
Masters, Robert *WhoMus 72*
Masters, Ruth 1899-1969 *WhScrn 74, -77, WhoHol B*
Masters, William Rush 1950- *AmSCAP 80*
Masterson, Bat *HalFC 80*
Masterson, Carroll 1913- *BiE&WWA,*

NotNAT
Masterson, Harris 1914- *BiE&WWA, NotNAT*
Masterson, Mary Stuart *WhoHol A*
Masterson, Peter *WhoHol A*
Masterson, Robbie Gowan 1918- *IntWWM 77, -80*
Masterson, Valerie 1937- *CmOp, IntWWM 77, -80, NewGrD 80, WhoOp 76*
Mastersounds *BiDAmM*
Mastilovic, Danica 1933- *CmOp, NewGrD 80, WhoOp 76*
Mastin, Will, Trio *BlksBF*
Mastini, Giovanni Battista 1700?-1771 *NewGrD 80*
Mastren, Carmen 1913- *AmSCAP 66, -80, CmpEPM, EncJzS 70, WhoJazz 72*
Mastripietri, Augusto *Film 2*
Mastro, Johnny *RkOn*
Mastrocinque, Camillo *WhoHrs 80*
Mastrogiovanni, Antonio 1936- *DcCM, NewGrD 80*
Mastrogiovanni, Attilio 1939- *IntWWM 80*
Mastroianni, Marcello 1923- *FilmAG WE[port], FilmEn, FilmgC, HalFC 80*
Mastroianni, Marcello 1924- *BiDFilm, -81, ForYSC, IntMPA 77, -75, -76, -78, -79, -80, MotPP, MovMk[port], OxFilm, WhoHol A, WorEFlm*
Mastroianni, Tony *ConAmTC*
Mastromei, Gian Piero 1932- *WhoOp 76*
Masucci, Jerry *ConMuA 80B*
Masuda, Mikio 1949- *EncJzS 70*
Masumura, Yasuzo 1924- *FilmEn*
Masuo, Yoshiaki 1946- *EncJzS 70*
Masur, Kurt 1927- *NewGrD 80*
Masurat, Theresa *WhoHol A*
Maszkowski, Rafal 1838-1901 *NewGrD 80*
Maszynski, Piotr 1855-1934 *Baker 78, NewGrD 80*
Mata, Eduardo 1942- *Baker 78, DcCM, IntWWM 77, -80, NewGrD 80*
Mata, Miguel P 1914-1956 *WhScrn 74, -77*
Mata, Ruth *CnOxB, DancEn 78[port]*
Mata, Yama *Film 2*
Mata And Hari *CnOxB, DancEn 78[port]*
Matacic, Lovro Von 1899- *CmOp, NewGrD 80*
Matalarte, Ioanne 1538?-1607 *NewGrD 80*
Matalon, Vivian 1929- *NotNAT, WhoThe 72, -77*
Matalon, Zack 1928- *BiE&WWA*
Matant, Jean-Baptiste *NewGrD 80*
Matau, Jean-Baptiste *NewGrD 80*
Matchett, Christine 1957- *WhoHol A*
Matchi *Film 2*
Matchinga, Caryn *WomWMM B*
Mate, Janos 1944- *IntWWM 80*
Mate, Rudolf 1898-1964 *DcFM*
Mate, Rudolph 1898-1964 *BiDFilm, -81, CmMov, FilmEn, OxFilm, WorEFlm*
Mate, Rudolph 1899-1964 *FilmgC, HalFC 80, WhoHrs 80*
Mateer, David Gordon 1946- *IntWWM 80*
Matej, Josef 1922- *Baker 78, NewGrD 80*
Mateja, Walter A 1944- *AmSCAP 66*
Matejka, Vaclav *NewGrD 80*
Matelart, Giovanni 1538?-1607 *NewGrD 80*
Matelart, Ioanne 1538?-1607 *NewGrD 80*
Matelart, Ioannes 1538?-1607 *NewGrD 80*
Matelart, Johannes 1538?-1607 *NewGrD 80*
Matelarte, Ioanne 1538?-1607 *NewGrD 80*
Matelartus, Ioanne 1538?-1607 *NewGrD 80*
Mateos, Hector 1901-1957 *WhScrn 74, -77*
Materassi, Sandro 1904- *WhoMus 72*
Matern, A W F d1789 *NewGrD 80*
Materna, Amalia 1844-1918 *NewEOp 71*
Materna, Amalie 1844-1918 *Baker 78, CmOp, NewGrD 80*
Matesky, Elizabeth Anne 1944- *WhoMus 72*
Matesky, Ralph 1913-1979 *AmSCAP 66, -80, IntWWM 77, -80*
Matesses, Antonios *REnWD[port]*
Mateuet, Mateo *NewGrD 80*
Mathalart, Ioanne *NewGrD 80*
Mathau, Jean-Baptiste *NewGrD 80*
Mathe, Carmen 1938- *CnOxB*
Mathe, Ed *Film 2*
Mathe, Edouard *Film 1*
Matheis, Nicholas *NewGrD 80*
Mather, Aubrey 1885-1958 *FilmEn, Film 2, FilmgC, HalFC 80, NotNAT B, Vers A[port], WhScrn 74, -77, WhThe, WhoHol B*
Mather, Betty Bang 1927- *IntWWM 77, -80*
Mather, Bruce 1939- *Baker 78, DcCM, NewGrD 80*
Mather, Christine Kyle 1929- *IntWWM 77, -80*
Mather, Cotton 1663-1728 *BiDAmM, OxMus*
Mather, Donald 1900- *WhThe*
Mather, Ernest Frederick *IntWWM 77, WhoMus 72*
Mather, Jack 1908-1966 *ForYSC, WhScrn 74, -77, WhoHol B*
Mather, Richard 1596-1669 *BiDAmM, OxMus*
Mather, Roger Frederick 1917- *IntWWM 80*
Mather, Sydney d1925 *NotNAT B*
Mathers, Jerry 1948- *ForYSC, What 4[port], WhoHol A*
Mathes, David Wayne 1933- *BiDAmM*
Mathes, Rachel 1941- *WhoOp 76*
Matheson, Don *WhoHol A*
Matheson, John 1928- *NewGrD 80, WhoMus 72, WhoOp 76*
Matheson, Murray 1910?- *HalFC 80*
Matheson, Murray 1912- *BiE&WWA, FilmgC, NotNAT, WhoHol A*
Matheson, Richard 1926- *CmMov, FilmgC, HalFC 80, NewYTET, WhoHrs 80, WorEFlm*
Matheson, Tim *HalFC 80, WhoHol A*
Matheson-Bruce, Graeme 1945- *IntWWM 77, -80*
Matheus De Brixia *NewGrD 80*
Matheus De Perusio *NewGrD 80*
Matheus De Sancto Johanne *NewGrD 80*
Matheus, John Frederick 1887- *BlkAmP, MorBAP*
Mathew, David 1945- *ConAmC*
Mathew, Gladys Hagee 1896- *IntWWM 77, -80*
Mathew, Ray 1929- *ConDr 73, -77*
Mathew, Richard d1660 *NewGrD 80*
Mathews *PupTheA*
Mathews, Carl d1959 *WhoHol B*
Mathews, Carmen *WhoHol A*
Mathews, Carmen 1914- *WhoThe 72, -77*
Mathews, Carmen 1918- *BiE&WWA, NotNAT*
Mathews, Carole 1920- *ForYSC, IntMPA 77, -75, -76, -78, -79, -80, WhoHol A*
Mathews, Charles 1776-1835 *EncWT, FamA&A[port], NotNAT A, -B, OxThe, PlP&P*
Mathews, Mrs. Charles, Sr. d1869 *NotNAT B*
Mathews, Mrs. Charles J d1899 *NotNAT B*
Mathews, Charles James 1803-1878 *EncWT, FamA&A[port], NotNAT A, -B, OxThe, PlP&P[port]*
Mathews, Dorothy *Film 2*
Mathews, Edwin A *ConMuA 80B*
Mathews, Emmett 1902?- *WhoJazz 72*
Mathews, Frances Aymar *WhThe*
Mathews, George 1911- *BiE&WWA, NotNAT, WhoHol A, WhoThe 72, -77*
Mathews, George H 1877-1952 *WhScrn 74, -77*
Mathews, James Snookie 1919- *AmSCAP 80*
Mathews, James W d1920 *WhThe*
Mathews, John Fenton 1926- *IntWWM 80*
Mathews, Joyce 1919- *ForYSC, WhoHol A*
Mathews, Justus Frederick 1945- *IntWWM 77, -80*
Mathews, Kerwin 1926- *FilmgC, ForYSC, HalFC 80, WhoHol A, WhoHrs 80*
Mathews, Lester 1900- *ForYSC*
Mathews, M V 1926- *ConAmC*
Mathews, Max V 1926- *BnBkM 80, DcCM*
Mathews, Patrick 1934- *AmSCAP 80*
Mathews, Ray *AmSCAP 80*
Mathews, Ronald Albert 1935- *BiDAmM, EncJzS 70*
Mathews, Ronnie 1935- *EncJzS 70*
Mathews, William Smith Babcock 1837-1912 *BiDAmM*
Mathews, William Smythe Babcock 1837-1912 *Baker 78*
Mathewson, Christy 1880-1925 *WhScrn 77*
Mathewson, Rognuald Andrew 1944- *IntWWM 77*
Mathey, Paul Andre 1909- *IntWWM 77, -80*
Mathez, Jean-Pierre 1938- *IntWWM 77, -80*
Mathias Fiamengo *NewGrD 80*
Mathias, Bob *WhoHol A*
Mathias, Franz Xaver 1871-1939 *Baker 78*
Mathias, Georges 1826-1910 *Baker 78*
Mathias, William 1934- *Baker 78, CpmDNM 78, -79, -80, IntWWM 77, -80, NewGrD 80, WhoMus 72*
Mathies, Charlene *WhoHol A*
Mathiesen, Aksel Helge 1931- *IntWWM 77, -80*
Mathieson, Dock 1914- *WhoMus 72*
Mathieson, Muir 1911-1975 *FilmEn, FilmgC, HalFC 80, IntMPA 75, NewGrD 80, WhScrn 77, WhoHol C, WhoMus 72*
Mathieu *NewGrD 80*
Mathieu, Emile 1844-1932 *Baker 78, NewGrD 80*
Mathieu, Julien-Amable 1734-1811 *NewGrD 80*
Mathieu, Michel 1689-1768 *NewGrD 80*
Mathieu, Michel-Julien 1740-1777? *NewGrD 80*
Mathieu, Rodolphe 1890-1962 *Baker 78*
Mathieu, Rodolphe 1894-1962 *CreCan 2*
Mathis, Bonnie 1942- *CnOxB*
Mathis, Edith 1938- *Baker 78, CmOp, IntWWM 77, -80, NewGrD 80, WhoMus 72, WhoOp 76*
Mathis, George Russell 1926- *IntWWM 77, -80*
Mathis, Johnny *AmPS A, -B*
Mathis, Johnny 1933- *BiDAmM*
Mathis, Johnny 1935- *BiDAmM, DrBlPA, RkOn[port]*
Mathis, June 1892-1927 *DcFM, FilmEn, FilmgC, HalFC 80, NotNAT B, TwYS A, WomWMM, WorEFlm*
Mathis, William 1934- *WhoMus 72*
Matho, Jean-Baptiste 1660?-1746 *NewGrD 80*
Mathot, Leon 1886-1968 *FilmEn*
Mathot, Leon 1896-1968 *Film 2, WhScrn 74, -77, WhoHol B*
Matias 1926- *WhoOp 76*
Matic-Marovic, Darinka 1937- *IntWWM 77, -80*
Maticic, Janez 1926- *Baker 78, NewGrD 80*
Matiegka, Vaclav Thomas 1773-1830 *NewGrD 80*
Matiegka, Wenzel Thomas 1773-1830 *NewGrD 80*
Matiesen, Otto 1873-1932 *WhScrn 74, -77, WhoHol B*
Matiesen, Otto 1893- *Film 1, -2, TwYS*
Matieson, Otto 1873- *ForYSC*
Matinsky, Mikhail Alexeyevich 1750-1825? *NewGrD 80*
Matisse, Henri 1869-1954 *CnOxB, DancEn 78*
Matkowsky, Adalbert d1909 *NotNAT B*
Matlack, Jack D 1914- *IntMPA 77, -75, -76, -78, -79, -80*
Matlaw, Myron 1924- *BiE&WWA, NotNAT*
Matlick, Jay Jeffries 1941- *AmSCAP 80*
Matlock, Julian Clifton 1907-1978 *AmSCAP 66, -80, BiDAmM*
Matlock, Julian Clifton 1909-1978 *EncJzS 70*
Matlock, Matty 1909-1978 *CmpEPM, EncJzS 70, WhoJazz 72*
Matofsky, Harvey 1933- *IntMPA 77, -75, -76, -78, -79, -80*
Matos, Alexander 1929- *AmSCAP 66, -80*
Matos, Jean-Baptiste *NewGrD 80*
Matos, Manuel Garcia 1904- *AmSCAP 66, -80*
Matos, Maria 1891-1952 *FilmAG WE[port]*
Matousek, Lukas 1943- *IntWWM 77, -80*
Matousek, Raymond Anthony 1926- *AmSCAP 80*
Matras, Christian 1903- *DcFM, FilmEn, FilmgC, HalFC 80, OxFilm, WorEFlm*
Matray, Gabor 1797-1875 *Baker 78, NewGrD 80*
Matshikiza, Todd T 1921-1968 *NewGrD 80*
Matson, Donna *WomWMM B*
Matson, Sigfred Christian 1917- *ConAmC, IntWWM 77, -80*
Matsoukas, Nicholas John 1903- *IntMPA 77, -75, -76, -78, -79, -80*
Matsudaira, Renko *AmSCAP 66, -80*

Matsudaira, Yori-Aki 1931- *Baker 78, DcCM, IntWWM 77, -80*
Matsudaira, Yoriaki 1931- *NewGrD 80*
Matsudaira, Yoritsune 1907- *Baker 78, NewGrD 80*
Matsui, Suisei 1900-1973 *WhScrn 77*
Matsumae, Norio 1931- *IntWWM 77, -80*
Matsumoto, Shigemi *IntWWM 77, -80, WhoOp 76*
Matsumura, Teizo 1929- *Baker 78, DcCM, NewGrD 80*
Matsumura, Vera Yoshi 1919- *IntWWM 77, -80*
Matsuoka, Tatsuo 1904- *IntMPA 75*
Matsushita, Hidemi 1954- *CpmDNM 74, -77*
Matsushita, Shin-Ichi 1922- *Baker 78, DcCM*
Matta, Domenico Del *NewGrD 80*
Mattan, Jean-Baptiste *NewGrD 80*
Mattei, Filippo *NewGrD 80, OxMus*
Mattei, Stanislao 1750-1825 *NewGrD 80*
Mattei, Tito 1841-1914 *Baker 78, OxMus*
Matteis, Nicholas 1670?-1749? *NewGrD 80*
Matteis, Nicholas 1670?-1749 *OxMus*
Matteis, Nicola *Baker 78, OxMus*
Matteis, Nicola d1707? *NewGrD 80*
Matteis, Nicola 1670?-1749? *NewGrD 80*
Matteo *DancEn 78[port]*
Matteo 1919- *CnOxB*
Matteo Da Perugia d1418 *Baker 78, NewGrD 80*
Mattern, A W F *NewGrD 80*
Mattern, Ludwig Anton Wilhelm *NewGrD 80*
Matters, Arnold 1903- *CmOp*
Matters, Arnold 1904- *NewGrD 80*
Matterstock, Albert 1912-1960 *WhScrn 74, -77, WhoHol B*
Matteson, Ruth 1909-1975 *BiE&WWA, NotNAT B, WhThe, WhoThe 72*
Matteson, Ruth 1910-1975 *WhScrn 77*
Mattey, Robert A *WhoHrs 80*
Mattfeld, Jacquelyn 1925- *NewGrD 80*
Mattfeld, Julius 1893-1968 *Baker 78, BiE&WWA, ConAmC*
Mattfeld, Victor Henry 1917- *Baker 78*
Matthaei, Conrad 1619-1667 *NewGrD 80*
Matthaei, Gay *WomWMM B*
Matthaei, Karl 1897-1960 *NewGrD 80*
Matthaei, Konrad *NotNAT*
Matthau, Walter 1920- *BiDFilm, -81, BiE&WWA, CmMov, CnThe, FilmEn, FilmgC, HalFC 80, MotPP, MovMk[port], NotNAT, OxFilm, WhoHol A, WhoThe 72, -77*
Matthau, Walter 1923- *ForYSC, IntMPA 77, -75, -76, -78, -79, -80, WorEFlm*
Matthay, Tobias 1858-1945 *Baker 78, BnBkM 80, NewGrD 80, OxMus*
Matthen, Lida Etta Rice 1936- *IntWWM 77, -80*
Matthen, Paul Seymour 1914- *IntWWM 77, -80*
Matthes, Betsy Durkin 1947- *AmSCAP 80*
Mattheson, Johann 1681-1764 *Baker 78, BnBkM 80, MusMk, NewGrD 80[port], OxMus*
Matthew, Jean Foster 1945- *IntWWM 77, -80*
Matthews, A E 1869-1960 *Film 2, FilmgC, HalFC 80, IlWWBF, -A, NotNAT A, -B, PlP&P, WhScrn 74, -77, WhThe, WhoHol B*
Matthews, Adelaide 1886- *WhThe*
Matthews, Albert Edward 1869-1960 *OxThe*
Matthews, Alexander 1879-1973 *Baker 78*
Matthews, Alice Tregoning 1898- *WhoMus 72*
Matthews, Bache 1876-1948 *NotNAT B, WhThe*
Matthews, Beatrice 1890-1942 *WhScrn 74, -77*
Matthews, Billy 1922- *BiE&WWA*
Matthews, Brander 1852-1929 *NotNAT A, -B, WhThe*
Matthews, Bruce R 1949- *IntWWM 77, -80*
Matthews, Christopher *WhoHol A*
Matthews, Clifford 1937- *IntWWM 80*
Matthews, Dave 1911- *CmpEPM, WhoJazz 72*
Matthews, David 1942- *EncJzS 70*
Matthews, David Henry 1949- *IntWWM 77, -80*
Matthews, Denis 1919- *IntWWM 77, -80, NewGrD 80, WhoMus 72*
Matthews, Donald Edward 1935- *AmSCAP 80*
Matthews, Dorcas *Film 2*
Matthews, Dorothy *Film 2*
Matthews, Enid Noel 1905- *IntWWM 80*
Matthews, Eric *WhoHol A*
Matthews, Ernest Leonard 1908- *WhoMus 72*
Matthews, Ethel 1870- *WhThe*
Matthews, Forrest 1908-1951 *WhScrn 77*
Matthews, Francis 1927- *FilmgC, HalFC 80, WhoHol A*
Matthews, George 1912- *IntWWM 77, WhoJazz 72*
Matthews, Glenn E 1897- *IntMPA 75, -76*
Matthews, Gloria *WhoHol A*
Matthews, H Alexander 1879-1973 *ConAmC*
Matthews, Harry Alexander 1879-1973 *AmSCAP 66, -80, BiDAmM*
Matthews, Holon 1904- *AmSCAP 66, ConAmC*
Matthews, Ian 1946- *ConMuA 80A, IlEncR*
Matthews, Inez 1917- *BiE&WWA, NotNAT*
Matthews, James Brander 1852-1929 *EncWT, OxThe*
Matthews, Jean D d1961 *WhScrn 74, -77, WhoHol B*
Matthews, Jessie 1907- *BiE&WWA, CmpEPM, CnThe, EncMT, FilmAG WE, FilmEn, Film 2, FilmgC, HalFC 80, IlWWBF[port], -A[port], IntMPA 77, -75, -76, -78, -79, -80, MotPP, MovMk, NotNAT, OxFilm, ThFT[port], What 2[port], WhoHol A, WhoThe 72, -77*
Matthews, John Sebastian 1870-1934 *ConAmC*
Matthews, Justus Frederick 1945- *ConAmC, IntWWM 77, -80*
Matthews, Lester 1900-1975 *FilmgC, HalFC 80, IlWWBF, WhScrn 77, WhThe, WhoHol A*
Matthews, Lewis 1885?- *NewOrJ*
Matthews, Marmaduke Matthews 1837-1913 *CreCan 1*
Matthews, Mary Ann 1922- *AmSCAP 80*
Matthews, Mary Jo *AmSCAP 80*
Matthews, Michael Gough 1932- *IntWWM 77, -80*
Matthews, Nathaniel 1890?-1961 *NewOrJ*
Matthews, Onzy D, Jr. 1936- *BiDAmM, EncJzS 70*
Matthews, Ramos 1886?-1958 *NewOrJ[port]*
Matthews, Stonewall 1889?- *NewOrJ*
Matthews, T *AmSCAP 80*
Matthews, Thomas 1907-1969 *NewGrD 80*
Matthews, Thomas 1915- *ConAmC*
Matthews, Walter E 1917- *ConAmC, WhoHol A*
Matthews, William *Film 2*
Matthews, William 1899-1964 *NewOrJ[port]*
Matthews, William 1950- *ConAmC*
Matthews, William Smythe Babcock 1837-1912 *BiDAmM*
Matthews Southern Comfort *RkOn 2[port]*
Matthias, Jack William 1915- *AmSCAP 80*
Matthias Hansen, Hans *NewGrD 80*
Matthison, Arthur d1883 *NotNAT B*
Matthison, Edith Wynne 1875-1955 *Film 1, NotNAT B, WhScrn 74, -77, WhThe, WhoHol B, WhoStg 1906, -1908*
Matthison-Hansen, Gottfred 1832-1909 *NewGrD 80*
Matthison-Hansen, Gottfried 1832-1909 *NewGrD 80*
Matthison-Hansen, Hans 1807-1890 *NewGrD 80*
Matthisson, Friedrich Von 1761-1831 *NewGrD 80*
Matthus, Siegfried 1934- *IntWWM 77, -80, NewGrD 80*
Matthys, Abel 1921- *IntWWM 77, -80*
Matthysz, Paulus 1613?-1684 *NewGrD 80*
Mattice, Hortense Crompton *CreCan 2*
Mattila, Edward Charles 1927- *ConAmC, IntWWM 77, -80*
Mattimore, Van *Film 2*
Mattingly, Hedley *WhoHol A*
Mattingly, Richard Egart 1950- *IntWWM 77, -80*
Mattioli, Andrea 1620?-1679 *NewGrD 80*
Mattioli, Lino 1853-1949 *BiDAmM*
Mattioli, Raf 1936-1960 *WhScrn 74, -77*
Mattiotti, Mario 1933- *WhoOp 76*
Mattis, Lillian 1924- *AmSCAP 80*
Mattis, Lillian 1925- *AmSCAP 66*
Mattison, Frank S 1890- *TwYS A*
Mattison, Hiram 1811-1868 *BiDAmM*
Mattlart, Ioanne *NewGrD 80*
Mattmann, Erwin 1942- *IntWWM 77, -80*
Mattocks, Isabella Hallam 1746-1826 *NotNAT B, OxThe*
Matton, Roger 1929- *Baker 78, CreCan 1, DcCM, NewGrD 80*
Mattoni, Andre *Film 2*
Mattox, Martha d1938 *Film 1, -2, TwYS*
Mattox, Martha 1879-1933 *ForYSC, WhScrn 74, -77, WhoHol B*
Mattox, Matt 1921- *BiE&WWA, CnOxB, DancEn 78, ForYSC, NotNAT, WhoHol A*
Mattraw, Scott 1885-1946 *Film 2, WhScrn 74, -77, WhoHol B*
Mattson, Eric 1908- *BiE&WWA, NotNAT*
Mattson, Julia *PupTheA*
Mattson, Sally Jeanne 1948- *IntWWM 77, -80*
Mattsson, Arne 1919- *DcFM, FilmEn, FilmgC, HalFC 80, OxFilm, WorEFlm*
Mattyasovsky, I *Film 2*
Matura, Mustapha 1939- *BlkAmP, ConDr 73, -77, WhoThe 77*
Maturana, Eduardo 1920- *DcCM, NewGrD 80*
Mature, Victor *MotPP, WhoHol A*
Mature, Victor 1915- *CmMov, FilmEn, FilmgC, ForYSC[port], HalFC 80, WhoHrs 80*
Mature, Victor 1916- *BiDFilm, -81, IntMPA 77, -75, -76, -78, -79, -80, MovMk[port], OxFilm, What 2[port], WorEFlm*
Maturin, Charles d1824 *NotNAT B*
Maturin, Eric 1883-1957 *Film 2, NotNAT B, WhThe*
Matusche, Alfred 1909- *CroCD*
Matuszczak, Bernadetta 1933- *NewGrD 80*
Matuszczak, Bernadetta 1937- *IntWWM 80*
Matyas, Maria 1927- *WhoOp 76*
Matys, Jiri 1927- *Baker 78*
Matys Brothers, The *RkOn*
Matz, Johanna 1932- *FilmAG WE*
Matz, Peter 1928- *BiDAmM*
Matz, Rudolf 1901- *Baker 78, IntWWM 77, -80*
Matzenauer, Margaret 1881-1963 *NewEOp 71, WhoHol B*
Matzenauer, Margarete 1881-1963 *Baker 78, BiDAmM, CmOp, MusSN[port], NewGrD 80*
Matzenauer, Margarette d1963 *NotNAT B*
Matzenauer, Marguerite 1881-1963 *WhScrn 77*
Matzka, George 1825-1883 *Baker 78*
Matzke, Hermann 1890-1976 *Baker 78*
Maubourg, Jeanne 1875- *BiDAmM*
Mauceri, John 1945- *Baker 78, WhoOp 76*
Mauceri, John Francis Peter 1945- *IntWWM 77, -80*
Mauch, Billy *ForYSC*
Mauch, Billy 1924- *WhoHol A*
Mauch, Billy 1925- *FilmgC, HalFC 80*
Mauch, Bobby *ForYSC*
Mauch, Bobby 1924- *WhoHol A*
Mauch, Bobby 1925- *FilmgC, HalFC 80*
Mauch Twins, The 1924- *What 5[port]*
Mauch Twins, The 1925- *MotPP*
Mauclair, Jacques 1919- *EncWT*
Maud, Arthur 1932- *IntWWM 77, -80*
Maud, Zuni *PupTheA*
Maude, Arthur *Film 1, IlWWBF*
Maude, Charles Raymond d1943 *NotNAT B, PlP&P, WhThe, WhoHol B*
Maude, Cyril 1862-1951 *Film 1, -2, NotNAT A, -B, OxThe, TwYS, WhScrn 74, -77, WhThe, WhoHol B*
Maude, Elizabeth 1912- *WhThe*
Maude, Gillian *WhThe*
Maude, Joan 1908- *Film 2, WhThe*
Maude, Margery 1889- *BiE&WWA, NotNAT, WhoHol A, WhoThe 72, -77*
Maude-Roxby, Roddy 1930- *WhoHol A, WhoThe 72, -77*
Maudrik, Lizzie 1898-1955 *CnOxB*
Mauduit, Jacques 1557-1627 *Baker 78, NewGrD 80*

Mauerhofer, Alois 1946- *IntWWM 77, -80*
Mauersberger, Erhard 1903- *NewGrD 80*
Mauersberger, Rudolf 1889-1971 *Baker 78, NewGrD 80*
Maugars, Andre 1580?-1645? *NewGrD 80*
Maugham, W Somerset 1874-1965 *HalFC 80*
Maugham, William Somerset 1874-1965 *BiE&WWA, CnMD, CnThe, EncWT, Ent, FilmgC, McGEWD[port], ModWD, NotNAT A, -B, OxThe, PlP&P[port], REnWD[port], WhScrn 77, WhThe*
Maughan, Jean Margaret 1935- *IntWWM 77*
Mauke, Wilhelm 1867-1930 *Baker 78*
Mauldin, Bill 1921- *JoeFr*
Mauldin, Bill 1922- *WhoHol A*
Mauldin, Michael 1947- *ConAmC*
Maule, Annabel 1922- *WhoThe 72, -77*
Maule, Donovan 1899- *WhoThe 72, -77*
Maule, Leroy Ernest 1904- *AmSCAP 80*
Maule, Michael 1926- *CnOxB, DancEn 78*
Maule, Robin 1924-1942 *NotNAT B, WhThe*
Maule, Vee *Film 2*
Maulnier, Thierry 1909- *McGEWD*
Maultsby, Carl *AmSCAP 80*
Maultsby, Portia 1947- *AmSCAP 80, IntWWM 77, -80*
Maunder, Dennis *WhoMus 72*
Maunder, John Henry 1858-1920 *Baker 78, NewGrD 80, OxMus*
Maunder, Peter Anthony 1936- *IntWWM 80, WhoMus 72*
Maunder, Wayne 1942- *FilmgC, HalFC 80, WhoHol A*
Maupain, Ernest 1881-1949 *WhScrn 77*
Maupassant, Guy De 1850-1893 *EncWT, NewEOp 71*
Maupin 1670-1707 *NewGrD 80*
Maupin, Bennie 1946- *EncJzS 70*
Maupin, Ernest *Film 2*
Maupin, Georges *Film 2*
Maupin, Rex 1886-1966 *AmSCAP 66, -80*
Maur, Meinhart *WhoHol A*
Mauracher *NewGrD 80*
Mauracher, Albert *NewGrD 80*
Mauracher, Andreas 1758-1824 *NewGrD 80*
Mauracher, Anton 1896-1962 *NewGrD 80*
Mauracher, Franz *NewGrD 80*
Mauracher, Hans d1900 *NewGrD 80*
Mauracher, Josef 1845-1907 *NewGrD 80*
Mauracher, Karl 1789-1844 *NewGrD 80*
Mauracher, Matthaus *NewGrD 80*
Mauracher, Matthaus 1859-1939 *NewGrD 80*
Mauracher, Matthaus 1885-1954 *NewGrD 80*
Mauracher, Matthias 1788-1857 *NewGrD 80*
Mauracher, Matthias 1818-1884 *NewGrD 80*
Maurada, Mac 1902-1963 *AmSCAP 66, -80*
Maurane, Camille 1911- *WhoMus 72*
Maureice, Ruth *Film 1*
Maurel, Michael 1931- *WhoMus 72*
Maurel, Victor 1848-1923 *Baker 78, BiDAmM, BnBkM 80, CmOp, NewEOp 71, NewGrD 80*
Maurer, Ludwig 1789-1878 *Baker 78, NewGrD 80*
Maurer, Maurice 1914- *IntMPA 77, -75, -76, -78, -79, -80*
Maurey, Max d1947 *NotNAT B, WhThe*
Maurey, Nicole 1925- *FilmEn, FilmgC, ForYSC, HalFC 80, IntMPA 77, -75, -76, -78, -79, -80, MotPP, WhoHol A*
Mauri, Rosita 1849-1923 *CnOxB, DancEn 78*
Mauriac, Francois 1885-1970 *CnMD, Ent, McGEWD[port], ModWD, REnWD[port]*
Mauriac, Francois 1885-1971 *EncWT*
Mauriac, Francois 1895- *BiE&WWA*
Mauriat, Paul *RkOn 2[port]*
Maurice d1927 *NotNAT B, WhScrn 77*
Maurice, Alphons 1862-1905 *Baker 78*
Maurice, Cecil *AmSCAP 80*
Maurice, Edmund d1928 *NotNAT B, WhThe*
Maurice, Glenda Ann 1939- *IntWWM 77*
Maurice, Mary 1844-1918 *Film 1, MotPP, NotNAT B, WhScrn 77, WhoHol B*
Maurice, Newman d1923 *NotNAT B*
Maurice, Pierre 1868-1936 *Baker 78, NewGrD 80*
Maurice-Amour, Lila Elisabeth 1906- *IntWWM 80*
Maurice-Jacquet, H 1886-1954 *AmSCAP 66, -80, ConAmC A*
Mauricio, Jose *NewGrD 80*
Mauricio, Jose 1752-1815 *Baker 78, NewGrD 80*
Mauriello, David Joseph 1936- *NatPD[port]*
Maurin, Jean-Pierre 1882-1894 *Baker 78*
Mauritius VonMenzingen 1654-1713 *NewGrD 80*
Mauro *NewGrD 80*
Mauro Di Firenze *NewGrD 80*
Mauro Fiorentino *NewGrD 80*
Mauro, Fra 1490?-1556 *NewGrD 80*
Mauro Matti, Fra 1545?-1621 *NewGrD 80*
Mauro, Alessandro *NewGrD 80, -80*
Mauro, Antonio *NewGrD 80*
Mauro, Domenico *NewGrD 80*
Mauro, Ermanno 1939- *WhoMus 72, WhoOp 76*
Mauro, Gaspare *NewGrD 80*
Mauro, Gerolamo *NewGrD 80*
Mauro, Gerolamo 1725-1766 *NewGrD 80*
Mauro, Giuseppe *NewGrD 80*
Mauro, Humberto 1897- *DcFM, FilmEn*
Mauro, Pietro *NewGrD 80*
Mauro, Romualdo *NewGrD 80*
Mauro, Tommaso De *NewGrD 80*
Mauro Family *OxThe*
Maurus, Gerda 1909-1968 *Film 2, WhScrn 74, -77, WhoHol B*
Maury, Lowndes 1911-1975 *AmSCAP 66, -80, Baker 78, ConAmC*
Maus, Octave 1856-1919 *Baker 78*
Maust, Ezma M 1914- *IntWWM 77, -80*
Mauti Nunziata, Elena 1946- *WhoOp 76*
Maves, David W 1937- *AmSCAP 80, CpmDNM 78, -80, ConAmC*
Maves, Victor Henry Arthur 1897- *AmSCAP 80*
Mavor, O H *PlP&P*
Maw, Nicholas 1935- *Baker 78, CmOp, DcCom&M 79, DcCM, IntWWM 77, -80, NewGrD 80, OxMus, WhoMus 72*
Mawby, Colin 1936- *IntWWM 80*
Mawdesley, Robert d1953 *NotNAT B, WhoHol B*
Mawer, Betty Oliphant *CreCan 1*
Mawson, Edward 1861-1917 *Film 1, NotNAT B, WhScrn 77, WhoHol B*
Max, Edouard Alexandre De 1869-1925 *NotNAT B, OxThe, WhThe*
Max, Edwin 1909- *Vers A[port], WhoHol A*
Max, Jean 1897-1971 *WhScrn 77*
Maxakova, Mariya 1902-1974 *NewGrD 80*
Maxam, Lola *Film 2*
Maxam, Louella Modie 1896-1970 *Film 1, -2, WhScrn 74, -77, WhoHol B*
Maxey, Leroy 1904- *WhoJazz 72*
Maxey, Paul 1908-1963 *ForYSC, NotNAT B, WhScrn 74, -77, WhoHol B*
Maxfield, Richard 1927-1969 *Baker 78, ConAmC, DcCM, NewGrD 80*
Maxilewicz, Wincenty *NewGrD 80*
Maxim, Abraham 1773-1829 *BiDAmM*
Maximilian I *NewGrD 80*
Maximilian III Joseph 1727-1777 *NewGrD 80*
Maximilian, Max *Film 2*
Maximo Lopez, Felix *NewGrD 80*
Maximoff, Richard Michael 1943- *IntWWM 77, -80*
Maximova, E *Film 2*
Maximova, Yekaterina 1939- *DancEn 78[port]*
Maximova, Yekaterina Sergeyevna 1939- *CnOxB*
Maximovna, Ita 1914- *EncWT*
Maximowna, Ita *WhoOp 76*
Maxson, Frederick 1862-1934 *Baker 78, BiDAmM*
Maxson, William Lynn 1930- *ConAmC*
Maxted, Billy 1917- *BgBands 74, CmpEPM*
Maxted, George Alfred 1911- *IntWWM 77, -80, WhoMus 72*
Maxted, Stanley 1900-1963 *WhScrn 74, -77, WhoHol B*
Maxtone-Graham, John 1929- *BiE&WWA, NotNAT*
Maxudian *Film 2*
Maxwell *Film 2*
Maxwell, Barbara 1941- *IntWWM 77, -80*
Maxwell, Charles 1892-1962 *AmSCAP 80*
Maxwell, Eddie 1912- *AmSCAP 66, -80*
Maxwell, Edwin d1948 *Film 1, ForYSC, NotNAT B, TwYS, WhoHol B*
Maxwell, Edwin 1886-1948 *HalFC 80, WhScrn 74, -77*
Maxwell, Edwin 1890-1948 *Film 2, FilmgC, Vers B[port]*
Maxwell, Elsa 1883-1963 *AmSCAP 66, -80, FilmgC, HalFC 80, NotNAT B, WhScrn 77, WhoHol B*
Maxwell, Everett *ConAmC*
Maxwell, Francis Kelly d1782 *NewGrD 80*
Maxwell, Frank *WhoHol A*
Maxwell, Gerald 1862-1930 *NotNAT B, WhThe*
Maxwell, Harry Philip 1901-1974 *AmSCAP 80*
Maxwell, Helen Purcell 1901- *AmSCAP 66*
Maxwell, Jacqueline Perkinson 1932- *ConAmC*
Maxwell, James Clerk 1831-1879 *OxMus*
Maxwell, James Kendrick 1917- *EncJzS 70*
Maxwell, Jenny *WhoHol A*
Maxwell, Jimmy 1917- *EncJzS 70*
Maxwell, John *ForYSC*
Maxwell, John d1806 *NewGrD 80*
Maxwell, John 1875-1940 *FilmgC, HalFC 80*
Maxwell, Linn 1945- *WhoOp 76*
Maxwell, Lois 1927- *FilmEn, FilmgC, ForYSC, HalFC 80, WhoHol A, WhoHrs 80*
Maxwell, Marilyn d1972 *MotPP, WhoHol B*
Maxwell, Marilyn 1921-1972 *FilmEn, FilmgC, ForYSC, HalFC 80*
Maxwell, Marilyn 1922-1972 *CmpEPM, MGM[port], MovMk, WhScrn 77*
Maxwell, Marina *MorBAP*
Maxwell, Mary Hamlin 1814-1853 *BiDAmM*
Maxwell, Meg d1955 *NotNAT B*
Maxwell, Melinda Sara 1953- *IntWWM 77, -80*
Maxwell, Michael 1936- *IntWWM 77, -80*
Maxwell, Michael Somerset Cullen 1921- *IntWWM 77, -80, WhoMus 72*
Maxwell, Peter 1921- *IlWWBF*
Maxwell, Philip 1901- *AmSCAP 66*
Maxwell, Richard Williams 1879-1953 *AmSCAP 66*
Maxwell, Richard Williams 1896-1954 *AmSCAP 80*
Maxwell, Robert 1921- *AmSCAP 66, -80, RkOn 2A*
Maxwell, Roberta *NotNAT*
Maxwell, Sanders 1917- *AmSCAP 80*
Maxwell, Spencer 1937- *AmSCAP 80*
Maxwell, Vera K d1950 *NotNAT B*
Maxwell, Victor *CreCan 2*
Maxwell, Walter 1877- *WhThe*
Maxwell Davies, Peter 1934- *BnBkM 80, DcCM*
Maxwell Street Jimmy *BluesWW*
Maxwell-Timmins, Donald 1927- *IntWWM 77, -80, WhoMus 72*
Maxylewicz, Vincentius 1685-1745 *NewGrD 80*
Maxylewicz, Wincenty 1685-1745 *NewGrD 80*
May, Ada 1900- *WhThe*
May, Akerman 1869-1933 *NotNAT B, WhThe*
May, Ann *Film 1, -2*
May, Billy 1916- *BgBands 74[port], CmpEPM, EncJzS 70, RkOn, WhoJazz 72*
May, Daryl 1936- *AmSCAP 80*
May, Donald *ForYSC, WhoHol A*
May, Doris *Film 1, -2, MotPP, TwYS*
May, E William 1916- *BiDAmM, EncJzS 70*
May, Earl Charles Barrington 1927- *BiDAmM*
May, Edna d1948 *AmPS B, Film 1, MotPP, WhoHol B*
May, Edna 1875-1948 *NotNAT B, WhoStg 1906, -1908*
May, Edna 1878-1948 *EncMT, WhThe*
May, Edna 1879-1948 *WhScrn 74, -77*
May, Edward Charles 1900- *AmSCAP 80*
May, Edward Collet 1806-1887 *Baker 78*
May, Edward Collett 1806-1887 *NewGrD 80*
May, Elaine *ForYSC, IntMPA 75, -76*
May, Elaine 1932- *BiE&WWA, ConDr 73, -77, ConLC 16, Ent, FilmEn, FilmgC, HalFC 80, IntMPA 77, -78, -79, -80, JoeFr[port], MotPP, NotNAT, PlP&P[port], WhoHol A, WhoThe 72, -77, WomWMM*
May, Ernest Dewey 1942- *IntWWM 77, -80*
May, Florence 1845-1923 *Baker 78, NewGrD 80*

May, Frederick 1911- *NewGrD 80*
May, Gisela 1924- *EncWT*
May, Gustav *Film 2*
May, Hans 1891-1959 *FilmgC, HalFC 80, NotNAT B, WhThe*
May, Harold R 1903-1973 *WhScrn 77, WhoHol B*
May, Henrietta Mabel 1884- *CreCan 1*
May, Jack 1922- *WhoThe 77*
May, James 1857-1941 *WhScrn 74, -77*
May, Jane *WhThe*
May, Joe 1880-1954 *BiDFilm, -81, DcFM, FilmEn, FilmgC, HalFC 80, OxFilm, WorEFlm*
May, Lola *Film 1*
May, Marty 1898-1975 *WhScrn 77*
May, Mia *Film 2*
May, Nina *MotPP*
May, Olive d1938 *NotNAT B, WhoStg 1908*
May, Olive d1947 *NotNAT B*
May, Pamela 1917- *CnOxB, DancEn 78, WhThe*
May, Paul 1909- *DcFM*
May, Robert Arden 1948- *AmSCAP 80*
May, Samuel Roderick 1910-1963 *WhScrn 74, -77*
May, Val 1927- *NotNAT, WhoThe 72, -77*
May, Walter B 1931- *ConAmC*
May-Czyzowska, Teresa 1935- *WhoOp 76*
Mayakovski, Vladimir 1893-1930 *CnMD*
Mayakovsky, Vladimir Vladimirovich 1893-1930 *CnThe, Ent, FilmEn, McGEWD[port], ModWD, REnWD[port]*
Mayakovsky, Vladimir Vladimirovich 1894-1930 *EncWT, NotNAT A, -B, OxFilm, OxThe, PlP&P*
Mayall, Herschel 1863-1941 *Film 1, -2, TwYS, WhoHol B*
Mayall, Hershell 1863-1941 *WhScrn 74, -77*
Mayall, John 1933- *BluesWW[port], ConMuA 80A, EncJzS 70, IlEncR[port], RkOn 2[port]*
Mayama, Miko *WhoHol A*
Mayberry, Lyndell H 1920- *IntMPA 75, -76*
Maybrick, Michael 1844-1913 *Baker 78, NotNAT B*
Maye, Bernyce d1962 *NotNAT B*
Maye, Jimsy 1894-1968 *WhScrn 77*
Mayeda, Akio 1935- *IntWWM 77*
Mayehoff, Eddie *IntMPA 77, -75, -76, -78, -79, -80, WhoHol A*
Mayehoff, Eddie 1911- *FilmgC, ForYSC, HalFC 80*
Mayehoff, Eddie 1914?- *BiE&WWA, NotNAT*
Mayer *NewGrD 80*
Mayer, Abby S 1928- *IntWWM 77, -80*
Mayer, Albert *Film 2*
Mayer, Alfred 1921- *IntWWM 77, -80*
Mayer, Arthur E 1918- *AmSCAP 66, -80*
Mayer, Arthur Loeb 1886- *IntMPA 79, -80*
Mayer, Arthur Loeb 1888- *IntMPA 77, -75, -76, -78*
Mayer, Ben 1925- *IntMPA 77, -75, -76, -78, -79, -80*
Mayer, Carl 1894-1944 *BiDFilm, -81, DcFM, FilmEn, FilmgC, HalFC 80, OxFilm, WorEFlm*
Mayer, Charles *WhoHol A*
Mayer, Charles 1799-1862 *Baker 78, NewGrD 80, OxMus*
Mayer, Daniel 1856-1928 *NotNAT B, WhThe*
Mayer, Doe *WomWMM B*
Mayer, Dorothy 1886-1974 *NewGrD 80*
Mayer, Dot d1964 *NotNAT B*
Mayer, Edwin Justus 1896?-1960 *FilmEn, McGEWD[port], ModWD, PlP&P, WhThe*
Mayer, Edwin Justus 1897-1960 *CnMD, NotNAT B*
Mayer, Frederic David 1931- *WhoOp 76*
Mayer, Frederick Christian 1882-1973 *Baker 78*
Mayer, Gaston 1869-1923 *NotNAT B, WhThe*
Mayer, George Louis 1929- *IntWWM 77, -80*
Mayer, Gerald 1919- *FilmEn, FilmgC, HalFC 80, IntMPA 77, -75, -76, -78, -79, -80*
Mayer, Lady Gertrude Dorothy 1886- *WhoMus 72*
Mayer, Giovanni Simone *NewGrD 80*
Mayer, Gunther 1930- *IntWWM 77, -80*
Mayer, Gyula *NewGrD 80*
Mayer, Henri d1941 *NotNAT B*
Mayer, Henry d1941 *WhThe*
Mayer, Ira 1952- *ConAmTC*
Mayer, Johann Baptist *NewGrD 80*
Mayer, Johann David 1636-1696 *NewGrD 80*
Mayer, Johannes Simon *NewGrD 80*
Mayer, John 1930- *IntWWM 80, NewGrD 80, WhoMus 72*
Mayer, Joseph Anton 1855-1936 *Baker 78*
Mayer, Josepha *NewGrD 80*
Mayer, Julius *NewGrD 80*
Mayer, Lori 1960- *AmSCAP 80*
Mayer, Louis B 1885-1957 *BiDFilm, -81, DcFM, FilmEn, FilmgC, HalFC 80, NotNAT B, OxFilm, TwYS B, WomWMM, WorEFlm*
Mayer, Louis B 1895-1957 *MGM A[port]*
Mayer, Lutz 1934- *ConAmC*
Mayer, Marcus d1918 *NotNAT B*
Mayer, Max 1859-1931 *Baker 78*
Mayer, Michael F 1917- *IntMPA 77, -75, -76, -78, -79, -80*
Mayer, Mike *ConMuA 80B*
Mayer, Natalie 1925- *AmSCAP 66*
Mayer, Nathaniel *RkOn*
Mayer, Paul M 1914-1968 *WhScrn 74, -77*
Mayer, Renee 1900- *WhThe*
Mayer, Robert 1879- *IntWWM 77, -80, NewGrD 80, WhoMus 72*
Mayer, Robert Alfred 1916- *IntWWM 77*
Mayer, Roger Laurance 1926- *IntMPA 80*
Mayer, Seymour R 1910- *IntMPA 77, -75, -76, -78, -79*
Mayer, Seymour R 1912- *IntMPA 80*
Mayer, Sylvain d1948 *NotNAT B*
Mayer, Thelma 1932- *AmSCAP 80*
Mayer, Werner *NewGrD 80*
Mayer, Wilhelm 1831-1898 *Baker 78, NewGrD 80*
Mayer, William 1925- *AmSCAP 66, Baker 78, CpmDNM 72, -75, -80, ConAmC, DcCM*
Mayer, William Robert 1925- *AmSCAP 80*
Mayer-Lismann, Else Mitia 1914- *IntWWM 77, -80, WhoMus 72*
Mayer-Mahr, Moritz 1869-1947 *Baker 78*
Mayer-Martin, Donna Jean 1947- *IntWWM 77, -80*
Mayer-Reinach, Albert 1876-1954 *Baker 78*
Mayer-Serra, Otto 1904-1968 *Baker 78, NewGrD 80*
Mayerl, Billy 1902-1959 *NewGrD 80, NotNAT B, WhThe*
Mayerl, William Joseph 1902-1959 *NewGrD 80*
Mayers, Benedict 1906- *AmSCAP 66, -80*
Mayers, Lloyd G 1929- *EncJzS 70*
Mayers, Wilmette K d1964 *NotNAT B*
Mayes, Ethel *BluesWW*
Mayes, Herbert 1910- *WhoMus 72*
Mayes, Wendell 1918- *CmMov, HalFC 80, IntMPA 77, -75, -76, -78, -79, -80, WorEFlm*
Mayeur, E F 1866- *WhThe*
Mayfield, Cleo 1897-1954 *CmpEPM, NotNAT B, WhScrn 74, -77, WhThe, WhoHol B*
Mayfield, Curtis 1942- *BiDAmM, ConMuA 80A, -80B, DrBlPA, IlEncR[port], RkOn 2[port]*
Mayfield, Julian 1928- *BlkAmP, DrBlPA, MorBAP*
Mayfield, Lida Louise Kendrick 1948- *IntWWM 77, -80*
Mayfield, Olga Gene 1928- *IntWWM 77*
Mayfield, Peggy Jean Jordan 1934- *IntWWM 77*
Mayfield, Percy 1920- *BluesWW[port]*
Mayger, Graham 1942- *IntWWM 77, -80, WhoMus 72*
Mayhall, Jerome d1964 *NotNAT B*
Mayhew, Charles 1908- *WhThe*
Mayhew, Henry 1812-1887 *DcPup, NotNAT B*
Mayhew, Horace d1872 *NotNAT B*
Mayhew, Kate 1853-1944 *Film 2, NotNAT B, WhScrn 74, -77, WhoHol B*
Mayhew, Nye *BgBands 74, CmpEPM*
Mayhew, Stella 1875-1934 *BiDAmM, NotNAT B, WhoHol B*
Mayhew, William 1889-1951 *AmSCAP 66, -80*
Mayhuet De Joan *NewGrD 80*
Maykapar, Samuil 1867-1938 *Baker 78*
Mayl, Gene 1928- *EncJzS 70*
Mayland, Jacob *NewGrD 80*
Mayland, Jakob *NewGrD 80*
Maylath, Heinrich 1827-1883 *Baker 78*
Mayleas, Ruth 1925- *BiE&WWA, NotNAT*
Maylon, Eily 1879-1961 *FilmgC, Vers B[port]*
Maynard, Bill 1928?- *HalFC 80*
Maynard, Claire 1912-1941 *WhScrn 74, -77, WhoHol B*
Maynard, Gertrude d1953 *NotNAT B*
Maynard, John 1577-1614? *NewGrD 80, OxMus*
Maynard, Ken 1885- *What 4[port]*
Maynard, Ken 1895-1973 *FilmEn, Film 2, FilmgC, ForYSC, HalFC 80, IlEncCM, MotPP, MovMk, TwYS, WhScrn 77, WhoHol B*
Maynard, Kermit 1898-1971 *FilmgC, HalFC 80*
Maynard, Kermit 1902-1971 *FilmEn, Film 2, ForYSC, WhScrn 74, -77, WhoHol B*
Maynard, Olga 1920- *CnOxB*
Maynard, Ruth 1913- *BiE&WWA, NotNAT*
Maynard, Tex *Film 2, TwYS*
Maynard, Walter *OxMus*
Mayne, Clarice 1886-1966 *OxThe, WhThe*
Mayne, Clarice 1890-1966 *WhScrn 77*
Mayne, Eric 1866-1947 *Film 2, NotNAT B, WhScrn 74, -77, WhoHol B*
Mayne, Ernie *WhThe*
Mayne, Ferdy *WhoHol A*
Mayne, Ferdy 1916- *FilmgC, HalFC 80*
Mayne, Ferdy 1920- *WhoThe 72, -77*
Mayne, Rutherford 1878-1967 *CnThe, OxThe, REnWD[port]*
Mayner, Giorgio *NewGrD 80*
Maynerius, Giorgio *NewGrD 80*
Maynor, Dorothy 1910- *Baker 78, BiDAmM, DrBlPA, MusSN[port], NewGrD 80*
Mayo, Albert 1887-1933 *WhScrn 74, -77*
Mayo, Archie L 1891-1968 *BiDFilm, -81, FilmEn, FilmgC, HalFC 80, WorEFlm*
Mayo, Archie L 1898-1968 *TwYS A, WhScrn 74, -77*
Mayo, Cass *AmSCAP 80*
Mayo, Christine *Film 2*
Mayo, Edna 1893-1970 *Film 1, MotPP, TwYS, WhScrn 77*
Mayo, Frank 1839-1896 *NotNAT B*
Mayo, Frank 1886-1963 *Film 1, -2, MotPP, NotNAT B, PlP&P, TwYS, WhScrn 74, -77, WhoHol B*
Mayo, Frank 1889-1963 *ForYSC*
Mayo, Mrs. Frank d1896 *NotNAT B*
Mayo, George 1891-1950 *WhScrn 74, -77, WhoHol B*
Mayo, Giovan Tomaso Di *NewGrD 80*
Mayo, Harry A 1898-1964 *NotNAT B, WhScrn 74, -77, WhoHol B*
Mayo, Joseph Anthony 1930-1966 *WhScrn 74, -77*
Mayo, Margaret 1882-1951 *NotNAT B, WhThe, WhoStg 1908*
Mayo, Nick 1922- *BiE&WWA, NotNAT*
Mayo, Nine *WomWMM*
Mayo, Sam 1881-1938 *NotNAT B, WhThe*
Mayo, Virginia *IntMPA 77, -75, -76, -78, -79, -80, MotPP*
Mayo, Virginia 1920- *FilmEn, FilmgC, HalFC 80[port], MovMk, WorEFlm*
Mayo, Virginia 1922- *BiDFilm, -81, ForYSC, WhoHol A*
Mayo, Whitman 1930- *DrBlPA*
Mayone, Ascanio 1565?-1627 *NewGrD 80*
Mayor, Agustin G 1935-1968 *WhScrn 74, -77*
Mayor, Augustin 1935-1968 *WhoHol B*
Mayorga, Margaret 1894- *BiE&WWA*
Mayr *NewGrD 80*
Mayr, Giovanni Simone 1763-1845 *NewGrD 80*
Mayr, Richard 1877-1935 *Baker 78, BnBkM 80, CmOp, MusSN[port], NewEOp 71, NewGrD 80*
Mayr, Rupert Erich 1926- *IntWWM 77, -80*
Mayr, Rupert Ignaz 1646-1712 *NewGrD 80*
Mayr, Simon 1763-1845 *Baker 78, NewGrD 80, OxMus*
Mayr, Simone 1763-1845 *MusMk*
Mayr, Wolfgang *NewGrD 80*

Mayron, Melanie *WhoHol A*
Mays, Carl W 1943- *AmSCAP 80*
Mays, Curley 1938- *BluesWW*
Mays, Livingston *BlksBF*
Mays, Lyle David 1953- *EncJzS 70*
Mays, Peyton *ConMuA 80B*
Mays, Sally Ann 1930- *IntWWM 80*
Mays, Walter A *ConAmC*
Mays, William Allen 1944- *AmSCAP 80*
Mayseder, Josef 1789-1863 *OxMus*
Mayseder, Joseph 1789-1863 *Baker 78, NewGrD 80*
Mayshuet *NewGrD 80*
Maysles, Al *OxFilm*
Maysles, Albert 1926- *ConLC 16, FilmEn, WorEFlm*
Maysles, Albert 1933- *DcFM, FilmgC, HalFC 80*
Maysles, David *OxFilm*
Maysles, David 1931- *DcFM, FilmgC, HalFC 80*
Maysles, David 1932- *ConLC 16, FilmEn, WorEFlm*
Maystre, Matthaeus Le *NewGrD 80*
Mayuto 1943- *EncJzS 70*
Mayuzumi, Toshiro 1929- *Baker 78, DcCM, NewGrD 80*
Maywood, Augusta 1825-1876 *CnOxB*
Maywood, Augusta 1825-1876? *DancEn 78[port]*
Mazak, Alberik 1609-1661 *NewGrD 80*
Mazarin, Cardinal 1602-1661 *OxMus*
Mazarin, Jules 1602-1661 *NewGrD 80*
Mazas, Jacques-Fereol 1782-1849 *Baker 78, NewGrD 80, OxMus*
Mazaud, Emile 1884- *McGEWD*
Mazel', Lev Abramovich 1907- *NewGrD 80*
Mazer, Henry *IntWWM 77, -80*
Mazer, Johan *OxMus*
Mazetti, Georgia *Film 2*
Mazilier, Joseph 1797-1868 *DancEn 78*
Mazilier, Joseph 1801-1868 *CnOxB*
Mazlen, Ann 1918- *AmSCAP 80*
Mazlen, Henry Gershwin 1912- *AmSCAP 66, -80*
Mazuel, Michel 1603-1676 *NewGrD 80*
Mazur, Albert 1929- *AmSCAP 66, -80*
Mazur, Krzyaztof Antoni 1929- *IntWWM 77, -80*
Mazur, Marion Claire 1920- *AmSCAP 80*
Mazura, Franz *WhoOp 76*
Mazurki, Mike 1909- *FilmEn, FilmgC, ForYSC, HalFC 80, HolCA[port], IntMPA 77, -75, -76, -78, -79, -80, Vers A[port], WhoHol A*
Mazurok, Yuri Antonovich 1931- *WhoOp 76*
Mazurok, Yury 1931- *NewGrD 80*
Mazursky, Paul 1930- *BiDFilm, -81, FilmEn, FilmgC, IntMPA 77, -75, -76, -78, -79, -80, MovMk[port], WhoHol A*
Mazursky, Paul 1938?- *HalFC 80*
Mazza, Jim *ConMuA 80B*
Mazza, Jose 1735?-1797 *NewGrD 80*
Mazza, Lynne S 1949- *IntWWM 80*
Mazza Ferrata, Giovanni Battista d1691 *NewGrD 80*
Mazzacurati, Benedetto 1898- *WhoMus 72*
Mazzaferrata, Giovanni Battista d1691 *NewGrD 80*
Mazzaferro, Giorgio *NewGrD 80*
Mazzarini, Giulio Raimondo *NewGrD 80*
Mazzarini, Giulio Raimondo 1602-1661 *NewGrD 80*
Mazzato, Umberto *Film 1*
Mazzeo, Rosario 1911- *IntWWM 77, -80*
Mazzetti, Lorenza *WomWMM*
Mazzi, Luigi *NewGrD 80*
Mazzi, Prospero *NewGrD 80*
Mazzinghi, Joseph 1765-1844 *Baker 78, NewGrD 80, OxMus*
Mazzini, Guido 1923- *WhoOp 76*
Mazzo, Kay 1946- *CnOxB*
Mazzocchi, Domenico 1592-1665 *Baker 78, NewGrD 80*
Mazzocchi, Virgilio 1597-1646 *Baker 78, NewGrD 80*
Mazzochi, Domenico 1592-1665 *OxMus*
Mazzochi, Virgilio 1597-1646 *OxMus*
Mazzola, John W 1928- *BiE&WWA, NotNAT*
Mazzolani, Antonio 1819-1900 *Baker 78*
Mazzoleni, Ettore 1905-1968 *Baker 78, CreCan 2, NewGrD 80*
Mazzoli, Ferruccio 1931- *WhoOp 76*
Mazzone, Marc'Antonio 1540?-1593? *NewGrD 80*
Mazzoni, Antonio 1717-1785 *NewGrD 80*
Mazzoni, Francesco d1576? *NewGrD 80*
Mazzucato, Alberto 1813-1877 *Baker 78, NewGrD 80*
Mazzucato, Daniela 1946- *WhoOp 76*
Mazzucato, Gian Andrea *NewGrD 80*
Mbande, Venancio Notico 1928- *IntWWM 77, -80*
M'Boom Re:percussion *EncJzS 70*
MC Five *BiDAmM*
McAdoo, Moira *WhoMus 72*
McAfee, Carlton Fred, Jr. 1938- *ConAmC*
McAfee, Don 1935- *CpmDNM 74, ConAmC*
McAfee, Johnny 1913- *CmpEPM*
McAlister, Mary *WhoHol A*
McAllister, Claude *Film 2, ForYSC*
McAllister, D C 1853-1920 *BiDAmM*
McAllister, David *AmSCAP 80*
McAllister, Forrest Lee 1912- *IntWWM 77, -80*
McAllister, Mary 1910- *Film 1, -2, TwYS*
McAllister, Maureen 1941- *IntWWM 77, -80*
McAllister, Paul 1875-1955 *WhScrn 77*
McAllister, Paul 1875-1959 *Film 1, -2, TwYS*
McAllister, Robert Charles 1935- *AmSCAP 80*
McAllister, Ward *Film 2*
McAlpin, Donald *Film 2*
McAlpin, Edith *Film 1*
McAlpine, Jane *Film 1*
McAlpine, William 1925- *WhoMus 72*
McAnally, Ray 1926- *WhoHol A, WhoThe 72, -77*
McAnaney, Harold 1948- *ConAmC*
McAndrew, Marianne 1938- *FilmgC, HalFC 80, WhoHol A*
McAndrew, William R d1968 *NewYTET*
McArdle, J F *WhThe*
McArthur, Edwin Douglas 1907- *AmSCAP 66, -80, WhoMus 72, WhoOp 76*
McArthur, Molly 1900- *WhThe*
McArthur, Peter 1866-1924 *CreCan 2*
M'Carthy, Justin Huntly 1860-1936 *WhThe*
McAtee, Ben 1903-1961 *NotNAT B, WhScrn 74, -77*
McAtee, Clyde 1880-1947 *Film 2, WhScrn 74, -77, WhoHol B*
McAuliff, Leon 1917- *CounME 74, -74A, EncFCWM 69*
McAuliffe, Eugene B 1893- *AmSCAP 66*
McAuliffe, Leon 1917- *AmSCAP 66, IlEncCM*
McAuliffe, William Leon 1917- *AmSCAP 80, BiDAmM*
McAvity, Thomas A d1972 *NewYTET*
McAvoy, Charles 1885-1953 *WhScrn 77*
McAvoy, May 1901- *FilmEn, Film 1, -2, ForYSC, HalFC 80, MotPP, MovMk, ThFT[port], TwYS, What 3[port], WhoHol A*
McBain, Diane 1941- *ForYSC, HalFC 80, MotPP, WhoHol A*
McBan, Mickey *Film 2*
McBay, A Douglas 1943- *IntWWM 77*
McBay, Alexander Douglas 1943- *IntWWM 80*
McBeath, Barry Mitchell 1921- *IntWWM 77*
McBee, Cecil 1935- *EncJzS 70*
McBeth, Edith *PupTheA*
McBeth, William Francis 1933- *AmSCAP 80, CpmDNM 80, ConAmC*
McBirney, Mara 1905- *CreCan 1*
McBirney, Mona 1905- *CreCan 1*
McBride, Carl 1894-1937 *WhScrn 74, -77*
McBride, Donald 1889-1957 *Film 1, ForYSC, WhScrn 74, -77*
McBride, Donald 1894-1957 *FilmgC, HalFC 80*
McBride, John S d1961 *NotNAT B*
McBride, Mary Margaret 1899- *What 3[port]*
McBride, Patricia *DancEn 78[port]*
McBride, Patricia 1942- *CnOxB, WhoHol A*
McBride, Robert *DancEn 78*
McBride, Robert Guyn 1911- *Baker 78, BiDAmM, ConAmC, DcCM, NewGrD 80, OxMus*
McBrien, Roger Ralph 1943- *AmSCAP 80*
McBroom, Marcia 1947- *DrBlPA*
McBrown, Gertrude Parthenic *BlkAmP*
McBrowne, Lenny 1933- *EncJzS 70*
McBrowne, Leonard Lewis 1933- *BiDAmM*
McBrowne, Leonard Louis 1933- *EncJzS 70*
McBryde, Donald M 1937- *NotNAT*
McCabe, Charles C 1836-1906 *BiDAmM*
McCabe, Charles Henry, III 1944- *AmSCAP 80*
McCabe, George d1917 *WhScrn 77*
McCabe, Harry 1881-1925 *WhScrn 74, -77, WhoHol B*
McCabe, John 1939- *Baker 78, CpmDNM 80, CnOxB, IntWWM 77, -80, MusMk, NewGrD 80, WhoMus 72*
McCabe, May 1873-1949 *NotNAT B, WhScrn 74, -77*
McCabe, Robin 1949- *IntWWM 77, -80*
McCadden, Margaret Cole *PupTheA*
McCain, Barry Reid 1951- *IntWWM 77, -80*
McCain, Jerry 1930- *BluesWW[port]*
McCaldin, Denis 1933- *IntWWM 77, -80*
McCaldin, Denis James 1933- *WhoMus 72*
McCall, C W 1928- *RkOn 2[port]*
McCall, C W 1929- *IlEncCM*
McCall, Daniel B, Jr. 1937- *IntWWM 77*
McCall, Harlo E 1909- *AmSCAP 66*
McCall, Leonard 1910- *AmSCAP 66, -80*
McCall, Lizzie d1942 *NotNAT B*
McCall, Mary Ann 1919- *CmpEPM*
McCall, Mitzi *WhoHol A*
McCall, Monica *BiE&WWA, NotNAT*
McCall, Sherrie Hughes 1947- *AmSCAP 80*
McCall, William 1879-1938 *Film 1, WhScrn 74, -77, WhoHol B*
McCalla, Irish *WhoHol A*
McCalla, Irish 1928- *ForYSC*
McCalla, Irish 1929- *WhoHrs 80*
McCalla, Vernon *BlksB&W C*
McCallin, Clement 1913- *WhoThe 72, -77*
McCallister, Lon 1923- *FilmEn, FilmgC, ForYSC, HalFC 80, HolP 40[port], MotPP, What 4[port], WhoHol A*
McCallister, Raymond E 1933- *IntWWM 77*
McCallum, David 1933- *FilmEn, FilmgC, ForYSC, HalFC 80, IlWWBF, IntMPA 77, -75, -76, -78, -79, -80, MotPP, MovMk[port], WhoHol A, WhoMus 72*
McCallum, John *WhoHol A*
McCallum, John 1917- *FilmgC, HalFC 80*
McCallum, John 1918- *IlWWBF, IntMPA 77, -75, -76, -78, -79, -80, WhoThe 72, -77*
McCallum, Neil 1929-1976 *HalFC 80, WhoHol A*
McCally, David 1935- *NotNAT*
McCalmon, George A 1909- *BiE&WWA*
McCambridge, Mercedes 1918- *BiE&WWA, FilmEn, FilmgC, ForYSC, HalFC 80, IntMPA 77, -75, -76, -78, -79, -80, MotPP, MovMk[port], NotNAT, OxFilm, WhoHol A*
McCammon, Bessie J d1964 *NotNAT B*
McCance, Larry 1917-1970 *CreCan 2*
McCandless, Paul 1947- *EncJzS 70*
McCandless, Stanley Russell 1897-1967 *BiE&WWA, NotNAT B*
McCann, Charles Andrew d1927 *WhScrn 74, -77, WhoHol B*
McCann, Chuck *WhoHol A*
McCann, Frances 1922-1963 *WhScrn 77*
McCann, John R 1933- *IntWWM 77, -80*
McCann, Les 1935- *AmSCAP 66, DrBlPA, EncJzS 70*
McCann, Leslie Coleman 1935- *BiDAmM, EncJzS 70*
McCann, Norman *WhoMus 72*
McCarey, Leo 1898-1969 *AmFD, AmSCAP 66, -80, BiDFilm, -81, DcFM, FilmEn, FilmgC, HalFC 80, MovMk[port], OxFilm, TwYS A, WorEFlm*
McCarey, Ray 1904-1948 *FilmEn, FilmgC, HalFC 80*
McCarroll, Frank d1954 *WhScrn 74, -77, WhoHol B*
McCarroll, Jesse Cornelius 1933- *IntWWM 77, -80*
McCarron, Charles 1891-1919 *AmSCAP 66, -80*

McCarten, John 1916-1974 *BiE&WWA, NotNAT B*
McCarthy, Charles J 1903-1960 *AmSCAP 66, -80*
McCarthy, Charlie *JoeFr*
McCarthy, Charlotte Ellen 1918- *AmSCAP 66, -80*
McCarthy, Daniel 1869- *WhThe*
McCarthy, David Wyn 1931- *WhoMus 72*
McCarthy, Dinitia Smith *WomWMM A, -B*
McCarthy, Earl *Film 2*
McCarthy, Eileen *IntWWM 77, -80*
McCarthy, Frank 1912- *FilmgC, HalFC 80, IntMPA 77, -75, -76, -78, -79, -80*
McCarthy, J P *Film 1*
McCarthy, John 1919- *NewGrD 80, WhoMus 72*
McCarthy, John P 1885- *TwYS A*
McCarthy, Joseph 1885-1943 *AmPS, AmSCAP 66, -80, BiDAmM, CmpEPM, EncMT, NewCBMT, Sw&Ld C*
McCarthy, Joseph 1905-1957 *FilmgC, HalFC 80*
McCarthy, Joseph Allan 1922-1975 *AmSCAP 66, -80*
McCarthy, Justin Huntly 1860-1936 *ModWD, NotNAT B*
McCarthy, Kevin 1914- *BiE&WWA, FilmEn, FilmgC, ForYSC, HalFC 80, IntMPA 77, -75, -76, -78, -79, -80, MovMk, NotNAT, WhoHol A, WhoHrs 80, WhoThe 72, -77*
McCarthy, Kevin James 1944- *AmSCAP 80*
McCarthy, Lillah 1875-1960 *NotNAT A, -B, OxThe, WhThe*
McCarthy, Lin *WhoHol A*
McCarthy, Margaret Patricia 1928- *IntWWM 80*
McCarthy, Mary 1912- *BiE&WWA, NotNAT*
McCarthy, Michael 1917-1959 *FilmgC, HalFC 80, IIWWBF*
McCarthy, Myles d1928 *Film 2, WhScrn 74, -77, WhoHol B*
McCarthy, Neil *WhoHol A*
McCarthy, Nobu *ForYSC, WhoHol A*
McCarthy, Pat 1911-1943 *WhScrn 74, -77*
McCarthy, Robert Sylvester, III 1949- *AmSCAP 80*
McCartney, Francine *PupTheA*
McCartney, John Paul 1942- *Baker 78*
McCartney, Paul 1942- *ConMuA 80A[port], -80B, FilmEn, ForYSC, IlEncR[port], IntWWM 77, MotPP, NewGrD 80, WhoHol A*
McCartney, Paul & Wings *RkOn 2[port]*
McCarty, E Clayton 1901- *BiE&WWA, NotNAT*
McCarty, Frank L 1941- *CpmDNM 72, ConAmC, IntWWM 77, -80*
McCarty, Joe Lawrence 1905- *AmSCAP 80*
McCarty, Mary 1923- *WhoHol A, WhoThe 72, -77*
McCarty, Mary Helen *ConAmC*
McCarty, Patrick 1928- *ConAmC*
McCaslin, Walter *ConAmTC*
McCathren, Don 1925- *AmSCAP 66*
McCathren, Donald Eugene 1924- *AmSCAP 80, IntWWM 77, -80*
McCauley, Edna d1919 *WhScrn 77*
McCauley, Jack 1900- *EncMT*
McCauley, Jackie *ConMuA 80B*
McCauley, John J 1937- *IntWWM 77, -80*
McCauley, William 1917- *Baker 78, CpmDNM 75*
McCaw, John 1918- *IntWWM 77, -80, WhoMus 72*
McCay, Peggy *WhoHol A*
McCay, Percy 1896- *NewOrJ[port]*
McCay, Thompson 1901-1963 *NewOrJ[port]*
McCay, Winsor 1886- *FilmEn, HalFC 80, WorEFlm*
McChesney, James 1941- *IntWWM 77, -80*
McClain, Billy *BlksB&W C*
McClain, Billy 1857-1950 *WhScrn 74, -77, WhoHol B*
McClain, Billy 1866-1949 *BlksBF[port]*
McClain, Charles S 1929- *IntWWM 77*
McClain, Floyd A 1917- *ConAmC*
McClain, John Wilcox 1904-1967 *BiE&WWA, NotNAT B*
McClain, Saundra *MorBAP*
McClanahan, David Russell 1948- *ConAmC*
McClanahan, Rue *WhoHol A, WhoThe 77*
McClarty, Jack 1938- *IntWWM 77, -80*
McClay, Clyde 1895-1939 *WhScrn 74, -77*
McClean, Richard 1898-1968 *NewOrJ*
McCleary, Diana Rae 1941- *IntWWM 77*
McCleary, Fiona 1900- *AmSCAP 66, -80, ConAmC A*
McCleary, Harriet 1947- *IntWWM 77*
McCleary, Millard A *ConAmC*
McCleery, Albert d1972 *NotNAT B*
McCleery, Janet Mary 1943- *IntWWM 77, -80*
McClellan, Hurd d1933 *WhScrn 74, -77*
McClellan, John Jasper 1874-1925 *Baker 78, ConAmC*
McClellan, Randall *ConAmC*
McClellan, William Monson 1934- *IntWWM 77, -80*
McClelland, Allan 1917- *WhoThe 72, -77*
McClelland, Curtis *PupTheA*
McClelland, Donald 1903-1955 *NotNAT B, WhScrn 77*
McClendon, Ernestine 1918- *BiE&WWA, DrBlPA, WhoHol A*
McClendon, Rose 1885-1936 *BlkAmP, DrBlPA, NotNAT B*
McClennan, Tommy 1908-1958? *BluesWW[port]*
McClennon, Rube *NewOrJ*
McCleod, Norman Z 1898-1964 *WorEFlm*
McClintic, Guthrie 1893-1961 *EncWT, NotNAT A, -B, OxThe, WhThe*
McClintic, Lambert Gerhardt, Jr. 1946- *AmSCAP 80*
McClintock, Ernie *DrBlPA*
McClintock, Harry Kirby 1882-1957 *AmSCAP 66, -80, CounME 74, -74A*
McClintock, Robert Bayles 1946- *IntWWM 77, -80*
McClinton, O B 1940- *CounME 74[port], -74A*
McClinton, O B 1942- *IlEncCM[port]*
McClinton, Osbie Burnett 1940- *AmSCAP 80*
McClory, Kevin 1926- *FilmgC, HalFC 80*
McClory, Sean *WhoHol A*
McClory, Sean 1923- *FilmgC, HalFC 80*
McClory, Sean 1924- *ForYSC, IntMPA 77, -75, -76, -78, -79, -80, Vers B[port]*
McCloskey, Elizabeth H 1870-1942 *WhScrn 74, -77*
McCloskey, James R 1918- *BiE&WWA*
McClung, Bobby 1921-1945 *WhScrn 74, -77*
McClung, Nellie Letitia 1873-1951 *CreCan 1*
McClung, Robert d1945 *WhoHol B*
McClure, A W *Film 1*
McClure, Bud 1886-1942 *WhScrn 74, -77, WhoHol B*
McClure, Doug 1934- *ForYSC*
McClure, Doug 1935- *FilmEn, HalFC 80, MotPP, WhoHol A*
McClure, Doug 1938- *WhoHrs 80*
McClure, Douglas 1935- *FilmgC*
McClure, Frank 1895-1960 *WhScrn 77, WhoHol B*
McClure, Greg 1918- *FilmgC, HalFC 80*
McClure, Gregg 1918- *ForYSC*
McClure, Irene d1928 *WhScrn 74, -77*
McClure, Michael 1932- *ConDr 73, -77, NatPD[port]*
McClure, Ron 1941- *EncJzS 70*
McClure, Ronald Dix 1941- *AmSCAP 80, BiDAmM, EncJzS 70*
McClure, Wendy 1934- *IntMPA 77, -75, -76, -78, -79, -80*
McClure, William K 1922- *IntMPA 77, -75, -76, -78, -79, -80*
McColl, William Duncan 1933- *IntWWM 77, -80*
McCollin, Frances 1892-1960 *AmSCAP 66, -80, BiDAmM, ConAmC*
McCollom, Thomas Oscar 1934- *IntWWM 77, -80*
McCollum, John Morris 1922- *WhoMus 72, WhoOp 76*
McComas, Annette *MorBAP*
McComas, Carroll d1962 *Film 1, NotNAT B*
McComas, Carroll 1886-1962 *WhScrn 74, -77, WhoHol B*
McComas, Carroll 1891-1962 *WhThe*
McComas, Glenn 1900-1959 *WhScrn 74, -77*
McComas, Lila 1906-1936 *WhScrn 74, -77*
McComb, Jeanne 1913- *AmSCAP 66*
McComb, Kate d1959 *NotNAT B*
McComb, William *MagIlD*
McConathy, Osbourne 1875-1949 *BiDAmM*
McConkey, Milton *PupTheA*
McConnaughey, George C d1966 *NewYTET*
McConnell, Forrest W d1962 *NotNAT B*
McConnell, Frederic *PlP&P[port]*
McConnell, George Burnham 1894- *AmSCAP 66, -80*
McConnell, Gladys 1907- *Film 2, TwYS, WhoHol A*
McConnell, Joseph H *NewYTET*
McConnell, Keith *WhoHol A*
McConnell, Lulu d1961 *NotNAT B*
McConnell, Lulu 1882-1962 *WhScrn 74, -77, WhoHol B*
McConnell, Mollie 1870-1920 *Film 1, WhoHol B*
McConnell, Molly 1870-1920 *WhScrn 74, -77*
McConville, Leo 1900-1968 *WhoJazz 72*
McCoo, Marilyn & Billy Davis, Jr. *RkOn 2[port]*
McCord, Betty *PupTheA*
McCord, Castor 1907-1963 *WhoJazz 72*
McCord, Kent *WhoHol A*
McCord, Mrs. Lewis d1917 *Film 1, WhScrn 77*
McCord, Nancy *WhThe*
McCord, Ted *IntMPA 75, -76*
McCord, Ted 1898-1976 *FilmEn*
McCord, Ted 1910-1976 *HalFC 80*
McCord, Ted 1912- *FilmgC, WorEFlm*
McCord, Vera *WomWMM*
McCord, William Patrick 1944- *AmSCAP 80*
McCorkle, Donald Macomber 1929-1978 *Baker 78, IntWWM 77, -80, NewGrD 80*
McCormac, Muriel *Film 2*
McCormack, Billie d1935 *WhScrn 74, -77*
McCormack, Frank *Film 2*
McCormack, Frank d1941 *NotNAT B*
McCormack, Hugh *Film 2*
McCormack, John 1884-1943 *CmOp*
McCormack, John 1884-1945 *Baker 78, BiDAmM, BnBkM 80[port], CmpEPM, FilmgC, HalFC 80, MusMk, MusSN[port], NewEOp 71, NewGrD 80, NotNAT B, WhScrn 74, -77, WhoHol B*
McCormack, Marni *WomWMM B*
McCormack, Patty 1945- *BiE&WWA, FilmEn, FilmgC, ForYSC, HalFC 80, MotPP, MovMk, NotNAT, WhoHol A, WhoHrs 80*
McCormack, Tom *BlkAmP*
McCormack, William M 1891-1953 *WhScrn 74, -77*
McCormick, Alyce 1904-1932 *WhScrn 74, -77, WhoHol B*
McCormick, Arthur Langdon d1954 *NotNAT B, WhThe*
McCormick, Clifford 1909- *AmSCAP 66, -80*
McCormick, F J d1948 *WhoHol B*
McCormick, F J 1891-1947 *FilmgC, HalFC 80, NotNAT B, WhScrn 74, -77*
McCormick, Loretta *PupTheA*
McCormick, Merrill d1953 *Film 2, WhoHol B*
McCormick, Myron 1907-1962 *FilmEn, WhThe*
McCormick, Myron 1908-1962 *FilmgC, ForYSC, HalFC 80, NotNAT B, WhScrn 74, -77, WhoHol B*
McCourt, Edward Alexander 1907-1972 *CreCan 2*
McCowan, Alex *PlP&P*
McCowan, Frances Hyland *CreCan 2*
McCowan, George *FilmgC, HalFC 80*
McCowen, Alec 1925- *CnThe, Ent[port], FilmgC, HalFC 80, MovMk, NotNAT, WhoHol A, WhoThe 72, -77*
McCown, Martha Rose *PupTheA*
McCoy, Bessie 1886?-1931 *AmPS B, CmpEPM*
McCoy, Bill d1975 *WhoHol C*
McCoy, Charles 1909-1950 *BluesWW*
McCoy, Charles R 1941- *AmSCAP 80*
McCoy, Charlie *IlEncR*
McCoy, Charlie 1941- *CounME 74[port], -74A, IlEncCM[port]*
McCoy, Clyde 1903- *AmPS A, BgBands 74, CmpEPM, Film 2, TwYS*

McCoy, D'Arcy *Film 2*
McCoy, Evelyn 1913- *Film 2*
McCoy, Frank d1947 *NotNAT B*
McCoy, Frederick Allan 1932- *BiDAmM*
McCoy, Gertrude 1896-1967 *Film 1, -2, TwYS, WhScrn 74, -77, WhoHol B*
McCoy, Hansen *Film 1*
McCoy, Harry 1894-1937 *FilmEn, Film 1, -2, TwYS, WhScrn 74, -77, WhoHol B*
McCoy, Hobart R 1897-1977 *AmSCAP 80*
McCoy, Joe 1905-1950 *BluesWW[port]*
McCoy, Kid *WhScrn 74, -77*
McCoy, Larry Gene 1940- *AmSCAP 80*
McCoy, Marvin M 1933- *IntWWM 77, -80*
McCoy, Minnie *BluesWW*
McCoy, Paul Bunyan 1930- *AmSCAP 80*
McCoy, Robert Edward 1910- *BluesWW*
McCoy, Robert Lee *BluesWW*
McCoy, Ruby *Film 2*
McCoy, Seth 1928- *BiDAmM*
McCoy, Sid *WhoHol A*
McCoy, Tim 1891-1978 *FilmEn, FilmgC, ForYSC, HalFC 80, IntMPA 77, -75, -76, -78, MotPP, TwYS, WhoHol A*
McCoy, Tim 1893- *Film 2*
McCoy, Van 1944- *ConMuA 80A, DrBlPA, RkOn 2[port]*
McCoy, Viola 1900?-1956? *BluesWW*
McCoy, Viola 1900?-1956 *CmpEPM*
McCoy, Violet *BluesWW[port]*
McCoy, Wesley Lawrence 1935- *IntWWM 77*
McCoy, William J 1848-1926 *Baker 78, BiDAmM*
McCoys *BiDAmM*
McCoys, The *RkOn 2[port]*
McCracken, Bob 1904- *EncJzS 70, WhoJazz 72*
McCracken, Esther 1902- *WhThe*
McCracken, James 1926- *BnBkM 80, CmOp, MusSN[port], NewGrD 80, WhoMus 72, WhoOp 76*
McCracken, Joan d1961 *MotPP, WhoHol B*
McCracken, Joan 1922-1961 *CmpEPM, EncMT, NotNAT B, WhThe*
McCracken, Joan 1923-1961 *CnOxB, DancEn 78, WhScrn 74, -77*
McCracken, John Eugene 1926- *NewEOp 71*
McCracken, Robert Edward 1904-1972 *BiDAmM, EncJzS 70*
McCracklin, Jimmy 1921- *BluesWW[port], RkOn*
McCrae, George & Gwen McCrae *RkOn 2[port]*
McCrae, John 1872-1918 *CreCan 2*
McCrary, Tex 1910- *IntMPA 77, -75, -76, -78, -79, -80*
McCray, Delbert H 1930- *AmSCAP 80*
McCray, James Joseph 1939- *WhoOp 76*
McCray, Joe *Film 2*
McCrea, Ann *ForYSC, WhoHol A*
McCrea, Bonnie *WomWMM*
McCrea, Jody *ForYSC, MotPP, WhoHol A*
McCrea, Joel 1905- *BiDFilm, -81, CmMov, FilmEn, Film 2, FilmgC, ForYSC, HalFC 80[port], IntMPA 77, -75, -76, -78, -79, -80, MotPP, MovMk[port], OxFilm, What 3[port], WhoHol A, WorEFlm*
McCrea, Minna 1895- *IntWWM 77*
McCrea, Susan 1956- *IntWWM 77*
McCreary, Bill 1933- *DrBlPA*
McCredie, Andrew Dalgarno 1930- *IntWWM 77, -80, NewGrD 80*
McCree, Junie 1865-1918 *AmSCAP 66, -80, BiDAmM, CmpEPM*
McCreery, Bud 1925- *BiE&WWA, NotNAT, WhoHol A*
McCreery, John Luckey 1835-1906 *BiDAmM*
McCreery, Walker 1921- *AmSCAP 66, -80*
McCrimmon, Daniel Bruce 1942- *AmSCAP 80*
McCrory, Martha 1920- *IntWWM 77, -80*
McCuaig, Ewen 1931- *IntWWM 77, -80*
McCue, Maureen *WomWMM B*
McCuller, Arnold 1950- *AmSCAP 80*
McCullers, Carson 1916-1967 *FilmgC, PlP&P*
McCullers, Carson 1917-1967 *BiE&WWA, CnMD, DcLB 7[port], EncWT, HalFC 80, McGEWD[port], ModWD, NotNAT B*
McCulloch, Andrew *WhoHol A*
McCullogh, Paul 1884-1926 *JoeFr*
McCulloh, Byron 1927- *AmSCAP 80, CpmDNM 78, -79, ConAmC, IntWWM 80*
McCullough, Charles Harold 1938- *IntWWM 77, -80*
McCullough, Jimmie B 1929- *IntMPA 80*
McCullough, John E 1832-1885 *FamA&A[port], NotNAT A, OxThe*
McCullough, John E 1837-1885 *NotNAT B*
McCullough, Oscar James 1922- *IntWWM 77, -80*
McCullough, Paul d1936 *WhoHol B*
McCullough, Paul 1883-1936 *WhThe*
McCullough, Paul 1884-1936 *FilmgC, HalFC 80, WhScrn 74, -77*
McCullough, Paul 1892-1936 *Film 2*
McCullough, Philo 1893- *Film 1, -2, ForYSC, TwYS, WhoHol A*
McCullum, Bartley d1916 *WhScrn 77*
McCullum, George, Jr. 1906?-1938 *NewOrJ*
McCullum, George, Sr. 1885-1920 *NewOrJ[port]*
McCurdy, Alexander 1905- *NewGrD 80*
McCurdy, Charles 1865?-1933 *NewOrJ*
McCurdy, Ed 1919- *AmSCAP 66, BiDAmM, EncFCWM 69*
McCurdy, Edward P 1919- *AmSCAP 80*
McCurdy, Racheal 1922- *IntWWM 77*
McCurdy, Roy Walter, Jr. 1936- *BiDAmM, EncJzS 70*
McCurry, John *DrBlPA, WhoHol A*
McCurry, John Gordon 1821-1886 *NewGrD 80*
McCutchan, Robert Guy 1877-1958 *Baker 78, BiDAmM*
McCutcheon, Bill *WhoHol A*
McCutcheon, George Barr 1866-1928 *WhScrn 77*
McCutcheon, Ralph 1899-1975 *WhScrn 77*
McCutcheon, Wallace 1881-1928 *Film 1, -2, NotNAT B, WhScrn 74, -77, WhoHol B*
McCutcheon, William Steven 1907- *IntWWM 77, WhoMus 72*
McDaniel, Barry 1930- *NewGrD 80, WhoOp 76*
McDaniel, Ellas 1928- *BluesWW[port]*
McDaniel, Etta 1890-1946 *WhScrn 77*
McDaniel, George 1886-1944 *Film 1, -2, WhScrn 74, -77, WhoHol B*
McDaniel, Hattie 1895-1952 *BluesWW[port], DrBlPA, FilmEn, FilmgC, ForYSC, HalFC 80, MotPP, MovMk[port], NotNAT B, OxFilm, ThFT[port], Vers A[port], WhScrn 74, -77, WhoHol B*
McDaniel, Mel H 1942- *AmSCAP 80*
McDaniel, Sam 1886-1962 *BlksB&W, -C, WhScrn 77, WhoHol B*
McDaniel, Sam 1887-1963 *ForYSC*
McDaniel, Sam 1896?-1962 *DrBlPA*
McDaniel, William J 1918- *CpmDNM 72, ConAmC*
McDaniel, William Theodore, Jr. *IntWWM 77*
McDaniels, Gene 1935- *RkOn*
McDermott, Aline d1951 *NotNAT B*
McDermott, Glenn *ConMuA 80B*
McDermott, Hugh 1908-1972 *FilmgC, HalFC 80, WhScrn 77, WhThe, WhoHol B*
McDermott, John 1892-1946 *WhoHol B*
McDermott, Joseph *Film 1*
McDermott, Marc 1880-1929 *Film 1*
McDermott, Marc 1881-1929 *WhScrn 74, -77*
McDermott, Thomas *NewYTET*
McDermott, Vincent 1933- *CpmDNM 80, ConAmC, IntWWM 77, -80*
McDermott, William F d1958 *NotNAT B*
McDevitt, Ruth 1895-1976 *BiE&WWA, ForYSC, HalFC 80, NotNAT, WhoHol A, WhoThe 72, -77*
McDiarmid, Don 1898-1977 *AmSCAP 66, -80*
McDonagh, Don 1932- *CnOxB*
McDonagh Sisters *WomWMM*
McDonald, Charles B 1886-1964 *WhScrn 74, -77, WhoHol B*
McDonald, Christie 1875-1962 *WhThe*
McDonald, Christine *AmPS B*
McDonald, Claire *Film 2*
McDonald, Country Joe *IlEncR[port]*
McDonald, Country Joe And The Fish *ConMuA 80A*
McDonald, Dan *Film 2*
McDonald, Donald Gordon 1925- *WhoMus 72*
McDonald, Edith *PupTheA*
McDonald, Elaine 1943- *CnOxB*
McDonald, Enos William 1915-1968 *BiDAmM*
McDonald, Eugene, Jr. d1958 *NewYTET*
McDonald, Francis 1891-1968 *FilmEn, Film 1, -2, ForYSC, TwYS, Vers B[port], WhScrn 74, -77, WhoHol B*
McDonald, Frank 1899- *FilmEn, FilmgC, HalFC 80, IntMPA 77, -75, -76, -78, -79, -80*
McDonald, Gerald 1913- *IntWWM 77, -80, WhoMus 72*
McDonald, Grace 1921- *ForYSC, HalFC 80*
McDonald, Harl 1899-1955 *AmSCAP 66, -80, Baker 78, BiDAmM, ConAmC, NewGrD 80, OxMus*
McDonald, Ian 1914- *ForYSC*
McDonald, Ian Donald 1937- *IntWWM 77, -80*
McDonald, Inez *Film 2*
McDonald, James 1886-1952 *WhScrn 74, -77*
McDonald, Joseph 1861-1935 *WhScrn 74, -77*
McDonald, Kenneth *TwYS A*
McDonald, Marie 1923-1965 *FilmEn, FilmgC, ForYSC, HalFC 80, MotPP, WhScrn 74, -77, WhoHol B*
McDonald, Melbourn *Film 2*
McDonald, Michael Hanley *AmSCAP 80*
McDonald, Ray 1920-1959 *FilmgC, HalFC 80*
McDonald, Ray 1924-1959 *NotNAT B, WhScrn 74, -77, WhoHol B*
McDonald, Ruth *PupTheA*
McDonald, Skeets 1968- *EncFCWM 69*
McDonald, Susan 1935- *WhoMus 72*
McDonald, Susann 1935- *Baker 78, IntWWM 80, NewGrD 80*
McDonald, Warren A *BlkAmP*
McDonald, Wilfred *Film 2*
McDonald, William *Film 2, WhoHol A*
McDonald, William 1820-1901 *BiDAmM*
McDonall, Lois Jeanette 1939- *NewGrD 80, WhoOp 76*
McDonell, A Eugene 1915- *ConAmC*
McDonell, Fergus 1910-1968 *FilmgC, HalFC 80*
McDonnel, G L *Film 2*
McDonnell, Richard Patrick, III 1945- *IntWWM 77*
McDonnell, Thomas Anthony 1940- *IntWWM 80, NewGrD 80, WhoOp 76*
McDonnell, Tom 1940- *NewGrD 80*
McDonough, Dick 1904-1938 *CmpEPM, WhoJazz 72*
McDonough, Gerald M 1945- *NatPD[port]*
McDonough, Jack 1944- *AmSCAP 80*
McDonough, Jerome 1946- *NatPD[port]*
McDonough, John E *PupTheA*
McDonough, Megan 1953- *AmSCAP 80*
McDonough, Michael 1876-1956 *WhScrn 74, -77*
McDonough, W S *Film 2*
McDougall, Gordon 1941- *WhoThe 77*
McDougall, Peter *ConDr 77C*
McDougall, Rex *Film 1, -2*
McDow, William Dayton 1930- *AmSCAP 80*
McDowall, Betty *IntMPA 77, -75, -76, -78, -79, -80*
McDowall, Malcolm 1943- *FilmAG WE, IntMPA 77, -75, -76, -78, -79, -80*
McDowall, Roddy 1928- *BiE&WWA, FilmAG WE, FilmEn, FilmgC, ForYSC, HalFC 80, IntMPA 77, -75, -76, -78, -79, -80, MotPP, MovMk, NotNAT, OxFilm, WhoHol A, WhoHrs 80[port], WhoThe 72, -77*
McDowell, Claire d1967 *WhoHol B*
McDowell, Claire 1877-1966 *FilmEn, WhScrn 74, -77*
McDowell, Claire 1877-1967 *ForYSC*
McDowell, Claire 1887-1967 *Film 1, -2, TwYS*
McDowell, Franklin Edgar Davey 1888-1965 *CreCan 2*
McDowell, Fred 1904-1972 *BluesWW[port]*
McDowell, Frederick 1904-1972 *BiDAmM*
McDowell, John H 1903- *BiE&WWA, NotNAT*
McDowell, John Herbert 1926- *Baker 78, CmpGMD, CnOxB, ConAmC, DcCM*
McDowell, Malcolm *WhoHol A*
McDowell, Malcolm 1943- *FilmEn, MovMk*

McDowell, Malcolm 1944- *FilmgC, HalFC 80, IlWWBF[port], WhoHrs 80[port]*
McDowell, Melbourne *Film 2*
McDowell, Melody *MorBAP*
McDowell, Nelson 1875-1947 *Film 2, WhScrn 74, -77, WhoHol B*
McDowell, Norman 1931- *CnOxB*
McDuff, Brother Jack 1926- *BiDAmM, EncJzS 70*
McDuff, Jack 1926- *AmSCAP 80*
McDuff, Lillie Mae 1907- *IntWWM 77*
McEachern, Murray 1915- *CmpEPM, EncJzS 70, WhoJazz 72*
McEachin, James *WhoHol A*
McEachin, James 1930- *DrBlPA*
McEachin, James 1931- *HalFC 80*
McEarchan, Malcolm d1945 *NotNAT B*
McEdward, Gordon *Film 2*
McElfresh, Clair Thomas 1931- *IntWWM 77, -80*
McElfresh, Tom 1935- *ConAmTC*
McElheran, Brock *ConAmC*
McElheran, N Brock 1918- *IntWWM 77, -80*
McElhern, James *Film 2*
McElhiney, Bill *AmSCAP 80*
McElrath, Randy *ConMuA 80B*
McElroy, Barbara Jo Harshman 1950- *IntWWM 77*
McElroy, Dorothy Lorie 1940- *IntWWM 77*
McElroy, Jack 1914-1959 *WhScrn 74, -77, WhoHol B*
McElroy, Leo F 1932- *AmSCAP 66, -80*
McElwaine, James William 1947- *AmSCAP 80*
McEnery, Dave 1914- *BiDAmM*
McEnery, David Largus 1914- *AmSCAP 66, -80*
McEnery, John 1945- *FilmgC, HalFC 80, WhoHol A*
McEnery, Peter 1940- *FilmgC, ForYSC, HalFC 80, MotPP, WhoHol A, WhoThe 72, -77*
McEnery, Red River Dave 1914- *IlEncCM[port]*
McEnery, Velma Lee 1929- *AmSCAP 80*
McEnroe, Robert E *BiE&WWA*
McEuen, Bill *ConMuA 80B*
McEuen, Mark *ConMuA 80B*
McEveety, Bernard *FilmgC, HalFC 80, IntMPA 77, -76, -78, -79, -80, NewYTET, TwYS A*
McEveety, Joseph L 1926-1976 *HalFC 80, IntMPA 77, -75, -76*
McEveety, Vince *FilmgC, HalFC 80*
McEveety, Vincent *HalFC 80, IntMPA 77, -75, -76, -78, -79, -80*
McEvilly, Burton *Film 2*
McEvoy, Charles 1879-1929 *NotNAT B, WhThe*
McEvoy, Dorothea d1976 *WhoHol C*
McEvoy, Ernest Simon 1894-1953 *WhScrn 74, -77*
McEvoy, J P 1894-1958 *NotNAT B, WhThe*
McEvoy, J P 1895-1958 *NewCBMT*
McEwan, Geraldine 1932- *BiE&WWA, NotNAT, PlP&P[port], WhoHol A, WhoThe 72, -77*
McEwan, Geraldine 1933- *HalFC 80*
McEwan, Isabelle 1897-1963 *WhScrn 74, -77*
McEwan, Jack *Film 2*
McEwen, Geraldine 1932- *CnThe*
McEwen, Jean Albert 1923- *CreCan 1*
McEwen, John 1923- *CreCan 1*
McEwen, Sir John Blackwood 1868-1948 *Baker 78, NewGrD 80, OxMus*
McEwen, Robert Finnie *OxMus*
McEwen, Terry *ConMuA 80B*
McEwen, Walter 1905- *Film 1, -2*
McFadden, Charles I 1888-1942 *WhScrn 74*
McFadden, Frank 1914- *IntMPA 77, -75, -76, -78, -79, -80*
McFadden, G Andrew *PupTheA*
McFadden, Hamilton 1901- *HalFC 80*
McFadden, Ira *Film 2*
McFadden, Ivor 1887-1942 *Film 1, -2, WhScrn 77*
McFarland, Dale H 1918- *IntMPA 77, -75, -76, -78*
McFarland, Gary 1933- *AmSCAP 80*
McFarland, Gary 1933-1971 *BiDAmM, EncJzS 70*
McFarland, J Patrick 1939- *IntWWM 77, -80*
McFarland, John Dennis 1946- *AmSCAP 80*
McFarland, John Thomas 1851-1913 *BiDAmM*
McFarland, Lester 1902- *BiDAmM*
McFarland, Olive *MotPP*
McFarland, Packy *WhoHol A*
McFarland, Spanky 1928- *FilmEn, FilmgC, ForYSC, HalFC 80, What 3[port], WhoHol A, MovMk*
McFarland Twins, The *BgBands 74[port]*
McFarlane, George 1877-1932 *Film 2, WhoHol B*
McFarlane, George 1887-1932 *NotNAT B*
McFarlane, Kenneth Ivor 1906- *WhoMus 72*
McFeeters, Raymond 1899- *AmSCAP 66, -80, ConAmC*
McFerrin, Robert 1921- *DrBlPA*
McFerrin, Sara Elizabeth Copper 1924- *IntWWM 77, -80*
McGann, William 1895-1977 *FilmEn, FilmgC, HalFC 80*
McGann, William 1898- *IlWWBF*
McGannon, Donald H 1920- *IntMPA 77, -75, -76, -78, -79, -80, NewYTET*
McGarity, Kent E 1940- *IntWWM 77*
McGarity, Lou 1917-1971 *CmpEPM, EncJzS 70, WhoJazz 72*
McGarity, Robert Louis 1917-1971 *BiDAmM*
McGarrigle, Kate 1946- *AmSCAP 80*
McGarrigle, Kate And Anna *ConMuA 80A, IlEncR*
McGarrity, Everett *Film 2*
McGarry, Vera *Film 1*
McGarvey, Cathal *Film 2*
McGaugh, Geneva *PupTheA*
McGaugh, Wilbur 1895-1965 *Film 2, WhScrn 74, -77, WhoHol B*
McGavin, Darren 1922- *BiE&WWA, FilmEn, FilmgC, ForYSC, HalFC 80, IntMPA 77, -75, -76, -78, -79, -80, MotPP, MovMk, NotNAT, WhoHol A*
McGaw, Charles 1910- *BiE&WWA, NotNAT*
McGeary, George L 1928- *IntWWM 77*
McGee, Fibber 1897- *FilmgC, HalFC 80, What 3[port]*
McGee, Fibber And Molly *JoeFr[port]*
McGee, Florence *PlP&P[port]*
McGee, Frank 1921-1974 *NewYTET*
McGee, Harold J d1955 *NotNAT B*
McGee, Kirk 1899- *BiDAmM, IlEncCM*
McGee, Pat 1906- *IntMPA 77, -75, -76, -78, -79, -80*
McGee, Patricia *Film 2*
McGee, Robin 1934- *IntWWM 77, -80*
McGee, Sam 1894-1975 *BiDAmM, IlEncCM*
McGee, Sam And Kirk *IlEncCM*
McGee, Timothy James 1936- *IntWWM 77*
McGee, Vonetta *DrBlPA, WhoHol A*
McGee, William James 1936- *ConAmC*
McGee Brothers *EncFCWM 69*
McGeehee, Gloria 1922-1964 *WhoHol B*
McGegan, Nicholas 1950- *IntWWM 77, -80*
McGehee, Helen *CnOxB, DancEn 78[port]*
McGhee, Andy 1927- *BiDAmM*
McGhee, Brownie 1914- *EncFCWM 69*
McGhee, Brownie 1915- *EncJzS 70*
McGhee, Gloria 1922-1964 *WhScrn 77*
McGhee, Granville H 1918-1961 *BluesWW[port]*
McGhee, Howard 1918- *AmSCAP 66, -80, BiDAmM, CmpEPM, EncJzS 70, IlEncJ*
McGhee, Johnny *BgBands 74*
McGhee, Paul A d1964 *NotNAT B*
McGhee, Walter Brown 1915- *BiDAmM, BluesWW[port], EncJzS 70*
McGibbon, William 1690?-1756 *NewGrD 80*
McGibeny, Ruth T 1896- *AmSCAP 66, -80*
McGill, Barney d1941 *HalFC 80*
McGill, Gwendolen Mary Finlayson 1910- *IntWWM 77, -80, WhoMus 72*
McGill, Josephine 1877-1919 *Baker 78*
McGilvray, Laura *WhoStg 1908*
McGinley, Laurence Joseph 1905- *BiE&WWA, NotNAT*
McGinn, Walter 1936-1977 *HalFC 80, NotNAT, PlP&P A[port], WhoHol A*
McGinnis, Donald R 1939- *AmSCAP 80*
McGinnis, James Doug 1922- *AmSCAP 80*
McGiveney, Owen 1884-1967 *WhScrn 74, -77, WhoHol B*
McGiver, John 1913-1975 *BiE&WWA, FilmgC, ForYSC, HalFC 80, MotPP, MovMk, NotNAT B, WhScrn 77, WhoHol C, WhoThe 72, -77*
McGivern, William P 1924- *HalFC 80*
McGlashan, Alexander 1740?-1797 *NewGrD 80*
McGlaughlin, William 1943- *IntWWM 77, -80*
McGlinn, Ann J 1922- *AmSCAP 66*
McGlynn, Frank 1866-1951 *NotNAT B, WhThe*
McGlynn, Frank 1867-1951 *Film 1, -2, ForYSC, HalFC 80, Vers A[port], WhScrn 74, -77, WhoHol B*
McGonigal, Alexander Andrew 1915- *AmSCAP 80*
McGonigle, Mary 1937- *AmSCAP 80*
McGoohan, Patrick 1928- *FilmAG WE, FilmEn, FilmgC, ForYSC, HalFC 80, IlWWBF[port], IntMPA 77, -75, -76, -78, -79, -80, MotPP, WhThe, WhoHol A*
McGough, Neil Vincent 1939- *IntWWM 77, -80*
McGovern, Bernard Francis 1940- *ConAmTC*
McGovern, John *BiE&WWA, NotNAT*
McGovern, Maureen 1949- *RkOn 2[port]*
McGowan, Bob *Film 1*
McGowan, Bryan *Film 2*
McGowan, Dorothy *Film 2*
McGowan, Dorrell *IntMPA 77, -78, -79, -80*
McGowan, J P 1880-1952 *FilmEn, Film 1, -2, ForYSC, TwYS, -A, WhoHol B*
McGowan, Jack *AmPS B*
McGowan, James Edward 1935- *AmSCAP 80*
McGowan, John P 1880-1952 *NotNAT B, WhScrn 74, -77*
McGowan, John W 1892- *BiE&WWA, NotNAT, WhThe*
McGowan, Oliver F 1907-1971 *BiE&WWA, NotNAT B, WhScrn 74, -77, WhoHol B*
McGowan, Robert A 1901- *HalFC 80, IntMPA 77, -75, -76, -78, -79, -80*
McGowan, Stuart *IntMPA 77, -78, -79, -80*
McGowan Brothers *IntMPA 75, -76, -79, -80*
McGowen, Adair *WhoOp 76*
McGowen, Frank S *AmSCAP 80*
McGrail, Walter d1970 *WhoHol B*
McGrail, Walter 1889-1970 *Film 1, -2, ForYSC, TwYS*
McGrail, Walter B 1899-1970 *WhScrn 74, -77*
McGranahan, James 1840-1907 *BiDAmM, NewGrD 80*
McGranary, Al 1902-1971 *WhScrn 77, WhoHol B*
McGrane, Paul James 1902- *AmSCAP 66, -80*
McGrane, Thomas J *Film 1*
McGrannahan, A Graydon, III 1951- *IntWWM 77*
McGrath, Barry 1941- *CnOxB*
McGrath, Bill *DancEn 78*
McGrath, David Fulton 1907-1958 *AmSCAP 80*
McGrath, Dennis 1875?-1955 *WhScrn 77*
McGrath, Earl *ConMuA 80B*
McGrath, Fidgy 1908-1958 *WhoJazz 72*
McGrath, Frank 1903-1967 *FilmgC, ForYSC, HalFC 80, WhScrn 74, -77, WhoHol B*
McGrath, Fulton 1907-1958 *AmSCAP 66*
McGrath, Joe 1930- *FilmgC, HalFC 80*
McGrath, John 1935- *CnThe, ConDr 73, -77, EncWT, Ent, WhoThe 72, -77*
McGrath, Joseph 1930- *IlWWBF*
McGrath, Joseph J 1889-1968 *ConAmC*
McGrath, Kathleen *WhoMus 72*
McGrath, Larry 1888-1960 *Film 2, WhScrn 77, WhoHol B*
McGrath, Michael d1976 *WhoHol C*
McGrath, Paul 1904- *BiE&WWA, ForYSC, NotNAT, WhoHol A, WhoThe 72, -77*
McGrath, Thomas J *IntMPA 77, -78, -79, -80*
McGraw, Cameron 1919- *AmSCAP 66, -80, ConAmC A*
McGraw, Charles 1914-1980 *FilmEn, FilmgC, ForYSC, HalFC 80, MotPP, WhoHol A*
McGraw, George Donald 1927-1969 *AmSCAP 66, -80*
McGraw, John 1873-1934 *WhScrn 77*
McGraw, John J *Film 1*
McGraw, Patricia Washington *MorBAP*
McGraw, William Ralph 1930- *BiE&WWA, NotNAT*

McGreal, E B 1905- *IntMPA 77, -76, -78, -79, -80*
McGregor, Bruce Howard 1952- *IntWWM 80*
McGregor, Charles 1927- *DrBlPA, IntMPA 77, -75, -76, -78, -79, -80*
McGregor, Chris *IlEncJ*
McGregor, Ernest Frank 1879-1946 *BiDAmM*
McGregor, Gordon *Film 2*
McGregor, Harmon d1948 *Film 2, WhoHol B*
McGregor, Irene Scott 1945- *WhoMus 72*
McGregor, Malcolm 1892-1945 *Film 2, ForYSC, MotPP, NotNAT B, TwYS, WhScrn 74, -77, WhoHol B*
McGregor, Parke 1907-1962 *NotNAT B, WhScrn 74, -77*
McGregor, Theodore Roosevelt 1902- *AmSCAP 80*
McGrew, Esther Gertrude Harris 1907- *IntWWM 77, -80*
McGriff, Jimmy 1936- *BiDAmM, EncJzS 70*
McGriff, Milton *BlkAmP, MorBAP*
McGuane, Thomas *HalFC 80*
McGuigan, Patrick 1933- *WhoMus 72*
McGuinn, Joe d1971 *WhoHol B*
McGuinn, Joseph Ford 1904-1971 *WhScrn 74, -77*
McGuinn, Roger 1942- *ConMuA 80A, IlEncR*
McGuinness Flint *IlEncR*
McGuire, Barbara 1940- *IntWWM 80*
McGuire, Barry 1935- *RkOn 2[port]*
McGuire, Benjamin 1875-1925 *WhScrn 74, -77, WhoHol B*
McGuire, Biff *WhoHol A*
McGuire, Biff 1926- *WhoThe 72, -77*
McGuire, Biff 1927- *BiE&WWA, NotNAT*
McGuire, Colin John 1947- *IntWWM 77, -80*
McGuire, Don 1919- *FilmEn, FilmgC, ForYSC, HalFC 80, IntMPA 77, -75, -76, -78, -79, -80, WhoHol A*
McGuire, Dorothy *MotPP, WhoHol A*
McGuire, Dorothy 1918- *BiDFilm, -81, BiE&WWA, FilmEn, MovMk[port], NotNAT, What 5[port], WhoThe 77, WorEFlm*
McGuire, Dorothy 1919- *FilmgC, ForYSC, HalFC 80, IntMPA 77, -75, -76, -78, -79, -80, OxFilm*
McGuire, Edward 1948- *IntWWM 77, -80*
McGuire, Harp 1921-1966 *WhScrn 77*
McGuire, Kathryn 1897-1978 *FilmEn, Film 2, ForYSC, TwYS, WhoHol A*
McGuire, Lois *BlkAmP*
McGuire, Maeve *WhoHol A*
McGuire, Michael *PlP&P A[port]*
McGuire, Mickey 1922- *Film 2, TwYS*
McGuire, Paddy *Film 1*
McGuire, Tom 1874-1954 *Film 2, WhScrn 74, -77, WhoHol B*
McGuire, William Anthony 1885-1940 *EncMT, NotNAT B, WhThe*
McGuire Sisters *AmPS A, -B, BiDAmM, RkOn[port]*
McGuirk, Harriet 1903-1975 *WhScrn 77, WhoHol C*
McGurk, Bob 1907-1959 *WhScrn 74, -77*
McGurk, J W *Film 2*
McGurk, Molly 1929- *IntWWM 80*
McGurk, Robert d1959 *WhoHol B*
McHaffie, Iain 1944- *IntWWM 80*
McHale, James d1973 *WhScrn 77*
McHale, Rosemary 1944- *WhoThe 77*
McHan, Don *EncFCWM 69*
McHarg, James 1908- *WhoMus 72*
McHargue, Rosy 1907- *CmpEPM, WhoJazz 72*
McHenry, Don 1908- *BiE&WWA, NotNAT*
McHenry, Nellie d1935 *NotNAT B*
McHose, Allen Irvine 1902- *ConAmC*
McHouston, Ed *BluesWW[port]*
McHugh, Catherine 1869-1944 *WhScrn 74, -77, WhoHol B*
McHugh, Charles Patrick d1931 *Film 2, WhScrn 74, -77, WhoHol B*
McHugh, Charles Russell 1940- *AmSCAP 80, ConAmC*
McHugh, Florence 1906- *WhThe*
McHugh, Frank *MotPP*
McHugh, Frank 1898- *BiE&WWA, FilmEn, Film 2, ForYSC, HolCA[port], NotNAT, WhoHol A*
McHugh, Frank 1899- *FilmgC, HalFC 80, IntMPA 77, -75, -76, -78, -79, -80, MovMk, Vers A[port]*
McHugh, Jack *Film 2*
McHugh, James 1894-1969 *NewGrD 80*
McHugh, James 1915- *IntMPA 77, -75, -76, -78, -79, -80*
McHugh, James Francis 1896-1969 *NotNAT B*
McHugh, Jimmy d1969 *WhoHol B*
McHugh, Jimmy 1894-1969 *AmSCAP 66, -80, Baker 78, BestMus, BiDAmM, CmpEPM, ConAmC, EncMT, FilmEn, NewCBMT, NewGrD 80, Sw&Ld C, WhScrn 74, -77*
McHugh, Jimmy 1895-1969 *AmPS, FilmgC, HalFC 80, PopAmC[port], PopAmC SUP*
McHugh, Jimmy 1896-1969 *BiE&WWA, NotNAT B*
McHugh, John 1914- *WhoMus 72*
McHugh, Matt 1894-1971 *Vers B[port], WhScrn 74, -77, WhoHol B*
McHugh, Therese *WhThe*
McIllwain, William A 1863-1933 *Film 2, WhScrn 74, -77, WhoHol B*
McIlrath, Patricia 1917- *BiE&WWA, NotNAT*
McIlvaine, Howard 1919- *AmSCAP 80*
McIlwaine, Frances Ellen 1945- *AmSCAP 80*
McIlwraith, Isa Roberta 1909- *ConAmC*
McIndoe, Sanna 1930- *IntWWM 80*
McInnes, Donald 1939- *IntWWM 77, -80*
McIntire, John 1907- *BiDFilm, -81, FilmEn, FilmgC, ForYSC, HalFC 80, IntMPA 77, -75, -76, -78, -79, -80, MotPP, WhoHol A, WorEFlm[port]*
McIntire, Lani 1904-1951 *AmSCAP 66, -80*
McIntire, Tim *WhoHol A*
McIntosh, Burr 1862-1942 *Film 1, -2, NotNAT B, TwYS, WhScrn 74, -77, WhoHol B*
McIntosh, David Cameron 1938- *WhoMus 72*
McIntosh, Ladd 1941- *ConAmC, EncJzS 70*
McIntosh, Madge 1875-1950 *NotNAT B, WhThe*
McIntosh, Michael D 1950- *AmSCAP 80*
McIntosh, Morris *Film 2*
McIntosh, Rigdon McCoy 1836-1899 *BiDAmM, NewGrD 80*
McIntosh, Stanley 1908- *IntMPA 77, -75, -76, -78, -79, -80*
McIntosh, Thomas 1948- *IntWWM 80*
McIntosh, Thomas S 1927- *BiDAmM, ConAmC, EncJzS 70*
McIntosh, Tom d1904 *BlksBF*
McIntosh, Tom 1927- *EncJzS 70*
McIntyre, Donald 1934- *IntWWM 77, -80, NewGrD 80, WhoMus 72, WhoOp 76*
McIntyre, Duncan 1907-1973 *WhScrn 77*
McIntyre, Earl P 1953- *EncJzS 70*
McIntyre, Frank d1949 *Film 1, MotPP, WhoHol B*
McIntyre, Frank 1878-1949 *WhScrn 74, -77*
McIntyre, Frank 1879-1949 *NotNAT B, WhThe*
McIntyre, Frank J 1880-1949 *JoeFr[port]*
McIntyre, Hal 1914-1959 *BgBands 74[port], BiDAmM, CmpEPM*
McIntyre, Harry J 1905- *IntMPA 75*
McIntyre, James T 1857-1937 *NotNAT B, WhoStg 1908*
McIntyre, John 1907- *Vers B[port]*
McIntyre, John 1938- *IntWWM 77*
McIntyre, John T d1951 *NotNAT B*
McIntyre, Joy 1938- *WhoOp 76*
McIntyre, Ken 1931- *EncJzS 70*
McIntyre, Kenneth Arthur 1931- *BiDAmM, EncJzS 70*
McIntyre, Lani *BgBands 74*
McIntyre, Leila 1882-1953 *NotNAT B, WhScrn 74, -77, WhoHol B*
McIntyre, Marion 1885-1975 *WhScrn 77, WhoHol C*
McIntyre, Mark W 1916-1970 *AmSCAP 66, -80*
McIntyre, Molly d1952 *NotNAT B*
McIntyre, Richard Rawlings 1914- *IntWWM 77, -80*
McIntyre, Robert John 1938- *IntWWM 80*
McIntyre, Tom *Film 2*
McIntyre And Heath *WhoStg 1908*
McIver, R *MorBAP*
McIver, Ray *BlkAmP, DrBlPA*
McIvor, Mary 1901-1941 *Film 2, WhScrn 74, -77, WhoHol B*
McKalip, Mansell Brown 1915- *AmSCAP 80*
McKay, Albert Phillip 1948- *AmSCAP 80*
McKay, Allison *WhoHol A*
McKay, Arthur Fortescue 1926- *CreCan 2*
McKay, David *ConAmC*
McKay, Francis Howard 1901- *AmSCAP 66, -80, ConAmC A*
McKay, Fred *Film 1, -2*
McKay, Frederick E d1944 *NotNAT B*
McKay, Gardner *WhoHol A*
McKay, George Frederick 1899-1970 *AmSCAP 66, -80, Baker 78, BiDAmM, ConAmC*
McKay, George W 1880-1945 *WhScrn 74, -77, WhoHol B*
McKay, Jim *NewYTET*
McKay, Michael *ConMuA 80B*
McKay, Neil 1924- *AmSCAP 66, ConAmC, IntWWM 77, -80*
McKay, Norman 1906-1968 *WhScrn 74, -77*
McKay, Paula F *PupTheA*
McKay, Roderick Neil 1924- *AmSCAP 80*
McKay, Scott 1915- *BiE&WWA, NotNAT, WhoHol A, WhoThe 77*
McKay, Todd *AmSCAP 80*
McKay, Wanda *ForYSC*
McKay, Winsor *Film 2*
McKayle, Donald 1930- *BiE&WWA, CmpGMD, CnOxB, DancEn 78[port], DrBlPA, NotNAT, WhoHol A*
McKean, Wilkin Joseph Martin 1952- *AmSCAP 80*
McKechnie, Donna 1940- *WhoHol A, WhoThe 77*
McKechnie, James d1964 *NotNAT B*
McKee, Arthur W 1891-1953 *AmSCAP 66, -80*
McKee, Bob *Film 2*
McKee, Buck 1865-1944 *WhScrn 74, -77*
McKee, Clive R 1883- *WhThe*
McKee, Donald M 1899-1968 *WhScrn 74, -77, WhoHol B*
McKee, Frank *Film 2*
McKee, Frank W 1867-1944 *AmSCAP 66, -80*
McKee, John *MorBAP*
McKee, John d1953 *NotNAT B*
McKee, Lafayette *Film 1*
McKee, Lafe 1872-1959 *Film 2, ForYSC, TwYS, Vers B[port], WhScrn 77, WhoHol B*
McKee, Lonette *WhoHol A*
McKee, Pat 1897-1950 *WhScrn 77*
McKee, Raymond *Film 1, -2, TwYS*
McKee, Richard 1941- *IntWWM 80, WhoOp 76*
McKee, Tom 1917-1960 *WhScrn 74, -77, WhoHol B*
McKeen, Lawrence D, Jr. 1925-1933 *WhScrn 74, -77*
McKeen, Sunny d1933 *Film 2, WhoHol B*
McKeever, Mike 1940-1967 *WhScrn 77*
McKellar, Hugh Christopher 1948- *IntWWM 77, -80*
McKellar, Kenneth 1927- *IntMPA 77, -75, -76, -78, -79, -80, IntWWM 77, -80, WhoMus 72*
McKellen, Ian *WhoHol A, WhoThe 72, -77*
McKellen, Ian 1935- *FilmgC, HalFC 80*
McKellen, Ian 1939- *CnThe*
McKelvey, Malcolm John 1926- *WhoMus 72*
McKelvie, Harold 1910-1937 *WhScrn 74, -77*
McKelvy, James Milligan 1917- *AmSCAP 80*
McKelvy, Lige William 1904-1965 *AmSCAP 66, -80*
McKendrick, Big Mike 1901-1965 *WhoJazz 72*
McKendrick, Little Mike 1903?-1961 *WhoJazz 72*
McKenna, Dave 1930- *EncJzS 70*
McKenna, David 1911- *IntWWM 77*
McKenna, David 1930- *BiDAmM*
McKenna, David 1949- *NotNAT*
McKenna, David J 1930- *AmSCAP 66, -80, EncJzS 70*
McKenna, Henry T 1894-1958 *WhScrn 74, -77*
McKenna, Kenneth 1899-1962 *MovMk*
McKenna, Peggy *WhoHol A*
McKenna, Siobhan *MotPP, PlP&P, WhoHol A*

McKenna, Siobhan 1922- *BiE&WWA, EncWT, ForYSC, NotNAT*
McKenna, Siobhan 1923- *CnThe, Ent, FilmEn, FilmgC, HalFC 80, IntMPA 77, -75, -76, -78, -79, -80, WhoThe 72, -77*
McKenna, T P *WhoHol A*
McKenna, T P 1929- *WhoThe 72, -77*
McKenna, T P 1931- *FilmgC, HalFC 80*
McKenna, Timothy 1948- *ConAmTC*
McKenna, Virginia 1931- *FilmAG WE, FilmEn, FilmgC, ForYSC, HalFC 80, IlWWBF[port], WhoHol A, WhoThe 72, -77*
McKenna, William J 1881-1950 *AmSCAP 66, -80, NotNAT B*
McKenney, Ruth 1911-1972 *NotNAT B*
McKenney, W Thomas 1938- *ConAmC*
McKennon, Dallas *WhoHol A*
McKenzie, Alexander 1886-1966 *WhScrn 74*
McKenzie, Bob d1949 *Film 2, WhoHol B*
McKenzie, Donald *TwYS A*
McKenzie, Ella *WhoHol A*
McKenzie, Eva B 1889-1967 *WhScrn 74, -77, WhoHol B*
McKenzie, Fay *ForYSC, WhoHol A*
McKenzie, Jack H 1930- *ConAmC*
McKenzie, James B 1926- *BiE&WWA, NotNAT, WhoThe 77*
McKenzie, Jean *DancEn 78*
McKenzie, Louis *WhoHol A*
McKenzie, Red 1899-1948 *CmpEPM, WhoJazz 72*
McKenzie, Robert *ForYSC*
McKenzie, Robert 1881-1949 *Vers B[port]*
McKenzie, Robert B 1883-1949 *WhScrn 74, -77*
McKenzie, Robert Tait 1867-1938 *CreCan 2*
McKenzie, Scott 1944- *BiDAmM, EncFCWM 69, RkOn 2[port]*
McKenzie, Wallace 1928- *ConAmC*
McKenzie, William 1907-1948 *BiDAmM*
McKern, Leo 1920- *CnThe, FilmEn, FilmgC, HalFC 80, IlWWBF, MovMk, WhoHol A, WhoThe 72, -77*
McKerrow, Rita *WhoMus 72*
McKetney, Edwin Charles *BlkAmP*
McKibbon, Al 1919- *CmpEPM*
McKibbon, Alfred Benjamin 1919- *BiDAmM, EncJzS 70*
McKie, Sir William Neil 1901- *IntWWM 77, -80, NewGrD 80, OxMus, WhoMus 72*
McKiernan, Arnold Thomas 1918- *WhoMus 72*
McKillen, Arch Alfred 1914- *AmSCAP 80*
McKim, Lucy *NewGrD 80*
McKim, Robert 1887-1927 *Film 1, -2, TwYS, WhScrn 74, -77, WhoHol B*
McKinley, Barry *CmpEPM*
McKinley, Bill *BluesWW*
McKinley, Carl 1895-1966 *Baker 78, BiDAmM, ConAmC*
McKinley, J Edward *WhoHol A*
McKinley, Ray 1910- *AmSCAP 66, BgBands 74[port], BiDAmM, CmpEPM, EncJzS 70, WhoJazz 72*
McKinley, Raymond Frederick 1910- *AmSCAP 80*
McKinley, Sharon 1941- *IntWWM 77, -80, WhoMus 72*
McKinley, William Thomas 1938- *IntWWM 77*
McKinley, William Thomas 1939- *CpmDNM 80, ConAmC*
McKinnel, Norman 1870-1932 *IlWWBF, NotNAT B, WhScrn 74, WhThe*
McKinnell, Norman 1870-1932 *Film 2, WhScrn 77, WhoHol B*
McKinney, Alene d1978 *AmSCAP 66, -80*
McKinney, Bill *IntMPA 79, -80, WhoHol A*
McKinney, Bill 1894- *WhoJazz 72*
McKinney, Elizabeth Richmond 1927- *IntWWM 77, -80*
McKinney, George W 1923- *BiE&WWA*
McKinney, Hal 1928- *EncJzS 70*
McKinney, Harold Walton 1928- *EncJzS 70*
McKinney, Howard D 1890- *AmSCAP 66, ConAmC*
McKinney, James Carroll 1921- *IntWWM 77, -80*
McKinney, John E, Jr. 1947- *AmSCAP 80*
McKinney, Mathilde 1904- *Baker 78, ConAmC*
McKinney, Nina Mae 1909-1967 *WhoHol B*
McKinney, Nina Mae 1909-1968 *FilmgC, HalFC 80, ThFT[port], WhScrn 74, -77*
McKinney, Nina Mae 1912-1967 *WhoJazz 72*
McKinney, Nina Mae 1913-1967 *BlksB&W[port], -C, DrBlPA*
McKinney, Nina May 1909-1968 *Film 2*
McKinney, Thomas 1946- *WhoOp 76*
McKinney's Cotton Pickers *BgBands 74, BiDAmM, CmpEPM*
McKinnon, Al *Film 1*
McKinnon, John *Film 1, -2*
McKinnor, Nadine Theresa 1941- *AmSCAP 80*
McKnight, Anna *WomWMM*
McKnight, Tom d1963 *NotNAT B*
McKuen, Rod *WhoHol A*
McKuen, Rod 1933- *AmSCAP 80, Baker 78, BiDAmM, ConAmC, EncFCWM 69, PopAmC SUP[port]*
McKuen, Rod 1938- *AmSCAP 66*
McKusick, Hal 1924- *CmpEPM*
McKusick, Harold Wilfred 1924- *BiDAmM*
McLaglen, Andrew 1925- *FilmgC, HalFC 80, MovMk[port]*
McLaglen, Andrew V 1920- *CmMov, FilmEn, IntMPA 77, -75, -76, -78, -79, -80, WorEFlm[port]*
McLaglen, Clifford *Film 2*
McLaglen, Cyril 1899- *Film 2, IlWWBF*
McLaglen, Victor d1959 *MotPP, WhoHol B*
McLaglen, Victor 1883-1957 *IlWWBF A*
McLaglen, Victor 1883-1959 *CmMov, FilmgC, HalFC 80[port], IlWWBF, TwYS*
McLaglen, Victor 1886-1959 *BiDFilm, -81, CmMov, FilmEn, Film 2, ForYSC, MovMk[port], NotNAT B, OxFilm, WhScrn 74, -77, WorEFlm*
McLain, Margaret Starr *ConAmC*
McLaine, Marilyn *Film 2*
McLane, Mary *Film 2*
McLane, Wilhelmina 1910- *IntWWM 77*
McLaren, Audrey *WomWMM*
McLaren, Joseph Dixon *PupTheA*
McLaren, Lorna J R 1953- *IntWWM 77, -80*
McLaren, Malcolm *ConMuA 80B*
McLaren, Marilyn *WomWMM B*
McLaren, Norman 1914- *CreCan 1, DcFM, FilmEn, FilmgC, HalFC 80, OxFilm, WhoHrs 80, WorEFlm*
McLauchlan, Katherine Hutchison *WhoMus 72*
McLauchlin, Beatrice Hall 1896- *IntWWM 77*
McLaughlin, Ed *Film 1*
McLaughlin, Gibb 1884-1960? *Film 2, FilmgC, HalFC 80, IlWWBF, WhoHol A*
McLaughlin, J B *Film 1*
McLaughlin, Jeff *Film 2*
McLaughlin, John 1897-1968 *AmSCAP 66, -80, NotNAT B*
McLaughlin, John 1942- *ConMuA 80A, EncJzS 70, IlEncR[port]*
McLaughlin, Leonard B 1892- *BiE&WWA*
McLaughlin, Mahavishnu John *IlEncJ*
McLaughlin, Marian 1923- *ConAmC*
McLaughlin, Millicent *WhoStg 1908*
McLaughlin, William *Film 2*
McLaughlin-Gill, Frances 1919- *WomWMM B*
McLaurin, Kate 1885- *WhoStg 1908*
McLean, Alastair 1922- *FilmgC*
McLean, Barbara *WomWMM*
McLean, Barbara P 1909- *HalFC 80*
McLean, Barton 1938- *AmSCAP 80, ConAmC, IntWWM 77, -80*
McLean, Charles 1712?-1765? *NewGrD 80*
McLean, D D *Film 2*
McLean, David *ForYSC*
McLean, Don 1945- *BiDAmM, ConMuA 80A, IlEncR, RkOn 2[port]*
McLean, Hamilton Gordon 1906- *AmSCAP 80*
McLean, Hugh John 1930- *CreCan 1, NewGrD 80*
McLean, Jackie 1931- *IlEncJ*
McLean, Jackie 1932- *EncJzS 70*
McLean, John Lenwood 1932- *EncJzS 70*
McLean, John Leonard 1932- *BiDAmM*
McLean, Phil *RkOn*
McLean, Priscilla Anne Taylor 1942- *CpmDNM 80, ConAmC, IntWWM 77, -80*
McLean, William *WhoHol A*
McLellan, C M S 1865-1916 *BiDAmM, EncMT, NotNAT B, WhThe, WhoStg 1908*
McLellan, G B d1932 *NotNAT B*
McLellan, Irene Mary 1928- *IntWWM 80*
McLellan, Joyce Anne Marriott *CreCan 1*
McLellan, Michael J 1941- *IntWWM 77, -80*
McLeod, Alice 1932- *EncJzS 70*
McLeod, Alice 1937- *BiDAmM*
McLeod, Archibald 1906- *BiE&WWA, NotNAT*
McLeod, Barbara 1908-1940 *WhScrn 74, -77*
McLeod, Catherine 1924?- *FilmgC, ForYSC, HalFC 80, MotPP, WhoHol A*
McLeod, Catherine 1925?- *FilmEn*
McLeod, Duncan *WhoHol A*
McLeod, Elsie *Film 1*
McLeod, Gordon *Film 2*
McLeod, Helen 1924-1964 *NotNAT B, WhScrn 74, -77*
McLeod, James 1912- *AmSCAP 80*
McLeod, Jennifer Helen 1941- *IntWWM 77, -80, NewGrD 80*
McLeod, John 1934- *IntWWM 77, -80, WhoMus 72*
McLeod, Keith 1894-1961 *AmSCAP 66, -80*
McLeod, Marilyn 1942- *AmSCAP 80*
McLeod, Norman Z 1898-1964 *BiDFilm, -81, DcFM, FilmEn, FilmgC, HalFC 80, MovMk[port]*
McLeod, Tex 1896-1973 *WhScrn 77*
McLerie, Allyn Ann 1926- *BiE&WWA, FilmgC, ForYSC, HalFC 80, IntMPA 77, -75, -76, -78, -79, -80, NotNAT, WhoHol A, WhoThe 72, -77*
McLiam, John 1920- *BiE&WWA, NatPD[port], NotNAT, WhoHol A*
McLin, Jimmy 1908- *WhoJazz 72*
McLin, Lena *ConAmC*
McLoud, Harry Haywood 1950- *AmSCAP 80*
McLuhan, Marshall 1911- *NewYTET*
McLuhan, T C *WomWMM B*
McMahan, Robert Young 1944- *ConAmC*
McMahon, Aline 1899- *PlP&P*
McMahon, Andrew 1926- *BluesWW[port]*
McMahon, David 1909-1972 *WhScrn 77, WhoHol B*
McMahon, Ed 1923- *IntMPA 77, -75, -76, -78, -79, -80, WhoHol A*
McMahon, Horace 1906-1971 *FilmEn*
McMahon, Horace 1907-1971 *BiE&WWA, ForYSC, MotPP, MovMk, NotNAT B, WhScrn 74, -77, WhoHol B*
McMahon, John G d1968 *WhScrn 77*
McMahon, John J 1932- *IntMPA 77, -75, -76, -78, -79, -80*
McManus, George d1954 *Film 2, WhScrn 77*
McManus, John L 1891-1963 *AmSCAP 80*
McManus, John L 1897-1963 *AmSCAP 66, NotNAT B*
McMarthy, Max *PupTheA*
McMartin, John *NotNAT, WhoHol A, WhoThe 77*
McMaster, Andrew *Film 2*
McMaster, Anew 1894-1962 *EncWT, NotNAT B, OxThe, WhThe*
McMaster, Gloria Bugni 1933- *IntWWM 77, -80*
McMeekin, Colleen 1917- *IntWWM 77, -80*
McMichen, Clayton 1900- *BiDAmM, CmpEPM, EncFCWM 69*
McMillan, Ann 1923- *ConAmC*
McMillan, Lida d1940 *NotNAT B*
McMillan, Roddy 1923- *WhoThe 77*
McMillan, Walter Kenneth 1917-1945 *WhScrn 74, -77*
McMillen, Violet 1885- *WhoStg 1908*
McMullan, Frank 1907- *BiE&WWA, NotNAT*
McMullan, Jim *WhoHol A*
McMullen, Dorothy 1926- *AmSCAP 66, -80*
McMullen, Edwin D 1911- *AmSCAP 66, -80*
McMullen, Patrick T 1939- *ConAmC*
McMurray, Lillian *Film 2*
McMurray, Richard *WhoHol A*
McMurray, Vance 1910- *AmSCAP 66, -80*
McNabb, Michael Don 1952- *AmSCAP 80*
McNair, A *PupTheA*
McNair, Barbara 1939- *BiE&WWA, DrBlPA, ForYSC, WhoHol A*
McNair, Harold 1931-1971 *BiDAmM, EncJzS 70*

McNair, Jacqueline Hanna 1931- *AmSCAP 80*
McNair, Sue *WomWMM*
McNally, Ed *WhoHol A*
McNally, Horace *ForYSC*
McNally, John J d1931 *NotNAT B*
McNally, Leonard 1752-1820 *OxMus*
McNally, Stephen 1913- *FilmEn, FilmgC, ForYSC, HalFC 80, IntMPA 77, -75, -76, -78, -79, -80, WhoHol A*
McNally, Terrence 1930- *CroCD*
McNally, Terrence 1939- *ConDr 73, -77, DcLB 7[port], McGEWD, NatPD[port], NotNAT, PlP&P, WhoThe 72, -77*
McNamar, John d1968 *WhScrn 77*
McNamara, Daniel I d1962 *NotNAT B*
McNamara, Edward C 1884-1944 *Film 2, WhScrn 74, -77, WhoHol B*
McNamara, Edward J d1944 *NotNAT B*
McNamara, Maggie 1928-1978 *FilmEn, FilmgC, ForYSC, HalFC 80, IntMPA 77, -75, -76, -78, MotPP, WhoHol A*
McNamara, Ray 1899- *AmSCAP 66*
McNamara, Robin *RkOn 2[port]*
McNamara, Ted d1928 *Film 2, WhScrn 74, -77, WhoHol B*
McNamara, Thomas J *IntMPA 78, -79, -80*
McNamara, Thomas J d1953 *WhScrn 74, -77*
McNamee, Donald 1897-1940 *WhScrn 74, -77, WhoHol B*
McNames, Dorothy *Film 2*
McNaught, Anthony Jonathan 1956- *IntWWM 80*
McNaught, Bob 1915- *FilmgC, HalFC 80*
McNaught, John Charles Kirkpatrick *CreCan 1*
McNaught, William Gray 1849-1918 *Baker 78, NewGrD 80, OxMus*
McNaught, William Gray 1883-1953 *Baker 78, NewGrD 80, OxMus*
McNaughton, Charles *Film 2*
McNaughton, Gus 1884-1969 *FilmgC, HalFC 80, IlWWBF, WhScrn 74, -77, WhThe, WhoHol B*
McNaughton, Harry 1897-1967 *WhScrn 74, -77, WhoHol B*
McNaughton, Jack *WhoHol A*
McNaughton, Tom 1867-1923 *WhThe*
McNaughtons, The *WhThe*
McNay, Evelyn d1944 *NotNAT B*
McNeal, Richard *NewOrJ[port]*
McNear, Howard 1905-1969 *ForYSC, HalFC 80, WhScrn 74, -77, WhoHol B*
McNeely, Big Jay 1928- *RkOn[port]*
McNeely, Jerry Clark 1928- *AmSCAP 80, NewYTET*
McNeely, Larry P 1948- *AmSCAP 80*
McNeil, Claudia 1917- *BiE&WWA, DrBlPA, NotNAT, WhoHol A, WhoThe 72, -77*
McNeil, J Charles 1902- *AmSCAP 66*
McNeil, James Charles 1902- *ConAmC A*
McNeil, Jan Pfischner 1945- *ConAmC*
McNeil, Laurence *PupTheA*
McNeil, Libby 1917- *AmSCAP 80*
McNeil, Robert A 1889- *IntMPA 77, -75, -76, -78, -79, -80*
McNeil, Stephen 1907-1980 *AmSCAP 80*
McNeill, Donald T 1907- *AmSCAP 80*
McNeill, Marguerite Grace 1935- *IntWWM 80*
McNellis, Maggi *IntMPA 77, -75, -76, -78, -79, -80*
McNeur, Lynda *WomWMM B*
McNichol, Eileen *BiE&WWA, NotNAT*
McNicoll, Helen Galloway 1879-1915 *CreCan 1*
McNulty, Daniel Aloysius 1920- *WhoMus 72*
McNulty, Dorothy *FilmEn, WhoHol A*
McNulty, Frank Fremont 1923- *AmSCAP 66, -80*
McNutt, Marshall 1935- *AmSCAP 80*
McNutt, Patterson d1948 *NotNAT B*
McNutt, Ronald Jan 1936- *ConAmC*
McPartland, James Dugald 1907- *BiDAmM, EncJzS 70*
McPartland, Jimmy 1907- *CmpEPM, Conv 2[port], EncJzS 70, WhoJazz 72*
McPartland, Marian 1918- *AmSCAP 66, -80, BiDAmM*
McPartland, Marian 1920- *CmpEPM, EncJzS 70*
McPeake, William Curtis 1927- *BiDAmM*
McPeters, Taylor 1900-1962 *NotNAT B, WhScrn 74, -77*
McPhail, Addie *Film 2*
McPhail, Douglas d1942 *ForYSC, WhoHol B*
McPhail, Douglas 1910-1944 *WhScrn 74, -77*
McPhail, Lenora Carpenter 1907- *AmSCAP 66*
McPhail, Lindsay 1895-1965 *AmSCAP 66, -80*
McPharlin, Paul 1903-1948 *DcPup, PupTheA*
McPhatter, Clyde *ConMuA 80A*
McPhatter, Clyde 1931-1972 *BiDAmM, DrBlPA, RkOn[port]*
McPhee, Colin 1900-1964 *NewGrD 80*
McPhee, Colin 1901-1964 *Baker 78, BiDAmM, ConAmC, DcCM, OxMus*
McPhee, George 1937- *IntWWM 77, -80*
McPhee, George McBeth 1937- *WhoMus 72*
McPhee, Joe *IlEncJ*
McPherson, Alexander 1937- *WhoOp 76*
McPherson, Charles 1939- *BiDAmM, EncJzS 70*
McPherson, Frances Marie 1912- *ConAmC*
McPherson, Margaret *WomWMM*
McPherson, Mervyn 1892- *WhThe*
McPherson, Quinton 1871-1940 *WhScrn 74, -77, WhoHol B*
McPherson, Richard Cecil 1883-1944 *ConAmC*
McPhillips, Hugh 1920- *IntMPA 75, -76*
McPugg, Cauliflower *JoeFr*
McQuade, Edward *Film 2*
McQuary, Charles S 1908-1970 *WhScrn 74, -77*
McQuattie, Sheila 1943- *IntWWM 80*
McQueen, Butterfly 1911- *BlksB&W C, DrBlPA, FilmEn, FilmgC, ForYSC, HalFC 80, MotPP, MovMk[port], ThFT[port], What 2[port], WhoHol A, WhoThe 72, -77*
McQueen, Jodi 1945- *AmSCAP 80*
McQueen, John Campbell 1931- *WhoMus 72*
McQueen, Steve *IntMPA 75, -76*
McQueen, Steve 1930- *BiDFilm, -81, FilmEn, FilmgC, ForYSC, HalFC 80, IntMPA 77, -78, -79, -80, MotPP, MovMk[port], OxFilm, WhoHol A, WhoHrs 80[port], WorEFlm*
McQueen, Steve 1932- *CmMov*
McQueen, Thelma *BlksB&W*
McQueeney, Robert *IntMPA 77, -75, -76, -78, -79, -80*
McQuiggan, Jack 1935- *BiE&WWA, NotNAT*
McQuire, Tom *Film 2*
McQuoid, Rose Lee 1887-1962 *NotNAT B, WhScrn 74, -77, WhoHol B*
McRae, Bruce 1867-1927 *Film 1, NotNAT B, WhScrn 74, -77, WhThe, WhoStg 1908*
McRae, Carmen 1922- *BiDAmM, DrBlPA, EncJzS 70*
McRae, Duncan d1931 *NotNAT B, WhScrn 77*
McRae, Edna *CnOxB*
McRae, Edna L *DancEn 78*
McRae, Ellen *FilmEn, WhoHol A*
McRae, Henry 1888- *TwYS A*
McRae, Teddy 1908- *AmSCAP 66*
McRae, Theodore 1908- *AmSCAP 80, WhoJazz 72*
McRea, Bruce 1867-1927 *WhoHol B*
M'Creery, John 1780?-1825 *BiDAmM*
McReynolds, Denny E 1929-1978 *AmSCAP 80*
McReynolds, James Monroe 1927- *BiDAmM*
McReynolds, Janet 1933- *ConAmTC*
McReynolds, Jesse 1929- *BiDAmM, IlEncCM[port]*
McReynolds, Jim 1927- *IlEncCM[port]*
McReynolds, Karen *AmSCAP 80*
McShane, Ian 1942- *FilmgC, HalFC 80, WhoHol A, WhoThe 72, -77*
McShane, Kitty 1898-1964 *IlWWBF, NotNAT B, WhScrn 74, -77, WhoHol B*
McShann, Hootie 1909- *EncJzS 70*
McShann, Jay *BgBands 74*
McShann, Jay 1909- *BiDAmM, CmpEPM, EncJzS 70, IlEncJ, WhoJazz 72*
McShann, Jay Columbus 1916- *AmSCAP 80*
McSpadden, C B *PupTheA*
McStay, Janetta 1919- *NewGrD 80*
McTaggart, James 1911-1949 *WhScrn 74, -77*
McTaggart, James 1928-1975 *HalFC 80*
McTell, Blind Willie 1898?-1962? *NewGrD 80*
McTell, Ralph *IlEncR*
McTell, Willie Samuel 1901-1959 *BluesWW[port]*
McTurk, Joe 1899-1961 *WhScrn 74, -77*
McTurk, Joe 1899-1967 *WhoHol B*
McVea, Jack 1914- *WhoJazz 72*
McVeagh, Diana M 1926- *IntWWM 77, -80, NewGrD 80, WhoMus 72*
McVeagh, Eve *WhoHol A*
McVey, Lucille *WhScrn 74, -77*
McVey, Lucille 1892- *WomWMM*
McVey, Lucille 1895- *Film 1*
McVey, Patrick 1910-1973 *WhScrn 77, WhoHol B*
McVey, Paul *ForYSC*
McVey, Tyler *ForYSC, WhoHol A*
McVicar, George Christie 1919- *IntWWM 77, -80, WhoMus 72*
McVicker, Horace d1931 *NotNAT B*
McVicker, J H d1896 *NotNAT B*
McVicker, Julius 1876-1940 *WhScrn 74, -77, WhoHol B*
McVicker, Mary *PlP&P*
McWade, Edward d1943 *Film 2, WhScrn 74, -77, WhoHol B*
McWade, Margaret d1956 *Film 2, WhoHol B*
McWade, Margaret 1872-1956 *WhScrn 77*
McWade, Margaret 1873-1956 *Vers B[port]*
McWade, Robert, Jr. 1882-1938 *Film 2, HolCA[port], NotNAT B, WhScrn 74, -77, WhThe, WhoHol B*
McWade, Robert, Sr. 1835-1913 *NotNAT B, WhScrn 77, WhoHol B*
McWatters, Arthur J 1871-1963 *WhScrn 74, -77*
McWhinnie, Donald 1920- *BiE&WWA, NotNAT, WhoThe 72, -77*
McWhood, Leonard Beecher 1870-1939 *BiDAmM, ConAmC*
McWhorter, Helen Thompson 1916- *IntWWM 77*
McWilliam, Clement Charles 1934- *IntWWM 77, -80*
McWilliams, Harry Kenneth 1907- *IntMPA 77, -75, -76, -78, -79, -80*
MC5 *ConMuA 80A, IlEncR*
Meacham *NewGrD 80*
Meacham, Anne 1925- *BiE&WWA, NotNAT, WhoHol A, WhoThe 72, -77*
Meacham, Frank W 1850?- *BiDAmM*
Meacham, Horace 1789-1861? *NewGrD 80*
Meacham, John, Jr. 1785-1844 *NewGrD 80*
Meachum, James H d1963 *NotNAT B*
Mead, Alice *PupTheA*
Mead, Andrew *ConAmC*
Mead, Edward Gould 1892- *AmSCAP 66, -80, ConAmC*
Mead, George 1902- *AmSCAP 66, -80, BiDAmM, ConAmC*
Mead, Sister Janet 1938- *RkOn 2[port]*
Mead, John Holstead 1937- *IntWWM 77*
Mead, Marjorie 1905- *WhoMus 72*
Mead, Robert 1940- *CnOxB, DancEn 78, NewYTET*
Mead, Taylor *WhoHol A*
Mead, Thomas 1904- *IntMPA 77, -75, -76, -78, -79, -80*
Meade, Bill d1941 *WhScrn 74, -77*
Meade, Claire 1883-1968 *WhScrn 77, WhoHol B*
Meade, E Kidder, Jr. *NewYTET*
Meade, Julia 1928- *BiE&WWA, ForYSC, NotNAT, WhoHol A*
Meader, Daniel *PupTheA*
Meader, Deborah *PupTheA*
Meader, George *ForYSC*
Meader, George 1888-1963 *Baker 78, WhScrn 77, WhThe*
Meader, George 1890-1963 *BiE&WWA, WhoHol B*
Meader, Vaughn 1936- *What 5[port]*
Meader, Vaughn 1937- *JoeFr[port]*
Meades, Kenneth Richardson 1943- *IntMPA 77, -75, -76, -78, -79, -80*
Meadow, Lynne 1946- *NotNAT*
Meadows, Audrey 1924- *ForYSC, MotPP, NewYTET, WhoHol A*
Meadows, Fred 1904- *AmSCAP 66, -80*
Meadows, George *Film 2*
Meadows, Jayne 1923- *ForYSC*
Meadows, Jayne 1926- *BiE&WWA, MotPP, WhoHol A*
Meadows, Joyce *ForYSC*

Meadows, Julia Ann 1939- *WhoMus 72*
Meadows White, Mrs. *OxMus*
Meadows White, Alice Mary *NewGrD 80*
Meagher, Aileen Alethea 1910- *CreCan 2*
Meakin, Charles 1880-1961 *Film 2, WhScrn 74, -77, WhoHol B*
Meakin, Ruth 1879-1939 *WhScrn 74, -77*
Meakins, Charles d1951 *NotNAT B*
Meale, Richard Graham 1932- *IntWWM 80, NewGrD 80, WhoMus 72*
Mealli, Giovanni Antonio Pandolfi *NewGrD 80*
Mealy, Norman Carleton 1923- *IntWWM 77*
Meaney, Donald V *IntMPA 78, -79, -80, NewYTET*
Meano, Cesare 1906-1958 *CnMD*
Means, Claude 1912- *BiDAmM, ConAmC*
Means, Thomas L 1918- *IntMPA 75, -76*
Meany, Donald V *IntMPA 77, -75, -76*
Meany, Stephen Joseph d1890 *OxMus*
Meara, Anne 1941?- *HalFC 80, WhoHol A*
Meares *NewGrD 80*
Mears *NewGrD 80*
Mears, Benjamin S 1872-1952 *WhScrn 74, -77*
Mears, J H d1956 *NotNAT B*
Mears, Marion 1899-1970 *WhScrn 74, -77*
Mears, Martha *WhoHol A*
Measor, Adela 1860-1933 *NotNAT B, WhThe*
Measor, Beryl 1908-1965 *WhThe*
Meat Loaf 1947- *RkOn 2[port]*
Meatloaf *ConMuA 80A[port]*
Meccoli, Domenico 1913- *IntMPA 75, -76*
Mech, Raymond Andrew 1923- *IntWWM 77, -80*
Mechem, Kirke Lewis 1925- *AmSCAP 80, ConAmC*
Mechetti *NewGrD 80*
Mechetti, Carlo 1748-1811 *NewGrD 80*
Mechetti, Karl 1811-1847 *NewGrD 80*
Mechetti, Pietro 1777-1850 *NewGrD 80*
Mechura, Leopold Eugen 1804-1870 *NewGrD 80*
Meck, Giuseppe 1690-1758 *NewGrD 80*
Meck, Joseph 1690-1758 *NewGrD 80*
Meck, Nadezhda Von 1831-1894 *Baker 78, OxMus*
Meckenheuser, Johann Georg 1666- *NewGrD 80*
Meckert, Ruth Louise 1927- *IntWWM 77, -80*
Meckna, Robert Michael 1945- *IntWWM 80*
Meco 1939- *RkOn 2[port]*
Meco, Richard *NewGrD 80*
Mecum, Dudley C 1896-1978 *AmSCAP 66, -80*
Medak, Peter *FilmgC, HalFC 80, IntMPA 78, -79, -80*
Medallions, The *RkOn*
Medavoy, Mike 1941- *IntMPA 78, -79, -80*
Medcraft, Russell Graham d1962 *NotNAT B*
Medcroft, Russell *Film 2*
Meddoks, Mikhail Egorovich 1747-1825 *OxThe*
Medecin, Pierre 1935- *WhoOp 76*
Medek, Tilo 1940- *IntWWM 77, -80, NewGrD 80*
Medema, Kenneth Peter 1943- *AmSCAP 80*
Meder, Johann Gabriel *NewGrD 80*
Meder, Johann Valentin 1649?-1719 *NewGrD 80*
Mederitsch, Johann 1752-1835 *NewGrD 80*
Medford, Don 1920?- *FilmgC, HalFC 80, IntMPA 77, -75, -76, -78, -79, -80*
Medford, Kay 1920- *BiE&WWA, ForYSC, NotNAT, WhoHol A, WhoThe 72, -77*
Medford, Mark d1914 *NotNAT B*
Medford, Sylvia *BlkWAB[port]*
Medhurst, Dorothy *PupTheA*
Medici *NewGrD 80*
Medici, Catherine De 1519-1589 *DancEn 78*
Medici, Cosimo 1389-1464 *NewGrD 80*
Medici, Cosimo 1519-1574 *NewGrD 80*
Medici, Giovanni Di Bicci De' 1360-1429 *NewGrD 80*
Medici, Lorenzino DiPier Francesco *OxThe*
Medici, Lorenzo 1395-1440 *NewGrD 80*
Medici, Lorenzo 1449?-1492 *OxThe*
Medici, Mario 1913- *NewGrD 80*
Medicine Head *IlEncR*
Medicus, Emil 1882- *IntWWM 77, WhoMus 72*
Medin, Harriet *WhoHol A*
Medina, Fernand Perez De *NewGrD 80*
Medina, Patricia *IntMPA 77, -75, -76, -78, -79, -80, MotPP*
Medina, Patricia 1919- *WhoHol A*
Medina, Patricia 1920- *FilmEn, FilmgC, ForYSC, MovMk*
Medina, Patricia 1921- *HalFC 80, IIWWBF*
Medina, Patricia 1923- *BiE&WWA*
Medina Mendez, Carmen 1919- *AmSCAP 80*
Medins *NewGrD 80*
Medins, Janis 1890-1966 *Baker 78, NewGrD 80*
Medins, Jazeps 1877-1947 *NewGrD 80*
Medins, Jekabs 1885-1971 *NewGrD 80*
Medley, Bill 1940- *RkOn 2[port]*
Medley, Cynthia Conwell 1929- *AmSCAP 66*
Medley, William Thomas 1940- *IntMPA 77, -75, -76, -78, -79, -80*
Medman, Edward A 1937- *IntMPA 79, -80*
Mednick, Murray 1939- *ConDr 73, -77, NotNAT*
Medoff, Mark 1940- *ConDr 77, DcLB 7[port], NatPD[port], NotNAT*
Medtner, Nicholas 1880-1951 *DcCom&M 79, OxMus*
Medtner, Nicolai 1880-1951 *DcCM*
Medtner, Nicolas 1880-1951 *CompSN[port]*
Medtner, Nikolai 1879?-1951 *BnBkM 80*
Medtner, Nikolai 1880-1951 *Baker 78, MusMk*
Medtner, Nikolay Karlovich *NewGrD 80*
Medvedeff, Dorothy *WhoMus 72*
Medvedkin, Alexander 1900- *OxFilm*
Medwall, Henry *McGEWD, OxThe*
Medwick, Joe d1975 *WhoHol C*
Medwin, Michael *WhoHol A*
Medwin, Michael 1923- *FilmgC, HalFC 80, IIWWBF*
Medwin, Michael 1925- *IntMPA 77, -75, -76, -78, -79, -80*
Mee, Charles Louis, Jr. 1938- *BiE&WWA*
Meech, Edward Montana d1952 *WhScrn 74, -77*
Meehan, Danny *AmSCAP 66, -80, WhoHol A*
Meehan, John d1963 *NotNAT B*
Meehan, John 1890-1954 *FilmEn, WhScrn 74, -77*
Meehan, John 1902- *FilmEn*
Meehan, Leo J *TwYS A*
Meehan, Lew 1891-1951 *Film 2, WhScrn 77, WhoHol B*
Meehan, Martha 1923- *AmSCAP 80*
Meehan, Nancy *CmpGMD*
Meehan, Thomas G 1895- *AmSCAP 66*
Meek, Donald 1880-1946 *FilmEn, Film 2, FilmgC, ForYSC, HalFC 80, HolCA[port], MotPP, MovMk[port], NotNAT B, Vers A[port], WhScrn 74, -77, WhThe, WhoHol B*
Meek, Frances McCullough 1934- *AmSCAP 80*
Meek, Kate d1925 *NotNAT B*
Meeker, Alfred 1901-1942 *WhScrn 74, -77*
Meeker, George 1888-1963 *Vers B[port]*
Meeker, George 1904?-1963 *Film 2, ForYSC, TwYS, WhScrn 74, WhoHol B*
Meeker, John *Film 2*
Meeker, Ralph 1920- *BiDFilm, -81, BiE&WWA, CmMov, FilmEn, FilmgC, ForYSC, HalFC 80, IntMPA 77, -75, -76, -78, -79, -80, MotPP, MovMk, NotNAT, WhoHol A, WhoHrs 80, WhoThe 72, -77, WorEFlm*
Meeks, Kate *Film 1*
Meeks, Larry Monroe 1930- *AmSCAP 66, -80*
Meeks, Quincy D 1910- *IntWWM 77, -80*
Meer, John Henry VanDer 1920- *NewGrD 80*
Meerens, Charles 1831-1909 *Baker 78*
Meeropol, Abel *AmSCAP 80*
Meers *NewGrD 80*
Meerson, Lazare 1900-1938 *DcFM, FilmEn, FilmgC, HalFC 80, OxFilm, WorEFlm*
Meerti, Elisa *NewGrD 80*
Meerts, Lambert 1800-1863 *Baker 78*
Meery, Ila *Film 2*
Mees, Arthur 1850-1923 *Baker 78, BiDAmM*
Mees, Joseph-Henri 1777-1858 *NewGrD 80*
Meester, Louis De 1904- *Baker 78, DcCM, NewGrD 80*
Meetz, Raymond 1785?- *BiDAmM*
Meeuwisse, Willy 1914-1952 *Baker 78*
Meeuws-Tonnaer, Henny 1944- *IntWWM 77, -80*
Mefano, Paul 1937- *Baker 78, DcCM, NewGrD 80*
Megard, Andree 1869- *WhThe*
Megatrons, The *RkOn*
Meged, Aharon 1920- *CnThe, REnWD[port]*
Megeney, Dorothy 1900- *WhoMus 72*
Megerle, Abraham 1607-1680 *NewGrD 80*
Megerlin, Alfred 1880- *BiDAmM*
Meggs, Mary d1691 *OxThe*
Meghor, Camillo 1935- *WhoOp 76*
Megli, Domenico Maria *NewGrD 80*
Meglin, Nick 1935- *AmSCAP 80*
Megna, John 1952- *BiE&WWA, WhoHol A*
Megowan, Don 1925?- *ForYSC, WhoHol A, WhoHrs 80[port]*
Megrue, Roi Cooper 1883-1927 *NotNAT B, WhThe*
Mehaffey, Blanche 1907-1968 *Film 2, WhScrn 77, WhoHol B*
Mehaffey, Harry S d1963 *NotNAT B*
Mehboob 1907-1964 *FilmEn, FilmgC, HalFC 80*
Mehboob 1909-1964 *WorEFlm*
Mehboob Khan, Ramjakhan 1907-1964 *DcFM*
Mehegan, John 1920- *ConAmC, EncJzS 70, IntWWM 77, -80*
Mehler, Friedrich Julius 1896- *IntWWM 80*
Mehr, Sheldon Marshall 1931- *AmSCAP 80*
Mehra, Lal Chand *WhoHol A*
Mehring, Margaret *WomWMM B*
Mehring, Walter 1896- *CnMD, EncWT, Ent*
Mehrkens, Friedrich Adolf 1840-1899 *Baker 78*
Mehrmann, Helen Alice d1934 *WhScrn 74, -77, WhoHol B*
Mehta, Mehli 1908- *Baker 78*
Mehta, Zubin 1936- *Baker 78, BiDAmM, BnBkM 80, CmOp, IntWWM 77, -80, MusMk, MusSN[port], NewEOp 71, NewGrD 80, WhoMus 72, WhoOp 76*
Mehul, Etienne Nicolas 1763-1817 *Baker 78, BnBkM 80, CmOp, GrComp[port], MusMk[port], NewEOp 71, NewGrD 80[port], OxMus*
Mei, Girolamo 1519-1594 *NewGrD 80*
Mei, Lan-Fang 1894-1943 *NotNAT A, -B*
Mei, Lan-Fang 1894-1961 *EncWT, NewGrD 80, OxThe, REnWD[port]*
Mei, Orazio 1731-1788 *NewGrD 80*
Mei, Lady Tsen *Film 1, MotPP*
Mei-Figner, Medea 1858-1952 *CmOp, NewGrD 80*
Meibach, Ina *ConMuA 80B*
Meibom, Marcus 1620?-1710 *Baker 78*
Meibom, Marcus 1620?-1711 *NewGrD 80*
Meibomius, Marcus 1620?-1711 *NewGrD 80*
Meiboom, Marcus 1620?-1711 *NewGrD 80*
Meier, Bernhard 1923- *IntWWM 80, NewGrD 80*
Meier, Don *NewYTET*
Meier, George B *ConMuA 80B*
Meier, Gustav 1929- *IntWWM 80, NewGrD 80*
Meier, Herbert 1928- *CnMD*
Meier, Johann David *NewGrD 80*
Meier, Johanna *WhoOp 76*
Meier, Norbert Al-Fred 1933- *IntWWM 77*
Meier, Peter *NewGrD 80*
Meifred, Pierre-Joseph Emile 1791-1867 *NewGrD 80*
Meigham, Margaret d1961 *WhScrn 74, -77*
Meighan, James, Jr. d1970 *WhoHol B*
Meighan, Thomas 1879-1936 *FilmEn, Film 1, -2, FilmgC, ForYSC, HalFC 80, MotPP, MovMk, NotNAT B, TwYS, WhScrn 74, -77, WhThe, WhoHol B*
Meignen, Leopold 1793-1873 *BiDAmM*
Meigret, Robert 1508-1568 *NewGrD 80*
Meijer, Axel 1940- *IntWWM 77, -80*
Meikle, William *OxMus*
Meiland, Jacob 1542-1577 *NewGrD 80*
Meiland, Jacob 1543?-1577 *MusMk*
Meiland, Jakob 1542-1577 *Baker 78, NewGrD 80*
Meilhac, Henri 1831-1897 *EncWT, McGEWD[port], NotNAT B, OxThe, PlP&P*
Meili, Max 1899-1970 *NewGrD 80*
Meilleur, Jacques *CreCan 1*
Meillon, John 1933- *FilmgC, HalFC 80, WhoHol A*

Meinardus, Ludwig Siegfried 1827-1896 *Baker 78, NewGrD 80*
Meineche, Annelise *WomWMM*
Meinecke, Christopher 1782-1850 *BiDAmM*
Meinert, John *OxMus*
Meinert, Rudolf *Film 2*
Meinhard, Edith *Film 2*
Meinken, Fred 1882-1958 *AmSCAP 66, -80*
Meinl, Ewald 1937- *NewGrD 80*
Meinl, Franz 1910- *NewGrD 80*
Meinrad, Josef 1913- *EncWT*
Meise, Heinrich Zur *NewGrD 80*
Meisel, Maribel 1936- *IntWWM 77, -80*
Meiser, Edith 1898- *BiE&WWA, NotNAT, WhoHol A, WhoThe 77*
Meisl, Karl 1775-1853 *OxThe*
Meisle, Kathryn 1895-1970 *BiDAmM*
Meisner, Philipp 1748-1816 *NewGrD 80*
Meisner, Randy 1946- *AmSCAP 80*
Meisner, Sanford 1905- *BiE&WWA, NotNAT, PlP&P[port]*
Meissner, Philipp 1748-1816 *NewGrD 80*
Meissonnier, Jean Antoine *NewGrD 80*
Meister, Barbara Ann *BiE&WWA, NotNAT*
Meister, Debbie *ConMuA 80B*
Meister, Hans 1937- *CnOxB, DancEn 78*
Meister, Johann Friedrich 1638?-1697 *NewGrD 80*
Meister, Otto L 1869-1944 *WhScrn 74, -77, WhoHol B*
Meister, Philip *NotNAT*
Meister, Scott R 1950- *ConAmC*
Meister, Theodore Henry 1940- *AmSCAP 80*
Meistre, Matthaeus Le *NewGrD 80*
Meiswinkel, Frank 1938- *WhoOp 76*
Meitus, Juli Sergeyevich 1903- *IntWWM 77, -80*
Meitus, Yuli 1903- *Baker 78*
Mejer, Johann David *NewGrD 80*
Mejia, Carlos Anthony 1923-1969 *AmSCAP 66, -80*
Mejuto, Andres *PupTheA*
Mekas, Adolfas 1922- *WorEFlm*
Mekas, Adolfas 1925- *FilmgC, HalFC 80, OxFilm*
Mekas, Jonas 1922- *FilmEn, FilmgC, HalFC 80, OxFilm, WorEFlm*
Mekeel, Joyce 1931- *ConAmC, IntWWM 77, -80*
Mekler, Mani *IntWWM 80*
Mel And Tim *RkOn 2[port]*
Mel, Gaudio *NewGrD 80*
Mel, Raynaldus Del 1554?-1598? *NewGrD 80*
Mel, Renatus Del 1554?-1598? *NewGrD 80*
Mel, Rene Del 1554?-1598? *NewGrD 80*
Mel, Renerus Del 1554?-1598? *NewGrD 80*
Mel, Rinaldo Del 1554?-1598? *NewGrD 80*
Mela, Eugenia *OxMus*
Melachrino, George 1909-1965 *Baker 78, NewGrD 80, WhScrn 74, -77, WhoMus 72*
Melamed, David J 1911- *IntMPA 77, -75, -76, -78, -79, -80*
Melamed, Nissan Cohen 1906- *IntWWM 77, -80*
Melanchthon, Philipp 1497-1560 *NewGrD 80*
Melander, Stina-Britta 1924- *WhoMus 72*
Melander, Sven 1924- *IntWWM 77*
Melani *NewGrD 80*
Melani, Alessandro 1639-1703 *NewGrD 80*
Melani, Atto 1626-1714 *NewGrD 80*
Melani, Jacopo 1623-1676 *Baker 78, NewGrD 80*
Melanie 1947- *ConMuA 80A, IlEncR[port], RkOn 2[port]*
Melanippides *NewGrD 80*
Melano, Fabrizio 1938- *WhoOp 76*
Melaro, H J M 1928- *AmSCAP 66*
Melaro, H J M 1931- *AmSCAP 80*
Melartin, Erik 1875-1937 *NewGrD 80*
Melartin, Erkki 1875-1937 *Baker 78, NewGrD 80, OxMus*
Melas, Spyros 1883- *CnMD, REnWD[port]*
Melato, Mariangela *WhoHol A*
Melba, Madame 1863- *WhoStg 1906, -1908*
Melba, Nellie 1859-1931 *Baker 78, BiDAmM, BnBkM 80[port], MusSN[port], NewEOp 71*
Melba, Nellie 1861-1931 *CmOp, MusMk[port], NewGrD 80[port], OxMus*
Melbourne, Victoria *OxMus*
Melby, John B 1941- *ConAmC*
Melcelius, Jiri 1624-1693 *NewGrD 80*
Melcer, Henryk 1869-1928 *Baker 78*
Melcer-Szczawinski, Henryk 1869-1928 *NewGrD 80*
Melcher, Martin 1915-1968 *FilmEn, FilmgC, HalFC 80, NewYTET*
Melchers, Henrik Melcher 1882-1961 *Baker 78*
Melchinger, Ulrich 1937- *WhoOp 76*
Melchior De Brissia *NewGrD 80*
Melchior, Georges *Film 2*
Melchior, Ib 1917- *FilmEn, FilmgC, HalFC 80, IntMPA 77, -75, -76, -78, -79, -80, WhoHrs 80*
Melchior, Lauritz 1890-1973 *Baker 78, BiDAmM, BnBkM 80, CmOp, FilmEn, FilmgC, ForYSC, HalFC 80, MGM[port], MovMk, MusMk, MusSN[port], NewEOp 71, NewGrD 80[port], WhScrn 77, WhoHol B, WhoMus 72*
Melchior, Lauritz 1913- *What 2[port]*
Melcl, Jiri *NewGrD 80*
Meldonian, Richard A 1930- *BiDAmM*
Mele, Frank 1921- *IntWWM 77, -80*
Mele, Giovanni Battista 1701-1752? *NewGrD 80*
Melendez, Bill *NewYTET*
Melesh, Alex 1890-1949 *Film 2, WhScrn 74, -77, WhoHol B*
Melesville 1787-1865 *NewEOp 71*
Melfi, Leonard 1935- *ConDr 73, -77, EncWT, NotNAT, PlP&P, WhoThe 72, -77*
Melfiche, Cola *NewGrD 80*
Melfio, Bastiano *NewGrD 80*
Melfio, Gioan Battista *NewGrD 80*
Melford, Austin 1884- *IntMPA 77, -75, -76, -78, -79, -80, WhThe*
Melford, George 1889-1961 *FilmEn, Film 1, ForYSC, TwYS A, WhScrn 74, -77, WhoHol B*
Melford, Jack 1899- *WhThe, WhoHol A*
Melford, Jill 1934- *WhoHol A, WhoThe 72, -77*
Melford, Louise 1880-1942 *WhScrn 74, -77, WhoHol B*
Melgarejo, Jesus 1876-1941 *WhScrn 74, -77*
Melgas, Diogo Dias 1638-1700 *NewGrD 80*
Melgaz, Diogo Dias 1638-1700 *NewGrD 80*
Meli, Pietro Paolo *NewGrD 80*
Melia, Joe *WhoThe 77*
Melichar, Alois 1896-1976 *Baker 78, WhoMus 72*
Melies, George 1861-1938 *TwYS A, WomWMM*
Melies, Georges 1861-1938 *BiDFilm, -81, DcFM, FilmEn, Film 1, FilmgC, HalFC 80, MovMk[port], OxFilm, WhScrn 77, WhoHrs 80, WorEFlm*
Melij, Pietro Paolo *NewGrD 80*
Melik-Aslanian, Emanuel 1915- *IntWWM 77, -80*
Melik-Pashayev, Alexander Shamil'yevich 1905-1964 *Baker 78, NewGrD 80*
Melikov, Arif 1933- *NewGrD 80*
Melikova, Genia 1930- *CnOxB, DancEn 78[port]*
Melikyan, Romanos Hovakimi 1883-1935 *NewGrD 80*
Melin, Bengt E 1928- *IntWWM 80*
Melin, William Eugene 1940- *IntWWM 77*
Meline, Florant 1790-1827 *BiDAmM*
Melis, Carmen 1885-1967 *Baker 78, BiDAmM*
Melis, Emanuel 1831-1916 *NewGrD 80*
Melis, Gyorgy 1923- *NewGrD 80*
Melis, Jose 1920- *AmSCAP 66, -80*
Melish, Fuller, Jr. *Film 2*
Melkikh, Dmitri 1885-1943 *Baker 78*
Melkonian, Zaban 1931- *IntWWM 77, -80*
Melkus, Eduard 1928- *IntWWM 77, -80, NewGrD 80*
Mell, David 1604-1662 *NewGrD 80*
Mell, Davie 1604-1662 *NewGrD 80*
Mell, Davis 1604-1662 *NewGrD 80*
Mell, Gaudio *NewGrD 80*
Mell, Gertrud Maria 1947- *IntWWM 77, -80*
Mell, Marisa 1929- *HalFC 80, WhoHol A*
Mell, Max 1882-1971 *CnMD, CroCD, McGEWD, ModWD, OxThe*
Melle, Gil *HalFC 80*
Melle, Rinaldo Del *NewGrD 80*
Mellenbruch, Giles Edward 1911- *AmSCAP 80*
Mellencamp, John J 1951- *AmSCAP 80*
Meller, Edith *Film 2*
Meller, Harro 1907-1963 *NotNAT B, WhScrn 74, -77, WhoHol B*
Meller, Raquel 1888-1962 *Film 2, NotNAT B, WhScrn 74, -77, WhoHol B*
Mellers, Wilfrid Howard 1914- *Baker 78, DcCM, IntWWM 77, -80, NewGrD 80, OxMus, WhoMus 72*
Melles, Carl 1926- *IntWWM 77, -80*
Melli, Domenico Maria *NewGrD 80*
Melli, Pietro Paolo *NewGrD 80*
Mellinger, Max 1906-1968 *WhScrn 77, WhoHol B*
Mellinina, Ardita *Film 1*
Mellion, John 1933- *MovMk*
Mellish, Colonel 1777?- *OxMus*
Mellish, Fuller *Film 1*
Mellish, Fuller 1865-1936 *NotNAT B, WhThe, WhoHol B, WhoStg 1908*
Mellish, Fuller, Jr. 1895-1930 *NotNAT B, WhScrn 74, -77, WhoHol B*
Mellnas, Arne 1933- *Baker 78, DcCM, IntWWM 77, -80, NewGrD 80*
Mello, Leonce 1888?-1941? *NewOrJ*
Mello, Manuel John 1886-1961 *NewOrJ*
Mello, Sanford 1901?- *NewOrJ*
Mello-Kings, The *RkOn*
Mello-Tones, The *RkOn[port]*
Mellon, Ada d1914 *NotNAT B*
Mellon, Mrs. Alfred 1824-1909 *NotNAT B, OxThe*
Mellon, Esther Lousie 1950- *BlkWAB*
Mellon, Harriot 1777-1837 *OxThe*
Mellor, Hugh *OxMus*
Mellor, William C 1904-1963 *FilmEn, FilmgC, HalFC 80, WorEFlm*
Melly, Andree 1932- *WhoHol A, WhoThe 72, -77*
Melly, George 1926- *IlEncJ, IlEncR, IntWWM 77, -80*
Melmerfelt, Sixten *Film 2*
Melmoth, Mrs. 1749-1823 *BiDAmM*
Melmoth, Charlotte 1749-1823 *NotNAT B, OxThe, PlP&P*
Melmoth, Courtney 1749-1814 *NotNAT B*
Melmuka, Radomir 1938- *IntWWM 77, -80*
Melngailis, Emilis 1874-1954 *NewGrD 80*
Melnick, Daniel 1934- *IntMPA 77, -76, -78, -79, -80, NewYTET*
Melnick, Linda Rodgers *AmSCAP 66*
Melniker, Benjamin 1913- *IntMPA 77, -75, -76, -78, -79, -80*
Melnikov, Ivan Alexandrovich 1832-1906 *Baker 78, CmOp, NewGrD 80*
Melnitz, William W 1900- *BiE&WWA, NotNAT*
Melnotte, Violet 1852-1935 *OxThe, WhThe*
Melnotte, Violet 1856-1935 *NotNAT B*
Melody Knights *BiDAmM*
Melody Masters, The *BiDAmM*
Melody Ranch Band *BiDAmM*
Meloy, Elizabeth 1904- *ConAmC*
Melrose, Frank 1907-1941 *CmpEPM, WhoJazz 72*
Melrose, Ronald Keith Lasonde 1954- *AmSCAP 80*
Melrose, Walter 1889-1968 *AmSCAP 66, -80, BiDAmM*
Melrose Band *BiDAmM*
Melross, Agnes Helen *WhoMus 72*
Melsher, Irving 1906-1962 *AmSCAP 66, -80*
Melson, John 1930- *IntMPA 79, -80*
Melton, Barry 1947- *IntWWM 77*
Melton, Frank 1907-1951 *WhScrn 74, -77, WhoHol B*
Melton, James d1961 *WhoHol B*
Melton, James 1904-1961 *Baker 78, BiDAmM, CmpEPM, FilmgC, ForYSC, HalFC 80*
Melton, James 1905-1961 *WhScrn 74, -77*
Melton, Sid *Vers A[port], WhoHol A*
Melton, Sidney *ForYSC*
Meltz, Valerie 1936- *IntWWM 77*
Meltzelius, Jiri *NewGrD 80*
Meltzer, Adam d1609 *NewGrD 80*
Meltzer, Charles Henry d1936 *NotNAT B, WhThe, WhoStg 1906, -1908*
Meltzer, Charles Henry 1852-1936 *Baker 78*

Meltzer, Charles Henry 1853-1936 *BiDAmM*
Meltzer, Harvey *ConMuA 80B*
Meltzer, Richard Bruce 1945- *AmSCAP 80*
Meluzzi, Salvatore 1813-1897 *Baker 78*
Melville, Alan 1910- *BiE&WWA, EncMT, NotNAT A, WhoThe 72, -77*
Melville, Andrew d1938 *NotNAT B*
Melville, Andrew 1912- *WhThe*
Melville, Clarissa Brayton 1941- *IntWWM 77, -80*
Melville, Derek *IntWWM 77, -80, WhoMus 72*
Melville, Emelie 1852-1932 *Film 2*
Melville, Emilie 1852-1932 *NotNAT B, WhScrn 77, WhoHol B*
Melville, Frederick 1876-1938 *NotNAT B, OxThe, WhThe*
Melville, Herman 1819-1891 *NewEOp 71*
Melville, Jean-Pierre 1917-1973 *BiDFilm, -81, DcFM, FilmEn, FilmgC, HalFC 80, OxFilm, WorEFlm*
Melville, Josie *Film 2*
Melville, June 1915-1970 *WhThe*
Melville, Kenneth 1929- *CnOxB*
Melville, Kenneth 1932- *DancEn 78*
Melville, Rose 1873-1946 *Film 1, NotNAT B, WhScrn 74, -77, WhThe, WhoHol B, WhoStg 1906, -1908*
Melville, Sam *WhoHol A*
Melville, Walter 1875-1937 *NotNAT B, OxThe, WhThe*
Melville, Winifred d1950 *NotNAT B*
Melville, Winnie d1937 *NotNAT B, WhThe*
Melvin, Donnie *WhoHol A*
Melvin, Duncan 1913- *WhThe*
Melvin, Harold *DrBlPA*
Melvin, Harold & The Bluenotes *RkOn 2[port]*
Melvin, John Redvers 1933- *WhoMus 72*
Melvin, Murray 1932- *FilmgC, HalFC 80, WhoHol A, WhoThe 72, -77*
Melvin, Sophia B 1916- *IntWWM 77, -80*
Melvoin, Michael 1937- *AmSCAP 80, BiDAmM*
Mely, Pietro Paolo *NewGrD 80*
Melyan, Theodore 1917- *AmSCAP 80*
Membree, Edmond 1820-1882 *Baker 78*
Meminger, Minna Shklar 1930- *IntWWM 77, -80*
Memmo, Dionisio *NewGrD 80*
Memo, Dionisio *NewGrD 80*
Memphis Blues Boy *BluesWW*
Memphis Jim *BluesWW*
Memphis Minnie 1896-1973 *BluesWW, CmpEPM, NewGrD 80*
Memphis Mose *BluesWW*
Memphis Slim 1915- *BiDAmM, BluesWW, IlEncJ*
Memphis Students *BiDAmM*
Memphis Willie B *BluesWW*
Mena, Gabriel *NewGrD 80*
Menager, Laurent 1835-1902 *Baker 78*
Menahan, Jean d1963 *WhScrn 77*
Menalt, Gabriel d1687 *NewGrD 80*
Menander 342BC-290?BC *NewGrD 80*
Menander 342?BC-291?BC *EncWT, NotNAT B*
Menander 342?BC-292?BC *CnThe, Ent, OxThe, REnWD[port]*
Menander 343?BC-291?BC *McGEWD[port]*
Menander 343BC-292BC *PlP&P[port]*
Menandros 342BC-290?BC *NewGrD 80*
Menantes *NewGrD 80*
Menard, Lucie *WomWMM*
Menard, Michael M 1898-1949 *WhScrn 74, -77*
Menasce, Jacques De 1905-1960 *Baker 78, BiDAmM, ConAmC, NewGrD 80*
Menault, Pierre-Richard 1644?-1694 *NewGrD 80*
Menchaca, Angel 1855-1924 *Baker 78*
Menchel, Don *NewYTET*
Mencher, Murray 1898- *AmSCAP 66, CmpEPM*
Mencher, T Murray 1904- *AmSCAP 80*
Mencken, Henry Louis 1880-1956 *NotNAT B*
Menckin, Thomas *NewGrD 80*
Mendel 1875- *WhThe*
Mendel, Arthur 1905-1979 *Baker 78, BiDAmM, IntWWM 77, -80, NewGrD 80, WhoMus 72*
Mendel, Deryk 1921- *CnOxB*
Mendel, Hermann 1834-1876 *Baker 78, OxMus*
Mendel, Johnny 1905-1966 *WhoJazz 72*
Mendel, Jules 1875-1938 *WhScrn 74, -77*
Mendelsohn, Alfred 1910-1966 *Baker 78, NewGrD 80*
Mendelsohn, Jack 1946- *IntWWM 77, -80*
Mendelsohn, Jacques Arko 1867-1940 *AmSCAP 66*
Mendelsohn, Oscar 1896- *WhoMus 72*
Mendelson, Lee *NewYTET*
Mendelson, Stanley 1923- *NewOrJ*
Mendelssohn, Arnold 1855-1933 *Baker 78, NewGrD 80*
Mendelssohn, Eleanora 1900-1951 *NotNAT B, WhoHol B*
Mendelssohn, Eleonora 1900-1951 *WhScrn 74, -77*
Mendelssohn, Fanny *Baker 78*
Mendelssohn, Fanny 1805-1847 *NewGrD 80*
Mendelssohn, Felix 1809-1847 *Baker 78, BnBkM 80[port], CmpBCM, DcCom 77[port], DcCom&M 79, GrComp[port], MusMk, NewEOp 71, NewGrD 80, NotNAT B, OxMus*
Mendelssohn, Felix Robert 1896-1951 *Baker 78*
Mendelssohn-Bartholdy, Felix 1809-1847 *CnOxB*
Mendelssohn Quintette Club Of Boston *BiDAmM*
Mendenhall, Ralph G 1921- *AmSCAP 66, -80*
Mendes, Catulle 1841-1909 *NewEOp 71, NewGrD 80, NotNAT B*
Mendes, Gilberto 1922- *DcCM, IntWWM 77, -80, NewGrD 80*
Mendes, John Prince 1919-1955 *WhScrn 74, -77, WhoHol B*
Mendes, Lothar 1894-1974 *FilmEn, FilmgC, HalFC 80, TwYS A, WhScrn 77*
Mendes, Manuel 1547?-1605 *NewGrD 80*
Mendes, Moses d1758 *NotNAT B*
Mendes, Sergio 1941- *BiDAmM, EncJzS 70*
Mendes, Sergio & Brasil '66 *RkOn 2[port]*
Mendez, Josefina 1940?- *CnOxB*
Mendez, Lola *Film 2*
Mendez, Lucila *Film 2*
Mendez, Luz Vieyre *PupTheA*
Mendez, Rafael G 1906- *AmSCAP 66, -80, CmpEPM*
Mendham, Geoffrey Leonard 1899- *WhoMus 72*
Mendham, Nelly *PupTheA*
Mendis, Angela 1941- *WhoMus 72*
Mendl, Robert W S 1892- *IntWWM 77, -80, WhoMus 72*
Mendoza, Anne Elizabeth 1914- *IntWWM 77, -80, WhoMus 72*
Mendoza, David 1894- *AmSCAP 66, -80*
Mendoza, Emilio 1953- *Baker 78*
Mendoza, Harry 1905-1970 *WhScrn 74, -77*
Mendoza, Vicente 1894-1964 *NewGrD 80*
Mendoza-Nava, Jaime 1925- *NewGrD 80*
Mendum, Georgie Drew d1957 *NotNAT B*
Mene *NewGrD 80*
Meneely, Sarah Suderley 1945- *ConAmC*
Menehou, Michel De *NewGrD 80*
Menestrier, Claude-Francois 1631-1705 *CnOxB, DancEn 78, NewGrD 80*
Mengal, Jean-Baptiste 1792-1878 *Baker 78*
Mengal, Martin-Joseph 1784-1851 *Baker 78, NewGrD 80*
Mengarelli, Julius 1920-1960 *CnOxB*
Mengarelli, Julius 1920-1961 *DancEn 78*
Mengarelli, Mario 1925- *CnOxB, DancEn 78*
Mengelberg *NewGrD 80*
Mengelberg, Karel 1902- *Baker 78, IntWWM 77, -80, NewGrD 80*
Mengelberg, Kurt Rudolf 1892-1959 *Baker 78*
Mengelberg, Misha 1935- *Baker 78, NewGrD 80*
Mengelberg, Misja 1935- *NewGrD 80*
Mengelberg, Rudolf 1892-1959 *NewGrD 80*
Mengelberg, Willem 1871-1951 *Baker 78, BnBkM 80, MusMk, MusSN[port], NewGrD 80[port]*
Menger, Reinhardt 1936- *IntWWM 77, -80*
Mengers, Sue *IntMPA 78, -79, -80*
Menges, Chris *FilmgC, HalFC 80*
Menges, Herbert 1902-1972 *Baker 78, NewGrD 80, WhThe, WhoMus 72, WhoThe 72*
Menges, Isolde 1893-1976 *Baker 78, NewGrD 80, WhoMus 72*
Menges, Joyce *WhoHol A*
Mengewein, Karl 1852-1908 *Baker 78*
Menhart, Alfred 1899-1955 *WhScrn 74, -77*
Menichelli, Pina 1893- *FilmAG WE*
Menil, Felicien De 1860-1930 *Baker 78*
Menippo, Carlo 1933- *WhoOp 76*
Menjou, Adolphe 1890-1963 *BiDFilm, -81, FilmEn, Film 1, -2, FilmgC, ForYSC, HalFC 80[port], MotPP, MovMk[port], NotNAT B, OxFilm, TwYS, WhScrn 74, -77, WhoHol B, WorEFlm*
Menjou, Henri *Film 2*
Menke, Werner 1907- *IntWWM 77, -80, OxMus*
Menken, Adah Isaacs 1835-1868 *Ent[port], FamA&A[port], NotNAT A, -B, OxThe*
Menken, Helen d1966 *PlP&P[port], WhoHol B*
Menken, Helen 1901-1966 *BiE&WWA, NotNAT B, WhThe*
Menken, Helen 1902-1966 *WhScrn 74, -77*
Menken, Marie 1909-1970 *WhScrn 74, -77, WomWMM*
Menken, Shepard *WhoHol A*
Menken, Shephard *ForYSC*
Menkes, Doris *AmSCAP 80*
Mennicke, Karl 1880-1917 *Baker 78*
Mennin, Peter 1923- *AmSCAP 66, -80, Baker 78, BiDAmM, BiE&WWA, BnBkM 80, CompSN[port], ConAmC, DcCom&M 79, DcCM, IntWWM 77, -80, MusMk, NewGrD 80, OxMus, WhoMus 72*
Mennini, Louis 1920- *AmSCAP 66, -80, Baker 78, ConAmC*
Mennini, Peter 1923- *BnBkM 80*
Menon, Bhaskar *ConMuA 80B*
Menon, Tuttovale 1510?- *NewGrD 80*
Menon, Tuttualle 1510?- *NewGrD 80*
Menon, Tutval 1510?- *NewGrD 80*
Menon, V K Narayana 1911- *NewGrD 80*
Menotti, Carlo 1909- *AmSCAP 80*
Menotti, Gian-Carlo 1911- *AmSCAP 66, Baker 78, BiDAmM, BiE&WWA, BnBkM 80, CmOp, CompSN[port], CnOxB, ConAmC, DancEn 78, DcCom 77[port], DcCom&M 79, DcCM, IntWWM 77, -80, McGEWD, MusMk[port], NewEOp 71, NewGrD 80[port], NotNAT, OxMus, WhoMus 72, WhoOp 76*
Menta, Francesco 1540?- *NewGrD 80*
Menter, Joseph 1808-1856 *Baker 78*
Menter, Sophie 1846-1918 *Baker 78, OxMus*
Mentzer, Larry Walter 1943- *IntWWM 77*
Menuhin *NewGrD 80*
Menuhin, Hephzibah 1920- *Baker 78, IntWWM 77, -80, NewGrD 80, WhoMus 72*
Menuhin, Jeremy 1951- *IntWWM 77, -80, NewGrD 80, WhoMus 72*
Menuhin, Yaltah *WhoMus 72*
Menuhin, Yaltah 1921- *IntWWM 77, -80*
Menuhin, Yaltah 1922- *NewGrD 80*
Menuhin, Yehudi 1916- *Baker 78, BnBkM 80[port], IntWWM 77, -80, MusMk, MusSN[port], NewGrD 80[port], OxMus, WhoHol A, WhoMus 72*
Menuhin, Yehudi 1917- *BiDAmM*
Menyhart, Jacqueline 1937- *CnOxB*
Menza, Don 1936- *EncJzS 70*
Menza, Donald Joseph 1936- *AmSCAP 80*
Menzel, Gerhard 1894- *ModWD*
Menzel, Jiri 1938- *DcFM, FilmEn, FilmgC, HalFC 80, OxFilm, WorEFlm*
Menzies, Archie 1904- *WhThe*
Menzies, William Cameron 1896-1957 *BiDFilm, -81, DcFM, FilmEn, FilmgC, HalFC 80, NotNAT B, OxFilm, WhoHrs 80, WorEFlm*
Menzingen, Mauritius Von *NewGrD 80*
Meo, Ascanio 157-?-1608? *NewGrD 80*
Mera, Edith d1935 *WhScrn 74, -77, WhoHol B*
Merande, Doro 1898?-1975 *BiE&WWA, ForYSC, HalFC 80, NotNAT, -B, WhScrn 77, WhThe, WhoHol C, WhoThe 72*

Merante, Louis 1828-1887 *CnOxB, DancEn 78, NotNAT B*
Merbecke, John 1505?-1585? *NewGrD 80*
Merbecke, John 1510?-1585? *OxMus*
Mercadante, Giuseppe Saverio Raffaele 1795-1870 *OxMus*
Mercadante, Saverio 1795-1870 *Baker 78, CmOp, DcCom 77, NewEOp 71, NewGrD 80[port]*
Mercadier, Jean Baptiste 1750-1815 *Baker 78*
Mercandotti, Maria 1801?- *CnOxB*
Mercanton, Louis 1879-1932 *FilmEn, OxFilm*
Mercantor, Jean *Film 2*
Mercator, Sir Michael 1491-1544 *NewGrD 80*
Mercer *PupTheA*
Mercer, Beryl 1882-1939 *FilmEn, Film 2, FilmgC, ForYSC, HalFC 80, HolCA[port], MotPP, MovMk, NotNAT B, ThFT[port], WhScrn 74, -77, WhThe, WhoHol B*
Mercer, David 1928- *CnThe, ConDr 73, -77, CroCD, EncWT, Ent, WhoThe 72, -77*
Mercer, Donald J *NewYTET*
Mercer, Frances *MotPP, WhoHol A*
Mercer, John H 1909-1976 *AmSCAP 66, -80, BiDAmM*
Mercer, Johnny d1976 *Sw&Ld C*
Mercer, Johnny 1909- *WhoThe 72*
Mercer, Johnny 1909-1976 *AmPS, Baker 78, BestMus, BiE&WWA, CmpEPM, EncMT, FilmEn, FilmgC, HalFC 80, IntMPA 75, -76, WhoHol A, WhoThe 77*
Mercer, Johnny 1910-1976 *NotNAT B*
Mercer, Mabel 1900- *CmpEPM, DrBlPA*
Mercer, Mae *DrBlPA, WhoHol A*
Mercer, Marian 1935- *BiE&WWA, NotNAT, WhoHol A, WhoThe 72, -77*
Mercer, Tommy 1925?- *CmpEPM*
Mercer, Tony 1922-1973 *WhScrn 77*
Mercer, W Elmo 1932- *AmSCAP 80*
Mercer, Will *BlkAmP*
Mercer, William Elmo 1932- *AmSCAP 66*
Merceur, John *NewGrD 80*
Merchant, David Lawson 1911- *WhoMus 72*
Merchant, Ismail *FilmEn*
Merchant, Jimmy 1941- *BiDAmM*
Merchant, Lawrence H, Jr. *IntMPA 77, -75, -76, -78, -79, -80*
Merchant, Vivien 1929- *FilmEn, FilmgC, HalFC 80, MotPP, OxFilm, PlP&P, WhoHol A, WhoThe 72, -77*
Mercher, Matthias *NewGrD 80*
Merchi, Joseph Bernard 1730?-1793 *NewGrD 80*
Merchy, Joseph Bernard 1730?-1793 *NewGrD 80*
Merci, Joseph Bernard 1730?-1793 *NewGrD 80*
Mercier, Sieur *PupTheA*
Mercier, Charles *BiDAmM*
Mercier, Louis *Film 2, WhoHol A*
Mercier, Louis-Sebastien 1740-1814 *McGEWD, NotNAT B, OxThe*
Mercier, Margaret 1937- *CnOxB, CreCan 1, DancEn 78[port]*
Mercier, Mary *NatPD[port]*
Mercier, Michele 1939- *FilmAG WE*
Mercier, Michele 1942- *FilmgC, HalFC 80, WhoHol A*
Mercier, Philipe 1940- *IntWWM 77*
Mercier, Philippe 1940- *IntWWM 80*
Merck, Daniel 1650?-1713 *NewGrD 80*
Mercker, Matthias *NewGrD 80*
Mercouri, Melina *IntMPA 77, -75, -76, -78, -79, -80, MotPP, WhoHol A*
Mercouri, Melina 1923- *FilmEn, FilmgC, HalFC 80*
Mercouri, Melina 1925- *ForYSC, MovMk[port], OxFilm, WorEFlm*
Mercure, John *NewGrD 80*
Mercure, Pierre 1927-1966 *Baker 78, CreCan 2, DcCM, NewGrD 80*
Mercurio, Paul *AmSCAP 80*
Mercurio, Vecchio *NewGrD 80*
Mercy *RkOn 2A*
Mercy, Lewis 1695?-1750? *NewGrD 80*
Mercy Dee *BluesWW*
Mere, Charles 1883- *WhThe*
Mereaux *NewGrD 80*
Mereaux, Jean-Amedee LeFroid De 1802-1874 *NewGrD 80*
Mereaux, Jean-Nicolas LeFroid De 1767-1838 *NewGrD 80*
Mereaux, Nicolas-Jean LeFroid De 1745-1797 *NewGrD 80*
Meredith, Burgess *MotPP, PlP&P, WhoHol A*
Meredith, Burgess 1907- *EncWT, MovMk[port], WorEFlm*
Meredith, Burgess 1908- *BiE&WWA, FilmEn, FilmgC, ForYSC, HalFC 80[port], HolP 30[port], NotNAT, WhoHrs 80, WhoThe 72, -77*
Meredith, Burgess 1909- *BiDFilm, -81, Ent[port], IntMPA 77, -75, -76, -78, -79, -80, OxFilm*
Meredith, Charles 1890-1964 *Film 1, -2, TwYS*
Meredith, Charles 1894-1964 *ForYSC, WhScrn 74, -77, WhoHol B*
Meredith, Cheerio 1890-1964 *ForYSC, WhScrn 74, -77, WhoHol B*
Meredith, Don *NewYTET*
Meredith, Geoffrey 1907- *WhoMus 72*
Meredith, Henry Morgan, Jr. 1946- *IntWWM 77, -80*
Meredith, Iris *ForYSC*
Meredith, Isaac H 1872-1962 *AmSCAP 66, -80, BiDAmM*
Meredith, Jo Anne *WhoHol A*
Meredith, Joan *WhoHol A*
Meredith, John 1933- *CreCan 2*
Meredith, Judi *WhoHol A*
Meredith, Lee *WhoHol A*
Meredith, Lois *Film 1, -2*
Meredith, Lu Anne *WhoHol A*
Meredith, Melba Melsing d1967 *WhoHol B*
Meredith, Morley *WhoOp 76*
Meredith, Victoria Steward 1949- *IntWWM 77, -80*
Meredyth, Bess 1890-1969 *FilmEn, Film 1, HalFC 80, WhScrn 74, -77, WhoHol B, WomWMM*
Merelle, Claude *Film 2*
Merelli, Bartolomeo 1794-1879 *NewGrD 80*
Meretta, Leonard V 1915- *AmSCAP 66, -80, ConAmC A*
Mergot, Franciscus *NewGrD 80*
Meri, La *CnOxB*
Meri, Veijo 1928- *CroCD*
Merian, Hans 1857-1905 *Baker 78*
Merian, Leon 1925- *AmSCAP 66, -80*
Merian, Wilhelm 1889-1952 *Baker 78, NewGrD 80*
Meric-Lalande, Henriette 1798-1867 *NewGrD 80*
Mericocke, Thomas *NewGrD 80*
Meriel, Paul 1818-1897 *Baker 78*
Meriggioli, Ileana *WhoOp 76*
Merighi, Antonia Margherita d1764? *NewGrD 80[port]*
Merighi, Giorgio 1939- *WhoOp 76*
Merikanto, Aarre 1893-1958 *Baker 78, NewGrD 80, OxMus*
Merikanto, Oskar 1868-1924 *Baker 78, NewGrD 80, OxMus*
Meril, Macha 1940- *FilmAG WE*
Merilainen, Usko 1930- *Baker 78, DcCM, NewGrD 80*
Merimee, Prosper 1803-1870 *EncWT, NewEOp 71, NewGrD 80, NotNAT B*
Merin, Jennifer *ConAmTC*
Merineau, Andre Henri 1929- *IntWWM 77, -80*
Merington, Edwin *PupTheA*
Merivale, Bernard 1882-1939 *NotNAT B, WhThe*
Merivale, Mrs. Herman d1932 *NotNAT B*
Merivale, Herman Charles 1839-1906 *NotNAT A, -B*
Merivale, John 1917- *BiE&WWA, ForYSC, NotNAT, WhoHol A*
Merivale, Philip d1946 *PlP&P, WhoHol B*
Merivale, Philip 1880-1946 *ForYSC, WhScrn 74, -77*
Merivale, Philip 1886-1946 *FilmgC, HalFC 80, NotNAT B, WhThe*
Meriwether, Lee 1935- *ForYSC, HalFC 80, WhoHol A*
Merk, Joseph 1795-1852 *Baker 78*
Merkel, Gustav 1827-1885 *Baker 78, NewGrD 80, OxMus*
Merkel, Una 1903- *BiE&WWA, FilmEn, Film 2, FilmgC, ForYSC, HalFC 80, HolCA[port], IntMPA 77, -75, -76, -78, -79, -80, MGM[port], MotPP, MovMk, NotNAT, ThFT[port], Vers A[port], What 3[port], WhThe, WhoHol A*
Merker, K Ethel 1923- *IntWWM 77, -80*
Merkher, Matthias *NewGrD 80*
Merklin, Joseph 1819-1905 *Baker 78, NewGrD 80*
Merku, Pavle 1927- *IntWWM 80*
Merku, Pavle 1929- *NewGrD 80*
Merkur, Jacob Louis 1895- *AmSCAP 80*
Merkyl, John *Film 1, -2*
Merkyl, Wilmuth 1885-1954 *Film 1, WhScrn 77*
Merle, George 1874-1945 *AmSCAP 66, -80*
Merle, John *AmSCAP 80*
Merlet, Dominique 1938- *IntWWM 80*
Merli, Francesco 1887-1976 *Baker 78, CmOp, NewGrD 80*
Merlin, Frank 1892-1968 *NotNAT B*
Merlin, Jan *ForYSC, WhoHol A*
Merlin, Joanna 1931- *BiE&WWA, NotNAT*
Merlin, John Joseph 1735-1803 *NewGrD 80*
Merlin, Joseph *OxMus*
Merlin, Olivier *DancEn 78*
Merlo, Alessandro 1530?-1594? *NewGrD 80*
Merlo, Alexander 1530?-1594? *NewGrD 80*
Merlo, Anthony *Film 2*
Merlotti, Claudio *NewGrD 80*
Merlow, Anthony *Film 1*
Merlow, Connie 1920- *AmSCAP 80*
Merlus, Alessandro *NewGrD 80*
Merlus, Alexander *NewGrD 80*
Merman, Ethel *AmPS B, MotPP, PlP&P[port], WhoHol A*
Merman, Ethel 1908- *FilmgC, HalFC 80, MovMk[port], ThFT[port]*
Merman, Ethel 1909- *BiDAmM, BiE&WWA, CmMov, CmpEPM, CnThe, EncMT, EncWT, Ent, FamA&A[port], FilmEn, ForYSC, IntMPA 77, -75, -76, -78, -79, -80, NotNAT, -A, WhoThe 72, -77*
Mermet, Auguste 1810-1889 *NewGrD 80*
Mero, Yolanda 1887-1963 *Baker 78*
Mero-Irion, Yolanda 1887-1963 *BiDAmM*
Meroff, Benny 1901-1973 *AmSCAP 66, -80, BgBands 74, CmpEPM*
Merola, Gaetano 1881-1953 *Baker 78, BiDAmM, NewEOp 71*
Merola, Mario Virgilio 1931- *CreCan 1*
Merques, Nicolas *NewGrD 80*
Merrall, Mary 1890-1973 *Film 2, FilmgC, HalFC 80, IntMPA 77, -75, -76, -78, -79, -80, WhThe, WhoHol B, WhoThe 72*
Merrelli, C *Film 2*
Merrett, James Edward 1912- *WhoMus 72*
Merriam, Alan P 1923-1980 *NewGrD 80*
Merriam, Charlotte *Film 2*
Merriam, Eve *BlkAmP*
Merrick, David 1911- *BiE&WWA, CnThe, EncMT, WhoThe 72, -77*
Merrick, Frank 1886- *Baker 78, IntWWM 77, -80, NewGrD 80, WhoMus 72*
Merrick, Leonard 1864-1939 *NotNAT B, WhThe*
Merrick, Lynn *ForYSC, WhoHol A*
Merricocke, Thomas *NewGrD 80*
Merrifield, Norman L 1906- *AmSCAP 66, ConAmC A*
Merrill, Abraham Dow 1796-1878 *BiDAmM*
Merrill, Amy 1898- *AmSCAP 66*
Merrill, Andrea O 1948- *IntWWM 77*
Merrill, Barbara *WhoHol A*
Merrill, Beth *PlP&P, WhThe*
Merrill, Bill 1921- *AmSCAP 66*
Merrill, Blanche 1895-1966 *AmSCAP 66, -80*
Merrill, Bob 1920- *BiE&WWA, NotNAT, WhoThe 72, -77*
Merrill, Bob 1921- *AmPS, AmSCAP 66, -80, CmpEPM, ConAmC, EncMT, NewCBMT, PopAmC[port], PopAmC SUP, Sw&Ld C*
Merrill, Buddy *AmSCAP 80*
Merrill, Dick *WhoHol A*
Merrill, Dina *IntMPA 75, -76, MotPP, WhoHol A*
Merrill, Dina 1925- *FilmEn, IntMPA 77, -78,*

-79, -80, *MovMk*
Merrill, Dina 1928- *FilmgC, ForYSC, HalFC 80*
Merrill, Frank 1892-1966 *Film 2*
Merrill, Frank 1894-1966 *WhScrn 74, -77, WhoHol B, WhoHrs 80*
Merrill, Gary *IntMPA 77, -75, -76, -78, -79, -80, MotPP, WhoHol A*
Merrill, Gary 1914- *FilmgC, HalFC 80, WhoHrs 80*
Merrill, Gary 1915- *BiE&WWA, FilmEn, ForYSC, MovMk[port], NotNAT*
Merrill, Helen 1929- *BiDAmM*
Merrill, Helen 1930- *EncJzS 70*
Merrill, Idaho *AmSCAP 80*
Merrill, John 1875- *NotNAT A*
Merrill, Lindsey 1925- *ConAmC*
Merrill, Louis 1911-1963 *NotNAT B, WhScrn 74, -77, WhoHol B*
Merrill, Nathaniel Chase 1927- *IntWWM 77, -80, WhoOp 76*
Merrill, Ray 1916- *AmSCAP 66, -80*
Merrill, Robert 1917- *Baker 78, CmOp, MusSN[port]*
Merrill, Robert 1919- *BiDAmM, CmpEPM, IntWWM 77, -80, NewEOp 71, NewGrD 80, WhoMus 72, WhoOp 76*
Merrill, Robert 1921- *BestMus, BiDAmM, HalFC 80*
Merrill, William Pierson 1867-1954 *BiDAmM*
Merriman, John d1974 *NewYTET*
Merriman, Katherine-Ann 1920- *NewGrD 80*
Merriman, Margarita 1927- *ConAmC*
Merriman, Nan 1920- *Baker 78, CmOp, IntWWM 77, -80, NewGrD 80*
Merriman, Thomas W 1924- *AmSCAP 80, ConAmC*
Merritt, A Tillman 1902- *NewGrD 80*
Merritt, Arthur Tillman 1902- *Baker 78*
Merritt, Charles *ConAmC*
Merritt, Dick *AmSCAP 80*
Merritt, Eva Kathleen *WhoMus 72*
Merritt, George 1890-1977 *FilmgC, HalFC 80, WhoHol A, WhoThe 72, -77*
Merritt, Grace 1881- *WhThe*
Merritt, James 1926- *BiDAmM*
Merritt, O O 1919- *AmSCAP 66, -80*
Merritt, Paul d1895 *NotNAT B*
Merritt, Theresa 1922- *DrBlPA, WhoHol A*
Merriweather, Major 1905-1953 *BluesWW[port]*
Merro, John *NewGrD 80*
Merrow, Jane 1941- *FilmgC, HalFC 80, IlWWBF, WhoHol A*
Merry, Mrs. 1769-1808 *OxThe*
Merry, Anne Brunton 1768-1808 *NotNAT A*
Merry, Anne Brunton 1769-1808 *FamA&A[port], PlP&P*
Merry, Hazel 1938- *CnOxB, DancEn 78*
Merry, Robert d1798 *NotNAT B*
Merry, Mrs. Robert 1763-1808 *NotNAT B*
Merry Macs, The *AmPS A, -B, CmpEPM*
Mersch, Mary *Film 2*
Merseburger *NewGrD 80*
Merseburger, Carl Wilhelm 1816-1885 *Baker 78, NewGrD 80*
Merseburger, Georg 1871-1958 *NewGrD 80*
Merseburger, Karl 1905-1978 *NewGrD 80*
Merseburger, Max 1853-1935 *NewGrD 80*
Merseburger, Otto 1822-1898 *NewGrD 80*
Mersenne, Marin 1588-1648 *Baker 78, NewGrD 80[port], OxMus*
Mersereau, Claire *Film 1*
Mersereau, Violet 1894- *Film 1, -2*
Mersey, Robert 1917- *AmSCAP 66, -80*
Mersirow-Minchin, Nina 1901- *WhoMus 72*
Mersmann, Hans 1891-1971 *Baker 78, NewGrD 80*
Merson, Billy 1881-1947 *Film 1, -2, IlWWBF, -A, OxThe, WhThe*
Merson, Marc 1931- *IntMPA 77, -78, -79, -80*
Mertel, Elias 1561?-1626 *NewGrD 80*
Mertelius, Elias 1561?-1626 *NewGrD 80*
Merten, Werner 1927- *IntWWM 77*
Mertens, Joseph 1834-1901 *Baker 78*
Mertins, Christa 1936- *CreCan 2*
Mertke, Eduard 1833-1895 *Baker 78*
Merton, Colette 1907-1968 *Film 2, WhoHol B*
Merton, Collette 1907-1968 *WhScrn 74, -77*
Merton, John 1901-1959 *Vers B[port], WhScrn 74, -77, WhoHol B*
Mertz, Franz 1897-1966 *EncWT*
Mertz, Joseph Kasper 1806-1856 *Baker 78*
Mertz, Paul Madeira 1904- *AmSCAP 66, -80, WhoJazz 72*
Meruco, Johannes De *NewGrD 80*
Merula, Tarquinio 1594?-1665 *NewGrD 80*
Merula, Tarquinio 1600?- *Baker 78*
Merulo, Claudio 1533-1604 *Baker 78, MusMk, NewGrD 80, OxMus*
Merulo, Giacinto 1595-1650 *NewGrD 80*
Merulus, Alessandro *NewGrD 80*
Merulus, Alexander *NewGrD 80*
Mervyn, Lee d1962 *NotNAT B*
Mervyn, William 1912-1976 *FilmgC, HalFC 80, WhoHol A, WhoThe 72, -77*
Mery, Andree *WhThe*
Merz, Karl 1836-1890 *Baker 78, BiDAmM*
Mesang, Ted 1904-1967 *AmSCAP 66, -80*
Mesang, Theodore L 1901- *ConAmC*
Mesangeau, Rene d1638 *NewGrD 80*
Mesangio, Rene d1638 *NewGrD 80*
Mescall, John 1899- *CmMov, FilmEn, FilmgC, HalFC 80*
Meschanson, Rene d1638 *NewGrD 80*
Meschke, Michael *DcPup*
Mesenge, Rene d1638 *NewGrD 80*
Mesengeot, Rene d1638 *NewGrD 80*
Mesereau, Violet 1894- *TwYS*
Meserve, Walter Joseph, Jr. 1923- *NotNAT*
Mesguich, Felix 1871-1949 *FilmEn*
Meshel, Billy *ConMuA 80B*
Meshel, Wilbur 1939- *AmSCAP 80*
Meshke, George Lewis 1930- *NotNAT*
Meskill, Jack 1897-1973 *AmSCAP 66, -80, CmpEPM*
Meskill, Katherine *WhoHol A*
Meskin, Aharon 1897-1974 *WhScrn 77*
Mesmer, Marie 1920- *IntMPA 77, -75, -76, -78, -79, -80*
Mesney, Dorothy Taylor 1916- *IntWWM 77, -80*
Mesomedes *NewGrD 80*
Mesple, Mady 1931- *NewGrD 80, WhoOp 76*
Mesquita, Henrique Alves De 1836-1906 *NewGrD 80*
Mesquita, Jose Joaquim Emerico Lobo De 1730?-1805 *NewGrD 80*
Mesrop-Mashtots d440 *NewGrD 80*
Mess, Philibert 1929- *IntWWM 77*
Mess, Suzanne *CreCan 2, WhoOp 76*
Messager, Andre 1853-1929 *Baker 78, BnBkM 80, CmOp, DcCom&M 79, NewEOp 71, NewGrD 80, OxMus, WhThe*
Messager, Charles *McGEWD[port], REnWD[port]*
Messangior, Rene *NewGrD 80*
Messarosh, Angelica *WhoMus 72*
Messaus, Guillaume 1589?-1640 *NewGrD 80*
Messchaert, Johannes Martinus 1857-1922 *Baker 78, NewGrD 80*
Messel, Oliver d1978 *PlP&P[port]*
Messel, Oliver 1904-1978 *BiE&WWA, EncWT, FilmgC, HalFC 80, NotNAT, WhoThe 77, WorEFlm*
Messel, Oliver 1905-1978 *CnThe, CnOxB, DancEn 78, Ent, OxThe, WhoOp 76, WhoThe 72*
Messemer, Hannes 1924- *EncWT, FilmAG WE, HalFC 80*
Messenger, Buddy 1909-1965 *TwYS, WhScrn 74, -77*
Messenger, Elsie Lily *WhoMus 72*
Messenger, Gary L 1941- *IntMPA 79, -80*
Messenger, Gertrude 1911- *ForYSC, TwYS*
Messenger, Joyce Eleanor 1922- *WhoMus 72*
Messenger, Thomas 1938- *IntWWM 77, -80, WhoMus 72*
Messenheimer, Sam 1898- *AmSCAP 66, -80*
Messenius, Johannes 1579-1636 *OxThe*
Messerer, Asaf Michailovich 1903- *CnOxB, DancEn 78[port]*
Messerer, Sulamith Michailovna 1908- *CnOxB, DancEn 78*
Messervy, George Thomas *IntWWM 77, -80, WhoMus 72*
Messiaen, Olivier 1908- *Baker 78, BnBkM 80[port], CompSN[port], CnOxB, DcCom 77, DcCom&M 79, DcCM, IntWWM 77, -80, MusMk[port], NewGrD 80[port], OxMus, WhoMus 72*
Messina, James M 1947- *AmSCAP 80*
Messina, Louis *ConMuA 80B*
Messina, Sylvester J 1917- *AmSCAP 80*
Messinger, Buddy 1909-1965 *Film 1, -2, WhoHol B*
Messinger, Gertrude 1911- *Film 1, -2*
Messinger, Josephine 1885-1968 *WhScrn 77, WhoHol B*
Messiter, Arthur Henry 1834-1916 *Baker 78, BiDAmM*
Messiter, Christine Marian 1948- *IntWWM 77, -80*
Messiter, Eric 1892-1960 *NotNAT B, WhScrn 74, -77, WhoHol B*
Messiter, Malcolm Cassan 1949- *IntWWM 77, -80*
Messner, Johnny 1909- *AmSCAP 66, -80, BgBands 74, CmpEPM*
Messner, Joseph 1893-1969 *Baker 78, NewGrD 80*
Messter, Oskar Eduard 1866-1943 *DcFM, FilmEn, OxFilm*
Mesta, Perle *What 5[port]*
Mestayer, Anna Maria d1881 *NotNAT B*
Mestayer, Harry *Film 1, -2, MotPP, TwYS*
Mestel, Jacob 1884-1958 *NotNAT B, WhScrn 74, -77*
Mester, Jorge 1935- *Baker 78, BnBkM 80, NewGrD 80, WhoMus 72*
Mestral, Armand *WhoHol A*
Mestral, Patrice 1945- *NewGrD 80*
Mestre, Goar *NewYTET*
Mestres-Quadreny, Josep M 1929- *Baker 78, DcCM, IntWWM 77, -80, NewGrD 80*
Mestrino, Nicola 1748-1789 *NewGrD 80*
Meszaros, Marta 1931- *OxFilm, WomWMM*
Metallo, Graminazio 1539?-1615? *NewGrD 80*
Metallo, Grammatico 1539?-1615? *NewGrD 80*
Metallo, Grammatio 1539?-1615? *NewGrD 80*
Metallov, Vasily Mikhaylovich 1862-1926 *NewGrD 80*
Metallov, Vassili 1862-1926 *Baker 78*
Metastasio 1698-1782 *NotNAT B, OxMus, OxThe*
Metastasio, Pietro 1698-1782 *Baker 78, BnBkM 80, CmOp, CnThe, Ent, McGEWD[port], NewEOp 71, NewGrD 80[port], REnWD[port]*
Metaxa, Georges 1899-1950 *NotNAT B, WhScrn 74, -77, WhThe, WhoHol B*
Metaxas, George 1899-1950 *HalFC 80*
Metayer, Monsieur *PupTheA*
Metcalf, Arthur *Film 2*
Metcalf, Earl 1889-1928 *Film 2, TwYS, WhScrn 74, -77*
Metcalf, Earle 1889-1928 *WhoHol B*
Metcalf, Frank J 1865-1945 *Baker 78*
Metcalf, John 1946- *WhoMus 72*
Metcalf, Louis 1905- *BiDAmM, WhoJazz 72*
Metcalf, Samuel Lytler 1798-1856 *BiDAmM*
Metcalf, William 1934- *WhoOp 76*
Metcalfe, Earle 1889-1928 *Film 1*
Metcalfe, James S 1901-1960 *WhScrn 74, -77, WhoHol B*
Metcalfe, James Stetson 1858-1927 *NotNAT B, WhThe*
Metcalfe, Jane Elizabeth 1951- *IntWWM 77*
Metenier, Oscar 1859-1913 *NotNAT B, WhThe*
Meters, The *IlEncR, RkOn 2[port]*
Metevier, Matilda *Film 2*
Methfessel, Albert Gottlieb 1785-1869 *Baker 78*
Method, Mayo 1904-1951 *MotPP*
Methodios d846 *NewGrD 80*
Methodius d846 *NewGrD 80*
Methot, Mayo 1904-1951 *ForYSC, HalFC 80, NotNAT B, ThFT[port], WhScrn 74, -77, WhoHol B*
Methven, William d1886 *NewGrD 80*
Metianu, Lucian 1937- *Baker 78, IntWWM 80*
Metis, Frank W 1925- *AmSCAP 66, -80*
Metivier, Paul Roberts 1915- *AmSCAP 80*
Metner, Nikolai *Baker 78*
Metner, Nikolay Karlovich 1880-1951 *NewGrD 80*
Metoyer, Arnold 1876?-1935 *NewOrJ[port]*
Metra 1830-1889 *Baker 78*

Metra, Olivier 1830-1889 *NewGrD 80*
Metrano, Art *WhoHol A*
Metru, Nicolas 1600?-1670? *Baker 78*
Metru, Nicolas 1610?-1663? *NewGrD 80*
Metsala, Juha Einari 1925- *IntWWM 77, -80*
Metsers, Hugo 1943- *FilmAG WE*
Metten, Charles 1927- *NotNAT*
Mettenleiter *NewGrD 80*
Mettenleiter, Bernhard 1822-1901 *NewGrD 80*
Mettenleiter, Dominicus 1822-1868 *Baker 78, NewGrD 80, OxMus*
Mettenleiter, Johann Georg 1812-1858 *Baker 78, NewGrD 80, OxMus*
Mettome, Doug 1925-1964 *CmpEPM*
Mettome, Douglas Voll 1925-1964 *BiDAmM*
Metty, Russell 1900- *CmMov*
Metty, Russell L 1906- *FilmgC, WorEFlm*
Metty, Russell L 1906-1978 *FilmEn*
Metty, Russell L 1906-1979 *HalFC 80*
Metz, Albert 1886-1940 *WhScrn 74, -77*
Metz, Donald Edward 1935- *IntWWM 77, -80*
Metz, Herbert Edward *ConAmTC*
Metz, Julius 1798?- *BiDAmM*
Metz, Louis 1910- *IntWWM 77*
Metz, Otto 1891-1949 *WhScrn 74, -77*
Metz, Theodore A 1848-1936 *AmSCAP 66, -80, BiDAmM, NotNAT B, PopAmC[port]*
Metzetti, Victor 1895-1949 *WhScrn 74, -77, WhoHol B*
Metzger, Ambrosius 1573-1632 *NewGrD 80*
Metzger, Heinz-Klaus 1932- *NewGrD 80*
Metzger, Marta 1947- *CnOxB*
Metzger, Radley 1930- *FilmEn, HalFC 80*
Metzger, Roswell William 1906- *AmSCAP 66*
Metzler *NewGrD 80*
Metzler, Friedrich 1910- *WhoMus 72*
Metzler, George Richard 1797-1867 *NewGrD 80*
Metzler, George Thomas 1835-1879 *NewGrD 80*
Metzler, Jakob *NewGrD 80*
Metzler, Richard 1948- *IntWWM 77, -80*
Metzler, Robert 1914- *IntMPA 77, -75, -76, -78, -79, -80*
Metzler, Valentin *NewGrD 80*
Metzler, Valentin d1833 *Baker 78*
Metzner, Erno 1892- *DcFM, FilmEn, OxFilm*
Meulemans, Arthur 1884-1966 *Baker 78, NewGrD 80*
Meulen, Servaes Vander 1525-1592? *NewGrD 80*
Meulen, Servais Vander 1525-1592? *NewGrD 80*
Meunier-Surcouf *Film 2*
Meurice, Paul d1905 *NotNAT B*
Meurisse, Paul 1912-1979 *FilmAG WE, FilmEn, FilmgC, HalFC 80*
Meursius, Johannes 1579-1639 *NewGrD 80*
Meuschel *NewGrD 80*
Meusel, Bob *Film 2*
Meusel, Irish *Film 2*
Meven, Franz Peter 1929- *WhoOp 76*
Mews, Eric Douglas Kelson 1918- *IntWWM 77, -80*
Mewton-Wood, Noel 1922-1953 *NewGrD 80*
Mexican Marimba Band Of Agua Caliente *Film 2*
Mexis, Konstantin Filotas 1913- *IntWWM 77, -80*
Mey, Kurt Johannes 1864-1912 *Baker 78*
Meybom, Marcus *Baker 78*
Meyer, Alan Haskel 1922- *AmSCAP 80*
Meyer, Andre 1884-1974 *NewGrD 80*
Meyer, Annie Nathan *BlkAmP, MorBAP*
Meyer, Berta *NewGrD 80*
Meyer, Bertie Alexander 1877-1967 *WhThe*
Meyer, Brigitte 1944- *IntWWM 77, -80*
Meyer, Caroline *PupTheA*
Meyer, Charles 1924- *AmSCAP 66, -80*
Meyer, Conrad d1881 *NewGrD 80, OxMus*
Meyer, David Harold 1931-1980 *AmSCAP 80*
Meyer, Don 1919- *AmSCAP 66, -80*
Meyer, Emile 1903- *CmMov, FilmEn, FilmgC, ForYSC, HalFC 80, WhoHol A*
Meyer, Ernest d1927 *NotNAT B*
Meyer, Ernst Hermann 1905- *Baker 78, IntWWM 80, NewGrD 80*
Meyer, Ernst Herrmann 1905- *DcCM*
Meyer, Eve Rose 1927- *IntWWM 77, -80*
Meyer, Frederic 1910-1973 *WhScrn 77*
Meyer, Frederick John 1906- *WhoMus 72*
Meyer, George *DcFM*
Meyer, George W 1884-1959 *AmPS, AmSCAP 66, -80, BiDAmM, CmpEPM, NotNAT B, PopAmC[port], Sw&Ld C*
Meyer, Greta *Film 2, ForYSC*
Meyer, Henry Edwin 1890- *IntWWM 77*
Meyer, Hyman 1875-1945 *Film 2, WhScrn 74, -77, WhoHol B*
Meyer, Johann David *NewGrD 80*
Meyer, Johannes *Film 2*
Meyer, John Lawrence 1911- *AmSCAP 66, -80*
Meyer, Joseph 1894- *AmPS, AmSCAP 66, -80, BiDAmM, CmpEPM, EncMT, PopAmC[port], Sw&Ld C*
Meyer, Kathi *NewGrD 80*
Meyer, Kerstin 1928- *CmOp, IntWWM 77, -80, NewGrD 80, WhoMus 72, WhoOp 76*
Meyer, Krzysztof 1943- *IntWWM 77, -80, NewGrD 80*
Meyer, Laverne 1935- *CnOxB, DancEn 78*
Meyer, Leonard B 1918- *Baker 78, NewGrD 80*
Meyer, Leopold Von 1816-1883 *Baker 78*
Meyer, Louis 1871-1915 *NotNAT B, WhThe*
Meyer, Lucy 1849-1922 *BiDAmM*
Meyer, Muffie *WomWMM, -A, -B*
Meyer, Ottowerner *WhoOp 76*
Meyer, Paul 1920- *DcFM*
Meyer, Philip James 1737-1819 *NewGrD 80*
Meyer, Philipp Jakob 1737-1819 *NewGrD 80*
Meyer, Philippe-Jacques 1737-1819 *NewGrD 80*
Meyer, Richard C 1920- *IntMPA 77, -75, -76, -78, -79, -80*
Meyer, Richard D 1928- *NotNAT*
Meyer, Rosalind *PupTheA*
Meyer, Russ 1923- *FilmEn, FilmgC, HalFC 80, IntMPA 77, -75, -76, -78, -79, -80, WhoHrs 80*
Meyer, Sigtenhorst *OxMus*
Meyer, Sol 1913-1964 *AmSCAP 66, -80*
Meyer, Stuart Thomas 1945- *WhoMus 72*
Meyer, Torben 1884-1975 *Film 2, Vers B[port], WhScrn 77, WhoHol C*
Meyer, Torben 1885-1965 *HalFC 80*
Meyer, Yvonne *CnOxB, DancEn 78*
Meyer-Baer, Kathi 1892- *Baker 78, NewGrD 80*
Meyer Beer, Giacomo 1791-1864 *NewGrD 80[port]*
Meyer Beer, Jakob Liebmann 1791-1864 *BnBkM 80[port]*
Meyer-Eppler, Werner 1913-1960 *Baker 78*
Meyer-Forster, Wilhelm d1934 *NotNAT B*
Meyer-Hanno, Andreas 1932- *WhoOp 76*
Meyer-Helmund, Erik 1861-1932 *Baker 78*
Meyer-Olbersleben, Max 1850-1927 *Baker 78*
Meyer-Siat, Pie 1913- *NewGrD 80*
Meyer VonSchauensee, Franz Joseph Leonti 1720-1789 *NewGrD 80*
Meyer-Wolff, Frido 1934- *WhoOp 76*
Meyerbeer, Giacomo 1791-1864 *Baker 78, BnBkM 80[port], CmOp, CmpBCM, CnOxB, DcCom 77, DcCom&M 79, GrComp[port], MusMk[port], NewEOp 71, NewGrD 80[port], OxMus*
Meyerhold, Vsevolod 1874-1940? *CnThe, Ent*
Meyerhold, Vsevolod Emilievich 1874-1942 *NotNAT A, -B*
Meyerhold, Vsevolod Emilievich 1874-1943? *OxThe, PlP&P[port]*
Meyerhold, Vsevolod Emilyevich 1874-1942 *EncWT*
Meyerinck, Victoria *WhoHol A*
Meyerkhold, Vsevolod 1874-1942 *Film 2, WhoHol B*
Meyerowitz, Jan 1913- *Baker 78, BiDAmM, ConAmC, DcCM, NewEOp 71, NewGrD 80, OxMus*
Meyerowitz, Michael 1926- *IntWWM 77, -80, WhoMus 72*
Meyers, Billy 1894- *AmSCAP 66, -80*
Meyers, Claudia D 1915- *AmSCAP 66*
Meyers, Denise *CreCan 1*
Meyers, Emerson 1910- *ConAmC, IntWWM 77, -80*
Meyers, Kathleen *Film 2*
Meyers, Lanny Douglas *AmSCAP 80*
Meyers, Laura *WomWMM B*
Meyers, Louie *BluesWW*
Meyers, Michael *WhoHol A*
Meyers, Nicholas *ConAmC*
Meyers, Patricia *CreCan 1*
Meyers, Robert 1934- *IntMPA 77, -75, -76, -78, -79, -80*
Meyers, Robert G 1932- *CpmDNM 75, ConAmC*
Meyers, Sidney 1894- *WorEFlm*
Meyers, Sidney 1906-1969 *DcFM, FilmEn*
Meyers, Warren B 1929- *AmSCAP 66, -80*
Meylan, Jean 1915- *IntWWM 77, -80, WhoMus 72*
Meylan, Pierre 1908-1974 *Baker 78, NewGrD 80*
Meylan, Raymond 1924- *IntWWM 77, NewGrD 80*
Meyland, Jacob *NewGrD 80*
Meyland, Jakob *NewGrD 80*
Meyn, Richard 1949- *IntWWM 77, -80*
Meyn, Robert 1896-1972 *WhScrn 77, WhoHol B*
Meyn, Theodore A 1901-1975 *AmSCAP 66, -80*
Meynell, Clyde 1867-1934 *NotNAT B, WhThe*
Meyner, Giorgio *NewGrD 80*
Meyrink, Gustav 1868-1932 *WhoHrs 80*
Meyrowitz, Bob *ConMuA 80B*
Meyrowitz, Selmar 1875-1941 *Baker 78*
Meyrowitz, Wally *ConMuA 80B*
Meytus, Yuly Sergeyevich 1903- *NewGrD 80*
Mezangeau, Rene *NewGrD 80*
Mezari, Maddalena *NewGrD 80*
Mezeray, Louis-Charles-Lazare-Costard De 1810-1887 *Baker 78*
Mezetti, Charles *Film 2*
Mezinescu, Alexa Dumitrache 1936- *CnOxB*
Meziniot, Rene *NewGrD 80*
Mezo, Laszlo 1939- *NewGrD 80*
Mezzo, Pietro De *NewGrD 80*
Mezzogori, Giovanni Nicolo d1623? *NewGrD 80*
Mezzogorri, Giovanni Nicolo d1623? *NewGrD 80*
Mezzrow, Mezz 1899-1972 *CmpEPM, EncJzS 70, WhoJazz 72*
Mezzrow, Milton 1899-1972 *BiDAmM*
MFSB *RkOn 2[port]*
M'Gilvray, Laura *WhoStg 1906*
M'Guckin, Barton 1852-1917 *NewGrD 80*
Mi Fiolo *NewGrD 80*
Miaco *PupTheA*
Miami, Joe *AmSCAP 80*
Miaskovsky, Nicolas 1881-1950 *OxMus*
Miaskovsky, Nikolai 1881-1950 *Baker 78, CompSN[port], MusMk*
Mica, Frantisek Adam 1746-1811 *NewGrD 80*
Mica, Frantisek Antonin 1694-1744 *NewGrD 80*
Micek, Isabelle Helen 1922- *IntWWM 77, -80*
Mich, Thomas Alexander, Jr. 1958- *AmSCAP 80*
Michael *NewGrD 80*
Michael I, King Of Rumania 1921- *What 2[port]*
Michael Modrekili *NewGrD 80*
Michael Scotus 1175?-1235 *NewGrD 80*
Michael, Christian 1593?-1637 *NewGrD 80*
Michael, Daniel *NewGrD 80*
Michael, David Moritz *ConAmC*
Michael, David Moritz 1751-1825 *Baker 78*
Michael, David Moritz 1751-1827 *NewGrD 80*
Michael, Edward 1853-1950 *NotNAT A, -B*
Michael, Elaine 1930- *AmSCAP 66, -80*
Michael, Friedrich 1892- *CnMD, McGEWD, ModWD*
Michael, Gertrude d1964 *MotPP, WhoHol B*
Michael, Gertrude 1910-1965 *ThFT[port], WhThe*
Michael, Gertrude 1911-1964 *FilmgC, HalFC 80, WhScrn 74, -77*
Michael, Gertrude 1911-1965 *FilmEn*
Michael, Gilbert F 1933- *AmSCAP 80*
Michael, Jeff *AmSCAP 80*
Michael, Kathleen 1917- *WhoThe 72, -77*
Michael, Mickie 1943-1973 *WhScrn 77*
Michael, Mike *AmSCAP 80*
Michael, Ralph 1907- *FilmgC, HalFC 80, WhoHol A, WhoThe 72, -77*
Michael, Robert 1901- *AmSCAP 80*

Michael, Rogier 1552?-1619 *NewGrD 80*
Michael, Samuel 1597?-1632 *NewGrD 80*
Michael, Tobias 1592-1657 *NewGrD 80*
Michael, Vivian *PupTheA*
Michaele, Antoninus De *NewGrD 80*
Michaeli, John Edward 1938- *IntMPA 77, -75, -76, -78, -79, -80*
Michaelian, Patricia Elyse 1949- *WhoMus 72*
Michaelides, Peter S 1930- *CpmDNM 76, ConAmC*
Michaelides, Solon 1905-1979 *Baker 78, NewGrD 80*
Michaelis, Robert 1884-1965 *WhThe*
Michaelis, Zanetto De *NewGrD 80*
Michaels, Beverly 1927- *FilmgC, ForYSC, HalFC 80, WhoHol A*
Michaels, D Z *AmSCAP 80*
Michaels, Dolores 1930- *FilmgC, ForYSC, HalFC 80, MotPP*
Michaels, Gertrude 1911-1964 *ForYSC*
Michaels, Lee 1945- *AmSCAP 80, ConMuA 80A, IlEncR, RkOn 2[port]*
Michaels, Lorne *ConMuA 80B, NewYTET*
Michaels, Sidney Ramon 1927- *CnMD SUP, ModWD*
Michaels, Stephen 1945- *AmSCAP 80*
Michaels, Sully 1917-1966 *WhScrn 74, -77, WhoHol B*
Michaels, Timothy Croak 1951- *IntWWM 77, -80*
Michaelson, Knut 1846- *WhThe*
Michailow, Boris *Film 2*
Michalak, Thomas *IntWWM 80*
Michalek, Allen S 1940- *IntWWM 80*
Michalesco, Michael d1957 *NotNAT B, WhoHol B*
Michalkov, Sergei 1913- *CnMD*
Michalove, Edwin B 1927- *AmSCAP 66, -80*
Michalove, Peter *ConAmC*
Michalowski, Aleksander 1851-1938 *NewGrD 80*
Michalowski, Kornel 1923- *IntWWM 77, -80, NewGrD 80*
Michalski, Raymond Charles 1933- *WhoOp 76*
Michalsky, Donal 1928- *ConAmC, DcCM*
Michalsky, Donal 1928-1975 *Baker 78*
Michalsky, Donal Ray 1928-1976 *AmSCAP 80*
Michau *OxThe*
Michaud, Armand Herve 1910- *IntWWM 77, -80*
Michaud, Henri 1912- *IntMPA 77, -75, -76, -78, -79, -80*
Michaud, Henry A 1914- *IntMPA 77, -75, -76, -78, -79, -80*
Michaut, Pierre 1895-1956 *CnOxB, DancEn 78*
Micheau, Janine 1914-1976 *CmOp, NewGrD 80*
Micheau, Janine 1915- *IntWWM 77*
Micheaux, Oscar 1884-1951 *DrBlPA, MorBAP*
Micheelsen, Hans Friedrich 1902-1973 *Baker 78*
Michel *NewGrD 80*
Michel Angelo DelViolino *NewGrD 80*
Michel De Toulouse *NewGrD 80*
Michel De Toulouze *NewGrD 80*
Michel, Andre 1910- *DcFM, FilmEn, WorEFlm*
Michel, Arthur *NewGrD 80*
Michel, Edward M 1936- *EncJzS 70*
Michel, Franny *WhoHol A*
Michel, Gaston 1856-1921 *WhScrn 77*
Michel, Georges 1926- *CroCD*
Michel, Guillaume *NewGrD 80*
Michel, Madelon 1939- *IntWWM 77, -80*
Michel, Micheline *FilmEn*
Michel, Paul 1918- *IntWWM 77, -80, NewGrD 80*
Michel, Paul-Baudouin 1930- *Baker 78, IntWWM 77, -80*
Michel, Stella *PupTheA*
Michel, Werner 1910- *IntMPA 77, -75, -76, -78, -79, -80, NewYTET*
Michelangeli 1920- *MusSN[port]*
Michelangeli, Arturo Benedetti 1920- *Baker 78, BnBkM 80, IntWWM 77, -80, MusMk, NewGrD 80[port]*
Michele *BluesWW*
Michelena, Beatrice 1890-1942 *WhScrn 74, -77*
Michelena, Beatriz 1890-1942 *Film 1, MotPP, WhoHol B*
Michelena, Vera 1884-1961 *CmpEPM, WhScrn 74, -77, WhoHol B*
Michelet, Michel *IntMPA 77, -76, -78, -79, -80*
Michelet, Michel 1894- *Baker 78*
Michelet, Michel 1899- *IntWWM 77, -80*
Micheletti, Gioseffo *NewGrD 80*
Micheli, Antonino Di *NewGrD 80*
Micheli, Benedetto 1700?-1784 *NewGrD 80*
Micheli, Domenico 1540?-1590? *NewGrD 80*
Micheli, Romano 1575?-1659? *NewGrD 80*
Michell, Keith *IntMPA 77, -75, -76, -78, -79, -80, WhoHol A*
Michell, Keith 1926- *FilmAG WE, FilmgC, HalFC 80, MovMk*
Michell, Keith 1928- *BiE&WWA, CnThe, EncMT, IlWWBF, NotNAT, WhoThe 72, -77*
Michelow, Sybil *IntWWM 77, -80, WhoMus 72*
Michels, Lloyd *AmSCAP 80*
Michels, Walter 1895- *AmSCAP 66, -80*
Michelsen, Hans Gunter 1920- *CnMD SUP, CroCD, McGEWD, ModWD*
Michelucci, Roberto 1922- *IntWWM 80*
Michener, James A 1907- *FilmgC, HalFC 80, PlP&P*
Michener, Marjorie Roop 1938- *IntWWM 77*
Michi, Horatio 1594?-1641 *NewGrD 80*
Michi, Orazio 1594?-1641 *NewGrD 80*
Michi, Orazio 1595?-1641 *Baker 78*
Michi Dell'Arpa, Horatio 1594?-1641 *NewGrD 80*
Michi Dell'Arpa, Orazio 1594?-1641 *NewGrD 80*
Michii, Makoto 1935- *IntWWM 77, -80*
Michl *NewGrD 80*
Michl, Ferdinand 1723-1754 *NewGrD 80*
Michl, Johann Joseph Ildefons 1708-1770 *NewGrD 80*
Michl, Joseph Willibald 1745-1816 *NewGrD 80*
Michl, Melchior Virgil 1735?-1795 *NewGrD 80*
Michlin, Spencer 1941- *AmSCAP 80*
Michna, Adam Vaclav 1600?-1676 *NewGrD 80*
Micho, Richard *NewGrD 80*
Michrovsky, Stefan *AmSCAP 80*
Micieces, Tomas 1624?-1662? *NewGrD 80*
Micieres, Tomas 1624?-1662? *NewGrD 80*
Micinski, Tadeusz 1873-1919 *CnMD*
Mick, Hettie Louise *PupTheA*
Mickelson, Jerry *ConMuA 80B*
Mickelson, Sig *NewYTET*
Mickey *BluesWW*
Mickey And Sylvia *RkOn[port]*
Mickiewicz, Adam Bernard 1798-1855 *EncWT, McGEWD[port], OxMus, OxThe, REnWD[port]*
Mickiewicz, Halina 1923- *IntWWM 77, -80*
Mickle, Elmon 1919-1977 *BluesWW[port]*
Mickle, William Julius 1734-1788 *OxMus*
Mico, Richard 1590?-1661 *NewGrD 80*
Micoe, Richard 1590?-1661 *NewGrD 80*
Micone, Ed *ConMuA 80B*
Miculi, Karol *NewGrD 80*
Miculs, Melita Luize 1945- *WhoOp 76*
Micunis, Gordon 1933- *WhoOp 76*
Micza, Frantisek Adam *NewGrD 80*
Micza, Frantisek Antonin *NewGrD 80*
Middaugh, Benjamin 1934- *IntWWM 77, -80*
Midday Merry-Go-Round *BiDAmM*
Middelschulte, Wilhelm 1863-1943 *Baker 78, OxMus*
Middendorf, John William, II 1924- *AmSCAP 80, ConAmC*
Middenway, Ralph 1932- *IntWWM 77, -80*
Middlebrok, Mamie 1899- *IntWWM 77*
Middlebrooks, Wilfred Roland 1933- *BiDAmM*
Middlemas, David 1919- *IntMPA 77, -75, -76, -78, -79, -80*
Middlemass, Robert M 1885-1949 *ForYSC, WhScrn 77*
Middleton, Charles B d1949 *MotPP*
Middleton, Charles B 1874-1949 *FilmgC, HalFC 80*
Middleton, Charles B 1878-1949 *HolCA[port]*
Middleton, Charles B 1879-1949 *FilmEn, Film 2, ForYSC, Vers A[port], WhScrn 74, -77, WhoHol B, WhoHrs 80*
Middleton, E Arthur *ConAmC*
Middleton, Edgar 1894-1939 *NotNAT B, WhThe*
Middleton, Eleanor *Film 2*
Middleton, Fay 1907- *WhoThe 72*
Middleton, George d1926 *NotNAT B*
Middleton, George 1880-1967 *BiE&WWA, NotNAT A, -B, WhThe*
Middleton, Mrs. George Edward *PupTheA*
Middleton, George William 1865-1946 *PupTheA*
Middleton, Guy d1973 *WhoHol B*
Middleton, Guy 1906-1973 *FilmgC, HalFC 80*
Middleton, Guy 1907-1973 *FilmEn, IlWWBF, NotNAT B, WhThe*
Middleton, Guy 1908-1973 *WhScrn 77*
Middleton, Henry James 1840?-1877 *PupTheA*
Middleton, Henry James 1858-1884 *PupTheA*
Middleton, Herman D 1925- *BiE&WWA, NotNAT*
Middleton, Hubert Stanley 1890-1959 *Baker 78*
Middleton, James Roland 1896- *WhoMus 72*
Middleton, Jaynne Claire 1947- *IntWWM 77, -80*
Middleton, Jean B *ConAmC*
Middleton, Josephine 1883-1971 *WhScrn 74, -77, WhThe, WhoHol B*
Middleton, Lavinia Joann 1934- *AmSCAP 80*
Middleton, Leora *WhScrn 74, -77*
Middleton, Marjory 1908- *CnOxB*
Middleton, Noelle 1928?- *HalFC 80, WhoHol A*
Middleton, Owen 1941- *AmSCAP 80*
Middleton, Ray *AmPS B, IntMPA 75, -76, -78, -79, -80*
Middleton, Ray 1907- *BiE&WWA, CmpEPM, EncMT, IntMPA 77, NotNAT, PlP&P, WhoHol A, WhoThe 77*
Middleton, Ray 1908- *HalFC 80*
Middleton, Robert 1911-1977 *FilmEn, FilmgC, ForYSC, HalFC 80, IntMPA 77, -75, -76, Vers A[port], WhoHol A*
Middleton, Robert 1920- *ConAmC*
Middleton, Thomas 1570?-1627 *CnThe, EncWT, NotNAT A, -B, OxThe, REnWD[port]*
Middleton, Thomas 1580-1627 *Ent, McGEWD[port]*
Middleton, Tom *WhoHol A*
Middleton, Velma 1917-1961 *BiDAmM, WhoJazz 72*
Midgely, Fannie 1877-1932 *Film 1, WhScrn 77*
Midgen, Chester L 1921- *IntMPA 80*
Midgley, Charles William 1899- *AmSCAP 80*
Midgley, Fannie 1877-1932 *Film 2*
Midgley, Florence 1890-1949 *Film 2, WhScrn 74, -77, WhoHol B*
Midgley, Leslie *NewYTET*
Midgley, Richard A 1910-1956 *WhScrn 74, -77, WhoHol B*
Midgley, Robin 1934- *WhoThe 77*
Midinet, Max 1948- *CnOxB*
Midler, Bette *ConMuA 80A*
Midler, Bette 1944- *JoeFr[port], WhoHol A*
Midler, Bette 1945- *IlEncR[port], RkOn 2[port]*
Midney, Barbara Joan 1954- *IntWWM 80*
Midnighters, The *RkOn[port]*
Midrolet, Roger 1926- *FilmAG WE*
Midwestern Hayride *BiDAmM*
Miechura, Leopold Eugen *NewGrD 80*
Miedel, Rainer 1938- *Baker 78*
Miedel, Rainer 1939- *WhoOp 76*
Miedke, Karl August *NewGrD 80*
Mieg, Peter 1906- *Baker 78, CpmDNM 80, IntWWM 80, NewGrD 80*
Miehler, Otto 1903- *IntWWM 77, -80*
Mieir, Audrey Mae 1916- *AmSCAP 80*
Mielck, Ernst 1877-1899 *Baker 78*
Mielczewski, Marcin d1651 *NewGrD 80*
Mielke, Antonia 1852?-1907 *Baker 78*
Mielorth *NewGrD 80*
Mielziner, Jo 1901-1976 *BiE&WWA, CnThe, EncWT, Ent, NotNAT, -B, OxThe, PlP&P[port], WhoThe 72, -77*
Miereanu, Costin 1943- *Baker 78, DcCM*
Mierendorff, Hans *Film 2*
Mierowski, Henryk 1905- *WhoMus 72*
Miersch, Carl Alexander Johannes 1865-1916 *BiDAmM*
Miersch, Paul Francis 1868-1956 *BiDAmM*
Miersch, Paul Friedrich Theodor 1868-1956 *Baker 78*

Mierzecka, Elzbieta 1943- *IntWWM 77, -80*
Mierzejewski, Mieczystaw 1905- *IntWWM 77, -80*
Mierzwinski, Wladyslaw 1850-1909 *NewGrD 80*
Mies, Paul 1889-1976 *Baker 78, IntWWM 77, -80, NewGrD 80*
Miescer, A Stephen 1903- *AmSCAP 66, -80*
Miessner, Benjamin Franklin 1890?-1976 *Baker 78*
Mietelski, Marek Stefan 1933- *IntWWM 77, -80*
Mifune, Toshiro 1920- *FilmEn, FilmgC, ForYSC, HalFC 80, IntMPA 77, -75, -76, -78, -79, -80, MotPP, MovMk, OxFilm, WhoHol A, WhoHrs 80, WorEFlm[port]*
Migden, Chester L 1921- *BiE&WWA, IntMPA 77, -75, -76, -78, -79*
Migliore, Tony 1944- *AmSCAP 80*
Mignan, Edouard-Charles-Octave 1884-1969 *Baker 78*
Mignon, Jean 1640?-1707? *NewGrD 80*
Mignone, Francisco 1897- *Baker 78, BiDAmM, CompSN[port], IntWWM 77, -80, NewGrD 80*
Mignot, DeLaVoye *NewGrD 80*
Mignot, Flore *WhThe*
Migot, Georges 1891-1976 *Baker 78, DcCM, IntWWM 77, NewGrD 80, OxMus, WhoMus 72*
Migret, Giacomo *NewGrD 80*
Miguel, Mariano Tafall Y *NewGrD 80*
Miguez, Leopoldo 1850-1902 *Baker 78, NewGrD 80*
Mihail, Alexandra 1947-1975 *WhScrn 77*
Mihaljinec, Stjepan 1935- *IntWWM 80*
Mihalka, Gyorgy 1924- *IntWWM 80*
Mihalovich, Edmund Von 1842-1929 *Baker 78*
Mihalovich, Odon Peter Jozsef De 1842-1929 *NewGrD 80*
Mihalovici, Marcel 1898- *Baker 78, DcCM, NewGrD 80, OxMus*
Mihaly, Andras 1917- *Baker 78, DcCM, IntWWM 77, -80, NewGrD 80*
Mihi, Orazio *NewGrD 80*
Mihleis, Alice *PupTheA*
Mihule, Jaroslav 1930- *IntWWM 77, -80*
Mihura, Miguel 1903- *ModWD*
Mihura, Miguel 1905- *CroCD*
Mihura Santos, Miguel 1905- *McGEWD[port]*
Mike And Meyer *JoeFr*
Mikell, F Eugene, Sr. 1880-1932 *WhoJazz 72*
Mikell, George *IntMPA 77, -75, -76, -78, -79, -80*
Mikels, Ted V *WhoHrs 80*
Mikelsons, Rudolfs Oskars 1905- *IntWWM 77, -80*
Mikes, Adolf 1864-1929 *NewGrD 80*
Miketta, Bob 1911-1975 *AmSCAP 66, -80*
Mikhailov, Maxim 1893-1971 *CmOp*
Mikhalkov, Sergei Vladimirovich 1913- *OxThe*
Mikhalkov, Sergey Vladimirovich 1913- *ModWD*
Mikhashoff, Yvar-Emilian 1944- *ConAmC*
Mikhaylov, Maxim 1893-1971 *NewGrD 80*
Mikhaylov-Stoyan, Konstantin Ivanovich 1853-1914 *NewGrD 80*
Mikhaylova, Maria 1866-1943 *NewGrD 80*
Mikhoels, Salomon 1890-1948 *NotNAT B, OxThe*
Mikhoels, Solomon 1890-1948 *WhoHol B*
Miki, Minoru 1930- *Baker 78, NewGrD 80*
Mikkelborg, Palle 1941- *EncJzS 70, IntWWM 77, -80*
Mikkelsen, Tove Bjorndal 1946- *IntWWM 77*
Mikley-Kemp, Barbara *NewGrD 80*
Miklosy, Margot 1938- *CnOxB*
Miko, Andras 1922- *IntWWM 80, WhoOp 76*
Mikolaj Z Krakowa *NewGrD 80*
Mikorey, Franz 1873-1947 *Baker 78*
Mikova, Alena 1928- *WhoMus 72, WhoOp 76*
Mikowsky, Solomon Gadles 1935- *IntWWM 77*
Mikowsky, Solomon Gadles 1936- *IntWWM 80*
Miksch, Johann Aloys 1765-1845 *Baker 78*
Mikula, Jacek Roman 1946- *IntWWM 77*
Mikulak, Marcia Lee 1948- *ConAmC*
Mikuli, Karl 1819-1897 *Baker 78*
Mikuli, Karol 1819-1897 *NewGrD 80*
Mila, Massimo 1910- *Baker 78, IntWWM 77, -80, NewGrD 80, WhoMus 72*
Miladinovitch, Dejan Dusan 1948- *WhoOp 76*
Miladinovitch, Dusan Slobodan 1924- *WhoOp 76*
Miladinovitch, Milica Dusan 1930- *WhoOp 76*
Miladowski, Florian Stanislaw 1819-1889 *NewGrD 80*
Milaidy, James *Film 2*
Milaine, Amille *Film 2*
Milam, Pauline 1912-1965 *WhScrn 74, -77, WhoHol B*
Milan, Lita *ForYSC, MotPP*
Milan, Luis 1500?-1561? *Baker 78, BnBkM 80, MusMk, NewGrD 80, OxMus*
Milan, Luys 1500?-1561? *NewGrD 80*
Milani, Francesco *NewGrD 80*
Milani, Joseph L *WhScrn 77*
Milano, Francesco Canova Da *NewGrD 80*
Milano, Frank d1962 *NotNAT B*
Milano, Robert 1936- *ConAmC*
Milanollo, Maria *NewGrD 80*
Milanollo, Teresa 1827-1904 *NewGrD 80*
Milanov, Zinka *IntWWM 77, -80*
Milanov, Zinka 1903- *WhoMus 72*
Milanov, Zinka 1906- *Baker 78, BnBkM 80, CmOp, MusSN[port], NewEOp 71, NewGrD 80[port]*
Milanova, Stoika 1945- *IntWWM 77, -80, NewGrD 80*
Milanova, Vanya Josifova 1954- *IntWWM 80*
Milanta, Giovanni Francesco 1607-1651? *NewGrD 80*
Milanuzii, Carlo d1647? *NewGrD 80*
Milanuzzi, Carlo d1647? *NewGrD 80, OxMus*
Milar, Adolph *Film 2, TwYS*
Milasch, Robert *Film 2*
Milash, Bib *Film 2*
Milash, Robert E 1885-1954 *WhScrn 74, -77, WhoHol B*
Milashkina, Tamara 1934- *NewGrD 80, WhoOp 76*
Milazzo, Charles Joseph 1909- *AmSCAP 80*
Milbert, Seymour 1915- *BiE&WWA*
Milbourne, Mister *PlP&P*
Milburn, Amos 1927- *BluesWW[port], RkOn*
Milburn, Ellsworth 1938- *AmSCAP 80, Baker 78, ConAmC*
Milburn, Richard 1845?-1900? *BiDAmM*
Milcheva-Nonov, Alexandrina 1939- *IntWWM 80*
Milcheva-Nonova, Alexandrina 1936- *WhoOp 76*
Milchevsky, Marcin *NewGrD 80*
Milcrest, Howard 1892-1920 *WhScrn 74, -77, WhoHol B*
Milde, Hans Feodor Von 1821-1899 *Baker 78*
Milde-Meissner, Hanson 1899- *WhoMus 72*
Mildenberg, Albert 1878-1918 *Baker 78, BiDAmM, ConAmC*
Mildenburg, Anna Von 1872-1947 *Baker 78, NewEOp 71, NewGrD 80*
Milder-Hauptmann, Anna 1785-1838 *NewGrD 80*
Milder-Hauptmann, Pauline Anna 1785-1838 *Baker 78, NewEOp 71*
Mildmay, Audrey 1900-1953 *CmOp, NewEOp 71, NewGrD 80*
Mildren, Margaret Joyce 1936- *IntWWM 77, WhoMus 72*
Miler, Zdenek 1929- *DcFM*
Milerta, John *Film 2*
Miles, Alfred Hart 1883-1956 *AmSCAP 66, -80*
Miles, Allan 1929- *BiE&WWA*
Miles, Art 1899-1955 *WhoHol B*
Miles, Arthur K 1899-1955 *WhScrn 74, -77*
Miles, Barry 1947- *AmSCAP 66, -80, Conv 2[port], EncJzS 70*
Miles, Sir Bernard 1907- *CnThe, EncWT, FilmAG WE, FilmEn, FilmgC, HalFC 80, IlWWBF, IntMPA 77, -75, -76, -78, -79, -80, OxThe, PlP&P, WhoHol A, WhoThe 72, -77*
Miles, Betty *WomWMM B*
Miles, Bob *Film 2*
Miles, Buddy 1946- *ConMuA 80A, IlEncR[port], RkOn 2[port]*
Miles, Buddy, Express *BiDAmM*
Miles, Butch 1944- *EncJzS 70*
Miles, C Austin 1868-1946 *AmSCAP 66, -80*
Miles, Carlton d1954 *NotNAT B*
Miles, Charles J 1944- *EncJzS 70*
Miles, Cherrily *BlkAmP*
Miles, Christopher 1939- *FilmEn, FilmgC, HalFC 80, IlWWBF*
Miles, Colin Lewis 1944- *IntWWM 80*
Miles, Daphne Denise Robson 1918- *IntWWM 77*
Miles, David d1915 *Film 1, WhScrn 77*
Miles, Elizabeth 1895-1963 *BluesWW[port]*
Miles, G H *PlP&P*
Miles, Garry *RkOn*
Miles, George 1946- *AmSCAP 80*
Miles, George Henry d1871 *NotNAT B*
Miles, H *Film 2*
Miles, Harold 1908- *ConAmC*
Miles, Herbert *Film 1*
Miles, Mrs. Herbert *Film 1*
Miles, Jackie 1913-1968 *JoeFr, NotNAT B, WhoHol B*
Miles, James 1949- *IntWWM 80*
Miles, Jane Mary *NewGrD 80*
Miles, Jennifer *WomWMM B*
Miles, Joanna 1949- *HalFC 80, WhoHol A*
Miles, John 1949- *IlEncR*
Miles, Josephine 1900?- *BluesWW[port]*
Miles, Julia *NotNAT*
Miles, Kenneth 1924- *WhoMus 72*
Miles, Lillian *WhoHol A*
Miles, Lizzie 1895-1963 *BiDAmM, CmpEPM, NewOrJ[port], WhoJazz 72*
Miles, Lotta 1899-1937 *WhScrn 74, -77, WhoHol B*
Miles, Luke 1925- *BiDAmM, BluesWW*
Miles, Luther *Film 2*
Miles, Maurice Edward 1908- *Baker 78, WhoMus 72*
Miles, Nelson Appleton 1839-1925 *WhScrn 77*
Miles, Peter 1938- *FilmgC, HalFC 80, WhoHol A*
Miles, Philip Napier 1865-1935 *Baker 78*
Miles, Richard 1916- *AmSCAP 66, -80*
Miles, Robert 1920- *AmSCAP 66, -80*
Miles, Rosalind *WhoHol A*
Miles, Sarah 1941- *BiDFilm, -81, FilmAG WE[port], FilmEn, FilmgC, ForYSC, HalFC 80, IlWWBF, IntMPA 77, -75, -76, -78, -79, -80, MotPP, MovMk[port], WhoHol A, WhoThe 72, -77*
Miles, Sherry *WhoHol A*
Miles, Sylvia 1926- *HalFC 80*
Miles, Sylvia 1932- *BiE&WWA, FilmEn, NotNAT, WhoHol A*
Miles, Vera *IntMPA 75, -76, MotPP, WhoHol A*
Miles, Vera 1929- *FilmEn, FilmgC, ForYSC, HalFC 80*
Miles, Vera 1930- *BiDFilm, -81, IntMPA 77, -78, -79, -80, MovMk, WorEFlm*
Miles, Walter E 1885-1961 *AmSCAP 66, -80*
Milestone, Lewis 1895-1980 *AmFD, BiDFilm, -81, CmMov, DcFM, FilmEn, FilmgC, HalFC 80, IntMPA 77, -75, -76, -78, -79, -80, MovMk[port], OxFilm, TwYS A, WorEFlm*
Miletic, Miroslav 1925- *Baker 78, IntWWM 77, -80*
Miley, Bubber 1903-1932 *CmpEPM, IlEncJ, NewGrD 80, WhoJazz 72*
Miley, James Wesley 1903-1932 *BiDAmM, NewGrD 80*
Miley, Jerry *Film 2*
Milford, Bliss *Film 1, MotPP*
Milford, Diana Ruth Marion 1931- *WhoMus 72*
Milford, John *IntMPA 79, -80*
Milford, Robin 1903-1959 *Baker 78, NewGrD 80, OxMus*
Milgram, David E 1907- *IntMPA 77, -75, -76, -78, -79, -80*
Milgram, Henry 1926- *IntMPA 77, -75, -76, -78, -79, -80*
Milhalesco *Film 2*
Milhaud, Darius 1892-1974 *Baker 78, BnBkM 80, CmOp, CompSN[port], CnOxB, DancEn 78, DcCom 77[port], DcCom&M 79, DcCM, DcFM,. FilmEn, MusMk[port], NewEOp 71, NewGrD 80[port], OxFilm, OxMus, WhoMus 72, WorEFlm*
Milhaud, Darius 1893-1974 *WhScrn 77*

Milhollin, James 1920- *FilmgC, HalFC 80*
Milhouse *NewGrD 80*
Milhouse, Richard 1725?- *NewGrD 80*
Milhouse, William 1753?- *NewGrD 80*
Milian, Thomas *WhoHol A*
Milian, Tomas *HalFC 80*
Milie, William 1929- *CnOxB*
Milioni, Pietro *NewGrD 80*
Military, Francis Philip 1926- *AmSCAP 80*
Military, Frank 1926- *AmSCAP 66*
Military, Pamela 1924- *AmSCAP 80*
Milius, John 1944- *BiDFilm 81*
Milius, John 1945- *HalFC 80, IntMPA 77, -75, -76, -78, -79, -80, MovMk[port]*
Miljakovic, Olivera 1939- *WhoOp 76*
Miljan, John 1892-1960 *FilmEn, HolCA[port]*
Miljan, John 1893-1960 *FilmgC, ForYSC, HalFC 80, MovMk, NotNAT B, Vers B[port], WhScrn 74, -77, WhoHol B*
Miljan, John 1899-1960 *Film 2, TwYS*
Milkey, Edward T 1908- *AmSCAP 66, -80, ConAmC*
Milkina, Nina 1919- *IntWWM 77, -80, NewGrD 80, WhoMus 72*
Mill, John Stuart 1806-1873 *OxMus*
Millaire, Albert 1935- *CreCan 2*
Millaire, Andree *DancEn 78*
Millan, Francisco *NewGrD 80*
Millan, Victor *WhoHol A*
Milland, Ray *MotPP, WhoHol A*
Milland, Ray 1905- *BiDFilm, -81, CmMov, FilmEn, FilmgC, ForYSC[port], HalFC 80[port], IlWWBF, -A[port], OxFilm, WhoHrs 80[port]*
Milland, Ray 1907- *Film 2, WorEFlm[port]*
Milland, Ray 1908- *IntMPA 77, -75, -76, -78, -79, -80, MovMk[port]*
Milland, Spike 1907- *Film 2*
Millar, Adelqui *Film 2*
Millar, Douglas 1875-1943 *NotNAT B, WhThe*
Millar, Edward *NewGrD 80*
Millar, Gertie 1879-1952 *EncMT, NotNAT B, OxThe, WhThe*
Millar, Jean Madeline *WhoMus 72*
Millar, Keith Hamilton Park 1946- *IntWWM 77, -80*
Millar, Lee 1888-1941 *WhScrn 74, -77, WhoHol B*
Millar, Mack d1962 *NotNAT B*
Millar, Marjie d1966 *WhScrn 77*
Millar, Marjie d1970 *WhoHol B*
Millar, Marjie 1930- *ForYSC*
Millar, Mary 1936- *WhoThe 72, -77*
Millar, Robins 1889-1968 *NotNAT B, WhThe*
Millar, Ronald 1919- *ConDr 73, -77, WhoThe 72, -77*
Millar, Stuart 1929- *FilmEn, FilmgC, HalFC 80, IntMPA 77, -75, -76, -78, -79, -80*
Millard, Edward R d1963 *NotNAT B*
Millard, Evelyn 1869-1941 *NotNAT B, WhThe*
Millard, Harrison 1829-1895 *Baker 78*
Millard, Harrison 1830-1895 *BiDAmM*
Millard, Harry W 1928-1969 *WhScrn 74, -77, WhoHol B*
Millard, Helene *Film 2*
Millard, Lyn *PupTheA*
Millard, Ursula 1901- *WhThe*
Millarde, Harry *Film 1, TwYS A, WhScrn 74, -77, WhoHol B*
Millaud, Albert d1892 *NotNAT B*
Millay, Edna St. Vincent 1892-1950 *AmSCAP 66, -80, CnMD, McGEWD, ModWD, NotNAT B*
Mille, Agnes De 1909- *CnOxB*
Miller, Mademoiselle 1770-1833 *DancEn 78*
Miller, Mrs. *RkOn 2[port]*
Miller, Adam S 1947- *AmSCAP 80*
Miller, Agnes *WhThe*
Miller, Albert *CreCan 2*
Miller, Alice Duer 1874-1942 *NotNAT B, WhoHol B*
Miller, Alice Moore *WhScrn 74, -77*
Miller, Ann 1919- *CmMov, CmpEPM, FilmEn, FilmgC, ForYSC, HalFC 80, MGM[port], MotPP, MovMk[port], NotNAT A, ThFT[port], WhoHol A, WhoThe 77, WorEFlm*
Miller, Ann 1923- *IntMPA 77, -75, -76, -78, -79, -80*
Miller, Anne Langdon 1908- *BiDAmM*
Miller, Arnold E, Jr. 1921- *AmSCAP 66, -80*
Miller, Arnold Louis 1922- *IlWWBF*
Miller, Arthur d1935 *NotNAT B*
Miller, Arthur 1915- *BiE&WWA, CnMD, CnThe, ConDr 73, -77, CroCD, DcFM, DcLB 7[port], EncWT, Ent, FilmEn, FilmgC, HalFC 80, McGEWD[port], ModWD, NatPD[port], NewEOp 71, NotNAT, -A, OxFilm, OxThe, PlP&P[port], REnWD[port], WhoThe 72, -77, WorEFlm*
Miller, Arthur C 1894-1971 *FilmgC, HalFC 80*
Miller, Arthur C 1895-1970 *DcFM, FilmEn, OxFilm, WorEFlm*
Miller, Ashley 1867-1949 *WhScrn 74, -77, WhoHol B*
Miller, Ashley 1877- *WhoStg 1908*
Miller, Beverly 1906- *IntMPA 77, -75, -76, -78, -79, -80*
Miller, Bill *CmpEPM*
Miller, Bob d1964 *NotNAT B*
Miller, Bob 1895-1955 *AmSCAP 66, -80, BiDAmM*
Miller, Buzz 1928- *BiE&WWA, CnOxB, NotNAT, WhoHol A*
Miller, Carl *Film 1, -2*
Miller, Carl S 1917- *AmSCAP 80*
Miller, Carlton *Film 2*
Miller, Carol M 1931- *IntWWM 77, -80*
Miller, Cecilia Ann 1922- *IntWWM 77*
Miller, Charles *TwYS A*
Miller, Charles 1899- *AmSCAP 66, -80, ConAmC*
Miller, Charles B 1891-1955 *WhScrn 74, -77, WhoHol B*
Miller, Charles Edward 1929- *AmSCAP 80*
Miller, Charlie K 1915-1962 *NewOrJ*
Miller, Cheryl 1943- *IntMPA 77, -75, -76, -78, -79, -80, WhoHol A*
Miller, Chris *ConMuA 80B*
Miller, Chuck *RkOn*
Miller, Clarence d1963 *NotNAT B*
Miller, Clarence H 1923- *BiDAmM*
Miller, Clarence Horatio 1922- *BluesWW[port]*
Miller, Claude 1942- *HalFC 80*
Miller, Clement A 1915- *IntWWM 77, -80*
Miller, Clifford Leonard *BlkAmP*
Miller, Clyde Elmer 1917- *IntWWM 77, -80*
Miller, Colleen 1932- *FilmEn, FilmgC, ForYSC, HalFC 80, WhoHol A*
Miller, Connie H 1920- *AmSCAP 80*
Miller, D Thomas *NewYTET*
Miller, David 1871-1933 *NotNAT B, WhThe*
Miller, David 1909- *BiDFilm, -81, FilmEn, FilmgC, HalFC 80, IntMPA 77, -75, -76, -78, -79, -80, MovMk[port], WorEFlm*
Miller, David Prince d1873 *NotNAT B*
Miller, Dayton Clarence 1866-1941 *Baker 78, NewGrD 80, OxMus*
Miller, Dean *ForYSC, WhoHol A*
Miller, Dennis 1935- *ForYSC*
Miller, Dennis Hayden 1951- *CpmDNM 80*
Miller, Denny 1935- *MotPP, WhoHol A, WhoHrs 80*
Miller, Dick 1928- *IntMPA 77, -75, -76, -78, -79, -80*
Miller, Dick 1930?- *WhoHrs 80[port]*
Miller, Doris *ConMuA 80B*
Miller, Douglas 1888- *WhoMus 72*
Miller, Douglas, Jr. 1951- *ConAmC*
Miller, E G 1883-1948 *WhScrn 77*
Miller, Ed E 1929- *AmSCAP 66*
Miller, Eddie 1891-1971 *BiDAmM, WhScrn 77, WhoHol B*
Miller, Eddie 1911- *CmpEPM, EncJzS 70, IlEncJ, NewOrJ[port], WhoJazz 72*
Miller, Eddie Piano *AmSCAP 80*
Miller, Edward 1730?-1807 *OxMus*
Miller, Edward 1735-1807 *NewGrD 80*
Miller, Edward 1930- *DcCM*
Miller, Edward G George 1883-1948 *WhScrn 74*
Miller, Edward J 1930- *ConAmC*
Miller, Edward R 1911- *AmSCAP 66, -80, BiDAmM*
Miller, Ella *Film 2*
Miller, Emily 1833-1913 *BiDAmM*
Miller, Ernest 1889-1971 *EncJzS 70*
Miller, Ernest 1894-1971 *NewOrJ[port]*
Miller, Ernest 1897- *BiDAmM*
Miller, Ernest Arthur 1925- *IntWWM 77, -80*
Miller, Ernest Louis *NewGrD 80*
Miller, Ethel *Film 2*
Miller, Eula Margie Bogans *IntWWM 77*
Miller, Eve 1925- *ForYSC*
Miller, Flournoy *BlkAmP, MorBAP*
Miller, Flournoy E d1971 *JoeFr*
Miller, Flournoy E 1887-1971 *AmSCAP 66, -80, DrBlPA, WhScrn 74, -77, WhoHol B*
Miller, Flournoy E 1889- *BlksB&W[port], -C*
Miller, Frank 1891- *IlWWBF*
Miller, Frankie *BiDAmM, ConMuA 80A, IlEncR[port]*
Miller, Franz *NewGrD 80*
Miller, Fred *WhoHol A*
Miller, Frederick S 1930- *AmSCAP 80, ConAmC*
Miller, George 1951- *JoeFr*
Miller, Gilbert Heron 1884-1969 *BiE&WWA, NotNAT B, PlP&P, WhThe*
Miller, Glenn 1904-1944 *AmPS A, -B, AmSCAP 66, -80, Baker 78, BgBands 74[port], BiDAmM, CmpEPM, FilmgC, HalFC 80, NewGrD 80, WhScrn 74, -77, WhoHol B, WhoJazz 72*
Miller, Glenn David 1940- *IntWWM 77, -80*
Miller, Grace Sadie 1917- *IntWWM 77*
Miller, H Thomas 1923- *AmSCAP 66, -80*
Miller, Hal 1923- *AmSCAP 66*
Miller, Harold d1972 *WhoHol B*
Miller, Harry M 1934- *WhoThe 77*
Miller, Harry S 1895- *AmSCAP 66, -80*
Miller, Harvey 1934- *ConAmC*
Miller, Helen *BlkAmP*
Miller, Henry 1859- *WhoStg 1906, -1908*
Miller, Henry 1860-1926 *FamA&A[port], NotNAT A, -B, OxThe, PlP&P[port], WhThe*
Miller, Henry Ned 1925- *BiDAmM*
Miller, Herb 1915- *AmSCAP 66, -80*
Miller, Herman *NewYTET*
Miller, Hugh 1889- *IlWWBF, WhThe*
Miller, Hugh J 1902-1956 *Film 2, WhScrn 74, -77, WhoHol B*
Miller, Irene Bliss d1962 *NotNAT B*
Miller, Irving 1907- *AmSCAP 66, -80*
Miller, J P 1919- *IntMPA 77, -75, -76, -78, -79, -80, NewYTET*
Miller, Jack 1888-1928 *WhScrn 74, -77*
Miller, Jack Shorty 1895-1941 *WhScrn 74, -77*
Miller, Jacques 1900- *AmSCAP 66, -80, ConAmC*
Miller, James *OxMus*
Miller, James d1744 *NotNAT B*
Miller, James E 1913- *NewOrJ*
Miller, James Hull 1916- *BiE&WWA, NotNAT*
Miller, James M 1907-1970 *AmSCAP 66, -80*
Miller, James Niven 1929- *WhoMus 72*
Miller, Jan *WhoHol A*
Miller, Janet 1916- *IntWWM 77, -80*
Miller, Jason *IntMPA 77, -75, -76, -78, -79, -80, NatPD[port], WhoHol A*
Miller, Jason 1932- *ConDr 73, -77*
Miller, Jason 1939- *DcLB 7[port], HalFC 80, NotNAT, PlP&P A[port], WhoThe 77*
Miller, Jeffrey *BlkAmP*
Miller, Jesse Paul 1935- *ConAmC*
Miller, Jim *BluesWW*
Miller, Joan 1910- *ConAmC, WhoHol A, WhoThe 72, -77*
Miller, Joaquin 1837-1913 *NotNAT B*
Miller, Jody 1941- *BiDAmM, CounME 74[port], -74A, EncFCWM 69, IlEncCM[port], RkOn 2[port]*
Miller, Joe *Film 2*
Miller, John Robert 1947- *IntWWM 77, -80*
Miller, Johnny 1897?- *NewOrJ*
Miller, Jonathan *WhoHol A*
Miller, Jonathan 1934- *BiE&WWA, EncWT, Ent, NotNAT, WhoOp 76, WhoThe 72, -77*
Miller, Jonathan 1936- *FilmgC, HalFC 80*
Miller, Joseph 1684-1738 *NotNAT B*
Miller, Joseph 1915- *AmSCAP 66, -80*
Miller, Josephine *Film 1*
Miller, Josias 1684-1738 *NotNAT B*
Miller, Juanita 1880-1970 *WhScrn 74, -77*

Miller, Julia WomWMM
Miller, Justin 1888- IntMPA 75, -76
Miller, Karl Frederick 1947- CpmDNM 78
Miller, Kevin WhoMus 72
Miller, Kid Punch 1889-1971 EncJzS 70
Miller, Kid Punch 1894-1971 IlEncJ
Miller, Kristine ForYSC
Miller, Lajos 1940- WhoOp 76
Miller, Laura Ann BlkAmP
Miller, Leon C 1902- BiE&WWA
Miller, Lewis Martin 1933- AmSCAP 80, ConAmC
Miller, Lillian Anne 1916- AmSCAP 66
Miller, Lou 1906-1941 WhScrn 74, -77
Miller, Louis Film 2
Miller, Lu 1906-1941 WhoHol B
Miller, M Leo 1905- IntMPA 75, -76
Miller, Malcolm E d1963 NotNAT B
Miller, Malloy 1918- ConAmC
Miller, Mandy 1944- FilmgC, HalFC 80, IlWWBF[port], WhoHol A
Miller, Marcianne WomWMM B
Miller, Margaret Faye Hefley 1930- IntWWM 77
Miller, Marilyn AmPS B
Miller, Marilyn 1896-1936 CnThe
Miller, Marilyn 1898-1936 BiDAmM, CmpEPM, EncMT, EncWT, Ent, FilmEn, Film 2, FilmgC, HalFC 80[port], MovMk, NotNAT B, PlP&P[port], ThFT[port], WhScrn 74, -77, WhoHol B
Miller, Marilyn 1899-1936 ForYSC
Miller, Marilynn 1898-1936 WhThe
Miller, Marion C 1928- AmSCAP 80
Miller, Mark ForYSC, WhoHol A
Miller, Martin 1899-1969 FilmgC, HalFC 80, WhScrn 74, -77, WhThe, WhoHol B
Miller, Marvin 1913- FilmgC, ForYSC, HalFC 80, IntMPA 77, -75, -76, -78, -79, -80, WhoHol A, WhoHrs 80
Miller, Mary Louise Film 2
Miller, Max 1895-1963 Ent, FilmEn, FilmgC, HalFC 80, IlWWBF, -A, NotNAT B, WhScrn 74, -77, WhoHol B
Miller, May BlkAmP, MorBAP
Miller, Michael Kenneth 1955- AmSCAP 80
Miller, Michael R 1932- AmSCAP 66, ConAmC
Miller, Mildred 1924- Baker 78
Miller, Mitch 1911- AmPS A, -B, BiDAmM, CmpEPM, RkOn[port]
Miller, Monique CreCan 2
Miller, Morris d1957 WhScrn 74, WhoHol B
Miller, Muriel Smock 1930- IntWWM 77
Miller, Nat 1909- IntMPA 77, -75, -76, -78, -79, -80
Miller, Ned RkOn
Miller, Ned 1899- AmSCAP 66, -80
Miller, Newton ConAmC
Miller, Niven 1929- IntWWM 77, -80
Miller, Patricia 1927- CnOxB, DancEn 78
Miller, Patsy MotPP
Miller, Patsy Ruth 1904- ForYSC, MovMk, TwYS
Miller, Patsy Ruth 1905- FilmEn, Film 1, -2, FilmgC, HalFC 80, ThFT[port], What 1[port], WhoHol A, WhoHrs 80
Miller, Paul 1925- AmSCAP 66
Miller, Paula BiE&WWA
Miller, Peggy WhoHol A
Miller, Philip Lieson 1906- Baker 78
Miller, Phyllis Margaret WhoMus 72
Miller, Punch 1894-1971 CmpEPM, WhoJazz 72
Miller, Rachel 1931- WhoMus 72
Miller, Ralph Dale 1909- IntWWM 77, -80
Miller, Ranger Bill 1878-1939 WhScrn 74, -77, WhoHol B
Miller, Ray CmpEPM
Miller, Reed 1880-1923 BiDAmM
Miller, Richard 1926- IntWWM 77, -80
Miller, Robert 1930- IntWWM 77, -80
Miller, Robert Beatson 1915- WhoMus 72
Miller, Robert Ellis 1927- FilmEn, FilmgC, HalFC 80, IntMPA 77, -76, -78, -79, -80
Miller, Robert Wiley 1925- AmSCAP 66, -80
Miller, Roger 1936- AmPS A, -B, BiDAmM, CounME 74[port], -74A, EncFCWM 69, IlEncCM[port], PopAmC SUP[port], RkOn 2[port], WhoHol A
Miller, Ron 1933- NewYTET
Miller, Ron D 1954- AmSCAP 80
Miller, Ron S 1936- AmSCAP 66, -80
Miller, Ronald 1934- AmSCAP 80
Miller, Ronald W 1933- IntMPA 77, -75, -76, -78, -79, -80
Miller, Rube Film 1
Miller, Ruby 1889-1976 IlWWBF, -A, WhThe, WhoHol C
Miller, Russell King 1871-1939 BiDAmM
Miller, Ruth Film 2
Miller, Ruth M IntMPA 75, -76
Miller, Scott ForYSC, WhoHol A
Miller, Seton I 1902-1974 CmMov, FilmEn, FilmgC, HalFC 80, WhScrn 77, WhoHol B, WorEFlm
Miller, Seymour 1908-1971 AmSCAP 66, -80
Miller, Shelley Robbins 1947- AmSCAP 80
Miller, Sidney 1916- AmSCAP 66, -80, ForYSC, WhoHol A
Miller, Silverius NewGrD 80
Miller, Steve 1943- ConMuA 80A, IlEncR, RkOn 2[port]
Miller, Steve, Band BiDAmM
Miller, Steven H AmSCAP 80
Miller, Sunnie Perlman 1929- AmSCAP 80
Miller, Susan 1944- NatPD[port]
Miller, T C 1944- NatPD[port]
Miller, Terrel W WhoOp 76
Miller, Terry Ellis 1945- IntWWM 80
Miller, Thomas 1872-1942 WhScrn 74, -77, WhoHol B
Miller, Thomas A 1941- ConAmC, IntWWM 77
Miller, Thomas W 1930- IntWWM 77, -80
Miller, Truman Gene d1963 NotNAT B
Miller, W Christy 1843-1922 WhScrn 77
Miller, W Christy 1892-1940 Film 1
Miller, Walter 1892-1940 Film 1, -2, NotNAT B, TwYS, WhScrn 74, -77, WhoHol B
Miller, Walter 1893-1940 ForYSC
Miller, Wesley C d1962 NotNAT B
Miller, Wilber H 1906- AmSCAP 66, -80
Miller, Willard Darnell 1937- BiDAmM
Miller, William Douglas 1888- IntWWM 77, -80
Miller, Winston 1910- Film 2, IntMPA 77, -75, -76, -78, -79, -80
Miller, Wyn d1932 NotNAT B
Miller, Wynne 1935- BiE&WWA, NotNAT
Miller And Lyles JoeFr
Miller-Milkis NewYTET
Milleran, Rene NewGrD 80
Millet, Jean 1618-1684 NewGrD 80
Millet, Kadish 1923- AmSCAP 66, -80
Millet, Luis 1867-1941 Baker 78
Millet, Luis Maria 1906- NewGrD 80
Millet, Nancy Lynne 1954- AmSCAP 80
Millet, Steven Richard 1956- AmSCAP 80
Milletaire, Carl WhoHol A
Millett, Arthur Film 1, -2
Millett, Kate 1934- WomWMM A, -B
Millett, Maude 1867-1920 NotNAT B, WhThe
Millette, Jean-Louis CreCan 1
Milleville NewGrD 80
Milleville Ferrarese 1565?-1639? NewGrD 80
Milleville, Alessandro 1521?-1589 NewGrD 80
Milleville, Francesco 1565?-1639? NewGrD 80
Milleville, Jean 1500?-1573? NewGrD 80
Milleville, Pierre NewGrD 80
Milleville, Pierreson NewGrD 80
Milley, Jane Film 1
Millhauser, Bertram 1892-1958 FilmgC, HalFC 80, TwYS A
Millhollin, James 1920- BiE&WWA, WhoHol A
Millhouse NewGrD 80
Milli, Robert WhoHol A
Millian, Baker 1908- WhoJazz 72
Millican, James 1910-1955 FilmEn, FilmgC, ForYSC, HalFC 80, Vers A[port], WhScrn 74, -77, WhoHol B
Millican, Jane 1902- WhThe
Millichip, Roy 1930- FilmgC, HalFC 80
Millico, Giuseppe 1737-1802 NewGrD 80
Milliet, Paul 1858- WhThe
Milligan, Andy WhoHrs 80
Milligan, Harold Vincent 1888-1951 Baker 78, BiDAmM, ConAmC
Milligan, James 1928-1961 CreCan 2
Milligan, James Lewis 1876- BiDAmM
Milligan, Mary Min 1882-1966 WhScrn 77
Milligan, Roy Hugh 1922- AmSCAP 66, -80, ConAmC A
Milligan, Spike 1918- EncWT, FilmgC, HalFC 80, IlWWBF, -A, WhoHol A, WhoThe 72, -77
Milligan, Thomas Braden, Jr. 1947- IntWWM 80
Milligen, Simon Van 1849-1929 NewGrD 80
Milliken, Robert Film 1
Milliken, Sandol WhoStg 1908
Millikin, Richard Alfred 1767-1815 OxMus
Millinder, Lucius 1900-1966 BiDAmM, EncJzS 70
Millinder, Lucky 1900-1966 BgBands 74, CmpEPM, DrBlPA, EncJzS 70, WhoJazz 72
Millington, Andrew 1952- IntWWM 77, -80
Millington, George Kenneth 1927- WhoMus 72
Millington, Rodney 1905- BiE&WWA, NotNAT, WhoThe 72, -77
Millioni, Pietro NewGrD 80
Milliot, Sylvette 1927- IntWWM 77, -80
Millitaire, Carl ForYSC
Millman, Jack M 1930- AmSCAP 66, -80
Millman, William 1883-1937 WhScrn 74, -77, WhoHol B
Millner, Franz NewGrD 80
Millner, Marietta Film 2
Millner, Silverius NewGrD 80
Millo, Josef 1916- EncWT
Millocker, Carl 1842-1899 NewGrD 80
Millocker, Karl 1842-1899 Baker 78, CmOp, NotNAT B, OxMus
Milloss, Aurel Von 1906- CnOxB, DancEn 78
Millot, Charles WhoHol A
Millot, Nicolas NewGrD 80
Millrose, Victor D 1935- AmSCAP 80
Mills NewGrD 80
Mills, A J 1872- WhThe
Mills, Alan 1914- CreCan 2
Mills, Alvin Marvin 1922- AmSCAP 80
Mills, Alyce Film 2
Mills, Annette d1955 NotNAT B
Mills, Bertram 1873-1938 NotNAT A
Mills, Bertram 1874-1938 Ent
Mills, Betty IntWWM 77, -80, WhoMus 72
Mills, Billy d1971 WhoHol B
Mills, Billy 1894-1971 CmpEPM
Mills, Bronwen Elizabeth 1951- IntWWM 80
Mills, Carley 1897-1962 AmSCAP 66, -80, NotNAT B
Mills, Charles 1914- Baker 78, ConAmC, NewGrD 80
Mills, Mrs. Clifford d1933 NotNAT B, WhThe
Mills, David 1929- IntWWM 80
Mills, Donn Laurence 1932- AmSCAP 80, IntWWM 80
Mills, Donna WhoHol A
Mills, Edgar 1915- ConAmC
Mills, Evelyn Film 2
Mills, Florence AmPS B
Mills, Florence d1927 BlksBF
Mills, Florence 1895-1927 BiDAmM, DrBlPA, EncMT, Ent, NotNAT B, WhoHol B
Mills, Florence 1901- WhThe
Mills, Frank Film 1, -2
Mills, Frank 1870-1921 NotNAT B, WhThe, WhoHol B
Mills, Frank 1891-1973 WhScrn 77
Mills, Frank 1942- IntWWM 77
Mills, Freddie 1919-1965 WhScrn 77, WhoHol B
Mills, Frederick Allen 1869-1948 AmSCAP 66, -80, Baker 78, BiDAmM
Mills, Gilbert 1909- AmSCAP 66
Mills, Gordon 1935- BiDAmM
Mills, Grant d1973 WhScrn 77, WhoHol B
Mills, Guy 1898-1962 NotNAT B, WhScrn 74, -77
Mills, Hayley 1945- ForYSC
Mills, Hayley 1946- FilmAG WE, FilmEn, FilmgC, HalFC 80, IlWWBF[port], IntMPA 77, -75, -76, -78, -79, -80, MotPP, MovMk, NotNAT A, RkOn, WhoHol A, WhoThe 77, WorEFlm
Mills, Henry 1757-1820 NewGrD 80

Mills, Henry 1786-1867 *BiDAmM*
Mills, Henry George 1914- *IntWWM 77, WhoMus 72*
Mills, Horace 1864-1941 *NotNAT B, WhThe*
Mills, Hugh 1913?- *FilmgC, HalFC 80*
Mills, Irene Ruth *WhoMus 72*
Mills, Irving 1894- *AmPS, AmSCAP 66, -80, BiDAmM, CmpEPM, Sw&Ld C*
Mills, Isabelle Margaret 1923- *IntWWM 77, -80*
Mills, Jackie 1922- *AmSCAP 80, BiDAmM*
Mills, James 1790-1844 *NewGrD 80*
Mills, Joe d1935 *Film 2, WhoHol B*
Mills, John 1812-1873 *NewGrD 80*
Mills, John 1908- *BiDFilm, -81, BiE&WWA, CmMov, EncMT, FilmAG WE[port], FilmEn, FilmgC, ForYSC, HalFC 80, IlWWBF[port], -A, IntMPA 77, -75, -76, -78, -79, -80, MotPP, MovMk[port], NotNAT A, OxFilm, PlP&P, WhoHol A, WhoThe 72, -77, WorEFlm*
Mills, John 1947- *IntWWM 77, -80*
Mills, John, Jr. 1910-1936 *WhScrn 77*
Mills, John, Sr. 1889-1967 *WhScrn 77*
Mills, Josefa Primo 1938- *AmSCAP 80*
Mills, Joseph S 1875-1935 *WhScrn 74, -77*
Mills, Juliet 1941- *BiE&WWA, FilmEn, FilmgC, ForYSC, HalFC 80, IlWWBF, MotPP, NotNAT A, WhoHol A, WhoThe 72, -77*
Mills, Kenneth Thomas 1928- *AmSCAP 80*
Mills, Kerry 1869-1948 *AmPS, CmpEPM, NotNAT B, PopAmC, Sw&Ld B*
Mills, Lincoln 1910-1957? *WhoJazz 72*
Mills, Louise *PupTheA*
Mills, Marilyn *Film 2*
Mills, Mort *WhoHol A*
Mills, Paul 1921- *AmSCAP 66, -80*
Mills, Richard 1798?-1870 *NewGrD 80*
Mills, Richard 1809-1844 *NewGrD 80, OxMus*
Mills, Richard 1840-1903 *NewGrD 80*
Mills, Sebastian Bach 1838-1898 *BiDAmM*
Mills, Stanley 1931- *AmSCAP 66, -80*
Mills, Stephanie 1959- *DrBlPA*
Mills, Taylor M 1908- *IntMPA 75, -76*
Mills, Thomas R 1878-1953 *Film 1, -2, WhScrn 74, -77, WhoHol B*
Mills, Verlye 1916- *AmSCAP 66, -80*
Mills, William R 1894-1971 *AmSCAP 66, -80*
Mills, Winifred H *PupTheA*
Mills Brothers, The *AmPS A, -B, BiDAmM, CmpEPM, RkOn[port], WhoHol A*
Mills-Cockell, John 1943- *Baker 78*
Mills Family *MotPP*
Millstein, Gilbert *BiE&WWA*
Millward, Charles d1892 *NotNAT B*
Millward, Jessie 1861-1932 *NotNAT A, -B, WhThe*
Millward, Jessie 1868- *WhoStg 1906, -1908*
Millward, Mike 1943-1966 *WhScrn 77*
Milly, Louise *Film 1*
Milman, Dean d1868 *NotNAT B*
Milne, A A 1882-1956 *DcPup, EncWT*
Milne, Alan Alexander 1882-1956 *CnMD, Ent, McGEWD[port], ModWD, NotNAT B, WhThe*
Milne, Alisdair *NewYTET*
Milne, Alison Sutherland 1914- *IntWWM 77, WhoMus 72*
Milne, David Brown 1882-1953 *CreCan 1*
Milne, Hamish 1939- *IntWWM 80*
Milne, Helen C 1897- *WhoMus 72*
Milne, Isabel *PupTheA*
Milne, Peter 1824-1908 *NewGrD 80*
Milne, Peter 1924- *WhoMus 72*
Milne, Peter James 1934- *WhoOp 76*
Milne-Home, Barbara Mary 1919- *WhoMus 72*
Milner, Anthony 1925- *Baker 78, DcCM, IntWWM 77, -80, NewGrD 80, OxMus, WhoMus 72*
Milner, Arthur Frederick 1894- *WhoMus 72*
Milner, Daniel Paul 1952- *AmSCAP 80*
Milner, Jack 1910- *IntMPA 77, -75, -76, -78, -79, -80*
Milner, Martin 1927- *FilmEn, FilmgC, ForYSC, HalFC 80, IntMPA 77, -75, -76, -78, -79, -80, MotPP, WhoHol A, WhoMus 72*
Milner, Ron 1938- *BlkAmP, ConDr 77, MorBAP, PlP&P A[port]*
Milner, Ronald 1938- *ConDr 73, DrBlPA*
Milner, Victor 1893- *CmMov, FilmEn, HalFC 80, WorEFlm*
Milnes, Sherrill 1935- *BiDAmM, BnBkM 80, CmOp[port], IntWWM 77, -80, MusSN[port], NewGrD 80, WhoOp 76*
Milnes, William Harold 1903- *IntWWM 77, -80, WhoMus 72*
Milo, George 1909- *IntMPA 77, -75, -76, -78, -79, -80*
Milo, Phil *AmSCAP 80*
Milo, Sandra 1935- *FilmEn, WhoHol A*
Milojevic, Miloje 1884-1946 *Baker 78, NewGrD 80*
Milon, Louis-Jacques 1766-1845 *CnOxB*
Milos, Milos 1941-1966 *WhScrn 77*
Milosavljevic, Radojica 1926- *IntWWM 80*
Milosevic, Predrag 1904- *IntWWM 77, -80, NewGrD 80*
Milovitch, Cordy *Film 2*
Milovsoroff, Basil *PupTheA*
Milovsoroff, Georgia *PupTheA*
Milowanoff, Sandra *Film 2*
Milsap, Ronald Lee *AmSCAP 80*
Milsap, Ronnie *CounME 74[port], -74A, IlEncCM*
Mil'shteyn, Yakov Isaakovich 1911- *NewGrD 80*
Milstein, Nathan 1904- *Baker 78, BiDAmM, BnBkM 80, IntWWM 77, -80, MusMk, MusSN[port], NewGrD 80, WhoMus 72*
Milstein, Yakov 1911- *Baker 78*
Miltern, John 1870-1937 *Film 2, NotNAT B, WhScrn 74, -77, WhThe, WhoHol B*
Milton, Mrs. Arthur d1936 *NotNAT B*
Milton, Billy 1905- *FilmgC, HalFC 80, IlWWBF, -A, WhThe, WhoHol A, WhoThe 72*
Milton, David Scott *NatPD[port]*
Milton, Ernest 1890-1974 *CnThe, Film 1, FilmgC, HalFC 80, PlP&P, WhScrn 77, WhThe, WhoHol B, WhoThe 72*
Milton, Ernest 1905- *NewOrJ*
Milton, Georges 1888-1970 *Film 2, WhScrn 74, -77, WhoHol B*
Milton, Harry 1900-1965 *WhScrn 74, -77, WhThe, WhoHol B*
Milton, Jay 1910- *AmSCAP 66, -80*
Milton, Joanna *WomWMM*
Milton, John 1563?-1647 *Baker 78, MusMk, NewGrD 80, OxMus*
Milton, John 1608-1674 *CnThe, EncWT, Ent, NewEOp 71, NotNAT B, OxMus, PlP&P, REnWD[port]*
Milton, Louette 1907-1930 *WhScrn 74, -77, WhoHol B*
Milton, Maud 1859-1945 *NotNAT B, WhThe, WhoHol B*
Milton, Meyrick *IlWWBF*
Milton, Robert 1890?-1956 *FilmEn, WhThe*
Milton, Roy 1907- *BluesWW[port]*
Milton, Royce *Film 2*
Miltou *NewGrD 80*
Milu 1926- *FilmAG WE*
Milveden, Ingmar 1920- *Baker 78, NewGrD 80*
Milveden, J Ingmar G 1920- *IntWWM 77, -80*
Milward, Dawson 1870-1926 *Film 2, NotNAT B, WhThe*
Milwid, Antoni *NewGrD 80*
Milyutin, Yury Sergeyevich 1903-1968 *NewGrD 80*
Mimaroglu, Ilhan 1926- *AmSCAP 80, Baker 78, CpmDNM 76, -79, -80, ConAmC, IntWWM 77, -80, NewGrD 80*
Mimica, Vatroslav 1923- *DcFM, OxFilm, WorEFlm*
Mimieux, Yvette *IntMPA 77, -75, -76, -78, -79, -80, MotPP, WhoHol A*
Mimieux, Yvette 1939- *FilmEn, FilmgC, ForYSC, HalFC 80, WhoHrs 80*
Mimieux, Yvette 1942- *MovMk*
Mimms, Garnet And The Enchanters *RkOn*
Mims, William *WhoHol A*
Mimura, Tsutomu 1924- *IntWWM 77, -80*
Minagawa, Tatsuo 1927- *IntWWM 77, -80, NewGrD 80*
Minardos, Nico *ForYSC, WhoHol A*
Minasi, Dom 1943- *EncJzS 70*
Minasi, Dominic 1943- *EncJzS 70*
Minato, Count Nicolo 1630?-1698 *NewGrD 80*
Mince, Johnny 1912- *CmpEPM, EncJzS 70, WhoJazz 72*
Minchejmer, Adam 1830-1904 *NewGrD 80*
Minchev, Georgi 1939- *Baker 78*
Minchi, John *NewGrD 80*
Minciotti, Esther 1883-1962 *HalFC 80*
Minciotti, Esther 1888-1962 *NotNAT B, Vers A[port], WhScrn 74, -77, WhoHol B*
Minciotti, Silvio 1883-1961 *HalFC 80, WhScrn 74, -77, WhoHol B*
Minde, Stefan 1936- *IntWWM 77, -80*
Minde, Stefan Paul 1936- *WhoOp 76*
Mindlin, Michael, Jr. *IntMPA 77, -75, -76, -78, -79, -80*
Mineau, Charlotte *Film 1, -2*
Minelli, Charles 1914- *AmSCAP 80*
Minelli, Liza 1946- *WomWMM*
Mineo, Antoinette 1926- *AmSCAP 66, -80*
Mineo, Attilio 1918- *AmSCAP 66, -80*
Mineo, Sal 1939-1976 *FilmEn, FilmgC, ForYSC, HalFC 80, IntMPA 75, -76, MotPP, MovMk, RkOn[port], WhoHol C*
Mineo, Samuel H 1909- *AmSCAP 66, -80*
Miner, Allen H *FilmgC, HalFC 80*
Miner, Daniel 1880-1938 *WhScrn 74, -77*
Miner, Henry Clay d1950 *NotNAT B*
Miner, Jan *WhoHol A*
Miner, Jan 1917- *WhoThe 77*
Miner, Jan 1919- *BiE&WWA, NotNAT*
Miner, Lawrence A 1943- *AmSCAP 80*
Miner, Worthington C 1900- *BiE&WWA, IntMPA 77, -75, -76, -78, -79, -80, NewYTET, NotNAT, WhThe*
Minerve, Geezil 1922- *EncJzS 70*
Minerve, Harold 1922- *EncJzS 70*
Mines, Anatole 1915- *IntWWM 77, -80*
Minetti, Bernhard 1905- *EncWT*
Minetti, Maria *WhThe*
Minevitch, Borrah 1904?-1955 *HalFC 80, NotNAT B, WhScrn 74, -77, WhoHol B*
Ming, Huang 685-762 *REnWD[port]*
Ming, James W 1918- *ConAmC*
Ming, Moy Luke 1863-1964 *WhScrn 77*
Minghino DalVioloncello *NewGrD 80*
Mingotti, Pietro 1702?-1759 *NewGrD 80*
Mingotti, Regina 1722-1808 *NewGrD 80*
Mingozzi, Gian Franco 1932- *WorEFlm*
Minguet Y Yrol, Pablo *NewGrD 80*
Mingus, Charles 1922-1979 *Baker 78, BiDAmM, CmpEPM, ConAmC, DrBlPA, EncJzS 70, IlEncJ, IntWWM 77, MusMk, NewGrD 80[port]*
Mini, Alessandro 1756?-1825 *NewGrD 80*
Minil, Renee Du 1868- *WhThe*
Miniscalchi, Guglielmo *NewGrD 80*
Minkoff, Frances Myra 1915- *AmSCAP 66, -80*
Minkofski-Garrigues, Horst 1925- *IntWWM 77, -80, WhoMus 72*
Minks, Wilfried 1931- *EncWT*
Minkus, Alois 1826-1917 *Baker 78*
Minkus, Barbara *WhoHol A*
Minkus, Leon 1826-1917 *NewGrD 80*
Minkus, Leon 1827-1890 *DancEn 78*
Minkus, Ludwig 1827-1907 *CnOxB*
Minnehaha *Film 2*
Minnelli, Lisa 1946- *ForYSC*
Minnelli, Liza 1946- *BiDAmM, BiDFilm, -81, BiE&WWA, EncMT, FilmEn, FilmgC, HalFC 80[port], IntMPA 77, -75, -76, -78, -79, -80, MotPP, MovMk[port], NotNAT, WhoHol A, WhoThe 77*
Minnelli, Vincente *IntMPA 77, -75, -76, -78, -79, -80, NotNAT, -A*
Minnelli, Vincente 1902- *AmFD*
Minnelli, Vincente 1910- *CmMov, FilmEn, FilmgC, HalFC 80*
Minnelli, Vincente 1913- *BiDFilm, -81, DcFM, EncMT, MovMk[port], OxFilm, WorEFlm*
Minner, Kathryn 1892-1969 *WhScrn 74, -77, WhoHol B*
Minney, R J 1895-1979 *HalFC 80*
Minney, Rubeigh James 1895- *FilmgC, WhThe*
Minogue, Dennis Michael 1941- *AmSCAP 80*
Minoja, Ambrogio 1752-1825 *NewGrD 80*
Minoja, Ambrosio 1752-1825 *Baker 78*
Minor, Alan James 1947- *IntWWM 77, -80*

Minor, Anderson 1901-1973 *NewOrJ SUP[port]*
Minor, Andrew C 1918- *IntWWM 80*
Minor, Donald 1935- *NewOrJ*
Minor, Fred 1913- *NewOrJ*
Minor, George *NewOrJ*
Minor, Roy 1905-1935 *WhScrn 74, -77*
Minor, Slamfoot 1909- *WhoJazz 72*
Minoret, Guillaume 1650?-1717 *NewGrD 80*
Minot, Anna *WhoHol A*
Minotis, Alexis 1900- *EncWT, OxThe*
Minotis, Alexis 1906- *BiE&WWA*
Minow, Newton N *NewYTET*
Minshull, George T d1943 *NotNAT B*
Minshull, Richard *NewGrD 80*
Minskoff, Jerome *NotNAT*
Minsky, Abraham Bennet 1881-1949 *NotNAT B*
Minsky, Howard G *IntMPA 77, -75, -76, -78, -79, -80*
Minsky, Mollie d1964 *NotNAT B*
Minster, Jack 1901-1966 *WhThe*
Minter, George 1911-1966 *FilmgC, HalFC 80*
Minter, Iverson 1936- *BluesWW[port]*
Minter, Mary Miles 1902- *FilmEn, Film 1, -2, FilmgC, HalFC 80, MotPP, MovMk[port], TwYS, WhThe, WhoHol A*
Minter, William F 1892-1937 *WhScrn 74, -77*
Minto, Dorothy 1891- *WhThe*
Minton, Yvonne 1938- *CmOp, IntWWM 77, -80, NewGrD 80, WhoMus 72, WhoOp 76*
Minturn, Harry L d1963 *NotNAT B*
Minty, Jeanette 1931- *DancEn 78*
Mintz, David *ConMuA 80B*
Mintz, Eli 1904- *NotNAT, WhoHol A*
Mintz, Shlomo 1957- *IntWWM 80*
Minucci, Ulpio 1921- *AmSCAP 80*
Minyard, Frank 1930- *NewOrJ SUP[port]*
Minzey, Frank 1879-1949 *NotNAT B, WhScrn 74, -77, WhoHol B*
Mioduszewski, Michal Marcin 1787-1868 *NewGrD 80*
Miolan, Marie *NewGrD 80*
Miolan-Carvalho, Marie 1827-1895 *CmOp, NewEOp 71*
Mion, Charles-Louis 1698-1775 *NewGrD 80*
Mioni, Fabrizio *WhoHol A*
Miou-Miou 1950- *FilmEn, WhoHol A*
Mir, David *Film 2*
Mir Y Llussa, Jose d1784? *NewGrD 80*
Mira, Leandro *NewGrD 80*
Mira DeAmescua, Antonio 1570?-1644 *McGEWD*
Miracle, Silas *Film 2*
Miracles, The *BiDAmM, RkOn[port]*
Miramova, Elena *WhThe*
Miranda, Ana-Maria 1937- *WhoOp 76*
Miranda, Carmen d1955 *AmPS B, MotPP, NotNAT B, WhoHol B*
Miranda, Carmen 1904-1955 *WhScrn 74, -77*
Miranda, Carmen 1909-1953 *BiDAmM*
Miranda, Carmen 1909-1955 *CmpEPM, FilmEn, MovMk[port]*
Miranda, Carmen 1913-1955 *HalFC 80, WorEFlm*
Miranda, Carmen 1914-1955 *FilmgC, ForYSC, OxFilm*
Miranda, Erasmo 1904- *AmSCAP 66*
Miranda, Francisco Sa De 1481-1558 *OxThe*
Miranda, Isa 1909- *BiDFilm, -81, FilmAG WE, FilmEn, FilmgC, HalFC 80, MovMk, OxFilm, WhoHol A*
Miranda, Isa 1912- *WorEFlm*
Miranda, Isa 1917- *ForYSC, IntMPA 77, -75, -76, -78, -79, -80*
Miranda, Jack 1908?-1959? *NewOrJ*
Miranda, Nicanor *DancEn 78*
Miranda, Susana *WhoHol A*
Mirande, Yves *WhThe*
Mirandy d1974 *WhScrn 77, WhoHol B*
Mirante, Thomas 1931- *ConAmC, IntWWM 77, -80, WhoMus 72*
Mirbeau, Octave 1848-1917 *CnMD, NotNAT B, OxThe, WhThe*
Mirbeau, Octave 1850-1917 *McGEWD, ModWD*
Mirchev, Zahari 1941- *IntWWM 77, -80*
Mirdita, Federik 1931- *WhoOp 76*
Mirea, Marina *WhoOp 76*
Mirecki, Franciszek Wincenty 1791?-1862 *NewGrD 80*
Mirecki, Franz 1791-1862 *Baker 78*
Mirell, Leon I *IntMPA 77, -75, -76, -78*
Miremont, Claude-Augustin 1827-1887 *NewGrD 80*
Mirikitani, Alan Masao 1955- *AmSCAP 80*
Mirisch, David 1935- *IntMPA 77, -75, -76, -78, -79, -80*
Mirisch, Harold 1907-1968 *FilmgC, HalFC 80*
Mirisch, Marvin E 1918- *FilmgC, HalFC 80, IntMPA 77, -75, -76, -78, -79, 80*
Mirisch, Walter 1921- *DcFM, FilmEn, FilmgC, HalFC 80, IntMPA 77, -75, -76, -78, -79, -80*
Mirisch Brothers, The *FilmgC, HalFC 80, WorEFlm[port]*
Miristus *NewGrD 80*
Mirkin, Barry W 1916- *AmSCAP 66, -80*
Miro, Joan 1893- *CnOxB, DancEn 78*
Miroglio, Francis 1924- *DcCM, NewGrD 80*
Miroglio, Jean-Baptiste 1725?-1785? *NewGrD 80*
Miroglio, Pierre *NewGrD 80*
Mirolybov, Peter 1918- *IntWWM 77, -80*
Miron, Issachar 1920- *AmSCAP 80, NewGrD 80*
Miron, Tsipora 1923- *AmSCAP 80*
Miroshnichenko, Evgeniya 1931- *NewGrD 80*
Miroslava d1955 *ForYSC*
Miroslava 1926-1955 *HalFC 80*
Miroslava 1930-1955 *FilmgC, WhScrn 74, -77, WhoHol B*
Mirouze, Marcel 1906-1957 *Baker 78*
Mirovitch, Alfred 1884-1959 *Baker 78*
Mirren, Helen 1946- *Ent[port], WhoHol A, WhoThe 72, -77*
Miry, Karel 1823-1889 *Baker 78, NewGrD 80*
Mirzoyan, Edvard Mik'aeli 1921- *Baker 78, NewGrD 80*
Misch, Ludwig 1887-1967 *Baker 78, NewGrD 80*
Misch, Margot *Film 2*
Mischa, Frantisek Adam *NewGrD 80*
Mischa, Frantisek Antonin *NewGrD 80*
Mischakoff, Anne 1942- *IntWWM 77, -80*
Mischakoff, Mischa 1895- *Baker 78*
Mischakoff, Mischa 1896- *NewGrD 80*
Mischiati, Oscar 1936- *NewGrD 80*
Misciagna, Louis 1938- *IntWWM 77*
Misciano, Alvinio 1915- *WhoOp 76*
Misener, Helen 1909-1960 *WhScrn 77*
Mishell, Kathryn Lee 1940- *CpmDNM 73, ConAmC*
Mishima, Masao 1906-1973 *WhScrn 77*
Mishima, Yukio 1925-1970 *CnMD, ModWD*
Mishima, Yukio 1925-1971 *EncWT, WhScrn 74, -77*
Mishori, Ya'acov 1937- *IntWWM 77, -80*
Miskiewicz, Maciej Arnulf d1685? *NewGrD 80*
Miskovitch, Milorad 1928- *CnOxB, DancEn 78[port]*
Mison, Luis d1766 *NewGrD 80*
Mison, Luis d1776 *Baker 78*
Misonne, Claude *WomWMM*
Misonne, Vincent 1490?-1550 *NewGrD 80*
Misra, Lalmani 1924- *IntWWM 80*
Misra, Mahapurush 1933- *Baker 78*
Misraki, Paul 1908- *DcFM, FilmEn, FilmgC, HalFC 80, IntWWM 77, -80, WhoMus 72, WorEFlm*
Miss America Of 1919 *What 1[port]*
Miss America Of 1941 *What 1[port]*
Miss America Of 1942 1923- *What 5[port]*
Miss America Of 1943 *What 5[port]*
Miss America Of 1948 1930- *What 4[port]*
Miss Frances 1908- *What 4[port]*
Miss Rhapsody *BluesWW*
Missa, Edmond Jean Louis 1861-1910 *Baker 78, NotNAT B*
Missal, Joshua M 1915- *AmSCAP 66, -80, ConAmC*
Missen, Oud Egede *Film 2*
Missimer, Howard *Film 1*
Missin, Russell Arthur 1922- *IntWWM 77, -80, WhoMus 72*
Missirio, Cenica *Film 2*
Mississippi *AmSCAP 80*
Mississippi Matilda *BluesWW*
Mississippi Mudder *BluesWW*
Misson, Luis *NewGrD 80*
Missonne, Vincent *NewGrD 80*
Missourians, The *BiDAmM*
Mistak, Alvin Frank 1930- *CpmDNM 72*
Misterly, Eugene 1926- *ConAmC*
Mistinguett 1873-1956 *EncWT, Ent[port]*
Mistinguett 1875-1956 *NotNAT A, -B, OxThe, WhThe*
Mistral, Frederic 1830-1914 *NewEOp 71*
Mistral, Jorge 1920- *FilmAG WE*
Mistral, Jorge 1923-1972 *WhScrn 77, WhoHol B*
Mita, Ura *Film 2*
Mitani, Yoko 1935- *IntWWM 77, -80*
Mitantier *NewGrD 80*
Mitchel, Les 1905-1975 *WhScrn 77*
Mitchelhill, J P 1879-1966 *WhThe*
Mitchell, Abbie 1884-1960 *BiDAmM, BlksBF, DrBlPA, NotNAT B*
Mitchell, Ada 1880- *WhoStg 1906, -1908*
Mitchell, Adrian 1932- *ConDr 77*
Mitchell, Alasdair 1947- *IntWWM 77, -80*
Mitchell, Alastair John Wingate 1939- *IntWWM 77, WhoMus 72*
Mitchell, Andrew 1925- *IntMPA 77, -75, -76, -78, -79, -80*
Mitchell, Arthur 1934- *CnOxB, DancEn 78[port], DrBlPA, NewOrJ*
Mitchell, Belle *Film 2, WhoHol A*
Mitchell, Betty 1896- *CreCan 1*
Mitchell, Billy 1926- *BiDAmM, EncJzS 70*
Mitchell, Blue 1930- *EncJzS 70*
Mitchell, Bob *ConMuA 80B*
Mitchell, Bob 1935- *EncJzS 70*
Mitchell, Bruce d1952 *Film 1, WhoHol B*
Mitchell, Bruce 1882-1952 *TwYS A*
Mitchell, Bruce 1883-1952 *WhScrn 74, -77*
Mitchell, Cameron 1918- *BiE&WWA, FilmEn, FilmgC, ForYSC, HalFC 80, IntMPA 77, -75, -76, -78, -79, -80, MotPP, MovMk, PlP&P[port], WhoHol A, WhoHrs 80*
Mitchell, Carolyn 1937-1966 *WhScrn 77*
Mitchell, Chad 1939- *RkOn*
Mitchell, Charles 1884-1929 *WhScrn 74, -77*
Mitchell, Charles 1910- *IntWWM 77*
Mitchell, Cyril John 1906- *WhoMus 72*
Mitchell, David *WhoThe 77*
Mitchell, David Ira 1932- *WhoOp 76*
Mitchell, Dobson 1868-1939 *WhScrn 77*
Mitchell, Dodson 1868-1939 *Film 1, -2, NotNAT B, WhThe, WhoHol B*
Mitchell, Don *AmSCAP 80, DrBlPA, WhoHol A*
Mitchell, Donald 1925- *Baker 78, IntWWM 77, -80, NewGrD 80, OxMus, WhoMus 72*
Mitchell, Doris *Film 1*
Mitchell, Dwike 1930- *Baker 78, BiDAmM*
Mitchell, Earle d1946 *NotNAT B*
Mitchell, Edna *NewOrJ*
Mitchell, Elizabeth *CreCan 1*
Mitchell, Ena *WhoMus 72*
Mitchell, Esther d1953 *NotNAT B*
Mitchell, Frank *JoeFr*
Mitchell, Geoffrey Roger 1936- *IntWWM 77, -80, WhoMus 72*
Mitchell, George 1899-1972 *BiDAmM, CmpEPM, EncJzS 70, IlEncJ, WhoJazz 72*
Mitchell, George 1905-1972 *BiE&WWA, NotNAT B, WhScrn 77, WhoHol B*
Mitchell, Gifford Jerome 1913- *IntWWM 80*
Mitchell, Gordon B 1932- *BiDAmM*
Mitchell, Grant d1957 *MotPP, WhoHol B*
Mitchell, Grant 1874-1957 *FilmEn, FilmgC, HalFC 80, HolCA[port], NotNAT B, WhScrn 74, -77, WhThe*
Mitchell, Grant 1875-1957 *ForYSC, MovMk, Vers A[port]*
Mitchell, Grover 1930- *BiDAmM, EncJzS 70*
Mitchell, Guy *AmPS A, -B, WhoHol A*
Mitchell, Guy 1925- *BiDAmM, FilmgC, HalFC 80*
Mitchell, Guy 1927- *CmpEPM, IntMPA 77, -75, -76, -78, -79, -80, RkOn[port]*
Mitchell, Gwenn *DrBlPA, WhoHol A*
Mitchell, Helen d1945 *WhScrn 74, -77, WhoHol B*
Mitchell, Helen Porter 1859-1931 *BnBkM 80[port]*

Mitchell, Howard 1883- *TwYS A*
Mitchell, Howard 1888-1958 *Film 1, WhScrn 74, -77, WhoHol B*
Mitchell, Howard 1911- *Baker 78, BiE&WWA, NewGrD 80, WhoMus 72*
Mitchell, Irving *Film 2*
Mitchell, Jack 1918- *IntMPA 77, -75, -76, -78, -79, -80*
Mitchell, Jack 1925- *CnOxB*
Mitchell, James 1920- *BiE&WWA, DancEn 78, ForYSC, HalFC 80, MotPP, MovMk, NotNAT, WhoHol A*
Mitchell, James Irving 1891-1969 *WhScrn 74, -77*
Mitchell, Jan 1916- *BiE&WWA*
Mitchell, Janet 1915- *CreCan 2*
Mitchell, John 1900?- *WhoJazz 72*
Mitchell, John 1919-1951 *WhScrn 74, -77*
Mitchell, John D 1917- *BiE&WWA, NotNAT*
Mitchell, John H 1918- *IntMPA 77, -75, -76, -78, -79, -80*
Mitchell, Johnny d1951 *WhoHol B*
Mitchell, Joni 1943- *ConMuA 80A, IlEncR[port], RkOn 2[port]*
Mitchell, Joseph d1738 *NotNAT B*
Mitchell, Joseph A *BlkAmP*
Mitchell, Julian 1854-1926 *EncMT, NotNAT B*
Mitchell, Julien 1884-1954 *FilmgC, HalFC 80*
Mitchell, Julien 1888-1954 *NotNAT B, WhScrn 74, -77, WhThe, WhoHol B*
Mitchell, Kathleen Mary 1911- *IntWWM 77*
Mitchell, Keith Moore 1927- *BiDAmM, EncJzS 70*
Mitchell, Langdon 1862-1935 *DcLB 7[port]*
Mitchell, Mrs. Langdon d1944 *NotNAT B*
Mitchell, Langdon Elwyn 1862-1933 *OxThe*
Mitchell, Langdon Elwyn 1862-1935 *CnMD, McGEWD[port], ModWD, NotNAT B, WhThe*
Mitchell, Laurie *WhoHrs 80*
Mitchell, Lee 1906- *BiE&WWA, NotNAT*
Mitchell, Leona 1949- *WhoOp 76*
Mitchell, Leonard *NewOrJ*
Mitchell, Les 1885-1965 *WhoHol B*
Mitchell, Leslie 1885-1965 *WhScrn 77*
Mitchell, Leslie 1905-1975 *FilmgC, HalFC 80, WhoHol C*
Mitchell, Loften 1919- *BiE&WWA, BlkAmP, ConDr 73, -77, DrBlPA, MorBAP, NotNAT*
Mitchell, Louis A 1885-1957 *WhoJazz 72*
Mitchell, Louis D 1928- *AmSCAP 80*
Mitchell, Lyndol 1923-1964 *ConAmC*
Mitchell, Lyndol Coleman 1923-1963 *AmSCAP 80*
Mitchell, Mae d1963 *NotNAT B*
Mitchell, Maggie 1832-1918 *FamA&A[port], NotNAT B, OxThe*
Mitchell, Malcolm 1926- *IntWWM 77*
Mitchell, Margaret 1900-1949 *FilmgC, HalFC 80*
Mitchell, Martin *Film 2*
Mitchell, Mary Ruth 1906-1941 *WhScrn 74, -77*
Mitchell, Maurine *BiE&WWA*
Mitchell, Max Allen 1914- *IntWWM 77, -80*
Mitchell, Melvin L *BlkAmP*
Mitchell, Millard 1900-1953 *FilmEn, FilmgC, HalFC 80, MotPP, WhScrn 74, -77, WhoHol B*
Mitchell, Millard 1903-1953 *ForYSC, NotNAT B*
Mitchell, Nahum 1769-1853 *BiDAmM*
Mitchell, Norma d1967 *WhScrn 74, -77, WhoHol B*
Mitchell, Norma Jean 1942- *IntWWM 77*
Mitchell, Oswald 1890?-1949 *FilmgC, HalFC 80, IlWWBF*
Mitchell, Patricia E 1943- *ConAmTC*
Mitchell, Priscilla 1941- *BiDAmM, EncFCWM 69*
Mitchell, Raymond Earle 1895- *AmSCAP 66, -80, ConAmC A*
Mitchell, Red 1927- *CmpEPM, EncJzS 70*
Mitchell, Rex 1929- *ConAmC*
Mitchell, Rhea *MotPP*
Mitchell, Rhea 1891-1957 *TwYS*
Mitchell, Rhea 1894-1957 *Film 1, -2, NotNAT B*
Mitchell, Rhea 1905-1957 *WhScrn 74, -77, WhoHol B*
Mitchell, Richard Allen 1930- *BiDAmM, EncJzS 70*
Mitchell, Robert E, Jr. 1935- *EncJzS 70*
Mitchell, Rodger Malcolm 1935- *AmSCAP 80*
Mitchell, Ronald E 1905- *BiE&WWA*
Mitchell, Roscoe 1940- *AmSCAP 80, EncJzS 70, IlEncJ*
Mitchell, Ruth 1919- *BiE&WWA, NotNAT, WhoThe 77*
Mitchell, Shirley *WhoHol A*
Mitchell, Sidney B 1888-1942 *AmPS*
Mitchell, Sidney D 1888-1942 *AmSCAP 66, -80, CmpEPM, Sw&Ld C*
Mitchell, Stephen 1907- *WhoThe 72, -77*
Mitchell, Steve *IntMPA 77, -75, -76, -78, -79, -80, WhoHol A*
Mitchell, Theodore -1938 *NotNAT B*
Mitchell, Thomas d1962 *MotPP, WhoHol B*
Mitchell, Thomas 1892-1962 *BiDFilm, -81, FilmEn, Film 2, FilmgC, HalFC 80, HolCA[port], MovMk[port], OxFilm, Vers A[port], WorEFlm*
Mitchell, Thomas 1893-1962 *ForYSC*
Mitchell, Thomas 1895-1962 *CmMov, NotNAT B, WhScrn 74, -77, WhThe*
Mitchell, Thomas Joseph 1926- *IntWWM 77*
Mitchell, Wallace Orlando 1951- *AmSCAP 80*
Mitchell, Warren 1926- *FilmgC, HalFC 80, WhoHol A, WhoThe 72, -77*
Mitchell, William 1798-1856 *NotNAT B, OxThe*
Mitchell, William 1907-1971 *BiDAmM*
Mitchell, William John 1906-1971 *Baker 78, NewGrD 80*
Mitchell, William L 1944- *AmSCAP 66, -80*
Mitchell, William Ormond 1914- *CreCan 1*
Mitchell, Willie *IlEncR, RkOn 2[port]*
Mitchell, Wirt McClintic 1914- *AmSCAP 66, -80*
Mitchell, Yvette *Film 1*
Mitchell, Yvonne 1925-1979 *FilmAG WE[port], FilmEn, FilmgC, HalFC 80, IlWWBF[port], -A, IntMPA 77, -75, -76, -78, -79, NotNAT A, OxFilm, WhoHol A, WhoThe 72, -77*
Mitchell And Durant *JoeFr*
Mitchill, Scoey 1930- *DrBlPA*
Mitchinson, John *IntWWM 77, -80, WhoMus 72, WhoOp 76*
Mitchum, Chris *WhoHol A*
Mitchum, Cindy *WhoHol A*
Mitchum, James 1938- *FilmgC, HalFC 80, MotPP*
Mitchum, Jim *WhoHol A*
Mitchum, Jim 1938- *ForYSC*
Mitchum, Jim 1941- *IntMPA 77, -78, -79, -80*
Mitchum, John *ForYSC, WhoHol A*
Mitchum, John Newman 1919- *AmSCAP 80*
Mitchum, Robert 1917- *AmSCAP 66, -80, BiDFilm, -81, CmMov, FilmEn, FilmgC, ForYSC, HalFC 80, IntMPA 77, -75, -76, -78, -79, -80, MotPP, MovMk[port], OxFilm, RkOn, WhoHol A, WorEFlm[port]*
Mitcoff, Elena d1943 *PupTheA*
Mitford, Mary Russell d1855 *NotNAT B*
Mithou *NewGrD 80*
Mitjana Y Gordon, Rafael 1869-1921 *Baker 78, NewGrD 80*
Mito, Mitsuko *WhoHol A*
Mitosky, Alan P 1934- *IntMPA 77, -78, -79, -80*
Mitra, Deenabandhu *REnWD[port]*
Mitra, Subatra 1931- *FilmEn*
Mitra, Subrata 1931- *WorEFlm*
Mitrale, Mari *AmSCAP 80*
Mitrea-Celarianu, Mihai 1935- *Baker 78*
Mitropoulos, Dimitri 1896-1960 *BnBkM 80, CmOp, NewEOp 71, NewGrD 80*
Mitropoulos, Dimtri 1896-1960 *MusSN[port]*
Mitropoulos, Dmitri 1896-1960 *BiDAmM*
Mitropoulus, Dimitri 1896-1960 *Baker 78*
Mitry, Jean 1907- *FilmEn, Film 2, HalFC 80, OxFilm, WorEFlm[port]*
Mitscha, Frantisek Adam *NewGrD 80*
Mitscha, Frantisek Antonin *NewGrD 80*
Mitsukuri, Shukichi 1895-1971 *Baker 78, NewGrD 80*
Mitsuoka, I *ConAmC*
Mitt, Tiina 1956- *IntWWM 80*
Mittantier *NewGrD 80*
Mittell, Lyn Donaldson 1892-1966 *WhScrn 74, -77*
Mittelmann, Norman 1932- *Baker 78, CreCan 1, WhoOp 76*
Mitterer, Ignaz Martin 1850-1924 *Baker 78*
Mitterhuber, Alois 1932- *CnOxB*
Mitterwurzer, Anton 1818-1876 *Baker 78*
Mitterwurzer, Friedrich 1844-1897 *EncWT*
Mittleman, Norman 1932- *CreCan 1*
Mittler, Franz 1893-1970 *Baker 78, ConAmC*
Mittmann, Paul 1868-1920 *Baker 78*
Mitton, Doreen *WhoMus 72*
Mitton, Mildred *PupTheA*
Mitzi 1891- *What 2[port]*
Mitzi, Little *Film 2*
Mitzi-Dalty, Mademoiselle *WhThe*
Mitzler DeKolof, Lorenz Christoph *NewGrD 80*
Miura, Tamaki 1884-1946 *CmOp*
Mix, Art d1972 *WhoHol B*
Mix, Ruth 1913- *Film 2, ForYSC*
Mix, Tom 1880-1940 *FilmEn, Film 1, -2, FilmgC, HalFC 80, MotPP, MovMk, NotNAT B, OxFilm, TwYS, WhScrn 74, -77, WhoHol B, WorEFlm*
Mix, Tom 1881-1940 *CmMov, ForYSC*
Mix, Wes 1946- *NewOrJ SUP[port]*
Mixa, Franz 1902- *WhoMus 72*
Mixon, Daniel Asbury 1949- *EncJzS 70*
Mixon, Danny 1949- *EncJzS 70*
Mixova, Ivana Hildegarda 1930- *WhoOp 76*
Mixter, Keith Eugene 1922- *IntWWM 77, -80*
Miyagawa, Kazuo 1908- *DcFM, FilmEn, WorEFlm*
Miyagi, Michio 1894-1956 *Baker 78, NewGrD 80*
Miyama, Toshiyuki 1921- *EncJzS 70*
Miyoshi, Akira 1933- *Baker 78, DcCM, NewGrD 80*
Mize, Billy 1932- *BiDAmM, EncFCWM 69*
Mize, Joann Alberta 1930- *AmSCAP 80*
Mizell, Alphonso James 1943- *AmSCAP 80*
Mizell, Laurence Clinton 1944- *AmSCAP 80*
Mizelle, Dary John 1940- *ConAmC*
Mizelle, John 1940- *Baker 78*
Mizerit, Klaro 1914- *IntWWM 77, -80*
Mizieres, Tomas *NewGrD 80*
Mizler, Lorenz Christoph 1711-1778 *Baker 78, OxMus*
Mizler VonKolof, Lorenz Christoph 1711-1778 *NewGrD 80*
Mizner, Wilson 1876-1933 *NotNAT B*
Mizoghuchi, Kenji 1898-1956 *WhScrn 74, -77*
Mizoguchi, Kenji 1898-1956 *BiDFilm, -81, DcFM, FilmEn, FilmgC, HalFC 80, MovMk[port], OxFilm, WorEFlm*
Mizonne, Vincent *NewGrD 80*
Mizuno, Shuko 1934- *DcCM, NewGrD 80*
Mizzy, Vic 1916- *CmpEPM*
Mizzy, Vic 1922- *AmSCAP 66, -80*
Mjoen, Reidar *OxMus*
M'Kin, Robert *WhScrn 74, -77*
Mladenovic, Ranko 1893-1947 *CnMD*
Mlakar, Pia 1908- *CnOxB, DancEn 78*
Mlakar, Pino 1907- *CnOxB, DancEn 78*
Mlakar, Veronika 1935- *CnOxB, DancEn 78[port]*
M'Lellan, C M S 1865-1916 *WhoStg 1906*
Mlynarski, Emil 1870-1935 *Baker 78, NewGrD 80*
Mngoma, Khabi 1922- *IntWWM 80*
Mnouchkine, Ariane 1939- *EncWT*
Moan, Patty *AmSCAP 80*
Moate, John 1940- *WhoMus 72*
Moats, Brenda Gail 1952- *IntWWM 77, -80*
Moatt, Christine *Film 2*
Mobbs, Kenneth William 1925- *IntWWM 77, -80, WhoMus 72*
Mobell, Sidney F 1926- *AmSCAP 66, -80*
Moberg, Carl-Allan 1896-1973 *Baker 78*
Moberg, Carl-Allan 1896-1978 *NewGrD 80*
Moberg, Vilhelm 1898-1973 *CnMD, ModWD*
Moberly, Connie *WomWMM B*
Moberly, Luke 1925- *IntMPA 77, -75, -76, -78, -79, -80*
Mobley, Hank 1930- *EncJzS 70, IlEncJ*
Mobley, Henry 1930- *BiDAmM, EncJzS 70*
Mobley, Mary Ann 1939- *FilmgC, ForYSC,*

HalFC 80, MotPP, WhoHol A
Mobley, Peggy J *WomWMM B*
Mobley, Roger *ForYSC*
Mobley, Sylvia Mae 1941- *AmSCAP 80*
Moby Grape *BiDAmM, ConMuA 80A, IlEncR*
Mocedades *RkOn 2[port]*
Moch, Fred *ConMuA 80B*
Mochalov, Pavel Stepanovich 1800-1848 *EncWT, OxThe*
Mociuk, Yar W 1927- *IntMPA 77, -78, -79*
Mock, Alice d1972 *WhScrn 77*
Mock, Flora Clar *WomWMM B*
Mock, Lewis E 1954- *AmSCAP 80*
Mocke, Antoine *NewGrD 80*
Mockridge, Cyril J 1896-1979 *FilmEn, FilmgC, HalFC 80, NewGrD 80, OxFilm, WorEFlm*
Mocky, Jean-Pierre 1929- *DcFM, FilmEn, FilmgC, HalFC 80, OxFilm, WorEFlm*
Mocque, Antoine *NewGrD 80*
Mocquereau, Andre 1849-1930 *Baker 78, NewGrD 80*
Model T Slim *BluesWW*
Modena, Leo Of *OxMus*
Modena, Giacomo 1766-1841 *NotNAT B, OxThe*
Modena, Gustavo 1803-1861 *EncWT, Ent, NotNAT B, OxThe*
Modena, Julio Da *NewGrD 80*
Modena, Leo Da *NewGrD 80*
Modena, Leone Da *NewGrD 80*
Modenos, John Philip 1930- *WhoMus 72, WhoOp 76*
Modern Jazz Quartet, The *BiDAmM, EncJzS 70, IlEncJ*
Modern Jazz Sextet *BiDAmM*
Modernaires, The *CmpEPM*
Moderne, Jacques 1495?-1562? *NewGrD 80*
Modiana, Horatio *NewGrD 80*
Modiana, Orazio *NewGrD 80*
Modie, Louella *WhScrn 74, -77*
Modjeska, Felix *Film 1*
Modjeska, Helen 1840-1909 *PlP&P*
Modjeska, Helena 1840-1909 *EncWT, Ent, FamA&A[port], NotNAT A, OxThe*
Modjeska, Helena 1844-1909 *CnThe, NotNAT B, WhoStg 1906, -1908*
Modl, Martha 1912- *CmOp, IntWWM 77, -80, NewEOp 71, NewGrD 80, WhoOp 76*
Modley, Albert 1891-1979 *HalFC 80*
Modlik, Helene Patricia 1907- *AmSCAP 80*
Modot, Gaston 1887-1970 *FilmAG WE, FilmEn, Film 2, HalFC 80, OxFilm, WhScrn 77, WorEFlm*
Modrekili, Michael *NewGrD 80*
Modugno, Anne Depardo *IntWWM 77, -80*
Modugno, Domenico 1929- *RkOn*
Modungo, Domenico *AmPS A*
Moe, Christian H 1929- *BiE&WWA, NotNAT*
Moe, Daniel 1926- *ConAmC*
Moeck *NewGrD 80*
Moeck, Hermann 1896- *Baker 78, NewGrD 80*
Moeck, Hermann 1922- *Baker 78, IntWWM 77, -80, NewGrD 80*
Moed, Pearl 1938- *AmSCAP 66*
Moehlmann, R L 1907-1972 *AmSCAP 66, -80*
Moehring, Kansas d1968 *WhScrn 77, WhoHol B*
Moelis, Fred *ConMuA 80B*
Moeller, Mathias 1855-1937 *Baker 78*
Moeller, Philip 1880-1958 *EncWT, ModWD, NotNAT B, PlP&P[port], WhThe*
Moeller, W E 1912- *EncFCWM 69*
Moen, Donald J 1950- *AmSCAP 80*
Moen, John Vincent 1928- *AmSCAP 80*
Moench VonSalzburg *NewGrD 80*
Moennig *NewGrD 80*
Moennig, William Heinrich 1883-1962 *NewGrD 80*
Moennig, William Herrman, Jr. 1905- *NewGrD 80*
Moer, De *NewGrD 80*
Moer, Paul 1916- *BiDAmM*
Moeran, E J 1894-1950 *NewGrD 80*
Moeran, Ernest John 1894-1950 *Baker 78, BnBkM 80, DcCom&M 79, MusMk, OxMus*
Moerdyk, Marie-Cecile 1929- *IntWWM 77, -80*
Moerk, Alice Anne 1936- *IntWWM 77, -80*
Moers, Hermann 1930- *CnMD, ModWD*
Moeschinger, Albert Jean 1897- *Baker 78, CpmDNM 80, DcCM, IntWWM 77, -80, NewGrD 80, WhoMus 72*
Moesser, Peter 1915- *WhoMus 72*
Moevs, Robert 1920- *AmSCAP 80, ConAmC, DcCM, IntWWM 77, -80, NewGrD 80*
Moevs, Robert W 1921- *Baker 78, CpmDNM 80*
Moffat, Alan Lyndon 1949- *IntWWM 80*
Moffat, Alfred 1866-1950 *NewGrD 80, OxMus*
Moffat, Alfred Edward 1863-1950 *Baker 78*
Moffat, Donald 1930- *BiE&WWA, NotNAT, WhoHol A, WhoThe 72, -77*
Moffat, Graham 1866-1951 *NotNAT A, -B, WhThe*
Moffat, Mrs. Graham 1873-1943 *NotNAT B, WhThe*
Moffat, Jeffrey 1942- *IntWWM 77*
Moffat, Kate *WhThe*
Moffat, Margaret d1942 *WhoHol B*
Moffat, Margaret 1882-1942 *NotNAT B, WhThe*
Moffat, Margaret 1892-1942 *WhScrn 74, -77*
Moffat, Winifred 1899- *WhThe*
Moffatt, Alice 1890- *WhThe*
Moffatt, Graham 1919-1965 *FilmgC, HalFC 80, IlWWBF, WhScrn 74, -77, WhoHol B*
Moffatt, James *AmSCAP 80*
Moffatt, John 1922- *BiE&WWA, NotNAT, WhoHol A, WhoThe 72, -77*
Moffatt, Joyce A 1936- *WhoOp 76*
Moffatt, Margaret 1882-1942 *WhThe*
Moffatt, Richard Cullen 1927- *AmSCAP 66, -80*
Moffatt, Sanderson d1918 *NotNAT B*
Moffet, Harold 1892-1938 *WhThe*
Moffett, Charles Mack 1929- *BiDAmM, EncJzS 70*
Moffett, Cleveland d1926 *NotNAT B*
Moffett, Harold 1892-1938 *NotNAT B*
Moffett, Percy S 1926- *AmSCAP 80*
Moffett, Sharyn 1936- *FilmgC, HalFC 80*
Moffitt, DeLoyce 1906-1976 *AmSCAP 66, -80*
Moffitt, Jefferson *Film 2*
Moffitt, John Craig *NewYTET*
Moffo, Anna *IntWWM 77, -80, WhoMus 72*
Moffo, Anna 1932- *Baker 78, MusSN[port]*
Moffo, Anna 1934- *NewEOp 71*
Moffo, Anna 1935- *BiDAmM, NewGrD 80, WhoHol A, WhoOp 76, CmOp*
Moga, Sorin *AmSCAP 80*
Mogavero, Antonio *NewGrD 80*
Moger, Art *IntMPA 77, -75, -76, -78, -79, -80*
Mogilevsky, Evgeny 1945- *NewGrD 80*
Mogin, Jean 1921- *ModWD*
Mogull, Ivan *ConMuA 80B*
Moguy, Leonide 1899-1976 *DcFM, FilmEn, FilmgC, HalFC 80*
Mohammed-Ben-Noni *Film 2*
Mohan, Chandra d1949 *WhScrn 77*
Mohan, Earl d1928 *WhScrn 74, -77, WhoHol B*
Mohatt, James L 1933- *IntWWM 77*
Mohaupt, Richard 1904-1957 *Baker 78, DancEn 78, NewGrD 80*
Mohler, Philipp 1908- *NewGrD 80*
Mohler, Ruth Ann *PupTheA*
Mohner, Carl 1921- *FilmgC, HalFC 80, WhoHol A*
Moholy-Nagy, Laszlo 1895-1946 *EncWT, OxFilm*
Mohr, Ernst 1902- *NewGrD 80*
Mohr, Gerald 1914-1968 *FilmEn, FilmgC, ForYSC, HalFC 80, NotNAT B, Vers A[port], WhScrn 74, -77, WhoHol B, WhoHrs 80[port]*
Mohr, Hal 1893- *WorEFlm*
Mohr, Hal 1894-1974 *CmMov, FilmEn, FilmgC, HalFC 80*
Mohr, Hermann 1830-1896 *BiDAmM*
Mohr, Max 1891-1944 *McGEWD*
Mohr, Wilhelm 1904- *IntWWM 77, -80*
Mohrhardt, Peter *NewGrD 80*
Mohringer, Karel Johannes Frederik 1937- *IntWWM 80*
Mohrmann, Margaret Nabors 1944- *IntWWM 77, -80*
Mohun, Michael 1620?-1684 *OxThe, PlP&P*
Mohyeddin, Zia 1933- *WhoHol A, WhoThe 72, -77*
Moineaux, Georges-Victor-Marcel *McGEWD*
Moinet, Monique *WomWMM*
Moir, David Macbeth 1798-1851 *DcPup*
Moire, Ephrem d1100? *NewGrD 80*
Moise, Dan 1943- *CnOxB*
Moise, Mina *WomWMM*
Moise, Warren 1953- *AmSCAP 80*
Moiseiwitch, Tanya 1914- *EncWT*
Moiseiwitsch, Benno 1890-1963 *Baker 78, BnBkM 80, MusSN[port], NewGrD 80[port]*
Moiseiwitsch, Tanya 1914- *BiE&WWA, CnThe, CreCan 2, NotNAT, WhoMus 72, WhoOp 76, WhoThe 72, -77*
Moiseyev, Igor Alexandrovich 1906- *CnOxB, DancEn 78[port]*
Moiseyeva, Olga Nicolayeva 1928- *CnOxB, DancEn 78[port]*
Moissi, Alexander 1880-1935 *EncWT, Ent, Film 2, NotNAT B, OxThe, WhScrn 74, -77, WhoHol B*
Moja, Hella 1898-1937 *Film 2, WhScrn 74, -77, WhoHol B*
Mojave, King d1973 *WhScrn 77, WhoHol B*
Mojica, Jose 1899-1974 *WhScrn 77, WhoHol B*
Mojo *BluesWW*
Mojsisovics, Roderich Von 1877-1953 *Baker 78, NewGrD 80*
Mok, Michel d1961 *NotNAT B*
Moke, Marie *OxMus*
Mokranjac, Stevan 1856-1914 *Baker 78, NewGrD 80*
Mokranjac, Vasilije 1923- *Baker 78*
Mokrejs, John 1875-1968 *Baker 78, ConAmC*
Mokrousov, Boris 1909-1968 *Baker 78*
Mokry, Ladislav 1932- *NewGrD 80*
Moksness, Ingrid Blakstad 1929- *IntWWM 80*
Mokuami, Kawatake 1816-1893 *CnThe, REnWD[port]*
Molaines, Pierre De *NewGrD 80*
Molander, Gustaf 1888-1973 *BiDFilm, -81, DcFM, FilmEn, FilmgC, HalFC 80, OxFilm*
Molander, Gustav 1888- *WorEFlm*
Molander, Karin 1890- *FilmEn, Film 1*
Molander, Olaf 1892-1966 *WhScrn 77*
Molander, Olof 1892-1966 *EncWT, FilmEn*
Molarsky, Osmond *PupTheA*
Molas, Zet *WomWMM*
Molberg, Karl-Theo 1951- *IntWWM 77, -80*
Molchanov, Kirill Vladimirovich 1922- *Baker 78, IntWWM 77, -80, NewGrD 80*
Moldavan, Nicolas 1891-1974 *Baker 78*
Moldenhauer, Hans 1906- *Baker 78, NewGrD 80*
Moldovan, Mihai 1937- *Baker 78*
Moldovan, Stefania 1931- *WhoOp 76*
Moldoveanu, Eugenia 1944- *WhoOp 76*
Moldoveanu, Vasile 1935- *WhoOp 76*
Mole, Francois-Rene 1734-1802 *OxThe*
Mole, Irving Milfred 1898-1961 *BiDAmM, NewGrD 80*
Mole, Miff 1898-1961 *CmpEPM, IlEncJ, NewGrD 80, WhoJazz 72*
Molenaar, Jan 1936- *IntWWM 77*
Molese, Michele 1936- *WhoOp 76*
Moleska, Paul *Film 2*
Molesworth, Ida d1951 *NotNAT B, WhThe*
Molette, Barbara 1940- *BlkAmP, MorBAP, NatPD[port]*
Molette, Carlton W, III 1939- *BlkAmP, MorBAP, NatPD[port]*
Molgaard, Torolf 1939- *IntWWM 77*
Moliere 1622-1673 *CnThe, CnOxB, EncWT, Ent, McGEWD[port], NewEOp 71, NewGrD 80, NotNAT A, -B, OxMus, OxThe, PlP&P[port], -A[port], REnWD[port]*
Moliere, Ernest 1902?- *NewOrJ*
Moliere, Frank 1914- *NewOrJ SUP[port]*

Moliere, Jean Baptiste Poquelin 1622-1673 *DcPup*
Moliere, Louis De *NewGrD 80*
Molin, James 1935- *AmSCAP 80*
Molina, Antonio J 1894- *Baker 78, NewGrD 80*
Molina, Bartolome De *NewGrD 80*
Molina, Carlos *WhoHol A*
Molina, Jose 1937- *CnOxB*
Molina, Tirso De 1571?-1648 *NotNAT B, OxThe*
Molina, Tirso De 1580?-1648 *McGEWD[port]*
Molina, Tirso De 1584-1648 *CnThe*
Molinari, Bernardino 1880-1952 *Baker 78, NewGrD 80*
Molinari, Doreen *WhoHol A*
Molinari, Guido 1933- *CreCan 2*
Molinari, Pietro 1626?-1679 *NewGrD 80*
Molinari-Pradelli, Francesco 1911- *Baker 78, CmOp, NewEOp 71, NewGrD 80, WhoOp 76*
Molinaro, Edouard 1928- *DcFM, FilmEn, FilmgC, HalFC 80, WorEFlm*
Molinaro, Simone 1565?-1615 *NewGrD 80*
Molinas, Richard *WhoHol A*
Moline, Pierre Louis 1740?-1821 *NewGrD 80*
Moline, Robert Lloyd 1938- *AmSCAP 80*
Molineux, Allen Walter 1950- *CpmDNM 76, ConAmC*
Molinie, Etienne *NewGrD 80*
Molino, Antonio 1495?-1571? *NewGrD 80*
Molins, P Des *NewGrD 80*
Molins, Pierre De *NewGrD 80*
Molique, Bernhard 1802-1869 *NewGrD 80*
Molique, Wilhelm Bernhard 1802-1869 *Baker 78, OxMus*
Molitor, Alexius 1730-1773 *NewGrD 80*
Molitor, Fidel 1627-1685 *NewGrD 80*
Molitor, Rapheal 1873-1948 *Baker 78*
Molitor, Valentin 1637-1713 *NewGrD 80*
Moll, Billy 1905-1968 *AmSCAP 66, -80, CmpEPM*
Moll, Elick 1907- *IntMPA 77, -75, -76, -78, -79, -80*
Moll, Georgia *ForYSC, WhoHol A*
Moll, Jaime 1926- *NewGrD 80*
Moll, Kurt Konrad 1938- *NewGrD 80, WhoOp 76*
Moll, Marques Juan 1936- *IntWWM 80*
Moll, Phillip 1943- *IntWWM 77, -80*
Moll Marques, Juan 1936- *IntWWM 77*
Mollajoli, Gustavo 1935- *CnOxB*
Mollandin, Henry M *Film 2*
Molle, Henry 1597?-1658 *NewGrD 80*
Mollendorff, Willi Von 1872-1934 *Baker 78*
Mollenhauer *NewGrD 80*
Mollenhauer, Bernhard 1944- *IntWWM 80*
Mollenhauer, Conrad 1876-1943 *NewGrD 80*
Mollenhauer, Eduard 1827-1914 *Baker 78*
Mollenhauer, Edward 1827-1914 *BiDAmM*
Mollenhauer, Emil 1855-1927 *Baker 78, BiDAmM*
Mollenhauer, Friedrich *Baker 78*
Mollenhauer, Gustav 1837-1914 *NewGrD 80*
Mollenhauer, Henry 1825-1889 *Baker 78*
Mollenhauer, Johannes 1875-1952 *NewGrD 80*
Mollenhauer, Johannes Andreas 1798-1871 *NewGrD 80*
Mollenhauer, Josef Nikolaus 1875-1964 *NewGrD 80*
Mollenhauer, Louis 1863-1926 *Baker 78*
Mollenhauer, Thomas 1840-1914 *NewGrD 80*
Mollenhauer, Thomas 1867-1938 *NewGrD 80*
Mollenhauer, Thomas 1908-1953 *NewGrD 80*
Moller *NewGrD 80*
Moller, Eberhard Wolfgang 1906- *McGEWD, ModWD*
Moller, Heinrich 1876-1958 *Baker 78*
Moller, Joachim *Baker 78, NewGrD 80*
Moller, Johann 1570?-1617 *NewGrD 80*
Moller, Johann Christoph 1755-1803 *NewGrD 80*
Moller, Johann Patroklus 1697?-1772 *NewGrD 80*
Moller, John Christopher 1755-1803 *Baker 78, BiDAmM, NewGrD 80*
Moller, M P *NewGrD 80*
Moller, Peter 1947- *IntWWM 80*
Moller, Wolfgang Michael *NewGrD 80*
Mollerstrom, Britta 1942- *WhoOp 76*
Mollerup, Mette 1931- *CnOxB, DancEn 78*
Mollica, Giovanni Leonardo *NewGrD 80*
Mollicone, Henry *ConAmC*
Mollier, Louis De 1615?-1688 *NewGrD 80*
Mollison, Bruce Bain 1939- *WhoMus 72*
Mollison, Clifford 1896- *IlWWBF*
Mollison, Clifford 1897- *WhoHol A, WhoThe 72, -77*
Mollison, Henry 1905- *WhThe*
Mollison, William 1893-1955 *NotNAT B, WhThe*
Mollo, Eduard *NewGrD 80*
Mollo, Tranquillo 1767-1837? *NewGrD 80*
Mollot, Yolande *WhoHol A*
Mollova, Millena 1940- *IntWWM 80*
Molloy, Charles d1767 *NotNAT B*
Molloy, J L d1909 *NotNAT B*
Molloy, James Lyman 1837-1909 *Baker 78*
Molloy, Michael 1917- *ConDr 77*
Molly Hatchet *ConMuA 80A*
Molnar, Albert Szenczi *NewGrD 80*
Molnar, Antal 1890- *Baker 78, NewGrD 80, WhoMus 72*
Molnar, Anthony 1890- *IntWWM 77, -80*
Molnar, Evamaria 1929- *WhoOp 76*
Molnar, Ferenc 1878-1952 *CnMD, CnThe, EncWT, Ent, HalFC 80, McGEWD[port], ModWD, NotNAT A, -B, OxThe, PlP&P, REnWD[port]*
Molnar, Ferenc 1896- *IntWWM 77, -80*
Molnar, Ferencz 1878-1952 *WhThe*
Molnar, John William 1909- *IntWWM 77, -80*
Molnar, Josef 1929- *IntWWM 77, -80, NewGrD 80*
Molnar, Julius, Jr. *Film 2*
Molnar, Lilly d1950 *WhoHol B*
Molnar, Lily d1950 *NotNAT B*
Molnar-Talajic, Liliana *WhoOp 76*
Moloney, John 1911-1969 *WhScrn 74, -77, WhoHol B*
Molt, Theodore Frederic 1795-1856 *NewGrD 80*
Molteni, Benedetta Emilia *NewGrD 80*
Molter, Johann Melchior 1696-1765 *NewGrD 80*
Moltzel, Jiri *NewGrD 80*
Molu, Pierre *NewGrD 80*
Molyneux, Christopher John 1941- *IntWWM 77, -80*
Molyneux, Eileen 1893-1962 *WhThe*
Molyneux, Kathleen Marie 1934- *WhoMus 72*
Molza, Tarquinia 1542-1617 *NewGrD 80*
Momai, Tetsu *Film 2*
Momary, Douglas R 1947- *AmSCAP 80*
Mombelli, Luisa *NewGrD 80*
Moments, The *RkOn 2[port]*
Momigny, Jerome-Joseph De 1762-1838 *Baker 78*
Momigny, Jerome-Joseph De 1762-1842 *NewGrD 80*
Momo, Alessandro 1953-1974 *WhScrn 77, WhoHol B*
Mompellio, Federico 1908- *NewGrD 80*
Mompfort, Hugo Von *NewGrD 80*
Mompou, Federico 1893- *Baker 78, DcCM, NewGrD 80, OxMus, WhoMus 72*
Monaca, Riccardo La *NewGrD 80*
Monachesi, Walter 1922- *WhoOp 76*
Monachus, Guillelmus *NewGrD 80*
Monaco, Princess Of *Film 1*
Monaco, Eitel 1903- *IntMPA 77, -75, -76, -78, -79, -80*
Monaco, James V 1885-1945 *AmPS, AmSCAP 66, -80, BiDAmM, CmpEPM, Sw&Ld C*
Monaco, Jimmy 1885-1945 *NotNAT B, PopAmC*
Monaco, Mario Del *Baker 78, MusSN[port]*
Monaco, Richard A 1930- *AmSCAP 80, ConAmC*
Monagas, Lionel *BlksB&W C*
Monagas, Natalie *NewGrD 80*
Monahan, Colleen *WomWMM B*
Monahan, James 1912- *CnOxB, DancEn 78*
Monahan, Kaspar J 1900- *BiE&WWA*
Monakhov, Nickolai Fedorovich 1875-1936 *NotNAT B*
Monakhov, Nikolai Fedorovich 1875-1936 *OxThe*
Monarchs *RkOn 2A*
Monari, Bartolomeo *NewGrD 80*
Monari, Clemente 1660?-1729? *NewGrD 80*
Monarino *NewGrD 80*
Monash, Paul 1916?- *HalFC 80, IntMPA 77, -75, -76, -78, -79, -80, NewYTET*
Monasterio, Jesus De 1836-1903 *Baker 78, NewGrD 80*
Monath, Norman 1920- *AmSCAP 80*
Monath, Norman 1930- *AmSCAP 66*
Monca, Georges 187-?-1940 *DcFM*
Moncada, Eduardo Hernandez *Baker 78*
Moncada, Francisco 1922- *NewGrD 80*
Moncayo, Jose Pablo 1912-1958 *Baker 78, DcCM*
Moncayo Garcia, Jose Pablo 1912-1958 *NewGrD 80*
Monch Von Salzburg *NewGrD 80*
Moncion, Francisco 1922- *CnOxB, DancEn 78[port], WhoHol A*
Monck, Nugent 1877-1958 *NotNAT B, OxThe, WhThe*
Monckton, Lionel d1924 *CmpEPM, NotNAT B*
Monckton, Lionel 1861-1924 *EncMT, NewGrD 80*
Monckton, Lionel 1862-1924 *WhThe*
Moncrieff, Gladys 1892-1976 *NewGrD 80*
Moncrieff, Gladys 1893- *WhThe*
Moncrieff, Margaret *IntWWM 80, WhoMus 72*
Moncrieff, Murri d1949 *NotNAT B*
Moncrieff, William Thomas 1794-1857 *NotNAT B, OxThe*
Moncries, Edward 1859-1938 *WhScrn 74, -77, WhoHol B*
Moncur, Grachan 1915- *WhoJazz 72*
Moncur, Grachan, III 1937- *BiDAmM, EncJzS 70, IlEncJ*
Moncur, Grachan, Jr. 1900- *BiDAmM*
Moncur, Pamela 1938- *DancEn 78*
Monday, John *NewGrD 80*
Monday, William *NewGrD 80*
Mondejar, Alonso De *NewGrD 80*
Mondello, Toots 1910?- *CmpEPM, WhoJazz 72*
Mondino, Nestor 1930- *CnOxB*
Mondo, Peggy *WhoHol A*
Mondolfi-Bossarelli, Anna 1907- *NewGrD 80*
Mondondone, Girolamo Da *NewGrD 80*
Mondonville, Jean-Joseph Cassanea De 1711-1772 *Baker 78, NewGrD 80[port], OxMus*
Mondose, Alex 1894-1972 *WhScrn 77*
Mondstein, Christian *NewGrD 80*
Mondy, Pierre 1925- *FilmgC, HalFC 80*
Mone, Franz Joseph 1796-1871 *NewGrD 80*
Monelle, Raymond 1937- *IntWWM 80*
Monello, Spartaco V 1909- *AmSCAP 66, -80, ConAmC A*
Monestel, Alejandro 1865-1950 *Baker 78*
Monet, Claude 1840-1926 *OxMus*
Monet, Gaby *WomWMM B*
Monet, Jean *NewGrD 80*
Monetarius, Stefan *NewGrD 80*
Money, David 1912- *IntWWM 77, -80, WhoMus 72*
Money, Eddie *ConMuA 80A*
Money-Chappelle, Kathleen Mary 1898- *IntWWM 77*
Monferrato, Natale 1603?-1685 *NewGrD 80*
Monfred, Avenir H De 1903-1974 *Baker 78*
Mong, William V 1875-1940 *Film 1, -2, ForYSC, MovMk, TwYS, WhScrn 74, -77, WhoHol B*
Mongberg, George *Film 2*
Mongeau, Jean-Guy 1931- *CreCan 1*
Mongini, Pietro 1830-1874 *CmOp, NewGrD 80*
Mongor, Ernest 1926- *IntWWM 77, -80*
Monhardt, Maurice *ConAmC*
Monicelli, Mario 1915- *DcFM, FilmEn, FilmgC, HalFC 80, IntMPA 77, -75, -76, -78, -79, -80, WorEFlm*
Moniglia, Giovanni Andrea 1624-1700 *NewGrD 80*
Monin, Janine 1934- *CnOxB*
Moniot D'Arras *NewGrD 80*
Moniot De Paris *NewGrD 80*
Moniuszko, Stanislaus 1819-1872 *GrComp[port], NewEOp 71*

Moniuszko, Stanislaw 1819-1872 *Baker 78, CmOp, MusMk, NewGrD 80[port], OxMus*
Monk, Allan James 1942- *WhoOp 76*
Monk, Christopher 1921- *NewGrD 80*
Monk, Edwin George 1819-1900 *Baker 78, NewGrD 80, OxMus*
Monk, Egon 1927- *EncWT*
Monk, Julius *WhoHol A*
Monk, Karin 1903- *IntWWM 77, -80*
Monk, Meredith *CmpGMD*
Monk, Meredith 1943- *CnOxB*
Monk, Meredith 1944- *ConAmC*
Monk, Meredith J 1942- *AmSCAP 80*
Monk, Noel *ConMuA 80B*
Monk, Thelonious 1917- *CmpEPM, EncJzS 70*
Monk, Thelonious 1918- *Baker 78, ConAmC, MusMk[port]*
Monk, Thelonious 1920- *BiDAmM, IlEncJ, NewGrD 80*
Monk, Thelonius *BnBkM 80*
Monk, Thelonius 1918- *DrBlPA*
Monk, William Henry 1823-1889 *Baker 78, NewGrD 80, OxMus*
Monk Of Bristol *NewGrD 80*
Monk Of Salzburg *NewGrD 80*
Monke, Josef 1882-1965 *NewGrD 80*
Monkees, The *BiDAmM, ConMuA 80A, FilmgC, HalFC 80, IlEncR, RkOn 2[port]*
Monkemeyer, Helmut 1905- *IntWWM 77, -80*
Monkhouse, Allan Noble 1858-1936 *ModWD, NotNAT B, OxThe, WhThe*
Monkhouse, Bob 1928- *FilmgC, HalFC 80, IlWWBF, IntMPA 77, -75, -76, -78, -79, -80, WhoHol A*
Monkhouse, Harry d1901 *NotNAT B*
Monkman, Phyllis 1892- *Film 2, WhThe*
Monks, James 1917- *WhThe, WhoHol A*
Monks, John, Jr. 1910- *BiE&WWA, IntMPA 77, -75, -76, -78, -79, -80, NotNAT*
Monks, Victoria 1884- *WhThe*
Monlaur, Yvonne 1938?- *WhoHrs 80*
Monleone, Domenico 1875-1942 *Baker 78*
Monmart, Berthe 1924?- *NewGrD 80*
Monn, Georg Matthias 1717-1750 *Baker 78, NewGrD 80, OxMus*
Monn, Giovanni Matteo *OxMus*
Monn, Johann *NewGrD 80*
Monn, Johann Christoph 1726-1782 *NewGrD 80, OxMus*
Monn, Matthias Georg 1717-1750 *NewGrD 80*
Monn-Iversen, Egil 1928- *IntWWM 80*
Monna-Delza, Mademoiselle d1921 *NotNAT B, WhThe*
Monnard, Jean-Francois 1941- *IntWWM 77, -80*
Monnet, Jean 1703-1785 *NewGrD 80, OxMus*
Monnier, Jackie *Film 2*
Monnikendam, Marius 1896- *IntWWM 77, -80*
Monnikendam, Marius 1896-1977 *Baker 78, NewGrD 80*
Monnot, Marguerite d1961 *NotNAT B*
Monod, Jacques-Louis 1927- *CpmDNM 80, ConAmC, IntWWM 77, -80, NewGrD 80*
Monod, Theodore 1836-1921 *BiDAmM*
Mononen, Sakari 1928- *Baker 78, NewGrD 80*
Monopoli, Giacomo *NewGrD 80*
Monosha, Coleman *AmSCAP 80*
Monosoff, Sonya 1927- *IntWWM 77, -80, NewGrD 80*
Monotones, The *RkOn[port]*
Monplaisir, Hippolyte 1821-1877 *DancEn 78*
Monpou, Hippolyte 1804-1841 *NewGrD 80*
Monrad Johansen, David 1888-1974 *Baker 78*
Monro, Harold 1879-1932 *DcPup*
Monro, Matt *RkOn*
Monroe, Bill 1911- *CmpEPM, CounME 74[port], -74A, EncFCWM 69, NewGrD 80, NewYTET*
Monroe, Charles Pendleton 1903- *BiDAmM*
Monroe, Charlie *EncFCWM 69*
Monroe, Charlie 1903- *IlEncCM*
Monroe, Frank d1937 *NotNAT B*
Monroe, George W d1932 *NotNAT B*
Monroe, James Frank 1908- *ConAmC*
Monroe, Marilyn 1926-1962 *BiDFilm, -81, CmMov, CmpEPM, FilmEn, FilmgC, HalFC 80, MotPP, MovMk[port], NotNAT B, OxFilm, WhScrn 74, -77, WhoHol B, WorEFlm[port]*
Monroe, Marilyn 1928-1962 *ForYSC[port]*
Monroe, Vaughan 1911-1973 *FilmgC, HalFC 80*
Monroe, Vaughn 1911-1973 *AmPS A, -B, AmSCAP 66, -80, BgBands 74[port], BiDAmM, CmpEPM, RkOn, What 4[port], WhScrn 77, WhoHol B*
Monroe, Vince *BluesWW*
Monroe, William 1911- *BiDAmM, IlEncCM[port], NewGrD 80*
Monroe Brothers *EncFCWM 69, IlEncCM[port]*
Mons, Filippo Di *NewGrD 80*
Mons, Philippe De *NewGrD 80, OxMus*
Mons, Philippus De *NewGrD 80*
Monsardus, Hieronymus *NewGrD 80*
Monserrate, Andres De *NewGrD 80*
Monsigny, Pierre-Alexandre 1729-1817 *Baker 78, GrComp[port], MusMk, NewEOp 71, NewGrD 80[port], OxMus*
Monson, Karen *ConAmTC*
Mont, Christina *Film 2*
Mont, Paul De 1895-1950 *ModWD*
Monta, Rudolph d1963 *NotNAT B*
Montagnana, Antonio *NewGrD 80*
Montagnana, Domenico 1687?-1750 *NewGrD 80*
Montagnana, Rinaldo Da *NewGrD 80*
Montagne, Edward J *IntMPA 77, -75, -76, -78, -79, -80*
Montagney, Joseph *NewGrD 80*
Montagu, Elizabeth 1909- *WhThe*
Montagu, Harry *PupTheA*
Montagu, Ivor 1904- *FilmEn, FilmgC, HalFC 80, IlWWBF A, OxFilm*
Montagu, Jeremy Peter Samuel 1927- *IntWWM 77, -80, WhoMus 72*
Montagu-Nathan, M 1877-1958 *NewGrD 80*
Montagu-Nathan, Montagu 1877-1958 *Baker 78*
Montague, Bertram 1892- *WhThe*
Montague, Charles Edward 1867-1928 *NotNAT B, OxThe, WhThe*
Montague, Duke *PupTheA*
Montague, Edna Woodruff *WhScrn 74, -77*
Montague, Emmeline d1910 *NotNAT B*
Montague, Fred *Film 1, WhoHol B*
Montague, Frederick 1864-1919 *WhScrn 77*
Montague, H J 1844-1878 *PlP&P[port]*
Montague, Harold 1874- *WhThe*
Montague, Harry d1927 *NotNAT B*
Montague, Henry James 1844-1878 *NotNAT B, OxThe*
Montague, Lee 1927- *FilmgC, HalFC 80, WhoHol A, WhoThe 72, -77*
Montague, Louise 1871-1906 *NotNAT B*
Montague, Monte d1959 *WhoHol B*
Montague, Monty *Film 2*
Montague, Rita 1884-1962 *NotNAT B, WhScrn 74, -77, WhoHol B*
Montal, Andre 1940- *WhoOp 76*
Montaland, Celine 1843-1891 *OxThe*
Montalban, Carlos *WhoHol A*
Montalban, Ricardo 1920- *BiE&WWA, CmpEPM, FilmEn, FilmgC, ForYSC, HalFC 80, IntMPA 77, -75, -76, -78, -79, -80, MGM[port], MotPP, MovMk[port], WhoHol A, WorEFlm*
Montalbano, Bartolomeo 1600?-1651 *NewGrD 80*
Mont'Albano, Bartolomeo 1600?-1651 *NewGrD 80*
Montalvan, Celia 1899-1958 *WhScrn 77*
Montana, Bull 1887-1950 *Film 1, -2, FilmgC, HalFC 80, TwYS, WhScrn 74, -77, WhoHol B, WhoHrs 80*
Montana, Montie 1910- *WhoHol A*
Montana, Patsy 1914- *AmSCAP 66, -80, BiDAmM, CmpEPM, CounME 74[port], -74A, EncFCWM 69, IlEncCM*
Montana, Vincent, Jr. 1928- *AmSCAP 80*
Montana Slim *CmpEPM, CounME 74, EncFCWM 69*
Montanari, Francesco d1730 *NewGrD 80*
Montand, Yves 1921- *BiDAmM, BiDFilm, -81, FilmAG WE[port], FilmEn, FilmgC, ForYSC, HalFC 80, IntMPA 77, -75, -76, -78, -79, -80, MotPP, MovMk[port], OxFilm, WhoHol A, WorEFlm*
Montane, Carlos 1941- *WhoOp 76*
Montani, Nicola Aloysius 1880-1948 *AmSCAP 66, -80, Baker 78, BiDAmM*
Montano, Signor *PupTheA*
Montano, A d1914 *WhScrn 77*
Montanos, Francisco De 1528?-1592? *NewGrD 80*
Montansier, Marguerite 1730-1820 *NotNAT B, OxThe*
Montanus *NewGrD 80*
Montanus, Edward *NewYTET*
Montarsolo, Paolo 1925- *WhoMus 72, WhoOp 76*
Montazel, Pierre 1911- *DcFM*
Montbuisson, Victor De 1575?-1638? *NewGrD 80*
Montbuysson, Victor De 1575?-1638? *NewGrD 80*
Montchretien, Antoine De 1575?-1621 *OxThe*
Montdory 1594-1651 *Ent, NotNAT B, OxThe*
Montdory, Guillaume 1594-1651 *CnThe*
Monte, Cola Nardo De *NewGrD 80*
Monte, Eric *BlkAmP, MorBAP*
Monte, Filippo Di 1521-1603 *NewGrD 80[port], OxMus*
Monte, Lodovico *NewGrD 80*
Monte, Lou 1917- *AmSCAP 66, RkOn[port]*
Monte, Philippe De 1521-1603 *Baker 78, BnBkM 80, GrComp[port], MusMk, NewGrD 80[port]*
Monte, Philippus De 1521-1603 *NewGrD 80[port]*
Monte, Toti Dal *Baker 78*
Monte Carmelo, Pater A *NewGrD 80*
Montecino, Alfonso Montalva 1924- *NewGrD 80*
Monteclair, Michel De 1667-1737 *MusMk*
Monteclair, Michel Pignolet De 1667-1737 *Baker 78, NewGrD 80*
Monteclair, Michel Pinolet De 1667?-1737 *NewGrD 80, OxMus*
Montefiore, Eade 1866-1944 *NotNAT B, WhThe*
Montefusco, Licinio 1936- *WhoOp 76*
Montegue, Sidney 1908-1969 *NewOrJ*
Monteiro, Pilar 1886-1962 *WhScrn 74, -77*
Monteiro, Stan *ConMuA 80B*
Montel, Blanche *Film 2*
Montel, Michael 1939- *NotNAT*
Montell, Lisa *ForYSC*
Montella, Giovanni Domenico 1570?-1607 *Baker 78, NewGrD 80*
Montelli, Giovanni Domenico *NewGrD 80*
Montemezzi, Italo 1875-1952 *Baker 78, BnBkM 80, CmOp, CompSN[port], NewEOp 71, NewGrD 80, OxMus*
Montenegro, Conchita 1912- *FilmEn, ForYSC, WhoHol A*
Montenegro, Hugo *RkOn 2A*
Montenelli, Bernardo *NewGrD 80*
Monterey, Carlotta 1888-1970 *Film 2, NotNAT B, WhScrn 77*
Montero *NewGrD 80*
Montero, Atanasio Bello *NewGrD 80*
Montero, Joaquin *NewGrD 80*
Montero, Jose Angel 1839-1881 *NewGrD 80*
Montero, Jose Lorenzo *NewGrD 80*
Montero, Jose Maria 1782-1869 *NewGrD 80*
Montero, Ramon d1878? *NewGrD 80*
Monterose, J R 1927- *IlEncJ*
Monterosso, Raffaello 1925- *NewGrD 80*
Montes, Lola 1818-1861 *FilmgC, HalFC 80*
Montesano, Alfonso 1595?-1624? *NewGrD 80*
Montesardo, Girolamo *NewGrD 80*
Montesole, Max d1942 *NotNAT B*
Montessu, Pauline 1805-1877 *CnOxB*
Monteux, Claude 1920- *NewGrD 80, WhoMus 72*
Monteux, Pierre 1874-1964 *CmOp*
Monteux, Pierre 1875-1964 *Baker 78, BiDAmM, BnBkM 80[port], CnOxB, MusMk, MusSN[port], NewEOp 71, NewGrD 80[port], NotNAT B*
Montevecchi, Liliane *ForYSC, WhoHol A*
Monteverde, Claudio 1567-1643 *NewGrD 80*
Monteverde, Maurizio 1933- *WhoOp 76*
Monteverdi, Claudio 1567-1643 *Baker 78, BnBkM 80[port], CmOp, CmpBCM,*

DcCom 77, DcCom&M 79, GrComp[port], MusMk[port], NewEOp 71, NewGrD 80, OxMus
Monteverdi, Francesco *NewGrD 80*
Monteverdi, Giulio Cesare 1573-1630? *Baker 78*
Monteverdi, Giulio Cesare 1573-1631? *NewGrD 80*
Montez, Chris 1944- *AmPS A, RkOn*
Montez, Lola 1818-1861 *CnOxB, DancEn 78, FamA&A[port], NotNAT A, -B*
Montez, Lola 1820?-1861 *Ent*
Montez, Maria d1951 *MotPP, WhoHol B*
Montez, Maria 1918-1951 *CmMov, FilmgC, ForYSC, WhScrn 74, -77, WhoHrs 80[port]*
Montez, Maria 1919-1951 *HalFC 80*
Montez, Maria 1920-1951 *FilmEn, MovMk, NotNAT B, WorEFlm*
Montfleury, Antoine-Jacob De 1639-1685 *Ent, OxThe*
Montfleury, Francoise 1640?-1708 *OxThe*
Montfleury, Louise 1649-1709 *OxThe*
Montfleury, Zacharie Jacob 1600?-1667 *OxThe*
Montford, Ivy *IIWWBF*
Montfort, Corneille De *NewGrD 80*
Montfort, Hugo Von *NewGrD 80*
Montgomerie, Hugh *NewGrD 80*
Montgomery, Baby Peggy 1918- *TwYS*
Montgomery, Barbara *DrBlPA*
Montgomery, Belinda J *WhoHol A*
Montgomery, Bruce 1921- *WhoMus 72*
Montgomery, Bruce 1927- *AmSCAP 66, -80, ConAmC A*
Montgomery, Buddy 1930- *EncJzS 70*
Montgomery, Charles F 1930- *BiDAmM, EncJzS 70*
Montgomery, David 1870-1917 *AmPS B, EncMT, JoeFr[port], NotNAT B, PlP&P[port]*
Montgomery, Doreen *IntMPA 77, -75, -76, -78, -79, -80*
Montgomery, Douglas 1908-1966 *WhScrn 74, -77*
Montgomery, Douglass d1966 *WhoHol B*
Montgomery, Douglass 1907-1966 *HalFC 80, HolP 30[port]*
Montgomery, Douglass 1908-1966 *FilmEn, FilmgC, NotNAT B*
Montgomery, Douglass 1909-1966 *WhThe*
Montgomery, Douglass 1912-1966 *BiE&WWA, ForYSC*
Montgomery, E *BluesWW*
Montgomery, Earl 1893-1966 *Film 2, WhScrn 77, WhoHol B*
Montgomery, Earl 1921- *BiE&WWA, NotNAT, WhoHol A, WhoThe 72, -77*
Montgomery, Edythe May 1908- *AmSCAP 66, -80*
Montgomery, Elizabeth 1902- *WhoThe 72, -77*
Montgomery, Elizabeth 1904- *BiE&WWA, NotNAT*
Montgomery, Elizabeth 1933- *FilmgC, ForYSC, HalFC 80, WhoHol A*
Montgomery, Eurreal 1907?- *NewOrJ*
Montgomery, Eurreal Wilford 1906- *BluesWW[port]*
Montgomery, Florence d1950 *NotNAT B*
Montgomery, Frank 1870-1944 *Film 2, WhScrn 77*
Montgomery, George 1916- *FilmEn, FilmgC, ForYSC, HalFC 80, HolP 40[port], IntMPA 77, -75, -76, -78, -79, -80, MotPP, MovMk, WhoHol A*
Montgomery, Jack 1892-1962 *WhScrn 74, -77, WhoHol B*
Montgomery, James 1882-1966 *WhThe*
Montgomery, Jean *PupTheA*
Montgomery, John Leslie 1925-1968 *BiDAmM, EncJzS 70*
Montgomery, Kandeda *AmSCAP 80*
Montgomery, Kenneth Mervyn 1943- *IntWWM 77, -80, NewGrD 80, WhoMus 72, WhoOp 76*
Montgomery, Lee Boyd, Jr. 1936- *IntWWM 77, -80*
Montgomery, Little Brother 1906- *WhoJazz 72*
Montgomery, Lucy Maud 1874-1942 *CreCan 2*
Montgomery, Marion 1934- *BiDAmM*
Montgomery, Marshall d1942 *NotNAT B*
Montgomery, Melba Joyce 1938- *BiDAmM, CounME 74[port], -74A, EncFCWM 69, IlEncCM[port]*
Montgomery, Merle 1904- *AmSCAP 66, -80, Baker 78, ConAmC*
Montgomery, Monk 1921- *EncJzS 70*
Montgomery, Peggy 1918- *FilmEn, Film 2, WhoHol A*
Montgomery, Peter Stephen 1909- *WhoMus 72*
Montgomery, Ray *ForYSC, WhoHol A*
Montgomery, Robert 1903- *WhThe*
Montgomery, Robert 1904- *BiDFilm, -81, BiE&WWA, CmMov, FilmEn, Film 2, FilmgC, ForYSC[port], HalFC 80[port], IntMPA 77, -75, -76, -78, -79, -80, MGM[port], MotPP, MovMk[port], NewYTET, NotNAT A, OxFilm, What 3[port], WhoHol A, WomWMM, WorEFlm[port]*
Montgomery, Robert Humphrey, Jr. 1923- *BiE&WWA*
Montgomery, Wes 1925-1968 *EncJzS 70, IlEncJ*
Montgomery, William Howard 1921- *BiDAmM, EncJzS 70*
Montgomery, William L 1934- *IntWWM 77, -80*
Montgomery And Stone *CmpEPM, JoeFr[port], NotNAT B*
Montgommery, David Craig 1870-1917 *WhThe*
Montherlant, Henri De 1896-1972 *OxThe*
Montherlant, Henry De 1896-1972 *CnMD, CnThe, CroCD, EncWT, Ent, McGEWD[port], ModWD, NotNAT A, REnWD[port]*
Monti *NewGrD 80*
Monti, Anna Maria 1704-1727? *NewGrD 80*
Monti, Gaetano 1750?-1816? *NewGrD 80*
Monti, Giacomo *NewGrD 80*
Monti, Grazia *NewGrD 80*
Monti, Laura 1704?-1760 *NewGrD 80*
Monti, Marianna 1704-1727? *NewGrD 80*
Monti, Marianna 1730-1814 *NewGrD 80*
Monti, Palola *Film 1*
Monti, Pier Maria *NewGrD 80*
Monti, Vincenzo 1754-1828 *McGEWD[port]*
Monti, Vittorio 1868-1922 *NewGrD 80*
Monticelli, Angelo Maria 1710?-1764 *NewGrD 80*
Montichiaro, Zanetto Di *NewGrD 80*
Montiel, Nelly d1951 *WhScrn 74, -77*
Montiel, Sara 1929- *WorEFlm*
Montiel, Sarita *ForYSC*
Montiel, Sarita 1927- *HalFC 80*
Montiel, Sarita 1928- *FilmEn*
Montiel, Sarita 1929- *WhoHol A, WorEFlm[port]*
Montiel, Urbano Gomez *AmSCAP 80*
Montisarduus, Hieronymus *NewGrD 80*
Montivedo, Signor *PupTheA*
Montivier, Monique *WomWMM*
Montmenil 1695-1743 *NotNAT B, OxThe*
Montoliu, Tete 1933- *EncJzS 70*
Montoliu, Vincente 1933- *EncJzS 70*
Montoya, Alex P 1907-1970 *ForYSC, WhScrn 77, WhoHol B*
Montoya, Carlos 1903- *AmSCAP 66, -80, BnBkM 80, WhoMus 72*
Montoya, Julia *WhoHol A*
Montoya Y Gadena, Francisca Tomasa *PupTheA*
Montplaisir, Hippolyte Georges 1821-1877 *CnOxB*
Montresor, Beni 1926- *WhoOp 76*
Montrose *IlEncR*
Montrose, Belle 1886-1964 *WhScrn 74, -77, WhoHol B*
Montrose, Helen *Film 2*
Montrose, Jack 1928- *AmSCAP 66, -80*
Montrose, Muriel *WhThe*
Montsalvatge, Bassols Xavier 1911- *Baker 78*
Montsalvatge, Xavier 1912- *CpmDNM 75, DcCM, NewGrD 80*
Montserrat, Andres De *NewGrD 80*
Montt, Christina 1897-1969 *WhScrn 74, -77, WhoHol B*
Montt, Christine *Film 2*
Montuori, Carlo 1885- *DcFM, FilmEn*
Montvila, Vytautas 1935- *DcCM*
Monty Python *WhoHrs 80[port]*
Mony, Walter Alexander 1930- *IntWWM 80*
Monza, Carlo 1735?-1801 *NewGrD 80*
Monza, Carlo Antonio d1736 *NewGrD 80*
Monza, Maria *NewGrD 80*
Monzani, Tebaldo 1762-1839 *NewGrD 80*
Monzani, Theobald 1762-1839 *NewGrD 80*
Monzino, Francesco Di *NewGrD 80*
Moock, Armando *OxThe*
Moode, Henry *NewGrD 80*
Moodie, Alma 1900-1943 *Baker 78*
Moodie, Louise M R d1934 *NotNAT B*
Moody, Clyde 1915- *BiDAmM, IlEncCM*
Moody, Dan 1890?-1959 *NewOrJ*
Moody, Fanny 1866-1945 *Baker 78, CmOp, NewGrD 80*
Moody, Harry *Film 1*
Moody, Helen Wills 1906- *What 1[port]*
Moody, James 1925- *BiDAmM, CmpEPM, EncJzS 70, IlEncJ*
Moody, King *WhoHol A*
Moody, Lynne *DrBlPA*
Moody, Michael Dorn 1944- *NatPD[port]*
Moody, Philip Trevor *AmSCAP 80*
Moody, Ralph 1887-1971 *ForYSC, WhScrn 74, -77, WhoHol B*
Moody, Richard 1911- *BiE&WWA, NotNAT*
Moody, Ron *WhoHol A*
Moody, Ron 1923- *ForYSC*
Moody, Ron 1924- *EncMT, FilmEn, FilmgC, HalFC 80, WhoMus 72, WhoThe 72, -77*
Moody, Ron 1926- *MovMk[port]*
Moody, Royston Everard 1907- *IntWWM 77*
Moody, Titus *JoeFr*
Moody, William Vaughan 1869-1910 *NotNAT B, PlP&P, WhoStg 1908*
Moody, William Vaughn 1869-1910 *CnThe, DcLB 7[port], EncWT, Ent, McGEWD, ModWD, NotNAT A, OxThe, REnWD[port]*
Moody And Sankey *OxMus*
Moody Blues, The *ConMuA 80A, IlEncR[port], RkOn 2[port]*
Mooers, DeSacia 1888-1960 *Film 2, WhScrn 74, -77, WhoHol B*
Moog, Robert A 1934- *Baker 78, MusMk, NewGrD 80*
Moog Synthesizers, G Kingsley And His *BiDAmM*
Mooke, Marie *OxMus*
Moomey, Katherine Walling 1917- *IntWWM 77, -80*
Moon, Anthony Joseph 1938- *AmSCAP 80*
Moon, Donna d1918 *WhScrn 77*
Moon, George 1886-1961 *WhScrn 74, WhoHol B*
Moon, George 1886-1967 *WhScrn 77*
Moon, Harry Edward 1937- *IntWWM 77, -80*
Moon, Jack *AmSCAP 80*
Moon, Joseph Frederick 1912- *AmSCAP 80*
Moon, Morse d1918 *WhScrn 77*
Moon, Vaughan Graham 1930- *WhoMus 72*
Moondaye, John *NewGrD 80*
Moondaye, William *NewGrD 80*
Moondog *AmSCAP 80*
Moonen, Janet Elisabeth 1937- *IntWWM 77, -80*
Mooney, Art *AmPS B, BgBands 74, CmpEPM, RkOn*
Mooney, Gerard Antony 1953- *IntWWM 80*
Mooney, Hal 1911- *CmpEPM*
Mooney, Harold 1911- *AmSCAP 66*
Mooney, Harold 1917- *AmSCAP 80*
Mooney, James A 1872-1951 *AmSCAP 66*
Mooney, Joe 1911-1975 *CmpEPM, EncJzS 70*
Mooney, Margaret *Film 1*
Mooney, Robert Daniel 1932- *IntWWM 77*
Moonglows, The *RkOn[port]*
Moonie, W B 1883-1961 *NewGrD 80*
Moonshiners *BiDAmM*
Moony, Art *AmPS A*
Moor, De *NewGrD 80*
Moor, Barbara Mary 1921- *WhoMus 72*
Moor, Emanuel 1863-1931 *Baker 78, MusMk, NewGrD 80, OxMus*
Moor, Karel 1873-1945 *Baker 78, NewGrD 80*
Moor, William *NewGrD 80*
Moorat, Gerard *WhoMus 72*
Moorat, Joseph 1864-1938 *NewGrD 80*
Moore, A P 1906- *WhThe*
Moore, Ada *BiE&WWA*
Moore, Adrienne *WhoHol A*

Moore, Alexander Herman 1899- BluesWW[port]
Moore, Alice 1916-1960 WhScrn 74, -77, WhoHol B
Moore, Allyson WomWMM B
Moore, Alvy ForYSC, WhoHol A, WhoHrs 80
Moore, Archie WhoHol A
Moore, Archie 1913- What 5[port]
Moore, Archie 1916?- DrBlPA
Moore, Arnold Dwight 1913- BluesWW
Moore, Art 1914- AmSCAP 66, -80
Moore, Barbara Hill 1942- IntWWM 77, -80
Moore, Barrie WhoMus 72
Moore, Big Chief 1912- WhoJazz 72
Moore, Bill 1901-1964 WhoJazz 72
Moore, Billy 1916- WhoJazz 72
Moore, Billy 1917- EncJzS 70
Moore, Bob 1932- RkOn
Moore, Bobby 1919- WhoJazz 72
Moore, Brew 1924-1973 EncJzS 70
Moore, Brian 1921- CreCan 2
Moore, Carlyle, Sr. 1875-1924 WhScrn 77, WhoStg 1908
Moore, Carman 1939- Baker 78
Moore, Carman Leroy 1936- AmSCAP 80, ConAmC, DrBlPA
Moore, Carole Torrence 1938- IntWWM 77, -80
Moore, Caroline Rudy 1943- BiDAmM
Moore, Carrie 1883-1956 NotNAT B, WhThe
Moore, Carroll 1913- BiE&WWA, NotNAT
Moore, Charles Film 2, WhoHol A
Moore, Charles 1928- DrBlPA
Moore, Charles 1938- ConAmC
Moore, Charles B, Jr. 1935- BiDAmM
Moore, Charles J d1962 NotNAT B
Moore, Charles L 1870-1919 BlksBF
Moore, Charles Werner 1920- BiE&WWA, NotNAT
Moore, Charles William 1918- AmSCAP 66, -80
Moore, Charlie d1961 NewOrJ
Moore, Claude Film 2
Moore, Clayton ForYSC
Moore, Clayton 1908- FilmgC, HalFC 80
Moore, Clayton 1914- FilmEn, WhoHol A
Moore, Clement Clarke 1779-1863 BiDAmM
Moore, Cleo 1928-1973 FilmgC, HalFC 80, WhScrn 77, WhoHol B
Moore, Cleo 1930-1973 FilmEn, ForYSC
Moore, Cleve d1961 Film 2, WhoHol B
Moore, Clive Film 2
Moore, Colleen 1900- FilmEn, Film 1, -2, FilmgC, ForYSC, HalFC 80, MotPP, ThFT[port], TwYS, WhoHol A
Moore, Colleen 1902- MovMk[port], What 2[port]
Moore, Constance MotPP
Moore, Constance 1919- FilmEn, FilmgC, HalFC 80
Moore, Constance 1920- CmpEPM, ForYSC, WhoHol A
Moore, Constance 1922- IntMPA 77, -75, -76, -78, -79, -80
Moore, Dale 1932- IntWWM 77, -80
Moore, Dallas 1929- AmSCAP 80
Moore, Daniel William 1941- EncJzS 70
Moore, Danny 1941- EncJzS 70
Moore, David A 1948- ConAmC
Moore, Decima 1871-1964 NotNAT B, WhThe, WhoStg 1908
Moore, Del 1917-1970 ForYSC, WhScrn 74, -77, WhoHol B
Moore, Dennie 1907- BiE&WWA, NotNAT, WhThe, WhoHol A
Moore, Dennis d1964 WhoHol B
Moore, Dick 1925- BiE&WWA, NotNAT
Moore, Dickie 1925- FilmEn, Film 2, FilmgC, ForYSC, HalFC 80, HolP 30[port], IntMPA 77, -75, -76, -78, -79, -80, MotPP, MovMk[port], What 3[port], WhoHol A
Moore, Donald Irving 1910- AmSCAP 80, ConAmC, IntWWM 77
Moore, Donald Lee 1910- AmSCAP 66, -80
Moore, Dora Mavor 1888- CreCan 2
Moore, Dorothy 1946- RkOn 2[port]
Moore, Dorothy Louise Sutton 1930-1967 BiDAmM
Moore, Douglas Stuart 1893-1969 AmSCAP 66, -80, Baker 78, BiDAmM, BnBkM 80, CompSN[port], ConAmC, DcCom&M 79, DcCM, NewEOp 71, NewGrD 80, OxMus
Moore, Dudley 1935- BiE&WWA, FilmEn, FilmgC, HalFC 80, NotNAT, WhoHol A, WhoThe 72, -77
Moore, Earl Vincent 1890- Baker 78, ConAmC, WhoMus 72
Moore, Edna Muriel 1904- WhoMus 72
Moore, Edward 1712-1757 NotNAT B, OxThe
Moore, Edward James 1935- NatPD[port], NotNAT
Moore, Eileen WhoHol A
Moore, Elizabeth Barrett Morgan 1937- IntWWM 77
Moore, Elizabeth Evelyn 1891- AmSCAP 66, -80
Moore, Ellis 1924- IntMPA 77, -75, -76, -78, -79, -80, NewYTET
Moore, Eloise Irene 1929- AmSCAP 80
Moore, Elsie WhoStg 1906, -1908
Moore, Elvie BlkAmP
Moore, Erin O'Brien WhoHol A
Moore, Eulabelle 1903-1964 BiE&WWA, NotNAT B, WhScrn 74, -77, WhoHol B
Moore, Eva 1870-1955 Film 2, FilmgC, HalFC 80, NotNAT A, -B, WhScrn 74, -77, WhThe, WhoHol B
Moore, F Frankfort d1931 NotNAT B
Moore, Florence 1886-1935 NotNAT B, WhScrn 74, -77, WhThe, WhoHol B
Moore, Francis 1886-1946 AmSCAP 66, -80
Moore, Francis John 1885- BiDAmM
Moore, Frank 1928- AmSCAP 66, -80
Moore, Frank F d1924 WhScrn 74, -77
Moore, Frank Ledlie 1923- AmSCAP 80
Moore, Freddie 1900- WhoJazz 72
Moore, Gar WhoHol A
Moore, Garry 1915- IntMPA 77, -76, -78, -79, -80, NewYTET
Moore, Gary 1915- BiDAmM
Moore, Gaylen WomWMM B
Moore, Geoff 1944- CnOxB
Moore, George Augustus 1852-1933 ModWD, NotNAT B, OxThe, REnWD[port], WhThe
Moore, George Philip, Jr. 1918- AmSCAP 80
Moore, Gerald 1899- Baker 78, IntWWM 77, -80, MusMk, NewGrD 80, WhoMus 72
Moore, Glen Richard 1941- AmSCAP 80, EncJzS 70
Moore, Grace AmPS B
Moore, Grace 1898-1947 Baker 78
Moore, Grace 1901-1947 BiDAmM, CmpEPM, EncMT, FilmEn, FilmgC, HalFC 80, MusSN[port], NewEOp 71, NewGrD 80, NotNAT A, -B, OxFilm, PlP&P[port], ThFT[port], WhScrn 74, -77, WhThe, WhoHol B
Moore, Grace 1902-1947 ForYSC
Moore, Grace 1903-1947 MovMk[port]
Moore, Grace 1904-1947 CmOp
Moore, Harry R 1888-1958 WhScrn 74, -77
Moore, Henrietta d1973 WhoHol B
Moore, Hilda d1929 Film 2, NotNAT B, WhScrn 77, WhThe, WhoHol B
Moore, Honor NatPD[port]
Moore, Howard MorBAP
Moore, Ida 1883-1964 FilmEn, Film 2, FilmgC, ForYSC, HalFC 80, WhScrn 74, -77, WhoHol B
Moore, Irene 1890- WhoStg 1908
Moore, Jack 1926- CmpGMD, CnOxB, DancEn 78
Moore, James 1909- WhoMus 72
Moore, James 1924-1970 BluesWW[port]
Moore, James 1930- CnOxB
Moore, James, III 1940- IntWWM 77, -80
Moore, James Mavor 1919- CreCan 1
Moore, Jessie d1910 NotNAT B, PupTheA
Moore, Joanna ForYSC, WhoHol A
Moore, Joe d1926 Film 1, -2, WhScrn 77
Moore, John Ralph 1924- WhoOp 76
Moore, John Weeks 1807-1889 Baker 78, BiDAmM
Moore, Johnny Belle 1950- BluesWW[port]
Moore, Joseph OxThe
Moore, Juanita 1922- DrBlPA, FilmgC, ForYSC, HalFC 80, HolCA[port], Vers A[port], WhoHol A
Moore, Kermit 1929- AmSCAP 80
Moore, Kieron 1925- FilmAG WE, FilmEn, FilmgC, ForYSC, HalFC 80, IlWWBF[port], IntMPA 77, -75, -76, -78, -79, -80, WhoHol A
Moore, Kingman T 1919- IntMPA 77, -75, -76, -78, -79, -80
Moore, Laurens 1919- NotNAT, WhoHol A
Moore, Leslie 1894-1942 AmSCAP 66
Moore, Lillian 1915- DancEn 78
Moore, Lillian 1917-1967 CnOxB
Moore, Lucia Film 1
Moore, Maggie 1847-1926 NotNAT B, WhThe
Moore, Marcia Film 1
Moore, Marjorie FilmEn, WhoHol A
Moore, Mary d1919 Film 1, WhScrn 77
Moore, Mary d1931 WhoHol B
Moore, Mary 1861-1931 NotNAT B, WhThe
Moore, Mary 1862-1931 OxThe
Moore, Mary Carr 1873-1957 AmSCAP 66, -80, Baker 78
Moore, Mary Carter 1873-1957 ConAmC
Moore, Mary Elaine Bell 1948- IntWWM 77
Moore, Mary Tyler MotPP, NewYTET, WhoHol A
Moore, Mary Tyler 1936- FilmgC, HalFC 80, IntMPA 77, -75, -76, -78, -79, -80, JoeFr[port]
Moore, Mary Tyler 1937- FilmEn, MovMk[port]
Moore, Mary Tyler 1938- ForYSC
Moore, Matt 1888-1960 FilmEn, Film 1, -2, ForYSC, HalFC 80, MotPP, TwYS, WhScrn 74, -77, WhoHol B
Moore, Matt 1890-1960 NotNAT B
Moore, Maurine Ricks 1908- ConAmC
Moore, Mavor 1919- ConDr 73, -77, CreCan 1
Moore, McElbert 1892-1974 AmSCAP 66, -80
Moore, Melba 1945- DrBlPA, PlP&P[port], -A[port], WhoHol A
Moore, Melvin 1923- BiDAmM
Moore, Michael WhoHol A
Moore, Michael Jackson 1945- AmSCAP 80
Moore, Mickey 1917- Film 2
Moore, Mildred Film 2
Moore, Milton Aubrey 1924-1973 BiDAmM, EncJzS 70
Moore, Miltona 1902- AmSCAP 66, -80
Moore, Monette d1961 NotNAT B
Moore, Monette 1902-1962 BluesWW[port], WhoJazz 72
Moore, Monette 1912-1962 WhScrn 74, -77, WhoHol B
Moore, Oscar Fred 1916- BiDAmM, CmpEPM
Moore, Oscar Frederic 1912- WhoJazz 72
Moore, Owen 1886-1939 FilmEn, Film 1, -2, ForYSC, NotNAT B, TwYS, WhScrn 74, -77, WhoHol B
Moore, Owen 1887-1939 HalFC 80
Moore, Pat Film 1
Moore, Pat 1917- Film 2
Moore, Patti 1901-1972 WhScrn 77
Moore, Paul Marvin, Jr. 1945- IntWWM 77
Moore, Percy 1878-1945 Film 2, NotNAT B, WhScrn 77, WhoHol B
Moore, Phil 1918- AmSCAP 66, CmpEPM, DrBlPA, EncJzS 70
Moore, Phil, III 1939- BiDAmM
Moore, Philip Douglas 1918- IntWWM 77, -80, WhoMus 72
Moore, Philip Harold 1921- WhoMus 72
Moore, Philip Hubert Hamond 1940- IntWWM 77
Moore, Philip John 1943- IntWWM 77, -80
Moore, Raymond AmPS B
Moore, Raymond d1940 NotNAT B
Moore, Rex d1975 WhoHol C
Moore, Rica Owen 1929- AmSCAP 66, -80
Moore, Richard FilmgC, HalFC 80
Moore, Richard A NewYTET
Moore, Robert HalFC 80, IntMPA 77, -78, -79, -80, WhoHol A
Moore, Robert 1898?-1966 NewOrJ
Moore, Robert 1927- WhoThe 72, -77
Moore, Robert 1929- NotNAT
Moore, Robert Francis d1964 NotNAT B
Moore, Robert L, Jr. 1925- AmSCAP 80

Moore, Robert S 1907- AmSCAP 66, -80
Moore, Robert Steele 1941- ConAmC
Moore, Roger IntMPA 77, -75, -76, -78, -79, -80, MotPP, WhoHol A
Moore, Roger 1928- FilmAG WE, FilmEn, FilmgC, HalFC 80[port], IlWWBF[port], -A, MovMk[port], WhoHrs 80[port]
Moore, Roger 1930- ForYSC
Moore, Ronald Gresham 1926- IntWWM 77, -80, WhoMus 72
Moore, Russell 1913- BiDAmM
Moore, Ruth Hart d1952 WhScrn 74, -77, WhoHol B
Moore, Scott 1889-1967 WhScrn 74, -77, WhoHol B
Moore, Sidney NewOrJ
Moore, Slim 1908- WhoJazz 72
Moore, Sonia BiE&WWA, NotNAT
Moore, Stephen WhoHol A
Moore, Stephen 1937- WhoThe 72, -77
Moore, Stephen Sidney 1902- IntWWM 77
Moore, Steven Richard 1942- AmSCAP 80
Moore, Sue 1916-1966 WhScrn 77
Moore, Ted 1914- CmMov, FilmEn, FilmgC, HalFC 80, WorEFlm
Moore, Terrence Film 2
Moore, Terry MotPP
Moore, Terry 1929- FilmEn, FilmgC, ForYSC, HalFC 80, WhoHol A, WhoHrs 80
Moore, Terry 1932- IntMPA 77, -75, -76, -78, -79, -80
Moore, Thelma AmSCAP 80
Moore, Thomas NewGrD 80, OxMus
Moore, Thomas 1779-1852 Baker 78, NewEOp 71, NewGrD 80, OxMus
Moore, Thomas 1933- CpmDNM 80, ConAmC
Moore, Thomas F 1911- AmSCAP 66, -80
Moore, Thomas W IntMPA 77, -75, -76, -78, -79, -80, NewYTET
Moore, Tim 1888-1958 BlksB&W, -C, BlksBF, DrBlPA, JoeFr
Moore, Timothy 1922- IntWWM 77, -80, WhoMus 72
Moore, Timothy Harrison AmSCAP 80
Moore, Tom d1955 MotPP, NotNAT B, WhoHol B
Moore, Tom 1883-1955 HalFC 80
Moore, Tom 1884-1955 Film 1, -2
Moore, Tom 1885-1955 FilmEn, ForYSC, MovMk[port], TwYS, WhScrn 74, -77
Moore, Undine Smith 1904- DrBlPA
Moore, Undine Smith 1905- BlkCS[port]
Moore, Victor 1876-1962 AmPS B, CmpEPM, EncMT, FilmEn, Film 1, -2, FilmgC, ForYSC, HalFC 80, JoeFr[port], MotPP, MovMk[port], NotNAT B, PlP&P, TwYS, Vers A[port], WhScrn 74, -77, WhThe, WhoHol B, WhoStg 1908
Moore, Vin 1878-1949 Film 1, -2, WhScrn 74, -77, WhoHol B
Moore, W Scott Film 1
Moore, Warren Thomas 1938- AmSCAP 80
Moore, William, Jr. 1916- BiDAmM
Moore, William, Jr. 1917- EncJzS 70
Moore, Willie C 1913-1971 BluesWW[port]
Moore, Wilma AmSCAP 80
Moorefield, Arthur A 1928- ConAmC
Moorehead, Agnes 1906-1974 BiDFilm, -81, BiE&WWA, CmMov, FilmEn, FilmgC, ForYSC, HalFC 80, MGM[port], MotPP, MovMk[port], NotNAT B, Vers A[port], WhScrn 77, WhoHol B, WhoHrs 80, WhoThe 72, -77, WorEFlm
Moorehead, Agnes 1918-1974 OxFilm
Moorehead, Consuela Lee 1926- BlkWAB
Moorehead, John 1760?-1804 NewGrD 80
Moorehouse, Bert Film 2
Moorehouse, Marie Film 2
Moorey, Stefa 1934-1972 WhScrn 77
Moorhead, Jean d1953 NotNAT B
Moorhead, John 1760?-1804 NewGrD 80
Moorhead, Natalie 1905- Film 2, ForYSC, ThFT[port]
Moorhouse, Bert 1895-1954 WhScrn 74, -77, WhoHol B
Moorhouse, Maryrose WhoMus 72
Moorland, Carol 1907- IntWWM 77, -80
Moorley, Thomas George 1906- WhoMus 72
Moors NewGrD 80
Moorse, George 1936- WorEFlm[port]
Moortgat, Alfons J I 1881- WhoMus 72
Moos, Paul 1863-1952 Baker 78, NewGrD 80
Moose John BluesWW[port]
Mooser, Aloys 1770-1839 Baker 78, NewGrD 80
Mooser, R-Aloys 1876-1969 Baker 78, NewGrD 80
Mootz, William Hoyt 1924- ConAmTC
Mopper, Irving 1914- AmSCAP 66, -80, ConAmC
Mora, Helene AmPS B
Mora, Vera 1908- IntWWM 77, -80
Moraes Pedroso, Manuel De NewGrD 80
Morago, Estevao Lopes 1575?-1630? NewGrD 80
Morahan, Christopher 1929- WhoThe 72, -77
Morahan, Christopher 1930?- FilmgC, HalFC 80
Moral, Pablo Del NewGrD 80
Morales, Abram 1939- IntWWM 80
Morales, Aida BlkAmP
Morales, Cristobal De 1500?-1553 Baker 78, BnBkM 80, GrComp[port], MusMk, NewGrD 80, OxMus
Morales, Esy Ishmael 1917-1950 WhScrn 74, WhoHol B
Morales, Hilda 1948- CnOxB
Morales, Ishmael Esy 1917-1950 WhScrn 77
Morales, Melesio 1838-1908 Baker 78, NewGrD 80
Morales, Noro 1911-1964 AmSCAP 66, -80, BiDAmM
Morales, Noro 1913-1964 NotNAT B
Morales, Olallo Juan Magnus 1874-1957 Baker 78, NewGrD 80, OxMus
Morales, Pedro Garcia 1879-1938 NewGrD 80, OxMus
Morali, Jacques ConMuA 80B
Moralt NewGrD 80
Moralt, Adam 1741?-1811 NewGrD 80
Moralt, Clementine 1797-1845 NewGrD 80
Moralt, Georg 1781-1818 Baker 78
Moralt, Johann Baptist 1777-1825 Baker 78, NewGrD 80
Moralt, Johann Wilhelm 1774-1842? NewGrD 80
Moralt, Joseph 1775-1855 Baker 78, NewGrD 80
Moralt, Peter 1814-1866? NewGrD 80
Moralt, Philipp 1780-1830 Baker 78
Moralt, Rudolf 1902-1958 NewGrD 80
Moralt, Wilhelm 1815-1874 NewGrD 80
Moran, Baby Film 2
Moran, Barber 1920- AmSCAP 66
Moran, Billy Film 1
Moran, Dolores 1926- ForYSC, IntMPA 77, -75, -76, -78, -79, -80, MotPP, WhoHol A
Moran, Edward P 1871-1956 AmSCAP 66, -80
Moran, Erin WhoHol A
Moran, Frank 1887-1967 WhScrn 77
Moran, George 1881-1949 NotNAT B
Moran, George 1882-1949 Film 2, WhScrn 74, -77, WhoHol B
Moran, Gerald 1926- IntWWM 77, -80
Moran, Gorgeous Gussie 1924- What 2[port]
Moran, Jackie 1925- ForYSC
Moran, Jaime AmSCAP 80
Moran, Jim 1909- BiE&WWA, NotNAT
Moran, Lee d1961 NotNAT B, WhoHol B
Moran, Lee 1888-1961 FilmEn, ForYSC
Moran, Lee 1889-1961 TwYS
Moran, Lee 1890-1961 WhScrn 74, -77
Moran, Lee 1899-1960 Film 1, -2
Moran, Lois 1907- PlP&P[port], ThFT[port], WhThe, WhoHol A
Moran, Lois 1908- FilmEn, ForYSC
Moran, Lois 1909- Film 2, TwYS
Moran, Mae BluesWW[port]
Moran, Manolo 1904-1967 WhScrn 74, -77
Moran, Pat 1901-1965 WhScrn 74, -77, WhoHol B
Moran, Patsy 1905-1968 NotNAT B, WhScrn 74, -77, WhoHol B
Moran, Peggy 1918- FilmEn, FilmgC, ForYSC, HalFC 80, WhoHol A
Moran, Percy d1958 IlWWBF
Moran, Percy 1886-1952 Film 1, -2
Moran, Peter K d1831 BiDAmM
Moran, Polly d1952 MotPP, WhoHol B
Moran, Polly 1883-1952 Funs[port], WhScrn 74, -77
Moran, Polly 1884-1952 FilmEn, FilmgC, ForYSC, HalFC 80, MovMk, ThFT[port], TwYS
Moran, Polly 1885-1952 Film 1, -2, NotNAT B
Moran, Polly 1886-1952 Vers A[port]
Moran, Priscilla Film 2
Moran, Robert Leonard 1937- Baker 78, ConAmC, DcCM, NewGrD 80
Moran, William Film 2
Moran And Mack JoeFr
Moran-Olden, Fanny 1855-1905 Baker 78
Morand, Edward Raymond 1938- AmSCAP 80
Morand, Eugene 1855-1930 NotNAT B, WhThe
Morand, Herb 1905-1952 NewOrJ[port], WhoJazz 72
Morand, Marcellus Raymond 1860-1922 NotNAT B, WhThe
Morand, Morris 1903?- NewOrJ SUP[port]
Morante, Joseph 1853-1940 WhScrn 74, -77
Morante, Milburn d1964 WhoHol B
Morante, Milburn 1887-1964 FilmEn, WhScrn 77
Morante, Milburn 1888-1964 Film 2, ForYSC, TwYS
Morari, Antonio d1597 NewGrD 80
Morata, Gines De NewGrD 80
Morata, Juan Jose Joachin 1769-1840 NewGrD 80
Moratelli, Sebastiano 1640-1706 NewGrD 80
Moratin OxThe
Moratin, Leandro Fernandez De 1760-1828 McGEWD[port]
Moratin, Nicolas Fernandez De 1737-1780 McGEWD[port]
Moratoria, Orosman 1859-1898 OxThe
Moravec, Ivan 1930- Baker 78, NewGrD 80
Moravia, Jerome Of NewGrD 80
Moravia, Alberto 1907- CnMD, FilmEn, WomWMM
Moraweck, Lucien 1901-1973 ConAmC
Morawetz, Oskar 1917- Baker 78, CreCan 1, DcCM, NewGrD 80
Morawski, Jerzy 1932- IntWWM 77, -80
Morawski-Dabrowa, Eugeniusz 1876-1948 NewGrD 80
Morax, Rene 1873-1963 ModWD
Mordant, Edwin 1868-1942 Film 1, NotNAT B, WhScrn 74, -77, WhoHol B
Mordant, Grace 1872-1952 WhScrn 74, -77, WhoHol B
Mordecai, Benjamin 1944- NotNAT
Mordente, Tony 1935- DancEn 78
Mordkin, Mikhail 1881-1944 DancEn 78[port]
Mordkin, Mikhail Mikhailovich 1880-1944 CnOxB, NotNAT B
Mordvinov, Nikolai Dmitrievich 1901-1966 OxThe
More, Hannah d1833 NotNAT B, OxMus
More, Kenneth 1914- CmMov, CnThe, FilmAG WE[port], FilmEn, FilmgC, ForYSC, HalFC 80, IlWWBF[port], -A, IntMPA 77, -75, -76, -78, -79, -80, WhoHol A, WhoThe 72, -77
More, Mal BlkAmP
More, Unity 1894- WhThe
More, William 1490?-1565 NewGrD 80
More O'Ferrall, George 1906?- FilmEn, FilmgC, HalFC 80, IlWWBF
Moreau PupTheA
Moreau, Angele d1897 NotNAT B
Moreau, Emile 1852- WhThe
Moreau, Felix 1922- IntWWM 77, -80
Moreau, Henri 1728?-1803 NewGrD 80
Moreau, Jacob Francois 1684?-1751 NewGrD 80
Moreau, Jacobus Franciscus 1684?-1751 NewGrD 80
Moreau, Jacqueline 1926- CnOxB, DancEn 78
Moreau, Jean 1928- IntMPA 77, -75, -76, -78
Moreau, Jean-Baptiste 1656-1733 Baker 78, MusMk, NewGrD 80, OxMus
Moreau, Jeanne 1928- BiDFilm, -81, FilmAG WE[port], FilmEn, FilmgC, ForYSC, HalFC 80, IntMPA 79, -80, MotPP, MovMk[port], OxFilm,

WhoHol A, WorEFlm[port]
Moreau, Leon 1870-1946 *Baker 78*
Moreau, Simon *NewGrD 80*
Moreau LeJeune 1741-1814 *OxThe*
Morecambe, Eric 1926- *FilmgC, HalFC 80, IlWWBF A[port]*
Morecock, Robert 1510?-1582 *NewGrD 80*
Morehead, Albert Hodges 1909-1966 *AmSCAP 66*
Morehead, James Turner 1906- *AmSCAP 66, -80*
Morehen, John Manley 1941- *IntWWM 77, WhoMus 72*
Morehouse, Chauncey 1902- *CmpEPM, WhoJazz 72*
Morehouse, Henry Lyman 1834-1917 *BiDAmM*
Morehouse, Ward 1898-1966 *NotNAT A, OxThe*
Morehouse, Ward 1899-1966 *NotNAT B, WhThe*
Morehouse, Ward 1906- *BiE&WWA*
Moreira, Antonio 1750?-1819 *Baker 78*
Moreira, Antonio Leal 1758-1819 *NewGrD 80*
Moreira, Maura *WhoOp 76*
Moreira DaRocha, Persio 1934- *IntWWM 77, -80*
Moreira Sa E Costa, Leonilde *NewGrD 80*
Morel *NewGrD 80*
Morel, Auguste-Francois 1809-1881 *Baker 78*
Morel, Clemens *NewGrD 80*
Morel, Clement *NewGrD 80*
Morel, Francois 1926- *Baker 78, CreCan 2, DcCM, NewGrD 80*
Morel, Genevieve *WhoHol A*
Morel, Jacques *NewGrD 80*
Morel, Jean 1903-1975 *Baker 78, NewGrD 80*
Morel, Jorge *AmSCAP 80*
Morel, Octave *NewGrD 80*
Morel, Paul 1946- *IntWWM 77*
Moreland, Barry 1943- *CnOxB*
Moreland, Mantan *ForYSC, JoeFr*
Moreland, Mantan d1973 *WhoHol B*
Moreland, Mantan 1901-1973 *BlksB&W[port], -C, BlksBF, HolCA[port], MovMk[port]*
Moreland, Mantan 1902-1973 *DrBlPA, FilmEn, FilmgC, HalFC 80, What 3[port], WhScrn 77*
Moreland, Margaret Elizabeth *WhoOp 76*
Morell, Andre 1909- *FilmgC, ForYSC, IntMPA 77, -75, -76, -78, -79, WhoHol A, WhoThe 72, -77*
Morell, Andre 1909-1978 *FilmEn*
Morell, Andre 1909-1979 *HalFC 80*
Morell, Barry 1927- *WhoMus 72, WhoOp 76*
Morell, John 1946- *EncJzS 70*
Morell, Marty 1944- *EncJzS 70*
Morell, Peter *MorBAP*
Morell, Sybil *Film 2*
Morell, Thomas 1703-1784 *NewGrD 80*
Morellati, Paolo 1740-1807 *NewGrD 80*
Morelle, Maureen 1934- *IntWWM 77, -80, WhoOp 76*
Morelli, Alamanno 1812-1893 *EncWT*
Morelli, Carlo 1897-1970 *Baker 78*
Morelli, Cesare *NewGrD 80*
Morelli, Giacomo 1745-1819 *Baker 78*
Morelli, Giuseppe 1907- *Baker 78*
Morelli, Maddalena *OxMus*
Morelli, Rina 1908-1976 *EncWT, Ent*
Morello, Joe 1928- *CmpEPM, EncJzS 70*
Morello, Joseph A 1928- *BiDAmM, EncJzS 70*
Morelot, Stephen 1820-1899 *Baker 78*
Morena, Berta 1878-1952 *Baker 78, CmOp, NewGrD 80*
Morena, Erna *Film 2*
Morency, Robert 1932-1937 *WhScrn 74, -77, WhoHol B*
Moreno, Antonio d1967 *MotPP, WhoHol B*
Moreno, Antonio 1886-1967 *Film 1, -2, FilmgC, HalFC 80*
Moreno, Antonio 1887-1967 *FilmEn, ForYSC, TwYS*
Moreno, Antonio 1888-1967 *WhScrn 74, -77*
Moreno, Antonio 1889-1967 *MovMk*
Moreno, Blanca 1931- *DancEn 78*
Moreno, Dario 1921-1968 *WhScrn 74, -77, WhoHol B*
Moreno, John Joseph 1917- *AmSCAP 80*
Moreno, Juan *NewGrD 80*
Moreno, Marcos *AmSCAP 80*
Moreno, Marguerite 1871-1948 *Film 2, NotNAT B, WhScrn 74, -77*
Moreno, Miguel Nava *PupTheA*
Moreno, Paco 1886-1941 *WhScrn 74, -77, WhoHol B*
Moreno, Rita 1931- *FilmEn, FilmgC, ForYSC, HalFC 80, IntMPA 77, -75, -76, -78, -79, -80, MotPP, MovMk, NotNAT, WhoHol A, WhoThe 77*
Moreno, Rosita *WhoHol A*
Moreno, Sara 1928- *IntWWM 77, -80*
Moreno, Segundo Luis 1882-1972 *Baker 78, NewGrD 80*
Moreno, Thomas 1895-1938 *WhScrn 74, -77*
Moreno, Victor 1928- *DancEn 78*
Moreno Gans, Jose 1897- *NewGrD 80*
Moreno Polo, Juan *NewGrD 80*
Moreno Torroba, Federico 1891- *NewGrD 80*
Moreno Y Polo, Juan *NewGrD 80*
Morera, Alberto *PupTheA*
Morera, Enric 1865-1942 *NewGrD 80*
Morera, Enrique 1865-1942 *Baker 78, NewGrD 80*
Morera, Francisco 1731-1793 *NewGrD 80*
Mores, Renaat 1909- *IntWWM 77, -80*
Moreschi, Alessandro 1858-1922 *Baker 78, NewGrD 80*
Moresco, Carlo 1905- *WhoOp 76*
Moret, Costante 1931- *WhoOp 76*
Moret, George 1870?-1924 *NewOrJ*
Moret, Neil 1878-1943 *AmSCAP 66, CmpEPM*
Moret, Norbert Eloi 1921- *IntWWM 77, -80*
Moreto Y Cabana, Agustin 1618-1669 *Ent, McGEWD[port], OxThe*
Moreto Y Cabana, Augustin 1618-1669 *EncWT*
Moreton, Ursula 1903-1973 *CnOxB, DancEn 78, WhThe*
Moretti, Eleanor *WhoStg 1908*
Moretti, Marcello 1910-1961 *EncWT*
Moretto, Nelly 1925- *IntWWM 77, -80*
Moretus, Jean 1543-1610 *NewGrD 80*
Morey, Edward *IntMPA 77, -75, -76*
Morey, Harry T d1936 *MotPP, WhoHol B*
Morey, Harry T 1873-1936 *WhScrn 74, -77*
Morey, Harry T 1879-1936 *Film 1, -2, TwYS*
Morey, Henry A 1848-1929 *WhScrn 74, -77, WhoHol B*
Morey, Larry 1905-1971 *AmSCAP 66, -80*
Morfogen, George *WhoHol A*
Morgan, Agnes 1901- *BiE&WWA, NotNAT*
Morgan, Al 1908-1974 *BiDAmM, CmpEPM, NewOrJ[port], WhoJazz 72*
Morgan, Al 1920- *BiE&WWA, NotNAT*
Morgan, Alan Richard 1925- *WhoMus 72*
Morgan, Andre 1953- *IntMPA 79, -80*
Morgan, Andrew 1903- *NewOrJ[port]*
Morgan, Arthur Derek Moore 1915- *WhoMus 72*
Morgan, Billie 1922- *BiDAmM*
Morgan, Bruce *AmSCAP 80*
Morgan, Carey 1885-1960 *AmSCAP 66, -80*
Morgan, Carole Montgomery 1939- *IntWWM 77, -80*
Morgan, Charles Langbridge 1894-1958 *CnMD, CnThe, CroCD, EncWT, ModWD, NotNAT B, OxThe, PlP&P, WhThe*
Morgan, Charles S, Jr. d1950 *NotNAT B*
Morgan, Christopher *NewYTET*
Morgan, Clark *WhoHol A*
Morgan, Claudia d1974 *WhoHol B*
Morgan, Claudia 1911-1974 *WhScrn 77*
Morgan, Claudia 1912-1974 *BiE&WWA, ForYSC, NotNAT B, WhThe, WhoThe 72*
Morgan, Dan d1975 *WhScrn 77, WhoHol A, -C*
Morgan, Daniel William 1947- *AmSCAP 80*
Morgan, David 1933- *WhoMus 72*
Morgan, David 1942- *AmSCAP 66, -80*
Morgan, David Sydney 1932- *IntWWM 77, -80, WhoMus 72*
Morgan, Dennis *MotPP*
Morgan, Dennis 1910- *CmpEPM, FilmEn, FilmgC, ForYSC, HalFC 80, MovMk[port], What 2[port], WhoHol A*
Morgan, Dennis 1920- *IntMPA 77, -75, -76, -78, -79, -80*
Morgan, Diana 1910- *WhoThe 72, -77, WomWMM*
Morgan, Dorinda 1909- *AmSCAP 66, -80*
Morgan, Edward P *NewYTET*
Morgan, Ernie 1945- *ConAmC*
Morgan, Frank 1890-1949 *EncMT, FilmEn, Film 1, -2, FilmgC, ForYSC, HalFC 80, HolCA[port], MGM[port], MotPP, MovMk[port], NotNAT B, PlP&P[port], TwYS, WhScrn 74, -77, WhThe, WhoHol B, WhoHrs 80[port]*
Morgan, Freddy 1910- *AmSCAP 66, -80*
Morgan, Gareth 1940- *WhoThe 72, -77*
Morgan, Gene 1892-1940 *WhScrn 74, -77*
Morgan, Gene 1892-1950 *WhoHol B*
Morgan, Genie Boinest 1897- *IntWWM 77, -80*
Morgan, Geoffrey David 1945- *IntWWM 77, -80*
Morgan, George *Film 2*
Morgan, George 1925-1975 *CounME 74, EncFCWM 69, IlEncCM*
Morgan, George Thomas 1924- *BiDAmM*
Morgan, George Washbourne 1822-1892 *BiDAmM*
Morgan, H A *Film 2*
Morgan, Harold Lansford 1934- *BiDAmM*
Morgan, Harry 1915- *FilmEn, FilmgC, HalFC 80, IntMPA 77, -75, -76, -78, -79, -80, MotPP, WhoHol A*
Morgan, Haydn 1898- *AmSCAP 66, -80, ConAmC*
Morgan, Helen 1900-1941 *AmPS B, BiDAmM, CmpEPM, EncMT, FamA&A[port], FilmEn, Film 2, FilmgC, ForYSC, HalFC 80[port], NotNAT A, -B, PlP&P, ThFT[port], WhScrn 74, -77, WhThe, WhoHol B*
Morgan, Helen 1922-1955 *WhScrn 77*
Morgan, Henry *ConAmC, FilmEn, WhoHol A*
Morgan, Henry 1915- *ForYSC, HolCA[port], JoeFr*
Morgan, Horace *Film 2*
Morgan, Howard 1936- *EncJzS 70*
Morgan, Howard 1945- *WhoMus 72*
Morgan, Inga Borgstrom *IntWWM 77*
Morgan, Isaiah 1897-1966 *NewOrJ*
Morgan, J C 1910- *AmSCAP 66*
Morgan, Jackie *Film 2*
Morgan, Jane *AmPS A, RkOn*
Morgan, Jane 1881-1972 *WhScrn 77, WhoHol B*
Morgan, Jane 1920- *BiDAmM*
Morgan, Jaye P *WhoHol A*
Morgan, Jaye P 1929- *BiDAmM*
Morgan, Jaye P 1932- *RkOn[port]*
Morgan, Jeanne *Film 2*
Morgan, Jesse Hilray, Jr. 1947- *AmSCAP 80*
Morgan, Jessica Emma 1929- *AmSCAP 66, -80*
Morgan, Joan d1962 *NotNAT B, WhoHol B*
Morgan, Joan 1905- *Film 1, -2, IlWWBF, WhoThe 72, -77*
Morgan, John Black 1938- *IntWWM 77*
Morgan, John Paul 1841-1879 *BiDAmM*
Morgan, Joseph 1901- *WhoMus 72*
Morgan, Justin 1747-1798 *BiDAmM, NewGrD 80*
Morgan, Kewpie *Film 2*
Morgan, Lee 1902-1967 *Film 2, WhScrn 77, WhoHol B*
Morgan, Lee 1938-1972 *BiDAmM, EncJzS 70, IlEncJ*
Morgan, Leon *Film 2*
Morgan, Marabel 1937- *AmSCAP 80*
Morgan, Margaret *Film 2*
Morgan, Margo 1897-1962 *WhScrn 74, -77, WhoHol B*
Morgan, Marilyn *FilmEn, WhoHol A*
Morgan, Marion 1924- *CmpEPM*
Morgan, Maud 1860-1941 *Baker 78*
Morgan, McKayla K 1927- *AmSCAP 66*
Morgan, Merlin d1924 *NotNAT B*
Morgan, Michele 1920- *BiDFilm, -81, FilmAG WE, FilmEn, FilmgC, ForYSC, HalFC 80, IntMPA 77, -75, -76, -78, -79, -80, MotPP, MovMk[port], OxFilm, WhoHol A, WorEFlm*
Morgan, Murray 1916- *ConAmTC*
Morgan, Paul d1939 *WhScrn 74, -77*
Morgan, Paula 1935- *IntWWM 80*

Morgan, Phalba *Film 2*
Morgan, Ralph d1956 *MotPP, WhoHol B*
Morgan, Ralph 1882-1956 *FilmEn, Film 2, FilmgC, ForYSC, HalFC 80, MovMk, WhoHrs 80*
Morgan, Ralph 1883-1956 *HolCA[port], NotNAT B, Vers A[port], WhScrn 74, -77*
Morgan, Ralph 1888-1956 *WhThe*
Morgan, Ray d1975 *WhScrn 77, WhoHol C*
Morgan, Read *WhoHol A*
Morgan, Richard Paul 1945- *IntWWM 77, -80*
Morgan, Robert B 1941- *AmSCAP 80, ConAmC*
Morgan, Robert Duke 1896- *AmSCAP 66, -80*
Morgan, Robert P 1934- *ConAmC, DcCM, IntWWM 77, -80*
Morgan, Robin *WhoHol A*
Morgan, Roger 1938- *WhoThe 77*
Morgan, Russ 1904-1969 *AmPS A, -B, AmSCAP 66, -80, Baker 78, BgBands 74[port], BiDAmM, CmpEPM, WhScrn 74, -77, WhoHol B, WhoJazz 72*
Morgan, Sam 1895-1936 *NewOrJ*
Morgan, Sidney d1931 *Film 2, WhoHol B*
Morgan, Sidney 1873-1946 *FilmEn, IlWWBF*
Morgan, Sonny 1936- *EncJzS 70*
Morgan, Sydney 1875?-1931 *WhScrn 77*
Morgan, Sydney 1885-1931 *NotNAT B, WhThe*
Morgan, Terence 1921- *FilmEn, FilmgC, ForYSC, HalFC 80, IlWWBF[port], IntMPA 77, -75, -76, -78, -79, -80, WhoHol A*
Morgan, Thelma *Film 2*
Morgan, Thomas *NewGrD 80*
Morgan, Thomas R 1936- *AmSCAP 66, -80*
Morgan, Tommy 1932- *AmSCAP 80, IntWWM 77*
Morgan, Viola Esther Wyatt 1908- *AmSCAP 66*
Morgan, Wallace *Film 2*
Morgan, William *Film 2*
Morgan, William d1944 *NotNAT B*
Morganfield, McKinley 1915- *BluesWW[port], NewGrD 80*
Morganthau, Rita Wallach 1880-1964 *BiE&WWA*
Morgenstern, Dan Michael 1929- *IntWWM 77, -80*
Morgenstern, Frank 1928- *IntWWM 77, -80*
Morgenstern, Jay *ConMuA 80B*
Morgenstern, Sam *ConAmC*
Morgenstern, Sheldon Jon 1939- *WhoMus 72*
Morgenthau, Rita Wallach 1880-1964 *NotNAT B*
Morgio, George A 1942- *AmSCAP 80*
Morhange *OxMus*
Morhange, Marcel *Film 1*
Morhange, Valentin *NewGrD 80*
Morhard, Peter d1685 *NewGrD 80*
Mori *NewGrD 80*
Mori, Angelo 1934- *WhoOp 76*
Mori, Francis 1820-1873 *NewGrD 80*
Mori, Frank 1820-1873 *Baker 78, NewGrD 80*
Mori, Iwao 1899- *IntMPA 77, -75, -76, -78, -79, -80*
Mori, Masayuki 1911- *FilmEn, WorEFlm*
Mori, Nicholas 1822-1890? *NewGrD 80*
Mori, Nicolas 1796-1839 *Baker 78, NewGrD 80*
Mori, Toshia *WhoHol A*
Mori DaViadana, Jacobi *NewGrD 80*
Moriana, Rocco Anthony 1927- *AmSCAP 80*
Moriani, Napoleone 1808-1878 *NewGrD 80*
Moriarty, Joanne 1939-1964 *WhScrn 74, -77, WhoHol B*
Moriarty, Marcus d1916 *WhScrn 77*
Moriarty, Michael *PlP&P A[port], WhoHol A*
Moriarty, Michael 1941- *FilmEn, HalFC 80, MovMk, WhoThe 77*
Moriarty, Michael 1942- *IntMPA 77, -75, -76, -78, -79, -80, NotNAT*
Morice, Gerald *DcPup*
Moriconi, Valeria 1931- *EncWT*
Moricz, Zsigmond 1879-1942 *OxThe*
Morigi, Angelo 1725-1801 *NewGrD 80*
Morike, Eduard 1804-1875 *NewGrD 80*
Morillo, Roberto Garcia 1911- *Baker 78, DancEn 78*
Morin, Alberto 1912- *Vers A[port], WhoHol A*
Morin, Charles *NewGrD 80*
Morin, Edgar 1921- *OxFilm*
Morin, Etienne *McGEWD[port]*
Morin, Eugene 1880?-1950? *NewOrJ*
Morin, Gosta 1900- *Baker 78*
Morin, Jean-Baptiste 1677-1754 *NewGrD 80*
Morin, Robert B *IntMPA 79, -80*
Morini, Elettra 1937- *CnOxB, DancEn 78*
Morini, Erica 1904- *Baker 78, MusSN[port], NewGrD 80*
Morini, Erica 1908?- *BnBkM 80*
Morini, Erica 1910- *WhoMus 72*
Morino, Egidius De *NewGrD 80*
Morisette, Johnnie *RkOn*
Morishita, Yoko 1948- *CnOxB*
Morison, Bradley G 1924- *BiE&WWA*
Morison, Duncan Matheson 1907- *WhoMus 72*
Morison, Elsie 1924- *CmOp, NewGrD 80, WhoMus 72*
Morison, Patricia *MotPP*
Morison, Patricia 1914- *FilmEn, HolP 40[port], ThFT[port]*
Morison, Patricia 1915- *BiE&WWA, CmpEPM, EncMT, FilmgC, ForYSC, HalFC 80, NotNAT, WhThe, WhoHol A, WhoThe 72*
Morissey, Betty *Film 2*
Moritt, Fred G 1905- *AmSCAP 66, -80*
Moritz, Landgrave Of Hessen-Kassel 1572-1632 *NewGrD 80*
Moritz, Carl Philipp 1757-1793 *OxMus*
Moritz, Edvard 1891-1974 *AmSCAP 66, -80, ConAmC, WhoMus 72*
Moritz, Max *Film 2*
Moritz, Milton I 1933- *IntMPA 77, -75, -76, -78, -79, -80*
Moriya, Shizu 1911-1961 *WhScrn 74, -77*
Mork, John Frithjof 1927- *IntWWM 80*
Morlacchi, Francesco 1784-1841 *Baker 78, NewGrD 80*
Morlacchi, Giuseppina 1843-1886 *CnOxB, DancEn 78*
Morlay, Gaby 1890-1964 *NotNAT B*
Morlay, Gaby 1896-1964 *WhThe*
Morlay, Gaby 1897-1964 *FilmEn, Film 1, -2, FilmgC, HalFC 80, OxFilm, WhScrn 74, -77, WhoHol B*
Morlaye, Guillaume 1510?-1558? *NewGrD 80*
Morley, Professor *PupTheA*
Morley, Christopher *CnThe, WhoThe 72, -77*
Morley, Christopher d1957 *NotNAT B*
Morley, Harry William d1953 *NotNAT B*
Morley, Henry 1822-1894 *DcPup, NotNAT B, OxThe*
Morley, John Edward 1936- *IntWWM 77*
Morley, Judith *NatPD[port]*
Morley, Karen 1905- *FilmEn, Film 2, FilmgC, ForYSC, HalFC 80, IntMPA 77, -75, -76, -78, -79, -80, MGM[port], MotPP, MovMk, ThFT[port], WhoHol A*
Morley, Kay *WhoHol A*
Morley, Malcolm 1890-1966 *WhThe*
Morley, Reginald *WhoMus 72*
Morley, Robert 1908- *BiE&WWA, CnThe, EncWT, Ent, FilmAG WE, FilmEn, FilmgC, ForYSC, HalFC 80, IlWWBF[port], -A, IntMPA 77, -75, -76, -78, -79, -80, MotPP, MovMk[port], NotNAT, -A, OxFilm, OxThe, PlP&P, Vers A[port], WhoHol A, WhoHrs 80, WhoThe 72, -77*
Morley, Robert James 1892-1952 *WhScrn 74, -77*
Morley, Ruth *BiE&WWA, NotNAT*
Morley, Thomas 1557-1602 *Baker 78, DcCom 77, GrComp, NewGrD 80*
Morley, Thomas 1557-1603 *BnBkM 80, CmpBCM, DcCom&M 79, MusMk, OxMus*
Morley, Victor d1953 *NotNAT B*
Morley, William d1721 *NewGrD 80*
Morley-Pegge, Reginald 1890-1972 *NewGrD 80*
Morlhon, Camille De d1945? *DcFM*
Mormon Tabernacle Choir *AmPS A*
Mornable, Anthoine 1515?- *NewGrD 80*
Mornable, Antoine 1515?- *NewGrD 80*
Morne, Maryland 1900-1935 *WhScrn 74, -77*
Morner, Carl-Gabriel Stellan 1915-1977 *NewGrD 80*
Morner, Stanley *FilmEn*
Morner, Stellan 1915- *IntWWM 77, -80*
Morningstar, Carter d1964 *NotNAT B*
Mornington, Earl Of 1735-1781 *OxMus*
Mornington, Garret Wesley, Earl Of 1735-1781 *NewGrD 80*
Mornington, Garrett C Wellesley, Earl Of 1735-1781 *Baker 78*
Moro *AmSCAP 80*
Moro, Il *NewGrD 80*
Moro, Giacomo *NewGrD 80*
Moro DaViadana, Giacomo *NewGrD 80*
Moroda, Derra De *CnOxB*
Moroder, Giorgio *ConMuA 80B*
Moroi, Makoto 1930- *Baker 78, DcCM, NewGrD 80*
Moroi, Saburo 1903-1977 *Baker 78, DcCM, NewGrD 80*
Moroney, Davitt 1950- *IntWWM 80*
Moroney, E J *WhoHol A*
Moroney, Edward Francis Pius 1949- *IntWWM 77, -80*
Moroney, Mary Emmeline 1942- *IntWWM 80*
Morosco, Oliver 1875-1945 *NotNAT A*
Morosco, Oliver 1876-1945 *NotNAT B, WhThe*
Morosco, Walter *Film 2*
Morosova, Olga *DancEn 78*
Moross, Jerome 1913- *AmSCAP 66, -80, Baker 78, BiDAmM, BiE&WWA, CmMov, ConAmC, DancEn 78, DcCM, EncMT, FilmgC, HalFC 80, NewGrD 80, NotNAT, WorEFlm*
Morozov, Boris Mikhailovich 1931- *WhoOp 76*
Morozov, Mikhail Nikolaevich 1897-1952 *OxThe*
Morozov, Sara *PlP&P*
Morpain *NewGrD 80*
Morphis, Robert C 1948- *AmSCAP 80*
Morphy, Guillermo, Conde De 1836-1899 *Baker 78*
Morphy, Lewis H 1904-1958 *WhScrn 74, -77*
Morpurgo, Nelly 1940- *WhoOp 76*
Morr, Skip 1912-1962 *BiDAmM*
Morra, Egidio 1906- *AmSCAP 66, -80*
Morra, Irene *WomWMM*
Morreau, Annette Scawen 1946- *IntWWM 80*
Morrell, George 1873-1955 *WhScrn 74, -77, WhoHol B*
Morrell, H H d1916 *NotNAT B*
Morrell, Margaret Evelyn *WhoMus 72*
Morrell, Valerie *WhoHol A*
Morrer, Carole *WomWMM B*
Morrice, James Wilson 1865-1924 *CreCan 2*
Morrice, Norman 1931- *CnOxB, DancEn 78*
Morricone, Ennio 1928- *FilmEn, FilmgC, HalFC 80, IntMPA 80, OxFilm*
Morrie, Margaret *Film 2*
Morrill, Dexter G 1938- *ConAmC*
Morrill, Priscilla 1927- *BiE&WWA, NotNAT*
Morris 1903-1971 *WhScrn 74, -77*
Morris, Adrian 1903-1940 *ForYSC, WhoHol B*
Morris, Adrian 1903-1941 *WhScrn 74, -77*
Morris, Aldyth *NatPD[port]*
Morris, Barboura 1932-1975 *WhScrn 77, WhoHol C, WhoHrs 80[port]*
Morris, Bernard *AmSCAP 80*
Morris, Charles Edward 1913- *AmSCAP 66, -80*
Morris, Chester 1901-1970 *BiE&WWA, FilmEn, Film 1, -2, FilmgC, ForYSC[port], HalFC 80, HolP 30[port], MotPP, MovMk, NotNAT B, WhScrn 74, -77, WhThe, WhoHol B, WhoHrs 80[port]*
Morris, Christopher John 1922- *IntWWM 77, -80, WhoMus 72*
Morris, Clara d1925 *PlP&P, WhoHol B*
Morris, Clara 1844-1925 *NotNAT A*
Morris, Clara 1846-1925 *EncWT, NotNAT B, OxThe, WhThe*
Morris, Clara 1847-1925 *FamA&A[port]*
Morris, Clara 1897-1925 *WhScrn 74, -77*
Morris, Mrs. Cleze Gill d1963 *NotNAT B*
Morris, Corbet 1881-1951 *WhScrn 77*
Morris, Cozette Marie 1952- *AmSCAP 80*
Morris, Dave *Film 2*

Morris, Deniese d1969 *WhScrn 77*
Morris, Denise d1969 *WhoHol B*
Morris, Diana 1907-1961 *WhScrn 74, -77, WhoHol B*
Morris, Dick *Film 2*
Morris, Dorothy 1922- *WhoHol A*
Morris, Doug *ConMuA 80B*
Morris, Earl J *BlksB&W C*
Morris, Eddie 1896- *NewOrJ*
Morris, Edmund *NatPD[port]*
Morris, Edmund Montague 1871-1913 *CreCan 1*
Morris, Edward 1896- *AmSCAP 66*
Morris, Elva Agnes 1917- *AmSCAP 80*
Morris, Ernest 1915- *FilmEn, FilmgC, HalFC 80, IlWWBF*
Morris, Felix 1850-1900 *NotNAT A, -B*
Morris, Mrs. Felix d1954 *NotNAT B*
Morris, Flora *IlWWBF*
Morris, Frances *Film 2, WhoHol A*
Morris, Franklin E 1920- *ConAmC*
Morris, Gareth 1920- *NewGrD 80, WhoMus 72*
Morris, Garrett 1937- *AmSCAP 66, DrBlPA, MorBAP*
Morris, George P 1802-1864 *BiDAmM*
Morris, Gladys *Film 1*
Morris, Glenn 1911-1974 *WhScrn 77, WhoHol B, WhoHrs 80*
Morris, Gordon 1899-1940 *WhScrn 74, -77, WhoHol B*
Morris, Greg 1934- *DrBlPA, WhoHol A*
Morris, Harold 1890-1964 *AmSCAP 66, -80, Baker 78, BiDAmM, ConAmC, NewGrD 80, OxMus*
Morris, Hayward 1922-1977 *AmSCAP 80*
Morris, Howard 1919- *FilmEn, FilmgC, ForYSC, HalFC 80, IntMPA 77, -75, -76, -78, -79, -80, JoeFr, WhoHol A*
Morris, Isaac *BlkAmP*
Morris, James 1947- *WhoOp 76*
Morris, Joe 1905?-1961 *NewOrJ*
Morris, John 1926- *AmSCAP 66, -80, BiE&WWA, NotNAT*
Morris, Johnnie 1886-1969 *Film 2, WhScrn 77*
Morris, Kathleen Moir 1893- *CreCan 2*
Morris, Kirk *WhoHrs 80*
Morris, Lana 1930- *FilmgC, HalFC 80, IlWWBF[port], IntMPA 77, -75, -76, -78, -79, -80, WhoHol A*
Morris, Lee 1912-1978 *AmSCAP 80*
Morris, Lee 1916- *AmSCAP 66, BiDAmM, Film 1*
Morris, Leigh E 1934- *BiE&WWA*
Morris, Lily d1952 *NotNAT B*
Morris, Margaret 1891- *CnOxB, DancEn 78, WhThe*
Morris, Margaret 1903-1968 *Film 2, WhScrn 77, WhoHol B*
Morris, Marion 1849-1924 *BiDAmM*
Morris, Mark Bennett 1942- *AmSCAP 80*
Morris, Marlowe 1915- *BiDAmM, WhoJazz 72*
Morris, Marnee 1946- *CnOxB*
Morris, Marshall 1946- *AmSCAP 80*
Morris, Mary 1895-1970 *BiE&WWA, FilmgC, HalFC 80, NotNAT B, PlP&P, WhThe, WhoHol B*
Morris, Mary 1896-1970 *WhScrn 74, -77*
Morris, Mary 1915- *FilmgC, HalFC 80, WhoHol A, WhoThe 72, -77*
Morris, Mary Eleanor 1938- *WhoMus 72*
Morris, Mary Smith 1940- *IntWWM 77*
Morris, Maynard d1964 *NotNAT B*
Morris, McKay 1891-1955 *NotNAT B, WhThe*
Morris, Melville 1888- *AmSCAP 66, -80*
Morris, Mildred *Film 1, WhoStg 1906, -1908*
Morris, Mowbray d1911 *NotNAT B*
Morris, Nelson 1920- *IntMPA 77, -75, -76, -78, -79, -80*
Morris, Oswald 1915- *FilmEn, FilmgC, HalFC 80, IntMPA 77, -76, -78, -79, -80, WorEFlm*
Morris, Ovvarean Lamaidy Dawsey 1908- *IntWWM 77*
Morris, Owen 1759-1790 *NotNAT B, OxThe*
Morris, Mrs. Owen 1753-1826 *NotNAT B, OxThe*
Morris, Paul 1938- *IntWWM 80*
Morris, Philip 1893-1949 *WhScrn 74, -77, WhoHol B*
Morris, Phyllis 1894- *WhoHol A, WhoThe 72, -77*
Morris, R A 1925- *IntMPA 77, -75, -76, -78, -79, -80*
Morris, R O 1886-1948 *NewGrD 80*
Morris, Reggie 1886-1928 *Film 1, WhScrn 77*
Morris, Reginald Owen 1886-1948 *Baker 78, OxMus*
Morris, Richard 1861-1924 *Film 2, WhScrn 77*
Morris, Richard 1924- *BiE&WWA, IntMPA 77, -75, -76, -78, -79, -80*
Morris, Robert *AmSCAP 80, CmpGMD*
Morris, Robert 1818-1888 *BiDAmM*
Morris, Robert Daniel 1943- *ConAmC, IntWWM 77, -80*
Morris, Rusty *WhoHol A*
Morris, Seymour 1906- *IntMPA 77, -75, -76, -78, -79, -80*
Morris, Stephen M 1944- *ConAmC*
Morris, Stevland 1950- *AmSCAP 80*
Morris, Thomas 1898?- *WhoJazz 72*
Morris, Tom *Film 2*
Morris, Walter Arthur 1932- *IntWWM 77*
Morris, Wayne 1914-1959 *FilmEn, FilmgC, ForYSC, HalFC 80, HolP 30[port], MotPP, MovMk[port], NotNAT B, WhScrn 74, -77, WhoHol B*
Morris, William d1932 *NotNAT B*
Morris, William 1861-1936 *NotNAT B, WhScrn 74, -77, WhThe, WhoHol B, WhoStg 1906, -1908*
Morris, William, Jr. 1899- *BiE&WWA, IntMPA 77, -75, -76, -78, -79, -80, NotNAT*
Morris, Wyn 1929- *IntWWM 77, -80*
Morris Brothers, The *IlEncCM*
Morrish, Alfred Southcott 1906- *WhoMus 72*
Morrison, Adrienne d1940 *NotNAT B*
Morrison, Alex *AmSCAP 80*
Morrison, Angus 1902- *IntWWM 77, NewGrD 80, WhoMus 72*
Morrison, Ann *WhoHol A*
Morrison, Anna Marie 1874-1972 *WhScrn 77, WhoHol B*
Morrison, Arthur 1880-1950 *Film 1, -2, WhScrn 74, -77, WhoHol B*
Morrison, Barbara *WhoHol A*
Morrison, Bill *ConDr 73, -77B*
Morrison, Bret *WhoHol A*
Morrison, Chester A 1922-1975 *WhScrn 77, WhoHol C*
Morrison, Chick d1968 *WhScrn 77*
Morrison, Chit d1968 *WhScrn 74, WhoHol B*
Morrison, Clifford *Film 2*
Morrison, Don *ConAmTC*
Morrison, Dorothy *Film 2*
Morrison, Duke *FilmEn*
Morrison, Effie 1917-1974 *WhScrn 77*
Morrison, Ernie *Film 2, WhoHol A*
Morrison, Florence *Film 2*
Morrison, George 1891- *BiDAmM*
Morrison, George E 1860-1930 *NotNAT B, WhThe*
Morrison, George Pete 1891-1973 *WhScrn 77*
Morrison, Harold Ralph 1931- *BiDAmM, EncFCWM 69*
Morrison, Henrietta Lee d1948 *NotNAT B*
Morrison, Hobe 1904- *BiE&WWA, ConAmTC, NotNAT, WhoThe 72, -77*
Morrison, Howard Priestly 1871-1938 *NotNAT B, WhThe*
Morrison, Jack 1887-1948 *NotNAT B, WhThe, WhoHol B*
Morrison, Jack 1912- *BiE&WWA, NotNAT*
Morrison, James 1888-1974 *Film 1, -2, TwYS, WhScrn 77, WhoHol B*
Morrison, James Douglas 1943-1971 *AmSCAP 80*
Morrison, James Douglas 1944-1971 *BiDAmM*
Morrison, Jeannine Romer 1930- *IntWWM 77, -80*
Morrison, Jim 1944-1971 *ConMuA 80A[port], WhScrn 77*
Morrison, Joe 1908- *CmpEPM*
Morrison, Joseph *Film 2*
Morrison, Julia *AmSCAP 80*
Morrison, Lewis 1845-1906 *NotNAT B*
Morrison, Louis *Film 1, -2*
Morrison, Marshall Lee, III 1944- *AmSCAP 80*
Morrison, Mary 1926- *CreCan 2*
Morrison, Paul 1906- *BiE&WWA, NotNAT*
Morrison, Pete d1973 *WhoHol B*
Morrison, Peter *Film 2*
Morrison, Ray 1946- *IntWWM 77, -80*
Morrison, Robert Edwin 1942- *AmSCAP 80*
Morrison, Ronald Alexander 1934- *IntWWM 77, -80*
Morrison, Sammy *BlksB&W C*
Morrison, Shelley *WhoHol A*
Morrison, Stuart Angus 1902- *IntWWM 80*
Morrison, Sunshine Sammy *Film 2*
Morrison, Van 1945- *ConMuA 80A, IlEncR[port], RkOn 2[port]*
Morriss, Ralph Alexander 1952- *AmSCAP 80*
Morrissey, Betty d1944 *Film 2, WhScrn 74, -77, WhoHol B*
Morrissey, John F d1941 *NotNAT B*
Morrissey, John J d1925 *NotNAT B*
Morrissey, John Joseph 1906- *AmSCAP 66, -80, ConAmC*
Morrissey, Paul 1939- *FilmEn, FilmgC, HalFC 80, IntMPA 77, -75, -76, -78, -79, -80, WhoHrs 80*
Morrissey, Will 1885-1957 *NotNAT B, WhScrn 74, -77, WhoHol B*
Morrissey, Will 1887-1957 *AmSCAP 66, -80*
Morritt, Charles 1860- *WhThe*
Morritt, Charles 1861-1936 *MagIlD*
Morrongiello, Lydia Anne 1942- *IntWWM 77, -80*
Morros, Boris 1891-1963 *FilmgC, HalFC 80, NotNAT B*
Morrow, Buddy 1919- *AmSCAP 66, -80, BgBands 74, CmpEPM, WhoJazz 72*
Morrow, Charles 1942- *ConAmC*
Morrow, Don *IntMPA 77, -75, -76, -78, -79, -80*
Morrow, Doretta d1968 *AmPS B, BiE&WWA, WhThe, WhoHol B*
Morrow, Doretta 1925-1968 *HalFC 80*
Morrow, Doretta 1926-1968 *NotNAT B*
Morrow, Doretta 1927-1968 *WhScrn 74, -77*
Morrow, Doretta 1928-1968 *EncMT*
Morrow, Grace Elizabeth Kline 1909- *IntWWM 77, -80*
Morrow, Jane d1925 *WhScrn 74, -77, WhoHol B*
Morrow, Jeff 1913- *FilmEn, FilmgC, ForYSC, HalFC 80, IntMPA 77, -75, -76, -78, -79, -80, WhoHol A, WhoHrs 80[port]*
Morrow, Jo 1940- *FilmgC, ForYSC, HalFC 80, MotPP, WhoHol A, WhoHrs 80*
Morrow, Michael 1929- *NewGrD 80*
Morrow, Morna-June Cecile 1943- *IntWWM 77*
Morrow, Patricia *WhoHol A*
Morrow, Ruth Elizabeth 1945- *IntWWM 77, -80*
Morrow, Sara Sprott 1905- *ConAmTC*
Morrow, Susan 1932- *ForYSC, WhoHol A*
Morrow, Vic 1932- *FilmEn, FilmgC, ForYSC, HalFC 80, IntMPA 77, -75, -76, -78, -79, -80, MotPP, WhoHol A*
Morrow, Walter 1850-1937 *NewGrD 80, OxMus*
Mors *NewGrD 80*
Mors, Rudolf Ernst Theodor 1920- *IntWWM 77, -80*
Morse, Anna Justina 1893- *BiDAmM*
Morse, Arthur D d1971 *NewYTET*
Morse, Barry 1918- *CreCan 1*
Morse, Barry 1919- *FilmgC, HalFC 80, NotNAT, WhThe, WhoHol A*
Morse, Carlton E 1901- *What 4[port]*
Morse, Charles Henry 1853-1927 *Baker 78, BiDAmM*
Morse, Dolly *AmSCAP 80*
Morse, Ella Mae *AmPS A, WhoHol A*
Morse, Ella Mae 1924- *CmpEPM*
Morse, Ella Mae 1925- *What 4[port]*
Morse, Grace *Film 2*
Morse, Hayward *WhoHol A*
Morse, Helen *HalFC 80*
Morse, John M 1911- *BiE&WWA*
Morse, Karl *Film 2*
Morse, Lee 1900?-1954 *CmpEPM*

Morse, Lee 1904-1954 *WhScrn 74, -77, WhoHol B*
Morse, Robert 1931- *BiDAmM, BiE&WWA, EncMT, FilmEn, FilmgC, ForYSC, HalFC 80, IntMPA 77, -75, -76, -78, -79, -80, MotPP, NotNAT, WhoHol A, WhoThe 77*
Morse, Robin 1915-1958 *WhScrn 74, -77, WhoHol B*
Morse, Terry 1906- *HalFC 80, IntMPA 77, -75, -76, -78, -79, -80, WhoHrs 80*
Morse, Theodora 1890-1953 *AmSCAP 66, -80, BiDAmM*
Morse, Theodore F 1873-1924 *AmPS, AmSCAP 66, -80, BiDAmM, CmpEPM, NotNAT B, PopAmC, Sw&Ld B*
Morse, Woolson 1858-1897 *BiDAmM, NotNAT B*
Morse-Boycott, Desmond Lionel 1892- *WhoMus 72*
Morsell, Fred *WhoHol A*
Morselli, Adriano d1692? *NewGrD 80*
Morselli, Ercole Luigi 1882-1921 *McGEWD[port], ModWD*
Morsi, Ahmad Kamel *DcFM*
Morsolino, Antonio *NewGrD 80*
Morsquini, Marie 1899- *Film 2*
Morss *NewGrD 80*
Mortari, Virgilio 1902- *Baker 78, NewGrD 80, OxMus*
Mortaro, Antonio *NewGrD 80*
Mortellari, Michele 1750?-1807 *NewGrD 80*
Mortelmans, Ivo 1901- *Baker 78*
Mortelmans, Lodewijk 1868-1952 *Baker 78, NewGrD 80*
Mortensen, Finn 1922- *Baker 78, DcCM, NewGrD 80*
Mortensen, Otto Jacob Hubertz 1907- *Baker 78, IntWWM 77, -80, NewGrD 80*
Mortensen, Tage 1932- *IntWWM 77, -80*
Morthenson, Jan W 1940- *Baker 78, DcCM, NewGrD 80*
Mortier, Pierre d1711 *NewGrD 80*
Mortimer, Charles d1864 *NotNAT B*
Mortimer, Charles d1913 *NotNAT B*
Mortimer, Charles 1885-1964 *WhScrn 74, -77, WhThe, WhoHol B*
Mortimer, Dorothy d1950 *NotNAT B*
Mortimer, Ed d1944 *WhoHol B*
Mortimer, Edmund 1875-1944 *WhScrn 74, -77*
Mortimer, Edmund 1883- *TwYS A*
Mortimer, Harry 1902- *WhoMus 72*
Mortimer, Henry 1875-1952 *WhScrn 74, -77, WhoHol B*
Mortimer, James d1911 *NotNAT B*
Mortimer, John Clifford 1923- *CnMD, CnThe, ConDr 73, -77, CroCD, EncWT, Ent, FilmgC, HalFC 80, McGEWD, ModWD, REnWD[port], WhoThe 72, -77*
Mortimer, Lee d1963 *NotNAT B*
Mortlock, Charles Bernard 1888-1967 *WhThe*
Morton, Annie Margaret *WhoMus 72*
Morton, Arthur 1908- *IntMPA 77, -75, -76, -78, -79, -80*
Morton, Benny 1907- *CmpEPM, DrBlPA, EncJzS 70, IlEncJ, WhoJazz 72*
Morton, Celia Franks *CreCan 1*
Morton, Charles 1819-1904 *OxThe*
Morton, Charles 1904- *Film 2, TwYS*
Morton, Charles 1907-1966 *FilmEn, ForYSC, WhScrn 77*
Morton, Clara d1948 *NotNAT B*
Morton, Clive 1904-1975 *FilmgC, HalFC 80, WhScrn 77, WhThe, WhoHol C, WhoThe 72*
Morton, Douglas Gibb 1926- *CreCan 1*
Morton, Drew 1855-1916 *WhScrn 77*
Morton, Edna *BlksB&W, -C, Film 2*
Morton, Edward d1922 *NotNAT B, WhThe*
Morton, Ferdinand 1885-1941 *AmSCAP 66, -80, BnBkM 80, MusMk, NewGrD 80, NewOrJ[port]*
Morton, Flutes Norvel E 1900?-1962 *WhoJazz 72*
Morton, Frank *AmSCAP 80*
Morton, Gary *NewYTET, WhoHol A*
Morton, George Shadow *IlEncR*
Morton, Gregory *WhoHol A*
Morton, Harry K d1956 *NotNAT B*
Morton, Henry Sterling 1907- *BiDAmM, EncJzS 70*
Morton, Hugh *EncMT, NotNAT B, WhThe*
Morton, James *ForYSC*
Morton, James C 1884-1942 *WhScrn 74, -77, WhoHol B*
Morton, James J d1938 *NotNAT B*
Morton, Jelly Roll 1885-1941 *Baker 78, BiDAmM, CmpEPM, DrBlPA, IlEncJ, NewGrD 80, WhoJazz 72*
Morton, Joe *PlP&P A[port]*
Morton, Joe 1947- *DrBlPA*
Morton, John 1930- *WhoMus 72*
Morton, John Maddison 1811-1891 *NotNAT B, OxThe*
Morton, Kitty d1927 *NotNAT B*
Morton, Lawrence 1942- *ConAmC*
Morton, Leon *WhThe*
Morton, Maggie d1939 *NotNAT B*
Morton, Marjorie *Film 2*
Morton, Martha 1870-1925 *NotNAT B, WhThe*
Morton, Maxine *WhScrn 74, -77*
Morton, Michael d1931 *NotNAT B, WhThe*
Morton, Mickey *WhoHol A*
Morton, Montague C *IntMPA 77, -75, -76, -78, -79, -80*
Morton, Richard 1948- *AmSCAP 80*
Morton, Richard Edward 1952- *IntWWM 80*
Morton, Robert 1430?-1476? *NewGrD 80*
Morton, Robert 1440?-1475 *Baker 78*
Morton, Sam d1941 *NotNAT B*
Morton, Thomas d1646 *OxMus*
Morton, Thomas d1879 *NotNAT B*
Morton, Thomas 1764?-1838 *NotNAT B, OxThe*
Morton, Vincent George 1933- *AmSCAP 80*
Morton, William 1838-1938 *NotNAT B*
Morton, William 1937- *IntWWM 77, -80, WhoMus 72*
Morungen, Heinrich Von *NewGrD 80*
Moryl, Richard 1929- *CpmDNM 79, ConAmC*
Mosaval, Johaar 1928- *CnOxB*
Mosaval, Johaar 1934- *DancEn 78*
Mosbacher, Carl E 1920- *IntWWM 77, -80*
Mosby, Curtis 1895- *WhoJazz 72*
Mosca, Giuseppe 1772-1839 *Baker 78, NewGrD 80*
Mosca, Luigi 1775-1824 *Baker 78, NewGrD 80*
Mosca, Salvatore Joseph 1927- *AmSCAP 80*
Moscaglia, Giovanni Battista *NewGrD 80*
Moscheles, Charlotte d1889 *Baker 78*
Moscheles, Ignaz 1794-1870 *Baker 78, BnBkM 80, MusMk, NewGrD 80[port], OxMus*
Moschin, Gastone 1929- *FilmAG WE*
Moscona, Nicola 1907-1975 *Baker 78, NewEOp 71*
Moscona, Nicolo 1907- *IntWWM 77*
Moscovitch, Maurice 1871-1940 *HolCA[port], NotNAT B, WhScrn 74, -77, WhThe, WhoHol B*
Moscovitz, Howard Samuel 1946- *ConAmC*
Moscovitz, Julianne 1951- *ConAmC*
Moscowitz, Jennie d1953 *NotNAT B*
Mosel, Giovanni Felice 1754-1812? *NewGrD 80*
Mosel, Ignaz Franz Von 1772-1844 *Baker 78, NewGrD 80*
Mosel, Tad 1922- *BiE&WWA, ConDr 77, McGEWD[port], ModWD, NewYTET, NotNAT*
Moseler, Karl Heinrich *NewGrD 80*
Moseley, Carlos 1914- *NewGrD 80*
Moseley, James Orville 1909- *AmSCAP 80*
Mosely, Richard *PupTheA*
Mosenthal, Joseph 1834-1896 *Baker 78, BiDAmM*
Mosenthal, Salomon Hermann Von 1821-1877 *NewEOp 71*
Mosenthal, Solomon Hermann d1877 *NotNAT B*
Moser *NewGrD 80*
Moser, Andreas 1859-1925 *Baker 78, NewGrD 80*
Moser, Artus *EncFCWM 69*
Moser, Claus 1922- *IntWWM 77, -80*
Moser, Edda *WhoMus 72*
Moser, Edda 1941- *NewGrD 80, WhoOp 76*
Moser, Edda Elisabeth 1942- *IntWWM 77, -80*
Moser, Gustav Von d1903 *NotNAT B*
Moser, Hans 1880-1964 *EncWT, FilmAG WE, NotNAT B, WhScrn 74, -77, WhoHol B*
Moser, Hans Joachim 1889-1967 *Baker 78, NewGrD 80*
Moser, Karl 1774-1851 *NewGrD 80*
Moser, Margot 1930- *BiE&WWA, NotNAT*
Moser, Roland 1943- *DcCM*
Moser, Rudolf 1892-1960 *Baker 78, NewGrD 80*
Moses, Bob 1948- *EncJzS 70*
Moses, Charles Alexander 1923- *IntMPA 77, -75, -76, -78, -79, -80*
Moses, Ethel *BlksB&W, -C, DrBlPA*
Moses, Gilbert *IntMPA 77, -75, -76, -78, -79, -80, MorBAP*
Moses, Gilbert 1942- *BlkAmP, DrBlPA, WhoThe 77*
Moses, Gilbert 1943- *NotNAT*
Moses, Harry d1937 *NotNAT B*
Moses, Joan Mary 1921- *WhoMus 72*
Moses, Lucia 1908- *BlksB&W[port]*
Moses, Montrose Jonas 1878-1934 *NotNAT B, OxThe, WhThe*
Moses, Raymond G *Film 2*
Moses, Robert 1888- *BiE&WWA*
Moses, Robert Laurence 1948- *EncJzS 70*
Mosewius, Johann Theodor 1788-1858 *Baker 78, NewGrD 80*
Moshay, Joe 1908- *AmSCAP 66, -80*
Mosheim, Grete 1905- *EncWT*
Mosheim, Grete 1907- *Film 2, WhThe*
Moshier, Carmen 1932- *AmSCAP 80*
Moshinsky, Elijah 1946- *IntWWM 77, -80*
Mosick, Marian Perry 1906-1973 *WhScrn 77, WhoHol B*
Mosier, Frank Moffett 1929- *NatPD[port]*
Mosjoukine *WorEFlm[port]*
Mosjoukine, Ivan 1889-1939 *FilmEn, Film 1, -2, FilmgC, HalFC 80, WhScrn 74, -77, WhoHol B*
Moskine, Ivan 1889-1939 *FilmEn, Film 2*
Mosko, Stephen 1948- *ConAmC*
Moskova, Joseph N Ney, Prince DeLa 1803-1857 *NewGrD 80*
Moskovitz, Harry H 1904- *IntWWM 77, -80*
Moskowa, Prince DeLa, Joseph Napoleon 1803-1857 *Baker 78*
Moskowitz, Art *ConMuA 80B*
Moskowitz, Henry d1936 *NotNAT B*
Moskowitz, Jennie *Film 2*
Moskowitz, Joseph H *IntMPA 77, -75, -76, -78*
Moskowitz, Maurice *NotNAT B*
Moskowitz, Seymour L 1926- *AmSCAP 80*
Moskvin, Andrei 1901-1961 *DcFM, FilmEn, OxFilm, WorEFlm*
Moskvin, Ivan Mikhailovich 1874-1946 *EncWT, NotNAT B, OxThe, PlP&P[port], WhScrn 74, -77*
Mosley, Baptiste 1893-1965 *NewOrJ*
Mosley, Edgar 1895-1962 *NewOrJ[port]*
Mosley, Fred 1854-1972 *WhScrn 74, -77*
Mosley, James P, II 1921- *IntWWM 77*
Mosley, Lawrence Leo 1905- *AmSCAP 80*
Mosley, Robert 1935- *WhoOp 76*
Mosley, Roger E *DrBlPA, WhoHol A*
Mosley, Snub 1909- *CmpEPM, DrBlPA, WhoJazz 72*
Mosolov, Alexandr Vasil'yevich 1900-1973 *NewGrD 80*
Mosolova, Vera 1876-1949 *DancEn 78*
Mosolova, Vera Ilyinina 1875-1949 *CnOxB*
Mosonyi 1814-1870 *OxMus*
Mosonyi, Mihaly 1814-1870 *Baker 78*
Mosonyi, Mihaly 1815-1870 *NewGrD 80[port]*
Mosonyi, Pierre 1918- *IntWWM 77, -80*
Mosquini, Maria 1899- *TwYS*
Mosquini, Marie 1899- *Film 2*
Moss, Arnold *IntMPA 75, -76, -78, -79, -80*
Moss, Arnold 1910- *BiE&WWA, FilmEn, FilmgC, ForYSC, HalFC 80, IntMPA 77, MovMk, NotNAT, WhoHol A, WhoThe 72, -77*
Moss, Arnold 1911- *Vers A[port]*
Moss, Arthur G d1932 *BlksBF*
Moss, Carleton 1910- *BlksB&W*
Moss, Carlton *MorBAP*
Moss, Charles B, Jr. 1944- *IntMPA 77, -78, -79, -80*

Moss, Earl 1940- AmSCAP 80
Moss, Sir Edward 1852-1912 NotNAT B, OxThe
Moss, Sir Edward 1854- WhThe
Moss, Eivind Roy 1909- AmSCAP 80
Moss, Ellsworth Francis 1904- AmSCAP 80
Moss, Eugene 1906- BluesWW[port]
Moss, F Carlton BlkAmP
Moss, Frances Pamela 1940- IntWWM 77
Moss, Frank L IntMPA 77, -75, -76, -78, -79, -80
Moss, George Film 1
Moss, Grant MorBAP
Moss, Hugh d1926 NotNAT B
Moss, Ira ConMuA 80B
Moss, Jeffrey Arnold AmSCAP 80
Moss, Jerry ConMuA 80B
Moss, John NewGrD 80
Moss, Lawrence Kenneth 1927- AmSCAP 80, Baker 78, CpmDNM 73, -74, -76, -78, -79, -80, ConAmC, DcCM, IntWWM 77, -80
Moss, Marshall OxMus
Moss, Michael ConAmC
Moss, Paul d1950 NotNAT B
Moss, Piotr 1949- Baker 78
Moss, Randolph Marshall 1908- IntWWM 77, -80
Moss, Stewart WhoHol A
Moss, W Keith 1892-1935 NotNAT B, WhThe
Moss, William 1942- IntWWM 80
Moss And Frye BlksBF
Mossafer-Rind, Bernice 1925- IntWWM 77
Mosse, John NewGrD 80
Mossenson, Yigal 1917- CnThe, REnWD[port]
Mosser, Thomas Richard 1946- IntWWM 77
Mossetti, Carlotta 1890- WhThe
Mossford, Lorna DancEn 78
Mossi, Giovanni NewGrD 80
Mossman, Bina Nieper 1893- AmSCAP 80
Mossman, Josef ConAmTC
Mossman, Merrily WomWMM B
Mossman, Ted 1914- AmSCAP 66, -80, ConAmC
Mossolof, Alexander 1900- OxMus
Mossolov, Alexander 1900-1973 Baker 78, MusMk
Mossop, Cyril Stephenson 1910- IntWWM 77
Mossop, Henry 1729-1774 NotNAT B, OxThe
Most, Abe 1920- CmpEPM, EncJzS 70
Most, Abraham 1920- EncJzS 70
Most, Mickie ConMuA 80B, IlEncR
Most, Sam 1930- EncJzS 70, IntWWM 77
Most, Samuel 1930- BiDAmM, EncJzS 70
Mostad, Jon 1942- IntWWM 80
Mostaert, David 1560?-1615 NewGrD 80
Mostar, Gerhart Hermann 1901- CnMD
Mostard, John 1942- IntWWM 77, -80
Mostart, David 1560?-1615 NewGrD 80
Mostel, Josh WhoHol A
Mostel, Zero 1915-1977 BiE&WWA, CmpEPM, EncMT, EncWT, Ent, FamA&A[port], FilmEn, FilmgC, ForYSC, HalFC 80, IntMPA 77, -75, -76, JoeFr[port], MotPP, MovMk[port], NotNAT, PlP&P[port], WhoHol A, WhoThe 72, -77
Mosto, Francesco 1550?-1590? NewGrD 80
Mosto, Giovanni Battista 1550?-1596 NewGrD 80
Mostras, Konstantin 1886-1965 NewGrD 80
Mosusova, Nadezda 1928- IntWWM 77
Moszato, Umberto Film 1
Moszkowicz, Imo 1925- WhoOp 76
Moszkowski, Alexander 1851-1934 Baker 78
Moszkowski, Moritz 1854-1925 Baker 78, BnBkM 80, GrComp[port], MusMk, NewGrD 80, OxMus
Moszumanska-Nazar, Krystyna 1924- Baker 78, IntWWM 77, -80, NewGrD 80
Mota, Jose Viana Da NewGrD 80
Moten, Benjamin 1894-1935 NewGrD 80
Moten, Bennie 1894-1935 BgBands 74, BiDAmM, CmpEPM, DrBlPA, IlEncJ, NewGrD 80, WhoJazz 72
Moten, Etta DrBlPA
Mother Earth BiDAmM
Motherlode RkOn 2[port]
Mothers Of Invention BiDAmM, ConMuA 80A
Motian, Stephen Paul 1931- BiDAmM, EncJzS 70
Motley BiE&WWA, WhoOp 76, WhoThe 77
Motley, John Lothrop PupTheA
Motojicho MorBAP
Motokiyo, Zeami 1363-1443 CnThe, EncWT, REnWD[port]
Motors, The ConMuA 80A
Motsev, Alexander 1900-1964 NewGrD 80
Mott IlEncR[port]
Mott, David Howard 1945- ConAmC
Mott, Harold 1908- AmSCAP 66, -80
Mott, Helga WhoMus 72
Mott The Hoople ConMuA 80A, RkOn 2[port]
Motta, Gilberto 1933- DancEn 78
Motta, Jose Vianna Da Baker 78, NewGrD 80
Motte, Claire 1937- CnOxB, DancEn 78
Motte, Diether DeLa 1928- NewGrD 80
Motte-Haber, Helga DeLa 1938- NewGrD 80
Motter, Charlotte Kay 1922- BiE&WWA, NotNAT
Motter, Margaret 1928- IntWWM 77
Mottershaw, Frank S IlWWBF
Motteux, Peter Anthony 1663-1718 NewGrD 80, NotNAT B
Motteux, Pierre Antoine 1663-1718 NewGrD 80
Mottl, Felix 1856-1911 Baker 78, BnBkM 80, CmOp, MusSN[port], NewEOp 71, NewGrD 80, OxMus
Mottl-Fassbender, Zdenka NewGrD 80
Mottley, John d1750 NotNAT B
Mottola, Anthony Charles 1918- AmSCAP 66, -80
Mottola, Tommy ConMuA 80B
Mottola, Tony 1918- CmpEPM
Mottram, Simon 1937- CnOxB
Mottu, Alexandre 1883-1943 Baker 78
Motz, Georg 1653-1733 NewGrD 80
Motz, Julie WomWMM B
Motzan, Otto 1880-1937 AmSCAP 66, -80
Moucque, Antoine NewGrD 80
Moud, Henry NewGrD 80
Mouezy-Eon, Andre 1880- WhThe
Mouillot, Frederick d1911 NotNAT B
Mouillot, Gertrude d1961 NotNAT B, WhThe
Moulaert, Pierre 1907-1967 Baker 78, NewGrD 80
Moulaert, Raymond 1875-1962 Baker 78, NewGrD 80
Moulan, Frank d1939 WhoHol B, WhoStg 1906, -1908
Moulan, Frank 1875-1939 NotNAT B, WhThe
Moulan, Frank 1876-1939 WhScrn 74, -77
Mould, Raymond Wesley 1905- WhThe
Moulder, Earline IntWWM 77, -80
Moulder, Walter C 1933-1967 WhScrn 74, -77, WhoHol B
Moulder Brown, John 1945- HalFC 80
Moule-Evans, David 1905- IntWWM 77, -80, NewGrD 80, WhoMus 72
Moulinie, Etienne 1600?-1669? NewGrD 80
Moulinier, Etienne 1600?-1669? NewGrD 80
Mouliniere, Etienne 1600?-1669? NewGrD 80
Mouloudji, Marcel 1922- FilmEn
Moulson, Robert Lewis 1932- WhoOp 76
Moulton, Edward Film 2, TwYS
Moulton, Robert 1922- BiE&WWA, NotNAT
Moulton Piper, Dorothy NewGrD 80
Moulu, Pierre 148-?-1550? NewGrD 80
Mound, Fred 1932- IntMPA 79, -80
Mound, Peter John 1929- IntWWM 77, WhoMus 72
Mound City Blue Blowers BiDAmM
Mounet, Jean Paul 1847-1922 NotNAT B, WhThe
Mounet, Jean Sully 1841-1916 OxThe
Mounet, Paul 1847-1922 OxThe
Mounet-Sully 1841-1916 EncWT, Film 1
Mounet-Sully, Jean 1841-1916 NotNAT B, WhThe, WhoHol B
Mounsey, Ann 1811-1891 NewGrD 80
Mounsey, Yvonne 1921- CnOxB, DancEn 78
Mount, Betty Copsey 1919- ConAmTC
Mount, Peggy 1916- FilmgC, HalFC 80, WhoHol A, WhoThe 72, -77
Mount-Edgcumbe, Richard 1764-1839 Baker 78
Mount-Edgcumbe, Richard, Earl Of 1764-1839 NewGrD 80
Mountain ConMuA 80A, IlEncR
Mountain, Earl B d1962 NotNAT B
Mountain, Peter 1923- IntWWM 77, -80, WhoMus 72
Mountford, Harry d1950 NotNAT B
Mountfort, Susanna Percival 1667-1703 NotNAT B, OxThe, PlP&P
Mountfort, William 1664-1692 NotNAT A, -B, OxThe, PlP&P
Mouque, Antoine 1659-1723 NewGrD 80
Mouquet, Jules 1867-1946 Baker 78
Mouradian, Sarky 1931- AmSCAP 80
Mourant, Violet Eliza WhoMus 72
Mourant, Walter 1910- CpmDNM 80, ConAmC
Mourao, Isabel 1936- IntWWM 77, -80
Mouret, Jean-Joseph 1682-1738 Baker 78, NewGrD 80, OxMus
Mourguet, Laurent 1745-1844 DcPup, Ent
Mourtois, Jean NewGrD 80
Mourton, Robert NewGrD 80
Mousjoukine OxFilm
Mousseau, Jean Paul 1927- CreCan 2
Moussinac, Leon 1890-1964 FilmEn, OxFilm, WorEFlm
Mousso, Dyne 1930- CreCan 1
Moussorgsky NewEOp 71
Moussorgsky, Modest Baker 78, GrComp, NewGrD 80
Moussorgsky, Modest Petrovitch 1835-1881 DancEn 78
Moussy, Marcel 1924- WorEFlm
Moustache WhoHol A
Mouth & MacNeal RkOn 2[port]
Mouton, Charles 1626-1699? NewGrD 80
Mouton, Jean d1522 OxMus
Mouton, Jean 1459?-1522 Baker 78, NewGrD 80
Mouton, Jean 1470?-1522 BnBkM 80
Moutsopoulos, Evanghelos A 1930- IntWWM 77, -80
Mouvet, Maurice d1927 NotNAT B
Mouzon, Alphonse 1948- AmSCAP 80, EncJzS 70
Movar, Dunja 1940-1963 WhScrn 74, -77, WhoHol B
Move, The ConMuA 80A, IlEncR
Mover, Bob 1952- EncJzS 70
Mover, Robert Alan 1952- EncJzS 70
Movin, Lisbeth WomWMM
Movita 1917- ForYSC, WhoHol A
Movius, Caspar NewGrD 80
Mowat, Anna Cora 1819-1870 NotNAT B
Mowat, David 1943- ConDr 73, -77
Mowat, Farley McGill 1921- CreCan 2
Mowatt, Anna Cora 1819-1870 FamA&A[port], McGEWD, NotNAT A, OxThe, REnWD[port]
Mowbray, Alan d1969 BiE&WWA, MotPP, WhoHol B
Mowbray, Alan 1893-1969 FilmgC, HalFC 80, HolCA[port], Vers A[port]
Mowbray, Alan 1896-1969 FilmEn, ForYSC, MovMk, WhScrn 74, -77
Mowbray, Alan 1897-1969 NotNAT B
Mowbray, Henry 1882-1960 WhScrn 77
Mowbray, Thomas d1900 NotNAT B
Mower, Jack 1890-1965 Film 1, -2, ForYSC, TwYS, WhScrn 74, -77, WhoHol B
Mower, Margaret PlP&P
Mower, Patrick 1940- HalFC 80
Mowery, Bobby Lee 1949- AmSCAP 80
Mowery, Carl Donald, Jr. 1941- ConAmC
Mowll, Katharine 1917- IntWWM 77
Mowrey, Margaret PupTheA
Moxey, John 1920- FilmEn, FilmgC, HalFC 80, IlWWBF, WhoHrs 80
Moxica NewGrD 80
Moy, Edgar 1893- WhoMus 72
Moy, William C C 1923- ConAmC
Moya, Natalie 1900- WhThe
Moye, Don 1946- EncJzS 70
Moye, Donald Franklin 1946- AmSCAP 80
Moyer, Birgitte Plesner 1938- IntWWM 77, -80
Moyer, J Harold 1927- ConAmC, IntWWM 77, -80
Moyer, Karl Eby 1937- IntWWM 77
Moyer, William Cassel 1929- IntWWM 77
Moyers, Bill D NewYTET
Moyes, Patricia 1923- BiE&WWA

Moylan, Mary Ellen 1926- *CnOxB, DancEn 78*
Moylan, William J *IntMPA 77, -75, -76, -78, -79, -80*
Moyle, Alice 1908- *NewGrD 80*
Moyle, Julian Kerr Scott 1927- *WhoOp 76*
Moyle, Richard Michael 1944- *IntWWM 77, -80*
Moyne, Jean-Baptiste *NewGrD 80*
Moynihan, Jane *WomWMM A, -B*
Moyse, Louis 1912- *Baker 78*
Moyse, Marcel 1889- *Baker 78, NewGrD 80*
Moyzes, Alexander 1906- *Baker 78, DcCM, IntWWM 77, -80, NewGrD 80*
Moyzes, Mikulas 1872-1944 *Baker 78, NewGrD 80*
Mozart *NewGrD 80*
Mozart, Anna 1751-1829 *Baker 78*
Mozart, Carl Thomas 1784-1858 *NewGrD 80*
Mozart, Constantia 1762-1842 *NewGrD 80[port]*
Mozart, Constanze 1762-1842 *NewGrD 80[port]*
Mozart, Franz Xaver Wolfgang 1791-1844 *NewGrD 80*
Mozart, George 1864-1947 *NotNAT A, -B, WhScrn 74, -77, WhThe, WhoHol B*
Mozart, Leopold 1719-1787 *Baker 78, NewGrD 80[port], OxMus*
Mozart, Maria Anna 1751-1829 *NewGrD 80[port]*
Mozart, Mickey *RkOn*
Mozart, Wolfgang Amadeus 1756-1791 *Baker 78, BnBkM 80[port], CmOp[port], CmpBCM, CnOxB, DcCom 77[port], DcCom&M 79, DcPup, GrComp[port], MusMk[port], NewEOp 71, NewGrD 80[port], OxMus*
Mozart, Wolfgang Amadeus 1791-1844 *Baker 78, NewGrD 80*
Mozeen, Mrs. *NewGrD 80*
Mozeen, Thomas d1768 *NotNAT B*
Mozhukhin, Ivan 1889-1939 *FilmEn, WorEFlm*
Mozhukin, Ivan 1890-1939 *OxFilm, WhScrn 77*
Mozian, Roger King 1925-1963 *AmSCAP 66, -80*
Mozisova, Bozena *WomWMM*
Mr. Bo *BluesWW[port]*
Mr. Bongo *AmSCAP 80*
Mr. Green Jeans *AmSCAP 80*
Mr. Honey *BluesWW[port]*
Mr. Rogers *AmSCAP 80*
Mr. Shortstuff *BluesWW[port]*
Mracek, Jaroslav John Stephen 1928- *IntWWM 77, -80*
Mracek, Joseph Gustav 1878-1944 *NewGrD 80*
Mraczek, Joseph Gustav 1878-1944 *Baker 78, NewGrD 80*
Mravik, Edward E 1917- *AmSCAP 66, -80*
Mravina, Evgeniya Konstantinovna 1864-1914 *NewGrD 80*
Mravinskaya, Evgeniya Konstantinovna 1864-1914 *NewGrD 80*
Mravinsky, Eugene 1903- *WhoMus 72*
Mravinsky, Evgeny 1906- *NewGrD 80*
Mravinsky, Evgheny 1903- *Baker 78*
Mravinsky, Yevgeni Alexsandrovich 1903- *IntWWM 77, -80*
Mraz, Barry *ConMuA 80B*
Mraz, George 1944- *EncJzS 70*
Mraz, Jiri 1944- *EncJzS 70*
Mrowiec, Karol 1919- *IntWWM 77, -80*
Mroz, Leonard Andrzej 1947- *WhoOp 76*
Mrozek, Slavomir 1930- *CnMD SUP*
Mrozek, Slawomir 1930- *CroCD, EncWT, McGEWD[port], ModWD, REnWD[port], WhoThe 72, -77*
Mrs. Ravenhall *AmSCAP 80*
Mrygon, Adam Wieslaw 1935- *IntWWM 77, -80*
Mshvelidze, Shalva Mikhaylovich 1904- *Baker 78, NewGrD 80*
Mt'acmideli, George d1065 *NewGrD 80*
Mucci, Eduliho *Film 2*
Muciuk, Yar W 1927- *IntMPA 80*
Muck, Carl 1859-1940 *NewGrD 80[port]*
Muck, Karl 1859-1940 *Baker 78, BnBkM 80, CmOp, MusMk, MusSN[port], NewEOp 71*
Muczynski, Robert 1929- *AmSCAP 66, -80, Baker 78, CpmDNM 78, -79, ConAmC*
Mud Dauber Joe *BluesWW[port]*
Mudarra, Alonso 1508?-1580 *Baker 78*
Mudarra, Alonso 1510?-1580 *NewGrD 80*
Mudd *NewGrD 80*
Mudd, John 1555-1631 *NewGrD 80*
Mudd, Roger *NewYTET*
Mudd, Thomas d1667 *NewGrD 80*
Mudd, Thomas 1560?-1619? *NewGrD 80*
Mudd And Trout *NewYTET*
Mudde *NewGrD 80*
Mudde, Harry d1588? *NewGrD 80*
Mudde, Henry d1588? *NewGrD 80*
Mudde, Thomas 1560?-1619? *NewGrD 80*
Muddy Waters 1915- *BluesWW[port], NewGrD 80*
Muddy Waters Junior *BluesWW[port]*
Mude, Hakurotwi 1938- *IntWWM 80*
Mudge, Enoch 1776-1850 *BiDAmM*
Mudge, Richard 1718-1763 *Baker 78, NewGrD 80, OxMus*
Mudie, George d1918 *NotNAT B*
Mudie, Leonard 1883-1965 *ForYSC*
Mudie, Leonard 1884-1965 *FilmgC, HalFC 80, Vers A[port], WhScrn 74, -77, WhThe, WhoHol B*
Mudie, Michael 1914-1962 *CmOp*
Mudie, Thomas Molleson 1809-1876 *NewGrD 80*
Mudie, Thomas Mollison 1809-1876 *Baker 78*
Muegel, Trudy Drummond 1936- *IntWWM 77, -80*
Muelas, Diego DeLas d1743 *NewGrD 80*
Muelen, Servais Vander *NewGrD 80*
Mueller, Allan 1941- *IntWWM 77*
Mueller, Barbara 1909-1967 *WhScrn 77*
Mueller, Carl Frank 1892- *AmSCAP 66, -80, ConAmC*
Mueller, Edward Charles 1912- *AmSCAP 80*
Mueller, Elizabeth 1926- *FilmgC, HalFC 80*
Mueller, Frank Frederick, Jr. 1937- *IntWWM 77*
Mueller, Frederick A 1921- *ConAmC, IntWWM 77, -80*
Mueller, Gustave 1890-1965 *NewOrJ[port], WhoJazz 72*
Mueller, H K *Film 2*
Mueller, Harold 1920- *IntWWM 80*
Mueller, Herbert Charles 1920- *WhoMus 72*
Mueller, Larry Ross 1939- *AmSCAP 80*
Mueller, Otto-Werner 1926- *IntWWM 77, -80*
Mueller, William F 1952- *AmSCAP 80*
Mueller, Wolfgang 1923-1960 *WhScrn 74, -77, WhoHol B*
Mueller VonAsow, Erich H 1892-1964 *NewGrD 80*
Muench, Gerhart 1907- *Baker 78*
Mueren, Florentijn Jan VanDer *NewGrD 80*
Muffat, Georg 1645?-1704 *BnBkM 80*
Muffat, Georg 1653-1704 *Baker 78, NewGrD 80, OxMus*
Muffat, Gottlieb 1690-1770 *Baker 78, MusMk, NewGrD 80, OxMus*
Muffat, Theophil 1690-1770 *NewGrD 80*
Mugellini, Bruno 1871-1912 *Baker 78*
Muggeridge, Malcolm 1903- *IntMPA 77, -75, -76, -78, -79, -80*
Muggs, J Fred *NewYTET*
Mugnone, Leopoldo 1858-1941 *Baker 78, CmOp, NewEOp 71, NewGrD 80*
Mugwana, Oshun *WomWMM B*
Mugwumps *BiDAmM*
Muhajir, El *BlkAmP*
Muhammad, Idris 1939- *EncJzS 70*
Muhammad Ibn Abd Al-Hamid *NewGrD 80*
Muhl, Edward E 1907- *FilmEn, FilmgC, HalFC 80, IntMPA 77, -75, -76, -78, -79, -80*
Muhlen, Raimund VonZur *NewGrD 80*
Muhlenberg, William Augustus 1796-1877 *BiDAmM*
Muhlfeld, Richard 1856-1907 *Baker 78, BnBkM 80, NewGrD 80, OxMus*
Muhling, August 1786-1847 *Baker 78*
Muhlstock, Louis 1904- *CreCan 1*
Muhssin, Ertugrul *Film 2*
Muir, Alexander *OxMus*
Muir, E Roger 1918- *IntMPA 75, -78, -79, -80*
Muir, Esther 1895- *FilmEn, FilmgC, ForYSC, HalFC 80*
Muir, Florabel 1889-1970 *WhScrn 77*
Muir, Gavin d1972 *WhoHol B*
Muir, Gavin 1907-1972 *FilmgC, HalFC 80, WhScrn 77*
Muir, Gavin 1909-1972 *FilmEn, ForYSC, Vers B[port]*
Muir, Graeme 1916- *IntMPA 77, -75, -76, -78, -79, -80*
Muir, Helen 1864-1934 *Film 1, WhScrn 74, -77, WhoHol B*
Muir, Jean 1911- *FilmEn, FilmgC, ForYSC, HalFC 80, ThFT[port], WhThe, WhoHol A*
Muir, Kenneth 1907- *BiE&WWA, NotNAT*
Muir, Lewis F 1884-1950 *AmSCAP 66, -80, BiDAmM, PopAmC, PopAmC SUP*
Muir, Roger E 1918- *IntMPA 77, -76*
Mukai, Shigeharu 1949- *EncJzS 70*
Mukes, Daniel 1901?-1956 *NewOrJ*
Mukherjee, Hemanta Kumar 1922- *IntWWM 77*
Mukhina, Tanya *Film 2*
Mul, Jan 1911-1971 *Baker 78, NewGrD 80*
Mulay, Vijaya *WomWMM*
Mulcaster *OxMus*
Mulcaster, G H 1891-1964 *Film 2, HalFC 80, NotNAT B, WhScrn 74, WhThe, WhoHol B*
Mulcaster, George H 1891-1964 *WhScrn 77*
Mulcay, Jimmy 1900-1968 *WhScrn 77, WhoHol B*
Muldaur, Diana 1943?- *FilmgC, HalFC 80, IntMPA 77, -75, -76, -78, -79, -80, WhoHol A*
Muldaur, Geoff *IlEncR*
Muldaur, Maria *ConMuA 80A[port]*
Muldaur, Maria 1942- *EncJzS 70*
Muldaur, Maria 1943- *IlEncR[port], RkOn 2[port]*
Muldener, Louise d1938 *NotNAT B*
Mulder, Ernest Willem 1898-1959 *Baker 78, NewGrD 80*
Mulder, Herman 1894- *Baker 78*
Mulder, Johannes Hermanus 1894- *IntWWM 77*
Muldofsky, Peri *WomWMM B*
Muldowney, Dominic 1952- *NewGrD 80*
Mule, Giuseppe 1885-1951 *Baker 78, NewGrD 80*
Mule, Marcel 1901- *Baker 78*
Mulet, Henri 1878-1967 *NewGrD 80, OxMus*
Mulet, Paul *BlkAmP*
Mulfinger, David Robert 1937- *IntWWM 77, -80*
Mulfinger, George Leonidas 1900- *ConAmC, WhoMus 72*
Mulfinger, Joan Elizabeth Wade 1933- *IntWWM 77, -80*
Mulford, Clarence E 1895-1970 *FilmgC, HalFC 80*
Mulford, Marilyn *WomWMM B*
Mulgan, Denis Mason 1915- *WhoMus 72*
Mulgan, Philip Anthony 1927- *IntWWM 77, -80*
Mulgrew, Thomas G 1889-1954 *WhScrn 74, -77*
Mulhall, Jack *MotPP*
Mulhall, Jack 1887-1979 *FilmEn, What 4[port]*
Mulhall, Jack 1888-1979 *HalFC 80*
Mulhall, Jack 1891- *Film 1, -2, FilmgC, MovMk, TwYS*
Mulhall, Jack 1894- *ForYSC, WhoHol A*
Mulhare, Edward 1923- *BiE&WWA, FilmEn, FilmgC, ForYSC, HalFC 80, MotPP, NotNAT, WhoHol A*
Mulhauser, James 1890-1939 *WhScrn 74, -77, WhoHol B*
Mulhern, Harry 1897- *BiE&WWA*
Mulholland, J B 1858-1925 *NotNAT B, WhThe*
Mulholland, John 1898-1970 *MagIlD*
Mulholland, Raymond 1928- *IntWWM 77, -80*
Mulholland, Robert E *IntMPA 79, -80, NewYTET*
Muling, Johannes *NewGrD 80*
Mulinus, Johannes *NewGrD 80*
Mull, Martin E 1943- *AmSCAP 80*
Mullally, Don d1933 *NotNAT B*
Mullaly, Jode *Film 1*

Mullaney, Jack *ForYSC, WhoHol A*
Mullard, Arthur 1920- *HalFC 80*
Mullavey, Greg *WhoHol A*
Mulle, Ida 1864?-1934 *NotNAT B, WhScrn 74, -77*
Mullen, Barbara 1914-1979 *FilmgC, HalFC 80, IlWWBF, WhoHol A, WhoThe 72, -77*
Mullen, Gordon *Film 1*
Mullen, Sadie *Film 2*
Mullens, Moon Edward 1916- *WhoJazz 72*
Muller *NewGrD 80*
Muller, Adolf, Jr. 1839-1901 *Baker 78*
Muller, Adolf, Sr. 1801-1886 *Baker 78, NewGrD 80*
Muller, Adolph 1801-1886 *NewGrD 80*
Muller, Andre 1926- *CreCan 1*
Muller, Artur 1909- *CnMD*
Muller, August Eberhard 1767-1817 *Baker 78, NewGrD 80*
Muller, Bernhard 1825-1895 *Baker 78*
Muller, Catherine *PupTheA*
Muller, Christian 1690-1763 *NewGrD 80*
Muller, Eduard 1912- *NewGrD 80*
Muller, Edward *PupTheA*
Muller, Ellen *Film 2*
Muller, Erich H *NewGrD 80*
Muller, Ernest Louis 1740-1811 *NewGrD 80*
Muller, Fidel *NewGrD 80*
Muller, Franz 1806-1876 *Baker 78, NewGrD 80*
Muller, Friedrich 1749-1825 *Ent, McGEWD*
Muller, Friedrich 1786-1871 *Baker 78*
Muller, Georg 1808-1855 *Baker 78*
Muller, Georg Gottfried 1762-1821 *Baker 78, NewGrD 80*
Muller, Gottfried 1914- *Baker 78*
Muller, Gunther 1933- *IntWWM 77, -80*
Muller, Gustav 1799-1855 *Baker 78*
Muller, Hajo 1931- *WhoOp 76*
Muller, Hans 1854-1897 *Baker 78*
Muller, Heiner 1928- *CnMD*
Muller, Heiner 1929- *CroCD, EncWT*
Muller, Heinrich 1631-1675 *NewGrD 80*
Muller, Heinrich Fidelis 1827-1905 *Baker 78*
Muller, Hermann 1868-1932 *Baker 78*
Muller, Hilde *Film 2*
Muller, Horst 1933- *CnOxB*
Muller, Hugo 1832-1886 *Baker 78*
Muller, Iwan 1786-1854 *Baker 78, NewGrD 80, OxMus*
Muller, Jennifer 1944- *CmpGMD, CnOxB*
Muller, Johann *NewGrD 80*
Muller, Johann Adam *NewGrD 80*
Muller, Johann Daniel *NewGrD 80*
Muller, Johann Michael 1683-1743 *NewGrD 80*
Muller, Johann Nicolaus 1700?-1749? *NewGrD 80*
Muller, Johann Patroklus *NewGrD 80*
Muller, Joseph 1877-1939 *Baker 78*
Muller, Karl 1797-1873 *Baker 78*
Muller, Karl 1829-1907 *Baker 78*
Muller, Karl Christian 1831-1914 *Baker 78*
Muller, Karl Franz 1922- *IntWWM 77, -80*
Muller, Maria 1898-1958 *Baker 78, CmOp, NewEOp 71, NewGrD 80*
Muller, Matthias *NewGrD 80*
Muller, Mette Vibeke 1930- *IntWWM 77, -80*
Muller, Paul 1898- *Baker 78, IntWWM 77, -80*
Muller, Per E 1932- *IntWWM 77, -80*
Muller, Peter 1791-1877 *Baker 78*
Muller, Renate 1907-1937 *FilmAG WE, FilmEn, FilmgC, HalFC 80, WhScrn 74, -77, WhoHol B*
Muller, Romeo *NewYTET*
Muller, Sigfrid Walther 1905-1946 *Baker 78*
Muller, Silverius 1745-1812 *NewGrD 80*
Muller, Sylvia Ruth Barbush 1935- *IntWWM 77, -80*
Muller, Theodor 1802-1875 *Baker 78*
Muller, Therese *NewGrD 80*
Muller, Traugott 1895-1944 *EncWT*
Muller, Valentin *NewGrD 80*
Muller, Wenzel 1767-1835 *Baker 78, MusMk, NewGrD 80, OxMus*
Muller, Wilhelm 1794-1827 *NewGrD 80*
Muller, Wilhelm 1834-1897 *Baker 78*
Muller, William 1834-1897 *BiDAmM*
Muller-Blattau, Josef M 1895-1976 *NewGrD 80*
Muller-Blattau, Joseph M 1895-1976 *NewGrD 80*
Muller-Blattau, Joseph Maria 1895-1976 *Baker 78*
Muller-Hartmann, Robert 1884-1950 *Baker 78, NewGrD 80*
Muller-Hermann, Johanna 1878-1941 *Baker 78, NewGrD 80*
Muller-Reuter, Theodor 1858-1919 *Baker 78*
Muller VonAsow, Erich Hermann 1892-1964 *Baker 78, NewGrD 80*
Muller VonKulm, Walter 1899-1967 *Baker 78, NewGrD 80*
Muller-Zurich, Paul 1898- *CpmDNM 79, -80, NewGrD 80*
Mullican, Aubrey Wilson 1909-1967 *BiDAmM*
Mullican, Moon 1909- *CounME 74A*
Mullican, Moon 1909-1967 *AmPS A, CounME 74, EncFCWM 69, IlEncCM*
Mulligan, Gerald Joseph 1927- *AmSCAP 66, -80, BiDAmM, EncJzS 70, NewGrD 80*
Mulligan, Gerry 1927- *BgBands 74[port], CmpEPM, EncJzS 70, IlEncJ, NewGrD 80, WhoHol A*
Mulligan, Jeru 1927- *EncJzS 70*
Mulligan, Moon d1967 *WhoHol B*
Mulligan, Richard 1932- *FilmgC, HalFC 80, WhoHol A, WhoThe 77*
Mulligan, Robert *IntMPA 77, -75, -76, -78, -79, -80*
Mulligan, Robert 1925- *BiDFilm, -81, FilmEn, FilmgC, HalFC 80, MovMk[port], WorEFlm*
Mulligan, Robert 1932- *OxFilm*
Mulliner, Thomas *NewGrD 80*
Mullings, Frank 1881-1953 *CmOp, NewGrD 80*
Mullins, Bascom Theodore 1934- *BiDAmM*
Mullins, Hugh 1922- *ConAmC*
Mullins, Hugh Englis 1922- *CpmDNM 74*
Mullins, Hugh Euglis 1922- *CpmDNM 77, -79*
Mullner, Amandus Gottfried Adolf 1774-1829 *McGEWD*
Mullner, Silverius *NewGrD 80*
Mulock, Al d1970? *WhScrn 77*
Mulvey, Jay *IntMPA 75*
Mulvey, Kay *IntMPA 77, -76, -78, -79*
Mulys, Gerard 1915- *CnOxB, DancEn 78*
Mumaw, Barton 1912- *DancEn 78[port]*
Mumbles *BluesWW[port]*
Mumby, Diana 1922-1974 *WhScrn 77, WhoHol B*
Mumby, Francis Smith 1915- *WhoMus 72*
Mumford, Jeff 1870?-1914? *NewOrJ*
Mumford, Thaddeus Quentin, Jr. 1951- *AmSCAP 80*
Mumler, Frederick 1772-1807 *BiDAmM*
Mumma, Gordon 1935- *Baker 78, BiDAmM, ConAmC, DcCM, NewGrD 80*
Mummert, Kenneth J 1939- *ConAmC*
Mumy, Billy 1954- *ForYSC, WhoHol A*
Munao, Susan *ConMuA 80B*
Muncaster, Clive 1936- *IntWWM 77, -80, WhoMus 72*
Muncey, Richard 1931- *WhoMus 72*
Munch, Andreas 1811-1884 *OxThe*
Munch, Charles 1891-1968 *Baker 78, BiDAmM, BnBkM 80, MusSN[port], NewGrD 80*
Munch, Edvard 1863-1944 *EncWT*
Munch, Ernst 1859-1928 *Baker 78*
Munch, Eugen *Baker 78*
Munch, Hans 1893- *Baker 78, NewGrD 80*
Munch, Richard 1916- *FilmAG WE*
Munchhausen, Adolph, Baron Von 1755?-1811 *NewGrD 80*
Munchhausen, August, Baron Von 1755?-1811 *NewGrD 80*
Munchhausen, Baron *JoeFr*
Munchheimer, Adam *NewGrD 80*
Munchinger, Karl 1915- *Baker 78, BnBkM 80, NewGrD 80, WhoMus 72*
Munck, Ernest, Chevalier De 1840-1915 *NewGrD 80*
Munclinger, Milan 1923- *NewGrD 80*
Mund, Uwe Claus 1941- *WhoOp 76*
Munday, Anthony 1553?-1633 *NotNAT B, OxThe*
Munday, Myron 1951- *IntWWM 77*
Munden, Joseph Shepherd 1758-1832 *NotNAT A, -B, OxThe*
Mundigl, Josef Otto 1942- *IntWWM 77, -80*
Mundin, Herbert d1939 *WhoHol B*
Mundin, Herbert 1889-1939 *ForYSC*
Mundin, Herbert 1898-1939 *FilmEn, Film 2, FilmgC, HalFC 80, HolCA[port], IlWWBF, NotNAT B, WhScrn 74, -77, WhThe*
Mundin, Herbert 1899-1939 *Vers A[port]*
Mundt, Richard 1936- *WhoOp 76*
Mundviller, Joseph-Louis 1886- *DcFM*
Mundy, Frank Jex *WhoMus 72*
Mundy, Helen *Film 2*
Mundy, James 1907- *CmpEPM*
Mundy, James L 1934- *AmSCAP 80*
Mundy, James R 1907- *AmSCAP 66, -80*
Mundy, Jimmy 1907- *BiDAmM, IlEncJ, WhoJazz 72*
Mundy, John 1555?-1630 *NewGrD 80, OxMus*
Mundy, John 1886- *AmSCAP 66, -80*
Mundy, Meg *BiE&WWA, NotNAT, WhThe*
Mundy, William 1529?-1591? *NewGrD 80, OxMus*
Munerat, Jean Le *NewGrD 80*
Munfurt, Hugo Von *NewGrD 80*
Munger, Dorothy M 1915- *IntWWM 80*
Munger, John *PupTheA*
Munger, Millicent Christner 1905- *ConAmC*
Munger, Shirley *ConAmC*
Munger, Thomas Charles 1950- *IntWWM 77*
Mungo Jerry *RkOn 2[port]*
Muni, Paul 1895-1967 *BiDFilm, -81, BiE&WWA, EncWT, Ent, FamA&A[port], FilmEn, Film 2, ForYSC, MotPP, MovMk[port], NotNAT A, -B, OxFilm, PlP&P, WhScrn 74, -77, WhThe, WhoHol B, WorEFlm*
Muni, Paul 1896-1967 *FilmgC, HalFC 80*
Muni, Scott *ConMuA 80B[port]*
Munier, Ferdinand 1889-1945 *Film 2, WhScrn 74, -77, WhoHol B*
Muniz, Carlos 1927- *CroCD*
Muniz, Juan DeDios 1906-1951 *WhScrn 74, -77*
Munk, Andrzej 1921-1961 *BiDFilm, -81, DcFM, FilmEn, FilmgC, HalFC 80, WorEFlm*
Munk, Andrzej 1921-1966 *OxFilm*
Munk, Kai 1898-1944 *CnMD*
Munk, Kaj 1898-1944 *CnThe, EncWT, Ent, McGEWD[port], ModWD, NotNAT B, OxThe, REnWD[port]*
Munkachy, Louis 1928- *IntWWM 77, -80*
Munker, Ariane *WhoHol A*
Munkittrick, Howard *NewGrD 80*
Munn, Alexandra Marguerite 1934- *IntWWM 77, -80*
Munn, Billy 1911- *WhoMus 72*
Munn, Charles *Film 1*
Munn, Frank 1895-1953 *AmPS B, CmpEPM*
Munn, Katrina Jeanette 1911- *IntWWM 77, -80*
Munn, Thomas John 1944- *WhoOp 76*
Munn, William O 1902- *AmSCAP 66, -80*
Munnich, Richard 1877-1970 *Baker 78, NewGrD 80*
Munns, Robert Ellis 1933- *IntWWM 77, -80, WhoMus 72*
Munoz, Eunice 1928- *FilmAG WE*
Munoz Molleda, Jose 1905- *NewGrD 80*
Munoz Seca, Pedro 1881-1936 *McGEWD[port]*
Munro, Alice Anne Laidlaw 1931- *CreCan 1*
Munro, Blanche *WhoMus 72*
Munro, C K 1889- *PlP&P, WhThe*
Munro, Caroline 1950?- *WhoHrs 80[port]*
Munro, Charles Kirkpatrick 1889- *CnMD, McGEWD*
Munro, Douglas *Film 2*
Munro, George d1968 *NotNAT B*
Munro, Grant 1923- *CreCan 1*
Munro, Janet 1934-1972 *FilmEn, FilmgC, ForYSC, HalFC 80, IlWWBF[port], MotPP, WhScrn 77, WhoHol B, WhoHrs 80[port]*
Munro, Nan 1905- *WhoHol A, WhoThe 72, -77*
Munro, Robert *Film 2*
Munro, William Henderson 1936- *IntWWM 77, -80*
Munrow, David 1942-1976 *BnBkM 80,*

NewGrD 80[port], WhoMus 72
Munsel, Patrice 1925- *Baker 78, BiDAmM, BiE&WWA, CmOp, FilmgC, HalFC 80, MusSN[port], NewEOp 71, WhoHol A, WhoMus 72*
Munsell, Warren P 1889- *BiE&WWA, NotNAT*
Munsell, Warren P, Jr. d1952 *NotNAT B*
Munsey, Joel Porter 1949- *AmSCAP 80*
Munshin, Jules d1970 *MotPP, WhoHol B*
Munshin, Jules 1913-1970 *CmMov*
Munshin, Jules 1915-1970 *BiE&WWA, CmpEPM, FilmEn, FilmgC, ForYSC, HalFC 80, NotNAT B, WhScrn 74, -77*
Munson, Audrey *Film 1*
Munson, Byron *Film 2*
Munson, Eugene Dale 1955- *AmSCAP 80*
Munson, Ona d1955 *MotPP, WhoHol B*
Munson, Ona 1903-1955 *ForYSC, WhScrn 74, -77*
Munson, Ona 1906-1955 *FilmEn, FilmgC, HalFC 80, MovMk, NotNAT B, ThFT[port], WhThe*
Munson, Ona 1908-1955 *Film 2, Vers A[port]*
Munster, Joseph Joachim Benedict 1694-1751? *NewGrD 80*
Munster, Robert 1928- *NewGrD 80*
Muntcho, Monique *WomWMM*
Munteanu, Petre *WhoMus 72*
Muntz, Laura *CreCan 1*
Muntz, Mad Man 1914- *What 4[port]*
Munz, Heinz-Rolf *Film 2*
Munz, Mieczyslaw 1900-1976 *Baker 78*
Munzer, Georg 1886-1908 *Baker 78*
Munzinger, Karl 1842-1911 *NewGrD 80*
Mura, Corinna d1965 *WhoHol B*
Mura, Corrine 1910-1965 *WhScrn 74, -77*
Mura, Peter 1924- *IntWWM 77, -80*
Murad, Jerry *RkOn*
Muradeli, Vano Il'ich 1908-1970 *Baker 78, NewGrD 80*
Muradian, Vazgen 1921- *AmSCAP 80, IntWWM 77, -80*
Murail, Tristan 1947- *IntWWM 80*
Muralter *NewGrD 80*
Muranyi, Joe 1928- *EncJzS 70*
Muranyi, Joseph Paul 1928- *BiDAmM, EncJzS 70*
Murat, Jean 1888-1968 *FilmEn, Film 2, WhScrn 77, WhoHol B*
Muratore, Lucian *Film 1*
Muratore, Lucien 1876-1954 *Baker 78, MusSN[port], NewEOp 71, NewGrD 80*
Muratore, Lucien 1878-1954 *WhScrn 77*
Muravyeva, Marfa Nicolayevna 1838-1879 *CnOxB*
Murcell, George 1925- *WhoHol A, WhoThe 72, -77*
Murchie, Leslie Graham 1918- *IntWWM 77, -80, WhoMus 72*
Murdaugh, Ella Lee 1910- *AmSCAP 66*
Murden, Eliza Crawly 1790?-1851? *BiDAmM*
Murdoch, Dennis 1914- *IntWWM 77, -80, WhoMus 72*
Murdoch, Frank Hitchcock d1872 *NotNAT B, OxThe*
Murdoch, Iris 1919- *ConDr 73, -77, PlP&P*
Murdoch, James Arthur 1930- *IntWWM 80*
Murdoch, James Edward 1811-1893 *FamA&A[port], NotNAT B, OxThe*
Murdoch, Mary Hersey 1931- *IntWWM 80*
Murdoch, Richard 1907- *FilmgC, HalFC 80, WhoHol A, WhoThe 72, -77*
Murdoch, Samuel 1838-1896 *PupTheA*
Murdoch, William 1888-1942 *NewGrD 80*
Murdock, Ann 1890- *Film 1, TwYS, WhThe*
Murdock, Frank *Film 1*
Murdock, George *WhoHol A*
Murdock, Henry d1971 *BiE&WWA, NotNAT B*
Murdock, Jack *WhoHol A*
Murdock, Jane *AmSCAP 80*
Murdock, Kermit *WhoHol A*
Mure, Eileen Davies 1918- *AmSCAP 80*
Mure, Sir William 1594-1657 *NewGrD 80*
Muresianu, Iacob 1857-1917 *NewGrD 80*
Muret, Marc-Antoine De 1526-1585 *NewGrD 80*
Muretus, Marc-Antoine De 1526-1585 *NewGrD 80*
Murfin, Jane 1893-1955 *FilmEn, HalFC 80, NotNAT B, WhThe, WomWMM*
Murgatroyd, Susan *WomWMM*
Murgier, Jacques 1912- *IntWWM 77, -80, WhoMus 72*
Muricy, Andrade 1895- *NewGrD 80*
Muriel, Roel *Film 2*
Muris, Jean De 1290?-1351? *BnBkM 80*
Muris, Johannes De 1290?-1351? *Baker 78, NewGrD 80, OxMus*
Murisiano, Jacob *OxMus*
Muristus *NewGrD 80*
Murmaids, The *RkOn*
Murnane, Allen *Film 1*
Murnau, F W 1888-1931 *FilmEn*
Murnau, F W 1889-1931 *AmFD, FilmgC, HalFC 80, TwYS A, WhoHrs 80, WomWMM*
Murnau, Friedrich Wilhelm 1888-1931 *DcFM, MovMk[port], OxFilm*
Murnau, Friedrich Wilhelm 1889-1931 *BiDFilm, -81*
Murnau, Friedrick Wilhelm 1889-1931 *WorEFlm*
Muro, Don 1951- *AmSCAP 80, IntWWM 77, -80*
Muro, Henri 1884-1967 *WhScrn 77*
Murphey, Michael *ConMuA 80A, IlEncR, RkOn 2[port]*
Murphy, Ada 1888-1961 *WhScrn 74, -77, WhoHol B*
Murphy, Arthur 1727-1805 *NotNAT B, OxThe*
Murphy, Arthur Lister 1906- *ConDr 73, -77*
Murphy, Audie 1924-1971 *BiDFilm, -81, CmMov, FilmEn, FilmgC, ForYSC, HalFC 80[port], MotPP, MovMk, WhScrn 74, -77, WhoHol B, WorEFlm*
Murphy, Ben 1941- *HalFC 80, IntMPA 78, -79, -80, WhoHol A*
Murphy, Beverly Kay 1947- *AmSCAP 80*
Murphy, Bob d1948 *WhoHol B*
Murphy, Bri *WomWMM B*
Murphy, Brian *ConMuA 80B, WhoHol A*
Murphy, Catherine *Film 2*
Murphy, Charles *WhoHol A*
Murphy, Charles Bernard 1884-1942 *Film 2, WhScrn 74, -77, WhoHol B*
Murphy, Charles Bernard, Jr. *Film 2*
Murphy, Dennis 1934- *IntWWM 77, -80*
Murphy, Dennis, Jr. 1944- *IntWWM 77*
Murphy, Donn B 1931- *NotNAT*
Murphy, Dudley 1897- *FilmEn*
Murphy, Edna 1904- *Film 2, ForYSC, MotPP, TwYS*
Murphy, Eileen *WhoHol A*
Murphy, Elliott *IlEncR*
Murphy, Estelle Prindle 1918- *AmSCAP 66*
Murphy, George *MotPP*
Murphy, George 1902- *CmpEPM, FilmEn, FilmgC, HalFC 80, IntMPA 77, -75, -76, -78, -79, -80, MGM[port], MovMk[port], WorEFlm*
Murphy, George 1904- *ForYSC, WhoHol A*
Murphy, Henry Lambert 1885-1954 *BiDAmM*
Murphy, Jack 1915- *Film 2*
Murphy, James d1759 *NotNAT B*
Murphy, James Francis 1910- *AmSCAP 80*
Murphy, Jimmy *WhoHol A*
Murphy, Joe 1877-1961 *Film 2, WhoHol B*
Murphy, John Daly 1873-1934 *Film 1, -2, NotNAT B, WhScrn 74, -77, WhoHol B*
Murphy, John F 1905- *IntMPA 77, -75, -76, -78, -79, -80*
Murphy, John T d1964 *NotNAT B*
Murphy, Joseph J 1877-1961 *WhScrn 74, -77*
Murphy, Julia *WomWMM*
Murphy, Kathleen G 1952- *IntWWM 80*
Murphy, Kevin Edgar 1928- *IntWWM 77, -80*
Murphy, Lambert 1885-1954 *Baker 78*
Murphy, Lyle 1908- *AmSCAP 66, -80, BiDAmM, ConAmC*
Murphy, Margaret *WomWMM B*
Murphy, Mark Howe 1932- *AmSCAP 80, BiDAmM, EncJzS 70*
Murphy, Mary 1931- *FilmEn, FilmgC, ForYSC, HalFC 80, IntMPA 77, -75, -76, -78, -79, -80, MotPP, WhoHol A*
Murphy, Matt *WhoHol A*
Murphy, Maurice *Film 2*
Murphy, Melvin E 1915- *BiDAmM, EncJzS 70*
Murphy, Michael *WhoHol A*
Murphy, Morris *Film 2*
Murphy, Owen 1893-1965 *AmSCAP 66, -80*
Murphy, Pamela *WhoHol A*
Murphy, Pat 1901-1954 *AmSCAP 66, -80*
Murphy, Paul 1928- *AmSCAP 80*
Murphy, Ralph 1895-1967 *FilmEn, FilmgC, HalFC 80*
Murphy, Richard 1912- *CmMov, FilmEn, FilmgC, HalFC 80, IntMPA 77, -75, -76, -78, -79, -80, WorEFlm*
Murphy, Robert 1889-1948 *WhScrn 74, -77*
Murphy, Rose 1913- *AmSCAP 66, -80, BlkWAB[port], CmpEPM, DrBlPA*
Murphy, Rosemary 1925- *HalFC 80*
Murphy, Rosemary 1927- *BiE&WWA, FilmgC, NotNAT, WhoHol A, WhoThe 72, -77*
Murphy, Spud 1908- *BgBands 74, CmpEPM, WhoJazz 72*
Murphy, Stanley 1875-1919 *AmSCAP 66, -80, BiDAmM*
Murphy, Stephen 1921- *IntMPA 75, -76*
Murphy, Steve *Film 2*
Murphy, Thomas 1935- *ConDr 73, -77*
Murphy, Tim d1928 *NotNAT B*
Murphy, Turk 1915- *CmpEPM, EncJzS 70*
Murphy, Walter & The Big Apple Band *RkOn 2[port]*
Murray *MagIID*
Murray, Alma 1854-1945 *NotNAT B, OxThe, WhThe*
Murray, Anita *Film 2*
Murray, Anne *CounME 74[port], -74A*
Murray, Anne 1946- *IlEncCM[port]*
Murray, Anne 1947- *ConMuA 80A, RkOn 2[port]*
Murray, Arthur 1895- *What 3[port]*
Murray, Bain 1926- *Baker 78, CpmDNM 79, ConAmC, IntWWM 80*
Murray, Barbara 1929- *FilmgC, HalFC 80, IlWWBF[port], IntMPA 77, -75, -76, -78, -79, -80, WhoHol A, WhoThe 72, -77*
Murray, Bert *AmSCAP 80*
Murray, Billy *CmpEPM*
Murray, Braham 1943- *WhoThe 72, -77*
Murray, Brian 1937- *NotNAT, WhoHol A, WhoThe 72, -77*
Murray, Charles d1821 *NotNAT B*
Murray, Charlie 1872-1941 *FilmEn, Film 1, -2, FilmgC, ForYSC, HalFC 80, MotPP, TwYS, WhScrn 74, -77, WhoHol B*
Murray, David 1955- *AmSCAP 80, EncJzS 70*
Murray, David Christie d1907 *NotNAT B*
Murray, David Mitchell 1853-1923 *WhScrn 74, -77, WhoHol B*
Murray, Don 1904?-1929 *CmpEPM, WhoJazz 72*
Murray, Don 1925- *ConAmC*
Murray, Don 1929- *BiDFilm, -81, BiE&WWA, FilmEn, FilmgC, ForYSC, HalFC 80, IntMPA 77, -75, -76, -78, -79, -80, MotPP, MovMk[port], WhoHol A, WorEFlm*
Murray, Doreen *WhoMus 72*
Murray, Douglas d1936 *NotNAT B, WhThe*
Murray, Edgar 1865-1932 *WhScrn 74, -77*
Murray, Edgar 1892-1959 *WhScrn 74, -77*
Murray, Elizabeth *AmPS B*
Murray, Elizabeth M 1871-1946 *Film 2, NotNAT B, WhScrn 74, -77, WhoHol B*
Murray, Eva VonGencsy *CreCan 2*
Murray, Francis 1915-1963 *NewOrJ*
Murray, Gaston d1889 *NotNAT B*
Murray, Mrs. Gaston d1891 *NotNAT B*
Murray, George Gilbert Aime 1866-1957 *WhThe*
Murray, Sir Gilbert Aime 1866-1957 *NotNAT B, OxThe, PlP&P*
Murray, Gilbert Donald, III 1930- *AmSCAP 66, -80*
Murray, Gordon *DcPup*
Murray, Gray *Film 2*
Murray, Gregory *OxMus*
Murray, Haya 1910- *AmSCAP 80*
Murray, Henry Valentine d1963 *NotNAT B*
Murray, J Christine 1939- *IntWWM 77*
Murray, J Harold 1891-1940 *CmpEPM,*

EncMT, Film 2, NotNAT B, WhScrn 74, -77, WhThe, WhoHol B
Murray, J K *WhoStg 1906, -1908*
Murray, Jack *AmSCAP 80*
Murray, Jack d1941 *WhScrn 74, -77*
Murray, James *MotPP*
Murray, James 1901- *ForYSC*
Murray, James 1901-1936 *FilmEn, FilmgC, HalFC 80, MovMk, WhScrn 74, -77, WhoHol B*
Murray, James 1901-1937 *Film 2, TwYS*
Murray, James Arthur 1927- *BiDAmM*
Murray, James Arthur 1937- *EncJzS 70, NewGrD 80*
Murray, James Orval 1929- *ConAmC*
Murray, James P 1946- *DrBlPA*
Murray, James Ramsey 1841-1905 *BiDAmM*
Murray, Jan 1917- *ForYSC, IntMPA 77, -75, -76, -78, -79, -80, JoeFr[port], MotPP, WhoHol A*
Murray, Jean d1966 *WhScrn 74, -77*
Murray, Jeremiah *ConAmC*
Murray, Joan 1941- *DrBlPA*
Murray, John *BlkAmP, BlksB&W C*
Murray, John 1906- *AmSCAP 66, BiE&WWA, NotNAT*
Murray, John A 1925- *AmSCAP 66, -80*
Murray, John J d1924 *NotNAT B*
Murray, John T *Film 2*
Murray, John T d1936 *WhoHol B*
Murray, John T 1886-1957 *WhScrn 74, -77*
Murray, Julian Bud 1888-1952 *WhScrn 74, -77*
Murray, Ken *IntMPA 77, -75, -76, -78, -79, -80, NewYTET*
Murray, Ken 1903- *FilmEn, FilmgC, ForYSC, HalFC 80, NotNAT A, WhoHol A*
Murray, Ken 1907- *Film 2*
Murray, Lola 1914-1961 *WhScrn 74, -77*
Murray, Lyn 1909- *AmSCAP 66, -80, ConAmC, HalFC 80*
Murray, M Gray *Film 2*
Murray, Mae d1965 *MotPP, WhoHol B*
Murray, Mae 1885-1965 *FilmEn, MovMk[port]*
Murray, Mae 1886?-1965 *WhScrn 77*
Murray, Mae 1889-1965 *CmpEPM, Film 1, -2, FilmgC, HalFC 80, NotNAT B, OxFilm, ThFT[port], TwYS*
Murray, Mae 1890-1965 *ForYSC, WhScrn 74*
Murray, Margaret 1921- *IntWWM 80, WhoMus 72*
Murray, Marie *Film 1*
Murray, Marion 1885-1951 *WhScrn 74, -77, WhoHol B*
Murray, Mark *AmSCAP 80*
Murray, Mary P *WomWMM*
Murray, Matthew H *WhoOp 76*
Murray, Michael 1932- *BiE&WWA, NotNAT*
Murray, Niall 1948- *IntWWM 80*
Murray, Paul 1885-1949 *NotNAT B, WhThe*
Murray, Paul 1927- *IntWWM 80*
Murray, Peg *WhoHol A, WhoThe 77*
Murray, Peter 1925- *WhThe*
Murray, Peter John Burns 1939- *WhoMus 72*
Murray, Rita *WomWMM*
Murray, Robert Gray 1936- *CreCan 1*
Murray, Robert Pfennig 1936- *IntWWM 77, -80*
Murray, Sonny 1937- *NewGrD 80*
Murray, Stephen 1912- *FilmAG WE, FilmEn, FilmgC, HalFC 80, IlWWBF, WhoHol A, WhoThe 72, -77*
Murray, Stephen Bruce 1941- *AmSCAP 80*
Murray, Sterling Ellis 1944- *IntWWM 77, -80*
Murray, Sunny 1937- *EncJzS 70, IlEncJ*
Murray, Thomas 1902-1961 *WhScrn 74, -77*
Murray, Thomas 1943- *IntWWM 77, -80*
Murray, Thomas C 1873-1959 *CnMD, ModWD, NotNAT B, OxThe, REnWD[port], WhThe*
Murray, Thomas Wilson 1925- *IntWWM 77, -80*
Murray, Tom 1875-1935 *Film 2, WhScrn 74, -77, WhoHol B*
Murray, Uncle *WhScrn 74, -77*
Murray, Walter *Film 1, OxThe, PlP&P*
Murray, Will d1955 *NotNAT B*
Murray, William Bruce 1935- *IntWWM 77, -80, WhoOp 76*
Murray, William H d1852 *NotNAT B*
Murray, Wynn d1957 *NotNAT B*
Murray-Hayden, E M 1942- *WhoMus 72*
Murray-Hill, Peter 1908-1957 *FilmgC, HalFC 80, WhScrn 74, -77, WhoHol B*
Murray-Robertson, Michael Stewart 1939- *IntWWM 77*
Murrell, Alys *Film 2*
Murrell, Irene Janet 1936- *AmSCAP 80*
Murrells, Joseph 1904- *IntWWM 77, -80, WhoMus 72*
Murrey, Charles *Film 2*
Murrill, Herbert Henry John 1909-1952 *Baker 78, NewGrD 80, OxMus*
Murrin, Jacobus *NewGrD 80*
Murrow, Edward R 1908-1965 *NewYTET, WhScrn 74, -77, WhoHol B*
Murry, Ted *AmSCAP 80*
Murschhauser, Franz Xaver Anton 1663-1738 *Baker 78, NewGrD 80*
Murska, Ilma Di 1836-1889 *Baker 78, NewGrD 80*
Mursky, Alexander *Film 2*
Murtagh, Cynthia *Film 2*
Murtagh, Kate *WhoHol A*
Murtaugh, John Edward 1927- *AmSCAP 66, -80, ConAmC*
Murth, Florence 1902-1934 *WhScrn 74, -77, WhoHol B*
Murton, Lionel 1915- *FilmgC, HalFC 80, WhoHol A*
Murtus *NewGrD 80*
Musa, Anthonius 1490?-1547 *NewGrD 80*
Musa Ibn-Maimun 1135-1204 *NewGrD 80*
Musahipzade, Celal 1868-1959 *REnWD[port]*
Musante, Joan *WomWMM B*
Musante, Tony *IntMPA 75, WhoHol A*
Musante, Tony 1936- *FilmEn, HalFC 80, IntMPA 77, -76, -78, -79, -80*
Musante, Tony 1941- *FilmgC*
Musaphia, Joseph 1935- *ConDr 77*
Musard, Philippe 1792-1859 *Baker 78*
Musard, Philippe 1793-1859 *NewGrD 80*
Musburger, Brent *NewYTET*
Muscarini, Girolamo *NewGrD 80*
Muschamp, Thomas 1917- *IntMPA 77, -75, -76, -78, -79, -80*
Musculus, Balthasar 1540?-1597? *NewGrD 80*
Muscutt, Leslie 1941- *NewOrJ SUP[port]*
Muse, Clarence 1889-1979 *AmSCAP 66, BlksB&W[port], -C, BlksBF, DrBlPA, FilmEn, Film 2, FilmgC, ForYSC, HalFC 80, HolCA[port], MovMk, Vers A[port], WhoHol A*
Muse, Lewis Anderson 1908- *BluesWW[port]*
Musel, Corneille *NewGrD 80*
Muset, Colin *NewGrD 80*
Musgrave, Madge Elizabeth 1940- *WhoMus 72*
Musgrave, Thea 1928- *Baker 78, BnBkM 80, CmOp, CpmDNM 79, -80, ConAmC, DcCom&M 79, DcCM, IntWWM 77, -80, MusMk, NewGrD 80[port], OxMus, WhoMus 72, WomCom[port]*
Musgrove, Alexander Johnston 1882-1952 *CreCan 2*
Musgrove, Gertrude 1912- *WhThe*
Mushanokoji, Saneatsu 1885- *ModWD*
Mushaqa, Mikha'il 1800-1888 *NewGrD 80*
Mushel', Georgy 1909- *NewGrD 80*
Music, Lorenzo 1937- *AmSCAP 80*
Music Explosion, The *BiDAmM, RkOn 2[port]*
Music Machine, The *RkOn 2[port]*
Music Makers *BiDAmM*
Musica Aeterna Orchestra *BiDAmM*
Musical Ramblers *BiDAmM*
Musicant, Samuel 1922- *AmSCAP 66, -80*
Musicescu, Gavriil 1847-1903 *Baker 78, NewGrD 80*
Musidora 1889-1957 *FilmEn, Film 1, OxFilm, WhScrn 74, -77, WhoHol B, WomWMM*
Musil, Karl 1939- *CnOxB, DancEn 78[port]*
Musil, Ludwig M 1941- *CnOxB*
Musil, Robert 1880-1942 *CnMD, McGEWD*
Musin *NewGrD 80*
Musin, Ovide 1854-1929 *Baker 78, BiDAmM*
Musiol, Robert Paul Johann 1846-1903 *Baker 78*
Musitz, Suzanne 1937- *DancEn 78*
Muskat, Thomas 1943- *IntWWM 80*
Muskerry, William d1918 *NotNAT B*
Muskett, Michael 1928- *IntWWM 77, -80, WhoMus 72*
Musolino, Angelo 1923- *AmSCAP 66, -80, ConAmC A*
Musorgsky, Modest Petrovich 1839-1881 *NewGrD 80[port]*
Mussato, Albertino 1261-1329 *McGEWD[port], OxThe*
Mussele, Corneille *NewGrD 80*
Musselman, Johnson J 1890-1958 *WhScrn 74, -77*
Musselwhite, Charles Douglas, III 1944- *BluesWW[port], EncJzS 70*
Musselwhite, Charlie 1944- *EncJzS 70*
Musser, Benjamin *PupTheA*
Musser, Clare *ConAmC*
Musser, Philip D 1943- *ConAmC*
Musser, Tharon 1925- *BiE&WWA, NotNAT, WhoOp 76, WhoThe 77*
Musser, Willard I 1913- *AmSCAP 66, -80, IntWWM 77, -80, WhoMus 72*
Musset, Alfred De 1810-1857 *CnThe, EncWT, Ent, McGEWD[port], NewEOp 71, NewGrD 80, NotNAT B, OxThe, REnWD[port]*
Mussett, Charles *Film 2*
Mussey, Francine d1933 *WhScrn 74, -77*
Mussiere, Luciene 1890-1972 *WhScrn 77*
Mussio, Emanuele *NewGrD 80*
Musso, Vido William 1913- *BiDAmM, CmpEPM, EncJzS 70, WhoJazz 72*
Mussolini *OxMus*
Mussolini, Cesare 1735- *Baker 78*
Mussolini, Romano 1927- *Baker 78*
Musson, Bennet 1866-1946 *WhScrn 74, -77, WhoHol B*
Mussorgsky, Modest 1839-1881 *Baker 78, BnBkM 80[port], CmOp, CmpBCM, CnOxB, GrComp[port], MusMk[port], NewEOp 71*
Mussorgsky, Modeste 1839-1881 *DcCom 77[port], DcCom&M 79, OxMus*
Mussulli, Boots 1917- *CmpEPM*
Mussulman, Joseph Agee 1928- *IntWWM 77, -80*
Mustafa, Domenico 1829-1912 *NewGrD 80*
Mustafa, Niazi 1903- *DcFM*
Mustapha, Matura *MorBAP*
Mustel, Victor 1815-1890 *Baker 78, NewGrD 80*
Mustillo, Lina 1905- *ConAmC*
Mustin, Burt 1884-1977 *FilmgC, HalFC 80, WhoHol A*
Musto, Michael J 1917- *IntMPA 77, -75, -76, -78, -79, -80*
Mustonen, Aimo Mainio 1909- *IntWWM 77, -80*
Musuraca, Nicholas 1890?- *FilmEn*
Musuraca, Nicholas 1900?- *HalFC 80*
Musuraca, Nicholas 1908- *CmMov, FilmgC, WorEFlm*
Mutchler, Ralph D 1929- *ConAmC*
Muthel, Johann Gottfried 1718-1788 *Baker 78*
Muthel, Johann Gottfried 1728-1788 *NewGrD 80*
Muthel, Lothar 1898-1965 *EncWT, Film 2*
Muti, Giovanni Vincenzo Macedonio Di *NewGrD 80*
Muti, Lorenzo 1951- *Baker 78*
Muti, Ornella 1956- *FilmAG WE*
Muti, Riccardo 1941- *Baker 78, BnBkM 80, IntWWM 80, MusSN[port], NewGrD 80, WhoOp 76*
Mutio, Giovanni Vincenzo Macedonio Di *NewGrD 80*
Mution, Ricardo 1884-1957 *WhScrn 77*
Mutis, Bartolomeo, Count Of Cesana 1575?-1623 *NewGrD 80*
Mutsu, Ian Yonosuke 1907- *IntMPA 77, -78, -79, -80*
Mutz, Frank 1900?- *NewOrJ*
Mutzel, Manfred 1943- *WhoOp 76*
Muybridge, Eadweard 1830-1904 *DcFM, FilmEn, OxFilm, WorEFlm*
Muybridge, Edward 1830-1904 *FilmgC, HalFC 80*
Muzik, Frantisek 1922- *NewGrD 80*
Muzio, Claudia 1889-1936 *Baker 78, CmOp, MusSN[port], NewEOp 71, NewGrD 80[port]*

Muzio, Emanuele 1821-1890 *NewGrD 80*
Muzio, Emanuele 1825-1890 *Baker 78*
Muzquiz, Carlos 1906-1960 *WhScrn 74, -77, WhoHol B*
Muzzarelli, Antonio 1744-1821 *CnOxB*
Muzzi, Edulilo *Film 2*
Muzzy, Robert *ConMuA 80B*
My Fancy 1878- *WhThe*
Myaskovsky, Nikolay Yakovlevich 1881-1950 *NewGrD 80*
Mycho, Richard *NewGrD 80*
Mycielski, Zygmunt 1907- *Baker 78, IntWWM 77, -80, NewGrD 80, WhoMus 72*
Myco, Richard *NewGrD 80*
Mycroft, Walter 1891-1959 *FilmgC, HalFC 80, IlWWBF*
Myer, Edmund John 1846-1934 *Baker 78, BiDAmM*
Myer, Torben *Film 2*
Myerberg, Michael 1906-1974 *BiE&WWA, NotNAT B, WhoHrs 80*
Myerov, Joseph 1928- *ConAmC*
Myers *PupTheA*
Myers, Amina Claudine 1942- *BlkWAB[port]*
Myers, Bessie Allen d1964 *NotNAT B*
Myers, Bumps 1912-1968 *EncJzS 70, WhoJazz 72*
Myers, Carl 1950- *CnOxB*
Myers, Carmel *MotPP, WhoHol A*
Myers, Carmel 1899-1966 *FilmEn, Film 1, -2, ForYSC, HalFC 80, TwYS*
Myers, Carmel 1901- *MovMk, ThFT[port]*
Myers, Carol *WomWMM*
Myers, Charles Arthur 1923- *WhoMus 72*
Myers, Claudia Margaret 1931- *WhoMus 72*
Myers, Farlan I 1918- *AmSCAP 66, -80*
Myers, Galene *PupTheA*
Myers, Gayther *BlkAmP, MorBAP*
Myers, Harry 1886-1938 *ForYSC, HalFC 80, WhScrn 74, -77, WhoHol B*
Myers, Harry C 1882-1938 *FilmEn, Film 1, -2, NotNAT B, TwYS*
Myers, Henry 1893- *AmSCAP 66, -80*
Myers, Herbert W 1943- *IntWWM 77, -80*
Myers, Hubert Maxwell 1912-1968 *EncJzS 70*
Myers, James E *AmSCAP 80*
Myers, Julian F 1918- *IntMPA 77, -75, -76, -78, -79, -80*
Myers, Kathleen *Film 2*
Myers, Louis 1929- *BluesWW[port]*
Myers, Margaret Helen 1947- *WhoMus 72*
Myers, Marion *PupTheA*
Myers, Paul 1917- *BiE&WWA, NotNAT*
Myers, Paulene *WhoHol A*
Myers, Pauline *DrBlPA*
Myers, Peter 1923- *WhoThe 72, -77*
Myers, Peter 1928-1968 *WhScrn 77, WhoHol B*
Myers, Peter S 1920- *IntMPA 77, -75, -76, -78, -79, -80*
Myers, Philip Frederick 1949- *IntWWM 77, -80*
Myers, Ray *Film 1, -2*
Myers, Raymond Geoffrey 1938- *NewGrD 80, WhoMus 72, WhoOp 76*
Myers, Richard 1901-1977 *AmSCAP 66, -80, BiE&WWA, CmpEPM, NotNAT, WhThe, WhoThe 72*
Myers, Rita Koors 1942- *IntWWM 77, -80*
Myers, Robert 1941- *CpmDNM 72, ConAmC*
Myers, Robert Francis 1925-1962 *WhScrn 74, -77*
Myers, Rollo Hugh 1892- *Baker 78, NewGrD 80, WhoMus 72*
Myers, Ronald Charles 1933- *AmSCAP 80*
Myers, Sammy 1936- *BluesWW[port]*
Myers, Serious Wilson Ernest 1906- *WhoJazz 72*
Myers, Sidney 1894- *FilmEn*
Myers, Stanley 1933- *IntWWM 77, -80*
Myers, Stanley A 1908- *AmSCAP 80*
Myers, Theldon 1927- *AmSCAP 80, CpmDNM 79, -80, ConAmC*
Myers, Warren 1930- *IntWWM 77*
Myerscough, Clarence Percy 1930- *IntWWM 77, -80, WhoMus 72*
Myerson, Bernard 1918- *IntMPA 77, -75, -76, -78, -79, -80*
Myerson, Bess 1924- *IntMPA 77, -75, -76, -78, -79, -80*
Myhers, John 1924- *BiE&WWA, WhoHol A*
Myhill, Jack *IntMPA 77, -76, -78, -79*
Myhren, Helge 1951- *IntWWM 80*
Mykietyn, Jerome 1942- *AmSCAP 80*
Myklegard, Age 1904- *IntWWM 77, -80*
Myles, Billy *RkOn*
Myles, Meg *WhoHol A*
Myles, Norbert *Film 2*
Myles, Warren 1920- *AmSCAP 80*
Mylius, Johann Daniel 1584?-1628? *NewGrD 80*
Mylius, Wolfgang Michael 1636-1713? *NewGrD 80*
Mylong, John 1893-1975 *WhScrn 77, WhoHol C*
Myltzewski, Marcin *NewGrD 80*
Mynniscus *OxThe*
Mynshall, Richard 1582?-1638 *NewGrD 80*
Myover, Max L 1924- *ConAmC*
Myrge, Mademoiselle *Film 2*
Myrick, Weldon Merle 1938- *BiDAmM*
Myriell, Thomas 1580?-1625 *NewGrD 80*
Myrow, Frederic 1939- *AmSCAP 66*
Myrow, Fredric 1939- *AmSCAP 80, ConAmC*
Myrow, Gerald 1923-1977 *AmSCAP 66, -80*
Myrow, Josef 1910- *AmSCAP 66, -80, CmpEPM, ConAmC*
Myrtil, Odette 1898-1978 *BiE&WWA, CmpEPM, ForYSC, HalFC 80, NotNAT, WhThe, WhoHol A*
Myrvik, Donald Arthur 1936- *IntWWM 77, -80*
Mysels, George 1912- *AmSCAP 80*
Mysels, George 1915- *AmSCAP 66*
Mysels, Maurice 1921- *AmSCAP 66, -80*
Mysels, Sammy 1906-1974 *AmSCAP 66, -80, CmpEPM*
Myslik, Antonin 1933- *IntWWM 77, -80*
Myslivecek, Josef 1737-1781 *NewGrD 80*
Mysliveczek, Joseph 1737-1781 *Baker 78*
Mysliviczek, Joseph 1737-1781 *OxMus*
Mysliweczek, Josef 1737-1781 *NewGrD 80*
Myssonne, Vincent *NewGrD 80*
Mystics, The *RkOn[port]*
Mysz-Gmeiner, Lula 1876-1948 *Baker 78, NewGrD 80*
Myszuga, Aleksander 1853-1922 *NewGrD 80*
Myton, Red *IntMPA 75, -76*
Mytou *NewGrD 80*

N

N Z Cracoviensis *NewGrD 80*
Nabarro, Margaret C Dalziel Nunes 1923- *IntWWM 80*
Nabbie, James Enoch 1920- *AmSCAP 80*
Nabokof, Nicolai 1903- *OxMus*
Nabokov, Nicholas 1903- *BiDAmM*
Nabokov, Nicolas 1903-1978 *Baker 78, CompSN[port], CnOxB, ConAmC, DancEn 78, DcCM, IntWWM 77, MusMk, NewGrD 80*
Nabokov, Nikolay 1903-1978 *NewGrD 80*
Nabors, James 1932- *BiDAmM*
Naccarato, John Thomas 1938- *WhoOp 76*
Nacchini, Pietro 1694?-1765 *NewGrD 80*
Nachbauer, Ernest *Film 2*
Nachbaur, Franz 1830-1902 *Baker 78*
Nachbaur, Franz 1835-1902 *NewEOp 71, NewGrD 80*
Nachez, Tivadar 1859-1930 *Baker 78*
Nachini, Pietro *NewGrD 80*
Nachtgall, Othmar *NewGrD 80*
Nachtigal, Sebald 1460?-1518 *NewGrD 80*
Nacio, H B *NewGrD 80*
Naclerio, Ruth 1924- *AmSCAP 80*
Nadajan d1974 *WhScrn 77*
Nadasi, Ferenc 1893-1966 *CnOxB*
Nadejdin, Serge 1880-1958 *DancEn 78*
Nadel, Arno 1878-1943 *Baker 78*
Nadel, Arthur *IntMPA 77, -75, -76, -78, -79, -80*
Nadel, Eli *Film 2*
Nadel, Norman 1915- *BiE&WWA, ConAmTC, NotNAT, WhoThe 72, -77*
Nadel, Warren 1930- *AmSCAP 66, -80*
Nademsky, Mikola *Film 2*
Nader, George 1921- *FilmEn, FilmgC, ForYSC, HalFC 80, IntMPA 77, -75, -76, -78, -79, -80, MotPP, WhoHol A, WhoHrs 80[port]*
Nader, Laura 1930- *WomWMM B*
Naderman *NewGrD 80*
Naderman, Francois-Joseph 1781-1835 *NewGrD 80*
Naderman, Henri 1780?-1835? *NewGrD 80*
Naderman, Jean-Henri 1735-1799 *NewGrD 80*
Nadermann, Francois-Joseph 1773?-1835 *BnBkM 80*
Nadermann, Francois Joseph 1781-1835 *Baker 78*
Nadezhdina, Nadezhda Sergeyevna 1908- *CnOxB, DancEn 78*
Nadi, Aldo 1899-1965 *Film 2, WhScrn 77*
Nadir, Moishe 1885-1943 *NotNAT B*
Nadir, Moses 1885-1943 *OxThe*
Nadler, Alexander *Film 2*
Naesteby, Kai J Angel 1920- *IntWWM 77, -80*
Naevius 270?BC-199?BC *Ent, PlP&P[port]*
Naevius, Gnaeus 270?BC-199?BC *NotNAT B, OxThe*
Nagan, Zvi Herbert 1912- *IntWWM 77, -80*
Nagano, Yonako 1933- *WhoOp 76*
Nagata, Masaichi 1906- *IntMPA 77, -75, -76, -78, -79, -80, WorEFlm*
Nagata, Mikifumi 1949- *CnOxB*
Nagaya, Kenzo *NewGrD 80*
Nagel *NewGrD 80*
Nagel, Adolph 1800-1873 *NewGrD 80*
Nagel, Ann *MotPP*
Nagel, Anne 1912-1966 *FilmEn, FilmgC, HalFC 80, WhScrn 74, -77, WhoHol B, WhoHrs 80*
Nagel, Anne 1916-1966 *ForYSC*
Nagel, Claire d1921 *NotNAT B*
Nagel, Conrad d1970 *MotPP, WhoHol B*
Nagel, Conrad 1896-1970 *Film 1, -2, FilmgC, HalFC 80, TwYS*
Nagel, Conrad 1897-1970 *BiE&WWA, FilmEn, ForYSC, MovMk[port], NotNAT B, WhScrn 74, -77, WhThe*
Nagel, Robert Earl, Jr. 1924- *CpmDNM 74, -76, ConAmC, IntWWM 77, -80*
Nagel, Wilibald 1863-1920 *OxMus*
Nagel, Wilibald 1863-1929 *Baker 78, NewGrD 80*
Nageli, Hans Georg 1773-1836 *NewGrD 80, OxMus*
Nageli, Johann Georg 1773-1836 *Baker 78*
Nagiah, V 1903-1973 *WhScrn 77*
Naginski, Charles 1909-1940 *Baker 78, BiDAmM, ConAmC*
Nagle, Mary Ellen 1928- *IntWWM 77, -80*
Nagle, Urban 1905-1965 *NotNAT B*
Nagler, A M 1907- *BiE&WWA, NotNAT*
Nagrin, Daniel 1917- *CmpGMD, CnOxB, DancEn 78[port]*
Nagy, Bill d1973 *WhScrn 77, WhoHol B*
Nagy, Frederick 1894- *AmSCAP 66, -80, ConAmC*
Nagy, Ivan 1943- *CnOxB*
Nagy, Kathe Von 1904-1973 *FilmAG WE*
Nagy, Kathe Von 1909- *FilmEn*
Nagy, Robert David 1929- *IntWWM 80, WhoOp 76*
Nagy, Stephen Istvan 1935- *WhoMus 72*
Nagy-Farkas, Peter 1933- *ConAmC*
Nah *Film 2*
Naharro, Bartolome DeTorres *OxThe*
Nahat, Dennis 1946- *CnOxB*
Nahatzki, Richard C 1949- *IntWWM 77, -80*
Nahmer, Wolfgang VanDer 1906- *IntWWM 80*
Nahmer, Wolfgang VonDer 1906- *IntWWM 77*
Naich, Hubert 1513?-1546? *NewGrD 80*
Naich, Hubertus 1513?-1546? *NewGrD 80*
Naich, Robertus 1513?-1546? *NewGrD 80*
Naidenov, Assen 1899- *NewGrD 80*
Naiditch-Cooper, Eva 1907- *IntWWM 80*
Naidoo, Bobby 1927-1967 *WhScrn 74, -77*
Naidu, S M Subbiah 1914- *IntWWM 77*
Naify, Marshall 1920- *IntMPA 77, -75, -76, -78, -79, -80*
Naify, Robert *IntMPA 77, -75, -76, -78, -79, -80*
Nail, Joanne *WhoHol A*
Naile, Linda Louise 1954- *AmSCAP 80*
Nainby, Robert 1869-1948 *NotNAT B, WhThe, WhoHol B*
Nairne, Baroness 1766-1845 *OxMus*
Naish, Archie 1878- *WhThe*
Naish, Bronwen 1939- *IntWWM 77, -80*
Naish, J Carrol 1900-1973 *FilmEn, FilmgC, ForYSC, HalFC 80[port], MovMk[port], WhScrn 77, WhoHol B*
Naish, J Carrol 1901-1973 *NotNAT B*
Naish, J Carroll 1897-1973 *HolCA[port]*
Naish, J Carroll 1900-1973 *MotPP, Vers A[port], WhoHrs 80*
Naismith, Laurence 1908- *BiE&WWA, FilmEn, FilmgC, ForYSC, HalFC 80, MovMk, NotNAT, WhoHol A, WhoThe 72, -77*
Naixh, Hubertus *NewGrD 80*
Najara, Israel *OxMus*
Najera, Edmund 1936- *ConAmC*
Nakada, Yoshinao 1923- *NewGrD 80*
Nakadai, Tatsuya 1930- *OxFilm, WorEFlm[port]*
Nakahira, Ko 1926- *FilmEn*
Nakajima, Haruo 1930?- *WhoHrs 80*
Nakamura, Kazuo 1926- *CreCan 2*
Nakamura, Kichizo 1877-1941 *ModWD*
Nakamura, Motohiko 1929- *IntMPA 77, -75, -76, -78, -79, -80*
Nakarai, Charles F T 1936- *IntWWM 77, -80*
Nakarenko, Dan *Film 2*
Nakas, Vytas 1947- *IntWWM 77, -80*
Nakashima, Jeanne Marie 1936- *AmSCAP 80*
Nakasuga Kengyo *NewGrD 80*
Nakay, Emma 1897- *IntWWM 77*
Nakayama, Teiichi 1920- *WhoOp 76*
Nakazawa, Katsura 1933- *WhoOp 76*
Nakic, Petar *NewGrD 80*
Naldi, Antonio *NewGrD 80*
Naldi, Giuseppe 1770-1820 *NewGrD 80*
Naldi, Hortensio *NewGrD 80*
Naldi, Nita d1961 *MotPP, WhoHol B*
Naldi, Nita 1889-1961 *Film 1, -2, TwYS*
Naldi, Nita 1897-1961 *NotNAT B*
Naldi, Nita 1899-1961 *FilmEn, FilmgC, HalFC 80, WhScrn 74, -77*
Naldi, Romolo d1612 *NewGrD 80*
Nalkowska, Zofia 1885-1954 *CnMD, ModWD*
Nalle, Billy *AmSCAP 66, -80, IntMPA 77, -75, -76, -78, -79, -80, IntWWM 77*
Nallinmaa, Eero Veikko 1917- *IntWWM 77, -80*
Nally, William *Film 2*
Namanworth, Phillip 1945- *AmSCAP 80*
Namara, Marguerite *Film 2*
Namath, Joe 1943- *FilmgC, HalFC 80, WhoHol A*
Nambu, K *Film 2*
Nameth, Martha J *AmSCAP 80*
Namieyski *NewGrD 80*
Namik, Kemal 1840-1888 *CnThe, REnWD[port]*
Namu d1966 *WhScrn 74, -77*
Namur, Jean De *NewGrD 80*
Namyslowski, Zbigniew 1939- *EncJzS 70*
Nanavaty, Daulat 1917- *IntWWM 80*
Nancarrow, Conlon 1912- *Baker 78, ConAmC, NewGrD 80*
Nance, Lonnie Bee 1938- *AmSCAP 80*

Nance, Ray 1913-1976 *CmpEPM, EncJzS 70, IlEncJ, WhoJazz 72*
Nance, Willis 1913-1976 *BiDAmM, EncJzS 70*
Nancekievill, Paul David 1952- *IntWWM 77, -80*
Nanchini, Pietro *NewGrD 80*
Nania, Salvatore 1915- *IntWWM 77, -80*
Nanino, Giovanni Bernardino 1550?-1623 *Baker 78*
Nanino, Giovanni Bernardino 1560?-1623 *NewGrD 80*
Nanino, Giovanni Maria 1543?-1607 *NewGrD 80*
Nanino, Giovanni Maria 1545?-1607 *Baker 78*
Nann, Nicholas T 1928- *AmSCAP 66*
Nanni, Fioravanti Domenico 1934- *WhoOp 76*
Nanook d1923 *Film 2, WhoHol B*
Nansen, Betty 1873-1943 *FilmEn*
Nansen, Betty 1876-1943 *Film 1, MotPP, NotNAT B, WhScrn 77, WhoHol B*
Nantermi *NewGrD 80*
Nantermi, Filiberto *NewGrD 80*
Nantermi, Michel'Angelo *NewGrD 80*
Nantermi, Orazio 1550?- *NewGrD 80*
Nanterni *NewGrD 80*
Nantier-Didiee, Constance 1831-1867 *NewGrD 80*
Nanton, Joe 1904-1948 *BiDAmM*
Nanton, Joseph 1904-1946 *IlEncJ*
Nanton, Morris Patrick 1929- *AmSCAP 66, -80*
Nanton, Tricky Sam 1904-1946 *CmpEPM, WhoJazz 72*
Nanut, Anton 1932- *IntWWM 77, -80*
Naogeorg *OxThe*
Napier, Alan 1903- *FilmEn, FilmgC, ForYSC, HalFC 80, IntMPA 77, -75, -76, -78, -79, -80, MovMk, Vers A[port], WhThe, WhoHol A*
Napier, Charles *WhoHol A*
Napier, Diana 1908- *FilmgC, HalFC 80, IlWWBF, WhoHol A*
Napier, Frank d1949 *NotNAT B*
Napier, John 1944- *WhoHol A, WhoThe 77*
Napier, Lonnie L *MorBAP*
Napier, Marita *IntWWM 80, WhoOp 76*
Napier, Paul *WhoHol A*
Napier, Russel 1910-1975 *WhoHol A*
Napier, Russell 1910-1974 *HalFC 80*
Napier, Russell 1910-1975 *FilmgC, WhScrn 77*
Napier, William 1740?-1812 *Baker 78, NewGrD 80*
Napierkowska *Film 1*
Napierkowska, Stacia *Film 2*
Napierkowska, Stanislawa *WhThe*
Napolean, Jo *WomWMM*
Napoleao DosSantos, Artur 1843-1925 *NewGrD 80*
Napoleon *Film 2*
Napoleon I, Emperor Of France 1769-1821 *NewGrD 80*
Napoleon, Art 1923- *FilmEn, FilmgC, HalFC 80, WorEFlm*
Napoleon, Marty 1921- *AmSCAP 66, -80, BiDAmM, CmpEPM, EncJzS 70*
Napoleon, Phil 1901-196-? *AmSCAP 66, -80, BgBands 74, BiDAmM, CmpEPM, WhoJazz 72*
Napoleon, Teddy George 1914-1964 *BiDAmM, CmpEPM, WhoJazz 72*
Napoleon XIV *RkOn[port], -2A*
Napoli, Gennaro 1881-1943 *Baker 78*
Napoli, Jacopo 1911- *Baker 78, IntWWM 77, -80, NewGrD 80, WhoOp 76*
Napravnik, Eduard 1839-1916 *Baker 78, BnBkM 80, CmOp, NewEOp 71, NewGrD 80[port]*
Napravnik, Edward 1839-1916 *OxMus*
Napton, Johnny 1924- *AmSCAP 66, -80*
Naquin, Bill 1900?- *NewOrJ*
Naranda, Ludmilla 1936- *CnOxB*
Naranjo, Ben *PupTheA*
Narayana Menon, Yatakke Kurupath 1911- *Baker 78*
Narbekova, O *Film 2*
Narcini, Deborah Antoinette 1953- *IntWWM 77, -80*
Narciso, Grazia d1967 *WhScrn 77*
Narcisse-Mair, Denise Lorraine 1940- *IntWWM 77, -80*
Nardelli, George d1973 *WhScrn 77*
Nardini, Pietro 1722-1793 *Baker 78, BnBkM 80, GrComp[port], MusMk, NewGrD 80, OxMus*
Nardini, Tom 1945- *FilmgC, HalFC 80, WhoHol A*
Nardino, Gary 1935- *BiE&WWA*
Nardo, Benedetto Serafico *NewGrD 80*
Nardo, Daniel C 1920-1968 *AmSCAP 66, -80*
Nares, Geoffrey 1917-1942 *NotNAT B, WhThe*
Nares, James 1715-1783 *Baker 78, NewGrD 80[port], OxMus*
Nares, Owen 1888-1943 *FilmEn, Film 1, -2, FilmgC, HalFC 80, IlWWBF[port], -A, NotNAT B, OxThe, WhScrn 74, -77, WhThe, WhoHol B*
Narholz, Gerhard Otto 1937- *WhoMus 72*
Narin, Gus *MorBAP*
Narizzano, Silvio 1927- *FilmEn, FilmgC, HalFC 80, IntMPA 77, -76, -78, -79, -80*
Narlay, R *Film 2*
Narmore, Edgar Eugene 1944- *AmSCAP 80*
Narrache, Jean *CreCan 2*
Naruse, Mikio 1905-1969 *DcFM, FilmEn, WorEFlm*
Narvaez, Luis De *Baker 78, OxMus*
Narvaez, Luys De *NewGrD 80*
Narvaez, Sara d1935 *WhScrn 74, -77*
Naschy, Paul *WhoHrs 80*
Nasci, Michele *NewGrD 80*
Nascimbene, Mario 1916- *HalFC 80*
Nascimbeni, Maria Francesca 1657?- *NewGrD 80*
Nascimbeni, Stefano *NewGrD 80*
Nasco, Gian 1510?-1561 *NewGrD 80*
Nasco, Giovanni 1510?-1561 *NewGrD 80*
Nasco, Jan 1510?-1561 *NewGrD 80*
Naseem, Banu 1922- *IntMPA 76*
Naseem, Mrs. Banu 1922- *IntMPA 75*
Naset, Clayton E 1895-1966 *AmSCAP 66, -80*
Nash, B A 1910- *AmSCAP 66*
Nash, Brian 1956- *WhoHol A*
Nash, Dick 1928- *CmpEPM*
Nash, Eugenia 1866-1937 *WhScrn 74, -77*
Nash, Florence 1888-1950 *NotNAT B, WhScrn 74, -77, WhThe, WhoHol B*
Nash, Frederick Ogden 1902-1971 *BiDAmM*
Nash, George 1865-1945 *Film 2*
Nash, George Frederick 1873-1944 *NotNAT B, WhScrn 74, -77, WhThe, WhoHol B*
Nash, Graham 1942- *AmSCAP 80, ConMuA 80A, IlEncR, RkOn 2[port]*
Nash, Harold 1931- *WhoMus 72*
Nash, Harold John *WhoMus 72*
Nash, Harold John 1931- *IntWWM 77, -80*
Nash, Heddle 1896-1961 *CmOp, NewGrD 80*
Nash, Ida Mae 1926- *AmSCAP 66*
Nash, Joey *CmpEPM*
Nash, John E *Film 2*
Nash, John Heddle *WhoMus 72*
Nash, John Lester, Jr. 1940- *AmSCAP 80*
Nash, Johnny 1940- *AmSCAP 66, DrBlPA, IlEncR[port], MorBAP, MotPP, RkOn*
Nash, June *Film 2*
Nash, Lemoine 1898-1969 *BluesWW*
Nash, Lemon 1898-1969 *NewOrJ*
Nash, Marilyn 1924?- *HalFC 80*
Nash, Mary 1885- *BiE&WWA, FilmgC, WhThe*
Nash, Mary 1885-1965 *ForYSC, NotNAT B, WhoHol B*
Nash, Mary 1885-1966 *WhScrn 74*
Nash, Mary 1885-1976 *HalFC 80, HolCA[port]*
Nash, Mary Evelyn d1965 *WhScrn 77*
Nash, Mary Frances Heddle 1928- *IntWWM 77, -80, WhoMus 72*
Nash, N Richard *AmSCAP 80, IntMPA 77, -75, -76, -78, -79, -80*
Nash, N Richard 1913- *BiE&WWA, EncWT, McGEWD, NotNAT, WhoThe 77*
Nash, N Richard 1916- *CnMD, ModWD*
Nash, Nancy *Film 2*
Nash, Noreen *ForYSC, WhoHol A*
Nash, Norman Graham 1940- *IntWWM 80*
Nash, Ogden 1902-1971 *AmSCAP 66, -80, BiE&WWA, EncMT, NotNAT B*
Nash, Percy 1880?- *FilmEn, IlWWBF*
Nash, Robert 1930- *AmSCAP 80*
Nash, Ted 1922- *CmpEPM*
Nashe, Thomas 1567-1601 *NotNAT B, OxThe, PlP&P*
Nashville Brass *BiDAmM, CounME 74A*
Nashville Students *BiDAmM*
Nashville Teens, The *RkOn 2[port]*
Nasidze, Sulkhan Ivanovich 1927- *Baker 78, NewGrD 80*
Nasimbeni, Stefano *NewGrD 80*
Nasirova, Khalima 1913- *NewGrD 80*
Nasja *Film 2*
Nasolini, Sebastiano 1768?-1816? *NewGrD 80*
Nason, Elias 1811-1887 *BiDAmM*
Nasr, Georges M *DcFM*
Nass, Elyse 1947- *NatPD[port]*
Nassan, Sander Alan 1947- *AmSCAP 80*
Nassarre, Pablo d1730 *NewGrD 80*
Nassau, Paul 1930- *BiE&WWA, NotNAT*
Nasser, Georges M 191-?- *DcFM*
Nasser, Jamil Sulieman 1932- *BiDAmM, EncJzS 70*
Nassif, S Joseph 1938- *NotNAT*
Nassiter, Marcia *WomWMM*
Nassour, Edward d1962 *NotNAT B*
Nastasijevic, Svetomir 1902- *Baker 78*
Nat, Marie-Jose 1940- *FilmAG WE, FilmEn*
Nat, Yves 1890-1956 *Baker 78, NewGrD 80*
Nat King Cole Trio *BiDAmM*
Natale, Pompeo d1681? *NewGrD 80*
Nataletti, Giorgio 1907-1972 *NewGrD 80*
Natali, Alfred Maxim 1915- *AmSCAP 80*
Natali, Pompeo d1681? *NewGrD 80*
Natalie, Angelo Michael 1952- *AmSCAP 80*
Natalis, N *NewGrD 80*
Natan, Emile d1962 *NotNAT B*
Natanson, Jacques 1901- *FilmEn, OxThe, WhThe*
Natanson, Tadeusz 1927- *Baker 78, IntWWM 77, -80*
Natchez *BluesWW[port]*
Nathan, Archibald *IlWWBF A*
Nathan, Ben 1857-1919 *NotNAT B, WhThe*
Nathan, Charles 1921- *AmSCAP 66, -80*
Nathan, George Jean 1882-1958 *EncWT, NotNAT A, -B, OxThe, WhThe*
Nathan, Hans 1910- *Baker 78, IntWWM 77, -80, NewGrD 80*
Nathan, Isaac 1790-1864 *Baker 78, NewGrD 80*
Nathan, Jack *IntWWM 77*
Nathan, Jerry *ConMuA 80B*
Nathan, Lane *AmSCAP 80*
Nathan, Montagu *Baker 78*
Nathan, Nancy *ConMuA 80B*
Nathan, Robert 1894- *AmSCAP 66, -80, ConAmC A*
Nathan, Vivian 1921- *BiE&WWA, NotNAT, WhoHol A, WomWMM*
Nathan, Wynn *IntMPA 77, -75, -76, -78, -79, -80*
Nathanson, Charles *Film 2*
Nathanson, Lucile Brahms *DancEn 78*
Nathanson, Morton 1918- *IntMPA 77, -75, -76, -78, -79, -80*
Nathanson, Nat *IntMPA 77, -75, -76, -78, -79, -80*
Nathanson, Ted *IntMPA 77, -75, -76, -78, -79, -80*
Natheaux, Louis 1898-1942 *Film 2, WhScrn 74, -77, WhoHol B*
Natiez, Max 1938- *DancEn 78*
Nation, Buck 1910- *IlEncCM*
Nation, Tex Ann 1916- *IlEncCM*
Nation, W H C 1843-1914 *NotNAT B, WhThe*
National Jazz Ensemble *EncJzS 70*
Natoli, Nat 1902?- *WhoJazz 72*
Natorp, Bernhard Christoph Ludwig 1774-1846 *Baker 78*
Natova, Natacha *Film 2*
Natra, Sergiu 1924- *Baker 78, DcCM, IntWWM 77, -80, NewGrD 80*
Natro, Jimmy 1908-1946 *WhScrn 74, -77*
Natschinski, Gerd 1928- *IntWWM 77, -80, NewGrD 80*
Natschinski, Thomas Michael 1947- *IntWWM 77*
Natte, Jean 1730?-1803 *PupTheA*
Nattiez, Jean-Jacques 1945- *NewGrD 80*
Natwick, Mildred 1908- *BiE&WWA, Ent, FilmEn, FilmgC, ForYSC, HalFC 80,*

HolCA[port], IntMPA 77, -75, -76, -78, -79, -80, MotPP, MovMk[port], NotNAT, Vers A[port], WhoHol A, WhoThe 72, -77
Nau, Etienne 1600?-1661? *NewGrD 80*
Nau, Maria Dolores Benedicta Josefina 1818-1891 *Baker 78, BiDAmM*
Nau, Simon *NewGrD 80*
Nau, Stephen 1600?-1661? *NewGrD 80*
Naudain, May 1880-1923 *NotNAT B, WhoStg 1908*
Naude, Gabriel 1600-1653 *NewGrD 80*
Naudin, Emilio 1823-1890 *Baker 78, NewEOp 71*
Naudot, Jacques-Christophe 1690?-1762 *NewGrD 80*
Naughton, Bill 1910- *CnThe, ConDr 73, -77, CroCD, EncWT, REnWD[port], WhoThe 72, -77*
Naughton, Bobby 1944- *EncJzS 70*
Naughton, Charles *FilmgC, HalFC 80*
Naughton, Charlie 1887-1976 *IlWWBF*
Naughton, James 1945- *HalFC 80, WhoHol A*
Naughton, Robert 1944- *EncJzS 70*
Naujalis, Juozas 1869-1934 *Baker 78*
Nault, Fernand 1921- *CnOxB, CreCan 1, DancEn 78*
Naumann *NewGrD 80*
Naumann, Emil 1827-1888 *Baker 78, NewGrD 80*
Naumann, Ernst 1832-1910 *NewGrD 80*
Naumann, Johann Gottlieb 1741-1801 *Baker 78, MusMk, NewGrD 80, OxMus*
Naumann, Karl Ernst 1832-1910 *Baker 78*
Naumann, Siegfried 1919- *Baker 78, NewGrD 80*
Naumberg, Nancy *WomWMM*
Naumbourg, Samuel 1815-1880 *NewGrD 80*
Naumov, Vladimir 1921- *DcFM*
Naumov, Vladimir 1927- *FilmEn*
Naundorf, Frank 1940- *NewOrJ SUP[port]*
Naura, Michael 1934- *EncJzS 70*
Nauss, Johann Xaver 1690?-1764 *NewGrD 80*
Nauwach, Johann 1595?-1630? *Baker 78, NewGrD 80*
Nava, Gaetano 1802-1875 *Baker 78*
Nava, Jose Maria *PupTheA*
Navara, Leon *AmSCAP 66, -80*
Navarra, Aimee *WomWMM*
Navarra, Andre 1911- *IntWWM 77, -80, NewGrD 80, WhoMus 72*
Navarra, Tina 1936- *AmSCAP 80*
Navarre, Avril 1928- *DancEn 78*
Navarro, Armando 1930- *CnOxB*
Navarro, Carlos 1922-1969 *WhScrn 74, -77, WhoHol B*
Navarro, Catherine *Film 2*
Navarro, Fats 1923-1950 *CmpEPM, IlEncJ, NewGrD 80*
Navarro, Jesus Garcia 1913-1960 *WhScrn 74, -77, WhoHol B*
Navarro, Joan *Film 2*
Navarro, Juan 1530?-1580 *Baker 78, NewGrD 80*
Navarro, Juan 1550?-1610? *NewGrD 80*
Navarro, Paul Louis 1943- *IntWWM 77, -80*
Navarro, Theodore 1923-1950 *BiDAmM, NewGrD 80*
Navarrus, Martinus *NewGrD 80*
Navas, Juan De *Baker 78, NewGrD 80*
Nave, Maria Luisa 1939- *WhoOp 76*
Navoigille, Guillaume 1745?-1811 *NewGrD 80*
Navoigille, Julien 1749?-1811? *NewGrD 80*
Navon, Shmuel 1904- *IntWWM 77, -80*
Navratil, Karel 1867-1936 *Baker 78*
Naw, Stephen *NewGrD 80*
Nawe, Izabella 1943- *WhoOp 76*
Nawm, Tom *Film 2*
Nawn, Tom *PupTheA*
Naww, Stephen *NewGrD 80*
Naxh, Hubertus *NewGrD 80*
Nay, Joseph *PupTheA*
Nayfack, Jules Joseph 1905- *IntMPA 77, -75, -76, -78*
Naylor *NewGrD 80*
Naylor, Bernard 1907- *Baker 78, NewGrD 80*
Naylor, E W *OxMus*
Naylor, Edward Woodall 1867-1934 *Baker 78, NewGrD 80*
Naylor, Jerry 1939- *IlEncCM*
Naylor, John 1838-1897 *Baker 78, NewGrD 80*
Naylor, John Duncan 1937- *WhoMus 72*
Naylor, Judy Anne 1956- *IntWWM 80*
Naylor, Kenneth Nicholson 1931- *WhoMus 72*
Naylor, Marjorie *PupTheA*
Naylor, Peter Russel 1933- *WhoMus 72*
Naylor, Peter Russell 1933- *IntWWM 77, -80*
Naylor, Robert 1899- *WhThe*
Naylor, Ruth 1908-1976 *Baker 78, WhoMus 72*
Nayo *BlkAmP*
Nayo, Nicholas Zinzendorf Kofi 1922- *IntWWM 77, -80*
Nazare, Ernesto 1863-1934 *NewGrD 80*
Nazareth *ConMuA 80A, IlEncR, RkOn 2[port]*
Nazareth, Ernesto 1863-1934 *Baker 78, NewGrD 80*
Nazarian, Bruce Charles 1949- *AmSCAP 80*
Nazarro, Cliff 1904-1961 *ForYSC, IntMPA 77, -75, -76, -78, -79, -80, WhScrn 77, WhoHol B*
Nazarro, Ray 1902- *FilmEn, FilmgC, HalFC 80, IntMPA 77, -75, -76, -78, -79, -80*
Nazim Hikmet Ran 1902-1963 *REnWD[port]*
Nazimova *WomWMM*
Nazimova, Alla 1879-1945 *CnThe, EncWT, Ent, FamA&A[port], FilmEn, Film 1, -2, FilmgC, ForYSC, HalFC 80, MotPP, MovMk, NotNAT B, OxFilm, OxThe, PlP&P, TwYS, WhScrn 74, -77, WhThe, WhoHol B, WhoStg 1908, WorEFlm*
Nazolin, Sebastiano *NewGrD 80*
Nazz *BiDAmM, RkOn 2[port]*
Nazzari, Amedeo 1907-1979 *FilmAG WE, FilmEn, FilmgC, HalFC 80, IntMPA 77, -75, -76, -78, -79, -80, WhoHol A*
Nazzaro, Lou 1936- *IntWWM 77*
Nazzaro, Lou 1939- *IntWWM 80*
Ndugu 1952- *EncJzS 70*
Neagle, Anna 1904- *BiDFilm, -81, BiE&WWA, EncMT, EncWT, FilmAG WE, FilmEn, FilmgC, ForYSC, HalFC 80, IlWWBF[port], -A[port], IntMPA 77, -75, -76, -78, -79, -80, MotPP, MovMk, NotNAT, -A, OxFilm, ThFT[port], WhoHol A, WhoThe 72, -77, WorEFlm*
Neagu, Aurelian 1929- *WhoOp 76*
Neal, Bob 1917- *EncFCWM 69*
Neal, Charles Taylor 1946- *ConAmC*
Neal, Frances *WhoHol A*
Neal, Frank 1917-1955 *WhScrn 74, -77, WhoHol B*
Neal, Gordon 1929- *IntWWM 77, -80*
Neal, Harold 1916- *IntWWM 77, -80*
Neal, Heinrich 1870-1940 *Baker 78*
Neal, Larry 1937- *BlkAmP, MorBAP*
Neal, Lenora Ford 1947- *IntWWM 77, -80*
Neal, Mary 1860-1944 *OxMus*
Neal, Patricia 1926- *BiDFilm, -81, BiE&WWA, FilmEn, FilmgC, ForYSC, HalFC 80, IntMPA 77, -75, -76, -78, -79, -80, MotPP, MovMk, NotNAT, -A, OxFilm, WhThe, WhoHol A, WhoHrs 80[port], WorEFlm*
Neal, Raful 1936- *BluesWW*
Neal, Richard *Film 2*
Neal, Tom 1914-1972 *FilmEn, FilmgC, ForYSC, HalFC 80, HolP 40[port], WhScrn 77, WhoHol B*
Neal, Walter 1920- *BiE&WWA, NotNAT*
Neal Smith, Denys John 1915- *IntWWM 77, -80, WhoMus 72*
Neale *NewGrD 80*
Neale, Frederick d1856 *NotNAT B*
Neale, John d1736 *NewGrD 80*
Neale, John Mason 1818-1866 *OxMus*
Neale, William d1769 *NewGrD 80*
Neals, Betty Harris 1934- *AmSCAP 80*
Neaman, Yfrah 1923- *IntWWM 77, -80, WhoMus 72*
Neame, Elwin *IlWWBF*
Neame, Ronald 1911- *BiDFilm, -81, DcFM, FilmEn, FilmgC, HalFC 80, IlWWBF, IntMPA 77, -75, -76, -78, -79, -80, MovMk[port], WorEFlm*
Neander, Alexius 1560?-1605? *NewGrD 80*
Neander, Joachim 1650-1680 *NewGrD 80*
Neander, Valentin 1540?-1584? *NewGrD 80*
Neander, Valentin 1575?-1619? *NewGrD 80*
Neapolitan, Ray 1940- *EncJzS 70*
Near, Gerald R A *ConAmC*
Near, Holly *WhoHol A*
Near, Holly Holmes 1949- *AmSCAP 80*
Nearing, Homer 1895- *AmSCAP 66*
Neary, Martin Gerard James 1940- *IntWWM 77, -80, NewGrD 80, WhoMus 72*
Neary, Patricia 1942- *CnOxB, DancEn 78[port]*
Neason, Hazel d1920 *WhScrn 77*
Neate, Charles 1784-1877 *Baker 78, NewGrD 80*
Neate, Kenneth 1914- *WhoMus 72*
Nebe, Michael 1947- *IntWWM 80*
Nebenzal, Seymour 1898-1961 *OxFilm*
Nebenzal, Seymour 1899-1961 *FilmEn, FilmgC, HalFC 80, IntMPA 77, -75, -76, -78, -79, -80*
Neblett, Carol 1946- *WhoOp 76*
Nebra, Jose De 1702-1768 *Baker 78, NewGrD 80*
Nebrada, Vincente 1932- *CnOxB*
Nechayev, Vasily 1895-1956 *Baker 78*
Necksten, Gart Bertil 1934- *IntWWM 77*
Ned, Louis 1858?-1895? *NewOrJ*
Nedbal, Karel 1888-1964 *Baker 78*
Nedbal, Manfred Josef Maria 1902- *IntWWM 77, -80, WhoMus 72*
Nedbal, Oscar 1874-1930 *OxMus*
Nedbal, Oskar 1874-1930 *Baker 78, NewGrD 80*
Nedd, Stuart d1971 *WhScrn 77*
Nedell, Alice Blakeney d1959 *WhScrn 74, -77, WhoHol B*
Nedell, Bernard 1898-1972 *BiE&WWA, Film 1, -2, HalFC 80, MotPP, Vers B[port], WhScrn 77, WhoHol B*
Nedell, Bernard 1899- *WhThe*
Nederlander, David T 1886-1967 *NotNAT B*
Nederlander, James 1922- *BiE&WWA, ConMuA 80B, NotNAT, WhoThe 77*
Nedrow, John Wilson 1912- *AmSCAP 80*
Nedyalkov, Hristo 1932- *IntWWM 80*
Needham, Hal *HalFC 80*
Needham, Hilary Margaret 1934- *IntWWM 77, -80*
Needham, Louise 1938- *IntWWM 77, -80*
Needham, Lucien 1929- *IntWWM 77, -80, WhoMus 72*
Needler, Henry 1685?-1760 *NewGrD 80*
Needles, Susan *WomWMM*
Neefe, Christian Gottlob 1748-1798 *Baker 78, MusMk, NewGrD 80, OxMus*
Neel, Boyd 1905- *Baker 78, CreCan 1, NewGrD 80*
Neel, Louis Boyd 1905- *CreCan 1, IntWWM 77, -80*
Neeley, Ted *WhoHol A*
Neely, Bennie E *BlkAmP*
Neely, Henry M d1963 *NotNAT B*
Neely, May *NewOrJ*
Neely, Neil *Film 2*
Neely, Sam 1948- *RkOn 2[port]*
Nees, Staf 1901-1965 *NewGrD 80*
Nees, Vic 1936- *IntWWM 77, -80*
Nef, Albert 1882-1966 *Baker 78*
Nef, Isabelle 1898-1976 *NewGrD 80*
Nef, Karl 1873-1935 *Baker 78, NewGrD 80*
Nef, Walter 1910- *NewGrD 80*
Neff, Fritz 1873-1904 *Baker 78*
Neff, Hildegard 1925- *FilmAG WE, HalFC 80, WorEFlm*
Neff, Hildegarde 1925- *BiDAmM, FilmEn, FilmgC, ForYSC, IntMPA 77, -75, -76, -78, -79, -80, MotPP, MovMk[port], OxFilm, WhoHol A*
Neff, Morty 1927- *AmSCAP 66, -80*
Neff, Pauline *Film 2*
Neff, Ralph d1973 *WhScrn 77*
Negin, Louis Mark 1932- *CreCan 1*
Negin, Mark 1932- *CreCan 1*
Neglia, Francesco Paolo 1874-1932 *NewGrD 80*
Neglia, Jose 1929-1971 *CnOxB*
Neglia, Jose 1935- *DancEn 78*
Negrea, Martian 1893-1973 *Baker 78, NewGrD 80*

Negrete, Jorge 1911-1953 *WhScrn 74, -77, WhoHol B*
Negri, Adelaida Graciela 1943- *WhoOp 76*
Negri, Cesare *DancEn 78*
Negri, Cesare 1535?-1604? *NewGrD 80*
Negri, Cesare 1536?-1604? *CnOxB*
Negri, Francesco 1609?-1635? *NewGrD 80*
Negri, Gino 1919- *Baker 78, NewGrD 80*
Negri, Giulio Santo Pietro De' *NewGrD 80*
Negri, Giuseppe 1920- *WhoOp 76*
Negri, Ippolito Chamatero Di *NewGrD 80*
Negri, Joseph 1926- *AmSCAP 66*
Negri, Marc'Antonio d1621? *NewGrD 80*
Negri, Maria Caterina *NewGrD 80*
Negri, Maria Rosa 1715?-1760 *NewGrD 80*
Negri, Massimiliano *NewGrD 80*
Negri, Pola *MotPP, What 1[port]*
Negri, Pola 1894- *BiDFilm, -81, FilmAG WE, FilmEn, Film 1, -2, ThFT[port], TwYS*
Negri, Pola 1897?- *FilmgC, ForYSC, HalFC 80, OxFilm, WhoHol A, WorEFlm[port]*
Negri, Pola 1899- *MovMk[port]*
Negri, Vittorio 1923- *IntWWM 80*
Negro, Giulio Santo Pietro De' *NewGrD 80*
Negroni, Baldassare 1877-1948 *DcFM, FilmEn*
Negroni, Joe 1940- *BiDAmM*
Negulesco, Jean 1900- *BiDFilm, -81, CmMov, FilmEn, FilmgC, HalFC 80, IntMPA 77, -75, -76, -78, -79, -80, MovMk[port], OxFilm, WomWMM, WorEFlm*
Negulesco, Julian 1946- *FilmAG WE*
Negus, Alfred Ainger 1905- *WhoMus 72*
Neher, Caspar 1897-1962 *EncWT, Ent, NewGrD 80, WhoMus 72*
Neher, John d1972 *WhoHol B*
Neher, Susan *WhoHol A*
Neiburg, Al J 1902-1978 *AmSCAP 66, -80, CmpEPM*
Neidhardt VonReuenthal 1180?-1240? *Baker 78*
Neidhardt, Johann Georg 1685?-1739 *NewGrD 80*
Neidhart Von Reuental 1180?-1237? *NewGrD 80[port]*
Neidhart Von Riuwental 1180?-1237? *NewGrD 80[port]*
Neidhart Von Rubental 1180?-1237? *NewGrD 80[port]*
Neidlinger, Buell 1936- *BiDAmM, EncJzS 70*
Neidlinger, Gustav 1912- *CmOp, IntWWM 77, -80, NewGrD 80*
Neidlinger, William Harold 1863-1924 *Baker 78, BiDAmM*
Neighborhood *RkOn 2A*
Neighbour, O W 1923- *NewGrD 80*
Neikrug, Marc E 1946- *AmSCAP 80, ConAmC*
Neil, Hildegarde 1939- *FilmgC, HalFC 80, WhoHol A*
Neil, Richard *Film 1*
Neil, Ross d1888 *NotNAT B*
Neil, Sandra 1932- *CnOxB*
Neil, Sara 1932- *DancEn 78*
Neilan, Marshal 1891-1958 *Film 1, FilmgC*
Neilan, Marshall 1891-1958 *BiDFilm, -81, FilmEn, Film 2, HalFC 80, MotPP, NotNAT B, OxFilm, TwYS A, WhScrn 74, -77, WhoHol B, WorEFlm*
Neild, Nancy Barbara 1915- *WhoMus 72*
Neill, Frank 1917- *IntMPA 77, -75, -76, -78, -79, -80*
Neill, James d1931 *Film 1, -2, NotNAT B, TwYS, WhoHol B*
Neill, James d1962 *NotNAT B*
Neill, James 1860-1931 *WhScrn 77*
Neill, James 1861-1931 *WhScrn 74*
Neill, Noel 1925?- *WhoHol A, WhoHrs 80[port]*
Neill, R William 1892-1946 *TwYS A*
Neill, Richard R 1876-1970 *Film 2, WhScrn 74, -77, WhoHol B*
Neill, Roy William 1886-1946 *FilmEn*
Neill, Roy William 1890-1946 *FilmgC, HalFC 80, IlWWBF, WhoHrs 80*
Neill, William *IntWWM 80, WhoOp 76*
Neillands, George 1900- *WhoMus 72*
Neillands, Isobel *WhoMus 72*
Neilsen-Terry, Dennis 1895-1932 *WhScrn 74, -77, WhoHol B*
Neilson, Ada 1846-1905 *NotNAT B*
Neilson, Adelaide 1846-1880 *OxThe*
Neilson, Adelaide 1848-1880 *FamA&A[port], NotNAT A*
Neilson, Agnes *Film 1*
Neilson, Asta 1883- *Film 2*
Neilson, Francis 1867-1961 *NotNAT B, WhThe*
Neilson, Harold V 1874-1956 *NotNAT B, WhThe*
Neilson, James 1910-1979 *FilmEn*
Neilson, James 1918-1979 *FilmgC, HalFC 80, WorEFlm*
Neilson, Julia 1868-1957 *OxThe, WhThe*
Neilson, Julia 1869-1957 *NotNAT A*
Neilson, Lilian Adelaide 1848-1880 *NotNAT B*
Neilson, Maud *WhoMus 72*
Neilson, Perlita 1933- *WhoHol A, WhoThe 72, -77*
Neilson-Fransen, Janis 1943- *IntWWM 80*
Neilson-Terry, Dennis 1895-1932 *NotNAT B, WhThe*
Neilson-Terry, Julia 1868-1957 *NotNAT B*
Neilson-Terry, Phyllis 1892- *BiE&WWA, WhThe, WhoHol A*
Neiman, John M 1935- *WhThe*
Neipris, Janet L *NatPD[port]*
Neischl *NewGrD 80*
Neise, George *WhoHol A*
Neisel, Edmund *Film 2*
Neisen, Gertrude 1910- *ForYSC*
Neithardt, Heinrich August 1793-1861 *NewGrD 80*
Neitz, Alvin J 1894- *TwYS A*
Neitzel, Otto 1852-1920 *Baker 78*
Nejedly, Vit 1912-1945 *Baker 78, NewGrD 80*
Nejedly, Zdenek 1878-1962 *Baker 78, NewGrD 80*
Nekes, Dore *WomWMM*
Nekes, Werner *WomWMM*
Nekola, Tassilo 1913- *WhoMus 72*
Nelbeland *NewGrD 80*
Nelhybel, Vaclav 1919- *AmSCAP 80, Baker 78, CpmDNM 79, ConAmC, NewGrD 80*
Nelidova, Lydia 1863-1929 *CnOxB*
Nelius, Louis *AmSCAP 80*
Nell, Louise M 1884-1944 *WhScrn 74, -77*
Nelle, Wilhelm 1849-1918 *Baker 78*
Nellhaus, Arlynn *ConAmTC*
Nelli, Piero 1926- *WorEFlm*
Nelligan, Kate 1951- *WhoThe 77*
Nelms, Henning 1900- *BiE&WWA*
Nelon, Rex Loyd 1932- *BiDAmM*
Nelson, Alice Brainerd d1963 *NotNAT B*
Nelson, Allison 1927- *WhoMus 72*
Nelson, Anne 1911-1948 *WhScrn 74, -77*
Nelson, Arthur *PupTheA*
Nelson, Barry *BiE&WWA, IntMPA 77, -75, -76, -78, -79, -80, MotPP, NotNAT, PlP&P A[port], WhoHol A, WhoThe 72*
Nelson, Barry 1920- *FilmEn, FilmgC, ForYSC, HalFC 80, MovMk*
Nelson, Barry 1925- *WhoThe 77*
Nelson, Big Eye Louis 1885-1949 *NewOrJ[port], WhoJazz 72*
Nelson, Bob 1944- *BluesWW*
Nelson, Bobby *Film 2*
Nelson, Boris *ConAmTC*
Nelson, Carrie d1916 *NotNAT B*
Nelson, Dave 1905-1946 *WhoJazz 72*
Nelson, David 1793-1844 *BiDAmM*
Nelson, David 1936- *ForYSC, IntMPA 77, -75, -76, -78, -79, -80, MotPP, What 5[port], WhoHol A*
Nelson, Davidson 1906?-1946 *NewOrJ*
Nelson, Don *ConAmTC*
Nelson, Dorothea Brandt *ConAmC*
Nelson, Douglas Raymond 1934- *IntWWM 77, -80*
Nelson, Dyer *AmSCAP 80*
Nelson, Ed 1928- *FilmgC, ForYSC, HalFC 80, WhoHol A, WhoHrs 80*
Nelson, Ed, Jr. 1916- *AmSCAP 66, -80*
Nelson, Ed G 1885- *AmSCAP 66, -80*
Nelson, Eddie Sunkist 1894-1940 *WhScrn 74, -77*
Nelson, Edgar *Film 2*
Nelson, Edward *PupTheA*
Nelson, Edward J 1911- *IntMPA 77, -78, -79, -80*
Nelson, Edward Warren 1922- *IntWWM 77*
Nelson, Eliza d1908 *NotNAT B*
Nelson, Eric Hilliard 1940- *BiDAmM*
Nelson, Erick 1949- *AmSCAP 80*
Nelson, Florence *Film 2*
Nelson, Frances *Film 1*
Nelson, Frank *Film 2*
Nelson, Frederic Jul 1923- *AmSCAP 66, -80*
Nelson, Gail 1946- *DrBlPA*
Nelson, Gene 1920- *CmMov, CmpEPM, FilmEn, FilmgC, ForYSC, HalFC 80, IntMPA 77, -75, -76, -78, -79, -80, MotPP, MovMk[port], NewYTET, PlP&P A[port], WhoHol A, WhoThe 77*
Nelson, George 1905- *NewOrJ*
Nelson, George Edward 1928- *IntWWM 77*
Nelson, Gordon d1956 *NotNAT B, WhoHol B*
Nelson, Gunvor *WomWMM A, -B*
Nelson, Harmon Oscar, Jr. 1907-1975 *AmSCAP 80*
Nelson, Harold d1937 *WhScrn 74, -77, WhoHol B*
Nelson, Harriet *ForYSC, IntMPA 77, -75, -76, -78, -79, -80, MotPP*
Nelson, Harry *ConMuA 80B*
Nelson, Havelock 1917- *IntWWM 77, -80, NewGrD 80, WhoMus 72*
Nelson, Helen *WomWMM B*
Nelson, Lord Horatio 1758-1805 *FilmgC, HalFC 80*
Nelson, Howard 1942- *WhoMus 72*
Nelson, Howard D 1930- *WhoOp 76*
Nelson, Howard Duane 1930- *WhoMus 72*
Nelson, Iromeio 1902-1974 *BluesWW[port]*
Nelson, J *Film 2*
Nelson, Jack 1882- *Film 1, -2, TwYS, -A*
Nelson, James C, Jr. 1921- *AmSCAP 66, -80*
Nelson, Jane *WhoOp 76*
Nelson, Jimmy 1928- *What 5[port]*
Nelson, John 1941- *Baker 78, WhoOp 76*
Nelson, Jon 1936- *IntWWM 77, -80*
Nelson, Judith 1939- *NewGrD 80*
Nelson, Ken 1911- *EncFCWM 69*
Nelson, Kenneth 1930- *BiE&WWA, NotNAT, WhoHol A, WhoThe 72, -77*
Nelson, Kristin *WhoHol A*
Nelson, Larry Alan 1944- *AmSCAP 80, CpmDNM 78, ConAmC*
Nelson, Lori 1933- *FilmEn, FilmgC, ForYSC, HalFC 80, IntMPA 77, -75, -76, -78, -79, -80, MotPP, WhoHol A, WhoHrs 80*
Nelson, Lottie 1875-1966 *WhScrn 74, -77, WhoHol B*
Nelson, Louis 1885-1949 *BiDAmM*
Nelson, Louis 1902- *NewOrJ[port], WhoJazz 72*
Nelson, Louise 1902- *IntWWM 77, -80*
Nelson, Malcolm George 1946- *IntWWM 77*
Nelson, Marcus *MorBAP*
Nelson, Monica Felicity 1932- *IntWWM 77*
Nelson, Natalie *MorBAP*
Nelson, Nick *PupTheA*
Nelson, Norman J 1943- *ConAmC*
Nelson, Novella 1939- *DrBlPA, NotNAT, PlP&P A[port]*
Nelson, Oliver Edward 1932-1975 *Baker 78, BiDAmM, BlkCS[port], ConAmC, DrBlPA, EncJzS 70, IlEncJ*
Nelson, Oswald George 1906-1975 *AmSCAP 66, -80, BiDAmM*
Nelson, Otto *Film 2*
Nelson, Ozzie d1975 *BgBands 74[port], IntMPA 75, MotPP, NewYTET, WhoHol C*
Nelson, Ozzie 1906-1975 *CmpEPM, HalFC 80, WhScrn 77*
Nelson, Ozzie 1907-1975 *FilmEn, FilmgC, ForYSC*
Nelson, Paul 1929- *AmSCAP 66, -80, ConAmC*
Nelson, Percy 1902- *WhoJazz 72*
Nelson, Peter 1932- *IntWWM 77, -80*
Nelson, Philip Francis 1928- *IntWWM 77, -80*
Nelson, Portia *WhoHol A*
Nelson, Portia 1920- *AmSCAP 80*
Nelson, Ralph 1916- *BiDFilm, -81, FilmEn, FilmgC, HalFC 80, IntMPA 77, -75, -76, -78, -79, -80, MovMk[port], NewYTET, WorEFlm[port]*

Nelson, Raymond 1898- *BiE&WWA, NotNAT*
Nelson, Raymond E 1907- *IntMPA 77, -75, -76, -78, -79, -80*
Nelson, Red *BluesWW[port]*
Nelson, Richard *NatPD[port]*
Nelson, Rick 1940- *ConMuA 80A, CounME 74[port], -74A, FilmgC, HalFC 80, IlEncCM[port], IlEncR[port], IntMPA 77, -75, -76, -78, -79, -80, MotPP, RkOn[port], WhoHol A*
Nelson, Ricky *AmPS B*
Nelson, Ricky 1940- *AmPS A, ForYSC*
Nelson, Robert *MagIlD, PupTheA*
Nelson, Robert 1902- *NewGrD 80*
Nelson, Robert E 1934- *AmSCAP 80*
Nelson, Robert U 1902- *Baker 78*
Nelson, Ron 1929- *AmSCAP 66, Baker 78, CpmDNM 72, -79, -80, ConAmC, DcCM*
Nelson, Ronald A 1927- *ConAmC*
Nelson, Ronald Jurez 1929- *AmSCAP 80*
Nelson, Ronald Jurez 1937- *AmSCAP 80*
Nelson, Ronnie *AmSCAP 80*
Nelson, Rosemary Muriel 1946- *IntWWM 77*
Nelson, Rudolf 1878-1960 *NewGrD 80*
Nelson, Ruth 1905- *PlP&P[port], WhoHol A, WhoThe 72, -77*
Nelson, Sam *Film 2*
Nelson, Sandy *AmSCAP 80*
Nelson, Sandy 1942- *RkOn*
Nelson, Sarah *CreCan 2*
Nelson, Seena 1936- *AmSCAP 80*
Nelson, Sheila Mary 1936- *WhoMus 72*
Nelson, Stanley 1933- *NatPD[port]*
Nelson, Steve Edward 1907- *AmSCAP 66, -80*
Nelson, Steven David 1947- *AmSCAP 80*
Nelson, Suzanne Janet 1951- *IntWWM 77*
Nelson, Sydney 1800-1862 *NewGrD 80*
Nelson, Tracy *IlEncCM, WhoHol A*
Nelson, Virginia Tallent 1911-1968 *WhScrn 77, WhoHol B*
Nelson, Willie 1933- *BiDAmM, ConMuA 80A[port], CounME 74[port], -74A, EncFCWM 69, IlEncCM, IlEncR*
Nelson Family *MotPP*
Nelsova, Zara *IntWWM 77, -80, WhoMus 72*
Nelsova, Zara 1918- *CreCan 2*
Nelsova, Zara 1919?- *NewGrD 80*
Nelsova, Zara 1924- *Baker 78*
Nembri, Damianus 1584-1649? *NewGrD 80*
Nemchinova, Vera 1899- *CnOxB, WhThe*
Nemec, Boyce 1918- *IntMPA 75*
Nemec, Jan 1936- *DcFM, FilmEn, FilmgC, HalFC 80, OxFilm, WorEFlm*
Nemec, Zdenek 1914-1945 *NewGrD 80*
Nemecek, Franz Xaver *Baker 78*
Nemecek, Jiri 1924- *CnOxB*
Nemenyi, Lili 1908- *IntWWM 77, -80*
Nemes, Katalin 1915- *IntWWM 77, -80*
Nemescu, Octavian 1940- *Baker 78, IntWWM 77, -80*
Nemet, Mary Ann 1936- *IntWWM 77, -80*
Nemeth, Carl 1926- *WhoOp 76*
Nemeth, Gyula 1930- *IntWWM 80*
Nemeth, Laszlo 1901-1975 *CroCD, McGEWD[port]*
Nemeth, Maria 1897-1967 *NewGrD 80*
Nemeth, Maria 1899-1967 *CmOp*
Nemeth, Ted *WomWMM*
Nemethy, Ella 1895-1961 *NewGrD 80*
Nemetz, Max *Film 2*
Nemiroff, Isaac 1912-1977 *AmSCAP 66, Baker 78, ConAmC*
Nemiroff, R *MorBAP*
Nemiroff, Robert *ConDr 77D, NotNAT*
Nemirovich-Danchenko, Vladimir Ivanovich 1858-1943 *EncWT, Ent[port], ModWD, NewGrD 80, NotNAT A, -B*
Nemirovich-Danchenko, Vladimir Ivanovich 1859-1943 *CnThe, OxThe, PlP&P[port]*
Nemo, Henry 1914- *AmSCAP 66, -80, CmpEPM*
Nemoy, Priscilla 1919- *AmSCAP 66, -80*
NeMoyer, Francis *Film 1*
Nemser, Sandy Rothenberg *WomWMM B*
Nemtchinova, Vera 1903- *DancEn 78*
Nemtin, Alexander 1936- *Baker 78*
Nemtzow, Lisa 1952- *AmSCAP 80*
Nemzo, Lisa *AmSCAP 80*
Nenasheva, L *Film 2*
Nendick, Josephine Anne *WhoMus 72*
Nendick, Josephine Anne 1931- *IntWWM 77, -80*
Nenna, Pomponio 1550?-1613? *NewGrD 80*
Nenna, Pomponio 1550?-1618? *Baker 78*
Nenning, Johann *NewGrD 80*
Nenov, Dimiter 1902-1953 *Baker 78, NewGrD 80*
Nentwig, Franz Ferdinand 1929- *WhoOp 76*
Neola, Princess *Film 2*
Neon Philharmonic *RkOn 2[port]*
Neophonic Orchestra *BiDAmM*
Nephelius, David *NewGrD 80*
Nepomuceno, Alberto 1864-1920 *Baker 78, NewGrD 80*
Nepomunceno, Luis 1930- *IntMPA 77, -75, -76, -78, -79, -80*
Nepotis *NewGrD 80*
Nepotis, Fleurquin 1495?-1537? *NewGrD 80*
Nepotis, Florens 1495?-1537? *NewGrD 80*
Nepotis, George 1530?-1567? *NewGrD 80*
Nepotis, Godefroid 1450?-1499 *NewGrD 80*
Nepotis, Govard 1450?-1499 *NewGrD 80*
Neralic, Tomislav 1917- *WhoOp 76*
Nerbe, Lennart 1917- *IntWWM 77, -80*
Nercom *NewGrD 80*
Nercome *NewGrD 80*
Neri, Donatelle *Film 2*
Neri, Filippo 1515-1595 *NewGrD 80*
Neri, Massimiliano 1615?-1666 *NewGrD 80*
Neri, Saint Donna Filippo 1515-1595 *Baker 78*
Neri, St. Philip *OxMus*
Neri De' Soldanieri, Niccolo Di *NewGrD 80*
Nericault, Philippe *REnWD[port]*
Nerina, Nadia 1927- *CnOxB, DancEn 78[port]*
Nerini, Emile 1882-1967 *Baker 78*
Neriti DaSalo, Vincenzo *NewGrD 80*
Nerito, Vincenzo *NewGrD 80*
Nernst, W *OxMus*
Nero 037-068 *NewGrD 80, OxThe*
Nero, Emperor *OxMus*
Nero, Charles *MorBAP*
Nero, Curtis *Film 2*
Nero, Franco *ForYSC*
Nero, Franco 1941- *FilmAG WE[port]*
Nero, Franco 1942- *FilmEn, FilmgC, HalFC 80, WhoHol A*
Nero, Paul 1917-1958 *AmSCAP 66, -80, CmpEPM, ConAmC*
Nero, Peter Bernard 1934- *BiDAmM, ConAmC*
Neron, Louis *NewGrD 80*
Neroni, Bartolomeo 1500?-1571? *OxThe*
Nerses IV Klayetsi 1112-1173 *NewGrD 80*
Neruda *NewGrD 80*
Neruda, Alois 1837-1899 *NewGrD 80*
Neruda, Franz Xaver 1843-1915 *Baker 78, NewGrD 80*
Neruda, Johann Baptist Georg 1707?-1780? *NewGrD 80*
Neruda, Josef 1807-1875 *NewGrD 80*
Neruda, Wilma 1838?-1911 *NewGrD 80*
Neruda, Wilma Maria Francisca 1839-1911 *Baker 78*
Nerudova, Amalie 1834-1890 *NewGrD 80*
Nerulos, Jacob Rizos 1778-1850 *NotNAT B*
Nerval, Gerard De 1808-1855 *NewEOp 71, NewGrD 80*
Nervig, Conrad A 1895- *HalFC 80*
Nervius, Leonardus 1585?-1652? *NewGrD 80*
Nervo, Jimmy *HalFC 80*
Nervo, Jimmy 1890-1975 *FilmgC, WhScrn 77, WhoHol C*
Nervo, Jimmy 1897-1975 *IlWWBF*
Nervo And Knox *Film 2*
Nes, Ole M 1888-1953 *Film 2*
Nesbet, John d1488? *NewGrD 80*
Nesbett, John d1488? *NewGrD 80*
Nesbit, Evelyn 1885-1967 *Film 1, -2, NotNAT A, -B, TwYS, WhScrn 74, -77, WhoHol B*
Nesbit, Evelyn 1886-1967 *HalFC 80*
Nesbit, John 1900-1938 *BiDAmM*
Nesbit, Pinna *Film 2*
Nesbitt, Cathleen *IlWWBF A, MotPP, PlP&P*
Nesbitt, Cathleen 1888- *BiE&WWA, FilmEn, ForYSC, HalFC 80, NotNAT, -A, WhoThe 77*
Nesbitt, Cathleen 1889- *FilmgC, MovMk, WhoHol A, WhoThe 72*
Nesbitt, Denis 1919- *WhoMus 72*
Nesbitt, Dennis 1919- *IntWWM 77, -80*
Nesbitt, Derren 1932?- *FilmgC, HalFC 80, WhoHol A*
Nesbitt, Edward Kerr 1919- *BiDAmM*
Nesbitt, John 1900?-1935 *WhoJazz 72*
Nesbitt, John 1910-1960 *WhScrn 77, WhoHol B*
Nesbitt, John 1911-1960 *HalFC 80*
Nesbitt, May *WhoMus 72*
Nesbitt, Miriam 1873-1954 *Film 1, MotPP, WhScrn 77, WhoHol B, WhoStg 1906, -1908*
Nesbitt, Miriam Anne 1879- *WhThe*
Nesbitt, Robert 1906- *EncMT, WhoThe 72, -77*
Nesbitt, Tom 1890-1927 *NotNAT B*
Neschling, John Luciano 1947- *IntWWM 77, -80*
Nesenus, Johann d1604 *NewGrD 80*
Neser, Johann 1560?-1602 *NewGrD 80*
Neseritis, Andreas 1897- *IntWWM 77, -80, NewGrD 80*
Nesin, Aziz 1915- *REnWD[port]*
Nesmith, Michael 1942- *ConMuA 80A, IlEncCM, IlEncR, WhoHol A*
Nesmith, Mike & The First National Band *RkOn 2[port]*
Nesmith, Ottola *ForYSC*
Nesmith, Ottola d1972 *Film 2, WhoHol B*
Nesmith, Ottola 1888-1972 *WhScrn 77*
Nesmith, Ottola 1893-1972 *WhThe*
Nesor, Al *WhoHol A*
Ness, Arthur J 1936- *IntWWM 77, -80*
Ness, Ed *WhoHol A*
Ness, Ole M 1888-1953 *Film 2, WhScrn 74, -77, WhoHol B*
Nessen, Ron *NewYTET*
Nessi, Giuseppe 1887-1961 *CmOp, NewGrD 80*
Nessler, Victor 1841-1890 *Baker 78, CmOp, NewEOp 71*
Nessler, Viktor 1841-1890 *NewGrD 80*
Nest, Loni *Film 2*
Nestaas, Eirik 1948- *IntWWM 77, -80*
Nestell, Bill 1895-1966 *MotPP, WhScrn 74, -77, WhoHol B*
Nesterenko, Evgeny 1938- *NewGrD 80*
Nesterenko, Yevgeni Yevgenievich 1938- *WhoOp 76*
Nestico, Sam 1924- *EncJzS 70*
Nestico, Sam 1931- *EncJzS 70*
Nestico, Samuel Louis 1924- *AmSCAP 80, ConAmC, EncJzS 70*
Nestor, John *FilmEn*
Nestroy, Johann Nepomuk 1801-1862 *CnThe, EncWT, Ent, McGEWD[port], NewGrD 80, NotNAT B, OxThe, REnWD[port]*
Nestyev, Izrail 1911- *Baker 78*
Nestyev Izrail Vladimirovich 1911- *NewGrD 80*
Nesvera, Josef 1842-1914 *NewGrD 80*
Netherclift, Joseph 1792-1863 *NewGrD 80*
Nethersole, Louis d1936 *NotNAT B*
Nethersole, Olga 1870-1951 *FamA&A[port], WhoStg 1906, -1908*
Nethersole, Olga Isabel 1863-1951 *OxThe*
Nethersole, Olga Isabel 1866-1951 *NotNAT B, WhThe*
Nethsingha, Lucian Alaric 1936- *IntWWM 77, -80*
Neto, Sebastiao Carvalho 1931- *AmSCAP 80*
Netolicka, Karel 1929- *IntWWM 77, -80*
Netsky, Ronald 1951- *AmSCAP 80*
Netsky, Steve 1951- *AmSCAP 80*
Nettel, Reginald 1899- *WhoMus 72*
Netter, Douglas 1921- *IntMPA 77, -75, -76, -78, -79, -80*
Netter, Leon D *IntMPA 75, -76*
Netti, Giovanni Cesare 1649-1686 *NewGrD 80*
Nettl, Bruno 1930- *Baker 78, IntWWM 77, -80, NewGrD 80*
Nettl, Paul 1889-1972 *Baker 78, BiDAmM, NewGrD 80*
Nettlefold, Archibald 1870-1944 *NotNAT B, WhThe*
Nettlefold, Frederick John 1867-1949 *NotNAT B, WhThe*

Nettles, Bill 1902?-1967 *BiDAmM*
Nettleton, Asahel 1783-1844 *BiDAmM*
Nettleton, John 1929- *WhoHol A, WhoThe 72, -77*
Nettleton, Lois 1929?- *BiE&WWA, FilmgC, ForYSC, HalFC 80, IntMPA 77, -75, -76, -78, -79, -80, NotNAT, WhoHol A, WhoThe 77*
Netto, Frank *NewOrJ*
Neu, Oscar F 1886-1957 *WhScrn 74, -77*
Neubauer, Franz Christoph 1750-1795 *Baker 78*
Neubauer, Franz Christoph 1760?-1795 *NewGrD 80*
Neubauer, Johann *NewGrD 80*
Neubauer, Vlastimil 1923- *IntWWM 77, -80*
Neubaur, Franz Christoph 1760?-1795 *NewGrD 80*
Neubaur, Johann *NewGrD 80*
Neuber, Caroline 1697-1760 *Ent[port]*
Neuber, Fredericka Carolina 1697-1760 *CnThe*
Neuber, Frederika Carolina 1697-1760 *NotNAT B, OxThe*
Neuber, Friedrike Caroline 1697-1760 *EncWT*
Neuber, Ulrich d1571 *NewGrD 80*
Neuber, Valentin d1590 *NewGrD 80*
Neubert, Bruce Alan 1954- *AmSCAP 80*
Neubert, Gunter 1936- *IntWWM 77, -80*
Neubrand, Heinz 1921- *IntWWM 77*
Neuburger, Hans 1934- *IntWWM 77, -80*
Neuchatel, Rudolf De *NewGrD 80*
Neuendorff, Adolf 1843-1897 *Baker 78, BiDAmM, NewEOp 71*
Neuer, Joann *WomWMM*
Neufeld, Mace 1928- *AmSCAP 66, -80*
Neufold, Max *Film 2*
Neufville, Johann Jacob De 1684-1712 *NewGrD 80*
Neugebauer, Hans 1923- *IntWWM 77, -80, WhoOp 76*
Neuhaus, Heinrich 1888-1964 *Baker 78, NewGrD 80*
Neuhaus, Max 1939- *ConAmC, IntWWM 77, -80, WhoMus 72*
Neuhaus, Rudolf 1914- *NewGrD 80, WhoOp 76*
Neuhoff *NewGrD 80*
Neukomm, Sigismund Ritter Von 1778-1858 *Baker 78, NewGrD 80*
Neukomm, Sigismund Von 1778-1858 *OxMus*
Neukrantz, Johann 1602-1654 *NewGrD 80*
Neuls-Bates, Carol 1939- *IntWWM 80*
Neuman, Alan 1924- *IntMPA 77, -75, -76, -78, -79, -80, NewYTET*
Neuman, E Jack *NewYTET*
Neumann, Alfred 1895-1952 *CnMD, McGEWD, ModWD*
Neumann, Alfred John 1928- *AmSCAP 80, ConAmC*
Neumann, Angelo 1838-1910 *Baker 78, NewEOp 71*
Neumann, Anton 1740-1776 *NewGrD 80*
Neumann, Dorothy *ForYSC, WhoHol A*
Neumann, Franz 1874-1929 *Baker 78*
Neumann, Freddie 1904- *NewOrJ*
Neumann, Frederick 1907- *NewGrD 80*
Neumann, Friedrich 1915- *IntWWM 77, -80*
Neumann, Gunter 1913- *WhoMus 72*
Neumann, Horst *NewGrD 80*
Neumann, Joanne K Nylund *AmSCAP 80*
Neumann, Karl 1903- *IntWWM 77, -80*
Neumann, Klaus L 1933- *IntWWM 80*
Neumann, Kurt 1906-1958 *FilmEn*
Neumann, Kurt 1908-1958 *FilmgC, HalFC 80, WhScrn 77, WhoHrs 80*
Neumann, Lotte *Film 2*
Neumann, Richard 1914- *ConAmC*
Neumann, Vaclav 1920- *IntWWM 77, -80, NewGrD 80[port], WhoOp 76*
Neumann, Veroslav 1931- *Baker 78, IntWWM 77, -80, NewGrD 80*
Neumann, Werner 1905- *NewGrD 80*
Neumann, Wolfgang 1945- *WhoOp 76*
Neumann-Spallart, Gottfried 1920- *WhoOp 76*
Neumark, Georg 1621-1681 *Baker 78, NewGrD 80*
Neumeier, John 1942- *CnOxB*
Neumeister, Erdmann 1671-1756 *NewGrD 80*
Neumeyer, Fritz 1900- *IntWWM 77, -80*
Neuner, Carl 1778-1830 *NewGrD 80*
Neunhaber, Anton *NewGrD 80*
Neupert *NewGrD 80*
Neupert, Edmund 1842-1888 *Baker 78*
Neupert, Hanns 1902- *IntWWM 77, -80, NewGrD 80*
Neupert, Johann Christoph 1848-1921 *NewGrD 80*
Neuroth, Freddie 1892?-1923 *NewOrJ[port]*
Neuschel *NewGrD 80*
Neuschl *NewGrD 80*
Neusidler *NewGrD 80*
Neusidler, Conrad 1541-1604? *NewGrD 80*
Neusidler, Hans 1508?-1563 *NewGrD 80*
Neusidler, Melchior 1531-1590 *NewGrD 80[port]*
Neuss, Heinrich Georg 1654-1716 *NewGrD 80*
Neusser, Eric 1902-1957 *WhScrn 74, -77*
Neuwirth, William 1915- *AmSCAP 80*
Nevada, Emma d1940 *NotNAT B*
Nevada, Emma 1859-1940 *Baker 78, BiDAmM, CmOp, MusSN[port], NewEOp 71, NewGrD 80*
Nevada, Mignon Mathilde Marie 1886-1971 *Baker 78, NewGrD 80*
Nevaro 1887-1941 *WhScrn 74, -77*
Nevel, Eva Mary 1924- *IntWWM 77, -80*
Nevens, Paul *WhoHol A*
Neves, Ignacio Parreiras 1730?-1793? *NewGrD 80*
Neveu 1750?- *NewGrD 80*
Neveu, Ginette 1919-1949 *Baker 78, NewGrD 80*
Neveu, Pierre Nicolas *BiDAmM*
Neveux, Georges 1900- *CnMD, McGEWD*
Neville, Aaron *RkOn 2[port]*
Neville, David James 1949- *IntWWM 80*
Neville, Diana Rosemary 1949- *IntWWM 80*
Neville, Edgar 1899- *McGEWD[port]*
Neville, Edgar 1900- *CroCD*
Neville, George *Film 2*
Neville, Harry d1945 *NotNAT B*
Neville, Henry Gartside 1837-1910 *NotNAT B, OxThe*
Neville, Jeffrey Edgar 1951- *IntWWM 77*
Neville, John 1925- *BiE&WWA, CnThe, FilmgC, HalFC 80, MotPP, NotNAT, -A, WhoHol A, WhoThe 72, -77*
Neville, John Gartside d1874 *NotNAT B*
Neville, Margaret 1939- *IntWWM 77, -80, WhoMus 72, WhoOp 76*
Neville, Michael Douglas 1942- *AmSCAP 80*
Neville, Phoebe *CmpGMD*
Neville, Rasunah Rosana 1938- *AmSCAP 80*
Nevin, Arthur Finley 1871-1943 *AmSCAP 66, -80, Baker 78, BiDAmM, ConAmC, NewGrD 80, OxMus*
Nevin, Edwin Henry 1814-1889 *BiDAmM*
Nevin, Ethelbert Woodbridge 1862-1901 *AmSCAP 66, -80, Baker 78, CmpEPM, NewGrD 80, OxMus*
Nevin, Ethelburt Woodbridge 1862-1901 *BiDAmM*
Nevin, George Balch 1859-1933 *AmSCAP 66, -80, BiDAmM*
Nevin, Gordon Balch 1892-1943 *AmSCAP 66, -80, Baker 78, BiDAmM, ConAmC*
Nevin, Mark *AmSCAP 80*
Nevins, Claudette *WhoHol A*
Nevins, Marian *OxMus*
Nevins, Morty 1917- *AmSCAP 66*
Nevins, Natalie 1943- *BiDAmM*
Nevins, Willard Irving 1890-1962 *AmSCAP 66*
Nevison, Howard S 1941- *WhoOp 76*
Nevius, John W 1774-1854 *BiDAmM*
New, George *PupTheA*
New, H *WhoMus 72*
New, Jimmy Ray 1938- *AmSCAP 80*
New, Leon John 1933- *IntWWM 80*
New Birth *RkOn 2[port]*
New Christy Minstrels *BiDAmM, EncFCWM 69, RkOn[port]*
New Colony Six, The *RkOn 2[port]*
New Grass Revival *IlEncCM[port]*
New Lost City Ramblers *BiDAmM, EncFCWM 69*
New Orleans All Stars *BiDAmM*
New Orleans Rhythm Kings *BiDAmM*
New Riders Of The Purple Sage *ConMuA 80A, IlEncCM, IlEncR, RkOn 2A*
New Seekers, The *RkOn 2[port]*
New Vaudeville Band, The *RkOn 2[port]*
New York Bass Choir *EncJzS 70*
New York City *RkOn 2[port]*
New York Dolls *ConMuA 80A, IlEncR*
New York Jazz Repertory Company *EncJzS 70*
New York Rock And Roll Ensemble *BiDAmM*
New York Saxophone Quartet *BiDAmM*
New York Syncopated Orchestra *BiDAmM*
Newall, Guy 1885-1927 *IlWWBF[port]*
Newall, Guy 1885-1937 *FilmEn, Film 1, -2, FilmgC, HalFC 80, NotNAT B, WhScrn 74, -77, WhThe, WhoHol B*
Newander, Mary Clarice 1935- *IntWWM 77, -80*
Newark, Derek *WhoHol A*
Newark, William 1450?-1509 *NewGrD 80*
Newarke, William 1450?-1509 *NewGrD 80*
Neway, Patricia 1919- *Baker 78, BiE&WWA, CmOp, NewEOp 71, NewGrD 80, NotNAT, WhoMus 72, WhoThe 72, -77*
Newbeats, The *RkOn 2[port]*
Newberg, Frank *Film 1, -2*
Newberry, Andrew 1949- *IntWWM 77, -80*
Newberry, Barbara 1910- *WhThe*
Newberry, Charles Bruce *IntMPA 80*
Newberry, Hazzard P 1907-1952 *WhScrn 74, -77*
Newbery, Charles Bruce *IntMPA 77, -75, -76, -78, -79*
Newbold, David *WhoMus 72*
Newborn, Abe 1920- *BiE&WWA*
Newborn, Ira 1949- *AmSCAP 80*
Newborn, Phineas, Jr. 1931- *BiDAmM*
Newborough, Gary 1955- *IntWWM 77*
Newbould, Herbert *OxMus*
Newbrook, Peter 1916- *FilmgC, HalFC 80, IntMPA 77, -75, -76, -78, -79, -80*
Newburg, Frank 1886-1969 *WhScrn 74, -77, WhoHol B*
Newbury, Kent Alan 1925- *AmSCAP 80, ConAmC*
Newbury, Mickey 1940- *CounME 74, -74A, IlEncCM[port]*
Newbury, Milton S, Jr. 1940- *AmSCAP 80*
Newcom, James E 1907- *IntMPA 77, -75, -76, -78, -79, -80*
Newcomb, Anthony 1941- *NewGrD 80*
Newcomb, Ethel 1875-1959 *Baker 78*
Newcomb, Ethel 1879-1959 *BiDAmM*
Newcomb, Mary d1967 *WhoHol B*
Newcomb, Mary 1894-1967 *WhScrn 74, -77*
Newcomb, Mary 1897-1966 *WhThe*
Newcombe, Caroline d1941 *NotNAT B*
Newcombe, Jessamine d1961 *WhScrn 74, -77*
Newcombe, Mary *PlP&P[port]*
Neweland *NewGrD 80*
Newell, David 1905- *Film 2*
Newell, John 1949- *ConAmC*
Newell, Raymond 1894- *WhThe*
Newell, Robert M 1940- *ConAmC*
Newell, Roy *AmSCAP 80*
Newell, Tom D d1935 *NotNAT B*
Newell, William 1894-1967 *ForYSC, WhScrn 74, -77, WhoHol B*
Newerk, William *NewGrD 80*
Newerk, William 1450?-1509 *NewGrD 80*
Newfeld, Sam 1900-1964 *FilmgC, HalFC 80*
Newfield, Sam 1899-1964 *FilmEn*
Newfield, Sam 1900-1964 *WhoHrs 80*
Newgard, Robert M 1925- *IntMPA 77, -75, -76, -78, -79, -80*
Newhall, Charles Stedman 1842-1935 *BiDAmM*
Newhall, Mayo 1890-1958 *WhScrn 74, -77, WhoHol B*
Newhall, Patricia *BiE&WWA, NotNAT, WhoHol A*
Newhart, Bob *IntMPA 75, -76, WhoHol A*
Newhart, Bob 1923- *FilmgC, HalFC 80*
Newhart, Bob 1929- *ForYSC, IntMPA 77, -78, -79, -80, JoeFr[port]*
Newill, James 1911- *ForYSC, WhoHol A*
Newlan, Paul Tiny *WhoHol A*
Newlan, Paul Tiny 1908- *Vers A[port]*
Newland, Anna Dewey 1881-1967 *WhScrn 74, -77*
Newland, John 1916?- *FilmgC, HalFC 80, IntMPA 77, -75, -76, -78, -79, -80, WhoHol A*
Newland, Mary 1905- *Film 2, IlWWBF, WhoHol A*
Newland, Paul 1903-1973 *WhScrn 77*

Newlands, Anthony 1926- *FilmgC, HalFC 80*
Newley, Anthony 1931- *BiDAmM, BiE&WWA, ConDr 73, -77D, EncMT, FilmAG WE, FilmEn, FilmgC, ForYSC, HalFC 80, IlWWBF[port], IntMPA 77, -75, -76, -78, -79, -80, MotPP, MovMk, NotNAT, OxFilm, WhoHol A, WhoThe 72, -77*
Newlin, Dika 1923- *Baker 78, ConAmC, NewGrD 80*
Newlove, John Herbert 1938- *CreCan 1*
Newman *NewGrD 80*
Newman, Al 1940- *IntMPA 77, -75, -76, -78, -79, -80*
Newman, Albert M 1900-1964 *AmSCAP 66, -80*
Newman, Alfred 1901-1970 *AmPS, AmSCAP 66, -80, Baker 78, BiDAmM, CmMov, CmpEPM, ConAmC, DcFM, FilmEn, FilmgC, HalFC 80, NewGrD 80, OxFilm, PopAmC[port], PopAmC SUP, WhScrn 74, -77, WhoHol B, WorEFlm*
Newman, Anthony 1941- *AmSCAP 80, BiDAmM, BnBkM 80, ConAmC*
Newman, Barbara Belle 1922- *AmSCAP 80*
Newman, Barry 1940- *FilmgC, HalFC 80, WhoHol A*
Newman, Candy 1945-1966 *WhScrn 77*
Newman, Charles 1901-1978 *AmSCAP 66, -80, BiDAmM, CmpEPM*
Newman, Claude 1903-1974 *CnOxB, DancEn 78, WhThe*
Newman, Danny 1919- *WhoOp 76*
Newman, David *ConDr 73*
Newman, David 1933- *BiDAmM, EncJzS 70*
Newman, David 1937- *ConDr 77A, FilmEn, IntMPA 77, -75, -76, -78, -79, -80*
Newman, Dwight 1902-1942? *NewOrJ*
Newman, Edwin 1919- *IntMPA 78, -79, -80, NewYTET*
Newman, Ernest 1868-1959 *Baker 78, DancEn 78, NewGrD 80, OxMus*
Newman, Eve *WomWMM*
Newman, Fathead 1933- *EncJzS 70*
Newman, Gerald 1939- *AmSCAP 80*
Newman, Gerald Miller 1926- *CreCan 2*
Newman, Greatrex 1892- *BiE&WWA, WhThe, WhoThe 72*
Newman, Harold H 1913- *IntMPA 75*
Newman, Herbert 1925- *AmSCAP 66, -80*
Newman, Howard 1911- *IntMPA 77, -75, -76, -78, NotNAT*
Newman, Jeanne Marjorie *PupTheA*
Newman, Jimmy 1927- *CounME 74, -74A, IlEncCM*
Newman, Jimmy C 1927- *BiDAmM, EncFCWM 69*
Newman, Joe 1909- *WorEFlm[port]*
Newman, Joe 1922- *CmpEPM, EncJzS 70*
Newman, John K 1864-1927 *Film 2, WhScrn 74, -77, WhoHol B*
Newman, Joseph Dwight 1922- *BiDAmM, EncJzS 70*
Newman, Joseph M 1909- *BiDFilm, -81, FilmEn, FilmgC, HalFC 80, IntMPA 77, -75, -76, -78, -79, -80, MovMk[port], WhoHrs 80, WorEFlm*
Newman, Lionel *CmpEPM, HalFC 80*
Newman, Lur Barden d1918 *WhScrn 77*
Newman, Martin H 1913- *IntMPA 77, -75, -76, -78, -79, -80*
Newman, Max 1914- *AmSCAP 66, -80*
Newman, Melissa *WhoHol A*
Newman, Nanette *FilmgC, IntMPA 77, -75, -76, -78, -79, -80, WhoHol A*
Newman, Nanette 1932- *IlWWBF[port]*
Newman, Nanette 1934- *HalFC 80*
Newman, Nanette 1935?- *FilmEn*
Newman, Nell 1881-1931 *WhScrn 74, -77*
Newman, Paul 1925- *BiDFilm, -81, BiE&WWA, CmMov, FilmEn, FilmgC, ForYSC, HalFC 80[port], IntMPA 77, -75, -76, -78, -79, -80, MotPP, MovMk[port], NotNAT A, OxFilm, WhThe, WhoHol A, WhoThe 72, WorEFlm[port]*
Newman, Peter Albert 1915- *WhoMus 72*
Newman, Phyllis 1935- *BiE&WWA, ForYSC, NotNAT, WhoHol A, WhoThe 77*
Newman, Randy 1943- *ConMuA 80A[port], IlEncR, RkOn 2[port]*
Newman, Randy 1944- *BiDAmM*
Newman, Robert *OxMus*
Newman, Robert V *IntMPA 77, -75, -76, -78, -79, -80*
Newman, Roger *WhoHol A*
Newman, Ruby 1902?- *BgBands 74, CmpEPM*
Newman, Samuel 1919- *IntMPA 77, -75, -76, -78, -79, -80*
Newman, Scott *WhoHol A*
Newman, Sidney 1917- *CreCan 2*
Newman, Sidney Thomas Mayow 1906- *IntWWM 77, WhoMus 72*
Newman, Sydney *IntMPA 77, -75, -76, -78, -79, -80, NewYTET*
Newman, Sydney 1917- *CreCan 2*
Newman, Theodore Simon 1933-1975 *AmSCAP 80, ConAmC*
Newman, Thomas *WhoHol A*
Newman, Walter Brown 1920- *HalFC 80, IntMPA 77, -75, -76, -78, -79, -80*
Newman, Widgey R 1900-1944 *IlWWBF*
Newman, William S 1912- *Baker 78, ConAmC, IntWWM 80, NewGrD 80, WhoMus 72*
Newman, Yvonne 1924- *IntWWM 77, -80, WhoMus 72*
Newmar, Julie *MotPP, WhoHol A*
Newmar, Julie 1930- *FilmgC, HalFC 80*
Newmar, Julie 1935- *BiE&WWA, FilmEn, ForYSC, NotNAT*
Newmarch, Rosa Harriet 1857-1940 *Baker 78, NewGrD 80*
Newmark, Hans 1904- *CreCan 1*
Newmark, John 1904- *Baker 78, CreCan 1, IntWWM 77, -80, NewGrD 80*
Newmark, Stewart 1916-1968 *WhScrn 77*
Newmeyer, Fred 1888- *FilmEn, TwYS A, WorEFlm*
Newnham-Davis, Nathaniel 1854-1917 *NotNAT B, WhThe*
Newsidler *NewGrD 80*
Newsom, Hugh Raymond 1891-1978 *Baker 78*
Newsom, Thomas Penn 1929- *AmSCAP 66, -80, BiDAmM, EncJzS 70*
Newsom, Tommy 1929- *EncJzS 70*
Newsome, Carman 1912-1974 *WhScrn 77*
Newsome, Carmen *BlksB&W C*
Newson, George John *WhoMus 72*
Newson, Roosevelt, Jr. 1946- *IntWWM 77, -80*
Newstone, Harry 1921- *NewGrD 80, WhoMus 72*
Newte, Horace Wykeham Can d1949 *NotNAT B*
Newton, Mrs. A *Film 2*
Newton, Betty 1922- *IntWWM 77, -80*
Newton, Charles d1926 *Film 2, WhScrn 74, -77, WhoHol B*
Newton, Edmund *ConAmTC*
Newton, Frances *CreCan 1*
Newton, Mrs. Frank 1896- *CreCan 1*
Newton, Frankie 1906-1954 *BiDAmM, CmpEPM, IlEncJ, WhoJazz 72*
Newton, George 1908- *IntWWM 77, -80*
Newton, Harold R 1906- *IntWWM 77, -80*
Newton, Henry Chance 1854-1931 *NotNAT B, WhThe*
Newton, Henry Jotham 1823-1895 *BiDAmM*
Newton, Sir Isaac 1642-1727 *NewGrD 80, OxMus*
Newton, Ivor 1892- *IntWWM 77, -80, NewGrD 80, WhoMus 72*
Newton, John *WhoHol A*
Newton, John d1625 *OxThe*
Newton, John 1725-1807 *OxMus*
Newton, Joy 1913- *CnOxB, DancEn 78*
Newton, Joyce Kathleen 1904- *WhoMus 72*
Newton, Kate d1940 *NotNAT B*
Newton, Lilias Torrance 1896- *CreCan 1*
Newton, Norma *WhoOp 76*
Newton, Raymond Nicholson 1944- *IntWWM 80*
Newton, Rhoda *AmSCAP 66*
Newton, Robert 1905-1956 *BiDFilm, -81, FilmAG WE[port], FilmEn, FilmgC, ForYSC, HalFC 80, IlWWBF[port], MotPP, MovMk[port], NotNAT B, OxFilm, Vers A[port], WhScrn 74, -77, WhThe, WhoHol B, WorEFlm*
Newton, Rodney Stephen 1945- *IntWWM 77, -80*
Newton, Theodore 1905-1963 *ForYSC, MotPP, NotNAT B, WhScrn 74, -77, WhoHol B*
Newton, Wayne *AmPS A, -B*
Newton, Wayne 1942- *RkOn*
Newton, Wayne 1944- *WhoHol A*
Newton, Willie 1885?-1921? *NewOrJ*
Newton-John, Olivia *ConMuA 80A[port]*
Newton-John, Olivia 1947- *RkOn 2[port]*
Newton-John, Olivia 1948- *AmSCAP 80, HalFC 80, IlEncCM[port], IlEncR[port]*
Newton Marsden, Ernest Octavius 1881-1954 *OxMus*
Nex, Andre *Film 2*
Ney, Elly 1882-1968 *Baker 78, NewGrD 80*
Ney, Joseph Napoleon *NewGrD 80*
Ney, Marie 1895- *HalFC 80, PlP&P, WhThe, WhoHol A*
Ney, Richard *IntMPA 77, -75, -76, -78, -79, -80, MotPP*
Ney, Richard 1916- *WhoHol A*
Ney, Richard 1917- *FilmgC, HalFC 80*
Ney, Richard 1918- *FilmEn, ForYSC*
Neyschl *NewGrD 80*
Neysidler *NewGrD 80*
Neytcheva-Milanova, Liliana 1945- *WhoOp 76*
Nez, Nita 1930- *AmSCAP 80*
Nezeritis, Andreas 1897- *CpmDNM 76, IntWWM 77, -80, NewGrD 80*
Nezhdanova, Antonina 1873-1950 *Baker 78, NewGrD 80[port]*
Nezval, Vitezslav 1900-1958 *FilmEn*
Ng, Marforie *WomWMM B*
Ngugi, James 1938- *ConDr 73, -77*
Nibbio, Stefano Venturi Del *NewGrD 80*
Nibelle, Adolphe-Andre 1825-1895 *Baker 78*
Nibley, Sloan *IntMPA 77, -75, -76, -78, -79, -80*
Niblo, Fred 1872-1948 *TwYS A*
Niblo, Fred 1874-1948 *BiDFilm 81, CmMov, DcFM, FilmEn, FilmgC, HalFC 80, MovMk[port], NotNAT B, OxFilm, WhScrn 74, -77, WhoHol B, WorEFlm*
Niblo, Fred, Jr. 1903-1973 *WhScrn 77*
Niblo, William d1878 *NotNAT B*
Niblock, James 1917- *AmSCAP 66, ConAmC*
Niblock, James F 1917- *AmSCAP 80, IntWWM 77, -80*
Nica, Grigore 1936- *IntWWM 80*
Nicander, Edwin 1876-1951 *NotNAT B, WhThe*
Nicaud, Philippe 1926- *FilmEn*
Niccodemi, Dario 1874-1934 *McGEWD[port]*
Niccolini, Dianora 1936- *WomWMM B*
Niccolini, Gian Battista 1782-1861 *McGEWD[port]*
Niccolini, Giuseppe *NewGrD 80*
Niccolo Da Perugia *NewGrD 80[port]*
Niccolo Del Proposto *NewGrD 80[port]*
Nice, The *ConMuA 80A, IlEncR*
Nice, Barbara Ann 1942- *IntWWM 77*
Nice, Carter 1940- *IntWWM 77, -80*
Nicetas, Bishop *OxMus*
Nichelmann, Christoph 1717-1762? *NewGrD 80*
Nichifor, Serban 1954- *IntWWM 80*
Nichol, Clarissa B 1895- *AmSCAP 66, -80*
Nichol, Emilie *Film 2*
Nichol, James W *BlkAmP*
Nichol, Margaret Kathleen *CreCan 1*
Nichol, Pegi *CreCan 1*
Nicholas De Merques *NewGrD 80*
Nicholas, Albert 1900-1973 *BiDAmM, CmpEPM, EncJzS 70, -70, IlEncJ, NewOrJ[port], WhoJazz 72*
Nicholas, Denise 1944?- *DrBlPA, WhoHol A*
Nicholas, Don 1913- *AmSCAP 66, -80*
Nicholas, Joan Maxwell 1928- *WhoMus 72*
Nicholas, John Kenneth 1923- *IntWWM 77, -80*
Nicholas, Joseph 1883-1957 *NewOrJ[port]*
Nicholas, Louis Thurston 1910- *IntWWM 77, -80*
Nicholas, Michael Bernard 1938- *IntWWM 77, -80*
Nicholas, Paul *RkOn 2[port], WhoHol A*
Nicholas, Robert Michael 1945- *IntWWM 77, -80*
Nicholas, Sarah Lacey 1908- *IntWWM 77*
Nicholas, William Arthur *WhoMus 72*
Nicholas, Wooden Joe 1883- *IlEncJ*
Nicholas Brothers, The *BlksBF, WhoHol A*

Nicholaus Prepositi De Perugia NewGrD 80
Nicholl, Don NewYTET
Nicholl, Horace Wadham 1848-1922 Baker 78, BiDAmM, NewGrD 80, OxMus
Nicholl, Joseph Weston 1875-1925 Baker 78
Nicholls, Agnes 1877-1959 Baker 78, CmOp, NewGrD 80
Nicholls, Agnes Margaret 1907- WhoMus 72
Nicholls, Anthony WhoHol A
Nicholls, Anthony 1902-1977 FilmgC, HalFC 80
Nicholls, Anthony 1907- WhoThe 72, -77
Nicholls, Fred J Film 2
Nicholls, George 1865-1927 HalFC 80, WhoHol B
Nicholls, George, Jr. 1897-1939 HalFC 80, WhoHol B
Nicholls, Gladys Lilian WhoMus 72
Nicholls, Harry 1852-1926 NotNAT B, WhThe
Nicholls, Horatio NewGrD 80
Nicholls, John NewGrD 80
Nicholls, John Whitburn 1916- IntWWM 77, -80, WhoMus 72
Nicholls, Leslie John 1948- IntWWM 80
Nicholo Del Proposto NewGrD 80
Nicholoff, Michael DancEn 78
Nichols, Alberta 1898-1957 AmSCAP 66, -80, ConAmC
Nichols, Alvin 1947- BluesWW[port]
Nichols, Anne 1891-1966 McGEWD, ModWD, NotNAT B, WhThe
Nichols, Anne 1896- BiE&WWA
Nichols, Barbara 1929-1976 FilmEn, HalFC 80
Nichols, Barbara 1932- FilmgC, ForYSC, MotPP, MovMk, WhoHol A
Nichols, Barbara 1932-1976 HolCA[port]
Nichols, Beverley 1898- WhThe
Nichols, Dandy 1907- FilmgC, HalFC 80, WhoHol A
Nichols, Dudley 1895-1960 BiDFilm 81, CmMov, DcFM, FilmEn, FilmgC, HalFC 80, OxFilm, WorEFlm
Nichols, Ernest Loring 1905-1965 AmSCAP 66, -80, Baker 78, BiDAmM, NewGrD 80, WhScrn 74, -77
Nichols, George 1864- Film 1, -2, TwYS
Nichols, George, Jr. 1897-1939 WhScrn 74, -77
Nichols, George, Sr. 1865-1927 WhScrn 74, -77
Nichols, George Ward 1831-1885 BiDAmM
Nichols, Guy d1928 NotNAT B
Nichols, Herbert Horatio 1919-1963 BiDAmM
Nichols, Herbie 1919-1963 IlEncJ
Nichols, Jack 1921- CreCan 2
Nichols, James Walker 1929- AmSCAP 80
Nichols, Jimmy BluesWW[port]
Nichols, Josephine WhoHol A
Nichols, Joy WhoHol A
Nichols, Leo FilmEn
Nichols, Lewis 1903- WhThe
Nichols, Margaret 1900-1941 WhScrn 74, -77, WhoHol B
Nichols, Marjorie J d1970 WhScrn 74, -77, WhoHol B
Nichols, Mike 1931- AmFD, BiDFilm 81, BiE&WWA, DcFM, EncWT, Ent, FilmEn, FilmgC, HalFC 80, IntMPA 77, -75, -76, -78, -79, -80, MovMk[port], NewYTET, NotNAT, OxFilm, WhoHol A, WhoThe 72, -77, WomWMM, WorEFlm
Nichols, Mike 1937- JoeFr[port]
Nichols, Nellie Margaret 1922- AmSCAP 80
Nichols, Nellie V 1885-1971 WhScrn 74, -77, WhoHol B
Nichols, Nichelle 1936?- DrBlPA, WhoHol A
Nichols, Norma Film 1
Nichols, Peter 1927- CnThe, ConDr 73, -77, EncWT, Ent, McGEWD, WhoThe 72, -77
Nichols, Red BgBands 74[port]
Nichols, Red 1905-1965 CmpEPM, NewGrD 80, WhoHol B, WhoJazz 72
Nichols, Red 1905-1966 IlEncJ
Nichols, Red And Five Pennies AmPS A
Nichols, Robert WhoHol A
Nichols, Robert Malise Bowyer 1893-1944 ModWD, NotNAT B
Nichols, Roger 1939- NewGrD 80
Nichols, Roger Stewart 1940- AmSCAP 80
Nichols, Ted 1928- AmSCAP 80
Nichols And May JoeFr[port]
Nichols-Bates, H Film 2
Nicholson, Anne P 1920- BiE&WWA, NotNAT
Nicholson, Charles 1795-1837 NewGrD 80
Nicholson, David 1919- IntWWM 77, -80
Nicholson, David Michael Prudhoe IntWWM 77, -80
Nicholson, Elizabeth Ann 1932- IntWWM 77, -80
Nicholson, Elwood J 1908- IntMPA 77, -75, -76, -78, -79, -80
Nicholson, Emrich 1913- IntMPA 77, -75, -76, -78, -79, -80
Nicholson, Eric WhoMus 72
Nicholson, H O 1868- WhThe
Nicholson, Jack IntMPA 75, -76, MotPP, WhoHol A
Nicholson, Jack 1936- IntMPA 77, -78, -79, -80, MovMk[port]
Nicholson, Jack 1937- BiDFilm 81, FilmEn, FilmgC, HalFC 80, OxFilm, WhoHrs 80
Nicholson, James 1946- NatPD[port]
Nicholson, James David 1917- BluesWW
Nicholson, James H 1916-1972 HalFC 80
Nicholson, James H 1916-1973 FilmgC, WhoHrs 80
Nicholson, John d1934 NotNAT B
Nicholson, Kenyon 1894- BiE&WWA, WhThe
Nicholson, Nora 1887-1973 FilmgC, WhoHol B
Nicholson, Nora 1889- WhoThe 72
Nicholson, Nora 1889-1973 WhThe
Nicholson, Nora 1892-1973 HalFC 80, WhScrn 77
Nicholson, Norman Cornthwaite 1914- CroCD
Nicholson, Paul 1877-1935 Film 2, TwYS, WhScrn 74, -77, WhoHol B
Nicholson, Ralph Ward 1907- IntWWM 77, -80, WhoMus 72
Nicholson, Richard 1570?-1639 NewGrD 80, OxMus
Nicholson, Robert IntMPA 77, -75, -76, -78, -79, -80
Nicholson, Sir Sydney 1875-1947 NewGrD 80
Nicholson, Sydney Hugo 1875-1947 OxMus
Nicholson, Sir William d1949 NotNAT B
Nicholson, William Joseph, Jr. 1948- IntWWM 77
Nichtern, Claire 1920- BiE&WWA, NotNAT
Nichtern, David M 1948- AmSCAP 80
Nick, Edmund 1891-1974 NewGrD 80
Nickel Von Hof NewGrD 80
Nickel, Gitta WomWMM
Nickel, Heinz 1935- IntWWM 77, -80
Nickel, Loren O 1942- IntWWM 77
Nickell, Paul IntMPA 77, -75, -76, -78, -79, -80
Nickerson, Camille 1888- BlkWAB, ConAmC
Nickerson, Dawn WhoHol A
Nickerson, Denise WhoHol A
Nickerson, Hammie BluesWW[port]
Nickerson, Philip 1886?- NewOrJ
Nickinson, Isabella 1847-1906 NotNAT B
Nickole, Leonidas 1929- BiE&WWA, NotNAT
Nickols, Walter 1853-1927 WhScrn 74, -77
Nicks, Walter 1925- CnOxB
Nickson, Noel John 1919- IntWWM 77, -80, WhoMus 72
Nico 1940?- ConMuA 80A, IlEncR
Nicode, Jean-Louis 1853-1919 Baker 78, NewGrD 80, OxMus
Nicodemi, Dario d1934 NotNAT B, WhThe
Nicodemo, Oswaldo 1915- IntWWM 77, -80
Nicol, Alex 1919- BiE&WWA, FilmEn, FilmgC, ForYSC, HalFC 80, IntMPA 77, -75, -76, -78, -79, -80, NotNAT, WhoHol A
Nicol, Emma d1877 NotNAT B
Nicol, Eric Patrick 1919- CreCan 2
Nicol, Harry N d1962 NotNAT B
Nicol, Joseph E 1856-1926 WhScrn 74, -77
Nicol, Pegi CreCan 1
Nicola Da Siena NewGrD 80
Nicola, The Great 1880-1946 MagIlD
Nicolai, Aldo 1920- CnMD
Nicolai, Carl Otto 1810-1849 NewEOp 71
Nicolai, Claudio 1929- WhoOp 76
Nicolai, David Traugott 1733-1799 NewGrD 80
Nicolai, Friedrich 1733-1811 NewGrD 80
Nicolai, Johann Michael 1629-1685 NewGrD 80
Nicolai, Johannes NewGrD 80
Nicolai, Karl Otto Ehrenfried 1810-1849 DcCom&M 79, OxMus
Nicolai, Otto 1810-1849 Baker 78, BnBkM 80, CmOp, CmpBCM, GrComp[port], MusMk, NewGrD 80[port]
Nicolai, Philipp 1556-1608 NewGrD 80
Nicolai, Valentin NewGrD 80
Nicolai, Valentino NewGrD 80
Nicolai, Willem 1829-1896 NewGrD 80, OxMus
Nicolas The Serb NewGrD 80
Nicolas, Ernest NewGrD 80
Nicolas, Guillaume NewGrD 80
Nicolau, Antoni 1858-1933 OxMus
Nicolau, Antonio 1858-1933 Baker 78, NewGrD 80
Nicolaus Capuanus NewGrD 80
Nicolaus Cracoviensis NewGrD 80
Nicolaus De Capua NewGrD 80
Nicolaus De Perugia NewGrD 80
Nicolaus De Radom NewGrD 80
Nicolaus De Senis NewGrD 80
Nicolaus Polonus NewGrD 80
Nicolescu, Antonius 1946- WhoOp 76
Nicolet, Aurele 1926- BnBkM 80, IntWWM 77, -80, NewGrD 80, WhoMus 72
Nicolet, Jean-Baptiste 1728-1796 EncWT, Ent, OxThe
Nicoletti, Filippo NewGrD 80
Nicoletti, Joseph 1947- AmSCAP 80
Nicoletti, Louis 1907-1969 WhScrn 77
Nicolini 1673-1732 NewEOp 71, NewGrD 80[port]
Nicolini 1834-1898 Baker 78
Nicolini, Ernest 1834-1898 NewGrD 80
Nicolini, Giuseppe 1762-1842 NewGrD 80
Nicoll, Allardyce 1894-1976 BiE&WWA, EncWT, NotNAT, OxThe, WhoThe 72, -77
Nicoll, Ellen 1927- WhoMus 72
Nicoll, James NewGrD 80
Nicoll, Marion 1909- CreCan 1
Nicolo NewGrD 80
Nicolo DeMalte NewGrD 80
Nicolson, Richard NewGrD 80, OxMus
Nicoly, Rene 1907-1971 NewGrD 80, OxMus
Nicomachus NewGrD 80
Nicosia, Paulo Caracciolo Da NewGrD 80
Nicostratos OxThe
Niculescu, Mariana IntWWM 80
Niculescu, Stefan 1927- Baker 78, DcCM, IntWWM 77, -80, NewGrD 80
Niday Canaday, Edna Veronica 1907- AmSCAP 80
Nidecki, Tomasz Napoleon 1807-1852 NewGrD 80
Niderlova, Milenka DancEn 78
Nides, Tina WomWMM
Nidetzky, Friedrich 1920- WhoOp 76
Nieberding, William Joseph 1948- AmSCAP 80
Niebuhr, Johann NewGrD 80
Niecks, Frederick 1845-1924 NewGrD 80, OxMus
Niecks, Friedrich 1845-1924 Baker 78, NewGrD 80
Niederdorfer, Otto Josef 1953- IntWWM 77, -80
Niederhoffer, Milton Lester 1943- IntWWM 77, -80
Niederholtzer, Rupert NewGrD 80
Niedermaier, Dale ConMuA 80B
Niedermeyer, Abraham Louis 1802-1861 OxMus
Niedermeyer, Louis 1802-1861 Baker 78, MusMk, NewGrD 80
Niedhammer, Ronald Edward 1930- AmSCAP 80
Niedt, Friedrich Erhard 1674-1708 NewGrD 80
Niedt, Nicolaus d1700 NewGrD 80
Niedzielski, Jozef 1793-1853 NewGrD 80
Niedzielski, Stanislaw 1842-1895 NewGrD 80
Niegehoff NewGrD 80
Nieh, Erh 1912-1935 NewGrD 80
Niehaus, Lennie 1929- EncJzS 70
Niehaus, Leonard 1929- BiDAmM, EncJzS 70

Niehaus, Manfred 1933- *DcCM, NewGrD 80*
Niehaus, Max 1888- *CnOxB, DancEn 78*
Niehoff *NewGrD 80*
Niel, Jean-Baptiste 1690?-1775? *NewGrD 80*
Niel, Pierre De *NewGrD 80*
Nieland, Christine *ConAmTC*
Nielsen, Alice *AmPS B*
Nielsen, Alice 1876-1943 *Baker 78, BiDAmM, NewEOp 71, NotNAT B, WhThe, WhoStg 1906, -1908*
Nielsen, Asta d1972 *Film 2, MotPP, WhoHol B*
Nielsen, Asta 1882-1972 *HalFC 80, WhScrn 77*
Nielsen, Asta 1883-1972 *BiDFilm 81, FilmEn, Film 1, FilmgC, OxFilm, WorEFlm[port]*
Nielsen, Augusta 1822-1902 *CnOxB*
Nielsen, Bjarne 1954- *IntWWM 80*
Nielsen, Carl 1865-1931 *Baker 78, BnBkM 80, CmOp, CompSN[port], DcCom 77, DcCom&M 79, DcCM, DcTwCC, -A, MusMk[port], NewGrD 80[port], OxMus*
Nielsen, Finn 1919- *IntWWM 77, -80*
Nielsen, Finn Fausing 1950- *IntWWM 80*
Nielsen, Flora 1900- *WhoMus 72*
Nielsen, Gertrude 1918-1975 *WhScrn 77*
Nielsen, Hans 1580?-1626? *NewGrD 80*
Nielsen, Hans 1911-1967 *WhScrn 77*
Nielsen, Ingvard d1975 *WhoHol C*
Nielsen, Karl *BiE&WWA*
Nielsen, Knud Leopold 1901- *IntWWM 77*
Nielsen, Leslie *IntMPA 75, -76, -78, -79, -80*
Nielsen, Leslie 1925- *FilmgC, HalFC 80, IntMPA 77, MotPP, MovMk, WhoHol A, WhoHrs 80*
Nielsen, Leslie 1926- *FilmEn, ForYSC*
Nielsen, Ludolf 1876-1939 *Baker 78, NewGrD 80*
Nielsen, Ludvig 1906- *NewGrD 80*
Nielsen, Margaret 1933- *NewGrD 80*
Nielsen, Mathilde *Film 2*
Nielsen, Niels Henrik 1935- *IntWWM 77, -80*
Nielsen, Riccardo 1908- *Baker 78, NewGrD 80*
Nielsen, Svend 1937- *Baker 78, CpmDNM 80, IntWWM 77, -80*
Nielsen, Tage 1929- *Baker 78, IntWWM 77, -80, NewGrD 80*
Nielson, Lewis James 1950- *CpmDNM 76*
Nielson, M Scott 1943- *AmSCAP 80*
Niemack, Ilza *ConAmC*
Nieman, Abbe 1913- *IntWWM 77*
Nieman, Alfred 1913- *IntWWM 80, WhoMus 72*
Niemann, Albert 1831-1917 *Baker 78, CmOp, NewEOp 71, NewGrD 80*
Niemann, Walter 1876-1953 *Baker 78, NewGrD 80*
Niemczyk, Waclaw 1907- *IntWWM 77, -80, WhoMus 72*
Niemetschek, Franz Xaver 1766-1849 *NewGrD 80*
Niemeyer, Harry 1909- *IntMPA 77, -75, -76, -78, -79, -80*
Niemeyer, Joseph H 1887-1965 *WhScrn 74, -77*
Niemoller, Klaus Wolfgang 1929- *NewGrD 80*
Niemotko-Brzezicka, Krystyna 1938- *IntWWM 80*
Niemtschek, Franz Xaver 1766-1849 *Baker 78*
Nienstedt, Gerd 1932- *WhoOp 76*
Niepce, Joseph-Nicephore 1765-1833 *DcFM, FilmEn*
Niepold, Mary Martin *ConAmTC*
Nierenberg, Roger 1947- *ConAmC*
Niert, Pierre De *NewGrD 80*
Niesen, Barney 1913- *AmSCAP 66*
Niesen, Gertrude d1975 *WhoHol C*
Niesen, Gertrude 1910- *CmpEPM, What 2[port], WhThe*
Niessen, Carl 1890-1969 *EncWT*
Niessen, Charly 1925- *IntWWM 77*
Niessen-Stone, Matja Von 1870-1948 *Baker 78*
Niessing, Paul 1917- *IntWWM 77, -80*
Nieto, Miguel 1844-1915 *NewGrD 80*
Nietzsche, Friedrich 1844-1900 *Baker 78, NewGrD 80, OxMus*
Nieva, Ignacio Morales 1928- *IntWWM 80*
Nieves Conde, Jose Antonio 1915- *FilmEn*
Niewiadomski, Stanislaw 1859-1936 *Baker 78, NewGrD 80*
Niewood, Gerry 1943- *EncJzS 70*
Nifosi, Alex *WhoMus 72*
Niger, Franciscus *NewGrD 80*
Nigetti, Francesco 1603-1681 *NewGrD 80*
Nigg, Serge 1924- *Baker 78, DcCM, NewGrD 80*
Niggli, Arnold 1843-1927 *Baker 78*
Niggli, Friedrich 1875-1959 *NewGrD 80*
Niggli, Josefina 1910- *NatPD[port]*
Nigh, Jane 1926- *FilmgC, ForYSC, HalFC 80, IntMPA 77, -75, -76, -78, -79, -80, WhoHol A, WhoHrs 80*
Nigh, William 1881-1955 *FilmEn, Film 1, -2, FilmgC, HalFC 80, TwYS A, WhScrn 77*
Night, Harry A Hank 1847-1930 *WhScrn 74, -77*
Nighthawk, Robert 1909-1967 *BluesWW[port]*
Nightingale, Alfred d1957 *NotNAT B*
Nightingale, C Leathley 1891- *WhoMus 72*
Nightingale, Florence 1820-1910 *HalFC 80*
Nightingale, James F 1948- *ConAmC*
Nightingale, Joe *WhThe*
Nightingale, Mae Wheeler 1898- *AmSCAP 66, -80, ConAmC*
Nightingale, Maxine 1952- *RkOn 2[port]*
Nigrin, Georg *NewGrD 80*
Nigyla, Cassandra *WomWMM B*
Nijazi 1912- *NewGrD 80*
Nijhoff, Martinus 1894-1953 *CnMD*
Nijinska, Bronislava Fominitshna 1891-1972 *CnOxB, DancEn 78[port], WhThe*
Nijinsky, Vaclav 1888-1950 *NewGrD 80*
Nijinsky, Vaslav 1890-1950 *DancEn 78[port], NotNAT A, -B, OxMus, WhThe*
Nijinsky, Vaslav Fomich 1888-1950 *CnOxB*
Nikandrov *Film 2*
Nikiprowetzky, Tolia 1916- *NewGrD 80*
Nikisch, Arthur 1855-1922 *Baker 78, BnBkM 80[port], MusMk, MusSN[port], NewEOp 71, NewGrD 80[port], OxMus*
Nikisch, Artur 1855-1922 *CmOp*
Nikitina, Alice 1909- *CnOxB, DancEn 78, WhThe*
Nikkonen, Harri Olavi 1933- *WhoOp 76*
Nikodemovich, Andry Maryanovich 1925- *NewGrD 80*
Nikolai, David Traugott *NewGrD 80*
Nikolaidi, Elena 1909- *Baker 78, MusSN[port], NewEOp 71*
Nikolaievic, Dusan 1885-1961 *CnMD*
Nikolais, Alwin 1912- *Baker 78, CmpGMD, CnOxB, ConAmC, ConDr 73, -77E, DancEn 78[port], DcCM*
Nikolaus Von Krakau *NewGrD 80*
Nikolayev, Alexander Alexandrovich 1903- *NewGrD 80*
Nikolayev, Alexey Alexandrovich 1931- *NewGrD 80*
Nikolayev, Leonid 1878-1942 *Baker 78, NewGrD 80*
Nikolayeva, Tatiana 1924- *Baker 78*
Nikolayeva, Tatyana 1924- *NewGrD 80*
Nikolic, Miomir 1944- *WhoOp 76*
Nikolov, Lazar 1922- *Baker 78, DcCM, NewGrD 80*
Nikolov, Ventseslav 1943- *IntWWM 80*
Nikolovski, Vlastimir 1925- *IntWWM 77, -80, NewGrD 80*
Nikomachos *NewGrD 80*
Nikonov, Vladimir Leonidovich 1937- *CnOxB*
Nile, Florian Martinez 1936-1959 *WhScrn 74, -77*
Niles, Fred A 1918- *IntMPA 77, -75, -76, -78, -79, -80*
Niles, John Jacob 1892- *AmSCAP 66, Baker 78, BiDAmM, ConAmC, EncFCWM 69, IntWWM 77, -80, WhoMus 72*
Nilges, Raymond Louis 1938- *AmSCAP 66*
Nilius, Rudolf 1883-1962 *Baker 78*
Nilles, Brad 1951- *AmSCAP 80*
Nillson, Alex *Film 1*
Nillson, Carlotta 1878?-1951 *Film 1, NotNAT B, WhThe, WhoStg 1908*
Nilovic, Janko 1941- *CpmDNM 79, -80*
Nilsen, Alexander 1903- *AmSCAP 66, -80*
Nilsen, Grethe 1952- *IntWWM 80*
Nilsen, Hans Jacob 1897-1957 *Ent[port]*
Nilson, Einar d1964 *NotNAT B*
Nilson, Leo 1939- *Baker 78*
Nilsson 1941- *RkOn 2[port]*
Nilsson, Anna Q 1888-1974 *WhScrn 77*
Nilsson, Anna Q 1889-1974 *HalFC 80*
Nilsson, Anna Q 1890- *What 3[port]*
Nilsson, Anna Q 1890-1974 *FilmEn, MotPP*
Nilsson, Anna Q 1893- *ForYSC*
Nilsson, Anna Q 1893-1974 *Film 1, -2, FilmgC, TwYS, WhoHol B*
Nilsson, Anna Q 1894-1974 *MovMk*
Nilsson, Birgit 1918- *Baker 78, BiDAmM, BnBkM 80[port], CmOp, IntWWM 77, -80, MusMk, MusSN[port], NewGrD 80[port], WhoHol A, WhoMus 72, WhoOp 76*
Nilsson, Birgit 1922- *NewEOp 71*
Nilsson, Bo 1937- *Baker 78, DcCom&M 79, DcCM, IntWWM 77, -80, NewGrD 80, WhoMus 72*
Nilsson, Christine 1843-1921 *BiDAmM, CmOp[port], NewEOp 71, NewGrD 80[port], NotNAT B, OxMus*
Nilsson, Erling Marten 1947- *IntWWM 77, -80*
Nilsson, Harry *WhoHol A*
Nilsson, Harry 1941- *IlEncR*
Nilsson, Harry 1942- *BiDAmM*
Nilsson, Kristina 1843-1921 *Baker 78, NewGrD 80[port]*
Nilsson, L 1939- *IntWWM 80*
Nilsson, Leopold Torre 1924- *FilmgC, HalFC 80*
Nilsson, Leopoldo Torre 1924- *BiDFilm, DcFM, FilmEn, WorEFlm[port]*
Nilsson, Maj-Britt 1924- *FilmEn*
Nilsson, Raymond 1920- *IntWWM 77, -80, WhoMus 72*
Nilsson, Torre 1924- *OxFilm*
Nilsson, Torsten 1920- *Baker 78, NewGrD 80*
Nimitz, Jack Jerome 1930- *BiDAmM, EncJzS 70*
Nimmo, Derek *WhoHol A*
Nimmo, Derek 1931- *FilmgC, HalFC 80*
Nimmo, Derek 1932- *WhoThe 72, -77*
Nimmons, Phil 1923- *CreCan 2, EncJzS 70*
Nimmons, Phillip Rista 1923- *BiDAmM, EncJzS 70*
Nimoy, Leonard 1931- *FilmEn, HalFC 80, IntMPA 80*
Nimoy, Leonard 1932- *FilmgC, ForYSC, WhoHol A, WhoHrs 80*
Nims, Ernest 1908- *IntMPA 77, -75, -76, -78, -79, -80*
Nims, Letha 1917- *BiE&WWA, NotNAT*
Nims, Walter Davis 1943- *AmSCAP 80*
Nimsgern, Siegmund 1940- *NewGrD 80, WhoOp 76*
Nimura, Yeichi 1897- *CnOxB*
Nimura, Yeichi 1908- *DancEn 78[port]*
Nin, Joaquin 1879-1949 *Baker 78, NewGrD 80, OxMus*
Nin-Culmell, Joaquin Maria 1908- *Baker 78, ConAmC, DcCM, IntWWM 77, -80, NewGrD 80, OxMus, WhoMus 72*
Ninchi, Ave *WhoHol A*
Ninchi, Carlo 1896-1974 *WhScrn 77, WhoHol B*
Nines, Patrick 1930- *WhoThe 72*
Nineteen Ten Fruitgum Company *BiDAmM*
Nineteen Ten Fruitgum Company, The *RkOn 2[port]*
Nini, Alessandro 1805-1880 *NewGrD 80*
Nino And The Ebb Tides *RkOn*
Ninot Le Petit d1502? *NewGrD 80*
Nioun, Mahoun Tien *DcFM*
Nirdlinger, Charles Frederic d1940 *NotNAT B*
Nisard, Theodore 1812-1888 *Baker 78, NewGrD 80*
Nisbet, J F d1899 *NotNAT B*
Nisbet, Joanne 1931- *CreCan 2*
Nisbett, Margaret 1930- *WhoMus 72*
Nisita, Giovanni d1962 *NotNAT B*
Niska, Maralin Fae 1930?- *IntWWM 80, NewGrD 80, WhoOp 76*
Nisle *NewGrD 80*
Nisle, Christian David 1772-1839? *NewGrD 80*
Nisle, Jean Frederic 1780-1861? *NewGrD 80*
Nisle, Johann Wilhelm Friedrich 1768-1839 *NewGrD 80*
Nisle, Johannes 1735-1788 *NewGrD 80*
Nisle, Martin 1780-1861? *NewGrD 80*

Nissel, Siegmund 1922- *WhoMus 72*
Nissen, Aud Egede *Film 2*
Nissen, Brian 1927- *WhThe*
Nissen, Constanze *NewGrD 80*
Nissen, Georg Nikolaus 1761-1826 *Baker 78, NewGrD 80*
Nissen, Greta 1906- *FilmEn, Film 2, FilmgC, ForYSC, HalFC 80, ThFT[port], TwYS, WhThe*
Nissen, Hans Hermann 1893- *Baker 78, CmOp, NewGrD 80*
Nissenson, Gloria Diane *AmSCAP 80*
Nissle *NewGrD 80*
Nistico, Sal 1940- *EncJzS 70*
Nistico, Salvatore 1940- *EncJzS 70*
Nite Hawks *BiDAmM*
Nite-Liters, The *RkOn 2[port]*
Nithart Von Reuental *NewGrD 80*
Nitrowski *NewGrD 80*
Nitrowski, Andrzej 1640?-1697 *NewGrD 80*
Nitrowski, Daniel 1635?-1683? *NewGrD 80*
Nitrowski, Jerzy 1605?-1673? *NewGrD 80*
Nitschke, Manfred 1926- *IntWWM 80*
Nitschmann, David 1696- *BiDAmM*
Nitty Gritty Dirt Band, The *BiDAmM, CounME 74[port], -74A, IlEncR, RkOn 2[port], ConMuA 80A,*
Nitzche, Jack 1937- *ConMuA 80B*
Nitzsche, Jack 1937- *AmSCAP 80, IlEncR, RkOn*
Niva, Rose *NewGrD 80*
Niven, David *IntMPA 77, -75, -76, -78, -79, -80, MotPP, WhoHol A*
Niven, David 1909- *FilmEn, FilmgC, HalFC 80[port], IlWWBF[port], -A, OxFilm, WhoHrs 80*
Niven, David 1910- *BiDFilm 81, ForYSC, MovMk[port], WorEFlm*
Niven, David, Jr. 1942- *IntMPA 78, -79, -80*
Niven, Frederick John 1878-1944 *CreCan 1*
Niven, Kip *WhoHol A*
Niverd, Raymond 1922- *IntWWM 77, -80*
Nivers, Guilaume 1632?-1714 *NewGrD 80*
Nivers, Guillaume Gabriel 1632?-1714 *NewGrD 80*
Nivert, Taffy *AmSCAP 80*
Niverville, Louis De 1933- *CreCan 1*
Nivoix, Paul 1889-1958 *McGEWD*
Niwa, Katsuumi 1938- *WhoOp 76*
Nix, Don 1941- *IlEncR*
Nix, Kenton T 1954- *AmSCAP 80*
Nix, Theo M 1910- *ConAmC*
Nix, William Patterson 1948- *IntMPA 78, -79, -80*
Nix, Willie 1922- *BluesWW[port]*
Nixon, Agnes *NewYTET*
Nixon, Allan *WhoHrs 80*
Nixon, Arundel 1907-1949 *WhScrn 77*
Nixon, Clint 1906-1937 *WhScrn 74, -77*
Nixon, David 1919-1978 *IntMPA 77, -75, -76, -78, -79, -80, MagIlD, PupTheA*
Nixon, Elmore 1933-1975? *BluesWW[port]*
Nixon, Hammie 1908- *BluesWW[port]*
Nixon, Hugh d1921 *NotNAT B*
Nixon, Marian 1904- *FilmEn, Film 2, FilmgC, ForYSC, HalFC 80, MotPP, ThFT[port], TwYS, WhoHol A*
Nixon, Marni *WhoMus 72*
Nixon, Marni 1929?- *FilmgC, HalFC 80, MotPP, WhoHol A*
Nixon, Marni 1930- *NewGrD 80*
Nixon, Roger A 1921- *AmSCAP 80, Baker 78, ConAmC*
Nixon-Nirdlinger, Fred G d1931 *NotNAT B*
Nizankowius, Andrzej 1591?-1655 *NewGrD 80*
Nizankowski, Andrzej 1591?-1655 *NewGrD 80*
Nizer, Louis 1902- *AmSCAP 66, -80, BiE&WWA, IntMPA 77, -75, -76, -78, -79, -80, NotNAT*
Nizhinsky, Vaclav 1888-1950 *NewGrD 80*
Njiric, Niksa 1927- *IntWWM 77, -80*
Nketia, Joseph Hanson Kwabena 1921- *IntWWM 77, -80*
Nkosi, Lewis 1936- *ConDr 73, -77*
Noa, Julian 1879-1958 *WhScrn 74, -77*
Noack, Eddie 1930- *IlEncCM*
Noack, Friedrich 1890-1958 *Baker 78*
Noack, Fritz 1935- *IntWWM 77, -80, NewGrD 80*
Noack, Kjeld *DancEn 78*
Noah, Mordecai Manuel 1785-1851 *EncWT, NotNAT B, OxThe*
Noak, Christian 1927- *CnMD*
Noakes, John *PlP&P[port]*
Noakova, Jana 1948-1968 *WhScrn 77*
Nobbe, Martha Johnson *PupTheA*
Nobel, Felix De 1907- *Baker 78, NewGrD 80*
Nobili, Laudivio De' *OxThe*
Noble, Ann 1955- *IntWWM 80*
Noble, Dennis 1898-1966 *WhThe*
Noble, Dennis 1899-1966 *CmOp, NewGrD 80*
Noble, Edward J d1958 *NewYTET*
Noble, Eulalie *WhoHol A*
Noble, Gil 1932- *DrBlPA, MorBAP*
Noble, Harry 1912-1966 *AmSCAP 66, -80*
Noble, James *WhoHol A*
Noble, Jeremy 1930- *IntWWM 77, -80, NewGrD 80, WhoMus 72*
Noble, John 1931- *IntWWM 77, -80, WhoMus 72*
Noble, John Avery 1892-1944 *AmSCAP 66, -80*
Noble, John W 1880- *TwYS A*
Noble, Lee G 1938- *IntWWM 77*
Noble, Leighton *BgBands 74, CmpEPM*
Noble, Milton 1844-1924 *Film 2*
Noble, Morag Jane *WhoMus 72*
Noble, Nick 1936- *AmSCAP 80*
Noble, Noel Alfred 1923- *IntWWM 77, -80*
Noble, Peter *IlWWBF A, IntMPA 77, -75, -76, -78, -79, -80*
Noble, Ray d1978 *BgBands 74[port], WhoHol A*
Noble, Ray 1903-1978 *Baker 78, CmpEPM, NewGrD 80, What 5[port]*
Noble, Ray 1907-1978 *BiDAmM*
Noble, Raymond 1903-1978 *NewGrD 80*
Noble, Richard Desmond Clunliffe 1930- *IntWWM 80*
Noble, Robert 1911- *WhoMus 72*
Noble, Ronald *IlWWBF A*
Noble, Tertius 1867-1953 *NewGrD 80*
Noble, Thomas Tertius 1867-1953 *AmSCAP 66, -80, Baker 78, OxMus*
Noble, Thomas Tertuis 1867-1953 *BiDAmM*
Noble, Weston *IntWWM 77, -80*
Noble, William 1921- *BiE&WWA, NotNAT*
Nobleman, Maurice 1927- *IntWWM 77, -80*
Nobles, Cliff & Co *RkOn 2A*
Nobles, Dollie d1930 *WhoHol B*
Nobles, Dolly d1930 *NotNAT B*
Nobles, Milton 1844-1924 *WhScrn 74, -77, WhoHol B, WhoStg 1908*
Nobles, Milton 1847-1924 *NotNAT B*
Nobles, Milton, Jr. d1925 *NotNAT B, WhoHol B*
Noblet, Charles 1715?-1769 *NewGrD 80*
Noblet, Lise 1801-1852 *CnOxB*
Noblitt, Katheryn McCall 1909- *AmSCAP 66, -80*
Nobre, Marlos 1939- *Baker 78, DcCM, IntWWM 77, -80, NewGrD 80*
Nobumitsu, Kwanze Kojiro *REnWD[port]*
Nobutaka *NewGrD 80*
Nobutoki, Kiyoshi 1887-1965 *Baker 78, NewGrD 80*
Noceti, Flaminio d1618? *NewGrD 80*
Nocetti, Flaminio d1618? *NewGrD 80*
Nock, Michael Anthony 1940- *AmSCAP 80, EncJzS 70*
Nocker, Hans Gunter 1927- *WhoOp 76*
Noda, Eva Saito 1921- *CpmDNM 78*
Noda, Ken 1962- *Baker 78*
Noda, Teruyuki 1940- *Baker 78, DcCM*
Nodalsky, Sonia *Film 2*
Nodari, Giovanni Paolo d1620? *NewGrD 80*
Nodell, Albert Charles *BlkAmP*
Nodell, Sonya *Film 2*
Nodermann, Preben 1867-1930 *Baker 78*
Noe, Stephen *NewGrD 80*
Noehren, Robert 1910- *BnBkM 80, ConAmC, NewGrD 80*
Noel *Film 2*
Noel, Barbara Hughes McMurtry 1929- *IntWWM 80*
Noel, Chris 1941- *ForYSC, WhoHol A*
Noel, Craig R 1915- *BiE&WWA, NotNAT*
Noel, Dick 1927- *AmSCAP 66, -80*
Noel, Jacques 1930- *IntWWM 77, -80*
Noel, Magali 1932- *FilmAG WE, FilmEn, FilmgC, HalFC 80, WhoHol A*
Noel, Rita 1943- *WhoOp 76*
Noel, Victoire *NewGrD 80*
Noel-Noel 1897- *FilmEn, HalFC 80, WhoHol A*
Noelli, Georg 1727-1789 *NewGrD 80*
Noelte, A Albert 1885-1946 *Baker 78*
Noelte, Rudolf 1921- *EncWT*
Noemi, Lea 1883-1973 *WhScrn 77, WhoHol B*
Noetel, Konrad Friedrich 1903-1947 *NewGrD 80*
Nofal, Emil 1926- *IntMPA 77, -75, -76, -78, -79, -80*
Nofere, Giovanni Battista *NewGrD 80*
Noferi, Giovanni Battista *NewGrD 80*
Nofieri, Giovanni Battista *NewGrD 80*
Noguchi, Isamu 1904- *CnOxB, DancEn 78, WomWMM*
Nohe, Beverly 1935- *ConAmC*
Nohl, Karl Friedrich Ludwig 1831-1885 *NewGrD 80*
Nohl, Ludwig 1831-1885 *Baker 78*
Noiret, Philippe 1931- *FilmAG WE[port], FilmEn, FilmgC, HalFC 80, IntMPA 79, -80, WhoHol A, WorEFlm*
Noisette, Katherine *BlksB&W C*
Noiseux-Labreque, Lise *WomWMM*
Nojima, Minoru *IntWWM 77, -80*
Nokes, James d1696 *OxThe, PlP&P*
Nola, Giovanni Domenico Da d1570 *OxMus*
Nola, Giovanni Domenico Del Giovane Da 151-?-1592 *NewGrD 80*
Nolan, Bill *Film 2*
Nolan, Bob *ForYSC*
Nolan, Dixie *BluesWW[port]*
Nolan, Doris 1916- *FilmEn, FilmgC, ForYSC, HalFC 80, ThFT[port], WhThe, WhoHol A*
Nolan, Gypo *Film 2*
Nolan, James *ForYSC, WhoHol A*
Nolan, Jeanette 1911?- *FilmEn, FilmgC, ForYSC, HalFC 80, WhoHol A*
Nolan, John *WhoHol A*
Nolan, Kathleen *WhoHol A*
Nolan, Kathy *ForYSC*
Nolan, Kenny *RkOn 2[port]*
Nolan, Lloyd *BiE&WWA, IntMPA 77, -75, -76, -78, -79, -80, MotPP, NotNAT, WhoHol A*
Nolan, Lloyd 1902- *FilmEn, FilmgC, ForYSC, HalFC 80[port], MovMk[port], WhThe, WorEFlm*
Nolan, Lloyd 1903- *CmMov, HolP 30[port]*
Nolan, Margaret *WhoHol A*
Nolan, Mary 1905-1940 *ForYSC*
Nolan, Mary 1905-1948 *FilmEn, Film 2, HalFC 80, TwYS, WhScrn 74, -77, WhoHol B*
Nolan, Mary 1906-1948 *NotNAT B*
Nolan, Poree *NewOrJ*
Nolan, Ronald Charles 1928- *WhoMus 72*
Nolan, Tom *WhoHol A*
Nolan, Walter *NewOrJ[port]*
Noland, James H 1918- *IntWWM 77*
Nolbandov, Sergei 1895-1971 *FilmgC, HalFC 80, IntMPA 77, -75, -76, -78, -79, -80*
Nolcini, Charles d1844 *BiDAmM*
Noldan, Svend *WomWMM*
Nolen, Charles R 1934- *IntWWM 77*
Nolen, Timothy 1941- *IntWWM 80, WhoOp 76*
Noll, Ernst-Diether 1934- *IntWWM 77, -80*
Nollekens, Joseph 1737-1823 *OxMus*
Nollet *NewGrD 80*
Nolletto *NewGrD 80*
Nolte, C Elmer, Jr. 1905- *IntMPA 77, -75, -76, -78, -79, -80*
Nolte, Charles 1926- *BiE&WWA, NotNAT, WhoHol A*
Nolte, Ewald Valentin 1909- *Baker 78, IntWWM 77, -80*
Nolte, Nick 1941- *FilmEn, HalFC 80*
Nolte, Nick 1942- *IntMPA 78, -79, -80*
Nolte, Roy E 1896-1979 *AmSCAP 66, -80, ConAmC*
Nolthenius, Helene 1920- *NewGrD 80*
Nomis, Leo d1932 *Film 2, WhScrn 74, -77, WhoHol B*

Nomis, Lou *AmSCAP 80*
Nomura, Yosio Francesco 1908- *IntWWM 77, -80, NewGrD 80*
Nonat, Joseph Waast Aubert *NewGrD 80*
Noni, Alda 1916- *CmOp, NewGrD 80*
Nono, Luigi 1924- *Baker 78, BnBkM 80, CompSN[port], CnOxB, DcCM, IntWWM 77, -80, MusMk[port], NewEOp 71, NewGrD 80[port], OxMus*
Nonot, Joseph Waast Aubert 1751-1840 *NewGrD 80*
Noon, David 1946- *AmSCAP 80, CpmDNM 74, -75, -77, -78, -79, -80, ConAmC, IntWWM 80*
Noon, Paisley 1897-1932 *WhScrn 74, -77, WhoHol B*
Noonan, John Ford 1943- *ConDr 73, -77, NotNAT*
Noonan, Patrick 1887-1962 *WhScrn 74, -77, WhoHol B*
Noonan, Tommy d1968 *MotPP, PupTheA, WhoHol B*
Noonan, Tommy 1921-1968 *FilmgC, HalFC 80*
Noonan, Tommy 1922-1968 *FilmEn, ForYSC, NotNAT B, WhScrn 74, -77*
Noone, Jimmie 1895-1944 *CmpEPM, IlEncJ, NewGrD 80, NewOrJ[port], WhoJazz 72*
Noone, Jimmy 1895-1944 *BiDAmM*
Noone, Lana M 1946- *IntWWM 77, -80*
Noone, Peter *WhoHol A*
Noord, Van *NewGrD 80*
Noordt, Van *NewGrD 80*
Noordt, Anthoni Van d1675 *NewGrD 80*
Noordt, Jacob Van 1619-1679? *NewGrD 80*
Noordt, Jacobus Van 1619-1679? *NewGrD 80*
Noordt, Sybrand Van d1705 *NewGrD 80*
Noort, Van *NewGrD 80*
Nopitsch, Christoph Friedrich Wilhelm 1758-1824 *NewGrD 80*
Noras, Arto Erkki 1942- *IntWWM 77, -80*
Norberg, Kevin Michael 1953- *AmSCAP 80*
Norbert, Frank *NewGrD 80*
Norbert, Henri 1904- *CreCan 1*
Norbert, Nat *PupTheA*
Norblin, Louis Pierre Martin 1781-1854 *NewGrD 80*
Norby, Erik 1936- *IntWWM 77, -80*
Norby, Irene Jellinek De *CreCan 1*
Norcliffe, Anthony 1939- *IntWWM 77*
Norcombe *NewGrD 80*
Norcombe, Daniel *NewGrD 80*
Norcombe, Daniel 1576-1626? *NewGrD 80*
Norcombe, John *NewGrD 80*
Norcome *NewGrD 80*
Norcome, Daniel 1576-1626? *OxMus*
Norcott, Beatrice *IntWWM 77*
Norcross, Frank 1856-1926 *NotNAT B, WhScrn 74, -77, WhoHol B*
Norcross, Hale d1947 *NotNAT B*
Norcross, Joseph M d1925 *NotNAT B*
Nord, Paul *REnWD[port]*
Nordal, Jon 1926- *Baker 78, NewGrD 80*
Nordblom, Johan Erik 1788-1848 *NewGrD 80*
Norden, Christine 1923- *FilmgC, HalFC 80*
Norden, Christine 1924- *IlWWBF*
Norden, Cliff 1923-1949 *WhScrn 74, -77*
Norden, Elfrida 1916- *AmSCAP 66, -80*
Norden, Hugo 1909- *ConAmC*
Norden, N Lindsay 1887-1956 *BiDAmM*
Norden, Norris Lindsay 1887-1956 *Baker 78, ConAmC*
Norden, Tommy *WhoHol A*
Nordenfelt, Dagmar 1908- *IntWWM 77, -80*
Nordenstrom, Gladys 1924- *ConAmC*
Nordgren, Erik 1913- *DcFM, FilmEn*
Nordgren, Herman Erik 1913- *IntWWM 77*
Nordgren, Pehr Henrik 1944- *Baker 78, IntWWM 77, -80, NewGrD 80*
Nordheim, Arne 1931- *Baker 78, DcCM, NewGrD 80*
Nordi, Cleo 1899- *CnOxB, DancEn 78*
Nordica, Lilian 1857-1914 *NewGrD 80[port]*
Nordica, Lillian 1857-1914 *Baker 78, BiDAmM, BnBkM 80, CmOp, MusSN[port], NewEOp 71, NewGrD 80[port], WhoStg 1906, -1908*
Nordin, Birgit 1934- *WhoMus 72, WhoOp 76*
Nordmo-Lovberg, Aase 1923- *CmOp*
Nordoff, Paul 1909-1977 *AmSCAP 66, Baker 78, BiDAmM, ConAmC, DancEn 78, DcCM, NewGrD 80, WhoMus 72*
Nordquist, Charles Paul 1947- *IntWWM 77, -80*
Nordquist, Johan Conrad 1840-1920 *Baker 78*
Nordqvist, Conrad 1840-1920 *NewGrD 80*
Nordqvist, Gustaf 1886-1949 *NewGrD 80*
Nordraach, Rikard 1842-1866 *NewGrD 80*
Nordraak, Richard 1842-1866 *OxMus*
Nordraak, Rikard 1842-1866 *Baker 78, NewGrD 80*
Nordstrom, Clarence 1893-1968 *NotNAT B, WhScrn 74, -77, WhoHol B*
Nordstrom, Frances *WhThe, WomWMM*
Nordstrom, Kristina *WomWMM B*
Nordstrom, Marie 1886- *WhoStg 1908*
Nordstrom, Tor Wilhelm 1944- *IntWWM 77, -80*
Nordyke, Kenneth *Film 2*
Noren, Heinrich Gottlieb 1861-1928 *Baker 78, NewGrD 80*
Norena, Eide 1884-1968 *Baker 78, BiDAmM, CmOp, NewEOp 71, NewGrD 80*
Norfolk, Edgar 1893- *WhThe*
Norfor, Avena Helen 1900- *WhoMus 72*
Norford, George 1918- *BlkAmP, DrBlPA, MorBAP*
Norgaard, Per 1932- *Baker 78, OxMus*
Norgard, Per 1932- *DcCM, IntWWM 77, -80, NewGrD 80*
Norgate, Edward d1650 *NewGrD 80*
Norgate, Matthew 1901- *WhoThe 72, -77*
Norheim, Thoralf Andreas 1912- *IntWWM 77, -80*
Norholm, Ib 1931- *Baker 78, NewGrD 80, OxMus*
Noricus, Johannes *NewGrD 80*
Noriega, Manolo 1880-1961 *WhScrn 74, -77*
Noriego, Eduardo *ForYSC*
Noringer, August *NewGrD 80*
Noris, Assia 1912- *FilmAG WE, FilmEn*
Noris, Matteo d1714 *NewGrD 80*
Norkin, Samuel N 1920- *ConAmTC*
Norlin, Lloyd B 1918- *AmSCAP 66, -80*
Norlind, Tobias 1879-1947 *Baker 78, NewGrD 80*
Norlund, Evy *WhoHol A*
Norma *PupTheA*
Norma Jean 1938- *IlEncCM[port]*
Norman, Amber *Film 2*
Norman, Barak 1670?-1740? *NewGrD 80*
Norman, Constance *AmSCAP 80*
Norman, E B d1930 *NotNAT B*
Norman, Evelyn Honor Richmond 1906- *WhoMus 72*
Norman, Frank *PlP&P*
Norman, Frank 1930- *ConDr 73, -77*
Norman, Frank 1931- *CroCD, EncWT, ModWD*
Norman, Fred 1910- *AmSCAP 66, -80, BiDAmM, WhoJazz 72*
Norman, Gary 1951- *CnOxB*
Norman, Gertrude 1848-1943 *Film 1, -2, WhScrn 74, -77, WhoHol B*
Norman, Jessye *IntWWM 80*
Norman, Jessye 1945- *BnBkM 80, DrBlPA, MusSN[port], NewGrD 80, WhoOp 76*
Norman, Jessye 1946- *BiDAmM*
Norman, John *NewGrD 80*
Norman, Josephine 1904-1951 *Film 2, WhScrn 74, -77, WhoHol B*
Norman, Karyl George d1947 *NotNAT B*
Norman, Leslie 1911- *FilmEn, FilmgC, HalFC 80, IlWWBF*
Norman, Louis *CreCan 1*
Norman, Lucille *ForYSC*
Norman, Ludvig 1831-1885 *Baker 78, NewGrD 80*
Norman, Maidie 1912- *DrBlPA, WhoHol A*
Norman, Monty 1928- *IntWWM 77, WhoMus 72*
Norman, Norman J 1870-1941 *NotNAT B, WhThe*
Norman, Norman V 1864-1943 *NotNAT B, WhThe*
Norman, Patricia 1916?- *CmpEPM*
Norman, Philip Keith 1949- *IntWWM 77*
Norman, Philip Thomas 1953- *IntWWM 80*
Norman, Robert *AmSCAP 80*
Norman, Rolf *AmSCAP 80*
Norman, Stanley 1921- *IntMPA 79, -80*
Norman, Theodore 1912- *AmSCAP 66, -80, ConAmC A*
Norman, Thyrza 1884- *WhThe*
Normand, Cisco 1936- *EncJzS 70*
Normand, Emile R 1936- *EncJzS 70*
Normand, Mabel d1930 *GrMovC[port]*
Normand, Mabel 1892-1930 *Funs[port]*
Normand, Mabel 1894-1930 *BiDFilm 81, FilmEn, Film 1, -2, FilmgC, HalFC 80, MotPP, MovMk, NotNAT B, OxFilm, TwYS, -A, WhScrn 74, -77, WhoHol B, WomWMM, WorEFlm*
Normand, Mabel 1895-1930 *JoeFr[port]*
Normand, Theodule Elzear Xavier *NewGrD 80*
Normansell, Ida Muriel 1906- *WhoMus 72*
Normiger, August 1560?-1613 *NewGrD 80*
Normington, John 1937- *WhoHol A, WhoThe 72, -77*
Norrenbrock, Paul Anthony 1947- *WhoOp 76*
Norreys, Rose d1946 *NotNAT B*
Norrie, Anna d1957 *NotNAT B, WhoHol B*
Norrington, Roger Arthur Carver 1934- *IntWWM 77, -80, NewGrD 80, WhoMus 72*
Norris, Al 1908- *WhoJazz 72*
Norris, Alexander *FilmEn, WhScrn 77*
Norris, Charles Glenn 1906- *IntMPA 77, -75, -76, -78, -79, -80*
Norris, Christopher *WhoHol A*
Norris, Edward 1910- *FilmEn, FilmgC, ForYSC, HalFC 80, IntMPA 77, -75, -76, -78, -79, -80, WhoHol A*
Norris, Ernest E d1935 *NotNAT B*
Norris, Geoffrey 1947- *IntWWM 77, -80*
Norris, Henry William Claudius 1887- *IntWWM 77*
Norris, Homer Albert 1860-1920 *BiDAmM*
Norris, John Wyatt 1893- *BiDAmM*
Norris, Karen *WhoHol A*
Norris, Kathi *IntMPA 77, -75, -76, -78, -79, -80*
Norris, Lee d1964 *NotNAT B*
Norris, Michael John 1934- *IntWWM 80*
Norris, Philip Eugene 1954- *AmSCAP 80*
Norris, Richard 1927- *IntWWM 80*
Norris, Robert 1924- *IntMPA 77, -75, -76, -78, -79, -80*
Norris, Thomas 1741-1790 *NewGrD 80*
Norris, Walter 1931- *EncJzS 70*
Norris, William d1929 *Film 1, -2, WhoHol B*
Norris, William 1669?-1702 *NewGrD 80*
Norris, William 1870-1929 *CmpEPM, NotNAT B, WhoStg 1906, -1908*
Norris, William 1872-1929 *WhScrn 74, -77, WhThe*
Norris, William James 1951- *BluesWW[port]*
North, Alex 1910- *AmSCAP 66, -80, Baker 78, BiE&WWA, CmpEPM, ConAmC, DancEn 78, DcCM, FilmEn, FilmgC, HalFC 80, IntMPA 77, -75, -76, -78, -79, -80, NewGrD 80, NotNAT, WorEFlm*
North, Bob 1881-1936 *WhScrn 74, -77*
North, Edmund H 1911- *CmMov, FilmEn, HalFC 80, IntMPA 77, -75, -76, -78, -79, -80*
North, Baron Francis 1637-1685 *NewGrD 80*
North, Francis, Lord Guilford 1637-1685 *OxMus*
North, Frank Mason 1850-1935 *BiDAmM*
North, Hattie *BluesWW[port]*
North, Jack King d1908- *AmSCAP 80*
North, Jay 1951- *ForYSC*
North, Jay 1952- *HalFC 80, WhoHol A*
North, Jay 1953- *FilmgC*
North, Joe d1945 *WhoHol B*
North, John Ringling 1903- *AmSCAP 66, -80*
North, Joseph B 1874-1945 *WhScrn 74, -77*
North, Michael 1920?- *HalFC 80, WhoHol A*
North, Nigel John 1954- *IntWWM 77, -80*
North, Robert 1945- *CnOxB*
North, Roger 1651?-1734 *NewGrD 80*
North, Roger 1653-1734 *Baker 78, OxMus*
North, Roger Dudley 1926- *IntWWM 77, -80, WhoMus 72*
North, Sheree *IntMPA 77, -75, -76, -78, -79, -80, MotPP*
North, Sheree 1930- *ForYSC, WhoHol A*
North, Sheree 1933- *FilmEn, FilmgC, HalFC 80*

North, Ted *ForYSC*
North, Wilfred 1853-1935 *Film 2, WhoHol B*
North, Wilfrid 1853-1935 *TwYS A, WhScrn 74, -77*
North, Zeme *WhoHol A*
Northcote, Anna 1907- *CnOxB*
Northcote, Anne *DancEn 78*
Northcote, Sidney Webber *IlWWBF*
Northcote, Sydney 1897-1968 *NewGrD 80*
Northcott, Bayan Peter 1940- *IntWWM 77, -80*
Northcott, Brian Richard 1944- *IntWWM 77, -80*
Northcott, John d1905 *NotNAT B*
Northcott, Richard 1871-1931 *NotNAT B, WhThe*
Northen, Michael 1921- *WhoThe 72, -77*
Northrup, Harry S 1877-1936 *Film 1, -2, MotPP, WhScrn 77*
Northshield, Robert *NewYTET*
Norton, Andrew 1786-1853 *BiDAmM*
Norton, Barry 1905-1956 *FilmEn, Film 2, ForYSC, MotPP, NotNAT B, TwYS, WhScrn 74, -77, WhoHol B*
Norton, Betty *Film 1*
Norton, Cecil A 1895-1955 *WhScrn 74, -77*
Norton, Cliff *WhoHol A*
Norton, E W 1915- *WhoMus 72*
Norton, Edgar *Film 2*
Norton, Elda 1891-1947 *WhScrn 74, -77*
Norton, Elliot 1903- *BiE&WWA, ConAmTC, NotNAT, WhoThe 72, -77*
Norton, Fletcher 1877-1941 *Film 2, WhScrn 74, -77, WhoHol B*
Norton, Frederic 1869-1946 *Film 2, NewGrD 80, NotNAT B, WhThe*
Norton, George A 1880-1923 *AmSCAP 66, -80, BiDAmM*
Norton, Henry Field 1899-1945 *WhScrn 74, -77*
Norton, Jack 1889-1958 *FilmEn, FilmgC, ForYSC, HalFC 80, HolCA[port], MotPP, MovMk, NotNAT B, Vers A[port], WhScrn 74, -77, WhoHol B*
Norton, Judy *WhoHol A*
Norton, Ken *WhoHol A*
Norton, Lillian 1857-1914 *BnBkM 80, NewGrD 80*
Norton, Lucille 1894-1959 *WhScrn 74, -77*
Norton, Richard *ConMuA 80B*
Norton, Robert Cecil *WhoMus 72*
Norton, Spencer 1909- *ConAmC*
Norton, Susan *WomWMM B*
Norton, Thomas 1532-1584 *Ent, McGEWD[port], NotNAT B, OxThe*
Norton, William *Film 2*
Norup, Bent 1936- *IntWWM 80, WhoOp 76*
Norvo, Kenneth 1908- *AmSCAP 66, -80*
Norvo, Red 1908- *BgBands 74[port], BiDAmM, CmpEPM, EncJzS 70, IlEncJ, NewGrD 80, WhoJazz 72*
Norvus, Nervous *RkOn*
Norwid, Cyprian Kamil 1821-1883 *CnThe, OxThe, REnWD[port]*
Norwood, Eille d1948 *CmMov, WhoHol B*
Norwood, Eille 1841-1948 *Film 1*
Norwood, Eille 1861-1948 *HalFC 80, IlWWBF[port], NotNAT B, WhThe*
Norwood, Ellie 1841-1948 *Film 2*
Norwood, Sam 1900?-1967? *BluesWW*
Norwood, Wayne Denzil, Jr. 1943- *AmSCAP 80*
Norworth, Jack 1879-1959 *AmSCAP 66, -80, BiDAmM, CmpEPM, EncMT, Film 2, NotNAT B, OxThe, WhScrn 74, -77, WhThe, WhoHol B*
Norworth, Ned 1889-1940 *WhScrn 74, -77*
Noske, Frits 1920- *NewGrD 80*
Noske, Willem 1918- *NewGrD 80*
Noskowski, Sigismund 1846-1909 *Baker 78*
Noskowski, Zygmunt 1846-1909 *NewGrD 80, OxMus*
Noss, Luther 1907- *IntWWM 77, -80, WhoMus 72*
Nossack, Hans Erich 1901- *CnMD*
Nosse, Carl E 1933- *ConAmC, IntWWM 77*
Nosseck, Max 1902-1972 *FilmEn, FilmgC, HalFC 80, IntMPA 77, -75, -76, -78, -79, -80, WhScrn 77*
Nosworthy, Marald Winnifred 1921- *AmSCAP 80*
Notari, Angelo 1566-1663 *NewGrD 80*
Notari, Guido 1894-1957 *WhScrn 74, -77, WhoHol B*
Noth *IntWWM 77*
Noth, Dominique Paul 1944- *ConAmTC*
Notker 840?-912 *Baker 78, NewGrD 80*
Notker III 950?-1022 *NewGrD 80*
Notker Labeo 950?-1022 *NewGrD 80*
Notker The German 950?-1022 *NewGrD 80*
Notman, Edith 1937- *ConAmTC*
Noto, Clara B *WomWMM B*
Noto, Lore 1923- *BiE&WWA, NotNAT*
Noto, Pat 1922- *AmSCAP 66, -80*
Noto, Sam 1930- *BiDAmM, EncJzS 70*
Notot, Joseph Waast Aubert *NewGrD 80*
Nott, Cicely d1900 *NotNAT B*
Nott, Douglas Duane 1944- *AmSCAP 80, CpmDNM 79, -80, ConAmC*
Nott-Bower, Jill *IntWWM 77, -80, WhoMus 72*
Nottara, Constantin 1890-1951 *NewGrD 80*
Nottebohm, Gustav 1817-1882 *NewGrD 80*
Nottebohm, Martin Gustav 1817-1882 *Baker 78, OxMus*
Nottingham, James Edward, Jr. 1925- *BiDAmM, EncJzS 70*
Nottingham, Jimmy 1925- *CmpEPM, EncJzS 70*
Nougues, Jean 1875-1932 *Baker 78, NewEOp 71*
Nouri, Michael 1945- *AmSCAP 80*
Nourrit, Adolphe 1802-1839 *Baker 78, BnBkM 80, CmOp, NewEOp 71, NewGrD 80[port]*
Nourrit, Auguste *NewGrD 80*
Nourrit, Louis 1780-1831 *BnBkM 80, NewGrD 80*
Nourse, Allen *WhoHol A*
Nourse, Dorothy *Film 2*
Nourse, Joan Thellusson 1921- *ConAmTC*
Nova, Alex *Film 2*
Nova, Hedda *Film 1, -2, TwYS*
Nova, Lou 1920?- *BiE&WWA, NotNAT, WhoHol A*
Novacek, Ottokar Eugen 1866-1900 *Baker 78, BiDAmM, NewGrD 80, OxMus*
Novacek, Rudolf 1860-1929 *Baker 78*
Novack, Shelly *WhoHol A*
Novaes, Guiomar 1895-1979 *BiDAmM, BnBkM 80, MusSN[port]*
Novaes, Guiomar 1896- *Baker 78, NewGrD 80*
Novak, Eva 1899- *Film 1, -2, FilmgC, ForYSC, HalFC 80, TwYS, WhoHol A*
Novak, Geza 1921- *IntWWM 80*
Novak, Jan 1921- *Baker 78, DcCM, NewGrD 80, WhoMus 72*
Novak, Jane 1896- *Film 1, -2, FilmgC, ForYSC, HalFC 80, MotPP, TwYS, WhoHol A*
Novak, Jiri 1924- *IntWWM 77, -80*
Novak, Johann Baptist 1756-1833 *Baker 78, NewGrD 80*
Novak, Kim 1933- *BiDFilm 81, FilmEn, FilmgC, ForYSC, HalFC 80, IntMPA 77, -75, -76, -78, -79, -80, MotPP, MovMk[port], OxFilm, WhoHol A, WhoHrs 80[port], WorEFlm*
Novak, Milan 1927- *Baker 78*
Novak, Nina 1927- *CnOxB, DancEn 78*
Novak, Viktor 1870-1949 *NewGrD 80[port]*
Novak, Viteszlav 1870-1949 *NewEOp 71*
Novak, Vitezlav 1870-1949 *CmOp*
Novak, Vitezslav 1870-1949 *Baker 78, BnBkM 80, CompSN[port], DcCM, NewGrD 80[port], OxMus*
Novak, William 1952- *ConAmC*
Novaro, Luciana 1923- *CnOxB, DancEn 78*
Novarro, Ramon *AmPS B*
Novarro, Ramon 1889-1968 *MovMk*
Novarro, Ramon 1899-1968 *BiDFilm 81, CmpEPM, FilmEn, Film 1, -2, FilmgC, ForYSC, HalFC 80, MotPP, OxFilm, TwYS, What 1[port], WhScrn 74, -77, WhoHol B, WorEFlm[port]*
Novarro, Ramon 1905-1968 *CmMov*
Novas, Himilce *WomWMM B*
Novelli, Amleto 1881-1924 *FilmEn*
Novelli, Amleto 1885-1924 *FilmAG WE[port]*
Novelli, Anna 1938- *WhoOp 76*
Novelli, Anthony *Film 1, -2*
Novelli, Antonio d1919 *WhoHol B*
Novelli, Augusto 1867-1927 *McGEWD[port]*
Novelli, Ermete 1851-1919 *EncWT, Ent, NotNAT B, OxThe, WhoStg 1908*
Novello *NewGrD 80*
Novello, Alfred 1810-1896 *NewGrD 80*
Novello, Clara Anastasia 1818-1908 *Baker 78, CmOp, NewGrD 80, OxMus*
Novello, Eugene Ralph 1912- *AmSCAP 66, -80*
Novello, Ivor 1893-1951 *BestMus, CnThe, EncMT, EncWT, Ent[port], FilmEn, Film 2, FilmgC, ForYSC, HalFC 80, IlWWBF[port], -A, McGEWD[port], ModWD, MotPP, MusMk[port], NewGrD 80, NotNAT A, -B, OxMus, OxThe, WhScrn 74, -77, WhThe, WhoHol B*
Novello, Jay 1904- *FilmEn, FilmgC, ForYSC, Vers B[port], WhoHol A*
Novello, Jay 1905- *HalFC 80*
Novello, Joseph Alfred 1810-1896 *Baker 78, OxMus*
Novello, Vincent 1781-1861 *Baker 78, BnBkM 80, NewGrD 80[port], OxMus*
Novello & Company *Baker 78*
Novello-Davies, Clara 1861-1943 *Baker 78*
November, Johnny *AmSCAP 80*
Noverre, Jean-Georges 1727-1810 *Baker 78, CnOxB, DancEn 78, NewGrD 80[port], NotNAT A, OxMus*
Novick, Julius 1939- *ConAmTC*
Novick, Melvyn J 1946- *IntWWM 80*
Novik, Ylda 1922- *IntWWM 77*
Novikoff, Laurent 1888-1956 *CnOxB, DancEn 78[port]*
Novikov, Anatoly Grigor'yevich 1896- *Baker 78, NewGrD 80*
Novinsky, Alexander 1878-1960 *WhScrn 77*
Novis, Donald 1906-1966 *CmpEPM*
Novis, Donald 1907-1966 *WhScrn 74, -77, WhoHol B*
Novius *OxThe*
Novo Portu, Francisco De *NewGrD 80*
Novoa, Salvador Antonio 1937- *WhoOp 76*
Novotna, Jarmila 1903- *Baker 78, MusSN[port]*
Novotna, Jarmila 1907- *CmOp, NewEOp 71, NewGrD 80, WhoMus 72*
Novotni, Franz Nikolaus 1743-1773 *NewGrD 80*
Novotny, Bretislav 1924- *IntWWM 77, -80*
Novotny, Franz Nikolaus 1743-1773 *NewGrD 80*
Novotny, Jan 1935- *IntWWM 77, -80*
Novotny, Jaroslav 1886-1918 *NewGrD 80*
Novotny, Vaclav Juda 1849-1922 *Baker 78, NewGrD 80*
Novy, Donald Andrew 1932- *ConAmC, IntWWM 77, -80*
Nowaczynski, Adolf 1876-1944 *CnMD, ModWD*
Nowak, Alison 1948- *ConAmC*
Nowak, Gerald C 1936- *ConAmC*
Nowak, Leopold 1904- *Baker 78, NewGrD 80*
Nowak, Lionel 1911- *Baker 78, ConAmC, DancEn 78, DcCM*
Nowak, Robert 1949- *ConAmC*
Nowak-Romanowicz, Alina 1907- *IntWWM 77, -80, NewGrD 80*
Nowakowski, Jozef 1800-1865 *NewGrD 80*
Nowakowski, Marian 1912- *WhoMus 72*
Nowakowski, Mieczyslaw 1934- *IntWWM 80*
Nowakowski, Perry Casey 1943- *AmSCAP 80*
Nowell, Wedgewood 1878-1957 *Film 1, TwYS, WhScrn 74, -77*
Nowell, Wedgwood 1878-1957 *Film 2, WhoHol B*
Nowka, Dieter 1924- *NewGrD 80*
Nowlan, Alden A 1933- *CreCan 2*
Nowlan, George 1925- *AmSCAP 66*
Nowotny, Franz Nikolaus *NewGrD 80*
Nowotny, Richard 1926- *CnOxB*
Nowowiejski, Feliks 1877-1946 *NewGrD 80*
Nowowiejski, Felix 1877-1946 *Baker 78, OxMus*
Nox, Andre *Film 2*
Noxon, Nicolas *NewYTET*
Noy, Wilfred 1882- *Film 2, IlWWBF*
Noyce, Barbara 1915- *WhoMus 72*

Noyers, Jean De *NewGrD 80*
Noyes, Joseph 1869-1936 *WhScrn 74, -77*
Noyes, Thomas 1922- *BiE&WWA, NotNAT*
Nozaki, Albert 1912- *WhoHrs 80*
Noziere, Fernand 1874-1931 *McGEWD, NotNAT B, WhThe*
Nsabe, Nia *MorBAP*
Ntshona, Winston *PlP&P A[port]*
Nu Tornados, The *RkOn[port]*
Nucci, Lucrezio *NewGrD 80*
Nucella *NewGrD 80*
Nuceti, Flaminio *NewGrD 80*
Nuceus *NewGrD 80*
Nucis, Johannes 1556?-1620 *NewGrD 80*
Nucius, Johannes 1556?-1620 *NewGrD 80*
Nucius, Johannes 1563?-1620 *Baker 78*
Nudleman, Nordyk *CreCan 2*
Nuemann, Charles 1873-1927 *WhScrn 74, -77*
Nuernberger, Louis Dean 1924- *ConAmC*
Nuffel, Jules Van 1883-1953 *NewGrD 80*
Nugent, Carol *ForYSC, WhoHol A*
Nugent, Eddie 1904- *Film 2*
Nugent, Edward 1904- *FilmEn, ForYSC, TwYS, WhoHol A*
Nugent, Elliot 1900-1980 *MovMk[port]*
Nugent, Elliott 1899-1980 *BiE&WWA, ConDr 73, -77, FilmEn, Film 2, FilmgC, ForYSC, HalFC 80, McGEWD, NotNAT, -A, WhThe, WhoHol A, WhoThe 72*
Nugent, Elliott 1900-1980 *BiDFilm 81, CnMD, IntMPA 77, -75, -76, -78, -79, -80, ModWD, What 3[port], WorEFlm*
Nugent, Frank S 1908-1965 *CmMov, FilmEn*
Nugent, Frank S 1908-1966 *FilmgC, HalFC 80, WorEFlm*
Nugent, J C 1875-1947 *WhScrn 74, -77, WhoHol B*
Nugent, J C 1878-1947 *ForYSC*
Nugent, John Charles 1878-1947 *NotNAT A, -B, WhThe*
Nugent, Maud *AmPS B*
Nugent, Maude 1873-1958 *BiDAmM*
Nugent, Moya 1901-1954 *NotNAT B, WhThe*
Nugent, Nancy 1933- *BiE&WWA*
Nugent, Nancy 1938- *NotNAT*
Nugent, Ted 1949- *ConMuA 80A[port], IlEncR[port], RkOn 2[port]*
Nugent, Theodore Anthony 1948- *AmSCAP 80*
Nuitter, Charles Louis Etienne 1828-1899 *Baker 78, CnOxB, DancEn 78, NewEOp 71, NewGrD 80*
Null, Cecil A 1927- *BiDAmM*
Numantino, Martin DeTapia *NewGrD 80*
Numes, Armand d1933 *NotNAT B*
Nummi, Seppo 1932- *NewGrD 80*
Nunes, Armando DaSilva *CreCan 1*
Nunes, Emanuel 1941- *NewGrD 80*
Nunes, Leon d1911 *NotNAT B*
Nunes, Margery Lambert *CreCan 2*
Nunes, Maxine *WomWMM*
Nunes DaSilva, Manuel d1704? *NewGrD 80*
Nunes Garcia, Jose Mauricio *NewGrD 80*
Nunez, Alcide 1892?-1933? *NewOrJ*
Nunez, Juan Manuel d1966 *WhScrn 77*
Nunez, Yellow Alcide 1884-1934 *WhoJazz 72*
Nunez DeArce, Gaspar 1834-1903 *McGEWD[port]*
Nunlist, Juli 1916- *ConAmC*
Nunn, Alice *WhoHol A*
Nunn, Alice May 1900- *WhoMus 72*
Nunn, Edward Cuthbert 1868-1914 *Baker 78*
Nunn, June Aubretta Linda 1929- *IntWWM 80, WhoMus 72*
Nunn, Thomas E 1946- *ConAmC*
Nunn, Trevor 1940- *CnThe, EncWT, Ent, WhoThe 72, -77*
Nunn, Wayne 1881-1947 *WhScrn 77*
Nunnallee, Ruth Burnette *IntWWM 77*
Nuno, Jaime 1824-1908 *Baker 78, BiDAmM, NewGrD 80*
Nuotio, Pekka 1929- *WhoOp 76*
Nurcombe *NewGrD 80*
Nurcome *NewGrD 80*
Nureyev, Rudolf 1938- *CnOxB, DancEn 78[port], HalFC 80, WhoHol A*
Nurmela, Kari 1937- *WhoOp 76*
Nurmimaa, Seppo Uolevi 1931- *WhoOp 76*
Nurnberger, Albert 1854-1931 *NewGrD 80*
Nurock, Kirk 1948- *ConAmC*
Nurullah, Shanta Sabriya Fermiye 1950- *BlkWAB[port]*
Nusic, Branislav 1864-1938 *EncWT*
Nussbaum, Mrs. 1909- *JoeFr, What 2[port]*
Nussbaum, Ted *ConMuA 80B*
Nussio, Otmar 1902- *Baker 78, NewGrD 80*
Nussle *NewGrD 80*
Nutley, Freda Ellen 1910- *WhoMus 72*
Nutley, Lionel Alfred 1907- *WhoMus 72*
Nutmegs, The *RkOn*
Nutt, Charles Edward Kenneth 1906- *WhoMus 72*
Nutt, Wayne 1940- *IlEncCM*
Nuttall, Michael 1935- *IntWWM 77*
Nutter, William Arthur 1909- *WhoMus 72*
Nutting, Dulcie Rhys 1896- *WhoMus 72*
Nutting, Geoffrey Howard 1936- *IntWWM 80*
Nutty Squirrels, The *RkOn*
Nuttycombe, Craig 1947- *AmSCAP 80*
Nux, Johannes *NewGrD 80*
Nuyen, France 1939- *BiE&WWA, FilmEn, FilmgC, ForYSC, HalFC 80, MotPP, WhoHol A*
Nuyts, Jan 1949- *CnOxB*
Nxumalo, Gideon N N 1929-1970 *NewGrD 80*
Nyberg, Gary B 1945- *IntWWM 80*
Nyborg, Anne Kristine 1938- *WhoOp 76*
Nyby, Christian 1919- *FilmEn, FilmgC, HalFC 80*
Nye, Anita Leonard *AmSCAP 80*
Nye, Ben *WhoHrs 80*
Nye, Carrie *BiE&WWA, NotNAT, WhoHol A, WhoThe 72, -77*
Nye, Carroll 1901-1968 *ForYSC, TwYS*
Nye, Carroll 1901-1974 *Film 2, WhScrn 77, WhoHol B*
Nye, Douglas Raymond 1930- *AmSCAP 80*
Nye, G Raymond *Film 1, -2*
Nye, Gerald P 1892- *What 1[port]*
Nye, Hermes 1908- *BiDAmM, EncFCWM 69*
Nye, Louis *ForYSC, WhoHol A*
Nye, Naomi Shihab 1952- *AmSCAP 80*
Nye, Pat 1908- *WhoHol A, WhoThe 72, -77*
Nye, Ruth *WhoMus 72*
Nye, Tom F d1925 *NotNAT B*
Nyert, Pierre De 1597?-1682 *NewGrD 80*
Nyeuwenhuys *NewGrD 80*
Nygaard, Eline 1913- *IntWWM 77, -80*
Nyght, Kim Alvin 1953- *IntWWM 77, -80*
Nygren, Samuel 1925- *IntWWM 77*
Nygryn, Georg *NewGrD 80*
Nyguist, Roger Thomas 1934- *ConAmC*
Nyhlen, Lennart 1936- *IntWWM 80*
Nyiregyhazi, Ervin 1903- *NewGrD 80*
Nyiregyhazi, Erwin 1903- *Baker 78*
Nyitray, Emil d1922 *NotNAT B*
Nykke, Thomas *NewGrD 80*
Nykvist, Sven 1922- *DcFM, FilmEn, FilmgC, HalFC 80, IntMPA 77, -75, -76, -78, -79, -80, WorEFlm*
Nykvist, Sven 1923- *OxFilm*
Nyla *Film 2*
Nylandensis, Theodoricus Petri *NewGrD 80*
Nyman, Amy Joyce Utting 1941- *IntWWM 77*
Nype, Russell 1924- *BiE&WWA, EncMT, NotNAT, WhoHol A, WhoThe 72, -77*
Nyquist, Morine A 1909- *ConAmC*
Nyren, David O 1924- *IntMPA 77, -75, -76, -78, -79, -80*
Nyro, Laura *ConMuA 80A*
Nyro, Laura 1947- *IlEncR[port], RkOn 2[port]*
Nyro, Laura 1949- *BiDAmM*
Nystedt, Knut 1915- *Baker 78, DcCM, IntWWM 80, NewGrD 80*
Nystroem, Gosta 1890-1966 *Baker 78, CompSN[port], DcCM, NewGrD 80, OxMus*
Nystroem, Margot 1935- *IntWWM 77, -80*
Nystrom, Alf 1927- *AmSCAP 66, -80*
Nyttenegger, Esther E 1941- *IntWWM 77, -80*
Nzewi, Meki Emeka 1938- *IntWWM 77, -80*

O

O Gallagher, Eamonn 1906- *NewGrD 80*
O Riada, Sean 1931-1971 *NewGrD 80*
Oak, Kilsung 1942- *ConAmC*
Oak Cliff T-Bone *BluesWW[port]*
Oak Ridge Boys *IlEncCM[port]*
Oak Ridge Quartet *BiDAmM*
Oakeley, Frederick *OxMus*
Oakeley, Sir Herbert Stanley 1830-1903 *Baker 78, NewGrD 80, OxMus*
Oaker, Jane 1880- *WhThe, WhoStg 1908*
Oaker, John *Film 1, NewGrD 80*
Oakes, Rodney Harland 1937- *AmSCAP 80, CpmDNM 78, -80, ConAmC, IntWWM 77, -80*
Oakes, Sarah Lawrence *WomWMM B*
Oakes, Sheila Margaret 1928- *WhoMus 72*
Oakes, Tom 1896- *AmSCAP 66*
Oakey, Emily Sullivan 1829-1883 *BiDAmM*
Oakie, Jack 1902?- *CmpEPM*
Oakie, Jack 1903-1978 *CmMov, FilmEn, Film 2, FilmgC, ForYSC, HalFC 80[port], HolP 30[port], IntMPA 77, -75, -76, -78, JoeFr[port], MotPP, MovMk[port], TwYS, What 2[port], WhoHol A*
Oakland, Ben 1907-1979 *AmSCAP 66, -80, CmpEPM*
Oakland, Ethel Mary *Film 1*
Oakland, Simon 1922- *FilmEn, FilmgC, ForYSC, HalFC 80, IntMPA 77, -75, -76, -78, -79, -80, WhoHol A*
Oakland, Vivian 1895-1958 *FilmEn, FilmgC, ForYSC, HalFC 80, TwYS, WhoHol B*
Oakland, Vivien 1895-1958 *Film 2, WhScrn 74, -77*
Oakland, Will 1883-1956 *NotNAT B, WhScrn 74, -77, WhoHol B*
Oakley, Annie d1926 *Film 1, WhoHol B*
Oakley, Annie 1859-1926 *FilmgC, HalFC 80*
Oakley, Annie 1860-1926 *Ent, WhScrn 77*
Oakley, Annie 1866-1926 *NotNAT A*
Oakley, Florence 1891-1956 *Film 2, WhScrn 74, -77, WhoHol B*
Oakley, Laura 1879-1957 *Film 1, WhScrn 77*
Oakley, Reginald Gordon Edmund 1907- *WhoMus 72*
Oakman, Wheeler 1890-1949 *Film 1, -2, ForYSC, NotNAT B, TwYS, WhScrn 74, -77, WhoHol B*
Oakum *BiDAmM*
Oates, Cicely d1934 *NotNAT B, WhoHol B*
Oates, Cicely d1935 *WhScrn 77*
Oates, J P *OxMus*
Oates, Ronnie O 1940- *AmSCAP 80*
Oates, Warren *ForYSC, IntMPA 75, -76, -78, -79, -80*
Oates, Warren 1928- *FilmEn*
Oates, Warren 1932- *BiDFilm 81, CmMov, FilmgC, HalFC 80, IntMPA 77, MovMk, WhoHol A*
Obadia, Heskel H 1924- *IntWWM 77, -80*
Obadiah The Proselyte *NewGrD 80*
Obaldia, Rene De 1918- *CnMD SUP, CroCD, EncWT, Ent, ModWD*
Obayani, Kambon *MorBAP*
O'Beck, Fred 1881-1929 *Film 2, WhScrn 74, -77, WhoHol B*
Obegi, Richard *AmSCAP 80*
Obelensky, W *Film 2*
Obelkevich, Mary Helen Rowen 1945- *IntWWM 80*
Ober, Carol Jean 1940- *IntWWM 80*
Ober, Christine *WomWMM B*
Ober, George d1912 *WhScrn 77*
Ober, Harold d1959 *NotNAT B*
Ober, Kirt 1875-1939 *WhScrn 74, -77*
Ober, Margaret Arndt 1885-1971 *CmOp*
Ober, Margarethe *NewGrD 80*
Ober, Philip 1902- *BiE&WWA, FilmgC, ForYSC, HalFC 80, IntMPA 77, -75, -76, -78, -79, -80, NotNAT, Vers A[port], WhThe, WhoHol A*
Ober, Phillip 1902- *FilmEn*
Ober, Robert d1950 *Film 2, WhoHol B*
Ober, Robert 1881-1950 *NotNAT B, WhoStg 1908*
Ober, Robert 1882-1950 *WhScrn 74, -77*
Oberg, Gustav *Film 2*
Oberg, Paul Matthews 1904- *WhoMus 72*
Oberhaus, Patricia *WomWMM B*
Oberhoffer, Emil Johann 1867-1933 *Baker 78, BiDAmM*
Oberle, Florence 1870-1943 *Film 2, WhScrn 74, -77, WhoHol B*
Oberle, Thomas d1906 *NotNAT B*
Oberleitner, Ewald 1937- *IntWWM 77*
Oberlin, James 1931-1962 *WhScrn 77*
Oberlin, Richard 1928- *NotNAT*
Oberlin, Russell 1928- *IntWWM 77, -80, NewGrD 80, WhoMus 72*
Obermayer, Joseph 1878-1966 *NewGrD 80*
Oberndorfer, David d1654? *NewGrD 80*
Oberndorffer, David d1654? *NewGrD 80*
Oberon, Merle d1979 *MotPP, WomWMM*
Oberon, Merle 1911-1979 *BiDFilm 81, CmMov, FilmAG WE, FilmEn, FilmgC, ForYSC, HalFC 80[port], IlWWBF, MovMk[port], OxFilm, ThFT[port], WhoHol A, WorEFlm[port]*
Oberon, Merle 1919-1979 *IntMPA 77, -75, -76, -78, -79, -80*
Oberthur, Charles 1819-1895 *NewGrD 80*
Oberthur, Karl 1819-1895 *Baker 78, NewGrD 80*
Oberwager, Jerome *PupTheA*
Obetz, John Wesley 1933- *IntWWM 77, -80*
Obey, Andre 1892-1975 *CnMD, CnThe, EncWT, McGEWD[port], ModWD, OxThe, WhThe*
Obidenna, Lara *DancEn 78*
Obilo *AmSCAP 80*
Obin, Louis-Henri 1820-1895 *Baker 78*
Obiols, Mariano 1809-1888 *NewGrD 80*
Obizzi, Domenico 1611?-1630? *NewGrD 80*
Oboler, Arch *IntMPA 77, -75, -76, -78, -79, -80*
Oboler, Arch 1907- *CnMD, ModWD*
Oboler, Arch 1909- *BiE&WWA, DcFM, FilmEn, FilmgC, HalFC 80, NotNAT, WhoHrs 80, WorEFlm[port]*
Oborin, Lev 1907-1974 *Baker 78, NewGrD 80*
Obouhof, Nicolas 1892-1954 *OxMus*
Obouhov, Nicolas 1892-1954 *Baker 78*
Oboukhoff, Anatole 1895-1962 *DancEn 78*
Oboukhoff, Anatole Nicolaievich 1896-1962 *CnOxB*
Oboussier, Robert 1900-1957 *Baker 78, NewGrD 80, OxMus*
Obradovic, Aleksandar 1927- *Baker 78, IntWWM 77, -80, NewGrD 80*
Obradovii, Aleksandar 1927- *DcCM*
O'Brady, Frederic *NotNAT A*
Obraztsov, Sergei Vladimirovich 1901- *DcPup, EncWT, OxThe, WhThe*
Obraztsova, Elena 1937- *Baker 78, NewGrD 80*
Obraztsova, Elena Vasilievna 1939- *BnBkM 80, WhoOp 76*
Obrecht, Eldon 1920- *ConAmC*
Obrecht, Jacob 1450?-1505 *Baker 78, NewGrD 80*
Obrecht, Jacob 1452-1505 *GrComp*
Obrecht, Jacob 1453-1505 *MusMk, OxMus*
Obrecht, Jakob 1452-1505 *BnBkM 80*
Obretenov, Svetoslav 1909- *Baker 78*
O'Brian, Hugh *AmSCAP 66, -80, MotPP, WhoHol A*
O'Brian, Hugh 1925- *FilmEn, FilmgC, ForYSC, HalFC 80, MovMk, WhoThe 77*
O'Brian, Hugh 1928- *BiE&WWA*
O'Brian, Hugh 1930- *IntMPA 77, -75, -76, -78, -79, -80*
O'Brian, Jack 1914- *IntMPA 77, -75, -76, -78, -79, -80*
O'Brian, Peter 1947- *IntMPA 77, -76, -78, -79, -80*
O'Brien, Barry 1893-1961 *Film 1, NotNAT B, WhThe, WhoHol B*
O'Brien, Bill *Film 2*
O'Brien, Charles 1882-1968 *Baker 78*
O'Brien, Chet 1911- *BiE&WWA, WhoHol A*
O'Brien, Clay *WhoHol A*
O'Brien, Dan *NewGrD 80*
O'Brien, Dave 1912-1969 *FilmEn, FilmgC, ForYSC, HalFC 80, Vers B[port], WhoHol B, WhoHrs 80*
O'Brien, David 1912-1969 *WhScrn 74, -77*
O'Brien, David 1930- *WhThe, WhoThe 72*
O'Brien, Donna Bray *IntWWM 77, -80*
O'Brien, Donnell d1970 *WhScrn 74, -77, WhoHol B*
O'Brien, Edmond 1915- *BiDFilm 81, FilmEn, FilmgC, ForYSC, HalFC 80, IntMPA 77, -75, -76, -78, -79, -80, MotPP, MovMk[port], OxFilm, WhoHol A, WhoHrs 80, WorEFlm[port]*
O'Brien, Erin *ForYSC, WhoHol A*
O'Brien, Eugene 1882-1966 *FilmEn, Film 1, -2, MotPP, TwYS, WhScrn 74, -77, WhoHol B*
O'Brien, Eugene 1945- *ConAmC*

O'Brien, Florence 1919- *BlksB&W*
O'Brien, Floyd 1904-1968 *CmpEPM, WhoJazz 72*
O'Brien, Floyd 1905- *BiDAmM*
O'Brien, Floyd 1907-1968 *EncJzS 70*
O'Brien, Frank *WhoHol A*
O'Brien, George 1900- *CmMov, FilmEn, Film 2, FilmgC, ForYSC, HalFC 80, IntMPA 77, -75, -76, -78, -79, -80, MotPP, MovMk, TwYS, What 4[port], WhoHol A, WorEFlm*
O'Brien, Gypsy *Film 2*
O'Brien, Hortense *Film 2*
O'Brien, Jack 1908- *Film 2, IntMPA 75*
O'Brien, Jack 1939- *AmSCAP 80*
O'Brien, James Joseph 1942- *AmSCAP 80*
O'Brien, Joan *ForYSC, WhoHol A*
O'Brien, John *Film 2*
O'Brien, John 1933- *CnOxB*
O'Brien, John 1938- *DancEn 78*
O'Brien, John Roger 1904- *AmSCAP 66*
O'Brien, Justin 1906-1968 *NotNAT B*
O'Brien, Kate 1897-1974 *BiE&WWA, NotNAT B, WhThe*
O'Brien, Katharine E 1901- *ConAmC*
O'Brien, Liam 1913- *BiE&WWA, IntMPA 77, -75, -76, -78, -79, -80, NotNAT*
O'Brien, Livia F *PupTheA*
O'Brien, Margaret 1937- *BiDFilm 81, FilmEn, FilmgC, ForYSC, HalFC 80, IntMPA 77, -75, -76, -78, -79, -80, MGM[port], MotPP, MovMk[port], What 2[port], WhoHol A, WorEFlm*
O'Brien, Maria *WhoHol A*
O'Brien, Marianne *WhoHol A*
O'Brien, Mary *Film 2*
O'Brien, Maureen 1943- *WhoThe 72, -77*
O'Brien, Neil d1909 *NotNAT B*
O'Brien, Pat 1899- *BiDFilm 81, BiE&WWA, FilmEn, Film 2, FilmgC, ForYSC, HalFC 80, IntMPA 77, -75, -76, -78, -79, -80, MotPP, MovMk[port], NotNAT, -A, OxFilm, TwYS, WhoHol A*
O'Brien, Peter Adrian 1936- *IntWWM 77, -80*
O'Brien, Richard *WhoHol A*
O'Brien, Robert Felix 1921- *AmSCAP 80, IntWWM 77, -80*
O'Brien, Robert H 1904- *IntMPA 75, -76*
O'Brien, Robert Owen 1941- *IntWWM 77*
O'Brien, Rory *WhoHol A*
O'Brien, Shots 1895-1961 *WhScrn 74, -77*
O'Brien, Sylvia *WhoHol A*
O'Brien, Teddy *WhoHol A*
O'Brien, Terence 1887-1970 *WhThe*
O'Brien, Timothy 1929- *WhoThe 72, -77*
O'Brien, Tom 1891-1947 *WhScrn 74, -77, WhoHol B*
O'Brien, Tom 1898- *Film 2, ForYSC, TwYS*
O'Brien, Vince *WhoHol A*
O'Brien, Virginia *IntMPA 77, -75, -76, -78, -79, -80, WhoHol A*
O'Brien, Virginia 1896- *WhThe*
O'Brien, Virginia 1921- *CmpEPM, FilmEn, FilmgC, ForYSC, HalFC 80, What 4[port]*
O'Brien, Virginia 1922- *MGM[port], MovMk*
O'Brien, William d1815 *NotNAT B*
O'Brien, Willis 1886-1962 *CmMov, FilmEn, FilmgC, HalFC 80, WhoHrs 80*
O'Brien-Moore, Erin 1908- *ForYSC, ThFT[port], WhThe, WhoHol A*
Obrist, Aloys 1867-1910 *Baker 78*
O'Bryant, Jimmy 1900?-1928 *BiDAmM, CmpEPM, WhoJazz 72*
O'Bryant, Joan 1923-1964 *BiDAmM, EncFCWM 69*
O'Bryen, W J 1898- *WhThe*
O'Bryne, Patsy 1886-1968 *WhoHol B*
Obscoenus, Paulus *NewGrD 80*
Obterre *NewGrD 80*
Obukhov, Nikolay 1892-1954 *NewGrD 80*
Obukhova, Nadezhda 1886-1961 *NewGrD 80*
O'Burrell, James *Film 1*
O'Byrne, Bryan *WhoHol A*
O'Byrne, Dermot *OxMus*
O'Byrne, Patsy 1886-1968 *Film 2, WhScrn 74, -77*
Ocadlik, Mirko 1904-1964 *NewGrD 80*
O'Callaghan, Ed *WhoHol A*
O'Callaghan, Richard 1940- *WhoHol A, WhoThe 77*
Ocampo, Silvina *PupTheA*
O'Carolan, Turlogh 1670-1738 *BnBkM 80*
O'Carolan, Turlough 1670-1738 *OxMus*
O'Casey, Sean 1880-1964 *BiE&WWA, CnThe, CroCD, EncWT, Ent, FilmgC, HalFC 80, McGEWD[port], ModWD, NotNAT A, -B, OxThe, PlP&P[port], REnWD[port], WhThe*
O'Casey, Sean 1884-1964 *CnMD*
Ocasio, Joe *WhoHol A*
Occum, Samson 1722-1779 *BiDAmM*
Ocean *RkOn 2[port]*
Ocenas, Andrej 1911- *Baker 78, DcCM, NewGrD 80*
Ochman, Wieslaw 1937- *IntWWM 77, NewGrD 80, WhoMus 72, WhoOp 76*
Ochs, Al d1964 *NotNAT B*
Ochs, Lillian d1964 *NotNAT B*
Ochs, Phil 1940-1976 *AmSCAP 66, -80, ConMuA 80A[port], EncFCWM 69, IlEncR[port]*
Ochs, Philip David 1940- *BiDAmM*
Ochs, Siegfried 1858-1929 *Baker 78, NewGrD 80*
Ochse, Orpha Caroline *ConAmC*
Ochsenkhun, Sebastian 1521-1574 *NewGrD 80*
Ochsenkun, Sebastian 1521-1574 *NewGrD 80*
Ochswald, Henrique *NewGrD 80*
Ockeghem, Jean 1410?-1497 *NewGrD 80*
Ockeghem, Jean D' 1420?-1495? *BnBkM 80*
Ockeghem, Jean De 1430?-1495? *OxMus*
Ockeghem, Jehan 1410?-1497 *NewGrD 80*
Ockeghem, Johannes 1410?-1497 *NewGrD 80*
Ockeghem, Johannes 1420?-1495? *BnBkM 80*
Ockeghem, Johannes 1420?-1496 *Baker 78*
Ockeghem, Johannes 1430-1495 *GrComp*
Ockeover, John *NewGrD 80*
Ocko, Dan *WhoHol A*
Oclande, Robert *NewGrD 80*
Ocnoff, Edward Ebber 1906- *AmSCAP 80*
O'Conaire, Deirdre 1938- *CnOxB*
O'Connell, Arthur 1908- *BiE&WWA, FilmEn, FilmgC, ForYSC, HalFC 80, IntMPA 77, -75, -76, -78, -79, -80, MovMk[port], NotNAT, WhoHol A, WhoHrs 80[port], WhoThe 77*
O'Connell, Bob *WhoHol A*
O'Connell, Charles 1900-1962 *Baker 78*
O'Connell, Gerald 1904- *BiE&WWA*
O'Connell, Harold *PupTheA*
O'Connell, Helen *AmPS B, WhoHol A*
O'Connell, Helen 1920- *CmpEPM*
O'Connell, Helen 1921- *What 3[port]*
O'Connell, Hugh 1898-1943 *NotNAT B, WhScrn 74, -77, WhThe, WhoHol B*
O'Connell, Jack *IntMPA 78, -79, -80*
O'Connell, L William 1890- *WorEFlm*
O'Connell, Louis P 1895- *AmSCAP 66, -80*
O'Connell, Patrick *WhoHol A*
O'Connell, Raymond 1922- *IntWWM 77, -80, WhoMus 72*
O'Connell, William *WhoHol A*
O'Conner, Edward 1862-1932 *WhScrn 77*
O'Connolly, Jim 1926- *FilmgC, HalFC 80, IlWWBF*
O'Connor, Bill 1919- *WhThe*
O'Connor, Carroll *ForYSC, IntMPA 75, -76, WhoHol A*
O'Connor, Carroll 1922- *FilmgC, HalFC 80*
O'Connor, Carroll 1923- *MovMk*
O'Connor, Carroll 1924- *AmSCAP 80*
O'Connor, Carroll 1925- *FilmEn, IntMPA 77, -78, -79, -80*
O'Connor, Charles William 1878-1955 *NotNAT B, WhThe*
O'Connor, Darren *WhoHol A*
O'Connor, Desmond *WhoMus 72*
O'Connor, Donald 1925- *AmSCAP 66, -80, CmMov, CmpEPM, FilmEn, FilmgC, ForYSC[port], HalFC 80, HolP 40[port], IntMPA 77, -75, -76, -78, -79, -80, MotPP, MovMk[port], OxFilm, WhoHol A, WhoHrs 80, WorEFlm*
O'Connor, Edward *Film 1, -2*
O'Connor, Edwin 1918-1968 *NotNAT B*
O'Connor, Frank 1888-1959 *TwYS A, WhScrn 74, -77, WhoHol B*
O'Connor, Frank 1903-1966 *CnMD, NotNAT B*
O'Connor, Giles 1908- *AmSCAP 66, -80*
O'Connor, Glynnis 1956- *HalFC 80, WhoHol A*
O'Connor, Harry M 1873-1971 *WhScrn 74, -77, WhoHol B*
O'Connor, James *Film 1*
O'Connor, James F d1963 *NotNAT B*
O'Connor, John 1874-1941 *WhScrn 74, -77, WhoHol B*
O'Connor, John J 1933- *WhThe, WhoThe 72*
O'Connor, Joseph 1916- *WhoThe 72*
O'Connor, Kathleen 1897-1957 *Film 1, -2, WhScrn 74, -77, WhoHol B*
O'Connor, Kathryn 1894-1965 *WhScrn 74, -77, WhoHol B*
O'Connor, Kevin 1938- *NotNAT, WhoHol A, WhoThe 77*
O'Connor, L J 1880-1959 *Film 2, WhoHol B*
O'Connor, Louis J 1880-1959 *WhScrn 74, -77*
O'Connor, Loyola *Film 1*
O'Connor, Robert d1947 *NotNAT B*
O'Connor, Robert Carl 1942- *AmSCAP 80*
O'Connor, Robert Emmett 1885-1962 *Film 1, -2, FilmgC, ForYSC, HalFC 80, NotNAT B, TwYS, WhScrn 74, -77, WhoHol B*
O'Connor, Rod d1964 *NotNAT B*
O'Connor, Thomas F 1896- *IntMPA 75, -76*
O'Connor, Una d1959 *MotPP, WhoHol B*
O'Connor, Una 1880-1959 *FilmEn, HolCA[port], NotNAT B, ThFT[port], WhScrn 74, -77, WhoHrs 80*
O'Connor, Una 1881-1959 *ForYSC, MovMk[port]*
O'Connor, Una 1893-1959 *FilmAG WE, Film 2, FilmgC, HalFC 80, Vers A[port], WhThe*
O'Conor, Joseph *WhoHol A*
O'Conor, Joseph 1910?- *FilmgC, HalFC 80*
O'Conor, Joseph 1916- *McGEWD, WhoThe 77*
Octobi, John *NewGrD 80*
O'Curran, Charles 1914- *AmSCAP 80*
Odak, Krsto 1888-1965 *Baker 78, NewGrD 80*
Odaka, Hisatada *Baker 78*
O'Daly, Cormac d1949 *NotNAT B*
O'Daniel, Lee *EncFCWM 69*
O'Daniel, W Lee 1890- *IlEncCM*
O'Daniel, Wilbert Lee 1890-1969 *BiDAmM*
O'Dare, Eileen *Film 2*
O'Dare, Peggy *Film 1, -2, TwYS*
O'Day, Alan Earle 1940- *AmSCAP 80, RkOn 2[port]*
O'Day, Alice d1937 *NotNAT B*
O'Day, Anita 1919- *BiDAmM, CmpEPM, EncJzS 70, WhoHol A*
O'Day, Dawn 1918- *FilmEn, Film 2, MotPP, MovMk[port], TwYS, WhoHol A*
O'Day, Molly 1911- *FilmEn, Film 2, ForYSC, TwYS, WhoHol A*
O'Day, Molly 1923- *IlEncCM*
O'Day, Peggy 1900-1964 *Film 2, WhScrn 74, -77, WhoHol B*
Oddie, Mildred Graham 1925- *IntWWM 77, WhoMus 72*
Oddo *NewGrD 80*
Oddone Sulli-Rao, Elisabetta 1878-1972 *Baker 78*
Ode, Jan 1906- *IntWWM 77*
O'Dea, Anne Caldwell 1867-1936 *BiDAmM*
O'Dea, Denis 1905-1978 *FilmgC, HalFC 80, WhThe, WhoHol A*
O'Dea, Jimmy 1899-1965 *HalFC 80, IlWWBF, WhScrn 74, -77, WhoHol B*
O'Dea, Joseph 1903-1968 *WhScrn 74, -77, WhoHol B*
Odegaard, Irene *PupTheA*
Odegard, Peter S *ConAmC*
Odei, Matthew Asare 1927- *IntWWM 77, -80*
O'Dell, Allen Doye 1912- *BiDAmM*
Odell, Caleb Sherwood 1827-1893 *NewGrD 80*
O'Dell, Digger 1904-1957 *WhScrn 74, -77, WhoHol B*
O'Dell, Doye *ForYSC*
Odell, E J d1928 *NotNAT B*
O'Dell, Garry *Film 2*
Odell, George *Film 1*
Odell, George Clinton Densmore 1866-1949 *NotNAT B, WhThe*
Odell, John Henry 1830-1899 *NewGrD 80*
O'Dell, Kenny *RkOn 2[port]*

O'Dell, Mac 1916- *BiDAmM*
Odell, Mamie *AmSCAP 80*
Odell, Maude d1937 *NotNAT B*
O'Dell, Seymour H 1863-1937 *WhScrn 74, -77*
Odell, Shorty 1874?-1924 *WhScrn 74, -77*
Odell, Thomas d1749 *NotNAT B*
Odemar, Fritz 1890-1955 *WhScrn 74, -77*
O'Dempsey, Brigit d1952 *NotNAT B*
Oden, James Burke 1903-1977 *BluesWW[port]*
Odenheimer, William Henry 1817-1879 *BiDAmM*
O'Denishawn, Florence *Film 2*
Oderman, Stuart Douglas *AmSCAP 80*
Odets, Clifford 1903-1963 *FilmgC, HalFC 80*
Odets, Clifford 1906-1963 *CnMD, CnThe, CroCD, DcFM, DcLB 7[port], EncWT, Ent, FilmEn, McGEWD, ModWD, NotNAT A, -B, OxFilm, OxThe, PlP&P[port], REnWD[port], WhThe, WorEFlm*
Odetta 1930- *BiDAmM, BluesWW[port], DrBlPA, EncFCWM 69, WhoHol A*
Odette, Mary 1901- *FilmEn, Film 1, -2, FilmgC, HalFC 80, IlWWBF[port], WhThe, WhoHol A*
O'Dette, Paul 1954- *IntWWM 80*
Odilon, Helene d1939 *NotNAT B*
Odin, Susan d1975 *WhScrn 77, WhoHol C*
Odingsells, Gabriel d1734 *NotNAT B*
Odington, Walter *Baker 78, NewGrD 80, OxMus*
Odle, Mary Arminda 1915- *AmSCAP 80*
Odlin, Richard *PupTheA*
Odnoposoff, Adolfo 1917- *Baker 78, WhoMus 72*
Odnoposoff, Ricardo 1914- *Baker 78, NewGrD 80*
Odo *NewGrD 80*
Odo De Corigiaria *NewGrD 80*
Odo DeCluny d942 *OxMus*
Odo DeCluny 879-942 *Baker 78*
Odo Of Arezzo *NewGrD 80*
Odo Of Cluny 878?-942 *NewGrD 80*
O'Doherty, Eileen 1891- *WhThe*
O'Doherty, Mignon 1890-1961 *WhThe*
Odom, Andrew 1936- *BluesWW[port]*
Odom, Selma *WomWMM B*
Odon De Paris *NewGrD 80*
O'Donnell, Cathy d1970 *MotPP, WhoHol B*
O'Donnell, Cathy 1923-1970 *FilmgC, HalFC 80*
O'Donnell, Cathy 1925-1970 *FilmEn, ForYSC, WhScrn 74, -77*
O'Donnell, Charles H 1886-1962 *NotNAT B, WhScrn 74, -77*
O'Donnell, Gene *WhoHol A*
O'Donnell, John David 1948- *IntWWM 80*
O'Donnell, Maire *WhoHol A*
O'Donnell, May 1909- *CmpGMD, CnOxB, DancEn 78[port]*
O'Donnell, Richard 1932- *NatPD[port]*
O'Donnell, Robert Edward 1943- *AmSCAP 80*
O'Donnell, Spec 1911- *Film 2, TwYS*
O'Donnell, William *IntMPA 77, -75, -76, -78, -79, -80*
O'Donovan, Desmond 1933- *WhoThe 72, -77*
O'Donovan, Elizabeth *WhoHol A*
O'Donovan, Frank 1900-1974 *WhScrn 77, WhoHol B*
O'Donovan, Fred 1889-1952 *NotNAT B, WhThe, WhoHol B*
O'Donovan, Una Margaret 1943- *IntWWM 77, -80*
Odoramnus Senonensis 985-1046 *NewGrD 80*
Odorannus De Sens 985-1046 *NewGrD 80*
O'Dowd, Mike *WhoHol A*
Odoyevsky, Prince Vladimir Fyodorovich 1804-1869 *NewGrD 80*
O'Driscoll, Martha 1922- *FilmEn, FilmgC, ForYSC, HalFC 80, WhoHol A*
O'Duinn, Proinnsias 1941- *IntWWM 80*
Odum, Howard Washington 1884- *OxMus*
O'Dunn, Irvin 1904-1933 *WhScrn 74, -77*
O'Dwyer, Robert 1862-1949 *Baker 78*
Odyssey *RkOn 2[port]*
Oede De La Couroierie d1294 *NewGrD 80*
Oeglin, Erhard d1520? *NewGrD 80*
Oehlenschlaeger, Adam Gottlob 1779-1850 *EncWT, NotNAT B, OxThe*
Oehlenschlager, Adam 1779-1850 *McGEWD[port], REnWD[port]*
Oehler, Dale Dixon 1941- *AmSCAP 80, ConAmC, EncJzS 70*
Oehlschlagel, Franz Joseph 1724-1788 *NewGrD 80*
Oehlschlegel, Franz Joseph 1724-1788 *NewGrD 80*
Oehmler, Leo Carl Martin 1867-1930 *BiDAmM*
Oehrle, Marie L *PupTheA*
Oelrichs, Blanche d1950 *NotNAT B*
Oelschlegel, Gerd 1926- *CnMD, McGEWD[port], ModWD*
Oenslager, Donald Mitchell 1902- *WhoThe 72*
Oenslager, Donald Mitchell 1902-1975 *BiE&WWA, NotNAT B, OxThe, PlP&P[port], WhThe*
Oenslager, Donald Mitchell 1902-1976 *EncWT*
Oesch, Hans 1926- *NewGrD 80*
Oeser, Fritz 1911- *NewGrD 80*
Oesterlein, Nikolaus 1842-1898 *Baker 78*
Oesterreicher, Georg 1563-1621 *NewGrD 80*
Oestreicher, Gerard 1916- *BiE&WWA, NotNAT*
Oestvig, Karl Aagaard 1889-1968 *CmOp, NewGrD 80*
Oettel, Wally *Film 2*
Oetting, William H 1875-1969 *Baker 78*
Oettingen, Arthur Joachim Von 1836-1920 *Baker 78, NewGrD 80*
Oettinger, Nancy *WomWMM*
Oevering, Rynoldus Popma Van *NewGrD 80*
O'Farrell, Bernadette 1926- *FilmgC, HalFC 80, WhoHol A*
O'Farrell, Broderick *Film 2*
O'Farrell, Mary 1892-1968 *WhThe, WhoHol B*
O'Farrell, Talbot d1952 *NotNAT B*
O'Farrill, Arturo 1921- *AmSCAP 66, -80, BiDAmM, EncJzS 70*
O'Farrill, Chico 1921- *EncJzS 70*
O'Ferrall, George More *FilmEn, IlWWBF*
Offenbach, Jacob 1819-1880 *NewGrD 80[port]*
Offenbach, Jacques 1819-1880 *Baker 78, BnBkM 80, CmOp, CmpBCM, CnOxB, DancEn 78, DcCom 77[port], DcCom&M 79, GrComp[port], MusMk, NewEOp 71, NewGrD 80[port], NotNAT B, OxMus, PlP&P*
Offenbach, Joseph 1905-1971 *WhScrn 74, -77*
Offenhauser, William H, Jr. 1904- *IntMPA 77, -75, -76, -78, -79, -80*
Offerman, George, Jr. 1917-1963 *NotNAT B, Vers B[port], WhScrn 74, -77, WhoHol B*
Offerman, George, Sr. 1880-1938 *Film 2, NotNAT B, WhScrn 74, -77, WhoHol B*
Offerman, Marie 1894-1950 *WhScrn 74, -77, WhoHol B*
Offitt, Lillian 1938- *BluesWW*
Offner, Debbie *PlP&P*
Offord, Bert *Film 2*
Oflazoglu, Turan 1932- *REnWD[port]*
O'Flynn, Carol Comer 1944- *AmSCAP 66*
O'Flynn, Charles 1897-1964 *AmSCAP 66, -80*
O'Flynn, Damian *ForYSC, WhoHol A*
O'Flynn, Honoria 1909- *AmSCAP 66, -80*
O'Flynn, Philip *WhoHol A*
Ofman, Lee 1946- *AmSCAP 80*
O'Fredericks, Alice *WomWMM*
Ofsdal, Steinar 1948- *IntWWM 80*
Ofterdingen, Heinrich Von *NewGrD 80*
Ofugi, Naburo d1960 *DcFM*
Ogal, T F *AmSCAP 80*
Oganesyan, Edgar Sergeyi *NewGrD 80*
O'Gatty, Jimmy Packy 1899-1966 *WhScrn 77*
Ogbe, George Korjosey 1932- *IntWWM 77, -80*
Ogden, Dave 1888?-1963 *NewOrJ*
Ogden, Jean Custer 1926- *ConAmTC*
Ogden, Rita *WomWMM*
Ogden, Vivia d1953 *Film 1, -2, WhScrn 77*
Ogdon, John 1937- *Baker 78, IntWWM 77, -80, MusMk[port], NewGrD 80, WhoMus 72*
Ogdon, Wilbur L 1921- *ConAmC*
Ogerman, Claus 1930- *EncJzS 70*
Ogier *NewGrD 80*
Ogier, Bulle 1939- *FilmAG WE[port]*
Ogihara, Toshitsugu 1910- *Baker 78*
Ogilby, John 1600-1676 *NewGrD 80*
Ogilvie, George 1931- *WhoThe 77*
Ogilvie, George Thomas Anderson 1912- *WhoMus 72*
Ogilvie, Glencairn Stuart 1858-1932 *NotNAT B, WhThe*
Ogilvie, Mary A H *PupTheA*
Ogilvie, Ruth Simmons 1920- *AmSCAP 66, -80*
Ogilvie, Will 1901- *CreCan 2*
Ogilvy, Ian 1943- *FilmgC, HalFC 80, IlWWBF, WhoHol A, WhoHrs 80*
Oginaga, Joaquin De *NewGrD 80*
Oginski *NewGrD 80*
Oginski, Franciszek Ksawery 1801-1837 *NewGrD 80*
Oginski, Prince Michael Cleophas 1765-1833 *Baker 78*
Oginski, Michal Kazimierz 1728-1800 *NewGrD 80*
Oginski, Michal Kleofas 1765-1833 *NewGrD 80*
Ogiwara, Toshitsugu 1910- *NewGrD 80*
Ogkeguam, Johannes *NewGrD 80*
Ogle, Arthur 1895?-1959 *NewOrJ*
Ogle, Charles 1865-1926 *FilmgC, HalFC 80*
Ogle, Charles 1865-1940 *WhScrn 77, WhoHol B, WhoHrs 80*
Ogle, Charles 1875- *Film 1, -2, TwYS*
Oglio, Domenico Dall' *NewGrD 80*
Oglio, Giovanni Battista Dall' *NewGrD 80*
Oglio, Giuseppe Dall' *NewGrD 80*
Ognivtsev, Alexander Pavlovich 1920- *NewGrD 80, WhoOp 76*
Ogolevets, Alexey Stepanovich 1894-1967 *NewGrD 80*
Ogoun, Lubos 1924- *CnOxB*
O'Grady, Monty *Film 2*
Ogrizovic, Milan 1877-1923 *CnMD*
Ogston, Bruce Robin 1944- *IntWWM 77, -80*
Ogterop, Bep Alberta Bernarda 1909- *IntWWM 77, -80*
Ogura, Roh 1916- *Baker 78, NewGrD 80*
O'Gwynn, James Leroy 1928- *BiDAmM, IlEncCM*
O'Gyla, Cassandra *WomWMM B*
Oh Gran, Gilbert 1886-1971 *WhScrn 77*
Oh Gran Gilbert 1886-1971 *WhScrn 74*
O'Hagan, Betsy *NewGrD 80*
O'Hagan, John Francis 1898- *WhoMus 72*
O'Haire, Patricia *ConAmTC*
Ohana, Maurice 1913- *WhoMus 72*
Ohana, Maurice 1914- *Baker 78, CpmDNM 80, IntWWM 77, -80, NewGrD 80*
Ohana, Maurice 1915- *DcCM*
Ohanesian, David 1927- *WhoOp 76*
O'Hanlon, George 1917- *FilmgC, ForYSC, HalFC 80, IntMPA 77, -75, -76, -78, -79, -80, WhoHol A*
O'Hanlon, George, Jr. *WhoHol A*
O'Hanlon, James *NewYTET*
O'Hanlon, Redmond L d1964 *NotNAT B*
O'Hara, Barry *WhoHol A*
O'Hara, Fiske 1878-1945 *NotNAT B, WhScrn 74, -77, WhoHol B*
O'Hara, Geoffrey 1882-1967 *AmSCAP 66, -80, Baker 78, BiDAmM, ConAmC, CreCan 2*
O'Hara, George 1899-1966 *Film 2, WhScrn 77, WhoHol B*
O'Hara, Gerry 1924- *FilmEn, IntMPA 77, -75, -76, -78, -79, -80*
O'Hara, Gerry 1925?- *FilmgC, HalFC 80, IlWWBF*
O'Hara, Jill 1947- *EncMT, WhoHol A*
O'Hara, Jim *WhoHol A*
O'Hara, John d1929 *NotNAT B*
O'Hara, John 1905- *BiE&WWA, PlP&P*
O'Hara, John 1905-1970 *BiDAmM, CnMD, FilmEn, HalFC 80, NotNAT A, -B, WorEFlm*
O'Hara, John 1905-1972 *FilmgC*
O'Hara, Kane 1711?-1782 *NewGrD 80, NotNAT B*
O'Hara, Karen 1933- *AmSCAP 80*
O'Hara, Kean 1711?-1782 *NewGrD 80*
O'Hara, Kene 1711?-1782 *NewGrD 80*
O'Hara, Linda 1948- *AmSCAP 80*
O'Hara, Maureen 1920- *BiDFilm 81, CmMov, FilmEn, FilmgC, ForYSC, HalFC 80, IlWWBF[port], IntMPA 77, -75, -76, -78, -79, -80, MotPP, MovMk[port], OxFilm, ThFT[port], WhoHol A, WomWMM, WorEFlm[port]*

O'Hara, Noelene 1935- IntWWM 77
O'Hara, Nolene 1935- IntWWM 80
O'Hara, Quinn WhoHol A
O'Hara, Shirley Film 2, WhoHol A
Ohardieno, Roger 1919-1959 WhScrn 74, -77, WhoHol B
O'Hare, Husk 1890?-1970 CmpEPM
Ohberg, Ake 1905- FilmEn
O'Hearn, Robert 1921- BiE&WWA, NotNAT, WhoOp 76
O'Herlihy, Dan IntMPA 75, -76, -78, -79, -80
O'Herlihy, Dan 1917- ForYSC
O'Herlihy, Dan 1919- FilmEn, FilmgC, HalFC 80, IntMPA 77, MovMk, WhoHol A
O'Herlihy, Michael 1929- FilmgC, HalFC 80
O'Higgins, Harvey J 1876-1929 NotNAT B, WhThe
Ohio Express, The BiDAmM, RkOn 2[port]
Ohio Players, The ConMuA 80A, IlEncR, RkOn 2[port]
Ohio Roscius OxThe, PlP&P[port]
Ohlberger, Karl 1912- NewGrD 80
Ohlson, Marion AmSCAP 66, -80, ConAmC
Ohlsson, Garrick 1948- Baker 78, BiDAmM, BnBkM 80, IntWWM 77, -80, MusSN[port], NewGrD 80
Ohlsson, Richard 1874-1940 NewGrD 80
Ohm, Georg Simon 1789-1854 NewGrD 80
Ohman, Frank 1939- CnOxB
Ohman, Phil 1896-1954 AmSCAP 66, -80, CmpEPM
Ohmart, Carol 1928- FilmgC, ForYSC, HalFC 80, IntMPA 77, -75, -76, -78, -79, -80, MotPP, WhoHol A, WhoHrs 80[port]
Ohmiya, Makoto 1924- IntWWM 77, -80
Ohms, Elisabeth 1888-1974 CmOp, NewGrD 80
Ohms, Fred 1918-1956 WhoJazz 72
Ohnet, Georges 1848-1918 McGEWD[port], NotNAT B, OxThe, WhThe
O'Hogan, Roger Matthew 1917- IntWWM 77, -80, WhoMus 72
O'Horgan, Thomas 1926- BiDAmM
O'Horgan, Tom IntMPA 77, -75, -76, -78, -79, -80, WhoThe 77
O'Horgan, Tom 1926- NotNAT
O'Horgan, Tom 1927- EncWT, Ent
O'Horgan, Tom 1928- EncMT
Ohren, Jacob NewGrD 80
Ohrlin, Glenn 1926- EncFCWM 69
Ohrn, Karen WomWMM B
Ohtani, Hiroshi 1910- IntMPA 77, -76, -78, -79, -80
Ohtani, Horishi 1910- IntMPA 75
Ohyama, Heiichiro 1947- IntWWM 77, -80
Oien, Ingegard 1940- IntWWM 77, -80
Oien, Per 1937- IntWWM 77, -80
Oiesen, Mabel Lucile 1904- IntWWM 77, -80
Oistrakh, David 1908-1974 Baker 78, BnBkM 80, MusMk[port], MusSN[port], NewGrD 80[port], WhoMus 72
Oistrakh, Igor Davidovich 1931- BnBkM 80, IntWWM 77, -80, NewGrD 80, WhoMus 72
O'Jays, The ConMuA 80A, IlEncR, RkOn 2[port]
Ojeda, Jesus Chucho 1892-1943 WhScrn 74, -77
Ojinaga, Joaquin De NewGrD 80
Oju, Abeodun AmSCAP 80
Okada, Eiji 1920- FilmEn
Okada, Hideki CreCan 2
O'Kalemo, Helen MotPP
Okamoto, Kelly G 1950- IntWWM 77, -80
Okamura, Takao 1931- IntWWM 77, -80, WhoOp 76
O'Kane, Tullius Clinton 1830-1912 BiDAmM
O'Kasions, The RkOn 2[port]
Okchem, Johannes NewGrD 80
O'Keefe, Allan J IntMPA 77, -75, -76, -78, -79, -80
O'Keefe, Arthur J 1874-1959 WhScrn 74, -77
O'Keefe, Bradshaw Dennis 1946- IntWWM 80
O'Keefe, Danny RkOn 2[port]
O'Keefe, Dennis 1908-1968 FilmEn, FilmgC, HalFC 80[port], HolP 40[port], MotPP, MovMk, WhScrn 74, -77, WhoHol B
O'Keefe, Dennis 1911-1968 ForYSC
O'Keefe, James Conrad 1892-1942 AmSCAP 66, -80
O'Keefe, Lester 1896-1977 AmSCAP 66, -80
O'Keefe, Paul C WhoHol A
O'Keefe, Walter Michael 1900- AmSCAP 66, -80
O'Keeffe, John 1747-1833 Ent, NotNAT A, -B, OxThe
Okeghem, Jan GrComp
Okeghem, Joannes 1430?-1495? MusMk
Okeghem, Johannes Baker 78, NewGrD 80
Okeland, Robert NewGrD 80
O'Kelly, Don WhScrn 77
O'Kelly, Seumas 1881-1918 REnWD[port]
Okeover, John 1590?-1663? NewGrD 80
Oker, John 1590?-1663? NewGrD 80
Okey, Jack d1963 NotNAT B
Okhlopkov, Nikolai Pavlovich 1900-1967 CnThe, DcFM, EncWT, FilmEn, OxThe, WhThe
Oki, Masao 1901-1971 Baker 78, NewGrD 80
Okinow, Harold ConMuA 80B
Okito 1875-1963 MagIID
Okon, Krzysztof 1939- IntWWM 77, -80
Okon, Ted 1929- IntMPA 77, -75, -76, -78, -79, -80
Okpaku, Joseph O O 1943- BlkAmP, DrBlPA
Oktay Rifat 1914- REnWD[port]
O'Kun, Lan 1932- AmSCAP 66, -80
Okun, Milt 1923- BiDAmM, EncFCWM 69
Okun, Milton Theodore 1923- AmSCAP 66, -80, ConMuA 80B
Olaf, Pierre 1928- BiE&WWA, NotNAT, WhoHol A, WhoThe 72, -77
Olafsson, Bjorn 1917- NewGrD 80
Olague, Bertolomeu De NewGrD 80
Olague, Martinho Garcia De NewGrD 80
Olah, Tiberiu 1928- Baker 78, DcCM, IntWWM 80, NewGrD 80
Olah, Tibor 1937- IntWWM 80
Oland, Edward WhoMus 72
Oland, Warner 1880-1938 CmMov, FilmEn, Film 1, -2, FilmgC, ForYSC, HalFC 80, MotPP, MovMk[port], NotNAT B, TwYS, WhScrn 74, -77, WhThe, WhoHol B, WhoHrs 80[port]
Olander, Pehr August 1824-1886 NewGrD 80
Olander, Per August 1824-1886 NewGrD 80
Olanova, Olga Film 1
Olatunji, Michael Babatunde DrBlPA
Olay, Ruth 1927- EncJzS 70
Olbrychski, Daniel 1945- FilmEn
Olchansky, Adolf Film 2
Olcott, Chauncey AmPS B
Olcott, Chauncey 1858-1932 AmPS, AmSCAP 80, BiDAmM, CmpEPM, NotNAT B, PopAmC[port]
Olcott, Chauncey 1860-1932 AmSCAP 66, NotNAT A, WhThe, WhoStg 1906, -1908
Olcott, Sidney 1873-1949 FilmEn, Film 1, FilmgC, HalFC 80, NotNAT B, OxFilm, WhScrn 74, -77, WhoHol B
Olcott, Sidney 1875-1949 TwYS A
Olczewska, Maria 1892-1969 Baker 78, CmOp, NewEOp 71, NewGrD 80
Oldaker, Max 1908-1972 WhScrn 77
Oldani, Luigi 1909- WhoOp 76
Oldberg, Arne 1874-1962 Baker 78, BiDAmM, ConAmC
Oldenburg, Claes 1929- ConDr 73, -77E
Oldfield, Anne 1683-1730 EncWT, Ent[port], NotNAT A, -B, OxThe, PlP&P[port]
Oldfield, Barney d1946 Film 1, WhoHol B
Oldfield, Barney 1877-1946 Film 2
Oldfield, Barney 1878-1946 FilmgC, HalFC 80, WhScrn 74, -77
Oldfield, Mike 1953- ConMuA 80A, IlEncR, RkOn 2[port]
Oldfield, Willard Alan 1935- ConAmC
Oldham, Andrew Loog ConMuA 80B, IlEncR
Oldham, Arthur William 1926- Baker 78, NewGrD 80, WhoMus 72
Oldham, Bill William 1909- WhoJazz 72
Oldham, Derek d1968 WhoHol B
Oldham, Derek 1892-1968 NotNAT B, WhThe
Oldham, Derek 1893-1968 WhScrn 74, -77
Oldis NewGrD 80
Oldis, Valentine 1620-1685 NewGrD 80
Oldland, Lilian 1905- Film 2, FilmgC, HalFC 80, WhThe
Oldland, Lillian IlWWBF
Oldman, C B 1894-1969 NewGrD 80
Oldman, Cecil Bernard 1894-1969 Baker 78, OxMus
Oldmixon, Mrs. d1835 NotNAT B, OxThe
Oldmixon, Georgina PlP&P[port]
Oldmixon, John d1742 NotNAT B
Oldmixon, Mrs. John d1836 FamA&A[port]
Oldring, Rube 1885-1961 WhScrn 77
Oldroyd, George 1886-1951 Baker 78
Olds, Gerry 1933- Baker 78, ConAmC
Olds, William Benjamin 1874-1948 AmSCAP 66, -80, ConAmC
Oldys NewGrD 80
O'Leary, Byron d1970 WhoHol B
O'Leary, Jane Strong 1946- IntWWM 77, -80
O'Leary, John WhoHol A
O'Leary, John 1926- NotNAT
O'Leary, Patsy Film 2
O'Leary, Thomas James 1924- WhoOp 76
Olembert, Theodora IntMPA 77, -78, -79
Olemert, Theodora IntMPA 80
Olenewa, Maria DancEn 78
Olenin, Alexander 1865-1944 Baker 78
Olenin, Boris Yulievich 1904-1961 OxThe
Olenina D'Alheim, Mariya Alexeyevna 1869-1970 NewGrD 80
Olenine D'Alheim, Marie 1869-1970 Baker 78
Olesen, Oscar 1916- BiE&WWA, NotNAT
Olesen, Otto K d1964 NotNAT B
Olesha, Yuri Karlovich 1899-1960 CnMD, CnThe, EncWT, ModWD, REnWD[port]
Olevsky, Estela Kersenbaum 1943- IntWWM 77, -80
Olevsky, Julian 1926- IntWWM 77, -80
Oley, Johann Christoph 1738-1789 NewGrD 80
Olfson, Lewy NatPD[port]
Olga, Duchess WhScrn 74, -77
Olgina, Y Film 2
Olgina-Mackiewicz, Olga 1904- IntWWM 77, -80
Olguim, Maria 1894- FilmAG WE
Oliac Y Serra, Juan 1708?-1780 NewGrD 80
Olian, Helen WomWMM B
Olias, Lotar IntWWM 77, -80
Oliffe, Geraldine WhThe
Oligny, Huguette CreCan 1
Olim, Dorothy 1934- BiE&WWA, NotNAT
Olin, Bob 1908-1956 WhScrn 74, -77
Olin, Milton E 1913- IntMPA 77, -75, -76, -78, -79, -80
Olin, Stig 1920- FilmEn
Oliosi, Eleonora 1939- DancEn 78
Oliphant, Betty 1918- CnOxB, CreCan 1
Oliphant, Grassella 1929- BiDAmM
Oliphant, Jack 1895- WhThe
Oliphant, Naomi Joyce 1953- IntWWM 80
Oliphant, Thomas 1799-1873 Baker 78, NewGrD 80
Olitzka, Rosa 1873-1949 Baker 78
Olitzki, Walter 1903-1949 Baker 78
Oliva NewGrD 80
Oliva, Frank F 1904- AmSCAP 66, -80
Olivadoti, Joseph 1893-1977 AmSCAP 66, -80
Olivares, Juan Manuel 1760-1797 NewGrD 80
Olive, Edyth d1956 NotNAT B, WhThe
Olive, Joan WomWMM B
Olive, Joseph P 1941- ConAmC, IntWWM 77
Oliveira, Aloysio 1914- AmSCAP 80
Oliveira, Elmar 1950- IntWWM 80
Oliveira, Jamary 1944- NewGrD 80
Oliveira, Jocy De 1936- Baker 78, IntWWM 77, -80
Oliveira, Manuel De 1905- DcFM
Oliveira, Manuel De 1908- FilmEn
Oliveira, Willy Correa De 1938- DcCM, IntWWM 77, -80, NewGrD 80
Oliveira Martins, Eduardo De 1911- FilmAG WE[port]
Oliver NewGrD 80
Oliver 1945- RkOn 2[port]
Oliver, Alexander 1944- WhoMus 72
Oliver, Anthony 1923- FilmgC, HalFC 80, IntMPA 77, -75, -76, -78, -79, -80, WhoHol A, WhoThe 72, -77
Oliver, Barrie 1900- WhThe
Oliver, Denise ConMuA 80B
Oliver, Eddie d1976 WhoHol C
Oliver, Eddie 1894- BiE&WWA
Oliver, Edith 1913- BiE&WWA, ConAmTC, NotNAT, WhoThe 72, -77

Oliver, Edna May d1942 *MotPP, WhoHol B*
Oliver, Edna May 1883-1942 *FilmEn, FilmgC, ForYSC, Funs[port], HalFC 80, HolCA[port], MovMk[port], OxFilm, ThFT[port], TwYS, WhScrn 74, -77, WorEFlm*
Oliver, Edna May 1884-1942 *Film 2, Vers A[port]*
Oliver, Edna May 1885-1942 *NotNAT B, WhThe*
Oliver, Fenwick *Film 2*
Oliver, Gordon 1910- *ForYSC*
Oliver, Guy 1875-1932 *Film 1, -2, ForYSC, TwYS, WhScrn 74, -77, WhoHol B*
Oliver, Harold Silas 1942- *CpmDNM 74, -78, ConAmC*
Oliver, Henry Kemble 1800-1885 *Baker 78, BiDAmM*
Oliver, Joe 1885-1938 *NewGrD 80*
Oliver, Joseph 1885-1938 *Baker 78, BiDAmM, NewOrJ[port]*
Oliver, Joseph King 1885-1938 *BnBkM 80, MusMk[port]*
Oliver, Kine *BluesWW[port]*
Oliver, King 1885-1938 *CmpEPM, DrBlPA, IlEncJ, MnPM[port], NewGrD 80, WhoJazz 72*
Oliver, Larry 1880-1973 *WhScrn 77, WhoHol B*
Oliver, Lynn 1921- *BiDAmM*
Oliver, Madra Emogene 1905- *AmSCAP 66, ConAmC*
Oliver, Melvin James 1910- *BiDAmM, EncJzS 70*
Oliver, Olive d1961 *NotNAT B*
Oliver, Richard 1927- *CpmDNM 72, ConAmC*
Oliver, Richard S 1936- *AmSCAP 80*
Oliver, Rochelle 1937- *BiE&WWA, NotNAT, WhoHol A*
Oliver, Sherling 1907-1971 *BiE&WWA*
Oliver, Shirling 1907-1971 *WhoHol B*
Oliver, Stephen *WhoHol A*
Oliver, Susan *MotPP, WhoHol A*
Oliver, Susan 1936- *BiE&WWA*
Oliver, Susan 1937- *FilmgC, ForYSC, HalFC 80*
Oliver, Suzanne *WomWMM*
Oliver, Sy *BgBands 74[port]*
Oliver, Sy 1910- *CmpEPM, DrBlPA, EncJzS 70, WhoJazz 72*
Oliver, Sy 1917- *Conv 2[port]*
Oliver, Ted 1895-1957 *WhScrn 74, -77, WhoHol B*
Oliver, Thelma *DrBlPA, WhoHol A*
Oliver, Thomas Edward, Jr. 1932- *AmSCAP 80*
Oliver, Vic 1898-1964 *FilmgC, HalFC 80, IlWWBF, -A, NotNAT A, -B, WhScrn 74, -77, WhThe, WhoHol B*
Oliver, William I 1926- *BiE&WWA*
Oliver-Sletten, Madra Imogene *AmSCAP 80*
Oliver Y Astorga, Juan 1733?-1830 *NewGrD 80*
Olivero, Magda 1912- *Baker 78*
Olivero, Magda 1913- *BiDAmM, MusSN[port], NewGrD 80*
Olivero, Magda 1914- *CmOp, NewEOp 71*
Olivero, Magda 1916- *WhoOp 76*
Olivero, Maria Maddalena 1913?- *NewGrD 80*
Oliveros, Pauline 1932- *AmSCAP 80, Baker 78, BnBkM 80, CpmDNM 78, -80, ConAmC, DcCM, NewGrD 80, WomCom[port]*
Olivette, Marie 1892-1959 *WhScrn 74, -77, WhoHol B*
Olivette, Nina 1908-1971 *WhScrn 74, -77, WhoHol B*
Olivier *NewGrD 80*
Olivier, Lord 1907- *IlWWBF[port], -A, IntMPA 77, -75, -76, -78, -79, -80*
Olivier, Adam 1865?- *NewOrJ*
Olivier, Adam 1870?- *BiDAmM*
Olivier, Gerrit Cornelius 1945- *IntWWM 77, -80*
Olivier, Jo *NewGrD 80*
Olivier, Sir Laurence 1907- *BiDFilm 81, BiE&WWA, CmMov, CnThe, DcFM, EncWT, Ent[port], FamA&A[port], FilmAG WE[port], FilmEn, FilmgC, ForYSC, HalFC 80, MotPP, MovMk[port], NotNAT, -A, OxFilm, OxThe, PlP&P[port], WhoHol A, WhoHrs 80, WhoThe 72, -77, WorEFlm[port]*
Olivieri, Angelo *NewGrD 80*
Olivieri, Giuseppe d1623? *NewGrD 80*
Oliviero, Angelo *NewGrD 80*
Olivo, Bruno F 1917- *AmSCAP 80*
Olivo, Sempliciano 1594-1680 *NewGrD 80*
Olivo, Simpliciano 1594-1680 *NewGrD 80*
Olkusnik, Joachim 1927- *IntWWM 77, -80*
Ollendorf, Paul d1920 *NotNAT B*
Ollendorff, Fritz 1912- *WhoOp 76*
Olleson, Edward 1937- *IntWWM 77, -80, NewGrD 80*
Olleta Mombiela, Domingo 1819-1890 *NewGrD 80*
Ollie Papa 1900?- *NewOrJ*
Ollivier, Paul *Film 2*
Ollone, Max D' 1875-1959 *Baker 78, NewGrD 80*
Olman, Abe 1888- *AmSCAP 66, -80, BiDAmM*
Olmeda, Federico 1865-1909 *NewGrD 80*
Olmeda DeSan Jose, Federico 1865-1909 *Baker 78*
Olmi, Ermanno 1931- *BiDFilm 81, DcFM, FilmEn, FilmgC, HalFC 80, OxFilm, WorEFlm*
Olmo, Lauro 1922- *McGEWD[port], ModWD*
Olmo, Lauro 1923- *CroCD*
Olmos, Pio d1965 *WhScrn 77*
Olmstead, Clarence 1892- *AmSCAP 66, ConAmC A*
Olmstead, Gary J 1941- *IntWWM 77, -80*
Olmstead, Gertrude 1897-1975 *FilmEn, Film 2, TwYS*
Olmstead, Gertrude 1904-1975 *ForYSC, WhScrn 77*
Olmstead, Timothy 1759-1848 *BiDAmM*
Olmsted, Gertrude 1897-1975 *FilmEn, WhoHol C*
Olney, Mary *PupTheA*
Olof, Efraim 1685-1735 *NewGrD 80*
Olof, Theo 1924- *NewGrD 80, WhoMus 72*
Olof, Victor 1898- *WhoMus 72*
O'Loughlin, Ed 1945- *AmSCAP 80*
O'Loughlin, Gerald S 1923- *HalFC 80*
O'Loughlin, Gerald Stuart 1921- *BiE&WWA, IntMPA 77, -75, -76, -78, -79, -80, NotNAT, WhoHol A*
Olsen, A Loran 1930- *ConAmC*
Olsen, Carl Gustav Sparre 1903- *IntWWM 80*
Olsen, Christopher 1947- *WhoHol A*
Olsen, Dorothy S 1917- *IntWWM 77*
Olsen, Ernst Bruun 1923- *CroCD*
Olsen, Esther Sigrid 1921- *AmSCAP 80*
Olsen, George 1893-1971 *BgBands 74[port], BiDAmM, CmpEPM, Film 2, WhScrn 74, -77, WhoHol B*
Olsen, Howard Stanley 1922- *IntWWM 77*
Olsen, Irene 1902-1931 *WhScrn 74, -77*
Olsen, Larry 1939- *WhoHol A*
Olsen, Lauritz *Film 2*
Olsen, Moroni 1889-1954 *FilmEn, FilmgC, ForYSC, HalFC 80, HolCA[port], MotPP, MovMk, NotNAT B, Vers A[port], WhScrn 74, -77, WhoHol B*
Olsen, Ole *ForYSC*
Olsen, Ole 1850-1927 *Baker 78, NewGrD 80, OxMus*
Olsen, Ole 1863- *FilmEn*
Olsen, Ole 1892-1963 *EncMT, FilmEn, MovMk, NotNAT B, WhScrn 74, -77, WhThe, WhoHol B*
Olsen, Ole 1892-1965 *FilmgC, HalFC 80, JoeFr[port]*
Olsen, Poul Rovsing 1922- *Baker 78, IntWWM 77, -80, NewGrD 80*
Olsen, Sparre 1903- *Baker 78, CpmDNM 80, IntWWM 77, NewGrD 80*
Olsen, Stephen 1900-1946 *WhScrn 74, -77*
Olsen, Susan 1961- *WhoHol A*
Olsen And Johnson *AmPS B, EncMT, JoeFr[port], WorEFlm*
Olshanetsky, Alexander 1892- *AmSCAP 66, -80*
Olson, Henry Russell 1913-1968 *AmSCAP 80*
Olson, Howard Stanley 1922- *IntWWM 80*
Olson, James 1932- *FilmgC, HalFC 80, WhoHol A*
Olson, Keith *ConMuA 80B*
Olson, Lynn Freeman 1938- *AmSCAP 80*
Olson, Mary 1928- *WomWMM*
Olson, Nancy 1928- *BiE&WWA, FilmEn, FilmgC, ForYSC, HalFC 80, IntMPA 77, -75, -76, -78, -79, -80, NotNAT, WhoHol A*
Olson, Richard 1943- *NatPD[port]*
Olson, Robert G 1913- *AmSCAP 66, -80, ConAmC A*
Olsson, Fredrik *Film 2*
Olsson, Hagar 1893- *CroCD*
Olsson, Mats Fredrik 1929- *IntWWM 77, -80*
Olsson, Otto Emanuel 1879-1964 *Baker 78, NewGrD 80*
Olsson, Rolf Nils Sture 1919- *IntWWM 77, -80*
Olsvai, Imre 1931- *NewGrD 80*
Olt, Arisztid *WhScrn 77*
Olthof, Statius 1555-1629 *NewGrD 80*
Olufsen, Otto Carl 1764-1827 *OxThe*
Olver, Hal d1963 *NotNAT B*
Olvera, Ernesto Hill 1937-1967 *WhScrn 74, -77*
Olympia Band *BiDAmM*
Olympia Orchestra *BiDAmM*
Olympics, The *RkOn[port]*
Olympus The Mysian *NewGrD 80*
Olyver *NewGrD 80*
O'Madigan, Isabel 1872-1951 *WhScrn 74, -77, WhoHol B*
O'Maille, Kit *Film 2*
O'Malley, Aileen *Film 2*
O'Malley, Charles *Film 2*
O'Malley, Ellen d1961 *WhThe*
O'Malley, Francis K 1896- *AmSCAP 66, -80*
O'Malley, Grania 1898-1973 *WhScrn 77*
O'Malley, J Pat d1966 *WhoHol A*
O'Malley, J Pat 1901- *ForYSC*
O'Malley, J Pat 1901-1966 *FilmgC*
O'Malley, J Pat 1901-1976 *HalFC 80*
O'Malley, J Pat 1904-1966 *BiE&WWA, MovMk[port], NotNAT*
O'Malley, J Patrick 1890-1966 *Vers A[port]*
O'Malley, J Patrick 1891-1966 *Film 1, -2*
O'Malley, James *Film 2*
O'Malley, John 1904-1945 *WhScrn 74, -77, WhoHol B*
O'Malley, John P 1916-1959 *WhScrn 74, -77, WhoHol B*
O'Malley, Kathleen *WhoHol A*
O'Malley, Pat d1966 *MotPP, WhoHol B*
O'Malley, Pat 1891-1966 *FilmEn, ForYSC, TwYS*
O'Malley, Pat 1892-1966 *WhScrn 74, -77*
O'Malley, Rex 1901-1976 *BiE&WWA, HalFC 80, NotNAT B, WhThe, WhoHol A, WhoThe 72*
O'Malley, Thomas E 1856-1926 *WhScrn 74, -77, WhoHol B*
Oman, Dorothy *PupTheA*
Oman, Julia Trevelyan 1930- *WhoOp 76, WhoThe 72, -77*
Oman, Lester *PupTheA*
Omar Khayyam 1050?-1123 *DcPup*
O'Mara, Joseph 1861-1927 *NewGrD 80*
O'Mara, Joseph 1866-1927 *CmOp*
O'Mara, Kate 1939- *FilmgC, HalFC 80, WhoHol A, WhoHrs 80, WhoThe 77*
Omarin *PupTheA*
Omartian, Stormie Sherric 1942- *AmSCAP 80*
Omata, Sumio 1947- *IntWWM 80*
Omatsu, Maryka *WomWMM*
O'Meagher, Hugh *ConAmC*
Omegna, Roberto 1876-1948 *FilmEn*
Omens, Estelle *WhoHol A*
Omerza, Mihael 1679-1742 *NewGrD 80*
Omitsu *Film 2*
Ommer, Andrea 1945- *IntWWM 77, -80*
Ommerle, Harry G d1976 *NewYTET*
O'Moore, Barry 1880-1945 *Film 1, WhScrn 74, -77, WhoHol B*
O'Moore, Patrick *ForYSC, WhoHol A*
O'Morrison, Kevin *NatPD[port], NotNAT*
Oncina, Juan 1925- *CmOp, NewGrD 80, WhoMus 72, WhoOp 76*
Ondek, Stephen 1899- *AmSCAP 66, -80*
Onderdenwyngaard, Toos A J 1926- *IntWWM 77, -80*
Onderdonk, Henry Ustick 1789-1858 *BiDAmM*
Ondra, Anny 1903- *FilmAG WE, FilmEn, Film 2, FilmgC, HalFC 80, OxFilm,*

WhoHol A
Ondricek NewGrD 80
Ondricek, Emanuel 1880-1958 NewGrD 80
Ondricek, Emanuel 1882-1958 Baker 78
Ondricek, Frantisek 1857-1922 NewGrD 80
Ondricek, Franz 1857-1922 Baker 78
Ondricek, Franz 1859-1922 OxMus
Ondricek, Ignac 1807-1871 NewGrD 80
Ondricek, Jan 1832-1900 Baker 78, NewGrD 80
Ondricek, Miroslav 1933- WorEFlm
Ondricek, Miroslav 1934- HalFC 80, OxFilm
Ondricek, Stanislav 1885-1953 NewGrD 80
One, Benny Film 2
One-Armed John BluesWW[port]
O'Neal, Barry 1942- CpmDNM 74, ConAmC
O'Neal, Christopher 1953- IntWWM 80
O'Neal, Frederick 1905- BiE&WWA, DrBlPA, FilmgC, HalFC 80, IntMPA 77, -75, -76, -78, -79, -80, MotPP, MovMk, NotNAT, WhoHol A, WhoThe 72, -77
O'Neal, John 1940- BlkAmP, MorBAP, NotNAT
O'Neal, Kevin WhoHol A
O'Neal, Patrick 1927- FilmEn, FilmgC, ForYSC, HalFC 80, IntMPA 77, -75, -76, -78, -79, -80, NotNAT, WhoHol A, WhoHrs 80, WhoThe 72, -77
O'Neal, Regina MorBAP
O'Neal, Ron 1937- DrBlPA, FilmEn, HalFC 80, IntMPA 77, -75, -76, -78, -79, -80, MorBAP, WhoHol A
O'Neal, Ryan WhoHol A
O'Neal, Ryan 1941- FilmEn, ForYSC, HalFC 80, IntMPA 77, -75, -76, -78, -79, -80, MovMk[port]
O'Neal, Ryan 1945- FilmgC
O'Neal, Tatum WhoHol A
O'Neal, Tatum 1962- HalFC 80
O'Neal, Tatum 1963- FilmEn, MovMk[port]
O'Neal, Tatum 1964- IntMPA 77, -78, -79, -80
O'Neal, William PlP&P[port]
O'Neal, William J 1898-1961 WhScrn 74, -77
O'Neal, Zelma 1907- CmpEPM, EncMT, WhThe
O'Neale, Margie Louise 1923- AmSCAP 66, -80
Onegin, Sigrid 1889-1943 Baker 78, NewGrD 80
Onegin, Sigrid 1891-1943 CmOp, NewEOp 71
Oneglia, Mario F 1927- AmSCAP 80
O'Neil, Barbara 1903- MovMk
O'Neil, Barbara 1909-1980 FilmEn, FilmgC, ForYSC, HalFC 80, WhoHol A
O'Neil, Barbara 1910- ThFT[port]
O'Neil, Barbara 1911-1980 HolCA[port]
O'Neil, Colette 1895-1975 WhScrn 77, WhoThe 77
O'Neil, George 1898-1940 CnMD
O'Neil, James Film 2
O'Neil, Jennifer 1947- FilmgC
O'Neil, Nance d1965 MotPP, WhoHol B
O'Neil, Nance 1874-1965 BiE&WWA, FamA&A[port]
O'Neil, Nance 1875-1965 Film 1, -2, ForYSC, HalFC 80, TwYS, WhScrn 74, -77
O'Neil, Nancy 1911- WhThe
O'Neil, Peggy 1898-1960 NotNAT B, WhThe
O'Neil, Sally d1968 WhoHol B
O'Neil, Sally 1908-1968 FilmEn, MovMk
O'Neil, Sally 1908-1969 ThFT[port]
O'Neil, Sally 1910-1968 Film 2, TwYS, WhScrn 74, -77
O'Neil, Sally 1912-1968 ForYSC
O'Neil, Sally 1913-1968 FilmgC, HalFC 80
O'Neil, Sue Film 2
O'Neil, Thomas F 1915- IntMPA 77, -75, -76, -78, -79, -80
O'Neil, Vincent 1912- AmSCAP 80
O'Neill, Charles 1882-1964 CreCan 2, NewGrD 80
O'Neill, Charles Edward 1930- WhoOp 76
O'Neill, Cheryl Lynn Boone 1954- AmSCAP 80
O'Neill, Dick WhoHol A
O'Neill, Dolores 1917- CmpEPM
O'Neill, Edward Film 2
O'Neill, Eileen WhoHol A
O'Neill, Eliza 1791-1872 OxThe
O'Neill, Eugene 1888-1953 CnMD, CnThe, CroCD, DcLB 7[port], DcPup, EncWT, Ent[port], FilmgC, HalFC 80, McGEWD[port], ModWD, NewEOp 71, NotNAT A, -B, OxThe, PlP&P[port], -A[port], REnWD[port], WhThe
O'Neill, Mrs. Eugene PlP&P
O'Neill, Eugene F 1888-1972 BiDAmM
O'Neill, Frank B 1869-1959 NotNAT B, WhThe
O'Neill, Harry Film 2
O'Neill, Henry 1891-1961 FilmEn, ForYSC, HolCA[port], MotPP, NotNAT B, PlP&P, Vers A[port], WhScrn 74, -77, WhThe, WhoHol B
O'Neill, Henry 1891-1964 Film 2, FilmgC, HalFC 80, MovMk
O'Neill, Iva PupTheA
O'Neill, Jack 1883-1957 WhScrn 74, -77
O'Neill, James d1938 WhScrn 77
O'Neill, James 1847-1920 FamA&A[port], Film 1, FilmgC, HalFC 80, NotNAT B, PlP&P, WhScrn 77
O'Neill, James 1848-1920 EncWT
O'Neill, James 1849-1920 WhThe, WhoStg 1906, -1908
O'Neill, James 1849-1938 WhScrn 74, WhoHol B
O'Neill, James, Jr. 1878-1923 NotNAT B, WhScrn 77, WhoHol B
O'Neill, James, Jr. 1920- BiE&WWA
O'Neill, James C 1876-1944 WhScrn 77
O'Neill, Jennifer WhoHol A
O'Neill, Jennifer 1947- FilmgC, HalFC 80
O'Neill, Jennifer 1948- FilmEn, MovMk[port]
O'Neill, Jimmy WhoHol A
O'Neill, Joseph J d1962 NotNAT B
O'Neill, Maire 1885-1952 FilmgC, HalFC 80, OxThe, PlP&P, WhThe, WhoHol B
O'Neill, Marie 1885-1952 Film 2, WhScrn 74, -77
O'Neill, Marie 1887-1952 NotNAT A, -B
O'Neill, Michael ConDr 77
O'Neill, Mickey 1903-1932 WhScrn 74, -77
O'Neill, Nance 1874-1965 WhThe
O'Neill, Nance 1875-1965 WhoStg 1908
O'Neill, Norman 1875-1934 Baker 78, NewGrD 80, NotNAT B, OxMus, WhThe
O'Neill, Norris 1939- AmSCAP 66, -80
O'Neill, Peggy 1924-1945 WhScrn 74, -77, WhoHol B
O'Neill, Raymond PlP&P
O'Neill, Robert A 1911-1951 WhScrn 74, -77, WhoHol B
O'Neill, Sally 1912-1968 NotNAT B
O'Neill, Selena 1899- AmSCAP 66
O'Neill, Sheila 1930- WhoHol A, WhoThe 72, -77
Ong, Dana Film 1
O'Niel, Colette 1895-1975 WhoHol C
Onions, Eileen Film 2
Onishi, Aiko 1930- IntWWM 77, -80
Onivas, D AmSCAP 80
Onley, Toni 1928- CreCan 1
Onna, Ferdinand Film 2
Ono, Yoko 1933- ConMuA 80A, IlEncR, WomWMM A, -B
Onodera, Sho d1974 WhoHol B
Onoe, Kikugoro 1885-1949 NotNAT B
Onofrei, Matilda 1932- WhoOp 76
Onofri, Alessandro 1874-1932 Baker 78
Onorati, Henry V 1912- AmSCAP 80
Onori, Romualdo NewGrD 80
Onorii, Romualdo NewGrD 80
Onslow, George 1784-1853 Baker 78, OxMus
Onslow, Georges 1784-1853 NewGrD 80
Ontkean, Michael 1950- HalFC 80, IntMPA 80, WhoHol A
Oord, Van NewGrD 80
Oort, Van NewGrD 80
Oost, Gert 1942- IntWWM 80
Oosterzee, Cornelie Van 1863-1943 Baker 78
Opatoshu, David IntMPA 77, -75, -76, -78, -79, -80, WhoHol A
Opatoshu, David 1918- BiE&WWA, FilmEn, FilmgC, ForYSC, HalFC 80, NotNAT, WhoThe 77
Opatoshu, David 1919- MovMk[port]
Openshaw, Charles Elton WhThe
Operti, LeRoi 1895-1971 BiDAmM, BiE&WWA, NotNAT B
Ophuls, Marcel 1927- BiDFilm 81, FilmEn, HalFC 80, OxFilm
Ophuls, Max 1902-1957 BiDFilm 81, DcFM, EncWT, FilmEn, FilmgC, HalFC 80, MovMk[port], OxFilm, WorEFlm[port]
Opie, Alan John 1945- WhoMus 72, WhoOp 76
Opie, Amelia OxMus
Opienski, Henryk 1870-1942 Baker 78, NewGrD 80
Opilionis, Othmar NewGrD 80
Opitiis, Benedictus De NewGrD 80
Opitz, Martin 1597-1639 CnThe, NewGrD 80, OxThe, REnWD[port]
Opler, Alfred M 1897- AmSCAP 66, -80
Opochinsky, David IntMPA 75
Opotowsky, Stan IntMPA 77, -75, -76, -78, -79, -80
Opp, Julie 1871-1921 NotNAT B, WhThe
Opp, Julie 1873-1921 WhoStg 1906, -1908
Opp, Paul F 1894- BiE&WWA, NotNAT
Oppenheim, David 1889-1961 AmSCAP 66, -80
Oppenheim, Hans 1892-1965 NewGrD 80
Oppenheim, Menasha d1973 WhScrn 77, WhoHol B
Oppenheimer, Alan WhoHol A
Oppenheimer, George 1900- BiE&WWA, ConAmTC, IntMPA 77, -75, -76, -78, -79, -80, NotNAT
Oppenheimer, Jess 1913- IntMPA 77, -76, -78, -79, -80
Oppenheimer, Jess 1918- IntMPA 75
Oppenheimer, Joseph L 1927- AmSCAP 66, -80
Oppenheimer, Peer J IntMPA 77, -78, -79, -80
Oppens, Ursula 1944- IntWWM 77, -80
Opper, Jacob 1935- IntWWM 77, -80
Opperman, Frank Film 1
O'Preska, John 1945- ConAmC
Opthof, Cornelis 1930- CreCan 2
Opthof, Cornelis 1932- WhoOp 76
Opuls, Max FilmEn
Oraffi, Pietro Marcellino NewGrD 80
Orafi, Pietro Marcellino NewGrD 80
Oram, Daphne Blake 1925- IntWWM 77, -80, WhoMus 72
O'Ramey, Georgia 1886-1928 CmpEPM, WhThe
Orange, Joseph 1941- BiDAmM
Orazio NewGrD 80
Orazio DellaViola NewGrD 80
Orbach, Jerry 1935- BiE&WWA, EncMT, NotNAT, WhoHol A, WhoThe 72, -77
Orbasany, Irma d1961 NotNAT B
Orben, Robert NewYTET
Orbin, Jack ConMuA 80B
Orbino, Il NewGrD 80
Orbison, Roy 1936- AmPS A, -B, BiDAmM, ConMuA 80A, CounME 74, -74A, EncFCWM 69, IlEncCM[port], IlEncR[port], PopAmC SUP[port], RkOn[port], WhoHol A
Orbon, Julian 1925- AmSCAP 80, Baker 78, DcCM, NewGrD 80
Orchard, Frank 1914- WhoJazz 72
Orchard, John WhoHol A
Orchard, Julian 1930-1979 FilmgC, HalFC 80, WhoHol A, WhoThe 77
Orchard, William Arundel 1867- Baker 78
Orcutt, David PupTheA
Orczy, Baroness Emmuska d1947 NotNAT B, WhThe
Ord, Bernhard 1897-1961 NewGrD 80
Ord, Boris 1897-1961 NewGrD 80
Ord, Robert WhThe
Ord, Simon 1874-1944 NotNAT B, WhThe
Ord-Hume, Arthur Wolfgang 1900- WhoMus 72
Orda, Alfred 1915- WhoMus 72
Orde, Beryl 1912-1966 WhScrn 74, -77, WhoHol B
Ordman, Jeannette 1935- CnOxB
Ordonetz, Carlo D' 1734-1786 NewGrD 80
Ordonez, Carlo D' 1734-1786 NewGrD 80
Ordonez, Carlos 1734-1786 Baker 78
Ordonez, Karl Von 1734-1786 NewGrD 80
Ordonez, Pedro 1510?-1585 NewGrD 80
Ordonneau, Maurice 1854-1916 NotNAT B, WhThe
Orduna, Juan 1908-1974 WhScrn 77
Ordung, Wyott WhoHrs 80

Ordway, John P 1824-1880 BiDAmM
Ordway, Sally NatPD[port]
Ordysnke, Richard Film 1
Ore, Charles William 1936- CpmDNM 73, -79, ConAmC
Ore, Harry 1885- WhoMus 72
Ore, John Thomas 1933- BiDAmM
O'Reare, James WhoHol A
Orefice, Antonio NewGrD 80
Orefice, Giacomo 1865-1922 Baker 78, NewGrD 80, OxMus
Orefici, Antonio NewGrD 80
O'Regan, Kathcrine 1904- Film 2
O'Regan, Kathleen 1903- WhThe
Oregon EncJzS 70
O'Reilly, Brendan WhoMus 72
O'Reilly, Erin WhoHol A
O'Reilly, Eugenia Nicks 1910- IntWWM 77
O'Reilly, John Samuel 1940- AmSCAP 80, ConAmC
O'Reilly, Miles OxMus
O'Reilly, Sally 1940- IntWWM 77, -80
O'Reilly, Sheilah 1931- CnOxB, DancEn 78
Orejon Y Aparicio, Jose De 1706-1765 NewGrD 80
Orel, Alfred 1889-1967 Baker 78, NewGrD 80
Orel, Dobroslav 1870-1942 Baker 78, NewGrD 80
Orell, Felix Film 2
Orellana, Carlos 1901-1960 WhScrn 74, -77
Orem, Preston Ware 1862-1938 BiDAmM
Orem, Preston Ware 1865-1938 Baker 78
Oren, Jacob NewGrD 80
Orendorff, George Robert 1906- WhoJazz 72
Orenstein, Harold ConMuA 80B
Orenstein, Larry 1918- AmSCAP 66, -80
Orent, Milton H 1918- AmSCAP 66, -80
Orentreich, Catherine WomWMM B
Oreste FilmgC, HalFC 80
Orff, Carl 1895- Baker 78, BnBkM 80, CmOp, CompSN[port], CnOxB, DancEn 78, DcCom 77[port], DcCom&M 79, DcCM, IntWWM 77, -80, MusMk, NewEOp 71, NewGrD 80[port], OxMus, WhoMus 72
Orfyn, Wedad WomWMM
Orga, Ates D'Arcy 1944- IntWWM 77, WhoMus 72
Orgad, Ben-Zion 1926- Baker 78, DcCM, NewGrD 80
Organi, Bartolomeo Degli NewGrD 80
Orgas, Annibale 1585?-1629 NewGrD 80
Orgeni, Aglaja 1841-1926 Baker 78, NewGrD 80
Orgiani, Teofilo d1725 NewGrD 80
Orgitano NewGrD 80
Orgitano, Paolo 1740?-1796 NewGrD 80
Orgitano, Raffaele 1770?-1812 NewGrD 80
Orgitano, Vincenzo 1735?-1807? NewGrD 80
Orhan Kemal 1914-1970 REnWD[port]
Oriani, Alfredo 1852-1909 McGEWD[port]
Orideyns, Johannes 151-?-1589? NewGrD 80
Oridijrus, Johannes 151-?-1589? NewGrD 80
Oridryus, Johannes 151-?-1589? NewGrD 80
Original Caste, The RkOn 2[port]
Original Creole Ragtime Band BiDAmM
Original Dixie Jubilee Singers BiDAmM
Original Dixieland Jazz Band BiDAmM, CmpEPM, IlEncJ, NewGrD 80
Original Jazz All-Stars BiDAmM
Original Memphis Five BiDAmM
Originals, The RkOn 2[port]
Orilo, V Film 1
Orinaga, Joaquin De NewGrD 80
Orio, C A 1912- AmSCAP 66, -80
Oriola, Pietro NewGrD 80
Orioles, The AmPS A, RkOn
Oriolo, Joseph 1913- IntMPA 77, -75, -76, -78, -79, -80
Orisicchio, Antonio NewGrD 80
Oristagno, Giulio D' 1543-1623 NewGrD 80
Orjasaeter, Tore 1886-1968 REnWD[port]
Orkeny, Istvan 1912- CroCD
Orkin, Ad 1922- IntMPA 78, -79, -80
Orkin, Harvey 1918-1975 NewYTET, WhScrn 77
Orkin, Ruth DcFM, WomWMM
Orkisz, Andrezj 1937- IntWWM 80
Orlamond, William 1867-1957 Film 2, TwYS, WhScrn 77
Orlamund, William 1867-1957 Film 2
Orland, Ferdinando 1774-1848 NewGrD 80
Orland, Henry 1918- AmSCAP 80, CpmDNM 76, -79, -80, ConAmC, IntWWM 77, -80
Orland, William Film 2
Orlandi, Camillo NewGrD 80
Orlandi, Felice WhoHol A
Orlandi, Ferdinando 1774-1848 NewGrD 80
Orlandi, Santi d1619 NewGrD 80
Orlandini, Giuseppe Maria 1675-1760 NewGrD 80
Orlando, Mariane 1934- CnOxB, DancEn 78[port]
Orlando, Tony 1944- RkOn[port]
Orlando, Tony & Dawn RkOn 2[port]
Orleans ConMuA 80A, IlEncR, RkOn 2[port]
Orlebeck, Lester 1907- IntMPA 77, -75, -76, -78, -79, -80
Orledge, Robert Francis Nicholas 1948- IntWWM 80
Orlenev, Pavel Nikolayevich 1869-1932 OxThe
Orles NewGrD 80
Orlick, Philip 1940- AmSCAP 66, -80
Orlik, Ivan A Vanya 1898-1953 WhScrn 74, -77
Orlikovsky, Vaslav 1921- DancEn 78
Orlikowsky, Vaslav 1921- CnOxB
Orlob, Harold 1885- AmSCAP 66, BiDAmM, BiE&WWA, NotNAT
Orlob, Harold F 1883- AmSCAP 80
Orloff, Nicholas 1914- CnOxB
Orloff, Vladimir 1928- IntWWM 77, -80, WhoMus 72
Orlons, The AmPS A, RkOn[port]
Orlov, Genrikh Alexandrovich 1926- NewGrD 80
Orlov, Nikolai 1892-1964 Baker 78
Orlov, Nikolay 1892-1964 NewGrD 80
Orlova, Lyubov 1902- FilmEn
Orlova, Lyubov 1903-1975 WhScrn 77, WhoHol C
Orlowski, Antoni 1811-1861 NewGrD 80
Orman, Felix 1884-1933 WhScrn 74, -77, WhoHol B
Orman, Roscoe 1944?- DrBlPA, WhoHol A
Ormandy, Eugene 1899- AmSCAP 66, -80, Baker 78, BiDAmM, BnBkM 80, IntWWM 77, -80, MusMk, MusSN[port], NewGrD 80[port], WhoMus 72
Orme, Daphnnie 1889-1970 AmSCAP 66, -80
Orme, Denise 1884-1960 NotNAT B, WhThe
Orme, Michael 1894-1944 NotNAT B, WhThe
Ormes, Gwendolyn BlkAmP
Ormestad, Caspar NewGrD 80
Ormonde, Eugene Film 1
Ormont, David 1898-1978 AmSCAP 80
Ormont, David 1905- AmSCAP 66
Orms, Howard R 1920- BiE&WWA
Ormslev, Gunnar 1928- IntWWM 77
Orn, Jacob d1653? NewGrD 80
Ornadel, Cyril 1924- HalFC 80, IntWWM 77, -80, WhoMus 72
Ornbo, Robert 1931- WhoThe 72, -77
Ornelas, Fernando 1948- CpmDNM 80
Ornell, Marty AmSCAP 80
Ornellas, Norman 1939-1975 WhScrn 77, WhoHol C
Ornest, Naomi 1924- WhoMus 72
Ornish, Natalie Gene 1926- AmSCAP 66, -80
Ornithoparchus, Andreas 1485?-1535? Baker 78
Ornithoparchus, Andreas 1490?- NewGrD 80
Ornithoparcus OxMus
Ornitz, Arthur J FilmgC, HalFC 80
Ornstein, George H 1918- IntMPA 77, -75, -76, -78
Ornstein, Leo 1892- Baker 78, ConAmC, DcCM, NewGrD 80
Ornstein, Leo 1895- BiDAmM, BnBkM 80, OxMus
Oro, Renee WomWMM
Orofino, Ruggero 1932- WhoOp 76
Orologio, Alessandro 1550?-1633? NewGrD 80
Orologio, Giovanni Dondi Dall' d1384 NewGrD 80
Orona, Vicente, Jr. 1931-1961 WhScrn 74, -77
Oropeza, Andrew L 1908-1971 WhScrn 77
O'Rorke, Brefni 1889-1946 NotNAT B, WhThe
O'Rorke, Peggy Film 2
Oros, Nancy 1951- IntWWM 77
Orosz, Adel 1938- CnOxB
O'Rourke, Brefni 1889-1945 FilmgC, HalFC 80
O'Rourke, Brefni 1889-1946 WhScrn 74, -77, WhoHol B
O'Rourke, Eugene 1863- WhoStg 1908
O'Rourke, J A d1937 NotNAT B, WhoHol B
O'Rourke, John J 1922- IntMPA 77, -75, -76, -78, -79, -80
O'Rourke, Michael PupTheA
O'Rourke, Tex d1963 NotNAT B
O'Rourke, Thomas 1872-1958 WhScrn 74, -77
O'Rourke, Tim 1933-1962 WhScrn 74, -77
O'Rourke, William Michael NewGrD 80
Orowan, Thomas F 1940- ConAmC
Orozco, Rafael 1946- IntWWM 77, -80, NewGrD 80, WhoMus 72
Orpheus RkOn 2[port]
Orr, Buxton Daeblitz 1924- CpmDNM 74, -75, -77, IntWWM 77, -80, NewGrD 80, WhoMus 72
Orr, C W 1893-1976 NewGrD 80, OxMus
Orr, Charles Wilfred 1893-1976 Baker 78, IntWWM 77, WhoMus 72
Orr, Christine d1963 NotNAT B
Orr, Forrest H d1963 NotNAT B, WhScrn 77, WhoHol B
Orr, Mary 1918- BiE&WWA, NotNAT, WhoHol A, WhoThe 72, -77
Orr, Robert 1909- NewGrD 80
Orr, Robin 1909- Baker 78, IntWWM 77, -80, NewGrD 80, OxMus, WhoMus 72
Orr, Terry 1943- CnOxB
Orr, Wendell Eugene 1930- IntWWM 77, -80
Orr, William T 1917- ForYSC, IntMPA 77, -75, -76, -78, -79, -80, NewYTET, WhoHol A
Orraca, Juan 1911-1956 WhScrn 74, -77
Orrego-Salas, Juan A 1919- Baker 78, CpmDNM 79, ConAmC, DcCM, IntWWM 77, -80, NewGrD 80
Orrery, Lord 1621-1679 OxThe
Orrey, Leslie 1908- NewGrD 80, WhoMus 72
Orrey, Leslie Gilbert 1908- IntWWM 77
Orrey, Leslie Gilbert 1909- IntWWM 80
Orry-Kelly 1897-1964 CmMov, FilmEn, FilmgC, HalFC 80, NotNAT B
Orsatti, Victor M 1905- IntMPA 77, -75, -76, -78, -79, -80
Orsborn, Victor R 1953- AmSCAP 80
Orselli, Cesare 1941- IntWWM 77, -80
Orshan, H Allen 1925- AmSCAP 66
Orshan, Herbert Allen 1925- AmSCAP 80
Orsi, Romeo 1843-1918 Baker 78
Orsina, Lucrezia NewGrD 80
Orsini, Valentino 1926- WorEFlm
Orska, Marie d1930 NotNAT B
Orso, Francesco d1567? NewGrD 80
Orsted Pedersen, Niels-Henning 1946- EncJzS 70
Orta Nadal, Enrique 1918- IntWWM 77, -80
Ortega, Anthony Robert 1928- BiDAmM, EncJzS 70
Ortega, Frank 1927- AmSCAP 80
Ortega, Frankie 1927- AmSCAP 66
Ortega, Sophie Film 2
Ortega, Tony 1928- EncJzS 70
Ortega DelVillar, Aniceto 1825-1875 NewGrD 80
Ortego, Art Film 1
Ortego, John Film 1
Ortells, Antonio Teodoro 1650?-1706 NewGrD 80
Ortes, Armand F 1880-1948 WhScrn 74
Orth, Frank 1880-1962 FilmEn, FilmgC, ForYSC, HalFC 80, MovMk, NotNAT B, Vers A[port], WhScrn 74, -77, WhoHol B
Orth, John 1850-1932 Baker 78
Orth, Louise Film 1, TwYS
Orth, Marion IntMPA 77, -75, -76, -78, -79, -80
Orthel, Leon 1905- Baker 78, CpmDNM 80, IntWWM 77, -80, NewGrD 80, WhoMus 72
Orthwine, Rudolf BiE&WWA
Ortico, Mario 1928- WhoMus 72
Ortigue, Joseph-Louis D' 1802-1866 Baker 78, NewGrD 80
Ortin, Leopoldo Chato 1893-1953 WhScrn 74,

-77
Ortiz, Cristina 1950- *IntWWM 77, -80*
Ortiz, Diego *OxMus*
Ortiz, Diego 1510?-1570? *NewGrD 80*
Ortiz, Diego 1525?- *Baker 78, MusMk*
Ortiz, Fernando 1881-1969 *NewGrD 80*
Ortiz, Thula 1894-1961 *WhScrn 74, -77*
Ortiz DeZarate, Domingo 1650?-1699? *NewGrD 80*
Ortlepp, Christa 1933- *IntWWM 77, -80*
Ortmann, Otto Rudolph 1889-1956 *Baker 78, BiDAmM*
Ortmans, Kay Muriel 1907- *IntWWM 77, -80*
Ortner, John Michael 1944- *IntWWM 77*
Orto, Marbriano De d1529 *Baker 78*
Orto, Marbrianus De 1460?-1529? *NewGrD 80*
Ortolani, Riz 1925- *HalFC 80*
Orton, J O C *IIWWBF*
Orton, Joe 1933-1967 *CnThe, ConDr 77F, CroCD, EncWT, Ent, McGEWD, ModWD, NotNAT B, REnWD[port]*
Orton, Richard 1940- *NewGrD 80*
Orus, Magdelena Laguna *PupTheA*
Orvieto, Ugolino Of *NewGrD 80*
Orwell, George 1903-1950 *HalFC 80*
Orwell, Virginia Wakelyn *CreCan 1*
Ory, Edward 1886-1973 *AmSCAP 66, -80, BiDAmM, EncJzS 70, NewGrD 80, NewOrJ[port]*
Ory, Edward Kid 1887-1973 *WhScrn 77, WhoHol B*
Ory, Kid 1886-1973 *CmpEPM, DrBlPA, EncJzS 70, IIEncJ, MusMk, NewGrD 80, WhoJazz 72*
Ory's Band, Kid *BiDAmM*
Orzazewski, Kasia 1888-1956 *WhScrn 77*
Orzello, Harry 1940- *NotNAT*
Osafo, Felix Onwona 1923- *IntWWM 77, -80*
Osato, Sono 1919- *BiE&WWA, CnOxB, DancEn 78[port], NotNAT*
Osaze, Ted Ernest *AmSCAP 80*
Osborn, Andrew 1912- *FilmgC, HalFC 80, IntMPA 77, -75, -76, -78, -79, -80, WhoHol A*
Osborn, Arthur H 1884-1965 *AmSCAP 66, -80*
Osborn, David Romaine 1941- *BiDAmM*
Osborn, E W 1860-1930 *NotNAT B, WhThe*
Osborn, Elizabeth 1928- *WhoMus 72*
Osborn, Franz 1905-1955 *NewGrD 80*
Osborn, John *NewGrD 80*
Osborn, Lyn 1923-1958 *WhScrn 74, WhoHol B*
Osborn, Lyn 1923-1959 *ForYSC*
Osborn, Lyn 1926-1958 *WhScrn 77, WhoHrs 80*
Osborn, Paul 1901- *BiE&WWA, CnMD, EncWT, FilmEn, McGEWD, ModWD, NotNAT, WhThe, WhoThe 72, WorEFlm*
Osborn-Hannah, Jane 1873-1943 *Baker 78, NewGrD 80*
Osborne, Adrienne 1873-1951 *Baker 78*
Osborne, Baby Marie 1911- *Film 1, -2, TwYS*
Osborne, Billy *Film 2*
Osborne, Bob 1931- *CounME 74, IIEncCM[port]*
Osborne, Bobby Van 1931- *BiDAmM*
Osborne, Bud d1964 *WhoHol B*
Osborne, Bud 1884-1964 *FilmEn*
Osborne, Bud 1888- *ForYSC*
Osborne, Charles 1927- *IntWWM 77, -80, NewGrD 80, WhoMus 72*
Osborne, Chester Gorham 1915- *AmSCAP 80, CpmDNM 79, IntWWM 77, -80*
Osborne, Conrad L 1934- *NewGrD 80*
Osborne, Don *AmSCAP 80*
Osborne, Gary *WhoMus 72*
Osborne, George 1938- *WhoOp 76*
Osborne, George Alexander 1806-1893 *NewGrD 80, OxMus*
Osborne, Gwendolen M S 1912- *IntWWM 77, -80*
Osborne, Gwendolyn *CreCan 2*
Osborne, Hubert *PlP&P*
Osborne, Jefferson 1871-1932 *WhScrn 74, -77*
Osborne, Jeffrey 1948- *AmSCAP 80*
Osborne, Jimmy 1923-1957 *BiDAmM*
Osborne, John 1792?-1835 *NewGrD 80*
Osborne, John 1929- *BiE&WWA, CnMD, CnThe, ConDr 73, -77, CroCD, EncWT, Ent[port], FilmEn, FilmgC, HalFC 80, IntMPA 77, -75, -76, -78, -79, -80, McGEWD[port], ModWD, NotNAT, -A, OxFilm, OxThe, PlP&P[port], REnWD[port], WhoHol A, WhoThe 72, -77, WorEFlm*
Osborne, Jose 1934- *IntWWM 80*
Osborne, Kipp 1944- *WhoThe 77*
Osborne, Lennie Bud 1881-1964 *NotNAT B, WhScrn 74, -77*
Osborne, Marie *WhoHol A*
Osborne, Mary 1921- *CmpEPM, EncJzS 70*
Osborne, Mike *IIEncJ*
Osborne, Miles Bud 1888-1964 *Film 1, -2, TwYS*
Osborne, Nat 1878-1954 *AmSCAP 66, -80*
Osborne, Neville 1928- *IntWWM 80, WhoMus 72*
Osborne, Nigel 1948- *Baker 78, NewGrD 80*
Osborne, Rosalynde R *PupTheA*
Osborne, Sonny 1937- *BiDAmM, CounME 74, IIEncCM[port]*
Osborne, Tony Roy Stuart 1947- *IntWWM 77, -80, WhoMus 72*
Osborne, Vivienne 1896-1961 *FilmEn, ThFT[port], WhScrn 77*
Osborne, Vivienne 1900-1961 *Film 2, ForYSC, HalFC 80, TwYS, WhoHol B*
Osborne, Vivienne 1905-1961 *WhThe*
Osborne, Will 1906- *AmSCAP 66, -80, BgBands 74, CmpEPM*
Osborne, Willson 1906- *ConAmC*
Osborne Brothers *CounME 74[port], -74A, IIEncCM[port]*
Osborne Brothers, The *EncFCWM 69*
Osbourne, Lloyd d1947 *NotNAT B*
Oscar *PupTheA*
Oscar, Henry 1891-1969 *IIWWBF, WhScrn 74, -77, WhThe, WhoHol B*
Oscar, Henry 1891-1970 *FilmgC, HalFC 80*
Oscard, Fifi 1921- *BiE&WWA*
Oscarsson, Per 1927- *FilmEn, FilmgC, HalFC 80, WhoHol A*
Osculati, Giulio d1615? *NewGrD 80*
Osculati, Iulio d1615? *NewGrD 80*
Osculatus, Iulius d1615? *NewGrD 80*
Ose, Jay 1911-1967 *WhScrn 77*
Osghian, Petar 1932- *Baker 78, NewGrD 80*
Osgood, Charles d1922 *NotNAT B*
Osgood, Donald 1921- *IntWWM 77, -80*
Osgood, George Laurie 1844-1922 *Baker 78, BiDAmM*
Osgood, Henry Osborne 1879-1927 *Baker 78, ConAmC*
Osgood, Lawrence 1929- *ConDr 73, -77*
Osgood, Mildred M *PupTheA*
Osgood, Richard E 1901- *ConAmTC*
Osgood, Stanton M *IntMPA 77, -75, -76, -78, -79, -80*
O'Shaughnessy *NewGrD 80*
O'Shaughnessy, John 1907- *BiE&WWA, NotNAT*
O'Shea, Black Jack 1906-1967 *Vers A[port], WhoHol B*
O'Shea, Cathy *AmSCAP 80*
O'Shea, Danny *Film 2*
O'Shea, Dennis *Film 2*
O'Shea, Jack Blackjack 1906-1967 *WhScrn 74, -77*
O'Shea, James J 1943- *AmSCAP 66*
O'Shea, Michael *MotPP*
O'Shea, Michael 1906-1973 *FilmEn, FilmgC, ForYSC, HalFC 80, WhScrn 77, WhoHol B*
O'Shea, Michael Sean 1922- *BiE&WWA*
O'Shea, Milo *WhoHol A*
O'Shea, Milo 1923?- *ForYSC*
O'Shea, Milo 1925- *FilmEn, MovMk*
O'Shea, Milo 1926- *FilmgC, HalFC 80, NotNAT*
O'Shea, Oscar 1882-1960 *WhScrn 74, -77, WhoHol B*
O'Shea, Tessie 1917- *FilmgC, HalFC 80, WhoHol A*
Oshima, Nagisa 1932- *BiDFilm 81, DcFM, FilmEn, OxFilm, WorEFlm*
Oshins, Julie d1956 *NotNAT B, WhoHol B*
Oshman, Irving L 1930- *IntMPA 75, -76*
Osiander, Irene 1903- *IntWWM 77, -80*
Osiander, Lucas 1534-1604 *NewGrD 80*
Osibisa *IIEncR*
Osieck, Hans 1910- *NewGrD 80*
Osinchuk, Juliana Lidia 1953- *IntWWM 77, -80*
Osipenko, Alla Yevgenyeva 1932- *CnOxB, DancEn 78*
Osipov, Nikolay 1901-1945 *NewGrD 80*
Oskamp, Gerard Hubertus Marinus 1950- *IntWWM 80*
Oskar I *NewGrD 80*
Oskar II *NewGrD 80*
Oskar, Keri Christine 1953- *AmSCAP 80*
Osman, Muhammed 1855-1900 *NewGrD 80*
Osmond, Cliff *HalFC 80, WhoHol A*
Osmond, Donny 1958- *IntMPA 79, -80*
Osmond, Hal *WhoHol A*
Osmond, Marie 1959- *IntMPA 79, -80*
Osmond, Miss V *Film 1*
Osmonds, The *ConMuA 80A, RkOn 2[port]*
Ossenbrink, Luther *IIEncCM*
Osser, Abe Arthur 1914- *AmSCAP 80*
Osser, Edna 1919- *AmSCAP 66, -80*
Osser, Glenn 1914- *AmSCAP 66, CmpEPM*
Ossewaarde, Jack Herman 1918- *AmSCAP 80, ConAmC*
Ossman, Vess *CmpEPM*
Ossoli, Sarah Margaret 1810-1850 *BiDAmM*
Ossovsky, Alexander Vyacheslavovich 1871-1957 *NewGrD 80*
Ossurarson, Bjarni 1954- *IntWWM 77*
Ost, Robert S 1951- *AmSCAP 80*
Ostadi, Nader Mortezapour 1951- *IntWWM 80*
Ostapiuk, Jerzy 1936- *WhoOp 76*
Ostbye, Rolf 1918- *IntWWM 80*
O'Steen, Sam 1923- *HalFC 80, NewYTET*
Osten, Eva VonDer 1881-1936 *CmOp, NewGrD 80*
Ostendorf, John Daniel 1945- *WhoOp 76*
Ostenso, Martha 1900-1963 *CreCan 1*
Osterberg, Jim *BiDAmM*
Osterberger, Georg d1602 *NewGrD 80*
Osterc, Slavko 1895-1941 *Baker 78, NewGrD 80*
Ostereng, Thorleif 1912- *IntWWM 80*
Ostergaard, Solveig 1939- *CnOxB, DancEn 78*
Ostergren, Eduardo Augusto 1943- *ConAmC*
Osterling, Eric Alfred 1926- *AmSCAP 66, -80, ConAmC*
Osterloh, Robert *WhoHol A*
Ostermaier, Andreas 1560?-1621 *NewGrD 80*
Osterman, Jack 1902- *JoeFr*
Osterman, Jack 1902-1939 *WhScrn 77, WhoHol B*
Osterman, Kathryn 1883-1956 *NotNAT B, WhScrn 77*
Osterman, Lester 1914- *BiE&WWA, NotNAT, WhoThe 72, -77*
Ostermayer, Andreas 1560?-1621 *NewGrD 80*
Ostermeier, Andreas 1560?-1621 *NewGrD 80*
Osterreich, Georg 1664?-1735 *NewGrD 80*
Ostertag, Barna 1902- *BiE&WWA, NotNAT*
Ostertag, Sandy *WomWMM B*
Osterwa, Juliusz 1885-1947 *NotNAT B*
Osterwald, Bibi 1920- *BiE&WWA, NotNAT, WhoHol A, WhoThe 72, -77*
Osterwald, Bibi 1921- *ForYSC*
Osthoff, Helmuth 1896- *Baker 78, IntWWM 77, -80, NewGrD 80*
Osthoff, Wolfgang 1927- *IntWWM 77, -80, NewGrD 80*
Ostiano, Vincenzo *NewGrD 80*
Ostin, Mo *ConMuA 80B*
Ostinelli, Sophie Henriette Hewitt d1846 *BiDAmM*
Ostler, William d1614 *NotNAT B, OxThe, PlP&P*
Ostlund, Island 1943- *EncJzS 70*
Ostlund, Petur David 1943- *EncJzS 70*
Ostova, Greta 1916- *IntWWM 80*
Ostrander, Bob *PupTheA*
Ostrander, Linda Woodaman 1937- *ConAmC*
Ostransky, Leroy *ConAmC*
Ostrcil, Otakar 1879-1935 *Baker 78, NewGrD 80*
Ostrcil, Ottokar 1879-1935 *OxMus*
Ostrer, Bertram 1913- *IntMPA 77, -75, -76, -78, -79, -80*
Ostriche, Muriel 1897- *Film 1, TwYS*
Ostroff, Esther 1909- *IntWWM 77*
Ostrove, Geraldine E 1938- *IntWWM 77, -80*
Ostrove, Michele Christine *WhoHol A*

Ostrovsky, Aleksandr 1823-1886 *McGEWD[port]*
Ostrovsky, Alexander 1823-1886 *CnThe, EncWT, Ent, NewGrD 80, NotNAT B, OxThe, REnWD[port]*
Ostrow, Herbert Ray 1911- *AmSCAP 66, -80*
Ostrow, Samuel 1919- *AmSCAP 66, -80*
Ostrow, Stuart 1932- *NotNAT, WhoThe 72, -77*
Ostrowski, Feliks 1802-1860 *NewGrD 80*
Ostrowsky, Avi 1939- *IntWWM 77, -80, WhoMus 72*
Ostrus, Merrill *AmSCAP 80*
Ostryniec, James Paul 1943- *IntWWM 77, -80*
Ostwald, David Frank 1943- *IntWWM 77, -80*
O'Sullivan, Anthony d1920 *Film 1, WhScrn 74, -77*
O'Sullivan, Denis 1868-1908 *BiDAmM, NewGrD 80*
O'Sullivan, Gilbert 1946- *RkOn 2[port]*
O'Sullivan, Gilbert 1947- *BiDAmM*
O'Sullivan, John 1878-1955 *CmOp*
O'Sullivan, Kevin P 1928- *IntMPA 77, -76, -78, -79, -80*
O'Sullivan, Maureen *IntMPA 75, -76, -78, -79, -80*
O'Sullivan, Maureen 1911- *BiE&WWA, CmMov, FilmEn, FilmgC, ForYSC, HalFC 80, IntMPA 77, MGM[port], MotPP, MovMk[port], OxFilm, ThFT[port], WhoHol A, WhoHrs 80, WorEFlm*
O'Sullivan, Maureen 1917- *WhoThe 72, -77*
O'Sullivan, Michael 1934-1971 *WhScrn 74, -77, WhoHol B*
O'Sullivan, Patrick 1871-1947 *Baker 78, ConAmC*
O'Sullivan, Richard 1943- *FilmgC, HalFC 80, WhoHol A*
O'Sullivan, Tony d1920 *WhoHol B*
Oswald Von Wolkenstein 1377?-1445 *NewGrD 80[port]*
Oswald, Andreas *NewGrD 80*
Oswald, Genevieve 1923- *BiE&WWA, CnOxB, DancEn 78, NotNAT*
Oswald, Gerd *IntMPA 77, -75, -76, -78, -79, -80*
Oswald, Gerd 1916- *BiDFilm 81, FilmEn, FilmgC, HalFC 80, MovMk[port]*
Oswald, Gerd 1919- *WorEFlm*
Oswald, Henrique 1852-1931 *NewGrD 80*
Oswald, James 1710?-1769 *OxMus*
Oswald, James 1711-1769 *NewGrD 80*
Oswald, Oscar *DcPup*
Oswald, Richard 1880-1963 *FilmEn, FilmgC, HalFC 80, IntMPA 77, -75, -76, -78, -79, -80, WorEFlm*
Oswald, Virginia 1926?- *BiE&WWA, NotNAT*
Oswalda, Ossi 1897-1948 *FilmEn*
Oswalda, Ossi 1899-1948 *FilmAG WE[port], Film 2, WhScrn 77*
Otaka, Hisatada 1911-1951 *Baker 78, NewGrD 80*
Otani, Takejiro 1877- *DcFM*
Otano, Nemesio 1880-1956 *Baker 78, NewGrD 80*
Otegui, Alberto 1913- *DancEn 78*
Oteo, Alfonso Esparza 1894- *IntWWM 77*
Otero, Caroline 1871- *WhoStg 1908*
Otero, Decio *DancEn 78*
Otescu, Ion Nonna 1888-1940 *Baker 78, NewGrD 80*
Otey, Orlando 1925- *IntWWM 80*
Otger *NewGrD 80*
Othegraven, August Von 1864-1946 *Baker 78*
Othmayr, Caspar 1515-1553 *Baker 78, NewGrD 80*
Otis And Carla *RkOn 2[port]*
Otis, Elita Proctor d1927 *Film 1, NotNAT B, WhoStg 1906, -1908*
Otis, Johnny 1921- *EncJzS 70*
Otis, Johnny 1924- *RkOn[port]*
Otis, Johnny, Jr. 1953- *EncJzS 70*
Otis, Philo Adams 1846-1930 *Baker 78*
Otis, Shuggie 1953- *EncJzS 70*
Otis, William R, Jr. *Film 2*
Otker Of Ratisbon *NewGrD 80*
Otker Of Regensburg *NewGrD 80*
Otloh Of St. Emmeram *NewGrD 80*
O'Toole, Catherine Mary *IntWWM 77, -80*
O'Toole, Peter *IntMPA 75, -76, MotPP, PlP&P, WhoHol A*
O'Toole, Peter 1932- *CnThe, EncWT, FilmAG WE[port], FilmEn, FilmgC, HalFC 80, IlWWBF[port], IntMPA 77, -78, -79, -80, MovMk[port], OxFilm, WhoThe 72, -77*
O'Toole, Peter 1933- *BiDFilm 81, ForYSC, WorEFlm*
Otowa, Nobuko *FilmEn*
Ots, Charles 1776-1845 *NewGrD 80*
Ots, Georg 1920-1975 *NewGrD 80*
Otsep, Fyodor *DcFM*
Otsuka, George 1938- *EncJzS 70*
Otsuka, Keiji 1938- *EncJzS 70*
Ott, Alexander 1888-1970 *WhScrn 77*
Ott, Alfons 1914-1976 *NewGrD 80*
Ott, Caroline *PupTheA*
Ott, Fred 1860-1936 *Film 1, HalFC 80, WhoHol B*
Ott, Frederick P 1860-1936 *WhScrn 74, -77*
Ott, Hans d1546 *NewGrD 80*
Ott, Horace 1933- *EncJzS 70*
Ott, Joseph Henry 1929- *AmSCAP 80, CpmDNM 79, ConAmC*
Ott, Lorenz Justinian 1748?-1805 *NewGrD 80*
Ott, Warrene *WhoHol A*
Ottani, Bernardino 1736?-1808 *NewGrD 80*
Ottani, Bernardo 1736-1827 *NewGrD 80*
Ottani, Gaetano 1736?-1808 *NewGrD 80*
Ottavio, Frate *NewGrD 80*
Ottaway, Hugh 1925-1979 *NewGrD 80*
Ottaway, James 1908- *WhoHol A, WhoThe 72, -77*
Otte, Hans 1926- *DcCM, NewGrD 80*
Ottel, Hans *NewGrD 80*
Otteman, Nicholas *NewGrD 80*
Otten, Daniel 1938- *IntWWM 77, -80*
Otten, Kees 1924- *IntWWM 77, -80, NewGrD 80*
Otter, Hens 1945- *IntWWM 77, -80*
Otter, Joseph 1760?-1836 *NewGrD 80*
Otterbach, Friedemann Gotthard 1942- *IntWWM 77, -80*
Otterloo, Willem Van 1907-1978 *Baker 78, NewGrD 80*
Ottesen, Milton F 1920- *AmSCAP 66, -80*
Ottiano, Rafaela 1894-1942 *Film 2, FilmgC, HalFC 80, ThFT[port], WhScrn 74, -77, WhoHol B, WhoHrs 80*
Ottiano, Rafaela 1895-1942 *ForYSC*
Ottinger, Leonora *Film 2*
Ottman, Robert W 1914- *Baker 78*
Otto, Arthur d1918 *WhScrn 77*
Otto, Eleanor *AmSCAP 80*
Otto, Georg 1550-1618 *NewGrD 80*
Otto, Georgius 1550-1618 *NewGrD 80*
Otto, H C 1901- *AmSCAP 66*
Otto, Hannskarl 1918- *WhoOp 76*
Otto, Hans *NewGrD 80*
Otto, Henry 1878-1952 *Film 2, TwYS A, WhScrn 74, -77, WhoHol B*
Otto, Henry Christian 1903- *AmSCAP 80*
Otto, Inga 1936- *AmSCAP 66, -80*
Otto, Irmgard 1912- *IntWWM 77, -80*
Otto, J Frank 1889- *AmSCAP 66*
Otto, Joseph Francis 1889- *AmSCAP 80*
Otto, Julius 1804-1877 *Baker 78*
Otto, Lisa 1919- *CmOp, IntWWM 77, -80, NewGrD 80*
Otto, Melitta 1842-1893 *NewGrD 80*
Otto, Paul *Film 2*
Otto, Stephan 1603?-1656 *NewGrD 80*
Otto, Theo 1904-1968 *EncWT*
Otto, Valerius 1579-1612? *NewGrD 80*
Ottobi, John *NewGrD 80*
Ottoboni, Pietro 1667-1740 *NewGrD 80*
Ottolini, Luigi 1928- *WhoOp 76*
Ottosen, Kirsten 1938- *IntWWM 80*
Ottosson, Robert A 1912-1974 *NewGrD 80*
Otvos, A Dorian 1890-1945 *AmSCAP 66, -80*
Otvos, Csaba 1943- *WhoOp 76*
Otvos, Gabor 1935- *WhoOp 76*
Otvos, Russell Emery 1954- *AmSCAP 80*
Otway, Grace d1935 *NotNAT B*
Otway, Thomas 1651-1685 *NotNAT B*
Otway, Thomas 1652-1685 *CnThe, EncWT, Ent, McGEWD[port], OxThe, PlP&P, REnWD[port]*
Otwell, Ronnie Ray 1929- *IntMPA 77, -75, -76, -78, -79, -80*
Oubradous, Fernand Robert 1903- *IntWWM 77, -80, NewGrD 80, WhoMus 72*
Oudal, Robert D 1930- *ConAmC*
Oudin, Eugene 1858-1894 *Baker 78, BiDAmM, NewGrD 80*
Oudot, Claude d1696 *NewGrD 80*
Oudrid, Cristobal 1825-1877 *Baker 78*
Oudrid Y Segura, Cristobal 1825-1877 *NewGrD 80*
Oudryns, Johannes *NewGrD 80*
Ouellette, Fernand 1930- *CreCan 1*
Ouellette, Paul E 1927- *BiE&WWA*
Oughtibridge, Enid Dorothea 1909- *WhoMus 72*
Oughton, Winifred 1890-1964 *WhThe*
Ouilliber, Emile 1921-1964 *NewOrJ*
Oukrainsky, Serge *CnOxB, DancEn 78*
Ould, Herman 1886-1951 *CnMD*
Ould, Hermon 1885-1951 *NotNAT B, WhThe*
Ould, Hermon 1886-1951 *ModWD*
Oulibicheff, Alexander Dmitryevich 1794-1858 *Baker 78, NewGrD 80*
Oulton, Brian 1908- *FilmgC, HalFC 80, WhoHol A, WhoThe 72, -77*
Oulton, W C d1820 *NotNAT B*
Our Gal Sunday *What 4[port]*
Our Gang Kids *Film 2*
Oursler, Fulton 1893-1952 *NotNAT B*
Oury, Anna Caroline 1808-1880 *Baker 78, NewGrD 80*
Oury, Antonio James 1800-1883 *NewGrD 80*
Oury, Gerard 1919- *FilmEn, FilmgC, HalFC 80, WhoHol A*
Ouseley, Sir Frederick Arthur Gore 1825-1889 *Baker 78, NewGrD 80, OxMus*
Ousley, Harold Lomax 1929- *BiDAmM, EncJzS 70*
Ousley, Timmy *WhoHol A*
Ouspenskaya, Maria 1867-1949 *HolCA[port]*
Ouspenskaya, Maria 1876-1949 *FilmEn, Film 1, -2, FilmgC, ForYSC, HalFC 80, MotPP, MovMk[port], NotNAT B, PlP&P[port], ThFT[port], Vers A[port], WhScrn 74, -77, WhThe, WhoHol B, WhoHrs 80, WorEFlm*
Ousset, Cecil 1936- *WhoMus 72*
Out, Johannes Adrianus 1911- *WhoMus 72*
Outeda, Tony *ConMuA 80B*
Outlaws, The *ConMuA 80A, IlEncR*
Outsiders, The *RkOn 2[port]*
Ouville, Antoine LeMetel D' 1590?-1656? *OxThe*
Ouvrard, Rene 1624-1694 *NewGrD 80*
Ovanin, Nikola 1911- *CpmDNM 79, ConAmC*
Ovanin, Nikola Leonard 1911- *AmSCAP 66, -80, CpmDNM 80*
Ovchinnikov, Viacheslav 1936- *Baker 78*
Oved, Margalit 1931?- *CnOxB*
Ovenden, Lionel H *WhoMus 72*
Ovens, Raymond John 1932- *IntWWM 77, -80*
Overall, Zan 1926- *AmSCAP 66, -80*
Overbeck, Bud d1970 *WhoHol B*
Overby, Karl Edvard 1938- *IntWWM 77, -80*
Overend, Dorothy *WhThe*
Overend, Marmaduke d1790 *NewGrD 80*
Overend, Susan Elizabeth 1955- *IntWWM 80*
Overgard, Graham T 1903- *AmSCAP 66, -80, IntWWM 77, -80*
Overholdt, Elaine Rosalie 1952- *IntWWM 80*
Overman, Jack 1916-1950 *WhScrn 74, -77, WhoHol B*
Overman, Lynn *MotPP*
Overman, Lynne 1887-1943 *CmMov, FilmEn, FilmgC, ForYSC, HalFC 80[port], HolCA[port], MovMk, NotNAT B, Vers B[port], WhScrn 74, -77, WhThe, WhoHol B*
Overskou, Thomas 1798-1873 *OxThe*
Overstreet, Tommy 1934- *CounME 74[port], -74A*
Overstreet, Tommy 1937- *IlEncCM[port]*
Overton, Bill 1947?- *DrBlPA*
Overton, Evart *Film 1*
Overton, Frank 1918-1967 *BiE&WWA, ForYSC, NotNAT B, WhScrn 74, -77, WhoHol B*
Overton, Hall 1920-1972 *Baker 78, BiDAmM, ConAmC, DcCM, EncJzS 70, NewGrD 80*

Overton, William J *WhoMus 72*
Ovey, George 1870-1951 *FilmEn, Film 1, -2, WhScrn 77*
Ovid 043BC-017AD *NewGrD 80*
Owa *MorBAP*
Owasso d1962 *WhScrn 77*
Owen, Alun 1925- *IntMPA 77, -78, -79, -80, WhoThe 77*
Owen, Alun 1926- *CnThe, ConDr 73, -77, CroCD, EncWT, Ent, IntMPA 75, -76, McGEWD, WhoThe 72*
Owen, Angela Maria 1928- *IntWWM 77, -80*
Owen, Barbara 1933- *IntWWM 77, -80*
Owen, Beti Mary *IntWWM 77, -80*
Owen, Bill *WhoHol A*
Owen, Bill 1914- *FilmgC, HalFC 80*
Owen, Bill 1915- *IntMPA 77, -75, 76, -78, -79, -80*
Owen, Bill 1916- *IlWWBF, WhoThe 72, -77*
Owen, Blythe 1898- *CpmDNM 73, -75, -78, -79, ConAmC, IntWWM 77, -80*
Owen, Catherine Dale 1900-1965 *FilmEn, ThFT[port], WhThe*
Owen, Catherine Dale 1903-1965 *Film 2, ForYSC, MovMk, WhScrn 74, -77, WhoHol B*
Owen, Chloe *WhoMus 72*
Owen, Cliff 1919- *FilmEn, FilmgC, HalFC 80, IlWWBF*
Owen, David 1720-1749 *OxMus*
Owen, Don 1934- *CreCan 1, WorEFlm*
Owen, Garry 1902-1951 *WhScrn 74, -77, WhoHol B*
Owen, Gary 1902-1951 *Vers A[port]*
Owen, Harold 1872-1930 *NotNAT B, WhThe*
Owen, Harold J 1931- *ConAmC, DcCM*
Owen, Harrison 1890- *WhThe*
Owen, Harry 1902- *AmSCAP 80*
Owen, Helen 1928- *AmSCAP 66, -80*
Owen, Jerry Michael 1944- *CpmDNM 79, -80, ConAmC*
Owen, John 1821-1883 *OxMus*
Owen, Lilian *PupTheA*
Owen, Lynn *WhoOp 76*
Owen, Lynn 1936- *WhoMus 72*
Owen, Mabel Burr 1902- *IntWWM 77*
Owen, Mary Jane 1886- *AmSCAP 80*
Owen, Milton d1969 *WhoHol B*
Owen, Reginald 1887-1972 *BiE&WWA, FilmEn, Film 2, FilmgC, ForYSC, HalFC 80, HolCA[port], MGM[port], MotPP, MovMk[port], NotNAT B, PlP&P, Vers A[port], WhScrn 77, WhThe, WhoHol B*
Owen, Richard 1922- *AmSCAP 80, ConAmC*
Owen, Seena d1966 *MotPP, WhoHol B*
Owen, Seena 1894-1966 *FilmEn, FilmgC, HalFC 80*
Owen, Seena 1895-1966 *Film 1, -2, TwYS*
Owen, Seena 1896-1966 *WhScrn 74, -77*
Owen, Tudor *Film 2, ForYSC*
Owen, William Henry 1845-1868 *OxMus*
Owens, Mr. *PupTheA*
Owens, Mrs. *PupTheA*
Owens, Alvis E, Jr. 1929- *BiDAmM*
Owens, Bonnie 1932- *CounME 74[port], -74A*
Owens, Bonnie 1933- *BiDAmM, EncFCWM 69, IlEncCM[port], WhoHol A*
Owens, Buck 1929- *CounME 74[port], -74A, EncFCWM 69, IlEncCM[port]*
Owens, Charles M 1939- *EncJzS 70*
Owens, D H 1892-1962 *AmSCAP 66, -80*
Owens, Daniel Walter 1948- *BlkAmP, MorBAP, NatPD[port]*
Owens, Donnie 1938- *RkOn*
Owens, Dorothy *AmSCAP 80*
Owens, Gary 1936- *IntMPA 77, -75, -76, -78, -79, -80, WhoHol A*
Owens, Harry 1902- *AmPS B, AmSCAP 66, BgBands 74, CmpEPM*
Owens, Jack Milton 1912- *AmSCAP 66, -80*
Owens, James Robert 1943- *BiDAmM, EncJzS 70*
Owens, Jerry Hubert 1944- *IntWWM 77, -80*
Owens, Jesse 1913- *What 1[port]*
Owens, Jimmy 1943- *EncJzS 70*
Owens, Joe *ConMuA 80B, PupTheA*
Owens, John Edmond 1823-1886 *NotNAT A, -B, OxThe*
Owens, Lloyd *PupTheA*
Owens, Margaret Ann *AmSCAP 80*
Owens, Patricia 1925- *FilmEn, FilmgC, ForYSC, HalFC 80, WhoHol A*
Owens, Peggy 1905-1931 *WhScrn 74, -77*
Owens, Reg 1928- *RkOn[port]*
Owens, Rochelle 1936- *AmSCAP 80, ConDr 73, -77, CroCD, EncWT, NatPD[port], NotNAT, PlP&P, WhoThe 72, -77*
Owens, Rose Mary 1937- *IntWWM 77*
Owens, Terry Winter 1936- *AmSCAP 80*
Owens, Tex 1892-1962 *IlEncCM[port]*
Owens, Tom *ConMuA 80B*
Owens, Virgil *BlksB&W C*
Owens, William 1863-1926 *NotNAT B, WhScrn 74, -77, WhoHol B*
Owens, William H 1922- *BiE&WWA*
Owings, Irene *PupTheA*
Owings, John 1943- *WhoMus 72*
Owomoyela, Oyekan *MorBAP*
Owsley, B Bristow 1882-1967 *AmSCAP 66, -80*
Owsley, Katherine N *AmSCAP 66*
Owsley, Monroe 1901-1937 *Film 2, WhScrn 74, -77, WhoHol B*
Owston, Charles Edward 1942- *AmSCAP 80*
Oxberry, John 1918- *IntMPA 77, -75, -76, -78, -79, -80*
Oxberry, William 1784-1824 *NotNAT B, OxThe*
Oxberry, William Henry 1808-1852 *NotNAT B, OxThe*
Oxenberg, Jan *WomWMM B*
Oxenbould, Moffatt Benjamin 1943- *WhoOp 76*
Oxenford, Edward d1929 *NotNAT B*
Oxenford, John 1812-1877 *NotNAT B*
Oxenham, Andrew William 1945- *CreCan 2*
Oxford, Vernon 1941- *BiDAmM, IlEncCM[port]*
Oxinaga, Joaquin De 1719?-1789 *NewGrD 80*
Oxinagas, Joaquin De 1719?-1789 *NewGrD 80*
Oxlade, John Stirling 1946- *WhoMus 72*
Oxley, Dave 1910-1974 *NewOrJ*
Oxley, David 1929?- *FilmgC, HalFC 80, WhoHol A*
Oxley, H R 1906- *IntMPA 77, -75, -76, -78, -79, -80*
Oxley, Harrison 1933- *IntWWM 80*
Oxley, John Ernest Barrington 1922- *IntWWM 77, -80*
Oxley, Thomas Frederick Harrison 1933- *WhoMus 72*
Oxley, Tony 1938- *EncJzS 70*
Oxman, Philip *ConDr 77B*
Oxonia, J *NewGrD 80*
Oya, Ichijiro 1894-1972 *WhScrn 77*
Oyama, Charles *EncFCWM 69*
Oyamo *NatPD*
Oyamo 1943- *BlkAmP, MorBAP*
Oyedele, Obamola *BlkAmP*
Oyewole, Abiodun *MorBAP*
Oyra, Jan 1888- *WhThe*
Oysher, Moishe 1907-1958 *NotNAT B, WhScrn 74, -77, WhoHol B*
Oysher, Moishe 1908-1958 *AmSCAP 66, -80*
Ozakman, Turgut 1930- *REnWD[port]*
Ozark Mountain Daredevils *ConMuA 80A, IlEncCM, IlEncR, RkOn 2[port]*
Ozark Quartet *BiDAmM*
Ozawa, Seiji 1935- *Baker 78, BiDAmM, BnBkM 80, IntWWM 77, -80, MusMk, MusSN[port], NewGrD 80, WhoMus 72*
Ozell, John d1743 *NotNAT B*
Ozep, Fedor 1895-1948 *DcFM*
Ozep, Fedor 1895-1949 *FilmEn, FilmgC, HalFC 80*
Ozeray, Madeleine 1910- *EncWT*
Ozerov, Vladislav Alexandrovich 1770-1816 *OxThe*
Ozga, Kazimierz 1931- *IntWWM 80*
Ozgijan, Petar 1932- *NewGrD 80*
Ozi, Etienne 1754-1813 *NewGrD 80*
Ozi, Pierre *NewGrD 80*
Ozim, Igor 1931- *IntWWM 77, -80, NewGrD 80, WhoMus 72*
Ozolins, Arthur Marcelo 1946- *IntWWM 80*
Ozolins, Egils 1945- *IntWWM 80*
Ozolins, Janis Alfreds 1919- *IntWWM 77, -80*
Ozu, Yasujiro 1903-1963 *BiDFilm 81, ConLC 16, DcFM, FilmEn, FilmgC, HalFC 80, OxFilm, WorEFlm*
Ozy, Etienne *NewGrD 80*
Ozy, Pierre *NewGrD 80*

P

P F M *IlEncR*
Paap, Wouter 1908- *Baker 78, NewGrD 80*
Paar, Jack 1918- *ForYSC, IntMPA 77, -75, -76, -78, -79, -80, JoeFr[port], NewYTET, WhoHol A*
Pabbruwe, Cornelis Thymanszoon *NewGrD 80*
Pablo, Juan *AmSCAP 80*
Pablo, Luis De 1930- *Baker 78, DcCM, NewGrD 80*
Pablo Cruise *ConMuA 80A, IlEncR, RkOn 2[port]*
Pabst, G W 1885-1967 *BiDFilm 81, FilmEn, HalFC 80*
Pabst, Georg Wilhelm 1885-1967 *DcFM, FilmgC, MovMk[port], TwYS A, WhScrn 77*
Pabst, Georg Wilhelm 1887-1967 *OxFilm*
Pabst, George Raymond 1916- *IntMPA 77, -75, -76, -78, -79, -80*
Pabst, George Wilhelm 1885-1967 *WorEFlm*
Pabst, Louis 1846-1903 *Baker 78*
Pabst, Paul 1854-1897 *Baker 78*
Pacak, Ludek 1902- *IntWWM 77*
Paccagnini, Angelo 1930- *DcCM, NewGrD 80*
Pacchiarotti, Gaspare 1740?-1821 *NewGrD 80*
Pacchiarotti, Gasparo 1740?-1821 *Baker 78, NewGrD 80*
Pacchierotti, Gaspare 1740?-1821 *NewGrD 80*
Pacchierotti, Gasparo 1740?-1821 *CmOp, NewEOp 71, NewGrD 80*
Pacchierotti, Gasparo 1744-1821 *OxMus*
Pacchierotti, Ubaldo 1875-1916 *Baker 78*
Pacchioni, Antonio Maria 1654?-1738 *NewGrD 80*
Pace, Antonio *NewGrD 80*
Pace, Antonio 1545-1589? *NewGrD 80*
Pace, Carmelo 1906- *IntWWM 77, -80*
Pace, David Allen 1954- *AmSCAP 80*
Pace, Giovanni Battista *NewGrD 80*
Pace, Judy 1946- *DrBlPA, FilmgC, HalFC 80, WhoHol A*
Pace, Max 1906-1942 *WhScrn 74, -77*
Pace, Pat Joseph 1930- *AmSCAP 80*
Pace, Pietro 1559-1622 *NewGrD 80*
Pace, Robert Joseph 1949- *ConAmC*
Pace, Thomas M 1949- *AmSCAP 80*
Pacelli, Asprilio 1570-1623 *NewGrD 80*
Paceri, Giuseppe *NewGrD 80*
Pache, Joseph 1861-1926 *Baker 78, BiDAmM*
Pache, William *NewGrD 80*
Pacheco, Assis 1903- *FilmAG WE[port]*
Pacheco, Assis 1914- *WhoOp 76*
Pacheco, Jose 1784-1865 *NewGrD 80*
Pachelbel, Carl Theodore 1690-1750 *OxMus*
Pachelbel, Carl Theodorus 1690-1750 *Baker 78*
Pachelbel, Johann 1653-1706 *Baker 78, BnBkM 80, GrComp, MusMk, NewGrD 80, OxMus*
Pachelbel, Wilhelm Hieronymus 1685?-1764 *OxMus*
Pachelbel, Wilhelm Hieronymus 1686?-1764 *Baker 78, NewGrD 80*
Pachelbell, Charles Theodor 1690-1750 *BiDAmM*
Pachler-Koschak, Marie Leopoldine 1792-1855 *Baker 78*
Pachman, Vladimir De 1848-1933 *NewGrD 80[port]*
Pachmann, Vladimir De 1848-1933 *Baker 78, BnBkM 80, MusSN[port], NewGrD 80[port]*
Pachschmidt, Carolomannus 1700-1734 *NewGrD 80*
Pachulski, Henryk 1859-1921 *NewGrD 80*
Pachymeres, Georgios 1242-1310? *NewGrD 80*
Paci, Francesco Maria 1716?- *NewGrD 80*
Paci, Pietro *NewGrD 80*
Pacieri, Giuseppe d1700? *NewGrD 80*
Pacific Gas & Electric *RkOn 2[port]*
Pacini, Andrea 1690?-1764 *NewGrD 80*
Pacini, Antonio Francesco Gaetano S 1778-1866 *NewGrD 80*
Pacini, Giovanni 1796-1867 *Baker 78, CmOp, NewEOp 71, NewGrD 80, OxMus*
Pacini, Leonardo 1885-1937 *Baker 78*
Pacini, Renato 1909- *IntWWM 80*
Pacino, Al *IntMPA 77, -75, -76, -78, -79, -80, WhoHol A*
Pacino, Al 1939- *FilmgC, HalFC 80*
Pacino, Al 1940- *BiDFilm 81, Ent, FilmEn, MovMk[port], WhoThe 77*
Paciorkiewicz, Tadeusz 1916- *Baker 78, IntWWM 77, -80, NewGrD 80*
Paciorkiewicz-Dutkiewicz, Antonina 1943- *IntWWM 77*
Paciotto, Pietro Paolo 1550?-1614? *NewGrD 80*
Pacius, F 1809-1891 *OxMus*
Pacius, Fredrik 1809-1891 *Baker 78, NewGrD 80*
Pacius, Friedrich 1809-1891 *NewGrD 80*
Pack, Gary Lee 1950- *EncJzS 70*
Pack, Lorenzo 1916- *AmSCAP 66, -80*
Pack, Marshall Thomas 1922- *BiDAmM*
Pack, Norman *Film 2*
Pack, Rowland 1927-1964 *NewGrD 80*
Pack, Simon 1654-1701 *NewGrD 80*
Pack, Thomas *NewGrD 80*
Packales, Joseph 1948- *ConAmC*
Packard, Albert 1909- *BiE&WWA*
Packard, Clayton L 1888-1931 *Film 2, WhScrn 74, -77, WhoHol B*
Packard, Frank Lucius 1877-1942 *CreCan 2*
Packard, Fred M 1919- *IntMPA 77, -75, -76, -78, -79, -80*
Packard, William *NatPD[port]*
Packe, Thomas *NewGrD 80*
Packer, Charles Sandys 1810-1883 *NewGrD 80*
Packer, Doris *WhoHol A*
Packer, Dorothy S 1923- *IntWWM 80*
Packer, George Leonard 1945- *ConAmC*
Packer, Netta 1897-1962 *NotNAT B, WhScrn 74, -77, WhoHol B*
Packford, Vincent Hubert 1922- *WhoMus 72*
Paclt, Jaromir 1927- *IntWWM 77, -80*
Pacuvius 220?BC-130BC *Ent*
Pacuvius, Marcus 220?BC-130BC *OxThe*
Padberg, Helen Swan 1919- *IntWWM 77, -80*
Padbrue, Cornelis Thymanszoon 1592?-1670 *NewGrD 80*
Padbrue, David Janszoon 1553?-1635 *NewGrD 80*
Padden, Sarah d1967 *Film 2, ForYSC, Vers B[port], WhScrn 77, WhoHol B*
Paddock, Charles *Film 2, TwYS*
Paddock, Ralph Austin 1921- *IntWWM 80*
Paddock, Robert Rowe 1914- *BiE&WWA*
Pade, Astrid *WomWMM*
Pade, Else Marie 1924- *IntWWM 77, -80*
Padellan, Irene H *AmSCAP 80*
Paderewski, Ignace Jan 1860-1941 *Baker 78, BiDAmM, FilmgC, HalFC 80, MusSN[port], WhScrn 74, -77, WhoHol B*
Paderewski, Ignacy Jan 1860-1941 *BnBkM 80[port], DcCom&M 79, MusMk[port], NewGrD 80[port], OxMus*
Padgen, Jack *Film 2*
Padgen, Leonard *Film 2*
Padgett, Stephen Thomas 1953- *AmSCAP 80*
Padgett-Chandler, David E 1945- *IntWWM 77, -80*
Padilla, Antoine 1944- *IntWWM 80*
Padilla, Ema 1900-1966 *WhScrn 74, -77*
Padilla, Jose 1889-1960 *NewGrD 80*
Padilla, Juan De 1605?-1673 *NewGrD 80*
Padilla, Juan Gutierrez De 1590?-1664 *NewGrD 80*
Padilla, Lola Artot De 1885-1933 *Baker 78*
Padilla, Manuel, Jr. 1956- *WhoHol A*
Padilla, Mario Rene 1949- *AmSCAP 80*
Padilla Y Ramos, Mariano 1842-1906 *Baker 78, NewGrD 80*
Padjan, Jack 1888-1960 *WhScrn 77*
Padjan, John *Film 2*
Padlewski, Roman 1915-1944 *NewGrD 80*
Padmore, Andrew Paul 1950- *IntWWM 77, WhoMus 72*
Padmore, Andrew Paul 1951- *IntWWM 80*
Padoano, Annibale 1527-1575 *NewGrD 80*
Padovani, Gianfranco 1928- *WhoOp 76*
Padovani, Lea 1920- *FilmEn, FilmgC, ForYSC, HalFC 80, WhoHol A*
Padovano, Annibale 1527-1575 *NewGrD 80*
Padovano, John 1916-1973 *WhScrn 77, WhoHol B*
Padre Barnaba *NewGrD 80*
Padre Raimo *NewGrD 80*
Padron, Bill 1903-1959 *NewOrJ*
Padros, Jaime 1926- *NewGrD 80*
Padt Brue, Cornelis Thymanszoon *NewGrD 80*
Padula, Edward 1916- *BiE&WWA, NotNAT*
Padula, Marguerita *Film 2*
Padula, Vincent 1900-1967 *WhScrn 77*
Padwa, Vladimir 1900- *AmSCAP 66, -80, ConAmC, IntWWM 77, -80*
Paepe, Andreas De *NewGrD 80*
Paer, Ferdinando 1771-1839 *Baker 78, BnBkM 80, CmOp, NewEOp 71, NewGrD 80[port], OxMus*
Paersch, Franz Friedrich 1857-1921 *NewGrD 80*

Paesiello, Giovanni 1740-1816 OxMus
Paesky, Efrain 1931- IntWWM 77, -80
Paetzold-Hrdlickova, Nadja IntWWM 77
Paetzoldp-Hrdlickova, Nadja IntWWM 80
Paff, Michael d1810? BiDAmM
Paffgen, Peter K 1950- IntWWM 77, -80
Pagan, Ricarda 1919- AmSCAP 80
Paganelli, Gioseffo Antonio 1710-1763? NewGrD 80
Paganelli, Giuseppe Antonio 1710-1762? Baker 78
Paganelli, Giuseppe Antonio 1710-1763? NewGrD 80
Paganelli, Sergio 1929- NewGrD 80
Pagani, Ernesto Film 1, -2
Paganini, Ercole 1770-1825 NewGrD 80
Paganini, Niccolo 1782-1840 Baker 78, BnBkM 80[port], CmpBCM, DancEn 78, DcCom 77[port], GrComp[port], MusMk[port], OxMus
Paganini, Nicolo 1782-1840 NewGrD 80[port]
Pagano, Bartolomeo 1878-1947 FilmAG WE
Pagano, Jo 1906- IntMPA 77, -75, -76, -78, -79, -80
Pagano, Tomaso 1635?-1690 NewGrD 80
Pagano, Tommaso 1635?-1690 NewGrD 80
Pagano, Tommasso 1635?-1690 NewGrD 80
Paganuzzi, Enrico 1921- IntWWM 77, -80
Pagava, Ethery 1931- CnOxB
Pagava, Ethery 1932- DancEn 78
Pagay, Sophie Film 2
Pagden, Leonard d1928 NotNAT B
Page, Andre CreCan 1
Page, Anita 1910- FilmEn, Film 2, ForYSC, MotPP, ThFT[port], TwYS, What 5[port], WhoHol A
Page, Annette 1932- CnOxB, DancEn 78
Page, Anthony d1905? NewOrJ
Page, Anthony 1935- FilmgC, HalFC 80, WhoThe 72, -77
Page, Arthur W 1885-1968 WhScrn 77
Page, Ashley d1934 NotNAT B
Page, Austin WhThe
Page, Bradley ForYSC
Page, Curtis C 1914- BiE&WWA
Page, Don FilmEn, WhScrn 74, -77
Page, Elizabeth S PupTheA
Page, Frederick 1905- NewGrD 80
Page, Gale 1913- FilmEn, FilmgC, HalFC 80, ThFT[port], WhoHol A
Page, Gale 1918- ForYSC, IntMPA 77, -75, -76, -78, -79, -80, MovMk
Page, Genevieve WhoHol A
Page, Genevieve 1930- FilmEn, ForYSC, MovMk[port]
Page, Genevieve 1931- FilmgC, HalFC 80
Page, Geraldine 1924- BiDFilm 81, BiE&WWA, CnThe, Ent[port], FamA&A[port], FilmEn, FilmgC, ForYSC, HalFC 80, IntMPA 77, -75, -76, -78, -79, -80, MotPP, MovMk[port], NotNAT, PlP&P, WhoHol A, WhoThe 72, -77, WorEFlm
Page, Harrison DrBlPA
Page, Helen Film 2
Page, Hot Lips 1908-1954 CmpEPM, DrBlPA, IlEncJ, WhoJazz 72
Page, James E 1870-1930 Film 2, WhScrn 77
Page, James Patrick 1944- AmSCAP 80
Page, Jimmy ConMuA 80A, -80B
Page, John 1760?-1812 Baker 78, NewGrD 80
Page, Joy Ann ForYSC, WhoHol A
Page, Kate Stearns 1873-1963 Baker 78
Page, Kenneth 1927- IntWWM 77, -80, WhoMus 72
Page, Lawanda 1920?- DrBlPA
Page, Louis 1905- DcFM, FilmEn
Page, Lucille 1871-1964 WhScrn 74, -77, WhoHol B
Page, Marco FilmEn
Page, Nathaniel Clifford 1866-1956 AmSCAP 66, -80, Baker 78, BiDAmM
Page, Nathen 1937- EncJzS 70
Page, Norman d1935 Film 2, NotNAT B, WhThe
Page, Oran Thaddeus 1908-1954 BiDAmM, BluesWW[port]
Page, Patricia Kathleen 1916- CreCan 1
Page, Patrick MagIlD
Page, Patti 1927- AmPS A, -B, BiDAmM, CmpEPM, FilmgC, ForYSC, HalFC 80, IntMPA 77, -75, -76, -78, -79, -80, RkOn[port], WhoHol A
Page, Paul 1903-1974 AmSCAP 80, Film 2, ForYSC, WhScrn 77, WhoHol B
Page, Paul F 1947- AmSCAP 80
Page, Paula Vivian WhoOp 76
Page, Philip P 1889-1968 NotNAT B, WhThe
Page, Raymond Edison 1929- AmSCAP 80
Page, Rita 1906-1954 NotNAT B, WhScrn 77, WhThe, WhoHol B
Page, Ronnie 1938- BiDAmM
Page, Ruth 1905- CnOxB, DancEn 78[port], WhoMus 72
Page, Tilsa 1926- WhThe
Page, Walter Sylvester 1900-1957 BiDAmM, CmpEPM, IlEncJ, NewGrD 80, WhoJazz 72
Page, Will A d1928 NotNAT B
Page Seven, The BiDAmM
Pagels, Jurgen Heinrich 1925- IntWWM 77, -80
Pagenstecher, Bernard 1907- AmSCAP 80
Pageot, Louis Simon NewGrD 80
Paget, Alfred 1880?-1925 FilmEn, Film 1, -2, TwYS, WhScrn 77, WhoHol B
Paget, Cecil d1955 NotNAT B, WhThe
Paget, Debra 1933- BiDFilm 81, FilmEn, FilmgC, ForYSC, HalFC 80, IntMPA 77, -75, -76, -78, -79, -80, MotPP, MovMk, WhoHol A, WhoHrs 80
Paget, Sir Richard Arthur Surtees 1869-1955 OxMus
Paget-Bowman, Cicely 1910- WhoHol A, WhoThe 72, -77
Pagett, Gary WhoHol A
Pagett, Nicola 1945- WhoThe 77
Pagett, Nicola 1948- HalFC 80
Pagholi, Bernardo NewGrD 80
Pagin, Andre-Noel 1721-1785? NewGrD 80
Pagliai, Vivienne 1928- IntWWM 77
Pagliardi, Giovanni Maria 1637-1702 NewGrD 80
Pagliaro, James Page 1902- IntMPA 77, -75, -76, -78, -79
Pagliero, Camilla 1859-1925 CnOxB
Pagliero, Marcello 1907- DcFM, FilmAG WE, FilmEn, OxFilm, WorEFlm
Pagliughi, Lina 1910- CmOp
Pagliughi, Lina 1911- NewGrD 80
Pagnol, Marcel 1894-1974 HalFC 80
Pagnol, Marcel 1895-1974 BiDFilm 81, BiE&WWA, CnMD, DcFM, EncWT, Ent, FilmEn, FilmgC, McGEWD[port], ModWD, MovMk[port], NotNAT A, -B, OxFilm, WhThe, WorEFlm
Pahissa, Jaime 1880-1969 Baker 78, NewGrD 80
Pahlen, Kurt 1907- Baker 78, NewGrD 80
Paia, John 1908-1954 WhScrn 74, -77
Paich, David Frank 1954- AmSCAP 80, ConMuA 80B
Paich, Martin Louis 1925- AmSCAP 66, -80, BiDAmM
Paich, Marty 1925- CmpEPM
Paien, Gioan NewGrD 80
Paige, Bob IntMPA 77, -75, -76, -78, -79, -80
Paige, Brydon CnOxB, CreCan 1, DancEn 78
Paige, Frances AmSCAP 80
Paige, Janis MotPP
Paige, Janis 1922- BiE&WWA, CmpEPM, EncMT, FilmEn, FilmgC, ForYSC, HalFC 80, WhoHol A, WhoThe 72, -77
Paige, Janis 1923- HolP 40[port], IntMPA 77, -75, -76, -78, -79, -80, MovMk, NotNAT
Paige, Jean Film 2
Paige, Mabel 1879-1954 FilmgC, HalFC 80
Paige, Mabel 1880?-1953 ForYSC, MovMk
Paige, Mabel 1880-1954 FilmEn, NotNAT B, Vers A[port], WhScrn 74, -77, WhoHol B
Paige, Norman 1935- IntWWM 77, -80, WhoOp 76
Paige, Patsy WhScrn 77
Paige, Paul 1934- IntWWM 77
Paige, Raymond 1900-1965 CmpEPM, WhScrn 77
Paige, Robert 1910- FilmEn, Film 2, FilmgC, ForYSC, HalFC 80, HolP 40[port], MotPP, WhoHol A
Paige, Roger 1928- AmSCAP 66, -80
Paige, Sheila WomWMM A, -B
Paik, Nam June 1932- Baker 78, ConAmC, DcCM, NewYTET
Paikov, Shaike 1937- IntWWM 77, -80
Pail, Edward Film 1
Paillard, Jean-Francois 1928- IntWWM 77, -80, NewGrD 80
Pailleron, Edouard 1834-1899 McGEWD[port], NotNAT B, OxThe
Pain, Lesley Joan 1933- WhoMus 72
Paine, Canio Francis 1920- ConAmTC
Paine, Charles F 1920- IntMPA 77, -75, -76, -78, -79, -80
Paine, Donald William McKenzie 1930- WhoMus 72
Paine, John EncFCWM 69
Paine, John Knowles 1839-1906 Baker 78, BiDAmM, BnBkM 80, NewGrD 80, OxMus
Paine, Thomas 1773-1811 BiDAmM
Paine, Thomas D 1813-1895 NewGrD 80
Painleve, Jean 1902- DcFM, FilmEn, FilmgC, HalFC 80, OxFilm, WorEFlm
Painter, Eleanor 1890-1947 CmpEPM, NotNAT B, WhThe
Paisable, James d1721? NewGrD 80
Paisible, James d1721? NewGrD 80
Paisible, Louis Henri 1745-1782 Baker 78
Paisible, Louis-Henry 1748-1782 NewGrD 80
Paisiello, Giovanni 1740-1816 Baker 78, BnBkM 80, CmOp, DcCom 77, GrComp[port], MusMk, NewEOp 71, NewGrD 80[port]
Paisley, William Merrell 1903- AmSCAP 66, -80
Paisner, Bruce NewYTET
Paisner, Dina WhoHol A
Paiste, Michael NewGrD 80
Paiste, Robert NewGrD 80
Paiste, Thomas NewGrD 80
Paita, Carlos 1932- IntWWM 80
Paiva, Heliodoro De 1502-1552 NewGrD 80
Paiva, Nestor 1905-1966 FilmEn, FilmgC, ForYSC, HalFC 80, HolCA[port], MotPP, Vers A[port], WhScrn 74, -77, WhoHol B, WhoHrs 80
Paix, Gilis NewGrD 80
Paix, Jakob 1556-1623? NewGrD 80
Pajaro, Eliseo M 1915- IntWWM 77, -80, NewGrD 80
Pajeaud, Willie 1895-1960 NewOrJ[port]
Pajeot, Louis Simon 1791-1849 NewGrD 80
Pakenham, Edward Arthur Henry McGEWD[port]
Pakhmutova, Alexandra Nikolayevna 1929- Baker 78, NewGrD 80
Pakke, Thomas NewGrD 80
Pakula, Alan J 1928- BiDFilm 81, FilmEn, FilmgC, HalFC 80, IntMPA 77, -75, -76, -78, -79, -80, MovMk[port], OxFilm
Pal 1915-1929 WhScrn 77
Pal, David 1935?- WhoHrs 80
Pal, George DcPup, IntMPA 77, -75, -76, -78, -79, -80, PupTheA
Pal, George 1900- DcFM
Pal, George 1908-1980 FilmEn, FilmgC, HalFC 80, WhoHrs 80, WorEFlm CmMov
Pala, Frantisek 1887-1964 NewGrD 80
Palacio, Ernesto 1946- WhoOp 76
Palacios Y Sojo, Pedro 1739-1799? NewGrD 80
Palad, Gelsa AmSCAP 80
Paladi, Radu 1927- IntWWM 77, -80
Paladilhe, Emile 1844-1926 Baker 78, NewGrD 80, OxMus
Paladin, Giovanni Paolo d1566? NewGrD 80
Paladin, Jean Paul d1566? NewGrD 80
Paladini, Ettore 1849- WhThe
Paladini-Ando, Celestina WhThe
Paladino, Gelsa Theresa 1944- AmSCAP 80
Paladino, Giovanni Paolo d1566? NewGrD 80
Paladino, Jean Paul d1566? NewGrD 80
Palaiol, Berenguier De NewGrD 80
Palamas, Costis REnWD[port]
Palance, Jack MotPP, WhoHol A
Palance, Jack 1919- FilmEn
Palance, Jack 1920- BiDFilm 81, CmMov, FilmgC, ForYSC, HalFC 80, IntMPA 77, -75, -76, -78, -79, -80, MovMk[port],

WhoHrs 80
Palance, Jack 1921- *CmMov, OxFilm, WorEFlm*
Palange, Louis Salvador 1917- *Baker 78, ConAmC*
Palange, Louis Salvador 1917-1979 *AmSCAP 66, -80*
Palanzi, Richard Bruno 1951- *ConAmC*
Palao, James A 1880?-1925? *NewOrJ*
Palao, Jimmy 1885?-1925? *WhoJazz 72*
Palaol, Berenguier De *NewGrD 80*
Palaprat, Jean DeBigot 1650-1721 *McGEWD, OxThe*
Palasthy, A *Film 2*
Palasty, Irene *Film 2*
Palatio, Paolo Jacopo *NewGrD 80*
Palau, Manuel 1893-1967 *Baker 78*
Palau Boix, Manuel 1893-1967 *NewGrD 80*
Palay, Elliot John 1948- *IntWWM 77, -80, WhoOp 76*
Palazol, Berenguier De *NewGrD 80*
Palazotto Tagliavia, Giuseppe 1587?-1633? *NewGrD 80*
Palazzo, Paolo Jacomo *NewGrD 80*
Palazzotti, Giuseppe 1587?-1633? *NewGrD 80*
Palazzotto E Tagliavia, Giuseppe 1587?-1633? *NewGrD 80*
Paleczny, Piotr Tadeusz 1946- *IntWWM 77, -80*
Palella, Antonio 1692-1761 *NewGrD 80*
Palenicek, Josef 1914- *Baker 78, NewGrD 80*
Palerme, Gina *Film 2, WhThe*
Palermitano, Il *NewGrD 80*
Palermitano, Bartolomeo Lieto *NewGrD 80*
Palermitano, Mauro *NewGrD 80*
Palermo, Alex 1929- *BiE&WWA, NotNAT*
Palero, Francisco Fernandez *NewGrD 80*
Palester, Roman 1907- *Baker 78, NewGrD 80*
Palestrina 1525?-1594 *Baker 78*
Palestrina, Giannetto 1525?-1594 *NewGrD 80[port]*
Palestrina, Giovanni Pierluigi Da 1525?-1594 *BnBkM 80[port], CmpBCM, DcCom 77[port], DcCom&M 79, GrComp[port], MusMk[port], NewGrD 80[port], OxMus*
Palette, Billy d1963 *NotNAT B*
Paletz, Darcy 1933- *WomWMM B*
Palevoda, Walter 1927- *WhoOp 76*
Paley, Herman 1879-1955 *AmSCAP 66, -80*
Paley, Thomas 1928- *BiDAmM*
Paley, Tom 1928- *EncFCWM 69*
Paley, William S 1901- *ConMuA 80B, IntMPA 77, -75, -76, -78, -79, -80, NewYTET*
Palfi, Lotta *WhoHol A*
Palfrey, May Lever 1867-1929 *NotNAT B, WhThe*
Paliashvili, Zakhary Petrovich 1871-1933 *NewGrD 80*
Paligon, Marcin *NewGrD 80*
Paligonius, Marcin *NewGrD 80*
Palikarova, Raina 1904-1960 *NewGrD 80*
Paling *NewGrD 80*
Paling, Anton Adriaan 1835-1922 *NewGrD 80*
Paling, Edwin John 1948- *IntWWM 77, -80*
Paling, Jan Hendrik 1796-1879 *NewGrD 80*
Paling, Willem Hendrik 1825-1895 *NewGrD 80*
Palisca, Claude Victor 1921- *Baker 78, IntWWM 77, -80, NewGrD 80*
Palisier, John 1885?- *NewOrJ*
Palitzsch, Peter 1918- *EncWT*
Palkovsky, Oldrich 1907- *Baker 78*
Palkovsky, Pavel 1939- *Baker 78*
Palladino, Ralph Francis 1938- *AmSCAP 80*
Palladio, Andrea 1508-1580 *EncWT, Ent*
Palladio, Andrea 1518-1580 *NotNAT B, OxThe, PlP&P*
Palladius, David *NewGrD 80*
Pallandios, Menelaos G 1914- *NewGrD 80*
Pallant, Walter d1904 *NotNAT B*
Pallante, Aladdin *WhScrn 74, -77*
Pallantios, Menelaos 1914- *Baker 78*
Pallardy, Thomas Patrick 1947- *AmSCAP 80*
Pallavicini, Carlo 1630-1688 *Baker 78, NewGrD 80*
Pallavicini, Stefano Benedetto 1672-1742 *NewGrD 80*
Pallavicini, Vincenzo d1756? *NewGrD 80*
Pallavicino, Benedetto 1551-1601 *Baker 78, NewGrD 80*
Pallavicino, Carlo d1688 *NewGrD 80*
Pallavicino, Germano 1545?-1610? *NewGrD 80*
Pallavicino, Stefano Benedetto 1672-1742 *NewGrD 80*
Pallemaerts, Edmundo 1867-1945 *Baker 78*
Pallenberg, Max 1877-1934 *EncWT, Ent, NotNAT B, OxThe, WhScrn 77*
Paller, Ingrid 1928- *IntWWM 77, -80*
Pallerini, Antonia 1790-1870 *CnOxB*
Pallette, Eugene 1889-1954 *FilmEn, Film 1, -2, FilmgC, ForYSC, HalFC 80, MotPP, MovMk, NotNAT B, OxFilm, TwYS, Vers A[port], WhScrn 74, -77, WhoHol B*
Pallette, Eugene 1899-1954 *HolCA[port]*
Palley, Xenia 1933- *CnOxB*
Palliser, Esther Walters 1872- *BiDAmM*
Pallo, Imre 1892- *NewGrD 80*
Pallock, Ruth 1926- *AmSCAP 80*
Pallos, Stephen 1902- *FilmgC, HalFC 80*
Pallos, Steven *IntMPA 77, -75, -76, -78, -79, -80*
Pallota, Matteo *NewGrD 80*
Pallotta, Lorraine 1934- *AmSCAP 66, -80*
Pallotta, Matteo *NewGrD 80*
Palm, Richard Dennis 1945- *IntWWM 77, -80*
Palm, Siegfried 1927- *IntWWM 77, -80, NewGrD 80*
Palm, Walter *Film 2*
Palma, Athos 1891-1951 *Baker 78, NewGrD 80*
Palma, Mona *Film 2*
Palma, Silvestro 1754-1834 *NewGrD 80*
Palma Ociosa *NewGrD 80*
Palmer *PupTheA*
Palmer, Lord 1858-1948 *OxMus*
Palmer, A H *PlP&P*
Palmer, Albert Marshman 1838-1905 *NotNAT B, OxThe*
Palmer, Anthony *WhoHol A*
Palmer, Archibald 1886- *AmSCAP 66*
Palmer, Barbara 1911- *WhThe*
Palmer, Bea *AmPS B*
Palmer, Belinda *WhoHol A*
Palmer, Betsy 1929- *BiE&WWA, FilmgC, ForYSC, HalFC 80, IntMPA 77, -75, -76, -78, -79, -80, MotPP, NewYTET, NotNAT, WhoHol A, WhoThe 77*
Palmer, Bissell B 1889- *AmSCAP 66, -80*
Palmer, Byron *ForYSC, WhoHol A*
Palmer, Carl Frederic 1954- *IntWWM 77*
Palmer, Cedric King 1913- *IntWWM 77, -80, WhoMus 72*
Palmer, Charles 1869-1920 *NotNAT B, WhThe*
Palmer, Charles Chuck d1976 *WhoHol C*
Palmer, Clement Charlton 1871-1944 *OxMus*
Palmer, Corliss *Film 2*
Palmer, Dawson 1937-1972 *WhScrn 77, WhoHol B*
Palmer, Earl C, Sr. 1924- *BiDAmM, EncJzS 70*
Palmer, Edward 1930- *IntMPA 77, -75, -76, -78, -79, -80*
Palmer, Effie d1942 *WhScrn 74, -77, WhoHol B*
Palmer, Elizabeth Ann *IntWWM 77, -80, WhoMus 72*
Palmer, Ernest 1885-1978 *CmMov, FilmEn, HalFC 80*
Palmer, Ethelyn 1879- *WhoStg 1908*
Palmer, Felicity Joan 1944- *IntWWM 77, -80, NewGrD 80*
Palmer, Francesca 1915- *WhoMus 72*
Palmer, Frank 1921- *CreCan 2*
Palmer, Frederik *NewGrD 80*
Palmer, George Arthur 1889- *WhoMus 72*
Palmer, George Herbert 1846-1926 *OxMus*
Palmer, Gregg 1927- *FilmEn, FilmgC, ForYSC, HalFC 80, IntMPA 77, -75, -76, -78, -79, -80, WhoHol A, WhoHrs 80*
Palmer, Harold G 1911- *IntWWM 77*
Palmer, Henry 159-?-166-? *NewGrD 80*
Palmer, Herbert Franklin *CreCan 2*
Palmer, Herbert Sydney 1881- *CreCan 2*
Palmer, Horatio Richmond 1834-1907 *Baker 78, BiDAmM*
Palmer, Irene *WhoMus 72*
Palmer, Jack 1900-1976 *AmSCAP 66, -80*
Palmer, Jimmy *CmpEPM*
Palmer, John *OxMus*
Palmer, John 1728-1768 *OxThe*
Palmer, John 1742-1798 *OxThe*
Palmer, John 1911- *WhoMus 72*
Palmer, John Leslie 1885-1944 *NotNAT B, WhThe*
Palmer, Jon Phillips *MorBAP*
Palmer, Larry Garland 1938- *IntWWM 77, -80*
Palmer, Lilli *IntMPA 75, -76, -78, -79, -80*
Palmer, Lilli 1911- *IIWWBF, -A*
Palmer, Lilli 1914- *BiDFilm 81, FilmAG WE[port], FilmEn, FilmgC, ForYSC, HalFC 80, IntMPA 77, MotPP, MovMk[port], NotNAT A, OxFilm, WhoHol A, WhoThe 72, -77, WorEFlm[port]*
Palmer, Lucile *AmSCAP 66*
Palmer, Maria 1924- *FilmgC, ForYSC, HalFC 80, IntMPA 77, -75, -76, -78, -79, -80, WhoHol A*
Palmer, Minnie 1857-1936 *WhThe*
Palmer, Minnie 1860-1936 *NotNAT B, WhoStg 1908*
Palmer, Patricia 1895-1964 *Film 2, WhScrn 77*
Palmer, Peggy 1912- *IntWWM 77, -80*
Palmer, Peter 1931- *BiE&WWA, FilmgC, ForYSC, HalFC 80, NotNAT, WhoHol A*
Palmer, Phoebe 1807-1874 *BiDAmM*
Palmer, Phyllis 1920- *WhoMus 72*
Palmer, Ray 1808-1887 *BiDAmM*
Palmer, Ray DaSilva *DcPup*
Palmer, Robert *ConMuA 80A, -80B, IlEncR, NewGrD 80, WhoHol A*
Palmer, Robert 1754-1817 *OxThe*
Palmer, Robert 1915- *Baker 78, BiDAmM, ConAmC, DcCM, NewGrD 80, OxMus*
Palmer, Roland Ford 1891- *BiDAmM*
Palmer, Roy 1892-1964 *BiDAmM, NewOrJ[port], WhoJazz 72*
Palmer, Ruby M *PupTheA*
Palmer, Shirley *Film 2*
Palmer, Singleton Nathaniel 1913- *WhoJazz 72*
Palmer, Solita Birdenia 1905- *AmSCAP 80*
Palmer, Thomas Moyer 1934- *WhoOp 76*
Palmer, Tony 1941- *IlEncR*
Palmer, Violet *Film 2*
Palmer, Willard A, Jr. 1917- *AmSCAP 66, -80*
Palmer, Willard Aldrich 1917- *IntWWM 80*
Palmer, William d1797 *OxThe*
Palmer, William J 1890- *AmSCAP 66, -80*
Palmer, Winthrop Bushnell 1899- *PupTheA*
Palmer, Zoe *Film 2*
Palmeri, Mimi *Film 2*
Palmerini, Giovanni Battista *NewGrD 80*
Palmerini, Luigi 1768-1842 *NewGrD 80*
Palmese, Rose Marie 1871-1953 *WhScrn 74, -77*
Palmgren, Selim 1878-1951 *Baker 78, MusMk, NewGrD 80, OxMus*
Palmier, Remo 1923- *EncJzS 70*
Palmieri, Edmund L 1907- *IntMPA 75*
Palmisano, Angelo *NewOrJ*
Palmiter, Lloyd Frank 1954- *IntWWM 80*
Paloczi Horvath, Adam 1760-1820 *NewGrD 80*
Palola, Elias Anter 1930- *IntWWM 77*
Palola, Juhani Antero 1952- *IntWWM 80*
Palomares, Juan De 1573?-1609? *NewGrD 80*
Palombo, Paul Martin 1937- *Baker 78, ConAmC, IntWWM 77, -80*
Palomino, Jose 1755-1810 *NewGrD 80*
Palon, Berenguier De *NewGrD 80*
Palos, Imre 1917- *WhoOp 76*
Palotai, Vilmos 1906- *WhoMus 72*
Palotay, Irene Banyay 1902- *IntWWM 77, -80*
Palotta, Matteo 1688?-1758 *NewGrD 80*
Palsa, Johann 1752-1792 *NewGrD 80*
Palsbo, Ole 1909-1952 *DcFM*
Palschau, Johann Gottfried Wilhelm 1742?-1813 *NewGrD 80*
Palsson, Halldor 1946- *IntWWM 77*
Palsson, Pall Pampichler 1928- *Baker 78, IntWWM 77, -80, NewGrD 80*
Paltenghi, David 1919-1961 *CnOxB, DancEn 78, WhScrn 77*
Paltenghi, Winthrop Bushnell 1899- *DancEn 78*
Paltridge, James Gilbert, Jr. 1942- *ConAmC*
Palucca, Gret 1902- *CnOxB, DancEn 78*
Palumbo, Camille Marie 1930- *AmSCAP 80*

Palumbo, John 1951- AmSCAP 80
Paluselli, Johann Anton 1748-1805 NewGrD 80
Paluselli, Stefan 1748-1805 NewGrD 80
Paluzzi, Luciana 1931- FilmEn, ForYSC
Paluzzi, Luciana 1939- FilmgC, HalFC 80, WhoHol A
Pam, Anita d1973 WhScrn 77
Pam, Jerry 1926- IntMPA 77, -75, -76, -78, -79, -80
Paminger, Leonhard 1495-1567 NewGrD 80
Pampani, Antonio Gaetano 1705?-1775 NewGrD 80
Pampanini, Rosetta 1896-1973 NewGrD 80
Pampanini, Rosetta 1900- CmOp
Pampanini, Silvana 1925- FilmEn, IntMPA 77, -75, -76, -78, -79, -80
Pampanini, Silvana 1933- HalFC 80
Pamphili, Benedetto 1653-1730 NewGrD 80
Pan, Hermes IntMPA 77, -75, -76, -78, -79, -80, WhoHol A
Pan, Hermes 1905- FilmgC, HalFC 80
Pan, Hermes 1910- CmMov, FilmEn
Panader, Carmen 1933- CnOxB, DancEn 78
Panaieff, Michel 1913- CnOxB, DancEn 78
Panama, Charles A 1925- IntMPA 77, -75, -76, -78, -79, -80
Panama, Norman 1914- BiE&WWA, CmMov, FilmEn, FilmgC, HalFC 80, IntMPA 77, -75, -76, -78, -79, -80, NotNAT, WorEFlm
Panassie, Hugues 1912-1974 Baker 78, EncJzS 70
Pancake, Roger WhoHol A
Pancho BgBands 74
Pancoast, Asa 1905- AmSCAP 66, -80
Pandel, Ted 1935- AmSCAP 66, -80
Pandi, Marianne 1924- IntWWM 77, -80
Pandolfi, Vito 1917- EncWT
Pandolfi Mealli, Giovanni Antonio NewGrD 80
Pandolfo, Joseph 1928- AmSCAP 80
Pandula, Dusan 1923- IntWWM 77
Pandula, Renata 1930- IntWWM 77
Pane, Domenico Dal NewGrD 80
Pane, Tullio 1935- WhoOp 76
Panenka, Jan 1922- NewGrD 80
Panerai, Rolando 1924- NewGrD 80, WhoOp 76
Paneral, Rolando 1924- CmOp
Panerio, Robert M ConAmC
Panetta, George 1915-1969 BiE&WWA, NotNAT B
Panetti, Joan ConAmC
Pangborn, Franklin d1958 WhoHol B
Pangborn, Franklin 1889-1958 ForYSC
Pangborn, Franklin 1893-1958 FilmEn, HolCA[port], Vers A[port]
Pangborn, Franklin 1894-1958 FilmgC, HalFC 80, MovMk, WhScrn 74, -77
Pangborn, Franklin 1896-1958 Film 2, NotNAT B, TwYS
Pangborn, Franklyn MotPP
Pangborn, Robert C 1934- IntWWM 77, -80
Panhofer, Walter 1910- IntWWM 77, -80
Panhormita, Maurus NewGrD 80
Panhormitano, Bartolomeo Lieto NewGrD 80
Pani, Corrado WhoHol A
Paniagua Y Vasques, Cenobio 1821-1882 NewGrD 80
Panicker, Chathunni DancEn 78
Panico, Frank Porky 1924- AmSCAP 66, -80
Panico, Louis BgBands 74
Panijel, Jacques 1921- DcFM
Panizza, Ettore 1875-1967 Baker 78, BiDAmM, CmOp, NewEOp 71, NewGrD 80
Panizza, Hector 1875-1967 NewGrD 80
Pankey, Aubrey 1905-1971 BiDAmM
Pankiewicz, Eugeniusz 1857-1898 NewGrD 80
Panko, William 1894-1948 CreCan 1
Pankow, James Carter 1947- AmSCAP 80
Pann, Anton 1796-1854 NewGrD 80
Pannaci, Charles 1904-1927 WhScrn 74, -77
Pannain, Guido 1891-1977 Baker 78, NewGrD 80
Pannel, Lynn BlkAmP
Pannell, Lynn K MorBAP
Pannella, Liliana 1932- IntWWM 77, -80
Panneton, Philippe 1895-1960 CreCan 2
Panni, Marcello 1940- DcCM, WhoOp 76
Panni, Nicoletta 1933- WhoOp 76
Panninger, Leonhard 1495-1567 NewGrD 80
Panny, Joseph 1794-1838 NewGrD 80
Panofka, Heinrich 1807-1887 Baker 78, NewGrD 80
Panormitano NewGrD 80
Panormitano, Bartolomeo Lieto NewGrD 80
Panormitano, Mauro NewGrD 80
Panormo, Vincenzo 1734-1813? NewGrD 80
Panou, Athanase Dimitrius 1933- IntWWM 77
Panov, Valeri Matvevich 1938- CnOxB
Panova, Vera Fyodorovna 1905-1973 ModWD
Panseron, Auguste 1796-1859 NewGrD 80
Panseron, Auguste-Mathieu 1795-1859 Baker 78, OxMus
Pansini, Rose WomWMM
Pantages, Clayton G 1927- IntMPA 77, -75, -76, -78, -79, -80
Pantaleoni, Hewitt 1929- IntWWM 77, -80
Pantaloncina, La NewGrD 80
Pantano-Salsbury AmSCAP 80
Panter, Joan 1909- WhThe
Panthulu, B R 1910-1974 WhScrn 77
Pantillon, Francois 1928- IntWWM 77, -80
Panton, Lawrence Arthur Colley 1894-1954 CreCan 2
Pantopuck The Puppetman DcPup
Panudla, Dusan 1923- IntWWM 80
Panufnik, Andrzej 1914- Baker 78, CompSN[port], DcCM, IntWWM 77, -80, MusMk, NewGrD 80, WhoMus 72
Panula, Forma Fuhani 1930- IntWWM 77, -80
Panula, Jorma 1930- Baker 78
Panum, Hortense 1856-1933 Baker 78
Panvini, Ron WhoHol A
Panzer, Paul 1867?-1937 WhScrn 74, -77
Panzer, Paul Wolfgang 1872-1948 Film 2
Panzer, Paul Wolfgang 1872-1958 FilmEn, Film 1, ForYSC, HalFC 80, MotPP, NotNAT B, WhScrn 74, -77, WhoHol B
Panzer, Paul Wolfgang 1873-1958 TwYS
Panzera, Charles 1896-1976 Baker 78, NewGrD 80
Panzner, Karl 1866-1923 Baker 78
Paoletti, Alberto 1905- WhoOp 76
Paoli, Raoul Film 2
Paolini, Aurelio NewGrD 80
Paolo Aretino NewGrD 80
Paolo Da Firenze d1419 NewGrD 80[port]
Paolo, Giampaolo De NewGrD 80
Paolone, Ernesto 1904- IntWWM 80
Paolucci, Giuseppe 1726-1776 NewGrD 80
Paoluzzi, Luciana FilmEn
Papa Charlie BluesWW[port]
Papa Chittlins BluesWW[port]
Papa George BluesWW[port]
Papa Schmid 1822-1912 DcPup
Papa Snow White BluesWW[port]
Papach, Gary 1944- IntWWM 80
Papadopoulos, Joannes NewGrD 80
Papaelias, John 1949- IntWWM 80
Papai, Ray Andrew 1932- AmSCAP 80, IntWWM 77, -80
Papaioannou, Iohannes G 1915- NewGrD 80
Papaioannou, John G 1915- NewGrD 80
Papaioannou, Yannis 1910- DcCM
Papaioannou, Yannis 1911- Baker 78, NewGrD 80
Papale, Henry ConAmC
Papalia, Anthony 1905-1974 NewOrJ[port]
Papalia, Giovanni Maria NewGrD 80
Papalia, Russ 1903-1972 NewOrJ[port]
Papandopulo, Boris 1906- Baker 78, NewGrD 80
Paparelli, Frank 1917-1973 AmSCAP 66, -80
Papas, Irene 1926- FilmEn, FilmgC, ForYSC, HalFC 80, IntMPA 77, -75, -76, -78, -79, -80, MotPP, MovMk[port], OxFilm, WhoHol A
Papas, Sophocles Thomas 1894- IntWWM 77, -80
Papasan, Mavour Ruth Gafford 1914- IntWWM 77
Papastefan, John James 1942- IntWWM 77, -80
Papatakis, Nico 1918- FilmEn
Papatakis, Niko 1918- WorEFlm
Papavasilion, Ernest John 1937- IntWWM 77, -80
Papavoine 1720?-1793 NewGrD 80
Papazian, Steven J 1944- IntMPA 80
Pape, Andre De 1552-1581 NewGrD 80
Pape, Edward Lionel 1867-1944 WhScrn 74, -77
Pape, Heinrich 1609-1663 NewGrD 80
Pape, Jean Henri 1789-1875 NewGrD 80
Pape, Johann Heinrich 1789-1875 NewGrD 80
Pape, Lionel d1944 WhoHol B
Pape, Louis Wayne 1939- ConAmC
Pape, Naomi 1907- IntWWM 77, -80
Paper Lace RkOn 2[port]
Papi, Genarro 1886-1941 NewEOp 71
Papi, Gennaro 1886-1941 Baker 78
Papier, Rosa 1858-1932 Baker 78
Papillon DeLaFerte, Denis Pierre Jean 1725-1794 NewGrD 80
Papin, Peter 1898- NewOrJ
Papineau-Couture, Jean 1916- Baker 78, CpmDNM 75, CreCan 1, DcCM, IntWWM 77, -80, NewGrD 80
Papini, Guido 1847-1912 NewGrD 80, OxMus
Papius, Andreas NewGrD 80
Papp, Geza 1915- NewGrD 80
Papp, Joseph 1921- BiE&WWA, CnThe, EncMT, EncWT, Ent, NewYTET, NotNAT, -A, OxThe, PlP&P[port], -A[port], WhoThe 72, -77
Papp, Lajos 1935- DcCM, NewGrD 80
Pappalardi, Felix Albert, Jr. 1939- AmSCAP 80, ConMuA 80A
Pappalardi, Gail Collins 1941- AmSCAP 80
Pappas, George PupTheA
Pappin, Malcolm C 1925- AmSCAP 80
Paprocki, Bohdan 1919- NewGrD 80
Papulkas, Soto 1943- WhoOp 76
Papvocki, Bogdan WhoOp 76
Paque, Desire 1867-1939 Baker 78, NewGrD 80, OxMus
Paque, Glyn Eric Glyn 1907-1953 WhoJazz 72
Paquerette, Madame Film 2
Paquet, Alfons 1881-1944 CnMD, ModWD
Paquette, Daniel 1930- IntWWM 77, -80
Paquette, Pauline Film 2
Parabosco, Girolamo 1524?-1557 McGEWD, NewGrD 80
Parabovi, Filippo Maria NewGrD 80
Parabovi, Francesco Maria NewGrD 80
Parada, Claudia Olinfa 1933- WhoOp 76
Paradeiser, Karl Marian 1747-1775 NewGrD 80
Paradeiser, Marian 1747-1775 NewGrD 80
Paradies, Domenico 1707-1791 NewGrD 80
Paradies, Maria Theresia Von 1759-1824 NewGrD 80
Paradies, Pietro Domenico 1707-1791 Baker 78, OxMus
Paradis, Maria Theresia Von 1759-1824 Baker 78, NewGrD 80
Paradis, Suzanne 1936- CreCan 1
Paradisi, Domenico NewGrD 80
Paradons, The RkOn
Paradossi, Giuseppe NewGrD 80
Paraga, Marco 1862-1929 NotNAT B
Paragons, The RkOn
Parain, Brice 1897-1971 WhScrn 77
Paramor, Norrie 1914- WhoMus 72
Paranjpe, Sai WomWMM
Paranov, Moshe 1895- Baker 78
Pararol, Berenguier De NewGrD 80
Pararols, Berenguier De NewGrD 80
Paratico, Giuliano 1550?-1617? NewGrD 80
Paratore, Ettore 1907- IntWWM 77, -80
Paray, Paul 1886-1979 Baker 78, BiDAmM, MusSN[port], NewGrD 80, OxMus
Parazol, Berenguier De NewGrD 80
Parazzini, Maria 1940- WhoOp 76
Parbury, Muriel 1890- IntWWM 77, WhoMus 72
Parc, Frantisek Xaver NewGrD 80
Parcher, Peter ConMuA 80B
Parchman, Gen Louis 1929- AmSCAP 80, CpmDNM 76, -78, -79, ConAmC
Parchman, Gene Louis 1929- AmSCAP 66
Parchman, William E 1936- NatPD[port]
Pard, Yvette WomWMM
Pardave, Joaquin 1901-1955 WhScrn 74, -77
Pardave, Jose 1902-1970 WhScrn 74, -77
Pardee, C W Doc 1885-1975 WhScrn 77
Pardee, Doc 1885-1975 WhoHol C
Pardee, Margaret 1920- IntWWM 77, -80
Pardis, Monique WomWMM

Pardo Tovar, Andres 1911-1972 *NewGrD 80*
Pardoll, David 1908- *BiE&WWA*
Pardon, Valerie Marcia 1937- *WhoMus 72*
Paredes, Juan *NewGrD 80*
Pareja, Bartolome Ramos De 1440?- *MusMk*
Pareja, Ramos De *OxMus*
Parella, Anthony 1915- *BiE&WWA, NotNAT*
Parelli, Attilio 1874-1944 *Baker 78*
Parent, Armand 1863-1934 *Baker 78, NewGrD 80*
Parent, Gail *WomWMM*
Parente, Alfredo 1905- *NewGrD 80*
Parente, Sister Elizabeth *AmSCAP 66, -80*
Parenteau, Zoel 1883-1972 *AmSCAP 66, BiDAmM, ConAmC*
Parenti, Anthony 1900-1972 *BiDAmM, EncJzS 70*
Parenti, Paolo Francesco 1764-1821 *NewGrD 80*
Parenti, Tony 1900-1972 *CmpEPM, EncJzS 70, IlEncJ, NewOrJ[port], WhoJazz 72*
Parepa, Euphrosyne 1836-1874 *NewGrD 80*
Parepa-Rosa, Euphrosyne 1836-1874 *Baker 78*
Parera, Grace Moore *WhScrn 74, -77*
Pares, Jose 1926- *CnOxB*
Pares, Philippe *IntWWM 77, -80, WhoMus 72*
Pareto, Graciela 1888- *NewGrD 80*
Pareto, Graziella 1888- *CmOp, NewGrD 80*
Paretzkin, Brita *WomWMM B*
Parfaict, Claude 1701-1777 *OxThe*
Parfaict, Francois 1698-1753 *NewGrD 80, OxThe*
Parfitt, Judy *WhoHol A, WhoThe 72, -77*
Parfrey, Raymond John 1928- *WhoMus 72*
Parfrey, Woodrow *WhoHol A*
Parham, Charles Valdez 1913- *BiDAmM*
Parham, Tiny 1900-1943 *CmpEPM, WhoJazz 72*
Parham, Truck 1913- *WhoJazz 72*
Pari, Claudio *NewGrD 80*
Pariati, Pietro 1665-1733 *NewGrD 80*
Paribeni, Giulio Cesare 1881-1960 *Baker 78*
Parigi, Alfonso d1656 *EncWT, OxThe*
Parigi, Francesco Da *NewGrD 80*
Parigi, Giulio 1580?-1636? *EncWT*
Parigi, Giulio 1590-1636 *OxThe*
Parik, Ivan 1936- *Baker 78, IntWWM 77, -80, NewGrD 80*
Parikian, Manoug 1920- *IntWWM 77, -80, NewGrD 80, WhoMus 72*
Parios, Gus *Film 2*
Paris, Aime 1798-1866 *NewGrD 80, OxMus*
Paris, Alain 1947- *IntWWM 77, -80*
Paris, Frank *PupTheA, PupTheA SUP*
Paris, Guillaume-Alexandre 1756?-1840 *NewGrD 80*
Paris, Guillaume-Alexis 1756?-1840 *NewGrD 80*
Paris, Henry *FilmEn*
Paris, Jackie 1926- *BiDAmM*
Paris, Jerry 1925- *FilmEn, FilmgC, ForYSC, HalFC 80, NewYTET, WhoHol A*
Paris, Juan 1759-1845 *NewGrD 80*
Paris, Manuel 1894-1959 *WhScrn 77*
Paris Sisters, The *RkOn[port]*
Parish, Eli 1808-1849 *NewGrD 80*
Parish, James *WhThe, WhoThe 72*
Parish, Mitchell 1900- *AmPS, AmSCAP 66, -80, BiDAmM, CmpEPM, Sw&Ld C*
Parish-Alvars, Elias 1808-1849 *Baker 78, NewGrD 80*
Parish-Alvars, Elias 1810-1849 *OxMus*
Parisi, Antonio *PupTheA*
Parisot, Aldo S 1920- *WhoMus 72*
Parissi, Robert W 1950- *AmSCAP 80*
Parisys, Marcelle *WhThe*
Parizot *NewGrD 80*
Parizot, Claude 1700-1750 *NewGrD 80*
Parizot, Henry 1730-1795 *NewGrD 80*
Parizot, Nicolas 1730-1792 *NewGrD 80*
Park *NewGrD 80*
Park, Custer B 1900-1955 *WhScrn 74, -77*
Park, E L *Film 2*
Park, Florence Oie Chan 1886-1967 *WhScrn 77*
Park, Ida May 1885?- *FilmEn, TwYS A, WomWMM*
Park, John 1804-1865 *NewGrD 80*
Park, John Edgar 1879-1956 *BiDAmM*
Park, Maria Hester 1775-1822 *NewGrD 80*
Park, Merle 1937- *CnOxB, DancEn 78*
Park, Philip James 1907- *WhoMus 72*
Park, Reg *WhoHrs 80*
Park, Robert H 1916- *IntMPA 77, -75, -76, -78, -79, -80*
Park, Roswell 1807-1869 *BiDAmM*
Park, Stephen 1911- *AmSCAP 66, -80, ConAmC*
Parke *NewGrD 80*
Parke, Harry *FilmEn*
Parke, John 1745-1829 *NewGrD 80*
Parke, MacDonald 1892-1960 *WhScrn 74, -77, WhoHol B*
Parke, Thomas *NewGrD 80*
Parke, Walter d1922 *NotNAT B*
Parke, William *TwYS A*
Parke, William, Sr. 1873-1941 *Film 2, WhScrn 74, -77, WhoHol B*
Parke, William Thomas 1762-1847 *NewGrD 80, OxMus*
Parkening, Christopher 1948- *BnBkM 80*
Parker *NewGrD 80*
Parker, Archbishop *OxMus*
Parker, Adele 1885-1966 *WhScrn 77*
Parker, Al 1889-1974 *IlWWBF*
Parker, Alan 1944- *HalFC 80*
Parker, Albert 1889- *Film 1, TwYS A*
Parker, Alfred David 1937- *IntWWM 77*
Parker, Alice 1925- *AmSCAP 66, -80, ConAmC*
Parker, Andrew Lindsay 1950- *IntWWM 77, -80*
Parker, Andy 1913- *IlEncCM*
Parker, Annette *WhoOp 76*
Parker, Anthony 1912- *WhThe*
Parker, Barnett d1941 *WhScrn 74, WhoHol B*
Parker, Barnett 1886-1941 *WhScrn 77*
Parker, Barnett 1890-1941 *FilmgC, HalFC 80*
Parker, Benjamin R 1909- *IntMPA 77, -75, -76, -78, -79, -80*
Parker, Bird 1920-1955 *NewGrD 80[port]*
Parker, Cecil 1897-1971 *FilmEn, FilmgC, ForYSC, HalFC 80, IlWWBF[port], MovMk, NotNAT B, Vers B[port], WhScrn 74, -77, WhThe, WhoHol B*
Parker, Cecilia *WhoHol A*
Parker, Cecilia 1905- *FilmEn, HalFC 80, MGM[port], MovMk, ThFT[port]*
Parker, Cecilia 1914- *What 5[port]*
Parker, Cecilia 1915?- *FilmgC, ForYSC*
Parker, Charles Christopher, Jr. 1920-1955 *BiDAmM, ConAmC, NewGrD 80[port]*
Parker, Charlie *BnBkM 80, Film 2*
Parker, Charlie 1920-1955 *Baker 78, CmpEPM, DrBlPA, IlEncJ, MusMk, NewGrD 80[port]*
Parker, Claire *FilmEn, WomWMM*
Parker, Clifton 1905- *CmMov, FilmgC, HalFC 80, WhoMus 72*
Parker, Craig Burwell 1951- *IntWWM 80*
Parker, Daniel *NewGrD 80*
Parker, David *WhoMus 72*
Parker, David 1929- *WhoMus 72*
Parker, Dennis Edward 1924- *WhoMus 72*
Parker, Dorothy 1893-1967 *AmSCAP 66, -80, BiE&WWA, FilmEn, HalFC 80, NotNAT A, -B*
Parker, Eddie 1900-1960 *WhoHrs 80*
Parker, Edward Robert 1906- *WhoMus 72*
Parker, Edwin 1900-1960 *WhScrn 77*
Parker, Edwin Pond 1836-1926 *BiDAmM*
Parker, Eleanor 1922- *BiDFilm 81, FilmEn, FilmgC, ForYSC, HalFC 80[port], IntMPA 77, -75, -76, -78, -79, -80, MotPP, MovMk[port], WhoHol A, WorEFlm*
Parker, Evan 1944- *EncJzS 70, IlEncJ, IntWWM 77*
Parker, Everett C *NewYTET*
Parker, Fess *AmPS A, IntMPA 75, -76, -78, -79, -80*
Parker, Fess 1921- *ForYSC*
Parker, Fess 1925- *AmSCAP 66, FilmgC, HalFC 80, IntMPA 77, MotPP, WhoHol A*
Parker, Fess 1926- *FilmEn*
Parker, Fess 1927- *RkOn[port]*
Parker, Flora d1950 *Film 2, NotNAT B, WhoHol B*
Parker, Francine *WomWMM, -B*
Parker, Frank 1862-1926 *NotNAT B*
Parker, Frank 1864-1926 *WhThe*
Parker, Frank 1906?- *CmpEPM*
Parker, Frank Pinky 1891-1962 *WhScrn 74, -77*
Parker, Franklin 1891-1962 *WhoHol B*
Parker, George Albert 1856-1939 *BiDAmM*
Parker, George D d1937 *NotNAT B*
Parker, Georgie 1905?-1959 *NewOrJ*
Parker, Gilbert 1927- *BiE&WWA, NotNAT*
Parker, Sir Gilbert d1932 *NotNAT B*
Parker, Graham *ConMuA 80A*
Parker, Graham & The Rumour *IlEncR*
Parker, Hazel H *IntMPA 77, -75, -76*
Parker, Helen K 1889-1954 *AmSCAP 80*
Parker, Henry Taylor 1867-1934 *Baker 78, BiDAmM, NotNAT A, -B, OxThe*
Parker, Herman 1927- *BiDAmM*
Parker, Herman 1932-1971 *BluesWW[port]*
Parker, Hilary Anita 1953- *IntWWM 80*
Parker, Horatio William 1863-1919 *AmSCAP 66, -80, Baker 78, BiDAmM, BnBkM 80, CompSN[port], MusMk, NewEOp 71, NewGrD 80, OxMus*
Parker, J C D 1828-1916 *NewGrD 80*
Parker, Jack *Film 2*
Parker, James Cutler Dunn 1828-1916 *Baker 78, BiDAmM*
Parker, Janet Lee *WhoHol A*
Parker, Jean *IntMPA 75, MotPP*
Parker, Jean 1912- *FilmEn, HalFC 80, MGM[port], ThFT[port]*
Parker, Jean 1915- *FilmgC, ForYSC, MovMk[port], What 5[port], WhoHol A*
Parker, John 1875-1952 *NotNAT B, OxThe, WhThe*
Parker, John Carl 1926- *AmSCAP 66, -80*
Parker, John William 1909- *BiE&WWA, NotNAT*
Parker, Jonathan 1922- *AmSCAP 80*
Parker, Joy 1924- *WhThe*
Parker, Katherine *Film 2*
Parker, Knocky 1918- *CmpEPM, WhoJazz 72*
Parker, Lady *Film 2*
Parker, Lara *WhoHol A*
Parker, Leo 1925-1962 *BiDAmM, CmpEPM, IlEncJ*
Parker, Leonard 1932- *DrBlPA, WhoHol A*
Parker, Lew d1972 *WhoHol B*
Parker, Lew 1906-1972 *WhThe, WhoThe 72*
Parker, Lew 1907-1972 *BiE&WWA, NotNAT B, WhScrn 77*
Parker, Lewis M *BlkAmP*
Parker, Linda Marlowe *AmSCAP 80*
Parker, Lottie Blair d1937 *NotNAT B, WhThe*
Parker, Louis Napoleon 1852-1944 *ModWD, NotNAT B, OxThe, WhThe, WhoStg 1908*
Parker, Margaret *IntWWM 77*
Parker, Marilyn Morris 1934- *IntWWM 77*
Parker, Martin *OxMus*
Parker, Mary *WhoHol A*
Parker, Mary 1915-1966 *WhScrn 74, -77, WhoHol B*
Parker, Murray 1896-1965 *WhScrn 74, -77*
Parker, P C *OxThe*
Parker, Roberson Frank, Jr. 1927- *IntWWM 77*
Parker, Robert 1930- *RkOn 2[port]*
Parker, Robert Clinton 1941- *IntWWM 77*
Parker, Seth d1975 *ForYSC, WhScrn 77, WhoHol C*
Parker, Shirley *WhoHol A*
Parker, Suzy *IntMPA 77, -75, -76, -78, -79, -80, MotPP, WhoHol A*
Parker, Suzy 1932- *FilmgC, HalFC 80, MovMk*
Parker, Suzy 1933- *FilmEn*
Parker, Suzy 1935- *ForYSC*
Parker, Thane 1907- *WhThe*
Parker, Theodore 1810-1860 *BiDAmM*
Parker, Uncle Murray d1965 *WhoHol B*
Parker, Vaninne Darynth 1949- *IntWWM 80*
Parker, Vivian d1974 *WhoHol B*
Parker, Vivien 1897-1974 *WhScrn 77*
Parker, W Oren 1911- *BiE&WWA, NotNAT*
Parker, Warren *ForYSC, WhoHol A*
Parker, Willard 1912- *FilmEn, FilmgC, ForYSC, HalFC 80, IntMPA 77, -75, -76,*

–78, –79, –80, *MotPP, WhoHol A*
Parker, William 1943- *WhoOp 76*
Parker, Willie 1875-1965 *NewOrJ*
Parker, Woody *PupTheA*
Parker, Yardbird 1920-1955 *NewGrD 80[port]*
Parkes, Alfred David 1937- *WhoMus 72*
Parkes, Gerard *WhoHol A*
Parkes, Joanna 1944- *IntWWM 80*
Parkes, Ross 1940- *CnOxB*
Parkhirst, Douglass d1964 *NotNAT B*
Parkhouse, David 1930- *IntWWM 77, –80, WhoMus 72*
Parkhurst, Frances d1969 *WhScrn 74, –77, WhoHol B*
Parkhurst, Howard Elmore 1848-1916 *Baker 78*
Parkhurst, Pearce 1919- *IntMPA 77, –75, –76, –78, –79, –80*
Parkin, Dean 1930?- *WhoHrs 80*
Parkin, Eric 1924- *IntWWM 77, –80, WhoMus 72*
Parkin, Florence W *PupTheA*
Parkin, Simon 1956- *IntWWM 80*
Parkington, Beulah d1958 *WhScrn 74, –77, WhoHol B*
Parkins, Barbara 1942- *FilmEn, FilmgC, HalFC 80, WhoHol A*
Parkins, Barbara 1944- *ForYSC*
Parkinson, Allen 1910- *IntMPA 77, –75, –76, –78, –79, –80*
Parkinson, Doris 1912- *IntWWM 77*
Parkinson, Edgar Mort 1927- *WhoMus 72*
Parkinson, Elizabeth 1882-1922 *BiDAmM*
Parkinson, Georgina 1938- *CnOxB, DancEn 78[port]*
Parkinson, H B 1884-1970 *IlWWBF*
Parkinson, John Alfred 1920- *IntWWM 77, –80, WhoMus 72*
Parkinson, Rhona Helen Evelyn *WhoMus 72*
Parkinson, Ruth-Christine 1956- *IntWWM 80*
Parkinson, William 1774-1848 *BiDAmM*
Parks, Anne Raiford 1935- *AmSCAP 80*
Parks, Bert *IntMPA 77, –75, –76, –78, –79, –80, NewYTET*
Parks, Carolyn *DancEn 78*
Parks, E L *Film 2*
Parks, Gordon *IntMPA 75, –76, –78, –79, –80, MorBAP*
Parks, Gordon 1912- *AmSCAP 80, BlkAmP, ConLC 16, DrBlPA, FilmEn, FilmgC, IntMPA 77*
Parks, Gordon 1925- *HalFC 80*
Parks, Gordon, Jr. 1934- *DrBlPA*
Parks, Gordon, Jr. 1948-1979 *FilmgC, HalFC 80*
Parks, Hildy *BiE&WWA, NotNAT, WhoHol A*
Parks, James Hays 1943- *IntWWM 77, –80*
Parks, Larry 1914-1975 *BiE&WWA, CmMov, FilmEn, FilmgC, ForYSC, HalFC 80, HolP 40[port], IntMPA 75, MotPP, MovMk, What 1[port], WhScrn 77, WhThe, WhoHol C, WhoThe 72*
Parks, Michael 1938- *FilmEn, FilmgC, ForYSC, HalFC 80, IntMPA 77, –75, –76, –78, –79, –80, MotPP, RkOn 2[port], WhoHol A*
Parks, Rick 1945- *AmSCAP 80*
Parks, Van Dyke 1941?- *ConMuA 80A, IlEncR*
Parkyakarkus 1904-1958 *FilmEn, FilmgC, ForYSC, HalFC 80, JoeFr, WhScrn 74, –77, WhoHol B*
Parkyn, Leslie *FilmgC, HalFC 80*
Parlan, Horace Louis 1931- *BiDAmM, EncJzS 70*
Parlasca, Bernardino *NewGrD 80*
Parlato, David Charles 1945- *EncJzS 70*
Parliament-Funkadelic *ConMuA 80A*
Parliaments, The *RkOn 2[port]*
Parlic, Dimitri 1919- *DancEn 78*
Parlic, Dimitrije 1919- *CnOxB*
Parlo, Dita *Film 2*
Parlo, Dita 1906-1971 *FilmEn, HalFC 80, OxFilm*
Parlo, Dita 1906-1972 *FilmAG WE, FilmgC, WhoHol B, WorEFlm*
Parlo, Dita 1907-1971 *WhScrn 77*
Parlow, Kathleen M 1890-1963 *Baker 78, BiDAmM, CreCan 2, NewGrD 80*
Parly, Ticho 1928- *NewGrD 80, WhoMus 72, WhoOp 76*
Parma, Ildebrando Da *NewGrD 80, OxMus*
Parma, Nicola *NewGrD 80*
Parma, Nicolo *NewGrD 80*
Parma, Santino Garsi Da *NewGrD 80*
Parmain, Martine 1942- *CnOxB*
Parman, Cliff *AmSCAP 66, –80*
Parmelee, Paul Frederick 1925- *IntWWM 77, –80*
Parmentier, C A J *AmSCAP 80*
Parmer, Edgar Alan 1928- *IntWWM 77, –80*
Parnas, Leslie 1932- *IntWWM 80*
Parnel, Ruth 1928- *CnOxB, DancEn 78*
Parnell, David Andrew 1954- *IntWWM 77, –80*
Parnell, Emory *IntMPA 75, –76, –78, –79*
Parnell, Emory 1894-1979 *FilmEn, FilmgC, HalFC 80, IntMPA 77, Vers A[port], WhoHol A*
Parnell, Emory 1900?- *ForYSC*
Parnell, Jack 1923- *CmpEPM, EncJzS 70*
Parnell, James 1923-1961 *NotNAT B, WhScrn 74, –77, WhoHol B*
Parnell, Lee Roy 1956- *AmSCAP 80*
Parnell, Val 1894- *WhThe*
Parnes, Paul 1925- *AmSCAP 66, –80*
Parnes, Sid *ConMuA 80B*
Parns, Leslie 1932- *IntWWM 77*
Parodi, Lorenzo 1856-1926 *Baker 78*
Paroisse-Pougin, Arthur *NewGrD 80*
Parolari, Egon 1924- *IntWWM 77, –80*
Parquet, Corinne *Film 1*
Parr, Colin 1938- *WhoMus 72*
Parr, Hector C 1927- *WhoMus 72*
Parr, Katherine *WhoHol A*
Parr, Peggy *Film 1*
Parr-Davies, Harry *NewGrD 80*
Parran *BluesWW[port]*
Parran, Antoine 1587-1650 *NewGrD 80*
Parratt, Sir Walter 1841-1924 *Baker 78, NewGrD 80[port], OxMus*
Parravicini, Florencio 1874-1941 *WhScrn 74, –77*
Parreiras Neves, Ignacio *NewGrD 80*
Parrenin, Jacques 1919- *NewGrD 80*
Parriott, James Deforis 1950- *AmSCAP 80*
Parris, Herman M 1903-1973 *AmSCAP 66, –80, ConAmC, OxMus*
Parris, Hermann M 1903- *Baker 78*
Parris, Marion *PupTheA*
Parris, Robert 1924- *Baker 78, ConAmC, DcCM, IntWWM 77, –80*
Parrish, Avery 1917-1959 *AmSCAP 66, –80, WhoJazz 72*
Parrish, Carl 1904-1965 *Baker 78, ConAmC, NewGrD 80*
Parrish, Gigi *WhoHol A*
Parrish, Helen d1959 *MotPP, NotNAT B, WhoHol B*
Parrish, Helen 1922-1959 *FilmEn, Film 2, FilmgC, ForYSC, HalFC 80, ThFT[port]*
Parrish, Helen 1924-1959 *WhScrn 74, –77*
Parrish, Judy 1916- *BiE&WWA*
Parrish, Julie *WhoHol A*
Parrish, Leslie *ForYSC, WhoHol A*
Parrish, Lillian Alberta 1917- *IntWWM 77, –80*
Parrish, Robert *IntMPA 75, –76, –78, –79, –80*
Parrish, Robert 1916- *BiDFilm 81, FilmEn, FilmgC, HalFC 80, IntMPA 77, MovMk[port], WorEFlm*
Parrott, Andrew Haden 1947- *IntWWM 77, –80*
Parrott, Barbara Violet 1925- *WhoMus 72*
Parrott, Charles *FilmEn, Film 1, WhScrn 74, –77*
Parrott, Ian 1916- *Baker 78, IntWWM 77, –80, NewGrD 80, OxMus, WhoMus 72*
Parrott, James 1892-1939 *CmMov, FilmEn, FilmgC, HalFC 80, WhScrn 74, –77*
Parrott, Jimmie *Film 2*
Parrott, Michael Ian Edwin 1942- *IntWWM 77, –80*
Parrott, Paul *Film 2*
Parrott, Paul Poll 1892-1939 *WhoHol B*
Parry, Sir Charles Hubert Hastings 1848-1918 *Baker 78*
Parry, Sir Edward Abbott d1943 *NotNAT B, WhThe*
Parry, Gordon 1908- *FilmEn, FilmgC, HalFC 80, IlWWBF, IntMPA 77, –75, –76, –78, –79, –80*
Parry, Harry 1912- *CmpEPM*
Parry, Harvey 1901- *Film 2*
Parry, Henry John *NewGrD 80*
Parry, Hubert 1848-1918 *BnBkM 80, MusMk[port], NewGrD 80[port], OxMus*
Parry, Jane Margaret 1908- *WhoMus 72*
Parry, John d1782 *OxMus*
Parry, John 1710?-1782 *Baker 78, NewGrD 80*
Parry, John 1776-1851 *Baker 78, NewGrD 80, OxMus*
Parry, John Orlando 1810-1879 *NewGrD 80, OxMus*
Parry, Joseph 1841-1903 *Baker 78, BiDAmM, NewGrD 80, OxMus*
Parry, Lee *Film 2*
Parry, Mhari Elisabeth Forbes 1921- *WhoMus 72*
Parry, Natasha 1930- *FilmgC, HalFC 80, IlWWBF, WhoHol A*
Parry, Paul 1908-1966 *WhScrn 77, WhoHol B*
Parry, Peggy *Film 1*
Parry, Roland 1897- *AmSCAP 66, ConAmC A*
Parry, Sefton Henry d1887 *NotNAT B*
Parry, Tom d1862 *NotNAT B*
Parry, Wilfrid 1908- *IntWWM 77, WhoMus 72*
Parry, Wilfrid 1909- *IntWWM 80*
Parry, William 1856- *WhoStg 1906, –1908*
Parry, William Stanley 1898- *IntWWM 77, WhoMus 72*
Parsch, Arnost 1936- *Baker 78, NewGrD 80*
Parshalle, Eve 1900- *AmSCAP 66*
Parsley, Osbert 1511-1585 *Baker 78, NewGrD 80, OxMus*
Parsley, Ruby *Film 2*
Parsloe, Charles T d1898 *NotNAT B*
Parson, Carol d1958 *WhScrn 74, –77*
Parsoneault, Catherine Jean 1950- *IntWWM 80*
Parsons *NewGrD 80*
Parsons, Alan *ConMuA 80B*
Parsons, Alan 1888-1933 *WhThe*
Parsons, Albert Ross 1847-1933 *Baker 78, BiDAmM*
Parsons, Allan 1888-1933 *NotNAT B*
Parsons, Bill 1934- *RkOn*
Parsons, Billy *Film 1*
Parsons, Sir Charles A 1854-1931 *OxMus*
Parsons, Donovan 1888- *WhThe*
Parsons, Ernest J 1882- *BiDAmM*
Parsons, Estelle *IntMPA 75, –76, –78, –79, –80*
Parsons, Estelle 1927- *BiE&WWA, Ent, FilmEn, FilmgC, HalFC 80, IntMPA 77, MovMk[port], NotNAT, WhoHol A, WhoThe 72, –77*
Parsons, Estelle 1928- *ForYSC*
Parsons, Frederick James 1891- *IntWWM 77, WhoMus 72*
Parsons, Geoffrey Penwill 1929- *IntWWM 77, –80, NewGrD 80, WhoMus 72*
Parsons, Gram 1946-1973 *ConMuA 80A, CounME 74[port], –74A, IlEncCM[port], IlEncR, WhScrn 77*
Parsons, Harriet *Film 1, IntMPA 77, –75, –76, –78, –79, –80, WomWMM*
Parsons, John 1575?-1623 *NewGrD 80*
Parsons, John Anthony 1938- *IntWWM 77, –80*
Parsons, Lindsley 1905- *IntMPA 77, –75, –76, –78, –79, –80*
Parsons, Louella d1972 *WhoHol B*
Parsons, Louella 1880-1972 *FilmgC, HalFC 80*
Parsons, Louella 1881?-1972 *Film 2, WhScrn 77*
Parsons, Louella 1890-1972 *OxFilm*
Parsons, Louella 1893-1972 *FilmEn, WorEFlm*
Parsons, Margaret Winifred 1929- *WhoMus 72*
Parsons, Michael 1938- *DcCM*
Parsons, Michael J *WhoHol A*
Parsons, Milton *HalFC 80, WhoHol A*
Parsons, Milton 1904- *WhoHrs 80*
Parsons, Muriel Mary 1907- *WhoMus 72*
Parsons, Nancie 1904- *WhThe*
Parsons, Nicholas 1928- *FilmgC, HalFC 80, WhoHol A*
Parsons, Percy 1878-1944 *NotNAT B, WhScrn 77, WhThe, WhoHol B*

Parsons, Robert d1570 *BnBkM 80, OxMus*
Parsons, Robert 1530?-1570 *NewGrD 80*
Parsons, Robert 1596-1676 *NewGrD 80*
Parsons, Smiling Billy 1878-1919 *WhScrn 77*
Parsons, William 1876-1919 *FilmEn*
Parsons, William 1933- *AmSCAP 66, -80, NewGrD 80*
Parsons, Sir William 1746-1817 *OxMus*
Part, Arvo 1935- *Baker 78, DcCM, NewGrD 80*
Partart, Antonio *NewGrD 80*
Partay, Lilla 1941- *CnOxB*
Partch, Harry 1901-1974 *Baker 78, BiDAmM, BnBkM 80, ConAmC, DcCM*
Partch, Harry 1901-1976 *NewGrD 80*
Parten, Peter *WhoHol A*
Partenico, Gian Domenico 1650?-1701 *NewGrD 80*
Partenico, Giovanni Domenico 1650?-1701 *NewGrD 80*
Partenio, Gian Domenico 1650?-1701 *NewGrD 80*
Partenio, Giovanni Domenico 1650?-1701 *NewGrD 80*
Partes, Frank 1901- *FilmEn*
Parthun, Paul R 1931- *ConAmC*
Partington, Kendrick John 1925- *WhoMus 72*
Partington, Rex *NotNAT*
Parton, Dolly 1946- *BiDAmM, CounME 74[port], -74A, IlEncCM[port], IlEncR[port], RkOn 2[port]*
Parton, Rosemary Patricia 1933- *IntWWM 77*
Partos, Gus *Film 2*
Partos, Odon 1907-1977 *NewGrD 80*
Partos, Oedoen 1907-1977 *Baker 78, DcCM, IntWWM 77, -80, NewGrD 80*
Partos, Oedon *OxMus*
Partridge, David 1919- *CreCan 1*
Partridge, Derek 1935- *IntMPA 79, -80*
Partridge, Ian 1938- *IntWWM 77, -80, NewGrD 80, WhoMus 72*
Partridge, Jennifer 1942- *IntWWM 77, -80*
Partridge, John Albert 1941- *IntWWM 77, -80*
Partridge Family, The *RkOn 2[port]*
Partsch, Frantisek Xaver 1760-1822 *NewGrD 80*
Partsch, Franz Xaver 1760-1822 *NewGrD 80*
Party Timers, The *BiDAmM, EncFCWM 69*
Parver, Michael 1936- *BiE&WWA*
Paryla, Karl 1905- *EncWT*
Pasatieri, Thomas 1943- *BiDAmM*
Pasatieri, Thomas 1945- *AmSCAP 80, Baker 78, CpmDNM 72, ConAmC, NewGrD 80*
Pascal, Andre *NotNAT B*
Pascal, Claude Rene Georges 1921- *IntWWM 80, NewGrD 80*
Pascal, Ernest 1896-1966 *FilmEn, NotNAT B*
Pascal, Florian *NewGrD 80*
Pascal, Gabriel 1894-1954 *FilmEn, FilmgC, HalFC 80, IlWWBF A, NotNAT A, -B, OxFilm, WorEFlm*
Pascal, Gisele 1923- *FilmEn*
Pascal, Giselle *WhoHol A*
Pascal, Jean-Claude 1927- *FilmEn*
Pascal, Jefferson *AmSCAP 80*
Pascal, Milton H 1908- *AmSCAP 66, -80*
Pascale, Francesco *NewGrD 80*
Pascale, Palma Anne 1950- *AmSCAP 80*
Pascan, Borislav Svetolik 1924- *WhoOp 76*
Pascarola, Giovanni T Benedictis Da *NewGrD 80*
Paschali, Francesco *NewGrD 80*
Pasche, William *NewGrD 80*
Paschke, Donald Vernon 1929- *IntWWM 77, -80*
Pasco, Richard 1926- *CnThe, FilmgC, HalFC 80, WhoHol A, WhoThe 72, -77*
Pascoal, Hermeto 1936- *EncJzS 70*
Pascoe, Charles Eyre d1912 *NotNAT B*
Pascoe, Richard W 1888-1968 *AmSCAP 66, -80*
Pascu, George 1912- *IntWWM 77, -80*
Pascual, Francisco 1683?-1743 *NewGrD 80*
Pasdeloup, Jules Etienne 1819-1887 *Baker 78, BnBkM 80, NewGrD 80, OxMus*
Pasek, Cepha *PupTheA*
Pasero, Tancredi 1893- *CmOp, NewEOp 71, NewGrD 80*
Pasetta, Marty *NewYTET*
Pasetto, Giordano *NewGrD 80*
Pasetus, Jordanus *NewGrD 80*
Pasfield, William Reginald 1909- *IntWWM 77, WhoMus 72*
Pasha, Kalla 1877-1933 *Film 2, TwYS, WhScrn 74, -77, WhoHol B*
Pashchenko, Andrei 1883-1972 *Baker 78*
Pashchenko, Andrey Filippovich 1885-1972 *NewGrD 80*
Pashe, William *NewGrD 80*
Pashennaya, Vera Nikolayevna 1887-1962 *OxThe*
Pashkalov, Viacheslav 1873-1951 *Baker 78*
Pashkevich, Vasiliy Alexeyevich 1742?-1797 *NewGrD 80*
Pashkevich, Vassily 1740?-1800 *Baker 78*
Pashley, Anne 1937- *IntWWM 77, -80, WhoMus 72, WhoOp 76*
Pashley, Frank *NewOrJ*
Pashley, Gloria *WhoMus 72*
Pashley, Newton H *ConAmC*
Pasinetti, Francesco 1911-1949 *FilmEn*
Pasino, Stefano d1679? *NewGrD 80*
Pask, Eric *WhoMus 72*
Paskalis, Kostas 1929- *NewGrD 80, WhoMus 72, WhoOp 76*
Paskman, Dailey 1897- *AmSCAP 66, -80*
Pasmore, Henry Bickford 1857-1944 *Baker 78, BiDAmM*
Paso, Alfonso 1926- *CnMD, CroCD, ModWD*
Paso Gil, Alfonso 1926- *McGEWD[port]*
Pasolini, Pier Paola 1922-1975 *WhScrn 77*
Pasolini, Pier Paolo 1922-1975 *BiDFilm 81, FilmEn, FilmgC, HalFC 80, MovMk[port], OxFilm, WorEFlm*
Pasolini, Piero Paolo 1922-1975 *DcFM*
Pasoti, Giovanni Giacomo *NewGrD 80*
Pasquale, Bonifacio d1585 *NewGrD 80*
Pasquali *OxMus*
Pasquali, Bonifacio d1585 *NewGrD 80*
Pasquali, Ernesto Maria 1883-1919 *FilmEn*
Pasquali, Francesco d1635? *NewGrD 80*
Pasquali, Francesco 1590?- *Baker 78*
Pasquali, Niccolo 1718?-1757 *NewGrD 80*
Pasquali, Nicolo 1718?-1757 *Baker 78*
Pasqualini, Marc'Antonio 1614-1691 *NewGrD 80*
Pasquall, Jerome Don 1902-1971 *WhoJazz 72*
Pasque, Ernest *Film 1*
Pasquet, Jean 1896-1977 *AmSCAP 66, -80, ConAmC*
Pasquier, Charles Bach 1881-1953 *WhScrn 74, -77*
Pasquini, Bernardo 1637-1710 *Baker 78, MusMk, NewGrD 80[port], OxMus*
Pasquini, Ercole d1619? *NewGrD 80*
Pasquini, Ercole d1620? *Baker 78*
Pasricha, Aruna 1942- *IntWWM 77, -80*
Pass, Joe 1929- *BiDAmM, EncJzS 70, IlEncJ*
Pass, Walter 1942- *NewGrD 80*
Passalaqua, Joseph A 1929- *AmSCAP 80*
Passani, Emile 1905- *WhoMus 72*
Passantino, Anthony *WhoHol A*
Passarge, Paul *Film 2*
Passarini, Camillo 1636-1694 *NewGrD 80*
Passarini, Francesco 1636-1694 *NewGrD 80*
Passche, William *NewGrD 80*
Passenger, Aegidius *NewGrD 80*
Passer, Ivan 1933- *HalFC 80, IntMPA 77, -76, -78, -79, -80, OxFilm, WorEFlm*
Passereau, Pierre *Baker 78, NewGrD 80*
Passerini, Christina *NewGrD 80*
Passerini, Francesco *NewGrD 80*
Passet *NewGrD 80*
Passetto, Giordano d1557 *NewGrD 80*
Passeur, Steve 1899-1966 *CnMD, McGEWD, ModWD, WhThe*
Passick, David *ConMuA 80B*
Passions, The *RkOn*
Passloff, Aileen *CmpGMD*
Passmore, Henry 1905- *IntMPA 77, -75, -76, -78, -79, -80*
Passmore, Walter 1867-1946 *NotNAT B, WhThe*
Passy, Edvard 1789-1870 *Baker 78*
Passy, Ludvig Anton Edmund 1789-1870 *NewGrD 80*
Pasta, Giovanni 1604-1664? *NewGrD 80*
Pasta, Giuditta 1797-1865 *Baker 78, NewGrD 80[port]*
Pasta, Giuditta 1798-1865 *BnBkM 80, CmOp, NewEOp 71*
Pasta, LaPiccola *NewGrD 80*
Pastel 6, The *RkOn*
Pastels, The *RkOn[port]*
Paster, Gary M 1943- *IntMPA 78, -79, -80*
Pasterla, La *NewGrD 80*
Pasternack, Josef Alexander 1881-1940 *Baker 78*
Pasternack, Joseph A 1881-1940 *BiDAmM*
Pasternacki, Stephan 1891- *AmSCAP 66, -80*
Pasternak, Joe 1901- *CmMov, FilmEn, FilmgC, HalFC 80, IntMPA 77, -75, -76, -78, -79, -80, WorEFlm*
Pasternak, Joseph H 1901- *AmSCAP 66, -80*
Pasterwitz, Georg Von 1730-1803 *Baker 78*
Pasterwiz, Georg 1730-1803 *NewGrD 80*
Pasterwiz, Robert 1730-1803 *NewGrD 80*
Pastine, Gianfranco 1937- *WhoOp 76*
Paston, Edward 1550?-1630 *NewGrD 80*
Paston, George d1936 *NotNAT B, WhThe*
Pastor, Antonio 1837-1908 *BiDAmM, WhoStg 1906, -1908*
Pastor, Tony 1837-1908 *FamA&A[port], NotNAT A, -B, OxThe*
Pastor, Tony 1907-1969 *BgBands 74[port], BiDAmM, CmpEPM, EncJzS 70, WhoHol B, WhoJazz 72*
Pastore, Giuseppe Alfredo 1915- *IntWWM 77, -80*
Pastore, John O 1907- *NewYTET*
Pastorius, Franz Daniel 1651-1719 *BiDAmM*
Pastorius, John Francis 1951- *AmSCAP 80*
Pastou, Etienne-Jean Baptiste 1784-1851 *Baker 78*
Pastrana, Pedro De 1480?-1559? *NewGrD 80*
Pastrone, Giovanni 1882-1959 *DcFM*
Pastrone, Giovanni 1883-1959 *FilmEn, OxFilm, WorEFlm*
Paszkiewicz, Andrzej *NewGrD 80*
Paszthory, Casimir Von 1886-1966 *NewGrD 80*
Pat And The Satellites *RkOn*
Patachich, Ivan 1922- *Baker 78, IntWWM 77, -80, NewGrD 80*
Patachou *WhoHol A*
Pataki, Michael *WhoHol A*
Pataky, Kalman 1896-1964 *NewGrD 80*
Patane, Giuseppe 1932- *Baker 78, NewGrD 80, WhoOp 76*
Patane, Vittorio 1933- *WhoOp 76*
Patard, Antonio 1560?-1605? *NewGrD 80*
Patart, Antonio 1560?-1605? *NewGrD 80*
Patarto, Antonio 1560?-1605? *NewGrD 80*
Patavino, Nicolo *NewGrD 80*
Patavinus, Antonius Stringarius *NewGrD 80*
Patbru, Cornelis Thymanszoon *NewGrD 80*
Patbrue, Cornelis Thymanszoon *NewGrD 80*
Patch, Wally 1888-1970 *Film 2, IlWWBF, WhScrn 74, -77, WhThe, WhoHol B*
Patch, Wally 1888-1971 *FilmgC, HalFC 80*
Patchett-Tarses *NewYTET*
Pate, Bob *ConAmTC*
Pate, John d1704 *NewGrD 80*
Pate, Michael 1920- *FilmEn, FilmgC, ForYSC, HalFC 80, MovMk, Vers B[port], WhoHol A, WhoHrs 80*
Patekar, Bhalchandra Vaman 1928- *IntWWM 77, -80*
Pateman, Robert 1840-1924 *NotNAT B, WhThe*
Patenaude, Joan 1941- *WhoOp 76*
Patenaude, Joan 1944- *IntWWM 80*
Pater A Monte Carmelo *NewGrD 80*
Paterno, Anton 1770-1839 *NewGrD 80*
Paterson, Jerry *Film 2*
Paterson, Neil 1915- *FilmEn*
Paterson, Neil 1916- *FilmgC, HalFC 80, IntMPA 77, -75, -76, -78, -79, -80*
Paterson, Pat 1911-1978 *FilmEn, IlWWBF[port], ThFT[port], WhoHol A*
Paterson, Robert d1859 *NewGrD 80*
Paterson, Robert Roy 1830-1903 *NewGrD 80*
Paterson, William 1919- *BiE&WWA*
Pates, Gennilla Atkins 1908- *IntWWM 77, -80*
Patey, Bent 1952- *IntWWM 80*
Patey, Edward Raymond 1940- *IntWWM 77, -80*
Patey, Janet Monach 1842-1894 *Baker 78, NewGrD 80*

Patey, John 1835-1901 *Baker 78*
Pathe, Charles 1863-1957 *DcFM, FilmEn, FilmgC, HalFC 80, NotNAT B, OxFilm, WorEFlm*
Pathfinders, The *BiDAmM*
Pathie, Roger 1510?-1565? *NewGrD 80*
Pathie, Rogier 1510?-1565? *NewGrD 80*
Patie, Roger 1510?-1565? *NewGrD 80*
Patie, Rogier 1510?-1565? *NewGrD 80*
Patience And Prudence *AmPS A, -B, RkOn[port]*
Patin, Jacques *DancEn 78*
Patino, Carlos d1675 *Baker 78, NewGrD 80*
Patist, Johan 1912- *IntWWM 77, -80*
Patnoe, Herbert Darrell 1928- *IntWWM 77*
Paton, Alan *PlP&P*
Paton, Charles *Film 2*
Paton, John Glenn 1934- *IntWWM 77, -80*
Paton, Mary Ann 1802-1864 *Baker 78*
Paton, Mary Anne 1802-1864 *NewGrD 80*
Paton, Stuart 1885-1944 *TwYS A, WhScrn 74, -77*
Patorzhinsky, Ivan 1896-1960 *NewGrD 80*
Patricij, Andrija *NewGrD 80*
Patricio, Andrea *NewGrD 80*
Patrick Campbell, Mrs. *EncWT*
Patrick, Benilde 1927- *BiE&WWA*
Patrick, Butch *WhoHol A*
Patrick, C L 1918- *IntMPA 77, -75, -76, -78, -79, -80*
Patrick, Corbin 1905- *ConAmTC*
Patrick, David Michael 1947- *IntWWM 77, -80*
Patrick, Dennis *WhoHol A*
Patrick, Dorothy *ForYSC*
Patrick, Ethel 1887-1944 *WhScrn 74, -77*
Patrick, Florence *PupTheA*
Patrick, Frederick 1896- *AmSCAP 66, -80*
Patrick, Gail d1980 *MotPP, What 5[port]*
Patrick, Gail 1911-1980 *FilmEn, FilmgC, HalFC 80, HolP 30[port], ThFT[port]*
Patrick, Gail 1912-1980 *ForYSC, WhoHol A*
Patrick, Gail 1915-1980 *MovMk[port]*
Patrick, George 1905- *IntMPA 77, -75, -76, -78, -79, -80*
Patrick, Jerome 1883-1923 *Film 1, -2, NotNAT B, WhScrn 74, -77, WhoHol B*
Patrick, John *Film 2*
Patrick, John 1902- *CnMD*
Patrick, John 1905- *FilmEn*
Patrick, John 1906- *DcLB 7[port], McGEWD[port]*
Patrick, John 1907- *BiE&WWA, ConDr 73, -77, EncWT, NotNAT, WhoThe 72, -77*
Patrick, John 1910- *ModWD*
Patrick, Julian 1927- *WhoOp 76*
Patrick, Kirk *AmSCAP 80*
Patrick, Lee *BiE&WWA, MotPP, NotNAT, What 5[port]*
Patrick, Lee 1906- *FilmgC, HalFC 80, HolCA[port]*
Patrick, Lee 1911- *FilmEn, Film 2, ForYSC, MovMk, Vers A[port], WhoHol A*
Patrick, Leonard *BiE&WWA*
Patrick, Lory *WhoHol A*
Patrick, Millar 1868-1951 *OxMus*
Patrick, Nathaniel d1595 *NewGrD 80, OxMus*
Patrick, Nelson Gray 1912- *IntWWM 77*
Patrick, Nigel 1913- *FilmAG WE, FilmEn, FilmgC, ForYSC, HalFC 80, IlWWBF, IntMPA 77, -75, -76, -78, -79, -80, MotPP, MovMk, WhoHol A, WhoThe 72, -77*
Patrick, Philip Howard 1946- *IntWWM 77, -80*
Patrick, Richard *OxMus*
Patrick, Robert 1937- *ConDr 73, -77, NotNAT*
Patricola, Tom d1950 *Film 2, WhoHol B*
Patricola, Tom 1891-1950 *NotNAT B, WhThe*
Patricola, Tom 1894-1950 *WhScrn 74, -77*
Patridge, William *PupTheA*
Patrinos, Harry *PupTheA*
Patroni Griffi, Giuseppe 1924- *WorEFlm*
Patry, Albert *Film 2*
Patry, Pierre 1933- *CreCan 2*
Patston, Doris 1904-1957 *NotNAT B, WhScrn 74, -77, WhoHol B*
Patt, Frank 1928- *BluesWW[port]*
Patta, Serafino *NewGrD 80*
Patten, Dorothy 1905-1975 *WhScrn 77, WhoHol C*
Patten, James 1936- *IntWWM 80, WhoMus 72*
Patten, Luana 1938- *FilmgC, ForYSC, HalFC 80, WhoHol A*
Patten, Mrs. Marc *PupTheA*
Patten, Robert *WhoHol A*
Patten, Robert Fletcher 1946- *AmSCAP 80*
Patterson, Colonel *Film 2*
Patterson, Ada d1939 *NotNAT B*
Patterson, Albert *WhoHol A*
Patterson, Albert d1975 *WhScrn 77, WhoHol C*
Patterson, Andy James 1929- *ConAmC, IntWWM 77, -80*
Patterson, Annie Wilson 1868-1934 *Baker 78, NewGrD 80*
Patterson, Benjamin *ConDr 73, -77E*
Patterson, Charles 1941- *BlkAmP, MorBAP*
Patterson, Cordelia M 1907- *AmSCAP 66*
Patterson, D H *PupTheA*
Patterson, Mrs. D H *PupTheA*
Patterson, David Nolte 1941- *ConAmC*
Patterson, Dick *WhoHol A*
Patterson, Don 1936- *BiDAmM, EncJzS 70*
Patterson, Elizabeth d1966 *MotPP, WhoHol B*
Patterson, Elizabeth 1874-1966 *BiE&WWA, FilmEn, ForYSC, HolCA[port], MovMk, NotNAT B, Vers A[port]*
Patterson, Elizabeth 1875-1966 *ThFT[port]*
Patterson, Elizabeth 1876-1966 *Film 2, FilmgC, HalFC 80, TwYS, WhScrn 74, -77*
Patterson, Frances H *PupTheA*
Patterson, Franklin Peale 1871-1966 *Baker 78, BiDAmM, ConAmC*
Patterson, Hank 1888-1975 *WhScrn 77, WhoHol C*
Patterson, Harry Thomas *CreCan 2*
Patterson, James 1932-1972 *NotNAT B, WhScrn 77, WhoHol B*
Patterson, James Hardy 1935- *IntWWM 77, -80*
Patterson, Jeremy David Kyle 1934- *IntWWM 77, -80*
Patterson, Jimmy Dale 1935- *BiDAmM*
Patterson, Joe 1898- *EncFCWM 69*
Patterson, John 1914- *IntWWM 77, WhoMus 72*
Patterson, Joseph Medill 1879-1946 *NotNAT B*
Patterson, Joy W 1906-1959 *WhScrn 74, -77, WhoHol B*
Patterson, Karin G 1950- *AmSCAP 80*
Patterson, Lee 1929- *FilmEn, FilmgC, ForYSC, HalFC 80, IlWWBF[port], WhoHol A*
Patterson, Lila *BluesWW[port]*
Patterson, Lindsay 1937- *DrBlPA*
Patterson, Marjorie d1948 *NotNAT B*
Patterson, Melody *WhoHol A*
Patterson, Neva 1922- *BiE&WWA, ForYSC, NotNAT, WhThe, WhoHol A*
Patterson, Neva 1925- *HalFC 80*
Patterson, Oscar *PupTheA*
Patterson, Ottilie 1932- *BluesWW[port], WhoMus 72*
Patterson, Pat *FilmgC, PupTheA, WhoHol A*
Patterson, Pat 1910-1978 *HalFC 80*
Patterson, Paul 1947- *ConAmC, IntWWM 77, -80, NewGrD 80, WhoMus 72*
Patterson, Richard L 1924- *IntMPA 77, -75, -76, -78, -79, -80*
Patterson, Russell *PupTheA*
Patterson, Russell 1928- *IntWWM 77, -80, WhoOp 76*
Patterson, Ruth Cleary *AmSCAP 80*
Patterson, Sam 1881- *BiDAmM*
Patterson, Strake *Film 2*
Patterson, T Richard 1917- *IntWWM 77, -80*
Patterson, Tom 1920- *CreCan 2, WhoThe 72, -77*
Patterson, Troy 1926-1975 *WhScrn 77, WhoHol C*
Patterson, Walter *Film 1*
Patterson, Wiley 1910- *AmSCAP 66*
Patti *NewGrD 80*
Patti, Adela 1843-1919 *NewGrD 80[port]*
Patti, Adelina 1843-1919 *Baker 78, BiDAmM, BnBkM 80, CmOp[port], MusMk[port], NewEOp 71, NewGrD 80[port], OxMus, WhoStg 1908*
Patti, Carlo 1842-1873 *BiDAmM, OxMus*
Patti, Carlotta 1835-1889 *Baker 78, NewGrD 80, OxMus*
Patti, Caterina Chiesa Barilli- d1870 *NewGrD 80*
Patti, Salvatore 1800-1869 *NewGrD 80*
Pattison, Bruce 1908- *IntWWM 77, -80*
Pattison, Evelyn *PupTheA*
Pattison, John Nelson 1845-1905 *Baker 78, BiDAmM*
Pattison, Lee 1890-1966 *Baker 78, BiDAmM, ConAmC*
Patto, Arcangelo *NewGrD 80*
Patton, Bill *Film 2, TwYS*
Patton, Charley 1887-1934 *BluesWW[port], NewGrD 80*
Patton, Charlie 1887-1934 *BluesWW[port]*
Patton, John 1936- *BiDAmM*
Patton, Mary *WhoHol A*
Patton, Phil 1911-1972 *WhScrn 77*
Patton, Roy E *PupTheA*
Patton, Virginia *ForYSC*
Patton, Willard 1853-1924 *Baker 78*
Patty & The Emblems *RkOn 2A[port]*
Patwardhan, Vinayakarao 1897-1975 *WhScrn 77*
Patye, Rogier *NewGrD 80*
Patzak, Julius 1898- *BnBkM 80, NewEOp 71, WhoMus 72*
Patzak, Julius 1898-1973 *CmOp*
Patzak, Julius 1898-1974 *Baker 78, NewGrD 80*
Patzschke, Christel *WhoOp 76*
Paudler, Maria *Film 2*
Pauer, Ernst 1825-1905 *OxMus*
Pauer, Ernst 1826-1905 *Baker 78, NewGrD 80*
Pauer, Fritz 1943- *EncJzS 70, IntWWM 77, -80*
Pauer, Jiri 1919- *Baker 78, NewGrD 80*
Pauer, Max Von 1866-1945 *Baker 78, NewGrD 80*
Pauk, Gyorgy 1936- *IntWWM 77, -80, NewGrD 80, WhoMus 72*
Pauker, Edmond d1962 *NotNAT B*
Pauker, Loretta *WomWMM B*
Paul And Paula *AmPS A, RkOn[port]*
Paul, Annette Av 1944- *CnOxB*
Paul, Barbarie 1945- *ConAmC*
Paul, Barberie 1946- *CpmDNM 75*
Paul, Bernard *PupTheA, PupTheA SUP*
Paul, Betty 1921- *BiE&WWA, WhThe, WhoHol A*
Paul, Billy 1934- *DrBlPA, RkOn 2[port]*
Paul, Byron *NewYTET*
Paul, Casimir *NewOrJ[port]*
Paul, Charles F 1902- *AmSCAP 80*
Paul, Charles Frederick 1912- *AmSCAP 66*
Paul, Doris A 1903- *AmSCAP 66, -80, ConAmC A*
Paul, Edith *PupTheA SUP*
Paul, Edmund *AmSCAP 80*
Paul, Edna *WomWMM*
Paul, Edward 1896- *AmSCAP 66, -80*
Paul, Emanuel 1904- *NewOrJ*
Paul, Ernst Julius 1907- *IntWWM 77, -80*
Paul, Fred 1880- *Film 2, IlWWBF*
Paul, Howard d1905 *NotNAT B*
Paul, Mrs. Howard d1879 *NotNAT B*
Paul, Jack 1925- *WhoMus 72*
Paul, James *IntWWM 77, -80*
Paul, Jimmy *AmSCAP 80*
Paul, John *AmSCAP 80, WhoHol A*
Paul, Lee *WhoHol A*
Paul, Les *AmPS A, -B, ConMuA 80A, WhoHol A*
Paul, Les 1906- *BiDAmM*
Paul, Les 1915- *IlEncCM*
Paul, Les 1916- *CmpEPM*
Paul, Les 1917- *IlEncR*
Paul, Les And Mary Ford *RkOn[port], What 4[port]*
Paul, Logan 1849-1932 *WhScrn 77*
Paul, Lynn *AmSCAP 80*
Paul, M B *IntMPA 77, -75, -76, -78, -79, -80*
Paul, Millie *WomWMM, -B*
Paul, Mimi *WhoHol A*
Paul, Mimi 1942- *CnOxB*

Paul, Mimi 1943- *DancEn 78[port]*
Paul, Oscar 1836-1898 *Baker 78, NewGrD 80*
Paul, Ouida Fay 1911- *IntWWM 77, -80*
Paul, Ralph 1920- *IntMPA 77, -75, -76, -78, -79, -80*
Paul, Reginald William 1894- *WhoMus 72*
Paul, Robert *WhoOp 76*
Paul, Robert William 1869-1943 *FilmEn, FilmgC, HalFC 80, OxFilm, WorEFlm*
Paul, Steven *WhoHol A*
Paul, Steven Everett 1937- *IntWWM 77, -80*
Paul, Taffy *FilmEn*
Paul, Thomas 1934- *WhoOp 76*
Paul, Wauna 1912-1973 *WhScrn 77*
Paula, Innocentio Di *NewGrD 80*
Paulas *Film 1*
Paulding, Fredcrick 1859-1937 *NotNAT B*
Paulet *NewGrD 80*
Pauletich, Aida *WomWMM B*
Paulette, Jane *AmSCAP 66, -80*
Pauley, Jane 1950- *IntMPA 79, -80, NewYTET*
Pauli, Hansjorg 1931- *IntWWM 77, -80, NewGrD 80*
Pauli-Winterstein, Hedwig *Film 2*
Paulig, Albert d1933 *Film 2, WhScrn 74, -77*
Paulin, Ernest 1902?- *NewOrJ SUP[port]*
Paulin, Frederic-Hubert 1678-1761 *NewGrD 80*
Pauline, J Robert *Film 2*
Pauline, Princess 1873- *WhThe*
Paulini, Joseph John 1925- *AmSCAP 80*
Paulirinus, Paulus 1413-1471? *NewGrD 80*
Paull, Alan *Film 2*
Paull, Barberi 1946- *Baker 78*
Paull, Barberi Platt 1945- *AmSCAP 80*
Paull, E T 1858-1924 *AmSCAP 66, -80*
Paull, Harry Major 1854-1934 *NotNAT B, WhThe*
Paull, Jennifer Irene 1944- *WhoMus 72*
Paull, Morgan *WhoHol A*
Paull, Muriel *Film 2*
Paull, Townsend D 1898-1933 *WhScrn 74, -77*
Paulli, Holger Simon 1810-1891 *Baker 78, CnOxB, NewGrD 80*
Paulo, Signor d1835 *NotNAT B*
Paulovics, Geza 1900- *WhoMus 72*
Pauls, Cherry-Willow 1946- *IntWWM 77, -80*
Paulsen, Albert *WhoHol A*
Paulsen, Arno 1900-1969 *WhScrn 74, -77, WhoHol B*
Paulsen, Harald 1895-1954 *WhScrn 74, -77*
Paulsen, Pat *WhoHol A*
Paulson, Arvid 1888- *NotNAT*
Paulson, Gustaf 1898-1966 *Baker 78, NewGrD 80*
Paulson, Guy *AmSCAP 80*
Paulson, Leone 1920- *IntWWM 77, -80*
Paulson, Martin A *ConMuA 80B*
Paulton, Edward Antonio d1939 *NotNAT B*
Paulton, Harry 1842-1917 *NotNAT B, WhThe*
Paulton, Tom d1914 *NotNAT B*
Paulus Abbas De Florentia *NewGrD 80*
Paulus De Praga *NewGrD 80*
Paulus, Olaf 1859-1912 *Baker 78*
Paulus, Stephen Harrison 1949- *ConAmC, IntWWM 77, -80*
Pauly, Reinhard G 1920- *IntWWM 80, NewGrD 80*
Pauly, Rosa 1894-1975 *Baker 78, CmOp*
Pauly, Rosa 1895-1975 *NewEOp 71*
Pauly, Rose 1894-1975 *NewGrD 80*
Pauly, Rose 1895-1975 *MusSN[port]*
Pauly-Dressen, Rose 1894-1975 *NewGrD 80*
Paumann, Conrad 1410?-1473 *Baker 78, MusMk, NewGrD 80, OxMus*
Paumgartner, Bernhard 1887-1971 *Baker 78, NewGrD 80*
Paumier, Alfred 1870-1951 *NotNAT B, WhThe*
Pauncefort, Claire d1924 *NotNAT B*
Pauncefort, George 1870-1942 *Film 2, NotNAT B, WhScrn 74, -77*
Pauncefort, Georgina d1895 *NotNAT B*
Paunetto, Robert Vincenzo 1944- *AmSCAP 80*
Paunovic, Milenko 1889-1924 *Baker 78*
Paupers, The *BiDAmM*
Paur, Emil 1855-1932 *Baker 78, NewEOp 71, NewGrD 80*
Paur, Maria Burger 1862-1899 *BiDAmM*
Pautza, Sabin 1943- *IntWWM 80*
Pauwels, Jean-Englebert 1768-1804 *NewGrD 80*
Pavageau, Alcide 1888-1968 *EncJzS 70*
Pavageau, Alcide 1888-1969 *NewOrJ[port]*
Pavageau, Slow Drag 1888-1968 *EncJzS 70*
Pavageau, Slow Drag 1888-1969 *WhoJazz 72*
Pavan, Marisa 1932- *FilmEn, FilmgC, ForYSC, HalFC 80, IntMPA 77, -75, -76, -78, -79, -80, MotPP, WhoHol A*
Pavanelli, Livio *Film 2*
Pavarana, Virginio 1941- *WhoMus 72*
Pavarotti, Luciano 1935- *BiDAmM, BnBkM 80, CmOp, MusSN[port], NewEOp 71, NewGrD 80, WhoMus 72, WhoOp 76*
Pavek, Janet 1936- *BiE&WWA*
Pavesi, Stefano 1779-1850 *NewGrD 80*
Pavetti, Sally Thomas 1936- *NotNAT*
Paviot, Paul 1925- *DcFM*
Paviour, Paul 1931- *IntWWM 77, -80*
Pavis, Marie *Film 1*
Pavitt, Matthew A 1917- *IntWWM 77*
Pavley, Andreas 1892-1931 *DancEn 78*
Pavlik, John M 1939- *IntMPA 77, -75, -76, -78, -79, -80*
Pavlova, Anna 1881-1931 *CnOxB, DancEn 78[port], NewGrD 80*
Pavlova, Anna 1882-1931 *NotNAT A*
Pavlova, Anna 1885-1931 *WhScrn 74, -77, WhThe, WhoHol B*
Pavlova, Nadezhda 1956- *CnOxB*
Pavlov's Dog *IlEncR*
Pavlow, Muriel *WhoHol A*
Pavlow, Muriel 1921- *FilmEn, FilmgC, HalFC 80, IlWWBF[port], WhoThe 72, -77*
Pavlow, Muriel 1924- *IntMPA 77, -75, -76, -78, -79, -80*
Pavlowa, Anna 1885-1931 *Film 1*
Pavon, Blanca Estela 1926-1949 *WhScrn 74, -77*
Pavona, Pietro Alessandro 1728-1786 *NewGrD 80*
Pavoni, Giuseppe *Film 2*
Pavy, Salathiel 1590-1603 *OxThe*
Pawassar, Klaus 1926- *WhoOp 76*
Pawle, J Lennox 1872-1936 *NotNAT B, WhThe*
Pawle, Lennox 1872-1936 *Film 1, -2, FilmgC, HalFC 80, WhScrn 74, -77, WhoHol B*
Pawley, Eric 1907- *BiE&WWA*
Pawley, Nancy 1901- *WhThe*
Pawley, Thomas 1917- *BlkAmP, MorBAP*
Pawley, William 1905-1952 *NotNAT B, WhScrn 74, -77, WhoHol B*
Pawlova, Vera *Film 2*
Pawlow, Pawel *Film 2*
Pawlowski, Walerian Henryk 1920- *IntWWM 77, -80*
Pawn, Doris 1896- *Film 1, -2, TwYS*
Pawson, Hargrave 1902-1945 *NotNAT B, WhThe*
Paxinou, Katina 1900- *ForYSC, WhoThe 72*
Paxinou, Katina 1900-1972 *OxFilm*
Paxinou, Katina 1900-1973 *BiE&WWA, CnThe, Ent[port], FilmEn, FilmgC, HalFC 80, MotPP, MovMk[port], OxThe, WhScrn 77, WhThe, WhoHol B, WorEFlm*
Paxinou, Katina 1900-1974 *EncWT*
Paxinov, Katina 1900-1973 *NotNAT B*
Paxman, Harry 1894-1965 *NewGrD 80*
Paxton, Gary S *AmSCAP 80*
Paxton, George d1914 *WhScrn 77*
Paxton, George 1916- *BgBands 74, CmpEPM*
Paxton, Glenn *AmSCAP 80*
Paxton, Glenn 1931- *BiE&WWA, NotNAT*
Paxton, Glenn G, Jr. 1921- *AmSCAP 66, ConAmC A*
Paxton, John 1911- *FilmEn, FilmgC, HalFC 80, IntMPA 77, -75, -76, -78, -79, -80, WorEFlm*
Paxton, Phoebe *PupTheA*
Paxton, Sidney 1861-1930 *WhScrn 74, -77, WhoHol B*
Paxton, Stephen 1735-1787 *NewGrD 80, OxMus*
Paxton, Steve *CmpGMD*
Paxton, Sydney 1860-1930 *Film 2, NotNAT B, WhThe*
Paxton, Thomas R 1937- *AmSCAP 66*
Paxton, Tom 1937- *AmSCAP 80, BiDAmM, ConMuA 80A, EncFCWM 69, IlEncR*
Paxton, William 1737-1781 *NewGrD 80, OxMus*
Pay, William *IntMPA 77, -75, -76, -78, -79, -80*
Paycheck, Johnny 1941- *BiDAmM, CounME 74, -74A, EncFCWM 69, IlEncCM[port]*
Payen, Colin 1512?-1559? *NewGrD 80*
Payen, Joc 1875?-1932 *NewOrJ*
Payen, Nicolas 1512?-1559? *NewGrD 80*
Payer, Premysl 1898- *IntWWM 77, -80*
Paymer, Ada 1896- *AmSCAP 66*
Paymer, Marvin E 1921- *AmSCAP 66, -80*
Payn, A A *AmSCAP 80*
Payn, G W *AmSCAP 80*
Payn, Graham 1918- *EncMT, WhoHol A, WhoThe 72, -77*
Payne, Albert 1842-1921 *Baker 78, OxMus*
Payne, Anthony 1936- *Baker 78, NewGrD 80*
Payne, Anthony Edward 1936- *IntWWM 77, -80, WhoMus 72*
Payne, B Iden 1881-1976 *BiE&WWA, NotNAT B*
Payne, Ben Iden 1881-1976 *OxThe*
Payne, Ben Iden 1888-1976 *CnThe, WhThe, WhoThe 72*
Payne, Benjamin *OxMus*
Payne, Bennie 1907- *DrBlPA, WhoJazz 72*
Payne, Benny 1907- *CmpEPM*
Payne, Bruce *ConMuA 80B*
Payne, Cecil McKenzie 1922- *BiDAmM, CmpEPM, EncJzS 70*
Payne, Celia Elizabeth 1907- *WhoMus 72*
Payne, Donald Ray 1933- *BiDAmM*
Payne, Douglas 1875-1965 *Film 2, IlWWBF, WhScrn 74, -77, WhoHol B*
Payne, Douglas 1927- *WhoMus 72*
Payne, Edmund 1865-1914 *NotNAT B, WhThe*
Payne, Edna 1891-1953 *Film 1, WhScrn 77*
Payne, Frank Lynn 1936- *AmSCAP 80, ConAmC*
Payne, Freda 1944?- *DrBlPA*
Payne, Freda 1945- *RkOn 2[port]*
Payne, George Adney d1907 *NotNAT B*
Payne, Jack 1899-1970 *CmpEPM*
Payne, Jimmy 1936- *BiDAmM, EncFCWM 69*
Payne, Jimmy 1939- *IlEncCM*
Payne, John 1912- *CmMov, CmpEPM, FilmEn, FilmgC, ForYSC, HalFC 80, IntMPA 77, -75, -76, -78, -79, -80, MotPP, MovMk[port], What 3[port], WhoHol A, WorEFlm*
Payne, John 1941- *Baker 78, ConAmC*
Payne, John Howard 1791-1852 *BiDAmM, NotNAT A, -B, OxMus, OxThe, PlP&P*
Payne, Julie *WhoHol A*
Payne, Laurence 1919- *FilmgC, HalFC 80, WhThe, WhoHol A*
Payne, Leon Roger 1917- *BiDAmM, EncFCWM 69*
Payne, Leon Roger 1917-1969 *CounME 74, -74A, IlEncCM*
Payne, Louis 1876-1953 *Film 2, WhScrn 74, -77, WhoHol B*
Payne, Millie *WhThe*
Payne, Norman *IntMPA 77, -75, -76, -78, -79, -80*
Payne, Percival 1926- *BiDAmM, EncJzS 70*
Payne, Richard 1880?- *NewOrJ*
Payne, Sally *WhoHol A*
Payne, Sam *CreCan 1*
Payne, Sonny 1926- *EncJzS 70*
Payne, Stanley Vincent *IntWWM 80*
Payne, Victor William 1924- *IntWWM 77, -80, WhoMus 72*
Payne, Walter d1949 *NotNAT B, WhThe*
Payne, William d1967 *WhScrn 77*
Payne, William H 1949- *AmSCAP 80*
Payne, William Louis 1876-1953 *NotNAT B, WhoStg 1906, -1908*
Payne, William McGuire 1943- *ConAmC*
Payne, Zodiac 1922- *EncJzS 70*
Payne-Jennings, Victor 1900-1962 *NotNAT B, WhThe*
Paynter, John Frederick 1931- *IntWWM 80,*

WhoMus 72
Paynton, Harry d1964 *NotNAT B*
Payshe, William *NewGrD 80*
Payson, Albert E 1934- *IntWWM 77*
Payson, Blanche 1881-1964 *Film 1, -2, NotNAT B, WhScrn 74, -77, WhoHol B*
Payton, Barbara 1927-1967 *FilmEn, FilmgC, HalFC 80, MotPP, NotNAT B, WhScrn 74, -77, WhoHol B, WhoHrs 80*
Payton, Barbara 1928-1967 *ForYSC*
Payton, Claude *Film 1*
Payton, Corse 1867-1934 *NotNAT A, -B, WhoHol B, WhoStg 1906, -1908*
Payton, Earlee 1923- *BluesWW[port]*
Payton, Gloria *Film 2*
Payton, Lenny 1921- *AmSCAP 66, -80*
Payton, Lew 1875-1945 *MorBAP, WhScrn 77*
Payton-Wright, Pamela 1941- *PlP&P A[port], WhoHol A, WhoThe 77*
Payvar, Faramarz 1932- *IntWWM 80*
Payvar, Faramarz 1933- *IntWWM 77*
Paz, Juan Carlos 1901-1972 *Baker 78, DcCM, NewGrD 80*
Pazdirek *NewGrD 80*
Pazdirek, Bohumil 1839-1919 *NewGrD 80*
Pazdirek, Frantisek 1848-1915 *NewGrD 80*
Pazdirek, Ludevit Raimund 1850-1914 *NewGrD 80*
Pazdirek, Oldrich 1887-1944 *NewGrD 80*
Pazovsky, Ariy Moiseyevich 1887-1953 *NewGrD 80*
Pchellas, John F W 1795?- *BiDAmM*
Peabody, Eddie 1901?-1970 *CmpEPM*
Peabody, Eddie 1912-1970 *WhoHol B*
Peabody, Eddy 1912-1970 *WhScrn 74, -77*
Peabody, Josephine Preston 1874-1922 *ModWD*
Peabody, Richard *WhoHol A*
Peabody, William Bourne Oliver 1799-1847 *BiDAmM*
Peace, Albert Lister 1844-1912 *Baker 78, OxMus*
Peace, George J 1909- *AmSCAP 66, -80*
Peace, Jakub Jan *NewGrD 80*
Peach, Mary 1934- *FilmgC, ForYSC, HalFC 80, IntMPA 77, -75, -76, -78, -79, -80, WhoHol A*
Peacham, Henry 1576?-1643? *NewGrD 80, OxMus*
Peachena 1948- *DrBlPA*
Peaches And Herb *BiDAmM, RkOn 2[port]*
Peacock, Bertram d1963 *AmPS B, NotNAT B*
Peacock, David 1924- *CreCan 1*
Peacock, Gary 1935- *BiDAmM*
Peacock, Ian Michael *NewYTET*
Peacock, Keith 1931-1966 *WhScrn 74, -77, WhoHol B*
Peacock, Kenneth Howard 1922- *CreCan 1, NewGrD 80*
Peacock, Kim 1901-1966 *WhScrn 74, -77, WhThe, WhoHol B*
Peacock, Lillian 1890?-1918 *WhScrn 77*
Peacock, Trevor 1931- *WhoThe 72, -77*
Peak, Edward Ernest 1951- *IntWWM 77, -80*
Peake, Donald G 1940- *AmSCAP 80*
Peake, Kathleen Hetty *IntWWM 77, WhoMus 72*
Peake, Luise Eitel 1925- *IntWWM 77, -80*
Peake, R B d1847 *NotNAT B*
Peaker, Charles 1899- *NewGrD 80*
Peaker, E J *IntMPA 77, -75, -76, -78, -79, -80, WhoHol A*
Peaks, Mary Jane *AmSCAP 80*
Peal, Gilbert d1964 *NotNAT B*
Peanut Butter Conspiracy *BiDAmM*
Pearce, Adele *FilmEn*
Pearce, Al d1961 *WhoHol B*
Pearce, Alice d1966 *MotPP, WhoHol B*
Pearce, Alice 1913-1966 *FilmEn, FilmgC, HalFC 80*
Pearce, Alice 1917-1966 *BiE&WWA, NotNAT B, WhThe*
Pearce, Alice 1919-1966 *WhScrn 74, -77*
Pearce, Alice 1919-1967 *ForYSC*
Pearce, Alison Margaret 1953- *IntWWM 80*
Pearce, Charles William 1856-1928 *OxMus*
Pearce, Connie 1920- *AmSCAP 66, -80*
Pearce, E H *OxMus*
Pearce, Edward 1560?-1613? *NewGrD 80*
Pearce, Elaine Julia 1946- *IntWWM 77, -80*
Pearce, George C 1865-1940 *Film 1, -2, WhScrn 74, -77, WhoHol B*
Pearce, George Geoffrey 1943- *IntWWM 77, -80*
Pearce, Jacqueline *WhoHrs 80*
Pearce, Judith 1947- *WhoMus 72*
Pearce, Max Macauley 1922- *IntWWM 77, -80*
Pearce, Melvin Michael 1943- *IntWWM 77, -80*
Pearce, Peggy *Film 1*
Pearce, Sam 1909-1971 *BiE&WWA, NotNAT B*
Pearce, Stephen Austen 1836-1900 *Baker 78, BiDAmM*
Pearce, Vera 1896-1966 *WhScrn 74, -77, WhThe, WhoHol B*
Pearcey, Leonard Charles 1938- *IntWWM 77, -80, WhoMus 72*
Pearl, Barry *WhoHol A*
Pearl, Cora *OxMus*
Pearl, Ernest 1902- *IntMPA 77, -75, -76, -78, -79, -80*
Pearl, Eula d1970 *WhScrn 77*
Pearl, Jack 1895- *BiE&WWA, EncMT, JoeFr, What 1[port], WhThe, WhoHol A*
Pearl, Leo J 1901-1977 *AmSCAP 80*
Pearl, Leo J 1907- *AmSCAP 66*
Pearl, Linda *WomWMM B*
Pearl, Louise 1937- *WhoOp 76*
Pearl, Minnie 1912- *BiDAmM, CounME 74[port], -74A, EncFCWM 69, IlEncCM*
Pearl, Minnie 1913- *WhoHol A*
Pearl, Ray *BgBands 74*
Pearl-Mann, Dora 1905- *AmSCAP 66*
Pearlman, Leonard Alexander 1928- *IntWWM 77, -80*
Pearlman, Richard Louis 1937- *WhoOp 76*
Pearlman, Sandy *ConMuA 80B*
Pearls Before Swine *BiDAmM, ConMuA 80A, IlEncR*
Pearlstein, David Bluefield 1947- *AmSCAP 80*
Pearmain, Andrew 1928- *WhoMus 72*
Pearman, Diana Frances 1923- *WhoMus 72*
Pears, Sir Peter 1910- *Baker 78, BnBkM 80, CmOp[port], IntWWM 77, -80, MusMk[port], MusSN[port], NewEOp 71, NewGrD 80[port], OxMus, WhoMus 72, WhoOp 76*
Pearsall, Robert Lucas De 1795-1856 *Baker 78, NewGrD 80, OxMus*
Pearson, Beatrice 1920- *FilmgC, HalFC 80, MotPP, WhThe, WhoHol A*
Pearson, Brett *WhoHol A*
Pearson, Columbus Calvin, Jr. 1932- *BiDAmM, EncJzS 70*
Pearson, Drew 1897-1969 *WhScrn 77*
Pearson, Duke 1932- *EncJzS 70*
Pearson, Fernando Antonio 1951- *AmSCAP 80*
Pearson, George 1875-1973 *FilmEn, FilmgC, HalFC 80, IlWWBF, -A, OxFilm*
Pearson, Henry Hugh *NewGrD 80*
Pearson, Henry Hugo *OxMus*
Pearson, Hesketh 1887-1964 *NotNAT B*
Pearson, Jesse 1936- *ForYSC, WhoHol A*
Pearson, John Frederick 1939- *IntWWM 77*
Pearson, Keith William 1938- *IntWWM 77, -80, WhoMus 72*
Pearson, Leon Morris 1899-1963 *NotNAT B*
Pearson, Lloyd 1897-1966 *FilmgC, HalFC 80, WhScrn 74, -77, WhThe, WhoHol B*
Pearson, Martin *NewGrD 80*
Pearson, Molly 1876-1959 *NotNAT B, WhScrn 77, WhThe, WhoHol B*
Pearson, Richard 1918- *HalFC 80, WhoHol A, WhoThe 72, -77*
Pearson, Robert *ConAmC*
Pearson, Susan G *WhoHol A*
Pearson, Ted d1961 *WhScrn 77*
Pearson, Virginia 1888-1958 *Film 1, -2, ForYSC, MotPP, NotNAT B, TwYS, WhScrn 74, -77, WhoHol B*
Pearson, W Blaine 1892-1918 *WhScrn 77*
Pearson, William Dean 1905- *IntWWM 77, -80, NewGrD 80, WhoMus 72*
Peart, Donald Richard 1909- *IntWWM 80, NewGrD 80, WhoMus 72*
Peary, Harold 1908- *ForYSC, HalFC 80, WhoHol A*
Peasable, James *NewGrD 80*
Pease, Alfred Humphries 1838-1882 *BiDAmM, NewGrD 80*
Pease, Edward 1930- *IntWWM 77, -80*
Pease, Frederick Taylor 1939- *AmSCAP 80*
Pease, Harry 1886-1945 *AmSCAP 66, -80*
Pease, James 1916-1967 *CmOp, NewEOp 71*
Pease, Kent *PupTheA*
Pease, Lois Joyce Elda *IntWWM 77, -80*
Peasible, James *NewGrD 80*
Peaslee, Richard C 1930- *ConAmC*
Peasley, Harriet *PupTheA*
Peattie, Yvonne *WhoHol A*
Pecaro, Daniel T *NewYTET*
Peccatte, Dominique 1810-1874 *NewGrD 80*
Pecci, Desiderio 1587?-1632 *NewGrD 80*
Pecci, Tomaso 1576?-1606 *NewGrD 80*
Peccopia, Pete d1950? *NewOrJ*
Pecelius, Johann Christoph *NewGrD 80*
Pecelli, Asprilio *NewGrD 80*
Pechacek, Franz Xaver 1793-1840 *NewGrD 80*
Pechel, Bartlomiej *NewGrD 80*
Pecheur, Bruce 1942-1973 *WhScrn 77*
Pechin, Gregor *NewGrD 80, -80*
Pechner, Gerhard 1903-1969 *Baker 78*
Pechon, Andre 1600?-1683? *NewGrD 80*
Pecile, Mirna 1943- *WhoOp 76*
Pecin, Gregor *NewGrD 80, -80*
Peck, Bert 1906- *NewOrJ*
Peck, Fletcher 1923- *AmSCAP 66*
Peck, Gregory 1916- *BiDFilm 81, BiE&WWA, CmMov, FilmEn, FilmgC, ForYSC, HalFC 80, IntMPA 77, -75, -76, -78, -79, -80, MotPP, MovMk[port], OxFilm, WhThe, WhoHol A, WhoHrs 80, WorEFlm[port]*
Peck, Murray 1903- *AmSCAP 66, -80*
Peck, Nat 1925- *BiDAmM*
Peck, Norman *Film 2*
Peck, Raymond W 1875-1950 *AmSCAP 66, -80*
Peck, Robert *Film 2*
Peck, Russell 1945- *AmSCAP 80, CpmDNM 78, -80, ConAmC*
Peck, Steven *WhoHol A*
Peckel, Bartlomiej *NewGrD 80*
Peckham, Frances Miles 1893-1959 *WhScrn 74, -77*
Peckham, Margaret 1939- *IntWWM 77, -80*
Peckinpah, Sam *NewYTET*
Peckinpah, Sam 1925- *FilmEn, IntMPA 77, -75, -76, -78, -79, -80*
Peckinpah, Sam 1926- *BiDFilm 81, CmMov, DcFM, FilmgC, HalFC 80, MovMk[port], OxFilm, WorEFlm*
Peckover, Alfred *NewGrD 80*
Pecman, Rudolf 1931- *NewGrD 80*
Pecora, Santo 1902- *CmpEPM, NewOrJ[port], WhoJazz 72*
Pecoraro, Santo 1906- *NewOrJ*
Pecour, Louis Guillaume 1651?-1729 *NewGrD 80*
Pecourt, Louis 1653?-1729 *CnOxB*
Pecourt, Louis 1655-1729 *DancEn 78*
Pecourt, Louis Guillaume 1651?-1729 *NewGrD 80*
Pecsi, Sebestyen 1910- *NewGrD 80*
Pedardo, Antonio *NewGrD 80*
Pedart, Antonio *NewGrD 80*
Peddie, Francis Grove *CreCan 2*
Peddie, Frank 1897-1959 *CreCan 2*
Pedelty, Donovan *IlWWBF*
Pedersen, Ann *WomWMM*
Pedersen, Gunner Moller 1943- *IntWWM 77, -80*
Pedersen, Maren *Film 2*
Pedersen, Mogens 1583?-1623 *NewGrD 80*
Pedersen, Paul Richard 1935- *IntWWM 77, -80*
Pedersen, Tove 1938- *IntWWM 77, -80*
Pederson, Mogens 1583?-1623 *NewGrD 80*
Pederson, Mogens 1585?-1623 *MusMk*
Pederson, Tommy 1920- *AmSCAP 80*
Pedery-Hunt, Dora De *CreCan 1*
Pederzini, Gianna 1906- *CmOp*
Pederzini, Gianna 1908- *WhoMus 72*
Pederzoli, Giovanni Battista d1692? *NewGrD 80*
Pederzuoli, Giovanni Battista d1692? *NewGrD 80*

Pedezzuoli, Giovanni Battista d1692? *NewGrD 80*
Pedgrift, Frederic Henchman *WhThe*
Pedi, Tom 1913- *BiE&WWA, NotNAT, WhoHol A*
Pedicin, Mike *RkOn*
Pedicord, Harry William 1912- *BiE&WWA, NotNAT*
Pedler, Gertrude *Film 2*
Pedrell, Carlos 1878-1941 *Baker 78, NewGrD 80*
Pedrell, Felipe 1841-1922 *Baker 78, BnBkM 80, CmOp, GrComp, NewGrD 80, OxMus*
Pedrick, Gale 1905-1970 *WhThe*
Pedro Del Puerto *NewGrD 80*
Pedrollo, Arrigo 1878-1964 *Baker 78, NewGrD 80*
Pedroski, Walter J 1948- *AmSCAP 80*
Pedroso, Manuel DeMoraes *NewGrD 80*
Pedrotti, Antonio 1901-1975 *Baker 78*
Pedrotti, Carlo 1817-1893 *Baker 78, NewGrD 80*
Peebles, Anthony Gavin Ian *IntWWM 80*
Peebles, Antony Gavin Ian 1946- *IntWWM 77*
Peebles, David d1592? *NewGrD 80*
Peebles-Meyers, Marjorie 1915- *BlkWAB*
Peek, Catherine Louise *AmSCAP 80*
Peek, Daniel Milton 1950- *AmSCAP 80*
Peek, Earl H 1921- *BiDAmM*
Peek, Joseph P *PupTheA*
Peek, Richard M 1927- *ConAmC*
Peek, Thomas Randall 1948- *AmSCAP 80*
Peel, David *ConMuA 80A*
Peel, David 1920?- *WhThe, WhoHrs 80*
Peel, David, And The Lower East Side *BiDAmM*
Peel, Eileen *WhoHol A, WhoThe 72, -77*
Peel, Graham 1877-1937 *OxMus*
Peel, John *OxMus*
Peele, George *PlP&P*
Peele, George 1557?-1596 *CnThe, McGEWD, REnWD[port]*
Peele, George 1558?-1597? *EncWT, Ent, OxThe*
Peele, George 1558?-1598? *NotNAT A, -B*
Peellaert, Augustin-Ghislain, Baron De 1793-1876 *Baker 78*
Peellaert, Augustin-Philippe, Baron de 1793-1876 *NewGrD 80*
Peepers, Mr. *JoeFr*
Peer, Beverly 1912?- *WhoJazz 72*
Peer, Helen 1898-1942 *WhScrn 74, -77, WhoHol B*
Peer, Monique I *ConMuA 80B*
Peer, Ralph 1892-1960 *IlEncCM*
Peer, Ralph Sylvester 1892-1960 *EncFCWM 69, NewGrD 80*
Peerce, Jan *IntWWM 77, -80, WhoMus 72*
Peerce, Jan 1904- *Baker 78, BnBkM 80, CmOp, CmpEPM, MusSN[port], NewEOp 71, NewGrD 80, WhoHol A*
Peerce, Jan 1906- *BiDAmM*
Peerce, Larry 1935?- *FilmEn, FilmgC, HalFC 80, IntMPA 77, -75, -76, -78, -79, -80*
Peerless Annabelle 1878-1961 *WhScrn 74, -77*
Peerless Quartet *CmpEPM*
Peers, Joan 1911-1975 *Film 2, ThFT[port], WhoHol C*
Peerson, Martin 1571?-1650 *MusMk*
Peerson, Martin 1571?-1651 *NewGrD 80*
Peerson, Martin 1572?-1651 *OxMus*
Peery, Rob Roy 1900-1973 *AmSCAP 66, -80, BiDAmM, ConAmC*
Peet, Creighton 1903- *ConAmTC*
Peeters, Flor 1903- *Baker 78, CpmDNM 80, DcCM, IntWWM 77, -80, NewGrD 80, OxMus, WhoMus 72*
Peeters, Giaches 1553?-1591? *NewGrD 80*
Peeters, Jacobus 1553?-1591? *NewGrD 80*
Peeters, Paul 1953- *IntWWM 77, -80*
Peetie Wheatstraw's Buddy *BluesWW[port]*
Peetie's Boy *BluesWW[port]*
Peetrino, Giaches 1553?-1591? *NewGrD 80*
Peetrino, Jacobus 1553?-1591? *NewGrD 80*
Peetrinus, Giaches 1553?-1591? *NewGrD 80*
Peetrinus, Jacobus 1553?-1591? *NewGrD 80*
Peffer, Crawford A d1961 *NotNAT B*
Peg-Leg Sam *BluesWW[port]*
Peg Pete *BluesWW[port]*
Pegasus *CreCan 2*
Pegay, Sophie *Film 2*
Pegg, Vester d1951 *Film 2, WhoHol B*
Peggy, Baby *Film 1*
Pegler, Westbrook 1894-1969 *WhScrn 77*
Pegolotti, Tomaso *NewGrD 80*
Pegram, Wayne Frank *AmSCAP 80*
Peguilhan, Aimeric De *NewGrD 80*
Peharda, Zdenko Ivan 1923- *IntWWM 77, -80, WhoOp 76*
Pehkonen, Elis 1942- *DcCM*
Pehrson, Joseph Ralph 1950- *AmSCAP 80*
Peiffer, Bernard 1922- *BiDAmM, EncJzS 70*
Peiko, Nicolai 1916- *Baker 78*
Peiko, Nikolai 1916- *DcCM*
Peil, Charles Edward d1962 *NotNAT B*
Peil, Ed 1888-1958 *TwYS*
Peil, Edward 1888-1958 *Film 1, -2, ForYSC, MotPP, NotNAT B, WhScrn 74, -77, WhoHol B*
Peil, Edward, Jr. 1908-1962 *Film 2, WhScrn 74, -77, WhoHol B*
Peile, Frederick Kinsey 1862-1934 *NotNAT A, -B, WhThe*
Peile, Kinsey *Film 2*
Peine, Josh *WhoHol A*
Peinemann, Edith 1939- *IntWWM 80, NewGrD 80*
Peirce, Evelyn *WhScrn 74, -77*
Peire Cardenal 1180?-1278? *NewGrD 80*
Peirick, Elyse Mach 1941- *IntWWM 77, -80*
Peirol 1160?-1221? *NewGrD 80*
Peiser, Judy 1945- *WomWMM B*
Peisley, Frederick 1904- *WhoHol A, WhoThe 72, -77*
Peixe, Cesar Guerra *DcCM*
Peixinho, Jorge 1940- *Baker 78, DcCM, NewGrD 80*
Peixoto, Mario 1912- *DcFM*
Pejman, Ahmad 1935- *IntWWM 77, -80*
Pejovic, Roksanda 1929- *IntWWM 77, -80*
Pekalski, Jozef Tadeusz Benedykt d1761? *NewGrD 80*
Pekel, Bartlomiej d1670? *NewGrD 80*
Pekelis, Mikhail Samoylovich 1899-1979 *NewGrD 80*
Pekell, Bartlomiej d1670? *NewGrD 80*
Pekiel, Bartlomiej d1670? *NewGrD 80*
Pekov, Mihail 1941- *Baker 78*
Pelagius II *OxMus*
Pelasula, Sonja 1949- *IntWWM 77*
Pelchat, Emma Naky 1897- *IntWWM 77*
Pele, Robert Le *NewGrD 80*
Pelemans, Willem 1901- *Baker 78, NewGrD 80*
Pelesier, Victor *NewGrD 80*
Pelham *DcPup*
Pelham, Meta d1948 *NotNAT B*
Pelikan, Maria 1920- *AmSCAP 80*
Pelinski, Ramon Adolfo 1932- *IntWWM 77, -80*
Pelio, Giovanni *NewGrD 80*
Pelish, Thelma *WhoHol A*
Peliso *NewGrD 80*
Pelissier, Anthony 1912- *FilmEn, FilmgC, HalFC 80, IlWWBF*
Pelissier, Harry Gabriel 1874-1913 *NotNAT B, OxThe, WhThe*
Pelissier, Marie 1707-1749 *NewGrD 80*
Pelissier, Victor *Baker 78, OxMus*
Pelissier, Victor 174-?-1820? *NewGrD 80*
Pelissier, Victor 1760-1820 *BiDAmM*
Pell, Dave 1925- *AmSCAP 80, CmpEPM*
Pell, David 1925- *AmSCAP 66*
Pellaert, Augustin-Philippe *NewGrD 80*
Pellan, Alfred 1906- *CreCan 2*
Pelland, Alfred *CreCan 2*
Pellant, Jiri 1950- *IntWWM 77, -80*
Pellatt, John *IntMPA 77, -75, -76, -78, -79, -80*
Pelleg, Frank 1910-1968 *NewGrD 80*
Pellegrin, Claude Mathieu 1682-1763 *NewGrD 80*
Pellegrin, Raymond 1925- *FilmEn*
Pellegrin, Simon-Joseph 1663-1745 *NewGrD 80*
Pellegrini, Al 1921- *AmSCAP 66, -80*
Pellegrini, Domenico d1662? *NewGrD 80*
Pellegrini, Ernesto P 1932- *CpmDNM 75, ConAmC*
Pellegrini, Eugene *WhoHol A*
Pellegrini, Ferdinando 1715?-1766? *NewGrD 80*
Pellegrini, Giulio *NewGrD 80*
Pellegrini, Maria *WhoMus 72, WhoOp 76*
Pellegrini, Pete 1885?-1940 *NewOrJ*
Pellegrini, Valeriano *NewGrD 80*
Pellegrini, Vincenzo d1632? *NewGrD 80*
Pellegrini, Vincenzo d1636 *Baker 78*
Pellegrino, Il *NewGrD 80*
Pellegrino, Alfred R 1921- *AmSCAP 80*
Pellegrino, Ferdinando *NewGrD 80*
Pellegrino, John 1930- *IntWWM 77, -80*
Pellegrino, Joseph Vito, Jr. 1944- *AmSCAP 80*
Pellegrino, Ronald 1940- *ConAmC*
Pellerin, Jean-Victor 1889- *McGEWD*
Pellerite, James John 1926- *IntWWM 77, -80, WhoMus 72*
Pellesier, Victor *NewGrD 80*
Pellesini, Giovanni 1526?-1612 *OxThe*
Pellesini, Vittoria Piissimi *OxThe*
Pelletier, Denise 1928- *CreCan 2*
Pelletier, Gilles *CreCan 1*
Pelletier, Louis Philippe 1945- *IntWWM 80*
Pelletier, Wilfred 1896- *BiDAmM*
Pelletier, Wilfrid 1896- *Baker 78, CreCan 2, IntWWM 77, -80, NewGrD 80*
Pelletier, Yvonne *Film 2*
Pellicani, Giovanni Battista Sanuti *NewGrD 80*
Pelliccia, Arrigo 1912- *NewGrD 80*
Pellicer, Pilar 1940-1964 *ForYSC*
Pellicer, Pina 1940-1964 *MotPP, WhScrn 74, -77, WhoHol B*
Pellico, Silvio 1789-1854 *McGEWD[port]*
Pellini, Giovanni 1912- *IntWWM 77, -80*
Pellio, Giovanni *NewGrD 80*
Pellish, Bert Jay 1914- *AmSCAP 66, -80*
Pellisson *NewGrD 80*
Pello, Giovanni *NewGrD 80*
Pelly, Farrell 1891-1963 *NotNAT B, WhScrn 74, -77, WhoHol B*
Pelnar, Ivana 1946- *IntWWM 77, -80*
Peloquin, C Alexander 1918- *ConAmC*
Peloubet, Chabrier 1806-1885 *NewGrD 80*
Pelton-Jones, Frances 1863-1946 *Baker 78*
Pelz, Walter L 1926- *ConAmC*
Pelzer, George *Film 2*
Peman, Jose Maria 1897- *CroCD, ModWD*
Peman Y Pemartin, Jose Maria 1897- *McGEWD[port]*
Pembaur, Joseph, Jr. 1875-1950 *Baker 78*
Pembaur, Joseph, Sr. 1848-1923 *Baker 78*
Pembaur, Karl Maria 1876-1939 *Baker 78*
Pember, Ron 1934- *WhoThe 72, -77*
Pemberton, Bill 1918- *EncJzS 70, WhoJazz 72*
Pemberton, Brock 1885-1950 *NotNAT B, WhThe, WhoHol B*
Pemberton, Henry W 1875-1952 *NotNAT B, WhScrn 74, -77, WhoHol B*
Pemberton, John Wyndham 1883-1947 *NotNAT B, WhThe*
Pemberton, Keith Rutland 1931- *WhoMus 72*
Pemberton, Sir Max 1863-1950 *NotNAT B, WhThe*
Pemberton, Reece 1914- *PlP&P, WhoThe 72, -77*
Pemberton, Roger *AmSCAP 80*
Pemberton, Sophie 1869-1959 *CreCan 1*
Pemberton, Thomas Edgar 1849-1905 *NotNAT B, OxThe*
Pemberton, William McLane 1918- *EncJzS 70*
Pemberton-Billing, Robin 1929- *WhoThe 72, -77*
Pembleton, Georgia *Film 2*
Pembroke, George d1972 *WhScrn 77, WhoHol B*
Pembroke, Percy *Film 2*
Pembroke, Scott *TwYS A*
Pembrook, P S *Film 1*
Pena, Angel 1921- *IntWWM 77, -80*
Pena, Julio 1912-1972 *WhScrn 77*
Pena, Martins 1815-1848 *CnThe, REnWD[port]*
Pena, Paul 1950- *AmSCAP 80*
Pena, Ralph R 1927-1969 *AmSCAP 66, -80, BiDAmM, EncJzS 70, WhScrn 74, -77*
Pena Costa, Joaquim 1873-1944 *NewGrD 80*
Pena Costa, Joaquin 1873-1944 *Baker 78, NewGrD 80*

Pena Y Goni, Antonio 1846-1896 *Baker 78, NewGrD 80*
Penalosa, Francisco De 1470?-1528 *NewGrD 80*
Penalosa, Juan De 1515?-1579 *NewGrD 80*
Penalva, Jose DeAlmeida 1924- *IntWWM 77, -80*
Penberthy, Beverly *WhoHol A*
Penberthy, James 1917- *NewGrD 80*
Penbroke, Clifford *Film 2*
Penbrook, Harry 1887-1960 *WhScrn 74, -77*
Penbrook, Henry d1952 *WhoHol B*
Pencerdd Gwalia *NewGrD 80*
Pencerdd Gwynedd *NewGrD 80*
Pencik, Jindrich 1930- *IntWWM 77, -80*
Penckel, Bartlomiej *NewGrD 80*
Penco DeLaVega, Joseph 1650-1703 *OxThe*
Pendarvis, Paul 1907- *BgBands 74, CmpEPM*
Pendennis, Rose d1943 *NotNAT B*
Pender, Doris 1900-1975 *WhScrn 77*
Penderecki, Krysztof 1933- *CompSN[port]*
Penderecki, Krzystof 1933- *CmOp, CnOxB, MusMk[port]*
Penderecki, Krzysztof 1933- *Baker 78, BnBkM 80, CpmDNM 78, DcCom&M 79, DcCM, IntWWM 77, -80, NewGrD 80[port]*
Pendergraft, Fred Albert 1938- *IntWWM 77*
Pendle, Karin Swanson 1938- *IntWWM 80*
Pendle, Karin Swanson 1939- *IntWWM 77*
Pendleton, Austin 1940- *HalFC 80, WhoHol A, WhoThe 77*
Pendleton, David 1937- *DrBlPA*
Pendleton, Gaylord *Film 2*
Pendleton, Nat d1967 *MotPP, WhoHol B*
Pendleton, Nat 1895-1967 *FilmEn, FilmgC, HalFC 80, HolCA[port], MovMk[port]*
Pendleton, Nat 1899-1967 *Film 2, ForYSC, WhScrn 74, -77*
Pendleton, Nat 1903-1967 *Vers A[port]*
Pendleton, Steve *WhoHol A*
Pendleton, Wyman 1916- *WhoHol A, WhoThe 72, -77*
Pene DuBois, Raoul 1914- *BiE&WWA, NotNAT*
Penella, Emma 1930- *FilmAG WE*
Penet, Hilaire 1501?- *NewGrD 80*
Penet, Hylaire 1501?- *NewGrD 80*
Penfield, Smith Newell 1837-1920 *Baker 78, BiDAmM*
Pengilly, Sylvia 1935- *ConAmC*
Penguins, The *AmPS A, RkOn[port]*
Penhaligon, Susan 1950- *HalFC 80, IlWWBF*
Penherski, Zbigniew 1935- *Baker 78, IntWWM 77, -80, NewGrD 80*
Penicka, Miloslav 1935- *IntWWM 77, -80*
Penigk, Johann Peter *NewGrD 80*
Peninger, James David 1929- *AmSCAP 80, ConAmC*
Penkethman, William d1725 *OxThe*
Penkova, Reni Todorova 1935- *WhoOp 76*
Penland, Arnold Clifford, Jr. 1933- *IntWWM 77, -80*
Penland, Ralph Morris 1953- *EncJzS 70*
Penley, Arthur 1881-1954 *WhThe*
Penley, Belville S d1940 *NotNAT B*
Penley, Sampson d1838 *NotNAT B*
Penley, William Sydney 1851-1912 *NotNAT B, WhThe*
Penley, William Sydney 1852-1912 *OxThe*
Penman, Lea 1895-1962 *ForYSC, NotNAT B, WhScrn 74, -77, WhoHol B*
Penn, Arthur 1922- *AmFD, BiDFilm 81, BiE&WWA, DcFM, FilmEn, FilmgC, HalFC 80, IntMPA 77, -75, -76, -78, -79, -80, MovMk[port], NotNAT, OxFilm, WhoThe 72, -77, WorEFlm*
Penn, Arthur A 1875-1941 *AmSCAP 66, -80, Baker 78, ConAmC*
Penn, Bill 1931- *WhThe, WhoThe 72*
Penn, Ernest *NewOrJ*
Penn, Leonard 1907-1975 *ForYSC, WhScrn 77, WhoHol C*
Penn, Sammy 1902-1969 *NewOrJ*
Penn, William d1946? *NewOrJ[port]*
Penn, William 1598?- *OxThe*
Penn, William Albert 1943- *AmSCAP 80, CpmDNM 77, ConAmC*
Penna, Dennis Roy 1947- *AmSCAP 80*
Penna, Lorenzo 1613-1693 *Baker 78, NewGrD 80*
Penna, Luiz Carlos Martins 1815-1848 *OxThe*
Penna, Nilson 1916- *DancEn 78*
Pennard *NewGrD 80*
Pennario, Leonard 1924- *AmSCAP 66, -80, Baker 78, ConAmC, MusSN[port], NewGrD 80, WhoMus 72*
Pennauer, Anton 1784?-1837 *NewGrD 80*
Penne, Antoine De d1616? *NewGrD 80*
Pennebaker, D A 1930- *FilmEn, WorEFlm*
Pennebaker, Donn Alan 1930- *OxFilm, WomWMM*
Pennell, Daniel *Film 2*
Pennell, Larry *ForYSC, WhoHol A*
Pennell, R O 1861-1934 *WhoHol B*
Pennell, Richard O 1861-1934 *Film 2, WhScrn 74, -77*
Pennequin, Jean *NewGrD 80*
Penner, Joe d1941 *MotPP, WhoHol B*
Penner, Joe 1904-1941 *FilmgC, ForYSC, HalFC 80[port]*
Penner, Joe 1905-1941 *JoeFr[port], WhScrn 74, -77*
Penney, Edward Joseph, Jr. 1925- *AmSCAP 66, -80*
Penney, Jennifer 1946- *CnOxB*
Pennick, Jack 1895-1964 *Film 2, ForYSC, HalFC 80, MotPP, TwYS, Vers B[port], WhScrn 74, -77, WhoHol B*
Pennick, Ronald Jack 1895-1964 *NotNAT B*
Penniman, Richard Wayne 1935- *BluesWW[port], DrBlPA*
Penningroth, Phil 1943- *NatPD[port]*
Pennington, Ann d1971 *AmPS B, CmpEPM, WhoHol B*
Pennington, Ann 1892-1971 *WhThe*
Pennington, Ann 1893-1971 *BiE&WWA, NotNAT B, What 2[port]*
Pennington, Ann 1894-1971 *EncMT, WhScrn 74, -77*
Pennington, Ann 1895-1971 *Film 1, -2, TwYS*
Pennington, Edith Mae d1974 *WhScrn 77, WhoHol B*
Pennington, John *ConAmC*
Pennington, Lily May 1917- *BiDAmM*
Pennington, Ray 1933- *BiDAmM, EncFCWM 69*
Pennington, Ron *ConAmTC*
Pennington, W H d1923 *NotNAT B*
Pennington-Richards, C M 1911- *FilmgC, HalFC 80, IlWWBF*
Pennino-Coppola, Italia 1918- *AmSCAP 80*
Pennisi, Francesco 1934- *NewGrD 80*
Pennsylvanians *BiDAmM*
Penny, Barbara 1929- *IntWWM 77*
Penny, Frank 1895-1946 *WhScrn 74, -77, WhoHol B*
Penny, Frederick David Linley 1896- *WhoMus 72*
Penny, George Barlow 1861-1934 *Baker 78, BiDAmM*
Penny, George Frederick 1915- *WhoMus 72*
Penny, Hank 1918- *IlEncCM*
Penny, Laura *PupTheA*
Penny, Lee *AmSCAP 80*
Pennycook, B 1949- *IntWWM 80*
Pennycuicke, Andrew 1620- *OxThe*
Penrod, Jerry Louis 1951- *AmSCAP 80*
Penrod, Mabel A *PupTheA*
Penrose, Charles d1952 *WhoHol B*
Penrose, John 1917- *WhThe*
Penrose, Timothy Nicholas 1949- *IntWWM 80*
Pensom, Beresford Alfred 1908- *WhoMus 72*
Penson, William 1776?-1829? *NewGrD 80*
Pentagons, The *RkOn*
Pentangle, The *ConMuA 80A, IlEncR*
Pente, Emilio 1860-1929 *Baker 78*
Pentenrieder, Franz Xaver 1813-1867 *Baker 78*
Pentland, Barbara 1912- *Baker 78, CreCan 1, DcCM, IntWWM 77, -80, NewGrD 80*
Penwarden, Duncan *Film 2*
Penzel, Christian Friedrich 1737-1801 *NewGrD 80*
Penzel, Erich 1930- *IntWWM 77, -80*
Penzoldt, Ernst 1892-1955 *CnMD, McGEWD[port], ModWD*
Peon, Ramon 190-?- *DcFM*
People, The *RkOn 2[port]*
People's Choice *RkOn 2A*
Pepa, Bonafe *Film 1*
Pepe, Carmine *ConAmC*
Peperara, Laura *NewGrD 80*
Pepin, Clermont 1926- *Baker 78, CreCan 2, DcCM, NewGrD 80*
Pepin, Jean Joseph Clermont *CreCan 2*
Pepito d1975 *WhoHol C*
Peple, Edward Henry 1867- *WhThe, WhoStg 1906, -1908*
Pepock, August 1887-1967 *Baker 78*
Pepoli, Carlo 1796-1881 *NewGrD 80*
Peppard, George *IntMPA 77, -75, -76, -78, -79, -80, MotPP, WhoHol A*
Peppard, George 1928- *FilmEn*
Peppard, George 1929- *FilmgC, ForYSC, HalFC 80*
Peppard, George 1933- *MovMk[port], WorEFlm*
Pepper *Film 1*
Pepper, Alan *ConMuA 80B*
Pepper, Art 1925- *CmpEPM, EncJzS 70, IlEncJ, NewGrD 80*
Pepper, Arthur Edward 1925- *BiDAmM, EncJzS 70*
Pepper, Barbara d1969 *MotPP, WhoHol B*
Pepper, Barbara 1912-1969 *HalFC 80, ThFT[port]*
Pepper, Barbara 1916-1969 *ForYSC, Vers B[port], WhScrn 74, -77*
Pepper, Buddy 1922- *AmSCAP 66, -80, WhoHol A*
Pepper, Cynthia *ForYSC, WhoHol A*
Pepper, George Douglas 1903-1962 *CreCan 1*
Pepper, John Henry 1821-1900 *MagIlD*
Pepper, L J *IntMPA 77, -75, -76, -78, -79, -80*
Pepper, Robert C 1916-1964 *WhScrn 74, -77*
Pepper Young's Family *What 4[port]*
Peppercorn, Carl *IntMPA 77, -75, -76, -78, -79, -80*
Peppermint Rainbow *RkOn 2A*
Peppers, William Andrew 1921-1961 *AmSCAP 80*
Peppiatt-Aylesworth *NewYTET*
Peppin, Geraldine *IntWWM 77, -80, WhoMus 72*
Peppin, Mary *IntWWM 77, -80, WhoMus 72*
Pepping, Ernst 1901- *Baker 78, DcCM, IntWWM 77, -80, NewGrD 80*
Pepusch, Johann Christoph 1667-1752 *BnBkM 80, MusMk, NewEOp 71, NewGrD 80[port]*
Pepusch, John Christopher 1667-1752 *Baker 78, BnBkM 80, NotNAT B, OxMus*
Pepys, Samuel 1633-1703 *DcPup, NewGrD 80, NotNAT B, OxMus, OxThe, PlP&P*
Peque, Paul 1906?- *NewOrJ*
Per, Il *NewGrD 80*
Perabo, Ernst 1845-1920 *Baker 78, NewGrD 80*
Perabo, Johann Ernst 1845-1920 *BiDAmM*
Perabovi, Filippo Maria *NewGrD 80*
Perabuoni, Filippo Maria *NewGrD 80*
Peragallo, Mario 1910- *Baker 78, NewGrD 80*
Perahia, Murray 1947- *Baker 78, BiDAmM, IntWWM 77, -80, NewGrD 80*
Perakos, Sperie P 1915- *IntMPA 77, -75, -76, -78, -79, -80*
Peralta, Angela 1845-1883 *NewGrD 80*
Peralta Escudero, Bernardo De d1617 *NewGrD 80*
Peranda, Marco Gioseppe 1625?-1675 *NewGrD 80*
Perande, Marco Gioseppe 1625?-1675 *NewGrD 80*
Perandi, Marco Gioseppe 1625?-1675 *NewGrD 80*
Perandreu, Jose *NewGrD 80*
Peraza *NewGrD 80*
Peraza, Armando 1924- *BiDAmM, EncJzS 70*
Peraza, Francisco De 1564-1598 *NewGrD 80*
Peraza, Francisco De 1597?-1636? *NewGrD 80*
Peraza, Jeronimo 1574-1604 *NewGrD 80*
Peraza, Jeronimo De 1550?-1617 *NewGrD 80*
Perazzo, Joseph William 1943- *AmSCAP 80*
Perceval, Julio 1903-1963 *Baker 78*
Perceval-Clark, Perceval 1881-1938 *NotNAT B, WhThe*
Perciful, Jack T 1925- *BiDAmM, EncJzS 70*
Percival, Allen Dain 1925- *IntWWM 77, -80, NewGrD 80, WhoMus 72*
Percival, Arlene *WhScrn 77*

Percival, Cyril *Film 2*
Percival, Horace d1961 *NotNAT B*
Percival, John 1927- *CnOxB*
Percival, Lance 1933- *FilmgC, HalFC 80, IntMPA 77, -75, -76, -78, -79, -80*
Percival, Walter C 1887-1934 *Film 2, NotNAT B, WhScrn 74, -77, WhoHol B*
Percy, Betty *PupTheA*
Percy, David *Film 2*
Percy, Edward 1891-1968 *BiE&WWA, NotNAT B, WhThe*
Percy, Eileen 1899-1973 *FilmEn, What 4[port]*
Percy, Eileen 1901-1973 *Film 1, -2, MotPP, TwYS, WhScrn 77, WhoHol B*
Percy, Esme Saville 1887-1957 *EncWT, FilmgC, HalFC 80, OxThe, PlP&P, WhScrn 74, -77, WhoHol B*
Percy, George d1962 *NotNAT B*
Percy, Richard Arthur 1944- *IntWWM 80*
Percy, S Esme 1887-1957 *NotNAT B, WhThe*
Percy, Staffan W 1946- *IntWWM 80*
Percy, Thomas 1729-1811 *OxMus*
Percy, William Alexander 1885-1942 *BiDAmM*
Percy, William Stratford 1872-1946 *NotNAT B, WhThe*
Percyval, T Wigney 1865- *WhThe*
Perdacher, Walter 1930- *WhoOp 76*
Perdeck, Rudolf 1925- *IntWWM 77, -80*
Perdeholtz, Lucas *NewGrD 80*
Perdigo *NewGrD 80*
Perdomo Escobar, Jose Ignacio 1917- *NewGrD 80*
Perdue, Derelys *TwYS, WhoHol A*
Perdue, Derlys *Film 2*
Peregrino Di Zanetto *NewGrD 80*
Pereira, Domingos Nunes d1729 *NewGrD 80*
Pereira, Hal 1910?- *FilmEn, IntMPA 77, -75, -76, -78, -79, -80, WhoHrs 80, WorEFlm*
Pereira, Marcos Soares 1595?-1655 *NewGrD 80*
Pereira, Mario 1934- *FilmAG WE*
Pereira-Arias, Antonio 1929- *IntWWM 80*
Pereira DosSantos, Nelson *DcFM*
Pereira-Salas, Eugenio 1904- *Baker 78, NewGrD 80*
Perelman, S J 1904-1979 *BiE&WWA, ConDr 73, -77, FilmEn, FilmgC, HalFC 80, McGEWD, NotNAT*
Perelmuth, Jacob Pincus *NewGrD 80*
Perenyi, Miklos 1948- *IntWWM 77, -80, NewGrD 80, WhoMus 72*
Perera, Ronald Christopher 1941- *AmSCAP 80, CpmDNM 72, -79, ConAmC*
Peress, Maurice 1930- *Baker 78, NewGrD 80*
Perestiani, Ivan *Film 2*
Peretola, Decimo Corinella Da *NewGrD 80*
Peretti, Hugo 1916- *AmSCAP 66, -80, ConMuA 80B*
Peretti, Serge 1910- *CnOxB, DancEn 78*
Peretz, Isaac Leib 1852-1915 *OxThe*
Peretz, Isaac Leob 1851-1915 *NotNAT B*
Peretz, Isaac Loeb 1852-1915 *CnMD, McGEWD*
Peretz, Susan *WhoHol A*
Peretz, Yitschok Leybush 1852-1915 *EncWT*
Peretz, Yitskhok Leybush 1852-1915 *CnThe, ModWD, REnWD[port]*
Pereyaslavec, Valentina 1907- *CnOxB*
Perez, David 1711-1778 *Baker 78, NewGrD 80*
Perez, Davide 1711-1778 *NewGrD 80*
Perez, Jose *WhoHol A*
Perez, Juan Gines 1548?-1612? *NewGrD 80*
Perez, Lou 1924- *AmSCAP 66*
Perez, Louis A 1928- *AmSCAP 80*
Perez, Manuel 1873-1946 *NewOrJ[port]*
Perez, Manuel 1879-1946 *BiDAmM*
Perez, Manuel 1880?-1946? *WhoJazz 72*
Perez, Pepito 1896-1975 *WhScrn 77*
Perez, Rudy 1929- *CmpGMD[port], CnOxB*
Perez Casas, Bartolomeo 1873-1956 *Baker 78*
Perez DeAlba, Alonso *NewGrD 80*
Perez DeAlbeniz, Mateo *NewGrD 80*
Perez Galdos, Benito 1843-1920 *CnMD, McGEWD[port], ModWD, OxThe*
Perez-Galdos, Benito 1845-1920 *NotNAT B*
Perez-Gutierrez, Mariano 1932- *IntWWM 80*
Perez Martinez, Vicente d1800 *NewGrD 80*
Perez Roldan, Juan 1610?-1671? *NewGrD 80*
Perfall, Karl, Freiherr Von 1824-1907 *Baker 78, NewGrD 80*
Perfect, Cyril Percy Absell 1905- *WhoMus 72*
Pergament, Harvey *IntMPA 77, -75, -76, -78, -79, -80*
Pergament, Moses 1893-1977 *Baker 78, NewGrD 80*
Pergament, Ruvim 1906-1965 *NewGrD 80*
Perger, Richard Von 1854-1911 *Baker 78*
Pergola, Domenico Evangelisti Dalla *NewGrD 80*
Pergola, Edith Della *CreCan 1*
Pergola, Luciano Della *CreCan 1*
Pergolese, Giovanni Battista 1710-1736 *DcPup, OxMus*
Pergolesi, Giovanni Battista 1710-1736 *Baker 78, BnBkM 80, CmOp, CmpBCM, DcCom&M 79, DcPup, GrComp[port], MusMk, NewEOp 71, NewGrD 80[port]*
Peri, Achille 1812-1880 *NewGrD 80*
Peri, Jacopo 1561-1633 *Baker 78, BnBkM 80, CmOp, CmpBCM, GrComp, MusMk, NewEOp 71, NewGrD 80[port], OxMus*
Perianez, Pedro 1540?-1613? *NewGrD 80*
Pericaud, Louis d1909 *NotNAT B*
Pericic, Vlastimir 1927- *Baker 78, IntWWM 77, -80, NewGrD 80*
Pericoli, Emilio 1928- *RkOn*
Perier, Etienne 1931- *FilmgC, HalFC 80*
Perier, Francois 1919- *EncWT, FilmEn, FilmgC, HalFC 80, OxFilm, WhoHol A*
Perier, Jean 1869-1954 *Baker 78, NewGrD 80*
Peries, Lester James 1921- *DcFM, WorEFlm*
Perile, Joseph *NewGrD 80*
Perinal, Georges 1897-1965 *CmMov, DcFM, FilmEn, FilmgC, HalFC 80, IntMPA 77, -75, -76, -78, -79, -80, OxFilm, WorEFlm*
Perinello, Carlo 1877-1942 *Baker 78*
Perinet *NewGrD 80*
Perini, Annibale 1560?-1596 *NewGrD 80*
Perino Degli Organi 1523-1552 *NewGrD 80*
Perino Fiorentino 1523-1552 *NewGrD 80*
Periolat, George d1960 *Film 1, -2, ForYSC, TwYS*
Periolat, George 1876-1940 *WhScrn 74, -77*
Periolot, George 1876-1940 *WhoHol B*
Periot, Arthur 1899-1929 *WhScrn 74, -77*
Periquin 1912-1957 *WhScrn 74, -77*
Peris, Malinee *WhoMus 72*
Perisson, Jean Marie 1924- *WhoOp 76*
Perissone, Cambio 1520?- *NewGrD 80*
Perissone, Francesco Bonardo *NewGrD 80*
Perito, Nick 1924- *AmSCAP 66, -80*
Peritz, Bernice Perry 1924- *AmSCAP 80*
Perkholtz, Lucas *NewGrD 80*
Perkin, Maimie 1919- *IntWWM 80*
Perkins, Anthony 1932- *BiDFilm 81, BiE&WWA, FilmEn, FilmgC, ForYSC, HalFC 80, IntMPA 77, -75, -76, -78, -79, -80, MotPP, MovMk[port], NotNAT, OxFilm, WhoHol A, WhoHrs 80, WhoThe 72, -77, WorEFlm*
Perkins, Bill 1924- *EncJzS 70*
Perkins, Carl *ConMuA 80A, WhoHol A*
Perkins, Carl 1928-1958 *IlEncJ*
Perkins, Carl 1932- *BiDAmM, CounME 74[port], -74A, EncFCWM 69, IlEncCM[port], IlEncR, RkOn[port]*
Perkins, Charles Callahan 1823-1886 *Baker 78, BiDAmM*
Perkins, Dave 1868?-1926 *NewOrJ*
Perkins, David Fessenden d1962 *NotNAT B*
Perkins, Dorothy Burrows 1884- *DancEn 78*
Perkins, Emily Swan 1866-1941 *BiDAmM*
Perkins, Eugene 1932- *BlkAmP, MorBAP*
Perkins, Francis Davenport 1897-1970 *Baker 78*
Perkins, Frank S 1908- *AmSCAP 66, -80, CmpEPM*
Perkins, Gary *ConMuA 80B*
Perkins, Gil *WhoHol A*
Perkins, Henry Southwick 1833-1914 *Baker 78, BiDAmM*
Perkins, Huel Davis 1924- *AmSCAP 80*
Perkins, Jean Edward 1899-1923 *WhScrn 74, -77, WhoHol B*
Perkins, Joe Willie 1913- *BluesWW[port]*
Perkins, John *MorBAP*
Perkins, John Henry Rowland, II 1934- *IntMPA 77, -75, -76, -78, -79, -80*
Perkins, John MacIvor 1935- *Baker 78, ConAmC*
Perkins, Julius Edson 1845-1875 *BiDAmM*
Perkins, Laurence 1954- *IntWWM 80*
Perkins, Leeman Lloyd 1932- *IntWWM 77, -80, NewGrD 80*
Perkins, Luther Monroe 1928-1968 *BiDAmM*
Perkins, Millie 1938- *FilmEn*
Perkins, Millie 1939- *FilmgC, ForYSC, HalFC 80, MotPP, WhoHol A*
Perkins, Orson 1802-1882 *BiDAmM*
Perkins, Osgood 1892-1937 *FamA&A[port], FilmgC, ForYSC, HalFC 80, NotNAT B, PlP&P, WhScrn 74, -77, WhThe, WhoHol B*
Perkins, Osgood 1893-1937 *Film 2*
Perkins, Ray 1896-1969 *AmSCAP 66, -80, Film 2*
Perkins, Richard 1585?-1650 *OxThe*
Perkins, Robert W *IntMPA 75, -76*
Perkins, Tony *MotPP*
Perkins, Voltaire *ForYSC, WhoHol A*
Perkins, Walter 1870-1925 *Film 1, -2, NotNAT B, WhScrn 74, -77, WhoHol B*
Perkins, Walter 1932- *BiDAmM*
Perkins, Walton 1847-1929 *Baker 78*
Perkins, William 1941- *Baker 78*
Perkins, William Oscar 1831-1902 *Baker 78, BiDAmM*
Perkins, William Reese 1924- *BiDAmM, EncJzS 70*
Perkinson, Coleridge-Taylor 1932- *AmSCAP 80, BiDAmM, BlkCS[port], ConAmC, DrBlPA*
Perkowski, Piotr 1901- *Baker 78, DcCM, IntWWM 77, -80, NewGrD 80*
Perl, Arnold 1914-1971 *BiE&WWA, NotNAT B*
Perl, Lothar 1910-1975 *AmSCAP 66, -80, ConAmC A*
Perla, Brenda *WomWMM*
Perla, Gene August 1940- *AmSCAP 80, EncJzS 70*
Perlasca, Bernardino *NewGrD 80*
Perlberg, William 1899-1968 *FilmgC, WorEFlm*
Perlberg, William 1899-1969 *FilmEn, HalFC 80*
Perle, George 1915- *AmSCAP 66, -80, Baker 78, BnBkM 80, CpmDNM 73, -74, -77, -79, ConAmC, DcCM, IntWWM 80, NewGrD 80, WhoMus 72*
Perlea, Jonel 1900-1970 *Baker 78, NewGrD 80, WhoMus 72*
Perlea, Junel 1900-1970 *CmOp*
Perlemuter, Vlado 1904- *IntWWM 77, -80, NewGrD 80, WhoMus 72*
Perley, Anna 1849-1937 *WhScrn 74, -77*
Perley, Charles 1886-1933 *WhScrn 74, -77, WhoHol B*
Perli, Lisa *NewGrD 80*
Perlis, Vivian 1928- *IntWWM 80*
Perlman, George *ConAmC*
Perlman, Itzhak 1945- *Baker 78, BnBkM 80, IntWWM 77, -80, MusSN[port], NewGrD 80, WhoMus 72*
Perlman, Morris 1894- *AmSCAP 66*
Perlman, Phyllis *BiE&WWA, NotNAT*
Perlman, William J d1954 *NotNAT B*
Perlmutter, David M 1934- *IntMPA 77, -76, -78, -79, -80*
Perlmutter, Leonard L *NatPD[port]*
Permain, Fred W d1933 *NotNAT B*
Perne, Francois-Louis 1772-1832 *Baker 78, NewGrD 80*
Pernel, Orrea 1906- *IntWWM 77, -80*
Pernes, Thomas 1956- *IntWWM 80*
Pernet, Andre 1894-1966 *NewGrD 80*
Perneth *NewGrD 80*
Pernye, Andras 1928- *IntWWM 77, -80, NewGrD 80*
Peron De Neele *NewGrD 80*
Peron, Eva 1919-1952 *FilmEn*
Peroni, Giovanni *NewGrD 80*
Peros De Neele *NewGrD 80*
Perosi, Don Lorenzo 1872-1956 *Baker 78*
Perosi, Lorenzo 1872-1956 *NewGrD 80, OxMus*
Perossier, James W 1785?- *BiDAmM*
Perotin *MusMk, NewGrD 80*
Perotin 1155?-1250? *Baker 78*
Perotin-Le-Grand 1160?-1220? *OxMus*

Perotinus Magnus NewGrD 80
Perottet, Philippe 1921- DancEn 78
Perotti, Giannagostino 1769-1855 NewGrD 80
Perotti, Giovanni Agostino 1769-1855 NewGrD 80
Perotti, Giovanni Domenico 1761-1825 NewGrD 80
Perper, James Douglas 1943- IntWWM 80
Perpessa, Harialaos ConAmC
Perpessas, Harilaos 1907- NewGrD 80
Perrachio, Luigi 1883-1966 NewGrD 80
Perrault, Charles 1628-1703 DcPup, NewEOp 71, NewGrD 80
Perrault, Claude 1613-1688 NewGrD 80
Perrault, John Paul 1942- AmSCAP 80
Perrault, Michel 1925- Baker 78, CreCan 1
Perrault, Pierre 1927- CreCan 2, OxFilm, WorEFlm
Perrault, Serge 1920- CnOxB
Perreard, Suzanne Louise Butler CreCan 2
Perreau, Gerald WhoHol A
Perreau, Gigi 1941- FilmEn, FilmgC, ForYSC, HalFC 80, IntMPA 77, -75, -76, -78, -79, -80, MotPP, WhoHol A
Perreau, Janine WhoHol A
Perredom, Luis 1882-1958 WhScrn 74, -77
Perrella, Robert NotNAT A
Perren, Christine Yarian 1944- AmSCAP 80
Perren, Freddie ConMuA 80B
Perren, Fredrick 1943- AmSCAP 80
Perret, Andre 1920- IntWWM 77, -80
Perret, Claudine 1935- IntWWM 77, -80
Perret, Denise 1942- IntWWM 77, -80
Perret, Leonce 1880-1935 DcFM, FilmEn, WorEFlm
Perret, Leonce 1882- TwYS A
Perret, Wilfred OxMus
Perretti, Claudine 1934- IntWWM 77, -80
Perrey, Mireille WhThe
Perri, Romano 1928- AmSCAP 80
Perrichon, Jean 1566-1600? NewGrD 80
Perrichon, Julien 1566-1600? NewGrD 80
Perrie, Ernestine 1912- BiE&WWA, NotNAT
Perrier, Claude 1918- WhoOp 76
Perriers, Daniele Bernadette 1945- WhoOp 76
Perrin D'Angicourt NewGrD 80
Perrin, Emile Cesare 1814-1885 NewEOp 71
Perrin, Harry Crane 1865-1953 Baker 78
Perrin, Jack 1896-1967 ForYSC, TwYS, WhScrn 74, -77, WhoHol B
Perrin, Jack 1896-1968 Film 1, -2
Perrin, Jacques WhoHol A
Perrin, Jean-Charles 1920- IntWWM 77, -80
Perrin, Juan 1927- AmSCAP 80
Perrin, Lesley Davison 1930- AmSCAP 80
Perrin, Nat IntMPA 77, -75, -76, -78, -79, -80
Perrin, Pierre 1620?-1675 Baker 78, NewGrD 80, OxMus
Perrin, Robert Henry 1924- IntWWM 77, -80
Perrin, Vic WhoHol A
Perrine d1698? NewGrD 80
Perrine, Valerie 1944- FilmEn, HalFC 80, IntMPA 77, -76, -78, -79, -80, WhoHol A
Perrinet NewGrD 80
Perrins, Leslie 1902-1962 FilmgC, HalFC 80, IlWWBF[port], NotNAT B, WhScrn 74, -77, WhThe, WhoHol B
Perris, Arnold B IntWWM 77, -80
Perron, Jean 1916- AmSCAP 80
Perron, Kurt ConAmC
Perron, Pierre 1935- IntWWM 77
Perrone, Frank 1928- AmSCAP 66
Perrone, Valentina 1906- AmSCAP 66, -80
Perronet Thompson, Thomas 1783-1869 OxMus
Perroni, Anna NewGrD 80
Perroni, Giovanni 1688-1748 NewGrD 80
Perrot De Neele NewGrD 80
Perrot, Irma Film 2
Perrot, Jules Joseph 1810-1892 CnOxB, DancEn 78, NewGrD 80
Perrott, Olive Madeline WhoMus 72
Perrotta, Sossio 1910- AmSCAP 80
Perry, Al ConMuA 80B
Perry, Albert H d1933 NotNAT B
Perry, Alfred 1910- AmSCAP 80
Perry, Alfred James 1931- AmSCAP 80
Perry, Annette 1932- WhoMus 72
Perry, Anthony 1929- IntMPA 77, -75, -76, -78, -79, -80
Perry, Antoinette 1888-1946 NotNAT B, WhScrn 74, -77, WhThe, WhoHol B
Perry, Arthur John 1906- WhThe
Perry, B Fisher 1940- NatPD[port]
Perry, Barbara WhoHol A
Perry, Bernice AmSCAP 80
Perry, Bob Film 2
Perry, Charles Emmett 1907-1967 WhScrn 77, WhoHol B
Perry, Charlotte 1890- BiE&WWA, DancEn 78
Perry, Desmond WhoHol A
Perry, Douglas Arthur 1953- IntWWM 77, -80
Perry, Earl 1921- IntMPA 77, -76, -78, -79, -80
Perry, Edward Baxter 1855-1924 Baker 78, BiDAmM
Perry, Elaine 1921- BiE&WWA, NotNAT
Perry, Eleanor ConDr 73, -77A, IntMPA 77, -75, -76, -78, -79, -80, WomWMM, -B
Perry, Esthryn Film 2
Perry, Felton DrBlPA, MorBAP, WhoHol A
Perry, Florence d1949 NotNAT B
Perry, Frank IntMPA 77, -75, -76, -78, -79, -80, WhoHol A
Perry, Frank 1930- FilmEn, FilmgC, HalFC 80, MovMk[port]
Perry, Frank 1933- BiDFilm 81, WorEFlm
Perry, George Frederick 1793-1862 Baker 78, NewGrD 80
Perry, Irma d1955 NotNAT B
Perry, Jack 1920- AmSCAP 66, -80, EncFCWM 69
Perry, Janet 1947- IntWWM 80, WhoOp 76
Perry, Joan ForYSC, WhoHol A
Perry, Joseph WhoHol A
Perry, Joyce WomWMM B
Perry, Julia 1924-1979 Baker 78, ConAmC, DcCM, NewGrD 80
Perry, Julia 1927- BiDAmM
Perry, Kathryn Film 2
Perry, Leslie D BlkAmP, MorBAP
Perry, Lincoln 1889- BlksB&W[port], -C
Perry, Manokai BlkAmP
Perry, Margaret 1913- BiE&WWA, NotNAT, WhThe, WhoHol A, WomWMM
Perry, Margaret Anne 1954- IntWWM 80
Perry, Martha BiE&WWA, NotNAT
Perry, Marvin Chapman, II 1948- IntWWM 80
Perry, Mary 1888-1971 NotNAT B, WhScrn 74, -77, WhoHol B
Perry, Mary Dean 1928- IntWWM 77
Perry, Paul P 1891-1963 FilmgC, HalFC 80
Perry, Phil 1914-1972 AmSCAP 66, -80
Perry, Quentin ConMuA 80B
Perry, Ray 1915-1950 WhoJazz 72
Perry, Richard ConMuA 80B, IlEncR
Perry, Robert E 1879-1962 Film 2, NotNAT B, TwYS, WhScrn 74, -77, WhoHol B
Perry, Rod 1941?- DrBlPA
Perry, Roger WhoHol A, WhoHrs 80
Perry, Roger Lee 1933- AmSCAP 80
Perry, Ronald d1963 NotNAT B
Perry, Sam A 1884-1936 AmSCAP 66, -80
Perry, Sara 1872-1959 WhScrn 74, -77, WhoHol B
Perry, Scott WhoHol A
Perry, Shauneille DrBlPA
Perry, Shaunielle MorBAP
Perry, Shauvneille BlkAmP
Perry, Victor 1920-1974 WhScrn 77, WhoHol B
Perry, Walter Film 2
Perry, Zenobia Powell 1914- ConAmC, IntWWM 77, -80
Perryman, Jill 1933- WhoThe 77
Perryman, Rufus G 1892-1973 BiDAmM, BluesWW[port]
Perryman, William Lee 1911- BluesWW[port]
Pers, Dirck Pieterszoon 1581-1662 NewGrD 80
Perschy, Maria 1940- ForYSC, IntMPA 79, -80, WhoHol A
Perse, Edward NewGrD 80
Perse, June 1927-1978 AmSCAP 80
Persiani, Fanny 1812-1867 Baker 78, CmOp, NewEOp 71, NewGrD 80
Persiani, Giuseppe 1799-1869 Baker 78, NewGrD 80
Persichetti, Vincent 1915- AmSCAP 66, -80, Baker 78, BiDAmM, BnBkM 80, CompSN[port], CpmDNM 72, -74, -75, -77, -78, ConAmC, DcCM, IntWWM 77, -80, MusMk, NewGrD 80, OxMus
Persico, Mario 1892- WhoMus 72
Persile, Giuseppe NewGrD 80
Persinger, Louis 1887-1966 Baker 78, NewGrD 80
Persinger, Louis 1888-1967 BiDAmM
Persip, Charles Lawrence 1929- EncJzS 70
Persip, Charli 1929- EncJzS 70
Perskin, Spencer Malcolm 1943- AmSCAP 80
Perskin, Susan Elizabeth 1946- AmSCAP 80
Persky, Lester 1927- IntMPA 78, -79, -80
Persky, Marilyn S WhoHol A
Persky, Stanley L 1941- ConAmC
Persky-Denoff NewYTET
Persoens, Josquino NewGrD 80
Persoff, Nehemiah 1920- BiE&WWA, FilmEn, FilmgC, ForYSC, HalFC 80, IntMPA 77, -75, -76, -78, -79, -80, MotPP, NotNAT, WhoHol A, WhoThe 72, -77
Persois 1800?-1850? NewGrD 80
Person, Gobelinus 1358-1421 NewGrD 80
Person, Houston 1934- EncJzS 70
Persona 1358-1421 NewGrD 80
Persones, Josquino NewGrD 80
Persons, Hal 1918- IntMPA 77, -75, -76, -78, -79
Persse, Thomas d1920 WhScrn 74, -77, WhoHol B
Persse, Tom Film 2
Persson, Aake 1932-1975 EncJzS 70
Persson, Edvard 1887-1957 WhScrn 74, -77
Persson, Essy 1945- FilmgC, HalFC 80, WhoHol A
Persson, Maria WhoHol A
Persuis, Louis-Luc Loiseau De 1769-1819 NewGrD 80
Perthen, Avis Ann 1951- IntWWM 77, -80
Perti, Giacomo Antonio 1661-1756 NewGrD 80
Perti, Jacopo Antonio 1661-1756 Baker 78
Perticaroli, Sergio 1930- WhoMus 72
Pertile, Aureliano 1885-1952 Baker 78, CmOp, NewEOp 71, NewGrD 80
Pertinaro, Francesco NewGrD 80
Pertis, Zsuzsa 1943- IntWWM 77, -80
Pertrovic, Radomir 1923- IntWWM 80
Pertwee, Jon 1919- FilmgC, HalFC 80, IntMPA 77, -75, -76, -78, -79, -80, WhoHol A, WhoHrs 80, WhoThe 72, -77
Pertwee, Michael 1916- FilmEn, FilmgC, HalFC 80, IntMPA 77, -75, -76, -78, -79, -80, WhoThe 72, -77
Pertwee, Roland IlWWBF A
Pertwee, Roland 1885-1963 WhThe, WhoHol A
Pertwee, Roland 1886?-1963 NotNAT A, -B
Perugia, Matteo Da NewGrD 80
Perugini, Signor d1914 NotNAT B
Perugini, Giulio 1927- CnOxB, DancEn 78
Perugini, Mark E 1876-1948 DancEn 78
Perusiis, Matheus De NewGrD 80
Perusinus, Matheus De NewGrD 80
Perusio, Matheus De NewGrD 80
Perusso, Mario 1936- Baker 78
Peruzzi, Baldassare 1481-1536 EncWT
Peruzzi, Baldassare 1481-1537 OxThe
Perz, Miroslaw 1933- IntWWM 77, -80
Perzynski, Wlodzimierz 1878-1930 CnMD, ModWD
Pesarino, Il NewGrD 80
Pescetti, Giovanni Battista 1704?-1766 NewGrD 80
Pesch, Gregor 1500?-1547? NewGrD 80
Peschek, James 1925- IntWWM 80, WhoMus 72
Pescheur NewGrD 80
Pescheur, Nicolas 1555?-1616 NewGrD 80
Pescheur, Pierre NewGrD 80
Pescheur, Pierre 1590?-1640? NewGrD 80
Peschin, Gregor 1500?-1547? NewGrD 80
Pesciolini, Biagio d1610? NewGrD 80
Pesek, Libor 1933- IntWWM 77, -80
Pesenti, Benedetto 1545?-1591? NewGrD 80
Pesenti, Martino 1600?-1648? NewGrD 80
Pesenti, Michele 1470?-1524? NewGrD 80
Peshkov, Aleksey Maksimovich McGEWD[port]
Peshkov, Alexei Maximovich REnWD[port]
Pesko NewGrD 80

Pesko, Gyorgy 1933- *NewGrD 80*
Pesko, Zoltan 1903-1967 *NewGrD 80*
Pesko, Zoltan 1937- *IntWWM 77, -80, NewGrD 80, WhoOp 76*
Pesonen, Olavi 1909- *NewGrD 80*
Pesori, Stefano d1650? *NewGrD 80*
Pessard, Emile-Louis-Fortune 1843-1917 *Baker 78, NewGrD 80*
Pestalozza, Luigi 1928- *NewGrD 80*
Pestalozzi, Heinrich 1878-1940 *Baker 78*
Pestelli, Giorgio 1938- *NewGrD 80*
Pesthin, Gregor *NewGrD 80*
Pestrino, Giulio Dal *NewGrD 80*
Petchey, Pamela 1922- *WhoMus 72*
Petchnikov, Alexander 1873-1949 *Baker 78*
Pete *Film 2*
Pete, Piute *AmSCAP 80*
Petelin, Jacob *NewGrD 80*
Petelle, Martha *Film 2*
Petelska, Eva *WomWMM*
Peter And Gordon *ConMuA 80A, RkOn 2[port]*
Peter Paul And Mary *AmPS A, -B, BiDAmM, ConMuA 80A[port], IlEncR, RkOn[port]*
Peter VanDenHove *NewGrD 80*
Peter, Christoph 1626-1669 *NewGrD 80*
Peter, Henry *NewGrD 80*
Peter, Johann Friedrich 1746-1813 *Baker 78, BiDAmM, NewGrD 80, OxMus*
Peter, John Desmond 1921- *CreCan 2*
Peter, John Frederik 1746-1813 *NewGrD 80*
Peter, Julius 1906- *WhoMus 72*
Peter, M *Film 2*
Peter, Simon 1743-1819 *Baker 78, NewGrD 80*
Peter The Great *Film 2*
Peterfi, Istvan 1884-1962 *NewGrD 80*
Peterik, James Michael 1950- *AmSCAP 80*
Peterkin, Norman 1886- *NewGrD 80, OxMus*
Peterlein, Johann *NewGrD 80*
Peters, Alan 1936- *WhoMus 72*
Peters, Ann 1920-1965 *WhScrn 77*
Peters, Audrey *WhoHol A*
Peters, Bernadette 1948- *EncMT, HalFC 80, NotNAT, WhoHol A, WhoThe 72, -77*
Peters, Brandon d1956 *NotNAT B*
Peters, Brock 1927- *BiE&WWA, DrBlPA, FilmEn, FilmgC, ForYSC, HalFC 80, IntMPA 77, -75, -76, -78, -79, -80, MotPP, MovMk[port], NotNAT, WhoHol A, WomWMM*
Peters, Brooke L *WhoHrs 80*
Peters, Carl Friedrich 1779-1827 *Baker 78, NewGrD 80*
Peters, Charles *MorBAP*
Peters, Charles Rollo 1892-1967 *NotNAT B*
Peters, Charley *BluesWW[port]*
Peters, Chris *ConMuA 80B*
Peters, Dale Hugh 1931- *IntWWM 77, -80*
Peters, Don 1921-1953 *WhScrn 77*
Peters, Elaine 1951- *IntWWM 77*
Peters, Fred 1884-1963 *Film 2, NotNAT B, WhScrn 74, -77, WhoHol B*
Peters, George David 1942- *IntWWM 77*
Peters, George J *WhoHol A*
Peters, Geroge David 1942- *IntWWM 80*
Peters, Gordon *WhoHol A*
Peters, Gordon Benes 1931- *IntWWM 77, -80*
Peters, Gunnar d1974 *WhScrn 77*
Peters, Gwendoline *WhoMus 72*
Peters, House d1967 *MotPP, WhoHol B*
Peters, House 1879-1967 *FilmEn*
Peters, House 1880?-1967 *FilmgC, HalFC 80, WhScrn 74, -77*
Peters, House 1888-1967 *Film 1, -2, TwYS*
Peters, House, Jr. *ForYSC, WhoHol A*
Peters, Howard *MagIlD*
Peters, Jean 1926- *BiDFilm 81, FilmEn, FilmgC, ForYSC, HalFC 80, IntMPA 75, MotPP, MovMk, WhoHol A, WorEFlm*
Peters, Johanna McLennan *IntWWM 80, WhoMus 72*
Peters, John d1940 *WhScrn 74, -77, WhoHol B*
Peters, John Rodie 1917- *WhoMus 72*
Peters, John S d1963 *Film 2, WhScrn 77*
Peters, Juanita Teal 1929- *IntWWM 77, -80*
Peters, Kay *WhoHol A*
Peters, Kelly Jean *WhoHol A*
Peters, Kurt 1915- *CnOxB, DancEn 78*
Peters, Lauri *WhoHol A*
Peters, Lynn *WhoHol A*
Peters, Mammy *Film 2*
Peters, Mattie *Film 2*
Peters, Mitchell Thomas 1935- *AmSCAP 80*
Peters, Page E d1916 *Film 1, WhScrn 77*
Peters, Paul *PlP&P*
Peters, Pauline 1896- *IlWWBF*
Peters, Peter 1926-1955 *WhScrn 74, -77*
Peters, Ralph 1903-1959 *Vers B[port], WhScrn 77, WhoHol B*
Peters, Reinhard 1926- *NewGrD 80, WhoOp 76*
Peters, Roberta 1930- *Baker 78, BiDAmM, CmOp, IntWWM 77, -80, MusSN[port], NewEOp 71, NewGrD 80, WhoHol A, WhoMus 72, WhoOp 76*
Peters, Rollo 1892-1967 *BiE&WWA, NotNAT B, PlP&P, WhThe*
Peters, Samuel *OxMus*
Peters, Scott *ForYSC, WhoHol A*
Peters, Susan 1921-1952 *FilmEn, FilmgC, ForYSC, HalFC 80, MGM[port], MotPP, MovMk, NotNAT B, WhScrn 74, -77, WhoHol B*
Peters, Ursula M 1920- *IntWWM 77, -80*
Peters, Werner 1918-1971 *FilmAG WE, HalFC 80*
Peters, Werner 1919-1971 *WhScrn 74, -77, WhoHol B*
Peters, William Cumming 1805-1866 *BiDAmM, NewGrD 80*
Peters, William Francis 1895- *AmSCAP 80*
Peters, William Frederick 1876-1938 *AmSCAP 66, ConAmC*
Petersen, Alf 1910- *IntWWM 77, -80*
Petersen, Cliff 1906- *IntMPA 77, -75, -76, -78, -79, -80*
Petersen, Colin 1946- *HalFC 80*
Petersen, David *NewGrD 80*
Petersen, Elsa d1974 *WhoHol B*
Petersen, Ernst *Film 2*
Petersen, Judith Ann Hellenberg 1935- *IntWWM 77, -80*
Petersen, Karen d1940 *NotNAT B*
Petersen, Kirsten 1936- *DancEn 78*
Petersen, Knud 1931- *IntWWM 77, -80*
Petersen, Lauritz Peter Corneliys *NewGrD 80*
Petersen, Marian F 1926- *ConAmC*
Petersen, Marie *AmSCAP 66, -80*
Petersen, Patricia Jeannette 1940- *IntWWM 77, -80*
Petersen, Paul 1944- *ForYSC, WhoHol A*
Petersen, Peter 1876-1956 *WhScrn 74, -77*
Petersen, Reinhard 1943- *WhoOp 76*
Petersen, Robert E 1937- *AmSCAP 80*
Petersen, Robert James 1934- *WhoOp 76*
Petersen, Wilhelm 1890-1957 *Baker 78, OxMus*
Petersilea, Carlyle 1844-1903 *Baker 78, BiDAmM*
Petersmeyer, C Wrede *NewYTET*
Peterson, Arthur *WhoHol A*
Peterson, Barr Edward 1924- *WhoOp 76*
Peterson, Bengt Olof 1923- *WhoOp 76*
Peterson, Betty J 1918- *AmSCAP 66, -80*
Peterson, Byron *PupTheA*
Peterson, Caleb 1917- *DrBlPA*
Peterson, Dorothy *ForYSC*
Peterson, Dorothy 1900?- *HalFC 80*
Peterson, Dorothy 1901- *MotPP, MovMk, ThFT[port], WhoHol A*
Peterson, Edgar 1913- *IntMPA 77, -75, -76, -78, -79, -80*
Peterson, Gil *WhoHol A*
Peterson, Glade 1928- *WhoOp 76*
Peterson, Hannibal Marvin Charles 1948- *EncJzS 70*
Peterson, Harold 1900?- *NewOrJ*
Peterson, Harold Vaughan 1948- *AmSCAP 80*
Peterson, Hazel Shirley 1952- *AmSCAP 80*
Peterson, Ileana Marija 1934- *WhoOp 76*
Peterson, Ina Mae *WomWMM B*
Peterson, Ivor 1905- *AmSCAP 66, -80*
Peterson, James Newell 1911-1967 *AmSCAP 80*
Peterson, John Willard 1921- *NewGrD 80*
Peterson, Kaj Harald Leininger *McGEWD[port]*
Peterson, Karen d1940 *WhScrn 77*
Peterson, Kirk 1951- *CnOxB*
Peterson, Leland Arnold 1911- *AmSCAP 80*
Peterson, Len 1917- *CreCan 1*
Peterson, Lenka 1925- *BiE&WWA, NotNAT, WhoHol A*
Peterson, Leonard Byron 1917- *CreCan 1*
Peterson, LeRoy Henry 1937- *IntWWM 77, -80*
Peterson, Louis 1922- *BiE&WWA, BlkAmP, DrBlPA, MorBAP, NotNAT*
Peterson, Margaret 1902- *CreCan 2*
Peterson, Marjorie d1974 *WhScrn 77, WhoHol B*
Peterson, Maurice 1952- *ConAmTC*
Peterson, Melody 1942- *ConAmC*
Peterson, Monica 1938- *DrBlPA, WhoHol A*
Peterson, Oscar Emmanuel 1925- *BiDAmM, CmpEPM, CreCan 1, DrBlPA, EncJzS 70, IlEncJ, IntWWM 77, -80, NewGrD 80*
Peterson, Oscar Emmanuel 1926- *MusMk[port]*
Peterson, Paul 1945- *IntMPA 77, -75, -76, -78, -79, -80, RkOn*
Peterson, Ray 1939- *RkOn[port]*
Peterson, Richard Trenholm 1934- *IntWWM 77, -80*
Peterson, Richard W 1949- *IntMPA 77, -75, -76, -78, -79, -80*
Peterson, Robert A 1936- *WhoOp 76*
Peterson, S Dean 1923- *IntMPA 78, -79, -80*
Peterson, Spencer C 1948- *AmSCAP 80*
Peterson, Vivian Woodward *WhoMus 72*
Peterson, Wayne Turner 1927- *AmSCAP 80, ConAmC*
Peterson, Wayne Turner 1937- *IntWWM 77, -80*
Peterson, Wilbur Pete 1915-1960 *WhScrn 74, -77*
Peterson-Berger, Olof Wilhelm 1867-1942 *OxMus*
Peterson-Berger, Wilhelm 1867-1942 *Baker 78, MusMk, NewGrD 80*
Peterszoon, Dirk *NewGrD 80*
Petey 1923-1930 *WhScrn 77*
Pethel, James 1936- *ConAmC, IntWWM 77, -80*
Petherbridge, Edward 1936- *WhoThe 72, -77*
Petin, Nikola 1920- *Baker 78, IntWWM 77, -80*
Petina, Irra 1914- *BiE&WWA, NotNAT*
Petipa, Jean Antoine 1796-1855 *CnOxB, DancEn 78*
Petipa, Lucien 1815-1898 *CnOxB, DancEn 78*
Petipa, Maria Mariusovna 1857-1930 *CnOxB*
Petipa, Maria Surovshchikova 1836-1882 *CnOxB*
Petipa, Marie 1836-1882 *DancEn 78*
Petipa, Marie 1857-1930 *DancEn 78*
Petipa, Marius 1818-1910 *CnOxB, NewGrD 80*
Petipa, Marius 1819-1910 *DancEn 78[port]*
Petipa, Marius 1822-1910 *NotNAT B*
Petit d1753? *NewGrD 80*
Petit, Albert 1887-1963 *WhScrn 77*
Petit, Buddie 1897?-1931 *WhoJazz 72*
Petit, Buddy 1887-1931 *BiDAmM, NewOrJ*
Petit, Francoise 1925- *IntWWM 77, -80*
Petit, Jean Louis 1937- *WhoMus 72*
Petit, Joseph 1880?-1946 *NewOrJ[port]*
Petit, Pascale 1938- *FilmAG WE, FilmEn, FilmgC, HalFC 80, WhoHol A*
Petit, Pierre 1922- *IntWWM 77, -80*
Petit, Raymond 1893- *Baker 78*
Petit, Roland 1924- *CnOxB, DancEn 78, WhThe, WhoHol A*
Petit Jean, Claude d1589 *NewGrD 80*
Petit Jehan, Claude d1589 *NewGrD 80*
Petite, E Dale 1926- *AmSCAP 80*
Petkanova, Magda *WomWMM*
Petkere, Bernice 1906- *AmSCAP 66, -80, CmpEPM*
Petkov, Dimiter 1919- *Baker 78, NewGrD 80*
Petkov, Dimiter 1938- *WhoOp 76*
Petkov, Dobrin 1923- *NewGrD 80*
Petkovic, Dragisa 1922- *IntWWM 77, -80*
Petley, E S d1945 *NotNAT B*
Petley, Frank E 1872-1945 *NotNAT B, WhThe, WhoHol B*
Petra-Basacopol, Carmen 1926- *Baker 78*
Petra-Basacopol, Carmen 1929- *IntWWM 80*

Petracchi, Francesco 1937- *NewGrD 80*
Petraeus, Christoph *NewGrD 80*
Petrak, Rudolf 1917-1972 *BiDAmM*
Petrakis, Thanos 1939- *WhoOp 76*
Petrarca, Francesco 1304-1374 *NewGrD 80*
Petrarch 1304-1374 *NewEOp 71, NewGrD 80, OxMus*
Petras, Peggy *WomWMM B*
Petrass, Sari 1890-1930 *NotNAT B, WhThe*
Petrassi, Goffredo 1904- *Baker 78, BnBkM 80, CompSN[port], DcCM, IntWWM 77, -80, MusMk, NewGrD 80[port], OxMus, WhoMus 72*
Petratti, Francesco *NewGrD 80*
Petrauskas, Kipras 1885-1968 *Baker 78*
Petrauskas, Mikas 1873-1937 *Baker 78*
Petre, Gio 1937- *FilmEn*
Petre, Henry *NewGrD 80*
Petreius, Johann 1497-1550 *NewGrD 80*
Petrejus, Johann 1497-1550 *NewGrD 80*
Petrella, Clara 1918- *NewGrD 80*
Petrella, Clara 1919- *CmOp*
Petrella, Enrico 1813-1877 *OxMus*
Petrella, Errico 1813-1877 *Baker 78, NewGrD 80*
Petrelli, Eleanora 1835-1904 *Baker 78*
Petreo, Magno *NewGrD 80*
Petresco *OxMus*
Petrescu, Camil 1894-1957 *McGEWD[port]*
Petrescu, Dinu Mircea Cristian 1939- *IntWWM 80*
Petrescu, Emilia 1925- *IntWWM 80*
Petrescu, Ioan D 1884-1970 *NewGrD 80*
Petri *NewGrD 80*
Petri, Balthasar Abraham 1704-1793 *NewGrD 80*
Petri, Christopher 1758- *NewGrD 80*
Petri, Egon 1881-1962 *Baker 78, BnBkM 80, MusSN[port], NewGrD 80*
Petri, Elio 1929-1979 *BiDFilm 81, DcFM, FilmEn, FilmgC, HalFC 80, WorEFlm*
Petri, Frantz 1935- *WhoOp 76*
Petri, Georg Gottfried 1715-1795 *NewGrD 80*
Petri, Johann *NewGrD 80*
Petri, Johann Samuel 1738-1808 *NewGrD 80*
Petri, Michala 1958- *IntWWM 77, -80*
Petri, Olavus 1493-1552 *OxThe*
Petri Nylandensis, Theodoricus *NewGrD 80*
Petric, Ivo 1931- *Baker 78, DcCM, IntWWM 80, NewGrD 80*
Petric, Joseph 1952- *IntWWM 80*
Petrides, Avra *NatPD[port]*
Petrides, Petro 1892-1978 *DcCM*
Petridis, Petro 1892-1978 *Baker 78*
Petridis, Petros 1892-1978 *NewGrD 80*
Petrie, Daniel 1920- *BiE&WWA, FilmEn, FilmgC, HalFC 80, IntMPA 77, -75, -76, -78, -79, -80, NewYTET, NotNAT*
Petrie, David Hay 1895-1948 *NotNAT B, WhThe*
Petrie, George *WhoHol A*
Petrie, George 1789-1866 *OxMus*
Petrie, Hay 1895-1948 *FilmgC, HalFC 80, WhScrn 74, -77, WhoHol B*
Petrie, Henry W 1857-1925 *AmSCAP 66, -80, BiDAmM*
Petrie, Howard A 1907-1968 *ForYSC, WhScrn 74, -77, WhoHol B*
Petrillo, Caesar 1898-1963 *AmSCAP 66, -80, CmpEPM*
Petrillo, Clement C 1914- *IntWWM 77, -80*
Petrillo, James C 1893?- *CmpEPM*
Petrillo, Sammy 1928?- *WhoHrs 80*
Petrini *NewGrD 80*
Petrini d1750 *NewGrD 80*
Petrini, Francesco 1744-1819 *NewGrD 80*
Petrini, Francois 1744-1819 *NewGrD 80*
Petrini, Franz 1744-1819 *NewGrD 80*
Petrini, Therese 1736-1800? *NewGrD 80*
Petrobelli, Francesco d1695 *NewGrD 80*
Petrobelli, Pierluigi 1932- *IntWWM 77, -80, NewGrD 80*
Petroff, Ossip 1807-1878 *NewEOp 71*
Petroff, Paul 1908- *CnOxB, DancEn 78*
Petrolini, Ettore 1886-1936 *EncWT, Ent[port]*
Petrone, Joseph 1928- *AmSCAP 80*
Petronella, Anthony J 1906- *AmSCAP 66*
Petros Peloponnesios 1730?-1778 *NewGrD 80*
Petrov, Andrei 1930- *Baker 78*
Petrov, Andrey Pavlovich 1930- *NewGrD 80*
Petrov, Ivan 1920- *Baker 78, CmOp, NewGrD 80*
Petrov, Nicolas 1933- *CnOxB*
Petrov, Nikolay 1943- *NewGrD 80*
Petrov, Osip 1806-1878 *NewGrD 80*
Petrov, Ossip 1806-1878 *Baker 78*
Petrov, Ossip 1807-1878 *CmOp*
Petrov, Stoyan 1916- *NewGrD 80*
Petrov, Vadim 1932- *IntWWM 77, -80*
Petrov, Vladimir 1896- *DcFM*
Petrov, Vladimir 1896-1965 *WorEFlm*
Petrov, Vladimir 1896-1966 *FilmEn, FilmgC, HalFC 80*
Petrov, Vladimir Nicolaevic 1926- *WhoOp 76*
Petrova, Elena *IntWWM 77*
Petrova, Ninel Alexandrovna 1924- *CnOxB*
Petrova, Olga 1886-1977 *FilmEn, Film 1, FilmgC, HalFC 80, MotPP, NotNAT A, TwYS, WhThe, WhoHol A*
Petrovic, Aleksander 1929- *FilmEn*
Petrovic, Bosko 1935- *EncJzS 70, IntWWM 77*
Petrovic, Danica 1945- *IntWWM 77, -80*
Petrovic, Milivoj 1938- *WhoOp 76*
Petrovic, Radmila 1923- *IntWWM 77, -80*
Petrovic, Radomir 1923- *Baker 78, IntWWM 77*
Petrovics, Emil 1930- *Baker 78, DcCM, IntWWM 77, -80, NewGrD 80*
Petrovitch, Ivan *Film 2*
Petrovitch, Jans *Film 2*
Petrovitch, Peter *Film 2*
Petrovsky, A *Film 2*
Petrucci, Brizio 1737-1828 *NewGrD 80*
Petrucci, Mary Jeanne 1952- *IntWWM 80*
Petrucci, Ottaviano Dei 1466-1539 *Baker 78, BnBkM 80, NewGrD 80, OxMus*
Petrus Abailardus *NewGrD 80*
Petrus Aponensis *NewGrD 80*
Petrus Bonus Ferrariensis *NewGrD 80*
Petrus Capuanus *NewGrD 80*
Petrus De Abano 1257-1315? *NewGrD 80*
Petrus De Amalfia *NewGrD 80*
Petrus De Cruce *NewGrD 80*
Petrus De Domarto *NewGrD 80*
Petrus De Picardia *NewGrD 80*
Petrus De Sancto Dionysio *NewGrD 80*
Petrus Frater Dictus Palma Ociosa *NewGrD 80*
Petrus Le Viser *NewGrD 80*
Petrus Optimus Notator, Magister *NewGrD 80*
Petrus Palma Ociosa *NewGrD 80*
Petrus Trothun Aurelianis, Magister *NewGrD 80*
Petrusanec, Franjo 1938- *WhoOp 76*
Petrushka, Shabtai Arieh 1903- *Baker 78, IntWWM 77, -80*
Petruzzi, Julian 1907-1967 *WhScrn 77*
Petryni, Michael *ConAmTC*
Petrzelka, Ivan 1928- *IntWWM 77, -80*
Petrzelka, Vilem 1889-1967 *Baker 78, NewGrD 80*
Pets, The *RkOn*
Petschler, Erik A *Film 2*
Pettan, Hubert 1912- *IntWWM 77, -80*
Pettersson, Allan G 1911-1980 *IntWWM 80, NewGrD 80*
Pettersson, Allan G 1919- *IntWWM 77*
Pettersson, Ann-Margret 1938- *WhoOp 76*
Pettersson, Brigitta *WhoHol A*
Pettersson, Gustaf Allan 1911- *Baker 78, BnBkM 80*
Pettersson, Hjordis *WhoHol A*
Pettet, Edwin Burr 1913- *BiE&WWA*
Pettet, Joanna 1944- *FilmEn, FilmgC, HalFC 80, WhoHol A*
Pettet, Joanne 1944- *ForYSC*
Pettey, Emma *PupTheA*
Petteys, The *PupTheA*
Petti, Anthony 1907- *IntMPA 77, -75, -76, -78, -79*
Petti, Emile *CmpEPM*
Petti, Paolo d1678 *NewGrD 80*
Petticolas, Philippe Abraham 1760-1841 *BiDAmM*
Pettiford, Oscar 1922-1960 *BiDAmM, CmpEPM*
Pettigrew, Leola B *BluesWW[port]*
Pettingell, Frank 1891-1966 *FilmgC, HalFC 80, IlWWBF, WhScrn 74, -77*
Pettingell, Frank 1891-1968 *WhThe*
Pettingill, Frank 1891-1966 *WhoHol B*
Pettis, Jack 1902- *CmpEPM, WhoJazz 72*
Pettit, Louise *PupTheA*
Pettit, Paul Bruce 1920- *BiE&WWA*
Pettitt, Henry d1893 *NotNAT B*
Pettle, Florence Muriel *WhoMus 72*
Petts, Frederick Thomas 1903- *WhoMus 72*
Petts, Pamela *WhoMus 72*
Petty, Frank 1916- *AmSCAP 66, -80*
Petty, James Carter 1928- *IntWWM 77, -80*
Petty, Roy Bynum 1943- *IntWWM 77*
Petty, Tom *IlEncR*
Petty, Violet Ann 1928- *AmSCAP 66, -80*
Petyr, Henry 1470?-1516? *NewGrD 80*
Petyrek, Felix 1892-1951 *Baker 78, NewGrD 80*
Petz, Johann Christoph 1664-1716 *Baker 78, NewGrD 80*
Petze, Lennie *ConMuA 80B*
Petzel, Johann Christoph *Baker 78, NewGrD 80*
Petzet, Walter 1866-1941 *Baker 78, BiDAmM*
Petzmayer, Johann 1803-1884 *NewGrD 80*
Petzold, Christian *NewGrD 80*
Petzold, Johann Christoph 1639-1694 *OxMus*
Petzold, Rudolf 1908- *Baker 78, NewGrD 80*
Petzoldt, Johann Christoph *NewGrD 80*
Petzoldt, Richard 1907-1974 *Baker 78, NewGrD 80*
Peudargent, Martin 1525?-1585? *NewGrD 80*
Peuerl, Paul 1570?-1625? *Baker 78, NewGrD 80*
Peukert, Leo *Film 2*
Peukert-Impekoven, Sabine 1890-1970 *WhScrn 74, -77*
Peutinger, Conrad 1465-1547 *NewGrD 80*
Peverall, John *IntMPA 80*
Peverara, Laura 1545?-1601 *NewGrD 80*
Pevernage, Andre 1543-1591 *NewGrD 80*
Pevernage, Andreas 1543-1591 *NewGrD 80, OxMus*
Pevernage, Andries 1543-1591 *Baker 78, NewGrD 80*
Pevney, Joseph *IntMPA 77, -75, -76, -78, -79, -80, WhoHol A*
Pevney, Joseph 1913- *WorEFlm*
Pevney, Joseph 1916?- *ForYSC*
Pevney, Joseph 1920- *BiDFilm 81, FilmEn, FilmgC, HalFC 80, MovMk[port]*
Pevsner, Leo 1906- *AmSCAP 66, -80*
Peyer, Andreas *NewGrD 80*
Peyer, Gervase De *NewGrD 80*
Peyer, Johann Baptist 1680?-1733 *NewGrD 80*
Peyerl, Paul *NewGrD 80*
Peyko, Nikolay Ivanovich 1916- *NewGrD 80*
Peyro, Jose *NewGrD 80*
Peyrol, Annie Mary 1948- *IntWWM 80*
Peyronel, Daniel Augusto 1953- *AmSCAP 80*
Peyser, Herbert Francis 1886-1953 *Baker 78*
Peyser, Joan 1931- *Baker 78*
Peyser, John 1916- *IntMPA 77, -75, -76, -78, -79, -80*
Peyser, Lois *WomWMM*
Peyton, Benny 1890?-1965 *WhoJazz 72*
Peyton, Charles *Film 2*
Peyton, Dave 1885?-1956 *WhoJazz 72*
Peyton, Henry *NewOrJ*
Peyton, Lawrence R d1918 *Film 1, WhScrn 77*
Peyton, Malcolm C 1932- *CpmDNM 79, ConAmC*
Pez, Johann Christoph 1664-1716 *NewGrD 80*
Pezel, Johann Christoph 1639-1694 *Baker 78, NewGrD 80*
Pezhuk-Romanoff, Ivan *CreCan 1*
Pezold, Christian 1677-1733 *NewGrD 80*
Pezold, Hans 1901- *IntWWM 77, -80*
Pezzetti, Emilia Cundari *CreCan 2*
Pezzetti, Sergio 1934- *WhoOp 76*
Pezzulo, Ted 1936- *NatPD[port]*
Pfaff, Philip Reginald *WhoMus 72*
Pfaff, Philip Reynold 1914- *WhoMus 72*
Pfaffl, Carolyn Sue *WomWMM B*
Pfanner, Adolf 1897- *IntWWM 77, -80*
Pfannhauser, Karl 1911- *NewGrD 80*
Pfannkuch, Wilhelm 1926- *IntWWM 77, -80*
Pfannmuller, Friedrich 1490?-1562? *NewGrD 80*
Pfannstiehl, Bernhard 1861-1940 *Baker 78*
Pfatteicher, Carl Friedrichs 1882-1957 *Baker 78*

Pfautsch, Lloyd Alvin 1921- *AmSCAP 66, –80, ConAmC, IntWWM 77, –80*
Pfeffinger, Philippe-Jacques 1765-1821? *NewGrD 80*
Pfeifer, Diane Patricia 1950- *AmSCAP 80*
Pfeiffer, Franz Anton 1754-1787 *NewGrD 80*
Pfeiffer, George 1790?- *BiDAmM*
Pfeiffer, Georges-Jean 1835-1908 *Baker 78, NewGrD 80*
Pfeiffer, Johann 1697-1761 *NewGrD 80*
Pfeiffer, John F 1920- *ConAmC*
Pfeiffer, Michael Traugott 1771-1849 *NewGrD 80*
Pfeiffer, Theodor 1853-1929 *Baker 78*
Pfeil, Clifford I 1931- *ConAmC*
Pfeil, V A *OxMus*
Pfendner, Heinrich 1590?-1631? *NewGrD 80*
Pfenninger, Rudolf *OxMus*
Pfiffner, Ernst 1922- *IntWWM 77, –80*
Pfischner, Jan *ConAmC*
Pfister, Hugo 1914-1969 *NewGrD 80*
Pfister, Johann Wolfgang Franciscus *NewGrD 80*
Pfister, Walter J, Jr. *NewYTET*
Pfitzner, Hans 1869-1949 *Baker 78, BnBkM 80, CmOp, CompSN[port], DcCom 77, DcCM, MusMk, NewEOp 71, NewGrD 80[port], OxMus*
Pfleger, Augustin 1635?-1686? *NewGrD 80*
Pflueger, Sidney 1905?- *NewOrJ*
Pflug, Jo Ann *WhoHol A*
Pflughaupt, Robert 1833-1871 *Baker 78*
Pfohl, Ferdinand 1862-1949 *Baker 78, NewGrD 80*
Pfohl, James Christian 1912- *IntWWM 77, –80*
Pfordten, Hermann Ludwig VonDer 1857-1933 *Baker 78*
Pfretzschner, Brigitte 1936- *WhoOp 76*
Pfrogner, Hermann 1911- *Baker 78, WhoMus 72*
Pfundmayr, Hedy 1899-1966 *CnOxB*
Pfundt, Ernst Gotthold Benjamin 1806-1871 *Baker 78*
Phagas, Dimitmos *AmSCAP 80*
Phair, Douglas *Film 2*
Phalese *NewGrD 80*
Phalese, Madeleine 1586?-1652 *NewGrD 80*
Phalese, Pierre 1510?-1573? *Baker 78*
Phalese, Pierre 1510?-1576? *NewGrD 80*
Phalese, Pierre 1550?-1629 *NewGrD 80*
Phalke, D G 1870-1944 *FilmEn*
Phalke, Dhundiraj Govind 1870-1944 *DcFM*
Phanmuller, Friedrich *NewGrD 80*
Pharar, Renee d1962 *NotNAT B*
Pharazyn, Professor *PupTheA*
Pharis, Gwen *CreCan 2*
Phelan, Brian *WhoHol A*
Phelps, Arthur 1890?-1933? *BluesWW[port]*
Phelps, Austin 1820-1890 *BiDAmM*
Phelps, Buster *Film 2*
Phelps, Christopher 1943- *IntWWM 80*
Phelps, Dodie d1963 *NotNAT B*
Phelps, Eleanor *WhoHol A*
Phelps, Ellsworth C 1827-1913 *Baker 78, BiDAmM*
Phelps, Fancher, Sr. d1972 *WhoHol B*
Phelps, Lawrence Irving 1923- *NewGrD 80*
Phelps, Lee d1952 *WhoHol B*
Phelps, Lee 1894-1953 *ForYSC, Vers B[port], WhScrn 74, –77*
Phelps, Leonard P d1924 *NotNAT B*
Phelps, Lewis Allen 1938- *CpmDNM 78*
Phelps, Lyon 1923- *BiE&WWA, NotNAT*
Phelps, Norman F 1911- *ConAmC*
Phelps, Samuel 1804-1878 *EncWT, Ent, NotNAT A, –B, OxThe, PlP&P[port]*
Phelps, Sandra Sue 1940- *AmSCAP 80*
Phelps, Sylvester Dryden 1816-1895 *BiDAmM*
Phelps, Vonda *Film 2*
Phelyppis, Thomas 1450?- *NewGrD 80*
Pherecrates *NewGrD 80, OxThe*
Phethean, David 1918- *WhoThe 72, –77*
Phetteplace, Jon 1940- *ConAmC*
Philbert *NewGrD 80*
Philbin, Jack *IntMPA 77, –75, –76, –78, –79, –80, NewYTET*
Philbin, Mary 1903- *FilmEn, Film 2, FilmgC, HalFC 80, MotPP, TwYS, WhoHol A, WhoHrs 80*
Philbrick, Herbert A 1915- *What 5[port]*
Philbrick, Norman 1913- *BiE&WWA, NotNAT*
Philbrook, James *ForYSC, WhoHol A*
Philburn, Al 1902-1972 *BiDAmM, CmpEPM, WhoJazz 72*
Phile, Philip 1734?-1793 *Baker 78, BiDAmM*
Philemon 361?BC-263BC *OxThe*
Philiba, Nicole 1937- *IntWWM 80*
Philidor *NewGrD 80*
Philidor, Alexandre Danican 1660?- *NewGrD 80*
Philidor, Andre Danican 1647?-1730 *Baker 78, NewGrD 80[port]*
Philidor, Anne Danican 1681-1728 *Baker 78, NewGrD 80*
Philidor, Francois Andre Danican 1726-1795 *Baker 78, GrComp[port], MusMk, NewEOp 71, NewGrD 80[port], OxMus*
Philidor, Jacques Danican 1657-1708 *Baker 78, NewGrD 80*
Philidor, Jean Danican 1620?-1679 *Baker 78, NewGrD 80*
Philidor, Michel Danican 1600?-1659 *NewGrD 80*
Philidor, Pierre Danican 1681-1731 *Baker 78, NewGrD 80*
Philip II 1527-1598 *NewGrD 80, OxMus*
Philip De Bourbon 1674-1723 *NewGrD 80*
Philip, Achille 1878-1959 *Baker 78*
Philip, James E d1910 *NotNAT B*
Philip, Joseph 1879-1960 *NewOrJ[port]*
Philip, Joseph, Jr. 1912-1968 *NewOrJ*
Philip, Robert Marshall 1945- *IntWWM 77, –80*
Philipe, Gerard 1922-1959 *BiDFilm 81, EncWT, Ent[port], FilmAG WE, FilmEn, FilmgC, HalFC 80, MotPP, MovMk[port], NotNAT B, OxFilm, OxThe, WhScrn 74, –77, WhoHol B, WorEFlm*
Philipoctus De Caserta *NewGrD 80*
Philipp, Adolph 1864-1936 *NotNAT B*
Philipp, Franz 1890-1972 *NewGrD 80*
Philipp, Isidor 1863-1958 *Baker 78, BiDAmM*
Philipp, Isidore 1863-1958 *BnBkM 80, NewGrD 80, OxMus*
Philippart, Nathalie *CnOxB, DancEn 78*
Philippe De Vitry 1291-1361 *Baker 78, BnBkM 80, NewGrD 80, OxMus*
Philippe The Chancellor 1160?-1236 *NewGrD 80*
Philippe, Andre *WhoHol A*
Philippe, Pierre *Film 2, NewGrD 80*
Philippe, Van Rans d1628? *NewGrD 80*
Philippi, Herbert M 1906-1958 *NotNAT B*
Philippin *OxThe*
Philippon *NewGrD 80*
Philippot, Michel Paul 1925- *Baker 78, DcCM, NewGrD 80*
Philippus De Caserta *NewGrD 80*
Philippus, Petrus *NewGrD 80*
Philips, Ambrose 1674-1749 *OxThe*
Philips, Augustus 1873- *WhoStg 1908*
Philips, Conrad 1930- *FilmgC, HalFC 80*
Philips, Francis Charles 1849-1921 *NotNAT A, –B, WhThe*
Philips, John Douglass 1932- *IntWWM 77, –80*
Philips, Lee 1927- *BiE&WWA, ForYSC, HalFC 80, NewYTET, WhoHol A*
Philips, Marie L 1925- *BiE&WWA, NotNAT*
Philips, Marvin James 1923- *BiE&WWA*
Philips, Mary 1900-1975 *HalFC 80*
Philips, Mary 1901-1975 *WhThe, WhoHol C*
Philips, Peter 1560?-1628 *BnBkM 80, NewGrD 80[port]*
Philips, Peter 1561-1628 *Baker 78, MusMk, OxMus*
Philips, Robin 1941- *FilmgC, HalFC 80*
Philips, William d1734 *NotNAT B*
Philipus *NewGrD 80*
Philliber, John 1872-1944 *HalFC 80, WhScrn 74, –77, WhoHol B*
Phillimore, Cynthia Frances Mary 1934- *IntWWM 77, –80*
Phillipe, Gerard 1922-1959 *CnThe*
Phillippe 1802-1878 *MagIID*
Phillippe, Roy Taylor 1950- *AmSCAP 80*
Phillipps, Adelaide 1833-1882 *Baker 78*
Phillipps, Peter *NewGrD 80*
Phillipps, Thomas *NewGrD 80*
Phillips, Acton d1940 *NotNAT B*
Phillips, Adelaide 1833-1882 *NewEOp 71*
Phillips, Ailne 1905- *CnOxB, DancEn 78*
Phillips, Albert 1875-1940 *NotNAT B, WhScrn 77*
Phillips, Alex 1901-1977 *DcFM, FilmEn*
Phillips, Mrs. Alfred d1876 *NotNAT B*
Phillips, Arthur 1605-1695 *NewGrD 80*
Phillips, Arthur A 1918- *ConAmC*
Phillips, Augustine d1605 *OxThe, PlP&P*
Phillips, Augustus *Film 1, MotPP*
Phillips, B Maude *PupTheA*
Phillips, Barney *WhoHol A*
Phillips, Barre 1934- *BiDAmM, ConAmC*
Phillips, Beau *ConMuA 80B*
Phillips, Bertram *IlWWBF*
Phillips, Bill 1936- *CounME 74, –74A, EncFCWM 69, IlEncCM, IntMPA 77, –75, –76, –78, –79, –80, Vers A[port]*
Phillips, Blanche *Film 1*
Phillips, Bryony 1948- *IntWWM 80*
Phillips, Burrill 1907- *AmSCAP 66, –80, Baker 78, BiDAmM, CpmDNM 78, –79, ConAmC, DcCM, IntWWM 77, –80, NewGrD 80, OxMus, WhoMus 72*
Phillips, Carmen 1895- *Film 1, –2, TwYS*
Phillips, Charles 1904-1958 *WhScrn 74, –77*
Phillips, Charles Allen 1940- *CpmDNM 72, ConAmC*
Phillips, Charles Don 1937- *BiDAmM*
Phillips, Clement K d1928 *WhScrn 74, –77*
Phillips, Conrad *WhoHol A*
Phillips, Cyril L 1894- *WhThe*
Phillips, D John *IntMPA 77, –75, –76, –78, –79, –80*
Phillips, D Valgene 1935- *ConAmC*
Phillips, Donald David 1919- *ConAmC, WhoMus 72*
Phillips, Dorothy 1892- *FilmEn, Film 1, –2, ForYSC, TwYS*
Phillips, E R *Film 1*
Phillips, Eddie 1899-1965 *Film 2, ForYSC, TwYS*
Phillips, Edna 1878-1952 *WhScrn 74, –77*
Phillips, Edward Eddie 1899-1965 *WhoHol B*
Phillips, Edward N 1899-1965 *WhScrn 74, –77*
Phillips, Edwin R d1915 *WhScrn 77*
Phillips, Elizabeth Ann 1946- *IntWWM 77*
Phillips, Esther 1925- *EncJzS 70*
Phillips, Esther 1935- *BiDAmM, BluesWW[port], DrBlPA*
Phillips, Evelyn Rose *WhoMus 72*
Phillips, Festus 1872-1955 *WhScrn 74, –77*
Phillips, Flip 1915- *CmpEPM, EncJzS 70, IlEncJ, WhoJazz 72*
Phillips, Frank *HalFC 80*
Phillips, Fred 1890-1956 *AmSCAP 66, –80*
Phillips, Gordon 1908- *WhoHol A, WhoMus 72*
Phillips, Guy Tom 1926- *IntWWM 77*
Phillips, Harry G *ConAmC*
Phillips, Harvey 1929- *Baker 78, IntWWM 77, –80, NewGrD 80, WhoMus 72*
Phillips, Helena 1875-1955 *Film 2, WhScrn 74, –77, WhoHol B*
Phillips, Henry 1801-1876 *NewGrD 80*
Phillips, Howard Baron 1909- *AmSCAP 66, –80, CmpEPM*
Phillips, Irna d1974 *NewYTET*
Phillips, J C 1953- *AmSCAP 80*
Phillips, Jack d1956 *NotNAT B*
Phillips, James *Film 2*
Phillips, Jane *DcPup*
Phillips, Jean d1970 *WhScrn 77, WhoHol A*
Phillips, Jean 1942- *IntWWM 77, –80*
Phillips, Jobyna *WhoHol A*
Phillips, Joe 1893- *NewOrJ[port]*
Phillips, John *EncFCWM 69, WhoHol A*
Phillips, John d1765? *NewGrD 80*
Phillips, John Charles 1921- *WhoMus 72*
Phillips, John E A 1941- *AmSCAP 80, BiDAmM*
Phillips, John Henry, Sr. 1877-1948 *NewOrJ*
Phillips, Joseph Edward 1915- *BiDAmM, EncJzS 70*
Phillips, Julia *IntMPA 77, –78, –79, –80*
Phillips, Karen 1942- *IntWWM 77, –80*
Phillips, Kate 1856-1931 *NotNAT B, WhThe*
Phillips, Katherine 1912- *AmSCAP 66, –80*
Phillips, Kenneth Edward 1916- *WhoMus 72*

Phillips, Kenneth Jay 1949- *AmSCAP 80*
Phillips, Lena Margaret 1944- *IntWWM 77, -80*
Phillips, Leslie 1924- *FilmgC, HalFC 80, IlWWBF, IntMPA 77, -75, -76, -78, -79, -80, WhoHol A, WhoThe 72, -77*
Phillips, Linda 1946- *IntWWM 77, -80, WhoMus 72, WhoOp 76*
Phillips, Lloyd 1905?- *WhoJazz 72*
Phillips, Lois 1926- *IntWWM 80, WhoMus 72*
Phillips, Lorraine *AmSCAP 80*
Phillips, Louis James 1942- *AmSCAP 80, NatPD[port]*
Phillips, MacKenzie 1960- *HalFC 80, MovMk, WhoHol A*
Phillips, Margaret 1923- *BiE&WWA, NotNAT, WhoHol A, WhoThe 72, -77*
Phillips, Marjorie D K *PupTheA*
Phillips, Mary 1901-1975 *WhScrn 77*
Phillips, Michael 1916- *IntMPA 77, -75, -76, -78, -79, -80, WomWMM*
Phillips, Michelle *WhoHol A*
Phillips, Mildred *AmSCAP 66, -80*
Phillips, Minna 1885-1963 *NotNAT B, WhScrn 74, -77, WhoHol B*
Phillips, Montague Fawcett 1885-1969 *Baker 78, NewGrD 80*
Phillips, Murray 1910- *AmSCAP 80*
Phillips, Nancy *Film 2*
Phillips, Noreen *Film 2*
Phillips, Norma 1893-1931 *Film 1, MotPP, NotNAT B, WhScrn 74, -77, WhoHol B*
Phillips, Norman, Sr. 1892-1931 *WhScrn 74, -77*
Phillips, Patricia Muriel 1933- *WhoMus 72*
Phillips, Paul *WhoHol A*
Phillips, Peggy *NatPD[port]*
Phillips, Peter *NewGrD 80*
Phillips, Peter 1930- *ConAmC, NewGrD 80*
Phillips, Phil 1931- *AmPS A, RkOn*
Phillips, Philip 1834-1895 *Baker 78, BiDAmM, NewGrD 80*
Phillips, Richard 1826-1941 *WhScrn 74, -77*
Phillips, Robert *ConAmC, WhoHol A*
Phillips, Robin 1942- *WhoHol A, WhoThe 72, -77*
Phillips, Sam 1923- *ConMuA 80B, IlEncR*
Phillips, Shawn 1943- *AmSCAP 80, ConMuA 80A*
Phillips, Sian 1934- *FilmgC, HalFC 80, WhoHol A, WhoThe 72, -77*
Phillips, Sid 1907-1973 *CmpEPM, WhoMus 72*
Phillips, Stephen 1864-1915 *EncWT, McGEWD, ModWD, NotNAT B, OxThe*
Phillips, Stephen 1866-1915 *WhThe*
Phillips, Stuart 1929- *IntWWM 77*
Phillips, Teddy 1917- *AmSCAP 66*
Phillips, Teddy Steve 1916- *AmSCAP 80*
Phillips, Thomas *NewGrD 80*
Phillips, Timothy William James 1949- *IntWWM 77*
Phillips, Van 1943- *WhoMus 72, WhoOp 76*
Phillips, Vivian D 1917- *ConAmC*
Phillips, Walter Joseph 1884-1963 *CreCan 1*
Phillips, Watts d1874 *NotNAT B*
Phillips, Wendell K 1907- *BiE&WWA, NotNAT, WhoHol A*
Phillips, Wendy *WomWMM B*
Phillips, William d1957 *ForYSC, WhScrn 74, -77, WhoHol B*
Phillips, William Clarence 1936- *BiDAmM*
Phillips, Willie 1885?- *NewOrJ*
Phillips, Wilma Susanne 1941- *AmSCAP 80*
Phillips, Woolf 1919- *WhoMus 72*
Phillips, Zoe *WomWMM*
Phillips-Watts, Curt 1949- *IntWWM 77*
Phillpots, Ambrosine 1912- *WhoHol A*
Phillpotts, Adelaide 1896- *WhThe*
Phillpotts, Ambrosine 1912- *WhoThe 72, -77*
Phillpotts, Eden 1862-1960 *EncWT, NotNAT B, OxThe, WhThe*
Philocles *OxThe*
Philodemus 110?BC-035?BC *NewGrD 80*
Philolaus *NewGrD 80*
Philotheos *NewGrD 80*
Philovalensis, Hieronim *NewGrD 80*
Philpot, Lucy *NewGrD 80*
Philpott, A R *DcPup*
Philpott, Violet M *DcPup*
Philpotts, Ambrosine 1912- *FilmgC, HalFC 80*
Phinot, Dominico 1510?-1555? *NewGrD 80*
Phinot, Dominique 1510?-1555? *NewGrD 80*
Phipps, Nicholas 1913- *FilmgC, HalFC 80, WhoHol A, WhoThe 72, -77*
Phipps, Sally *Film 2, WhoHol A*
Phipps, William *ForYSC, WhoHol A*
Phizacklea, Thomas Islym 1906- *WhoMus 72*
Phoebus, Frank Coleman 1899-1968 *AmSCAP 80*
Phrynichos 541?BC-470?BC *Ent*
Phrynichus *OxThe*
Phrynis Of Mitylene *NewGrD 80*
Phrynis Of Mytilene *NewGrD 80*
Phylypps *NewGrD 80*
Physioc, Joseph Allen d1951 *NotNAT B*
Physioc, Wray 1890- *TwYS A*
Pi, Rosario *WomWMM*
Piacenti, Enrico *Film 2*
Piacentini, Vincent 1922- *NotNAT*
Piacenza, Domenico Da *NewGrD 80*
Piacenza, Giuseppe Allevi *NewGrD 80*
Piaf, Edith d1963 *WhoHol B*
Piaf, Edith 1915-1963 *Baker 78, CmpEPM, MusMk[port], NewGrD 80, NotNAT B, OxThe*
Piaf, Edith 1916-1963 *WhScrn 74, -77*
Piaggi, Anthony Francis 1952- *IntWWM 80*
Pialat, Maurice 1925- *FilmEn, HalFC 80*
Piamenta, Abraham 1938- *IntWWM 77, -80*
Piamor, John *NewGrD 80*
Piana, Giovanni Antonio *NewGrD 80*
Pianelaio DeFirence, Jachopo *NewGrD 80*
Piani, Giovanni Antonio 1678-1757? *NewGrD 80*
Piano, Anthony A 1926- *AmSCAP 66, -80*
Piano, Giovanni Antonio *NewGrD 80*
Piano Choir *EncJzS 70*
Piano Red *BluesWW[port]*
Piantadosi, Al 1884-1955 *AmPS, AmSCAP 66, -80, BiDAmM, CmpEPM*
Piantanida, Giovanni 1705-1782 *NewGrD 80*
Piastro, Josef 1889-1964 *Baker 78, ConAmC*
Piastro, Michel 1891-1970 *Baker 78*
Piatigorsky, Gregar 1903-1976 *BiDAmM*
Piatigorsky, Gregor 1903-1976 *Baker 78, BnBkM 80, IntWWM 77, MusMk, MusSN[port], NewGrD 80, WhoMus 72*
Piatti, Alfredo Carlo 1822-1901 *Baker 78, BnBkM 80, NewGrD 80[port], OxMus*
Piave, Francesco Maria 1810-1876 *NewEOp 71*
Piave, Francesco Mario 1810-1876 *NewGrD 80*
Piavko, Vladislav Ivanovich 1941- *WhoOp 76*
Piazza, Ben 1934- *BiE&WWA, FilmgC, HalFC 80, MotPP, NotNAT, WhoHol A, WhoThe 72, -77*
Piazza, Dario 1904-1974 *WhScrn 77*
Piazza, Giovanni Battista *NewGrD 80*
Piazza, Jim *WhoHol A*
Pibernik, Zlatko 1926- *NewGrD 80*
Pibrac, Guy DuFaur De 1528?-1584 *NewGrD 80*
Pica, Tina 1884-1968 *FilmAG WE*
Pica, Tina 1888-1968 *WhScrn 74, -77, WhoHol B*
Picabia, Francis *Film 2*
Picander *NewGrD 80*
Picanol, Jose d1769? *NewGrD 80*
Picanyol, Jose d1769? *NewGrD 80*
Picard *NewGrD 80*
Picard, Le *NewGrD 80*
Picard, Andre 1874-1926 *McGEWD[port], NotNAT B, WhThe*
Picard, Louis Baptiste 1769-1828 *NotNAT B, OxThe*
Picard, Nicolas *NewGrD 80*
Picardi, Andreas *NewGrD 80*
Picardi, Rudolph 1927- *IntWWM 77, -80*
Picardia, Petrus De *NewGrD 80*
Picardo, Thomas R 1942- *AmSCAP 80*
Picardus, Anthonius *NewGrD 80*
Picariello, Frederick Anthony 1922- *AmSCAP 80*
Picart *NewGrD 80*
Picart, Nicolas *NewGrD 80*
Picasso, Pablo Ruiz 1881-1973 *CnOxB, DancEn 78, DcFM, EncWT, Ent, WhScrn 77*
Picavet *NewGrD 80*
Picazo, Miguel 1929- *WorEFlm*
Piccardia *NewGrD 80*
Piccardo *NewGrD 80*
Piccaver, Alfred 1884-1958 *CmOp, NewEOp 71, NewGrD 80*
Picchardo *NewGrD 80*
Picchardo, Ant *NewGrD 80*
Picchi, Giovanni *NewGrD 80, OxMus*
Picchi, Mirto 1915- *NewGrD 80, WhoOp 76*
Picchi, Silvano 1922- *Baker 78, IntWWM 77, -80*
Piccinato, Carlo Ferdinando 1907- *WhoOp 76*
Piccini, Signor *DcPup*
Piccini, Niccolo 1728-1800 *GrComp[port]*
Piccini, Nicola 1728-1800 *OxMus*
Piccinini, Alessandro 1566-1638? *NewGrD 80*
Piccininni, Jeanette M 1956- *AmSCAP 80*
Piccinni *NewGrD 80*
Piccinni, Lodovico 1764-1827 *NewGrD 80*
Piccinni, Lodovico Alessandro 1779-1850 *NewGrD 80*
Piccinni, Louis Alexandre 1779-1850 *NewGrD 80*
Piccinni, Luigi 1764-1827 *NewGrD 80*
Piccinni, Luigi Alessandro 1779-1850 *NewGrD 80*
Piccinni, Niccolo 1728-1800 *Baker 78, BnBkM 80, CmOp, MusMk[port], NewGrD 80[port]*
Piccinni, Nicola 1728-1800 *NewEOp 71, NewGrD 80[port]*
Piccioli, Giacomo Antonio *NewGrD 80*
Piccioli, Jacomo Antonio *NewGrD 80*
Piccioni, Giovanni 1550?-1619? *NewGrD 80*
Piccioni, Piero 1921- *WorEFlm*
Piccola Pasta, La *NewGrD 80*
Piccoli, Michel 1925- *BiDFilm 81, FilmAG WE[port], FilmEn, FilmgC, HalFC 80, MovMk[port], OxFilm, WhoHol A, WorEFlm*
Piccolo, Anthony 1946- *ConAmC*
Piccolo, Ottavia 1949- *FilmAG WE*
Piccolomini, Enea Silvio 1405-1464 *OxThe*
Piccolomini, Marietta 1834-1899 *CmOp, NewGrD 80*
Piccolomini, Nicolo *NewGrD 80*
Picerli, Silverio *NewGrD 80*
Picerni, Paul 1922- *FilmEn, FilmgC, ForYSC, HalFC 80, IntMPA 77, -75, -76, -78, -79, -80, WhoHol A*
Picha, Frantisek 1893-1964 *NewGrD 80*
Picha, Hermann *Film 2*
Pichardo, Filippo *NewGrD 80*
Pichel, Irving 1891-1954 *BiDFilm 81, FilmEn, FilmgC, ForYSC, HalFC 80, HolCA[port], MovMk[port], NotNAT B, PlP&P, WhScrn 74, -77, WhoHol B, WhoHrs 80, WorEFlm*
Pichel, Vaclav 1741-1805 *NewGrD 80*
Picher, Claude 1927- *CreCan 2*
Pichette, Henri 1923- *REnWD[port]*
Pichette, Henri 1924- *McGEWD, ModWD*
Pichl, Vaclav 1741-1805 *NewGrD 80*
Pichl, Wenzel 1741-1805 *Baker 78*
Pichler, Guenter 1940- *WhoMus 72*
Pichler, Gusti 1893- *CnOxB*
Pichon, Fats 1906-1967 *EncJzS 70, WhoJazz 72*
Pichon, Walter 1905-1957 *NewOrJ[port]*
Pichon, Walter 1906-1967 *BluesWW[port], EncJzS 70*
Picht-Axenfeld, Edith Maria 1914- *IntWWM 77, -80, NewGrD 80, WhoMus 72*
Pichteler VonGreiffenthal, Matthias S *NewGrD 80*
Pick, Karl Heinz 1929- *IntWWM 77, -80*
Pick, Lupe 1886-1931 *WhScrn 74, -77*
Pick, Lupu 1886-1931 *BiDFilm, -81, DcFM, FilmEn, Film 2, HalFC 80, OxFilm, WhoHol B*
Pick, Richard Samuel Burns 1915- *ConAmC, IntWWM 77, -80*
Pick-Hieronimi, Monica 1943- *WhoOp 76*
Pick-Mangiagalli, Riccardo 1882-1949 *Baker 78, NewGrD 80, OxMus*
Picka, Frantisek 1873-1918 *Baker 78*
Pickar, Arnold *NewGrD 80*
Pickard, Alan Henry 1942- *IntWWM 80*

Pickard, Charles Gilbert *WhoMus 72*
Pickard, Christine Frances *WhoMus 72*
Pickard, Helena d1959 *WhoHol B*
Pickard, Helena 1899-1959 *OxThe*
Pickard, Helena 1900-1959 *NotNAT B, WhScrn 74, -77, WhThe*
Pickard, John *WhoHol A*
Pickard, Mae d1946 *NotNAT B*
Pickard, Margery 1911- *WhThe*
Pickard, Obey d1958 *BiDAmM*
Pickart *NewGrD 80*
Pickel, Conrad *NewGrD 80*
Pickelherring *OxThe*
Pickell, Edward Ray 1934- *AmSCAP 80*
Picken, Laurence 1909- *NewGrD 80*
Pickens, Edwin Goodwin 1916-1964 *BluesWW*
Pickens, Helen Jean *PupTheA*
Pickens, Jane *CmpEPM, EncMT*
Pickens, Slim 1919- *BluesWW, FilmEn, FilmgC, ForYSC, HalFC 80, HolCA[port], IntMPA 77, -75, -76, -78, -79, -80, MovMk[port], Vers A[port], WhoHol A*
Pickens Sisters, The *CmpEPM, What 4[port]*
Picker, Arnold M 1913- *IntMPA 77, -75, -76, -78, -79, -80*
Picker, David V 1931- *IntMPA 77, -75, -76, -78, -79, -80*
Picker, Eugene D 1903- *IntMPA 77, -75, -76, -78, -79, -80*
Picker, Geraldine Lee 1945- *AmSCAP 80*
Picker, Martin 1929- *NewGrD 80*
Pickering, Edward A 1871- *WhThe*
Pickering, J Russell d1947 *NotNAT B*
Pickett, Bill *BlksB&W C*
Pickett, Bobby Boris 1940- *RkOn*
Pickett, Elizabeth *WomWMM*
Pickett, Ingram B 1899-1963 *NotNAT B, WhScrn 74, -77, WhoHol B*
Pickett, Jess 1860?-1922? *BiDAmM*
Pickett, Wilson 1941- *BiDAmM, ConMuA 80A[port], DrBlPA, RkOn[port]*
Pickford, Jack 1896-1933 *FilmEn, Film 1, -2, FilmgC, HalFC 80, NotNAT B, TwYS, WhScrn 74, -77, WhoHol B*
Pickford, Lottie 1895-1936 *Film 1, -2, NotNAT B, TwYS, WhScrn 74, -77, WhoHol B*
Pickford, Mary 1893-1979 *BiDFilm, -81, FilmEn, Film 1, -2, FilmgC, HalFC 80[port], IntMPA 77, -75, -76, -78, -79, MotPP, MovMk[port], OxFilm, PlP&P, ThFT[port], TwYS, WhThe, WhoHol A, WomWMM, WorEFlm[port]*
Pickhart, Arnold *NewGrD 80*
Pickles, Christina *WhoHol A*
Pickles, Vivian 1933- *FilmgC, HalFC 80, WhoHol A*
Pickles, Wilfred 1904-1978 *FilmgC, HalFC 80, IntMPA 77, -75, -76, -78, WhoHol A*
Pickman, Jerome 1916- *IntMPA 77, -75, -76, -78, -79, -80*
Pickman, Milton Eugene *IntMPA 77, -75, -76, -78, -79, -80*
Pickthall, Marjorie Lowry Christie 1883-1922 *CreCan 1*
Pickup, Ronald 1941- *WhoHol A, WhoThe 72, -77*
Pickus, Albert M 1903- *IntMPA 77, -75, -76, -78, -79, -80*
Pico, Foriano *NewGrD 80*
Picon, Molly 1898- *AmSCAP 66, BiE&WWA, HalFC 80, NotNAT, -A, WhoHol A, WhoThe 72, -77*
Picot, Eustache 1575?-1651 *NewGrD 80*
Picou, Alphonse 1880-1961 *NewOrJ[port]*
Picou, Alphonse Floristan 1878-1961 *BiDAmM, WhoJazz 72*
Picquet *NewGrD 80*
Picquigny, Gerardus *NewGrD 80*
Pidal, Jose 1896-1956 *WhScrn 74, -77*
Piddington, Lesley *MagIlD*
Piddington, Sydney *MagIlD*
Piddock, J C d1919 *NotNAT B*
Pidgeon, Edward Everett d1941 *NotNAT B*
Pidgeon, John *PupTheA*
Pidgeon, Walter *MotPP*
Pidgeon, Walter 1897- *BiDFilm, -81, BiE&WWA, CmMov, CmpEPM, FilmEn, Film 2, FilmgC, HalFC 80, MGM[port], OxFilm, TwYS, WhoHol A, WhoHrs 80, WhoThe 72, -77, WorEFlm*
Pidgeon, Walter 1898- *ForYSC, IntMPA 77, -75, -76, -78, -79, -80, MovMk[port]*
Pidoux, Pierre 1905- *NewGrD 80*
Pie DeDieu, Pierre *NewGrD 80*
Piechelr, Arthur 1896- *IntWWM 77*
Piechler, Arthur 1896- *IntWWM 80*
Piechowska, Alina 1937- *IntWWM 77, -80*
Pied Pipers, The *BiDAmM, CmpEPM*
Pieete, Koos 1947- *IntWWM 77*
Piehtler VonGreiffenthal, Matthias S *NewGrD 80*
Piekarz, Ladislaus 1930- *IntWWM 77, -80*
Piel, Edward 1888-1958 *Film 2, WhScrn 74, -77*
Piel, Edward, Jr. 1908-1962 *Film 2, WhScrn 74, -77*
Piel, Harry 1892-1963 *FilmAG WE, WhScrn 77*
Piel, Walter Karl 1939- *IntWWM 77, -80*
Piela, Andrzej 1938- *IntWWM 77*
Pieltain, Dieudonne-Pascal 1754?-1833 *NewGrD 80*
Pieplu, Claude 1923- *FilmAG WE[port]*
Pieranti, Diva Francisca E 1931- *WhoOp 76*
Pieranzovini, Pietro 1814-1885 *OxMus*
Pierat, Marie Therese d1934 *NotNAT B, WhThe*
Pierce, Alexandra 1934- *AmSCAP 80, CpmDNM 78, -79, -80*
Pierce, Barbara *Film 2*
Pierce, Bettye *AmSCAP 80*
Pierce, Billie 1905-1974 *EncJzS 70*
Pierce, Billie 1907-1974 *BluesWW[port], NewOrJ[port]*
Pierce, Bobby 1942- *EncJzS 70*
Pierce, Charlotte *Film 2*
Pierce, Curtis *Film 2*
Pierce, Dede 1904-1973 *EncJzS 70*
Pierce, Don 1915- *EncFCWM 69*
Pierce, Edward *NewGrD 80*
Pierce, Elnora Retledge Cooper *IntWWM 77, -80*
Pierce, Evelyn 1908-1960 *Film 2, WhScrn 74, -77, WhoHol B*
Pierce, Frederick S *IntMPA 77, -76, -78, -79, -80, NewYTET*
Pierce, George *Film 1, -2, WhScrn 74, -77*
Pierce, Jack 1889-1968 *DcFM, FilmEn, FilmgC, HalFC 80, WhoHrs 80[port]*
Pierce, James 1905- *WhoHol A*
Pierce, James H 1900- *Film 2*
Pierce, Jane Gail Illingworth 1948- *IntWWM 77, -80*
Pierce, Jerry Dale 1937- *IntWWM 77, -80*
Pierce, Jim 1900- *WhoHrs 80*
Pierce, Joseph DeLacrois 1904-1973 *BiDAmM, EncJzS 70*
Pierce, Joseph DeLaCroix 1904-1973 *NewOrJ[port]*
Pierce, Judith *WhoMus 72*
Pierce, Maggie *WhoHol A*
Pierce, Nat 1925- *AmSCAP 66, -80, BiDAmM, CmpEPM, EncJzS 70*
Pierce, Ponchitta 1942- *DrBlPA*
Pierce, Webb 1926- *AmSCAP 80, BiDAmM, CmpEPM, CounME 74[port], -74A, EncFCWM 69, IlEncCM[port], RkOn*
Pierce, Wilhelmina Goodson 1905-1974 *EncJzS 70*
Pierce, Wilhelmina Goodson 1907-1974 *BlkWAB*
Pierchala, Ryszard 1920- *IntWWM 77*
Pierlot, Denis *NewGrD 80*
Pierlot, Francis 1876-1953 *ForYSC*
Pierlot, Francis 1876-1955 *HalFC 80, MotPP, NotNAT B, WhScrn 74, -77, WhoHol B*
Pierlot, Pierre 1921- *NewGrD 80*
Piermarini, Clito L 1927- *AmSCAP 80*
Piernay, Rudolf 1943- *IntWWM 77, -80*
Pierne, Gabriel 1863-1937 *Baker 78, CompSN[port], DcCom&M 79, MusMk, NewEOp 71, NewGrD 80, OxMus*
Pierne, Paul 1874-1952 *Baker 78*
Piero *NewGrD 80[port]*
Piero Degli Organi *NewGrD 80*
Pierpont, James S 1822-1893 *Baker 78, BiDAmM*
Pierpont, John 1785-1866 *BiDAmM*
Pierpont, Laura 1881-1972 *WhScrn 77*
Pierray, Claude *NewGrD 80*
Pierre Bonnel *NewGrD 80*
Pierre De Corbeil d1222 *NewGrD 80*
Pierre De Corbie d1195? *NewGrD 80*
Pierre De La Croix *NewGrD 80*
Pierre De Molaines *NewGrD 80*
Pierre De Molins *NewGrD 80*
Pierre, Anatole d1926 *WhScrn 74, -77*
Pierre, Andre 1884-1975 *WhScrn 77*
Pierre, Constant 1855-1918 *Baker 78, NewGrD 80*
Pierre, Dorothi Bock *DancEn 78*
Pierre, Francis 1931- *NewGrD 80*
Pierre, Paul DeLa *NewGrD 80*
Pierrekin De La Coupele *NewGrD 80*
Pierrequin De Therache *NewGrD 80*
Pierreson Cambio *NewGrD 80*
Pierront, Noelie Marie Antoinette 1899- *WhoMus 72*
Pierrot De Neele *NewGrD 80*
Pierrot, Noelie Marie Antoinette 1899- *IntWWM 77, -80*
Piersall, Jimmy 1929- *What 5[port]*
Piersel, David Thomas 1937- *IntWWM 77*
Piersen, Arthur 1891?-1975 *WhoHol C*
Pierson, Arthur 1891?-1975 *WhScrn 77*
Pierson, Arthur Tappan 1837-1911 *BiDAmM*
Pierson, Eddie 1904-1958 *NewOrJ*
Pierson, Edward 1931- *IntWWM 77, -80, WhoOp 76*
Pierson, Frank 1925- *FilmgC, IntMPA 77, -78, -79, -80, NewYTET*
Pierson, Frank 1945- *HalFC 80*
Pierson, Henry Hugh 1815-1873 *Baker 78*
Pierson, Henry Hugo 1815-1873 *NewGrD 80, OxMus*
Pierson, Herbert 1914- *IntWWM 77, -80*
Pierson, Hugh 1815-1873 *NewGrD 80*
Pierson, Robert Morey 1930- *BiDAmM*
Pierson, Suzy *Film 2*
Pierson, Thomas Claude 1922- *IntWWM 77, -80*
Pierszynski, Kasper *NewGrD 80*
Piestrup, Donald J 1937- *AmSCAP 80*
Piestrup, Donall James 1937- *EncJzS 70*
Pietarinen, Riitta Annikki 1939- *WhoOp 76*
Pieterszoon, Adriaan 1400?-1480 *NewGrD 80*
Pietkin, Lambert 1613?-1696 *NewGrD 80*
Pieton, Aloysis *NewGrD 80*
Pieton, Louys *NewGrD 80*
Pieton, Loys *NewGrD 80*
Pieton, Loyset *NewGrD 80*
Pietragrua *NewGrD 80*
Pietrangeli, Antonio 1919-1968 *OxFilm, WorEFlm*
Pietrequin Bonnel *NewGrD 80*
Pietri, Giuseppe 1886-1946 *Baker 78*
Pietrich, Roger T *ConAmC*
Pietro Dei Rossi *NewGrD 80*
Pietrobelli, Francesco *NewGrD 80*
Pietrobono 1417?-1497 *NewGrD 80*
Pietrobono Del Chitarino 1417?-1497 *NewGrD 80*
Pietrowski, Karol *NewGrD 80*
Pietruszynska, Jadwiga *NewGrD 80*
Pietsch, Edna Frida 1894- *ConAmC*
Pifait *NewGrD 80*
Pifaro, Marc'Antonio 1500?- *NewGrD 80*
Pifaro, Nicolo *NewGrD 80*
Pifay *NewGrD 80*
Pifet *NewGrD 80*
Piffard, Frederic 1902- *WhThe, WhoThe 72*
Piffet *NewGrD 80*
Piffet, Joseph-Antoine 1710?- *NewGrD 80*
Piffet, Louis-Francois-Barthelemy 1734-1779 *NewGrD 80*
Piffet, Pierre d1760? *NewGrD 80*
Piffet, Pierre-Louis 1706?-1773 *NewGrD 80*
Pig 'n' Whistle Red *BluesWW*
Pigeaud, Francois Andre Jean Robert 1943- *IntWWM 80*
Piggot, Tempe 1884-1962 *Film 2*
Piggott, Audrey Margaret *IntWWM 77, -80, WhoMus 72*
Piggott, Patrick *WhoMus 72*
Piggott, Tempe 1884-1962 *TwYS*
Pigmeat *DrBlPA*
Pigmeat Pete *BluesWW*
Pignati, Pietro Romulo d1700 *NewGrD 80*

Pignatta, Pietro Romulo d1700? *NewGrD 80*
Pigneguy, John Joseph 1945- *IntWWM 77, -80*
Pigonitis, Joannes Laskaris *NewGrD 80*
Pigorsch, Phyllis *WomWMM B*
Pigott, A S *WhThe*
Pigott, Francis 1665?-1704 *NewGrD 80*
Pigott, Raymond 1935- *IntWWM 77, -80, WhoMus 72*
Pigott, Tempe 1884-1962 *ForYSC, HalFC 80, NotNAT B, WhScrn 74, -77, WhoHol B*
Piguet, Michel 1932- *IntWWM 77, -80, NewGrD 80*
Pihl, Christine R *WomWMM B*
Piispanen, Sylvi Elisabet *IntWWM 77, -80*
Pijper, Willem 1894-1947 *Baker 78, CompSN[port], DcCM, MusMk, NewGrD 80[port], OxMus*
Pikayzen, Viktor Alexandrovich 1933- *NewGrD 80*
Pike, Albert 1809-1891 *BiDAmM*
Pike, Alfred 1913- *ConAmC*
Pike, Dave 1938- *EncJzS 70*
Pike, David Samuel 1938- *BiDAmM, EncJzS 70*
Pike, Eleanor B Franklin *WhoMus 72*
Pike, Harry J d1919 *WhScrn 77*
Pike, Lionel John 1939- *IntWWM 80*
Pike, Nita 1913-1954 *WhScrn 74, -77, WhoHol B*
Pike, William *Film 1*
Piket, Frederick 1903-1974 *AmSCAP 66, -80, ConAmC*
Pikler, Charles Robert 1951- *IntWWM 77, -80*
Pikler, Robert 1909- *NewGrD 80*
Pila, Maximo 1886-1939 *WhScrn 74, -77*
Piland, Jeanne Smith 1945- *IntWWM 77, -80*
Pilarczyk, Helga 1925- *Baker 78, CmOp, NewGrD 80, WhoMus 72*
Pilati, Mario 1903-1938 *Baker 78, NewGrD 80*
Pilato, Boris 1921- *CnOxB*
Pilbeam, Nova 1919- *FilmAG WE, FilmgC, HalFC 80, IlWWBF, OxFilm, ThFT[port], WhThe, WhoHol A*
Pilbrow, Richard 1933- *WhoThe 72, -77*
Pilcer, Harry 1885-1961 *Film 1, NotNAT B, WhScrn 77, WhThe*
Pilcher, Gerard W *NewGrD 80*
Pilcher, Henry 1798-1880 *NewGrD 80*
Pilcher, Henry, Jr. 1828-1890 *NewGrD 80*
Pilcher, J V *NewGrD 80*
Pilcher, Paul B *NewGrD 80*
Pilcher, R E *NewGrD 80*
Pilcher, Tony 1936- *IntMPA 77, -75, -76, -78, -79, -80*
Pilcher, William 1830- *NewGrD 80*
Pilcher, William E *NewGrD 80*
Pilcher, William E, Jr. *NewGrD 80*
Piletta, Georges 1945- *CnOxB*
Pilgrim, Jack Alfred 1929- *IntWWM 77, -80*
Pilgrim, James 1825-1877 *NotNAT B*
Pilhofer, Herb *ConMuA 80B*
Pilhofer, Phil *ConAmC*
Pilia, Paolo 1933- *WhoMus 72*
Pilikhina, Margarita *WomWMM*
Pilinski, Stanislaw 1839-1905 *NewGrD 80*
Pilkington, Charles Vere 1905- *IntWWM 77, -80*
Pilkington, Constance *WhoMus 72*
Pilkington, Francis d1638? *BnBkM 80*
Pilkington, Francis 1562?-1638 *Baker 78, OxMus*
Pilkington, Francis 1570?-1638 *NewGrD 80*
Pilkington, Michael Charles 1928- *IntWWM 80*
Pillays, Johannes *NewGrD 80*
Piller, Eugene Seymour 1918- *AmSCAP 80*
Pillin, Boris William 1940- *AmSCAP 80, CpmDNM 73, -76, ConAmC*
Pillney, Karl Hermann 1896- *IntWWM 80, NewGrD 80*
Pillois, Jacques 1877-1935 *Baker 78, BiDAmM*
Pillot, Leo *IntMPA 75, -76*
Pillow, Ray 1937- *BiDAmM, CounME 74, -74A, IlEncCM[port]*
Pillow, Ray 1940?- *EncFCWM 69*
Pilobolus Dance Theater *CmpGMD*
Pilon, Jean-Guy 1930- *CreCan 2*
Pilon, Raymonde *WomWMM*
Pilos, Joanna 1931- *NewGrD 80*
Pilot *RkOn 2[port]*
Pilot, Bernice *Film 2*
Pilot, Robert W 1898-1967 *CreCan 1*
Pilotti-Schiavonetti, Elisabetta d1742 *NewGrD 80*
Pilotto, Camillo 1883?-1963 *WhScrn 77*
Pilou, Jeannette *NewEOp 71*
Pilou, Jeannette 1931- *NewGrD 80*
Pilou, Jeannette 1937- *WhoOp 76*
Pilss, Karl 1902- *CpmDNM 74, -75, -76, IntWWM 77, -80, OxMus*
Piltch, Bernie *CreCan 2*
Piltz, George d1968 *WhScrn 77*
Piltzecker, Ted 1950- *AmSCAP 80*
Pimley, John 1919-1972 *WhScrn 77*
Pimsleur, Solomon 1900-1962 *Baker 78, ConAmC*
Pinacci, Giovanni Battista *NewGrD 80*
Pinaire *NewGrD 80*
Pinard, Lancelot Victor 1902- *AmSCAP 80*
Pincherle, Marc 1888-1974 *Baker 78, NewGrD 80, OxMus, WhoMus 72*
Pinches, George *IntMPA 77, -75, -76, -78, -79, -80*
Pinchot, Rosamond d1936 *WhoHol B*
Pinchot, Rosamond 1904-1938 *NotNAT B*
Pinchot, Rosamond 1905-1938 *WhScrn 77*
Pincus, Buck *AmSCAP 80*
Pincus, Herman *AmSCAP 80*
Pincus, Irving *IntMPA 77, -75, -76, -78, -79, -80*
Pindar 522?BC-436?BC *NewGrD 80*
Pindaros 522?BC-436?BC *NewGrD 80*
Pindemonte, Giovanni 1751-1812 *McGEWD*
Pindemonte, Ippolito 1753-1828 *McGEWD[port]*
Pinder, Arthur Thomas 1917- *IntWWM 77, -80, WhoMus 72*
Pinder, Powis d1941 *NotNAT B*
Pine, Arthur 1917- *AmSCAP 80*
Pine, Ed 1904-1950 *WhScrn 74, -77*
Pine, Howard 1917- *IntMPA 77, -75, -76, -78, -79, -80*
Pine, Linda *Film 2*
Pine, Philip *WhoHol A*
Pine, Ralph 1939- *NotNAT*
Pine, Tina *WomWMM*
Pine, Virginia *WhoHol A*
Pine, William H 1896-195-? *CmMov, FilmEn, FilmgC, HalFC 80*
Pineapple, Johnny *AmSCAP 66, -80*
Pineda, Francisco DeAtienza Y *NewGrD 80*
Pineda-Duque, Roberto 1910- *NewGrD 80*
Pinel, Germain d1661 *NewGrD 80*
Pinelli, Ettore 1843-1915 *NewGrD 80*
Pinelli, Tullio 1908- *FilmEn*
Pinello DiGherardi, Giovanni Battista 1544?-1587 *NewGrD 80*
Pinello DiGhirardi, Giovanni Battista 1544?-1587 *NewGrD 80*
Pinellus DeGerardis, Giovanni Battista 1544?-1587 *NewGrD 80*
Pinera, Michael Carlos 1948- *AmSCAP 80*
Pinero, Anthony 1887-1958 *WhScrn 74, -77*
Pinero, Sir Arthur Wing 1855-1934 *CnThe, EncWT, Ent, HalFC 80, McGEWD[port], ModWD, NotNAT A, -B, OxThe, PlP&P, REnWD[port], WhScrn 77, WhThe, WhoStg 1906, -1908*
Pinero, Frank 1906?-1967 *NewOrJ*
Pinero, Jose Juan 1942- *AmSCAP 80*
Pinero, Miguel *MorBAP, PlP&P A[port]*
Pinetti, Giuseppe 1750-1800 *Ent*
Pinetti, Guiseppe 1750?-1800 *MagIlD*
Pinewood Tom *BluesWW*
Pingatore, Frank J 1930- *AmSCAP 66, -80*
Pinget, Robert 1919- *EncWT, McGEWD[port]*
Pinget, Robert 1920- *CnMD, CroCD, ModWD, REnWD[port]*
Pingirolo, Gabriele *NewGrD 80*
Pingirolo, Paolo *NewGrD 80*
Pingoud, Ernest 1888-1942 *Baker 78, NewGrD 80*
Pingree, Earl *Film 2*
Pinheiro, Antonio 1550?-1617 *NewGrD 80*
Pini, Anthony 1902- *NewGrD 80, WhoMus 72*
Pini, Carlos Antonio 1902- *NewGrD 80*
Pini, Eugene *WhoMus 72*
Pini-Corsi, Antonio 1858-1918 *CmOp, NewGrD 80[port]*
Pinilla, Enrique 1927- *DcCM, NewGrD 80*
Pink, Sidney 1916- *HalFC 80, IntMPA 77, -75, -76, -78, -79, -80, WhoHrs 80*
Pink, Wal d1922 *NotNAT B, WhThe*
Pink Fairies *IlEncR*
Pink Floyd *ConMuA 80A, IlEncR, RkOn 2[port]*
Pinkard, Edna Belle 1892- *AmSCAP 66, -80*
Pinkard, Maceo 1897-1962 *AmSCAP 66, -80, CmpEPM, NotNAT B*
Pinkert, Herb *AmSCAP 80*
Pinkerton, William Charles 1936- *AmSCAP 80*
Pinkett, Ward 1906-1937 *CmpEPM, WhoJazz 72*
Pinkett, William Ward 1906-1937 *BiDAmM*
Pinkham, Daniel 1923- *Baker 78, BnBkM 80, CpmDNM 72, -73, -79, -80, ConAmC, DcCM, NewGrD 80*
Pinkham, Richard R 1914- *IntMPA 77, -75, -76, -78, -79, -80, NewYTET*
Pinkser, Allen 1930- *IntMPA 75*
Pinkston, Gladys *IntWWM 77*
Pinnell, Janice Smith 1929- *IntWWM 77, -80*
Pinnell, Richard Tilden 1942- *IntWWM 80*
Pinnell, Ruth 1917- *IntWWM 77, -80*
Pinner, Clay 1895-1969 *NewOrJ*
Pinner, David 1940- *ConDr 73, -77*
Pinney, Charles *WhoHol A*
Pinnock, Trevor David 1946- *IntWWM 77, -80*
Pino, Rosario d1933 *NotNAT B, WhThe*
Pinos, Alois 1925- *Baker 78, DcCM, NewGrD 80*
Pinschof, Thomas 1948- *IntWWM 77, -80*
Pinsent, Gordon 1933- *FilmgC, HalFC 80, WhoHol A*
Pinsker, Allen 1930- *IntMPA 77, -76, -78, -79, -80*
Pinski, David 1872-1959 *CnMD, McGEWD, ModWD, REnWD[port]*
Pinsonneault, Bernard 1930- *WhoMus 72*
Pinsuti, Ciro 1829-1888 *Baker 78, NewGrD 80*
Pinsuto, Circo 1829-1888 *OxMus*
Pinta, Pamela *WhoHol A*
Pinter, Harold 1930- *BiE&WWA, CnThe, ConDr 73, -77, CroCD, DcFM, EncWT, Ent[port], FilmEn, FilmgC, HalFC 80, McGEWD, ModWD, NotNAT, OxFilm, OxThe, PlP&P[port], REnWD[port], WhoThe 72, -77, WorEFlm*
Pinter, Harold 1932- *CnMD*
Pintgen, Hans-Werner 1940- *WhoOp 76*
Pinto, Mrs. *NewGrD 80*
Pinto, Alejandro 1922- *IntWWM 77, -80*
Pinto, Alfredo 1891-1968 *Baker 78*
Pinto, Carlo D 1925- *IntWWM 77, -80*
Pinto, Francisco Antonio N DosSantos 1815-1860 *NewGrD 80*
Pinto, George Frederick 1785-1806 *NewGrD 80*
Pinto, Guiomar *NewGrD 80*
Pinto, Julia *NewGrD 80*
Pinto, Luiz Alvares 1719-1789? *NewGrD 80*
Pinto, Maurice 1907- *AmSCAP 80*
Pinto, Octavio 1890-1950 *Baker 78*
Pinto, Thomas 1714-1783 *NewGrD 80*
Pintoff, Ernest 1931- *DcFM, FilmEn, FilmgC, HalFC 80, OxFilm, WorEFlm*
Pinxy, Madame *PupTheA*
Pinz, Shelley 1943- *AmSCAP 80*
Pinza, Ezio d1957 *AmPS B, PlP&P[port], WhoHol B*
Pinza, Ezio 1892-1957 *Baker 78, BiDAmM, BnBkM 80, CmOp, CmpEPM, EncMT, FilmEn, ForYSC, MusSN[port], NewEOp 71, NewGrD 80[port], NotNAT B, WhScrn 74, -77*
Pinza, Ezio 1893-1957 *FilmgC, HalFC 80*
Pinzarrone, Nina Vacketta 1947- *IntWWM 80*
Pinzauti, Leonardo 1926- *NewGrD 80*
Pio, Elith *Film 2*
Pio, Francesco 1590?-1660? *NewGrD 80*
Piochi, Cristofano d1675? *NewGrD 80*
Piochi, Cristoforo d1675? *NewGrD 80*
Piollet, Wilfride 1943- *CnOxB*
Piombino, Rich *ConMuA 80B*
Pionerio, Joannes d1573 *NewGrD 80*
Pionnier, Joannes d1573 *NewGrD 80*

Pious, Minerva 1909-1979 *HalFC 80*
Piozzi, Gabriele Mario 1740-1809 *NewGrD 80*
Pipegrop, Heinrich *NewGrD 80*
Pipeiro, Roberto d1963 *WhScrn 77*
Pipelare, Matthaeus 1450?-1512? *Baker 78*
Pipelare, Matthaeus 1450?-1515? *NewGrD 80*
Piper, Alan 1926- *IntWWM 77*
Piper, Anne *WomWMM*
Piper, Elsie B 1903- *IntWWM 77*
Piper, Franco *WhThe*
Piper, Frederick 1902-1979 *FilmgC, HalFC 80, IntMPA 77, -75, -76, -78, -79, -80, WhoHol A*
Piper, John 1903- *CnOxB, DancEn 78*
Pipes, William *BlkAmP*
Pipgrop, Heinrich *NewGrD 80*
Pipgroppe, Heinrich *NewGrD 80*
Pipia, Mimmo 1902- *AmSCAP 66, -80*
Pipkins, The *RkOn 2[port]*
Pipkov, Lubomir 1904-1974 *Baker 78, DcCM*
Pipkov, Lyubomir 1904-1974 *NewGrD 80*
Pipkov, Panayot 1871-1942 *NewGrD 80*
Pipo *NewGrD 80*
Pipo 1902-1970 *WhScrn 74, -77*
Pippin, Don *NotNAT*
Pippin, Donald W 1930- *AmSCAP 66*
Piquart, Joannes Robert Dit *NewGrD 80*
Pique, Francois-Louis 1758-1822 *NewGrD 80*
Piquigny, Robert De *NewGrD 80*
Pirandello, Luigi 1867-1936 *CnMD, CnThe, EncWT, Ent[port], McGEWD[port], ModWD, NotNAT A, -B, OxThe, PlP&P, -A[port], REnWD[port], WhThe*
Piranesi, Giovanni Battista 1720-1778 *NotNAT B*
Pirani, Eugenio 1852-1939 *Baker 78*
Pirani, Max Gabriel 1898- *WhoMus 72*
Pirchan, Emil 1884-1957 *EncWT*
Pirck, Wenzel Raimund 1718?-1763 *NewGrD 80*
Pirckh, Wenzel Raimund 1718?-1763 *NewGrD 80*
Pirenne, Maurice Maria 1928- *IntWWM 77, -80*
Pires, Filipe 1934- *Baker 78, DcCM, NewGrD 80*
Pires, Vasco *NewGrD 80*
Pirie, Peter John 1916- *IntWWM 77, -80, NewGrD 80, WhoMus 72*
Pirner, Gitti 1943- *IntWWM 77, -80*
Pirogov, Alexander 1899-1964 *CmOp, NewGrD 80*
Pirogov, Alexandr 1899-1964 *Baker 78*
Pirogov, Grigory 1885-1931 *NewGrD 80*
Piron, Alexis 1689-1773 *Ent, McGEWD, OxThe*
Piron, Armand John 1888-1943 *AmSCAP 66, -80, NewOrJ[port], WhoJazz 72*
Pironkov, Simeon 1927- *Baker 78, NewGrD 80*
Pirosh, Robert 1910- *CmMov, FilmEn, FilmgC, HalFC 80, IntMPA 77, -75, -76, -78, -79, -80*
Pirot, Andre *NewGrD 80*
Piroye, Charles 1668?-1730? *NewGrD 80*
Pirro, Andre 1869-1943 *Baker 78, NewGrD 80*
Pirrot, Andre 1869-1943 *NewGrD 80*
Pirrotta, Antonino 1908- *NewGrD 80*
Pirrotta, Nino 1908- *Baker 78, NewGrD 80*
Pirsson, William 1780?- *BiDAmM*
Pirszczynski, Kasper *NewGrD 80*
Pisa, Agostino *Baker 78, NewGrD 80*
Pisacane, Marci 1946- *AmSCAP 80*
Pisador, Diego 1509?-1557? *Baker 78, NewGrD 80*
Pisanelli, Pompilio d1606? *NewGrD 80*
Pisani, Nicola *NewGrD 80*
Pisano, Bernardo 1490-1548 *NewGrD 80*
Pisano, John 1931- *EncJzS 70*
Pisano, Nicola *NewGrD 80*
Pisari, Pasquale 1725-1778 *Baker 78, NewGrD 80*
Pisaroni, Benedetta Rosmunda 1793-1872 *NewGrD 80*
Pisarri, Alessandro *NewGrD 80*
Piscaer, Anny Petronella Henrica Maria 1902- *IntWWM 77, -80*
Piscator, Erwin 1893-1966 *BiE&WWA, CnThe, CroCD, DcFM, EncWT, Ent[port], NotNAT A, -B, OxThe, WorEFlm*
Piscator, Georg *NewGrD 80*
Piscator, Maria Ley *BiE&WWA, NotNAT*
Pischek, Jan Krtitel *NewGrD 80*
Pischna, Josef 1826-1896 *Baker 78*
Pischner, Hans 1914- *IntWWM 80, NewGrD 80*
Pisek, Jan Krtitel 1814-1873 *NewGrD 80*
Pisek, Johann Baptist 1814-1873 *NewGrD 80*
Pisemsky, Aleksey Feofilaktovich 1820-1881 *McGEWD*
Pisemsky, Alexei Feofilaktovich 1820-1881 *NotNAT B*
Pisendel, Johann Georg 1687-1755 *Baker 78, NewGrD 80*
Piseri, Pasquale *NewGrD 80*
Pisier, Marie-France 1944- *FilmEn, HalFC 80*
Pising, William *NewGrD 80*
Pisinge, William *NewGrD 80*
Pisistratus d528BC *OxThe*
Pisk, Paul Amadeus 1893- *Baker 78, BiDAmM, ConAmC, DcCM, IntWWM 77, -80, NewGrD 80, OxMus, WhoMus 72*
Piskacek, Rudolf 1884-1940 *NewGrD 80*
Pisoni, Giovanni *NewGrD 80*
Pistilli, Gene 1947- *AmSCAP 80*
Pistocchi, Francesco Antonio Mamiliano 1659-1726 *Baker 78, NewGrD 80*
Piston, Walter 1894-1976 *Baker 78, BiDAmM, BnBkM 80, CompSN[port], ConAmC, DcCom&M 79, DcCM, IntWWM 77, MusMk, NewGrD 80[port], OxMus, WhoMus 72*
Pistone, Daniele 1946- *IntWWM 80*
Pistoni, Mario 1932- *CnOxB, DancEn 78*
Pistorius, Steve 1954- *NewOrJ SUP[port]*
Pistritto, John 1920- *AmSCAP 80*
Pitanus, Friedrich *NewGrD 80*
Pitcairn, Jack *Film 2*
Pitcathley, John 1955- *IntWWM 77, -80*
Pitcher, Oliver *BlkAmP*
Pitchford, Joan 1918- *IntWWM 77, -80*
Pitfield, Thomas Baron 1903- *Baker 78, IntWWM 77, -80, NewGrD 80, OxMus, WhoMus 72*
Pithey, Wensley 1914- *HalFC 80, WhoHol A, WhoThe 72, -77*
Piticchio, Francesco *NewGrD 80*
Pitkin, William 1925- *BiE&WWA, NotNAT, WhoThe 72, -77*
Pitlik, Noam *WhoHol A*
Pitman, Richard d1941 *NotNAT B*
Pitman, William *AmSCAP 80*
Pitney, Gene 1941- *AmPS A, RkOn*
Pitoeff, Georges 1884-1939 *EncWT, Ent*
Pitoeff, Georges 1885-1939 *NotNAT B, OxThe*
Pitoeff, Georges 1886-1939 *WhThe*
Pitoeff, Georges 1887-1939 *CnThe*
Pitoeff, Ludmilla 1895-1951 *EncWT*
Pitoeff, Ludmilla 1896-1951 *CnThe, NotNAT B, OxThe, WhThe*
Pitoeff, Sacha *EncWT*
Pitoni, Giuseppe Ottavio 1657-1743 *Baker 78, NewGrD 80*
Pitot, Genevieve *BiE&WWA, NotNAT*
Pitou, Augustus 1843-1915 *NotNAT A, -B, WhThe*
Pitra, Jean Baptiste 1812-1889 *NewGrD 80*
Pitrot, Antoine Bonaventura *CnOxB*
Pitrou, Robert 1879-1963 *NewGrD 80*
Pitschner, Gregor *NewGrD 80*
Pitsiladis, Evangelos 1943- *IntWWM 77*
Pitt *OxThe*
Pitt, Archie 1885-1940 *NotNAT B, WhThe*
Pitt, Archie 1895-1940 *WhScrn 74, -77, WhoHol B*
Pitt, Fanny Addison d1937 *NotNAT B*
Pitt, Felix d1922 *NotNAT B*
Pitt, Ingrid 1944- *FilmgC, WhoHol A, WhoHrs 80[port]*
Pitt, Ingrid 1945- *IlWWBF[port]*
Pitt, Isabel *PupTheA*
Pitt, Percy 1869-1932 *NewGrD 80*
Pitt, Percy 1870-1932 *Baker 78, CmOp, NewEOp 71*
Pitt, Tom d1924 *WhThe*
Pittaluga, Gustavo 1906- *Baker 78*
Pittanus, Friedrich 1568?-1606? *NewGrD 80*
Pittar, Fanny Krumpholtz *NewGrD 80*
Pittendrigh, Margaret Henrietta Broome 1926- *WhoMus 72*
Pittman, Bob *ConMuA 80B*
Pittman, Booker Taliaferro 1909-1969 *WhoJazz 72*
Pittman, C Earl 1914- *IntWWM 77, -80*
Pittman, Evelyn Larue 1910- *AmSCAP 80*
Pittman, Josiah 1816-1886 *NewGrD 80*
Pittman, Monte 1918-1962 *WhScrn 74, -77*
Pittman, Richard 1935- *IntWWM 77, -80*
Pittman, Tom 1933-1958 *WhScrn 74, -77, WhoHol B*
Pittman, Tom 1933-1959 *ForYSC*
Pittrich, George Washington 1870-1934 *Baker 78*
Pitts, Alfred *BluesWW*
Pitts, Gertrude Elizabeth 1932- *AmSCAP 80*
Pitts, Lucia Mae *BlkAmP*
Pitts, Ruth Eleanor Landes 1939- *IntWWM 77, -80*
Pitts, Vincent Clifford 1935- *AmSCAP 66, -80*
Pitts, William S 1830-1918 *BiDAmM*
Pitts, Zasu d1963 *MotPP, WhoHol B*
Pitts, Zasu 1898-1963 *BiDFilm, -81, FilmEn, Film 1, -2, FilmgC, Funs[port], HalFC 80, MovMk[port], NotNAT B, ThFT[port], TwYS, WhScrn 74, -77, WorEFlm[port]*
Pitts, Zasu 1900-1963 *ForYSC, JoeFr, OxFilm, Vers A[port], WhThe*
Pittschau, Warner 1903-1928 *Film 2*
Pittschau, Werner 1903-1928 *WhScrn 74, -77*
Pitz, Wilhelm 1897-1973 *NewGrD 80, WhoMus 72*
Pitzinger, Gertrude 1904- *Baker 78*
Pius IV *OxMus*
Pius IX *OxMus*
Pius X *OxMus*
Pius XI *OxMus*
Pius, Francesco *NewGrD 80*
Piutti, Carl 1846-1902 *OxMus*
Piutti, Karl 1846-1902 *Baker 78*
Pivnick, Anitra *WomWMM B*
Pivoda, Frantisek 1824-1898 *NewGrD 80*
Pixerecourt, Guilbert De 1773-1844 *Ent*
Pixerecourt, Rene Charles Guilbert De 1773-1844 *CnThe, McGEWD, NotNAT B, OxThe, REnWD[port]*
Pixis *NewGrD 80*
Pixis, Francilla 1816- *NewGrD 80*
Pixis, Friedrich Wilhelm 1755- *NewGrD 80*
Pixis, Friedrich Wilhelm 1785-1842 *NewGrD 80*
Pixis, Johann Peter 1788-1874 *Baker 78, NewGrD 80, OxMus*
Pixis, Theodor 1831-1856 *NewGrD 80*
Pixley, Frank 1867-1919 *EncMT, NotNAT B, WhThe*
Pixley, Gus 1874-1923 *WhScrn 77*
Pizarro, David 1931- *IntWWM 80, WhoMus 72*
Pizer, Larry *FilmgC, HalFC 80*
Pizer, Russell A 1935- *IntWWM 77*
Pizer, Theresa Lizzie 1907- *WhoMus 72*
Pizor, Lewen *IntMPA 77, -75, -76, -78*
Pizza, Patt *WhoHol A*
Pizzarelli, Bucky 1926- *EncJzS 70*
Pizzarelli, John 1926- *EncJzS 70*
Pizzetti, Ildebrando 1880-1968 *Baker 78, CmOp, CompSN[port], DcCom&M 79, DcCM, DcFM, NewEOp 71, NewGrD 80[port], OxMus, WorEFlm*
Pizzi, Emilio 1861-1940 *Baker 78*
Pizzi, Emilio 1862-1940 *NewGrD 80*
Pizzi, Pier Luigi 1930- *EncWT, WhoOp 76*
Pizzi, Ray 1943- *EncJzS 70*
Pizzini, Carlo Alberto 1905- *Baker 78, NewGrD 80*
Pizzioni, Giovanni *NewGrD 80*
Pla, Mirta 1940?- *CnOxB*
Plabilischikov, Peter Alexeivich 1760-1812 *OxThe*
Place, Harvey *PupTheA*
Place, Mary Kay 1947- *AmSCAP 80*
Place, Vivika *PupTheA*
Placek, Robert Walter 1932- *IntWWM 77, -80*
Placide, Madame *DancEn 78*
Placide, Alexandre d1812 *OxThe, PlP&P[port]*

Placide, Mrs. Alexandre *PlP&P*
Placide, Caroline d1881 *NotNAT B*
Placide, Henry 1799-1870 *FamA&A[port], NotNAT B, OxThe*
Placker, Christiaan De 1613-1691 *NewGrD 80*
Placuzzi, Gioseffo Maria *NewGrD 80*
Placzek, Czeslaw 1934- *IntWWM 77*
Plaetner, Jorgen 1930- *DcCM*
Plaichinger, Thila 1868-1939 *NewGrD 80*
Plaidy, Louis 1810-1874 *Baker 78, OxMus*
Plain, Gerald 1940- *ConAmC*
Plainsmen Quartet *BiDAmM*
Plaisted, Ronald *DancEn 78*
Plaistow, Stephen 1937- *IntWWM 77, -80, WhoMus 72*
Plaja, Alonso De *NewGrD 80*
Plamenac, Dragan 1895- *Baker 78, NewGrD 80*
Planchart, Alejandro Enrique 1935- *ConAmC, DcCM*
Planche, Gustave 1808-1857 *OxThe*
Planche, James Robinson 1796-1880 *BnBkM 80, EncWT, NotNAT A, -B, OxThe, PlP&P*
Planchet, Dominique-Charles 1857-1946 *Baker 78*
Planchon, Roger 1931- *CnMD SUP, CnThe, EncWT, Ent, OxThe, WhThe*
Planck, Gerd 1915- *IntWWM 80*
Planck, Robert 1894- *FilmEn, FilmgC, HalFC 80, IntMPA 77, -75, -76, -78, -79, -80*
Plancken, Corneille Vander 1772-1849 *NewGrD 80*
Planckenmuller, Georg *NewGrD 80*
Planco, George *WhoHol A*
Plancon, Jean *NewGrD 80*
Plancon, Jehan *NewGrD 80*
Plancon, Pol 1851-1914 *Baker 78, BnBkM 80, MusSN[port], NewGrD 80[port]*
Plancon, Pol 1854-1914 *CmOp*
Plancon, Pol-Henri 1854-1914 *NewEOp 71*
Planer, Franz F 1894-1963 *FilmEn, FilmgC, HalFC 80, WorEFlm*
Planiciczky, Josef Antonin 1690?-1732 *NewGrD 80*
Planicky, Josef Antonin 1690?-1732 *NewGrD 80*
Planicky, Joseph Anton 1690?-1732 *NewGrD 80*
Planiczky, Josef Antonin 1690?-1732 *NewGrD 80*
Planitzky, Josef Antonin 1690?-1732 *NewGrD 80*
Plank, Melinda *WhoHol A*
Plank, Thomas C d1962 *NotNAT B*
Plano, Gerald Peter 1938- *AmSCAP 80*
Planquette, Jean-Robert 1848-1903 *Baker 78, NewEOp 71*
Planquette, Robert 1848-1903 *NewGrD 80, OxMus*
Planson, Jean 1559?-1612? *NewGrD 80*
Planson, Jehan 1559?-1612? *NewGrD 80*
Plant, Joe *Film 2*
Plant, Philip Paul *BlkAmP*
Plant, Robert Anthony 1948- *AmSCAP 80*
Plantade, Charles-Henri 1764-1839 *Baker 78, NewGrD 80*
Plante, Francis 1839-1934 *Baker 78, BnBkM 80, NewGrD 80*
Plantin, Christopher 1520?-1589 *NewGrD 80*
Plantinga, Leon Brooks 1935- *IntWWM 77, -80, NewGrD 80*
Planyavsky, Alfred 1924- *NewGrD 80*
Planyavsky, Peter Felix 1947- *IntWWM 77, -80*
Plaschke, Friedrich 1875-1951 *NewGrD 80*
Plaskett, Joseph Francis 1918- *CreCan 2*
Plass, Ludwig 1864-1946 *Baker 78*
Plasson, Michel *WhoOp 76*
Platania, Pietro 1828-1907 *Baker 78, NewGrD 80*
Plate, Wilfried 1937- *WhoOp 76*
Plateau, Joseph Antoine Ferdinand 1801-1883 *DcFM, FilmEn, OxFilm*
Platel, Nicolas-Joseph 1777-1835 *NewGrD 80*
Platen, Emil 1925- *IntWWM 77, -80*
Platen, Karl *Film 2*
Plater, Alan 1935- *ConDr 73, -77, EncWT, WhoThe 72, -77*
Plater, Bobby 1914- *WhoJazz 72*
Plater, Robert 1914- *BiDAmM*
Plath, Wolfgang 1930- *IntWWM 77, -80, NewGrD 80*
Plato *OxThe*
Plato 422?BC-348BC *DcPup*
Plato 427BC-347BC *Baker 78*
Plato 427BC-348BC *OxThe*
Plato 428?BC-347?BC *NotNAT B*
Plato 429?BC-347BC *NewGrD 80*
Platoff, Marc 1915- *CnOxB, DancEn 78*
Platon 429?BC-347BC *NewGrD 80*
Platt, Agnes *WhThe*
Platt, Alma *WhoHol A*
Platt, Billy *Film 2*
Platt, Ed 1916-1974 *WhScrn 77, WhoHol B*
Platt, Eddie *RkOn*
Platt, Edward 1916-1974 *FilmEn, FilmgC, HalFC 80, MotPP*
Platt, Edward C 1926- *ForYSC*
Platt, Howard *WhoHol A*
Platt, Jack E 1914- *AmSCAP 66*
Platt, John Curtis 1929- *IntWWM 77*
Platt, Joseph B 1895-1968 *NotNAT B*
Platt, Livingston *WhThe*
Platt, Louise 1914- *FilmgC, HalFC 80*
Platt, Louise 1915- *FilmEn, ForYSC, ThFT[port], WhoHol A*
Platt, Marc 1913- *FilmgC, ForYSC, HalFC 80, MotPP, WhoHol A*
Platt, Marc 1915- *DancEn 78[port]*
Platt, Milt *IntMPA 77, -75, -76, -78, -79, -80*
Platt, Norman 1920- *WhoMus 72*
Platt, Peter 1924- *NewGrD 80*
Platt, Raymond *NatPD[port]*
Platt, Ronald Lee 1929- *IntMPA 75, -76*
Platters, The *AmPS A, -B, BiDAmM, RkOn[port]*
Platthy, Jeno 1920- *AmSCAP 80, IntWWM 80*
Platti, Giovanni 1697-1763 *Baker 78*
Platti, Giovanni Benedetto 1700?-1763 *NewGrD 80*
Plattner, Augustin *NewGrD 80*
Platts, Kenneth Michael 1946- *IntWWM 77, -80*
Platts-Mills, Barney 1944- *HalFC 80, OxFilm*
Plaut, Jonathan 1936- *ConAmTC*
Plautius, Gabriel d1641 *NewGrD 80*
Plautus 251?BC-184BC *CnThe, McGEWD[port], REnWD[port]*
Plautus 252?BC-184BC *Ent*
Plautus 254?BC-184BC *NotNAT B, OxThe, PlP&P*
Plautus, Titus Maccius 251?BC-184BC *EncWT*
Plautus, Titus Maccius 254?BC-184?BC *NewGrD 80*
Plautz, Gabriel d1641 *NewGrD 80*
Plautzius, Gabriel d1641 *NewGrD 80*
Plavec, Joseph 1905- *IntWWM 77, -80, WhoMus 72*
Playboys, The *BiDAmM, RkOn*
Player *RkOn 2[port]*
Playfair, Arthur 1869-1918 *NotNAT B, WhThe*
Playfair, Sir Nigel 1874-1934 *CnThe, EncMT, EncWT, NotNAT A, -B, OxThe, PlP&P, WhScrn 77, WhThe, WhoHol B*
Playford *NewGrD 80*
Playford, Henry 1657-1706 *OxMus*
Playford, Henry 1657?-1707? *NewGrD 80*
Playford, Henry 1657-1709? *BnBkM 80*
Playford, Henry 1657-1720 *Baker 78*
Playford, John 1623-1686 *Baker 78, BnBkM 80, CnOxB, DancEn 78, MusMk, NewGrD 80[port], OxMus*
Playford, John 1655-1685 *NewGrD 80, OxMus*
Playman, Gordon 1922- *AmSCAP 80*
Playmates, The *AmPS A, RkOn[port]*
Playten, Alice *WhoHol A*
Playter, Wellington *Film 2*
Playter, Wellington 1879-1937 *WhScrn 77*
Playter, Wellington 1883- *Film 1, TwYS*
Plaza, Juan Bautista 1898-1964 *Baker 78*
Plaza, Juan Bautista 1898-1965 *NewGrD 80*
Plaza, Ramon DeLa 1835?-1886 *NewGrD 80*
Ple-Caussade, Simone 1897- *Baker 78*
Pleasance, Donald 1919- *FilmAG WE, FilmEn, FilmgC, PlP&P[port]*
Pleasant, Cousin Joe *BluesWW[port]*
Pleasant, Richard d1961 *NotNAT B*
Pleasant, Richard 1906-1961 *CnOxB*
Pleasant, Richard 1909-1961 *DancEn 78*
Pleasant Joe *BluesWW*
Pleasant Valley Boys, The *BiDAmM, EncFCWM 69*
Pleasants, Henry 1910- *NewGrD 80*
Pleasants, Jack 1874- *WhThe*
Pleasence, Angela *WhoHol A, WhoThe 72, -77*
Pleasence, Donald 1919- *BiE&WWA, Ent, ForYSC, HalFC 80, IntMPA 77, -75, -76, -78, -79, -80, MotPP, MovMk, NotNAT, OxFilm, WhoHol A, WhoHrs 80[port]*
Pleasence, Donald 1921- *IlWWBF[port], WhoThe 72, -77*
Pleasure, King 1922- *IlEncJ*
Pledath, Werner *Film 2*
Pleeth, Anthony Michael 1948- *IntWWM 77, -80, WhoMus 72*
Pleeth, William 1916- *IntWWM 77, -80, NewGrD 80, WhoMus 72*
Pleis, Jack K 1920- *AmSCAP 66, -80*
Pleschette, Suzanne 1937- *BiE&WWA*
Pleschkes, Otto 1931- *FilmgC, HalFC 80*
Pleschkoff, Michael *Film 2*
Pleshakov, Vladimir 1934- *Baker 78, IntWWM 77, -80*
Pleshcheev, Alexander 1858-1945 *DancEn 78*
Pleshette, Eugene *IntMPA 77, -75, -76, -78, -79, -80*
Pleshette, John *WhoHol A*
Pleshette, Suzanne 1937- *FilmEn, FilmgC, ForYSC, HalFC 80, IntMPA 77, -75, -76, -78, -79, -80, MotPP, MovMk, WhoHol A, WorEFlm*
Pleskow, Eric *IntMPA 77, -75, -76, -78, -79, -80*
Pleskow, Raoul 1931- *CpmDNM 79, -80, ConAmC, DcCM*
Plesnicar, David 1942- *ConAmC*
Plessis *NewGrD 80*
Plessis, Hubert Du 1922- *Baker 78, NewGrD 80*
Pletcher, Stew 1907- *CmpEPM, WhoJazz 72*
Plettner, Arthur Rudolph 1904- *ConAmC, IntWWM 77, -80*
Pleydell, George 1868- *WhThe*
Pleyel *NewGrD 80*
Pleyel, Madame *OxMus*
Pleyel, Camille 1788-1855 *Baker 78, NewGrD 80, OxMus*
Pleyel, Ignace Joseph 1757-1831 *NewGrD 80[port]*
Pleyel, Ignaz Joseph 1757-1831 *Baker 78, BnBkM 80, MusMk, OxMus*
Pleyel, Marie Moke 1811-1875 *BnBkM 80, NewGrD 80*
Plicka, Karel 1894- *NewGrD 80*
Plievier, Theodor 1892-1955 *CnMD, ModWD*
Plimmer, Walter, Jr. *Film 2*
Plimpton, George 1927- *WhoHol A*
Plimpton, Job 1784-1864 *BiDAmM*
Plimpton, Shelley *WhoHol A*
Plinge, Walter *WhThe*
Plinkiewisch, Helen Edwina 1908- *IntWWM 77, -80*
Plinthamer, Adolf *NewGrD 80*
Pliny *OxMus*
Plisetskaya, Maya 1925- *CnOxB, DancEn 78[port], WhoHol A*
Plishka, Paul Peter 1941- *Baker 78, NewGrD 80, WhoOp 76*
Plitt, Henry G 1918- *IntMPA 77, -75, -76, -78, -79, -80*
Plivova-Simkova, Vera *WomWMM*
Plocek, Alexandr 1914- *NewGrD 80*
Plocek, Vaclav 1923- *NewGrD 80*
Plocka, Marek Z *NewGrD 80*
Ploder, Katherin Norine Olivia *IntWWM 77, -80, WhoMus 72*
Plog, Anthony Clifton 1947- *CpmDNM 80*
Plomer, John *NewGrD 80*
Plomer, William *BlkAmP, BnBkM 80*
Plonsky, Peter 1943- *Baker 78*
Plotnikov, Eugene 1877-1951 *Baker 78*
Plott, Stefan Julius Johannes 1939- *IntWWM 77, -80*
Plourmel, John *NewGrD 80*
Plousiadenos, Joannes *NewGrD 80*

Plousiadenus, Joannes *NewGrD 80*
Plowden, Roger S 1902-1960 *WhScrn 74, -77, WhoHol B*
Plowman, Michael John 1950- *IntWWM 77*
Plowright, Hilda *WhoHol A*
Plowright, Joan 1929- *BiE&WWA, CnThe, EncWT, Ent, HalFC 80, NotNAT, OxThe, PlP&P, WhoHol A, WhoThe 72, -77*
Plowright, Rosalind Anne 1949- *IntWWM 77, -80*
Ployhar, James D *ConAmC*
Plucis, Harijs 1900-1970 *CnOxB, DancEn 78*
Pluddemann, Martin 1854-1897 *Baker 78, NewGrD 80*
Pludermacher, Georges 1944- *IntWWM 77, NewGrD 80, WhoMus 72*
Plues, George L 1895-1953 *WhScrn 74, -77, WhoHol B*
Plugge, Mary Lou 1906- *BiE&WWA, NotNAT*
Plumb, E Hay 1883-1960 *WhScrn 77*
Plumb, Edward H 1907-1958 *AmSCAP 80*
Plumb, Hay 1883-1960 *IlWWBF*
Plumb, Neely 1912- *AmSCAP 66, -80*
Plumby, Donald 1919- *AmSCAP 66, -80, ConAmC A*
Plumer, Lincoln 1876-1928 *WhScrn 77*
Plumer, Rose Lincoln d1955 *WhScrn 77*
Plumere, John 1410?-1484? *NewGrD 80*
Plumley, Don *WhoHol A*
Plummer, Arthur Christopher Orme 1929- *CreCan 2*
Plummer, Christopher *IntMPA 77, -75, -76, -78, -79, -80, MotPP, PlP&P, WhoHol A*
Plummer, Christopher 1927- *Ent, FilmEn, FilmgC, ForYSC, HalFC 80, MovMk[port], WhoThe 77*
Plummer, Christopher 1929- *BiE&WWA, CnThe, CreCan 2, EncWT, FilmAG WE, NotNAT, WhoThe 72, WorEFlm[port]*
Plummer, Eldora Fite 1915- *AmSCAP 80*
Plummer, Howard 1921- *AmSCAP 66, -80*
Plummer, Jean Vincent 1913- *AmSCAP 66, -80*
Plummer, John 1410?-1484? *NewGrD 80*
Plummer, Lincoln 1876-1928 *Film 2, WhScrn 74, WhoHol B*
Plummer, Rose Lincoln d1955 *WhScrn 74, WhoHol B*
Plummer, Susan Jennifer 1943- *WhoOp 76*
Plummer, William 1938- *BiDAmM*
Plumstead, Mary 1905- *WhoMus 72*
Plunkett, Adeline 1824-1910 *CnOxB*
Plunkett, Edward John Morton Drax *McGEWD[port]*
Plunkett, Patricia *WhoHol A*
Plunkett, Patricia 1926- *IlWWBF, WhThe*
Plunkett, Patricia 1928- *FilmgC, HalFC 80, IntMPA 77, -75, -76, -78, -79, -80*
Plunkett, Walter 1902- *FilmEn, FilmgC, HalFC 80, IntMPA 77, -75, -76, -78, -79, -80*
Plutarch 050-120 *Baker 78, NewGrD 80*
Plutzik, Roberta 1948- *ConAmTC*
Plympton, Eben 1853-1915 *NotNAT B, WhThe, WhoStg 1906, -1908*
Pniak, Jan 1944- *IntWWM 77*
Po Sein *REnWD[port]*
Po' Boys *EncFCWM 69*
Poakwa, Daniel Anim 1936- *IntWWM 77, -80*
Pobbe, Marcella 1927- *WhoMus 72*
Pober, Leon 1920-1971 *AmSCAP 66, -80*
Pobliner, Harriet 1943- *AmSCAP 80*
Pocci, Count Frank Graf 1807-1876 *DcPup*
Pocci, Franz, Graf Von 1807-1876 *Baker 78, NewGrD 80*
Pochon, Alfred 1878-1959 *AmSCAP 66, -80, Baker 78, ConAmC A*
Pociej, Bohdan 1933- *NewGrD 80*
Pocknall, Harold George 1890- *WhoMus 72*
Pockorny, Franz Xaver *NewGrD 80*
Pockrich, Richard *OxMus*
Pockriss, Lee 1924- *AmPS*
Pockriss, Lee J 1927- *AmSCAP 66, -80, BiE&WWA, NotNAT, PopAmC SUP[port]*
Poco *ConMuA 80A, IlEncCM[port], IlEncR, RkOn 2[port]*
Pocock, Isaac 1782-1835 *NotNAT B, OxThe*
Pocock, Lewis John 1903- *WhoMus 72*
Pod, Captain *DcPup*
Poddany, Eugene Frank 1919- *AmSCAP 80*
Podell, Albert N 1937- *IntMPA 77, -75, -76, -78, -79, -80*
Podell, Arthur M 1936- *AmSCAP 80*
Podell, Jon *ConMuA 80B*
Podest, Ludvik 1921-1968 *Baker 78, NewGrD 80*
Podesta, Italo d1964 *NotNAT B*
Podesta, Jose J *OxThe*
Podesta, Rosanna 1934- *MotPP*
Podesta, Rossana 1934- *FilmAG WE, FilmgC, ForYSC, HalFC 80, IntMPA 77, -75, -76, -78, -79, -80, WhoHol A*
Podesta, Rossanna 1934- *FilmEn*
Podesva, Jaromir 1927- *Baker 78, DcCM, NewGrD 80*
Podhorzer, Munio *IntMPA 77, -75, -76, -78, -79, -80*
Podhorzer, Nathan 1919- *IntMPA 77, -75, -76, -78, -79, -80*
Podio, Francesco *NewGrD 80*
Podio, Guillermo De *NewGrD 80*
Podius, Francesco *NewGrD 80*
Podolski, Michel 1928- *IntWWM 77, -80*
Podolsky, Leo S 1891- *AmSCAP 80*
Podrecca, Vittorio 1883-1959 *DcPup, PupTheA*
Poduschka, Ludwig 1913- *IntWWM 77*
Poe, Edgar Allan 1809-1849 *DancEn 78, DcPup, FilmgC, HalFC 80, NewEOp 71, NewGrD 80, WhoHrs 80*
Poe, Edgar Allen 1809-1849 *NotNAT B*
Poe, Elizabeth 1787-1811 *BiDAmM*
Poe, Frances R 1937- *IntWWM 77*
Poe, Horace Coy 1907- *AmSCAP 80*
Poe, James *IntMPA 77, -75, -76, -78, -79, -80*
Poe, James 1921-1980 *FilmEn*
Poe, James 1923- *FilmgC, HalFC 80, WorEFlm*
Poeira, Barreto 1901- *FilmAG WE[port]*
Poel, William 1852-1934 *CnThe, EncWT, NotNAT A, -B, OxThe, PlP&P, WhThe*
Poelchau, Georg Johann Daniel 1773-1836 *NewGrD 80*
Poell, Alfred *IntWWM 77, -80*
Poelvoorde, Rita 1951- *CnOxB*
Poelzig, Hans 1869-1936 *EncWT, WorEFlm*
Poenicke, Johann Peter *NewGrD 80*
Poff, Lon 1870-1952 *Film 1, -2, TwYS, WhScrn 77*
Poff, Louis *Film 2*
Pogacic, Vladimir 1918- *DcFM*
Pogany, Willy d1955 *NotNAT B*
Poggioli, Antonio 1580?-1673 *NewGrD 80*
Poggioli, Ferdinando Maria 1897-1944 *WorEFlm*
Pogl, Peregrinus 1711-1788 *NewGrD 80*
Poglietti, Alessandro d1683 *Baker 78, NewGrD 80*
Pogodin, Nikolai F 1900-1962 *CnMD, CnThe, EncWT, Ent, ModWD, NotNAT B, OxThe*
Pogodin, Nikolay Fyodorovich 1900-1962 *McGEWD[port]*
Pogostin, S Lee 1926- *FilmgC, HalFC 80*
Pogue, Thomas 1876-1941 *WhoHol B*
Pogue, Tom 1876-1941 *WhScrn 74, -77*
Pohanka, Jaroslav 1924-1964 *NewGrD 80*
Pohjola, Erkki 1931- *IntWWM 77, -80*
Pohjola, Maija-Liisa 1936- *IntWWM 80*
Pohjola, Paavo 1934- *IntWWM 77, -80*
Pohl, Carl Ferdinand 1819-1887 *Baker 78, NewGrD 80*
Pohl, Claus *Film 2*
Pohl, David *NewGrD 80*
Pohl, Gisela 1937- *WhoOp 76*
Pohl, Madeleine 1925- *WhoMus 72*
Pohl, Max *Film 2*
Pohl, Richard 1826-1896 *Baker 78, NewGrD 80*
Pohl, William Francis 1937- *IntWWM 77, -80*
Pohle, David 1624-1695 *NewGrD 80*
Pohlen, David 1624-1695 *NewGrD 80*
Pohlig, Karl 1858-1928 *Baker 78*
Pohlman, M Ray 1930- *AmSCAP 80*
Pohlmann, Eric 1913- *FilmEn, FilmgC, ForYSC, HalFC 80, WhoHol A*
Pohlmann, Johannes *NewGrD 80*
Pohlreich, Ferdinand 1917- *IntWWM 77, -80*
Poindexter, Norwood 1926- *BiDAmM, EncJzS 70*
Poindexter, Pony 1926- *EncJzS 70*
Pointer, Anita 1948- *EncJzS 70*
Pointer, Bonnie 1950- *EncJzS 70*
Pointer, June 1953- *EncJzS 70*
Pointer, Patricia 1950- *EncJzS 70*
Pointer, Ruth 1946- *EncJzS 70*
Pointer, Sidney d1955 *NotNAT B, WhoHol B*
Pointer Sisters, The *ConMuA 80A[port], EncJzS 70, IlEncR, RkOn 2[port]*
Pointner, Anton *Film 2*
Pointon, Barbara 1939- *IntWWM 77, -80*
Poiree, Gabriel 1850-1925 *Baker 78*
Poirier, Anne-Claire *WomWMM*
Poirier, Gerard 1930- *CreCan 2*
Poirier, Leon 1876?-1968 *DcFM*
Poirier, Leon 1884-1968 *FilmEn*
Poise, Ferdinand 1828-1892 *Baker 78, NewGrD 80*
Poissl, Johann Nepomuk 1783-1865 *Baker 78, NewGrD 80*
Poisson, Angelique 1657-1756 *OxThe*
Poisson, Francois Arnould 1696-1753 *OxThe*
Poisson, Jakub Jan *NewGrD 80*
Poisson, Madeleine-Angelique 1684-1770 *OxThe*
Poisson, Paul 1658-1735 *NotNAT B, OxThe*
Poisson, Philippe 1682-1743 *OxThe*
Poisson, Raymond 1630?-1690 *NotNAT B, OxThe*
Poitevin, Guillaume 1646-1706 *NewGrD 80*
Poitier, Sidney 1924- *BiDFilm, -81, BiE&WWA, FilmEn, FilmgC, ForYSC, HalFC 80, IntMPA 77, -75, -76, -78, -79, -80, MotPP, MovMk[port], NotNAT, WhoHol A, WhoThe 72, -77*
Poitier, Sidney 1927- *DrBlPA, OxFilm*
Poitier, Sydney 1924- *WorEFlm*
Pojar, Bretislav 1923- *DcFM, FilmEn, WorEFlm*
Pokorny *NewGrD 80*
Pokorny, Frantisek d1797 *NewGrD 80*
Pokorny, Frantisek 1729-1794 *NewGrD 80*
Pokorny, Frantisek Xaver Jan 1797-1850 *NewGrD 80*
Pokorny, Franz 1797-1850 *NewGrD 80*
Pokorny, Franz Xaver 1728-1794 *Baker 78*
Pokorny, Franz Xaver 1729-1794 *NewGrD 80*
Pokorny, Gotthard 1733-1802 *NewGrD 80*
Pokorny, Jan 1689-1783 *NewGrD 80*
Pokorny, Johann Ferdinand 1797-1870 *NewGrD 80*
Pokorny, Petr 1932- *IntWWM 77, -80*
Pokorny, Stephan Johann 1740?-1792 *NewGrD 80*
Pokras, Barbara *WomWMM*
Pokrass, Dimitri 1899- *Baker 78*
Pokrovsky, Boris *WhoOp 76*
Pol *NewGrD 80*
Pol, David *NewGrD 80*
Pol, Talitha 1940-1971 *WhScrn 74, -77*
Pola, Bruno 1943- *WhoOp 76*
Pola, Edward 1907- *AmSCAP 66, -80, CmpEPM*
Pola, Isa 1909- *FilmAG WE*
Polacca *NewGrD 80*
Polacchina, La *NewGrD 80*
Polacco, Giorgio 1873-1960 *Baker 78*
Polacco, Giorgio 1875-1960 *BiDAmM, CmOp, NewEOp 71, NewGrD 80*
Polacek, Louis Vask 1920-1963 *NotNAT B*
Polaczek, Dietmar 1942- *NewGrD 80*
Polaire, Mademoiselle 1879-1939 *NotNAT B, WhThe*
Polajenko, Nicholas 1932- *CnOxB, DancEn 78*
Polak, Jacob *OxMus*
Polak, Jakub *NewGrD 80*
Polak, Jan *NewGrD 80*
Polakoff, Abe *WhoOp 76*
Polan, Barron 1914- *BiE&WWA*
Polan, Lou 1904-1976 *BiE&WWA, NotNAT, -B, WhoHol C, WhoThe 72, -77*
Polani, Girolamo *NewGrD 80*
Polanski, Roman 1933- *BiDFilm, -81, ConLC 16, DcFM, FilmEn, FilmgC, HalFC 80, IntMPA 77, -75, -76, -78, -79, -80, MovMk[port], OxFilm, WhoHrs 80, WorEFlm*
Polansky, Roman 1933- *WhoHol A*
Polasek, Barbara 1939- *WhoMus 72*
Polbero *NewGrD 80*

Polcer, Ed 1937- *EncJzS 70*
Polcer, Edward Joseph 1937- *EncJzS 70*
Poldini, Ede 1869-1957 *Baker 78, NewGrD 80*
Poldini, Eduard 1869-1957 *DcPup*
Poldowski 1879-1932 *Baker 78*
Poldowski 1880-1932 *OxMus*
Pole, David *NewGrD 80*
Pole, Hans *NewGrD 80*
Pole, William 1814-1900 *Baker 78, NewGrD 80, OxMus*
Polednak, Ivan 1931- *NewGrD 80*
Poledouris, Basil Konstantine 1945- *AmSCAP 80*
Polen, Nat *WhoHol A*
Polewheel *NewGrD 80*
Polewska, Ludmilla 1898- *IntWWM 77, -80*
Polewska, Zoia 1929- *IntWWM 77, -80*
Polgar, Alfred 1875-1955 *EncWT, NotNAT B*
Polgar, Tibor 1907- *Baker 78, IntWWM 77, -80*
Polglase, Joseph 1940- *IntWWM 77, -80*
Polglase, Van Nest 1898-1968 *FilmEn, FilmgC, HalFC 80*
Poli, Paolo 1929- *Ent*
Poliakoff, Stephen 1952- *Ent[port]*
Poliakoff, Stephen 1953- *ConDr 77*
Poliakoff, Vera *WhThe*
Poliakova, Elena 1884-1972 *CnOxB*
Policci, Giovanni Battista *NewGrD 80*
Police *ConMuA 80A[port]*
Policki *NewGrD 80*
Policreti, Giuseppe *NewGrD 80*
Policreto, Giuseppe *NewGrD 80*
Policretto, Giuseppe *NewGrD 80*
Polidori, Ortensio *NewGrD 80*
Polier, Dan A *IntMPA 77, -75, -76, -78, -79, -80*
Polifrone, Jon Joseph 1937- *CpmDNM 76, ConAmC*
Polignac, Armande De 1876-1962 *Baker 78*
Polin, Claire 1926- *AmSCAP 80, CpmDNM 72, -74, -76, -78, -79, ConAmC, IntWWM 77, -80*
Polini, Emily d1927 *NotNAT B*
Polini, G M d1914 *NotNAT B*
Polini, Marie d1960 *NotNAT B, WhThe*
Polinski, Aleksander 1845-1916 *NewGrD 80*
Polinski, Alexander 1845-1916 *Baker 78*
Polistina, Anthony Thomas 1944- *AmSCAP 80*
Polite, Charlene *WhoHol A*
Politian 1454-1491 *OxThe*
Politis, Photos 1890-1934 *OxThe*
Polito, Gene *HalFC 80*
Polito, Sol 1892-1960 *FilmEn, FilmgC, HalFC 80, WorEFlm*
Polito, Sol 1894-1960 *CmMov*
Politoske, Daniel T 1935- *IntWWM 77, -80*
Politte, Charlotte *AmSCAP 80*
Politzer, Robert 1939- *IntWWM 77*
Polivka, Vladimir 1896-1948 *Baker 78*
Poliziano 1454-1491 *OxThe*
Poliziano, Angelo 1454-1494 *McGEWD[port], NewGrD 80*
Polk, Gordon 1924-1960 *WhScrn 74, -77, WhoHol B*
Polk, Hersholt Calvin 1942- *AmSCAP 80*
Polk, Lucy Ann *CmpEPM*
Polk, Mary Jane 1916- *AmSCAP 66, -80*
Polk, Oscar *BlksB&W, DrBlPA*
Polka Dot Slim *BluesWW*
Polko, Elise 1822-1899 *Baker 78*
Poll, Heinz 1926- *CnOxB*
Poll, Martin H 1922- *FilmgC, HalFC 80, IntMPA 77, -75, -76, -78, -79, -80*
Poll, Melvyn 1941- *IntWWM 77, -80, WhoOp 76*
Poll, Ruth 1899-1955 *AmSCAP 66, -80*
Polla, Pauline M 1868-1940 *WhScrn 74, -77, WhoHol B*
Polla, W C 1876-1939 *AmSCAP 66, -80*
Pollack, Ben d1971 *BgBands 74[port], WhoHol B*
Pollack, Ben 1903-1971 *AmSCAP 66, -80, Baker 78, BiDAmM, CmpEPM, EncJzS 70, IlEncJ, WhoJazz 72*
Pollack, Ben 1904-1971 *WhScrn 74, -77*
Pollack, Egon 1879-1933 *Baker 78, NewEOp 71*
Pollack, Emma *AmPS B*
Pollack, Jeff *ConMuA 80B*
Pollack, Joe 1931- *ConAmTC*
Pollack, Lew 1895-1946 *AmSCAP 66, -80, CmpEPM, NotNAT B*
Pollack, Lew 1896-1946 *AmPS*
Pollack, Mimi *WomWMM*
Pollack, Sidney *IntMPA 75*
Pollack, Sidney 1934- *WorEFlm*
Pollack, Sydney *FilmgC, HalFC 80, IntMPA 77, -76, -78, -79, -80*
Pollack, Sydney 1930- *MovMk[port]*
Pollack, Sydney 1934- *BiDFilm, -81, FilmEn*
Pollak, Anna 1912- *IntWWM 77, -80, NewGrD 80, WhoMus 72*
Pollak, Anna 1915- *CmOp*
Pollak, Frank *NewGrD 80*
Pollak, Helen Charlotte Schiller 1932- *IntWWM 77, -80*
Pollak, Robert 1880-1962 *Baker 78*
Pollak, Rose *NewGrD 80*
Pollak, William Thomas 1900- *ConAmC*
Pollar, Gene 1892- *Film 2, WhoHol B, WhoHrs 80*
Pollard, Anthony Cecil 1929- *IntWWM 77, -80*
Pollard, Brian Joseph 1930- *IntWWM 77, -80*
Pollard, Bud 1887-1952 *WhScrn 74, -77, WhoHol B*
Pollard, Daphne 1890-1978 *HalFC 80, WhThe*
Pollard, Daphne 1894- *Film 2, ForYSC, TwYS*
Pollard, Harry *Film 1, MotPP*
Pollard, Harry 1883-1934 *FilmEn, FilmgC, HalFC 80, NotNAT B, TwYS A, WhScrn 74, -77, WhoHol B*
Pollard, Harry Snub 1886-1962 *FilmEn, NotNAT B, TwYS, WhScrn 74, -77*
Pollard, Kathleen Vera 1926- *IntWWM 77*
Pollard, Laura *Film 2*
Pollard, Michael J 1939- *BiE&WWA, FilmEn, FilmgC, ForYSC, HalFC 80, MotPP, MovMk[port], WhoHol A*
Pollard, Shackleton 1887- *WhoMus 72*
Pollard, Snub 1886-1962 *Film 1, -2, FilmgC, ForYSC, HalFC 80, WhoHol B*
Pollard, Terry 1931- *BlkWAB*
Pollard, Thomas *OxThe*
Pollaroli, Carlo 1653-1722 *MusMk*
Pollaroli, Carlo Francesco 1653-1732 *OxMus*
Pollarolo, Antonio 1676-1746 *NewGrD 80*
Pollarolo, Antonio 1680-1746 *Baker 78*
Pollarolo, Carlo Francesco 1653-1722 *Baker 78*
Pollarolo, Carlo Francesco 1653?-1723 *NewGrD 80*
Polledro, Giovanni Battista 1781-1853 *NewGrD 80*
Pollet *NewGrD 80*
Pollet, Albert *Film 2*
Pollet, Benoit 1753-1823 *NewGrD 80*
Pollet, Charles-Francois-Alexandre 1748-1815 *NewGrD 80*
Pollet, Jean-Daniel 1936- *WorEFlm*
Pollet, Joseph 1803-1883 *NewGrD 80*
Pollexfen, Jack 1918- *IntMPA 77, -75, -76, -78, -79, -80, WhoHrs 80*
Pollier, Mathias *NewGrD 80*
Pollini, Bernhard 1838-1897 *Baker 78*
Pollini, Cesare, Cavaliere De' 1858-1912 *Baker 78*
Pollini, Francesco 1762-1846 *Baker 78, NewGrD 80*
Pollini, Franz 1762-1846 *NewGrD 80*
Pollini, Maurizio 1942- *Baker 78, IntWWM 77, -80, NewGrD 80, WhoMus 72*
Pollitt, Arthur W 1878-1933 *Baker 78*
Pollitzer, Adolf 1832-1900 *NewGrD 80*
Pollitzer, Adolphe 1832-1900 *NewGrD 80*
Pollius, Daniel *NewGrD 80*
Pollock, Allan d1942 *NotNAT B*
Pollock, Anna d1946 *NotNAT B*
Pollock, Arthur 1886- *WhThe*
Pollock, Benjamin 1856-1937 *DcPup*
Pollock, Bert D 1923- *AmSCAP 66, -80*
Pollock, Channing 1880-1946 *AmSCAP 66, -80, MagIID, ModWD, NotNAT A, -B, WhThe, WhoStg 1908*
Pollock, Dee *WhoHol A*
Pollock, Edith *PupTheA*
Pollock, Elizabeth 1898-1970 *WhThe*
Pollock, Ellen 1903- *HalFC 80, PlP&P, WhoHol A, WhoThe 72, -77*
Pollock, George 1907- *FilmEn, FilmgC, HalFC 80, IlWWBF*
Pollock, Gordon W d1956 *NotNAT B*
Pollock, Horace d1964 *NotNAT B*
Pollock, John d1945 *NotNAT B*
Pollock, John 1878-1963 *WhThe*
Pollock, Louis d1964 *NotNAT B*
Pollock, Martin *AmSCAP 80*
Pollock, Muriel d1971 *AmSCAP 66, -80*
Pollock, Nancy R *WhoHol A*
Pollock, Nancy R 1905- *WhoThe 72, -77*
Pollock, Nancy R 1907- *BiE&WWA, NotNAT*
Pollock, Robert Emil 1946- *Baker 78, CpmDNM 79, -80, ConAmC, IntWWM 77, -80*
Pollock, Ted L 1936- *IntWWM 77*
Pollock, William 1881-1944 *NotNAT B, WhThe*
Polmier, John *NewGrD 80*
Polo, Danny 1901-1949 *CmpEPM, WhoJazz 72*
Polo, Eddie 1875-1961 *FilmEn, Film 1, -2, MotPP, NotNAT B, TwYS, WhScrn 74, -77, WhoHol B*
Polo, Malvine *Film 2*
Polo, Robert d1968 *WhScrn 74, -77*
Polo, Sam 1873-1966 *Film 1, -2, WhScrn 77, WhoHol B*
Pologe, Steven 1952- *IntWWM 77, -80*
Pololanik, Zdenek 1935- *Baker 78, DcCM, NewGrD 80*
Polon, Matty 1913- *IntMPA 75, -76*
Polon, Vicki 1948- *WomWMM B*
Polone, Gerald L 1931- *IntMPA 75, -76*
Polonsky, Abraham 1910- *BiDFilm, -81, ConDr 73, -77A, FilmEn, FilmgC, HalFC 80, IntMPA 75, -76, -78, -79, -80, MovMk[port], OxFilm, WorEFlm*
Polonus, Johannes *NewGrD 80*
Polovinkin, Leonid Alexeyevich 1894-1949 *Baker 78, NewGrD 80*
Polston, Jean Jerrett *AmSCAP 80*
Poltinger, Friedl 1919- *WhoMus 72*
Poltronieri, Alberto 1894- *WhoMus 72*
Polumier, John *NewGrD 80*
Polunin, Elizabeth Margaret 1943- *WhoMus 72*
Polunin, Tanya 1917- *IntWWM 77, -80*
Polus *Ent, OxThe*
Poluskis, The *WhThe*
Polyakin, Miron Borislovich 1895-1941 *NewGrD 80*
Polyakova, Lyudmila Viktorovna 1921- *NewGrD 80*
Polymnestus Of Colophon *NewGrD 80*
Polyzoides, Christos 1931- *IntWWM 77, -80*
Polyzoides, Katherina *IntWWM 77, -80*
Polzelli, Luigia 1760?-1832 *NewGrD 80*
Pomare, Eleo 1937- *CmpGMD, CnOxB, DrBlPA*
Pomares, Jean 1943- *CnOxB*
Pomeranz, David Hyman 1951- *AmSCAP 80*
Pomeranz, Felice 1957- *IntWWM 77*
Pomeroy, Herb 1930- *BiDAmM, EncJzS 70*
Pomeroy, Jay 1895-1955 *NotNAT B, WhThe*
Pomius, Francesco *NewGrD 80*
Pommer, Erich 1889-1966 *DcFM, FilmEn, FilmgC, HalFC 80, OxFilm, TwYS B, WorEFlm*
Pommer, Josef 1845-1918 *NewGrD 80*
Pommer, Max Conrad Wolfgang 1936- *IntWWM 77, -80*
Pommier, Jean-Bernard 1944- *IntWWM 77, -80, NewGrD 80*
Pomo, Francesco Del *NewGrD 80*
Pompadur, I Martin *NewYTET*
Pompeati, Signora *NewGrD 80*
Pompilo, Jan *CpmDNM 78*
Pomponius *OxThe*
Pomykalo, Igor 1946- *IntWWM 77, -80*
Ponc, Miroslav 1902-1976 *Baker 78, NewGrD 80*
Poncar, Josef 1902- *IntWWM 77*
Ponce, Ethel *AmSCAP 66, -80*
Ponce, Juan *OxMus*
Ponce, Juan 1480?-1521? *NewGrD 80*
Ponce, Manuel 1882-1948 *MusMk, NewGrD 80*
Ponce, Manuel M 1882-1948 *Baker 78, OxMus*
Ponce, Manuel M 1886-1948 *DcCM*

Ponce, Phil 1886-1945 *AmSCAP 66, -80*
Ponce DeLeon, Jose Maria *NewGrD 80*
Ponchielli, Amilcare 1834-1886 *Baker 78, BnBkM 80, CmOp, CmpBCM, DcCom 77, DcCom&M 79, GrComp[port], MusMk, NewEOp 71, NewGrD 80[port], OxMus*
Poncia, Vini *ConMuA 80B*
Poncin, Marcel d1953 *NotNAT B, WhoHol B*
Pond, Albert Edward *Baker 78*
Pond, Anson Phelps d1920 *NotNAT B*
Pond, George Warren *Baker 78*
Pond, Helen Barbara 1924- *WhoOp 76, WhoThe 77*
Pond, Sylvanus Billings 1792-1871 *Baker 78*
Pond, Sylvester Billings 1792-1871 *BiDAmM*
Pond, William A *Baker 78*
Pond, William A, Jr. d1884 *Baker 78*
Pondelli, Jo *NewGrD 80*
Ponder, James Willis 1946- *EncJzS 70*
Ponder, Jimmy 1946- *EncJzS 70*
Ponderoso, Louis *WhoHol A*
Pong, Grace 1955- *IntWWM 80*
Pong, Lily 1913- *WhoMus 72*
Pongor, Ildiko 1953- *CnOxB*
Pongracz, Zoltan 1912- *Baker 78, NewGrD 80*
Poni-Tails, The *RkOn[port]*
Poniatowski, Josef 1816-1873 *Baker 78*
Poniatowski, Joseph Michael X F John 1816-1873 *OxMus*
Poniatowski, Jozef Michal Ksawery F J 1816-1873 *NewGrD 80*
Ponick, Johann Peter *NewGrD 80*
Poniridis, Georges 1892- *Baker 78*
Poniridy, Georges 1892- *DcCM*
Ponisi, Madame 1818-1899 *NotNAT B*
Ponnelle, Jean-Pierre 1932- *CmOp, CnOxB, WhoOp 76*
Ponomaryov, Vladimir Ivanovich 1892-1951 *CnOxB, DancEn 78*
Pons DeCapdoil 1165?-1215? *NewGrD 80*
Pons D'Ortafas *NewGrD 80*
Pons, Alice Josephine 1898-1976 *BnBkM 80*
Pons, Arthur 1913-1973 *NewOrJ[port]*
Pons, Charles 1870-1957 *Baker 78*
Pons, Helene *BiE&WWA, NotNAT*
Pons, Jose 1768?-1818 *NewGrD 80*
Pons, Lily d1976 *WhoHol C*
Pons, Lily 1895-1976 *FilmgC*
Pons, Lily 1898-1976 *Baker 78, BnBkM 80, FilmEn, NewGrD 80, ThFT[port]*
Pons, Lily 1904-1976 *BiDAmM, CmOp, CmpEPM, ForYSC, HalFC 80, MusMk, MusSN[port], NewEOp 71, What 2[port]*
Ponsard, Francois 1814-1867 *NotNAT B, OxThe*
Ponse, Luctor 1914- *Baker 78, NewGrD 80*
Ponselle, Carmela 1892-1977 *Baker 78, NewEOp 71*
Ponselle, Rosa 1894- *NewEOp 71*
Ponselle, Rosa 1897- *Baker 78, BiDAmM, BnBkM 80, CmOp, IntWWM 77, -80, MusSN[port], NewGrD 80[port], What 4[port], WhoMus 72*
Ponset DeCapdoil *NewGrD 80*
Ponsetc DeCapdoil *NewGrD 80*
Ponsett DeCapdoil *NewGrD 80*
Ponsonby, Charles Garrett *NewGrD 80*
Ponsonby, Eustace d1924 *NotNAT B*
Pont, Jacques Du 1500?-1564? *NewGrD 80*
Pont, Kenneth Graham 1937- *IntWWM 77, -80*
Ponta, Adamus De *NewGrD 80*
Pontac, Diego De 1603-1654 *NewGrD 80*
Pontanus, Adamus *NewGrD 80*
Ponte, Giaches De *NewGrD 80*
Ponte, Jacques Du *NewGrD 80*
Ponte, Lorenzo Da 1749-1838 *BnBkM 80, CmOp, NewGrD 80, OxMus*
Pontecorvo, Gillo 1919- *BiDFilm, -81, DcFM, FilmEn, FilmgC, HalFC 80, MovMk[port], OxFilm, WorEFlm*
Pontecoulant, Louis-Adolphe, Marquis De 1794-1882 *Baker 78*
Pontelibero, Ferdinando 1770-1835 *NewGrD 80*
Ponti, Carlo 1910- *FilmEn, OxFilm, WorEFlm*
Ponti, Carlo 1913- *DcFM, FilmgC, HalFC 80, IntMPA 77, -75, -76, -78, -79, -80*
Ponti, Diana Da *OxThe*
Pontiflet, Sudan *BlkAmP*
Ponting, Herbert George 1870-1935 *DcFM, FilmgC, HalFC 80, WorEFlm*
Pontio, Pietro 1532-1595 *NewGrD 80*
Pontious, Melvin F 1931- *IntWWM 77*
Ponto, Erich d1957 *WhScrn 74, -77, WhoHol B*
Pontoglio, Cipriano 1831-1892 *Baker 78*
Pontois, Noella 1943- *CnOxB*
Pontoppidan, Clara *Film 2*
Pontsler, Clark W 1931- *IntWWM 77*
Ponty, Jean-Luc 1942- *ConMuA 80A, EncJzS 70, IlEncJ, IlEncR, NewGrD 80*
Ponzillo, Rosa 1897- *BnBkM 80, NewGrD 80*
Ponzio, Giuseppe *NewGrD 80*
Ponzio, Pietro *NewGrD 80*
Ponzo, Giuseppe *NewGrD 80*
Pool, Elwood J *Film 2*
Pool, F C d1944 *NotNAT B*
Pool, Jeannie Gayle 1951- *IntWWM 80*
Pool, Robert David 1954- *IntWWM 80*
Poole, Anthony *NewGrD 80*
Poole, Charles D, Jr. 1931- *AmSCAP 66*
Poole, Charlie 1892-1931 *IlEncCM*
Poole, David 1925- *CnOxB, DancEn 78*
Poole, Donn H 1945- *AmSCAP 80*
Poole, Elizabeth 1820-1906 *Baker 78*
Poole, Frank S 1913- *IntMPA 77, -75, -76, -78, -79, -80*
Poole, Geoffrey Richard 1949- *IntWWM 80*
Poole, George E 1904- *AmSCAP 66, -80*
Poole, Henry Ward 1825-1890 *BiDAmM*
Poole, John d1872 *NotNAT B*
Poole, John Charles 1934- *IntWWM 77, -80, WhoMus 72*
Poole, Roy 1924- *NotNAT, WhoHol A*
Pooler, Frank 1926- *AmSCAP 80*
Pooler, Marie 1928- *ConAmC*
Pooley, Olaf *WhThe, WhoHol A, WhoThe 72*
Poor Bob *BluesWW*
Poor Boy *BluesWW*
Poor Charlie *BluesWW*
Poor Jim *BluesWW*
Poot, Marcel 1901- *Baker 78, CompSN[port], DcCM, NewGrD 80, OxMus*
Poot, Sonja *WhoOp 76*
Pop, Iggy 1947- *ConMuA 80A, IlEncR[port]*
Popa, Magdalena 1941- *CnOxB*
Popa, Temistocle 1921- *IntWWM 77*
Pope, Alexander d1835 *NotNAT B*
Pope, Alexander 1688-1744 *NewGrD 80, OxMus, PlP&P*
Pope, Conrad 1951- *CpmDNM 80, ConAmC*
Pope, Curtis L 1919- *BiE&WWA, NotNAT*
Pope, Edward J 1919- *IntMPA 77, -75, -76, -78, -79, -80*
Pope, Elizabeth d1797 *NotNAT B*
Pope, H Lefevre 1911- *IntWWM 77, -80*
Pope, Isabel 1901- *NewGrD 80*
Pope, Jane 1742-1818 *NotNAT B, OxThe*
Pope, John Kenneth 1928- *IntWWM 77*
Pope, Karl Theodore 1937- *NotNAT*
Pope, L E 1906- *IntMPA 75, -76*
Pope, Maria Ann d1803 *NotNAT B*
Pope, Michael Douglas 1927- *IntWWM 77, -80*
Pope, Muriel *WhThe*
Pope, Norman Denes Kelway 1932- *WhoMus 72*
Pope, Peggy *WhoHol A*
Pope, Peter Searson 1917- *IntWWM 77, -80*
Pope, Roger John 1942- *IntWWM 77*
Pope, Stanley 1916- *WhoMus 72*
Pope, T L 1904- *AmSCAP 66, -80*
Pope, T Michael d1930 *NotNAT B*
Pope, Thomas d1604 *NotNAT B, OxThe, PlP&P*
Pope, Unola B 1884-1938 *WhScrn 74, -77*
Pope, Mrs. W Coleman 1809-1880 *NotNAT B*
Pope, William Coleman d1868 *NotNAT B*
Pope, William T 1924- *AmSCAP 66, -80*
Popescu, Gabriel 1932- *CnOxB*
Popescu, Paul 1929- *IntWWM 80*
Popescu-Gopo, Ion 1923- *DcFM, FilmEn, OxFilm*
Popescu-Judetz, Eugenia 1925- *IntWWM 77*
Popiolkowski, Louis John 1927- *AmSCAP 66, -80*
Popkin, Harry M *FilmgC, HalFC 80, IntMPA 77, -75, -76, -78, -79, -80*
Popko, Nicolai Mikhailovich 1911-1966 *CnOxB*
Poplavskaya, Irina *WomWMM*
Pople, Peter Ravenhill 1943- *IntWWM 77, -80*
Pople, Ross 1945- *IntWWM 80*
Poplin Family *IlEncCM*
Popma VanOevering, Reinolt 1692-1782 *NewGrD 80*
Popma VanOevering, Rynoldus 1692-1782 *NewGrD 80*
Popov, Alexander 1927- *Baker 78, OxMus*
Popov, Alexei Dmitrevich 1892-1961 *EncWT, OxThe*
Popov, Gavriil Nikolayevich 1904-1972 *Baker 78, NewGrD 80*
Popov, N *Film 2*
Popov, Oleg Konstantinovich 1930- *EncWT, Ent[port]*
Popov, Stojan *WhoOp 76*
Popov, Todor 1921- *NewGrD 80*
Popov, V *Film 2*
Popov, Valery 1937- *NewGrD 80*
Popova, Constance 1947- *IntWWM 77*
Popova, Nina 1922- *CnOxB, DancEn 78*
Popova, Vera 1899- *WhoMus 72*
Popovic, Berislav 1931- *IntWWM 77, -80*
Popovic-Gordan, Dusan 1927- *WhoOp 76*
Popovich, Mira 1935- *IntWWM 77*
Popovich, Steve *ConMuA 80B*
Popovici, Doru 1932- *Baker 78*
Popovici, Timotei 1870-1950 *NewGrD 80, OxMus*
Popp, Lucia 1939- *IntWWM 77, -80, NewGrD 80, WhoMus 72, WhoOp 76*
Poppa Hop *BluesWW*
Poppe, Nils 1908- *FilmEn*
Poppele, J R 1898- *IntMPA 75, -76*
Popper, David 1843-1913 *Baker 78, BnBkM 80, NewGrD 80, OxMus*
Popper, Felix 1908- *IntWWM 80, WhoOp 76*
Poppies, The *RkOn 2[port]*
Popplewell, Jack 1911- *WhoThe 72, -77*
Popplewell, Kenneth Arthur 1914- *IntWWM 77, -80*
Popplewell, Mary Page 1920- *AmSCAP 66, -80*
Popplewell, Richard John 1935- *IntWWM 77, -80*
Poppy Family, The *RkOn 2[port]*
Poppy Hop *BluesWW[port]*
Popwell, Albert *DrBlPA, WhoHol A*
Popwell, Johnny *WhoHol A*
Popwell, Robert Lee *AmSCAP 80*
Poquelin, Jean-Baptiste *McGEWD, NewGrD 80, REnWD[port]*
Poradowski, Stefan Boleslaw 1902-1967 *Baker 78, NewGrD 80*
Porat, Yoram 1939- *AmSCAP 80*
Porcaro, Vincent *PupTheA*
Porcasi, Paul 1880-1946 *Film 2, FilmgC, HalFC 80, HolCA[port], WhScrn 74, -77, WhoHol B*
Porcelain, Bessie Petts d1968 *WhScrn 77*
Porcelijn, David 1947- *Baker 78, NewGrD 80*
Porcelli, Fred *WhoHol A*
Porcher, Nananne 1922- *WhoOp 76*
Porchov-Lynch, Tao *WomWMM B*
Porcile, Giuseppe *NewGrD 80*
Porcino, Al 1925- *BiDAmM, EncJzS 70*
Pordenon, Marc'Antonio Da 1535-158-? *NewGrD 80*
Poree, Ernest 1908- *NewOrJ[port]*
Porel, Marc 1949- *FilmAG WE[port], WhoHol A*
Porel, Paul 1843-1917 *NotNAT B, WhThe*
Porena, Boris 1927- *NewGrD 80*
Porfetye, Andreaa 1927- *IntWWM 77, -80*
Porfiri, Pietro *NewGrD 80*
Porfirii, Pietro *NewGrD 80*
Porges, Heinrich 1837-1900 *Baker 78*
Pork Chop *NewOrJ*
Porphyrios 234?-301? *NewGrD 80*
Porphyrius 234?-301? *NewGrD 80*
Porphyry 234?-301? *NewGrD 80*
Porpora, Niccolo Antonio 1686-1766 *DcCom&M 79, NewEOp 71, OxMus*
Porpora, Nicola Antonio 1686-1766 *MusMk[port]*
Porpora, Nicola Antonio 1686-1768 *Baker 78, BnBkM 80, NewGrD 80[port]*

Porrino, Ennio 1910-1959 Baker 78, NewGrD 80
Porro, Gian Giacomo 1590?-1656 NewGrD 80
Porro, Giovanni Giacomo 1590?-1656 NewGrD 80
Porro, Pierre-Jean 1750-1831 Baker 78
Porro, Pierre Jean 1759?-1831 NewGrD 80
Porrot, Pierre Jean 1759?-1831 NewGrD 80
Porsile, Giuseppe 1680-1750 Baker 78, NewGrD 80
Porsille, Giuseppe 1680-1750 NewGrD 80
Porta, Bernardo 1758-1829 NewGrD 80
Porta, Constanzo 1529?-1601 Baker 78
Porta, Costanzo 1528?-1601 NewGrD 80[port]
Porta, Costanzo 1530?-1601 MusMk
Porta, Ercole 1585-1630 NewGrD 80
Porta, Francesco Della NewGrD 80
Porta, Gasparo Della NewGrD 80
Porta, Giambattista Della OxThe
Porta, Giovanni 1690?-1755 NewGrD 80
Porta, Giovanni Battista NewGrD 80
Porta, Hercole 1585-1630 NewGrD 80
Portal, Michel 1935- EncJzS 70
Portefaix, Loulou 1935?- DancEn 78
Porten, Henny 1888-1960 FilmAG WE, FilmEn, Film 2
Porten, Henny 1890-1960 HalFC 80, NotNAT B, OxFilm, WhScrn 74, -77, WhoHol B
Portenaro, Francesco NewGrD 80
Porteous, Gilbert 1868-1928 NotNAT B, WhThe
Porter, Andrew 1928- AmSCAP 80, CnOxB, IntWWM 77, -80, NewGrD 80, WhoMus 72
Porter, B L AmSCAP 80
Porter, Caleb 1867-1940 NotNAT B, WhThe
Porter, Cole BnBkM 80
Porter, Cole 1891-1964 AmPS, AmSCAP 80, Baker 78, BestMus[port], BiE&WWA, CmMov, EncMT, FilmgC, NewGrD 80, NotNAT A, -B, OxFilm, Sw&Ld C
Porter, Cole 1892-1964 BiDAmM, CmpEPM, ConAmC, DancEn 78, EncWT, Ent[port], FilmEn, MnPM[port], MusMk[port], NewCBMT, PopAmC SUP
Porter, Cole 1893-1964 AmSCAP 66, HalFC 80, McGEWD, PlP&P[port], PopAmC[port], WhThe
Porter, Don 1912- FilmEn, FilmgC, ForYSC, HalFC 80, IntMPA 77, -75, -76, -78, -79, -80, NotNAT, WhoHol A, WhoThe 72, -77
Porter, Edward D 1881-1939 WhScrn 74, -77, WhoHol B
Porter, Edwin S WomWMM
Porter, Edwin S 1869-1941 CmMov, FilmEn, FilmgC, HalFC 80, TwYS A, WhoHrs 80, WorEFlm
Porter, Edwin S 1870-1941 AmFD, DcFM, OxFilm
Porter, Ellen Jane Lorenz ConAmC
Porter, Eric 1928- CnThe, FilmEn, FilmgC, ForYSC, HalFC 80, IlWWBF, WhoHol A, WhoThe 72, -77
Porter, Evelyn IntWWM 77, -80, WhoMus 72
Porter, Gene 1910- WhoJazz 72
Porter, Hal 1911- ConDr 73, -77
Porter, Harold B 1896-1939 WhScrn 74, -77
Porter, Harry A d1920 NotNAT B
Porter, Henry d1599 McGEWD[port], OxThe, REnWD[port]
Porter, Hugh ConAmC
Porter, J Robert WhoHol A
Porter, Jake 1910?- WhoJazz 72
Porter, Jean ForYSC, WhoHol A
Porter, John 1890?-1958 NewOrJ
Porter, Lee 1930- AmSCAP 66
Porter, Leo Bernard 1930- AmSCAP 80
Porter, Lew 1892-1956 AmSCAP 66, -80
Porter, Lillian WhoHol A
Porter, Lulu WhoHol A
Porter, Mary Ann d1765 OxThe
Porter, Neil 1895-1944 NotNAT B, WhThe
Porter, Nyree Dawn 1940- FilmgC, HalFC 80, WhoHol A
Porter, Pansy Film 2
Porter, Paul Film 2
Porter, Paul A d1975 NewYTET
Porter, Quincy 1897-1966 Baker 78, BiDAmM, CompSN[port], ConAmC, DcCM, IntWWM 77, -80, NewGrD 80, NotNAT B, OxMus
Porter, Rand 1933- IntMPA 77, -76, -78, -79, -80
Porter, Robert Douglas 1932- BiDAmM
Porter, Robert Morris 1924- AmSCAP 80
Porter, Ronald Fowler 1928- IntWWM 77, -80
Porter, Rosalind 1950- IntWWM 77, -80
Porter, Roy L 1923- AmSCAP 80
Porter, Samuel 1733-1810 NewGrD 80
Porter, Stephen 1925- NotNAT, WhoThe 72, -77
Porter, Steven Clark 1943- IntWWM 77, -80
Porter, Viola Adele 1879-1942 WhScrn 74, -77
Porter, Walter d1659 OxMus
Porter, Walter 1587?-1559 NewGrD 80
Porter, Walter 1595?-1659 MusMk
Porter, Yank 1895?-1944 WhoJazz 72
Porterfield, Robert H 1905-1971 BiE&WWA, NotNAT B, WhScrn 74, -77, WhThe, WhoHol B, WhoThe 72
Porteus, Beilby 1731-1808 OxMus
Portia Faces Life What 4[port]
Portillo, Frank PupTheA
Portillo, Rafael Lopez WhoHrs 80
Portinarius, Francesco 1520?-1578? NewGrD 80
Portinaro, Francesco 1520?-1578? NewGrD 80
Portman, Eric 1903-1969 BiE&WWA, CnThe, FilmEn, FilmgC, ForYSC, HalFC 80, IlWWBF, -A, MotPP, PlP&P, WhScrn 74, -77, WhThe, WhoHol B
Portman, Eric 1903-1970 FilmAG WE, NotNAT B
Portman, Eric 1904-1969 MovMk
Portman, James Bickle 1935- ConAmTC
Portman, Julie BlkAmP
Portman, Richard d1655? NewGrD 80
Portner, Paul 1925- CroCD
Portnoff, Mischa 1901- AmSCAP 66, -80, ConAmC A
Portnoff, Wesley 1910- AmSCAP 66, ConAmC A
Portnor, Ralph B 1919- AmSCAP 80
Portnoy, Eddie ConMuA 80B
Portnoy, Neil ConMuA 80B
Porto, Allegro NewGrD 80
Porto-Riche, George De 1849-1930 NotNAT B
Porto-Riche, Georges De 1849-1930 CnMD, McGEWD, ModWD, WhThe
Portogallo, Marcos Antonio NewGrD 80
Portu, Francisco DeNovo NewGrD 80
Portugal, Marcos Antonio DaFonseca 1762-1830 Baker 78, NewGrD 80
Portugal, Simao Victorino 1774-1842? NewGrD 80
Portugheis, Alberto 1941- IntWWM 77, -80, WhoMus 72
Porumbescu, Ciprian 1853-1883 Baker 78, NewGrD 80
Posch, Isaac d1623? NewGrD 80
Pose, Richard E PupTheA
Posegate, Maxcine Woodbridge 1924- AmSCAP 80
Poseidonius Of Apamea OxMus
Poser, Hans 1917-1970 NewGrD 80
Posey, Phillip Carl 1937- IntWWM 77
Posey, Sandy CounME 74
Posey, Sandy 1947- RkOn 2[port]
Posford, George 1906-1976 BestMus, NewGrD 80, WhThe
Posin, Kathryn CmpGMD
Posnack, Blanche 1912- AmSCAP 66, -80
Posnack, George 1904- AmSCAP 66, -80
Posner, Mel ConMuA 80B
Pospekhin, Lev Alexandrovich 1909- CnOxB
Pospisil, Frantisek 1933- IntWWM 77, -80
Pospisil, Juraj 1931- Baker 78, NewGrD 80
Pospisil, Ladislav 1935- IntWWM 77, -80
Pospisil, Vilem 1911- IntWWM 77, -80
Poss, Georg 1570?-1633? NewGrD 80
Possart, Ernst Von 1841-1921 EncWT, NotNAT B, OxThe, WhThe
Posse, Wilhelm 1852-1925 NewGrD 80
Posselt, Ruth 1914- Baker 78
Possenti, Pellegrino NewGrD 80
Post, Buddy Film 2
Post, Carl 1910- AmSCAP 66
Post, Charles A Film 2
Post, Don 1902-1979 WhoHrs 80
Post, Guy Bates d1968 WhoHol B
Post, Guy Bates 1875-1946 NotNAT B
Post, Guy Bates 1875-1968 NotNAT B, WhScrn 74, -77, WhThe, WhoStg 1906, -1908
Post, Guy Bates 1876-1968 Film 2, ForYSC, TwYS
Post, Joseph Mozart 1906-1972 NewGrD 80, WhoMus 72
Post, Mike RkOn 2[port]
Post, Nora 1949- IntWWM 77, -80
Post, Ted IntMPA 77, -75, -76, -78, -79, -80
Post, Ted 1918- FilmEn
Post, Ted 1925- FilmgC, HalFC 80
Post, Wiley d1935 WhScrn 74, -77, WhoHol B
Post, William, Jr. WhoHol A
Post, Wilmarth H d1930 WhScrn 74, -77
Posta, Adrienne 1948- FilmgC, HalFC 80, WhoHol A
Posta, Frantisek 1919- WhoMus 72
Postel, Christian Heinrich 1658-1705 NewGrD 80
Posthius, Johannes 1537-1597 NewGrD 80
Postigo, Augusto PupTheA
Postlewate, Charles Willard 1941- IntWWM 77, -80
Postnikova, Victoria 1944- NewGrD 80, WhoMus 72
Postnikova, Viktoria 1944- NewGrD 80
Postolka, Milan 1932- IntWWM 77, -80, NewGrD 80
Poston, Doc 1895?-1942 WhoJazz 72
Poston, Elizabeth 1905- Baker 78, NewGrD 80, OxMus, WhoMus 72
Poston, Tom WhoHol A
Poston, Tom 1921- WhoThe 72, -77
Poston, Tom 1927- BiE&WWA, FilmgC, ForYSC, HalFC 80, NotNAT
Posznanski, Alfred McGEWD
Pot, Cornelius OxMus
Poteaught, Ben PupTheA
Potechina, Lydia Film 2
Potel, Victor 1889-1947 Film 1, -2, ForYSC, NotNAT B, TwYS, Vers B[port], WhScrn 74, -77, WhoHol B
Potger, Keith EncFCWM 69
Potheinos DcPup
Pothier, Joseph 1835-1923 Baker 78, BnBkM 80, NewGrD 80, OxMus
Potier, Matthias NewGrD 80
Potier DesCailletieres, Charles-Gabriel 1774-1838 OxThe
Potiers, Matthias NewGrD 80
Potiron, Henri 1882-1972 NewGrD 80
Potmesilova, Jaroslava 1936- IntWWM 77, -80
Pott, August Friedrich 1806-1883 NewGrD 80
Pottebaum, William G 1930- ConAmC, IntWWM 77, -80
Pottenger, Harold Paul 1932- ConAmC, IntWWM 77, -80
Potter NewGrD 80
Potter, A J 1918-1980 NewGrD 80
Potter, Archibald James 1918- IntWWM 77, -80, WhoMus 72
Potter, Arthur Wayne 1953- AmSCAP 80
Potter, Betty WhoHol A
Potter, Bob WhoHol A
Potter, Brian ConMuA 80B
Potter, Charles Thomas 1918- BiDAmM, EncJzS 70
Potter, Cipriani 1792-1871 MusMk, NewGrD 80
Potter, Cora Urquhart 1857-1936 FamA&A[port], WhThe
Potter, David Kinsman 1932- IntWWM 77, -80
Potter, Dennis 1935- ConDr 73, -77, WhoThe 77
Potter, H C 1904-1977 BiE&WWA, DcFM, FilmEn, FilmgC, HalFC 80, IntMPA 77, -75, -76, MovMk[port], NotNAT, WhThe, WorEFlm
Potter, Mrs. James Brown 1859-1936 OxThe, WhoStg 1906, -1908
Potter, John 1734?-1813? NewGrD 80
Potter, Malcolm Frederick 1933- IntWWM 77, -80
Potter, Martin 1944- FilmgC, HalFC 80,

WhoHol A
Potter, Maureen *WhoHol A*
Potter, Nettie *BluesWW*
Potter, Neville 1941- *AmSCAP 80*
Potter, Paul M 1853-1921 *NotNAT B, WhThe, WhoStg 1906, -1908*
Potter, Peter *WhoMus 72*
Potter, Philip Cipriani Hambly 1792-1871 *Baker 78, OxMus*
Potter, Raeschelle Julian 1946- *WhoOp 76*
Potter, Richard 1726-1806 *NewGrD 80*
Potter, Richard Huddleston 1755-1821 *NewGrD 80*
Potter, Tommy 1918- *CmpEPM, EncJzS 70*
Potter, William Henry 1760-1848 *NewGrD 80*
Pottgen, Ernst *WhoOp 76*
Pottgiesser, Heinrich Wilhelm Theodor 1766-1829 *NewGrD 80*
Pottier, Eugene *OxMus*
Pottier, Mathieu 1553?-1629 *NewGrD 80*
Pottier, Matthias 1553?-1629 *NewGrD 80*
Pottiers, Mathieu 1553?-1629 *NewGrD 80*
Pottiers, Matthias 1553?-1629 *NewGrD 80*
Pottle, Bonnie 1910?-1940 *NewOrJ[port]*
Pottle, Sam 1934-1978 *AmSCAP 66, -80*
Potts, John R *AmSCAP 80*
Potts, June E 1935- *IntWWM 77, -80*
Potts, Nadia 1948- *CnOxB*
Potts, Nancy *NotNAT, WhoThe 77*
Potts, Nell *WhoHol A*
Potts, William Orie 1928- *AmSCAP 80*
Potucek, Jura 1923- *NewGrD 80*
Pouctal, Henri 1856-1922 *DcFM, FilmEn*
Poueigh, Jean 1876-1958 *Baker 78, NewGrD 80*
Pougin, Arthur 1834-1921 *Baker 78, NewGrD 80, NotNAT B*
Pougnet, Jean 1907-1968 *NewGrD 80*
Pouhe, Joseph Frank *ConAmC*
Pouishnoff, Lev 1891-1959 *NewGrD 80*
Pouishnov, Lev 1891-1959 *NewGrD 80*
Poujouly, Georges 1940- *FilmgC, HalFC 80*
Poul, Anthony *NewGrD 80*
Poulenc, Francis 1889-1963 *NotNAT B*
Poulenc, Francis 1899-1963 *Baker 78, BnBkM 80, CmOp, CompSN[port], CnOxB, DancEn 78, DcCom 77[port], DcCom&M 79, DcCM, DcFM, DcTwCC, -A, FilmEn, MusMk, NewEOp 71, NewGrD 80[port], OxMus*
Poulet, Gaston 1892-1974 *Baker 78, NewGrD 80*
Poulet, Gerard Georges 1938- *Baker 78, WhoMus 72*
Poulsen, Aage 1943- *CnOxB*
Poulsen, Johannes d1938 *NotNAT B*
Poulsen, Ulla 1905- *CnOxB, DancEn 78*
Poulsen, Valdemar *OxMus*
Poulter, Eileen Margaret *WhoMus 72*
Poulton, A G 1867- *WhThe*
Poulton, Diana 1903- *IntWWM 77, -80, NewGrD 80, WhoMus 72*
Poulton, Mabel 1903- *Film 2*
Poulton, Mabel 1905- *FilmgC, HalFC 80, WhoHol A*
Poulton, Mabel 1906- *IlWWBF*
Poumay, Juliette 1934- *IntWWM 77, -80*
Pouncey, Denys Duncan Rivers 1906- *WhoMus 72*
Pound, Ezra 1884-1972 *DcCM*
Pound, Ezra 1885-1972 *CnMD, EncWT, NewGrD 80*
Pounds, Charles Courtice 1862-1927 *NotNAT B, WhThe*
Pounds, Jessie Brown 1861-1921 *BiDAmM*
Pounds, Louie *WhThe*
Poupard, Henri-Pierre *NewGrD 80*
Poupeliniere, Alexandre LeRiche DeLa 1692-1762 *NewEOp 71*
Poupet, Michel 1926- *IntWWM 77, -80*
Poupliniere *Baker 78*
Poupon, Michele 1940- *CnOxB*
Pourcel, Frank 1928- *RkOn*
Pourtales, Guido James De 1881-1940 *NewGrD 80*
Pourtales, Guy De 1881-1940 *NewGrD 80*
Pourtales, Guy De 1881-1941 *Baker 78*
Pousse, Marcel 1920- *IntWWM 77, -80*
Pousseur, Henri 1929- *Baker 78, BnBkM 80, DcCM, MusMk, NewGrD 80*
Pousson, Rose 1904- *IntWWM 77*
Pouteau, Joseph 1739-1823 *NewGrD 80*
Pouyet, Eugene *Film 1, -2*
Povah, Phyllis 1920- *BiE&WWA, NotNAT, WhThe, WhoHol A*
Powell *PlP&P[port]*
Powell, Addison *WhoHol A*
Powell, Alma Webster 1874-1930 *BiDAmM*
Powell, Arlene Karr *IntWWM 77, -80*
Powell, Baden *Film 1*
Powell, Bellendom *Film 2*
Powell, Benjamin Gordon 1930- *BiDAmM, EncJzS 70*
Powell, Benny 1930- *EncJzS 70*
Powell, Brychan B 1896- *AmSCAP 66, -80*
Powell, Bud 1924-1966 *CmpEPM, IlEncJ, NewGrD 80*
Powell, Charles M 1934- *IntMPA 77, -75, -76, -78, -79, -80*
Powell, Charles Stuart d1811 *NotNAT B*
Powell, David *MotPP*
Powell, David d1925 *WhScrn 74, -77, WhoHol B*
Powell, David 1887-1923 *Film 1, -2, TwYS*
Powell, David 1934- *AmSCAP 80*
Powell, Dawn 1900- *PlP&P[port]*
Powell, Dick *AmPS B*
Powell, Dick d1948 *WhScrn 74, -77, WhoHol B*
Powell, Dick 1904-1962 *ForYSC*
Powell, Dick 1904-1963 *BiDAmM, BiDFilm, -81, CmMov, CmpEPM, FilmEn, FilmgC, HalFC 80[port], MotPP, MovMk[port], NewYTET, NotNAT B, WhScrn 74, -77, WhoHol B, WorEFlm*
Powell, Dick, Jr. *WhoHol A*
Powell, Dilys *IntMPA 77, -75, -76, -78, -79, -80*
Powell, Earl 1924-1966 *Baker 78, BiDAmM, DrBlPA, NewGrD 80*
Powell, Eddie *WhoHrs 80*
Powell, Edward Soldene 1865- *WhoStg 1908*
Powell, Eleanor *AmPS B, MotPP*
Powell, Eleanor 1910- *EncMT, FilmgC, HalFC 80, WhoHol A*
Powell, Eleanor 1912- *BiE&WWA, CmMov, CmpEPM, FilmEn, ForYSC, MGM[port], MovMk[port], OxFilm, ThFT[port], WhThe*
Powell, Eleanor 1913- *What 2[port]*
Powell, Ellis d1963 *NotNAT B*
Powell, Everard Stephen, Sr. 1907- *BiDAmM*
Powell, Felix *ConAmC*
Powell, Frank *Film 1, TwYS A*
Powell, George 1668-1714 *NotNAT B, OxThe*
Powell, Jack 1941- *AmSCAP 80*
Powell, James 1930- *IntWWM 77*
Powell, Jane *AmPS B, IntMPA 77, -75, -76, -78, -79, -80, MotPP*
Powell, Jane 1928- *CmMov*
Powell, Jane 1929- *CmpEPM, FilmEn, FilmgC, ForYSC, HalFC 80, MGM[port], MovMk, WhoHol A, WorEFlm*
Powell, Jimmie 1914- *WhoJazz 72*
Powell, John 1882-1963 *AmSCAP 66, -80, Baker 78, BiDAmM, ConAmC, MusMk, NewGrD 80, OxMus*
Powell, John Leonard 1944- *AmSCAP 80*
Powell, Laurence 1899- *AmSCAP 66, -80, Baker 78, ConAmC*
Powell, Lee 1896-1954 *WhScrn 74, -77*
Powell, Lee 1912-1944 *WhoHol B*
Powell, Lee B 1908-1944 *WhScrn 74, -77*
Powell, Lovelady *WhoHol A*
Powell, Martin *DcPup, Ent, OxThe*
Powell, Maud 1868-1920 *Baker 78, BiDAmM, MusSN[port]*
Powell, Mel 1923- *AmSCAP 66, -80, Baker 78, CmpEPM, ConAmC, DcCM, EncJzS 70, NewGrD 80, WhoHol A*
Powell, Melvin 1923- *EncJzS 70*
Powell, Michael 1905- *BiDFilm, -81, CmMov, ConDr 73, -77A, DcFM, FilmEn, Film 2, FilmgC, HalFC 80, IlWWBF, -A, IntMPA 77, -75, -76, -78, MovMk[port], OxFilm, WhoHrs 80, WorEFlm*
Powell, Morgan E 1938- *AmSCAP 80, CpmDNM 77, -79, ConAmC, IntWWM 77, -80*
Powell, Nicholas 1940- *WhoMus 72*
Powell, Norman James 1930- *IntWWM 80*
Powell, Pat *WomWMM A, -B*
Powell, Paul *TwYS A*
Powell, Peter 1908- *WhThe*
Powell, Ray 1925- *CnOxB, DancEn 78*
Powell, Richard *MorBAP*
Powell, Richard 1897-1937 *WhScrn 74, -77, WhoHol B*
Powell, Robert *WhoHol A*
Powell, Robert 1941- *CnOxB, DancEn 78*
Powell, Robert 1944- *WhoThe 77*
Powell, Robert 1946- *FilmgC, HalFC 80*
Powell, Robert J 1932- *AmSCAP 80, CpmDNM 79, -80, ConAmC*
Powell, Rudy 1907- *CmpEPM, WhoJazz 72*
Powell, Russ 1875-1950 *WhScrn 77*
Powell, Russell *Film 2*
Powell, Sandy 1898- *FilmgC, HalFC 80*
Powell, Sandy 1900- *IlWWBF, -A*
Powell, Seldon 1928- *CmpEPM*
Powell, Sheldon 1928- *BiDAmM*
Powell, Specs 1922- *CmpEPM*
Powell, Teddy *BgBands 74[port]*
Powell, Teddy 1905- *CmpEPM, WhoJazz 72*
Powell, Teddy 1906- *AmSCAP 66, -80*
Powell, Templar *Film 2*
Powell, Vance 1928?- *BluesWW[port]*
Powell, Verne Q 1879-1968 *NewGrD 80*
Powell, Virginia d1959 *BiDAmM*
Powell, Walter 1697-1744 *NewGrD 80*
Powell, Walter Templer d1949 *NotNAT B*
Powell, William 1735-1769 *NotNAT B, OxThe*
Powell, William 1892- *BiDFilm, -81, CmMov, FilmEn, Film 1, -2, FilmgC, ForYSC, HalFC 80[port], IntMPA 77, -75, -76, -78, -79, -80, MGM[port], MotPP, MovMk[port], OxFilm, TwYS, What 2[port], WhThe, WhoHol A, WorEFlm*
Power, Clavering d1931 *NotNAT B*
Power, Sir George d1928 *NotNAT B*
Power, Hartley 1894-1966 *BiE&WWA, FilmgC, HalFC 80, WhScrn 74, -77, WhThe, WhoHol B*
Power, James 1766-1836 *NewGrD 80*
Power, John 1874-1951 *WhScrn 74, -77*
Power, Jules *Film 1, -2*
Power, Leonel d1445 *BnBkM 80, NewGrD 80*
Power, Leonelle d1445 *NewGrD 80*
Power, Leonellus d1445 *NewGrD 80*
Power, Lionel d1445 *Baker 78, NewGrD 80, OxMus*
Power, Lyonel d1445 *NewGrD 80*
Power, Mala 1921- *IntMPA 80*
Power, Nelly d1887 *NotNAT B*
Power, Paul 1902-1968 *WhScrn 74, -77, WhoHol B*
Power, Romina *WhoHol A*
Power, Rosine 1840-1932 *NotNAT B*
Power, Tyrone d1958 *MotPP, WhoHol B*
Power, Tyrone 1795-1841 *EncWT, Ent, OxThe*
Power, Tyrone 1797-1841 *FamA&A[port], NotNAT A, -B*
Power, Tyrone 1913-1958 *BiDFilm, -81, CmMov, FilmEn, FilmgC, HalFC 80, MovMk[port], NotNAT B, OxFilm*
Power, Tyrone 1914-1958 *CmMov, EncWT, ForYSC[port], OxThe, WhScrn 74, -77, WhThe, WorEFlm*
Power, Tyrone, Sr. 1866-1931 *WhThe, WhoStg 1906, -1908*
Power, Tyrone, Sr. 1869-1931 *EncWT, FilmEn, Film 1, -2, FilmgC, HalFC 80, NotNAT A, -B, OxThe, TwYS, WhScrn 74, -77, WhoHol B*
Power, Victor 1930- *NatPD[port]*
Power, William *NewGrD 80*
Powers, Adrian Peter 1945- *IntWWM 77, -80*
Powers, Arba Eugene d1935 *NotNAT B*
Powers, Beverly *WhoHol A*
Powers, C F, Jr. 1923- *IntMPA 77, -76, -78, -79, -80*
Powers, Eddie 1900?-1955? *NewOrJ*
Powers, Eugene 1872- *WhThe*
Powers, Francis *Film 2*
Powers, Francis Gary 1929- *What 5[port]*
Powers, George 1917- *ConAmC*
Powers, Harold S 1928- *NewGrD 80*

Powers, Harry J d1941 *NotNAT B*
Powers, James T 1862-1943 *CmpEPM, NotNAT A, -B, WhThe, WhoStg 1906, -1908*
Powers, Jimmy *IntMPA 76*
Powers, Joey 1939- *RkOn*
Powers, John 1935- *WhoThe 77*
Powers, John H 1885-1941 *WhScrn 74, -77, WhoHol B*
Powers, Joyce 1931- *IntWWM 77*
Powers, Jule d1932 *WhScrn 74, -77*
Powers, Julia *BluesWW*
Powers, Julius *BluesWW*
Powers, Leona 1896-1970 *BiE&WWA, NotNAT B, WhoHol B*
Powers, Leona 1898-1967 *WhThe*
Powers, Lucille *Film 2*
Powers, Mala *HalFC 80, MotPP, WomWMM*
Powers, Mala 1921- *IntMPA 77, -75, -76, -78, -79*
Powers, Mala 1931- *FilmEn, FilmgC, ForYSC, WhoHol A, WhoHrs 80[port]*
Powers, Marie d1973 *BiE&WWA, NotNAT B, WhScrn 77, WhoHol B*
Powers, Mary Gare d1961 *WhScrn 77, WhoHol B*
Powers, Maurine *Film 2*
Powers, Maxwell 1911- *AmSCAP 66, ConAmC*
Powers, Melvin 1932- *AmSCAP 80*
Powers, Nelson *PupTheA*
Powers, Ollie 1890?-1928 *WhoJazz 72*
Powers, Richard d1963 *FilmEn, WhScrn 74, -77, WhoHol B*
Powers, Rod *AmSCAP 80*
Powers, Stefanie 1942- *FilmgC, ForYSC, HalFC 80, MotPP, MovMk, WhoHol A*
Powers, Stephanie 1942- *FilmEn*
Powers, Thomas Edward 1948- *AmSCAP 80*
Powers, Tom 1890-1955 *FilmEn, Film 1, FilmgC, ForYSC, HalFC 80, HolCA[port], NotNAT B, PlP&P, Vers A[port], WhScrn 74, -77, WhThe, WhoHol B*
Powers, William 1941- *WhoOp 76*
Powley, Bryan 1871-1962 *Film 2, WhScrn 77*
Pownall, Mrs. *PlP&P*
Pownall, Mary Ann 1751-1796 *Baker 78, BiDAmM*
Powning, Graham Francis 1949- *IntWWM 80*
Powrozniak, Jozef 1902- *IntWWM 77, -80*
Powys, Stephen 1907- *BiE&WWA, NotNAT, WhThe, WhoThe 72*
Poy, Nardo 1948- *IntWWM 77, -80*
Poynt *NewGrD 80*
Poynte *NewGrD 80*
Poynter, P Kingsley *PupTheA*
Poynts *NewGrD 80*
Poyntz *NewGrD 80*
Pozajic, Mladen 1905- *IntWWM 77, -80*
Pozar, Cleve F 1941- *ConAmC*
Pozdro, John Walter 1923- *AmSCAP 80, Baker 78, ConAmC, IntWWM 77, -80*
Pozner, Vladimir 1905- *DcFM*
Pozniak, Bronislaw 1887-1953 *Baker 78*
Pozniak, Piotr 1939- *IntWWM 77, -80*
Pozniak, Wlodzimierz 1904-1967 *NewGrD 80*
Pozo-Seco Singers *RkOn 2A*
Pozzi, Mrs. *Film 2*
Pozzi, Luigi *NewGrD 80*
Pozzi Escot 1931- *NewGrD 80*
Pozzoli, Ettore 1873-1957 *NewGrD 80*
Praagh, Peggy Van 1910- *CnOxB*
Prac, Jan Bohumir *NewGrD 80*
Prach, Ivan *NewGrD 80*
Pracht, Mary Ellen 1936- *WhoOp 76*
Prada, Jose Maria *FilmAG WE*
Pradas Gallen, Jose 1689-1757 *NewGrD 80*
Prade, Marie *Film 2*
Prado, Jose-Antonio 1943- *DcCM*
Prado, Jose DeAlmeida 1943- *NewGrD 80*
Prado, Perez 1922- *AmPS A, -B, BgBands 74, RkOn[port]*
Prado Peraita, German 1891- *NewGrD 80*
Pradon, Jacques 1644-1698 *McGEWD, OxThe*
Pradot, Marcelle *Film 2*
Praeger, Ferdinand 1815-1891 *NewGrD 80*
Praelisauer *NewGrD 80*
Praelisauer, Andreas Benedikt 1699?-1743 *NewGrD 80*
Praelisauer, Anton Simon Ignaz 1692?-1746 *NewGrD 80*
Praelisauer, Coelestin 1694?-1745 *NewGrD 80*
Praelisauer, Columban 1703?-1753 *NewGrD 80*
Praelisauer, Franz Idelfons 1694?-1745 *NewGrD 80*
Praelisauer, Josef Bernhard 1703?-1753 *NewGrD 80*
Praelisauer, Martin Aemilianus 1708?-1771 *NewGrD 80*
Praelisauer, Robert 1708?-1771 *NewGrD 80*
Praetorius *NewGrD 80*
Praetorius, Abraham *NewGrD 80*
Praetorius, Bartholomaeus 1590?-1623 *NewGrD 80*
Praetorius, Bartholomaus 1590?-1623 *NewGrD 80*
Praetorius, Christian Andreas *NewGrD 80*
Praetorius, Christoph d1609 *NewGrD 80*
Praetorius, Conrad 1515?-1555 *NewGrD 80*
Praetorius, Ernst 1880-1946 *Baker 78*
Praetorius, Hieronymus 1560-1629 *Baker 78, NewGrD 80*
Praetorius, Jacob 1530?-1586 *NewGrD 80*
Praetorius, Jacob 1586-1651 *NewGrD 80*
Praetorius, Jacobus 1586-1651 *Baker 78*
Praetorius, Johannes 1595?-1660 *NewGrD 80*
Praetorius, Konrad 1515?-1555 *NewGrD 80*
Praetorius, Michael 1571-1621 *Baker 78, BnBkM 80, NewGrD 80[port]*
Praga, Marco 1862-1929 *McGEWD[port], ModWD, REnWD[port], WhThe*
Prager, Alice Heinecke 1930- *IntMPA 77, -75, -76, -78, -79, -80*
Prager, Bud *ConMuA 80B*
Prager, Carl 1913- *IntMPA 77, -75, -76, -78, -79*
Prager, Samuel 1907- *AmSCAP 66, -80*
Prager, Stanley 1917-1972 *BiE&WWA, NotNAT B, WhScrn 77, WhoHol B*
Prager, Willy 1877-1956 *WhScrn 74, -77*
Prahacs, Margit 1893-1974 *NewGrD 80*
Prairie Ramblers, The *IlEncCM*
Prampolini, Enrico 1894-1956 *EncWT*
Prandelli, Giacinto 1916- *CmOp*
Prant, Jobst Vom *NewGrD 80*
Prasch, Auguste *Film 2*
Prata, Joaquim 1882-1953 *WhScrn 74, -77*
Pratella, Balilla 1880-1955 *OxMus*
Pratella, Francesco Balilla 1880-1955 *Baker 78, DcCM, NewEOp 71, NewGrD 80*
Pratensis, Jodocus *NewGrD 80*
Prater, Johnnie Lee 1906- *AmSCAP 80*
Prather, Harry 1906- *WhoJazz 72*
Prather, Lee 1890-1958 *WhScrn 74, -77, WhoHol B*
Prati, Alessio 1750-1788 *NewGrD 80*
Pratinas *OxThe*
Pratinas Of Phlius *NewGrD 80*
Pratley, Geoffrey Charles 1940- *WhoMus 72*
Pratley, Gerald *IntMPA 77, -75, -76, -78, -79, -80*
Prato, Johannes De *NewGrD 80*
Prato, Lorenzo Da *NewGrD 80*
Pratoneri, Gaspero *NewGrD 80*
Pratsch, Johann Gottfried 1750?-1818? *NewGrD 80*
Pratt, Alfred 1908-1960? *WhoJazz 72*
Pratt, Andrew Sears 1947- *AmSCAP 80*
Pratt, Andy *IlEncR*
Pratt, Bobby 1926- *EncJzS 70*
Pratt, Carroll C 1894- *NewGrD 80*
Pratt, Charles A 1923- *IntMPA 77, -78, -79, -80*
Pratt, Charles E 1841-1902 *BiDAmM*
Pratt, Edwin John 1883-1964 *CreCan 2*
Pratt, Eleanor Janet Lockhart 1938- *IntWWM 77*
Pratt, George 1935- *IntWWM 77, -80, WhoMus 72*
Pratt, Henry 1777-1849 *BiDAmM*
Pratt, Jack *Film 2*
Pratt, John Christopher 1935- *CreCan 1*
Pratt, Judson 1916- *ForYSC, WhoHol A*
Pratt, Louis Truett 1949- *AmSCAP 80*
Pratt, Lynn 1863-1930 *Film 2, WhScrn 74, -77, WhoHol B*
Pratt, Michael *WhoHol A*
Pratt, Muriel d1945 *NotNAT B, WhThe*
Pratt, Ned *CreCan 2*
Pratt, Neil 1890-1934 *WhScrn 74, -77*
Pratt, Purnell B 1882-1941 *Film 2, TwYS, WhoHol B*
Pratt, Purnell B 1882-1951 *ForYSC*
Pratt, Purnell B 1886-1941 *WhScrn 74, -77*
Pratt, Ross 1916- *WhoMus 72*
Pratt, Samuel Jackson d1814 *NotNAT B*
Pratt, Samuel Orson 1925- *AmSCAP 80*
Pratt, Silas Gamaliel 1846-1916 *Baker 78, BiDAmM, NewGrD 80, OxMus*
Pratt, Theodore 1901-1969 *NotNAT B*
Pratt, Tom Michael 1930- *WhoMus 72*
Pratt, Waldo Selden 1857-1939 *Baker 78, NewGrD 80, OxMus*
Pratt & McClain *RkOn 2[port]*
Praupner, Jan 1751-1824? *NewGrD 80*
Praupner, Vaclav 1745-1807 *NewGrD 80*
Praupner, Venceslaus 1745-1807 *NewGrD 80*
Prausnitz, Frederick 1920- *NewGrD 80*
Prausnitz, Frederik W 1920- *IntWWM 77, -80, NewGrD 80*
Prautner, Jan *NewGrD 80*
Prautner, Vaclav *NewGrD 80*
Prautner, Venceslaus *NewGrD 80*
Pravecek, Jindrich 1909- *IntWWM 77*
Pravov, Ivan *WomWMM*
Praxy, Raoul 1892-1967 *WhScrn 77*
Pray, Anna M 1891-1971 *WhScrn 74, -77*
Pray, Isaac Clark d1869 *NotNAT B*
Pray, Lewis Glover 1793- *BiDAmM*
Prazak, Premysl 1908-1966 *NewGrD 80*
Prebil, Zarko 1934- *CnOxB*
Prebilic, Elizabeth J 1918- *IntWWM 77, -80*
Precht, Robert *NewYTET*
Prechtel, Franz Joachim *NewGrD 80*
Predieri *NewGrD 80*
Predieri, Angelo 1655-1731 *NewGrD 80*
Predieri, Antonio 1650?-1710 *NewGrD 80*
Predieri, Giacomo 1611-1695 *NewGrD 80*
Predieri, Giacomo Cesare 1671-1753 *NewGrD 80*
Predieri, Giovanni Battista *NewGrD 80*
Predieri, Luca Antonio 1688-1767 *Baker 78, NewGrD 80*
Predieri, Tommaso 1655-1731 *NewGrD 80*
Predonce, Johnny 1895?-1939 *NewOrJ*
Preece, Tim 1938- *WhoThe 72, -77*
Preece, Vera *WhoMus 72*
Preedy, George R 1888-1952 *NotNAT B, WhThe*
Preer, Evalyn d1932 *WhoHol B*
Preer, Evelyn 1896-1932 *BlksB&W, -C, DrBlPA, WhScrn 74, -77*
Preetorius, Emil 1883-1973 *EncWT*
Prefontaine, Claude *CreCan 2*
Prefontaine, Yves-G 1947- *IntWWM 77*
Preger, Leo 1907-1965 *Baker 78*
Prehauser, Gottfried 1699-1769 *EncWT, NotNAT B, OxThe*
Preindl, Josef 1756-1823 *NewGrD 80*
Preindl, Joseph 1756-1823 *Baker 78*
Preiner, Johann Jacob *NewGrD 80*
Preininger, John A 1947- *IntWWM 77, -80*
Preiss, Cornelius 1884-1944 *Baker 78*
Preisser, Cherry d1964 *NotNAT B, WhoHol B*
Preisser, June *ForYSC*
Preisser, June 1920?- *FilmEn*
Preisser, June 1921- *HalFC 80*
Preisser, Suse 1920?- *CnOxB, DancEn 78*
Prejean, Albert 1893?-1979 *FilmEn, OxFilm*
Prejean, Albert 1894- *WhoHol A, WorEFlm*
Prejean, Albert 1898- *FilmAG WE, Film 2, FilmgC, HalFC 80*
Prejzner, Tadeusz 1925- *IntWWM 77, -80*
Prek, Stanko 1915- *IntWWM 77, -80*
Prelia, Claire *Film 2*
Prelle, Micheline *FilmEn, WhoHol A*
Prelleur, Peter *NewGrD 80*
Prelleur, Pierre *NewGrD 80*
Prelock, Edward P 1934- *IntMPA 77, -78, -79, -80*
Prelude *RkOn 2[port]*
Premice, Josephine 1926- *BiE&WWA, DrBlPA, NotNAT*
Premiers, The *RkOn 2[port]*
Preminger, Ingo *FilmgC, HalFC 80*
Preminger, Otto 1906- *AmFD, BiDFilm, -81,*

BiE&WWA, CmMov, DcFM, FilmEn, FilmgC, ForYSC, HalFC 80, IntMPA 77, -75, -76, -78, -79, -80, MovMk[port], NotNAT, -A, OxFilm, WhoHol A, WorEFlm
Premru, Raymond Eugene 1934- *IntWWM 77, -80*
Premysler, Francine *WomWMM*
Prencourt, F De *NewGrD 80*
Prendcourt, F De *NewGrD 80*
Prendergast, John Xavier *IntMPA 77, -75, -76, -78, -79, -80*
Prendergast, Roy Martin 1943- *CpmDNM 78, ConAmC*
Prenestino, Giovanni Pierluigi Da *NewGrD 80*
Prenner, Georg d1590 *NewGrD 80*
Prenshaw, Eric Richard 1930- *IntWWM 77*
Prensky, Lester H *BiE&WWA, NotNAT*
Prentes, Henry d1514 *NewGrD 80*
Prentice, Charles W 1898- *WhThe*
Prentice, George *PupTheA*
Prentice, Herbert M 1890- *WhThe*
Prentice, Keith *WhoHol A*
Prentis, Lewis R 1905-1967 *WhScrn 74, -77*
Prentiss, Ann *WhoHol A*
Prentiss, Ed *WhoHol A*
Prentiss, Elizabeth 1818-1878 *BiDAmM*
Prentiss, Paula 1939- *BiDFilm, FilmEn, FilmgC, ForYSC, HalFC 80, IntMPA 77, -75, -76, -78, -79, -80, MotPP, MovMk[port], WhoHol A*
Prentner, Johann Joseph Ignaz *NewGrD 80*
Prentyce, Henry d1514 *NewGrD 80*
Preobrajenska 1871-1962 *OxMus*
Preobrajenska, Olga 1871-1962 *DancEn 78[port]*
Preobrajenska, Olga Josifovna 1870-1962 *CnOxB*
Preobrajenska, Vera Nicolaevna 1926- *ConAmC, IntWWM 77*
Preobrajensky, Vladimir Alexeievich 1912- *CnOxB*
Preobrazhenskaya, Olga 1885-1966 *FilmEn, WomWMM*
Preobrazhensky, Anatoly Viktorovich 1870-1929 *NewGrD 80*
Preobrazhensky, Anton 1870-1929 *Baker 78*
Preponitus Brisiensis *NewGrD 80*
Prepositus Brixiensis *NewGrD 80*
Preprek, Stanislav 1900- *IntWWM 80*
Preprek, Stansilav 1900- *IntWWM 77*
Pres, Josquin Des *NewGrD 80, OxMus*
Presano, Rita d1935 *NotNAT B*
Presbrey, Eugene Wyley 1853-1931 *NotNAT B, WhThe*
Presbrey, Otis F 1820-1901 *BiDAmM*
Preschner, Paul *NewGrD 80*
Prescott, Abraham 1789-1858 *NewGrD 80*
Prescott, Dewey *NewOrJ*
Prescott, Norm 1927- *AmSCAP 80*
Prescott, Thomas Mayhew 1951- *IntWWM 77, -80*
Prescott, Vivian *Film 1*
Presidents *RkOn 2A*
Presle, Micheline 1922- *BiDFilm, -81, FilmAG WE[port], FilmEn, FilmgC, ForYSC, HalFC 80, IntMPA 77, -75, -76, -78, -79, -80, MotPP, MovMk, OxFilm, WhoHol A, WorEFlm*
Presley, Elvis 1935-1977 *AmPS A, -B, Baker 78, BiDAmM, BiDFilm, -81, CmMov, ConMuA 80A[port], CounME 74[port], -74A, EncFCWM 69, FilmEn, FilmgC, ForYSC, HalFC 80, IlEncCM[port], IlEncR[port], IntMPA 77, -75, -76, MotPP, MovMk[port], MusMk[port], NewGrD 80, OxFilm, RkOn[port], -2[port], WhoHol A, WorEFlm[port]*
Presnell, Harve 1933- *FilmEn, FilmgC, ForYSC, HalFC 80, MotPP, WhoHol A*
Presnell, Robert, Sr. 1894- *FilmgC, HalFC 80*
Presnell, Robert R, Jr. 1914- *FilmgC, HalFC 80, IntMPA 77, -75, -76, -78, -79, -80*
Press, Jacques 1903- *AmSCAP 66, -80, ConAmC*
Press, Marvin 1915-1968 *WhScrn 77*
Press, Michael 1872-1938 *BiDAmM*
Press, Percy *DcPup*
Press, Seymour Red 1924- *IntWWM 77, -80*
Pressburger, Arnold 1885-1951 *FilmEn, FilmgC, HalFC 80*
Pressburger, Emeric 1902- *DcFM, FilmEn, FilmgC, HalFC 80, IlWWBF, OxFilm, WorEFlm*
Pressenda, Joannes Franciscus 1777?-1854 *NewGrD 80*
Presser, Andre 1933- *IntWWM 77, -80*
Presser, Theodore 1848-1925 *Baker 78, BiDAmM, NewGrD 80*
Presser, William Henry 1916- *AmSCAP 80, CpmDNM 72, -74, -75, -76, -77, -78, -79, -80, ConAmC*
Pressl, Hermann Markus 1939- *IntWWM 77*
Pressler, Menahem *IntWWM 77, -80*
Pressley, Allen Andrew 1918- *AmSCAP 80*
Pressman, Ailene *AmSCAP 80*
Pressman, David 1913- *BiE&WWA, NotNAT*
Pressman, Edward R *IntMPA 77, -75, -76, -78, -79, -80*
Pressman, Harry 1907-1973 *AmSCAP 66, -80*
Pressman, Lawrence *WhoHol A*
Pressman, Lynn *WomWMM*
Pressman, Mildred *AmSCAP 80*
Pressnell, Constance Elizabeth *CreCan 2*
Presten, Georgio d1553 *NewGrD 80*
Presten, Jorgen d1553 *NewGrD 80*
Preston, Billy *ConMuA 80A*
Preston, Billy 1946- *IlEncR, RkOn 2[port]*
Preston, Billy 1947?- *DrBlPA*
Preston, Christopher *NewGrD 80*
Preston, Don 1932- *EncJzS 70*
Preston, Donald Ward 1932- *EncJzS 70*
Preston, Edna 1892-1960 *WhScrn 74, -77*
Preston, George Hamish Hew 1929- *IntWWM 77, -80*
Preston, Harold *PupTheA*
Preston, J A *DrBlPA*
Preston, Jean 1925- *IntWWM 77, -80*
Preston, Jessie d1928 *NotNAT B*
Preston, John d1798 *NewGrD 80*
Preston, John E *ConAmC*
Preston, Johnny 1939- *AmPS A, RkOn[port]*
Preston, Jorgen *NewGrD 80*
Preston, Joyce Mary *WhoMus 72*
Preston, Robert *AmPS B, IntMPA 77, -75, -76, -78, -79, -80, MotPP*
Preston, Robert 1917- *CmMov, CmpEPM, FilmgC, ForYSC, HalFC 80, HolP 40[port]*
Preston, Robert 1918- *BiE&WWA, EncMT, FamA&A[port], FilmEn, MovMk[port], NotNAT, WhoHol A, WhoThe 72, -77, WorEFlm*
Preston, Robert 1942- *IntWWM 77, -80*
Preston, Simon John 1938- *BnBkM 80, IntWWM 80, NewGrD 80, WhoMus 72*
Preston, Stephen John 1945- *IntWWM 77, -80, NewGrD 80*
Preston, Terry *EncFCWM 69*
Preston, Thomas *McGEWD[port], OxThe, REnWD[port]*
Preston, Thomas d1559? *NewGrD 80*
Preston, Tony *BlkAmP*
Preston, Walter 1880?- *NewOrJ SUP[port]*
Preston, Walter H 1901- *AmSCAP 66, -80*
Preston, Wayde *ForYSC, WhoHol A*
Preston, William d1807 *NotNAT B*
Pretal, Camillus *Film 2*
Preti, Alfonso *NewGrD 80*
Pretorius, Conrad *NewGrD 80*
Pretre, Georges 1924- *Baker 78, CmOp, IntWWM 77, -80, NewEOp 71, NewGrD 80, WhoOp 76*
Pretty, Arline 1893- *Film 1, -2, TwYS, WhoHol A*
Pretty, Sharman Ellen 1951- *IntWWM 77, -80*
Pretty Things, The *ConMuA 80A, IlEncR*
Preumayr *NewGrD 80*
Preumayr, Carl Josef 1780-1849 *NewGrD 80*
Preumayr, Frans Carl 1782-1853 *NewGrD 80*
Preumayr, Johan Conrad 1775-1819 *NewGrD 80*
Preussner, Carltheodor 1895- *IntWWM 77, -80*
Preussner, Eberhard 1899-1964 *NewGrD 80*
Prevedi, Bruno 1928- *WhoOp 76*
Prevert, Jacques 1900-1977 *DcFM, FilmEn, FilmgC, HalFC 80, OxFilm, WorEFlm*
Prevert, Pierre 1906- *DcFM, FilmEn, HalFC 80, OxFilm, WorEFlm*
Preville 1721-1799 *NotNAT B, OxThe*
Previn, Andre 1929- *AmPS, AmSCAP 66, -80, Baker 78, BiDAmM, BnBkM 80, CmMov, CmpEPM, CpmDNM 80, ConAmC, DcCom&M 79, EncJzS 70, FilmEn, FilmgC, HalFC 80, IntMPA 77, -75, -76, -78, -79, -80, MusSN[port], NewGrD 80, OxFilm, PlP&P, PopAmC[port], PopAmC SUP, WhoHol A, WhoMus 72, WorEFlm*
Previn, Andre 1930- *IntWWM 77, -80, WhoOp 76*
Previn, Charles 1888- *AmSCAP 66, -80*
Previn, Dory Langdon 1925- *AmSCAP 66, IlEncR*
Previn, Steve 1925- *IntMPA 77, -75, -76, -78, -79, -80*
Previtali, Fernando 1907- *Baker 78, CmOp, NewEOp 71, NewGrD 80, WhoMus 72, WhoOp 76*
Prevost, Abbe 1697-1763 *NewEOp 71*
Prevost, Andre 1934- *Baker 78, CreCan 2, NewGrD 80*
Prevost, Eddie 1942- *EncJzS 70*
Prevost, Eugene-Prosper 1809-1872 *Baker 78, BiDAmM, NewGrD 80*
Prevost, Francois 1680-1741 *NewGrD 80*
Prevost, Francoise 1680-1741 *CnOxB, DancEn 78*
Prevost, Francoise 1929- *HalFC 80*
Prevost, Francoise 1930- *FilmAG WE, OxFilm, WhoHol A*
Prevost, Frank G 1894-1946 *WhScrn 74, -77*
Prevost, James 1919- *NewOrJ SUP[port]*
Prevost, Marcel 1862-1941 *NotNAT B, WhThe*
Prevost, Marie 1893-1937 *HalFC 80*
Prevost, Marie 1898-1937 *FilmEn, Film 1, -2, FilmgC, ForYSC, MotPP, MovMk[port], NotNAT B, ThFT[port], TwYS, WhScrn 74, -77, WhoHol B*
Prevost, Robert *CreCan 1*
Prevosti, Carlos *PupTheA*
Prewett, Eda Valerga d1964 *NotNAT B*
Prey, Claude 1925- *Baker 78, NewGrD 80*
Prey, Hermann 1929- *Baker 78, BnBkM 80, CmOp, IntWWM 77, -80, MusSN[port], NewEOp 71, NewGrD 80, WhoMus 72, WhoOp 76*
Preyer, Carl Adolph 1863-1947 *Baker 78*
Preyer, Gottfried Von 1807-1901 *Baker 78*
Preziosi, Remo J 1911- *AmSCAP 80*
Priano, Aldo 1895- *IntWWM 80*
Pribyl, Vilem 1925- *NewGrD 80*
Price, Alan 1942- *ConMuA 80A, IlEncR[port], WhoHol A*
Price, Albert John 1943- *AmSCAP 66*
Price, Alonzo 1888-1962 *WhScrn 77, WhoHol B*
Price, Benton *AmSCAP 80*
Price, Carl F 1881-1948 *BiDAmM*
Price, Darryl *AmSCAP 80*
Price, Dennis 1915-1973 *BiE&WWA, FilmAG WE, FilmEn, FilmgC, ForYSC, HalFC 80, IlWWBF[port], MovMk, NotNAT B, OxFilm, WhScrn 77, WhThe, WhoHol B, WhoThe 72*
Price, Doris *BlkAmP*
Price, Dorothea Mildred *WhoMus 72*
Price, Eleazer D d1935 *NotNAT B*
Price, Enrique 1819-1863 *Baker 78*
Price, Evadne 1896- *WhThe*
Price, Florence Anne 1931- *AmSCAP 80*
Price, Florence B 1888-1953 *AmSCAP 66, -80, Baker 78, BiDAmM*
Price, Florence B 1898-1953 *ConAmC*
Price, Fonce *NewOrJ*
Price, Frank 1930- *IntMPA 79, -80, NewYTET*
Price, George *AmPS B*
Price, George E 1900-1964 *AmSCAP 66, -80, NotNAT B*
Price, George N d1962 *NotNAT B*
Price, Georgie 1900-1964 *CmpEPM, JoeFr, WhScrn 74, -77, WhoHol B*
Price, Gilbert 1942- *DrBlPA*
Price, Hal 1886-1964 *Film 2, WhScrn 77, WhoHol B*
Price, Harry 1881-1948 *MagIID*

Price, Harvey Alan 1947- *AmSCAP 80*
Price, Henry Paschal 1945- *WhoOp 76*
Price, Jack 1910- *AmSCAP 66*
Price, James 1761-1805 *DancEn 78*
Price, Janet *IntWWM 77, -80, WhoMus 72*
Price, Jesse 1910-1974 *CmpEPM, EncJzS 70, WhoJazz 72*
Price, Joe Allen *PupTheA*
Price, John d1641 *NewGrD 80, OxMus*
Price, John 1946- *WhoMus 72*
Price, John Elwood 1935- *AmSCAP 80, ConAmC, IntWWM 77, -80*
Price, John L, Jr. 1920- *BiE&WWA, NotNAT*
Price, Jorge Wilson 1853-1953 *Baker 78, NewGrD 80*
Price, Juliette 1831-1906 *DancEn 78*
Price, Kate d1942 *WhoHol B*
Price, Kate 1872-1942 *ForYSC*
Price, Kate 1872-1943 *TwYS, WhScrn 74, -77*
Price, Kate 1873-1943 *Film 1, -2, NotNAT B*
Price, Kenny 1931- *BiDAmM, CounME 74[port], -74A, EncFCWM 69, IlEncCM[port]*
Price, Kerry 1939- *BluesWW[port]*
Price, Leontyne 1927- *Baker 78, BiDAmM, BiE&WWA, BnBkM 80, CmOp[port], DrBlPA, IntWWM 77, -80, MusMk, MusSN[port], NewEOp 71, NewGrD 80[port], PlP&P, WhoMus 72, WhoOp 76*
Price, Lloyd *AmPS A, ConMuA 80A*
Price, Lloyd 1932- *BiDAmM*
Price, Lloyd 1933- *AmSCAP 80, RkOn[port]*
Price, Lorain M d1963 *NotNAT B*
Price, Lorin Ellington 1921- *NotNAT*
Price, Maire d1958 *OxThe*
Price, Margaret 1941- *Baker 78, BnBkM 80, CmOp, IntWWM 77, -80, NewGrD 80, WhoMus 72, WhoOp 76*
Price, Marion James 1913- *AmSCAP 80*
Price, Mark d1917 *Film 1, WhScrn 77*
Price, Milburn 1938- *ConAmC*
Price, Nancy 1880-1970 *Film 2, FilmgC, HalFC 80, OxThe, PlP&P, WhScrn 74, -77, WhThe, WhoHol B*
Price, Nancy 1890-1970 *IlWWBF*
Price, Norman Frederick 1931- *WhoMus 72*
Price, Paul William 1921- *ConAmC*
Price, Penny *AmSCAP 80*
Price, Perry 1942- *WhoOp 76*
Price, Ray 1926- *BiDAmM, CounME 74, -74A, EncFCWM 69, IlEncCM[port], RkOn*
Price, Robert d1761 *NewGrD 80*
Price, Roger 1920- *IntMPA 77, -75, -76, -78, -79, -80, JoeFr[port], WhoHol A*
Price, Ruth 1938- *BiDAmM*
Price, Sam 1908- *CmpEPM, WhoJazz 72*
Price, Sammy 1908- *IlEncJ*
Price, Sherwood *WhoHol A*
Price, Stanley L 1900-1955 *NotNAT B, WhScrn 74, -77, WhoHol B*
Price, Stephen 1783-1840 *EncWT, NotNAT B, OxThe, PlP&P*
Price, Stephen 1940- *AmSCAP 66*
Price, Valdemar 1836-1908 *DancEn 78*
Price, Vincent 1911- *BiDFilm, -81, BiE&WWA, CmMov, FilmEn, FilmgC, ForYSC, HalFC 80, IntMPA 77, -75, -76, -78, -79, -80, MotPP, MovMk[port], NotNAT, OxFilm, WhoHol A, WhoHrs 80[port], WhoThe 72, -77, WorEFlm[port]*
Price, Walter *AmSCAP 80, WhoHol A*
Price, Walter J 1942- *AmSCAP 66*
Price, Walter Travis 1917- *BluesWW[port]*
Price, Will d1962 *NotNAT B*
Price, William Thompson d1920 *NotNAT B*
Price-Drury, W d1949 *NotNAT B*
Price Family *DancEn 78*
Prickett, Maudie *ForYSC*
Prickett, Oliver B 1905- *BiE&WWA, ForYSC, NotNAT, WhoHol A*
Pricope, Eugen 1927- *IntWWM 80*
Pride, Charley 1938- *BiDAmM, ConMuA 80A, CounME 74[port], -74A, DrBlPA, EncFCWM 69, IlEncCM[port], RkOn 2[port]*
Pride, Malcolm 1930- *WhoThe 72, -77*
Prideaux, James 1935- *NatPD[port]*
Prideaux, Tom 1908- *BiE&WWA, NotNAT*
Prieberg, Fred K 1928- *Baker 78*
Pries, Ralph W 1919- *IntMPA 77, -75, -76, -78, -79, -80*
Priesing, Dorothy 1910- *AmSCAP 66, -80, ConAmC*
Priest, Dan *WhoHol A*
Priest, Janet 1881- *WhoStg 1908*
Priest, John 1931- *WhoOp 76*
Priest, Joseph d1734 *NewGrD 80*
Priest, Josiah d1734 *NewGrD 80*
Priest, Josias d1734 *CnOxB, NewGrD 80, OxMus*
Priest, Natalie *WhoHol A*
Priest, Pat *WhoHol A*
Priester, Julian Anthony 1935- *EncJzS 70*
Priestley, J B 1894- *BiE&WWA, CnThe, ConDr 73, -77, CroCD, DcPup, HalFC 80, IntMPA 77, -75, -76, -78, -79, -80, McGEWD[port], ModWD, NotNAT, PlP&P, REnWD[port], WhoThe 72, -77, WorEFlm*
Priestley, John Boynton 1894- *CnMD, EncWT, Ent[port], NotNAT A, OxThe*
Priestman, Brian 1927- *Baker 78, IntWWM 77, -80, NewGrD 80, WhoMus 72*
Prieto, Antonio 1915-1965 *WhScrn 74, -77*
Prieto, Claudio 1934- *NewGrD 80*
Prieto Arrizubieta, Jose Ignacio 1900- *NewGrD 80*
Priggen, Norman 1924- *FilmgC, HalFC 80*
Prigmore, James 1943- *AmSCAP 80*
Prigmore, Nancy Nielson 1947- *IntWWM 77*
Prigozhin, Lucian 1926- *DcCM*
Prigozhin, Lyutsian Abramovich 1926- *NewGrD 80*
Prihoda, Vasa 1900-1960 *Baker 78, NewGrD 80*
Prikopa, Herbert 1935- *WhoOp 76*
Prill, Emil 1867-1940 *Baker 78*
Prill, Karl 1864-1931 *Baker 78*
Prill, Paul 1860-1930 *Baker 78*
Prim, Suzy 1895- *FilmEn*
Prima, Leon 1907- *NewOrJ[port]*
Prima, Louis *BgBands 74[port]*
Prima, Louis 1911-1978 *AmSCAP 66, -80, BiDAmM, CmpEPM, NewOrJ, WhoJazz 72*
Prima, Louis 1912-1978 *RkOn*
Prima, Louis 1913?-1978 *WhoHol A*
Primas, Hugh *NewGrD 80*
Primato, Frank Peter 1956- *AmSCAP 80*
Primavera, Giovan Leonardo 1540?-1585? *NewGrD 80*
Prime, Harry *CmpEPM*
Primm, Frances *Film 2*
Primo, Al *NewYTET*
Primosch, James Thomas 1956- *CpmDNM 80*
Primrose *NewGrD 80*
Primrose, Dorothy 1916- *WhoHol A, WhoThe 72, -77*
Primrose, George *AmPS B*
Primrose, William 1903- *Baker 78, MusSN[port], NewGrD 80*
Primrose, William 1904- *BnBkM 80, WhoMus 72*
Primus, Barry *HalFC 80, WhoHol A*
Primus, Constance Merrill 1931- *IntWWM 77, -80*
Primus, Marc *BlkAmP*
Primus, Pearl 1919- *CmpGMD[port], CnOxB, DancEn 78, DrBlPA*
Prin, Jean-Baptiste 1669?-1742? *NewGrD 80*
Prince, Adelaide 1866-1941 *NotNAT B, WhThe, WhoStg 1908*
Prince, Arthur 1881- *WhThe*
Prince, Elsie 1902- *WhThe*
Prince, George A 1818-1890 *NewGrD 80*
Prince, Harold 1924- *FilmgC, HalFC 80*
Prince, Harold 1928- *BiE&WWA, CnThe, EncMT, Ent[port], IntMPA 77, -75, -76, -78, -79, -80, NotNAT, -A, PlP&P A[port], WhoThe 72, -77*
Prince, Hugh Denham 1906-1960 *AmSCAP 66*
Prince, Hugh Durham 1906-1960 *AmSCAP 80*
Prince, Jessie *Film 2*
Prince, John T 1871-1937 *Film 2, WhScrn 74, -77, WhoHol B*
Prince, Lillian d1962 *NotNAT B*
Prince, Robert 1929- *AmSCAP 80, BiDAmM, ConAmC*
Prince, Roland Don Matthew 1946- *EncJzS 70*
Prince, Thomas 1687-1758 *BiDAmM*
Prince, William 1912- *ForYSC, WhoHol A*
Prince, William 1913- *BiE&WWA, FilmEn, FilmgC, HalFC 80, IntMPA 77, -75, -76, -78, -79, -80, NotNAT, WhoThe 72, -77*
Prince, William F 1938- *AmSCAP 80*
Prince Randian 1871?-1934? *WhScrn 77*
Princess Kanza Omar 1912-1958 *WhScrn 74, -77*
Principal, Victoria *WhoHol A*
Prine, Andrew 1935- *ForYSC*
Prine, Andrew 1936- *BiE&WWA, FilmgC, HalFC 80, NotNAT, WhoHol A, WhoHrs 80*
Prine, John 1946- *ConMuA 80A[port], IlEncCM, IlEncR*
Pring, Gerald *Film 2*
Pring, Katherine 1940- *CmOp, NewGrD 80, WhoOp 76*
Pringle, Aileen 1885?- *ForYSC*
Pringle, Aileen 1895- *FilmEn, Film 1, -2, FilmgC, HalFC 80, MotPP, MovMk, ThFT[port], TwYS, What 2[port], WhoHol A*
Pringle, Bryan 1935- *FilmgC, HalFC 80, WhoHol A*
Pringle, Della *Film 1*
Pringle, Joan *DrBlPA, WhoHol A*
Pringle, John d1929 *WhScrn 74, -77, WhoHol B*
Pringle, John David 1938- *WhoOp 76*
Pringle, Ronald J *BlkAmP*
Pringsheim, Klaus 1883-1972 *Baker 78*
Prinner, Johann Jacob 1624-1694 *NewGrD 80*
Prins-Buttle, Ida Mary *WhoMus 72*
Prinsen, Jaap Anton 1942- *IntWWM 77, -80*
Prinsep, Anthony Leyland 1888-1942 *WhThe*
Prinsep, Val d1904 *NotNAT B*
Printemps, Yvonne *CnThe*
Printemps, Yvonne 1894-1977 *HalFC 80*
Printemps, Yvonne 1895- *EncMT, OxFilm, OxThe, WhThe, WhoHol A*
Printemps, Yvonne 1898- *BiE&WWA*
Printz, Wolfgang Caspar 1641-1717 *Baker 78, NewGrD 80*
Prinz, Alfred 1930- *IntWWM 77, -80*
Prinz, John 1946- *CnOxB*
Prinz, LeRoy 1895- *CmMov, FilmEn, FilmgC, HalFC 80, IntMPA 77, -75, -76, -78, -79, -80, WorEFlm*
Prinze, Freddie 1954- *IntMPA 77*
Prinzmetal, I H 1906- *IntMPA 77, -75, -76, -78, -79*
Prioli, Giovanni *NewGrD 80*
Prioli, Marieta Morosina *NewGrD 80*
Priolo, Christopher 1949- *ConAmC*
Priolo, Joseph P 1918- *AmSCAP 66, -80*
Prior, Allan *WhThe*
Prior, Beatrix *Film 2*
Prior, Herbert 1867-1954 *Film 1, -2, TwYS, WhScrn 77, WhoHol B*
Prior, Robert *Film 2*
Prior, Susan Jane 1946- *IntWWM 80*
Prioris, Johannes 1460?-1514? *NewGrD 80*
Prisadsky, Marjorie *WomWMM B*
Prisco, Al *Film 2*
Prisco, Thomas Matthews 1931- *AmSCAP 80*
Priscoe, Albert *Film 2*
Prister, Bruno 1909- *IntWWM 77, -80*
Pritchard, Arthur J 1908- *IntWWM 77, -80, WhoMus 72*
Pritchard, Barry *NatPD[port]*
Pritchard, Brian William 1942- *IntWWM 77*
Pritchard, Brian William 1943- *IntWWM 80*
Pritchard, David *PupTheA*
Pritchard, David 1949- *EncJzS 70*
Pritchard, Dick d1963 *NotNAT B*
Pritchard, Hannah 1711-1768 *OxThe, PlP&P*
Pritchard, John Michael 1921- *CmOp, IntWWM 77, -80, NewEOp 71, NewGrD 80, WhoMus 72, WhoOp 76*
Pritchard, Robert Paul 1927- *WhoMus 72*
Pritchard, Roger 1940- *ConAmC*
Pritchard, William Dalzel 1913- *IntWWM 77, WhoMus 72*
Pritchett, Paula *WhoHol A*
Pritner, Calvin Lee 1935- *NotNAT*

Pritts, Roy A 1936- *AmSCAP 80, IntWWM 77*
Priuli, Giovanni 1575?-1629 *NewGrD 80*
Priuli, Marieta Morosina *NewGrD 80*
Prival, Lucien 1900- *Film 2, ForYSC, TwYS*
Prival, Max 1889-1957 *AmSCAP 66, -80*
Privin, Bernie 1919- *CmpEPM, WhoJazz 72*
Prizek, Mario 1922- *IntMPA 77, -75, -76, -78, -79, -80*
Pro, Serafin 1906- *NewGrD 80*
Probert, George *Film 2*
Probert, George Arthur, Jr. 1927- *AmSCAP 80, EncJzS 70*
Probst, Leonard 1921- *ConAmTC*
Probst, Robert J 1929- *AmSCAP 66*
Proby, David d1964 *NotNAT B*
Proby, P J 1938- *BiDAmM, RkOn 2[port]*
Proch, Heinrich 1809-1878 *Baker 78*
Prochazka, Rudolf 1864-1936 *Baker 78*
Prochazka, Zdenek Horymir 1915- *IntWWM 77, -80*
Prochnicka, Lidia *WhoHol A*
Prochut, Louis, Jr. 1931- *AmSCAP 80*
Proclemer, Anna 1923- *EncWT*
Procol Harum *ConMuA 80A[port], IlEncR, RkOn 2[port]*
Procope, Russell 1908- *BiDAmM, CmpEPM, EncJzS 70, IlEncJ, WhoJazz 72*
Procopius Von Templin 1607-1690 *NewGrD 80*
Procter, Alice McElroy 1915- *Baker 78*
Procter, Ivis Goulding 1906-1973 *WhScrn 77*
Procter, Jessie Olive 1874-1975 *WhScrn 77*
Procter, Leland 1914- *Baker 78, ConAmC, IntWWM 77, -80*
Procter, Norma 1928- *IntWWM 77, -80, NewGrD 80, WhoMus 72*
Procter-Gregg, Humphrey 1895- *IntWWM 77, -80, WhoMus 72*
Proctor, Bryan Waller d1874 *NotNAT B*
Proctor, Catherine *Film 2*
Proctor, Cathrine *WhoStg 1908*
Proctor, Charles 1906- *IntWWM 77, -80, WhoMus 72*
Proctor, David 1878- *WhoStg 1908*
Proctor, Edith M *PupTheA*
Proctor, Ellen *PupTheA, PupTheA SUP*
Proctor, F F *WhoStg 1906, -1908*
Proctor, Frederick Francis 1851-1929 *NotNAT B, OxThe*
Proctor, Frederick Freeman 1851-1929 *NotNAT A*
Proctor, George Alfred 1931- *IntWWM 80*
Proctor, Hester *PupTheA*
Proctor, James D 1907- *BiE&WWA, NotNAT*
Proctor, Joseph d1897 *NotNAT B*
Proctor, Marland *WhoHol A*
Proctor, Philip *WhoHol A*
Proctor, Robin John Faraday 1935- *WhoMus 72*
Proctor, Romain 1899-1961 *DcPup, PupTheA, PupTheA SUP*
Proctor, Roy *ConAmTC*
Prod'homme, J G 1871-1956 *NewGrD 80*
Prod'homme, Jacques-Gabriel 1871-1956 *Baker 78*
Profanato, Gene *WhoHol A*
Profe, Ambrosius 1589-1661 *Baker 78, NewGrD 80*
Professor Longhair *BluesWW*
Profeta, Laurentiu 1925- *Baker 78, IntWWM 77, -80, NewGrD 80*
Proffer, Spencer *ConMuA 80B*
Proffitt, Frank 1913-1965 *BiDAmM, EncFCWM 69*
Proffitt, Josephine Moore *AmSCAP 80*
Profit, Clarence 1912-1944 *WhoJazz 72*
Profius, Ambrosius 1589-1661 *NewGrD 80*
Profumo, John 1915- *What 4[port]*
Prohaska, Carl 1869-1927 *Baker 78*
Prohaska, Felix 1912- *Baker 78, IntWWM 77, -80, NewGrD 80*
Prohaska, Janos 1921-1974 *WhScrn 77, WhoHrs 80*
Prohaska, Jaro 1891-1965 *CmOp, NewGrD 80*
Prohaska, Karl 1869-1927 *NewGrD 80*
Prohaska, Robert d1974 *WhScrn 77*
Prohut, Lou 1931- *AmSCAP 66*
Prokhorova, Violetta *DancEn 78*
Prokhovenko, Shanna *WhoHol A*
Prokofief, Serge 1891-1953 *OxMus*
Prokofiev, Serge 1891-1953 *CnOxB, DcTwCC, -A, MusMk[port], NewEOp 71*
Prokofiev, Sergei 1891-1953 *Baker 78, CompSN[port], DancEn 78[port], DcCom 77[port], DcCom&M 79, DcCM, DcFM, DcPup, FilmEn, OxFilm, WorEFlm*
Prokofiev, Sergey 1891-1953 *BnBkM 80[port], CmOp, NewGrD 80[port]*
Prokopiev, Trajko 1909- *NewGrD 80*
Prokoviev, Sergei 1891-1953 *FilmgC, HalFC 80*
Prokovsky, Andre 1939- *CnOxB, DancEn 78[port]*
Proks, Josef 1794-1864 *NewGrD 80*
Proks, Joseph 1794-1864 *NewGrD 80*
Proksch, Josef 1794-1864 *Baker 78, NewGrD 80*
Proksch, Joseph 1794-1864 *NewGrD 80*
Prometheus Gemini *AmSCAP 80*
Promio, Alexandre 1870-1927 *DcFM, FilmEn*
Promis, Flo 1884-1956 *WhScrn 74, -77*
Pronomos *NewGrD 80*
Pronomus *NewGrD 80*
Prony, Gaspard-Claire-F-Riche, Baron De 1755-1839 *Baker 78*
Prophet, Ronnie *IlEncCM[port]*
Prophets, The *BiDAmM*
Propiac, Girard De 1759-1823 *NewGrD 80*
Prosdocimus De Beldemandis d1428 *NewGrD 80*
Proser, Monte *BiE&WWA*
Prosev, Ioma 1931- *IntWWM 77*
Prosev, Toma 1931- *Baker 78, IntWWM 80, NewGrD 80*
Proske, Carl 1794-1861 *Baker 78, NewGrD 80*
Proske, Karl 1794-1861 *NewGrD 80, OxMus*
Prosniz, Adolf 1829-1917 *Baker 78*
Prosperi, Carlo 1921- *NewGrD 80*
Prosser, Hugh 1906-1952 *WhScrn 74, -77, WhoHol B*
Prosser, Reese T 1927- *IntWWM 77*
Prostakoff, Joseph 1911- *ConAmC*
Prostejovsky, Michael 1948- *IntWWM 77*
Proszynski, Stanislaw 1926- *IntWWM 77, -80*
Prot, Felix-Jean 1747-1823 *NewGrD 80*
Prota *NewGrD 80*
Prota, Gabriele 1755-1843 *NewGrD 80*
Prota, Giovanni 1786?-1843 *NewGrD 80*
Prota, Giuseppe 1737-1807 *NewGrD 80*
Prota, Ignazio 1690-1748 *NewGrD 80*
Prota, Tommaso d1768? *NewGrD 80*
Prota-Giurleo, Ulisse 1886-1966 *Baker 78, NewGrD 80*
Protazanov, Yakov 1881-1945 *DcFM, FilmEn, OxFilm*
Protazonov, Yakov 1881-1945 *WorEFlm*
Protero, Dodi 1937- *WhoOp 76*
Protheroe, Daniel 1866-1934 *Baker 78, BiDAmM, NewGrD 80*
Protheroe, Guy 1947- *IntWWM 80*
Protic, Predrag Zivojin 1945- *WhoOp 76*
Proto, Frank 1941- *AmSCAP 80, ConAmC*
Protopopov, Vladimir Vasil'yevich 1908- *NewGrD 80*
Prott, Egon Max 1932- *IntWWM 77, -80*
Protti, Aldo 1920- *WhoOp 76*
Proulx, Richard *ConAmC*
Prout, Ebenezer 1835-1909 *Baker 78, NewGrD 80, OxMus*
Prout, Eva *Film 1*
Prouty, Jed 1879-1956 *FilmEn, Film 2, FilmgC, ForYSC, HalFC 80, HolCA[port], MotPP, MovMk, NotNAT B, TwYS, Vers A[port], WhScrn 74, -77, WhoHol B*
Prouty, Olive Higgins 1882-1974 *HalFC 80*
Provedi, Francesco 1710?-1755 *NewGrD 80*
Provenzale, Francesco 1626?-1704 *NewGrD 80*
Provenzale, Francesco 1627-1704 *Baker 78*
Provenzano, Aldo 1930- *ConAmC*
Provenzano, Johnny 1878?-1962? *NewOrJ*
Provenzano, Pasquale *PupTheA*
Providence, Wayne *MorBAP*
Provine, Dorothy 1937- *FilmEn, FilmgC, ForYSC, HalFC 80, IntMPA 77, -75, -76, -78, -79, -80, MotPP, MovMk, WhoHol A*
Provisor, Dennis Errol 1943- *AmSCAP 80*
Provost, Jeanne *WhThe*
Provost, Jon 1949- *ForYSC, MotPP, WhoHol A*
Prowett, Stephen 1495?- *NewGrD 80*
Prowo, Pierre 1697-1757 *NewGrD 80*
Prowse, David 1941- *WhoHrs 80*
Prowse, Juliet 1936- *FilmEn, ForYSC*
Prowse, Juliet 1937- *FilmgC, HalFC 80, MotPP, WhoHol A*
Prowse, Keith *OxMus*
Pruck, Arnold De *NewGrD 80*
Pruden, Larry 1925- *NewGrD 80*
Prudence Penny 1889-1974 *WhScrn 77*
Prudent d1780? *NewGrD 80*
Prudent, Emile 1817-1863 *Baker 78, NewGrD 80*
Prudenzani, Simone d1440? *NewGrD 80*
Prud'homme, Cameron 1892-1967 *BiE&WWA, ForYSC, MotPP, NotNAT B, WhScrn 74, -77, WhoHol B*
Prud'homme, George 1901-1972 *WhScrn 77, WhoHol B*
Pruett, James W 1932- *Baker 78*
Pruett, Jeanne *CounME 74[port], -74A, IlEncCM[port]*
Pruett, Jerome 1941- *WhoOp 76*
Pruett, Lilian Pibernik 1930- *IntWWM 77, -80*
Pruett Twins *BiDAmM*
Pruette, William *WhoStg 1908*
Pruever, Julius 1874-1943 *BiDAmM*
Prufer, Arthur 1860-1944 *Baker 78*
Prugg, Jacob De *NewGrD 80*
Prujan, Turk 1909- *AmSCAP 66, -80*
Prumier, Ange-Conrad 1820-1884 *Baker 78*
Prumier, Antoine 1794-1868 *Baker 78, NewGrD 80*
Prunieres, Henry 1886-1942 *Baker 78, NewGrD 80, OxMus*
Pruslin, Stephen Lawrence 1940- *IntWWM 80*
Prussing, Louise 1897- *Film 2, WhThe*
Pruwer, Julius 1874-1943 *Baker 78*
Pryce, John Maxwell 1936- *IntWWM 77, -80, WhoMus 72*
Pryce, Richard d1942 *NotNAT B, WhThe*
Pryce-Jones, Alan 1908- *BiE&WWA, NotNAT*
Pryce-Jones, John 1946- *WhoOp 76*
Pryde, Peggy 1869- *WhThe*
Pryde, Ted d1963 *NotNAT B*
Prynne, William d1669 *NotNAT B*
Pryor, Ainslie 1921-1958 *ForYSC, WhScrn 74, -77, WhoHol B*
Pryor, Arthur 1870-1942 *AmSCAP 66, -80, Baker 78, BiDAmM, NotNAT B*
Pryor, Beatrix *Film 2*
Pryor, Gwenneth Ruth 1941- *IntWWM 77, -80, WhoMus 72*
Pryor, Hugh 1925-1963 *WhScrn 77*
Pryor, Jacqueline 1930-1963 *WhScrn 77*
Pryor, James Edward 1921- *BluesWW[port]*
Pryor, Martha *BluesWW*
Pryor, Maureen *WhoHol A*
Pryor, Nicholas 1935- *BiE&WWA, NotNAT, WhoHol A*
Pryor, Richard *IntMPA 78, -79, -80*
Pryor, Richard 1940- *DrBlPA, FilmEn, HalFC 80, JoeFr[port]*
Pryor, Richard 1941- *FilmgC, MovMk, WhoHol A*
Pryor, Roger d1974 *WhoHol B*
Pryor, Roger 1900-1974 *FilmgC*
Pryor, Roger 1901-1974 *CmpEPM, FilmEn, HalFC 80, HolP 30[port], What 4[port], WhScrn 77, WhThe*
Pryor, Roger 1903- *Vers A[port]*
Pryor, Roger 1903-1954 *ForYSC*
Pryor, Thomas M 1912- *ConMuA 80B, IntMPA 77, -75, -76, -78, -79, -80*
Prys, Edmund 1541?-1624 *OxMus*
Pryse, Hugh 1910-1955 *NotNAT B, WhThe, WhoHol B*
Prysock, Arthur 1929- *BiDAmM, CmpEPM, DrBlPA, RkOn 2A*
Prysock, Red *RkOn*
Przyblski, Bronislaw 1941- *Baker 78*
Przybyszewski, Stanislaus 1868-1927 *CnMD*
Przybyszewski, Stanislaw 1868-1927 *McGEWD[port], ModWD*
Przylubski, Kazimierz 1945- *IntWWM 77, -80*
Przystas, Czeslaw 1907- *IntWWM 77, -80*

Psacharopoulos, Nikos 1928- *BiE&WWA, IntWWM 77, -80, NotNAT*
Pscherer, Kurt 1915- *WhoOp 76*
Psellos, Konstantin 1018-1080? *NewGrD 80*
Psellos, Michael 1018-1080? *NewGrD 80*
Psellus, Konstantin 1018-1080? *NewGrD 80*
Psellus, Michael 1018-1080? *NewGrD 80*
Pseudo-Aristoteles *NewGrD 80*
Pseudo-Guido Caroli Loci *NewGrD 80*
Psota, Ivo Vana 1908-1952 *CnOxB*
Ptacnik, Jiri 1921- *IntWWM 77, -80*
Ptaszynska, Marta 1943- *Baker 78, ConAmC, IntWWM 77, -80*
Ptolemaeus 083?-161 *NewGrD 80*
Ptolemaios, Klaudius 083?-161 *NewGrD 80*
Ptolemy, Claudius 083?-161 *Baker 78, NewGrD 80*
Ptushko, Alexander 1900- *DcFM, FilmEn*
Publilius Syrus *OxThe*
Puccini *NewGrD 80*
Puccini, Antonio 1747-1832 *NewGrD 80*
Puccini, Domenico 1772-1815 *NewGrD 80*
Puccini, Giacomo 1712?-1781 *NewGrD 80*
Puccini, Giacomo 1858-1924 *Baker 78, BnBkM 80[port], CmOp[port], CmpBCM, CompSN[port], DcCom 77[port], DcCom&M 79, DcTwCC, -A, MusMk, NewEOp 71, NewGrD 80[port], OxMus, PlP&P*
Puccini, Michele 1813-1864 *NewGrD 80*
Puccitelli, Virgilio 1599-1654 *NewGrD 80*
Puccitta, Vincenzo 1778-1861 *NewGrD 80*
Pucek, Anna 1943- *IntWWM 80*
Puchalsky, Vladimir 1848-1933 *Baker 78*
Puchat, Max 1859-1919 *Baker 78*
Puchi, Rebecca *WomWMM*
Puchner, Hans *NewGrD 80*
Pucitta, Vincenzo 1778-1861 *Baker 78, NewGrD 80*
Puck, Harry 1890-1964 *AmSCAP 66, NotNAT B*
Puckeridge, Richard *OxMus*
Puckett, Gary *BiDAmM*
Puckett, Gary & The Union Gap *RkOn 2[port]*
Puckett, George Riley 1890-1946 *BiDAmM, EncFCWM 69*
Puckett, Riley d1946 *CmpEPM*
Puckett, Riley 1894-1946 *IlEncCM*
Puckhaber, Ralph L 1921- *IntMPA 79, -80*
Puco, Philip Milo 1926- *AmSCAP 80*
Puddles d1912 *WhScrn 77*
Puddy, Keith A 1935- *IntWWM 77, -80, WhoMus 72*
Pudney, John 1909- *IntMPA 77, -75, -76, -78*
Pudoffstin, J *Film 2*
Pudovkin, V 1893-1953 *HalFC 80*
Pudovkin, Vsevolod I 1893-1952 *BiDFilm, -81*
Pudovkin, Vsevolod I 1893-1953 *DcFM, FilmEn, FilmgC, MovMk[port], OxFilm, WhScrn 74, -77, WhoHol B, WorEFlm[port]*
Puecher, Virginio 1927- *EncWT, WhoOp 76*
Puel, Christoph *NewGrD 80*
Puente, Ernest Anthony 1923- *AmSCAP 80*
Puente, Gioseppe De *NewGrD 80*
Puente, Giuseppe Del *NewEOp 71, NewGrD 80*
Puente, Giuseppe Del 1841-1900 *Baker 78*
Puente, Giuseppe Del 1845-1900 *BiDAmM*
Puerling, Eugene Thomas 1929- *EncJzS 70*
Puerling, Gene 1929- *EncJzS 70*
Puerto, Diego Del *NewGrD 80*
Pueyo, Eduardo Del 1905- *NewGrD 80*
Pueyo, Salvador 1935- *NewGrD 80*
Puffer, Deena *AmSCAP 66*
Puffer, Merle 1915- *AmSCAP 66*
Puffy, Charles *Film 2*
Puget *NewGrD 80*
Puget, Claude-Andre 1905- *CnMD, McGEWD, ModWD*
Puget, Eugene 1838-1892 *NewGrD 80*
Puget, Jean-Baptiste 1849-1940 *NewGrD 80*
Puget, Loisa 1810-1889 *NewGrD 80*
Puget, Louise-Francoise 1810-1889 *NewGrD 80*
Puget, Maurice 1884-1960 *NewGrD 80*
Puget, Paul-Charles-Marie 1848-1917 *Baker 78*
Puget, Theodore 1799-1883 *NewGrD 80*
Puggelli, Lamberto 1938- *WhoOp 76*
Pugh, Donald Wagner 1931- *IntWWM 77, -80*
Pugh, James Edward 1950- *EncJzS 70*
Pugh, Joe Bennie 1926-1960 *BluesWW*
Pugh, Leonard 1929- *IntWWM 77, -80, WhoMus 72*
Pugh, Sally *WomWMM B*
Puglia, Frank d1975 *WhoHol C*
Puglia, Frank 1892- *MovMk, Vers A[port]*
Puglia, Frank 1892-1962 *FilmgC*
Puglia, Frank 1892-1975 *FilmEn, HalFC 80, WhScrn 77*
Puglia, Frank 1894-1962 *Film 2, ForYSC, TwYS*
Pugliese, Carlos Anibal 1944- *AmSCAP 80*
Pugliese, Rudolph E 1918- *BiE&WWA, NotNAT*
Pugliesi, Constance M *PupTheA*
Pugnani, Gaetano 1731-1798 *Baker 78, BnBkM 80, MusMk, NewGrD 80, OxMus*
Pugni, Cesare 1802-1870 *Baker 78, DancEn 78, NewGrD 80*
Pugni, Cesare 1805?-1870 *CnOxB*
Pugno, Raoul 1852-1914 *Baker 78, BnBkM 80, NewGrD 80*
Puhel, Christoph *NewGrD 80*
Puhler, Johann 1550?-1591? *NewGrD 80*
Puig, Bernardo Calvo 1819-1880 *NewGrD 80*
Puig, Eva G 1894-1968 *WhScrn 77*
Puig, Guillermo De *NewGrD 80*
Puilloys, Johannes *NewGrD 80*
Puishnov, Lev *NewGrD 80*
Pujman, Ferdinand 1889-1961 *NewGrD 80*
Pujol, David 1894- *NewGrD 80*
Pujol, Emilio 1886- *OxMus*
Pujol, Francesc 1878-1945 *Baker 78*
Pujol, Francisco 1878-1945 *NewGrD 80*
Pujol, Jose *NewGrD 80*
Pujol, Juan 1573?-1626 *Baker 78, NewGrD 80, OxMus*
Pujol, Juan Bautista 1835-1898 *OxMus*
Pujol Vilarrubi, Emilio 1886- *NewGrD 80*
Pukhal'sky, Vladimir 1848-1933 *NewGrD 80*
Pulaski, Jack d1948 *NotNAT B*
Pulgar Vidal, Francisco Bernardo 1929- *NewGrD 80*
Puliaschi, Gian Domenico *NewGrD 80*
Puliaschi, Giovan Domenico *NewGrD 80*
Puliaschi, Giovanni Domenico *NewGrD 80*
Puliti, Gabriello 1575?-1644? *NewGrD 80*
Puliti, Leto 1818-1875 *Baker 78*
Puliti, Ornella *NewGrD 80*
Pullaer, Louis Van 1475?-1528 *NewGrD 80*
Pullen, Mrs. Claude E *ConAmC*
Pullen, Don Gabriel 1944- *EncJzS 70, IlEncJ*
Pullen, Mary Money 1907- *WhoMus 72*
Pullen, Olive Dungan 1903- *AmSCAP 80*
Pullen, William *ForYSC*
Pulli, Pietro 1710?-1759? *NewGrD 80*
Pulliam, John Arthur 1925- *IntWWM 77*
Pulliam, Lucille E 1909- *IntWWM 77, -80*
Pullin, Audrey 1927- *WhoMus 72*
Pullin, Audrey 1929- *IntWWM 77, -80*
Pulling, M J L 1906- *IntMPA 77, -75, -76, -78, -79, -80*
Pullins, Carl Leroy 1940- *AmSCAP 80*
Pullis, Jimmy *ConMuA 80B*
Pullois, Jean d1478 *NewGrD 80*
Pullois, Jehan d1478 *NewGrD 80*
Pullois, Johannes d1478 *NewGrD 80*
Pully, B S 1911-1972 *JoeFr, PlP&P, WhScrn 77, WhoHol B*
Puls, Gerd 1927- *IntWWM 77, -80*
Pulver, Jeffrey 1884- *Baker 78, NewGrD 80, OxMus*
Pulver, Lilo 1929- *FilmgC, ForYSC, HalFC 80*
Pulver, Liselotte *WhoHol A*
Pulver, Liselotte 1929- *FilmAG WE, FilmEn*
Pulver, Liselotte 1939?- *ForYSC*
Puma, Joe 1927- *EncJzS 70*
Puma, Joseph J 1927- *EncJzS 70*
Puma, Salvatore 1920- *WhoOp 76*
Pumiglio, Pete *CmpEPM*
Pumphrey, Byron *NatPD[port]*
Pumpian, Paul H 1928- *AmSCAP 80*
Punsley, Bernard *ForYSC, WhoHol A*
Punter, Melanie 1952- *BlkWAB*
Punto' *OxMus*
Punto, Giovanni 1746-1803 *NewGrD 80[port]*
Punto, Giovanni 1748-1803 *BnBkM 80*
Puppo, Giuseppe 1749-1827 *Baker 78, NewGrD 80*
Purcell *NewGrD 80*
Purcell, Charles 1883-1962 *CmpEPM, EncMT, WhThe*
Purcell, Daniel 1660?-1717 *Baker 78, NewGrD 80, OxMus*
Purcell, Dick 1908-1944 *FilmEn, FilmgC, ForYSC, HalFC 80, WhoHol B*
Purcell, Edward 1689-1740 *NewGrD 80*
Purcell, Edward 1928- *AmSCAP 66*
Purcell, Edward Henry d1765 *NewGrD 80*
Purcell, Gertrude d1963 *NotNAT B*
Purcell, Harold 1907- *WhThe*
Purcell, Henry d1664 *NewGrD 80*
Purcell, Henry 1658?-1695 *OxMus*
Purcell, Henry 1659?-1695 *Baker 78, BnBkM 80[port], CmOp, CmpBCM, CnOxB, DcCom 77, DcCom&M 79, DcPup, GrComp[port], MusMk[port], NewEOp 71, NewGrD 80*
Purcell, Henry 1742-1802 *BiDAmM*
Purcell, Irene d1972 *WhoHol B*
Purcell, Irene 1902-1972 *FilmEn, WhScrn 77*
Purcell, Irene 1903-1972 *WhThe*
Purcell, Lee *WhoHol A*
Purcell, Noel 1900- *FilmgC, HalFC 80, IntMPA 77, -75, -76, -78, -79, -80, WhoHol A*
Purcell, Patricia 1925- *IntWWM 77, -80*
Purcell, Richard 1908-1944 *WhScrn 74, -77*
Purcell, Thomas d1682 *NewGrD 80*
Purck, Wenzel Raimund *NewGrD 80*
Purday *NewGrD 80*
Purday, Charles Henry 1799-1885 *NewGrD 80, OxMus*
Purday, Thomas Edward *NewGrD 80*
Purdell, Reginald 1896-1953 *FilmgC, HalFC 80, NotNAT B, WhScrn 74, -77, WhThe, WhoHol B*
Purdell, Reginald 1896-1963 *IlWWBF*
Purdie, Bernard 1939- *EncJzS 70*
Purdie, John d1891 *NewGrD 80*
Purdie, Pretty 1939- *EncJzS 70*
Purdie, Robert *NewGrD 80*
Purdom, C B 1883-1965 *BiE&WWA, WhThe*
Purdom, Edmund *IntMPA 77, -75, -76, -78, -79, -80, MotPP*
Purdom, Edmund 1924- *FilmEn, FilmgC, HalFC 80, WhoHol A*
Purdom, Edmund 1925- *ForYSC*
Purdon, Richard *Film 1*
Purdy, Alfred Wellington 1918- *CreCan 2*
Purdy, Constance 1885?-1960 *WhScrn 77*
Purdy, James *PlP&P*
Purdy, Rai 1910- *IntMPA 77, -75, -76, -78, -79, -80*
Purdy, William T 1882-1918 *AmSCAP 80*
Pure Prairie League *ConMuA 80A, IlEncCM[port], IlEncR*
Purifoy, John David 1952- *AmSCAP 80*
Purifoy, Lydia M 1942- *AmSCAP 80*
Purify, James & Bobby *RkOn 2[port]*
Purim, Flora 1942- *EncJzS 70*
Purk, Wenzel Raimund *NewGrD 80*
Purkine, Jan Evangelista 1787-1869 *DcFM*
Purkiss, Anthony John 1943- *IntWWM 77, WhoMus 72*
Purl, Linda *HalFC 80*
Purnell, Alton 1911- *AmSCAP 66, -80, NewOrJ[port], WhoJazz 72*
Purnell, Keg 1915-1965 *WhoJazz 72*
Purnell, Louise 1942- *WhoHol A, WhoThe 72, -77*
Purnell, Theodore 1903?-1974 *NewOrJ*
Purnell, William 1915-1965 *BiDAmM*
Purney, Wilfrid 1914- *WhoMus 72*
Purpura, Craig John 1951- *AmSCAP 80*
Pursell, Bill *RkOn[port]*
Pursell, William 1926- *ConAmC*
Purser, John Whitley 1942- *IntWWM 77, -80, WhoMus 72*
Purswell, Patrick W 1939- *ConAmC*
Purtill, Maurice 1916- *CmpEPM*
Purtill, Moe 1916- *WhoJazz 72*
Purviance, Edna 1894-1958 *FilmEn, Film 1, -2, FilmgC, HalFC 80, MotPP, MovMk[port], OxFilm, TwYS, WhScrn 74, -77, WhoHol B, WorEFlm*
Purviance, Edna 1895-1958 *NotNAT B*
Purvin, Theodore V 1918- *AmSCAP 80*

Purvis, Charlie 1909- *AmSCAP 66, -80*
Purvis, Jack 1906-1962 *CmpEPM, WhoJazz 72*
Purvis, Richard 1915- *BiDAmM, ConAmC*
Puschman, Adam 1532-1600 *NewGrD 80*
Puschmann, Adam 1532-1600 *Baker 78*
Puschmann, Josef 1740?-1794 *NewGrD 80*
Puschmann, Zacharias *Baker 78*
Pusey, Arthur *Film 2, WhThe*
Pushkin, Aleksandr Sergeyevich 1799-1837 *McGEWD[port]*
Pushkin, Alexander 1799-1837 *DancEn 78, Ent[port], NewEOp 71*
Pushkin, Alexander Ivanovich 1907-1970 *CnOxB*
Pushkin, Alexander Sergeivich 1799-1837 *OxThe*
Pushkin, Alexander Sergeyevich 1799-1837 *CnThe, NewGrD 80, REnWD[port]*
Pushkin, Alexander Sergeyevitch 1799-1837 *NotNAT B*
Pushkin, Alexandr Sergeyevich 1799-1837 *EncWT*
Pusina, Jan 1940- *ConAmC*
Pustelak, Kazimierz 1930- *WhoOp 76*
Pustet *NewGrD 80*
Pustet, Friedrich 1798-1882 *Baker 78, NewGrD 80*
Pusztai, Tibor 1946- *ConAmC*
Puteanus, Ericus 1574-1646 *NewGrD 80*
Puteanus, Erycius 1574-1646 *NewGrD 80*
Puteus, Vincentius *NewGrD 80*
Putman, George d1974 *WhScrn 77*
Putnam, Ashley 1952- *IntWWM 80*
Putnam, Bill *ConMuA 80B*
Putnam, Curly 1930- *BiDAmM*
Putnam, George d1975 *WhoHol C*
Putnam, Jill *WhoMus 72*
Putnam, Norbert *ConMuA 80B*
Putnik, Edwin Vincent 1924- *IntWWM 77, -80*
Putsche, Thomas 1929- *AmSCAP 80, ConAmC*
Puttar-Gold, Nada 1923- *WhoOp 76*
Putter, Alice Mildred *Film 2*
Putz *NewGrD 80*
Putz, Andreas *NewGrD 80*
Putz, Georg d1694 *NewGrD 80*
Putz, Jakob d1706 *NewGrD 80*
Putz, Martin d1700 *NewGrD 80*
Putz, Ruth Margaret 1933- *WhoMus 72*
Putz, Ruth-Margret 1932- *WhoOp 76*
Puxol, Lucas *NewGrD 80*
Puy, Henry Du *NewGrD 80*
Puyana, Rafael 1931- *IntWWM 77, -80, NewGrD 80*
Puzhnaya, R *Film 2*
Puzzi, Giovanni 1792-1876 *NewGrD 80*
Py, Gilbert 1933- *WhoOp 76*
Pyamour, John d1431 *Baker 78, NewGrD 80*
Pyatnitsky, Mitrofan Efimovich 1864-1927 *NewGrD 80*
Pybrac, Guy DuFaur De *NewGrD 80*
Pybus, Josephine Anne 1936- *IntWWM 77, WhoMus 72*
Pycard *Baker 78, NewGrD 80*
Pychard, Thomas *NewGrD 80*
Pycharde, Thomas *NewGrD 80*
Pye, Charlotte Alington *NewGrD 80*
Pye, Henry James d1813 *NotNAT B*
Pygot, Richard *NewGrD 80*
Pygott, Richard *NewGrD 80*
Pyke, Harold Irvine 1903- *AmSCAP 80*
Pyke, Harry 1903- *AmSCAP 66*
Pyke, Irene 1912- *WhoMus 72*
Pykini *NewGrD 80*
Pykke, Thomas *NewGrD 80*
Pylades *OxThe*
Pyle, Denver 1920- *FilmEn, FilmgC, ForYSC, HalFC 80, MovMk[port], WhoHol A*
Pyle, Francis Johnson 1901- *AmSCAP 66, -80, ConAmC*
Pyle, Harry C 1894- *AmSCAP 66*
Pyle, Russell 1941- *NotNAT*
Pylkkanen, Tauno Kullervo 1918- *Baker 78, DcCM, IntWWM 77, -80, NewGrD 80*
Pyllois, Johannes *NewGrD 80*
Pylloys, Johannes *NewGrD 80*
Pylois, Johannes *NewGrD 80*
Pyloys, Johannes *NewGrD 80*
Pyne *NewGrD 80*
Pyne, James Kendrick 1852-1938 *Baker 78, BiDAmM, NewGrD 80*
Pyne, Joe 1925-1970 *WhScrn 74, -77, WhoHol B*
Pyne, Louisa 1832-1904 *NewGrD 80*
Pyonnier, Joannes *NewGrD 80*
Pyper, Nancy Phillips 1893- *CreCan 1*
Pyrenaeus, Georg *NewGrD 80*
Pyriev, Ivan 1901-1968 *DcFM, FilmEn*
Pyrison, Cambio *NewGrD 80*
Pyros, John *NatPD[port]*
Pyrszynski, Gasparus 1718-1758 *NewGrD 80*
Pyrszynski, Kasper 1718-1758 *NewGrD 80*
Pysing, William 1605?-1684 *NewGrD 80*
Pythagoras 582?BC-500?BC *Baker 78, NewGrD 80*

Q

Quaal, Ward L *NewYTET*
Quaciari, Gene L *AmSCAP 80*
Quade, John *WhoHol A*
Quadflieg, Will 1914- *EncWT, Ent, WhoHol A*
Quadling, Lew 1908- *AmSCAP 66, -80*
Quadreny, Josep M Mestres *DcCM*
Quadri, Argeo 1911- *CmOp*
Quadris, Johannes De *NewGrD 80*
Quaglia, Giovanni Battista 1625?-1700 *NewGrD 80*
Quagliati, Paolo 1555?-1628 *Baker 78, MusMk, NewGrD 80*
Quaglio *NewGrD 80, OxThe*
Quaglio, Angelo 1784-1815 *NewGrD 80*
Quaglio, Angelo 1828-1890 *EncWT*
Quaglio, Angelo 1829-1890 *NewGrD 80*
Quaglio, Domenico 1708-1773 *NewGrD 80*
Quaglio, Domenico 1787-1837 *EncWT, NewGrD 80*
Quaglio, Eugen 1857-1942 *EncWT*
Quaglio, Giovanni Maria 1700?-1765? *NewGrD 80*
Quaglio, Giovanni Maria 1772-1813 *NewGrD 80*
Quaglio, Giulio 1668-1751 *NewGrD 80*
Quaglio, Giulio 1764-1801 *NewGrD 80*
Quaglio, Giuseppe 1747-1828 *NewGrD 80*
Quaglio, Lorenzo 1730-1805 *NewGrD 80*
Quaglio, Lorenzo 1793-1869 *NewGrD 80*
Quaglio, Lorenzo I 1730-1804 *EncWT*
Quaglio, Martin *NewGrD 80*
Quaglio, Simon 1795-1837 *EncWT*
Quaglio, Simon 1795-1878 *NewGrD 80*
Quaid, Randy 1953- *HalFC 80, IntMPA 77, -75, -76, -78, -79, -80, MovMk[port], WhoHol A*
Quaile, Elizabeth 1874-1951 *Baker 78*
Quaker City Boys, The *RkOn*
Quaker City Four *AmPS B*
Quale, Anthony *MotPP*
Qualemberg, Johann Michael 1726?-1786 *NewGrD 80*
Qualen, John *IntMPA 77, -75, -76, -78, -79, -80, MotPP*
Qualen, John 1899- *FilmEn, FilmgC, HalFC 80, HolCA[port], MovMk, Vers A[port], WhoHol A*
Qualen, John 1908- *ForYSC*
Qualenberg, Johann Michael 1726?-1786 *NewGrD 80*
Quality, Gertrude *Film 2*
Quallenberg, Johann Michael 1726?-1786 *NewGrD 80*
Qualters, Tot 1895-1974 *WhScrn 77, WhoHol B*
Qualtinger, Helmut 1928- *EncWT, WhoHol A*
Quantz, Johann Joachim 1697-1773 *Baker 78, BnBkM 80, MusMk[port], NewGrD 80[port], OxMus*
Quaranta, Letizia 1892- *OxFilm*
Quaranta, Lydia 1891-1928 *FilmEn, Film 1, OxFilm, WhScrn 77*
Quare, Daniel *OxMus*
Quarenghi, Guglielmo 1826-1882 *Baker 78, NewGrD 80*
Quarles, Charles d1717? *NewGrD 80*
Quarles, Charles d1727? *NewGrD 80*
Quarles, James Thomas 1877-1954 *Baker 78, BiDAmM, ConAmC*
Quarles, Norma 1936- *DrBlPA*
Quarm, Joan Helana Phelan *ConAmTC*
Quarry, Robert 1923- *FilmgC, HalFC 80, WhoHol A*
Quarry, Robert 1928- *WhoHrs 80*
Quartaro, Nena 1911- *ForYSC, TwYS*
Quartaro, Nina 1911- *Film 2*
Quartermaine, Charles 1877-1958 *NotNAT B, OxThe, WhThe, WhoHol B*
Quartermaine, Leon 1876-1967 *BiE&WWA, NotNAT B, OxThe, WhScrn 74, -77, WhThe, WhoHol B*
Quarterman, Leonora *PupTheA*
Quartette Tres Bien *BiDAmM*
Quartieri, Pietro Paolo 1560?-1601? *NewGrD 80*
Quartiero, Pietro Paolo 1560?-1601 *NewGrD 80*
Quatremere DeQuincy, Antoine-Chrysostome 1755-1849 *Baker 78, NewGrD 80*
Quatris, Johannes De *NewGrD 80*
Quatro, Suzi 1950- *ConMuA 80A, IlEncR*
Quattlebaum, Douglas Elijah 1927- *BluesWW[port]*
Quattrini, Jan Ludwik 1822-1893 *NewGrD 80*
Quayle, Anna *WhoHol A*
Quayle, Anna 1936- *BiE&WWA, NotNAT*
Quayle, Anna 1937- *FilmgC, HalFC 80, WhoThe 72, -77*
Quayle, Anthony 1913- *BiE&WWA, CnThe, Ent, FilmAG WE, FilmEn, FilmgC, ForYSC, HalFC 80, IlWWBF[port], IntMPA 77, -75, -76, -78, -79, -80, MovMk[port], NotNAT, OxThe, PlP&P, WhoHol A, WhoThe 72, -77*
Quayle, Antony 1913- *EncWT*
Quayle, Calvin 1927- *BiE&WWA, NotNAT*
Quayle, Leo Gordon 1918- *WhoOp 76*
Quealey, Chelsea 1905-1950 *WhoJazz 72*
Quebec, Ike Abrams 1918-1963 *BiDAmM, CmpEPM*
Quebedo, Bartolome De *NewGrD 80*
Quedens, Eunice *FilmEn, Film 2, WhoHol A*
Queen *ConMuA 80A[port], IlEncR, RkOn 2[port]*
Queen, Dorothea Mitchell 1913- *IntWWM 77, -80*
Queen, Robert I 1919- *IntMPA 77, -75, -76, -78, -79, -80*
Queen, Virginia 1921- *ConAmC*
Queen City Concert Band *BiDAmM*
Queener, Charles Conant 1921- *AmSCAP 80, BiDAmM*
Queener, Charlie 1921- *CmpEPM*
Queeny, Mary 190-?- *DcFM, WomWMM*
Quef, Charles 1873-1931 *Baker 78*
Queffelec, Anne 1948- *IntWWM 80, NewGrD 80*
Queiroz, Gloria 1930- *WhoOp 76*
Queldryk *NewGrD 80*
Queler, Eve 1936- *WhoOp 76, WomCom[port]*
Quellmalz, Alfred 1899- *IntWWM 77, -80*
Quello, James H *NewYTET*
Queneau, Raymond 1903-1976 *DcFM, FilmEn, OxFilm, WorEFlm*
Quensel, Isa *WhoHol A*
Quentin, Bertin d1767? *NewGrD 80*
Quentin, Jean-Baptiste *NewGrD 80*
Quenzer, Arthur 1905- *AmSCAP 66, -80*
Queralt, Francisco 1740-1825 *NewGrD 80*
Quercu, Simon De *NewGrD 80*
Querol, Miguel 1912- *NewGrD 80*
Querol Gavalda, Miguel 1912- *Baker 78*
Quesada, Virginia 1951- *ConAmC*
Quesne, Joseph 1746-1809 *NewGrD 80*
Quesnel, Steven R 1950- *CpmDNM 79, IntWWM 77*
Questel, Mae 1910- *BiE&WWA, WhoHol A*
Question Mark & The Mysterians *RkOn 2[port]*
Quevedo, Bartolome De 1510?-1569 *NewGrD 80*
Quica, La 1907?-1967 *CnOxB*
Quick, John 1748-1831 *OxThe, PlP&P[port]*
Quick, Robert E 1917- *IntMPA 77, -75, -76, -78, -79, -80*
Quicksell, Howdy 1901-1953 *WhoJazz 72*
Quicksilver Messenger Service *BiDAmM, ConMuA 80A, IlEncR, RkOn 2[port]*
Quigley, Charles 1906-1964 *WhScrn 77*
Quigley, Don *WhoHol A*
Quigley, Godfrey *WhoHol A*
Quigley, Juanita 1931- *MotPP, ThFT[port], WhoHol A*
Quigley, Martin 1890-1964 *NotNAT B*
Quigley, Martin, Jr. 1917- *IntMPA 77, -75, -76, -78, -79, -80*
Quigley, Rita 1923- *WhoHol A*
Quigley, William J 1951- *IntMPA 79, -80*
Quilici, Folco 1930- *DcFM, FilmEn, WorEFlm*
Quilico, Louis *CmOp*
Quilico, Louis 1926- *CreCan 2*
Quilico, Louis 1929- *NewGrD 80*
Quilico, Louis 1930- *WhoOp 76*
Quill, Daniel Eugene 1927- *BiDAmM*
Quill, Gene 1927- *CmpEPM*
Quill, Gynter Clifford 1915- *ConAmTC*
Quillan, Eddie 1907- *FilmEn, Film 2, FilmgC, ForYSC, HalFC 80, IntMPA 77, -75, -76, -78, -79, -80, MovMk, TwYS, Vers A[port], What 4[port], WhoHol A*
Quillan, Sarah 1879-1969 *WhScrn 77, WhoHol B*
Quillen, Charles W 1938- *AmSCAP 80*
Quilley, Denis 1927- *CnThe, WhoHol A, WhoThe 72, -77*
Quillian, Joseph F 1884-1952 *WhScrn 74, -77*
Quillian, Joseph F 1884-1962 *WhoHol B*
Quilling, Howard L 1935- *CpmDNM 72, ConAmC*
Quilter, Bryan 1928- *IntMPA 75, -76*
Quilter, Roger 1877-1953 *Baker 78,*

DcCom&M 79, MusMk, NewGrD 80, NotNAT B, OxMus
Quimby, Fred 1886-1965 *FilmEn, FilmgC, HalFC 80, WorEFlm*
Quimby, Helen Sherwood 1870- *BiDAmM*
Quimby, Margaret d1965 *Film 2, TwYS, WhScrn 77*
Quimby, Margerie *Film 2*
Quin, Carol Lynelle 1947- *IntWWM 77*
Quin, James 1693-1766 *CnThe, Ent, NotNAT A, -B, OxThe, PlP&P[port]*
Quin-Tones, The *RkOn*
Quinard, Jean 1582?-1670 *NewGrD 80*
Quinard, Jesson 1582?-1670 *NewGrD 80*
Quinart, Jean 1582?-1670 *NewGrD 80*
Quinart, Jesson 1582?-1670 *NewGrD 80*
Quinault *OxThe*
Quinault, Jean-Baptiste-Maurice 1685?-1744 *Baker 78*
Quinault, Jean-Baptiste Maurice 1687-1745 *NewGrD 80*
Quinault, Marie-Anne-Catherine 1695-1791 *NewGrD 80*
Quinault, Philippe 1635-1688 *Baker 78, BnBkM 80, CnOxB, DancEn 78, Ent, McGEWD, NewEOp 71, NewGrD 80, NotNAT B, OxThe, REnWD[port]*
Quinault, Phillipe 1635-1688 *CmOp, CnThe*
Quinby, Benjamin F 1830-1890 *NewGrD 80*
Quinby, George H 1901- *BiE&WWA, NotNAT*
Quince, Louis Veda 1900-1954 *WhScrn 74, -77*
Quincey, Thomas De 1785-1859 *OxMus*
Quinchette, Paul 1921- *BiDAmM*
Quincy, George 1944- *AmSCAP 80*
Quine, Hector 1926- *IntWWM 77, -80, WhoMus 72*
Quine, Richard 1920- *AmSCAP 66, -80, BiDFilm, -81, CmMov, DcFM, FilmEn, FilmgC, ForYSC, HalFC 80, IntMPA 77, -75, -76, -78, -79, -80, MotPP, MovMk[port], OxFilm, WhoHol A, WorEFlm*
Quinet, Fernand 1898-1971 *Baker 78, NewGrD 80, WhoMus 72*
Quinet, Marcel 1915- *Baker 78, DcCM, IntWWM 77, -80, NewGrD 80*
Quiney, Enid Joyce 1928- *IntWWM 77, -80, WhoMus 72*
Quinichette, Paul 1916- *EncJzS 70*
Quinichette, Paul 1921- *CmpEPM*
Quinlan, Fred J 1925- *AmSCAP 80*
Quinlan, Gertrude 1875-1963 *NotNAT B, WhThe, WhoStg 1908*
Quinlan, John C d1954 *NotNAT B*
Quinlan, Kathleen *HalFC 80, IntMPA 80*
Quinlivan, Charles 1924-1974 *WhScrn 77, WhoHol B*
Quinn, Adelle *AmSCAP 80*
Quinn, Alan J 1889-1944 *WhScrn 74, -77*
Quinn, Allen d1944 *Film 1, WhoHol B*
Quinn, Andrew J 1931- *AmSCAP 66*
Quinn, Anthony 1915- *BiDFilm, -81, BiE&WWA, CmMov, FilmEn, FilmgC, ForYSC, HalFC 80[port], IntMPA 77, -75, -76, -78, -79, -80, MotPP, NotNAT A, OxFilm, WhoHol A, WhoHrs 80, WhoThe 77, WorEFlm[port]*
Quinn, Anthony 1916- *MovMk[port]*
Quinn, Arthur Hobson 1875-1960 *NotNAT B*
Quinn, Bill *WhoHol A*
Quinn, Charles *Film 2*
Quinn, Don 1900- *AmSCAP 66, -80*
Quinn, Edwin McIntosh 1906-1952 *NewOrJ[port]*
Quinn, J Mark 1936- *ConAmC*
Quinn, James 1884-1919 *WhScrn 77*
Quinn, James Francis, III 1952- *AmSCAP 80*
Quinn, James Jimmie 1885-1940 *WhScrn 74, -77*
Quinn, Jerrel H 1934- *AmSCAP 80*
Quinn, Jimmie *Film 2*
Quinn, Jimmy 1885-1940 *WhoHol B*
Quinn, Joe 1899-1974 *WhScrn 77, WhoHol B*
Quinn, Joe 1917-1971 *WhScrn 74, -77*
Quinn, John 1851-1916 *WhScrn 77*
Quinn, Lawrence A 1952- *AmSCAP 80*
Quinn, Louis *WhoHol A*
Quinn, Mary d1947 *NotNAT B*
Quinn, Pat *WhoHol A*
Quinn, Paul 1870-1936 *WhScrn 74, -77*
Quinn, Peter *CreCan 1*
Quinn, Ray *ConMuA 80B*
Quinn, Regina *Film 2*
Quinn, Ruth *PupTheA*
Quinn, Sally *NewYTET*
Quinn, Snoozer 1906-1952? *WhoJazz 72*
Quinn, Stanley J, Jr. 1915- *IntMPA 77, -75, -76, -78, -79, -80*
Quinn, Teddy 1959- *WhoHol A*
Quinn, Tony 1899-1967 *WhScrn 74, -77, WhThe, WhoHol B*
Quinn, William *Film 1, -2*
Quinones DeBenavente, Luis 1589?-1651 *McGEWD*
Quinska *AmSCAP 80*
Quint, Michael 1950- *IntWWM 77, -80*
Quintanar, Hector 1936- *Baker 78, DcCM, NewGrD 80*
Quintavalle, Antonio *NewGrD 80*
Quintero, The Brothers *OxThe*
Quintero, Joaquin Alvarez 1873-1944 *McGEWD[port], NotNAT B, WhThe*
Quintero, Jose 1924- *BiE&WWA, CnThe, EncWT, Ent, NotNAT, -A, PlP&P, -A[port], WhoThe 72, -77*
Quintero, Serafin Alvarez 1871-1938 *CnMD, CnThe, McGEWD, NotNAT B, WhThe*
Quinteros, Abelardo 1923- *NewGrD 80*
Quintet Of The Hot Club Of France *CmpEPM*
Quintiani, Giulio Cesare 1550?-1600? *NewGrD 80*
Quintiani, Lucrezio 1555?-1595? *NewGrD 80*
Quintiere, Jude 1939- *ConAmC*
Quintilian 030?- *NewGrD 80*
Quintilianus, Aristides *NewGrD 80*
Quinton, Mark d1891 *NotNAT B*
Quinziani, Giulio Cesare *NewGrD 80*
Quinziani, Lucrezio *NewGrD 80*
Quirk, Billie *TwYS*
Quirk, Billy *TwYS A*
Quirk, Billy 1881-1926 *FilmEn, WhoHol B*
Quirk, Billy 1888-1926 *Film 1, -2*
Quirk, William 1881-1926 *WhScrn 74, -77*
Quiroga, Manuel 1890-1961 *Baker 78*
Quiroz, Salvador 1881-1956 *WhScrn 74, -77*
Quirsfeld, Johann 1642-1686 *NewGrD 80*
Quitin, Jose 1915- *NewGrD 80*
Quitschreiber, Georg 1569-1638 *NewGrD 80*
Quittard, Henri Charles Etienne 1864-1919 *Baker 78, NewGrD 80*
Quittenton, Martin 1945- *AmSCAP 80*
Quivey, Marvel *Film 2*
Quo, Beulah *WhoHol A*
Quon, Maple *WhoMus 72*
Quotations, The *RkOn[port]*
Qutb Al-Din 1236-1312 *NewGrD 80*
Qweldryk *NewGrD 80*

R

Raab, Franz DePaula 1763-1804 *NewGrD 80*
Raabe, Christoph *NewGrD 80*
Raabe, Peter 1872-1945 *Baker 78, NewGrD 80*
Raaben, Lev Nikolayevich 1913- *NewGrD 80*
Raabeova, Hedvika *WomWMM*
Raad, Virginia 1925- *IntWWM 77, -80, WhoMus 72*
Raaff, Anton 1714-1797 *Baker 78, BnBkM 80, NewGrD 80[port]*
Raalte, Albert Van 1890-1952 *Baker 78*
Raasted, Niels Otto 1888-1966 *Baker 78*
Raats, Jaan 1932- *Baker 78, DcCM, NewGrD 80*
Rab, Christoph 1552-1620 *NewGrD 80*
Rab, Christopher 1552-1620 *NewGrD 80*
Rab, Corvinus 1552-1620 *NewGrD 80*
Rab, Phyllis *BiE&WWA*
Rab, Valentin 1522?-1596 *NewGrD 80*
Rab, Valentinus 1522?-1596 *NewGrD 80*
Rabagliati, Alberto 1906-1974 *Film 2, WhScrn 77, WhoHol B*
Rabal, Francisco *WhoHol A*
Rabal, Francisco 1925- *FilmAG WE, FilmEn*
Raban, Jonathan *ConDr 73, -77B*
Rabassa, Pedro 1683-1767 *NewGrD 80*
Rabaud, Henri 1873-1949 *Baker 78, CompSN[port], NewEOp 71, NewGrD 80, OxMus*
Rabb, Ellis 1930- *BiE&WWA, PlP&P, WhoThe 72, -77*
Rabbit, Samuel 1911- *AmSCAP 66, -80*
Rabbit Foot Minstrels *BiDAmM*
Rabbitt, Eddie *ConMuA 80A*
Rabbitt, Eddie 1941- *IlEncCM*
Rabe, Christiaan 1915- *IntWWM 77, -80*
Rabe, Christoph *NewGrD 80*
Rabe, David 1940- *ConDr 73, -77, DcLB 7[port], EncWT, Ent, NotNAT, PlP&P A[port], WhoThe 77*
Rabe, Folke 1935- *Baker 78, DcCM, IntWWM 77, -80, NewGrD 80*
Rabe, Valentin *NewGrD 80*
Rabelais, Francois 1494?-1553? *NewEOp 71*
Rabelais, Francois 1494-1554? *NewGrD 80*
Rabello, Manuel *NewGrD 80*
Rabelo, Joao Soares *NewGrD 80*
Rabenalt, Arthur Maria 1905- *DcFM*
Rabes, Lennart 1938- *IntWWM 77, -80*
Rabich, Ernst 1856-1933 *Baker 78*
Rabie, Ilva Katherine 1927- *IntWWM 80*
Rabier, Jean 1927- *FilmEn, FilmgC, HalFC 80, OxFilm, WorEFlm*
Rabin, Jack 1910?- *WhoHrs 80*
Rabin, Michael 1936-1972 *Baker 78, BiDAmM*
Rabinof, Benno 1910-1975 *Baker 78*
Rabinof, Sylvia *AmSCAP 66, ConAmC*
Rabinovich, David 1900- *Baker 78*
Rabinovich, Isaac Moiseivich 1894-1961 *OxThe*
Rabinovitch, Fishel *AmSCAP 80*
Rabinovitz, Jason 1921- *IntMPA 80*
Rabinowitz, Harry 1916- *IntWWM 77, -80, WhoMus 72*
Rabinowitz, Sholem *McGEWD, REnWD[port]*
Rabl, Walter 1873-1940 *Baker 78*
Raborg, Frederick A, Jr. 1934- *NatPD[port]*
Rabovsky, Istvan 1930- *CnOxB, DancEn 78*
Raby, Derek *ConDr 77B*
Racamato, Claire Durand 1936- *IntWWM 77*
Racan, Honorat DeBueil, Marquis De 1589-1670 *OxThe*
Racchiano, Giovanni Battista *NewGrD 80*
Race, Steve 1921- *IntWWM 77, -80, WhoMus 72*
Racek, Fritz 1911-1975 *NewGrD 80*
Racek, Jan 1905-1979 *IntWWM 77, -80, NewGrD 80, WhoMus 72*
Racette, Vicki 1956- *IntWWM 77, -80*
Rach, John *PupTheA*
Rachel 1820-1858 *CnThe, FamA&A[port], OxThe*
Rachel 1821-1858 *EncWT, Ent, NotNAT A*
Rachel, Madame 1820-1858 *NotNAT B*
Rachel, Mademoiselle 1820-1858 *PlP&P*
Rachel, Lydia d1915 *NotNAT B*
Rachell, James 1910- *BluesWW[port]*
Rachmaninof, Sergei Vassilievich 1873-1943 *OxMus*
Rachmaninoff, Sergei 1873-1943 *AmSCAP 66, -80, Baker 78, BiDAmM, BnBkM 80[port], CompSN[port], ConAmC, MusSN[port], NewEOp 71*
Rachmaninoff, Sergei Vassilievitch 1873-1943 *DancEn 78*
Rachmaninoff, Sergey *NewGrD 80*
Rachmaninov, Sergei 1873-1943 *DcCom 77[port], DcCom&M 79, DcTwCC, -A, MusMk[port]*
Rachmaninov, Sergey 1873-1943 *CmOp, DcCM, NewGrD 80*
Rachmil, Lewis J 1908- *FilmEn, IntMPA 77, -75, -76, -78, -79, -80*
Rachmilovich, Jacques 1895-1956 *Baker 78*
Rachoen, Stefan 1906- *IntWWM 80*
Racholdinger, Elias *NewGrD 80*
Rachonn, Stefan 1906- *IntWWM 77*
Rachow, Louis A 1927- *NotNAT*
Racimo, Victoria *WhoHol A*
Racine, Jean 1639-1699 *CnThe, EncWT, Ent, McGEWD[port], NewEOp 71, NewGrD 80, NotNAT A, -B, OxThe, PlP&P, REnWD[port]*
Raciunas, Antanas 1906- *NewGrD 80*
Rackham, Arthur 1867-1939 *DcPup*
Rackin, Martin 1918-1976 *FilmEn, FilmgC, HalFC 80, IntMPA 75, -76, WorEFlm*
Rackley, Lawrence 1932- *AmSCAP 80, CpmDNM 72, -79, ConAmC*
Rackmil, Milton R *IntMPA 77, -75, -76, -78, -79, -80*
Rackstraw, William *NewGrD 80*
Racquet, Charles 1597-1664 *NewGrD 80*
Radamm, Monika 1950- *CnOxB*
Radau S-Prager, Piroska 1910- *IntWWM 77*
Radauer, Irmfried 1928- *IntWWM 77, -80*
Raday, Imre *Film 2*
Radcliff, Jack 1900-1967 *WhScrn 74, WhoHol B*
Radcliffe, E J 1893- *Film 2, TwYS*
Radcliffe, Jack 1900-1967 *WhScrn 77*
Radcliffe, P Sterling 1929- *AmSCAP 80*
Radcliffe, Philip Fitzhugh 1905- *IntWWM 77, -80, NewGrD 80, WhoMus 72*
Radcliffe, Violet *Film 1*
Radd, Ronald *WhoHol A*
Radd, Ronald 1924-1976 *HalFC 80*
Radd, Ronald 1926?- *FilmgC*
Radd, Ronald 1929-1976 *WhoThe 72, -77*
Raddall, Thomas Head 1903- *CreCan 1*
Raddatz, Carl 1911- *FilmAG WE*
Raddatz, Otto Wilhelm Richard 1917- *IntWWM 77, -80*
Radeck, Johann Martin 1623?-1684 *NewGrD 80*
Radeck, Johann Rudolf d1662 *NewGrD 80*
Radecke, Ernst 1866-1920 *Baker 78*
Radecke, Robert 1830-1911 *Baker 78*
Radecke, Rudolf 1829-1893 *Baker 78*
Rademakers, Fons 1920- *FilmEn, OxFilm*
Rademakers, Fons 1921- *FilmgC, HalFC 80, WorEFlm*
Radenkovic, Milutin 1921- *Baker 78*
Rader, Don 1935- *EncJzS 70*
Rader, Donald Arthur 1935- *BiDAmM, EncJzS 70*
Rader, Gene *WhoHol A*
Rader, Jack *WhoHol A*
Radesca DiFoggia, Enrico d1625 *NewGrD 80*
Radford, Basil 1897-1952 *FilmEn, Film 2, FilmgC, HalFC 80, IlWWBF, NotNAT B, OxFilm, WhScrn 74, -77, WhThe, WhoHol B*
Radford, Dave 1884- *AmSCAP 66, -80*
Radford, Geoffrey Paul 1939- *WhoMus 72*
Radford, Maisie *WhoMus 72*
Radford, Robert 1874-1933 *CmOp*
Radford, Winifred 1901- *IntWWM 77, -80, WhoMus 72*
Radic, Dusan 1923- *DcCM*
Radic, Dusan 1929- *Baker 78, NewGrD 80*
Radic, Marija 1939- *IntWWM 77*
Radica, Ruben 1931- *Baker 78, DcCM, IntWWM 77, -80, NewGrD 80*
Radicati, Felice Alessandro 1775-1820 *NewGrD 80*
Radicati, Teresa *NewGrD 80*
Radice, Anthea Mulso 1917- *IntWWM 80, WhoMus 72*
Radice, Attilia 1913- *DancEn 78*
Radice, Attilia 1914- *CnOxB*
Radice, Mark 1957- *AmSCAP 80*
Radiciotti, Giuseppe 1858-1931 *Baker 78, NewGrD 80*
Radics, Bela *OxMus*
Radilak, Charles H 1907-1972 *WhScrn 77*
Radin, Paul *IntMPA 77, -76, -78, -79, -80*
Radino, Giovanni Maria d1607? *NewGrD 80*
Radino, Giulio d1607? *NewGrD 80*
Radius, Alexandra 1942- *CnOxB*
Radlov, Sergei Yevgenyevich 1892-1958 *OxThe*
Radmall, Peggy *WhoMus 72*

Radnai, Miklos 1892-1935 *Baker 78, NewGrD 80*
Radnay, George 1920- *WhoOp 76*
Radnay, Hilda *Film 2*
Radnitz, Robert B 1925- *FilmEn, FilmgC, HalFC 80, IntMPA 77, -75, -76, -78, -79, -80*
Rado, Agi 1931- *IntWWM 77, -80*
Rado, Aladar 1882-1914 *Baker 78*
Rado, James *AmSCAP 80, ConDr 73, -77D, PlP&P[port]*
Rado, James 1932- *NotNAT*
Rado, James 1939- *EncMT*
Radocchia, Emil 1932- *AmSCAP 80*
Radok, Alfred 1914-1976 *EncWT, FilmEn*
Radok, Alfred 1914-1979 *DcFM, OxFilm, WorEFlm*
Radolt, Baron Wenzel Ludwig Von 1667?-1716 *NewGrD 80*
Radoluski, Nicolaus De *NewGrD 80*
Radom, Mikolaj *NewGrD 80*
Radom, Nicolaus De *NewGrD 80*
Radomski, James 1942- *AmSCAP 80*
Radomski, Jan *NewGrD 80*
Radomski, Nicolaus De *NewGrD 80*
Radoux, Charles 1877-1952 *Baker 78*
Radoux, Jean-Theodore 1835-1911 *Baker 78, NewGrD 80*
Radoux-Rogier, Charles 1877-1952 *NewGrD 80*
Radovan, Ferdinand 1938- *WhoOp 76*
Radovanovic, Vladan 1932- *Baker 78*
Radshenko, Serge Nikolaievich 1944- *CnOxB*
Radulphus Laudunensis *NewGrD 80*
Radunsky, Alexander Ivanovich 1912- *CnOxB, DancEn 78*
Radvanyi, Geza Von 1907- *DcFM, FilmEn*
Rady, Simon 1909-1965 *AmSCAP 66, -80*
Radzina, Medea *Film 2*
Radzina, Remea *Film 2*
Radziwill, Prince Anton Heinrich 1775-1833 *Baker 78*
Radziwill, Prince Antoni Henryk 1775-1833 *NewGrD 80*
Radziwill, Prince Maciej 1751?-1800 *NewGrD 80*
Radziwill, Marcelina *NewGrD 80*
Rae, Allan McLean 1942- *Baker 78, IntWWM 80*
Rae, Charlotte 1926- *BiE&WWA, NotNAT, WhoHol A, WhoThe 72, -77*
Rae, Claire 1889-1938 *WhScrn 74, -77, WhoHol B*
Rae, Eric 1899- *WhThe*
Rae, Isabel *Film 1*
Rae, Jack 1899-1957 *WhScrn 74, -77*
Rae, John 1934- *BiDAmM, EncJzS 70, WhoHol A*
Rae, Kenneth 1901- *BiE&WWA, WhThe, WhoThe 72*
Rae, Melba 1922-1971 *WhScrn 74, -77*
Rae, Raida *Film 2*
Rae, Zoe *Film 1*
Raebeck, Lois Rupp 1921- *IntWWM 77, -80*
Raeburn, Boyd 1913-1966 *BgBands 74[port], BiDAmM, CmpEPM*
Raeburn, Henzie *WhoHol A*
Raeburn, Henzie 1900- *WhThe, WhoThe 72*
Raeburn, Henzie 1901-1973 *WhScrn 77*
Raecke, Hans-Karsten 1941- *NewGrD 80*
Raedler, Dorothy 1917- *BiE&WWA, NotNAT, WhoThe 72, -77*
Raeli, Vito 1880-1970 *Baker 78, NewGrD 80*
Raesel, Andreas *NewGrD 80*
Raevsky, Iosif Moiseevich 1900- *WhThe*
Rafanelli, Flora 1930- *WhoOp 76*
Rafelson, Bob *BiDFilm*
Rafelson, Bob 1934- *BiDFilm 81, FilmEn*
Rafelson, Bob 1935- *FilmgC, HalFC 80, IntMPA 77, -78, -79, -80*
Rafelson, Bob 1938- *MovMk[port]*
Rafelson, Toby *WomWMM*
Rafetto, Mike *Film 2*
Raff, Joachim 1822-1882 *BnBkM 80, GrComp[port], NewGrD 80, OxMus*
Raff, Joseph Joachim 1822-1882 *Baker 78*
Raff, Matthew *NewYTET*
Raff, William Jourdan *MorBAP*
Raffaelli, Michel 1929- *EncWT*
Rafferty, Chips 1909-1971 *FilmEn, FilmgC, ForYSC, HalFC 80, MovMk, OxFilm, WhScrn 74, -77, WhoHol B*
Rafferty, Frances 1922- *FilmEn, FilmgC, ForYSC, HalFC 80, IntMPA 77, -75, -76, -78, -79, -80, MGM[port], MotPP, MovMk, WhoHol A*
Rafferty, Gerry *ConMuA 80A*
Rafferty, Pat 1861-1952 *NotNAT B, WhThe*
Raffin, Deborah 1953- *FilmEn, HalFC 80, IntMPA 77, -75, -76, -78, -79, -80, WhoHol A*
Raffles, Sir Thomas Stamford 1781-1826 *DcPup*
Raffles Bill 1895-1940 *WhScrn 74, -77*
Raffman, Relly 1921- *CpmDNM 76, ConAmC*
Rafi, Claude 1515-1553 *NewGrD 80*
Rafkin, Alan *FilmgC, HalFC 80*
Raft, George *IntMPA 77, -75, -76, -78, -79, -80, MotPP*
Raft, George 1895- *CmMov, FilmEn, FilmgC, HalFC 80[port], MovMk[port], What 3[port]*
Raft, George 1903- *BiDFilm, -81, Film 2, ForYSC, OxFilm, WhoHol A, WorEFlm[port]*
Rafter, Leonard 1911- *WhoMus 72*
Raftor, Catherine *NewGrD 80*
Ragabliati, Alberto *Film 2*
Ragaini, Aurora 1906- *IntWWM 77*
Ragan, Bronson 1915-1971 *BiDAmM*
Ragan, Ruth d1962 *WhScrn 74, -77*
Ragas, Henry 1897-1919 *BiDAmM, CmpEPM, NewOrJ*
Ragas, Herman *NewOrJ[port]*
Ragazzi, Angelo 1680?-1750 *NewGrD 80*
Ragazzoni, Ottavio *NewGrD 80*
Ragazzoni, Pietro Paolo 1499-1580? *NewGrD 80*
Ragazzono, Ottavio *NewGrD 80*
Ragazzono, Pietro Paolo 1499-1580? *NewGrD 80*
Ragin, John S *WhoHol A*
Raglan, James 1901-1961 *NotNAT B, WhScrn 74, -77, WhThe, WhoHol B*
Ragland, Esther 1912-1939 *WhScrn 74, -77*
Ragland, Larry 1948- *DrBlPA*
Ragland, Rags 1905-1946 *FilmEn, FilmgC, HalFC 80, HolCA[port], MGM[port], MotPP, MovMk, NotNAT B, Vers A[port], WhScrn 74, -77, WhoHol B*
Ragland, Rags 1906-1946 *ForYSC*
Ragland, Robert Oliver 1931- *AmSCAP 66, -80*
Ragland, Robert Oliver 1933- *ConAmC A*
Raglin, Alvin 1917-1955 *BiDAmM*
Raglin, Junior 1917-1955 *WhoJazz 72*
Ragni, Gerome *ConDr 73, -77D, NotNAT, PlP&P[port]*
Ragni, Gerome 1936- *AmSCAP 80*
Ragni, Gerome 1942- *EncMT*
Ragno, Joseph *WhoHol A*
Rago, Alexis 1930- *Baker 78*
Ragonese, Don 1920- *AmSCAP 80*
Ragossnig, Konrad 1932- *IntWWM 80, WhoMus 72*
Ragotzy, Jack 1921- *BiE&WWA, NotNAT*
Ragovoy, Jerry 1930- *AmSCAP 80*
Ragozina, Galina 1949- *CnOxB*
Ragsdale, Carl V 1925- *IntMPA 77, -75, -76, -78, -79, -80*
Ragsdale, John David 1932- *IntWWM 77, -80*
Ragtime Band *BiDAmM*
Ragtime Jug Stompers *BiDAmM*
Ragtimers *BiDAmM*
Rague, Louis-Charles 1760?-1793? *NewGrD 80*
Raguenet, Francois 1660?-1722 *NewGrD 80*
Rahbari, Ali 1948- *IntWWM 77, -80*
Rahere d1144 *OxThe, PlP&P[port]*
Rahim, Emmanuel Khaliq 1934- *AmSCAP 80*
Rahlwes, Alfred 1878-1946 *Baker 78*
Rahm, Knute 1876-1957 *WhScrn 77*
Rahman, Aishah *BlkAmP, MorBAP*
Rahman, Yusuf Nafeesur 1942- *AmSCAP 80*
Rahn, John 1944- *ConAmC, IntWWM 77, -80*
Rahn, Muriel 1911-1961 *BlksBF, DrBlPA*
Rai, Himansu *Film 2*
Raiani, Albert George 1917-1962 *AmSCAP 80*
Raichev, Alexander 1922- *Baker 78, NewGrD 80*
Raichev, Russlan 1919- *NewGrD 80*
Raichl, Miroslav 1930- *Baker 78*
Raick, Dieudonne 1703-1764 *NewGrD 80*
Raics, Istvan 1912- *IntWWM 77, -80*
Raida, Karl Alexander 1852-1923 *Baker 78*
Raider, Nat 1929- *IntWWM 77, -80*
Raiders, The *BiDAmM*
Raidestinos, David *NewGrD 80*
Raidy, William Anthony 1923- *ConAmTC, NotNAT*
Raik, Etienne 1904- *DcFM*
Railroad Bill *BluesWW*
Railton, John 1929- *IntWWM 77, -80, WhoMus 72*
Railton, Ruth 1915- *IntWWM 77, -80*
Railton, Ruth 1916- *WhoMus 72*
Raimann, Ferdinand *NewGrD 80*
Raimann, Rudolf 1861-1913 *Baker 78*
Raimbaut De Vaqeiras 115-?-1207 *NewGrD 80*
Raimbaut De Vaqueiras 115-?-1207 *NewGrD 80*
Raimo, Padre *NewGrD 80*
Raimon De Miraval *NewGrD 80*
Raimondi, Gianni 1923- *Baker 78, NewGrD 80, WhoOp 76*
Raimondi, Gianni 1925- *CmOp*
Raimondi, Ignazio 1735?-1813 *NewGrD 80*
Raimondi, Ignazio 1737?-1813 *Baker 78*
Raimondi, Pietro 1786-1853 *Baker 78, NewGrD 80, OxMus*
Raimondi, Ruggero 1941- *CmOp, IntWWM 77, -80, NewGrD 80*
Raimondi, Ruggero 1942- *BiDAmM*
Raimondi, Ruggero 1944- *WhoOp 76*
Raimu 1883-1946 *CnThe, EncWT, Ent, FilmAG WE, FilmEn, FilmgC, HalFC 80, MotPP, MovMk[port], OxFilm, WhoHol B, WorEFlm*
Raimu, Jules 1883-1946 *NotNAT B, WhScrn 74, -77*
Raimu, M 1883-1946 *WhThe*
Raimund, Carl 1871-1951 *CnOxB*
Raimund, Ferdinand 1790-1836 *CnThe, EncWT, Ent[port], McGEWD[port], NewGrD 80, NotNAT B, OxThe, REnWD[port]*
Rain, Cunz *NewGrD 80*
Rain, Douglas *CreCan 1, WhoHol A, WhoHrs 80, WhoThe 72, -77*
Rain, Martha Buhs *CreCan 1*
Rainaldi, Carlo 1611-1691 *NewGrD 80*
Rainbow, Bernard 1914- *WhoMus 72*
Rainbow, Bernarr 1914- *IntWWM 77, -80, NewGrD 80*
Rainbow, Frank 1913- *WhoThe 72, -77*
Rainbows, The *RkOn*
Raindrops, The *RkOn*
Raine, Jack 1895-1979 *HalFC 80*
Raine, Jack 1897- *BiE&WWA, NotNAT, WhThe, WhoHol A, WhoThe 72*
Raine, Norman Reilly 1895-1971 *FilmEn, FilmgC, HalFC 80*
Rainer, Jacob *NewGrD 80*
Rainer, Jeff 1947- *IntWWM 77, -80*
Rainer, Luise *MotPP, What 1[port]*
Rainer, Luise 1909- *FilmgC, HalFC 80*
Rainer, Luise 1910- *FilmEn, ForYSC, MGM[port], MovMk[port], ThFT[port], WhoHol A*
Rainer, Luise 1912- *BiDFilm, -81, OxFilm, WhThe, WorEFlm[port]*
Rainer, Yvonne 1934- *CmpGMD, CnOxB, WomWMM B*
Raines, Christina *WhoHol A*
Raines, Ella 1921- *FilmEn, FilmgC, ForYSC, HalFC 80, HolP 40[port], IntMPA 77, -75, -76, -78, -79, -80, MotPP, MovMk, WhoHol A*
Raines, Jack William 1929- *IntWWM 80*
Raines, Lester *PupTheA*
Raines, Walter 1940- *CnOxB*
Rainey, Charles W, III 1940- *EncJzS 70*
Rainey, Chuck 1940- *EncJzS 70*
Rainey, Ford 1908- *BiE&WWA, ForYSC, NotNAT, WhoHol A*
Rainey, Gertrude 1886-1939 *BiDAmM, BluesWW[port], NewGrD 80*
Rainey, Ma 1886-1939 *CmpEPM, DrBlPA, IlEncJ, MusMk[port], NewGrD 80, WhoJazz 72*
Rainey, Norman 1888-1960 *WhScrn 77*
Rainey, Paul J *Film 1*

Rainey, Thomas, Jr. 1947- *IntWWM 77, -80*
Rainforth, Elizabeth 1814-1877 *NewGrD 80*
Rainger, Ralph d1942 *Sw&Ld C*
Rainger, Ralph 1900-1942 *AmSCAP 80*
Rainger, Ralph 1901-1942 *AmPS, AmSCAP 66, Baker 78, BestMus, BiDAmM, CmpEPM, FilmEn, NewGrD 80, NotNAT B, PopAmC*
Rainier, Priaulx 1903- *Baker 78, MusMk, NewGrD 80, OxMus, WhoMus 72*
Rainier, Priaux 1903- *IntWWM 77, -80*
Raino, Alfredo 1938- *CnOxB*
Rainoldi, Paolo 1781?-1853 *CnOxB*
Rains, Claude 1889-1967 *BiDFilm, -81, BiE&WWA, FilmEn, FilmgC, ForYSC, HalFC 80[port], MotPP, MovMk[port], NotNAT B, OxFilm, WhScrn 74, -77, WhThe, WhoHol B, WhoHrs 80, WorEFlm*
Rains, Claude 1890-1967 *CmMov*
Rains, Fred 1875-193-? *Film 2, IlWWBF*
Rains, Jessica *WhoHol A*
Rains, Leon 1870-1954 *Baker 78, BiDAmM*
Rains, Robert De *NewGrD 80*
Rains, Robert H 1921- *IntMPA 77, -75, -76, -78, -79, -80*
Rainsford, Peter 1952- *IntWWM 80*
Rainwater, Marvin 1925- *BiDAmM, CounME 74, -74A, EncFCWM 69, IlEncCM[port], RkOn*
Rainy, Al *AmSCAP 80*
Rainy, Ron *ConMuA 80B*
Rais, Jakub De *NewGrD 80*
Raisa, Rosa 1893-1963 *Baker 78, BiDAmM, BnBkM 80, CmOp, MusSN[port], NewEOp 71, NewGrD 80*
Raisa, Rose 1878-1963 *WhScrn 77*
Raisin, Catherine 1650-1701 *OxThe*
Raisin, Francoise Pitel DeLongchamp 1661-1721 *OxThe*
Raisin, Jacques 1653-1702 *OxThe*
Raisin, Jean-Baptiste 1655-1693 *NotNAT B, OxThe*
Raisman, Yuli 1903- *FilmEn*
Raison, Andre 1650?-1719 *Baker 78, NewGrD 80*
Raison, Charles W 1936- *NotNAT*
Raiss, Renzo 1927- *CnOxB*
Raiter, Frank *WhoHol A*
Raithel, Ute 1944- *WhoOp 76*
Raitio, Pentti 1930- *NewGrD 80*
Raitio, Vaino 1891-1945 *Baker 78, NewGrD 80*
Raitt, Bonnie *ConMuA 80A[port]*
Raitt, Bonnie 1949- *AmSCAP 80, BluesWW[port], RkOn 2[port]*
Raitt, Bonnie 1950- *IlEncR*
Raitt, John *AmPS B, WhoHol A*
Raitt, John 1917- *BiE&WWA, CmpEPM, EncMT, NotNAT, WhoThe 72, -77*
Raitt, John 1921- *FilmgC, HalFC 80*
Raizman, Yuli 1903- *DcFM, FilmEn*
Raizman, Yuri 1903- *FilmEn*
Rajah, Raboid d1962 *NotNAT B*
Rajapur, Gayathri 1938- *IntWWM 77, -80*
Rajeczky, Benjamin 1901- *NewGrD 80*
Rajicic, Stanojlo 1910- *Baker 78, DcCM, IntWWM 77, -80, NewGrD 80*
Rajna, Elizabeth Faith 1929- *IntWWM 80*
Rajna, Thomas 1928- *IntWWM 80, NewGrD 80, WhoMus 72*
Rajonski, Milton M *NewGrD 80*
Rajter, L'udovit 1906- *NewGrD 80*
Raju 1937-1972 *WhScrn 77*
Raker, Lorin 1891-1959 *Film 2, WhScrn 77*
Rakhlin, Natan Grigor'yevich 1906- *NewGrD 80*
Rakhmaninov, Sergey 1873-1943 *NewGrD 80[port]*
Raki, Laya 1927- *HalFC 80, WhoHol A*
Rakier, Rene Alphons 1936- *IntWWM 77, -80*
Rakine, Marthe *CreCan 2*
Rakoff, Alvin 1927- *FilmgC, HalFC 80, IntMPA 77, -75, -76, -78, -79, -80*
Rakosi, Geza Rezso 1938- *IntWWM 80*
Rakosi, Jeno 1842-1929 *OxThe*
Rakov, Nicolai 1908- *Baker 78*
Rakov, Nikolay Petrovich 1908- *NewGrD 80*
Rakov, Philip H 1903- *AmSCAP 66, -80*
Raksin, David 1912- *AmSCAP 66, -80, Baker 78, CmpEPM, ConAmC, FilmEn, FilmgC, HalFC 80, IntMPA 77, -75, -76, -78, -79, -80, IntWWM 77, WorEFlm*
Rale, M W *Film 1, -2*
Raleigh, Cecil 1856-1914 *Film 1, NotNAT B, WhThe*
Raleigh, Mrs. Cecil d1923 *NotNAT B*
Raleigh, Joe *Film 2*
Raleigh, Saba d1923 *Film 2, WhThe*
Raleigh, Stuart W 1940- *ConAmC, IntWWM 77, -80*
Raley, Glenn 1944- *AmSCAP 80*
Ralf *NewGrD 80*
Ralf, Einar 1888-1971 *NewGrD 80*
Ralf, Oscar 1881-1964 *NewGrD 80*
Ralf, Richard K 1897- *Baker 78, IntWWM 77, -80*
Ralf, Torsten 1901-1954 *Baker 78, CmOp, NewEOp 71, NewGrD 80*
Ralfe, Kenneth Harry 1935- *IntWWM 80*
Ralke, Donald Edward *AmSCAP 80*
Rall, Tommy 1929- *BiE&WWA, CnOxB, DancEn 78, MotPP, NotNAT*
Ralli, Giovanna 1935- *FilmEn, FilmgC, HalFC 80, WhoHol A*
Ralli, Paul 1905-1953 *Film 2, WhScrn 74, -77, WhoHol B*
Ralov, Borge 1908- *CnOxB, DancEn 78*
Ralov, Kirsten 1922- *CnOxB, DancEn 78*
Ralph, Hanna *Film 2*
Ralph, James 1698-1762 *BiDAmM*
Ralph, Jesse 1864-1944 *MovMk*
Ralph, Jessie d1944 *NotNAT B, WhoHol B*
Ralph, Jessie 1864-1944 *FilmEn, FilmgC, HalFC 80, HolCA[port], ThFT[port]*
Ralph, Jessie 1865-1944 *Vers A[port]*
Ralph, Jessie 1876-1944 *ForYSC, WhScrn 74, -77*
Ralph, Julia *Film 2*
Ralph, Louis *Film 2*
Ralph, Ralph J *AmSCAP 80*
Ralston, Alfred *WhoMus 72*
Ralston, Esther 1902- *FilmEn, Film 2, FilmgC, ForYSC, HalFC 80, MotPP, MovMk, ThFT[port], TwYS, What 2[port], WhoHol A, WomWMM*
Ralston, Gil 1912- *IntMPA 77, -75, -76, -78, -79, -80*
Ralston, Gilbert A 1912- *AmSCAP 66, -80*
Ralston, Howard *Film 2*
Ralston, Jobyna d1967 *MotPP, WhoHol B*
Ralston, Jobyna 1901-1967 *FilmgC, HalFC 80, MovMk*
Ralston, Jobyna 1902-1967 *FilmEn, Film 2, TwYS*
Ralston, Jobyna 1904-1967 *WhScrn 74, -77*
Ralston, Rudy 1918- *IntMPA 77, -75, -76, -78, -79, -80*
Ralston, Vera Hruba *MotPP*
Ralston, Vera Hruba 1919- *FilmEn, ForYSC, WhoHol A*
Ralston, Vera Hruba 1921- *FilmgC, HalFC 80, MovMk[port], What 4[port]*
Ram, Buck 1909- *AmSCAP 66*
Ram, Ralla 1924- *IntWWM 77, -80*
Ram, Samuel 1907- *AmSCAP 80*
Rama, Rau E *Film 2*
Rama Rau, Santha 1923- *BiE&WWA*
Ramage, Cecil B 1895- *WhThe*
Ramakers, Christiane Josee 1914- *IntWWM 80*
Ramalho, Elba Braga 1940- *IntWWM 77, -80*
Ramann, Lina 1833-1912 *Baker 78, NewGrD 80*
Rambal, Enrique 1924-1971 *WhScrn 74, -77*
Rambaldi, Carlo 1926- *WhoHrs 80*
Rambeau, Eddie 1943- *RkOn 2[port]*
Rambeau, Marjorie 1889-1970 *FilmEn, Film 1, -2, FilmgC, ForYSC, HalFC 80, HolCA[port], MotPP, MovMk[port], ThFT[port], TwYS, Vers B[port], WhScrn 74, -77, WhThe, WhoHol B*
Ramberg, Miriam 1888- *NewGrD 80*
Rambert, Marie 1888- *CnOxB, DancEn 78[port], NewGrD 80, NotNAT A, WhThe*
Ramblin' Bob *BluesWW*
Rambling Mountaineers *BiDAmM*
Rambo, Dack *WhoHol A*
Rambo, Dirk d1967 *WhoHol B*
Rambo, Joyce Reba 1934- *AmSCAP 80*
Rambos, The Singing *BiDAmM*
Rambousek, Joseph 1845-1901 *Baker 78*
Rambova, Natacha 1897-1966 *Film 1, -2, HalFC 80, TwYS, WhScrn 74, -77, WhoHol B*
Rambova, Natasha *FilmEn*
Rameau, Emil *Film 2*
Rameau, Jean-Philippe 1683-1764 *Baker 78*
Rameau,-Jean Philippe 1683-1764 *BnBkM 80[port]*
Rameau, Jean-Philippe 1683-1764 *CmOp, CmpBCM, CnOxB, DcCom 77[port], DcCom&M 79, GrComp[port], MusMk, NewEOp 71, NewGrD 80[port], OxMus*
Rameau, Pierre *CnOxB, DancEn 78, NewGrD 80*
Ramel, Povel Karl Henric 1922- *IntWWM 77*
Ramella, Elvina 1931- *WhoOp 76*
Ramella, Giovanni Francesco *NewGrD 80*
Ramey, Daralyn 1952- *BlkWAB*
Ramey, Eugene Glasco 1913- *BiDAmM*
Ramey, Gene 1913- *WhoJazz 72*
Ramey, Philip 1939- *ConAmC*
Ramey, Phillip 1939- *DcCM*
Ramey, Samuel 1942- *IntWWM 77, -80, WhoOp 76*
Rami De Pareia, Bartolomeo *NewGrD 80*
Ramin, Gunther 1898-1956 *Baker 78, NewGrD 80*
Ramin, Jordan S 1932- *AmSCAP 66*
Ramin, Jordan Stanley 1930- *AmSCAP 80*
Ramin, Sid 1924- *AmSCAP 66, -80, BiE&WWA, IntWWM 77, NotNAT*
Ramirex, Roger J 1913- *AmSCAP 66*
Ramirez, Carlos *WhoHol A*
Ramirez, Gilberto *PupTheA*
Ramirez, Luis Antonio 1923- *Baker 78, IntWWM 77, -80*
Ramirez, Pepita 1902-1927 *WhScrn 74, -77*
Ramirez, Ram 1913- *WhoJazz 72*
Ramirez, Roger J 1913- *AmSCAP 80*
Ramirez, Rosita *Film 2*
Ramler, Karl Wilhelm 1725-1798 *NewGrD 80*
Ramm, Kathryn Joan 1938- *IntWWM 77*
Ramnoth, K 1912- *DcFM*
Ramon *Film 2*
Ramon Llull *NewGrD 80*
Ramon, Elizabeth T B 1894- *AmSCAP 66*
Ramon, Laon *Film 2*
Ramon Y Rivera, Luis Felipe 1913- *NewGrD 80*
Ramona 1909?- *CmpEPM*
Ramondon, Lewis *NewGrD 80*
Ramone, Phil *ConMuA 80B*
Ramoneda, Ignacio 1735?-1781 *NewGrD 80*
Ramones, The *ConMuA 80A, IlEncR*
Ramos, Florenzo 1865?-1931 *NewOrJ*
Ramos, Jesus Maza 1911-1955 *WhScrn 74, -77*
Ramos, Richard *WhoHol A*
Ramos, Sou Sou *NewOrJ*
Ramos DePareia, Bartolomeo 1440?-1491? *NewGrD 80*
Ramos DePareja, Bartolome 1440?- *Baker 78*
Ramous, Gianni 1930- *Baker 78*
Ramovs, Primoz 1921- *Baker 78, DcCM, IntWWM 77, -80, NewGrD 80*
Rampal, Jean-Pierre 1922- *Baker 78, BnBkM 80, IntWWM 77, -80, MusSN[port], NewGrD 80, WhoMus 72*
Rampazetto, Francesco d1577? *NewGrD 80*
Rampini, Domenico 1765?-1816 *NewGrD 80*
Rampini, Giacomo d1811 *NewGrD 80*
Rampini, Giacomo 1680-1760 *NewGrD 80*
Rampini, Vincenzo *NewGrD 80*
Rampling, Charlotte *WhoHol A*
Rampling, Charlotte 1945- *FilmEn, FilmgC, HalFC 80*
Rampling, Charlotte 1946- *IntMPA 77, -75, -76, -78, -79, -80*
Rampollini, Mattia 1497-1553? *NewGrD 80*
Rampollini, Mattio 1497-1553? *NewGrD 80*
Ramponi, Virginia *NewGrD 80*
Ramrods, The *RkOn*
Ramsay, Allan 1686-1758 *OxMus*
Ramsay, Eugene Spurgeon 1918- *AmSCAP 66, -80*
Ramsay, G Clark 1915- *IntMPA 77, -75, -76, -78*
Ramsay, John 1877-1962 *MagIlD*
Ramsay, Lisa *CreCan 1*
Ramsay, Patrick 1926- *IntMPA 80*

Ramsay, Remak 1937- *WhoThe 77*
Ramsaye, Terry d1954 *NotNAT B*
Ramsbotham, Alexander 1862-1932 *OxMus*
Ramsbotham, Alexander 1870-1932 *NewGrD 80*
Ramsbottom, Derek 1933- *IntWWM 80*
Ramsden, Dennis 1918- *WhoThe 72, -77*
Ramsden, Lawrence Earl 1939- *IntWWM 77, -80*
Ramseier, Paul 1927- *AmSCAP 66*
Ramsell, Hilary Keith 1933- *IntWWM 80*
Ramsell, Kenneth 1904- *IntWWM 77, -80*
Ramsey, Alicia d1933 *NotNAT B, WhThe*
Ramsey, Anne *WhoHol A*
Ramsey, Basil 1929- *WhoMus 72*
Ramsey, C Frederic, Jr. 1915- *IntWWM 77*
Ramsey, Curtis Lynford 1916- *AmSCAP 80*
Ramsey, Cyril Ernest 1904- *WhoMus 72*
Ramsey, George *BluesWW*
Ramsey, Gloria C 1926- *IntWWM 77, -80*
Ramsey, John Nelson d1929 *WhScrn 74, -77*
Ramsey, Logan 1921- *BiE&WWA, NotNAT, WhoHol A*
Ramsey, Nelson d1929 *NotNAT B, WhoHol B*
Ramsey, Norman *AmSCAP 80*
Ramsey, Peter 1921- *NatPD[port]*
Ramsey, Robert 1595?- *Baker 78, NewGrD 80*
Ramsey, Ward *ForYSC*
Ramsey, Willis Alan 1951- *AmSCAP 80*
Ramsier, Paul *AmSCAP 80*
Ramsier, Paul 1927- *AmSCAP 66, ConAmC*
Ramsier, Paul 1937- *IntWWM 77, -80*
Ramsing, Pamella *WomWMM B*
Ran, Schulamit 1949- *IntWWM 77, -80*
Ran, Shulamit 1949- *AmSCAP 80, Baker 78, CpmDNM 79, ConAmC, NewGrD 80*
Rana, Johannes *NewGrD 80*
Ranaldi, Frank 1905-1933 *WhScrn 74, -77, WhoHol B*
Ranalow, Frederick Baring 1873-1953 *CmOp, NewGrD 80, NotNAT B, WhThe, WhoHol B*
Ranbrugh, Irene *PIP&P*
Rancalli, Ludovico *NewGrD 80*
Ranch, Hieronymus Justesen 1539-1607 *OxThe*
Rancourt, Jules *Film 2*
Rand, Ande *AmSCAP 80*
Rand, Bill d1961 *NotNAT B*
Rand, Harold 1928- *IntMPA 77, -75, -76, -78, -79, -80*
Rand, John F 1872-1940 *Film 1, -2, WhScrn 74, -77, WhoHol B*
Rand, Lionel 1909-1942 *WhScrn 74, -77*
Rand, Lionel 1910-1942 *AmSCAP 80*
Rand, Odell 1905?-1960 *WhoJazz 72*
Rand, Sally 1903-1979 *FilmEn, Film 2, ForYSC, TwYS, WhoHol A*
Rand, Sally 1904-1979 *FilmgC, HalFC 80, What 1[port]*
Rand, Sumner G, Jr. 1923- *ConAmTC*
Rand, Mrs. William W, Jr. 1927- *BiE&WWA*
Randall, Addison 1907-1945 *FilmEn, WhScrn 74, -77, WhoHol B*
Randall, Anne *WhoHol A*
Randall, Bernard 1884-1954 *Film 2, WhScrn 74, -77, WhoHol B*
Randall, Bob 1937- *ConDr 77D, NatPD[port], NotNAT*
Randall, Bruce *AmSCAP 80*
Randall, Carl d1965 *CmpEPM, WhThe*
Randall, Gerald Robert 1936- *AmSCAP 80*
Randall, Greenwood d1645? *NewGrD 80*
Randall, Harry 1860-1932 *NotNAT A, OxThe, WhThe*
Randall, J K 1929- *ConAmC*
Randall, Jack *ForYSC*
Randall, James K 1929- *Baker 78, DcCM, NewGrD 80*
Randall, James Ryder 1839-1908 *BiDAmM, OxMus*
Randall, Jerry *WhoHol A*
Randall, John 1717-1799 *NewGrD 80*
Randall, Larry 1920-1951 *WhScrn 74, -77*
Randall, Leslie 1924- *WhThe, WhoHol A, WhoThe 72*
Randall, Meg *ForYSC*
Randall, Pat *WhoHol A*
Randall, Paul E 1902- *BiE&WWA*
Randall, Peter *NewGrD 80*
Randall, Rae 1909-1934 *WhScrn 74, -77, WhoHol B*
Randall, Rebel *ForYSC*
Randall, Stuart *ForYSC, WhoHol A*
Randall, Tony *IntMPA 75, -76, -78, -79, -80*
Randall, Tony 1920- *BiE&WWA, FilmEn, FilmgC, ForYSC, HalFC 80, IntMPA 77, MotPP, MovMk[port], NotNAT, WhoHol A, WhoHrs 80[port], WhoThe 77*
Randall, Tony 1924- *WorEFlm[port]*
Randall, William d1604? *NewGrD 80*
Randall, William 1728?-1776 *NewGrD 80*
Randall, William 1877-1939 *WhScrn 74, -77*
Randazzo, Arlene 1943- *IntWWM 80, WhoOp 76*
Randazzo, Teddy 1937- *RkOn, WhoHol A*
Randegger, Alberto 1832-1911 *Baker 78, NewGrD 80*
Randegger, Alberto, Jr. 1880-1918 *Baker 78*
Randegger, Giuseppe Aldo 1874-1946 *Baker 78*
Randegger, Guisseppe Aldo 1874-1946 *ConAmC*
Randel, Andreas 1806-1864 *NewGrD 80*
Randel, Don M 1940- *NewGrD 80*
Randell, Ron *WhoHol A*
Randell, Ron 1918- *FilmEn, FilmgC, ForYSC, HalFC 80, MovMk*
Randell, Ron 1923- *BiE&WWA, NotNAT, WhoThe 72, -77*
Randell, Sheila 1930- *IntWWM 77, -80*
Randhartinger, Benedikt 1802-1893 *NewGrD 80*
Randi, Don 1937- *BiDAmM, EncJzS 70*
Randi, Ermanno d1951 *WhScrn 77*
Randi, James *MagIlD*
Randle, Annie K *BlkAmP*
Randle, Dodie *AmSCAP 80*
Randle, Edward Earl 1947- *AmSCAP 80*
Randle, Frank 1901-1957 *FilmgC, HalFC 80, IlWWBF[port], WhScrn 74, -77, WhoHol B*
Rando, Doc *NewOrJ*
Randol, George 1895- *BlksB&W[port], -C*
Randolf, Anders 1875-1930 *Film 1, -2, TwYS*
Randoll, William *NewGrD 80*
Randolph, Amanda 1902-1967 *BlksB&W, -C, BlksBF, DrBlPA, WhScrn 74, -77, WhoHol B*
Randolph, Anders d1930 *WhoHol B*
Randolph, Anders 1875-1930 *Film 2*
Randolph, Anders 1876-1930 *HalFC 80, WhScrn 74, -77*
Randolph, Anders 1876-1931 *ForYSC*
Randolph, Boots *CounME 74[port], -74A, IlEncCM, RkOn*
Randolph, David 1914- *IntWWM 77, -80*
Randolph, David Mark 1945- *IntWWM 80*
Randolph, Don *WhoHol A*
Randolph, Donald *ForYSC*
Randolph, Dorothy d1918 *WhScrn 77*
Randolph, Dorothy Overn 1928- *IntWWM 77, -80*
Randolph, Elsie 1904- *EncMT, FilmgC, HalFC 80, IlWWBF, IntMPA 77, -75, -76, -78, -79, -80, WhoHol A, WhoThe 72, -77*
Randolph, Eva d1927 *NotNAT B*
Randolph, Harold 1861-1927 *Baker 78, BiDAmM*
Randolph, Innes 1837-1887 *BiDAmM*
Randolph, Irving 1909- *BiDAmM, CmpEPM*
Randolph, Isabel 1890-1973 *ForYSC, WhScrn 77, WhoHol B*
Randolph, James 1934- *DrBlPA*
Randolph, Jane 1919- *FilmEn, FilmgC, HalFC 80, WhoHol A*
Randolph, Jeremy *BlkAmP*
Randolph, John *NotNAT, WhoHol A*
Randolph, John 1915- *BiE&WWA*
Randolph, John 1917- *FilmgC, HalFC 80*
Randolph, Lillian *BlksB&W C, DrBlPA, ForYSC, WhoHol A*
Randolph, Louise d1953 *NotNAT B, WhoStg 1908*
Randolph, May 1873-1956 *WhScrn 74, -77*
Randolph, Mouse 1909- *WhoJazz 72*
Randolph, Robert 1926- *BiE&WWA, NotNAT, WhoThe 72, -77*
Randolph, Thomas 1605-1635 *NotNAT B, REnWD[port]*
Randolph, Virginia 1882- *WhoStg 1908*
Randolph, Zilmer Trenton 1899- *BiDAmM*
Randolph, Zilner Trenton 1899- *WhoJazz 72*
Random, Bob *WhoHol A*
Randone, Salvo *WhoHol A*
Randone, Salvo 1906- *EncWT, Ent*
Randova, Eva *WhoOp 76*
Rands, Bernard 1934- *Baker 78, CpmDNM 80*
Rands, Bernard 1935- *DcCM, IntWWM 77, -80, NewGrD 80, WhoMus 72*
Randulf, Earl *OxMus*
Randy And The Rainbows *RkOn*
Ranelli, J *NatPD[port]*
Ranevsky, Boris 1891- *Film 2, WhThe*
Raney, Carolyn 1924- *AmSCAP 80, IntWWM 77, -80*
Raney, James Elbert 1927- *BiDAmM, ConAmC, EncJzS 70*
Raney, Jim 1927- *EncJzS 70*
Raney, Jimmy 1927- *CmpEPM, EncJzS 70, IlEncJ*
Raney, Sue 1939- *AmSCAP 66*
Raney, Wayne T 1921- *BiDAmM*
Ranft, Albert Adam 1858- *WhThe*
Ranga Rao, S V 1918-1974 *WhScrn 77*
Ranganathan, Tanjore 1925- *IntWWM 77, -80*
Rangel, Arturo Soto 1882-1965 *WhScrn 74, -77, WhoHol B*
Ranger, Claude 1941- *EncJzS 70*
Ranger Bill *WhScrn 77*
Rangers Trio *BiDAmM*
Rangstrom, Ture 1884-1947 *Baker 78, MusMk, NewGrD 80, OxMus*
Rani, Paul *Film 2*
Ranier, Richard Robert 1889-1960 *WhScrn 77*
Ranieri, Giovanni Simone 1590?-1649 *NewGrD 80*
Ranin, Helge 1897-1952 *WhScrn 74, -77*
Ranish, John Frederick 1692?-1777 *NewGrD 80*
Ranisien, Sigismund d1653? *NewGrD 80*
Ranisius, Sigismund d1653? *NewGrD 80*
Rank, Lord *IlWWBF A*
Rank, Bill 1904- *CmpEPM, WhoJazz 72*
Rank, J Arthur 1888-1972 *DcFM, FilmEn, FilmgC, HalFC 80, OxFilm, WorEFlm*
Ranken, Frederick W d1905 *NotNAT B*
Ranki, Dezso 1951- *IntWWM 80, NewGrD 80*
Ranki, Gyorgy 1907- *Baker 78, IntWWM 77, -80, NewGrD 80, WhoMus 72*
Rankin, Arthur 1900-1947 *Film 2, NotNAT B, TwYS, WhScrn 74, -77, WhoHol B*
Rankin, Arthur McKee 1841-1914 *NotNAT B, OxThe, WhThe, WhoStg 1908*
Rankin, Caroline *Film 1, -2*
Rankin, Catherine *Film 2*
Rankin, Doris d1946 *Film 2, NotNAT B, TwYS, WhoHol B*
Rankin, Dorothy Louise *PupTheA*
Rankin, Gil *WhoHol A*
Rankin, Gladys d1914 *NotNAT B*
Rankin, Herbert 1876-1946 *WhScrn 74, -77*
Rankin, Hughie *NewOrJ*
Rankin, Jeannette 1880- *What 2[port]*
Rankin, Jeremiah Eames 1828-1904 *BiDAmM*
Rankin, John *IntWWM 77, -80, WhoMus 72*
Rankin, Kitty Blanchard 1847-1911 *OxThe*
Rankin, McKee 1841-1914 *FamA&A[port]*
Rankin, Mrs. McKee 1847-1911 *NotNAT B*
Rankin, Molly *WhThe*
Rankin, Nell 1926- *CmOp, MusSN[port], WhoOp 76*
Rankin, Phyllis 1874-1934 *NotNAT B, WhThe, WhoHol B, WhoStg 1906, -1908*
Rankin, R S 1933- *BluesWW[port]*
Rankins, Sam d1971 *NewOrJ*
Rankl, Karl 1898-1968 *Baker 78, CmOp, NewGrD 80*
Ranney, Frank 1863- *WhoStg 1906, -1908*
Ranno, Richard B 1950- *AmSCAP 80*
Ranody, Laszlo 1919- *FilmEn, OxFilm, WorEFlm*
Ranoe, Cecilia d1870 *NotNAT B*
Ranous, Dora d1916 *NotNAT A*
Ranous, William V 1847-1915 *WhScrn 77*
Rans, Van *NewGrD 80*
Rans, Aert Van *NewGrD 80*
Rans, Gaspar Van d1641 *NewGrD 80*
Rans, Jaspar Van d1641 *NewGrD 80*

Rans, Nicolas 1548?- *NewGrD 80*
Rans, Nicolas Van d1641 *NewGrD 80*
Rans, Philips Van d1628? *NewGrD 80*
Rans, Philips Van 1541?-1628 *NewGrD 80*
Ransford, Maurice 1896- *FilmEn*
Ransley, Angela Jane 1946- *IntWWM 77*
Ransley, Peter 1931- *ConDr 73, –77*
Ransohoff, Martin 1927- *FilmEn, FilmgC, HalFC 80, IntMPA 77, –75, –76, –78, –79, –80, NewYTET*
Ransom, Charles *PupTheA*
Ransom, Edith *Film 2*
Ransom, Raymond L, Jr. 1950- *AmSCAP 80*
Ransome, Antony 1940- *IntWWM 77, –80*
Ransome, John W d1929 *NotNAT B*
Ransome, Prunella 1943- *FilmgC, HalFC 80, WhoHol A*
Ranson, Herbert 1889- *WhThe*
Ranson, Lois *ForYSC*
Ranst, Van *NewGrD 80*
Ranta, Sulho 1901-1960 *Baker 78, NewGrD 80*
Rants, Pamela Cohick 1952- *IntWWM 77, –80*
Rao, Enakshi Rama *Film 2*
Rao, Saluru Hanumantha 1916- *IntWWM 77*
Rao, Shanta 1930- *CnOxB, DancEn 78*
Raoul De Beauvais *NewGrD 80*
Raoul De Ferrieres *NewGrD 80*
Raoul De Soissons 1210?-1270? *NewGrD 80*
Raoux *NewGrD 80*
Raoux, Joseph 1725?-1800? *NewGrD 80*
Raoux, Lucien-Joseph 1753-1826? *NewGrD 80*
Raoux, Marcel-Auguste 1795-1871 *NewGrD 80*
Rapalo, Ugo 1914- *WhoOp 76*
Rapaport, N Rosemary P 1918- *WhoMus 72*
Rapaport, Rosemary 1918- *IntWWM 77, –80*
Rapee, Erno 1891-1945 *AmPS, AmSCAP 66, –80, Baker 78, BiDAmM, CmpEPM, WorEFlm*
Rapf, Kurt 1922- *Baker 78, IntWWM 77, –80*
Rapf, Matthew 1920- *IntMPA 77, –75, –76, –78, –79, –80*
Raph, Alan 1933- *AmSCAP 66, –80, ConAmC*
Raph, Theodore E 1905- *AmSCAP 66, –80*
Raphael 1483-1520 *EncWT*
Raphael, Bernard 1883?- *NewOrJ*
Raphael, Enid d1964 *NotNAT B, WhScrn 74, –77*
Raphael, Frederic 1931- *ConDr 73, –77A, FilmEn, FilmgC, HalFC 80, IntMPA 77, –75, –76, –78, –79, –80*
Raphael, Gunter 1903-1960 *NewGrD 80*
Raphael, Gunther 1903-1960 *Baker 78*
Raphael, John N 1868-1917 *NotNAT B, WhThe*
Raphael, Lennox *BlkAmP, MorBAP*
Raphael, Mark 1900- *IntWWM 80, WhoMus 72*
Raphael, Peter 1905-1963 *NewOrJ SUP[port]*
Raphael, Roger Bernard 1929- *IntWWM 77, –80*
Raphael, William 1858- *WhThe*
Raphaelson, Samson *IntMPA 77, –75, –76, –78, –79, –80*
Raphaelson, Samson 1896- *FilmEn, FilmgC, HalFC 80, McGEWD, WhThe, WorEFlm*
Raphaelson, Samson 1899- *BiE&WWA, NotNAT*
Raphel, David 1925- *IntMPA 77, –75, –76, –78, –79, –80*
Raphel, Jerome *WhoHol A*
Raphelengius, Christopher *NewGrD 80*
Raphling, Sam 1910- *AmSCAP 66, –80, Baker 78, ConAmC, IntWWM 77, –80*
Rapley, Edmund Felton 1907- *WhoMus 72*
Rapley, Felton *ConAmC*
Rapley, Rose *Film 2*
Rapoport, Eda *ConAmC*
Raposo, Joseph G 1937- *AmSCAP 80*
Rapp, Augustus *PupTheA*
Rapp, Barney d1970 *BgBands 74, CmpEPM*
Rapp, Butler 1898?-1931 *NewOrJ*
Rapp, George *NewGrD 80*
Rapp, Jacques 1930- *WhoOp 76*
Rapp, Richard *DancEn 78, WhoHol A*
Rappaport, Herbert *FilmEn*
Rappaport, Jonathan Charles 1947- *IntWWM 77*
Rappaport, Shloyme Zaynvl *REnWD[port]*
Rappe, Virginia d1921 *Film 2, WhScrn 74, –77, WhoHol B*
Rappeneau, Jean-Paul 1932- *HalFC 80, WorEFlm*
Rapper, Irving *IntMPA 77, –75, –76, –78, –79, –80*
Rapper, Irving 1898- *BiDFilm, –81, CmMov, FilmEn, HalFC 80, MovMk[port], WorEFlm*
Rapper, Irving 1904?- *FilmgC*
Rappold, Marie 1873?-1957 *Baker 78*
Rappold, Marie Winteroth 1880-1957 *BiDAmM*
Rappoldi *NewGrD 80*
Rappoldi, Adrian 1876-1949 *NewGrD 80*
Rappoldi, Eduard 1831-1903 *Baker 78, NewGrD 80*
Rappoldi, Laura 1853-1925 *NewGrD 80*
Rappolo *WhoJazz 72*
Rappolo, Joseph Leon 1902-1943 *BiDAmM*
Rappolo, Leon 1902-1943 *CmpEPM*
Rappoport, Gerald J 1925- *IntMPA 77, –75, –76, –78, –79, –80*
Rappoport, Shloyme Zanul *McGEWD*
Raptakis, Kleon 1905- *AmSCAP 66, –80, ConAmC A*
Raqua, Charles *Film 2*
Rare Earth *RkOn 2[port]*
Rarig, John *ConAmC*
Ras, Eva *WhoHol A*
Rasa, Lina Bruna 1907- *CmOp, NewGrD 80*
Rasar, William 1488?- *NewGrD 80*
Rasbach, Oscar 1888-1975 *AmSCAP 66, –80, Baker 78, BiDAmM, ConAmC*
Rascals, The *BiDAmM, ConMuA 80A, IlEncR, RkOn 2[port]*
Rascarini, Francesco Maria d1706 *NewGrD 80*
Rascel, Renato 1912- *FilmAG WE*
Rasch, Albertina d1967 *Film 2, WhThe*
Rasch, Albertina 1891-1967 *WhScrn 77*
Rasch, Albertina 1896-1967 *BiE&WWA, CnOxB, EncMT, NotNAT B*
Rasch, Ellen 1920- *DancEn 78*
Rasch, Franz 1922- *WhoMus 72*
Rasch, Johann 1540?-1612? *NewGrD 80*
Rasch, Kurt 1912- *IntWWM 77, –80*
Rasch, Raymond P 1919-1964 *AmSCAP 66, –80*
Rascher, Sigurd Manfred 1907- *Baker 78, IntWWM 77, –80, NewGrD 80*
Raschi, Eugene G 1929- *AmSCAP 66, –80*
Raschig, Kraft *Film 2*
Rascoe, Burton 1892-1957 *NotNAT B, WhThe*
Rascoe, Judith *WomWMM*
Raselius, Andreas 1563?-1602 *Baker 78, NewGrD 80*
Rasely, Charles W 1921- *ConAmC*
Rasely, Thomas E 1951- *ConAmC*
Raser, William *NewGrD 80*
Rasetti, Amedeo 1754-1799 *NewGrD 80*
Rasheed, Hassan 1896-1969 *NewGrD 80*
Rashevskaya, Natalya *WomWMM*
Rasi, Francesco 1574-1620? *NewGrD 80*
Raskatoff *Film 2*
Raskie, Barney *Film 2*
Raskin, Eugene 1909- *AmSCAP 80*
Raskin, Gene 1909- *AmSCAP 66*
Raskin, Judith 1928- *Baker 78, IntWWM 77, –80, MusSN[port]*
Raskin, Judith 1932- *NewEOp 71, NewGrD 80*
Raskin, Milton William 1916- *AmSCAP 66, BiDAmM*
Raskin, William 1896-1942 *AmSCAP 66, –80*
Raskind, Philip *AmSCAP 66*
Rasley, John M 1913- *AmSCAP 66, ConAmC A*
Rasmussen, Arne Skjold 1921- *IntWWM 77, –80, WhoMus 72*
Rasmussen, Fritz 1917- *IntWWM 80*
Rasmussen, Henning Bro 1924- *IntWWM 77, –80*
Rasmussen, Jane Edith 1928- *IntWWM 77, –80*
Rasmussen, Karl Aage 1947- *Baker 78, IntWWM 77, –80*
Rasmussen, Niels Christian 1950- *IntWWM 77, –80*
Rasor, William *NewGrD 80*
Rasp, Fritz 1891-1977 *FilmAG WE[port], FilmEn, Film 2, FilmgC, HalFC 80, WhoHol A*
Raspberries, The *ConMuA 80A, RkOn 2[port]*
Raspe, Paul 1942- *IntWWM 77, –80*
Rasputin, Maria 1898- *What 4[port]*
Rassadin, Konstantin Alexandrovich 1937- *CnOxB*
Rasse, Francois 1873-1955 *Baker 78, NewGrD 80*
Rassine, Alexis 1919- *CnOxB, DancEn 78*
Rastall, Richard 1940- *IntWWM 77, –80*
Rastell, John 1475?-1536 *NewGrD 80, OxMus, OxThe*
Rastrelli, Gioseffo 1799-1842 *NewGrD 80*
Rastrelli, Giuseppe 1799-1842 *NewGrD 80*
Rastrelli, Joseph 1799-1842 *Baker 78, NewGrD 80*
Rastrelli, Vincenzo 1760-1839 *NewGrD 80*
Rasulala, Thalmus 1939- *DrBlPA, HalFC 80, WhoHol A*
Rasumny, Alexander 1891- *FilmEn*
Rasumny, Mikhail d1938 *NotNAT B*
Rasumny, Mikhail 1890-1956 *FilmEn, FilmgC, HalFC 80, MovMk, Vers A[port], WhScrn 74, –77, WhoHol B*
Rasumny, Mikhail 1893-1956 *ForYSC*
Rasumovsky *Baker 78*
Rat, Le *NewGrD 80*
Ratcliff, Onamae *IntWWM 77*
Ratcliffe, Desmond Hayward 1917- *IntWWM 77, –80*
Ratcliffe, E J 1893- *ForYSC*
Ratcliffe, Edward J 1893- *Film 2*
Ratcliffe, Guy Nicholas 1935- *WhoMus 72*
Ratcliffe, John 1929- *IntMPA 77, –75, –76, –78, –79, –80*
Ratdolt, Erhard 1447-1527? *NewGrD 80*
Ratez, Emile-Pierre 1851-1934 *Baker 78*
Rath, Felix Vom 1866-1905 *Baker 78*
Rath, George Richard 1944- *IntWWM 77*
Rath, John Frederic 1946- *IntWWM 80*
Rathaus, Karel 1895-1954 *BiDAmM*
Rathaus, Karol 1895-1954 *AmSCAP 66, –80, Baker 78, ConAmC, DcCM, NewGrD 80, OxMus*
Rathbone, Basil 1892-1967 *BiDFilm, –81, BiE&WWA, CmMov, FamA&A[port], FilmEn, Film 2, FilmgC, ForYSC, HalFC 80[port], IlWWBF A, MotPP, MovMk[port], NotNAT A, –B, OxFilm, WhScrn 74, –77, WhThe, WhoHol B, WhoHrs 80[port], WorEFlm[port]*
Rathbone, Christopher Bruce 1947- *IntWWM 77, –80*
Rathbone, Guy B 1884-1916 *NotNAT B, WhThe*
Rathbone, Joyce 1929- *IntWWM 77, –80, WhoMus 72*
Rathbone, Ouida 1887-1974 *BiE&WWA, NotNAT B*
Rathbun, Janet d1975 *WhoHol C*
Rathburn, Eldon Davis 1916- *Baker 78, CpmDNM 76, –78, CreCan 1*
Rather, Dan *IntMPA 79, –80, NewYTET*
Rathgeber, Johann Valentin 1682-1750 *NewGrD 80*
Rathner, Wilhelmine 1863-1913 *CnOxB*
Rathsckoff *PupTheA*
Ratisbonne, George De *NewGrD 80*
Ratiu, Adrian 1928- *Baker 78, IntWWM 77, –80, NewGrD 80*
Ratjen, Hans Georg 1909- *IntWWM 77, –80*
Ratnam, Kali N d1950 *WhScrn 77*
Ratner, Anna 1892-1967 *WhScrn 74, –77, WhoHol B*
Ratner, Leonard Gilbert 1916- *Baker 78, ConAmC, NewGrD 80*
Ratoff, Gregory d1960 *MotPP, WhoHol B*
Ratoff, Gregory 1893-1960 *NotNAT B, WhThe*
Ratoff, Gregory 1897-1960 *BiDFilm, –81, FilmEn, FilmgC, ForYSC, HalFC 80, MovMk, Vers A[port], WhScrn 74, –77, WorEFlm*
Raton, Doris *Film 2*
Rattenbach, Augusto 1927- *Baker 78*
Rattenberry, Harry 1860-1925 *WhScrn 74, –77, WhoHol B*
Rattenbury, Harry *Film 1*
Rattenbury, Kenneth Miller 1920- *IntWWM 77*
Ratter, Thomas 1929- *WhoMus 72*

Ratti, Bartolomeo 1565-1634 *NewGrD 80*
Ratti, Lorenzo 1590?-1630 *NewGrD 80*
Rattigan, Terence 1911- *BiE&WWA, CnMD, CnThe, ConDr 73, -77, CroCD, EncWT, IntMPA 77, -75, -76, -78, McGEWD[port], ModWD, NotNAT, OxFilm, OxThe, PlP&P[port], WhoThe 72, -77, WorEFlm[port]*
Rattigan, Terence 1911-1977 *FilmEn*
Rattigan, Terence 1911-1979 *Ent*
Rattigan, Terence 1912- *FilmgC*
Rattigan, Terence 1912-1977 *HalFC 80*
Rattle, Simon 1954- *IntWWM 80*
Rattle, Simon 1955- *NewGrD 80*
Ratz, Erwin 1898-1973 *NewGrD 80*
Ratzenberger, Theodor 1840-1879 *Baker 78*
Rau, J Eblen 1898- *NewOrJ[port]*
Rau, Santha Rama 1923- *BiE&WWA*
Rauch *NewGrD 80*
Rauch, Andreas 1592-1656 *NewGrD 80*
Rauch, Billy 1910- *CmpEPM*
Rauch, Caspar 1558-1618? *NewGrD 80*
Rauch, Frantisek 1910- *NewGrD 80*
Rauch, Johann Baptist *NewGrD 80*
Rauch, Johann Georg d1710 *NewGrD 80*
Rauch, Johann Georg 1702-1779 *NewGrD 80*
Rauch, Joseph 1904- *IntWWM 77, -80*
Rauch, Joseph Michel 1685?-1738 *NewGrD 80*
Rauch, Siegfried *WhoHol A*
Rauch VonSchratt, Hans *NewGrD 80*
Rauche, Michael *NewGrD 80*
Rauchenecker, Georg Wilhelm 1844-1906 *Baker 78*
Raucourt 1756-1815 *OxThe*
Raucourt, Jules d1967 *WhoHol B*
Raucourt, Jules 1890-1967 *Film 1, -2, TwYS*
Raucourt, Jules 1891-1967 *WhScrn 77*
Raudenbush, George King 1899-1956 *Baker 78*
Rauet *Film 2*
Raugel, Felix 1881-1975 *Baker 78, NewGrD 80, WhoMus 72*
Rauhe, Hermann 1930- *IntWWM 77, -80*
Raulin De Vaux *NewGrD 80*
Rault, Felix 1736-1800? *NewGrD 80*
Raupach *NewGrD 80*
Raupach, Christoph 1686-1744 *NewGrD 80*
Raupach, Ernst 1784-1852 *EncWT*
Raupach, Ernst Benjamin Salomo 1784-1848 *NewGrD 80*
Raupach, Hermann Friedrich 1728-1778 *NewGrD 80*
Rausch *Film 2*
Rausch, Carlos 1924- *ConAmC, IntWWM 77, -80*
Rausch, Edgar Leon 1927- *BiDAmM*
Rausch, Friedrich 1755-1823 *BiDAmM*
Rausch, Leon 1927- *EncFCWM 69*
Rauschenberg, Dale E 1938- *ConAmC*
Rauschenberg, Robert 1925- *CmpGMD, CnOxB, ConDr 73, -77E*
Rauscher, Hans *Film 2*
Rauscher, Henry *ConAmC*
Raussi, Paavo 1901- *IntWWM 80*
Rautavaara, Einojuhani 1928- *Baker 78, DcCM, IntWWM 77, -80, NewGrD 80*
Rautenstein, Julius Ernst 1590?-1654? *NewGrD 80*
Rauthner, Christian Peganius *NewGrD 80*
Rautio, Erkki Ilmari 1931- *IntWWM 77, -80*
Rautio, Matti 1922- *Baker 78, NewGrD 80*
Rautioaho, Asko A J 1936- *IntWWM 77, -80*
Rauzzini, Matteo 1754-1791 *NewGrD 80*
Rauzzini, Venanzio 1746-1810 *MusMk, NewGrD 80[port], OxMus*
Rava, Enrico 1943- *EncJzS 70*
Ravaglia, Emilia 1936- *WhoOp 76*
Raval, Sebastian 1550?-1604? *NewGrD 80*
Ravalle, Sebastian 1550?-1604? *NewGrD 80*
Ravan, Genya 1941- *BiDAmM*
Ravanello, Oreste 1871-1938 *Baker 78*
Ravasenga, Carlo 1891-1964 *Baker 78*
Ravazza, Carl 1912?-1968 *BgBands 74, CmpEPM*
Ravazzi, Gabriella 1942- *WhoOp 76*
Ravel, Maurice 1875-1937 *Baker 78, BnBkM 80[port], CmOp, CompSN[port], CnOxB, DancEn 78, DcCom 77[port], DcCom&M 79, DcCM, DcPup, DcTwCC, -A, MusMk[port], NewEOp 71, NewGrD 80[port], OxMus*
Ravel, Sandra d1954 *WhScrn 74, -77, WhoHol B*
Ravelle, Ray *WhScrn 74, -77*
Ravelomanantsoa, Glen Anthony 1948- *BlkAmP*
Raven, Eddy *AmSCAP 80, IlEncCM[port]*
Raven, Elsa *WhoHol A*
Raven, Grey Eagle *AmSCAP 80*
Raven, Mike 1927?- *WhoHol A, WhoHrs 80*
Ravenel, Florence d1975 *WhScrn 77*
Ravenel, John 1912-1950 *WhScrn 74, -77*
Ravens, The *RkOn*
Ravenscroft, Edward *NotNAT B, OxThe*
Ravenscroft, John d1708? *Baker 78, NewGrD 80*
Ravenscroft, John d1745? *NewGrD 80*
Ravenscroft, Thomas 1582?-1635? *NewGrD 80*
Ravenscroft, Thomas 1583?-1633? *BnBkM 80*
Ravenscroft, Thomas 1590?-1633? *Baker 78, MusMk, OxMus*
Raverii, Alessandro *NewGrD 80*
Ravetch, Irving 1915?- *FilmEn, FilmgC, HalFC 80, IntMPA 77, -75, -76, -78, -79, -80*
Ravina, Jean-Henri 1818-1906 *Baker 78*
Ravitz, Myrna *WomWMM A, -B*
Ravitz, Ron *ConMuA 80B*
Ravn, Hans Mikkelsen 1610?-1663 *NewGrD 80*
Ravnik, Janko 1891- *IntWWM 77*
Ravosa, Carmino C 1930- *AmSCAP 66, -80*
Rawdon, Lord *OxMus*
Rawhide *CreCan 1*
Rawi, Ousama 1940- *HalFC 80*
Rawitz, Steven Jeffrey 1954- *AmSCAP 80*
Rawley, James *WhoHol A*
Rawling, Sylvester d1921 *NotNAT B*
Rawlings *NewGrD 80*
Rawlings, Alice *WhoHol A*
Rawlings, Margaret 1906- *WhoHol A, WhoThe 72, -77*
Rawlings, Robert 1742-1814 *NewGrD 80*
Rawlings, Thomas 1703?-1767 *NewGrD 80*
Rawlings, Thomas A 1775-1850? *NewGrD 80*
Rawlins *NewGrD 80*
Rawlins, Caroline Bessie 1898- *IntWWM 77, -80*
Rawlins, Herbert d1947 *WhScrn 74, -77*
Rawlins, John 1902- *FilmEn, FilmgC, HalFC 80*
Rawlins, Joseph Thomas 1936- *IntWWM 77, -80*
Rawlins, Judith 1936-1974 *WhScrn 77*
Rawlins, Judy d1974 *WhoHol B*
Rawlins, Lester 1924- *BiE&WWA, NotNAT, WhoHol A, WhoThe 72, -77*
Rawlins, W H d1927 *NotNAT B*
Rawlinson, A R 1894- *IntMPA 77, -75, -76, -78, -79, -80, WhThe*
Rawlinson, Griselda Maxwell 1930- *IntWWM 77, -80*
Rawlinson, Harold 1891- *WhoMus 72*
Rawlinson, Herbert 1885-1953 *FilmEn, Film 1, -2, ForYSC, MotPP, MovMk, NotNAT B, TwYS, WhScrn 74, -77, WhoHol B*
Rawls, Eugenia 1916- *BiE&WWA, NotNAT, WhoThe 77*
Rawls, Lou 1935- *BiDAmM, DrBlPA, EncJzS 70, WhoHol A*
Rawls, Lou 1936- *RkOn 2[port]*
Rawls, Louis Allen 1935- *BluesWW[port]*
Rawls, Richard B 1908- *IntMPA 75, -76*
Rawlston, Zelma d1915 *NotNAT B, WhoStg 1908*
Rawnsley, David 1909- *FilmgC, HalFC 80*
Rawson, Graham 1890-1955 *NotNAT B, WhThe*
Rawson, Tristan 1888- *WhThe*
Rawsthorne, Alan 1905- *CompSN[port]*
Rawsthorne, Alan 1905-1971 *Baker 78, BnBkM 80, DcCom&M 79, DcCM, FilmgC, HalFC 80, MusMk, NewGrD 80[port], OxMus, WorEFlm*
Rawsthorne, Alan 1905-1973 *OxFilm*
Rawsthorne, Noel 1924- *IntWWM 77, -80*
Rawsthorne, Noel 1929- *NewGrD 80, WhoMus 72*
Raxach, Enrique 1932- *Baker 78, DcCM, NewGrD 80*
Ray, Albert 1883- *Film 2, TwYS A*
Ray, Aldo 1926- *BiDFilm, -81, FilmEn, FilmgC, ForYSC, HalFC 80, IntMPA 77, -75, -76, -78, -79, -80, MotPP, MovMk, OxFilm, WhoHol A, WorEFlm*
Ray, Allene 1901- *FilmEn, Film 2, TwYS*
Ray, Andrew 1939- *BiE&WWA, FilmgC, HalFC 80, NotNAT, WhoHol A*
Ray, Anthony *WhoHol A*
Ray, Arthur *BlksB&W C*
Ray, Barbara 1914-1955 *WhScrn 74, -77, WhoHol B*
Ray, Bobby *Film 2*
Ray, Carline 1925- *BlkWAB[port]*
Ray, Charles 1891-1943 *FilmEn, Film 1, -2, FilmgC, ForYSC, HalFC 80, MotPP, NotNAT B, TwYS, -A, WhScrn 74, -77, WhoHol B*
Ray, Charles 1894-1943 *MovMk*
Ray, Danny 1934- *BiDAmM*
Ray, Diane 1942- *RkOn*
Ray, Don Brandon 1926- *Baker 78, ConAmC*
Ray, Donald Edwin 1928- *IntWWM 77*
Ray, Ellen *BiE&WWA, WhoHol A*
Ray, Emma 1871-1935 *WhScrn 74, -77, WhoHol B*
Ray, Estelle Goulding 1888-1970 *WhScrn 74, -77*
Ray, Ford 1935- *IntWWM 77*
Ray, Gabrielle 1883- *WhThe*
Ray, Hal *ConMuA 80B*
Ray, Harmon 1914- *BluesWW[port]*
Ray, Helen 1879-1965 *WhScrn 74, -77, WhoHol B*
Ray, Ian Patrick 1946- *IntWWM 77, -80*
Ray, Isom *BluesWW*
Ray, Jack 1917-1975 *WhScrn 77, WhoHol C*
Ray, James 1932- *BiE&WWA, NotNAT, WhoThe 72, -77*
Ray, James 1941- *RkOn*
Ray, Jimmy 1915?- *CmpEPM*
Ray, John Alvin 1927- *AmSCAP 66, -80*
Ray, John William d1871 *NotNAT B*
Ray, Johnnie 1927- *AmPS A, -B, BiDAmM, FilmgC, HalFC 80, RkOn[port], WhoHol A*
Ray, Johnny 1859-1927 *WhScrn 74, -77, WhoHol B*
Ray, Larry 1940- *AmSCAP 80*
Ray, Leah *WhoHol A*
Ray, Man 1890-1976 *DcFM, FilmEn, Film 2, FilmgC, HalFC 80, OxFilm*
Ray, Marc B 1940- *AmSCAP 80*
Ray, Marjorie 1900-1924 *WhScrn 74, -77, WhoHol B*
Ray, Mary Dominic 1913- *IntWWM 80*
Ray, Michel 1945- *IntMPA 77, -75, -76, -78, -79, -80, WhoHol A*
Ray, Mona *Film 2*
Ray, Naomi 1893-1966 *WhScrn 74, -77*
Ray, Nicholas 1911-1979 *BiDFilm, -81, DcFM, FilmEn, FilmgC, HalFC 80, IntMPA 77, -75, -76, -78, -79, MovMk[port], OxFilm, WorEFlm[port]*
Ray, Phil 1872- *WhThe*
Ray, Phil 1888?- *NewOrJ*
Ray, Rene 1912- *Film 2, FilmgC, HalFC 80, IlWWBF[port], WhThe, WhoHol A*
Ray, Robert J 1919- *AmSCAP 66*
Ray, Ruby *WhoStg 1908*
Ray, Ruth 1899- *IntWWM 77, -80*
Ray, Satyajit 1921- *BiDFilm, -81, ConLC 16, DcFM, FilmEn, FilmgC, HalFC 80, MovMk[port], OxFilm, WorEFlm*
Ray, Ted *IntMPA 77, -75, -76, -78, WhoHol A*
Ray, Ted 1906-1977 *HalFC 80*
Ray, Ted 1909-1977 *FilmgC, IlWWBF, -A[port]*
Ray, Wade 1913- *BiDAmM, EncFCWM 69*
Ray, Wallace *Film 2*
Ray, William B *NewYTET*
Rayam, Curtis 1951- *WhoOp 76*
Raybould, Clarence 1886-1972 *NewGrD 80, WhoMus 72*
Raybould, Harry *ForYSC*
Rayburn, Gene *IntMPA 77, -75, -76, -78, -79, -80*
Rayburn, John M 1928- *IntWWM 77*
Rayburn, Margie *AmSCAP 66, -80, RkOn*
Rayburn, Mark Lynn 1947- *AmSCAP 80*
Raye, Carol 1923- *FilmgC, HalFC 80,*

WhThe, WhoHol A
Raye, Don 1909- *AmSCAP 66, –80, CmpEPM, Sw&Ld C*
Raye, Martha 1916- *BiDAmM, BiE&WWA, CmpEPM, EncMT, FilmEn, FilmgC, ForYSC, Funs[port], HalFC 80, IntMPA 77, –75, –76, –78, –79, –80, JoeFr[port], MotPP, MovMk[port], NewYTET, ThFT[port], WhoHol A, WhoThe 72, –77*
Raye, Susan 1944- *CounME 74, –74A, IlEncCM[port]*
Raye, Thelma *WhoStg 1908*
Rayel, Robert Michael 1949- *IntWWM 77*
Rayet, Jacqueline 1932- *CnOxB, DancEn 78*
Rayfield, Curt *Film 2*
Rayford, Alma *Film 2*
Raygada, Carlos 1898-1953 *NewGrD 80*
Rayleigh, Baron John William Strutt 1842-1919 *NewGrD 80*
Raym, Mrs. Max *PupTheA*
Raymaker, Herman C 1893-1944 *TwYS A*
Raymond, Charles d1911 *NotNAT B*
Raymond, Charles 1858-1930 *FilmEn, IlWWBF*
Raymond, Cyril 1897?-1973 *Film 2, FilmgC, HalFC 80, WhThe, WhoHol B, WhoThe 72*
Raymond, Edwin Matthew 1920- *IntWWM 77, –80, WhoMus 72*
Raymond, Ford 1900-1960 *WhScrn 74, –77, WhoHol B*
Raymond, Frances 1869-1961 *Film 2, WhScrn 74, –77, WhoHol B*
Raymond, Frankie *Film 2*
Raymond, Fred 1900-1954 *NewGrD 80*
Raymond, Gary 1935- *FilmgC, ForYSC, HalFC 80, MotPP, WhoHol A*
Raymond, Gene 1908- *BiDAmM, BiE&WWA, FilmEn, FilmgC, ForYSC, HalFC 80, HolP 30[port], IntMPA 77, –75, –76, –78, –79, –80, MotPP, MovMk, What 5[port], WhoHol A, WhoThe 72, –77*
Raymond, George 1903- *AmSCAP 66, –80*
Raymond, Glenda 1922- *WhoMus 72*
Raymond, Guy *ForYSC, WhoHol A*
Raymond, Harold Newell 1884-1957 *AmSCAP 66, –80*
Raymond, Helen 1885?-1965 *BiE&WWA, Film 2, WhScrn 74, –77, WhThe, WhoHol B*
Raymond, Henry 1895?-1949 *NewOrJ*
Raymond, Jack 1886-1953 *FilmEn, IlWWBF*
Raymond, Jack 1892-1953 *FilmgC, HalFC 80*
Raymond, Jack 1901-1951 *Film 2, WhScrn 74, –77, WhoHol B*
Raymond, John T 1836-1887 *NotNAT B, OxThe*
Raymond, Lewis 1908- *AmSCAP 66*
Raymond, Lewis 1908-1956 *ConAmC*
Raymond, Lewis 1908-1966 *AmSCAP 80*
Raymond, Maud d1961 *NotNAT B, WhoStg 1906, –1908*
Raymond, Paula *IntMPA 77, –75, –76, –78, –79, –80, MotPP, WhoHol A*
Raymond, Paula 1923- *FilmEn, FilmgC, WhoHrs 80*
Raymond, Paula 1928?- *ForYSC*
Raymond, Robin *ForYSC, WhoHol A*
Raymond, Royal 1916-1949 *WhScrn 77*
Raymond, Walker X *AmSCAP 80*
Raymond, Whitney *Film 1*
Raymond, William *Film 1*
Raymonde, Frankie 1874- *WhoStg 1906, –1908*
Raymundi, Daniel 1558?-1634 *NewGrD 80*
Raynal, Jackie *WomWMM*
Raynal, Paul *WhThe*
Raynal, Paul 1885-1971 *EncWT, McGEWD*
Raynal, Paul 1890- *CnMD, ModWD*
Raynaud, Fernand d1973 *WhScrn 77*
Rayne, Leonard 1869-1925 *NotNAT B, WhThe*
Rayner, Alfred d1898 *NotNAT B*
Rayner, Christine *Film 2*
Rayner, Clare Grill 1931- *IntWWM 77, –80*
Rayner, Gordon 1935- *CreCan 1*
Rayner, John *WhoHol A*
Rayner, Lionel Benjamin d1855 *NotNAT B*
Rayner, Minnie 1869-1941 *NotNAT B, WhThe, WhoHol B*
Raynero DeScarsellis *NewGrD 80*
Raynham, Frederick *Film 2*
Raynor, Henry Broughton 1917- *IntWWM 77, –80, WhoMus 72*
Raynor, Lynn S 1940- *IntMPA 77, –75, –76, –78, –79, –80*
Raynore, Katherine *WhoStg 1908*
Rayo, Mirra *Film 2*
Rays, The *AmPS A, RkOn[port]*
Razador, Jose 1935- *WhoOp 76*
Razaf, Andy 1895-1973 *AmPS, AmSCAP 66, –80, BiDAmM, BlkAmP, CmpEPM, DrBlPA, EncJzS 70, MorBAP, Sw&Ld C*
Razafkeriefo, Andrea Paul *AmSCAP 80*
Razeto, Stella *Film 1*
Razetti, Amedeo *NewGrD 80*
Razetto, Stella 1881-1948 *WhScrn 77*
Razumovsky, Count Andrei 1752-1836 *Baker 78*
Razumovsky, Count Andrey Kyrillovich 1752-1836 *NewGrD 80*
Razumovsky, Dmitry Vasil'yevich 1818-1889 *NewGrD 80*
Razzetti, Amedeo *NewGrD 80*
Razzi, Fausto 1932- *Baker 78, NewGrD 80*
Razzi, Giovanni 1531-1611 *NewGrD 80*
Razzi, Girolamo *McGEWD*
Razzi, Giulio 1904- *WhoMus 72*
Re, Peter 1919- *ConAmC*
Rea, Alec L 1878-1953 *NotNAT B, WhThe*
Rea, David Ernest 1946- *AmSCAP 80*
Rea, Isabel *Film 1*
Rea, John 1944- *Baker 78*
Rea, Mabel Lillian 1932-1968 *WhScrn 74, –77, WhoHol B*
Rea, Oliver 1923- *BiE&WWA, NotNAT*
Rea, Peggy *WhoHol A*
Rea, Virginia *CmpEPM*
Rea, William 1827-1903 *OxMus*
Rea, William J 1884-1932 *NotNAT B, WhThe*
Reach, Alice Scanlon *AmSCAP 66, –80*
Reach, Angus B d1856 *NotNAT B*
Read, Barbara 1917-1963 *WhScrn 77, WhoHol B*
Read, Daniel 1757-1836 *Baker 78, BiDAmM, NewGrD 80*
Read, Dolly *WhoHol A*
Read, Donald William 1914- *AmSCAP 66, –80, IntWWM 77, –80*
Read, Doris *WhoMus 72*
Read, Ernest 1879-1965 *NewGrD 80, OxMus*
Read, Gardner 1913- *AmSCAP 66, –80, Baker 78, BiDAmM, CompSN[port], CpmDNM 72, –75, –79, –80, ConAmC, DcCM, IntWWM 77, –80, NewGrD 80, OxMus, WhoMus 72*
Read, Helen Frieda 1902- *IntWWM 77, –80, WhoMus 72*
Read, Joel 1753-1837 *BiDAmM*
Read, John 1920- *IntMPA 77, –75, –76*
Read, Sir John 1918- *IntMPA 77, –76, –78, –79, –80*
Read, John William 1933- *CpmDNM 72, –79, –80*
Read, Lillian *MotPP*
Read, Piers Paul 1941- *ConDr 73, –77B*
Read, Richard *NewGrD 80*
Read, Thomas Lawrence 1938- *ConAmC, IntWWM 77, –80*
Read, Vernon Sydney 1886- *WhoMus 72*
Reade, Charles 1814-1884 *EncWT, NotNAT A, –B, OxThe*
Reade, Charles Faso 1911- *AmSCAP 66, –80*
Reade, Hamish *CreCan 2*
Reade, Paul Geoffrey 1943- *IntWWM 77, –80*
Reade, Richard *NewGrD 80*
Reade, Timothy *OxThe*
Reader, Ralph 1903- *BiE&WWA, IlWWBF A, IntMPA 77, –75, –76, –78, –79, –80, NotNAT, –A, WhoHol A, WhoThe 72, –77*
Readick, Frank M 1861-1924 *WhScrn 77*
Readick, Robert 1926- *IntMPA 77, –75, –76, –78, –79, –80*
Reading, John *NewGrD 80*
Reading, John 1645?-1692 *Baker 78, NewGrD 80, OxMus*
Reading, John 1677-1764 *Baker 78*
Reading, John 1685?-1764 *NewGrD 80*
Reagan, Charles M 1896- *IntMPA 79, –80*
Reagan, Maureen *WhoHol A*
Reagan, Ronald *IntMPA 77, –75, –76, –78, –79, –80, MotPP, NewYTET*
Reagan, Ronald 1911- *FilmEn, FilmgC, HalFC 80, MovMk[port]*
Reagan, Ronald 1912- *BiDFilm, –81, ForYSC[port], OxFilm, WhoHol A, WorEFlm*
Reagon, Bernice *MorBAP*
Reaks, Brian Harold James 1920- *IntWWM 77, –80, WhoMus 72*
Real, Betty d1969 *WhScrn 74, –77, WhoHol B*
Real, Louis Albert, II 1951- *AmSCAP 80*
Real, Louise *Film 1*
Reale, Marcella *WhoOp 76*
Reale, Paul 1943- *CpmDNM 76, ConAmC, IntWWM 77, –80*
Reals, Nancy *WomWMM*
Reaney, Gilbert 1924- *IntWWM 77, –80, NewGrD 80*
Reaney, James Crerar 1926- *CnThe, ConDr 73, –77, CreCan 1, McGEWD, REnWD[port]*
Reardon, Caspar 1907-1941 *CmpEPM*
Reardon, Casper 1907-1941 *BiDAmM, WhoJazz 72*
Reardon, Dennis J 1944- *ConDr 77, NatPD[port]*
Reardon, Frank C 1925- *AmSCAP 80*
Reardon, Jack 1934- *AmSCAP 66, –80*
Reardon, James *IlWWBF*
Reardon, John 1930- *Baker 78, BiE&WWA, MusSN[port], NewGrD 80, WhoOp 76*
Reardon, Michael *WhoHol A*
Reardon, Mildred *Film 1, –2, MotPP*
Reardon, William R *BlkAmP*
Rearick, Martha Nell 1938- *IntWWM 77, –80*
Reason, Lionel 1909?- *NewOrJ[port]*
Reason, Rex 1928- *FilmEn, FilmgC, ForYSC, HalFC 80, IntMPA 77, –75, –76, –78, –79, –80, WhoHol A, WhoHrs 80*
Reason, Rhodes 1930- *FilmgC, ForYSC, HalFC 80, WhoHol A*
Reasoner, Harry 1923- *IntMPA 77, –75, –76, –78, –79, –80, NewYTET*
Reavey, Jean *NatPD[port]*
Reay, Samuel 1822-1905 *OxMus*
Rebel *NewGrD 80*
Rebel, Anne-Renee 1663?-1722 *NewGrD 80*
Rebel, Francois 1701-1775 *Baker 78, MusMk, NewGrD 80, OxMus*
Rebel, Jean d1692 *NewGrD 80*
Rebel, Jean-Baptiste-Ferry 1666-1747 *NewGrD 80[port]*
Rebel, Jean-Fery 1661-1747 *MusMk, OxMus*
Rebel, Jean-Fery 1666-1747 *NewGrD 80[port]*
Rebel, Renee Anne 1663-1722 *NewGrD 80*
Rebello, Joao Lourenco 1610-1661 *Baker 78*
Rebello, Joao Soares 1610-1661 *NewGrD 80*
Rebello, Manoel 1575?-1647 *NewGrD 80*
Rebello, Manuel 1575?-1647 *NewGrD 80*
Rebelo, Joao Lourenco 1610-1661 *NewGrD 80*
Rebelo, Joao Soares 1610-1661 *NewGrD 80*
Rebelo, Manuel 1575?-1647 *NewGrD 80*
Rebels Quartet *BiDAmM*
Rebenlein *NewGrD 80*
Rebenlein, Georg 1575-1657 *NewGrD 80*
Reber, Henri 1807-1880 *NewGrD 80*
Reber, Mrs. Lloyd *PupTheA*
Reber, Napoleon-Henri 1807-1880 *Baker 78*
Rebhuhn, Paul 1500?-1546? *NewGrD 80*
Rebhun, Paul 1500?-1546 *OxThe*
Rebicek, Josef 1844-1904 *Baker 78*
Rebikof, Vladimir 1866-1920 *OxMus*
Rebikov, Vladimir 1866-1920 *Baker 78, MusMk, NewEOp 71, NewGrD 80*
Rebille, Philbert *NewGrD 80*
Rebille, Philibert *NewGrD 80*
Rebillot, Pat 1935- *EncJzS 70*
Rebillot, Patrick Earl 1935- *AmSCAP 80, EncJzS 70*
Rebling, Eberhard 1911- *IntWWM 77, –80*
Rebling, Gustav 1821-1902 *Baker 78*
Rebmann, Liselotte 1935- *WhoOp 76*
Rebner, Adolf 1876-1967 *Baker 78*
Rebner, Wolfgang Edward 1910- *Baker 78, IntWWM 77*
Rech, Geza 1910- *IntWWM 77, –80, NewGrD 80, WhoMus 72*
Rechberger, Hermann 1947- *IntWWM 77, –80*

Recio, Mademoiselle *OxMus*
Reck, David 1935- *ConAmC, DcCM*
Recklaw, Betty *Film 2*
Reckless, Arthur *WhoMus 72*
Reckless, Margaret Mary *WhoMus 72*
Reckord, Barry *ConDr 73, -77*
Reckow, Fritz 1940- *NewGrD 80*
Record, Lucy Dean 1924- *IntWWM 77*
Record Boys *BiDAmM*
Rectanus, Hans 1935- *IntWWM 77, -80*
Rector, Eddie 189-?-1962 *BlksBF[port]*
Rector, William Eugene 1929- *BiDAmM*
Red Devil *BluesWW*
Red Hot Peppers *BiDAmM*
Red Hot Willie *BluesWW*
Red Nelson *BluesWW*
Red River Dave *AmSCAP 80*
Red Wing d1974 *WhScrn 77, WhoHol B*
Red Wing, Princess *Film 1*
Reda, Siegfried 1916-1968 *DcCM, NewGrD 80*
Redbone *RkOn 2[port]*
Redbone, Leon *IlEncR*
Redd, Alonza Thomas 1950- *AmSCAP 80*
Redd, Elvira 1930- *BlkWAB, EncJzS 70*
Redd, Freddie 1928- *BiDAmM*
Redd, Mary-Robin *WhoHol A*
Redd, Vi *EncJzS 70*
Reddick, William J 1890-1965 *AmSCAP 66, -80, ConAmC A*
Redding *NewGrD 80*
Redding, Edward C 1917- *AmSCAP 66*
Redding, Edward Carolan 1915- *AmSCAP 80*
Redding, Eugene 1870- *WhoStg 1908*
Redding, Noel David 1945- *AmSCAP 80*
Redding, Otis 1941-1967 *BiDAmM, ConMuA 80A, DrBlPA, IlEncR[port], RkOn[port], WhScrn 77*
Reddy, Helen *ConMuA 80A, HalFC 80*
Reddy, Helen 1941- *RkOn 2[port]*
Reddy, Helen 1942- *IlEncR[port], IntMPA 77, -75, -76, -78, -79, -80, WhoHol A*
Rede, Leman Tertius 1799-1832 *OxThe*
Rede, Thomas Leman 1799-1832 *NotNAT B*
Rede, William Leman 1802-1847 *NotNAT B, OxThe*
Redeker, Quinn *WhoHol A*
Redel, Kurt 1918- *NewGrD 80*
Redel, Martin Christoph 1947- *NewGrD 80*
Redelings, Lowell E *IntMPA 77, -75, -76, -78, -79, -80*
Reder, Philip 1924- *IntWWM 80*
Redestinos, David *NewGrD 80*
Redfern, Philip Edwin 1908- *WhoMus 72*
Redfern, W B d1923 *NotNAT B*
Redfield, William *WhoHol A*
Redfield, William 1927-1976 *BiE&WWA, FilmEn, ForYSC, HalFC 80, NotNAT A, -B, WhoThe 72, -77*
Redfield, William 1928- *FilmgC*
Redford, Barbara *Film 2*
Redford, George Alexander d1916 *NotNAT B*
Redford, John d1547 *Baker 78, NewGrD 80, OxMus*
Redford, Jonathan Alfred Clawson 1953- *AmSCAP 80*
Redford, Robert *MotPP, WhoHol A*
Redford, Robert 1936- *FilmgC, HalFC 80, OxFilm*
Redford, Robert 1937- *BiDFilm, -81, BiE&WWA, FilmEn, ForYSC, IntMPA 77, -75, -76, -78, -79, -80, MovMk[port], WorEFlm*
Redgrave, Colin 1939- *ForYSC*
Redgrave, Corin 1939- *CnThe, EncWT, FilmEn, FilmgC, HalFC 80, WhoHol A, WhoThe 72, -77*
Redgrave, Lynn *CnThe, MotPP, WhoHol A*
Redgrave, Lynn 1943- *FilmAG WE, FilmEn, FilmgC, ForYSC, HalFC 80, IlWWBF[port], IntMPA 77, -75, -76, -78, -79, -80, MovMk, NotNAT, WhoThe 72, -77*
Redgrave, Lynn 1944- *EncWT, OxFilm*
Redgrave, Sir Michael 1908- *BiDFilm, -81, BiE&WWA, CmMov, CnThe, EncWT, Ent, FilmAG WE, FilmEn, FilmgC, ForYSC, HalFC 80, IlWWBF[port], -A, IntMPA 77, -75, -76, -78, -79, -80, MotPP, MovMk[port], NotNAT, -A, OxFilm, OxThe, PlP&P, WhoHol A, WhoHrs 80, WhoThe 72, -77, WorEFlm*
Redgrave, Rachel Kempson 1910- *EncWT*
Redgrave, Vanessa 1937- *BiDFilm, -81, CnThe, EncWT, Ent, FilmAG WE[port], FilmEn, FilmgC, ForYSC, HalFC 80, IlWWBF[port], IntMPA 77, -75, -76, -78, -79, -80, MotPP, MovMk[port], OxFilm, OxThe, WhoHol A, WhoThe 72, -77, WorEFlm*
Redgrave Family *MotPP*
Redhead, Richard 1820-1901 *Baker 78, NewGrD 80*
Redi, Tommaso 1675?-1738 *NewGrD 80*
Rediske, Johannes Paul Samuel 1926-1975 *EncJzS 70, WhoMus 72*
Redlich, Don 1933- *CmpGMD, CnOxB*
Redlich, Hans Ferdinand 1903-1968 *Baker 78, NewGrD 80, OxMus*
Redman, Ben Ray 1896-1962 *NotNAT B*
Redman, Dewey 1931- *IlEncJ*
Redman, Don 1900-1964 *AmSCAP 66, -80, BgBands 74[port], CmpEPM, IlEncJ, NewGrD 80, WhoJazz 72*
Redman, Donald Mathew 1900-1964 *NewGrD 80*
Redman, Donald Matthew 1900-1964 *BiDAmM*
Redman, Frank *Film 1, -2*
Redman, Harry Newton 1869-1958 *Baker 78*
Redman, Joan Dorothea 1929- *IntWWM 77, -80, WhoMus 72*
Redman, Joyce 1918- *BiE&WWA, CnThe, FilmEn, FilmgC, HalFC 80, NotNAT, PlP&P[port], WhoHol A, WhoThe 72, -77*
Redman, Joyce 1919- *ForYSC*
Redman, Reginald 1892- *WhoMus 72*
Redman, Roy Alvin 1938- *IntWWM 77, -80*
Redman, Walter Dewey 1931- *AmSCAP 80, EncJzS 70*
Redmond *PupTheA*
Redmond, Eugene B 1937- *BlkAmP, MorBAP*
Redmond, John 1906- *AmSCAP 66, -80*
Redmond, Liam 1913- *FilmgC, ForYSC, HalFC 80, WhoHol A, WhoThe 72, -77*
Redmond, Marge *WhoHol A*
Redmond, Moira *HalFC 80, WhoHol A, WhoThe 72, -77*
Redmond, T C d1937 *NotNAT B*
Redmond, William d1915 *NotNAT B*
Redmont, Bernard *NewYTET*
Redner, Lewis H 1831-1908 *BiDAmM*
Redstone, Edward S 1928- *IntMPA 77, -75, -76, -78, -79, -80*
Redstone, Michael 1902- *IntMPA 77, -75, -76, -78, -79, -80*
Redstone, Sumner M 1923- *IntMPA 77, -75, -76, -78, -79, -80*
Redstone, Willy d1949 *NotNAT B*
Redwine, Wilbur 1926- *AmSCAP 66, -80*
Redwing, Rodd 1905-1971 *ForYSC, WhScrn 74, -77, WhoHol B*
Redwood, John *BlkAmP*
Ree, Anton 1820-1886 *Baker 78*
Ree, Louis 1861-1939 *Baker 78*
Reece, Alphonso Son 1931- *BiDAmM*
Reece, Arley R 1945- *WhoOp 76*
Reece, Brian d1962 *NotNAT B, WhoHol B*
Reece, Brian 1913-1962 *FilmgC, HalFC 80, WhThe*
Reece, Brian 1914-1962 *WhScrn 74, -77*
Reece, Robert d1891 *NotNAT B*
Reed, Adam *WhoHol A*
Reed, Alaina 1946- *DrBlPA*
Reed, Alan 1907-1977 *AmSCAP 66, FilmEn, ForYSC, IntMPA 77, -75, -76, Vers A[port], WhoHol A*
Reed, Alan 1908-1977 *HalFC 80*
Reed, Alan, Jr. *ForYSC, WhoHol A*
Reed, Albert *DrBlPA*
Reed, Alfred 1921- *AmSCAP 66, -80, CpmDNM 80, ConAmC, IntWWM 77, -80*
Reed, Alfred German d1895 *NotNAT B*
Reed, Billy 1914-1974 *WhScrn 77*
Reed, Carl D d1962 *NotNAT B*
Reed, Sir Carol 1906-1976 *BiDFilm, -81, CmMov, DcFM, FilmEn, FilmgC, HalFC 80, IlWWBF, IntMPA 75, -76, MovMk[port], OxFilm, WhThe, WorEFlm*
Reed, Dave 1872-1946 *WhScrn 74, -77*
Reed, David 1872-1946 *AmSCAP 66, -80*
Reed, Diana LaDean 1947- *WhoOp 76*
Reed, Don Sterling 1929- *AmSCAP 66*
Reed, Donald 1905-1973 *FilmEn*
Reed, Donald 1907-1973 *Film 2, WhScrn 77, WhoHol B*
Reed, Donna 1921- *BiDFilm, -81, FilmEn, FilmgC, ForYSC, HalFC 80, IntMPA 77, -75, -76, -78, -79, -80, MGM[port], MotPP, MovMk[port], What 5[port], WhoHol A, WorEFlm[port]*
Reed, Florence d1967 *MotPP, WhoHol B*
Reed, Florence 1863-1967 *Film 1, TwYS*
Reed, Florence 1883-1967 *BiE&WWA, Film 2, ForYSC, NotNAT B, WhScrn 74, -77, WhThe*
Reed, Geoffrey *WhoHol A*
Reed, George d1952 *BlksB&W C, WhoHol B*
Reed, George 1867-1952 *Vers B[port]*
Reed, George E d1952 *WhScrn 74, -77, WhoHol B*
Reed, George H *Film 2*
Reed, George H 1866-1952 *WhScrn 77*
Reed, Mrs. German d1895 *NotNAT B*
Reed, Gus 1880-1965 *WhScrn 74, -77*
Reed, H Owen 1910- *AmSCAP 80, CpmDNM 79, -80, ConAmC, DcCM, IntWWM 77, -80*
Reed, Henry *ConDr 73, -77B*
Reed, Henry Philip Howell 1906- *WhoMus 72*
Reed, Herbert Owen 1910- *AmSCAP 66, Baker 78*
Reed, Howard 1906- *NewOrJ*
Reed, Isaac d1807 *NotNAT B*
Reed, Ishmael *MorBAP*
Reed, Jane *Film 2*
Reed, Janet 1916- *CnOxB, DancEn 78*
Reed, Jared d1962 *NotNAT B*
Reed, Jerry 1937- *CounME 74[port], -74A, IlEncCM, RkOn[port]*
Reed, Jimmy *RkOn[port]*
Reed, Joel M *NatPD[port]*
Reed, John *PlP&P*
Reed, John Marshall 1954- *AmSCAP 80*
Reed, Jordan *WhoHol A*
Reed, Joseph d1787 *NotNAT B*
Reed, Joseph Verner, Sr. 1902-1973 *BiE&WWA, NotNAT A, -B, WhThe, WhoThe 72*
Reed, Lou 1944- *ConMuA 80A, IlEncR[port], RkOn 2[port]*
Reed, Lucy 1921- *BiDAmM*
Reed, Luther 1888-1961 *FilmEn, TwYS A*
Reed, Margaret *PupTheA*
Reed, Mark 1890- *BiE&WWA, McGEWD*
Reed, Mark 1893- *WhThe*
Reed, Marshall 1917- *ForYSC, IntMPA 77, -75, -76, -78, -79, -80, WhoHol A*
Reed, Mathis James 1925-1976 *BluesWW[port]*
Reed, Maxwell d1974 *WhoHol B*
Reed, Maxwell 1919-1974 *IlWWBF[port], WhScrn 77*
Reed, Maxwell 1920-1974 *FilmgC, ForYSC, HalFC 80, IntMPA 77, -75, -76, -78, -79, -80*
Reed, Mel *PupTheA*
Reed, Michael 1929- *HalFC 80*
Reed, Nancy 1928- *AmSCAP 66, -80*
Reed, Nancy Binns 1924- *AmSCAP 80*
Reed, Nora *BluesWW, Film 2*
Reed, Oliver 1938- *FilmAG WE, FilmEn, FilmgC, ForYSC, HalFC 80, IlWWBF[port], -A, IntMPA 77, -75, -76, -78, -79, -80, MovMk, OxFilm, WhoHol A, WhoHrs 80*
Reed, Paul *WhoHol A*
Reed, Peter *IntMPA 77, -75, -76, -78, -79, -80*
Reed, Peter Hugh 1892-1969 *Baker 78*
Reed, Philip *IntMPA 77, -75, -76, -78, -79, -80*
Reed, Philip 1900- *ForYSC, WhoHol A*
Reed, Philip 1908- *FilmEn, FilmgC, HalFC 80*
Reed, Rex 1938- *ConAmTC*
Reed, Rex 1939- *WhoHol A*
Reed, Richard *NewGrD 80*
Reed, Robert 1932- *ForYSC, WhoHol A*
Reed, Robert B 1900-1968 *AmSCAP 66, -80, ConAmC A*
Reed, Roland 1852-1901 *NotNAT B*
Reed, Susan 1927- *BiDAmM, EncFCWM 69,*

WhoHol A
Reed, Theodore 1887-1959 *FilmEn*
Reed, Thomas German 1817-1888 *Baker 78, NewGrD 80, NotNAT B*
Reed, Tracy 1949?- *DrBlPA, WhoHol A*
Reed, Vivian *DrBlPA, Film 1*
Reed, Walter *ForYSC, WhoHol A, WhoHrs 80*
Reed, William Henry 1876-1942 *Baker 78, NewGrD 80*
Reed, William Leonard 1910- *Baker 78, IntWWM 77, -80, NewGrD 80, WhoMus 72*
Reehm, George *Film 2*
Reeker, Cecilia 1897- *AmSCAP 80*
Reeks, Kathleen Doris 1902- *WhoMus 72*
Reel, Edward *Film 1*
Reel, Frank A 1907- *IntMPA 77, -75, -76, -78, -79*
Reemhber, Arthur O *AmSCAP 80*
Reemtsma, Mrs. H J *PupTheA*
Reenberg, Annelise *WomWMM*
Rees, Abraham 1743-1825 *OxMus*
Rees, Angharad 1949- *HalFC 80*
Rees, Ann 1935- *IntWWM 77, -80*
Rees, David *OxMus*
Rees, Edward Randolph d1976 *WhoHol C*
Rees, Eric Vernon 1919- *IntWWM 77, -80*
Rees, J T 1857-1949 *NewGrD 80*
Rees, Llewellyn 1901- *WhoHol A, WhoThe 72, -77*
Rees, Olive Gwendoline *WhoMus 72*
Rees, Roger 1944- *WhoThe 77*
Rees, Winifred Emily 1900- *WhoMus 72*
Rees-Davies, Barbara *IntWWM 77, WhoMus 72*
Reese, Claude *AmSCAP 80*
Reese, Della *WhoHol A*
Reese, Della 1931- *AmSCAP 80*
Reese, Della 1932- *BiDAmM, DrBlPA, RkOn[port]*
Reese, Gustave 1899-1977 *Baker 78, NewGrD 80, OxMus*
Reese, James W d1960 *NotNAT B, WhoHol B*
Reese, Lizette Woodworth 1856-1935 *BiDAmM*
Reese, Roberta Lea 1953- *IntWWM 77*
Reese, Tom 1930- *FilmgC, HalFC 80, WhoHol A*
Reese, W James 1898-1960 *WhScrn 74, -77*
Reese, Wendel *AmSCAP 80*
Reeser, Eduard 1908- *IntWWM 77, -80*
Reeser, H Eduard 1908- *NewGrD 80*
Reesor, Frederick Alan Edwin 1936- *IntWWM 77, -80*
Reeve, Ada 1874-1966 *EncMT, FilmgC, HalFC 80, IlWWBF A, WhScrn 74, -77, WhThe, WhoHol B*
Reeve, Alex 1900- *BiE&WWA, NotNAT*
Reeve, Christopher 1952- *HalFC 80, IntMPA 80, WhoHrs 80[port]*
Reeve, Douglas George William 1901- *WhoMus 72*
Reeve, Eve Lynne Joan 1935- *IntWWM 77, -80*
Reeve, Fox *AmSCAP 80*
Reeve, Geoffrey 1932- *HalFC 80*
Reeve, Robert Graham 1947- *IntWWM 80*
Reeve, William 1757-1815 *Baker 78, NewGrD 80*
Reeve, Wybert d1906 *NotNAT B*
Reeves, Alfred 1876-1946 *FilmEn*
Reeves, Betty 1913- *IntWWM 77, -80, WhoMus 72*
Reeves, Billie *Film 1, -2*
Reeves, Billy 1864-1943 *WhScrn 74, -77, WhoHol B*
Reeves, Bob d1960 *WhoHol B*
Reeves, Charlene *PupTheA*
Reeves, David Wallace 1838-1900 *Baker 78*
Reeves, Del 1933- *CounME 74[port], -74A, EncFCWM 69*
Reeves, Del 1934- *IlEncCM[port]*
Reeves, Delano 1933- *BiDAmM*
Reeves, Donald Lee 1934- *AmSCAP 66*
Reeves, Gabor 1928- *IntWWM 80*
Reeves, Gabor 1929- *WhoMus 72*
Reeves, Geoffrey 1939- *WhoThe 72, -77*
Reeves, George 1914-1959 *FilmEn, FilmgC, ForYSC, HalFC 80, MotPP, NotNAT B, WhScrn 74, -77, WhoHol B, WhoHrs 80[port]*
Reeves, Goebel 1899-1959 *IlEncCM*
Reeves, Hazard E 1906- *IntMPA 77, -75, -76, -78, -79, -80*
Reeves, J Harold *Film 2*
Reeves, James Mathew 1919- *IntWWM 77*
Reeves, James Travis 1924-1964 *BiDAmM*
Reeves, Jim 1923- *IlEncCM[port]*
Reeves, Jim 1924- *CounME 74A*
Reeves, Jim 1924-1964 *AmPS A, CounME 74[port], EncFCWM 69, NotNAT B, RkOn[port], WhScrn 74, -77, WhoHol B*
Reeves, John Sims 1818-1900 *Baker 78*
Reeves, Kynaston 1893- *WhThe, WhoThe 72*
Reeves, Kynaston 1893-1971 *HalFC 80, WhScrn 74, -77, WhoHol B*
Reeves, Kynaston 1893-1972 *FilmgC*
Reeves, Michael 1944-1969 *FilmgC, HalFC 80, WhoHrs 80*
Reeves, Red 1905- *WhoJazz 72*
Reeves, Richard 1912-1967 *WhScrn 77, WhoHol B*
Reeves, Robert Henry, III 1941- *IntWWM 77*
Reeves, Robert Jasper 1892-1960 *Film 1, -2, WhScrn 74, -77*
Reeves, Sims 1818-1900 *CmOp, NewGrD 80*
Reeves, Steve 1926- *FilmEn, Film 2, FilmgC, ForYSC, HalFC 80, IntMPA 77, -75, -76, -78, -79, -80, MotPP, MovMk[port], WhoHol A, WhoHrs 80[port], WorEFlm*
Reeves, Talcott 1904- *WhoJazz 72*
Reeves, Theodore 1910-1973 *BiE&WWA, NotNAT B, WomWMM*
Reeves-Smith, H d1938 *Film 2, WhoHol B*
Reeves-Smith, H 1862-1938 *WhThe*
Reeves-Smith, H 1863-1938 *WhScrn 74, -77*
Reeves-Smith, Harry 1862-1938 *NotNAT B*
Reeves-Smith, Olive 1894-1972 *BiE&WWA, NotNAT B, WhoHol B*
Refardt, Edgar 1877-1968 *Baker 78, NewGrD 80*
Refice, Licinio 1883-1954 *Baker 78*
Refice, Licinio 1885-1954 *NewGrD 80*
Reflections, The *RkOn 2[port]*
Regamey, Constantin 1907- *Baker 78, DcCM, IntWWM 77, -80, NewGrD 80*
Regan, Anna 1841-1902 *NewGrD 80*
Regan, Berry 1914-1956 *WhScrn 74, -77*
Regan, Christopher Peter William 1929- *WhoMus 72*
Regan, Edgar J d1938 *WhScrn 74, -77*
Regan, Joseph 1896-1931 *WhScrn 74, -77, WhoHol B*
Regan, Norah 1899- *WhoMus 72*
Regan, Patti *WhoHol A*
Regan, Phil 1906- *CmpEPM, ForYSC, IntMPA 77, -75, -76, -78, -79, -80, WhoHol A*
Regan, Sylvia 1908- *BiE&WWA, NatPD[port], NotNAT*
Regas, George 1890-1940 *Film 2, WhScrn 74, -77, WhoHol B*
Regas, Pedro 1882-1974 *WhScrn 77, WhoHol B*
Regents, The *RkOn*
Regeny, Rudolf Wagner *OxMus*
Reger, Max 1873-1916 *Baker 78, BnBkM 80, CompSN[port], DcCom 77, DcCom&M 79, MusMk, NewGrD 80[port], OxMus*
Reggiani, Serge 1922- *BiDFilm, -81, FilmAG WE[port], FilmEn, FilmgC, HalFC 80, OxFilm, WhoHol A, WorEFlm*
Reggio, Fattorin Da *NewGrD 80*
Reggio, Hoste *NewGrD 80*
Reggio, Pietro 1632? 1685 *NewGrD 80*
Regino Of Prum 842?-915 *NewGrD 80*
Regis, Johannes 1430?-1485? *Baker 78, NewGrD 80*
Regitz, Hartmut 1943- *CnOxB*
Regli, Francesco 1802-1866 *Baker 78*
Regnal *OxMus*
Regnard, Jean Francois 1655-1709 *CnThe, Ent, McGEWD[port], NotNAT B, OxThe, REnWD[port]*
Regnard, Jean Francois 1655-1710 *EncWT*
Regnart, Florence *Film 2*
Regnart, Jacob 1540?-1599 *Baker 78, NewGrD 80*
Regnart, Jacques 1540?-1599 *MusMk, NewGrD 80*
Regnault, Madame d1887 *NotNAT B*
Regnault, Pierre *NewGrD 80*
Regner, Otto Friedrich 1913-1963 *CnOxB, DancEn 78*
Regnes, Nicole *NewGrD 80*
Regnier 1807-1885 *NotNAT B, OxThe*
Regnier, Francois *PlP&P*
Regnier, Marthe 1880- *WhThe*
Regnier, Nicolas *NewGrD 80*
Rego, Maria DelCarmen Sanchez *PupTheA*
Rego, Pedro Vaz 1673?-1736 *NewGrD 80*
Regondi, Giulio 1822-1872 *NewGrD 80, OxMus*
Regt, Hendrik De 1950- *Baker 78*
Regua, Charles *Film 2*
Reguera, Rogelio 1926- *IntWWM 77, -80*
Rehak, Frank James 1926- *BiDAmM, EncJzS 70*
Rehan, Ada 1860-1916 *EncWT, Ent, FamA&A[port], NotNAT A, -B, OxThe, PlP&P, WhThe, WhoStg 1906, -1908*
Rehan, Mary 1887-1963 *NotNAT B, WhScrn 74, -77, WhoHol B*
Rehberg, Hans 1901-1963 *CnMD, EncWT, ModWD*
Rehberg, Walter 1900-1957 *Baker 78*
Rehfeld, Curt *Film 2*
Rehfeldt, Phillip R 1939- *IntWWM 77, -80*
Rehfisch, Hans Jose 1891-1960 *CnMD, EncWT, McGEWD, ModWD*
Rehfuss, Heinz J 1917- *IntWWM 77, NewGrD 80*
Rehfuss, Heniz J 1917- *IntWWM 80*
Rehim, Gamal *NewGrD 80*
Rehkopf, Paul *Film 2*
Rehm, Wolfgang 1929- *IntWWM 77, -80, NewGrD 80*
Reibel, Guy 1936- *DcCM*
Reiber, Mina Franke 1905- *IntWWM 77, -80*
Reich, Bruce 1948- *ConAmC*
Reich, George 1926- *CnOxB, DancEn 78*
Reich, Gunter *WhoOp 76*
Reich, John 1906- *BiE&WWA, NotNAT*
Reich, Richard *NatPD[port]*
Reich, Stephen 1936- *NewGrD 80*
Reich, Steve 1936- *Baker 78, BiDAmM, BnBkM 80, ConAmC, DcCM, IntWWM 80, NewGrD 80*
Reich, Willi 1898-1980 *Baker 78, IntWWM 77, -80, NewGrD 80*
Reicha, Antoine 1770-1836 *MusMk, NewGrD 80*
Reicha, Anton 1770-1836 *Baker 78, NewGrD 80, OxMus*
Reicha, Antonin 1770-1836 *NewGrD 80*
Reicha, Josef 1752-1795 *NewGrD 80*
Reichard, Heinrich Gottfried 1742-1801 *NewGrD 80*
Reichard, Johann Georg 1710-1782 *NewGrD 80*
Reichardt, Bernhard 1840-1907 *NewGrD 80*
Reichardt, Johann Friedrich 1752-1814 *Baker 78, MusMk[port], NewEOp 71, NewGrD 80[port], OxMus*
Reichardt, Louise 1779-1826 *NewGrD 80[port]*
Reichardt, Luise 1779-1826 *Baker 78*
Reiche, Gottfried 1667-1734 *BnBkM 80, NewGrD 80, OxMus*
Reiche, Gwendolyn 1912- *WhoMus 72*
Reicheg, Richard 1937- *AmSCAP 80*
Reichel, Bernard 1901- *NewGrD 80*
Reichel, Friedrich 1833-1889 *Baker 78*
Reichel, Kathe 1926- *EncWT*
Reichenbach, Francois 1922- *DcFM, FilmEn, FilmgC, HalFC 80, OxFilm, WorEFlm*
Reicher, Emanuel 1849-1924 *EncWT*
Reicher, Emmanuel 1849-1924 *NotNAT B*
Reicher, Ernest *Film 2*
Reicher, Frank 1875-1965 *FilmEn, Film 2, FilmgC, HalFC 80, HolCA[port], MotPP, MovMk, TwYS, Vers B[port], WhScrn 74, -77, WhThe, WhoHol B, WhoHrs 80*
Reicher, Frank 1876-1965 *ForYSC, TwYS A*
Reicher, Hedwiga *Film 2*
Reicher-Kindermann, Hedwig 1853-1883 *Baker 78, CmOp, NewGrD 80*
Reichert, Arno Julius 1866-1933 *Baker 78*

Reichert, Georg 1910-1966 NewGrD 80
Reichert, Heinz 1877-1940 AmSCAP 66, -80
Reichert, James A 1932- AmSCAP 66, -80, ConAmC
Reichert, Johannes 1876-1942 Baker 78
Reichert, Julia WomWMM A, -B
Reichert, Kittens Film 1, -2
Reichman, Joe 1898?-1970 BgBands 74, CmpEPM
Reichmann, Theodor 1848-1903 NewEOp 71
Reichmann, Theodor 1849-1903 Baker 78, CmOp, NewGrD 80
Reichner, S Bickley 1905- AmSCAP 66, -80
Reichow, Otto 1904- Vers A[port]
Reichow, Werner 1922-1973 WhScrn 77, WhoHol B
Reichwein, Leopold 1878-1945 Baker 78
Reid, Ada Beatrice WhoMus 72
Reid, Alastair 1939- FilmgC, HalFC 80
Reid, Beryl ForYSC, WhoHol A
Reid, Beryl 1918- FilmAG WE[port], FilmgC, HalFC 80
Reid, Beryl 1920- FilmEn, IlWWBF, WhoThe 72, -77
Reid, Carl Benton d1973 WhoHol B
Reid, Carl Benton 1893-1973 FilmEn, MovMk, Vers A[port]
Reid, Carl Benton 1894-1973 FilmgC, HalFC 80, WhScrn 77
Reid, Carl Benton 1895- ForYSC
Reid, Charles Stuart 1900- IntWWM 77, -80
Reid, Charlotte T NewYTET
Reid, Daphne Kate CreCan 2
Reid, Don EncFCWM 69
Reid, Don 1914- AmSCAP 66
Reid, Don S 1945- BiDAmM
Reid, Donald 1915- AmSCAP 80
Reid, Dorothy Davenport FilmEn, WomWMM
Reid, Elliott 1920- BiE&WWA, FilmEn, ForYSC, HalFC 80, MotPP, NotNAT, Vers A[port], WhoHol A
Reid, Frances 1918- BiE&WWA, NotNAT, WhThe, WhoHol A
Reid, Francis WomWMM B
Reid, Francis Ellison d1933 NotNAT B
Reid, George Agnew 1860-1947 CreCan 2
Reid, Hal d1920 Film 1, NotNAT B, WhScrn 77, WhThe, WhoHol B
Reid, Harold W 1939- BiDAmM, EncFCWM 69
Reid, Hazel BlkAmP
Reid, Helen Ann 1959- IntWWM 80
Reid, Ira A BlkAmP
Reid, Isaac Erret 1916- IntWWM 77
Reid, James Hallek 1860-1920 FilmEn
Reid, John ConMuA 80B
Reid, John 1721-1807 Baker 78, NewGrD 80, OxMus
Reid, John Stanley 1948- IntWWM 80
Reid, John William 1946- CpmDNM 73, ConAmC, IntWWM 77
Reid, Joyce Green 1903- AmSCAP 80
Reid, Kate 1930- BiE&WWA, CreCan 2, HalFC 80, NotNAT, WhoHol A, WhoThe 72, -77
Reid, Mary Hiester 1854-1921 CreCan 2
Reid, Max 1903-1969 WhScrn 77
Reid, Milton WhoHol A, WhoHrs 80
Reid, Neil 1912- WhoJazz 72
Reid, Peggy MotPP
Reid, Reidy 1889-1946 AmSCAP 66, -80
Reid, Rex DancEn 78
Reid, Sheila WhoHol A
Reid, Terry 1949- ConMuA 80A, IlEncR
Reid, Theodate N PupTheA
Reid, Thomas Michael 1946- IntWWM 77
Reid, Trevor 1909-1965 WhScrn 74, -77, WhoHol B
Reid, Virginia FilmEn
Reid, Wallace d1923 MotPP, WhoHol B
Reid, Wallace 1890-1923 Film 1, -2, FilmgC, HalFC 80, MovMk
Reid, Wallace 1891-1923 FilmEn, WhScrn 74, -77, WhThe
Reid, Wallace 1892-1923 NotNAT A, -B, TwYS
Reid, Mrs. Wallace WhoHol A
Reid, Wallace, Jr. WhoHol A
Reid, Willis Wilfred 1910- AmSCAP 80
Reidel, Judy WomWMM B
Reidemeister, Peter 1942- IntWWM 77, -80
Reidy, Kitty 1902- WhThe
Reif, Paul 1910-1978 AmSCAP 66, -80, Baker 78, CpmDNM 76, -77, ConAmC
Reiffarth, Jennie 1848- WhoStg 1908
Reifsneider, Robert 1912- BiE&WWA, NotNAT
Reigbert, Otto 1890-1957 EncWT
Reiger, Margie Film 1
Reighard, Catherine PupTheA
Reilich, Gabriel 1630?-1677 NewGrD 80
Reilly, Anastasia d1961 NotNAT B
Reilly, Charles E, Jr. IntMPA 77, -75, -76, -78, -79, -80
Reilly, Charles Nelson 1931- BiE&WWA, NotNAT, PlP&P A[port], WhoHol A, WhoThe 72, -77
Reilly, Dean Edwin 1926- BiDAmM
Reilly, Dominick Film 1
Reilly, Edward R 1929- NewGrD 80
Reilly, Hugh WhoHol A
Reilly, J Terrance 1945- BlkAmP
Reilly, Jack 1932- AmSCAP 80, ConAmC
Reilly, Jacqueline Ivings CreCan 1
Reilly, Jane WhoHol A
Reilly, Michael 1933-1962 WhScrn 74, -77
Reilly, Paul Cameron 1948- IntWWM 77, -80
Reilly, Thomas 1919- NewGrD 80
Reilly, Tommy 1919- IntWWM 77, -80, NewGrD 80
Reiman, Elise CnOxB, DancEn 78
Reimann, Albert 1925- IntWWM 80
Reimann, Aribert 1936- Baker 78, IntWWM 77, -80, NewGrD 80
Reimann, Heinrich 1850-1906 Baker 78, NewGrD 80
Reimann, Ignaz 1820-1885 Baker 78
Reimann, Margarete Hildegard 1907- IntWWM 80, NewGrD 80
Reimann, Matthias NewGrD 80
Reimar Von Hagenouwe NewGrD 80
Reimer, Johannes Film 2
Reimers, Ed ForYSC, WhoHol A
Reimers, Georg d1936 NotNAT B, WhoHol B
Reimers, K Lennart 1928- IntWWM 77, -80
Reimers, Paul 1878-1942 Baker 78
Reimherr, George Film 2
Reimoser, Jan 1904- CnOxB
Reims, Clifford Waldemar 1923- IntWWM 77, -80
Reimueller, Ross Carl 1937- IntWWM 77, -80
Rein, Conrad 1475?-1522 NewGrD 80
Rein, Cunz 1475?-1522? NewGrD 80
Rein, Walter 1893-1955 Baker 78, NewGrD 80
Reina, Sisto d1664? NewGrD 80
Reinach, Edward Film 2
Reinach, Enrico 1851- WhThe
Reinach, Jacquelyn 1930- AmSCAP 66, -80
Reinach, Theodore 1860-1928 Baker 78, NewGrD 80
Reinagle NewGrD 80
Reinagle, Alexander 1756-1809 Baker 78, BiDAmM, NewGrD 80, PlP&P
Reinagle, Alexander Robert 1799-1877 NewGrD 80
Reinagle, Hugh 1764?-1785 NewGrD 80
Reinagle, Joseph d1775? NewGrD 80
Reinagle, Joseph 1762-1825 NewGrD 80
Reinauer, Richard 1926- IntMPA 77, -75, -76, -78, -79, -80
Reinberger, Jiri 1914-1977 NewGrD 80
Reinblatt, Moe 1917- CreCan 1
Reinblatt, Moses CreCan 1
Reincken, Jan Adams 1623-1722 NewGrD 80
Reincken, Johann Adam 1623-1722 NewGrD 80
Reindel, Carl WhoHol A
Reindl, Constantin 1738-1799 NewGrD 80
Reinecke, Abraham 1712-1760 BiDAmM
Reinecke, Carl 1824-1910 Baker 78, BnBkM 80, NewGrD 80[port], OxMus
Reinecke, Hans-Peter 1926- IntWWM 77, -80, NewGrD 80
Reiner, Adam NewGrD 80
Reiner, Ambrosius 1604-1672 NewGrD 80
Reiner, Carl NewYTET, WhoHol A, WomWMM
Reiner, Carl 1920- ForYSC
Reiner, Carl 1922- BiE&WWA, FilmEn, FilmgC, HalFC 80, JoeFr, MovMk
Reiner, Carl 1923- IntMPA 77, -75, -76, -78, -79, -80
Reiner, Ethel Linder d1971 BiE&WWA, NotNAT B
Reiner, Fritz 1888-1963 Baker 78, BiDAmM, BnBkM 80[port], CmOp, MusSN[port], NewEOp 71, NewGrD 80, NotNAT B, WhScrn 77
Reiner, Jacob 1560?-1606 NewGrD 80
Reiner, Jules NewOrJ
Reiner, Karel 1910-1979 Baker 78, DcCM, IntWWM 77, -80, NewGrD 80, WhoMus 72
Reiner, Manny d1974 NewYTET
Reiner, Rob WhoHol A
Reingolds, Kate d1911 NotNAT B
Reinhard NewGrD 80
Reinhard, Andreas d1614? NewGrD 80
Reinhard, John Film 1, -2
Reinhard, Karol 1929- IntWWM 77, -80
Reinhard, Kurt August Georg 1914-1979 IntWWM 77, -80, NewGrD 80
Reinhardt NewGrD 80
Reinhardt, Delia 1892-1974 CmOp, NewGrD 80
Reinhardt, Django 1910-1953 CmpEPM, IlEncJ, NewGrD 80[port]
Reinhardt, Georg 1911- WhoOp 76
Reinhardt, Gottfried IntMPA 77, -75, -76, -78, -79, -80
Reinhardt, Gottfried 1911- FilmEn, FilmgC, HalFC 80
Reinhardt, Gottfried 1914- WorEFlm
Reinhardt, Harry Film 2
Reinhardt, Heinrich 1865-1922 Baker 78, NewGrD 80
Reinhardt, Jean Baptiste 1910-1953 NewGrD 80[port]
Reinhardt, Jean Django 1910-1953 MusMk
Reinhardt, Johann Franz 1713?-1761 NewGrD 80
Reinhardt, Johann Georg 1676?-1742 NewGrD 80
Reinhardt, John 1901-1953 WhScrn 74, -77, WhoHol B
Reinhardt, Joseph Franz 1684?-1727 NewGrD 80
Reinhardt, Karl Mathias 1710?-1767 NewGrD 80
Reinhardt, Kilian 1653?-1729 NewGrD 80
Reinhardt, Max 1873-1943 BiDAmM, CmOp, CnThe, DcFM, EncWT, Ent, FilmEn, FilmgC, HalFC 80, NewGrD 80, NotNAT A, -B, OxFilm, OxThe, PlP&P, WhThe, WorEFlm
Reinhardt, Walter 1915- IntWWM 77, -80
Reinhart, Alice IntMPA 80
Reinhart, Carole Dawn 1941- IntWWM 77, -80
Reinhart, Charles Lawrence 1930- CnOxB
Reinheart, Alice IntMPA 77, -75, -76, -78, -79
Reinheimer, Howard E 1899- BiE&WWA
Reinhold, Frederick Charles 1737-1815 NewGrD 80
Reinhold, Helmut 1925- IntWWM 77
Reinhold, Henry Theodore d1751 NewGrD 80
Reinhold, Hugo 1854-1935 Baker 78
Reinhold, Otto 1899-1965 NewGrD 80
Reinhold, Theodor Christlieb 1682-1755 NewGrD 80
Reinholm, Gert 1926- CnOxB, DancEn 78
Reiniger, Lotte 1899- DcFM, DcPup, FilmEn, Film 2, FilmgC, HalFC 80, OxFilm, WomWMM, -B, WorEFlm
Reiniger, Meredith NewGrD 80
Reinike, Johann Adam NewGrD 80
Reining, Maria 1903- NewGrD 80
Reining, Maria 1905- CmOp
Reininger, Johnny 1908- NewOrJ
Reinitz, Bela 1878-1943 NewGrD 80
Reinken, Jan Adams 1623-1722 Baker 78
Reinken, Johann Adam 1623-1722 MusMk, NewGrD 80, OxMus
Reinking, Wilhelm 1896- WhoOp 76
Reinmann, Matthias NewGrD 80
Reinmar Der Brannenburger d1276? NewGrD 80
Reinmar Der Bremberger d1276? NewGrD 80
Reinmar Der Brenneberger d1276? NewGrD 80
Reinmar Von Brennenberg d1276? NewGrD 80
Reinmar Von Hagenau d1205? NewGrD 80

Reinmar Von Hagenouwe d1205? *NewGrD 80*
Reinmar Von Zweter 1200?-1260? *NewGrD 80*
Reinold, Bernard d1940 *WhScrn 77*
Reinold, Helmut 1926- *IntWWM 80*
Reinsch, J Leonard *NewYTET*
Reinspeck, Michael *NewGrD 80*
Reinstein, Jack *ConMuA 80B*
Reinthaler, Karl 1822-1896 *Baker 78, NewGrD 80*
Reinwald, Greta *Film 2*
Reinwald, Otto *Film 2*
Reis, Alberto 1902-1953 *WhScrn 74, -77*
Reis, Faye Louise 1934- *AmSCAP 66*
Reis, Irving 1906-1953 *BiDFilm, -81, FilmEn, FilmgC, HalFC 80, NotNAT B, WorEFlm*
Reis, Jakub *NewGrD 80*
Reis, Joan Sachs 1922- *IntWWM 80*
Reisch, Gregor 1465?-1525 *NewGrD 80*
Reisch, Walter 1900- *FilmgC, HalFC 80*
Reisch, Walter 1903- *FilmEn*
Reischius, Georgium 1465?-1525 *NewGrD 80*
Reisdorf, Helen E *PupTheA*
Reisenauer, Alfred 1863-1907 *Baker 78, NewGrD 80*
Reisenbach, Sanford E *IntMPA 80*
Reisenfeld, Hugo 1883- *WorEFlm*
Reisenhofer, Maria *Film 2*
Reiser, Alois 1884- *AmSCAP 66, BiDAmM, ConAmC*
Reiser, Violet 1915- *AmSCAP 66, -80*
Reisfeld, Bert 1906- *AmSCAP 66, -80*
Reisinger, Barbara *NewGrD 80*
Reisinger, Julius *DancEn 78*
Reisinger, Wenzel 1827-1892 *CnOxB*
Reisman, Jane Maritza 1937- *WhoOp 76*
Reisman, Joe 1924- *AmSCAP 66, -80, RkOn*
Reisman, Judith 1935- *AmSCAP 80*
Reisman, Leo 1897-1961 *AmPS A, BgBands 74, CmpEPM, WhoJazz 72*
Reisner, Allen *FilmgC, HalFC 80, IntMPA 77, -75, -76, -78, -79, -80*
Reisner, Charles F 1887-1962 *FilmEn, Film 1, -2, FilmgC, HalFC 80, TwYS A, WhScrn 74, -77*
Reisner, Dean *IntMPA 80*
Reiss, Albert 1870-1940 *Baker 78, NewEOp 71, NewGrD 80*
Reiss, Alvin 1932- *ConAmTC*
Reiss, Barry *ConMuA 80B*
Reiss, Georg 1861-1914 *OxMus*
Reiss, Jeffrey C 1942- *IntMPA 77, -76, -78, -79, -80*
Reiss, Josef Wladyslaw 1879-1956 *Baker 78*
Reiss, Jozef 1879-1956 *NewGrD 80*
Reiss, Stuart A 1921- *IntMPA 77, -75, -76, -78, -79, -80*
Reisserova, Julie 1888-1938 *Baker 78*
Reissiger, Carl Gottlieb 1798-1859 *Baker 78*
Reissiger, Karl Gottlieb 1798-1859 *NewGrD 80, OxMus*
Reissinger, Marianne 1945- *IntWWM 77, -80*
Reissmann, August 1825-1903 *Baker 78, NewGrD 80*
Reiswig, David Earl 1945- *IntWWM 77*
Reisz, Karel 1926- *BiDFilm, -81, FilmEn, FilmgC, HalFC 80, IlWWBF, IntMPA 77, -75, -76, -78, -79, -80, MovMk[port], OxFilm, WorEFlm*
Reisz, Karl 1926- *DcFM*
Reiter, Franz DePaula Von *NewGrD 80*
Reiter, Josef 1862-1939 *Baker 78*
Reiter, Melvyn T 1938- *AmSCAP 80*
Reiter, Ronny 1939- *WhoOp 76*
Reiter, Virginia *WhThe*
Reiter-Soffer, Domy 1943- *CnOxB*
Reith, Lord John C W d1968 *NewYTET*
Reithe, Aloise D 1890-1943 *WhScrn 74, 77*
Reitherman, Wolfgang *HalFC 80*
Reitter, Rose B 1934- *AmSCAP 80*
Reitz, Heiner 1925- *IntWWM 77, -80*
Reiz, Jakub De *NewGrD 80*
Reizen, Mark 1895- *CmOp, NewGrD 80*
Reizenstein, Franz 1911-1968 *Baker 78, NewGrD 80, OxMus*
Reizner, June *AmSCAP 80*
Rejane 1856-1920 *EncWT, Ent*
Rejane 1857-1920 *CnThe, OxThe*
Rejane, Madame 1857-1920 *NotNAT B*
Rejane, Gabriella 1857-1920 *WhScrn 74, -77*
Rejane, Gabrielle 1857-1920 *Film 1, -2, PlP&P, WhThe, WhoHol B*
Rejcha, Anton *NewGrD 80*
Rejcha, Antonin *NewGrD 80*
Rejcha, Josef *NewGrD 80*
Rejto, Gabor 1916- *IntWWM 77, -80*
Rejto, Peter A 1948- *IntWWM 77, -80*
Relfe, John 1763-1837? *Baker 78*
Reliance Brass Band *BiDAmM*
Relley, Gina *Film 2*
Rellstab, Johann Carl Friedrich 1759-1813 *NewGrD 80*
Rellstab, Johann Karl Friedrich 1759-1813 *Baker 78*
Rellstab, Ludwig 1799-1860 *Baker 78, NewGrD 80*
Relniger, Lotte *Film 2*
Relph, George 1888-1960 *FilmgC, HalFC 80, NotNAT B, PlP&P, WhScrn 74, -77, WhThe, WhoHol B*
Relph, Michael 1915- *FilmEn, FilmgC, HalFC 80, IlWWBF[port], IntMPA 77, -75, -76, -78, -79, -80, WhThe*
Relph, Phyllis 1888- *WhThe*
Relyea, Robert E 1930- *IntMPA 79, -80*
Remacha, Fernando 1898- *NewGrD 80*
Remains, The *BiDAmM*
Remarque, Erich Maria 1898-1970 *FilmgC, HalFC 80, NotNAT B, WhScrn 77*
Rembt, Johann Ernst 1749-1810 *NewGrD 80*
Rembusch, Trueman T 1909- *IntMPA 77, -75, -76, -78, -79, -80*
Remd, Johann Ernst 1749-1810 *NewGrD 80*
Remedios, Alberto 1935- *CmOp[port], IntWWM 77, -80, NewGrD 80, WhoMus 72, WhoOp 76*
Remenkov, Stefan 1923- *Baker 78*
Remenyi, Ede 1828-1898 *NewGrD 80*
Remenyi, Eduard 1828-1898 *NewGrD 80*
Remenyi, Eduard 1830-1898 *Baker 78, BiDAmM, OxMus*
Remer *NewGrD 80*
Remick, Jerome H d1931 *BiDAmM*
Remick, Lee *BiE&WWA, IntMPA 75, -76, MotPP, WhoHol A*
Remick, Lee 1935- *BiDFilm, -81, FilmEn, FilmgC, ForYSC, HalFC 80, MovMk[port], NotNAT, OxFilm, WorEFlm*
Remick, Lee 1937- *IntMPA 77, -78, -79, -80*
Remigio De' Girolami 1245?-1319 *NewGrD 80*
Remigius Autissiodorensis *NewGrD 80*
Remigius Florentinus 1245?-1319 *NewGrD 80*
Remington, Barbara 1936- *CnOxB, DancEn 78*
Remington, Emory 1891-1971 *NewGrD 80*
Remington, Emory 1892-1971 *BiDAmM*
Remley, Frank 1902-1967 *WhScrn 74, -77*
Remley, Ralph McHugh 1885-1939 *WhScrn 74, -77, WhoHol B*
Remmer *NewGrD 80*
Remnant, Mary Elizabeth Teresa 1935- *IntWWM 77, -80, WhoMus 72*
Remondon, Suzanne 1884- *WhoMus 72*
Remoortel, Edouard Van 1926-1977 *Baker 78, NewGrD 80*
Remouchamps, Henri De 1600?-1639 *NewGrD 80*
Rempt, Johann Ernst *NewGrD 80*
Remsen, Alice 1896- *AmSCAP 66*
Remsen, Bert *WhoHol A*
Remunde, Christophe Van 1475?-1531 *NewGrD 80*
Remusat, Jean 1815-1880 *Baker 78*
Remy Of Auxerre *NewGrD 80*
Remy, Albert 1912-1967 *WhScrn 74, -77, WhoHol B*
Remy, Alfred 1870-1937 *Baker 78*
Remy, Dick, Sr. 1873-1947 *WhScrn 74, -77, WhoHol B*
Remy, Dominique 1886- *NewOrJ*
Remy, Guillaume 1856-1932 *Baker 78*
Remy, W A 1831-1898 *NewGrD 80*
Rena, Henry 1898-1949 *NewOrJ[port]*
Rena, Henry 1900-1949 *BiDAmM*
Rena, Joseph 1897-1973 *NewOrJ*
Rena, Kid Henry 1898-1949 *WhoJazz 72*
Renad, Frederick d1939 *NotNAT B*
Renaissance *ConMuA 80A, IlEncR*
Renaldi, Giulio d1576 *NewGrD 80*
Renaldis, Giulio De d1576 *NewGrD 80*
Renaldo, Duncan 1904-1980 *FilmEn, Film 2, FilmgC, ForYSC, HalFC 80, IntMPA 77, -75, -76, -78, -79, -80, MotPP, MovMk, What 3[port], WhoHol A*
Renan, Emile 1913- *WhoOp 76*
Renar, Helmuth *Film 2*
Renard, David 1921-1973 *WhScrn 77, WhoHol A, -B*
Renard, Ervin *Film 2*
Renard, Jacques *CmpEPM*
Renard, Jules 1864-1910 *CnMD, Ent, McGEWD, ModWD, NotNAT B*
Renard, Kaye *Film 2*
Renard, Ken *DrBlPA, WhoHol A*
Renard, Maurice 1885-1940 *WhoHrs 80*
Renaud, Emiliano 1875-1932 *CreCan 2*
Renaud, Henri 1925- *EncJzS 70*
Renaud, Madeleine *CnThe, WhThe*
Renaud, Madeleine 1900- *BiE&WWA, NotNAT*
Renaud, Madeleine 1903- *EncWT, Ent, FilmAG WE, FilmEn, OxThe*
Renaud, Maurice 1861-1933 *Baker 78, CmOp, MusSN[port], NewEOp 71, NewGrD 80[port]*
Renault, Francis d1955 *NotNAT B*
Renault, Jack *Film 2*
Renault, Michel 1927- *CnOxB, DancEn 78[port]*
Renavent, George 1894-1969 *Film 2, WhScrn 74, -77, WhoHol B*
Renavent, Georges 1893-1969 *ForYSC*
Renay, Diane *RkOn 2[port]*
Renay, Liz *WhoHol A*
Rencher, Derek 1932- *CnOxB*
Rencher, Derek 1935- *DancEn 78*
Rendall, David 1948- *IntWWM 80*
Rendall, Geoffrey 1890-1952 *NewGrD 80*
Rendano, Alfonso 1853-1931 *NewGrD 80*
Rendell, Barbara *WhoMus 72*
Rendell, Don 1926- *IntWWM 77, -80*
Rendell, Robert *Film 2*
Rendle, Thomas McDonald 1856-1926 *NotNAT B, WhThe*
Rene, Googie *RkOn*
Rene, Henri *CmpEPM*
Rene, Ida *WhThe*
Rene, Jean 1935- *IntWWM 80*
Rene, Joseph 1920- *AmSCAP 66, -80*
Rene, Leon T 1902- *AmSCAP 66, -80*
Rene, Natalia 1907- *CnOxB, DancEn 78*
Rene, Otis J, Jr. 1898-1970 *AmSCAP 66, -80*
Rene & Rene *RkOn 2A*
Renee, Renate *Film 2*
Renee And Calvert *PupTheA*
Renek, Morris *NatPD[port]*
Renela, Rita *Film 2*
Renella, Pat *WhoHol A*
Rener, Adam 1485?-1520? *NewGrD 80*
Renesse, George Van 1909- *NewGrD 80*
Renevant, George *Film 1*
Renfeld, C *Film 1*
Renfro, Rennie 1893-1962 *Film 2, TwYS, WhScrn 74, -77, WhoHol B*
Reni *Film 2*
Renick, Ruth *Film 2, TwYS*
Renicke, Volker 1929- *WhoOp 76*
Renie, Henriette 1875-1956 *Baker 78*
Renier, Nicolas d1731? *NewGrD 80*
Renieri, Giovanni Simone *NewGrD 80*
Renison, Herbert J 1915- *IntWWM 77, -80*
Renn, Katharina 1913-1975 *WhScrn 77, WhoHol A, -C*
Renn, Samuel 1786-1845 *NewGrD 80*
Renna, Richard Joseph 1920- *AmSCAP 80*
Rennagel, Johann Wilhelm *NewGrD 80*
Rennahan, Ray 1896-1980 *FilmEn, FilmgC, HalFC 80*
Rennahan, Ray 1898-1980 *CmMov*
Rennahan, Raymond 1896-1980 *WorEFlm*
Renner, Josef 1832-1895 *Baker 78*
Rennert, Gunther 1911-1978 *CmOp, EncWT, NewEOp 71, NewGrD 80, WhoMus 72*
Rennert, Gunther Peter 1911- *WhoOp 76*
Rennert, Jonathan 1952- *IntWWM 77, -80*
Rennert, Wolfgang 1928- *WhoOp 76*
Rennes *NewGrD 80*
Rennes, Catharina Van 1858-1940 *NewGrD 80*
Rennick, Nancy *WhoHol A*
Rennie, Guy *WhoHol A*

Rennie, Hugh d1953 *NotNAT B*
Rennie, James d1965 *WhoHol B*
Rennie, James 1889-1965 *Film 2, ForYSC, TwYS, WhScrn 74, -77*
Rennie, James 1890-1965 *BiE&WWA, FilmgC, HalFC 80, NotNAT B, WhThe*
Rennie, John d1952 *NotNAT B*
Rennie, Michael 1909-1971 *BiE&WWA, FilmAG WE[port], FilmEn, FilmgC, ForYSC, HalFC 80, IlWWBF[port], MotPP, MovMk[port], NotNAT B, WhScrn 74, -77, WhoHol B, WhoHrs 80[port]*
Rennie, Susan Elizabeth 1956- *IntWWM 80*
Rennoldson, Reginald Charles *WhoMus 72*
Reno, Bob *ConMuA 80B*
Renoir, Claude 1913- *WorEFlm*
Renoir, Claude 1914- *DcFM, FilmEn, FilmgC, HalFC 80, OxFilm*
Renoir, Jean 1894-1979 *BiDFilm, -81, DcFM, FilmEn, FilmgC, HalFC 80, IntMPA 77, -75, -76, -78, -79, MovMk[port], OxFilm, WhoHol A, WorEFlm*
Renoir, Marguerite *OxFilm, WomWMM*
Renoir, Pierre 1885-1952 *EncWT, FilmEn, FilmgC, HalFC 80, NotNAT B, OxFilm, WhScrn 74, -77, WhoHol B, WorEFlm*
Renoir, Rita *OxFilm*
Renosto, Paolo 1935- *DcCM, NewGrD 80*
Renotte, Hubert 1704-1745? *NewGrD 80*
Renouardt, Jeanne *WhThe*
Renoudet, Pete *WhoHol A*
Renouf, David 1928- *IntWWM 77, -80, WhoMus 72*
Renouf, Henry d1913 *NotNAT B*
Rensch, Gabrielle 1944- *IntWWM 80*
Renshaw, Edyth 1901- *BiE&WWA, NotNAT*
Rensin, Hymen 1904- *IntWWM 77, -80*
Renthall, Charles H Lawyer *BiE&WWA*
Rentia, Anna *NewGrD 80*
Rentius De Ponte Curvo *NewGrD 80*
Renton, Barbara Hampton 1937- *IntWWM 80*
Renton, Edward 1912- *WhoMus 72*
Renvoisy, Richard De 1520?-1586 *NewGrD 80*
Renvoysy, Richard De 1520?-1586 *NewGrD 80*
Renwick, Ruth *Film 2*
Renwick, Wilke Richard 1921- *AmSCAP 80*
Renzi, Anna 1620?-1660? *NewGrD 80[port]*
Renzi, Emma *WhoOp 76*
Renzi, Eva 1944- *FilmgC, ForYSC, HalFC 80, WhoHol A*
Renzini, Anna 1620?-1660? *NewGrD 80[port]*
Reo Speedwagon *ConMuA 80A*
Reome, Aurelian Of *NewGrD 80*
Reparata & The Delrons *RkOn 2A*
Rephuhn, Paul *NewGrD 80*
Repnikova *Film 2*
Repp, Ed Earl *IntMPA 77, -75, -76, -78, -79, -80*
Repp, Stafford 1918-1974 *WhScrn 77, WhoHol B*
Reppa, David 1926- *WhoOp 76*
Reppel, Carmen 1941- *WhoOp 76*
Reppen, Jack 1933-1964 *CreCan 2*
Reppen, John Richard *CreCan 2*
Repper, Charles 1886- *ConAmC*
Repper, Charles 1889- *AmSCAP 66, BiDAmM*
Requa, Charles *Film 2*
Requeno, Vicente 1743-1811 *NewGrD 80*
Requeno, Vincenzo 1743-1811 *NewGrD 80*
Rescher, Gayne *FilmgC, HalFC 80*
Reschke, Heinz 1926- *WhoOp 76*
Reschofsky, Alex 1887- *WhoMus 72*
Rescigno, Nicola *WhoOp 76*
Reser, Harry d1965 *CmpEPM*
Resin, Dan *WhoHol A*
Resinarius, Balthasar 1485?-1544 *NewGrD 80*
Resinarius, Balthasar 1486?-1544 *Baker 78*
Resnais, Alain 1922- *BiDFilm, -81, ConLC 16, DcFM, FilmEn, FilmgC, HalFC 80, IntMPA 78, -79, -80, MovMk[port], OxFilm, WomWMM, WorEFlm*
Resnick, Lee 1923- *AmSCAP 80*
Resnick, Leo *IntMPA 75, -76*
Resnick, Leon 1923- *AmSCAP 66*
Resnicoff, Ethel 1947- *AmSCAP 80*
Resnik, Muriel *BiE&WWA, NotNAT, -A*
Resnik, Regina 1922- *Baker 78, IntWWM 77, -80, MusSN[port], NewEOp 71, NewGrD 80*
Resnik, Regina 1923- *BiDAmM*
Resnik, Regina 1924- *CmOp, WhoMus 72, WhoOp 76*
Reson, Johannes *NewGrD 80*
Resor, Stanley Burnet d1962 *NotNAT B*
Respighi, Ottorino 1879-1936 *Baker 78, BnBkM 80, CmOp, CompSN[port], DancEn 78, DcCom 77, DcCom&M 79, DcPup, MusMk[port], NewEOp 71, NewGrD 80, OxMus*
Ress, Sabine 1904- *CnOxB*
Ressler, Benton Crews d1963 *NotNAT B*
Resta, Agostino 1550?-1586? *NewGrD 80*
Resta, Francis Eugene 1894-1968 *AmSCAP 80, WhScrn 74, -77*
Resta, Natale *NewGrD 80*
Restori, Antonio 1859-1928 *Baker 78*
Restout, Denise 1915- *IntWWM 77, -80*
Restz, Jakub De *NewGrD 80*
Reszke *NewEOp 71*
Reszke, Edouard De *Baker 78*
Reszke, Jean De 1850-1925 *Baker 78, MusMk, NotNAT B*
Reszke, Radomir 1920- *IntWWM 77, -80*
Retallick, Robert Henry 1935- *IntWWM 77, -80*
Retchin, Norman 1919- *IntMPA 77, -75, -76, -78, -79, -80*
Retchitzky, Marcel 1924- *IntWWM 77, -80*
Retford, Ella d1962 *NotNAT B, WhThe*
Retford, William Charles 1875-1970 *NewGrD 80*
Rethberg, Elisabeth 1894-1976 *Baker 78, CmOp, MusSN[port], NewGrD 80*
Rethberg, Elizabeth 1894- *NewEOp 71*
Reti, Rudolf 1885-1957 *Baker 78, BiDAmM, ConAmC, NewGrD 80*
Reti, Rudolph 1885-1957 *NewGrD 80*
Reties, Jill *Film 2*
Rettich, Wilhelm 1892- *Baker 78, IntWWM 77, -80, NewGrD 80*
Rettig, Richard *PupTheA*
Rettig, Tommy 1941- *FilmEn, FilmgC, ForYSC, HalFC 80, IntMPA 77, -75, -76, -78, -79, -80, What 4[port], WhoHol A*
Rettino, Ernest W 1949- *AmSCAP 80*
Retty, Wolf Albach 1908-1967 *WhScrn 77*
Return To Forever *EncJzS 70, IlEncJ, IlEncR*
Retz, Jakub De *NewGrD 80*
Retzel, Frank 1948- *ConAmC, IntWWM 77, -80*
Reubke *NewGrD 80*
Reubke, Adolf 1805-1875 *Baker 78, NewGrD 80*
Reubke, Emil 1836-1885 *Baker 78*
Reubke, Julius 1834-1858 *Baker 78, BnBkM 80, MusMk, NewGrD 80, OxMus*
Reubke, Otto 1842-1913 *Baker 78, NewGrD 80*
Reuchsel, Amedee 1875-1931 *Baker 78*
Reuchsel, Maurice 1880-1968 *Baker 78*
Reuental, Neidhart Von *NewGrD 80*
Reuental, Nithart Von *NewGrD 80*
Reufer-Eichberg, Adele *Film 2*
Reuling, Wilhelm 1802-1879 *Baker 78*
Reulx, Anselme De *NewGrD 80*
Reulx, Anselmo De *NewGrD 80*
Reumert, Poul 1883-1968 *Ent*
Reunion *RkOn 2[port]*
Reusch, Johann 1525?-1582 *NewGrD 80*
Reusch, Johannes 1525?-1582 *NewGrD 80*
Reuschel, Johann Georg *NewGrD 80*
Reusner, Esaias d1680? *NewGrD 80*
Reusner, Esaias 1636-1679 *NewGrD 80*
Reusner, Esajas 1636-1679 *Baker 78*
Reuss, Allan 1915- *BiDAmM, CmpEPM, WhoJazz 72*
Reuss, August 1871-1935 *Baker 78, NewGrD 80*
Reuss, Eduard 1851-1911 *Baker 78, BiDAmM*
Reuss, Wilhelm Franz 1886-1945 *Baker 78*
Reuss-Belce, Luise 1860-1945 *Baker 78*
Reussner, Esaias *NewGrD 80*
Reuter, Florizel Von 1890- *Baker 78, BiDAmM*
Reuter, Fritz 1896-1963 *NewGrD 80*
Reuter, Rudolf 1920- *IntWWM 77, -80*
Reutter, Georg Von, Jr. 1708-1772 *Baker 78, NewGrD 80*
Reutter, Georg Von, Sr. 1656-1738 *Baker 78, NewGrD 80*
Reutter, Hermann 1900- *Baker 78, CmOp, DcCM, NewGrD 80, OxMus*
Reux, Anselme De *NewGrD 80*
Rev, Livia *WhoMus 72*
Revalles, Flora *Film 2*
Revel, Gary Neal 1949- *AmSCAP 80*
Revel, Harry 1905-1958 *AmPS, AmSCAP 66, -80, BestMus, BiDAmM, CmpEPM, HalFC 80, NewGrD 80, NotNAT B, PopAmC, Sw&Ld C*
Revel, Linda Marie 1957- *AmSCAP 80*
Revela, Rita *Film 2*
Revelator Quartet *BiDAmM*
Revelers, The *CmpEPM*
Revell, Dorothy 1879- *WhoStg 1908*
Revelle, Arthur Hamilton 1872-1958 *NotNAT B, WhThe, WhoStg 1908*
Revelle, Hamilton 1872-1958 *Film 1, -2, WhoHol B, WhoStg 1906*
Revelli, William D 1902- *Baker 78*
Revels, The *RkOn*
Revere *NewGrD 80*
Revere, Ann 1903- *MovMk, Vers A[port]*
Revere, Anne *MotPP, PlP&P[port], WhoHol A*
Revere, Anne 1903- *BiE&WWA, FilmEn, FilmgC, ForYSC, HalFC 80, HolCA[port], NotNAT, What 1[port]*
Revere, Anne 1906- *WhThe*
Revere, Anne 1907- *IntMPA 77, -75, -76, -78, -79, -80*
Revere, Giuseppe 1812-1889 *OxThe*
Revere, Paul 1735-1818 *BiDAmM, OxMus*
Revere, Paul And The Raiders *BiDAmM, ConMuA 80A, RkOn[port]*
Revertz *NewGrD 80*
Revesz, Geza 1878-1955 *Baker 78, NewGrD 80*
Revesz, Gyorgy 1927- *FilmEn, WorEFlm*
Revicki, Roberto *ConAmC*
Revier, Dorothy 1904- *FilmEn, Film 2, ThFT[port], TwYS, WhoHol A*
Revier, Dorothy 1909- *ForYSC*
Revier, Harry J 1889- *FilmEn, TwYS A*
Revill, Clive 1930- *BiE&WWA, EncMT, FilmEn, FilmgC, ForYSC, HalFC 80, IntMPA 77, -75, -76, -78, -79, -80, WhoHol A, WhoThe 72, -77*
Reville, Alma 1900- *FilmEn, FilmgC, HalFC 80, WomWMM, WorEFlm*
Reville, Robert d1893 *NotNAT B*
Revitt, Peter 1916-1968 *CnOxB, DancEn 78*
Revol, Claude *WomWMM*
Revolutionary Ensemble, The *BiDAmM*
Revueltas, Silvestre 1899-1940 *AmSCAP 66, -80, Baker 78, BiDAmM, BnBkM 80, CompSN[port], DcCM, NewGrD 80, OxMus*
Revutsky, Lev 1889-1977 *Baker 78*
Revutsky, Lev Nikolayevich 1889-1977 *NewGrD 80*
Revutsky, Levko Mykolayevich 1889-1977 *NewGrD 80*
Rex *Film 2, TwYS*
Rex, Eugen *Film 2*
Rex, Harley 1930- *ConAmC, IntWWM 77*
Rex, Ludwig *Film 2*
Rexford, Eben E 1841-1916 *BiDAmM*
Rexroth, Kenneth 1905- *ConDr 73, -77*
Rexroth-Berg, Natanael *NewGrD 80*
Rey *NewGrD 80*
Rey, Alejandro *ForYSC, HalFC 80, MotPP, WhoHol A*
Rey, Alvino *BgBands 74[port]*
Rey, Alvino 1911- *CmpEPM*
Rey, Alvino 1918?- *BiDAmM*
Rey, Antonia *WhoHol A*
Rey, Cemal Reshid 1904- *Baker 78*
Rey, Cemal Resit 1904- *NewGrD 80*
Rey, Fernando *WhoHol A*
Rey, Fernando 1915- *FilmEn, FilmgC, HalFC 80*
Rey, Fernando 1917- *FilmAG WE*
Rey, Fernando 1919- *MovMk[port]*
Rey, Florian 189-?-1961 *DcFM*
Rey, Jean-Baptiste 1734-1810 *Baker 78, NewGrD 80*

Rey, Jean-Baptiste 1760?-1822? NewGrD 80
Rey, Kathleen Film 2
Rey, Louis-Charles-Joseph 1738-1811 Baker 78, NewGrD 80
Rey, Roberto 1905-1972 WhScrn 77
Rey, Rosa d1969 WhScrn 77, WhoHol B
Reyer, Carolyn 1919- WhoMus 72
Reyer, Ernest 1823-1909 CmOp, GrComp, NewEOp 71, NewGrD 80, OxMus
Reyer, Louis-Etienne-Ernest 1823-1909 Baker 78
Reyes, Efren 1924-1968 WhScrn 77
Reyes, Eva 1915-1970 WhScrn 74, -77, WhoHol B
Reyes, Lucha 1908-1944 WhScrn 77
Reymann, Matthias 1565?-1625? NewGrD 80
Reymann, Rita Marie 1939- IntWWM 77, -80
Reymar Von Zwetel NewGrD 80
Reymar Von Zweten NewGrD 80
Reyn, Judith 1944- CnOxB
Reyna, Ferdinando 1899-1969 CnOxB
Reynaldus Tenorista NewGrD 80
Reynaldus, Fr NewGrD 80
Reynaldus, Franciscus NewGrD 80
Reynaldus, Frate NewGrD 80
Reynaud, Emile 1844-1918 DcFM, OxFilm, WorEFlm
Reynaud, Emile 1884-1918 FilmEn
Reyneau, Gacian 1370?- NewGrD 80
Reynish, Timothy John 1938- IntWWM 77, -80, WhoMus 72
Reynolds OxMus
Reynolds, Abe 1884-1955 WhScrn 74, -77, WhoHol B
Reynolds, Adeline DeWalt 1862-1961 FilmEn, FilmgC, HalFC 80, MotPP, NotNAT B, Vers A[port], WhScrn 74, -77, WhoHol B
Reynolds, Adeline DeWalt 1863-1961 ForYSC
Reynolds, Alfred 1884-1969 WhThe
Reynolds, Ann 1931?- NewGrD 80
Reynolds, Anna 1931?- CmOp, IntWWM 77, -80, NewGrD 80, WhoMus 72, WhoOp 76
Reynolds, Ben FilmEn, WorEFlm
Reynolds, Burt 1936- BiDFilm 81, FilmEn, FilmgC, ForYSC, HalFC 80, IntMPA 77, -75, -76, -78, -79, -80, MotPP, MovMk[port], WhoHol A
Reynolds, Charles H 1931- AmSCAP 80
Reynolds, Charles Heath 1924- ConAmC
Reynolds, Clarke IntMPA 77, -75, -76, -78, -79, -80
Reynolds, Craig 1907-1949 ForYSC, NotNAT B, WhScrn 74, -77, WhoHol B
Reynolds, Dale WhoHol A
Reynolds, Debbie 1932- AmPS A, -B, BiDFilm, -81, CmMov, CmpEPM, EncMT, FilmEn, FilmgC, ForYSC, HalFC 80, IntMPA 77, -75, -76, -78, -79, -80, MGM[port], MotPP, MovMk[port], OxFilm, PlP&P A[port], RkOn, WhoHol A, WorEFlm
Reynolds, Dorothy 1913- WhoThe 72, -77
Reynolds, E Vivian 1866-1952 NotNAT B, WhThe
Reynolds, Eileen Mary 1908- WhoMus 72
Reynolds, Ely Film 2
Reynolds, Erma 1922- ConAmC
Reynolds, Frank NewYTET
Reynolds, Frank E d1962 NotNAT B
Reynolds, Frederick 1764-1841 NotNAT A, -B, OxThe
Reynolds, Gene 1925- ForYSC, HalFC 80, NewYTET, WhoHol A
Reynolds, George B 1951- ConAmC
Reynolds, George Earl 1921- AmSCAP 66
Reynolds, George Francis 1880- WhThe
Reynolds, George French 1927- AmSCAP 80
Reynolds, Gordon 1921- IntWWM 77, -80, WhoMus 72
Reynolds, Harold 1896-1972 WhScrn 77
Reynolds, Herbert AmSCAP 80
Reynolds, Hunter L 1903- AmSCAP 66
Reynolds, Jack 1904- AmSCAP 66, -80
Reynolds, James d1957 NotNAT B
Reynolds, Jane Louisa d1907 NotNAT B
Reynolds, Jimmy James Russel 1907?-1963 WhoJazz 72
Reynolds, Jody RkOn
Reynolds, John T NewYTET
Reynolds, Joseph WhoHol A
Reynolds, Joyce 1924- FilmEn, FilmgC, ForYSC, HalFC 80, IntMPA 77, -75, -76, -78, -79, -80, MotPP
Reynolds, Judy WomWMM B
Reynolds, Kay WhoHol A
Reynolds, Lake 1889-1952 WhScrn 74, -77
Reynolds, Lee AmSCAP 80
Reynolds, Linda Melick 1952- ConAmTC
Reynolds, Lynn E 1889-1927 TwYS A
Reynolds, Malvina ConMuA 80B
Reynolds, Malvina 1900-1978 AmSCAP 66, -80, BiDAmM
Reynolds, Malvina 1901- EncFCWM 69
Reynolds, Marjorie 1921- FilmEn, FilmgC, ForYSC, HalFC 80, IntMPA 77, -75, -76, -78, -79, -80, MotPP, MovMk, WhoHol A
Reynolds, Michael John 1930- IntWWM 77, -80, WhoMus 72
Reynolds, Nick 1933- BiDAmM
Reynolds, Noah d1948 WhScrn 74, -77
Reynolds, Peter 1926-1975 FilmgC, HalFC 80, IlWWBF[port], WhScrn 77, WhoHol A
Reynolds, Quentin 1903-1965 WhScrn 77
Reynolds, Randall Film 2
Reynolds, Robert OxThe
Reynolds, Roger 1934- Baker 78, BiDAmM, CpmDNM 72, -80, ConAmC, DcCM, NewGrD 80
Reynolds, Samuel D 1938- IntWWM 77
Reynolds, Sheldon 1923- FilmgC, HalFC 80, IntMPA 77, -75, -76, -78, -79, -80, WorEFlm
Reynolds, Stephen Charles 1947- IntWWM 77, -80
Reynolds, Steve BlksB&W C
Reynolds, Stuart 1907- IntMPA 77, -75, -76, -78, -79, -80
Reynolds, Thomas d1947 NotNAT B, WhThe
Reynolds, Thomas A 1917- BiDAmM
Reynolds, Tom Film 2
Reynolds, Tom 1866-1942 NotNAT B, WhThe
Reynolds, Tommy BgBands 74
Reynolds, Tommy 1915?- CmpEPM
Reynolds, Tommy 1917- AmSCAP 66
Reynolds, Vera 1900-1962 FilmEn, ForYSC
Reynolds, Vera 1905-1962 Film 2, MotPP, NotNAT B, TwYS. WhScrn 74, -77, WhoHol B
Reynolds, Verne 1926- AmSCAP 80, Baker 78, CpmDNM 74, -78, ConAmC
Reynolds, Walter d1941 NotNAT B
Reynolds, William 1931?- ForYSC, WhoHol A, WhoHrs 80
Reynolds, William H 1910- HalFC 80
Reynolds, William Jensen 1920- AmSCAP 66, -80
Reynolds, Wilson Film 2
Reynoldson, T H d1888 NotNAT B
Reys, Jacob 1540?-1605? NewGrD 80
Reys, Jakub 1540?-1605? NewGrD 80
Reyser, Georg NewGrD 80
Reyzen, Mark 1895- NewGrD 80
Rezac, Ivan 1924-1977 Baker 78, IntWWM 77, -80, NewGrD 80
Rezits, Joseph 1925- IntWWM 80, WhoMus 72
Reznicek, E N Von 1860-1945 NewGrD 80
Reznicek, Emil Nicolaus Von 1860-1945 CmOp
Reznicek, Emil Nikolaus Von 1860-1945 Baker 78, OxMus
Reznicek, Emil Von 1860-1945 MusMk, NewEOp 71
Rezon, Johannes NewGrD 80
Rezzuto, Tom 1929- BiE&WWA
Rhau, Georg 1488-1548 NewGrD 80[port]
Rhauma, Gypsy Film 2
Rhaw, Georg 1488-1548 Baker 78, NewGrD 80[port]
Rhazes NewGrD 80
Rhea, Arthur D, Jr. 1919- IntWWM 77
Rhea, Claude Hiram, Jr. 1927- AmSCAP 80, IntWWM 77, -80
Rhea, Raymond 1910-1970 AmSCAP 66, -80, ConAmC
Rheinberger, Josef Gabriel 1839-1901 GrComp[port], OxMus
Rheinberger, Joseph 1839-1901 Baker 78, BnBkM 80, NewGrD 80
Rheineck, Christoph 1748-1797 NewGrD 80
Rheiner, Judith Diane 1940- IntMPA 77, -78, -79, -80
Rheiner, Samuel IntMPA 77, -75, -76, -78, -79, -80
Rheinhardt NewGrD 80
Rhekopf, Paul Film 2
Rhemann, Eugene Evans 1941- IntWWM 77
Rhene-Baton 1879-1940 Baker 78, OxMus
Rhete, George 1600-1645? NewGrD 80
Rhete, Jerzy NewGrD 80
Rhett, Alicia WhoHol A
Rhetus, Georg 1600-1645? NewGrD 80
Rhetus, Jerzy 1600-1645? NewGrD 80
Rhiemann, Jacob NewGrD 80
Rhine, Jack 1911-1951 WhScrn 74, -77
Rhinehart, Charles Bennett, Jr. 1929- IntWWM 77
Rhinehart, Raymond Patrick 1942- ConAmTC
Rhines, Howard M 1912- AmSCAP 66, -80
Rhinoceros BiDAmM, IlEncR
Rho, Stella 1886- WhThe
Rhoades, Barbara WhoHol A
Rhoads, Patricia 1945- IntWWM 77
Rhoads, William Earl 1918- AmSCAP 80, ConAmC
Rhoda, Sybil Film 2
Rhoden, Elmer C 1893- IntMPA 77, -75, -76, -78, -79, -80
Rhodes, Alfred Dusty d1948 WhScrn 77
Rhodes, Barbara ForYSC
Rhodes, Betty Jane 1921- CmpEPM, ForYSC, HalFC 80
Rhodes, Billie 1906- FilmEn, Film 1, TwYS, WhoHol A
Rhodes, Billy 1906- Film 2
Rhodes, Burt 1923- IntWWM 80
Rhodes, Cherry 1943- IntWWM 77, -80
Rhodes, Christopher WhoHol A
Rhodes, David 1917- AmSCAP 66
Rhodes, Donnelly WhoHol A
Rhodes, E A 1900- IntMPA 77, -75, -76, -78, -79, -80
Rhodes, Elizabeth Film 2
Rhodes, Emma Dora 1899- IntWWM 80, WhoMus 72
Rhodes, Erik 1906- BiE&WWA, FilmEn, FilmgC, ForYSC, HalFC 80, HolCA[port], MovMk, NotNAT, PlP&P[port], WhoHol A
Rhodes, George A 1918- DrBlPA
Rhodes, Grandon ForYSC, WhoHol A
Rhodes, Grayson AmSCAP 80
Rhodes, Hari 1932- DrBlPA, WhoHol A
Rhodes, Harriet WomWMM
Rhodes, Harrison 1871-1929 NotNAT B, WhThe
Rhodes, Helen NewGrD 80
Rhodes, Jane 1929- NewGrD 80
Rhodes, John 1606?- OxThe, PlP&P
Rhodes, Jordan WhoHol A
Rhodes, Joseph William 1901- AmSCAP 80
Rhodes, Keith 1930- WhoMus 72
Rhodes, Lawrence 1939- CnOxB, DancEn 78[port]
Rhodes, Leon S 1916- AmSCAP 66
Rhodes, Leonard William 1952- IntWWM 80
Rhodes, Marjorie WhoHol A
Rhodes, Marjorie 1902- FilmgC, HalFC 80
Rhodes, Marjorie 1903- IntMPA 75, -76, WhoThe 72, -77
Rhodes, Michael 1923- IntWWM 77, -80
Rhodes, Percy William d1956 NotNAT B
Rhodes, Phillip 1940- CpmDNM 79, -80, ConAmC, DcCM
Rhodes, Raymond Compton 1887-1935 NotNAT B
Rhodes, Raymond Crompton 1887-1935 WhThe
Rhodes, Red 1930- IlEncCM
Rhodes, Robert Milford 1931- AmSCAP 80
Rhodes, Stan 1924- AmSCAP 66, -80
Rhodes, Taylor AmSCAP 80
Rhodes, Terry ConMuA 80B
Rhodes, Thomas Anthony 1957- AmSCAP 80
Rhodes, Todd Washington 1900-1965 BiDAmM, WhoJazz 72
Rhodes, Vivian WhoHol A
Rhodes, Willard 1901- Baker 78, IntWWM 77, -80, NewGrD 80
Rhodin, Teddy 1919- CnOxB, DancEn 78

Rhone, Trevor *BlkAmP, MorBAP*
Rhoten, Kenneth Dale 1950- *AmSCAP 80*
Rhudin, Fridolf 1895-1935 *WhScrn 74, -77*
Rhue, Madlyn 1934- *FilmgC, HalFC 80, MotPP, WhoHol A*
Rhue, Madlyn 1938- *ForYSC*
Rhynsburger, H Donovan 1903- *BiE&WWA, NotNAT*
Rhys, Philip Ap *NewGrD 80*
Rhys-Davies, Jennifer 1953- *IntWWM 80*
Rhythm Boys *BiDAmM*
Rhythm Heritage *RkOn 2[port]*
Riabouchinska, Tatiana 1916- *WhThe*
Riabouchinska, Tatiana 1917- *CnOxB, DancEn 78[port]*
Riabynkina, Yelena 1941- *CnOxB, DancEn 78*
Riadis, Emile 1885-1935 *Baker 78*
Riadis, Emile 1886-1935 *DcCM*
Riadis, Emilios 1886-1935 *NewGrD 80*
Rial, Louise d1940 *NotNAT B*
Riann, Paul *ConMuA 80B*
Rianne, Patricia 1943- *CnOxB*
Riano, Juan Facundo 1828-1901 *Baker 78*
Riano, Renie 1899-1971 *ForYSC, HalFC 80, Vers A[port], WhScrn 74, -77, WhoHol B*
Riavme, Helen *Film 1*
Ribafrecha, Martin De *NewGrD 80*
Ribakov, Sergey Gavrilovich 1867-1921 *NewGrD 80*
Ribari, Antal 1924- *Baker 78, NewGrD 80*
Ribary, Antal 1924- *IntWWM 80*
Ribaupierre, Andre De 1893-1955 *NewGrD 80*
Ribayaz, Lucas Ruiz De *NewGrD 80*
Ribbing, Bo Carl Stig 1904- *IntWWM 80*
Ribeirinho 1911- *FilmAG WE[port]*
Ribeiro, Alberto 1920- *FilmAG WE[port]*
Ribeiro, Joy 1956-1972 *WhScrn 77*
Ribeiro, Mario Luis DeSampayo *NewGrD 80*
Ribemont-Dessaignes, Georges 1884- *ModWD*
Riber, Anders 1937- *IntWWM 80*
Riber, Jean-Claude 1934- *IntWWM 77, -80, WhoOp 76*
Ribera, Antonio 1873-1956 *Baker 78*
Ribera, Antonio De *NewGrD 80*
Ribera, Bernardino De d1570? *NewGrD 80*
Ribera, Julian 1858-1934 *Baker 78, NewGrD 80*
Ribgy, Edward 1879-1951 *WhScrn 74*
Ribla, Gertrude 1914- *IntWWM 77, -80*
Ribman, Ronald 1932- *ConDr 73, -77, CroCD, MorBAP, NatPD[port], NotNAT, WhoThe 72, -77*
Ribner, Irving 1921-1972 *BiE&WWA, NotNAT B*
Ribniczki, Jacobo Christophoro *NewGrD 80*
Ribo, Jesus A *NewGrD 80*
Ribock, Justus Johannes Heinrich 1743-1785? *NewGrD 80*
Ribot, Rhoda *AmSCAP 80*
Ribouillault-Bibron, Danielle Marie 1952- *IntWWM 80*
Ricard, Andre 1938- *CreCan 1*
Ricarda, Ana *CnOxB, DancEn 78*
Ricardel, Joe *BgBands 74*
Ricardel, Molly d1963 *NotNAT B*
Ricartsvorde, Jean *NewGrD 80*
Ricaux, Gustave 1884-1961 *CnOxB*
Ricca, John Albert 1900- *AmSCAP 80*
Ricca, Louis 1909- *AmSCAP 66, -80*
Riccati, Count Giordano 1709-1790 *NewGrD 80*
Ricchezza, Donato 1648-1716 *NewGrD 80*
Ricchio, Frank Theodore 1923- *AmSCAP 80*
Ricci, Cesarina *NewGrD 80*
Ricci, Corrado 1858-1934 *Baker 78*
Ricci, Emma *Baker 78*
Ricci, Federico 1809-1877 *Baker 78, NewGrD 80, OxMus*
Ricci, Francesco Pasquale 1732-1817 *NewGrD 80*
Ricci, Giorgio *Baker 78*
Ricci, Luigi 1805-1859 *Baker 78, NewGrD 80, OxMus*
Ricci, Paul J 1914- *CmpEPM, WhoJazz 72*
Ricci, Renzo 1899- *EncWT*
Ricci, Robert J 1938- *ConAmC, IntWWM 77, -80*
Ricci, Ruggiero 1918- *Baker 78, BnBkM 80, IntWWM 77, MusSN[port], NewGrD 80*
Ricci, Ruggiero 1920- *BiDAmM, WhoMus 72*
Ricciardello, Joseph A 1911- *AmSCAP 66, -80*
Ricciardi, William *Film 2*
Ricciarelli, Katia 1946- *CmOp, IntWWM 77, -80, NewGrD 80, WhoOp 76*
Riccieri, Giovanni Antonio *NewGrD 80*
Riccio, Benedetto 1678?-1710? *NewGrD 80*
Riccio, David *NewGrD 80*
Riccio, Giovanni Battista *NewGrD 80*
Riccio, Patrick Joseph 1918- *BiDAmM*
Riccio, Teodore 1540?-1600? *NewGrD 80*
Riccio, Teodoro 1540?-1600? *NewGrD 80*
Ricciotti, Carlo 1681?-1756 *NewGrD 80*
Riccitelli, Elizabeth *WomWMM B*
Riccitelli, Primo 1875-1941 *Baker 78*
Riccius, August Ferdinand 1819-1886 *Baker 78*
Riccius, Karl August 1830-1893 *Baker 78*
Riccoboni *PlP&P*
Riccoboni, Antonio Francesco 1707-1772 *EncWT, OxThe*
Riccoboni, Francois 1707-1772 *CnOxB*
Riccoboni, Luigi 1675?-1753 *NotNAT B, OxThe*
Riccoboni, Luigi Andrea 1676-1753 *EncWT*
Riccoboni, Marie-Jeanne DeLaBoras 1713-1792 *EncWT*
Rice, Professor *PupTheA*
Rice, Andy d1963 *NotNAT B*
Rice, Andy, Jr. *Film 2*
Rice, Bobby G 1944- *CounME 74, -74A, IlEncCM[port]*
Rice, Charles d1880 *NotNAT B*
Rice, Chester 1895- *AmSCAP 66*
Rice, Daddy 1808-1860 *NewGrD 80*
Rice, Dan *PupTheA*
Rice, Dan 1823-1900 *Ent, NotNAT A*
Rice, Darlene *WhoHol A*
Rice, Darol A 1917- *AmSCAP 66*
Rice, Douglas 1942- *ConAmC*
Rice, Edward E 1849-1924 *EncMT*
Rice, Edward Everett *WhoStg 1906, -1908*
Rice, Edward Everett 1848-1924 *NewGrD 80, NotNAT B, WhThe*
Rice, Edward Henry 1900- *WhoMus 72*
Rice, Elmer 1892-1967 *AmSCAP 66, BiE&WWA, CnMD, CnThe, DcLB 7[port], EncWT, Ent[port], FilmgC, HalFC 80, McGEWD, ModWD, NotNAT A, -B, OxThe, PlP&P[port], REnWD[port], WhThe*
Rice, Fanny d1936 *NotNAT B*
Rice, Fenelon Bird 1841-1901 *BiDAmM*
Rice, Florence d1974 *WhoHol B*
Rice, Florence 1907-1974 *FilmEn, HalFC 80, ThFT[port]*
Rice, Florence 1911-1974 *FilmgC, ForYSC, WhScrn 77*
Rice, Frank 1892-1936 *Film 2, TwYS, WhScrn 77, WhoHol B*
Rice, Freddie 1898-1956 *WhScrn 74*
Rice, Gitz Ingraham 1891-1947 *AmSCAP 66, NotNAT B*
Rice, Grantland 1881-1954 *HalFC 80, WhScrn 74, -77, WhoHol B*
Rice, Howard *WhoHol A*
Rice, Jack 1893-1968 *Vers B[port], WhScrn 77*
Rice, Jennifer Madge Celia *WhoMus 72*
Rice, Joan 1930- *FilmEn, FilmgC, ForYSC, HalFC 80, IlWWBF, WhoHol A*
Rice, John 1596?- *OxThe*
Rice, John 1720?-1795 *BiDAmM*
Rice, John C 1858-1915 *FilmEn, Film 1, WhScrn 77*
Rice, Myron B 1864- *WhoStg 1906, -1908*
Rice, Norman 1910-1957 *WhScrn 74, -77, WhoHol B*
Rice, Mrs. P E *PupTheA*
Rice, Peter 1928- *WhoThe 72, -77*
Rice, Robert 1913-1968 *WhScrn 77*
Rice, Robert Gene 1944- *AmSCAP 80*
Rice, Ron 1935-1964 *WorEFlm*
Rice, Sam 1874-1946 *WhScrn 74, -77, WhoHol B*
Rice, Tandy *ConMuA 80B*
Rice, Thomas *AmPS B*
Rice, Thomas Dartmouth 1808-1860 *BiDAmM, Ent, FamA&A[port], NewGrD 80, NotNAT B, OxThe, PlP&P[port]*
Rice, Thomas Nelson 1933- *ConAmC, IntWWM 77, -80*
Rice, Thomas Nelson 1943- *CpmDNM 76*
Rice, Tim 1944- *ConDr 73, -77D, Ent, WhoThe 77*
Rice, Tim & Andrew Lloyd Webber *IlEncR*
Rice, Vernon d1954 *NotNAT B*
Rice, Virginia *PupTheA*
Rice, William Gorham 1856-1945 *Baker 78*
Rice-Davies, Mandy 1944- *What 3[port]*
Rice Paddy Ranger *EncFCWM 69*
Rich, Alan 1924- *ConAmTC*
Rich, Allan *WhoHol A*
Rich, Bernard 1917- *BiDAmM, EncJzS 70, NewGrD 80*
Rich, Brenda Kittredge *PupTheA*
Rich, Buddy 1917- *BgBands 74[port], CmpEPM, EncJzS 70, IlEncJ, NewGrD 80, WhoJazz 72*
Rich, Charles Allan 1934- *AmSCAP 80*
Rich, Charles J 1855-1921 *NotNAT B*
Rich, Charlie 1932- *ConMuA 80A, CounME 74[port], -74A, IlEncR, RkOn[port]*
Rich, Charlie 1934- *IlEncCM[port]*
Rich, Christopher d1714 *NotNAT B, OxThe, PlP&P*
Rich, Claude 1929- *EncWT, FilmAG WE, WhoHol A*
Rich, David Earl 1936- *BiDAmM*
Rich, David Lowell 1923?- *FilmEn, FilmgC, HalFC 80*
Rich, Dick 1909-1967 *WhScrn 77, WhoHol B*
Rich, Don *EncFCWM 69*
Rich, Don 1941- *IlEncCM*
Rich, Doris d1971 *WhoHol B*
Rich, Eddie 1926- *BiE&WWA*
Rich, Frances *WhoHol A*
Rich, Fred 1898-1956 *CmpEPM, WhoJazz 72*
Rich, Freddie 1898-1956 *AmSCAP 66, -80, WhScrn 77, WhoHol B*
Rich, Gladys 1892- *AmSCAP 66, ConAmC*
Rich, Helen d1963 *NotNAT B, WhoHol B*
Rich, Irene *MotPP*
Rich, Irene 1891- *FilmEn, FilmgC, HalFC 80, MovMk[port], ThFT[port], What 1[port], WhoHol A*
Rich, Irene 1894- *Film 1, -2, TwYS*
Rich, Irene 1897- *ForYSC, IntMPA 77, -75, -76, -78, -79, -80*
Rich, John *PlP&P[port]*
Rich, John 1682?-1761 *CnThe, CnOxB, NotNAT B, OxMus*
Rich, John 1691?-1761 *NewGrD 80*
Rich, John 1692?-1761 *DancEn 78, Ent, OxThe*
Rich, John 1925- *FilmEn, FilmgC, HalFC 80, IntMPA 77, -75, -76, -78, -79, -80, NewYTET*
Rich, Lee *NewYTET*
Rich, Lillian d1954 *MotPP, NotNAT B, WhoHol B*
Rich, Lillian 1900-1954 *FilmEn, WhScrn 74, -77*
Rich, Lillian 1902-1954 *Film 1, -2, TwYS*
Rich, Lillian 1905-1954 *ForYSC*
Rich, Martin 1908- *WhoOp 76*
Rich, Max 1897- *AmSCAP 66, -80*
Rich, Michael William 1943- *WhoMus 72*
Rich, Phil 1896-1956 *WhScrn 74, -77*
Rich, Ron 1938- *DrBlPA, WhoHol A*
Rich, Roy 1909-1969 *FilmgC, WhThe*
Rich, Roy 1909-1970 *HalFC 80*
Rich, Ruthanne 1941- *IntWWM 77, -80*
Rich, Selma *AmSCAP 80*
Rich, Thaddeus 1885-1969 *BiDAmM*
Rich, Vivian *Film 1, MotPP*
Richafort, Jean 1480?- *MusMk*
Richafort, Jean 1480?-1547? *NewGrD 80*
Richafort, Jean 1480?-1548 *Baker 78*
Richam, Carl *BlkAmP*
Richard I 1157-1199 *MusMk, NewGrD 80, OxMus*
Richard II 1367-1400 *OxMus*
Richard III 1452-1485 *OxMus*
Richard De Bellengues *NewGrD 80*
Richard, Al d1962 *NotNAT B*
Richard, Balthazar 1600?-1660? *NewGrD 80*
Richard, Cliff 1940- *ConMuA 80A, FilmAG WE, FilmEn, FilmgC, HalFC 80, IlEncR, IlWWBF[port], -A, IntMPA 77, -75, -76, -78, -79, -80, NewGrD 80,*

RkOn 2[port], WhoHol A
Richard, Edmund *ConAmC*
Richard, Etienne 1621?-1669? *NewGrD 80*
Richard, Francois d1650 *NewGrD 80*
Richard, Frida *Film 2*
Richard, Frieda 1873-1946 *WhScrn 74, -77, WhoHol B*
Richard, Fritz *Film 2*
Richard, George N 1892- *BiE&WWA*
Richard, Georges d1891 *NotNAT B*
Richard, Jean-Charles Andre Daniel 1922- *IntWWM 77, -80*
Richard, Jean-Louis 1927- *WorEFlm*
Richard, Keith *ConMuA 80B*
Richard, Lawrence 1942- *IntWWM 77, -80, WhoMus 72*
Richard, Little 1932- *IlEncR[port], WhoHol A*
Richard, Mae *AmSCAP 80*
Richard, Viola *Film 2, TwYS*
Richard-Willm, Pierre 1895- *FilmEn*
Richardinus, Robertus *NewGrD 80*
Richards, A Bate d1876 *NotNAT B*
Richards, Addison d1964 *MotPP, NotNAT B, WhoHol B*
Richards, Addison 1887-1964 *FilmEn, FilmgC, ForYSC, HalFC 80, WhScrn 74, -77*
Richards, Addison 1902-1964 *HolCA[port]*
Richards, Addison 1903-1964 *MovMk, Vers A[port]*
Richards, Angela 1944- *WhoThe 77*
Richards, Ann *MotPP*
Richards, Ann 1918- *FilmEn, FilmgC, ForYSC, HalFC 80, MovMk*
Richards, Ann 1919- *MGM[port], WhoHol A*
Richards, Ann 1935- *BiDAmM*
Richards, Antony John 1930- *IntWWM 77, -80*
Richards, Aubrey *WhoHol A*
Richards, Beah *BiE&WWA, BlkAmP, DrBlPA, HalFC 80, MorBAP, NotNAT, WhoHol A*
Richards, Bernard Roland 1913- *IntWWM 77, WhoMus 72*
Richards, Brinley 1817-1885 *Baker 78*
Richards, Brinley 1819-1885 *NewGrD 80*
Richards, Burt *WhoHol A*
Richards, Charles 1899-1948 *WhScrn 74, -77, WhoHol B*
Richards, Charles 1912- *BiDAmM, EncJzS 70*
Richards, Charles Herbert 1839-1925 *BiDAmM*
Richards, Cicely d1933 *NotNAT B, WhThe*
Richards, Cully 1908- *AmSCAP 66*
Richards, Dave *AmSCAP 80*
Richards, David Bryant 1942- *ConAmTC, NotNAT*
Richards, Denby 1924- *IntWWM 77, -80, WhoMus 72*
Richards, Denis George 1910- *WhoMus 72*
Richards, Dianne 1934- *CnOxB, DancEn 78*
Richards, Dick 1936?- *HalFC 80*
Richards, Don *AmSCAP 80*
Richards, Donald d1953 *NotNAT B*
Richards, Eddie *AmSCAP 80*
Richards, Emil 1932- *AmSCAP 66, -80, BiDAmM, EncJzS 70*
Richards, Frank *WhoHol A*
Richards, George 1755?-1816 *BiDAmM*
Richards, Gordon 1893-1964 *NotNAT B, WhScrn 74, -77, WhoHol B*
Richards, Gordon 1894-1964 *ForYSC*
Richards, Grant 1916-1963 *ForYSC, WhScrn 74, -77, WhoHol B*
Richards, Henry Brinley 1817-1885 *OxMus*
Richards, Howard L, Jr. 1927- *AmSCAP 66, -80, ConAmC*
Richards, James E 1918- *IntWWM 77*
Richards, Jay 1917- *AmSCAP 66, -80*
Richards, Jean *WomWMM*
Richards, Jeff 1922- *FilmEn, ForYSC, HalFC 80, IntMPA 77, -75, -76, -78, -79, -80*
Richards, Jerald R 1918- *AmSCAP 66*
Richards, John Kell 1918- *IntWWM 77, -80*
Richards, Johnny 1911-1968 *BgBands 74, BiDAmM, CmpEPM, EncJzS 70*
Richards, Jon *WhoHol A*
Richards, Julian D 1917- *IntMPA 77, -75, -76, -78, -79, -80*
Richards, Kathleen 1895- *WhoMus 72*
Richards, Keith *ForYSC, WhoHol A*
Richards, Ken *WhoHol A*
Richards, Kim *WhoHol A*
Richards, Lewis Loomis 1881-1940 *Baker 78*
Richards, Lloyd *BiE&WWA, DrBlPA, NotNAT*
Richards, Mary *Film 1*
Richards, Michael Stuart 1928- *WhoMus 72*
Richards, N *PlP&P*
Richards, Norman 1931- *AmSCAP 66, -80*
Richards, Paul 1924-1974 *ForYSC, HalFC 80, WhScrn 77, WhoHol B*
Richards, Pennington *IlWWBF*
Richards, Red 1912- *EncJzS 70, WhoJazz 72*
Richards, Richard R d1925 *NotNAT B*
Richards, Rosa *Film 2*
Richards, Stanley 1918- *BlkAmP, IntMPA 77, -75, -76, -78, -79, -80*
Richards, Stephen *FilmEn, ForYSC, WhoHol A*
Richards, Stephen 1908- *AmSCAP 66, -80*
Richards, Stephen 1935- *AmSCAP 80, ConAmC*
Richards, Susan 1898- *WhThe, WhoHol A*
Richards, Terry *AmSCAP 80*
Richards, Vincent *WhoHol A*
Richards, William Henry 1924- *IntWWM 77*
Richards, William John 1919- *WhoMus 72*
Richardson, Alan 1904-1978 *IntWWM 77, NewGrD 80, WhoMus 72*
Richardson, Alfred Madeley 1868-1949 *Baker 78*
Richardson, Arnold 1914-1973 *NewGrD 80, WhoMus 72*
Richardson, Arthur 1899-1963 *AmSCAP 66, -80*
Richardson, Baury Bradford *Film 2*
Richardson, Ben 1910?- *WhoJazz 72*
Richardson, Carol *WhoOp 76*
Richardson, Charlotte Smith 1775- *BiDAmM*
Richardson, Claiborne Foster 1929- *AmSCAP 66, -80*
Richardson, Clarence Clifford 1918- *BluesWW[port]*
Richardson, Clive 1909- *IntWWM 77, -80*
Richardson, Darrell Ervin 1911- *AmSCAP 80, ConAmC*
Richardson, David Vivian 1941- *IntWWM 77, -80*
Richardson, Dorothy *IntWWM 77, -80*
Richardson, Doug C *PupTheA*
Richardson, Eddie 1903- *NewOrJ*
Richardson, Edward *Film 2*
Richardson, Enid Dorothy 1905- *IntWWM 77, -80, WhoMus 72*
Richardson, Esther *PupTheA*
Richardson, Evelyn May Fox 1902- *CreCan 2*
Richardson, Ferdinand 1558?-1618 *NewGrD 80*
Richardson, Ferdinando Heybourne 1558?-1618 *OxMus*
Richardson, Florence *Film 2*
Richardson, Foster d1942 *NotNAT B*
Richardson, Frank d1913 *WhScrn 77*
Richardson, Frank 1871-1917 *NotNAT B, WhThe*
Richardson, Frank 1898-1962 *Film 2, WhoHol B*
Richardson, Frank A 1892- *IlWWBF*
Richardson, Frankie 1898-1962 *NotNAT B, WhScrn 74, -77*
Richardson, Grace Barrons 1909- *WhoMus 72*
Richardson, Hal Ainslie 1913-1978 *AmSCAP 66, -80*
Richardson, Howard 1917- *BiE&WWA, McGEWD, NotNAT*
Richardson, Ian 1934- *CnThe, PlP&P, WhoHol A, WhoThe 72, -77*
Richardson, J P 1935-1959 *BiDAmM*
Richardson, Jack *ConMuA 80B*
Richardson, Jack 1883- *Film 1, -2, ForYSC, TwYS*
Richardson, Jack 1935- *BiE&WWA, CnMD, CnThe, ConDr 73, -77, CroCD, DcLB 7[port], McGEWD, ModWD, NotNAT, PlP&P, REnWD[port]*
Richardson, James 1817-1863 *BiDAmM*
Richardson, Jerome 1920- *CmpEPM*
Richardson, Jerome C 1920- *BiDAmM*
Richardson, Jerome G 1920- *EncJzS 70*
Richardson, John *Film 2*
Richardson, John 1936- *FilmgC, ForYSC, HalFC 80, WhoHol A, WhoHrs 80[port]*
Richardson, Karl *ConMuA 80B*
Richardson, Kenneth *PupTheA*
Richardson, Larry 1941- *CnOxB*
Richardson, Leander 1856-1918 *NotNAT B, WhThe*
Richardson, Lee 1926- *BiE&WWA, NotNAT*
Richardson, Louis S 1924- *ConAmC*
Richardson, Marilyn Ann 1936- *IntWWM 77, -80, NewGrD 80*
Richardson, Mel *BlkAmP*
Richardson, Myrtle *WhThe*
Richardson, Norman Maurice 1905- *WhoMus 72*
Richardson, Philip John Sampey 1875-1963 *CnOxB, DancEn 78*
Richardson, Sir Ralph 1902- *BiDFilm, -81, BiE&WWA, CnThe, EncWT, Ent[port], FamA&A[port], FilmAG WE[port], FilmEn, FilmgC, ForYSC, HalFC 80, IlWWBF[port], -A, IntMPA 77, -75, -76, -78, -79, -80, MotPP, MovMk[port], NotNAT, -A, OxFilm, OxThe, PlP&P, WhoHol A, WhoHrs 80, WhoThe 72, -77, WorEFlm*
Richardson, Randell 1921- *AmSCAP 66*
Richardson, Ruth Pauline 1930- *IntWWM 77*
Richardson, Samuel 1689-1761 *NewEOp 71*
Richardson, Sharon 1948- *ConAmC*
Richardson, Thomas *MorBAP*
Richardson, Tony 1928- *BiDFilm, -81, BiE&WWA, DcFM, EncWT, Ent, FilmEn, FilmgC, HalFC 80, IlWWBF, IntMPA 77, -75, -76, -78, -79, -80, MovMk[port], NotNAT, OxFilm, WhoThe 72, -77, WomWMM, WorEFlm*
Richardson, Vaughan 1670?-1729 *NewGrD 80*
Richardson, Virgil *MorBAP*
Richardson, William 1876-1937 *WhScrn 77*
Richardson, William Henry 1883- *WhoMus 72*
Richardson, Willis 1889- *BlkAmP, DrBlPA, MorBAP*
Richardson, Woodrow P 1919- *AmSCAP 80*
Richart De Fournival d1260 *NewGrD 80*
Richart De Semilli *NewGrD 80*
Richauffort, Jean *NewGrD 80*
Richault *NewGrD 80*
Richault, Charles-Simon 1780-1866 *Baker 78, NewGrD 80*
Richault, Guillaume-Simon 1805-1877 *NewGrD 80*
Richault, Leon 1839-1895 *NewGrD 80*
Riche, Anthoine Le *NewGrD 80*
Riche, Robert *NatPD[port]*
Richee, Philipp Franz LeSage De *NewGrD 80*
Richelieu 1585-1642 *EncWT*
Richelieu, Cardinal Armand-Jean DuP De 1585-1642 *Ent, OxThe*
Richens, James William 1936- *AmSCAP 80, ConAmC*
Richepin, Elaine *IntWWM 77*
Richepin, Eliane *IntWWM 80*
Richepin, Jacques 1880-1946 *NotNAT B, WhThe*
Richepin, Jean 1849-1926 *McGEWD, ModWD, NewEOp 71, NotNAT B, OxThe, WhThe*
Richers, Herbert 1923- *IntMPA 77, -75, -76, -78, -79*
Riches, Edgar David 1935- *WhoMus 72*
Richey, Angela 1931- *IntWWM 77, -80*
Richfield, Edwin *WhoHol A*
Richings, Peter 1798-1871 *BiDAmM*
Richler, Mordecai 1931- *CreCan 1*
Richman, Abraham Samuel 1921- *BiDAmM*
Richman, Al 1885-1936 *WhScrn 74, -77*
Richman, Arthur 1886-1944 *NotNAT B, WhThe*
Richman, Boomie 1921- *CmpEPM*
Richman, Charles 1870-1940 *ForYSC, NotNAT B, Vers B[port], WhScrn 74, -77, WhThe, WhoHol B, WhoStg 1906, -1908*
Richman, Charles 1879-1940 *Film 1, -2, TwYS*
Richman, David Alan 1947- *AmSCAP 80*
Richman, Harry 1895-1972 *AmPS B, AmSCAP 66, -80, BiE&WWA, CmpEPM, EncMT, HalFC 80, NotNAT A, -B, What 1[port], WhScrn 77, WhThe, WhoHol B*

Richman, Jonathan 1952- *ConMuA 80A, IlEncR*
Richman, Marian 1922-1956 *WhScrn 77*
Richman, Mark 1927- *BiE&WWA, FilmgC, ForYSC, HalFC 80, IntMPA 77, -75, -76, -78, -79, -80, MotPP, NotNAT*
Richman, Peter Mark 1927- *WhoHol A*
Richman, Stella *NewYTET*
Richmann, Jacob d1720 *NewGrD 80*
Richmond, Al *Film 2*
Richmond, Albert *IntWWM 77, -80*
Richmond, Charles Daniel 1935- *BiDAmM*
Richmond, Dannie 1935- *EncJzS 70*
Richmond, Edna *Film 2*
Richmond, James Erskine 1915- *AmSCAP 80*
Richmond, June *BlksB&W C*
Richmond, June 1915-1962 *CmpEPM, WhoJazz 72*
Richmond, Kane 1906-1973 *FilmEn, FilmgC, ForYSC, HalFC 80, WhScrn 77, WhoHol B, WhoHrs 80*
Richmond, Kim Robert 1940- *AmSCAP 80*
Richmond, Louis B 1942- *IntWWM 77, -80*
Richmond, Miles C 1930- *BiDAmM*
Richmond, Paul David 1941- *AmSCAP 80*
Richmond, Susan 1894-1959 *NotNAT B, WhThe*
Richmond, Ted 1912- *FilmgC, HalFC 80, IntMPA 77, -75, -76, -78, -79, -80*
Richmond, Thomas L 1935- *ConAmC*
Richmond, Tony 1942- *HalFC 80*
Richmond, Virginia 1932- *AmSCAP 66, -80*
Richmond, Warner 1895-1948 *Film 1, -2, ForYSC, TwYS, WhScrn 74, -77, WhoHol B*
Richner, Thomas Benjamin 1911- *WhoMus 72*
Richter, Ada *AmSCAP 66, -80, IntWWM 77*
Richter, Alfred 1846-1919 *Baker 78*
Richter, Anton Karl *NewGrD 80*
Richter, Caspar 1944- *WhoOp 76*
Richter, Clifford G 1917- *AmSCAP 80*
Richter, Ellen *Film 2*
Richter, Ernst Friedrich 1808-1879 *Baker 78, NewGrD 80, OxMus*
Richter, Ferdinand Tobias 1651-1711 *Baker 78, NewGrD 80*
Richter, Francis William 1888-1938 *Baker 78*
Richter, Franz Xaver 1709-1789 *Baker 78, MusMk[port], NewGrD 80[port]*
Richter, Frederico 1932- *IntWWM 77, -80*
Richter, George *Film 2*
Richter, Hans 1843-1916 *Baker 78, BnBkM 80, CmOp, MusMk, MusSN[port], NewEOp 71, NewGrD 80[port], OxMus*
Richter, Hans 1888-1976 *DcFM, FilmEn, FilmgC, HalFC 80, MovMk[port], OxFilm, WhoHol C, WorEFlm*
Richter, Harmann Lukas 1923- *IntWWM 80*
Richter, Hedi 1936- *CnOxB*
Richter, Hermann Luka 1923- *IntWWM 77*
Richter, Johann Christoph 1700-1785 *NewGrD 80*
Richter, Johann Paul Friedrich *NewGrD 80*
Richter, John *Film 2*
Richter, Karl 1926- *BnBkM 80, IntWWM 77, -80, NewGrD 80*
Richter, Lukas 1923- *NewGrD 80*
Richter, Marga *WomCom*
Richter, Marga 1926- *AmSCAP 66, -80, CpmDNM 78, -79, ConAmC, IntWWM 77, -80*
Richter, Marion Morrey 1900- *ConAmC, IntWWM 77, -80*
Richter, Nico Max 1915-1945 *Baker 78, NewGrD 80*
Richter, Paul 1896-1961 *Film 2, NotNAT B, WhScrn 74, -77, WhoHol B*
Richter, Sviatoslav 1914- *MusMk[port], MusSN[port]*
Richter, Sviatoslav 1915- *Baker 78, BnBkM 80, NewGrD 80[port], WhoMus 72*
Richter, Svyatoslav Theofilovich 1915- *IntWWM 77, -80*
Richter, W D *IntMPA 80*
Richter, William B 1901- *AmSCAP 66*
Richter-Haaser, Ernst Max Hans 1912- *IntWWM 77, -80*
Richter-Haaser, Hans 1912- *NewGrD 80, WhoMus 72*
Richter-Herf, Franz 1920- *IntWWM 77, -80*
Ricieri, Giovanni Antonio 1679-1746 *NewGrD 80*
Rick And The Keens *RkOn*
Rickaby, J W *WhThe*
Rickard, Tex *Film 2*
Rickardsson, Paul Gotthard 1929- *IntWWM 77*
Rickenbacher, Karl Anton 1940- *IntWWM 77, -80*
Ricker, Earl D 1926- *AmSCAP 80*
Ricker, Ramon Lee 1943- *AmSCAP 80, IntWWM 77*
Rickerson, Martha 1942- *IntWWM 77*
Ricketson, Frank H, Jr. *IntMPA 77, -75, -76, -78, -79, -80*
Ricketts, Charles 1866-1931 *NotNAT A, -B, OxThe, PlP&P, WhThe*
Ricketts, Frederick Joseph *NewGrD 80*
Ricketts, Frederick Joseph 1881-1945 *Baker 78, BiDAmM*
Ricketts, Joan D 1926- *IntWWM 77*
Ricketts, John Bill 1760-1799 *Ent*
Ricketts, Thomas 1853-1939 *WhScrn 74, -77*
Ricketts, Tom d1938 *ForYSC*
Ricketts, Tom d1939 *Film 1, -2, TwYS, WhoHol B*
Rickles, Don 1926- *FilmgC, ForYSC, HalFC 80, JoeFr[port], WhoHol A, WhoHrs 80*
Ricks, Archie *Film 2*
Ricks, James d1974 *WhScrn 77*
Ricks, Lee *AmSCAP 80*
Ricksecker, Peter 1791-1873 *BiDAmM*
Ricksen, Lucille 1907-1925 *Film 2, WhoHol B*
Rickson, Joe *Film 2*
Rickson, Lucille 1907-1925 *WhScrn 74, -77*
Rico, Mona *Film 2, WhoHol A*
Ricordi *BnBkM 80, NewGrD 80*
Ricordi, Giovanni 1785-1853 *Baker 78, NewEOp 71, NewGrD 80*
Ricordi, Giulio 1840-1912 *NewGrD 80*
Ricordi, Guilio 1840-1912 *Baker 78*
Ricordi, Tito 1811-1888 *Baker 78, NewGrD 80*
Ricordi, Tito 1865-1933 *Baker 78, NewGrD 80*
Riddell, Don 1928- *IntWWM 77*
Riddell, Donald 1930- *IntWWM 77*
Riddell, George d1944 *NotNAT B*
Riddell, Joyce 1921- *IntWWM 77, -80, WhoMus 72*
Ridderbusch, Karl 1932- *CmOp, NewGrD 80, WhoOp 76*
Ridderstrom, Bo 1937- *IntWWM 77, -80*
Riddick, Jeff 1907- *NewOrJ[port]*
Riddick, Johnny 1901- *NewOrJ*
Riddick, Kathleen 1907- *WhoMus 72*
Riddick, Richard 1904- *NewOrJ*
Riddick, Tom 1900- *NewOrJ*
Riddle, Frederick Craig 1912- *NewGrD 80, WhoMus 72*
Riddle, Hal *WhoHol A*
Riddle, Jim d1976? *WhScrn 77*
Riddle, Nelson 1921- *AmPS A, -B, BiDAmM, CmpEPM, ConAmC, FilmgC, HalFC 80, RkOn*
Riddle, Pauline Peck 1932- *IntWWM 77, -80*
Riddle, Peter H 1939- *IntWWM 77, -80*
Riddle, R Richard 1936- *AmSCAP 66*
Riddle, R Richard 1940- *AmSCAP 80*
Riddle, Richard *WhScrn 74, -77*
Ridenour, Valerie Dunn *AmSCAP 80*
Rideout, Patricia 1931- *CreCan 2*
Rider-Kelsey, Corinne 1877-1947 *Baker 78*
Rider-Kelsey, Corinne 1880-1947 *BiDAmM*
Ridett, Reginald Edgar *WhoMus 72*
Ridge, Bradley B 1926- *AmSCAP 80*
Ridge, Clyde Herman 1914- *AmSCAP 80*
Ridge, Walter J 1900-1968 *WhScrn 74, -77*
Ridgeley, John 1909-1968 *FilmgC, HalFC 80, MotPP*
Ridgely, Cleo d1962 *NotNAT B, WhoHol B*
Ridgely, Cleo 1893-1962 *Film 1, -2, TwYS*
Ridgely, Cleo 1894-1962 *WhScrn 74, -77*
Ridgely, John 1909-1968 *FilmEn, ForYSC, MovMk, Vers B[port], WhScrn 74, -77, WhoHol B*
Ridgely, Richard 1910- *AmSCAP 66*
Ridgely, Robert *WhoHol A*
Ridges, Stanley d1951 *NotNAT B, WhoHol B*
Ridges, Stanley 1891-1951 *Film 2, HolCA[port]*
Ridges, Stanley 1892-1951 *FilmEn, FilmgC, ForYSC, HalFC 80, MovMk, Vers A[port], WhScrn 74, -77*
Ridgeway, Frank 1931- *IntWWM 77, -80*
Ridgeway, Fritz *Film 2*
Ridgeway, Fritzi 1898-1960 *ForYSC*
Ridgeway, Fritzi 1898-1961 *WhScrn 74, -77, WhoHol B*
Ridgeway, Fritzie 1898-1960 *Film 1, -2, TwYS*
Ridgeway, Peter d1938 *NotNAT B*
Ridgeway, Philip 1891-1954 *NotNAT B, WhThe*
Ridgeway, Philip 1920- *WhThe*
Ridgewell, Audrey 1904-1968 *WhScrn 77*
Ridgewell, George 1870?-1935 *FilmEn*
Ridgley, Tommy 1925- *BluesWW[port]*
Ridgley, William 1882-1961 *NewOrJ[port]*
Ridgway, Jack *Film 1*
Ridgwell, George 1870?-1935 *IlWWBF*
Ridky, Jaroslav 1897-1956 *Baker 78, NewGrD 80*
Ridler, Anne Barbara 1912- *ConDr 73, -77*
Ridler, Philipp Jakob *NewGrD 80*
Ridley, Arnold 1896- *WhoThe 72, -77*
Ridley, Clifford Anthony 1935- *ConAmTC*
Ridley, Larry *EncJzS 70*
Ridley, Laurence Howard, II 1937- *IntWWM 77, -80*
Ridley, Laurence Howard, Jr. 1935- *EncJzS 70*
Ridley, Michael Hunter 1948- *IntWWM 77*
Ridley, Robert 1901-1958 *WhScrn 74, -77*
Ridout, Alan John 1934- *IntWWM 77, -80, NewGrD 80, WhoMus 72*
Ridout, Godfrey 1918- *Baker 78, CreCan 2, DcCM, IntWWM 77, -80, NewGrD 80*
Riechers, August 1836-1893 *Baker 78*
Riechers, Helene 1869-1957 *WhScrn 74, -77*
Rieck, Carl Friedrich d1704 *NewGrD 80*
Rieck, Karl Friedrich d1704 *NewGrD 80*
Riecker, Charles J 1934- *WhoOp 76*
Rieckhoff, Gustav John, Jr. 1926- *IntWWM 77*
Riedel, Carl 1827-1888 *NewGrD 80*
Riedel, Friedrich Wilhelm 1929- *IntWWM 77, -80, NewGrD 80*
Riedel, Georg 1676-1738 *NewGrD 80*
Riedel, Georg 1934- *EncJzS 70*
Riedel, Karl 1827-1888 *Baker 78*
Riederer, Johann Bartholomaus 1720?-1771 *NewGrD 80*
Riedl, Josef Anton 1927- *NewGrD 80*
Riedt, Friedrich Wilhelm 1710-1783 *Baker 78, NewGrD 80*
Riefenstahl, Leni 1902- *BiDFilm, -81, ConLC 16, DcFM, FilmEn, Film 2, FilmgC, HalFC 80, OxFilm, WhoHol A, WomWMM, WorEFlm*
Rieffler, Monsieur *Film 2*
Riefling, Robert 1911- *IntWWM 77, -80, WhoMus 72*
Riegal, Charles *Film 2*
Riegel *NewGrD 80*
Riegel, Antoine 1745?-1807? *NewGrD 80*
Riegel, Anton 1745?-1807? *NewGrD 80*
Riegel, Heinrich Joseph 1741-1799 *Baker 78*
Riegel, Kenneth 1938- *WhoOp 76*
Rieger *NewGrD 80*
Rieger, Franz 1812-1885 *NewGrD 80*
Rieger, Fritz 1910- *WhoMus 72*
Rieger, Gottfried 1764-1855 *NewGrD 80*
Rieger, Gustav 1848-1905 *NewGrD 80*
Rieger, Otto 1847-1903 *NewGrD 80*
Rieger, Otto 1880-1920 *NewGrD 80*
Riegger, Wallingford 1885-1961 *Baker 78, BiDAmM, BnBkM 80, CompSN[port], CnOxB, ConAmC, DancEn 78, DcCM, MusMk, NewGrD 80[port], OxMus*
Riegle, Barbara Katherine Rickard 1931- *WomWMM B*
Riegler, Francois Sav *NewGrD 80*
Riegler, Frantisek Pavel *NewGrD 80*
Riegler, Franz Paul *NewGrD 80*
Riegler, Franz Xaver *NewGrD 80*
Riego, Teresa Clotilde Del 1876-1968 *OxMus*
Riehl, Kate *WhoHol A*
Riehl, Wilhelm Heinrich Von 1823-1897 *Baker 78*
Riehm, Diethard 1940- *IntWWM 77, -80*

Riehm, Rolf 1937- *NewGrD 80*
Riekelt, Gustave *Film 2*
Riel, Alex Poul 1940- *EncJzS 70*
Riem, Friedrich Wilhelm 1779-1857 *Baker 78*
Rieman, Johannes *Film 2*
Riemann, Hugo 1849-1919 *Baker 78, NewGrD 80, OxMus*
Riemann, Jacob *NewGrD 80*
Riemann, Johannes 1887-1959 *WhScrn 74, -77*
Riemann, Ludwig 1863-1927 *Baker 78*
Riemann, Margarete Hildegard 1907- *IntWWM 77*
Riemenschneider, Albert 1878-1950 *Baker 78, BiDAmM, NewGrD 80*
Riemenschneider, Johann Gottfried *NewGrD 80*
Riemer, Otto 1902-1977 *NewGrD 80*
Riemer, Rudolf 1935- *WhoOp 76*
Riemersma, Coby 1905- *IntWWM 77, -80*
Riemschneider, Johann Gottfried *NewGrD 80*
Riemsdijk, Johan Cornelis Marius Van 1841-1895 *NewGrD 80*
Riepe, Russell Casper 1945- *AmSCAP 80, CpmDNM 80, ConAmC, IntWWM 77, -80*
Riepel, Joseph 1709-1782 *Baker 78, NewGrD 80*
Riepp, Karl Joseph 1710-1775 *NewGrD 80*
Rierson, Richard D 1929- *AmSCAP 66, -80*
Ries *NewGrD 80*
Ries, Adolph 1837-1899 *NewGrD 80*
Ries, Anna Maria 1745?-1794? *NewGrD 80*
Ries, Ferdinand 1784-1838 *Baker 78, NewGrD 80, OxMus*
Ries, Franz 1755-1846 *NewGrD 80*
Ries, Franz 1846-1932 *Baker 78, NewGrD 80*
Ries, Franz Anton 1755-1846 *Baker 78, OxMus*
Ries, Hubert 1802-1886 *Baker 78, NewGrD 80, OxMus*
Ries, Johann 1723-1784 *NewGrD 80*
Ries, Joseph 1791-1882 *NewGrD 80*
Ries, Louis 1830-1913 *NewGrD 80*
Ries, William J 1895-1955 *WhScrn 74, -77*
Riesel, Victor *ConAmTC*
Riesemann, Oscar Von 1880-1934 *Baker 78*
Riesemann, Oskar Von 1880-1934 *NewGrD 80*
Riesenfeld, Hugo 1879-1939 *AmSCAP 66, -80, BiDAmM, ConAmC A*
Riesner, Charles Francis 1887-1962 *AmSCAP 66, -80, FilmEn, Film 2*
Riesner, Chuck 1887-1962 *WhoHol B*
Riesner, Dean 1930?- *HalFC 80, IntMPA 77, -75, -76, -78, -79, WhoHol A*
Rieter-Biedermann, J Melchior 1811-1876 *Baker 78*
Rieter-Biedermann, Jakob Melchior 1811-1876 *NewGrD 80*
Riethmuller, Heinrich 1921- *IntWWM 77, WhoMus 72*
Riethof, Peter W *IntMPA 77, -75, -76, -78, -79*
Rieti, Vittorio 1898- *Baker 78, CpmDNM 80, CnOxB, ConAmC, DancEn 78, DcCM, IntWWM 77, MusMk, NewGrD 80, OxMus, WhoMus 72*
Rietsch, Heinrich 1860-1927 *Baker 78, NewGrD 80*
Rietschel, Georg Christian 1842-1914 *Baker 78*
Rietstap, Ine 1929- *DancEn 78*
Rietti, Victor 1888-1963 *NotNAT B, WhScrn 74, -77, WhThe, WhoHol B*
Rietty, Robert 1923- *WhoHol A, WhoThe 72, -77*
Rietz, Eduard 1802-1832 *NewGrD 80*
Rietz, Julius 1812-1877 *Baker 78, NewGrD 80*
Rieu, Anselmo De *NewGrD 80*
Rieunier, Jean-Paul Michel Andre Marie 1933- *IntWWM 80*
Riezler, Walter 1878-1956 *Baker 78*
Rifbjerg, Klaus 1931- *CroCD*
Rifkin, Joshua 1944- *EncJzS 70, IlEncR, NewGrD 80*
Rifkin, Julian 1915- *IntMPA 77, -75, -76, -78, -79, -80*
Rifkin, Maurice J 1915- *IntMPA 77, -75, -76, -78, -79*
Rifkin, Ron *WhoHol A*
Rifkind, Julie *ConMuA 80B*
Rifkind, Marilyn A 1949- *IntWWM 77, -80*
Riga, Nadine 1909-1968 *WhScrn 74, -77, WhoHol B*
Rigacci, Bruno 1921- *WhoOp 76*
Rigas, George *Film 2*
Rigatti, Giovanni Antonio 1615-1649 *NewGrD 80*
Rigaud, George *WhoHol A*
Rigaud, Louis De *NewGrD 80*
Rigby, Arthur d1971 *WhoHol A, -B*
Rigby, Arthur 1870-1944 *NotNAT B, WhThe*
Rigby, Arthur 1900-1971 *WhScrn 77, WhoThe 72, -77*
Rigby, Arthur 1901-1971 *WhScrn 74*
Rigby, Edward 1879-1951 *FilmgC, HalFC 80, IlWWBF, NotNAT B, WhScrn 77, WhThe, WhoHol B*
Rigby, Frank J d1963 *NotNAT B*
Rigby, Harry 1925- *EncMT, NotNAT*
Rigby, Terence *WhoHol A*
Rigel *NewGrD 80*
Rigel, Antoine 1745?-1807? *NewGrD 80*
Rigel, Henri-Jean 1772-1852 *Baker 78, NewGrD 80*
Rigel, Henri-Joseph 1741-1799 *NewGrD 80*
Rigel, Louis 1769-1811 *NewGrD 80*
Rigg, Diana 1938- *FilmEn, FilmgC, ForYSC, HalFC 80, IlWWBF, IntMPA 77, -75, -76, -78, -79, -80, MotPP, PlP&P, WhoHol A, WhoHrs 80[port], WhoThe 72, -77*
Riggenbach, Marie Bond 1916- *IntWWM 77*
Riggins, Herbert L 1948- *ConAmC*
Riggs, John Frederick *AmSCAP 80*
Riggs, Lynn 1899-1954 *CnMD, McGEWD, ModWD, NotNAT B, PlP&P, WhThe*
Riggs, Ralph d1951 *NotNAT B, WhoHol B*
Riggs, Sarah *WomWMM*
Riggs, Tommy 1908-1967 *WhScrn 74, -77, WhoHol B*
Riggs, William d1975 *WhScrn 77*
Righetti, Geltrude 1793-1862 *NewGrD 80*
Righi, Gioseffo *NewGrD 80*
Righi, Giovanni 1577-1613 *NewGrD 80*
Righi, Giuseppe Maria *NewGrD 80*
Righini, Pietro 1907- *NewGrD 80*
Righini, Vincenzo 1756-1812 *Baker 78, NewGrD 80*
Righteous Brothers, The *BiDAmM, ConMuA 80A, IlEncR[port], RkOn*
Rightmire, William H 1857-1933 *WhScrn 74, -77*
Righton, Edward C d1899 *NotNAT B*
Rigler, Francois Sav 1747?-1796 *NewGrD 80*
Rigler, Franz Paul 1747?-1796 *NewGrD 80*
Rigler, Franz Xaver 1747?-1796 *NewGrD 80*
Rignold, George d1912 *NotNAT B, WhThe*
Rignold, Harry *Film 2*
Rignold, Henry d1873 *NotNAT B*
Rignold, Hugo 1905-1976 *Baker 78, NewGrD 80, WhoMus 72*
Rignold, Lionel d1919 *NotNAT B, WhThe*
Rignold, Marie d1932 *NotNAT B*
Rignold, Susan d1895 *NotNAT B*
Rignold, William d1904 *NotNAT B*
Rignold, William Henry d1910 *NotNAT B*
Rigor, Laura Frances 1920- *IntWWM 77, -80*
Riha, Bobby 1958- *WhoHol A*
Rihani, Neguib 1891-1949 *WhScrn 74, -77*
Rihovsky, Vojtech 1871-1950 *NewGrD 80*
Rihtman, Cvjetko 1902- *IntWWM 80, NewGrD 80*
Riis, Donald L 1938- *AmSCAP 80*
Riisager, Knudage 1897-1974 *Baker 78, CompSN[port], CnOxB, DcCM, NewGrD 80, WhoMus 72*
Riisna, Ene *WomWMM B*
Rijavec, Andrej 1937- *IntWWM 77, -80*
Rijspoort, Jan *NewGrD 80*
Riker, Franklin Wing 1876-1958 *BiDAmM*
Rilchard, Frida *Film 2*
Rilety, Anna *Film 2*
Riley, Amos 1879?-1925 *NewOrJ[port]*
Riley, Ann Marion 1928- *ConAmC*
Riley, Ben 1933- *EncJzS 70*
Riley, Benjamin A 1933- *EncJzS 70*
Riley, Brooks *WomWMM*
Riley, Clayton 1935- *DrBlPA, MorBAP*
Riley, Dennis 1943- *CpmDNM 80, ConAmC, IntWWM 77, -80, NewGrD 80*
Riley, Doctor Music 1945- *EncJzS 70*
Riley, Doug 1945- *EncJzS 70*
Riley, Edna Goldsmith d1962 *NotNAT B*
Riley, Edward 1769-1829 *BiDAmM*
Riley, Edward C 1800?-1871 *BiDAmM*
Riley, George 1900-1972 *WhScrn 77, WhoHol B*
Riley, Herman 1940- *EncJzS 70*
Riley, Howard 1943- *EncJzS 70, IntWWM 77, WhoMus 72*
Riley, Jack *WhoHol A*
Riley, Jack Slim 1895-1933 *WhScrn 74, -77, WhoHol B*
Riley, James 1922- *IntWWM 77*
Riley, James R 1938- *AmSCAP 80, CpmDNM 79, ConAmC*
Riley, James Whitcomb 1849-1916 *AmSCAP 66, -80*
Riley, Jean 1916- *NatPD[port]*
Riley, Jeannie C 1945- *CounME 74[port], -74A, IlEncCM, RkOn 2[port]*
Riley, Jeannine *WhoHol A*
Riley, John Arthur 1920- *Baker 78, ConAmC, IntWWM 77, -80*
Riley, John Howard 1943- *IntWWM 80*
Riley, Lawrence 1891-1975 *BiE&WWA, NotNAT B*
Riley, Lawrence 1897- *NotNAT*
Riley, Marin *WhoHol A*
Riley, Mike 1904- *AmSCAP 66, -80, CmpEPM*
Riley, Mike 1907?- *WhoJazz 72*
Riley, Nancy *WomWMM*
Riley, Ron *ConMuA 80B*
Riley, Ronald H 1908- *IntMPA 77, -75, -76, -78*
Riley, Stanley 1901- *IntWWM 77, WhoMus 72*
Riley, Terry 1935- *Baker 78, ConAmC, DcCM, NewGrD 80*
Riley, Theodore 1924- *NewOrJ*
Riley, William *Film 2, OxMus*
Riley And Farley *BgBands 74*
Rill, Eli 1926- *BiE&WWA, NotNAT*
Rilla, Walter 1895- *FilmEn, Film 2, FilmgC, HalFC 80, IntMPA 77, -75, -76, -78, -79, -80, WhoHol A*
Rilla, Wolf 1920- *FilmEn, FilmgC, HalFC 80, IlWWBF, WhoHrs 80*
Rilling, Helmuth 1933- *BnBkM 80, NewGrD 80*
Rillon, John T *Film 2*
Rim, Carlo *DcFM, FilmEn*
Rimac, Ciro Campos 1894-1973 *WhScrn 77*
Rimbaud, Arthur *OxMus*
Rimbault, Edward Francis 1816-1876 *Baker 78, NewGrD 80, OxMus*
Rimbault, Stephen Francis 1773-1837 *Baker 78*
Rimington, A Wallace *OxMus*
Rimini, Ruggero 1947- *WhoOp 76*
Rimmer, Frederick William 1914- *IntWWM 77, -80, WhoMus 72*
Rimmer, John Francis 1939- *IntWWM 77, -80*
Rimmer, Roy Edward 1930- *WhoMus 72*
Rimon, Meir 1946- *IntWWM 77, -80*
Rimonte, Pedro 1570?-1618? *NewGrD 80*
Rimskaya-Korsakova, Yuliya Lazarevna *NewGrD 80*
Rimsky, Nicholas *Film 2*
Rimsky-Korsakof, Nicholas 1844-1908 *OxMus*
Rimsky-Korsakov, Andrei 1878-1940 *Baker 78*
Rimsky-Korsakov, Andrey Nikolayevich 1878-1940 *NewGrD 80*
Rimsky-Korsakov, Georgi 1901-1965 *Baker 78*
Rimsky-Korsakov, Georgy Mikhaylovich 1901-1965 *NewGrD 80*
Rimsky-Korsakov, Nicholas Andreievitch 1844-1908 *DancEn 78*
Rimsky-Korsakov, Nicolai 1844-1908 *CnOxB, DcCom 77[port]*
Rimsky-Korsakov, Nikolai 1844-1908 *Baker 78, CmpBCM, GrComp[port], MusMk[port], NewEOp 71*
Rimsky-Korsakov, Nikolas 1844-1908 *DcCom&M 79*
Rimsky-Korsakov, Nikolay 1844-1908 *BnBkM 80[port], CmOp, NewGrD 80[port]*
Rimur *OxMus*
Rin Tin Tin 1916-1930 *Film 2, TwYS*
Rin Tin Tin 1916-1932 *FilmEn, FilmgC, ForYSC, HalFC 80, WhScrn 74, -77, WhoHol B*

Rin Tin Tin 1918-1932 *OxFilm*
Rin Tin Tin, Jr. *WhScrn 74, -77*
Rinaldi *PupTheA*
Rinaldi, Alberto 1939- *WhoOp 76*
Rinaldi, Margherita 1935- *NewGrD 80, WhoOp 76*
Rinaldi, Mario 1903- *WhoMus 72*
Rinaldi, Maurizio 1937- *WhoOp 76*
Rinaldi, Tina C *Film 2*
Rinaldi, William *Film 2*
Rinaldo 1884- *WhThe*
Rinaldo Dall'Arpa d1603 *NewGrD 80*
Rinaldo DiCapua 1705?-1780? *NewGrD 80*
Rinaldo DiCapua 1710?- *Baker 78*
Rinaldo, Duncan 1904- *Film 2, TwYS*
Rinaldo, Rinaldini *Film 2*
Rinaudo, Mario 1936- *WhoOp 76*
Rinch-Smiles, Frank *Film 2*
Rinck, Johann Christian Heinrich 1770-1846 *Baker 78, NewGrD 80, OxMus*
Rinckart, Martin 1586-1648 *NewGrD 80*
Rindell, Matti A 1934- *IntWWM 77, -80*
Rindler, Milton 1898- *BiE&WWA, NotNAT*
Rinehardt, Harry *Film 2*
Rinehart, John 1937- *ConAmC*
Rinehart, Marilyn *ConAmC*
Rinehart, Mary Roberts 1876-1958 *HalFC 80, ModWD, NotNAT B, WhThe*
Rines, Joseph 1902- *AmSCAP 66, -80*
Rinfret, Jean-Claude 1929- *CreCan 2*
Ring, Blanche d1961 *AmPS B, Film 1, WhoHol B*
Ring, Blanche 1871-1961 *EncMT*
Ring, Blanche 1872-1961 *BiDAmM, Film 2*
Ring, Blanche 1876-1961 *NotNAT B, WhScrn 74, -77, WhoStg 1908*
Ring, Blanche 1877-1961 *CmpEPM, WhThe*
Ring, Cyril 1893-1967 *Film 2, ForYSC, WhScrn 74, -77, WhoHol B*
Ring, Frances 1882-1951 *NotNAT B, WhScrn 74, -77, WhThe, WhoStg 1906, -1908*
Ring, Guy Layton 1922- *IntWWM 77, -80, WhoMus 72*
Ring, Sutherland *Film 1*
Ringbom, Nils-Eric 1907- *Baker 78, IntWWM 77, -80, NewGrD 80*
Ringer, Alexander L 1921- *Baker 78, NewGrD 80*
Ringham, Maisie *WhoMus 72*
Ringle, Dave 1893-1965 *AmSCAP 66, -80*
Ringling, Al *PupTheA*
Ringling, Albert 1852-1916 *Ent*
Ringo, James 1926- *ConAmC*
Ringuet *CreCan 2*
Ringwald, Roy 1910- *AmSCAP 66, -80*
Ringwood, Gwen Pharis 1910- *CreCan 2*
Rinker, Al 1907- *AmSCAP 66, -80, CmpEPM*
Rinker, Alton 1907- *ConAmC*
Rinker, Charles Donald 1911- *AmSCAP 66, -80*
Rinky-Dinks, The *RkOn*
Rinoldi, Antonio *NewGrD 80*
Rintels, David W *NewYTET*
Rintzler, Marius Adrian 1932- *WhoOp 76*
Rinuccini, Cino 1350?-1417 *NewGrD 80*
Rinuccini, Ottavio *BnBkM 80*
Rinuccini, Ottavio 1562-1621 *NewEOp 71, NewGrD 80*
Rinuccini, Ottavio 1563-1621 *Baker 78*
Rinzler, Ralph *EncFCWM 69*
Rio, Anita 1873-1971 *BiDAmM*
Rio, Rita *BgBands 74*
Rio, Rosa 1914- *AmSCAP 66, -80*
Riopelle, Jean-Paul 1923- *CreCan 1*
Riordan, Monica Lynn 1953- *AmSCAP 80*
Riordan, Robert J 1913-1968 *WhScrn 74, -77, WhoHol B*
Rios, Alvaro DeLos 1580?-1623 *NewGrD 80*
Rios, Consuelo *DancEn 78*
Rios, James 1931- *AmSCAP 66, -80*
Rios, Lalo 1927-1973 *WhScrn 77, WhoHol B*
Rios, Miguel *RkOn 2A*
Riotte, Philipp Jakob 1776-1856 *Baker 78, NewGrD 80*
Rip d1941 *NotNAT B*
Rip, Georges d1941 *WhThe*
Rip Chords, The *RkOn*
Ripa, Alberto Da 1480?-1551 *Baker 78*
Ripa, Alberto Da 1500?-1551 *NewGrD 80*
Ripa, Antonio 1720?-1795 *NewGrD 80*
Ripere, Jean-Jacques *NewGrD 80*
Ripert, Jean-Jacques *NewGrD 80*
Riperton, Minnie *IlEncR[port]*
Riperton, Minnie 1947?- *DrBlPA*
Riperton, Minnie 1948- *RkOn 2[port]*
Ripin, Edwin M 1930-1975 *NewGrD 80*
Ripley, Arthur 1895-1961 *FilmEn, FilmgC, HalFC 80*
Ripley, Charles *Film 1*
Ripley, Heather *WhoHol A*
Ripley, Patricia 1926- *BiE&WWA, NotNAT*
Ripley, Ray 1891-1938 *WhoHol B*
Ripley, Raymond 1891-1938 *WhScrn 74, -77*
Ripley, Robert L 1893-1949 *WhScrn 74, -77, WhoHol B*
Ripley, Thomas Baldwin 1795-1876 *BiDAmM*
Ripman, Olive 1886- *CnOxB, DancEn 78*
Ripolles, Vicente 1867-1943 *NewGrD 80*
Riposo, Joseph 1933- *AmSCAP 80*
Rippe, Albert De *NewGrD 80*
Ripper, Michael 1913- *FilmgC, HalFC 80, WhoHol A, WhoHrs 80*
Ripper, Theodore William 1925- *CpmDNM 74, ConAmC*
Rippert, Jean-Jacques *NewGrD 80*
Rippon, Angela *NewYTET*
Rippon, John 1751-1836 *OxMus*
Rippon, Michael George 1938- *IntWWM 77, -80, WhoMus 72, WhoOp 76*
Rippy, Rodney Allen 1968?- *DrBlPA, WhoHol A*
Riquier, Guiraut 1230?-1300? *NewGrD 80*
Rischbieter, Wilhelm Albert 1834-1910 *Baker 78*
Riscoe, Arthur 1896-1954 *FilmgC, HalFC 80, NotNAT B, WhScrn 74, -77, WhThe, WhoHol B*
Risdon, Edward Mark 1902- *WhoMus 72*
Risdon, Elisabeth 1887-1958 *HolCA[port]*
Risdon, Elizabeth 1887-1958 *FilmEn, Film 1, FilmgC, HalFC 80, IlWWBF[port], MotPP, MovMk, NotNAT B, ThFT[port], Vers A[port], WhScrn 74, -77, WhThe, WhoHol B*
Risdon, Elizabeth 1888-1958 *ForYSC*
Riseley, George 1845-1932 *Baker 78*
Rishell, Myrtle 1877-1942 *WhScrn 77*
Risi, Dino 1916- *FilmgC, HalFC 80*
Risi, Dino 1917- *FilmEn, WorEFlm*
Rising, W *Film 2*
Rising, William S 1851-1930 *WhScrn 74, -77, WhoHol B*
Risinger, Karel 1920- *NewGrD 80*
Riskin, Robert 1897-1955 *CmMov, DcFM, FilmEn, FilmgC, HalFC 80, OxFilm, WorEFlm*
Rislakki, Ensio 1896- *CroCD*
Risler, Edouard 1873-1929 *Baker 78*
Riso, Rick 1950- *AmSCAP 80*
Rispoli, Salvatore 1736?-1812 *NewGrD 80*
Risque, W H d1916 *NotNAT B*
Riss, Dan 1910-1970 *WhScrn 74, -77, WhoHol B*
Risser, Bryce Nathan 1943- *AmSCAP 80*
Risset, Jean-Claude 1938- *NewGrD 80*
Rissien, Edward L *IntMPA 77, -75, -76, -78, -79*
Rissmiller, Jim *ConMuA 80B*
Rissmiller, Lawson J 1914-1953 *WhScrn 74, -77*
Risso, Attilio 1913-1967 *WhScrn 74, -77, WhoHol B*
Risso, Roberto *WhoHol A*
Rist, Johann 1607-1667 *Baker 78, NewGrD 80*
Rist, Robbie *WhoHol A*
Ristenpart, Karl 1900-1967 *NewGrD 80*
Ristic, Milan 1908- *Baker 78, DcCM, IntWWM 77, -80, NewGrD 80*
Ristori, Adelaide 1821-1906 *NotNAT A*
Ristori, Adelaide 1822-1906 *CnThe, EncWT, Ent, FamA&A[port], NotNAT B, OxThe, PlP&P*
Ristori, Giovanni Alberto 1692-1753 *Baker 78, NewGrD 80*
Ristow, Roderick 1937- *WhoOp 76*
Ritch, David 1932- *WhoOp 76*
Ritchard, Cyril *WhoHol A*
Ritchard, Cyril 1896-1977 *Film 2, FilmgC, HalFC 80*
Ritchard, Cyril 1897-1977 *BiE&WWA, EncMT, IlWWBF, NotNAT, WhoThe 72, -77*
Ritchard, Viola *Film 2*
Ritchie, Adele 1874-1930 *CmpEPM, NotNAT B, WhThe, WhoStg 1908*
Ritchie, Billie 1877-1921 *FilmEn*
Ritchie, Billie 1879-1921 *Film 1, WhScrn 74, -77, WhoHol B*
Ritchie, Clint *WhoHol A*
Ritchie, Elisabeth 1933- *WhoMus 72*
Ritchie, Elizabeth *IntWWM 80*
Ritchie, Elizabeth Nicol *WhoMus 72*
Ritchie, Franklin d1918 *Film 1, WhScrn 77*
Ritchie, Jean 1922- *AmSCAP 66, -80, BiDAmM, EncFCWM 69*
Ritchie, John Anthony 1921- *IntWWM 77, -80*
Ritchie, June 1939- *FilmgC, HalFC 80, IlWWBF, WhoHol A, WhoThe 77*
Ritchie, Larry *WhoHol A*
Ritchie, Margaret 1903-1969 *NewGrD 80, WhoMus 72*
Ritchie, Michael *FilmgC*
Ritchie, Michael 1936- *OxFilm*
Ritchie, Michael 1938- *FilmEn, IntMPA 77, -76, -78, -79, -80*
Ritchie, Michael 1939- *BiDFilm 81, HalFC 80, IntMPA 75*
Ritchie, Terry V 1887-1918 *WhScrn 77*
Ritchie, Tom Vernon 1922- *ConAmC*
Ritchie Family, The *EncFCWM 69, RkOn 2[port]*
Ritchings-Bernard Old Folks Company *BiDAmM*
Ritenour, John Donald 1950- *AmSCAP 80*
Ritenour, Lee Mack 1952- *AmSCAP 80, EncJzS 70*
Ritman, William *NotNAT, WhoThe 77*
Ritschel *NewGrD 80*
Ritschel, Franz Joseph d1763 *NewGrD 80*
Ritschel, Georg 1744-1805 *NewGrD 80*
Ritschel, Georg Wenzel 1680?-1757 *NewGrD 80*
Ritschel, Johannes 1739?-1766 *NewGrD 80*
Ritt, Martin *IntMPA 77, -75, -76, -78, -79, -80, WhoHol A*
Ritt, Martin 1919- *FilmgC, HalFC 80, MovMk[port]*
Ritt, Martin 1920- *BiDFilm, -81, BiE&WWA, DcFM, FilmEn, NotNAT, OxFilm, WorEFlm*
Rittau, Gunther 1893-1971 *DcFM, FilmEn*
Rittau, Gunther 1897-1971 *WorEFlm*
Rittenberg, Saul N 1912- *IntMPA 75, -76*
Rittenhouse, Elizabeth Mae 1915- *AmSCAP 66, -80*
Rittenhouse, Florence d1929 *NotNAT B*
Ritter *NewGrD 80*
Ritter, Alexander 1833-1896 *Baker 78, NewGrD 80, OxMus*
Ritter, August Gottfried 1811-1885 *Baker 78*
Ritter, Carol *WomWMM B*
Ritter, Charity Lee 1917- *AmSCAP 80*
Ritter, Christian 1645?-1717? *NewGrD 80*
Ritter, Esther 1902-1925 *WhScrn 74, -77, WhoHol B*
Ritter, Frederic Louis 1834-1891 *Baker 78, BiDAmM*
Ritter, Georg Wenzel 1748-1808 *NewGrD 80*
Ritter, George d1919 *WhScrn 77*
Ritter, Heinrich *NewGrD 80*
Ritter, Hermann 1849-1926 *Baker 78, NewGrD 80*
Ritter, Johann Christoph 1715-1767 *NewGrD 80*
Ritter, Johann Nikolaus 1702-1782 *NewGrD 80*
Ritter, John *WhoHol A*
Ritter, John P d1920 *NotNAT B*
Ritter, Maurice Woodward 1906- *BiDAmM*
Ritter, Melvin 1923- *WhoMus 72*
Ritter, Paul J d1962 *WhScrn 74, -77*
Ritter, Peter 1763-1846 *Baker 78, NewGrD 80*
Ritter, Sascha *NewGrD 80*
Ritter, Tex d1974 *WhoHol B*
Ritter, Tex 1905-1973 *IlEncCM[port]*
Ritter, Tex 1905-1974 *FilmEn*
Ritter, Tex 1906-1974 *CmpEPM, EncFCWM 69, RkOn, WhScrn 77*
Ritter, Tex 1907- *CounME 74A*
Ritter, Tex 1907-1974 *CounME 74[port], FilmgC, ForYSC, HalFC 80*

Ritter, Thelma 1905-1969 *BiDFilm, -81, BiE&WWA, FilmEn, FilmgC, ForYSC, HalFC 80, MotPP, MovMk[port], NotNAT B, OxFilm, Vers A[port], WhScrn 74, -77, WhoHol B, WorEFlm*
Ritter, Theodore 1841-1886 *Baker 78*
Ritterband, Gerhard 1905-1959 *WhScrn 74, -77*
Rittler, Philipp Jakob 1637?-1690 *NewGrD 80*
Rittman, Trude *BiE&WWA, NotNAT*
Rittner, Rudolf *Film 2*
Rittner, Rudolf 1869-1943 *EncWT*
Rittner, Tadeusz 1873-1921 *CnMD, McGEWD, ModWD*
Ritz, Al 1901-1965 *FilmEn, Film 1, FilmgC, HalFC 80, MotPP, OxFilm, WhScrn 74, -77, WhoHol B*
Ritz, Al 1903-1965 *ForYSC, Funs[port], JoeFr[port]*
Ritz, Harry 1906- *FilmEn, FilmgC, HalFC 80, MotPP, OxFilm*
Ritz, Harry 1908- *ForYSC, Funs[port], JoeFr[port]*
Ritz, Jim 1903- *FilmEn, FilmgC, HalFC 80, OxFilm*
Ritz, Jim 1905- *ForYSC*
Ritz, Jimmy *MotPP*
Ritz, Jimmy 1905- *Funs[port]*
Ritz, Jimmy 1906- *JoeFr[port]*
Ritz, Lyle Joseph 1930- *AmSCAP 80, BiDAmM*
Ritz, Sally *BluesWW*
Ritz Brothers, The *FilmEn, FilmgC, ForYSC, Funs[port], HalFC 80, JoeFr[port], MotPP, MovMk[port], OxFilm, WhoHol A*
Riuwental, Neidhart Von *NewGrD 80*
Riva, Emmanuele *MotPP, WhoHol A*
Riva, Emmanuele 1927- *WorEFlm*
Riva, Emmanuele 1932- *FilmgC, HalFC 80, OxFilm*
Riva, Emmanuelle 1927- *BiDFilm, -81, FilmAG WE, FilmEn*
Riva, Giulio *NewGrD 80*
Riva, Maria *WhoHol A*
Rivadavia, Comodoro *PupTheA*
Rivaflecha, Martin De d1528 *NewGrD 80*
Rivafrecha, Martin De d1528 *NewGrD 80*
Rivali, Tina *Film 2*
Rivander, Paul 1570?-1621? *NewGrD 80*
Rivard, William H 1928- *ConAmC*
Rivarde, Serge Achille 1865-1940 *BiDAmM*
Rivas, Duke Of *McGEWD*
Rivas, Duque De *OxThe*
Rivas, Bimbo *PIP&P A[port]*
Rivas, Carlos *ForYSC, WhoHol A*
Rivas, Jose M L 1901-1955 *WhScrn 74, -77*
Rive, Kenneth 1919- *IntMPA 77, -75, -76, -78, -79, -80*
Rive-King, Julie 1854-1937 *Baker 78*
Rive-King, Julie 1857-1937 *BiDAmM*
Rivelli, Pauline 1939- *AmSCAP 80*
Rivemale, Alexandre 1918- *CnMD, McGEWD*
Rivera, Chita 1933- *BiE&WWA, CnOxB, DancEn 78, EncMT, HalFC 80, NotNAT, WhoHol A, WhoThe 72, -77*
Rivera, Geraldo 1943- *IntMPA 78, -79, -80, NewYTET*
Rivera, Graciela 1921- *IntWWM 77, -80*
Rivera, Lawrence 1930- *AmSCAP 80*
Rivera, Linda *WomWMM B*
Rivera, Luis *WhoHol A*
Rivera, Ray A 1929- *AmSCAP 66, -80*
Rivera, Roberto 1924- *IntWWM 77, -80*
Rivera, Ronald M 1949- *ConAmC*
Rivero, Jorge *WhoHol A*
Rivero, Julian 1890-1976 *Vers A[port], WhoHol C*
Rivero, Lorraine *Film 2*
Rivers, Alfred d1955 *NotNAT B*
Rivers, Conrad Kent 1933-1968 *BlkAmP*
Rivers, Earl G, Jr. 1944- *IntWWM 77*
Rivers, Joan 1935- *JoeFr[port], WhoHol A*
Rivers, Johnnie 1942- *IlEncR*
Rivers, Johnny 1942- *ConMuA 80A, RkOn 2[port]*
Rivers, Louis 1922- *BlkAmP, DrBlPA, NatPD[port]*
Rivers, Malcolm 1937- *WhoOp 76*
Rivers, Mavis *CmpEPM*
Rivers, Patrick Charles 1932- *WhoMus 72*
Rivers, Sam 1930- *EncJzS 70, IlEncJ*
Rivers, Samuel Carthorne 1930- *EncJzS 70*
Rivers, Steve *ConMuA 80B*
Rives, Amelie d1945 *NotNAT B*
Rivett-River, Jackie *WomWMM B*
Rivette, Jacques 1928- *BiDFilm, -81, DcFM, FilmEn, FilmgC, HalFC 80, OxFilm, WorEFlm*
Rivier, Jean 1896- *Baker 78, CompSN[port], DcCM, IntWWM 77, -80, NewGrD 80*
Riviera, Jake *ConMuA 80B*
Rivieras, The *RkOn, -2A[port]*
Riviere, Fred Curly 1875-1935 *WhScrn 74, -77, WhoHol B*
Riviere, Gaston *Film 1*
Rivingtons, The *RkOn[port]*
Rivkin, Allen 1903- *IntMPA 77, -75, -76, -78, -79, -80*
Rivkin, Joe 1912- *IntMPA 77, -75, -76, -78, -79, -80*
Rivoire, Andre *NotNAT B*
Rivoli, Benedict *PupTheA*
Rivoli, Gianfranco *WhoOp 76*
Rivoli, Ludwika 1814-1878 *NewGrD 80*
Rivoli, Paulina 1823?-1881 *NewGrD 80*
Rivortorto, Il *NewGrD 80*
Rivotorto *NewGrD 80*
Rivulo, Franziscus De *NewGrD 80*
Rix, Brian 1924- *CnThe, Ent, FilmgC, HalFC 80, IlWWBF, -A, IntMPA 77, -75, -76, -78, -79, -80, PIP&P, WhoHol A, WhoThe 72, -77*
Rixon, Benjamin R *WhoHol A*
Rixon, Morris L *WhoHol A*
Rizhkin, Iosif Yakovlevich 1907- *NewGrD 80*
Rizo, Marco 1916- *AmSCAP 66, -80, ConAmC*
Rizza, George Joseph 1925- *IntWWM 77, -80*
Rizza, Gilda Dalla *NewGrD 80*
Rizzi, Alberto 1889-1945 *AmSCAP 66, -80*
Rizzi, Tony 1923- *EncJzS 70*
Rizzi, Trefoni 1923- *AmSCAP 80, BiDAmM, EncJzS 70*
Rizzio, David 1525?-1566 *NewGrD 80*
Rizzio, David 1533?-1566 *OxMus*
Rizzo, Alfredo *WhoHol A*
Rizzo, Bob 1937- *AmSCAP 66*
Rizzo, Francis 1936- *WhoOp 76*
Rizzo, Gianni *WhoHol A*
Rizzo, Giovanni Battista *NewGrD 80*
Rizzo, Joe 1917- *AmSCAP 66, -80*
Rizzoli, Angelo 1889-1970 *FilmEn*
Roach, Bert 1891-1971 *Film 1, -2, FilmgC, ForYSC, HalFC 80, TwYS, Vers B[port], WhScrn 77, WhoHol B*
Roach, Christine English 1952- *AmSCAP 80*
Roach, E *MorBAP*
Roach, Freddie *BlkAmP*
Roach, Hal 1892- *CmMov, DcFM, FilmEn, FilmgC, HalFC 80, OxFilm, TwYS B, WorEFlm*
Roach, Hal, Jr. *IntMPA 77, -75, -76, -78, -79, -80*
Roach, Joseph Maloy 1913- *AmSCAP 66*
Roach, Margaret 1921-1964 *WhScrn 74, -77, WhoHol B*
Roach, Marjorie *Film 2*
Roach, Max 1925- *CmpEPM, DrBlPA, EncJzS 70, IlEncJ, NewGrD 80*
Roach, Maxine 1950- *BlkWAB*
Roach, Maxwell 1925- *BiDAmM, EncJzS 70, NewGrD 80*
Roach, Thomas A d1962 *NotNAT B*
Roache, Viola d1961 *WhoHol B*
Roache, Viola 1885-1961 *NotNAT B, WhThe*
Roache, Viola 1886-1961 *WhScrn 74, -77*
Road, Anne Selina *WhoMus 72*
Road, Mike *WhoHol A*
Roadrunners *BiDAmM*
Roan, Barbara *CmpGMD*
Roane, Kenneth A 1902?- *WhoJazz 72*
Roanne, Andre *Film 2*
Roar, Leif *WhoOp 76*
Roarke, Adam *WhoHol A*
Robards, Jason, Jr. *MotPP, PIP&P[port], -A[port], WhoHol A*
Robards, Jason, Jr. 1920- *FilmgC, ForYSC, HalFC 80[port]*
Robards, Jason, Jr. 1922- *BiDFilm 81, BiE&WWA, CnThe, Ent[port], FilmEn, IntMPA 77, -75, -76, -78, -79, -80, MovMk[port], NotNAT, WhoThe 72, -77*
Robards, Jason, Sr. d1963 *MotPP, NotNAT B, WhoHol B*
Robards, Jason, Sr. 1892-1963 *FilmEn, WhScrn 74, -77*
Robards, Jason, Sr. 1893-1963 *Film 2, FilmgC, ForYSC, HalFC 80, MovMk, TwYS*
Robards, Willis *Film 2*
Robarge, John F *BiDAmM*
Robb, Dodi *WomWMM*
Robb, John Donald 1892- *AmSCAP 66, -80, CpmDNM 78, -79, ConAmC, NewGrD 80*
Robb, Kathryn *PupTheA*
Robb, Lori *WhoHol A*
Robbe-Grillet, Alain 1922- *DcFM, FilmEn, FilmgC, HalFC 80, OxFilm, WorEFlm[port]*
Robberts, Oriell *AmSCAP 80*
Robbie, Seymour Mitchell *IntMPA 77, -75, -76, -78, -79, -80, NewYTET*
Robbin, Peter 1956- *WhoHol A*
Robbinne *Film 1*
Robbins, Sir Alfred 1856-1931 *NotNAT B, WhThe*
Robbins, Archie 1913-1975 *WhScrn 77, WhoHol C*
Robbins, Burton E 1920- *IntMPA 77, -75, -76, -78, -79, -80*
Robbins, Carrie Fishbein 1943- *NotNAT, WhoThe 77*
Robbins, Chandler 1810-1882 *BiDAmM*
Robbins, Cindy *WhoHol A*
Robbins, Corky *AmSCAP 80*
Robbins, Daniel 1947- *ConAmC*
Robbins, David Paul 1946- *ConAmC*
Robbins, Eduard Rubini 1910- *WhoMus 72*
Robbins, Edward E 1930- *BiE&WWA, NotNAT*
Robbins, Edward John 1920- *IntWWM 80*
Robbins, Edwina *Film 1*
Robbins, Gale 1924-1980 *FilmEn, ForYSC, HalFC 80, WhoHol A*
Robbins, Gale 1932- *IntMPA 77, -75, -76, -78, -79, -80*
Robbins, Gerald Martin 1945- *IntWWM 77, -80*
Robbins, Harold 1916- *FilmgC, HalFC 80*
Robbins, Howard Chandler 1876-1952 *BiDAmM*
Robbins, Ira A *ConMuA 80B*
Robbins, Jane Marla *WhoHol A*
Robbins, Jerome 1918- *BiE&WWA, CmMov, CnThe, CnOxB, DancEn 78[port], EncMT, EncWT, Ent, FilmEn, FilmgC, HalFC 80, NotNAT, OxFilm, PIP&P, WhoThe 72, -77, WorEFlm*
Robbins, Jesse *Film 1*
Robbins, Josie *PupTheA SUP*
Robbins, Marc 1868-1931 *Film 2, WhoHol B*
Robbins, Marcus B 1868-1931 *WhScrn 74, -77*
Robbins, Marty 1925- *AmPS A, -B, BiDAmM, CounME 74[port], -74A, EncFCWM 69, IlEncCM[port], PopAmC SUP[port], RkOn*
Robbins, Matthew *IntMPA 79, -80*
Robbins, Mrs. R B *PupTheA*
Robbins, Richard 1919-1969 *WhScrn 74, -77, WhoHol B*
Robbins, Sheila *WhoHol A*
Robbins, Walt *Film 2*
Robbins Landon, H C *NewGrD 80*
Robbio DiSanRafaele *NewGrD 80*
Robbs, The *BiDAmM*
Robe, Annie d1922 *NotNAT B*
Robe, Harold Athol 1881-1946 *AmSCAP 66, -80*
Rober, Richard 1906-1952 *FilmgC, ForYSC, HalFC 80, NotNAT B, WhScrn 74, -77, WhoHol B*
Roberday, Francois 1624?-1680 *NewGrD 80*
Roberdeau, John Peter d1815 *NotNAT B*
Roberds, Fred Allen 1941- *AmSCAP 66, -80*
Robers, Edith *Film 2*
Roberson, Arthur *BlkAmP*
Roberson, Chuck *WhoHol A*
Roberson, Lou 1921-1966 *WhScrn 74, -77*
Roberson, Richard M 1935- *IntWWM 77*
Roberson, William *BlkAmP*
Roberston, Duncan 1924- *IntWWM 80*
Robert And Johnny *RkOn*

Robert Ap Huw *NewGrD 80*
Robert De Blois *NewGrD 80*
Robert De Castel *NewGrD 80*
Robert De Handlo *NewGrD 80*
Robert De La Piere d1258 *NewGrD 80*
Robert De Rains La Chievre *NewGrD 80*
Robert De Reins *NewGrD 80*
Robert De Reins La Chievre *NewGrD 80*
Robert Du Chastel *NewGrD 80*
Robert Le Pele *NewGrD 80*
Robert, Camille *OxMus*
Robert, Eugene 1877- *WhThe*
Robert, Frederic 1932- *NewGrD 80*
Robert, Marika *CreCan 1*
Robert, Patricia Harrison 1939- *IntMPA 77, -75, -76, -78, -79, -80*
Robert, Pierre 1618?-1699 *NewGrD 80*
Robert, Walter 1908- *WhoMus 72*
Robert, Yves 1920- *DcFM, FilmEn, FilmgC, HalFC 80, WhoHol A*
Robert-Blunn, John 1936- *IntWWM 77, -80*
Robert DeSabilon *OxMus*
Robert-Houdin, Jean Eugene 1805-1871 *Ent[port], MagIlD[port]*
Robert Junior *BluesWW[port]*
Roberti, Costantino 1700-1773 *NewGrD 80*
Roberti, Girolamo Frigimelica *NewGrD 80*
Roberti, Giulio 1829-1891 *NewGrD 80*
Roberti, Lyda *AmPS B*
Roberti, Lyda 1906-1938 *FilmEn, ThFT[port], WhoHol B*
Roberti, Lyda 1909-1938 *JoeFr[port], NotNAT B, WhScrn 74, -77, WhThe*
Roberti, Lyda 1910-1938 *CmpEPM, FilmgC, ForYSC, HalFC 80*
Roberto *PupTheA*
Roberto, Constantino 1700-1773 *NewGrD 80*
Roberton, Sir Hugh S 1874-1952 *Baker 78, OxMus*
Roberton, Kenneth Bantock 1913- *IntWWM 77, -80*
Roberts, A Cledge 1905-1957 *WhScrn 74, -77*
Roberts, Albert G 1902-1941 *WhScrn 74, -77, WhoHol B*
Roberts, Alice *Film 2*
Roberts, Allan 1905-1966 *AmSCAP 66, -80, CmpEPM*
Roberts, Allene 1928- *ForYSC, MotPP*
Roberts, Arthur 1852-1933 *NotNAT B, OxThe, WhThe, WhoStg 1908*
Roberts, Arthur 1912- *IntWWM 77, -80*
Roberts, Austin *AmSCAP 80, RkOn 2A*
Roberts, Bart *FilmEn, WhoHol A*
Roberts, Ben 1916- *FilmgC, HalFC 80, IntMPA 77, -75, -76, -78, -79, -80, WorEFlm*
Roberts, Bernard 1933- *IntWWM 77, -80, WhoMus 72*
Roberts, Beryl *Film 2*
Roberts, Beverly 1914- *BiE&WWA, FilmEn, ForYSC, NotNAT, ThFT[port], WhoHol A*
Roberts, Billy Joe *AmSCAP 80*
Roberts, Brenda 1945- *WhoOp 76*
Roberts, C Luckeyth 1893- *AmSCAP 80*
Roberts, C Luckeyth 1893-1948 *BlksBF*
Roberts, C Luckeyth 1893-1968 *AmSCAP 66, NotNAT B*
Roberts, Carol E 1935- *IntWWM 77*
Roberts, Sir Charles George Douglas 1860-1943 *CreCan 2*
Roberts, Charles J 1868-1957 *AmSCAP 66, -80*
Roberts, Charles Luckeyeth 1890-1968 *BiDAmM*
Roberts, Charles Luckeyeth 1895-1968 *EncJzS 70*
Roberts, Charles Luckeyth *NewGrD 80*
Roberts, Christian *WhoHol A*
Roberts, Christopher Morrell 1943- *IntWWM 80*
Roberts, Cledge 1905-1957 *NotNAT B, WhoHol B*
Roberts, Clifford *WhoMus 72*
Roberts, Curtis *IntMPA 77, -75, -76, -78, -79, -80*
Roberts, Dagmar 1910- *IntWWM 77, -80*
Roberts, Daniel Crane 1841-1907 *BiDAmM*
Roberts, David Brian 1935- *AmSCAP 80*
Roberts, Davis 1917- *DrBlPA, WhoHol A*
Roberts, Desmond 1894- *ForYSC, WhoHol A*
Roberts, Dick 1897-1966 *WhScrn 74, -77, WhoHol B*
Roberts, Donald Lowell 1938- *IntWWM 77, -80*
Roberts, Doris 1930- *NotNAT, WhoHol A, WhoThe 77*
Roberts, Dorothy 1906- *CreCan 1*
Roberts, Dorothy F Diamond *AmSCAP 66*
Roberts, Edith 1899-1935 *FilmEn, WhScrn 74, -77, WhoHol B*
Roberts, Edith 1901-1935 *Film 1, -2, TwYS*
Roberts, Edwin *ConAmC*
Roberts, Eleazer 1825-1912 *NewGrD 80*
Roberts, Elliot *ConMuA 80B*
Roberts, Eric 1905- *IntWWM 77, -80*
Roberts, Evelyn 1886-1962 *WhThe*
Roberts, Ewan 1914- *WhoHol A, WhoThe 72, -77*
Roberts, Florence d1940 *WhoHol B*
Roberts, Florence 1860-1940 *FilmgC, HalFC 80*
Roberts, Florence 1861-1940 *ForYSC, NotNAT B, WhScrn 74, -77*
Roberts, Florence 1871-1927 *Film 1, NotNAT B, WhScrn 74, -77, WhThe, WhoHol B, WhoStg 1906, -1908*
Roberts, Florence Smythe d1925 *NotNAT B*
Roberts, Gene 1918-1970 *AmSCAP 66, -80*
Roberts, George 1845-1930 *Film 2, WhScrn 77*
Roberts, George E Theodore Goodridge 1877-1953 *CreCan 1*
Roberts, George M 1928- *AmSCAP 66, -80*
Roberts, Gertrud Hermine Kunzel 1906- *IntWWM 77, -80*
Roberts, Gertrud Kuenzel 1906- *ConAmC*
Roberts, Glen 1921-1974 *WhScrn 77, WhoHol B*
Roberts, Goodridge 1904- *CreCan 2*
Roberts, Hans d1954 *NotNAT B*
Roberts, Helen 1888- *BluesWW, NewGrD 80*
Roberts, Henry *NewGrD 80*
Roberts, Herbert Arthur 1900- *WhoMus 72*
Roberts, Hi *WhoHol A*
Roberts, Howard Alfred 1924- *AmSCAP 80*
Roberts, Howard Mancel 1929- *BiDAmM, EncJzS 70*
Roberts, J H 1884-1961 *Film 2, NotNAT B, WhThe, WhoHol B*
Roberts, J Henry 1856-1920 *BiDAmM*
Roberts, Jason *AmSCAP 80*
Roberts, Jean 1926- *CreCan 1*
Roberts, Jerry *AmSCAP 80*
Roberts, Jim 1933- *BiDAmM*
Roberts, Jimmy d1962 *NotNAT B*
Roberts, Joan 1918- *WhThe*
Roberts, Joan 1922- *BiE&WWA, NotNAT, -A*
Roberts, Joann Nancy 1933- *IntWWM 77*
Roberts, John *ConAmTC, ConMuA 80B, NewGrD 80*
Roberts, John 1822-1877 *NewGrD 80, OxMus*
Roberts, John 1916- *WhoThe 72, -77*
Roberts, John Bransby 1937- *WhoMus 72*
Roberts, John Henry 1848-1924 *NewGrD 80*
Roberts, John Peter Lee 1930- *IntWWM 80*
Roberts, John Varley 1841-1920 *OxMus*
Roberts, Jon *AmSCAP 80*
Roberts, Joseph *Film 2*
Roberts, Kathleen 1941- *WhoOp 76*
Roberts, Kay George 1950- *BlkWAB[port]*
Roberts, Keith *WhoHol A*
Roberts, Kenny 1927- *BiDAmM, IlEncCM*
Roberts, Lee S 1884-1949 *AmSCAP 66, -80, BiDAmM*
Roberts, Leona 1880-1954 *ForYSC, WhScrn 74, -77, WhoHol B*
Roberts, Linda 1901- *AmSCAP 66, -80*
Roberts, Lloyd 1884-1966 *CreCan 2*
Roberts, Lois *WhoHol A*
Roberts, Lou *AmSCAP 80*
Roberts, Louise 1911- *NotNAT*
Roberts, Luanne *WhoHol A*
Roberts, Luckey 1887?-1968 *NewGrD 80, WhoJazz 72*
Roberts, Luckey 1895-1968 *EncJzS 70*
Roberts, Lynn 1919- *FilmEn, ForYSC*
Roberts, Lynne 1919- *WhoHol A*
Roberts, Lynne 1922- *FilmgC, HalFC 80, IntMPA 77, -75, -76, -78, -79, -80*
Roberts, Margaret Christie 1908- *IntWWM 77*
Roberts, Marguerite *IntMPA 77, -75, -76, -78, -79, -80, WomWMM*
Roberts, Marilyn *WhoHol A*
Roberts, Marion Earl, Jr. 1945- *AmSCAP 80*
Roberts, Mark *WhoHol A*
Roberts, Meade 1930- *BiE&WWA, NotNAT, WhoHol A*
Roberts, Megan 1952- *Baker 78*
Roberts, Merrill 1885-1940 *WhScrn 74, -77*
Roberts, Mervyn 1906- *NewGrD 80*
Roberts, Muriel *AmSCAP 80*
Roberts, Myron J 1912- *ConAmC*
Roberts, Nancy 1892-1962 *NotNAT B, WhScrn 77, WhoHol B*
Roberts, Paul 1915- *AmSCAP 66, -80*
Roberts, Paul Anthony 1949- *IntWWM 77, -80*
Roberts, Pernell *WhoHol A*
Roberts, Pernell 1928- *ForYSC*
Roberts, Pernell 1930- *HalFC 80*
Roberts, R A 1870- *WhThe*
Roberts, Rachel *IntMPA 75, -76, -78, -79, -80*
Roberts, Rachel 1927- *CnThe, EncMT, FilmEn, FilmgC, HalFC 80, IlWWBF, IntMPA 77, MotPP, OxFilm, WhoHol A, WhoThe 72, -77*
Roberts, Rachel 1931?- *ForYSC*
Roberts, Ralph *Film 2, WhoHol A*
Roberts, Ralph d1944 *NotNAT B, WhThe*
Roberts, Ralph Arthur 1884-1940 *WhScrn 77*
Roberts, Sir Randal d1899 *NotNAT B*
Roberts, Rebecca 1948- *WhoOp 76*
Roberts, Rhoda *AmSCAP 66, -80*
Roberts, Roy 1900-1975 *FilmEn, FilmgC, ForYSC, HalFC 80, WhScrn 77, WhoHol C*
Roberts, Ruth *WhoHol A*
Roberts, Ruth 1926- *AmSCAP 66*
Roberts, Ruth 1930- *AmSCAP 80*
Roberts, Sally *BluesWW*
Roberts, Sara Jane 1924-1968 *WhScrn 74, -77, WhoHol B*
Roberts, Snitcher *BluesWW*
Roberts, Stanley 1916- *IntMPA 77, -75, -76, -78, -79, -80*
Roberts, Stephen *IntMPA 77, -75, -76, -78, -79, WhoHol A*
Roberts, Stephen 1895-1936 *FilmEn, HalFC 80, WhScrn 74, -77*
Roberts, Stephen Pritchard 1949- *IntWWM 80*
Roberts, Thayer 1903-1968 *WhScrn 74, -77, WhoHol B*
Roberts, Theodore 1861-1928 *FilmEn, Film 1, -2, HalFC 80, MotPP, NotNAT B, TwYS, WhScrn 74, -77, WhThe, WhoHol B, WhoStg 1908*
Roberts, Theodore Goodridge 1877-1953 *CreCan 1*
Roberts, Tom *WhoHol A*
Roberts, Tony 1939- *FilmEn, NotNAT, WhoHol A, WhoThe 77*
Roberts, Tracey *ForYSC, WhoHol A*
Roberts, Velma Irene Tate 1904- *IntWWM 77*
Roberts, Vera Mowry 1918- *BiE&WWA, NotNAT*
Roberts, Verna Dean Smith 1925- *IntWWM 77, -80*
Roberts, Victoria *BlkAmP*
Roberts, Walter Buchanan 1893- *WhoMus 72*
Roberts, Wilfred Bob 1921- *AmSCAP 80, IntWWM 77, -80*
Roberts, William *IntMPA 77, -75, -76, -78, -79, -80*
Roberts, William Goodridge *CreCan 2*
Roberts, William Harris Lloyd *CreCan 2*
Roberts, William Herbert Mervyn 1906- *IntWWM 77, -80, WhoMus 72*
Roberts, Winifred *IntWWM 77, -80, WhoMus 72*
Robertshaw, Jerrold 1866-1941 *Film 1, -2, FilmgC, HalFC 80, NotNAT B, WhScrn 74, -77, WhThe, WhoHol B*
Robertson, Agnes 1833-1916 *FamA&A[port], NotNAT B, PlP&P*
Robertson, Alec 1892- *NewGrD 80, WhoMus 72*
Robertson, Alex d1964 *NotNAT B*
Robertson, Alexander *NewGrD 80*
Robertson, Alexander 1892- *NewGrD 80*
Robertson, Beatrice Forbes- *WhThe*

Robertson, C Alvin 1891-1943 *NewOrJ[port]*
Robertson, Cliff 1925- *BiDFilm, -81, BiE&WWA, CmMov, FilmEn, FilmgC, ForYSC, HalFC 80, IntMPA 77, -75, -76, -78, -79, -80, MotPP, MovMk[port], WhoHol A, WhoHrs 80, WorEFlm*
Robertson, Dale *IntMPA 79*
Robertson, Dale 1920- *ForYSC*
Robertson, Dale 1923- *AmSCAP 66, FilmEn, FilmgC, HalFC 80, IntMPA 77, -75, -76, -78, -80, MotPP, WhoHol A*
Robertson, Dennis *WhoHol A*
Robertson, Dick 1903- *AmSCAP 66, -80, CmpEPM, WhoJazz 72*
Robertson, Don 1922- *AmSCAP 66, EncFCWM 69, RkOn*
Robertson, Don 1942- *AmSCAP 80*
Robertson, Donald d1926 *NotNAT B, WhoStg 1908*
Robertson, Donald Irwin 1922- *AmSCAP 80, BiDAmM*
Robertson, Donna Nagey 1935- *CpmDNM 73, -78, ConAmC, IntWWM 77, -80*
Robertson, Doris S *WhoHol A*
Robertson, Duncan 1924- *IntWWM 77, WhoMus 72*
Robertson, Duncan D 1940- *ConAmC*
Robertson, E Arnot 1903-1961 *OxFilm*
Robertson, East d1916 *NotNAT B*
Robertson, Eck 1880?- *EncFCWM 69*
Robertson, Eck 1887- *IlEncCM*
Robertson, Edwin C 1938- *ConAmC*
Robertson, F J 1916- *IntMPA 77, -75, -76, -78, -79, -80*
Robertson, George 1929- *CreCan 1*
Robertson, George Austin, Jr. 1945- *AmSCAP 80*
Robertson, Guy 1892- *CmpEPM, EncMT, ForYSC, WhThe*
Robertson, Henry P 1890?- *NewOrJ[port]*
Robertson, Hermine d1962 *NotNAT B*
Robertson, Hugh A *DrBlPA*
Robertson, Hugh Sterling, II 1940-1973 *ConAmC*
Robertson, Ian 1858-1936 *NotNAT B, WhThe*
Robertson, Ian 1947- *IntWWM 77, -80*
Robertson, Imogene 1905-1948 *Film 2, WhScrn 74, -77, WhoHol B*
Robertson, J Francis *Film 2*
Robertson, James 1912- *CmOp, IntWWM 77, -80, WhoMus 72*
Robertson, James B 1910- *AmSCAP 66*
Robertson, James Scotty 1859-1936 *WhScrn 74, -77, WhoHol B*
Robertson, Jean 1894-1967 *WhScrn 74, -77, WhoHol B*
Robertson, Jerome d1962 *NotNAT B*
Robertson, Jetta 1925- *WhoMus 72*
Robertson, John *Film 2*
Robertson, John d1962 *NotNAT B*
Robertson, John Seymour 1938- *IntWWM 77, -80*
Robertson, John Stuart 1878-1964 *FilmEn, TwYS A, WhScrn 74, -77, WhoHol B*
Robertson, Sir Johnston Forbes *WhThe, WhoStg 1908*
Robertson, Lauri *WomWMM B*
Robertson, Leroy 1896-1971 *AmSCAP 66, -80, Baker 78, ConAmC, DcCom&M 79, WhoMus 72*
Robertson, Lolita *Film 1*
Robertson, Malcolm 1933- *WhoThe 77*
Robertson, Mary *WhScrn 74, -77*
Robertson, Maud d1930 *NotNAT B*
Robertson, Max *IntMPA 77, -75, -76, -78, -79, -80*
Robertson, Orie O 1881-1964 *NotNAT B, WhScrn 74, -77, WhoHol B*
Robertson, Paul Allan Reuben 1952- *IntWWM 77, -80*
Robertson, Pax d1948 *NotNAT B*
Robertson, Rae 1893-1956 *Baker 78, NewGrD 80*
Robertson, Sarah Margaret 1891-1948 *CreCan 1*
Robertson, Stuart 1901-1958 *WhScrn 74, -77, WhoHol B*
Robertson, Mrs. Thomas d1855 *NotNAT B*
Robertson, Thomas William 1829-1871 *CnThe, EncWT, Ent, McGEWD[port], NotNAT A, -B, OxThe, REnWD[port]*
Robertson, Thomas William Shafto d1895 *NotNAT B*
Robertson, Toby 1928- *WhoThe 72, -77*
Robertson, Tom 1829-1871 *PlP&P*
Robertson, W Graham 1867-1948 *NotNAT A, -B, WhThe*
Robertson, Walt 1928- *EncFCWM 69*
Robertson, Walter 1928- *BiDAmM*
Robertson, Willard 1886-1948 *FilmEn, ForYSC, HolCA[port], WhScrn 77, WhoHol B*
Robertson, William *WhoHol A*
Robertson, Zue C Alvin 1891-1943 *WhoJazz 72*
Robertson-Justice, James 1905-1975 *FilmEn*
Robertus De Anglia *NewGrD 80*
Robertus De Brunham *NewGrD 80*
Robertus De Burnham *NewGrD 80*
Robertus De Sabilone *NewGrD 80*
Robeson, Lila P 1880-1960 *Baker 78, BiDAmM*
Robeson, Orlando 1910?- *WhoJazz 72*
Robeson, Paul 1898-1976 *Baker 78, BiDAmM, BiE&WWA, BlksB&W C, BnBkM 80, CmpEPM, CnThe, DrBlPA, EncMT, EncWT, Ent, FilmEn, FilmgC, ForYSC, HalFC 80, IlWWBF[port], -A, MovMk, MusMk, NewGrD 80, NotNAT A, -B, OxFilm, OxThe, PlP&P, What 2[port], WhThe, WhoHol C, WhoMus 72*
Robey, Sir George 1869-1954 *CnThe, EncMT, EncWT, Ent, Film 1, -2, FilmgC, HalFC 80, IlWWBF[port], -A, NotNAT A, OxFilm, OxThe, WhScrn 74, -77, WhThe, WhoHol B*
Robic, Ivo 1927- *IntWWM 77*
Robic, Ivo 1931- *RkOn*
Robichaux, Joe 1900-1965 *NewOrJ[port]*
Robichaux, John 1866-1939 *NewOrJ*
Robichaux, John 1915- *NewOrJ[port]*
Robichaux, Joseph 1900-1965 *WhoJazz 72*
Robijns, Jozef 1920- *NewGrD 80*
Robilant, Claire H De 1915- *CnOxB*
Robin, Dany 1927- *FilmEn, FilmgC, HalFC 80, IntMPA 77, -75, -76, -78, -79, -80, WhoHol A*
Robin, Henri 1805?-1875 *MagIlD*
Robin, Joann Cohan 1928- *IntWWM 77, -80*
Robin, Leo 1899- *BiE&WWA, FilmEn, FilmgC, HalFC 80, NotNAT*
Robin, Leo 1900- *AmPS, AmSCAP 66, -80, BestMus, BiDAmM, CmpEPM, EncMT, IntMPA 77, -75, -76, -78, -79, -80, NewCBMT, Sw&Ld C*
Robin, Mado 1918-1960 *CmOp*
Robin, Melville Woodrow 1921- *WhoMus 72*
Robin, Sydney 1912- *AmSCAP 66, -80*
Robina, Fanny d1927 *NotNAT B*
Robina, Florrie d1953 *NotNAT B*
Robineau, Alexandre-Auguste 1747-1828 *NewGrD 80*
Robinet De La Magdalaine 1415-1478 *NewGrD 80*
Robinette, Joseph Allen 1939- *AmSCAP 80*
Robins, The *RkOn*
Robins, Barry *WhoHol A*
Robins, Edward H 1880-1955 *NotNAT B, WhScrn 77, WhThe, WhoHol B*
Robins, Elisabeth 1862-1952 *EncWT*
Robins, Elizabeth 1862-1952 *NotNAT A, -B, OxThe*
Robins, Elizabeth 1865-1952 *WhThe*
Robins, Gertrude L d1917 *NotNAT B, WhThe*
Robins, John Daniel 1884-1952 *CreCan 2*
Robins, Robert Edwin 1927- *IntWWM 77*
Robins, Toby *WhoHol A*
Robins, William A d1948 *NotNAT B*
Robinson *NewGrD 80, 80*
Robinson, Miss *NewGrD 80*
Robinson, Albert Henry 1881-1956 *CreCan 1*
Robinson, Alvan, Jr. 1802-1865 *BiDAmM*
Robinson, Amy 1948- *MovMk*
Robinson, Anastasia 1692?-1755 *NewGrD 80[port]*
Robinson, Andy *WhoHol A*
Robinson, Ann 1927- *WhoHol A, WhoHrs 80[port]*
Robinson, Ann Turner d1741 *NewGrD 80*
Robinson, Anna d1917 *NotNAT B*
Robinson, Arthur *Film 1*
Robinson, Arthur Langmead 1910- *WhoMus 72*
Robinson, Avery 1878-1965 *AmSCAP 66, -80*
Robinson, Banjo Ikey L 1904- *WhoJazz 72*
Robinson, Bartlett *ForYSC, WhoHol A*
Robinson, Bernard 1912- *CmMov*
Robinson, Bernard Wheeler 1904- *IntWWM 77, -80*
Robinson, Bertrand d1959 *NotNAT B*
Robinson, Betsy Julia *MorBAP*
Robinson, Betty Jean *AmSCAP 80*
Robinson, Bill 1878-1949 *BlksB&W[port], -C, BlksBF[port], CmpEPM, CnOxB, DancEn 78, DrBlPA, EncMT, Ent[port], FilmEn, FilmgC, ForYSC, HalFC 80, MovMk[port], NotNAT B, WhScrn 74, -77, WhThe, WhoHol B*
Robinson, Casey 1903-1979 *CmMov, FilmEn, FilmgC, HalFC 80, IntMPA 77, -75, -76, -78, -79, -80*
Robinson, Charles Knox 1909- *BiE&WWA, ForYSC, NotNAT, WhoHol A*
Robinson, Charles Seymour 1829-1899 *BiDAmM*
Robinson, Chris 1940- *ForYSC, WhoHol A*
Robinson, Christine *WomWMM*
Robinson, Daisy *Film 1*
Robinson, David *ConMuA 80B, WhoHol A*
Robinson, David Gerald 1931- *WhoMus 72*
Robinson, David Peter Francis 1937- *WhoMus 72*
Robinson, Del *MorBAP*
Robinson, Dewey 1898-1950 *ForYSC, Vers B[port], WhScrn 74, -77, WhoHol B*
Robinson, Douglas 1912- *WhoMus 72*
Robinson, Douglas 1913- *IntWWM 77, -80*
Robinson, E M 1855-1932 *NotNAT B*
Robinson, Earl *Film 2*
Robinson, Earl 1910- *AmSCAP 66, -80, Baker 78, BiDAmM, ConAmC, EncFCWM 69, IntWWM 77*
Robinson, Ed 1882?- *NewOrJ*
Robinson, Edward 1905- *AmSCAP 66, -80, ConAmC A*
Robinson, Edward Alfred 1921- *AmSCAP 80*
Robinson, Edward G 1893- *BiE&WWA, ForYSC, MotPP, WhThe, WorEFlm[port]*
Robinson, Edward G 1893-1972 *FilmgC, OxFilm*
Robinson, Edward G 1893-1973 *BiDFilm, -81, CmMov, FilmEn, Film 2, HalFC 80[port], MovMk[port], NotNAT A, WhScrn 77, WhoHol B, WhoHrs 80*
Robinson, Edward G, Jr. 1934-1974 *WhScrn 77, WhoHol B*
Robinson, Eli 1908- *WhoJazz 72*
Robinson, Eli 1911-1972 *BiDAmM, EncJzS 70*
Robinson, Eric 1908- *WhoMus 72*
Robinson, Esme Stuart Lennox 1886-1958 *NotNAT B*
Robinson, Ethan M d1919 *NotNAT B*
Robinson, Fanny Arthur 1831-1879 *NewGrD 80*
Robinson, Faye 1943- *WhoOp 76*
Robinson, Fention 1935- *BluesWW[port]*
Robinson, Fenton 1935- *BluesWW[port]*
Robinson, Floyd *RkOn*
Robinson, Forbes 1926- *CmOp, IntWWM 77, -80, NewGrD 80, WhoMus 72, WhoOp 76*
Robinson, Forest *Film 1*
Robinson, Forrest 1859-1924 *Film 2, NotNAT B, WhScrn 74, -77, WhoHol B*
Robinson, Frances 1916-1971 *FilmgC, ForYSC, HalFC 80, WhScrn 74, -77, WhoHol B*
Robinson, Francis *NewGrD 80*
Robinson, Francis 1910- *WhoOp 76*
Robinson, Francis, I *OxMus*
Robinson, Francis, II 1800?-1872 *OxMus*
Robinson, Francis James 1799?-1872 *NewGrD 80*
Robinson, Frank *NewOrJ*
Robinson, Frankie 1940- *What 2[port]*
Robinson, Franklin Whitman 1875-1946 *Baker 78, BiDAmM*
Robinson, Fred 1901- *CmpEPM, WhoJazz 72*
Robinson, Fred Leroy 1939- *EncJzS 70*
Robinson, Frederic Charles Patey 1832-1912 *NotNAT B*
Robinson, Frederick L 1901- *BiDAmM*
Robinson, Gail 1946- *WhoOp 76*
Robinson, Garrett *BlkAmP, MorBAP*

Robinson, George *FilmEn*
Robinson, Gertrude R 1891-1962 *Film 1, WhScrn 74, -77, WhoHol B*
Robinson, Glen O *NewYTET*
Robinson, Gordon W 1908- *AmSCAP 66, -80*
Robinson, Harry I 1888-1954 *AmSCAP 66, -80*
Robinson, Helene Margaret 1914- *IntWWM 77, -80*
Robinson, Herbert *IntMPA 77, -75, -76, -78, -79*
Robinson, Herman Lee 1939- *AmSCAP 66*
Robinson, Horace 1909- *BiE&WWA, NotNAT*
Robinson, Hubbell d1974 *NewYTET*
Robinson, Irwin *ConMuA 80B*
Robinson, Isaiah 1892-1962 *NewOrJ*
Robinson, J Russel 1892-1963 *AmSCAP 66, -80, CmpEPM, NotNAT B, WhoJazz 72*
Robinson, J Russell 1892-1963 *BiDAmM*
Robinson, Jackie 1919-1972 *WhScrn 77, WhoHol B*
Robinson, James 1892-1976 *BiDAmM, EncJzS 70*
Robinson, James 1903-1957 *BluesWW*
Robinson, Janice Elaine 1951- *BlkWAB[port]*
Robinson, Jay 1930- *BiE&WWA, FilmgC, ForYSC, HalFC 80, NotNAT, WhoHol A*
Robinson, Jessie Mae 1919- *AmSCAP 66, -80*
Robinson, Jim *ConMuA 80B*
Robinson, Jim 1892-1976 *CmpEPM, EncJzS 70, IlEncJ, WhoJazz 72*
Robinson, Jimmy Lee 1931- *BluesWW[port]*
Robinson, Joan Lee 1954- *IntWWM 77*
Robinson, Joe *WhoHol A*
Robinson, John 1682?-1762 *NewGrD 80, OxMus*
Robinson, John 1812?-1844 *NewGrD 80, OxMus*
Robinson, John 1908-1979 *FilmgC, HalFC 80, WhoHol A, WhoThe 72, -77*
Robinson, John 1940- *NatPD[port]*
Robinson, Joseph 1816-1898 *NewGrD 80, OxMus*
Robinson, Judith *PlP&P[port]*
Robinson, Kathleen 1909- *WhThe*
Robinson, Keith *ConAmC*
Robinson, Lennox 1886-1958 *CnMD, CnThe, EncWT, McGEWD[port], ModWD, NotNAT A, OxThe, PlP&P, REnWD[port], WhThe*
Robinson, Les 1914- *CmpEPM*
Robinson, Lisa *ConMuA 80B*
Robinson, Lloyd E 1908- *AmSCAP 66*
Robinson, Louis Charles 1915-1976 *BluesWW[port]*
Robinson, Lucy 1949- *IntWWM 77, -80*
Robinson, M Louise *PupTheA*
Robinson, Madeleine 1908- *WhThe*
Robinson, Madeleine 1916- *EncWT, FilmEn, FilmgC, HalFC 80*
Robinson, Marie 1940- *WhoOp 76*
Robinson, Mary Darby 1758-1800 *NotNAT A, OxThe*
Robinson, Matt 1937- *DrBlPA*
Robinson, Matthew Thomas, Jr. 1937- *AmSCAP 80*
Robinson, Michael Finlay 1933- *IntWWM 77, -80, NewGrD 80*
Robinson, Michelle *ConMuA 80B*
Robinson, Muriel *IntWWM 77*
Robinson, Nathan 1892-1976 *NewOrJ[port]*
Robinson, Norah 1901- *WhThe*
Robinson, Oscar 1888?- *NewOrJ*
Robinson, Paul E 1940- *IntWWM 80*
Robinson, Percy 1889-1967 *WhThe*
Robinson, Perdita 1758-1800 *NotNAT B*
Robinson, Perry Morris 1938- *EncJzS 70*
Robinson, Pete 1950- *EncJzS 70*
Robinson, Prince 1902-1960 *CmpEPM*
Robinson, Prince 1904- *BiDAmM*
Robinson, Richard d1648 *OxThe*
Robinson, Richard 1923- *ConAmC*
Robinson, Roger 1941- *DrBlPA*
Robinson, Ruth 1888-1966 *WhScrn 77, WhoHol B*
Robinson, S Garrett 1939- *NatPD[port]*
Robinson, Sam *NewOrJ*
Robinson, Shari 1942- *WhoHol A*
Robinson, Smokey 1940- *ConMuA 80A, DrBlPA, IlEncR, RkOn 2[port]*
Robinson, Spike 1884-1942 *Film 1, -2, WhScrn 74, -77, WhoHol B*
Robinson, Stamford 1904- *IntWWM 77*
Robinson, Stanford 1904- *Baker 78, IntWWM 80, NewGrD 80, WhoMus 72*
Robinson, Stuart *DcPup*
Robinson, Stuart 1936- *BiE&WWA*
Robinson, Sugar Chile 1940- *DrBlPA*
Robinson, Sugar Ray 1920- *DrBlPA*
Robinson, Sugar Ray 1921- *WhoHol A*
Robinson, Sugarchile 1940- *WhoHol A*
Robinson, Thelma Frances 1914- *WhoMus 72*
Robinson, Thomas *NewGrD 80, OxMus*
Robinson, Tom, Band *ConMuA 80A*
Robinson, Vicki Sue 1955- *RkOn 2[port]*
Robinson, Virginia Morgan 1910- *IntWWM 77, -80*
Robinson, W C *Film 1*
Robinson, Wayne 1916- *BiE&WWA, NotNAT*
Robinson, William 1805?- *NewGrD 80, OxMus*
Robinson, William, Jr. 1940- *AmSCAP 80*
Robinson, Sir William Cleaver Francis 1834-1897 *NewGrD 80*
Robinson, William Ellsworth *MagIlD*
Robinson, Woody *MorBAP*
Robinson-Cleaver, Harold Arthur 1907- *WhoMus 72*
Robinson-Duff, Frances d1951 *NotNAT B*
Robison, Arthur 1888-1935 *DcFM, FilmEn, FilmgC, HalFC 80, OxFilm*
Robison, Carson J 1890-1957 *AmSCAP 66, -80, BiDAmM, CmpEPM, CounME 74, EncFCWM 69, IlEncCM*
Robison, Charles Wright 1925- *IntWWM 77, -80*
Robison, Paula 1941- *IntWWM 77, -80, NewGrD 80*
Robison, Willard 1894-1968 *AmSCAP 66, -80, CmpEPM*
Robjohn, W J 1843-1920 *NewGrD 80*
Robledo, Juan Ruiz De *NewGrD 80*
Robledo, Melchor 1520?-1587? *NewGrD 80*
Robles, Daniel Alomias 1871-1942 *Baker 78*
Robles, Emmanuel Francois 1913- *CnMD*
Robles, German *WhoHrs 80*
Robles, Maria Esther 1921- *IntWWM 77, -80*
Robles, Marisa 1937- *IntWWM 77, -80, NewGrD 80, WhoMus 72*
Robles, Richard 1902-1940 *WhScrn 74, -77, WhoHol B*
Robles, Rudy 1910-1970 *WhScrn 74, -77, WhoHol B*
Robles, Walter *WhoHol A*
Robletti, Giovanni Battista *NewGrD 80*
Robotham, Barbara 1936- *IntWWM 77, -80, WhoMus 72*
Robredo, Manuel Saumell *NewGrD 80*
Robson, Andrew 1867-1921 *Film 1, -2, WhScrn 74, -77, WhoHol B*
Robson, E M 1855-1932 *WhThe*
Robson, Eleanor Elise 1879- *NotNAT A, WhThe, WhoStg 1906, -1908*
Robson, Elizabeth 1939- *IntWWM 77, -80, WhoOp 76*
Robson, Flora 1902- *BiE&WWA, CnThe, EncWT, Ent, FilmAG WE, FilmEn, FilmgC, ForYSC, HalFC 80, IlWWBF[port], -A, IntMPA 77, -75, -76, -78, -79, -80, MotPP, MovMk, NotNAT, -A, OxFilm, OxThe, PlP&P, ThFT[port], Vers A[port], WhoHol A, WhoThe 72, -77*
Robson, Frederick d1919 *NotNAT B*
Robson, Frederick 1821-1864 *NotNAT A, -B, OxThe*
Robson, Jean-Jacques 1723?-1785 *NewGrD 80*
Robson, June 1922-1972 *WhScrn 77*
Robson, Mark 1913-1978 *BiDFilm, -81, CmMov, DcFM, FilmEn, FilmgC, HalFC 80, IntMPA 77, -75, -76, -78, MovMk[port], OxFilm, WhoHrs 80, WomWMM, WorEFlm*
Robson, Mary 1893- *WhThe*
Robson, Mat d1899 *NotNAT B*
Robson, May d1942 *MotPP, PlP&P, WhoHol B, WhoStg 1906, -1908*
Robson, May 1858-1942 *FilmEn, HalFC 80, HolCA[port], ThFT[port], WhScrn 74, -77*
Robson, May 1859-1942 *FilmgC*
Robson, May 1864-1942 *MovMk[port]*
Robson, May 1865-1942 *Film 1, -2, ForYSC, NotNAT B, OxFilm, TwYS, Vers A[port], WhThe*
Robson, Philip d1919 *WhScrn 77*
Robson, Stuart 1836-1903 *FamA&A[port], NotNAT B, OxThe, PlP&P*
Robson, Mrs. Stuart d1924 *NotNAT B, WhoHol B*
Robson, Stuart, Jr. d1946 *NotNAT B*
Robson, William *NotNAT B*
Roby, Lavelle *DrBlPA, WhoHol A*
Roby, Paul Edward 1935- *IntWWM 77, -80*
Robyn, Alfred George 1860-1935 *AmSCAP 66, -80, Baker 78, BiDAmM, NotNAT B*
Robyn, Gay 1912-1942 *WhScrn 74, -77*
Robyns *NewGrD 80*
Robyns, William 1855-1936 *Film 2, WhScrn 74, -77, WhoHol B*
Roc, Patricia 1918- *FilmAG WE, FilmEn, FilmgC, HalFC 80, IlWWBF[port], WhoHol A*
Roca, Matheo Tollis DeLa *NewGrD 80*
Rocca, Daniela *WhoHol A*
Rocca, Gino 1891-1941 *McGEWD*
Rocca, Giuseppe 1807-1865 *NewGrD 80*
Rocca, Lodovico 1895- *Baker 78, IntWWM 77, -80, NewEOp 71, NewGrD 80, WhoMus 72*
Roccardi, Albert 1864-1934 *Film 1, -2, WhScrn 77*
Rocchi, Aldo 1921- *WhoOp 76*
Rocchi, Manlio 1935- *WhoOp 76*
Rocchigiani, Giovanni Battista d1632? *NewGrD 80*
Roccia *NewGrD 80*
Roccia, Aurelio 1540?-1571? *NewGrD 80*
Roccia, Dattilo 1570?-1617? *NewGrD 80*
Roccia, Francesco 1582-1613? *NewGrD 80*
Roccisano, Joe 1939- *EncJzS 70*
Roccisano, Joseph Lucian 1939- *EncJzS 70*
Rocco, Alex *WhoHol A*
Rocco, Maurice 1915-1976 *BiDAmM, DrBlPA, EncJzS 70, WhoHol C*
Roch, Madeleine d1930 *NotNAT B, WhThe*
Rocha, Francisco Gomes Da d1808 *NewGrD 80*
Rocha, Glauber 1938- *DcFM, FilmEn, OxFilm, WorEFlm*
Rocha, Miguel F d1961 *WhScrn 74, -77*
Rochat, Andree 1900- *IntWWM 77, -80*
Rochay, Joe *Film 2*
Rochberg, A George 1918- *AmSCAP 80*
Rochberg, George 1918- *AmSCAP 66, Baker 78, BnBkM 80, CpmDNM 72, -77, -78, -79, DcCom&M 79, DcCM, IntWWM 77, -80, NewGrD 80, OxMus*
Rochberg, George 1919- *ConAmC*
Roche, Clara Darley *Film 2*
Roche, Eugene 1934?- *HalFC 80, WhoHol A*
Roche, Frank d1963 *WhoHol B*
Roche, Franklyn D 1904-1963 *WhScrn 74, -77*
Roche, Guillaume *McGEWD[port]*
Roche, Jerome Laurence Alexander 1942- *IntWWM 77, -80, NewGrD 80*
Roche, John 1896-1952 *Film 2, ForYSC, TwYS, WhScrn 74, -77, WhoHol B*
Roche, Mary Elizabeth 1920- *BiDAmM*
Roche, Michel Sylvain Nizier 1936- *IntWWM 77, -80*
Rochefort, Jean 1930- *FilmEn, WhoHol A*
Rochefort, Jean Baptiste 1746-1819 *NewGrD 80*
Rochell And The Candles *RkOn*
Rochelle, Claire *ForYSC*
Rochelle, Edward d1908 *NotNAT B*
Rochemont, Louis De *DcFM*
Rocher, Rene 1890- *WhThe*
Rocherolle, Eugenie Ricau 1936- *AmSCAP 80, ConAmC*
Rochers, Joseph Alfred Houle Des *CreCan 1*
Rochester 1905-1977 *DrBlPA, ForYSC, IntMPA 77, -76, -78, -79, -80, JoeFr[port], WhoHol A*
Rochetti, Filippo *NewGrD 80*
Rochin, Paul 1889-1964 *NotNAT B, WhScrn 74, -77*
Rochinski, Stanley J 1906- *AmSCAP 80*
Rochinski, Stanley R 1906- *AmSCAP 66*
Rochlin, Diane *WomWMM, -B*
Rochlin, Irv 1926- *EncJzS 70*

Rochlin, Irvin 1926- *EncJzS 70*
Rochlitz, Friedrich 1769-1842 *NewGrD 80*
Rochlitz, Johann Friedrich 1769-1842 *Baker 78*
Rochois, Marthe Le *NewGrD 80*
Rochon, Roger *DancEn 78*
Rock, Blossom *FilmEn, ForYSC, WhoHol A*
Rock, Charles 1866-1919 *Film 1, NotNAT B, WhScrn 77, WhThe, WhoHol B*
Rock, Chris *AmSCAP 80*
Rock, Felippa *WhoHol A*
Rock, Joseph V 1936- *AmSCAP 66, -80*
Rock, William d1922 *NotNAT B*
Rock, William T 1853-1916 *WhScrn 77*
Rock-A-Teens, The *RkOn*
Rockefeller, John D, III 1906- *BiE&WWA*
Rockefeller, Kay 1918- *NotNAT*
Rockefeller, Martha Baird 1895-1971 *BiDAmM*
Rockel *NewGrD 80*
Rockel, August 1814-1876 *NewGrD 80*
Rockel, Eduard 1816-1899 *NewGrD 80*
Rockel, Josef 1783-1870 *NewGrD 80*
Rockel, Joseph 1783-1870 *NewGrD 80*
Rockel, Joseph Leopold 1838-1923 *NewGrD 80*
Rockert, John F 1924- *IntMPA 79, -80*
Rockin' Rebels, The *RkOn*
Rockin' Red *BluesWW*
Rockin' Sydney *BluesWW*
Rockland, Jeffrey *WhoHol A*
Rockstro, William Smyth 1823-1895 *Baker 78, NewGrD 80, OxMus*
Rockwell, Donald Shumway 1895- *AmSCAP 66*
Rockwell, Ed *Film 2*
Rockwell, Florence 1880-1964 *NotNAT B, WhoStg 1906, -1908*
Rockwell, Jack d1946 *ForYSC*
Rockwell, Jack d1947 *Film 2, WhScrn 77, WhoHol B*
Rockwell, John *ConMuA 80B*
Rockwell, Mary *WhScrn 74, -77*
Rockwell, Robert *ForYSC, WhoHol A*
Rockwood, Roy *Film 2*
Rocky Fellers, The *RkOn*
Rocour, Pierre De *NewGrD 80*
Rocourt, Pierre De *NewGrD 80*
Rocquemore, Henry 1909- *AmSCAP 80*
Rocquemore, Henry 1915- *AmSCAP 66*
Roczek, Paul 1947- *IntWWM 77, -80*
Rod, Einar *Film 2*
Roda, Cecilio De 1865-1912 *NewGrD 80*
Roda Y Lopez, Cecilio De 1865-1912 *Baker 78*
Rodan, Mendi 1929- *IntWWM 77, -80, NewGrD 80, WhoMus 72*
Rodann, Ziva 1933?- *ForYSC, WhoHol A, WhoHrs 80*
Rodber, John D *PupTheA*
Rodby, John Leonard 1944- *CpmDNM 73, -78, ConAmC*
Rodby, Walter 1917- *AmSCAP 66, ConAmC*
Rodby, Walter 1920- *AmSCAP 80*
Rodd, Marcia 1940- *NotNAT, PlP&P[port], WhoHol A, WhoThe 72, -77*
Rodda, John 1940- *IntWWM 80*
Rodde, Leroy William 1919- *AmSCAP 80*
Roddenberry, Gene *FilmgC, HalFC 80, NewYTET*
Roddie, John W 1903- *AmSCAP 66, -80*
Roddie, Vin 1918- *AmSCAP 66*
Roddy, Ruben 1906-1960 *NewOrJ*
Rode, Helge 1870-1937 *NotNAT B, OxThe*
Rode, Jacques Pierre Joseph 1774-1830 *OxMus*
Rode, Lizzie 1933- *CnOxB, DancEn 78*
Rode, Pierre 1774-1830 *Baker 78, BnBkM 80, GrComp[port], NewGrD 80*
Rode, Walter d1973 *WhScrn 77, WhoHol B*
Rode, Wilhelm 1887-1959 *CmOp, NewGrD 80*
Rodeheaver, Homer Alvan 1880-1955 *AmSCAP 66, -80, Baker 78, BiDAmM, NewGrD 80*
Rodemich, Gene *CmpEPM*
Roden, Anthony 1937- *IntWWM 80, WhoOp 76*
Roden, Jess *IlEncR*
Rodenbach, Georges 1855-1898 *NotNAT B*
Rodensteen *NewGrD 80*
Rodensteen, Hermann d1583 *NewGrD 80*
Rodensteen, Israel *NewGrD 80*
Rodensteen, Raphael d1552? *NewGrD 80*
Roder, Carl Gottlieb 1812-1883 *Baker 78, NewGrD 80*
Roder, Johann Michael *NewGrD 80*
Roder, Martin 1851-1895 *Baker 78*
Roder, Milan 1878-1956 *AmSCAP 66, -80, ConAmC*
Roderick, George *WhoHol A*
Roderick, Leslie 1907-1927 *WhScrn 74, -77*
Roderick Jones, Richard Trevor 1947- *IntWWM 77, -80*
Rodericus *NewGrD 80*
Rodetsky, Samuel 1906- *IntWWM 77, -80*
Rodgers, Anton *WhoHol A*
Rodgers, Anton 1927- *FilmgC, HalFC 80*
Rodgers, Anton 1933- *WhoThe 72, -77*
Rodgers, Bob 1924- *BiE&WWA*
Rodgers, Carrie Cecil d1961 *NotNAT B*
Rodgers, Eileen 1933- *BiE&WWA, NotNAT, RkOn[port]*
Rodgers, G W *PupTheA*
Rodgers, Gaby 1928- *IntMPA 77, -75, -76, -78, -79, -80*
Rodgers, Gene 1910- *WhoJazz 72*
Rodgers, Ilona *WhoHol A*
Rodgers, James d1890 *NotNAT B*
Rodgers, James Charles 1897-1933 *BluesWW[port], NewGrD 80*
Rodgers, James Frederick 1933- *AmSCAP 80, BiDAmM*
Rodgers, Jimmie *Film 2*
Rodgers, Jimmie 1897-1933 *AmSCAP 66, -80, Baker 78, BiDAmM, CmpEPM, CounME 74[port], EncFCWM 69, NewGrD 80*
Rodgers, Jimmie 1933- *AmPS A, -B, EncFCWM 69, RkOn[port]*
Rodgers, Jimmie Charles 1897-1933 *CounME 74A, IlEncCM[port]*
Rodgers, Jimmy 1897-1933 *NotNAT B*
Rodgers, John 1917- *AmSCAP 66, -80, ConAmC*
Rodgers, John Wesley *WhoHol A*
Rodgers, Marty 1948- *AmSCAP 80*
Rodgers, Mary *AmSCAP 80*
Rodgers, Mary 1931- *AmSCAP 66, BiE&WWA, ConAmC, EncMT, NewCBMT, NotNAT*
Rodgers, Nile *ConMuA 80B*
Rodgers, Pamela *WhoHol A*
Rodgers, Richard *BnBkM 80, IntMPA 77, -75, -76, -78, -79, -80, WhoHol A*
Rodgers, Richard 1901-1979 *CmMov, FilmgC, HalFC 80*
Rodgers, Richard 1902-1979 *AmPS, AmSCAP 66, -80, Baker 78, BiDAmM, BiE&WWA, CmpEPM, ConAmC, EncMT, EncWT, FilmEn, IntWWM 77, McGEWD, MnPM[port], MusMk, NewCBMT, NewGrD 80, NotNAT, -A, OxFilm, PlP&P[port], PopAmC[port], PopAmC SUP, Sw&Ld C, WhoMus 72, WhoThe 72, -77*
Rodgers, Rod 1938?- *CmpGMD, CnOxB, DrBlPA*
Rodgers, Thomas Edward 1927- *IntMPA 77, -75, -76, -78, -79*
Rodgers, Walter 1887-1951 *Film 1, -2, WhScrn 74, -77, WhoHol B*
Rodham, Robert 1939- *CnOxB, DancEn 78*
Rodilak, Charles d1972 *WhoHol B*
Rodin, Gil 1906-1974 *CmpEPM, EncJzS 70, WhoJazz 72*
Rodin, Gilbert A 1906-1974 *BiDAmM, EncJzS 70*
Rodin, Margot Kerstin Birgitta 1935- *WhoOp 76*
Rodio, Jolanda Caterina Letizia 1914- *IntWWM 77, -80*
Rodio, Rocco 1530?-1615? *Baker 78*
Rodio, Rocco 1535?-1615? *NewGrD 80*
Rodman, Howard *NewYTET*
Rodman, Nancy *WhoHol A*
Rodman, Victor 1893-1965 *Film 2, WhScrn 77*
Rodney, Don 1920- *AmSCAP 66, -80*
Rodney, Earl *Film 1, -2*
Rodney, Earle 1891-1932 *TwYS, WhScrn 74, -77, WhoHol B*
Rodney, Frank d1902 *NotNAT B*
Rodney, Jack 1916-1967 *WhScrn 74, -77, WhoHol B*
Rodney, Joseph B 1917- *AmSCAP 80*
Rodney, Lynne d1937 *WhScrn 77*
Rodney, Red 1927- *BiDAmM, CmpEPM, EncJzS 70, IlEncJ*
Rodney, Stratton d1932 *NotNAT B*
Rodolphe, Jean Joseph 1730-1812 *Baker 78, NewGrD 80*
Rodolphe, Johann Joseph *CnOxB*
Rodomista, Vincent 1918- *AmSCAP 80*
Rodrigo, Joaquin 1901- *NewGrD 80*
Rodrigo, Joaquin 1902- *Baker 78, BnBkM 80, DcCom&M 79, DcCM, MusMk*
Rodrigo DeLedesma, Mariano 1779-1848 *Baker 78*
Rodrigues, Alfred 1921- *CnOxB, DancEn 78*
Rodrigues, Amalia 1920- *FilmAG WE*
Rodrigues, Luis 1906- *IntWWM 77, -80*
Rodrigues, Nelson 1912- *CnThe, REnWD[port]*
Rodrigues, Percy 1924- *DrBlPA, FilmgC, HalFC 80*
Rodrigues Coelho, Manuel 1555?-1635? *NewGrD 80*
Rodriguez, Alex 1940- *EncJzS 70*
Rodriguez, Augusto 1904- *Baker 78*
Rodriguez, Charles J *WhoHol A*
Rodriguez, Estelita 1915-1966 *ForYSC, WhScrn 74, -77, WhoHol B*
Rodriguez, Felipe 1759-1814 *Baker 78*
Rodriguez, Johnny 1951- *CounME 74[port], -74A*
Rodriguez, Johnny 1952- *IlEncCM[port]*
Rodriguez, Percy *WhoHol A*
Rodriguez, Robert Xavier 1946- *AmSCAP 80, CpmDNM 74, -76, ConAmC*
Rodriguez, Rod Nicholas Goodwin 1904?- *WhoJazz 72*
Rodriguez, Rodolfo 1935- *DancEn 78*
Rodriguez, Tito 1923-1973 *WhScrn 77*
Rodriguez, Vicente d1760 *NewGrD 80*
Rodriguez, Vicente 1685?-1761 *Baker 78*
Rodriguez, Zhandra 1947- *CnOxB*
Rodriguez Alvarez, Alejandro *McGEWD*
Rodriguez Buded, Ricardo *CroCD*
Rodriguez DeHita, Antonio 1724?-1787 *Baker 78, NewGrD 80*
Rodriguez DeLedesma, Mariano 1779-1847 *NewGrD 80*
Rodulfus Saint Trudonis *NewGrD 80*
Rodulfus Sancti Trudonis 1070?-1138 *NewGrD 80*
Rodulfus Van St. Truiden 1070?-1138 *NewGrD 80*
Rodway, Norman 1929- *WhoHol A, WhoThe 72, -77*
Rodway, Philip 1876-1932 *NotNAT A, -B*
Rodwell, G H d1852 *NotNAT B*
Rodwell, George 1800-1852 *NewGrD 80*
Rodzinski, Artur d1958 *NotNAT B*
Rodzinski, Artur 1892-1958 *Baker 78, BnBkM 80, MusSN[port], NewGrD 80[port]*
Rodzinski, Artur 1894-1958 *BiDAmM, NewEOp 71*
Rodzinski, Richard 1945- *WhoOp 76*
Roe, Bassett 1860-1934 *NotNAT B, WhThe*
Roe, Betty Eileen 1930- *WhoMus 72*
Roe, Charles Richard 1940- *IntWWM 77, -80, WhoOp 76*
Roe, Christopher John 1940- *WhoMus 72*
Roe, Eileen Betty 1930- *IntWWM 80*
Roe, Gloria Ann 1935- *AmSCAP 66*
Roe, Gloria Kliewer 1940- *AmSCAP 80*
Roe, Helen Mary Gabrielle 1955- *IntWWM 77, -80*
Roe, Hilda Joan 1922- *WhoMus 72*
Roe, Joan Mary 1910- *WhoMus 72*
Roe, Patricia 1932- *BiE&WWA, NotNAT, WhoHol A*
Roe, Pauline Cicely 1937- *IntWWM 77*
Roe, Tex 1922- *BiDAmM*
Roe, Tommy 1943- *RkOn*
Roebling, Paul 1934- *BiE&WWA, NotNAT, WhoThe 72, -77*
Roebuck, Disney d1885 *NotNAT B*
Roeckel *NewGrD 80*
Roeckel, August 1814-1876 *Baker 78, OxMus*
Roeckel, Edward 1816-1899 *OxMus*
Roeckel, Joseph August 1783-1870 *OxMus*
Roeckel, Joseph Leopold 1838-1923 *OxMus*
Roecker, Dorothy *WomWMM B*
Roeckle, Charles Albert 1942- *IntWWM 77*

Roeder, Benjamin F d1943 *NotNAT B*
Roeder, Martin 1851-1895 *BiDAmM*
Roederer, Juan G 1929- *IntWWM 77, -80*
Roedl, Linda L 1944- *IntWWM 80*
Roeg, Nicholas 1928- *BiDFilm, DcFM, IlWWBF, IntMPA 77, -75, -76, -78, -79, -80, OxFilm, WorEFlm*
Roeg, Nicolas 1928- *BiDFilm 81, FilmEn, FilmgC, HalFC 80, WhoHrs 80*
Roel DelRio, Antonio Ventura *NewGrD 80*
Roelle, Valdemar Zbigniew 1935- *IntWWM 80*
Roels, Marcel 1893-1973 *WhScrn 77*
Roels, Marcel 1894-1974 *FilmAG WE*
Roelstraete, Herman 1925- *NewGrD 80*
Roemer, Michael 1928- *FilmEn*
Roemheld, Heinz 1901- *AmSCAP 66, -80*
Roerich, Nicholas 1874 1947 *DancEn 78*
Roerick, William 1912- *NotNAT, WhoHol A, WhoThe 72, -77*
Roes, Carol Lasater *AmSCAP 80*
Roesborg, Nikolai *Film 2*
Roeser, Donald 1947- *AmSCAP 80*
Roeser, Valentin 1735?-1782? *NewGrD 80*
Roesgen-Champion, Marguerite 1894-1976 *Baker 78*
Roessler, Ernst Karl 1909- *IntWWM 77, -80*
Roeter, Ada 1906- *AmSCAP 80*
Roeterdink, Hubertus Johannus Albertus 1948- *IntWWM 77*
Roethinger *NewGrD 80*
Roethinger, Andre 1928- *NewGrD 80*
Roethinger, Edmond Alexandre 1866-1953 *NewGrD 80*
Roethinger, Max 1897- *NewGrD 80*
Roetscher, Konrad Felix 1910- *IntWWM 80*
Roettger, Dorye 1932- *IntWWM 77, -80*
Roettger, Heinz Martin Albert 1909- *IntWWM 80*
Roff, Joseph 1910- *AmSCAP 80, ConAmC*
Roffman, Frederick S 1945- *IntWWM 77, -80*
Roffman, Julian *WhoHrs 80*
Roffredi, Guglielmo *NewGrD 80*
Rogalski, Theodor 1901-1954 *Baker 78, NewGrD 80*
Rogan, Beth *WhoHol A*
Rogan, Florence *Film 2*
Rogan, James Edward 1908- *AmSCAP 80*
Rogan, Jimmy 1908- *AmSCAP 66*
Rogan, John *WhoHol A*
Rogatis, Pascual De 1880- *Baker 78*
Rogatis, Pascual De 1881- *NewGrD 80*
Roge, Pascal 1951- *IntWWM 77, -80, NewGrD 80*
Rogel, Jose 1829-1901 *Baker 78, NewGrD 80*
Rogell, Albert S 1901- *FilmEn, FilmgC, HalFC 80, IntMPA 77, -75, -76, -78, -79, -80, TwYS A*
Rogell, Irma *IntWWM 77, -80*
Roger, Estienne 1665?-1722 *NewGrD 80*
Roger, Gustave-Hippolyte 1815-1879 *Baker 78, NewGrD 80*
Roger, Jeanne 1692-1722 *NewGrD 80*
Roger, Lee *WhoHol A*
Roger, Victor 1853-1903 *NewGrD 80*
Roger, Victor 1854-1903 *Baker 78*
Roger, William d1482 *NewGrD 80*
Roger-Ducasse, Jean-Jules Aimable 1873-1954 *Baker 78, BnBkM 80, NewGrD 80, OxMus*
Roger-Ferdinand 1898- *McGEWD*
Rogeri, Giovanni Baptista *NewGrD 80*
Rogers, Alex d1930 *BlkAmP, BlksBF*
Rogers, Ann *AmSCAP 80*
Rogers, Anne 1933- *BiE&WWA, EncMT, NotNAT, WhoThe 72, -77*
Rogers, Benjamin 1614-1698 *NewGrD 80, OxMus*
Rogers, Bernard 1893-1968 *AmSCAP 66, -80, Baker 78, BiDAmM, ConAmC, DcCM, NewGrD 80, OxMus*
Rogers, Billie 1919?- *CmpEPM*
Rogers, Blake *WhoHol A*
Rogers, Brian 1932- *IntWWM 77*
Rogers, Brooks *WhoHol A*
Rogers, Budd 1891- *IntMPA 75*
Rogers, Buddy *BgBands 74, MotPP*
Rogers, Calvin Y 1922- *IntWWM 77, -80*
Rogers, Carl D 1900-1965 *WhScrn 74, -77, WhoHol B*
Rogers, Charles 1904- *AmPS B, CmpEPM, FilmEn, Film 2, FilmgC, ForYSC, HalFC 80[port], IntMPA 77, -75, -76, -78, -79, -80, MovMk[port], TwYS, What 3[port], WhoHol A*
Rogers, Charles R d1957 *NotNAT B*
Rogers, Charley *Film 2*
Rogers, Clara Kathleen Barnett 1844-1931 *Baker 78, BiDAmM*
Rogers, Clyde *CmpEPM*
Rogers, David *BlkAmP*
Rogers, David 1936- *CounME 74[port], -74A, IlEncCM*
Rogers, David Claude 1939- *IntWWM 80*
Rogers, Delmer Dalzell 1928- *IntWWM 77, -80*
Rogers, Dick 1912-1970 *AmSCAP 66, -80, BgBands 74*
Rogers, Donald Brent Rankin 1934- *IntWWM 77*
Rogers, Dora *Film 1*
Rogers, Earl *ConAmC*
Rogers, Eddy *AmSCAP 80*
Rogers, Eddy 1907-1964 *AmSCAP 66, ConAmC*
Rogers, Emmett 1898?-1947? *NewOrJ[port]*
Rogers, Emmett 1915-1965 *BiE&WWA, NotNAT B*
Rogers, Eric G 1921- *IntWWM 77, -80*
Rogers, Ernest 1891-1956 *NewOrJ[port]*
Rogers, Ethel Tench 1914- *ConAmC*
Rogers, Eugene 1867?-1919 *WhScrn 77*
Rogers, Everett 1891-1952 *NewOrJ*
Rogers, Frances Octavia 1912- *AmSCAP 80*
Rogers, Francis 1870-1951 *Baker 78, BiDAmM*
Rogers, Fred 1928- *AmSCAP 66, -80*
Rogers, Gene *Film 1*
Rogers, George 1911- *IntWWM 77, -80, WhoMus 72*
Rogers, Gil *WhoHol A*
Rogers, Ginger 1911- *AmPS B, BiDAmM, BiDFilm, -81, BiE&WWA, CmMov, CmpEPM, CnOxB, DancEn 78, EncMT, FilmEn, Film 2, FilmgC, ForYSC, HalFC 80, IntMPA 77, -75, -76, -78, -79, -80, MotPP, MovMk[port], OxFilm, ThFT[port], WhoHol A, WhoThe 77, WorEFlm*
Rogers, Gus 1869-1908 *NotNAT B, WhoStg 1906*
Rogers, Harlan Dale 1943- *AmSCAP 80*
Rogers, Harriet *WhoHol A*
Rogers, Henry C 1914- *IntMPA 77, -75, -76, -78, -79, -80*
Rogers, Herbert 1929- *IntWWM 77, -80*
Rogers, Ira *MorBAP*
Rogers, James 1924- *BluesWW[port]*
Rogers, James Douglas 1947- *IntWWM 80*
Rogers, James Henderson 1852-1933 *Baker 78*
Rogers, James Hotchkiss 1857-1940 *AmSCAP 66, -80, Baker 78, BiDAmM*
Rogers, Jean *MotPP*
Rogers, Jean 1916- *FilmEn, ForYSC, WhoHol A, WhoHrs 80*
Rogers, John *Film 2, WhoHol A*
Rogers, John 1605?-1676 *NewGrD 80*
Rogers, John E 1938- *ConAmC*
Rogers, John R d1932 *NotNAT B*
Rogers, John W 1916- *IntMPA 77, -75, -76, -78, -79, -80*
Rogers, John Willis 1929- *IntWWM 77*
Rogers, Joseph 1871-1942 *WhScrn 74, -77*
Rogers, Kasey *WhoHol A*
Rogers, Keith 1943- *WhoMus 72*
Rogers, Kenneth *AmSCAP 80*
Rogers, Kenneth Ray *AmSCAP 80*
Rogers, Kenny 1941?- *ConMuA 80A[port], IlEncCM[port]*
Rogers, Kenny & The First Edition *RkOn 2[port]*
Rogers, Larry Thomas *AmSCAP 80*
Rogers, Lawrence H, II 1921- *IntMPA 77, -75, -76, -78, -79, -80*
Rogers, Lee *AmSCAP 80*
Rogers, Lela Emogen 1890- *AmSCAP 66, WhoHol A*
Rogers, Lora d1948 *NotNAT B*
Rogers, Louise Mackintosh d1933 *NotNAT B*
Rogers, Maclean 1899- *FilmgC, HalFC 80*
Rogers, Marshall d1934 *BlksBF*
Rogers, Max d1932 *NotNAT B, WhThe, WhoStg 1906*
Rogers, Mildred 1899-1973 *WhScrn 77, WhoHol B*
Rogers, Milt 1925- *AmSCAP 66, -80*
Rogers, Milton 1914- *AmSCAP 80*
Rogers, Milton 1924- *AmSCAP 66, -80, BiDAmM, NewGrD 80*
Rogers, Molly *Film 2*
Rogers, Nigel David 1935- *IntWWM 77, -80, NewGrD 80*
Rogers, Noelle *WhoOp 76*
Rogers, Otto Donald 1935- *CreCan 2*
Rogers, P Maclean 1899-1962 *IlWWBF*
Rogers, Paul 1917- *BiE&WWA, CnThe, FilmgC, HalFC 80, MotPP, MovMk, NotNAT, -A, PlP&P, WhoHol A, WhoThe 72, -77*
Rogers, Peter 1916- *FilmgC, HalFC 80, IntMPA 77, -75, -76, -78, -79, -80*
Rogers, Ralph D *NewYTET*
Rogers, Rena 1901-1966 *WhScrn 74, -77*
Rogers, Rene 1901-1966 *Film 1, WhoHol B*
Rogers, Richard 1902- *BestMus[port]*
Rogers, Richard H 1926- *IntMPA 77, -75, -76, -78, -79, -80*
Rogers, Robert C 1862-1912 *BiDAmM*
Rogers, Robert L 1947- *IntWWM 77*
Rogers, Roddy *IntMPA 77, -75, -76, -78, -79, -80*
Rogers, Roy *AmPS B, AmSCAP 66, -80, MotPP, WhoHol A*
Rogers, Roy d1967 *WhScrn 77*
Rogers, Roy 1911- *IlEncCM[port], IntMPA 77, -75, -76, -78, -79, -80*
Rogers, Roy 1912- *BiDAmM, CmMov, CmpEPM, CounME 74[port], -74A, EncFCWM 69, FilmEn, FilmgC, ForYSC, HalFC 80, MovMk, OxFilm, WorEFlm*
Rogers, Roy, Jr. *WhoHol A*
Rogers, Sharon Elery 1929- *AmSCAP 80*
Rogers, Shorty 1924- *CmpEPM, IlEncJ, NewGrD 80*
Rogers, Stanwood d1963 *NotNAT B*
Rogers, Susan Whipple 1943- *ConAmC*
Rogers, Ted 1920- *IntMPA 77, -75, -76, -78, -79, -80*
Rogers, Timmie 1915- *BiDAmM, DrBlPA, RkOn[port]*
Rogers, Timothy Louis Aiverum 1915- *AmSCAP 66, -80*
Rogers, Twyla Fern 1909- *WhoMus 72*
Rogers, Victor *WhoHol A*
Rogers, W F *BlkAmP*
Rogers, Walter *Film 2*
Rogers, Warren *Film 2*
Rogers, Wayne 1940?- *AmSCAP 80, HalFC 80, WhoHol A*
Rogers, Will d1935 *GrMovC[port]*
Rogers, Will 1874-1935 *ForYSC*
Rogers, Will 1878-1935 *JoeFr*
Rogers, Will 1879-1935 *BiDFilm, -81, EncMT, Ent, FilmEn, Film 1, -2, FilmgC, Funs[port], HalFC 80[port], MotPP, MovMk[port], NotNAT A, -B, OxFilm, PlP&P, TwYS, WhScrn 74, -77, WhThe, WhoHol B, WorEFlm*
Rogers, Will, Jr. 1911- *What 3[port]*
Rogers, Will, Jr. 1912- *Film 2, ForYSC, IntMPA 77, -75, -76, -78, -79, -80, WhoHol A*
Rogers, William *NewGrD 80, OxMus*
Rogers, William Forrest, Jr. 1938- *IntWWM 77*
Rogers, William Keith *ConAmC*
Rogers, William Penn Adair 1879-1935 *OxThe*
Rogers, William Webster 1888- *IntWWM 77*
Rogers, Williams Webster 1888- *WhoMus 72*
Rogers And Owens *PupTheA*
Rogers Brothers *WhoStg 1908*
Roget, Henriette 1910- *Baker 78*
Rogg, Lionel 1936- *BnBkM 80, IntWWM 77, -80, NewGrD 80, WhoMus 72*
Rogge, Florence 1904- *DancEn 78*
Rogge, Lola 1908- *CnOxB*
Roggenkamp, Peter 1935- *NewGrD 80*
Roggius, Nicolaus 1518?-1567 *NewGrD 80*
Rogier *NewGrD 80*
Rogier, Philippe 1561?-1596 *NewGrD 80*
Rogister, Jean 1879-1964 *Baker 78, NewGrD 80*

Rognan, Jean Lorraine 1912-1969 *WhScrn 77*
Rognan, Lorraine 1912-1969 *WhoHol B*
Rogne, Sture 1947- *IntWWM 80*
Rogniono *NewGrD 80*
Rognone *NewGrD 80*
Rognoni *NewGrD 80*
Rognoni d1943 *WhScrn 77*
Rognoni, Luigi 1913- *NewGrD 80*
Rognoni, Riccardo d1620? *NewGrD 80*
Rognoni Taeggio *NewGrD 80*
Rognoni Taeggio, Francesco d1626? *NewGrD 80*
Rognoni Taeggio, Giovanni Domenico d1626? *NewGrD 80*
Rogoff, Gordon 1931- *BiE&WWA, NotNAT*
Rogosin, Lionel 1924- *DcFM, FilmEn, OxFilm, WorEFlm*
Rogowski, Ludomir Michal 1881-1954 *Baker 78, NewGrD 80*
Roguski, Gustav 1839-1921 *Baker 78*
Rohaczewski, Andrzej *NewGrD 80*
Rohan, Brian *ConMuA 80B*
Rohan, Jindrich 1919- *IntWWM 77, -80*
Rohard, Jutta 1927- *IntWWM 77, -80*
Rohde, Volker 1939- *WhoOp 76*
Rohde, Wilhelm 1856-1928 *Baker 78*
Rohe, Robert Kenneth 1916- *AmSCAP 80, ConAmC*
Rohe, Robert Kenneth 1920- *AmSCAP 66*
Rohlfs, Eckart 1929- *IntWWM 80*
Rohlig, Harald *ConAmC*
Rohloff, Ernst 1899- *Baker 78, IntWWM 77, -80, NewGrD 80*
Rohm, Maria 1949- *IntMPA 77, -78, -79, -80, WhoHol A*
Rohm, Wilhelm 1903- *WhoMus 72*
Rohmann, Imre 1953- *IntWWM 80*
Rohmer, Eric 1920- *BiDFilm, -81, ConLC 16, FilmEn, FilmgC, HalFC 80, MovMk[port], OxFilm, WorEFlm*
Rohmer, Harriet *WomWMM B*
Rohmer, Sax 1886-1959 *HalFC 80, NotNAT B, WhThe, WhoHrs 80*
Rohner, Wilhelmine Georgine 1908- *IntWWM 77, -80*
Rohr, Hugo 1866-1937 *Baker 78*
Rohrig, Emil 1882-1954 *Baker 78*
Rohrig, Walter 1893- *DcFM, FilmEn, OxFilm, WorEFlm*
Rohrl, Manfred 1935- *IntWWM 80, WhoOp 76*
Rohwer, Jens 1914- *DcCM, IntWWM 77, -80, NewGrD 80*
Roi, Bartolomeo *NewGrD 80*
Roig, Gonzalo 1890-1970 *Baker 78*
Roiha, Eino 1904-1955 *NewGrD 80*
Roikjer, Kjell Maale 1901- *IntWWM 77, -80*
Roince, Aloisio d1597 *NewGrD 80*
Roince, Luigi d1597 *NewGrD 80*
Roince, Luisio d1597 *NewGrD 80*
Roitman, David 1884-1944 *BiDAmM*
Roizman, Owen *HalFC 80*
Rojas, Fernando De 1465?-1541 *EncWT, McGEWD, OxThe*
Rojas Zorilla, Francisco De 1607-1648 *NotNAT B*
Rojas Zorrilla, Francisco De 1607-1648 *McGEWD[port], OxThe*
Roje, Ana 1909- *CnOxB, DancEn 78*
Rojo, Casiano 1877-1931 *Baker 78*
Rojo, Gustavo *ForYSC, WhoHol A*
Rojo Olalla, Casiano 1877-1931 *NewGrD 80*
Roka, Istvan 1941- *WhoOp 76*
Roker, Granville William 1932- *EncJzS 70*
Roker, Mickey 1932- *EncJzS 70*
Roker, Renny *DrBlPA, WhoHol A*
Roker, Roxie *DrBlPA, NotNAT*
Rokitansky, Hans Von 1835-1909 *NewGrD 80*
Rokitansky, Victor Von *NewGrD 80*
Rokk, Marika 1913- *FilmAG WE[port]*
Rokseth, Yvonne 1890-1948 *Baker 78, NewGrD 80*
Roland, Alan 1930- *NatPD[port]*
Roland, Claude-Robert 1935- *Baker 78, IntWWM 77, -80*
Roland, Frederick 1886-1936 *WhScrn 74, -77*
Roland, Fredric d1936 *WhoHol B*
Roland, Gene 1921- *BiDAmM, EncJzS 70*
Roland, Gilbert 1905- *FilmEn, Film 2, FilmgC, ForYSC, HalFC 80, HolP 30[port], IntMPA 77, -75, -76, -78, -79, -80, MotPP, MovMk[port], TwYS, WhoHol A, WorEFlm*
Roland, Gyl *WhoHol A*
Roland, Ida 1881-1951 *NotNAT B*
Roland, Joe 1920- *CmpEPM*
Roland, Joseph Alfred 1920- *BiDAmM*
Roland, Kathleen *WhoHol A*
Roland, Marc 1894- *WhoMus 72*
Roland, Marion *WhScrn 74, -77*
Roland, Rita *WomWMM*
Roland, Ruth d1937 *MotPP, WhoHol B*
Roland, Ruth 1892-1937 *FilmEn, TwYS, WhScrn 74, -77*
Roland, Ruth 1893-1937 *Film 1, -2, FilmgC, HalFC 80, NotNAT B*
Roland, Steve *WhoHol A*
Roland Holst, Henriette 1869-1952 *CnMD*
Roland-Manuel 1891-1966 *NewGrD 80*
Roland-Manuel, Alexis 1891-1966 *Baker 78*
Rolane, Andree *Film 2*
Roldan, Amadeo 1900-1939 *Baker 78, DcCM, NewGrD 80*
Roldan, Enrique 1901-1954 *WhScrn 74, -77*
Roldan, Juan Perez *NewGrD 80*
Roldan, Washington 1921- *IntWWM 77*
Roleff, Peter 1906- *CnOxB*
Roley, Sutton *IntMPA 77, -75, -76, -78, -79, -80*
Rolf, Erik d1957 *WhScrn 77*
Rolf, Frederick 1926- *BiE&WWA, NotNAT*
Rolfe *NewGrD 80*
Rolfe, B A 1879-1956 *CmpEPM*
Rolfe, Guy 1915- *FilmEn, FilmgC, ForYSC, HalFC 80, IlWWBF, WhoHol A, WhoHrs 80*
Rolfe, Sam H *NewYTET*
Rolfe, Walter 1880-1944 *AmSCAP 66, -80*
Rolfe, William *NewGrD 80*
Roll, John Michael Frederick 1946- *WhoMus 72*
Rolla *NewGrD 80*
Rolla, Alessandro 1757-1841 *Baker 78, NewGrD 80*
Rolla, Antonio 1798-1837 *Baker 78*
Rolla, Carlo Francesco *NewGrD 80*
Rolla, Giorgio d1651? *NewGrD 80*
Rollan, Henri *Film 2*
Rolland, Jean-Claude 1933-1967 *WhScrn 74, -77*
Rolland, Paul 1911- *IntWWM 77, -80*
Rolland, Romain 1866-1944 *Baker 78, CnMD, EncWT, Ent, McGEWD[port], ModWD, NewEOp 71, NewGrD 80, NotNAT B, OxMus*
Rolle, Esther 1922- *DrBlPA, IntMPA 79, -80, NotNAT, WhoThe 77*
Rolle, Georges d1916 *NotNAT B, WhThe*
Rolle, Johann Heinrich 1716-1785 *Baker 78, NewGrD 80*
Rolle, Liselotte *Film 2*
Rollens, Jacques *Film 2*
Roller, Alfred 1864-1935 *EncWT, NewEOp 71, NewGrD 80*
Roller, Cleve *WhoHol A*
Roller, Johannes *NewGrD 80*
Roller Coasters *BiDAmM*
Rolleri, William *MorBAP*
Rollet, Johannes *NewGrD 80*
Rollet, Marie Francois L Gand Leblanc *NewGrD 80*
Rollett, Raymond 1907-1961 *WhScrn 74, -77, WhoHol B*
Rollette, Jane *Film 2*
Rolli, Paolo Antonio 1687-1765 *NewGrD 80*
Rollig, Carl Leopold 1735?-1804 *Baker 78*
Rollig, Johann Georg 1710-1790 *NewGrD 80*
Rollig, K L *OxMus*
Rollig, Karl Leopold d1804 *NewGrD 80*
Rollin, Georges d1964 *WhScrn 77*
Rollin, Jean 1906- *Baker 78*
Rollin, Jean 1940- *WhoHrs 80*
Rollin, Robert Leon 1947- *AmSCAP 80, CpmDNM 74, ConAmC*
Rolling Stones, The *BiDAmM, ConMuA 80A[port], IlEncR[port], NewGrD 80, RkOn 2[port]*
Rollini, Adrian 1904-1956 *BiDAmM, CmpEPM, IlEncJ, WhoJazz 72*
Rollini, Arthur 1912- *CmpEPM, WhoJazz 72*
Rollins, Bryant 1937- *BlkAmP*
Rollins, David d1952 *WhoHol B*
Rollins, David 1908-1952 *WhScrn 74, -77*
Rollins, David 1909-1952 *Film 2*
Rollins, Glenn *AmSCAP 80*
Rollins, Jack *BiE&WWA, Film 1, IntMPA 77, -76, -78, -79, -80*
Rollins, Jack 1906- *AmSCAP 66*
Rollins, Lanier 1937- *AmSCAP 80*
Rollins, Sonny 1929- *CmpEPM, EncJzS 70*
Rollins, Sonny 1930- *DrBlPA, IlEncJ, NewGrD 80*
Rollins, Theodore Walter 1929- *BiDAmM, EncJzS 70*
Rollins, Theodore Walter 1930- *NewGrD 80*
Rollins, Walter E 1906-1973 *AmSCAP 80*
Rollins, Walter E 1907-1973 *BiDAmM*
Rollo, Billy d1964 *NotNAT B*
Rollow, Preston J 1871-1947 *WhScrn 74, -77, WhoHol B*
Rolly, Jeanne d1929 *NotNAT B, WhThe*
Rolon, Jose 1883-1945 *Baker 78, DcCM, NewGrD 80*
Rolph, Gwendoline Mary 1915- *WhoMus 72*
Rolston, William d1964 *NotNAT B*
Rolt, Richard d1770 *NotNAT B*
Rolyat, Dan 1872-1927 *NotNAT B, WhThe*
Roma, Caro *WhoStg 1906, -1908*
Roma, Caro 1866-1937 *BiDAmM*
Roma, Clarice 1902-1947 *WhScrn 74, -77*
Roma, Giovannino Da *NewGrD 80*
Roma, Vinny *AmSCAP 80*
Romagnesi, Brigida Bianchi 1613-1703? *OxThe*
Romagnesi, Carlo Virgilio 1670-1708 *OxThe*
Romagnesi, Marc'Antonio 1633?-1706 *OxThe*
Romagnesi, Niccolo d1660 *OxThe*
Romain, George E d1929 *Film 2, WhScrn 77*
Romain, Yvonne 1938- *FilmgC, ForYSC, HalFC 80, WhoHol A, WhoHrs 80*
Romaine, Claire 1873-1964 *WhThe*
Romains, Jules 1885-1942 *NotNAT B*
Romains, Jules 1885-1972 *CnMD, EncWT, Ent, McGEWD, ModWD, OxThe, WhThe*
Roman DeFauvel *NewGrD 80*
Roman, Elly 1905- *IntWWM 77*
Roman, Greg *WhoHol A*
Roman, Hanna *WomWMM B*
Roman, Hugh *Film 2*
Roman, J H 1694-1758 *OxMus*
Roman, Johan Helmich 1694-1758 *Baker 78, MusMk, NewGrD 80*
Roman, Lawrence 1921- *BiE&WWA, IntMPA 77, -75, -76, -78, -79, -80, NotNAT*
Roman, Leticia 1939- *FilmgC, HalFC 80, WhoHol A*
Roman, Murray d1973 *WhScrn 77*
Roman, Ric *WhoHol A*
Roman, Ruth *IntMPA 77, -75, -76, -78, -79, -80, MotPP*
Roman, Ruth 1923- *WhoHol A*
Roman, Ruth 1924- *FilmEn, FilmgC, ForYSC, HalFC 80, MovMk*
Roman, Ruth 1925- *WorEFlm*
Roman, Stella 1910- *NewGrD 80*
Romance, Viviane 1909?- *FilmgC, WhoHol A*
Romance, Viviane 1912- *FilmAG WE, FilmEn, WorEFlm*
Romance, Vivianne 1909- *HalFC 80*
Romanella, Nelly 1938- *WhoOp 76*
Romanelli, Luigi *BgBands 74*
Romanelli, Luigi 1751-1839 *NewGrD 80*
Romanelli Of Mantua, Samuel 1757-1814 *OxThe*
Romani, Carlo 1824-1875 *Baker 78*
Romani, Felice 1788-1865 *Baker 78, BnBkM 80, CmOp, NewEOp 71, NewGrD 80, NotNAT B, OxThe*
Romani, G 1917- *WhoMus 72*
Romani, Pietro 1791-1877 *Baker 78, NewGrD 80*
Romani, Stefano 1778-1850? *NewGrD 80*
Romanic, Teodor 1926- *IntWWM 77, -80*
Romanina, La *NewGrD 80*
Romanini, Giorgio 1935- *IntWWM 77, -80*
Romaniuk, Jerzy 1943- *IntWWM 80*
Romano, Il *NewGrD 80*
Romano, Alessandro *NewGrD 80*
Romano, Alexander *NewGrD 80*
Romano, Andy *WhoHol A*

Romano, Charles d1937 NotNAT B
Romano, Eustachio NewGrD 80
Romano, Filippo NewGrD 80
Romano, Giulio NewGrD 80
Romano, Jane d1962 NotNAT B
Romano, Joe 1932- EncJzS 70
Romano, John 1896-1957 WhScrn 74, -77
Romano, Joseph 1932- EncJzS 70
Romano, Marcantonio 1552?-1636 NewGrD 80
Romano, Nick 1922- AmSCAP 66, -80
Romano, Nina Film 2
Romano, Ralph 1928- AmSCAP 66, -80
Romano, Thomas M 1923- AmSCAP 66
Romano, Thomas Matthew 1929- AmSCAP 80
Romano, Tony 1915- AmSCAP 66, -80
Romanoff, Constance Film 2
Romanoff, Constantine Film 2
Romanoff, Dimitri 1907- CnOxB, DancEn 78[port]
Romanoff, Ivan 1915- CreCan 1
Romanoff, Michael 1890?-1971 WhScrn 74, -77
Romanoff, Mike 1890- What 3[port]
Romanoff, Mike 1890-1971 WhoHol B
Romanoff, Mike 1890-1972 FilmgC, HalFC 80
Romanos The Melode d555? NewGrD 80
Romanov NewGrD 80
Romanov, Boris 1891-1957 CnOxB, DancEn 78[port]
Romanova, Maria 1886-1954 DancEn 78
Romanovsky, Erich Maria 1929- IntWWM 77, -80, WhoMus 72
Romanowicz, Alina NewGrD 80
Romanska-Gabrys, Jadwiga 1928- IntWWM 80
Romanus, Christiane Mariane Von NewGrD 80
Romanus, Richard WhoHol A
Romanzini, Maria Theresa NewGrD 80
Romashov, Boris Sergeivich 1895-1958 OxThe
Romay, Lina ForYSC, WhoHol A
Romberg NewGrD 80
Romberg, Andreas Jakob 1767-1821 Baker 78, NewGrD 80, OxMus
Romberg, Angelica 1775-1803? NewGrD 80
Romberg, Anton 1771-1842 NewGrD 80
Romberg, Bernhard 1767-1841 Baker 78, BnBkM 80, OxMus
Romberg, Bernhard Anton 1742-1814 NewGrD 80
Romberg, Bernhard Heinrich 1767-1841 NewGrD 80, -80[port]
Romberg, Gerhard Heinrich 1745-1819 NewGrD 80
Romberg, Sigmund 1887-1951 AmPS, AmSCAP 66, -80, Baker 78, BestMus, BiDAmM, BnBkM 80, CmpEPM, ConAmC, EncMT, EncWT, FilmEn, FilmgC, HalFC 80, MusMk, NewCBMT, NewGrD 80, NotNAT A, -B, OxMus, PlP&P[port], PopAmC[port], Sw&Ld C, WhThe
Rombouts, Pieter NewGrD 80
Rome, Bert Film 2
Rome, Fred 1874- WhThe
Rome, Harold 1908- AmPS, AmSCAP 66, -80, BestMus, BiDAmM, BiE&WWA, CmpEPM, EncMT, NewCBMT, NewGrD 80, NotNAT, PopAmC[port], PopAmC SUP, WhoMus 72
Rome, J Gus AmSCAP 80
Rome, Stewart d1965 WhoHol B
Rome, Stewart 1886-1965 FilmEn, Film 1, IlWWBF[port], WhScrn 74, -77
Rome, Stewart 1887-1965 FilmgC, HalFC 80
Rome, Stuart 1886-1965 Film 2
Rome, Sydne 1947- FilmEn
Romea, Alberto 1883-1960 WhScrn 74, -77
Romeo, James Joseph 1955- AmSCAP 80, CpmDNM 79, -80
Romer NewGrD 80
Romer, Andreas 1704-1750? NewGrD 80
Romer, Anne d1852 NotNAT B
Romer, Anton 1724-1779 NewGrD 80
Romer, Emma 1814-1868 NewGrD 80
Romer, Ferdinand Josef 1657?-1723 NewGrD 80
Romer, Johann Ulrich 1650?- NewGrD 80
Romer, Leila 1878-1944 WhScrn 74, -77, WhoHol B
Romer, Robert d1874 NotNAT B
Romer, Tomi 1924-1969 WhScrn 74, -77, WhoHol B
Romer VonZwickau NewGrD 80
Romero, Angel 1946- BnBkM 80
Romero, Angelo 1940- WhoOp 76
Romero, Carlos ForYSC, WhoHol A
Romero, Celedonio 1918- AmSCAP 80, BnBkM 80, IntWWM 77, -80
Romero, Celin 1940- BnBkM 80
Romero, Cesar 1907- BiDFilm, -81, FilmEn, FilmgC, ForYSC, HalFC 80, HolP 30[port], IntMPA 77, -75, -76, -78, -79, -80, MotPP, MovMk, WhoHol A, WhoHrs 80[port], WorEFlm
Romero, Eddie WhoHrs 80
Romero, Florita 1931-1961 WhScrn 74, -77
Romero, Gary 1912- AmSCAP 66, -80
Romero, George 1939- HalFC 80
Romero, George 1940- WhoHrs 80
Romero, Jesus C 1893-1958 NewGrD 80
Romero, John J 1920- IntWWM 80
Romero, Juan NewGrD 80
Romero, Mateo 1575-1647 Baker 78, NewGrD 80
Romero, Nancy WomWMM
Romero, Ned WhoHol A
Romero, Pepe 1944- BnBkM 80
Romero, Redentor L 1929- IntWWM 77, -80
Romero DeAvila, Manuel Jeronimo 1717-1779 NewGrD 80
Romero Family BnBkM 80
Romeu, Luis 1874-1937 Baker 78
Romeyn, Jane 1901-1963 NotNAT B, WhScrn 74, -77
Romhild, Johann Theodor 1684-1756 NewGrD 80
Romhildt, Johann Theodor 1684-1756 NewGrD 80
Romhildt, Johann Theodor 1684-1757 Baker 78
Romieu, Jean-Baptiste 1723-1766 NewGrD 80
Romine, Latosca S 1900- AmSCAP 66
Romiti, Richard A 1940- ConAmC
Romm, Mikhail 1901-1971 BiDFilm, -81, DcFM, FilmEn, FilmgC, HalFC 80, OxFilm, WorEFlm
Rommer NewGrD 80
Rommer, Clare Film 2
Romney, Edana 1919- FilmgC, HalFC 80, WhThe, WhoHol A
Romney, Hans Charles 1911- IntWWM 77, -80
Romoff, Colin 1924- AmSCAP 66, -80
Romoff, Woody 1918- BiE&WWA, NotNAT
Ron, Martin De 1789-1817 NewGrD 80
Ron, Rahamim 1944- CnOxB
Rona, Viktor 1936- CnOxB
Ronald, Landon 1873-1938 OxMus
Ronald, Sir Landon 1873-1938 Baker 78, NewEOp 71, NewGrD 80, WhThe
Ronald, William 1926- CreCan 1
Ronaldson, James 1930- CreCan 1
Ronay, Edina WhoHol A
Ronayne, John Edward Joseph 1931- IntWWM 77, -80
Roncaglia, Gino 1883-1968 Baker 78, NewGrD 80
Roncal, Simeon 1870-1953 NewGrD 80
Roncalli, Ludovico NewGrD 80
Ronchetti, Martin 1940- WhoMus 72
Ronconi, Domenico 1772-1839 Baker 78
Ronconi, Giorgio 1810-1890 BiDAmM, NewGrD 80
Ronconi, Luca 1913- EncWT
Rondelli, Jo NewGrD 80
Rondi, Brunello 1924- WorEFlm
Rondiris, Dimitrios 1899- BiE&WWA, OxThe
Rondo, Don RkOn
Ronell, Ann AmPS, AmSCAP 66, -80, BiE&WWA, CmpEPM, NotNAT
Ronet, Maurice 1927- BiDFilm, -81, FilmAG WE[port], FilmEn, FilmgC, HalFC 80, OxFilm, WhoHol A, WorEFlm
Ronettes, The ConMuA 80A, RkOn[port]
Roney, Irene Salemka CreCan 2
Ronga, Luigi 1901- Baker 78, NewGrD 80
Ronge, Jean-Baptiste 1825-1882 Baker 78
Ronger, Florimond NewGrD 80
Ronghe, Albericus De NewGrD 80
Ronghe, Michael De 1620-1696 NewGrD 80
Roni, Luigi 1942- WhoOp 76
Ronka, Elmer 1905- AmSCAP 66
Ronka, Ilmari 1905- AmSCAP 80
Ronly-Riklis, Shalom 1922- NewGrD 80
Ronnagel, Johann Wilhelm 1690-1759 NewGrD 80
Ronnblom, Anders F 1946- IntWWM 80
Ronnefeld, Peter 1935-1965 Baker 78, NewGrD 80
Ronnel, Ann WomWMM
Ronnie & The Daytonas RkOn 2A
Ronnie And The Hi-Lites RkOn
Ronnow, Ola 1952- IntWWM 80
Ronsard, Pierre De 1524-1585 NewGrD 80, OxMus
Ronshein, John 1927- ConAmC
Ronson, Mick IlEncR
Ronson, Raoul R 1931- IntWWM 77, -80
Ronstadt, Linda 1946- BiDAmM, ConMuA 80A[port], IlEncCM, IlEncR[port], RkOn 2[port]
Rontani, Rafaello d1622 NewGrD 80
Rontani, Raffaello d1622 NewGrD 80
Rontgen NewGrD 80
Rontgen, Engelbert 1829-1897 NewGrD 80
Rontgen, Engelbert 1886-1958 NewGrD 80
Rontgen, Joachim 1906- IntWWM 77, -80, NewGrD 80
Rontgen, Johannes 1898-1969 NewGrD 80
Rontgen, Julius 1855-1932 Baker 78, NewGrD 80, OxMus
Rontgen, Julius 1881-1951 NewGrD 80
Ronzi DeBegnis, Giuseppina 1800-1853 NewGrD 80
Roobenian, Amber 1905- AmSCAP 66, -80, ConAmC, WhoMus 72
Roocroft, Stanley James 1937- IntWWM 77, -80
Rood, Hale 1923- AmSCAP 66, -80
Rooftop Singers AmPS A, BiDAmM, EncFCWM 69, RkOn
Rook, Heidi WhoHol A
Rook, John ConMuA 80B
Rooke, Arthur H IlWWBF
Rooke, Irene 1878-1958 Film 2, NotNAT B, OxThe, WhScrn 77, WhThe
Rooke, Valentine 1912- WhThe
Rooke, William Michael 1794-1847 NewGrD 80
Rooklyn, Maurice MagIlD
Rooks, Conrad HalFC 80, WhoHol A
Rooley, Anthony 1944- IntWWM 77, -80, NewGrD 80
Room, Abraham 1894-1976 WorEFlm
Room, Abram 1894-1976 DcFM, FilmEn, FilmgC, HalFC 80, OxFilm
Room, Alexander 1894-1976 FilmEn, OxFilm, WorEFlm
Room, Avram 1894-1976 FilmEn
Roomates, The RkOn
Rooner, Charles 1901-1954 WhScrn 74, -77, WhoHol B
Rooney, Andrew A NewYTET
Rooney, Gilbert Film 2
Rooney, James Kevin 1938- AmSCAP 80
Rooney, Mercy WhoHol A
Rooney, Mickey AmPS B, AmSCAP 80, MotPP, WhoHol A
Rooney, Mickey 1920- AmSCAP 66, CmMov, CmpEPM, FilmEn, Film 2, FilmgC, HalFC 80, MGM[port], MovMk[port], WhoHrs 80
Rooney, Mickey 1922- BiDFilm, -81, ForYSC, IntMPA 77, -75, -76, -78, -79, -80, OxFilm, WorEFlm
Rooney, Pat AmPS B, IntMPA 78, -79, -80
Rooney, Pat 1880-1962 AmSCAP 66, DancEn 78, Film 2, NotNAT B, WhScrn 74, -77, WhoHol B
Rooney, Pat 1891-1933 WhScrn 74, -77, WhoHol B
Rooney, Pat, Sr. 1880-1962 AmSCAP 80, CmpEPM
Rooney, Pat B 1925- IntMPA 77, -75, -76
Rooney, Teddy 1950- ForYSC, WhoHol A
Rooney, Tim WhoHol A
Rooney, Timmy 1947- ForYSC
Rooney, Wallace WhoHol A
Roope, Clover 1937- CnOxB, DancEn 78
Roope, Fay 1893-1961 WhScrn 74, -77, WhoHol B
Roope, Jesse William Thomas 1903- IntWWM 80

Rooper, Jasper 1898- *IntWWM 77, -80, WhoMus 72*
Roos, Barbara *WomWMM A, -B*
Roos, Ingemar 1945- *IntWWM 80*
Roos, Joanna 1901- *BiE&WWA, BlkAmP, NotNAT, PlP&P, WhThe, WhoHol A*
Roos, Jorgen 1922- *DcFM, FilmEn*
Roos, Lars Anders 1945- *IntWWM 77*
Roos, Lisa *WomWMM*
Roos, Nel 1914- *DancEn 78*
Roos, Robert De 1907-1976 *Baker 78, NewGrD 80*
Roose, Olwen 1900- *WhThe*
Roose-Evans, James 1927- *WhoThe 72, -77*
Roosegaarde Bisschop, Eugene 1916- *IntWWM 77, -80*
Roosevelt, Blanche 1853-1898 *BiDAmM*
Roosevelt, Buddy 1898-1973 *Film 1, -2, ForYSC, TwYS, WhScrn 77, WhoHol A*
Roosevelt, Franklin Delano 1882-1945 *FilmgC, HalFC 80*
Roosevelt, Hilborne Lewis 1849-1886 *NewGrD 80*
Roosevelt, Hilbourne Lewis 1849-1886 *BiDAmM*
Roosevelt, Leila *WomWMM*
Roosevelt, Theodore 1858-1919 *FilmgC, HalFC 80, OxMus*
Roosters *BiDAmM*
Root, E Tower 1822-1896 *BiDAmM*
Root, Frederic Woodman 1846-1916 *BiDAmM*
Root, Frederick Woodman 1846-1916 *Baker 78*
Root, G F *OxMus*
Root, George Frederick 1820-1895 *AmPS, Baker 78, BiDAmM, NewGrD 80, NotNAT B, PopAmC[port], Sw&Ld A*
Root, Lynn 1905- *BiE&WWA, NotNAT*
Root, Robert *WhoHol A*
Root, Wells *IntMPA 77, -75, -76, -78, -79, -80*
Rootham, Cyril Bradley 1875-1938 *Baker 78, NewGrD 80, OxMus*
Rooy, Anton Van *NewEOp 71, NewGrD 80*
Ropartz, Guy 1864-1955 *Baker 78, DcCom&M 79, OxMus*
Ropartz, Joseph Guy 1864-1955 *NewGrD 80*
Ropek, Jiri 1922- *IntWWM 77, -80, NewGrD 80, WhoMus 72*
Roper, Brian *WhoHol A*
Roper, Edgar Stanley 1878-1953 *OxMus*
Roper, Jack 1904-1966 *Film 2, WhScrn 77, WhoHol B*
Roper, June *CreCan 1*
Roper, Nellie 1901- *WhoMus 72*
Roper, Steve *AmSCAP 80*
Roppolo, Leon J 1902-1943 *NewOrJ[port], WhoJazz 72*
Roquemore, Henry 1888-1943 *Film 2, WhScrn 74, -77, WhoHol B*
Roqueta, Jaime Moll *NewGrD 80*
Roquevert, Noel 1892-1973 *WhScrn 77, WhoHol B*
Roquevert, Noel 1894-1973 *FilmAG WE, FilmEn*
Rore, Cipriano De 1515?-1565 *NewGrD 80[port]*
Rore, Cipriano De 1516-1565 *Baker 78, OxMus*
Rore, Cipriano Di 1516-1565 *MusMk*
Rorem, Ned 1923- *AmSCAP 66, -80, Baker 78, BiDAmM, BnBkM 80, CompSN[port], CpmDNM 72, -73, -79, -80, ConAmC, DcCM, IntWWM 77, -80, MusMk, NewEOp 71, NewGrD 80, WhoMus 72*
Rorie, Yvonne 1907-1959 *NotNAT B, WhThe*
Rork, Al *Film 2*
Rork, Anne *Film 2*
Rorke, Hayden *ForYSC*
Rorke, J E *Film 1*
Rorke, John d1957 *NotNAT B*
Rorke, Kate 1866-1945 *NotNAT B, OxThe, WhThe*
Rorke, Margaret Hayden 1884-1969 *WhScrn 74, -77, WhoHol B*
Rorke, Mary 1858-1938 *NotNAT B, WhThe*
Rory, Rosanna *ForYSC*
Rory, Rossana *WhoHol A*
Ros, Edmundo 1910- *IntWWM 77, NewGrD 80, WhoMus 72*
Rosa, Carl d1889 *NotNAT B*
Rosa, Carl 1842-1889 *Baker 78, MusMk, NewEOp 71, NewGrD 80*
Rosa, Carl August Nicolas 1842-1889 *OxMus*
Rosa, Carlantonio De 1762-1847 *NewGrD 80*
Rosa, Nera d1920 *NotNAT B*
Rosa, Salvator 1615-1673 *NewGrD 80, OxMus*
Rosa, Salvatore 1615-1673 *Baker 78, NewGrD 80*
Rosada, Luciano 1923- *WhoOp 76*
Rosado, Peggy Moran *WhoHol A*
Rosado Fernandes, Cremilde 1940- *IntWWM 80*
Rosales, Antonio 1740?-1801 *NewGrD 80*
Rosales, Marco Fidel 1913- *AmSCAP 66, -80*
Rosales, Sylvia 1917- *AmSCAP 66, -80*
Rosamonde, Miss *Film 1*
Rosand, Aaron 1927- *IntWWM 77, -80, WhoMus 72*
Rosanova, Rosa 1883- *Film 2, TwYS*
Rosapepe, Lucia-Lena 1947- *IntWWM 77*
Rosar, Annie 1888-1963 *NotNAT B, WhScrn 74, -77, WhoHol B*
Rosario 1918- *CnOxB*
Rosario 1920- *DancEn 78*
Rosas, Enrique *DcFM, FilmEn*
Rosas, Fernando 1915-1959 *WhScrn 74, -77*
Rosas, John 1908- *NewGrD 80*
Rosas, Juventino 1868-1894 *NewGrD 80*
Rosati, Carolina 1826-1905 *CnOxB*
Rosati, Carolina 1827-1905 *DancEn 78*
Rosay, Francoise 1891-1974 *BiE&WWA, FilmAG WE, FilmEn, Film 2, FilmgC, ForYSC, HalFC 80, IlWWBF A, MotPP, MovMk, OxFilm, WhScrn 77, WhThe, WhoHol B, WhoThe 72, WorEFlm*
Rosay, Madeleine *DancEn 78*
Rosbaud, Hans d1962 *NotNAT B*
Rosbaud, Hans 1895-1962 *Baker 78, BnBkM 80, CmOp, NewEOp 71, NewGrD 80[port]*
Rosca, Gabriel *Film 2*
Roscelli, Francesco *NewGrD 80*
Rosch, Friedrich 1862-1925 *Baker 78*
Roscher, Wolfgang 1927- *IntWWM 80*
Roscius d062BC *PlP&P*
Roscius 115?BC-062BC *Ent*
Roscius 125?BC-062BC *EncWT*
Roscius, Quintus d062BC *CnThe, OxThe*
Roscius Gallus, Quintus 126?BC-062BC *NotNAT B*
Roscoe, Alan 1888-1933 *WhScrn 74, -77, WhoHol B*
Roscoe, Albert 1887-1925? *WhScrn 77*
Roscoe, Albert 1887-1931 *Film 1, -2, TwYS*
Roscoe, B Jeanie 1932- *AmSCAP 80*
Roscoe, Lee *WhoHol A*
Roscoe, Martin 1952- *IntWWM 80*
Rose Marie *AmSCAP 66, -80, WhoHol A*
Rose, Adrian 1859-1933 *NotNAT B*
Rose, Al *WhoHol A*
Rose, Alex *IntMPA 79, -80*
Rose, Alexander *WhoHol A*
Rose, Arnold 1863-1946 *Baker 78, NewGrD 80*
Rose, Barry Michael 1934- *NewGrD 80, WhoMus 72*
Rose, Beatrice Schroeder 1922- *IntWWM 77, -80*
Rose, Bernard 1916- *NewGrD 80*
Rose, Bernard Norman 1947- *IntWWM 77*
Rose, Bernard William George 1916- *IntWWM 77, -80, WhoMus 72*
Rose, Betty Clarke d1947 *NotNAT B*
Rose, Billy 1899-1966 *AmPS, AmSCAP 66, -80, BiE&WWA, CmpEPM, EncMT, HalFC 80, NotNAT A, -B, Sw&Ld C, WhThe*
Rose, Blanche 1878-1953 *WhScrn 74, -77, WhoHol B*
Rose, Carl *NewGrD 80*
Rose, Carla Valentine 1945- *WomWMM B*
Rose, Clarkson 1890-1968 *NotNAT B, OxThe, WhThe*
Rose, Clifford *WhoHol A*
Rose, David *AmPS A*
Rose, David 1910- *AmSCAP 66, BiDAmM, CmpEPM, FilmgC, HalFC 80, IntMPA 77, -75, -76, -78, -79, -80, PopAmC[port], RkOn*
Rose, David 1919- *AmSCAP 80*
Rose, David E 1895- *FilmgC, HalFC 80, IntMPA 77, -75, -76, -78, -79, -80*
Rose, Earl Alexander 1946- *AmSCAP 80, IntWWM 77, -80*
Rose, Ed 1875-1935 *AmSCAP 66, -80, BiDAmM*
Rose, Edward d1904 *NotNAT B*
Rose, Edward Everett 1862-1939 *NotNAT B, WhThe*
Rose, Fred 1897-1954 *AmSCAP 66, -80, BiDAmM, CmpEPM, EncFCWM 69, IlEncCM[port]*
Rose, Freddie 1892?- *NewOrJ*
Rose, George 1920- *BiE&WWA, FilmgC, HalFC 80, MovMk[port], NotNAT, WhoHol A, WhoThe 72, -77*
Rose, Gloria 1933-1974 *NewGrD 80*
Rose, Griffith Wheeler 1936- *AmSCAP 80, CpmDNM 79, ConAmC*
Rose, Harry d1975 *WhoHol C*
Rose, Harry 1888?-1962 *NotNAT B, WhScrn 74, -77*
Rose, Harry 1893- *AmSCAP 66, -80*
Rose, Jack *HalFC 80*
Rose, Jack 1897- *IntMPA 77, -75, -76, -78, -79, -80*
Rose, Jack 1911- *FilmEn, FilmgC, IntMPA 77, -75, -76, -78, -79, -80*
Rose, Jane *BiE&WWA, WhoHol A*
Rose, Jennifer *WhoHol A*
Rose, Jerome 1938- *WhoMus 72*
Rose, Jewel d1970 *WhScrn 77, WhoHol B*
Rose, John *NewGrD 80*
Rose, John 1948- *IntWWM 77, -80*
Rose, John C 1905- *IntMPA 77, -75, -76, -78, -79, -80*
Rose, John Luke 1933- *IntWWM 77, -80, WhoMus 72*
Rose, Juanelva Marie 1937- *IntWWM 77, -80*
Rose, Juergen *WhoOp 76*
Rose, Jurgen *NewGrD 80*
Rose, Jurgen 1937- *CnOxB*
Rose, L Arthur 1887-1958 *WhThe*
Rose, Laurie *WhoHol A*
Rose, Leonard 1918- *Baker 78, BiDAmM, BnBkM 80, IntWWM 77, -80, MusSN[port], NewGrD 80, WhoMus 72*
Rose, Louisa *WomWMM*
Rose, Margo *PupTheA SUP*
Rose, Michael Edward 1934- *IntWWM 77, -80*
Rose, Michael Paul 1945- *IntWWM 77, -80*
Rose, Norman *WhoHol A*
Rose, Peter *ConDr 77D*
Rose, Peter Gregory 1948- *WhoMus 72*
Rose, Philip 1921- *BiE&WWA, NotNAT, WhoThe 72, -77*
Rose, Ralph, Jr. 1911- *AmSCAP 66*
Rose, Reginald *NewYTET*
Rose, Reginald 1920- *BiE&WWA, NotNAT*
Rose, Reginald 1921- *FilmgC, HalFC 80, IntMPA 77, -75, -76, -78, -79, -80, WorEFlm*
Rose, Reve *WhoHol A*
Rose, Robert *Film 2*
Rose, Ronald Frederick 1940- *AmSCAP 80*
Rose, Rubye B 1914- *AmSCAP 80*
Rose, Rufus *PupTheA, PupTheA SUP*
Rose, Ruth 1900?- *WhoHrs 80*
Rose, Stephen *IntMPA 77, -76, -78, -79, -80*
Rose, Thomas William 1918- *AmSCAP 66*
Rose, Tim 1940- *IlEncR*
Rose, Vincent 1880-1944 *AmSCAP 66, -80, BiDAmM, CmpEPM*
Rose, Virginia *WhoHol A*
Rose, Wally 1913- *CmpEPM*
Rose, Wesley 1918- *ConMuA 80B, EncFCWM 69, IlEncCM*
Rose, Wesley H 1918- *IntWWM 77*
Rose, William 1899-1966 *BiDAmM*
Rose, William 1918- *CmMov, FilmEn, FilmgC, HalFC 80, IntMPA 77, -75, -76, -78, -79, -80*
Rose, William H 1926- *IntWWM 77, -80*
Rose, Zelma 1873-1933 *WhScrn 74, -77*
Rose Garden, The *RkOn 2[port]*
Rose Marie *ForYSC*
Rose Royce *RkOn 2[port]*
Roseberry, Eric Norman 1930- *IntWWM 77, -80, WhoMus 72*
Rosebery, Arthur d1928 *NotNAT B*

Rosebery, Lilian *WhThe*
Roseblade, Christine Margaret 1947- *IntWWM 77*
Roseblade, Emily Garrett 1879- *WhoMus 72*
Rosecrans, Carol *PupTheA*
Roseingrave *NewGrD 80*
Roseingrave, Daniel d1727 *NewGrD 80, OxMus*
Roseingrave, Ralph 1695-1747 *NewGrD 80, OxMus*
Roseingrave, Thomas 1688-1766 *NewGrD 80*
Roseingrave, Thomas 1690-1766 *Baker 78, MusMk, OxMus*
Rosel, Artur 1859-1934 *Baker 78*
Rosel, Peter 1945- *WhoMus 72*
Roseleigh, Jack 1887?-1940 *WhScrn 74, -77, WhoHol B*
Roselius, Ludwig 1902-1977 *Baker 78*
Rosell, Lars-Erik 1944- *Baker 78*
Roselle, Amy 1854-1895 *NotNAT B*
Roselle, William 1878-1945 *Film 1, NotNAT B, WhScrn 74, -77, WhoHol B*
Rosellen, Henri 1811-1876 *Baker 78*
Roseman, Edward F *Film 1, -2*
Roseman, Ronald Ariah 1933- *IntWWM 80*
Rosemarin, Jacob I 1892- *IntWWM 77*
Rosemboom, David 1947- *DcCM*
Rosemond, Anna *Film 1*
Rosemond, Clinton C 1883-1966 *BlksB&W C, DrBlPA, WhScrn 74, -77, WhoHol B*
Rosemond, Henri *MorBAP*
Rosemont, Norman *NewYTET*
Rosemont, Walter Louis 1895-1969 *AmSCAP 66, -80, ConAmC A*
Rosen, Albert 1924- *WhoMus 72, WhoOp 76*
Rosen, Arthur M 1928- *IntMPA 75, -76*
Rosen, Carole Margaret 1934- *IntWWM 77, -80*
Rosen, Charles 1927- *Baker 78, BnBkM 80, IntWWM 77, -80, NewGrD 80, WhoMus 72*
Rosen, David B 1938- *IntWWM 77, -80*
Rosen, Elsa Marianne Von 1927- *CnOxB, DancEn 78*
Rosen, Ethel *IntMPA 75, -76*
Rosen, Heinz 1908-1972 *CnOxB, DancEn 78*
Rosen, Ida 1922- *IntWWM 77*
Rosen, James 1885-1940 *WhScrn 74, -77*
Rosen, Jerome 1921- *Baker 78, ConAmC, NewGrD 80*
Rosen, Jerome 1939- *Baker 78*
Rosen, Jerome William 1921- *IntWWM 77, -80*
Rosen, Julius *PlP&P*
Rosen, Kenneth M d1976 *NewYTET*
Rosen, Marjorie *WomWMM*
Rosen, Mary K 1918- *IntWWM 77, -80*
Rosen, Max 1900-1956 *Baker 78, BiDAmM*
Rosen, Michael 1942- *IntWWM 77*
Rosen, Milton Sonnett 1906- *AmSCAP 66, -80, IntWWM 77*
Rosen, Myor 1917- *IntWWM 80*
Rosen, Nathaniel Kent 1948- *IntWWM 80*
Rosen, Oscar 1906- *WhoMus 72*
Rosen, Phil 1888-1951 *FilmEn, FilmgC, HalFC 80, WhoHrs 80*
Rosen, Philip 1888-1951 *TwYS A*
Rosen, Theodore 1918- *AmSCAP 66, -80*
Rosenbaum, Carl *ConMuA 80B*
Rosenbaum, Edward, Sr. d1927 *NotNAT B*
Rosenbaum, Maria Therese *NewGrD 80*
Rosenbaum, Samuel 1919- *AmSCAP 66, -80*
Rosenberg, Aaron 1912-1979 *CmMov, FilmEn, FilmgC, HalFC 80, IntMPA 77, -75, -76, -78, -79, -80, WorEFlm*
Rosenberg, Emanuel 1910- *ConAmC*
Rosenberg, Frank P 1913- *IntMPA 77, -75, -76, -78, -79, -80*
Rosenberg, George *AmSCAP 80*
Rosenberg, Herbert 1904- *IntWWM 77, -80, NewGrD 80*
Rosenberg, Hilding 1892- *Baker 78, CompSN[port], DcCM, IntWWM 80, NewEOp 71, NewGrD 80, OxMus*
Rosenberg, Jacob 1896-1946 *AmSCAP 66, -80*
Rosenberg, James L *NatPD[port]*
Rosenberg, Joseph Arnold 1951- *AmSCAP 80*
Rosenberg, Kenyon Charles 1933- *IntWWM 80*
Rosenberg, Marvin 1912- *BiE&WWA, NotNAT*
Rosenberg, Meta *NewYTET*
Rosenberg, Rick *IntMPA 79, -80*
Rosenberg, Royanne *WomWMM B*
Rosenberg, Sarah 1874-1964 *NotNAT B, WhScrn 74, -77, WhoHol B*
Rosenberg, Seymour S 1933- *AmSCAP 80*
Rosenberg, Stuart 1925- *FilmgC, HalFC 80, MovMk[port]*
Rosenberg, Stuart 1928- *FilmEn, IntMPA 77, -75, -76, -78, -79, -80, WorEFlm*
Rosenberger, Margaret A 1921- *AmSCAP 66, -80*
Rosenblatt, Adrian *WomWMM B*
Rosenblatt, Ed *ConMuA 80B*
Rosenblatt, Josef 1882-1933 *Film 2, WhScrn 77*
Rosenblatt, Joseph 1882-1933 *BiDAmM*
Rosenblatt, Rose *WomWMM B*
Rosenblith, Eric 1920- *IntWWM 77, -80*
Rosenbloom, Maxie *IntMPA 76, -75,*
Rosenbloom, Maxie 1903- *ForYSC, What 4[port]*
Rosenbloom, Maxie 1906-1976 *HalFC 80, MotPP, MovMk[port]*
Rosenbloom, Slapsey Maxey 1903- *JoeFr*
Rosenbloom, Slapsie Maxie 1903-1976 *FilmEn*
Rosenbloom, Slapsie Maxie 1906-1976 *FilmgC, WhoHol C*
Rosenbloom, Sydney 1889-1967 *Baker 78*
Rosenblum, Jack Irwin 1924- *IntWWM 77*
Rosenblum, M Edgar 1932- *BiE&WWA, NotNAT*
Rosenblum, Myron 1933- *IntWWM 77, -80*
Rosenblum, Peter 1941- *IntMPA 75*
Rosenblum, Ralph 1925- *HalFC 80*
Rosenblut, Hans *OxThe*
Rosenbluth, Leo 1904- *IntWWM 77, -80*
Rosenboom, David 1947- *Baker 78, ConAmC, IntWWM 77, -80*
Rosencrans, Leo S *IntMPA 77, -75, -76, -78, -79, -80*
Rosencrantz, Margareta *WomWMM*
Rosene, Paul E 1930- *IntWWM 77*
Rosenfeld, David 1933- *AmSCAP 80*
Rosenfeld, Gerhard Klaus 1931- *Baker 78, IntWWM 77, -80, NewGrD 80*
Rosenfeld, Jayn 1938- *IntWWM 77, -80*
Rosenfeld, Jerome M *BiE&WWA*
Rosenfeld, Leopold 1850-1909 *Baker 78*
Rosenfeld, Maurice 1867-1939 *BiDAmM*
Rosenfeld, Monroe H 1861-1918 *BiDAmM, Sw&Ld B*
Rosenfeld, Pamela Jean 1950- *IntWWM 77, -80*
Rosenfeld, Paul 1890-1946 *Baker 78, NewGrD 80*
Rosenfeld, Sydney 1855-1931 *NotNAT B, WhThe, WhoStg 1906, -1908*
Rosenfelt, Frank E 1921- *IntMPA 77, -76, -78, -79, -80*
Rosenfield, Jonas, Jr. *IntMPA 77, -75, -76, -78, -79, -80*
Rosenfield, Joseph J 1906- *IntMPA 75, -76*
Rosenfield, Lois *WomWMM*
Rosengarden, Bobby 1924- *EncJzS 70*
Rosengarden, Robert M 1924- *EncJzS 70*
Rosenhain, Eduard 1818-1861 *Baker 78*
Rosenhain, Jacob 1813-1894 *Baker 78, NewGrD 80*
Rosenhain, Jacques 1813-1894 *NewGrD 80*
Rosenhain, Jakob 1813-1894 *NewGrD 80*
Rosenhart, Kees 1939- *IntWWM 77, -80*
Rosenhaus, Matthew B *IntMPA 79, -80*
Rosenheim, Richard *PupTheA*
Rosenheim, Mrs. Richard *PupTheA*
Rosenman, Joel *ConMuA 80B*
Rosenman, Leonard 1924- *AmSCAP 66, -80, Baker 78, ConAmC, FilmEn, HalFC 80, NewGrD 80, WorEFlm*
Rosenmiller, Giovanni 1619?-1684 *NewGrD 80*
Rosenmuller, Johann 1619?-1684 *Baker 78, NewGrD 80*
Rosenmuller, Johann 1620?-1684 *OxMus*
Rosenow, Emil 1871-1904 *McGEWD*
Rosenroth, Christian Knorr Von *NewGrD 80*
Rosenstein, Gertrude *IntMPA 77, -75, -76, -78, -79, -80*
Rosenstiel, Leonie 1947- *IntWWM 77, -80*
Rosenstock, Joseph 1895- *Baker 78, BiDAmM, CmOp, IntWWM 77, -80, MusSN[port], NewEOp 71, WhoMus 72*
Rosenstock, Milton 1917- *AmSCAP 80, BiE&WWA, NotNAT*
Rosenthal, Albi 1914- *IntWWM 80, NewGrD 80*
Rosenthal, Andrew 1917- *BiE&WWA, NotNAT*
Rosenthal, Bud 1934- *IntMPA 77, -75, -76, -78, -79, -80*
Rosenthal, Carl A 1904- *IntWWM 77, -80*
Rosenthal, David 1952- *ConAmC*
Rosenthal, Harold David 1917- *Baker 78, IntWWM 80, NewGrD 80, WhoMus 72*
Rosenthal, Harry 1900-1953 *NotNAT B, WhScrn 74, -77, WhoHol B*
Rosenthal, Irving *ConAmC*
Rosenthal, J J d1923 *NotNAT B*
Rosenthal, Jack *ConDr 73, -77C*
Rosenthal, Jean 1912-1969 *BiE&WWA, CnOxB, DancEn 78, NotNAT B*
Rosenthal, Laurence 1926- *AmSCAP 66, -80, BiE&WWA, ConAmC, FilmEn, IntWWM 77, -80, NotNAT*
Rosenthal, Manuel 1904- *Baker 78, DcCM, IntWWM 77, -80, MusMk, NewGrD 80, WhoMus 72*
Rosenthal, Mara d1975 *WhoHol C*
Rosenthal, Mark *NewGrD 80*
Rosenthal, Moriz 1862-1946 *Baker 78, BiDAmM, BnBkM 80, MusSN[port], NewGrD 80[port], OxMus*
Rosenthal, Robert M 1936- *IntMPA 77, -75, -76, -78, -79, -80*
Rosenthal, Roberta *AmSCAP 80*
Roser, Franz DePaula 1779-1830 *NewGrD 80*
Roser, Johann Georg 1740-1797 *NewGrD 80*
Rosete Aranda, Leandro *PupTheA*
Rosette, Marion Savage *AmSCAP 66, -80*
Rosetti, Antonio 1750?-1792 *NewGrD 80*
Rosetti, Francesco Antonio 1750?-1792 *Baker 78*
Rosetti, Frantisek Antonin 1750?-1792 *NewGrD 80*
Rosetti, Franz Anton 1750?-1792 *NewGrD 80*
Rosety, Antonio 1750?-1792 *NewGrD 80*
Rosevear, Robert Allan 1915- *IntWWM 77, -80*
Rosewig, Albert H 1846-1929 *BiDAmM*
Rosey, George 1864-1936 *AmSCAP 66, -80*
Rosey, Joe 1882-1943 *AmSCAP 66, -80*
Roshal, Gregori *WomWMM*
Roshal, Grigori 1898- *DcFM*
Roshal, Grigori 1899- *FilmEn*
Roshanara d1926 *NotNAT B*
Rosher, Charles 1885-1974 *CmMov, FilmEn, FilmgC, HalFC 80, WomWMM*
Rosher, Dorothy *WhoHol A*
Roshkind, Michael *ConMuA 80B*
Rosi, Francesco 1922- *BiDFilm, -81, DcFM, FilmEn, FilmgC, HalFC 80, OxFilm, WorEFlm*
Rosian, Peter F 1902- *IntMPA 77, -75, -76, -78, -79, -80*
Rosie And The Originals *RkOn*
Rosier, Carl 1640-1725 *Baker 78, NewGrD 80*
Rosier, Charles 1640-1725 *NewGrD 80*
Rosiers, Andre, Sieur De Beaulieu *NewGrD 80*
Rosiers, Carl 1640-1725 *NewGrD 80*
Rosimond 1640?-1686 *OxThe*
Rosin, Armin O 1939- *NewGrD 80*
Rosina, Rose *AmSCAP 80*
Rosing, Bodil 1878-1942 *Film 2, ForYSC, TwYS, WhScrn 74, -77, WhoHol B*
Rosing, Vladimir 1890-1963 *Baker 78, CmOp, NewEOp 71*
Rosini, Carl 1882- *MagIlD*
Rosinska-Szklarzewicz, Maria 1915- *IntWWM 80*
Rosita, Eva *Film 2*
Rositsky, Jacek *NewGrD 80*
Roskelly, William 1919- *IntWWM 77, -80*
Roskin, Sheldon *ConMuA 80B*
Roskott, Carl 1953- *ConAmC*
Roslavets, Nikolai 1881-1930 *OxMus*
Roslavets, Nikolay Andreyevich 1881-1944 *NewGrD 80*
Roslavetz, Nikolai 1881-1944 *Baker 78*
Roslavleva *CnOxB*
Rosler, Anton *NewGrD 80*

Rosler, Endre 1904-1963 *NewGrD 80*
Rosler, Frantisek Antonin *NewGrD 80*
Rosler, Franz Anton *Baker 78, NewGrD 80*
Rosler, Gregorius *NewGrD 80*
Rosler, Jan Josef 1771-1813 *NewGrD 80*
Rosler, Johann Josef 1771-1813 *Baker 78, OxMus*
Rosler, Jozef 1771-1813 *NewGrD 80*
Rosley, Adrian 1890-1937 *WhScrn 74, -77, WhoHol B*
Rosmarin, Charles 1911- *IntMPA 77, -75, -76, -78, -79, -80*
Rosmarin, Mathieu *NewGrD 80*
Rosmer, Milton 1881-1971 *FilmEn, Film 1, -2, FilmgC, HalFC 80, IlWWBF, WhScrn 74, -77, WhoHol B*
Rosmer, Milton 1882- *WhThe*
Rosner, Arnold 1945- *AmSCAP 80, Baker 78, ConAmC*
Rosner, Francis 1916- *IntWWM 77, -80*
Rosner, George 1909- *AmSCAP 80*
Rosner, Jack *ConMuA 80B*
Rosness, Juanita M 1897-1967 *AmSCAP 66, -80*
Rosoff, Charles 1898- *AmSCAP 66, -80*
Rosolino, Frank 1926- *CmpEPM, EncJzS 70*
Rosowsky, Salomon 1878-1962 *BiDAmM*
Rosowsky, Solomon 1878-1962 *Baker 78, NewGrD 80, OxMus*
Rospigliosi, Giulio 1600-1669 *NewGrD 80*
Rosqui, Tom 1928- *BiE&WWA, NotNAT, WhoHol A*
Ross, Adrian 1859-1933 *CmpEPM, EncMT, WhThe*
Ross, Annie *IlEncJ*
Ross, Annie 1930- *EncJzS 70, WhoThe 77*
Ross, Anthony 1906-1955 *ForYSC, NotNAT B, WhScrn 74, -77, WhThe, WhoHol B*
Ross, Arnold 1921- *AmSCAP 80, CmpEPM, EncJzS 70*
Ross, Barney 1907-1967 *WhScrn 74, -77, WhoHol B*
Ross, Barry Fred 1944- *IntWWM 77, -80*
Ross, Ben 1911-1958 *AmSCAP 66, -80*
Ross, Benny 1912- *AmSCAP 66, -80*
Ross, Bertram 1920- *CnOxB, DancEn 78*
Ross, Betsy King 1923- *WhoHol A*
Ross, Betty *PupTheA*
Ross, Betty 1880-1947 *Film 2, WhScrn 74, -77, WhoHol B*
Ross, Beverly 1937- *AmSCAP 66*
Ross, Beverly Morgan 1914- *BiDAmM*
Ross, Bill 1915- *BiE&WWA*
Ross, Billy 1948- *IntWWM 77*
Ross, Burt *Film 2*
Ross, Carol *ConMuA 80B*
Ross, Charles Cowper 1929- *WhoThe 72, -77*
Ross, Charles Isaih 1925- *BluesWW[port]*
Ross, Charles J 1859-1918 *NotNAT B, WhoStg 1908*
Ross, Charles Ramsay Murray 1888- *WhoMus 72*
Ross, Chester Monroe 1917- *IntMPA 77, -76, -78, -79*
Ross, Chris 1946-1970 *WhScrn 74, WhoHol B*
Ross, Christopher 1946-1970 *WhScrn 77, WhoHol A*
Ross, Churchill 1901-1961 *WhScrn 77*
Ross, Churchill 1901-1962 *Film 2, WhoHol B*
Ross, Clifford 1879- *BlksBF*
Ross, Colin Archibald Campbell 1911- *IntWWM 77, -80, WhoMus 72*
Ross, Corinne Heath Sumner 1879-1965 *WhScrn 74, -77*
Ross, David 1891-1975 *WhScrn 77, WhoHol C*
Ross, David 1922-1966 *BiE&WWA, NotNAT B*
Ross, Diana 1944- *DrBlPA, HalFC 80, IlEncR, IntMPA 77, -75, -76, -78, -79, -80, MovMk[port], RkOn 2[port], WhoHol A*
Ross, Don *WhoHol A*
Ross, Dorothy 1912- *BiE&WWA, NotNAT*
Ross, Earle 1888-1961 *WhScrn 77*
Ross, Ed *WhoHol A*
Ross, Edna *Film 1*
Ross, Edward *AmSCAP 80, PupTheA*
Ross, Elinor 1932- *WhoOp 76*
Ross, Elizabeth 1928- *BiE&WWA, NotNAT*
Ross, Etna *Film 2*
Ross, Frances *Film 2*
Ross, Frank *Film 2*
Ross, Frank 1904- *FilmEn, FilmgC, HalFC 80, IntMPA 77, -75, -76, -78, -79, -80*
Ross, Frederick 1879- *WhThe*
Ross, George 1911- *BiE&WWA, NotNAT*
Ross, George I 1907- *WhoThe 72, -77*
Ross, Gilbert 1903- *IntWWM 77, -80, WhoMus 72*
Ross, Glynn 1914- *WhoOp 76*
Ross, Harry 1913- *WhThe*
Ross, Hector 1915- *WhThe*
Ross, Helen 1912- *AmSCAP 66, -80*
Ross, Herbert *IntMPA 79, -80*
Ross, Herbert d1934 *WhoHol B*
Ross, Herbert 1865-1934 *NotNAT B, WhThe*
Ross, Herbert 1866-1934 *WhScrn 77*
Ross, Herbert 1926- *CnOxB, DancEn 78*
Ross, Herbert 1927- *BiE&WWA, CmMov, FilmEn, FilmgC, HalFC 80, IntMPA 77, -75, -76, -78, NotNAT, WorEFlm*
Ross, Hugh 1898- *Baker 78*
Ross, Jackie *RkOn 2A*
Ross, James B *Film 1*
Ross, James Sinclair *CreCan 2*
Ross, Jane *OxMus*
Ross, Jerold 1926-1955 *BiDAmM*
Ross, Jerrold 1935- *IntWWM 77, -80*
Ross, Jerry *NewGrD 80*
Ross, Jerry 1926-1955 *AmPS, AmSCAP 66, -80, EncMT, NewCBMT, NotNAT B*
Ross, Joe E *WhoHol A*
Ross, John *NewGrD 80*
Ross, John 1763-1837 *NewGrD 80*
Ross, John M *BlkAmP, MorBAP*
Ross, John Marshall 1944- *IntWWM 77*
Ross, Julie *WhoHol A*
Ross, Katharine *IntMPA 75, -76, MotPP, WhoHol A*
Ross, Katharine 1942- *FilmEn, FilmgC, HalFC 80, MovMk[port], WhoHrs 80[port]*
Ross, Katharine 1943- *ForYSC, IntMPA 77, -78, -79, -80*
Ross, Kenneth 1941- *IntMPA 77, -76, -78, -79, -80*
Ross, Lancelot Patrick 1906- *AmSCAP 80*
Ross, Lanny 1906- *AmPS B, AmSCAP 66, CmpEPM, ForYSC, IntMPA 77, -75, -76, -78, -79, -80, What 1[port], WhoHol A*
Ross, Leonard Q *FilmEn*
Ross, Mabel Fenton d1931 *NotNAT B*
Ross, Marion 1898-1966 *WhScrn 74, -77, WhoHol A, -B*
Ross, Martin *NotNAT B*
Ross, Mary *Film 1*
Ross, Michael *ForYSC, NewYTET, WhoHol A*
Ross, Milton *Film 1, -2*
Ross, Myrna 1939-1975 *WhScrn 77, WhoHol A, -C*
Ross, Oriel 1907- *WhThe*
Ross, Orvin *ConAmC*
Ross, Richard *CpmDNM 80*
Ross, Robert d1954 *NotNAT B*
Ross, Robert S 1938- *NatPD[port]*
Ross, Ronald 1933- *EncJzS 70*
Ross, Ronnie 1933- *EncJzS 70*
Ross, Sam 1878?-1921 *NewOrJ*
Ross, Shirley d1975 *AmPS B, MotPP*
Ross, Shirley 1909-1975 *FilmEn, ForYSC, HalFC 80, WhScrn 77*
Ross, Shirley 1914-1975 *ThFT[port], WhoHol C*
Ross, Shirley 1915- *CmpEPM*
Ross, Sinclair 1908- *CreCan 2*
Ross, Spencer *RkOn*
Ross, Stan *WhoHol A*
Ross, Stanley 1935- *AmSCAP 66*
Ross, Stanley Ralph 1940- *AmSCAP 80*
Ross, Steve *ConMuA 80B*
Ross, Susanna 1950- *IntWWM 77, -80*
Ross, Sylvia Lucy 1930- *IntWWM 77*
Ross, Tayloe *WomWMM B*
Ross, Ted *DrBlPA*
Ross, Thomas W d1959 *Film 1, WhoHol B, WhoStg 1906*
Ross, Thomas W 1875-1959 *Film 2, NotNAT B, WhScrn 74, -77, WhThe*
Ross, Thomas W 1878-1959 *WhoStg 1908*
Ross, Tom *ConMuA 80B*
Ross, Wallace Michael 1920- *WhoMus 72*
Ross, Walter Beghtol 1936- *AmSCAP 80, Baker 78, CpmDNM 72, -73, -75, -78, -79, -80, ConAmC*
Ross, William *WhoHol A*
Ross, William 1925-1963 *NotNAT B, WhScrn 74, -77*
Ross, William Wrightson Eustace 1894-1966 *CreCan 1*
Ross-Clarke, Betty *WhThe*
Ross-Oliver, Charmion June *WhoMus 72*
Ross-Russell, Noel 1931- *WhoMus 72*
Rossana, Augustine S 1922- *AmSCAP 66*
Rossana, Augustine S 1932- *AmSCAP 80*
Rossana, Noel 1931- *DancEn 78*
Rossano, Nino *AmSCAP 80*
Rosse, Frederick 1867-1940 *NewGrD 80, NotNAT B*
Rosse, Russell d1910 *NotNAT B*
Rosseau, Norbert 1907- *WhoMus 72*
Rosseau, Norbert 1907-1975 *Baker 78, NewGrD 80*
Rosseels, Gustave A 1911- *IntWWM 77, -80*
Rossel, Roger 1930- *WhoOp 76*
Rossel-Majdan, Hildegard 1921- *IntWWM 77, -80*
Rosselle, William *Film 2*
Rosselli, Francesco *NewGrD 80*
Rossellini, Isabella *WhoHol A*
Rossellini, Renzo 1908- *Baker 78, DcFM, IntWWM 77, -80, NewEOp 71, NewGrD 80, WhoHol A, WhoMus 72, WhoOp 76*
Rossellini, Roberto 1906-1977 *BiDFilm, -81, DcFM, FilmEn, FilmgC, HalFC 80, IntMPA 77, -75, -76, MovMk[port], OxFilm, WorEFlm*
Rossen, Carol *WhoHol A*
Rossen, Robert 1908-1966 *AmFD, BiDFilm, -81, CmMov, DcFM, FilmEn, FilmgC, HalFC 80, MovMk[port], OxFilm, WorEFlm[port]*
Rosset, Barney 1922- *BiE&WWA, NotNAT*
Rosseter, Philip 1567?-1623 *NewGrD 80*
Rosseter, Philip 1568-1623 *MusMk*
Rosseter, Philip 1575?-1623 *OxMus, OxThe*
Rossetti, Antonio *NewGrD 80*
Rossetti, Biagio d1547? *NewGrD 80*
Rossetti, Pietro 1659-1709 *NewGrD 80*
Rossetti, Stefano *NewGrD 80*
Rossetto, Il *NewGrD 80*
Rossetto, Stefano *NewGrD 80*
Rossi, Abbate Francesco 1645?- *Baker 78*
Rossi, Alfred *WhoHol A*
Rossi, Ernesto 1827-1896 *EncWT, Ent[port]*
Rossi, Ernesto Fortunato Giovanni Maria 1827-1896 *OxThe*
Rossi, Ernesto Fortunato Giovanni Maria 1827-1897 *NotNAT B*
Rossi, Francesco *NewGrD 80*
Rossi, Franco 1919- *FilmEn, FilmgC, HalFC 80, OxFilm, WorEFlm*
Rossi, Gaetano 1774-1855 *NewGrD 80*
Rossi, Gaetano 1780-1855 *NewEOp 71*
Rossi, Giacomo *NewGrD 80*
Rossi, Giovan Carlo 1617?-1692 *NewGrD 80*
Rossi, Giovanni *NewGrD 80*
Rossi, Giovanni 1828-1886 *NewGrD 80*
Rossi, Giovanni Battista *NewGrD 80*
Rossi, Giovanni Gaetano 1828-1886 *Baker 78*
Rossi, Giovanni Maria De 1522?-1590 *NewGrD 80*
Rossi, Giulio 1865-1931 *Baker 78*
Rossi, Giuseppe De d1720? *NewGrD 80*
Rossi, John L 1927- *IntWWM 77, -80*
Rossi, Lauro 1810-1885 *Baker 78*
Rossi, Lauro 1812-1885 *NewGrD 80*
Rossi, Lemme 1602?-1673 *NewGrD 80*
Rossi, Luigi 1597?-1653 *NewGrD 80, OxMus*
Rossi, Luigi 1598?-1653 *Baker 78, MusMk*
Rossi, Mario 1902- *NewGrD 80, WhoMus 72, WhoOp 76*
Rossi, Massimo 1933- *IntWWM 77, -80*
Rossi, Michel Angelo 1602-1656 *Baker 78*
Rossi, Michelangelo 1601?-1656 *NewGrD 80*
Rossi, Nick 1924- *IntWWM 77, -80*
Rossi, Rita *Film 2*

Rossi, Robert Ralph 1933- *IntWWM 77, -80*
Rossi, Salamon De' 1570-1630? *NewGrD 80*
Rossi, Salamone 1570-1630? *NewGrD 80*
Rossi, Salomone 1570-1630? *Baker 78, NewGrD 80, OxMus*
Rossi, Shlomo 1570-1630? *NewGrD 80*
Rossi, Steve *WhoHol A*
Rossi, Tino 1907- *FilmEn*
Rossi, Vittorio 1936- *WhoOp 76*
Rossi, Walter 1914- *AmSCAP 66, -80*
Rossi-Drago, Eleanora 1925- *FilmAG WE, FilmEn, MotPP, WhoHol A, WorEFlm*
Rossi-Drago, Eleonora 1925- *FilmgC, HalFC 80*
Rossi-Lemeni, Nicola 1920- *Baker 78, CmOp, IntWWM 77, -80, NewEOp 71, NewGrD 80, WhoMus 72, WhoOp 76*
Rossif, Frederic 1922- *DcFM, FilmEn, FilmgC, HalFC 80, OxFilm, WorEFlm*
Rossignol, Felix Ludger *Baker 78, NewGrD 80*
Rossington, Norman 1928- *FilmgC, HalFC 80, WhoHol A*
Rossini, Carlo 1890-1975 *AmSCAP 66, -80, BiDAmM, ConAmC*
Rossini, Gioacchino 1792-1868 *Baker 78, BnBkM 80[port], CmOp, CmpBCM, CnOxB, DcCom 77[port], DcCom&M 79, GrComp[port], MusMk[port], NewEOp 71, OxMus*
Rossini, Gioachino 1792-1868 *NewGrD 80[port]*
Rossini, Giocchimo 1792-1868 *DcPup*
Rossino Mantovano *NewGrD 80*
Rossinto, Angelo *Film 2*
Rossiter, David Kensett 1952- *ConAmC*
Rossiter, Leonard 1926- *WhoHol A, WhoThe 72, -77*
Rossiter, Leonard 1927- *HalFC 80*
Rossiter, Will 1867-1954 *AmSCAP 66*
Rossitto, Angelo 1905?- *WhoHrs 80*
Rossius, Raymond 1926- *WhoOp 76*
Rossler, Anton *NewGrD 80*
Rossler, Ernestine *NewGrD 80*
Rossler, Frantisek Antonin *NewGrD 80*
Rossler, Franz Anton *NewGrD 80*
Rossler, Johann Joseph *NewGrD 80*
Rosslyn, Elaine d1964 *NotNAT B*
Rossmann, Hermann 1902- *CnMD*
Rosso De Chollegrana *NewGrD 80*
Rosso, Il *NewGrD 80*
Rosso, Giovanni Maria Del *NewGrD 80*
Rosso, Girolamo *NewGrD 80*
Rosso, Hieronymus *NewGrD 80*
Rosso, Lewis T 1911- *IntMPA 77, -75, -76, -78, -79, -80*
Rosso DiSan Secondo, Pier Luigi Maria 1887-1956 *CnThe, McGEWD[port], ModWD, OxThe, REnWD[port]*
Rosso DiSanSecondo, Pier Maria 1887-1956 *EncWT*
Rosson, Arthur d1960 *Film 1, WhoHol B*
Rosson, Arthur 1887-1960 *TwYS A*
Rosson, Arthur H 1889-1960 *FilmEn, WhScrn 74, -77*
Rosson, Hal 1895- *FilmEn, FilmgC, HalFC 80*
Rosson, Harold 1895- *CmMov, WorEFlm*
Rosson, Helene *Film 1*
Rosson, Keith 1937- *CnOxB, DancEn 78*
Rosson, Queenie *Film 1*
Rosson, Richard *Film 1, -2*
Rosson, Richard 1893-1953 *WhScrn 77*
Rosson, Richard 1894-1953 *FilmEn, TwYS A*
Rossoni, Giulio *NewGrD 80*
Rossum, Frederik Van 1939- *NewGrD 80*
Rost, Franz 1640?-1688 *NewGrD 80*
Rost, Nicolaus *NewGrD 80*
Rostal, Max 1905- *IntWWM 77, -80, NewGrD 80, WhoMus 72*
Rostand, Claude 1912-1970 *Baker 78, NewGrD 80*
Rostand, Edmond 1868-1918 *CnMD, CnThe, EncWT, Ent, McGEWD[port], ModWD, NotNAT B, OxThe, REnWD[port], WhThe*
Rostand, Maurice 1891-1968 *CnMD, EncWT, ModWD*
Rosten, Irwin *NewYTET*
Rosten, Leo 1908- *FilmEn*
Rosten, Norman 1914- *AmSCAP 80, BiE&WWA, NotNAT*
Rostetter, Alice *PupTheA*
Rosthius, Nicolaus 1542?-1622 *NewGrD 80*
Rostirolla, Giancarlo 1941- *IntWWM 77, -80*
Rostrom, Jan 1941- *IntWWM 77*
Rostropovich, Leopold 1892-1942 *Baker 78*
Rostropovich, Mstislav 1927- *Baker 78, BnBkM 80[port], IntWWM 77, -80, MusMk[port], MusSN[port], NewGrD 80, WhoMus 72, WhoOp 76*
Rostworowski, Karol Hubert 1877-1938 *CnMD, ModWD*
Rosvaenge, Helge 1897-1972 *NewGrD 80*
Roswaenge, Helge 1896-1972 *WhScrn 77*
Roswaenge, Helge 1897-1972 *Baker 78, CmOp, NewEOp 71, NewGrD 80*
Roswitha *NewGrD 80*
Roswitha 935?-1001? *CnThe, OxThe, REnWD[port]*
Rota, Andrea 1553?-1597 *NewGrD 80*
Rota, Antonio *NewGrD 80*
Rota, Giuseppe 1822-1865 *CnOxB*
Rota, Nino 1911-1979 *Baker 78, DcFM, FilmEn, FilmgC, HalFC 80, MusMk, NewGrD 80, OxFilm, RkOn 2A, WorEFlm*
Rotardier, Kelvin 1936- *CnOxB*
Rote, Kyle 1928- *AmSCAP 66, -80*
Rotella, John W 1920- *AmSCAP 80*
Rotella, Johnny 1920- *AmSCAP 66*
Rotenbucher, Erasmus 1525?-1586 *NewGrD 80*
Roters, Ernst 1892-1961 *Baker 78*
Roth, Andy *WhoHol A*
Roth, Ann *WhoThe 77*
Roth, Bernard 1923- *AmSCAP 80*
Roth, Bertrand 1855-1938 *Baker 78*
Roth, Christian 1585?-1640? *NewGrD 80*
Roth, Cy 1912- *IntMPA 77, -75, -76, -78, -79, -80*
Roth, Daniel 1942- *IntWWM 77, -80*
Roth, David Robert 1936- *IntWWM 77, -80*
Roth, Elliott *Film 2*
Roth, Ernst 1896-1971 *NewGrD 80*
Roth, Feri 1899-1969 *Baker 78*
Roth, Gene 1901-1976 *WhoHol A, WhoHrs 80[port]*
Roth, George 1904- *IntWWM 77, -80, WhoMus 72*
Roth, Ghitta Caiserman *CreCan 1*
Roth, Gunter 1925- *WhoOp 76*
Roth, Herman 1882-1938 *Baker 78*
Roth, Hieronymus *NewGrD 80*
Roth, Leon 1919- *IntMPA 75, -76*
Roth, Lillian *AmPS B, PlP&P*
Roth, Lillian 1910-1980 *BiE&WWA, FilmEn, FilmgC, ForYSC, HalFC 80, NotNAT, -A, ThFT[port], What 3[port], WhoHol A, WhoThe 77*
Roth, Lillian 1911-1980 *CmpEPM, Film 1, -2, MovMk*
Roth, Martin 1580?-1610 *NewGrD 80*
Roth, Michael Steven 1954- *AmSCAP 80*
Roth, Nicholas 1910- *IntWWM 77, -80, WhoMus 72*
Roth, Paul A 1930- *IntMPA 77, -75, -76, -78, -79, -80*
Roth, Pete 1893- *AmSCAP 66, -80*
Roth, Philipp 1779-1850 *NewGrD 80*
Roth, Richard A 1943- *IntMPA 77, -75, -76, -78, -79, -80*
Roth, Robert N *ConAmC*
Roth, Sandy 1889-1943 *WhScrn 74, -77, WhoHol B*
Roth, Wilhelm August Traugott 1720?-1765 *NewGrD 80*
Roth, Wolfgang 1910- *WhoOp 76*
Rotha, Paul 1907- *DcFM, FilmEn, FilmgC, HalFC 80, IIWWBF, IntMPA 77, -75, -76, -78, -79, -80, OxFilm, WorEFlm*
Rotha, Wanda *WhoHol A, WhoThe 72, -77*
Rothafel, S L Roxy 1882-1931 *WorEFlm*
Rothauser, Eduard *Film 2*
Rothberg, Bob 1901-1938 *AmSCAP 66, -80*
Rothberg, Gerald *ConMuA 80B*
Rothchild, Paul *ConMuA 80B*
Rothe, Anita d1944 *NotNAT B*
Rothe, Hans 1894- *EncWT*
Rothenberg, David 1933- *BiE&WWA*
Rothenberger, Anneliese 1924- *Baker 78, CmOp, NewGrD 80*
Rothenberger, Anneliese 1926- *IntWWM 77, -80, WhoMus 72, WhoOp 76*
Rothenpucher, Erasmus *NewGrD 80*
Rothenstein, Albert Daniel 1883- *WhThe*
Rother, Artur 1885-1972 *NewGrD 80*
Rothgarber, Herbert 1930- *ConAmC*
Rothgardt, Wanda *Film 1*
Rothier, Leon *Film 1*
Rothier, Leon 1874-1951 *Baker 78, BiDAmM, MusSN[port], NewEOp 71*
Rothkirch, Edward V 1919- *IntMPA 77, -75, -76, -78, -79, -80*
Rothlisberger, Max 1914- *IntWWM 80*
Rothman, Joel 1938- *IntWWM 77*
Rothman, Lawrence 1934- *BiE&WWA, NotNAT*
Rothman, Marion *WomWMM*
Rothman, Mo 1919- *IntMPA 77, -75, -76, -78, -79, -80*
Rothman, Stephanie *WhoHrs 80, WomWMM, -B*
Rothmueller, Aron Marko 1918- *BiDAmM*
Rothmuller, Marko 1908- *Baker 78, CmOp, IntWWM 77, -80, NewEOp 71, NewGrD 80*
Rothmund, Doris *IntWWM 77, -80*
Rothschild, Amalie R *WomWMM A, -B*
Rothschild, Eileen *ConMuA 80B*
Rothschild, Myrtle 1936- *IntWWM 80*
Rothstein, Albert Jeffrey 1947- *IntWWM 77, -80*
Rothstein, Arnold 1923- *ConAmC*
Rothstein, Jack *WhoMus 72*
Rothwell, Evelyn 1911- *NewGrD 80, WhoMus 72*
Rothwell, Michael *WhoHol A*
Rothwell, Robert *WhoHol A*
Rothwell, Walter Henry 1872-1927 *Baker 78, BiDAmM, NewEOp 71*
Rotis, Joe 1917-1965 *NewOrJ*
Rotman, Johan 1923- *IntWWM 77, -80*
Rotmund, Ernest 1887-1955 *WhScrn 77*
Rotmund, Ernst 1887-1955 *WhScrn 74*
Rotoli, Augusto 1847-1904 *BiDAmM*
Rotron, Jean De 1609-1650 *NotNAT B*
Rotrou, Jean De 1609-1650 *CnThe, EncWT, Ent, McGEWD, OxThe, REnWD[port]*
Rott, Hans 1858-1884 *NewGrD 80*
Rott, Josef 1929- *IntWWM 80*
Rotta, Antonio 1495?-1549 *NewGrD 80*
Rottenberg, Ludwig 1864-1932 *Baker 78*
Rottenbucher, Erasmus *NewGrD 80*
Rottenburgh *NewGrD 80*
Rottenburgh, Godefroid-Adrien-Joseph 1642-1720 *NewGrD 80*
Rottenburgh, Jean-Hyacinth-Joseph 1672-1765 *NewGrD 80*
Rottenstein-Pock *NewGrD 80*
Rotter, Fritz *BiE&WWA*
Rottger, Heinz 1909-1977 *NewGrD 80*
Rottura, Joseph James 1929- *AmSCAP 66, ConAmC A*
Rottura, Joseph James 1929-1980 *AmSCAP 80*
Rotunda, Marjorie *WomWMM B*
Rotundo, Emil 1928- *IntWWM 80*
Rotunno, Giuseppe *HalFC 80*
Rotunno, Giuseppe 1923- *FilmEn*
Rotunno, Giuseppe 1926- *DcFM, FilmgC, WorEFlm*
Rouart, Alexander 1869-1921 *Baker 78*
Rouart-Lerolle *NewGrD 80*
Rouault, Georges 1871-1958 *DancEn 78*
Roubakine, Boris 1908- *CreCan 1*
Roubert, Matty *Film 1, -2*
Roubleau, Ernest 1897?-1973 *NewOrJ*
Rouch, Jean 1917- *BiDFilm, -81, DcFM, FilmEn, OxFilm, WorEFlm[port]*
Rouche, Jacques 1862-1957 *DancEn 78*
Rouchon, Tete 1860?-1932? *NewOrJ*
Roucourt, Pierre De *NewGrD 80, -80*
Roude, Neil *WhoHol A*
Roudenko, Vladimir *Film 2*
Rouer, Germaine *Film 2*
Rougas, Michael *WhoHol A*
Rouge, Filippo *NewGrD 80*
Rouge, Guillaume 1385?-1456? *NewGrD 80*
Rouget, Gilbert 1916- *IntWWM 77, -80, NewGrD 80*

Rouget DeLisle, Claude-Joseph 1760-1836 *Baker 78*
Rouget DeLisle, Claude Joseph 1760-1836 *MusMk[port]*
Rouget DeLisle, Claude-Joseph 1760-1836 *NewGrD 80*
Rouget DeLisle, Claude Joseph 1760-1836 *OxMus*
Rough, Cecil Emilie Sarah *WhoMus 72*
Roughwood, Owen 1876-1947 *Film 2, NotNAT B, WhThe, WhoHol B*
Rouince, Luigi *NewGrD 80*
Rouleau, Joseph Alfred 1929- *CmOp, IntWWM 77, -80, NewGrD 80, WhoMus 72, WhoOp 76*
Rouleau, Raymond 1904- *FilmEn, WorEFlm*
Roulien, Raul *WhoHol A*
Roullet, Johannes *NewGrD 80*
Roullet, Marie F L G Leblanc 1716-1786 *NewGrD 80*
Round, Thomas 1918- *WhoMus 72*
Rounders, The *Film 2*
Rounds, David 1930- *NotNAT, WhoHol A*
Roundtree, Richard *IntMPA 75, -76, -78, -79, -80*
Roundtree, Richard 1937- *HalFC 80*
Roundtree, Richard 1942- *DrBlPA, FilmEn, FilmgC, IntMPA 77, MovMk, WhoHol A*
Rounesville, Robert 1914-1974 *WhScrn 77*
Rounitch, Joseph *Film 2*
Rounseville, Robert 1914-1974 *BiE&WWA, EncMT, HalFC 80, NotNAT B, WhoHol B, WhoThe 72, -77*
Rouquier, Georges 1909- *DcFM, FilmEn, FilmgC, HalFC 80, OxFilm, WorEFlm*
Rourke, M E 1867-1933 *BiDAmM*
Rourke, Michael Elder 1867-1933 *AmSCAP 66, -80*
Rourke, William Michael *NewGrD 80*
Rous, Francis 1579-1659 *OxMus*
Rous, Helen d1934 *NotNAT B, WhThe*
Rousanne, Madame 1894-1958 *CnOxB, DancEn 78*
Rousby, William Wybert d1907 *NotNAT B*
Rouse, Charles 1924- *EncJzS 70*
Rouse, Charlie 1924- *CmpEPM, EncJzS 70*
Rouse, Christopher Chapman 1949- *CpmDNM 80, ConAmC*
Rouse, Ervin Thomas 1917- *AmSCAP 80*
Rouse, Hallock 1897-1930 *WhScrn 74, -77, WhoHol B*
Rouse, Morris *NewOrJ*
Rouse, Russel 1916?- *HalFC 80*
Rouse, Russell 1916- *BiDFilm, -81, FilmEn, FilmgC, IntMPA 77, -75, -76, -78, -79, -80, WorEFlm[port]*
Rouse, Simon *WhoHol A*
Rousee, Jean *NewGrD 80*
Roussakis, Nicolas 1934- *ConAmC, IntWWM 77, -80*
Rousseau, August 1894?-1956? *NewOrJ*
Rousseau, Eugene Ellsworth 1932- *WhoMus 72*
Rousseau, Jean 1644-1700? *NewGrD 80*
Rousseau, Jean-Baptiste 1671-1741 *NewGrD 80, OxThe*
Rousseau, Jean-Jacques 1712-1778 *Baker 78, CmOp, MusMk[port], NewEOp 71, NewGrD 80, OxMus, OxThe*
Rousseau, Jean-Marie d1784 *NewGrD 80*
Rousseau, Marcel 1882-1955 *Baker 78, NewGrD 80*
Rousseau, Samuel-Alexandre 1853-1904 *Baker 78*
Roussel, Albert 1869-1937 *Baker 78, BnBkM 80, CompSN[port], CnOxB, DcCom&M 79, DcCM, DcTwCC, -A, MusMk, NewEOp 71, NewGrD 80[port], OxMus*
Roussel, Francois 1510?-1577? *NewGrD 80*
Roussier, Pierre-Joseph 1716-1790? *Baker 78*
Roussier, Pierre-Joseph 1716?-1792 *NewGrD 80*
Roussin, Andre 1911- *BiE&WWA, CnMD, CnThe, Ent, McGEWD[port], ModWD, NotNAT*
Routch, Robert 1917- *IntWWM 77, -80*
Routers, The *RkOn*
Routh, Francis John 1927- *IntWWM 77, -80, NewGrD 80, WhoMus 72*
Routier, Simone 1901- *CreCan 1*
Routledge, Calvert d1916 *NotNAT B*
Routledge, Patricia 1929- *EncMT, WhoHol A, WhoThe 72, -77*
Routley, Erik 1917- *NewGrD 80*
Rouverol, Mrs. Aurania d1955 *NotNAT B*
Rouverol, Jean *ForYSC, WhoHol A*
Rouwizer, Francois Leonard 1737-1827 *NewGrD 80*
Rouwyzer, Francois Leonard 1737-1827 *NewGrD 80*
Roux, Aline 1935- *CnOxB*
Roux, Jacques *WhoHol A*
Roux, Jean-Louis 1923- *CreCan 2*
Roux, Michel 1924- *WhoOp 76*
Rouzon, Oscar 1912- *NewOrJ SUP[port]*
Rove, Billie *Film 2*
Rovelle, Camille *Film 2*
Rovelli, Pietro 1793-1838 *Baker 78, NewGrD 80*
Rovenski, Josef 189-?-1936 *DcFM*
Rovensky, Joseph *Film 2*
Rovensky, Vaclav Karel Holan *NewGrD 80*
Rover Boys, The *RkOn*
Rovere, Gina *WhoHol A*
Rovescio, Al *NewGrD 80*
Rovetta, Gerolamo 1851-1910 *McGEWD*
Rovetta, Giovanni 1595?-1668 *NewGrD 80*
Rovetta, Giovanni Battista *NewGrD 80*
Rovetta, Girolamo 1850- *WhThe*
Rovettino, Giovanni Battista *NewGrD 80*
Rovics, Howard 1936- *ConAmC, IntWWM 77, -80*
Rovigo, Franceschino 1541?-1597 *NewGrD 80*
Rovigo, Francesco 1541?-1597 *NewGrD 80*
Rovin, Felix A 1912- *AmSCAP 80, IntWWM 77, -80*
Rovince, Luigi *NewGrD 80*
Rovitti, Olerto *NewGrD 80*
Rovsing Olsen, Poul *NewGrD 80*
Row, Richard D 1899- *AmSCAP 66*
Rowal, Jack *Film 2*
Rowaldt, Johann Jacob 1718-1775 *NewGrD 80*
Rowan, Dan 1922- *FilmgC, ForYSC, HalFC 80, JoeFr[port], WhoHol A*
Rowan, Dan And Dick Martin *ForYSC*
Rowan, Don d1966 *WhoHol B*
Rowan, Donald W 1906-1966 *WhScrn 74, -77*
Rowan, Ernest 1886-1960 *WhScrn 74, -77*
Rowan, Frank M 1897- *AmSCAP 66*
Rowan, Irwin 1897- *AmSCAP 66*
Rowan And Martin *JoeFr[port]*
Rowbotham, John Frederick 1854-1925 *Baker 78*
Rowden, Walter Courtenay *IlWWBF*
Rowe, Earl *WhoHol A*
Rowe, Eileen Florence 1914- *WhoMus 72*
Rowe, Fanny 1913- *WhThe*
Rowe, George *Film 2*
Rowe, George Fawcett 1834-1889 *NotNAT B, OxThe*
Rowe, Marilyn 1946- *CnOxB*
Rowe, Misty *WhoHol A*
Rowe, Mitchell L 1948- *AmSCAP 80*
Rowe, Nellie *AmSCAP 80*
Rowe, Nicholas 1674-1718 *CnThe, DcPup, EncWT, Ent, McGEWD[port], NotNAT B, OxThe, REnWD[port]*
Rowe, Nicolas *PlP&P[port]*
Rowe, Sir Reginald d1945 *NotNAT B*
Rowe, Roy 1905- *IntMPA 77, -75, -76, -78, -79, -80*
Rowe, Walter d1647? *NewGrD 80*
Rowe, Winston Hugh 1900- *WhoMus 72*
Rowell, Glenn 1899-1965 *AmSCAP 66, -80*
Rowell, Kenneth 1922- *CnOxB, DancEn 78*
Rowen, Ruth Halle 1918- *AmSCAP 66, -80, Baker 78*
Rowicki, Witold 1914- *Baker 78, IntWWM 77, NewGrD 80*
Rowin, John William 1945- *AmSCAP 80*
Rowland, Adele *AmPS B, CmpEPM, Film 2*
Rowland, Betty *What 5[port]*
Rowland, Christopher 1946- *IntWWM 77, -80*
Rowland, Gerald *WhoHol A*
Rowland, H W d1937 *NotNAT B*
Rowland, Helen *Film 2*
Rowland, Henry *ForYSC, WhoHol A*
Rowland, James G d1951 *WhScrn 74, -77*
Rowland, Mabel d1943 *NotNAT B*
Rowland, Margery 1910-1945 *NotNAT B, WhThe*
Rowland, Michael 1936- *WhoMus 72*
Rowland, Roy 1910- *BiDFilm, -81, CmMov, FilmEn, FilmgC, HalFC 80, IntMPA 77, -75, -76, -78, -79, -80, WorEFlm[port]*
Rowland, Steve *WhoHol A*
Rowland, Thomas Horsfall 1913- *WhoMus 72*
Rowland, Toby 1916- *WhoThe 72, -77*
Rowland, William 1900- *IntMPA 77, -75, -76, -78, -79, -80*
Rowland, Winifred Maude *IntWWM 77*
Rowland-Entwistle, Theodore 1925- *IntWWM 77*
Rowlands, Alan 1929- *WhoMus 72*
Rowlands, Art 1898-1944 *WhScrn 74, -77, WhoHol B*
Rowlands, David *WhoHol A*
Rowlands, Gaynor d1906 *NotNAT B*
Rowlands, Gena 1934- *FilmEn, HalFC 80*
Rowlands, Gena 1936- *BiE&WWA, FilmgC, ForYSC, IntMPA 77, -76, -78, -79, -80, MotPP, NotNAT, WhoHol A*
Rowlands, Lady *WhoHol A*
Rowlands, Patsy 1935- *WhoHol A, WhoThe 72, -77*
Rowlandson, Thomas 1756-1827 *DcPup*
Rowlard *NewGrD 80*
Rowles, James George 1918- *AmSCAP 66, -80, EncJzS 70*
Rowles, Jimmy 1918- *CmpEPM, EncJzS 70*
Rowles, John 1947- *BiDAmM*
Rowles, Polly 1914- *BiE&WWA, NotNAT, WhoHol A, WhoThe 72, -77*
Rowley, Alec 1892-1958 *Baker 78, NewGrD 80, OxMus*
Rowley, Gordon Samuel 1943- *IntWWM 77, -80*
Rowley, J W d1925 *NotNAT B, WhThe*
Rowley, John H 1917- *IntMPA 77, -75, -76, -78, -79, -80*
Rowley, Naomi Jean 1943- *IntWWM 77, -80*
Rowley, Samuel 1575?-1624 *CnThe, NotNAT B, OxThe, REnWD[port]*
Rowley, William *McGEWD[port]*
Rowley, William 1585?-1626 *EncWT*
Rowley, William 1585?-1637? *OxThe*
Rowley, William 1585?-1638? *NotNAT B*
Rowley, William 1585?-1642? *CnThe, Ent, REnWD[port]*
Rowling, Red 1894?- *NewOrJ*
Rowlinson, Mark 1948- *IntWWM 80*
Rowntree, John Pickering 1937- *IntWWM 77, -80*
Rowser, James Edward 1926- *EncJzS 70*
Rowser, Jimmy 1926- *EncJzS 70*
Rowson, Susanna Haswell d1824 *NotNAT B*
Rowson, Susannah 1762-1824 *BiDAmM*
Rox, John Jefferson d1957 *NotNAT B*
Roxanne *WhoHol A*
Roxborough, Picton d1932 *NotNAT B*
Roxburgh, Edwin 1937- *IntWWM 77, -80, NewGrD 80, WhoMus 72*
Roxbury, Ronald 1946- *ConAmC*
Roxy Music *ConMuA 80A, IlEncR*
Roy Henry *NewGrD 80*
Roy, Alexander 1935- *CnOxB*
Roy, Alphonse 1906- *IntWWM 77, -80*
Roy, Bartolomeo 1530?-1599 *NewGrD 80*
Roy, Bimal 1909-1966 *FilmEn, WorEFlm*
Roy, Bimal 1912-1966 *DcFM*
Roy, Charu *Film 2*
Roy, Colin Maitland 1942- *IntWWM 77, -80*
Roy, D L *REnWD[port]*
Roy, Dan *Film 2, WhScrn 74, -77*
Roy, Derek 1922- *WhoMus 72*
Roy, Gabrielle 1909- *CreCan 2*
Roy, Harry 1904-1971 *WhScrn 74, -77, WhoHol B, WhoMus 72*
Roy, Jessie H *BlkAmP*
Roy, John 1899-1975 *WhScrn 77*
Roy, Klaus George 1924- *ConAmC*
Roy, Nardo 1948- *IntWWM 77, -80*
Roy, Teddy 1905-1966 *EncJzS 70, WhoJazz 72*
Roy, Theodore Gerald 1905-1966 *EncJzS 70*
Roy, Will *IntWWM 80, WhoOp 76*
Roy, William 1928- *AmSCAP 66, -80*
Royaards, Wilhem d1929 *WhThe*
Royaards, William d1929 *NotNAT B*
Royal, Billy Joe 1945- *RkOn 2[port]*

Royal, Ernest Andrew 1921- *EncJzS 70*
Royal, Ernie 1921- *BiDAmM, CmpEPM, EncJzS 70*
Royal, John F d1974 *NewYTET*
Royal, Marshall 1912- *CmpEPM, EncJzS 70, WhoJazz 72*
Royal, Ted 1904- *AmSCAP 66, -80, BiE&WWA, NotNAT*
Royal Guardsmen, The *RkOn 2[port]*
Royal Hawaiians *BiDAmM*
Royal Scots Dragoon Guards, The *RkOn 2[port]*
Royal Teens, The *RkOn[port]*
Royale, Harry M d1963 *NotNAT B*
Royalettes, The *RkOn 2A[port]*
Royaltones, The *RkOn*
Royce, Brigham d1933 *NotNAT B, WhoHol B*
Royce, Mrs. E W *Film 2*
Royce, Edward 1870-1964 *EncMT, NotNAT B, WhThe*
Royce, Edward 1886-1963 *Baker 78, BiDAmM, ConAmC*
Royce, Edward William 1841-1926 *NotNAT B, WhThe*
Royce, Forrest Frosty 1911-1965 *WhScrn 74, -77*
Royce, Julian 1870-1946 *NotNAT B, WhThe, WhoHol B*
Royce, Lionel 1891-1946 *WhScrn 74, -77, WhoHol B*
Royce, Riza *WhoHol A*
Royce, Rosita 1918-1954 *WhScrn 74, -77*
Royce, Ruth *Film 2*
Royce, Virginia 1932-1962 *NotNAT B, WhScrn 74, -77, WhoHol B*
Royde, Frank 1882- *WhThe*
Royde-Smith, Naomi d1964 *NotNAT B, WhThe*
Roye, Phillip *WhoHol A*
Roye, Ruth *AmPS B*
Royed, Beverly *Film 2*
Royer, Etienne 1882-1928 *Baker 78*
Royer, Harry Missouri 1889-1951 *WhScrn 74, -77, WhoHol B*
Royer, Joseph-Nicolas-Pancrace 1700-1755 *Baker 78*
Royer, Joseph-Nicolas-Pancrace 1705?-1755 *NewGrD 80*
Royer, Paul H 1922- *ConAmC*
Royle, Edwin Milton 1862-1942 *McGEWD[port], NotNAT B, WhThe, WhoStg 1908*
Royle, Josephine *WhThe*
Royle, May Alexander *WhoMus 72*
Royle, Selena 1904- *FilmEn, ForYSC, HalFC 80, IntMPA 77, -75, -76, -78, -79, -80, MGM[port], Vers B[port], WhThe, WhoHol A*
Royle, Selena Fetter d1955 *NotNAT B*
Royle, Stanley 1888-1962 *CreCan 1*
Royllart, Philippus *NewGrD 80*
Roynci, Luigi *NewGrD 80*
Royston, Julius d1935 *WhScrn 74, -77*
Royston, Roy 1899- *WhThe*
Royton, Verna d1974 *WhoHol B*
Royzman, Leonid 1916- *NewGrD 80*
Rozakis, Greg *WhoHol A*
Rozan, Micheline *WomWMM*
Rozanov, Sergey 1870-1937 *NewGrD 80*
Rozanova, Berta *DancEn 78*
Rozario, Bob 1933- *AmSCAP 80*
Roze, Marie-Hippolyte 1846-1926 *Baker 78, NewEOp 71*
Roze, Nicolas 1745-1819 *NewGrD 80*
Roze, Raymond 1875-1920 *Baker 78, NotNAT B, WhThe*
Rozenberg, Lucien *WhThe*
Rozet, Monsieur *Film 2*
Rozet, Francois *CreCan 2*
Rozet, Sonia *IntWWM 77*
Rozewicz, Tadeusz 1921- *CroCD, ModWD, REnWD[port]*
Rozhdestvensky, Gennadi 1930- *CmOp, WhoMus 72*
Rozhdestvensky, Gennadi Nikolayevich 1931- *IntWWM 77, -80*
Rozhdestvensky, Gennady 1931- *BnBkM 80, NewGrD 80[port]*
Rozhdestvensky, Gennady Nikolaevich 1930- *WhoOp 76*
Rozier, Jacques 1926- *DcFM, FilmEn, OxFilm, WorEFlm*
Roziers, Andre *NewGrD 80*
Roziewicz, Tadeusz 1921- *EncWT*
Rozin, Albert 1906- *AmSCAP 66, -80*
Rozkosny, Josef Richard 1833-1913 *Baker 78, NewGrD 80*
Rozmarynowicz, Andrzej 1928- *IntWWM 77, -80*
Rozmiarek, Joseph *ConAmTC*
Rozo Contreras, Jose 1894- *NewGrD 80*
Rozov, Victor Sergeevich 1913- *CnMD, CnThe, ModWD*
Rozov, Victor Sergeyevich 1913- *EncWT*
Rozsa, Bela 1905- *ConAmC*
Rozsa, Miklos 1907- *Baker 78, CmMov, CmpEPM, CpmDNM 76, -79, -80, ConAmC, DcCM, FilmEn, FilmgC, HalFC 80, IntMPA 77, -76, -78, -79, -80, IntWWM 77, -80, NewGrD 80, OxFilm, OxMus, WhoHrs 80, WhoMus 72, WorEFlm*
Rozsa, Suzanne 1927- *WhoMus 72*
Rozsa, Suzanne 1929- *IntWWM 77, -80*
Rozsa, Vera *WhoMus 72*
Rozsavolgyi, Mark 1789-1848 *NewGrD 80*
Rozsnyai *NewGrD 80*
Rozsnyai, Karoly *NewGrD 80*
Rozsos, Istvan 1944- *WhoOp 76*
Rozycki, Aleksander 1845-1914 *NewGrD 80*
Rozycki, Jacek d1697? *NewGrD 80*
Rozycki, Ludomir 1883-1953 *OxMus*
Rozycki, Ludomir 1884-1953 *Baker 78, NewGrD 80*
RR Ranch Boys *BiDAmM*
Ruanne, Patricia 1945- *CnOxB*
Ruano, Candido Jose 1760?-1803 *NewGrD 80*
Ruanova, Maria 1912- *CnOxB, DancEn 78*
Ruark, Robert C 1915-1965 *WhScrn 77*
Rub, Christian 1887-1956 *FilmEn, Film 1, FilmgC, HalFC 80, Vers B[port], WhScrn 74, -77, WhoHol B*
Rubach, Keith Edward 1944- *IntWWM 77, -80*
Rubber, Violla 1910- *BiE&WWA*
Rubbert, Johann Martin *NewGrD 80*
Rubbra, Edmund 1901- *Baker 78, BnBkM 80, CompSN[port], DcCom&M 79, DcCM, IntWWM 77, -80, MusMk, NewGrD 80[port], OxMus, WhoMus 72*
Rubell, Steve *ConMuA 80B*
Ruben, Aaron *AmSCAP 80, NewYTET*
Ruben, J Walter 1899-1942 *FilmEn*
Ruben, Jose d1969 *WhoHol B*
Ruben, Jose 1886-1969 *Film 2*
Ruben, Jose 1888-1969 *NotNAT B, WhThe*
Ruben, Jose 1889-1969 *PlP&P, WhScrn 74, -77*
Ruben And The Jets *BiDAmM*
Rubens, Alma 1897-1931 *FilmEn, Film 1, -2, FilmgC, HalFC 80, MotPP, MovMk, TwYS, WhScrn 74, -77, WhoHol B*
Rubens, Alma 1898-1931 *NotNAT B*
Rubens, Hugo 1905- *AmSCAP 66, -80, ConAmC A*
Rubens, Maurie 1893-1948 *AmSCAP 66, -80, NotNAT B*
Rubens, Paul *CmpEPM*
Rubens, Paul A 1875-1917 *Baker 78, EncMT, NewGrD 80, NotNAT B*
Rubens, Paul A 1876-1917 *OxMus, WhThe*
Rubenson, Albert 1826-1901 *Baker 78*
Rubenstein, Ida *Film 2*
Rubenstein, Louis Urban 1908- *AmSCAP 66, -80*
Rubenstein, Nancy 1929- *ConAmTC*
Rubental, Neidhart Von *NewGrD 80*
Rubert, Johann Martin 1614-1680 *NewGrD 80*
Ruberti, Costantino *NewGrD 80*
Rubes, Jan 1920- *CreCan 1, WhoOp 76*
Rubeus, Petrus 1374-1438 *NewGrD 80*
Rubiconi, Grisostomo 1576- *NewGrD 80*
Rubin, Ada 1906- *AmSCAP 66, -80*
Rubin, Al I 1928- *AmSCAP 80*
Rubin, Benny 1899- *FilmEn, Film 2, ForYSC, TwYS, Vers A[port], WhoHol A*
Rubin, Diane Gail *AmSCAP 80*
Rubin, Doris Anne 1921- *AmSCAP 80*
Rubin, Ed *ConMuA 80B*
Rubin, Mrs. Harry 1906- *EncFCWM 69*
Rubin, Joan Alleman 1931- *ConAmTC*
Rubin, Joel E 1928- *BiE&WWA*
Rubin, Marcel 1905- *Baker 78, IntWWM 77, -80*
Rubin, Menachem d1962 *NotNAT B*
Rubin, Nathan 1929- *IntWWM 77, -80*
Rubin, Pedro d1938 *WhScrn 74, -77*
Rubin, Robert Jacob 1911- *IntMPA 75, -76*
Rubin, Ronald *WhoHol A*
Rubin, Ruth 1906- *AmSCAP 66, -80, BiDAmM*
Rubin, Stanley 1917- *IntMPA 77, -75, -76, -78, -79, -80*
Rubin, Syd 1912- *IntMPA 75, -76*
Rubinet *NewGrD 80*
Rubini, Giacomo *NewGrD 80*
Rubini, Giovanni Battista 1794-1854 *Baker 78, CmOp, NewEOp 71, NewGrD 80[port], OxMus*
Rubini, Giovanni Battista 1795-1854 *BnBkM 80*
Rubini, Michel 1942- *AmSCAP 66*
Rubini, Nicolo 1584-1625 *NewGrD 80*
Rubinoff 1896- *What 2[port]*
Rubinoff, Dave 1897- *CmpEPM*
Rubinshteyn, Anton 1829-1894 *NewGrD 80[port]*
Rubinstein, Anton 1829-1894 *Baker 78, BnBkM 80[port], DancEn 78, GrComp[port], MusMk[port], NewEOp 71, NewGrD 80[port], OxMus*
Rubinstein, Anton 1830-1894 *CmOp*
Rubinstein, Arthur 1887- *MusSN[port], NewGrD 80[port]*
Rubinstein, Artur 1886- *BiDAmM, MusMk[port]*
Rubinstein, Artur 1887- *Baker 78, BnBkM 80[port], IntWWM 77, -80, NewGrD 80[port], WhoHol A*
Rubinstein, Artur 1890- *WhoMus 72*
Rubinstein, Beryl 1898-1952 *Baker 78, ConAmC*
Rubinstein, Beryl 1898-1953 *BiDAmM*
Rubinstein, Harold F 1891- *WhThe*
Rubinstein, Ida 1885?-1960 *CnOxB, DancEn 78, EncWT, WhThe*
Rubinstein, John Arthur 1946- *AmSCAP 80, WhoHol A*
Rubinstein, Joseph 1847-1884 *Baker 78*
Rubinstein, Lubov 1910- *IntWWM 80*
Rubinstein, Nicholas 1835-1881 *BnBkM 80, OxMus*
Rubinstein, Nicolai 1835-1881 *Baker 78*
Rubinstein, Nikolay 1835-1881 *NewGrD 80[port]*
Rubinstein, Stanley Jack 1890- *WhoMus 72*
Rubinus *NewGrD 80*
Rubio, David 1934- *NewGrD 80*
Rubio, Hilarion 1902- *NewGrD 80*
Rubio, Paul 1943- *IntMPA 75, -76*
Rubio, Samuel 1912- *NewGrD 80*
Rubio Piqueras, Felipe 1881-1936 *Baker 78*
Rubiola, Joe 1906-1939 *WhScrn 74, -77*
Rubner, Cornelius *Baker 78*
Rubsamen, Walter H 1911-1973 *Baker 78, NewGrD 80*
Ruby And The Romantics *RkOn*
Ruby, Ellalee *Film 2*
Ruby, Guillaume *NewGrD 80*
Ruby, Harry d1974 *Sw&Ld C*
Ruby, Harry 1895- *AmPS*
Ruby, Harry 1895-1959 *BiDAmM*
Ruby, Harry 1895-1974 *AmSCAP 66, -80, BiE&WWA, CmpEPM, EncMT, HalFC 80, NewCBMT, NotNAT B, PopAmC[port], PopAmC SUPN, WhThe*
Ruby, Herman 1891-1959 *AmSCAP 66, -80*
Ruby, Mary *Film 1*
Ruby, Thelma 1925- *WhoHol A, WhoThe 72, -77*
Ruccolo, James S 1943- *ConAmC*
Rucellai *PlP&P*
Rucellai, Giovanni 1475-1525 *McGEWD, OxThe*
Ruck, Hermann 1897- *IntWWM 77, -80*
Ruckaert *NewGrD 80*
Ruckaerts *NewGrD 80*
Ruckauf, Anton 1855-1903 *Baker 78*
Rucker, John 1866- *BlksBF[port]*
Ruckers *NewGrD 80*

Ruckers, Andreas *Baker 78*
Ruckers, Andreas d1654? *Baker 78*
Ruckers, Andreas 1579?-1645? *NewGrD 80*
Ruckers, Andreas 1607?-1667? *NewGrD 80*
Ruckers, Andries 1579?-1645? *NewGrD 80*
Ruckers, Andries 1607?-1667? *NewGrD 80*
Ruckers, Christoffel *Baker 78*
Ruckers, Hans d1643 *Baker 78*
Ruckers, Hans 1540?-1598 *NewGrD 80*
Ruckers, Hans 1550?-1598? *Baker 78*
Ruckers, Hans 1555?-1623? *MusMk*
Ruckers, Joannes 1578?-1643 *NewGrD 80*
Ruckert, Ernest *Film 2*
Ruckert, Friedrich 1788-1866 *NewGrD 80*
Rucqueer *NewGrD 80*
Ructis, Ar De *NewGrD 80*
Rudami, Rosa 1899-1966 *WhScrn 74, -77*
Rudani, Rosa d1966 *WhoHol B*
Rudbeck, Olaus 1630?-1702 *NewGrD 80*
Rudbeck, Olof 1630?-1702 *NewGrD 80*
Rudbeckius, Olof 1630?-1702 *NewGrD 80*
Rudd, Enid *NatPD[port]*
Rudd, Hughes *NewYTET*
Rudd, Paul *WhoHol A*
Rudd, Roswell Hopkins, Jr. 1935- *EncJzS 70, IlEncJ*
Ruddick, Joe 1917- *IntMPA 75, -76*
Ruddock, John 1897- *WhoHol A, WhoThe 72, -77*
Ruddy, Albert S 1934- *HalFC 80, IntMPA 77, -75, -76, -78, -79, -80*
Rude, Johann 1555?-1615? *NewGrD 80*
Rudel, Hugo 1868-1934 *Baker 78*
Rudel, Jaufre *NewGrD 80*
Rudel, Jofre 1921- *NewGrD 80*
Rudel, Julius 1921- *Baker 78, BiDAmM, BiE&WWA, BnBkM 80, CmOp, IntWWM 80, MusSN[port], NewEOp 71, NewGrD 80, WhoOp 76*
Rudel De Blaja, Jaufre *NewGrD 80*
Ruden, Jan Olof 1937- *NewGrD 80*
Rudenius, Johann *NewGrD 80*
Rudenko, Bela 1933- *NewGrD 80*
Rudenus, Johann *NewGrD 80*
Ruderman, Seymour George 1926- *AmSCAP 66, -80*
Rudersdorff, Hermine 1822-1882 *Baker 78, BiDAmM*
Rudge, Peter *ConMuA 80B*
Rudhyar, Dane 1895- *Baker 78, BiDAmM, ConAmC, DcCM, Film 2, IntWWM 77, -80, NewGrD 80, OxMus*
Rudiakov, Michael 1934- *IntWWM 77, -80*
Rudie, Evelyn 1947- *ForYSC, IntMPA 77, -75, -76, -78, -79, -80, What 1[port], WhoHol A*
Rudie, Robert 1919- *IntWWM 77, -80*
Rudin, Andrew 1939- *ConAmC*
Rudinger, Gottfried 1886-1946 *Baker 78, NewGrD 80*
Rudkin, David 1936- *ConDr 73, -77, CroCD, EncWT, McGEWD, REnWD[port], WhoThe 77*
Rudley, Herbert 1911- *FilmgC, ForYSC, HalFC 80, Vers A[port], WhoHol A*
Rudman, Kal *ConMuA 80B*
Rudman, Michael 1939- *WhoThe 77*
Rudnick, Wilhelm 1850-1927 *Baker 78*
Rudnicki, Marian Teofil 1888-1944 *Baker 78*
Rudnitsky, Antin 1902-1975 *ConAmC*
Rudnytsky, Antin 1902-1975 *Baker 78, IntWWM 77*
Rudnytsky, Roman 1942- *IntWWM 77, -80, WhoMus 72*
Rudolf Of St. Trond 1070?-1138 *NewGrD 80*
Rudolf Von Fenis-Neuenburg 1150?-1196? *NewGrD 80*
Rudolf, Leopold 1911- *EncWT*
Rudolf, Max 1902- *Baker 78, BnBkM 80, IntWWM 77, -80, NewEOp 71, NewGrD 80, WhoOp 76*
Rudolf, Perak 1891- *WhoMus 72*
Rudolph II *OxMus*
Rudolph, Archduke Of Austria 1788-1831 *NewGrD 80*
Rudolph, Johann Joseph 1730-1812 *CnOxB, NewGrD 80*
Rudolph, Johanna 1902-1974 *NewGrD 80*
Rudolph, Louis *IntMPA 77, -75, -76, -78, -79*
Rudolph, Oscar *Film 2*
Rudorf, Gunther 1921- *CnMD*
Rudorff, Ernst Friedrich Karl 1840-1916 *Baker 78, NewGrD 80*
Rudow, Vivian Adelberg 1936- *ConAmC*
Rudy Sisters, The *BiDAmM*
Rudzinski, Witold 1913- *Baker 78, DcCM, IntWWM 77, -80, NewGrD 80, WhoMus 72*
Rudzinski, Zbigniew 1935- *Baker 78, DcCM, IntWWM 77, -80, NewGrD 80*
Rue, Pierre DeLa *NewGrD 80*
Rueckers *NewGrD 80*
Rueckert, Ernst *Film 2*
Rueda, Jose *Film 2*
Rueda, Lope De 1505?-1565 *OxThe*
Rueda, Lope De 1510?-1565 *McGEWD[port], NotNAT B*
Ruederer, Josef 1861-1915 *McGEWD, ModWD*
Ruegger, Elsa 1881-1924 *BiDAmM*
Ruehmann, Heinz *WhoHol A*
Ruekaerts *NewGrD 80*
Ruelle, Charles Emile 1833-1912 *Baker 78*
Rues, Marga 1926- *DancEn 78*
Ruette, Jean-Louis La *NewGrD 80*
Ruettino, Giovanni Battista *NewGrD 80*
Ruetz, Caspar 1708-1755 *NewGrD 80*
Rufart, Carlos 1887-1957 *WhScrn 74, -77*
Rufer, Josef 1893- *Baker 78, NewGrD 80*
Rufer, Philippe 1844-1919 *Baker 78*
Ruff, Albert E 1851-1948 *BiDAmM*
Ruff, Herbert A 1918- *IntWWM 77, -80*
Ruff, Willie 1931- *Baker 78*
Ruff-Stoehr, Herta Maria Klara 1904- *IntWWM 77, -80*
Ruffa, Girolamo *NewGrD 80*
Ruffalo, Joseph *ConMuA 80B*
Ruffer, Magdi 1924- *IntWWM 77, -80*
Ruffin, David 1941- *RkOn 2[port]*
Ruffin, Jimmy 1939- *RkOn 2[port]*
Ruffini, Gene *NatPD[port]*
Ruffino D'Assisi 1490?-1532? *NewGrD 80*
Ruffino, Tony *ConMuA 80B*
Ruffo, Edgar 1925- *IntWWM 77, -80*
Ruffo, Tito d1953 *WhoHol B*
Ruffo, Titta 1877-1953 *Baker 78, BnBkM 80, CmOp, MusSN[port], NewEOp 71, NewGrD 80[port], WhScrn 74, -77*
Ruffo, Vincenzo 1505-1587 *OxMus*
Ruffo, Vincenzo 1508?-1587 *NewGrD 80*
Ruffolo, Lucretio 1550?-1612? *NewGrD 80*
Ruffulo, Lucretio 1550?-1612? *NewGrD 80*
Rufilo, Matteo *NewGrD 80*
Rufolo, Matteo *NewGrD 80*
Rufty, Hilton 1909- *BiDAmM, ConAmC*
Rufus *ConMuA 80A, IlEncR, RkOn 2[port]*
Ruge, Filippo 1725?-1767? *NewGrD 80*
Ruger, Morris Hutchins 1902- *ConAmC*
Rugeri, Francesco 1620-1695? *NewGrD 80*
Rugge, Filippo *NewGrD 80*
Ruggeri, Francesco 1620-1695? *NewGrD 80*
Ruggeri, Giovanni Maria *NewGrD 80*
Ruggeri, Roger 1939- *IntWWM 77, -80*
Ruggeri, Ruggero 1871-1953 *EncWT, NotNAT B, OxThe, WhoHol B*
Ruggi, Filippo *NewGrD 80*
Ruggi, Francesco 1767-1845 *Baker 78, NewGrD 80*
Ruggieri, Alexander F 1952- *IntWWM 80*
Ruggieri, Edmond 1907-1964 *AmSCAP 80*
Ruggieri, Giovanni Maria *NewGrD 80*
Ruggiero, Charles Howard 1947- *ConAmC, IntWWM 80*
Ruggle, George 1575-1622 *OxThe*
Ruggles, Carl 1876-1971 *AmSCAP 80, Baker 78, BiDAmM, BnBkM 80, CompSN[port], ConAmC, DcCM, MusMk, NewGrD 80[port], OxMus*
Ruggles, Charles d1970 *WhThe, WhoHol B*
Ruggles, Charles 1876-1971 *NewGrD 80[port]*
Ruggles, Charles 1886-1970 *FilmEn, FilmgC, HalFC 80[port]*
Ruggles, Charles 1890-1970 *Film 1, -2, MovMk[port], OxFilm, WhScrn 74, -77*
Ruggles, Charles 1891- *ForYSC*
Ruggles, Charles 1892-1970 *BiE&WWA, WorEFlm*
Ruggles, Charlie *MotPP*
Ruggles, Charlie 1886-1970 *Funs[port]*
Ruggles, Charlie 1892- *Vers A[port]*
Ruggles, Wesley 1889-1972 *CmMov, FilmEn, Film 1, FilmgC, HalFC 80, OxFilm, TwYS A, WhScrn 77, WhoHol B, WorEFlm*
Rugi, Filippo *NewGrD 80*
Rugieri, Francesco *NewGrD 80*
Rugoff, Donald S 1927- *IntMPA 77, -75, -76, -78, -79, -80*
Rugolo, Pete 1915- *CmpEPM, IntMPA 77, -75, -76, -78, -79, -80*
Rugolo, Peter 1915- *ConAmC*
Rugstad, Gunnar 1921- *IntWWM 77, -80*
Rugtvedt, Unni 1934- *WhoOp 76*
Ruhl, Arthur Brown d1935 *NotNAT B*
Ruhling, Johannes 1550?-1615 *NewGrD 80*
Ruhlmann, Francois 1868-1948 *NewEOp 71*
Ruhlmann, Frans 1868-1948 *Baker 78*
Ruhlmann, Franz 1896-1945 *Baker 78*
Ruhlmann, Julius 1816-1877 *Baker 78*
Ruhmann, Heinz 1902- *EncWT, FilmAG WE[port], FilmgC, HalFC 80*
Ruhmann, Heinz 1912- *FilmEn*
Ruhnke, Martin 1921- *NewGrD 80*
Ruick, Barbara 1932-1974 *ForYSC, HalFC 80, MotPP, WhScrn 77, WhoHol B*
Ruick, Melville d1972 *WhoHol B*
Ruijkers *NewGrD 80*
Ruimonte, Pedro *NewGrD 80, OxMus*
Ruince, Luigi *NewGrD 80*
Ruisi, Giuseppe Ferdinando 1914- *WhoOp 76*
Ruiter, Wim De 1943- *Baker 78*
Ruiz, Antonio *WhoHol A*
Ruiz, Brunilda 1936- *CnOxB, DancEn 78[port]*
Ruiz, Enrique 1908-1975 *AmSCAP 66, -80*
Ruiz, Federico d1961 *NotNAT B*
Ruiz, Hilton 1952- *EncJzS 70*
Ruiz, Jose Rivero 1896-1948 *WhScrn 74, -77*
Ruiz, Juan *NewGrD 80*
Ruiz, Matias d1708? *NewGrD 80*
Ruiz Azner, Valentin 1902-1972 *NewGrD 80*
Ruiz DeAlarcon, Juan 1580?-1639 *McGEWD[port]*
Ruiz DeAlarcon Y Mendoza, Juan 1581?-1639 *OxThe*
Ruiz DeRibayaz, Lucas 1650?- *NewGrD 80*
Ruiz DeRobledo, Juan d1644? *NewGrD 80*
Ruiz Iriarte, Victor 1912- *CroCD, McGEWD[port]*
Ruk-Focic, Bozena 1937- *WhoOp 76*
Rukeyser, Bud *NewYTET*
Rukkers *NewGrD 80*
Rule, Beverly C *WomWMM*
Rule, Elton H 1917- *IntMPA 80, NewYTET*
Rule, James S 1896- *AmSCAP 66*
Rule, Janice 1928- *ForYSC*
Rule, Janice 1931- *BiDFilm, -81, BiE&WWA, FilmEn, FilmgC, HalFC 80, IntMPA 77, -75, -76, -78, -79, -80, MotPP, NotNAT, WhoHol A, WhoThe 77*
Ruloffs, Bartholomeus 1741-1801 *NewGrD 80*
Ruman, Siegfried 1885-1967 *WhScrn 74, -77*
Ruman, Sig d1967 *MotPP, NotNAT B*
Ruman, Sig 1884-1967 *FilmEn, FilmgC, HalFC 80, OxFilm, Vers A[port]*
Ruman, Sig 1885-1967 *Film 2*
Rumann, Sig d1967 *WhoHol B*
Rumann, Sig 1884-1967 *HolCA[port], MovMk[port]*
Rumann, Sig 1885-1967 *ForYSC*
Rumbley, Jack Edward 1930- *IntWWM 77*
Rumford, Kennerley *NewGrD 80*
Rumley, Jerry 1930- *BiE&WWA, NotNAT*
Rummeister, Augusta *Film 2*
Rummel *NewGrD 80*
Rummel, Christian 1787-1849 *Baker 78, NewGrD 80*
Rummel, Franz 1853-1901 *Baker 78*
Rummel, Franziska 1821- *NewGrD 80*
Rummel, Joseph 1818-1880 *NewGrD 80*
Rummel, Josephine 1812-1877 *NewGrD 80*
Rummel, Walter Morse 1887-1953 *Baker 78*
Rumoro, Joe Louis 1923- *AmSCAP 66, -80*
Rumowsko-Machnikowska, Hanna *WhoOp 76*
Rump, Alan George 1947- *IntWWM 80*
Rumsey, Bert 1892-1968 *WhScrn 77*
Rumsey, David Edward 1939- *IntWWM 77, -80*
Rumsey, Howard 1917- *CmpEPM, EncJzS 70*
Rumsey, Murray *AmSCAP 80*

Rumsey, Murray 1907- *AmSCAP 66*
Rumshinsky, Joseph M 1881-1956 *AmSCAP 80, NotNAT B*
Rumshinsky, Joseph M 1881-1963 *AmSCAP 66*
Rumshinsky, Murray 1907- *AmSCAP 80*
Runacre, Jenny 1943- *HalFC 80*
Runanin, Boris 1917- *DancEn 78*
Runaways *ConMuA 80A*
Runcie, Constance Faunt LeRoy 1836-1911 *BiDAmM*
Runciman, Alex 1924- *IntMPA 77, -75, -76, -78, -79, -80*
Runciman, John F 1866-1916 *Baker 78*
Rundans, Anita 1943- *IntWWM 77, -80*
Rundgren, Bengt Erik 1931- *WhoOp 76*
Rundgren, Todd 1948- *ConMuA 80A, -80B, IlEncR[port], RkOn 2[port]*
Rung, Frederik 1854-1914 *Baker 78, NewGrD 80*
Rung, Henrik 1807-1871 *Baker 78*
Runge *NewGrD 80*
Runge, Georg d1639 *NewGrD 80*
Runge, Paul 1848-1911 *Baker 78*
Runge, Peter-Christoph 1939- *WhoMus 72, WhoOp 76*
Rungenhagen, Carl Friedrich 1778-1851 *Baker 78*
Runkel, Kenneth E 1882- *BiDAmM*
Runkel, Kenneth Eldon 1881- *ConAmC*
Runnel, Albert F 1892-1974 *WhScrn 77*
Runner, David Clark 1948- *IntWWM 77, -80*
Runner, Steve *ConMuA 80B*
Runningbrook, Jim *AmSCAP 80*
Runolfsson, Karl Otto 1900-1970 *Baker 78, NewGrD 80*
Runsten, Lars E I 1931- *WhoOp 76*
Runyan, William Marion 1870-1957 *AmSCAP 80*
Runyon, Damon 1884-1946 *Film 2, FilmgC, HalFC 80, ModWD, NotNAT A, -B, PlP&P, WhScrn 77, WhoHol B*
Runze, Maximilian 1849-1931 *Baker 78*
Ruodolf De Neuchatel *NewGrD 80*
Ruohonen, Seppo Juhani 1946- *WhoOp 76*
Ruolz-Montchal, Henri, Comte De 1808-1887 *Baker 78*
Rupert Of Deutz 1070?-1130? *NewGrD 80*
Rupertus Tuitensis *NewGrD 80*
Rupff, Conrad *NewGrD 80*
Rupin, Ivan Alexeyevich 1790?-1850 *NewGrD 80*
Rupnik, Ivan 1911- *Baker 78, IntWWM 80*
Rupp, Anna T 1909- *AmSCAP 66, -80*
Rupp, Carl 1892- *AmSCAP 66, -80*
Rupp, Marjorie J 1943- *IntWWM 80*
Ruppe, Christian Friedrich 1753-1826 *NewGrD 80*
Ruppe, Fredrik 1753-1826 *NewGrD 80*
Ruppe, Friedrich Christian 1771-1834 *NewGrD 80*
Ruppel, Karl Heinrich 1900- *NewGrD 80*
Ruppich, Conrad *NewGrD 80*
Ruprecht *NewGrD 80*
Ruprecht, Conrad *NewGrD 80*
Ruprecht, Hieronymus *NewGrD 80*
Ruprecht, Johannes *NewGrD 80*
Ruprecht, Martin 1758?-1800 *NewGrD 80*
Rupsch, Conrad 1475?-1530? *NewGrD 80*
Ruremunde, Christophe Van *NewGrD 80*
Rusca, Francesco *Baker 78*
Rusch, Harold W 1908- *AmSCAP 66, -80, ConAmC A*
Rusch, Jerome Anthony 1943- *AmSCAP 80*
Rusconi, Gerardo 1922-1974 *Baker 78*
Ruse, Robert Louis 1919- *AmSCAP 80*
Rush *ConMuA 80A*
Rush, Alvin *NewYTET*
Rush, Barbara 1927- *FilmEn, FilmgC, ForYSC[port], HalFC 80, IntMPA 77, -75, -76, -78, -79, -80, MotPP, MovMk, WhoHol A, WhoHrs 80[port], WorEFlm*
Rush, Dick *Film 2*
Rush, George *NewGrD 80*
Rush, Herman *IntMPA 75, -76, NewYTET*
Rush, Jerry *AmSCAP 80*
Rush, Lawrence R 1938- *AmSCAP 80*
Rush, Loren 1935- *Baker 78, ConAmC*
Rush, Mary Jo 1909- *AmSCAP 66, -80*
Rush, Merilee & The Turnabouts *RkOn 2[port]*
Rush, Otis 1934- *BluesWW[port]*
Rush, Richard *FilmgC, HalFC 80, IntMPA 77, -75, -76, -78, -79, -80*
Rush, Richard 1930?- *FilmEn*
Rush, Tom 1941- *BiDAmM, ConMuA 80A, EncFCWM 69, IlEncR[port]*
Rushby-Smith, John 1936- *IntWWM 80*
Rushen, Patrice Louise 1954- *BlkWAB[port], EncJzS 70*
Rushing, James Andrew 1902-1972 *AmSCAP 66, -80, BiDAmM, BluesWW[port]*
Rushing, James Andrew 1903-1972 *EncJzS 70, NewGrD 80*
Rushing, Jimmy 1903-1972 *CmpEPM, EncJzS 70, IlEncJ, NewGrD 80, WhScrn 77, WhoJazz 72*
Rushnell, Squire D *NewYTET*
Rushton, Joe 1907-1964 *CmpEPM, WhoJazz 72*
Rushton, Julian Gordon 1941- *IntWWM 77, -80*
Rushton, Lucy 1844- *OxThe*
Rushton, Russell *Film 2*
Rushworth, William James Lyon 1913- *IntWWM 77, -80, WhoMus 72*
Rusincky, Paul 1903-1979 *AmSCAP 66, -80*
Rusinol, Santiago 1861-1931 *ModWD*
Rusinyol, Santiago 1861-1931 *NotNAT B*
Ruskaja, Jia 1902-1970 *CnOxB*
Ruskin, Coby *NewYTET*
Ruskin, Daniel Francis 1935- *IntWWM 77*
Ruskin, Harry 1894- *AmSCAP 66, -80*
Ruskin, John 1819-1900 *DcPup*
Ruskin, Shimen *Film 2, WhoHol A*
Ruskin, Sybil d1940 *NotNAT B*
Rusoff, Lou *WhoHrs 80*
Ruspoli, Francesco Maria 1672-1731 *NewGrD 80*
Ruspoli, Mario 1925- *DcFM, OxFilm*
Russ, Henry 1903- *NewOrJ*
Russ, Paula 1893-1966 *WhScrn 74, -77*
Russel, Del 1952- *WhoHol A*
Russel, Tony *WhoHol A*
Russell d1745? *NewGrD 80*
Russell, Agnes d1947 *NotNAT B*
Russell, Alexander 1880-1953 *AmSCAP 66, -80, ConAmC*
Russell, Alice B *BlksB&W C*
Russell, Andy *CmpEPM, ForYSC, WhoHol A*
Russell, Ann d1955 *WhScrn 74, -77*
Russell, Anna 1911- *AmSCAP 66, -80, BiE&WWA, JoeFr, NotNAT, OxThe, WhoHol A*
Russell, Annie 1864-1936 *FamA&A, NotNAT B, OxThe, PlP&P[port], WhThe, WhoStg 1906, -1908*
Russell, Armand King 1932- *AmSCAP 80, ConAmC, IntWWM 77, -80*
Russell, Benee 1902-1961 *AmSCAP 66, -80*
Russell, Billy d1956 *WhScrn 74, -77*
Russell, Bing *WhoHol A*
Russell, Bob 1914-1970 *AmSCAP 66, -80, CmpEPM, Sw&Ld C*
Russell, Bobby 1941- *AmSCAP 80*
Russell, Bud *NewOrJ*
Russell, Byron 1884-1963 *Film 2, NotNAT B, WhScrn 74, -77, WhoHol B*
Russell, Charles Ellsworth 1906-1969 *AmSCAP 66, -80, BiDAmM, NewGrD 80*
Russell, Charles Elsworth 1906-1969 *EncJzS 70*
Russell, Charles W 1918- *IntMPA 77, -75, -76, -78, -79, -80*
Russell, Charlie 1932- *BlkAmP, DrBlPA, MorBAP*
Russell, Connie *WhoHol A*
Russell, Craig H 1951- *ConAmC*
Russell, Curly 1920- *CmpEPM*
Russell, Dorothy 1881- *WhoStg 1908*
Russell, Edd X 1878-1966 *WhScrn 74, -77*
Russell, Sir Edward Richard 1834-1920 *WhThe*
Russell, Eleanor 1931- *IntWWM 77, -80*
Russell, Elizabeth *WhoHol A*
Russell, Ella 1864-1935 *BiDAmM*
Russell, Ernest *PupTheA*
Russell, Evangeline *Film 2*
Russell, Evelyn d1976 *WhoHol C*
Russell, Francia 1938- *CnOxB, DancEn 78*
Russell, Francis 1895- *WhoMus 72*
Russell, Fred 1862-1957 *OxThe, WhThe*
Russell, Gail 1924-1961 *FilmEn, FilmgC, ForYSC, HalFC 80, HolP 40[port], MotPP, MovMk, NotNAT B, WhScrn 74, -77, WhoHol B*
Russell, Gene 1932- *EncJzS 70*
Russell, George 1923- *ConAmC, IlEncJ, NewGrD 80*
Russell, George Alexander 1880-1953 *Baker 78*
Russell, George Allan 1923- *BlkCS[port], EncJzS 70*
Russell, George Allen 1923- *IntWWM 77, -80*
Russell, George H 1919- *AmSCAP 80*
Russell, George Horne 1861-1933 *CreCan 2*
Russell, George William 1867-1935 *McGEWD, ModWD, PlP&P*
Russell, Gibson Howard 1939- *IntWWM 77*
Russell, H Scott 1868-1949 *NotNAT B, WhThe*
Russell, Hanon W 1947- *AmSCAP 66, -80*
Russell, Harold *WhoStg 1908*
Russell, Harold 1914- *FilmEn, FilmgC, HalFC 80, What 2[port], WhoHol A*
Russell, Helen Eugenia 1956- *AmSCAP 80*
Russell, Henry 1812-1900 *AmPS, Baker 78, BiDAmM, NewGrD 80, NotNAT B, OxMus, PopAmC[port], Sw&Ld A*
Russell, Henry 1871-1937 *Baker 78, NewEOp 71*
Russell, Henry 1913-1968 *AmSCAP 66, -80, NotNAT B*
Russell, Howard d1914 *NotNAT B*
Russell, Irene 1901- *Film 2, WhThe*
Russell, Iris 1922- *WhoThe 72, -77*
Russell, J Gordon 1883-1935 *Film 2, WhScrn 74, -77, WhoHol B*
Russell, Jack 1919- *IntMPA 77, -75, -76, -78, -79, -80*
Russell, Jackie *WhoHol A*
Russell, James *Film 2*
Russell, James Reagan 1935- *IntWWM 80*
Russell, Jane 1921- *BiDFilm, -81, CmMov, CmpEPM, FilmEn, FilmgC, ForYSC, HalFC 80[port], IntMPA 77, -75, -76, -78, -79, -80, MotPP, MovMk[port], OxFilm, WhoHol A, WorEFlm[port]*
Russell, Jean d1922 *WhScrn 74, -77*
Russell, Joey 1920- *AmSCAP 66*
Russell, John 1921- *ConAmC, FilmEn, FilmgC, ForYSC, HalFC 80, IntMPA 77, -75, -76, -78, -79, -80, MotPP, MovMk[port], WhoHol A*
Russell, John Hugh 1914- *WhoMus 72*
Russell, John L *WorEFlm[port]*
Russell, John Lowell 1875-1937 *WhScrn 77*
Russell, John Wentworth 1879-1959 *CreCan 1*
Russell, Johnny *CounME 74, -74A*
Russell, Johnny 1909- *WhoJazz 72*
Russell, Joseph E 1920- *AmSCAP 80*
Russell, Julia Theresa *BlksB&W C*
Russell, Kathlyn Wilson 1927- *ConAmTC*
Russell, Ken 1921- *ConLC 16*
Russell, Ken 1927- *BiDFilm, -81, FilmEn, FilmgC, HalFC 80, IlEncR, IlWWBF[port], -A, IntMPA 77, -75, -76, -78, -79, -80, OxFilm, WhoHrs 80, WorEFlm*
Russell, Kurt 1942- *ForYSC*
Russell, Kurt 1947- *FilmgC, HalFC 80, WhoHrs 80*
Russell, Kurt 1951- *WhoHol A*
Russell, Lee 1920- *AmSCAP 66, -80*
Russell, Leon 1941- *ConMuA 80A, IlEncR, RkOn 2[port]*
Russell, Leslie 1901- *WhoMus 72*
Russell, Lewis 1885-1961 *NotNAT B, WhScrn 74, -77, WhoHol B*
Russell, Lilian d1922 *FilmgC*
Russell, Lilian 1861-1922 *Film 1*
Russell, Lillian *AmPS B*
Russell, Lillian d1922 *WhoHol B*
Russell, Lillian 1860-1922 *WhScrn 74, -77*
Russell, Lillian 1861-1922 *BiDAmM, CmpEPM, EncMT, FamA&A[port], HalFC 80, NotNAT A, -B, OxThe, PlP&P, WhThe, WhoStg 1906, -1908*
Russell, Lois Roberta Langley 1932- *IntWWM 77, -80*
Russell, Louis Arthur 1854-1925 *Baker 78, BiDAmM*
Russell, Luis 1902-1962? *NewOrJ*

Russell, Luis 1902-1963 *AmSCAP 80, BiDAmM, CmpEPM, IlEncJ, NewGrD 80, WhoJazz 72*
Russell, Mabel d1908 *NotNAT B*
Russell, Mabel 1887-1951 *NotNAT B, WhThe*
Russell, Marie Booth d1911 *NotNAT B*
Russell, Martha *Film 1*
Russell, Nipsey 1920- *JoeFr*
Russell, Nipsey 1924?- *DrBlPA*
Russell, Pat *WomWMM B*
Russell, Paul 1947- *CnOxB*
Russell, Pee Wee 1906-1969 *CmpEPM, EncJzS 70, IlEncJ, NewGrD 80, WhoHol B, WhoJazz 72*
Russell, Philip 1928- *WhoMus 72*
Russell, Ray *Film 1*
Russell, Ray 1924- *WhoHrs 80*
Russell, Raymond Anthony 1922-1964 *NewGrD 80*
Russell, Reb 1905- *WhoHol A*
Russell, Robert *ConAmC, Film 2, IntMPA 77, -75, -76, -78, -79, -80*
Russell, Robert Wallace 1912- *BiE&WWA, NatPD[port]*
Russell, Rosalind *IntMPA 77, -75, -76, MotPP, WhoHol A, WomWMM*
Russell, Rosalind 1907-1976 *MovMk[port], ThFT[port]*
Russell, Rosalind 1908-1976 *FilmEn, FilmgC, HalFC 80, MGM[port]*
Russell, Rosalind 1911-1976 *WorEFlm*
Russell, Rosalind 1912-1976 *BiDFilm, -81, BiE&WWA, EncMT, ForYSC[port], NotNAT, OxFilm, WhoThe 72, -77*
Russell, Samuel Thomas d1845 *NotNAT B*
Russell, Sheridan 1900- *WhoMus 72*
Russell, Sol Smith 1848-1902 *FamA&A[port], NotNAT B, OxThe*
Russell, Sydney King 1897- *AmSCAP 66*
Russell, Sylvester d1930 *BlksBF[port]*
Russell, T J *PupTheA*
Russell, Theresa *WhoHol A*
Russell, Violet *IntWWM 77, WhoMus 72*
Russell, William *MotPP, OxMus, WhoHol A*
Russell, William d1915? *WhScrn 77*
Russell, William 1777-1813 *NewGrD 80*
Russell, William 1798-1873 *BiDAmM*
Russell, William 1884-1929 *FilmEn, Film 1, -2, NotNAT B, TwYS, WhoHol B*
Russell, William 1886-1929 *WhScrn 74, -77*
Russell, William 1905- *ConAmC, NewOrJ SUP[port]*
Russell, William Clark d1911 *NotNAT B*
Russell, William D 1908-1968 *FilmEn, FilmgC, HalFC 80*
Russell, William Eugene 1932- *EncJzS 70*
Russell-Dadds, Richard 1906- *WhoMus 72*
Russell Of Liverpool, Lord 1834-1920 *NotNAT B*
Russell-Smith, Geoffry Edwin 1927- *WhoMus 72*
Russillo, Joseph 1941- *CnOxB*
Russin, Babe 1911- *CmpEPM, WhoJazz 72*
Russin, Irving 1911- *AmSCAP 66, -80*
Russo, Bill 1928- *CmpEPM*
Russo, Dan 1885-1956 *AmSCAP 66, -80*
Russo, Frank *ConMuA 80B*
Russo, John Peter 1943- *CpmDNM 80, ConAmC*
Russo, Lillian *WomWMM B*
Russo, Matt *WhoHol A*
Russo, Salvatore 1940- *WhoOp 76*
Russo, William 1928- *AmSCAP 66, -80, Baker 78, CpmDNM 75, ConAmC, DcCM*
Russolo, Luigi 1885-1947 *Baker 78, DcCM, NewGrD 80, OxMus*
Russotto, Leo 1896- *AmSCAP 66, ConAmC*
Rust *NewGrD 80*
Rust, Frank 1907- *WhoMus 72*
Rust, Friedrich Wilhelm 1739-1796 *Baker 78, NewGrD 80, OxMus*
Rust, Giacomo 1741-1786 *NewGrD 80*
Rust, Gordon A 1908- *BiE&WWA*
Rust, John Frederick 1921- *WhoMus 72*
Rust, Mildred *PupTheA*
Rust, Richard *WhoHol A*
Rust, Wilhelm 1822-1892 *Baker 78, NewGrD 80, OxMus*
Rust, Wilhelm Karl 1787-1855 *NewGrD 80, OxMus*
Rusti, Giacomo 1741-1786 *NewGrD 80*
Rustichelli, Carlo 1916- *HalFC 80*
Rustman, Sven Rune Werner 1925- *IntWWM 77*
Rusu, Liviu 1908- *IntWWM 80*
Rut, Josef 1926- *IntWWM 77, -80*
Rutan, Harold Duane 1927- *IntWWM 80*
Rutebeuf 1230?-1285? *OxThe*
Rutebeuf 1248?-1285? *McGEWD*
Rutge, Daniel *NewGrD 80*
Rutgers, Franciscus Marinus 1948- *IntWWM 77, -80*
Ruth, Babe 1895-1948 *Film 2, WhScrn 74, -77, WhoHol B*
Ruth, Barbara F *AmSCAP 66*
Ruth, Dan *ConAmTC*
Ruth, James Richard 1940- *ConAmTC*
Ruth, Jim 1880?-1957 *NewOrJ[port]*
Ruth, Marshall 1898-1953 *Film 2, WhScrn 74, -77, WhoHol B*
Ruth, Patsy *Film 2*
Ruthardt, Adolf 1849-1934 *Baker 78*
Ruthenberg, Jane Catherine *AmSCAP 80*
Ruthenburg, Grace Dorcas *PupTheA*
Ruthenfranz, Robert 1905-1970 *NewGrD 80*
Rutherford, Ann *MotPP*
Rutherford, Ann 1917- *FilmEn, HalFC 80, MGM[port], MovMk[port], ThFT[port]*
Rutherford, Ann 1920- *FilmgC, ForYSC, What 4[port], WhoHol A*
Rutherford, Ann 1924- *IntMPA 77, -75, -76, -78, -79, -80*
Rutherford, David *OxMus*
Rutherford, Elman 1912- *EncJzS 70*
Rutherford, John *OxMus*
Rutherford, Margaret 1892-1972 *BiE&WWA, CnThe, EncWT, Ent[port], FilmAG WE[port], FilmEn, FilmgC, ForYSC, HalFC 80, IlWWBF[port], -A, MotPP, MovMk[port], NotNAT A, -B, OxFilm, OxThe, WhScrn 77, WhThe, WhoHol B, WhoThe 72*
Rutherford, Mary 1945- *WhoThe 77*
Rutherford, Michael F 1926- *IntWWM 77*
Rutherford, Paris N, III 1934- *AmSCAP 80*
Rutherford, Paul William 1940- *IntWWM 77*
Rutherford, Richard *CnOxB, CreCan 2, DancEn 78*
Rutherford, Rudy 1912- *EncJzS 70, WhoJazz 72*
Rutherford, Tom d1973 *WhScrn 77*
Rutherfurd, Tom d1973 *WhoHol B*
Rutherston, Albert Daniel 1883-1953 *NotNAT B, WhThe*
Ruthstrom, Julius 1877-1944 *Baker 78, NewGrD 80*
Rutini, Ferdinando 1764?-1827 *NewGrD 80*
Rutini, Giovanni Marco 1723-1797 *NewGrD 80*
Rutini, Giovanni Maria 1723-1797 *NewGrD 80*
Rutini, Giovanni Placido 1723-1797 *NewGrD 80*
Rutkowski, Antoni Wincenty 1859-1886 *NewGrD 80*
Rutkowski, Bronislaw 1898-1964 *NewGrD 80*
Rutland, Harold 1900- *IntWWM 77, -80, WhoMus 72*
Rutledge, George E 1928- *IntWWM 77, -80*
Rutman, Leo 1938- *NatPD[port]*
Rutten, Gary Donald 1942- *AmSCAP 80*
Rutten, Gerard *DcFM*
Ruttenberg, Joseph 1889- *FilmEn, FilmgC, HalFC 80*
Ruttenberg, Joseph 1898- *WorEFlm*
Rutters, Matthias 1929- *IntWWM 77, -80*
Ruttis, Ar De *NewGrD 80*
Ruttman, Walter 1887-1941 *FilmgC, HalFC 80*
Ruttmann, Walter 1887-1941 *BiDFilm, -81, FilmEn, OxFilm, WorEFlm*
Ruttmann, Walther 1887-1941 *DcFM*
Rutz, Ottmar 1881-1952 *Baker 78*
Ruud, Bos 1936- *IntWWM 77*
Ruud, Tomm 1943- *CnOxB*
Ruuli, Rinaldo *NewGrD 80*
Ruuth, Gustaf 1920- *IntWWM 77, -80*
Ruutha, Didrik Persson *NewGrD 80*
Ruvinskis, Wolf *WhoHrs 80*
Ruvo, Giulio *NewGrD 80*
Ruwet, Nicolas 1932- *NewGrD 80*
Ruygrok, Leo 1889-1944 *Baker 78*
Ruymonte, Pedro *NewGrD 80*
Ruyneman, Daniel 1886-1963 *Baker 78, DcCM, NewGrD 80, OxMus*
Ruysdael, Basil d1959 *Film 2, ForYSC*
Ruysdael, Basil 1888-1960 *FilmgC, HalFC 80, WhScrn 74, -77, WhoHol B*
Ruzante 1502?-1543 *EncWT, NewGrD 80*
Ruzdjak, Vladimir 1922- *IntWWM 77, -80, WhoOp 76*
Ruzicka, Peter 1948- *Baker 78, NewGrD 80*
Ruzicka, Rudolf 1941- *Baker 78*
Ruzickova, Zuzana 1928- *NewGrD 80, WhoMus 72*
Ruziski, Jacek *NewGrD 80*
Ruzitska, Gyorgy 1789-1869 *NewGrD 80*
Ruzitska, Ignac 1777-1833 *NewGrD 80*
Ruzitska, Jozsef 1775?-1823? *NewGrD 80*
Ruzsch, Conrad *NewGrD 80*
Ruzsicska, Wencelas *OxMus*
Ruzzante 1502-1542 *Ent, OxThe*
Ruzzante, Il 1502-1542 *McGEWD[port], REnWD[port]*
Rwtha, Didrik Persson *NewGrD 80*
Ryall, Joan 1934- *WhoMus 72*
Ryan, Father Abram J 1838-1886 *BiDAmM*
Ryan, Annie 1865-1943 *Film 2, WhScrn 74, -77, WhoHol B*
Ryan, Anthony Wayne 1951- *IntWWM 80*
Ryan, Arthur N *IntMPA 77, -76, -78, -79, -80*
Ryan, Arthur Q 1872-1955 *ForYSC*
Ryan, Ben 1892-1968 *AmSCAP 66, -80*
Ryan, Bill *PupTheA*
Ryan, Charles V 1913- *BiE&WWA*
Ryan, Charlie *RkOn[port]*
Ryan, Colin A 1953- *IntWWM 80*
Ryan, Conny d1963 *NotNAT B*
Ryan, Dick 1897-1969 *WhScrn 74, -77, WhoHol B*
Ryan, Don *Film 2*
Ryan, Eddie *MotPP*
Ryan, Edmon *WhoHol A*
Ryan, Fran *WhoHol A*
Ryan, Frank 1907-1947 *FilmEn, FilmgC, HalFC 80*
Ryan, Irene d1973 *WhoHol B*
Ryan, Irene 1902-1973 *MovMk[port]*
Ryan, Irene 1903-1973 *FilmEn, FilmgC, ForYSC, HalFC 80, WhScrn 77*
Ryan, J Harold d1961 *NewYTET*
Ryan, James Edmund 1946- *AmSCAP 80*
Ryan, Joan Mary 1940- *AmSCAP 80*
Ryan, Joe 1887-1944 *Film 1, -2, WhScrn 77*
Ryan, John 1939?- *HalFC 80, WhoHol A*
Ryan, Kate d1922 *NotNAT B*
Ryan, Kathleen 1922- *FilmEn, FilmgC, HalFC 80, IlWWBF, WhoHol A*
Ryan, Lacy 1694-1760 *NotNAT B, OxThe*
Ryan, Lillian *PupTheA*
Ryan, Madge 1919- *WhoHol A, WhoThe 72, -77*
Ryan, Marthinus Johannes 1951- *IntWWM 80*
Ryan, Mary 1885-1948 *NotNAT B, WhThe, WhoHol B*
Ryan, Maurice *Film 2*
Ryan, Michael M *WhoHol A*
Ryan, Mildred *Film 2*
Ryan, Mitchell 1928- *HalFC 80, IntMPA 77, -75, -76, -78, -79, -80, WhoHol A*
Ryan, Nancy *Film 2*
Ryan, Peggy 1924- *FilmEn, FilmgC, ForYSC, HalFC 80, HolP 40[port], IntMPA 77, -75, -76, -78, -79, -80, MotPP, WhoHol A*
Ryan, Robert d1973 *MotPP, PlP&P A[port], WhoHol B*
Ryan, Robert 1909-1973 *FilmEn, FilmgC, HalFC 80, MovMk[port], NotNAT B, WhScrn 77*
Ryan, Robert 1910-1973 *Film 2*
Ryan, Robert 1913-1973 *BiDFilm, -81, BiE&WWA, CmMov, ForYSC[port], OxFilm, WhThe, WhoThe 72, WorEFlm[port]*
Ryan, Robert Francis 1930- *AmSCAP 80*
Ryan, Sam *Film 1, -2*
Ryan, Sheila 1921-1975 *FilmEn, FilmgC, ForYSC, HalFC 80, IntMPA 77, -75, -76, -78, -79, -80, WhScrn 77, WhoHol C*
Ryan, T E d1920 *NotNAT B*
Ryan, Thomas 1827-1903 *Baker 78, BiDAmM*
Ryan, Thomas H *IntMPA 75, -76*

Ryan, Tim d1956 *FilmEn, ForYSC*
Ryan, Tim 1889-1956 *FilmgC, HalFC 80*
Ryan, Tim 1899-1956 *Vers B[port], WhScrn 74, -77, WhoHol B*
Ryan, Tommy *CmpEPM*
Ryba, Jakub Jan 1765-1815 *NewGrD 80*
Ryba, Jan Jakub 1765-1815 *Baker 78*
Rybach, Ladislaus 1935- *IntWWM 77, -80*
Rybar, Peter 1913- *IntWWM 77, -80*
Rybaric, Richard 1930- *NewGrD 80*
Rybaville, Jakub Jan *NewGrD 80*
Ryberg, Flemming 1940- *CnOxB*
Rybicki, Feliks 1899- *IntWWM 77, -80*
Rybkowski, Jan 1912- *DcFM, FilmEn*
Rybner, Cornelius 1855-1929 *Baker 78*
Rybner, Peter Martin Cornelius 1855-1929 *BiDAmM*
Rybnicky, Jakub Krystof 1600?-1639 *NewGrD 80*
Rycardt *NewGrD 80*
Ryce, Joel 1933- *IntWWM 77, -80, WhoMus 72*
Rycefort, Jean *NewGrD 80*
Rychlik, Jan 1916-1964 *Baker 78, NewGrD 80*
Rychlik, Josef Henryk 1946- *IntWWM 77, -80*
Rychlik, Jozef 1946- *Baker 78*
Rychnovsky, Ernst 1879-1934 *Baker 78*
Rychtarik, Richard Waslav 1894- *WhoOp 76*
Rycke, Antonius *NewGrD 80*
Ryckman, Chester 1897-1918 *WhScrn 77*
Rycroft, Marjorie Elizabeth 1946- *IntWWM 80*
Ryde, Doris *CreCan 1*
Rydel, Lucjan 1870-1918 *CnMD, ModWD*
Rydell, Bobby 1942- *AmPS A, -B, BiDAmM, FilmgC, HalFC 80, RkOn[port], WhoHol A*
Rydell, Mark 1934- *FilmEn, FilmgC, HalFC 80, IntMPA 77, -75, -76, -78, -79, -80, WhoHol A*
Ryden, Hope *WomWMM A, -B*
Ryder, Alfred 1919- *BiE&WWA, MotPP, NotNAT, WhoHol A, WhoThe 72, -77*
Ryder, Arthur Hilton 1875-1944 *Baker 78, ConAmC*
Ryder, Arthur W d1938 *NotNAT B*
Ryder, Georgia Atkins 1924- *IntWWM 77, -80*
Ryder, Kenneth Stanley 1940- *IntWWM 77, -80*
Ryder, Loren L 1900- *IntMPA 77, -75, -76, -78, -79, -80*
Ryder, Mary E 1924- *AmSCAP 80*
Ryder, Mitch *ConMuA 80A*
Ryder, Mitch & The Detroit Wheels *RkOn 2[port]*
Ryder, Noah F 1914-1964 *AmSCAP 66, -80, BiDAmM, ConAmC*
Ryder, Thomas Philander 1836-1887 *Baker 78, BiDAmM*
Rydge, Sir Norman 1900- *IntMPA 77, -75, -76, -78, -79, -80*
Rydge, Norman Bede, Jr. 1928- *IntMPA 77, -75, -76, -78, -79, -80*
Rydholm, Ralph Williams 1937- *AmSCAP 80*
Rydl, Kurt 1947- *WhoOp 76*
Rydman, Kari 1936- *Baker 78, DcCM, NewGrD 80*
Rydzeski, Burnhart John 1937- *IntWWM 77, -80*
Rye, Daphne 1916- *WhThe*
Rye, Sven 1926- *AmSCAP 66, -80*
Ryelandt, Joseph 1870-1965 *Baker 78*
Ryer, Pierre Du 1600?-1658 *OxThe*
Ryerson, Adna Mary 1907- *IntWWM 77, -80*
Ryerson, Florence 1892-1965 *BiE&WWA, NotNAT B*
Ryerson, Frank Layton 1905- *AmSCAP 66, -80*
Ryga, George 1932- *ConDr 73, -77*
Rygert, Torsten 1904- *IntWWM 77, -80*
Ryland, Cliff 1856- *WhThe*
Rylander, Alexander S 1941- *IntMPA 77, -75, -76, -78, -79, -80*
Rylands, George 1902- *WhoThe 72, -77*
Ryley, J H d1922 *NotNAT B*
Ryley, Madeleine Lucette 1865-1934 *NotNAT B, WhThe*
Ryley, Madeline Lucette *WhoStg 1906, -1908*
Ryley, Samuel William 1759-1837 *NotNAT A, -B*
Ryling, Franciszek 1902- *IntWWM 77*
Ryman, Bryan 1933- *AmSCAP 80*
Ryman, Tyra *Film 2*
Rynearson, Paul Franklin 1945- *AmSCAP 80, ConAmC, IntWWM 77*
Rypdal, Terje 1947- *EncJzS 70, NewGrD 80*
Rysanek, Leonie *WhoMus 72*
Rysanek, Leonie 1926- *Baker 78, CmOp, NewEOp 71, NewGrD 80*
Rysanek, Leonie 1928- *IntWWM 77, -80, MusSN[port], WhoOp 76*
Rysanek, Lotte 1929- *WhoOp 76*
Ryse, Philipp *NewGrD 80*
Ryskind, Morrie 1895- *BiE&WWA, ConDr 73, -77D, EncMT, FilmEn, FilmgC, HalFC 80, IntMPA 77, -75, -76, -78, -79, -80, ModWD, NewCBMT, NotNAT, WhThe*
Ryskind, Morris *PIP&P*
Rytel, Piotr 1884-1970 *Baker 78, NewGrD 80*
Ryterband, Roman 1914- *AmSCAP 66, Baker 78, ConAmC A*
Rywacka-Morozewicz, Ludwika 1817-1858 *NewGrD 80*
Ryweck, Charles *ConAmTC*
Rzepko, Adolf 1825-1892 *NewGrD 80*
Rzepko, Wladyslaw 1854-1932 *NewGrD 80*
Rzewski, Frederic 1938- *Baker 78, ConAmC, DcCM, IntWWM 80, NewGrD 80*

S

S Uciredor *NewGrD 80*
Sa DeMiranda, Francisco De 1485-1558 *OxThe, REnWD[port]*
Sa E Costa, Helena *NewGrD 80*
Sa E Costa, Leonilde Moreira *NewGrD 80*
Sa E Costa, Madalena *NewGrD 80*
Saad, Margit *WhoHol A*
Sa'adya Gaon *NewGrD 80*
Saal, Alfred, Jr. *PupTheA*
Saal, Alfred P *PupTheA*
Saar, Louis Victor 1868-1937 *AmSCAP 66, -80, Baker 78, BiDAmM, NewGrD 80*
Saar, Mart 1882-1963 *NewGrD 80*
Saare, Arla *WomWMM*
Saari, Charles 1944- *BiE&WWA, NotNAT*
Saari, Jouko Erik Sakari 1944- *IntWWM 77, -80*
Saarinen, Eero *PlP&P*
Saarinen, Gloria Edith 1934- *WhoMus 72*
Saastamoinen, Iipo Erkki Aslak 1942- *IntWWM 80*
Saastamoinen, Ilpo Erkki Asiak 1942- *IntWWM 77*
Saavedra, Angel De, Duque DeRivas 1791-1865 *McGEWD[port], NotNAT B, OxThe*
SaBacon, Jose Pereira De *NewGrD 80*
Sabadini, Bernardo d1718 *NewGrD 80*
Sabaneef, Leonid Leonidovich 1881-1968 *OxMus*
Sabaneyev, Leonid Leonidovich 1881-1968 *Baker 78, NewGrD 80*
Sabat, Antoni 1935- *IntWWM 77, -80*
Sabata, Victor De 1892-1967 *Baker 78, MusSN[port], NewEOp 71, NewGrD 80, OxMus*
Sabath, Bernard *NatPD[port]*
Sabatini, Bernardo *NewGrD 80*
Sabatini, Ernesto 1878-1954 *WhScrn 74, -77*
Sabatini, Nicola 1708?-1796 *NewGrD 80*
Sabatini, Rafael 1875-1950 *FilmgC, HalFC 80, NotNAT B, WhThe*
Sabatini, Renzo 1905- *WhoMus 72*
Sabatino, Nicola 1708?-1796 *NewGrD 80*
Sabato, Alfredo *Film 2*
Sabato, Antonio *WhoHol A*
Sabbatini, Galeazzo 1595?-1662 *Baker 78*
Sabbatini, Galeazzo 1597-1662 *NewGrD 80*
Sabbatini, Luigi Antonio 1732-1809 *Baker 78, NewGrD 80*
Sabbatini, Niccolo 1574-1654 *EncWT*
Sabbatini, Pietro Paolo 1600?-1657? *NewGrD 80*
Sabbatino, Nicola *NewGrD 80*
Sabbattini, Nicola 1574-1654 *NotNAT B, OxThe*
Sabbe, Herman L 1937- *IntWWM 77, -80*
Sabel, Josephine 1866-1945 *AmPS B, NotNAT B, WhScrn 74, -77, WhoStg 1906, -1908*
Sabilon, Robert De *OxMus*
Sabin, Catherine Jerome 1879-1943 *WhScrn 74, -77, WhoHol B*
Sabin, Robert 1912-1969 *Baker 78*
Sabin, Wallace Arthur 1860-1937 *Baker 78*
Sabine, Martin 1876- *WhThe*
Sabine, P E *OxMus*
Sabine, Wallace C 1868-1919 *NewGrD 80*
Sabini, Frank *Film 2*
Sabini, Ippolito *NewGrD 80*
Sabini, Nicola 1675?-1705 *NewGrD 80*
Sabinina, Marina Dmitriyevna 1917- *NewGrD 80*
Sabino *NewGrD 80*
Sabino, Antonino d1650 *NewGrD 80*
Sabino, Antonio d1650 *NewGrD 80*
Sabino, Francesco *NewGrD 80*
Sabino, Giovanni Francesco *NewGrD 80*
Sabino, Giovanni Maria d1649 *NewGrD 80*
Sabino, Ippolito 1550?-1593 *NewGrD 80*
Sabino, Nicola *NewGrD 80*
Sabinson, Harvey B 1924- *BiE&WWA, NotNAT*
Sabinson, Lee 1911- *BiE&WWA, NotNAT, WhThe*
Sabirova, Malika 1942- *CnOxB*
Sable, Antoine DeLa *NewGrD 80*
Sable, Barbara Kinsey 1927- *IntWWM 77, -80*
Sablieres, Grenouillet 1627-1700? *NewGrD 80*
Sablieres, Jean Granouilhet 1627-1700? *NewGrD 80*
Sabline, Oleg 1925- *CnOxB, DancEn 78*
Sabljic, Mladen 1921- *WhoOp 76*
Sablon, Jean 1909- *BiE&WWA*
Sabogal, Ernesto *WomWMM*
Saboly, Nicolas 1614-1675 *NewGrD 80*
Sabor, Rudolph 1919- *WhoMus 72*
Sabouret, Marie d1960 *WhScrn 74, -77, WhoHol B*
Sabourin, Marcel 1935- *CreCan 1*
Sabra, Wadi' 1876-1952 *NewGrD 80*
Sabrina *WhoHol A*
Sabu 1924-1963 *CmMov, FilmEn, FilmgC, HalFC 80, HolP 40[port], IlWWBF[port], MotPP, MovMk, NotNAT B, WhScrn 74, -77, WhoHol B, WhoHrs 80[port], WorEFlm*
Sabu 1925-1963 *OxFilm*
Sabu 1927-1963 *ForYSC*
Sacadas Of Argos *NewGrD 80*
Saccaggio, Adelina Luisa N 1918- *IntWWM 77, -80*
Saccente, Roberto 1928- *IntWWM 77, -80*
Sacchetti, Carl Salvatore 1915- *AmSCAP 80*
Sacchetti, Franco 1332?-1400 *NewGrD 80*
Sacchetti, Liberio Antonovich 1852-1916 *NewGrD 80*
Sacchetti, Liberius 1852-1916 *Baker 78*
Sacchi, Giovenale 1726-1789 *Baker 78, NewGrD 80*
Sacchi, Leo Joseph 1934- *IntWWM 77, -80*
Sacchini, Antonio 1730-1786 *Baker 78, MusMk, NewEOp 71, NewGrD 80[port], OxMus*
Sacco, Anthony 1908- *AmSCAP 66, -80*
Sacco, John Charles 1905- *AmSCAP 66, -80, ConAmC*
Sacco, P Peter 1928- *AmSCAP 80, Baker 78, ConAmC*
Sacco, Tony 1908- *CmpEPM*
Saccomani, Lorenzo 1938- *WhoOp 76*
Sacconi, Fernando 1895-1973 *NewGrD 80*
Sacerdote, David *NewGrD 80*
Sacerdote, Delia 1920- *IntWWM 77*
Sacerdoti, Davit De *NewGrD 80*
Sacharoff, Alexander *CnOxB*
Sacharow, Lawrence 1937- *NotNAT*
Sacher, Paul 1906- *Baker 78, IntWWM 77, -80, NewGrD 80[port], WhoMus 72*
Sachs, Aaron 1923- *CmpEPM*
Sachs, Curt 1881-1959 *Baker 78, CnOxB, DancEn 78, NewGrD 80*
Sachs, David *WhoHol A*
Sachs, Hans 1494-1576 *Baker 78, CnThe, DcPup, EncWT, Ent, McGEWD[port], NewEOp 71, NewGrD 80[port], NotNAT B, OxMus, OxThe, REnWD[port]*
Sachs, Henry Everett 1881- *AmSCAP 66*
Sachs, Klaus-Jurgen 1929- *IntWWM 80, NewGrD 80*
Sachs, Kurt 1881-1959 *OxMus*
Sachs, Leo 1856-1930 *Baker 78*
Sachs, Leonard 1909- *WhoHol A, WhoThe 72, -77*
Sachs, Sharon J *WomWMM B*
Sachse, Leopold 1880-1961 *Baker 78, NewEOp 71*
Sachse, Peter 1940-1966 *WhScrn 77*
Sachse, Raymond H 1899- *AmSCAP 66*
Sachsenskjold, Henrik 1918- *IntWWM 77, -80*
Sack, Albert E 1911-1947 *AmSCAP 80*
Sack, Erna 1898-1972 *Baker 78*
Sack, Erna 1903-1972 *WhScrn 77, WhoHol A*
Sack, Johann Philipp 1722-1763 *NewGrD 80*
Sack, Michael Louis 1934- *WhoOp 76*
Sack, Nathaniel 1882-1966 *Film 1, WhScrn 74, -77*
Sack, Theodor 1910- *IntWWM 77, -80*
Sackett, Ernest *PupTheA*
Sackheim, Jerry *FilmgC, HalFC 80*
Sackheim, William B 1919- *FilmgC, HalFC 80, IntMPA 77, -75, -76, -78, -79, NewYTET*
Sackler, Howard 1929- *ConDr 73, -77, DcLB 7[port], McGEWD, NotNAT, PlP&P[port]*
Sacks, Joseph Leopold 1881-1952 *NotNAT B, WhThe*
Sacks, Michael *WhoHol A*
Sacks, Robert D 1931- *IntWWM 77*
Sacks, Samuel 1908- *IntMPA 77, -75, -76, -78, -79, -80*
Sacks, Stuart 1941- *Baker 78, ConAmC*
Sackville, Gordon d1926 *Film 1, -2, WhScrn 74, -77, WhoHol B*
Sackville, Thomas 1536-1608 *Ent, McGEWD, OxThe*
Sacramento, Lucino 1908- *NewGrD 80*
Sacrati, Francesco 1600?-1650 *Baker 78*
Sacrati, Francesco 1605?-1650 *NewGrD 80*
Sacro Buscho *NewGrD 80*
Sadai, Yitzhak 1935- *DcCM*

Sadai, Yizhak 1935- Baker 78, NewGrD 80
Sadanji, Ichi Kawa 1881-1940 WhThe
Saddler, Donald 1920- BiE&WWA, CnOxB, DancEn 78, EncMT, NotNAT, WhoThe 77
Sadecky, Zdenek 1925-1971 NewGrD 80
Sadelar, Johan 1550-1610 NewGrD 80
Sadi, Fats 1926- EncJzS 70
Sadi, Lallemand 1926- EncJzS 70
Sadie, Stanley 1930- Baker 78, IntWWM 80, NewGrD 80
Sadie, Stanley John 1930- WhoMus 72
Sadistic Mika Band IlEncR[port]
Sadler, Barry 1941- AmPS A, RkOn 2[port], WhoHol A
Sadler, Charles R 1875-1950 WhScrn 74, -77
Sadler, Dudley, Jr. d1951 WhScrn 74, -77, WhoHol B
Sadler, Haskell Robert 1935- BluesWW[port]
Sadler, Ian 1902-1971 WhScrn 74, -77, WhoHol B
Sadler, Michael ConDr 73, -77B
Sadlo, Milos 1912- NewGrD 80
Sado, Keiji 1926-1964 WhScrn 77
Sadoff, Fred E 1926- BiE&WWA, NotNAT, WhoHol A
Sadoff, Melissa M 1933- AmSCAP 66, -80
Sadoff, Robert 1920- AmSCAP 66, -80
Sadoff, Simon 1919- CnOxB, DancEn 78
Sadoul, Georges 1904-1967 FilmEn, OxFilm
Sadour, Ben Film 2
Sadovsky, Elisaveta Mikhailovna 1870-1934 EncWT
Sadovsky, Mikhail Provich 1847-1910 EncWT
Sadovsky, Olga Osipovna Sadovskaya 1850-1919 EncWT
Sadovsky, Prov Michailovich 1818-1872 NotNAT B
Sadovsky, Prov Mikhailovich 1818-1872 EncWT, OxThe
Sadovsky, Prov Mikhailovich 1874-1947 EncWT
Sadowski, Krzystof Jan 1936- IntWWM 77
Sadowsky, Reah 1918- IntWWM 80
Sadusk, Maureen WhoHol A
Sadze, Christianus NewGrD 80
Sa'Earp, Elenita DancEn 78
Saeden, Erik 1924- NewGrD 80, WhoOp 76
Saenger, Gustav 1865-1935 AmSCAP 66, -80, Baker 78, BiDAmM
Saenger, Oscar 1868-1926 BiDAmM
Saenger, Oscar 1868-1929 Baker 78
Saenz, Pedro 1915- Baker 78, IntWWM 77, -80, NewGrD 80
Saerchinger, Cesar 1884-1971 Baker 78
Saeverud, Harald 1897- Baker 78, CompSN[port], DcCM, IntWWM 77, -80, NewGrD 80
Saeverud, Ketil 1939- Baker 78
Safan, Mark 1951- AmSCAP 80
Safane, Clifford Jay 1947- ConAmC
Safaris, The RkOn
Safer, Morley IntMPA 79, -80, NewYTET
Saffer, Bob 1910- AmSCAP 66, -80
Saffian, Sol ConMuA 80B
Saffir, Kurt 1929- IntWWM 77, -80
Saffle, M W 1923- IntMPA 78, -79, -80
Safford, Edwin Ruthven, III 1924- ConAmTC
Safi Al-Din d1294 NewGrD 80
Safier, Gloria 1921- BiE&WWA
Safir, Sidney 1923- IntMPA 77, -75, -76, -78, -79, -80
Safka, Melanie 1947- AmSCAP 80
Safonof, Vassily 1852-1918 OxMus
Safonov, Vasily Il'ich 1852-1918 NewGrD 80
Safonov, Vassily 1852-1918 Baker 78
Safran, Arno M 1932- ConAmC
Safranek-Kavic, Lujo 1882-1940 Baker 78
Safranski, Eddie 1918-1974 CmpEPM, EncJzS 70
Safranski, Edward 1918-1974 EncJzS 70
Sagaev, Dimiter 1915- Baker 78
Sagal, Boris 1923- FilmEn, FilmgC, HalFC 80, NewYTET
Sagall, Solomon NewYTET
Sagan, Francoise 1935- FilmEn, FilmgC, HalFC 80
Sagan, Gene Hill 1936- CnOxB
Sagan, Leontine d1974 WomWMM
Sagan, Leontine 1889-1974 FilmEn, WhThe, WorEFlm
Sagan, Leontine 1899-1974 HalFC 80, OxFilm
Sagarra Y Castellarnau, Jose Maria De d1961 NotNAT B
Sagau, Jayme De La Te' Y NewGrD 80
Sage, Byron d1974 Film 2, WhoHol B
Sage, Frances 1915-1963 WhScrn 77
Sage, Stuart Film 2
Sage, Willard 1922-1974 WhScrn 77, WhoHol B
Sager, Johann Baptista NewGrD 80
Sager, Peggy DancEn 78
Sager, Sidney 1917- WhoMus 72
Sager, Sue WomWMM B
Sagert, Horst 1934- EncWT
Saggion NewGrD 80
Saggione NewGrD 80
Saggittarus MorBAP
Sagittarius Baker 78
Sagittarius, Henricus NewGrD 80
Saguer, Louis 1907- NewGrD 80
Saguet, Henri 1901- DcFM
Sahai, Pandit Sharda 1935- IntWWM 77, -80
Sahak I 387-439 NewGrD 80
Sahkoor, Salahudin MorBAP
Sahl, Michael 1934- AmSCAP 80, ConAmC
Sahl, Mort 1926- FilmEn, FilmgC, HalFC 80, WhoHol A
Sahl, Mort 1927- Ent, JoeFr[port]
Sahlin, Don PupTheA, PupTheA SUP, WhoHrs 80
Sahm, Doug 1941- ConMuA 80A, IlEncCM[port], IlEncR
Sahni, Balraj 1913-1973 WhScrn 77
Saibe NewGrD 80
Saidenberg, Daniel 1906- IntWWM 77, -80, WhoMus 72
Saidy, Fred 1907- BiE&WWA, ConDr 73, -77D, EncMT, NatPD[port], NewCBMT, NotNAT
Saigal, K L d1947 WhScrn 77
Saikkola, Lauri 1906- Baker 78, NewGrD 80
Sailcat RkOn 2A
Sailer, Leonard 1656-1696? NewGrD 80
Sailer, Sebastian 1714-1777 NewGrD 80
Saillard, M G Film 2
Saillard, Ninette Film 2
Sailor IlEncR
Sainct-Gelays, Mellin De NewGrD 80
Sainer, Arthur 1924- ConAmTC, ConDr 73, -77, NatPD[port]
Sainne NewGrD 80
Sainne, Lambert De 1500?-1564? NewGrD 80
Sainpolis, John 1887-1942 Film 2, WhScrn 77
Sainsbury, John H NewGrD 80
Saint, Eva Marie IntMPA 75, -76, MotPP, WhoHol A
Saint, Eva Marie 1924- FilmEn, FilmgC, ForYSC, HalFC 80, IntMPA 77, -78, -79, -80, MovMk[port], WorEFlm[port]
Saint, Eva Marie 1929- BiDFilm, -81, BiE&WWA
Saint-Amand, Louis Joseph 1749-1820? NewGrD 80
Saint-Amans, Louis Joseph 1749-1820? NewGrD 80
Saint-Amant, Louis Joseph 1749-1820? NewGrD 80
St. Angel, Michael WhoHol A
St. Angelo, Robert Film 2
St. Audrie, Stella d1925 Film 2, NotNAT B, WhoHol B
St. Cecilia OxMus
Saint-Charles, Joseph 1868-1956 CreCan 2
Saint Circ, Uc De NewGrD 80
St. Clair, Cyrus 1890-1955 WhoJazz 72
St. Clair, Elizabeth WhoHol A
St. Clair, Eric Film 2
St. Clair, F V 1860- WhThe
St. Clair, Floyd J 1871-1942 AmSCAP 66, -80, ConAmC A
St. Clair, Lydia d1970 WhoHol B
St. Clair, Lydia d1974 WhScrn 77
St. Clair, Mal 1897-1952 Film 1, TwYS A
St. Clair, Malcolm 1897-1952 BiDFilm, -81, FilmEn, FilmgC, HalFC 80, MotPP, MovMk[port], WhScrn 77, WorEFlm
St. Clair, Maurice 1903-1970 WhScrn 74, -77, WhoHol B
St. Clair, Michael WhoHol A
St. Clair, Richard 1946- ConAmC
St. Clair, Robert 1910-1967 WhScrn 74, -77
St. Clair, Sylvia AmSCAP 80
St. Clair, Sylvie AmSCAP 66
St. Clair, Wesley BlkAmP
St. Clair, Yvonne 1914-1971 WhScrn 74, -77, WhoHol B
St. Claire, Adah 1854-1928 WhScrn 74, -77
St. Cyr, John Alexander 1890-1966 BiDAmM
St. Cyr, Johnny IlEncJ
St. Cyr, Johnny 1889-1966 NewOrJ[port]
St. Cyr, Johnny 1890-1966 CmpEPM, WhoJazz 72
St. Cyr, Lili 1917- What 5[port]
St. Cyr, Lili 1920- ForYSC, WhoHol A
St. Cyr, Lillian Red Wing 1873-1974 WhScrn 77
Saint-Cyr, Renee 1907- FilmEn
St. Dan, Deborah PlP&P A[port]
St. Denis, Joe 1928-1968 WhScrn 74, -77, WhoHol B
Saint-Denis, Michel 1897-1971 BiE&WWA, CnThe, EncWT, NotNAT B, OxThe, PlP&P, WhThe, WhoThe 72
St. Denis, Ruth CmpGMD[port]
St. Denis, Ruth 1877-1968 DancEn 78[port], NewGrD 80, NotNAT B
St. Denis, Ruth 1878-1968 WhScrn 74, -77, WhoHol B
St. Denis, Ruth 1880?-1968 CnOxB
St. Denis, Teddie 1909- WhThe
St. Dennis, Ruth 1877- Film 1
Saint-Denys Garneau, Hector De CreCan 1
Saint-Denys Garneau, Henri De CreCan 1
Saint-Evremond, Sieur De 1610-1703 NotNAT B
Saint-Evremond, Charles DeSaint-Denis 1614?-1703 NewGrD 80
Saint-Exupery, Antoine De 1900-1943 DcPup
Saint-Foix, Georges De 1874-1954 Baker 78, NewGrD 80
Saint-Gelais, Mellin De 1491-1558 NewGrD 80
Saint-Gelais, Merlin De 1491-1558 NewGrD 80
St. Gelasius Of Helioppolis d297 NotNAT B
St. Genesius d297 Ent
St. Genesius The Comedian d286? NotNAT B
Saint-George, Boulogne, Chevalier De 1739?-1799 NewGrD 80[port]
Saint-George, Chevalier OxMus
St. George, Eleanor 1929- WhoMus 72
Saint-George, George 1841-1924 Baker 78
Saint-George, Henry 1866-1917 Baker 78
St. George, Julia d1903 NotNAT B
Saint-Georges, Boulogne, Chevalier De 1739?-1799 NewGrD 80[port]
Saint-Georges, Joseph Boulogne 1739-1799 Baker 78
Saint-Georges, Jules Henri Vernoy De 1801-1875 NewEOp 71
Saint Germain, Count Of d1784 NewGrD 80
St. Germain, Teresa PupTheA
St. Germaine, Kay CmpEPM
St. Gregory OxMus
St. Helier, Ivy d1971 WhScrn 74, -77, WhThe, WhoHol B
Saint-Huberti, Madame De 1756-1812 NewGrD 80
Saint-Huberty, Madame De 1756-1812 NewGrD 80
St. Jacques, Raymond 1930- DrBlPA, FilmEn, FilmgC, ForYSC, HalFC 80, IntMPA 77, -75, -76, -78, -79, -80, MovMk, WhoHol A
St. James, Susan 1946- FilmEn, FilmgC, ForYSC
Saint James, Susan 1946- HalFC 80
St. James, Susan 1946- IntMPA 77, -75, -76, -78, -79, -80
Saint James, Susan 1946- WhoHol A
St. John, Adela Rogers 1893- HalFC 80
St. John, Al 1893-1963 FilmEn, Film 1, -2, FilmgC, ForYSC, HalFC 80, MotPP, NotNAT B, TwYS, Vers B[port], WhScrn 74, -77, WhoHol B
St. John, Betta IntMPA 75, -76, -78, -79, -80
St. John, Betta 1929- FilmEn, ForYSC
St. John, Betta 1930- FilmgC, HalFC 80, IntMPA 77, WhoHol A
St. John, Christopher DrBlPA, WhoHol A
St. John, Christopher Marie d1960 NotNAT B, WhThe

St. John, Florence 1854-1912 *NotNAT B, WhThe*
St. John, Howard *WhoThe 72*
St. John, Howard 1905- *ForYSC*
St. John, Howard 1905-1974 *BiE&WWA, FilmEn, FilmgC, HalFC 80, MovMk, NotNAT B, WhScrn 77, WhThe, WhoHol B*
St. John, Jane Lee 1912-1957 *WhScrn 74*
St. John, Jill 1940- *FilmEn, FilmgC, ForYSC, HalFC 80, MotPP, MovMk, WhoHol A*
St. John, John *Film 2*
St. John, Kathleen Louise 1942- *AmSCAP 80*
St. John, Lily 1895- *WhThe*
St. John, Marguerite d1940 *Film 2, NotNAT B, WhoHol B*
St. John, Norah d1962 *NotNAT B*
St. John, Richard *WhoHol A*
St. John, Rosemary Innes 1926- *WhoMus 72*
St. John, Valerie *WhoHol A*
Saint-Lambert, Michel De *NewGrD 80*
Saint-Leon, Arthur 1821-1870 *CnOxB, NewGrD 80*
Saint-Leon, Arthur Michel 1815?-1870 *DancEn 78*
St. Leonard, Florence *Film 2*
Saint-Lubin, Leon De 1805-1850 *Baker 78*
Saint-Luc, Jacques De 1616-1684? *NewGrD 80*
Saint-Luc, Jean De *CreCan 2*
Saint-Luc, Laurent De 1663-1700? *NewGrD 80*
Saint-Marcoux, Micheline Coulombe 1938- *Baker 78*
St. Martini, Giovanni Battista *NewGrD 80*
St. Martini, Giuseppe *NewGrD 80*
St. Maur, Adele 1888-1959 *WhScrn 74, -77, WhoHol B*
St. Onge, Bill *AmSCAP 80*
St. Peters, Crispian 1944- *RkOn 2[port]*
St. Pierre, Clara 1866-1942 *WhScrn 74, -77*
Saint-Pierre, Denyse *CreCan 2*
Saint-Pierre, Jacques Henri Bernardin De 1737-1814 *NewEOp 71*
St. Polis, John d1946 *WhoHol B*
St. Polis, John 1873-1946 *WhScrn 77*
St. Polis, John 1887-1942 *Film 1, ForYSC, TwYS*
Saint-Requier, Leon 1872-1964 *Baker 78*
St. Roch, Christian 1948- *IntWWM 77*
Saint-Saens, Camille 1835-1921 *Baker 78, BnBkM 80[port], CmOp, CmpBCM, DcCom 77[port], DcCom&M 79, DcPup, GrComp[port], MusMk[port], NewEOp 71, NewGrD 80[port], NotNAT B, OxMus*
Saint-Saens, Charles Camille 1835-1921 *DancEn 78*
Saint-Sevin *NewGrD 80*
St. Sixt *NewGrD 80*
Saint-Subber, Arnold 1918- *BiE&WWA, NotNAT, WhoThe 72, -77*
St. Trond, Rudolph Of *NewGrD 80*
Sainte-Beuve, Charles-Augustin 1804-1869 *EncWT, NotNAT B, OxThe*
Sainte-Colombe d1701? *NewGrD 80*
Sainte-Croix, A *CreCan 1*
Sainte-Marie, Buffy 1941- *AmSCAP 80, BiDAmM, EncFCWM 69, IlEncCM[port], IlEncR[port], RkOn 2[port]*
Sainthill, Loudon 1919-1969 *EncWT*
Sainton, Prosper 1813-1890 *Baker 78, NewGrD 80*
Sainton-Dolby, Charlotte 1821-1885 *NewGrD 80*
Saintsbury, H A 1869-1939 *NotNAT B, WhThe*
Saione *NewGrD 80*
Saioni *NewGrD 80*
Saire, David *WhoHol A*
Sais, Marin 1888- *FilmEn, Film 1, -2, ForYSC, TwYS, WhoHol A*
Saito, Bill *WhoHol A*
Saito, Hideo 1902-1974 *Baker 78*
Saive *NewGrD 80*
Sakac, Branimir 1918- *Baker 78, NewGrD 80*
Sakadas Of Argos *NewGrD 80*
Sakai, Claire Hatsue 1951- *IntWWM 77*
Sakall, S Z 1884-1955 *FilmEn, Film 2, FilmgC, ForYSC, HalFC 80, MotPP, MovMk[port], WhScrn 74, -77, WhoHol B*
Sakall, S Z 1887-1955 *Funs[port]*
Sakall, S Z 1888-1955 *NotNAT B, Vers A[port]*
Sakamaki, Ben 1921- *AmSCAP 80*
Sakamoto, Kyu 1941- *RkOn*
Sakata, Harold *WhoHol A, WhoHrs 80*
Sakayama, Bob 1947- *AmSCAP 80*
Saker, Annie 1882-1932 *NotNAT B, WhThe*
Saker, Edward d1883 *NotNAT B*
Saker, Mrs. Edward 1847-1912 *NotNAT B, WhThe*
Saker, Horace d1861 *NotNAT B*
Saker, Horatio d1902 *NotNAT B*
Saker, Maria d1902 *NotNAT B*
Saker, Richard Henry d1870 *NotNAT B*
Saker, Rose d1923 *NotNAT B*
Saker, William d1849 *NotNAT B*
Sakharoff, Alexander 1886-1963 *CnOxB*
Sakharov, Alexandre 1886-1963 *DancEn 78*
Sakketti, Liberio Antonovich *NewGrD 80*
Sakowski, Helmut 1924- *CroCD*
Saks, Benny *AmSCAP 80*
Saks, Gene 1921- *BiE&WWA, FilmEn, FilmgC, HalFC 80, IntMPA 77, -75, -76, -78, -79, -80, NotNAT, WhoHol A, WhoThe 72, -77*
Saks, Gitle Langner *AmSCAP 80*
Saks, Matthew *WhoHol A*
Sala, George Augustus d1895 *NotNAT B*
Sala, Giuseppe *NewGrD 80*
Sala, Josquino Della *NewGrD 80*
Sala, Nicola 1713-1801 *Baker 78, NewGrD 80*
Sala, Oskar 1910- *IntWWM 77, -80*
Sala, Vittorio 1918- *WorEFlm*
Salaam, Kalamu Ya 1947- *BlkAmP, MorBAP*
Salabert *NewGrD 80*
Salabert, Edouard 1838-1903 *NewGrD 80*
Salabert, Francis 1884-1946 *Baker 78*
Salabova, Libuse 1929- *IntWWM 77, -80*
Salabue, Ignazio Alessandro Cozio Di *NewGrD 80*
Salacrou, Armand 1899- *CnMD, CnThe, CroCD, EncWT, Ent, McGEWD[port], ModWD, OxThe, REnWD[port], WhThe, WhoThe 72*
Salaets, Ruth Elizabeth Swanson 1913- *IntWWM 77*
Salah, Rehba Ben *Film 2*
Salaman, Charles Kensington 1814-1901 *Baker 78, NewGrD 80, OxMus*
Salaman, Esther Sarah *IntWWM 77, -80, WhoMus 72*
Salaman, Malcolm C d1940 *NotNAT B*
Salaman, William Herbert 1940- *IntWWM 77*
Salamon, Ed *ConMuA 80B*
Salant, Richard S 1914- *IntMPA 77, -75, -76, -78, -79, -80, NewYTET*
Salari, Francesco 1751-1828 *NewGrD 80*
Salas, Juan Orrego *DcCM*
Salas, Nancy 1910- *IntWWM 77, -80*
Salas, Paco 1875-1964 *WhScrn 74, -77*
Salas Viu, Vicente 1911-1967 *Baker 78, NewGrD 80*
Salas Y Castro, Esteban 1725-1803 *NewGrD 80*
Salat, Howard 1928- *AmSCAP 66, -80*
Salaverde, Bartolome DeSelma Y *NewGrD 80*
Salavisa, Jorge *CnOxB*
Salaway, Lowell 1921- *AmSCAP 66*
Salazar, Adolfo 1890-1958 *Baker 78, NewGrD 80, OxMus*
Salazar, Antonio De 1650?-1715? *NewGrD 80*
Salazar, Diego Jose De d1709 *NewGrD 80*
Salazar, Diego Joseph De d1709 *NewGrD 80*
Salazar, Juan Garcia d1710 *OxMus*
Salberg, Derek S 1912- *WhoThe 72, -77*
Salberg, Leon d1937 *NotNAT B*
Salbinger, Sigmund *NewGrD 80*
Salblinger, Sigmund *NewGrD 80*
Salce, Luciano 1922- *FilmEn, WorEFlm*
Saldari, Luciano 1934- *WhoOp 76*
Saldivar, Gabriel 1909- *NewGrD 80*
Saldoni, Baltasar 1807-1889 *Baker 78, NewGrD 80*
Sale *NewGrD 80*
Sale, Adrien Trudo 1722?-1782 *NewGrD 80*
Sale, Adrien Trudon 1722?-1782 *NewGrD 80*
Sale, Charles 1885-1936 *ForYSC, NotNAT B, WhScrn 74, -77, WhThe, WhoHol B*
Sale, Charles 1885-1937 *HalFC 80*
Sale, Chic *MotPP*
Sale, Chic 1885-1936 *JoeFr*
Sale, Chic Charles *Film 2*
Sale, Frances 1892-1969 *WhScrn 74, -77, WhoHol B*
Sale, Francois *NewGrD 80*
Sale, Franz *NewGrD 80*
Sale, Giovanni Battista Del 1575?-1615 *NewGrD 80*
Sale, John 1934- *DancEn 78*
Sale, Richard 1911- *FilmEn, FilmgC, HalFC 80, IntMPA 77, -75, -76, -78, -79, -80*
Sale, Virginia *Film 2, ForYSC, MotPP, TwYS, WhoHol A*
Salemka, Irene 1931- *CreCan 2, WhoOp 76*
Salerni, Giuliano 1942- *AmSCAP 80*
Sales, Franz 1550?-1599 *NewGrD 80*
Sales, Grover 1919- *ConAmTC*
Sales, Nikolaus 1550?-1606 *NewGrD 80*
Sales, Pietro Pompeo 1729-1797 *Baker 78, NewGrD 80*
Sales, Soupy *MotPP, NewYTET, WhoHol A*
Sales, Soupy 1926- *FilmgC, HalFC 80*
Sales, Soupy 1930- *AmSCAP 66, -80*
Sales, Vicente Mercado 1918- *IntWWM 77, -80*
Saleski, Gdal 1888-1966 *Baker 78*
Salesky, Brian 1952- *IntWWM 80*
Saletan, Anthony David 1931- *IntWWM 77*
Saletri, Frank R 1928- *IntMPA 77, -75, -76, -78, -79, -80*
Saletz, Franz *NewGrD 80*
Saleza, Albert 1867-1916 *Baker 78, NewGrD 80*
Salgado, Luis H 1903- *DcCM*
Salici, Enrico *PupTheA*
Salici, Ferdinando *PupTheA*
Salieri, Antonio 1750-1825 *Baker 78, BnBkM 80, CmOp, MusMk, NewEOp 71, NewGrD 80[port], OxMus*
Salignac, Eustase Thomas 1867-1945 *NewEOp 71*
Salignac, Thomas 1867-1945 *CmOp*
Salim *MorBAP*
Salim, Kamel 191-?-1945 *DcFM*
Salimbene Da Parma 1221-1288 *NewGrD 80*
Salimbene De Adam 1221-1288 *NewGrD 80*
Salimu *BlkAmP, MorBAP*
Salin, Klaus 1919- *CnOxB*
Salinas, Francisco 1513-1590 *OxMus*
Salinas, Francisco De 1513-1590 *Baker 78, NewGrD 80*
Salinger, Conrad d1962 *NotNAT B*
Salinis, Huberty *NewGrD 80*
Salinis, Hymbert De *NewGrD 80*
Salis, Brindes De *OxMus*
Salis, Rodolphe 1852-1897 *Ent*
Salisbury, Frank 1930- *NatPD[port]*
Salisbury, Ian Patrick *WhoMus 72*
Salisbury, James-Earl 1951- *IntWWM 77, -80*
Salisbury, Leah d1975 *BiE&WWA, NotNAT B*
Salisbury, Monroe d1935 *MotPP, WhoHol B*
Salisbury, Monroe 1876-1935 *WhScrn 74, -77*
Salisbury, Monroe 1879-1935 *Film 1, -2, TwYS*
Salisbury-Jones, Raymond Arthur 1933- *IntWWM 80*
Salkeld, Robert 1920- *IntWWM 80, WhoMus 72*
Salkind, Alexander *IntMPA 80*
Salkind, Ilya *IntMPA 80*
Salkov, Abraham A 1921- *ConAmC*
Salkow, Sidney 1909- *FilmEn, FilmgC, HalFC 80, WhoHrs 80*
Salkow, Sidney 1911- *IntMPA 77, -75, -76, -78, -79, -80*
Sallantin, Francois 1755-1816? *NewGrD 80*
Sallas, Dennis *WhoHol A*
Salle, Mademoiselle *PlP&P*
Salle, Adrien Trudo *NewGrD 80*
Salle, Marie 1707-1756 *CnOxB, DancEn 78, NewGrD 80*
Salle, Marie 1710-1756 *OxMus*
Sallentin, Francois 1755-1816? *NewGrD 80*
Salley, Helen M 1921- *IntWWM 77*
Sallinen, Aulis 1935- *Baker 78, DcCM, NewGrD 80*

Sallinen, Aulis Heikki 1935- *IntWWM 77, -80*
Sallis, Peter 1921- *FilmgC, HalFC 80, WhoHol A, WhoThe 72, -77*
Sallis, Zoe *WhoHol A*
Sallo, Jacob 1920- *AmSCAP 80*
Salmanov, Vadim Nikolayevich 1912- *Baker 78, NewGrD 80*
Salmanova, Lyda *Film 2*
Salmen, Walter 1926- *NewGrD 80*
Salmenhaara, Erkki 1941- *Baker 78, DcCM, NewGrD 80*
Salmhofer, Franz 1900-1975 *Baker 78, NewGrD 80*
Salmhoffer, Franz 1900-1975 *CmOp*
Salmi, Albert 1928- *BiE&WWA, FilmEn, FilmgC, ForYSC, HalFC 80, IntMPA 77, -75, -76, -78, -79, -80, NotNAT, WhoHol A*
Salmi, Vexi 1942- *IntWWM 77, -80*
Salminen, Matti Kalervo 1945- *WhoOp 76*
Salminger, Sigmund 1500?-1554? *NewGrD 80*
Salmon, Alvan Glover 1868-1917 *Baker 78*
Salmon, Christopher David Baker 1940- *IntWWM 77, -80*
Salmon, Eliza 1787-1849 *NewGrD 80*
Salmon, Jacques 1545?- *NewGrD 80*
Salmon, Karel 1897-1974 *NewGrD 80*
Salmon, Karl 1897-1974 *NewGrD 80*
Salmon, Thomas 1648-1706 *NewGrD 80, OxMus*
Salmond, Felix 1888-1952 *Baker 78, MusSN[port], NewGrD 80*
Salmond, Norman d1914 *NotNAT B*
Salmonova, Lyda 1889-1968 *WhScrn 77*
Salo, Gasparo Da *Baker 78, NewGrD 80*
Saloio, Carlos H 1931- *IntWWM 77, -80*
Salom, Jaime 1925- *CroCD*
Saloman, Ora Frishberg 1938- *IntWWM 77, -80*
Saloman, Siegfried 1816-1899 *Baker 78*
Salome, Helene Berthe Elisabeth 1924- *IntWWM 80*
Salome, Theodor Cesar 1834-1896 *OxMus*
Salomon *Baker 78*
Salomon, Henry, Jr. d1957 *NewYTET*
Salomon, Horst 1929- *CroCD*
Salomon, Johann Peter 1745-1815 *Baker 78, MusMk, NewGrD 80[port], OxMus*
Salomon, Joseph-Francois 1649?-1732 *NewGrD 80*
Salomon, Jules Auguste *NewGrD 80*
Salomon, Karel *NewGrD 80*
Salomon, Karl *OxMus*
Salomon, Lee *ConMuA 80B*
Salomon, Siegfried 1885-1962 *NewGrD 80*
Salonen, Sulo 1899-1976 *Baker 78, IntWWM 77, NewGrD 80*
Salpeter, Sophie 1916- *AmSCAP 66, -80*
Salsbury, Hubert Ivan 1938- *AmSCAP 80*
Salsbury, Nathan 1846-1902 *NotNAT B*
Salsbury, Ronald Foster 1950- *AmSCAP 80*
Salsoul Orchestra, The *RkOn 2[port]*
Salstone, Milt *ConMuA 80B*
Salt, Jennifer 1944- *FilmEn, WhoHol A*
Salt, Ruth 1945- *IntWWM 77*
Salt, Valerie Jean 1956- *IntWWM 80*
Salt, Waldo 1914- *FilmEn, FilmgC, HalFC 80, IntMPA 77, -75, -76, -78, -79, -80*
Salta, Anita Maria 1937- *WhoOp 76*
Salta, Menotti 1893- *AmSCAP 66, ConAmC A*
Salten, Alfred 1914- *IntWWM 77, -80*
Salter, Hans J 1896- *AmSCAP 66, -80, FilmEn, HalFC 80, IntMPA 77, -75, -76, -78, -79, -80, IntWWM 77, WhoHrs 80*
Salter, Harold d1928 *Film 2, WhScrn 74, -77*
Salter, Harry d1928 *Film 1, TwYS, WhoHol B*
Salter, Humphrey *NewGrD 80*
Salter, Lionel Paul 1914- *IntWWM 77, -80, NewGrD 80, WhoMus 72*
Salter, Mary Elizabeth Turner 1856-1938 *Baker 78*
Salter, Mary Turner 1856-1938 *AmSCAP 66, -80, BiDAmM*
Salter, Maud 1898- *IntWWM 77*
Salter, Richard 1943- *WhoOp 76*
Salter, Sumner 1856-1944 *Baker 78, BiDAmM*
Salter, Thelma d1953 *Film 1, -2, WhScrn 74, -77, WhoHol B*
Salter, Timothy John 1942- *IntWWM 77, -80, WhoMus 72*
Salter, William 1936- *AmSCAP 80*
Salthouse, Graham 1941- *ConAmC*
Saltikov-Schedrin, Mikhail Yevgrafovich 1826-1889 *EncWT*
Saltikov-Shchedrin, Mikhail Evgrafovich 1826-1889 *OxThe*
Saltikow, N *Film 1*
Saltmarsh, Anthony Clive 1935- *WhoMus 72*
Salty Dog Sam *BluesWW*
Saltzman, Harry 1915- *FilmEn, FilmgC, HalFC 80, IntMPA 77, -75, -76, -78, -79, -80, WhoHrs 80*
Saltzman, Harry 1916- *WorEFlm*
Saltzman, Herbert Royce 1928- *IntWWM 77, -80*
Saltzmann-Stevens, Minnie 1874-1950 *CmOp, NewGrD 80*
Salucci, Joseph James 1956- *AmSCAP 80*
Salva, Tadeas 1937- *Baker 78, NewGrD 80*
Salvador, Mario 1917- *IntWWM 77, -80*
Salvador, Sal 1925- *AmSCAP 66, -80, BgBands 74, CmpEPM*
Salvador-Daniel *NewGrD 80*
Salvadori, Andrea 1591-1635 *NewGrD 80*
Salvadori, Angelo *NewGrD 80*
Salvai, Maria Maddalena *NewGrD 80*
Salvatore, Giovanni d1688? *NewGrD 80*
Salvatori, Adolph 1908- *AmSCAP 66, -80*
Salvatori, Paul 1912- *AmSCAP 66, -80*
Salvatori, Renato 1933- *FilmEn, MotPP, WhoHol A*
Salvayre, Gaston 1847-1916 *Baker 78, NewGrD 80*
Salvayre, Gervais Bernard 1847-1916 *NewGrD 80*
Salver, Lianna *Film 2*
Salverson, Laura Goodman 1890- *CreCan 1*
Salvi, Antonio d1742 *NewGrD 80*
Salvi, Lola *Film 2*
Salvi, Victor 1921- *NewGrD 80*
Salvini, Alessandro *Film 2*
Salvini, Alessandro 1860-1896 *NotNAT B*
Salvini, Alexander *Film 1*
Salvini, Alexander 1860-1896 *NotNAT B*
Salvini, Guido 1893- *EncWT*
Salvini, Gustavo 1859-1930 *EncWT, NotNAT B*
Salvini, Tomasso 1829-1915 *WhThe*
Salvini, Tommaso 1829-1915 *EncWT, Ent*
Salvini, Tommaso 1829-1916 *CnThe, FamA&A[port], NotNAT A, -B, OxThe, PlP&P[port]*
Salvini-Donatelli, Fanny 1815?-1891 *NewGrD 80*
Salvioni, Guglielma 1842- *CnOxB*
Salvioni, Guglielmina 1842- *DancEn 78*
Salviucci, Giovanni 1907-1937 *Baker 78, NewGrD 80*
Salviuolo, Joseph Anthony 1940- *AmSCAP 80*
Salvor, Lianne *Film 2*
Salvotti, Vera *Film 2*
Salwasser, Lynda Bybee *WomWMM B*
Salway, Thomas 1706?-1743 *NewGrD 80*
Salwitz, Hardy 1930- *AmSCAP 66, -80*
Salzburg, Joseph S 1917- *IntMPA 77, -75, -76, -78, -79, -80*
Salzburg, Milton J 1912- *IntMPA 77, -75, -76, -78, -79, -80*
Salzedo, Carlos 1885-1961 *AmSCAP 66, -80, Baker 78, BiDAmM, BnBkM 80, ConAmC, DcCM, MusMk, MusSN[port], NewGrD 80, OxMus*
Salzedo, Leonard 1921- *CnOxB, IntWWM 77, -80, NewGrD 80, WhoMus 72*
Salzer, Beeb 1933- *WhoOp 76*
Salzer, Eugene d1964 *NotNAT B*
Salzer, Felix 1904- *Baker 78, NewGrD 80*
Salzilli, Crescentio 1580?-1621? *NewGrD 80*
Salzman, Eric 1933- *AmSCAP 80, Baker 78, BiDAmM, ConAmC, DcCM, NewGrD 80*
Salzman, Pnina 1924- *NewGrD 80, WhoMus 72*
Sam And Dave *BiDAmM, ConMuA 80A, RkOn 2[port]*
Sam 'n' Henry *JoeFr*
Sam The Sham & The Pharaohs *RkOn 2[port]*
Saman, Rene *NewGrD 80*
Samand, Rene *NewGrD 80*
Samane, Rene *NewGrD 80*
Samar, Devi Lal *DcPup*
Samar, Pari 1937- *WhoOp 76*
Samara, Spiro 1861-1917 *Baker 78, OxMus*
Samaras, Spyridon 1863-1917 *NewGrD 80*
Samaritani, Pierluigi 1942- *WhoOp 76*
Samaroff, Olga 1882-1948 *Baker 78, BiDAmM, BnBkM 80, MusSN[port], NewGrD 80*
Samaropoulo, Persephone 1941- *CnOxB*
Samary, Jeanne d1890 *NotNAT B*
Samary, Marie d1941 *NotNAT B*
Samatowicz, D *WomWMM B*
Samazeuilh, Gustave 1877-1967 *Baker 78, NewGrD 80, OxMus*
Samber, Johann Baptist 1654?-1717 *NewGrD 80*
Samberg, Arnold 1899-1936 *WhScrn 74, -77*
Samborski, I I Koval *Film 2*
Sambson, Giovanni *NewGrD 80*
Samel, Morey 1909- *WhoJazz 72*
Samela, Gustavo Gerardo Andres 1940- *IntWWM 77, -80*
Sameth, Jack *IntMPA 77, -75, -76, -78, -79, -80*
Samin, Vulfran *NewGrD 80*
Saminsky, Lazar 1882-1959 *OxMus*
Saminsky, Lazare 1882-1959 *AmSCAP 66, -80, Baker 78, BiDAmM, ConAmC, DcCM, NewGrD 80*
Samish, Adrian d1976 *NewYTET*
Sammarco, Mario 1868-1930 *Baker 78, CmOp, NewEOp 71, NewGrD 80*
Sammartini, Gioseffo 1695-1750 *NewGrD 80*
Sammartini, Giovanni Battista 1698-1775 *BnBkM 80, GrComp*
Sammartini, Giovanni Battista 1700?-1775 *NewGrD 80[port]*
Sammartini, Giovanni Battista 1701-1775 *Baker 78, OxMus*
Sammartini, Giuseppe 1693?-1750? *Baker 78, MusMk*
Sammartini, Giuseppe 1693?-1751 *BnBkM 80, OxMus*
Sammartini, Giuseppe 1695-1750 *NewGrD 80*
Sammartini, Pietro *NewGrD 80*
Sammis, George W d1927 *NotNAT B*
Sammons, Albert Edward 1886-1957 *Baker 78, NewGrD 80*
Sammons, Donald E 1940- *WhoMus 72*
Samoilova, Tatania 1934- *HalFC 80*
Samoilova, Tatiana 1934- *OxFilm*
Samoilova, Tatyana 1934- *FilmEn, WhoHol A*
Samokhalova, Maria Nicolaievna 1929- *CnOxB*
Samon, Grico *AmSCAP 80*
Samosud, Samuil Abramovich 1884-1964 *Baker 78, NewGrD 80*
Samotulinus, Venceslaus *NewGrD 80*
Sampayo Ribeiro, Mario Luis De 1898-1966 *NewGrD 80*
Samper, Gabriela *WomWMM*
Samper, Rico Frances 1926- *IntWWM 80*
Sampion *NewGrD 80*
Sample, Joe 1939- *EncJzS 70*
Sample, John Robert 1923- *IntWWM 77*
Sample, Joseph Leslie 1939- *EncJzS 70*
Samples, Junior *IlEncCM*
Sampley, Arthur McCullough 1903- *AmSCAP 66*
Samponi, Gioseffo *NewGrD 80*
Sampson d1554 *NewGrD 80*
Sampson, David Charles 1951- *ConAmC*
Sampson, Edgar M 1907-1973 *AmSCAP 66, -80, BiDAmM, CmpEPM, DrBlPA, EncJzS 70, IlEncJ*
Sampson, Edgar Melvin 1907-1973 *WhoJazz 72*
Sampson, George 1861-1949 *Baker 78*
Sampson, James 1930- *AmSCAP 80*
Sampson, John Patterson 1837- *BlkAmP*
Sampson, Larry Carl 1942- *AmSCAP 80*
Sampson, Leonard E 1918- *IntMPA 80*
Sampson, Peggie 1912- *IntWWM 77, -80, WhoMus 72*
Sampson, Robert *WhoHol A*
Sampson, Sammy *BluesWW*
Sampson, Teddy 1895-1970 *Film 2, TwYS, WhScrn 77*
Sampson, Will *HalFC 80*
Sampson, William d1922 *NotNAT B*

Samrock, Victor 1907- *BiE&WWA, NotNAT*
Sams, Eric 1926- *Baker 78, NewGrD 80*
Samsing, Freddy 1946- *IntWWM 77, -80*
Samson, Ivan d1963 *WhoHol B*
Samson, Ivan 1894-1963 *NotNAT B, WhThe*
Samson, Ivan 1895-1963 *WhScrn 74, -77*
Samson, Joseph-Isidore 1793-1871 *NotNAT B, OxThe*
Samson, Teddy 1895- *Film 1*
Samson, Valerie Brooks 1947- *IntWWM 80*
Samson, Valerie Brooks 1948- *ConAmC*
Samson-Francois 1924-1970 *NewGrD 80*
Samsonov, Samson 1921- *DcFM, FilmEn, WorEFlm[port]*
Samsony, Giovanni *NewGrD 80*
Samsova, Galina 1937- *CnOxB*
Samtsova *CnOxB*
Samtsova, Galina 1937- *DancEn 78*
Samuel, Adolphe 1824-1898 *Baker 78, NewGrD 80*
Samuel, Claude 1931- *NewGrD 80*
Samuel, Gerhard 1924- *AmSCAP 80, Baker 78, ConAmC, NewGrD 80*
Samuel, Harold 1879-1937 *Baker 78, NewGrD 80, OxMus*
Samuel, Harold E 1924- *IntWWM 77, -80*
Samuel, Harry Cecil 1927- *IntWWM 77, -80, WhoMus 72*
Samuel, Leopold 1883-1975 *NewGrD 80*
Samuel-Holeman, Eugene 1863-1942 *NewGrD 80*
Samuel-Rousseau, Marcel *Baker 78*
Samuel-Rousseau, Marcel 1882-1955 *NewGrD 80*
Samuels, Abram 1920- *IntMPA 77, -75, -76, -78, -79, -80*
Samuels, Bernhard *OxMus*
Samuels, David Alan 1948- *AmSCAP 80*
Samuels, Gertrude *NatPD[port]*
Samuels, Jacob *Film 2*
Samuels, Lesser *IntMPA 77, -75, -76, -78, -79, -80*
Samuels, Maurice 1885-1964 *WhScrn 77*
Samuels, Maxine *WomWMM*
Samuels, Milton Isadore 1904- *AmSCAP 66, -80*
Samuels, Patrick Stephen 1940- *IntWWM 77, -80*
Samuels, Walter Gerald 1908- *AmSCAP 66, -80, CmpEPM*
Samuelsen, Roy 1933- *IntWWM 77, -80, WhoOp 76*
Samuelson, David W 1924- *IntMPA 77, -75, -76, -78, -79, -80*
Samuelson, G B 1887-1945 *FilmgC, HalFC 80*
Samuelson, G B 1888-1947 *FilmEn*
Samuelson, George Berthold 1888-1947 *IlWWBF*
Samuelson, Kathryn Allen 1921- *IntWWM 77, -80*
Samuelson, Kristine *WomWMM B*
Samuelson, Peter George Wylie 1951- *IntMPA 80*
Samuelson, Sydney W 1925- *IntMPA 75, -76, -77, -78, -79, -80*
San, Herman Van 1929- *NewGrD 80*
San Diego Marine Base Band *Film 2*
San Fernando Red *JoeFr*
San Gallo, Bastiano Da 1481-1551 *OxThe*
San-Giorgiu, Ion 1893-1950 *CnMD*
San Juan, Olga 1927- *FilmgC, ForYSC, What 5[port], WhoHol A*
San Martin, Carlos *Film 2*
San Martini *Baker 78*
San Martini, Giovanni Battista *NewGrD 80*
San Remo Golden Strings *RkOn 2A*
San Sebastian, Padre Jose Antonio De *Baker 78*
San Secondo, Pier Maria Rosso Di 1887-1956 *Ent*
San Secondo, Rosso Di 1887-1956 *CnMD*
Sanasardo, Paul 1928- *CmpGMD, CnOxB, DancEn 78*
Sanborn, Dave 1945- *EncJzS 70*
Sanborn, David William 1945- *EncJzS 70*
Sanborn, Fred C 1899-1961 *WhScrn 74, -77, WhoHol B*
Sanborn, John Pitts 1879-1941 *BiDAmM*
Sanborn, Pitts 1879-1941 *Baker 78*
Sances, Giovanni Felice 1600?-1679 *NewGrD 80*
Sanchez, Florencio 1875-1910 *CnThe, McGEWD, ModWD, OxThe, REnWD[port]*
Sanchez, Florencio 1875-1917 *NotNAT B*
Sanchez, Jaime *WhoHol A*
Sanchez, Joaquin 1923-1966 *WhScrn 77*
Sanchez, Juan 1945- *CnOxB*
Sanchez, Marguerite *Film 2*
Sanchez, Pedro *WhoHol A*
Sanchez, Ramon Diaz 1903- *CnMD*
Sanchez, Sonia 1934- *BlkAmP, DrBlPA, MorBAP*
Sanchez DeBadajoz, Diego 1479?-1550? *McGEWD*
Sanchez DeFuentes, Eduardo 1874-1944 *Baker 78, NewGrD 80*
Sanchez Malaga, Carlos 1904- *NewGrD 80*
Sancho, Fernando 1916- *FilmAG WE, WhoHol A*
Sancho Marraco, Jose 1879-1960 *NewGrD 80*
Sancta Maria, Thomas De *NewGrD 80*
Sancta Maria, Tomas De *NewGrD 80*
Sand, George 1804-1876 *DcPup, NotNAT B*
Sand, Georges 1804-1876 *NewEOp 71*
Sand, Inge 1928-1974 *CnOxB, DancEn 78*
Sand, Maurice 1823-1889 *DcPup*
Sand, Monique 1944- *CnOxB*
Sand, Paul 1935- *NotNAT, WhoHol A, WhoThe 77*
Sanda, Dominique *WhoHol A*
Sanda, Dominique 1948- *FilmAG WE, FilmEn, FilmgC, HalFC 80*
Sanda, Dominique 1952- *MovMk*
Sandbach, Mary 1904- *WhoMus 72*
Sandberg, Anders Wilhelm 1887-1938 *DcFM, FilmEn*
Sandberg, Lars 1955- *IntWWM 80*
Sandberg, Mordecai 1897-1973 *Baker 78, ConAmC*
Sandberg, Willy 1929- *DancEn 78*
Sandberger, Adolf 1864-1943 *Baker 78, NewGrD 80*
Sandblom, Jorgen 1945- *IntWWM 77*
Sandbrook, June 1938- *DancEn 78*
Sandburg, Carl 1878-1967 *AmSCAP 66, -80, BiDAmM, OxMus*
Sandburg, Carl August 1878-1967 *EncFCWM 69*
Sandby, Herman 1881-1965 *Baker 78*
Sandby, Hermann 1881-1965 *NewGrD 80*
Sande, Earle *Film 2*
Sande, Walter 1906-1972 *FilmgC, ForYSC, HalFC 80, Vers A[port], WhScrn 77, WhoHol B*
Sandeau, Jules 1811-1883 *McGEWD[port]*
Sandelewski, Wiaroslaw Jozef 1912- *IntWWM 77, -80*
Sander *NewGrD 80*
Sander, F S 1760?-1796 *NewGrD 80*
Sander, Ian *WhoHol A*
Sander, Peter 1933- *IntWWM 77, -80, WhoMus 72*
Sanderling, Kurt 1912- *NewGrD 80*
Sanders, Alma M 1882-1956 *AmSCAP 66, -80, ConAmC*
Sanders, Anita *WhoHol A*
Sanders, Ann *WhoHol A*
Sanders, Bonnie *AmSCAP 80*
Sanders, Branch Stevens 1947- *AmSCAP 80*
Sanders, Denis 1929- *FilmEn, FilmgC, HalFC 80, IntMPA 77, -75, -76, -78, -79, -80*
Sanders, Dick 1933- *CnOxB, DancEn 78*
Sanders, Dorothea K *PupTheA*
Sanders, Ernest H 1918- *IntWWM 77, -80, NewGrD 80*
Sanders, Fareil *AmSCAP 80*
Sanders, Farrell 1940- *EncJzS 70*
Sanders, George 1906-1972 *BiDFilm, -81, FilmEn, Film 2, FilmgC, ForYSC, HalFC 80, IlWWBF, -A, MotPP, MovMk[port], NotNAT A, OxFilm, WhScrn 77, WhoHol B, WhoHrs 80, WorEFlm*
Sanders, Helke *WomWMM*
Sanders, Honey *IntMPA 77, -75, -76, -78, -79, -80*
Sanders, Hugh 1912-1966 *WhScrn 77, WhoHol B*
Sanders, Jessica *WomWMM B*
Sanders, Job 1929- *CnOxB, DancEn 78*
Sanders, Joe L 1896-1965 *AmSCAP 66, -80, CmpEPM, WhoJazz 72*
Sanders, John Derek 1933- *IntWWM 77, -80*
Sanders, Marlene *NewYTET, WomWMM, -B*
Sanders, Nat 1892- *IntMPA 77, -75, -76, -78, -79, -80*
Sanders, Neill Joseph 1923- *WhoMus 72*
Sanders, Paul 1915- *AmSCAP 66, -80*
Sanders, Paul Florus 1891- *Baker 78, IntWWM 77, -80*
Sanders, Pharoah 1940- *DrBlPA, EncJzS 70, IlEncJ*
Sanders, R Denis 1929- *WorEFlm*
Sanders, Richard Charles 1949- *AmSCAP 80*
Sanders, Robert L 1906-1974 *AmSCAP 66, -80, Baker 78, BiDAmM, ConAmC, NewGrD 80*
Sanders, Scott 1885-1956 *HalFC 80, NotNAT B, WhoHol B*
Sanders, Shepherd *WhoHol A*
Sanders, Terry Barrett 1931- *FilmgC, HalFC 80, IntMPA 77, -75, -76, -78, -79, -80, WorEFlm*
Sanderson, Anne *PupTheA*
Sanderson, Challis *IlWWBF*
Sanderson, Joey *Film 2*
Sanderson, John *PupTheA*
Sanderson, Julia *AmPS B, Film 1*
Sanderson, Julia 1887-1975 *BiE&WWA, CmpEPM, EncMT, NotNAT B, WhThe, WhoStg 1908*
Sanderson, Julia 1888-1975 *WhScrn 77*
Sanderson, Kent *Film 2*
Sanderson, Lora *Film 2*
Sanderson, Mary d1712 *OxThe*
Sanderson, Ronda Beryl 1921- *IntWWM 80*
Sanderson, Sibyl 1865-1903 *Baker 78, BiDAmM, NewGrD 80*
Sanderson, Sybil 1865-1903 *CmOp, NewEOp 71*
Sandford, Christopher 1939- *FilmgC, HalFC 80, WhoHol A*
Sandford, Marjorie 1910- *WhThe*
Sandford, Samuel *OxThe*
Sandford, Tiny 1894-1961 *HalFC 80, WhScrn 77*
Sandgren, Clyde D 1910- *AmSCAP 80*
Sandholm, Kaj-Gustav Arvid 1944- *IntWWM 77*
Sandi, Luis 1905- *Baker 78, NewGrD 80*
Sandifur, Ann Elizabeth 1949- *ConAmC, IntWWM 80*
Sandison, Gordon 1913-1958 *NotNAT B, WhThe*
Sandle, Floyd 1913- *BiE&WWA, NotNAT*
Sandley *NewGrD 80*
Sandlin, Dorothy Southerland Johnson 1927- *IntWWM 77, -80*
Sandlin, Johnny *ConMuA 80B*
Sandner, Arwed Ernst 1929- *WhoOp 76*
Sandon, Nicholas John 1948- *IntWWM 80*
Sandonato, Barbara 1943- *CnOxB*
Sandoni, Pietro Giuseppe 1685-1748 *NewGrD 80*
Sandor, Alfred 1918- *BiE&WWA, NotNAT*
Sandor, Anna 1950- *IntWWM 77, -80*
Sandor, Arpad 1896-1972 *Baker 78*
Sandor, Frigyes 1905- *IntWWM 77, -80*
Sandor, Gyorgy 1912- *Baker 78, BnBkM 80, IntWWM 77, -80, NewGrD 80, WhoMus 72*
Sandor, Janos 1933- *IntWWM 80, WhoMus 72*
Sandor, John Carson 1946- *WhoOp 76*
Sandor, Steve *WhoHol A*
Sandoval, Che *WomWMM B*
Sandoval, Miguel 1903-1953 *AmSCAP 66, -80, Baker 78, ConAmC*
Sandow, Eugene 1867-1924? *Ent*
Sandow, Eugene 1867-1925 *Film 1, WhScrn 77*
Sandoz, May Jacqueline *IntWWM 77, -80, WhoOp 76*
Sandoz, Paul 1906- *IntWWM 77, -80*
Sandpipers, The *RkOn 2[port]*
Sandquist, Kathryn Simpson 1937- *IntWWM 77, -80*

Sandqvist, Olof Ingmar 1927- *IntWWM 77, -80*
Sandrelli, Stefania 1946- *FilmAG WE, FilmEn, WhoHol A*
Sandresky, Margaret Vardell 1921- *ConAmC*
Sandrey, Irma *WhoHol A*
Sandri, Anna-Maria *WhoHol A*
Sandrich, Jay *NewYTET*
Sandrich, Mark 1900-1945 *BiDFilm, -81, CmMov, DcFM, FilmEn, FilmgC, HalFC 80, WorEFlm*
Sandrich, Mark, Jr. 1928- *AmSCAP 80*
Sandrin 1490?-1561? *NewGrD 80*
Sandrock, Adele 1863-1937 *EncWT*
Sandrock, Adele 1864-1937 *NotNAT B, WhScrn 77, WhoHol B*
Sandry, Vin 1902- *AmSCAP 66, -80*
Sands, Billy *WhoHol A*
Sands, Bobby 1907- *WhoJazz 72*
Sands, Diana 1934-1973 *BiE&WWA, DrBlPA, EncWT, FilmEn, MotPP, NotNAT B, WhScrn 77, WhThe, WhoHol B, WhoThe 72, WomWMM*
Sands, Dorothy 1893- *BiE&WWA, NotNAT, PlP&P[port], WhoThe 72, -77*
Sands, Ernest 1924- *IntMPA 77, -75, -76, -78, -79, -80*
Sands, Evie *AmSCAP 80*
Sands, George 1900-1933 *WhScrn 74, -77*
Sands, Gillian *WhoMus 72*
Sands, Jodie *RkOn*
Sands, Johnny 1927- *ForYSC, IntMPA 77, -75, -76, -78, -79, -80, MotPP, WhoHol A*
Sands, Leslie 1921- *WhoHol A, WhoThe 72, -77*
Sands, Thomas Adrian 1937- *AmSCAP 66*
Sands, Tommy *AmPS A, -B, MotPP*
Sands, Tommy 1936- *ForYSC, WhoHol A*
Sands, Tommy 1937- *BiDAmM, FilmEn, FilmgC, HalFC 80, IntMPA 77, -75, -76, -78, -79, -80, RkOn*
Sandstrom, Sven-David 1942- *Baker 78, IntWWM 77, -80, NewGrD 80*
Sandt, Maximilian VanDe 1863-1934 *Baker 78*
Sandunova, Elizaveta Semyonovna 1772?-1826 *NewGrD 80*
Sandvik, Ole Mork 1875-1976 *Baker 78, NewGrD 80*
Sandvold, Arild Edvin 1895- *IntWWM 77, -80*
Sandy 1938- *HalFC 80*
Sandy, Baby 1938- *HalFC 80*
Sandys, George 1578-1644 *OxMus*
Sanelli, Gualtiero 1816-1861 *NewGrD 80*
Sanes, Giovanni Felice *NewGrD 80*
Sanfilippo, Josephine Ann 1918- *AmSCAP 80*
Sanfilippo, Margherita Marie 1927- *AmSCAP 80*
Sanford, Agnes d1955 *WhScrn 74, -77*
Sanford, Albert, Jr. 1893-1953 *WhScrn 74, -77, WhoHol B*
Sanford, Alexandra *PupTheA*
Sanford, Charles 1905- *IntMPA 77, -75, -76, -78, -79, -80*
Sanford, Dick 1896- *AmSCAP 66, -80*
Sanford, Edward Clark 1948- *AmSCAP 80*
Sanford, Erskine 1880-1950 *FilmgC, HalFC 80, PlP&P, WhoHol B*
Sanford, Harold Bryant 1879-1945 *Baker 78*
Sanford, Herbert C 1905- *AmSCAP 80*
Sanford, Isabel *WhoHol A*
Sanford, Isabell *DrBlPA*
Sanford, Joseph G *FilmEn*
Sanford, Ralph 1899-1963 *FilmgC, HalFC 80, Vers B[port], WhScrn 74, -77, WhoHol B*
Sanford, Robert 1904- *BiE&WWA*
Sanford, Samuel Simons 1849-1910 *Baker 78*
Sanford, Stanley 1894-1961 *Film 1, -2*
Sanford, Tiny 1894-1961 *Film 2*
Sang, Lani 1916-1977 *AmSCAP 66, -80*
Sang, Leonard B 1900- *NotNAT*
Sang, Leonard B 1904- *BiE&WWA*
Sang, Samantha 1953- *RkOn 2[port]*
Sangalli, Rita 1850-1909 *CnOxB*
Sangalli, Rita 1851-1909 *DancEn 78*
Sanger, Bert 1894-1969 *WhScrn 74, -77, WhoHol B*
Sanger, David John 1947- *IntWWM 77, -80*
Sanger, Fred d1923 *NotNAT B*
Sanger, George 1827-1911 *Ent, NotNAT A*
Sanger, Gerald 1898- *IntMPA 77, -75, -76, -78, -79, -80*
Sanger, Zedekiah 1771-1821 *BiDAmM*
Sangiovanni, Antonio 1831-1892 *Baker 78*
Sangster, Alfred 1880- *WhThe*
Sangster, Jimmy *IntMPA 77, -75, -76, -78, -79, -80*
Sangster, Jimmy 1924- *FilmEn, FilmgC, HalFC 80, WhoHrs 80*
Sangster, Jimmy 1925- *CmMov*
Sanicola, Henry W 1914-1974 *AmSCAP 80*
Sanicola, Henry W 1915- *AmSCAP 66*
Sanicola, John Joseph 1917- *AmSCAP 66, -80*
Sanina, Mira 1922- *DancEn 78*
Sanipoli, Vittorio 1915- *FilmAG WE*
Sanjines, Jorge 1936- *OxFilm*
SanJuan, Olga 1927- *FilmEn, HalFC 80*
Sanjuan, Pedro 1886-1976 *Baker 78, BiDAmM, ConAmC*
Sanjust, Filippo 1925- *EncWT, WhoOp 76*
Sankey, Ira David 1840-1908 *Baker 78, BiDAmM, NewGrD 80*
Sankovskaya, Ekaterina 1816-1878 *NewGrD 80*
Sankovskaya, Yekaterina 1816-1878 *CnOxB*
Sanmartini, Giuseppe *NewGrD 80*
Sanmartini, Pietro 1636-1701 *NewGrD 80*
Sannella, Andy 1900-1961 *CmpEPM*
Sannella, Andy 1900-1961? *WhoJazz 72*
SanPedro, Lucio 1913- *NewGrD 80*
Sanquirico, Alessandro 1777-1849 *NewGrD 80*
Sanquirico, Alessandro 1780-1849 *OxThe*
SanRafaele, Benvenuto Robbio, Count Of 1735-1797 *NewGrD 80*
Sanroma, Jesus Maria 1902- *Baker 78*
Sanromano, Carlo Giuseppe 1630?-1680? *NewGrD 80*
Sanserre, Pierre *NewGrD 80*
Sanseverino, Benedetto *NewGrD 80*
Sansom, Gillian *WhoMus 72*
Sansom, Lester A *IntMPA 77, -75, -76, -78, -79, -80*
Sanson, Yvonne 1926- *FilmEn*
Sansone, Giovanni 1593-1648 *NewGrD 80*
Sansoni, Giovanni 1593-1648 *NewGrD 80*
Santa Croce, Francesco 1487?-1556? *NewGrD 80*
Santa Cruz, Dominga 1899- *OxMus*
Santa Cruz, Domingo 1899- *Baker 78, DcCM, NewGrD 80[port]*
Santa Maria, Fray Tomas De 1510?-1570 *Baker 78*
Santa Maria, Jorge De *NewGrD 80*
Santa Maria, Salvatore *NewGrD 80*
Santa Maria, Tomas De d1570 *NewGrD 80*
Sant'Agata, Tommaso Da *NewGrD 80*
Santamaria, Mongo *IlEncJ, RkOn[port]*
Santamarie, Manuel d1960 *WhScrn 74, -77*
Santana *ConMuA 80A, IlEncR, RkOn 2[port]*
Santana, Vasco 1890-1958 *WhScrn 74, -77*
Santana, Vasco 1898-1958 *FilmAG WE*
Santana Blues Band *BiDAmM*
Santangelo, John, Jr. *ConMuA 80B*
Sant'Anna, Jose Pereira De 1696-1759 *NewGrD 80*
Santarpia, Ralph C 1951- *AmSCAP 80*
Sante, Sophia Van 1925- *NewGrD 80*
Santell, Al 1895- *TwYS A*
Santell, Alfred 1895- *FilmEn, FilmgC, HalFC 80, IntMPA 77, -75, -76, -78, -79, WorEFlm*
Santelli, Giovanna 1937- *WhoOp 76*
Santelmann, William Henry 1863-1932 *Baker 78*
Santelton, Frederick *Film 2*
Santerre, Pierre d1567? *NewGrD 80*
Santestevan, Maria 1933- *CnOxB, DancEn 78*
Santi, Nello 1931- *WhoOp 76*
Santi, Padre Angelo De 1847-1922 *Baker 78*
Santiago, Burnell 1915-1944 *NewOrJ[port]*
Santiago, Francisco 1889-1947 *NewGrD 80*
Santiago, Francisco De 1578?-1644 *NewGrD 80*
Santiago, Herman 1940- *BiDAmM*
Santiago, Lester 1909-1965 *NewOrJ[port]*
Santiago, Willie 1887?-1945 *NewOrJ*
Santiago-Felipe, Vilma R 1932- *IntWWM 77, -80*
Santina, Bruno Della d1968 *WhScrn 77*
Santini, Abbate Fortunato 1778-1861 *Baker 78*
Santini, Fortunato 1778-1861 *NewGrD 80*
Santini, Gabriele 1886-1964 *NewGrD 80*
Santini, Gabriele 1886-1965 *CmOp*
Santini, Prospero *NewGrD 80*
Santino *NewGrD 80*
Santley, Sir Charles 1834-1922 *Baker 78, CmOp, NewGrD 80[port], OxMus*
Santley, Fred d1953 *WhoHol B*
Santley, Frederic d1953 *Film 1*
Santley, Frederic 1887-1953 *WhThe*
Santley, Frederic 1888-1953 *WhScrn 74, -77*
Santley, Fredric d1953 *NotNAT B*
Santley, Joseph 1889-1971 *EncMT, FilmEn, FilmgC, HalFC 80, WhScrn 74, -77, WhThe, WhoHol B*
Santley, Joseph 1890- *CmpEPM*
Santley, Joseph And Sawyer, Ivy *AmPS B*
Santley, Kate d1923 *NotNAT B, WhThe*
Santlow, Hester d1778 *NotNAT B*
Santly, Henry 1890-1934 *AmSCAP 66, -80*
Santly, Joseph H 1886-1962 *AmSCAP 66, -80, NotNAT B*
Santly, Lester 1894- *AmSCAP 66, -80*
Santo *WhoHrs 80*
Santo And Johnny *AmPS A, RkOn[port]*
Santoliquido, Francesco 1883-1971 *Baker 78, NewGrD 80*
Santoliquido, Ornella 1906-1977 *NewGrD 80*
Santon, Penny *WhoHol A*
Santoni, Joel 1943- *FilmEn*
Santoni, Linda R 1936- *AmSCAP 66*
Santoni, Reni 1939- *FilmgC, HalFC 80, WhoHol A*
Santora, Jack *Film 2*
Santorini, Lorenz *NewGrD 80*
Santoro, Claudio 1919- *Baker 78, DcCM, IntWWM 77, -80, NewGrD 80*
Santoro, Paul 1915- *AmSCAP 80*
Santorsola, Guido Antonio 1904- *CpmDNM 75, DcCM, IntWWM 77, -80, NewGrD 80*
Santos, Bert *WhoHol A*
Santos, Clovis Pereira 1932- *IntWWM 77, -80*
Santos, Joe *WhoHol A*
Santos, Joly Braga 1924- *Baker 78, NewGrD 80*
Santos, Jose Joaquim Dos 1747?-1801 *NewGrD 80*
Santos, Lawrence E 1941- *AmSCAP 80*
Santos, Luciano Xavier Dos 1734-1808 *NewGrD 80*
Santos, Murillo 1931- *IntWWM 77, -80*
Santos, Nelson Pereira Dos 1928- *DcFM*
Santos, Ramon Pagayon 1941- *NewGrD 80*
Santos, Rosendo 1922- *NewGrD 80*
Santos, Tiki d1974 *WhScrn 77*
Santos, Tony *AmSCAP 80*
Santos, Turibio 1943- *IntWWM 80, WhoMus 72*
Santos Ocampo, Amada 1925- *NewGrD 80*
Santos Pinto, Francisco A Norberto Dos *NewGrD 80*
Santschi, Thomas 1882-1931 *Film 1, -2*
Santschi, Tom d1931 *WhoHol B*
Santschi, Tom 1878-1931 *FilmEn*
Santschi, Tom 1879-1931 *FilmgC, ForYSC, HalFC 80, WhScrn 74, -77*
Santschi, Tom 1882-1931 *TwYS*
Santucci, Marco 1762-1843 *Baker 78, NewGrD 80*
Santunione, Orianna 1934- *WhoOp 76*
Santurini, Francesco 1627-1682 *OxThe*
Sanuti Pellicani, Giovanni Battista 1632?-1697 *NewGrD 80*
Sanz, C Moneo *PupTheA*
Sanz, Gaspar *Baker 78, NewGrD 80, OxMus*
Sanzogno, Nino 1911- *Baker 78, CmOp, NewGrD 80, OxMus, WhoMus 72, WhoOp 76*
Saorgin, Rene 1928- *NewGrD 80*
Sapeinikov, Vassily 1867-1941 *Baker 78*
Sapelli, Domingo d1961 *WhScrn 77*
Saper, Jack *IntMPA 77, -75, -76, -78*
Saperstein, David 1948- *Baker 78, ConAmC*
Saperstein, Henry G 1918- *IntMPA 77, -75, -76, -78, -79, -80, NewYTET, WhoHrs 80*
Saperton, David 1889-1970 *Baker 78, BiDAmM*
Sapia, Patrick L, Jr. 1941- *AmSCAP 66*
Sapieyevski, Jerzy 1945- *CpmDNM 72, -73, -74, -77, -78, ConAmC*
Sapin, Louis *MorBAP*
Sapio, Romualdo 1858-1943 *Baker 78, BiDAmM*

Saporiti, Teresa 1763-1869 *NewGrD 80*
Saporta, Marc *OxMus*
Sapp, Allen Dwight 1922- *Baker 78, ConAmC, NewGrD 80*
Sapp, Gary J 1944- *ConAmC*
Sapper *NotNAT B*
Sapphires *RkOn 2A*
Sappho 612?BC- *NewGrD 80*
Sappington, Margo 1947- *CnOxB*
Sara, Sandor 1933- *OxFilm*
Sarabhai, Mrinalini 1923- *CnOxB, DancEn 78[port]*
Sarabia, Guillermo 1937- *WhoOp 76*
Saraceni, Francesco Maria 1911-1961 *NewGrD 80*
Saraceni, Raymond R 1932- *AmSCAP 80*
Saraceno, Joseph 1931- *AmSCAP 66*
Saraceno, Joseph 1936- *AmSCAP 80*
Sarach, Marian *CmpGMD*
Saracinelli, Ferdinando 1590?-1640? *NewGrD 80*
Saracini, Claudio 1586-1649? *MusMk, NewGrD 80*
Saradzhev, Konstantin 1877-1954 *NewGrD 80*
Saradzhian, Konstantin 1877-1954 *NewGrD 80*
Sarafian, Richard C 1925?- *FilmEn*
Sarafian, Richard C 1927?- *FilmgC, HalFC 80*
Sarai, Tibor 1919- *Baker 78, IntWWM 77, -80, NewGrD 80*
Sarakatsannis, Leonidas Nicholas 1929- *IntWWM 80*
Saram, Rohan De 1939- *WhoMus 72*
Saran, Franz Ludwig 1866-1931 *Baker 78*
Sarandon, Chris 1942- *HalFC 80, WhoHol A*
Sarandon, Susan 1946- *FilmEn, HalFC 80, IntMPA 79, -80, WhoHol A*
Sarasate, Pablo De 1844-1908 *Baker 78, BnBkM 80, DcCom&M 79, GrComp[port], MusMk, NewGrD 80[port], OxMus*
Sarat, Agnan d1613 *OxThe*
Sarauer, Alois 1901- *IntWWM 77*
Sarauw, Paul 1883- *CnMD*
Sarcey, Francisque 1827-1899 *EncWT, NotNAT A, -B, OxThe*
Sarche, Ed 1907- *AmSCAP 66, -80*
Sarda, Albert 1943- *IntWWM 77, -80*
Sardaby, Michel 1935- *EncJzS 70*
Sardella, Edward A 1928- *AmSCAP 66, -80*
Sardena, Orazio 1550?-1638 *NewGrD 80*
Sardi, Dorothea *NewGrD 80*
Sardi, Giuseppe *NewGrD 80*
Sardi, Ivan 1930- *WhoOp 76*
Sardi, Vincent, Jr. 1915- *BiE&WWA*
Sardinero, Vicente 1937- *NewGrD 80*
Sardinero, Vincenzo 1937- *NewGrD 80, WhoOp 76*
Sardo, Cosmo *WhoHol A*
Sardonius, Jean *NewGrD 80*
Sardou, Fernand *WhoHol A*
Sardou, Victorien 1831-1908 *CnThe, EncWT, Ent, McGEWD[port], ModWD, NewEOp 71, NewGrD 80, NotNAT A, -B, OxThe, PlP&P, REnWD[port], WhoStg 1908*
Sarecky, Barney 1895- *IntMPA 77, -75, -76, -78, -79*
Sarg, Tony 1880-1942 *DcPup, PupTheA*
Sargant, James Edmund 1935- *WhoOp 76*
Sargeant, Winthrop 1903- *Baker 78*
Sargent, Alfred Maxwell 1881-1949 *WhScrn 74, -77*
Sargent, Alvin *FilmEn, HalFC 80, IntMPA 77, -75, -76, -78, -79, -80*
Sargent, Dick *FilmgC, WhoHol A*
Sargent, Dick 1933- *IntMPA 80*
Sargent, Dick 1937?- *HalFC 80*
Sargent, Epes Winthrop d1938 *NotNAT B*
Sargent, Evelyn *IntWWM 77, WhoMus 72*
Sargent, Franklin H d1923 *NotNAT B*
Sargent, Frederic 1879- *WhThe*
Sargent, George *TwYS A*
Sargent, Herbert C 1873- *WhThe*
Sargent, Joseph 1925- *FilmEn, FilmgC, HalFC 80, IntMPA 78, -79, -80, WhoHrs 80*
Sargent, Karen *AmSCAP 80*
Sargent, Kenny 1906-1969 *CmpEPM, WhoHol B*
Sargent, Lewis 1904- *Film 1, -2, TwYS, WhoHol A*
Sargent, Sir Malcolm 1895-1967 *Baker 78, BnBkM 80, MusSN[port], NewEOp 71, NewGrD 80[port], OxMus, WhScrn 77*
Sargent, Malcolm B 1933- *WhoMus 72*
Sargent, Pamela J 1946- *IntWWM 77, -80*
Sargent, Paul 1910- *AmSCAP 66, -80, ConAmC*
Sargent, Thornton 1902- *IntMPA 77, -75, -76, -78, -79, -80*
Sargon, Simon 1938- *AmSCAP 80*
Sargous, Harry Wayne 1948- *IntWWM 77, -80*
Sargoy, Edward A *IntMPA 77, -75, -76, -78, -79, -80*
Sari, Ada 1886-1968 *Baker 78*
Saridis, Saverio 1933- *RkOn*
Sarkadi, Imre 1921-1961 *CroCD*
Sarkissian, Rousanne *DancEn 78*
Sarkozy, Istvan 1920- *Baker 78, IntWWM 77, -80, NewGrD 80*
Sarle, Regina *Film 1*
Sarlow, Mary K 1912- *AmSCAP 66*
Sarlui, Ed 1925- *IntMPA 77, -75, -76, -78, -79, -80*
Sarly, Henry 1883-1954 *Baker 78*
Sarmanto, Heikki Veli Uolevi 1939- *EncJzS 70, IntWWM 77*
Sarment, Jean 1897- *CnMD, McGEWD, ModWD, WhThe*
Sarmento, William Edward 1946- *ConAmTC*
Sarna, Mohinder Singh 1926- *IntWWM 77, -80*
Sarne, Michael *WhoHol A*
Sarne, Michael 1939- *FilmEn, FilmgC, HalFC 80*
Sarne, Mike 1940- *OxFilm*
Sarner, Alexander 1892-1948 *NotNAT B, WhThe, WhoHol B*
Sarner, Sylvia *WomWMM, -B*
Sarnette, Eric Antoine Joseph Andre 1898- *Baker 78*
Sarno, Hector V 1880-1953 *Film 1, -2, WhScrn 74, -77, WhoHol B*
Sarno, Janet *WhoHol A*
Sarno, Tom *Film 2*
Sarnoff, David d1971 *NewYTET*
Sarnoff, Dorothy 1919- *BiE&WWA, NotNAT*
Sarnoff, Janyce Lois 1928- *AmSCAP 66, -80*
Sarnoff, Robert W 1918- *IntMPA 77, -75, -76, -78, -79, -80, NewYTET*
Sarnoff, Thomas 1927- *IntMPA 77, -75, -76, -78, -79, -80, NewYTET*
Saro, J Heinrich 1827-1891 *Baker 78*
Sarony, Leslie 1897- *WhThe*
Sarosi, Balint 1925- *IntWWM 77, -80, NewGrD 80*
Saroyan, Lucy *WhoHol A*
Saroyan, William 1908- *BiE&WWA, CnMD, CnThe, ConDr 73, -77, DcLB 7[port], EncWT, Ent, FilmEn, FilmgC, HalFC 80, McGEWD, ModWD, NotNAT, -A, OxThe, PlP&P[port], REnWD[port], WhoThe 72, -77*
Sarracco, John M 1956- *IntWWM 77*
Sarracini, Gerald d1957 *NotNAT B*
Sarracino, Ernest *WhoHol A*
Sarrafian, Richard C *IntMPA 77, -75, -76, -78, -79, -80*
Sarrazin, Maurice 1925- *EncWT*
Sarrazin, Michael 1940- *FilmEn, FilmgC, HalFC 80, IntMPA 77, -75, -76, -78, -79, -80, WhoHol A*
Sarrazin, Michael 1941- *ForYSC*
Sarrette, Bernard 1765-1858 *Baker 78, NewGrD 80*
Sarri, Domenico Natale 1679-1744 *NewGrD 80*
Sarris, Andrew *OxFilm*
Sarro, Domenico Natale 1679-1744 *NewGrD 80*
Sarroca, Suzanne 1927- *WhoOp 76*
Sarry, Christine 1947- *CnOxB*
Sarstadt, Marian 1942- *CnOxB*
Sarta, Mary *Film 2*
Sartain, John, Jr. *AmSCAP 80*
Sarthou, Jacques 1920- *OxThe*
Sarti, Andre *Film 2*
Sarti, Giovanni Vincenzo *NewGrD 80*
Sarti, Giuseppe 1729-1802 *Baker 78, BnBkM 80, MusMk, NewEOp 71, NewGrD 80[port], OxMus*
Sarti, Laura *WhoMus 72*
Sarto, Johannes De *NewGrD 80*
Sartori, Claudio 1913- *Baker 78, NewGrD 80*
Sartorio, Angiola 1903- *DancEn 78*
Sartorio, Antonio 1620?-1681 *Baker 78*
Sartorio, Antonio 1630-1680 *NewGrD 80*
Sartorio, Gasparo 1625?-1680 *NewGrD 80*
Sartorius, Christian d1676 *NewGrD 80*
Sartorius, Erasmus 1577-1637 *NewGrD 80*
Sartorius, Paul 1569-1609 *Baker 78, NewGrD 80*
Sartory, Eugene 1871-1946 *NewGrD 80*
Sartov, Hendrik *HalFC 80*
Sartre, Jean-Paul 1905-1980 *BiE&WWA, CnMD, CnThe, CroCD, EncWT, Ent, FilmEn, FilmgC, HalFC 80, McGEWD[port], ModWD, NotNAT, -A, OxThe, PlP&P, REnWD[port], WhoThe 72, -77*
Sary, Laszlo 1940- *Baker 78, NewGrD 80*
Saryan, Ghazar 1920- *NewGrD 80*
Sas, Andre 1900-1967 *OxMus*
Sas, Andres 1900-1967 *Baker 78, NewGrD 80*
Sasdy, Peter 1934- *FilmgC, HalFC 80, IlWWBF, WhoHrs 80*
Saslav, Isidor 1938- *IntWWM 77, -80*
Saslavsky, Alexander 1876-1924 *Baker 78, BiDAmM*
Saslavsky, Luis 1906- *WorEFlm[port]*
Saslavsky, Luis 1908- *DcFM, FilmEn*
Sass, Edward d1916 *NotNAT B, WhThe*
Sass, Enid 1889-1959 *NotNAT B, WhThe*
Sass, Sylvia 1951- *NewGrD 80, WhoOp 76*
Sassard, Jacqueline 1940- *FilmEn, FilmgC, HalFC 80, WhoHol A*
Sasse, Konrad 1926- *NewGrD 80*
Sassetti *NewGrD 80*
Sassetti, Joao Baptista 1817-1889 *NewGrD 80*
Sasseville *PupTheA*
Sassola, Renato Pablo Carlos 1927- *WhoOp 76*
Sassoli, Ada 1886-1946 *Baker 78*
Sassoli, Dina *WhoHol A*
Sassower, Harvey L 1945- *IntMPA 77, -75, -76, -78, -79, -80*
Sassu, Aligi 1912- *WhoOp 76*
Sastre, Alfonso 1926- *CnMD, CroCD, EncWT, McGEWD[port], ModWD*
Satanowski, Robert 1928- *NewGrD 80*
Satchmo *DrBlPA, NewGrD 80*
Satenstein, Frank 1924- *IntMPA 77, -75, -76, -78, -79, -80*
Sateren, Leland B 1913- *ConAmC*
Satherley, Art 1889- *IlEncCM*
Sathyanarayana, R 1929- *IntWWM 77, -80*
Satie, Eric 1866-1925 *NewGrD 80[port]*
Satie, Erik 1866-1925 *Baker 78, BnBkM 80, CmpBCM, CompSN[port], CnOxB, DancEn 78, DcCom 77[port], DcCom&M 79, DcCM, DcTwCC, -A, MusMk[port], NewEOp 71, NewGrD 80[port], OxFilm, OxMus, WhScrn 77, WorEFlm[port]*
Satikov-Shchedrin, Mikhail Evgrafavich 1826-1889 *NotNAT B*
Sato, Eishi *NewGrD 80*
Sato, Keijiro 1927- *Baker 78*
Sato, Masahiko 1941- *EncJzS 70*
Sato, Reiko *WhoHol A*
Satoh 1941- *EncJzS 70*
Satoh, Toyohiko 1943- *NewGrD 80*
Satra, Antonin 1901- *WhoMus 72*
Satre, Ana-Raquel 1933- *WhoMus 72*
Satter, Gustav 1832-1879 *Baker 78, BiDAmM*
Satterlee, Bruce *WhoHol A*
Satterwhite, Collen Gray 1920-1978 *AmSCAP 66, -80*
Sattin, Lonnie *BiE&WWA, DrBlPA*
Sattin, Tina *DrBlPA*
Sattinger, Celia C 1903- *AmSCAP 80*
Sattler, Heinrich 1811-1891 *Baker 78*
Sattler, Lisbeth *NewGrD 80*
Satton, Lon *WhoHol A*
Saturen, David Haskell 1939- *IntWWM 77, -80*
Satz, Ilya 1875-1912 *Baker 78*
Satz, Lillie 1896-1974 *WhScrn 77*
Satz, Ludwig 1891-1944 *WhScrn 74, -77, WhoHol B*
Satzel, Christoph d1655 *NewGrD 80*
Satzl, Christoph d1655 *NewGrD 80*
Saucedo, Victor 1937- *CpmDNM 77, -80,*

ConAmC
Saucier, Gene Allen 1929- *CpmDNM 78, -79*
Saudek, Robert *NewYTET*
Sauer *NewGrD 80*
Sauer, Colin 1924- *WhoMus 72*
Sauer, Emil Von 1862-1942 *Baker 78, BnBkM 80, NewGrD 80*
Sauer, Ignaz 1759-1833 *NewGrD 80*
Sauer, Oscar 1856-1918 *EncWT*
Sauer, Robert 1872-1944 *AmSCAP 66, -80*
Sauer, Wolfgang 1928- *IntWWM 77, -80*
Sauerman, Carl 1868-1924 *Film 1, WhScrn 77*
Sauguet, Henri 1901- *Baker 78, CompSN[port], CnOxB, DancEn 78, DcCM, NewEOp 71, NewGrD 80, OxMus, WhoMus 72*
Saul, Oscar 1912- *FilmEn, IntMPA 77, -75, -76, -78, -79, -80*
Saulesco, Mircea Petre 1926- *IntWWM 77, -80*
Saulnier, Jacques 1928- *FilmEn, WorEFlm*
Saum, Cliff 1883-1943 *Film 2, WhoHol B*
Saum, Clifford 1883-1943 *WhScrn 74, -77*
Saum, Grace *Film 1*
Saumell Robredo, Manuel 1817-1870 *NewGrD 80*
Saunders, Ada 1952- *BlkWAB*
Saunders, Antony Jefferies 1935- *WhoMus 72*
Saunders, Arlene *WhoOp 76*
Saunders, Bryon C *MorBAP*
Saunders, Carrie Lou 1893- *AmSCAP 66*
Saunders, Charles 1904- *FilmEn, FilmgC, HalFC 80, IlWWBF*
Saunders, Charlotte d1899 *NotNAT B*
Saunders, Dudley *ConAmTC*
Saunders, E G d1913 *NotNAT B*
Saunders, Florence d1926 *Film 2, NotNAT B, PlP&P, WhThe*
Saunders, Frank G *MorBAP*
Saunders, Gertrude *BlksBF*
Saunders, Hazel 1907- *WhoMus 72*
Saunders, Jackie d1954 *MotPP, WhoHol B*
Saunders, Jackie 1893-1954 *Film 1, -2, TwYS*
Saunders, Jackie 1898-1954 *WhScrn 74, -77*
Saunders, James A 1925- *CnThe, ConDr 73, -77, CroCD, EncWT, Ent, McGEWD, WhoThe 72, -77*
Saunders, Janet *WomWMM*
Saunders, Janet Winifred 1929- *WhoMus 72*
Saunders, John *Film 1*
Saunders, John d1895 *NotNAT B*
Saunders, John Monk 1895-1940 *FilmgC, HalFC 80*
Saunders, John Monk 1897-1940 *FilmEn*
Saunders, Lawrence Ira 1943- *IntWWM 77, -80*
Saunders, Lori *WhoHol A*
Saunders, Madge 1894-1967 *WhThe*
Saunders, Mary Jane *MotPP, WhoHol A*
Saunders, Milton 1913- *AmSCAP 66, -80*
Saunders, Neil 1918- *IntWWM 77, -80, WhoMus 72*
Saunders, Nellie Peck 1869-1942 *WhScrn 74, -77, WhoHol B*
Saunders, Orville 1954- *EncJzS 70*
Saunders, Otis 1872- *BiDAmM*
Saunders, Pat *WomWMM B*
Saunders, Percy George 1902- *WhoMus 72*
Saunders, Peter 1911- *BiE&WWA, WhoThe 72, -77*
Saunders, Red 1912- *WhoJazz 72*
Saunders, Reginald Charles 1900- *WhoMus 72*
Saunders, Richard Thomas 1935- *IntWWM 77*
Saunders, Rosamond Metta 1909- *IntWWM 77, -80, WhoMus 72*
Saunders, Ruby Constance 1939- *BlkAmP*
Saupe, Christian Gottlob 1763-1819 *NewGrD 80*
Saupicquet *NewGrD 80*
Saura, Carlos 1932- *FilmEn, WorEFlm*
Sauret, Emile 1852-1920 *Baker 78, NewGrD 80*
Saurin, Bernard-Joseph 1706-1781 *OxThe*
Saurindramohana Thakura *NewGrD 80*
Saursbi *NewGrD 80*
Saussy, Tupper *ConAmC*
Sautell, Al 1895- *WorEFlm[port]*
Sauter, Ed 1914- *BiDAmM*
Sauter, Eddie 1914- *CmpEPM, IlEncJ, WhoJazz 72*
Sauter, Edward Ernest 1914- *AmSCAP 66, -80, ConAmC A*
Sauter, Ernest 1928- *IntWWM 80*
Sauter, William *Film 1*
Sauter-Finegan *BgBands 74[port]*
Sautet, Claude 1924- *FilmEn, FilmgC, HalFC 80, WorEFlm*
Sauvajon, Marc Gilbert 1909- *CnMD*
Sauveur, Joseph 1653-1716 *Baker 78, NewGrD 80*
Sauzay, Eugene 1809-1901 *Baker 78, NewGrD 80*
Sava, Helen 1941- *IntWWM 77, -80*
Savadove, Laurence D 1931- *AmSCAP 80*
Savage, Ann 1921- *FilmEn, ForYSC, MotPP, WhoHol A*
Savage, Anne 1896- *CreCan 1*
Savage, Annie Douglas *CreCan 1*
Savage, Archie *DrBlPA*
Savage, Brad *WhoHol A*
Savage, David 1924- *IntMPA 77, -75, -76, -78, -79, -80*
Savage, George 1904- *BiE&WWA, NotNAT*
Savage, Henry Wilson 1859-1927 *Baker 78, BiDAmM, EncMT, NewEOp 71, NotNAT B, WhThe*
Savage, Houston *WhScrn 77*
Savage, Jane *NewGrD 80*
Savage, John 1953?- *HalFC 80, IntMPA 80, WhoHol A*
Savage, Margaret Cecilia 1928- *IntWWM 77*
Savage, Nelly *Film 2*
Savage, Richard *AmSCAP 80*
Savage, Richard d1743 *NotNAT B*
Savage, Richard Temple 1909- *IntWWM 77, -80*
Savage, Roger Bentham 1949- *IntWWM 77*
Savage, Stephen 1942- *IntWWM 77, -80, WhoMus 72*
Savage, Turner *Film 2*
Savage, William 1720-1789 *NewGrD 80*
Savagnone, Giuseppe 1902- *NewGrD 80*
Saval, Dany 1940- *FilmEn, WhoHol A*
Savalas, George *WhoHol A*
Savalas, Telly 1924- *FilmgC, ForYSC, HalFC 80, IntMPA 77, -75, -76, -78, -79, -80, MotPP, MovMk[port], WhoHol A, WhoHrs 80*
Savalas, Telly 1925- *FilmEn*
Savall, Jordi 1941- *IntWWM 77, -80*
Savan, Bruce 1927- *BiE&WWA, NotNAT*
Savard, Augustin 1814-1881 *Baker 78*
Savard, Claude 1941- *IntWWM 77, -80*
Savard, Marie-Emmanual-Augustin 1861-1942 *Baker 78*
Savart, Felix 1791-1841 *Baker 78, NewGrD 80*
Savary, Jean Nicolas 1786-1853 *NewGrD 80*
Savary, Louis Michael 1936- *AmSCAP 80*
Savasta, Rosario *PupTheA*
Savattier, Gerard 1932- *IntWWM 77, -80*
Savchenko, Igor 1906-1950 *DcFM, FilmEn*
Saveiiev, I *Film 2*
Savery, Carl Maria 1897- *IntWWM 77, WhoMus 72*
Savery, Finn 1933- *IntWWM 77, -80*
Savery, Janne 1938- *IntWWM 80*
Savetta, Antonio *NewGrD 80*
Savignano, Luciana 1943- *CnOxB*
Savile, Isabel *WhoMus 72*
Savile, Jeremy *NewGrD 80, OxMus*
Savill, Patrick Stanley 1909- *IntWWM 77, -80, WhoMus 72*
Saville, DeSacia *Film 2*
Saville, Mrs. E Faucit d1879 *NotNAT B*
Saville, Edmund Faucit 1811-1857 *NotNAT B*
Saville, Eugenia Curtis 1913- *IntWWM 77, -80*
Saville, Frances 1863-1935 *Baker 78*
Saville, Gus 1857-1934 *Film 2, WhScrn 74, -77, WhoHol B*
Saville, J Faucit d1855 *NotNAT B*
Saville, Mrs. J Faucit d1889 *NotNAT B*
Saville, Jack *Film 1*
Saville, Kate d1922 *NotNAT B*
Saville, Reginald John 1922- *WhoMus 72*
Saville, T G d1934 *NotNAT B*
Saville, Victor 1897-1979 *BiDFilm, -81, FilmEn, FilmgC, HalFC 80, IlWWBF, -A, IntMPA 77, -75, -76, -78, -79, OxFilm, WorEFlm*
Savin, Francisco 1929- *Baker 78, DcCM*
Savina, Maria d1915 *NotNAT B*
Savina, Vera *CnOxB*
Savine, Alexander 1881-1949 *Baker 78*
Savini, Tom *WhoHrs 80*
Savinio, Alberto 1891-1956 *NewGrD 80*
Savino, Domenico 1882- *AmSCAP 66, -80, ConAmC A*
Savino, Jo 1935- *CnOxB*
Savio, Isaias 1900- *IntWWM 77, -80*
Savio, Johann Baptist *NewGrD 80*
Savioli, Alessandro 1544-1623? *NewGrD 80*
Savion *NewGrD 80*
Savioni, Mario 1608-1685 *NewGrD 80*
Savits, Jocza 1847-1915 *EncWT*
Savitsky, Viacheslav *Film 2*
Savitsyew, P *WhoMus 72*
Savitt, Jan d1948 *BgBands 74[port]*
Savitt, Jan 1908-1948 *BiDAmM*
Savitt, Jan 1913-1948 *AmSCAP 66, -80, CmpEPM*
Savo, Jimmie 1895-1960 *Ent*
Savo, Jimmy d1960 *AmPS B, PlP&P[port], WhoHol B*
Savo, Jimmy 1895-1960 *EncMT, HalFC 80, NotNAT A, -B, WhThe*
Savo, Jimmy 1896-1960 *BiDAmM, JoeFr[port], WhScrn 74, -77*
Savoie, Andre Sebastien 1935- *IntWWM 77*
Savoie, Robert 1927- *WhoOp 76*
Savoir, Alfred 1883-1934 *McGEWD, NotNAT B*
Savonese, Il *NewGrD 80*
Savory, Gerald 1909- *CnMD, WhoThe 72, -77*
Savouret, Alain Louis Camille 1942- *IntWWM 80*
Savoy, Houston *WhScrn 77*
Savoy, James *AmSCAP 80*
Savoy Brown *ConMuA 80A, IlEncR*
Savoy Sultans *BiDAmM*
Sawa, Victor Norman 1950- *IntWWM 77*
Sawallisch, Wolfgang 1923- *Baker 78, CmOp, IntWWM 77, -80, MusSN[port], NewEOp 71, NewGrD 80, WhoMus 72, WhoOp 76*
Sawamura, Kunitaro 1905-1974 *WhScrn 77*
Sawbridge, Edward Hugh Frere 1932- *WhoMus 72*
Sawelson, Mel 1929- *IntMPA 77, -75, -76, -78, -79, -80*
Sawerthal *NewGrD 80*
Sawicka, Olga 1932- *CnOxB*
Sawtell, Paul *HalFC 80*
Sawtell, Paul 1906- *AmSCAP 66, -80*
Sawyer, Carl 1921- *BiE&WWA, NotNAT*
Sawyer, Charles Carrol 1833- *BiDAmM*
Sawyer, Charles P d1935 *NotNAT B*
Sawyer, Connie *WhoHol A*
Sawyer, Dorie 1897- *WhThe*
Sawyer, Ivy 1896- *CmpEPM, EncMT, WhThe*
Sawyer, Jean *AmSCAP 66*
Sawyer, Joe 1901- *HolCA[port]*
Sawyer, Joe 1908- *ForYSC, MovMk, Vers B[port], WhoHol A*
Sawyer, Joseph 1901- *FilmgC, HalFC 80*
Sawyer, Laura 1885-1970 *Film 1, WhScrn 74, -77, WhoHol B*
Sawyer, Pamela Joan *AmSCAP 80*
Sawyer, Philip John 1948- *IntWWM 77, -80*
Sax *NewGrD 80*
Sax, Adolphe 1814-1894 *Baker 78, BnBkM 80, MusMk, NewGrD 80*
Sax, Alphonse 1822-1874 *NewGrD 80*
Sax, Antoine 1822-1874 *NewGrD 80*
Sax, Antoine Joseph 1814-1894 *BnBkM 80*
Sax, Antoine-Joseph 1814-1894 *NewGrD 80*
Sax, Charles-Joseph 1791-1865 *Baker 78, NewGrD 80*
Sax, S *WhoMus 72*
Saxby, Joseph 1910- *WhoMus 72*
Saxby, Thomas Church 1880- *WhoMus 72*
Saxe, Templar d1935 *WhoHol B*
Saxe, Templar 1865-1935 *WhScrn 77*
Saxe, Templar 1866-1935 *NotNAT B*
Saxe, Temple *Film 1, -2*
Saxe, Templer *TwYS*
Saxe, Templer 1866-1935 *WhoStg 1906, -1908*
Saxe-Meiningen, Georg II, Duke Of 1826-1914 *NotNAT B*
Saxon, Christian Karl *NewGrD 80*

Saxon, David 1919- *AmSCAP 66, -80*
Saxon, Grace 1912- *AmSCAP 66, -80*
Saxon, Hugh A 1869-1945 *Film 2, WhScrn 74, -77, WhoHol B*
Saxon, John 1935- *FilmgC, ForYSC, HalFC 80, IntMPA 77, -75, -76, -78, -79, -80, MotPP, MovMk, WhoHol A, WhoHrs 80[port]*
Saxon, Marie 1904-1941 *NotNAT B, WhScrn 77*
Saxon-Snell, H *Film 2*
Saxton, Beryl 1934- *IntWWM 80*
Saxton, S Earl 1919- *IntWWM 77, -80*
Saxton, Stanley 1904- *AmSCAP 66, -80, ConAmC A*
Say, Edith Joan 1915- *WhoMus 72*
Sayao, Balduina DeOliveira 1902- *BnBkM 80, NewGrD 80*
Sayao, Bidu 1902- *Baker 78, BnBkM 80, CmOp, MusSN[port], NewEOp 71, NewGrD 80*
Sayer, Leo 1948- *ConMuA 80A, IlEncR, RkOn 2[port]*
Sayers, Dorothy Leigh 1893-1957 *CnMD, ModWD, NotNAT B, WhThe*
Sayers, Harry d1934 *NotNAT B*
Sayers, Henry J 1854-1932 *BiDAmM*
Sayers, Jo Ann 1918- *WhoHol A*
Sayers, Peter Esmonde 1942- *AmSCAP 80*
Sayers, Vera Winifred 1912- *IntWWM 77, -80, WhoMus 72*
Saygun, Ahmed Adnan 1907- *Baker 78, CpmDNM 75, DcCM*
Saygun, Ahmet Adnan 1907- *NewGrD 80*
Sayin, Hidayet 1929- *REnWD[port]*
Sayler, Oliver Martin 1887-1958 *WhThe*
Sayles, Charles 1948- *BluesWW[port]*
Sayles, Emanuel 1905- *NewOrJ[port]*
Sayles, Francis H 1892-1944 *WhScrn 74, -77, WhoHol B*
Sayles, George 1880?- *NewOrJ[port]*
Sayles, Manny 1907- *WhoJazz 72*
Saylor, Bruce Stuart 1946- *AmSCAP 80, ConAmC, IntWWM 77, -80*
Saylor, Katie *WhoHol A*
Saylor, Oliver Martin 1887-1958 *NotNAT B*
Saylor, Richard 1926- *ConAmC*
Saylor, Sid 1895-1962 *FilmEn*
Saylor, Syd 1895-1862 *ForYSC*
Saylor, Syd 1895-1962 *FilmEn, Film 2, NotNAT B, Vers B[port], WhScrn 74, -77, WhoHol B*
Sayn-Wittgenstein-Berleburg, Count F E 1837-1915 *Baker 78*
Sayne, Lambert De *NewGrD 80*
Sayre, Bigelow d1975 *WhScrn 77, WhoHol C*
Sayre, C Bigelow *WhoHol A*
Sayre, Jeffrey 1901-1974 *WhScrn 77, WhoHol B*
Sayre, Theodore Burt 1874- *WhThe, WhoStg 1906, -1908*
Sayve, De *NewGrD 80*
Sayve, Arnold De 1574?-1618 *NewGrD 80*
Sayve, Erasme De 1563?-1632? *NewGrD 80*
Sayve, Lambert De 1548?-1614 *NewGrD 80*
Sayve, Lambert De 1594-1614 *Baker 78*
Sayve, Lampertus De 1548?-1614 *NewGrD 80*
Sayve, Mathias De 154-?-1619 *NewGrD 80*
Sayve, Mathias De 1576?-1616? *NewGrD 80*
Sayve, Mathieu De 154-?-1619 *NewGrD 80*
Sayve, Raso De 1563?-1632? *NewGrD 80*
Sazandarian, Tatevik 1916- *NewGrD 80*
Sazarina, Maria 1914-1959 *WhScrn 74, -77*
Sazonova, Julia *PupTheA*
Sbarbaro, Anthony 1897-1969 *AmSCAP 66, -80*
Sbarbaro, Tony 1897-1969 *NewOrJ*
Sbarra, Francesco 1611-1668 *NewGrD 80*
Sbriglia, Giovanni 1832-1916 *Baker 78, NewEOp 71*
Scabazzi, Petronio Maria Pio *NewGrD 80*
Scacchi, Marco 1600?-1687? *NewGrD 80*
Scaccia, Angelo Maria 1690?-1761 *NewGrD 80*
Scacciati, Bianca 1894-1948 *Baker 78*
Scadding, Thomas Joseph 1911- *WhoMus 72*
Scaduto, Joseph 1898-1943 *WhScrn 74, -77, WhoHol B*
Scaffen, Henricus *NewGrD 80*
Scafuro, Anthony Philip 1948- *AmSCAP 80*
Scaggs, Boz 1944- *ConMuA 80A, IlEncR[port], RkOn 2[port]*
Scaggs, William Royce 1944- *AmSCAP 80*
Scaglione, Nunzio 1890-1935 *NewOrJ*
Scaife, Edward 1912- *FilmEn*
Scaife, Gillian *WhThe*
Scaife, Ted 1912- *FilmgC, HalFC 80*
Scala, Flaminio *OxThe, PlP&P*
Scala, Francis 1819-1903 *BiDAmM*
Scala, Francis Maria 1819-1903 *Baker 78*
Scala, Gia 1933- *ForYSC*
Scala, Gia 1934-1972 *FilmEn, FilmgC, HalFC 80, MotPP, MovMk, WhScrn 77, WhoHol B*
Scala, Paulus *NewGrD 80*
Scalabrini, Paolo 1713-1806? *NewGrD 80*
Scalchi, Sofia 1850-1922 *Baker 78, NewEOp 71, NewGrD 80*
Scalcotas, Nikolaos *NewGrD 80*
Scalero, Rosario 1870-1954 *Baker 78, BiDAmM, ConAmC*
Scales, Prunella 1932- *WhoHol A, WhoThe 72, -77*
Scaletta, Orazio 1550?-1630 *NewGrD 80*
Scalichius, Paulus *NewGrD 80*
Scaliger, Julius Ceasar 1484-1588 *NotNAT B*
Scalitz, Paulus *NewGrD 80*
Scalzi, Carlo *NewGrD 80[port]*
Scalzi, Cichion *NewGrD 80[port]*
Scalzi, Edward Anthony 1918- *AmSCAP 66, -80*
Scammacca, Ortensio 1562-1648 *OxThe*
Scammon, P R *Film 2*
Scammon, Richard *PupTheA*
Scamozzi, Vicenzo 1552-1616 *EncWT*
Scamozzi, Vincenzo 1552-1616 *NotNAT B, OxThe, PlP&P*
Scampion *NewGrD 80*
Scandello, Antonio 1517-1580 *NewGrD 80*
Scandellus, Antonius 1517-1580 *NewGrD 80*
Scandrani, Fatma *WomWMM*
Scanlan, W James 1856-1898 *NotNAT B*
Scanlan, William J 1856-1898 *AmPS, -B, BiDAmM, PopAmC*
Scanlon, E *Film 2*
Scannell, Frank *ForYSC, WhoHol A*
Scannell, William J 1912-1963 *WhScrn 74, -77*
Scantlin, Ray 1947- *AmSCAP 80*
Scapita, Vincenzo d1656 *NewGrD 80*
Scapitta, Vincenzo d1656 *NewGrD 80*
Scappettone, Sandra *WomWMM*
Scarabelli, Damiano d1598? *NewGrD 80*
Scarabelli, Diamante Maria *NewGrD 80*
Scarabeus, Damiano d1598? *NewGrD 80*
Scarabino, Guillermo 1940- *IntWWM 77, -80*
Scaramella, Bernardino *NewGrD 80*
Scaramuccia, Filisteo *NewGrD 80*
Scarani, Giuseppe *NewGrD 80*
Scarborough, George 1875- *WhThe*
Scarborough, Linda Gail 1953- *IntWWM 77*
Scarborough, Mary Joanna 1932- *IntWWM 77*
Scardino, Don *WhoHol A*
Scardon, Paul d1954 *Film 1, MotPP, NotNAT B, WhoHol B*
Scardon, Paul 1875-1954 *ForYSC, TwYS A*
Scardon, Paul 1878-1954 *WhScrn 74, -77*
Scarfiotti, Ferdinando 1941- *WhoOp 76*
Scaria, Emil 1838-1886 *Baker 78, NewEOp 71, NewGrD 80*
Scaria, Emilia 1838-1886 *CmOp*
Scarlata *NewGrD 80*
Scarlatesco, Ion 1872-1922 *Baker 78*
Scarlatti *NewGrD 80*
Scarlatti, Alessandro 1660-1725 *Baker 78, BnBkM 80, CmOp, CmpBCM, DcCom 77[port], DcCom&M 79, GrComp[port], MusMk[port], NewEOp 71, NewGrD 80[port], OxMus*
Scarlatti, Anna Maria 1661-1703 *NewGrD 80*
Scarlatti, Domenico 1685-1757 *Baker 78, BnBkM 80[port], CmpBCM, CnOxB, DancEn 78, DcCom 77[port], DcCom&M 79, GrComp[port], MusMk, NewGrD 80[port], OxMus*
Scarlatti, Francesco 1666-1741? *NewGrD 80*
Scarlatti, Giuseppe 1718?-1777 *Baker 78, NewGrD 80*
Scarlatti, Melchiorra Brigida 1663-1736 *NewGrD 80*
Scarlatti, Pietro Filippo 1679-1750 *NewGrD 80*
Scarlatti, Tommaso 1669?-1760 *NewGrD 80*
Scarlet, John *PupTheA*
Scarmolin, A Louis 1890-1969 *AmSCAP 66, -80, ConAmC*
Scarmolin, Louis 1890-1969 *Baker 78*
Scarne, John *MagIID*
Scarpa, Salvatore 1918- *AmSCAP 66, -80*
Scarpinati, Nicholas Joseph 1944- *WhoOp 76*
Scarpini, Pietro 1911- *Baker 78, NewGrD 80*
Scarratt, Charles, III 1927- *AmSCAP 66*
Scarron, Paul 1610-1660 *CnThe, EncWT, Ent, McGEWD, OxThe, REnWD[port]*
Scarselli, Rinieri d1642? *NewGrD 80*
Scarselli, Riniero d1642? *NewGrD 80*
Scastelain, Jean *NewGrD 80*
Scatigna, Angelo *Film 2*
Scattolin, Pier Paolo 1949- *IntWWM 80*
Scavarda, Donald 1928- *ConAmC*
Scek, Ivan 1925- *IntWWM 77, -80*
Scelba, Anthony J 1947- *ConAmC*
Scellery, Pierre Borjon De *NewGrD 80*
Scelsi, Giacinto 1905- *Baker 78, NewGrD 80*
Scemana Chikly 1872-1950? *DcFM*
Schaab, Robert 1817-1887 *Baker 78*
Schaad, Roar 1941- *CpmDNM 78, -79, -80*
Schaaf, Edward Oswald 1869-1939 *Baker 78*
Schaal, Richard 1922- *NewGrD 80*
Schaale, Christian Friedrich *NewGrD 80*
Schaap, Jan 1928- *IntWWM 77, -80*
Schable, Robert 1873-1947 *Film 1, -2, WhScrn 74, -77, WhoHol B*
Schachinger, Hans 1485-1558? *NewGrD 80*
Schachinger, Johann 1485-1558? *NewGrD 80*
Schachner, Rudolf Joseph 1821-1896 *Baker 78*
Schacht, Al *JoeFr*
Schacht, Matthias Henriksen 1660-1700 *Baker 78, NewGrD 80*
Schacht, Theodor, Freiherr Von 1748-1823 *NewGrD 80*
Schacht, Theodor Von 1748-1823 *Baker 78*
Schachtel, Irving I 1909- *AmSCAP 66, -80*
Schachteli, Werner 1927- *WhoOp 76*
Schachteli, Werner 1934- *DancEn 78*
Schachter, Leon 1900-1974 *WhScrn 77*
Schachtschneider, Herbert 1919- *IntWWM 77, -80*
Schack, Benedikt 1758-1826 *Baker 78, CmOp, NewGrD 80*
Schack, David 1947- *ConAmC*
Schackelford, Floyd *Film 2*
Schacker, Marshall 1922- *IntMPA 77, -75, -76, -78, -79, -80*
Schad, Joseph 1812-1879 *Baker 78*
Schad, Walter C 1889-1966 *AmSCAP 66, -80, ConAmC*
Schadaeus, Abraham 1566-1626 *NewGrD 80*
Schadaus, Abraham 1566-1626 *NewGrD 80*
Schade, Abraham 1566-1626 *NewGrD 80*
Schade, Betty *Film 1, -2, TwYS*
Schade, Fritz *Film 1*
Schader, Freddie d1962 *NotNAT B*
Schadewitz, Carl 1887-1945 *Baker 78*
Schadlich, David *NewGrD 80*
Schaefer, Albert 1916-1942 *WhScrn 74, -77, WhoHol B*
Schaefer, Andre Jacques 1942- *IntWWM 77*
Schaefer, Anne *Film 1, -2*
Schaefer, Billy Kent *Film 2*
Schaefer, Carl *IntMPA 77, -75, -76, -78, -79, -80*
Schaefer, Carl Fellman 1903- *CreCan 2*
Schaefer, Charles N 1864-1939 *WhScrn 74, -77, WhoHol B*
Schaefer, Eugene V 1911- *IntWWM 77*
Schaefer, George 1920- *BiE&WWA, FilmEn, FilmgC, HalFC 80, IntMPA 77, -75, -76, -78, -79, -80, NewYTET, NotNAT, WhoThe 72, -77*
Schaefer, George J 1888- *IntMPA 77, -75, -76, -78, -79*
Schaefer, George McCord 1928- *WhoOp 76*
Schaefer, Hal 1925- *AmSCAP 80*
Schaefer, Hans Joachim 1923- *WhoOp 76*
Schaefer, Hansjurgen 1930- *NewGrD 80*
Schaefer, Harold Herman 1925- *AmSCAP 66, ConAmC A*
Schaefer, Jack 1907- *IntMPA 77, -75, -76, -78, -79, -80*
Schaefer, Karl Ludolf 1866-1931 *Baker 78*
Schaefer, Mary Cherubin 1886- *BiDAmM*
Schaefer, Natalie 1912- *MovMk[port]*

Schaefer, Patricia 1930- *IntWWM 77, -80*
Schaefer, Robert E 1926- *AmSCAP 80*
Schaefer, Theodor 1904-1969 *Baker 78, NewGrD 80*
Schaefer, William Arkwell 1918- *AmSCAP 66, -80, IntWWM 77, -80*
Schaefer, Willis H 1928- *AmSCAP 66, -80, ConAmC*
Schaeffer, A L *Film 2*
Schaeffer, Don 1935- *AmSCAP 80*
Schaeffer, Donald 1935- *AmSCAP 66*
Schaeffer, Mary 1893-1977 *AmSCAP 66, -80*
Schaeffer, Paul *NewGrD 80, OxMus*
Schaeffer, Pierre 1910- *Baker 78, BnBkM 80, DcCM, NewGrD 80*
Schaeffer, Pierre 1911- *DcFM*
Schaeffner, Andre 1895- *Baker 78, NewGrD 80*
Schaenen, Lee 1925- *WhoOp 76*
Schaeuble, Hans-Joachim 1906- *NewGrD 80, WhoMus 72*
Schafer, Bob 1897-1943 *AmSCAP 66, -80*
Schafer, Daniel Joseph 1952- *AmSCAP 80*
Schafer, Dirk 1873-1931 *Baker 78, NewGrD 80, OxMus*
Schafer, Helen Schafmeister *AmSCAP 80*
Schafer, Lawrence 1940- *CreCan 1, WhoOp 76*
Schafer, Milton 1920- *AmSCAP 66, -80, BiE&WWA*
Schafer, Murray 1933- *CreCan 2*
Schafer, Natalie 1912- *BiE&WWA, FilmEn, FilmgC, ForYSC, HalFC 80, HolCA[port], IntMPA 77, -75, -76, -78, -79, -80, NotNAT, WhThe, WhoHol A*
Schafer, R Murray 1933- *Baker 78, CreCan 2, DcCM, IntWWM 80, NewGrD 80[port]*
Schafer, Reuben *WhoHol A*
Schafer, Walter Erich 1901- *CnMD*
Schaff, Jan 1903- *AmSCAP 66, -80*
Schaff, Sylvia 1916- *AmSCAP 66, -80*
Schaffen, Heinrich *NewGrD 80*
Schaffen, Henri *NewGrD 80*
Schaffen, Henrichus *NewGrD 80*
Schaffen, Henricus *NewGrD 80*
Schaffer, August 1814-1879 *Baker 78*
Schaffer, Boguslaw 1929- *Baker 78, DcCM, NewGrD 80*
Schaffer, Jane *WomWMM*
Schaffer, Johann Wilhelm *NewGrD 80*
Schaffer, Julius 1823-1902 *Baker 78*
Schaffer, Michael 1937-1978 *NewGrD 80*
Schaffer, Paul *NewGrD 80*
Schaffer, Peggy *Film 2*
Schaffner, Franklin 1920- *HalFC 80, IntMPA 75, -76, -78, -79, -80*
Schaffner, Franklin J 1920- *BiDFilm, -81, FilmEn, FilmgC, IntMPA 77, MovMk[port], NewYTET, WorEFlm*
Schaffner, Franklin L 1920- *OxFilm*
Schaffrath, Christoph 1709-1763 *Baker 78, NewGrD 80*
Schafhautl, Karl Franz Emil Von 1803-1890 *Baker 78*
Schafmeister, Helen Louise 1900- *AmSCAP 80*
Schafrat, Christoph 1709-1763 *NewGrD 80*
Schafrath, Christoph 1709-1763 *NewGrD 80*
Schaik-Willing, Jeanne Van 1895- *CnMD*
Schak, Benedikt *NewGrD 80*
Schale, Christian Friedrich 1713-1800 *NewGrD 80*
Schalit, Heinrich 1886-1943 *BiDAmM, ConAmC, DcCM*
Schalk, Franz 1863-1931 *Baker 78, CmOp, NewEOp 71, NewGrD 80*
Schalk, Josef 1857-1900 *Baker 78*
Schall, Claus 1757-1835 *Baker 78, CnOxB*
Schall, Claus Nielsen 1757-1835 *NewGrD 80*
Schall, Ekkehard 1930- *EncWT*
Schalla, Hans 1904- *EncWT*
Schallert, William 1925- *ForYSC, WhoHol A, WhoHrs 80[port]*
Schamel, Johann Martin 1668-1742 *NewGrD 80*
Schamelius, Johann Martin 1668-1742 *NewGrD 80*
Schamotulinus, Venceslaus *NewGrD 80*
Schanfield, Moses *JoeFr*
Schang, Frederick 1893- *DancEn 78*
Schanke, Einar L 1927- *IntWWM 77*
Schankman, Sidney 1919- *IntWWM 77*
Schankman, Steve *ConMuA 80B*
Schanne, Margrethe 1921- *CnOxB, DancEn 78[port]*
Schanppecher, Melchior 1480?- *NewGrD 80*
Schantz, David Mathew 1953- *AmSCAP 80*
Schantz, Johan Filip Von 1835-1865 *NewGrD 80*
Schanzer, Wolfgang 1924- *IntWWM 77, -80*
Schanzlin, Hans Peter 1916- *NewGrD 80*
Schapiro, Herb *NatPD[port]*
Schappert, Edna 1934- *NatPD[port]*
Scharf, Herman 1901-1963 *NotNAT B, WhScrn 74, -77, WhoHol B*
Scharf, Walter 1910- *AmSCAP 66, -80, HalFC 80*
Scharfe, Gustav 1835-1892 *Baker 78*
Scharfenberg, William 1819-1895 *Baker 78, BiDAmM*
Scharff, Lester *Film 2*
Scharfman, Nitra 1938- *AmSCAP 80*
Scharlach, Ed 1943- *AmSCAP 80*
Scharrer, August 1866-1936 *Baker 78*
Scharrer, Irene 1888-1971 *Baker 78, NewGrD 80*
Scharres, Barbara *WomWMM B*
Scharwenka, Ludwig Philipp 1847-1917 *OxMus*
Scharwenka, Philipp 1847-1917 *Baker 78, NewGrD 80*
Scharwenka, Xaver 1850-1924 *Baker 78, NewGrD 80[port], OxMus*
Schary, Dore 1905-1980 *BiDFilm, -81, BiE&WWA, ConDr 73, -77, DcFM, FilmEn, FilmgC, HalFC 80, IntMPA 77, -75, -76, -78, -79, -80, MGM A[port], ModWD, NatPD[port], NotNAT, OxFilm, WhoThe 72, -77, WorEFlm*
Schary, Elke 1947- *WhoOp 76*
Schastelain, Jean *NewGrD 80*
Schat, Peter 1935- *Baker 78, DcCM, IntWWM 80, NewGrD 80*
Schattenberg, Thomas 1580?-1622? *NewGrD 80*
Schattner, Meyer 1911- *BiE&WWA, NotNAT*
Schatz, Albert 1839-1910 *Baker 78*
Schatzberg, Jerry *FilmEn, FilmgC, HalFC 80, IntMPA 77, -75, -76, -78, -79, -80*
Schau, Michael P 1945- *ConAmTC*
Schaub, Hans Ferdinand 1880-1965 *Baker 78*
Schauer, Patricia Kay 1947- *AmSCAP 80*
Schauffler, Elsie T d1935 *NotNAT B*
Schauffler, Robert Haven 1879-1964 *Baker 78*
Schaufuss, Frank 1921- *CnOxB, DancEn 78*
Schaufuss, Peter 1949- *CnOxB*
Schauler, Eileen *WhoOp 76*
Schaum, John W 1905- *AmSCAP 66, -80, Baker 78, ConAmC*
Schaumburg, John Hays 1923- *AmSCAP 66*
Schavran, Henrietta *IntWWM 77, -80*
Schayer, Richard 1882- *FilmEn*
Schayk, Toer Van 1936- *CnOxB*
Schear, Robert 1936- *BiE&WWA, NotNAT*
Schebek, Edmund 1819-1895 *Baker 78*
Schebest, Agnese 1813-1869 *Baker 78*
Schechinger, Johann *NewGrD 80*
Schechner, Anna 1806-1860 *NewGrD 80*
Schechner, Nanette 1806-1860 *NewGrD 80*
Schechner, Richard 1934- *BiE&WWA, NotNAT, WhoThe 72, -77*
Schechner-Waagen, Nanette 1806-1860 *NewGrD 80*
Schechtman, Carolyn R 1924- *AmSCAP 80*
Schechtman, Saul 1924- *AmSCAP 80, BiE&WWA, NotNAT*
Scheck, George 1911- *AmSCAP 66, -80*
Scheck, Gustav 1901- *NewGrD 80*
Schede, Paul Melissus 1539-1602 *NewGrD 80*
Schedl, Gerhard 1957- *IntWWM 80*
Schedlich, David 1607-1687 *NewGrD 80*
Scheeder, Louis W 1946- *NotNAT*
Scheel, Fritz 1852-1907 *Baker 78, BiDAmM*
Scheepers, Martin 1933- *DancEn 78*
Scheer, Philip *WhoHrs 80*
Scheerer, Maud d1961 *NotNAT B*
Scheerer, Theophil *NewGrD 80*
Schefer, Mandy *WomWMM*
Scheff, Fritzi 1879-1954 *AmPS B, Baker 78, CmOp, CmpEPM, EncMT, Film 1, NewEOp 71, NewGrD 80, NotNAT B, WhScrn 74, -77, WhThe, WhoHol B, WhoStg 1906, -1908*
Scheffel, Herb *PupTheA*
Scheffel, Oswald *Film 2*
Scheffel-Stein, Renata *WhoMus 72*
Scheffel-Stein, Renata 1914- *IntWWM 77, -80*
Scheffer, Eric Johan George 1909- *IntWWM 80*
Scheffer, Johann Wilhelm *NewGrD 80*
Scheffer, Paul *NewGrD 80*
Scheffler, Johannes *NewGrD 80*
Scheffler, Siegfried 1892-1969 *Baker 78*
Schehade, Georges 1906- *CnMD*
Schehade, Georges 1910- *CroCD, EncWT, Ent, McGEWD[port], ModWD, REnWD*
Schehl, J Alfred 1882-1937 *BiDAmM*
Scheib, Charles J 1891- *AmSCAP 66, -80*
Scheibe, Johann 1680?-1748 *NewGrD 80*
Scheibe, Johann Adolf 1708-1776 *Baker 78*
Scheibe, Johann Adolph 1708-1776 *NewGrD 80*
Scheibel, Gottfried Ephraim 1696-1759 *NewGrD 80*
Scheibler, Johann Heinrich 1777-1837 *Baker 78, NewGrD 80*
Scheibler, Johann Heinrich 1777-1838 *OxMus*
Scheid, Paul 1938- *IntWWM 77, -80*
Scheid, Peter 1938- *IntWWM 77*
Scheidemann, David *NewGrD 80*
Scheidemann, Heinrich 1595?-1663 *NewGrD 80*
Scheidemann, Heinrich 1596?-1663 *Baker 78, MusMk, OxMus*
Scheidemantel, Karl 1859-1923 *Baker 78, CmOp, NewGrD 80[port]*
Scheider, Georg Abraham 1770-1839 *NewGrD 80*
Scheider, Roy *IntMPA 77, -75, -76, -78, -79, -80*
Scheider, Roy 1934- *FilmgC, HalFC 80, WhoHol A, WhoHrs 80*
Scheider, Roy 1935- *FilmEn*
Scheidler, Johann David 1748-1802 *NewGrD 80*
Scheidt, Gottfried 1593-1661 *NewGrD 80*
Scheidt, Samuel 1587-1654 *Baker 78, BnBkM 80, GrComp[port], MusMk, NewGrD 80[port], OxMus*
Scheier, Mary *PupTheA*
Scheiffelhuet, Jakob 1647-1709 *NewGrD 80*
Scheiffelhut, Jacob 1647-1709 *NewGrD 80*
Scheiffelhut, Jakob 1647-1709 *NewGrD 80*
Schein, Ann 1939- *WhoMus 72*
Schein, Johann Hermann 1586-1630 *Baker 78, GrComp, MusMk, NewGrD 80[port], OxMus*
Schein, Julius 1910-1969 *AmSCAP 66, -80*
Scheinpflug, Paul 1875-1937 *Baker 78, NewGrD 80*
Scheinpflugova, Olga 1902-1968 *WhScrn 74, -77*
Schelb, Josef 1894- *NewGrD 80*
Schelble, Johann Nepomuk 1789-1837 *Baker 78, NewGrD 80*
Schelkopf, Anton 1914- *IntMPA 77, -75, -78, -79*
Schell, Carl *ForYSC*
Schell, Catherine *WhoHol A*
Schell, Karl *WhoHol A*
Schell, Maria 1926- *BiDFilm, -81, FilmAG WE, FilmEn, FilmgC, ForYSC, HalFC 80, IntMPA 80, MotPP, MovMk[port], WhoHol A, WorEFlm*
Schell, Maximilian 1930- *BiE&WWA, FilmAG WE[port], FilmEn, FilmgC, ForYSC, HalFC 80, IntMPA 77, -75, -76, -78, -79, -80, MotPP, MovMk[port], WhoHol A, WorEFlm*
Schell, Norman Clark 1944- *AmSCAP 80*
Schell, Ronnie *JoeFr*
Schellang, August 1905-1958 *NewOrJ*
Schelle, Johann 1648?-1701 *NewGrD 80*
Schelle, Karl Eduard 1816-1882 *Baker 78*
Schelle, Michael 1950- *AmSCAP 80*
Schellen, Fernando 1934- *WhoOp 76*
Schellendorf, Hans Bronsart Von *NewGrD 80*
Scheller, George *Film 2*
Scheller, Stanley 1940- *IntWWM 77, -80*
Schelling, Ernest 1876-1939 *AmSCAP 66, -80, Baker 78, BiDAmM, ConAmC, NewGrD 80, OxMus*
Schelling, F W J 1775-1854 *NewGrD 80*
Schellow, Erich 1915- *EncWT, WhThe*

Schemelli, Georg Christian 1676?-1762 *NewGrD 80*
Schemmel, Georg Christian 1676?-1762 *NewGrD 80*
Schemper, Raul 1921- *IntWWM 77, -80*
Schenck, Aubrey 1908- *FilmEn, FilmgC, HalFC 80, IntMPA 77, -75, -76, -78, -79, -80*
Schenck, Earl *Film 1, -2*
Schenck, Jan 1660?-1712? *NewGrD 80[port]*
Schenck, Jean d1715? *Baker 78*
Schenck, Joan 1660?-1712? *NewGrD 80[port]*
Schenck, Joe 1892-1930 *JoeFr, NotNAT B, WhoHol B*
Schenck, Johann 1660?-1712? *NewGrD 80[port]*
Schenck, Johann 1753-1836 *Baker 78*
Schenck, Johannes 1660?-1712? *NewGrD 80[port]*
Schenck, Joseph 1877-1961 *OxFilm*
Schenck, Joseph M 1878-1961 *FilmEn, FilmgC, HalFC 80, TwYS B*
Schenck, Joseph T 1891-1930 *WhScrn 74, -77*
Schenck, Nicholas M 1881-1969 *DcFM, FilmEn, FilmgC, HalFC 80, MGM A[port], OxFilm*
Schenck, Nicolas 1881-1969 *WorEFlm*
Schenck, Pyotr 1870-1915 *Baker 78*
Schenfeld, Rina 1938- *CnOxB*
Schenk, Dorothy Ellen 1941- *IntWWM 77*
Schenk, Erich 1902-1974 *Baker 78, NewGrD 80*
Schenk, Johann Baptist 1753-1836 *NewGrD 80[port]*
Schenk, Johannes *NewGrD 80*
Schenk, Joseph M 1877-1961 *DcFM*
Schenk, Manfred *WhoOp 76*
Schenk, Otto 1930- *CmOp, EncWT, NewGrD 80, WhoOp 76*
Schenkel, Bernard 1941- *IntWWM 77, -80*
Schenkel, Chris *NewYTET*
Schenker, Friedrich 1942- *IntWWM 77, -80, NewGrD 80*
Schenker, Heinrich 1868-1935 *Baker 78, NewGrD 80, OxMus*
Schenker, Joel 1903- *BiE&WWA, NotNAT*
Schenkman, Peter 1937- *IntWWM 77, -80*
Schenstrom, Carl 1881-1942 *FilmEn, Film 2*
Schentzer, Hans *NewGrD 80*
Schentzer, Johannes *NewGrD 80*
Schepard, Eric *BiE&WWA*
Schepp, Dieter d1962 *NotNAT B*
Scher, John *ConMuA 80B*
Scher, William 1900-1975 *AmSCAP 66, -80*
Scherbaum, Adolf 1909- *NewGrD 80*
Scherchen, Hermann 1891-1966 *Baker 78, BnBkM 80, CmOp, MusSN[port], NewEOp 71, NewGrD 80[port]*
Scherchen-Hsiao, Tona 1938- *NewGrD 80*
Scheremetiev, Alexander *Baker 78*
Scherer *NewGrD 80*
Scherer, B L 1949- *IntWWM 77, -80*
Scherer, Barry 1949- *ConAmC*
Scherer, Frank H 1897- *AmSCAP 66, -80, ConAmC A*
Scherer, Hans *NewGrD 80*
Scherer, Hans d1611 *NewGrD 80*
Scherer, Jakob d1574? *NewGrD 80*
Scherer, Michael *NewGrD 80*
Scherer, N *NewGrD 80*
Scherer, Ray *NewYTET*
Scherer, Sebastian Anton 1631-1712 *NewGrD 80*
Scherffenstein, Martin Kinner Von *NewGrD 80*
Scherffer VonScherffenstein, Wencel 1603-1674 *NewGrD 80*
Scherffer VonScherffenstein, Wenceslaus 1603-1674 *NewGrD 80*
Scherffer VonScherffenstein, Wenzel 1603-1674 *NewGrD 80*
Scherick, Edgar J *IntMPA 77, -76, -78, -79, -80, NewYTET*
Schering, Arnold 1877-1941 *Baker 78, NewGrD 80*
Scherler, Barbara 1938- *WhoOp 76*
Scherley, Joseph *NewGrD 80*
Scherman, Barbara d1935 *WhScrn 74, -77*
Scherman, Robert 1920- *AmSCAP 66, -80*
Scherman, Thomas 1917-1979 *Baker 78, NewGrD 80*
Schermer, Jules *IntMPA 77, -75, -76, -78, -79, -80*
Schermerhorn, Kenneth 1929- *Baker 78, CnOxB, DancEn 78, IntWWM 77, -80, NewGrD 80, WhoMus 72*
Schermerhorn, Kenneth 1930- *BiDAmM*
Schermerhorn, Maja 1934- *IntWWM 77, -80*
Scherndorp, Philipp *NewGrD 80*
Scherreiks, Herbert Theodor 1930- *WhoOp 76*
Scherrer, N *NewGrD 80*
Schertzer, Hymie 1909- *CmpEPM*
Schertzinger, Victor 1880-1941 *FilmEn, FilmgC, HalFC 80*
Schertzinger, Victor 1888-1941 *WorEFlm*
Schertzinger, Victor 1889-1941 *TwYS A*
Schertzinger, Victor 1890-1941 *AmPS, AmSCAP 66, -80, BestMus, BiDAmM, CmpEPM, NotNAT B, PopAmC*
Scherzer *NewGrD 80*
Scherzer, Kurt 1895-1962 *NewGrD 80*
Scherzer, Manfred 1933- *IntWWM 77, -80*
Scherzer, Otto 1821-1886 *Baker 78*
Schesch, Elizabeth Yassin 1913- *IntWWM 77*
Schetky 1776-1831 *Baker 78*
Schetky, J George 1776-1831 *NewGrD 80*
Schetky, Johann Georg Christoff 1740-1824 *Baker 78*
Schetky, Johann Georg Christoph 1737-1824 *NewGrD 80*
Schetky, John George 1776-1831 *BiDAmM*
Scheu, Just 1903-1956 *WhScrn 74, -77*
Scheuenstuhl, Michael 1705-1770 *NewGrD 80*
Scheuer, Constance 1910-1962 *WhScrn 74, -77*
Scheuer, Philip K 1902- *BiE&WWA, IntMPA 75*
Scheuerle, Paul Norman 1926- *IntWWM 77, -80*
Scheuermann, Georg Caspar *NewGrD 80*
Scheuermann, Lilly 1945- *CnOxB*
Scheurleer, Daniel Francois 1855-1927 *Baker 78, NewGrD 80*
Scheurwater, Marinus 1924- *IntWWM 77, -80*
Scheve, Edward Benjamin 1865-1924 *BiDAmM*
Schevill, James 1920- *ConDr 73, -77, NatPD[port]*
Schiaffino, Rosanna 1939- *FilmEn, FilmgC, ForYSC, HalFC 80, WhoHol A*
Schiaffino, Rosanna 1940- *FilmAG WE*
Schiafino, Carlos 1932- *CnOxB, DancEn 78*
Schiassi, Gaetano Maria 1698-1754 *NewGrD 80*
Schiavetti, Giulio d1565? *NewGrD 80*
Schiavetto, Giulio d1565? *NewGrD 80*
Schiavi, Felice Rolando 1931- *WhoOp 76*
Schiavone, James 1917- *IntMPA 77, -75, -76, -78, -79, -80*
Schiavone, John Sebastian 1947- *ConAmC*
Schibler, Armin 1920- *Baker 78, DcCM, IntWWM 80, NewGrD 80, WhoMus 72*
Schic, Anna Stella *WhoMus 72*
Schichart, Johann Christian *NewGrD 80*
Schicht, Johann Gottfried 1753-1823 *Baker 78, NewGrD 80*
Schichtl, Carl *PupTheA*
Schick, Elliot 1924- *IntMPA 79, -80*
Schick, Ernst 1756-1815 *NewGrD 80*
Schick, George 1908- *Baker 78*
Schick, Margarete Luise 1773-1809 *Baker 78, NewGrD 80*
Schickaneder *NewGrD 80*
Schickele, Peter 1935- *AmSCAP 66, -80, Baker 78, CpmDNM 78, -79, ConAmC, NewGrD 80*
Schickele, Rene 1883?-1940 *CnMD*
Schickhard, Johann Christian 1682?-1762 *NewGrD 80*
Schickhardt, Johann Christian 1682?-1762 *NewGrD 80*
Schickhart, Johann Christian 1682?-1762 *NewGrD 80*
Schidlof, Peter 1922- *IntWWM 77, -80, WhoMus 72*
Schidlowsky, Leon 1931- *Baker 78, DcCM, NewGrD 80*
Schiebe, Ernst Friedemann 1942- *IntWWM 77, -80*
Schiebler, Beverly Beasley 1937- *IntWWM 77, -80*
Schiebler, Carl Robert 1937- *IntWWM 77, -80*
Schiedermair, Ludwig 1876-1957 *Baker 78, NewGrD 80*
Schiedermayer, Johann Baptist 1779-1840 *Baker 78*
Schiedler, John *PupTheA*
Schiedmayer *NewGrD 80*
Schiedmayer, Adolf 1819-1890 *Baker 78*
Schiedmayer, Adolf 1820-1890 *NewGrD 80*
Schiedmayer, Balthasar 1711-1781 *Baker 78, NewGrD 80*
Schiedmayer, Hermann 1820-1891 *Baker 78*
Schiedmayer, Hermann 1821-1861 *NewGrD 80*
Schiedmayer, Johann David 1753-1805 *Baker 78, NewGrD 80*
Schiedmayer, Johann Lorenz 1786-1860 *Baker 78, NewGrD 80*
Schiedmayer, Julius 1822-1878 *Baker 78, NewGrD 80*
Schiedmayer, Max Julius *Baker 78*
Schiedmayer, Paul 1829-1890 *Baker 78, NewGrD 80*
Schieferdecker, Johann Christian 1679-1732 *NewGrD 80*
Schiefferdecker, Johann Christian 1679-1732 *NewGrD 80*
Schier, Ernest 1918- *ConAmTC*
Schier-Tiessen, Anneliese 1923- *IntWWM 77, -80*
Schierbeck, Poul 1888-1949 *NewGrD 80, OxMus*
Schieri, Fritz Franz 1922- *IntWWM 77*
Schieske, Alfred 1909-1970 *WhScrn 74, -77, WhoHol B*
Schiesser, Karen Ann 1938- *AmSCAP 80*
Schieti, Cesare d1600 *NewGrD 80*
Schietti, Cesare d1600 *NewGrD 80*
Schiever, Ernst 1844-1915 *NewGrD 80*
Schiff, Andras 1953- *IntWWM 77, -80*
Schiff, Heinrich 1952- *IntWWM 80*
Schiff, Larry *NatPD[port]*
Schiff, Suzanna *WomWMM B*
Schiffman, Harold 1928- *ConAmC*
Schiffman, Suzanne *WomWMM B*
Schifrin, Boris 1932- *EncJzS 70*
Schifrin, Lalo 1932- *Baker 78, BiDAmM, ConAmC, EncJzS 70, HalFC 80, IntMPA 77, -75, -76, -78, -79, -80, NewGrD 80, RkOn 2A, WorEFlm*
Schikaneder *NewGrD 80*
Schikaneder, Anna 1767-1862 *NewGrD 80*
Schikaneder, Emanuel 1751-1812 *Baker 78, BnBkM 80, EncWT, Ent[port], NewGrD 80[port], OxMus, OxThe*
Schikaneder, Johann Emanuel 1748-1812 *NewEOp 71*
Schikaneder, Karl 1770-1845 *NewGrD 80*
Schikaneder, Nanette 1767-1862 *NewGrD 80*
Schikaneder, Nanny 1767-1862 *NewGrD 80*
Schikaneder, Urban 1746-1818 *NewGrD 80*
Schikardt, Johann Christian *NewGrD 80*
Schikhart, Johann Christian *NewGrD 80*
Schildberger, Herman 1899- *WhoMus 72*
Schilder, Marie 1903- *IntWWM 77, -80*
Schildhause, Sol *NewYTET*
Schildkraut, Joseph d1964 *MotPP, WhoHol B*
Schildkraut, Joseph 1895-1964 *EncWT, FilmEn, Film 2, FilmgC, HalFC 80, HolCA[port], MovMk, NotNAT B, TwYS*
Schildkraut, Joseph 1896-1964 *BiE&WWA, FamA&A[port], ForYSC, NotNAT A, WhScrn 74, -77, WhThe*
Schildkraut, Rudolf 1862-1930 *EncWT, FilmEn*
Schildkraut, Rudolph 1862-1930 *FilmEn, Film 1, -2, TwYS*
Schildkraut, Rudolph 1865-1930 *NotNAT B, WhScrn 74, -77, WhoHol B*
Schildt, Melchior 1592?-1667 *NewGrD 80*
Schilke, Renold O 1910- *NewGrD 80*
Schillaci, Joseph John 1906- *AmSCAP 66, -80*
Schiller, Allan 1943- *IntWWM 77, -80, WhoMus 72*
Schiller, Fred *IntMPA 77, -75, -76, -78, -79, -80*
Schiller, Friedrich Von 1750-1805 *DcPup*
Schiller, Friedrich Von 1759-1805 *Baker 78, CnThe, EncWT, Ent[port], McGEWD[port], NewEOp 71, NewGrD 80, REnWD[port]*
Schiller, Henryk 1931- *NewGrD 80*

Schiller, Johann Christoph Friedrich Von 1759-1805 NotNAT A, -B, OxThe
Schiller, Leon 1887-1954 EncWT, Ent, NotNAT B, OxThe
Schiller, Norbert WhoHol A
Schiller, Thomas Bennett 1949- AmSCAP 80
Schilling, August E Gus 1908-1957 WhScrn 74, -77
Schilling, Bertha Agnes Lisette NewGrD 80
Schilling, Charles Walter 1915- IntWWM 77, -80
Schilling, George, Jr. NewOrJ
Schilling, George, Sr. 1886-1964 NewOrJ
Schilling, Gus 1908-1957 FilmgC, ForYSC, HalFC 80, Vers A[port], WhoHol B
Schilling, Gustav 1803-1880 Baker 78
Schilling, Gustav 1805-1880 NewGrD 80
Schilling, Hans Ludwig 1927- NewGrD 80
Schilling, Tom 1928- CnOxB
Schillinger, Joseph 1895-1943 Baker 78, BiDAmM, ConAmC, DcCM, NewGrD 80, OxMus
Schillings, Max Von 1868-1933 Baker 78, NewEOp 71, NewGrD 80, OxMus
Schillio, Emile Jacques 1909- AmSCAP 80
Schilson, Baron Janos 1750?-1809? NewGrD 80
Schimbraczky, Johannes NewGrD 80
Schimel, Adolph 1904- IntMPA 77, -75, -76, -78, -79, -80
Schiml, Marga 1945- WhoOp 76
Schimmel NewGrD 80
Schimmel, Herbert D 1927- IntMPA 77, -75, -76, -78, -79, -80
Schimmel, William Michael 1946- ConAmC, IntWWM 77, -80
Schimon, Adolf 1820-1887 Baker 78, NewGrD 80
Schimon-Regan, Anna 1841-1902 Baker 78
Schimpff, Mary Frances PupTheA
Schimrack, Johannes NewGrD 80
Schimrag, Johannes NewGrD 80
Schimrak, Johannes NewGrD 80
Schindel, Seymore 1907-1948 WhScrn 74, -77
Schindell, Cy 1907-1948 WhScrn 77
Schindelmeisser, Louis 1811-1864 NewGrD 80
Schindelmeisser, Ludwig 1811-1864 Baker 78
Schindler, Allan 1944- ConAmC
Schindler, Anton Felix 1795-1864 Baker 78, NewGrD 80, OxMus
Schindler, Hollis 1930- IntWWM 77, -80
Schindler, Kurt 1882-1935 Baker 78, BiDAmM, NewGrD 80, OxMus
Schindler, Poul Christian 1648-1740 NewGrD 80
Schindler, Walter 1909- IntWWM 77, -80
Schine, G David IntMPA 79, -80
Schine, Hildegarde Feldman 1903- AmSCAP 80
Schinelli, Achille 1882- WhoMus 72
Schinkel, Karl Friedrich 1781-1841 EncWT, NewGrD 80
Schinn, Georg Johann 1768-1833 NewGrD 80
Schinstine, William Joseph 1922- AmSCAP 80, CpmDNM 78, ConAmC
Schinstine, William Joseph 1923- AmSCAP 66
Schioler, Bolette 1901- IntWWM 77
Schioler, Victor 1899-1967 Baker 78
Schiorring, Niels 1743?-1798 NewGrD 80
Schiorring, Nils 1910- NewGrD 80
Schiotz, Aksel 1906-1975 Baker 78, MusSN[port], NewGrD 80, WhoHol C
Schipa, Carlo Film 2
Schipa, Tito 1888-1965 CmOp, NewGrD 80[port]
Schipa, Tito 1889-1965 Baker 78, MusSN[port], NewEOp 71, WhScrn 74, -77, WhoHol B
Schipper, Emil 1882-1957 CmOp, NewGrD 80
Schipper, Lee 1947- IntWWM 77
Schippers, Thomas 1930-1977 Baker 78, BiDAmM, BnBkM 80, CmOp, IntWWM 77, -80, MusSN[port], NewEOp 71, NewGrD 80, WhoMus 72, WhoOp 76
Schira, Francesco 1809-1883 NewGrD 80
Schirle, John PupTheA
Schirmer NewGrD 80
Schirmer, Astrid 1942- WhoOp 76
Schirmer, Ernest Charles 1865-1958 Baker 78, NewGrD 80
Schirmer, Ernst Ludwig Rudolf 1784- Baker 78
Schirmer, Gus, Jr. 1918- BiE&WWA, NotNAT
Schirmer, Gustav 1829-1893 Baker 78, NewGrD 80
Schirmer, Gustave 1864-1907 Baker 78
Schirmer, Gustave, III 1890-1965 Baker 78
Schirmer, Johann Georg Baker 78
Schirmer, Rudolf Ernest 1859-1919 BiDAmM
Schirmer, Rudolph Edward 1859-1919 Baker 78
Schirmer, Rudolph Edward 1919- AmSCAP 66, -80, Baker 78
Schirmer, Rudolphe BiE&WWA
Schiro, Luke 1903?- NewOrJ
Schiro, Tony 1899- NewOrJ[port]
Schiroli, Gregorio NewGrD 80
Schisgal, Murray 1926- BiE&WWA, CnMD SUP, ConDr 73, -77, CroCD, EncWT, Ent, McGEWD, ModWD, NotNAT, WhoThe 72, -77
Schiske, Karl 1916-1969 Baker 78, NewGrD 80, WhoMus 72
Schissler, Henry ConMuA 80B
Schiuma, Alfredo 1885-1963 Baker 78
Schjelderup, Gerhard 1859-1933 Baker 78, NewGrD 80
Schjelderup-Ebbe, Dag 1926- NewGrD 80
Schkraup, Franz 1801-1862 OxMus
Schlabach, Errol Weiss 1942- ConAmC
Schlacter, Marvin ConMuA 80B
Schladebach, Julius 1810-1872 Baker 78
Schlaf, Johannes 1862-1941 CnMD, ModWD
Schlag NewGrD 80
Schlag, Bruno 1879-1952 NewGrD 80
Schlag, Christian Gottlieb 1803-1889 NewGrD 80
Schlag, Johann Karl 1808-1869? NewGrD 80
Schlag, Oskar 1848-1918 NewGrD 80
Schlag, Reinhold 1874-1952? NewGrD 80
Schlag, Theodor 1847-1918 NewGrD 80
Schlager, Hans 1820-1885 Baker 78
Schlager, Karlheinz 1938- NewGrD 80
Schlaifer, Charles 1909- IntMPA 77, -75, -76, -78, -79, -80
Schlaks, Stephen David 1940- AmSCAP 80
Schlang, Joseph 1911- IntMPA 77, -75, -76, -78, -79, -80
Schlanger, Ben 1904-1971 BiE&WWA, NotNAT B
Schlatter, George NewYTET
Schlecker, Max 1930- IntWWM 77, -80
Schlegel NewGrD 80
Schlegel, August Wilhelm Von 1767-1845 EncWT, Ent[port], NotNAT B, OxThe, REnWD[port]
Schlegel, Friedrich Von 1772-1829 REnWD[port]
Schlegel, Johann Elias Von 1719-1749 EncWT, McGEWD, NotNAT B, OxThe
Schlegel, Leander 1844-1913 Baker 78, NewGrD 80
Schlegel, Margarete Film 2
Schleicher, Neil Clark 1931- IntWWM 80
Schleifer, Eliyahu Arieh 1939- IntWWM 77, -80
Schlein, Irving 1905- AmSCAP 66, -80, ConAmC
Schleinitz, Heinrich Conrad 1803-1881 Baker 78
Schlemm, Gustav Adolf 1902- IntWWM 77, -80, WhoMus 72
Schlemmer, Oskar 1888-1943 CnOxB, EncWT, Ent[port]
Schlenter, Paul d1916 NotNAT B
Schlenther, Paul 1854-1916 EncWT
Schlesinger NewGrD 80
Schlesinger, Adolf Martin 1769-1838 Baker 78
Schlesinger, Adolph Martin 1769-1838 NewGrD 80
Schlesinger, Carl 1808-1831 NewGrD 80
Schlesinger, Daniel 1799-1839 BiDAmM
Schlesinger, Heinrich 1810-1879 NewGrD 80
Schlesinger, Isidore d1949 NotNAT B
Schlesinger, John IntMPA 77, -75, -76, -78, -79, -80
Schlesinger, John 1925- OxFilm
Schlesinger, John 1926- BiDFilm, -81, DcFM, FilmEn, FilmgC, HalFC 80, IlWWBF, MovMk, WhoThe 72, -77, WorEFlm[port]
Schlesinger, Kathleen 1862-1953 Baker 78
Schlesinger, Leon 1884-1949 WorEFlm
Schlesinger, Maurice 1797-1871 Baker 78
Schlesinger, Maurice 1798-1871 NewGrD 80
Schlesinger, Moritz Adolf 1798-1871 NewGrD 80
Schlesinger, Riva WomWMM
Schlesinger, Sebastian Benson 1837-1917 Baker 78
Schlesinger, Sigmund 1835-1906 BiDAmM
Schletter, Annie d1944 NotNAT B
Schletterer, Hans Michel 1824-1893 Baker 78
Schlettow, Hans Adelbert 1888-1945 Film 2, WhScrn 77
Schlichter, Joseph CmpGMD
Schlichting, Fred Paul 1922- IntWWM 77, -80
Schlick, Arnolt 1460?-1521? NewGrD 80
Schlick, Arnolt 1460?-1525? Baker 78
Schlick, Rudolf NewGrD 80
Schlicker, Herman Leonhard 1902-1974 NewGrD 80
Schlieder, Frederick William 1873-1953 Baker 78, BiDAmM
Schlimbach NewGrD 80
Schlimbach, Johann Caspar 1777-1861 NewGrD 80
Schlindel, Valentin 1580?-1631? NewGrD 80
Schlissel, Jack 1922- BiE&WWA
Schlitt, John William 1950- AmSCAP 80
Schlitten, Don 1932- EncJzS 70
Schlitz, Don 1952- AmSCAP 80
Schloezer, Boris De 1881-1969 Baker 78
Schlogel, Xavier 1854-1889 Baker 78
Schlom, Herman IntMPA 75, -76
Schlondorff, Volker 1939- BiDFilm, -81, FilmEn, OxFilm
Schlossberg, Julian 1942- IntMPA 77, -76, -78, -79, -80
Schlosser, Adolf 1830-1913 Baker 78
Schlosser, Herbert S IntMPA 77, -75, -76, -78, -79, -80, NewYTET
Schlosser, Louis 1800-1886 Baker 78
Schlottmann, Louis 1826-1905 Baker 78
Schlumpf, Martin 1947- IntWWM 77, -80
Schlundel, Valentin NewGrD 80
Schluntz, Freddy 1918- IntWWM 77
Schlusnus, Heinrich 1888-1952 Baker 78, CmOp, NewEOp 71, NewGrD 80
Schlusselberg, Martin 1936- IntMPA 77, -75, -76, -78, -79, -80
Schmahl NewGrD 80
Schmahl, Christoph Friedrich 1739-1814 NewGrD 80
Schmahl, Georg Friedrich 1700-1773 NewGrD 80
Schmahl, Johann Adam 1704-1757 NewGrD 80
Schmahl, Johann Friedrich 1693-1737 NewGrD 80
Schmahl, Johann Michael 1654-1725 NewGrD 80
Schmaltzl, Wolfgang NewGrD 80
Schmalzle, Gerhard 1930- IntWWM 77, -80
Schmedes, Erik 1866-1931 CmOp, NewEOp 71, NewGrD 80
Schmedes, Erik 1868-1931 Baker 78
Schmeling, Gertrud Elisabeth NewEOp 71, NewGrD 80
Schmeling, Max 1905- What 1[port], WhoHol A
Schmeltzer, Andreas Anton 1653?-1701 NewGrD 80
Schmeltzer, Johann Heinrich NewGrD 80
Schmeltzer, Johann Heinrich 1620?-1680 NewGrD 80
Schmeltzl, Wolfgang 1500?-1566? NewGrD 80
Schmelzer, Andreas Anton 1653?-1701 NewGrD 80
Schmelzer, Johann Heinrich 1620?-1680 NewGrD 80
Schmelzer, Johann Heinrich 1623?-1680 Baker 78, BnBkM 80
Schmelzer, Peter Clemens NewGrD 80
Schmelzer VonEhrenruef, Andreas Anton 1653?-1701 NewGrD 80
Schmelzer VonEhrenruef, Johann Heinrich 1620?-1680 NewGrD 80
Schmelzl, Wolfgang 1500?-1561? Baker 78
Schmersal, Arthur H 1935- AmSCAP 80
Schmetzer, Georg 1642-1697 NewGrD 80
Schmezer, Georg 1642-1697 NewGrD 80
Schmicorer, Johann Abraham NewGrD 80

Schmid, Adolf 1868-1958 *AmSCAP 66, -80, Baker 78, NewGrD 80*
Schmid, Anton 1787-1857 *Baker 78, NewGrD 80*
Schmid, Balthasar 1705-1749 *NewGrD 80*
Schmid, Bernhard 1535-1592 *NewGrD 80*
Schmid, Bernhard 1567-1625 *NewGrD 80*
Schmid, Erich 1907- *IntWWM 77, -80, NewGrD 80*
Schmid, Ernst Fritz 1904-1960 *Baker 78, NewGrD 80*
Schmid, Ferdinand 1694?-1756 *NewGrD 80*
Schmid, Gretl 1910- *IntWWM 77, -80*
Schmid, Hans 1920- *IntWWM 77, -80*
Schmid, Heinrich Kaspar 1874-1953 *Baker 78, NewGrD 80*
Schmid, Johann C 1870-1951 *AmSCAP 80*
Schmid, Johann C 1890-1951 *AmSCAP 66*
Schmid, Johann Michael 1720?-1792 *NewGrD 80*
Schmid, Joseph Leonhard 1822-1912 *DcPup*
Schmid, Manfred Hermann 1947- *IntWWM 77, -80*
Schmid, Oscar 1936- *IntWWM 77, -80*
Schmid, Otto 1858-1931 *Baker 78*
Schmid-Gagnebin, Ruth 1921- *IntWWM 77, -80*
Schmidbauer, Hans-Benno 1934- *IntWWM 77, -80*
Schmidl, Carlo 1859-1943 *Baker 78, NewGrD 80*
Schmidli, Johannes 1722-1772 *NewGrD 80*
Schmidlin, Johannes 1722-1772 *NewGrD 80*
Schmidt *PupTheA*
Schmidt, Alexandra *Film 2*
Schmidt, Arthur P 1846-1921 *NewGrD 80*
Schmidt, Arthur Paul 1846-1921 *Baker 78, BiDAmM, OxMus*
Schmidt, Bernhard *NewGrD 80, OxMus*
Schmidt, Beverly *CmpGMD, DancEn 78*
Schmidt, Charles A 1923- *BiE&WWA, NotNAT*
Schmidt, Christian Martin 1942- *IntWWM 77, -80*
Schmidt, Dale 1942- *IntWWM 77, -80*
Schmidt, Diane Louise 1948- *ConAmC*
Schmidt, Douglas W 1942- *NotNAT, WhoOp 76, WhoThe 72, -77*
Schmidt, Erwin R 1890-1966 *AmSCAP 66, -80*
Schmidt, Franz 1874-1939 *Baker 78, DcCom 77, NewGrD 80, OxMus*
Schmidt, Gisele *CreCan 1*
Schmidt, Gustav 1816-1882 *Baker 78, NewGrD 80*
Schmidt, Hans 1930- *IntWWM 77, -80*
Schmidt, Harvey 1929- *AmSCAP 66, -80, BestMus, BiE&WWA, EncMT, NewCBMT, NewGrD 80, NotNAT, PopAmC SUP[port]*
Schmidt, Heinrich 1861-1923 *Baker 78*
Schmidt, Heinrich 1904- *WhoMus 72*
Schmidt, Jan *WomWMM B*
Schmidt, Jochen 1936- *CnOxB*
Schmidt, Johann Christoph *NewGrD 80*
Schmidt, Johann Christoph 1664-1728 *NewGrD 80*
Schmidt, Johann Michael *NewGrD 80*
Schmidt, Johann Michael 1728-1799 *NewGrD 80*
Schmidt, Johann Michael 1741-1793 *NewGrD 80*
Schmidt, Johann Philipp Samuel 1779-1853 *Baker 78, NewGrD 80*
Schmidt, John Henry *Baker 78*
Schmidt, Joseph 1904-1942 *Baker 78*
Schmidt, Kai *Film 2*
Schmidt, Karl 1869-1948 *Baker 78*
Schmidt, Kenneth Julius 1923- *IntWWM 77, -80*
Schmidt, Leopold 1860-1927 *Baker 78*
Schmidt, Liselotte Martha 1933- *IntWWM 77, -80*
Schmidt, Lloyd John 1924- *IntWWM 77, -80*
Schmidt, Manfred 1928- *WhoMus 72*
Schmidt, Manfred 1929- *WhoOp 76*
Schmidt, Nickel *NewGrD 80*
Schmidt, Ole 1928- *Baker 78, IntWWM 77, -80, NewGrD 80*
Schmidt, Peer *WhoHol A*
Schmidt, Peter *NewGrD 80*
Schmidt, Robert Louis *NewYTET*
Schmidt, Sharon Yvonne Davis 1937- *AmSCAP 80*
Schmidt, Trudeliese *WhoOp 76*
Schmidt, Warren F 1921- *ConAmC*
Schmidt, Willi 1910- *EncWT*
Schmidt, William Joseph, Jr. 1926- *AmSCAP 80, Baker 78, CpmDNM 75, -76, -77, -78, -79, -80, ConAmC, IntWWM 80*
Schmidt, Yves Rudner 1933- *IntWWM 77, -80*
Schmidt And Jones *BestMus*
Schmidt-Boelcke, Werner 1903- *IntWWM 77, -80*
Schmidt-Boelcke, Werner 1905- *WhoMus 72*
Schmidt-Gorg, Joseph 1897- *Baker 78, NewGrD 80*
Schmidt-Isserstedt, Hans 1900-1973 *Baker 78, BnBkM 80, CmOp, NewEOp 71, NewGrD 80, WhoMus 72*
Schmidt-Scheepmaker, Ernestine Augusta 1895- *IntWWM 77, -80*
Schmidtbonn, Wilhelm 1876-1952 *CnMD, ModWD, NotNAT B*
Schmidtmer, Christiane *WhoHol A*
Schmiedeknecht, Johann Matthaus 1660-1715 *NewGrD 80*
Schmiedel, Gottfried 1920- *IntWWM 77, -80*
Schmieder, Willy *Film 2*
Schmieder, Wolfgang 1901- *Baker 78, NewGrD 80*
Schmiedt, Siegfried 1756?-1799 *NewGrD 80*
Schmierer, Johann Abraham 1661-1719 *NewGrD 80*
Schmikerer, Johann Abraham 1661-1719 *NewGrD 80*
Schminke, Oscar Eberhard 1881-1969 *Baker 78, ConAmC*
Schmirer, Johann Abraham 1661-1719 *NewGrD 80*
Schmit, Camille 1908-1976 *NewGrD 80*
Schmit, Jean-Pierre 1904- *IntWWM 77, WhoMus 72*
Schmitke, Olive Marion 1920- *IntWWM 77*
Schmitt, Aloys 1788-1866 *Baker 78, OxMus*
Schmitt, Beate Gabriela 1949- *IntWWM 77, -80*
Schmitt, Bernhard *NewGrD 80*
Schmitt, Camille 1908-1976 *Baker 78*
Schmitt, Cecilia 1928- *IntWWM 77, -80*
Schmitt, Florent 1870-1958 *Baker 78, BnBkM 80, CompSN[port], MusMk, NewGrD 80, OxMus*
Schmitt, Georg Aloys 1827-1902 *Baker 78*
Schmitt, Georgius Adamus Josephus *NewGrD 80*
Schmitt, Hans 1835-1907 *Baker 78*
Schmitt, Homer Carl Christian 1911- *IntWWM 77, -80*
Schmitt, Jacob 1803-1853 *Baker 78*
Schmitt, Jacqueline *NewGrD 80*
Schmitt, Joseph 1734?-1791 *NewGrD 80*
Schmitt, Joseph 1871-1935 *WhScrn 74, -77*
Schmitt, Meinrad 1935- *IntWWM 80*
Schmitt, Saladin 1883-1951 *EncWT*
Schmitt-Sentner, Willy d1964 *NotNAT B*
Schmittbauer, Joseph Aloys 1718-1809 *NewGrD 80*
Schmittbaur, Joseph Aloys 1718-1809 *NewGrD 80*
Schmitts, Charles *PupTheA*
Schmitts, Hazel *PupTheA*
Schmitz, Arnold 1893- *Baker 78, NewGrD 80*
Schmitz, Claude M 1919- *IntWWM 77, -80*
Schmitz, E Robert 1889-1949 *BiDAmM, NewGrD 80*
Schmitz, Elie Robert 1889-1949 *Baker 78*
Schmitz, Eugen 1882-1959 *Baker 78, NewGrD 80*
Schmitz, Hans-Peter 1916- *IntWWM 77, -80*
Schmitz, Hans Wolfgang 1928- *IntWWM 80*
Schmitz, Ludwig 1884-1954 *WhScrn 74, -77*
Schmitz, Sybille 1909-1955 *FilmAG WE*
Schmitz, Sybille 1912-1955 *WhScrn 74, -77*
Schmitzer, Henrietta *Film 2*
Schmoele, Blanche Baum 1925- *IntWWM 77*
Schmolzer, Jakob Eduard 1812-1886 *NewGrD 80*
Schmucker, Beale Melanchthon 1827-1888 *BiDAmM*
Schmucki, Norbert 1940- *CnOxB*
Schmugel, Johann Christoph 1727?-1798 *NewGrD 80*
Schmuller, Alexander 1880-1933 *Baker 78*
Schmutz, Albert Daniel 1887- *AmSCAP 66, ConAmC*
Schnabel, Artur 1882-1951 *Baker 78, BnBkM 80[port], MusMk, MusSN[port], NewGrD 80[port], OxMus*
Schnabel, Ekke *ConMuA 80B*
Schnabel, Joseph Ignaz 1767-1831 *Baker 78, NewGrD 80*
Schnabel, Karl Ulrich 1909- *Baker 78, IntWWM 77, -80, NewGrD 80, WhoMus 72*
Schnabel, Stefan 1912 *ForYSC, NotNAT, WhoHol A, WhoThe 77*
Schnapka, Georg 1932- *WhoOp 76*
Schnapper, Edith B 1909- *NewGrD 80*
Schnebel, Dieter 1930- *DcCM, NewGrD 80*
Schneckenburger, Frederick 1922-1967 *DcPup, Ent*
Schneckenburger, Max *OxMus*
Schnee, Bill *ConMuA 80B*
Schnee, Charles 1916-1963 *FilmEn, FilmgC, HalFC 80*
Schnee, Charles 1918-1962 *WorEFlm*
Schnee, Joel 1935- *CnOxB*
Schnee, Thelma *WhThe*
Schneeberger, Hansheinz 1926- *NewGrD 80*
Schneegass, Cyriacus 1546-1597 *NewGrD 80*
Schneegass, Cyriak 1546-1597 *NewGrD 80*
Schneemann, Carolee *CmpGMD, ConDr 73, -77E, WomWMM B*
Schneer, Charles H 1920- *FilmEn, FilmgC, HalFC 80, IntMPA 77, -75, -76, -78, -79, -80, WhoHrs 80*
Schneerson, Grigory 1901- *Baker 78*
Schneevoigt, Georg Lennart 1872-1947 *Baker 78, NewGrD 80*
Schneeweis, Jan 1904- *WhoMus 72*
Schneickher, Paul *NewGrD 80*
Schneideman, Robert Ivan 1926- *BiE&WWA, NotNAT*
Schneider *NewGrD 80*
Schneider, A 1905- *IntMPA 77, -75, -76, -78, -79*
Schneider, Alan 1917- *BiE&WWA, EncWT, NewYTET, NotNAT, WhoThe 72, -77*
Schneider, Alexander 1908- *Baker 78, BiDAmM, BnBkM 80, NewGrD 80*
Schneider, Andreas 1640?-1685 *NewGrD 80*
Schneider, Bert 1934- *BiDFilm 81*
Schneider, Clarence J *IntMPA 77, -75, -76, -78*
Schneider, Conrad Michael 1673?-1752 *NewGrD 80*
Schneider, Dick *IntMPA 77, -75, -76, -78, -79, -80*
Schneider, Dorothy Fay 1932- *AmSCAP 80*
Schneider, Dorothy Louise *IntWWM 77*
Schneider, Edward Faber 1872-1950 *Baker 78, BiDAmM, ConAmC*
Schneider, Franz 1737?-1812 *NewGrD 80*
Schneider, Friedrich *Film 2*
Schneider, Friedrich 1786-1853 *Baker 78, NewGrD 80*
Schneider, Georg Abraham 1770-1839 *Baker 78*
Schneider, George Herbert 1943- *AmSCAP 80*
Schneider, Gottlieb 1797-1856 *NewGrD 80*
Schneider, Hannes *Film 2*
Schneider, Hans 1921- *IntWWM 77, -80*
Schneider, Hortense 1833-1922? *NewGrD 80*
Schneider, James 1882-1967 *MotPP, WhScrn 74, -77, WhoHol B*
Schneider, Johann 1702?-1788 *NewGrD 80*
Schneider, Johann 1789-1864 *Baker 78, NewGrD 80*
Schneider, Johann Christian Friedrich *OxMus*
Schneider, Johann Gottlob 1753-1840 *Baker 78*
Schneider, John A 1926- *IntMPA 77, -75, -76, -78, -79, -80, NewYTET*
Schneider, Julius 1805-1885 *Baker 78*
Schneider, Jurgen 1936- *CnOxB*
Schneider, Karl Ernst 1819-1893 *Baker 78*
Schneider, Laura 1947- *IntWWM 77, -80*
Schneider, Louis 1861-1934 *Baker 78*
Schneider, Magda *WhoHol A*
Schneider, Magda 1908- *FilmEn*
Schneider, Magda 1909- *FilmAG WE*

Schneider, Maria 1952- *FilmEn, HalFC 80*
Schneider, Maria 1953- *MovMk[port], WhoHol A*
Schneider, Marion *WomWMM B*
Schneider, Marius 1903- *Baker 78, NewGrD 80*
Schneider, Martin *NewGrD 80*
Schneider, Max 1875-1967 *Baker 78, NewGrD 80*
Schneider, Melvin Frederick 1904- *IntWWM 77, -80*
Schneider, Michael 1909- *NewGrD 80*
Schneider, Paul *NewGrD 80*
Schneider, Peter 1939- *WhoOp 76*
Schneider, Reinhold 1903-1958 *CnMD*
Schneider, Richard Stanley 1952- *IntWWM 77, -80*
Schneider, Rolf 1932- *CroCD*
Schneider, Romy 1938- *BiDFilm, -81, FilmAG WE, FilmEn, FilmgC, ForYSC, HalFC 80, IntMPA 77, -75, -76, -78, -79, -80, MotPP, MovMk, OxFilm, WhoHol A, WorEFlm*
Schneider, Rosalind *WomWMM B*
Schneider, Stanley *IntMPA 75*
Schneider, Theodor 1827-1909 *Baker 78, NewGrD 80*
Schneider, Urs Peter 1939- *DcCM, IntWWM 77, -80, -80*
Schneider-Cuvay, Maria Michaela Olga 1933- *IntWWM 77, -80*
Schneider-Siemssen, Gunther 1926- *EncWT, NewGrD 80, WhoOp 76*
Schneider-Trnavsky, Mikulas 1881-1958 *Baker 78, NewGrD 80*
Schneiderhan, Walther 1901- *WhoMus 72*
Schneiderhan, Wolfgang 1915- *IntWWM 77, -80, NewGrD 80, WhoMus 72*
Schneiderman, George 1890?-1964 *HalFC 80*
Schneidermann, Dina 1931- *IntWWM 80, NewGrD 80, WhoMus 72*
Schneidewind, Hellmut 1928- *NewGrD 80*
Schneier, Frederick 1927- *IntMPA 77, -75, -76, -78, -79, -80*
Schneitzhoeffer, Jean-Madeleine 1785-1852 *CnOxB*
Schneitzhoeffer, Jean-Madeline 1785-1852 *Baker 78*
Schnell, G H *Film 2*
Schnell, Johann Jakob 1687-1754 *NewGrD 80*
Schnerich, Alfred 1859-1944 *Baker 78*
Schnetzler, Johann *NewGrD 80*
Schnherr, Karl 1867-1943 *NotNAT B*
Schnicke, Maxie Cleere 1915- *IntWWM 77*
Schnickelfritz *WhScrn 77*
Schnifis, Laurentius Von *NewGrD 80*
Schnitger *NewGrD 80*
Schnitger, Arp 1648-1719 *Baker 78, NewGrD 80*
Schnitger, Franz Caspar 1693?-1729 *NewGrD 80*
Schnitger, Johann Georg 1690?-1733? *NewGrD 80*
Schnitke, Alfred 1934- *DcCM*
Schnittelbach, Nathanael 1633-1667 *NewGrD 80*
Schnitter, David Bertram 1948- *EncJzS 70*
Schnittke, Alfred 1934- *Baker 78*
Schnitzer *NewGrD 80*
Schnitzer, Albrecht d1525? *NewGrD 80*
Schnitzer, Franz 1740-1785 *NewGrD 80*
Schnitzer, Germaine 1889- *BiDAmM*
Schnitzer, Robert C 1906- *BiE&WWA, NotNAT*
Schnitzke, Gregor 1580?-1627? *NewGrD 80*
Schnitzkius, Gregor 1580?-1627? *NewGrD 80*
Schnitzky, Gregor 1580?-1627? *NewGrD 80*
Schnitzler *PlP&P*
Schnitzler, Arthur 1862-1931 *CnMD, CnThe, EncWT, Ent, FilmgC, HalFC 80, McGEWD[port], ModWD, NotNAT A, -B, OxThe, REnWD[port]*
Schnitzler, Michael 1944- *IntWWM 77, -80*
Schnizer, Franz *NewGrD 80*
Schnoor, Hans 1893-1976 *Baker 78, NewGrD 80*
Schnorr, Klemens 1949- *IntWWM 77, -80*
Schnorr VonCarolsfeld, Ludwig 1836-1865 *Baker 78, BnBkM 80, CmOp, NewEOp 71, NewGrD 80[port]*
Schnorr VonCarolsfeld, Malwine 1832-1904 *Baker 78*
Schnuffis, Laurentius Von *NewGrD 80*
Schnufis, Laurentius Von *NewGrD 80*
Schnur, Esther *WomWMM B*
Schnur, Jerome 1923- *IntMPA 77, -75, -76, -78, -79, -80*
Schnyder VonWartensee, Xaver 1786-1868 *Baker 78, NewGrD 80*
Schoberlechner, Franz 1797-1843 *Baker 78, NewGrD 80*
Schobert, Jean 1735?-1767 *NewGrD 80*
Schobert, Johann 1720?-1767 *MusMk, OxMus*
Schobert, Johann 1735?-1767 *NewGrD 80*
Schobert, Johann 1740-1767 *Baker 78*
Schock, Rudolf 1915- *IntWWM 77, -80*
Schodler, Dave *Film 2*
Schoebel, Elmer 1896-1970 *AmSCAP 66, -80, BiDAmM, CmpEPM, EncJzS 70, WhoJazz 72*
Schoeck, Othmar 1886-1957 *Baker 78, BnBkM 80, DcCom&M 79, DcCM, NewEOp 71, NewGrD 80[port], OxMus*
Schoedsack, Ernest B 1893-1979 *HalFC 80*
Schoedsack, Ernest Beaumont 1893- *CmMov, DcFM, FilmgC, OxFilm, TwYS A, WorEFlm*
Schoedsack, Ernest Beaumont 1893-1979 *BiDFilm, -81, FilmEn, WhoHrs 80*
Schoeffer, Peter, Jr. 1475?-1547 *NewGrD 80*
Schoeffler, Paul 1897- *BnBkM 80, CmOp, NewEOp 71*
Schoelcher, Victor 1804-1893 *Baker 78, NewGrD 80, OxMus*
Schoemacher, Maurice *OxMus*
Schoemaker, Maurice 1890-1964 *Baker 78, NewGrD 80*
Schoen, Margaret *Film 2*
Schoen, Vic 1917?- *CmpEPM*
Schoen, Victor 1916- *AmSCAP 80*
Schoen-Rene, Anna E 1864-1942 *Baker 78, NewEOp 71*
Schoenbach, Sol 1915- *NewGrD 80*
Schoenbaum, Camillo 1925- *NewGrD 80*
Schoenbaum, Donald 1926- *NotNAT*
Schoenberg, Alex d1945 *WhoHol B*
Schoenberg, Arnold 1874-1951 *AmSCAP 66, -80, Baker 78, BnBkM 80[port], CmOp, CompSN[port], CnOxB, ConAmC, DcCom 77[port], DcCom&M 79, DcCM, DcTwCC, -A, MusMk[port], NewEOp 71, NewGrD 80*
Schoenbrun, David *NewYTET*
Schoendoerffer, Pierre 1928- *WorEFlm*
Schoendorff, Philipp 1565?-1617? *NewGrD 80*
Schoene, Mary *Film 2*
Schoenefeld, Heinrich 1857-1936 *BiDAmM*
Schoenefeld, Henry 1857-1936 *Baker 78*
Schoenfeld, Bernard C *WomWMM*
Schoenfeld, Joe 1907- *IntMPA 77, -75, -76, -78, -79, -80*
Schoenfeld, Lester 1916- *IntMPA 77, -75, -76, -78, -79, -80*
Schoenfeld, William C 1893-1969 *AmSCAP 66, -80*
Schoenfield, Paul *ConAmC*
Schoening, Alwina *NewGrD 80*
Schoenleben, Ralph 1915- *AmSCAP 80*
Schoenstedt, Friedrich Wilhelm Arno 1913- *IntWWM 77, -80*
Schoep, Arthur Paul 1920- *IntWWM 77, -80*
Schoettle, Elmer 1910-1973 *ConAmC*
Schofer, Ottokar 1930- *WhoOp 76*
Schoffer, Peter *NewGrD 80*
Schoffler, Paul 1897-1977 *Baker 78, NewGrD 80*
Schoffler, Paul 1907- *WhoMus 72*
Schofield, Albert Y 1905- *AmSCAP 66*
Schofield, Bertram 1896- *NewGrD 80*
Schofield, Johnny d1921 *NotNAT B*
Schofield, Paul 1922- *WorEFlm[port]*
Schol, Dirk *NewGrD 80*
Scholczer, Thomas *NewGrD 80*
Scholem, Richard Jay 1931- *ConAmTC*
Scholes, Percy Alfred 1877-1958 *Baker 78, NewGrD 80, OxMus*
Scholin, C Albert 1896-1958 *AmSCAP 66, -80, ConAmC A*
Scholl, Danny *WhoHol A*
Scholl, Dirk 1641-1727 *NewGrD 80*
Scholl, Jack 1903- *AmSCAP 66, CmpEPM*
Scholl, Jack Trevor 1903- *AmSCAP 80*
Scholl, Nicolas *OxMus*
Schollar, Ludmila Franzevna 1888- *CnOxB*
Schollenberger, Kaspar 1673-1735 *NewGrD 80*
Scholler, William *Film 2*
Schollum, Robert 1913- *Baker 78, DcCM, IntWWM 77, -80, NewGrD 80*
Scholtz, Herrmann 1845-1918 *Baker 78*
Scholz, Bernard E 1835-1916 *Baker 78*
Scholz, Bernhard 1835-1916 *NewGrD 80*
Scholz, Erwin Christian 1910- *WhoMus 72*
Scholz, Hans 1879-1953 *NewGrD 80*
Scholz, Janos 1903- *WhoMus 72*
Scholz, Paul 1894- *AmSCAP 66, -80*
Scholz, Robert *Film 2*
Scholz, Tom *ConMuA 80B*
Scholz, Wenzel 1787-1857 *EncWT*
Scholz, Werner 1926- *IntWWM 77, -80*
Scholz, Wilhelm Von 1874-1969 *CnMD, McGEWD, ModWD*
Scholze, Johann Sigismund *NewGrD 80*
Schomacker, Johann Heinrich 1800-1875 *BiDAmM*
Schomberg, Martin 1944- *WhoOp 76*
Schon, Margarete *Film 2*
Schonbach, Dieter 1931- *Baker 78, DcCM, NewGrD 80*
Schonberg, Alexander 1886-1945 *WhScrn 74, -77*
Schonberg, Arnold 1874-1951 *Baker 78, BiDAmM, DancEn 78, OxMus*
Schonberg, Chris M 1890-1957 *AmSCAP 66, -80*
Schonberg, Harold C 1915- *Baker 78, BiDAmM, IntWWM 77, -80, NewGrD 80, OxMus*
Schonberg, Ib 1902-1955 *WhScrn 74, -77, WhoHol B*
Schonberg, Stig Gustav 1933- *Baker 78, IntWWM 77, -80, NewGrD 80*
Schonberger, Benno 1863-1930 *Baker 78*
Schonberger, John 1892- *AmSCAP 66, -80, BiDAmM*
Schondorf, Johannes 1833-1912 *Baker 78*
Schondorpp, Philipp *NewGrD 80*
Schone, Lotte 1891-1977 *CmOp, NewGrD 80*
Schoneck *NewGrD 80*
Schonemann, Johann Friedrich 1704-1782 *EncWT, Ent, NotNAT B, OxThe*
Schonenberger, Georges 1808-1856 *NewGrD 80*
Schoner, Ingeborg 1935- *FilmAG WE[port]*
Schonfeld, Johann Philipp 1742-1790 *NewGrD 80*
Schonfelder, Gerd 1936- *IntWWM 77, -80, NewGrD 80*
Schonfelder, Jorg *NewGrD 80*
Schonherr, Karl 1867-1943 *CnMD, EncWT, McGEWD[port], ModWD, OxThe*
Schonherr, Max 1903- *IntWWM 77, -80, NewGrD 80, WhoMus 72*
Schonig *NewGrD 80*
Schonig, Hans Ulrich 1589-1655 *NewGrD 80*
Schonig, Johann 1616-1680 *NewGrD 80*
Schonig, Johann Jakob 1657-1694 *NewGrD 80*
Schonig, Valentin 1544-1614 *NewGrD 80*
Schonsleder, Wolfgang 1570-1651 *NewGrD 80*
Schonstedt, Friedrich Wilhelm Arno 1913- *WhoMus 72*
Schonstein, Karl 1797-1876 *Baker 78*
Schonthal, Ruth Esther 1924- *CpmDNM 78, -80, ConAmC*
Schonthal-Seckel, Ruth Esther 1924- *CpmDNM 77, IntWWM 80*
Schonthan, Franz Von 1849-1913 *EncWT*
Schonwald, Albert *NewGrD 80*
Schonzeler, Hans-Hubert 1925- *IntWWM 77, -80, NewGrD 80, WhoMus 72*
Schoof, Manfred 1936- *EncJzS 70, NewGrD 80*
Schoolboy Cleve *BluesWW*
Schoolboys, The *RkOn[port]*
Schooley, Anne 1943- *IntWWM 77, -80*
Schooley, John Heilman 1943- *AmSCAP 80, CpmDNM 76, ConAmC, IntWWM 77, -80*
Schooling, Elisabeth 1918- *DancEn 78*
Schoonbroodt, Hubert Laurens 1941- *IntWWM 77*
Schoonmaker, Lloyd 1939- *AmSCAP 80*

Schoonmaker, Thelma *WomWMM*
Schoop, Hans 1934- *IntWWM 77, -80*
Schoop, Jack 1909- *ConAmC A*
Schoop, Paul 1907-1976 *IntWWM 77, -80*
Schoop, Paul 1909-1976 *AmSCAP 66, -80, Baker 78*
Schoop, Trudi 1903- *CnOxB, DancEn 78*
Schop *NewGrD 80*
Schop, Albert 1632?-1667? *NewGrD 80*
Schop, Johann d1667 *NewGrD 80*
Schop, Johann 1626-1670? *NewGrD 80*
Schopenhauer, Arthur 1788-1860 *Baker 78, NewGrD 80*
Schopick, Sonya Turitz 1917- *IntWWM 77*
Schorer, Suki 1939- *CnOxB, DancEn 78[port]*
Schorm, Evald 1931- *DcFM, FilmEn, OxFilm*
Schorm, Ewald 1931- *WorEFlm[port]*
Schornburg, Heinrich 1533-1596 *NewGrD 80*
Schorr, Daniel *NewYTET*
Schorr, Friedrich 1888-1953 *Baker 78, BiDAmM, CmOp, MusSN[port], NewEOp 71, NewGrD 80*
Schorr, Hortense *IntMPA 77, -75, -76, -78*
Schorr, Jose *IntMPA 77, -75, -76, -78, -79, -80*
Schorr, Lonnie *JoeFr*
Schorsch, Josepha 1915- *IntWWM 77*
Schory, Richard *ConMuA 80B*
Schott *NewGrD 80*
Schott, Andreas 1781-1840 *Baker 78*
Schott, Anton 1846-1913 *Baker 78, NewEOp 71*
Schott, Bernhard 1748-1809 *Baker 78, NewGrD 80*
Schott, Franz Philip 1811-1874 *Baker 78*
Schott, Franz Philipp 1811-1874 *NewGrD 80*
Schott, Georg Balthasar 1686-1736 *NewGrD 80*
Schott, Howard 1923- *IntWWM 77, -80*
Schott, Johann Andreas 1781-1840 *NewGrD 80*
Schott, Johann Georg 1548?-1614 *NewGrD 80*
Schott, Johann Joseph 1782-1855 *Baker 78, NewGrD 80*
Schott, Peter d1894 *Baker 78*
Schott, Peter, Jr. *Baker 78*
Schottelius, Renate 1921- *CnOxB, DancEn 78*
Schou, Dagmar 1906- *IntWWM 77, -80*
Schoumacher, David *NewYTET*
Schousboe, Torben 1937- *IntWWM 77, -80, NewGrD 80*
Schouten, Joop 1907- *IntWWM 77*
Schouwman, Hans 1902-1967 *Baker 78*
Schoyen, Einar 1952- *IntWWM 80*
Schrade, Leo 1903-1964 *Baker 78, NewGrD 80*
Schrade, Rolande Young *AmSCAP 80*
Schrader, Barry 1945- *ConAmC*
Schrader, Frederich Franklin 1857-1943 *NotNAT B*
Schrader, Frederick Franklin 1857-1943 *WhoStg 1908*
Schrader, Frederick Franklin 1859- *WhThe*
Schrader, Lynn Gordon 1949- *IntWWM 77*
Schrader, Paul 1946- *FilmEn, HalFC 80, IntMPA 77, -78, -79, -80*
Schradick, Henry 1846-1918 *BiDAmM*
Schradieck, Heinrich 1846-1918 *NewGrD 80*
Schradieck, Henry 1846-1918 *Baker 78, NewGrD 80*
Schram, Violet 1898- *Film 1, -2, TwYS*
Schramm, Ernst Gerold 1938- *WhoOp 76*
Schramm, Harold 1935- *AmSCAP 66, -80, ConAmC*
Schramm, Johann Jacob 1724-1808 *NewGrD 80*
Schramm, Karla *Film 1, -2, TwYS*
Schramm, Melchior 1553?-1619 *NewGrD 80*
Schramm, Rudolf R A 1902- *AmSCAP 66, -80*
Schrammel, Johann 1850-1893 *NewGrD 80*
Schrank, Joseph *NatPD[port]*
Schrat, Katharina d1940 *NotNAT B*
Schratt, Hans Rauch Von *NewGrD 80*
Schraubstader, Carl 1902- *AmSCAP 66, -80*
Schreck, Gustav 1849-1918 *Baker 78*
Schreck, Max 1870-1936 *FilmAG WE*
Schreck, Max 1879-1936 *FilmEn, Film 2, FilmgC, HalFC 80, WhScrn 77, WhoHol B, WhoHrs 80*
Schrecker, Bruno 1928- *IntWWM 77, -80, WhoMus 72*
Schreder, Carol *WomWMM B*
Schreiber, Alfred *Film 2*
Schreiber, Avery *WhoHol A*
Schreiber, Edward 1913- *IntMPA 77, -75, -76, -78, -79, -80*
Schreiber, Frederick C 1895- *AmSCAP 66, -80, Baker 78*
Schreiber, Friedrich Gustav 1817-1889 *Baker 78*
Schreiber, Johann Evangelist 1716?-1800 *NewGrD 80*
Schreiber, Johannes Evangelista 1716?-1800 *NewGrD 80*
Schreiber, Nancy *WomWMM*
Schreiber, Ottmar 1906- *NewGrD 80*
Schreiber, Sally *WhoHol A*
Schreiber, Sidney 1905- *IntMPA 77, -75, -76, -78, -79*
Schreibman, Alexander 1910- *AmSCAP 80*
Schreider, Christopher *NewGrD 80*
Schreier, Peter Max 1935- *IntWWM 77, -80, NewGrD 80, WhoOp 76*
Schreiner, Alexander 1901- *AmSCAP 66, -80, BnBkM 80, IntWWM 77, -80, WhoMus 72*
Schreiner, Elissa Paulette 1934- *AmSCAP 80*
Schreiner, Ona Eileen 1922- *IntWWM 77*
Schreiner, Tony 1912?- *NewOrJ SUP[port]*
Schreker, Franz 1878-1934 *Baker 78, CmOp, CompSN[port], DcCom 77, NewEOp 71, NewGrD 80, OxMus*
Schrems, Joseph 1815-1872 *Baker 78*
Schreuder, Frans G 1930- *IntWWM 77*
Schreyber, Heinrich *NewGrD 80*
Schreyer, Annie *Film 2*
Schreyer, Gregor 1720?-1768 *NewGrD 80*
Schreyvogel, Josef 1768-1832 *OxThe*
Schreyvogel, Joseph 1768-1832 *EncWT, NotNAT B*
Schreyvogl, Friedrich 1899- *CnMD, CroCD, McGEWD, ModWD*
Schrider, Christoph d1751 *NewGrD 80*
Schrider, Christopher d1751 *NewGrD 80*
Schrift, Benjamin R 1906- *IntMPA 77, -75, -76, -78, -79*
Schrock, Sophia 1931- *WhoOp 76*
Schroder *NewGrD 80*
Schroder, Alwin 1855-1920 *BiDAmM*
Schroder, Alwin 1855-1928 *Baker 78, NewGrD 80*
Schroder, Carl 1848-1935 *Baker 78*
Schroder, Christopher *NewGrD 80*
Schroder, Ernst 1915- *EncWT, WhoHol A*
Schroder, Friedrich 1910- *NewGrD 80*
Schroder, Friedrich Ludwig 1744-1816 *CnThe, EncWT, Ent, NotNAT B, OxThe*
Schroder, Hanning 1896- *Baker 78*
Schroder, Hermann 1843-1909 *Baker 78, NewGrD 80*
Schroder, Jaap 1925- *BnBkM 80, IntWWM 77, -80*
Schroder, Jens 1909- *IntWWM 77, -80*
Schroder, Johannes d1677 *NewGrD 80*
Schroder, Karl 1816-1890 *NewGrD 80*
Schroder, Karl 1848-1935 *NewGrD 80*
Schroder, Lorentz d1647? *NewGrD 80*
Schroder-Devrient, Wilhelmine 1804-1860 *Baker 78, BnBkM 80, CmOp, NewEOp 71, NewGrD 80[port]*
Schroder-Feinen, Ursula *WhoOp 76*
Schroder-Feinen, Ursula 1936- *NewGrD 80*
Schroeder *NewGrD 80*
Schroeder, Aaron Harold 1926- *AmSCAP 66, -80, ConMuA 80B*
Schroeder, Anne *Film 2*
Schroeder, Arthur *Film 2*
Schroeder, Barbet 1941- *FilmEn*
Schroeder, Eugene Charles 1915-1975 *EncJzS 70*
Schroeder, Gene 1915-1975 *CmpEPM, EncJzS 70, WhoJazz 72*
Schroeder, Gerald H 1936- *IntWWM 77, -80*
Schroeder, Hanning 1896- *WhoMus 72*
Schroeder, Harry W 1906- *IntMPA 77, -75, -76, -78, -79*
Schroeder, Hermann 1904- *DcCM, IntWWM 77, -80, NewGrD 80*
Schroeder, Linda Ann 1954- *IntWWM 80*
Schroeder, Raymond Lee 1936- *IntWWM 77, -80*
Schroeder, Sophia Charlotta 1714-1792 *NotNAT B*
Schroeder, William A 1888-1960 *AmSCAP 66, ConAmC A*
Schroeder, William A 1921- *ConAmC*
Schroell, N *Film 2*
Schroen, B *OxMus*
Schroeter *NewGrD 80*
Schroeter, Christoph Gottlieb 1699-1782 *OxMus*
Schroeter, Johann Samuel 1750-1788 *OxMus*
Schroeter, Johann Samuel 1752?-1788 *NewGrD 80*
Schroeter, Leonhard 1532?-1601? *NewGrD 80*
Schroff, William 1889-1964 *WhScrn 74, -77*
Schron, Cania *Film 2*
Schrooth, Heinrich *Film 2*
Schroter *NewGrD 80*
Schroter, Christoph Gottlieb 1699-1782 *Baker 78, NewGrD 80*
Schroter, Corona 1751-1802 *Baker 78, EncWT, NewGrD 80*
Schroter, Heinrich 1760?-1782? *NewGrD 80*
Schroter, Johann Friedrich 1724-1811 *NewGrD 80*
Schroter, Johann Georg 1683-1750? *NewGrD 80*
Schroter, Johann Samuel 1750?-1788 *Baker 78*
Schroter, Leonhard *NewGrD 80*
Schroter, Leonhart 1532?-1601? *Baker 78*
Schroter, Marie Henriette 1766-1804? *NewGrD 80*
Schroth, Gerhard Otto 1937- *IntWWM 77, -80*
Schroth, Godfrey 1927- *ConAmC*
Schroyens, Raymond Jean Joseph 1933- *IntWWM 77, -80*
Schryock, Buren 1881-1974 *Baker 78, ConAmC*
Schub, Esther *DcFM*
Schuba, Konrad Philipp 1929- *NewGrD 80*
Schuback, Jacob 1726-1784 *NewGrD 80*
Schubart, Christian Friedrich Daniel 1739-1791 *NewGrD 80, OxMus*
Schubart, Daniel 1739-1791 *Baker 78*
Schubaur, Johann Lukas 1749-1815 *Baker 78, NewGrD 80*
Schubel, Max 1932- *ConAmC*
Schubert *NewGrD 80*
Schubert, Christian John 1870-1953 *BiDAmM*
Schubert, Ferdinand 1794-1859 *Baker 78, NewGrD 80*
Schubert, Franz 1797-1828 *Baker 78, BnBkM 80[port], CmOp, CmpBCM, CnOxB, DancEn 78, DcCom 77[port], DcCom&M 79, GrComp[port], MusMk[port], NewEOp 71, NewGrD 80[port], NotNAT B, OxMus*
Schubert, Franz 1808-1878 *Baker 78, NewGrD 80, OxMus*
Schubert, Franz Anton 1768-1827 *NewGrD 80*
Schubert, Georgine 1840-1878 *NewGrD 80*
Schubert, Johann Friedrich 1770-1811 *NewGrD 80*
Schubert, Joseph 1757-1837 *NewGrD 80*
Schubert, Karin 1944- *FilmAG WE*
Schubert, Kathryn *WomWMM B*
Schubert, Lia 1926- *CnOxB, DancEn 78*
Schubert, Louis 1828-1884 *Baker 78, NewGrD 80*
Schubert, Manfred 1937- *IntWWM 80, NewGrD 80*
Schubert, Reinhold 1928- *WhoOp 76*
Schubert, Zenon 1934- *IntWWM 77, -80*
Schuberth *NewGrD 80*
Schuberth, Carl 1811-1863 *NewGrD 80*
Schuberth, Friedrich 1817-1890? *NewGrD 80*
Schuberth, Gottlob 1778-1846 *NewGrD 80*
Schuberth, Julius 1804-1875 *Baker 78, NewGrD 80*
Schuberth, Karl 1811-1863 *Baker 78*
Schuberth, Ludwig 1806-1850 *NewGrD 80*
Schubiger, Anselm 1815-1888 *Baker 78, NewGrD 80*
Schuch, Ernst Von 1846-1914 *Baker 78, CmOp, NewEOp 71, NewGrD 80*
Schuch, Franz 1716?-1764 *EncWT, OxThe*
Schuch, Liesel Von 1891- *Baker 78*
Schuch-Proska, Clementine 1850-1932 *NewGrD 80*
Schuchardt, Theodor 1601-1677 *NewGrD 80*
Schuchart, J J 1695?-1758 *NewGrD 80*
Schucht, Jean F 1822-1894 *Baker 78*
Schuchter, Gilbert 1919- *IntWWM 77, -80*
Schuchter, Wilhelm 1911-1974 *NewGrD 80*

Schuck, John *HalFC 80, WhoHol A*
Schuckett, Ralph Dion 1948- *AmSCAP 80*
Schudel, Thomas Michael 1937- *Baker 78, IntWWM 77, -80*
Schudi, Burkat *NewGrD 80*
Schudson, Howard M 1942- *AmSCAP 80*
Schudy, Frank d1963 *NotNAT B*
Schuecker *NewGrD 80*
Schuecker, Edmund 1860-1911 *Baker 78, NewGrD 80*
Schuecker, Heinrich 1867-1913 *Baker 78, NewGrD 80*
Schuecker, Joseph E 1886-1938 *Baker 78, NewGrD 80*
Schueller, Rudolf 1884-1949 *Baker 78*
Schuenzel, Reinhold 1886-1954 *NotNAT B*
Schuessler, Roy Ayres 1910- *IntWWM 77*
Schuetz, Heinrich 1585-1672 *CmpBCM, GrComp*
Schufftan, Eugen 1893-1977 *DcFM, FilmEn, OxFilm, WorEFlm*
Schufftan, Eugene 1893-1977 *FilmgC, HalFC 80*
Schuftan, Eugene 1893-1977 *FilmEn*
Schuh, Marie 1922- *AmSCAP 66, -80*
Schuh, Oscar Fritz 1904- *CmOp, EncWT, WhoOp 76*
Schuh, Willi 1900- *Baker 78, NewGrD 80*
Schuhmacher, Gerhard 1939- *IntWWM 77, -80*
Schuijt, Cornelis *NewGrD 80*
Schukat, Peter *ConMuA 80B*
Schuke *NewGrD 80*
Schuke, Carl Alexander 1870-1933 *NewGrD 80*
Schukin, Boris 1894-1939 *WhScrn 74, -77*
Schukow, A *Film 2*
Schulberg, B P 1892-1957 *FilmEn, FilmgC, HalFC 80, NotNAT B, OxFilm, TwYS B*
Schulberg, Ben P 1892-1957 *WorEFlm*
Schulberg, Budd 1914- *AmSCAP 66, -80, BiE&WWA, ConDr 73, -77D, DcFM, FilmEn, FilmgC, HalFC 80, IntMPA 77, -75, -76, -78, -79, -80, NotNAT, OxFilm, WorEFlm*
Schulberg, Stuart *NewYTET*
Schuldt, Agnes Crawford 1902- *IntWWM 77, -80*
Schule, Bernard E 1909- *ConAmC, IntWWM 77, -80*
Schuler, Arnold Louis 1933- *IntWWM 77*
Schuler, Billy *Film 2*
Schuler, Johannes 1894-1966 *CmOp*
Schuler, Richard Joseph 1920- *IntWWM 77, -80*
Schuler, Robert C 1920- *IntMPA 77, -75, -76, -78, -79*
Schulhoff, Ervin 1894-1942 *NewGrD 80*
Schulhoff, Erwin 1894-1942 *Baker 78, OxMus*
Schulhoff, Julius 1825-1898 *Baker 78, OxMus*
Schull, John Joseph *CreCan 2*
Schull, Joseph 1910- *CreCan 2*
Schuller, Gunther 1925- *Baker 78, BiDAmM, BnBkM 80, CompSN[port], CpmDNM 77, -78, -80, ConAmC, DcCM, EncJzS 70, IntWWM 77, -80, MusMk, NewEOp 71, NewGrD 80, OxMus*
Schuller, Stefan 1943- *CnOxB*
Schulman, Arnold 1925- *BiE&WWA, NotNAT*
Schulman, Bernard H 1923- *IntMPA 75, -76*
Schulman, Billy Revel 1950- *AmSCAP 66, -80*
Schulman, Ira 1926- *EncJzS 70*
Schulman, Nina *WomWMM, -A, -B*
Schulman, Samuel 1910- *IntMPA 77, -75, -76, -78, -79*
Schulman, Sylvia 1925- *IntWWM 77, -80, WhoMus 72*
Schulman, William B 1916- *IntMPA 77, -75, -76, -78, -79, -80*
Schulmeister, Mary 1950- *IntWWM 77*
Schulps, Dave *ConMuA 80B*
Schulte, Mary Jo 1932- *IntWWM 77*
Schulte, Minnie *AmPS B*
Schultheiss, Benedict 1653-1693 *NewGrD 80*
Schultheiss, Michael *NewGrD 80*
Schulthesius, Johann Paul 1748-1816 *NewGrD 80*
Schulthess, Walter 1894-1971 *Baker 78, NewGrD 80*
Schultz *NewGrD 80*
Schultz, Albert *ConMuA 80B*
Schultz, Barbara *NewYTET*
Schultz, Bartold *NewGrD 80*
Schultz, Carl Allen 1934- *WhoOp 76*
Schultz, Mrs. Cecil E 1905-1953 *WhScrn 74, -77*
Schultz, Edwin 1827-1907 *Baker 78*
Schultz, Floyd VanNest 1910- *IntWWM 77*
Schultz, Harry 1883-1935 *Film 2, WhScrn 74, -77, WhoHol B*
Schultz, Helmut 1904-1945 *Baker 78, NewGrD 80*
Schultz, Johann 1747-1800 *MusMk, NewGrD 80*
Schultz, Johannes 1582?-1653 *NewGrD 80*
Schultz, Maurice *Film 2*
Schultz, Michael A 1938- *DrBlPA, FilmEn, WhoThe 72, -77*
Schultz, Norbert 1911- *WhoMus 72*
Schultz, Ralph C 1932- *ConAmC*
Schultz, Sheldon *ConMuA 80B*
Schultz, Svend S 1913- *Baker 78, IntWWM 77, -80, NewGrD 80*
Schultz, William Eben 1887- *OxMus*
Schultz-Hauser, Karlheinz 1907- *IntWWM 77, -80*
Schultze *NewGrD 80*
Schultze, Christoph 1606?-1683 *NewGrD 80*
Schultze, Michael *NewGrD 80*
Schultze, Nobert 1911- *IntWWM 80*
Schultze, Norbert 1911- *Baker 78, NewGrD 80*
Schultze, William 1827-1888 *BiDAmM*
Schulz *NewGrD 80*
Schulz, August 1837-1909 *Baker 78*
Schulz, Charles 1922- *NewYTET*
Schulz, Claus 1934- *CnOxB*
Schulz, Ferdinand 1821-1897 *Baker 78*
Schulz, Fritz 1896-1972 *WhScrn 77*
Schulz, J A P 1747-1800 *OxMus*
Schulz, Johann Abraham Peter 1747-1800 *Baker 78, NewGrD 80*
Schulz, Johann Philipp Christian 1773-1827 *Baker 78, NewGrD 80*
Schulz, Leo 1865-1944 *Baker 78, BiDAmM*
Schulz-Beuthen, Heinrich 1838-1915 *Baker 78*
Schulz-Dornburg, Rudolf 1891-1949 *Baker 78*
Schulz-Evler, Andrei 1852-1905 *Baker 78*
Schulz-Schwerin, Karl 1845-1913 *Baker 78*
Schulze *NewGrD 80*
Schulze, Christian Andreas 1660?-1699 *NewGrD 80*
Schulze, Eduard 1830-1880 *NewGrD 80*
Schulze, Hans-Joachim 1934- *NewGrD 80*
Schulze, Heinrich Edmund 1824-1878 *NewGrD 80*
Schulze, Herward 1830?-1908 *NewGrD 80*
Schulze, Johann Andreas 1740?-1810 *NewGrD 80*
Schulze, Johann Friedrich 1793-1858 *NewGrD 80*
Schulze, Werner 1952- *IntWWM 80*
Schumacher, Harold 1921- *IntMPA 75, -76*
Schumacher, Max 1925-1966 *WhScrn 77*
Schumacher, Max 1927-1966 *WhScrn 74*
Schumacher, Stanley E 1942- *CpmDNM 75, ConAmC, IntWWM 80*
Schumacher, Thomas 1937- *IntWWM 77, -80, WhoMus 72*
Schumacher, Timothy Albert 1945- *AmSCAP 80*
Schuman, Edward L 1916- *IntMPA 77, -75, -76, -78, -79, -80*
Schuman, William Howard 1910- *Baker 78, BiDAmM, BiE&WWA, BnBkM 80, CompSN[port], CpmDNM 72, -73, -78, -80, CnOxB, ConAmC, DancEn 78, DcCom&M 79, DcCM, IntWWM 77, -80, MusMk, NewGrD 80, OxMus, WhoMus 72*
Schumann, Camillo 1872-1946 *Baker 78*
Schumann, Clara 1819-1896 *Baker 78, BnBkM 80, NewGrD 80[port], OxMus*
Schumann, Elisabeth 1885-1952 *Baker 78, BnBkM 80, CmOp, MusSN[port], NewEOp 71*
Schumann, Elisabeth 1888-1952 *NewGrD 80[port]*
Schumann, Elizabeth 1891-1952 *BiDAmM*
Schumann, Erik *WhoHol A*
Schumann, Frederic Theodor *NewGrD 80*
Schumann, Georg 1866-1952 *Baker 78, NewGrD 80*
Schumann, Robert 1810-1856 *Baker 78, BnBkM 80[port], CmOp, CmpBCM, CnOxB, DancEn 78, DcCom 77[port], DcCom&M 79, GrComp[port], MusMk[port], NewEOp 71, NewGrD 80[port], OxMus*
Schumann, Walter 1913-1958 *AmSCAP 66, -80, Baker 78, ConAmC, NotNAT B*
Schumann, Wolfgang 1927- *IntWWM 80*
Schumann-Heink, Madame 1861-1936 *WhoStg 1906, -1908*
Schumann-Heink, Ernestine 1861-1936 *Baker 78, BiDAmM, BnBkM 80[port], CmOp, ForYSC, MusSN[port], NewEOp 71, NewGrD 80[port], WhScrn 74, -77, WhoHol B*
Schumann-Heink, Ferdinand 1893-1955 *Film 2, ForYSC, TwYS*
Schumann-Heink, Ferdinand 1893-1958 *WhScrn 74, -77, WhoHol B*
Schumer, Henry 1914- *BiE&WWA*
Schumer, Yvette 1921- *BiE&WWA, NotNAT*
Schumm, Harry W 1878-1953 *Film 1, TwYS, WhScrn 74, -77, WhoHol B*
Schunemann, Georg 1884-1945 *Baker 78, NewGrD 80*
Schunke, Karl 1801-1839 *Baker 78*
Schunke, Ludwig 1810-1834 *Baker 78*
Schunzel, Reinhold 1886-1954 *FilmEn, Film 2, FilmgC, HalFC 80, WhScrn 74, -77, WhoHol B*
Schuppanzigh, Ignaz 1776-1830 *Baker 78, NewGrD 80*
Schure, Edouard 1841-1929 *Baker 78*
Schureck, Ralph John 1931- *IntWWM 80*
Schurer, Johann Georg 1720?-1786 *NewGrD 80*
Schuricht, Carl 1880-1967 *Baker 78, MusSN[port], NewGrD 80*
Schurig, Arthur 1870-1929 *Baker 78*
Schurig, Volkmar 1822-1899 *Baker 78*
Schuring, William *PupTheA*
Schurman, Nona *DancEn 78*
Schurmann, Georg Caspar 1672?-1751 *Baker 78, NewGrD 80*
Schurmann, Gerard 1928- *Baker 78, IntWWM 77, -80, NewGrD 80, WhoMus 72*
Schuster, Bernhard 1870-1934 *Baker 78*
Schuster, Georg 1915- *NewGrD 80*
Schuster, Giora 1915- *NewGrD 80*
Schuster, Harold 1902- *FilmEn, FilmgC, HalFC 80, IntMPA 77, -75, -76, -78, -79, -80*
Schuster, Harry *WomWMM*
Schuster, Ignaz 1779-1835 *EncWT, NewGrD 80, OxThe*
Schuster, Ira 1889-1945 *AmSCAP 66, -80*
Schuster, Irwin *ConMuA 80B*
Schuster, Josef 1748-1812 *Baker 78*
Schuster, Joseph 1748-1812 *NewGrD 80*
Schuster, Joseph 1896-1959 *AmSCAP 66, -80*
Schuster, Joseph 1903-1969 *Baker 78*
Schuster, Joseph 1905-1969 *BiDAmM*
Schuster, Joseph 1908- *WhoMus 72*
Schuster, Robert Joseph, Jr. 1950- *AmSCAP 80*
Schuster, Vincent *OxMus*
Schute, Martin *IntMPA 79, -80*
Schutt, Arthur 1902-1965 *CmpEPM, WhoJazz 72*
Schutt, Eduard 1856-1933 *Baker 78, OxMus*
Schutte, Marcus Kamehameha, Jr. 1931- *AmSCAP 80*
Schutz *NewGrD 80*
Schutz, Francoise Jeanne *NewGrD 80*
Schutz, Franz 1892-1962 *Baker 78*
Schutz, Gabriel 1633-1710 *NewGrD 80*
Schutz, Georg Gabriel 1670-1716 *NewGrD 80*
Schutz, Heinrich 1585-1672 *Baker 78, BnBkM 80[port], DcCom 77[port], DcCom&M 79, GrComp[port], MusMk, NewEOp 71, NewGrD 80[port], OxMus*
Schutz, Henrich 1585-1672 *NewGrD 80[port]*
Schutz, Jacob Balthasar 1661-1700 *NewGrD 80*
Schutz, Maurice *Film 2*
Schutzendorf *NewGrD 80*
Schutzendorf, Alfons 1882-1946 *Baker 78, NewGrD 80*

Schutzendorf, Guido 1880-1967 *Baker 78, NewGrD 80*
Schutzendorf, Gustav 1883-1937 *Baker 78, NewEOp 71, NewGrD 80*
Schutzendorf, Leo 1886-1931 *Baker 78, NewGrD 80*
Schuyler, Philippa 1931-1967 *DrBlPA*
Schuyler, Philippa Duke *AmSCAP 80*
Schuyler, Philippa Duke 1934-1967 *AmSCAP 66*
Schuyler, Phillipa Duke 1932-1967 *ConAmC A*
Schuyler, Sonny 1913- *CmpEPM*
Schuyt, Cornelis 1557-1616 *Baker 78, NewGrD 80*
Schuyt, Nico 1922- *NewGrD 80*
Schuyt, Nicolaas 1922- *Baker 78*
Schuyten, Ernest Eugene Emile 1881- *ConAmC, WhoMus 72*
Schwaarz, Heidrun 1943- *CnOxB*
Schwab, Albert L 1926- *AmSCAP 80*
Schwab, Bonifacius 1611?-1661? *NewGrD 80*
Schwab, Felician 1611?-1661? *NewGrD 80*
Schwab, Frederick *OxMus*
Schwab, Laurence 1893-1951 *EncMT, NotNAT B, WhThe*
Schwab, Laurence, Jr. 1922- *IntMPA 77, -75, -76, -78, -79, -80*
Schwabacher, H Simon *McGEWD[port]*
Schwadron, Abraham A 1925- *ConAmC*
Schwaen, Kurt 1909- *IntWWM 77, -80, NewGrD 80*
Schwager, Myron August 1937- *IntWWM 80*
Schwaiger, Georg d1581 *NewGrD 80*
Schwalb, Ben 1901- *IntMPA 77, -75, -76, -78, -79*
Schwalm, Oskar 1856-1936 *Baker 78*
Schwalm, Robert 1845-1912 *Baker 78*
Schwam, Lynne Sue Ockner 1950- *IntWWM 77*
Schwamm, George S Tony 1903-1966 *WhScrn 74, -77*
Schwanbeck, Bodo 1935- *IntWWM 77, -80, WhoOp 76*
Schwanberg, Johann Gottfried 1740?-1804 *NewGrD 80*
Schwanberger, Johann Gottfried 1740?-1804 *NewGrD 80*
Schwandt, Erich Paul 1935- *IntWWM 77, -80*
Schwandt, Wilbur 1914- *AmSCAP 66*
Schwandt, Wilbur Clyde 1904- *AmSCAP 80*
Schwanenberg, Johann Gottfried 1740?-1804 *Baker 78*
Schwanenberger, Johann Gottfried 1740?-1804 *NewGrD 80*
Schwann, William 1913- *Baker 78*
Schwanneke, Ellen d1972 *WhScrn 77*
Schwanter, Joseph 1943- *CpmDNM 77, -80, ConAmC*
Schwantner, Joseph 1943- *IntWWM 77, -80*
Schwarbrick, Thomas d1753? *NewGrD 80*
Schwarbrook, Thomas d1753? *NewGrD 80*
Schwartz, Abe d1963 *NotNAT B*
Schwartz, Arthur 1900- *AmPS, AmSCAP 66, -80, BestMus, BiDAmM, BiE&WWA, CmpEPM, EncMT, EncWT, FilmEn, FilmgC, HalFC 80, IntMPA 77, -75, -76, -78, -79, -80, NewCBMT, NewGrD 80, NotNAT, PlP&P, PopAmC[port], PopAmC SUP, Sw&Ld C, WhoThe 77*
Schwartz, Arthur H 1903- *IntMPA 77, -75, -76, -78, -79, -80*
Schwartz, Bermuda *IntMPA 77, -75, -76, -78, -79, -80*
Schwartz, Bert *ConMuA 80B*
Schwartz, Charles *AmSCAP 80*
Schwartz, Charles M *IntWWM 77, -80*
Schwartz, Elliot 1936- *DcCM*
Schwartz, Elliott 1936- *AmSCAP 80, Baker 78, CpmDNM 72, -73, -74, -76, -78, -79, -80, ConAmC, NewGrD 80*
Schwartz, Emile *Film 2*
Schwartz, Francis 1940- *AmSCAP 80, Baker 78, CpmDNM 72, ConAmC*
Schwartz, James *ConMuA 80B*
Schwartz, Jean 1878-1956 *AmPS, AmSCAP 66, -80, BiDAmM, CmpEPM, EncMT, NewCBMT, NotNAT B, PopAmC[port], Sw&Ld C, WhThe*
Schwartz, Joan M *WomWMM B*
Schwartz, John *Film 2*
Schwartz, Judith Leah 1943- *IntWWM 80*
Schwartz, Julie 1947- *ConAmC*
Schwartz, Leslie R 1915- *IntMPA 77, -75, -76, -78, -79, -80*
Schwartz, Lillian *WomWMM B*
Schwartz, Marvin Robert 1937- *ConAmC, IntWWM 77, -80*
Schwartz, Maurice d1960 *Film 2, WhoHol B*
Schwartz, Maurice 1889-1960 *OxThe*
Schwartz, Maurice 1890-1960 *FilmEn, NotNAT B, WhThe*
Schwartz, Maurice 1891-1960 *WhScrn 74, -77*
Schwartz, Milton M 1924- *AmSCAP 66, -80*
Schwartz, Nan Louise 1953- *AmSCAP 80*
Schwartz, Paul 1907- *ConAmC, IntWWM 80*
Schwartz, Rudolf 1859-1935 *Baker 78, NewGrD 80*
Schwartz, Ruth 1908- *BiE&WWA*
Schwartz, Sam *WhoHol A*
Schwartz, Seymour 1917- *AmSCAP 66, -80*
Schwartz, Sherwood *NewYTET*
Schwartz, Sherwood 1916- *AmSCAP 80*
Schwartz, Sol A *IntMPA 77, -75, -76, -78, -79, -80*
Schwartz, Stephen 1948- *AmSCAP 80, BiDAmM, ConAmC, EncMT, WhoThe 77*
Schwartz, Stephen 1950- *NotNAT*
Schwartz, Stu *ConMuA 80B*
Schwartz, Theodora 1914- *AmSCAP 80*
Schwartz, Vera 1929- *IntWWM 80*
Schwartz, Walter A *IntMPA 75, -76, NewYTET*
Schwartz, Wendie Lee 1923-1968 *WhScrn 74, -77*
Schwartz, Wilbur 1918- *CmpEPM*
Schwartz, Wilfred 1923- *IntWWM 77, -80*
Schwartzkopf, Elisabeth *WhoHol A*
Schwartzkopff, Theodor 1659-1732 *NewGrD 80*
Schwartzman, Seymour 1930- *WhoOp 76*
Schwarz, Boris 1906- *Baker 78, IntWWM 80, NewGrD 80*
Schwarz, Gerard 1947- *BnBkM 80, NewGrD 80*
Schwarz, Gerhard 1902- *NewGrD 80*
Schwarz, Helmut 1928- *CroCD*
Schwarz, Ira Paul 1922- *CpmDNM 72, ConAmC*
Schwarz, Joseph 1880-1926 *NewGrD 80*
Schwarz, Joseph 1883-1945 *BiDAmM*
Schwarz, Maurice 1891-1960 *FilmgC, HalFC 80*
Schwarz, Rudolf 1905- *Baker 78, IntWWM 77, -80, NewGrD 80, WhoMus 72*
Schwarz, Solange 1910- *CnOxB, DancEn 78*
Schwarz, Thomas Jakob 1695-1754 *NewGrD 80*
Schwarz, Tracy 1938- *BiDAmM*
Schwarz, Vera 1889-1964 *Baker 78*
Schwarz, Vera 1929- *IntWWM 77, -80*
Schwarz, Wilhelm 1825-1878 *Baker 78*
Schwarz, Yevgeni 1896-1958 *CnMD*
Schwarz DuBrusle DeRouvroy, Jean 1939- *IntWWM 77, -80*
Schwarz-Schilling, Reinhard 1904- *IntWWM 77, -80*
Schwarze, Margarethe 1912- *IntWWM 77*
Schwarzenberg, Elisabeth 1933- *WhoOp 76*
Schwarzendorf, Johann Paul Aegidius *NewGrD 80*
Schwarzerd, Philipp *NewGrD 80*
Schwarzkopf, Elisabeth 1915- *Baker 78, BnBkM 80[port], CmOp, MusMk, MusSN[port], NewEOp 71, NewGrD 80[port]*
Schwarzkopf-Legge, Elisabeth 1915- *IntWWM 77, -80*
Schwarzwald, Arnold 1918- *AmSCAP 80*
Schwarzwald, Milton 1891-1950 *AmSCAP 66, -80*
Schwedler, Maximilian 1853-1940 *Baker 78*
Schweher, Krystop *NewGrD 80*
Schweiger, Georg *NewGrD 80*
Schweikart, Hans 1895-1975 *CnMD, EncWT*
Schweikert, Ernest G 1921- *AmSCAP 80*
Schweikert, Norman Carl 1937- *IntWWM 77, -80*
Schweisthal, Helen *WhScrn 74, -77*
Schweitzer, Albert 1875-1965 *Baker 78, BnBkM 80, MusMk, MusSN[port], NewGrD 80, OxMus*
Schweitzer, Anton 1735-1787 *Baker 78, NewGrD 80*
Schweitzer, Anton 1898- *IntWWM 77, -80*
Schweizelsberg, Casimir 1668-1722? *NewGrD 80*
Schweizelsperg, Casimir 1668-1722? *NewGrD 80*
Schweizelsperg, Caspar 1668-1722? *NewGrD 80*
Schweizelsperger, Casimir 1668-1722? *NewGrD 80*
Schweizer, Klaus 1939- *NewGrD 80*
Schwemmer, Heinrich 1621-1696 *NewGrD 80*
Schwencke *NewGrD 80*
Schwencke, Carl 1797-1870 *NewGrD 80*
Schwencke, Christian Friedrich Gottlieb 1767-1822 *Baker 78, NewGrD 80*
Schwencke, Friedrich Gottlieb 1823-1896 *Baker 78, NewGrD 80*
Schwencke, Fritz 1792-1852 *NewGrD 80*
Schwencke, Johann Friedrich 1792-1852 *Baker 78, NewGrD 80*
Schwencke, Johann Gottlieb 1744-1823 *Baker 78, NewGrD 80*
Schwencke, Karl 1797-1870 *NewGrD 80*
Schwenke, Johann Gottlieb 1744-1823 *NewGrD 80*
Schwentker, Mrs. O H *PupTheA*
Schwerdtfeger, E Anne 1930- *ConAmC*
Schwerin, Doris Halpern 1925- *AmSCAP 80*
Schwerke, Irving 1893-1975 *Baker 78, NewGrD 80*
Schwertsik, Kurt 1935- *DcCM, IntWWM 77, -80, NewGrD 80*
Schwezoff, Igor 1904- *CnOxB, DancEn 78*
Schwiefert, Fritz 1890- *CnMD*
Schwieger, Hans 1906- *Baker 78*
Schwieger, Hans 1910- *IntWWM 77, -80, WhoMus 72*
Schwieger, Jacob 1624-1660? *NewGrD 80*
Schwiegerling, P *PupTheA*
Schwiger, Jacob 1624-1660? *NewGrD 80*
Schwilge, Andreas 1608?-1688 *NewGrD 80*
Schwilgi, Andreas 1608?-1688 *NewGrD 80*
Schwiller, Elisabeth *IntWWM 77, -80, WhoMus 72*
Schwimmer, Walter *NewYTET*
Schwindel, Friedrich 1737-1786 *MusMk, NewGrD 80*
Schwindl, Friedrich 1737-1786 *NewGrD 80, OxMus*
Schwinger, Eckart 1934- *IntWWM 77, -80*
Schwinger, Wolfram 1928- *NewGrD 80, WhoOp 76*
Schytte, Ludvig 1848-1909 *Baker 78, NewGrD 80*
Scialla, Alessandro *NewGrD 80*
Sciambra, Jacob 1910- *NewOrJ[port]*
Sciammarella, Valdo 1924- *Baker 78*
Scianni, Joseph 1928- *AmSCAP 66, -80, ConAmC*
Sciapiro, Michel 1891-1962 *AmSCAP 66, -80, ConAmC*
Sciarrino, Salvatore 1947- *NewGrD 80*
Scibetta, Anthony James 1926- *AmSCAP 66, -80*
Scibona, Jorge 1931- *AmSCAP 80*
Scigalski, Franciszek 1782-1846 *NewGrD 80*
Scimone, Claudio 1934- *NewGrD 80*
Scinelli, Emilio 1905- *AmSCAP 66*
Scioneaux, Louis 1931?- *NewOrJ*
Scionte, Joseph *PupTheA*
Scionti, Isabel Laughlin *IntWWM 77, -80*
Sciroli, Gregorio 1722-1781? *NewGrD 80*
Sciutti, Graziella 1932- *Baker 78, CmOp, IntWWM 77, -80, NewGrD 80, WhoOp 76*
Sckroder, Greta *Film 2*
Sclater, James Stanley 1943- *AmSCAP 80, CpmDNM 80, ConAmC*
Scob, Edith *WhoHol A, WhoHrs 80*
Scobey, Bob 1916-1963 *CmpEPM*
Scobie, James d1968 *WhScrn 77*
Scoffield, William Eric 1940- *IntWWM 77, -80*
Scofield, Paul 1922- *BiE&WWA, CnThe, EncMT, EncWT, Ent[port], FilmEn, FilmgC, ForYSC, HalFC 80, IIWWBF, MotPP, MovMk[port], NotNAT, -A, OxFilm, OxThe, PlP&P[port], WhoHol A, WhoThe 72, -77*

Scoglio, Joseph 1943- *CnOxB*
Scognamillo, Gabriel A 1906- *IntMPA 77, -75, -76, -78, -79, -80*
Scola, Adamo *NewGrD 80*
Scola, Ettore 1931- *FilmEn*
Scola, Katherine *WomWMM*
Scolari, Giuseppe 1720?-1774? *NewGrD 80*
Scolari, Henri Louis 1923- *IntWWM 77, -80*
Scollard, Clinton 1860-1932 *BiDAmM*
Scollay, Fred J *WhoHol A*
Scontrino, Antonio 1850-1922 *Baker 78, NewGrD 80, OxMus*
Scooler, Zvee *WhoHol A*
Scopes, John T *What 1[port]*
Scoppettone, Sandra *NatPD[port]*
Scordino, Judith Marie 1952- *IntWWM 77*
Scordino-Hayes, Judith Marie 1952- *IntWWM 80*
Scorpione, Domenico *NewGrD 80*
Scorrer, Muriel *WhoMus 72*
Scorsese, Martin *HalFC 80, IntMPA 75, -76, -78, -79, -80*
Scorsese, Martin 1940- *IntMPA 77, MovMk[port], WhoHol A, WomWMM*
Scorsese, Martin 1942- *BiDFilm 81, FilmEn*
Scorsoni, Renzo 1929- *WhoOp 76*
Scorzuto, Giovanni Maria *NewGrD 80*
Scot, Reginald 1538-1599 *MagIID*
Scotland, J H 1873- *WhThe*
Scott *PupTheA*
Scott, A C 1909- *BiE&WWA, DcPup, NotNAT*
Scott, Adrian 1912- *IntMPA 75, -76, -78, -79, -80*
Scott, Adrian 1912-1972 *HalFC 80*
Scott, Adrian 1912-1973 *FilmEn, FilmgC, IntMPA 77*
Scott, Agnes *WhoStg 1908*
Scott, Alan *WhoHol A*
Scott, Alan Robert 1922- *AmSCAP 80*
Scott, Alex *WhoHol A*
Scott, Alex 1895?-1943? *NewOrJ*
Scott, Alexander Robert Crawford 1932- *IntWWM 80*
Scott, Allan 1909- *BiE&WWA, IntMPA 77, -75, -76, -78, -79, -80, NotNAT*
Scott, Anthony Leonard Winstone 1911- *IntWWM 77, -80, WhoMus 72*
Scott, Arthur 1890-1949 *BiDAmM, NewOrJ[port]*
Scott, Avis *WhoHol A*
Scott, Barbara *IntMPA 77, -75, -76, -78, -79, -80, What 2[port]*
Scott, Barry *WhoHol A*
Scott, Bennett 1875- *WhThe*
Scott, Bobby 1937- *RkOn*
Scott, Bonnie 1941- *BiE&WWA, WhoHol A*
Scott, Brenda *WhoHol A*
Scott, Bruce *WhoHol A*
Scott, Bud 1890-1949 *CmpEPM, WhoJazz 72*
Scott, C Calo 1920- *IntWWM 77*
Scott, Carrie *Film 2*
Scott, Cecil Xavier 1905-1964 *CmpEPM, WhoJazz 72*
Scott, Charles Hepburn 1886-1964 *CreCan 1*
Scott, Charles Kennedy 1876-1965 *AmSCAP 80, Baker 78, NewGrD 80, OxMus*
Scott, Charles Russell 1898- *IntWWM 77, -80, WhoMus 72*
Scott, Clement William 1841-1904 *BiDAmM, NotNAT B, OxThe*
Scott, Connie *WhoHol A*
Scott, Cynthia *WomWMM*
Scott, Cyril 1866-1945 *Film 1, NotNAT B, WhScrn 74, -77, WhThe, WhoHol B, WhoStg 1906, -1908*
Scott, Cyril 1879-1970 *Baker 78, BnBkM 80, CompSN[port], MusMk, NewGrD 80, OxMus*
Scott, Darby *OxMus*
Scott, Dave 1939-1964 *WhScrn 77*
Scott, David *WhoHol A*
Scott, David 1928- *DancEn 78*
Scott, David Robert 1928- *CreCan 2*
Scott, Debralee *WhoHol A*
Scott, Derek Brian 1950- *IntWWM 80*
Scott, Dick 1903-1961 *WhScrn 74, -77*
Scott, Douglas Frazer *Film 2*
Scott, Douglas Michael 1938- *IntWWM 77, -80*
Scott, Duncan Campbell 1862-1947 *CreCan 2*
Scott, E L *OxMus*
Scott, Edward Noble 1919- *AmSCAP 80*
Scott, Estelle *Film 1*
Scott, Evelyn *WhoHol A*
Scott, F Wayne *ConAmC*
Scott, Francis George 1880-1958 *Baker 78, NewGrD 80*
Scott, Francis Reginald 1899- *CreCan 1*
Scott, Frank 1899- *CreCan 1*
Scott, Frank R 1921- *AmSCAP 66, -80*
Scott, Fred 1902- *FilmEn, Film 2, WhoHol A*
Scott, Freddy 1933- *RkOn*
Scott, Frederick George 1861-1944 *CreCan 2*
Scott, Frederick T d1942 *WhScrn 74, -77, WhoHol B*
Scott, Genevia *BluesWW*
Scott, George C *MotPP, PlP&P A[port], WhoHol A*
Scott, George C 1926- *FilmgC, HalFC 80*
Scott, George C 1927- *BiDFilm, -81, BiE&WWA, Ent, FilmEn, ForYSC, IntMPA 77, -75, -76, -78, -79, -80, NotNAT, OxFilm, WhoThe 72, -77, WorEFlm*
Scott, George C 1929- *MovMk[port]*
Scott, Gertrude d1951 *NotNAT B, WhThe*
Scott, Gordon 1927- *FilmEn, FilmgC, ForYSC, HalFC 80, IntMPA 77, -75, -76, -78, -79, -80, WhoHol A, WhoHrs 80[port]*
Scott, Gordon L T 1920- *FilmgC, HalFC 80, IntMPA 77, -75, -76, -78, -79, -80*
Scott, Gregory 1879- *Film 2, IlWWBF[port]*
Scott, Harold 1891-1964 *NotNAT B, WhScrn 74, -77, WhThe, WhoHol B*
Scott, Harold 1935- *BiE&WWA, DrBlPA*
Scott, Harry d1947 *NotNAT B*
Scott, Hazel 1920- *AmPS B, AmSCAP 66, -80, BiDAmM, BlkWAB, CmpEPM, DrBlPA, WhoHol A*
Scott, Helena *BiE&WWA, NotNAT*
Scott, Henri Guest 1876-1942 *BiDAmM*
Scott, Henry G 1944- *IntWWM 77, -80*
Scott, Henry Lawrence 1908- *WhoMus 72*
Scott, Howard *Film 1, What 2[port]*
Scott, Ian *IntMPA 77, -75, -76, -78, -79, -80*
Scott, Isabella *NewGrD 80*
Scott, Ivy 1886-1947 *NotNAT B, WhScrn 77, WhoHol B*
Scott, Jack 1936- *RkOn[port]*
Scott, Jacob Richardson 1815-1861 *BiDAmM*
Scott, Jacqueline *WhoHol A*
Scott, James 1925- *IntWWM 80*
Scott, James A *AmSCAP 80*
Scott, James D 1939-1964 *WhScrn 74, -77, WhoHol B*
Scott, James Sylvester 1886-1938 *BiDAmM, NewGrD 80*
Scott, Janette 1938- *FilmAG WE, FilmEn, FilmgC, ForYSC, HalFC 80, IlWWBF[port], -A, IntMPA 77, -75, -76, -78, -79, -80, WhoHol A*
Scott, Jay *WhoHol A*
Scott, Jay Hutchinson 1924- *WhoThe 72, -77*
Scott, Jimmie *BlkAmP*
Scott, Joan *WhoHol A*
Scott, Joan Clement *WhThe*
Scott, Joanne Nisbet *CreCan 2*
Scott, John *BlkAmP*
Scott, John 1775?-1815 *NewGrD 80*
Scott, John 1930- *IntWWM 77, -80*
Scott, John 1937- *NatPD[port]*
Scott, Lady John Douglas 1810-1900 *OxMus*
Scott, John Gavin 1956- *IntWWM 77, -80*
Scott, John Newhall 1907-1963 *AmSCAP 66, ConAmC*
Scott, John Prindle 1877-1932 *AmSCAP 66, -80, BiDAmM, ConAmC*
Scott, John R d1856 *NotNAT B*
Scott, Johnie *MorBAP*
Scott, Johnnie Newhall 1907-1963 *AmSCAP 80*
Scott, Joseph *AmSCAP 80*
Scott, Kathryn Leigh *WhoHol A*
Scott, Kay 1928-1971 *WhScrn 74, -77, WhoHol B*
Scott, Ken *ForYSC, HalFC 80, WhoHol A*
Scott, Kenneth Irving *AmSCAP 80*
Scott, Kevin *WhoHol A*
Scott, Le *PupTheA*
Scott, Lee *WhoHol A*
Scott, Leonard 1908- *IntWWM 77, -80*
Scott, Leslie 1921-1969 *DrBlPA, WhScrn 74, -77, WhoHol B*
Scott, Linda 1945- *RkOn, WhoHol A*
Scott, Lizabeth *IntMPA 75, -76, -78, -79, -80*
Scott, Lizabeth 1922- *FilmEn, FilmgC, HalFC 80, IntMPA 77, MotPP, MovMk, What 3[port], WhoHol A, WorEFlm*
Scott, Lizabeth 1924- *ForYSC*
Scott, Mabel Juliene 1898- *Film 1, -2*
Scott, Mabel Julienna 1898- *TwYS*
Scott, Maidie *WhThe*
Scott, Malcolm 1872-1929 *NotNAT B, WhThe*
Scott, Margaret 1922- *CnOxB, DancEn 78*
Scott, Margaret Clement- *WhThe*
Scott, Margaretta 1912- *FilmgC, HalFC 80, IlWWBF, IntMPA 77, -75, -76, -78, -79, -80, WhoHol A, WhoThe 72, -77*
Scott, Marilyn Lang *AmSCAP 80*
Scott, Marion 1922- *CmpGMD, DancEn 78*
Scott, Marion Margaret 1877-1953 *Baker 78, NewGrD 80*
Scott, Mark 1915-1960 *WhScrn 74, -77, WhoHol B*
Scott, Markie d1958 *WhoHol B*
Scott, Markle 1873-1958 *WhScrn 74, -77*
Scott, Martha 1914- *BiE&WWA, FilmEn, FilmgC, ForYSC, HalFC 80, HolP 40[port], MotPP, MovMk, NotNAT, WhoHol A, WhoThe 72, -77*
Scott, Martha 1916- *IntMPA 77, -75, -76, -78, -79, -80*
Scott, Marty *ConMuA 80B*
Scott, Mary Bichard 1947- *IntWWM 77*
Scott, Maxyne Mathisen 1924- *IntWWM 77*
Scott, Molly 1938- *AmSCAP 80*
Scott, Morton W *IntMPA 77, -75, -76, -78, -79, -80*
Scott, Nathan George 1915- *AmSCAP 66, -80*
Scott, Noel 1889-1956 *NotNAT B, WhThe*
Scott, Norman 1920-1968 *NewEOp 71*
Scott, Norman 1921-1968 *BiDAmM*
Scott, Orange 1800-1847 *BiDAmM*
Scott, Oscar Emanuel 1929- *AmSCAP 80*
Scott, Paul 1894-1944 *WhScrn 74, -77*
Scott, Peter 1932- *WhThe*
Scott, Peter Graham 1923- *FilmgC, HalFC 80, IlWWBF*
Scott, Peter Stewart 1945- *WhoMus 72*
Scott, Pippa 1935- *BiE&WWA, FilmgC, ForYSC, HalFC 80, MotPP, WhoHol A*
Scott, Randolph 1903- *BiDFilm, -81, CmMov, FilmEn, Film 2, FilmgC, ForYSC, HalFC 80[port], IntMPA 77, -75, -76, -78, -79, -80, MotPP, MovMk[port], OxFilm, What 3[port], WhoHol A, WorEFlm[port]*
Scott, Raymond *AmSCAP 80, BgBands 74[port]*
Scott, Raymond 1909- *AmSCAP 66, BiDAmM, CmpEPM, MnPM[port], PopAmC[port]*
Scott, Raymond 1910- *WhoJazz 72*
Scott, Richard L d1962 *NotNAT B*
Scott, Ridley 1938- *HalFC 80, WhoHrs 80*
Scott, Robert Balgarnie Young 1899- *BiDAmM*
Scott, Robert Charles 1935- *IntWWM 77, -80*
Scott, Robert W 1937- *AmSCAP 66, -80, ConAmC*
Scott, Ronald 1927- *NewGrD 80*
Scott, Ronnie 1927- *EncJzS 70, IlEncJ, IntWWM 80, NewGrD 80*
Scott, Rosemary 1914- *WhThe*
Scott, Rupert Nicolas Boileau 1945- *IntWWM 80*
Scott, Samuel Hurley 1919- *IntWWM 77, -80*
Scott, Seret 1947- *BlkAmP*
Scott, Sherman *FilmEn*
Scott, Shirley 1934- *BlkWAB, EncJzS 70*
Scott, Simon *WhoHol A*
Scott, Sondra *WhoHol A*
Scott, Stephen 1944- *ConAmC*
Scott, Stuart John 1949- *IntWWM 77, -80*
Scott, Thomas Wright 1948- *EncJzS 70*
Scott, Timothy *WhoHol A*
Scott, Tom 1912-1961 *Baker 78, BnBkM 80, ConAmC*
Scott, Tom 1948- *ConMuA 80A, EncJzS 70*

Scott, Tommy Lee 1917- *AmSCAP 66, -80*
Scott, Tony 1921- *BiDAmM, CmpEPM, EncJzS 70*
Scott, Wallace d1970 *Film 1, WhScrn 77*
Scott, Sir Walter 1771-1832 *DcPup, HalFC 80, NewEOp 71, NewGrD 80, OxMus, PlP&P*
Scott, Walter D *IntMPA 77, -75, -76, NewYTET*
Scott, Walter G *PupTheA*
Scott, Walter M 1906- *IntMPA 77, -75, -76, -78, -79, -80*
Scott, William *Film 1, -2*
Scott, William Gregory 1934- *IntWWM 77*
Scott, Zachary 1914-1965 *BiE&WWA, FilmEn, FilmgC, ForYSC, HalFC 80, HolP 40[port], MotPP, MovMk[port], NotNAT B, WhScrn 74, -77, WhoHol B*
Scott-Gatty, Alexander 1876-1937 *NotNAT B, WhThe*
Scott-Heron, Gil 1948- *EncJzS 70*
Scott-Heron, Gil 1949- *AmSCAP 80, DrBlPA, IlEncR*
Scott-Hunter, Hortense *ConAmC*
Scott-Maddocks, Daniel James Vincent 1932- *WhoMus 72*
Scotti, Antonio 1866-1936 *Baker 78, BiDAmM, CmOp, MusSN[port], NewEOp 71, NewGrD 80*
Scotti, Ben And Tony *ConMuA 80B*
Scotti, Vito *ForYSC, WhoHol A*
Scotti, William 1895- *AmSCAP 66, -80*
Scottigena, Johannes *NewGrD 80*
Scottish Roscius *OxThe*
Scotto *NewGrD 80*
Scotto, Girolamo 1505?-1572 *NewGrD 80*
Scotto, Marchio *NewGrD 80*
Scotto, Marchiore *NewGrD 80*
Scotto, Melchiorre *NewGrD 80*
Scotto, Ottaviano *NewGrD 80*
Scotto, Ottaviano d1498 *NewGrD 80*
Scotto, Renata *WhoMus 72*
Scotto, Renata 1934- *Baker 78, CmOp, NewEOp 71, NewGrD 80*
Scotto, Renata 1935- *MusSN[port], WhoOp 76*
Scotto, Vincent 1874-1952 *NewGrD 80*
Scotto, Vincent 1876-1952 *DcFM, FilmEn*
Scotto, Vincente 1876-1952 *FilmgC, HalFC 80*
Scottoline, Angelo 1908- *AmSCAP 66*
Scottoline, Mary Rosalia 1923- *AmSCAP 66, -80*
Scotus, Joannes 815?-881? *Baker 78*
Scouarnec, Claudette 1942- *CnOxB*
Scoular, Angela *WhoHol A*
Scourby, Alexander *MotPP, NewYTET, WhoHol A*
Scourby, Alexander 1908- *MovMk*
Scourby, Alexander 1913- *BiE&WWA, FilmEn, FilmgC, ForYSC, HalFC 80, NotNAT, WhoThe 72, -77*
Scourby, Helen *WhoHol A*
Scourfield, Emily Gwendoline Rees *WhoMus 72*
Scoville, Margaret 1944- *ConAmC*
Scovotti, Jeanette 1938- *IntWWM 77, -80*
Scovotti, Jeanette Louise 1936- *WhoOp 76*
Scozzese, Agostino 1550?-1584? *NewGrD 80*
Scragg, Thomas William 1940- *IntWWM 77, -80*
Scranton Sirens *BiDAmM*
Scrase, David Bernard 1932- *IntWWM 80*
Screaming Lord Sutch *IlEncR[port]*
Screiber, Frederick C 1895- *ConAmC*
Scriabin, Aleksandr 1871?-1915 *BnBkM 80*
Scriabin, Alexander 1872-1915 *Baker 78, CompSN[port], CnOxB, DcCom 77, DcCM, MusMk[port], NewGrD 80, OxMus*
Scriabine, Marina 1911- *Baker 78*
Scribanus, Iohannes *NewGrD 80*
Scribe, August-Eugene 1791-1861 *NewEOp 71*
Scribe, Eugene 1791-1861 *Baker 78, BnBkM 80, CmOp, CnThe, CnOxB, EncWT, Ent[port], McGEWD[port], NewGrD 80, NotNAT A, -B, OxThe, REnWD[port]*
Scribner, Samuel A d1941 *NotNAT B*
Scripps, Douglas Jerry 1942- *IntWWM 77, -80*
Scrivano, Juan *NewGrD 80*
Scriven, R C *ConDr 77B*
Scronx, Gerard *NewGrD 80*
Scronx, Lambert *NewGrD 80*
Scruffy *IlWWBF A*
Scruggs, Earl 1924- *BiDAmM, CmpEPM, CounME 74[port], -74A, EncFCWM 69, IlEncCM[port]*
Scruggs, Irene 1901- *BluesWW*
Scruggs, Linda *WhoHol A*
Scrutton, Maud E *PupTheA*
Scudamore, Frank A d1904 *NotNAT B*
Scudamore, Margaret 1884-1958 *NotNAT B, WhThe*
Scudder, Eliza 1821-1896 *BiDAmM*
Scudder, Moses L 1814-1891 *BiDAmM*
Scudder, Virgil Elmer 1936- *ConAmTC*
Scudder, Wallace M *AmSCAP 66, -80*
Scudery, Georges De 1601-1667 *OxThe*
Scudo, P 1806-1864 *NewGrD 80*
Scudo, Paul 1806-1864 *NewGrD 80*
Scudo, Paulo 1806-1864 *NewGrD 80*
Scudo, Pierre 1806-1864 *Baker 78, NewGrD 80*
Scudo, Pietro 1806-1864 *NewGrD 80*
Scudus, Aegidius *NewGrD 80*
Scull, Harold Thomas 1898- *WhoMus 72*
Scullion, James H J d1920 *NotNAT B*
Scully, Frank *ForYSC*
Scully, Joe 1926- *IntMPA 77, -75, -76, -78, -79, -80*
Scully, Peter R 1920- *IntMPA 77, -75, -76, -78, -79, -80*
Scully, William A 1894- *IntMPA 77, -75, -76, -78*
Sculthorpe, Peter 1929- *Baker 78, DcCM, IntWWM 77, -80, MusMk, NewGrD 80, WhoMus 72*
Scuse, Dennis George 1921- *IntMPA 77, -75, -76, -78, -79, -80*
Scutta, Andreas 1806-1863 *NewGrD 80*
Sea, Bernie *AmSCAP 80*
Sea Island Singers *EncFCWM 69*
Sea Train *BiDAmM, IlEncR*
Seabrook, Jeremy 1939- *ConDr 77*
Seabrook, Thomas Q *AmPS B*
Seabrooke, Terry *MagIlD*
Seabrooke, Thomas Quigley 1860-1913 *NotNAT B, WhThe, WhoStg 1906, -1908*
Seabury, Forest *Film 1, -2*
Seabury, Ynez 1909-1973 *Film 2, WhScrn 77, WhoHol B*
Seaby, Clifford Bird 1908- *IntWWM 77*
Seaby, Mary Dorothy 1916- *IntWWM 77*
Seacombe, Dorothy 1905- *Film 2, WhThe*
Seacombe, Dorothy 1906- *IlWWBF*
Seader, Richard 1923- *BiE&WWA*
Seadler, Silas F *IntMPA 77, -75, -76, -78, -79, -80*
Seaforth, Susan *WhoHol A*
Seager, Gerald *ConAmC*
Seagle, Oscar 1877-1945 *Baker 78*
Seagram, Lisa *WhoHol A*
Seagram, Wilfrid 1884-1938 *NotNAT B, WhThe*
Seagull, Barbara 1948- *FilmEn, HalFC 80, WhoHol A*
Seal, Elizabeth 1933- *BiE&WWA, EncMT, NotNAT, WhoThe 72, -77*
Seal, Elizabeth 1935- *FilmgC, HalFC 80, WhoHol A*
Seal, Richard Godfrey 1935- *IntWWM 77, -80*
Sealby, Mabel 1885- *WhThe*
Seale, Carl 1936- *CpmDNM 80*
Seale, Douglas 1913- *BiE&WWA, NotNAT, WhoThe 72, -77*
Seale, Kenneth 1916- *WhoThe 77*
Seals, Frank Junior 1942- *BluesWW[port]*
Seals, Gladys O'Farrell *BlkWAB[port]*
Seals, Howard E *MorBAP*
Seals, Troy 1938- *CounME 74[port], -74A, IlEncCM[port]*
Seals & Crofts *IlEncR[port], RkOn 2[port]*
Seaman, Christopher 1942- *IntWWM 80, WhoMus 72*
Seaman, David John 1943- *IntWWM 77, -80*
Seaman, Eugene I 1925- *ConAmC*
Seaman, Gerald Roberts 1934- *IntWWM 77, -80, WhoMus 72*
Seaman, Isaac d1923 *NotNAT B*
Seaman, Julia d1909 *NotNAT B*
Seaman, Sir Owen 1861-1936 *NotNAT B, WhThe*
Seaman, Phil 1926-1972 *EncJzS 70, IlEncJ*
Seaman, Phillip William 1926-1972 *EncJzS 70*
Seaman, William Hyland 1910- *AmSCAP 80*
Seami, Motokiyo 1363-1443 *McGEWD, REnWD[port]*
Sear, Walter 1930- *ConAmC*
Search, Frederick Preston 1899- *ConAmC*
Searchers, The *BiDAmM, RkOn 2[port]*
Searchfield, J W 1930- *IntWWM 77*
Searchfield, John W 1930- *IntWWM 80*
Searcy, Dale Lanning 1905- *AmSCAP 66*
Searcy, George 1881-1949 *JoeFr*
Searl, Jackie 1920- *FilmEn, Film 2, MotPP*
Searle, Francis 1909- *FilmgC, HalFC 80*
Searle, Francis A 1909- *IlWWBF*
Searle, Humphrey 1915- *Baker 78, DcCM, IntWWM 77, -80, MusMk, NewEOp 71, NewGrD 80, OxMus, WhoMus 72*
Searle, Jackie 1920- *FilmEn, FilmgC, ForYSC, HalFC 80, WhoHol A*
Searle, Judith *WhoHol A*
Searle, Kamuela C 1890-1920 *Film 2, WhoHol B*
Searle, Kamuela C 1890-1924 *WhScrn 77*
Searle, Laura 1928- *IntWWM 77*
Searle, Sam *Film 1*
Searle, Victor Clark 1929- *IntWWM 80*
Searles, Barbara *WomWMM B*
Searles, Cora 1859-1935 *WhScrn 74, -77*
Searley, Bill *Film 2*
Sears, A D *Film 1*
Sears, Al 1910- *CmpEPM, IlEncJ, WhoJazz 72*
Sears, Allan 1887-1942 *Film 2, TwYS, WhScrn 74, -77, WhoHol B*
Sears, Blanche 1870-1939 *WhScrn 74, -77*
Sears, David *PlP&P*
Sears, Edmund Hamilton 1810-1876 *BiDAmM*
Sears, Fred F *ForYSC*
Sears, Fred F 1913-1957 *FilmEn, FilmgC, HalFC 80, WhScrn 77, WhoHol B, WhoHrs 80, WorEFlm*
Sears, Heather 1935- *FilmEn, FilmgC, ForYSC, HalFC 80, IlWWBF, IntMPA 77, -75, -76, -78, -79, -80, MotPP, WhoHol A, WhoThe 72, -77*
Sears, Ilene Hanson 1938- *ConAmC*
Sears, Ted 1900-1958 *AmSCAP 66, -80*
Sears, Zelda 1873-1935 *Film 2, NotNAT B, WhScrn 74, -77, WhThe, WhoHol B*
Seashore, Carl Emil 1866-1949 *Baker 78, NewGrD 80, OxMus*
Seastrom, Dorothy *Film 2*
Seastrom, Victor 1879-1960 *AmFD, BiDFilm, -81, DcFM, FilmEn, Film 1, -2, FilmgC, HalFC 80, NotNAT B, OxFilm, TwYS A, WhScrn 74, -77, WhoHol B*
Seaton, Douglass 1950- *IntWWM 77, -80*
Seaton, George 1911-1979 *BiDFilm, -81, DcFM, FilmEn, FilmgC, HalFC 80, IntMPA 77, -75, -76, -78, -79, MovMk[port], WorEFlm*
Seaton, Scott 1878-1968 *WhScrn 74, -77, WhoHol B*
Seatrain *ConMuA 80A*
Seave *NewGrD 80*
Seaver, Blanche Ebert 1891- *AmSCAP 66, -80, ConAmC*
Seaver, Frank A 1910- *IntMPA 77, -75, -76, -78, -79*
Seaver, Harry A 1909- *ConAmC*
Seawell, Brent *ConAmC*
Seawell, Donald R *WhoThe 72, -77*
Seay, Albert 1916- *NewGrD 80*
Seay, Billy *Film 2*
Seay, James *ForYSC, WhoHol A*
Sebald, Alexander 1869-1934 *BiDAmM*
Sebastian The Lute Player *OxMus*
Sebastian Z Felsztyna 148-?-1543? *NewGrD 80*
Sebastian, Adele Stephanie 1956- *BlkWAB*
Sebastian, Dorothy d1957 *MotPP, NotNAT B, WhoHol B*
Sebastian, Dorothy 1903-1957 *FilmEn, ThFT[port], WhScrn 74, -77*
Sebastian, Dorothy 1904-1957 *Film 2, ForYSC, TwYS*
Sebastian, George 1903- *CmOp, NewEOp 71*
Sebastian, Georges 1903- *Baker 78,*

NewGrD 80, WhoMus 72, WhoOp 76
Sebastian, John 1944- *ConMuA 80A, -80B, IlEncR[port], RkOn 2[port], WhoHol A*
Sebastian, Mihail 1907-1945 *McGEWD[port]*
Sebastiani, Claudius *NewGrD 80*
Sebastiani, Johann 1622-1683 *Baker 78, NewGrD 80*
Sebastiani, Sylva 1942- *WhoOp 76*
Sebell, Tellervo 1915- *IntWWM 77, -80*
Sebenico, Giovanni 1640?-1705 *NewGrD 80*
Seberg, Jean 1938-1979 *BiDFilm, -81, FilmAG WE, FilmEn, FilmgC, ForYSC, HalFC 80, IntMPA 77, -75, -76, -78, -79, MotPP, MovMk[port], OxFilm, WhoHol A, WorEFlm[port]*
Sebesky, Don 1937- *EncJzS 70*
Sebesky, Donald J 1937- *AmSCAP 80, EncJzS 70*
Sebesky, Gerald John 1941- *AmSCAP 80, ConAmC*
Sebestyen, Georges *NewGrD 80*
Sebestyen, Janos 1931- *IntWWM 80*
Sebestyen, Katalin 1943- *IntWWM 77, -80*
Sebiniano, Michael P 1927- *AmSCAP 66, -80*
Sebok, Gyorgy 1922- *WhoMus 72*
Sebor, Karl 1843-1903 *Baker 78*
Sebree, Charles 1914- *BlkAmP, DrBlPA, MorBAP*
Sebring, Jay 1933-1969 *WhScrn 77*
Secchi, Niccolo 1500?-1560 *McGEWD*
Sechan, Edmond 1919- *DcFM, WorEFlm*
Sechter, Simon 1788-1867 *Baker 78, NewGrD 80*
Seckendorff, Carl Siegmund Von 1744-1785 *Baker 78*
Seckendorff, Karl Siegmund, Freiherr Von 1744-1785 *NewGrD 80*
Seckler, Beatrice *CnOxB, DancEn 78*
Secombe, Harry 1921- *EncMT, FilmgC, HalFC 80, IlWWBF[port], IntMPA 77, -75, -76, -78, -79, -80, WhoHol A, WhoMus 72, WhoThe 72, -77*
Second, Sarah *NewGrD 80*
Secondari, John H d1975 *NewYTET*
Secrest, Andy 1907- *CmpEPM, WhoJazz 72*
Secrest, James *WhoHol A*
Secretan, Lance 1939- *WhThe*
Secrets, The *RkOn*
Secrist, Harley Walter 1890- *AmSCAP 66, -80*
Secrt, Josef *NewGrD 80*
Secter, David 1943- *CreCan 2*
Section, The *ConMuA 80A*
Secunda, Sheldon 1929- *AmSCAP 66, -80*
Secunda, Sholom 1894-1974 *AmSCAP 66, -80, ConAmC, WhoMus 72*
Sedaine, Michel-Jean 1719-1797 *CnThe, McGEWD, NewEOp 71, NewGrD 80, OxThe, REnWD[port]*
Sedaka, Neil 1939- *AmPS B, ConMuA 80A, IlEncR[port], RkOn[port], -2[port]*
Sedan, Rolfe 1896- *Film 2, ForYSC, TwYS, Vers A[port]*
Seddon, Margaret 1872-1968 *Film 2, WhScrn 77, WhoHol B*
Sedgwick, Edie 1943-1971 *WhScrn 74, -77, WhoHol B*
Sedgwick, Edward d1953 *WhoHol B*
Sedgwick, Edward 1892-1933? *TwYS A*
Sedgwick, Edward 1892-1953 *FilmEn*
Sedgwick, Edward 1893-1953 *FilmgC, HalFC 80*
Sedgwick, Edward, Jr. 1889?-1953 *WhScrn 77*
Sedgwick, Eileen 1895- *FilmEn*
Sedgwick, Eileen 1897- *Film 1, -2, TwYS, WhoHol A*
Sedgwick, Josie d1973 *MotPP, WhoHol B*
Sedgwick, Josie 1895-1973 *FilmEn*
Sedgwick, Josie 1898-1973 *WhScrn 77*
Sedgwick, Josie 1900-1973 *Film 1, -2, TwYS*
Sedgwick, Russell *Film 2*
Sedie, Enrico Delle *NewEOp 71*
Sedillo, Juan *Film 2*
Sedivka, Jan 1917- *IntWWM 80, WhoMus 72*
Sedlak, John 1942- *NatPD[port]*
Sedlak, Wenzel 1776-1851 *NewGrD 80*
Sedley, Sir Charles 1639?-1701 *Ent, NotNAT B, OxThe*
Sedley, Henry *Film 2*
Sedley-Smith, William Henry 1806-1872 *NotNAT B, OxThe*
Sedores, Sil *AmSCAP 80*
Sedova, Julia 1880-1969 *DancEn 78*
Sedova, Julie 1880-1969 *CnOxB*
Sedric, Eugene 1907-1963 *CmpEPM*
Sedric, Honey Bear 1907-1963 *WhoJazz 72*
Sedulius *NewGrD 80*
See, Edmond 1875-1959 *McGEWD[port], WhThe*
Seebass, Tilman 1939- *IntWWM 77, -80*
Seeber, Guido 1879-1940 *DcFM, FilmEn*
Seeberg *Film 2*
Seeboeck, William Charles Ernest 1859-1907 *BiDAmM*
Seebohm, E V d1888 *NotNAT B*
Seed, Donald 1913- *WhoMus 72*
Seedo 1700?-1754? *Baker 78, NewGrD 80*
Seedo, Maria *NewGrD 80*
Seeds, The *BiDAmM, ConMuA 80A, RkOn 2[port]*
Seefehlner, Egon 1912- *WhoOp 76*
Seefried, Irmgard 1919- *Baker 78, BnBkM 80, CmOp, IntWWM 77, -80, MusSN[port], NewEOp 71, NewGrD 80, WhoMus 72*
Seegar, Miriam 1909- *Film 2, WhoHol A*
Seegar, Sara *WhoHol A*
Seeger *NewGrD 80*
Seeger, Charles Louis, Jr. 1886-1979 *Baker 78, BiDAmM, ConAmC, EncFCWM 69, NewGrD 80*
Seeger, Horst 1926- *IntWWM 77, -80, NewGrD 80, WhoOp 76*
Seeger, Johann Baptista *NewGrD 80*
Seeger, Josef *NewGrD 80*
Seeger, Joseph 1716-1782 *Baker 78*
Seeger, Judith *WomWMM B*
Seeger, Margaret 1935- *BiDAmM, NewGrD 80*
Seeger, Michael 1933- *BiDAmM, IntWWM 77, -80, NewGrD 80*
Seeger, Mike 1933- *EncFCWM 69*
Seeger, Peggy 1935- *EncFCWM 69, NewGrD 80*
Seeger, Pete 1919- *Baker 78, CmpEPM, ConMuA 80A, EncFCWM 69, IlEncR, MusMk, NewGrD 80, WhoHol A*
Seeger, Peter R *PupTheA*
Seeger, Peter R 1919- *BiDAmM*
Seeger, Ruth Crawford 1901-1953 *Baker 78, BnBkM 80, ConAmC, DcCM, NewGrD 80*
Seeger, Sanford *WhoHol A*
Seekers, The *EncFCWM 69, RkOn 2[port]*
Seel, Charles *WhoHol A*
Seel, Jeanne N 1898-1964 *WhScrn 74, -77*
Seelen, Arthur 1923- *BiE&WWA, NotNAT*
Seelen, Jerry 1912- *AmSCAP 66, -80*
Seelen, Johann Heinrich Von 1688-1762 *NewGrD 80*
Seeley, Blossom 1891-1974 *CmpEPM, What 4[port]*
Seeley, Blossom 1892-1974 *BiE&WWA, HalFC 80, NotNAT B, WhoHol B*
Seeley, James d1943 *NotNAT B, WhoHol B*
Seeley, Lewis *Film 2*
Seeley, Paul David 1949- *IntWWM 80*
Seeley, S K *FilmEn*
Seelig, Arthur, Jr. 1929- *NewOrJ*
Seelig, Arthur, Sr. 1908- *NewOrJ[port]*
Seelig, Virginia Garrett 1922- *IntWWM 77*
Seeling, Hans 1828-1862 *Baker 78*
Seeling, Josef Antonin *NewGrD 80*
Seelkopf, Martin 1942- *IntWWM 80*
Seelos, Annette 1891-1918 *WhScrn 77*
Seely, Blossom 1892-1974 *WhScrn 77*
Seely, Jeannie 1940- *CounME 74[port], -74A, IlEncCM*
Seely, Marilyn Jeanne 1940- *BiDAmM*
Seely, Scott Buckley 1911- *AmSCAP 66, -80*
Seely, Tim *WhoHol A*
Seferian, Edward 1931- *IntWWM 77, -80*
Seff, Richard 1927- *BiE&WWA, NatPD[port], NotNAT*
Sefton, Alfred 1935- *IntWWM 77*
Sefton, Ernest d1954 *NotNAT B, WhoHol B*
Segal, Alex 1915-1977 *BiE&WWA, EncWT, FilmEn, FilmgC, HalFC 80, IntMPA 77, -75, -76, NewYTET, NotNAT*
Segal, Ben 1919- *BiE&WWA, NotNAT*
Segal, Bernard 1868-1940 *WhScrn 74, WhoHol B*
Segal, David F 1943- *NotNAT*
Segal, Erich 1937- *AmSCAP 66, -80, WhoHol A*
Segal, George 1934- *BiDFilm, -81, FilmEn, FilmgC, HalFC 80[port], IntMPA 77, -75, -76, -78, -79, -80, MotPP, MovMk[port], WhoHol A*
Segal, George 1936- *WorEFlm*
Segal, George 1939- *ForYSC*
Segal, Jack 1918- *AmSCAP 66, -80*
Segal, Maurice 1921- *IntMPA 77, -75, -76, -78, -79, -80*
Segal, Uri 1944- *IntWWM 77, NewGrD 80*
Segal, Uriel 1944- *IntWWM 80*
Segal, Vivienne 1897- *AmPS B, BiDAmM, BiE&WWA, CmpEPM, EncMT, FilmEn, Film 2, ForYSC, HalFC 80, MotPP, NotNAT, ThFT[port], What 3[port], WhThe, WhoHol A*
Segall, Bernardo 1911- *AmSCAP 66, -80, ConAmC, DancEn 78*
Segall, Don 1933- *AmSCAP 80*
Segall, Donald 1933- *AmSCAP 66*
Segall, Harry 1897-1975 *FilmgC, HalFC 80*
Segall, Richard Robert 1947- *AmSCAP 80*
Segar, Lucia 1874-1962 *Film 2, WhScrn 74, -77, WhoHol B*
Segarra, Ramon 1939- *CnOxB*
Segelstein, Irwin B *NewYTET*
Seger, Bob 1945- *ConMuA 80A[port], IlEncR, RkOn 2[port]*
Seger, Johann Baptista *NewGrD 80*
Seger, Josef 1716?-1782 *NewGrD 80*
Seger, Lucia 1874-1962 *NotNAT B*
Seger, Robert Clark 1945- *AmSCAP 80*
Segers, Henry Louis 1921- *WhoMus 72*
Segerstam, Leif Selim 1944- *Baker 78, DcCM, IntWWM 77, -80, NewGrD 80, WhoOp 76*
Segerstrom, Per Arthur 1952- *CnOxB*
Seghers, Francois-Jean-Baptiste 1801-1881 *Baker 78*
Segni, Julio 1498-1561 *NewGrD 80*
Segnitz, Eugen 1862-1927 *Baker 78*
Sego Brothers And Naomi *BiDAmM*
Segond, Pierre 1913- *NewGrD 80*
Segond-Weber, Eugenie-Caroline 1867- *WhThe*
Segovia, Andres 1893- *Baker 78, BnBkM 80[port], MusMk[port], MusSN[port], NewGrD 80, OxMus*
Segovia, Andres 1894- *IntWWM 77, WhoMus 72*
Segovia, Rosita 1926- *CnOxB*
Seguin, Arthur Edward S 1809-1852 *BiDAmM NewGrD 80*
Seguin, Denys 1937- *CreCan 1*
Segura, Leticia Espinosa d1956 *WhScrn 74, -77*
Sehlbach, Erich 1898- *DcCM, IntWWM 77, -80, NewGrD 80*
Sehling, Josef Antonin 1710-1756 *NewGrD 80*
Sehnal, Jiri 1931- *IntWWM 77, -80, NewGrD 80*
Seibel, Klauspeter 1936- *IntWWM 80, WhoOp 76*
Seiber, Matyas 1905-1960 *Baker 78, DcCom&M 79, DcCM, MusMk[port], NewGrD 80[port], OxMus*
Seibert, Bob *ConAmC*
Seibert, Peter Clarendon 1936- *IntWWM 77*
Seible, Lynda Suzanne 1949- *IntWWM 77*
Seickard, Joseph *Film 2*
Seidel, Diana E *WomWMM A, -B*
Seidel, Friedrich Ludwig 1765-1831 *Baker 78, NewGrD 80*
Seidel, Jan 1908- *Baker 78, NewGrD 80*
Seidel, Johann Julius 1810-1856 *Baker 78*
Seidel, Richard D 1925- *ConAmC*
Seidel, Samuel 1610?-1665 *NewGrD 80*
Seidel, Toscha 1899-1962 *Baker 78, MusSN[port]*
Seidelman, Robert 1925- *IntMPA 77, -75, -76, -78, -79*
Seidelmann, Franz *NewGrD 80*
Seideman, Wladyslaw 1849-1890? *NewGrD 80*
Seiden, Stanley 1922- *BiE&WWA*
Seider, Harold *ConMuA 80B*
Seidewitz, Marie d1929 *WhScrn 74, -77*
Seidl, Anton 1850-1898 *Baker 78, BiDAmM, BnBkM 80, CmOp, NewEOp 71,*

NewGrD 80, OxMus
Seidl, Arthur 1863-1928 *Baker 78*
Seidl, Jan *NewGrD 80*
Seidl, Lea 1902- *WhThe*
Seidman, J S 1901- *BiE&WWA, NotNAT*
Seidman, Lloyd 1913- *IntMPA 77, -75, -76, -78, -79, -80*
Seidman, William 1953- *AmSCAP 80*
Seidner, Irene 1880-1959 *WhScrn 77*
Seifarth, Johann Gabriel *NewGrD 80*
Seifert *NewGrD 80*
Seifert, Ernst Hubertus 1855-1928 *NewGrD 80*
Seifert, F A *PupTheA*
Seifert, Johann Caspar *NewGrD 80*
Seifert, Johann Gottfried *NewGrD 80*
Seifert, Louis 1884- *AmSCAP 66*
Seifert, M J 1864-1947 *BiDAmM*
Seifert, Otto Erich 1912- *IntWWM 77, -80*
Seifert, Patricia Diane 1941- *IntWWM 77*
Seifert, Uso 1852-1912 *Baker 78*
Seifert, Zbigniew 1946- *EncJzS 70*
Seiffert, Elaine 1941- *IntWWM 80*
Seiffert, Max 1868-1948 *Baker 78, NewGrD 80*
Seiffert, Stephen Lyons 1938- *IntWWM 77, -80*
Seifriz, Max 1827-1885 *Baker 78*
Seigenfeld, Edward P 1937- *IntMPA 77, -75, -76, -78, -79, -80*
Seigenthaler, William Robert 1934- *AmSCAP 80*
Seiger, Marvin L 1924- *BiE&WWA, NotNAT*
Seigfred, Earl C *PupTheA*
Seighman, William Henry 1938- *AmSCAP 80*
Seigmann, George 1884-1928 *Film 1, -2, TwYS*
Seigner, Louis 1903- *FilmEn*
Seigneuret, Michele 1934- *CnOxB, DancEn 78*
Seiler, Conrad *BlkAmP, MorBAP*
Seiler, Edward 1911-1952 *AmSCAP 66, -80*
Seiler, Lew *TwYS A*
Seiler, Lewis 1891-1963 *FilmEn*
Seiler, Lewis 1891-1964 *FilmgC, HalFC 80, NotNAT B*
Seiler, Mimy 1906- *IntWWM 77, -80*
Seillier, Daniel Fernand 1926- *CreCan 1*
Seillier, Daniel Fernard 1926- *CnOxB*
Sein, Kenneth *REnWD[port]*
Seinberg, Lillian 1907- *AmSCAP 80*
Seinemeyer, Meta 1895-1929 *Baker 78, CmOp, NewGrD 80*
Seiner, Katinka 1937- *IntWWM 80*
Seiss, Isodor 1840-1905 *Baker 78*
Seiter, Bill *Film 1*
Seiter, William A 1891-1964 *FilmgC, HalFC 80*
Seiter, William A 1892-1964 *FilmEn, WhScrn 74, -77*
Seiter, William S 1895-1964 *TwYS A*
Seitter, Charles F 1892- *AmSCAP 66, -80*
Seitz, Dran 1928- *BiE&WWA, NotNAT, WhoHol A*
Seitz, George B d1944 *Film 1, WhoHol B*
Seitz, George B 1880-1944 *WorEFlm*
Seitz, George B 1883-1944 *TwYS A*
Seitz, George B 1888-1944 *FilmEn, Film 2, FilmgC, HalFC 80, MovMk[port], WhScrn 74, -77*
Seitz, Gerhard 1922- *IntWWM 77, -80*
Seitz, John 1899-1979 *CmMov*
Seitz, John F 1892-1979 *WorEFlm*
Seitz, John F 1893-1979 *FilmEn, FilmgC, HalFC 80*
Seitz, Robert 1837-1889 *Baker 78*
Seitz, Tani 1928- *BiE&WWA, NotNAT, WhoHol A*
Seitz, Wayne T 1932- *BiE&WWA, NotNAT*
Seivewright, Robert Andrew 1926- *IntWWM 77, -80, WhoMus 72*
Seixas, Carlos De 1704-1742 *Baker 78, MusMk, NewGrD 80*
Sejan, Nicolas 1745-1819 *Baker 78, NewGrD 80*
Sejean, Nicolas 1745-1819 *NewGrD 80*
Sejna, Karel 1896- *NewGrD 80*
Sejour, Victor 1817-1874 *BlkAmP, DrBlPA*
Sekely, Irene Agay 1914-1950 *WhScrn 74, -77, WhoHol B*
Sekely, Steve 1899-1979 *FilmEn, FilmgC, HalFC 80, IntMPA 77, -75, -76, -78, -79, WhoHrs 80*
Sekert, Josef *NewGrD 80*
Sekh, Yaroslav 1930- *CnOxB, DancEn 78*
Sekigawa, Hideo 1908- *FilmEn*
Sekka, Johnny 1939- *DrBlPA, WhoHol A*
Sekles, Bernhard 1872-1934 *Baker 78, NewGrD 80, OxMus*
Seklucjan, Jan 1510?-1578 *NewGrD 80*
Sekulidis, Donna 1949- *AmSCAP 80*
Selander, Concordia *Film 1, -2*
Selander, Hjalmar *Film 1*
Selander, Lesley 1900-1979 *FilmEn, FilmgC, HalFC 80, IntMPA 77, -75, -76, -78, -79, -80, WhoHrs 80*
Selbie, Evelyn 1882-1950 *Film 1, -2, TwYS, WhScrn 74, -77, WhoHol B*
Selbiger, Liselotte *WhoMus 72*
Selbit, P T 1879-1938 *MagIlD[port]*
Selbourne, David 1937- *ConDr 73, -77*
Selbst, George 1917- *ConAmC*
Selby, Bertram Luard 1853-1918 *Baker 78*
Selby, Charles d1963 *NotNAT B*
Selby, Mrs. Charles d1873 *NotNAT B*
Selby, David *IntMPA 77, -75, -76, -78, -79, -80, WhoHol A*
Selby, Kid McCoy 1874-1940 *WhScrn 74*
Selby, Nicholas 1925- *WhoHol A, WhoThe 72, -77*
Selby, Norman 1874-1940 *Film 1, -2, WhScrn 77, WhoHol B*
Selby, Percival M 1886-1955 *NotNAT B, WhThe*
Selby, Peter Hollinshead 1914- *AmSCAP 66, -80*
Selby, Sarah *ForYSC, WhoHol A*
Selby, Tony 1938- *WhoHol A, WhoThe 72, -77*
Selby, William *NewGrD 80*
Selby, William 1738?-1798 *Baker 78, NewGrD 80, OxMus*
Selby, William 1739?-1798 *BiDAmM*
Selby Brothers *ConMuA 80B*
Selch, Frederick Richard 1930- *IntWWM 80*
Selch, Grant W *PupTheA*
Selden, Albert W 1922- *AmSCAP 66, BiE&WWA, NotNAT*
Selden, Fred Laurence 1945- *EncJzS 70*
Selden, Margery Stomne *IntWWM 80*
Selden, Neil 1931- *NatPD[port]*
Selden, Samuel 1899- *BiE&WWA, NotNAT*
Seldes, Gilbert 1893-1970 *BiE&WWA, NotNAT B, OxFilm*
Seldes, Marian 1928- *BiE&WWA, ForYSC, NotNAT, WhoHol A, WhoThe 72, -77*
Selen, Paul Ebbe 1920- *IntWWM 77, -80*
Selesses, Jacopinus *NewGrD 80*
Seletsky, Harold *ConAmC*
Self, Charles *BlkAmP*
Self, George 1921- *IntWWM 77, -80*
Self, William 1921- *ForYSC, IntMPA 77, -75, -76, -78, -79, -80, NewYTET*
Selfridge-Field, Eleanor Anne 1940- *IntWWM 80*
Selich, Daniel 1581?-1626 *NewGrD 80*
Selichius, Daniel 1581?-1626 *NewGrD 80*
Selig, Robert 1939- *ConAmC*
Selig, Robert William *IntMPA 77, -75, -76, -78, -79, -80*
Selig, William Nicholas 1864-1946 *FilmgC*
Selig, William Nicholas 1864-1948 *FilmEn, HalFC 80, NotNAT B*
Seligman, Marjorie 1900- *BiE&WWA*
Seligman, Nat Jeffrey 1950- *AmSCAP 80*
Seligman, Selig J d1969 *NewYTET*
Seligmann, Hippolyte-Prosper 1817-1882 *Baker 78*
Seligmann, Lilias Hazewell MacLane d1964 *NotNAT B*
Selinder, Anders 1806-1874 *CnOxB*
Seling, Josef Antonin *NewGrD 80*
Selinsky, Wladimir 1910- *AmSCAP 66, -80*
Selk, George W 1893-1967 *WhScrn 77, WhoHol B*
Selkin, Margaret *PupTheA*
Sell, David Frank 1930- *IntWWM 77, -80*
Sell, Henry G *Film 1, -2*
Sell, Janie 1941- *WhoThe 77*
Sellar, Robert J B d1960 *NotNAT B*
Sellars, Elizabeth 1923- *FilmEn, FilmgC, ForYSC, HalFC 80, IlWWBF, IntMPA 77, -75, -76, -78, -79, -80, WhoHol A, WhoThe 72, -77*
Sellars, Vera Arnold 1897- *IntWWM 77*
Sellars, Winifred Treasure *WhoMus 72*
Selle, Maude Marshall 1906- *AmSCAP 66*
Selle, Thomas 1599-1663 *Baker 78, NewGrD 80[port]*
Selleck, John *ConAmC*
Selleck, Tom *WhoHol A*
Seller, Jane *WomWMM B*
Seller, Thomas *IntMPA 77, -75, -76, -78, -79, -80*
Sellers, Arlene *IntMPA 79, -80*
Sellers, Brother John 1924- *AmSCAP 80, DrBlPA*
Sellers, Catherine *WhoHol A*
Sellers, Charles Emmett 1887-1934 *JoeFr*
Sellers, John B 1924- *AmSCAP 66, BluesWW[port]*
Sellers, Peter 1924-1980 *ForYSC*
Sellers, Peter 1925-1980 *BiDFilm, -81, CmMov, FilmAG WE[port], FilmEn, FilmgC, HalFC 80, IlWWBF[port], -A, IntMPA 77, -75, -76, -78, -79, -80, JoeFr[port], MotPP, MovMk[port], OxFilm, WhoHol A, WorEFlm[port]*
Sellers, Ronnie *WhoHol A*
Sellers, Sallie *PupTheA*
Sellers, Thomas *PupTheA*
Sellick, Phyllis 1911- *IntWWM 77, -80, NewGrD 80, WhoMus 72*
Selling, Caj 1935- *DancEn 78*
Sellitto, Giuseppe 1700-1777 *NewGrD 80*
Sellman, Hunton D 1900- *BiE&WWA, NotNAT*
Sellner, Gustav Rudolf 1905- *EncWT, WhoOp 76*
Sellner, Johann *NewGrD 80*
Sellner, Joseph 1787-1843 *Baker 78*
Sellon, Charles 1878-1937 *Film 2, ForYSC, TwYS, WhScrn 74, -77, WhoHol B*
Selma Y Salaverde, Bartolome De *NewGrD 80*
Selmer *NewGrD 80*
Selmer, Johan Peter 1844-1910 *Baker 78, NewGrD 80*
Selmer, Kathryn Lande 1930- *AmSCAP 66, -80, ConAmC A*
Selmer, Mildred 1900- *IntWWM 77*
Selneccer, Nikolaus 1528-1592 *NewGrD 80*
Selnecker, Nikolaus 1528-1592 *NewGrD 80*
Selner, Johann 1525?-1583 *NewGrD 80*
Selner, Johannes 1525?-1583 *NewGrD 80*
Selsman, Victor 1908-1958 *AmSCAP 66, -80*
Selten, Morton 1860-1939 *NotNAT B, WhScrn 74, -77, WhThe, WhoHol B*
Selten, Morton 1860-1940 *FilmgC, HalFC 80*
Seltzer, David *HalFC 80*
Seltzer, Jules 1908- *IntMPA 77, -75, -76, -78, -79, -80*
Seltzer, Walter 1914- *FilmgC, HalFC 80, IntMPA 77, -75, -76, -78, -79, -80*
Selucky, Rosalie Anne 1943- *IntWWM 77, -80*
Selva, Blanche 1884-1942 *Baker 78, NewGrD 80*
Selvaggi, Rito 1898-1972 *Baker 78*
Selvaggio, John Ralph 1937- *AmSCAP 66, -80*
Selvin, Ben 1900?- *AmPS A, BgBands 74, CmpEPM*
Selvin, Robert Brian 1957- *AmSCAP 80*
Selwart, Tonio 1896- *BiE&WWA, NotNAT, WhThe, WhoHol A, WhoThe 72*
Selwood, Maureen *WomWMM B*
Selwyn, Archibald d1959 *NotNAT B, WhThe*
Selwyn, Clarissa *Film 1, -2*
Selwyn, Edgar 1875-1944 *FilmEn, Film 1, FilmgC, HalFC 80, NotNAT B, WhThe, WhoStg 1908*
Selwyn, Edward *WhoMus 72*
Selwyn, Ruth 1905-1954 *NotNAT B, WhScrn 74, -77, WhoHol B*
Selwynne, Clarissa *TwYS*
Selzer, Milton *WhoHol A*
Selzick, Stephen *Film 2*
Selznick, David O 1902-1965 *BiDFilm, -81, DcFM, FilmEn, FilmgC, HalFC 80, MGM A[port], OxFilm, TwYS B, WorEFlm*
Selznick, Irene Mayer 1910- *BiE&WWA, NotNAT*
Selznick, Joyce *WomWMM*

Selznick, Lewis 1870-1932 OxFilm
Selznick, Lewis 1870-1933 FilmEn, NotNAT B
Selznick, Myron 1898-1944 FilmEn, NotNAT B
Sembello, John Anthony 1945- AmSCAP 80
Sembello, Michael Andrew 1954- AmSCAP 80
Sembene, Ousmane 1923- DrBlPA
Semberova, Zora 1913- CnOxB
Sembrich, Marcella 1858-1935 Baker 78, BiDAmM, BnBkM 80, CmOp, MusSN[port], NewEOp 71, NewGrD 80[port]
Semegen, Daria 1946- CpmDNM 79, -80, ConAmC, IntWWM 77, -80
Semegen, Daria W 1946- CpmDNM 76
Semel, Terry 1943- IntMPA 77, -78, -79, -80
Semele, Harry 1887-1946 Film 1, -2
Semels, Harry 1887-1946 ForYSC, WhScrn 77
Semenoff, Simon 1908- CnOxB, DancEn 78
Semenov, Nicholas DancEn 78
Semenova, Ekaterina Semenovna 1786-1849 NotNAT B, OxThe
Semenyaka, Ludmila 1952- CnOxB
Semet, Theophile 1824-1888 Baker 78
Semien, Lee 1931- BluesWW
Semien, Sidney 1938- BluesWW
Seminiati, Santino NewGrD 80
Seminiato, Santino NewGrD 80
Seminole, Paul 1904-1932 BiDAmM
Semkow, Georg 1928- Baker 78, NewGrD 80
Semkow, Jerzy 1928- IntWWM 77, -80, NewGrD 80, WhoMus 72
Semler, Sonny E 1947- IntWWM 80
Semmler, Alexander 1900-1977 Baker 78, ConAmC
Semmler, Gustav Film 2
Semmler, Rudolf Heinrich Mathias 1904- IntWWM 80
Semola, Alfonse J 1919- AmSCAP 80
Semon, Larry 1889-1928 FilmEn, Film 1, -2, FilmgC, HalFC 80, JoeFr[port], OxFilm, TwYS, -A, WhScrn 74, -77, WhoHol B, WorEFlm
Semon, Zera PupTheA
Semos, Murray 1913- AmSCAP 66, -80
Semper, Gottfried 1803-1879 EncWT, OxThe
Semper, Jean 1928- IntWWM 77, -80
Semple, Lorenzo, Jr. FilmgC, HalFC 80
Semsey, Maria 1943- IntWWM 77, -80
Semyonov, Victor 1893-1942 DancEn 78
Semyonov, Victor Alexandrovich 1892-1944 CnOxB
Semyonov, Vladilen Grigorievich 1932- CnOxB, DancEn 78
Semyonova, Marina Timofeyevna 1908- CnOxB, DancEn 78
Sen, Bachoo 1934- IntMPA 79, -80
Senaille, Jean Baptiste 1687-1730 Baker 78, MusMk
Senaille, Jean Baptiste 1688?-1730 NewGrD 80
Senaillie, Jean Baptiste 1688?-1730 NewGrD 80
Senaillier, Jean Baptiste 1688?-1730 NewGrD 80
Senallie, Jean Baptiste 1687-1730 OxMus
Senallie, Jean Baptiste 1688?-1730 NewGrD 80
Senallier, Jean Baptiste 1688?-1730 NewGrD 80
Senart NewGrD 80
Senart, Maurice 1878-1962 Baker 78, NewGrD 80
Senator, Ronald 1926- IntWWM 77
Senator, Ronald 1928- IntWWM 80
Senator Bobby RkOn 2[port]
Senators Quartet BiDAmM
Sendak, Maurice Bernard 1928- AmSCAP 80
Sender, Ramon 1934- DcCM
Sendrey, Aladar 1884-1976 NewGrD 80
Sendrey, Albert 1921- IntMPA 77, -75, -76, -78, -79, -80
Sendrey, Albert Richard 1900- ConAmC
Sendrey, Albert Richard 1911- Baker 78
Sendrey, Albert Richard 1922- AmSCAP 66, -80
Sendrey, Alfred 1884-1976 Baker 78, BiDAmM, ConAmC, NewGrD 80
Seneca 004?BC-065AD Ent, McGEWD[port], PlP&P[port]
Seneca, Lucius Annaeus 004?BC-065AD CnThe, EncWT, NotNAT B, OxThe, REnWD[port]
Senechal, Michel 1927- NewGrD 80
Senefelder, Alois 1771-1834 NewGrD 80, OxMus
Senensky, Bernard Melvyn 1944- EncJzS 70
Senensky, Bernie 1944- EncJzS 70
Senese NewGrD 80
Senesino d1759 NewGrD 80[port]
Senesino 1680-1750 CmOp, NewEOp 71
Senesino, Francesco 1680?-1750? Baker 78
Senfelius, Ludwig 1486?-1543 NewGrD 80[port]
Senff, Bartholf 1815-1900 Baker 78
Senff, Bartolf Wilhelm 1815-1900 NewGrD 80
Senfl, Ludwig 1486?-1543 Baker 78, NewGrD 80[port]
Senfl, Ludwig 1490?-1543 OxMus
Senger, Hugo Von 1832-1892 NewGrD 80
Sengstchmid, Johann 1936- IntWWM 80
Sengtschmid, Johann 1936- IntWWM 77
Senia, Paul Anthony 1925- CpmDNM 74, -76
Senilov, Vladimir 1875-1918 Baker 78
Senior, Evan 1907- WhoMus 72
Senior, John 1958- IntWWM 77, -80
Senior, Milton 1900?-1948? WhoJazz 72
Senk, Radimir IntWWM 77
Senkrah, Arma Leorette Hoffman Harkness 1864-1900 BiDAmM
Senleches, Jacob De NewGrD 80
Senn, Herbert Charles 1924- WhoOp 76, WhoThe 77
Senn, Kurt Wolfgang 1905-1965 NewGrD 80
Senn, Walter 1904- IntWWM 77, -80, NewGrD 80, WhoMus 72
Sennett, Mack 1880-1960 AmFD, CmMov, DcFM, FilmEn, Film 1, -2, FilmgC, HalFC 80, JoeFr[port], MotPP, TwYS, -A, WhScrn 74, -77, WhoHol B, WorEFlm[port]
Sennett, Mack 1884-1960 OxFilm, TwYS B
Sennewald NewGrD 80
Sennewald, Gustaw Adolf 1804-1860 NewGrD 80
Sennfl, Ludwig NewGrD 80
Senofsky, Berl 1925- WhoMus 72
Senoga-Zake, George William 1920- WhoMus 72
Sens, Al 1933- CreCan 1
Sens, Ginetta NewGrD 80
Sensational Alex Harvey Band IlEncR[port]
Sensations, The RkOn
Sensenderfer, Robert E P d1957 NotNAT B
Sensenschmidt, Johannes d1491? NewGrD 80
Senserre, Pierre NewGrD 80
Sent M'ahesa CnOxB
Sentenat 1896- WhoMus 72
Senter, Boyd Langdon 1898- AmSCAP 80
Senter, Boyd Langdon 1899- CmpEPM, WhoJazz 72
Senterre, Pierre NewGrD 80
Seprodi, Janos 1874-1923 NewGrD 80
Sequeiros, Juan DeLima 1655?-1726? NewGrD 80
Sequi, Sandro 1935- IntWWM 77, -80, WhoOp 76
Serafin, Santo NewGrD 80
Serafin, Tulio 1878-1968 Baker 78
Serafin, Tullio 1878-1968 BnBkM 80, CmOp, MusSN[port], NewEOp 71, NewGrD 80[port]
Serafino Aquilano 1466-1500 NewGrD 80
Serafino De' Ciminelli Dall'Aquila 1466-1500 NewGrD 80
Serafino, Santo 1650?-1740? Baker 78, NewGrD 80
Serandrei, Mario 1907- FilmEn
Seraphin, Dominique 1747-1800 DcPup, Ent
Seraphin, Sanctus 1699-1758? NewGrD 80
Seraphin, Santo 1699-1758? NewGrD 80
Seraphine, Daniel Peter 1948- AmSCAP 80
Seraphine, Nicola PupTheA
Serassi NewGrD 80
Serassi, Andrea Luigi 1725-1799 NewGrD 80
Serassi, Giuseppe 1694-1760 Baker 78, NewGrD 80
Serassi, Giuseppe 1750-1817 NewGrD 80
Serato, Arrigo 1877-1948 Baker 78, NewGrD 80
Serato, Massimo 1916- FilmAG WE
Serato, Massimo 1917- FilmEn
Serauky, Walter 1903-1959 Baker 78, NewGrD 80
Serbo, Rico Frank 1940- WhoOp 76
Serda, Julia Film 2
Sere, Octave NewGrD 80
Serebier, Jose 1938- IntWWM 77
Serebrier, Jose 1938- Baker 78, ConAmC, DcCM, IntWWM 80, NewGrD 80
Serebrier, Jose 1939- CpmDNM 75
Serebrinsky, Tito 1937- WhoOp 76
Serebryakov, Pavel 1909- NewGrD 80
Seregi, Laszlo 1929- CnOxB
Serena, Sigmund Film 2
Serendero, David 1934- IntWWM 77, -80
Serendero-Proust, David 1934- Baker 78
Serendipity Singers, The RkOn 2[port]
Sereni, Mario 1928- WhoOp 76
Sereny, Marika Robert CreCan 1
Seres, William NewGrD 80
Seress, Rezso 1899-1968 Baker 78
Seretan, Stephen Howard 1948- AmSCAP 80
Sergava, Katherine DancEn 78
Serge, John WhoMus 72
Sergeant, Desmond Charles 1929- WhoMus 72
Sergeant, Lewis Film 2
Sergeyev, Konstantin Mikhailovich 1910- CnOxB, DancEn 78[port], NewGrD 80
Sergeyev, Nicholas 1876-1951 CnOxB, DancEn 78
Sergi, Arturo 1927- WhoOp 76
Sergine, Vera d1946 NotNAT B, WhThe
Sergyl, Yvonne Film 2
Seria, Joel 1944- HalFC 80
Serieyx, Auguste 1865-1949 Baker 78, NewGrD 80
Sering, Friedrich Wilhelm 1822-1901 Baker 78
Serini, Giovanni Battista 1724?- Baker 78, NewGrD 80
Serjeantson, Kate d1918 NotNAT B, WhThe
Serkin, Peter 1947- Baker 78, BnBkM 80, NewGrD 80
Serkin, Peter A 1947- WhoMus 72
Serkin, Rudolf 1903- Baker 78, BiDAmM, BnBkM 80[port], IntWWM 77, MusMk, MusSN[port], NewGrD 80[port], WhoMus 72
Serkin, Rudolph 1903- IntWWM 80
Serkoyan, Gerard 1922- WhoOp 76
Serle, T J d1889 NotNAT B
Serlen, Bruce 1947- NatPD[port]
Serlin, Bernard M IntMPA 77, -75, -76, -78, -79
Serlin, Oscar 1901-1971 BiE&WWA, NotNAT B, WhThe
Serling, Rod 1924-1975 ConDr 73, FilmEn, FilmgC, HalFC 80, IntMPA 75, -76, NewYTET, WhScrn 77, WhoHrs 80[port], WorEFlm
Serlio, Sebastiano 1473?-1554 NotNAT B
Serlio, Sebastiano 1475-1554 EncWT, Ent, OxThe, PlP&P
Serlo Of Wilton 1110?-1181? NewGrD 80
Serly, Tibor 1900-1978 AmSCAP 66, -80, Baker 78, BiDAmM, CpmDNM 75, ConAmC
Serly, Tibor 1901-1978 NewGrD 80, WhoMus 72
Sermila, Jarmo Kalevi 1939- Baker 78, IntWWM 77, -80
Sermisy, Claude De 1490?-1562 Baker 78, NewGrD 80
Sermisy, Claudin De 1490?-1562 NewGrD 80
Serna, Estacio DeLa 1570?-1616? NewGrD 80
Serna, Pepe WhoHol A
Sernas, Jacques 1925- FilmEn, FilmgC, ForYSC, HalFC 80, IntMPA 77, -75, -76, -78, -79, -80, MotPP, WhoHol A
Sernklef, Harry Torild Wladimir 1923- IntWWM 77, -80
Serocki, Kazimierz 1922- Baker 78, DcCM, IntWWM 77, -80, NewGrD 80, OxMus
Seroen, Berthe 1882-1957 NewGrD 80
Serof, Alexander 1820-1871 OxMus
Seroff, George Film 2
Seroff, Muni 1903- BiE&WWA, NotNAT, WhoHol A
Seroff, Victor 1902- Baker 78, WhoMus 72
Serov, Alexander 1820-1871 Baker 78, CmOp, NewEOp 71, NewGrD 80[port]
Serpe, Ralph B 1914- IntMPA 77, -75, -76, -78,

–79, –80
Serpette, Gaston 1846-1904 *Baker 78, NewGrD 80*
Serpico, Dominick, Jr. 1953- *CpmDNM 80*
Serqueira, Juan De *NewGrD 80*
Serra, Luis 1680?-1759 *NewGrD 80*
Serra, Michelangelo 1571-1628? *NewGrD 80*
Serrano, Emilio 1850-1939 *Baker 78*
Serrano, Jose 1873-1941 *NewGrD 80*
Serrano, Lupe 1930- *CnOxB, DancEn 78[port]*
Serrano, Marta 1936- *WhoOp 76*
Serrano, Mercedes 1930- *DancEn 78*
Serrano, Nina *WomWMM B*
Serrano, Vincent d1935 *Film 1, –2, WhoHol B*
Serrano, Vincent 1867-1935 *WhScrn 74, –77*
Serrano, Vincent 1870-1935 *NotNAT B, WhThe*
Serrano Y Ruiz, Emilio 1850-1939 *NewGrD 80*
Serranus, Johann Baptista 1540-1600 *NewGrD 80*
Serrao, Paolo 1830-1907 *Baker 78, NewGrD 80*
Serrato, Massimo *HalFC 80*
Serre, Jean-Adam 1704-1788 *NewGrD 80*
Serres, Louis De 1864-1942 *Baker 78*
Serres, Marthe Des *CreCan 2*
Serrett, James 1948- *AmSCAP 80*
Serrlya, Sivia *WhoOp 76*
Serrurier, Georges *NewGrD 80*
Sersen, Fred 1890-1962 *FilmEn, FilmgC, HalFC 80*
Sert, Jose Maria 1876-1945 *CnOxB*
Sert, Jose Maria 1876-1947 *DancEn 78*
Sertel, Neela 1901-1969 *WhScrn 74, –77*
Sertic, Ivan 1927- *CnOxB*
Sertorio, Antonio *NewGrD 80*
Sertorio, Gasparo *NewGrD 80*
Servadei, Annette Elizabeth 1945- *IntWWM 80*
Servaes, Dagny *Film 2*
Servaes, William Reginald 1921- *WhoOp 76*
Servais *NewGrD 80*
Servais, Adrien Francois 1807-1866 *NewGrD 80, OxMus*
Servais, Francois 1807-1866 *Baker 78*
Servais, Francois 1847?-1901 *Baker 78*
Servais, Francois Mathieu 1846-1901 *NewGrD 80*
Servais, Franz 1846-1901 *NewGrD 80*
Servais, Jean 1910-1976 *FilmAG WE, FilmEn, FilmgC, ForYSC, HalFC 80, OxFilm, WhoHol C*
Servais, Joseph 1850-1885 *Baker 78, NewGrD 80, OxMus*
Servandony, Jean-Nicolas 1695-1766 *NotNAT B, OxThe*
Servanti, Luigi *Film 2*
Servent, Arthur 1904- *WhoMus 72*
Service, Robert William 1874?-1958 *CreCan 1*
Servieres, Georges 1858-1937 *Baker 78, NewGrD 80*
Servin, Jean 1530?-1596? *NewGrD 80*
Servoss, Mary 1908-1968 *BiE&WWA, WhScrn 74, –77, WhThe, WhoHol B*
Servyn, Jean 1530?-1596? *NewGrD 80*
Serwaczynski, Stanislaw 1791-1859 *NewGrD 80*
Sese Y Balaguer, Juan De *NewGrD 80*
Sesini, Ugo 1899-1945 *NewGrD 80*
Sessa D'Aranda *NewGrD 80*
Sesse Y Balaguer, Juan De 1736-1801 *NewGrD 80*
Sessions, Almira 1888-1974 *ForYSC, HalFC 80, WhScrn 77, WhoHol B*
Sessions, Kermit J 1932- *IntMPA 77, –75, –76, –78, –79*
Sessions, Roger 1896- *Baker 78, BiDAmM, BnBkM 80, CompSN[port], CpmDNM 73, –76, –77, –78, ConAmC, DcCom&M 79, DcCM, IntWWM 77, –80, MusMk, NewGrD 80[port], OxMus, WhoMus 72*
Sestairo, Albertet De *NewGrD 80*
Sestak, Tomislav 1931- *IntWWM 77, –80*
Sestak, Zdenek 1925- *Baker 78, IntWWM 77, –80*
Sestaro, Albertet De *NewGrD 80*
Sestarron, Albertet De *NewGrD 80*
Sesterhenn, Peter Bernhard 1937- *IntWWM 77, –80*
Sestini-Palli, Tina *WhoOp 76*
Setaccioli, Giacomo 1868-1925 *Baker 78*
Setaro, Peter D 1924- *AmSCAP 80*
Setchell, Martin Philip 1949- *IntWWM 77*
Sete, Bola 1928- *EncJzS 70*
Seter, Mordecai 1916- *Baker 78, DcCM, NewGrD 80*
Seth, Will d1964 *NotNAT B*
Seton, Sir Bruce 1909-1969 *FilmgC, HalFC 80, WhScrn 74, –77, WhoHol B*
Seton, Ernest Thompson 1860-1946 *CreCan 2*
Seton-Thompson, Ernest *CreCan 2*
Setti, Giulio 1869-1938 *NewEOp 71*
Settle, Elkanah 1648-1724 *NotNAT B, OxThe, PlP&P*
Settle, Maurice 1912- *BiE&WWA*
Settle, Mike *EncFCWM 69*
Setto, Kilza 1932- *IntWWM 77*
Setto, Kliza 1932- *IntWWM 80*
Setton, Maxwell 1909- *FilmgC, HalFC 80, IntMPA 77, –75, –76, –78, –79, –80*
Seuffert, Johann Caspar *NewGrD 80*
Seuffert, Johann Gottfried *NewGrD 80*
Seurat, Pilar *ForYSC, WhoHol A*
Seval, Nevin 1920-1958 *WhScrn 74, –77*
Sevareid, Eric 1912- *IntMPA 77, –75, –76, –78, –79, –80, NewYTET*
Sevastianov, German 1906- *DancEn 78*
Sevcik, Otakar 1852-1934 *Baker 78, NewGrD 80*
Sevcik, Ottokar 1852-1934 *OxMus*
Seveilhac, Pauline Lightstone *CreCan 1*
Seven, Johnny *ForYSC, WhoHol A*
Seven Little Foys, The *What 5[port]*
Sevening, Dora 1883- *WhThe*
Sevening, Nina *WhThe*
Sevenstern, Jan 1949- *IntWWM 77, –80*
Seventeen Interns *BiDAmM*
Sever, Albert 1891-1953 *WhoHol B*
Sever, Alfred 1891-1953 *WhScrn 74, –77*
Severac, Deodat De 1872-1921 *Baker 78, NewGrD 80*
Severac, Deodat De 1873-1921 *OxMus*
Severance, Julia G *PupTheA*
Severen, Maida *WhoHol A*
Severi, Francesco d1630 *NewGrD 80*
Severijn, Andre 1605?-1673 *NewGrD 80*
Severin, Andre 1605?-1673 *NewGrD 80*
Severin, Andries 1605?-1673 *NewGrD 80*
Severin, Andry 1605?-1673 *NewGrD 80*
Severin, Peder *IntWWM 77, –80*
Severin-Mara, M d1920 *NotNAT B*
Severin-Mars d1921 *Film 2, WhScrn 74, –77*
Severin-Mars, M d1921 *WhoHol B*
Severino, Giulio d1601? *NewGrD 80*
Severinsen, Carl H 1927- *AmSCAP 66, –80, BiDAmM, EncJzS 70*
Severinsen, Doc 1927- *CmpEPM, EncJzS 70*
Severn, Billy *MotPP*
Severn, Edmund 1862-1942 *AmSCAP 66, –80, Baker 78*
Severn, Gerry *DancEn 78*
Severo, Raul 1929- *DancEn 78*
Severo DiLuca, Antonio *NewGrD 80*
Severos Of Antioch 465?-538 *NewGrD 80*
Severskaya, Anna *DancEn 78*
Severson, Anne *WomWMM B*
Severson, Marie 1913- *AmSCAP 66, –80*
Severus Of Antioch 465?-538 *NewGrD 80*
Severy, Violet Cavell 1912- *ConAmC*
Sevilla, Carmen 1930- *FilmAG WE, FilmEn*
Seville, Clifford *WhoMus 72*
Seville, David 1919-1972 *AmPS A, –B, AmSCAP 80, BiDAmM, RkOn*
Sevilles, The *RkOn*
Sevitzky, Fabian 1893-1967 *BiDAmM*
Sevitzky, Fabien 1891-1967 *Baker 78*
Sevitzky, Fabien 1893-1967 *AmSCAP 66, –80, ConAmC, WhoMus 72*
Sevitzky, Mary 1924- *WhoMus 72*
Sewall, Barbara Jean *IntMPA 77, –75, –76, –78, –79, –80*
Sewall, Frank 1837-1915 *BiDAmM*
Sewall, Mary 1927- *IntWWM 77*
Sewall, Rachel *PupTheA*
Sewall, Samuel 1652-1730 *OxMus*
Seward, Alexander T 1902-1972 *BluesWW[port]*
Seward, Theordore Frelinghuysen 1835-1902 *BiDAmM*
Sewell, Allen D 1883-1954 *WhScrn 74, –77, WhoHol B*
Sewell, Audrey *Film 2*
Sewell, Blanche *WomWMM*
Sewell, David Kendall 1933- *WhoMus 72*
Sewell, George 1924- *HalFC 80, WhoHol A*
Sewell, Hetty Jane d1961 *NotNAT B*
Sewell, Vernon 1903- *FilmEn, FilmgC, HalFC 80, IlWWBF, WhoHrs 80*
Sex Pistols *ConMuA 80A, IlEncR*
Sexauer, Arwin F B Garelick 1921- *AmSCAP 80*
Sexton, Carter *Film 2*
Sexton, Mildred B *PupTheA*
Sextus Empiricus *NewGrD 80*
Seybold, Artur 1868-1948 *Baker 78*
Seydelmann, Franz 1748-1806 *Baker 78, NewGrD 80*
Seyfert, Johann Caspar 1697?-1767 *NewGrD 80*
Seyfert, Johann Gottfried 1731-1772 *NewGrD 80*
Seyferth, Wilfried 1908-1954 *WhScrn 74, –77, WhoHol B*
Seyffardt, Ernst Hermann 1859-1942 *Baker 78*
Seyffarth, Johann Gabriel 1711-1796 *NewGrD 80*
Seyffert, Dietmar 1943- *CnOxB*
Seyffertitz, Gustav Von 1863-1943 *FilmEn*
Seyfried, Ignaz Von 1776-1841 *NewGrD 80*
Seyfried, Ignaz Xaver, Ritter Von 1776-1841 *Baker 78*
Seyfried, Ignaz Xavier Ritter Von 1776-1841 *OxMus*
Seyfrit, Michael Eugene 1947- *ConAmC*
Seyler, Abel 1730-1800 *EncWT, NewGrD 80*
Seyler, Abel 1730-1801 *OxThe*
Seyler, Athene 1889- *Film 2, FilmgC, HalFC 80, IlWWBF[port], –A, OxThe, PlP&P, WhoHol A, WhoThe 72, –77*
Seyler, Athene 1899- *EncWT*
Seyler, Leonard *NewGrD 80*
Seymour, Alan 1927- *ConDr 73, –77*
Seymour, Anne 1909- *BiE&WWA, FilmEn, FilmgC, ForYSC, HalFC 80, MotPP, MovMk, NotNAT, WhoHol A*
Seymour, Caroline *WhoHol A*
Seymour, Clarine d1920 *MotPP, WhScrn 74, WhoHol B*
Seymour, Clarine 1900-1919 *NotNAT B*
Seymour, Clarine 1900-1920 *Film 1, –2, TwYS*
Seymour, Clarine 1901-1920 *WhScrn 77*
Seymour, Dan 1915- *FilmEn, FilmgC, ForYSC, HalFC 80, IntMPA 77, –75, –76, –78, –79, –80, MotPP, MovMk, Vers A[port], WhoHol A*
Seymour, David Leslie 1945- *IntWWM 77*
Seymour, Deryck John 1913- *WhoMus 72*
Seymour, George *BluesWW*
Seymour, Harry d1967 *Film 2, WhoHol B*
Seymour, Harry 1890-1967 *WhScrn 74, –77*
Seymour, Harry 1891-1967 *AmSCAP 66, –80*
Seymour, James 1823-1864 *NotNAT B, OxThe*
Seymour, Jane 1899-1956 *NotNAT B, WhScrn 74, –77, WhoHol B*
Seymour, Joan Dorothy 1930- *IntWWM 77, –80, WhoMus 72*
Seymour, John D 1897- *BiE&WWA, NotNAT, WhoHol A*
Seymour, John Laurence 1893- *AmSCAP 66, –80, Baker 78, BiDAmM, ConAmC, IntWWM 77*
Seymour, Johnny 1865-1942 *BiDAmM*
Seymour, Katherine *PupTheA*
Seymour, Laura d1879 *NotNAT B*
Seymour, Lynn 1939- *CnOxB, CreCan 2, DancEn 78[port]*
Seymour, Madeline 1891- *Film 2, WhThe*
Seymour, May Davenport 1883-1967 *BiE&WWA, NotNAT B*
Seymour, Tot d1966 *AmSCAP 66, –80, CmpEPM*
Seymour, William Gorman 1855-1933 *NotNAT B, OxThe, WhThe, WhoStg 1906, –1908*
Seyrig, Delphine 1932- *BiDFilm, –81, EncWT, Ent[port], FilmAG WE[port], FilmEn, FilmgC, HalFC 80, WhoHol A, WorEFlm*
Seyve, De *NewGrD 80*
Sezbie, Evelyn *Film 2*
Sfetsas, Kyriacos 1945- *NewGrD 80*

Sforza *NewGrD 80*
Sgabazzi, Petronio Maria Pio 1716-1740? *NewGrD 80*
Sgambati, Giovanni 1841-1914 *Baker 78, GrComp, NewGrD 80, OxMus*
Sgambellone, Guido Vincent 1904- *AmSCAP 80*
Sgatberoni, Johann Anton 1708?-1795 *NewGrD 80*
Sgourda, Antigone 1938- *IntWWM 77, -80, WhoOp 76*
Sgrizzi, Luciano 1910- *IntWWM 77, -80, NewGrD 80*
Sha Na Na *IlEncR, RkOn 2[port]*
Shabelevski, Yurek 1911- *DancEn 78*
Shabelevsky, Yurek 1911- *CnOxB*
Shacham, Nathan 1925- *REnWD[port]*
Shackelford, Rudolph Owens 1944- *AmSCAP 80*
Shackelford, Rudy 1944- *CpmDNM 78, ConAmC*
Shackford, Charles Reeve 1918- *ConAmC, IntWWM 77, -80*
Shackleton, Allan 1937-1979 *WhoHrs 80, WomWMM*
Shackleton, Robert W 1914-1956 *NotNAT B, WhScrn 74, -77, WhoHol B*
Shackley, George H 1890-1959 *AmSCAP 66, -80*
Shacklock, Constance 1913- *CmOp, IntWWM 77, -80, WhoMus 72*
Shackson, Margo *WomWMM B*
Shadbolt, Jack Leonard 1909- *CreCan 2*
Shadburne, Susan *WomWMM B*
Shade, Betty *Film 1*
Shade, Ellen Gertrude *WhoOp 76*
Shade, Jamesson 1895-1956 *WhScrn 74, -77, WhoHol B*
Shade, Lillian d1962 *NotNAT B*
Shade, Nancy *WhoOp 76*
Shade, Will 1898-1966 *BluesWW*
Shades Of Blue *RkOn 2A*
Shadow, The *What 4[port]*
Shadow, Bert 1890-1936 *WhScrn 74, -77*
Shadows, The *ConMuA 80A, IlEncR, IntMPA 77, -75, -76, -78, -79, -80*
Shadows Of Knight, The *RkOn 2[port]*
Shadur, Lawrence S 1938- *WhoOp 76*
Shadwell, C M *WhoMus 72*
Shadwell, Charles d1726 *NotNAT B*
Shadwell, Thomas 1641?-1692 *CnThe, McGEWD[port], REnWD[port]*
Shadwell, Thomas 1642?-1692 *EncWT, Ent, NewGrD 80, NotNAT B, OxThe*
Shaefer, Anna *Film 2*
Shafer, Mollie B 1872-1940 *WhScrn 74, -77, WhoHol B*
Shaff, Monroe 1908- *IntMPA 77, -75, -76, -78, -79*
Shaff, Monty *BiE&WWA*
Shaffer, Anthony 1926- *ConDr 73, -77, EncWT, NotNAT, WhoThe 72, -77*
Shaffer, Deborah *WomWMM B*
Shaffer, Elaine *WhoMus 72*
Shaffer, Jeanne Ellison 1925- *AmSCAP 80, CpmDNM 79, IntWWM 77, -80*
Shaffer, Lloyd M 1901- *AmSCAP 66, -80*
Shaffer, Max 1925- *AmSCAP 66, -80*
Shaffer, Peter 1926- *BiE&WWA, CnMD, CnThe, ConDr 73, -77, CroCD, EncWT, Ent, McGEWD, ModWD, MorBAP, NotNAT, PlP&P, -A[port], REnWD[port], WhoThe 72, -77*
Shaffer, Sherwood 1934- *ConAmC, IntWWM 77, -80*
Shaffner, Lillian *Film 1*
Shaffner, Roberta Rose 1937- *AmSCAP 80*
Shafir, Shulamith *WhoMus 72*
Shafran, Daniel 1923- *Baker 78*
Shafran, Daniil Borisovich 1923- *NewGrD 80*
Shaftel, Arthur 1916- *AmSCAP 80*
Shaftel, Josef 1919- *IntMPA 77, -75, -76, -78, -79, -80*
Shaftel, Selig Sidney *AmSCAP 80*
Shafter, Bert *WhoHol A*
Shaftesbury, Lord 1671-1713 *NewGrD 80*
Shagan, Steve *IntMPA 77, -78, -79, -80*
Shah, Chandulal J 1900- *IntMPA 77, -75, -76, -78, -79*
Shahan, Paul 1923- *AmSCAP 66, -80, ConAmC*
Shahdoodakian, Tatiezam *Film 2*
Shahin, Raymond Joseph 1930- *IntWWM 77*
Shahin, Youssef 1926- *DcFM*
Shahverdyan, Alexander Isaakovich 1903-1954 *NewGrD 80*
Shaiffer, Howard Charles *MotPP*
Shaiffer, Tiny 1918-1967 *WhScrn 74, -77, WhoHol B*
Shainberg, Maurice *NatPD[port]*
Shairp, Alexander Mordaunt 1887-1939 *WhThe*
Shairp, Mordaunt 1887-1939 *ModWD, NotNAT B*
Shakarian, Roupen 1950- *ConAmC*
Shakeshaft, Stephen *IntWWM 77, -80, WhoMus 72*
Shakespeare, Frank J *NewYTET*
Shakespeare, John 1923- *IntWWM 77*
Shakespeare, William 1564-1616 *CnThe, DcPup, EncWT, Ent, FilmgC, HalFC 80, McGEWD[port], NewEOp 71, NewGrD 80, NotNAT A, -B, OxFilm, OxMus, OxThe, PlP&P[port], -A[port], REnWD[port], WhoHrs 80*
Shakespeare, William 1849-1931 *Baker 78, OxMus*
Shakey Jake *BluesWW*
Shakey Walter *BluesWW*
Shakhovsky, Alexander Alexandrovich 1777-1846 *NotNAT B, OxThe*
Shakti *IlEncJ*
Shale, Thomas Augustin 1867-1953 *NotNAT B, WhThe*
Shalek, Bertha 1884- *WhoStg 1908*
Shalet, Diane *WhoHol A*
Shalit, Carl H *IntMPA 77, -75, -76, -78, -79*
Shalit, Gene 1932- *IntMPA 77, -78, -79, -80, NewYTET*
Shalyapin, Fyodor Ivanovich 1873-1938 *NewGrD 80[port]*
Shamir, Moshe 1921- *CnThe, REnWD[port]*
Shamotulinus, Venceslaus *NewGrD 80*
Shamrock, Mary Stringham 1937- *IntWWM 80*
Shamroy, Leon 1901-1974 *CmMov, FilmEn, FilmgC, HalFC 80, IntMPA 77, -75, -76, -78, -79, -80, OxFilm, WorEFlm*
Shanafelt, Marjorie *PupTheA, PupTheA SUP*
Shanaphy, Edward John 1938- *AmSCAP 80*
Shand, Ernest 1868- *WhThe*
Shand, John 1901-1955 *NotNAT B, WhThe*
Shand, Phyllis 1894- *WhThe*
Shand, Terry 1904- *AmSCAP 66, -80, BgBands 74, CmpEPM*
Shand, William 1902- *AmSCAP 80*
Shandoff, Zachari *DcFM*
Shane, Bob 1934- *BiDAmM*
Shane, Gillian 1943- *CnOxB*
Shane, Maxwell 1905- *FilmEn, FilmgC, HalFC 80, IntMPA 77, -75, -76, -78, -79, -80*
Shane, Rita Frances *IntWWM 77, -80, WhoOp 76*
Shane, Sara *ForYSC, WhoHol A*
Shanet, Howard 1918- *Baker 78, IntWWM 77, -80, NewGrD 80*
Shange, Ntozake 1948- *DrBlPA, MorBAP, NatPD[port]*
Shangri-Las, The *ConMuA 80A, RkOn 2[port]*
Shank, Bud 1926- *CmpEPM, EncJzS 70, IlEncJ*
Shank, Clifford Everett, Jr. 1926- *AmSCAP 66, -80, EncJzS 70*
Shank, John d1636 *OxThe*
Shank, Theodore 1929- *BiE&WWA, NotNAT*
Shankar, Ravi 1920- *AmSCAP 80, Baker 78, BnBkM 80, IntWWM 77, -80, MusMk[port], NewGrD 80, WhoHol A, WhoMus 72, WorEFlm*
Shankar, Uday *DcPup*
Shankar, Uday 1900-1977 *CnOxB, DcFM, NewGrD 80*
Shankar, Uday 1902?- *DancEn 78[port]*
Shankland, Richard 1904-1953 *WhScrn 74, -77, WhoHol B*
Shanklin, Wayne, Sr. 1916- *AmSCAP 66, -80*
Shanks, Alec 1904- *WhoThe 72, -77*
Shanks, Ann Zane Kushner *WomWMM B*
Shanks, Bob *NewYTET*
Shanks, Clare Louise 1939- *IntWWM 77, -80*
Shanks, Donald 1940- *NewGrD 80*
Shanley, Robert d1968 *WhScrn 74, -77, WhoHol B*
Shannaw, Phyllis *Film 2*
Shannon, Alex K *Film 1*
Shannon, Cora 1869?-1957 *WhScrn 77*
Shannon, Mrs. Dale d1923 *WhScrn 74, -77, WhoHol B*
Shannon, Del 1939- *AmPS A, RkOn[port]*
Shannon, Effie 1867-1954 *Film 1, -2, NotNAT B, PlP&P, TwYS, WhScrn 74, -77, WhThe, WhoHol B, WhoStg 1906, -1908*
Shannon, Elizabeth S 1914-1959 *WhScrn 74, -77, WhoHol B*
Shannon, Ethel 1898-1951 *Film 1, -2, TwYS, WhScrn 74, -77, WhoHol B*
Shannon, Frank Connolly 1875-1959 *Film 2, WhScrn 74, -77, WhThe, WhoHol B, WhoHrs 80*
Shannon, Harry 1885- *NewOrJ*
Shannon, Harry 1890-1964 *FilmEn, FilmgC, ForYSC, HalFC 80, MovMk[port], NotNAT B, Vers A[port], WhScrn 74, -77, WhoHol B*
Shannon, Harry 1948- *AmSCAP 80*
Shannon, Irene *AmSCAP 66*
Shannon, Jack 1892-1968 *WhScrn 74, -77, WhoHol B*
Shannon, James Royce 1881-1946 *AmSCAP 66, -80, BiDAmM*
Shannon, Kathleen *WomWMM*
Shannon, Peggy d1941 *MotPP, WhoHol B*
Shannon, Peggy 1907-1941 *FilmEn, NotNAT B, ThFT[port], WhThe*
Shannon, Peggy 1909-1941 *WhScrn 74, -77*
Shannon, Peggy 1911-1941 *ForYSC*
Shannon, Ray 1895-1971 *WhScrn 74, -77*
Shannon, Scott *ConMuA 80B*
Shannon, Tony *NewOrJ*
Shannon, Winona d1950 *NotNAT B*
Shanor, Peggy d1935 *Film 1, -2, WhScrn 74, -77, WhoHol B*
Shansky, Daniel 1920- *IntWWM 77, -80*
Shantaram, Rajaram Vanakudre 1901- *DcFM*
Shaper, Hal David 1931- *IntWWM 77*
Shaper, Harold David *WhoMus 72*
Shapero, Harold Samuel 1920- *AmSCAP 66, -80, Baker 78, BiDAmM, ConAmC, DcCom&M 79, DcCM, MusMk, NewGrD 80, OxMus, WhoMus 72*
Shapey, Ralph 1921- *AmSCAP 66, -80, Baker 78, BiDAmM, BnBkM 80, CpmDNM 79, -80, ConAmC, DcCom&M 79, DcCM, NewGrD 80*
Shapinsky, Aaron 1925- *IntWWM 77, -80*
Shapiro, Art 1916- *CmpEPM, WhoJazz 72*
Shapiro, Beverly Myers *AmSCAP 80*
Shapiro, Byron M 1918- *IntMPA 78, -79, -80*
Shapiro, Carl Frederick 1938- *AmSCAP 66, -80*
Shapiro, Dan 1910- *AmSCAP 66, -80*
Shapiro, Gerald 1942- *DcCM*
Shapiro, Herman 1898- *BiE&WWA*
Shapiro, Irvin *IntMPA 77, -75, -76, -78, -79, -80*
Shapiro, Jacob 1928- *IntMPA 77, -75, -76, -78, -79, -80*
Shapiro, Jason *ConMuA 80B*
Shapiro, Jerry *ConMuA 80B*
Shapiro, Joel 1934- *IntWWM 77, -80, WhoMus 72*
Shapiro, Ken 1943- *IntMPA 77, -76, -78, -79, -80*
Shapiro, Kenneth Steven 1943- *AmSCAP 80*
Shapiro, Laurence David 1941- *IntWWM 77, -80*
Shapiro, Lionel Sebastion Berk 1908-1958 *CreCan 1*
Shapiro, Marvin L *NewYTET*
Shapiro, Maurice 1906- *AmSCAP 66, -80*
Shapiro, Mel *PlP&P A[port]*
Shapiro, Michael Jeffrey 1951- *AmSCAP 80*
Shapiro, Michael Joseph 1940- *AmSCAP 80*
Shapiro, Mickey *ConMuA 80B*
Shapiro, Norman R 1930- *ConAmC*
Shapiro, Robert K *IntMPA 77, -75, -76, -78, -79, -80*
Shapiro, Robert W 1938- *IntMPA 77, -75, -76,*

-78, -79, -80
Shapiro, Stanley 1925- *CmMov, FilmEn, FilmgC, HalFC 80*
Shapiro, Susan 1923- *AmSCAP 66, -80*
Shapiro, Ted 1899- *AmSCAP 66, -80*
Shapiro, Thomas M 1923- *AmSCAP 66*
Shapleigh, Bertram 1871-1940 *Baker 78, NewGrD 80*
Shaporin, Yuri 1887-1966 *Baker 78*
Shaporin, Yuri 1889-1966 *OxMus*
Shaporin, Yury 1889-1966 *CmOp*
Shaporin, Yury Alexandrovich 1887-1966 *NewGrD 80*
Shaposhnikov, Adrian Grigor'yevich 1888?-1967 *NewGrD 80*
Shaps, Cyril *WhoHol A*
Sharaf, Frederic *ConAmC*
Sharaff, Irene 1910?- *BiE&WWA, CnOxB, DancEn 78[port], FilmgC, HalFC 80, NotNAT, WhoThe 72, -77*
Sharaku, Toshusai *REnWD[port]*
Sharalee *AmSCAP 80*
Sharbutt, Del 1912- *AmSCAP 66, WhoHol A*
Sharbutt, Delbert Eugene 1912- *AmSCAP 80*
Share, Robert 1928- *AmSCAP 66*
Sharie, Bonnie *WhoHol A*
Sharif, Omar *IntMPA 75, -76*
Sharif, Omar 1924- *ForYSC*
Sharif, Omar 1932- *BiDFilm, -81, CmMov, FilmEn, FilmgC, HalFC 80, IntMPA 77, -78, -79, -80, MotPP, MovMk[port], OxFilm, WhoHol A, WorEFlm[port]*
Sharif, Tarek *WhoHol A*
Sharkey *NewOrJ*
Sharkey, Jack *Film 1, NatPD[port]*
Sharkey, Jack 1902- *What 3[port]*
Sharkey, Sailor *Film 2*
Sharkey, Tom *MorBAP*
Sharkey, Tom 1873-1953 *WhScrn 77*
Sharland, Reginald d1944 *Film 2, WhoHol B*
Sharland, Reginald 1886-1944 *NotNAT B, WhThe*
Sharland, Reginald 1887-1944 *WhScrn 74, -77*
Sharlin, William 1920- *ConAmC*
Sharma, Pyarelal Ramprasad 1940- *IntWWM 77, -80*
Sharnik, John *NewYTET*
Sharon, Ann *PupTheA*
Sharon, Muriel 1920- *BiE&WWA, NotNAT*
Sharon, Ralph 1923- *CmpEPM*
Sharon, William E d1968 *WhScrn 77*
Sharp, Alan *IntMPA 77, -75, -76, -78, -79, -80*
Sharp, Anthony 1915- *WhoHol A, WhoThe 72, -77*
Sharp, Barbara Lou 1944- *AmSCAP 80*
Sharp, Cecil 1859-1924 *Baker 78, BnBkM 80, DancEn 78, MusMk, NewGrD 80, OxMus*
Sharp, Christopher William 1948- *ConAmTC*
Sharp, Dee Dee 1945- *RkOn*
Sharp, Don 1922- *FilmEn, FilmgC, HalFC 80, IlWWBF, IntMPA 77, -75, -76, -78, -79, -80, WhoHrs 80*
Sharp, Eileen 1900- *WhThe*
Sharp, F B J 1874- *WhThe*
Sharp, Frederick *CmOp, WhoMus 72*
Sharp, Geoffrey 1914-1974 *Baker 78, NewGrD 80, WhoMus 72*
Sharp, Henry 1887-1964 *NotNAT B, WhScrn 74, -77, WhoHol B*
Sharp, Henry 1890?-1966 *HalFC 80*
Sharp, Henry 1892-1966 *FilmEn*
Sharp, James H *PupTheA*
Sharp, Joseph Pershing *AmSCAP 80*
Sharp, Len 1890-1958 *WhScrn 74*
Sharp, Leonard 1890-1958 *WhScrn 77, WhoHol B*
Sharp, Margery *WhThe*
Sharp, Mary 1907- *IntWWM 80*
Sharp, Robert Louis, Jr. 1924- *AmSCAP 80*
Sharp, Ronald William 1929- *IntWWM 77, -80*
Sharp, Saundra 1943?- *DrBlPA, MorBAP*
Sharp, William 1924- *BiE&WWA, NotNAT*
Sharp-Bolster, Anita *WhoHol A*
Sharpe, Albert *WhoHol A*
Sharpe, Cedric *WhoMus 72*
Sharpe, Claude 1905- *AmSCAP 66, -80*
Sharpe, Cornelia *WhoHol A*
Sharpe, Dave 1911-1980 *WhoHol A, WhoHrs 80*
Sharpe, Edith 1894- *WhThe, WhoHol A, WhoThe 72*
Sharpe, Gyda 1908-1973 *WhScrn 77*
Sharpe, Herbert Francis 1861-1925 *Baker 78*
Sharpe, John Rufus, III 1909- *AmSCAP 66, -80*
Sharpe, Karen *ForYSC, WhoHol A*
Sharpe, Lester 1895-1962 *WhScrn 77*
Sharpe, Ray 1938- *RkOn*
Sharpe, Richard 1602?-1632 *OxThe*
Sharpe, S H *MagIlD*
Sharpe, Terence 1933- *WhoOp 76*
Sharpham, Edward d1608 *NotNAT B*
Sharples, Robert 1913- *IntWWM 77*
Sharples, Winston S 1909-1978 *AmSCAP 66, -80*
Sharplin, John 1916-1961 *WhScrn 74, -77*
Sharps, Wallace S 1927- *IntMPA 77, -75, -76, -78, -79, -80*
Sharrock, Linda 1949- *EncJzS 70*
Sharrock, Sonny 1940- *EncJzS 70*
Shartels, Wally *Film 2*
Sharvit, Uri 1939- *IntWWM 77, -80, NewGrD 80*
Shasby, Anne 1945- *IntWWM 77, -80*
Shashoua, Salim Samuel 1930- *IntWWM 77, -80*
Shatal, Miriam 1903- *IntWWM 77*
Shaternikova, Nina *Film 2*
Shatin, Judith 1949- *ConAmC*
Shatner, William 1931- *BiE&WWA, FilmEn, FilmgC, ForYSC, HalFC 80, MotPP, MovMk, NotNAT, WhoHol A, WhoHrs 80, WhoThe 77*
Shatterell *OxThe*
Shatto, Charles *ConAmC*
Shattuck, Arthur 1881-1951 *Baker 78, BiDAmM*
Shattuck, Edward F 1890-1948 *WhScrn 74, -77*
Shattuck, Ethel d1963 *NotNAT B*
Shattuck, Truly 1876-1954 *Film 2, NotNAT B, WhScrn 74, -77, WhThe, WhoHol B, WhoStg 1906, -1908*
Shatzky, Yevgeny 1941- *IntWWM 77, -80*
Shaughnessy, Alfred 1916- *FilmgC, HalFC 80*
Shaughnessy, Ed 1929- *EncJzS 70*
Shaughnessy, Eddie 1929- *CmpEPM*
Shaughnessy, Edwin Thomas 1929- *EncJzS 70*
Shaughnessy, Mickey 1920- *FilmEn, FilmgC, ForYSC, HalFC 80, MovMk[port], WhoHol A*
Shaughnessy, Robert Michael 1925- *ConAmC*
Shave, Peter Stanley 1944- *IntWWM 77, -80*
Shavelson, Melville 1917- *CmMov, FilmEn, FilmgC, HalFC 80, IntMPA 77, -75, -76, -78, -79, -80, WorEFlm*
Shaver, Billy Joe *CounME 74[port], -74A, IlEncCM[port]*
Shaver, Bob *WhoHol A*
Shaver, C L 1905- *BiE&WWA, NotNAT*
Shaver, Floyd Herbert 1905- *AmSCAP 66, -80*
Shavers, Charles 1917-1971 *AmSCAP 66, -80, EncJzS 70*
Shavers, Charlie 1917-1971 *BiDAmM, CmpEPM, EncJzS 70, IlEncJ, WhoHol B, WhoJazz 72*
Shaverzashvili, Alexander 1919- *Baker 78*
Shavitch, Vladimir 1888-1947 *Baker 78, BiDAmM*
Shavitz, Carl 1940- *IntWWM 77, -80*
Shavrova, Tamaia *Film 2*
Shaw *NewGrD 80*
Shaw, Alexander 1650?-1706 *NewGrD 80*
Shaw, Alma *PupTheA*
Shaw, Anabel *WhoHol A*
Shaw, Anthony *WhoHol A*
Shaw, Anthony 1897- *WhThe*
Shaw, Arnold 1909- *AmSCAP 66, -80, Baker 78, ConAmC*
Shaw, Arthur W d1946 *NotNAT B*
Shaw, Artie *AmPS A, -B, BgBands 74[port]*
Shaw, Artie 1904?- *HalFC 80*
Shaw, Artie 1910- *AmSCAP 66, -80, Baker 78, BiDAmM, CmpEPM, IlEncJ, NewGrD 80, What 2[port], WhoHol A, WhoJazz 72*
Shaw, Arvell 1923- *EncJzS 70*
Shaw, Barnett 1911- *AmSCAP 66*
Shaw, Barnett 1914- *AmSCAP 80*
Shaw, Belinda Dianne 1954- *BlkWAB[port]*
Shaw, Bernard 1856-1950 *FilmgC, HalFC 80, ModWD, NewGrD 80, REnWD[port], WhThe*
Shaw, Brian 1928- *CnOxB, DancEn 78*
Shaw, Brinsley *Film 1, -2*
Shaw, C Montague 1884-1968 *ForYSC, WhScrn 74, -77*
Shaw, Charles 1906-1963 *AmSCAP 66, -80*
Shaw, Christopher Graham 1924- *IntWWM 77, -80, NewGrD 80, WhoMus 72*
Shaw, Clifford 1911- *AmSCAP 66, ConAmC*
Shaw, Clifford 1911-1976 *AmSCAP 80*
Shaw, David Ferguson 1926- *ConAmC*
Shaw, David T *AmPS B*
Shaw, Dennis 1921-1971 *WhScrn 74, -77*
Shaw, Edward S 1938- *IntMPA 78*
Shaw, Edward S 1939- *IntMPA 79, -80*
Shaw, Elliott 1887-1973 *WhScrn 77*
Shaw, Francis Richard 1942- *IntWWM 80*
Shaw, Frank Holcomb 1884-1959 *Baker 78*
Shaw, Frank M 1894-1937 *WhScrn 74, -77*
Shaw, G Tito *MorBAP*
Shaw, Geoffrey 1879-1943 *NewGrD 80*
Shaw, Geoffrey Edward 1927- *IntWWM 77, -80, WhoMus 72*
Shaw, Geoffrey Turton 1879-1943 *OxMus*
Shaw, George Bernard 1856-1950 *Baker 78, CnMD, CnThe, DcPup, EncWT, Ent[port], Film 2, IlWWBF A, McGEWD[port], NotNAT A, -B, OxMus, OxThe, PlP&P[port], WhScrn 77, WhoStg 1906, -1908*
Shaw, Mrs. George Bernard 1857-1943 *NotNAT B*
Shaw, Glen Byam 1904- *BiE&WWA, CmOp, CnThe, EncWT, NotNAT, OxThe, WhoHol A, WhoOp 76, WhoThe 72, -77*
Shaw, Greg *ConMuA 80B*
Shaw, Harlan 1922- *NotNAT*
Shaw, Harold M 1875?-1926 *FilmEn, Film 1, WhScrn 77*
Shaw, Harold Marvin 1926- *IlWWBF*
Shaw, Harold Watkins 1911- *IntWWM 80*
Shaw, Hilda 1922- *IntWWM 77, -80*
Shaw, Irwin *PlP&P[port]*
Shaw, Irwin 1912- *FilmgC, HalFC 80*
Shaw, Irwin 1913- *BiE&WWA, CnMD, CnThe, ConDr 73, -77, EncWT, Ent, FilmEn, McGEWD, ModWD, NotNAT, WhoThe 72, -77, WorEFlm*
Shaw, Jack d1970 *WhoHol B*
Shaw, James R 1930- *ConAmC*
Shaw, Jean *WomWMM B*
Shaw, Jeremy Howard 1956- *IntWWM 80*
Shaw, John 1921- *CmOp, WhoMus 72*
Shaw, Keith Latham 1934- *WhoMus 72*
Shaw, Kenneth Raymond 1927- *IntWWM 77, -80*
Shaw, Kerry *NatPD[port]*
Shaw, Lewis 1910- *Film 2, WhThe*
Shaw, Lige 1900- *WhoJazz 72*
Shaw, Lucretia Faye 1941- *IntWWM 77, -80*
Shaw, Marlena 1944- *DrBlPA, EncJzS 70*
Shaw, Martin 1875-1958 *Baker 78, ConAmC, NewGrD 80, OxMus*
Shaw, Mary 1814-1876 *Baker 78, NewGrD 80*
Shaw, Mary 1854-1929 *NotNAT B, PlP&P, WhThe, WhoStg 1906, -1908*
Shaw, Milt *BgBands 74*
Shaw, Montague 1884-1968 *Film 2, MotPP, TwYS, WhoHol B*
Shaw, Oliver 1779-1848 *Baker 78, BiDAmM, NewGrD 80*
Shaw, Oscar d1967 *AmPS B, Film 2, MotPP, WhoHol B*
Shaw, Oscar 1889-1967 *EncMT*
Shaw, Oscar 1891-1967 *CmpEPM, WhScrn 74, -77*
Shaw, Oscar 1899-1967 *WhThe*
Shaw, Peggy *Film 2*
Shaw, Peter *WhoHol A*
Shaw, Ralph *WhoHol A*
Shaw, Reta 1912- *ForYSC, WhoHol A*
Shaw, Richard *WhoHol A*
Shaw, Richard Randall 1941- *AmSCAP 80*
Shaw, Robert 1908- *BluesWW[port]*
Shaw, Robert 1916- *Baker 78, BiDAmM, BnBkM 80, IntWWM 80, MusSN[port], NewGrD 80*

Shaw, Robert 1927- *BiE&WWA, ConDr 73, -77, CroCD, EncWT, FilmAG WE[port], FilmgC, ForYSC, IlWWBF[port], McGEWD, MovMk[port], NotNAT, PlP&P, -A[port], WhoHol A, WhoThe 72, -77*
Shaw, Robert 1927-1978 *BiDFilm 81, FilmEn*
Shaw, Robert 1927-1979 *HalFC 80*
Shaw, Robert 1928- *IntMPA 77, -75, -76, -78*
Shaw, Robert Gould d1931 *NotNAT B, OxThe*
Shaw, Sandie 1947- *RkOn 2[port]*
Shaw, Sebastian 1903- *IlWWBF*
Shaw, Sebastian 1905- *FilmEn, FilmgC, HalFC 80, IntMPA 77, -75, -76, -78, -79, -80, WhoHol A, WhoThe 72, -77*
Shaw, Serena *AmSCAP 66, -80*
Shaw, Susan 1929- *FilmgC, IlWWBF, WhoHol A*
Shaw, Susan 1929-1978 *FilmEn*
Shaw, Susan 1929-1979 *HalFC 80*
Shaw, Sydney 1923-1969 *AmSCAP 66, -80*
Shaw, Thomas 1760?-1830? *NewGrD 80*
Shaw, Thomas Edgar 1908-1977 *BluesWW[port]*
Shaw, Tommy *AmSCAP 80*
Shaw, Victoria 1935- *FilmEn, FilmgC, ForYSC, HalFC 80, MotPP, MovMk, WhoHol A*
Shaw, Watkins 1911- *IntWWM 77, NewGrD 80, WhoMus 72*
Shaw, Wini *MotPP*
Shaw, Wini 1899- *FilmgC, HalFC 80*
Shaw, Wini 1900?- *CmpEPM*
Shaw, Wini 1910- *ThFT[port], WhoHol A*
Shaw, Winifred 1899- *FilmEn*
Shaw, Woody 1944- *EncJzS 70*
Shawe-Taylor, Desmond 1907- *IntWWM 77, -80, NewGrD 80, WhoMus 72*
Shawhan, April 1940- *NotNAT*
Shawlee, Joan 1929- *FilmEn, FilmgC, ForYSC, HalFC 80, IntMPA 77, -75, -76, -78, -79, -80, WhoHol A*
Shawn, Dick 1929?- *FilmEn, FilmgC, ForYSC, HalFC 80, IntMPA 77, -75, -76, -78, -79, -80, MotPP, MovMk, WhoHol A, WhoThe 77*
Shawn, Nelson A 1898-1945 *AmSCAP 66, -80*
Shawn, Philip d1972 *WhoHol B*
Shawn, Ted *CmpGMD[port]*
Shawn, Ted 1891-1972 *CnOxB, DancEn 78[port], NewGrD 80*
Shawn, Ted 1892-1972 *Film 1, WhScrn 77, WhoHol B*
Shawn, Wallace 1943- *ConDr 77, NatPD[port]*
Shawwan, Aziz 1916- *NewGrD 80*
Shaxon, Alan *MagIlD*
Shay, Dorothy 1923- *AmPS B, CmpEPM, IlEncCM, WhoHol A*
Shay, Earl R 1945- *IntWWM 77*
Shay, Larry 1897- *AmSCAP 66, -80, CmpEPM*
Shay, Patricia d1966 *WhScrn 77*
Shay, William E *Film 1, -2*
Shayne, Bob 1945- *AmSCAP 80*
Shayne, Edith *Film 1*
Shayne, Konstantin *FilmEn, ForYSC, WhoHol A*
Shayne, Larry 1909- *AmSCAP 66, -80*
Shayne, Robert 1905- *WhoHrs 80[port]*
Shayne, Robert 1910?- *FilmEn, FilmgC, ForYSC, HalFC 80, IntMPA 77, -75, -76, -78, -79, -80, Vers B[port], WhoHol A*
Shayne, Tamara 1897- *ForYSC, HalFC 80, WhoHol A*
Shchedrin, Rodion Konstantinovich 1932- *Baker 78, CnOxB, DcCM, NewGrD 80*
Shchepkin, Mikhail 1788-1863 *Ent*
Shchepkin, Mikhail Semenovich 1788-1863 *CnThe, NotNAT B, OxThe*
Shchepkin, Mikhail Semyonovich 1788-1863 *EncWT*
Shcherbachev, Vladimir 1889-1952 *Baker 78*
Shcherbachov, Andrey Vladimirovich 1869-1916 *NewGrD 80*
Shcherbachov, Nikolay Vladimirovich 1854- *NewGrD 80*
Shcherbachov, Vladimir Vladimirovich 1889-1952 *NewGrD 80*
Shchukin, Boris Vasilievich 1894-1939 *EncWT, NotNAT B, OxThe, WhoHol B*
Shea, Bird d1924 *WhScrn 74, -77*
Shea, Bird d1925 *WhoHol B*
Shea, George Beverly 1909- *BiDAmM*
Shea, Jack 1900-1970 *NewYTET, WhoHol B*
Shea, John Jack 1900-1970 *WhScrn 74, -77*
Shea, Mike 1952- *WhoHol A*
Shea, Olive *Film 2*
Shea, Steven *NatPD[port]*
Shea, Thomas E d1940 *NotNAT B*
Shea, William J d1918 *Film 1, WhScrn 77*
Shead, Herbert Arthur 1906- *IntWWM 77, -80, WhoMus 72*
Sheafe, Alex *WhoHol A*
Sheafe, Alfonso Josephs 1874-1956 *DancEn 78*
Sheaff, Donald J 1925- *IntMPA 77, -75, -76, -78, -79, -80*
Sheaffer, Louis 1912- *NotNAT*
Shean, Al 1868-1949 *EncMT, Ent, Film 2, FilmgC, ForYSC, HalFC 80, JoeFr, NotNAT B, WhScrn 74, -77, WhThe, WhoHol B*
Shean, David Charles 1934- *IntWWM 77, -80*
Shear, Barry *IntMPA 77, -75, -76, -78, -79*
Shear, Barry 1920?-1979 *FilmEn*
Shear, Barry 1923-1979 *HalFC 80*
Shear, Pearl *WhoHol A*
Shear, Virginia M 1950- *IntWWM 77*
Shearer, Aaron 1919- *IntWWM 77*
Shearer, Benjamin B, Sr. 1913- *AmSCAP 66*
Shearer, Clarence Maynard 1940- *CpmDNM 80*
Shearer, Dick 1940- *EncJzS 70*
Shearer, Douglas 1899-1971 *FilmEn, FilmgC, HalFC 80*
Shearer, Edith Norma 1904- *BiDFilm, -81*
Shearer, Juanita 1919- *BiE&WWA*
Shearer, Moira 1926- *CnOxB, DancEn 78[port], FilmEn, FilmgC, ForYSC, HalFC 80, MotPP, WhThe, WhoHol A*
Shearer, Norma *MotPP, What 1[port]*
Shearer, Norma 1900- *CmMov, FilmEn, Film 2, FilmgC, HalFC 80, MGM[port], ThFT[port]*
Shearer, Norma 1904- *ForYSC, MovMk[port], OxFilm, TwYS, WhoHol A, WorEFlm[port]*
Shearer, Richard Bruce 1940- *EncJzS 70*
Shearer, Sybil 1918?- *CmpGMD, CnOxB, DancEn 78[port]*
Shearing, George 1919- *Baker 78, BiDAmM, CmpEPM, EncJzS 70, IntWWM 80, MusMk, WhoHol A*
Shearn, David 1940- *IntWWM 77*
Shearn, Edith 1870-1968 *WhScrn 74, -77, WhoHol B*
Shearouse, Florine W 1898- *AmSCAP 66*
Shebalin, Vissarion Yakovlevich 1902-1963 *Baker 78, NewGrD 80, OxMus*
Sheckler, Lewis Raymond 1930- *IntWWM 77*
Shedd, Elizabeth Ann Wakefield 1929- *IntWWM 77*
Shedlo, Ronald 1940- *IntMPA 77, -75, -76, -78, -79*
Shedlock, J S 1843-1919 *NewGrD 80*
Shedlock, John South 1843-1919 *Baker 78, OxMus*
Sheehan, Bobbie d1974 *WhScrn 77*
Sheehan, David *ConAmTC*
Sheehan, Jack 1890-1958 *NotNAT B*
Sheehan, John J 1890-1952 *WhScrn 74, -77, WhoHol B*
Sheehan, Joseph F *WhoStg 1906, -1908*
Sheehan, Neil Joseph 1946- *AmSCAP 80*
Sheehan, Tess 1888-1972 *WhScrn 77*
Sheehan, William 1925- *IntMPA 78, -79, NewYTET*
Sheehan, Winfield 1883-1945 *FilmEn*
Sheehy, Thomas Joseph Michael 1912- *IntMPA 75*
Sheekman, Arthur 1891-1978 *HalFC 80*
Sheekman, Arthur 1892- *FilmgC*
Sheekman, Arthur 1901-1978 *FilmEn, IntMPA 77, -75, -76, -78*
Sheeler, Mark 1923- *IntMPA 77, -75, -76, -78, -79, -80*
Sheen, Bishop Fulton J 1895- *NewYTET, WhoHol A*
Sheen, Martin 1940- *FilmEn, HalFC 80, IntMPA 77, -75, -76, -78, -79, -80, MovMk, NotNAT, WhoHol A, WhoThe 72, -77*
Sheen, Mickey 1927- *AmSCAP 66, -80*
Sheer, Anita 1938- *IntWWM 77*
Sheer, Philip 1915- *AmSCAP 66, -80*
Sheerer, Will E d1915 *MotPP, WhScrn 77*
Sheets, Walter Kester 1911- *AmSCAP 80*
Sheff, Robert Nathan 1945- *ConAmC, IntWWM 77*
Sheffield, Flora 1902- *WhThe*
Sheffield, John 1931- *IntMPA 77, -75, -76, -78, -79, -80*
Sheffield, Johnny 1931- *FilmEn, FilmgC, HalFC 80, MovMk[port], What 2[port], WhoHrs 80*
Sheffield, Johnny 1932- *ForYSC, WhoHol A*
Sheffield, Leo 1873-1951 *NotNAT B, WhThe, WhoHol B*
Sheffield, Maceo B *BlksB&W, -C*
Sheffield, Nellie d1957 *NotNAT B*
Sheffield, Reginald 1901-1957 *FilmEn, Film 2, MotPP, NotNAT B, TwYS, WhScrn 74, -77, WhThe, WhoHol B*
Shefield, Reginald 1901-1957 *ForYSC*
Shefter, Bert 1904- *AmSCAP 66, -80, IntMPA 77, -76, -78, -79, -80*
Shehade, Georges 1910- *REnWD[port]*
Sheikh, Kamal El *DcFM*
Sheil, Richard Lalor d1851 *NotNAT B*
Sheils, Peter *ConMuA 80B*
Sheina, Svetlana 1918- *DancEn 78*
Sheina, Svetlana Konstantinovna 1918- *CnOxB*
Sheinberg, Sidney Jay 1935- *IntMPA 80*
Sheiner, David *WhoHol A*
Sheiness, Marsha *NatPD[port]*
Sheinfeld, David 1910- *ConAmC*
Sheinkman, Mordecai 1926- *ConAmC*
Shekhter, Boris 1900-1961 *Baker 78, NewGrD 80*
Shelby, Charlotte d1957 *WhScrn 77*
Shelby, James 1927- *BluesWW*
Shelby, Juliet *FilmEn*
Shelby, Margaret 1900-1939 *Film 2, WhScrn 77*
Shelby, Miriam *Film 1*
Shelbye, William d1561? *NewGrD 80*
Shelden, Paul M 1941- *IntWWM 77, -80*
Sheldo, Ronald 1940- *IntMPA 80*
Sheldon, Brewster 1886-1946 *CnThe*
Sheldon, Connie 1921-1947 *WhScrn 74*
Sheldon, David 1931- *BiE&WWA*
Sheldon, Earl 1915-1977 *AmSCAP 66, -80*
Sheldon, Edward Brewster 1886-1946 *CnMD, DcLB 7[port], EncWT, McGEWD[port], ModWD, NotNAT A, -B, OxThe, PlP&P, REnWD[port], WhThe*
Sheldon, Ernie *AmSCAP 80, EncFCWM 69*
Sheldon, Ernie 1930- *AmSCAP 66, IntWWM 77*
Sheldon, Gene 1909?- *ForYSC, HalFC 80, WhoHol A*
Sheldon, Hardy *PupTheA*
Sheldon, Harry Sophus d1940 *NotNAT B, WhThe*
Sheldon, Herb d1964 *NotNAT B*
Sheldon, Jack 1931- *EncJzS 70*
Sheldon, James *Film 2, IntMPA 77, -75, -76, -78, -79, -80*
Sheldon, Jerome 1891-1962 *NotNAT B, WhScrn 74, -77*
Sheldon, Jerry 1901-1962 *NotNAT B, WhScrn 74, -77, WhoHol B*
Sheldon, Marie d1939 *NotNAT B*
Sheldon, Marion W 1886-1944 *WhScrn 74, -77, WhoHol B*
Sheldon, Robin Treeby 1932- *IntWWM 77, -80, WhoMus 72*
Sheldon, Sidney 1917- *AmSCAP 66, -80, BiE&WWA, FilmEn, FilmgC, HalFC 80*
Sheldon, Suzanne 1875-1924 *NotNAT B, WhThe, WhoStg 1908*
Shelesnova, Eleonora 1932?- *CnOxB*
Shelest, Alla 1919- *CnOxB, DancEn 78*
Sheley, Wayne McDowell 1940- *IntWWM 77, -80*
Shelle, Eileen *WhoOp 76*
Shelle, Lori *WhoHol A*
Shelley, Miss *PupTheA*

Shelley, Barbara 1933- FilmEn, FilmgC, HalFC 80, IlWWBF[port], WhoHol A, WhoHrs 80[port]
Shelley, Carole 1939- NotNAT, WhoHol A, WhoThe 72, -77
Shelley, Gladys AmSCAP 66, -80, BiDAmM
Shelley, Harry Rowe 1858-1947 AmSCAP 66, Baker 78, BiDAmM, OxMus
Shelley, Herbert d1921 NotNAT B
Shelley, Howard 1950- IntWWM 77, -80
Shelley, Joshua BiE&WWA, NotNAT, WhoHol A
Shelley, Margot 1933- IntWWM 77
Shelley, Mary Wollstonecraft 1797-1851 FilmgC, HalFC 80
Shelley, Mary Wollstonecraft 1797-1851 WhoHrs 80
Shelley, Miriam Film 1
Shelley, Percy Bysshe 1792-1822 CnThe, DcPup, EncWT, McGEWD[port], NotNAT B, OxThe, REnWD[port]
Shells, The RkOn
Shelly, Louis Edward 1898-1957 AmSCAP 66, -80
Shelly, Maxine Film 2
Shelly, Norman WhoHol A
Shelton, Abigail WhoHol A
Shelton, Connie 1921-1947 WhScrn 77
Shelton, Don WhoHol A
Shelton, Earl ConMuA 80B
Shelton, Eleanor Film 2
Shelton, George 1852-1932 NotNAT A, -B, WhThe
Shelton, George 1884-1971 WhScrn 74, -77, WhoHol B
Shelton, Hugh Norman Arthur 1925- IntWWM 77, -80
Shelton, James 1913-1975 WhScrn 77, WhoHol C
Shelton, James H 1912-1975 AmSCAP 66, -80
Shelton, Jerline Odell 1948- AmSCAP 80
Shelton, John 1917-1972 FilmEn, WhoHol B
Shelton, Joy 1922- FilmgC, HalFC 80, IlWWBF, WhoHol A
Shelton, Kenneth E d1962 NotNAT B
Shelton, Larry Zane 1950- AmSCAP 80
Shelton, Louie ConMuA 80B
Shelton, Maria Film 2
Shelton, Sloane WhoHol A, WomWMM B
Shelving, Paul d1968 NotNAT B, WhThe
Shenandoah Boys BiDAmM
Shenburn, Archibald A 1905-1954 NotNAT B, WhThe
Shengelaya, Eldar 1933- FilmEn
Shengelaya, Nikolai 1901-1943 DcFM, FilmEn
Shenshin, Alexander 1890-1944 Baker 78
Shenson, Walter IntMPA 77, -75, -76, -78, -79, -80
Shenson, Walter 1919- FilmEn
Shenson, Walter 1921?- FilmgC, HalFC 80
Shentall, Susan 1934- HalFC 80, WhoHol A
Shep Film 1
Shep And The Limelites RkOn[port]
Shepard, Alice WhoHol B
Shepard, Ann AmSCAP 80
Shepard, Dick PupTheA
Shepard, Elaine WhoHol A
Shepard, Frank Hartson 1863-1913 Baker 78, BiDAmM
Shepard, Iva Film 1
Shepard, Jan WhoHol A
Shepard, Jean 1933- BiDAmM, CounME 74[port], -74A, EncFCWM 69, IlEncCM[port]
Shepard, Jean Ellen 1949- ConAmC
Shepard, Joan 1933- AmSCAP 80
Shepard, Lucille PupTheA
Shepard, Richard WhoHol A
Shepard, Robert Bloomfield 1927- AmSCAP 80
Shepard, Sam IntMPA 80, PlP&P
Shepard, Sam 1942- NotNAT
Shepard, Sam 1943- ConDr 73, -77, CroCD, DcLB 7[port], EncWT, Ent, NatPD[port], WhoThe 77
Shepard, Sam 1953?- HalFC 80
Shepard, Thomas Griffen 1848-1905 BiDAmM
Shepard, Vendla Lorentzon AmSCAP 66, -80
Shepeard, Jean 1904- WhThe
Shephard, Firth 1891-1949 NotNAT B, WhThe
Shephard, Richard James 1949- IntWWM 77, -80
Shepheard, Jean WhoHol A
Shepheard, John OxMus
Shepherd, Adrian 1939- IntWWM 80
Shepherd, Arthur 1880-1958 AmSCAP 66, -80, Baker 78, BiDAmM, CompSN[port], ConAmC, NewGrD 80, OxMus
Shepherd, Christine 1948- IntWWM 77, -80
Shepherd, Cybill IntMPA 77, -75, -76, -78, -79, -80, WhoHol A
Shepherd, Cybill 1949- HalFC 80, MovMk[port], WomWMM
Shepherd, Cybill 1950- FilmEn
Shepherd, Donald Paul 1917- IntWWM 77, -80
Shepherd, Edward 1670?-1747 OxThe
Shepherd, Ivy Film 1
Shepherd, Jack 1940- WhoHol A, WhoThe 72, -77
Shepherd, Jean 1923- JoeFr
Shepherd, John NewGrD 80, OxMus
Shepherd, Leonard 1872- WhThe, WhoStg 1908
Shepherd, Paul 1935- IntWWM 77, -80
Shepherd, Richard 1927- IntMPA 77, -75, -76, -78, -79, -80
Shepherd, Russell 1917- WhoMus 72
Shepherd Sisters, The RkOn
Shepitka, Larissa WomWMM
Shepley, Ida d1975 WhScrn 77, WhoMus 72
Shepley, Michael 1907-1961 FilmgC, HalFC 80, NotNAT B, WhScrn 74, -77, WhThe, WhoHol B
Shepley, Ruth 1889-1951 Film 2, WhScrn 74, -77, WhoHol B
Shepley, Ruth 1892-1951 NotNAT B, WhThe
Shepodd, Jon 1926- AmSCAP 66, ForYSC
Shepp, Archie 1937- BiDAmM, BlkAmP, BlkCS[port], DrBlPA, EncJzS 70, IlEncJ, MorBAP
Sheppard, Buddy 1903- AmSCAP 66, -80
Sheppard, Charles 1918- IntWWM 77
Sheppard, Elizabeth Honor IntWWM 77, -80
Sheppard, Franklin Lawrence 1852-1930 BiDAmM
Sheppard, Honor IntWWM 77, -80, WhoMus 72
Sheppard, John ForYSC, MovMk[port]
Sheppard, John 1515?-1560? NewGrD 80, OxMus
Sheppard, Joseph Stanley 1915- AmSCAP 66, -80
Sheppard, Russell John 1914- WhoMus 72
Sheppard, T G IlEncCM[port]
Sheppard, Timothy Edsel 1954- AmSCAP 80
Shepperd, John 1907- FilmEn, FilmgC, HalFC 80, WhoHol A
Sher, Abbott J 1918- IntMPA 77, -75, -76, -78, -79, -80
Sher, Daniel Paul 1943- IntWWM 77
Sher, Jack 1913- AmSCAP 66, -80, FilmEn, FilmgC, HalFC 80, IntMPA 77, -75, -76, -78, -79, -80
Sher, Louis K 1914- IntMPA 77, -75, -76, -78, -79, -80
Sher, Rebecca 1950- IntWWM 80
Sher, Rose NatPD[port]
Shera, Frank Henry 1882-1956 Baker 78, NewGrD 80, OxMus
Sherard, Giacomo 1666-1738 NewGrD 80
Sherard, James 1666-1738 NewGrD 80
Sherart, Georgia Film 2
Sherberg, Jon Alfred 1951- AmSCAP 80
Sherbrooke, Michael 1874-1957 NotNAT B, WhThe
Sherdeman, Ted IntMPA 77, -75, -76, -78, -79, -80, WhoHrs 80
Shere, Charles 1935- ConAmC, IntWWM 77, -80
Sherek, Henry 1900-1967 BiE&WWA, NotNAT B, WhThe
Sheremetiev, Count Alexander 1859-1931 Baker 78
Sheridan, Ann 1915-1967 BiDFilm, -81, FilmEn, Film 2, FilmgC, HalFC 80, MotPP, MovMk[port], ThFT[port], WhScrn 74, -77, WhoHol B, WorEFlm
Sheridan, Ann 1916-1967 ForYSC
Sheridan, Dan 1916-1963 WhScrn 77
Sheridan, Dinah 1920- FilmgC, HalFC 80, IlWWBF[port], WhoHol A, WhoThe 77
Sheridan, Elizabeth Ann 1754-1792 NotNAT B
Sheridan, Frances Chamberlayne 1724-1766 NotNAT B
Sheridan, Frank 1869-1943 Film 2, NotNAT B, WhScrn 74, -77, WhoHol B
Sheridan, Frank 1898-1962 Baker 78
Sheridan, Margaret 1889-1958 CmOp, NewGrD 80
Sheridan, Mark d1917 OxThe, WhThe
Sheridan, Mary 1903- WhThe
Sheridan, Richard Brinsley 1751-1816 CnThe, EncWT, Ent, McGEWD[port], NewEOp 71, NotNAT A, -B, OxThe, PlP&P[port], REnWD[port]
Sheridan, Thomas 1719-1788 NotNAT A, PlP&P
Sheridan, William Edward 1840-1887 NotNAT B, OxThe
Sheriff, Noam 1935- Baker 78, DcCM, NewGrD 80
Sheriff, Paul 1903-1962 FilmgC, HalFC 80
Sheriff, Paul 1903-1965 FilmEn
Sherin, Edwin 1930- FilmgC, HalFC 80, NotNAT, WhoThe 77
Sheringham, George 1885-1937 NotNAT B, WhThe
Sherlie, Joseph NewGrD 80
Sherlock, Maureen WomWMM B
Sherlock, William OxThe
Sherly, Joseph NewGrD 80
Sherman, Al IntMPA 77, -75, -76, -78, -79, -80
Sherman, Al 1897-1973 AmSCAP 66, -80, CmpEPM
Sherman, Alida WomWMM
Sherman, Allan 1924-1973 AmSCAP 66, -80, JoeFr[port], RkOn
Sherman, Arthur 1920- AmSCAP 66
Sherman, Bobby 1945- RkOn 2[port]
Sherman, Edward 1903- IntMPA 77, -75, -76, -78, -79, -80
Sherman, Elna ConAmC
Sherman, Enoch 1945- WhoOp 76
Sherman, Evelyn Film 2
Sherman, Fred E 1905-1969 WhScrn 74, -77, WhoHol B
Sherman, Garry 1933- AmSCAP 80
Sherman, George 1908- CmMov, FilmEn, FilmgC, HalFC 80, IntMPA 77, -75, -76, -78, -79, -80
Sherman, Geraldine WhoHol A
Sherman, Herman E 1923- NewOrJ SUP[port]
Sherman, Hiram 1908- BiE&WWA, EncMT, WhoHol A, WhoThe 72, -77
Sherman, Ingrid 1919- IntWWM 77, -80
Sherman, Jane Film 2
Sherman, Jenny WhoHol A
Sherman, Jimmie BlkAmP, MorBAP
Sherman, Jimmy 1908- WhoJazz 72
Sherman, Joe 1926- AmSCAP 66
Sherman, John K 1898-1969 BiE&WWA, NotNAT B
Sherman, Joseph D 1926- AmSCAP 80
Sherman, Lena Janice 1938- IntWWM 80
Sherman, Lois Film 2
Sherman, Lowell 1885-1933 TwYS A
Sherman, Lowell 1885-1934 BiDFilm, -81, FilmEn, Film 1, -2, FilmgC, ForYSC, HalFC 80, MotPP, NotNAT B, TwYS, WhScrn 74, -77, WhThe, WhoHol B, WorEFlm
Sherman, Margaret BiE&WWA
Sherman, Martin NatPD[port]
Sherman, Noel 1930-1972 AmSCAP 66, -80
Sherman, Norman 1926- Baker 78
Sherman, Orville WhoHol A
Sherman, Paula Film 1
Sherman, Ransom ForYSC, WhoHol A
Sherman, Richard M 1928- BestMus, FilmEn, FilmgC, HalFC 80, IntMPA 77, -75, -76, -78, -79, -80, PlP&P A[port]
Sherman, Robert B 1925- BestMus, FilmEn, FilmgC, HalFC 80, IntMPA 77, -75, -76, -78, -79, -80, PlP&P A[port]
Sherman, Robert M IntMPA 77, -75, -76, -78, -79, -80
Sherman, Robert William 1921- ConAmC
Sherman, Russell 1930- BnBkM 80
Sherman, Samuel M IntMPA 77, -75, -76, -78,

-79, -80
Sherman, Sean *WhoHol A*
Sherman, Seymour M 1929- *IntWWM 77, -80*
Sherman, Sylvan Robert *WhoHol A*
Sherman, Vincent 1906- *FilmEn, FilmgC, ForYSC, HalFC 80, IntMPA 77, -75, -76, -78, -79, -80, WhoHol A, WomWMM, WorEFlm*
Sherman, William 1924- *BiE&WWA*
Sherman Sisters, The *Film 2*
Shermet, Hazel *WhoHol A*
Sherock, Shorty 1915- *BgBands 74, CmpEPM, WhoJazz 72*
Sheron, Andre *Film 2*
Sherratt, Colin George 1936- *IntWWM 77*
Sherric, Stormie *AmSCAP 80*
Sherriff, R C 1896-1975 *FilmEn, FilmgC, HalFC 80, IntMPA 75, -76, PlP&P*
Sherriff, Robert Cedric 1896-1975 *BiE&WWA, CnMD, CnThe, ConDr 73, CroCD, EncWT, Ent, McGEWD[port], ModWD, NotNAT A, -B, OxThe, WhThe, WhoThe 72*
Sherril, Joya *DrBlPA*
Sherrill, Billy *IlEncCM[port]*
Sherrill, Jack *Film 1*
Sherrill, Joya 1927- *CmpEPM*
Sherrin, Ned 1931- *ConDr 73, -77D, FilmgC, HalFC 80, IntMPA 77, -75, -76, -78, -79, -80, WhoThe 72, -77*
Sherrod, Ronald J 1945- *IntWWM 77, -80*
Sherry, Craighall *Film 2*
Sherry, Ernest H *NewYTET*
Sherry, J Barney 1872-1944 *WhScrn 74, -77, WhoHol B*
Sherry, J Barney 1874-1944 *Film 1, -2, TwYS, -A*
Sherrys, The *RkOn*
Shertzer, James Melton 1943- *ConAmTC*
Sherwin, Jeannette d1936 *NotNAT B, WhThe*
Sherwin, Manning 1902-1974 *AmSCAP 66, -80, BiDAmM, EncMT*
Sherwin, Manning 1903-1974 *WhThe*
Sherwin, Sterling *AmSCAP 80*
Sherwin, William Fiske 1826-1888 *BiDAmM*
Sherwood, Bob *ConMuA 80B*
Sherwood, Bobby 1914- *BgBands 74, CmpEPM*
Sherwood, C L *Film 2*
Sherwood, Gale *ForYSC, WhoHol A*
Sherwood, Garrison P 1902-1963 *NotNAT B, WhThe*
Sherwood, Gary 1941- *CnOxB*
Sherwood, Henry *Film 2*
Sherwood, Henry d1967 *WhoHol B*
Sherwood, Henry 1931- *WhoThe 72, -77*
Sherwood, James *WhoHol A*
Sherwood, James Peter 1894- *WhThe, WhoThe 72*
Sherwood, John *WhoHrs 80*
Sherwood, Josephine *WhoStg 1908*
Sherwood, Lew *CmpEPM*
Sherwood, Lydia 1906- *WhThe, WhoHol A*
Sherwood, Madeleine 1926- *BiE&WWA, FilmEn, FilmgC, HalFC 80, MotPP, WhoHol A, WhoThe 72, -77*
Sherwood, Millige G 1876-1958 *WhScrn 74, -77*
Sherwood, Robert Emmet 1896-1955 *CnMD, CnThe, DcLB 7[port], EncWT, Ent, FilmEn, FilmgC, HalFC 80, McGEWD[port], ModWD, NotNAT B, OxThe, PlP&P[port], REnWD[port], WhThe*
Sherwood, Robert Emmett 1896-1955 *NotNAT A*
Sherwood, Roberta 1912- *AmPS B, ForYSC, WhoHol A*
Sherwood, William Hall 1854-1911 *Baker 78, BiDAmM*
Sherwood, Yorke 1873-1958 *Film 2, WhScrn 74, -77, WhoHol B*
Sherzer, George 1916- *AmSCAP 66, -80*
Sheta, Reda 1949- *CnOxB*
Shetky, J George *NewGrD 80*
Shevelove, Burt 1915- *BiE&WWA, ConDr 73, -77D, EncMT, NotNAT, WhoThe 72, -77*
Shevey, Sandra *WomWMM B*
Shevitz, Arnold 1921- *AmSCAP 80*
Shew, Bobby 1941- *EncJzS 70*
Sheybal, Vladek 1928- *FilmgC, HalFC 80, WhoHol A*
Shibata, George *ForYSC*
Shibata, Minao 1916- *Baker 78, DcCM, NewGrD 80*
Shibuya, Minoru 1907- *FilmEn*
Shield, Fred d1974 *WhoHol B*
Shield, LeRoy 1893-1962 *AmSCAP 80*
Shield, LeRoy 1898-1962 *AmSCAP 66*
Shield, William 1748-1829 *Baker 78, NewGrD 80[port], OxMus*
Shields, The *RkOn*
Shields, Alice 1943- *ConAmC*
Shields, Arthur d1970 *MotPP, Vers A[port], WhoHol B*
Shields, Arthur 1895-1970 *FilmgC, HalFC 80, WhoHrs 80*
Shields, Arthur 1896-1970 *FilmEn, HolCA[port], WhScrn 74, -77*
Shields, Arthur 1900-1970 *ForYSC, MovMk, WhThe*
Shields, Bernard Saxon 1893- *NewOrJ*
Shields, Brooke 1965- *FilmEn, HalFC 80, IntMPA 79, -80*
Shields, David 1935- *CreCan 1, DancEn 78*
Shields, Eddie 1896-1938 *NewOrJ[port]*
Shields, Ella 1879- *WhThe*
Shields, Ernest *Film 1, -2*
Shields, Frank 1910-1975 *WhScrn 77, WhoHol C*
Shields, Frederick 1904-1974 *WhScrn 77*
Shields, Harry 1899-1971 *NewOrJ[port]*
Shields, Helen d1963 *NotNAT B, WhScrn 74, -77, WhoHol B*
Shields, Larry 1893-1953 *BiDAmM, CmpEPM, NewOrJ[port], WhoJazz 72*
Shields, Leroy 1898-1962 *ConAmC A*
Shields, Pat 1891?- *NewOrJ*
Shields, Ren 1868-1913 *AmSCAP 66, -80, BiDAmM, CmpEPM*
Shields, Sammy 1874- *WhThe*
Shields, Sandy 1873-1923 *WhScrn 74, -77*
Shields, Sidney 1888-1960 *Film 1*
Shields, Sydney 1888-1960 *NotNAT B, WhScrn 74, -77, WhoHol B*
Shields, William A 1946- *IntMPA 77, -78, -79, -80*
Shields Family *NewOrJ[port]*
Shiels, George 1886-1949 *ModWD, NotNAT B, OxThe, REnWD[port], WhThe*
Shiels, Una *Film 2*
Shiffrin, Irving 1909- *IntMPA 77, -75, -76, -78, -79*
Shifrin, Seymour J 1926- *Baker 78, BnBkM 80, CpmDNM 79, ConAmC, DcCM, NewGrD 80*
Shigekawa, Joan 1936- *WomWMM, -B*
Shigeoka, Keni Kinuko *IntWWM 77, -80*
Shigeoka, Raymond M 1948- *IntWWM 80*
Shigeta, James 1933- *FilmEn, FilmgC, ForYSC, HalFC 80, MovMk, WhoHol A*
Shih, Mei *WomWMM*
Shihab, Sahib 1925- *CmpEPM, EncJzS 70*
Shilkret, Jack 1896-1964 *AmSCAP 66, -80, CmpEPM, NotNAT B*
Shilkret, Nat 1895- *CmpEPM*
Shilkret, Nathaniel 1895- *AmSCAP 66, -80, Baker 78, BiDAmM, ConAmC, OxMus*
Shilling, Eric 1920- *CmOp, IntWWM 77, -80, WhoMus 72, WhoOp 76*
Shilling, Ivy *WhThe*
Shillitto, Walter William 1927- *IntWWM 77, -80*
Shillo, Michael *WhoHol A*
Shiloah, Amnon 1928- *NewGrD 80*
Shima, Koji *IntMPA 77, -75, -76, -78, -79, -80*
Shimada, Haruo *MagIlD*
Shimada, Teru *ForYSC, WhoHol A*
Shimazu, Yasujiro 1897- *FilmEn*
Shimizu, Hiroshi 1903- *FilmEn*
Shimizu, Masashi 1901- *IntMPA 77, -75, -76, -78, -79, -80*
Shimizu, Osamu 1911- *Baker 78, NewGrD 80*
Shimkin, Bonnie Lee 1941- *AmSCAP 80*
Shimkus, Joanna 1943- *FilmAG WE[port], FilmEn, FilmgC, ForYSC, HalFC 80, WhoHol A*
Shimono, Sab *WhoHol A*
Shimoyama, Hifumi 1930- *Baker 78*
Shimura, Takashi 1905- *FilmEn, HalFC 80, MovMk, OxFilm*
Shinall, Vern 1936- *WhoMus 72, WhoOp 76*
Shinbach, Bruce D 1939- *IntMPA 79, -80*
Shinbrot, Mark S 1945- *CpmDNM 76, -78, ConAmC*
Shindelman, Arkady 1954- *IntWWM 80*
Shindle, William Richard 1930- *IntWWM 77, -80*
Shindo, Kaneto 1912- *DcFM, FilmEn, FilmgC, HalFC 80, OxFilm, WorEFlm*
Shindo, Tak 1922- *AmSCAP 66, -80, Baker 78, ConAmC*
Shine, Bill 1911- *FilmgC, HalFC 80, WhoHol A, WhoThe 72, -77*
Shine, Billy *Film 2*
Shine, John L 1854-1930 *Film 1, NotNAT B, WhThe, WhoHol B*
Shine, Ted 1936- *BlkAmP, DrBlPA, MorBAP*
Shine, Wilfred 1863-1939 *WhScrn 74, -77*
Shine, Wilfred E d1939 *Film 2*
Shine, Wilfred E 1864-1939 *NotNAT B, WhThe*
Shiner, Ronald 1903-1966 *FilmAG WE, FilmEn, FilmgC, HalFC 80, IlWWBF[port], WhScrn 74, -77, WhThe, WhoHol B*
Shines, John Ned 1915- *BluesWW[port]*
Shines, Johnny 1915- *BiDAmM*
Shingler, Helen 1919- *WhThe, WhoHol A*
Shingles, Stephen *WhoMus 72*
Shinn, Frederick G 1867-1950 *OxMus*
Shinn, Randall 1944- *AmSCAP 80, CpmDNM 74, -76, ConAmC*
Shinoda, Masahiro 1931- *FilmEn*
Shinohara, Makota 1931- *Baker 78*
Shinohara, Makoto 1931- *DcCM, NewGrD 80*
Shipley, Donald Walter 1945- *IntWWM 77, -80*
Shipley, Joseph T 1893- *ConAmTC, NotNAT, WhoThe 72, -77*
Shipman, Barry 1912- *IntMPA 77, -75, -76, -78, -79, -80*
Shipman, Daniel Walter 1957- *IntWWM 77*
Shipman, Ernest 1871- *WhThe*
Shipman, Gertrude *Film 1*
Shipman, Kenneth 1930- *IntMPA 77, -75, -76, -78, -79, -80*
Shipman, Louis Evan 1869-1933 *NotNAT B, WhThe, WhoStg 1908*
Shipman, Nell d1970 *WhoHol B, WomWMM*
Shipman, Nell 1892-1970 *Film 1, -2, TwYS*
Shipman, Nell 1893-1970 *WhScrn 77*
Shipman, Nina *ForYSC, WhoHol A*
Shipman, Samuel 1883-1937 *NotNAT B, WhThe*
Shipman, Willie B *BlkAmP*
Shipp, Cameron d1961 *NotNAT B*
Shipp, J A *BlkAmP, MorBAP*
Shipp, Jesse A 1859?-1934 *BlksBF, DrBlPA*
Shipp, John Arthur 1938- *IntWWM 77*
Shipp, Julia Lowande d1962 *NotNAT B*
Shipp, Olivia Sophie L'Ange 1880-1980 *BlkWAB[port]*
Shippy, Richard W 1927- *ConAmTC*
Shipstad, Roy 1911-1975 *WhScrn 77, WhoHol C*
Shira, Francesco 1808-1883 *Baker 78*
Shirart, Georgia 1862-1929 *WhScrn 74, -77, WhoHol B*
Shire, David 1937- *AmSCAP 66, HalFC 80, IntMPA 80*
Shire, Talia 1947- *FilmEn, HalFC 80, IntMPA 78, -79, -80, WhoHol A*
Shirelles, The *AmPS A, BiDAmM, RkOn[port]*
Shires, Norman 1920- *IntWWM 77*
Shirinian, Hampartzoum 1948- *IntWWM 77, -80*
Shirinsky, Vasily Petrovich 1901-1965 *NewGrD 80*
Shirinsky, Vassily 1901-1965 *Baker 78*
Shirl, Jimmy 1909- *AmSCAP 66, -80*
Shirle, John *PupTheA*
Shirley And Lee *RkOn*
Shirley, Anne 1918- *FilmEn, Film 2, FilmgC, ForYSC, HalFC 80, MotPP, MovMk[port], ThFT[port], WhoHol A*
Shirley, Anne 1919- *What 5[port]*

Shirley, Arthur 1853-1925 *Film 1, NotNAT B, WhThe*
Shirley, Bill 1921- *BiE&WWA, ForYSC, WhoHol A*
Shirley, Bobbie d1970 *WhScrn 77, WhoHol B*
Shirley, Don 1926- *DrBlPA*
Shirley, Donald 1927- *BiDAmM, ConAmC, WhoMus 72*
Shirley, Dorinea *Film 2*
Shirley, Florence 1893-1967 *WhScrn 74, -77, WhoHol B*
Shirley, George 1934- *BiDAmM, CmOp, DrBlPA, IntWWM 77, -80, MusSN[port], NewEOp 71, NewGrD 80, WhoMus 72, WhoOp 76*
Shirley, James 1596-1666 *CnThe, EncWT, Ent, McGEWD, NewGrD 80, NotNAT A, -B, OxMus, OxThe, PlP&P, REnWD[port]*
Shirley, Jimmy 1913- *WhoJazz 72*
Shirley, John *PupTheA*
Shirley, Mrs. John *PupTheA*
Shirley, Joseph *NewGrD 80*
Shirley, Lenna Landes *PupTheA*
Shirley, Peg *WhoHol A*
Shirley, Sam 1881- *IntMPA 77, -75, -76, -78, -79*
Shirley, Thomas P d1961 *NotNAT B*
Shirley, Tom 1900-1962 *WhScrn 74, -77, WhoHol B*
Shirley, Walter, Sr. d1963 *NotNAT B*
Shirley, William 1739-1780 *NotNAT B*
Shirley & Company *RkOn 2[port]*
Shirley-Quirk, John 1931- *Baker 78, CmOp, IntWWM 77, -80, NewGrD 80[port], WhoMus 72, WhoOp 76*
Shirly, Joseph *NewGrD 80*
Shirma, Grigory Romanovich 1892- *NewGrD 80*
Shirra, Edmonston d1861 *NotNAT B*
Shirtcliff, James Stanley 1899- *WhoMus 72*
Shirvell, James 1902- *WhThe*
Shishov, Ivan 1888-1947 *Baker 78*
Shisler, Charles P 1882- *AmSCAP 66*
Shiva, H B *AmSCAP 80*
Shivas, Mark *IntMPA 77, -78, -79, -80*
Shkvarkin, Vasili Vasilevich 1893- *ModWD*
Shlifshteyn, Semyon Isaakovich 1903-1975 *NewGrD 80*
Shlonsky, Verdina 1913- *NewGrD 80*
Shlyen, Ben *IntMPA 77, -75, -76, -78, -79*
Shmuckler, Gregori 1899- *AmSCAP 80*
Shmueli, Herzl 1920- *NewGrD 80*
Shneerson, Grigory Mikhaylovich 1901- *NewGrD 80*
Shnitke, Alfred 1934- *Baker 78, NewGrD 80*
Shockey, Christian Allen 1910- *AmSCAP 66, -80*
Shocking Blue, The *RkOn 2[port]*
Shockley, Marian *WhoHol A*
Shoe Shine Johnny *BluesWW[port]*
Shoemake, Charles Edward 1937- *EncJzS 70*
Shoemake, Charlie 1937- *EncJzS 70*
Shoemaker, Ann d1979 *Vers B[port]*
Shoemaker, Ann 1891-1979 *BiE&WWA, ForYSC, NotNAT, ThFT[port], WhoHol A, WhoThe 72, -77*
Shoemaker, Ann 1895-1979 *FilmgC, HalFC 80, MovMk*
Shoffner, Bob 1900- *WhoJazz 72*
Sholdar, Mickey 1949- *WhoHol A*
Sholem, Lee 1900?- *FilmgC, HalFC 80, WhoHrs 80*
Sholem Aleichem 1859-1916 *CnMD, CnThe, EncWT, McGEWD[port], ModWD, REnWD[port]*
Sholes, Steve 1911-1968 *EncFCWM 69, IlEncCM*
Sholin, Dave *ConMuA 80B*
Shollar, Ludmila *CnOxB, DancEn 78*
Shomoda, Yuki *WhoHol A*
Shondell, Troy 1944- *RkOn*
Shonfeld, Phil *IntMPA 80*
Shonteff, Lindsay *FilmgC, HalFC 80, WhoHrs 80*
Shook, Ben 1874- *BiDAmM*
Shook, Karel 1920?- *CnOxB*
Shoop, Pamela *WhoHol A*
Shooshan, Harry M, III *NewYTET*
Shooting Star 1890-1966 *WhScrn 74, -77, WhoHol B*
Shor, Elaine *PlP&P[port]*
Shor, Pat 1928- *AmSCAP 80*
Shore *NewGrD 80*
Shore, Andrew 1952- *IntWWM 80*
Shore, Bernard 1896- *IntWWM 77, -80, NewGrD 80, WhoMus 72*
Shore, Catherine 1668?-1730 *NewGrD 80, OxMus*
Shore, Dinah *AmPS A, -B, MotPP, NewYTET, WhoHol A*
Shore, Dinah 1917- *CmpEPM, FilmEn, FilmgC, ForYSC, HalFC 80, RkOn[port]*
Shore, Dinah 1920- *BiDAmM, IntMPA 77, -75, -76, -78, -79, -80*
Shore, Elaine *WhoHol A*
Shore, Jean *WhoHol A*
Shore, John 1662?-1752 *Baker 78, NewGrD 80, OxMus*
Shore, Mary Catherine 1943- *IntWWM 77, -80*
Shore, Mathias d1700 *OxMus*
Shore, Matthew d1700 *NewGrD 80*
Shore, Matthias d1700 *NewGrD 80*
Shore, Paul *ConMuA 80B*
Shore, Roberta 1942- *ForYSC, WhoHol A*
Shore, Samuel Royle 1856-1946 *Baker 78, NewGrD 80*
Shore, Sig *IntMPA 77, -75, -76, -78, -79, -80*
Shore, William d1707 *NewGrD 80, OxMus*
Shores, Byron L 1907-1957 *WhScrn 74, -77, WhoHol B*
Shores, Lynn *Film 2, TwYS*
Shores, Richard *AmSCAP 66, -80, ConAmC*
Shorey, Kenneth J 1947- *WhoMus 72*
Shorey, Kenneth Paul 1937- *ConAmTC*
Short, Antrim 1900-1972 *Film 1, -2, ForYSC, TwYS, WhScrn 77, WhoHol B*
Short, Bobby 1924- *DrBlPA*
Short, Bobby 1926- *EncJzS 70*
Short, Ernest Henry d1959 *NotNAT B*
Short, Florence 1889-1946 *Film 1, -2, WhScrn 74, -77, WhoHol B*
Short, Frank Lea d1949 *NotNAT B*
Short, Gertrude 1902-1968 *Film 1, -2, ForYSC, MotPP, TwYS, WhScrn 74, -77, WhoHol B*
Short, Gregory Norman 1938- *ConAmC*
Short, Harry 1876-1943 *Film 2, WhScrn 77*
Short, Hassard d1956 *Film 1, -2, TwYS, WhoHol B*
Short, Hassard 1877-1956 *EncMT, NotNAT B, WhThe*
Short, Hassard 1878-1956 *WhScrn 74, -77*
Short, Horace *OxMus*
Short, J D 1902-1962 *BluesWW[port]*
Short, Lew 1875-1958 *TwYS, WhoHol B*
Short, Lewis W 1875-1958 *WhScrn 74, -77*
Short, Lou 1875-1958 *Film 1, -2*
Short, Michael 1937- *IntWWM 77, -80, WhoMus 72*
Short, Nancye *AmSCAP 80*
Short, Penelope *WhoMus 72*
Short, Peter d1603 *NewGrD 80*
Short, Robert Waltrip 1926- *EncJzS 70*
Short, Sylvia 1927- *BiE&WWA, NotNAT*
Shortall, Harrington 1895- *BiDAmM, ConAmC*
Shorte, Dino 1947- *DrBlPA*
Shorter, Wayne 1933- *EncJzS 70, IlEncJ*
Shorty George *BluesWW[port]*
Shostakovich, Dmitri 1906-1975 *Baker 78, BnBkM 80[port], CmOp, CompSN[port], CnOxB, DcCom 77[port], DcCom&M 79, DcCM, DcFM, FilmEn, HalFC 80, NewEOp 71, OxFilm, OxMus, WorEFlm*
Shostakovich, Dmitri 1906-1977 *MusMk[port]*
Shostakovich, Dmitry 1906-1975 *NewGrD 80[port], WhoMus 72*
Shostakovich, Maxim 1938- *NewGrD 80*
Shostakovitch, Dimitri 1906- *DancEn 78*
Shostakovitch, Dmitri 1906-1975 *FilmgC*
Shott, Michael John 1928- *AmSCAP 80*
Shotter, Winifred 1904- *FilmgC, HalFC 80, IlWWBF[port], WhThe, WhoHol A*
Shotwell, Marie d1934 *Film 1, -2, NotNAT B, TwYS, WhScrn 77, WhoHol B, WhoStg 1908*
Show *NewGrD 80*
Showalter, A J 1858-1924 *NewGrD 80*
Showalter, A J 1858-1929 *BiDAmM*
Showalter, Max 1917- *AmSCAP 66, -80, FilmEn, FilmgC, ForYSC, HalFC 80, IntMPA 77, -75, -76, -78, -79, -80, WhoHol A*
Shower, Hudson 1919- *BluesWW*
Showers *NewGrD 80*
Showmen, The *RkOn*
Shows, Charles W 1912- *AmSCAP 66, -80*
Shows, Ernestine McCarty 1929- *IntWWM 77*
Shpetner, Stan *NewYTET*
Shrader, David Lewis 1939- *CpmDNM 75, ConAmC*
Shrader, Frederick Franklin 1859- *WhThe*
Shrader, Frederick P d1943 *NotNAT B*
Shrager, Pyta *IntWWM 77, WhoMus 72*
Shrager, Pytha *IntWWM 80*
Shram, Violet *Film 2*
Shrapnel, Hugh Michael 1947- *DcCM*
Shreve, Bobbie Jean 1931- *IntWWM 77*
Shreve, Susan E 1952- *ConAmC*
Shreve, Tiffany d1964 *NotNAT B*
Shrimpton, Jean *WhoHol A*
Shriner, Herb 1918-1970 *AmSCAP 66, BiE&WWA, JoeFr, NewYTET, WhScrn 74, -77, WhoHol B*
Shriner, Herb 1918-1976 *NotNAT B*
Shrog, Maurice *WhoHol A*
Shropshire, Anne *WhoHol A*
Shrubsole, William 1760-1806 *NewGrD 80*
Shtein, Aleksandr Petrovich 1906- *ModWD*
Shteyn, Alexander Petrovich 1906- *OxThe*
Shteynberg, Maximilian Oseyevich 1883-1946 *NewGrD 80*
Shteynpress, Boris Solomonovich 1908- *NewGrD 80*
Shtogarenko, Andrei 1902- *Baker 78*
Shtogarenko, Andriy Yakovlevich 1902- *NewGrD 80*
Shtraukh, Maxim 1901-1974 *Film 2, WhScrn 77*
Shtraukh, Maxim Maximovich 1900-1974 *EncWT*
Shu, Eddie 1918- *CmpEPM*
Shu, Shuen *WomWMM*
Shu-Hu *Film 2*
Shuard, Amy 1924-1975 *CmOp, NewGrD 80, WhoMus 72*
Shub, Esther Ilyanichna 1894-1949 *FilmEn*
Shub, Esther Ilyanichna 1894-1959 *DcFM, OxFilm, WomWMM, WorEFlm*
Shubert, Eddie 1898-1937 *WhScrn 74, -77, WhoHol B*
Shubert, Jacob J 1880-1963 *CnThe, EncWT, NotNAT A, -B, OxThe, PlP&P[port], WhThe*
Shubert, John 1908-1962 *NotNAT B*
Shubert, Lee 1875-1935 *EncWT*
Shubert, Lee 1875-1953 *CnThe, NotNAT A, -B, OxThe, PlP&P[port], WhThe, WhoStg 1908*
Shubert, Milton I d1967 *NotNAT B*
Shubert, Sam S 1875-1905 *NotNAT A, -B*
Shubert, Sam S 1876-1905 *CnThe, EncWT, OxThe, PlP&P[port]*
Shubert Brothers *EncMT, PlP&P[port]*
Shudi, Burkat 1702-1773 *NewGrD 80*
Shudi, Burkhardt 1702-1773 *NewGrD 80, OxMus*
Shufflin' Sam *BluesWW[port]*
Shuftan, Eugen *IntMPA 77, -75, -76, -78*
Shuftan, Eugene *FilmEn*
Shugard, Amy V *WomWMM B*
Shugrue, J Edward 1909- *IntMPA 77, -75, -76, -78*
Shuken, Leo 1906-1976 *AmSCAP 66, -80, HalFC 80*
Shukshin, Vasily 1929-1974 *WhScrn 77*
Shull, Leo 1913- *BiE&WWA, ConAmTC, NotNAT, WhoThe 72, -77*
Shull, Margaret *PupTheA*
Shull, Richard B *WhoHol A*
Shuller, Florence Anita 1906- *IntWWM 77*
Shulman, Alan M 1915- *AmSCAP 66, -80, Baker 78, ConAmC*
Shulman, Harry 1916-1971 *BiDAmM*
Shulman, Max 1919- *BiE&WWA, IntMPA 77, -75, -76, -78, -79, -80, NotNAT*
Shulman, Milton 1913- *WhoThe 72, -77*
Shultz, Harry *Film 2*
Shulze, Frederick B 1935- *ConAmC*

Shuman, Alden 1924- AmSCAP 80
Shuman, Earl Stanley 1923- AmSCAP 66, -80
Shuman, Francis K 1908- AmSCAP 66, -80
Shuman, Harry Film 2
Shuman, Mark Orrin 1951- IntWWM 80
Shuman, Mort NotNAT
Shuman, Roy 1925-1973 WhScrn 77, WhoHol B
Shumate, Harold IntMPA 77, -75, -76, -78, -79, -80
Shumiatcher, Bella IntWWM 80
Shumley, Walter Film 2
Shumlin, Herman 1896- BiE&WWA, WorEFlm
Shumlin, Herman 1898-1979 FilmEn, FilmgC, HalFC 80, NotNAT, WhoThe 72, -77
Shumsky, Oscar 1917- CreCan 2, NewGrD 80
Shumway, Lee C 1884-1959 Film 1, -2, ForYSC, TwYS, WhScrn 77
Shumway, Walter Film 2
Shunmugham, T K 1912-1973 WhScrn 77
Shupert, George T 1904- IntMPA 77, -75, -76, -78, -79, -80
Shure, Leonard 1910- Baker 78
Shure, R Deane 1885- AmSCAP 66, -80
Shure, Ralph Deane 1885- ConAmC A
Shurey, Dinah WomWMM
Shurlock, Geoffrey 1895-1976 HalFC 80
Shurpin, Sol 1914- IntMPA 77, -75, -76, -78, -79, -80
Shurr, Alan 1912- AmSCAP 66, -80
Shurr, Gertrude CnOxB, DancEn 78
Shurr, Louis BiE&WWA
Shurtleff, Ernest Warburton 1862-1917 BiDAmM
Shurtleff, Lynn Richard 1939- ConAmC
Shurtleff, Michael BiE&WWA, NatPD[port], NotNAT
Shusherin, Yakov Emelyanovich 1753-1813 OxThe
Shuster, Frank 1916- CreCan 2
Shute, Nevil 1899-1960 FilmgC, HalFC 80
Shuter, Edward 1728-1776 NotNAT B, OxThe, PlP&P[port]
Shutler, Dorothy Kate WhoMus 72
Shutta, Ethel 1896-1976 BiDAmM, WhThe, WhoHol C, WhoThe 72
Shutta, Ethel 1897- CmpEPM
Shutta, Jack 1899-1957 WhScrn 74, -77, WhoHol B
Shuttleworth, Anna Lee 1927- IntWWM 77, -80, WhoMus 72
Shuttleworth, Gisele CreCan 2
Shuttleworth, Obadiah d1734 NewGrD 80
Shvarts, Yevgeni Lvovich 1896-1958 EncWT, ModWD
Shwartz, Evgenyi Lvovich 1896-1961 OxThe
Shwartz, Martin 1923- BiE&WWA, NotNAT
Shy, Gus 1894-1945 NotNAT B, WhScrn 74, -77, WhoHol B
Shyam d1951 WhScrn 77
Shylen, Ben IntMPA 80
Shyman, Mona WomWMM
Shyre, Paul 1929- BiE&WWA, NotNAT, WhoThe 72, -77
Si Stebbins MagIlD
Sib BluesWW[port]
Sibbald, Laurie WhoHol A
Sibbing, Robert 1929- ConAmC
Sibbritt, Gerard 1942- CnOxB
Sibelius, Jan 1865-1957 DancEn 78
Sibelius, Jean 1865-1957 Baker 78, BnBkM 80[port], CompSN[port], CnOxB, DcCom 77[port], DcCom&M 79, DcCM, DcTwCC, -A, MusMk[port], NewGrD 80[port], NotNAT B, OxMus
Sibelius, Johan 1865-1957 NewGrD 80[port]
Sibelli, Giovanni Antonio NewGrD 80
Sibencanin, Ivan NewGrD 80
Siber, Max PupTheA
Siberau, Wolfgang Conrad Andreas 1688-1766 NewGrD 80
Siberskaia, Nadia Film 2
Sibert, Paul NewGrD 80
Sibilla d1766? NewGrD 80
Sibley, Antoinette 1939- CnOxB, DancEn 78[port], WhoHol A
Sibley, Lucy d1945 NotNAT B
Siboni, Erik Anthon Valdemar 1828-1892 Baker 78, NewGrD 80
Siboni, Giuseppe 1780-1839 NewGrD 80
Sibson, Arthur Robert 1906- IntWWM 77, -80, WhoMus 72
Sicard, Jean NewGrD 80
Sicari, Joseph R WhoHol A
Sicher, Fridolin 1490-1546 NewGrD 80
Sichra, Andrey Osipovich NewGrD 80
Sicignano, Albert J 1912- IntMPA 77, -76, -78, -79, -80
Siciliani, Francesco 1911- NewGrD 80
Sicilianos, Yorgo 1922- Baker 78, DcCM
Sicilianos, Yorgos 1922- NewGrD 80
Sickert, Walter Richard d1942 NotNAT B
Sicot, Irene Marie-Therese 1930- WhoOp 76
Sicurella, Joseph Paul 1949- AmSCAP 80
Sidaris, Andrew W NewYTET
Sidaris, Andy 1932- IntMPA 77, -75, -76, -78, -79, -80
Siddelley, Barbara IntWWM 77, -80
Siddons, Harriett d1844 NotNAT B
Siddons, Henry d1815 NotNAT B
Siddons, James 1948- IntWWM 77, -80
Siddons, Sarah Kemble 1755-1831 CnThe, EncWT, Ent, NotNAT A, -B, OxThe, PlP&P[port]
Siddons, William PlP&P
Sidel'nikov, Nikolay Nikolayevich 1930- NewGrD 80
Sideman, William AmSCAP 80
Sider, Ronald Ray 1933- IntWWM 77, -80
Sides, Carolyn WomWMM B
Sidey, John Wear 1933- IntWWM 77
Sidgwick, John Robert Lindsay 1923- CreCan 2
Sidi, Yizhak NewGrD 80
Sidimus, Joysanne 1938- CreCan 2
Sidlow, Carol ConMuA 80B
Sidman, Sam Film 2
Sidney, Fred W WhoStg 1906, -1908
Sidney, George 1876-1945 FilmEn, NotNAT B, WhScrn 74, -77
Sidney, George 1878-1945 Film 2, FilmgC, ForYSC, Funs[port], HalFC 80, TwYS, WhoHol B
Sidney, George 1911- BiDFilm, -81, CmMov, FilmgC, HalFC 80, MovMk[port], WorEFlm
Sidney, George 1916- DcFM, FilmEn, IntMPA 77, -75, -76, -78, -79, -80
Sidney, Mabel 1884-1969 WhScrn 74, -77
Sidney, P J DrBlPA
Sidney, Philip OxMus
Sidney, Scott 1872-1928 TwYS A, WhScrn 74, -77, WhoHol B
Sidney, Sylvia 1910- BiDFilm, -81, BiE&WWA, FilmEn, Film 2, FilmgC, ForYSC, HalFC 80[port], IntMPA 77, -75, -76, -78, -79, -80, MotPP, MovMk[port], NotNAT, OxFilm, ThFT[port], What 3[port], WhoHol A, WhoThe 72, -77, WomWMM, WorEFlm
Sidon, Samuel Peter 1630?- NewGrD 80
Sidow NewGrD 80
Sidran, Ben H 1943- AmSCAP 80
Sidwell, Martindale 1916- WhoMus 72
Siebel, Peter 1884-1949 WhScrn 74, -77
Siebel, Richard 1896- IntWWM 77
Siebeneicher, Mateusz d1582 NewGrD 80
Siebenhaar, Malachias 1616-1685 NewGrD 80
Siebenkas, Johann 1714-1781 NewGrD 80
Siebenkees, Johann 1714-1781 NewGrD 80
Sieber, Ferdinand 1822-1895 Baker 78
Sieber, Georges-Julien 1775-1847 NewGrD 80
Sieber, Jean-Georges 1738-1822 NewGrD 80
Siebert, David ConMuA 80B
Siebert, Lynn Laitman 1946- IntWWM 77, -80
Siebert, Wilhelm Dieter 1931- IntWWM 77, -80
Siebner, Herbert Johannes Josef 1925- CreCan 1
Siedlecki, Agnes WomWMM B
Siefert, Paul 1586-1666 NewGrD 80
Sieg, Jerry Paul 1943- ConAmC
Siegel, Al 1898- AmSCAP 66, -80
Siegel, Arsene 1897- AmSCAP 66, ConAmC A
Siegel, Arthur 1923- AmSCAP 66, -80, BiE&WWA, IntWWM 77, NotNAT
Siegel, Benjamin 1919- ConAmC
Siegel, Bernard 1868-1940 Film 1, -2, TwYS, WhScrn 77
Siegel, Carl F W 1869- Baker 78
Siegel, Don 1912- FilmEn, FilmgC, HalFC 80, IntMPA 77, -75, -76, -78, -79, -80, MovMk[port], OxFilm, WhoHrs 80
Siegel, Don 1913- CmMov
Siegel, Donald 1912- BiDFilm, -81, DcFM, WorEFlm
Siegel, Harro DcPup
Siegel, Henry 1906- CpmDNM 80, ConAmC
Siegel, Jeffrey 1942- WhoMus 72
Siegel, Marcia B 1932- CnOxB
Siegel, Marian WomWMM B
Siegel, Max d1958 NotNAT B
Siegel, Norman ConAmC
Siegel, Paul 1914- AmSCAP 66, -80, ConAmC
Siegel, Ralph Maria WhoMus 72
Siegel, Rudolf 1878-1948 Baker 78
Siegel, Sidney Edward 1927- AmSCAP 66, -80
Siegel, Simon B IntMPA 77, -75, -76, -78, -79, -80, NewYTET
Siegel, Sol C 1903- CmMov, FilmEn, FilmgC, HalFC 80, IntMPA 77, -75, -76, -78, -79, -80, WorEFlm
Siegel, Wayne Perry 1953- IntWWM 80
Siegele, Ulrich 1930- NewGrD 80
Siegenthaler, Robert NewYTET
Siegfried, Francoise 1914- IntWWM 77, -80
Siegl, Otto 1896- Baker 78, IntWWM 77, -80, NewGrD 80, WhoMus 72
Siegler, Al Film 1
Siegman, Diane Marie 1951- IntWWM 77
Siegmann, George d1928 Film 2, WhoHol B
Siegmann, George 1883-1928 WhScrn 74, -77
Siegmann, George 1884-1928 Film 1
Siegmeister, Elie 1909- AmSCAP 66, -80, Baker 78, BiDAmM, BiE&WWA, BnBkM 80, CompSN[port], CpmDNM 73, -79, -80, ConAmC, DcCM, IntWWM 77, -80, MusMk, NewGrD 80, NotNAT, OxMus, WhoMus 72
Siegmund-Schultze, Walther 1916- IntWWM 77, -80, NewGrD 80
Sieh, Eleanor Anne Becker 1936- IntWWM 77
Siekmann, Frank Herman 1925- CpmDNM 76, -78, IntWWM 77, -80
Sielanski, Stanley d1955 WhScrn 74, -77
Siemon, Carl 1918- AmSCAP 80
Siems, Margarethe 1879-1952 CmOp, NewGrD 80
Sienkiewicz, Henryk 1846-1916 NotNAT A, -B
Siennicki, Edmund John 1920- AmSCAP 80, ConAmC, IntWWM 77
Siepi, Cesare 1923- Baker 78, BiE&WWA, BnBkM 80, CmOp, IntWWM 77, -80, MusSN[port], NewEOp 71, NewGrD 80, WhoHol A, WhoMus 72, WhoOp 76
Sieradza, Cyprian Z NewGrD 80
Sierakowski, Waclaw 1741-1806 NewGrD 80
Sierck, Detlaf FilmEn
Sierck, Dietlef 1900- WorEFlm[port]
Sierra, Gregorio Martinez OxThe
Sierra, Margarita d1963 WhoHol B
Sies, Johannes d1534? NewGrD 80
Siess, Johannes d1534? NewGrD 80
Sietz, Reinhold 1895-1973 NewGrD 80
Sieveking, Margot WhThe
Sieveking, Martinus 1867-1950 Baker 78, BiDAmM
Sievers, Gerd 1915- IntWWM 77, -80, NewGrD 80
Sievers, Heinrich 1908- IntWWM 80, NewGrD 80
Sievers, Johann Friedrich Ludwig 1742-1806 NewGrD 80
Sievert, Ludwig 1887-1966 NewGrD 80
Sievert, Ludwig 1887-1968 EncWT
Siewinski, Andrzej NewGrD 80
Siface NewGrD 80
Siface, Giovanni Francesco 1653-1697 Baker 78
Sifler, Paul John 1911- AmSCAP 80, ConAmC
Sifnios, Dusanka 1934- DancEn 78
Sifnios, Duska 1934- CnOxB
Sifonia, Firmino 1917- NewGrD 80
Sifton, Claire 1898- PlP&P
Sifton, Paul 1898-1972 CnMD, ModWD, PlP&P[port]
Sigefrid, Cornelius 1550?-1605? NewGrD 80
Sigelius, Rufinus 1601-1675 NewGrD 80

Siggins, Julia Williams *WhScrn 74, -77*
Sighele, Mietta *WhoOp 76*
Sighvatsson, Karl Johann 1950- *IntWWM 77*
Sigismondi, Giuseppe 1739-1826 *Baker 78*
Sigismondo, Giuseppe 1739-1826 *NewGrD 80*
Sigl, Rufinus *NewGrD 80*
Sigler, Bunny *RkOn 2[port]*
Sigler, James Henry 1930- *AmSCAP 80*
Sigler, John M 1891- *AmSCAP 66*
Sigler, Maurice 1901-1961 *AmSCAP 66, -80, CmpEPM*
Sigman, Carl 1909- *AmPS, AmSCAP 66, -80, CmpEPM, Sw&Ld C*
Sigman, Mike *ConMuA 80B*
Sigmund, Oskar 1919- *IntWWM 77, -80*
Signac 1600?-1630? *NewGrD 80*
Signorelli, Frank 1901- *AmSCAP 66, -80, CmpEPM, WhoJazz 72*
Signorelli, Michael 1906- *IntWWM 77, -80*
Signorelli, Tom *WhoHol A*
Signoret, Gabriel 1873-1937 *Film 1, -2, WhScrn 74, -77, WhThe, WhoHol B*
Signoret, Gabriel 1878-1937 *NotNAT B*
Signoret, Simone 1921- *BiDFilm, -81, FilmAG WE[port], FilmEn, FilmgC, ForYSC, HalFC 80, IntMPA 77, -75, -76, -78, -79, -80, MotPP, MovMk[port], OxFilm, WhoHol A, WorEFlm[port]*
Signoretti, Aurelio 1567-1635 *NewGrD 80*
Signorucci, Pompeo *NewGrD 80*
Sigourney, Lydia Howard Huntley 1791-1865 *BiDAmM*
Sigtenhorst-Meyer, Bernhard VanDen 1888-1953 *Baker 78, NewGrD 80, OxMus*
Sigurbjornsson, Thorkell 1938- *Baker 78, DcCM, NewGrD 80*
Sigurd, Jacques 1920- *FilmEn*
Sigurdsson, Elisabeth Gudrun 1931- *IntWWM 77, -80*
Sigwart, Botho 1884-1915 *Baker 78*
Sihmada, Ihamu d1965 *WhScrn 77*
Sijalowa-Vogel, Irena 1927- *IntWWM 77, -80*
Sikes, Virginia Lee 1941- *IntWWM 77*
Sikevitz, Gail *WomWMM B*
Sikhra, Andrey Osipovich 1773?-1850 *NewGrD 80*
Siki, Bela 1923- *IntWWM 77, -80, NewGrD 80, WhoMus 72*
Sikking, James *WhoHol A*
Sikla, Ferry *Film 2*
Siklos, Albert 1878-1942 *Baker 78, NewGrD 80*
Sikorski *NewGrD 80*
Sikorski, Hans 1899-1972 *NewGrD 80*
Sikorski, Jozef 1813-1896 *NewGrD 80*
Sikorski, Kazimierz 1895- *Baker 78, IntWWM 77, NewGrD 80*
Sikorski, Tomasz 1939- *Baker 78, DcCM, IntWWM 77, -80, NewGrD 80*
Siks, Geraldine B 1912- *BiE&WWA, NotNAT*
Sil-Vara, G d1938 *NotNAT B*
Silas, Edouard 1827-1909 *NewGrD 80, OxMus*
Silas, Eduard 1827-1909 *Baker 78*
Silber, Arthur 1919- *IntMPA 77, -75, -76, -78, -79, -80*
Silber, Euchario *NewGrD 80*
Silber, Irwin 1925- *EncFCWM 69*
Silberkleit, William B *IntMPA 77, -78, -79, -80*
Silbermann *NewGrD 80*
Silbermann, Alphons 1909- *IntWWM 77, -80, WhoMus 72*
Silbermann, Andreas 1678-1734 *Baker 78, NewGrD 80*
Silbermann, Gottfried 1683-1753 *Baker 78, NewGrD 80, OxMus*
Silbermann, Johann Andreas 1712-1783 *Baker 78, NewGrD 80*
Silbermann, Johann Daniel 1717-1766 *Baker 78*
Silbermann, Johann Friedrich 1762-1817 *Baker 78*
Silbermann, Johann Heinrich 1727-1799 *Baker 78*
Silbert, Lisa 1880-1965 *WhScrn 74, -77, WhoHol B*
Silbert, Liza *Film 2*
Silbert, Theodore *Film 2*
Silberta, Rhea 1900-1959 *AmSCAP 66, -80, ConAmC*
Silcher, Friedrich 1789-1860 *Baker 78, NewGrD 80*
Silcock, Norman 1915- *IntWWM 77, -80, WhoMus 72*
Silesius, Angelus *NewGrD 80*
Siletti, Mario G 1904-1964 *NotNAT B, WhScrn 74, -77, WhoHol B*
Silfen, Martin *ConMuA 80B*
Silhouettes, The *AmPS A, RkOn[port]*
Silipigni, Alfredo 1931- *IntWWM 77, -80, WhoOp 76*
Silja, Anja 1940- *CmOp, NewGrD 80, WhoOp 76*
Silk, Dorothy 1883-1942 *NewGrD 80*
Silkie, The *RkOn 2[port]*
Silkoff, David Michael 1949- *IntWWM 80*
Sill, Edward Rowland 1841-1887 *BiDAmM*
Sill, Lester *ConMuA 80B*
Sill, William Raymond 1869-1922 *NotNAT B, WhoStg 1906, -1908*
Sillamy, Jean-Claude 1932- *IntWWM 77, -80*
Sillas, Harry *PupTheA*
Sillaway, Ward 1909-1965 *CmpEPM*
Sillem, Maurits 1929- *WhoMus 72*
Silliman, A Cutler 1922- *ConAmC*
Silliphant, Sterling 1918- *FilmgC, HalFC 80, WorEFlm*
Silliphant, Stirling 1918- *CmMov, FilmEn, IntMPA 77, -75, -76, -78, -79, -80, NewYTET*
Silliphant, Tiana *WhoHol A*
Sillito, Kenneth *WhoMus 72*
Sillitoe, Alan 1928- *HalFC 80*
Sillman, June *AmSCAP 80*
Sillman, Leonard 1908- *BiE&WWA, EncMT, NotNAT, -A, WhoThe 72, -77*
Silloway, Ward 1909-1965 *WhoJazz 72*
Sills, Berenice *AmSCAP 66, -80*
Sills, Beverly 1929- *Baker 78, BiDAmM, BnBkM 80, CmOp[port], IntWWM 77, -80, MusMk, MusSN[port], NewEOp 71, NewGrD 80[port], WhoOp 76*
Sills, Beverly 1931- *WhoMus 72*
Sills, Milton 1882-1930 *FilmEn, Film 1, -2, FilmgC, ForYSC, HalFC 80, MovMk, NotNAT B, TwYS, WhScrn 74, -77, WhoHol B*
Sills, Paul *NotNAT*
Sillward, Edward d1930 *NotNAT B*
Silly Kid, The *BluesWW[port]*
Silo, Susan *WhoHol A*
Silone, Ignazio 1900- *CnMD*
Siloti, Alexander 1863-1945 *Baker 78, BiDAmM, MusSN[port], NewGrD 80*
Silsbee, Ann Loomis 1930- *CpmDNM 78, -80, ConAmC, IntWWM 80*
Silsbee, Joshua 1813-1855 *FamA&A[port]*
Silsbury, Elizabeth Alice 1931- *IntWWM 80*
Silva, Andreas De *NewGrD 80*
Silva, Antonio *FilmAG WE*
Silva, Antonio Joao 1870-1954 *WhScrn 74, -77*
Silva, Antonio Jose Da 1705-1739 *CnThe, NotNAT B, OxThe, REnWD[port]*
Silva, Francisco DaCosta E *NewGrD 80*
Silva, Francisco Manuel Da 1795-1865 *Baker 78, NewGrD 80*
Silva, Henry 1928- *FilmEn, FilmgC, ForYSC, HalFC 80, MovMk[port], WhoHol A*
Silva, Jesus Bermudez *NewGrD 80*
Silva, Joao Cordeiro Da 1735?-1808? *NewGrD 80*
Silva, Jose DaCosta E *NewGrD 80*
Silva, Jose DeSanta Rita Marques E 1778?-1837 *NewGrD 80*
Silva, Luis Antonio 1943- *AmSCAP 80*
Silva, Manuel Nunes Da *NewGrD 80*
Silva, Oscar Da 1870-1958 *Baker 78*
Silva, Poll Da 1834-1875 *Baker 78*
Silva, Simone 1928-1957 *WhScrn 74, -77, WhoHol B*
Silva, Stella 1948- *WhoOp 76*
Silva, Tristao Da *NewGrD 80*
Silva, Yvan J 1936- *AmSCAP 80*
Silva Leite, Antonio Da *NewGrD 80*
Silva Nunes, Armando Da *CreCan 1*
Silvain, Eugene Charles Joseph 1851-1930 *NotNAT B, WhThe*
Silvain, Falconetti *Film 2*
Silvain, James d1856 *CnOxB*
Silvani, Aldo 1891-1964 *WhScrn 74, -77, WhoHol B*
Silvani, Francesco 1660?- *NewGrD 80*
Silvani, Giuseppe Antonio 1672-1727? *NewGrD 80*
Silvani, Marino d1711 *NewGrD 80*
Silver, Abner *Sw&Ld C*
Silver, Abner 1895- *AmPS*
Silver, Abner 1899-1966 *AmSCAP 66, -80, CmpEPM*
Silver, Alfred Lindsey Leigh *IntWWM 77, -80, WhoMus 72*
Silver, Bassett 1909- *WhoMus 72*
Silver, Borah *WhoHol A*
Silver, Charles 1868-1949 *Baker 78*
Silver, Charles L 1948- *AmSCAP 80*
Silver, Christine d1960 *WhoHol B*
Silver, Christine 1884-1960 *WhThe*
Silver, Christine 1885-1960 *WhScrn 74, -77*
Silver, Dorothy *MorBAP*
Silver, Frank 1896-1960 *AmSCAP 66, -80, BiDAmM*
Silver, Fred 1936- *AmSCAP 66*
Silver, Frederick 1936- *AmSCAP 80, ConAmC*
Silver, Horace 1928- *AmSCAP 66, -80, BiDAmM, CmpEPM, EncJzS 70, IlEncJ, NewGrD 80*
Silver, Joan *WomWMM, -B*
Silver, Joan Macklin *HalFC 80*
Silver, Joan Micklin 1935- *IntMPA 78, -79, -80*
Silver, Joe 1922- *BiE&WWA, NotNAT, WhoHol A, WhoThe 77*
Silver, Johnny *WhoHol A*
Silver, Len *ConMuA 80B*
Silver, Leon J 1918- *IntMPA 77, -75, -76, -78, -79, -80*
Silver, Mark 1892-1965 *AmSCAP 66, -80*
Silver, Mary S *PupTheA*
Silver, Millicent *WhoMus 72*
Silver, Milton *IntMPA 77, -75, -76, -78, -79, -80*
Silver, Monty 1933- *BiE&WWA, NotNAT*
Silver, Pat *AmSCAP 66, IntMPA 77, -75, -76, -78, -79, -80*
Silver, Pauline 1888-1969 *WhScrn 74, -77, WhoHol B*
Silver, Phil 1911- *AmSCAP 80*
Silver, Phillip Alan 1946- *IntWWM 80*
Silver, Phillip Jack 1943- *WhoOp 76*
Silver, Raphael D 1930- *IntMPA 78, -79, -80*
Silver, Ronald *WhoHol A*
Silver, Sheila J 1946- *ConAmC*
Silver, Stuart 1947- *NatPD[port]*
Silver Apples *BiDAmM*
Silver Convention *RkOn 2[port]*
Silvera, Frank 1914-1970 *BiE&WWA, BlkAmP, DrBlPA, FilmEn, FilmgC, ForYSC, HalFC 80, MorBAP, MovMk, NotNAT B, WhScrn 74, -77, WhoHol B*
Silvera, John *BlkAmP*
Silverbach, Alan M *NewYTET*
Silverberg, Frederick Irwin 1936- *AmSCAP 80*
Silverheels, Jay 1919-1980 *FilmEn*
Silverheels, Jay 1920- *FilmgC, ForYSC, HalFC 80, WhoHol A*
Silveri, Paolo 1913- *CmOp, IntWWM 77, -80, NewGrD 80, WhoMus 72*
Silverlight, Terry Bennet 1957- *AmSCAP 80*
Silverman, Belle Miriam 1929- *BnBkM 80*
Silverman, Dave *Film 2*
Silverman, Faye-Ellen 1947- *AmSCAP 80, CpmDNM 74, -76, -77, -78, -79, -80, ConAmC, IntWWM 77, -80*
Silverman, Fred 1937- *IntMPA 77, -76, -78, -79, -80, NewYTET*
Silverman, Ron 1933- *IntMPA 77, -75, -76, -78, -79, -80*
Silverman, Sam *ConMuA 80B*
Silverman, Sid 1898-1950 *NotNAT B*
Silverman, Sime 1872-1933 *NotNAT B*
Silverman, Sime 1873-1933 *NotNAT A*
Silverman, Stanley 1938- *BnBkM 80, ConAmC*
Silverman, Syd 1932- *BiE&WWA, ConMuA 80B, IntMPA 77, -75, -76, -78, -79, -80, NotNAT*
Silvers, Doc *AmSCAP 80*
Silvers, Dolores *AmSCAP 66, -80*
Silvers, Ed *ConMuA 80B*
Silvers, Lou *Film 2*

Silvers, Louis 1889-1954 *AmSCAP 66, -80, BiDAmM, NotNAT B*
Silvers, Maurice *PupTheA*
Silvers, Phil *MotPP, NewYTET*
Silvers, Phil 1911- *AmSCAP 66, BiE&WWA, CmpEPM, EncMT, Ent, ForYSC, Funs[port], NotNAT, -A, WhoHol A, WhoThe 77*
Silvers, Phil 1912- *CmMov, FilmEn, FilmgC, HalFC 80, IntMPA 77, -75, -76, -78, -79, -80, JoeFr[port], MovMk[port]*
Silvers, Sid 1907-1976 *AmSCAP 66, -80*
Silvers, Sid 1908-1976 *Film 2, ForYSC, IntMPA 77, -75, -76, -78, -79, -80*
Silverstein, Eliot 1925?- *FilmgC, HalFC 80, MovMk[port]*
Silverstein, Elliot 1927- *FilmEn, WorEFlm*
Silverstein, Helen *WomWMM*
Silverstein, Herman 1910- *AmSCAP 80*
Silverstein, Joseph 1932- *Baker 78, NewGrD 80*
Silverstein, Maurice 1912- *IntMPA 77, -75, -76, -78, -79, -80*
Silverstein, Shel *IlEncCM[port]*
Silverstone, Jonas T 1906- *BiE&WWA, NotNAT*
Silverthorne, Paul Adam 1951- *IntWWM 77, -80*
Silvester II *NewGrD 80*
Silvester, Frederick Caton 1901-1966 *CreCan 1*
Silvester, Victor 1900-1978 *IntMPA 77, -75, -76, -78, -79, -80, IntWWM 77, -80, NewGrD 80, WhoMus 72*
Silvestre *NewGrD 80*
Silvestre, Ami *WhoHol A*
Silvestre, Armando *WhoHol A*
Silvestre, Hippolyte 1808-1879 *NewGrD 80*
Silvestre, Hippolyte Chretien 1845-1913 *NewGrD 80*
Silvestre, Lourival 1949- *IntWWM 77, -80*
Silvestre, Pierre 1801-1859 *NewGrD 80*
Silvestri, Constantin 1913-1969 *Baker 78, NewGrD 80*
Silvestri, Florido De d1672? *NewGrD 80*
Silvestri, Renzo 1899- *IntWWM 77, -80, WhoMus 72*
Silvestrino, Francesco *NewGrD 80*
Silvestris, Florido De d1672? *NewGrD 80*
Silvestrov, Valentin 1937- *Baker 78, DcCM, NewGrD 80*
Silzer, Giorgio W 1920- *IntWWM 77, -80*
Sim, Alastair 1900-1976 *CmMov, FilmAG WE, FilmEn, FilmgC, ForYSC, HalFC 80, IlWWBF[port], IntMPA 75, -76, MotPP, MovMk[port], WhoHol A, WhoThe 72, -77*
Sim, Alistair 1900-1976 *CnThe*
Sim, Gerald 1925- *HalFC 80, WhoHol A*
Sim, Millie 1895- *WhThe*
Sim, Sheila 1922- *FilmgC, HalFC 80, IlWWBF, WhThe, WhoHol A*
Sima, Oskar *Film 2*
Sima, William Richard, Sr. 1892-1965 *AmSCAP 66, -80*
Simacek, Oldrich 1919- *WhoOp 76*
Simai, Pavol 1930- *Baker 78*
Siman, E E, Jr. 1921- *EncFCWM 69*
Simandl, Franz 1840-1912 *Baker 78*
Simandl, Josef 1903- *IntWWM 77, -80*
Simandy, Joszef 1916- *NewGrD 80*
Simanek, Otto 1901-1967 *WhScrn 74, -77, WhoHol B*
Simard, Jean 1916- *CreCan 1*
Simbracky, Jan *NewGrD 80*
Simcock, John *OxMus*
Simeanuer, Peter W 1931- *IntWWM 80*
Simenon, Georges 1903- *FilmgC, HalFC 80*
Simeon, Omer 1902-1959 *BiDAmM, CmpEPM, IlEncJ, NewOrJ[port], WhoJazz 72*
Simeone, Harry 1911- *AmSCAP 66, -80, ConAmC*
Simeone, Harry 1914- *RkOn*
Simeonov, Konstantin Arsen'yevich 1910- *NewGrD 80*
Simeonova, Nedyalka 1901-1959 *NewGrD 80*
Simic, Borivoje 1920- *Baker 78, IntWWM 77, -80*
Simila, Martti 1898-1958 *Baker 78*
Simionato, Giuletta 1910- *CmOp*
Simionato, Giulietta 1910- *Baker 78, BnBkM 80, MusSN[port], NewEOp 71, NewGrD 80*
Simionato, Giulletta 1916- *IntWWM 77, -80*
Simionato, Guilietta *WhoMus 72*
Simionescu, Elena 1937- *WhoOp 76*
Simkins, Cyril Frank 1902- *WhoMus 72*
Simmes, William *NewGrD 80*
Simmonds, Annette 1918-1959 *WhScrn 74, -77, WhoHol B*
Simmonds, Kim 1947- *BiDAmM*
Simmonds, Paul Edward 1949- *IntWWM 80*
Simmonds, Stanley *WhoHol A*
Simmonds, William *DcPup*
Simmons, Anthony 1924?- *FilmgC, HalFC 80, WorEFlm*
Simmons, Calvin 1950- *IntWWM 77, -80*
Simmons, Chester R *NewYTET*
Simmons, David *WhoMus 72*
Simmons, Donald E 1929- *IntWWM 80*
Simmons, Elsie *AmSCAP 66, -80*
Simmons, Gwendolyn Annette 1940- *IntWWM 77*
Simmons, H C *Film 2*
Simmons, Homer 1900-1971 *AmSCAP 66, -80, ConAmC*
Simmons, Huey 1933- *EncJzS 70*
Simmons, Jean 1929- *BiDFilm, -81, CmMov, FilmAG WE[port], FilmEn, FilmgC, ForYSC, HalFC 80, IlWWBF[port], IntMPA 77, -75, -76, -78, -79, -80, MotPP, MovMk[port], OxFilm, WhoHol A, WorEFlm*
Simmons, John *IntMPA 77, -75, -76, -78, -79, -80*
Simmons, John 1918- *BiDAmM, CmpEPM, EncJzS 70, WhoJazz 72*
Simmons, Jumpin' Gene *RkOn 2A*
Simmons, Lonnie 1915?- *WhoJazz 72*
Simmons, Mack 1934- *BluesWW[port]*
Simmons, Otis Davis 1928- *IntWWM 77*
Simmons, Richard 1918- *ForYSC, WhoHol A*
Simmons, Sonny 1933- *EncJzS 70, IlEncJ*
Simmons, Stanley 1915- *IntMPA 77, -75, -76, -78, -79, -80*
Simmons, William Benjamin Dearborn 1823-1876 *NewGrD 80*
Simms, Alice D 1920- *AmSCAP 66, -80*
Simms, David Michael 1954- *IntWWM 77*
Simms, Frank 1921- *IntMPA 77, -75, -76, -78, -79, -80*
Simms, Ginny 1915- *CmpEPM*
Simms, Ginny 1916- *FilmgC, HalFC 80, MotPP*
Simms, Ginny 1918- *ForYSC*
Simms, Hilda 1920- *BiE&WWA, DrBlPA, NotNAT, WhoHol A, WhoThe 72, -77*
Simms, Joe *BlksBF*
Simms, Larry 1934- *FilmgC, ForYSC, HalFC 80, What 5[port], WhoHol A*
Simms, Philip 1935- *WhoMus 72*
Simms, Tedd *AmSCAP 80*
Simms, Willard *WhoStg 1908*
Simms, William *NewGrD 80*
Simms, Winnie Lee 1925- *AmSCAP 80*
Simola, Liisa *WomWMM B*
Simon *NewGrD 80*
Simon A Scto Bartholomaeo *NewGrD 80*
Simon D'Authie 118-?-1235? *NewGrD 80*
Simon D'Autie 118-?-1235? *NewGrD 80*
Simon De Insula *NewGrD 80*
Simon Le Breton d1473 *NewGrD 80*
Simon Van Eijcken *NewGrD 80*
Simon, Abbey 1922- *Baker 78, IntWWM 77, -80, WhoMus 72*
Simon, Abram Robert 1903- *IntMPA 77, -75, -76, -78, -79*
Simon, Alice 1879-1957 *NewGrD 80*
Simon, Alicia 1879-1957 *Baker 78*
Simon, Alicja 1879-1957 *NewGrD 80*
Simon, Anton 1850-1916 *Baker 78, NewGrD 80*
Simon, Bernard 1904- *BiE&WWA, NotNAT*
Simon, Carly 1945- *AmSCAP 80, BiDAmM, ConMuA 80A[port], IlEncR, RkOn 2[port]*
Simon, Charles d1910 *NotNAT B*
Simon, Delbert Richard 1935- *IntWWM 77, -80*
Simon, Edward G 1871-1934 *AmSCAP 66, -80*
Simon, Emil 1936- *IntWWM 77, -80*
Simon, Ernest Arthur 1862-1950 *BiDAmM*
Simon, Francois 1917- *FilmAG WE*
Simon, Frederick Victor 1914- *IntWWM 77*
Simon, George R 1910- *AmSCAP 66*
Simon, George Thomas 1912- *AmSCAP 80*
Simon, Hans Arno 1919- *WhoMus 72*
Simon, Harry 1926- *IntWWM 77*
Simon, Howard 1901-1961 *AmSCAP 66, -80*
Simon, J Elizabeth *WhoMus 72*
Simon, James 1880-1944 *Baker 78*
Simon, Joanna 1940- *WhoOp 76*
Simon, Joe 1941?- *DrBlPA*
Simon, Joe 1945- *RkOn 2[port]*
Simon, Johann Caspar 1701-1776 *NewGrD 80*
Simon, John 1925- *BiE&WWA, ConAmTC, NotNAT, WhoThe 72, -77*
Simon, John Spier 1941- *AmSCAP 80*
Simon, Joseph 1594-1671 *OxThe*
Simon, Lou *ConMuA 80B*
Simon, Louis M 1906- *NotNAT, WhoThe 72, -77*
Simon, Lucy *AmSCAP 80*
Simon, Maurice 1929- *EncJzS 70*
Simon, Melvin 1926- *IntMPA 80*
Simon, Michel 1895-1975 *BiDFilm, -81, FilmAG WE, FilmEn, Film 2, FilmgC, HalFC 80, MovMk, OxFilm, WhScrn 77, WhoHol C, WorEFlm*
Simon, Nat 1900-1979 *AmSCAP 66, -80, CmpEPM*
Simon, Neil 1927- *BiE&WWA, CnThe, ConDr 73, -77, CroCD, DcLB 7[port], EncMT, EncWT, Ent[port], FilmEn, FilmgC, HalFC 80, IntMPA 77, -75, -76, -78, -79, -80, McGEWD[port], ModWD, NewCBMT, NewYTET, NotNAT, PlP&P[port], -A[port], WhoThe 72, -77*
Simon, Norman J 1925- *AmSCAP 66, -80*
Simon, P *NewGrD 80*
Simon, Paul *ConMuA 80A*
Simon, Paul 1941- *IlEncR[port]*
Simon, Paul 1942- *BiDAmM, PopAmC SUP[port]*
Simon, Pazuza 1908?-1960 *WhoJazz 72*
Simon, Peggy *AmSCAP 80*
Simon, Pierre 1808-1882 *NewGrD 80*
Simon, Prosper-Charles 1788-1866 *NewGrD 80*
Simon, Richard Dages 1922- *ConAmTC*
Simon, Richard George 1921- *IntWWM 77*
Simon, Robert A 1897- *AmSCAP 66, -80*
Simon, Robert F *ForYSC, WhoHol A*
Simon, Roger Hendricks 1942- *NotNAT*
Simon, S Sylvan 1910-1951 *FilmEn, FilmgC, HalFC 80*
Simon, Seymour F 1915- *IntMPA 77, -75, -76, -78, -79*
Simon, Simon 1735?-1780? *NewGrD 80*
Simon, Simone *MotPP*
Simon, Simone 1910- *FilmgC, HalFC 80, HolP 30[port], ThFT[port], WhoHol A, WhoHrs 80*
Simon, Simone 1911- *BiDFilm, -81, FilmEn, OxFilm, WorEFlm*
Simon, Simone 1914- *FilmAG WE, ForYSC, IntMPA 77, -75, -76, MovMk[port], What 2[port]*
Simon, Sol S 1864-1940 *Film 2, WhScrn 74, -77, WhoHol B*
Simon, Stephen 1937- *BiDAmM, NewGrD 80*
Simon, Stephen Anthony 1937- *IntWWM 77, -80*
Simon, Victoria 1939- *DancEn 78*
Simon, Walter Cleveland 1884-1958 *AmSCAP 66, -80*
Simon, William Louis 1920- *AmSCAP 66, -80*
Simon, William N 1916- *AmSCAP 66, -80*
Simon And Garfunkel *ConMuA 80A[port], EncFCWM 69, RkOn 2[port]*
Simon-Girard, Aime *Film 2*
Simonds, Bruce 1895- *Baker 78, ConAmC, WhoMus 72*
Simone DiGolino DiPrudenzano *NewGrD 80*
Simone, Madame 1880- *WhThe*
Simone, Carl *AmSCAP 80*
Simone, Elaine *AmSCAP 80*
Simone, Joe *ConMuA 80B*
Simone, Kirsten 1934- *CnOxB, DancEn 78[port]*
Simone, Nina 1933- *AmSCAP 66, -80, BiDAmM, DrBlPA, EncJzS 70, IlEncR,*

RkOn[port]
Simone, Simone 1914- *IntMPA 78, -79, -80*
Simoneau, Leopold 1918- *Baker 78, CreCan 1, NewGrD 80*
Simoneau, Leopold 1919- *IntWWM 77, -80*
Simoneau, Leopold 1920- *CmOp*
Simoneau, Pierrette Alarie *CreCan 1*
Simonella, Liborio 1933- *WhoOp 76*
Simonelli, Charles F 1923- *IntMPA 77, -75, -76, -78, -79*
Simonelli, Matteo 1618?-1696 *NewGrD 80*
Simonetti, Achille 1857-1928 *Baker 78, NewGrD 80*
Simonetti, Leonardo d1630? *NewGrD 80*
Simonetti, Ted Eddy 1904- *AmSCAP 80*
Simonffy, Kalman 1831-1888 *NewGrD 80*
Simoni, Renato 1875-1952 *EncWT*
Simonian, Roy *PupTheA*
Simonini, Piercarlo 1927- *WhoOp 76*
Simonis, Jean-Marie 1931- *Baker 78, IntWWM 77, -80*
Simoniti, Rado Jacobus 1914- *IntWWM 77, -80*
Simonkova, Dagmar 1939- *IntWWM 77, -80*
Simonov, Konstantin Mikhailovich 1915- *CnMD, CroCD, EncWT, McGEWD, ModWD, OxThe, PlP&P[port]*
Simonov, Nikolai 1902-1973 *WhScrn 77*
Simonov, Reuben Nikolaievich 1899-1969 *EncWT*
Simonov, Reuben Nikolaivich 1899-1968 *OxThe*
Simonov, Yuri Ivanovich 1941- *IntWWM 77, -80, WhoOp 76*
Simonov, Yury Ivanovich 1941- *NewGrD 80*
Simons, Beverley 1938- *ConDr 77*
Simons, John 1911- *IntWWM 77, -80, WhoMus 72*
Simons, Julie *NewGrD 80*
Simons, Netty *ConAmC*
Simons, Netty 1913- *IntWWM 80*
Simons, Netty 1923- *CpmDNM 75, -76, -78*
Simons, Rudy 1928- *AmSCAP 80*
Simons, Seymour 1896-1949 *AmSCAP 66, -80, CmpEPM, NotNAT B*
Simons, Ted 1933- *AmSCAP 66*
Simons, Thomas 1943- *ConAmC*
Simonsen, Anker Fjeld 1944- *IntWWM 80*
Simonsen, Dag 1946- *WhoOp 76*
Simonsen, Rudolph 1889-1947 *NewGrD 80*
Simonsen Fjeld, Anker 1944- *IntWWM 77*
Simonson, Ernest Lowell 1953- *AmSCAP 80*
Simonson, Lee 1888-1967 *BiE&WWA, EncWT, NotNAT A, -B, OxThe, PlP&P[port], WhThe*
Simonx, S S *Film 2*
Simov, Victor Andreyevich 1858-1935 *OxThe, PlP&P*
Simper, Douglas Alan 1944- *IntWWM 77*
Simpkins, Andrew 1932- *EncJzS 70*
Simpkins, Andy 1932- *EncJzS 70*
Simpson, Adrienne Marie 1943- *IntWWM 80*
Simpson, Alan 1929- *FilmgC, HalFC 80*
Simpson, Allan *Film 2*
Simpson, Arthur *OxMus*
Simpson, Carl *PupTheA*
Simpson, Cassino Wendell 1909-1952 *WhoJazz 72*
Simpson, Charles Walter 1878-1942 *CreCan 2*
Simpson, Cheridah d1922 *NotNAT B*
Simpson, Christopher d1669 *OxMus*
Simpson, Christopher 1605?-1669 *NewGrD 80[port]*
Simpson, Christopher 1610?-1669 *Baker 78, BnBkM 80*
Simpson, Derek 1928- *WhoMus 72*
Simpson, Doctor *Film 2*
Simpson, Donald Alan 1929- *IntWWM 77*
Simpson, Dudley George 1922- *IntWWM 77, -80*
Simpson, Duke *NewOrJ*
Simpson, Edmund Shaw 1784-1848 *NotNAT B, OxThe*
Simpson, Edward Burton 1916- *WhoMus 72*
Simpson, Eugene Thamon 1932- *AmSCAP 80*
Simpson, Faith *PupTheA*
Simpson, Garry *IntMPA 77, -75, -76, -78, -79, -80*
Simpson, George Elliott 1876-1958 *Baker 78, ConAmC*
Simpson, Grant 1884-1932 *WhScrn 74, -77*
Simpson, Harold *WhThe*
Simpson, Ivan 1875-1951 *Film 1, -2, ForYSC, HalFC 80, HolCA[port], NotNAT B, WhScrn 74, -77, WhoHol B*
Simpson, J D 1928- *BiDAmM*
Simpson, J Palgrave d1887 *NotNAT B*
Simpson, Jim *NewYTET*
Simpson, John d1749? *NewGrD 80*
Simpson, John Lawrence 1933- *WhoMus 72*
Simpson, John Michael 1933- *IntWWM 77, -80, WhoMus 72*
Simpson, Margaret *WhoMus 72*
Simpson, Marian Carlyn 1915- *IntWWM 77*
Simpson, Martin Bland, III 1948- *AmSCAP 80*
Simpson, Mary Jean 1941- *IntWWM 77, -80*
Simpson, Mary K *WomWMM B*
Simpson, N F 1919- *BiE&WWA, CnMD SUP, ConDr 77, CroCD, McGEWD, ModWD, NotNAT, WhoThe 72, -77*
Simpson, Norman Frederick 1919- *CnThe, ConDr 73, EncWT*
Simpson, O J 1947- *DrBlPA, HalFC 80, WhoHol A*
Simpson, Peggy *WhThe*
Simpson, Red *CounME 74[port], -74A*
Simpson, Robert 1910- *IntMPA 77, -75, -76, -78, -79*
Simpson, Robert 1921- *Baker 78, IntWWM 77, -80, NewGrD 80, WhoMus 72*
Simpson, Robert 1924- *NatPD[port]*
Simpson, Ron 1935- *NewOrJ SUP[port]*
Simpson, Ronald 1896-1957 *NotNAT B, WhThe, WhoHol B*
Simpson, Ronald West 1940- *AmSCAP 80*
Simpson, Russell d1959 *MotPP, NotNAT B, WhoHol B*
Simpson, Russell 1878-1959 *FilmgC, HalFC 80, TwYS*
Simpson, Russell 1880-1959 *Film 1, -2, ForYSC, HolCA[port], MovMk[port], Vers A[port], WhScrn 74, -77*
Simpson, Sloan 1917- *What 4[port]*
Simpson, Thomas 1582-1630? *Baker 78, NewGrD 80, OxMus*
Simpson, Valerie R 1946- *AmSCAP 80*
Simpson, W Kenneth *IntWWM 77, -80, WhoMus 72*
Simpson, Winifred Nellie 1899- *WhoMus 72*
Simrock *NewGrD 80*
Simrock, Friedrich August 1837-1901 *NewGrD 80*
Simrock, Heinrich *NewGrD 80*
Simrock, Johann Baptist 1861-1910 *NewGrD 80*
Simrock, Nicolaus 1751-1832 *NewGrD 80*
Simrock, Nikolaus 1751-1832 *Baker 78*
Simrock, Peter Joseph 1792-1868 *NewGrD 80*
Sims, Ezra 1928- *Baker 78, CpmDNM 78, -79, -80, ConAmC, DcCM, IntWWM 77, -80, NewGrD 80*
Sims, Frankie Lee 1917-1970 *BluesWW[port]*
Sims, Gary Wayne 1949- *IntWWM 77*
Sims, George 1872?- *NewOrJ*
Sims, George Robert 1847-1922 *NotNAT B, WhThe, WhoStg 1908*
Sims, Ginny 1916- *What 3[port]*
Sims, Harry 1908- *AmSCAP 66, -80*
Sims, Jack 1925- *BiDAmM*
Sims, James Christopher 1949- *AmSCAP 80*
Sims, Joan 1930- *FilmgC, HalFC 80, IntMPA 77, -75, -76, -78, -79, -80, WhoHol A, WhoThe 72, -77*
Sims, John Haley 1925- *AmSCAP 80, EncJzS 70, IntWWM 77*
Sims, Jon Reed 1947- *IntWWM 77*
Sims, Lee 1898-1966 *AmSCAP 66, -80, CmpEPM*
Sims, Mac *BluesWW[port]*
Sims, Phillip Weir 1925- *IntWWM 77, -80*
Sims, Ray 1921- *CmpEPM*
Sims, Sylvia *WhoHol A*
Sims, Zoot 1925- *CmpEPM, EncJzS 70, IlEncJ*
Sims Twins, The *RkOn*
Simun, Francis George 1944- *AmSCAP 80*
Simutis, Leonard J 1920- *ConAmC*
Sin, Otakar 1881-1943 *Baker 78, NewGrD 80*
Sin-Nui, Hung 1920-1966 *WhScrn 77*
Sin-Nul, Hung 1920-1966 *WhScrn 74*
Sina, Sandy 1927- *IntMPA 77, -75, -76, -78, -79*
Sinasi, Ibrahim 1826-1871 *REnWD[port]*
Sinatra, Francis Albert 1915- *AmSCAP 80, BiDAmM, EncJzS 70, NewGrD 80, WhoMus 72*
Sinatra, Frank 1915- *AmPS A, -B, AmSCAP 66, Baker 78, BiDFilm, -81, CmMov, CmpEPM, FilmEn, FilmgC, ForYSC, HalFC 80[port], IntMPA 77, -75, -76, -78, -79, -80, MGM[port], MotPP, MovMk[port], MusMk[port], NewGrD 80, NewYTET, OxFilm, RkOn, WhoHol A, WorEFlm*
Sinatra, Frank, Jr. *WhoHol A*
Sinatra, Frank, Jr. 1943- *ForYSC*
Sinatra, Frank W 1944- *AmSCAP 80*
Sinatra, Nancy *AmPS A*
Sinatra, Nancy 1940- *FilmgC, ForYSC, HalFC 80, RkOn 2[port], WhoHol A*
Sinatra, Nancy 1941- *BiDAmM*
Sinatra, Ray 1904- *AmSCAP 66, -80, ConAmC A*
Sinceretti, Francis 1942- *CnOxB*
Sinchak, Michael 1919- *IntWWM 77*
Sinclair, Andrew 1935- *HalFC 80, IntMPA 77, -75, -76, -78, -79, -80*
Sinclair, Arthur 1883-1951 *NotNAT B, OxThe, WhScrn 74, -77, WhThe, WhoHol B*
Sinclair, Barry 1911- *WhoHol A, WhoThe 72, -77*
Sinclair, Betty *WhoHol A*
Sinclair, Daisy 1878-1929 *WhScrn 74, -77*
Sinclair, Eleanor *Film 2*
Sinclair, George Robertson 1863-1917 *Baker 78, NewGrD 80*
Sinclair, Gordon 1900- *RkOn 2[port]*
Sinclair, Horace 1884-1949 *WhScrn 74, -77, WhoHol B*
Sinclair, Hugh 1903-1962 *FilmgC, HalFC 80, IlWWBF, NotNAT B, WhScrn 74, -77, WhThe, WhoHol B*
Sinclair, Jeannette *IntWWM 77, -80, WhoMus 72*
Sinclair, Jerry *Film 2*
Sinclair, Jerry Wayne 1943- *AmSCAP 80*
Sinclair, John 1791-1857 *NewGrD 80*
Sinclair, Johnny *Film 2*
Sinclair, Lister Shedden 1921- *CreCan 1*
Sinclair, Madge 1940- *DrBlPA, WhoHol A*
Sinclair, Mary *IntMPA 77, -75, -76, -78, -79, -80*
Sinclair, Maud *Film 2*
Sinclair, Monica 1925- *IntWWM 77, -80, WhoMus 72*
Sinclair, Moray d1964 *NotNAT B*
Sinclair, Robert B 1905-1970 *BiE&WWA, FilmEn, FilmgC, HalFC 80, NotNAT B*
Sinclair, Ronald 1924- *ForYSC*
Sinclair, Ruth *Film 2*
Sinclair, Upton Beall 1878-1968 *OxFilm, WorEFlm*
Sinde Ramallal, Clara 1935- *IntWWM 77, -80*
Sindelar, Pearl *Film 1*
Sindell, Bernard I 1912- *IntMPA 77, -75, -76, -78, -79, -80*
Sinden, Donald 1923- *CnThe, Ent, FilmAG WE, FilmEn, FilmgC, HalFC 80, IlWWBF, IntMPA 77, -75, -76, -78, -79, -80, WhoHol A, WhoThe 72, -77*
Sinden, Topsy 1878- *WhThe*
Sindik, Anka 1943- *WhoOp 76*
Sindilaru, Maria 1927- *WhoOp 76*
Sinding, Christian 1856-1941 *Baker 78, CompSN[port], MusMk, NewGrD 80[port], OxMus*
Sinding, Ellen *Film 2*
Singelee, Jean-Baptiste 1812-1875 *Baker 78*
Singenberger, John Baptist 1848-1924 *BiDAmM*
Singer, A 1927- *IntMPA 77, -75, -76, -78, -79, -80*
Singer, Alexander 1932- *FilmEn, FilmgC, HalFC 80, WorEFlm*
Singer, Amy *AmSCAP 80*
Singer, Arthur 1919- *AmSCAP 66, -80*
Singer, Aubrey E *NewYTET*
Singer, Bob 1930- *AmSCAP 66*
Singer, Campbell 1909- *FilmgC, HalFC 80, WhoHol A, WhoThe 72, -77*
Singer, Deborah Anne 1953- *ConAmTC*
Singer, Dolph 1900-1942 *AmSCAP 66, -80*

Singer, Edmund 1830-1912 *Baker 78*
Singer, Emmy Heim *CreCan 2*
Singer, George 1908- *NewGrD 80*
Singer, Guy *AmSCAP 80*
Singer, Hal 1919- *EncJzS 70, WhoJazz 72*
Singer, Harold 1919- *EncJzS 70*
Singer, Izzy *WhoHol A*
Singer, Jack *Film 2*
Singer, Jeanne 1924- *AmSCAP 80, IntWWM 77, -80*
Singer, John *NotNAT B, PlP&P*
Singer, Judith *WomWMM*
Singer, Kurt 1885-1944 *Baker 78*
Singer, Louis C 1912- *AmSCAP 66, -80*
Singer, Malcolm John 1940- *IntWWM 77, -80*
Singer, Otto 1833-1894 *Baker 78, BiDAmM*
Singer, Otto, Jr. 1863-1931 *Baker 78*
Singer, Peter 1810-1882 *Baker 78, NewGrD 80*
Singer, Richard 1879-1940 *BiDAmM*
Singer, Robert Morris 1930- *AmSCAP 80*
Singer, Samuel Bart 1913- *IntMPA 77, -75, -76, -78, -79*
Singer, Samuel L 1911- *IntWWM 77*
Singer, Werner 1903- *AmSCAP 66*
Singerling, Jan Willem 1920- *IntWWM 77, -80*
Singh, Bhogwan 1883-1962 *WhScrn 77*
Singh, Gurdial 1944- *IntWWM 77*
Singh, Prabhu 1937- *IntWWM 77, -80, WhoMus 72*
Singh, Ram *Film 2*
Singh, Ranveer 1931- *IntMPA 77, -75, -76, -78, -79*
Singh, Sarain 1888-1952 *WhScrn 74, -77*
Singher, Martial 1904- *Baker 78, MusSN[port], NewEOp 71, NewGrD 80, WhoMus 72*
Singin' Sam *CmpEPM*
Singing Brakeman, The *EncFCWM 69*
Singing Christian, The *BluesWW[port]*
Singing Nun, The *RkOn*
Singing Rambos, The *BiDAmM*
Singletary, Robert Thomas 1935- *IntWWM 77, -80*
Singleton *PupTheA*
Singleton, Alvin *ConAmC A*
Singleton, Arthur James 1898-1975 *BiDAmM, EncJzS 70, NewGrD 80, NewOrJ*
Singleton, Catherine 1904-1969 *WhScrn 74, -77, WhoHol B*
Singleton, Doris *ForYSC, WhoHol A*
Singleton, Esther 1865-1930 *Baker 78*
Singleton, Geoffrey 1929- *WhoMus 72*
Singleton, George 1900- *IntMPA 77, -75, -76, -78, -79, -80*
Singleton, Joe E *Film 1, -2*
Singleton, Joseph *Film 1*
Singleton, Margaret Louise 1935- *BiDAmM*
Singleton, Penny *IntMPA 75, -76, -78, -79, -80, What 2[port]*
Singleton, Penny 1908- *FilmEn, FilmgC, HalFC 80, HolP 30[port], IntMPA 77, MotPP, MovMk, ThFT[port], WhoHol A*
Singleton, Penny 1912- *ForYSC*
Singleton, Shelby 1931- *EncFCWM 69, IlEncCM*
Singleton, Trinette 1945- *CnOxB*
Singleton, Zutty 1898-1975 *CmpEPM, EncJzS 70, IlEncJ, NewGrD 80, WhScrn 77, WhoHol C, WhoJazz 72*
Singoni, Giovanni Battista *NewGrD 80*
Siniavine, Alec 1916- *IntWWM 77, -80, WhoMus 72*
Sinico, Francesco 1810-1865 *Baker 78*
Sinigaglia, Leone 1868-1944 *Baker 78, MusMk, NewGrD 80, OxMus*
Sini'letta, Vic d1921 *WhScrn 74, -77*
Sinisalo, Helmer-Rayner 1920- *NewGrD 80*
Sink, Kuldar 1942- *DcCM, NewGrD 80*
Sinko, George 1923- *IntWWM 80*
Sinn, Robert S 1930- *IntMPA 77, -75, -76, -78, -79, -80*
Sinnicam, Don *AmSCAP 80*
Sinnone, Ileana *WhoOp 76*
Sinnott, Patricia *WhoHol A*
Sinoel 1868-1949 *WhScrn 74, -77, WhoHol B*
Sinopoli, Giuseppe 1946- *NewGrD 80*
Sinyavskaya, Tamara Ilinichna 1943- *WhoOp 76*
Sinzheimer, Max 1894- *ConAmC*
Siodmak, Curt 1902- *CmMov, FilmEn, FilmgC, HalFC 80, IntMPA 77, -75, -76, -78, -79, -80, WhoHrs 80*
Siodmak, Robert 1900-1973 *BiDFilm, -81, CmMov, DcFM, FilmEn, FilmgC, HalFC 80, MovMk[port], OxFilm, WhScrn 77, WhoHrs 80, WorEFlm*
Siohan, Robert-Lucien 1894- *Baker 78, NewGrD 80*
Sion, Georges S 1913- *ModWD*
Sipherd, Clara *PupTheA*
Sipila, Eero 1918-1972 *Baker 78, NewGrD 80*
Sipperley, Ralph 1890-1928 *NotNAT B, WhScrn 77*
Sipperly, Ralph 1890-1928 *Film 2, WhoHol B*
Siqueira, Jose DeLima 1907- *Baker 78, NewGrD 80*
Sir, Neil *ConAmC*
Sir Douglas Quintet, The *BiDAmM, RkOn 2[port]*
Sir Lancelot *DrBlPA*
Siras, John *AmSCAP 80*
Siravo, George 1916- *AmSCAP 80, CmpEPM*
Sircom, Arthur R 1899- *BiE&WWA, NotNAT*
Sire, Henry B d1917 *NotNAT B*
Siret, Nicholas 1663-1754 *NewGrD 80*
Siriscevic, Nada *WhoOp 76*
Sirk, Douglas 1900- *BiDFilm, -81, CmMov, DcFM, FilmEn, FilmgC, HalFC 80, IntMPA 77, -75, -76, -78, -79, -80, OxFilm, WorEFlm*
Sirmay, Albert d1967 *AmSCAP 66, -80, NewGrD 80*
Sirmen, Maddalena Laura 1735-1785? *NewGrD 80*
Sirokay, Zsuzsanna 1941- *IntWWM 77, -80, WhoMus 72*
Sirola, Bozidar 1889-1956 *Baker 78, NewGrD 80*
Sirola, Joseph *WhoHol A*
Siroli, Gregorio *NewGrD 80*
Sirone 1940- *EncJzS 70*
Sironen, Doretha May E *IntWWM 80*
Sironen, Dorothea May E *IntWWM 77*
Sironi, Irene 1873-1961? *CnOxB*
Sirote, Stanley *ConMuA 80B*
Sirucek, Jerry Edward 1922- *IntWWM 80*
Siscart, Solango *Film 2*
Sissle, Noble 1889-1975 *AmSCAP 66, -80, BgBands 74[port], BiDAmM, BlkAmP, BlksB&W[port], -C, BlksBF[port], CmpEPM, DrBlPA, EncMT, MorBAP, WhScrn 77, WhoJazz 72*
Sisson, Kenn 1898-1947 *AmSCAP 66, -80*
Sisson, Vera 1891-1954 *WhScrn 77, WhoHol B*
Sisson, Vera 1895-1954 *Film 1, -2, TwYS*
Sistermans, Anton 1865-1926 *Baker 78*
Sistinus, Theodoricus *NewGrD 80*
Sita-Bella, Therese *WomWMM*
Sitgreaves, Beverley 1867-1943 *WhThe*
Sitgreaves, Beverly 1867-1943 *NotNAT B, WhoStg 1906, -1908*
Sithole, Elkin Thamsanqa 1931- *IntWWM 77, -80*
Sitka, Emil *WhoHol A*
Sitsky, Larry 1934- *Baker 78, DcCM, IntWWM 77, -80, NewGrD 80*
Sitt, Hans 1850-1922 *Baker 78, NewGrD 80*
Sittard, Alfred 1878-1942 *Baker 78*
Sittard, Josef 1846-1903 *Baker 78*
Sittig, Robert Donald 1919- *AmSCAP 66, -80*
Sitting Bull 1831-1890 *HalFC 80*
Sittner, Hans 1903- *NewGrD 80*
Sitwell, Edith 1887-1964 *OxMus*
Sitwells, The *DancEn 78*
Siunetsi, Step'annos *NewGrD 80*
Sivec, Joze 1930- *IntWWM 80*
Sivelli, Giovanni Antonio *NewGrD 80*
Siverson, Glenn Keith 1939- *IntWWM 77*
Sivert, Paul *NewGrD 80*
Sivic, Pavel 1908- *NewGrD 80*
Sivieri, Enrique Cesar Manlio 1915- *WhoOp 76*
Sivo, Josef *IntWWM 77, -80, WhoMus 72*
Sivori, Camillo 1815-1894 *Baker 78, BnBkM 80, NewGrD 80[port]*
Sivori, Ernesto Camillo 1815-1894 *OxMus*
Sivuca 1930- *EncJzS 70*
Siwe, Thomas 1935- *ConAmC*
Siwek, Roman 1935- *AmSCAP 80*
Siwertz, Sigfrid 1882- *ModWD*
Siwinski, Andrzej *NewGrD 80*
Six, Les *BnBkM 80, DancEn 78, NewGrD 80*
Six, Herbert L *ConAmC*
Six, Jack 1930- *EncJzS 70*
Six Teens, The *RkOn*
Sixt, Giovanni August 1757-1797 *NewGrD 80*
Sixt, Johann Abraham 1757-1797 *Baker 78, NewGrD 80*
Sixt VonLerchenfels, Johann 155-?-1629 *NewGrD 80*
Sixt Z Lerchenfelsu, Jan 155-?-1629 *NewGrD 80*
Sixta, Jozef 1940- *Baker 78, IntWWM 77, -80*
Sizemore, Arthur 1891-1954 *AmSCAP 66, 80*
Sizemore, Asher 1906- *BiDAmM, IlEncCM[port]*
Sizemore, Gordon 1909- *BiDAmM*
Sizemore, Little Jimmy 1928- *IlEncCM[port]*
Sizova, Alla Ivanova 1939- *DancEn 78*
Sizova, Alla Ivanovna 1939- *CnOxB*
Sjoberg, Alf 1903-1980 *BiDFilm, -81, DcFM, EncWT, FilmEn, FilmgC, HalFC 80, OxFilm*
Sjoberg, Svante Leonard 1873-1935 *Baker 78*
Sjogren, Albert Johannes Richard 1934- *IntWWM 80*
Sjogren, Emil 1853-1918 *Baker 78, NewGrD 80, OxMus*
Sjoman, Vilgot 1924- *FilmEn, FilmgC, HalFC 80, MovMk[port], OxFilm, WorEFlm*
Sjostedt, Sten Johan Kristian 1945- *IntWWM 80*
Sjosten, Lars 1941- *EncJzS 70*
Sjostrom, Nils Gunnar 1928- *IntWWM 77, -80*
Sjostrom, Victor 1879-1960 *BiDFilm, -81, DcFM, FilmEn, Film 1, FilmgC, HalFC 80, MovMk[port], OxFilm, WhoHol B, WorEFlm*
Sjostron, Victor 1879-1960 *Film 2*
Skabrada, Jaroslav 1919- *IntWWM 77, -80*
Skadden, Vanda Sue Sydenham 1942- *IntWWM 77*
Skaff, George *WhoHol A*
Skagestad, Tormod 1920- *EncWT*
Skaggs, Hazel Ghazarian 1924- *AmSCAP 66, -80, IntWWM 77, -80*
Skala, Lilia *ForYSC, HalFC 80, WhoHol A, WhoThe 77*
Skalic, Pavao 1534-1575 *NewGrD 80*
Skalicki, Amrei 1935- *WhoOp 76*
Skalicki, Wolfram 1925- *WhoOp 76*
Skalicky, Jan *WhoOp 76*
Skalicky, Mary Elizabeth Moore 1931- *IntWWM 77*
Skalkottas, Nicos 1904-1949 *NewGrD 80[port]*
Skalkottas, Nikolaos 1904-1949 *NewGrD 80[port]*
Skalkottas, Nikos 1904-1949 *Baker 78, BnBkM 80, DcCM, MusMk, NewGrD 80[port], OxMus*
Skall, William V 1898-1976 *HalFC 80*
Skalova, Olga 1928- *CnOxB*
Skalovski, Todor 1909- *NewGrD 80*
Skarda, Elsa *PupTheA*
Skeaping, Adam 1940- *WhoMus 72*
Skeaping, Mary 1902- *CnOxB, DancEn 78[port]*
Skeath, Harold R 1899-1942 *AmSCAP 66, -80*
Skeffington, Sir Lumley d1850 *NotNAT B*
Skei, Allen Bennet 1935- *IntWWM 77, -80*
Skellern, Peter 1947- *IlEncR*
Skellorn, Marjorie Alice Janette *WhoMus 72*
Skelly, Hal 1891-1934 *AmPS B, CmpEPM, Film 2, ForYSC, HalFC 80, WhScrn 74, -77, WhThe, WhoHol B*
Skelly, James 1936-1969 *WhScrn 74, -77, WhoHol B*
Skelly, Joseph P 1850?- *BiDAmM*
Skelly, Madge 1904- *BiE&WWA, NotNAT*
Skelton, Geoffrey 1916- *WhoMus 72*
Skelton, John 1460?-1529 *McGEWD, OxThe*
Skelton, Marlys *WomWMM B*
Skelton, Red *GrMovC[port], IntMPA 77, -75, -76, -78, -79, -80, MotPP, NewYTET*
Skelton, Red 1910- *CmMov, FilmgC,*

HalFC 80
Skelton, Red 1913- *FilmEn, Funs[port], JoeFr[port], MGM[port], MovMk[port], WhoHol A*
Skelton, Red 1914- *ForYSC*
Skelton, Richard 1913- *AmSCAP 66, -80*
Skelton, Thomas *WhoThe 77*
Skepton, Howard 1947- *DcCM*
Skeris, Robert A 1935- *IntWWM 80*
Skerjanc, Lucian Maria 1900- *WhoMus 72*
Skerjanc, Lucijan Marija 1900-1973 *Baker 78, NewGrD 80*
Skerl, Dane 1931- *Baker 78, NewGrD 80*
Skerritt, Tom *WhoHol A*
Sketchley, Leslie *Film 2*
Skewis, Margaret *PupTheA*
Skiba, John Christopher 1949- *IntWWM 77, -80*
Skibine, George Borisovich 1920- *CnOxB, DancEn 78[port]*
Skidmore, Alan Richard James 1942- *EncJzS 70, IntWWM 77*
Skidmore, Will E 1880-1959 *AmSCAP 66, -80*
Skidmore, William R 1941- *IntWWM 77, -80*
Skiles, Marlin 1906- *AmSCAP 66, -80, HalFC 80, IntMPA 77, -75, -76, -78, -79, -80, IntWWM 77*
Skillan, George 1893- *WhThe*
Skillet Lickers *BiDAmM, EncFCWM 69, IlEncCM*
Skilton, Charles Sanford 1868-1941 *AmSCAP 66, -80, Baker 78, BiDAmM, CompSN[port], NewGrD 80, OxMus*
Skinner, Al 1906- *AmSCAP 66*
Skinner, Bill *IntWWM 80*
Skinner, Cornelia Otis 1901-1979 *BiE&WWA, EncWT, FilmgC, ForYSC, HalFC 80, NotNAT, -A, WhoHol A, WhoThe 72, -77*
Skinner, Cornelia Otis 1902-1979 *OxThe*
Skinner, Dorothy *PupTheA*
Skinner, Edith Warman 1904- *BiE&WWA, NotNAT*
Skinner, Edward 1891-1971 *BiDAmM*
Skinner, Eileen Sweezey 1946- *IntWWM 77*
Skinner, Ernest M 1866-1960 *Baker 78*
Skinner, Ernest M 1886-1961 *NewGrD 80*
Skinner, Frank 1897-1968 *AmSCAP 66, -80, CmpEPM, NotNAT B*
Skinner, Frank 1898-1968 *HalFC 80*
Skinner, Gladys d1968 *WhoHol B*
Skinner, Harold Otis d1922 *NotNAT B*
Skinner, James R 1923- *AmSCAP 80*
Skinner, James Scott 1843-1927 *NewGrD 80*
Skinner, Jimmie *EncFCWM 69, IlEncCM*
Skinner, John York 1949- *IntWWM 80*
Skinner, Lynn J 1940- *IntWWM 77*
Skinner, Marion *Film 2*
Skinner, Otis d1942 *WhoHol B*
Skinner, Otis 1857-1942 *WhScrn 74, -77*
Skinner, Otis 1858-1942 *EncWT, FamA&A[port], Film 1, -2, FilmgC, HalFC 80, NotNAT A, -B, OxThe, PlP&P[port], TwYS, WhThe*
Skinner, Otis 1865- *WhoStg 1906, -1908*
Skinner, Richard 1900-1971 *BiE&WWA, NotNAT B*
Skinner, Ted 1911- *BiE&WWA, NotNAT*
Skinner, Wilbur Albert 1906- *AmSCAP 80*
Skip And Flip *RkOn*
Skipper, Joan 1924- *IntWWM 77*
Skipworth, Alison d1952 *WhoHol B*
Skipworth, Alison 1863-1948 *HolCA[port]*
Skipworth, Alison 1863-1952 *FilmEn, Funs[port], NotNAT B, ThFT[port], WhThe*
Skipworth, Alison 1865?-1952 *WhScrn 74, -77*
Skipworth, Alison 1870-1952 *MovMk[port], Vers B[port]*
Skipworth, Alison 1871-1952 *WhoStg 1908*
Skipworth, Alison 1875-1952 *Film 2, FilmgC, ForYSC, HalFC 80[port]*
Skipworth, Allison *MotPP*
Skirball, Jack H 1896- *FilmEn, FilmgC, HalFC 80, IntMPA 77, -75, -76, -78, -79, -80*
Skirball, William N *IntMPA 77, -75, -76, -78, -79, -80*
Skirpan, Stephen J 1930- *BiE&WWA, NotNAT*
Skjaer, Henry 1899- *IntWWM 80*
Skjavetic, Julije *NewGrD 80*
Skjeveland, Helge 1950- *ConAmC*
Skladanovsky, Max 1863-1939 *WorEFlm*
Skladanowsky, Max 1863-1939 *DcFM, FilmEn*
Sklar, George 1908- *BiE&WWA, McGEWD, ModWD, NotNAT, PlP&P*
Sklar, Michael *IntMPA 77, -75, -76, -78, -79, -80*
Sklavos, George 1888-1976 *NewGrD 80*
Sklavos, Georges 1888- *Baker 78*
Sklerov, Gloria J *AmSCAP 80*
Skold, Bengt-Goran 1936- *IntWWM 77, -80*
Skold, Berit 1939- *CnOxB, DancEn 78*
Skold, Yngve 1899- *Baker 78, NewGrD 80*
Skolimowski, Jerzy 1938- *BiDFilm, 81, DcFM, FilmEn, FilmgC, HalFC 80, OxFilm, WorEFlm*
Skolnik, Walter 1934- *CpmDNM 78, -79, -80, ConAmC*
Skolovsky, Zadel 1926- *IntWWM 77, -80*
Skolsky, Sidney 1905- *IntMPA 77, -75, -76, -78, -79, -80*
Skomal, Margaret Elaine 1958- *IntWWM 77, -80*
Skomrlj, Ike Franciska 1936- *WhoOp 76*
Skorik, Irene 1928- *CnOxB, DancEn 78*
Skorik, Irene Angele Nina 1930- *WhoMus 72*
Skornicka, Joseph E 1902-1972 *AmSCAP 66, -80, ConAmC A*
Skoronel, Vera 1906-1932 *CnOxB*
Skorr, Michael 1912- *AmSCAP 80*
Skorzeny, Fritz 1900- *IntWWM 77, -80, WhoMus 72*
Skouen, Arne 1913- *WorEFlm*
Skouras, George P d1964 *NotNAT B*
Skouras, Spyros P 1893-1971 *DcFM, FilmEn, FilmgC, HalFC 80, OxFilm, WorEFlm*
Skouras, Spyros S 1923- *IntMPA 75*
Skouratoff, Vladimir 1925- *CnOxB, DancEn 78*
Skowroneck, Martin 1926- *NewGrD 80*
Skram, Knut 1937- *IntWWM 77, -80, WhoOp 76*
Skramstad, Hans 1797-1839 *NewGrD 80*
Skraup, Jan Nepomuk *NewGrD 80*
Skrebkov, Sergey Sergeyevich 1905-1967 *NewGrD 80*
Skrepek, Roman 1931- *IntWWM 77, -80*
Skriabin, Alexander 1872-1915 *Baker 78, DcCom&M 79, NewGrD 80*
Skriptschenko, Clara 1923- *IntWWM 77, -80*
Skrjabin, Alexander Nikolayevich *NewGrD 80*
Skrobela, Katherine Creelman 1941- *IntWWM 77, -80*
Skroblin, Gislinde 1944- *CnOxB*
Skroski, Linda Ann 1951- *IntWWM 77*
Skroup, Frantisek Jan 1801-1862 *MusMk, NewGrD 80*
Skroup, Franz 1801-1862 *Baker 78*
Skroup, Jan Nepomuk 1811-1892 *Baker 78, NewGrD 80*
Skrowaczewski, Stanislaw 1923- *AmSCAP 80, Baker 78, BnBkM 80, IntWWM 77, -80, MusSN[port], NewGrD 80, WhoMus 72, WhoOp 76*
Skryabin, Alexander 1872-1915 *NewGrD 80[port]*
Skuhersky, Frantisek Zdenek 1830-1892 *Baker 78, NewGrD 80*
Skuhrova, Irma 1925- *IntWWM 77, -80*
Skulnik, Menasha 1892-1970 *NotNAT B, WhScrn 77*
Skulnik, Menasha 1894-1970 *WhThe*
Skulnik, Menasha 1898-1970 *BiE&WWA*
Skulte, Adolfs 1909- *NewGrD 80*
Skupa, Josef 1892-1957 *DcPup*
Skurkoy, Mary *Film 2*
Skuszanka, Krystyna 1924- *EncWT*
Skwara, Zdziskaw Feliks 1920- *IntWWM 80*
Skwara, Zdziskaw Felix 1920- *IntWWM 77*
Skwierawski, Edward R *IntWWM 77, -80*
Sky, Jack *AmSCAP 80*
Sky, Pat 1940- *EncFCWM 69*
Sky, Patrick 1940- *BiDAmM*
Skydell, Barbara *ConMuA 80B*
Skye, Diane S 1945- *AmSCAP 80*
Skylar, Joanne Alex *WhoHol A*
Skylar, Sunny 1913- *AmSCAP 66, -80*
Skylark *RkOn 2[port]*
Skyliners, The *RkOn[port]*
Skyllstad, Kjell Muller 1928- *IntWWM 77, -80*
Skyttegaard, Jorgen 1940- *IntWWM 80*
Slack, Freddie 1910-1965 *AmSCAP 66, CmpEPM, WhScrn 74, -77, WhoHol B*
Slack, Freddy *BgBands 74*
Slack, Frederic Charles 1910-1965 *AmSCAP 80*
Slack, Lyle 1946- *ConAmTC*
Slack, Roy 1912- *IntWWM 77, -80, WhoMus 72*
Slade *ConMuA 80A, IlEncR*
Slade, Bernard *NewYTET*
Slade, Heather Anne 1947- *IntWWM 77, -80*
Slade, Julian 1930- *BestMus, EncMT, NewGrD 80, WhoMus 72, WhoThe 72, -77*
Slade, Mark *WhoHol A*
Slade, Mary Bridges 1826-1882 *BiDAmM*
Slade, Olga d1949 *NotNAT B, WhoHol B*
Slade, Scott *ConMuA 80B*
Sladek, Paul 1896- *AmSCAP 66, -80, ConAmC*
Sladen, Victoria 1910- *CmOp, WhoMus 72*
Slades, The *RkOn*
Slane, Eva Weith 1929- *BiE&WWA*
Slaney, Amy *WhoMus 72*
Slapp Happy *IlEncR*
Slate, Henry *WhoHol A*
Slate, Jeremy 1925- *FilmgC, ForYSC, HalFC 80, WhoHol A*
Slater, Barney 1923- *IntMPA 77, -75, -76, -78, -79*
Slater, Bill 1903- *IntMPA 77, -75, -76, -78, -79, -80*
Slater, Bob *Film 2*
Slater, Daphne 1928- *IntMPA 77, -75, -76, -78, -79, -80, WhThe*
Slater, Frank *Film 2*
Slater, George M d1949 *NotNAT B*
Slater, Gerald *NewYTET*
Slater, Gordon Archbold 1896- *IntWWM 77, WhoMus 72*
Slater, Hartley d1964 *NotNAT B*
Slater, John 1916-1975 *FilmgC, HalFC 80, IntMPA 75, -76, WhScrn 77, WhThe, WhoHol C, WhoThe 72*
Slater, Lucille 1916- *IntWWM 77*
Slater, M 1826-1899 *NewGrD 80*
Slater, Neil *ConAmC*
Slater, Richard Wesley 1931- *AmSCAP 80*
Slater, Robert 1869-1930 *BlksBF*
Slater Brothers, The *Film 2*
Slates, Philip M 1924-1966 *ConAmC*
Slatford, Rodney Gerald Yorke 1944- *IntWWM 77, -80, WhoMus 72*
Slatin, Sonia 1910- *IntWWM 77*
Slatin, Steve *ConMuA 80B*
Slatin-Lewis, Sonia 1910- *IntWWM 80*
Slatinaru, Maria 1938- *WhoOp 76*
Slatkin, Felix 1915-1963 *NewGrD 80, NotNAT B*
Slatkin, Leonard 1944- *AmSCAP 80, Baker 78, IntWWM 77, -80*
Slatkonia, Georg 1456-1522 *NewGrD 80*
Slattegard, Gunilla Lovisa 1938- *WhoOp 76*
Slattegard, Tord 1933- *WhoOp 76*
Slatter, Charles *Film 2*
Slatter, Mary Arton *WhoMus 72*
Slattery, Charles *Film 2*
Slattery, Daniel G d1964 *NotNAT B*
Slattery, Joe *ConMuA 80B*
Slattery, Richard X *WhoHol A*
Slattery, Thomas Carl 1935- *IntWWM 77, -80*
Slatyer, William 1587-1647 *NewGrD 80*
Slatzer, Robert Franklin 1927- *IntMPA 77, -75, -76, -78, -79*
Slaughter, A Walter 1860-1908 *Baker 78*
Slaughter, Bessie 1879- *WhThe*
Slaughter, Henry T 1927- *BiDAmM*
Slaughter, Marion Try *NewGrD 80*
Slaughter, Minnie B T 1956- *IntWWM 77*
Slaughter, N Carter 1885-1956 *NotNAT B, WhThe*
Slaughter, Tod 1885-1956 *FilmAG WE, FilmgC, ForYSC, HalFC 80, WhScrn 74, -77, WhoHol B, WhoHrs 80*
Slaughter, Tod 1885-1962 *IlWWBF[port]*
Slaughter, Walter d1908 *NotNAT B*
Slavenska, Mia 1914- *CnOxB*
Slavenska, Mia 1916- *DancEn 78[port]*

Slavenski, Josip 1896-1955 *Baker 78, NewGrD 80*
Slavicky, Klement 1910- *Baker 78, DcCM, IntWWM 77, -80, NewGrD 80*
Slavik, Josef 1806-1833 *Baker 78, NewGrD 80*
Slavin, Bob *ConMuA 80B*
Slavin, George 1916- *IntMPA 77, -75, -76, -78, -79, -80*
Slavin, John C d1940 *NotNAT B*
Slavinsky, Tadeo 1901-1945 *CnOxB*
Slawinski, Adam 1935- *IntWWM 77, -80*
Slawson, Wayne 1932- *ConAmC*
Slay, Frank Conley, Jr. 1930- *AmSCAP 66, -80, IntWWM 77*
Slayden, Anne 1945- *IntWWM 77, -80*
Sleath, Herbert 1870-1921 *NotNAT B, WhThe, WhoStg 1906, -1908*
Slechta, Milan 1923- *IntWWM 77, -80, NewGrD 80*
Sledd, Patsy 1944- *IlEncCM*
Sledge, Percy 1941- *RkOn 2[port]*
Sledzinski, Stefan 1897- *IntWWM 77, -80*
Slee, Raymond 1923- *IntWWM 77, -80, WhoMus 72*
Sleek, Earl Forest 1946- *AmSCAP 80*
Sleeman, Philip *Film 2*
Sleep, Wayne 1948- *CnOxB*
Sleeper, Henry Dike 1865-1948 *Baker 78*
Sleeper, Martha 1901- *Film 2, TwYS*
Sleeper, Martha 1907- *FilmEn*
Sleeper, Martha 1910- *BiE&WWA, ForYSC, NotNAT, WhoHol A*
Sleeper, Martha 1911- *WhThe*
Sleeth, Natalie Wakeley 1930- *AmSCAP 80, ConAmC*
Slegel *NewGrD 80*
Slegel, Cornelis d1593 *NewGrD 80*
Slegel, Jan d1604? *NewGrD 80*
Slegel, Jan d1684? *NewGrD 80*
Slegel, Jorrien d1568? *NewGrD 80*
Slegel, Jorrien d1615? *NewGrD 80*
Slegel, Michiel d1585? *NewGrD 80*
Slenczynska, Ruth 1925- *Baker 78, IntWWM 77, -80, WhoMus 72*
Slenczynski, Ruth 1925- *BiDAmM*
Slendzinska, Julitta 1927- *IntWWM 77, -80*
Slesin, Aviva *WomWMM, -A, -B*
Sletten, M Rix *AmSCAP 80*
Slevogt, Max 1868-1932 *EncWT*
Slezak, Leo 1873-1946 *Baker 78, BnBkM 80, CmOp, MusSN[port], NewEOp 71, NewGrD 80[port]*
Slezak, Leo 1875-1946 *WhScrn 74, -77, WhoHol B*
Slezak, Margarete 1901-1953 *WhScrn 74, -77, WhoHol B*
Slezak, Walter 1902- *BiDAmM, BiE&WWA, CmMov, EncMT, FilmEn, Film 2, FilmgC, ForYSC, HalFC 80, IntMPA 77, -75, -76, -78, -79, -80, MotPP, MovMk, NotNAT, -A, Vers A[port], WhoHol A, WhoThe 72, -77*
Slezinger, Herbert Edwin 1918- *AmSCAP 80*
Slice, Karilyn Slye 1936- *IntWWM 77*
Slick, Grace 1940- *BiDAmM*
Slick, Grace 1943- *ConMuA 80A[port]*
Slifka, Lewis *AmSCAP 80*
Slim, H Colin 1929- *NewGrD 80*
Slim Harpo *BluesWW[port]*
Slim Pickens *BluesWW[port]*
Slingsby, Simon *CnOxB*
Slippery, Ralph *Film 2*
Slivka, Meyer 1923- *IntWWM 77, -80*
Sloan, Alfred Baldwin 1872-1925 *NotNAT B*
Sloan, Blanding *PupTheA, PupTheA SUP*
Sloan, David W 1937- *IntWWM 77, -80*
Sloan, Isobel *PupTheA*
Sloan, John R *IntMPA 77, -75, -76, -78, -79, -80*
Sloan, Ken *AmSCAP 80*
Sloan, Ted *Film 2*
Sloane, A Baldwin 1872-1925 *AmSCAP 66, -80, CmpEPM, EncMT*
Sloane, A Baldwin 1872-1926 *AmPS, BiDAmM, NewCBMT, PopAmC*
Sloane, Alfred Baldwin 1872- *WhoStg 1906, -1908*
Sloane, Alfred Baldwin 1872-1925 *WhThe*
Sloane, Barton *WhoHrs 80*
Sloane, Everett d1965 *MotPP, WhoHol B*
Sloane, Everett 1909-1965 *BiDFilm, -81, FilmEn, FilmgC, HalFC 80, HolCA[port], MovMk, NotNAT B, WhScrn 74, -77*
Sloane, Everett 1910-1965 *ForYSC, Vers A[port]*
Sloane, Olive 1896-1963 *FilmgC, HalFC 80, IlWWBF, WhScrn 74, -77, WhThe, WhoHol B*
Sloane, Patricia Hermine 1934- *WomWMM B*
Sloane, Paul 1893- *FilmEn, TwYS A*
Slobodianik, Alexander 1941- *Baker 78*
Slobodskaya, Oda 1888-1970 *Baker 78, NewGrD 80[port]*
Slobodskaya, Oda 1895-1970 *CmOp*
Slocombe, Douglas 1913- *DcFM, FilmEn, FilmgC, HalFC 80, IntMPA 80, WorEFlm*
Slocum, Earl A 1902- *AmSCAP 66, -80*
Slocum, Tex 1902-1963 *WhScrn 74, -77*
Slocum, William Bennett 1936- *ConAmC*
Slogrove, William 1948- *IntWWM 77*
Slokar, Branimir 1946- *IntWWM 80*
Sloman, Charles 1808-1870 *OxThe*
Sloman, Edward 1885-1972 *Film 1, TwYS A, WhScrn 77*
Sloman, Edward 1887- *FilmEn*
Sloman, Jan Mark 1949- *IntWWM 77, -80*
Slomen, Hilda *Film 1*
Slonimsky, Nicolas 1894- *AmSCAP 66, -80, Baker 78, BiDAmM, ConAmC, DcCM, NewGrD 80, OxMus, WhoMus 72*
Slonimsky, Sergei 1932- *Baker 78, DcCM*
Slonimsky, Sergey Mikhaylovich 1932- *NewGrD 80*
Slonimsky, Yuri 1902-1978 *Baker 78, CnOxB, DancEn 78*
Slonov, Mikhail 1869-1930 *Baker 78*
Sloop, Jean C 1931- *IntWWM 77*
Sloper, Lindsay 1826-1887 *Baker 78*
Slote, Gilbert Monroe 1929- *AmSCAP 66, -80*
Sloughton, Mabel *Film 1*
Slous, A R d1883 *NotNAT B*
Slovak, Ladislav 1919- *NewGrD 80*
Slowacki, Juliusz 1809-1849 *CnThe, EncWT, McGEWD[port], OxThe, REnWD[port]*
Slowakiewicz-Wolanska, Alicja Maria 1942- *IntWWM 77, -80*
Slowinski, Wladyslaw 1930- *IntWWM 77, -80*
Slowitzky, Michael *AmSCAP 80*
Sluchin, Benjamin 1948- *IntWWM 77*
Sluchin, Benny 1948- *IntWWM 80*
Sluefoot Joe *BluesWW[port]*
Sluszny, Naum 1914- *WhoMus 72*
Sly, William d1608 *NotNAT B, OxThe*
Sly And The Family Stone *BiDAmM, ConMuA 80A, IlEncR, RkOn 2[port]*
Slydini, Tony *MagIlD*
Slye, Leonard 1911- *AmSCAP 80*
Smailovc, Avdo 1917- *IntWWM 80*
Smailovic, Avdo 1917- *IntWWM 77*
Smakwitz, Charles A *IntMPA 77, -75, -76, -78, -79, -80*
Smalacombe, John *CreCan 2*
Smale, George Albert 1905- *IntWWM 77*
Smale, Robert Claire 1931- *AmSCAP 66, -80*
Smales, Kathleen Ann 1943- *IntWWM 77, -80*
Small, Allan *AmSCAP 80*
Small, Dick d1972 *WhoHol B*
Small, Edna 1898-1917 *WhScrn 77*
Small, Edward 1891-1977 *FilmEn, FilmgC, HalFC 80, IntMPA 77, -75, -76*
Small, Freddie 1898?- *NewOrJ*
Small, Jack d1962 *NotNAT B*
Small, Lillian Schary d1961 *NotNAT B*
Small, Michael 1939- *BiE&WWA*
Small, Millie 1946- *RkOn 2[port]*
Small, Milton Noel 1895- *AmSCAP 66*
Small, Paul *CmpEPM*
Small, Paul d1954 *NotNAT B*
Small, Richard B *WhoHol A*
Small, Rosemary 1943- *IntWWM 77, -80*
Small, William J *NewYTET*
Small, Winifred 1896- *WhoMus 72*
Small Faces, The *IlEncR, RkOn 2[port]*
Smallbone, Graham 1934- *IntWWM 77, -80, WhoMus 72*
Smallens, Alexander 1889-1972 *Baker 78, BiDAmM, DancEn 78, MusSN[port], NewEOp 71, NewGrD 80*
Smalley, Cardo Brooks 1910- *IntWWM 77, -80*
Smalley, Denis Arthur 1946- *IntWWM 80*
Smalley, Phillips d1939 *WhoHol B, WomWMM*
Smalley, Phillips 1870-1939 *Film 1, -2, TwYS*
Smalley, Phillips 1875-1939 *FilmEn, ForYSC, WhScrn 74, -77*
Smalley, Roger 1943- *Baker 78, NewGrD 80, WhoMus 72*
Smalley, Webster 1921- *NotNAT*
Smallman, Frederic Basil Rowley 1921- *IntWWM 77, -80, WhoMus 72*
Smalls, C *MorBAP*
Smalls, Cliff 1918- *EncJzS 70*
Smalls, Clifton Arnold 1918- *EncJzS 70*
Smallwood, Ray C 1888- *TwYS A*
Smallwood, Williams 1831-1897 *Baker 78*
Smareglia, Antonio 1854-1929 *Baker 78, NewGrD 80, OxMus*
Smart *NewGrD 80*
Smart, Bobby *BlksB&W C*
Smart, Charles Drewett 1897- *WhoMus 72*
Smart, Christopher d1771 *NotNAT B*
Smart, Clive Frederick *IntWWM 80*
Smart, Gary L 1943- *ConAmC*
Smart, George d1805? *NewGrD 80*
Smart, Sir George Thomas 1776-1867 *Baker 78, NewGrD 80[port], OxMus*
Smart, Harold Charles Norbert 1921- *WhoMus 72*
Smart, Henry 1778-1823 *NewGrD 80*
Smart, Henry Thomas 1813-1879 *Baker 78, NewGrD 80, OxMus*
Smart, J Scott 1903-1960 *WhScrn 74, -77, WhoHol B*
Smart, Ralph 1908- *FilmgC, HalFC 80, IlWWBF, IntMPA 77, -75, -76, -78, -79, -80*
Smart, Roy L *IntMPA 77, -75, -76, -78, -79, -80*
Smart, Shirley Anne Grear 1923- *IntWWM 77*
Smathers, Ben 1928- *BiDAmM*
Smeck, Roy 1900- *AmSCAP 66, -80, CmpEPM*
Smedeby, Sune 1934- *IntWWM 77, -80*
Smedley, Morgan T d1964 *NotNAT B*
Smedley, Peter Francis 1932- *IntWWM 77, -80, WhoMus 72*
Smedley-Aston, E M 1912- *FilmgC, HalFC 80*
Smeets, Leon Joseph Hubert 1899- *IntWWM 77, -80*
Smegergill, William *NewGrD 80*
Smekal, Mojmir 1920- *IntWWM 77*
Smelker, Mary 1909-1933 *WhScrn 74, -77*
Smelser, Daniel Richard 1944- *IntWWM 77*
Smeltzer, Mary Susan 1941- *CpmDNM 80*
Smend, Friedrich 1893-1980 *NewGrD 80*
Smendzianka, Regina 1924- *IntWWM 77, -80, NewGrD 80*
Smert, Richard *NewGrD 80*
Smetacek, Pavel 1940- *IntWWM 77, -80*
Smetacek, Vaclav 1906- *Baker 78, IntWWM 77, -80, NewGrD 80*
Smetana, Bedrich 1824-1884 *Baker 78, BnBkM 80, CmOp, CmpBCM, DcCom 77[port], DcCom&M 79, DcPup, GrComp[port], MusMk, NewEOp 71, NewGrD 80[port], OxMus*
Smetana, Frantisek 1914- *IntWWM 77, -80*
Smetana, Friedrich 1824-1884 *NewGrD 80[port]*
Smetana, Robert 1904- *NewGrD 80*
Smeterlin, Jan 1892-1967 *Baker 78*
Smethergell, William *NewGrD 80*
Smiah, C C *Film 2*
Smid, Miroslav 1932- *IntWWM 77, -80*
Smidd, Gorm *Film 2*
Smight, Jack 1926- *FilmEn, FilmgC, HalFC 80, IntMPA 77, -75, -76, -78, -79, -80, WhoHrs 80, WorEFlm*
Smijers, Albert Anton 1888-1957 *Baker 78, NewGrD 80*
Smiles, Finch *Film 2*
Smiley, Arthur Lee, Jr. 1925-1972 *BiDAmM*
Smiley, Helen A *PupTheA*
Smiley, Joseph W 1881-1945 *Film 1, -2, WhScrn 74, -77, WhoHol B*
Smiley, Pril 1943- *ConAmC, IntWWM 77, -80*
Smiley, Ralph *WhoHol A*
Smilin' Joe *NewOrJ[port]*

Smiling Joe *BluesWW[port]*
Smiljanic, Radmila 1940- *WhoOp 76*
Smiljanich, Dorothy Weik 1947- *ConAmTC*
Smillie, Thomson John 1942- *WhoOp 76*
Smirczeck, Josef Blazej *NewGrD 80*
Smirnov, Dmitry 1882-1944 *NewGrD 80*
Smirnova, Dina *Film 2*
Smirnova, Yelena Alexandrovna 1888-1934 *CnOxB*
Smirnova, Yelena Alexandrovna 1888-1935 *DancEn 78*
Smis, A K *NewGrD 80*
Smit, Andre-Jean 1926- *IntWWM 77, -80*
Smit, Johannes 1913- *ConAmC*
Smit, Leo 1900-1943 *NewGrD 80*
Smit, Leo 1900-1944? *Baker 78*
Smit, Leo 1921- *AmSCAP 66, -80, Baker 78, BiDAmM, CpmDNM 79, ConAmC, DcCM, IntWWM 77, -80, NewGrD 80, WhoMus 72*
Smith *NewGrD 80, RkOn 2[port]*
Smith, Father 1630?-1708 *NewGrD 80, OxMus*
Smith, A Berkeley 1918- *IntMPA 77, -75, -76, -78, -79, -80*
Smith, Al K *BluesWW[port]*
Smith, Alan 1940- *IntWWM 80*
Smith, Alan Benson 1930- *IntWWM 80*
Smith, Albert 1816-1860 *NotNAT A, -B, OxThe*
Smith, Albert E 1875-1958 *WhScrn 77*
Smith, Albert J 1894-1939 *WhScrn 74, -77, WhoHol B*
Smith, Alexis 1921- *FilmEn, FilmgC, ForYSC, HalFC 80, IntMPA 77, -75, -76, -78, -79, -80, MotPP, MovMk[port], PlP&P A[port], WhoHol A, WhoThe 77, WorEFlm*
Smith, Alfred Jesse 1941- *AmSCAP 80*
Smith, Alfred Morton 1879- *BiDAmM*
Smith, Alice Mary 1839-1884 *Baker 78, NewGrD 80, OxMus*
Smith, Alicia 1931- *AmSCAP 66, -80*
Smith, Alison 1914- *IntWWM 80*
Smith, Anderson *Film 2*
Smith, Anita 1922- *AmSCAP 66, ConAmC*
Smith, Anne *BluesWW[port]*
Smith, Anthony Edmund 1929- *WhoMus 72*
Smith, Archie *WhoHol A*
Smith, Art 1899-1973 *HalFC 80*
Smith, Art 1900-1973 *PlP&P[port], WhScrn 77, WhoHol B*
Smith, Arthur *EncFCWM 69*
Smith, Arthur 1921- *BiDAmM, EncFCWM 69, IlEncCM[port]*
Smith, Arthur Corbett d1945 *NotNAT B*
Smith, Arthur James Marshall 1902- *CreCan 2*
Smith, Arthur Leonard 1913- *WhoMus 72*
Smith, Sir Aubrey 1863-1948 *WhThe*
Smith, Augustus J *BlkAmP, MorBAP*
Smith, Barbara Barnard 1920- *IntWWM 77, -80*
Smith, Barbara L *WomWMM A, -B*
Smith, Barry 1939- *DcPup, IntWWM 77, -80*
Smith, Beasley 1901-1968 *AmSCAP 66, -80, BgBands 74, CmpEPM, NotNAT B*
Smith, Beatrice Lieb 1862-1942 *WhScrn 74, -77*
Smith, Ben 1905- *WhoJazz 72*
Smith, Bernard 1630?-1708 *Baker 78, NewGrD 80*
Smith, Bernard 1905?- *FilmgC, HalFC 80*
Smith, Bessie *BlksB&W C*
Smith, Bessie 1894-1937 *Baker 78, BluesWW[port], DrBlPA, NewGrD 80, WhScrn 77*
Smith, Bessie 1894?-1938 *IlEncJ*
Smith, Bessie 1895-1937 *BiDAmM, CmpEPM, MusMk[port], WhoJazz 72*
Smith, Betty 1906-1972 *BiE&WWA, NotNAT B*
Smith, Billy d1963 *NotNAT B*
Smith, Billye-Mullins *IntWWM 80*
Smith, Blaine 1915- *BiDAmM*
Smith, Branson 1921- *ConAmC*
Smith, Bruce d1942 *NotNAT B*
Smith, Buddy *Film 2*
Smith, Buffalo Bob *NewYTET, What 2[port]*
Smith, Buster 1904- *CmpEPM, WhoJazz 72*
Smith, C Aubrey d1948 *MotPP, WhoHol B*
Smith, C Aubrey 1862-1948 *WhoStg 1908*
Smith, C Aubrey 1863-1948 *FilmAG WE, FilmEn, Film 1, -2, FilmgC, ForYSC, HalFC 80, HolCA[port], IlWWBF, MovMk[port], NotNAT B, PlP&P, Vers A[port], WhScrn 74, -77*
Smith, C Charles *ConMuA 80B*
Smith, C Ray *PupTheA*
Smith, C U 1901- *AmSCAP 80*
Smith, Cal 1932- *BiDAmM, CounME 74[port], -74A, IlEncCM[port]*
Smith, Calvin L 1950- *IntWWM 77, -80*
Smith, Carl 1927- *BiDAmM, CounME 74, -74A, EncFCWM 69, IlEncCM[port]*
Smith, Carleton Sprague 1905- *Baker 78, IntWWM 80, NewGrD 80*
Smith, Carol 1926- *WhoOp 76*
Smith, Carol Taylor 1935- *IntWWM 77*
Smith, Caroline Louisa Sprague 1827-1886 *BiDAmM*
Smith, Carrie 1941- *BluesWW[port]*
Smith, Cary 1934- *ConAmC*
Smith, Catherine Parsons 1933- *IntWWM 77, -80*
Smith, Cecil 1906-1956 *Baker 78*
Smith, Charles 1920?- *FilmgC, ForYSC, HalFC 80, WhoHol A*
Smith, Charles Ellis *PupTheA*
Smith, Charles H 1866-1942 *Film 2, WhScrn 74, -77, WhoHol B*
Smith, Charles Martin *WhoHol A*
Smith, Charles Thomas 1887- *WhoMus 72*
Smith, Charles Warren 1936- *ConAmC*
Smith, Charlie Martin 1955- *IntMPA 77, -75, -76, -78, -79, -80*
Smith, Charlotte 1873-1928 *WhScrn 77*
Smith, Chris 1879-1949 *AmPS, AmSCAP 66, -80, BiDAmM, CmpEPM, NotNAT B, PopAmC, Sw&Ld B*
Smith, Christopher Alan 1947- *AmSCAP 80*
Smith, Chuck *MorBAP*
Smith, Cladys 1908- *BiDAmM, EncJzS 70*
Smith, Clara 1894-1935 *BluesWW[port], CmpEPM, WhoJazz 72*
Smith, Clarence 1904-1929 *BiDAmM, BluesWW*
Smith, Claude Thomas 1932- *AmSCAP 80, ConAmC*
Smith, Clay 1877-1930 *AmSCAP 66, -80*
Smith, Clay 1885- *WhThe*
Smith, Cliff 1894-1937 *FilmEn, Film 1*
Smith, Clifford d1937 *TwYS A*
Smith, Clifford 1945- *AmSCAP 80, ConAmC*
Smith, Connie 1941- *BiDAmM, CounME 74[port], -74A, EncFCWM 69, IlEncCM[port]*
Smith, Constance *IntMPA 77, -75, -76, -78, -79, -80, WhoHol A*
Smith, Constance 1929- *FilmgC, HalFC 80*
Smith, Constance 1930- *ForYSC*
Smith, Craig Edward 1941- *IntWWM 80*
Smith, Crickett 1883-1943 *WhoJazz 72*
Smith, Cyril 1892-1963 *Film 1, -2, FilmgC, HalFC 80, NotNAT B, WhScrn 74, -77, WhThe, WhoHol B*
Smith, Cyril 1909-1974 *NewGrD 80, WhoMus 72*
Smith, D A Clarke *Film 2*
Smith, Daniel C 1954- *IntWWM 77*
Smith, Darwood K *WhoHol A*
Smith, David *TwYS A*
Smith, David Charles Morgan 1929- *IntWWM 77, -80*
Smith, David Leroy 1915- *AmSCAP 80*
Smith, David Stanley 1877-1949 *Baker 78, BiDAmM, ConAmC, NewGrD 80, OxMus*
Smith, Dean *WhoHol A*
Smith, Delos V, Jr. *WhoHol A*
Smith, Demon *BlkAmP*
Smith, Derek 1927- *WhoThe 77*
Smith, Derek G 1931- *AmSCAP 80*
Smith, Dexter 1839-1909 *BiDAmM*
Smith, Diane Hartman 1935- *AmSCAP 80*
Smith, Dick *WhoHrs 80*
Smith, Djeni Ba *BlkAmP*
Smith, Dodie 1896- *BiE&WWA, ConDr 77, McGEWD, NotNAT, PlP&P, WhoThe 72, -77*
Smith, Donald *Film 2, MorBAP*
Smith, Donald Aumont 1922- *AmSCAP 66, -80*
Smith, Donald Sydney *WhoOp 76*
Smith, Doreen Wilhelmina 1931- *IntWWM 77*
Smith, Dorothy Dumbrille *CreCan 2*
Smith, Dorothy E *BlkWAB*
Smith, Dorothy Maud 1907- *WhoMus 72*
Smith, Doug 1935- *ConAmTC*
Smith, Douglas 1939- *IntWWM 77, -80*
Smith, Douglas Alton 1944- *IntWWM 77, -80*
Smith, Doyle R 1924- *BiE&WWA, NotNAT*
Smith, Drifting *BluesWW[port]*
Smith, Dudley *Film 2*
Smith, Dwan *WhoHol A*
Smith, Dwight 1857-1949 *WhScrn 74, -77*
Smith, Earl Hobson 1898- *NatPD[port]*
Smith, Earle Francis 1929- *AmSCAP 80*
Smith, Eddie d1964 *NotNAT B*
Smith, Edgar 1857-1938 *AmPS, AmSCAP 66, -80, CmpEPM, EncMT, NewCBMT, NotNAT B, Sw&Ld B, WhThe, WhoStg 1906, -1908*
Smith, Edna Marilyn 1924- *BlkWAB[port]*
Smith, Edward 1585?-1612 *NewGrD 80*
Smith, Edward 1927- *AmSCAP 80*
Smith, Edward Tyrrell 1804-1877 *OxThe*
Smith, Edwin William 1914- *IntWWM 77, -80, WhoMus 72*
Smith, Elihu Hubbard 1771-1798 *BiDAmM*
Smith, Elizabeth *WhoHol A*
Smith, Elizabeth Lee Allen 1817-1877 *BiDAmM*
Smith, Elmer d1963 *NotNAT B*
Smith, Elsie Linehan d1964 *NotNAT B*
Smith, Ethel *AmPS B, BlksB&W C*
Smith, Ethel 1910- *AmSCAP 66, -80, CmpEPM, What 3[port], WhoHol A*
Smith, Ethel 1921- *BiDAmM, ForYSC*
Smith, Fabian 1908- *WhoMus 72*
Smith, Felix 1935- *DancEn 78*
Smith, Fiddlin' Arthur *EncFCWM 69, IlEncCM*
Smith, Florence *Film 1*
Smith, Floyd 1917- *CmpEPM, WhoJazz 72*
Smith, Francesca *WhoHol A*
Smith, Frank L d1953 *NotNAT B*
Smith, Frank M 1906-1976 *AmSCAP 66, -80*
Smith, Freda 1904- *IntWWM 77, -80*
Smith, Freddie Lawrence 1935- *IntWWM 77*
Smith, Frederick Theodore 1919- *AmSCAP 66, -80*
Smith, Frederick Wilson d1944 *NotNAT B*
Smith, Funny Papa *BluesWW[port]*
Smith, Funny Paper *BluesWW[port]*
Smith, G A 1864-1959 *FilmgC, HalFC 80*
Smith, G Alan 1947- *ConAmC*
Smith, G Albert 1898-1959 *NotNAT B, WhScrn 74, -77, WhoHol B*
Smith, Gary Milton 1943- *AmSCAP 80*
Smith, Gayle 1943- *IntWWM 77, -80*
Smith, Geoffrey Charles 1955- *WhoMus 72*
Smith, George 1924- *BluesWW[port]*
Smith, George Albert 1864-1959 *DcFM, FilmEn, IlWWBF, OxFilm, WorEFlm*
Smith, George M 1912- *AmSCAP 66, -80*
Smith, George T d1947 *NotNAT B*
Smith, George W d1946 *WhoHol B*
Smith, George W 1899-1947 *WhScrn 74, -77*
Smith, George Washington 1820?-1899 *CnOxB, DancEn 78*
Smith, Gerald Christopher 1913- *WhoMus 72*
Smith, Gerald L 1921- *IntWWM 77, -80*
Smith, Gerald L K *What 1[port]*
Smith, Gerald Oliver 1896-1974 *Film 2, WhScrn 77, WhoHol B*
Smith, Gerrit 1859-1912 *Baker 78, BiDAmM*
Smith, Glanville 1901- *ConAmC*
Smith, Glenn Parkhurst 1912- *IntWWM 77, -80*
Smith, Gord 1937- *CreCan 2*
Smith, Gordon Appelbe 1919- *CreCan 1*
Smith, Gregg 1931- *AmSCAP 66, -80, BnBkM 80, CpmDNM 80, ConAmC*
Smith, Gregory James 1952- *IntWWM 80*
Smith, Gunboat *Film 2*
Smith, Guy *BluesWW[port]*
Smith, H Reeves *Film 2, WhThe*
Smith, H Wakefield 1865-1956 *AmSCAP 66, -80*
Smith, Hal *ForYSC, WhoHol A*
Smith, Hale 1925- *Baker 78, BiDAmM, BlkCS[port], ConAmC, DrBlPA, NewGrD 80*

Smith, Harry Bache 1860-1936 *AmPS, AmSCAP 66, -80, BiDAmM, CmpEPM, EncMT, NewCBMT, NotNAT A, -B, Sw&Ld B, WhThe, WhoStg 1906, -1908*
Smith, Harvey 1904- *BiE&WWA*
Smith, Heisel *PupTheA*
Smith, Helen Creeger 1924- *ConAmTC*
Smith, Helen S 1909- *BiE&WWA*
Smith, Henry Charles 1931- *IntWWM 80*
Smith, Henry More *PupTheA*
Smith, Herbert 1901- *IlWWBF*
Smith, Herbert Arnold 1887- *WhoMus 72*
Smith, Hezekiah Leroy Gordon 1909-1967 *AmSCAP 66, BiDAmM, EncJzS 70*
Smith, Hobart 1897-1965 *EncFCWM 69*
Smith, Honey Boy *BluesWW[port]*
Smith, Houston 1910- *AmSCAP 66, -80*
Smith, Howard *WomWMM*
Smith, Howard 1910- *CmpEPM, WhoJazz 72*
Smith, Howard I 1893-1968 *Vers A[port], WhScrn 74, -77, WhoHol B*
Smith, Howard I 1894-1968 *NotNAT B, WhThe*
Smith, Howard I 1895-1968 *BiE&WWA*
Smith, Howard K 1914- *IntMPA 77, -75, -76, -78, -79, -80*
Smith, Howard Russell 1949- *AmSCAP 80*
Smith, Howard W, Jr. *PupTheA*
Smith, Howlin' *BluesWW[port]*
Smith, Huey Piano 1924- *RkOn*
Smith, Hurricane 1923- *RkOn 2[port]*
Smith, Hy 1934- *IntMPA 77, -75, -76, -78, -79, -80*
Smith, Ira Alexander 1903-1965 *AmSCAP 80*
Smith, J Agustus 1891- *BlksB&W, -C, BlksBF*
Smith, J Lewis 1906-1964 *WhScrn 77*
Smith, J Sebastian 1869-1948 *NotNAT B, WhThe*
Smith, J Stanley 1905-1974 *WhScrn 77*
Smith, Jabbo 1908- *CmpEPM, EncJzS 70, WhoJazz 72*
Smith, Jack 1898-1950 *NotNAT B*
Smith, Jack 1901- *WhoMus 72*
Smith, Jack 1918?- *CmpEPM*
Smith, Jack 1932- *OxFilm*
Smith, Jack C 1896-1944 *WhScrn 74, -77, WhoHol B*
Smith, Jaclyn *IntMPA 78, -79, -80*
Smith, Jacqueline 1933- *IntMPA 77, -75, -76, -78, -79, -80*
Smith, James Howard 1938- *EncJzS 70*
Smith, James Oscar 1925- *EncJzS 70*
Smith, Jane *BluesWW[port]*
Smith, Janet Carol 1941- *AmSCAP 80*
Smith, Jay R *Film 2*
Smith, Jean *BlkAmP*
Smith, Jennie *AmSCAP 80*
Smith, Jerome 1895- *NewOrJ*
Smith, Jerry Neil 1935- *AmSCAP 80, ConAmC*
Smith, Jimmie 1938- *EncJzS 70*
Smith, Jimmy 1925- *EncJzS 70, IlEncJ, RkOn*
Smith, Joe *ConMuA 80B, Film 2*
Smith, Joe 1884- *WhoHol A*
Smith, Joe 1900-1952 *NotNAT B, WhScrn 74, -77, WhoHol B*
Smith, Joe 1902-1937 *BiDAmM, CmpEPM, IlEncJ, WhoJazz 72*
Smith, John *OxMus*
Smith, John d1612 *OxMus*
Smith, John 1880?-1918 *NewOrJ*
Smith, John 1910- *NewOrJ*
Smith, John 1931- *FilmgC, ForYSC, HalFC 80, WhoHol A*
Smith, John Brodie Gurney 1909- *WhoMus 72*
Smith, John Cameron 1927- *WhoMus 72*
Smith, John Christopher 1712-1795 *Baker 78, NewGrD 80, OxMus*
Smith, John Frank 1950- *IntWWM 77, -80*
Smith, John Ivor 1927- *CreCan 2*
Smith, John Meredith *CreCan 2*
Smith, John Shaffer, Jr. 1913- *AmSCAP 66, ConAmC*
Smith, John Stafford 1750-1836 *Baker 78, MusMk, NewGrD 80, OxMus*
Smith, John Sydney 1932- *IntWWM 77*
Smith, John T 1890- *BluesWW*
Smith, John Thomas *OxMus*
Smith, Johnny 1922- *CmpEPM*
Smith, Joseph C *CmpEPM*
Smith, Joseph Coyal, Jr. 1924- *AmSCAP 80*
Smith, Joseph P *IntMPA 79, -80*
Smith, Josephine Rinaldo 1931- *IntWWM 77*
Smith, Judy *WomWMM B*
Smith, Julia 1911- *AmSCAP 66, -80, Baker 78, BiDAmM, CpmDNM 72, ConAmC, DcCM, NewGrD 80*
Smith, Julian Bricknell 1944- *WhoOp 76*
Smith, Julian John Hamling 1929- *IntWWM 77, -80, WhoMus 72*
Smith, June *WomWMM B*
Smith, Justin *WhoHol A*
Smith, Karen *WhoHol A*
Smith, Kate 1909- *AmPS A, -B, BiDAmM, CmpEPM, IntMPA 77, -76, -78, -79, -80, NewYTET, PlP&P, ThFT[port], WhoHol A*
Smith, Kathleen 1942- *CnOxB*
Smith, Kay 1911- *CreCan 1*
Smith, Keely 1932- *AmSCAP 66, BiDAmM, CmpEPM, ForYSC, WhoHol A*
Smith, Keith Hamilton 1928- *IntWWM 77, -80*
Smith, Kenneth 1920- *WhoMus 72*
Smith, Kenneth Leslie 1946- *IntWWM 80*
Smith, Kent *ConAmC*
Smith, Kent 1907- *BiE&WWA, FilmEn, FilmgC, ForYSC, HalFC 80, HolP 40[port], IntMPA 77, -75, -76, -78, -79, -80, MovMk, NotNAT, WhoHol A, WhoHrs 80, WhoThe 72, -77*
Smith, Kermit Stephen 1948- *AmSCAP 80*
Smith, Kevin 1942- *IntWWM 80*
Smith, L *Film 2*
Smith, Lane *WhoHol A*
Smith, Lani 1934- *ConAmC*
Smith, Larry Michael 1939- *AmSCAP 66*
Smith, Laurence Fabian 1908- *IntWWM 77*
Smith, Laurence Fabian 1909- *IntWWM 80*
Smith, Lawrence 1936- *Baker 78*
Smith, Lawrence Rackley 1932- *AmSCAP 80*
Smith, Leigh R *Film 2*
Smith, Lela *WomWMM A, -B*
Smith, Leland 1925- *Baker 78, ConAmC, NewGrD 80*
Smith, Leo 1881-1952 *NewGrD 80*
Smith, Leo 1941- *EncJzS 70*
Smith, Leona May 1914- *AmSCAP 66*
Smith, Leonard Bingley 1915- *AmSCAP 66, -80*
Smith, Leonard Henry Francis 1929- *WhoMus 72*
Smith, Leonard O *WhoHol A*
Smith, Leonard R 1889-1958 *WhScrn 74, -77*
Smith, Leopold 1881-1952 *NewGrD 80*
Smith, Lester 1898-1952 *NewOrJ[port]*
Smith, Linda Kay 1949- *BlkWAB*
Smith, Linda Lee 1948- *IntWWM 80*
Smith, Lois 1930- *BiE&WWA, NotNAT, WhoHol A, WhoThe 77*
Smith, Lois Irene 1929- *CnOxB, CreCan 1, DancEn 78*
Smith, Lonnie Liston 1940- *DrBlPA, EncJzS 70*
Smith, Loring 1895- *BiE&WWA, NotNAT, WhThe, WhoHol A, WhoThe 72*
Smith, Louise 1928- *IntWWM 77, -80*
Smith, Lowell James 1936- *IntWWM 77, -80*
Smith, Lydia Sutton *PupTheA*
Smith, Lynn *WomWMM B*
Smith, Mabel 1924-1972 *BluesWW[port], EncJzS 70, WhScrn 77*
Smith, Madeline 1950- *WhoHol A, WhoHrs 80*
Smith, Maggie 1934- *BiDFilm, -81, CnThe, EncMT, EncWT, Ent, FilmAG WE, FilmEn, FilmgC, ForYSC, HalFC 80, IlWWBF, IntMPA 77, -75, -76, -78, -79, -80, MotPP, MovMk[port], PlP&P[port], WhoHol A, WhoThe 72, -77*
Smith, Malcolm Sommerville 1933- *WhoOp 76*
Smith, Malcolm Wallace 1944- *IntWWM 80*
Smith, Mamie *BlksB&W, -C, BlksBF*
Smith, Mamie 1883?-1946 *BluesWW[port], CmpEPM, WhoJazz 72*
Smith, Mandy *BluesWW[port]*
Smith, Marcus 1829-1874 *OxThe*
Smith, Margaret Ann 1941- *IntWWM 77*
Smith, Margaret Lillias 1930- *IntWWM 80*
Smith, Margaret Louise 1908- *WhoMus 72*
Smith, Margaret M 1881-1960 *WhScrn 74, -77, WhoHol B*
Smith, Mark 1829-1874 *NotNAT B*
Smith, Mark 1886-1944 *NotNAT B, WhScrn 77*
Smith, Martha Ann 1949- *ConAmTC*
Smith, Martha E *PupTheA*
Smith, Mary Cecelia 1913- *AmSCAP 66, -80*
Smith, Mary Lasswell 1905- *AmSCAP 80*
Smith, Mary Louise 1843-1927 *BiDAmM*
Smith, Mary Stewart *WomWMM B*
Smith, Matthew 1905-1953 *WhScrn 74, -77, WhoHol B*
Smith, Maureen Felicity *IntWWM 77, -80, WhoMus 72*
Smith, Maurice 1939- *IntMPA 77, -75, -76, -78, -79, -80*
Smith, Maybelle 1924-1972 *BiDAmM*
Smith, Melville 1898- *ConAmC*
Smith, Meribel 1902- *IntWWM 77, -80*
Smith, Meryl Coulson 1918- *IntWWM 77*
Smith, Michael 1935- *ConDr 73, -77*
Smith, Michael John 1937- *IntWWM 77, -80*
Smith, Michael Joseph 1938- *EncJzS 70, IntWWM 80*
Smith, Mildred Joanne 1923- *DrBlPA*
Smith, Milton 1890- *BiE&WWA, NotNAT*
Smith, Moses 1901-1964 *Baker 78, NotNAT B*
Smith, Moses 1932- *BluesWW[port]*
Smith, Muriel 1923- *BiE&WWA, DrBlPA, NotNAT, WhoHol A*
Smith, Nayland *Film 2*
Smith, Nicholas Richard Norman 1948- *IntWWM 77, -80*
Smith, Noel 1923- *WhoMus 72*
Smith, Noel Mason 1890?- *FilmEn, TwYS A*
Smith, Norman Edward 1921- *IntWWM 77, -80*
Smith, Norwood 1915- *BiE&WWA, NotNAT, WhoHol A*
Smith, O C 1932- *DrBlPA, RkOn*
Smith, Ocie Lee 1937- *BiDAmM*
Smith, Olive Kent 1904- *WhoMus 72*
Smith, Oliver 1918- *BiE&WWA, CnOxB, DancEn 78, EncWT, Ent, NotNAT, PlP&P, WhoOp 76, WhoThe 72, -77*
Smith, Oscar *Film 2*
Smith, Oswald Jeffrey 1889- *AmSCAP 66, -80*
Smith, Otis *BlkAmP*
Smith, Patricia 1930- *BiE&WWA, NotNAT, WhoHol A*
Smith, Patricia L 1946- *AmSCAP 80*
Smith, Patrick John 1932- *IntWWM 77, -80*
Smith, Patti 1946- *ConMuA 80A[port], IlEncR[port]*
Smith, Paul *ConMuA 80B, WhoHol A*
Smith, Paul 1922- *CmpEPM*
Smith, Paul G 1894-1968 *NotNAT B*
Smith, Paul Gerald d1968 *WhScrn 77*
Smith, Paul Gerard 1894- *BiE&WWA*
Smith, Paul Girard *WhThe*
Smith, Paul Joseph 1906- *AmSCAP 66, -80*
Smith, Paulene Rhoda 1943- *WhoMus 72*
Smith, Pete 1892-1979 *FilmEn, FilmgC, HalFC 80, IntMPA 77, -75, -76, -78, -79, What 4[port]*
Smith, Peter Melville 1943- *IntWWM 77*
Smith, Pine Top 1904-1929 *BluesWW[port], CmpEPM, NewGrD 80, WhoJazz 72*
Smith, Pleasant 1886-1969 *WhScrn 74, -77*
Smith, Pops 1890-1966 *WhoJazz 72*
Smith, Portia 1950- *BlkWAB*
Smith, Putter *WhoHol A*
Smith, Queenie *AmPS B*
Smith, Queenie 1898- *CmpEPM, ForYSC, WhoHol A*
Smith, Queenie 1902- *EncMT, WhThe*
Smith, R A 1780-1829 *OxMus*
Smith, Ralph G 1906- *IntMPA 77, -75, -76, -78, -79*
Smith, Ray 1938- *RkOn*
Smith, Ray E 1908- *IntMPA 77, -75, -76, -78, -79, -80*
Smith, Rebecca Dianna *WhoHol A*
Smith, Reed 1881-1943 *Baker 78*
Smith, Reid *WhoHol A*
Smith, Richard B 1901-1935 *AmSCAP 66, -80*
Smith, Richard Drew 1949- *AmSCAP 80*
Smith, Richard Harrison 1937- *ConAmC*

Smith, Richard J 1909- *WhoJazz 72*
Smith, Richard Langham 1947- *IntWWM 77, –80*
Smith, Richard Lemon 1952- *AmSCAP 80*
Smith, Richard Penn 1799-1854 *NotNAT B, OxThe*
Smith, Richard Penn 1799-1858 *PlP&P*
Smith, Richard Roy 1928- *WhoMus 72*
Smith, Rick *ConMuA 80B*
Smith, Robert d1647 *NewGrD 80*
Smith, Robert 1648?-1675 *NewGrD 80*
Smith, Robert 1689-1768 *NewGrD 80*
Smith, Robert 1922- *IntWWM 77, –80, WhoMus 72*
Smith, Robert Archibald 1780-1829 *NewGrD 80*
Smith, Robert Bache 1875-1951 *AmPS, AmSCAP 66, –80, BiDAmM, CmpEPM, EncMT, NewCBMT, NotNAT B, Sw&Ld B, WhThe*
Smith, Robert Edward 1946- *IntWWM 77, –80*
Smith, Robert Kimmel 1930- *NatPD[port]*
Smith, Robert Lee 1940- *AmSCAP 80*
Smith, Robert Paul 1915- *BiE&WWA, NotNAT*
Smith, Robert W, Jr. 1929- *AmSCAP 66*
Smith, Roger 1932- *FilmgC, ForYSC, HalFC 80, IntMPA 77, –75, –76, –78, –79, –80, MotPP, MovMk, WhoHol A*
Smith, Roger 1949- *IntWWM 80*
Smith, Roger Montgomery 1915-1975 *AmSCAP 66, –80*
Smith, Ronald 1922- *IntWWM 77, –80, WhoMus 72*
Smith, Ronald Aubrey 1928- *IntWWM 77, –80, WhoMus 72*
Smith, Ronald Hugh 1930- *WhoMus 72*
Smith, Ruby Mae 1902- *AmSCAP 66*
Smith, Russell 1927- *AmSCAP 80, ConAmC, DcCM*
Smith, S F 1808-1895 *OxMus*
Smith, Sammi 1943- *CounME 74[port], –74A, IlEncCM[port], RkOn 2[port]*
Smith, Sammy *WhoHol A*
Smith, Samuel Francis 1808-1895 *BiDAmM*
Smith, Samuel J 1771-1835 *BiDAmM*
Smith, Sharon *WomWMM B*
Smith, Sid 1892-1928 *Film 1, –2, WhoHol B*
Smith, Sidney d1935 *WhThe*
Smith, Sidney 1892-1928 *WhScrn 74, –77*
Smith, Sidney F R *NewYTET*
Smith, Sol 1801-1869 *EncWT, NotNAT B*
Smith, Solomon Franklin 1801-1869 *NotNAT A, OxThe*
Smith, Somethin' And The Redheads *RkOn[port]*
Smith, Sonelius Larel 1942- *EncJzS 70*
Smith, Stanley 1905-1974 *Film 2, WhoHol B*
Smith, Stuart S 1948- *AmSCAP 80, CpmDNM 76, –77, ConAmC*
Smith, Stuff 1909-1965 *CmpEPM*
Smith, Stuff 1909-1967 *EncJzS 70, IlEncJ, WhoJazz 72*
Smith, Sue Ellen French 1947- *IntWWM 77*
Smith, Susie *BluesWW[port]*
Smith, Sydney *WhoHol A*
Smith, Sydney d1935 *NotNAT B*
Smith, Sydney 1839-1889 *Baker 78, NewGrD 80, OxMus*
Smith, Sydney 1908- *WhoMus 72*
Smith, Tab 1909-1971 *CmpEPM, EncJzS 70, WhoJazz 72*
Smith, Talmadge 1909-1971 *EncJzS 70*
Smith, Tatti 1908?- *WhoJazz 72*
Smith, Ted *Film 2*
Smith, Theodore 1740?-1810? *NewGrD 80, OxMus*
Smith, Thomas *NewGrD 80*
Smith, Thomas Allen 1946- *AmSCAP 80*
Smith, Thomas C 1892-1950 *WhScrn 74, –77, WhoHol B*
Smith, Thorne 1892-1934 *FilmgC, HalFC 80*
Smith, Thorne 1893-1934 *WhoHrs 80*
Smith, Tom d1976 *WhoHol C*
Smith, Trefor Leslie 1948- *IntWWM 77*
Smith, Trixie 1895-1943 *BluesWW[port]*
Smith, Truman *WhoHol A*
Smith, Vernon *PupTheA*
Smith, Vincent *WhoHol A*
Smith, Vincent L, III 1947- *IntWWM 77*
Smith, Viola *Film 1*
Smith, Vivian *Film 2*
Smith, Vivienne Grace 1920- *IntWWM 77*
Smith, Wallace 1923- *BiE&WWA, NotNAT*
Smith, Walter A 1930- *AmSCAP 80*
Smith, Walter Wallace 1894-1948 *AmSCAP 66, –80*
Smith, Warren 1908- *CmpEPM*
Smith, Warren 1934- *EncJzS 70*
Smith, Warren Doyle 1908-1975 *EncJzS 70, WhoJazz 72*
Smith, Warren Storey 1885-1971 *Baker 78*
Smith, Warren Story 1885-1971 *ConAmC*
Smith, Wayne C 1953- *IntWWM 80*
Smith, Welton *BlkAmP*
Smith, Wentworth 1601-1620 *NotNAT B*
Smith, Whispering *BluesWW[port]*
Smith, Whispering Jack *AmPS B*
Smith, Whispering Jack 1898-1950 *Film 2, WhScrn 77*
Smith, Whispering Jack 1899-1951 *CmpEPM*
Smith, Wilford Davis 1913- *IntWWM 77, –80*
Smith, Wilfred 1911- *IntWWM 77, –80, WhoMus 72*
Smith, Wilfred Elmar 1916- *WhoMus 72*
Smith, William *NewGrD 80, WhoHol A*
Smith, William d1696 *OxThe*
Smith, William 1603?-1645 *NewGrD 80*
Smith, William 1730-1819 *NotNAT B, OxThe*
Smith, William 1754-1821 *BiDAmM*
Smith, William C 1881-1972 *NewGrD 80, OxMus*
Smith, William H 1897-1973 *AmSCAP 66, –80, BiDAmM, EncJzS 70*
Smith, William Henry d1872 *NotNAT B*
Smith, William McLeish 1908- *BiDAmM*
Smith, William McLeish 1910-1967 *EncJzS 70*
Smith, William O 1926- *Baker 78, ConAmC, NewGrD 80*
Smith, William Ronald *CreCan 1*
Smith, William Thurlow 1910- *WhoMus 72*
Smith, Willie 1910-1967 *CmpEPM, EncJzS 70, IlEncJ, WhoJazz 72*
Smith, Willie The Lion 1897-1973 *Baker 78, CmpEPM, EncJzS 70, IlEncJ, WhoJazz 72*
Smith, Wilson George 1855-1929 *Baker 78, BiDAmM*
Smith, Winchell 1871-1933 *CnMD, ModWD*
Smith, Winchell 1872-1933 *NotNAT B, WhThe*
Smith, Wonderful *WhoHol A*
Smith And Dale *JoeFr[port], What 2[port]*
Smith Brindle, Reginald 1917- *DcCM, NewGrD 80*
Smither, Arthur Biggs 1922- *WhoMus 72*
Smither, Howard E 1925- *Baker 78, IntWWM 77, –80, NewGrD 80*
Smithers, Don 1933- *NewGrD 80*
Smithers, Florence *WhThe*
Smithers, Jan *WhoHol A*
Smithers, William *WhoHol A*
Smithson, Florence 1884-1936 *NotNAT B, WhThe*
Smithson, Frank d1949 *NotNAT B*
Smithson, Harriet Constance 1800-1854 *CnThe, OxMus, OxThe*
Smithson, Henrietta Constance 1800-1854 *NotNAT B*
Smithson, Laura 1878-1963 *WhScrn 77, WhThe*
Smithson, Will d1927 *NotNAT B*
Smits *NewGrD 80*
Smits, Franciscus Cornelius 1800-1876 *NewGrD 80*
Smits, Franciscus Cornelius 1834-1918 *NewGrD 80*
Smits, Henricus Wilhelmus Josephus 1871-1944 *NewGrD 80*
Smits, Nicolaas Lambertus 1790-1831 *NewGrD 80*
Smits VanWaesberghe, Joseph 1901- *NewGrD 80*
Smitterick, Grover d1914 *WhScrn 77*
Smok, Pavel 1927- *CnOxB*
Smokehouse Charley *BluesWW[port]*
Smoker, Paul Alva 1941- *IntWWM 77*
Smokey Mountain Boys *BiDAmM, EncFCWM 69*
Smoktunovsky, Innokenti 1925- *FilmEn, FilmgC, HalFC 80*
Smoky Babe *BluesWW[port]*
Smolanoff, Michael Louis 1942- *AmSCAP 80, ConAmC, IntWWM 77, –80*
Smoldon, W L 1892-1974 *NewGrD 80*
Smoldon, William Lawrence 1892- *WhoMus 72*
Smolen, Donald E 1923- *IntMPA 77, –75, –76, –78, –79, –80*
Smolensky, Stepan Vasil'yevich 1848-1909 *Baker 78, NewGrD 80*
Smolian, Arthur 1856-1911 *Baker 78*
Smolka, Jaroslav 1933- *IntWWM 77, –80, NewGrD 80*
Smoller, Dorothy 1901-1926 *WhScrn 74, –77*
Smollett, Molly *WomWMM B*
Smollett, Tobias *OxMus*
Smollett, Tobias George 1721-1771 *NotNAT B*
Smolover, Raymond 1921- *ConAmC*
Smoothies, The *CmpEPM*
Smorgacheva, Ludmila 1950- *CnOxB*
Smotherman, Micheal Wayne 1952- *AmSCAP 80*
Smothers, Dick 1939- *JoeFr[port], WhoHol A*
Smothers, Otis 1929- *BluesWW[port]*
Smothers, Richard 1938- *BiDAmM*
Smothers, Thomas B 1937- *AmSCAP 80, BiDAmM*
Smothers, Tom 1937- *JoeFr[port], WhoHol A*
Smothers Brothers, The *EncFCWM 69, JoeFr[port]*
Smout, Adrian Joriszoon 1579?-1646 *NewGrD 80*
Smrcek, Josef Blazej 1751-1813 *NewGrD 80*
Smrschek, Josef Blazej 1751-1813 *NewGrD 80*
Smrtzek, Josef Blazej 1751-1813 *NewGrD 80*
Smrzek, Josef Blazej 1751-1813 *NewGrD 80*
Smuin, Michael 1938- *CnOxB*
Smulders, Charles 1863-1934 *Baker 78*
Smutny, Jiri 1932- *NewGrD 80*
Smyrl, David Langston *MorBAP*
Smyth *NewGrD 80*
Smyth, Brian Mills 1928- *IntWWM 80, WhoMus 72*
Smyth, Edward *NewGrD 80*
Smyth, Eleanore M *PupTheA*
Smyth, Ethel 1858-1944 *Baker 78, CmOp, DcCom&M 79, MusMk, NewEOp 71, NewGrD 80, OxMus*
Smyth, Felix Joseph *PupTheA*
Smyth, Richard *NewGrD 80*
Smyth, Thomas *NewGrD 80*
Smyth, William *NewGrD 80*
Smythe, Florence 1878-1925 *WhScrn 74, –77, WhoHol B*
Smythe, James Moore d1734 *NotNAT B*
Smythe, Michael Alan 1932- *IntWWM 77*
Smythe, William G d1921 *NotNAT B*
Snadowsky, Stanley *ConMuA 80B*
Snaer, Albert Joseph 1902-1962? *NewOrJ, WhoJazz 72*
Snaer, Samuel 1833- *BiDAmM*
Snape, John 1936- *WhoMus 72*
Snaper, Wilbur 1911- *IntMPA 77, –75, –76, –78, –79, –80*
Snave, Elmas *BlkAmP*
Snavely, Jack 1929- *IntWWM 77, –80*
Sneed, Floyd C 1942- *IntWWM 77*
Snegoff, Leonid 1883-1974 *Film 2, WhScrn 77*
Snel, Billy 1938- *AmSCAP 66*
Snel, Joseph-Francois 1793-1861 *Baker 78, NewGrD 80*
Snell, David L 1897-1967 *AmSCAP 66, –80*
Snell, Paul 1904- *IntMPA 77, –75, –76, –78, –79*
Snelling, Minnette 1878-1945 *WhScrn 74, –77, WhoHol B*
Snellings, Sidney Lockhart 1934- *IntWWM 77*
Snep, Johan *NewGrD 80*
Sneppe, Jean *NewGrD 80*
Snerd, Mortimer *JoeFr*
Snesrud, Arlin Duane 1939- *AmSCAP 80*
Snetzler, Johann 1710-1785 *Baker 78*
Snetzler, John 1710-1785 *NewGrD 80, OxMus*
Snider, Ralph E 1903- *IntMPA 77, –75, –76, –78, –79*
Snider, Ronald Joe 1947- *IntWWM 77, –80*
Snijders, Ronald 1937- *CnOxB, DancEn 78*
Snipes, Margaret Ford Taylor *MorBAP*
Snitil, Vaclav 1928- *NewGrD 80*
Snitzer, Jimmy 1926-1945 *WhScrn 77*

Snitzer, Miriam 1922-1966 *WhScrn 77*
Snizkova, Jitka 1924- *IntWWM 77*
Snizkova-Skrhova, Jitka 1924- *IntWWM 80*
Snoddy, Glen *ConMuA 80B*
Snodgress, Carrie *IntMPA 77, -75, -76, -78, -79, -80, WhoHol A*
Snodgress, Carrie 1945- *MovMk[port]*
Snodgress, Carrie 1946- *FilmEn, HalFC 80*
Snodham, Thomas d1624 *NewGrD 80*
Snoeck, Kenneth Maurice 1946- *AmSCAP 80*
Snoek, Hans 1906- *CnOxB, DancEn 78*
Snoer, Johannes 1868-1936 *Baker 78*
Snooks, Baby *JoeFr*
Snookums *WhScrn 74, -77*
Snooky *BluesWW[port]*
Snorrason, Askell 1888-1970 *NewGrD 80*
Snow, Clarence Eugene 1914- *BiDAmM*
Snow, Eliza Roxey 1804-1887 *BiDAmM*
Snow, Hank 1914- *CmpEPM, CounME 74[port], -74A, EncFCWM 69, IlEncCM*
Snow, John Harold Thomas 1911- *CreCan 2*
Snow, Joyce Wieland *CreCan 1*
Snow, Leida *AmSCAP 80*
Snow, Marguerite d1958 *MotPP, NotNAT B, WhoHol B*
Snow, Marguerite 1888-1958 *Film 1, -2, TwYS*
Snow, Marguerite 1889-1958 *FilmEn, WhScrn 74, -77*
Snow, Mary McCarty 1928- *CpmDNM 79, ConAmC*
Snow, Michael James Aleck 1929- *CreCan 1, OxFilm*
Snow, Mortimer 1869-1935 *Film 2, WhScrn 74, -77, WhoHol B*
Snow, Moses d1702 *NewGrD 80*
Snow, Phoebe 1952- *ConMuA 80A[port], EncJzS 70, IlEncR, RkOn 2[port]*
Snow, Terry *AmSCAP 80*
Snow, Ursula Mary 1927- *IntWWM 77, -80, WhoMus 72*
Snow, Valaida d1956 *NotNAT B*
Snow, Valaida 1900?-1956 *DrBlPA, WhoJazz 72*
Snow, Valaida 1903-1957 *BlksBF*
Snow, Valaida 1909?-1956 *BlkWAB[port]*
Snow, Valentine d1770 *NewGrD 80*
Snowball, Elizabeth 1939- *IntWWM 77, -80*
Snowden, Alec Crawford *IntMPA 77, -75, -76, -78, -79*
Snowden, Alex Crawford *IntMPA 80*
Snowden, Carolynne *Film 2*
Snowden, Elmer Chester 1900-1973 *CmpEPM, EncJzS 70, WhScrn 77, WhoJazz 72*
Snowden, Eric *ForYSC*
Snowden, James Wyn 1943- *IntWWM 77, -80*
Snowden, Leigh 1932- *ForYSC, IntMPA 77, -75, -76, -78, -79, WhoHol A*
Snowden, Leigh 1933?- *WhoHrs 80*
Snowden, Philip 1864-1936 *OxMus*
Snowden, Pops 1900-1973 *EncJzS 70*
Snowdon, Leigh 1932- *IntMPA 80*
Snowdon, Roger *WhoHol A*
Snowflake *ForYSC*
Snowhill, George H 1911- *AmSCAP 66, -80*
Snowman, M Nicholas 1944- *IntWWM 77, -80*
Snowman, Nicholas 1944- *WhoMus 72*
Snyder, Barry 1944- *IntWWM 77, -80*
Snyder, Denton 1915- *BiE&WWA*
Snyder, Don *PupTheA*
Snyder, Edward Abraham 1919- *AmSCAP 66, -80*
Snyder, Frederick 1922- *IntWWM 77*
Snyder, Gene d1953 *NotNAT B*
Snyder, Jack *ConMuA 80B*
Snyder, John LeRoy 1950- *IntWWM 77*
Snyder, John Michael 1945- *IntWWM 77*
Snyder, Kenneth C T 1925- *AmSCAP 80*
Snyder, Mary Susan Smeltzer 1941- *IntWWM 80*
Snyder, Matt d1917 *Film 1, WhScrn 77*
Snyder, Randall 1944- *ConAmC, IntWWM 77*
Snyder, Ted 1881-1965 *AmPS, AmSCAP 66, -80, BiDAmM, CmpEPM, PopAmC, PopAmC SUP*
Snyder, Theodore 1924- *ConAmC*
Snyder, Tom 1936- *IntMPA 77, -78, -79, -80, NewYTET*
Snyder, William 1916- *AmSCAP 66, ConAmC A*
Snyder, William 1929- *ConDr 73, -77*
Snyder, William L 1920- *IntMPA 77, -75, -76, -78, -79, -80*
Snyder, William Paul 1920- *AmSCAP 80*
Soames, Arthur *Film 2*
Soames, Cynthia Elizabeth 1946- *IntWWM 77, -80*
Soames, Rene 1903- *WhoMus 72*
Soane, George d1860 *NotNAT B*
Soares Netto, Calimerio Augusto 1944- *IntWWM 77, -80*
Soares Pereira, Marcos *NewGrD 80*
Soares Rebelo, Joao *NewGrD 80*
Sobeka *CnOxB*
Sobel, Bernard 1887-1964 *BiE&WWA, NotNAT B, WhThe*
Sobel, Robert Murray 1925- *ConAmTC*
Soberg, Alf 1903- *WorEFlm*
Sobieska, Jadwiga 1909- *NewGrD 80*
Sobieski, Marian 1908-1967 *NewGrD 80*
Sobinov, Leonid 1873-1934 *CmOp*
Sobinov, Leonid Vital'yevich 1872-1934 *NewGrD 80[port]*
Sobinova, Natasha *CreCan 2*
Soble, Ron 1932- *IntMPA 77, -75, -76, -78, -79, -80, WhoHol A*
Sobol, Edward d1962 *NotNAT B*
Sobol, Lawrence Paul 1946- *IntWWM 77, -80*
Sobol, Louis 1896- *IntMPA 77, -75, -76, -78, -79, -80*
Sobolevsky, Pyotr *Film 2*
Sobolewski, Friedrich Eduard De 1808-1872 *Baker 78*
Sobolewski, Fryderyk Edward 1808-1872 *NewGrD 80*
Sobolewski, J Fredrich Eduard 1808-1872 *BiDAmM*
Soboloff, Arnold 1930- *BiE&WWA, NotNAT, WhoHol A, WhoThe 77*
Sobotka, Ruth 1925-1967 *NotNAT B, WhScrn 77*
Socarras, Alberto *WhoJazz 72*
Socas, Roberto D 1895- *IntMPA 75, -76*
Socci, Gianni 1939- *WhoOp 76*
Sochet, Win H *AmSCAP 80*
Sochin, Irving 1910- *IntMPA 77, -75, -76, -78, -79, -80*
Socolow, Sanford *NewYTET*
Socor, Matei 1908- *Baker 78*
Socrates *PlP&P[port]*
Sodders, Carl d1958 *WhScrn 74, -77*
Soderbaum, Kristina 1912- *FilmAG WE*
Soderbaum, Ulla *CnOxB*
Soderberg, Hjalmar 1869-1941 *CnMD*
Soderblom, Ulf Arne 1930- *WhoOp 76*
Soderholm, Valdemar 1909- *IntWWM 77, -80*
Soderini, Agostino *NewGrD 80*
Soderino, Agostino *Baker 78*
Soderlind, Ragnar 1945- *Baker 78*
Soderling, Walter d1968 *WhoHol B*
Soderling, Walter 1872-1948 *Vers A[port], WhScrn 77*
Soderlund, Gustav Frederic 1881-1972 *Baker 78*
Soderlund, Gustave Frederic 1881-1972 *ConAmC, NewGrD 80*
Soderman, August Johann 1832-1876 *Baker 78, OxMus*
Soderman, Jackie 1927- *DancEn 78*
Soderman, Johan August 1832-1876 *NewGrD 80*
Sodero, Cesare 1886-1947 *AmSCAP 66, -80, Baker 78, BiDAmM, ConAmC A, NewEOp 71*
Sodersten, Gunno 1920- *IntWWM 80*
Soderstrom, Elisabeth 1927- *CmOp, IntWWM 77, -80, NewGrD 80[port], WhoMus 72, WhoOp 76*
Soderstrom, Gunilla *WhoOp 76*
Sodi, Carlo 1715?-1788 *NewGrD 80*
Sodi, Carmen Sordo *NewGrD 80*
Sodi, Charles 1715?-1788 *NewGrD 80*
Sodi, Pietro d1775? *CnOxB*
Sody, Carlo 1715?-1788 *NewGrD 80*
Sody, Charles 1715?-1788 *NewGrD 80*
Soegijo, Paul Gutama 1934- *NewGrD 80*
Soehnel, Ray 1900- *AmSCAP 66, -80*
Soehnel, Zelma 1909- *AmSCAP 66*
Soehner, Barbara *AmSCAP 80*
Soell, John B 1911-1965 *AmSCAP 66, -80*
Soellner, Glenn Earl 1929- *IntWWM 77*
Soest, Johannes Von 1448-1506 *NewGrD 80*
Sofaer, Abraham 1896- *FilmEn, FilmgC, ForYSC, HalFC 80, IntMPA 77, -75, -76, -78, -79, -80, Vers B[port], WhoHol A, WhoThe 72, -77*
Soffici, Mario 1900- *DcFM*
Soffing, Tilly 1932- *CnOxB*
Soffredini, Alfredo 1854-1923 *Baker 78*
Sofras, Polychronis George 1930- *IntWWM 77, -80*
Sofronitsky, Vladimir 1901-1961 *NewGrD 80*
Sofronitzky, Vladimir 1901-1961 *Baker 78*
Sofronov, Anatol Vladimirovich 1911- *CnMD, OxThe*
Sofronov, Anatoli Vladimirovich 1911- *ModWD*
Soft Machine *ConMuA 80A, IlEncR*
Sogner, Pasquale 1793-1842 *NewGrD 80*
Sogner, Tommaso 1762-1821? *NewGrD 80*
Soh, Tomotada 1943- *IntWWM 77*
Soh, Tomotada 1948- *IntWWM 80*
Sohal, Naresh 1939- *NewGrD 80*
Soherr, Hermann H F 1924- *WhoOp 76*
Sohi, Valentin *NewGrD 80*
Sohier, Charles-Joseph-Balthazar 1728?-1759 *NewGrD 80*
Sohier, Jean *NewGrD 80*
Sohier, Mathieu d1560? *NewGrD 80*
Sohier, Valentin *NewGrD 80*
Sohlke, Gus 1865-1924 *NotNAT B, WhThe*
Sohn, Joseph 1876-1935 *Baker 78*
Sohngen, Oskar 1900- *NewGrD 80*
Sohren, Peter 1630?-1692 *NewGrD 80*
Sohyer, Mathieu *NewGrD 80*
Soicka, Matej 1740-1817 *NewGrD 80*
Soicka, Matous 1740-1817 *NewGrD 80*
Sojberg, Gunnar *WhoHol A*
Sojin 1884-1954 *HalFC 80*
Sojin 1891-1954 *ForYSC, TwYS, WhScrn 77, WhoHol B, WhoHrs 80*
Sojin, Kamiyama 1891-1954 *Film 2*
Sojka, Matej 1740-1817 *NewGrD 80*
Sojka, Matous 1740-1817 *NewGrD 80*
Sojo, Pedro *NewGrD 80*
Sojo, Vicente Emilio 1887- *NewGrD 80*
Soka, Ladislav 1931- *IntWWM 77, -80*
Sokalsky, Pyotr Petrovich 1832-1887 *Baker 78, NewGrD 80*
Sokhor, Arnol'd Naumovich 1924- *NewGrD 80*
Sokol, Marilyn *WhoHol A*
Sokol, Vilem 1915- *IntWWM 77, -80*
Sokola, Milos 1913- *Baker 78, IntWWM 77, -80, WhoMus 72*
Sokola, Milos 1913-1976 *NewGrD 80*
Sokole, Lucy Bender *AmSCAP 66, -80*
Sokoloff, David 1910- *AmSCAP 66, -80*
Sokoloff, Nicolai Grigorovitch 1886-1965 *BiDAmM*
Sokoloff, Nikolai 1886-1965 *Baker 78*
Sokoloff, Noel 1923- *ConAmC*
Sokoloff, Vladimir 1889-1962 *FilmEn, FilmgC, HalFC 80, HolCA[port], MovMk, NotNAT B, Vers A[port], WhScrn 74, -77*
Sokoloff, Vladimir 1890-1962 *Film 2, ForYSC, MotPP, WhoHol B*
Sokolov, Harry *IntMPA 75, -76*
Sokolov, Nikolai 1859-1922 *Baker 78*
Sokolov, Nikolay Alexandrovich 1859-1922 *NewGrD 80*
Sokolov, Oleg Germanovich 1936- *CnOxB*
Sokolova, Eugenie 1854-1926 *DancEn 78*
Sokolova, Evgenia Pavlovna 1850-1925 *CnOxB*
Sokolova, Lydia 1896-1974 *CnOxB, DancEn 78, WhThe*
Sokolova, Natasha 1917- *WhThe*
Sokolove, Richard *IntMPA 75*
Sokolove, Samuel 1914- *AmSCAP 66*
Sokolovsky, Mikhail Matveyevich *NewGrD 80*
Sokolow, Anna *CmpGMD[port]*
Sokolow, Anna 1912- *BiE&WWA, CnOxB, NotNAT*
Sokolow, Anna 1915- *DancEn 78[port]*
Sokolow, Ethel d1970 *WhScrn 77*
Sokolowska, Anna *WomWMM*
Sokolowski, Marek Konrad 1818-1883 *NewGrD 80*
Sokorska, Bogna 1937- *WhoOp 76*
Sokorski, Jerzy 1916- *IntWWM 77, -80*

Sola, Andres De 1634?-1696 *NewGrD 80*
Solage *NewGrD 80*
Solal, Martial 1927- *EncJzS 70, NewGrD 80*
Solana, Jose 1643?-1712 *NewGrD 80*
Solano, Francisco Ignacio 1720?-1800 *Baker 78, NewGrD 80*
Solar, Willie d1956 *NotNAT B, WhoHol B*
Solares, Enrique 1910- *Baker 78, DcCM*
Solari, Rudy *WhoHol A*
Solc, Karel 1893- *IntWWM 77, -80*
Soldani, Charles L 1893-1968 *WhScrn 77*
Soldanieri, Niccolo 1325?-1385 *NewGrD 80*
Soldano, Anthony 1927- *AmSCAP 66*
Soldat, Marie 1863-1955 *Baker 78*
Soldati, Mario 1905- *OxFilm*
Soldati, Mario 1906- *DcFM, FilmEn, FilmgC, HalFC 80, IntMPA 77, -75, -76, -78, -79, -80, WorEFlm*
Soldene, Emily 1840-1912 *NotNAT A, -B, OxThe*
Soldi, Luca Antonio *NewGrD 80*
Soldi, Stephen d1974 *WhScrn 77*
Solem, Delmar E 1915- *BiE&WWA, NotNAT*
Solemn Ol' Judge, The *EncFCWM 69*
Soleniere, Eugene De 1872-1904 *Baker 78*
Soler, Antonio 1729-1783 *BnBkM 80, MusMk, NewGrD 80, OxMus*
Soler, Antonio Ruiz 1927- *WhThe*
Soler, Domingo 1902-1961 *WhScrn 77*
Soler, Francisco 1625?-1688 *NewGrD 80*
Soler, Jose 1935- *NewGrD 80*
Soler, Josep 1935- *Baker 78, IntWWM 77, -80*
Soler, Martin Y *OxMus*
Soler, Padre Antonio 1729-1783 *Baker 78*
Soler, Pedro Genard 1938- *IntWWM 77, -80*
Soler, Vicente Martin Y *NewGrD 80*
Solera, Temistocle 1815-1878 *NewGrD 80*
Solerti, Angelo 1865-1907 *Baker 78, NewGrD 80*
Solie, Jean-Pierre 1755-1812 *NewGrD 80*
Solier, Jean-Pierre 1755-1812 *NewGrD 80*
Solin, Vladimir 1911- *IntWWM 77, -80*
Soling, Josef Antonin *NewGrD 80*
Solino, Antonio 1638-1704 *NewGrD 80*
Solis, Javier 1931-1966 *WhScrn 74, -77*
Solis, Max 1913- *AmSCAP 66, -80*
Solis Taiana, Elsa Ines 1938- *IntWWM 80*
Solis Y Rivadeneyra, Antonio De 1610-1686 *McGEWD[port]*
Solito DeSolis, Aldo 1905-1973 *AmSCAP 66, -80, ConAmC A*
Soliva, Carlo Evasio 1792-1851 *NewGrD 80*
Sollberger, Harvey 1938- *Baker 78, CpmDNM 80, ConAmC, DcCM*
Sollberger, Harvey 1939- *NewGrD 80*
Sollertinsky, Ivan Ivanovich 1902-1944 *Baker 78, NewGrD 80*
Solleveld, Coen *ConMuA 80B*
Solley, Marvin 1937- *BiDAmM*
Sollie, Jean-Pierre *NewGrD 80*
Sollis, Linda Jane 1952- *IntWWM 77*
Sollner, Johann Gottlieb 1732-1798 *NewGrD 80*
Sollnitz, Anton Wilhelm *NewGrD 80*
Sollors, Daniel Michael 1941- *WhoOp 76*
Solly, Bill 1931- *AmSCAP 80*
Solm, Fred *Film 2*
Solman, Alfred 1868-1937 *AmSCAP 66, -80*
Solnado, Raul 1929- *FilmAG WE*
Solnerus, Johannes *NewGrD 80*
Solnik, Tania 1956- *AmSCAP 80*
Solnitz, Anton Wilhelm 1708?-1758? *NewGrD 80*
Solntseva, Yulia 1901- *FilmEn, WomWMM, WorEFlm*
Solo, Robert H *IntMPA 77, -75, -76, -78, -79, -80*
Solodovnikov, Alexandr Vasilievich 1904- *WhThe*
Soloff, Lew 1944- *EncJzS 70*
Soloff, Lewis Michael 1944- *EncJzS 70*
Sologne, Madeleine 1912- *FilmEn*
Sologub, Fyodor 1863-1927 *CnMD, McGEWD, ModWD*
Solomon 1902- *Baker 78, BnBkM 80, IntWWM 77, -80, NewGrD 80[port]*
Solomon Cutner 1902- *BnBkM 80*
Solomon, A B *WhoMus 72*
Solomon, Alan 1938- *IntWWM 77, -80*
Solomon, C B E 1902- *WhoMus 72*
Solomon, Edward 1855-1895 *NewGrD 80, NotNAT B*
Solomon, Edward 1932- *CpmDNM 79, -80*
Solomon, Florence *IntMPA 77, -75, -76, -78, -79, -80*
Solomon, Harold 1903- *AmSCAP 66, -80*
Solomon, Izler 1910- *Baker 78, BiDAmM, MusSN[port], WhoMus 72*
Solomon, John 1856-1953 *NewGrD 80*
Solomon, Joseph 1897-1947 *AmSCAP 66, -80*
Solomon, L *WhoMus 72*
Solomon, Larry Joseph 1940- *IntWWM 77, -80*
Solomon, Maureen C *WomWMM B*
Solomon, Melvin Ira 1947- *CpmDNM 80, ConAmC*
Solomon, Michael Jay 1938- *IntMPA 80*
Solomon, Paul Marshall *AmSCAP 80*
Solomon, Russ *ConMuA 80B*
Solomon, Seymour *ConMuA 80B*
Solomon, Shirley 1919- *AmSCAP 80*
Solomon, Theodore George 1920- *IntMPA 77, -75, -76, -78, -79, -80*
Solomon, Tina *WhoHol A*
Solomon, Yonty 1937- *WhoMus 72*
Solomon, Yonty 1938- *NewGrD 80*
Solomons, Gus, Jr. 1940?- *CmpGMD, CnOxB*
Solon, Ewen 1923?- *FilmgC, HalFC 80, WhoHol A*
Solorzano, Carlos 1922- *ModWD*
Solov, Zachary 1923- *CnOxB, DancEn 78[port]*
Soloviev, Nikolai 1846-1916 *Baker 78*
Soloviev, Yuri Vladimirovich 1940- *CnOxB*
Solovyev-Sedoy, Vassily 1907- *Baker 78*
Solov'yov, Nikolay Feopemptovich 1846-1916 *NewGrD 80*
Solovyov, Vladimir Aleksandrovich 1907- *ModWD*
Solovyov, Yuri 1940- *DancEn 78*
Solov'yov-Sedoy, Vasily Pavlovich 1907-1979 *NewGrD 80*
Solow, Sidney Paul 1910- *IntMPA 77, -75, -76, -78, -79, -80*
Soloway, Leonard 1928- *BiE&WWA*
Sols Taiana, Elsa Ines 1938- *IntWWM 77*
Solski, Ludwik 1854-1954 *NotNAT B*
Solt, Andrew 1916- *IntMPA 77, -75, -76, -78, -79, -80*
Solters, Larry *ConMuA 80B*
Solters, Lee 1919- *BiE&WWA*
Solti, Sir Georg 1912- *BnBkM 80[port], CmOp[port], IntWWM 77, -80, MusMk[port], MusSN[port], NewEOp 71, NewGrD 80[port], WhoMus 72, WhoOp 76*
Solti, Sir George 1912- *Baker 78*
Solti, Sir Gyorgy 1912- *NewGrD 80[port]*
Soltntseva, Yulia 1901- *DcFM*
Soltyk, Count Franciszek 1783-1865 *NewGrD 80*
Soltyk, Count Karol 1791-1831? *NewGrD 80*
Soltys, Adam 1890-1968 *Baker 78*
Soltys, Mieczyslaw 1863-1929 *Baker 78, NewGrD 80*
Soltz, Charlene E *IntMPA 77, -78, -79, -80*
Soltz, Rose d1973 *WhScrn 77*
Solveg, Maria *Film 2*
Solway, Kenneth David 1954- *IntWWM 80*
Solymos, Peter 1910- *IntWWM 77, -80, WhoMus 72*
Solyom, Janos 1938- *IntWWM 77, -80, WhoMus 72*
Solyom-Nagy, Sandor 1941- *WhoOp 76*
Som, Laszio 1934- *IntWWM 77, -80*
Somack, Jack *WhoHol A*
Soman, Claude 1897-1960 *NotNAT B, WhThe*
Sombert, Claire 1935- *CnOxB, DancEn 78[port], WhoHol A*
Somer, Avo 1934- *ConAmC*
Somer, Hilde 1930- *Baker 78*
Somers, Barbara Chilcott Davis *CreCan 1*
Somers, Brett *WhoHol A*
Somers, Bud *Film 2*
Somers, Carole d1974 *WhScrn 77*
Somers, Fred d1970 *WhScrn 77, WhoHol B*
Somers, Harry Stewart 1925- *Baker 78, CreCan 1, DancEn 78, DcCM, NewGrD 80*
Somers-Cocks, John 1907- *WhoMus 72*
Somersaloni, Urho *Film 2*
Somerset, C W 1847-1929 *NotNAT B, WhThe*
Somerset, Pat 1897-1974 *Film 2, WhScrn 77, WhoHol B, WomWMM*
Somerset, Patrick 1897-1974 *WhThe*
Somervell, Sir Arthur 1863-1937 *Baker 78, MusMk, NewGrD 80, OxMus*
Somerville, Christopher Charles *DcPup*
Somerville, J A C 1872- *OxMus*
Somerville, John Baxter 1907-1963 *WhThe*
Somerville, Kevin John 1954- *IntWWM 77*
Somerville, Slim 1892- *TwYS*
Somes, A Edwin *WhoMus 72*
Somes, Michael 1917- *CnOxB, DancEn 78[port], WhThe, WhoHol A*
Somfai, Laszlo 1934- *IntWWM 77, -80, NewGrD 80*
Somi, Leone Ebreo Di 1527-1592 *OxThe*
Somis, Ardy 1688-1775 *NewGrD 80*
Somis, Francesco Lorenzo 1663-1736 *Baker 78*
Somis, Giovanni Battista 1686-1763 *Baker 78, NewGrD 80*
Somis, Lorenzo Giovanni 1688-1775 *Baker 78, NewGrD 80*
Somkin, Steven 1941- *NatPD[port]*
Somlo, Josef 1885-1973 *FilmgC, HalFC 80*
Somlyo, Roy A 1925- *BiE&WWA*
Somma, Antonio 1809-1865 *NewGrD 80*
Sommars, Julie *ForYSC, WhoHol A*
Sommer, Edith *BiE&WWA, NotNAT*
Sommer, Elke *MotPP, WhoHol A*
Sommer, Elke 1940- *FilmAG WE[port], FilmEn, FilmgC, HalFC 80, MovMk*
Sommer, Elke 1941- *ForYSC, IntMPA 77, -75, -76, -78, -79, -80*
Sommer, Hans 1837-1922 *Baker 78, NewGrD 80*
Sommer, Johann d1627 *NewGrD 80*
Sommer, Raphael 1937- *IntWWM 77, -80, WhoMus 72*
Sommer, Ted 1924- *IntWWM 77*
Sommer, Vladimir 1921- *Baker 78, DcCM, NewGrD 80*
Sommerfeldt, Oistein 1919- *Baker 78, IntWWM 77, -80*
Sommerfield, David Fredric 1941- *IntWWM 80*
Sommerkamp, Helga 1937- *CnOxB, DancEn 78*
Sommerlatte, Ulrich 1914- *WhoMus 72*
Sommers, Ben 1906- *BiE&WWA*
Sommers, Harry G d1953 *NotNAT B*
Sommers, Henry J 1918- *AmSCAP 66*
Sommers, Joanie 1942- *ForYSC, RkOn[port], WhoHol A*
Sommers, John Martin 1940- *AmSCAP 80*
Sommerschield, Rose Neiditch *WomWMM B*
Sommerville, Thomas 1916- *WhoMus 72*
Somnes, George d1956 *NotNAT B*
Somogi, Judith 1943- *IntWWM 77, -80*
Somohamo, Arturo 1910-1977 *ConAmC A*
Somohano, Arturo 1910-1977 *AmSCAP 66, -80*
Son *BluesWW[port]*
Son, Babe 1897?- *NewOrJ*
Son Joe *BluesWW[port]*
Son Of Man Hammer *Film 2*
Sonal, Marc 1858- *WhThe*
Sondergaard, Gale *BiE&WWA, IntMPA 77, -75, -76, -78, -79, -80, MotPP, NotNAT, Vers A[port], What 1[port]*
Sondergaard, Gale 1899- *FilmEn, FilmgC, HalFC 80[port], HolCA[port], MovMk[port], ThFT[port], WhoHrs 80[port]*
Sondergaard, Gale 1900- *ForYSC, WhoHol A*
Sondergaard, Gale 1901- *WhoThe 72, -77*
Sondheim, Stephen 1930- *AmPS, AmSCAP 66, -80, Baker 78, BestMus, BiDAmM, BiE&WWA, BnBkM 80, ConAmC, EncMT, EncWT, Ent[port], HalFC 80, IntWWM 77, NatPD[port], NewCBMT, NewGrD 80, NotNAT, -A, PlP&P, -A[port], PopAmC SUP[port], WhoThe 72, -77*
Sondheimer, Hans 1901- *BiE&WWA, NotNAT, WhoOp 76*
Sondheimer, Robert 1881-1956 *Baker 78, NewGrD 80*
Sonenberg, David *ConMuA 80B*
Sonenfeld, Otto *IntMPA 77, -75, -76, -78, -79, -80*
Sones, Carol *WomWMM B*

Sonevytsky, Ihor 1926- *IntWWM 80*
Songayllo, Raymond Thaddeus 1930- *IntWWM 77, -80*
Songer, Ernestine *PupTheA*
Songer, Lewis A 1935- *ConAmC*
Songier, Leo *NewOrJ*
Sonja, Magda *Film 2*
Sonneck, Oscar George Theodore 1873-1928 *Baker 78, BiDAmM, ConAmC, NewGrD 80, OxMus*
Sonnemann, Emmy d1974 *WhoHol B*
Sonnenburg, Friedrich Von *NewGrD 80*
Sonnenfeld, Adolf Gustaw 1837-1914 *NewGrD 80*
Sonnenfeld, Kurt 1921- *IntWWM 77, -80*
Sonnenfels, Josef Von 1733-1817 *EncWT, OxThe*
Sonnenthal, Adolf Von 1834-1909 *EncWT*
Sonneveld, Wim 1918-1974 *WhScrn 77, WhoHol B*
Sonnichsen, Soren 1765-1826 *NewGrD 80*
Sonnier, Joel 1946- *AmSCAP 80*
Sonninen, Ahti 1914- *Baker 78, IntWWM 77, -80, NewGrD 80*
Sonnleithner *NewGrD 80*
Sonnleithner, Christoph 1734-1786 *NewGrD 80*
Sonnleithner, Ignaz 1770-1831 *NewGrD 80*
Sonnleithner, Joseph 1766-1835 *Baker 78, NewGrD 80*
Sonnleithner, Leopold Von 1797-1873 *NewGrD 80*
Sonnleitner *NewGrD 80*
Sonntag, Gertrud Walburga 1806-1854 *BnBkM 80*
Sonntag, Henriette *NewGrD 80*
Sonntag, Stanley 1921- *IntWWM 77, -80*
Sonny *BluesWW[port]*
Sonny And Cher *BiDAmM, ConMuA 80A, IlEncR, RkOn 2[port]*
Sonny T *BluesWW[port]*
Sons, Maurice 1857-1942 *NewGrD 80*
Sons Of Champlin *IlEncR*
Sons Of The Pioneers *BiDAmM, CmpEPM, CounME 74[port], -74A, EncFCWM 69, IlEncCM*
Sons Of The Pioneers And Bob Nolan *ForYSC*
Sonstevold, Elisabeth 1942- *IntWWM 77, -80*
Sonstevold, Gunnar 1912- *DcCM, NewGrD 80*
Sonstevold, Knut 1945- *IntWWM 80*
Sonstevold, Maj 1917- *IntWWM 77, -80*
Sontag, Art *PupTheA*
Sontag, Henriette 1806-1854 *Baker 78, BnBkM 80, CmOp, NewEOp 71, NewGrD 80[port]*
Sontag, Susan 1933- *OxFilm, WomWMM*
Sonyer, Tomas *NewGrD 80*
Sony'r Ra, Le *NewGrD 80*
Sonzogno *NewGrD 80*
Sonzogno, Edoardo 1836-1920 *Baker 78, NewEOp 71, NewGrD 80*
Sonzogno, Francesco *NewGrD 80*
Sonzogno, Giovan Battista *NewGrD 80*
Sonzogno, Giulio Cesare 1906-1976 *Baker 78, WhoMus 72*
Sonzogno, Lorenzo *NewGrD 80*
Sonzogno, Renzo 1877-1920 *NewGrD 80*
Sonzogno, Riccardo d1915 *NewGrD 80*
Soo, Jack *MotPP, WhoHol A*
Soo, Jack 1916-1979 *HalFC 80*
Soo, Jack 1934- *ForYSC*
Soomil, Stephan 1940- *ConAmC*
Soot, Friedrich 1878-1965 *NewGrD 80*
Soot, Fritz 1878-1965 *NewGrD 80*
Sooter, Edward 1934- *WhoOp 76*
Sopanen, Jeri *WomWMM*
Sopena, Federico 1917- *Baker 78, NewGrD 80*
Soper, Mary Therese Janiczek 1926- *IntWWM 77*
Soper, Paul 1906- *BiE&WWA, NotNAT*
Soper, Tut 1910?- *WhoJazz 72*
Soph, Edward B 1945- *EncJzS 70*
Sophia Elisabeth 1613-1676 *NewGrD 80*
Sophie Elisabeth 1613-1676 *NewGrD 80*
Sophocles 496?BC-406?BC *CnThe, Ent[port], McGEWD[port], NewEOp 71, NewGrD 80, NotNAT A, -B, OxThe, PlP&P[port], REnWD[port]*
Sophocles 497?BC-406BC *EncWT*
Sophokles 496?BC-406BC *NewGrD 80*
Sophron *OxThe*
Sopkin, Henry 1903- *AmSCAP 66, -80, Baker 78*
Soproni, Jozsef 1930- *Baker 78, IntWWM 77, -80, NewGrD 80*
Sopuerta, Miguel De *NewGrD 80*
Sopwith Camel *RkOn 2[port]*
Sor, Fernando 1778-1839 *Baker 78, NewGrD 80, OxMus*
Sor, Fernando 1780-1839 *BnBkM 80[port]*
Soraa, Jarle 1932- *IntWWM 80*
Sorabji, Kaikhosru 1892- *Baker 78, MusMk, NewGrD 80, OxMus*
Sorano, Daniel 1920-1962 *EncWT, OxThe*
Soray, Turkan *WomWMM*
Sorbi *NewGrD 80*
Sorcar, P C 1913-1971 *MagIID*
Sorce, Richard 1943- *AmSCAP 80, ConAmC*
Sordello, Enzo 1931- *WhoOp 76*
Sorden, Milo Taylor 1906- *AmSCAP 80*
Sordi, Alberto *MotPP, WhoHol A*
Sordi, Alberto 1919- *FilmEn, FilmgC, HalFC 80, MovMk*
Sordi, Alberto 1920- *OxFilm, WorEFlm[port]*
Sordo Sodi, Carmen 1932- *NewGrD 80*
Sore, Martin *NewGrD 80, OxMus*
Sorel, Cecile d1966 *WhoHol B*
Sorel, Cecile 1873-1966 *WhThe*
Sorel, Cecile 1874-1966 *WhScrn 74, -77*
Sorel, Cecile 1875-1966 *NotNAT A*
Sorel, Claudette Marguerite 1932- *IntWWM 77, -80*
Sorel, George S 1899-1948 *WhScrn 74, -77, WhoHol B*
Sorel, Guy 1914- *NotNAT, WhoHol A*
Sorel, Jean 1934- *FilmgC, HalFC 80, WhoHol A*
Sorel, Jeanne *WhoHol A*
Sorel, Louise 1944- *FilmgC, HalFC 80, WhoHol A*
Sorel, Ruth *CnOxB, CreCan 2*
Sorell, Christiane 1936- *WhoOp 76*
Sorell, Walter 1905- *DancEn 78*
Sorelle, William *Film 1*
Sorensen, Arne Kjaer 1944- *IntWWM 77*
Sorensen, Inger 1944- *IntWWM 80*
Sorensen, Jens 1895- *IntWWM 77, -80*
Sorensen, Linda *WhoHol A*
Sorensen, Paul *WhoHol A*
Sorensen, Soren 1920- *NewGrD 80*
Sorenson, John Roger 1945- *ConAmC*
Sorenson, Richard A 1940- *IntWWM 77*
Sorenson, Torsten Napoleon 1908- *Baker 78, IntWWM 77, -80*
Soreny, Eva *WhoHol A*
Sorere, Gabrielle *WomWMM*
Soresi, Carl D 1916- *AmSCAP 66*
Soresina, Alberto 1911- *Baker 78*
Sorey, Vincent 1897-1977 *AmSCAP 80*
Sorey, Vincent 1900- *AmSCAP 66*
Sorge, Georg Andreas 1703-1778 *Baker 78, NewGrD 80*
Sorge, Reinhard Johannes 1892-1916 *CnMD, EncWT, McGEWD, ModWD, OxThe*
Sorgo, Antonio *NewGrD 80*
Sorgo, Luca *NewGrD 80*
Soria, Madeleine *WhThe*
Sorian, Jack *WhoHol A*
Soriano, Alberto 1915- *Baker 78*
Soriano, Dale 1918- *IntMPA 77, -75, -76, -78, -79, -80*
Soriano, Francesco *Baker 78*
Soriano, Francesco 1548?-1621 *NewGrD 80*
Soriano, Francesco 1549-1620 *OxMus*
Soriano, Gonzalo 1913-1972 *NewGrD 80, WhoMus 72*
Soriano DeAndia, Vicente *McGEWD*
Soriano Fuertes, Mariano 1817-1880 *Baker 78*
Soriano Fuertes Y Piqueras, Mariano 1817-1880 *NewGrD 80*
Sorin, Louis 1893-1961 *NotNAT B*
Sorin, Louis 1894-1961 *Film 2, WhScrn 74, -77, WhoHol B*
Sorina, Alexandra *Film 2*
Sorkin, Barney 1903-1973 *WhScrn 77*
Sorkocevic, Antun 1775-1841 *NewGrD 80*
Sorkocevic, Luka 1734-1789 *NewGrD 80*
Sorley, Edward *Film 2*
Sorley Walker, Kathrine *DancEn 78*
Sorm, Pavel 1935- *IntWWM 77, -80*
Sorma, Agnes 1865-1927 *EncWT, Ent, NotNAT B, OxThe*
Sormann, Alfred 1861-1913 *Baker 78*
Sornoff, Sidney 1921-1962 *AmSCAP 66, -80*
Soro, Enrique 1884-1954 *Baker 78, DcCM, NewGrD 80*
Soro, Jose *Baker 78*
Sorokina, Nina Ivanovna 1942- *CnOxB*
Sorosina, Benedetta *NewGrD 80*
Sorozabal, Pablo 1897- *NewGrD 80*
Sorrell, Graham Henry Norman 1933- *WhoMus 72*
Sorrell, Helena *IntMPA 77, -75, -76, -78, -79, -80*
Sorrell, Walter 1905- *CnOxB*
Sorrells, Robert *WhoHol A*
Sorrentina d1973 *WhScrn 77*
Sorrentino, Charles 1906- *AmSCAP 66, -80, ConAmC A*
Sorrin, Ellen *WomWMM B*
Sors, Fernando 1780-1839 *BnBkM 80[port], NewGrD 80, OxMus*
Sorte, Bartolomeo d1601? *NewGrD 80*
Sortes *NewGrD 80*
Sorvino, Paul 1939- *FilmEn, HalFC 80, IntMPA 80, PlP&P A[port], WhoHol A, WhoThe 77*
Sosa, Geo Anne *WhoHol A*
Sosa, Susan *WhoHol A*
Sosenko, Anna 1910- *AmSCAP 66, -80*
Sosnik, Harry 1906- *AmSCAP 66, -80, CmpEPM, ConAmC*
Sotelo, Joaquin Calvo 1905- *CnMD*
Sothern, Ann *AmSCAP 66, -80, MotPP*
Sothern, Ann 1909- *CmpEPM, EncMT, FilmEn, Film 2, FilmgC, HalFC 80, MGM[port], MovMk[port], ThFT[port], WhThe, WorEFlm*
Sothern, Ann 1911- *ForYSC, WhoHol A*
Sothern, Ann 1912?- *OxFilm*
Sothern, Ann 1923- *IntMPA 77, -75, -76, -78, -79, -80*
Sothern, David Annerley 1921- *IntWWM 77, -80*
Sothern, E A 1826-1881 *NotNAT B, PlP&P*
Sothern, E H 1859-1933 *Film 1, WhoHol B*
Sothern, Edward Askew 1826-1881 *EncWT, FamA&A[port], NotNAT A, OxThe*
Sothern, Edward Hugh 1859-1933 *FamA&A[port], NotNAT A, -B, OxThe, WhScrn 74, -77, WhThe, WhoStg 1906, -1908*
Sothern, Edwin Hugh 1859-1933 *EncWT, PlP&P*
Sothern, Ethel 1882-1957 *WhScrn 74, -77*
Sothern, Eve 1898- *Film 1*
Sothern, Georgia 1917?- *What 4[port]*
Sothern, Harry 1883-1957 *NotNAT B*
Sothern, Harry 1884-1957 *Film 2, WhScrn 74, -77, WhoHol B*
Sothern, Hugh 1881-1947 *NotNAT B, WhScrn 74, -77, WhoHol B*
Sothern, Janet Evelyn *WhThe*
Sothern, Jean d1964 *NotNAT B*
Sothern, Jean 1895-1924 *Film 1, WhScrn 74, -77, WhoHol B*
Sothern, Sam 1870-1920 *NotNAT B, WhThe, WhoHol B*
Sotin, Hans 1939- *NewGrD 80, WhoOp 76*
Soto, Luchy 1920-1970 *WhScrn 74, -77*
Soto, Roberto 1888-1960 *WhScrn 74, -77, WhoHol B*
Soto DeLanga, Francisco 1534-1619 *Baker 78, NewGrD 80*
Sotomayor, Jose 1905-1967 *WhScrn 74, -77*
Soubies, Albert 1846-1918 *Baker 78, NewGrD 80*
Soubre, Etienne-Joseph 1813-1871 *Baker 78, NewGrD 80*
Souchay, Marc-Andre 1906- *IntWWM 80*
Souchet, H A Du *WhThe*
Souchon, Doc 1897-1968 *EncJzS 70*
Souchon, Edmond, II 1897-1968 *EncJzS 70, NewOrJ*
Soucy, Jean-Baptiste 1915- *CreCan 2*
Soudeikine, Serge d1946 *NotNAT B*
Soudeikine, Serge 1882-1946 *DancEn 78*
Soudeikine, Serge 1883-1946 *CnOxB*
Souers, Mildred 1894- *AmSCAP 66, ConAmC*
Souesby *NewGrD 80*

Souffriau, Arsene 1926- *NewGrD 80, WhoMus 72*
Souhaitty, Jean-Jacques 1650?- *Baker 78, NewGrD 80*
Soul, David *IntMPA 78, -79, -80, RkOn 2[port], WhoHol A*
Soul, Jimmy 1942- *RkOn*
Soul Stirrers *BiDAmM*
Soul Survivors, The *BiDAmM, RkOn 2[port]*
Soulage, Marcelle 1894- *WhoMus 72*
Soule, Edmund Foster 1915- *AmSCAP 80, CpmDNM 72, -78, -79, ConAmC*
Soule, Olan *ForYSC, WhoHol A*
Soule, Robert 1926- *BiE&WWA, NotNAT*
Soules, Dale *WhoHol A*
Soulie, Jean-Pierre *NewGrD 80*
Soulier, Jean-Pierre *NewGrD 80*
Souliotis, Elena 1943- *WhoOp 76*
Soulten, Graham *Film 2*
Soumagnas, Jean-Louis 1938- *WhoOp 76*
Soumagne, Henri 1891-1951 *ModWD*
Sounds Orchestral *RkOn 2A*
Sounova, Daniela 1943- *WhoOp 76*
Soupault, Philippe 1897- *ModWD*
Souper, G Kay d1947 *NotNAT B*
Souper, Kay d1947 *WhoHol B*
Sour, Robert 1905- *BiDAmM*
Sourek, Otakar 1883-1956 *Baker 78, NewGrD 80*
Souresby, John *NewGrD 80*
Souris, Andre 1890-1970 *NewGrD 80*
Souris, Andre 1899-1970 *Baker 78, DcCM*
Souritz, Elizabeth 1923- *CnOxB*
Sourlier, Matthias 1944- *IntWWM 77, -80*
Souroujon, Leon 1913- *IntWWM 80*
Soursby *NewGrD 80*
Sousa, John Philip 1854-1932 *AmSCAP 66, -80, Baker 78, BiDAmM, BnBkM 80, CmpEPM, EncMT, HalFC 80, MusMk[port], NewGrD 80, NotNAT B, OxMus, PopAmC[port], WhThe, WhoStg 1906, -1908*
Sousa Carvalho, Joao De *NewGrD 80*
Soussanin, Nicholas 1909-1975 *Film 2, WhScrn 77, WhoHol C*
Soussman, H *CpmDNM 78*
Souster, Raymond 1921- *CreCan 1*
Souster, Tim 1943- *Baker 78, DcCM, IntWWM 77, -80, NewGrD 80*
Souster, Timothy Andrew James 1943- *WhoMus 72*
Soutar, Alexander Anderson 1913- *WhoMus 72*
Soutar, Andrew d1941 *NotNAT B*
Soutar, J Farren 1870-1962 *WhThe*
Soutar, Robert d1908 *NotNAT B*
South, Eddie 1904-1962 *BiDAmM, CmpEPM, DrBlPA, NotNAT B, WhoJazz 72*
South, Eddie 1906-1962 *IlEncJ*
South, Joan Mary 1915- *IntWWM 77, -80, WhoMus 72*
South, Joe *CounME 74, -74A*
South, Joe 1940- *RkOn*
South, Joe 1942- *IlEncR*
South, Robert Henry Slater 1912- *IntWWM 77, -80, WhoMus 72*
Southall, Mitchell B 1922- *ConAmC*
Southard, Harry D 1881-1939 *WhScrn 74, -77, WhoHol B*
Southard, Lucien H 1827-1881 *Baker 78, BiDAmM*
Southard, Mary Ann 1926- *AmSCAP 80*
Souther, John David *ConMuA 80A*
Souther-Hillman-Furay Band, The *IlEncR, RkOn 2[port]*
Southern, Eileen 1920- *Baker 78, IntWWM 80, NewGrD 80*
Southern, Eve 1898- *Film 2, TwYS*
Southern, Helenclair Kelly 1916- *IntWWM 77*
Southern, Jeri 1926- *CmpEPM*
Southern, John 1893- *WhThe*
Southern, Richard *WhoHol A*
Southern, Sam 1870-1920 *Film 1, -2, TwYS, WhScrn 74, -77*
Southern, Sheila *WhoMus 72*
Southern, Terry 1924- *ConDr 73, -77A*
Southern, Virginia *Film 2*
Southern Gentlemen, The *EncFCWM 69*
Southern Syncopated Orchestra *BiDAmM*
Southerne, Thomas 1659-1746 *EncWT*
Southerne, Thomas 1660-1746 *Ent, NotNAT B, OxThe, PlP&P[port]*
Southerners, The *BiDAmM*
Southers, Leroy William, Jr. 1941- *ConAmC*
Southgate, Charles d1818 *BiDAmM*
Southgate, Elsie 1890- *WhThe*
Southgate, Howard S 1895-1971 *WhScrn 74, -77*
Southgate, Thomas 1814-1868 *BiDAmM*
Southside Johnny And The Asbury Jukes *ConMuA 80A, IlEncR*
Southwell, William 1756-1842 *NewGrD 80*
Southwick, Dale 1913-1968 *WhScrn 74, -77, WhoHol B*
Soutsos, Alexandros *REnWD[port]*
Soutsos, Panayiotis *REnWD[port]*
Souvairan, Pierre J A 1911- *IntWWM 77*
Souvall, George *ConMuA 80B*
Souvariran, Pierre J A 1911- *IntWWM 80*
Souza, Jose Alves 1935- *IntWWM 77, -80*
Souza, Noemi 1929- *WhoOp 76*
Souzay, Gerald 1920- *NewEOp 71*
Souzay, Gerard 1920- *Baker 78, IntWWM 77, -80, MusMk, MusSN[port], NewGrD 80[port], WhoMus 72, WhoOp 76*
Sovern, Clarence 1900-1929 *WhScrn 74, -77, WhoHol B*
Sovey, Raymond 1897-1966 *BiE&WWA, NotNAT B, PlP&P[port], WhThe*
Soviero, Diana *IntWWM 80, WhoOp 76*
Sovine, Red 1918- *CounME 74, -74A, EncFCWM 69, IlEncCM, RkOn 2A*
Sovine, Woodrow W 1918- *BiDAmM*
Sowande, Fela 1905- *Baker 78, ConAmC, NewGrD 80*
Sowards, George Albert 1888-1975 *WhScrn 77*
Sowards, Len 1893-1962 *NotNAT B, WhScrn 74, -77*
Sowell, Laven 1933- *IntWWM 77, -80*
Sowerby, Katherine Githa *WhThe*
Sowerby, Leo 1895-1968 *AmSCAP 66, -80, Baker 78, BiDAmM, BnBkM 80, CompSN[port], ConAmC, DcCom&M 79, DcCM, MusMk, NewGrD 80, OxMus*
Sowinski, John 1947- *CnOxB*
Sowinski, Wojciech 1803-1880 *Baker 78*
Sowinski, Wojciech 1805?-1880 *NewGrD 80*
Sowresby, John *NewGrD 80*
Soya, Carl-Erik 1896- *CnMD, CnThe, McGEWD[port], ModWD, OxThe, REnWD[port]*
Soye, Charles-Joseph-Balthazar *NewGrD 80*
Soyer, Charles-Joseph-Balthazar *NewGrD 80*
Soyer, David 1923- *IntWWM 77, -80*
Soyer, Mathieu *NewGrD 80*
Soyer, Roger 1939- *CmOp, NewGrD 80, WhoOp 76*
Soyez, Charles-Joseph-Balthazar *NewGrD 80*
Soyinka, Wole 1934- *CnThe, ConDr 73, -77, DrBlPA, EncWT, Ent, ModWD, REnWD[port]*
Soyka, Matej *NewGrD 80*
Spaak, Agnes *WhoHol A*
Spaak, Catherine 1945- *FilmEn, FilmgC, ForYSC, HalFC 80, MotPP, WhoHol A, WorEFlm*
Spaak, Charles 1903-1975 *DcFM, FilmEn, FilmgC, HalFC 80, OxFilm, WhoHol C, WorEFlm*
Space, Arthur *ForYSC, WhoHol A*
Spacek, Sissy *IntMPA 78, -79, -80, WhoHol A*
Spacek, Sissy 1949- *FilmEn*
Spacek, Sissy 1950- *HalFC 80, WhoHrs 80*
Spacemen, The *RkOn*
Spacey, John G 1895-1940 *WhScrn 74, -77, WhoHol B*
Spach, Barrett 1898- *BiDAmM*
Spada, Pietro Salvatore 1935- *WhoMus 72*
Spada, Vincenzo *NewGrD 80*
Spadario, Giovanni *NewGrD 80*
Spadaro, Odoardo 1894-1965 *WhScrn 77*
Spadavecchia, Antonio Emmanuilovich 1907- *Baker 78, IntWWM 80, NewGrD 80*
Spadavekkia, Antonio Emmanuilovich 1907- *IntWWM 77*
Spade, Marcello *Film 2*
Spaeth, Merrie 1949?- *WhoHol A*
Spaeth, Sigmund 1885-1965 *AmSCAP 66, -80, Baker 78, BiDAmM, CmpEPM, OxMus*
Spafford, Horatio Gates 1829-1888 *BiDAmM*
Spagna, Arcangelo 1631?-1720? *NewGrD 80*
Spagnoletti, Paolo 1768-1834 *NewGrD 80*
Spagnoletto, Il *NewGrD 80*
Spagnoli, Genaro *Film 2*
Spahr, Lani Ray 1947- *IntWWM 77, -80*
Spaic, Kosta 1923- *EncWT*
Spain, Elsie *WhThe*
Spain, Fay *ForYSC, MotPP, WhoHol A*
Spain, Nancy 1918-1964 *WhScrn 77*
Spain, Verna Gale *AmSCAP 80*
Spaink Abbink, Pierre Francois 1931- *IntWWM 77*
Spalding, Albert 1888-1953 *AmSCAP 66, -80, Baker 78, BiDAmM, BnBkM 80, ConAmC, MusSN[port]*
Spalding, Graydon 1911- *NotNAT*
Spalding, Walter Raymond 1865-1962 *Baker 78*
Spalenza, Hortensio *NewGrD 80*
Spalenza, Pietr'Antonio 1545?-1577? *NewGrD 80*
Spalla, Joseph Salvatore 1923- *IntMPA 77, -75, -76, -78, -79, -80*
Span, Norman *AmSCAP 66, -80*
Spandaro, Odoardo 1894-1965 *WhScrn 74*
Spange, Svend Aage 1920- *IntWWM 77, -80*
Spangenberg *NewGrD 80*
Spangenberg, Cyriac 1528-1604 *NewGrD 80*
Spangenberg, Heinrich 1861-1925 *Baker 78*
Spangenberg, Johann 1484-1550 *NewGrD 80*
Spangenberg, Wolfhart *NewGrD 80*
Spangler *NewGrD 80*
Spangler, Dale 1919- *AmSCAP 80*
Spangler, Ignaz 1757-1811 *NewGrD 80*
Spangler, Johann Georg 1752-1802 *NewGrD 80*
Spangler, Johann Michael 1721?-1794 *NewGrD 80*
Spangler, Maria Magdalena 1750-1794 *NewGrD 80*
Spani, Hina 1896-1969 *CmOp*
Spaniels, The *RkOn*
Spanier, Francis 1906-1966 *BiDAmM*
Spanier, Francis Joseph 1906-1967 *EncJzS 70, MusMk, NewGrD 80*
Spanier, Herbert Anthony Charles 1928- *EncJzS 70*
Spanier, Herbie 1928- *EncJzS 70*
Spanier, Muggsy d1966 *BgBands 74[port]*
Spanier, Muggsy 1903-1967 *WhScrn 74, -77, WhoHol B*
Spanier, Muggsy 1906-1967 *CmpEPM, EncJzS 70, IlEncJ, NewGrD 80, WhoJazz 72*
Spanke, Hans 1884-1944 *NewGrD 80*
Spanky And Our Gang *BiDAmM, RkOn 2[port]*
Spann, Lucille 1938- *BluesWW[port]*
Spann, Meno *PupTheA*
Spann, Otis 1930-1970 *BluesWW[port], EncJzS 70*
Spann, Otis 1931- *BiDAmM*
Spannheimer, Franz Erasmus 1946- *IntWWM 77, -80*
Spano, Donato Antonio 1585?-1609? *NewGrD 80*
Spanoghe, Jean Justin 1945- *IntWWM 77, -80*
Spanon, Alonso *NewGrD 80*
Spanuth, August 1857-1920 *Baker 78*
Sparacciari, Giovanni Giorgio d1630? *NewGrD 80*
Sparacino, Angelo 1914- *AmSCAP 66, -80*
Sparemblek, Milko 1928- *CnOxB, DancEn 78*
Sparer, Paul *NotNAT, WhoHol A, WhoThe 77*
Sparger, Celia d1973 *CnOxB*
Sparger, Rex *NewYTET*
Spargo, Tony 1897-1969 *AmSCAP 80, CmpEPM, EncJzS 70, NewOrJ[port], WhoJazz 72*
Spark, Muriel 1918- *HalFC 80*
Spark, William 1823-1897 *Baker 78, NewGrD 80, OxMus*
Sparkletones, The *RkOn*
Sparks *ConMuA 80A, IlEncR*
Sparks, Edgar H 1908- *NewGrD 80*
Sparks, Felton 1931- *AmSCAP 80*
Sparks, Jeff 1905- *AmSCAP 80*
Sparks, Joseph M 1856- *WhoStg 1906, -1908*
Sparks, Judith Rosemary *CreCan 2*
Sparks, Martha Lee *Film 2*

Sparks, Ned d1957 MotPP, NotNAT B, WhoHol B
Sparks, Ned 1883-1957 FilmEn, Film 1, -2, FilmgC, HalFC 80, MovMk, TwYS, WhScrn 74, -77
Sparks, Ned 1884-1957 ForYSC, HolCA[port], Vers A[port]
Sparks, Randy 1933- AmSCAP 66, -80, BiDAmM, EncFCWM 69, ForYSC, WhoHol A
Sparks, Robert IntMPA 77, -75, -76, -78, -79, -80
Sparkuhl, Theodor 1894-1945 FilmEn, HalFC 80, WorEFlm
Sparkuhl, Theodore 1894- FilmgC
Sparnaay, Harry Willem 1944- Baker 78, IntWWM 80
Sparrow, Andrew Nigel 1949- IntWWM 80
Sparrow, Bili 1954- AmSCAP 80
Sparrow, Harry PupTheA
Sparry, Franz 1715-1767 NewGrD 80
Sparv, Camilla 1943- FilmgC, ForYSC, HalFC 80, WhoHol A
Spasov, Ivan 1934- Baker 78
Spataro, Giovanni 1458?-1541 NewGrD 80
Spath, Franz Jakob 1714-1786 NewGrD 80
Spatz, Christa Mertins CreCan 2
Spaulding, George 1881-1959 WhScrn 74, -77, WhoHol B
Spaulding, Jack AmSCAP 80
Spaulding, James Ralph 1937- AmSCAP 80, EncJzS 70
Spaulding, Jimmy 1937- EncJzS 70
Spaulding, Nellie Parker Film 2
Spazier, Johann Gottlieb Carl 1761-1805 Baker 78
Spazier, Johann Gottlieb Karl 1761-1805 NewGrD 80
Speaight, George DcPup[port]
Speaight, Joseph 1868-1947 Baker 78
Speaight, Robert 1904- PlP&P, WhoThe 72, -77
Speakman, W J 1903- IntMPA 77, -75, -76
Speaks, Oley 1874-1948 AmSCAP 66, -80, Baker 78, BiDAmM, CmpEPM, ConAmC, NotNAT B, OxMus, PopAmC[port]
Spear, Anne AmSCAP 80
Spear, Harry 1921-1969 Film 2, TwYS, WhScrn 74, -77, WhoHol B
Spear, Jack 1928- AmSCAP 66, -80
Spear, Lee Seaman 1945- IntWWM 77
Spear, Sammy 1910-1975 WhScrn 77
Spear, Thomas Truman 1803-1882 BiDAmM
Speare, Patricia Follett 1923- IntWWM 77, -80
Spearing, Robert Michael 1950- IntWWM 80
Spearman, Kenneth NewGrD 80
Spearman, Rawn W 1923- DrBlPA
Spears, A B d1965 NewOrJ
Spears, Billy Jo IlEncCM[port]
Spears, Jared Tozier 1936- AmSCAP 80, ConAmC, IntWWM 77, -80
Spech, Janos 1767?-1836 NewGrD 80
Specht, Donald David 1929- AmSCAP 80
Specht, Paul 1895?-1954 BgBands 74, CmpEPM
Specht, Richard 1870-1932 Baker 78, NewGrD 80
Specht, Robert John, Jr. 1937- IntWWM 77, -80
Spechtshart, Hugo 1285?-1360? NewGrD 80
Speckled Red BluesWW[port]
Specktor, Frederick 1933- IntMPA 77, -76, -78, -79, -80
Spector, Edward BiE&WWA
Spector, Frederick 1933- IntMPA 75
Spector, Irwin 1916- ConAmC, IntWWM 77, -80
Spector, Joel BiE&WWA
Spector, Martin ConMuA 80B
Spector, Phil ConMuA 80A, -80B
Spector, Phil 1940- IlEncR[port], MusMk
Spector, Phil 1941- BiDAmM
Spedding, Chris 1943- IlEncR
Spedding, Frank Donald 1929- IntWWM 77, -80, WhoMus 72
Spedding, Rosemary 1934- WhoMus 72
Spee VonLangenfeld, Friedrich 1591-1635 NewGrD 80
Speechley, Billy 1911- WhThe
Speed, Carol DrBlPA, WhoHol A
Speer, Daniel 1636-1707 Baker 78, NewGrD 80
Speer, George Thomas 1891-1966 BiDAmM
Speer, Klaus 1911- IntWWM 77, -80
Speer, Lena Brock d1967 BiDAmM
Spehr, Johann Peter 1770?-1860? NewGrD 80
Speidel, Wilhelm 1826-1899 Baker 78
Speier, Wilhelm NewGrD 80
Speight, John Anthony 1945- IntWWM 77, -80
Speight, Johnny 1921- ConDr 73, -77
Speight, Johnny 1922- McGEWD
Speirs, John V 1916- AmSCAP 80
Speiser, Elisabeth 1940- IntWWM 77, -80
Speizman, Morris 1905- AmSCAP 66, -80
Spelda, Antonin 1904- IntWWM 77, -80
Spell, George DrBlPA, WhoHol A
Spell, Wanda WhoHol A
Speller, Frank N ConAmC
Speller, Robert WhoHol A
Spelling, Aaron IntMPA 77, -76, -78, -79, -80, NewYTET, WhoHol A
Spellman, Leora 1891-1945 WhScrn 74, -77, WhoHol B
Spelman, Timothy Mather 1891-1970 Baker 78, BiDAmM, ConAmC, NewGrD 80
Spelvin, George 1886?- BiE&WWA, NotNAT
Spelvin, George S Film 2
Spelvin, Georgina 1937- WhoHol A, WhoHrs 80
Spence, Edward F 1860-1932 NotNAT B, WhThe
Spence, Eulalie 1894- BlkAmP, DrBlPA, MorBAP
Spence, Joyce Ann 1945- AmSCAP 80
Spence, Keith Graham Frederick 1930- WhoMus 72
Spence, Lew 1920- AmSCAP 66, -80
Spence, Ralph 1889-1949 NotNAT B, WhScrn 74, -77, WhoHol B
Spencer, Allen Hervey 1870-1950 Baker 78, BiDAmM
Spencer, Bud HalFC 80, WhoHol A
Spencer, Christine DrBlPA
Spencer, Colin 1933- ConDr 73, -77, EncWT
Spencer, Dorothy 1909- HalFC 80, WomWMM
Spencer, Douglas 1910-1960 WhScrn 74, -77, WhoHol B
Spencer, Edmund 1552?-1599 DcPup
Spencer, Eleanor 1890- BiDAmM
Spencer, Emile-Alexis-Xavier 1859-1921 Baker 78
Spencer, Fleta Jan Brown 1883-1938 AmSCAP 66, -80
Spencer, Frank Woolley Sim 1911- WhoMus 72
Spencer, Fred d1952 WhScrn 74, -77
Spencer, Gabriel d1598 NotNAT B, OxThe
Spencer, George Soule Film 1
Spencer, Glenn J 1910-1970 AmSCAP 66, -80
Spencer, Harold A 1936- AmSCAP 80
Spencer, Helen 1903- WhThe
Spencer, Helen Walker 1936- IntWWM 80
Spencer, Herbert 1878-1944 AmSCAP 66, -80
Spencer, James Film 2
Spencer, James Houston 1895-1967 AmSCAP 66, -80, ConAmC
Spencer, Jessica 1919- WhThe
Spencer, Joan 1921- IntWWM 77, -80, WhoMus 72
Spencer, Joan Mary 1922- IntWWM 77, -80
Spencer, John OxThe
Spencer, Judy AmSCAP 80
Spencer, Kenneth 1913-1964 DrBlPA, HalFC 80, NotNAT B, WhScrn 74, -77, WhoHol B
Spencer, Kevin Bion 1955- AmSCAP 80
Spencer, Lucy 1884- WhoStg 1906, -1908
Spencer, Mabel WhoStg 1908
Spencer, Marguerita 1892- IntWWM 77
Spencer, Marian 1905- WhoHol A, WhoThe 72, -77
Spencer, Mary Ann WomWMM B
Spencer, Norman Film 2, IntMPA 77, -75, -76, -78
Spencer, O'Neill 1909-1944 CmpEPM, WhoJazz 72
Spencer, Otis 1890-1958 AmSCAP 66
Spencer, Palmer Florence Margaret 1900- WhoMus 72
Spencer, Philipp Jakob 1635-1705 NewGrD 80
Spencer, Robert Film 2
Spencer, Robert 1932- IntWWM 77, -80, WhoMus 72
Spencer, Robert E 1902-1946 AmSCAP 66, -80
Spencer, Robert Lamar 1938- IntWWM 77, -80
Spencer, Robert Nelson 1877- BiDAmM
Spencer, S Reid 1872-1945 Baker 78, ConAmC
Spencer, T Guy, Jr. 1933- IntMPA 77, -75, -76, -78, -79, -80
Spencer, Terry 1895-1954 WhScrn 74, -77
Spencer, Tim ConMuA 80B
Spencer, Tim 1908- BiDAmM, EncFCWM 69
Spencer, Tim 1909-1974 WhScrn 77, WhoHol B
Spencer, Vernon 1875-1949 Baker 78, ConAmC
Spencer, Willard 1852-1933 NotNAT B
Spencer, William O'Neill 1909-1944 BiDAmM
Spencer, Williametta 1932- ConAmC, IntWWM 77, -80
Spencer Davis Group, The IlEncR[port]
Spencer Palmer, Florence Margaret 1900- IntWWM 77
Spender, Stephen 1909- CnMD, ModWD
Spendiarov, Alexander 1871-1928 Baker 78
Spendiaryan, Alexander Afanasii 1871-1928 NewGrD 80
Spener, Robert 1932- NewGrD 80
Spengel, Julius Heinrich 1853-1936 Baker 78
Spengler, Pierre 1947- IntMPA 80
Spenser, Jeremy 1937- FilmgC, HalFC 80, IntMPA 77, -75, -76, -78, -79, -80, WhoHol A
Spenser, Willard 1852-1933 BiDAmM
Spensley, Philip BlkAmP
Speranza, Alessandro 1728?-1797 NewGrD 80
Speranza, Giovanni Antonio 1811-1850 NewGrD 80
Sperati, Carleton 1918- IntWWM 77, -80
Speratus, Paul 1484-1551 NewGrD 80
Sperger, Johannes 1750-1812 NewGrD 80
Sperl, Gary Robert 1950- IntWWM 77, -80
Sperling, Hazel Film 2
Sperling, Jack 1922- CmpEPM
Sperling, Johann Peter Gabriel 1671-1720 NewGrD 80
Sperling, Karen WhoHol A, WomWMM, -B
Sperling, Milton 1912- FilmEn, FilmgC, HalFC 80, IntMPA 77, -75, -76, -78, -79, -80, WorEFlm
Spero, Bette 1944- ConAmTC
Speroni, Sperone 1500-1588 McGEWD, OxThe
Sperontes 1705-1750 Baker 78, NewGrD 80
Sperr, Martin 1944- CroCD, EncWT, Ent
Sperry, Don Ray 1947- CpmDNM 72, -73, ConAmC
Spervogel NewGrD 80, -80
Spervogel, Der Junge NewGrD 80
Spervogel, Alterer NewGrD 80
Spessivtseva, Olga Alexandrovna 1895- CnOxB
Spessivtzeva, Olga 1895- DancEn 78[port]
Speth, Johannes 1664-1720? NewGrD 80
Spetrino, Francesco 1857-1948 NewGrD 80
Speuy, Henderick 1575?-1625 NewGrD 80
Speuy, Hendrick 1575?-1625 NewGrD 80
Speuy, Hendrik 1575?-1625 NewGrD 80
Spewack, Bella 1899- BiDAmM, BiE&WWA, ConDr 73, -77D, EncMT, IntMPA 77, -75, -76, -78, -79, -80, McGEWD[port], ModWD, NewCBMT, NotNAT, WhThe, WomWMM
Spewack, Sam 1899-1971 EncMT, FilmgC, HalFC 80
Spewack, Samuel 1899-1971 BiDAmM, BiE&WWA, CnMD, FilmEn, McGEWD[port], ModWD, NewCBMT, NotNAT B, WhThe
Speyer, Eduard NewGrD 80
Speyer, Eve Film 2
Speyer, Wilhelm 1790-1878 Baker 78, NewGrD 80
Speziale, Marie 1942- IntWWM 77, -80
Spezzaferri, Laszlo Elio 1912- WhoMus 72
Spheeris, Penelope WomWMM B
Spheeris, Penny WomWMM A
Spialek, Hans 1894- AmSCAP 66, -80, Baker 78, ConAmC
Spicer, Earle WhoMus 72
Spicer, Harold William 1888- WhoMus 72

Spicer, Joanna 1907- *IntMPA 75, -76*
Spicer, L Randall 1914- *IntWWM 77*
Spicer, Paul Cridland 1952- *IntWWM 77, -80*
Spicker, Max 1858-1912 *Baker 78, BiDAmM*
Spickett, Ronald J 1926- *CreCan 1*
Spickol, Max 1913- *AmSCAP 66, -80*
Spider Sam *BluesWW[port]*
Spiders, The *RkOn*
Spiegel, Larry 1938- *IntMPA 77, -75, -76, -78, -79, -80*
Spiegel, Laurie 1945- *AmSCAP 80, Baker 78, ConAmC, IntWWM 77, -80*
Spiegel, Olga *WomWMM B*
Spiegel, Sam 1901- *FilmgC, HalFC 80*
Spiegel, Sam 1903- *FilmEn, IntMPA 77, -75, -76, -78, -79, -80*
Spiegel, Sam 1904- *BiDFilm, -81, OxFilm, WorEFlm*
Spiegel, Ted *IntMPA 77, -75, -76, -78, -79, -80*
Spiegelberg, Christian d1732 *OxThe*
Spiegelman, Joel 1933- *AmSCAP 80, Baker 78, CpmDNM 78, ConAmC, DcCM*
Spiegl, Fritz 1926- *IntWWM 77, -80, WhoMus 72*
Spiegler, Matthias 1595?-1631? *NewGrD 80*
Spielberg, David *WhoHol A*
Spielberg, Steven 1946- *FilmgC, HalFC 80*
Spielberg, Steven 1947- *BiDFilm 81, FilmEn, IntMPA 77, -75, -76, -78, -79, -80*
Spielberg, Steven 1948- *WhoHrs 80*
Spielman, Fred *AmSCAP 66*
Spielman, Fritz *AmSCAP 80, IntWWM 77*
Spielter, Hermann 1860-1925 *Baker 78*
Spier, Dorothy 1938- *AmSCAP 80*
Spier, Harry R 1888-1952 *AmSCAP 66, -80, ConAmC*
Spier, Larry 1901-1956 *AmSCAP 66, -80*
Spier, William *IntMPA 77, -75, -76, -78, -79, -80*
Spiering, Theodor 1871-1925 *BiDAmM*
Spiering, Theodore 1871-1925 *Baker 78*
Spies, Claudio 1925- *AmSCAP 66, -80, ConAmC, DcCM, IntWWM 77, -80, NewGrD 80*
Spies, Daisy 1905- *CnOxB*
Spies, Hermine 1857-1893 *Baker 78*
Spies, Leo 1899-1965 *NewGrD 80*
Spiess, Lincoln Bunce 1913- *NewGrD 80*
Spiess, Ludovic 1938- *NewGrD 80, WhoOp 76*
Spiess, Matthaus 1683-1761 *NewGrD 80*
Spiess, Meinrad 1683-1761 *Baker 78, NewGrD 80*
Spiessens, Godelieve Jozefina Adolf 1932- *IntWWM 77*
Spieth, Noelle 1950- *IntWWM 80*
Spigelgass, Leonard 1908- *BiE&WWA, IntMPA 77, -76, -78, -79, -80, NotNAT, WhoThe 72, -77*
Spigener, Tommy Ray 1931- *IntWWM 77*
Spighi, Bartolomeo d1641? *NewGrD 80*
Spiker, Ray 1902-1964 *NotNAT B, WhScrn 74, -77, WhoHol B*
Spikes, Benjamin 1888- *AmSCAP 66, -80*
Spikes, John C 1882-1955 *AmSCAP 66, -80*
Spikings, Barry 1939- *IntMPA 78, -79, -80*
Spilka, Frantisek 1887-1960 *Baker 78*
Spillane, Mickey 1918- *FilmgC, HalFC 80, WhoHol A*
Spillard, William J 1888- *AmSCAP 66*
Spiller, Emily d1941 *NotNAT B*
Spiller, Isabele Taliaferro 1888-1974 *BlkWAB[port]*
Spiller, Ljerko 1908- *IntWWM 77, -80*
Spilman, Jonathan E 1812-1896 *BiDAmM*
Spils, Mai *WomWMM*
Spina, Carl Anton *NewGrD 80*
Spina, Harold 1906- *AmSCAP 66, -80, CmpEPM*
Spinacino, Francesco *NewGrD 80*
Spinazzari, Alessandro *NewGrD 80*
Spindel, Jerry 1944- *NatPD[port]*
Spindle, Louise Cooper *AmSCAP 66, ConAmC*
Spindler, Fritz 1817-1905 *Baker 78*
Spindler, Stanislaus 1763-1819 *NewGrD 80*
Spinelli, Andree 1891- *WhThe*
Spinelli, Nicola 1865-1909 *Baker 78, NewGrD 80*
Spinelli, Salvatore Vincent 1896-1978 *AmSCAP 80*
Spinetti, Victor *WhoHol A*
Spinetti, Victor 1932- *FilmgC, HalFC 80*
Spinetti, Victor 1933- *WhoThe 72, -77*
Spingler, Harry 1890-1953 *WhScrn 74, -77, WhoHol B*
Spink, Ian 1932- *IntWWM 77, -80, NewGrD 80, WhoMus 72*
Spinks, Donald 1921- *IntWWM 77*
Spinks, Garland 1908- *AmSCAP 66*
Spinner, Leopold 1906- *NewGrD 80*
Spinners, The *ConMuA 80A, RkOn*
Spinney, Bradley 1915- *IntWWM 77, -80*
Spino, Pasquale J 1942- *ConAmC*
Spinosa, Tom 1922- *AmSCAP 66, -80*
Spinozza, David 1949- *EncJzS 70*
Spira, Camilla 1906- *FilmAG WE, Film 2*
Spira, Francoise d1965 *WhScrn 74, -77*
Spira, Phyllis 1943- *CnOxB*
Spiral Starecase *RkOn 2A*
Spire, Charles A 1929- *AmSCAP 80*
Spirea, Andrei 1932- *IntWWM 77, -80*
Spires, Arthur 1912- *BluesWW[port]*
Spires, John B *IntMPA 77, -75, -76, -78, -79, -80*
Spiridion 1615-1685 *NewGrD 80*
Spirit *BiDAmM, ConMuA 80A, IlEncR, RkOn 2[port]*
Spirito Da Reggio *NewGrD 80*
Spiro, Demon *AmSCAP 80*
Spisak, Michal 1914-1965 *Baker 78, NewGrD 80*
Spitalny, H Leopold 1887- *AmSCAP 66*
Spitalny, Maurice 1893- *AmSCAP 66, -80*
Spitalny, Phil *BgBands 74[port], What 1[port]*
Spitalny, Phil 1889-1970 *Baker 78*
Spitalny, Phil 1890-1970 *AmSCAP 66, -80, BiDAmM, CmpEPM, WhScrn 74, -77, WhoHol B*
Spitlera, Joseph P, Jr. 1938?- *NewOrJ*
Spitta, Friedrich 1852-1924 *Baker 78*
Spitta, Julius August Philipp 1841-1894 *NewGrD 80*
Spitta, Julius Auguste Philipp 1841-1894 *OxMus*
Spitta, Philipp 1841-1894 *Baker 78, BnBkM 80*
Spitz, Henry 1905- *IntMPA 77, -75, -76, -78, -79, -80*
Spitz, Willy 1936- *IntWWM 77, -80*
Spitzenberger, Herbert 1927- *IntWWM 77, -80*
Spitzer, Cordelia *AmSCAP 80*
Spitzer, Marian *Film 2, IntMPA 77, -75, -76, -78, -79, -80*
Spitzer, Murray *NatPD[port]*
Spitzmueller, Alexander 1894-1962 *Baker 78*
Spitzmuller, Alexander, Freiherr Von 1894-1962 *NewGrD 80*
Spivack, Larry S 1954- *AmSCAP 80*
Spivacke, Harold 1904-1977 *Baker 78, NewGrD 80*
Spivak, Alice *WhoHol A*
Spivak, Charlie *BgBands 74[port]*
Spivak, Charlie 1905?- *WhoJazz 72*
Spivak, Charlie 1906- *CmpEPM*
Spivak, Charlie 1907- *Conv 2[port]*
Spivak, Joseph 1948- *ConAmC*
Spivak, Lawrence E *IntMPA 77, -75, -76, -78, -79, -80*
Spivakosky, Tossy 1907- *IntWWM 77, -80*
Spivakovsky, Tossy 1907- *Baker 78*
Spivakowsky, Tossy 1907- *BiDAmM*
Spivery, William 1930- *AmSCAP 66*
Spivey, Addie 1910-1943 *BluesWW[port]*
Spivey, Beverly F 1950- *IntWWM 77*
Spivey, Elton Island 1900-1971 *BluesWW*
Spivey, Victoria 1910?- *CmpEPM, Film 2, WhoJazz 72*
Spivey, Victoria Regina 1906-1976 *BluesWW[port]*
Spivy 1907-1971 *WhScrn 74, WhoHol B*
Spivy, Madame 1907-1971 *WhScrn 77*
Spizizen, Louise 1928- *ConAmC*
Splane, Elza K 1905-1968 *WhScrn 74, -77*
Splettstober, Erwin *Film 2*
Spodick, Robert C 1919- *IntMPA 77, -75, -76, -78, -79, -80*
Spoerl, Dorothy T *PupTheA*
Spoerli, Heinz 1941- *CnOxB*
Spofford, Charles M 1902- *BiE&WWA*
Spofford, Grace Harriet *WhoMus 72*
Spofforth, Reginald 1768?-1827 *NewGrD 80*
Spofforth, Reginald 1770-1827 *OxMus*
Spohn, Charles L 1926- *IntWWM 77*
Spohr, Arnold *DancEn 78*
Spohr, Arnold 1920?- *CnOxB, CreCan 2*
Spohr, Louis 1784-1859 *BnBkM 80, CmOp, CmpBCM, GrComp[port], MusMk, NewGrD 80[port], OxMus*
Spohr, Ludewig 1784-1859 *NewGrD 80[port]*
Spohr, Ludwig 1784-1859 *Baker 78, DcCom 77, NewEOp 71, NewGrD 80[port]*
Spohrer, Thomas *NewGrD 80*
Spoliansky, Mischa 1898- *FilmgC, HalFC 80, OxFilm*
Spolidoro, Ascanio *PupTheA*
Spoljaric, Vlado 1926- *IntWWM 77, -80*
Spong, Hilda 1875-1955 *NotNAT B, WhScrn 74, -77, WhThe*
Spong, Hilda 1875-1966 *WhoHol B, WhoStg 1906, -1908*
Spong, Jon Curtis 1933- *ConAmC, IntWWM 77, -80*
Spong, W B d1929 *NotNAT B*
Sponga, Francesco *NewGrD 80*
Sponga, Gabriel *NewGrD 80*
Spongia, Francesco *NewGrD 80*
Sponsel, Johann Ulrich 1721?-1788 *NewGrD 80*
Spontaneous Music Ensemble *IlEncJ*
Spontini, Gaspare 1774-1851 *Baker 78, NewGrD 80[port]*
Spontini, Gasparo 1774-1851 *BnBkM 80, CmOp, DcCom 77, DcCom&M 79, GrComp[port], MusMk, NewEOp 71, OxMus*
Spontone, Alessandro 1549?-1590? *NewGrD 80*
Spontone, Bartolomeo 1530?-1592? *NewGrD 80*
Spontoni, Ludovico 1555?-1609? *NewGrD 80*
Sponza, Francesco *NewGrD 80*
Sponza, Gabriel *NewGrD 80*
Spooky Tooth *ConMuA 80A, IlEncR*
Spoon *BluesWW[port]*
Spooner, Cecil *Film 1, WhThe*
Spooner, Edna May d1953 *NotNAT B, WhThe, WhoHol B*
Spooner, William *PupTheA*
Spoorenberg, Erna 1926- *NewGrD 80*
Sporck, Count Franz Anton 1662-1738 *NewGrD 80*
Sporck, Georges 1870-1943 *Baker 78*
Sporer, Thomas 1490?-1534 *NewGrD 80*
Sporrer, Thomas 1490?-1534 *NewGrD 80*
Sport *WhScrn 77*
Sportonio, Marc'Antonio 1631?-1680? *NewGrD 80*
Spottiswoode, Raymond 1913-1970 *FilmEn, OxFilm*
Spotts, Roger Hamilton 1928- *AmSCAP 80*
Spottswood, James 1882-1940 *Film 2, NotNAT B, WhScrn 74, -77, WhoHol B*
Spradlin, G D 1925?- *ForYSC*
Spradling, G D *WhoHol A*
Sprague, Carl T 1895- *IlEncCM[port]*
Sprague, William Hackman, Jr. 1945- *IntWWM 77, -80*
Spranger, Barry 1719-1777 *Ent*
Spratlan, Lewis 1940- *Baker 78, ConAmC*
Spratley, Tom *WhoHol A*
Spratt, Edward Robert 1926- *IntWWM 77, -80*
Spratt, Geoffrey Kenneth 1950- *IntWWM 80*
Spratt, Jack *ConAmC A*
Spratt, John F 1914- *IntWWM 77*
Sprayberry, Robert Jones 1952- *ConAmC*
Sprecher, Gunther William 1924- *AmSCAP 80*
Sprenger, Eugen 1882-1953 *NewGrD 80*
Sprenkle, Elam R 1948- *IntWWM 77*
Sprigge, Elizabeth 1900- *BiE&WWA, NotNAT*
Spriggs, Elizabeth 1929- *CnThe, WhoHol A, WhoThe 77*
Spring, Glenn E, Jr. 1939- *ConAmC*
Spring, Helen *WhoHol A*
Spring, Howard 1889-1965 *HalFC 80*
Spring, Morton A *IntMPA 75, -76*
Spring, Samuel *IntMPA 75, -76*
Spring, Sylvia *WomWMM, -B*
Springbett, Lynn Berta *CreCan 2*

Springer, A L 1911- *AmSCAP 80*
Springer, Gary *WhoHol A*
Springer, Hermann 1872-1945 *Baker 78*
Springer, John *IntMPA 75, -76*
Springer, Joseph R 1897- *IntMPA 77, -75, -76, -78, -79*
Springer, Lorene H 1927- *IntWWM 77*
Springer, Max 1877-1954 *Baker 78*
Springer, Philip 1926- *AmSCAP 66, -80*
Springett, Freddie 1915- *WhThe*
Springfield, Dusty 1939- *BiDAmM, ConMuA 80A, IlEncR[port], RkOn 2[port]*
Springfield, Rick 1949- *RkOn 2[port]*
Springfields, The *RkOn*
Springford, Norma Linton *CreCan 1*
Springford, Ruth *CreCan 1*
Springsteen, Bruce 1949- *AmSCAP 80, ConMuA 80A[port], IlEncR[port], RkOn 2[port]*
Springsteen, R G 1904- *FilmEn, FilmgC, HalFC 80, IntMPA 77, -75, -76, -78, -79, -80, WorEFlm*
Springuel, France-Virgine 1956- *IntWWM 77, -80*
Sproles, Victor 1927- *EncJzS 70*
Sprongl, Norbert 1892- *IntWWM 77, -80, WhoMus 72*
Spronk, Gonnie 1946- *IntWWM 77*
Spross, Charles Gilbert 1874-1961 *Baker 78*
Spross, Charles Gilbert 1874-1962 *AmSCAP 66, -80, BiDAmM, ConAmC*
Sprott, Horace 1890?- *BluesWW[port]*
Sprotte, Bert 1871-1949 *Film 2, WhScrn 77*
Sproule, Ruth 1910-1968 *WhScrn 77*
Sprout, John Wells, Jr. 1952- *AmSCAP 80*
Sprout, Sarah Bigelow 1936- *IntWWM 77*
Sprung, David R 1931- *ConAmC*
Spry, Constance Elsie 1914- *WhoMus 72*
Spry, Henry d1904 *NotNAT B*
Spry, Walter 1868-1953 *Baker 78*
Spurgeon, Charles Haddon 1834-1892 *OxMus*
Spurgeon, Jack 1918- *DancEn 78*
Spurling, John 1936- *ConDr 73, -77*
Spurrell, Elizabeth Joyce 1932- *IntWWM 80*
Squair, Jean 1925- *IntWWM 80*
Squarcialupi, Antonio 1416-1480 *Baker 78, NewGrD 80*
Squarzina, Luigi 1922- *CnMD, EncWT, McGEWD[port], WhoOp 76*
Squibb, David 1935- *WhoMus 72*
Squibb, June 1935- *BiE&WWA, NotNAT*
Squire, Sir John Collings 1884-1958 *ModWD*
Squire, Katherine 1903- *BiE&WWA, NotNAT, WhoHol A, WhoThe 72, -77*
Squire, Ronald 1886-1958 *FilmgC, ForYSC, HalFC 80, IlWWBF, NotNAT B, WhScrn 74, -77, WhThe, WhoHol B*
Squire, Russel Nelson 1908- *IntWWM 77, -80*
Squire, W H 1871-1963 *NewGrD 80*
Squire, William 1920- *BiE&WWA, NotNAT, PlP&P[port], WhoHol A, WhoThe 72, -77*
Squire, William Barclay 1855-1927 *Baker 78, NewGrD 80, OxMus*
Squire, William Henry 1871-1963 *Baker 78, OxMus*
Squires, Emily *WomWMM B*
Squires, Harry D 1897-1961 *AmSCAP 66*
Squires, Harry D 1898-1960 *AmSCAP 80*
Squires, Ruth *PupTheA*
Squires, Shelagh Marion *IntWWM 77, -80*
Sramek, Vladimir 1923- *Baker 78*
Srb, Josef 1836-1904 *NewGrD 80*
Srb-Debrnov, Josef 1836-1904 *NewGrD 80*
Srebotnjak, Alojz 1931- *Baker 78, DcCM, IntWWM 77, NewGrD 80*
Srebotnjak, Alonjz 1931- *IntWWM 80*
Sreenivos, Prathivadi Bhayankaram 1930- *IntWWM 77*
Sri Chinmoy 1931- *IntWWM 77, -80*
Srinivasan, Manamadurai Balakrishnan 1925- *IntWWM 77*
Sritrange, Wandee 1950-1975 *WhScrn 77*
Srnka, Jiri 1907- *Baker 78, IntWWM 77, -80, NewGrD 80*
Srom, Karel 1904- *Baker 78, IntWWM 77, -80, NewGrD 80*
Srubar, Teodor 1917- *WhoOp 76*
St. Louis Jimmy *BluesWW[port]*
St. Louis Mac *BluesWW[port]*
Staar, Rene 1951- *IntWWM 80*
Staats, Leo 1877-1952 *CnOxB, DancEn 78*
Stabile, Annibale 1535?-1595 *NewGrD 80*
Stabile, Dick 1909- *BgBands 74[port], CmpEPM*
Stabile, James 1937- *AmSCAP 80, ConAmC*
Stabile, Mariano 1888-1968 *Baker 78, CmOp, NewEOp 71, NewGrD 80[port]*
Stabile, Pompeo *NewGrD 80*
Stabinger, Mathias 1750?-1815? *NewGrD 80*
Stabinger, Mattia 1750?-1815? *NewGrD 80*
Stabingher, Mathias 1750?-1815? *NewGrD 80*
Stabingher, Mattia 1750?-1815? *NewGrD 80*
Stablein, Bruno 1895-1978 *Baker 78, IntWWM 77, -80, NewGrD 80*
Stabulas, Nicholas 1929-1973 *EncJzS 70*
Stabulas, Nick 1929-1973 *EncJzS 70*
Stach, Matthaus 1711-1787 *BiDAmM*
Stachowicz, Damian 1658-1699 *NewGrD 80*
Stachowski, Marek 1936- *Baker 78, IntWWM 77, -80, NewGrD 80*
Stack, Robert 1919- *BiDFilm, -81, FilmEn, FilmgC, ForYSC, HalFC 80[port], IntMPA 77, -75, -76, -78, -79, -80, MotPP, MovMk[port], WhoHol A, WorEFlm[port]*
Stack, William 1882- *WhThe*
Stackhouse, Houston 1910- *BluesWW[port]*
Stackridge *IlEncR*
Stacy, James *WhoHol A*
Stacy, Jess 1904- *BiDAmM, CmpEPM, EncJzS 70, IlEncJ, WhoJazz 72*
Stacy, Thomas 1938- *IntWWM 77, -80*
Stade, Frederica Von *MusSN[port], NewGrD 80*
Stade, Friedrich 1844-1928 *Baker 78*
Stade, Heinrich Bernhard 1816-1882 *Baker 78*
Stade, Wilhelm 1817-1902 *Baker 78*
Stadelmaier, Johann *NewGrD 80*
Stadelman, Egon P 1911- *ConAmTC*
Stadelmayer, Johann *NewGrD 80*
Stadelmeyer, Johann *NewGrD 80*
Staden, Adam *NewGrD 80*
Staden, Johann 1581-1634 *Baker 78, MusMk, NewGrD 80[port]*
Staden, Sigmund Gottlieb 1607-1655 *NewGrD 80[port]*
Staden, Sigmund Theophil 1607-1655 *NewGrD 80[port]*
Staden, Sigmund Theophilus 1607-1655 *Baker 78*
Stader, Maria *IntWWM 77, -80, WhoMus 72*
Stader, Maria 1911- *NewGrD 80*
Stader, Maria 1915- *MusSN[port]*
Stadlen, Lewis J 1947- *NotNAT, PlP&P A[port], WhoThe 77*
Stadlen, Peter 1910- *IntWWM 80, NewGrD 80*
Stadler, Anton 1753-1812 *Baker 78, BnBkM 80, NewGrD 80, OxMus*
Stadler, Heiner 1942- *EncJzS 70*
Stadler, Irmgard *WhoOp 76*
Stadler, Johann Wilhelm 1747-1819 *NewGrD 80*
Stadler, Maximilian 1748-1833 *Baker 78, NewGrD 80, OxMus*
Stadlmair, Johann 1575?-1648 *NewGrD 80*
Stadlmayr, Johann 1575?-1648 *NewGrD 80*
Stadtfeld, Alexander 1826-1853 *NewGrD 80*
Stadtfeld, Alexandre 1826-1853 *Baker 78*
Staedtler, R Darrell 1940- *AmSCAP 80*
Staehelin, Marguerite Martha 1916- *IntWWM 77, -80*
Staehelin, Martin 1937- *IntWWM 77, -80, NewGrD 80*
Staempfli, Edward 1908- *Baker 78, CpmDNM 80, DcCM, NewGrD 80*
Staempfli, Jakob 1934- *IntWWM 77, -80*
Staern, Gunnar 1922- *WhoMus 72*
Staern, Gunner Oscar 1922- *IntWWM 77, -80*
Staes, Ferdinand 1748-1809 *NewGrD 80*
Staff, Charles *ConAmTC*
Staff, Frank 1918-1971 *CnOxB, DancEn 78*
Staff, John Gavin 1933- *IntWWM 80, WhoMus 72*
Staff, May *PlP&P*
Staffani, Agostino *NewGrD 80*
Stafford, Barbara *WomWMM B*
Stafford, Brendan J *IntMPA 77, -75, -76, -78, -79, -80*
Stafford, Frederick 1928- *FilmgC, HalFC 80, WhoHol A*
Stafford, George 1898?-1936 *WhoJazz 72*
Stafford, Hanley 1898-1968 *WhScrn 74, -77, WhoHol B*
Stafford, Hanley 1899-1968 *ForYSC*
Stafford, James E 1933- *ConAmC*
Stafford, James W *AmSCAP 80*
Stafford, Jim 1944- *RkOn 2[port]*
Stafford, Jo *AmPS A, -B*
Stafford, Jo 1918- *BiDAmM*
Stafford, Jo 1920- *CmpEPM, RkOn[port]*
Stafford, John Michael 1928- *IntWWM 80*
Stafford, Judith Wolper 1950- *IntWWM 80*
Stafford, Mary 1895?-1938? *BluesWW[port]*
Stafford, Terry *RkOn 2[port]*
Stafford, Tim *WhoHol A*
Stafford-Clark, Max 1941- *WhoThe 72, -77*
Stagg, Alan 1952- *AmSCAP 80*
Stagg, Charles d1735 *NotNAT B, OxThe, PlP&P*
Stagg, Mary *OxThe*
Staggins, Nicholas d1700 *NewGrD 80*
Staggs, Jack E 1920- *IntMPA 79, -80*
Stagnelius, Erik Johann 1793-1823 *OxThe*
Stagno, Roberto 1840-1897 *Baker 78*
Stahel, Johann *NewGrD 80*
Stahl, Al *IntMPA 77, -75, -76, -78, -79, -80*
Stahl, David 1949- *EncJzS 70, IntWWM 80*
Stahl, Grace *PupTheA*
Stahl, Herbert M 1914- *BiE&WWA, NotNAT*
Stahl, Howard M 1948- *ConAmC*
Stahl, Jockel 1911-1957 *CnOxB*
Stahl, Johann *NewGrD 80*
Stahl, John M 1886-1950 *BiDFilm, -81, CmMov, DcFM, FilmEn, FilmgC, HalFC 80, MovMk[port], TwYS A, WorEFlm*
Stahl, Max *BiE&WWA*
Stahl, Rose *Film 1*
Stahl, Rose 1870-1955 *WhThe*
Stahl, Rose 1875?-1955 *NotNAT B, WhoStg 1908*
Stahl, Stanley *BiE&WWA*
Stahl, Steffy 1919- *DancEn 78*
Stahl, Walter O 1884-1943 *WhScrn 74, -77, WhoHol B*
Stahl, Wilhelm 1872-1953 *Baker 78*
Stahl, Willy 1896-1963 *BiDAmM, ConAmC*
Stahl-Nachbauer, Ernst *Film 2*
Stahl-Nachbaur, Ernest 1886-1960 *WhScrn 74, -77, WhoHol B*
Stahlbeg, Fritz 1877-1937 *Baker 78*
Stahlberg, Fritz 1877- *ConAmC*
Stahle, Anna Greta 1913- *CnOxB, DancEn 78*
Stahlhut, Judith L 1941- *IntWWM 77*
Stahlin, Jacob Von 1709-1785 *NewGrD 80*
Stahlin, Jakob Von 1709-1785 *Baker 78*
Stahuljak, Dubravko 1920- *IntWWM 77, -80*
Stahuljak, Juraj 1901- *IntWWM 77*
Stahuljak, Mladen 1914- *IntWWM 77, -80*
Staicu, Paul 1937- *IntWWM 80*
Staiger, Libi 1928- *BiE&WWA, NotNAT, WhoHol A*
Staimitz *NewGrD 80*
Stainer, Jacob 1617?-1683 *NewGrD 80*
Stainer, Jacob 1621-1683 *MusMk*
Stainer, Jakob 1617?-1683 *NewGrD 80*
Stainer, Jakob 1621-1683 *Baker 78*
Stainer, Joan Ranald 1915- *WhoMus 72*
Stainer, Sir John 1840-1901 *Baker 78, BnBkM 80, MusMk, NewGrD 80, OxMus*
Stainer, Markus *Baker 78, NewGrD 80*
Staines, Franklin *CreCan 1*
Staingaden, Constantin *NewGrD 80*
Stainlein, Louis C G Corneille, Comte De 1819-1867 *Baker 78*
Stainov, Petko 1896- *Baker 78*
Stainton, Philip 1908-1961 *FilmgC, WhThe, WhoHol A*
Stainton, Philip 1908-1963 *HalFC 80*
Stair, Patty 1869-1926 *Baker 78, BiDAmM*
Stairs, Louise E 1892- *BiDAmM, ConAmC*
Stajnc, Jaroslav 1943- *WhoOp 76*
Stalder, Hans Rudolf 1930- *IntWWM 77, -80*
Stalder, Joseph Franz Xaver Dominik 1725-1765 *NewGrD 80*
Stalenin, Evan *Film 2*
Staley, Joan *ForYSC, WhoHol A*
Stalker, Richard Bruce 1945- *IntWWM 77*

Stalker, William Hugh 1928- *WhoMus 72*
Stall, Karl 1871-1947 *WhScrn 77*
Stallings, Charles Kendall 1940- *AmSCAP 80*
Stallings, Laurence 1894-1968 *BiE&WWA, DcLB 7[port], FilmEn, FilmgC, HalFC 80, McGEWD, ModWD, NotNAT B, PlP&P, WhThe*
Stallone, Michael Sylvester 1946- *BiDFilm 81*
Stallone, Sylvester 1946- *FilmEn, HalFC 80, IntMPA 78, -79, -80*
Stalman, Roger Claude 1927- *IntWWM 77, -80, WhoMus 72*
Stalmann, Joachim 1931- *IntWWM 80*
Stalmaster, Hal *WhoHol A*
Stalvey, Dorrance 1930- *AmSCAP 80, ConAmC, IntWWM 77, -80*
Stam, Edward 1916- *IntWWM 77, -80*
Stam, Henk 1922- *Baker 78, CpmDNM 76, IntWWM 77, -80*
Stam, Joop 1934- *IntWWM 77, -80*
Stamac, Ivan 1936- *IntWWM 77, -80*
Stamaty, Camille-Marie 1811-1870 *Baker 78, NewGrD 80*
Stambaugh, Jack *Film 2*
Stamegna, Nicolaus 1615?-1685 *NewGrD 80*
Stamegna, Nicolo 1615?-1685 *NewGrD 80*
Stamenova, Galina 1958- *IntWWM 80*
Stamford, John Scott 1923- *WhoOp 76*
Stamic, Jan Vaclav Antonin 1717-1757 *BnBkM 80*
Stamic, Karel 1745-1801 *BnBkM 80*
Stamigna, Nicolaus 1615?-1685 *NewGrD 80*
Stamigna, Nicolo 1615?-1685 *NewGrD 80*
Stamitz *NewGrD 80*
Stamitz, Anton *Baker 78*
Stamitz, Anton 1750-1809? *NewGrD 80*
Stamitz, Anton 1754-1809? *OxMus*
Stamitz, Carl 1745-1801 *Baker 78, BnBkM 80, NewGrD 80*
Stamitz, Jan Waczlaw Antonin 1717?-1757 *NewGrD 80[port]*
Stamitz, Johann 1717-1757 *Baker 78, BnBkM 80, CmpBCM, GrComp, MusMk[port], NewGrD 80[port], OxMus*
Stamitz, Karl 1745-1801 *OxMus*
Stamm, Harald 1938- *WhoOp 76*
Stamm, Marvin Louis 1939- *EncJzS 70*
Stammers, Edward d1802 *BiDAmM*
Stammers, Frank d1921 *NotNAT B*
Stamp, Terence *MotPP, WhoHol A*
Stamp, Terence 1938- *IntMPA 77, -78, -79, -80*
Stamp, Terence 1939- *FilmAG WE[port], ForYSC*
Stamp, Terence 1940- *FilmEn, FilmgC, HalFC 80, IlWWBF[port], IntMPA 75, -76, MovMk[port], OxFilm, WorEFlm*
Stamp-Taylor, Enid 1904-1946 *Film 2, FilmgC, HalFC 80, IlWWBF, WhScrn 74, -77, WhThe, WhoHol B*
Stampeders, The *RkOn 2[port]*
Stamper, Dave 1883-1963 *AmPS, CmpEPM, NewCBMT, PopAmC, PopAmC SUP, WhThe*
Stamper, David 1883-1963 *AmSCAP 66, -80, BiDAmM, NotNAT B*
Stamper, F Pope 1880-1950 *NotNAT B, WhThe*
Stamper, Wallace Logan 1930- *BiDAmM*
Stampfel, Hermann 1946- *AmSCAP 80*
Stampfer, Simon Ritter Von *DcFM*
Stampiglia, Silvio 1664-1725 *NewGrD 80*
Stampley, Joe *CounME 74[port], -74A, IlEncCM[port]*
Stamps, V O 1892-1940 *NewGrD 80*
Stamps Quartet *BiDAmM*
Stan, Radu 1928- *IntWWM 77, -80*
Stanback, Thurman W *BlkAmP*
Stancheva-Brashovanova, Lada *NewGrD 80*
Stanchinsky, Alexey Vladimirovich 1888-1914 *NewGrD 80*
Standells, The *RkOn 2[port]*
Standen, Richard *IntWWM 77, -80, WhoMus 72*
Stander, Lionel 1908- *BiE&WWA, FilmEn, FilmgC, ForYSC, HalFC 80, HolCA[port], IntMPA 77, -75, -76, -78, -79, -80, MotPP, MovMk, NotNAT, Vers A[port], WhoHol A*
Standford, Patric John 1939- *IntWWM 77, NewGrD 80, WhoMus 72*
Standfuss, J C d1759? *NewGrD 80*
Standing, Charlene 1921-1957 *WhScrn 74, -77*
Standing, Charles Wyndham 1880- *WhThe*
Standing, Ellen d1906 *NotNAT B*
Standing, Emily d1899 *NotNAT B*
Standing, Frank H *NewGrD 80*
Standing, Gordon d1927 *Film 2, WhScrn 74, -77, WhoHol B*
Standing, Sir Guy 1873-1937 *FilmEn, FilmgC, ForYSC, HalFC 80, HolCA[port], MotPP, NotNAT B, WhScrn 74, -77, WhThe, WhoHol B, WhoStg 1906, -1908*
Standing, Guy, Jr. d1954 *WhScrn 74, -77, WhoHol B*
Standing, Herbert *Film 1*
Standing, Herbert 1846-1923 *NotNAT B, WhScrn 77, WhThe, WhoStg 1906, -1908*
Standing, Herbert 1846-1928 *WhScrn 74*
Standing, Herbert 1884-1955 *Film 2, NotNAT B, WhScrn 74, -77, WhoHol B*
Standing, Jack 1886-1917 *Film 1, WhScrn 77*
Standing, Joan 1903- *Film 2*
Standing, John 1934- *FilmgC, HalFC 80, WhoHol A, WhoThe 77*
Standing, Percy Darnell *Film 1, -2*
Standing, Percy Darrell *WhoHrs 80*
Standing, Wyndham 1880-1963 *Film 1, -2, ForYSC, TwYS, WhScrn 77*
Standish, Myles 1907- *IntMPA 75, -76*
Standish, Orlando *NewGrD 80*
Standish, Pamela 1920- *WhThe*
Standley *NewGrD 80*
Standly *NewGrD 80*
Stane *NewGrD 80*
Stanek, Alan Edward 1939- *IntWWM 77, -80*
Stanesby *NewGrD 80*
Stanesby, Thomas 1668?-1734 *NewGrD 80*
Stanesby, Thomas 1692-1754 *NewGrD 80*
Stanescu, Lucia *WhoOp 76*
Stanfield, Clarkson 1793-1867 *NotNAT B, OxThe*
Stanfield, Doreen *IntWWM 77, -80, WhoMus 72*
Stanfield, Milly Bernardine *WhoMus 72*
Stanfill, Dennis C 1927- *IntMPA 77, -75, -76, -78, -79, -80, NewYTET*
Stanford, Benjamin 1949- *IntWWM 77*
Stanford, Charles Villiers 1852-1924 *Baker 78, BnBkM 80, CmOp, DcCom&M 79, MusMk[port], NewEOp 71, NewGrD 80[port], OxMus*
Stanford, E Thomas 1929- *IntWWM 77, -80*
Stanford, Henry 1872-1921 *NotNAT B, WhThe, WhoHol B, WhoStg 1906, -1908*
Stanford, Patric John 1939- *IntWWM 80*
Stanford, Stanley *Film 2*
Stang, Arnold *WhoHol A*
Stang, Arnold 1925- *AmSCAP 66, BiE&WWA, FilmEn, ForYSC*
Stang, Arnold 1926- *Vers A[port]*
Stang, Arnold 1927- *AmSCAP 80, IntMPA 77, -75, -76, -78, -79, -80*
Stang, Betsy *WomWMM B*
Stange, Claude Richard 1913- *CnMD*
Stange, Hermann 1835-1914 *Baker 78*
Stange, Max 1856-1932 *Baker 78*
Stange, Stanislaus d1917 *EncMT, NotNAT B, WhThe*
Stangeland, Robert Alan 1930- *IntWWM 77*
Stanger, Russell T 1924- *AmSCAP 80*
Stanhope, David Richard 1952- *IntWWM 77, -80*
Stanhope, Ted *WhoHol A*
Stanhope, Warren *WhoHol A*
Stanis, Bernnadette 1953- *DrBlPA*
Stanislaus, Frederick d1891 *NotNAT B*
Stanislav, Josef 1897-1971 *NewGrD 80*
Stanislavska, Marie Lilina *PlP&P*
Stanislavsky, Constantin Sergeievich 1865-1938 *DcPup*
Stanislavsky, Constantin Sergeivich 1863-1938 *NotNAT B*
Stanislavsky, Konstantin 1863-1938 *Ent*
Stanislavsky, Konstantin Sergeivich 1863-1938 *OxThe*
Stanislavsky, Konstantin Sergeyevich 1863-1938 *EncWT, NewGrD 80, OxFilm*
Stanislavsky, Konstantin Sergeyevich 1865-1938 *CnThe*
Stanislawski, Constantine 1863-1938 *WhThe*
Stanko, Tomasz 1942- *EncJzS 70*
Stanlaws, Penrhyn d1923 *TwYS A*
Stanley, Adelaide 1906- *WhThe*
Stanley, Aileen 1897- *CmpEPM*
Stanley, Albert Augustus 1851-1932 *Baker 78, BiDAmM*
Stanley, Alma 1854-1931 *NotNAT B, WhThe*
Stanley, Carter Glen 1925-1966 *BiDAmM*
Stanley, Charles *CmpGMD*
Stanley, Charles 1922- *AmSCAP 66*
Stanley, Donald Arthur 1937- *IntWWM 77, -80*
Stanley, Edwin 1880-1944 *WhScrn 74, -77, WhoHol B*
Stanley, Eric 1884- *WhThe*
Stanley, Florence *WhoHol A, WhoThe 77*
Stanley, Forest 1889-1969 *Film 1, -2*
Stanley, Forrest 1889-1969 *TwYS, WhScrn 77*
Stanley, Frances Kniffin 1914- *IntWWM 77, -80*
Stanley, George *Film 1*
Stanley, Glen 1925- *IlEncCM[port]*
Stanley, Harry *MagIlD*
Stanley, Helen Camille 1930- *ConAmC, IntWWM 77, -80*
Stanley, Henry *Film 1*
Stanley, Jack *WhoHol A*
Stanley, Jack 1890-1936 *AmSCAP 66, -80*
Stanley, Jerome 1941- *IntWWM 77*
Stanley, John 1712-1786 *NewGrD 80[port]*
Stanley, John 1713-1786 *Baker 78, MusMk, OxMus*
Stanley, Ken *WhoHol A*
Stanley, Kim *MotPP*
Stanley, Kim 1921- *Ent, FilmgC, HalFC 80, WhoThe 77*
Stanley, Kim 1925- *BiE&WWA, CnThe, FilmEn, ForYSC, MovMk, NotNAT, WhoHol A, WhoThe 72*
Stanley, Lilian d1943 *NotNAT B*
Stanley, Marion *WhoStg 1908*
Stanley, Martha 1879- *WhThe*
Stanley, Maxfield *Film 1*
Stanley, Norris *WhoMus 72*
Stanley, Pamela 1909- *WhThe*
Stanley, Pat 1931- *BiE&WWA, NotNAT, WhoHol A*
Stanley, Paul 1952- *AmSCAP 80*
Stanley, Phyllis 1914- *IntMPA 77, -75, -76, -78, -79, -80, WhThe*
Stanley, Ralph Edmond 1927- *BiDAmM, IlEncCM[port]*
Stanley, Ralph Nick 1914-1972 *WhScrn 77, WhoHol A*
Stanley, Richard *FilmEn*
Stanley, Robert 1902- *AmSCAP 66, -80*
Stanley, S Victor 1892-1939 *NotNAT B, WhScrn 74, -77, WhThe*
Stanley Brothers *IlEncCM[port]*
Stanley Brothers *EncFCWM 69*
Stanmore, Frank d1943 *WhoHol B*
Stanmore, Frank 1877-1943 *Film 2, IlWWBF*
Stanmore, Frank 1878-1943 *NotNAT B, WhThe*
Stannar, William *NewGrD 80*
Stannard, Don 1916-1949 *HalFC 80, IlWWBF*
Stannard, Heather 1928- *WhThe*
Stano, Henry 1908- *AmSCAP 66, -80*
Stano, Janina 1919- *IntWWM 80*
Stansby, William d1638 *NewGrD 80*
Stantley, Ralph d1964 *NotNAT B*
Stantley, Ralph d1972 *WhoHol B*
Stanton, Betty *WhoHol A*
Stanton, Edmund C d1901 *BiDAmM*
Stanton, Francis Hayward 1913- *AmSCAP 66, -80, NatPD[port]*
Stanton, Frank 1908- *BiE&WWA, IntMPA 75, -76, NewYTET*
Stanton, Frank Lebby 1857-1927 *AmSCAP 66, -80*
Stanton, Frank Libby 1857-1927 *BiDAmM*
Stanton, Fred R 1881-1925 *Film 1, -2, WhoHol B*
Stanton, Frederick R 1881-1925 *WhScrn 74, -77*
Stanton, Harry *WhoHol A*
Stanton, Harry Dean *WhoHol A*
Stanton, Jane C *WomWMM*
Stanton, Joseph 1906- *ConAmC*

Stanton, Larry T d1955 WhScrn 74, -77
Stanton, Paul 1884-1955 ForYSC, WhScrn 77
Stanton, Richard Film 1, TwYS A
Stanton, Rosemary Brown 1924- AmSCAP 80
Stanton, Royal Waltz 1916- AmSCAP 66, -80, ConAmC A, IntWWM 77, -80
Stanton, Walter Kendall 1891- OxMus, WhoMus 72
Stanton, Will 1885-1969 Film 2, WhScrn 77
Stanwood, Rita Film 1
Stanwyck, Barbara 1907- BiDFilm, -81, BiE&WWA, CmMov, FilmEn, Film 2, FilmgC, ForYSC[port], HalFC 80, IntMPA 77, -75, -76, -78, -79, -80, MotPP, MovMk[port], OxFilm, ThFT[port], WhThe, WhoHol A, WorEFlm
Stanyon, Ellis 1871-1951 MagIlD
Stanzler, Meyer 1908- IntMPA 77, -75, -76, -78, -79
Staple Singers, The BiDAmM, IlEncR, RkOn 2[port]
Staplehurst, David Ernest 1913- WhoMus 72
Stapleton, Bill 1945- EncJzS 70
Stapleton, Cyril RkOn, WhoMus 72
Stapleton, Eric William 1917- WhoMus 72
Stapleton, Jean 1923- BiE&WWA, FilmEn, ForYSC, HalFC 80, IntMPA 77, -75, -76, -78, -79, -80, NotNAT, WhoHol A, WhoThe 77
Stapleton, Maureen 1925- BiE&WWA, CnThe, Ent, FamA&A[port], FilmEn, FilmgC, ForYSC, HalFC 80, IntMPA 77, -75, -76, -78, -79, -80, MotPP, MovMk, NotNAT, WhoHol A, WhoThe 72, -77
Stapleton, Sir Robert d1669 NotNAT B
Stapleton, Vivian WhoHol A
Stapleton, William John 1945- EncJzS 70
Stapley, Richard FilmgC, HalFC 80, WhoHol A
Stapp, Marjorie WhoHol A
Stapp, Olivia 1940- WhoOp 76
Stappen, Crispin Van 1470?-1532 NewGrD 80
Star, Cheryl M 1947- IntWWM 77, -80
Star, Frederick Film 2
Starbuck RkOn 2[port]
Starbuck, Betty WhScrn 77
Starbuck, James BiE&WWA, CnOxB, DancEn 78, NotNAT
Starcher, Buddy Edgar 1910- BiDAmM
Starck, Claude 1928- IntWWM 77, -80
Starck, Ingeborg NewGrD 80
Starczewski, Felix 1868-1945 Baker 78
Starek, Jiri 1928- NewGrD 80
Starenios, Dimos WhoHol A
Starer, Robert 1924- AmSCAP 66, -80, Baker 78, CpmDNM 80, ConAmC, DancEn 78, DcCM, IntWWM 80, NewGrD 80
Starevich, Irene WomWMM
Starevitch, Ladislas 1892-1965 DcFM, OxFilm
Starewicz, Wladyslaw 1892-1965 FilmEn
Starger, Martin IntMPA 77, -76, -78, -79, -80, NewYTET
Staricius, Johann NewGrD 80
Staricius, Johannes NewGrD 80
Starikoff, Ireyne IntWWM 77, -80
Stark NewGrD 80
Stark, Abraham 1659-1709 NewGrD 80
Stark, Bobbie Robert Victor 1906-1945 WhoJazz 72
Stark, Bobby 1906-1945 BiDAmM, CmpEPM
Stark, Douglas WhoHol A
Stark, Edward Josef 1858-1918 BiDAmM
Stark, Ethel 1916- CreCan 2, IntWWM 77, -80
Stark, Graham 1922- FilmgC, HalFC 80, WhoHol A
Stark, Herald Ira 1907- IntWWM 77
Stark, Howard ConMuA 80B
Stark, James C 1939- AmSCAP 80
Stark, John Stillwell 1841-1927 BiDAmM
Stark, Leighton d1924 Film 1, WhScrn 77
Stark, Ludwig 1831-1884 Baker 78
Stark, Mabel 1889-1968 WhScrn 74, -77, WhoHol B
Stark, Phil 1929- WhoOp 76
Stark, Ray FilmEn, IntMPA 77, -75, -76, -78, -79, -80, WorEFlm
Stark, Ray 1914?- FilmgC, HalFC 80, WomWMM
Stark, Ray 1915- BiE&WWA
Stark, Robert 1847-1922 Baker 78
Stark, Wenzel 1670-1757 NewGrD 80
Stark, Wilbur IntMPA 77, -75, -76, -78, -79
Stark, William Joseph 1925- IntWWM 77
Stark-Gstettenbaur, Gustl Film 2
Starke, Arthur George WhoMus 72
Starke, Johanne Christiane 1731-1809 OxThe
Starke, Pauline 1900-1977 FilmEn, Film 1, -2, ForYSC, MotPP, TwYS, WhoHol A
Starke, Pauline 1901- HalFC 80
Starke, Tod 1961- WhoHol A
Starker, Janos 1924- Baker 78, BnBkM 80, IntWWM 77, -80, MusSN[port], NewGrD 80, WhoMus 72
Starkes, Jaison MorBAP
Starkey, Bert 1880-1939 Film 2, WhScrn 74, -77, WhoHol B
Starkie, Martin 1925- WhoThe 72, -77
Starkie, Walter Fitzwilliam 1894-1976 NewGrD 80, WhoMus 72
Starks, Howard F 1928- ConAmC
Starks, Robert 1952- AmSCAP 80
Starkweather, David 1935- ConDr 73, -77, DcLB 7[port]
Starland Vocal Band RkOn 2[port]
Starling, Lynn 1891-1955 NotNAT B, WhThe
Starmer, William Wooding 1866-1927 Baker 78
Starnes, Carroll Moore 1926- IntWWM 77
Starokadomsky, Mikhail 1901-1954 Baker 78
Staromieyski, J NewGrD 80
Starovolscius, Szymon 1588-1656 NewGrD 80
Starowolski, Szymon 1588-1656 NewGrD 80
Staroyanis, Stratis N 1937- AmSCAP 80
Starr, Belle 1848-1889 HalFC 80
Starr, Edwin 1942- RkOn 2[port]
Starr, Eve IntMPA 77, -75, -76, -78, -79, -80
Starr, Frances 1881-1973 NotNAT B, WhScrn 77
Starr, Frances 1886-1973 BiE&WWA, PlP&P, ThFT[port], WhThe, WhoHol B, WhoStg 1906, -1908
Starr, Fred 1878-1921 Film 1, -2
Starr, Frederick 1878-1921 WhScrn 74, -77, WhoHol B
Starr, Helen 1940- CnOxB
Starr, Irving 1905- IntMPA 77, -75, -76, -78, -79
Starr, Jack WhoHol A
Starr, Jane Film 2
Starr, Kay 1922- AmPS A, BiDAmM, CmpEPM, RkOn[port]
Starr, Kenny 1953- IlEncCM[port]
Starr, Mark 1942- AmSCAP 80
Starr, Muriel 1888-1950 NotNAT B, WhThe
Starr, Randy AmSCAP 80
Starr, Randy 1930- RkOn
Starr, Randy 1931-1970 WhScrn 74, -77
Starr, Ringo 1940- Baker 78, ConMuA 80A[port], FilmEn, ForYSC, IlEncR, MotPP, NewGrD 80, RkOn 2[port], WhoHol A
Starr, Sally Film 2
Starr, Steven ConMuA 80B
Starr, Susan 1942- IntWWM 77, -80, WhoMus 72
Starr, Sylvia 1879- WhoStg 1906, -1908
Starr, Tama Lynn 1946- AmSCAP 80
Starr, Tony AmSCAP 80
Starr, Tony 1914-1971 AmSCAP 66, -80
Starrett, Charles IntMPA 75
Starrett, Charles 1903- FilmEn, What 5[port]
Starrett, Charles 1904- Film 2, FilmgC, ForYSC, HalFC 80, WhoHol A
Starrett, Claude E, Jr. WhoHol A
Starrett, Jack FilmEn, HalFC 80, WhoHol A
Starrett, Jennifer WhoHol A
Starrett, Susan 1940- WhoMus 72
Starrett, Valerie WhoHol A
Starreveld, Rogier 1941- IntWWM 77
Stary, Emanuel 1843-1906 NewGrD 80
Staryk, Steven 1932- Baker 78, IntWWM 80, NewGrD 80, WhoMus 72
Starz RkOn 2[port]
Starzer, Josef 1726-1787 Baker 78
Starzer, Joseph 1726-1787 CnOxB, NewGrD 80
Stasheff, Edward 1909- BiE&WWA
Stasio, Marilyn L ConAmTC
Stasny, Carl Richard 1855-1920 Baker 78
Stasny, Ludwig 1823-1883 Baker 78
Stasov, Vladimir 1824-1906 Baker 78, NewGrD 80
Stastny NewGrD 80
Stastny, Bernard 1760?-1835? NewGrD 80
Stastny, Jan d1779? NewGrD 80
Stastny, Jan 1764?-1826? NewGrD 80
Staten, Pat MorBAP
Staten, Vince ConAmTC
Statesman Quartet BiDAmM
Statham, Heathcote D 1889-1973 NewGrD 80
Statham, Keith 1934- IntWWM 80
Stather, Frank Film 1
Statius 219?BC-166BC Ent
Statkowski, Roman 1859-1925 NewGrD 80
Statkowski, Roman 1860-1925 Baker 78, OxMus
Statler, Darrell AmSCAP 80
Statler Brothers, The BiDAmM, CounME 74[port], -74A, EncFCWM 69, IlEncCM[port], RkOn 2[port]
Staton, Barbara 1933- AmSCAP 80
Staton, Candi RkOn 2[port]
Staton, Dakota 1932- BiDAmM, DrBlPA, EncJzS 70
Staton, Merrill 1919- AmSCAP 66, -80
Statues, The RkOn
Status Quo ConMuA 80A, IlEncR, RkOn 2[port]
Staub, August W 1931- NotNAT
Staub, Ralph d1969 WhoHol B
Staubinger, Mathias NewGrD 80
Staudigl, Josef, Jr. 1850-1916 Baker 78
Staudigl, Josef, Sr. 1807-1861 Baker 78
Staudigl, Joseph, Jr. 1850-1916 NewGrD 80
Staudigl, Joseph, Sr. 1807-1861 NewGrD 80
Staudt, Johann Bernhard 1654-1712 NewGrD 80
Staudte, Wolfgang 1906- DcFM, FilmEn, HalFC 80, WorEFlm
Staudte, Wolfgang 1909- OxFilm
Stauffer, Donald Wesley 1919- AmSCAP 66, -80, ConAmC, IntWWM 77
Stauffer, George B 1947- IntWWM 77, -80
Staughton, William 1770-1829 BiDAmM
Staulz, Lorenzo 1880?-1928? NewOrJ
Staunton, Ann WhoHol A
Staunton, William 1803-1889 BiDAmM
Staveley, Colin 1942- IntWWM 77, -80, WhoMus 72
Stavenhagen, Bernhard 1862-1914 Baker 78, BnBkM 80
Staver, Robert B 1916- AmSCAP 66
Stavis, B MorBAP
Stavis, Barrie 1906- AmSCAP 80, BiE&WWA, BlkAmP, ConDr 73, -77, NotNAT
Stavru, Cornel 1929- WhoOp 76
Stawinski, Jerzy Stefan 1921- DcFM, FilmEn
Stayden, Gail WomWMM
Staynov, Petko 1896-1977 NewGrD 80
Stayton, Frank 1874-1951 NotNAT B, WhThe
Stcherbatchef, Vladimir 1889-1952 OxMus
Stead, Estelle PlP&P
Stead, James Henry d1886 OxThe
Stead, Maurice Oliver 1939- IntWWM 77, -80
Stead, Robert James Campbell 1880-1959 CreCan 2
Steade, Douglas Film 2
Steadman, Jack William 1920- IntWWM 77, -80, WhoMus 72
Steadman, Vera 1900-1966 Film 1, -2, TwYS, WhScrn 74, -77, WhoHol B
Steadman-Allen, Raymond Victor 1922- IntWWM 77, -80, WhoMus 72
Steagall, Red CounME 74[port], -74A, IlEncCM[port]
Stealer's Wheel IlEncR, RkOn 2[port]
Steals, Mervin H 1946- AmSCAP 80
Steam RkOn 2[port]
Steamboat Four, The BiDAmM
Stear, Ronald Charles WhoMus 72
Stearman, David J, III 1949- AmSCAP 80
Stearns, Agnes June 1939- BiDAmM
Stearns, Edith Bond d1961 NotNAT B
Stearns, Linda CreCan 1
Stearns, Louis Film 1
Stearns, M Eunice 1919- AmSCAP 80
Stearns, Myron Morris d1963 NotNAT B

Stearns, Peter Pindar 1931- *CpmDNM 79, ConAmC, IntWWM 77, -80*
Stearns, Theodore 1880-1935 *Baker 78, BiDAmM, ConAmC*
Stebbings, Ruth 1956- *IntWWM 80*
Stebbins, George Coles 1846-1945 *AmSCAP 66, -80, BiDAmM, NewGrD 80*
Stebbins, George Waring 1869-1930 *Baker 78, BiDAmM*
Stebbins, J A *AmSCAP 80*
Stebbins, Robert *DcFM*
Stebbins, Robert A 1938- *IntWWM 77, -80*
Stebbins, Rowland 1882-1948 *NotNAT B*
Steber, Eleanor 1916- *Baker 78, BiDAmM, BnBkM 80, CmOp, MusSN[port], NewEOp 71, NewGrD 80, WhoMus 72*
Stecher, Melvin 1931- *IntWWM 77, -80, WhoMus 72*
Steck, George 1829-1897 *BiDAmM*
Steck, Hazel *WhoHol A*
Steck, Olga d1935 *NotNAT B*
Steckel, Leonard 1901-1971 *EncWT*
Stecker, Karel 1861-1918 *Baker 78, NewGrD 80*
Steckler, Anne-Marie *NewGrD 80*
Steckler, Ray Dennis 1939- *WhoHrs 80*
Stecman, Phil *AmSCAP 80*
Steddom, Art 1925- *AmSCAP 80*
Stedman, Fabian *OxMus*
Stedman, Lincoln 1900-1941 *Film 2, TwYS*
Stedman, Lincoln 1907-1948 *NotNAT B, WhScrn 74, -77, WhoHol B*
Stedman, Marshall 1874-1943 *WhScrn 74, -77, WhoHol B*
Stedman, Myrtle d1938 *WhoHol B*
Stedman, Myrtle 1887-1938 *TwYS*
Stedman, Myrtle 1888-1938 *Film 1, -2, ForYSC, NotNAT B*
Stedman, Myrtle 1889-1938 *WhScrn 74, -77*
Stedman, Ursula 1927- *IntWWM 80*
Stedron *NewGrD 80*
Stedron, Bohumir 1905- *Baker 78, IntWWM 80, NewGrD 80*
Stedron, Milos 1942- *Baker 78, NewGrD 80*
Stedron, Vladimir 1900- *Baker 78, IntWWM 77, NewGrD 80*
Steed, Graham 1913- *IntWWM 77, -80*
Steed, Judy *WomWMM*
Steedman, Heather 1953- *IntWWM 80*
Steeg, Bruce 1938- *IntWWM 77, -80*
Steeg, Rosemary 1937- *IntWWM 80*
Steeg, Ted H 1930- *AmSCAP 80*
Steel, Alan *WhoHrs 80*
Steel, Anthony 1920- *FilmEn, FilmgC, ForYSC, HalFC 80, IlWWBF[port], IntMPA 77, -75, -76, -78, -79, -80, WhoHol A*
Steel, Barbara 1938- *ForYSC*
Steel, Christopher Charles 1939- *IntWWM 77, -80, NewGrD 80, WhoMus 72*
Steel, Edward 1897-1965 *WhScrn 77*
Steel, John 1900-1971 *AmPS B, BiDAmM, CmpEPM, EncMT*
Steel, John 1936- *IntWWM 77, -80*
Steel, June Mary *WomWMM B*
Steel, Susan d1959 *NotNAT B*
Steel, Vernon 1882-1955 *WhThe*
Steele, Barbara 1938- *FilmEn, FilmgC, HalFC 80, MotPP, WhoHol A, WhoHrs 80[port]*
Steele, Basse Byron 1918- *IntWWM 77*
Steele, Bill 1889-1966 *Film 2, WhScrn 74, WhoHol A*
Steele, Blanche d1944 *NotNAT B*
Steele, Blue *CmpEPM*
Steele, Bob 1906- *FilmEn, Film 2, TwYS, Vers A[port]*
Steele, Bob 1907- *FilmgC, ForYSC, HalFC 80, WhoHol A*
Steele, Clifford 1878-1940 *WhScrn 74, -77*
Steele, Daniel 1772-1828 *BiDAmM*
Steele, Helen 1904- *AmSCAP 66, -80, ConAmC A*
Steele, Hubert John 1929- *IntWWM 80*
Steele, James Eugene *IntWWM 80*
Steele, Joe Joseph A 1900?-1964 *WhoJazz 72*
Steele, John 1929- *IntWWM 77, NewGrD 80*
Steele, Jon 1912- *AmSCAP 66, -80*
Steele, Jon And Sandra *AmPS A*
Steele, Joshua 1700-1791 *NewGrD 80*
Steele, Karen 1934- *ForYSC, WhoHol A*
Steele, Lanny 1933- *ConAmC*
Steele, Lee *WhoHol A*
Steele, Lois 1910- *AmSCAP 66, -80*
Steele, Lou *WhoHol A*
Steele, Louis Thornton 1911- *AmSCAP 66, -80*
Steele, Marjorie *WhoHol A*
Steele, Minnie 1881-1949 *Film 2, WhScrn 74, -77, WhoHol B*
Steele, Patricia Joudry *CreCan 2*
Steele, Philip John 1936- *IntWWM 77, -80*
Steele, Pippa *WhoHol A*
Steele, Porter 1880-1966 *BiDAmM, ConAmC*
Steele, R V *Film 1*
Steele, Richard *BlkAmP*
Steele, Richard 1672-1729 *Ent*
Steele, Sir Richard 1672-1729 *CnThe, EncWT, McGEWD[port], NotNAT A, -B, OxThe, PlP&P, REnWD[port]*
Steele, Robert Michael 1942- *ConAmTC*
Steele, Ronald Arthur 1934- *WhoMus 72*
Steele, Ted 1917- *AmSCAP 66, -80*
Steele, Tom *WhoHrs 80*
Steele, Tommy 1936- *EncMT, FilmAG WE[port], FilmEn, FilmgC, ForYSC, HalFC 80, IlWWBF, -A, IntMPA 77, -75, -76, -78, -79, -80, MotPP, WhoHol A, WhoThe 72, -77*
Steele, Tommy 1937- *BiDAmM*
Steele, Vernon 1882-1955 *NotNAT B*
Steele, Vernon 1883-1955 *Film 1, -2, MotPP, WhScrn 74, -77, WhoHol B*
Steele, Vickie Fee 1947-1975 *WhScrn 77*
Steele, Wilbur Daniel 1886-1970 *NotNAT B*
Steele, William 1889-1966 *Film 2, WhScrn 77, WhoHol B*
Steeleye Span *ConMuA 80A, IlEncR*
Steelman, Hosea *Film 1*
Steely Dan *ConMuA 80A, IlEncR, RkOn 2[port]*
Steen, Al *IntMPA 77, -75, -76, -78*
Steen, Bernt Anker 1943- *IntWWM 80*
Steen, Marguerite 1894-1975 *WhScrn 77*
Steen-Noekleberg, Einar 1944- *IntWWM 77, -80*
Steenburgen, Mary 1952?- *HalFC 80*
Steenland, Thomas Haynes 1950- *CpmDNM 80*
Steenwick, Gisbert d1679 *NewGrD 80*
Steer, John Wesley 1824-1900 *NewGrD 80*
Steere, Clifton *WhoHol A*
Steere, John Wesley 1824-1900 *NewGrD 80*
Steers, Larry 1881-1951 *Film 1, -2, ForYSC, TwYS, WhScrn 74, -77, WhoHol B*
Steevens, George d1800 *NotNAT B*
Stefan The Serb *NewGrD 80*
Stefan, Paul 1879-1943 *Baker 78, NewGrD 80*
Stefan, Virginia 1926-1964 *NotNAT B, WhScrn 74, -77, WhoHol B*
Stefan-Grunfeldt, Paul 1879-1943 *NewGrD 80*
Stefanescu, Barbu *McGEWD[port]*
Stefanescu, Marinel 1947- *CnOxB*
Stefani, Agostino *NewGrD 80*
Stefani, Andrea *NewGrD 80*
Stefani, Giovanni *NewGrD 80*
Stefani, Jan 1746?-1829 *Baker 78, NewGrD 80*
Stefani, Jozef 1800-1867 *Baker 78*
Stefani, Jozef 1800-1876 *NewGrD 80*
Stefanini, Giovanni Battista 1574-1630 *NewGrD 80, OxMus*
Stefanis, Gaetano De d1710? *NewGrD 80*
Stefano Di Cino *NewGrD 80*
Stefano, Giuseppe Di *MusSN[port], NewGrD 80*
Stefano, Joseph *WhoHrs 80*
Stefano, Joseph 1922- *AmSCAP 66, -80*
Stefanov, Ivan 1927- *WhoOp 76*
Stefanov, Vassil 1913- *NewGrD 80*
Stefanova, Nina 1943- *WhoOp 76*
Stefanovic, Dimitrije 1929- *IntWWM 77, -80, NewGrD 80*
Stefanovic, Pavle 1901- *IntWWM 77, -80*
Stefanschi, Sergiu 1941- *CnOxB*
Stefansdottir, Thora Ingibjorg 1941- *IntWWM 77*
Stefanska-Lukowicz, Elzbieta 1943- *IntWWM 77, -80*
Stefansson, Fjolnir 1930- *Baker 78, NewGrD 80*
Steffan, Geary *WhoHol A*
Steffan, Josef Antonin *NewGrD 80*
Steffan, Joseph Anton 1726-1797 *Baker 78*
Steffani, Abbate Agostino 1654-1728 *Baker 78*
Steffani, Agostino 1654-1728 *BnBkM 80, MusMk, NewEOp 71, NewGrD 80[port], OxMus*
Steffani, Josef Antonin *NewGrD 80*
Steffano, Agostino 1654-1728 *NewGrD 80[port]*
Steffe, Edwin 1907- *BiDAmM*
Steffe, William 1830?-1890? *BiDAmM*
Steffek, Hanny 1927- *WhoOp 76*
Steffen, Albert 1884-1963 *CnMD, ModWD, NotNAT B*
Steffen, Frederick John 1949- *ConAmC*
Steffen, Gerhard 1924- *IntWWM 80*
Steffen, Wolfgang 1923- *Baker 78, NewGrD 80*
Steffens, Johann 1560?-1616? *NewGrD 80*
Steffens, Johannes 1560?-1616? *NewGrD 80*
Steffens, Walter 1934- *NewGrD 80*
Steffkin, Theodore d1673? *NewGrD 80*
Steffkins, Theodore d1673? *NewGrD 80*
Stefkins, Theodore d1673? *NewGrD 80*
Stegall, Richard Carroll 1941- *IntWWM 77*
Steger, Hanns Hermann 1940- *IntWWM 77, -80*
Steger, Ingrid *WhoOp 76*
Steger, Julius d1959 *NotNAT B, WhoStg 1908*
Steger, Werner 1932- *NewGrD 80*
Steggall, Charles 1826-1905 *Baker 78, OxMus*
Steggall, Reginald 1867-1938 *Baker 78, OxMus*
Steglich, Hermann 1929- *IntWWM 77, -80*
Steglich, Rudolf 1886-1976 *Baker 78, NewGrD 80*
Stegmann, Carl David 1751-1826 *NewGrD 80*
Stegmayer, Ferdinand 1803-1863 *Baker 78*
Stegmayer, Matthaeus 1771-1820 *Baker 78*
Stegmayer, Matthaus 1771-1820 *NewGrD 80*
Stegmeyer, Bill 1916-1968 *CmpEPM, WhoJazz 72*
Stegmeyer, William John 1916-1968 *AmSCAP 66, -80*
Steguweit, Heinz d1964 *NotNAT B*
Stehle, J Gustav Eduard 1839-1915 *Baker 78*
Stehle, Sophie 1838-1921 *Baker 78, CmOp*
Stehli, Edgar 1884-1973 *BiE&WWA, NotNAT B, WhScrn 77, WhoHol B*
Stehlik, Miroslav 1916- *CnMD*
Stehman, Jacques 1912-1975 *Baker 78, NewGrD 80*
Steibelt, Daniel 1765-1823 *Baker 78, NewGrD 80, OxMus*
Steidl, Brigitta Margareta Kindler 1925- *IntWWM 77*
Steier, Sylvester *NewGrD 80*
Steiffkin, Theodore *NewGrD 80*
Steig, Jeremy 1942- *AmSCAP 80, EncJzS 70, IlEncJ*
Steiger, Jimmy 1896-1930 *AmSCAP 66, -80*
Steiger, Rod 1925- *BiDFilm, -81, BiE&WWA, CmMov, FilmEn, FilmgC, ForYSC, HalFC 80, IntMPA 77, -75, -76, -78, -79, -80, MotPP, MovMk[port], OxFilm, WhoHol A, WhoHrs 80, WorEFlm[port]*
Steigleder *NewGrD 80*
Steigleder, Adam 1561-1633 *NewGrD 80*
Steigleder, Johann Ulrich 1593-1635 *Baker 78, NewGrD 80*
Steigleder, Utz d1581 *NewGrD 80*
Steigman, Joyce Barthelson *AmSCAP 80*
Steijen, P Hakan H 1949- *IntWWM 80*
Stein, Alan 1949- *ConAmC*
Stein, Alexander 1906- *CnMD*
Stein, Andreas *Baker 78*
Stein, Arlene C 1935- *IntWWM 77, -80*
Stein, Carol *WomWMM B*
Stein, Carol Eden 1927-1958 *WhScrn 74, -77*
Stein, Erwin 1885-1958 *Baker 78, NewGrD 80*
Stein, Fritz 1879-1961 *Baker 78, NewGrD 80*
Stein, Gertrude 1874-1946 *CnMD, EncWT, ModWD, NewEOp 71, NotNAT A, -B*
Stein, Gertrude Emilie *IntWWM 77, -80*
Stein, Gladys Marie 1900- *IntWWM 77, -80*
Stein, Harlene Sharon 1932- *AmSCAP 80*
Stein, Hedwig 1907- *WhoMus 72*
Stein, Herman *WhoHrs 80*
Stein, Herman 1915- *AmSCAP 80,*

CpmDNM 72, ConAmC
Stein, Horst 1928- *Baker 78, NewEOp 71, NewGrD 80, WhoMus 72, WhoOp 76*
Stein, Jerry J 1941- *ConAmTC*
Stein, Jim 1943- *AmSCAP 80*
Stein, Johann Andreas 1728-1792 *Baker 78, NewGrD 80*
Stein, Johnny 1891-1962 *NewOrJ*
Stein, Joseph *IntMPA 75, -76, -78, -79, -80*
Stein, Joseph 1912- *BiE&WWA, ConDr 73, -77D, EncMT, IntMPA 77, NatPD[port], NewCBMT, NotNAT, WhoThe 72, -77*
Stein, Jules C 1896- *IntMPA 77, -75, -76, -78, -79, -80*
Stein, Julian 1924- *AmSCAP 66*
Stein, Julius *NewGrD 80*
Stein, Leon 1910- *Baker 78, BiDAmM, CpmDNM 78, -79, -80, ConAmC, IntWWM 77, -80, NewGrD 80, WhoMus 72*
Stein, Leonard 1916- *Baker 78, NewGrD 80*
Stein, Lotte *Film 2*
Stein, Lou 1922- *CmpEPM*
Stein, Mini *AmSCAP 66*
Stein, Nanette 1769-1838 *OxMus*
Stein, Nikolaus d1629 *NewGrD 80*
Stein, Paul 1891-1952 *FilmgC, HalFC 80*
Stein, Paul L 1892-1951 *FilmEn*
Stein, Paul L 1892-1952 *IlWWBF, TwYS A*
Stein, Ralph 1919- *AmSCAP 80*
Stein, Richard Heinrich 1882-1942 *Baker 78, NewGrD 80, OxMus*
Stein, Ronald *WhoHrs 80*
Stein, Ronald 1930- *AmSCAP 66, -80, IntMPA 77, -75, -76, -78, -79, -80*
Stein, Sam Sammy 1906-1966 *WhScrn 77*
Stein, Sammy 1906-1966 *WhoHol B*
Stein, Sarah *WomWMM B*
Stein, Seymour *ConMuA 80B*
Stein, William 1918- *AmSCAP 66, -80*
Steinbach, Emil 1849-1919 *NewGrD 80*
Steinbach, Fritz 1855-1916 *Baker 78, NewGrD 80*
Steinbacher, Johann Michael *NewGrD 80*
Steinbauer, Othmar 1895-1962 *Baker 78*
Steinbauer, Robert Andrus 1926- *IntWWM 77*
Steinbeck, Hans David 1925- *IntWWM 77, -80*
Steinbeck, John 1902-1968 *BiE&WWA, CnMD, CnThe, DcLB 7[port], EncWT, FilmEn, FilmgC, HalFC 80, McGEWD[port], ModWD, NotNAT B, OxFilm, OxThe, WhThe*
Steinbeck, Wolfram 1945- *IntWWM 77, -80*
Steinberg, Abraham 1897- *AmSCAP 66, -80*
Steinberg, Amy d1920 *NotNAT B*
Steinberg, David *WhoHol A*
Steinberg, David J *ConMuA 80B*
Steinberg, Hans Wilhelm 1899-1978 *BnBkM 80*
Steinberg, Herb 1921- *IntMPA 77, -75, -76, -78, -79, -80*
Steinberg, Irwin *ConMuA 80B*
Steinberg, Maximilian 1883-1946 *Baker 78, NewGrD 80, OxMus*
Steinberg, Michael 1928- *Baker 78, NewGrD 80*
Steinberg, Roslyn *WomWMM B*
Steinberg, Susan *WomWMM B*
Steinberg, Wilhelm 1899-1978 *NewGrD 80*
Steinberg, William 1899-1978 *Baker 78, BiDAmM, BnBkM 80, CmOp, IntWWM 77, MusSN[port], NewEOp 71, NewGrD 80*
Steinberg, Zeev 1918- *Baker 78, NewGrD 80*
Steinberg, Ze'ev Wolfgang 1918- *IntWWM 77, -80*
Steinberger, Gabor *NewGrD 80*
Steinbrecher, Marcia *WomWMM B*
Steinbrook, David Herman 1941- *ConAmC*
Steindel, Bruno 1896-1949 *BiDAmM*
Steindler, Alma *WhoMus 72*
Steinecke, Wolfgang 1910-1961 *NewGrD 80*
Steiner, Elio 1905-1965 *WhScrn 74, -77*
Steiner, Elisabeth 1940- *WhoOp 76*
Steiner, Emma 1850-1928 *Baker 78*
Steiner, Frances Josephine 1937- *IntWWM 77, -80*
Steiner, Frederick 1923- *AmSCAP 80, ConAmC, IntWWM 77, -80*
Steiner, Gary A d1966 *NewYTET*
Steiner, George 1900-1967 *AmSCAP 66, -80, ConAmC A*
Steiner, Gitta Hana 1932- *AmSCAP 80, CpmDNM 76, ConAmC, IntWWM 77, -80*
Steiner, Herbert 1895-1964 *AmSCAP 66, -80*
Steiner, Howard Irving 1896- *AmSCAP 66, -80*
Steiner, Ira 1915?- *BiE&WWA*
Steiner, Johann Ludwig 1688-1761 *NewGrD 80*
Steiner, Joseph *IntMPA 77, -75, -76, -78*
Steiner, Max 1888- *AmSCAP 66, CmpEPM, WorEFlm*
Steiner, Max 1888-1971 *AmSCAP 80, Baker 78, ConAmC, FilmEn, HalFC 80, NewGrD 80, NotNAT B, OxFilm, PopAmC[port]*
Steiner, Max 1888-1972 *CmMov, DcFM, FilmgC, WhoHrs 80*
Steiner, Maximilian Raoul 1888-1971 *BiDAmM*
Steiner, Ralph 1899- *WorEFlm[port]*
Steiner, Rudolf *OxMus*
Steiner, Ruth 1931- *NewGrD 80*
Steiner, Sigmund Anton *NewGrD 80*
Steinert, Alexander Lang 1900- *AmSCAP 66, -80, Baker 78, BiDAmM, ConAmC, OxMus*
Steinert, Moritz 1831-1912 *NewGrD 80*
Steinert, Morris 1831-1912 *NewGrD 80, OxMus*
Steinfort, Robert Edwin 1946- *AmSCAP 80*
Steingaden, Constantin 1618?-1675 *NewGrD 80*
Steingraber *NewGrD 80*
Steingraber, Burkhard 1866-1945 *NewGrD 80*
Steingraber, Eduard 1823-1906 *NewGrD 80*
Steingraber, Georg 1858- *NewGrD 80*
Steingraber, Johann Georg 1858-1932 *Baker 78*
Steingraber, Theodor Leberecht 1830-1904 *Baker 78, NewGrD 80*
Steingrimsson, Gudmundur 1929- *IntWWM 77, -80*
Steingruber, Ilona 1912-1962 *Baker 78*
Steingruber-Wildgans, Ilona *IntWWM 77*
Steinhard, Erich 1886-1942? *Baker 78*
Steinhardt, Herschel 1910- *NatPD[port]*
Steinhardt, Milton Jacob 1909- *Baker 78, IntWWM 77, -80, NewGrD 80*
Steinhausen, Friedrich Adolf 1859-1910 *OxMus*
Steinhoff, Hans 1882-1945 *DcFM, FilmEn, WorEFlm*
Steininger, Frank K W 1906- *ConAmC A*
Steininger, Franz K W 1906- *AmSCAP 66*
Steininger, Franz K W 1910-1974 *AmSCAP 80*
Steinitz, Charles Paul Joseph 1909- *IntWWM 77, -80, WhoMus 72*
Steinitz, Paul 1909- *NewGrD 80*
Steinitz, Richard John 1938- *IntWWM 80*
Steinitzer, Max 1864-1936 *Baker 78*
Steinkamp, Fredric *HalFC 80*
Steinke, Greg A 1942- *AmSCAP 80, CpmDNM 74, -76, -77, -79, -80, ConAmC*
Steinke, Hans 1893-1971 *WhScrn 74, -77, WhoHol B, WhoHrs 80*
Steinkellner, Hans 1925- *NatPD[port]*
Steinkopf, Otto 1904-1980 *NewGrD 80*
Steinmann, Conrad Michael 1951- *IntWWM 80*
Steinmetz *NewGrD 80*
Steinmetz, Earl 1915-1942 *WhScrn 74, -77*
Steinmetz, Johann Erhard *NewGrD 80*
Steinmetz, Lee *PupTheA*
Steinmeyer, Georg Friedrich 1819-1901 *NewGrD 80*
Steinmez *NewGrD 80*
Steinpress, Boris Solomonovich *NewGrD 80*
Steinrisck, Albert *Film 2*
Steinruck, Albert 1872-1929 *EncWT, Film 2, WhScrn 77*
Steinrueck, Albert 1872-1929 *WhoHol B*
Steinway, Albert 1840-1877 *Baker 78*
Steinway, Charles 1829-1865 *Baker 78*
Steinway, Heinrich Engelhard 1797-1871 *NewGrD 80*
Steinway, Heinrich Engelhardt 1797-1871 *BiDAmM*
Steinway, Henry *Baker 78*
Steinway, Henry 1830-1865 *Baker 78*
Steinway, Theodore 1825-1889 *Baker 78, NewGrD 80*
Steinway, Theodore E d1957 *Baker 78*
Steinway, William 1835-1896 *Baker 78*
Steinweg *Baker 78*
Steinweg, C F Theodor 1825-1889 *NewGrD 80, -80*
Steinweg, Heinrich Engelhard 1797-1871 *Baker 78, NewGrD 80*
Stekel, Eric Paul 1898- *IntWWM 77, -80, WhoMus 72*
Stekke, Leon 1904-1970 *Baker 78*
Stekl, Konrad 1901- *IntWWM 77, -80, WhoMus 72*
Stekly, Karel 1903- *DcFM*
Stella, Alfred *NewGrD 80*
Stella, Antonietta 1929- *CmOp, WhoMus 72, WhoOp 76*
Stella, Scipione 1559?-1630? *NewGrD 80*
Stella Dallas *What 3[port]*
Stellfeld, Jean-Auguste 1881-1952 *Baker 78, NewGrD 80*
Stellings, Ernest G *IntMPA 77, -75, -76, -78, -79, 80*
Stelloff, Skip 1925- *IntMPA 77, -75, -76, -78, -79, -80*
Stellovsky, Fyodor Timofeyevich 1826-1875 *NewGrD 80*
Stellwagen *NewGrD 80*
Stellwagen, Friedrich d1659 *NewGrD 80*
Steloff, Frances 1887- *BiE&WWA, NotNAT*
Stelzer, Frances C 1895- *AmSCAP 66, -80*
Stembler, John H 1913- *IntMPA 77, -75, -76, -78, -79, -80*
Stemmele, Gregor d1619 *NewGrD 80*
Stemmelius, Gregor d1619 *NewGrD 80*
Stempel, Michael Lloyd 1953- *AmSCAP 80*
Sten, Anna *MotPP, WomWMM*
Sten, Anna 1907?- *ForYSC, WhoHol A*
Sten, Anna 1908- *FilmEn, FilmgC, HalFC 80, HolP 30[port], MovMk[port], ThFT[port], WorEFlm*
Sten, Anna 1910- *Film 2, OxFilm, What 1[port]*
Stenback, Kirsten *WomWMM*
Stenberg, Jordan 1947- *Baker 78, ConAmC*
Stenberg, Sigvard 1933- *IntWWM 77, -80*
Stenborg, Carl 1752-1813 *Baker 78, NewGrD 80*
Stendhal 1783-1842 *Baker 78, DcPup, NewGrD 80*
Stenermann, Salka *Film 2*
Stengel, Casey 1890-1975 *WhScrn 77, WhoHol C*
Stengel, Leni *Film 2*
Stenger, Nicolaus 1609-1680 *NewGrD 80*
Stenger, Nikolaus 1609-1680 *NewGrD 80*
Stenhammar, Per Ulrik 1828-1875 *Baker 78*
Stenhammar, Vilhelm Eugen 1871-1927 *OxMus*
Stenhammar, Wilhelm 1871-1927 *Baker 78, NewGrD 80*
Stenholm, Katherine Alee Corne 1917- *WomWMM A, -B*
Stenholm, Rolf 1937- *IntWWM 77, -80*
Stenhouse, William 1773-1827 *NewGrD 80*
Stenings, Henry *NewGrD 80*
Stenner, Olive Dunning 1907- *WhoMus 72*
Steno 1915- *FilmEn*
Steno 1917- *WorEFlm*
Stensgaard, Yutte 1948?- *WhoHrs 80*
Stensvold, Terje 1943- *WhoOp 76*
Stent, Keith Geoffrey 1934- *IntWWM 80, WhoMus 72*
Stenton, Paul *NewGrD 80*
Stentzsch, Rosine *NewGrD 80*
Stenzl, Jurg Thomas 1942- *IntWWM 77, -80, NewGrD 80*
Step 'n' Fetchit 1896- *ForYSC*
Stepan, Giuseppe Antonio 1726?-1797 *NewGrD 80*
Stepan, Josef Antonin 1726?-1797 *NewGrD 80*
Stepan, Joseph Anton 1726?-1797 *NewGrD 80*
Stepan, Pavel 1925- *IntWWM 77, -80, NewGrD 80*
Stepan, Vaclav 1889-1944 *Baker 78, NewGrD 80*
Stepanek, Karel 1899- *FilmgC, ForYSC, HalFC 80, MovMk, WhThe, WhoHol A, WhoThe 72*
Stepanian, Aro 1897-1966 *Baker 78*
Step'annos Siunetsi *NewGrD 80*
Stepanoff, Vladimir 1866-1896 *DancEn 78*
Stepanov, Lev 1908- *Baker 78*
Stepanov, Vladimir Ivanovich 1866-1896 *CnOxB*
Stepanova, Elena Andreyevna 1891- *NewGrD 80*

Step'anyan, Haro Levoni 1897-1966 *NewGrD 80*
Stephan, Clemens *NewGrD 80*
Stephan, John *OxMus*
Stephan, Josef Antonin *NewGrD 80*
Stephan, Rudi 1887-1915 *Baker 78, NewGrD 80*
Stephan, Rudolf 1925- *IntWWM 80, NewGrD 80*
Stephane, Nicole *WomWMM*
Stephanescu, George 1843-1925 *Baker 78, NewGrD 80*
Stephani, Agostino *NewGrD 80*
Stephani, Clemens 1530?-1592 *NewGrD 80*
Stephani, Hermann 1877-1960 *Baker 78, NewGrD 80*
Stephani, Johann *NewGrD 80*
Stephani, Josef Antonin *NewGrD 80*
Stephanie, Gottlieb 1741-1800 *NewGrD 80*
Stephanus, Clemens *NewGrD 80*
Stephen Of Liege *NewGrD 80*
Stephen, David 1869-1946 *OxMus*
Stephen, Edith 1929- *CnOxB*
Stephen, Edward 1822-1885 *NewGrD 80, OxMus*
Stephen, John 1912-1974 *WhScrn 77*
Stephen, Susan 1931- *FilmgC, HalFC 80, IntMPA 77, -75, -76, -78, -79, -80, WhoHol A*
Stephen, Susan 1932- *IlWWBF*
Stephens *PupTheA*
Stephens, Ann 1931- *FilmgC, HalFC 80, WhoHol A*
Stephens, Catherine 1794-1882 *NewGrD 80*
Stephens, Charles Cole 1938- *ConAmC*
Stephens, Charles Edward 1821-1892 *Baker 78*
Stephens, Edward *NewGrD 80*
Stephens, Frances 1906- *WhThe*
Stephens, George d1851 *NotNAT B*
Stephens, Glyndwr 1918- *WhoMus 72*
Stephens, H Pottinger d1903 *NotNAT B*
Stephens, Helen *WhoHol A*
Stephens, Howard 1921- *IntWWM 77, -80, WhoMus 72*
Stephens, J Frank d1950 *NotNAT B*
Stephens, Joe d1974 *NewOrJ*
Stephens, John 1720?-1780 *NewGrD 80*
Stephens, John Anthony 1947- *IntWWM 80*
Stephens, John William 1932- *WhoMus 72*
Stephens, Jud 1888-1935 *WhScrn 74, -77*
Stephens, Laraine *WhoHol A*
Stephens, Martin 1949- *FilmgC, HalFC 80, WhoHrs 80[port]*
Stephens, Marvin 1949- *WhoHol A*
Stephens, Mike 1885?-1927? *NewOrJ*
Stephens, Norris Lynn 1930- *IntWWM 77, -80*
Stephens, Paul Day, Jr. 1946- *IntWWM 77, -80*
Stephens, Phillip Rodd 1940- *NatPD[port]*
Stephens, Rachel *WhoHol A*
Stephens, Rex 1913- *IntWWM 77, -80, WhoMus 72*
Stephens, Robert 1931- *CnThe, FilmAG WE, FilmEn, FilmgC, HalFC 80, IlWWBF, WhoHol A, WhoThe 72, -77*
Stephens, Roy *WhoHol A*
Stephens, Sheila *WhoHol A*
Stephens, Socorro *WhoHol A*
Stephens, Stephanie 1900- *WhThe*
Stephens, Mrs. W H d1896 *NotNAT B*
Stephens, Ward 1869-1940 *AmSCAP 66, -80*
Stephens, William Raymond 1916- *IntWWM 77, -80*
Stephens, Yorke 1862-1937 *NotNAT B, WhThe*
Stephensen, B C d1906 *NotNAT B*
Stephenson, Christina Elizabeth 1931- *WhoMus 72*
Stephenson, Donald James 1947- *IntWWM 80*
Stephenson, Edward 1759-1833 *NewGrD 80*
Stephenson, Eric William 1930- *IntWWM 77, -80, WhoMus 72*
Stephenson, Henry 1871-1956 *CmMov, FilmEn, Film 1, -2, FilmgC, HalFC 80, HolCA[port], MotPP, MovMk[port], NotNAT B, Vers A[port], WhScrn 74, -77, WhoHol B*
Stephenson, Henry 1874-1956 *ForYSC, WhThe*
Stephenson, James 1888-1941 *FilmgC, HalFC 80, MotPP, NotNAT B, WhScrn 74, -77, WhoHol B*
Stephenson, James 1903-1941 *ForYSC, IlWWBF*
Stephenson, John d1963 *NotNAT B, WhoHol B*
Stephenson, John W 1922- *AmSCAP 66, -80*
Stephenson, Kurt 1899- *IntWWM 77, -80, NewGrD 80*
Stephenson, Loran Dean 1925- *IntWWM 77, -80*
Stephenson, Mark 1950- *ConAmC*
Stephenson, Robert 1931- *IntWWM 77*
Stephenson, Robert Robinson 1901-1970 *WhScrn 74, -77, WhoHol B*
Stephenson, Skip *JoeFr*
Stephkins, Theodore *NewGrD 80*
Stepin Fetchit 1892- *WhoHol A*
Stepin Fetchit 1896- *Film 2*
Stepin Fetchit 1902- *What 1[port]*
Stepka, Karel Vaclav 1908- *IntWWM 77, -80, WhoMus 72*
Stepleton, James Irvin 1941- *AmSCAP 80, ConAmC*
Steppat, Ilse 1900-1970 *HalFC 80*
Steppat, Ilse 1917-1969 *WhScrn 74, -77, WhoHol B*
Steppat, Ilse 1917-1970 *FilmgC*
Steppenwolf *BiDAmM, ConMuA 80A, IlEncR, RkOn 2[port]*
Stepper, Martin Paul 1948- *ConAmC, IntWWM 77*
Steppling, John C 1869-1932 *Film 1, -2, WhScrn 74, -77, WhoHol B*
Stept, Sam H 1897-1964 *AmPS, AmSCAP 66, -80, BiDAmM, CmpEPM, Sw&Ld C*
Steptoe, Roger Guy 1953- *IntWWM 80*
Steptoe, Rogert Guy 1953- *IntWWM 77*
Sterbini, Cesare 1784-1831 *NewGrD 80*
Stereos, The *RkOn*
Sterk, Ienske 1940- *IntWWM 77, -80*
Sterke, Jeanette *WhoHol A*
Sterkel, Johann Franz Xaver 1750-1817 *Baker 78, NewGrD 80*
Sterler, Hermine *Film 2*
Sterling, Andrew B 1874-1955 *AmPS, AmSCAP 66, -80, BiDAmM, CmpEPM, Sw&Ld B*
Sterling, Antoinette 1850-1904 *Baker 78, BiDAmM, NewGrD 80*
Sterling, Bruce *Film 2*
Sterling, Dick *WhoHol A*
Sterling, Edythe 1887-1962 *Film 2, NotNAT B, WhScrn 74, -77, WhoHol B*
Sterling, Ford 1880-1939 *WhScrn 74, -77*
Sterling, Ford 1883-1939 *FilmEn, FilmgC, ForYSC, HalFC 80, MovMk[port], TwYS, -A*
Sterling, Ford 1884?-1939 *NotNAT B, WhoHol B*
Sterling, Ford 1885-1939 *Film 1, -2*
Sterling, Harriet *Film 2*
Sterling, Jan 1923- *BiE&WWA, FilmEn, FilmgC, HalFC 80, IntMPA 77, -75, -76, -78, -79, -80, MotPP, MovMk, NotNAT, WhoHol A, WhoThe 77*
Sterling, Jane 1923- *ForYSC*
Sterling, Jean *AmSCAP 80*
Sterling, Larry 1935-1958 *WhScrn 74, -77, WhoHol B*
Sterling, Lee 1904-1951 *WhScrn 74, -77*
Sterling, Merta 1883-1944 *Film 2, WhScrn 74, -77, WhoHol B*
Sterling, Phil *WhoHol A*
Sterling, Raymond Andrew 1898- *AmSCAP 66, -80*
Sterling, Richard 1880-1959 *NotNAT B, WhThe*
Sterling, Robert 1917- *BiE&WWA, FilmEn, FilmgC, HalFC 80, IntMPA 77, -75, -76, -78, -79, -80, MGM[port], MotPP, WhoHol A*
Sterling, Tisha 1945- *ForYSC, WhoHol A*
Sterling, Winthrop Smith 1859-1943 *Baker 78, BiDAmM*
Stern *NewGrD 80*
Stern, Adolf 1835-1907 *Baker 78*
Stern, Alfred Bernard 1910- *ConAmC*
Stern, Alfred Bernard 1920- *AmSCAP 80*
Stern, Alfred E F *IntMPA 77, -75, -76, -78, -79, -80*
Stern, Bert *IntMPA 77, -75, -76, -78, -79*
Stern, Bill 1907-1971 *IntMPA 77, -75, -76, -78, -79, WhScrn 74, -77, WhoHol B*
Stern, Carl 1902-1971 *BiDAmM*
Stern, Eddie 1917- *IntMPA 77, -75, -76, -78, -79, -80*
Stern, Edward J 1916- *IntMPA 75, -76*
Stern, Edward J 1946- *NotNAT*
Stern, Ernest 1876-1954 *NotNAT A, -B, WhThe*
Stern, Ernst 1876-1954 *EncWT*
Stern, Ezra E 1908- *IntMPA 77, -75, -76, -78, -79, -80*
Stern, G B 1890- *WhThe*
Stern, Harold *BgBands 74*
Stern, Harry 1902- *IntMPA 75*
Stern, Heinrich 1592-1665 *NewGrD 80*
Stern, Henry 1874-1966 *AmSCAP 66, -80*
Stern, Isaac 1920- *Baker 78, BiDAmM, BnBkM 80, IntWWM 77, -80, MusMk, MusSN[port], NewGrD 80, WhoHol A, WhoMus 72*
Stern, Jack 1896- *AmSCAP 66, -80*
Stern, Jeanne 1908- *DcFM*
Stern, Joan Keller *WomWMM B*
Stern, Johann d1614 *NewGrD 80*
Stern, Johann d1656 *NewGrD 80*
Stern, Johann 1633-1712 *NewGrD 80*
Stern, Joseph W 1870-1934 *AmPS, BiDAmM, NotNAT B, PopAmC[port]*
Stern, Julius 1820-1883 *Baker 78, NewGrD 80*
Stern, Kurt 1907- *DcFM*
Stern, Leo 1862-1904 *Baker 78, NewGrD 80*
Stern, Leonard B *NewYTET*
Stern, Louis 1860-1941 *Film 2, WhScrn 74, -77, WhoHol B*
Stern, Max 1947- *AmSCAP 80, ConAmC*
Stern, Robert Lewis 1934- *AmSCAP 66, -80, ConAmC*
Stern, Sam 1883- *WhThe*
Stern, Stanley L 1917- *IntMPA 77, -78, -79, -80*
Stern, Stewart 1922- *ConDr 73, -77A, FilmEn, IntMPA 77, -75, -76, -78, -79, -80, WorEFlm*
Stern, Tom *WhoHol A*
Stern, Toni Kathrin 1950- *AmSCAP 80*
Stern, Wes *WhoHol A*
Sternad, Rudolph 1905-1963 *IntMPA 77, -75, -76, -78, -79, -80, NotNAT B*
Sternbach, David Joel 1934- *IntWWM 77, -80*
Sternberg, Constantin 1852-1924 *Baker 78, BiDAmM*
Sternberg, Erich Walter 1891-1974 *Baker 78, NewGrD 80*
Sternberg, Jonathan 1919- *IntWWM 77, -80, WhoMus 72*
Sternberg, Josef Von 1894-1969 *AmFD, DcFM, FilmEn, OxFilm*
Sternbergh, Beverly Kelley 1927- *IntWWM 77*
Sternburg, Janet *WomWMM A, -B*
Sterndale-Bennett, Barry Monkhouse 1939- *IntWWM 77, -80, WhoMus 72*
Sterndale-Bennett, T C 1882-1944 *NotNAT B, WhThe*
Sterne, Colin C 1921- *ConAmC, IntWWM 77, -80*
Sterne, Kenneth *AmSCAP 80*
Sterne, Morgan 1926- *BiE&WWA, NotNAT, WhoHol A*
Sternefeld, Daniel 1905- *Baker 78, IntWWM 77, -80, NewGrD 80, WhoMus 72*
Sternfeld, F W 1914- *NewGrD 80*
Sternfeld, Frederick William 1914- *Baker 78, IntWWM 77, -80, WhoMus 72*
Sternfeld, Richard 1858-1926 *Baker 78*
Sternfield, Allen *NatPD[port]*
Sternhagen, Frances 1930- *BiE&WWA, NotNAT, WhoHol A, WhoThe 72, -77*
Sternheim, Carl 1878-1942 *CnMD, CnThe, EncWT, Ent, McGEWD[port], ModWD, REnWD[port]*
Sternheim, Carl 1878-1943 *NotNAT B, OxThe*
Sternhold, Thomas d1549 *OxMus*
Sternhold And Hopkins *OxMus*
Sternklar, Avraham 1930- *AmSCAP 80, ConAmC*
Sternroyd, Vincent 1857-1948 *NotNAT B, WhThe*
Sterrall, Gertrude *Film 2*

Sterrett, Thomas *Film 1*
Stesichorus 610?BC-535?BC *NewGrD 80*
Steszewski, Jan Maria 1929- *IntWWM 77, -80, NewGrD 80*
Stettheimer, Florine d1944 *NotNAT B*
Stettith, Olive d1937 *NotNAT B*
Stettner, Fred 1927- *IntMPA 75, -76*
Steuart, Douglas 1927- *DancEn 78*
Steuart, Richard Carson 1956- *IntWWM 77, -80*
Steuccius, Heinrich 1579-1645 *NewGrD 80*
Steucke, Heinrich 1579-1645 *NewGrD 80*
Steude, Wolfram 1931- *NewGrD 80*
Steuerlein, Johann 1546-1613 *Baker 78, NewGrD 80*
Steuerlein, Johannes 1546-1613 *NewGrD 80*
Steuermann, Eduard 1892-1964 *Baker 78, BnBkM 80, DcCM, NewGrD 80*
Steuermann, Edward 1892-1964 *ConAmC, NewGrD 80*
Steve And Eydie *RkOn[port]*
Steven, Boyd 1875-1967 *WhScrn 74, -77, WhoHol B*
Steven, Gary *WhoHol A*
Stevens, Alex *WhoHol A*
Stevens, Allan Stanley Herbert 1924- *WhoMus 72*
Stevens, Andrew 1955- *HalFC 80*
Stevens, Andrew 1956- *IntMPA 79, -80*
Stevens, Angela *ForYSC*
Stevens, Arthur *NewOrJ*
Stevens, Ashton 1872-1951 *NotNAT B, WhThe*
Stevens, Bernard 1916- *Baker 78, ConAmC, IntWWM 77, -80, NewGrD 80, OxMus*
Stevens, Bernard George 1916- *WhoMus 72*
Stevens, Byron E 1904-1964 *WhScrn 74, -77, WhoHol B*
Stevens, Casandra Mayo d1966 *AmSCAP 66, -80*
Stevens, Cat *ConMuA 80A*
Stevens, Cat 1947- *IlEncR*
Stevens, Cat 1948- *BiDAmM, RkOn 2[port]*
Stevens, Charles 1893-1964 *Film 1, -2, ForYSC, NotNAT B, TwYS, Vers B[port], WhScrn 74, -77, WhoHol B*
Stevens, Charlotte *Film 2*
Stevens, Clancey *Film 2*
Stevens, Clifford 1936- *BiE&WWA, NotNAT*
Stevens, Connie 1938- *AmPS A, BiDAmM, FilmEn, FilmgC, ForYSC, HalFC 80, IntMPA 77, -75, -76, -78, -79, -80, MotPP, RkOn[port], WhoHol A*
Stevens, Craig 1918- *BiE&WWA, FilmEn, FilmgC, ForYSC, HalFC 80, HolP 40[port], IntMPA 77, -75, -76, -78, -79, -80, MotPP, MovMk, WhoHol A*
Stevens, Cy d1974 *WhoHol B*
Stevens, Cye d1974 *WhScrn 77*
Stevens, David Kilburn 1860-1946 *AmSCAP 66, -80*
Stevens, Denis William 1922- *Baker 78, IntWWM 77, -80, NewGrD 80, OxMus, WhoMus 72*
Stevens, Dodie *WhoHol A*
Stevens, Dodie 1947- *RkOn*
Stevens, Edward Gale 1941- *AmSCAP 80*
Stevens, Edwin 1860-1923 *Film 1, -2, TwYS, WhScrn 77, WhThe*
Stevens, Emily 1882-1928 *Film 1, NotNAT B, WhScrn 74, -77, WhThe, WhoHol B*
Stevens, Emily Favela *WomWMM B*
Stevens, Evelyn 1891-1938 *WhScrn 74, -77, WhoHol B*
Stevens, Floyd Euon 1944- *IntWWM 77*
Stevens, Fran *WhoHol A*
Stevens, Garry 1916- *CmpEPM*
Stevens, Geoffrey *WhoHol A*
Stevens, George *Film 1*
Stevens, George 1803-1894 *NewGrD 80*
Stevens, George 1904-1975 *BiDFilm, -81, CmMov, DcFM, FilmEn, FilmgC, HalFC 80, IntMPA 75, MovMk[port], OxFilm, WhScrn 77, WorEFlm*
Stevens, George 1905-1975 *AmFD, Film 2*
Stevens, George, Jr. 1932- *FilmEn, IntMPA 77, -75, -76, -78, -79, -80*
Stevens, George Alexander d1784 *NotNAT B*
Stevens, Georgia Cooper *WhScrn 74, -77*
Stevens, Glenn 1899-1974 *AmSCAP 66, -80, ConAmC*
Stevens, H C G 1892-1967 *WhThe*
Stevens, Halsey 1908- *Baker 78, CpmDNM 74, -79, -80, ConAmC, DcCM, IntWWM 77, -80, NewGrD 80, OxMus, WhoMus 72*
Stevens, Harvey *ForYSC*
Stevens, Harvey 1971- *WhoHrs 80*
Stevens, Horace 1876-1950 *NewGrD 80*
Stevens, Inger d1970 *MotPP, WhoHol B*
Stevens, Inger 1934-1970 *BiE&WWA, FilmEn, ForYSC, NotNAT B*
Stevens, Inger 1935-1970 *FilmgC, HalFC 80, WhScrn 74, -77*
Stevens, Inger 1936-1970 *MovMk*
Stevens, Ira S 1922- *IntMPA 77, -75, -76*
Stevens, J E 1921- *IntWWM 80*
Stevens, James 1928- *WhoMus 72*
Stevens, James 1930- *IntWWM 77, -80*
Stevens, Joan Frances 1921- *IntWWM 77, -80*
Stevens, John *IlEncJ*
Stevens, John 1921- *NewGrD 80*
Stevens, John A d1916 *NotNAT B*
Stevens, John Edgar 1921- *WhoMus 72*
Stevens, John William Eric 1931- *WhoMus 72*
Stevens, John Wright *WhoOp 76*
Stevens, Josephine *Film 1*
Stevens, Julie *WhoHol A*
Stevens, K T 1919- *FilmEn, FilmgC, HalFC 80, IntMPA 77, -75, -76, -78, -79, -80, WhThe, WhoHol A*
Stevens, Katherine 1919- *ForYSC*
Stevens, Kaye *WhoHol A*
Stevens, Lander 1877-1940 *WhoHol B*
Stevens, Landers 1877-1940 *Film 2, WhScrn 74, -77*
Stevens, Lee 1930- *IntMPA 77, -75, -76, -78, -79, -80*
Stevens, Leith 1909-1970 *CmpEPM, EncJzS 70, FilmEn, HalFC 80, WhoHrs 80, WorEFlm*
Stevens, Leith 1910-1970 *FilmgC*
Stevens, Len *WhoMus 72*
Stevens, Lenore *WhoHol A*
Stevens, Leslie 1924- *BiE&WWA, FilmEn, FilmgC, HalFC 80, IntMPA 77, -75, -76, -78, -79, -80, NewYTET, NotNAT, WorEFlm*
Stevens, Lester *Film 2*
Stevens, Lynn 1898-1950 *WhScrn 74, -77, WhoHol B*
Stevens, Mark *IntMPA 77, -75, -76, -78, -79, -80, MotPP*
Stevens, Mark 1915- *FilmEn, ForYSC, WhoHol A*
Stevens, Mark 1916- *FilmgC, HalFC 80*
Stevens, Marsha Jeanne 1952- *AmSCAP 80*
Stevens, Martin *PupTheA*
Stevens, Morton 1929- *AmSCAP 66, -80*
Stevens, Morton L 1890-1959 *NotNAT B, WhScrn 74, -77, WhoHol B*
Stevens, Nan 1921- *BiE&WWA*
Stevens, Naomi *WhoHol A*
Stevens, Olga *PupTheA*
Stevens, Onslow *IntMPA 77, -75, -76*
Stevens, Onslow 1902-1977 *FilmEn, FilmgC, ForYSC, HalFC 80, MovMk, Vers A[port], WhoHol A, WhoHrs 80*
Stevens, Onslow 1906- *BiE&WWA, NotNAT, WhThe*
Stevens, Oren *WhoHol A*
Stevens, Paul 1924- *BiE&WWA, NotNAT, WhoHol A*
Stevens, Perry 1928- *AmSCAP 80*
Stevens, Ray 1939- *IlEncCM[port]*
Stevens, Ray 1941- *RkOn*
Stevens, Richard John Samuel 1757-1837 *Baker 78, NewGrD 80, OxMus*
Stevens, Rise 1913- *Baker 78, BiDAmM, BnBkM 80, CmOp, CmpEPM, FilmgC, ForYSC, HalFC 80, IntMPA 75, -76, MusSN[port], NewEOp 71, NewGrD 80, What 4[port], WhoHol A*
Stevens, Robert 1880?-1963 *NotNAT B, WhScrn 74, -77*
Stevens, Robert 1882-1963 *WhoHol B*
Stevens, Robert 1925?- *FilmEn, FilmgC, HalFC 80*
Stevens, Robert T 1899- *What 4[port]*
Stevens, Roger L 1910- *BiE&WWA, NotNAT, WhoThe 72, -77*
Stevens, Ron 1940- *WhoOp 76*
Stevens, Ronnie 1925- *FilmgC, HalFC 80, WhoHol A, WhoThe 72, -77*
Stevens, Stella *IntMPA 75, -76*
Stevens, Stella 1936- *FilmEn, ForYSC, HalFC 80, WhoHrs 80*
Stevens, Stella 1938- *BiDFilm, -81, FilmgC, IntMPA 77, -78, -79, -80, MotPP, WhoHol A*
Stevens, Thomas Wood d1942 *NotNAT B*
Stevens, Vi 1892-1967 *WhoHol B*
Stevens, Victor d1925 *NotNAT B*
Stevens, Violet 1892-1967 *WhScrn 74, -77*
Stevens, Warren 1919- *FilmgC, ForYSC, HalFC 80, WhoHol A*
Stevens, William Jervis 1921- *IntWWM 77, -80*
Stevenson, Adlai E 1900-1965 *WhScrn 77*
Stevenson, B W 1949- *RkOn 2[port]*
Stevenson, Barbara Thorne 1919- *IntWWM 77, -80*
Stevenson, Ben 1937- *CnOxB*
Stevenson, Burke 1899- *NewOrJ*
Stevenson, Charles A 1851-1929 *NotNAT B, WhScrn 74, -77, WhoHol B*
Stevenson, Charles E 1888-1943 *Film 2, WhScrn 74, -77, WhoHol B*
Stevenson, Douglas 1883-1934 *Film 2, NotNAT B, WhScrn 77, WhoHol B*
Stevenson, George Edward 1906-1970 *EncJzS 70, WhoJazz 72*
Stevenson, Harry Payne 1916- *AmSCAP 66*
Stevenson, Hayden *Film 2, TwYS*
Stevenson, Houseley 1879-1953 *FilmgC, ForYSC, HalFC 80, Vers B[port], WhScrn 74, -77, WhoHol B*
Stevenson, Houseley, Jr. *WhoHol A*
Stevenson, Hugh 1910-1946 *CnOxB*
Stevenson, Hugh 1910-1956 *DancEn 78*
Stevenson, John d1922 *WhScrn 74, -77*
Stevenson, Sir John Andrew 1761-1833 *NewGrD 80, OxMus*
Stevenson, Louis C 1949- *AmSCAP 80*
Stevenson, Margot *WhoHol A*
Stevenson, Margot 1914- *WhoThe 72, -77*
Stevenson, Margot 1918- *BiE&WWA, NotNAT*
Stevenson, McLean *WhoHol A*
Stevenson, Nora Ann Carroll 1924- *IntWWM 77, -80*
Stevenson, Parker *IntMPA 79, -80*
Stevenson, Peter Anthony Stanley 1928- *WhoMus 72*
Stevenson, Phyllis Diane Miles 1944- *IntWWM 77, -80*
Stevenson, Robert *NewGrD 80*
Stevenson, Robert 1905- *FilmEn, FilmgC, HalFC 80, IlWWBF, IntMPA 77, -75, -76, -78, -79, -80, MovMk[port], WhoHrs 80, WorEFlm*
Stevenson, Robert E Lee 1924- *AmSCAP 66*
Stevenson, Robert J 1915-1975 *WhScrn 77, WhoHol C*
Stevenson, Robert Louis 1850-1894 *DcPup, FilmgC, HalFC 80, OxMus, WhoHrs 80*
Stevenson, Robert Murrell 1916- *Baker 78, IntWWM 77, -80, NewGrD 80*
Stevenson, Ronald 1928- *Baker 78, DcCM, IntWWM 77, -80, NewGrD 80, WhoMus 72*
Stevenson, Steve Tommy 1914?-1944 *WhoJazz 72*
Stevenson, Venetia *ForYSC, WhoHol A*
Stevenson, William 1521-1575 *CnThe, McGEWD, NotNAT B, OxThe*
Stevenson, William Thomas 1929- *AmSCAP 80*
Steventon, G H 1914- *AmSCAP 80*
Stever, Hans *Film 2*
Steward, Cliff 1916- *AmSCAP 66, -80*
Steward, Ernest *HalFC 80*
Steward, Herbie 1926- *CmpEPM*
Steward, Kenny *PlP&P A[port]*
Steward, Leslie *Film 2*
Steward, Redd *BiDAmM*
Stewart, Al 1945- *AmSCAP 80, ConMuA 80A, IlEncR, RkOn 2[port]*
Stewart, Alexandra 1939- *FilmAG WE, FilmEn, FilmgC, HalFC 80, WhoHol A*
Stewart, Alonzo 1919- *NewOrJ SUP[port]*
Stewart, Andy 1934- *IntMPA 77, -75, -76, -78,*

-79
Stewart, Anita d1961 *MotPP, NotNAT B, WhoHol B*
Stewart, Anita 1895-1961 *FilmEn, Film 1, -2, FilmgC, HalFC 80, WhScrn 74, -77*
Stewart, Anita 1896-1962 *TwYS*
Stewart, Athole 1879-1940 *FilmgC, HalFC 80, NotNAT B, WhScrn 74, -77, WhThe, WhoHol B*
Stewart, Barbara D 1941- *IntWWM 77, -80*
Stewart, Barry *WhoHol A*
Stewart, Betty 1912-1944 *WhScrn 74, -77*
Stewart, Betty Jean 1935- *IntWWM 77*
Stewart, Billy d1970 *RkOn[port]*
Stewart, Blanche d1952 *WhScrn 77*
Stewart, Buddy 1921?-1950 *CmpEPM*
Stewart, Charles 1887- *BiE&WWA*
Stewart, Charles Hylton 1884-1932 *OxMus*
Stewart, Charlotte *WhoHol A*
Stewart, Cray 1924-1961 *WhScrn 74, -77*
Stewart, Daniel Kalauawa 1907-1961 *AmSCAP 80*
Stewart, Danny 1907-1962 *NotNAT B, WhScrn 74, -77, WhoHol B*
Stewart, David J d1966 *WhoHol B*
Stewart, David J 1914-1966 *WhScrn 74, -77*
Stewart, David J 1919-1966 *BiE&WWA, NotNAT B*
Stewart, David N *ConAmC*
Stewart, Dona Jean 1939-1961 *WhScrn 74, -77*
Stewart, Donald 1911-1966 *WhScrn 74, -77, WhoHol B*
Stewart, Donald George 1935- *AmSCAP 80, ConAmC*
Stewart, Donald Ogden 1894-1980 *BiE&WWA, Conv 1[port], FilmEn, FilmgC, HalFC 80, NotNAT, WhThe, WorEFlm*
Stewart, Doris *PupTheA*
Stewart, Dorothy M 1897-1954 *AmSCAP 66, -80*
Stewart, Douglas Alexander 1913- *ConDr 73, -77*
Stewart, Douglas MacDonald 1892- *WhoMus 72*
Stewart, Earl 1906- *IntWWM 77*
Stewart, Elaine 1929- *FilmEn, FilmgC, ForYSC, HalFC 80, IntMPA 77, -75, -76, -78, -79, -80, MotPP, WhoHol A*
Stewart, Eldean *Film 1*
Stewart, Ellen 1931- *DrBlPA, NotNAT, PlP&P, WhoThe 77*
Stewart, Frank Graham 1920- *AmSCAP 80, CpmDNM 73, -76, -80, ConAmC, IntWWM 77, -80*
Stewart, Fred d1970 *WhoHol B*
Stewart, Fred 1906-1970 *BiE&WWA, NotNAT B, WhThe, WhoThe 72*
Stewart, Fred 1907-1970 *WhScrn 74, -77*
Stewart, G Wauchope *OxMus*
Stewart, Gary *IlEncCM[port]*
Stewart, George *NewOrJ*
Stewart, George 1888-1945 *Film 2, WhScrn 74, -77, WhoHol B*
Stewart, Grant d1929 *NotNAT B, WhoStg 1908*
Stewart, Hascal Vaughan 1898- *ConAmC*
Stewart, Herbert G 1909- *AmSCAP 66, -80*
Stewart, Hugh 1910- *FilmgC, HalFC 80, IntMPA 77, -75, -76, -78, -79, -80*
Stewart, Humphrey John 1856-1932 *Baker 78, BiDAmM*
Stewart, Jack 1914-1966 *WhScrn 74, -77, WhoHol B*
Stewart, James *IntMPA 77, -75, -76, -78, -79, -80, WhoHol A*
Stewart, James d1860? *NewGrD 80*
Stewart, James 1908- *BiDFilm, -81, BiE&WWA, CmMov, FilmEn, FilmgC, ForYSC, HalFC 80[port], MGM[port], MotPP, MovMk[port], OxFilm, PlP&P, WhoHrs 80[port], WhoThe 77, WorEFlm[port]*
Stewart, James 1909- *CmMov*
Stewart, James Otto 1937- *AmSCAP 80, EncJzS 70*
Stewart, James Richard 1950- *AmSCAP 80*
Stewart, James T *BlkAmP*
Stewart, Jay *IntMPA 79, -80*
Stewart, Jean *Film 1*
Stewart, Jean Elinor 1914- *IntWWM 77, -80, WhoMus 72*
Stewart, Jimmy 1937- *EncJzS 70*
Stewart, Joan Beatrice *AmSCAP 80*
Stewart, John *ConMuA 80A, IntWWM 80*
Stewart, John d1957 *NotNAT B, OxThe*
Stewart, John 1939- *IlEncCM[port], IlEncR*
Stewart, John Harger 1940- *WhoOp 76*
Stewart, Johnny *WhoHol A*
Stewart, Joseph Anthony 1924- *AmSCAP 80*
Stewart, Julia *Film 1, WhScrn 77*
Stewart, Katharine 1891- *WhoMus 72*
Stewart, Katherine d1949 *NotNAT B*
Stewart, Kay *WhoHol A*
Stewart, Kensey D *ConAmC*
Stewart, Larry *WhoHol A*
Stewart, Larry 1914- *CmpEPM*
Stewart, Larry Joe 1940- *IntWWM 77, -80*
Stewart, Leroy Elliott 1914- *AmSCAP 80, BiDAmM, EncJzS 70*
Stewart, Leslie *Film 1*
Stewart, Lock *Film 1*
Stewart, Lucille Lee 1894- *Film 1, -2, TwYS, WhoHol A*
Stewart, M Dee 1935- *IntWWM 77, -80*
Stewart, Marianne *WhoHol A*
Stewart, Marilyn *IntMPA 77, -75, -76, -78, -79, -80*
Stewart, Martha 1921?- *CmpEPM*
Stewart, Martha 1922- *IntMPA 77, -75, -76, -78, -79, -80, WhoHol A*
Stewart, Mel *DrBlPA, WhoHol A*
Stewart, Meredith A 1951- *AmSCAP 80*
Stewart, Michael *ConDr 73, -77D, ConMuA 80B*
Stewart, Michael 1924- *IntMPA 77, -75, -76, -78, -79*
Stewart, Michael 1929- *BiE&WWA, EncMT, NewCBMT, NotNAT, WhoThe 77*
Stewart, N Coe 1837-1921 *BiDAmM*
Stewart, Nancye 1893- *WhThe*
Stewart, Nellie 1858-1931 *WhScrn 77*
Stewart, Nellie 1860-1931 *NotNAT B, WhThe*
Stewart, Nicholas *WhoHol A*
Stewart, Nicodemus *BlksB&W C*
Stewart, Olive Elsie *WhoMus 72*
Stewart, Ora Pate 1910- *AmSCAP 80*
Stewart, Patrick 1940- *WhoHol A, WhoThe 72, -77*
Stewart, Paul 1908- *FilmEn, FilmgC, ForYSC, HalFC 80, HolCA[port], MovMk, Vers A[port], WhoHol A*
Stewart, Paula 1933- *BiE&WWA, NotNAT, WhoHol A, WomWMM*
Stewart, Peggy 1923- *FilmEn, ForYSC, IntMPA 77, -75, -76, -78, -79, -80, WhoHol A*
Stewart, Perry 1942- *ConAmTC*
Stewart, Peter *FilmEn*
Stewart, Priscilla Kay 1948- *IntWWM 80*
Stewart, Redd *EncFCWM 69*
Stewart, Redd 1921- *IlEncCM[port]*
Stewart, Reginald 1900- *Baker 78, CreCan 1*
Stewart, Reginald George 1902- *WhoMus 72*
Stewart, Rex 1907-1967 *AmSCAP 66, -80, BiDAmM, CmpEPM, EncJzS 70, IlEncJ, WhoJazz 72*
Stewart, Richard *ConAmC*
Stewart, Richard d1938? *WhScrn 74, -77*
Stewart, Richard d1939 *WhoHol B*
Stewart, Richard Murray 1954- *IntWWM 77, -80*
Stewart, Robert 1918- *ConAmC, IntWWM 77, -80*
Stewart, Robert J 1932- *ConAmC*
Stewart, Sir Robert Prescott 1825-1894 *Baker 78, NewGrD 80, OxMus*
Stewart, Robin *WhoHol A*
Stewart, Rod 1945- *AmSCAP 80, ConMuA 80A[port], IlEncR[port], RkOn 2[port]*
Stewart, Ron *BlkAmP, MorBAP*
Stewart, Roy d1933 *MotPP, WhoHol B*
Stewart, Roy 1884-1933 *Film 1, -2, TwYS*
Stewart, Roy 1889-1933 *ForYSC, WhScrn 74, -77*
Stewart, Ruth Finnemore 1932- *WhoMus 72*
Stewart, S S 1855-1898 *NewGrD 80*
Stewart, Sam *WhoHol A*
Stewart, Sammy 1890-1960 *WhoJazz 72*
Stewart, Sandy 1937- *AmPS A, -B, RkOn*
Stewart, Slam 1914- *CmpEPM, EncJzS 70, WhoJazz 72*
Stewart, Sophie 1908- *WhoHol A, WhoThe 72, -77*
Stewart, Sophie 1909-1977 *FilmgC, HalFC 80*
Stewart, Susan Kaye 1953- *IntWWM 77*
Stewart, Ted *Film 2*
Stewart, Thomas 1928- *Baker 78, BiDAmM, CmOp, IntWWM 77, -80, MusSN[port], NewEOp 71, NewGrD 80*
Stewart, Thomas James 1928- *WhoOp 76*
Stewart, Tom *WhoHol A*
Stewart, Virginia Lee *Film 2*
Stewart, William G 1870-1941 *NotNAT B, WhoStg 1906, -1908*
Stewart, William H 1923- *AmSCAP 66*
Stewart, Wynn 1934- *BiDAmM, CounME 74, -74A, EncFCWM 69, IlEncCM[port]*
Stewart, Yvonne *WhoHol A*
Steyer, Matej Vaclav 1630-1692 *NewGrD 80*
Sthoken, Johannes De *NewGrD 80*
Stiasny *NewGrD 80, -80*
Stiastny *NewGrD 80, -80*
Stibilj, Milan 1929- *Baker 78, DcCM, NewGrD 80*
Stice, Johnnie Mae 1943- *IntWWM 77*
Stich, J W *OxMus*
Stich, Jan Vaclav 1746-1803 *Baker 78*
Stich, Johann Wenzel *NewGrD 80*
Stich, Patricia *WhoHol A*
Stich-Randall, Teresa 1927- *CmOp, IntWWM 77, -80, NewEOp 71, NewGrD 80, WhoMus 72*
Stickl, Franz *NewGrD 80*
Stickland, William *MagIID*
Stickle, David V R 1916- *IntMPA 77, -75, -76, -78, -79*
Stickles, William C 1882-1971 *AmSCAP 66, -80, BiDAmM*
Stickney, Dorothy 1900- *BiE&WWA, ForYSC, MotPP, NotNAT, WhoHol A, WhoThe 72, -77*
Stickney, John 1744-1827 *BiDAmM*
Stickney, Kimball Philip 1953- *AmSCAP 80*
Stidfole, Arthur *ConAmC*
Stidham, Arbee 1917- *BluesWW[port]*
Stidman, Bobby 1953- *AmSCAP 80*
Stiebler, Ernstalbrecht 1934- *NewGrD 80*
Stiebler, Mary *AmSCAP 80*
Stiebner, Hans 1899-1958 *WhScrn 74, -77*
Stieda, Heinz *Film 2*
Stiedry, Fritz 1883-1968 *Baker 78, BiDAmM, CmOp, MusSN[port], NewEOp 71, NewGrD 80*
Stief, Bo 1946- *IntWWM 77*
Stiefel, Milton 1900- *BiE&WWA, NotNAT*
Stieff *NewGrD 80*
Stieff, Charles d1917 *NewGrD 80*
Stieff, Charles Maximilian 1805-1862 *NewGrD 80*
Stieff, Frederick Philip 1845-1918 *NewGrD 80*
Stieff, Frederick Philip, Jr. *NewGrD 80*
Stieff, George Waters *NewGrD 80*
Stieff, John L 1831-1901 *NewGrD 80*
Stiehl, Carl Johann Christian 1826-1911 *Baker 78, NewGrD 80*
Stiehl, Heinrich 1829-1886 *Baker 78, NewGrD 80*
Stiehl, Johann Dietrich 1800-1873 *Baker 78*
Stiehl, Karl 1826-1911 *NewGrD 80*
Stieler, Caspar Von 1632-1707 *NewGrD 80*
Stierlein, Johann Christoph d1693 *NewGrD 80*
Stierlein, Philipp David *NewGrD 80*
Stierlin, Adolf 1859-1930 *Baker 78*
Stierlin, Johann Christoph *NewGrD 80*
Stiernhielm, Georg 1598-1672 *OxThe*
Stievenard, Alexandre 1767?-1855 *NewGrD 80*
Stiff, Wilfred Charles 1918- *WhoMus 72*
Stifter, Magnus *Film 2*
Stigelli, Giorgio 1815-1868 *Baker 78*
Stigler, Eric 1917- *AmSCAP 80*
Stiglic, France 1919- *DcFM, WorEFlm*
Stignani, Ebe 1903- *MusSN[port]*
Stignani, Ebe 1904-1974 *CmOp, NewGrD 80[port]*
Stignani, Ebe 1907-1974 *BnBkM 80, NewEOp 71*
Stigwood, Robert *ConMuA 80B*
Stigwood, Robert 1930- *CnThe*
Stigwood, Robert 1934- *IlEncR, IntMPA 79,*

-80
Stigwood, Robert 1939?- *HalFC 80*
Stiles, Frank 1924- *IntWWM 77, -80*
Stiles, James Everett 1949- *CpmDNM 79, -80*
Stiles, Leslie 1876- *WhThe*
Stiles, Norman B 1942- *AmSCAP 80*
Stiles, Thelma Jackson 1939- *BlkAmP*
Stilinovic, Branka 1926- *WhoOp 76*
Still, Franc *PupTheA*
Still, John d1607 *NotNAT B, OxThe*
Still, Robert 1910-1971 *Baker 78, NewGrD 80*
Still, William Grant 1895-1978 *AmSCAP 66, -80, Baker 78, BiDAmM, BnBkM 80, CompSN[port], ConAmC, DcCM, DrBlPA, NewEOp 71, NewGrD 80, OxMus, WhoMus 72*
Stiller, Andrew Philip 1946- *ConAmC*
Stiller, Jerry *WhoHol A*
Stiller, Mauritz 1883-1928 *BiDFilm, -81, DcFM, FilmEn, FilmgC, HalFC 80, MovMk[port], OxFilm, TwYS A, WhScrn 77, WorEFlm*
Stillfried, Eleonore Auersperg De 1919- *IntWWM 77, -80*
Stillingfleet, Benjamin 1702-1771 *NewGrD 80*
Stillman, Al 1906-1979 *AmPS, AmSCAP 66, -80, CmpEPM, Sw&Ld C*
Stillman, David B d1963 *NotNAT B*
Stillman, Marsha d1962 *NotNAT B*
Stillman, Mildred 1890-1950 *BiDAmM*
Stillman, Mitya 1892-1936 *Baker 78, ConAmC*
Stillman-Kelley, Edgar *Baker 78*
Stills, Stephen 1945- *AmSCAP 80, ConMuA 80A, IlEncR[port]*
Stills, William Grant *MorBAP*
Stilman, Julia 1937- *IntWWM 77, -80*
Stilwell, F Raymond 1932- *IntWWM 77, -80*
Stilwell, John Grant 1895- *WhoMus 72*
Stilwell, Richard 1942- *NewGrD 80, WhoOp 76*
Stilwell, Sandra Sykora 1941- *IntWWM 77*
Stimson, John W 1946- *NatPD[port]*
Stine, Clifford *WhoHrs 80*
Stine, Lawrence 1912- *BiE&WWA, NotNAT*
Stinfalico, Eterio *NewGrD 80*
Stingl, Anton 1908- *IntWWM 77, -80*
Stingle, David Ellot 1948- *AmSCAP 80*
Stinnett, Stephanie Gayle 1954- *IntWWM 77, -80*
Stinnette, Juanita 1899-1932 *BlksBF*
Stinson, Albert Forrest, Jr. 1944-1969 *EncJzS 70*
Stinton, Elsie *WhoMus 72*
Stipe, Eula Mae 1933- *IntWWM 77*
Stipe, Thomas R, II 1950- *AmSCAP 80*
Stipo, Carmine *WhoHol A*
Stires, Ernest 1926- *AmSCAP 80*
Stirling, Edward 1809-1894 *NotNAT B, OxThe*
Stirling, Edward 1892-1948 *WhScrn 77, WhoHol B*
Stirling, Elizabeth 1819-1895 *Baker 78, OxMus*
Stirling, Fanny 1813-1895 *NotNAT A, -B*
Stirling, Fanny 1815-1895 *OxThe*
Stirling, Helen *WhoHol A*
Stirling, Ian *WhoMus 72*
Stirling, Linda 1921- *ForYSC, What 5[port], WhoHol A, WhoHrs 80[port]*
Stirling, Pamela *WhoHol A*
Stirling, W Edward 1891-1948 *NotNAT A, -B, WhThe*
Stites, Frank 1882-1915 *WhScrn 77*
Stites, Gary 1940- *RkOn*
Stith, Laurence 1933- *AmSCAP 66, -80*
Stith, Marice W 1926- *IntWWM 77, -80*
Stitt, Edward 1924- *BiDAmM, EncJzS 70*
Stitt, Irene C 1925- *IntWWM 77, -80*
Stitt, Milan 1941- *NotNAT*
Stitt, Sonny 1924- *CmpEPM, DrBlPA, EncJzS 70, IlEncJ*
Stitz, Harry 1905- *AmSCAP 66*
Stitzel, Mel 1903-1953 *WhoJazz 72*
Stitzel, Melville J 1902-1952 *AmSCAP 66, -80*
Stivell, Alan 1943- *IlEncR*
Stivers, Duskal *Film 2*
Stivin, Jiri 1942- *EncJzS 70*
Stivori, Francesco 1550?-1605 *NewGrD 80*
Stix, John 1920- *BiE&WWA, NotNAT*
Stjepan, Zlatica 1929- *DancEn 78*
Stobaeus, Johann 1580-1646 *Baker 78, MusMk, NewGrD 80*
Stobaeus, Johannes 1580-1646 *NewGrD 80*
Stobart, James William 1938- *IntWWM 80, WhoMus 72*
Stobaus, Johann 1580-1646 *NewGrD 80*
Stobeus, Johann 1580-1646 *NewGrD 80*
Stoboeus, Johann 1580-1646 *NewGrD 80*
Stoccken, Johannes De *NewGrD 80*
Stochem, Johannes De *NewGrD 80*
Stochs, Georg *NewGrD 80*
Stochs, Johann d1546? *NewGrD 80*
Stock, Alfred Robert 1888- *WhoMus 72*
Stock, David 1947- *AmSCAP 80*
Stock, David Frederick 1939- *Baker 78, CpmDNM 76, -77, ConAmC, DcCM*
Stock, Frederick A 1872-1942 *Baker 78, BiDAmM, BnBkM 80, ConAmC, MusSN[port], NewGrD 80, OxMus*
Stock, Friedrich August 1872-1942 *NewGrD 80*
Stock, Gailene 1946- *CnOxB*
Stock, Jack d1954 *NotNAT B*
Stock, Larry 1896- *AmSCAP 66*
Stock, Lawrence 1896- *AmSCAP 80*
Stock, Nigel 1919- *FilmgC, HalFC 80, WhoHol A, WhoThe 72, -77*
Stock, Valeska *Film 2*
Stockard, Sharon *BlkAmP, MorBAP*
Stockbridge, Fanny *Film 2*
Stockbridge, Henry *Film 2*
Stockdale, Carl 1874-1942 *Film 1, ForYSC, TwYS*
Stockdale, Carl 1874-1953 *Vers B[port], WhScrn 77, WhoHol B*
Stockdale, Carlton 1874-1942 *Film 2*
Stockem, Johannes De *NewGrD 80*
Stocker, Caspar *NewGrD 80*
Stocker, Constance Jeannette *WhoMus 72*
Stocker, Markus 1945- *IntWWM 77, -80*
Stockfeld, Betty 1905-1966 *IlWWBF[port]*
Stockfield, Betty 1905-1966 *FilmgC, HalFC 80, WhScrn 74, -77, WhThe, WhoHol B*
Stockfisch *OxThe*
Stockhausen *NewGrD 80*
Stockhausen, Franz, Jr. 1839-1926 *Baker 78, NewGrD 80*
Stockhausen, Franz, Sr. 1789-1868 *Baker 78, NewGrD 80*
Stockhausen, Julius 1826-1906 *Baker 78, NewGrD 80*
Stockhausen, Karlheinz 1928- *Baker 78, BnBkM 80[port], CompSN[port], CnOxB, DcCom 77, DcCom&M 79, DcCM, IntWWM 77, -80, MusMk[port], NewGrD 80[port], OxMus, WhoMus 72*
Stockhausen, Margarethe 1803-1877 *NewGrD 80*
Stockhoff, Walter William 1876-1968 *Baker 78*
Stockhoff, Walter William 1887-1968 *ConAmC*
Stockigt, Siegfried 1929- *IntWWM 80*
Stocking, Jay Thomas 1870-1936 *BiDAmM*
Stocklassa, Erik *Film 1*
Stockmann, Doris 1929- *NewGrD 80*
Stockmann, Erich 1926- *IntWWM 77, -80, NewGrD 80*
Stockmeier, Wolfgang 1931- *IntWWM 80*
Stocksdale, Howard Melvin 1905- *AmSCAP 80*
Stockton, Edith *Film 2, TwYS*
Stockton, John Hart 1813-1877 *BiDAmM*
Stockton, Martha Matilda Brustar 1821-1885 *BiDAmM*
Stockton, Richard 1932- *NatPD[port]*
Stockwell, Dean *IntMPA 75, -76, -78, -79, -80*
Stockwell, Dean 1936- *FilmEn, FilmgC, ForYSC, IntMPA 77, MGM[port], MotPP, MovMk[port], WhoHol A*
Stockwell, Dean 1938- *HalFC 80*
Stockwell, Guy 1936- *HalFC 80*
Stockwell, Guy 1938- *FilmgC, ForYSC, WhoHol A*
Stockwell, Harry *WhoHol A*
Stockwell, Jeremy *WhoHol A*
Stockwell, Samuel 1788-1816 *BiDAmM*
Stodare, Colonel 1831-1866 *MagIlD*
Stodart *NewGrD 80*
Stodart, Robert *NewGrD 80*
Stodart, William *NewGrD 80*
Stoddard, Belle 1869-1950 *Film 2, WhScrn 74, -77, WhoHol B*
Stoddard, Betsy 1884-1959 *WhScrn 74, -77*
Stoddard, Brandon *IntMPA 77, -75, -76, -78, -79, -80*
Stoddard, George D 1897- *BiE&WWA*
Stoddard, Haila 1913- *BiE&WWA, NotNAT, WhoThe 72, -77*
Stoddard, Harry 1892-1951 *AmSCAP 66, -80*
Stoddart, James Henry 1827-1907 *NotNAT A, -B*
Stoddart, John Stewart 1936- *WhoOp 76*
Stodden, Patricia Callaway 1944- *IntWWM 77*
Stodola, Ivan 1888- *CnThe, REnWD[port]*
Stoeckel, Carl 1858-1925 *Baker 78*
Stoeckel, Gustav Jakob 1819-1907 *Baker 78*
Stoeckel, Joe 1894-1959 *WhScrn 74, -77*
Stoeckl, Boniface 1745-1784 *NewGrD 80*
Stoeckl, Johann Evangelist 1745-1784 *NewGrD 80*
Stoeffken, Ditrich *NewGrD 80*
Stoehr, Moritz *OxMus*
Stoelzel, Heinrich *NewGrD 80*
Stoepel, Richard d1887 *NotNAT B*
Stoeppelmann, Janet 1948- *ConAmC, IntWWM 77, -80*
Stoessel, Albert 1894-1943 *AmSCAP 66, -80, Baker 78, BiDAmM, ConAmC, NewGrD 80, OxMus*
Stoeving, Paul 1861-1948 *Baker 78*
Stohr, Richard 1874-1967 *Baker 78, ConAmC, NewGrD 80*
Stoian, Ion 1927- *WhoOp 76*
Stoianov, Konstantin Kolev 1961- *IntWWM 77, -80*
Stoica, Mariana 1933- *WhoOp 76*
Stoin, Elena 1915- *NewGrD 80*
Stoin, Vassil 1880-1938 *NewGrD 80*
Stojanov, Stojan 1929- *WhoOp 76*
Stojanovic, Petar 1877-1957 *NewGrD 80*
Stojanovits, Peter Lazar 1877-1957 *Baker 78*
Stojowski, Sigismond 1870-1946 *BiDAmM*
Stojowski, Sigismund 1869-1946 *Baker 78, OxMus*
Stojowski, Zygmunt 1870-1946 *NewGrD 80*
Stok, Isidor *DcPup*
Stokem, Johannes De 1445?-1501? *NewGrD 80*
Stoken, Johannes De 1445?-1501? *NewGrD 80*
Stoker, Austin *DrBlPA*
Stoker, Bram 1847-1912 *FilmgC, HalFC 80, NotNAT B, WhoHrs 80*
Stoker, H G 1885-1966 *WhScrn 74, -77, WhoHol B*
Stoker, Hew Gordon Dacre 1885-1966 *WhThe*
Stoker, Richard 1938- *Baker 78, IntWWM 77, -80, NewGrD 80, WhoMus 72*
Stoker, Willard 1905- *WhoThe 72, -77*
Stokes, Byron D 1886- *BiDAmM*
Stokes, Dorothy *Film 2*
Stokes, Eric 1930- *AmSCAP 80, ConAmC, IntWWM 77, -80*
Stokes, Ernest L 1907-1964 *NotNAT B, WhScrn 74, -77*
Stokes, Frank 1888-1955 *BluesWW[port]*
Stokes, Herbert *BlkAmP, MorBAP*
Stokes, Ida Christine 1889- *WhoMus 72*
Stokes, Jack *MorBAP*
Stokes, Roberta 1927- *AmSCAP 80*
Stokes, Sewell 1902- *WhThe*
Stokes, William James Nicks 1940- *IntWWM 77, -80*
Stokhem, Johannes De *NewGrD 80*
Stokowski, Leopold 1882- *OxMus*
Stokowski, Leopold 1882-1977 *AmSCAP 66, Baker 78, BiDAmM, BnBkM 80[port], ConAmC, FilmEn, FilmgC, HalFC 80, IntWWM 77, MusMk[port], MusSN[port], NewEOp 71, NewGrD 80[port], WhoHol A*
Stokowski, Leopold 1887- *WhoMus 72*
Stolarik, Ivo 1923- *IntWWM 77, -80*
Stolber, Dean 1944- *IntMPA 79, -80*
Stolcer, Josip *NewGrD 80*
Stolczer, Thomas *NewGrD 80*
Stoler, Shirley *WhoHol A*
Stoll, Dennis Gray 1912- *IntWWM 77, -80, WhoMus 72*
Stoll, George 1905- *CmMov, FilmEn, FilmgC, HalFC 80, IntMPA 77, -75, -76, -78, -79, -80*
Stoll, Georgie *CmpEPM*
Stoll, John 1913- *FilmEn*
Stoll, Sir Oswald 1866-1942 *NotNAT B,*

OxThe, WhThe
Stoll, Rand *ConMuA 80B*
Stollberg, Oskar 1903- *IntWWM 77, -80*
Stolle, Der Junge *NewGrD 80*
Stolle, Johann 1566?-1614 *NewGrD 80*
Stolle, Philipp 1614-1675 *NewGrD 80*
Stoller, Alvin 1925- *CmpEPM*
Stoller, Michael Endore 1933- *AmSCAP 80*
Stoller, Mike *ConMuA 80B*
Stoller, Morris 1915- *IntMPA 77, -75, -76, -78, -79, -80*
Stollery, David *WhoHol A*
Stolnitz, Art 1928- *IntMPA 77, -75, -76, -78, -79, -80*
Stoloff, Ben 1895- *FilmEn*
Stoloff, Benjamin 1895- *TwYS A*
Stoloff, Morris *AmPS A, -B, IntMPA 77, -75, -76, -78, -79, -80*
Stoloff, Morris 1893-1980 *CmMov, FilmEn, FilmgC, HalFC 80*
Stoloff, Morris 1898- *AmSCAP 66, -80, RkOn*
Stoloff, Victor *IntMPA 77, -75, -76, -78, -79, -80*
Stolow, Benjamin 1929- *IntWWM 77, -80*
Stolow, Meyer 1929- *IntWWM 77, -80*
Stolp, James *PupTheA*
Stolpe, Antoni 1851-1872 *NewGrD 80*
Stolper, Alexander 1907- *FilmEn*
Stolte, Siegfried 1925- *IntWWM 77, -80*
Stoltz, Arnold T *IntMPA 77, -75, -76, -78, -79, -80*
Stoltz, Rosine 1815-1903 *Baker 78, NewEOp 71, NewGrD 80[port]*
Stoltze, Robert H 1910- *ConAmC*
Stoltzel, Gottfried Heinrich *NewGrD 80*
Stoltzenberg, Christoph 1690-1764 *NewGrD 80*
Stoltzer, Thomas 1475?-1526 *Baker 78*
Stoltzer, Thomas 1480?-1526? *NewGrD 80*
Stoltzman, Richard Leslie 1942- *IntWWM 77, -80*
Stolyarsky, Pyotr Solomonovich 1871-1944 *NewGrD 80*
Stolz, Don 1919- *BiE&WWA, NotNAT*
Stolz, Robert 1880-1975 *Baker 78, BiDAmM, BiE&WWA, IntWWM 77, NewGrD 80, NotNAT B, WhoMus 72*
Stolz, Robert 1886- *WhThe*
Stolz, Teresa 1834-1902 *Baker 78, CmOp, NewEOp 71, NewGrD 80[port]*
Stolz, Teresina 1834-1902 *NewGrD 80[port]*
Stolz, Terezie 1834-1902 *NewGrD 80[port]*
Stolze, Gerhard 1926-1979 *CmOp, NewGrD 80, WhoOp 76*
Stolze, Kurt-Heinz 1930-1970 *CnOxB*
Stolzel, Gottfried Heinrich 1690-1749 *Baker 78, NewGrD 80*
Stolzel, Heinrich 1772-1844 *NewGrD 80*
Stolzel, Heinrich 1780-1844 *OxMus*
Stolzenberg, Christoph *NewGrD 80*
Stolzenberger, Christoph *NewGrD 80*
Stolzer, Josip *NewGrD 80*
Stolzova, Teresa *NewGrD 80*
Stomius, Johannes 1502-1562 *NewGrD 80*
Stonard, William 1550?-1630 *NewGrD 80*
Stone *NewGrD 80*
Stone, Alix *WhoThe 72, -77*
Stone, Amelia 1879- *WhoStg 1906, -1908*
Stone, Andrew L 1902- *BiDFilm, -81, CmMov, FilmEn, FilmgC, HalFC 80, IntMPA 77, -75, -76, -78, -79, -80, WomWMM, WorEFlm*
Stone, Arnold *ConMuA 80B*
Stone, Arthur 1884-1940 *WhScrn 74, -77, WhoHol B*
Stone, Arthur 1897- *Film 2, ForYSC, TwYS*
Stone, Barbara *WomWMM B*
Stone, Bentley 1908?- *CnOxB, DancEn 78*
Stone, Billy 1884-1931 *AmSCAP 66, -80*
Stone, Brian *ConMuA 80B*
Stone, Burton S 1928- *IntMPA 77, -75, -76, -78, -79, -80*
Stone, Butch 1913?- *CmpEPM*
Stone, Carol 1915- *BiE&WWA, WhThe, WhoHol A*
Stone, Charles *WhThe*
Stone, Christopher *WhoHol A*
Stone, Christopher Reynolds 1882-1965 *OxMus*
Stone, Cliffie 1917- *BiDAmM, CounME 74[port], -74A, EncFCWM 69, IlEncCM*
Stone, Cyril Hubert *WhoMus 72*
Stone, Danny *WhoHol A*
Stone, David Clifford 1936- *IntWWM 77, -80, WhoMus 72*
Stone, David Elphinstone 1922- *IntWWM 77*
Stone, David Leon 1916- *WhoMus 72*
Stone, Doc *Film 2*
Stone, Don *PupTheA*
Stone, Mrs. Don *PupTheA*
Stone, Dorothy 1905-1974 *BiE&WWA, NotNAT B, WhScrn 77, WhThe, WhoHol B*
Stone, Dorothy Alexandra 1903- *WhoMus 72*
Stone, Dwight Donald *ConAmC*
Stone, Eddie 1907?- *BgBands 74, CmpEPM*
Stone, Edward Durell 1902- *BiE&WWA*
Stone, Ezra C 1917- *BiE&WWA, ForYSC, IntMPA 77, -75, -76, -78, -79, -80, NewYTET, NotNAT, WhoHol A*
Stone, Florence Oakley d1956 *NotNAT B*
Stone, Fred *AmPS B*
Stone, Fred 1874-1959 *ForYSC*
Stone, Fred 1935- *EncJzS 70*
Stone, Fred Andrew 1873-1959 *EncMT, FilmEn, Film 1, -2, NotNAT A, -B, PlP&P[port], TwYS, Vers A[port], WhScrn 74, -77, WhThe, WhoHol B*
Stone, Gage C 1919- *AmSCAP 66*
Stone, Gene *Film 2*
Stone, George *AmSCAP 80*
Stone, George 1877-1939 *WhScrn 77*
Stone, George E 1903-1967 *FilmEn, Film 1, -2, FilmgC, HalFC 80, HolCA[port], MotPP, MovMk, TwYS, Vers A[port], WhScrn 74, WhoHol B*
Stone, George E 1904-1966 *ForYSC*
Stone, George E 1904-1967 *WhScrn 77*
Stone, Gregory 1900- *AmSCAP 66, -80, ConAmC A*
Stone, Harold *NotNAT*
Stone, Harold J 1911- *FilmgC, ForYSC, HalFC 80, WhoHol A*
Stone, Harry *AmSCAP 80, Film 1*
Stone, Harvey 1913-1974 *WhScrn 77*
Stone, Helen *Film 2*
Stone, Henry *ConMuA 80B*
Stone, Ira *AmSCAP 80*
Stone, Jack *Film 2*
Stone, James F 1901-1969 *WhScrn 77, WhoHol B*
Stone, James Y 1929- *AmSCAP 66, -80*
Stone, Jean 1914- *AmSCAP 66*
Stone, Jeffrey *WhoHol A*
Stone, Jesse 1901- *WhoJazz 72*
Stone, John *NewGrD 80, WhoHol A*
Stone, John 1903- *IntWWM 77, -80, WhoMus 72*
Stone, John Augustus 1801-1834 *NotNAT B, OxThe, PlP&P*
Stone, Jon 1931- *AmSCAP 80*
Stone, Joseph 1920- *AmSCAP 66, -80*
Stone, Joseph C 1758-1837 *BiDAmM*
Stone, Justin Federman 1916- *AmSCAP 80, BgBands 74*
Stone, Kirby 1918- *AmSCAP 66, -80*
Stone, Kurt 1911- *AmSCAP 80, Baker 78, IntWWM 77, -80, NewGrD 80*
Stone, Leonard *WhoHol A*
Stone, Lew *BgBands 74*
Stone, Lew 1898-1969 *NewGrD 80*
Stone, Lew 1899?-1969 *CmpEPM*
Stone, Lewis 1878- *WhThe*
Stone, Lewis 1879-1953 *FilmEn, Film 1, -2, FilmgC, ForYSC, HalFC 80, HolCA[port], MGM[port], MotPP, MovMk[port], NotNAT B, TwYS, Vers B[port], WhScrn 74, -77, WhoHol B, WhoHrs 80*
Stone, Malcolm A 1934- *ConAmC*
Stone, Margaret Dorothy 1927- *WhoMus 72*
Stone, Marianne 1920?- *HalFC 80, IntMPA 77, -75, -76, -78, -79, -80, WhoHol A*
Stone, Maxine *AmSCAP 80*
Stone, Maxine 1910-1964 *WhScrn 74, -77, WhoHol B*
Stone, Milburn 1904-1980 *FilmEn, FilmgC, ForYSC, HalFC 80, HolCA[port], MotPP, WhoHol A, WhoHrs 80*
Stone, Miriam Scadron 1916- *AmSCAP 80*
Stone, Norman Millard, Jr. 1946- *AmSCAP 80*
Stone, Paddy 1924- *WhoHol A, WhoThe 72, -77*
Stone, Paula 1916- *BiE&WWA, ForYSC, NotNAT, WhThe, WhoHol A*
Stone, Paula 1945- *AmSCAP 80*
Stone, Peter 1930- *BiE&WWA, ConDr 73, -77D, EncMT, FilmEn, FilmgC, HalFC 80, IntMPA 79, -80, NotNAT, WhoThe 72, -77*
Stone, Phil *TwYS A*
Stone, Robert 1516-1613 *NewGrD 80*
Stone, Robert 1941- *IntWWM 77*
Stone, Mrs. Robert E d1916 *WhScrn 77*
Stone, Robin Domnic Alexander *IntWWM 77, -80, WhoMus 72*
Stone, Roger Hayes 1946- *AmSCAP 66*
Stone, Sid *NewYTET*
Stone, Sly 1944?- *BiDAmM, DrBlPA*
Stone, Suzie Kay *WhoHol A*
Stone, Virginia *WomWMM*
Stone, William 1915- *IntWWM 77, -80*
Stone, William C 1921- *ConAmC*
Stone, William Henry 1830-1891 *NewGrD 80*
Stone, Wilson 1927- *AmSCAP 80*
Stone Country *BiDAmM*
Stone Poneys, The *BiDAmM, RkOn 2[port]*
Stone The Crows *IlEncR*
Stoneham, Jean 1929- *DancEn 78*
Stonehouse, Ruth *MotPP*
Stonehouse, Ruth d1941 *WhoHol B, WomWMM*
Stonehouse, Ruth 1891-1940 *TwYS*
Stonehouse, Ruth 1893-1941 *FilmEn, WhScrn 74, -77*
Stonehouse, Ruth 1894-1941 *Film 1, -2, NotNAT B*
Stoneman, Ernest V 1893-1968 *BiDAmM, CmpEPM*
Stoneman, James M 1927- *IntMPA 77, -75, -76, -78, -79, -80*
Stoneman, Pop *EncFCWM 69*
Stoneman Family *EncFCWM 69, IlEncCM*
Stoner, Michael S 1911- *AmSCAP 66, -80*
Stoner, William *NewGrD 80*
Stonerd, William *NewGrD 80*
Stones, Joseph 1928- *WhoMus 72*
Stoney, George *OxFilm*
Stoney Mountain Cloggers *BiDAmM*
Stoning, Henry *NewGrD 80*
Stoninges, Henry *NewGrD 80*
Stonnard, William *NewGrD 80*
Stonninge, Henry *NewGrD 80*
Stonum, Harry Francis 1924- *AmSCAP 80*
Stooge, Iggy *BiDAmM*
Stooges *BiDAmM*
Stooges, The Three *FilmEn, FilmgC, IntMPA 75*
Stookey, Noel Paul 1937- *AmSCAP 66, -80, BiDAmM*
Stookey, Paul *EncFCWM 69*
Stoopnagle, Colonel 1897- *JoeFr*
Stoopnagle, Lemuel Q 1897-1950 *WhScrn 77*
Stopel, Franz 1794-1836 *Baker 78*
Stoppa, Paolo 1902- *EncWT*
Stoppa, Paolo 1906- *FilmEn, FilmgC, HalFC 80, MovMk, WhoHol A*
Stoppard, Tom 1937- *CnThe, ConDr 73, -77, CroCD, EncWT, Ent, McGEWD[port], ModWD, NotNAT, PlP&P A[port], WhoThe 72, -77*
Stoppelaer, Michael 1710?-1777 *NewGrD 80*
Stoquerus, Gaspar *NewGrD 80*
Stor, Carl 1814-1889 *Baker 78*
Storace *NewGrD 80*
Storace, Ann Selina 1765-1817 *NewGrD 80[port]*
Storace, Ann Selina 1766-1817 *CmOp*
Storace, Anna 1765-1817 *NewGrD 80[port]*
Storace, Bernardo *NewGrD 80*
Storace, Nancy 1765-1817 *Baker 78, NewGrD 80[port]*
Storace, Stephano 1725?-1781? *NewGrD 80*
Storace, Stephen 1725?-1781? *NewGrD 80*
Storace, Stephen 1762-1796 *NewGrD 80, OxMus*
Storace, Stephen 1763-1796 *Baker 78, MusMk*
Storch, Arthur 1925- *BiE&WWA, ForYSC, NotNAT, WhoHol A, WhoThe 72, -77*

Storch, Larry 1923- *BiE&WWA, ForYSC, HalFC 80, MotPP, NotNAT, WhoHol A*
Storch, M Anton 1813-1888 *Baker 78*
Storchio, Rosina 1876-1945 *Baker 78, CmOp, NewGrD 80*
Storck, Henri 1907- *DcFM, FilmEn, FilmgC, HalFC 80, OxFilm, WorEFlm*
Storck, Karl G L 1873-1920 *Baker 78, NewGrD 80*
Stordahl, Alex 1913-1963 *WhScrn 77*
Stordahl, Axel 1913-1963 *AmSCAP 66, -80, CmpEPM, NotNAT B*
Storer *OxThe*
Storer, George B 1899-1975 *IntMPA 75, -76, NewYTET*
Storer, Henry Johnson 1860-1935 *BiDAmM*
Storer, John 1858-1930 *Baker 78*
Storer, Maria 1750?-1795 *BiDAmM*
Storey, Cheryl Denise 1952- *CpmDNM 80*
Storey, David 1923- *CroCD*
Storey, David 1933- *CnThe, ConDr 73, -77, EncWT, Ent, NotNAT, PlP&P, -A[port], WhoThe 72, -77*
Storey, Edith 1892- *FilmEn, Film 1, -2, MotPP, TwYS*
Storey, Fred 1861-1917 *NotNAT B, WhThe*
Storey, Frederick 1909- *IntMPA 77, -75, -76, -78, -79, -80*
Storey, June *ForYSC*
Storey, Ralph *BlkAmP*
Storey, Rex *Film 2*
Storey, Sylvia Lilian d1947 *NotNAT B*
Stories *RkOn 2[port]*
Storioni, Lorenzo 1751-1800? *NewGrD 80*
Storjohann, Helmut 1920- *IntWWM 77, -80*
Stork, George Frederick 1913- *AmSCAP 66, -80*
Storke, William F *IntMPA 77, -76, -78, -79, -80, NewYTET*
Storl, Johann Georg Christian 1675-1719 *NewGrD 80*
Storm, Billy 1938- *RkOn*
Storm, Gale *AmPS A, MotPP*
Storm, Gale 1921- *What 5[port], WhoHol A*
Storm, Gale 1922- *BiDAmM, FilmEn, FilmgC, ForYSC, HalFC 80, HolP 40[port], IntMPA 77, -75, -76, -78, -79, -80, MovMk, RkOn[port]*
Storm, Jerome *Film 1, TwYS A*
Storm, Lesley 1903-1975 *BiE&WWA, NotNAT B, WhThe, WhoThe 72*
Storm, Olaf *Film 2*
Stormont, Leo d1923 *Film 2, NotNAT B*
Storry, Jean Margaret Cunningham 1907- *WhoMus 72*
Storti, Mauro 1937- *IntWWM 77, -80*
Storup, Carl 1908- *IntWWM 77, -80*
Story, Aubrey d1963 *NotNAT B*
Story, Carl Moore 1916- *BiDAmM*
Story, Nat 1905-1968 *WhoJazz 72*
Story, Rosalyn Marie 1950- *BlkWAB*
Story, Van Dyck 1917- *AmSCAP 66, -80*
Stossel, Ludwig 1883-1973 *FilmEn, FilmgC, ForYSC, HalFC 80, Vers A[port], WhScrn 77, WhoHol B*
Stothart, Herbert d1949 *NotNAT B, WhThe*
Stothart, Herbert 1884-1949 *WorEFlm*
Stothart, Herbert 1885-1949 *AmPS, AmSCAP 66, -80, BestMus, CmMov, CmpEPM, ConAmC A, EncMT, FilmEn, HalFC 80, NewCBMT, NewGrD 80*
Stotijn, Haakon 1915-1964 *NewGrD 80*
Stotijn, Jaap 1891-1970 *NewGrD 80*
Stotijn, Louis 1918- *WhoMus 72*
Stott, Judith 1929- *WhThe, WhoThe 72*
Stott, Kathryn Linda 1958- *IntWWM 80*
Stott, Mike 1944- *ConDr 77*
Stoue *NewGrD 80*
Stouffer, Paul M 1916- *AmSCAP 66, -80, ConAmC*
Stoughton, Bonita Adele 1949- *IntWWM 77, -80*
Stoughton, Michael Gordon 1942- *IntWWM 77, -80*
Stoughton, Roy Spaulding 1884-1953 *AmSCAP 66, -80, ConAmC A*
Stourton *NewGrD 80*
Stout, Alan 1932- *Baker 78, CpmDNM 79, ConAmC, DcCM, NewGrD 80*
Stout, Archie 1886- *FilmEn, FilmgC, HalFC 80, WorEFlm*
Stout, Clarence 1892-1960 *AmSCAP 66, -80*
Stout, Donald 1956- *IntWWM 80*
Stout, Gordon Bryan 1952- *AmSCAP 80*
Stout, Herbert E 1905- *AmSCAP 66, -80*
Stout, Louis James 1924- *IntWWM 77, -80*
Stout, Mary Frances *PupTheA*
Stout, Rex 1886-1975 *HalFC 80*
Stoutamire, Albert Lucian 1921- *AmSCAP 80, IntWWM 77*
Stoutz, Edmond De 1920- *NewGrD 80*
Stovall, Don 1913-1970 *CmpEPM, WhoJazz 72*
Stovall, Jewell 1907-1974 *BluesWW[port]*
Stovall, Vern 1928- *BiDAmM, EncFCWM 69*
Stover, Chester A 1925- *AmSCAP 80*
Stover, Franklin Howard 1953- *ConAmC*
Stover, Harold M 1946- *AmSCAP 80, ConAmC*
Stow, Baron 1801-1869 *BiDAmM*
Stow, John *PlP&P[port]*
Stow, John 1525?-1605 *OxMus*
Stow, Percy *IlWWBF, WhoHrs 80*
Stowe, Charlotte Wilhelmine Caroline *NewGrD 80*
Stowe, Gustav 1835-1891 *Baker 78*
Stowe, Harriet Beecher 1811-1896 *BiDAmM, DcPup, FilmgC, HalFC 80, NotNAT B, PlP&P*
Stowe, Leslie 1886-1949 *Film 1, -2, WhScrn 77*
Stowe, Lester *Film 2*
Stowell, C W 1878-1940 *WhoHol B*
Stowell, Clarence W 1878-1940 *WhScrn 74, -77*
Stowell, Kent 1939- *CnOxB*
Stowell, William H 1885-1919 *Film 1, WhScrn 77*
Stowitz *Film 2*
Stoyanov, Andrei *Baker 78*
Stoyanov, Pancho 1931- *Baker 78*
Stoyanov, Stoyan 1912- *NewGrD 80*
Stoyanov, Veselin 1902-1969 *Baker 78*
Stoyanov, Vesselin 1902-1969 *NewGrD 80*
Stozl, Gottfried Heinrich *NewGrD 80*
Straatmann, Verle F 1930- *IntWWM 77*
Stracciari, Riccardo 1875-1955 *CmOp, NewEOp 71, NewGrD 80*
Strachan, Alan 1946- *WhoThe 77*
Strachan, Lucille *AmSCAP 80*
Strachey, Jack 1894- *WhThe*
Stracke, Win 1908- *BiDAmM, EncFCWM 69*
Strada, Giovanni Battista *NewGrD 80*
Strada DelPo, Anna Maria *CmOp, NewGrD 80*
Stradal, August 1860-1930 *Baker 78*
Stradella, Alessandro 1642-1682 *CmOp, MusMk, NewEOp 71*
Stradella, Alessandro 1644-1682 *Baker 78, NewGrD 80, OxMus*
Stradella, Alessandro 1645?-1682 *BnBkM 80*
Strader, Rodger Allan 1952- *AmSCAP 80*
Stradivari, Antonio 1644-1737 *Baker 78, BnBkM 80, MusMk, NewGrD 80, OxMus*
Stradivari, Francesco 1671-1743 *OxMus*
Stradivari, Omobono 1679-1742 *OxMus*
Stradling, Harry 1901-1970 *CmMov, DcFM*
Stradling, Harry 1902-1970 *FilmEn*
Stradling, Harry 1907-1970 *FilmgC, HalFC 80*
Stradling, Harry 1910-1970 *OxFilm*
Stradling, Harry, Jr. 1925- *CmMov, DcFM, FilmEn, FilmgC, HalFC 80*
Stradling, Walter *Film 1*
Stradner, Rose 1913-1958 *FilmgC, HalFC 80, NotNAT B, WhScrn 74, -77, WhoHol B*
Stradner, Rose 1916-1958 *ForYSC*
Straesser, Joep 1934- *Baker 78, CpmDNM 76, -80, IntWWM 77, -80, NewGrD 80*
Straeten, Edmond Vander 1826-1895 *NewGrD 80*
Straeten, Edmund *Baker 78*
Straeten, Edmund S J VanDer 1855-1934 *NewGrD 80*
Straeter, Ted 1914?- *BgBands 74, CmpEPM*
Strahl, Dorothy Elizabeth 1942- *IntWWM 77, -80*
Strahl, Margaret A 1933- *IntWWM 77*
Straight, Beatrice 1916- *HalFC 80*
Straight, Beatrice 1918- *BiE&WWA, IntMPA 80, NotNAT, WhoHol A, WhoThe 72, -77*
Straight, Charley 1891-1940 *AmSCAP 66, -80, CmpEPM*
Straight, Willard 1930- *AmSCAP 66, -80, ConAmC*
Straigis, Roy J 1931- *AmSCAP 66*
Strain, Thayer *Film 2*
Strait, Pauline Alice 1928- *IntWWM 80*
Straker, John A 1908- *AmSCAP 66*
Strakosch, Maurice 1825-1887 *Baker 78, NewEOp 71*
Strakosch, Max 1834-1892 *BiDAmM*
Strakova, Theodora 1915- *NewGrD 80*
Stramer, Hugo *IntMPA 77, -75, -76, -78, -79, -80*
Stramm, August 1874-1915 *ModWD*
Stranack, Wallace d1950 *NotNAT B*
Strand, Chick *WomWMM A, -B*
Strand, David 1908- *AmSCAP 66*
Strand, Les 1924- *EncJzS 70*
Strand, Paul 1890-1976 *DcFM, FilmEn, OxFilm, WorEFlm*
Strandberg, Newton 1921- *ConAmC*
Strandgaard, Charlotte *WomWMM*
Strandmark, Erik 1919-1963 *WhScrn 77*
Strang, Gerald 1908- *Baker 78, BiDAmM, ConAmC, DcCM, NewGrD 80, OxMus*
Strang, Harry d1972 *Film 2, Vers B[port], WhScrn 77, WhoHol B*
Strange, Le *NewGrD 80*
Strange, Allen 1943- *ConAmC*
Strange, Charles Edward 1902- *WhoMus 72*
Strange, Glenn 1899-1973 *FilmEn, FilmgC, HalFC 80, Vers A[port], WhScrn 77, WhoHol B, WhoHrs 80[port]*
Strange, Glenn 1911- *ForYSC*
Strange, Justin *AmSCAP 80*
Strange, Michael 1890-1950 *NotNAT A, -B*
Strange, Philip *Film 2*
Strange, Richard Eugene 1928- *IntWWM 77, -80*
Strange, Robert 1882-1952 *Vers B[port], WhScrn 74, -77, WhThe, WhoHol B*
Strange, William E 1930- *AmSCAP 80, BiDAmM*
Strangeloves, The *RkOn 2[port]*
Strangis, Jane 1932-1966 *WhScrn 74, -77*
Strangis, Judy *WhoHol A*
Stranglers, The *IlEncR*
Strangways, A H Fox *NewGrD 80*
Stranitzky, Anton Joseph 1676-1726 *EncWT*
Stranitzky, Joseph Anton 1676-1726 *Ent, OxThe*
Stransky, Josef 1872-1936 *Baker 78, NewGrD 80*
Stransky, Joseph 1872-1936 *BiDAmM*
Straram, Walther 1876-1933 *Baker 78*
Strasberg, Lee 1901- *BiE&WWA, CnThe, EncWT, Ent, FilmEn, FilmgC, HalFC 80, NotNAT, PlP&P[port], WhoHol A, WhoThe 72, -77*
Strasberg, Paula d1966 *BiE&WWA, NotNAT B*
Strasberg, Susan 1938- *BiE&WWA, FilmEn, FilmgC, ForYSC, HalFC 80, IntMPA 77, -75, -76, -78, -79, -80, MotPP, MovMk[port], NotNAT, WhoHol A, WhoHrs 80*
Strasfogel, Ian 1940- *IntWWM 77, -80, WhoOp 76*
Strasfogel, Ignace 1909- *WhoMus 72, WhoOp 76*
Strassberg, Morris 1898-1974 *Film 2, WhScrn 77, WhoHol B*
Strassberg, Stephen *IntMPA 77, -75, -76, -78, -79, -80*
Strassburg, Robert 1915- *AmSCAP 66, Baker 78, CpmDNM 77, ConAmC*
Strasser, Ewald 1867-1933 *Baker 78*
Strasser, Hugo 1922- *WhoMus 72*
Strasser, Janos 1900- *WhoMus 72*
Strasser, Robin *WhoHol A*
Strassler, Paul Gene 1925- *IntWWM 77*
Strassny, Fritz *Film 2*
Strata, Giovanni Battista *NewGrD 80*
Stratakis, Anastasia *CreCan 2*
Stratakos, Ellis 1904-1961 *NewOrJ*
Stratas, Teresa 1938- *Baker 78, CreCan 2, MusSN[port], NewGrD 80, WhoMus 72, WhoOp 76*

Strate, Grant Elroy 1927- *CnOxB, CreCan 2, DancEn 78*
Strategier, Herman 1912- *Baker 78, NewGrD 80*
Stratford, William *NewGrD 80*
Stratico, Michele 1721?-1782? *NewGrD 80*
Stratta, Ettore 1933- *AmSCAP 66, -80*
Strattner, Georg Christoph 1644?-1704 *NewGrD 80*
Stratton, Caleb B *IntMPA 75, -76*
Stratton, Charles Sherwood 1838-1883 *NotNAT A*
Stratton, Chester 1913-1970 *WhScrn 74, -77*
Stratton, Chet 1913-1970 *WhoHol B*
Stratton, Donald 1928- *AmSCAP 66*
Stratton, Eugene 1861-1918 *NotNAT B, OxThe, WhThe*
Stratton, Gene *Film 2*
Stratton, George 1897-1954 *Baker 78, NewGrD 80*
Stratton, Gil, Jr. *ForYSC*
Stratton, Harry 1898-1955 *WhScrn 74, -77*
Stratton, John 1925- *HalFC 80, IntMPA 77, -75, -76, -78, -79, -80, WhoHol A, WhoThe 72, -77*
Stratton, John F 1832-1912 *NewGrD 80*
Stratton, Stephen Samuel 1840-1906 *Baker 78*
Straub, Agnes 1890-1941 *EncWT*
Straub, Jean-Marie 1933- *BiDFilm, -81, FilmEn, HalFC 80, OxFilm, WomWMM, -B, WorEFlm*
Straub, Mary E 1884-1951 *WhScrn 74, -77*
Straub, Solomon W 1842-1899 *BiDAmM*
Straube, Karl 1873-1950 *Baker 78, BnBkM 80, NewGrD 80, OxMus*
Straube, Rudolf 1717-1780? *NewGrD 80*
Strauch, I *Film 2*
Strauch, Maxim *Film 2*
Straus, Ivan 1937- *IntWWM 77, -80*
Straus, Oscar 1870-1954 *Baker 78, CmpEPM, MusMk, NewGrD 80, NotNAT B, WhThe*
Straus, Oskar 1870-1954 *OxMus*
Strausbaugh, Warren L 1909- *BiE&WWA*
Strausberg, Solomon M 1907- *IntMPA 77, -75, -76, -78, -79, -80*
Strauss *NewGrD 80*
Strauss, Christoph 1575?-1631 *NewGrD 80*
Strauss, Clement 1886-1915 *WhScrn 77*
Strauss, Eduard 1835-1916 *Baker 78, DcCom 77[port], NewGrD 80[port], OxMus*
Strauss, Eduard 1910-1969 *NewGrD 80*
Strauss, Franz 1822-1905 *Baker 78, BnBkM 80*
Strauss, George R 1951- *ConAmC*
Strauss, Helen M *BiE&WWA, WomWMM*
Strauss, Herbert 1929- *AmSCAP 66, -80*
Strauss, Isaac 1806-1888 *NewGrD 80*
Strauss, Johann 1804-1849 *Baker 78, BnBkM 80, DcCom 77[port], NewGrD 80[port], NotNAT B, OxMus*
Strauss, Johann 1825-1899 *Baker 78, BnBkM 80, CmOp, CmpBCM, CnOxB, DancEn 78, DcCom 77[port], DcCom&M 79, GrComp[port], MusMk[port], NewEOp 71, NewGrD 80[port], NotNAT B, OxMus*
Strauss, Johann 1866-1939 *NewGrD 80, NotNAT B, OxMus, PlP&P*
Strauss, John 1913- *IntMPA 77, -75, -76, -78, -79, -80*
Strauss, John 1920- *AmSCAP 66, -80, BiE&WWA, ConAmC A, NotNAT*
Strauss, Josef 1827-1870 *Baker 78, DcCom 77[port], NewGrD 80[port]*
Strauss, Joseph 1827-1870 *NewGrD 80[port], NotNAT B, OxMus*
Strauss, Melvin *IntWWM 77, -80*
Strauss, Peter 1942- *HalFC 80*
Strauss, Peter 1947- *IntMPA 77, -78, -79, -80, WhoHol A*
Strauss, Peter E 1940- *IntMPA 77, -75, -76, -78, -79, -80*
Strauss, Richard *IntMPA 77, -75, -76, -78, -79, -80*
Strauss, Richard 1864-1949 *Baker 78, BnBkM 80[port], CmOp[port], CmpBCM, CompSN[port], CnOxB, DancEn 78, DcCom 77[port], DcCom&M 79, DcCM, DcTwCC, -A, MusMk, MusSN[port], NewEOp 71, NewGrD 80[port], NotNAT B, OxMus*
Strauss, Robert 1913- *ForYSC, IntMPA 75*
Strauss, Robert 1913-1974 *NotNAT B*
Strauss, Robert 1913-1975 *BiE&WWA, FilmEn, FilmgC, HalFC 80, HolCA[port], MovMk[port], WhScrn 77, WhoHol C*
Strauss, Robert 1915- *Vers A[port]*
Strauss, Robert Irwin 1949- *AmSCAP 80*
Strauss, William H 1885-1943 *Film 2, TwYS, WhScrn 74, -77, WhoHol B*
Stravinsky, Feodor 1843-1902 *Baker 78*
Stravinsky, Fyodor Ignat'yevich 1843-1902 *NewGrD 80*
Stravinsky, Igor 1882-1971 *AmSCAP 80, Baker 78, BiDAmM, BnBkM 80[port], CmOp, CompSN[port], CnOxB, ConAmC, DcCom 77[port], DcCom&M 79, DcCM, DcPup, DcTwCC, -A, MusMk[port], NewEOp 71, NewGrD 80[port], OxMus*
Stravinsky, Soulima 1910- *Baker 78, CpmDNM 80*
Straw, Arlein Ford 1920- *AmSCAP 80*
Strawberry Alarm Clock, The *BiDAmM, RkOn 2[port]*
Strawbridge, Edwin d1957 *CmpGMD, DancEn 78*
Strawbs *ConMuA 80A, IlEncR*
Strayer, Frank 1891-1964 *FilmEn, FilmgC, HalFC 80, TwYS A*
Strayhorn, Billy 1915-1967 *AmSCAP 66, -80, CmpEPM, DrBlPA, EncJzS 70, IlEncJ, NewGrD 80, WhoJazz 72*
Strayhorn, Swee'Pea 1915-1967 *EncJzS 70*
Strayhorn, William 1915-1967 *Baker 78, BiDAmM, ConAmC, EncJzS 70, NewGrD 80*
Strazzeri, Frank John 1930- *EncJzS 70*
Streater, Robert 1624-1680 *OxThe*
Streatfeild, Richard Alexander 1866-1919 *Baker 78, NewGrD 80*
Streatfeild, Simon Nicholas 1929- *IntWWM 77, -80*
Streatfield, Simon Nicholas 1929- *WhoMus 72*
Streator, George *BlkAmP*
Strecker, Heinrich 1893- *IntWWM 77*
Streep, Meryl 1950- *Ent*
Streep, Meryl 1951- *FilmEn*
Streep, Meryl 1953?- *HalFC 80*
Street, David 1917-1971 *WhScrn 74, -77, WhoHol B*
Street, George A 1869-1956 *WhScrn 74, -77*
Street, George Slythe 1867-1936 *WhThe*
Street, Jill B 1945- *IntWWM 77*
Street, Joye *AmSCAP 80*
Street, Julian 1880-1947 *WhScrn 77*
Street, Tison 1943- *Baker 78, ConAmC*
Street People *RkOn 2A*
Streeter, Edward 1892-1976 *HalFC 80*
Streeter, Thomas Wayne 1943- *IntWWM 77, -80*
Streets, John 1928- *IntWWM 77, -80, WhoMus 72*
Strehler, Giorgio 1921- *CmOp, CnThe, EncWT, Ent, NewGrD 80, WhoOp 76*
Streich, Rita *WhoMus 72*
Streich, Rita 1920- *CmOp, NewGrD 80, WhoOp 76*
Streich, Rita 1926- *IntWWM 77, -80*
Streicher, Emil 1836-1916 *NewGrD 80*
Streicher, Johann Andreas 1761-1833 *Baker 78, NewGrD 80, OxMus*
Streicher, Johann Baptist 1796-1871 *NewGrD 80*
Streicher, Nannette Stein 1769-1833 *NewGrD 80*
Streicher, Theodor 1874-1940 *Baker 78, NewGrD 80*
Streinikov, Nicolai 1888-1939 *Baker 78*
Streisand, Barbra 1942- *AmPS A, -B, AmSCAP 80, BiDAmM, BiDFilm, -81, BiE&WWA, CmMov, ConMuA 80A[port], EncMT, FilmEn, FilmgC, ForYSC, HalFC 80, IntMPA 77, -75, -76, -78, -79, -80, MotPP, MovMk[port], NotNAT, -A, OxFilm, PlP&P, RkOn 2[port], WhoHol A, WhoThe 72, -77, WomWMM*
Strelezki, Anton 1859-1907 *Baker 78, BiDAmM, OxMus*
Strelling, Frank Denys 1926- *IntWWM 77, -80*
Strengthfeild, Thomas *NewGrD 80*
Strens, Jules 1892-1971 *Baker 78, OxMus*
Strepponi, Giuseppina 1815-1897 *Baker 78, CmOp, NewEOp 71, NewGrD 80[port]*
Stretton, Thomas *NewGrD 80*
Strevens, Patrick Keir 1928- *IntWWM 77, -80*
Stribling, Melissa *WhoHol A, WhoHrs 80*
Stribolt, Oscar *Film 2*
Striccius, Wolfgang 1555?-1615? *NewGrD 80*
Strick, Joseph 1923- *BiDFilm, -81, FilmEn, FilmgC, HalFC 80, OxFilm, WorEFlm*
Stricker, Augustin Reinhard d1720? *NewGrD 80*
Stricker, Remy 1936- *IntWWM 77, -80*
Strickfaden, Ken 1900?- *WhoHrs 80*
Strickland, Amzie *WhoHol A*
Strickland, Connie *WhoHol A*
Strickland, Enfield Rube d1964 *NotNAT B*
Strickland, Helen 1863-1938 *NotNAT B, WhScrn 77, WhoHol B*
Strickland, Kathy *WomWMM B*
Strickland, Lily Teresa 1887-1958 *AmSCAP 66, -80, Baker 78, BiDAmM, ConAmC*
Strickland, William *ConAmC*
Strickland, William 1914- *Baker 78*
Strickland, William Bradley 1929- *AmSCAP 80*
Strickland, Willy *ConAmC*
Strickler, Benny 1917?-1946 *WhoJazz 72*
Strickler, Jerry 1939- *BiE&WWA, NotNAT*
Stricklyn, Ray 1930- *FilmgC, ForYSC, HalFC 80, IntMPA 77, -78, -79, -80, MotPP, WhoHol A*
Stride, Harry 1903- *AmSCAP 66, -80*
Stride, John 1936- *FilmgC, HalFC 80, WhoHol A, WhoThe 72, -77*
Strider, Phil *ConMuA 80B*
Striegler, Kurt 1886-1958 *Baker 78, NewGrD 80*
Striepke, Dan *WhoHrs 80*
Striesfield, Herb 1946- *NotNAT*
Striggio, Alessandrino 1573?-1630 *NewGrD 80*
Striggio, Alessandro 1535?-1595? *Baker 78, BnBkM 80*
Striggio, Alessandro 1540?-1592 *NewGrD 80*
Striggio, Alessandro 1573?-1630 *NewGrD 80*
Strigi, Alessandro 1540?-1592 *NewGrD 80*
Strigia, Alessandro 1540?-1592 *NewGrD 80*
Strike, Lois 1948- *CnOxB*
Strike, Maurice 1945- *CreCan 2*
Striker, Joseph 1900-1974 *Film 2, WhScrn 77, WhoHol B*
Strilko, Anthony 1931- *ConAmC*
Strimer, Joseph 1881-1962 *Baker 78*
Strimpell, Stephen *WhoHol A*
Strimple, Nick 1946- *IntWWM 77*
Strina Sacchi, Regina 1764-1839 *NewGrD 80*
Strinasacchi, Regina 1764-1839 *NewGrD 80, OxMus*
Strindberg, Arthur *PlP&P*
Strindberg, August 1849-1912 *CnMD, CnThe, EncWT, Ent, McGEWD[port], ModWD, NewEOp 71, NotNAT A, -B, OxThe, PlP&P A[port], REnWD[port]*
Strindberg, Axel 1910- *CnMD*
Strindberg, Goran 1917- *WorEFlm*
String-A-Longs, The *RkOn*
Stringari, Antonio *NewGrD 80*
Stringbean 1915-1973 *BiDAmM, CounME 74[port], -74A, EncFCWM 69, IlEncCM[port]*
Stringer, Alan 1938- *ConAmC*
Stringer, Arthur John Arbuthnott 1874-1950 *CreCan 2*
Stringer, Michael *WhoHol A*
Stringer, Robert 1911- *AmSCAP 66, -80*
Stringfield, Lamar 1897-1959 *AmSCAP 66, -80, Baker 78, BiDAmM, ConAmC, NewGrD 80*
Stringham, Edwin John 1890-1974 *Baker 78, BiDAmM, ConAmC, OxMus, WhoMus 72*
Stringham, Mary Elizabeth 1937- *IntWWM 77*
Strini, Tom 1949- *ConAmC*
Stripling, Jan 1941- *CnOxB*
Stripp, Alan Alfred Martyn 1924- *IntWWM 77, -80, WhoMus 72*
Stritch, Elaine *MotPP*
Stritch, Elaine 1922- *FilmgC*

Stritch, Elaine 1925- *BiE&WWA, EncMT, ForYSC, NotNAT, WhoHol A*
Stritch, Elaine 1926- *FilmEn, HalFC 80, WhoThe 72, -77*
Strittmatter, Erwin 1912- *CnMD, CroCD, EncWT*
Strnad, Oskar 1879-1935 *EncWT*
Strobel, Fredric 1936- *CreCan 1, DancEn 78*
Strobel, Heinrich 1898-1970 *Baker 78, NewGrD 80*
Strobel, Otto 1895-1953 *Baker 78, NewGrD 80*
Strobel, Valentin 1575?-1640 *NewGrD 80*
Strobel, Valentin 1611?-1669? *NewGrD 80*
Strobl, Rudolf 1831-1915 *NewGrD 80*
Strock, Herbert L 1918- *FilmEn, FilmgC, HalFC 80, IntMPA 78, -79, -80, WhoHrs 80*
Strode, Warren Chetham 1897- *PlP&P, WhThe*
Strode, Woody *WhoHol A*
Strode, Woody 1914- *DrBlPA, FilmEn*
Strode, Woody 1923- *CmMov, FilmgC, ForYSC, HalFC 80*
Stroe, Aurel 1932- *Baker 78, DcCM, IntWWM 77, -80, NewGrD 80*
Stroganova, Nina 1920- *CnOxB, DancEn 78*
Strogers, Nicholas *NewGrD 80*
Stroheim, Erich Von 1885-1957 *AmFD, DcFM, FilmEn, OxFilm*
Strohm, Reinhard 1942- *IntWWM 77, -80, NewGrD 80*
Strohn, Albert J 1888- *BiDAmM*
Strolka, Egbert 1935- *DancEn 78*
Stroll, Edson *ForYSC, WhoHol A*
Strollo, Angie d1964 *NotNAT B*
Strom, Terrye *AmSCAP 80*
Stromberg, Hunt 1894-1968 *FilmEn, FilmgC, HalFC 80*
Stromberg, John 1853-1902 *AmPS, BiDAmM, NewCBMT, NotNAT B, PopAmC[port], Sw&Ld B*
Stromberg, Ole-Jergen 1946- *IntWWM 77, -80*
Strombergs, Alfred 1922- *IntWWM 77, -80*
Stromholm, Folke 1941- *IntWWM 77*
Strong, Austin 1881-1952 *ModWD, NotNAT B, WhThe*
Strong, Barrett 1941- *RkOn*
Strong, Benny 1911- *CmpEPM*
Strong, Bob *BgBands 74*
Strong, Carl E 1907-1965 *WhScrn 74, -77*
Strong, David *WhoHol A*
Strong, Eugene *Film 1, -2*
Strong, George Templeton 1856-1948 *Baker 78, BiDAmM, NewGrD 80, OxMus*
Strong, Jay 1896-1953 *NotNAT B, WhScrn 74, -77, WhoHol B*
Strong, Jimmy 1906- *WhoJazz 72*
Strong, Joyce Elizabeth 1933- *IntWWM 77, -80*
Strong, Leonard *Vers B[port]*
Strong, Mark *Film 1*
Strong, Michael *WhoHol A*
Strong, Nathan 1748-1816 *BiDAmM*
Strong, Porter 1879-1923 *Film 1, -2, WhScrn 77, WhoHol B*
Strong, Romaner Jack *BlkAmP*
Strong, Steve d1975 *WhScrn 77, WhoHol C*
Strong, Susan 1875- *BiDAmM*
Strongheart 1916-1929 *Film 2, TwYS, WhScrn 77*
Strongheart, Nipo 1891-1966 *WhoHol B*
Strongheart, Nipo 1891-1967 *Film 2, ForYSC, MotPP, TwYS*
Stronghili, Miranda 1929- *IntWWM 77, -80*
Stroock, Bianca 1896- *BiE&WWA, NotNAT*
Stroock, Gloria *WhoHol A*
Stroock, James E 1891-1965 *BiE&WWA, NotNAT, -B*
Stros, Ladislav 1926- *WhoOp 76*
Strosky, Rose Kathryn 1912- *AmSCAP 66*
Stross, Raymond 1916- *FilmgC, HalFC 80, IntMPA 77, -75, -76, -78, -79, -80*
Stross, Raymond 1917- *WorEFlm*
Strothers, Bill *Film 2*
Stroud, Clarence 1907-1973 *WhScrn 77*
Stroud, Claude *ForYSC, WhoHol A*
Stroud, Don 1937- *FilmEn, FilmgC, HalFC 80, WhoHol A*
Stroud, Don 1942- *ForYSC*
Stroud, Gregory 1892- *WhThe*
Stroud, Richard 1929- *ConAmC*
Stroud, Sally Ann *WhoHol A*
Stroup, Don *WhoHol A*
Strouse, Charles 1928- *AmPS, AmSCAP 66, -80, BiDAmM, BiE&WWA, EncMT, NewCBMT, NewGrD 80, NotNAT, PopAmC SUP[port], WhoThe 72, -77*
Strouse, Charles 1929- *BestMus*
Strouse And Adams *BestMus*
Strout, Mrs. Alan *PupTheA*
Strouth, Penelope *WomWMM B*
Stroux, Karl Heinz 1908- *EncWT*
Strow-Piccolo, Lynne 1943- *IntWWM 80*
Strowger, E *NewGrD 80*
Strowger, Nicholas *NewGrD 80*
Strowgers, Nicholas *NewGrD 80*
Stroyberg, Annette *WhoHol A*
Stroyeva, Vera 1903- *DcFM, FilmEn, WomWMM*
Strozier, Frank R 1937- *EncJzS 70*
Strozzi, Barbara 1619-1664? *NewGrD 80*
Strozzi, Giulio 1583-1652 *NewGrD 80[port]*
Strozzi, Gregorio 1615?-1687? *NewGrD 80*
Strozzi, Kay *WhThe, WhoHol A*
Strozzi, Piero 1550?-1609? *NewGrD 80*
Strozzi, Pietro *Baker 78*
Strub, Harald 1923- *WhoMus 72*
Strube, Gustav 1867-1953 *Baker 78, BiDAmM, NewGrD 80*
Struble, Larry J 1940- *IntWWM 77, -80*
Struchkova, Raisa 1925- *DancEn 78[port]*
Struchkova, Raissa Stepanovna 1925- *CnOxB*
Struck, Paul 1776-1820 *NewGrD 80*
Strudwick, Nancy 1921- *IntWWM 77, -80, WhoMus 72*
Strudwick, Sheppard 1907- *MovMk*
Strudwick, Shepperd 1907- *BiE&WWA, FilmEn, FilmgC, ForYSC, HalFC 80, IntMPA 77, -75, -76, -78, -79, -80, NotNAT, WhoHol A, WhoThe 72, -77*
Struewe, Hans *Film 2*
Strukoff, Rudolf Stephen 1938- *CpmDNM 75, ConAmC*
Strum, Hans *Film 2*
Strummer, Peter 1948- *WhoOp 76*
Strumway, Lee *Film 2*
Strunck, Delphin 1600?-1694 *NewGrD 80*
Strunck, Nicolaus Adam 1640-1700 *NewGrD 80*
Strungk, Delphin 1600?-1694 *NewGrD 80*
Strungk, Nicolaus Adam 1640-1700 *Baker 78, NewGrD 80*
Strunk, Jud 1936- *RkOn 2[port]*
Strunk, Oliver 1901-1980 *Baker 78, NewGrD 80*
Strunk, Steven 1943- *ConAmC, IntWWM 77, -80*
Strunz, Wolfgang 1936- *CnOxB*
Strus, George *WhoHol A*
Struss, Karl *IntMPA 77, -75, -76, -78, -79*
Struss, Karl 1886- *WhoHrs 80*
Struss, Karl 1890- *CmMov, FilmgC*
Struss, Karl 1891- *FilmEn, HalFC 80, WorEFlm*
Struthers, Sally 1947- *HalFC 80*
Struthers, Sally 1948- *WhoHol A*
Strutt, John William *NewGrD 80*
Strutt, Joseph 1749-1802 *DcPup*
Strutz, Thomas 1621?-1678 *NewGrD 80*
Struwer, Astrid 1942- *CnOxB*
Struzick, Edward Hugh, II 1951- *AmSCAP 80*
Stryczek, Karl-Heinz 1937- *WhoOp 76*
Stryja, Karol 1915- *IntWWM 77, -80*
Stryker, Gustave 1866-1943 *WhScrn 74, -77*
Stryker, Joseph *Film 2*
Stryker, Melancthon Woolsey 1851-1929 *BiDAmM*
Strzelecki, Henry P 1939- *AmSCAP 80*
Stuart *NewGrD 80*
Stuart, Aimee *IntMPA 77, -75, -76, -78, -79, -80, WhThe*
Stuart, Amy *WhoHol A*
Stuart, Arlen *WhoHol A*
Stuart, Barbara *WhoHol A*
Stuart, Binkie 1932?- *FilmgC, HalFC 80, WhoHol A*
Stuart, C Douglas 1864- *WhThe*
Stuart, Cora d1940 *NotNAT B*
Stuart, Cosmo 1868- *WhoStg 1908*
Stuart, Cosmo 1869- *WhThe*
Stuart, Donald 1898-1944 *Film 2, WhScrn 74, -77, WhoHol B*
Stuart, Eleanor *CreCan 2*
Stuart, Gil *WhoHol A*
Stuart, Gina *WhoHol A*
Stuart, Gloria *MotPP, What 5[port]*
Stuart, Gloria 1909- *FilmgC, HalFC 80, MovMk[port], WhoHrs 80*
Stuart, Gloria 1910- *FilmEn, HolP 30[port], ThFT[port]*
Stuart, Gloria 1911- *ForYSC, WhoHol A*
Stuart, Henry *Film 2*
Stuart, Hugh M 1917- *ConAmC*
Stuart, Iris 1903-1936 *Film 2, MotPP, WhScrn 77, WhoHol B*
Stuart, James Fortier 1928- *IntWWM 77, -80*
Stuart, Jean 1904-1926 *Film 1, WhScrn 74, -77, WhoHol B*
Stuart, Jeanne 1908- *WhThe*
Stuart, Joan Pauline 1925- *WhoMus 72*
Stuart, John 1898- *Film 2, FilmgC, IlWWBF[port], -A, WhoHol A, WhoThe 72, -77*
Stuart, John 1898-1972? *HalFC 80*
Stuart, John 1898-1979 *FilmEn*
Stuart, Leslie 1864-1928 *CmpEPM, EncMT, HalFC 80, NewGrD 80, NotNAT B, WhThe*
Stuart, Leslie 1866-1928 *Baker 78, OxMus*
Stuart, Madge 1897- *Film 2, IlWWBF, WhThe*
Stuart, Margaret *WhoHol A*
Stuart, Martha *WomWMM B*
Stuart, Mary *AmSCAP 80, WhoHol A*
Stuart, Maxine *WhoHol A*
Stuart, Mel 1926?- *FilmgC, HalFC 80, NewYTET*
Stuart, Muriel 1903- *CnOxB, DancEn 78*
Stuart, Nick 1904-1973 *FilmEn, Film 2, WhScrn 77, WhoHol B*
Stuart, Nick 1906-1973 *ForYSC, TwYS*
Stuart, Otho 1865-1930 *NotNAT B, WhThe*
Stuart, Philip 1887-1936 *NotNAT B, WhThe*
Stuart, Ralph R 1890-1952 *Film 1, WhScrn 74, -77, WhoHol B*
Stuart, Randy *ForYSC*
Stuart, Roberta *AmSCAP 80*
Stuart, Simeon *Film 2*
Stuart, Thomas Gilmore 1948- *AmSCAP 80*
Stuart, Tom 1878- *WhThe*
Stuart, Walter 1925- *AmSCAP 66, -80*
Stuarti, Enzo 1925- *AmSCAP 66, -80*
Stubbington, Vera Kathleen *WhoMus 72*
Stubbs, George Edward 1857-1937 *BiDAmM*
Stubbs, Harry 1874-1950 *Film 2, WhScrn 77*
Stubbs, Louise *DrBlPA*
Stubbs, Simon *NewGrD 80*
Stubbs, Una *WhoThe 77*
Stuber, Conrad 1550?-1605? *NewGrD 80*
Stuberus, Conrad 1550?-1605? *NewGrD 80*
Stuchs, Georg d1520 *NewGrD 80*
Stuchs, Johann d1546? *NewGrD 80*
Stuck, Jean-Baptiste 1680-1755 *Baker 78, NewGrD 80*
Stucken, Frank Valentin VanDer 1858-1929 *Baker 78, NewGrD 80, OxMus*
Stuckenschmidt, Hans Heinz 1901- *Baker 78, IntWWM 77, -80, NewGrD 80*
Stuckey, Henry 1897-1966 *BluesWW*
Stuckey, Nat 1937- *CounME 74[port], -74A, IlEncCM[port]*
Stuckey, Nathan Wright 1937- *BiDAmM*
Stuckey, Phyllis *WhThe*
Stuckgold, Grete 1895-1977 *Baker 78, NewEOp 71*
Stuckgold, Jacques 1877-1953 *Baker 78*
Stucki, Hans *NewGrD 80*
Stucki, Johannes *NewGrD 80*
Stuckmann, Werner 1936- *WhoOp 76*
Stucky, Steven 1949- *CpmDNM 73, -74, ConAmC, IntWWM 80*
Studakevich, Anna *Film 2*
Studdiford, Grace *Film 2*
Studebaker, Howard James 1920- *AmSCAP 80*
Studebaker, Julia Marlene 1951- *IntWWM 80*
Studer, Hans 1911- *NewGrD 80*
Studer, Pierre Andre 1941- *IntWWM 77, -80*
Studholm, Marie 1875-1930 *NotNAT B*
Studholme, Marie 1875-1930 *WhThe*

Studholme, Marion 1927- *CmOp, WhoMus 72*
Study, Lomax *WhoHol A*
Studzinska-Marczewska, Wiktoria 1818-1881 *NewGrD 80*
Studzinski *NewGrD 80*
Studzinski, Kajetan 1832-1855 *NewGrD 80*
Studzinski, Karol 1828-1883 *NewGrD 80*
Studzinski, Piotr 1826-1869 *NewGrD 80*
Studzinski, Wincenty 1815-1854 *NewGrD 80*
Stueber, Conrad *NewGrD 80*
Stueckgold, Grete 1895- *BiDAmM*
Stuessy, Clarence Joseph, Jr. 1943- *AmSCAP 80*
Stuessy, Joseph 1943- *ConAmC*
Stuhec, Igor 1932- *NewGrD 80*
Stukalov, Nikolay Fyodorovich *McGEWD[port]*
Stukolkin, Timofei Alexeievich 1829-1894 *CnOxB*
Stulberg, Gordon 1923- *IntMPA 77, -75, -76, -78, -79, -80*
Stull, Donald Earl 1927- *AmSCAP 80*
Stull, Walter *Film 1*
Stults, R M 1861-1923 *BiDAmM*
Stumm *NewGrD 80*
Stumm, Johann Heinrich d1788 *NewGrD 80*
Stumm, Johann Michael 1683-1747 *NewGrD 80*
Stumm, Johann Philipp 1705-1776 *NewGrD 80*
Stumpf, Carl 1848-1936 *Baker 78, NewGrD 80*
Stumpf, Johann Christian 1740?-1801? *NewGrD 80*
Stumpff, Carolus *NewGrD 80*
Stuntz, Joseph Hartmann 1793-1859 *Baker 78, NewGrD 80*
Stupan VonEhrenstein, Johann Jakob 1664-1739 *NewGrD 80*
Sturchio, Frank G 1894-1971 *ConAmC*
Sturcken, Frank W 1929- *BiE&WWA*
Sturdivant, B Victor 1901- *IntMPA 77, -75, -76, -78, -79, -80*
Sturgeon, N d1454 *NewGrD 80*
Sturgeon, Nicholas d1454 *Baker 78*
Sturgeon, Rollin d1925 *TwYS A*
Sturgeon, Russell M 1921- *AmSCAP 80*
Sturges *NewGrD 80*
Sturges, John 1911- *AmFD, BiDFilm, -81, CmMov, DcFM, FilmEn, FilmgC, HalFC 80, MovMk[port], OxFilm, WorEFlm*
Sturges, John Eliot *IntMPA 77, -75, -76, -78, -79, -80*
Sturges, Preston 1898-1959 *AmFD, BiDFilm, -81, CmMov, DcFM, FilmEn, FilmgC, HalFC 80[port], ModWD, MovMk[port], OxFilm, WhThe, WorEFlm*
Sturges, Solomon *WhoHol A*
Sturgess, Arthur d1931 *NotNAT B*
Sturgis, Eddie 1881-1947 *Film 2, WhScrn 77*
Sturgis, Edwin *Film 2*
Sturgis, Norman 1922- *IntMPA 77, -75, -76, -78, -79, -80*
Sturm, Erna *Film 2*
Sturm, Hannes *Film 2*
Sturm, Kaspar d1599? *NewGrD 80*
Sturm, Maurice 1899- *AmSCAP 80*
Sturm, Murray 1899- *AmSCAP 66*
Sturman, Marjorie 1902- *CnOxB*
Sturman, Paul 1943- *IntWWM 80*
Sturmer, Bruno 1892-1958 *Baker 78, NewGrD 80*
Sturt, John *NewGrD 80*
Sturt, Lois *Film 2*
Sturton *NewGrD 80*
Stury, Alfred *PupTheA*
Sturzenegger, Richard 1905-1976 *Baker 78, NewGrD 80*
Stutenroth, Gene 1903- *Vers A[port]*
Stutschewsky, Joachim 1891- *Baker 78, NewGrD 80*
Stutschewsky, Yehoyachin 1891- *NewGrD 80*
Stutsman, Grace May *BiDAmM*
Stutz, Carlton Franklin 1915- *AmSCAP 80*
Stutzmann, Christiane 1939- *WhoOp 76*
Stuyf, Koert 1938- *CnOxB*
Styles, Beverly *AmSCAP 80*
Styles, Dorothy Geneva 1922- *IntWWM 77, -80*
Styles, Edwin 1899-1960 *NotNAT B, WhThe, WhoHol A, -B*
Styles, John Ernest Fredric 1913- *IntWWM 77, -80, WhoMus 72*
Styles, Ronald Arthur 1917- *IntWWM 77*
Stylistics, The *IlEncR[port], RkOn 2[port]*
Styman, Barbara *WomWMM B*
Styne, Jule 1905- *AmPS, AmSCAP 66, -80, Baker 78, BestMus, BiDAmM, BiE&WWA, CmpEPM, ConAmC, EncMT, FilmEn, FilmgC, HalFC 80, IntMPA 77, -76, -78, -79, -80, NewCBMT, NewGrD 80, NotNAT, PopAmC[port], PopAmC SUP, Sw&Ld C, WhoThe 72, -77*
Styne, Stanley 1940- *AmSCAP 66*
Styne, Stanley H 1930- *AmSCAP 80*
Styx *ConMuA 80A[port], RkOn 2[port]*
Suard, Jean Baptiste Antoine 1735-1817 *NewGrD 80*
Suarez Couto, Cesar-Antonio 1952- *IntWWM 80*
Suarez Rebelo, Joao *NewGrD 80*
Suart, George Frederick 1910- *WhoMus 72*
Suart, Richard Martin 1951- *IntWWM 80*
Suassuna, Arina 1920- *EncWT*
Subbulakshmi, Madurai Shanmukhavadivu 1916- *NewGrD 80*
Subira, Jose 1882- *Baker 78, NewGrD 80*
Subject, Evelyn d1975 *WhScrn 77, WhoHol C*
Sublett, John Bubbles *WhoHol A*
Sublett, John William *BlksBF[port]*
Sublette, Walter 1940- *BlkAmP*
Subligny, Marie 1666-1736 *DancEn 78*
Subligny, Marie-Therese 1666-1735? *CnOxB*
Subota, Dorothy Lapell 1897- *AmSCAP 80*
Subotnick, Joan Lotz LaBarbara 1947- *AmSCAP 80*
Subotnick, Morton 1933- *AmSCAP 80, Baker 78, BnBkM 80, ConAmC, DcCM, IntWWM 77, -80, NewGrD 80*
Subotnik, Morton 1933- *BiDAmM*
Subotsky, Milton 1921- *FilmgC, HalFC 80, IntMPA 77, -75, -76, -78, -79, -80, WhoHrs 80*
Subramaniam, Lakshminarayana 1947- *IntWWM 80*
Subramaniam, Lakshminatayana 1947- *IntWWM 77*
Subramanian, Jane M 1950- *IntWWM 77*
Such, Percy Frederick 1878-1959 *Baker 78*
Sucher, Henry 1900- *IntMPA 77, -75, -76, -78, -79, -80, WhoHrs 80*
Sucher, Josef 1843-1908 *NewGrD 80*
Sucher, Joseph 1843-1908 *Baker 78*
Sucher, Rosa 1849-1927 *Baker 78, CmOp, NewEOp 71, NewGrD 80*
Suchoff, Benjamin 1918- *AmSCAP 66, -80*
Suchon, Eugen 1908- *Baker 78, DcCM, IntWWM 77, -80, NewGrD 80*
Suchy, Frantisek 1891-1973 *NewGrD 80*
Suchy, Frantisek 1902-1977 *NewGrD 80*
Suchy, Gregoria Karides *ConAmC*
Suck, Charles J *NewGrD 80*
Suckling, Sir John 1609-1642 *CnThe, OxThe, REnWD[port]*
Suckling, Norman Charles 1904- *Baker 78, WhoMus 72*
Sucksdorff, Arne 1917- *DcFM, FilmEn, FilmgC, HalFC 80, OxFilm, WhoHol A, WorEFlm*
Sucoff, Herbert 1938- *ConAmC, IntWWM 77*
Suda, Stanislav 1865-1931 *Baker 78*
Sudakevich, Annel *Film 2*
Sudakov, Ilya Yakovleivich 1890-1969 *OxThe*
Sudan, Nazzam A 1944- *BlkAmP*
Sudbury, Graham 1925- *IntWWM 77, -80*
Suddaby, Elsie *WhoMus 72*
Suddermann, Hermann 1857-1928 *CnThe*
Suddoth, J Guy *BluesWW[port]*
Sudds, William 1843-1920 *Baker 78*
Suderburg, Robert 1936- *AmSCAP 80, CpmDNM 72, -78, -80, ConAmC*
Suderman, David H 1909- *IntWWM 77*
Sudermann, Herman 1857-1928 *NotNAT B*
Sudermann, Hermann 1857-1928 *CnMD, EncWT, Ent, McGEWD[port], ModWD, OxThe*
Sudhalter, Dick 1938- *EncJzS 70*
Sudhalter, Richard Merrill 1938- *EncJzS 70*
Sudkamp, Sister Augustine 1914- *IntWWM 77*
Sudlow, Bessie d1928 *NotNAT B*
Sudlow, Joan 1892-1970 *WhScrn 74, -77, WhoHol B*
Sudy, Joseph *CmpEPM*
Sue, Eugene 1804-1857 *OxThe*
Suedo, Julie 1904- *Film 2, IlWWBF*
Sues, Leonard 1921-1971 *AmSCAP 66, WhScrn 74, -77, WhoHol B*
Suess, John G 1929- *IntWWM 77, -80*
Suessdorf, Karl 1911- *AmSCAP 66*
Suessdorf, Karl 1921- *AmSCAP 80*
Suesse, Dana 1909- *AmSCAP 80*
Suesse, Dana 1911- *AmSCAP 66, Baker 78, CmpEPM, ConAmC*
Suessenguth, Walther d1964 *NotNAT B, WhoHol B*
Suett, Richard 1755-1805 *OxThe*
Suevus, Felician *NewGrD 80*
Suffield, Raymond Herbert Alfred 1906- *WhoMus 72*
Suga, Michio *NewGrD 80*
Sugano, Kunihiko 1935- *EncJzS 70*
Sugar, Clara Steele 1932- *IntWWM 77*
Sugar, Joseph M 1919- *IntMPA 77, -75, -76, -78, -79, -80*
Sugar, Joseph Robert 1928- *IntWWM 77*
Sugar, Rezso 1919- *Baker 78, DcCM, IntWWM 77, -80, NewGrD 80*
Sugarloaf *RkOn 2[port]*
Sugarman, Burt *ConMuA 80B*
Sugarman, Harold 1905- *IntMPA 77, -75, -76, -78, -79, -80*
Sugden, Charles 1850-1921 *NotNAT B, WhThe*
Sugden, Mrs. Charles *WhThe*
Suggia, Guilhermina 1888-1950 *Baker 78, NewGrD 80*
Suggs, James Douglas 1886-1955 *BluesWW*
Suggs, Peter 1909- *WhoJazz 72*
Sugimori, Nobumori *McGEWD[port]*
Sugrue, Frank 1927- *BiE&WWA, NotNAT*
Suhit, Suzanne Bergeron *CreCan 1*
Suhl, Johann Matthias *NewGrD 80*
Suhosky, Bob 1928- *IntMPA 77, -75, -76, -78, -79, -80*
Suhrs, Susan H *PupTheA*
Suib, Leonard W *PupTheA*
Suisse *NewGrD 80*
Suiter, Arlendo D 1919- *AmSCAP 66*
Suitner, Otmar 1922- *IntWWM 77, -80, NewGrD 80, WhoMus 72, WhoOp 76*
Suitner, Peter 1928- *IntWWM 80*
Suitor, M Lee 1942- *ConAmC*
Suk, Josef 1874-1935 *Baker 78, DcCom&M 79, NewGrD 80[port], OxMus*
Suk, Josef 1929- *Baker 78, IntWWM 77, -80, NewGrD 80, WhoMus 72*
Suk, Joseph 1874-1935 *CompSN[port], DcCM, MusMk*
Suk, Vaclav 1861-1933 *NewGrD 80*
Suk, Vasa 1861-1933 *Baker 78*
Sukardi, Kotot *DcFM*
Sukegawa, Toshiya 1930- *Baker 78*
Sukhovo-Kobylin, Aleksandr Vasilevich 1817-1903 *McGEWD, ModWD*
Sukhovo-Kobylin, Alexander 1817-1903 *Ent*
Sukhovo-Kobylin, Alexander Vasileivich 1817-1903 *CnThe, OxThe, REnWD[port]*
Sukhovo-Kobylin, Alexander Vasilievich 1817-1903 *EncWT*
Sukis, Lilian 1942- *CreCan 2, WhoOp 76*
Sukman, Frances Paley *AmSCAP 80*
Sukman, Harry 1912- *AmSCAP 66, -80*
Sul-Te-Wan, Madame d1959 *Film 2, WhoHol B*
Sulc, Miroslav 1927- *IntWWM 77, -80*
Sulcova, Brigita 1937- *IntWWM 77, -80*
Sulek, Stjepan 1914- *Baker 78, DcCM, NewGrD 80*
Sulerzhitsky, Leopold Antonovich 1872-1916 *EncWT*
Sulich, Vasili 1929- *DancEn 78*
Sulich, Vassili 1929- *CnOxB*
Sulieman, Idrees Dawud 1923- *EncJzS 70*
Suliotis, Elena 1943- *IntWWM 77, -80, WhoMus 72*
Sulka, Elaine *NotNAT*
Sullavan, Margaret d1960 *MotPP, WhoHol B*
Sullavan, Margaret 1909-1960 *ThFT[port]*
Sullavan, Margaret 1911-1960 *BiDFilm, -81, CmMov, FilmEn, FilmgC, ForYSC,*

HalFC 80[port], MGM[port], MovMk[port], NotNAT B, OxFilm, OxThe, WhScrn 74, -77, WhThe
Sullivan, Alexander 1885-1956 *AmSCAP 66, -80*
Sullivan, Sir Arthur Seymour 1842-1900 *Baker 78, BnBkM 80, CmOp, DcCom 77[port], DcCom&M 79, EncWT, GrComp[port], MusMk, NewEOp 71, NewGrD 80[port], NotNAT A, -B, OxMus, REnWD[port]*
Sullivan, Barry 1821-1891 *NotNAT B, OxThe*
Sullivan, Barry 1824-1891 *NotNAT A*
Sullivan, Barry 1912- *BiE&WWA, FilmEn, FilmgC, ForYSC, HalFC 80, IntMPA 77, -75, -76, -78, -79, -80, MotPP, MovMk[port], NotNAT, WhoHol A*
Sullivan, Bartholomew Thomas 1902- *IntWWM 77, -80, WhoMus 72*
Sullivan, Betty Somers 1919- *IntWWM 77, -80*
Sullivan, Billy *Film 2*
Sullivan, Brian 1915-1969 *BiDAmM*
Sullivan, Brian 1919-1969 *WhScrn 74, -77, WhoHol B*
Sullivan, C Gardner *WomWMM*
Sullivan, C Gardner 1879-1965 *DcFM, FilmEn*
Sullivan, C Gardner 1885-1965 *HalFC 80, OxFilm*
Sullivan, Charles *Film 2*
Sullivan, Charles Henry 1944- *EncJzS 70*
Sullivan, Dan 1875-1948 *AmSCAP 66, -80*
Sullivan, Dan 1940- *WhoOp 76*
Sullivan, Dane 1950- *AmSCAP 80*
Sullivan, Daniel d1764 *NewGrD 80*
Sullivan, Daniel Joseph 1935- *ConAmTC*
Sullivan, David *WhoHol A*
Sullivan, David L *Film 1*
Sullivan, Don 1938?- *WhoHrs 80*
Sullivan, Ed 1902-1974 *IntMPA 75, NewYTET, PlP&P, WhScrn 77, WhoHol B*
Sullivan, Elliott d1974 *WhoHol B*
Sullivan, Elliott 1907-1974 *BiE&WWA, NotNAT B*
Sullivan, Elliott 1908-1974 *WhScrn 77*
Sullivan, Francis Loftus 1903-1956 *FilmAG WE, FilmEn, FilmgC, ForYSC, HalFC 80, IlWWBF, MotPP, NotNAT B, PlP&P, Vers A[port], WhScrn 74, -77, WhThe, WhoHol B*
Sullivan, Fred 1872-1937 *Film 2, WhoHol B*
Sullivan, Frederick R 1872-1937 *WhScrn 74, -77*
Sullivan, Gala 1939- *AmSCAP 80*
Sullivan, Gerald Warden 1891- *AmSCAP 80*
Sullivan, Gwynne 1937- *IntWWM 80*
Sullivan, Helene *Film 2*
Sullivan, Henry 1893- *AmSCAP 66, -80, BiDAmM*
Sullivan, Ira Brevard 1931- *EncJzS 70*
Sullivan, James E 1864-1931 *Film 2, WhScrn 74, -77, WhThe, WhoHol B*
Sullivan, James Francis 1880- *WhoStg 1908*
Sullivan, James Maurice d1949 *WhoHol B*
Sullivan, Jean 1923- *ForYSC, WhoHol A*
Sullivan, Jenny *WhoHol A*
Sullivan, Jeremiah *WhoHol A*
Sullivan, Jeri Kelli 1924- *AmSCAP 80*
Sullivan, Jerry 1891- *AmSCAP 66*
Sullivan, Jo *BiE&WWA, NotNAT*
Sullivan, Joe d1971 *ConMuA 80B, IlEncJ*
Sullivan, Joe 1906-1971 *BiDAmM, CmpEPM, EncJzS 70, WhoJazz 72*
Sullivan, Joe 1910-1971 *WhScrn 74, -77*
Sullivan, John *WhoHol A*
Sullivan, John 1917-1967 *BiDAmM*
Sullivan, John A d1964 *NotNAT B*
Sullivan, John Laurence 1940- *IntWWM 77, -80*
Sullivan, John Maurice 1876-1949 *WhScrn 74, -77*
Sullivan, Joseph J *AmPS B*
Sullivan, Joseph Michael 1906-1971 *AmSCAP 66, -80*
Sullivan, Liam 1923- *AmSCAP 80, ForYSC, WhoHol A*
Sullivan, Maxine 1911- *BiDAmM, CmpEPM, DrBlPA, EncJzS 70, IlEncJ, WhoJazz 72*
Sullivan, Mella d1963 *NotNAT B*
Sullivan, Pat 1887-1933 *FilmEn, HalFC 80*
Sullivan, Pat 1888-1933 *WorEFlm*
Sullivan, Patrick J 1920- *IntMPA 77, -75, -76, -78, -79, -80*
Sullivan, Rollin 1919- *BiDAmM*
Sullivan, Ruth Irene 1921- *IntWWM 77*
Sullivan, Sean *WhoHol A*
Sullivan, Sylvia Ingeborg Vivian 1909- *WhoMus 72*
Sullivan, Thomas Joseph, Jr. 1947- *AmSCAP 80*
Sullivan, Thomas Russell 1849-1916 *NotNAT B*
Sullivan, Timothy 1939- *ConAmC*
Sullivan, William *Film 2*
Sullivan, William M 1922- *AmSCAP 66*
Sullivan, William Michael 1925- *AmSCAP 80*
Sully, Daniel 1855-1910 *NotNAT B, WhoStg 1906, -1908*
Sully, Frank 1908-1975 *WhScrn 77, WhoHol C*
Sully, Frank 1910-1975 *ForYSC, HalFC 80, IntMPA 75, -76, Vers B[port]*
Sully, Janet Miller *Film 1*
Sully, Mariette 1878- *WhThe*
Sultan, Arne 1925- *AmSCAP 66, -80*
Sultan, June 1912- *AmSCAP 66*
Sultan, Roger H *IntMPA 77, -75, -76, -78, -79, -80*
Sultzbach, Russell 1952- *CnOxB*
Sultzberger, Johann Ulrich 1638-1701 *NewGrD 80*
Sultzer, Joe 1884- *JoeFr*
Sulyok, Imre 1912- *IntWWM 77, -80*
Sulzberger, Nikolaus 1938- *WhoOp 76*
Sulzer, Balduin 1932- *IntWWM 80*
Sulzer, Johann Anton 1752-1828 *NewGrD 80*
Sulzer, Johann Georg 1720-1779 *NewGrD 80*
Sulzer, Julius Salomon 1834-1891 *Baker 78*
Sulzer, Salomon 1804-1890 *Baker 78, NewGrD 80*
Sumac, Yma 1922- *ForYSC, WhoHol A*
Sumac, Yma 1927- *Baker 78, What 4[port]*
Sumac, Yma 1928- *HalFC 80, WhoMus 72*
Sumarokov, Alexei Petrovich 1718-1777 *NotNAT B, OxThe*
Sumaya, Manuel De *NewGrD 80*
Sumen, Meric 1943- *CnOxB*
Sumer, Guner 1936- *REnWD[port]*
Sumerlin, Macon D 1919- *AmSCAP 66, -80, ConAmC*
Sumikura, Ichiro 1932- *IntWWM 77, -80*
Sumlin, Hubert 1931- *BluesWW[port]*
Summer, Donna 1948- *AmSCAP 80, ConMuA 80A[port], RkOn 2[port]*
Summer, Robert *ConMuA 80B*
Summerall, Pat *NewYTET*
Summerfield, Eleanor 1921- *FilmgC, HalFC 80, IntMPA 77, -75, -76, -78, -79, -80, WhThe, WhoHol A*
Summerfield, Sidney Charles 1889- *AmSCAP 80*
Summerland, Augusta *WhoHol A*
Summerlin, Ed 1928- *EncJzS 70*
Summerlin, Edgar E 1928- *ConAmC, EncJzS 70*
Summers, Reverend 1880-1948 *NotNAT B*
Summers, Andrew Rowan 1912-1968 *BiDAmM, EncFCWM 69*
Summers, Ann 1920-1974 *WhScrn 77, WhoHol B*
Summers, Dorothy d1964 *NotNAT B, WhScrn 77, WhoHol B*
Summers, Eddie 1903- *NewOrJ*
Summers, Elaine 1925- *CmpGMD, CnOxB, WomWMM A, -B*
Summers, Hope *WhoHol A*
Summers, Jeremy 1931- *FilmgC, HalFC 80, IlWWBF*
Summers, Jerry *WhoHol A*
Summers, Jesse *ConMuA 80B*
Summers, Joseph 1843- *OxMus*
Summers, Madlyn Jane *WhoStg 1906, -1908*
Summers, Manuel 1935- *WorEFlm*
Summers, Montague 1880-1946 *OxThe*
Summers, Montague 1880-1948 *WhThe*
Summers, Robert Eugene 1929- *AmSCAP 80*
Summers, Shari *WhoHol A*
Summers, Stanley *ConAmC*
Summers, Thomas Osmond 1812-1882 *BiDAmM*
Summers, Walter 1896- *FilmEn, FilmgC, HalFC 80, IlWWBF*
Summerson, Patrick Eugene 1951- *AmSCAP 80*
Summerton, Benjamin 1908- *WhoMus 72*
Summerville, Amelia 1862-1934 *Film 1, -2, WhoHol B, WhoStg 1906, -1908*
Summerville, Amelia 1863-1934 *WhScrn 77*
Summerville, George 1892-1946 *ForYSC, Vers A[port]*
Summerville, Slim d1946 *MotPP, NotNAT B, WhoHol B*
Summerville, Slim 1892-1946 *FilmEn, Film 1, -2, FilmgC, HalFC 80, HolCA[port], MovMk, TwYS*
Summerville, Slim 1896-1946 *WhScrn 74, -77*
Summey, James Clell *IlEncCM*
Summonte, Antonio d1637 *NewGrD 80*
Sumner, Carol 1940- *CnOxB, DancEn 78*
Sumner, Corinne Heath *WhScrn 74, -77*
Sumner, Geoffrey 1908- *HalFC 80, WhoHol A, WhoThe 72, -77*
Sumner, John David 1924- *BiDAmM, WhoThe 77*
Sumner, Kathryn *Film 2*
Sumner, Mary 1888-1956 *NotNAT B, WhThe*
Sumner, Oonah R 1883- *IntWWM 77*
Sumner, Sarah *ConAmC*
Sumner, Verlyn 1897-1935 *WhScrn 77*
Sumner, William Leslie 1904-1973 *NewGrD 80, WhoMus 72*
Sumsion, Herbert Whitton 1899- *IntWWM 80, NewGrD 80*
Sun Ra *DrBlPA*
Sun Ra 1915- *EncJzS 70*
Sun Ra 1928?- *IlEncJ, NewGrD 80[port]*
Sundberg, Clinton *IntMPA 77, -75, -76, -78, -79, -80, Vers B[port], WhoHol A*
Sundberg, Clinton 1906- *BiE&WWA, FilmEn, ForYSC, NotNAT*
Sundberg, Clinton 1919- *FilmgC, HalFC 80, MovMk*
Sundberg, Johan E F 1936- *IntWWM 77, -80, NewGrD 80*
Sundelius, Marie 1884-1958 *Baker 78*
Sunderland, Ethel *PupTheA*
Sunderland, Nan d1973 *NotNAT B, WhScrn 77, WhoHol B*
Sunderland, Scott 1883- *WhThe*
Sunderman, F William *IntWWM 80*
Sunderman, William *IntWWM 77*
Sundgaard, Arnold 1909- *AmSCAP 66, -80, BiE&WWA, NotNAT*
Sundgren-Schneevoigt, Sigrid Ingeborg 1878-1953 *Baker 78*
Sundholm, Bill d1971 *WhoHol B*
Sundholm, William Bill d1971 *WhScrn 77*
Sundin, Jerre *Film 2*
Sundman, Ulf Johan 1929- *IntWWM 77, -80*
Sundmark, Betty *WhScrn 74, -77*
Sundsten, John 1899- *ConAmC*
Sundstrom, Florence 1918- *BiE&WWA, NotNAT, WhoHol A*
Sundstrom, Frank *WhoHol A*
Suneburg, Friedrich Von *NewGrD 80*
Sung, Alexander 1947- *IntWWM 77, -80*
Sung-Tai, Kim 1907- *IntWWM 77, -80*
Sunnenburg, Friedrich Von *NewGrD 80*
Sunny And The Sunglows *RkOn*
Sunny Jim *BluesWW[port]*
Sunny Land Slim *BluesWW[port]*
Sunny South Quartet *BiDAmM*
Sunnyland Slim *BluesWW[port]*
Sunol, Gregorio Maria 1879-1946 *NewGrD 80*
Sunol Y Baulenas, Dom Gregorio Maria 1879-1946 *Baker 78*
Sunset Royal Serenaders, The *BgBands 74*
Sunshine, Baby 1915-1917 *WhScrn 77*
Sunshine, Madeline 1948- *AmSCAP 80*
Sunshine, Marion d1963 *AmSCAP 80, Film 1, NotNAT B, WhoHol B*
Sunshine, Marion 1894-1963 *AmSCAP 66, FilmEn*
Sunshine, Marion 1897-1963 *WhScrn 74, -77*
Sunshine, Morton 1915- *IntMPA 77, -75, -76, -78, -79, -80*
Sunshine Boys Quartet *BiDAmM*
Sunshine Company, The *BiDAmM, RkOn 2A*
Suolahti, Heikki 1920-1936 *Baker 78*
Supa, Richard *AmSCAP 80*
Supersax *EncJzS 70*
Supertramp *ConMuA 80A[port], IlEncR*
Supervia, Conchita 1895-1936 *Baker 78,*

CmOp, NewGrD 80[port]
Supervia, Conchita 1899-1936 NewEOp 71
Supervielle, Jules 1884-1960 CnMD, McGEWD, ModWD
Supicic, Ivo 1928- NewGrD 80
Suppa, Carl M 1925- WhoOp 76
Suppan, Jakob NewGrD 80
Suppan, Wolfgang 1933- IntWWM 77, -80, NewGrD 80
Suppe, Franz Von 1819-1895 Baker 78, BnBkM 80, CmOp, CmpBCM, DcCom 77, GrComp[port], MusMk, NewEOp 71, NewGrD 80, OxMus
Suppe Demelli, Francesco Ezechiele E 1819-1895 BnBkM 80
Supplee, Esther Ritter WhScrn 74, -77
Supremes, The BiDAmM, ConMuA 80A, RkOn[port]
Supries, Joseph 1761-1822 NewGrD 80
Supuerta, Miguel De NewGrD 80
Sur, Donald 1935- ConAmC, IntWWM 77, -80
Suratt, Valeska 1882-1962 Film 1, TwYS, WhScrn 77, WhoHol B
Surdin, Morris 1914- Baker 78, CreCan 2, IntWWM 80
Surette, Thomas Whitney 1861-1941 Baker 78
Surette, Thomas Whitney 1862-1941 BiDAmM
Surfaris, The BiDAmM, RkOn
Surgal, Jon 1949- AmSCAP 80
Surgenor, Ingrid 1946- IntWWM 77, -80
Surgi, Stanley 1907- NewOrJ
Surian, Elvidi 1940- IntWWM 77
Surian, Elvidio 1940- IntWWM 80
Suriani, Francesco NewGrD 80
Suriano, Francesco 1549-1621 Baker 78, NewGrD 80
Surianus, Francesco NewGrD 80
Surinach, Carlos 1915- Baker 78, CpmDNM 80, CnOxB, ConAmC, DancEn 78, DcCM, IntWWM 77, -80, NewGrD 80
Surman, John 1944- EncJzS 70, IlEncJ, NewGrD 80
Surmejan, Hazaros 1943- CnOxB, CreCan 2
Surov, Anatol CnMD
Surov, Anatoli Alekseevich 1910- ModWD
Surovy, Nick WhoHol A
Surowiak-Poliszewska, Bozena Maria 1949- IntWWM 77
Surplice, Reginald Alwyn 1906- WhoMus 72
Surrey, Philip Henry 1910- CreCan 2
Surrey, Richard CreCan 1
Surtees, Bruce FilmEn, FilmgC, HalFC 80, IntMPA 77, -76, -78, -79, -80
Surtees, Robert L 1906- CmMov, FilmEn, FilmgC, HalFC 80, IntMPA 77, -75, -76, -78, -79, -80, OxFilm, WorEFlm
Surzynski NewGrD 80
Surzynski, Jozef 1851-1919 Baker 78, NewGrD 80
Surzynski, Mieczyslaw 1866-1924 NewGrD 80
Surzynski, Stefan 1855-1919 NewGrD 80
Susa, Conrad 1935- AmSCAP 80, Baker 78, ConAmC
Susana CnOxB
Susands, Cecil Film 2
Susann, Jacqueline 1921-1974 HalFC 80, WhScrn 77, WhoHol B
Susarion OxThe
Susato, Johannes De 1448-1506 Baker 78, NewGrD 80
Susato, Tielman 1500?-1561? Baker 78
Susato, Tylman 1500?-1564? NewGrD 80, OxMus
Susay, Jo NewGrD 80
Suschitsky, Peter FilmgC, HalFC 80
Suschitsky, Wolfgang 1912- FilmgC, HalFC 80
Suschitzky, Peter FilmEn
Suschitzky, Wolfgang 1912- FilmEn
Susie BluesWW[port]
Susil, Frantisek 1804-1868 NewGrD 80
Susman, Todd WhoHol A
Sussan, Herbert 1921- IntMPA 77, -75, -76, -78, -79, -80
Sussenguth, Walther 1900-1964 WhScrn 74, -77
Sussin, Mathilde Film 2
Susskind, David 1920- BiE&WWA, FilmEn, FilmgC, HalFC 80, NewYTET, NotNAT
Susskind, Peter 1944- IntWWM 80
Susskind, Walter 1913- Baker 78, CreCan 2, IntWWM 77, MusMk, WhoMus 72, WhoOp 76
Susskind, Walter 1918-1980 NewGrD 80
Sussman, David Ethan 1951- IntWWM 77, -80
Sussman, Samuel 1913- NatPD[port]
Sussman, Sharron 1943- ConAmTC
Sussman, Stanley Barton 1938- AmSCAP 80, IntWWM 77
Sussmayer, Franz Xaver 1766-1803 NewGrD 80
Sussmayr, Franz Xaver 1766-1803 Baker 78, NewGrD 80
Sust, Johannes Von NewGrD 80
Sutch, Herbert Film 1, -2
Sutch, Lord ConMuA 80A
Sutch, Marion Adams PupTheA
Sutcliffe, Doris 1911- WhoMus 72
Sutcliffe, George Henry 1911- WhoMus 72
Sutcliffe, James 1929- ConAmC
Sutcliffe, James Thomas 1943- WhoMus 72
Sutcliffe, Sidney Clement 1918- IntWWM 77, -80, WhoMus 72
Sutej, Josip 1920- WhoOp 76
Suter, Hermann 1870-1926 Baker 78, NewGrD 80
Suter, Louis-Marc 1928- IntWWM 80
Suter, Marion 1903?-1974 NewOrJ SUP[port]
Suter, Paul 1930- AmSCAP 80
Suter, Robert 1919- Baker 78, CpmDNM 80, DcCM, NewGrD 80
Suter, W E d1882 NotNAT B
Sutermeister, Heinrich 1910- Baker 78, CmOp, CompSN[port], CpmDNM 80, DcCM, IntWWM 77, -80, NewEOp 71, NewGrD 80, WhoMus 72
Suthaus, Ludwig 1906-1971 CmOp, NewGrD 80
Sutherin, Wayne WhoHol A
Sutherland, A Edward 1895-1973 FilmgC, WhScrn 77
Sutherland, A Edward 1895-1974 HalFC 80
Sutherland, Allene PupTheA
Sutherland, Anne 1867-1942 Film 1, NotNAT B, WhoHol B
Sutherland, Annie 1867-1942 WhThe
Sutherland, Birdie d1955 NotNAT B
Sutherland, Bruce ConAmC, IntWWM 77, -80
Sutherland, David 1941- CnOxB
Sutherland, Dick 1882-1934 Film 2, WhScrn 74, -77, WhoHol B
Sutherland, Donald IntMPA 77, -75, -76, -78, -79, -80, WhoHol A, WomWMM
Sutherland, Donald 1934- FilmEn, MovMk[port]
Sutherland, Donald 1935- BiDFilm, -81, FilmgC, HalFC 80, WhoHrs 80
Sutherland, Donald S 1939- IntWWM 80
Sutherland, Eddie 1897- Film 1, TwYS
Sutherland, Eddie 1897-1973 Film 2
Sutherland, Edward 1895-1974 BiDFilm, -81, FilmEn
Sutherland, Edward 1897-1974 TwYS A, WhoHol B
Sutherland, Efua 1924- BlkAmP, ConDr 73, -77, WomWMM
Sutherland, Evelyn Greenleaf 1855-1908 NotNAT B, WhoStg 1908
Sutherland, Francilda PupTheA
Sutherland, Hope Film 2
Sutherland, Iain 1936- IntWWM 77, -80
Sutherland, Joan 1926- Baker 78, BiDAmM, BnBkM 80[port], CmOp[port], IntWWM 77, -80, MusMk[port], MusSN[port], NewGrD 80[port], WhoOp 76
Sutherland, Joan 1928- WhoMus 72
Sutherland, Joan 1929- NewEOp 71
Sutherland, John 1845-1921 Film 1, WhScrn 77
Sutherland, Joseph Film 1
Sutherland, Kennett Bruce 1939- AmSCAP 80
Sutherland, Margaret 1897- Baker 78, DcCM, NewGrD 80
Sutherland, Oriel IntWWM 77, -80
Sutherland, Paul 1935- CnOxB, DancEn 78
Sutherland, Robert IntWWM 77, -80
Sutherland, Robert C d1962 NotNAT B
Sutherland, Victor 1889-1968 Film 1, MotPP, WhScrn 74, -77, WhoHol B
Sutherland Brothers & Quiver IlEncR
Suthern, Orrin Clayton, II 1912- IntWWM 77, -80
Sutin, Marci AmSCAP 80
Sutowski, Thor 1945- CnOxB
Sutro, Alfred 1858- WhoStg 1906
Sutro, Alfred 1863-1933 McGEWD[port], ModWD, NotNAT A, -B, WhThe, WhoStg 1908
Sutro, Florence Edith 1865-1906 Baker 78
Sutro, Rose Laura 1870-1957 Baker 78, BiDAmM
Sutt, Grzegorz 1938- IntWWM 77, -80
Sutter, Milton Joseph, Jr. 1940- IntWWM 77, -80
Sutterer, Karen Jerelle 1949- IntWWM 77, -80
Suttie, Alan 1938- IntWWM 77, -80, WhoMus 72, WhoOp 76
Suttle, Ernest Frank Arnold 1914- IntWWM 77, -80, WhoMus 72
Sutto, Jeanine CreCan 2
Sutton, Charles Film 2
Sutton, David C, Sr. 1925- AmSCAP 80
Sutton, Dolores WhoHol A
Sutton, Dudley 1933- FilmgC, HalFC 80, WhoHol A
Sutton, Ernest E 1886-1963 AmSCAP 66
Sutton, Frank 1923-1974 WhScrn 77, WhoHol B
Sutton, Gertrude Film 2
Sutton, Grady 1908- FilmEn, Film 2, FilmgC, ForYSC, HalFC 80, HolCA[port], MotPP, MovMk, Vers A[port], WhoHol A
Sutton, James T IntMPA 77, -75, -76, -78, -79, -80
Sutton, John NewGrD 80
Sutton, John 1908-1963 FilmEn, FilmgC, ForYSC, HalFC 80, IntMPA 77, -75, -76, -78, -79, -80, MotPP, MovMk, WhScrn 74, -77, WhoHol B
Sutton, Julia WhoHol A
Sutton, Julia Sumberg 1928- IntWWM 80
Sutton, Kay ForYSC
Sutton, Paul 1912-1970 WhScrn 74, -77, WhoHol B
Sutton, Ralph Earl 1922- BiDAmM, CmpEPM, EncJzS 70, IlEncJ
Sutton, Reginald 1916- IntMPA 77, -75, -76, -78, -79, -80
Sutton, Sandra WomWMM B
Sutton, Sondra K 1942- AmSCAP 80
Sutton, Susie BlksB&W C
Sutton, Vern 1938- WhoOp 76
Sutton, Wadham Francis 1935- WhoMus 72
Sutton, William 1877-1955 WhScrn 74, -77
Sutton-Vane, Vane 1888-1963 WhThe
Suttonn, Reginald 1922- IntWWM 77
Suycott, Forrest D 1922- ConAmC
Suys, Hans NewGrD 80
Suzman, Janet 1939- CnThe, Ent[port], FilmAG WE, FilmgC, HalFC 80, WhoHol A, WhoThe 72, -77
Suzor-Cote, Aurele DeFoy 1869-1937 CreCan 1
Suzor-Cote, Marcus Aurele DeFoy CreCan 1
Suzoy, Johannes NewGrD 80
Suzuki, Hidetero 1937- IntWWM 80
Suzuki, Isao 1936- EncJzS 70
Suzuki, Pat AmPS B, WhoHol A
Suzuki, Shin'ichi 1898- NewGrD 80[port]
Suzuki, Shinichi 1901- MusMk
Svacov, Vladan 1930- WhoOp 76
Svanberg, Carsten 1945- IntWWM 80
Svanesoe, Robert 1921- IntWWM 77, -80
Svanholm, Set 1904-1964 Baker 78, CmOp, MusSN[port], NewEOp 71, NewGrD 80[port]
Svanoe, Bill EncFCWM 69
Svara, Danilo 1902- DcCM, NewGrD 80
Svarda, William Ernest 1941- AmSCAP 80
Svashenko, Semyon Film 2
Svecenski, Louis 1862-1926 Baker 78, BiDAmM
Sved, Alexander 1904- NewGrD 80
Sved, Sandor 1904- NewGrD 80
Svedbom, Vilhelm 1843-1904 NewGrD 80
Svehla, Zdenek 1924- WhoOp 76
Sveinbjornsson, Sveinbjorn 1847-1927 NewGrD 80
Sveinsson, Atli Heimer 1938- DcCM

Sveinsson, Atli Heimir 1938- *Baker 78, IntWWM 77, -80, NewGrD 80*
Sveinsson, Gunnar Reynir 1933- *IntWWM 77, NewGrD 80*
Svejda, Miroslav 1939- *WhoOp 76*
Svendsen, Johan 1840-1911 *Baker 78, GrComp, NewGrD 80[port], OxMus*
Svendsen, Olga *Film 2*
Svendsen, Oluf 1832-1888 *NewGrD 80*
Svennberg, Tore 1852- *Film 2, WhThe*
Svenson, Bo 1941- *HalFC 80, WhoHol A*
Svensson, Reinhold 1919- *CmpEPM*
Sverdlin, Lev N 1902-1969 *WhScrn 74, -77*
Sverrisson, Hjalmar 1950- *IntWWM 77, -80*
Sveshnikov, Alexander Vasil'yevich 1890- *NewGrD 80*
Svetlanov, Eugeni Pyodorovich 1928- *IntWWM 77, -80*
Svetlanov, Evgeny 1928- *Baker 78, NewGrD 80[port]*
Svetlev, Michail 1943- *WhoOp 76*
Svetlov, Valerian 1860-1934 *DancEn 78*
Svetlova, Marina 1922- *CnOxB, DancEn 78[port], IntWWM 77*
Sviridov, Georgy 1915- *Baker 78, DcCM, NewGrD 80*
Svoboda, Jiri 1897- *WhoMus 72*
Svoboda, Josef 1920- *EncWT, Ent, NewGrD 80, NotNAT, -A, WhoOp 76, WhoThe 77*
Svoboda, Tomas 1939- *AmSCAP 80, Baker 78, CpmDNM 72, -78, -80, ConAmC, IntWWM 77, -80, NewGrD 80*
Svorc, Antonin 1933- *WhoMus 72*
Svorc, Antonin 1934- *IntWWM 77, -80, WhoOp 76*
Svosovsky Z Lorbenthalu, Jan Petr *NewGrD 80*
Swack, Irwin 1919- *CpmDNM 75, ConAmC*
Swack, Irwin 1928- *AmSCAP 80*
Swaen, Guilielmus De 1610?-1674 *NewGrD 80*
Swaen, Willem De 1610?-1674 *NewGrD 80*
Swaffer, Hannen 1879-1962 *NotNAT A, -B, WhThe*
Swafford, Thomas J *NewYTET*
Swain, Freda Mary 1902- *IntWWM 77, -80, OxMus, WhoMus 72*
Swain, Leonard 1821-1869 *BiDAmM*
Swain, Mack 1876-1935 *FilmEn, Film 1, -2, FilmgC, ForYSC, HalFC 80, JoeFr, MotPP, MovMk, TwYS, WhScrn 74, -77, WhoHol B*
Swain, Paul Stevens 1911- *AmSCAP 80*
Swaine, Alexander Freiherr Von 1905- *CnOxB*
Swainson, Anthony Robin 1947- *IntWWM 77, -80*
Swale, David 1928- *NewGrD 80*
Swalin, Benjamin F 1901- *IntWWM 77, -80*
Swallow, Margaret 1896-1932 *NotNAT B, WhThe*
Swallow, Norman 1921- *IntMPA 77, -75, -76, -78, -79, -80*
Swallow, Stephen W 1940- *EncJzS 70*
Swallow, Steve 1940- *EncJzS 70*
Swallows, The *RkOn*
Swan, Alfred Julius 1890-1970 *Baker 78, ConAmC, NewGrD 80*
Swan, Anna 1846-1888 *Ent*
Swan, Aunt Alice *MorBAP*
Swan, Billy 1944- *IlEncCM[port], IlEncR, RkOn 2[port]*
Swan, Don *AmSCAP 80*
Swan, Dottie 1916- *BiDAmM*
Swan, Einar Aaron 1904-1940 *AmSCAP 66, -80*
Swan, Jabez 1800-1884 *BiDAmM*
Swan, Judith 1946- *WhoMus 72*
Swan, Judy 1946- *IntWWM 77, -80*
Swan, Laurence *MorBAP*
Swan, Lew d1964 *NotNAT B*
Swan, Marcus Lafayette 1837?-1869 *NewGrD 80*
Swan, Mark Elbert 1871-1942 *NotNAT B, WhThe*
Swan, Paul 1883-1972 *CnOxB*
Swan, Paul 1884-1972 *Film 1, WhScrn 77, WhoHol B*
Swan, Paul 1889?- *DancEn 78*
Swan, Robert *WhoHol A*
Swan, Timothy 1758-1842 *Baker 78, BiDAmM, NewGrD 80*
Swan, W H *NewGrD 80*
Swan, William *WhoHol A*
Swanborough, Mrs. d1889 *NotNAT B*
Swanborough, Ada d1893 *NotNAT B*
Swank, Patsy 1919- *ConAmTC*
Swann, Caroline Burke *BiE&WWA*
Swann, Darius Leander *BlkAmP*
Swann, Donald 1923- *BiE&WWA, IntWWM 77, -80, JoeFr, NotNAT, OxThe, WhoMus 72, WhoThe 72, -77*
Swann, Elaine *WhoHol A*
Swann, Francis 1913- *BiE&WWA, IntMPA 77, -75, -76, -78, -79, -80, NotNAT*
Swann, Frederick Lewis 1931- *WhoMus 72*
Swann, Gloria Sheinberg 1926- *IntWWM 77, -80*
Swann, Jeffrey 1951- *ConAmC*
Swann, Lynn *WhoHol A*
Swann, Sir Michael *NewYTET*
Swann, Robert *WhoHol A*
Swanson, Gloria *AmPS B, MotPP, WomWMM*
Swanson, Gloria 1897- *FilmEn, FilmgC, HalFC 80, ThFT[port]*
Swanson, Gloria 1898- *BiDFilm, -81, Film 1, -2, ForYSC, MovMk[port], OxFilm, TwYS, WorEFlm[port]*
Swanson, Gloria 1899- *BiE&WWA, IntMPA 77, -75, -76, -78, -79, -80, WhoHol A, WhoThe 77*
Swanson, Hazel S *PupTheA*
Swanson, Howard 1907- *ConAmC*
Swanson, Howard 1907-1978 *Baker 78, NewGrD 80*
Swanson, Howard 1909- *BiDAmM, BlkCS[port], OxMus*
Swanson, Maureen 1932- *FilmgC, HalFC 80, WhoHol A*
Swanson, Robert E 1920- *IntMPA 77, -75, -76, -78, -79, -80*
Swanson, Walter Donald 1903- *IntWWM 77, -80, WhoMus 72*
Swanson, Wyn *AmSCAP 80*
Swanston, Edwin S 1922- *AmSCAP 66, -80*
Swanston, Eliard d1651 *OxThe*
Swanston, Hilliard d1651 *OxThe*
Swanston, Roderick Brian 1948- *IntWWM 77, -80*
Swanstram, Karin *Film 2*
Swanstrom, Arthur 1888-1940 *AmSCAP 66, -80*
Swanwick, Keith 1937- *IntWWM 77, -80*
Swanwick, Peter 1912-1968 *WhScrn 77*
Swarbutt, Thomas d1753? *NewGrD 80*
Swarowsky, Hans 1899-1975 *Baker 78, NewGrD 80*
Swarsbrick, Thomas d1753? *NewGrD 80*
Swart, Peter Janszoon De 1536-1597 *NewGrD 80*
Swarthout, Donald Malcolm 1884-1962 *BiDAmM*
Swarthout, Gladys *AmPS B*
Swarthout, Gladys 1900-1969 *Baker 78*
Swarthout, Gladys 1904-1969 *BiDAmM, CmOp, FilmEn, FilmgC, ForYSC, HalFC 80, MusSN[port], NewEOp 71, NewGrD 80, ThFT[port], What 2[port], WhScrn 74, -77, WhoHol B, WhoMus 72*
Swartley, Wilmer C 1908- *IntMPA 77, -75, -76*
Swartout, Gladys 1904-1969 *CmpEPM*
Swarts, Sara 1899-1949 *WhScrn 74, -77, WhoHol B*
Swartz, Harvie J 1948- *AmSCAP 80, EncJzS 70*
Swartz, Herbert 1926- *AmSCAP 66, -80*
Swartz, Jack Paul 1920- *IntWWM 77, -80*
Swash, Bob 1929- *WhoThe 77*
Swayne, Giles Oliver Cairnes 1946- *IntWWM 77, -80*
Swayne, Julia d1933 *WhoHol B*
Swayze, John Cameron 1906- *IntMPA 77, -75, -76, -78, -79, -80, NewYTET*
Swayzee, King 1903-1935 *WhoJazz 72*
Swears, Herbert d1946 *NotNAT A, -B*
Sweatman, Wilbur C 1882-1961 *AmSCAP 66, -80, BiDAmM, CmpEPM, WhoJazz 72*
Swedien, Bruce Frederik 1934- *AmSCAP 80*
Swedlund, Helga 1904- *CnOxB*
Swedroe, Jerome D 1925- *IntMPA 77, -75, -76, -78, -79, -80*
Sweelinck, Dirck Janszoon 1591?-1652 *NewGrD 80*
Sweelinck, Jan 1562-1621 *Baker 78, BnBkM 80, CmpBCM, DcCom 77[port], DcCom&M 79, GrComp[port], MusMk[port], NewGrD 80[port], OxMus*
Sweeney, Augustin *Film 2*
Sweeney, Barbara B 1937- *WhoOp 76*
Sweeney, Bob *ForYSC, NewYTET, WhoHol A*
Sweeney, Cecily Pauline 1932- *IntWWM 77, -80*
Sweeney, Charles F, Jr. 1924- *AmSCAP 66, -80*
Sweeney, Edward C 1906-1967 *WhScrn 74, -77*
Sweeney, Eric John 1948- *IntWWM 77, -80*
Sweeney, Fred C 1894-1954 *WhScrn 74, -77*
Sweeney, Jack 1889-1950 *WhScrn 74, -77, WhoHol B*
Sweeney, Jacob *PupTheA*
Sweeney, Joel W 1810-1860 *BiDAmM*
Sweeney, Joseph d1963 *WhScrn 77, WhoHol B*
Sweeny, Anna Trehearne 1941- *IntWWM 77*
Sweet *ConMuA 80A, IlEncR[port], RkOn 2[port]*
Sweet, Blanche *MotPP*
Sweet, Blanche 1895- *FilmEn, FilmgC, HalFC 80, TwYS, What 1[port]*
Sweet, Blanche 1896- *BiE&WWA, Film 1, -2, ForYSC, MovMk[port], NotNAT, OxFilm, WhoHol A*
Sweet, David Kevin 1954- *AmSCAP 80*
Sweet, Dolph 1920- *BiE&WWA, NotNAT, WhoHol A*
Sweet, Gwen *AmSCAP 66, -80*
Sweet, Harry 1901-1933 *Film 2, WhScrn 77*
Sweet, Jeffrey Warren 1950- *NatPD[port]*
Sweet, Katie 1957- *WhoHol A*
Sweet, Lonn Milford 1940- *IntWWM 77, -80*
Sweet, Milo Allison 1899- *AmSCAP 66, -80*
Sweet, Reginald Lindsay 1885-1950 *BiDAmM, ConAmC*
Sweet, Sam d1948 *NotNAT B*
Sweet, Sheila *WhoHol A*
Sweet, Tom 1933-1967 *WhScrn 74, -77, WhoHol B*
Sweet Inspirations, The *BiDAmM, RkOn 2[port]*
Sweet Peas *BluesWW[port]*
Sweet Pease *BluesWW[port]*
Sweet Thangs *BiDAmM*
Sweetser, Joseph Emerson 1825-1873 *BiDAmM*
Sweigerling *PupTheA*
Sweitzl *NewGrD 80*
Swelinck, Jan Pieterszoon *NewGrD 80*
Sweling, Jan Pieterszoon *NewGrD 80*
Swelingh, Jan Pieterszoon *NewGrD 80*
Swem, E Hez 1860?-1912 *BiDAmM*
Sweney, John R 1837-1899 *NewGrD 80*
Swenson, Alfred G 1883-1941 *WhScrn 74, -77, WhoHol B*
Swenson, Inga *BiE&WWA, NotNAT, WhoHol A*
Swenson, Inga 1932- *EncMT, FilmgC, HalFC 80*
Swenson, Inga 1934- *WhoThe 72, -77*
Swenson, Inga 1935- *ForYSC*
Swenson, John *ConMuA 80B*
Swenson, Karl *ForYSC, WhoHol A*
Swenson, Linda *WhoHol A*
Swenson, S A G *IntMPA 77, -75, -76, -78, -79, -80*
Swenson, Sven *WhoHol A*
Swenson, Swen 1932- *WhoThe 72, -77*
Swenson, Swen 1934- *BiE&WWA, NotNAT*
Swenson, Warren Arthur 1937- *ConAmC*
Swentzel, Betty Lou *IntWWM 77*
Swere, E Lyall 1865-1930 *WhThe*
Swerling, Jo 1894- *FilmgC, HalFC 80, WorEFlm*
Swerling, Jo 1897- *BiE&WWA, FilmEn, IntMPA 77, -75, -76, -78, -79, -80, NotNAT*
Swerling, Jo, Jr. *HalFC 80, NewYTET*
Swert, Isidore De *NewGrD 80*
Swert, Jules De 1843-1891 *Baker 78, NewGrD 80*
Swet, Peter 1942- *NatPD[port]*
Swets, E Lyall 1865-1930 *NotNAT B*

Sweval, Pieter H 1948- *AmSCAP 80*
Sweys, Liebing *NewGrD 80*
Swiatek, Lucie 1906- *IntWWM 77, -80*
Swick, George E 1918- *AmSCAP 66*
Swickard, Charles F 1861-1929 *TwYS A, WhScrn 74, -77, WhoHol B*
Swickard, Josef 1867-1940 *TwYS*
Swickard, Joseph 1866-1940 *WhScrn 74, -77*
Swickard, Joseph 1867-1940 *Film 1, -2, ForYSC, WhoHol B*
Swickard, Josie *Film 2*
Swickard, Ralph 1922- *ConAmC*
Swida-Szacilowska, Helena Maria 1928- *IntWWM 77, -80*
Swieten, Gottfried, Baron Von 1733-1803 *NewGrD 80*
Swietly, Hermann Karl 1943- *IntWWM 77, -80*
Swift, Allen 1924- *IntMPA 77, -75, -76, -78, -79, -80*
Swift, Basil J 1919- *AmSCAP 66, -80*
Swift, Clive 1936- *WhoHol A, WhoThe 72, -77*
Swift, David 1919- *FilmEn, FilmgC, HalFC 80, IntMPA 77, -75, -76, -78, -79, -80, WorEFlm*
Swift, Frederic Fay 1907- *AmSCAP 80*
Swift, Jonathan 1667-1745 *DcPup, HalFC 80, OxMus, PlP&P*
Swift, Kay 1905- *AmSCAP 66, -80, CmpEPM, ConAmC, EncMT*
Swift, Lela *IntMPA 77, -75, -76, -78, -79, -80, NewYTET*
Swift, Richard 1927- *AmSCAP 80, Baker 78, ConAmC, DcCM, IntWWM 77, -80, NewGrD 80*
Swift, Robert F 1940- *IntWWM 77*
Swift, Tom 1928- *WhoOp 76*
Swift Cowboys *BiDAmM*
Swijssen, Joos *NewGrD 80*
Swilling, Daphne Annette 1953- *AmSCAP 80*
Swimmer, Bob d1971 *WhScrn 77*
Swimmer, Saul *IntMPA 77, -75, -76, -78, -79, -80*
Swinarski, Konrad 1929-1975 *EncWT*
Swinburne, Algernon Charles 1837-1909 *NotNAT B*
Swinburne, Sir James 1858-1958 *OxMus*
Swinburne, Mercia 1900- *WhThe*
Swinburne, Nora 1902- *FilmEn, Film 2, FilmgC, HalFC 80, IlWWBF[port], IntMPA 77, -75, -76, -78, -79, -80, WhoHol A, WhoThe 72, -77*
Swindell, Archie 1931- *AmSCAP 80*
Swindell, Warren C 1934- *IntWWM 80*
Swineford, Merle *PupTheA*
Swiney, Owen 1675?-1754 *OxThe*
Swing, Peter Gram 1922- *IntWWM 77, -80*
Swing, Raymond Gram 1887- *ConAmC*
Swing Brother *BluesWW[port]*
Swingers, The *BiDAmM*
Swingin' Bluejeans, The *RkOn 2[port]*
Swingin' Medallions, The *RkOn 2[port]*
Swingle, Ward Lemar 1927- *NewGrD 80*
Swingle Singers *NewGrD 80*
Swingsters, The *BiDAmM*
Swink, Robert E 1918- *IntMPA 77, -75, -76, -78, -79, -80*
Swinley, Ian 1892-1937 *PlP&P*
Swinley, Ion d1937 *Film 2, WhoHol B*
Swinley, Ion 1891-1937 *NotNAT B, WhThe*
Swinley, Ion 1892-1937 *WhScrn 77*
Swinson, Cyril 1910-1962 *DancEn 78*
Swinson, Cyril 1910-1963 *CnOxB*
Swinstead, Felix Gerald 1880-1959 *OxMus*
Swinstead, Joan 1903- *WhThe*
Swinton, George 1917- *CreCan 1*
Swinyard, Laurence 1901- *WhoMus 72*
Swisher, Arden 1910- *AmSCAP 66*
Swisher, Gloria Agnes Wilson 1935- *ConAmC, IntWWM 77, -80*
Swit, Loretta 1947?- *HalFC 80, WhoHol A*
Swital, Chet L 1904- *IntMPA 77, -75, -76, -78, -79, -80*
Switzer, Carl 1926-1959 *FilmEn, FilmgC, ForYSC, HalFC 80, MotPP, NotNAT B, WhScrn 74, -77, WhoHol B*
Swoboda, Adalbert 1828-1902 *Baker 78*
Swoboda, Henry 1897- *Baker 78, IntWWM 77, -80, WhoMus 72*
Swoboda, Maria *DancEn 78*
Swoboda, Vecheslav 1892-1948 *DancEn 78*
Swofford, Ken *WhoHol A*
Swoger, Harry 1919-1970 *WhScrn 77*
Swope, Earl 1922-1968 *CmpEPM, EncJzS 70*
Swope, Herbert Bayard, Jr. *BiE&WWA, IntMPA 77, -75, -76, -78, -79, -80, NotNAT*
Swope, Martha 1933?- *CnOxB*
Swope, Topo *WhoHol A*
Swor, Bert 1878-1943 *Film 2, WhScrn 74, -77, WhoHol B*
Swor, Bert, Jr. *Film 2*
Swor, John 1883-1965 *WhScrn 74, -77, WhoHol B*
Swor, Mabel *Film 2*
Swybbertszoon, Peter *NewGrD 80*
Swynford *NewGrD 80*
Syberberg, Hans-Jurgen 1935- *BiDFilm 81*
Syberg, Franz 1904-1955 *NewGrD 80*
Sybil, Ailene *AmSCAP 80*
Sybil, Fern *AmSCAP 80*
Sychra, Andrey Osipovich *NewGrD 80*
Sychra, Antonin 1918-1969 *Baker 78, NewGrD 80*
Sychra, Josef Cyril 1859-1935 *NewGrD 80*
Sydeman, William 1928- *AmSCAP 80, Baker 78, BiDAmM, CompSN[port], CpmDNM 79, ConAmC, DcCM, NewGrD 80*
Sydney, Basil d1968 *MotPP, WhoHol B*
Sydney, Basil 1894-1967 *ForYSC*
Sydney, Basil 1894-1968 *BiE&WWA, FilmEn, FilmgC, HalFC 80, IlWWBF, MovMk, NotNAT B, PlP&P, WhScrn 74, -77, WhThe*
Sydney, Basil 1897-1968 *Film 2, Vers A[port]*
Sydney, Bruce 1889-1942 *WhScrn 74, -77, WhoHol B*
Sydney, Jon 1933- *WhoOp 76*
Sydnor, Earl *WhoHol A*
Sydow, Jack 1921- *BiE&WWA, NotNAT*
Sydow, Max Von 1929- *EncWT, FilmEn*
Syer, Warren B *ConMuA 80B*
Syers, Martyn Edward 1951- *IntWWM 77*
Syfert, Paul *NewGrD 80*
Sygar, John *NewGrD 80*
Sygietynski, Antoni 1850-1923 *NewGrD 80*
Sygietynski, Tadeusz 1896-1955 *Baker 78*
Sykes, Brenda 1949?- *DrBlPA, WhoHol A*
Sykes, Eric *WhoHol A*
Sykes, Eric 1923- *FilmgC, HalFC 80*
Sykes, Eric 1924- *IlWWBF, IntMPA 77, -75, -76, -78, -79, -80*
Sykes, James Andrews 1908- *Baker 78, IntWWM 80, WhoMus 72*
Sykes, Jerome d1903 *NotNAT B*
Sykes, Malcolm 1946- *IntWWM 77, -80*
Sykes, Peter *WhoHrs 80*
Sykes, Roosevelt 1906- *BluesWW[port]*
Sykora, Bogumil 1890-1953 *Baker 78*
Sykora, Peter Narziss 1944- *WhoOp 76*
Sykora, Vaclav Jan 1918- *IntWWM 80*
Sylbert, Richard *FilmgC, HalFC 80*
Syle, Edwin A d1964 *NotNAT B*
Sylos, Frank Paul 1900- *IntMPA 77, -75, -76, -78, -79*
Sylva, Andreas De *NewGrD 80*
Sylva, Ilena 1916- *WhThe*
Sylva, Marguerita 1876-1957 *NotNAT B*
Sylva, Marguerite 1876-1957 *WhScrn 77*
Sylva, Tristam De *NewGrD 80*
Sylva, Vesta 1907- *Film 1, -2, WhThe*
Sylvain, Louise d1930 *NotNAT B*
Sylvain, M *Film 2*
Sylvaine, Vernon 1897-1957 *NotNAT B, WhThe*
Sylvane, Andre 1850- *WhThe*
Sylvani, Gladys 1885-1953 *WhScrn 74, -77, WhoHol B*
Sylvani, Gladys 1886-1953 *IlWWBF[port]*
Sylvanus, Erwin 1917- *CnMD, ModWD*
Sylvern, Hank *IntMPA 77, -75, -76, -78, -79*
Sylvern, Henry 1908-1964 *AmSCAP 66, -80*
Sylvers, The *RkOn 2[port]*
Sylvers, Edmund Theodore 1957- *AmSCAP 80*
Sylvester, Saint *OxMus*
Sylvester, Charles *Film 2*
Sylvester, Erich *AmSCAP 80*
Sylvester, Frank L 1868-1931 *WhScrn 74, -77*
Sylvester, Hanna 1900?-1973 *BluesWW[port]*
Sylvester, Hannah 1900?-1973 *BluesWW[port]*
Sylvester, Henry 1882-1961 *WhScrn 77*
Sylvester, Lillian *Film 2*
Sylvester, William 1922- *FilmgC, HalFC 80, IlWWBF[port], WhThe, WhoHol A, WhoThe 72*
Sylvestris, Floridus De d1672? *NewGrD 80*
Sylvia 1936- *RkOn 2[port]*
Sylvia, Marguerita d1957 *WhoHol B*
Sylvie d1970 *WhoHol B*
Sylvie 1882-1970 *WhScrn 74, -77*
Sylvie 1883-1970 *FilmEn, OxFilm*
Sylvie 1885-1970 *FilmAG WE*
Sylvie 1887-1970 *FilmgC, HalFC 80*
Sylvie, Louise 1885- *WhThe*
Sylwan, Kari 1940- *DancEn 78*
Sym, Igo *Film 2*
Symcox, Peter John Fortune 1925- *WhoOp 76*
Symeon Of Thessaloniki *NewGrD 80*
Symes, Marty 1904-1953 *AmSCAP 66, -80, BiDAmM, CmpEPM*
Symington, James Wadsworth 1927- *AmSCAP 66, -80*
Symmes, Thomas 1678-1725 *BiDAmM, OxMus*
Symon *NewGrD 80*
Symon Britonis *NewGrD 80, -80*
Symon Brytonis *NewGrD 80*
Symon De Insula *NewGrD 80*
Symon De Sacaglia, Magister *NewGrD 80*
Symon Le Breton *NewGrD 80*
Symon, P *NewGrD 80*
Symon, Rea Janet *AmSCAP 80*
Symonds, Augustin 1869-1944 *WhScrn 77*
Symonds, Augustine *Film 2*
Symonds, Norm 1920- *CreCan 2*
Symonds, Norman 1920- *Baker 78, DcCM, IntWWM 80*
Symonds, Robert 1926- *BiE&WWA, NotNAT, WhoThe 72, -77*
Symonds, Stewart 1937- *IntWWM 80*
Symons, Arthur d1945 *NotNAT B*
Symons, Oliver 1936- *CnOxB, DancEn 78*
Sympson, Christopher *NewGrD 80*
Sympson, Marthe *PupTheA*
Sympson, Tony 1906- *IntWWM 77, WhoMus 72, WhoThe 72, -77*
Syms, Algernon d1915 *NotNAT B*
Syms, Sylvia *RkOn*
Syms, Sylvia 1934- *FilmAG WE, FilmEn, FilmgC, HalFC 80, IlWWBF, IntMPA 77, -75, -76, -78, -79, -80, MotPP, WhoHol A*
Syna, Seymour Meyer 1928- *ConAmTC*
Synadinos, Theodoros *REnWD[port]*
Syncopated Orchestra, New York *BiDAmM*
Syndeconde *Film 1*
Syndicate Of Sound, The *RkOn 2[port]*
Synge, John Millington 1871-1909 *CnMD, CnThe, EncWT, Ent, McGEWD[port], ModWD, NewEOp 71, NotNAT A, -B, OxThe, PlP&P[port], REnWD[port]*
Synnestvedt, Viggo Redmond 1918- *IntWWM 77, -80*
Sypher, Wylie 1905- *BiE&WWA, NotNAT*
Syrcher, Madeleine B 1896-1973 *AmSCAP 66, -80*
Syreeta *DrBlPA*
Syrmen, Maddalena Laura *NewGrD 80*
Sysak, Juliette Augustina *CreCan 2*
Syse, Glenna 1927- *BiE&WWA, ConAmTC, NotNAT*
Syverud, Stephen Luther 1938- *CpmDNM 79, -80, ConAmC*
Szabados, Bela Antal 1867-1936 *Baker 78, NewGrD 80*
Szabelski, Boleslaw 1896-1979 *Baker 78, IntWWM 77, -80, NewGrD 80*
Szabo, Albert Edward 1931- *AmSCAP 80, IntWWM 80*
Szabo, Antal 1938- *IntWWM 77, -80*
Szabo, Burt Edward 1931- *ConAmC, IntWWM 77*
Szabo, Csaba 1936- *IntWWM 80, NewGrD 80*
Szabo, Ferenc 1902-1969 *Baker 78, DcCM, NewGrD 80*
Szabo, Frank J 1952- *EncJzS 70*
Szabo, Gabor 1936- *EncJzS 70*

Szabo, Istvan 1938- *FilmEn, FilmgC, HalFC 80, OxFilm*
Szabo, Magda 1917- *CroCD*
Szabo, Miklos 1931- *IntWWM 77, -80*
Szabo, Rozsa 1932- *WhoOp 76*
Szabo, Sandor *WhoHol A*
Szabo, Sandor 1906-1966 *WhScrn 77*
Szabo, Sandor 1915- *BiE&WWA, NotNAT*
Szabolcsi, Bence 1899-1973 *Baker 78, NewGrD 80, WhoMus 72*
Szadek, Tomasz d1612 *NewGrD 80*
Szajner, Robert Martin 1938- *AmSCAP 80*
Szakall, Szoke *FilmEn*
Szalma, Ferenc Jozsef 1923- *WhoOp 76*
Szalonek, Witold 1927- *Baker 78, DcCM, IntWWM 77, -80, NewGrD 80*
Szalowski, Antoni 1907-1973 *Baker 78, NewGrD 80*
Szamotul, Waclaw Z 1524?-1560? *NewGrD 80*
Szamotulczyk, Waclaw Z 1524?-1560? *NewGrD 80*
Szamotulski, Waclaw Z 1524?-1560? *NewGrD 80*
Szaniawski, Jerzy 1886-1970 *CnMD, CroCD, ModWD*
Szanto, Theodor 1877-1934 *Baker 78*
Szarfenberg, Maciej d1547 *NewGrD 80*
Szarfenberger, Maciej d1547 *NewGrD 80*
Szarffemberg, Maciej d1547 *NewGrD 80*
Szarffenberck, Maciej d1547 *NewGrD 80*
Szarth, Georg *NewGrD 80*
Szarvas, Leslie L 1930- *AmSCAP 80*
Szarzynski, Stanislaw Sylwester *NewGrD 80*
Szathmary, Albert 1909-1975 *WhScrn 77, WhoHol C*
Szczawinski, Henryk Melcer- *NewGrD 80*
Szczepanowski, Stanislaw 1814-1877 *NewGrD 80*
Szczepanska, Krystyna 1917- *WhoOp 76*
Szczepanska, Maria 1902-1962 *NewGrD 80*
Szczepanski, Zygmunt 1909- *IntWWM 77, -80*
Szczurowski, Jacek 1716?-1773? *NewGrD 80*
Szczurowski, Jan Nepomucen 1771-1849 *NewGrD 80*
Sze, Yi-Kwei 1917- *IntWWM 77, -80*
Szekely, Endre 1912- *Baker 78, NewGrD 80*
Szekely, Istvan *FilmEn*
Szekely, Mihaly 1901-1963 *CmOp, NewGrD 80*
Szekely, Zoltan 1903- *NewGrD 80*
Szekelyhidy, Ferenc 1885-1954 *NewGrD 80*
Szekeres, Ferenc 1927- *IntWWM 77, -80*
Szelenyi, Istvan 1904-1972 *Baker 78, IntWWM 80, NewGrD 80*
Szelenyi, Laszlo 1935- *IntWWM 77, -80*
Szelenyi, Stephen 1904- *IntWWM 77, WhoMus 72*
Szeligowski, Tadeusz 1896-1963 *Baker 78, NewGrD 80*
Szell, Georg 1897-1970 *CmOp, ConAmC, MusMk, NewGrD 80[port]*
Szell, George 1897-1970 *Baker 78, BiDAmM, BnBkM 80[port], MusSN[port], NewGrD 80[port]*
Szeluto, Apolinary 1884-1966 *NewGrD 80*
Szemes, Marianne *WomWMM*
Szenci Molnar, Albert 1574-1634 *NewGrD 80*
Szendrei, Aladar 1884-1976 *Baker 78, ConAmC*
Szendrei, Alfred *NewGrD 80*
Szendy, Arpad 1863-1922 *Baker 78, NewGrD 80*
Szenik, Ilona 1927- *NewGrD 80*
Szenkar, Eugen 1891-1977 *Baker 78, NewEOp 71*
Szervanszky, Endre 1911-1977 *Baker 78, DcCM, NewGrD 80*
Szervanszky, Endrew 1911- *IntWWM 77, -80, WhoMus 72*
Szeryng, Henryk 1918- *Baker 78, BnBkM 80, IntWWM 77, -80, MusSN[port], NewGrD 80[port], WhoMus 72*
Szewczyk, Jan 1934- *IntWWM 77*
Szidon, Roberto 1941- *IntWWM 77, -80*
Szigeti, Joseph 1882-1973 *BiDAmM*
Szigeti, Joseph 1892- *WhoMus 72*
Szigeti, Joseph 1892-1972 *MusSN[port]*
Szigeti, Joseph 1892-1973 *Baker 78, BnBkM 80, MusMk, NewGrD 80[port]*
Szigeti, Joseph 1893-1973 *WhScrn 77, WhoHol B*
Szigety, Paul 1919- *AmSCAP 80*
Szigligeti, Ede 1814-1878 *NotNAT B*
Szigligeti, Eduard 1814-1878 *McGEWD[port]*
Sziklay, Erika 1936- *NewGrD 80*
Szilagyi, Deszo *DcPup*
Szilard, Paul 1919- *DancEn 78*
Szirmai, Albert 1880-1967 *NewGrD 80*
Szirmay, Marta 1939- *IntWWM 77, -80*
Szirtes, Andrew Peter 1952- *IntWWM 80*
Szirtes, Gyorgy 1923- *WhoOp 76*
Szkodzinski, Louise 1921- *IntWWM 77, -80*
Szmczyk, Bill *ConMuA 80B*
Szmolyan, Walter 1929- *IntWWM 77, -80*
Szokolay, Sandor 1931- *Baker 78, DcCM, IntWWM 77, -80, NewGrD 80*
Szold, Bernard 1894-1960 *WhScrn 74, -77, WhoHol B*
Szollosy, Andras 1921- *Baker 78, IntWWM 77, -80, NewGrD 80*
Szolowski, K *WomWMM*
Szomjas-Schiffert, Gyorgy 1910- *IntWWM 77, -80, NewGrD 80*
Szomory, Dezso 1869-1945 *NotNAT B*
Szonyi, Elisabeth 1924- *NewGrD 80*
Szonyi, Erzsebet 1924- *Baker 78, IntWWM 77, -80, NewGrD 80*
Szonyi, Ferenc 1929- *WhoMus 72*
Szonyi, Nora 1953- *CnOxB*
Szonyi, Olga 1936- *WhoOp 76*
Szopski, Felicjan 1865-1939 *NewGrD 80*
Szoreghi, Julius V *Film 2*
Szostek-Radkowa, Krystyna 1933- *NewGrD 80*
Szostek-Radkowa, Krystyna 1936- *WhoOp 76*
Szpilman, Wladyslaw 1911- *IntWWM 77, -80*
Szpinalski, Antoni 1901- *IntWWM 77, -80*
Sztaudynger, Jan Izydor *DcPup*
Sztompka, Henryk 1901-1964 *NewGrD 80*
Szu, Shih 1953- *WhoHrs 80*
Szulc *NewGrD 80*
Szulc, Bronislaw 1881-1955 *NewGrD 80*
Szulc, Henryk 1836-1903 *NewGrD 80*
Szulc, Josef Zygmunt 1875-1956 *Baker 78*
Szulc, Joseph Sigismond 1875-1956 *NewGrD 80*
Szulc, Jozef 1893- *NewGrD 80*
Szulc, Jozef Zygmunt 1875-1956 *NewGrD 80*
Szumowska, Antoinette 1868-1938 *Baker 78, BiDAmM*
Szumrak, Vera 1938- *CnOxB*
Szurma-Hasani, Marianne 1949- *IntWWM 77, -80*
Szuster, Julja Isabel 1946- *IntWWM 77, -80*
Szwarc, Jeannot *HalFC 80, WhoHrs 80*
Szwed, Jozef 1929- *IntWWM 77, -80*
Szweykowski, Zygmunt Marian 1929- *IntWWM 77, -80, NewGrD 80*
Szydlovita *NewGrD 80*
Szydlowita *NewGrD 80*
Szyfman, Arnold 1882-1967 *EncWT*
Szymanowska, Maria Agata 1789-1831 *Baker 78, NewGrD 80*
Szymanowski, Karol 1882-1937 *Baker 78, BnBkM 80, CompSN[port], DcCom 77[port], DcCM, MusMk, NewEOp 71, NewGrD 80[port], OxMus*
Szymanowski, Karol 1883-1937 *DcCom&M 79*
Szymanska, Iwonka Bogumiia 1943- *IntWWM 77, -80*
Szymanski, Stanislaw 1930- *CnOxB*
Szymonowicz, Zbigniew 1922- *IntWWM 77, -80*
Szymulska, Halina 1921- *IntWWM 77, -80*
Szyrocki, Jan 1931- *IntWWM 77, -80*

T

T-Bones *RkOn 2A*
T I M E, The *BiDAmM*
T Rex *RkOn 2[port]*
T V Slim *BluesWW[port]*
Taafe, Alice *Film 1*
Tabach, Brian Henry 1943- *AmSCAP 80*
Tabachnick, Arthur *IntWWM 77, -80*
Tabachnik, Michel 1942- *Baker 78, IntWWM 77, -80, NewGrD 80*
Tabackin, Lew 1940- *EncJzS 70*
Tabackin, Lewis Barry 1940- *EncJzS 70*
Tabakov, Mikhail Innokent'yevich 1877-1956 *NewGrD 80*
Tabane, Philip Nchipi 1940- *IntWWM 77*
Tabaret, Pierre d1711? *NewGrD 80*
Tabarin d1626 *OxThe*
Tabarroni, Adelmo 1899- *WhoMus 72*
Tabart, Pierre d1711? *NewGrD 80*
Tabary, Louis 1773-1831 *BiDAmM*
Tabat, Sister Joan 1921- *IntWWM 77*
Tabbert, William 1921-1974 *BiE&WWA, CmpEPM, EncMT, NotNAT B, WhThe*
Tabel, Hermann d1738? *NewGrD 80*
Tabelak, John-Michael *ConDr 77D*
Tabelin, Alan 1927- *WhoMus 72*
Taber, Richard 1885-1957 *Film 1, -2, NotNAT B, TwYS, WhScrn 74, -77, WhoHol B*
Taber, Robert Schell 1865-1904 *NotNAT B*
Tabet, Georges 1905- *WhoMus 72*
Table, Hermann *NewGrD 80*
Tabler, P Dempsey *WhoHol B*
Tabler, P Dempsey 1880-1953 *Film 2, WhoHrs 80*
Tabler, P Dempsey 1880-1963 *WhScrn 77*
Taboada, Julio, Jr. 1926-1962 *NotNAT B, WhScrn 74, -77*
Tabor, Disiree d1957 *NotNAT B*
Tabor, Joan 1933-1968 *WhScrn 74, -77, WhoHol B*
Tabori, George 1914- *BiE&WWA, ConDr 73, -77, NotNAT, WhoThe 72, -77*
Tabori, Kristoffer *NotNAT, WhoHol A*
Tabori, Paul 1908- *IntMPA 75*
Taborowski, Stanislaw 1830- *NewGrD 80*
Tabourot, Jehan *Baker 78, NewGrD 80, OxMus*
Tabuteau, Marcel 1887-1966 *BnBkM 80, NewGrD 80*
Tacchella, Jean-Charles 1926- *FilmEn*
Tacchinardi, Niccolo 1772-1859 *NewGrD 80*
Tacchinardi, Nicola 1772-1859 *Baker 78, NewGrD 80*
Tacchinardi-Persiani, Fanny 1812-1867 *NewGrD 80*
Tacchino, Gabriel 1934- *NewGrD 80*
Tachezi, Herbert 1930- *NewGrD 80*
Tachikawa, Sumito 1929- *WhoOp 76*
Tackney, Stanley 1909- *BiE&WWA, NotNAT, WhoHol A*
Tackova, Jarmila d1971 *WhoHol B*
Taconis, Atze 1900- *AmSCAP 66, -80*
Tacuchian, Ricardo 1939- *IntWWM 77, -80*
Taddei, Gino 1943- *WhoOp 76*
Taddei, Giuseppe 1916- *CmOp, NewEOp 71, NewGrD 80, WhoMus 72, WhoOp 76*
Tadei, Alessandro 1585?-1667 *NewGrD 80*
Tadema, Sir Lawrence Alma- 1836-1912 *OxThe*
Tadeo, Giorgio 1929- *WhoOp 76*
Tadolini, Eugenia 1809- *NewGrD 80[port]*
Tadolini, Giovanni 1785-1872 *Baker 78*
Tadolini, Giovanni 1789?-1872 *NewGrD 80*
Taeger, Ralph 1935- *ForYSC, WhoHol A*
Taeggio *NewGrD 80*
Taegio *NewGrD 80*
Tafall Y Miguel, Mariano 1813?-1874 *NewGrD 80*
Taffanel, Paul 1844-1908 *Baker 78, BnBkM 80, NewGrD 80*
Taffner, Donald L *IntMPA 77, -75, -76, -78, -79, -80*
Taffs, Anthony 1916- *ConAmC*
Tafler, Sidney 1916-1979 *FilmgC, HalFC 80*
Tafler, Sydney 1916-1979 *IlWWBF, WhoHol A*
Taft, Billy *Film 2*
Taft, Jerry *WhoHol A*
Taft, Sara d1973 *WhScrn 77*
Taft, Vincent 1946- *AmSCAP 80*
Tafur, Robert *WhoHol A*
Tag, Christian Gotthilf 1735-1811 *Baker 78, NewGrD 80*
Tag, Christian Traugott 1777-1839 *NewGrD 80*
Tagawa, Rick M 1947- *ConAmC*
Tagg, Alan 1928- *WhoThe 72, -77*
Taggart, Barbara Budlong *AmSCAP 80*
Taggart, Ben L 1889-1947 *WhScrn 77*
Taggart, Charles F, Jr. 1930- *AmSCAP 66*
Taggart, Hal 1892-1971 *WhScrn 74, -77, WhoHol B*
Taggart, Patrick Ewing 1949- *ConAmTC*
Taggart, William 1926- *AmSCAP 66, -80*
Tagger, Nicola 1930- *WhoOp 76*
Tagger, Theodor *McGEWD[port]*
Taggert, Brian *NatPD[port]*
Tagi-zade-Hajibeyov, Nijazi Z *NewGrD 80*
Taglia, Pietro *NewGrD 80*
Tagliabue, Carlo 1898-1978 *CmOp, NewGrD 80*
Tagliafico, Joseph 1821-1900 *NewGrD 80*
Tagliapietra, Gino 1887-1954 *Baker 78, NewGrD 80*
Tagliapietra, Giovanni 1846-1921 *Baker 78*
Tagliavini, Ferruccio 1913- *Baker 78, CmOp, IntWWM 77, -80, MusSN[port], NewEOp 71, NewGrD 80, WhoMus 72*
Tagliavini, Franco 1934- *WhoOp 76*
Tagliavini, Luigi Ferdinando 1929- *NewGrD 80, WhoMus 72*
Taglichsbeck, Thomas 1799-1867 *NewGrD 80*
Taglietti, Giulio 1660?-1718 *NewGrD 80*
Taglietti, Luigi 1668-1715 *NewGrD 80*
Taglioni *CnOxB*
Taglioni, Filippo 1777-1871 *CnOxB, NotNAT B*
Taglioni, Filippo 1778-1871 *DancEn 78*
Taglioni, Maria 1804-1884 *DancEn 78[port]*
Taglioni, Marie 1804-1884 *CnOxB, NewGrD 80, NotNAT B*
Taglioni, Marie 1833-1891 *CnOxB*
Taglioni, Marie Paul 1830-1891 *DancEn 78*
Taglioni, Paul 1808-1884 *CnOxB, DancEn 78, NotNAT B*
Taglioni, Salvatore 1789-1868 *CnOxB*
Taglioni, Salvatore 1790-1868 *DancEn 78*
Tagore, Sir Rabindranath 1861-1941 *CnMD, CnThe, EncWT, Ent, McGEWD[port], ModWD, NewGrD 80, NotNAT B, OxThe, REnWD[port]*
Tagore, Sir Sourindro Mohun 1840-1914 *NewGrD 80*
Tagore, Sir Surindro Mohun 1840-1914 *Baker 78*
Taguchi, Kosuke 1941- *WhoOp 76*
Tahourdin, Peter Richard 1928- *IntWWM 80, NewGrD 80*
Tahse, Martin 1930- *BiE&WWA*
Taiani, Hugo Edward 1912- *AmSCAP 66, -80*
Taiber *NewGrD 80*
Taikeff, Stanley 1940- *NatPD[port]*
Tailer, Daniel *NewGrD 80*
Tailer, John d1569? *NewGrD 80*
Tailhandier, Pierre *NewGrD 80*
Taillade, Paul d1898 *NotNAT B*
Taillandier, Pierre *NewGrD 80*
Tailleferre, Germaine 1892- *Baker 78, BnBkM 80, IntWWM 77, -80, NewGrD 80, OxMus*
Tailler, Simon *NewGrD 80, OxMus*
Tailler, Symon *NewGrD 80*
Taillerus, Simon *NewGrD 80*
Taillerus, Symon *NewGrD 80*
Taillon, Angus D 1888-1953 *WhScrn 74, -77*
Taillon, Gus d1953 *WhoHol B*
Taillon, Jocelyne Jeanne 1941- *WhoOp 76*
Tailour, Robert d1637? *NewGrD 80*
Taira, Yoshihisa *CpmDNM 79*
Tairov, Aleksandr 1885-1950 *Ent*
Tairov, Alexander Yakovlevich 1885-1950 *CnThe, EncWT, NotNAT B, OxThe, PlP&P[port]*
Taishoff, Sol J *NewYTET*
Tait, Andrew 1710?-1778 *NewGrD 80*
Tait, E J d1947 *NotNAT B*
Tait, Malcolm James 1931- *IntWWM 80*
Tait, Marion 1950- *CnOxB*
Tait, Walter *Film 2*
Tajcevic, Marko 1900- *Baker 78, NewGrD 80*
Tajiri, Larry S 1914- *BiE&WWA*
Tajo, Italo 1915- *CmOp, IntWWM 77, -80, NewEOp 71, NewGrD 80, WhoOp 76*
Tajvidi, Ali 1927- *IntWWM 77, -80*
Taka, Miiko *ForYSC, WhoHol A*
Takacs, Eugene 1902- *NewGrD 80*
Takacs, Jeno 1902- *Baker 78, ConAmC, IntWWM 77, -80, NewGrD 80*
Takacs, Lisa Ann 1934- *IntWWM 77*
Takagi, Toroku 1904- *Baker 78*
Takahashi, Yoriko 1937- *IntWWM 77, -80*
Takahashi, Yuji 1938- *Baker 78, DcCM, NewGrD 80*
Takala, Aino Sisko 1928- *WhoOp 76*

Takamura, Kiyoshi 1902- IntMPA 77, -75, -76, -78, -79, -80
Takas, Bill 1932- EncJzS 70
Takas, William J 1932- EncJzS 70
Takashima, Shizuye Violet 1928- CreCan 2
Takata, Saburo 1913- Baker 78, NewGrD 80
Takata, Shin-Ichi 1920- Baker 78
Takeda, Izumo 1688-1756 NotNAT B
Takeda, Y 1933- IntWWM 77, -80
Takei, George WhoHol A
Takei, Kei CmpGMD, CnOxB
Takemitsu, Toru 1930- Baker 78, BnBkM 80, DcCM, IntWWM 77, -80, NewGrD 80
Taki, Rentaro 1879-1903 NewGrD 80
Takiff, Jonathan Henry 1946- ConAmTC
Takimoto, Yuzo 1932- IntWWM 77
Taktakishvili, Otar Vasil'yevich 1924- Baker 78, NewGrD 80
Taktakishvili, Shalva Mikhailovich 1900-1965 Baker 78, NewGrD 80
Taku, Koji 1904- Baker 78
Tal, Josef 1910- DcCM, IntWWM 77, -80, NewGrD 80
Tal, Joseph 1910- Baker 78
Talagrand, Jacques McGEWD[port]
Talamo, Gino Film 2
Talankin, Igor 1927- FilmEn
Talarczyk, Joseph 1919- IntWWM 77, -80
Talarico, Noel 1925- IntWWM 77
Talarico, Rita 1941- WhoOp 76
Talazac, Odette d1948 OxFilm, WhScrn 77
Talbert, Elmer 1900-1950 NewOrJ[port]
Talbert, Fred Douglas 1926- AmSCAP 80
Talbert, Homer Alexander, Jr. 1948- AmSCAP 80
Talbert, Patricia 1948- AmSCAP 80
Talbert, Ted AmSCAP 80
Talbot, Desiree Ruth 1926- IntWWM 80
Talbot, Howard 1865-1928 Baker 78, EncMT, NewGrD 80, NotNAT B, WhThe
Talbot, Irvin 1896- IntMPA 75, -76
Talbot, James 1665-1708 NewGrD 80
Talbot, Joseph T 1938- IntMPA 77, -75, -76, -78, -79, -80
Talbot, Lyle MotPP
Talbot, Lyle 1902- BiE&WWA, FilmEn, HolCA[port], NotNAT
Talbot, Lyle 1904- FilmgC, ForYSC, HalFC 80, IntMPA 77, -75, -76, -78, -79, -80, MovMk[port], Vers B[port], WhoHol A, WhoHrs 80
Talbot, Mae 1869-1942 WhScrn 74, -77
Talbot, Margaret Aimee Eileen 1925- IntWWM 77, -80
Talbot, Michael Owen 1943- IntWWM 77, -80, WhoMus 72
Talbot, Nita 1930- FilmgC, ForYSC, HalFC 80, WhoHol A
Talbot, Peter Henry 1948- AmSCAP 80
Talbot, Richard, Earl Of Tyrconnel 1630-1691 OxMus
Talbot, Slim 1896-1973 WhScrn 77, WhoHol B
Talbot, Toby WomWMM B
Talbott, Gloria 1932?- ForYSC, WhoHrs 80[port]
Talbott, Howard 1865-1928 BiDAmM
Talcove, Rick 1948- ConAmTC
Talent, Leo Robert 1906- AmSCAP 66, -80
Talent, Ziggy 1925- CmpEPM
Taler, Daniel NewGrD 80
Talesio, Pedro NewGrD 80
Talfourd, Frances d1862 NotNAT B
Talfourd, Sir Thomas Noon 1795-1854 NotNAT B, OxThe
Talhanderius, Pierre NewGrD 80
Taliaferro, Edith d1958 Film 1, TwYS, WhoHol B
Taliaferro, Edith 1892-1958 Film 2
Taliaferro, Edith 1893-1958 NotNAT B, WhThe
Taliaferro, Edith 1894-1958 WhScrn 74, -77
Taliaferro, Hal 1895- FilmEn, Film 2, ForYSC
Taliaferro, Kerry 1938- WhoOp 76
Taliaferro, Mabel 1887-1979 BiE&WWA, FilmEn, Film 1, -2, MotPP, NotNAT, TwYS, WhoHol A, WhoStg 1908
Taliaferro, Mabel 1889-1979 WhThe
Talich, Vaclav 1883-1961 Baker 78, CmOp, NewGrD 80
Talisman, David Michael 1944- AmSCAP 80
Talking Heads ConMuA 80A
Tallafangi Calabr, Andreas NewGrD 80
Tallarico, Pasquale 1891-1974 ConAmC
Tallat-Kelpsa, Juozas 1889-1949 NewGrD 80
Tallchief, Maria 1925- CnOxB, DancEn 78[port], WhThe, WhoHol A, WhoMus 72
Tallchief, Marjorie 1927- CnOxB, DancEn 78[port]
Talles, Thomas 1505?-1585 NewGrD 80
Talley, Frank AmSCAP 80
Talley, James IlEncCM
Talley, Marion 1907- Baker 78, BiDAmM, ForYSC, WhoHol A
Talli, Carloni Film 2
Talli, Virgilio 1857- WhThe
Talli, Virgilio 1858-1928 EncWT
Tallichet, Margaret WhoHol A
Tallis, Sir George 1867-1948 NotNAT B, WhThe
Tallis, Thomas 1505?-1585 Baker 78, BnBkM 80, DcCom 77[port], DcCom&M 79, GrComp[port], MusMk[port], NewGrD 80, OxMus
Tallman, Ellen d1963 NotNAT B
Tallmer, Jerry 1920- BiE&WWA, NotNAT
Tallon, John Ernest 1937- WhoMus 72
Tallys, Thomas 1505?-1585 NewGrD 80
Talma, Mademoiselle WhThe
Talma, Francois-Joseph 1763-1826 CnThe, EncWT, Ent, NotNAT A, -B, OxThe
Talma, Louise 1906- AmSCAP 66, -80, Baker 78, BiDAmM, CpmDNM 78, -79, -80, ConAmC, DcCM, IntWWM 77, -80, NewGrD 80, WomCom[port]
Talma, Zolya WhoHol A
Talmadge, Constance d1973 MotPP, WhoHol B
Talmadge, Constance 1898-1973 HalFC 80, MovMk[port], WhScrn 77
Talmadge, Constance 1899-1973 FilmgC, Funs[port], OxFilm
Talmadge, Constance 1900-1973 FilmEn, Film 1, -2, TwYS, What 1[port], WorEFlm
Talmadge, Joseph Keaton Film 2
Talmadge, Natalie d1969 FilmEn, WhoHol B
Talmadge, Natalie 1898-1969 Film 1, -2, FilmgC, TwYS
Talmadge, Natalie 1899-1969 HalFC 80, WhScrn 74, -77
Talmadge, Norma d1957 MotPP, WhoHol B
Talmadge, Norma 1893-1957 FilmgC, HalFC 80, WhScrn 77
Talmadge, Norma 1896-1957 Film 1, -2, TwYS
Talmadge, Norma 1897-1957 BiDFilm, -81, FilmEn, ForYSC, MovMk[port], NotNAT B, OxFilm, ThFT[port], WhScrn 74, WorEFlm
Talmadge, Richard 1892- WhoHol A
Talmadge, Richard 1896- FilmEn, Film 1, -2, FilmgC, HalFC 80
Talmadge, Richard 1898- ForYSC, TwYS
Talman, Lloyd Film 2
Talman, William 1915-1968 FilmgC, ForYSC, HalFC 80, MotPP, WhScrn 74, -77, WhoHol B
Talmi, Yoav 1943- IntWWM 80
Talmon, Zvi 1922- IntWWM 77, -80
Talmy, Shel 1938- IlEncR
Talon, Pierre 1721-1785 NewGrD 80
Talsma, Willem Retza 1927- IntWWM 77
Talsma, Willem Retze 1927- IntWWM 80
Taltabull, Cristofor 1888-1964 Baker 78
Talton, Alix WhoHol A
Talvela, Marrti Olavi 1935- WhoMus 72
Talvela, Martti 1935- MusSN[port], NewEOp 71, NewGrD 80, WhoOp 76
Talvela, Martti Olavi 1934- IntWWM 77, -80
Talvo, Tyyne 1919- CnOxB
Tamagno, Francesco 1850-1905 Baker 78, BnBkM 80, CmOp, NewEOp 71, NewGrD 80[port]
Tamara 1907-1943 AmPS B, EncMT, Film 2, NotNAT B, WhScrn 77, WhThe, WhoHol B
Tamarin, Alfred H 1913- IntMPA 77, -75, -76, -78, -79
Tamarin, B P Film 2
Tamas, Janos 1936- IntWWM 77, -80
Tamasi, Aron 1897-1966 CnMD
Tamassy, Eva 1936- IntWWM 80
Tamassy, Eva 1937- WhoOp 76
Tamassy, Zdenko 1921- IntWWM 77, -80
Tamayo Y Baus, Manuel 1829-1898 McGEWD[port], NotNAT B, OxThe
Tamba, Tetsuro 1929?- FilmgC, HalFC 80, WhoHol A
Tamberg, Eino 1930- Baker 78, NewGrD 80
Tamberlick, Enrico 1820-1889 NewGrD 80[port]
Tamberlik, Enrico 1820-1889 Baker 78, BnBkM 80, CmOp, NewGrD 80[port]
Tamblyn, Eddie 1907-1957 WhoHol B
Tamblyn, Edward 1907-1957 WhScrn 74, -77
Tamblyn, Russ IntMPA 77, -75, -76, -78, -79, -80, MotPP
Tamblyn, Russ 1934- CmMov, FilmEn, FilmgC, HalFC 80, MovMk, WhoHrs 80
Tamblyn, Russ 1935- ForYSC, WhoHol A
Tamblyn, William 1941- IntWWM 77, -80, WhoMus 72
Tamburini NewGrD 80
Tamburini, Antonio 1800-1876 Baker 78, BnBkM 80, CmOp, NewEOp 71, NewGrD 80[port]
Tamburini, Giovanni 1857-1942 NewGrD 80
Tamburini, Giuseppe NewGrD 80
Tamburini, Pietro Antonio 1589?-1635 NewGrD 80
Tamias, Dimitrios NewGrD 80
Tamir, Alexander NewGrD 80
Tamiris, Helen 1905-1966 BiE&WWA, CmpGMD[port], CnOxB, DancEn 78[port], EncMT, NotNAT B, WhThe
Tamiroff, Akim d1972 MotPP, WhoHol B
Tamiroff, Akim 1898-1972 HolCA[port]
Tamiroff, Akim 1899-1972 BiDFilm, -81, FilmEn, FilmgC, ForYSC, HalFC 80[port], OxFilm, WhScrn 77, WhoHrs 80, WorEFlm
Tamiroff, Akim 1901-1972 BiE&WWA, MovMk[port], NotNAT B, Vers A[port]
Tamkin, David 1906-1975 Baker 78
Tamla Motown IlEncR
Tammaro, Ferruccio 1947- IntWWM 80
Tammy, Mark d1975 WhScrn 77
Tampa Red 1900- BluesWW[port], CmpEPM
Tams, The RkOn[port]
Tamu DrBlPA, WhoHol A
T'an, Hsin-P'ei 1847-1917 NewGrD 80
Tan, Margaret Hee-Leng 1945- IntWWM 77, -80
Tan, Melvyn 1956- IntWWM 80
Tanabe, Hisao 1883- NewGrD 80
Tanabe, Takao 1926- CreCan 2
Tanaglia, Antonio Francesco NewGrD 80
Tanaglino, Antonio Francesco NewGrD 80
Tanaka, Kinuyo 1910-1977 FilmEn, WomWMM
Tanaka, Nadyoshi 1900- IntMPA 77, -75, -76, -78, -79
Tanaka, Shoji 1886-1918 WhScrn 77
Tanaka, Toshimitsu 1930- Baker 78
Tanchuck, Nat 1912- IntMPA 77, -75, -76, -78
Tancredi, Ralph Anthony 1921- ConAmC
Tandy, Donald WhoHol A
Tandy, Jessica 1909- BiE&WWA, CnThe, FilmEn, FilmgC, ForYSC, HalFC 80, IntMPA 77, -75, -76, -78, -79, -80, MotPP, MovMk[port], NotNAT, PlP&P[port], WhoHol A, WhoThe 72, -77
Tandy, Valerie 1921-1965 WhThe
Tandy, Valerie 1923-1965 WhScrn 74, -77
Tanega, Norma Cecilia 1939- AmSCAP 80, RkOn 2A
Taneief, Alexander 1850-1918 OxMus
Taneief, Serge 1856-1915 OxMus
Taneiev, Sergei 1856-1915 GrComp
Tanel NewGrD 80
Tanen, Ned IntMPA 78, -79, -80
Tanenbaum, Elias 1924- ConAmC
Taner, Haldun 1916- REnWD[port]
Tanev, Alexander 1928- Baker 78, NewGrD 80

Taneyev, Alexander Sergeyevich 1850-1918 *Baker 78, NewGrD 80*
Taneyev, Sergei 1856-1915 *Baker 78, MusMk*
Taneyev, Sergey Ivanovich 1856-1915 *BnBkM 80, NewGrD 80[port]*
Tang, Jordan Cho-Tung 1948- *AmSCAP 80, CpmDNM 76, -79, -80, ConAmC, IntWWM 77, -80*
Tangerine Dream *IlEncR*
Tanggaard, Svend Erik 1942- *IntWWM 80*
Tangle Eye *BluesWW[port]*
Tango, Egisto 1873-1951 *Baker 78*
Tanguay, Eva *AmPS B*
Tanguay, Eva 1878-1947 *Ent, Film 1, NotNAT B, WhScrn 74, -77, WhThe, WhoHol B, WhoStg 1908*
Tanguay, Eva 1878-1948 *CmpEPM*
Tanguy, Josephine 1905- *WhoMus 72*
Tanhuser, Der *NewGrD 80*
Tani, Al *AmSCAP 80*
Tani, Yoko 1932- *FilmgC, HalFC 80, WhoHol A*
Tani, Yoko 1933?- *ForYSC*
Tanisha, Ta *DrBlPA*
Tankersley, Robert K 1927- *IntMPA 78, -79, -80*
Tannahill, Robert *OxMus*
Tanneberg, David 1728-1804 *NewGrD 80*
Tanneberger, David 1728-1804 *BiDAmM, NewGrD 80*
Tannen, Julius 1881-1965 *JoeFr, MotPP, WhScrn 74, -77, WhoHol B*
Tannen, Michael *ConMuA 80B*
Tannen, William *ForYSC*
Tannenbaum, Samuel W 1890- *IntMPA 75, -76*
Tannenberg, David 1728-1804 *Baker 78, NewGrD 80*
Tanner, Alain 1929- *FilmEn*
Tanner, Annie Louise d1921 *NotNAT B*
Tanner, Bill *ConMuA 80B*
Tanner, Clay *WhoHol A*
Tanner, Elmo 1904- *CmpEPM*
Tanner, Gid 1885-1960 *CmpEPM, EncFCWM 69*
Tanner, Gordon *WhoHol A*
Tanner, Haldun 1916- *CnThe*
Tanner, James Gideon 1885-1960 *BiDAmM*
Tanner, James J 1873-1934 *WhScrn 74, -77*
Tanner, James T d1915 *NotNAT B, WhThe*
Tanner, Jerre Eugene 1939- *AmSCAP 80, ConAmC, IntWWM 80*
Tanner, Marc Lee 1952- *AmSCAP 80*
Tanner, Paul O W 1917- *AmSCAP 66, -80, ConAmC, EncJzS 70, IntWWM 77, -80*
Tanner, Peter 1914- *HalFC 80*
Tanner, Peter H 1936- *ConAmC*
Tanner, Richard 1948- *CnOxB*
Tanner, Stella *WhoHol A*
Tanner, Tony 1932- *FilmgC, HalFC 80, WhoHol A*
Tanner, William H *MorBAP*
Tanner, Winston R 1905- *IntMPA 77, -75, -76, -78, -79, -80*
Tannhauser 1200?- *Baker 78*
Tannhauser, Der 1205?-1270? *NewGrD 80*
Tanny, Mark d1975 *WhoHol C*
Tano, Guy 1914-1952 *WhScrn 74, -77*
Tanser, Julia *WomWMM*
Tansey, Emma 1884-1942 *WhScrn 74, -77, WhoHol B*
Tansey, Johnny *Film 1*
Tansey, Sheridan *Film 2*
Tansley, Michael Stuart 1943- *IntWWM 77*
Tansman, Aleksander 1897- *NewGrD 80*
Tansman, Alexander 1897- *CompSN[port]*
Tansman, Alexandre 1897- *Baker 78, DcCom&M 79, DcCM, IntWWM 77, -80, NewGrD 80, WhoMus 72*
Tans'ur, William 1700-1783 *NewGrD 80*
Tans'ur, William 1706-1783 *Baker 78, OxMus*
Tanswell, Bertram 1908- *BiE&WWA, NotNAT*
Tanto, Gyula Pal 1927- *IntMPA 77, -75, -76, -78, -79, -80*
Tanvser, Der *NewGrD 80*
Tanymarian *NewGrD 80*
Tanzer, William *NewGrD 80*
Tanzy, Jeanne *WhoHol A*
Tapales, Ramon 1906- *NewGrD 80*
Taperay, Jean-Francois *NewGrD 80*
Taperet, Jean-Francois *NewGrD 80*
Taphouse, Thomas William 1838-1905 *NewGrD 80*
Tapia, Jose 1942- *BlkAmP*
Tapia, Martin De *NewGrD 80*
Tapissier, Johannes 1370?-1410? *NewGrD 80*
Tapkov, Dimiter 1929- *NewGrD 80*
Tapley, Colin 1911- *HalFC 80*
Tapley, Rolland Sylvester 1901- *IntWWM 77, -80*
Tapley, Rose 1883-1956 *Film 1, -2, MotPP, TwYS, WhScrn 74, -77, WhoHol B*
Taplin, Terence *PlP&P[port]*
Taplinger, Robert S 1909- *IntMPA 75, -76*
Tappan, William Bingham 1794-1849 *BiDAmM*
Tapper, Bertha Feiring 1859-1915 *BiDAmM*
Tapper, Thomas 1864-1958 *Baker 78*
Tappert, Wilhelm 1830-1907 *Baker 78, NewGrD 80*
Tapping, Alfred B d1928 *NotNAT B, WhThe*
Tapping, Mrs. Alfred B 1852-1926 *NotNAT B, WhThe*
Tappolet, Willy 1890- *Baker 78, NewGrD 80*
Tappy, Eric 1931- *NewGrD 80, WhoOp 76*
Tapray, Jean-Francois 1738-1819? *NewGrD 80*
Taps, Jonie *IntMPA 77, -75, -76, -78, -79, -80*
Tapscott, Horace 1934- *EncJzS 70*
Tapsony, Veronica 1938- *IntWWM 77, -80*
Taptuka, Clarence S 1898-1967 *WhScrn 77*
Taraba, Bohuslav 1894- *IntWWM 77, -80*
Tarack, Gerald 1929- *IntWWM 77, -80*
Taradash, Daniel 1913- *CmMov, FilmEn, FilmgC, HalFC 80, IntMPA 77, -75, -76, -78, -79, -80, OxFilm, WorEFlm*
Tarade, Theodore-Jean 1731-1788 *NewGrD 80*
Tarakanov, Mikhail Evgen'yevich 1928- *NewGrD 80*
Taranow, Gerda *NotNAT*
Taranto, Joe *NewOrJ*
Taranto, Vernon Anthony, Jr. 1946- *ConAmC, IntWWM 77, -80*
Taranu, Cornel 1934- *Baker 78, DcCM, IntWWM 77, -80, NewGrD 80*
Taras, John 1919- *CnOxB, DancEn 78*
Tarasava, Alla 1898-1973 *WhoHol B*
Tarasov, Ivan 1878-1954 *DancEn 78*
Tarasov, Nicolai Ivanovich 1902- *CnOxB, DancEn 78*
Tarasova, Alla Konstantinovna 1898-1973 *EncWT, WhScrn 77, WhThe*
Tarbat, Lorna 1916-1961 *WhScrn 74, -77*
Tarbill, Cindy *WomWMM B*
Tarbutt, Frazer 1894-1918 *WhScrn 77*
Tarcan, Haluk 1931- *IntWWM 77, -80*
Tarchi, Angelo 1755-1814 *Baker 78*
Tarchi, Angelo 1760?-1814 *NewGrD 80*
Tarchi, Angiolo 1760?-1814 *NewGrD 80*
Tardieu, Jean 1903- *CnMD, CnThe, EncWT, Ent, McGEWD, ModWD, REnWD[port]*
Tarditi, Giovanni 1857-1935 *Baker 78*
Tarditi, Orazio 1602-1677 *NewGrD 80*
Tarditi, Paolo d1649? *NewGrD 80*
Tardos, Bela 1910-1966 *Baker 78, NewGrD 80*
Tardy, John Edward 1927- *IntWWM 77*
Tarell, Anthony 1912- *IntMPA 75, -76*
Tarheel Slim *BluesWW[port]*
Tariol-Bauge, Anna 1872- *WhThe*
Tarisio, Luigi 1790?-1854 *NewGrD 80*
Tarisio, Luigi 1795?-1854 *Baker 78*
Tarita *WhoHol A*
Tarjan, George 1910-1973 *WhScrn 77*
Tarjani, Ferenc 1938- *NewGrD 80*
Tarkam, Ella 1938- *IntWWM 77, -80*
Tarkhanov, Mikhail d1948 *WhScrn 77*
Tarkington, Booth 1869-1946 *FilmgC, HalFC 80, McGEWD, ModWD, OxThe, PlP&P*
Tarkington, Newton Booth 1862-1946 *WhThe*
Tarkington, Newton Booth 1869-1946 *NotNAT B*
Tarkington, Rockne *DrBlPA, WhoHol A*
Tarkington, William O d1962 *NotNAT B*
Tarkovsky, Andrei 1932- *BiDFilm, -81, FilmEn, HalFC 80, OxFilm*
Tarlarni, Madame *Film 1*
Tarleton, Jimmie 1892- *EncFCWM 69*
Tarleton, Johnny James Rimbert 1892- *BiDAmM*
Tarleton, Richard d1588 *CnThe, EncWT, Ent, NotNAT B, OxThe, PlP&P*
Tarlow, Florence *WhoHol A*
Tarlow, Karen Anne 1947- *CpmDNM 76, -77, ConAmC*
Tarlton, Jimmie 1892-1973 *IlEncCM*
Tarlton, Richard d1588 *OxMus*
Tarn, Colin 1939- *IntWWM 77*
Tarnapol, Nat *ConMuA 80B*
Tarnay, Gyula 1928- *WhoOp 76*
Tarner, Evelyn Fern 1912- *AmSCAP 80*
Tarner, Stanley Philip 1923- *AmSCAP 80*
Tarnoff, John B 1952- *IntMPA 80*
Tarnowski, Count Wladyslaw 1841-1878 *NewGrD 80*
Taroni, Antonio *NewGrD 80*
Tarp, Svend Erik 1908- *Baker 78, IntWWM 77, -80, NewGrD 80, OxMus, WhoMus 72*
Tarplin, Marvin 1941- *AmSCAP 80*
Tarr, David Eugene 1932- *IntWWM 77, -80*
Tarr, Edward Hankins 1936- *IntWWM 77, -80, NewGrD 80*
Tarr, Florence 1907-1951 *AmSCAP 80*
Tarr, Florence 1908-1951 *AmSCAP 66*
Tarr, Justin *WhoHol A*
Tarrant, L Newell 1911- *BiE&WWA, NotNAT*
Tarrega, Francisco 1852-1909 *Baker 78, BnBkM 80, NewGrD 80, OxMus*
Tarreria, Francesco *NewGrD 80*
Tarres, Enriqueta *WhoOp 76*
Tarri, Suzette d1955 *NotNAT B*
Tarride, Abel 1867- *WhThe*
Tarriers, The *BiDAmM, EncFCWM 69, RkOn*
Tarron, Elsie *Film 2*
Tarroni, Antonio *NewGrD 80*
Tarsia, Joe *ConMuA 80B*
Tarski, Alexander 1921- *WhoOp 76*
Tartaglia, John Andrew 1944- *AmSCAP 80*
Tartaglino, Hippolito 1539?-1582 *NewGrD 80*
Tartini, Giuseppe 1692-1770 *Baker 78, BnBkM 80, CmpBCM, DcCom 77, GrComp[port], MusMk, NewGrD 80[port], OxMus*
Tarto, Joe 1902- *AmSCAP 80, CmpEPM, WhoJazz 72*
Tarver, James L 1916- *AmSCAP 66, -80*
Tarvers, Jim *Film 1*
Tarzia, Peter 1908- *AmSCAP 80*
Tasaka, Tomotaka 1902- *FilmEn*
Tasca, Jules 1938- *NatPD[port]*
Tasco, Rai 1917- *IntMPA 77, -75, -76, -78, -79, -80*
Tashamira *DancEn 78[port]*
Tashlin, Frank 1913-1972 *BiDFilm, -81, CmMov, DcFM, FilmEn, FilmgC, HalFC 80, OxFilm, WorEFlm*
Tashman, Lilyan d1934 *MotPP, WhoHol B*
Tashman, Lilyan 1899-1934 *FilmEn, Film 2, FilmgC, HalFC 80, MovMk[port], NotNAT B, ThFT[port], WhThe*
Tashman, Lilyan 1900-1934 *ForYSC, TwYS, WhScrn 74, -77*
Tasker, William Decatur, Jr. 1943- *IntWWM 77, -80*
Taskin, Alexandre 1853-1897 *Baker 78*
Taskin, Pascal 1723-1793 *Baker 78, NewGrD 80*
Taskova, Slavka 1940- *WhoOp 76*
Tasku, V *Film 2*
Tasso, Gioan Maria *NewGrD 80*
Tasso, Torquato 1544-1595 *CnThe, EncWT, Ent, McGEWD, NewEOp 71, NewGrD 80, NotNAT B, OxThe, PlP&P[port], REnWD[port]*
Tastavin, Geronimo *NewGrD 80*
Tata, Paul M, Sr. 1883-1962 *WhScrn 74, -77, WhoHol B*
Tatam, John Alfred 1894- *IntWWM 77*
Tate, Beth 1890- *WhThe*
Tate, Buddy 1914- *CmpEPM, WhoJazz 72*
Tate, Buddy 1915- *EncJzS 70, IlEncJ*
Tate, Charles Henry 1916-1972 *BluesWW[port]*
Tate, Erskine 1895- *CmpEPM, WhoJazz 72*
Tate, George Holmes 1915- *EncJzS 70*
Tate, Grady 1932- *EncJzS 70*
Tate, Hal 1912- *AmSCAP 66*
Tate, Harry 1872-1940 *EncWT, Ent, HalFC 80, IlWWBF[port], WhScrn 74,*

Teague, Bob 1929- *BlkAmP, DrBlPA*
Teague, Brian 1937-1970 *WhScrn 74, -77*
Teague, Frances *Film 2*
Teague, Guy d1970 *WhScrn 74, -77, WhoHol B*
Teague, Thurman 1910- *WhoJazz 72*
Teague, Tony *MorBAP*
Teague, William Chandler, Sr. 1922- *IntWWM 77, -80*
Teal, Ben d1917 *NotNAT B*
Teal, Ray 1902-1976 *FilmEn, FilmgC, ForYSC, HalFC 80, HolCA[port], IntMPA 75, -76, Vers A[port], WhoHol C*
Teale, Perry Wendel 1923- *IntWWM 77, -80*
Tear, Robert 1922- *CmOp*
Tear, Robert 1939- *IntWWM 77, -80, NewGrD 80, WhoMus 72, WhoOp 76*
Teare, Ethel 1894-1959 *Film 1, WhScrn 74, -77, WhoHol B*
Tearle, Constance *Film 2*
Tearle, Conway d1938 *MotPP, WhoHol B*
Tearle, Conway 1878-1938 *FilmEn, FilmgC, ForYSC, HalFC 80, NotNAT B, WhScrn 74, -77, WhThe*
Tearle, Conway 1882-1938 *Film 1, -2, MovMk, TwYS*
Tearle, David *Film 2*
Tearle, Edmund 1856-1913 *NotNAT B*
Tearle, Sir Godfrey 1884-1953 *CnThe, FilmAG WE, FilmEn, Film 1, -2, FilmgC, HalFC 80, IlWWBF, NotNAT B, OxThe, WhScrn 74, -77, WhThe, WhoHol B*
Tearle, Malcolm 1888-1935 *NotNAT B, WhScrn 74, -77*
Tearle, Noah *Film 2*
Tearle, Osmond 1852-1901 *NotNAT B, OxThe*
Teasdale, Sara 1884-1933 *BiDAmM*
Teasdale, Veree 1897?- *Film 2, ForYSC*
Teasdale, Verree *WhoHol A*
Teasdale, Verree 1904- *FilmgC, HalFC 80*
Teasdale, Verree 1906- *FilmEn, HolCA[port], ThFT[port], WhThe*
Teather, Ida d1954 *WhScrn 74, -77*
Tebaldi, Renata 1922- *Baker 78, BnBkM 80, CmOp, IntWWM 77, -80, MusMk, MusSN[port], NewEOp 71, NewGrD 80[port], WhoHol A, WhoMus 72, WhoOp 76*
Tebaldini, Giovanni 1864-1952 *Baker 78, NewGrD 80*
Tebaldini, Nicolo *NewGrD 80*
Tebelak, John Michael 1948- *AmSCAP 80*
Tebet, David 1920- *IntMPA 75, -76*
Tebet, David W *NewYTET*
Tecchler, David 1666?-1747? *NewGrD 80*
Tecer, Ahmet Kutsi 1901-1967 *REnWD[port]*
Tech A Curia, Nikolaus *NewGrD 80*
Techelmann, Franz Matthias 1649?-1714 *NewGrD 80*
Techine, Andre 1943- *FilmEn*
Teck, Katherine 1939- *IntWWM 77, -80*
Tedder, Gary E 1952- *AmSCAP 80*
Teddy *Film 1, -2*
Teddy Bears, The *RkOn*
Teddybears *AmPS A*
Tedeschi, Luigi Maurizio 1867-1944 *NewGrD 80*
Tedeschi, Simplicio *NewGrD 80*
Tedeschino, Il *NewGrD 80*
Tedescho, Simplicio *NewGrD 80*
Tedesco, Fredric 1906- *AmSCAP 80*
Tedesco, Ignaz 1817-1882 *Baker 78*
Tedesco, Jean 1895-1958 *OxFilm*
Tedesco, Jean 1895-1959 *DcFM*
Tedesco, Lou *NewYTET*
Tedesco, Pat Louis 1934- *AmSCAP 80*
Tedesco, Sergio 1934- *WhoOp 76*
Tedeyev, Vadim 1946- *CnOxB*
Tedmarsh, W J *Film 1*
Tedrow, Irene 1907- *ForYSC, WhoHol A*
Tee, Richard 1943- *AmSCAP 80*
Tee Set, The *RkOn 2[port]*
Teed, John 1911- *WhThe*
Teed, Roy Norman 1928- *Baker 78, IntWWM 77, WhoMus 72*
Teegarden & VanWinkle *RkOn 2A[port]*
Teege, Joachim 1925-1969 *WhScrn 74, -77, WhoHol B*
Teen Agers *BiDAmM*
Teen Queens, The *RkOn[port]*
Teer, Barbara Ann 1937- *BlkAmP, DrBlPA, MorBAP, NotNAT*
Teetor, Macy O 1898- *AmSCAP 66, -80*
Teeus *NewGrD 80*
Teff, Joyce *WomWMM*
Tefft, Al *PupTheA*
Teggin, Maggie L 1946- *IntWWM 80*
Teghi, Pietro *NewGrD 80*
Teghze-Gerber, Miklos *AmSCAP 80*
Teiber *NewGrD 80*
Teicher, Louis 1924- *AmSCAP 66, -80*
Teichmann, Howard 1916- *BiE&WWA, McGEWD[port], NatPD[port], NotNAT*
Teichmuller, Robert 1863-1939 *Baker 78*
Teifer, Gerald E 1922- *AmSCAP 66, -80*
Teike, Carl 1864-1922 *Baker 78, NewGrD 80*
Teilich, Philipp *NewGrD 80*
Teinturier, Johannes *NewGrD 80*
Teirlinck, Herman 1879-1967 *CnMD, ModWD*
Teitel, Carol 1929- *BiE&WWA, NotNAT, WhoThe 72, -77*
Teitelbaum, Jack 1902-1964 *AmSCAP 66, -80*
Teitelbaum, Mashel 1921- *CreCan 1*
Teitelbaum, Pedro 1922- *IntMPA 77, -78, -79, -80*
Teitelbaum, Richard 1939- *ConAmC*
Teixeira, Antonio 1707?-1759? *NewGrD 80*
Teixeira, Virgilio 1917- *FilmAG WE[port]*
Teixeira DeMattos, Alexander Louis 1865-1921 *NotNAT B, WhThe*
Teje, Tora 1893- *FilmEn, Film 2*
Tejeda, Alonso De 1556?-1628 *NewGrD 80*
Tejon, Jose Ignacio 1920- *IntWWM 77, -80*
Tekahionwake *CreCan 2*
TeKanawa, Kiri *IntWWM 77, -80, WhoOp 76*
TeKanawa, Kiri 1944- *BnBkM 80, CmOp, NewGrD 80*
TeKanawa, Kiri 1945?- *MusSN[port]*
Tekeliev, Alexander 1942- *Baker 78*
Telasko, Ralph 1911- *WhoOp 76*
Telbin, William 1813-1873 *NotNAT B, OxThe*
Telbin, William Lewis 1846-1931 *NotNAT B, OxThe*
Telemann, Georg Michael 1748-1831 *Baker 78, NewGrD 80*
Telemann, Georg Philipp 1681-1767 *Baker 78, BnBkM 80[port], CmOp, CmpBCM, DcCom 77[port], DcCom&M 79, GrComp[port], MusMk[port], NewGrD 80[port], OxMus*
Telerman, Estela 1946- *IntWWM 77, -80*
Teleshova, Elizabeth d1943 *NotNAT B*
Television *IlEncR*
Telford, John Henry 1911- *WhoMus 72*
Telford, Robert S 1923- *BiE&WWA, NotNAT*
Tell, Alma 1892-1937 *Film 1, -2, NotNAT B, TwYS, WhScrn 74, -77, WhThe, WhoHol B*
Tell, Arthur *WhoHol A*
Tell, Olive 1894-1951 *Film 1, -2, NotNAT B, TwYS, WhScrn 74, -77, WhThe, WhoHol B*
Tell, Olive 1896-1951 *ForYSC*
Telle, Karl 1826-1895 *CnOxB*
Tellefsen, Arve 1936- *WhoMus 72*
Tellefsen, Thomas Dyke 1823-1874 *Baker 78, NewGrD 80, OxMus*
Tellegen, Lou 1881-1934 *FilmEn, Film 1, -2, FilmgC, HalFC 80, MotPP, NotNAT B, TwYS, WhScrn 77, WhThe, WhoHol B*
Tellegen, Lou 1883-1934 *NotNAT A*
Tellegen, Lou 1884-1934 *WhScrn 74*
Teller, Al *ConMuA 80B*
Teller, Florian Johann *NewGrD 80*
Teller, Ira 1940- *IntMPA 77, -75, -76, -78, -79, -80*
Teller, Marcus *NewGrD 80*
Tellez, Gabriel *McGEWD[port]*
Telloli, Bruno 1937- *CnOxB*
Tellstrom, Anders Theodore 1919- *IntWWM 77, -80*
Telmanyi, Emil 1892- *Baker 78, IntWWM 77, -80, NewGrD 80, WhoMus 72*
Telmanyi, Ilona Dorothea Antoinette 1937- *IntWWM 77, -80*
Telva, Marian 1897-1962 *Baker 78*
Telva, Marion 1897-1962 *NewEOp 71*
Telva, Marion 1897-1965 *BiDAmM*
Telyakovsky, Vladimir A 1860-1924 *DancEn 78*
Telzlaff, Teddy *Film 1*
Temary, Elza *Film 2, WhScrn 74, -77*
Temerson, Leon 1904- *IntWWM 77, -80, WhoMus 72*
Temianka, Henri 1906- *Baker 78, NewGrD 80, WhoMus 72*
Temkin, Ascher M 1938- *IntWWM 77, -80*
Temkin, Harold P 1949- *AmSCAP 80*
Temperley, Jean *IntWWM 77, -80*
Temperley, Joe 1929- *EncJzS 70*
Temperley, Joseph 1929- *EncJzS 70*
Temperley, Nicholas Mark 1932- *IntWWM 77, -80, NewGrD 80*
Tempest, Doreen *DancEn 78*
Tempest, Francis Adolphus Vane- *WhThe*
Tempest, Marie d1942 *Film 1, WhoHol B*
Tempest, Marie 1862-1942 *WhoStg 1906, -1908*
Tempest, Marie 1864-1942 *CnThe, EncMT, EncWT, Ent[port], FamA&A[port], FilmgC, HalFC 80, OxThe, PlP&P, WhScrn 74, -77, WhThe*
Tempest, Marie 1866-1942 *NotNAT A*
Tempest, Pierce 1635-1717 *OxMus*
Tempesto, Louis Michael 1905- *AmSCAP 66, -80*
Templar, Joan *ConAmC*
Temple, Edward P d1921 *NotNAT B*
Temple, Helen 1894- *WhThe*
Temple, Hope *OxMus*
Temple, Joan d1965 *WhThe*
Temple, Johnny 1906-1968 *BluesWW[port]*
Temple, Jonnie 1906-1968 *BluesWW[port]*
Temple, Lorraine *Film 2*
Temple, Madge d1943 *NotNAT B, WhThe*
Temple, Nat *WhoMus 72*
Temple, Richard 1847- *WhThe*
Temple, Richard Burdette 1931- *IntWWM 77*
Temple, Shirley *AmPS B, MotPP*
Temple, Shirley 1927- *ForYSC, WhoHol A*
Temple, Shirley 1928- *BiDAmM, BiDFilm, -81, CmMov, CmpEPM, FilmEn, FilmgC, HalFC 80, MovMk[port], OxFilm, ThFT[port]*
Temple, Shirley 1929- *IntMPA 77, -75, -76, -78, -79, -80, WorEFlm*
Temple Savage, Richard 1909- *WhoMus 72*
Templeman, Ted *ConMuA 80B*
Templeton, Alec 1909-1963 *Baker 78, ConAmC*
Templeton, Alec 1910-1963 *AmSCAP 66, -80, BiDAmM, CmpEPM, NotNAT B, WhoHol B*
Templeton, Fay *AmPS B*
Templeton, Fay 1865-1939 *CmpEPM, EncMT, NotNAT B, WhThe, WhoStg 1906, -1908*
Templeton, Fay 1866-1939 *WhScrn 74, -77, WhoHol B*
Templeton, John d1907 *NotNAT B*
Templeton, John 1802-1886 *Baker 78, CmOp, NewGrD 80*
Templeton, Pearl 1898- *AmSCAP 66*
Templeton, W P 1913- *WhThe*
Templeton, W P 1915- *BiE&WWA*
Templeton, William B 1918- *AmSCAP 66, -80*
Templin, Procopius Von *NewGrD 80*
Tempo, Nino 1935- *AmSCAP 66, -80*
Tempo, Nino 1937- *RkOn[port]*
Tempo, Nino And April Stevens *RkOn[port]*
Tempo Club Orchestra *BiDAmM*
Tempos, The *RkOn*
Temptations, The *BiDAmM, ConMuA 80A, RkOn, -2[port]*
Ten, Ichi *MagIID*
Ten cc *ConMuA 80A, IlEncR[port], RkOn 2[port]*
Ten Years After *ConMuA 80A, IlEncR*
Tenaglia, Antonio Francesco 161-?-1661? *NewGrD 80, OxMus*
TenBokum, Jan Gerardus Arend 1942- *IntWWM 77, -80*
Tenbrook, Harry 1887-1960 *Film 2, WhScrn 77*
Tenbrook, James *Film 2*
Tenducci, Giusto 1736?-1790 *CmOp*
Tenducci, Giusto Ferdinando 1735?-1790 *NewGrD 80[port]*
Tenducci, Giusto Ferdinando 1736?-1790 *Baker 78*
Tenenholtz, Nettie *Film 2*

Tener, Martin Jack 1935- *AmSCAP 80*
TenEyck, Lillian *Film 2*
TenEyck, Melissa *Film 2*
TenEyck, Mills, Jr. 1920- *BiE&WWA*
Teniers, Guillaume Albert 1748-1820 *NewGrD 80*
Teniers, Willem 1748-1820 *NewGrD 80*
Tennant, Barbara *Film 1, -2, TwYS*
Tennant, Veronica 1946- *CnOxB, CreCan 1*
Tennant, William *IntMPA 77, -78, -79, -80*
Tennberg, Jean-Marc 1924-1971 *WhScrn 77*
Tennenbaum, Jeff *ConMuA 80B*
Tennent, Henry M 1879-1941 *NotNAT B, WhThe*
Tennessee Gabriel *BluesWW[port]*
Tennessee Mountain Boys, The *BiDAmM, EncFCWM 69*
Tennessee Students *BiDAmM*
Tennessee Three, Johnny Cash's *BiDAmM*
Tenneva Ramblers, The *EncFCWM 69, IlEncCM*
Tenney, Del *WhoHrs 80*
Tenney, Gena *NewGrD 80*
Tenney, Jack B 1898-1970 *AmSCAP 66, -80*
Tenney, James 1934- *ConAmC, DcCM, IntWWM 77, -80*
Tenniel, Sir John 1820-1914 *DcPup*
Tennstedt, Klaus 1926- *Baker 78, NewGrD 80, WhoOp 76*
Tenny, Marion H d1964 *NotNAT B*
Tennyson, Alfred 1809-1892 *CnThe, DcPup, McGEWD[port], NewEOp 71, NotNAT B, OxMus, OxThe, REnWD[port]*
Tennyson, Gladys *Film 1, -2*
Tennyson, James J 1898- *AmSCAP 66, -80*
Tennyson, Jean 1905- *WhoMus 72*
Tennyson, Pen 1912-1941 *IlWWBF*
Tennyson, Pen 1918-1941 *HalFC 80*
Tennyson, Penrose 1912-1941 *IlWWBF A*
Tennyson, Walter *Film 2*
Tennyson, William J, Jr. 1923-1959 *AmSCAP 66, -80*
Tenredus *NewGrD 80*
Tenschert, Roland 1894-1970 *Baker 78, NewGrD 80*
Tenser, Tony 1920- *IntMPA 77, -75, -76*
Teo, Li-Lin 1953- *IntWWM 80*
Teodorian, Valentin 1928- *WhoOp 76*
Teodorini, Elena 1857-1926 *NewGrD 80*
Teodorini, Helena 1857-1926 *Baker 78*
Teodoro Del Carmine *NewGrD 80*
Teoli, Albert G 1915- *AmSCAP 66, -80*
Teoli, Gertrude H 1925- *AmSCAP 80*
Tepper, Albert 1921- *AmSCAP 80, ConAmC, IntWWM 77, -80*
Tepper, Saul Joel 1899- *AmSCAP 66, -80*
Tepper, Sid 1918- *AmSCAP 66, -80*
Ter-Arutunian, Rouben 1920- *BiE&WWA, CnOxB, DancEn 78, EncWT, NewEOp 71, NotNAT, WhoOp 76, WhoThe 72, -77*
Ter-T'at'evosyan, Hovhannes Gurgeni 1926- *NewGrD 80*
Ter Weeme, Mascha *CnOxB, DancEn 78*
Terabust, Elisabetta 1946- *CnOxB*
Terale, Noel *Film 2*
Terascon, Albertet De *NewGrD 80*
Terebey, Raisa *WomWMM B*
Terence 190?BC-159BC *CnThe, EncWT, Ent, McGEWD, NewGrD 80, NotNAT B, OxThe, PlP&P[port]*
Terence 195?BC-159BC *REnWD[port]*
Terenyi, Ede 1935- *NewGrD 80*
Terenyi, Eduard 1935- *Baker 78*
Teresa 1929- *CnOxB, DancEn 78*
Terey-Smith, Mary *IntWWM 77, -80*
Terhune, Anice Potter 1873-1964 *Baker 78, ConAmC*
Terhune, Max 1890-1973 *HalFC 80*
Terhune, Max 1891-1973 *FilmEn, FilmgC, ForYSC, HolCA[port], WhScrn 77, WhoHol B*
Terian, Mikhail 1905- *NewGrD 80*
Terker, Arthur 1899- *AmSCAP 66, -80*
Termer, Helga Elisabeth 1938- *WhoOp 76*
Termini, Joe d1964 *NotNAT B*
Termini, Olga 1930- *IntWWM 77, -80*
Ternan, Thomas d1846 *NotNAT B*
Ternaux, Victoire *NewGrD 80*
Ternick, Frank 1895-1966 *WhScrn 77*
Ternina, Milka 1863-1941 *Baker 78, CmOp, MusSN[port], NewEOp 71, NewGrD 80*
Terpander *NewGrD 80*
Terpis, Max 1889-1958 *CnOxB, DancEn 78*
Terr, Al 1893-1967 *WhScrn 77*
Terr, Max 1890-1951 *AmSCAP 66, -80*
Terr, Mischa Richard 1899- *AmSCAP 66, -80*
Terrabugio, Giuseppe 1842-1933 *Baker 78*
Terradeglias, Domenico 1713?-1751 *NewGrD 80*
Terradellas, Domingo 1713-1751 *Baker 78, NewGrD 80*
Terranova, Bastian *PupTheA*
Terranova, Carolina *PupTheA*
Terranova, Dan *WhoHol A*
Terranova, Dino 1904-1969 *WhScrn 74, -77, WhoHol B*
Terranova, Joseph A 1941- *AmSCAP 80*
Terranova, Vittorio Antonio 1945- *WhoOp 76*
Terrasse, Claude 1867-1923 *Baker 78, NewGrD 80*
Terrasson, Rene-Pierre 1924- *WhoOp 76*
Terraux, L H Du d1878 *NotNAT B*
Terrayova, Maria Jana 1922- *IntWWM 77, -80*
Terrell, Charles Wayne 1948- *IntWWM 77*
Terrell, Ken 1904-1966 *WhScrn 77*
Terrell, Mary E Church 1863-1954 *BiDAmM*
Terrell, Pha Elmer 1910-1945 *CmpEPM, WhoJazz 72*
Terrell, St. John 1916- *BiE&WWA, NotNAT*
Terrell, Steven *ForYSC*
Terrell, Tammi 1970- *RkOn 2[port]*
Terrell, Vincent *BlkAmP*
Terresco, Michael *AmSCAP 80*
Terri, Salli Clementina *AmSCAP 80*
Terribill, Giovanni *Film 2*
Terriera, Francesco *NewGrD 80*
Terrieria, Francesco *NewGrD 80*
Terrill, Vincent *MorBAP*
Terris, Ellaline d1971 *WhoHol B*
Terris, Norma 1904- *EncMT, Film 2, WhThe, WhoHol A*
Terris, Tom *Film 1*
Terriss, Dorothy *AmSCAP 80*
Terriss, Ellaine 1871-1971 *Film 2*
Terriss, Ellaline 1871-1971 *EncMT, FilmgC, HalFC 80, OxThe, WhScrn 74, -77, WhThe*
Terriss, Tom 1874-1964 *WhThe*
Terriss, Tom 1887-1964 *TwYS A, WhScrn 77*
Terriss, William 1847-1897 *NotNAT A, -B, OxThe*
Terriss, Mrs. William d1898 *NotNAT B*
Terron, Carlo 1913- *McGEWD[port]*
Terroni, Raphael 1945- *IntWWM 77, -80*
Terry, Al 1922- *BiDAmM, IlEncCM*
Terry, Alice *MotPP*
Terry, Alice 1896- *Film 1, -2, TwYS*
Terry, Alice 1899- *FilmEn, FilmgC, HalFC 80, MovMk*
Terry, Alice 1901- *WhoHol A*
Terry, Beatrice 1890- *OxThe, WhThe*
Terry, Benjamin 1818-1896 *NotNAT B, OxThe*
Terry, Mrs. Benjamin 1819-1892 *NotNAT B*
Terry, Charles d1933 *NotNAT B*
Terry, Charles Sanford 1864-1936 *Baker 78, NewGrD 80, OxMus*
Terry, Clark 1920- *BiDAmM, CmpEPM, EncJzS 70, IlEncJ*
Terry, Daniel 1789-1829 *NotNAT B, OxThe*
Terry, Dennis 1895-1932 *NotNAT B, OxThe*
Terry, Doc 1921- *BluesWW[port]*
Terry, Don 1902- *FilmEn, Film 2, FilmgC, ForYSC, HalFC 80, WhoHol A*
Terry, Douglas Fairchild 1921- *WhoMus 72*
Terry, Edward O'Connor 1844-1912 *NotNAT B, OxThe, WhThe, WhoStg 1908*
Terry, Eliza d1878 *NotNAT B*
Terry, Ellen Alice d1928 *Film 1, WhoHol B*
Terry, Ellen Alice 1847-1928 *CnThe, EncWT, Ent[port], FamA&A[port], OxThe, PlP&P[port]*
Terry, Ellen Alice 1848-1928 *Film 2, HalFC 80, NotNAT A, -B, WhScrn 74, -77, WhThe, WhoStg 1906, -1908*
Terry, Ethel Grey 1898-1931 *Film 1, -2, TwYS, WhScrn 74, -77, WhoHol B*
Terry, Ethelind 1900- *CmpEPM, EncMT, WhThe*
Terry, Florence 1854-1896 *NotNAT B, OxThe*
Terry, Frances 1884- *ConAmC*
Terry, Francis *Film 2*
Terry, Fred 1863-1933 *CnThe, NotNAT B, OxThe, WhScrn 74, -77, WhThe, WhoHol B, WhoStg 1908*
Terry, George d1928 *NotNAT B*
Terry, George N 1906- *AmSCAP 66, -80*
Terry, Gordon 1931- *BiDAmM*
Terry, Harry *Film 2*
Terry, Hazel 1918-1974 *WhScrn 77, WhThe, WhoHol B*
Terry, J E Harold 1885-1939 *NotNAT B, WhThe*
Terry, Jack *Film 2*
Terry, James Arlie 1948- *AmSCAP 80*
Terry, Joe *AmSCAP 80*
Terry, Sir John 1913- *IntMPA 77, -75, -76, -78, -79, -80*
Terry, Julia Emilie Neilson 1868-1957 *OxThe*
Terry, Kate 1844-1924 *NotNAT B, OxThe, WhThe, WhoStg 1908*
Terry, Kenton F 1909- *IntWWM 77, -80*
Terry, Mabel Gwynedd Terry-Lewis 1872-1957 *OxThe*
Terry, Marion 1852-1930 *NotNAT B, OxThe*
Terry, Marion 1856-1930 *WhThe, WhoStg 1908*
Terry, Megan 1932- *ConDr 73, -77, CroCD, DcLB 7[port], EncWT, NotNAT, PlP&P, WhoThe 77*
Terry, Minnie 1882-1964 *OxThe, WhThe*
Terry, Nigel *WhoHol A*
Terry, Olive 1884- *WhThe*
Terry, Paul 1887-1971 *DcFM, FilmEn, FilmgC, HalFC 80*
Terry, Paul Michael 1949- *IntWWM 80*
Terry, Phil 1909- *FilmEn*
Terry, Philip 1909- *FilmgC, HalFC 80*
Terry, Philip 1912?- *ForYSC*
Terry, Phillip 1909- *FilmEn, MotPP, WhoHol A*
Terry, Phyllis 1892- *OxThe*
Terry, Sir R R 1865-1938 *NewGrD 80*
Terry, Ralph *PupTheA*
Terry, Sir Richard Runciman 1865-1938 *Baker 78, OxMus*
Terry, Robert *WhoHol A*
Terry, Robert 1928- *AmSCAP 66, -80*
Terry, Robert E Huntington 1867-1953 *AmSCAP 66, -80*
Terry, Ron 1920- *AmSCAP 66*
Terry, Ruth *ForYSC*
Terry, Sanders *BluesWW[port]*
Terry, Sarah Ballard 1817-1892 *OxThe*
Terry, Sheila 1910-1957 *ForYSC, WhScrn 77, WhoHol B*
Terry, Sonny 1911- *BiDAmM, BluesWW[port], CmpEPM, EncFCWM 69, EncJzS 70, IlEncJ*
Terry, Walter d1932 *NotNAT B*
Terry, Walter 1913- *CnOxB, DancEn 78*
Terry, William Patrick 1952- *AmSCAP 80*
Terry, Zela 1957- *BlkWAB*
Terry-Lewis, Mabel 1872-1957 *NotNAT B, WhThe, WhoHol B*
Terry-Thomas 1911- *FilmEn, FilmgC, ForYSC, HalFC 80, IlWWBF[port], IntMPA 77, -75, -76, -78, -79, -80, MotPP, MovMk[port], WhoHol A, WhoHrs 80[port]*
Terschak, Adolf 1832-1901 *Baker 78*
Tersmeden, Gerard 1920- *IntWWM 80*
Terson, Peter 1932- *CnThe, ConDr 73, -77, CroCD, EncWT, REnWD[port], WhoThe 77*
Terteryan, Avet 1929- *NewGrD 80*
Tertis, Lionel *OxMus*
Tertis, Lionel 1876-1975 *Baker 78, BnBkM 80, MusSN[port], NewGrD 80[port]*
Tertis, Lionel 1876-1976 *MusMk*
Tervalon, Clement 1915- *NewOrJ*
Tervapaa, Juhani *CroCD*
Terwilliger, George 1882- *TwYS A*
Terzagi, Bernardinus *NewGrD 80*
Terzago, Bernardino *NewGrD 80*
Terzago, Bernardinus *NewGrD 80*
Terzagus, Bernardinus *NewGrD 80*
Terzakis, Dimitri 1938- *CpmDNM 78, -79, -80,*

DcCM, NewGrD 80
Terzakis, Dimitris 1938- *Baker 78*
Terzi, Giovanni Antonio *NewGrD 80*
Terzian, Anita 1947- *WhoOp 76*
Terziani, Eugenio 1824-1889 *Baker 78, NewGrD 80*
Terziani, Pietro 1765-1831 *NewGrD 80*
Terzieff, Laurent 1935- *EncWT, FilmEn, FilmgC, HalFC 80, WhoHol A*
Teschau, Walter E *PupTheA*
Teschemacher, Frank 1906-1932 *BiDAmM, CmpEPM, IlEncJ, NewGrD 80, WhoJazz 72*
Teschemacher, Margarete 1903-1959 *NewGrD 80*
Teschemacher, Marguerite 1903-1959 *CmOp, NewEOp 71*
Teschler, Fred Fritz 1926- *WhoOp 76*
Teschner, Gustav Wilhelm 1800-1883 *Baker 78, NewGrD 80*
Teschner, Melchior 1584-1635 *NewGrD 80*
Teschner, Richard 1879-1948 *DcPup, Ent*
Teshigahara, Hiroshi 1927- *BiDFilm, -81, DcFM, OxFilm, WorEFlm*
Teshighara, Hiroshi 1927- *FilmEn*
Tesi, Vittoria 1700-1775 *Baker 78, NewGrD 80*
Tess, Giulia 1889-1976 *NewGrD 80*
Tessari, Duccio 1926- *WorEFlm*
Tessarini, Carlo 1690?-1766? *Baker 78, NewGrD 80*
Tessier, Albert Denis 1900- *AmSCAP 80*
Tessier, Andre 1886-1931 *Baker 78, NewGrD 80*
Tessier, Carles *NewGrD 80*
Tessier, Charles 1550?- *Baker 78, NewGrD 80*
Tessier, Guillaume *NewGrD 80*
Tessier, Robert *WhoHol A*
Tessier, Roger 1939- *Baker 78*
Tessiery, Carles *NewGrD 80*
Tessiery, Charles *NewGrD 80*
Tessmer, Hans 1895-1943 *Baker 78*
Testa, Joseph 1933- *IntWWM 77*
Testagrossa, Giovanni Angelo 1470-1530 *NewGrD 80*
Tester, Desmond 1919- *FilmgC, HalFC 80, WhThe*
Testi, Flavio 1923- *NewGrD 80*
Testoni, Alfredo 1856-1931 *McGEWD*
Testore *NewGrD 80*
Testore, Carlo Antonio *NewGrD 80*
Testore, Carlo Giuseppe 1660?-1720? *Baker 78, NewGrD 80*
Testore, Guglielmo *NewGrD 80*
Testore, Paolo Antonio *NewGrD 80*
Testore, Pietro *NewGrD 80*
Testori, Carlo Giovanni 1714-1782 *Baker 78, NewGrD 80*
Testori, Guglielmo *NewGrD 80*
Testorius, Johann *NewGrD 80*
Testrup, Alice 1929- *IntWWM 80*
Teternikov, Fyodor Kusmich *McGEWD[port]*
Tetley, Dorothy *WhThe*
Tetley, Glen 1926- *CmpGMD, CnOxB, DancEn 78[port]*
Tetley, Walter 1915-1975 *ForYSC, WhScrn 77, WhoHol C*
Tetrazzini, Eva 1862-1938 *Baker 78*
Tetrazzini, Luisa 1871-1940 *Baker 78, BiDAmM, BnBkM 80[port], CmOp, MusSN[port], NewEOp 71, NewGrD 80[port], OxMus*
Tetz *NewGrD 80*
Tetzel, Joan 1921- *BiE&WWA, ForYSC, MotPP, NotNAT, WhoHol A, WhoThe 72, -77*
Tetzel, Joan 1924-1977 *FilmgC, HalFC 80*
Tetzlaff, Ted 1903- *BiDFilm, -81, FilmEn, FilmgC, HalFC 80, IntMPA 77, -75, -76, -78, -79, -80, WorEFlm*
Tetzlaff, Toni *Film 2*
Teuber *NewGrD 80*
Teuber, Tom *ConMuA 80B*
Teuber, Ulrich J 1920- *IntWWM 80*
Teutsch, Walter 1909- *IntWWM 77, -80*
Teverner, William d1731 *NotNAT B*
Tevis, Carol 1907-1965 *WhScrn 77*
Tevo, Zaccaria 1651-1712? *NewGrD 80*
Tewkesbury, Joan *IntMPA 77, -76, -78, -79, -80, WomWMM*
Tewkesbury, Peter 1924- *WorEFlm[port]*
Tewksbury, Peter 1924- *FilmEn, FilmgC, HalFC 80*
Tex, Joe 1933- *RkOn 2[port]*
Texans, The *BiDAmM*
Texas Guitar Slim *BluesWW[port]*
Texas Longhorns *EncFCWM 69*
Texas Longhorns, Billie Walker's *BiDAmM*
Texas Medley Quartette *BiDAmM*
Texas Playboys, The *BiDAmM, EncFCWM 69*
Texas Slim *BiDAmM, BluesWW[port], EncFCWM 69*
Texas Sons *BiDAmM*
Texas Tessie *BluesWW[port]*
Texas Tommy *BluesWW[port]*
Texas Troubadours *BiDAmM, EncFCWM 69*
Textor, Keith V 1921- *AmSCAP 80*
Textoris, Guglielmo *NewGrD 80*
Teyber *NewGrD 80*
Teyber, Anton 1754-1822 *Baker 78*
Teyber, Anton 1756-1822 *NewGrD 80*
Teyber, Elisabeth 1744-1816 *NewGrD 80*
Teyber, Franz 1756-1810 *Baker 78*
Teyber, Franz 1758-1810 *NewGrD 80*
Teyber, Matthaus 1711?-1785 *NewGrD 80*
Teyber, Therese 1760-1830 *NewGrD 80*
Teyte, Maggie 1888-1976 *Baker 78, BnBkM 80, CmOp, MusSN[port], NewEOp 71, NewGrD 80[port]*
Teyte, Maggie 1889- *EncMT, WhThe*
Tgettis, Nicholas Chris 1933- *AmSCAP 80, CpmDNM 76, -77, -80, ConAmC*
Tgettis, Nicholas Cris 1933- *CpmDNM 78, -79*
Thacher, Anita *WomWMM B*
Thacher, Russell *IntMPA 80*
Thackeray, William Makepeace 1811-1863 *DcPup*
Thackery, Bud 1903- *FilmgC, HalFC 80*
Thackray, Thomas *NewGrD 80*
Thadewaldt, Hermann 1827-1909 *Baker 78*
Thaillandier, Antoni *NewGrD 80*
Thakura, Saurindramohana *NewGrD 80*
Thalasso, Arthur *Film 2*
Thalben-Ball, George Thomas 1896- *IntWWM 80, NewGrD 80, WhoMus 72*
Thalberg, Irving 1899-1936 *BiDFilm, -81, DcFM, FilmEn, FilmgC, HalFC 80, MGM A[port], OxFilm, TwYS B, WorEFlm*
Thalberg, Sigismond 1812-1871 *Baker 78, BnBkM 80, MusMk, NewGrD 80[port], OxMus*
Thalberg, T B d1947 *NotNAT B*
Thalberg, Zare 1858-1915 *NewGrD 80*
Thaler, Doug *ConMuA 80B*
Thalesio, Pedro 1563?-1629? *NewGrD 80*
Thalhimer, Morton G, Jr. 1924- *IntMPA 77, -75, -76, -78, -79, -80*
Thalhimer, Morton Gustavus 1889- *IntMPA 77, -75, -76*
Thall, Peter *ConMuA 80B*
Thallaug, Edith *IntWWM 80, WhoOp 76*
Thaller, Johann Babtist 1872-1952 *NewGrD 80*
Thallon, Robert 1852-1910 *Baker 78*
Thalman, Marilynn Carstens *IntWWM 77, -80*
Thamant, Johannes *NewGrD 80*
Thamon, Eugene *AmSCAP 80*
Thane, Adele 1904- *BiE&WWA*
Thane, Edward d1954 *WhScrn 77*
Thane, Elswyth *WhThe*
Thane, Gibson *Film 2*
Tharp, Grahame 1912- *IntMPA 77, -75, -76*
Tharp, Twyla 1942- *CmpGMD[port], CnOxB*
Tharp, Winston Collins 1905-1961 *AmSCAP 80*
Tharpe, Sister Rosetta 1915-1973 *NewGrD 80*
Tharpe, Sister Rosetta 1921-1973 *BiDAmM, DrBlPA, EncJzS 70*
Thatcher, Eva 1862-1942 *Film 1, WhoHol B*
Thatcher, Evelyn 1862-1942 *WhScrn 74, -77*
Thatcher, Heather *Film 1, -2, ForYSC, IlWWBF[port], IntMPA 77, -75, -76, -78, -79, -80, WhThe, WhoHol A*
Thatcher, Heather 1897- *HalFC 80*
Thatcher, Heather 1898?- *FilmEn*
Thatcher, Howard Rutledge 1878-1973 *AmSCAP 66, -80, ConAmC*
Thatcher, Noel *AmSCAP 80*
Thatcher, Torin 1905- *BiE&WWA, FilmEn, FilmgC, ForYSC, HalFC 80, HolCA[port], IntMPA 77, -75, -76, -78, -79, -80, MovMk, NotNAT, WhThe, WhoHol A, WhoHrs 80[port], WhoThe 72*
Thau, Marty *ConMuA 80B*
Thau, Pierre-Eugene 1933- *WhoOp 76*
Thauer, Anja 1945- *IntWWM 77, -80, WhoMus 72*
Thaw, David Martin 1928- *WhoOp 76*
Thaw, Evelyn Nesbit 1885-1967 *Film 1, WhScrn 74, -77, WhoHol B*
Thaw, John 1942- *HalFC 80, WhoHol A, WhoThe 72, -77*
Thaw, Russell *Film 1, -2*
Thawl, Evelyn 1915-1945 *WhScrn 74, -77*
Thaxter, Phyllis *BiE&WWA, MotPP, NotNAT, WhoThe 72*
Thaxter, Phyllis 1920- *WhoThe 77*
Thaxter, Phyllis 1921- *FilmEn, FilmgC, ForYSC, HalFC 80, IntMPA 77, -75, -76, -78, -79, -80, MGM[port], MovMk[port], WhoHol A*
Thayer, Alexander Wheelock 1817-1897 *Baker 78, NewGrD 80, OxMus*
Thayer, Arthur Wilder 1857-1934 *Baker 78*
Thayer, Eugene 1838-1889 *Baker 78, NewGrD 80*
Thayer, Fred M 1941- *ConAmC*
Thayer, Julia *WhoHol A*
Thayer, Lorna *WhoHol A*
Thayer, Lucien Hamilton 1890- *AmSCAP 66*
Thayer, Merewyn *Film 2*
Thayer, Tina *ForYSC*
Thayer, Whitney Eugene 1838-1889 *BiDAmM*
Thayer, William Armour 1874-1933 *Baker 78, BiDAmM, ConAmC*
Theadore, Ralph *Film 2*
Theaker, Mavis Glendora *WhoMus 72*
Theard, Sam 1904- *AmSCAP 66, -80*
Thebom, Blanche 1918- *Baker 78, MusSN[port], NewGrD 80*
Thebom, Blanche 1919- *BiDAmM, IntWWM 77, -80, NewEOp 71*
Theburn, Robert *Film 2*
Theby, Rosemary 1885- *Film 1, -2, MotPP, TwYS*
Theeuwes *NewGrD 80*
Theeuwes, Jacob *NewGrD 80*
Theeuwes, Lodewijk *NewGrD 80*
Theewes *NewGrD 80*
Theilade, Nini 1915- *WhThe*
Theilade, Nini 1916- *CnOxB, DancEn 78*
Theile, Johann 1646-1724 *Baker 78, NewGrD 80, OxMus*
Theilmann, Helen d1956 *NotNAT B*
Theimer, Axel 1946- *IntWWM 77, -80*
Theinred Of Dover *NewGrD 80*
Theis, Alfred 1899-1951 *WhScrn 74, -77*
Theise, Mortimer M 1866- *WhoStg 1908*
Thelin, Eje 1938- *EncJzS 70*
Them *RkOn 2[port]*
Themeli, Georges 1915- *WhoMus 72*
Themelis, Dimitris 1931- *IntWWM 80*
Themen, Art *IlEncJ*
Themmen, Ivana Marburger 1936- *CpmDNM 76, -80*
Theobald, James Chester 1950- *ConAmC*
Theobald, Jim 1950- *CpmDNM 79, -80*
Theobald, Lewis d1944 *NotNAT B*
Theobalde *NewGrD 80*
Theobaldus *NewGrD 80*
Theobaldus Gallicus *NewGrD 80*
Theobold, Jim 1950- *CpmDNM 78*
Theocritus 308?BC-240?BC *NewGrD 80*
Theodericus, Sixt *NewGrD 80*
Theodonus De Caprio d1434 *NewGrD 80*
Theodorakis, Mikis 1925- *Baker 78, FilmEn, IntWWM 80, MusMk[port], NewGrD 80, OxFilm, WorEFlm*
Theodore *JoeFr*
Theodore, Mademoiselle 1760-1796 *CnOxB, DancEn 78*
Theodore, Elton 1897-1972 *NewOrJ*
Theodorici, Sixt *NewGrD 80*
Theodoricus *NewGrD 80*
Theodoricus De Campo *NewGrD 80*
Theodoricus Petri Nylandensis 1560?-1617? *NewGrD 80*
Theodoricus Sistinus *NewGrD 80*

Theodoricus, Georg NewGrD 80
Theodorus OxThe, PlP&P[port]
Theodorus Petrejus NewGrD 80
Theofanidis, Iraklis B 1926- AmSCAP 80
Theogerus Of Metz 1050?-1120 NewGrD 80
Theognis OxThe
Theokritos NewGrD 80
Theon Of Smyrna NewGrD 80
Theophile DeViau 1590-1626 OxThe
Theoret, Sandy Mason 1944- AmSCAP 80
Therache, Pierrequin De 1465?-1526? NewGrD 80
Theremin, Leon 1896- Baker 78, NewGrD 80
Theriault, Yves 1916- CreCan 1
Thern, Karoly 1817-1886 NewGrD 80
Theron, Anna Margaretha 1918- IntWWM 80
Thesiger, Ernest 1879-1961 CnThe, FilmEn, Film 2, FilmgC, ForYSC, HalFC 80, IlWWBF, -A, NotNAT B, Vers B[port], WhScrn 74, -77, WhThe, WhoHol B, WhoHrs 80[port]
Thesmar, Ghislaine 1943- CnOxB
Thespis EncWT, Ent, NotNAT B, OxThe
Thesselius, Johann NewGrD 80
Thessier, Charles NewGrD 80
Thessier, Guillaume NewGrD 80
Theta, Shirley Crane WomWMM B
Thevenard, Gabriel-Vincent 1669-1741 NewGrD 80
Thevenin, Francis 1930- IntWWM 77, -80
Thevet, Lucien Andre 1914- IntWWM 77, -80
Thew, Manora Film 1
Thew, Warren 1927- IntWWM 80
Theyard, Harry 1939- WhoOp 76
T'Hezan, Helia 1934- WhoOp 76
Thiard, Pontus De NewGrD 80
Thibaud, Jacques 1880-1953 Baker 78, BnBkM 80, MusSN[port], NewGrD 80
Thibaud, Pierre 1929- NewGrD 80
Thibault, Charles 1794?-1853 BiDAmM
Thibault, Conrad 1906- CmpEPM
Thibault, Genevieve 1902-1975 Baker 78, NewGrD 80
Thibault DeCourville, Joachim NewGrD 80
Thibaut IV 1201-1253 Baker 78, MusMk, NewGrD 80
Thibaut De Blaison d1229? NewGrD 80
Thibaut De Blason d1229? NewGrD 80
Thibaut De Blazon d1229? NewGrD 80
Thibaut DeCourville, Joachim OxMus
Thibaut, Anton Friedrich Justus 1772-1840 Baker 78, NewGrD 80
Thibaut, Anton Friedrich Justus 1774-1840 OxMus
Thibaut, Jean-Baptiste 1872-1938 NewGrD 80, OxMus
Thibodeaux, Carole 1937- IntWWM 77
Thibodeaux, Richard BlkAmP
Thibon, Nanon 1944- CnOxB, DancEn 78
Thibouville NewGrD 80
Thibouville, Andre 1831- NewGrD 80
Thibouville, Desire 1861- NewGrD 80
Thibouville, Henri 1863- NewGrD 80
Thibouville, Martin NewGrD 80
Thibouville, Martin Victor Gustave 1856- NewGrD 80
Thibouville-Lamy, Jerome 1833-1890? NewGrD 80
Thick, Henricus NewGrD 80
Thiel, Carl 1862-1939 Baker 78
Thiel, Joern 1921- IntWWM 77, -80
Thiel, Wolfgang 1947- IntWWM 77, -80
Thiel-Phillips, Vivian D ConAmC
Thiele, Bob 1922- EncJzS 70
Thiele, Douglas M 1944- AmSCAP 80
Thiele, Louis 1816-1848 Baker 78
Thiele, Robert 1922- AmSCAP 66, -80, EncJzS 70
Thiele, Rolf 1918- DcFM, FilmEn, HalFC 80, WorEFlm
Thiele, Siegfried 1934- IntWWM 77, -80, NewGrD 80
Thiele, Walter Joachim 1931- IntWWM 77
Thiele, Wilhelm J 1890-1975 DcFM, FilmEn, OxFilm
Thiele, William J 1890-1975 FilmEn, FilmgC, HalFC 80, WhScrn 77
Thielemans, Jean 1922- EncJzS 70
Thielemans, Toots 1922- CmpEPM, EncJzS 70
Thielman, Robert CpmDNM 79
Thielman, Ronald 1936- AmSCAP 66, -80, ConAmC
Thielo, Carl August 1707-1763 NewGrD 80
Thiem, Clemens 1631-1668 NewGrD 80
Thieme, Clemens 1631-1668 NewGrD 80
Thieme, Darius L 1928- IntWWM 77
Thieme, Ernst Maria Hermann 1924- IntWWM 77, WhoMus 72
Thieme, Frederic 1750-1802 Baker 78, NewGrD 80
Thieme, Friedrich 1750-1802 NewGrD 80
Thieme, Hermann Ernst Maria 1924- IntWWM 77, -80
Thieme, Ulrich 1950- IntWWM 77, -80
Thienen, Marcel Van 1922- Baker 78, NewGrD 80
Thierfelder, Albert 1846-1924 Baker 78
Thierri De Soissons NewGrD 80
Thierry NewGrD 80
Thierry, Alexandre 1646?-1699 NewGrD 80
Thierry, Edouard d1894 NotNAT B
Thierry, Francois 1677-1749 NewGrD 80
Thierry, Pierre 1604-1665 NewGrD 80
Thierstein, Eldred A 1935- IntWWM 77
Thiery NewGrD 80
Thies, Albert Christoph NewGrD 80
Thies, Henry 1893-1935 CmpEPM
Thiess, Frank 1890- CnMD
Thiess, Manuela WhoHol A
Thiess, Ursula 1920- ForYSC
Thiess, Ursula 1924- FilmEn
Thiess, Ursula 1929- FilmgC, HalFC 80, MotPP, WhoHol A
Thigpen, Ben 1908-1971 WhoJazz 72
Thigpen, Ben 1909-1971 EncJzS 70
Thigpen, Ed 1930- EncJzS 70
Thigpen, Edmund Leonard 1930- EncJzS 70
Thigpen, Helen d1966 WhScrn 77, WhoHol B
Thigpen, Lynne WhoHol A
Thijs, Johan NewGrD 80
Thijsse, Wilhelmus Hermanus 1916- IntWWM 80
Thill, Georges 1897- CmOp, NewEOp 71, NewGrD 80
Thilliere, Joseph Bonaventure NewGrD 80
Thillon, Sophie Anna 1819-1903 NewGrD 80
Thillon, Sophie Anne 1819-1903 NewGrD 80
Thilman, Johannes Paul 1906-1973 NewGrD 80
Thiman, Eric Harding 1900-1975 Baker 78, NewGrD 80, WhoMus 72
Thime, Clemens NewGrD 80
Thimey, Erika DancEn 78
Thimig, Hans 1900- EncWT
Thimig, Helen ForYSC
Thimig, Helene 1889-1974 EncWT, HalFC 80, WhScrn 77, WhoHol B
Thimig, Hermann 1890-1976 EncWT, Film 2
Thimig, Hugo 1854-1944 EncWT
Thimm, Daisy WhThe
Thimmig, Leslie 1943- CpmDNM 79, ConAmC
Thimus, Albert, Freiherr Von 1806-1878 Baker 78, NewGrD 80
Thin Lizzy ConMuA 80A, IlEncR[port], RkOn 2[port]
Thingnaes, Frode Sverre 1940- IntWWM 77
Think RkOn 2[port]
Thinnes, Roy 1938- FilmgC, ForYSC, HalFC 80, WhoHol A
Thirard, Armand 1899- DcFM, FilmEn, FilmgC, HalFC 80, WorEFlm
Thirer, Irene d1964 NotNAT B
Thiriet, Maurice 1906-1972 Baker 78, DcFM, FilmEn, NewGrD 80, WhoMus 72
Thirkield, Rob 1936- NotNAT
Thirlwell, George Film 2
Thistle, Lauretta DancEn 78
Thliveris, Elizabeth Hope 1939- AmSCAP 80
Thoburn, Helen 1885-1932 BiDAmM
Thoday, Gillian 1948- IntWWM 80
Thoedorakis, Mikis 1925- IntWWM 77
Thoene, Walter 1928- IntWWM 77, -80
Thoinan, Ernest 1827-1894 Baker 78, NewGrD 80
Thollary, Jan Krtitel NewGrD 80
Thom, Eitelfriedrich 1933- IntWWM 77, -80
Thoma, Helge 1936- WhoOp 76
Thoma, Ludwig 1867-1921 CnMD, EncWT, McGEWD[port], ModWD, NotNAT B
Thoma, Mike 1926- BiE&WWA
Thomae, R L Film 1
Thoman, Istvan 1862-1940 Baker 78, NewGrD 80
Thomas Aquinas 1226-1274 OxMus
Thomas Aquinas 1227-1274 Baker 78, NewGrD 80
Thomas De Sancto Juliano NewGrD 80
Thomas Of Celano OxMus
Thomas, A E 1872-1947 WhThe
Thomas, A F Leighton 1927- IntWWM 80, WhoMus 72
Thomas, A Goring d1892 NotNAT B
Thomas, Agnes WhThe
Thomas, Al ConMuA 80B
Thomas, Alan ConAmC
Thomas, Albert Ellsworth 1872-1947 NotNAT B
Thomas, Ambroise 1811-1896 Baker 78, BnBkM 80, CmOp, CmpBCM, DcCom 77, DcCom&M 79, GrComp[port], MusMk, NewEOp 71, NewGrD 80[port], NotNAT B, OxMus
Thomas, Andrew 1939- CpmDNM 80, ConAmC
Thomas, Ann WhoHol A
Thomas, Anna I WomWMM B
Thomas, Arthur Goring 1850-1892 Baker 78, NewGrD 80, OxMus
Thomas, Augustus 1857-1934 CnThe, McGEWD[port], ModWD, NotNAT A, -B, OxThe, PlP&P[port], REnWD[port], WhThe
Thomas, Augustus 1859- WhoStg 1906, -1908
Thomas, Austin Woodgate 1902- WhoMus 72
Thomas, B J 1942- RkOn 2[port]
Thomas, Barbara 1945- ConAmTC
Thomas, Basil 1912-1957 NotNAT B, WhThe
Thomas, Beal 1940- IntWWM 77, -80
Thomas, Bill 1921- IntMPA 77, -75, -76, -78, -79, -80
Thomas, Blanche 1922-1977 BluesWW, NewOrJ SUP[port]
Thomas, Bob 1898?-1960 NewOrJ[port]
Thomas, Brandon 1856-1914 McGEWD[port], ModWD, NotNAT A, -B, WhThe
Thomas, Brian Keith 1957- AmSCAP 80
Thomas, Brian L 1937- IntWWM 77, -80
Thomas, C Edward 1935- ConAmC
Thomas, Carla 1942- BiDAmM
Thomas, Carla 1947- RkOn
Thomas, Chapman Snead 1909- AmSCAP 66, -80
Thomas, Charles 1925- BluesWW[port]
Thomas, Charles Columbus 1940- IntWWM 77, -80
Thomas, Charles Henry d1941 NotNAT B
Thomas, Christian Friedrich Theodore 1835-1905 BiDAmM
Thomas, Christian Gottfried 1748-1806 Baker 78, NewGrD 80
Thomas, Christine WhoHol A
Thomas, Christopher 1894- AmSCAP 66, ConAmC A
Thomas, Clive 1934- WhoMus 72
Thomas, Cotton BluesWW[port]
Thomas, Dan 1904- IntMPA 75, -76
Thomas, Danny 1914- BiDAmM, CmpEPM, FilmEn, FilmgC, ForYSC, HalFC 80, IntMPA 77, -75, -76, -78, -79, -80, JoeFr[port], MotPP, NewYTET, WhoHol A
Thomas, David WhoHol A
Thomas, David Wynne NewGrD 80
Thomas, Daxon WhoHol A
Thomas, Dick 1915- AmSCAP 66, -80
Thomas, Donald Edward 1943- AmSCAP 80
Thomas, Dorothy 1882- WhThe, WhoStg 1908
Thomas, Dyfrig Rhys 1921- IntWWM 77
Thomas, Dylan 1914-1953 CnMD, EncWT, HalFC 80, McGEWD, ModWD, NotNAT B, PlP&P
Thomas, Earl Morgan 1925- IntWWM 77, -80
Thomas, Edgar Abraham Treharne 1928- WhoMus 72
Thomas, Edna 1886-1974 WhScrn 77, WhoHol B
Thomas, Edward Film 2
Thomas, Edward 1924- AmSCAP 80
Thomas, Edward Francis 1929- WhoMus 72
Thomas, Elizabeth Eva WhoMus 72

Thomas, Elvera 1912- *IntWWM 80*
Thomas, Ernst 1916- *IntWWM 77, -80, NewGrD 80*
Thomas, Eugen 1863-1922 *Baker 78*
Thomas, Evan 1890?-1931 *NewOrJ*
Thomas, Evan 1891- *WhThe*
Thomas, Evan Tom *WhoMus 72*
Thomas, Fathead d1930 *WhoJazz 72*
Thomas, Fatisha *BlkAmP*
Thomas, Foots 1907- *WhoJazz 72*
Thomas, Frank 1889- *Film 2, Vers A[port], WhoHol A*
Thomas, Frank, Jr. 1926- *BiE&WWA, ForYSC, NotNAT*
Thomas, Frank M 1922- *ForYSC*
Thomas, Frank Victor 1916- *IntWWM 77, WhoMus 72*
Thomas, Frankie 1922- *WhoHol A*
Thomas, Gene Eden 1938- *AmSCAP 80*
Thomas, George 1914- *IntMPA 77, -75, -76, -78, -79, -80*
Thomas, George W 1885?- *NewOrJ*
Thomas, Gerald 1920- *FilmEn, FilmgC, HalFC 80, IlWWBF, IntMPA 77, -75, -76, -78, -79, -80*
Thomas, Glynne 1934- *WhoMus 72*
Thomas, Gretchen 1897-1964 *WhScrn 74, -77, WhoHol B*
Thomas, Gunter 1932- *IntWWM 80*
Thomas, Gus 1865-1926 *WhScrn 74, -77*
Thomas, Gustav Adolf 1842-1870 *Baker 78*
Thomas, Gwyn 1913- *ConDr 73, -77, CroCD, EncWT, WhoThe 72, -77*
Thomas, Harry E 1920- *IntMPA 77, -75, -76, -78, -79, -80*
Thomas, Harry H 1892- *IntMPA 75, -76*
Thomas, Helen d1973 *AmSCAP 66, -80, ConAmC*
Thomas, Helga *Film 2*
Thomas, Henry *BluesWW*
Thomas, Henry 1874- *BluesWW*
Thomas, Herbert 1868- *WhThe*
Thomas, Hociel 1904-1952 *BluesWW[port]*
Thomas, Howard *IlWWBF A, IntMPA 77, -75, -76, -78, -79, -80*
Thomas, Irma 1941- *BluesWW[port], RkOn 2[port]*
Thomas, Isaiah 1749-1831 *BiDAmM, NewGrD 80*
Thomas, J W d1878 *NotNAT B*
Thomas, James 1922- *IntMPA 77, -75, -76, -78, -79, -80*
Thomas, James 1926- *BluesWW[port]*
Thomas, Jameson d1939 *WhoHol B*
Thomas, Jameson 1889-1939 *FilmEn, WhScrn 74, -77*
Thomas, Jameson 1892-1939 *Film 2, FilmgC, ForYSC, HalFC 80*
Thomas, Jameson 1893-1939 *IlWWBF[port]*
Thomas, Jamieson d1939 *NotNAT B*
Thomas, Jane *Film 2*
Thomas, Jess 1927- *BiDAmM, CmOp[port], IntWWM 77, -80, MusSN[port], NewEOp 71, NewGrD 80, WhoMus 72, WhoOp 76*
Thomas, Joe 1902- *NewOrJ*
Thomas, Joe 1909- *CmpEPM, EncJzS 70, WhoJazz 72*
Thomas, Joel *WhoHol A*
Thomas, John 1795-1871 *OxMus*
Thomas, John 1826-1913 *Baker 78, NewGrD 80, OxMus*
Thomas, John 1839-1922 *OxMus*
Thomas, John Charles *AmPS B*
Thomas, John Charles 1887-1960 *Film 2, NotNAT B, WhScrn 74, -77, WhoHol B*
Thomas, John Charles 1891-1960 *Baker 78, MusSN[port], NewEOp 71*
Thomas, John Charles 1892-1960 *BiDAmM, CmpEPM*
Thomas, John Hugh 1946- *IntWWM 77*
Thomas, John L 1902-1971 *WhoJazz 72*
Thomas, John Meredith 1930- *IntWWM 77*
Thomas, John Patrick 1941- *ConAmC*
Thomas, John R 1829-1896 *Baker 78, BiDAmM, OxMus*
Thomas, Joseph Lewis 1909- *EncJzS 70*
Thomas, Josephine *BluesWW[port]*
Thomas, Joyce Carol *MorBAP*
Thomas, Juan Maria 1896-1966 *NewGrD 80*
Thomas, Judith 1938- *IntWWM 77, -80*
Thomas, Julius Earl 1953- *AmSCAP 80*
Thomas, Kid *BluesWW[port], NewOrJ[port]*
Thomas, Kurt 1904-1973 *Baker 78, NewGrD 80*
Thomas, Lafayette Jerl 1928-1977 *BluesWW[port]*
Thomas, Larry *AmSCAP 80*
Thomas, Leon Amos 1935- *AmSCAP 80*
Thomas, Leone 1937- *EncJzS 70*
Thomas, Lionel Arthur John 1915- *CreCan 2*
Thomas, Lowell 1892- *FilmgC, HalFC 80, IntMPA 77, -75, -76, -78, -79, -80, NewYTET, WhoHol A*
Thomas, Lowell, Jr. *WhoHol A*
Thomas, Lyndon 1942- *IntWWM 80*
Thomas, Mama Lee *EncFCWM 69*
Thomas, Mansel 1909- *NewGrD 80*
Thomas, Margaret Ann 1942- *IntWWM 80*
Thomas, Marie *WhoHol A*
Thomas, Marjorie *WhoMus 72*
Thomas, Mark Stanton 1931- *AmSCAP 80, IntWWM 77, -80*
Thomas, Marlo *IntMPA 75, -76*
Thomas, Marlo 1937- *FilmEn*
Thomas, Marlo 1938- *IntMPA 77, -78, -79, -80, WhoHol A*
Thomas, Marlo 1944?- *HalFC 80*
Thomas, Mary 1935- *NewGrD 80, WhoMus 72*
Thomas, Mary Virginia *AmSCAP 66, -80*
Thomas, Max *AmSCAP 80*
Thomas, Michael Tilson 1944- *Baker 78, BnBkM 80, MusSN[port], NewGrD 80*
Thomas, Michael Tilson 1945- *BiDAmM*
Thomas, Neville Aubrey 1921- *IntWWM 77, -80*
Thomas, Normearleasa 1957- *BlkWAB*
Thomas, Olive d1920 *MotPP, WhoHol B*
Thomas, Olive 1884-1920 *FilmEn, WhScrn 74, -77*
Thomas, Olive 1888-1920 *FilmgC*
Thomas, Olive 1898-1920 *Film 1, -2, HalFC 80, NotNAT B, TwYS*
Thomas, Pascal 1945- *FilmEn, HalFC 80*
Thomas, Paul Lindsley 1929- *AmSCAP 80, CpmDNM 77, ConAmC*
Thomas, Peter 1925- *IntWWM 80*
Thomas, Peter 1944- *WhoMus 72*
Thomas, Peter Evan *Film 2*
Thomas, Philip M 1949- *DrBlPA, WhoHol A*
Thomas, Phill *AmSCAP 80*
Thomas, Phyllis 1904- *WhThe*
Thomas, Piri *MorBAP*
Thomas, Powys 1925- *CreCan 2*
Thomas, Queenie 1898- *IlWWBF[port]*
Thomas, Queenie 1900- *Film 1, -2*
Thomas, Ralph 1915- *FilmEn, FilmgC, HalFC 80, IlWWBF, IntMPA 77, -75, -76, -78, -79, -80, WhoHol A, WorEFlm*
Thomas, Randy Keith 1954- *AmSCAP 80*
Thomas, Rene 1927- *EncJzS 70*
Thomas, Richard 1951- *FilmgC, HalFC 80, IntMPA 77, -75, -76, -78, -79, -80, WhoHol A*
Thomas, Richard Vaughan 1949- *IntWWM 77, -80*
Thomas, Robert 1944- *CnOxB*
Thomas, Robert Arthur 1919- *WhoMus 72*
Thomas, Robert G 1943- *IntMPA 78, -79, -80*
Thomas, Robert J 1922- *IntMPA 77, -75, -76, -78, -79, -80*
Thomas, Robert L 1929- *WhoOp 76*
Thomas, Rufus 1917- *AmSCAP 80, BiDAmM, BluesWW[port], RkOn*
Thomas, Ruth 1911-1970 *WhScrn 74, -77*
Thomas, Sarah 1942- *WhoMus 72*
Thomas, Scott *WhoHol A*
Thomas, Sippie *BluesWW[port]*
Thomas, Son 1903?-1933? *NewOrJ*
Thomas, Stan *BlkAmP*
Thomas, Stephen d1961 *NotNAT B*
Thomas, Susan Marie 1946- *AmSCAP 80*
Thomas, Sylvia 1931- *NatPD[port]*
Thomas, Terry *FilmgC, HalFC 80, IlWWBF*
Thomas, Theodore 1835-1905 *Baker 78, BnBkM 80[port], NewEOp 71, NewGrD 80, OxMus*
Thomas, Thomas 1829-1913 *OxMus*
Thomas, Thomas Donley 1929- *IntWWM 77*
Thomas, Timmy 1944- *RkOn 2[port]*
Thomas, Tony *WhoHol A*
Thomas, Villesta *WhoHol A*
Thomas, Virginia *Film 2*
Thomas, W Moy d1910 *NotNAT B*
Thomas, Walter Brandon 1856-1914 *EncWT, OxThe*
Thomas, Walter Foots 1907- *CmpEPM*
Thomas, William 1918-1948 *WhScrn 77*
Thomas, William Buckwheat d1968 *WhScrn 74*
Thomas, William C *HalFC 80*
Thomas, William C 1892- *FilmgC*
Thomas, William C 1903- *AmSCAP 66, -80, FilmEn, IntMPA 77, -75, -76, -78, -79, -80*
Thomas, William Sherwood 1944- *AmSCAP 80*
Thomas, Willie B 1912- *BluesWW[port]*
Thomas, Wolfgang Alexander 1874-1918 *Baker 78*
Thomas, Worthia 1907- *NewOrJ[port]*
Thomas, Wyndham Harwood 1938- *IntWWM 77, -80*
Thomas, Yvonne *Film 2*
Thomas Jubilee Singers *BiDAmM*
Thomaschke, Thomas Michael 1943- *WhoOp 76*
Thomashefsky, Bessie d1962 *NotNAT B*
Thomashefsky, Boris 1868-1939 *NotNAT B*
Thomashefsky, Max 1872-1932 *WhScrn 74, -77*
Thomason, Alexander 1926- *AmSCAP 80*
Thomassin, Jeanne *WhThe*
Thome, Diane 1942- *CpmDNM 77, ConAmC, IntWWM 77, -80*
Thome, Francis 1850-1909 *Baker 78, NewGrD 80, NotNAT B*
Thome, Francois Luc Joseph 1850-1909 *NewGrD 80*
Thome, Joel 1939- *ConAmC*
Thome, Karen *WomWMM*
Thomelin, Jacques-Denis 1640?-1693 *NewGrD 80*
Thomish, Frantisek Vaclav *NewGrD 80*
Thommen, Edward *BiE&WWA*
Thommen, Johannes 1711-1783 *NewGrD 80*
Thommessen, Reidar 1889- *IntWWM 77, -80*
Thomolin, Jacques-Denis *NewGrD 80*
Thomopoulos, Anthony D 1938- *IntMPA 79, -80*
Thompkins, Eddie 1908-1943 *WhoJazz 72*
Thompsom, Lotus *Film 2*
Thompson *NewGrD 80*
Thompson, Al *Film 2*
Thompson, Alastair M 1944- *IntWWM 80*
Thompson, Alex *FilmgC, HalFC 80*
Thompson, Alexander M 1861-1948 *NotNAT A, -B, WhThe*
Thompson, Alfred d1895 *NotNAT B*
Thompson, Alfreda Lydia 1911- *AmSCAP 66, -80*
Thompson, Alma I 1912- *AmSCAP 80*
Thompson, Anita *BlksB&W, -C*
Thompson, Ann *AmSCAP 80, NewGrD 80*
Thompson, Arthur Charles 1942- *DrBlPA*
Thompson, Baird M 1950- *ConAmTC*
Thompson, Barbara Gatwood 1923- *IntWWM 77, -80*
Thompson, Benjamin d1816 *NotNAT B*
Thompson, Betty Hermione 1921- *WhoMus 72*
Thompson, Bill d1971 *WhoHol B*
Thompson, Blanche *BlksB&W C*
Thompson, Bob 1924- *AmSCAP 80*
Thompson, Bobby *EncFCWM 69*
Thompson, Brian Michael 1946- *AmSCAP 80*
Thompson, Brian Raymond 1939- *IntWWM 77, -80*
Thompson, Bruce Alfred 1937- *IntWWM 77*
Thompson, Carl G 1931- *IntWWM 77, -80*
Thompson, Carlos *IntMPA 77, -75, -76, -78, -79, -80, WhoHol A*
Thompson, Carlos 1916- *FilmEn, FilmgC, HalFC 80*
Thompson, Carlos 1920?- *ForYSC*
Thompson, Charles *NewGrD 80*
Thompson, Sir Charles 1918- *CmpEPM, EncJzS 70*
Thompson, Clarence *Film 2*
Thompson, Clive 1940- *CnOxB, DrBlPA*
Thompson, Danielle *WomWMM*
Thompson, Dave *ConMuA 80B*
Thompson, David H 1886-1957 *WhScrn 74, -77, WhoHol B*

Thompson, David William 1925- *IntWWM 77, -80*
Thompson, Dean K 1940- *AmSCAP 80*
Thompson, Denman 1833-1911 *ModWD, NotNAT B, WhoStg 1908*
Thompson, Denton *Film 2*
Thompson, Don *EncJzS 70*
Thompson, Donald Bryce 1925- *ConAmC*
Thompson, Donald Winston 1940- *EncJzS 70*
Thompson, Duane 1905- *Film 2, TwYS, WhoHol A*
Thompson, Eddie 1925- *AmSCAP 66*
Thompson, Edward *BlksB&W C*
Thompson, Edward Ian 1931- *IntWWM 77, -80, WhoMus 72*
Thompson, Eli 1924- *BiDAmM, EncJzS 70*
Thompson, Elizabeth Zinn 1941- *IntWWM 77, -80*
Thompson, Eloise Bibb *BlkAmP, MorBAP*
Thompson, Eric 1922- *WhoMus 72*
Thompson, Eric 1929- *WhoThe 77*
Thompson, Eric 1936- *NatPD[port]*
Thompson, Ernest Evan Seton *CreCan 2*
Thompson, Evan *WhoHol A*
Thompson, Evan 1931- *AmSCAP 80*
Thompson, Frank *WhoThe 77*
Thompson, Fred 1884-1949 *EncMT, NotNAT B, WhThe*
Thompson, Fred 1890-1928 *Film 2*
Thompson, Fred W 1901-1969 *AmSCAP 66, -80*
Thompson, Frederick A 1870-1925 *WhScrn 74, -77, WhoHol B*
Thompson, Frederick W 1872-1919 *NotNAT B, WhThe*
Thompson, Garland Lee 1938- *BlkAmP, DrBlPA*
Thompson, George 1868-1929 *Film 2, WhScrn 74, -77, WhoHol B*
Thompson, Gerald Marr 1856-1938 *NotNAT B, WhThe*
Thompson, Grace *Film 1*
Thompson, H S 1825?- *BiDAmM*
Thompson, Hal 1894-1966 *WhScrn 77*
Thompson, Hank 1925- *AmPS A, AmSCAP 66, CounME 74[port], -74A, EncFCWM 69, IlEncCM[port]*
Thompson, Harlan 1890- *AmSCAP 66, -80*
Thompson, Henry William 1925- *BiDAmM*
Thompson, Herbert 1856-1945 *NewGrD 80*
Thompson, Hilarie *WhoHol A*
Thompson, Hugh *Film 1, -2, MotPP*
Thompson, Hugh R 1915- *WhoOp 76*
Thompson, J Denton *Film 2*
Thompson, J Lee 1914- *BiDFilm, -81, DcFM, FilmEn, OxFilm, WhThe, WorEFlm*
Thompson, James 1700-1748 *PlP&P*
Thompson, Jay 1927- *AmSCAP 66, BiE&WWA, NotNAT*
Thompson, Jeff *WhoHol A*
Thompson, Jennings L, Jr. 1927- *AmSCAP 80*
Thompson, Jimmy *WhoHol A*
Thompson, Joan Shepard *AmSCAP 80*
Thompson, John d1634 *OxThe*
Thompson, John Edd, Jr. 1942- *AmSCAP 80*
Thompson, John Herman 1896- *IntMPA 75, -76*
Thompson, John Sylvanus 1889-1963 *Baker 78*
Thompson, John Winter 1867-1951 *Baker 78*
Thompson, Johnny *Film 2*
Thompson, Kay 1913- *AmSCAP 66, -80, CmpEPM, MotPP, WhoHol A*
Thompson, Kenneth *Film 2*
Thompson, Kenneth 1926- *WhoMus 72*
Thompson, Larry 1950- *BlkAmP*
Thompson, Lee *IlWWBF*
Thompson, Leonard *Film 2*
Thompson, Leslie Stephen 1948- *AmSCAP 80*
Thompson, Lotus *Film 2, TwYS*
Thompson, Lucky 1924- *CmpEPM, EncJzS 70*
Thompson, Lydia 1836-1908 *AmPS B, Ent, FamA&A[port], NotNAT B, OxThe*
Thompson, Madeleine d1964 *NotNAT B*
Thompson, Marcus Aurelius 1946- *IntWWM 80*
Thompson, Margaret *Film 1, WomWMM*
Thompson, Marshall *IntMPA 77, -75, -76, -78, -79, -80, MotPP, WhoHol A*
Thompson, Marshall 1925- *FilmEn, HalFC 80, MGM[port]*
Thompson, Marshall 1926- *FilmgC, ForYSC, MovMk, WhoHrs 80[port]*
Thompson, Molly 1879-1928 *WhScrn 74, -77, WhoHol B*
Thompson, Nick *Film 2*
Thompson, Oscar 1887-1945 *Baker 78, BiDAmM, NewGrD 80*
Thompson, Peter d1757? *NewGrD 80*
Thompson, Polly d1933 *WhScrn 77*
Thompson, Randall 1899- *AmSCAP 66, -80, Baker 78, BiDAmM, BnBkM 80, CompSN[port], ConAmC, IntWWM 77, -80, MusMk, NewGrD 80, OxMus*
Thompson, Reginald Milton 1929- *WhoMus 72*
Thompson, Rex *WhoHol A*
Thompson, Richard And Linda *ConMuA 80A, IlEncR*
Thompson, Richard D 1933- *BiE&WWA*
Thompson, Richard Wayne 1948- *IntWWM 77*
Thompson, Robert C 1937- *AmSCAP 80*
Thompson, Robert Ian 1943- *IntWWM 80*
Thompson, Robert Wickens, II 1949- *AmSCAP 80*
Thompson, Ron S *MorBAP*
Thompson, Roy *Film 2*
Thompson, Sada 1929- *BiE&WWA, HalFC 80, IntMPA 79, -80, NotNAT, PlP&P A[port], WhoHol A, WhoThe 72, -77*
Thompson, Samuel d1795 *NewGrD 80*
Thompson, Sheila 1917- *WhoMus 72*
Thompson, Sheila Margaret 1938- *IntWWM 77*
Thompson, Stanley *PupTheA*
Thompson, Sue *IlEncCM[port]*
Thompson, Sue 1926- *BiDAmM, EncFCWM 69, RkOn[port]*
Thompson, Therese 1876-1936 *WhScrn 74, -77*
Thompson, Thomas Perronet 1783-1869 *OxMus*
Thompson, Ulu M 1873-1957 *WhScrn 74, -77, WhoHol B*
Thompson, Ulysses 1888- *BlksBF*
Thompson, Uncle Jimmy 1848-1931 *IlEncCM*
Thompson, Van Denman 1890- *BiDAmM, ConAmC*
Thompson, Victoria *WhoHol A*
Thompson, Virgil 1896- *WorEFlm*
Thompson, W H 1852-1923 *WhThe*
Thompson, W T d1940 *NotNAT B*
Thompson, Will Lamartine 1847-1909 *Baker 78, BiDAmM*
Thompson, William 1913-1971 *WhScrn 74, -77*
Thompson, William H 1852-1923 *Film 1, -2, NotNAT B, WhScrn 77, WhoHol B*
Thompson, Woodman d1955 *NotNAT B*
Thoms, Paul Edward 1936- *IntWWM 77, -80*
Thoms, Virginia *BiE&WWA*
Thoms, William John 1803-1885 *OxMus*
Thoms, William M 1850-1913 *BiDAmM*
Thomsen, Geraldine 1917- *WhoMus 72*
Thomsen, Niels 1945- *IntWWM 77, -80*
Thomson, Alan *IntMPA 77, -75, -76, -78, -79, -80*
Thomson, Andrew Graham 1944- *WhoMus 72*
Thomson, Andrew Mitchell 1779-1831 *OxMus*
Thomson, Beatrix 1900- *WhThe*
Thomson, Bryden 1929- *IntWWM 80, WhoMus 72*
Thomson, Cesar 1857-1931 *Baker 78, NewGrD 80, OxMus*
Thomson, Edward William 1849-1924 *CreCan 2*
Thomson, Fred 1890-1928 *FilmEn, MotPP, TwYS, WhScrn 74, -77, WhoHol B*
Thomson, George 1757-1851 *Baker 78, NewGrD 80, OxMus*
Thomson, Harold 1906- *IntWWM 80, WhoMus 72*
Thomson, Heather 1940- *WhoOp 76*
Thomson, James 1700-1748 *NotNAT B, OxMus, OxThe*
Thomson, James Cutting 1909- *IntWWM 77, -80*
Thomson, Joan Lewis 1940- *IntWWM 77, -80*
Thomson, John 1805-1841 *Baker 78, NewGrD 80, OxMus*
Thomson, Kenneth d1967 *MotPP, WhoHol B*
Thomson, Kenneth 1889-1967 *Film 2*
Thomson, Kenneth 1899-1967 *ForYSC, IntMPA 75, -76, TwYS, WhScrn 74, -77*
Thomson, Mary Ann 1834-1923 *BiDAmM*
Thomson, Millard S 1918- *ConAmC*
Thomson, Pat *WomWMM A, -B*
Thomson, Rick Michael 1954- *AmSCAP 80*
Thomson, Thomas John 1877-1917 *CreCan 1*
Thomson, Tom 1877-1917 *CreCan 1*
Thomson, Virgil 1896- *AmSCAP 66, -80, Baker 78, BiDAmM, BiE&WWA, BnBkM 80, CmOp, CompSN[port], CpmDNM 75, -80, ConAmC, DancEn 78, DcCom 77, DcCom&M 79, DcCM, IntWWM 77, -80, MusMk, NewEOp 71, NewGrD 80[port], NotNAT, OxFilm, OxMus, WhoMus 72*
Thomson, Warren Milton 1935- *IntWWM 77, -80*
Thomson, William 1684?-1760? *NewGrD 80*
Thomson, William Ennis 1927- *AmSCAP 66, ConAmC*
Thonger, Aubrey *WhoMus 72*
Thooft, Willem Frans 1829-1900 *Baker 78*
Thopul, Timolphus *NewGrD 80*
Thor, Jerome 1915- *ForYSC*
Thor, Jerome 1920- *IntMPA 77, -75, -76, -78, -79, -80, WhoHol A*
Thor, Larry d1976 *ForYSC, WhoHol C*
Thorarinsson, Jon 1917- *NewGrD 80*
Thorarinsson, Leifur 1934- *Baker 78, IntWWM 77, -80, NewGrD 80*
Thorberg, Kerstin 1896-1970 *CmOp*
Thorborg, Kerstin 1896-1970 *Baker 78, MusSN[port], NewGrD 80*
Thorborg, Kirsten 1896-1970 *NewEOp 71*
Thorburn, H M 1884-1924 *NotNAT B, WhThe*
Thorburn, June 1931-1967 *FilmgC, HalFC 80, MotPP, WhScrn 74, -77, WhoHol B*
Thordal, Vagn 1918- *IntWWM 77, -80*
Thordarson, Sigurdur 1895-1968 *NewGrD 80*
Thordsen, Kelly *IntMPA 77, -75, -76, -78, WhoHol A*
Thoren, Kenneth Alexander 1926- *AmSCAP 80*
Thoresby, Ralph 1658-1725 *OxMus*
Thorette, Pierre 1620?-1684 *NewGrD 80*
Thorgersen, Ed *IntMPA 77, -75, -76, -78, -79*
Thori, Hermogene Da 1555?-1623? *NewGrD 80*
Thorley, Victor *WhoHol A*
Thorn, Geoffrey d1905 *NotNAT B*
Thorn, Lee E 1919- *IntMPA 77, -75, -76, -78, -79*
Thornburgh, Donald Wayne 1894- *IntMPA 75, -76*
Thornby, Robert T 1889- *TwYS A*
Thorndike, Andrew 1909- *DcFM, FilmgC, HalFC 80, OxFilm, WorEFlm*
Thorndike, Annelie 1925- *OxFilm, WomWMM, WorEFlm[port]*
Thorndike, Arthur Russell 1885- *WhThe*
Thorndike, Eileen 1891-1953 *OxThe, PlP&P*
Thorndike, Eileen 1891-1954 *NotNAT B, WhThe*
Thorndike, Lucille d1935 *Film 2, WhoHol B*
Thorndike, Oliver 1918-1954 *WhScrn 74, -77, WhoHol B*
Thorndike, Russell 1885- *Film 2*
Thorndike, Russell 1885-1972 *OxThe, PlP&P, WhScrn 77, WhoHol B*
Thorndike, Russell 1885-1973 *CnThe*
Thorndike, Sybil 1882- *BiE&WWA, CnThe, MotPP, MovMk, NotNAT A, OxThe, WhoHol A*
Thorndike, Sybil 1882-1975 *Film 2*
Thorndike, Sybil 1882-1976 *EncWT, Ent[port], FilmEn, FilmgC, HalFC 80, IlWWBF, -A, NotNAT B, PlP&P, WhoThe 72, -77*
Thorndyke, Lucyle 1885-1935 *WhScrn 74, -77*
Thorndyke, Sybil 1882-1976 *FilmAG WE*
Thorne, Ann Maria Mestayer d1881 *OxThe*
Thorne, Charles Robert, Jr. 1840-1883 *NotNAT B, OxThe*
Thorne, Charles Robert, Sr. 1814-1893 *OxThe*
Thorne, Clara d1915 *NotNAT B*
Thorne, Dick 1905-1957 *WhScrn 74, -77*
Thorne, Dyanne *WhoHol A*
Thorne, Edward Henry 1834-1916 *Baker 78*
Thorne, Eric d1922 *NotNAT B*
Thorne, Francis 1922- *AmSCAP 66, Baker 78, CpmDNM 77, -80, ConAmC, DcCM, IntWWM 77, -80, NewGrD 80*
Thorne, George Hope *WhoMus 72*
Thorne, George Tyrrel 1856-1922 *NotNAT B, OxThe*

Thorne, John 1519?-1573 *NewGrD 80, OxMus*
Thorne, Joy Coghill *CreCan 2*
Thorne, Phillip Martin 1951- *IntWWM 80*
Thorne, Robert 1881-1965 *Film 2, WhScrn 74, -77, WhoHol B*
Thorne, Sarah 1836-1899 *NotNAT B*
Thorne, Sarah 1837-1899 *OxThe*
Thorne, Sylvia d1922 *NotNAT B*
Thorne, Thomas 1841-1918 *NotNAT B, OxThe, WhThe*
Thorne, Mrs. Thomas d1884 *NotNAT B*
Thorne, William L *Film 2*
Thornecroft, John Keith 1936- *IntWWM 77*
Thorner, Helmut 1903- *IntWWM 77, -80*
Thorneycroft, G B 1893- *IntMPA 75*
Thornhill, Claude d1965 *BgBands 74[port]*
Thornhill, Claude 1908-1965 *AmSCAP 66, -80, BiDAmM, WhScrn 74, -77, WhoHol B*
Thornhill, Claude 1909-1965 *Baker 78, CmpEPM, IlEncJ, WhoJazz 72*
Thornhill, Margaret Louise 1950- *IntWWM 77, -80*
Thornsby, Lee *AmSCAP 80*
Thornton, Bonnell 1724-1768 *OxMus*
Thornton, Bonnie *AmPS B*
Thornton, Clifford Edward, III 1936- *EncJzS 70*
Thornton, Dennison S 1909- *IntMPA 77, -75, -76, -78*
Thornton, Edith *Film 2, TwYS*
Thornton, Edna 1880?-1964 *CmOp*
Thornton, F Martin *IlWWBF*
Thornton, Frank d1918 *NotNAT B*
Thornton, Frank 1921- *HalFC 80, WhoHol A, WhoThe 72, -77*
Thornton, Gene *PupTheA*
Thornton, Gladys 1899-1964 *WhScrn 74, -77, WhoHol B*
Thornton, James 1861-1938 *AmPS, AmSCAP 66, -80, BiDAmM, NotNAT B, PopAmC, Sw&Ld B*
Thornton, William 1919- *ConAmC*
Thornton, Willie Mae 1926- *BluesWW[port], RkOn*
Thornwall, Francis *Film 2*
Thorogood, Alfreda 1942- *CnOxB*
Thorp, Joseph Peter 1873- *WhThe*
Thorpe, George 1891-1961 *WhThe*
Thorpe, Gordon *Film 2*
Thorpe, Jerry 1930?- *FilmgC, HalFC 80, NewYTET*
Thorpe, Jim 1888-1953 *HalFC 80, WhScrn 74, -77, WhoHol B*
Thorpe, Jim 1889-1953 *ForYSC*
Thorpe, Jonathan 1943- *CnOxB*
Thorpe, Marion *IntWWM 77, -80*
Thorpe, Morgan *Film 1*
Thorpe, Raymond 1931- *WhoMus 72*
Thorpe, Richard 1896- *CmMov, FilmEn, Film 2, FilmgC, HalFC 80, IntMPA 77, -75, -76, -78, -79, -80, TwYS A, WhoHol A, WorEFlm*
Thorpe, Ted 1917-1970 *WhScrn 77*
Thorpe-Bates, Peggy 1914- *WhoHol A, WhoThe 72, -77*
Thorpe Davie, Cedric 1913- *NewGrD 80*
Thorson, Russell *WhoHol A*
Thorsteinsdottir-Stross, Asdis 1939- *IntWWM 77, -80*
Thorsteinsson, Bjarni 1861-1938 *NewGrD 80, OxMus*
Thorue, Anna V *BlkAmP*
Thouret, Georg 1855-1924 *Baker 78*
Thow, George Albert 1908- *AmSCAP 66, -80, CmpEPM*
Thrall, Roy Summers 1917- *IntWWM 77*
Thrane, Carl 1837-1916 *NewGrD 80*
Thrane, Valdemar 1790-1828 *OxMus*
Thrane, Waldemar 1790-1828 *Baker 78, NewGrD 80*
Thrasher, Ethelyn 1912- *BiE&WWA, NotNAT*
Threadgill, Francis Dycus, Jr. 1939- *WhoMus 72*
Threatte, Charles 1940- *ConAmC*
Three Degrees, The *RkOn 2[port]*
Three Dog Night *BiDAmM, ConMuA 80A, IlEncR, RkOn 2[port]*
Three Friends, The *RkOn*
Three Keys, The *BiDAmM*
Three Sounds, The *BiDAmM*
Three Stooges, The *FilmEn, ForYSC, Funs[port], GrMovC[port], JoeFr[port], MotPP, What 4[port], WhoHrs 80[port]*
Three Suns, The *CmpEPM*
Threlkeld, Budge 1922- *BiE&WWA*
Thring, Edward 1821-1887 *OxMus*
Thring, Frank *CmMov, FilmgC, ForYSC, HalFC 80, WhoHol A*
Throckmorton, Cleon 1897-1965 *BiE&WWA, NotNAT B, PlP&P, WhThe*
Throckmorton, James Fron 1941- *AmSCAP 80*
Throne, Malachi *WhoHol A*
Thropp, Clara d1960 *NotNAT B*
Thrower, Fred M 1910- *IntMPA 77, -75, -76*
Thuille, Ludwig 1861-1907 *Baker 78, NewGrD 80, OxMus*
Thuillier, Emilio *WhThe*
Thulin, Ingrid 1929- *BiDFilm, -81, EncWT, FilmEn, FilmgC, ForYSC, HalFC 80, IntMPA 77, -75, -76, -78, -79, -80, MotPP, MovMk, OxFilm, WhoHol A, WomWMM, WorEFlm[port]*
Thuma, Frantisek Ignac Antonin *NewGrD 80*
Thumb, Tom d1926 *WhScrn 77*
Thumb, Tom 1838-1883 *Ent[port], NotNAT B*
Thumb, Mrs. Tom 1841-1919 *WhScrn 77*
Thummler, David Gotthilf 1801-1847 *NewGrD 80*
Thumont, Burk *NewGrD 80*
Thumoth, Burk *NewGrD 80, OxMus*
Thuna, Lee *BlkAmP*
Thunder *Film 2*
Thunder, Henry Gordon, Jr. 1865-1958 *BiDAmM*
Thunder, Henry Gordon, Sr. 1832-1881 *BiDAmM*
Thunder, Johnny 1941- *RkOn*
Thunder Cloud, Chief 1889-1955 *HolCA[port]*
Thunder Cloud, Chief 1899-1955 *IntMPA 77, -76, -79, -80*
Thunderclap Newman *ConMuA 80A, IlEncR[port], RkOn 2[port]*
Thundercloud, Chief 1899-1955 *FilmEn, ForYSC, IntMPA 75, -78*
Thundercloud, Chief 1900-1955 *FilmgC, Vers A[port]*
Thunen, Tommy 1908- *IntWWM 77*
Thurber, J Kent 1892-1957 *WhScrn 74, -77*
Thurber, James 1894-1961 *FilmgC, HalFC 80, McGEWD[port], NotNAT A, -B*
Thurburn, Gwynneth 1899- *WhoThe 72, -77*
Thuren, Hjalmar Lauritz 1873-1912 *Baker 78, NewGrD 80*
Thuring, Joachim *NewGrD 80*
Thuring, Johann d1635 *NewGrD 80*
Thuringus, Joachim *NewGrD 80*
Thurinomarus *NewGrD 80*
Thurlings, Adolf 1844-1915 *Baker 78*
Thurlow, Alan John 1947- *IntWWM 77*
Thurm, Joachim 1927- *IntWWM 80*
Thurman, Bill *WhoHol A*
Thurman, Mary 1894-1925 *Film 1, -2, MotPP, TwYS, WhScrn 74, -77, WhoHol B*
Thurman, Wallace 1901-1934 *BlkAmP, MorBAP*
Thurman, Wallace 1902- *DrBlPA*
Thurn Und Taxis *NewGrD 80*
Thurner, Frederic Eugene De 1785-1827 *Baker 78*
Thurner, Georges d1910 *NotNAT B*
Thurnmaier, John *NewGrD 80*
Thurnmayer, Jean *NewGrD 80*
Thursby, Emma 1845-1931 *Baker 78*
Thursby, Emma Cecilia 1857-1931 *BiDAmM*
Thurschmidt, Carl *NewGrD 80*
Thurston, Carol 1923-1969 *ForYSC, IntMPA 77, -75, -76, -78, -79, -80, WhScrn 77, WhoHol B*
Thurston, Charles E 1869-1940 *Film 2, WhScrn 74, -77, WhoHol B*
Thurston, Elsie *WhoMus 72*
Thurston, Ernest Temple 1879-1933 *NotNAT B, WhThe*
Thurston, Ethel Holbrooke 1911- *IntWWM 77, -80*
Thurston, Frederick 1901-1953 *NewGrD 80*
Thurston, Harry d1955 *NotNAT B, WhScrn 77*
Thurston, Helene *PupTheA*
Thurston, Howard 1869-1936 *MagIID*
Thurston, Jane Jacquelin 1915- *AmSCAP 80*
Thurston, Muriel 1875-1943 *WhScrn 74, -77*
Thurston, Ted *WhoHol A*
Thury, Ilona d1953 *NotNAT B*
Thurzo, Gabor 1912- *CroCD*
Thyard, Pontus De *NewGrD 80*
Thybo, Leif 1922- *Baker 78, NewGrD 80*
Thyiades *NewGrD 80*
Thym, Jurgen 1943- *IntWWM 77, -80*
Thysius, Johan 1621-1653 *NewGrD 80*
Thyssen, Greta 1935?- *ForYSC, WhoHol A, WhoHrs 80[port]*
Tiazza, Dario d1974 *WhoHol B*
Tibaldi, Giuseppe 1729-1790? *NewGrD 80*
Tibaldi Chiesa, Maria 1896- *Baker 78*
Tibay, Zoltan 1910- *WhoMus 72*
Tibbet, Lawrence 1896-1960 *NewGrD 80*
Tibbett, Lawrence 1896-1960 *AmPS B, Baker 78, BiDAmM, BnBkM 80, CmOp, CmpEPM, FilmEn, Film 2, FilmgC, ForYSC, HalFC 80[port], MGM[port], MusSN[port], NewEOp 71, NewGrD 80, NotNAT B, WhScrn 74, -77, WhThe, WhoHol B*
Tibbits, George 1933- *NewGrD 80*
Tibbles, George F 1913- *AmSCAP 66*
Tibbles, George F 1923- *AmSCAP 80*
Tibbs, Casey *WhoHol A*
Tiberi, Frank 1928- *EncJzS 70*
Tiberti, Giacomo 1631-1689 *NewGrD 80*
Tiburce, Francois *NewGrD 80*
Tiburtino, Giuliano 1510?-1569 *NewGrD 80*
Tiburtius Van Brussel 1605?-1669 *NewGrD 80*
Tiby, Ottavio 1891-1955 *Baker 78, NewGrD 80*
Ticciati, Niso 1924- *WhoMus 72*
Tice, Steve *WhoHol A*
Ticehurst, Marguerite *WhoMus 72*
Tich, Little 1868-1928 *Ent, WhThe*
Tichacek, Josef 1807-1886 *NewGrD 80[port]*
Tichatschek, Joseph A 1807-1886 *Baker 78, BnBkM 80, CmOp, NewEOp 71, NewGrD 80[port]*
Tichenor, Edna *Film 2, WhoHrs 80[port]*
Tichenor, Tom 1923- *BiE&WWA, NotNAT*
Tichy, Georg 1949- *WhoOp 76*
Tickell, Richard d1793 *NotNAT B*
Tickle, Frank 1893-1955 *NotNAT B, WhThe, WhoHol B*
Tickner, Ronald 1920- *IntWWM 77, WhoMus 72*
Tico And The Triumphs *RkOn*
Tidblad, Inga 1901-1975 *EncWT, Ent[port]*
Tidblad, Inga 1902-1975 *WhScrn 77, WhoHol C*
Tidboald, David 1926- *WhoOp 76*
Tiden, Fritz d1931 *NotNAT B*
Tiden, Zelma *Film 2*
Tidmarsh, Ferdinand 1883-1922 *Film 1, WhScrn 77*
Tidmarsh, Vivian 1896-1941 *NotNAT B, WhThe*
Tidyman, Ernest *HalFC 80, IntMPA 77, -76, -78, -79, -80*
Tieck, Johann Ludwig 1773-1853 *McGEWD[port]*
Tieck, Ludwig 1773-1853 *CnThe, EncWT, Ent, NewGrD 80, NotNAT B, OxThe, REnWD[port]*
Tiedtke, Jacob 1875-1960 *WhoHol B*
Tiedtke, Jakob 1875-1960 *Film 2, WhScrn 74, -77*
Tieffenbrucker *Baker 78, NewGrD 80*
Tieffenbrucker, Gaspar, The Elder 1514-1571 *NewGrD 80[port]*
Tieffenbrucker, Gaspar, The Younger *NewGrD 80*
Tieffenbrucker, Jachomo *NewGrD 80*
Tieffenbrucker, Jacob *NewGrD 80*
Tieffenbrucker, Jean *NewGrD 80*
Tieffenbrucker, Johann *NewGrD 80*
Tieffenbrucker, Leonardo, The Elder *NewGrD 80*
Tieffenbrucker, Leonardo, The Younger *NewGrD 80*
Tieffenbrucker, Magno, The Elder *NewGrD 80*
Tieffenbrucker, Magno, The Younger *NewGrD 80*
Tieffenbrucker, Michael d1585? *NewGrD 80*

Tieffenbrucker, Ulrich *NewGrD 80*
Tieffenbrucker, Wendelin *NewGrD 80*
Tiehsen, Otto 1817-1849 *Baker 78*
Tielke, Joachim 1641-1719 *NewGrD 80*
Tiella, Marco 1930- *IntWWM 77, -80*
Tieme, Clemens *NewGrD 80*
T'ien, Han 1898- *REnWD[port]*
Tienot, Yvonne 1897- *NewGrD 80*
Tiensuu, Jukka 1948- *Baker 78, IntWWM 77, -80*
Tiercelin, Louis 1849- *WhThe*
Tierney, Gene 1920- *BiDFilm, -81, CmMov, FilmEn, FilmgC, ForYSC, HalFC 80, IntMPA 77, -75, -76, -78, -79, -80, MotPP, MovMk[port], What 5[port], WhoHol A, WorEFlm[port]*
Tierney, Harry 1890-1965 *AmSCAP 66, -80, Baker 78, BiDAmM, BiE&WWA, CmpEPM, ConAmC, EncMT, HalFC 80, NewCBMT, NewGrD 80, NotNAT B*
Tierney, Harry 1894-1965 *WhThe*
Tierney, Harry 1895-1965 *AmPS, BestMus, PopAmC[port], PopAmC SUP*
Tierney, Harry Austin, Jr. 1934- *AmSCAP 80*
Tierney, Lawrence 1919- *FilmEn, FilmgC, ForYSC, HalFC 80, IntMPA 77, -75, -76, -78, -79, -80, MotPP, MovMk, WhoHol A*
Tierney, Thomas John 1942- *AmSCAP 80*
Tiersch, Otto 1838-1892 *Baker 78*
Tiersot, Julien 1857-1936 *Baker 78, NewGrD 80*
Tiessen, Heinz 1887-1971 *Baker 78, DcCM, NewGrD 80*
Tietjen, Andrew 1911-1953 *BiDAmM*
Tietjen, Heinz 1881-1967 *CmOp, NewEOp 71*
Tietjens, Paul 1877-1943 *AmSCAP 66, -80, ConAmC, NotNAT B*
Tietjens, Therese 1831-1877 *CmOp*
Tietjens, Therese 1831-1887 *NewGrD 80[port]*
Tietjens, Therese Cathline Johanna 1831-1877 *OxMus*
Tietjens, Therese Johanne Alexandra 1831-1877 *Baker 78*
Tietz, Anton Ferdinand *NewGrD 80*
Tiffin, Pamela 1942- *FilmEn, FilmgC, ForYSC, HalFC 80, IntMPA 77, -75, -76, -78, -79, -80, MotPP, WhoHol A*
Tigerman, Gary *WhoHol A*
Tiggeler, Steffen 1931- *WhoOp 76*
Tighe, Harry 1885?-1935 *NotNAT B, WhScrn 74, -77, WhoHol B*
Tighe, Kevin 1944- *AmSCAP 80, WhoHol A*
Tigranian, Armen 1879-1950 *Baker 78*
Tigranyan, Armen Tigran 1879-1950 *NewGrD 80*
Tigranyan, Nikoghayos Fadeyi 1856-1951 *NewGrD 80*
Tigrini, Orazio 1535?-1591 *NewGrD 80*
Tijardovic, Ivo 1895- *Baker 78*
Tik, Henricus *NewGrD 80*
Tikhomirnova, Irina Victorovna 1917- *CnOxB*
Tikhomirov, Vassili Dimitrievich 1876-1956 *CnOxB*
Tikhomirov, Vassily 1876-1956 *DancEn 78*
Tikhonov, Vladimir Petrovich 1935- *CnOxB*
Tikka, Kari 1946- *Baker 78, IntWWM 77, -80*
Tikotsky, Evgeny Karlovich 1893-1970 *Baker 78, NewGrD 80*
Tilbury, Adelina *NewGrD 80*
Tilbury, Dorothy Elizabeth 1946- *IntWWM 80*
Tilbury, John 1936- *IntWWM 77, -80, NewGrD 80*
Tilbury, Zeffie 1863- *Film 1*
Tilbury, Zeffie 1863-1945 *Film 2, ForYSC, TwYS*
Tilbury, Zeffie 1863-1950 *FilmgC, HalFC 80, NotNAT B, Vers B[port], WhScrn 74, -77, WhThe, WhoHol B*
Tilden, Beau *WhoHol A*
Tilden, Bill 1893-1953 *NotNAT B, WhScrn 74, -77, WhoHol B*
Tilden, Milano C d1951 *NotNAT B*
Tilden, William T *Film 2*
Tildsley, Peter d1962 *NotNAT B*
Tilghman, William Matthew 1854-1924 *WhScrn 77*
Tilkin, Felix *NewGrD 80*
Till, Eric 1929- *CreCan 2, FilmgC, HalFC 80*
Till, George William 1866-1947 *BiDAmM*
Till, Jakob 1713-1783 *BiDAmM*
Till, Jenny *WhoHol A*
Till, Johann Christian 1762-1844 *Baker 78, NewGrD 80*
Till, John *PupTheA*
Till, Louisa *PupTheA*
Till, Maurice 1926- *NewGrD 80*
Tiller, John d1925 *NotNAT B*
Tiller, Mrs. John *CnOxB*
Tiller, Nadia *WhoHol A*
Tiller, Nadja 1929- *FilmAG WE, FilmEn, HalFC 80, WorEFlm*
Tiller, Najda 1929- *FilmgC*
Tilles, Ken 1912-1970 *WhScrn 77*
Tillett, Jeffery Nicholas Lewis 1927- *WhoMus 72*
Tillett, Wilbur Fisk 1854-1936 *BiDAmM*
Tilley, John d1935 *NotNAT B*
Tilley, Vesta 1864-1952 *Ent, NotNAT A, -B, OxThe, PlP&P, WhThe*
Tillier, Joseph Bonaventure 1750?-1790? *NewGrD 80*
Tilliere, Joseph Bonaventure 1750?-1790? *NewGrD 80*
Tillis, Frederick Charles 1930- *BiDAmM, CpmDNM 75, -79, ConAmC, DrBlPA, IntWWM 77, -80*
Tillis, Mel 1932- *BiDAmM, CounME 74[port], -74A, EncFCWM 69, IlEncCM[port]*
Tillius, Sven-Gunnar Carl 1937- *WhoOp 76*
Tillman, Cornelius 1887?- *NewOrJ*
Tillman, Edwin Earl 1900- *AmSCAP 66, -80*
Tillman, Floyd 1914- *BiDAmM, EncFCWM 69, IlEncCM[port]*
Tillman, John 1916- *IntMPA 75*
Tillman, Katherine Davis *BlkAmP*
Tillman, Wilbert 1898-1967 *NewOrJ[port]*
Tillotson, Johnny 1939- *RkOn*
Tillstrom, Burr 1917- *AmSCAP 66, -80, IntMPA 77, -75, -76, -78, -79, -80, PupTheA, PupTheA SUP*
Tilly, Vesta 1864-1952 *WhoStg 1906, -1908*
Tillyard, H J W 1881-1968 *NewGrD 80*
Tillyard, Henry Julius Wetenhall 1881-1968 *Baker 78, OxMus*
Tilman, Alfred 1848-1895 *Baker 78*
Tilmant, Alexandre *NewGrD 80*
Tilmant, Theophile 1799-1878 *Baker 78, NewGrD 80*
Tilmouth, Michael 1930- *IntWWM 77, -80, NewGrD 80, WhoMus 72*
Tilney, Colin 1933- *NewGrD 80, WhoMus 72*
Tilney, Sir Edmund *OxThe*
Tilson Thomas, Michael 1944- *IntWWM 77, -80, WhoMus 72*
Tilton, Edwin Booth 1860-1926 *Film 1, -2, WhScrn 74, -77, WhoHol B*
Tilton, George 1922- *AmSCAP 66, -80*
Tilton, James A *Film 2*
Tilton, James F 1937- *NotNAT, WhoThe 72, -77*
Tilton, Liz *CmpEPM*
Tilton, Martha *WhoHol A*
Tilton, Martha 1915- *HalFC 80, What 5[port]*
Tilton, Martha 1918?- *CmpEPM*
Tilton, Webb 1915- *BiE&WWA*
Tim, Tiny 1930?- *BiDAmM*
Timante, Bernardo Delle Girandole *NewGrD 80*
Timari, Frank J 1948- *IntWWM 77*
Timberg, Anders Richard Vilhelm 1905- *WhoMus 72*
Timberg, Herman 1892-1952 *WhScrn 74, -77, WhoHol B*
Timberg, Sammy 1903- *AmSCAP 66, -80*
Timberliners *BiDAmM*
Timblin, Slim d1962 *NotNAT B*
Timbrooke, Harry *Film 2*
Time, Clemens *NewGrD 80*
Time-Tones, The *RkOn*
Timer *NewGrD 80*
Timm, Henry Christian 1811-1892 *Baker 78, BiDAmM, NewGrD 80*
Timm, Jeanne Margaret *IntWWM 77, -80*
Timm, Kenneth N 1934- *AmSCAP 80, IntWWM 77, -80*
Timm, Wladimir 1885-1958 *AmSCAP 66, -80*
Timmer *NewGrD 80*
Timmer, Anton 1706-1764 *NewGrD 80*
Timmer, Joseph 1696-1750 *NewGrD 80*
Timmer, Joseph Carl 1698-1785 *NewGrD 80*
Timmer, Joseph Ferdinand 1708-1771 *NewGrD 80*
Timmer, Leopold 1701-1757 *NewGrD 80*
Timmer, Mathias 1662?-1742 *NewGrD 80*
Timmermans, Ferdinand 1891- *Baker 78*
Timmermans, Ferdinandus 1891- *IntWWM 77, -80*
Timmons, Bobby 1935- *EncJzS 70*
Timmons, Joseph 1897-1933 *WhScrn 74, -77*
Timmons, Robert Henry 1935- *EncJzS 70*
Timms, Nigel Frederick Ernest 1953- *IntWWM 77*
Timofeyeva, Nina 1935- *DancEn 78[port]*
Timofeyeva, Nina Vladimirovna 1935- *CnOxB*
Timontayev, A *Film 2*
Timotheus 450?BC-360?BC *NewGrD 80*
Timpano, Paola Francesca 1924- *AmSCAP 80*
Tin Tin *RkOn 2[port]*
Tinayre, Yves 1891-1972 *Baker 78*
Tinazzoli, Agostino d1723? *NewGrD 80*
Tincher, Fay *Film 1, -2, MotPP, TwYS*
Tinctor, Johannes 1435?-1511? *NewGrD 80*
Tinctoris, Johannes 1435-1511 *Baker 78, NewGrD 80*
Tinctoris, Johannes 1436?-1511 *BnBkM 80*
Tindal, Mary Klugh Garner 1920- *IntWWM 77*
Tindale, Franklin M 1871-1947 *WhScrn 74, -77*
Tindall, Loren 1921-1973 *WhScrn 77, WhoHol B*
Tindley, Charles Albert 1851-1933 *NewGrD 80*
Tinel, Edgar 1854-1912 *Baker 78, NewGrD 80, OxMus*
Tinel, Emiel Jozef 1885- *IntWWM 77, WhoMus 72*
Ting-Liang-Tchao *Film 2*
Tingley, Christopher 1950- *IntWWM 77*
Tingwell, Charles 1917- *FilmgC, HalFC 80, WhoHol A*
Tini *NewGrD 80*
Tinker, Christopher Geoffrey 1950- *IntWWM 77*
Tinker, Grant A 1926- *IntMPA 77, -75, -76, -78, -79, -80, NewYTET*
Tinley, Ned *Film 1*
Tinling, James 1889-1955 *IntMPA 77, -75, -76, -78, -79, -80*
Tinling, James 1889-1967 *FilmEn*
Tinling, James 1899?-1955 *FilmgC, HalFC 80*
Tinne, Alex *WhoHol A*
Tinney, Cal 1908- *JoeFr*
Tinney, Frank 1878-1940 *CmpEPM, JoeFr, NotNAT B, WhThe, WhoHol B*
Tinodi, Sebestyen 1505?-1556 *NewGrD 80*
Tinsley, Pauline Cecilia 1940- *CmOp[port], IntWWM 77, -80, NewGrD 80, WhoMus 72, WhoOp 76*
Tinsman, Sylvia McKaye 1916-1975 *WhScrn 77*
Tinti, Gabriele *WhoHol A*
Tintner, Georg 1917- *NewGrD 80*
Tinturin, Peter 1910- *AmSCAP 66, -80, CmpEPM*
Tiny Alice *BiDAmM*
Tiny Tim 1930?- *WhoHol A*
Tiny Tim 1933- *RkOn 2[port]*
Tio, Lorenzo, Jr. 1880-1934 *BiDAmM*
Tio, Lorenzo, Jr. 1884-1933 *NewOrJ, WhoJazz 72*
Tio, Lorenzo, Sr. 1865?-1920 *BiDAmM, NewOrJ*
Tio, Louis 1863-1927 *BiDAmM*
Tio, Luis 1863?-1927 *NewOrJ*
Tiomkin, Dimitri *IntMPA 77, -75, -76, -78, -79, -80*
Tiomkin, Dimitri 1894-1979 *NewGrD 80*
Tiomkin, Dimitri 1899-1979 *AmPS, BiDAmM, CmMov, DcFM, FilmEn, IntWWM 77, MusMk, PopAmC[port], PopAmC SUP, WhoHrs 80*
Tiomkin, Dmitri 1894-1979 *Baker 78, ConAmC*
Tiomkin, Dmitri 1899-1979 *CmpEPM, FilmgC, HalFC 80, OxFilm, WorEFlm*
Tipei, Sever 1943- *ConAmC*
Tipler, Brian Archer 1933- *WhoMus 72*
Tippe, William *NewGrD 80*
Tippett, Elizabeth 1939- *WhoMus 72*
Tippett, Sir Michael 1905- *Baker 78,*

BnBkM 80, CmOp, CompSN[port], DcCom 77[port], DcCom&M 79, DcCM, IntWWM 77, -80, MusMk[port], NewEOp 71, NewGrD 80[port], OxMus, WhoMus 72
Tippit, Wayne *WhoHol A*
Tipple, Colin John 1942- *IntWWM 77, -80*
Tipton, Carl B 1925- *BiDAmM*
Tipton, Clyde 1934- *ConAmC*
Tipton, George Aliceson 1932- *AmSCAP 80*
Tipton, Julius R, III 1942- *ConAmC*
Tipton, Thomas 1926- *WhoOp 76*
Tirabassi, Antonio 1882-1947 *Baker 78*
Tircuit, Heuwell 1931- *Baker 78, ConAmC*
Tirella, Eduardo 1924-1966 *WhScrn 77*
Tirimo 1942- *IntWWM 80*
Tirimo, Martino 1942- *IntWWM 77*
Tirindelli, Pier Adolfo 1858-1937 *Baker 78*
Tiroff, James d1975 *WhScrn 77*
Tirrell, Audrey Nordin *PupTheA*
Tirro, Frank Pascale 1935- *AmSCAP 80, ConAmC, IntWWM 80*
Tirso DeMolina 1571?-1648 *EncWT, OxThe, REnWD[port]*
Tirso DeMolina 1584?-1648 *Ent*
Tisch, Laurence A 1922- *IntMPA 77, -75, -76*
Tisch, Laurence A 1923- *IntMPA 78, -79, -80*
Tisch, Preston Robert 1926- *IntMPA 77, -75, -76, -78, -79, -80*
Tischer, Gerhard 1877-1959 *Baker 78*
Tischer, Johann Nikolaus 1707-1774 *NewGrD 80*
Tischhauser, Franz 1921- *Baker 78, IntWWM 80, WhoMus 72*
Tischler, Hans 1915- *Baker 78, IntWWM 77, -80, NewGrD 80*
Tisdale, Clarence 1900?- *NewOrJ*
Tisdale, William *NewGrD 80*
Tishchenko, Boris Ivanovich 1939- *Baker 78, NewGrD 80*
Tishingham, Rita 1940- *ForYSC*
Tishman, Fay 1913- *AmSCAP 66, -80*
Tisne, Antoine 1932- *Baker 78, NewGrD 80*
Tisse, Edouard 1897-1961 *FilmgC, HalFC 80*
Tisse, Eduard Kasimirovich 1897-1961 *DcFM*
Tisse, Edvard 1897-1961 *OxFilm*
Tisse, Edward 1897-1961 *FilmEn, WorEFlm*
Tissier, Jean 1896-1973 *FilmAG WE, FilmEn, WhScrn 77, WhoHol B*
Tissot, Alice 1890-1971 *Film 2, WhScrn 74, -77, WhoHol B*
Titayna *WomWMM*
Titcomb, Caldwell 1926- *ConAmTC, IntWWM 77, -80*
Titcomb, Everett 1884-1968 *ConAmC*
Titcomb, H Everett 1884- *BiDAmM*
Titelouze, Jean 1563-1633 *Baker 78, MusMk, OxMus*
Titelouze, Jehan 1562?-1633 *NewGrD 80*
Titheradge, Dion 1879-1934 *WhScrn 74, -77*
Titheradge, Dion 1889-1934 *NotNAT B, WhThe*
Titheradge, George S 1848-1916 *NotNAT B, WhThe*
Titheradge, Lily d1937 *NotNAT B*
Titheradge, Madge 1887-1961 *NotNAT B, WhScrn 74, -77, WhThe, WhoHol B*
Titl, Anton Emil 1809-1882 *Baker 78, NewGrD 80*
Titmuss, Phyllis 1900-1946 *Film 2, NotNAT B, WhThe*
Titof, Nicholas 1800-1875 *OxMus*
Titon, Jeff Todd 1943- *IntWWM 77, -80*
Titon DuTillet, Evrard 1677-1762 *NewGrD 80*
Titov *NewGrD 80*
Titov, Alexei 1769-1827 *Baker 78*
Titov, Alexey Nikolayevich 1769-1827 *NewGrD 80*
Titov, Mikhail Alexeyevich 1804-1853 *NewGrD 80*
Titov, Nicolai 1800-1875 *Baker 78*
Titov, Nikolay Alexeyevich 1800-1875 *NewGrD 80*
Titov, Nikolay Sergeyevich 1798-1843 *NewGrD 80*
Titov, Sergey Nikolayevich 1770-1825 *NewGrD 80*
Titov, Vasily Polikarpovich 1650?-1715? *NewGrD 80*
Titt, Michael George 1939- *IntWWM 77, -80*
Titta, Ruffo Cafiero *NewGrD 80*
Titta Ruffo *Baker 78*
Tittel, Ernst 1910-1969 *NewGrD 80*
Tittell, Charlotte d1941 *NotNAT B*
Titterton, William Richard 1876-1963 *WhThe*
Tittle, John Stephen 1935- *ConAmC*
Titus, Alan Witkowski 1945- *NewGrD 80, WhoOp 76*
Titus, Antoine *CnOxB*
Titus, Frank *PupTheA*
Titus, Graham 1949- *IntWWM 77, -80*
Titus, Lydia Yeamans d1929 *TwYS, WhoHol B*
Titus, Lydia Yeamans 1866-1929 *WhScrn 74, -77*
Titus, Lydia Yeamans 1874 1929 *Film 1, -2*
Titus, Tom Warren 1938- *ConAmTC*
Titz *NewGrD 80*
Titz, Anton Ferdinand 1742?-1810 *NewGrD 80*
Titz, August Ferdinand 1742?-1810 *NewGrD 80*
Titz, Heinrich d1759 *NewGrD 80*
Titz, Johannes Henricus 1745-1826 *NewGrD 80*
Titz, Wilhelm d1775 *NewGrD 80*
Titze, Robert 1920- *WhoMus 72*
Tivey, Roger James 1942- *IntWWM 80*
Tixier, Guillaume *NewGrD 80*
Tizol, Juan 1900- *AmSCAP 66, -80, BiDAmM, CmpEPM, EncJzS 70, WhoJazz 72*
Tjader, Cal 1925- *CmpEPM, EncJzS 70*
Tjader, Callen 1893- *AmSCAP 66, -80*
Tjader, Callen Radcliffe 1925- *EncJzS 70*
Tobani, Theodore Moses 1855-1933 *Baker 78, BiDAmM*
Toberen, Charles *PupTheA*
Tobey, Dan *Film 2*
Tobey, Ken 1919- *ForYSC, WhoHol A*
Tobey, Kenneth 1919- *HalFC 80, MotPP, WhoHrs 80[port]*
Tobias, Charles 1898-1970 *AmPS, AmSCAP 66, -80, BiDAmM, CmpEPM, Sw&Ld C*
Tobias, Fred 1928- *AmSCAP 66, -80*
Tobias, George *IntMPA 77, -75, -76, -78, -79, -80, MotPP*
Tobias, George 1901-1980 *FilmEn, FilmgC, ForYSC, HalFC 80, HolCA[port], MovMk, WhoHol A*
Tobias, George 1905- *BiE&WWA, NotNAT, Vers A[port]*
Tobias, Harry 1895- *AmSCAP 66, -80, BiDAmM, CmpEPM, Sw&Ld C*
Tobias, Henry 1905- *AmSCAP 66, -80, BiDAmM, CmpEPM*
Tobias, Ken 1945- *IntWWM 77*
Tobias, Oliver 1947- *HalFC 80*
Tobias, Roy 1927?- *CnOxB, DancEn 78*
Tobias, Sally Brayley *CreCan 2*
Tobie, Charlotte *PupTheA*
Tobin, Ashleigh Hambridge 1939- *IntWWM 80*
Tobin, Candida 1926- *IntWWM 80*
Tobin, Caroline 1941- *IntWWM 77, -80*
Tobin, Dan 1909?- *FilmgC, ForYSC, HalFC 80, PlP&P, WhoHol A*
Tobin, Darra Lyn *WhoHol A*
Tobin, Genevieve *MotPP*
Tobin, Genevieve 1901- *FilmEn, FilmgC, HalFC 80, HolP 30[port], ThFT[port], WhoHol A*
Tobin, Genevieve 1902- *WhThe*
Tobin, Genevieve 1904- *ForYSC, MovMk[port]*
Tobin, Genevieve 1905?- *What 4[port]*
Tobin, John d1804 *NotNAT B*
Tobin, John 1891- *NewGrD 80, WhoMus 72*
Tobin, Lenore 1912- *BiE&WWA*
Tobin, Lew 1904- *AmSCAP 66, -80*
Tobin, Michele *WhoHol A*
Tobin, Richard Lawrence 1932- *ConAmTC*
Tobin, Robert L B 1934- *WhoOp 76*
Tobin, Vivian 1904- *WhThe*
Tobitt, Janet E 1898- *AmSCAP 66*
Toboggan, Christopher *AmSCAP 80*
Toby, Harriet 1929-1952 *DancEn 78*
Toca, Lawrence 1900?-1972 *NewOrJ[port]*
Tocchi, Gian-Luca 1901- *Baker 78, IntWWM 77, NewGrD 80, WhoMus 72*
Toch, Ernest 1887-1964 *BiDAmM*
Toch, Ernst 1887-1964 *AmSCAP 66, -80, Baker 78, BnBkM 80, CompSN[port], ConAmC, DcCM, IntWWM 77, -80, NewEOp 71, NewGrD 80, OxMus*
Toche, Raoul d1895 *NotNAT B*
Tocher, Helen Lucie 1894- *WhoMus 72*
Toczyska, Stefania Maria 1943- *IntWWM 77*
Tod, Dorothy *WomWMM A, -B*
Tod, Malcolm *Film 2*
Toda, Kunio 1915- *Baker 78, IntWWM 77, -80, NewGrD 80*
Todaro, Tony 1915-1976 *AmSCAP 66, -80*
Todd, Ann *IntMPA 77, -75, -76, -78, -79, -80, MotPP, WhoThe 72, -77*
Todd, Ann 1909- *FilmAG WE, FilmEn, FilmgC, HalFC 80, IlWWBF[port], MovMk, OxFilm, WhoHol A*
Todd, Ann 1910- *BiE&WWA, ForYSC*
Todd, Ann 1932- *FilmEn, FilmgC, ForYSC, HalFC 80*
Todd, Art And Dotty *AmPS A, RkOn*
Todd, Arthur W 1920- *AmSCAP 66, -80*
Todd, Beverly 1946- *DrBlPA, WhoHol A*
Todd, Bob 1922- *FilmgC, HalFC 80, WhoHol A*
Todd, Bob 1941- *AmSCAP 80*
Todd, Camilla 1888?-1969 *NewOrJ*
Todd, Christine *WhoHol A*
Todd, Clarence E 1897- *AmSCAP 66, -80*
Todd, D S *AmSCAP 80*
Todd, Dana *Film 2*
Todd, Diana R 1943- *IntWWM 77, -80*
Todd, Dick 1914?- *CmpEPM*
Todd, Dotty 1923- *AmSCAP 66, -80*
Todd, George Bennett 1935- *ConAmC*
Todd, Harry 1865-1935 *Film 1, -2, WhScrn 74, -77, WhoHol B*
Todd, J Garrett *WhThe*
Todd, James 1908-1968 *WhScrn 77, WhoHol B*
Todd, James Paul 1937- *IntWWM 77*
Todd, Lawrence Edwin Jerome 1919- *IntWWM 77, -80*
Todd, Lida Elizabeth Roberts 1918- *IntWWM 77, -80*
Todd, Lisa *WhoHol A*
Todd, Lola *Film 2, TwYS, WhoHol A*
Todd, Michael 1907-1958 *EncMT, FilmEn, NotNAT A, -B, WhThe, WorEFlm*
Todd, Mike 1907-1958 *DcFM, FilmgC, HalFC 80, OxFilm*
Todd, Nick *RkOn*
Todd, R Larry 1952- *IntWWM 77*
Todd, Richard 1919- *CmMov, FilmAG WE, FilmEn, FilmgC, ForYSC, HalFC 80, IlWWBF[port], IntMPA 77, -75, -76, -78, -79, -80, MotPP, MovMk[port], WhoHol A, WhoThe 77*
Todd, Ross *ConMuA 80B*
Todd, Thelma d1935 *MotPP, WhoHol B*
Todd, Thelma 1905-1935 *FilmEn, Film 2, FilmgC, ForYSC, Funs[port], HalFC 80, JoeFr, MovMk, NotNAT B, ThFT[port], WhScrn 74, -77, WhoHrs 80[port]*
Todd, Thelma 1908-1935 *TwYS*
Todd, Tom T 1923- *AmSCAP 66, -80*
Todd, William Vivian 1904- *WhoMus 72*
Todds, Walter Henry 1920- *IntWWM 77, -80*
Toddy, Ted 1912- *IntMPA 77, -75, -76, -78, -79, -80*
Todeschi, Simplicio 1600?- *NewGrD 80*
Todeschini, Francesco *NewGrD 80*
Todhunter, John d1916 *NotNAT B*
Todi, Jacopone Da *NewGrD 80*
Todi, Luisa 1753-1833 *NewGrD 80*
Todi, Luiza Rosa DeAguilar 1753-1833 *Baker 78, NewGrD 80*
Todini, Michele 1625?-1689? *NewGrD 80*
Todino, Cesare *NewGrD 80*
Todisco, Nunzio 1942- *WhoOp 76*
Todman, Howard 1920- *IntMPA 77, -75, -76, -78, -79, -80*
Todman, William S 1916- *IntMPA 77, -75, -76, -78, -79*
Todris, Murray 1918- *AmSCAP 66, -80*
Todt, Giovanni Christoforo *NewGrD 80*
Todt, Johann Christoph *NewGrD 80*
Toduja, Sigismund 1908- *NewGrD 80*
Toduta, Sigismund 1908- *Baker 78*
Toebosch, Louis Christiaan 1916- *Baker 78, IntWWM 77, -80, NewGrD 80*

Toensing, Richard 1940- *ConAmC*
Toeplitz, Jerzy *WomWMM*
Toepper-Mixa, Hertha *WhoMus 72*
Toeschi *NewGrD 80*
Toeschi, Alessandro 1700?-1758 *Baker 78, NewGrD 80*
Toeschi, Carl Joseph 1731-1788 *NewGrD 80*
Toeschi, Carlo Giuseppe 1723?-1788 *OxMus*
Toeschi, Carlo Giuseppe 1731-1788 *Baker 78*
Toeschi, Johann Baptist 1735-1800 *Baker 78*
Toeschi, Johann Christoph 1735-1800 *NewGrD 80*
Toeschi, Johann DeCastellamonte 1735-1800 *NewGrD 80*
Toeschi, Karl Theodor 1768-1843 *NewGrD 80*
Tofano, Sergio 1886- *EncWT*
Toffolo, Luigi 1909- *WhoOp 76*
Tofft, Alfred 1865-1931 *Baker 78*
Toft, Lars Esben 1928- *IntWWM 77, -80*
Tofte-Hansen, Paul 1914- *IntWWM 77, -80*
Tofts, Catherine 1685?-1756 *NewGrD 80*
Tognazzi, Ugo 1922- *FilmEn, FilmgC, HalFC 80, IntMPA 80, WhoHol A*
Togni, Camillo 1922- *Baker 78, DcCM, NewGrD 80*
Togstad, John Olav 1947- *IntWWM 80*
Toguri, David *WhoThe 77*
Toivola, Antti Olavi 1935- *IntWWM 77, -80*
Tokar, Norman 1920-1979 *FilmEn, FilmgC, HalFC 80, IntMPA 77, -75, -76, -78, -79*
Tokatyan, Armand 1896-1960 *Baker 78*
Tokatyan, Armand 1899-1960 *NewEOp 71*
Tokens, The *AmPS A, RkOn[port]*
Tokieda, Toshie *WomWMM, -B*
Tokonaga, Frank *Film 1, -2*
Tokyo Rose 1916- *What 3[port]*
Tolan, Kathleen *WhoHol A*
Tolan, Michael *BiE&WWA, NotNAT, WhoHol A*
Toland, Gregg 1904-1948 *DcFM, FilmEn, FilmgC, HalFC 80, OxFilm, WorEFlm*
Tolansky, Jonathan Paul 1948- *IntWWM 77, -80*
Tolar, Jan Krtitel *NewGrD 80*
Tolar, Johann Baptist *NewGrD 80*
Tolbecque *NewGrD 80*
Tolbecque, Auguste 1830-1919 *Baker 78, NewGrD 80*
Tolbecque, Auguste-Joseph 1801-1869 *NewGrD 80*
Tolbecque, Charles-Joseph 1806-1835 *NewGrD 80*
Tolbecque, Jean-Baptiste-Joseph 1797-1869 *Baker 78, NewGrD 80*
Tolbert, Berlinda 1949- *DrBlPA*
Tolbert, Gregory Jerome 1953- *AmSCAP 80*
Tolchin, Arthur M 1914- *IntMPA 75*
Toldra, Eduardo 1895-1962 *Baker 78, NewGrD 80*
Toler, Hooper 1891-1922 *WhScrn 74, -77, WhoHol B*
Toler, Sidney 1874-1947 *FilmEn, Film 2, FilmgC, ForYSC, HalFC 80, HolCA[port], MotPP, MovMk[port], NotNAT B, WhScrn 74, -77, WhThe, WhoHol B, WhoHrs 80*
Tolgesy, Victor 1928- *CreCan 1*
Tolgyesy, Victor 1928- *CreCan 1*
Tolis DeLaRoca, Matheo *NewGrD 80*
Toliver, Juanita Darlene 1951- *BlkWAB*
Tolkan, James *WhoHol A*
Tolkowsky, Denise 1918- *WhoMus 72*
Toll, Michael *WhoMus 72*
Toll, Pamela *WhoHol A*
Tollaire, August *Film 2*
Tollar, Jan Krtitel *NewGrD 80*
Tollefsen, Augusta Schnabel 1885-1955 *BiDAmM*
Tollefsen, Carl H 1882-1963 *Baker 78*
Tollefsen, Toralf Louis 1914- *IntWWM 77*
Tollefson, Arthur Ralph 1942- *IntWWM 77, -80*
Tollenaere, Joachim De *NewGrD 80*
Toller, Ernst 1893-1939 *CnMD, CnThe, EncWT, Ent, McGEWD[port], ModWD, NotNAT B, OxThe, PlP&P, REnWD[port], WhThe*
Toller, Florian Johann *NewGrD 80*
Toller, Rosalie 1885- *WhThe*
Toller-Bond, D H *ConMuA 80B*
Tollet, Thomas d1696? *NewGrD 80*
Tollett, George *NewGrD 80*
Tollett, Thomas d1696? *NewGrD 80*
Tolley, Jean *Film 2*
Tollio, Giovanni *NewGrD 80*
Tollis DeLaRoca, Mathco 1710?-1781 *NewGrD 80*
Tollit, Thomas *NewGrD 80*
Tollius, Jan 1550?-1603? *NewGrD 80*
Tolliver, Charles 1942- *EncJzS 70, IlEncJ*
Tolliver, Melba 1939- *DrBlPA*
Tolly, Frank d1924 *WhScrn 77*
Tolmage, Gerald *AmSCAP 80*
Tolmie, Frances *OxMus*
Tolo, Leland Stanford 1943- *IntWWM 77, -80*
Tolo, Marilu 1943- *FilmAG WE*
Tolonen, Jouko Paavo Kalervo 1912- *Baker 78, IntWWM 77, -80, NewGrD 80*
Tolsky, Susan *WhoHol A*
Tolson, Melvin Beavnorus 1900-1966 *BlkAmP, MorBAP*
Tolstoi, Countess 1846-1919 *WhScrn 77*
Tolstoi, Aleksei Nikolaevich 1883-1945 *ModWD*
Tolstoi, Leo 1828-1910 *ModWD*
Tolstoy, A K 1817-1875 *McGEWD*
Tolstoy, Aleksey Nikolayevich 1883-1945 *McGEWD*
Tolstoy, Alexandra 1884- *What 3[port]*
Tolstoy, Alexei Konstantinovich 1817-1875 *EncWT, Ent, OxThe, PlP&P*
Tolstoy, Alexei Nikolaivich 1882-1945 *OxThe*
Tolstoy, Alexei Nikolayevich 1882-1945 *EncWT, Ent*
Tolstoy, Alexei Nikolayevich 1883-1945 *CnMD*
Tolstoy, Alexey Konstantinovich 1817-1875 *NewGrD 80*
Tolstoy, Alexie Nikolayevich 1882-1945 *NotNAT B*
Tolstoy, Dmitri 1923- *Baker 78*
Tolstoy, Count Illya *Film 2*
Tolstoy, Leo 1828-1910 *Ent[port], FilmgC, HalFC 80, McGEWD[port], NewEOp 71, PlP&P[port], REnWD[port]*
Tolstoy, Leo Nikolaivich 1828-1910 *OxThe*
Tolstoy, Leo Nikolayevich 1828-1910 *EncWT, NewGrD 80, NotNAT B*
Tolstoy, Leo Nikolayevitch 1828-1910 *CnMD*
Tolstoy, Lev Nikolayevich 1828-1910 *CnThe, NewGrD 80*
Tolstoy, Countess Tamara *Film 2*
Tolveno, Arricha Del *NewGrD 80*
Tom And Jerry *RkOn*
Tom, Blind *OxMus*
Tom, C Y 1907- *IntMPA 77, -75, -76, -78, -79*
Toma, Peter 1922- *AmSCAP 66*
Tomack, Sid 1907-1962 *ForYSC, NotNAT B, Vers A[port], WhScrn 74, -77, WhoHol B*
Tomadini, Jacopo 1820-1883 *NewGrD 80*
Tomamoto, Thomas 1879-1924 *WhScrn 74, -77*
Toman, Gerald John 1937- *AmSCAP 66, -80*
Tomarchio, Ludovico 1886-1947 *WhScrn 77*
Tomas, Guillermo M 1868-1933 *NewGrD 80*
Tomas Pares, Juan 1896-1967 *NewGrD 80*
Tomaschek, Johann Wenzel 1774-1850 *Baker 78, OxMus*
Tomaschek, Wenzel Johann 1774-1850 *NewGrD 80[port]*
Tomasek, Andrija 1919- *IntWWM 77, -80*
Tomasek, Jan Vaclav 1774-1850 *MusMk*
Tomasek, Jaroslav 1896-1970 *Baker 78*
Tomasek, Vaclav Jan Krtitel 1774-1850 *NewGrD 80[port]*
Tomaselli, Bruno Adam 1932- *WhoOp 76*
Tomasi, Biagio 1585?-1640 *NewGrD 80*
Tomasi, Giovanni Battista *NewGrD 80*
Tomasi, Henri 1901-1971 *Baker 78, DcCM, NewGrD 80, OxMus*
Tomasini *NewGrD 80*
Tomasini, Alois 1779-1858 *NewGrD 80*
Tomasini, Alois Luigi 1741-1808 *NewGrD 80*
Tomasini, Anton 1775-1824 *NewGrD 80*
Tomasini, George 1900?-1964 *HalFC 80*
Tomasini, George 1910-1965 *CmMov*
Tomasini, Luigi 1741-1808 *Baker 78*
Tomasini, Luigi 1779-1858 *NewGrD 80*
Tomasson, Helgi 1942- *CnOxB*
Tomasson, Jonas 1946- *Baker 78, NewGrD 80*
Tomaszewski, Henryk 1925- *CnOxB*
Tombelle, Fernand DeLa *Baker 78*
Tombes, Andrew *IntMPA 77, -75, -76, -78, -79, -80, WhScrn 77*
Tombes, Andrew 1889-197-? *FilmEn, FilmgC, HalFC 80*
Tombes, Andrew 1891?- *ForYSC, MovMk, WhoHol A*
Tomblings, Philip Benjamin 1902- *IntWWM 77, -80, WhoMus 72*
Tombragel, Maurice *IntMPA 77, -75, -76, -78, -79, -80*
Tomc, Matija 1899- *IntWWM 77, -80*
Tomei, Luigi 1910-1955 *WhScrn 74, -77*
Tomek, Otto 1928- *IntWWM 77, -80, NewGrD 80*
Tomelty, Joseph 1910- *FilmgC, HalFC 80, WhoHol A*
Tomeoni *NewGrD 80*
Tomeoni, Erminia 1783?-1845? *NewGrD 80*
Tomeoni, Florido 1755-1820 *NewGrD 80*
Tomeoni, Irene 1763-1830 *NewGrD 80*
Tomeoni, Nicola Felice d1830 *NewGrD 80*
Tomeoni, Pellegrino 1729?-1816? *NewGrD 80*
Tomer, William Gould 1832-1896 *BiDAmM*
Tomes, Francesco Vaclav 1759-1796? *NewGrD 80*
Tomes, Francois Vaclav 1759-1796? *NewGrD 80*
Tomes, Frantisek Vaclav 1759-1796? *NewGrD 80*
Tomescu, Vasile 1929- *IntWWM 77, -80, NewGrD 80*
Tomich, Frantisek Vaclav *NewGrD 80*
Tomick, Frantisek Vaclav *NewGrD 80*
Tomilin, Victor 1908-1941 *Baker 78*
Tomin, Jorge 1915- *DancEn 78*
Tomisch, Frantisek Vaclav *NewGrD 80*
Tomita 1932- *IlEncR*
Tomkins *NewGrD 80*
Tomkins, Don *WhoHol A*
Tomkins, Eddie 1908-1943 *BiDAmM*
Tomkins, Giles 1587?-1668 *NewGrD 80*
Tomkins, John 1586-1638 *NewGrD 80*
Tomkins, Nathaniel 1599-1681 *NewGrD 80*
Tomkins, Robert *NewGrD 80*
Tomkins, Thomas 1572-1656 *Baker 78, BnBkM 80, MusMk, NewGrD 80*
Tomkins, Thomas 1573-1656 *OxMus*
Tomkins, William Vaughan 1941- *IntWWM 77*
Tomkis, Thomas *NotNAT B*
Tomkison, Thomas *NewGrD 80*
Tomlan, Gwynne *WhoHol A*
Tomlin, Blanche 1889- *WhThe*
Tomlin, Lily *IntMPA 76, -78, -79, -80*
Tomlin, Lily 1936- *IntMPA 77, WhoHol A*
Tomlin, Lily 1939- *AmSCAP 80, HalFC 80, JoeFr[port]*
Tomlin, Pinky 1908- *AmSCAP 66, -80, CmpEPM, WhoHol A*
Tomlins, Frederick Guest d1867 *NotNAT B*
Tomlins, William Lawrence 1844-1930 *Baker 78, BiDAmM*
Tomlinson, Daniel G *Film 2*
Tomlinson, David 1917- *FilmEn, FilmgC, HalFC 80, IlWWBF[port], IntMPA 77, -75, -76, -78, -79, -80, WhoHol A, WhoHrs 80, WhoThe 72, -77*
Tomlinson, Ernest 1924- *IntWWM 77, -80, NewGrD 80, WhoMus 72*
Tomlinson, John 1946- *IntWWM 77, -80*
Tomlinson, Kellom *NewGrD 80*
Tomlinson, Kenelm *NewGrD 80*
Tomlinson, Leslie *Film 2*
Tommasini, Vincenzo 1878-1950 *Baker 78, CompSN[port], NewGrD 80, OxMus*
Tommasini, Vincenzo 1880-1950 *DancEn 78*
Tommy *IlEncR*
Tommy, Tony *Film 2*
Tomowa-Sintow, Anna 1941- *WhoOp 76*
Tompall And The Glaser Brothers *BiDAmM, EncFCWM 69, IlEncCM[port]*
Tompkins, Angel *WhoHol A*
Tompkins, Beatrice 1918- *CnOxB, DancEn 78*
Tompkins, Darlene *WhoHol A*
Tompkins, Eddic *WhoJazz 72*
Tompkins, Eugene d1909 *NotNAT B*
Tompkins, Joan *WhoHol A*
Tompkins, Ross 1938- *EncJzS 70*
Toms, Carl 1927- *IntWWM 77, -80, NotNAT, WhoMus 72, WhoOp 76, WhoThe 72, -77*
Toms, Gary, Empire *RkOn 2[port]*
Toms, Graydon Arthur 1957- *AmSCAP 80*

Toms, Ricky *NewOrJ*
Tomsic, Dubravka 1940- *IntWWM 77, -80, WhoMus 72*
Tomsky, Alexander Romanovich 1905-1970 *CnOxB*
Toncray, Kate *Film 1, -2, TwYS*
Tondino, Gentile 1923- *CreCan 2*
Tone, Franchot *MotPP, PIP&P[port]*
Tone, Franchot d1968 *WhoHol B*
Tone, Franchot 1905- *BiE&WWA*
Tone, Franchot 1905-1968 *FilmEn, FilmgC, ForYSC, HalFC 80, MGM[port], NotNAT B, WhScrn 74, -77*
Tone, Franchot 1905-1969 *MovMk*
Tone, Franchot 1906-1968 *OxFilm, WhThe, WorEFlm*
Tone, Franchot 1906-1969 *BiDFilm, -81, CmMov*
Tonelli, Antonio 1686-1765 *NewGrD 80*
Tonello, Antonio *NewGrD 80*
Tonelus *NewGrD 80*
Tonemasters *BiDAmM*
Toner, Tom *WhoHol A*
Toney, James d1973 *WhScrn 77*
Toney, Kevin Kraig 1953- *AmSCAP 80, EncJzS 70*
Toney, Lemuel Gordon *AmSCAP 80*
Tong, Kam 1907-1969 *WhScrn 74, -77, WhoHol B*
Tong, Sammee 1901-1964 *MotPP, WhScrn 74, -77, WhoHol B*
Tong, Sammee 1905-1966 *ForYSC*
Tonge, H Asheton d1927 *NotNAT B*
Tonge, Lillian Bernard *Film 2*
Tonge, Philip d1959 *WhoHol B*
Tonge, Philip 1892-1959 *NotNAT B, WhThe*
Tonge, Philip 1897-1961 *ForYSC*
Tonge, Philip 1898-1959 *WhScrn 74, -77, WhoHrs 80*
Tonger, P J *NewGrD 80*
Tongue, Alan *IntWWM 77*
Toni, Alceo 1884-1969 *Baker 78, NewGrD 80*
Toni, Olivier 1926- *IntWWM 77, -80*
Tonin-Nikic, Boris 1933- *CnOxB*
Tonini, Bernardo 1666?-1727? *NewGrD 80*
Tonking, Henry Charles 1863-1926 *NewGrD 80*
Tonkinson, Steven Earl 1950- *IntWWM 77*
Tonna, Charlotte Elizabeth 1780-1846 *OxMus*
Tonnancour, Jacques Godefroy De 1917- *CreCan 2*
Tonnesen, Terje 1955- *IntWWM 80*
Tonning, Gerard 1860-1940 *Baker 78, BiDAmM*
Tonning, Merrill D, Sr. 1910- *AmSCAP 66, -80*
Tonnolini, Giovanni Battista *NewGrD 80*
Tononi *NewGrD 80*
Tononi, Carlo d1730? *NewGrD 80*
Tononi, Giovanni d1713 *NewGrD 80*
Tonson, Jacob d1736 *NotNAT B*
Tonsor, Michael 1546?-1607? *NewGrD 80*
Tonti, Aldo 1910- *DcFM, FilmEn, FilmgC, HalFC 80, WorEFlm*
Tonto 1920- *What 3[port]*
Tonto, Charlie *AmSCAP 80*
Tony 1909-1942 *WhScrn 77*
Too Tight Henry *BluesWW[port]*
Toobin, Jerome *NewYTET*
Toohey, John L 1916- *BiE&WWA*
Toohey, John Peter d1947 *NotNAT B*
Tooker, William 1875- *Film 1, -2, TwYS*
Tooker, William H 1864-1936 *WhScrn 74, -77, WhoHol B*
Toole, John Laurence 1830-1906 *NotNAT B, OxThe*
Toole, John Lawrence 1830-1906 *NotNAT A*
Tooley, Sir John 1924- *NewGrD 80*
Tooley, Nicholas 1575?-1623 *NotNAT B, OxThe*
Toombes, Andrew 1889- *Vers A[port]*
Toomer, Jean 1894-1967 *BlkAmP, MorBAP*
Toomey, Regis 1902- *FilmEn, Film 2, FilmgC, ForYSC, HalFC 80, HolCA[port], IntMPA 77, -75, -76, -78, -79, -80, MotPP, MovMk, Vers A[port], WhoHol A*
Toon, Christopher 1935- *WhoMus 72*
Toone, Geoffrey 1910- *IlWWBF, WhoHol A, WhoThe 72, -77*
Toones, Fred *ForYSC*
Toop, Richard William 1945- *IntWWM 80*
Toots And The Maytals *ConMuA 80A, IlEncR*
Top Hatters *BiDAmM*
Topart, Jean *WhoHol A*
Topart, Lise 1930-1952 *WhScrn 74, -77*
Topaz, Muriel 1932- *BiE&WWA, NotNAT*
Toperczer, Peter 1944- *IntWWM 80*
Topfer, Johann Gottlob 1791-1870 *Baker 78, NewGrD 80*
Topfer, Wolfgang *NewGrD 80*
Topham, Edward d1820 *NotNAT B*
Topham, William *NewGrD 80*
Toplady, Augustus Montague 1740-1778 *OxMus*
Toplansky, Herman 1907- *IntWWM 77, -80*
Topliff, Roger *CpmDNM 78*
Topol 1935- *FilmEn, FilmgC, HalFC 80, WhoHol A*
Topol, Chaim *ForYSC*
Topol, Haym 1935- *MovMk*
Topol, Josef 1935- *CnThe, CroCD, EncWT, REnWD[port]*
Toporkov, Vasily Osipovich 1889- *WhThe*
Topper, Barbara Blake 1942- *IntWWM 77*
Topper, Burt 1934- *FilmEn, FilmgC, HalFC 80, WhoHol A*
Topper, Hertha 1924- *CmOp, NewGrD 80, WhoOp 76*
Toradze, David Alexandrovich 1922- *Baker 78, NewGrD 80*
Torbett, Dave 1908- *AmSCAP 66, -80*
Torcaso, Enrico 1936- *ConAmC*
Torch, Sidney *WhoMus 72*
Torchi, Luigi 1858-1920 *Baker 78, NewGrD 80*
Torchinsky, Abe 1920- *IntWWM 77, -80*
Tordesilla, Jesus 1893-1973 *WhScrn 77*
Tordesillas, Pedro De *NewGrD 80*
Torelli, Achille 1841-1922 *McGEWD[port]*
Torelli, Gasparo *Baker 78, NewGrD 80*
Torelli, Gasparo d1613? *NewGrD 80*
Torelli, Giacomo 1608-1678 *CnThe, Ent, NewGrD 80, NotNAT B, OxThe*
Torelli, Giuseppe 1658-1709 *Baker 78, BnBkM 80, GrComp[port], NewGrD 80, OxMus*
Torelli, Guasparri d1613? *NewGrD 80*
Torelli, Jacopo 1608-1678 *NewGrD 80*
Toremans, August 1926- *WhoMus 72*
Toren, Marta 1926-1957 *FilmEn, FilmgC, HalFC 80, MotPP, NotNAT B, WhScrn 74, -77, WhoHol B*
Toren, Marta 1927-1957 *ForYSC*
Toren, Torvald 1945- *IntWWM 77, -80*
Torenbosch, Chris 1930- *DancEn 78*
Torf, Silva *Film 2*
Torgh, Roberto *NewGrD 80*
Torgrimson, Paul Edward 1918- *IntWWM 77, -80*
Torices, Benito Bello De *NewGrD 80*
Torigi, Richard 1917- *WhoOp 76*
Torjussen, Trygve 1885-1977 *Baker 78*
Tork, Peter 1942- *WhoHol A*
Torkanowsky, Werner 1926- *Baker 78*
Torlez *NewGrD 80*
Torme, Mel *IlEncJ, IntMPA 77, -75, -76, -78, -79, -80, WhoHol A*
Torme, Mel 1923- *FilmgC, HalFC 80*
Torme, Mel 1925- *CmpEPM, EncJzS 70, ForYSC, RkOn[port]*
Torme, Melvin Howard 1925- *AmSCAP 66, -80, BiDAmM, EncJzS 70*
Tormis, Velio 1930- *NewGrD 80*
Tormo, Antonio *NewGrD 80*
Torn, Rip 1931- *BiE&WWA, FilmEn, FilmgC, ForYSC, HalFC 80, IntMPA 77, -75, -76, -78, -79, -80, MovMk, NotNAT, WhoHol A, WhoThe 72, -77*
Tornadoes, The *RkOn*
Tornar, Roberto 1587?-1629? *NewGrD 80*
Tornatore, Joe *WhoHol A*
Tornbech, Svend *Film 2*
Torne, Bengt Von 1891-1967 *Baker 78, NewGrD 80*
Tornek, Jack d1974 *WhScrn 77*
Torner, Eduado Martinez 1888-1955 *Baker 78*
Torner, Eduardo Martinez 1888-1955 *NewGrD 80*
Torner, Joseph Nicolaus 1700?-1762 *NewGrD 80*
Tornerr, Joseph Nicolaus 1700?-1762 *NewGrD 80*
Torning, Alice *Film 2*
Tornioli, Marcantonio d1617? *NewGrD 80*
Torns, Raymond G 1943- *IntWWM 77*
Toro, Puli 1947- *IntWWM 77, -80*
Torok, Mitchell *RkOn*
Torrance, George William 1835-1907 *Baker 78, NewGrD 80*
Torrance, Mrs. Joe Taylor 1899- *AmSCAP 66*
Torre, Alfonso DeLa *NewGrD 80*
Torre, Francisco DeLa *NewGrD 80*
Torre, Janice *AmSCAP 66, -80*
Torre, Jeronimo DeLa *NewGrD 80*
Torre, Pietro Paolo *NewGrD 80*
Torre Nilsson, Leopoldo 1924-1978 *BiDFilm 81, DcFM, FilmEn, FilmgC*
Torre-Nilsson, Leopoldo 1924-1978 *HalFC 80*
Torre Nilsson, Leopoldo 1924-1978 *OxFilm, WorEFlm*
Torre Rios, Leopoldo 189-?-1960 *DcFM*
Torrefranca, Fausto 1883-1955 *Baker 78, NewGrD 80*
Torregano, Joseph C 1952- *NewOrJ SUP[port]*
Torrejon Y Velasco, Tomas De 1644-1728 *NewGrD 80*
Torrelhas, Joseph *NewGrD 80*
Torrellas, Joseph *NewGrD 80*
Torrence, David 1864-1951 *WhScrn 77*
Torrence, David 1870-1942 *HalFC 80, WhThe*
Torrence, David 1880-1942 *FilmEn, Film 1, -2, ForYSC, TwYS, WhoHol B*
Torrence, Ernest 1878-1933 *FilmEn, Film 2, FilmgC, ForYSC, HalFC 80, HolCA[port], MotPP, MovMk[port], NotNAT B, TwYS, WhScrn 74, -77, WhThe, WhoHol B*
Torrence, Lena *BlksB&W C*
Torrentes, Andres De 1510?-1580 *NewGrD 80*
Torres, Cancino 1935- *IntWWM 77*
Torres, Cathie *Film 1*
Torres, Felipe *PIP&P A[port]*
Torres, Joan *WomWMM*
Torres, Jose *WhoHol A*
Torres, Juan De 1596?-1679 *NewGrD 80*
Torres, Liz *WhoHol A*
Torres, Melchior De *NewGrD 80*
Torres, Raquel 1908- *FilmEn, Film 2, FilmgC, ForYSC, HalFC 80, MotPP, TwYS, WhoHol A*
Torres, Ricardo 1947- *AmSCAP 80*
Torres Contreras, Miguel *FilmEn*
Torres Naharro, Bartolome De d1524? *OxThe*
Torres Naharro, Bartolome De d1531? *EncWT*
Torres Naharro, Bartolome De 1476?-1531? *McGEWD*
Torres Naharro, Bartolome De 1485?-1524? *Ent*
Torres Y Martinez Bravo, Jose De 1665?-1738 *NewGrD 80*
Torres Y Martinez Bravo, Joseph De 1665?-1738 *NewGrD 80*
Torresano, Andrea *NewGrD 80*
Torrey, Bradford 1843-1912 *BiDAmM*
Torrey, Mary Ide 1817-1869 *BiDAmM*
Torrey, Roger *WhoHol A*
Torri, Pietro 1650?-1737 *Baker 78, NewGrD 80*
Torriani, Aimee 1890-1963 *WhScrn 74, -77, WhoHol B*
Torricella, Christoph 1715?-1798 *NewGrD 80*
Torrijos, Diego De 1640?-1691 *NewGrD 80*
Torrington, Frederick Herbert 1837-1917 *Baker 78, BiDAmM, NewGrD 80*
Torrini 1770?-1820? *Ent, MagIID*
Torrio, Ermogine *NewGrD 80*
Torruco, Miguel 1920-1956 *WhScrn 74, -77, WhoHol B*
Tors, Ivan 1916- *FilmEn, FilmgC, HalFC 80, IntMPA 77, -75, -76, -78, -79, -80, NewYTET, WhoHrs 80*
Torstensson, Thorleif S G 1949- *IntWWM 80*
Tort, Cesar 1929- *Baker 78*
Tortamano, Nicola 158-?-1627? *NewGrD 80*
Tortelier, Paul 1914- *Baker 78, IntWWM 77, -80, MusMk[port], NewGrD 80[port], WhoMus 72*
Tortelier, Yan Pascal 1947- *IntWWM 80*
Torti, Ludovico 1547-1615? *NewGrD 80[port]*
Torto, Luigi 1547-1615 *NewGrD 80[port]*
Tortorella, Adalberto 1927- *IntWWM 77, -80*
Tortorich, Mary A 1914- *IntWWM 77, -80*
Tortorich, Tony 1900?- *NewOrJ*

Tortoriello, Vincent Joseph 1902- *AmSCAP 80*
Torvay, Jose d1973 *WhScrn 77*
Tosar, Hector 1923- *Baker 78, NewGrD 80*
Tosar-Errecart, Hector 1923- *DcCM*
Tosatti, Vieri 1920- *Baker 78, NewGrD 80*
Toscanini, Arthuro 1867-1957 *NotNAT B*
Toscanini, Arturo 1867-1957 *Baker 78, BiDAmM, BnBkM 80[port], CmOp[port], MusMk[port], MusSN[port], NewEOp 71, NewGrD 80[port], OxMus, WhScrn 77*
Toscano, Carmen *WomWMM*
Toscano, Carol 1941- *WhoOp 76*
Toscano, Nicolo 1530?-1605 *NewGrD 80*
Toscano, Salvador *WomWMM*
Toscano Barragan, Salvador 1873-1947 *DcFM*
Toselli, Enrico 1883-1926 *Baker 78, NewGrD 80, OxMus*
Toser, David *NotNAT*
Tosh, Peter 1944- *ConMuA 80A*
Toshevas, Nevena *WomWMM*
Tosi, Giuseppe Felice *NewGrD 80*
Tosi, Pier Francesco 1653?-1732 *NewGrD 80*
Tosi, Pier Francesco 1654-1732 *Baker 78*
Tosi, Piero 1928- *DcFM*
Toso, Otello d1966 *WhScrn 74, -77, WhoHol B*
Tosone, Marcello d1624? *NewGrD 80*
Tosoni, Marcello d1624? *NewGrD 80*
Tosso, Joseph 1802-1887 *BiDAmM*
Tosti, Francesco Paolo 1846-1916 *OxMus*
Tosti, Sir Francesco Paolo 1846-1916 *Baker 78, GrComp*
Tosti, Francesco Paulo 1846-1916 *DcCom 77*
Tosti, Sir Paolo 1846-1916 *NewGrD 80*
Toszeghi, Andras 1945- *IntWWM 77, -80*
Totenberg, Roman *IntWWM 77, -80, WhoMus 72*
Totenberg, Roman 1911- *NewGrD 80*
Totenberg, Roman 1913- *Baker 78*
Toth, Aladar 1898-1968 *NewGrD 80, WhoMus 72*
Toth, Edra 1952- *CnOxB*
Toth, Margit 1920- *IntWWM 77, -80*
Toth, Sandor 1937- *CnOxB*
Totheroh, Dan 1894- *ModWD, WhThe*
Totheroh, Dan 1898- *CnMD*
Totheroh, Rolland H 1890-1967 *FilmEn*
Totheroh, Rollie 1890- *WorEFlm*
Totheroh, Rollie 1891-1967 *FilmgC, HalFC 80*
Toto *ConMuA 80A, FilmAG WE, Film 1, MotPP*
Toto 1897-1967 *FilmgC, HalFC 80, MovMk[port], WhScrn 74, -77, WhoHol B, WhoHrs 80*
Toto 1898-1967 *EncWT, Ent, FilmEn, WorEFlm*
Toto The Clown 1888-1938 *WhScrn 77*
Totten, Joseph Byron d1946 *NotNAT B*
Totter, Audrey *IntMPA 77, -75, -76, -78, -79, -80, MotPP*
Totter, Audrey 1918- *FilmEn, FilmgC, ForYSC, HalFC 80, MGM[port], MovMk*
Totter, Audrey 1919?- *WhoHol A*
Tottmann, Albert 1837-1917 *Baker 78*
Tottola, Leone d1831 *NewGrD 80*
Toubas, Maurice 1902- *WhoMus 72*
Touchagues *Film 2*
Touchemoulin, Joseph 1727-1801 *NewGrD 80*
Touchin, Colin Michael 1953- *IntWWM 80*
Touchmolin, Joseph 1727-1801 *NewGrD 80*
Touff, Cy 1927- *CmpEPM*
Tough, Dave 1908-1948 *BiDAmM, CmpEPM, IlEncJ, WhoJazz 72*
Toughey, John *Film 2*
Toukermine, Doris *WomWMM*
Touliatos, George 1929- *BiE&WWA*
Toulmouche, Fredeic d1909 *NotNAT B*
Toulmouche, Frederic 1850-1909 *Baker 78*
Touloubieva, Z *WomWMM*
Toulouse, Michel De *NewGrD 80*
Toulouse-Lautrec, Henri De 1864-1901 *EncWT*
Toulout, Jean *Film 2*
Touma, Habib Hassan 1934- *DcCM, IntWWM 77, -80, NewGrD 80*
Toumanova, Tamara 1917- *FilmgC, HalFC 80, WhThe, WhoHol A*
Toumanova, Tamara 1919- *CnOxB, DancEn 78[port]*
Toumarkine, Doris *WomWMM B*
Toumine, Nesta Williams 1912- *CreCan 1, DancEn 78*
Toumonova, Tamara 1918- *ForYSC*
Tourangeau, Huguette 1938- *WhoOp 76*
Tourel, Jennie 1900-1973 *Baker 78, BnBkM 80, MusSN[port], NewGrD 80*
Tourel, Jennie 1910-1973 *BiDAmM, CmOp, NewEOp 71, WhScrn 77, WhoHol B*
Tourjansky, Victor 1891- *FilmEn*
Tourjee, Eben 1834-1891 *Baker 78, BiDAmM, NewGrD 80*
Tournell, Joseph Nicolaus *NewGrD 80*
Tournemire, Charles Arnould 1870-1939 *Baker 78, BnBkM 80, MusMk, NewGrD 80, OxMus*
Tourner, Joseph Nicolaus *NewGrD 80*
Tourneur, Andree *Film 2*
Tourneur, Cyril 1575-1626 *CnThe, EncWT, Ent, McGEWD, NotNAT B, OxThe, REnWD[port]*
Tourneur, Jacques 1904- *BiDFilm, CmMov, DcFM, FilmgC, OxFilm, WorEFlm*
Tourneur, Jacques 1904-1977 *BiDFilm 81, FilmEn, HalFC 80*
Tourneur, Jacques 1904-1978 *WhoHrs 80*
Tourneur, Maurice 1876-1961 *AmFD, BiDFilm, -81, DcFM, FilmEn, FilmgC, HalFC 80, OxFilm, TwYS A, WorEFlm*
Tourneur, Maurice 1878-1961 *MovMk[port]*
Touro, Pinchback 1870?- *NewOrJ*
Touront, Johannes *NewGrD 80*
Tours, Berthold 1838-1897 *Baker 78, NewGrD 80, OxMus*
Tours, Frank E 1877-1963 *Baker 78, ConAmC, NotNAT B, WhThe*
Tourte *NewGrD 80*
Tourte, Francois 1747-1835 *Baker 78, MusMk, NewGrD 80, OxMus*
Tourtelot, Madeline *WomWMM B*
Tousignant, Claude 1932- *CreCan 1*
Tousignant, Serge 1942- *CreCan 2*
Toussaint, Allan 1938- *ConMuA 80B*
Toussaint, Allen 1938- *ConMuA 80A, IlEncR*
Toussaint, Richard *BlkAmP*
Toutain, Blanche d1932 *NotNAT B, WhThe*
Touzet, Rene 1916- *AmSCAP 66, -80*
Tovar, Francisco d1522 *NewGrD 80*
Tovar, Lupita 1911- *ForYSC, WhoHol A*
Tover, Leo 1902- *FilmgC, HalFC 80*
Tover, Leo 1902-1964 *FilmEn*
Tover, May 1911-1949 *WhScrn 74, -77, WhoHol B*
Tovey, Sir Donald Francis 1875-1940 *Baker 78, BnBkM 80, MusMk, NewGrD 80, OxMus*
Tovey, Sir Donald Francis 1950- *IntWWM 77*
Tovstonogov, Georgii Alexandrovich 1915- *EncWT*
Tovstonogov, Georgyi Alexandrovich 1915- *OxThe*
Towb, Harry 1925- *WhoHol A, WhoThe 72, -77*
Towbin, Cyril 1897-1971 *BiDAmM*
Towbin, Marion Fredi *NatPD[port]*
Towell, Philip Patrick 1930- *WhoMus 72*
Tower, Allen d1963 *NotNAT B*
Tower, Ibrook 1948- *IntWWM 77, -80*
Tower, Joan 1938- *CpmDNM 78, ConAmC, IntWWM 77, -80*
Tower Of Power, The *ConMuA 80A, IlEncR, RkOn 2[port]*
Towers, Constance 1933- *ForYSC, MotPP, WhoHol A, WhoThe 77*
Towers, Harry Alan 1920- *FilmgC, HalFC 80, IntMPA 77, -75, -76, -78, -79, -80*
Towers, Harry P 1873- *WhThe*
Towers, Johnson d1891 *NotNAT B*
Towers, Samuel *OxThe*
Towersey, Phyllis Mary 1914- *WhoMus 72*
Towles, Nat 1900?- *NewOrJ*
Towles, Nat 1905-1963 *WhoJazz 72*
Town, Christopher 1945- *IntWWM 77, -80*
Town, Harold Barling 1924- *CreCan 2*
Town, Robert Lloyd 1937- *IntWWM 77, -80*
Towne, Aline *ForYSC, WhoHol A*
Towne, Charles Hanson 1877-1949 *AmSCAP 66, -80, NotNAT B*
Towne, Edward Owings 1869- *WhoStg 1908*
Towne, Gene 1904-1979 *HalFC 80, IntMPA 77, -75, -76, -78, -79*
Towne, Robert *HalFC 80, IntMPA 77, -76, -78, -79, -80, WhoHrs 80*
Towne, Rosella 1919- *Film 2, ForYSC*
Towneley, Simon P Edmund Cosmo William 1921- *IntWWM 80*
Townend, Joseph Thomas 1912- *IntWWM 77*
Towner, Daniel Brink 1850-1919 *NewGrD 80*
Towner, Ralph N 1940- *EncJzS 70*
Townes, Christopher *WhoHol A*
Townes, Harry 1918- *ForYSC, NotNAT, WhoHol A*
Townhill, Dennis William 1925- *IntWWM 77, -80, WhoMus 72*
Townley, Jack 1897- *IntMPA 75, -76*
Townley, James d1778 *NotNAT B*
Townley, Robin *Film 1*
Townley, Toke *WhoHol A*
Towns, George A *BlkAmP*
Townsend, Anna d1923 *Film 2, WhScrn 74, -77, WhoHol B*
Townsend, Aurelian *NotNAT B*
Townsend, Brigham 1907- *AmSCAP 80*
Townsend, Brigham 1909- *AmSCAP 66*
Townsend, Colleen 1928- *ForYSC, WhoHol A*
Townsend, David Michael 1942- *AmSCAP 80, IntWWM 77, -80*
Townsend, Douglas 1921- *Baker 78, ConAmC*
Townsend, Ed 1929- *RkOn[port]*
Townsend, Genevieve *Film 2*
Townsend, Henry 1909- *BluesWW[port]*
Townsend, Jill *WhoHol A*
Townsend, K C *WhoHol A*
Townsend, Leo 1908- *IntMPA 77, -75, -76, -78, -79, -80*
Townsend, Pauline Swanson *IntMPA 77, -75, -76, -78, -79, -80*
Townsend, Peter 1914- *What 3[port]*
Townsend, Thompson d1870 *NotNAT B*
Townsend, Willa A *BlkAmP*
Townson, Ron 1933- *BiDAmM*
Towse, John Ranken 1845-1927 *OxThe*
Towse, John Ranken 1845-1933 *NotNAT B*
Towsey, Vera Josephine *WhoMus 72*
Toy, Beatrice d1938 *NotNAT B*
Toy, Noel *WhoHol A*
Toyama, Yoshio 1944- *NewOrJ SUP[port]*
Toyama, Yuzo 1931- *Baker 78*
Toye, Francis 1883-1964 *Baker 78, NewGrD 80, OxMus*
Toye, Geoffrey 1889-1942 *Baker 78, NewEOp 71, NewGrD 80, OxMus, WhThe*
Toye, Wendy 1917- *CnOxB, EncMT, FilmEn, FilmgC, HalFC 80, IlWWBF, IntMPA 77, -75, -76, -78, -79, -80, WhoThe 72, -77, WomWMM*
Toyne, Gabriel 1905-1963 *NotNAT B, WhThe, WhoHol B*
Toyoda, Shiro 1906- *FilmEn*
Toys, The *RkOn 2[port]*
Tozer, H V *DcPup*
Tozere, Frederic 1901-1972 *BiE&WWA, NotNAT B, WhScrn 77, WhThe, WhoHol B, WhoThe 72*
Tozzi, Antonio 1736?-1812? *NewGrD 80*
Tozzi, Fausto 1921- *FilmAG WE, WhoHol A*
Tozzi, Francesco *NewGrD 80*
Tozzi, George 1923- *NewGrD 80*
Tozzi, Giorgio 1923- *Baker 78, CmOp, MusSN[port], NewEOp 71, NewGrD 80, WhoMus 72, WhoOp 76*
Tozzi, Vincenzo 1612?-167-? *NewGrD 80*
Tozzo, Vincent J 1929- *AmSCAP 80*
Trabaci, Giovanni Maria 1575?-1647 *Baker 78, NewGrD 80*
Trabattone *NewGrD 80*
Trabattone, Bartolomeo *NewGrD 80*
Trabattone, Egidio *NewGrD 80*
Trabattone, Giovanni Battista *NewGrD 80*
Trabert, Tony *WhoHol A*
Trabichoff, Geoffrey Colin 1946- *IntWWM 77, -80*
Trace, Al 1900- *CmpEPM*
Trace, Albert J *AmSCAP 66, -80*
Trace, Ben L 1897- *AmSCAP 66, -80*
Tracey, Andrew T N 1936- *IntWWM 77, -80*
Tracey, Bradford 1951- *IntWWM 77, -80*
Tracey, Edmund 1927- *IntWWM 77, -80, WhoMus 72, WhoOp 76*

Tracey, Hugh 1903-1977 NewGrD 80, OxMus
Tracey, Paul Hugh Lawrence 1939- AmSCAP 80
Tracey, Stan 1926- EncJzS 70, IlEncJ, NewGrD 80
Tracey, Thomas F 1880-1961 NotNAT B, WhScrn 77
Tracey, William G 1893-1957 AmSCAP 66, -80
Track, Ernst 1911- IntWWM 77, -80
Track, Gerhard 1934- ConAmC, IntWWM 77, -80
Track, Micaela Maihart 1934- IntWWM 77, -80
Tracy, Arthur AmPS B, What 1[port]
Tracy, Arthur 1900?- CmpEPM
Tracy, Arthur 1903- FilmgC, ForYSC, HalFC 80, WhoHol A
Tracy, Dennis Arthur 1948- AmSCAP 80
Tracy, Helen Film 1, -2, WhoStg 1908
Tracy, Lee 1898-1968 BiE&WWA, FilmEn, Film 2, FilmgC, ForYSC, HalFC 80, HolP 30[port], MotPP, MovMk, NotNAT B, WhScrn 74, -77, WhThe, WhoHol B
Tracy, Spencer 1900-1967 BiDFilm, -81, BiE&WWA, CmMov, Ent, FilmEn, FilmgC, ForYSC[port], HalFC 80[port], MGM[port], MotPP, MovMk[port], NotNAT B, OxFilm, PlP&P, WhScrn 74, -77, WhThe, WhoHol B, WhoHrs 80, WorEFlm[port]
Tracy, Virginia d1946 NotNAT B
Tracy, William 1917-1967 FilmEn, FilmgC, ForYSC, HalFC 80, MotPP, WhScrn 74, -77, WhoHol B
Trade Winds, The RkOn 2[port]
Trader, Bill 1922- AmSCAP 66
Trader, William Marvin 1922- AmSCAP 80
Traeg, Johann 1747-1805 NewGrD 80
Traeger, Elinor Meissner 1906- IntWWM 77
Traeger, Rick WhoHol A
Traerup, Birthe 1930- IntWWM 77, -80
Traetta, Filippo 1777-1854 Baker 78, BiDAmM, NewGrD 80
Traetta, Tommaso 1727-1779 Baker 78, MusMk, NewEOp 71, NewGrD 80[port], OxMus
Traffic ConMuA 80A, IlEncR, RkOn 2[port]
Trafford, Edmund ConAmC
Traficante, Frank Anthony 1937- IntWWM 77, -80
Trago, Jose 1856-1934 Baker 78
Traguth, Fred 1932- CnOxB
Trailine, Boris 1921- CnOxB, DancEn 78
Trailine, Helene 1928- CnOxB, DancEn 78
Traill, Eric Sinclair 1904- IntWWM 77, -80
Traill, Peter 1896- WhThe
Train, Jack 1902-1966 IlWWBF A, WhScrn 74, -77, WhoHol B
Trainer, David 1947- NatPD[port]
Trainor, Leonard 1879-1940 WhScrn 74, -77, WhoHol B
Trainor, Thomas Walter 1928- AmSCAP 80
Trajan Turnovsky, Jan NewGrD 80
Trajanus Turnovinus, Johannes NewGrD 80
Trajetta, Filippo 1777-1854 NewGrD 80
Trajetta, Tommaso NewGrD 80
Trajkovic, Vlastimir 1947- IntWWM 77, -80
Traktman, Peggy Simon 1932- AmSCAP 80
Trama, Ugo 1932- WhoOp 76
Trambitsky, Victor 1895-1970 Baker 78
Trambitsky, Viktor Nikolayevich 1895-1970 NewGrD 80
Trambukis, William J 1926- IntMPA 79, -80
Trammel, Niles d1973 NewYTET
Trammps, The ConMuA 80A, RkOn 2[port]
Trampeli NewGrD 80
Trampeli, Christian Wilhelm 1748-1803 NewGrD 80
Trampeli, Friedrich Wilhelm 1790-1832 NewGrD 80
Trampeli, Johann Gottlob 1742-1812 NewGrD 80
Trampeli, Johann Paul 1708-1764 NewGrD 80
Trampler, Walter 1915- Baker 78, BnBkM 80, IntWWM 77, -80, MusSN[port], NewGrD 80, WhoMus 72
Tran, Quang Hai 1944- IntWWM 77, -80
Tran Van Khe 1921- IntWWM 77, -80, NewGrD 80
Tranah, Alan 1920- IntWWM 77, WhoMus 72
Tranchell, Peter Andrew 1922- Baker 78, IntWWM 77, -80, NewGrD 80, WhoMus 72
Tranovsky, Jiri 1592-1637 NewGrD 80
Tranovsky, Juraj 1592-1637 NewGrD 80
Tranowsky, Jirik 1592-1637 NewGrD 80
Trant, Leonard Brian WhoMus 72
Trantham, William Eugene 1929- IntWWM 77, -80
Trantow, Herbert 1903- WhoMus 72
Tranum, Charles B 1916- BiE&WWA
Trapassi, Antonio Domenico Bonaventura NewGrD 80
Trapassi, Pietro Antonio Domenico McGEWD[port]
Trapido, Joel 1913- BiE&WWA
Trapp, Max 1887-1971 Baker 78, NewGrD 80
Trappan, Ruth PupTheA
Trappier, Traps 1910- WhoJazz 72
Trarieux, Gabriel 1870- WhThe
Trashmen, The RkOn
Trask, Diana 1940- CounME 74[port], -74A, IlEncCM[port]
Trask, Franklin 1907- BiE&WWA, NotNAT
Trask, Wayland 1887-1918 Film 1, TwYS, WhScrn 77
Trass, Vel MorBAP
Trasuntino NewGrD 80
Trasuntino, Alessandro NewGrD 80
Trasuntino, Giovanni Francesco NewGrD 80
Trasuntino, Giulio NewGrD 80
Trasuntino, Vito NewGrD 80
Trattner, Johann Thomas 1717-1798 NewGrD 80
Traube, Shepard 1907- BiE&WWA, NotNAT, WhoThe 72, -77
Traubel, Helen 1899-1972 Baker 78, BnBkM 80, CmOp, FilmgC, HalFC 80, NewEOp 71, NewGrD 80
Traubel, Helen 1903-1972 BiDAmM, ForYSC, MusSN[port], WhScrn 77, WhoHol B
Trauberg, Ilya Zakharovich 1905?-1948 DcFM, FilmEn, OxFilm, WorEFlm
Trauberg, Leonid Zakharovich 1902- DcFM, FilmEn, Film 2, OxFilm, WorEFlm
Trauffer, Barbara Olive 1940- IntWWM 77, -80
Trauner, Alexander 1906- FilmEn, FilmgC, HalFC 80, OxFilm, WorEFlm
Trauner, Alexandre 1906- DcFM
Traunfellner, Peter Carl 1930- IntWWM 77, -80, WhoMus 72
Trautman, Ludwig 1886-1957 WhScrn 74, -77
Trautsch, Leonhard 1693-1762 NewGrD 80
Trautwein, Friedrich 1888-1956 Baker 78, NewGrD 80
Trautwein, Traugott Baker 78
Traux, Maude Film 2
Travelers 3 BiDAmM, EncFCWM 69
Travellers BiDAmM
Traven, B 1882?-1955? HalFC 80
Travener, Jo WomWMM B
Travenol, Louis-Antoine 1698?-1783 NewGrD 80
Traver, James Ferris 1929- ConAmC
Travernier, Albert Film 2
Travers, Alfred 1906- IlWWBF
Travers, Anthony 1920-1959 WhScrn 74, -77
Travers, Ben IlWWBF A
Travers, Ben 1886- BiE&WWA, ConDr 73, -77, CroCD, EncWT, Ent, FilmgC, HalFC 80, McGEWD[port], NotNAT, -A, WhoThe 72, -77
Travers, Ben 1889- CnThe
Travers, Bill 1922- FilmEn, FilmgC, HalFC 80, IlWWBF, IntMPA 77, -75, -76, -78, -79, -80, MovMk, WhoHol A
Travers, Dick MotPP
Travers, George Film 2
Travers, Henry 1874-1965 FilmEn, FilmgC, ForYSC, HalFC 80, HolCA[port], MotPP, MovMk[port], PlP&P, Vers B[port], WhScrn 74, -77, WhThe, WhoHol B
Travers, Jim Film 1
Travers, John 1703?-1758 Baker 78, NewGrD 80, OxMus
Travers, Linden 1913- FilmgC, HalFC 80, IlWWBF, WhThe, WhoHol A
Travers, Madalaine 1875-1964 Film 1, -2, TwYS
Travers, Mary EncFCWM 69
Travers, Mary Allin 1937- AmSCAP 66, -80
Travers, Mary Ellin 1936- BiDAmM
Travers, Richard C 1890-1935 Film 1, -2, TwYS, WhScrn 74, -77, WhoHol B
Travers, Roxy WomWMM
Travers, Roy Film 2
Travers, Susan WhoHol A
Travers, Sy WhoHol A
Travers, Tony d1959 WhoHol B
Travers, William 1922- ForYSC
Traverse, Alan 1938- WhoMus 72
Traverse, Madaline 1876-1964 WhoHol B
Traverse, Madlaine 1876-1964 MotPP, NotNAT B, WhScrn 74, -77
Traviesas, Herminio NewYTET
Travis And Bob RkOn[port]
Travis, Bob ConMuA 80B
Travis, Carolynn D 1922- AmSCAP 80
Travis, Charles W 1861-1917 WhScrn 77
Travis, Francis Irving 1921- WhoMus 72
Travis, June 1914- FilmEn, ForYSC, WhoHol A
Travis, Merle 1917- BiDAmM
Travis, Merle Robert 1917- CmpEPM, CounME 74[port], -74A, EncFCWM 69, IlEncCM
Travis, Michael 1928- BiE&WWA, NotNAT
Travis, Nick 1925-1964 CmpEPM
Travis, Richard 1913- FilmEn, FilmgC, ForYSC, HalFC 80, IntMPA 77, -75, -76, -78, -79, -80, Vers B[port], WhoHol A
Travis, Roy 1922- AmSCAP 80, CpmDNM 80, ConAmC, DcCM, IntWWM 77, -80
Travolta, John 1954- BiDFilm 81, FilmEn, HalFC 80, RkOn 2[port]
Travolta, John 1955- IntMPA 78, -79, -80
Trawinska Moroz, Urszula 1937- WhoOp 76
Traylor, Rudolph 1918- WhoJazz 72
Traylor, William WhoHol A
Trazegniers, Francois-Joseph De 1744-1820 NewGrD 80
Trazegnies, Francois-Joseph De 1744-1820 NewGrD 80
Treacher, Arthur d1975 MotPP
Treacher, Arthur 1893-1975 Vers B[port]
Treacher, Arthur 1894-1975 BiE&WWA, FilmEn, Film 2, FilmgC, ForYSC, HalFC 80, HolCA[port], MovMk[port], NotNAT B, WhScrn 77, WhoHol C
Treacher, Arthur V IntMPA 75, -76
Treacher, Graham Martin 1932- WhoMus 72
Treacy, Emerson 1905-1967 MotPP, WhScrn 74, -77, WhoHol B
Treador, Marie Film 1
Treadway, Charlotte 1895-1963 NotNAT B, WhScrn 74, -77, WhoHol B
Treadwell, George 1919- DrBlPA
Treadwell, Laura B 1879-1960 WhScrn 74, -77, WhoHol B
Treadwell, Sophie 1890-1970 CnMD, McGEWD, ModWD
Trebaol, Edouard Film 2
Trebaol Children Film 2
Trebelli, Zelia 1838-1892 Baker 78, CmOp, NewGrD 80
Trebitsch, Siegfried 1869-1956 ModWD
Treble, Sepha 1908- WhThe
Trebor NewGrD 80
Trebor, Robert AmSCAP 80
Trechoffuet, Gregorius NewGrD 80
Trechoven, Gregorius NewGrD 80
Trechovius, Gregorius NewGrD 80
Trechsel NewGrD 80
Treckman, Emma 1909- WhThe
Trecu, Pirmin 1930- CnOxB, DancEn 78
Trede, Yngve Jan 1933- IntWWM 77, -80
Tredici, David Del DcCM
Tredinnick, Noel Harwood 1949- IntWWM 77, -80
Tree, Lady 1863-1937 NotNAT B, WhScrn 74, -77, WhThe, WhoHol B
Tree, Beerbohm 1853-1917 WhoStg 1908
Tree, Chief Big ForYSC
Tree, David 1915- EncWT, FilmgC, HalFC 80, WhThe, WhoHol A

Tree, Dorothy 1909- *FilmEn, ForYSC, IntMPA 77, -75, -76, -78, -79, -80, WhoHol A*
Tree, E Wayne *MorBAP*
Tree, Ellen 1805-1880 *FamA&A[port]*
Tree, Ellen 1806-1880 *OxThe*
Tree, Helen Maud Holt 1863-1937 *EncWT, OxThe*
Tree, Sir Herbert Beerbohm d1917 *Film 1, WhoHol B*
Tree, Sir Herbert Beerbohm 1852-1917 *EncWT, WhScrn 77*
Tree, Sir Herbert Beerbohm 1853-1917 *CnThe, FamA&A[port], NotNAT A, -B, OxThe, PlP&P[port], WhThe*
Tree, Maria d1862 *NotNAT B*
Tree, Michael 1934- *IntWWM 77, -80*
Tree, Rose *PupTheA*
Tree, Viola 1884-1938 *EncWT, NotNAT A, -B, OxThe, WhScrn 74, -77, WhThe, WhoHol B*
Treen, Mary Lou 1907- *FilmEn, FilmgC, ForYSC, HalFC 80, IntMPA 77, -75, -76, -78, -79, -80, MotPP, Vers A[port], WhoHol A*
Trefilova, Vera Alexandrovna 1875-1943 *CnOxB, DancEn 78*
Tregaskis, Herbert Alan 1918- *IntWWM 77, -80*
Tregian, Francis 1574-1619 *Baker 78, NewGrD 80, OxMus*
Treharne, Bryceson 1879-1948 *AmSCAP 66, -80, Baker 78, BiDAmM, ConAmC A*
Trehou, Gregorius 154-?-1621 *NewGrD 80*
Treiber, Friedrich Georg 1909- *IntWWM 77, -80*
Treiber, Johann Friedrich 1642-1719 *NewGrD 80*
Treiber, Johann Philipp 1675-1727 *NewGrD 80*
Treichlinger, Jozsef 1807-1866? *NewGrD 80*
Treigle, Norman 1927-1975 *Baker 78, MusSN[port], NewGrD 80, WhoMus 72*
Treigle, Norman 1928-1975 *CmOp*
Treitler, Leo 1931- *NewGrD 80*
Treloff, John *NewGrD 80*
Tremain, Ronald 1923- *IntWWM 77, -80, NewGrD 80, WhoMus 72*
Tremaine, Ann Kafoury 1929- *IntWWM 77, -80*
Tremaine, Betty Pitt 1906- *AmSCAP 66*
Tremaine, Paul *BgBands 74, CmpEPM*
Tremais, De *NewGrD 80*
Tremayne, Les *HalFC 80*
Tremayne, Les 1910- *WhoHrs 80[port]*
Tremayne, Les 1913- *ForYSC, IntMPA 77, -75, -76, -78, -79, -80, WhoHol A*
Tremblay, George 1911- *Baker 78, ConAmC, DcCM, NewGrD 80*
Tremblay, Gilles 1932- *Baker 78, CreCan 1, DcCM, NewGrD 80*
Tremblay, Jean-Louis 1939- *CreCan 1*
Tremblay, Monique *CreCan 2, NewGrD 80*
Tremeloes, The *RkOn 2[port]*
Trempont, Michel Fernand 1928- *WhoOp 76*
Trench, Herbert 1865-1923 *NotNAT B, WhThe*
Trenchard-Smith, Brian 1946- *HalFC 80*
Trend, J B 1887-1958 *NewGrD 80*
Trend, John Brande 1887-1958 *Baker 78, OxMus*
Trenev, Konstantin Andreivich 1884-1945 *OxThe*
Trenholme, Helen 1911-1962 *NotNAT B, WhThe, WhoHol B*
Trenier, Diane *BlkAmP*
Trenker, Luis 1892?- *OxFilm*
Trenker, Luis 1893- *DcFM, FilmEn*
Trenker, Luis 1896- *Film 2*
Trenkle, Joseph 1840?-1878 *BiDAmM*
Trenner, Donn 1927- *AmSCAP 66, -80*
Trent, Alphonse 1905-1959 *NewGrD 80*
Trent, Alphonso E 1905-1959 *NewGrD 80, WhoJazz 72*
Trent, Bob *Film 2*
Trent, Bruce *WhoThe 72, -77*
Trent, Jo 1892-1954 *AmSCAP 66, -80*
Trent, John 1897-1961 *WhScrn 77*
Trent, John 1906-1966 *Film 2, WhScrn 77, WhoHol B*
Trent, John 1935- *IntMPA 77, -76, -78, -79, -80*
Trent, Sheila d1954 *NotNAT B*
Trent, Tom *Film 1*
Trent, Tommy *PupTheA*
Trenti, Madame *NewGrD 80*
Trentini, Emma 1885-1959 *AmPS B, CmpEPM, EncMT, NotNAT B, PlP&P, WhThe*
Trento, Guido *Film 2*
Trento, Vittorio 1761-1833 *Baker 78, NewGrD 80*
Trenton, Louise 1882- *WhoMus 72*
Trenton, Pell *Film 1, -2*
Trenyov, Konstantin Andreevich 1878?-1945 *ModWD*
Trenyov, Konstantin Andreevich 1884-1945 *CnMD*
Trepagnier, Ernest 1885?-1968 *NewOrJ[port]*
Treptow, Gunther 1907- *CmOp, NewGrD 80*
Tersahar, John d1936 *NotNAT B*
Tresahar, John d1936 *WhThe*
Treschault, Gregorius *NewGrD 80*
Treseniers, Francois-Joseph De *NewGrD 80*
Tresgot, Annie *WomWMM*
Tresham, Jennie 1881-1913 *WhScrn 77*
Tresignier, Francois-Joseph De *NewGrD 80*
Treskoff, Olga 1902-1938 *WhScrn 74, -77, WhoHol B*
Tresmand, Ivy 1898- *WhThe*
Tresor, Jonas *NewGrD 80*
Tressel, George *PupTheA*
Tressel, Mary Ann *PupTheA*
Tressler, Georg 1917- *WorEFlm*
Tresti, Flaminio 1560?-1613? *NewGrD 80*
Tresure, Jonas *NewGrD 80*
Trethowan, Ian *NewYTET*
Tretyakov, Sergei Mikhailovich 1892-1937 *CnMD*
Tretyakov, Sergei Mikhailovich 1892-1939 *EncWT, ModWD, OxThe, PlP&P*
Tret'yakov, Viktor Viktorovich 1946- *NewGrD 80*
Tretzel *NewGrD 80*
Tretzscher, Matthias 1626-1686 *NewGrD 80*
Treu, Abdias 1597-1669 *NewGrD 80*
Treu, Daniel Gottlieb 1695-1749 *Baker 78*
Treu, Daniel Gottlob 1695-1749 *NewGrD 80*
Trevarthen, Noel *WhoHol A*
Trevarthen, Robert Richard *ConAmC*
Trevelyan, Hilda 1880-1959 *NotNAT B, OxThe, WhThe, WhoHol B*
Trevelyan, Jean 1928- *IntWWM 77*
Trevelyan, John 1903- *IntMPA 75, -76*
Trevelyan, John 1904- *FilmgC, HalFC 80*
Trevelyan, Una *Film 2*
Trevens, Francine L 1932- *ConAmTC, NatPD[port]*
Treveque, Jack 1899?- *NewOrJ*
Trevi, Christina 1930-1956 *WhScrn 74, -77*
Treville, Roger 1903- *WhThe*
Treville, Yvonne De 1881-1954 *Baker 78, BiDAmM*
Trevison, Hank 1923- *AmSCAP 66*
Trevor, Ann 1918-1970 *Film 2, WhThe, WhoHol B*
Trevor, Anne 1918-1970 *WhScrn 77*
Trevor, Austin 1897-1978 *FilmgC, HalFC 80, IlWWBF, WhThe, WhoHol A, WhoThe 72*
Trevor, C H 1895-1976 *NewGrD 80*
Trevor, Claire *IntMPA 77, -75, -76, -78, -79, -80, MotPP, WomWMM*
Trevor, Claire 1909- *BiDFilm, -81, CmMov, FilmEn, FilmgC, ForYSC, HalFC 80, MovMk[port], OxFilm, ThFT[port], WhThe, WhoHol A, WorEFlm[port]*
Trevor, Claire 1912- *CmMov*
Trevor, Howard *WhoHol A*
Trevor, Hugh 1903-1933 *Film 2, ForYSC, TwYS, WhScrn 74, -77, WhoHol B*
Trevor, Jack *Film 2*
Trevor, Leo d1927 *NotNAT B, WhThe*
Trevor, Norman 1877-1929 *Film 1, -2, ForYSC, NotNAT B, TwYS, WhScrn 74, -77, WhThe, WhoHol B*
Trevor, Spencer 1875-1945 *Film 2, NotNAT B, WhThe, WhoHol B*
Trevor, Van 1940- *AmSCAP 80, BiDAmM*
Trevor, Violet *WhoMus 72*
Trevor, Walter 1931- *CnOxB*
Trevor, William 1928- *ConDr 73, -77*
Trew, Abdias *NewGrD 80*
Trew, Daniel Gottlob *NewGrD 80*
Trewin, John Courtenay 1908- *WhoThe 72, -77*
Trewin, Mary Worthy 1935- *IntWWM 77*
Trexler, Charles B 1916- *IntMPA 77, -76, -78, -79, -80*
Trexler, Georg Max 1903- *IntWWM 77, -80, NewGrD 80*
Trexlor, Charles B 1916- *IntMPA 75*
Treybenreif, Peter *NewGrD 80*
Treyz, Oliver E *NewYTET*
Trial *NewGrD 80*
Trial, Antoine 1737-1795 *NewGrD 80*
Trial, Armand-Emmanuel 1771-1803 *NewGrD 80*
Trial, Jean-Claude 1732-1771 *Baker 78, NewGrD 80*
Trial, Marie-Jeanne 1746-1818 *NewGrD 80*
Triana, Jose 1931- *EncWT*
Triana, Juan De *NewGrD 80*
Tribble, Andrew 1879-1935 *BlksBF[port]*
Tribble, Fredric 1912- *AmSCAP 66*
Tribolet, Marianne De *NewGrD 80*
Tribot *NewGrD 80*
Tricarico, Antonio *NewGrD 80*
Tricarico, Giuseppe 1623-1697 *NewGrD 80*
Trice, Richard 1917- *BluesWW[port]*
Trice, William Augusta 1910-1976 *BluesWW[port]*
Trichet, Pierre 1586?-1644? *NewGrD 80*
Trick, Martha *Film 1*
Trickler, Jean Balthasar 1750-1813 *NewGrD 80*
Tricklir, Jean Balthasar 1750-1813 *NewGrD 80*
Tricoli, Carlo d1966 *WhScrn 77*
Triebensee, Josef 1772-1846 *NewGrD 80*
Triebert *NewGrD 80*
Triebert, Charles-Louis 1810-1867 *NewGrD 80*
Triebert, Frederic 1813-1878 *NewGrD 80*
Triebert, Guillaume 1770-1848 *NewGrD 80*
Trier, Johann 1716-1790 *NewGrD 80*
Trier, Stephen Luke 1930- *IntWWM 77, -80, WhoMus 72*
Triesault, Ivan *WhoHol A*
Triesault, Ivan 1900-1980 *Vers A[port]*
Triesault, Ivan 1902-1980 *FilmEn, FilmgC, HalFC 80*
Trieste, Leopoldo 1919- *CnMD, WhoHol A*
Trietsch, Paul *JoeFr*
Trietsch, Rudy *JoeFr*
Trifunovic, Vitomir 1916- *Baker 78*
Trifunovich, Vitomir 1916- *IntWWM 77, -80*
Trigg, William *OxThe*
Trigger 1932-1965 *WhScrn 74, -77*
Trigger, Ian *WhoHol A*
Triggs, Aubrey Leigh 1921- *AmSCAP 80*
Triggs, Dudley *PupTheA*
Triggs, Harold 1900- *ConAmC*
Triklir, Jean Balthasar *NewGrD 80*
Trikonis, Gus *WhoHol A*
Trillat, Ennemond 1890- *WhoMus 72*
Triller, Valentin d1573? *NewGrD 80*
Trilling, Ossia 1913- *WhoThe 72, -77*
Trimarchi, Domenico 1940- *WhoOp 76*
Trimble, Arthur *Film 2*
Trimble, Jessie d1957 *NotNAT B*
Trimble, Joan *WhoMus 72*
Trimble, Larry 1885-1954 *Film 1, IlWWBF, WhScrn 77*
Trimble, Laurence 1885-1954 *FilmEn, TwYS A*
Trimble, Lawrence 1885-1954 *NotNAT B*
Trimble, Lester 1920- *Baker 78*
Trimble, Lester 1923- *ConAmC, DcCM, NewGrD 80*
Trimble, Samuel, Jr. 1942- *IntWWM 77*
Trimble, Valerie 1917- *IntWWM 77, -80, WhoMus 72*
Trimmingham, Ernest d1942 *NotNAT B*
Trinder, Tommy 1909- *FilmgC, HalFC 80, IlWWBF[port], IntMPA 77, -75, -76, -78, -79, -80, WhoHol A, WhoThe 72, -77*
Trinkaus, George J 1878-1960 *AmSCAP 66, -80, ConAmC A*
Trinkaus, Marilyn Miller *WomWMM B*
Trintignant, Jean-Louis 1930- *BiDFilm, -81, FilmAG WE, FilmEn, FilmgC, HalFC 80, IntMPA 77, -75, -76, -78, -79, -80, MotPP, MovMk[port], OxFilm, WhoHol A, WorEFlm[port]*

Trintignant, Marie *WhoHol A*
Trintignant, Nadine Marquand 1934- *FilmEn, WomWMM*
Triola, Anne *WhoHol A*
Tripod, Irene *Film 2*
Tripp, Alva 1937- *WhoOp 76*
Tripp, Paul 1911- *AmSCAP 66, WhoHol A*
Tripp, Paul 1916- *AmSCAP 80*
Trisler, Joyce 1934- *CmpGMD, CnOxB, DancEn 78[port]*
Trissino, Gian Giorgio 1478-1550 *OxThe, PlP&P*
Trissino, Giangiorgio 1478-1550 *McGEWD[port]*
Tristabocca, Pasquale *NewGrD 80*
Tristan L'Hermite 1601?-1655 *Ent*
Tristan, Dorothy *WhoHol A*
Tristan L'Hermite, Francois 1600?-1655 *REnWD[port]*
Tristan L'Hermite, Francois 1601?-1655 *McGEWD[port], OxThe*
Tristani *NewGrD 80*
Tristano, Lennie 1919-1978 *CmpEPM, EncJzS 70, IlEncJ, NewGrD 80*
Tristano, Leonard Joseph 1919-1978 *BiDAmM, EncJzS 70, NewGrD 80*
Tritonius, Petrus 1465?-1525? *NewGrD 80*
Tritt, Johnnie *AmSCAP 80*
Tritta, Giacomo 1733-1824 *NewGrD 80*
Tritto, Giacomo 1733-1824 *Baker 78, NewGrD 80*
Trivas, Victor 1896-1970 *FilmEn, FilmgC, HalFC 80*
Trivas, Viktor 1896-1970 *DcFM*
Trivers, Barry 1912- *AmSCAP 66, -80*
Trivers, John *AmSCAP 80*
Trivett, Vincent William 1882- *WhoMus 72*
Trix, Helen 1892-1951 *AmSCAP 66, NotNAT B*
Trnecek, Hans 1858-1914 *NewGrD 80*
Trnecek, Hanus 1858-1914 *Baker 78, NewGrD 80*
Trnecek, Johann 1858-1914 *NewGrD 80*
Trnina, Milka *NewGrD 80*
Trninic, Dusan 1929- *CnOxB, DancEn 78*
Trnka, Jiri *DcPup*
Trnka, Jiri 1910-1969 *FilmgC, HalFC 80*
Trnka, Jiri 1912-1969 *DcFM, FilmEn, OxFilm, WorEFlm*
Trobian, Helen Reed 1918- *IntWWM 77*
Trodd, Gerald Edward 1915- *WhoMus 72*
Troell, Jan 1931- *FilmEn, HalFC 80, IntMPA 77, -75, -76, -78, -79, -80, MovMk[port], WorEFlm*
Trofeo, Ruggier 1550?-1614 *NewGrD 80*
Trofimov, Serge 1899- *IntWWM 77*
Trofimova, Natasha *DancEn 78*
Trofimowa, Natascha 1924?- *CnOxB*
Trogan, Roland 1933- *ConAmC*
Trogen, Stanley *ConAmC*
Troggs, The *ConMuA 80A, RkOn 2[port]*
Troglodytes *BiDAmM*
Troiano, Massimo d1570? *NewGrD 80*
Troili, Giuseppe *NewGrD 80*
Troilo, Antonio *NewGrD 80*
Troilus A Lessoth, Franciscus Godefridus *NewGrD 80*
Troisi, Mario Carlos 1910- *WhoOp 76*
Trojan, Vaclav 1907- *Baker 78, NewGrD 80*
Trojan Turnovsky, Jan 1550?-1595? *NewGrD 80*
Trojano, John *Film 1*
Trojano, Massimo *NewGrD 80*
Troker, Katherine Beaton 1891- *AmSCAP 66, -80*
Trolda, Emilian 1871-1949 *NewGrD 80*
Trollens, Charlotte *OxMus*
Trolli, Giuseppe *NewGrD 80*
Trollope, Anthony *PlP&P*
Trombecin, Bartolomeo *NewGrD 80*
Trombetta, Gayle M 1947- *AmSCAP 80*
Trombetta, Teresa *NewGrD 80*
Trombetta, Vincent John 1940- *AmSCAP 80, IntWWM 77, -80*
Trombetti, Agostino d1658? *NewGrD 80*
Trombetti, Ascanio 1544-1590 *NewGrD 80*
Trombetti, Girolamo 1557-1624 *NewGrD 80*
Tromble, William Warner 1932- *IntWWM 77, 80*
Tromblee, Maxell Ray 1935- *IntWWM 77, -80*
Trombley, Rosalie *ConMuA 80B*
Trombly, Preston A 1945- *ConAmC*
Tromboncino, Bartolomeo 1470?-1535? *NewGrD 80*
Trombone, Il *NewGrD 80*
Trombonzin, Bartolomeo *NewGrD 80*
Tromlitz, Johann Georg 1725-1805 *Baker 78, NewGrD 80*
Tronson, Robert 1924- *FilmgC, HalFC 80, IlWWBF, IntMPA 77, -75, -76, -78, -79, -80*
Troobnick, Eugene 1926- *WhoThe 77*
Troobnick, Gene *WhoHol A*
Tropea, Giacomo 159-?-1622? *NewGrD 80*
Troschel, Wilhelm *NewGrD 80*
Trosper, Guy d1963 *IntMPA 77, -75, -76, -78, -79, -80, NotNAT B*
Trossarello, Pietro 1550?-1570? *NewGrD 80*
Trost, Caspar d1651 *NewGrD 80*
Trost, Johann Baptist Matthaus *NewGrD 80*
Trost, Russel G 1910- *AmSCAP 66, -80*
Trost, Tobias Heinrich Gottfried 1673-1759 *NewGrD 80*
Troszel, Wilhelm 1823-1887 *NewGrD 80*
Trotere, Henry 1855-1912 *Baker 78*
Trotman, William C 1930- *BiE&WWA, NotNAT*
Trotsky, Leon 1879-1940 *Film 1, WhScrn 77, WhoHol B*
Trotta, Raymond 1896- *AmSCAP 66, -80*
Trotter, James Monroe 1842-1892 *NewGrD 80*
Trotter, John Scott 1908-1975 *AmSCAP 66, -80, CmpEPM, WhScrn 77, WhoHol C*
Trotter, Linda *WhoOp 76*
Trotter, Thomas Henry Yorke 1854-1934 *Baker 78*
Trotti, Lamar 1900-1952 *FilmEn, FilmgC, HalFC 80, WorEFlm*
Trottier, Gerald 1925- *CreCan 1*
Trottier, Pierre 1925- *CreCan 2*
Troughton, Patrick 1920- *FilmgC, HalFC 80, WhoHol A*
Trouhanova, Natalia Vladimirovna 1885-1956 *CnOxB*
Trouillon-Lacombe, Louis *NewGrD 80*
Trouluffe, John *NewGrD 80*
Trouncer, Cecil 1898-1953 *FilmgC, HalFC 80, NotNAT B, OxThe, WhScrn 74, -77, WhThe, WhoHol B*
Trounson, Marilyn 1947- *CnOxB*
Troup, Beatrice Ellen Joyce 1905- *WhoMus 72*
Troup, Bobby 1918- *CmpEPM, ForYSC, WhoHol A*
Troup, Kenneth Hugh 1906- *AmSCAP 80*
Troup, Malcolm 1930- *IntWWM 77, -80, WhoMus 72*
Troup, Robert William, Jr. 1918- *AmSCAP 66, -80*
Troupe, Tom *WhoHol A*
Troupenas, Eugene-Theodore 1799-1850 *NewGrD 80*
Trout, Francis Dink 1898-1950 *WhScrn 74, -77, WhoHol B*
Trout, Robert 1908- *NewYTET*
Troutbeck, John 1832-1899 *Baker 78, NewGrD 80*
Troutman, Ivy 1883- *WhThe, WhoStg 1906, -1908*
Troutman, John *AmSCAP 80*
Trow, William 1891-1973 *WhScrn 77, WhoHol B*
Trowbridge, Charles 1882-1967 *Film 1, FilmgC, ForYSC, HalFC 80, HolCA[port], MotPP, Vers B[port], WhScrn 74, -77, WhoHol B*
Trowbridge, Charlotte *DancEn 78*
Trowbridge, John Eliot 1845-1912 *BiDAmM*
Trowbridge, Luther 1892- *ConAmC*
Trowbridge, Lynn Mason 1942- *IntWWM 77, -80*
Trowell, Arnold 1887-1966 *OxMus*
Trowell, Brian 1931- *NewGrD 80, WhoMus 72*
Trowell, Robertus *NewGrD 80*
Trower, Robin 1945- *ConMuA 80A, IlEncR*
Troxell, Jerry 1936- *CpmDNM 73, ConAmC*
Troy, Doris 1937- *RkOn*
Troy, Elinor d1949 *WhScrn 77*
Troy, Hector *WhoHol A*
Troy, Helen 1905-1942 *WhScrn 74, -77, WhoHol B*
Troy, Henry 1908-1962 *AmSCAP 80, BlkAmP*
Troy, Louise *BiE&WWA, NotNAT, WhoHol A, WhoThe 72, -77*
Troyanos, Tatiana 1938- *CmOp, NewGrD 80, WhoMus 72, WhoOp 76*
Troyanova, I *WomWMM*
Troyanovsky, Boris 1883-1957 *NewGrD 80*
Troyer, Carlos 1837-1920 *NewGrD 80*
Trozel, Paul F 1918- *IntWWM 77*
Truax, John d1969 *WhScrn 77*
Truax, Maude *Film 2, TwYS*
Truax, Sarah 1877- *WhThe, WhoStg 1908*
Trubar, Primus 1508-1587 *NewGrD 80*
Trube, Adolph 1815-1857 *NewGrD 80*
Trubensee, Josef *NewGrD 80*
Truber, Primus *NewGrD 80*
Trubetzskoy, Youcca 1905- *Film 1, -2, TwYS*
Trubitt, Allen Roy 1931- *AmSCAP 80, ConAmC*
Trubshawe, Michael *WhoHol A*
Trudeau, Alfred H 1906- *ConAmC*
Trudeau, Yves 1930- *CreCan 2*
Trudic, Bozidar 1911- *Baker 78, IntWWM 77, -80*
True, Alan Harding 1939- *IntWWM 80*
True, Andrea, Connection *RkOn 2[port]*
True, Bess *Film 2*
True, Christopher Mark 1954- *AmSCAP 80*
True, Virginia *PupTheA*
Trueba, Don d1835 *NotNAT B*
Trued, S Clarence 1895- *AmSCAP 66, -80, ConAmC*
Trueheart, John 1900?-1949 *WhoJazz 72*
Truelove, John *NewGrD 80*
Trueman, Brian William 1930- *IntWWM 80, WhoMus 72*
Trueman, Paula 1907- *BiE&WWA, NotNAT, WhoHol A, WhoThe 72, -77*
Truesdale, Howard 1870- *Film 2, TwYS*
Truesdale, Tod *MorBAP*
Truesdell, F Donald 1920- *ConAmC*
Truesdell, Fred C *Film 1*
Truesdell, Frederick C 1873-1937 *Film 2, NotNAT B, WhScrn 77, WhoHol B*
Truex, Ernest d1973 *MotPP, WhoHol B*
Truex, Ernest 1889-1973 *BiE&WWA, EncMT, ForYSC, HolCA[port], MovMk[port], NotNAT B, TwYS, WhScrn 77, WhThe, WhoThe 72*
Truex, Ernest 1890-1973 *FilmEn, Film 1, -2, FilmgC, HalFC 80, Vers A[port]*
Truex, Philip *WhoHol A*
Trufanoff, Sergios *Film 1*
Truffaut, Francois 1932- *BiDFilm, -81, DcFM, FilmEn, FilmgC, HalFC 80, IntMPA 77, -75, -76, -78, -79, -80, MovMk[port], OxFilm, WhoHol A, WhoHrs 80, WorEFlm[port]*
Truffier, Jules 1856- *WhThe*
Truglio, Mario Thomas 1942- *AmSCAP 80*
Truhn, Friedrich Hieronymus 1811-1886 *Baker 78*
Truinet *Baker 78*
Truinet, Charles-Louis-Etienne *NewGrD 80*
Truitte, James 1925?- *CmpGMD, CnOxB, DancEn 78*
Trujillo, Allen Eugene *AmSCAP 80*
Trujillo, Estelita *PupTheA*
Trujillo, Lorenzo Chel 1906-1962 *WhoHol B*
Trujillo, Lorenzo L 1906-1962 *NotNAT B, WhScrn 74, -77*
Truman, Edward Crane 1915- *AmSCAP 66, -80, IntWWM 77*
Truman, Ernest Edwin Phillip 1870-1948 *NewGrD 80*
Truman, Mary Margaret 1924- *BiDAmM*
Truman, Michael 1916- *FilmgC, HalFC 80, IlWWBF, IntMPA 77, -75, -76, -78, -79, -80*
Truman, Ralph 1900-1977 *FilmgC, HalFC 80, WhoHol A*
Trumbauer, Frank 1901-1956 *AmSCAP 66, -80*
Trumbauer, Frankie *BgBands 74*
Trumbauer, Frankie 1900?-1956 *CmpEPM*
Trumbauer, Frankie 1901-1956 *BiDAmM, WhoJazz 72*
Trumbauer, Frankie 1902-1956 *IlEncJ*
Trumble, Robert William 1919- *IntWWM 77, -80*

Trumbo, Dalton 1905-1976 *ConDr 73, -77A, DcFM, FilmEn, FilmgC, HalFC 80, IntMPA 75, -76, OxFilm, WorEFlm*
Trumbull, Douglas 1943?- *WhoHrs 80*
Trump *CreCan 1*
Trumper, Michael 1603-1670 *NewGrD 80*
Trumperus, Michael 1603-1670 *NewGrD 80*
Trumps *Film 2*
Trumpy, Balz 1946- *IntWWM 77, -80*
Trundy, Natalie 1942- *FilmgC, ForYSC, HalFC 80, WhoHol A*
Trunk, Peter 1936-1973 *EncJzS 70*
Trunk, Richard 1879-1968 *Baker 78, NewGrD 80*
Trunnelle, Mabel *FilmEn, Film 1, WhoHol A*
Trunoff, Vassili 1929- *DancEn 78*
Trunoff, Vassilie 1929- *CnOxB*
Truppi, Danny 1919-1970 *WhScrn 77*
Truscott, Anna 1940- *DancEn 78*
Truscott, Harold 1914- *IntWWM 77, -80*
Trusdell, Richard V, Jr. *PupTheA*
Trusler, Ivan 1925- *AmSCAP 66, -80*
Trussel, Jack 1943- *WhoOp 76*
Trussell, Fred 1858-1923 *NotNAT B, WhThe*
Trustman, Susan *WhoHol A*
Trutovsky, Vasiliy Fyodorovich 1740?-1810 *NewGrD 80*
Trutovsky, Vasily 1740?-1810 *Baker 78*
Truyol, Antonio 1933- *CnOxB, DancEn 78*
Try, Charles De *OxMus*
Trydell, John 1715?-1776 *NewGrD 80*
Tryk, Christian Maureen 1951- *IntWWM 77, -80*
Trylova, Hermina *WomWMM*
Tryon, Glenn d1970 *MotPP, WhoHol B*
Tryon, Glenn 1894-1970 *FilmEn, ForYSC*
Tryon, Glenn 1897-1970 *Film 2, TwYS*
Tryon, Glenn 1899-1970 *WhScrn 77*
Tryon, Tom 1919- *FilmgC, HalFC 80*
Tryon, Tom 1926- *FilmEn, ForYSC, IntMPA 77, -75, -76, -78, -79, -80, WhoHol A, WhoHrs 80[port]*
Tryon, Valerie Ann 1934- *IntWWM 77, -80, WhoMus 72*
Trythall, Gilbert 1930- *ConAmC*
Trythall, Richard Aaker 1939- *AmSCAP 80, ConAmC, IntWWM 77, -80*
Trzaskowski, Andrzej 1933- *EncJzS 70, IntWWM 77, -80*
Trzcinski, Edmund 1921- *BiE&WWA*
Trzcinski, Krysztof *NewGrD 80*
Trzcinski, Krzysztof 1931-1969 *AmSCAP 80*
Tsai, Tsou-Sen 190-?- *DcFM*
Ts'ao, Yu 1905- *ModWD*
Tsappi, V *Film 2*
Tsapralis, Nancye Faye 1953- *AmSCAP 80*
Tschachtli, Marie-Madeleine 1925- *IntWWM 77, -80*
Tschaikov, Alan 1933- *IntWWM 77, -80*
Tschaikov, Basil Nichols 1925- *IntWWM 77, -80, WhoMus 72*
Tschaikovsky, Boris Alexandrovich *NewGrD 80*
Tschaikovsky, Peter Ilich 1840-1893 *GrComp*
Tschaikovsky, Peter Illich 1840-1893 *NewGrD 80*
Tschaikowski, Boris Alexandrovich *NewGrD 80*
Tschaikowsky *Baker 78*
Tschaikowsky, Peter Illich *NewGrD 80*
Tschaikowsky, Peter Illich 1840-1893 *NotNAT B*
Tschantz, Eddie 1911- *NewOrJ[port]*
Tschechowa, Olga 1896- *FilmAG WE*
Tschekowa, Olga *Film 2*
Tschernichin-Larsson, Jenny *Film 1*
Tschirch, Wilhelm 1818-1892 *Baker 78*
Tschortsch, Johann Georg 1681?-1737? *NewGrD 80*
Tschudi *Baker 78*
Tschudi, Aegidius 1505-1572 *NewGrD 80*
Tschudi, Burkat *NewGrD 80*
Tschudi, Gilg 1505-1572 *NewGrD 80*
Tschudy, Aegidius 1505-1572 *NewGrD 80*
Tschudy, Gilg 1505-1572 *NewGrD 80*
Tsegaye Gabre-Medhin 1936- *ConDr 73, -77*
Tsessarskaya, Emma *Film 2*
Tseytlin, Lev Moiseyevich 1881-1952 *NewGrD 80*
Tsfasman, Alexander 1906-1971 *Baker 78*
Tshudi, Burkat *NewGrD 80*
Tsiang, H T 1899-1971 *WhScrn 74, -77, WhoHol B*
Tsiganov, Dmitry Mikhaylovich 1903- *NewGrD 80*
Tsikotski, Evgeny Karlovich *NewGrD 80*
Tsingh, Hurri *Film 1*
Tsinguirides, Georgette 1933- *CnOxB*
Tsintsadze, Sulkhan Fyodorovich 1925- *Baker 78, NewGrD 80*
Ts'ong, Fou *NewGrD 80*
Tsopel, Corinna *WhoHol A*
Tsou, Se-Ling *DcFM*
Tsouleas, Harry *PupTheA*
Tsouyopoulos, Georges S 1930- *Baker 78, DcCM*
Tsu, Irene 1943- *FilmgC, HalFC 80, WhoHol A*
Tsuburaya, Eiji 1901-1970 *FilmEn*
Tsuburuya, Eiji 1901-1970 *WhoHrs 80*
Tsuchida, Sadao 1908- *IntWWM 77, -80*
Tsuji, Shoichi 1895- *NewGrD 80*
Tsukamoto, Raynum K 1889-1974 *WhScrn 77*
Tsukasa, Yoko 1934- *FilmEn, IntMPA 77, -75, -76, -78, -79, -80*
Tsukatani, Akihiro 1919- *Baker 78*
Tsukiji, Yonesaburo *WhoHrs 80*
Tsukimori, Sennosuke 1908- *IntMPA 77, -75, -76, -78, -79, -80*
Tsukkerman, Viktor Abramovich 1903- *NewGrD 80*
Tsur, Chaim Asher 1939- *IntWWM 77, -80*
Tsutsumi, Tsuyoshi 1942- *IntWWM 80, WhoMus 72*
Tsvetanov, Tsvetan 1931- *NewGrD 80*
Tsvetanov, Tsvetau 1931- *IntWWM 80*
Tsytovich, Vladimir 1931- *DcCM*
Tua, Teresina 1867-1955 *Baker 78*
Tual, Denise *WomWMM*
Tuala, Mario 1924-1961 *WhScrn 74, -77*
Tubal, Adrian *NewGrD 80*
Tubau, Maria *WhThe*
Tubb, Caroline 1876-1976 *NewGrD 80*
Tubb, Carrie 1876-1976 *Baker 78, NewGrD 80*
Tubb, Ernest 1914- *BiDAmM, CmpEPM, CounME 74[port], -74A, EncFCWM 69, IlEncCM[port], NewGrD 80*
Tubb, Glenn Douglas 1935- *BiDAmM*
Tubb, Justin Wayne 1935- *BiDAmM, CounME 74, -74A, EncFCWM 69, IlEncCM*
Tubb, Monte 1933- *ConAmC*
Tubbs *NewGrD 80*
Tubbs, Alfred d1912 *NewGrD 80*
Tubbs, Bill 1908-1953 *WhoHol B*
Tubbs, Edward *NewGrD 80*
Tubbs, Hubert Allen 1947- *AmSCAP 80*
Tubbs, James 1835-1919 *NewGrD 80*
Tubbs, Thomas *NewGrD 80*
Tubbs, Vincent 1915- *DrBlPA*
Tubbs, William d1878? *NewGrD 80*
Tubbs, William 1908-1953 *WhScrn 74, -77*
Tubbs, William 1909-1953 *HalFC 80*
Tubert, Bob 1932- *EncFCWM 69*
Tubert, Robert 1932- *BiDAmM*
Tubes, The *ConMuA 80A, IlEncR*
Tubin, Eduard 1905- *Baker 78, IntWWM 77, -80, NewGrD 80*
Tucapsky, Antonin 1928- *IntWWM 77, -80*
Tucci, Gabriela 1929- *Baker 78*
Tucci, Gabriella 1932- *CmOp, MusSN[port], NewGrD 80, WhoOp 76*
Tucci, Joseph William 1953- *AmSCAP 80*
Tucci, Maria 1941- *WhoThe 77*
Tuccio, Stefano 1540-1597 *OxThe*
Tucek *NewGrD 80*
Tucek, Frantisek 1782-1850 *NewGrD 80*
Tucek, Franz 1782-1850 *NewGrD 80*
Tucek, Jan 1743?-1783 *NewGrD 80*
Tucek, Vincenc 1773-1821? *NewGrD 80*
Tucher, Gottlieb, Freiherr Von 1798-1877 *Baker 78*
Tuchner, Michael *FilmgC, HalFC 80*
Tuchock, Wanda *IntMPA 77, -75, -76, -78, -79, -80, WomWMM*
Tucholsky, Kurt 1890-1935 *Ent*
Tucic, Srdan 1873-1940 *CnMD*
Tucker, Annette May *AmSCAP 80*
Tucker, Cy 1889-1952 *WhScrn 74, -77*
Tucker, David L 1937- *IntWWM 77*
Tucker, Edmund *NewGrD 80*
Tucker, Edna Mae 1907- *AmSCAP 66*
Tucker, Edward *NewGrD 80*
Tucker, Eliot 1950- *AmSCAP 80*
Tucker, Forrest 1919- *BiE&WWA, FilmEn, FilmgC, ForYSC, HalFC 80, IntMPA 77, -75, -76, -78, -79, -80, MotPP, MovMk[port], WhoHol A, WhoHrs 80[port]*
Tucker, Francis Bland 1895- *BiDAmM*
Tucker, Gaylord Bob 1915- *BiDAmM*
Tucker, George Loane d1921 *MotPP, NotNAT B, WhoHol B*
Tucker, George Loane 1872-1921 *IlWWBF, TwYS A, WhScrn 77*
Tucker, George Loane 1881-1921 *DcFM, FilmEn, HalFC 80*
Tucker, Gillian Margaret 1951- *IntWWM 77*
Tucker, Glenn *ConAmTC*
Tucker, Gregory *DancEn 78*
Tucker, Gregory 1908-1971 *ConAmC*
Tucker, Gregory 1909-1971 *BiDAmM*
Tucker, Harlan *Film 2*
Tucker, Harland d1949 *WhScrn 77*
Tucker, Joan 1927- *DancEn 78*
Tucker, John A 1896- *AmSCAP 66, -80*
Tucker, John Bartholomew *WhoHol A*
Tucker, John Ireland 1819-1895 *BiDAmM*
Tucker, Larry *WhoHol A*
Tucker, Lem 1938- *DrBlPA*
Tucker, Lillian *Film 1*
Tucker, Lorenzo 1907- *BlksB&W[port], -C, DrBlPA*
Tucker, Luther 1936- *BluesWW[port]*
Tucker, Melville 1916- *IntMPA 77, -75, -76, -78, -79, -80*
Tucker, Michael B 1941- *EncJzS 70*
Tucker, Mickey 1941- *EncJzS 70*
Tucker, Norman 1910-1978 *NewGrD 80*
Tucker, Orrin 1911- *AmSCAP 66, -80, BgBands 74[port], BiDAmM, CmpEPM*
Tucker, Paula McKinney *WomWMM B*
Tucker, Phil 1927?- *WhoHrs 80*
Tucker, Richard 1869-1942 *FilmEn, Film 1, -2, ForYSC, TwYS, WhoHol B*
Tucker, Richard 1884-1942 *WhScrn 74, -77*
Tucker, Richard 1913-1975 *Baker 78, MusSN[port], NewEOp 71, NewGrD 80*
Tucker, Richard 1914-1975 *BiDAmM, BnBkM 80[port], CmOp, WhScrn 77*
Tucker, Sophie *AmPS B*
Tucker, Sophie 1884-1966 *BiDAmM, CmpEPM, EncMT, Film 2, FilmgC, ForYSC, HalFC 80, JoeFr, NotNAT A, ThFT[port], WhScrn 74, -77, WhThe, WhoHol B*
Tucker, Sophie 1887-1966 *NotNAT B*
Tucker, Sophie 1888-1966 *BiE&WWA*
Tucker, Tanya 1958- *CounME 74[port], -74A, IlEncCM[port], RkOn 2[port], WhoHol A*
Tucker, Tommy *BgBands 74[port], RkOn 2A*
Tucker, Tommy 1903- *IntWWM 77*
Tucker, Tommy 1908- *AmSCAP 66, -80, BiDAmM, CmpEPM, WhoMus 72*
Tucker, Tommy 1933- *BluesWW[port]*
Tucker, Tui St. George *ConAmC*
Tucker, Viola 1921- *WhoMus 72*
Tucker, William d1679 *NewGrD 80*
Tucker, William H *Film 2*
Tuckerman, Maury 1905-1966 *BiE&WWA, NotNAT B*
Tuckerman, Samuel Parkman 1819-1890 *Baker 78, BiDAmM, NewGrD 80*
Tucket, Richard 1915- *WhoMus 72*
Tuckey, William 1708-1781 *Baker 78, BiDAmM, NewGrD 80*
Tucknott, Jean Lilian 1927- *WhoMus 72*
Tuckwell, Barry 1931- *Baker 78, BnBkM 80, IntWWM 77, -80, NewGrD 80, WhoMus 72*
Tuczek *NewGrD 80*
Tuczek-Ehrenburg, Leopoldine 1821-1883 *NewGrD 80*
Tuder, John *NewGrD 80*
Tuderto, Jacopus De *NewGrD 80*
Tudino, Cesare 1530?-1590? *NewGrD 80*
Tudor *NewGrD 80*
Tudor, Anthony 1909- *WhThe*
Tudor, Antony 1908- *CnOxB*
Tudor, Antony 1909- *BiE&WWA,*

DancEn 78[port]
Tudor, David 1926- *Baker 78, ConAmC, DcCM, NewGrD 80*
Tudor, John *NewGrD 80*
Tudor, Kenneth *WhoMus 72*
Tudor, Rowan 1905- *BiE&WWA, NotNAT*
Tudor, Valerie 1910- *WhThe*
Tudual *NewGrD 80*
Tudway, Thomas 1650-1726 *Baker 78, NewGrD 80, OxMus*
Tuerk, John d1951 *NotNAT B*
Tuerlinckx *NewGrD 80*
Tuerlinckx, Corneille Jean Joseph 1783-1855 *NewGrD 80*
Tuerlinckx, Jean Arnold Antoine 1753-1827 *NewGrD 80*
Tufano, Dennis S 1946- *AmSCAP 80*
Tufares, Deno Athan, Jr. 1948- *CpmDNM 80*
Tufnell, Arthur Tregoning 1934- *WhoMus 72*
Tufnell, Herbert Percy 1900- *WhoMus 72*
Tufts, John 1689-1750 *Baker 78, BiDAmM, NewGrD 80*
Tufts, John Wheeler 1825-1908 *Baker 78, BiDAmM*
Tufts, Paul 1924- *CpmDNM 77*
Tufts, Sonny d1970 *MotPP, WhoHol B*
Tufts, Sonny 1911-1970 *FilmEn, FilmgC, HalFC 80, HolP 40[port], What 2[port], WhoHrs 80*
Tufts, Sonny 1912-1970 *ForYSC, MovMk[port], WhScrn 74, -77*
Tugal, Pierre 1883-1964 *CnOxB*
Tugal, Pierre 1895-1964 *DancEn 78*
Tugarinova, Tatiana Fedorovna 1925- *WhoOp 76*
Tugend, Harry 1898- *FilmEn*
Tughin, Hans 1460?-1519 *NewGrD 80*
Tugi, Hans 1460?-1519 *NewGrD 80*
Tugy, Hans 1460?-1519 *NewGrD 80*
Tuitama, Kuka Leupena 1901- *AmSCAP 80*
Tujague, Joe *NewOrJ*
Tujague, Jon *NewOrJ*
Tuke, Sir Samuel d1674 *OxThe*
Tulan, Frederick Thomas 1934- *IntWWM 77, -80*
Tulikov, Serafim 1914- *NewGrD 80*
Tulindberg, Erik 1761-1814 *Baker 78, NewGrD 80*
Tulipan, Ira H 1934- *IntMPA 77, -75, -76, -78, -79, -80*
Tull, Fisher Aubrey 1934- *AmSCAP 80, CpmDNM 78, -80, ConAmC*
Tull, Jethro *BiDAmM*
Tullar, Grant Colfax 1870-1950 *BiDAmM*
Tulley, Ethel 1898-1968 *WhScrn 74, WhoHol B*
Tully, Ethel 1898-1968 *WhScrn 77*
Tully, George F 1876-1930 *NotNAT B, WhThe*
Tully, Jim 1891-1947 *WhScrn 77*
Tully, May d1924 *NotNAT B, WomWMM*
Tully, Montgomery 1904- *FilmEn, FilmgC, HalFC 80, IlWWBF, IntMPA 77, -75, -76, -78, -79, -80*
Tully, Richard Walton 1877-1945 *NotNAT B, WhThe*
Tully, Sydney Strickland 1860-1911 *CreCan 1*
Tully, Tom *IntMPA 77, -75, -76, -78, -79, -80, MotPP*
Tully, Tom 1896- *FilmgC, HalFC 80, WhoHol A*
Tully, Tom 1902?- *ForYSC, MovMk*
Tully, Tom 1908- *FilmEn, HolCA[port], Vers A[port]*
Tulou, Jean-Louis 1786-1865 *Baker 78, NewGrD 80*
Tulsa Red *BluesWW[port]*
Tuma, Frantisek Ignac Antonin 1704-1774 *NewGrD 80*
Tuma, Franz 1704-1774 *Baker 78*
Tuma, Mirko 1921- *ConAmTC*
Tumanina, Nadezhda Vasil'yevna 1909-1968 *NewGrD 80*
Tumanov, Joseph Mikhailovich 1905- *OxThe*
Tumarin, Boris 1910- *BiE&WWA, NotNAT, WhoThe 72, -77*
Tumbleson, J Raymond 1922- *IntWWM 77, -80*
Tuminello, Phil J 1921- *AmSCAP 66, -80*
Tunberg, Karl *IntMPA 77, -75, -76, -78, -79, -80*
Tunberg, Karl 1907- *FilmEn*
Tunberg, Karl 1908- *FilmgC, HalFC 80*
Tunbridge, Joseph A 1886-1961 *NotNAT B, WhThe*
Tunc, Irene *WhoHol A*
Tunder, Franz 1614-1667 *Baker 78, MusMk, NewGrD 80*
Tune, Tommy 1939- *CnOxB, WhoHol A*
Tune Rockers, The *RkOn*
Tune Weavers, The *RkOn[port]*
Tunesters *BiDAmM*
Tunick, Eugene 1920- *IntMPA 77, -75, -76, -78, -79, -80*
Tunick, Irve *IntMPA 77, -75, -76, -78, -79, -80*
Tunick, Jonathan 1938- *AmSCAP 80*
Tunis, Fay 1890-1967 *Film 1, WhScrn 74, -77, WhoHol B*
Tunley, David Evatt 1930- *IntWWM 80, NewGrD 80*
Tunnard, Viola *WhoMus 72*
Tunnell, Bon Bon George N 1903- *WhoJazz 72*
Tunnell, Charles Jeremy 1941- *WhoMus 72*
Tunnell, John 1936- *IntWWM 77, -80, WhoMus 72*
Tunnell, Susan Mary 1933- *IntWWM 77, -80*
Tunney, Gene 1897- *What 1[port]*
Tunney, Gene 1898- *Film 2*
Tunstall, Anthony Richard 1924- *WhoMus 72*
Tunsted, Simon d1369? *OxMus*
Tunstede, Simon d1369 *NewGrD 80*
Tuohy, William Joseph 1941- *AmSCAP 80*
Tuominen, Harri Olavi 1944- *IntWWM 77, -80*
Tuotilo d915 *NewGrD 80*
Tuotti, Joseph Dolan *MorBAP*
Tupin, Wasil 1922- *CnOxB, DancEn 78*
Tupine, Oleg 1920- *DancEn 78*
Tupkov, Dimiter 1929- *Baker 78*
Tupou, Manu 1935- *WhoThe 77*
Tupper, James 1819-1868 *BiDAmM*
Tupper, Lois Ann *WomWMM B*
Tupper, Martin 1810-1889 *OxMus*
Tupper, Mary d1964 *NotNAT B*
Tupper, Pearl *Film 2*
Tur, Leonid Davidovich 1905-1961 *ModWD*
Tur, Pyotr Davidovich 1907- *ModWD*
Turan, Jerry *AmSCAP 80*
Turati, Antonio Maria 1608-1650 *NewGrD 80*
Turbans, The *RkOn[port]*
Turcar, Elemir 1919- *IntWWM 77*
Turchaninof, Peter 1779-1856 *OxMus*
Turchaninov, Piotr 1779-1856 *Baker 78*
Turchaninov, Pyotr Ivanovich 1779-1856 *NewGrD 80*
Turchi, Guido 1916- *Baker 78, NewGrD 80, OxMus*
Turckheim, Edith *CnOxB*
Turco, Giovanni Del *NewGrD 80*
Turco, Lorenzo Del *NewGrD 80*
Tureck, Rosalyn 1914- *Baker 78, BnBkM 80, IntWWM 77, -80, MusSN[port], NewGrD 80, WhoMus 72, WomCom[port]*
Turell, Saul J 1921- *IntMPA 77, -75, -76, -78, -79, -80*
Turellier, Jean 1923- *IntWWM 77*
Turetzky, Bertram Jay 1933- *AmSCAP 80, NewGrD 80*
Turfkruyer, Marc *IntMPA 77, -75, -76, -78, -79, -80*
Turfler, James *Film 2*
Turgenev, Ivan 1818-1883 *Ent, NewEOp 71*
Turgenev, Ivan Sergeivich 1818-1883 *PlP&P[port]*
Turgenev, Ivan Sergeyevich 1818-1883 *CnThe, EncWT, McGEWD[port], NewGrD 80, NotNAT A, -B, REnWD[port]*
Turgeniev, Ivan Sergeivich 1818-1883 *OxThe*
Turgeon, Bernard 1932- *CreCan 2, WhoOp 76*
Turgeon, Peter 1919- *BiE&WWA, WhoHol A*
Turges, Edmund 1450?- *NewGrD 80*
Turich, Felipe *WhoHol A*
Turich, Rosa *WhoHol A*
Turin, Victor 1895-1945 *DcFM, WorEFlm*
Turina, Joaquin 1882-1949 *Baker 78, BnBkM 80, CompSN[port], DcCom&M 79, DcCM, MusMk, NewGrD 80, OxMus*
Turini, Francesco 1589?-1656 *NewGrD 80*
Turini, Francesco 1595?-1656 *MusMk*
Turini, Gregorio 1560?-1600? *NewGrD 80*
Turini, Ronald 1934- *NewGrD 80*
Turja, Ilmari 1901- *CroCD*
Turk, Arlene M *WhoHol A*
Turk, Daniel Gottlieb 1756-1813 *OxMus*
Turk, Daniel Gottlob 1750-1813 *NewGrD 80*
Turk, Daniel Gottlob 1756-1813 *Baker 78*
Turk, Hans Peter 1940- *IntWWM 80*
Turk, Roy 1892-1934 *AmSCAP 66, -80, CmpEPM, Sw&Ld C*
Turk, Roy 1892-1949 *AmPS*
Turk, William 1866?-1911? *BiDAmM*
Turkel, Ann *HalFC 80, WhoHol A*
Turkel, Joseph *WhoHol A*
Turkin, Marshall W *ConAmC*
Turknett, Clifford *NatPD[port]*
Turle, James 1802-1882 *Baker 78, NewGrD 80, OxMus*
Turleigh, Veronica 1903-1971 *PlP&P, WhScrn 77, WhThe, WhoHol A*
Turleron, Hilaire *NewGrD 80*
Turley, Dianne *WhoHol A*
Turlupin 1587?-1637 *NotNAT B, OxThe*
Turlur, Englebert 1560?-1598 *NewGrD 80*
Turmair, Johann *NewGrD 80*
Turman, Glynn 1946?- *DrBlPA, WhoHol A*
Turman, Laurence 1926- *FilmgC, HalFC 80*
Turman, Lawrence 1926- *FilmEn, IntMPA 77, -75, -76, -78, -79, -80*
Turnau, Joseph 1888-1954 *BiDAmM*
Turnbull, David Middleton 1931- *IntWWM 80*
Turnbull, Sister Fedora 1895- *WhoMus 72*
Turnbull, Florence Jessie *WhoMus 72*
Turnbull, Graham Morrison 1931- *AmSCAP 66, -80*
Turnbull, John 1880-1956 *NotNAT B, WhThe, WhoHol B*
Turnbull, Julia 1822-1887 *CnOxB, DancEn 78*
Turnbull, Percy Purvis 1902- *WhoMus 72*
Turnbull, Stanley d1924 *Film 2, NotNAT B, WhThe*
Turner, Alfred 1870-1941 *NotNAT B, WhThe*
Turner, Alfred Dudley 1854-1888 *Baker 78, BiDAmM*
Turner, Alfred Vernon 1913- *IntWWM 77*
Turner, Annie Mae 1939- *BiDAmM*
Turner, Anthony *OxThe*
Turner, Babe Kyro Lemon 1907-1972 *BluesWW[port]*
Turner, Baby *Film 2*
Turner, Barbara *WhoHol A*
Turner, Benny 1908?-1973 *NewOrJ*
Turner, Bert *Film 1*
Turner, Beth *MorBAP, NatPD[port]*
Turner, Big Joe 1911- *CmpEPM, EncJzS 70, IlEncJ, WhoJazz 72*
Turner, Blind Squire *BluesWW[port]*
Turner, Bowditch *Film 2*
Turner, Bridget *WhoHol A, WhoThe 77*
Turner, Bruce 1922- *IlEncJ, IntWWM 77, -80*
Turner, Cecil James 1906- *WhoMus 72*
Turner, Charles *WhoHol A*
Turner, Charles 1921- *AmSCAP 66, -80, Baker 78, ConAmC*
Turner, Cicely d1940 *NotNAT B*
Turner, Claramae 1920- *BiE&WWA, NewEOp 71, WhoHol A, WhoOp 76*
Turner, Clifford 1913- *IntMPA 77, -75, -76, -78, -79, -80*
Turner, Cyril *McGEWD[port]*
Turner, David 1927- *ConDr 73, -77, CroCD, McGEWD, WhoThe 72, -77*
Turner, David Bruce 1948- *IntWWM 77*
Turner, Dennis Lance *BlkAmP, NatPD*
Turner, Dianne Gross 1938- *AmSCAP 80*
Turner, Doreen *Film 2*
Turner, Dorothy 1895-1969 *WhThe*
Turner, Douglas *WhoHol A, WhoThe 72, -77*
Turner, Eardley d1929 *NotNAT B*
Turner, Emanuel 1884-1941 *WhScrn 74, -77*
Turner, Eva *WhoMus 72*
Turner, Eva 1892- *CmOp, NewEOp 71, NewGrD 80[port]*
Turner, Eva 1899- *IntWWM 77, -80*
Turner, F A 1842?-1923 *WhScrn 77*
Turner, Florence d1946 *MotPP, WhoHol B*
Turner, Florence 1877-1946 *NotNAT B*
Turner, Florence 1885-1946 *FilmEn, WhScrn 74, -77*

Turner, Florence 1887-1946 *Film 1, -2, FilmgC, HalFC 80, TwYS*
Turner, Florence 1888-1946 *IlWWBF[port], MovMk*
Turner, Fred 1938- *WhoMus 72*
Turner, Fred A *Film 1, -2*
Turner, Geneva C *BlkAmP*
Turner, George 1902-1968 *BiE&WWA, Film 2, NotNAT B, WhScrn 77, WhoHol A*
Turner, Godfrey 1913-1948 *Baker 78, ConAmC*
Turner, Hal 1930- *AmSCAP 66*
Turner, Harold 1909-1962 *CnOxB, DancEn 78, NotNAT B, WhThe*
Turner, Harold Joseph 1930- *AmSCAP 80*
Turner, Helene *WomWMM*
Turner, Henry B 1904- *WhoJazz 72*
Turner, Herbert Barclay 1852-1927 *BiDAmM*
Turner, Ike 1934- *BiDAmM, WhoHol A*
Turner, Ike And Tina *ConMuA 80A[port], IlEncR[port], RkOn*
Turner, J W d1913 *NotNAT B*
Turner, Jet Elton 1928- *IntWWM 77*
Turner, Joe 1907- *BiDAmM, EncJzS 70, WhoJazz 72*
Turner, Joe 1911- *RkOn[port]*
Turner, John *NewGrD 80*
Turner, John 1932- *FilmgC, HalFC 80*
Turner, John C 1896-1949 *AmSCAP 66, -80*
Turner, John David, Jr. 1930- *AmSCAP 80*
Turner, John Godfrey 1935- *IntWWM 77*
Turner, John Hastings 1892- *WhThe*
Turner, John R *IntWWM 77, -80, WhoMus 72*
Turner, Joseph *BlkAmP*
Turner, Joseph Vernon 1911- *BluesWW[port], EncJzS 70*
Turner, L Godfrey- *WhThe*
Turner, Lana *MotPP*
Turner, Lana 1920- *CmMov, FilmEn, FilmgC, ForYSC, HalFC 80, MGM[port], MovMk[port], ThFT[port], WhoHol A, WorEFlm*
Turner, Lana 1921- *BiDFilm, -81, IntMPA 77, -75, -76, -78, -79, -80, OxFilm*
Turner, Laurance 1901- *WhoMus 72*
Turner, Leland Smith, Jr. 1936- *AmSCAP 80*
Turner, Lynne Alison 1941- *IntWWM 77, -80*
Turner, Maidel 1888-1953 *Film 2, NotNAT B, WhScrn 74, -77, WhoHol B*
Turner, Malcolm 1939- *IntWWM 77, -80*
Turner, Margarita Joy 1943- *WhoOp 76*
Turner, Marion 1920- *AmSCAP 66*
Turner, Marion M 1929- *IntWWM 77, -80*
Turner, Maude *Film 2*
Turner, Michael 1921- *WhoHol A, WhoThe 72, -77*
Turner, Mildred Cozzens 1897- *AmSCAP 66, -80, ConAmC*
Turner, Myra Brooks *ConAmC*
Turner, Norah 1912- *IntWWM 77, WhoMus 72*
Turner, Otis Daddy 1862-1918 *TwYS A, WhScrn 77*
Turner, Pamela Ann Morgan 1928- *IntWWM 77, -80*
Turner, Raymond *Film 2*
Turner, Richard Julian 1936- *CreCan 1*
Turner, Robert Comrie 1920- *Baker 78, CreCan 1, IntWWM 80, NewGrD 80*
Turner, Roger David 1946- *WhoMus 72*
Turner, Roscoe 1896-1970 *WhScrn 74, -77, WhoHol B*
Turner, Sally Margaret Tudsbery 1945- *IntWWM 77, -80*
Turner, Sammy 1932- *RkOn[port]*
Turner, Scott *AmSCAP 80*
Turner, Spyder *RkOn 2[port]*
Turner, Thomas G 1937- *ConAmC, IntWWM 77, -80*
Turner, Thomas Sample 1941- *ConAmC*
Turner, Tim 1924- *IntMPA 75, -76, WhoHol A*
Turner, Tina 1939- *DrBlPA, WhoHol A*
Turner, Titus *RkOn*
Turner, Tom *WhoHol A*
Turner, Vickery *WhoHol A*
Turner, W J 1889-1946 *CnMD, NewGrD 80, NotNAT B*
Turner, Walter James 1889-1946 *Baker 78*
Turner, Wedgwood *Film 1*
Turner, William *NewGrD 80*
Turner, William 1651-1740 *Baker 78, MusMk, NewGrD 80, OxMus*
Turner, William H 1861-1942 *Film 1, -2, WhScrn 74, -77, WhoHol B*
Turner, Willis Lloyd 1927- *BiE&WWA*
Turner Robinson, Ann *NewGrD 80*
Turney, Catherine 1906- *BiE&WWA, NotNAT*
Turney, Edward 1816-1872 *BiDAmM*
Turney, Matt *CnOxB, DancEn 78*
Turney, Norris William 1921- *EncJzS 70*
Turnhout, Gerard De 1520?-1580 *Baker 78, NewGrD 80*
Turnhout, Jan-Jacob Van 1545?-1618? *NewGrD 80*
Turnhout, Jean-Jacques De 1545?-1618? *NewGrD 80*
Turnick, Clement Joseph 1913- *AmSCAP 80*
Turnier, Gary Richard 1954- *AmSCAP 80*
Turnis, Arthur *NewOrJ*
Turnovius, Jan *NewGrD 80*
Turnovsky, Jan Trojan *NewGrD 80*
Turnovsky, Martin 1928- *IntWWM 77, -80, NewGrD 80, WhoMus 72, WhoOp 76*
Turnowski, Jan 1567-1629 *NewGrD 80*
Turofsky, Riki 1944- *WhoOp 76*
Turok, Paul Harris 1929- *AmSCAP 80, Baker 78, CpmDNM 76, -79, -80, ConAmC, IntWWM 77, -80*
Turp, Andre *WhoMus 72*
Turp, Andre 1925- *CreCan 2*
Turp, Andre 1926- *NewGrD 80*
Turpilius *OxThe*
Turpin, Ben 1869-1940 *Funs[port], WhScrn 77*
Turpin, Ben 1873-1940 *JoeFr[port]*
Turpin, Ben 1874-1940 *FilmEn, Film 1, -2, FilmgC, ForYSC, HalFC 80, MotPP, MovMk[port], NotNAT B, TwYS, WhScrn 74, WhoHol B, WorEFlm[port]*
Turpin, Carrie 1882-1925 *WhScrn 77, WhoHol B*
Turpin, Dick 1705-1739 *FilmgC, HalFC 80*
Turpin, Edmund Hart 1835-1907 *Baker 78, NewGrD 80*
Turpin, Gerry 1930?- *FilmgC, HalFC 80*
Turpin, Thomas Million 1873-1922 *BiDAmM*
Turpin, Waters *MorBAP*
Turpio, Ambivius *OxThe*
Turrano, Joe 1918- *AmSCAP 66*
Turrano, Joseph A 1918- *AmSCAP 80*
Turre, Steve 1949- *EncJzS 70*
Turrell, Frances 1903- *IntWWM 77, -80*
Turrentine, Stanley 1934- *EncJzS 70*
Turrin, Joseph Edigio 1947- *AmSCAP 80*
Turrin, Joseph Egidio 1947- *ConAmC*
Turrschmidt, Carl 1753-1797 *NewGrD 80*
Turrschmidt, Karl 1753-1797 *NewGrD 80*
Turrschmiedt, Carl 1753-1797 *NewGrD 80*
Turrschmiedt, Karl 1753-1797 *NewGrD 80*
Turschmit, Carl 1753-1797 *NewGrD 80*
Turschmit, Karl 1753-1797 *NewGrD 80*
Turska, Irena 1912- *CnOxB*
Turski, Zbigniew 1908- *Baker 78, IntWWM 77, -80, NewGrD 80*
Turteltaub-Orenstein *NewYTET*
Turtles, The *BiDAmM, ConMuA 80A, IlEncR, RkOn 2[port]*
Turton, Gervaise Mary 1899- *IntWWM 80*
Turton, Peter Arthur 1925- *WhoMus 72*
Tuscano, Nicolo *NewGrD 80*
Tushingham, Rita *MotPP, WhoHol A*
Tushingham, Rita 1940- *FilmAG WE[port], FilmgC, HalFC 80*
Tushingham, Rita 1942- *FilmEn, IlWWBF[port], IntMPA 77, -75, -76, -78, -79, -80, MovMk, OxFilm, WhoThe 72, -77, WorEFlm*
Tushinsky, Irving 1912- *IntMPA 75, -76*
Tushinsky, Joseph S 1910- *IntMPA 75, -76*
Tusler, Robert Leon 1920- *Baker 78, IntWWM 77, -80*
Tusmole, Joseph *NewGrD 80*
Tussaud, Madame 1761-1850 *DcPup*
Tustain, George *Film 2*
Tustin, Whitney *AmSCAP 66, -80, ConAmC*
Tuthill, B C *OxMus*
Tuthill, Burnet Corwin 1888- *AmSCAP 66, -80, Baker 78, BiDAmM, CpmDNM 75, -77, ConAmC, IntWWM 77, -80, NewGrD 80, WhoMus 72*
Tutin, Dorothy 1930- *BiE&WWA, CnThe, EncWT, Ent, FilmgC, HalFC 80, IlWWBF, IntMPA 77, -75, -76, -78, -79, -80, NotNAT, OxFilm, WhoHol A, WhoThe 72, -77*
Tutmarc, Paul H d1972 *WhScrn 77*
Tutor, John *NewGrD 80*
Tutschek *NewGrD 80*
Tutt, Homer J *MorBAP*
Tutt, J Homer *BlkAmP, BlksB&W, -C*
Tuttle, Day 1902- *BiE&WWA, NotNAT*
Tuttle, Eugenia *Film 2*
Tuttle, Frank 1892-1963 *BiDFilm, -81, FilmEn, FilmgC, HalFC 80, WorEFlm*
Tuttle, Frank 1893-1963 *TwYS A*
Tuttle, Lurene *ForYSC, Vers A[port], WhoHol A*
Tuttle, Thelma Kent 1902- *IntWWM 77, -80*
Tuttle, Wesley *IlEncCM*
Tuttle, William 1911- *WhoHrs 80*
Tuttman, Alice 1895- *AmSCAP 66*
Tutuual *NewGrD 80*
Tuukkanen, Kalervo 1909- *Baker 78, IntWWM 77, -80, NewGrD 80*
Tuvelle, Howard Jesse 1934- *IntWWM 77*
Tuvim, Abe 1895-1958 *AmSCAP 66, -80*
Tuxedo Brass Band *BiDAmM*
Tuxen, Erik 1902-1957 *Baker 78, NewGrD 80*
Tuzer, Tanju 1944- *CnOxB*
Tuzun, Ferit 1929-1977 *NewGrD 80*
Tveit, Geirr 1908- *NewGrD 80*
Tveitt, Geirr 1908- *Baker 78, IntWWM 77, -80, NewGrD 80*
Tvermoes, Ruth Vibeke 1907- *IntWWM 77, -80*
Twain, Mark 1835-1910 *FilmgC, HalFC 80, NotNAT B, OxMus*
Twain, Norman 1930- *BiE&WWA, NotNAT*
Twaits, William 1781-1814 *BiDAmM, NotNAT B, OxThe, PlP&P[port]*
Twardowski, Romuald 1930- *Baker 78, IntWWM 77, -80, NewGrD 80*
Tweddell, Frank 1895-1971 *WhScrn 74, -77*
Tweddell, Fritz d1971 *WhoHol B*
Tweed, Frank *Film 2*
Tweed, Thomas William 1908-1971 *CreCan 1*
Tweed, Tommy 1907-1971 *WhScrn 77, WhoHol B*
Tweed, Tommy 1908-1971 *CreCan 1*
Tweedy, Donald Nichols 1890-1948 *Baker 78, BiDAmM, ConAmC*
Tweedy, Henry Hallam 1868-1953 *BiDAmM*
Twelvetrees, Helen d1958 *MotPP, NotNAT B, WhoHol B*
Twelvetrees, Helen 1907-1958 *FilmEn, ThFT[port]*
Twelvetrees, Helen 1908-1958 *Film 2, FilmgC, ForYSC, HalFC 80, HolP 30[port], MovMk, WhScrn 74, -77, WhoHrs 80*
Twerefoo, Gustav Oware 1934- *IntWWM 80*
Twiggy *IlWWBF A, WhoHol A*
Twiggy 1946- *FilmgC, HalFC 80*
Twiggy 1949- *IntMPA 77, -75, -76, -78, -79, -80*
Twine, Bobby *AmSCAP 80*
Twist, Derek 1905- *FilmgC, HalFC 80, IlWWBF, IntMPA 77, -75, -76, -78, -79*
Twist, John 1895-1976 *HalFC 80*
Twist, John 1898-1976 *FilmEn*
Twist, John 1902- *IntMPA 75, -76*
Twist, John Stuart 1898-1976 *FilmEn*
Twitchell, A R Archie 1906-1957 *WhScrn 74, -77*
Twitchell, Archie 1906-1957 *WhoHol B*
Twitchell, Archie 1907-1957 *ForYSC*
Twitty, Conway *EncFCWM 69, WhoHol A*
Twitty, Conway 1933- *CounME 74[port], -74A, ForYSC, IlEncCM[port]*
Twitty, Conway 1935- *BiDAmM, RkOn[port]*
Two Black Crows *JoeFr*
Twohig, Daniel S 1883-1961 *AmSCAP 80*
Twohig, Daniel S 1883-1962 *AmSCAP 66*
Twombly, Mary Lynn 1935- *ConAmC*
Twomey, Kathleen Greeley 1914- *AmSCAP 66, -80*
Tworek, Wandy 1913- *IntWWM 77, -80*
Tworkov, Jack *PupTheA*
Twyman, Alan P 1934- *IntMPA 77, -78, -79,*

–80
Tyard, Pontus De 1521-1605 *NewGrD 80*
Tyars, Frank 1848-1918 *NotNAT B, WhThe*
Tye, Christopher *MusMk*
Tye, Christopher 1497?-1572? *OxMus*
Tye, Christopher 1500?-1572? *Baker 78*
Tye, Christopher 1500?-1573? *BnBkM 80*
Tye, Christopher 1505?-1572? *NewGrD 80*
Tye, Robbie Wynona Rea 1906- *IntWWM 77*
Tyers, Jonathan d1767 *OxMus*
Tyers, Jonathan d1792 *OxMus*
Tyers, Thomas 1726-1787 *OxMus*
Tyers, William H 1876-1924 *AmSCAP 66, –80, BiDAmM*
Tyes, J *NewGrD 80*
Tyes, John *Baker 78*
Tyke, John 1895-1940 *WhScrn 77*
Tyl, Josef Kajetan 1808-1856 *CnThe, REnWD[port]*
Tyl, Noel 1936- *WhoOp 76*
Tyler, Beverly 1924- *FilmgC, HalFC 80*
Tyler, Beverly 1928- *ForYSC, IntMPA 77, –75, –76, –78, –79, –80, WhoHol A*
Tyler, Bonnie *ConMuA 80A*
Tyler, George Crouse 1867-1946 *NotNAT A, –B, WhThe, WhoStg 1908*
Tyler, Gladys C 1893-1972 *WhScrn 77, WhoHol B*
Tyler, Goldie 1925- *AmSCAP 66, –80*
Tyler, Harry 1888-1961 *Film 2, ForYSC, Vers A[port], WhScrn 74, –77, WhoHol B*
Tyler, James Henry 1940- *IntWWM 77, –80, NewGrD 80*
Tyler, John Malcolm 1929- *IntWWM 77, –80, WhoMus 72*
Tyler, Joseph 1751-1823 *BiDAmM*
Tyler, Judy 1933-1957 *MotPP, NotNAT B, WhScrn 77, WhoHol B*
Tyler, Odette 1869-1936 *NotNAT B, WhThe*
Tyler, Odette 1872- *WhoStg 1906, –1908*
Tyler, Parker 1904-1974 *HalFC 80, OxFilm*
Tyler, Royall 1757-1826 *CnThe, EncWT, McGEWD, NotNAT B, OxThe, PlP&P, REnWD[port]*
Tyler, Royall 1758-1826 *BiDAmM*
Tyler, T Texas 1916-1972 *BiDAmM, CounME 74, –74A, EncFCWM 69, IlEncCM[port]*
Tyler, Tom 1903-1954 *FilmEn, Film 2, FilmgC, HalFC 80, MotPP, NotNAT B, TwYS, WhScrn 74, –77, WhoHol B, WhoHrs 80[port]*
Tyler, Tom 1904-1954 *ForYSC*
Tyler, Willie *DrBlPA*
Tyling *NewGrD 80*
Tylkowski, Wojciech 1624?-1695 *NewGrD 80*
Tymes, The *AmPS A, RkOn[port]*
Tympany Five *BiDAmM*
Tynan, Brandon 1879-1967 *Film 2, ForYSC, WhScrn 74, –77, WhThe, WhoHol B*
Tynan, Kenneth 1927- *BiE&WWA, CroCD, EncWT, NotNAT, WhoThe 72, –77*
Tyndale, William d1530 *OxMus*
Tyndall, Jeremy Peter 1950- *IntWWM 80*
Tyndall, John 1820-1893 *Baker 78*
Tyndall, Kate d1919 *NotNAT B*
Tyne, George *WhoHol A*
Tyner, Alfred McCoy 1938- *EncJzS 70*
Tyner, Charles *WhoHol A*
Tyner, McCoy 1938- *IlEncJ*
Tynes, Margaret 1929- *DrBlPA, WhoOp 76*
Typp, W *Baker 78, NewGrD 80*
Tyra, Thomas Norman 1933- *AmSCAP 66, –80, IntWWM 77, –80*
Tyree, Elizabeth *WhoStg 1906, –1908*
Tyree, Ronald Wayne 1932- *IntWWM 77, –80*
Tyrell, Susan *WhoHol A*
Tyren, Arne 1928- *WhoMus 72, WhoOp 76*
Tyrlova, Hermina 1900- *DcFM*
Tyrol, Jacques *TwYS A*
Tyroler, William *Film 2*
Tyron, Max *Film 2*
Tyrrell, Agnes 1846-1883 *NewGrD 80*
Tyrrell, Jim *ConMuA 80B*
Tyrrell, Rose d1934 *NotNAT B*
Tyrrell, Susan 1946- *FilmEn, HalFC 80, IntMPA 77, –75, –76, –78, –79, –80*
Tyrwhitt, Gerald *Baker 78, OxMus*
Tyson, Alan 1926- *IntWWM 77, –80, NewGrD 80*
Tyson, Cicely 1932?- *FilmEn*
Tyson, Cicely 1933- *HalFC 80, MovMk[port], NotNAT, WhoHol A, WhoThe 77*
Tyson, Cicely 1939- *DrBlPA*
Tyson, Ian 1933- *BiDAmM*
Tyson, Ian D 1936- *AmSCAP 80*
Tyson, J H *PupTheA*
Tyson, Margaret Lynn 1948- *IntWWM 80*
Tyson, Mildred Lund 1901- *AmSCAP 66, –80, ConAmC*
Tyson, Sylvia Fricker 1940- *AmSCAP 80*
Tyszkowski, Jerzy Stanislaw 1930- *IntWWM 77, –80*
Tytgat, Martin Marie Nicholas 1911- *IntWWM 77, –80*
Tyulin, Yury Nikolayevich 1893- *NewGrD 80*
Tyven, Gertrude 1924-1966 *CnOxB, DancEn 78*
Tyzack, Margaret 1933- *FilmgC, HalFC 80, WhoHol A, WhoThe 72, –77*
Tzaknopoulos, Joannes *NewGrD 80*
Tzamen, Thomas *NewGrD 80*
Tzara, Tristan 1896-1963 *ModWD*
Tzarth, Georg 1708-1778 *Baker 78, NewGrD 80*
Tzavellas, George 1916-1976 *FilmEn*
Tzavellas, Georges 1916- *DcFM*
Tzelniker, Meier 1894- *FilmgC, HalFC 80*
Tzipine, Georges 1907- *NewGrD 80*
Tzivin, Mikhail 1949- *CnOxB*
Tzvetanov, Tzvetan 1931- *Baker 78*
Tzybin, Vladimir 1877-1949 *Baker 78*

U

U Ku *REnWD[port]*
U Kyin U d1853 *REnWD[port]*
U Pok Ni 1849- *REnWD[port]*
U Pon Nya *REnWD[port]*
U Su Tha *REnWD[port]*
Ubeda, Jose Maria 1839-1909 *NewGrD 80*
Uber *NewGrD 80*
Uber, Alexander 1783-1824 *NewGrD 80*
Uber, Christian Benjamin 1746-1812 *NewGrD 80*
Uber, Christian Friedrich Hermann 1781-1822 *Baker 78, NewGrD 80*
Uber, David Albert 1921- *AmSCAP 66, -80, CpmDNM 78, -79, -80, ConAmC*
Uberti, Antonio 1697-1783 *Baker 78*
Uberti, Mauro 1936- *IntWWM 77, -80*
Ubertus De Psalinis *NewGrD 80*
Uboldi, Christian 1932- *CnOxB*
Uboldi, Oscar 1925- *DancEn 78*
Uc De Saint Circ 1190-1253? *NewGrD 80*
Uccellini, Marco 1603?-1680 *Baker 78, NewGrD 80*
Uccellini, Ugo *Film 2*
Uchatius, Franz Von *DcFM*
Uchida, Ruriko 1920- *IntWWM 77, -80*
Uchida, Tomu 1897-1970 *DcFM*
Uchida, Tomu 1898-1970 *FilmEn*
Uciredor, S *NewGrD 80*
Udaeta, Jose 1919- *CnOxB*
Udall, Lyn *AmSCAP 80*
Udall, Nicholas 1505-1556 *CnThe, EncWT, Ent, McGEWD, NotNAT B, OxThe*
Udalscalcus Of Maisach d1151? *NewGrD 80*
Udbye, Martin Andreas 1820-1889 *Baker 78, NewGrD 80*
Udden, Ake 1903- *NewGrD 80*
Udden, Olof Wilhelm 1799-1868 *NewGrD 80*
Ude, Armin 1933- *WhoOp 76*
Udell, Budd 1934- *ConAmC*
Udell, Peter David 1934- *AmSCAP 66, -80, ConDr 77D*
Udine, Girolamo Da *NewGrD 80*
Udine, Jean D' 1870-1938 *Baker 78*
Udoff, Yale M 1935- *NatPD[port]*
Udow, Michael William 1949- *ConAmC*
Uffenbach, Johann Friedrich Armand Von 1687-1769 *NewGrD 80*
Ufferer, Giovanni Damascenus *NewGrD 80*
Ufferer, Johann Damascenus *NewGrD 80*
UFO *ConMuA 80A, IlEncR*
Ugalde, Delphine 1829-1910 *Baker 78*
Ugarte, Floro M 1884-1975 *Baker 78, NewGrD 80*
Ugarte, Floro M 1885- *DancEn 78*
Uggams, Eloise *BlksBF*
Uggams, Leslie *WhoHol A*
Uggams, Leslie 1943- *BiDAmM, DrBlPA, EncMT, IntMPA 77, -75, -76, -78, -79, -80, NotNAT*
Uggams, Leslie 1945- *FilmgC, HalFC 80*
Ugo De Lantinis *NewGrD 80*
Ugolini, Vincenzo 1570?-1638 *Baker 78*
Ugolini, Vincenzo 1580?-1638 *NewGrD 80*
Ugolino DeOrvieto 1380?-1457? *Baker 78*
Ugolino Di Francesco Urbevetano 1380?-1457 *NewGrD 80*
Ugolino Of Orvieto 1380?-1457 *NewGrD 80*
Ugolino, Biagio *NewGrD 80*
Ugolinus, Blasius 1700?-1771 *NewGrD 80*
Ugoni, Francesco *NewGrD 80*
Ugray, Klotild 1932- *CnOxB*
Uhde, Hermann 1914-1965 *CmOp, NewEOp 71, NewGrD 80*
Uhde, Johann Otto 1725-1766 *NewGrD 80*
Uhl, Albert Alexander, Jr. 1930- *AmSCAP 80*
Uhl, Alfred 1909- *Baker 78, DcCM, IntWWM 77, -80, NewGrD 80*
Uhl, Fritz 1928- *IntWWM 77, -80, WhoMus 72, WhoOp 76*
Uhl, Richard Rathvon 1918- *AmSCAP 66, -80*
Uhl, Ruth *AmSCAP 80*
Uhlig, Max E 1896-1958 *WhScrn 74, -77*
Uhlig, Theodor 1822-1853 *Baker 78, NewGrD 80*
Uhr, William 1907-1976 *AmSCAP 80*
Uhrmacher, Hildegard *WhoOp 76*
Uissel, Gui D' *NewGrD 80*
Ujfalussy, Jozsef 1920- *IntWWM 77, -80, NewGrD 80*
Ujj, Bela 1873-1942 *Baker 78*
Ukelele, Johnny *BiDAmM*
Ukil, Sarada *Film 2*
Ukmar, Vilko 1905- *IntWWM 80, NewGrD 80*
Ukulele Kid *BluesWW*
Ulanova, Galina 1910- *CnOxB, DancEn 78[port], NewGrD 80, WhoHol A*
Ulbrich, Maximilian 1741?-1814 *NewGrD 80*
Ulbrich, Maximilian 1752?-1814 *Baker 78*
Ulbrich, Siegfried 1922- *WhoMus 72*
Ulbrich, Werner 1928- *DancEn 78*
Ulehla, Ludmila 1923- *ConAmC*
Ulenberg, Kaspar 1549-1617 *NewGrD 80*
Ulfik, Richard Joseph 1949- *AmSCAP 80*
Ulfrstad, Marius Moaritz 1890-1968 *Baker 78, NewGrD 80*
Ulfrung, Ragnar 1927- *CmOp*
Ulfung, Ragnar Sigurd 1927- *NewGrD 80, WhoOp 76*
Ulhard, Philipp d1568? *NewGrD 80*
Ulhart, Philipp d1568? *NewGrD 80*
Ulibishev, Alexander Dmitryevich 1794-1858 *NewGrD 80*
Ulitskaya, Olga *WomWMM*
Ullate, Victor 1947- *CnOxB*
Ullinger, Augustin 1746-1781 *NewGrD 80*
Ullman, Chinita 1908- *DancEn 78*
Ullman, Daniel 1920- *FilmgC, HalFC 80, IntMPA 77, -75, -76, -78, -79, -80*
Ullman, Elwood *IntMPA 77, -75, -76, -78, -79, -80*
Ullman, Ethel *Film 1*
Ullman, Greta d1972 *WhoHol B*
Ullman, Liv 1938- *OxFilm*
Ullman, Liv 1939- *FilmgC*
Ullman, Marvin *BlkAmP*
Ullman, Robert 1928- *BiE&WWA*
Ullmann, Lisa 1907- *CnOxB*
Ullmann, Liv *IntMPA 77, -75, -76, -78, -79, -80, PlP&P A, WhoHol A*
Ullmann, Liv 1939- *BiDFilm, -81, FilmEn, HalFC 80*
Ullmann, Liv 1940- *MovMk[port]*
Ullmann, Louis Gustave 1937- *WhoMus 72*
Ullmann, Viktor 1898-1944? *Baker 78, NewGrD 80*
Ulloa, Pedro De 1663-1721 *NewGrD 80*
Ullom, Jack Ralph 1944- *IntWWM 77, -80*
Ullrich, Beverly Ann McFaddin Brandon 1928- *IntWWM 77*
Ullrich, Hermann 1888- *NewGrD 80*
Ullstein, Vladimir Mark 1898- *AmSCAP 66, -80*
Ulmar, Geraldine 1862-1932 *NotNAT B, WhThe*
Ulmer, Edgar Georg 1900-1972 *BiDFilm, -81, DcFM, FilmgC, HalFC 80, WhScrn 77*
Ulmer, Edgar Georg 1904-1972 *FilmEn, WhoHrs 80, WorEFlm*
Ulmer, Fritz *Film 2*
Ulrey, Charles Franklin 1923- *IntWWM 77*
Ulric, Lenore 1892-1970 *BiE&WWA, FamA&A[port], FilmEn, Film 1, -2, FilmgC, ForYSC, MotPP, MovMk, ThFT[port], TwYS, WhThe, WhoHol B*
Ulric, Lenore 1894-1970 *WhScrn 74, -77*
Ulric, Leonore 1892-1970 *HalFC 80*
Ulrich Von Lichtenstein 1198-1276 *NewGrD 80*
Ulrich Von Liechtenstein 1198-1276 *NewGrD 80*
Ulrich Von Liehtenstein 1198-1276 *NewGrD 80*
Ulrich, Barry R *ConAmC*
Ulrich, Boris 1935- *IntWWM 77, -80*
Ulrich, Eugene J 1921- *ConAmC*
Ulrich, Florence *Film 2*
Ulrich, Homer 1906- *Baker 78, IntWWM 80, NewGrD 80*
Ulrich, Hugo 1827-1872 *Baker 78*
Ulrich, Jochen 1944- *CnOxB*
Ulrich, Jurgen 1939- *IntWWM 77, -80*
Ulrych, Lucy *WomWMM*
Ultan, Lloyd 1929- *CpmDNM 76, -80, ConAmC, IntWWM 77, -80*
Ultimate Spinach *BiDAmM*
Ultra Violet *WhoHol A*
Ulybyshev, Alexander *Baker 78*
Um-Kalthoum, Ibrahim *NewGrD 80*
Umbrico, Judy Loman *CreCan 1*
Umeki, Miyoshi 1929- *FilmEn, FilmgC, ForYSC, HalFC 80, MotPP, MovMk, WhoHol A*
Umeko, Miyoshi 1929- *BiE&WWA*
Uminska, Eugenia 1910- *IntWWM 80, NewGrD 80*
Umlauf, Carl Ignaz Franz 1824-1902 *NewGrD 80*
Umlauf, Ignaz 1746-1796 *Baker 78, NewGrD 80*
Umlauf, Michael 1781-1842 *Baker 78, NewGrD 80*
Umlauff, Ignaz 1746-1796 *NewGrD 80*

Umlauff, Michael 1781-1842 *NewGrD 80*
Umstatt, Joseph 1711-1762 *NewGrD 80*
Unamuno, Miguel De 1864-1936 *CnMD, EncWT, McGEWD[port], ModWD, OxThe*
Unamunoy, Jugo Miguel De 1864-1936 *NotNAT B*
Uncle Henry's Original Kentucky M *IlEncCM*
Uncle Lumpy *AmSCAP 80*
Uncle Morris *AmSCAP 80*
Uncle Murray *WhScrn 74, -77*
Uncle Skipper *BluesWW*
Unda, Emilie *Film 2*
Underdown, Edward 1908- *FilmgC, HalFC 80, IlWWBF, IntMPA 77, -75, -76, -78, -79, -80, WhoHol A*
Underhill, Cave 1634?-1710? *OxThe*
Underhill, Edward d1964 *NotNAT B*
Underhill, Georgina *WomWMM B*
Underhill, John Garrett d1946 *NotNAT B*
Underhill, Viola *BluesWW*
Underholtzer, Rupert *NewGrD 80*
Underwood, Brian 1939- *WhoMus 72*
Underwood, Franklin 1877-1940 *WhoHol B*
Underwood, Franklin 1877-1963 *Film 2*
Underwood, Franklin Roosevelt 1935- *AmSCAP 80*
Underwood, Franklyn d1940 *NotNAT B*
Underwood, Ian *WhoHol A*
Underwood, Isabelle *WhoStg 1906, -1908*
Underwood, John 1590?-1624 *OxThe, PlP&P*
Underwood, Lawrence 1871-1939 *Film 2, WhScrn 74, -77, WhoHol B*
Underwood, Loyal *Film 1, -2*
Underwood, Lucas 1902- *ConAmC*
Underwood, Mark Cecil 1952- *IntWWM 77, -80*
Underwood, Miles *CreCan 2*
Underwood, Ruth Komanoff 1946- *EncJzS 70*
Underwood, William L 1940- *ConAmC*
Undisputed Truth, The *RkOn 2[port]*
Ung, Chinary 1942- *ConAmC*
Unger, Alvin E 1911-1975 *IntMPA 75, NewYTET*
Unger, Andreas 1605?-1657 *NewGrD 80*
Unger, Anthony B 1940- *IntMPA 77, -75, -76, -78, -79, -80*
Unger, Carolina 1803-1877 *NewGrD 80*
Unger, Caroline 1803-1877 *Baker 78, CmOp, NewEOp 71, NewGrD 80*
Unger, Georg 1837-1887 *Baker 78, CmOp, NewGrD 80*
Unger, Gerhard 1916- *NewGrD 80, WhoOp 76*
Unger, Gladys Buchanan d1940 *NotNAT B, WhThe*
Unger, Gunnar *Film 2*
Unger, Gustaf 1920- *AmSCAP 80*
Unger, Heinz 1895-1965 *Baker 78, NewGrD 80*
Unger, Hermann 1886-1958 *Baker 78, NewGrD 80*
Unger, Karoline 1803-1877 *NewGrD 80*
Unger, Kurt 1922- *IntMPA 77, -75, -76, -78, -79, -80*
Unger, Leigh James 1945- *ConAmC*
Unger, Max 1883-1959 *Baker 78, NewGrD 80*
Unger, Oliver A 1914- *IntMPA 77, -75, -76, -78, -79, -80*
Unger, Robert *NatPD[port]*
Unger, Stella 1905- *AmSCAP 66, -80*
Ungher, Karoline *NewGrD 80*
Ungler, Florian d1536 *NewGrD 80*
Ungvary, Tamas 1936- *IntWWM 77, -80*
Uninsky, Alexander 1910-1972 *Baker 78*
Union Gap, Gary Puckett And The *BiDAmM*
Unit Four Plus Two *RkOn 2[port]*
United States Of America *BiDAmM, ConMuA 80A*
Unruh, Fritz Von 1885-1970 *CnMD, McGEWD[port], ModWD, REnWD[port]*
Unruh, Fritz Von 1885-1971 *EncWT*
Unruh, Stan 1939- *WhoOp 76*
Unruh, Walter 1898-1973 *NotNAT B*
Unruh, Walther 1898-1973 *BiE&WWA, EncWT*
Unsworth, Geoffrey 1914-1978 *FilmEn, FilmgC, HalFC 80, WorEFlm*
Unterholtzer, Rupert 1505?- *NewGrD 80*
Unterholtzer, Ruprecht 1505?- *NewGrD 80*
Unterkirchen, Hans *Film 2*
Untershiak, J *Film 2*
Untersteiner, Alfredo 1859-1918 *Baker 78*
Unverdorben, Marx *NewGrD 80*
Unverdorben, Max *NewGrD 80*
Unverricht, Hubert Johannes 1927- *IntWWM 77, -80*
Unverricht, Hubert Johnannes 1927- *NewGrD 80*
Unverzagte, Der *NewGrD 80*
Unvuortzaghete, Der *NewGrD 80*
Unzelmann, Friederike Bethmann- *EncWT*
Unzelmann, Karl Wilhelm Ferdinand 1753-1832 *EncWT*
Unzelmann, Karl Wolfgang 1786-1843 *EncWT*
Uolrich Von Liehtenstein *NewGrD 80*
Upchurch, Phil 1941- *EncJzS 70*
Upchurch, Philip *RkOn*
Updegraff, Henry 1889-1936 *WhScrn 74, -77*
Updyke, Hubert *JoeFr*
Uphagen, Erika *WhoOp 76*
Uppard, Peter Garth 1944- *IntWWM 77, -80*
Uppington, Francis Walter Alexander 1899- *WhoMus 72*
Uppman, Theodor 1920- *CmOp, IntWWM 77, -80, NewEOp 71, NewGrD 80, WhoOp 76*
Upshaw, Patricia 1951- *BlkWAB[port]*
Upsher, Peter d1963 *NotNAT B*
Upson, Virginia *PupTheA*
Upton, Anne *AmSCAP 66*
Upton, Donald Niles 1925-1978 *AmSCAP 80*
Upton, Frances 1904-1975 *WhScrn 77, WhoHol C*
Upton, George Putnam 1834-1919 *Baker 78, BiDAmM, NewGrD 80*
Upton, Kathleen Louise 1933- *IntWWM 77*
Upton, Leonard 1901- *WhThe*
Upton, William Treat 1870-1961 *Baker 78, NewGrD 80*
Upwood, Dorothy Lilian 1930- *IntWWM 77*
Uraneff, Vadim *Film 2*
Uranova *NewGrD 80*
Uray, Ernst Ludwig 1906- *IntWWM 77, -80, WhoMus 72*
Urbach, Otto 1871-1927 *Baker 78*
Urbain, James 1943- *CnOxB*
Urban VIII *NewGrD 80*
Urban, Charles 1870?-1942 *DcFM*
Urban, Charles 1871-1942 *FilmEn, HalFC 80, OxFilm*
Urban, Dorothy K 1869-1961 *WhScrn 74, -77, WhoHol B*
Urban, Friedrich Julius 1838-1918 *Baker 78*
Urban, Heinrich 1837-1901 *Baker 78*
Urban, Joseph 1872-1933 *EncWT, NewEOp 71, NotNAT B, OxThe*
Urbanek, Frantisek Augustin 1842-1919 *NewGrD 80*
Urbanek, Mojmir 1873-1919 *Baker 78, NewGrD 80*
Urbani, Giuseppe 1928- *CnOxB*
Urbani, Peter 1749-1816 *NewGrD 80*
Urbani, Valentini *NewGrD 80*
Urbani, Valentino *NewGrD 80*
Urbaniak, Michal 1943- *AmSCAP 80, EncJzS 70*
Urbanner, Erich 1936- *Baker 78, IntWWM 77, -80, NewGrD 80*
Urbano, Alfred J 1911- *AmSCAP 66, -80*
Urbano, Tony *PupTheA SUP*
Urbansky, Yevgeny 1931-1965 *WhScrn 74, -77*
Urbanyi-Krasnodebska, Zofia Jadwiga 1936- *IntWWM 77, -80*
Urbini, Pierluigi 1929- *WhoOp 76*
Urbont, Dorothy 1903- *AmSCAP 80*
Urbont, Jacques 1930- *IntWWM 77*
Urbont, Rosalind Zeins 1942- *AmSCAP 80*
Urcelay, Nicolas 1920-1959 *WhScrn 74, -77*
Ure, Mary 1933-1975 *BiE&WWA, EncWT, FilmAG WE, FilmEn, FilmgC, ForYSC, HalFC 80, IntMPA 75, MotPP, MovMk, NotNAT B, PlP&P[port], WhScrn 77, WhThe, WhoHol C, WhoThe 72*
Urecal, Minerva d1966 *MotPP, WhoHol B*
Urecal, Minerva 1894-1966 *ForYSC, WhScrn 74, -77, WhoHrs 80[port]*
Urecal, Minerva 1896-1966 *FilmgC, HalFC 80, Vers B[port]*
Urede, Johannes *NewGrD 80*
Urfey, Thomas D' 1653-1723 *Baker 78, NewGrD 80*
Urhan, Chretien 1790-1845 *Baker 78, NewGrD 80*
Urho, Ellen Alli Marjatta Helefuo 1920- *IntWWM 77, -80*
Uriah Heep *ConMuA 80A, IlEncR, RkOn 2[port]*
Uriarte, Father Eustaquio De 1863-1900 *Baker 78, NewGrD 80*
Uribe, Justa *Film 2*
Uribe-Holguin, Guillermo 1880-1971 *Baker 78, NewGrD 80, OxMus*
Urich, Jean 1849-1939 *Baker 78*
Urio, Francesco Antonio 1631?-1719? *NewGrD 80*
Urio, Francesco Antonio 1660?- *Baker 78*
Urlus, Jacobus 1867-1935 *NewGrD 80*
Urlus, Jacques 1867-1935 *Baker 78, NewEOp 71, NewGrD 80*
Urner, Catherine Murphy 1891-1942 *NewGrD 80*
Urquhart, Alasdair 1914-1954 *WhScrn 74, -77, WhoHol B*
Urquhart, Anthony Morse 1934- *CreCan 1*
Urquhart, Dan Murdock 1944- *IntWWM 77, -80*
Urquhart, Gordon 1922-1957 *WhScrn 77*
Urquhart, Isabelle 1865-1907 *NotNAT B, WhoStg 1906, -1908*
Urquhart, Molly *WhThe, WhoHol A*
Urquhart, Robert 1922- *FilmgC, HalFC 80, IlWWBF, IntMPA 77, -75, -76, -78, -79, -80, WhoHol A*
Urquhart, Thomas *NewGrD 80*
Urquhart, Tony 1934- *CreCan 1*
Urquhart, Wilkinson *WhoMus 72*
Urreda, Johannes *NewGrD 80*
Urrede, Johannes *NewGrD 80*
Urreta, Alicia 1935- *Baker 78*
Urrila, Irma Kristiina 1943- *WhoOp 76*
Urros, Joseph *NewGrD 80*
Urroz, Jose *NewGrD 80*
Urrueta, Chano 189-?- *DcFM*
Urrutia-Blondel, Jorge 1905- *Baker 78, NewGrD 80*
Urseanu, Tilde 1923- *CnOxB*
Ursianu, Malvina *WomWMM*
Ursillo, Fabio d1759 *NewGrD 80*
Ursino, Gennaro 1650-1715? *NewGrD 80*
Ursinus, Johann *NewGrD 80*
Urso, Camilla 1842-1902 *Baker 78, BiDAmM*
Urspruch, Anton 1850-1907 *Baker 78, NewGrD 80*
Ursprung, Otto 1879-1960 *Baker 78, NewGrD 80*
Urstein, Carl 1905- *AmSCAP 80*
Ursuleac, Viorica 1894- *NewGrD 80[port]*
Ursuleac, Viorica 1899- *Baker 78, CmOp, NewEOp 71*
Ursuliak, Alexander 1937- *CnOxB*
Ursus, Johann *NewGrD 80*
Urup, Henning 1931- *IntWWM 77, -80*
Urusevsky, Sergei 1908- *DcFM*
Urwick, Phyllis Joyce *WhoMus 72*
Urwin, Gary Lee 1955- *AmSCAP 80*
Urwin, Stanley George 1937- *WhoMus 72*
Urzi, Saro 1913- *FilmAG WE*
Usandizaga, Jose Maria 1887-1915 *Baker 78, NewGrD 80*
Usher, Graham 1938-1975 *CnOxB, DancEn 78*
Usher, Guy 1875-1944 *WhScrn 74, -77, WhoHol B*
Usher, Harry 1887-1950 *WhScrn 74, -77*
Usher, Julia 1945- *IntWWM 80*
Usher, Luke *PlP&P*
Ushioda, Masuko 1942- *NewGrD 80*
Usigli, Rodolfo *OxThe*
Usigli, Rodolfo 1903- *CroCD*
Usigli, Rodolfo 1905- *CnThe, McGEWD, ModWD, REnWD[port]*
Usiglio, Emilio 1841-1910 *Baker 78, NewGrD 80*
Usmanbas, Ilhan 1921- *Baker 78, NewGrD 80*
Uspensky, Nikolay Dmitriyevich 1900- *NewGrD 80*
Uspensky, Victor 1879-1949 *Baker 78*
Uspensky, Viktor Alexandrovich 1879-1949 *NewGrD 80*
Usper, Francesco 1570?-1641 *NewGrD 80*

Usper, Gabriel *NewGrD 80*
Ussachevsky, Vladimir 1911- *Baker 78, BiDAmM, CpmDNM 79, ConAmC, DcCM, NewGrD 80*
Ussel, Gui D' *NewGrD 80*
Ustinoff, Nicolai *NewGrD 80*
Ustinov, Peter 1921- *BiDFilm, -81, BiE&WWA, CmMov, CnMD, CnThe, ConDr 73, -77, CroCD, EncWT, Ent[port], FilmAG WE[port], FilmEn, FilmgC, ForYSC, HalFC 80, IlWWBF[port], -A, IntMPA 77, -75, -76, -78, -79, -80, JoeFr[port], McGEWD[port], ModWD, MotPP, MovMk[port], NotNAT, -A, OxFilm, OxThe, PlP&P, WhoHol A, WhoOp 76, WhoThe 72, -77, WorEFlm*
Ustinov, Tamara *WhoHol A*
Ustvol'skaia, Galina 1919- *DcCM*
Ustvolskaya, Galina 1919- *Baker 78*
Ustvol'skaya, Galina Ivanovna 1919- *NewGrD 80*
Uszycka, Walentyna *WomWMM*
Utagawa, Anne 1948- *IntWWM 77, -80*
Uten, Eugeen 1919- *IntWWM 80*
Utendal, Alexander 1530?-1581 *Baker 78, NewGrD 80*
Utenthal, Thal 1530?-1581 *NewGrD 80*
Utgaard, Merton Blaine 1914- *IntWWM 77, -80*
Uthman, Muhammed *NewGrD 80*
Uthoff, Ernst 1904- *CnOxB, DancEn 78*
Uthoff, Michael 1943- *CnOxB*
Uthup, Usha 1947- *IntWWM 77, -80*
Utley, Garrick *NewYTET*
Utopia *ConMuA 80A*
Utrecht, Heinrich d1634? *NewGrD 80*
Utrede, Johannes *NewGrD 80*
Utsui, Ken *WhoHrs 80*
Uttal, Fred 1905-1963 *WhScrn 77*
Uttal, Larry *ConMuA 80B*
Uttini, Francesco Antonio Baldassare 1723-1795 *NewGrD 80*
Uttini, Francesco Antonio Baltassare 1723-1795 *Baker 78*
Uustalu, Uve-Holger 1933- *IntWWM 77, -80*
Uwen, Nathan *MorBAP*
Uys, Jamie 1921- *FilmgC, HalFC 80, IntMPA 77, -75, -76, -78, -79, -80, WhoHol A*
Uyttenhove, Henry J *CmMov*
Uyttenhove, Yolande 1925- *IntWWM 77, -80*

V

Vaatainen, Teuvo Uolevi 1925- *IntWWM 77*
Vacares, Bertrandus *NewGrD 80*
Vaccai, Nicola 1790-1848 *Baker 78, NewGrD 80*
Vaccaro, Brenda *WhoHol A*
Vaccaro, Brenda 1939- *BiE&WWA, FilmEn, HalFC 80, IntMPA 77, -76, -78, -79, -80, NotNAT, WhoThe 72, -77*
Vaccaro, Brenda 1940- *FilmgC*
Vacchelli, Giovanni Battista 1625?-1667? *NewGrD 80*
Vacchiano, William 1912- *NewGrD 80*
Vacek, Karel 1902- *IntWWM 77*
Vacek, Milos 1928- *Baker 78*
Vach, Ferdinand 1860-1939 *Baker 78*
Vachalova, Libuse 1932- *IntWWM 77, -80*
Vache, Alphonse *NewOrJ*
Vachell, Horace Annesley 1861-1955 *NotNAT B, WhThe*
Vachon, Jean *Film 2*
Vachon, Pierre 1731-1802 *Baker 78*
Vachon, Pierre 1731-1803 *NewGrD 80*
Vacio, Natividad *WhoHol A*
Vackar *NewGrD 80*
Vackar, Dalibor C 1906- *Baker 78, IntWWM 77, -80, NewGrD 80*
Vackar, Tomas 1945-1963 *Baker 78, NewGrD 80*
Vackar, Vaclav 1881-1954 *NewGrD 80*
Vackova, Jarmila 1908-1971 *WhScrn 74, -77*
Vackova, Jirlina Marie 1912- *IntWWM 77, -80*
Vacqueras, Bertrandus *NewGrD 80*
Vactor, David Van 1906- *MusMk*
Vaczek, Karl *OxMus*
Vad, Knud 1936- *IntWWM 77, -80*
Vadas, Agnes 1929- *IntWWM 77, -80*
Vade, Jean-Joseph 1719-1757 *NewGrD 80*
Vadeboncoeur, Joan E *ConAmTC*
Vader, Hans 1942- *IntWWM 77, -80*
Vadim, Annette *WhoHol A*
Vadim, Roger *WhoHol A*
Vadim, Roger 1927- *FilmgC, HalFC 80, WhoHrs 80*
Vadim, Roger 1928- *BiDFilm, -81, DcFM, FilmEn, MovMk, OxFilm, WorEFlm[port]*
Vado, Juan Del d1675? *NewGrD 80*
Vaerwere, Johannes De *NewGrD 80*
Vaet, Jacobus 1529-1567 *Baker 78, NewGrD 80*
Vagabonds, The *IlEncCM*
Vaganova, Agrippina 1879-1951 *CnOxB, DancEn 78[port]*
Vagares, Bertrandus *NewGrD 80*
Vagner, Genrikh Matusovich 1922- *NewGrD 80*
Vagramian, Aram 1921- *AmSCAP 66, -80*
Vagrants, The *BiDAmM*
Vague, Vera d1974 *HalFC 80, JoeFr*
Vague, Vera 1904- *ForYSC*
Vague, Vera 1904-1974 *FilmgC, WhScrn 77, WhoHol B*
Vague, Vera 1905-1974 *FilmEn*
Vail, James H 1929- *IntWWM 77, -80*
Vail, Lester 1900-1959 *NotNAT B, WhScrn 77, WhThe, WhoHol B*
Vail, Myrtle 1888- *What 3[port]*
Vail, Olive 1904-1951 *WhScrn 74, -77, WhoHol B*
Vail, Silas Jones 1818-1884 *BiDAmM*
Vaillancourt, Armand 1931- *CreCan 2*
Vailland, Roger 1907-1965 *CnMD, DcFM*
Vaillant, Jehan *NewGrD 80*
Vaillant, Johannes *NewGrD 80*
Vaillat, Leandre 1876-1952 *CnOxB*
Vainberg, Moisei 1919- *Baker 78*
Vainio, Matti Olavi 1946- *IntWWM 80*
Vainonen, Vasily 1898-1964 *NewGrD 80*
Vainonen, Vasily Ivanovich 1901-1964 *CnOxB*
Vainonen, Vassily 1898-1964 *DancEn 78*
Vaisanen, Armas Otto 1890-1969 *NewGrD 80*
Vajda *PlP&P*
Vajda, Ernest 1887-1954 *FilmEn, NotNAT B, WhThe*
Vajda, Igor 1935- *IntWWM 77, -80*
Vajda, Ladislao 1905-1965 *DcFM, WorEFlm*
Vajda, Ladislao 1906-1965 *FilmEn*
Vajda, Ladislas 1905-1965 *IlWWBF, WorEFlm*
Vajda, Ladislaus 1880?-1933 *FilmEn*
Vajnar, Frantisek 1930- *WhoOp 76*
Vakhnyanyn, Anatol' 1841-1908 *NewGrD 80*
Vakhnyanyn, Natal' 1841-1908 *NewGrD 80*
Vakhtangov, Eugen V 1883-1922 *NotNAT A, -B*
Vakhtangov, Eugene V 1883-1922 *EncWT, Ent, OxThe, PlP&P*
Vakhtangov, Yevgeny 1883-1922 *CnThe*
Val, Jack 1897- *AmSCAP 66, -80*
Val, Paul d1962 *NotNAT B*
Vala, Do *NewGrD 80*
Valabrega, Cesare 1898-1965 *Baker 78, NewGrD 80*
Valabregue, Albin *WhThe*
Valach, Jan 1925- *IntWWM 77, -80*
Valaida *WhThe*
Valaitis, Vladimir Antonovich 1923- *WhoOp 76*
Valante, Harrison R 1936- *IntWWM 77, -80*
Valavani, Tasso George 1928- *IntWWM 80*
Valavanis, Tassos George 1928- *IntWWM 77*
Valberg, Birgitta *WhoHol A*
Valberkh, Ivan 1766-1819 *CnOxB*
Valcarcel, Edgar 1932- *Baker 78, DcCM, NewGrD 80*
Valcarcel, Luis E 1891- *NewGrD 80*
Valcarcel, Teodoro 1900-1942 *Baker 78*
Valcarcel, Theodoro 1900-1942 *NewGrD 80*
Valcourt, Jean *CreCan 2*
Valda, Guilia 1855-1925 *BiDAmM*
Valdambrini, Oscar 1924- *EncJzS 70*
Valdare, Sunny Jim d1962 *NotNAT B*
Valdemar, Tania 1904-1955 *WhScrn 74, -77*
Valdemar, Thais *Film 2*
Valdengo, Giuseppe 1914- *CmOp, NewEOp 71, NewGrD 80*
Valdengo, Guiseppe 1920- *IntWWM 77, -80*
Valderabano, Enrique Enriquez De *Baker 78*
Valderrabano, Enriquez De *NewGrD 80*
Valderrama, Carlos 1887-1950 *Baker 78*
Valdes, Miguel Francisco Letelier *DcCM*
Valdes, Santino Detto *NewGrD 80*
Valdis, Sigrid *WhoHol A*
Valdivielso, Jose De 1560-1638 *McGEWD*
Valdivieso, No *PupTheA*
Valdombre *CreCan 2*
Valdrighi, Luigi Francesco 1827-1899 *Baker 78*
Valdrighi, Count Luigi Francesco 1837-1899 *NewGrD 80*
Vale, Eugene 1916- *IntMPA 77, -75, -76, -78, -79, -80*
Vale, Jerry 1932- *AmPS A, -B, RkOn[port]*
Vale, Louise d1918 *Film 1, WhScrn 77*
Vale, Martin *BiE&WWA, NotNAT*
Vale, Travers 1865- *TwYS A*
Vale, Viola *Film 2*
Vale, Virginia *ForYSC*
Vale, Vola *Film 1, TwYS*
Valedon, Lora 1884-1946 *WhScrn 74, -77*
Valek, Jiri 1923- *Baker 78*
Valek, Jiri 1940- *IntWWM 77, -80*
Valek, Vladimir 1935- *IntWWM 77, -80*
Valen, Fartein 1887-1952 *Baker 78, DcCM, MusMk, NewGrD 80*
Valen, Ritchie 1941-1959 *WhScrn 77*
Valencia, Antonio Maria 1902-1952 *Baker 78, NewGrD 80*
Valencin, Senor *PupTheA*
Valency, Maurice 1903- *AmSCAP 66, -80, BiE&WWA, NotNAT*
Valene, Nanette *Film 2*
Valens, Richie *ConMuA 80A*
Valens, Ritchie *AmPS A*
Valens, Ritchie 1940-1959 *BiDAmM*
Valens, Ritchie 1941-1959 *RkOn[port]*
Valent, Joseph Arthur 1955- *CpmDNM 78*
Valenta, Vladimir *WhoHol A*
Valente, Antonio 1520?- *Baker 78, NewGrD 80*
Valente, Benita *WhoOp 76*
Valente, Caterina *IntMPA 77, -75, -76, -78, -79, -80, WhoHol A*
Valente, Giorgio *Baker 78*
Valente, Saverio *NewGrD 80*
Valente, Vincenzo 1855-1921 *Baker 78*
Valenti, Fernando 1926- *NewGrD 80*
Valenti, Jack A 1921- *FilmEn*
Valenti, Jack J 1921- *FilmgC, HalFC 80, IntMPA 77, -75, -76, -78, -79, -80, NewYTET*
Valenti, Michael *ConAmC*
Valentin *CroCD*
Valentin, Bouboul 1870?-1925? *NewOrJ*
Valentin, Erich 1906- *Baker 78, NewGrD 80*
Valentin, Karl 1882-1948 *EncWT, Ent*
Valentin, Karl Fritiof 1853-1918 *NewGrD 80*
Valentin, Karl Fritjof 1853-1918 *NewGrD 80*
Valentin, Punkie 1866?-1951? *NewOrJ*
Valentin, Regina *NewGrD 80*
Valentine *NewGrD 80*
Valentine 1876- *WhThe*
Valentine, Anthony *WhoHol A*
Valentine, Barbara *WhoHol A*
Valentine, Carla *WomWMM A*

Valentine, Dickie d1971 WhoHol B
Valentine, Elizabeth d1971 WhScrn 77
Valentine, Elmer ConMuA 80B
Valentine, Grace 1884-1964 WhThe
Valentine, Grace 1890-1964 Film 1, -2, TwYS, WhScrn 77
Valentine, John Film 2
Valentine, John 1710-1791 NewGrD 80
Valentine, Joseph 1900-1949 FilmEn, HalFC 80
Valentine, Joseph 1903-1948 FilmgC
Valentine, Leila Film 2
Valentine, Mary 1922- WhoMus 72
Valentine, Paul d1924 NotNAT B
Valentine, Paul 1919- BiE&WWA, NotNAT
Valentine, Robert ConAmC, OxMus
Valentine, Robert 1680?-1735? NewGrD 80
Valentine, Syd Raymond 1908- WhoJazz 72
Valentine, Sydney 1865-1919 NotNAT B, WhThe
Valentine, Thomas 1896- NewOrJ[port]
Valentine, Vangie Film 1
Valentines, The RkOn
Valentini NewGrD 80
Valentini, Giovanni 1582-1649 Baker 78, NewGrD 80, OxMus
Valentini, Giuseppe 1680?-1740 OxMus
Valentini, Giuseppe 1680?-1746? Baker 78
Valentini, Giuseppe 1680?-1759? NewGrD 80
Valentini, Lucia 1948- WhoOp 76
Valentini, Michelangelo 1720?-1768? NewGrD 80
Valentini, Michele Angelo 1720?-1768? NewGrD 80
Valentini, Pier Francesco 1570?-1654 Baker 78, NewGrD 80, OxMus
Valentini, Pierfrancesco 1570?-1654 NewGrD 80
Valentini, Pietro Francesco 1570?-1654 NewGrD 80
Valentini, Roberto OxMus
Valentino, Francesco 1907- NewEOp 71
Valentino, Henri-Justin-Armand-Joseph 1785-1865 Baker 78
Valentino, Henri Justin Armand Joseph 1785-1865 NewGrD 80
Valentino, Mark 1942- RkOn
Valentino, Michelangelo 1720?-1768? NewGrD 80
Valentino, Michele Angelo 1720?-1768? NewGrD 80
Valentino, Pier Francesco 1570?-1654 NewGrD 80
Valentino, Pierfrancesco 1570?-1654 NewGrD 80
Valentino, Pietro Francesco 1570?-1654 NewGrD 80
Valentino, Rodolph 1895-1926 FilmEn
Valentino, Rudolph 1895-1926 BiDFilm, -81, CmMov, FilmEn, Film 1, -2, FilmgC, HalFC 80, MotPP, MovMk, NotNAT B, OxFilm, TwYS, WhScrn 74, -77, WhoHol B, WomWMM, WorEFlm[port]
Valentino, Thomas J 1907- IntMPA 77, -76, -78, -79, -80
Valentinos, The RkOn
Valentova, Ivona 1944- WhoOp 76
Valenty, Lili ForYSC, WhoHol A
Valenzola, Pietro NewGrD 80
Valenzuela, Pedro NewGrD 80
Valere, Jean 1925- WorEFlm
Valere, Simone 1923- EncWT
Valeri, Gaetano 1760-1822 NewGrD 80
Valeriano NewGrD 80
Valerie, Gladys Film 2
Valerie, Jeanne WhoHol A
Valerie, Olive Film 2
Valerio OxThe
Valerio, Albano 1889-1961 WhScrn 74, -77, WhoHol B
Valerio, Theresa d1964 NotNAT B
Valerius, Adriaen 1575-1625 NewGrD 80
Valerius, Adrianus 1575-1625 Baker 78, NewGrD 80
Valero, Albano Film 2
Valery, Estelle WhoMus 72
Valery, Olga WhoHol A
Valery, Paul Ambroise 1871-1945 CnMD, EncWT
Valesi, Fulgenzio 1565?-1614? NewGrD 80
Valesi, Giovanni 1735-1816 NewGrD 80
Valet, Nicholas NewGrD 80
Valetti, Cesare 1922- CmOp
Valgaeren, Marcel J F 1938- IntWWM 77, -80
Valia, Mademoiselle Film 2
Valiants, The RkOn
Valignani, Achille 1910- IntMPA 77, -75, -76, -78, -79
Valjakka, Taru 1938- WhoOp 76
Valjean RkOn
Valk, Alexis 1945- IntWWM 77
Valk, Frederick 1895-1956 Ent
Valk, Frederick 1901-1956 CnThe, FilmgC, HalFC 80, NotNAT B, WhScrn 74, -77, WhThe, WhoHol B
Valkan, Nick AmSCAP 80
Valkare, Gunnar 1943- Baker 78
Valkyrien 1894-1953 Film 1
Valkyrien, Valda 1894-1953 WhScrn 74, -77, WhoHol B
Valla, Domenico NewGrD 80
Valla, Giorgio 1447-1500 NewGrD 80
Valla, Pellegrino NewGrD 80
Valla, Peregrino NewGrD 80
Vallade, Johann Baptist Anton 1722?-1780? NewGrD 80
Vallara, Francesco Maria 1687-1740 NewGrD 80
Vallas, Leon 1879-1956 Baker 78, NewGrD 80
Valle DePaz Baker 78
Valle, Felix Film 2
Valle, Marcos Kostenbader 1943- AmSCAP 80
Valle, Pietro Della NewGrD 80
Valle-Inclan, Ramon Maria Del 1866-1936 CnMD SUP, EncWT, Ent, McGEWD[port], ModWD, OxThe
Valle-Riestra, Jose Maria 1859-1925 Baker 78
Valledor Y LaCalle, Jacinto 1744-1809? NewGrD 80
Vallee, Arthur A 1916- AmSCAP 66
Vallee, Fay Webb WhScrn 74, -77
Vallee, Herbert Prior 1901- BiDAmM
Vallee, Hubert Prior 1901- AmSCAP 80, NewGrD 80
Vallee, Marcel Film 2
Vallee, Rudy 1901- AmPS, -A, -B, AmSCAP 66, BgBands 74[port], BiE&WWA, CmpEPM, EncMT, FilmEn, Film 2, FilmgC, ForYSC, HalFC 80, IntMPA 77, -75, -76, -78, -79, -80, MotPP, MovMk[port], NewGrD 80, OxMus, WhoHol A
Vallee, Yvonne Film 2
Vallentin, Hermann Film 2
Valleran-Lecomte OxThe
Vallerand, Jean 1915- Baker 78, CreCan 2, NewGrD 80
Valleria, Alwina 1848-1925 Baker 78, BiDAmM, NewEOp 71, NewGrD 80
Vallerius, Harald 1646-1716 NewGrD 80
Valles, Dave Film 2
Vallesi, Giovanni NewGrD 80
Vallet, Nicolas 1583-1626? Baker 78
Vallet, Nicolas 1583?-1642? NewGrD 80
Vallette, Pierre 1525?- NewGrD 80
Valletti, Cesare 1922- NewEOp 71, NewGrD 80, WhoMus 72
Valli, Alida 1921- BiDFilm, -81, FilmAG WE[port], FilmEn, FilmgC, ForYSC, HalFC 80, IntMPA 77, -75, -76, -78, -79, -80, MotPP, MovMk, OxFilm, WhoHol A, WorEFlm[port]
Valli, Frankie 1937- RkOn, -2[port]
Valli, June 1930- RkOn
Valli, Romolo WhoHol A
Valli, Romolo 1924- WhoOp 76
Valli, Romolo 1925- EncWT
Valli, Valli 1882-1927 Film 1, WhScrn 77, WhThe, WhoHol B
Valli, Virginia d1968 MotPP, WhoHol B
Valli, Virginia 1895-1968 FilmEn, ForYSC, TwYS
Valli, Virginia 1898-1968 Film 1, -2, FilmgC, HalFC 80, MovMk
Valli, Virginia 1900-1968 WhScrn 74, -77
Vallier, John WhoMus 72
Vallin, Ninon 1886-1961 CmOp, NewGrD 80
Vallin, Rick ForYSC, IntMPA 77, -75, -76, -78, -79, -80, WhoHol A
Vallin-Pardo, Eugenie 1886-1961 NewGrD 80
Vallis, Robert d1932 Film 2, WhScrn 74, -77
Vallon, Larry ConMuA 80B
Vallone, Raf IntMPA 77, -75, -76, -78, -79, -80, WhoHol A
Vallone, Raf 1916- FilmAG WE, FilmgC, ForYSC, HalFC 80, MovMk, WorEFlm
Vallone, Raf 1917- FilmEn
Vallotti, Francesco Antonio 1697-1780 Baker 78, NewGrD 80[port]
Valls, Francisco 1665-1747 NewGrD 80
Valls, Jose 1904- NewGrD 80
Valls, Manuel 1920- DcCM, NewGrD 80
Valois NewGrD 80
Valois, Ninette De 1898- CnOxB, NewGrD 80
Valray, Maria Film 2
Valsini, F NewGrD 80
Valsted, Myrtle 1910-1928 WhScrn 74, -77
Valtasaari, Tapani Heikki 1941- WhoOp 76
Valton, Peter d1784 BiDAmM
Valtz, Lynn Berta Springbett CreCan 2
Valvasensi, Lazaro 1585-1661 NewGrD 80
Valvasensi, Lazaro 1600- Baker 78
Valvasensis, Lazaro 1585-1661 NewGrD 80
Valverda, Rafael Film 2
Valverde, Balbina WhThe
Valverde, Joaquin 1846-1910 Baker 78, NewGrD 80
Vamos, Gyorgy 1946- CnOxB
Vampira 1921- ForYSC, JoeFr, WhoHrs 80[port]
Van Tony Free III 1951- IntWWM 77
Van, Beatrice Film 1
Van, Billy 1912-1973 WhScrn 77, WhoHol B
Van, Billy B 1870-1950 WhThe
Van, Billy B 1878-1950 NotNAT B, WhScrn 74, -77, WhoHol B
Van, Bobby WhoHol A
Van, Bobby 1916- ForYSC
Van, Bobby 1930-1980 EncMT, FilmEn, FilmgC, HalFC 80, WhoThe 77
Van, Bobby 1932-1980 WhoThe 72
Van, Bobby 1935-1980 NotNAT
Van, Charley d1963 NotNAT B
Van, Connie 1909-1961 WhScrn 74, -77
Van, Guillaume De 1906-1949 NewGrD 80
Van, Gus d1968 NotNAT B, WhoHol B
Van, Gus 1887- AmSCAP 80
Van, Gus 1887-1968 AmSCAP 66, JoeFr[port]
Van, Gus 1888-1968 WhScrn 74, -77
Van, Jeffrey Wylie 1941- IntWWM 80
Van, Wally 1885-1974 Film 1, -2, TwYS A, WhoHol B
Van And Schenck AmPS B, CmpEPM, JoeFr[port]
VanAaitern, Truus Film 2
VanAckere, Jules-Emile 1914- IntWWM 77, -80
VanAerde, Raymond 1876-1944 Baker 78
Vanaire, Jacques Film 2
Vanal, Charles 1892- FilmAG WE
VanAllan, Richard 1935- IntWWM 77, -80, NewGrD 80, WhoMus 72, WhoOp 76
VanAllen, Neil 1929- WhoMus 72
VanAlstyne, Egbert 1882-1951 AmPS, BiDAmM, CmpEPM, PopAmC[port], Sw&Ld B
VanAlstyne, Egbert Aanson 1882-1951 NotNAT B
VanAlstyne, Egbert Anson 1882-1951 AmSCAP 66, -80
VanAlstyne, Frances C BiDAmM
VanAmburgh, Isaac 1801-1865 Ent[port]
VanAmelsvoort, Adriaan Johannes Maria 1910- IntWWM 77
VanAmerongen, Alexander 1920- IntWWM 77, -80
VanAmmelrooy, Willeke 1944- FilmAG WE
VanAntwerp, Albert Film 2
VanAppledorn, Mary Jean 1927- ConAmC
VanAppledorn, Mary Jeanne 1927- AmSCAP 80, CpmDNM 72, -73, -78, -79, -80
Vanarelli, Francesco Antonio NewGrD 80
VanArk, Joan WhoHol A
VanAsperen, Bob 1947- IntWWM 80
VanAuker, C K d1938 WhScrn 74, -77, WhoHol B
VanBailey, Polly d1952 WhScrn 74, -77
VanBakergem, Frits 1923- IntWWM 77, -80
VanBarthold, Kenneth 1927- IntWWM 77, -80

VanBeers, Sonja 1940- *DancEn 78*
VanBeers, Stanley 1911-1961 *WhScrn 74, -77, WhThe, WhoHol B*
VanBeinum, Eduard 1901-1959 *Baker 78, MusSN[port], NewGrD 80[port]*
VanBergijk, Johannes *NewGrD 80*
VanBiene, Auguste 1850-1913 *NotNAT B, WhThe*
VanBlerk, Gerardus J M 1924- *IntWWM 77, -80*
VanBousen, H *Film 2*
VanBrakle, John 1903- *AmSCAP 66, -80*
VanBranteghem, Luc 1910- *IntWWM 77, -80*
VanBree, Joannes *Baker 78*
VanBrock, Florence *AmSCAP 66*
Vanbrugh, Biolet 1867-1942 *WhThe*
Vanbrugh, George *NewGrD 80*
Vanbrugh, Irene 1872-1949 *EncWT, FilmgC, HalFC 80, IIWWBF, -A, NotNAT A, -B, OxThe, PIP&P, WhScrn 74, -77, WhThe, WhoHol B*
Vanbrugh, Sir John 1664-1726 *CnThe, EncWT, Ent[port], McGEWD[port], NotNAT A, -B, OxThe, PIP&P[port], REnWD[port]*
Vanbrugh, Prudence 1902- *WhThe*
Vanbrugh, Violet *EncWT*
Vanbrugh, Violet Augusta Mary 1865-1942 *WhoStg 1908*
Vanbrugh, Violet Augusta Mary 1867-1942 *NotNAT A, -B, OxThe, WhoHol B*
Vanbrughe, George *NewGrD 80*
VanBunnen, Hermann *NewGrD 80*
VanBuren, A H *Film 1*
VanBuren, Mabel 1878-1947 *Film 1, -2, NotNAT B, TwYS, WhScrn 74, -77, WhoHol B*
Vanburgh, Irene 1872-1949 *Film 2*
VanBuskirk, June 1880- *WhoStg 1908*
VanBuskirk, June 1882- *WhThe*
VanCamp, Leonard Ward 1934- *AmSCAP 80*
VanCampen, Jacob 1590?-1657 *OxThe*
Vance The Great 1839-1888 *OxThe*
Vance, Alfred Glanville *PIP&P*
Vance, Ann Stockton 1950- *IntWWM 80*
Vance, Bobbye Marie Booker 1943- *BlkAmP*
Vance, Charles 1929- *WhoThe 72, -77*
Vance, Clarice *Film 2*
Vance, Dennis 1924- *IntMPA 77, -75, -76, -78, -79, -80*
Vance, Dick 1915- *CmpEPM, EncJzS 70, WhoJazz 72*
Vance, Jane *Film 1*
Vance, Leigh 1922- *IntMPA 77, -75, -76, -78, -79, -80*
Vance, Lucile 1893-1974 *WhoHol B*
Vance, Lucille 1893-1974 *WhScrn 77*
Vance, N Noble 1915- *IntWWM 77*
Vance, Nina *BiE&WWA, NotNAT*
Vance, Norma 1927-1956 *DancEn 78*
Vance, Paul J 1929- *AmSCAP 66, -80*
Vance, Richard Thomas 1915- *EncJzS 70*
Vance, Samuel 1939- *BlkAmP*
Vance, Virginia 1902-1942 *Film 2, WhScrn 74, -77, WhoHol B*
Vance, Vivian d1979 *IntMPA 77, -75, -76, -78, -79, JoeFr, MotPP*
Vance, Vivian 1903-1979 *FilmgC, HalFC 80*
Vance, Vivian 1912- *ForYSC, WhoHol A*
Vancea, Zeno 1900- *Baker 78, DcCM, NewGrD 80*
Vancini, Florestano 1926- *WorEFlm*
VanCleave, Nathan 1910-1970 *AmSCAP 66, -80, ConAmC*
VanCleef, Lee 1925- *CmMov, FilmEn, FilmgC, ForYSC, HalFC 80, IntMPA 77, -75, -76, -78, -79, -80, MotPP, MovMk[port], OxFilm, WhoHol A, WhoHrs 80[port]*
VanCleemput, Werner F P 1930- *IntWWM 77, -80*
VanCleve, Bert 1899- *AmSCAP 66*
VanCleve, Bertram Dorian 1899- *AmSCAP 80*
VanCleve, Edith 1903- *BiE&WWA, NotNAT, WhoHol A*
VanCleve, John Smith 1851-1917 *Baker 78, BiDAmM*
Vancura, Arnost 1750?-1801? *NewGrD 80*
Vancura, Ernest 1750?-1801? *NewGrD 80*
Vancy, Joseph-Francois Duche De *NewGrD 80*
Vandal, Marion *WomWMM*
VanDam, Albert 1920- *AmSCAP 66, -80*
VanDam, Alfred 1902- *WhoMus 72*
VanDam, Jose 1940- *CmOp, NewGrD 80, WhoOp 76*
VanDamm, Arnold *WhoHrs 80*
Vandamm, Florence d1966 *NotNAT B*
VanDamm, Vivian 1889-1960 *Ent, IIWWBF A, NotNAT B*
VanDamme, Art 1920- *AmSCAP 80, CmpEPM*
VanDamme, Joseph 1940- *NewGrD 80*
VanDantzig, Rudi 1933- *DancEn 78*
VanDeele, Edmond *Film 2*
VanDeerlin, Lionel *NewYTET*
VanDelden, Lex 1919- *Baker 78, IntWWM 77, -80, NewGrD 80*
VanDeMoortel, Arie 1918-1976 *Baker 78, WhoMus 72*
VanDenBerg, Johann *NewGrD 80*
VanDenBerg, Pieter 1928- *WhoOp 76*
VanDenBerg, Sanet 1953- *IntWWM 80*
VanDenBerghe, Frans *NewGrD 80*
VanDenBooren, Jo 1935- *IntWWM 77, -80*
VanDenBoorn-Coclet, Henriette 1866-1945 *Baker 78*
VanDenBorren, Charles 1874-1966 *Baker 78, NewGrD 80*
VanDenBosch-Schmidt, Johanna W E 1900- *WhoMus 72*
VanDenBril, Hendrik 1948- *IntWWM 80*
Vandenbroek, Othon Joseph 1758-1832 *NewGrD 80*
VanDenBurg, William 1901- *IntWWM 80*
Vandenburgh, Mildred M 1898- *AmSCAP 80*
VanDenEeden, Jean-Baptiste *Baker 78*
Vandeneet, Aegidius *NewGrD 80*
Vandeneet, Gilles *NewGrD 80*
VanDenGhein *NewGrD 80*
VanDenGheyn *NewGrD 80*
VanDenGheyn, Matthias 1721-1785 *NewGrD 80*
VanDenHeuvel, Johannes R, Jr. 1946- *IntWWM 80*
Vandenhoff, Charles H d1890 *NotNAT B*
Vandenhoff, Charlotte Elizabeth 1818-1860 *NotNAT B, OxThe*
Vandenhoff, George 1813-1884 *NotNAT B*
Vandenhoff, George 1813-1885 *OxThe*
Vandenhoff, George 1820-1884 *NotNAT A*
Vandenhoff, George 1820-1885 *FamA&A[port]*
Vandenhoff, Henry d1888 *NotNAT B*
Vandenhoff, Mrs. Henry d1870 *NotNAT B*
Vandenhoff, John 1790-1861 *NotNAT B, OxThe*
Vandenhoff, Kate d1942 *NotNAT B*
VanDenHorst, Herman 1911- *WorEFlm*
VanDenHove, Joachim *NewGrD 80*
VanDenKerckhoven, Abraham *NewGrD 80*
VanDenVondel, Joost 1587-1679 *Ent, OxThe*
VanDerBeek, Andrew Theodorus 1946- *IntWWM 77, -80*
Vanderbilt, Gertrude 1887?-1960 *CmpEPM, NotNAT B*
Vanderbilt, Gloria 1924- *BiE&WWA, NotNAT*
VanDerBilt, Peter *WhoOp 76*
Vanderbur, Angelyn Elizabeth 1909- *IntWWM 77*
Vanderburg, Gordon J 1913- *AmSCAP 66, -80*
Vandercook, John W d1963 *NotNAT B*
VanDerElst, Johannes *NewGrD 80*
VanDerGeest, Simon 1935- *WhoOp 76*
Vandergould, Charles W *PupTheA*
VanDerGraaf Generator *ConMuA 80A, IlEncR*
Vandergrift, J Monte 1893-1939 *WhScrn 74, -77*
Vandergrift, Monte 1893-1939 *WhoHol B*
VanDerGroen, Dora 1927- *FilmAG WE*
Vanderhagen, Amand 1753-1822 *NewGrD 80*
VanDerHallen, Arnold Joseph Gustaaf 1923- *IntWWM 77, -80*
VanDerHorst, Anthon *Baker 78*
VanderLinden, Albert 1913- *IntWWM 77, -80, NewGrD 80*
VanDerLinden, Cornelis 1839-1918 *Baker 78*
Vandermaesbrugge, Max 1933- *Baker 78*
VanDerMeer, Antonious Wiebe 1908- *IntWWM 80*
VanDerMeer, Antonius Wiebe 1908- *IntWWM 77*
VanDerMeer, John Henry 1920- *IntWWM 77, -80*
VanDerMeer, Rudolf Cornelius Adrianus 1936- *IntWWM 77, -80*
VanDerMerwe, Derik 1924- *IntWWM 77, -80*
VanDerMerwe, Jaco *WhoOp 76*
VanDerMueren, Florentijn Jan 1890-1966 *NewGrD 80*
VanDerMueren, Floris Jan 1890-1966 *NewGrD 80*
Vanderpool, Frederick W 1877-1947 *AmSCAP 66, -80*
VanDerPump, Charles Lyndon 1925- *WhoMus 72*
VanDerPutten, Hendrik *NewGrD 80*
Vanders, Warren *WhoHol A*
VanDerSlice, John 1940- *ConAmC*
VanDerSloot, Pieter 1926- *DancEn 78*
Vanderspar, Elizabeth 1921- *WhoMus 72*
VanDerSpuy, Herman Hubert 1942- *IntWWM 77*
VanDerStraeten, Edmond 1826-1895 *Baker 78*
VanderStraeten, Edmond 1826-1895 *NewGrD 80*
VanDerStraeten, Edmund S Joseph 1855-1934 *Baker 78, NewGrD 80*
VanDerStucken *OxMus*
VanDerStucken, Frank Valentin 1858-1929 *Baker 78, BiDAmM*
VanDerValk, Nettie *DancEn 78*
VanDerVelden, Renier *NewGrD 80*
VanDerVelden, Renier 1910- *Baker 78, IntWWM 77, -80*
VanDerVinck, Herman *NewGrD 80*
VanDerVlis, Diana 1935- *BiE&WWA, NotNAT, WhoHol A*
Vandervoort, Paul, II 1903- *AmSCAP 66, -80*
Vandervoort, Phil *WhoHol A*
VanderWielen, Jan Pieterszoon *NewGrD 80*
VanDerWyk, Jack A 1929- *IntWWM 77, -80*
Vanderzand, Charles 1932- *WhoMus 72*
VanDeVate, Nancy Hayes 1930- *AmSCAP 80, CpmDNM 75, -76, -77, -78, -79, -80, ConAmC, IntWWM 77, -80, WomCom[port]*
VanDeVelde, Anton 1895- *ModWD*
VanDeVen, Monique 1952- *FilmAG WE*
Vandever, Michael *WhoHol A*
VanDevere, Trish *WhoHol A*
VanDevere, Trish 1943- *FilmgC, HalFC 80*
VanDevere, Trish 1944- *MovMk*
VanDevere, Trish 1945- *FilmEn*
VanDeWeetering, Conrad 1929- *DancEn 78*
Vandewoestijn, David *NewGrD 80*
VanDeWoestijne, David 1915- *Baker 78*
VanDieren, Bernard *Baker 78*
VanDijk, Peter 1929- *DancEn 78*
VanDine, S S 1888-1939 *FilmgC, HalFC 80*
Vandini, Antonio 1690?-1771? *NewGrD 80*
Vandis, Titos *WhoHol A*
Vandivere, Elinor *Film 2*
VanDobeneck, Baron *Film 2*
VanDommelen, Caroline 1874-1957 *Film 2*
VanDommelen, Jan 1878-1942 *FilmAG WE*
VanDongen, Helen *OxFilm, WomWMM*
VanDoorslaer, Georges 1864-1940 *Baker 78*
Vandor, Sandor 1901-1945 *NewGrD 80*
VanDoren, Charles *NewYTET*
VanDoren, Mamie *MotPP*
VanDoren, Mamie 1931- *FilmEn, WhoHol A*
VanDoren, Mamie 1933- *FilmgC, ForYSC, HalFC 80, IntMPA 77, -75, -76, -78, -79, -80, MovMk, WhoHrs 80*
VanDoren, Mark 1894- *BiE&WWA*
VanDoren, Meta Westfall 1902- *IntWWM 77*
VanDorn, Mildred *Film 2*
VanDreelan, John *ForYSC*
VanDreelen, John *WhoHol A*
VanDresser, Marcia 1877-1937 *Baker 78*
VanDresser, Marcia 1880-1937 *BiDAmM*
VanDriem, Adriann Julius August 1901- *IntWWM 77, -80*
Vandross, Luther R 1951- *AmSCAP 80*
VanDruten, John 1901-1957 *CnMD, CnThe, EncWT, Ent, FilmgC, HalFC 80, McGEWD[port], ModWD, NotNAT A, -B, OxThe, PIP&P, WhThe*
VanDurme, Jef 1907-1965 *Baker 78,*

NewGrD 80
VanDusen, Granville *WhoHol A*
VanDuyse, Flor *NewGrD 80*
VanDuyze, Florimond 1843-1910 *Baker 78*
VanDyck, Ernest 1861-1923 *Baker 78, MusSN[port], NewEOp 71, NewGrD 80*
VanDyck, Jeannette 1925- *IntWWM 80*
VanDyk, James 1895-1951 *WhScrn 74, -77*
VanDyke, Conny *WhoHol A*
VanDyke, Dick 1925- *FilmEn, FilmgC, ForYSC, Funs[port], HalFC 80, IntMPA 77, -75, -76, -78, -79, -80, JoeFr[port], MotPP, MovMk[port], WhoHol A, WorEFlm*
VanDyke, Henry 1852-1933 *BiDAmM*
VanDyke, Jan *CmpGMD[port]*
VanDyke, Jerry 1931- *ForYSC, MotPP, WhoHol A*
VanDyke, Leroy Frank 1929- *BiDAmM, CounME 74[port], -74A, EncFCWM 69, IlEncCM, RkOn*
VanDyke, Truman 1897- *Film 1, -2, TwYS*
VanDyke, W S *Film 1*
VanDyke, W S 1887-1943 *BiDFilm, -81, WhScrn 77, WorEFlm*
VanDyke, W S 1887-1944 *DcFM, MovMk[port]*
VanDyke, W S 1889-1943 *FilmEn, HalFC 80*
VanDyke, W S 1889-1944 *CmMov, FilmgC*
VanDyke, W S 1899-1943 *OxFilm, TwYS A*
VanDyke, W S 1899-1944 *AmFD*
VanDyke, Willard 1906- *DcFM, FilmEn, OxFilm, WomWMM, WorEFlm*
VanDyke, Woody 1887-1943 *WorEFlm*
Vane, Charles *Film 2*
Vane, Denton 1890-1940 *WhScrn 74, -77, WhoHol B*
Vane, Dorothy d1947 *NotNAT B*
Vane, Edwin T *NewYTET*
Vane, Helen d1840 *NotNAT B*
Vane, Myrtle *Film 2*
Vane, Norman Thaddeus 1931- *IntMPA 77, -75, -76*
Vane, Sutton d1913 *NotNAT B*
Vane, Sutton 1888-1963 *McGEWD[port], ModWD, NotNAT B*
Vane-Tempest, Francis Adolphus 1863-1932 *NotNAT B, WhThe*
Vanecek, Jaroslav 1920- *IntWWM 77, -80*
Vaneck, Florence M *PupTheA*
Vaneck, Pierre *WhoHol A*
Vaneck, Pierre 1931- *EncWT*
Vanek, Matthew F 1941- *IntWWM 77*
Vanel, Charles *Film 2*
Vanel, Charles 1885- *WorEFlm*
Vanel, Charles 1892- *FilmEn, FilmgC, HalFC 80, WhoHol A*
Vanelli, Gino *ConMuA 80A*
VanEnger, Charles J 1890- *HalFC 80, IntMPA 77, -75, -76, -78, -79*
VanEps, George 1913- *AmSCAP 66, -80, CmpEPM, EncJzS 70, WhoJazz 72*
VanEps, Robert 1909- *AmSCAP 80*
VanEss, Connie *WhoHol A*
VanEss, Donald Harrison 1926- *IntWWM 77, -80*
Vaneuf, Andre *AmSCAP 80, ConAmC*
VanEyck, Jacob *NewGrD 80*
VanEyck, Peter 1911-1969 *FilmgC, HalFC 80*
VanEyck, Peter 1912-1969 *FilmAG WE[port]*
VanEyck, Peter 1913-1969 *FilmEn, ForYSC, MovMk, Vers A[port], WhScrn 74, -77, WhoHol B*
VanEyssen, John 1925- *FilmgC, HalFC 80, WhoHol A*
VanFleet, Jo *BiE&WWA, IntMPA 77, -75, -76, -78, -79, -80, MotPP, NotNAT, WhoHol A, WhoThe 72*
VanFleet, Jo 1919- *FilmEn, FilmgC, ForYSC, HalFC 80, HolCA[port]*
VanFleet, Jo 1922- *MovMk, Vers A[port], WhoThe 77*
VanForst, Kathy 1904- *AmSCAP 66, -80*
VanFrachen, Victor 1924- *IntWWM 80*
VanGastern, Louis 1922- *DcFM*
VanGelder, Hans 1919- *IntWWM 77, -80*
VanGelder, Holtropp *WhThe*
Vangelis *IlEncR*
Vangeon, Henri *McGEWD*
VanGhelen *NewGrD 80*
VanGhelen, Jakob Anton d1782 *NewGrD 80*
VanGhelen, Johann Leopold *NewGrD 80*
VanGhelen, Johann Peter 1673-1754 *NewGrD 80*
VanGilse, Jan *Baker 78*
VanGinkel, Peter 1932- *WhoOp 76*
VanGogh, Lucy *CreCan 1*
VanGool, Albertus Bernardus A Maria 1912- *IntWWM 77*
VanGordon, Cyrena 1896-1967 *BiDAmM*
VanGorkom, Karel 1946- *IntWWM 77, -80*
VanGriethuysen, Ted 1934- *BiE&WWA, NotNAT, WhoThe 72, -77*
Vangsaa, Mona 1920- *DancEn 78*
Vangsaae, Mona 1920- *CnOxB*
VanGucht, Georges 1934- *IntWWM 77, -80*
VanGyseghem, Andre 1906- *WhoThe 72, -77*
VanHaden, Anders 1876-1936 *WhScrn 74, -77, WhoHol B*
VanHagen, Peter *OxMus*
VanHagen, Peter Albrecht, Jr. 1781-1837 *BiDAmM, NewGrD 80*
VanHagen, Peter Albrecht, Sr. 1750-1803 *Baker 78, BiDAmM*
Vanhal, Jan 1739-1813 *MusMk*
VanHal, Johann Baptist 1739-1813 *Baker 78*
Vanhal, Johann Baptist 1739-1813 *NewGrD 80*
VanHalen *ConMuA 80A*
Vanhall, Johann Baptist 1739-1813 *NewGrD 80, OxMus*
VanHamel, Martine 1945- *CreCan 2*
VanHarmelen, Rita 1933- *IntWWM 77, -80*
VanHasselt, Luc 1936- *IntWWM 77, -80*
VanHeerden, Stephen 1950- *IntWWM 80*
VanHemel, Oscar Louis 1892- *IntWWM 77, -80*
VanHessen, Ro 1913- *WhoMus 72*
VanHeusen, James 1913- *AmPS, AmSCAP 66, -80, BiDAmM, BiE&WWA, FilmEn, NewGrD 80, NotNAT, Sw&Ld C, WhoThe 72, -77*
VanHeusen, Jimmy 1913- *BestMus, CmpEPM, NewGrD 80, PopAmC[port], PopAmC SUP*
VanHeusen, Jimmy 1919- *FilmgC, HalFC 80, IntMPA 77, -75, -76, -78, -79, -80*
VanHeyningen, Judy *WomWMM*
VanHoecke, Daniel Marin 1926- *IntWWM 77, -80*
VanHoek, Jan-Anton 1936- *IntWWM 77, -80*
VanHoogstraten, Willem *Baker 78*
VanHool, Roger 1940- *FilmAG WE*
VanHoose, Ellison 1868-1936 *Baker 78*
VanHoose, Ellison 1869-1936 *BiDAmM*
VanHorn, Emile d1967 *WhScrn 77*
VanHorn, James 1917-1966 *WhScrn 74, -77*
VanHorn, Jimmy 1917-1966 *WhoHol B*
VanHorn, Rollin Weber 1882-1964 *BiE&WWA, NotNAT B*
VanHorne, Harry Randall 1924- *AmSCAP 66, -80*
VanHulse, Camil 1897- *AmSCAP 66, -80, ConAmC*
VanHulsteyn, Jeannine *WomWMM B*
VanHulsteyn, Joai'n C 1869-1947 *BiDAmM*
VanIjzer-Vincent, Jo *NewGrD 80*
Vanilla Fudge *BiDAmM, ConMuA 80A, IlEncR, RkOn 2[port]*
VanImmerseel, Jos 1945- *IntWWM 80*
VanImmerseel, Joseph 1945- *IntWWM 77*
VanInderstine, Arthur Prentice 1920- *AmSCAP 80*
Vanini, Bernardino *NewGrD 80*
VanItallie, Jean-Claude 1936- *ConDr 73, -77, CroCD, DcLB 7[port], Ent, McGEWD, ModWD, NatPD[port], NotNAT, PlP&P, WhoThe 72, -77*
Vanity Fare *RkOn 2[port]*
VanJueten, Grit 1944- *WhoOp 76*
VanKampen, Bernhardt Anthony 1943- *IntWWM 77, -80*
VanKampen, Christopher Francis Royle 1945- *IntWWM 77*
VanKatwijk, Paul 1885- *Baker 78, WhoMus 72*
VanKatwijk, Viola Edna Beck 1894- *ConAmC*
VanKerckhove, Abraham *NewGrD 80*
VanKesteren, John 1921- *WhoMus 72, WhoOp 76*
VanKeulen, Geert Synco 1943- *IntWWM 77, -80*
VanLeer, Arnold 1895-1975 *IntMPA 75, WhScrn 77*
VanLeeuwen, Andrianus Cornelis 1887- *IntWWM 77, -80*
VanLennep, William 1906-1962 *DancEn 78, NotNAT B*
VanLent, Lucille *Film 2*
VanLier, Bertus 1906-1972 *Baker 78, NewGrD 80*
VanLier, Jacques 1875-1951 *Baker 78*
VanLoan, Paul S 1892-1963 *AmSCAP 80*
Vanloo, Albert d1920 *NotNAT B, WhThe*
VanLoon, Gerard Willem 1911- *AmSCAP 66, -80*
VanLove, Ludy *AmSCAP 80*
VanLuin, Maria Hillegonde 1911- *IntWWM 80*
VanMaldeghem, Robert Julien *Baker 78*
VanMaldere, Pierre *Baker 78*
VanManen, Hans 1932- *DancEn 78*
VanMeter, Harry *Film 1, TwYS*
VanMever, Pieter Adriaan 1899- *IntWWM 77, -80*
VanMilaan-Christiaanse, Loekie Elsje 1932- *IntWWM 77, -80*
VanMill, Arnold 1921- *WhoOp 76*
VanMill, Rucky 1922- *IntWWM 77, -80, WhoMus 72*
Vann, Al 1899- *AmSCAP 66, -80*
Vann, Polly 1882-1952 *Film 2, WhScrn 77*
Vann, William Stanley 1910- *IntWWM 77, -80*
Vanna, Nina *Film 2*
VanName, Elsie *Film 1*
Vannarelli, Francesco Antonio 1615?-1676? *NewGrD 80*
Vanne, Marda d1970 *WhScrn 74, -77, WhThe, WhoHol B*
Vannelli, Gino 1952- *AmSCAP 80*
Vanneo, Steffano 1493-1540? *NewGrD 80*
Vanneo, Stephano 1493-1540? *NewGrD 80*
Vannes, Rene 1888-1956 *NewGrD 80*
Vanneschi, Francesco 1660?-1735? *NewGrD 80*
VanNeste, Etienne 1918- *WhoMus 72*
Vanni, Helen Elizabeth 1924- *WhoOp 76*
Vanni, Renata *WhoHol A*
Vanni-Marcoux *Baker 78*
Vanni-Marcoux 1877-1962 *NewGrD 80*
Vannini, Bernardino 1590?-1666? *NewGrD 80*
Vannini, Elia 1660?-1699? *NewGrD 80*
Vannius, Johannes *NewGrD 80*
VanNoordt *NewGrD 80*
VanNostrand, Burr *ConAmC*
VanNostrand, Morris Abbott 1911- *BiE&WWA, NotNAT*
Vannoy, Cheryl 1953- *ConAmTC*
Vannucci, Domenico Francesco 1718?-1775 *NewGrD 80*
Vannuccini, Luigi 1828-1911 *Baker 78*
VanNutter, Rik *WhoHol A*
Vanocur, Sander *NewYTET, WhoHol A*
Vanoff, Nick *NewYTET*
VanOle, Rhea *Film 1*
VanOostveen, Klaas 1911- *IntWWM 77, -80*
VanOrden, Christina 1945- *IntWWM 77*
VanOrden, Edith *PupTheA*
VanOtterloo, Jan Willem 1907- *IntWWM 77*
VanOtterloo, Willem *Baker 78*
VanOverberghe, Malvina J P Felicite *NewGrD 80*
VanPallandt, Nina *WhoHol A*
VanParys, Georges 1902-1970 *WorEFlm*
VanParys, Georges 1902-1971 *DcFM, FilmEn, FilmgC, HalFC 80, OxFilm*
VanPatten, Dick 1928- *BiE&WWA, FilmEn, HalFC 80, IntMPA 77, -75, -76, -78, -79, -80, NotNAT, WhoHol A, WhoThe 72, -77*
VanPatten, Joyce 1934- *BiE&WWA, FilmEn, FilmgC, HalFC 80, NotNAT, WhoHol A, WhoThe 72, -77*
VanPatten, Joyce 1935- *ForYSC*
VanPatten, Vincent *WhoHol A*
VanPeebles, Melvin 1932- *AmSCAP 80, BlkAmP, ConDr 77D, DrBlPA, FilmEn, FilmgC, HalFC 80, IntMPA 77, -75, -76, -78, -79, -80, MorBAP, NotNAT, PlP&P A, WhoHol A, WhoThe 77*
VanPoole, Virginia Cromwell 1955- *IntWWM 77, -80*
VanPraag, William 1924- *IntMPA 77, -75, -76,*

-78, -79, -80
VanPraagh, Peggy 1910- *DancEn 78[port]*
VanProoijen, Cornelius Anton 1939- *IntWWM 77, -80*
VanPuijenbroeck, Victor 1932- *IntWWM 77*
VanPut, Hendrik *NewGrD 80*
VanQuaille, Jacqueline 1938- *WhoOp 76*
VanRaalte, Albert *Baker 78*
Vanrans *NewGrD 80*
VanRee, Jean 1943- *WhoOp 76*
VanRee-Bernard, Nelly 1923- *IntWWM 77, -80*
VanRemoortel, Edouard-William 1926- *IntWWM 77, -80*
VanRiel, Raimondo *Film 2*
VanRikfoord, Harold C 1935- *IntMPA 77, -75, -76, -78, -79, -80*
VanRonk, Dave 1936- *EncFCWM 69*
VanRonk, David 1936- *AmSCAP 66, -80, BiDAmM, BluesWW[port]*
VanRooten, Luis 1906-1973 *BiE&WWA, FilmEn, FilmgC, ForYSC, HalFC 80, Vers B[port], WhScrn 77, WhoHol B*
VanRooy, Anton d1932 *NotNAT B*
VanRooy, Anton 1870-1932 *Baker 78, NewEOp 71, NewGrD 80*
VanRooy, Anton 1879-1932 *MusSN[port]*
VanRossum, Frederic 1939- *Baker 78*
VanRossum, Frederik 1939- *IntWWM 77, -80, NewGrD 80*
VanRoyen, Everard Jacob 1913- *WhoMus 72*
Vanrrans *NewGrD 80*
VanSaher, Lilla A 1912-1968 *NotNAT B, WhScrn 74, -77, WhoHol B*
VanSciver, Esther 1907-1952 *AmSCAP 66, -80*
VanScott, Glory *BlkAmP, DrBlPA*
VanScoyk, Robert 1928- *BiE&WWA*
VanSertima, Theresia Elizabeth 1935- *WhoMus 72*
VanSickel, Dale *WhoHrs 80[port]*
VanSickle, Dale *WhoHol A*
VanSickle, Raymond d1964 *NotNAT B*
Vansittart, Sir Robert G 1881- *WhThe*
VanSloan, Edward 1881-1964 *HolCA[port]*
VanSloan, Edward 1882-1964 *FilmEn, FilmgC, ForYSC, HalFC 80, NotNAT B, WhScrn 74, -77, WhoHol B, WhoHrs 80[port]*
VanSlyck, Nicholas 1922- *AmSCAP 80, Baker 78, CpmDNM 80, ConAmC*
VanSpall, Peter Alexander 1913- *AmSCAP 66, -80*
VanSpengen, Lilly N H 1911- *IntWWM 77, -80*
VanStappen, Crispin *NewGrD 80*
VanSteeden, Peter, Jr. 1904- *AmSCAP 66, -80, CmpEPM*
VanSteenbergen, Anna 1928- *IntWWM 77, -80*
VanStolk, Mary *WomWMM*
VanStralen, Anton *WhoHol A*
VanStuddiford, Grace 1873-1927 *NotNAT B, WhThe*
VanTaalingen, J Th 1921- *IntMPA 77, -75, -76, -78, -79, -80*
Vantaggio, Giancarlo 1936- *CnOxB*
VanTassel, Charles 1937- *WhoOp 76*
VanTassell, David William 1954- *IntWWM 77*
VanThal, Dennis 1909- *IntMPA 77, -75, -76, -78, -79, -80, WhThe*
VanTine, Margaret *PupTheA*
VanTress, Mabel 1873-1962 *WhScrn 77, WhoHol B*
VanTrump, Jessalyn 1885-1939 *Film 1, WhScrn 74, -77, WhoHol B*
VanTuly, Helen d1964 *NotNAT B*
Vantus, Istvan 1935- *IntWWM 80*
VanTuyi, Hellen d1964 *WhoHol B*
VanTuyl, Helen 1891-1964 *WhScrn 74, -77*
VanTuyl, Marian 1907- *DancEn 78*
VanUpp, Virginia 1902-1970 *FilmEn, WhScrn 74, -77, WhoHol B, WomWMM*
VanUpp, Virginia 1912-1970 *FilmgC, HalFC 80*
Vanura, Ceslaus 1694-1736 *NewGrD 80*
Vanura, Ceslav 1694-1736 *NewGrD 80*
VanVactor, David 1906- *AmSCAP 66, -80, Baker 78, BiDAmM, CpmDNM 75, -76, -77, ConAmC, DcCM, IntWWM 77, -80, OxMus, WhoMus 72*
VanVechten, Carl 1880-1964 *Baker 78, BiDAmM, DancEn 78[port], NotNAT B*
VanVeelen, Paul 1939- *IntWWM 77, -80*
VanVleck, Jacob 1751-1831 *Baker 78, NewGrD 80*
VanVliet, Cornelius 1886-1973 *Baker 78*
VanVliet, Jean *Film 2*
VanVliet, Trudy Ann 1955- *IntWWM 77, -80*
VanVlijmen, Jan 1935- *DcCM*
VanVolkenburg, Ellen *PupTheA, WhThe*
VanVolkenburg, J L 1903- *IntMPA 77, -75, -76, -78, -79, -80, NewYTET*
VanVooren, Monique 1933- *BiE&WWA, ForYSC, MotPP, WhoHol A, WhoHrs 80*
VanVoorhis, Westbrook 1903-1968 *WhScrn 77, WhoHol B*
VanVoorthuysen, Jan 1911- *IntWWM 77, -80*
VanVorhees, Westbrook *HalFC 80*
VanVrooman, Richard Clyde 1936- *WhoOp 76*
VanVulpen *NewGrD 80*
VanVulpen, Adrianus 1922- *NewGrD 80*
VanVulpen, Rijk 1921- *NewGrD 80*
Vanwally *Film 2*
VanWerkhoven, Huber B M 1944- *IntWWM 80*
VanWessel, Bernadus Gerhardus 1931- *IntWWM 77, -80*
VanWesterhout, Niccolo 1857-1898 *Baker 78*
VanWickevoort Crommelin, Ankie 1903- *IntWWM 77, -80*
VanWilder, Philip *NewGrD 80*
VanWilgenburg, Margot *DancEn 78*
VanWilgenburg, Wouter Antonie 1944- *IntWWM 77*
VanWinkle, Harold E 1939- *AmSCAP 66, -80*
VanWinterstein, Edward *Film 2*
VanWormer, Gordon W 1937- *IntWWM 77, -80*
VanWormer, Randall Edwin 1955- *AmSCAP 80*
VanWyck, Wilfrid Charles 1904- *WhoMus 72*
VanWyk, Arnold 1916- *Baker 78, IntWWM 80*
VanWyk, Carl Albert 1942- *IntWWM 80*
Vanya, Elsie *Film 2*
VanZandt, Marie 1861-1919 *Baker 78, NewEOp 71, NewGrD 80*
VanZandt, Mary O'Sullivan 1903- *AmSCAP 66, -80*
VanZandt, Philip 1904-1951 *ForYSC, WhoHol B*
VanZandt, Philip 1904-1958 *FilmEn, FilmgC, HalFC 80, MovMk, Vers A[port], WhScrn 74, -77, WhoHrs 80*
VanZandt, Porter 1923- *BiE&WWA, NotNAT*
VanZandt, Steven 1950- *AmSCAP 80*
Vanzant, Clinton E 1929- *AmSCAP 66*
VanZant, Marie 1861-1920 *BiDAmM*
VanZanten, Cornelia 1855-1946 *Baker 78*
Vanzina, Stefano *FilmEn*
Vanzo, Alain 1928- *NewGrD 80, WhoOp 76*
Vanzo, Vittorio Mario 1862-1945 *NewGrD 80*
VanZyl, Lorett Elizabeth 1949- *IntWWM 80*
Vaquedano, Jose De d1711 *NewGrD 80*
Vaquer, Dorothea Joyce Buchalter 1943- *AmSCAP 80*
Vaqueras, Bertrandus 1450?-1507? *NewGrD 80*
Varady, Julia 1941- *NewGrD 80, WhoOp 76*
Varady, Ladislaus 1908- *WhoMus 72*
Varcoe, Jonathan Philip 1941- *IntWWM 77, -80*
Varcoe, William 1925- *WhoMus 72*
Varconi, Victor 1896- *FilmgC, MovMk*
Varconi, Victor 1896-1958 *Film 2, ForYSC, TwYS*
Varconi, Victor 1896-1976 *FilmEn, HalFC 80, WhoHol B*
Varda, Agnes 1928- *BiDFilm, -81, ConLC 16, DcFM, FilmEn, FilmgC, HalFC 80, IntMPA 79, -80, OxFilm, WhoHol A, WomWMM, WorEFlm*
Vardell, Charles Gildersleeve 1893-1958 *BiDAmM*
Vardell, Charles Gildersleeve, Jr. 1893-1962 *ConAmC*
Varden, Evelyn d1958 *MotPP, WhoHol B*
Varden, Evelyn 1893-1958 *Vers A[port]*
Varden, Evelyn 1895-1958 *FilmgC, ForYSC, HalFC 80, NotNAT B, WhScrn 74, -77, WhThe*
Varden, Norma 1898?- *FilmgC, ForYSC, HalFC 80, MovMk[port], WhoHol A*
Vardi, Emanuel 1917- *ConAmC*
Vardi, Pietro *NewGrD 80*
Vardina, Pietro *NewGrD 80*
Vardy, Stella Marguerite 1901- *WhoMus 72*
Varela, Dante A 1917- *AmSCAP 66, -80*
Varella, Jane 1936- *IntWWM 77, -80*
Varella-Cid, Sergio 1935- *WhoMus 72*
Varese, Edgar 1883-1965 *Baker 78, BnBkM 80, DcTwCC, NewGrD 80[port], OxMus*
Varese, Edgar 1885-1965 *DcCom 77[port]*
Varese, Edgard 1883-1965 *BiDAmM, BnBkM 80, CompSN[port], CnOxB, ConAmC, DcCM, NewGrD 80[port]*
Varese, Edgard 1885-1965 *MusMk*
Varesi, Elena Boccabadati- *NewGrD 80*
Varesi, Felice 1813-1889 *CmOp, NewEOp 71, NewGrD 80*
Varesi, Gilda 1887- *WhThe*
Varey, J E *PupTheA*
Varga, Laszlo 1924- *WhoMus 72*
Varga, Ovidiu 1913- *Baker 78*
Varga, Tibor 1921- *Baker 78, IntWWM 80, NewGrD 80, WhoMus 72*
Varga-Dinicu, Carolina *WhoHol A*
Vargas, Darwin 1925- *NewGrD 80*
Vargas, Manolo *CnOxB, DancEn 78*
Vargas, Urban De d1656 *NewGrD 80*
Vargyas, Lajos 1914- *IntWWM 77, -80, NewGrD 80*
Vari, John *WhoHol A*
Variadis, Serge 1926- *WhoOp 76*
Varien, Dorothea L 1893- *IntWWM 77*
Varischini, Giovanni *NewGrD 80*
Varischino, Giovanni *NewGrD 80*
Varisco, Tito 1915- *WhoOp 76*
Varius Rufus, Lucius 074?BC-014BC *OxThe*
Varlamov, Alexander Egorovich 1801-1848 *Baker 78, NewGrD 80*
Varlamov, Konstantin Alexandrovitch d1915 *NotNAT B*
Varlay, Rene G 1927- *AmSCAP 80*
Varley, Beatrice 1896-1969 *FilmgC, HalFC 80, WhoHol B*
Varley, Frederick Horsman 1881-1969 *CreCan 1*
Varley, Patricia *WhoMus 72*
Varlund, Rudolf 1900-1945 *ModWD*
Varmalov, Leonid Vassilievich 1907-1962 *DcFM*
Varna, Victo *Film 2*
Varnado, Allean 1947- *AmSCAP 80*
Varnai, Peter P 1922- *IntWWM 77, -80, NewGrD 80*
Varnay, Astrid 1918- *Baker 78, BiDAmM, BnBkM 80, CmOp, IntWWM 77, -80, MusSN[port], NewEOp 71, NewGrD 80, WhoMus 72, WhoOp 76*
Varnel, Marcel 1894-1947 *FilmEn, FilmgC, HalFC 80, IlWWBF, NotNAT B, WhThe*
Varnel, Max 1925- *FilmgC, HalFC 80, IlWWBF*
Varney, Louis 1844-1908 *Baker 78, NewGrD 80*
Varney, Pierre Joseph Alphonse 1811-1879 *Baker 78*
Varney, Reg 1922- *FilmgC, HalFC 80, WhoHol A*
Varnick, Ted 1913- *AmSCAP 66, -80*
Varnlund, Rudolf 1900-1945 *CnMD*
Varon, Neil 1950- *IntWWM 80*
Varon, Nelson 1928- *AmSCAP 66*
Varona, Jose Luciano 1930- *WhoOp 76*
Varoter, Francesco *NewGrD 80*
Varotti, P Albino 1925- *IntWWM 77*
Varotto, Michele 1550?-1599? *NewGrD 80*
Varrey, Edwin d1907 *NotNAT B*
Varro, Marcus Terentius 116BC-027BC *NewGrD 80*
Varro, Marie-Aimee 1915-1971 *Baker 78*
Vars, Henry 1902-1977 *AmSCAP 66, -80, ConAmC*
Varsi, Diane 1937- *FilmEn*
Varsi, Diane 1938- *FilmgC, ForYSC, HalFC 80, MotPP, MovMk, WhoHol A*
Varsi, Dinorah 1939- *IntWWM 77*
Vartan, Sylvie *WhoHol A*
Vartian, Thomas *Film 2*
Varvarande, Robert Emile 1922- *CreCan 1*

Varvarow, Feodor *Film 2*
Varviso, Silvio 1924- *Baker 78, NewEOp 71, NewGrD 80, WhoOp 76*
Varvoglis, Mario 1885-1967 *Baker 78, DcCM, NewGrD 80*
Vary, Ferenc 1928- *IntWWM 77*
Vas, Judit *WomWMM*
Vasan, S S 1900- *DcFM*
Vasara, Oiva Llmari 1939- *IntWWM 77*
Vasarhelyi, Zoltan 1900-1977 *NewGrD 80*
Vasari, Giorgio 1511-1574 *EncWT*
Vasaroff, Michael *Film 2*
Vasary, Tamas 1933- *IntWWM 77, -80, NewGrD 80, WhoMus 72*
Vasconcellos, Joaquim De 1849-1936 *Baker 78, NewGrD 80*
Vasconcellos Correa, Sergio Oliveira De 1934- *IntWWM 80*
Vasconcelos, Jorge Croner De 1910- *Baker 78*
Vasek, Marisha *WhoHol A*
Vasilenko, Sergey Nikiforovich 1872-1956 *NewGrD 80*
Vasilescu, Ion 1903-1960 *NewGrD 80*
Vasiliev, Georgi 1899-1945 *WorEFlm*
Vasiliev, Georgi 1899-1946 *DcFM, OxFilm*
Vasiliev, Georgy 1899-1945 *FilmEn*
Vasiliev, Sergei 1900-1959 *DcFM, FilmEn, OxFilm, WorEFlm*
Vasiliev, Vladimir Victorovich 1940- *CnOxB*
Vasiliov, Vladimir Lubovich 1931- *CnOxB*
Vasina-Grossman, Vera Andreyevna 1908- *NewGrD 80*
Vasquez, Juan 1510?-1560? *NewGrD 80*
Vasquez, Juan 1550?-1604 *Baker 78*
Vass, Lulu 1877-1952 *WhScrn 74, -77*
Vassallo, Aldo Mirabella 1915- *WhoOp 76*
Vassar, Queenie 1870-1960 *NotNAT B, WhScrn 74, -77, WhoHol B*
Vasseli, Judith *Film 2*
Vasseur, Leon 1844-1917 *Baker 78, NewGrD 80*
Vassilenko, Sergei 1872-1956 *Baker 78, NewEOp 71*
Vassiliadis, Stefanos T 1933- *CpmDNM 78*
Vassiliev, Vladimir 1940- *DancEn 78*
Vassiliev-Buglay, Dmitri 1888-1956 *Baker 78*
Vasson, Pierre *NewGrD 80*
Vatatzes, Joannes *NewGrD 80*
Vatatzis, Joannes *NewGrD 80*
Vatelot, Etienne 1925- *NewGrD 80*
Vater, Christian 1679-1756 *NewGrD 80*
Vatielli, Francesco 1876-1946 *NewGrD 80*
Vatielli, Francesco 1877-1946 *Baker 78*
Vaubourgoin, Jean-Fernand 1880-1952 *NewGrD 80*
Vaubourgoin, Marc 1907- *NewGrD 80*
Vaucaire, Maurice 1865-1918 *NotNAT B, WhThe*
Vauclain, Constant 1908- *ConAmC*
Vaucorbeil, Auguste-Emmanuel 1821-1884 *Baker 78, NewGrD 80*
Vaudreuil, Guy De *CreCan 1*
Vaughan, Bernard *Film 2*
Vaughan, Clifford 1893- *AmSCAP 66, -80, ConAmC, IntWWM 77, -80*
Vaughan, David 1924- *CnOxB*
Vaughan, Denis 1926- *Baker 78, IntWWM 77, -80, NewGrD 80, WhoMus 72*
Vaughan, Dorothy 1889-1955 *WhScrn 74, -77, WhoHol B*
Vaughan, Elizabeth 1937- *CmOp, IntWWM 77, -80, NewGrD 80, WhoMus 72*
Vaughan, Elizabeth 1938- *WhoOp 76*
Vaughan, Frank, Jr. 1944- *AmSCAP 80*
Vaughan, Frankie 1928- *FilmgC, HalFC 80, IlWWBF[port], IntMPA 75, -76, WhoHol A*
Vaughan, Gillian *WhoHol A*
Vaughan, Gladys *BiE&WWA, NotNAT*
Vaughan, Hilda 1898-1957 *WhThe*
Vaughan, James D 1864-1941 *NewGrD 80*
Vaughan, John Forbes 1921- *AmSCAP 66*
Vaughan, Kate 1852?-1903 *NotNAT B, OxThe*
Vaughan, Margery 1927- *IntWWM 77, -80*
Vaughan, Peter 1923- *ConAmTC, FilmgC, HalFC 80, WhoHol A*
Vaughan, Robert Alfred 1823-1857 *DcPup*
Vaughan, Rodger Dale 1932- *AmSCAP 80, ConAmC*
Vaughan, Sarah 1924- *AmPS A, -B, BiDAmM, CmpEPM, DrBlPA, EncJzS 70, IlEncJ, NewGrD 80, RkOn[port]*
Vaughan, Stuart 1925- *BiE&WWA, NatPD[port], NotNAT, WhoThe 72, -77*
Vaughan, Susie 1853-1950 *NotNAT B, WhThe*
Vaughan, T B d1928 *NotNAT B*
Vaughan, Thomas David 1873-1934 *NewGrD 80*
Vaughan, Vivian *Film 1*
Vaughan Williams, Ralph 1872-1958 *Baker 78, BnBkM 80, CmOp, CompSN[port], DcCom 77[port], DcCom&M 79, DcCM, DcTwCC, -A, MusMk[port], NewEOp 71, NewGrD 80, OxFilm, OxMus*
Vaughan Williams, Ursula 1911- *IntWWM 77, -80, WhoMus 72*
Vaughn, Ada Mae 1906-1943 *Film 2*
Vaughn, Adamae 1906-1943 *WhScrn 74, -77, WhoHol B*
Vaughn, Alberta 1906- *ForYSC, TwYS, WhoHol A*
Vaughn, Alberta 1908- *Film 2*
Vaughn, Billy *AmPS A, -B, AmSCAP 66*
Vaughn, Billy 1919- *BiDAmM*
Vaughn, Billy 1931- *RkOn[port]*
Vaughn, Dorothy 1889-1955 *ForYSC, Vers B[port]*
Vaughn, Frankie 1928- *ForYSC*
Vaughn, Hilda 1898-1957 *Film 2, ForYSC, NotNAT B, WhScrn 74, -77, WhoHol B*
Vaughn, Jack 1925- *AmSCAP 66, -80*
Vaughn, Julie Ramm 1940- *IntWWM 77*
Vaughn, Richard Smith 1919- *AmSCAP 80*
Vaughn, Robert 1932- *FilmEn, FilmgC, ForYSC, HalFC 80, IntMPA 77, -75, -76, -78, -79, -80, MotPP, MovMk, WhoHol A, WhoHrs 80[port], WorEFlm*
Vaughn, Sammy *WhoHol A*
Vaughn, Thomas Wade 1936- *EncJzS 70*
Vaughn, Tom 1936- *EncJzS 70*
Vaughn, Vivian 1902-1966 *WhScrn 74, -77*
Vaughn, William d1946 *Film 2, WhScrn 74, -77, WhoHol B*
Vaulthier, Georges d1926 *WhScrn 74, -77*
Vausden, Val *Film 2*
Vaussard, Christiane 1923- *CnOxB, DancEn 78*
Vauthier, Jean 1910- *CnMD, CroCD, EncWT, McGEWD, ModWD, REnWD[port]*
Vautier, Elmire *Film 2*
Vautier, Rene 1928- *DcFM*
Vautor, Thomas 1590?- *Baker 78, NewGrD 80, OxMus*
Vautrollier, Thomas d1587 *NewGrD 80*
Vaverka, Anton d1937 *Film 2, WhScrn 74, -77, WhoHol B*
Vavitch, Michael *Film 2, ForYSC, TwYS*
Vavra, Otakar 1911- *DcFM, FilmEn, OxFilm, WorEFlm*
Vavrineck, Elaine *PupTheA*
Vavrinecz, Bela 1925- *IntWWM 77, -80*
Vayllant, Jehan *NewGrD 80*
Vaynberg, Moyssey Samuilovich 1919- *NewGrD 80*
Vaz, Francois R 1931- *EncJzS 70*
Vaz DaCosta, Afonso *NewGrD 80*
Vaz DaCosta, Alfonso *NewGrD 80*
Vaz DeAcosta, Afonso *NewGrD 80*
Vaz DeAcosta, Alfonso *NewGrD 80*
Vaz Dias, David *AmSCAP 80*
Vaz Dias, Selma 1911- *WhThe, WhoHol A, WhoThe 72*
Vaz Rego, Pedro *NewGrD 80*
Vazem, Yekaterina Ottovna 1848-1937 *CnOxB*
Vazquez, Juan *NewGrD 80*
Vazquez, Myrna 1935-1975 *WhScrn 77*
Vazquez, Roland *WhoHol A*
Vazsonyi, Balint 1936- *IntWWM 77, -80, WhoMus 72*
Vazzana, Anthony E 1922- *AmSCAP 66, -80, ConAmC*
Vea, Ketil 1932- *IntWWM 80*
Veal, Arthur Edwin *IntWWM 77, -80, WhoMus 72*
Veal, Margaret 1935- *IntWWM 77, -80, WhoMus 72*
Veale, John 1922- *NewGrD 80, WhoMus 72*
Veasey, Josephine 1930- *IntWWM 77, -80, NewGrD 80, WhoOp 76*
Veasey, Josephine 1931- *CmOp, WhoMus 72*
Veazie, Carol *WhoHol A*
Veazie, George Augustus 1835-1915 *Baker 78, BiDAmM*
Veber, Gyula 1929- *IntWWM 80*
Veber, Pierre 1869-1942 *McGEWD*
Veca, Lawrence 1889-1911 *NewOrJ[port]*
Vecchi, Giuseppe 1912- *IntWWM 77, -80, NewGrD 80*
Vecchi, Horatio 1550-1605 *NewGrD 80[port]*
Vecchi, Lorenzo 1564?-1628 *NewGrD 80*
Vecchi, Orazio 1550-1605 *Baker 78, BnBkM 80, CmpBCM, DcPup, GrComp[port], MusMk, NewGrD 80[port], OxMus*
Vecchi, Orfeo 1550-1604? *Baker 78, NewGrD 80*
Vecchione, Al *NewYTET*
Veccoli *NewGrD 80*
Vecheslova, Tatiana 1910- *DancEn 78*
Vechten, Carl Van 1880-1964 *CnOxB*
Vecla, Djema *NewGrD 80*
Vecoli *NewGrD 80*
Vecoli, Francesco *NewGrD 80*
Vecoli, Pietro *NewGrD 80*
Vecoli, Regolo *NewGrD 80*
Vecsei, Desider Josef 1882-1966 *AmSCAP 66, Baker 78, ConAmC*
Vecsey, Franz Von 1893-1935 *Baker 78*
Vecsey, Jeno 1909-1966 *Baker 78, NewGrD 80*
Vedder, William H 1872-1961 *WhScrn 74, -77, WhoHol B*
Vedernikov, Alexander Filipovich 1927- *WhoOp 76*
Vedrenne, John E 1867-1930 *EncWT, NotNAT B, OxThe, WhThe*
Vedres, Nicole 1911-1965 *DcFM, FilmEn, FilmgC, HalFC 80, OxFilm, WomWMM, WorEFlm*
Vedreune, J E *PlP&P[port]*
Vee, Bobby 1943- *AmPS A, BiDAmM, RkOn[port], WhoHol A*
Veen, Jan 1908- *DancEn 78*
Veen, Jan VanDer 1923- *NewGrD 80*
Veeninga, Jennie Jantina 1936- *WhoOp 76*
Veenstra, Piet 1929- *IntWWM 77, -80*
Veerhoff, Carlos 1926- *Baker 78, NewGrD 80*
Veg, Willem De *NewGrD 80*
Vega *NewGrD 80*
Vega, Al *AmSCAP 80*
Vega, Aurelio DeLa 1925- *Baker 78, ConAmC, NewGrD 80*
Vega, Carlos 1898-1966 *Baker 78, NewGrD 80*
Vega, Carpio 1562-1635 *OxMus*
Vega, Isela *WhoHol A*
Vega, Jose 1920- *BiE&WWA, NotNAT*
Vega, Lope De 1562-1635 *CnThe, REnWD[port]*
Vega, Rose *Film 2*
Vega, Ventura DeLa 1807-1865 *McGEWD[port], OxThe*
Vega Carpio, Lope Felix De 1562-1635 *McGEWD[port], NotNAT A, -B, OxThe*
Veggio, Claudio Maria 1510?- *NewGrD 80*
Vegh, Sandor 1905- *IntWWM 77, -80, NewGrD 80*
Vegoda, Joseph 1910- *IntMPA 77, -75, -76, -78, -79, -80*
Vehe, Michael 1480?-1539 *NewGrD 80*
Veichtner, Franz Adam 1741-1822 *NewGrD 80*
Veidt, Conrad d1943 *MotPP, WhoHol B*
Veidt, Conrad 1892-1943 *TwYS, WorEFlm[port]*
Veidt, Conrad 1893-1943 *BiDFilm, -81, FilmAG WE, FilmEn, Film 1, -2, FilmgC, ForYSC, HalFC 80, IlWWBF, MovMk[port], NotNAT B, OxFilm, WhScrn 74, -77, WhoHrs 80[port]*
Veidt, Lily *BiE&WWA, NotNAT*
Veiga *NewGrD 80*
Veigl, Eva Maria *CnOxB*
Veiller, Anthony 1903-1965 *FilmEn, FilmgC, HalFC 80*
Veiller, Bayard 1869-1943 *NotNAT A, -B, WhThe*
Veillot, Jean d1662 *NewGrD 80*

Veinert, Antoni *NewGrD 80*
Veinus, Abraham 1916- *Baker 78, NewGrD 80*
Veit, Huns *NewGrD 80*
Veit, Vaclav Jindrich 1806-1864 *NewGrD 80*
Veit, Wenzel Heinrich 1806-1864 *Baker 78*
Veit, Wenzell Heinrich 1806-1864 *NewGrD 80*
Veitch, Joyce Clara 1933- *WhoMus 72*
Vejar, Harry J 1890-1968 *Film 2, WhScrn 74, -77, WhoHol B*
Vejvanovsky, Pavel Josef 1633?-1693 *NewGrD 80*
Vekroff, Perry 1881-1937 *TwYS A, WhScrn 74, -77, WhoHol B*
Velaise, Robert *IntMPA 77, -75, -76, -78, -79, -80*
Velasco, Conchita *FilmAG WE*
Velasco, Jerry *WhoHol A*
Velasco, Nicolas Doizi De *NewGrD 80*
Velasco, Sebastian Lopez De *NewGrD 80*
Velasco-Llanos, Santiago 1915- *Baker 78*
Velasco Maidana, Jose Maria 1899- *Baker 78*
Velasco Maidana, Jose Maria 1901- *NewGrD 80*
Velasques, Jose Francisco *NewGrD 80*
Velasquez, Glauco 1884-1914 *NewGrD 80*
Velasquez, Jose Francisco *NewGrD 80*
Velazco, Robert E 1924- *IntMPA 77, -75, -76, -78, -79, -80*
Velazquez, Higinio 1926- *Baker 78*
Velazquez, Jose Francisco *NewGrD 80*
Veld, Henry 1895- *IntWWM 77*
Velde, Donald L 1902- *IntMPA 77, -75, -76, -78, -79, -80*
Velde, James R *IntMPA 77, -75, -76, -78, -79, -80*
Veldeke, Hendrik Van *NewGrD 80*
Velden, Renier VanDer 1910- *NewGrD 80*
Velebny, Karel 1931- *IntWWM 77*
Veleris, Mabel 1937- *WhoOp 76*
Veleta, Richard Kenneth 1929- *IntWWM 77*
Velez, Lupe d1944 *MotPP, WhoHol B*
Velez, Lupe 1908-1944 *FilmEn, FilmgC, ForYSC, HalFC 80, NotNAT B, ThFT[port], WhScrn 74, -77*
Velez, Lupe 1909-1944 *CmpEPM, Film 2, MovMk, TwYS, WhThe*
Velez DeGuevara, Luis 1579-1644 *McGEWD*
Velezdy, Joseph 1912- *AmSCAP 80*
Velezdy, Mary 1912- *AmSCAP 80*
Velickova, Ljuba *NewGrD 80*
Velie, Janet *AmPS B*
Velikanoff, Ivan 1890-1971 *BiDAmM*
Velimirovic, Milos 1922- *Baker 78, NewGrD 80*
Velis, Andrea 1931?- *BiDAmM*
Velis, Andrea 1932- *WhoOp 76*
Veliz, Andy C 1943- *AmSCAP 80*
Velke, Fritz 1930- *AmSCAP 66, -80, ConAmC*
Vella, Joseph Paul 1942- *IntWWM 77, -80*
Vella, Michelangelo 1715?-1792 *NewGrD 80*
Vella, Oliver *WhoMus 72*
Velle, Gaston *DcFM*
Vellekoop, Cornelis Kees 1940- *IntWWM 77, -80*
Vellekoop, Gerrit 1907- *IntWWM 80*
Velleman, Dora *PupTheA SUP*
Velleman, Leo *PupTheA SUP*
Vello DeTorices, Benito *NewGrD 80*
Velluti, Giovanni Battista 1780-1861 *CmOp, NewEOp 71*
Velluti, Giovanni Battista 1781-1861 *NewGrD 80, OxMus*
Velmont, James *AmSCAP 80*
Velo, Carlos 1905- *DcFM, WorEFlm*
Velona, Anthony 1920- *AmSCAP 66, -80*
Veloso, Robert Florendo 1947- *AmSCAP 80*
Velours, The *RkOn*
Veloz And Yolanda *WhoHol A*
Veloz And Yolande Orchestra *BiDAmM*
Veltchek, Vaslav 1896?- *DancEn 78*
Velten, Johannes 1640-1692 *OxThe*
Velten, Johannes 1640-1693? *Ent*
Velthen, Johannes 1640-1693 *EncWT*
Veltri, Michelangelo 1940- *WhoOp 76*
Velut, Egidius *NewGrD 80*
Velut, Gilet *NewGrD 80*
Velvet Underground *BiDAmM, ConMuA 80A, IlEncR[port]*
Velvets, The *RkOn[port]*
Velvette, Helene *AmSCAP 80*
Venable, Evelyn 1913- *FilmEn, Film 2, FilmgC, ForYSC, HalFC 80, MotPP, MovMk, ThFT[port], What 3[port], WhoHol A*
Venable, Reginald 1926-1974 *WhScrn 77, WhoHol B*
Venatorini *Baker 78*
Vencelius *NewGrD 80*
Vender, Jheronimus *NewGrD 80*
Venders, Jheronimus *NewGrD 80*
Vendome, Richard Andrew John 1949- *IntWWM 77, -80*
Vene, Ruggero 1897-1961 *AmSCAP 66, -80, ConAmC*
Venechanos, S Samuel 1924- *AmSCAP 66*
Venegas DeHenestrosa, Luis 1500?- *Baker 78*
Venegas DeHenestrosa, Luis 1510?-1557? *NewGrD 80*
Venema, Mea 1946- *CnOxB*
Vener, Victor 1945- *IntWWM 77, -80*
Veneri, Gregorio 1602?-1631? *NewGrD 80*
Venesile, John A 1937- *IntWWM 77*
Veness, Amy 1876-1960 *Film 1, FilmgC, HalFC 80, NotNAT B, WhScrn 74, -77, WhoHol B*
Venetus, Franciscus *NewGrD 80*
Venezianer, Sandor *NewGrD 80*
Veneziani, Gaetano 1656-1716 *NewGrD 80*
Veneziano, Gaetano 1656-1716 *NewGrD 80*
Veneziano, Giovanni 1683-1742 *NewGrD 80*
Vengerova, Isabelle 1877-1956 *Baker 78, BiDAmM*
Venhoda, Miroslav 1915- *IntWWM 77, -80, NewGrD 80*
VenHorst, Sister St. John 1908- *IntWWM 77, -80*
Venier, Jean Baptiste *NewGrD 80*
Venier, Marie 1590-1619 *NotNAT B, OxThe*
Venieris, Calliope *DancEn 78*
Vening, Alan Peter 1934- *WhoMus 72*
Venkataramaya, Relangi 1910-1975 *WhScrn 77*
Venkatesh, Guruzala Krishnadas 1927- *IntWWM 77*
Venn, Paul A 1943- *IntWWM 77, -80*
Vennard, William D 1909-1971 *Baker 78*
Venne, Lottie 1852-1928 *NotNAT B, OxThe, WhThe*
Venneker, Klaas 1931- *IntWWM 77*
Venning, Una 1893- *WhThe*
Venora, Lee 1932- *BiE&WWA, NotNAT*
Vent, Jan *NewGrD 80*
Ventapane, Lorenzo *NewGrD 80*
Vente, Maarten Albert 1915- *NewGrD 80*
Venth, Carl 1860-1938 *Baker 78*
Vento, Ivo De 1543?-1575 *NewGrD 80*
Vento, Marc 1936- *WhoOp 76*
Vento, Matthias 1735-1776 *NewGrD 80*
Vento, Mattia 1735-1776 *NewGrD 80*
Vento, Yvo De 1543?-1575 *NewGrD 80*
Ventre, Frank L 1895-1966 *AmSCAP 66, -80*
Ventriglia, Franco 1927- *WhoMus 72*
Ventura, Angelo Benedetto 1781?-1856 *NewGrD 80*
Ventura, Charlie 1916- *BgBands 74, CmpEPM, EncJzS 70, WhoJazz 72*
Ventura, Giuseppe 1702?-1751 *NewGrD 80*
Ventura, Jose 1817-1875 *NewGrD 80*
Ventura, Leno *WhoHol A*
Ventura, Lino 1918- *FilmgC, HalFC 80, WorEFlm*
Ventura, Lino 1919- *FilmEn*
Ventura, Ray 1908-1979 *FilmEn*
Ventura, Viviane *WhoHol A*
Venture, Jo A La *NewGrD 80*
Venture, Richard *WhoHol A*
Venturelli, Giuseppe 1711-1775 *NewGrD 80*
Ventures, The *AmPS A, RkOn*
Venturi, Pompilio *NewGrD 80*
Venturi DelNibbio, Stefano *NewGrD 80*
Venturin, Margaret Ross *AmSCAP 80*
Venturini, Dante A 1922- *AmSCAP 80*
Venturini, Edward *TwYS A*
Venturini, Francesco 1675?-1745 *NewGrD 80*
Venuta, Benay 1911- *CmpEPM, WhoThe 72, -77*
Venuta, Benay 1912- *BiE&WWA, Film 2, ForYSC, NotNAT, WhoHol A*
Venuti, Giuseppe 1898-1978 *EncJzS 70*
Venuti, Giuseppe 1903-1978 *BiDAmM*
Venuti, Joe d1978 *BgBands 74*
Venuti, Joe 1898-1978 *EncJzS 70, IlEncJ*
Venuti, Joe 1899-1978 *WhoJazz 72*
Venuti, Joe 1903-1978 *AmSCAP 66, -80*
Venuti, Joe 1904- *CmpEPM*
Venza, Jac *NewYTET*
Venzano, Luigi 1814-1878 *Baker 78*
Venzuella, Peter *Film 2*
Vep, Irma *Film 1*
Veprik, Alexander Moiseyevich 1899-1958 *NewGrD 80*
Veprik, Alexandr 1899-1958 *Baker 78*
Vera, Billy *AmSCAP 80*
Vera, Billy & Judy Clay *RkOn 2[port]*
Vera-Ellen *MotPP*
Vera-Ellen 1920- *ForYSC, WhoHol A*
Vera-Ellen 1926- *CmMov, CmpEPM, FilmEn, FilmgC, HalFC 80, MovMk[port], WorEFlm*
Vera Vague *What 5[port]*
Veracini, Antonio *OxMus*
Veracini, Antonio 1650?- *MusMk*
Veracini, Antonio 1659-1733 *NewGrD 80*
Veracini, Francesco Maria 1690-1750 *GrComp[port], MusMk, OxMus*
Veracini, Francesco Maria 1690-1768 *Baker 78, NewGrD 80[port]*
Veras, Ph F *NewGrD 80*
VerBecke, W Edwin *NatPD[port]*
Verben, Jo *NewGrD 80*
Verber, Pierre 1869- *WhThe*
Verbesselt, August Frans 1919- *Baker 78, WhoMus 72*
Verbit, Helen *WhoHol A*
Verbonnet, Johannes *NewGrD 80*
Verbruggen, Mrs. *OxThe*
Verbrugghen, Henri 1873-1934 *Baker 78, NewGrD 80*
Verbrughen, Henri 1873-1934 *BiDAmM*
Verbytsky, Mykhaylo 1815-1870 *NewGrD 80*
Verchaly, Andre Paul Joseph 1903-1976 *IntWWM 77, -80, NewGrD 80*
Verchi, Nino Giovanni 1921- *WhoOp 76*
Verchinina, Nina *CnOxB, DancEn 78[port], WhThe*
Vercoe, Barry Lloyd 1937- *ConAmC, IntWWM 77, -80*
Vercoe, Elizabeth 1941- *CpmDNM 80*
Vercore, Mathias Herman *NewGrD 80*
Vercore, Matthias Herman *NewGrD 80*
Verdalonga, Jose *NewGrD 80*
Verdehr, Walter 1941- *IntWWM 77, -80*
Verdeil, Raina *NewGrD 80*
Verdelot, Philippe 1470?-1552? *Baker 78, NewGrD 80[port], OxMus*
Verdi, Giuseppe 1813-1901 *Baker 78, BnBkM 80[port], CmOp[port], CmpBCM, CnOxB, DcCom 77[port], DcCom&M 79, GrComp[port], MusMk[port], NewEOp 71, NewGrD 80[port], OxMus*
Verdi, Joe 1885-1957 *WhoHol B*
Verdi, Joseph 1885-1957 *WhScrn 74, -77*
Verdi, Pietro *NewGrD 80*
Verdi, Ralph Carl 1944- *IntWWM 77, -80*
Verdier, Pierre 1627-1706 *NewGrD 80*
Verdina, Pietro 1600?-1643 *NewGrD 80*
Verdon, Gwen *AmPS B, MotPP, WhoHol A*
Verdon, Gwen 1925- *DancEn 78, FilmEn, HalFC 80, WhoThe 77*
Verdon, Gwen 1926- *BiE&WWA, CnOxB, EncMT, ForYSC, NotNAT, WhoThe 72*
Verdonch, Cornelis 1563-1625 *NewGrD 80*
Verdonck, Cornelis 1563-1625 *NewGrD 80*
Verdonck, Cornelius 1563-1625 *MusMk*
Verdoncq, Cornelis 1563-1625 *NewGrD 80*
Verdonk, Cornelis 1563-1625 *NewGrD 80*
Verducci, John S 1912-1977 *AmSCAP 66, -80*
Verdugo, Elena 1926- *FilmEn, FilmgC, ForYSC, HalFC 80, MovMk, WhoHol A*
Verdugo, Sebastian Martinez *NewGrD 80*
Verdy, Violette 1933- *CnOxB, DancEn 78[port], WhoHol A*
Vere, Clementine Duchene De 1864-1954 *Baker 78, BiDAmM*
Vere, Diana 1942- *CnOxB*
Verebes, Ernest *Film 2*
Verebes, Erno 1904- *IntMPA 75, -76*
Verebes, Robert 1934- *IntWWM 80*
Verecore, Mathias Hermann *NewGrD 80*

Verecore, Matthias Hermann *NewGrD 80*
Veredon, Gray 1943- *CnOxB*
Vereen, Ben 1946- *DrBlPA, EncMT, HalFC 80, NotNAT, WhoHol A, WhoThe 77*
Veremans, Renaat 1894-1969 *Baker 78*
Veress, Sandor 1907- *Baker 78, ConAmC, DcCM, IntWWM 77, -80, NewGrD 80*
Veretti, Antonio 1900- *Baker 78, NewGrD 80, WhoMus 72*
Verevka, Grigory 1895-1964 *Baker 78*
Verga, Giovanni 1840-1922 *CnThe, EncWT, McGEWD[port], ModWD, OxThe, REnWD[port], WhThe*
Vergano, Aldo 1894-1957 *DcFM, FilmEn*
Verge, Cyril A 1921- *AmSCAP 66*
Vergerio, Pier Paolo 1370-1444 *OxThe*
Verges, Joe 1892-1964 *AmSCAP 66, -80*
Vergez-Tricom *WomWMM*
Vergil *NewGrD 80*
Verhaalen, Marion 1930- *IntWWM 77, -80*
Verhaar, Ary 1900- *CpmDNM 76, IntWWM 77, -80, NewGrD 80*
Verhaeren, Emile Adolphe Gustave 1855-1916 *ModWD*
Verheul, Koos 1927- *IntWWM 77, -80*
Verhey, Emmy 1949- *WhoMus 72*
Verheyden, Edward 1878-1959 *Baker 78*
Verheyen, Pierre Emmanuel 1750?-1819 *NewGrD 80*
Verhoeff, Nicolaas Theodorus 1904- *IntWWM 77, -80*
Verhoeven, Paul 1901-1975 *WhScrn 77*
Verhulst, Edu 1940- *IntWWM 77*
Verhulst, Johannes Josephus Herman 1816-1891 *Baker 78, NewGrD 80, OxMus*
Verikivsky, Mykhaylo 1896-1962 *NewGrD 80*
Verikovsky, Mikhail Ivanovich 1896-1962 *NewGrD 80*
Verio, Juan *NewGrD 80*
Veritophilus *NewGrD 80*
Verjus *NewGrD 80*
Verjus 1435?-1499 *NewGrD 80*
Verjust 1435?-1499 *NewGrD 80*
Verkoff, Perry N 1887-1937 *WhScrn 77*
Verkouteren, John Adrian 1950- *AmSCAP 80*
Verlaine, Paul 1844-1896 *NewGrD 80, OxMus*
Verley, Bernard 1939- *FilmAG WE, WhoHol A*
Verley, Renaud *WhoHol A*
Verlit, Gaspar De 1625?-1673? *NewGrD 80*
Verlith, Gaspar De 1625?-1673? *NewGrD 80*
Verloge, Hilaire d1734 *NewGrD 80*
Verly, Michele *Film 2*
Vermeeren, Anthoni 1640?-1668? *NewGrD 80*
Vermeeren, Anthonis 1640?-1668? *NewGrD 80*
Vermeersch, Jef 1928- *WhoOp 76*
Vermeren, Anthoni 1640?-1668? *NewGrD 80*
Vermeren, Anthonis 1640?-1668? *NewGrD 80*
Vermeulen, Matthijs 1888-1967 *Baker 78, NewGrD 80, OxMus*
Vermeulen, Matthys 1888-1967 *DcCM*
Vermilyea, Harold 1889-1958 *FilmgC, ForYSC, HalFC 80, NotNAT B, WhScrn 74, -77, WhThe, WhoHol B*
Vermont, Pernot d1558 *NewGrD 80*
Vermont, Pierre d1532 *NewGrD 80*
Vermont Primus d1532 *NewGrD 80*
Vermorel, Claude 1909- *DcFM*
Vermoyal, Paul d1925 *Film 2, WhScrn 77*
Vernart, Esteban *NewGrD 80*
Verne, Adela 1877-1952 *Baker 78*
Verne, Alice Bredt 1868-1958 *Baker 78*
Verne, Jules 1828-1905 *DcPup, FilmgC, HalFC 80, WhoHrs 80*
Verne, Kaaren 1918-1967 *ForYSC, WhoHol B*
Verne, Karen 1915?-1967 *FilmgC, HalFC 80, WhScrn 74*
Verne, Karen 1918-1967 *WhScrn 77*
Verne, Larry 1936- *RkOn*
Verne, M *Film 2*
Verne, Mathilde 1865-1936 *Baker 78*
Verne, Robert *AmSCAP 80*
Vernengo, Marisa Serrano *PupTheA*
Verneuil *OxThe*
Verneuil, Henri 1920- *FilmEn, FilmgC, HalFC 80, WorEFlm*
Verneuil, Louis 1893-1952 *CnMD, EncWT, McGEWD[port], ModWD, NotNAT B, WhThe*
Verneuil, Raoul De 1899- *Baker 78*
Verney, Guy d1970 *WhScrn 74, -77, WhoHol B*
Verney, Myra *IntWWM 77, -80, WhoMus 72*
Vernici, Ottavio *NewGrD 80*
Vernier, Jean Aime 1769-1838? *NewGrD 80*
Vernillat, France 1912- *NewGrD 80*
Vernizzi, Ottavio 1569-1649 *NewGrD 80*
Verno, Jerry 1895-1975 *FilmgC, HalFC 80, IlWWBF, WhThe, WhoHol A, WhoThe 72*
Vernoff, Robert Arnold 1944- *AmSCAP 80*
Vernon, Agnes *Film 1, -2*
Vernon, Anne 1925- *FilmEn, FilmgC, HalFC 80, IntMPA 77, -75, -76, -78, -79, -80, WhoHol A, WorEFlm*
Vernon, Barbara 1918- *DancEn 78*
Vernon, Bobby 1895-1939 *Film 1, -2, TwYS*
Vernon, Bobby 1896-1939 *HalFC 80*
Vernon, Bobby 1897-1939 *FilmEn, WhScrn 74, -77, WhoHol B*
Vernon, Dai *MagIlD[port]*
Vernon, Dorothy 1875-1970 *Film 2, WhScrn 77*
Vernon, Frank 1875-1940 *NotNAT B, WhThe*
Vernon, Glen 1923- *WhoHol A*
Vernon, Harriett d1923 *NotNAT B, WhThe*
Vernon, Harry M 1878- *WhThe*
Vernon, Howard *WhoHol A*
Vernon, Ida 1843-1923 *NotNAT B, WhoStg 1906, -1908*
Vernon, Jackie *WhoHol A*
Vernon, John 1932- *FilmEn*
Vernon, John 1935- *FilmgC, HalFC 80, WhoHol A*
Vernon, Joseph 1739?-1782 *NewGrD 80*
Vernon, Kate Olga d1939 *NotNAT B*
Vernon, Knight 1934- *ConAmC*
Vernon, Konstanze 1939- *CnOxB*
Vernon, Lou 1888-1971 *WhScrn 77*
Vernon, Richard *WhoHol A*
Vernon, Richard 1907?- *FilmgC*
Vernon, Richard 1925- *HalFC 80, WhoThe 72, -77*
Vernon, Virginia 1894- *WhThe*
Vernon, Vivian *Film 2*
Vernon, Wally 1904-1970 *FilmgC, ForYSC, HalFC 80, Vers B[port], WhScrn 74, -77, WhoHol B*
Vernon, William 1912-1971 *WhScrn 77*
Vernor, F Dudleigh 1892-1974 *AmSCAP 66, -80, BiDAmM*
Verocai, Giovanni 1700?-1745 *NewGrD 80*
Veron, Louis-Desire 1798-1867 *DancEn 78*
Verona, Michael Ross *WhoHol A*
Verona, Stephen *MorBAP*
Veronensis, Peregrinus Cesena *NewGrD 80*
Verovio, Simone *NewGrD 80*
VerPlanck, John Fenno 1930- *AmSCAP 66, -80*
Verrall, John 1908- *Baker 78, BiDAmM, CpmDNM 78, ConAmC, DcCM, NewGrD 80*
Verreau, Richard 1926- *CreCan 2*
Verrecore, Mathias Hermann *NewGrD 80*
Verrecore, Matthias Hermann *NewGrD 80*
Verrees, Emiel Constant 1892- *WhoMus 72*
Verret, Irving 1906?- *NewOrJ[port]*
Verrett, Harrison 1907-1965 *NewOrJ*
Verrett, Shirley *CmOp[port]*
Verrett, Shirley 1931- *BnBkM 80, DrBlPA, IntWWM 77, -80, MusSN[port], NewGrD 80, WhoOp 76*
Verrett, Shirley 1933- *BiDAmM, NewEOp 71*
Verrijt, Jan Baptist 1610?-1650 *NewGrD 80*
Verrit, Jan Baptist 1610?-1650 *NewGrD 80*
Verrith, Jan Baptist 1610?-1650 *NewGrD 80*
Verryt, Jan Baptist 1610?-1650 *NewGrD 80*
Versatile Sextet *BiDAmM*
Verscharen, Joseph W 1940- *AmSCAP 80*
Verschraegen, Herman Elie Bertha 1936- *IntWWM 77, -80*
Verseghy, Ferenc 1757-1822 *NewGrD 80, OxMus*
Verso, Antonio Il *NewGrD 80*
Verso, Edward 1941- *CnOxB*
Versois, Odile 1930-1980 *FilmEn, FilmgC, HalFC 80, IntMPA 77, -75, -76, -78, -79, -80, WhoHol A*
Verst, Ruth 1930- *AmSCAP 66, -80*
Verstegen, Aart 1920- *CnOxB, DancEn 78*
Verstovsky, Alexei 1799-1862 *Baker 78*
Verstovsky, Alexey Nikolayevich 1799-1862 *NewGrD 80*
Verstovsky, Alexis 1799-1862 *OxMus*
Versus, Antonio Il *NewGrD 80*
Vert, Jacques De *OxMus*
Vertes, Marcel 1895-1961 *DancEn 78, NotNAT B*
Vertov, Dziga 1896-1954 *BiDFilm, -81, DcFM, FilmEn, FilmgC, HalFC 80, OxFilm, WomWMM, WorEFlm*
Vertue, Beryl *NewYTET*
Verulus *NewGrD 80*
Verushka *WhoHol A*
VerValin *PupTheA*
Vervenne, Frans 1945- *CnOxB*
Verwayen, Percy *BlksB&W C*
Very, Jones 1813-1880 *BiDAmM*
Very, Washington 1815-1853 *BiDAmM*
Vesaas, Tarjei 1897-1970 *REnWD[port]*
Vesak, Norbert 1936- *CnOxB*
Vesala, Edward 1945- *EncJzS 70*
Vesco, Eleonore *DancEn 78*
Vescovo, Bruno 1949- *CnOxB*
Vesela, Alena 1923- *NewGrD 80*
Vesela, Marie 1935- *WhoOp 76*
Veselka, Josef 1910- *NewGrD 80*
Vesely, Jan Pavel *NewGrD 80*
Vesely, Jindrich 1885-1939 *DcPup*
Vesely, Raimund Friedrich *NewGrD 80*
Vesi, Simone 1610?-1667? *NewGrD 80*
Vesmas, Tamas 1944- *IntWWM 80*
VeSota, Bruno 1922-1976 *WhScrn 77, WhoHrs 80[port]*
Vespa, Girolamo 1540?-1596? *NewGrD 80*
Vespermann, Kurt 1887-1957 *Film 2, WhScrn 74, -77*
Vesque VonPuttlingen, Johann 1803-1883 *Baker 78, NewGrD 80*
Vessel, Anne Marie 1949- *CnOxB*
Vest, James M 1941- *AmSCAP 80*
Vest, Phyllis Parker 1916- *IntWWM 77*
Vestal, Don *PupTheA*
Vester, Frans 1922- *IntWWM 80*
Vestergaard-Pedersen, Christian 1913- *IntWWM 77, -80*
Vestfali, Felicja 1824-1880 *NewGrD 80*
Vestoff, Floria 1918-1963 *AmSCAP 66, -80, NotNAT B*
Vestoff, Virginia *WhoHol A*
Vestri *NewGrD 80*
Vestri, Gaetano Apollo Baldassare 1825-1862 *DancEn 78*
Vestris *NewGrD 80*
Vestris, Madame 1797-1856 *EncWT, Ent, NotNAT A, OxMus, PlP&P[port]*
Vestris, Angiolo Maria Gasparo 1730-1809 *CnOxB, NewGrD 80, OxMus*
Vestris, Armand 1786-1825 *CnOxB*
Vestris, Armand 1787-1825 *DancEn 78*
Vestris, Armand 1788-1825 *OxMus*
Vestris, Auguste 1760-1842 *CnOxB, DancEn 78, NewGrD 80, OxMus*
Vestris, Auguste-Armand *DancEn 78*
Vestris, Auguste-Armand 1788-1825 *NewGrD 80*
Vestris, Bartolozzi, Madame 1797-1856 *NotNAT B*
Vestris, Charles 1797- *DancEn 78, NewGrD 80*
Vestris, Eliza Lucy 1797-1856 *FamA&A[port], NewGrD 80*
Vestris, Francoise Gourgaud 1743-1804 *OxThe*
Vestris, Francoise-Rose 1743-1804 *EncWT, Ent*
Vestris, Gaetan Apolline Balthasar 1729-1808 *DancEn 78, NewGrD 80*
Vestris, Gaetano 1729-1808 *NewGrD 80, OxMus*
Vestris, Gaetano Apolline Baldassare 1728-1808 *CnOxB*
Vestris, Giovanni Battista 1725-1801 *NewGrD 80*
Vestris, Jean-Baptiste 1725-1801 *NewGrD 80*
Vestris, Lucia Elizabeth 1787-1856 *CmOp, NewEOp 71*
Vestris, Lucia Elizabeth 1797-1856 *NewGrD 80*
Vestris, Lucia Elizabetta 1797-1856 *OxThe*

Vestris, Maria Teresa Francesca 1726-1808 NewGrD 80
Vestris, Marie Francoise Therese 1726-1808 NewGrD 80
Vestris, Marie-Jean-Augustin 1760-1842 NewGrD 80
Vestris, Teresa 1726-1808 CnOxB
Vestris, Teresina 1726-1808 OxMus
Vestris, Therese 1726-1808 DancEn 78
Vestris, Violante 1732?-1791 NewGrD 80, OxMus
Vestris, Violantina 1732?-1791 NewGrD 80
Vetcheslova, Tatiana Mikhailovna 1910- CnOxB
Vetri, Victoria 1944- FilmgC, HalFC 80, WhoHrs 80
Vetter, Conrad 1546-1622 NewGrD 80
Vetter, Daniel 1657?-1721 NewGrD 80
Vetter, Michael 1943- DcCM, NewGrD 80
Vetter, Nicolaus 1666-1734 NewGrD 80
Vetter, Richard 1928- IntMPA 77, -75, -76, -78, -79, -80
Vetter, Walther 1891-1967 Baker 78, NewGrD 80
Vetterl, Karel 1898-1979 NewGrD 80
Vetulus DeAnagnia, Johannes NewGrD 80
Veyron-Lacroix, Robert 1922- IntWWM 77, -80, NewGrD 80, WhoMus 72
Veysberg, Yuliya Lazarevna 1880-1942 NewGrD 80
Veyvoda, Gerald Joseph 1948- ConAmC
Vezin, Arthur 1878- WhThe
Vezin, Hermann 1829-1910 NotNAT B, OxThe
Vezin, Mrs. Hermann d1902 NotNAT B
Vezin, Jane Elizabeth Thomson 1827-1902 OxThe
Vezina, Joseph 1849-1924 NewGrD 80
Viadana, Berardo NewGrD 80
Viadana, Giacomo Moro Da NewGrD 80
Viadana, Jacobi Mori Da NewGrD 80
Viadana, Lodovico Da 1560-1627 Baker 78, NewGrD 80[port]
Viaera, Fredericus NewGrD 80
Viafore, S Victor 1910-1970 AmSCAP 80
Viala, Claude 1922- IntWWM 77, -80
Vian, Boris 1920-1959 CnMD SUP, CnThe, CroCD, EncWT, Ent, McGEWD, ModWD, REnWD[port]
Viana, Frutuoso 1896-1976 NewGrD 80
Viana DaMota, Jose 1868-1948 NewGrD 80
Vianesi, Auguste-Charles-L-Francis 1837-1908 NewGrD 80
Vianesi, Auguste-Charles-L-Francois 1837-1908 Baker 78, BiDAmM
Vianna, Fructuoso 1896- Baker 78
Vianna DaMotta, Jose 1868-1948 Baker 78, NewGrD 80
Viardot, Pauline 1821-1910 BnBkM 80, NewGrD 80[port], NotNAT B
Viardot-Garcia, Pauline 1821-1910 Baker 78, CmOp[port], NewEOp 71
Vibart, Henry 1863-1939 Film 2, WhThe
Vibert, Marcel Film 2
Vibert, Mathieu 1920- IntWWM 77, -80
Vibert, Nicolas 1710?-1772 NewGrD 80
Vibrations, The RkOn[port]
Viby, Marguerite WomWMM
Vic And Sade What 5[port]
Vicar, Anthony Arnold 1914- AmSCAP 66, -80
Vicar, Del AmSCAP 80
Vicari, Josephine M 1930- AmSCAP 80
Vicars, Harold d1922 AmSCAP 66, -80, BiDAmM
Vicary, Margaret Eva 1927- WhoMus 72
Vicas, Victor 1918- FilmEn, FilmgC, HalFC 80
Viccajee, Victor Framjee 1903- IntWWM 77, -80
Viccola, Giovanni Film 2
Vicenot, Joh NewGrD 80
Vicente, Gil 1465?-1536? CnThe, EncWT, Ent, NewGrD 80, REnWD[port]
Vicente, Gil 1465?-1537? OxThe
Vicente, Gil 1470?-1536? McGEWD
Vicentino, Michele NewGrD 80
Vicentino, Nicola 1511-1572 Baker 78, OxMus
Vicentino, Nicola 1511-1576? NewGrD 80[port]
Vick, Danny AmSCAP 80
Vick, Harold Edward 1936- EncJzS 70
Vickers, J WhoMus 72
Vickers, James Edward 1942- AmSCAP 80
Vickers, Jon 1926- Baker 78, BnBkM 80, CmOp[port], CreCan 1, IntWWM 77, -80, MusSN[port], NewEOp 71, NewGrD 80[port], WhoOp 76
Vickers, Jon 1929- WhoMus 72
Vickers, Martha 1925-1971 FilmEn, FilmgC, ForYSC, HalFC 80, HolP 40[port], WhScrn 74, -77, WhoHol B
Vickers, Wendy 1938?- AmSCAP 80
Vickers, Yvette WhoHol A
Vickers, Yvette 1938?- WhoHrs 80[port]
Vickerstaff, Lorna Doreen 1927- WhoMus 72
Vico, Diana NewGrD 80
Victor, Benjamin d1778 NotNAT B
Victor, Charles 1896-1965 FilmgC, HalFC 80, WhScrn 74, -77, WhThe, WhoHol B
Victor, David NewYTET
Victor, Edward 1885-1964 MagIlD
Victor, Harvey L IntMPA 77, -75, -76, -78, -79, -80
Victor, Henry 1898-1945 FilmEn, Film 1, -2, FilmgC, HalFC 80, IlWWBF[port], WhScrn 74, -77, WhoHol B, WhoHrs 80
Victor, James WhoHol A
Victor, Josephine 1885- WhThe, WhoStg 1908
Victor, Katherine 1928- WhoHrs 80[port]
Victor, Lionel d1940 NotNAT B
Victor, Lucia BiE&WWA, NotNAT
Victor, Mary Anne d1907 NotNAT B
Victoria, Queen OxMus
Victoria, Tomas Luis De 1548-1611 BnBkM 80, CmpBCM, GrComp, MusMk[port], NewGrD 80
Victoria, Tomas Luis De 1549-1611 Baker 78, OxMus
Victoria, Vesta 1873-1951 AmPS B, NotNAT B, WhThe, WhoStg 1906, -1908
Victorica, Victoria Garcia 1922- DancEn 78
Victorinus, Georg d1631? NewGrD 80
Victorius, Lauretus NewGrD 80
Victory, Gerard 1921- Baker 78, IntWWM 77, -80, NewGrD 80, WhoMus 72
Victory, Jim NewYTET
Victrix, Claudia Film 2
Vida, Frank J 1894- AmSCAP 66
Vidacovich, I J 1904-1966 AmSCAP 66, -80
Vidacovich, Irvine d1966 WhoHol B
Vidacovich, Irvine 1905-1966 NewOrJ[port]
Vidacovich, Irving J 1905-1966 WhScrn 74, -77
Vidacovich, Pinky 1904-1966 WhoJazz 72
Vidakovic, Albe 1914-1964 NewGrD 80
Vidal, Augustus Olatunji 1942- IntWWM 77, -80
Vidal, Gore 1925- BiE&WWA, CnMD, ConDr 73, -77, CroCD, EncWT, FilmEn, McGEWD, ModWD, NotNAT, -A, WhoThe 72, -77, WorEFlm
Vidal, Henri 1919-1959 FilmEn, FilmgC, ForYSC, HalFC 80, MotPP, NotNAT B, WhScrn 74, -77, WhoHol B
Vidal, Louis-Antoine 1820-1891 Baker 78, NewGrD 80
Vidal, Paul Antonin 1863-1931 Baker 78, NewGrD 80, OxMus
Vidal, Peire NewGrD 80
Vidame De Chartres 1145?-1204 NewGrD 80
Vidar, Jorunn 1918- NewGrD 80
Vidas, Patrick Joseph 1953- AmSCAP 80
Vide, Jacobus NewGrD 80
Viderkehr, Jacques NewGrD 80
Videro, Finn 1906- NewGrD 80
Vidor, Catherine Film 2
Vidor, Charles 1900-1959 BiDFilm, -81, DcFM, FilmEn, FilmgC, HalFC 80, MovMk[port], OxFilm, WomWMM, WorEFlm
Vidor, Florence 1895-1977 FilmEn, Film 1, -2, FilmgC, HalFC 80, MotPP, MovMk[port], TwYS, WhoHol A
Vidor, King Film 1
Vidor, King 1894- AmFD, DcFM, FilmEn, Film 2, FilmgC, HalFC 80, MovMk[port], TwYS A, What 3[port]
Vidor, King 1895- IntMPA 77, -75, -76, -78, -79, -80, WorEFlm
Vidor, King 1896- BiDFilm, -81, CmMov, OxFilm
Vidovszky, Laszlo 1944- IntWWM 77, -80
Vidu, Ion 1863-1931 Baker 78, NewGrD 80
Viduus, Robert NewGrD 80
Vie, Florence d1939 NotNAT B
Viehman, Theodore 1889- BiE&WWA
Vieira, Ernesto 1848-1915 Baker 78, NewGrD 80
Viel, Marguerite WomWMM
Vielart De Corbie NewGrD 80
Vienne, Marie-Louise De 1905- WhoMus 72
Vierdanck, Hans 1605?-1646 NewGrD 80
Vierdanck, Johann 1605-1646? Baker 78
Vierdanck, Johann 1605?-1646 NewGrD 80
Vierdanck, Johannes 1605?-1646 NewGrD 80
Vierling, Georg 1820-1901 Baker 78
Vierling, Jacob 1796-1867 Baker 78
Vierling, Johann Gottfried 1750-1813 Baker 78, NewGrD 80
Vierne, Louis 1870-1937 Baker 78, BnBkM 80, MusMk, NewGrD 80, OxMus
Vierne, Rene 1878-1918 OxMus
Vierny, Sacha 1919- DcFM, FilmEn, FilmgC, HalFC 80, OxFilm, WorEFlm
Vierra, M L ConAmC
Viertel, Berthold 1885-1953 FilmEn, FilmgC, HalFC 80
Viertel, Berthold 1885-1954 OxThe
Viertel, Berthold 1885-1955 EncWT
Viertel, Karl-Heinz Rudolph 1929- IntWWM 77, -80
Vieru, Anatol 1926- Baker 78, DcCM, IntWWM 80, NewGrD 80
Vietheer, Erich Walter 1930- IntWWM 80
Vietheer, George C 1910- IntMPA 77, -75, -76, -78, -79, -80
Vietinghoff-Scheel, Baron Boris 1829-1901 Baker 78
Vieuille, Felix 1872-1953 Baker 78
Vieulle, Felix 1872-1953 CmOp
Vieuxtemps NewGrD 80
Vieuxtemps, Ernest 1832-1896 NewGrD 80
Vieuxtemps, Henri 1820-1881 Baker 78, BnBkM 80, CmpBCM, GrComp[port], MusMk, OxMus
Vieuxtemps, Henry 1820-1881 NewGrD 80[port]
Vieuxtemps, Lucien 1828-1901 NewGrD 80
Vieville, Jean Laurent LeCerf DeLa NewGrD 80
Vieyra, Paulin 1923- DcFM
Vig, Roger 1972- IntWWM 77
Vig, Rudolf 1929- IntWWM 77, -80
Vig, Tommy 1938- AmSCAP 80, EncJzS 70, IntWWM 77
Vigano, Giulio 1739-1811 CnOxB
Vigano, Onorato 1739-1811 NewGrD 80
Vigano, Salvatore 1769-1821 Baker 78, CnOxB, DancEn 78[port], NewGrD 80
Vigarani, Carlo OxThe
Vigarani, Carlo 1622-1713 DancEn 78
Vigarani, Carlo 1623?-1713? NewGrD 80
Vigarani, Gaspare 1586-1663 NewGrD 80, NotNAT B, OxThe
Vigay, Denis 1926- IntWWM 77, -80, WhoMus 72
Vigay, Edgar WhoMus 72
Vigeland, Hans ConAmC
Viglione-Borghese, Domenico 1877-1957 NewGrD 80
Vignali, Francesco NewGrD 80
Vignanelli, Ferruccio 1903- WhoMus 72
Vignati, Giuseppe d1768 NewGrD 80
Vigne, Antoine De NewGrD 80
Vigne, John 1865?- NewOrJ
Vigne, John 1885?- NewOrJ
Vigne, Sidney 1903?-1925 NewOrJ
Vigneault, Gilles 1928- CreCan 2, NewGrD 80
Vignola, Giuseppe 1662-1712 NewGrD 80
Vignola, Robert 1882-1953 WhoHol B
Vignola, Robert C 1882-1953 Film 1
Vignola, Robert G 1882-1953 FilmEn, NotNAT B, TwYS A, WhScrn 74, -77
Vignoles, Roger Hutton 1945- IntWWM 77, -80
Vignon, Hierosme NewGrD 80
Vignon, Jean-Paul WhoHol A
Vignon, Jerome NewGrD 80
Vigny, Alfred De 1797-1863 CnThe, Ent, McGEWD[port], NotNAT B, REnWD[port]

Vigny, Alfred De 1799-1863 NewEOp 71
Vigny, Alfred-Victor, Comte De 1797-1863 EncWT
Vigo, Jean 1905-1934 BiDFilm, -81, DcFM, FilmEn, FilmgC, HalFC 80, MovMk[port], OxFilm, WorEFlm
Vigoda, Abe WhoHol A
Vigoda, Johannan ConMuA 80B
Vigone NewGrD 80
Vigoni NewGrD 80
Vigoni, Carlo Federico 1658-1693? NewGrD 80
Vigoni, Francesco 1624?-1699 NewGrD 80
Vigoni, Giuseppe NewGrD 80
Vigorito, Gabe ConMuA 80B
Vigran, Herb 1910- Vers A[port], WhoHol A
Vigri, Girolamo Di NewGrD 80
Viguerie, Bernard 1761?-1819 NewGrD 80
Viharo, Robert WhoHol A
Vihtol, Joseph 1863-1948 OxMus
Viitanen, Usko Samuel 1928- WhoOp 76
Vikar, Laszlo 1929- IntWWM 77, -80, NewGrD 80
Viking, Vonceil d1929 WhScrn 74, -77
Vikulov, Serge Vasilievich 1937- CnOxB
Vila, Pedro Alberto 1517-1582 Baker 78, NewGrD 80
Vila, Sabra DeShon 1850-1917 WhScrn 77
Vilano, Gabriele NewGrD 80
Vilanova, Ramon 1801-1870 NewGrD 80
Vilar, Francisco d1770 NewGrD 80
Vilar, Jean d1971 WhoHol B
Vilar, Jean 1912-1970 EncWT
Vilar, Jean 1912-1971 BiE&WWA, CnThe, Ent, FilmEn, NotNAT B, OxThe, WhThe
Vilar, Jean 1913-1971 WhScrn 74, -77
Vilar, Jose Teodor 1836-1905 NewGrD 80
Vilas, William H IntMPA 77, -75, -76, -78, -79, -80
Vilback, Renaud De 1829-1884 Baker 78, NewGrD 80
Vilbert, Henri WhoHol A
Vilboa, Konstantin 1817-1882 Baker 78
Vilches, Ernesto d1954 WhScrn 74, -77
Vildrac, Charles Messager 1882-1971 CnMD, McGEWD[port], ModWD, REnWD[port]
Vilec, Michal 1902- IntWWM 77, -80, NewGrD 80
Vilers, Antoine De NewGrD 80
Vilhar, Franz 1852-1928 Baker 78
Vilko, Ukmar 1905- IntWWM 77
Villa, Antoine De NewGrD 80
Villa, Joseph ConAmC
Villa, Manuel 1917- AmSCAP 66, -80
Villa, Ricardo 1873-1935 Baker 78
Villa-Lobos, Heitor 1887-1959 Baker 78, BnBkM 80, CompSN[port], DcCom 77[port], DcCom&M 79, DcCM, MusMk[port], NewGrD 80[port], OxMus
Villa-Lobos, Heitor 1890-1959 DancEn 78
Villaespesa, Francisco 1877-1936 McGEWD[port]
Villafane, Javier PupTheA
Villafranca, Luis De NewGrD 80
Village People ConMuA 80A[port]
Village Stompers, The BiDAmM, RkOn[port]
Villagrossi, Ferruccio Ferdinando 1937- WhoOp 76
Villalar, Andres De 1530?-1593? NewGrD 80
Villalba Munoz, Luis 1872-1921 NewGrD 80
Villalba Munoz, Luis 1873-1921 Baker 78
Villalpando, Alberto 1940- DcCM, NewGrD 80
Villani, Filippo 1325-1405 NewGrD 80
Villani, Gabriele NewGrD 80
Villani, Gabrielle NewGrD 80
Villani, Gabriello NewGrD 80
Villani, Gasparo 1550?-1619? NewGrD 80
Villanis, Luigi Alberto 1863-1906 Baker 78, NewGrD 80
Villano, Gasparo 1550?-1619? NewGrD 80
Villanueva, Martin De d1605 NewGrD 80
Villar, Carlos Villarias WhoHrs 80
Villar, Rogelio Del 1875-1937 Baker 78, NewGrD 80
Villard, Frank 1917- FilmEn, FilmgC, HalFC 80, WhoHol A
Villard, Juliette 1945-1971 WhScrn 77
Villareal, Edmund 1947- AmSCAP 80
Villaret, Joao 1913-1961 FilmAG WE[port]
Villaret, Joao 1914-1961 WhScrn 74, -77
Villarosa, Marquis Of NewGrD 80
Villarreal, Julio 1885-1958 WhScrn 74, -77, WhoHol B
Villate, Gaspar 1851-1891 NewGrD 80
Villaume, Jack Waldemar 1907- IntWWM 77, -80
Villaurutia, Xavier OxThe
Villechaize, Herve 1943- HalFC 80, WhoHol A, WhoHrs 80
Villella, Edward 1936- DancEn 78[port]
Villella, Edward 1937- CnOxB, WhoHol A
Villeneuve, Alexandre De 1677-1756? NewGrD 80
Villeneuve, Josse De NewGrD 80
Villers, Antoine De NewGrD 80
Villesavoye, Paul 1683-1760 NewGrD 80
Villetard, Edmond d1890 NotNAT B
Villetard, Henri 1869-1955 NewGrD 80
Villiers, Claude Deschamps De 1600-1681 OxThe
Villiers, Edwin d1904 NotNAT B
Villiers, George, Duke Of Buckingham 1628-1687 Ent[port], McGEWD, NotNAT B, OxThe
Villiers, James WhoHol A
Villiers, James 1930?- FilmgC, HalFC 80
Villiers, James 1933- WhoThe 72, -77
Villiers, Jean DeVilliers 1648-1701 OxThe
Villiers, Marguerite Beguet d1670 OxThe
Villiers, P De NewGrD 80
Villiers DeL'Isle-Adam, Jean Marie 1838-1889 REnWD[port]
Villifranchi, Giovanni Cosimo 1646-1699 NewGrD 80
Villines, Virginia 1912- AmSCAP 80
Villines, Virginia 1917- AmSCAP 66
Villis, Marjorie IlWWBF
Villoing, Alexander 1804-1878 Baker 78
Villoing, Vassily 1850-1922 Baker 78
Villon, Francois 1431-1463? NewEOp 71
Villone, Larry Paul 1948- AmSCAP 80
Villot, Jean NewGrD 80
Villoteau, Guillaume-Andre 1759-1839 Baker 78, NewGrD 80
Villoud, Hector Iglesias NewGrD 80
Vilma, Michele WhoOp 76
Vilzak, Anatole Josifovich 1898- CnOxB, DancEn 78
Vimmerstedt, Sarah Germaine 1904- AmSCAP 80
Vina, Facundo DeLa 1876-1952 Baker 78
Vina, Victo Film 2
Vinaccesi, Benedetto 1670?-1719? NewGrD 80
Vinacese, Benedetto 1670?-1719? NewGrD 80
Vinacesi, Benedetto 1670?-1719? NewGrD 80
Vinaldi PupTheA
Vinard, F N AmSCAP 80
Vinay, Ramon 1912- NewEOp 71, NewGrD 80
Vinay, Ramon 1914- CmOp
Vinayak, Master d1947 WhScrn 77
Vincenci, Giacomo NewGrD 80
Vincencio Da Imola NewGrD 80
Vincenet, Johannes NewGrD 80
Vincenot, Louis 1884-1967 WhScrn 77, WhoHol B
Vincent d1650? NewGrD 80
Vincent DeBeauvais 1190?-1264 NewGrD 80
Vincent, Alexandre-Joseph Hydulphe 1797-1868 Baker 78
Vincent, Allen Film 2
Vincent, Billy 1896-1966 WhScrn 77
Vincent, Bob 1918- AmSCAP 66, -80
Vincent, Caspar NewGrD 80
Vincent, Charles John 1852-1934 Baker 78
Vincent, Charles T d1935 NotNAT B
Vincent, Clarence 1899-1960 NewOrJ
Vincent, Evelyn Dorothea 1894- WhoMus 72
Vincent, Francis T, Jr. IntMPA 79, -80
Vincent, Gene 1935-1971 BiDAmM, ConMuA 80A, IlEncR, RkOn, WhScrn 74, -77, WhoHol B
Vincent, Gene And The Blue Caps 1935-1971 RkOn[port]
Vincent, Heinrich Joseph 1819-1901 Baker 78, OxMus
Vincent, Henry Bethuel 1872-1941 Baker 78, ConAmC
Vincent, J J 1894- WhoMus 72
Vincent, James d1957 NotNAT B, WhoHol B
Vincent, Jan-Michael 1944- FilmEn, HalFC 80, IntMPA 77, -75, -76, -78, -79, -80, WhoHol A
Vincent, Jo 1898- NewGrD 80
Vincent, John 1902- AmSCAP 66, ConAmC, DcCM
Vincent, John 1902-1977 AmSCAP 80, Baker 78, NewGrD 80
Vincent, June 1919- ForYSC, HalFC 80, IntMPA 77, -75, -76, -78, -79, -80, WhoHol A
Vincent, Katharine 1919- IntMPA 77, -75, -76, -78, -79, -80
Vincent, Larry WhoHol A
Vincent, Larry 1901-1977 AmSCAP 66, -80
Vincent, Larry 1925-1975 WhScrn 77
Vincent, Lina 1923- IntWWM 77, -80
Vincent, Madge 1884- WhThe
Vincent, Mary Ann 1818-1887 NotNAT A, -B, OxThe
Vincent, Mildred Film 2
Vincent, Monroe 1919- BluesWW[port]
Vincent, Nathaniel Hawthorne 1889-1979 AmSCAP 66, -80, BiDAmM
Vincent, Robbie d1968 WhoHol B
Vincent, Robert William 1941- IntWWM 77, -80, WhoMus 72
Vincent, Romo WhoHol A
Vincent, Ruth 1877-1955 NotNAT B, WhThe, WhoStg 1908
Vincent, Sailor Billy 1896-1966 WhScrn 77
Vincent, Thomas 1720?-1783 NewGrD 80, OxMus
Vincent, Vernon Lee 1946- IntWWM 77
Vincent, Virginia WhoHol A
Vincent, Walter BluesWW
Vincent, Walter 1868-1959 NotNAT B
Vincent, Warren Edward 1925- AmSCAP 66, -80
Vincent, Yves WhoHol A
Vincenti, Alessandro NewGrD 80
Vincenti, Giacomo d1619 NewGrD 80
Vincentius Bellovacensis NewGrD 80
Vincentius, Caspar 1580?-1624 NewGrD 80
Vincenz, Lilli WomWMM B
Vincenzi, Edo 1921- WhoOp 76
Vincenzi, Giacomo NewGrD 80
Vincenzo Da Rimini NewGrD 80[port]
Vincenzo Di Pasquino NewGrD 80
Vinci, Leonardo 1690-1730 Baker 78, BnBkM 80, MusMk, NewGrD 80[port], OxMus
Vinci, Leonardo Da NewGrD 80
Vinci, Pietro 1535?-1584? NewGrD 80
Vinci, Pietro 1540-1584 Baker 78
Vinco, Ivo 1927- WhoOp 76
Vincson, Walter BluesWW
Vincze, Imre 1926-1969 Baker 78, NewGrD 80
Vincze, Otto 1906- IntWWM 77, -80
Vinders, Jheronimus NewGrD 80
Vine, Billy 1915-1958 WhScrn 74, -77, WhoHol B
Vinea, Antoine De NewGrD 80
Viner, Edward Film 1
Viner, William d1716 NewGrD 80
Viner, William Letton 1790-1867 BiDAmM
Vines, Margaret 1910- WhThe
Vines, Ricardo 1875-1943 Baker 78, NewGrD 80, OxMus
Vinholes, L C 1933- IntWWM 77, -80
Vinier, Guillaume Li NewGrD 80
Vinier, Guille Li NewGrD 80
Vining, Fanny d1891 NotNAT B
Vining, Frederick d1871 NotNAT B
Vining, George J d1875 NotNAT B
Viniziana NewGrD 80
Vinnegar, Leroy 1928- EncJzS 70
Vinogradov, Oleg Mikhailovich 1937- CnOxB
Vinogradsky, Alexander 1855-1912 Baker 78
Vinquist, Mary 1938- IntWWM 77, -80
Vinson, Cleanhead 1917- EncJzS 70
Vinson, Eddie 1885?- NewOrJ
Vinson, Eddie 1917- BluesWW[port], CmpEPM, EncJzS 70, IlEncJ
Vinson, Gary WhoHol A
Vinson, Harvey Lee 1943- IntWWM 77, -80
Vinson, Helen 1907- FilmEn, FilmgC, ForYSC, HalFC 80, HolCA[port],

MovMk, ThFT[port], WhThe, WhoHol A
Vinson, Walter Jacobs 1901-1975 *BluesWW[port]*
Vint, Alan *WhoHol A*
Vint, Bill *WhoHol A*
Vint, Jesse *WhoHol A*
Vinter, Gilbert 1909- *WhoMus 72*
Vintila, George 1924- *IntWWM 77, -80*
Vinton, Arthur Rolfe d1963 *ForYSC, NotNAT B, WhScrn 74, -77, WhoHol B*
Vinton, Bobby *AmPS A, -B*
Vinton, Bobby 1935- *AmSCAP 66, BiDAmM, WhoHol A*
Vinton, Bobby 1941- *RkOn[port]*
Vinton, John 1937- *IntWWM 77, -80, NewGrD 80*
Vinzing, Ute *WhoOp 76*
Viola, Al 1919- *EncJzS 70*
Viola, Alessandro Della *NewGrD 80*
Viola, Alexander Della *NewGrD 80*
Viola, Alfonso Alfred 1919- *EncJzS 70*
Viola, Alfonso Della 1508-1570 *Baker 78*
Viola, Dalla *NewGrD 80*
Viola, Della *NewGrD 80*
Viola, Elizabeth 1952- *IntWWM 77, -80*
Viola, Francesco *Baker 78, NewGrD 80*
Viola, Giovanni Domenico 1540?-1601? *NewGrD 80*
Viola, Orazio Della *NewGrD 80*
Viola, P Anselm 1738-1798 *Baker 78*
Viola, W N *PupTheA*
Violante, Madame *PlP&P*
Viole, Rudolf 1825-1867 *Baker 78, NewGrD 80*
Violette, Eva Maria 1724-1822 *CnOxB*
Violino, Il *NewGrD 80*
Violino, Carlo Del *NewGrD 80*
Violinsky, Solly Sol Ginsberg d1963 *NotNAT B*
Viollier, Renee Marguerite 1894- *IntWWM 77, -80, NewGrD 80*
Violoncello, Giovannino Del *NewGrD 80*
Viotta, Henri 1848-1933 *Baker 78, NewGrD 80*
Viotta, Johannes Josephus 1814-1859 *Baker 78, NewGrD 80*
Viotti, Gino *Film 2*
Viotti, Giovanni Battista 1755-1824 *Baker 78, BnBkM 80, CmpBCM, GrComp[port], MusMk, NewGrD 80[port], OxMus*
Viozzi, Giulio 1912- *IntWWM 77, -80, NewGrD 80*
Virche, Girolamo Di 1523?-1574? *NewGrD 80*
Virchi, Girolamo Di 1523?-1574? *NewGrD 80*
Virchi, Paolo 1550?-1610 *NewGrD 80*
Virchinus, Girolamo Di *NewGrD 80*
Virchis, Girolamo De *NewGrD 80*
Virdanck, Johann *NewGrD 80*
Virdung, Sebastian 1465- *Baker 78, NewGrD 80, OxMus*
Virga, Girolamo Di *NewGrD 80*
Virgelli, Emilio *NewGrD 80*
Virghi, Girolamo Di *NewGrD 80*
Virgil 070BC-019BC *NewEOp 71, NewGrD 80*
Virgil, Helen *Film 2*
Virginia, Barbara *WomWMM*
Virginia Boys *BiDAmM, EncFCWM 69*
Virginia Minstrels *BiDAmM*
Virginia Serenaders *BiDAmM*
Virgis, Girolamo Di *NewGrD 80*
Virgo, Clement H 1940- *IntWWM 77*
Virgo, Peter *WhoHol A*
Virgo, Peter, Jr. *WhoHol A*
Virizlay, Mihaly 1931- *ConAmC, IntWWM 77, -80*
Virizlay, Paula Skolnick 1945- *IntWWM 77, -80*
Virkahaus, Taavo 1934- *IntWWM 80*
Virkhaus, Taavo 1934- *ConAmC, IntWWM 77*
Virneisel, Wilhelm 1902- *NewGrD 80*
Virsowitz, Daniel *NewGrD 80*
Virta, Nikilai Yevgenievich 1906- *OxThe*
Virta, Nikolai Evgenievich 1906- *CroCD*
Virtue, Robert Francis 1930- *IntWWM 77, -80*
Virtues, The *RkOn*
Virtuoso, Frank 1923- *AmSCAP 66, -80*
Virues, Cristobal De 1550?-1614? *McGEWD*
Virues, Jose 1770-1840 *NewGrD 80*
Visakhadatta *REnWD[port]*
Visaroff, Michael d1951 *WhoHol B*
Visaroff, Michael 1890-1951 *Film 2, ForYSC, TwYS*
Visaroff, Michael 1892-1951 *WhScrn 74, -77*
Visaroff, Nina 1888-1938 *WhScrn 77*
Viscarra Monje, Humberto 1898-1971 *Baker 78*
Visconti, Domenico d1626 *NewGrD 80*
Visconti, Gasparo 1683-1713? *NewGrD 80*
Visconti, Giulio 1750-1829 *NewGrD 80*
Visconti, Luchino 1906-1976 *BiDFilm, -81, CmOp, CnThe, ConLC 16, DcFM, EncWT, Ent, FilmEn, FilmgC, HalFC 80, IntMPA 75, -76, MovMk[port], NewEOp 71, NewGrD 80, OxFilm, OxThe, WhoOp 76, WorEFlm*
Viscount, Bill Martin *CreCan 2*
Viscounts, The *RkOn*
Viscuglia, Felix Alfred 1927- *IntWWM 77, -80*
Visee, Robert De 1650?-1725? *Baker 78, NewGrD 80, OxMus*
Visetti, Albert 1846-1928 *OxMus*
Visetti, Alberto Antonio 1846-1928 *Baker 78*
Vishnegradsky, Ivan Alexandrovich 1893- *NewGrD 80*
Vishnevskaya, Galina 1926- *Baker 78, BnBkM 80, CmOp, IntWWM 77, -80, MusSN[port], NewEOp 71, NewGrD 80[port], WhoOp 76*
Vishnevski, Vsevolod Vitalevich 1901-1951 *CnMD*
Vishnevsky, Vsevolod Vitalevich 1900-1951 *CroCD, DcFM, ModWD, OxThe*
Vishnevsky, Vsevolod Vitalievich 1900-1951 *EncWT, McGEWD*
Viski, Janos 1906-1961 *Baker 78, NewGrD 80*
Vismari, Filippo 1635?-1706? *NewGrD 80*
Vismarri, Filippo 1635?-1706? *NewGrD 80*
Visotsky, Mikhail Timofeyevich 1791-1837 *NewGrD 80*
Vissenaecken, Willem Van *NewGrD 80*
Visser, Lieuwe 1940- *WhoOp 76*
Visser, Piet 1898- *WhoMus 72*
Visser, Ruth Arienne 1948- *IntWWM 80*
Visser, Schalk 1927- *IntWWM 77*
Vita, Perlo *FilmEn*
Vitale, Angelo *NewGrD 80*
Vitale, Costantino *NewGrD 80*
Vitale, Edoardo 1872-1937 *NewGrD 80*
Vitale, Joseph A 1901- *IntMPA 78, -79, -80*
Vitale, Joseph A 1905- *IntMPA 77, -75, -76*
Vitale, Mario *WhoHol A*
Vitale, Milly 1928- *HalFC 80*
Vitale, Milly 1932- *FilmEn*
Vitale, Milly 1938- *FilmgC, ForYSC, IntMPA 77, -75, -76, -78, -79, -80, WhoHol A*
Vitale, Vincent Albert 1942- *IntWWM 77, -80*
Vitale, William Nicholas *AmSCAP 80*
Vitali *NewGrD 80*
Vitali, Angelo *NewGrD 80*
Vitali, Bernardino *NewGrD 80*
Vitali, Dominique *PupTheA*
Vitali, Filippo 1580?-1653 *MusMk*
Vitali, Filippo 1590?-1653 *Baker 78, NewGrD 80, OxMus*
Vitali, Giovanni Battista 1632-1692 *Baker 78, NewGrD 80, OxMus*
Vitali, Giovanni Battista 1644?-1692 *GrComp, MusMk*
Vitali, Tomaso Antonio 1663-1745 *NewGrD 80, OxMus*
Vitalian, Pope *OxMus*
Vitaliani, Italia *Film 2*
Vitalini, Alberico 1921- *Baker 78*
Vitalis, George 1895-1959 *Baker 78*
Vitaly, Georges 1917- *EncWT*
Vitasek, Jan August 1770-1839 *NewGrD 80*
Vitasek, Johann Matthias 1770-1839 *NewGrD 80*
Vitelli, Vitellozzo *NewGrD 80*
Viterbo, Patricia 1943-1966 *WhScrn 74, -77*
Vitkova, Blanka 1948- *WhoOp 76*
Vito, Signor *PupTheA*
Vito And The Salutations *RkOn[port]*
Vitoch, Pavel 1934- *IntWWM 77*
Vitolins, Jekabs 1898- *NewGrD 80*
Vitols, Jazeps 1863-1948 *NewGrD 80*
Vitous, Miroslav Ladislav 1947- *EncJzS 70*
Vitrac, Roger 1899-1952 *CnThe, EncWT, Ent, McGEWD, ModWD, OxThe, REnWD[port]*
Vitriaco *NewGrD 80*
Vitruvius *PlP&P*
Vitruvius 084?BC-014?BC *NewGrD 80*
Vitruvius 088BC-026BC *EncWT*
Vitruvius Pollio 084?BC-014?BC *NewGrD 80*
Vitruvius Pollio, Marcus *NotNAT B, OxThe*
Vitry, Philippe De 1291-1361 *Baker 78, BnBkM 80, MusMk, NewGrD 80, OxMus*
Vittadini, Franco 1884-1948 *Baker 78, NewGrD 80*
Vitte, Ray *DrBlPA*
Vittes, Louis *WhoHrs 80*
Vitti, Monica *MotPP, WhoHol A*
Vitti, Monica 1931- *FilmAG WE[port], FilmEn, MovMk[port], OxFilm, WorEFlm*
Vitti, Monica 1933- *BiDFilm, -81, FilmgC, ForYSC, HalFC 80, WhoHrs 80*
Vittori, Loreto 1600?-1670 *NewGrD 80*
Vittoria, Tomas Luis De *NewGrD 80*
Vittoria, Tommaso Luigi Da *Baker 78*
Vittorij, Loreto 1600?-1670 *NewGrD 80*
Vittriaco *NewGrD 80*
Vitzthumb, Ignace 1720-1816 *NewGrD 80*
Vitzthumb, Ignaz 1720-1816 *NewGrD 80*
Viva *WhoHol A*
Vivaldi, Antonio 1669-1741 *CmpBCM, GrComp[port]*
Vivaldi, Antonio 1675?-1741 *CmOp, DcCom&M 79, MusMk[port], NewEOp 71*
Vivaldi, Antonio 1678-1741 *Baker 78, BnBkM 80[port], DcCom 77[port], NewGrD 80[port], OxMus*
Vivaldi, Giovanni Battista *Baker 78*
Vivanco, Sebastian De 1551?-1622 *NewGrD 80*
Vivarino, Innocentio 1575?-1626 *NewGrD 80*
Vivas, Marta *WomWMM B*
Vivell, Colestin 1846-1923 *Baker 78, NewGrD 80*
Vives, Amadeo 1871-1932 *Baker 78, NewGrD 80, OxMus*
Vivian, Anthony Crespigny Claud 1906- *WhThe*
Vivian, Lila *BluesWW*
Vivian, Percival 1890-1961 *NotNAT B, WhScrn 77, WhoHol B*
Vivian, Robert 1859-1944 *NotNAT B, WhScrn 77, WhoHol B*
Vivian, Robert 1885-1944 *Film 1, -2*
Vivian, Ruth d1949 *NotNAT B, WhScrn 77, WhoHol B*
Vivian, Violet d1960 *NotNAT B*
Vivian-Rees, Joan *WhThe*
Viviani, Antonio Maria 1630?-1687? *NewGrD 80*
Viviani, Giovanni Buonaventura 1638-1692? *NewGrD 80*
Viviani, Raffaele 1888-1950 *McGEWD[port]*
Vivienne, Hazel 1934- *IntWWM 77, -80, WhoOp 76*
Vivier, Albert-Joseph 1816-1903 *Baker 78*
Vivier, Claude 1948- *Baker 78, IntWWM 80*
Vivier, Eugene-Leon 1817-1900 *Baker 78, BnBkM 80, NewGrD 80*
Vivyan, John *WhoHol A*
Vix, Genevieve 1879-1939 *Baker 78*
Viyel'gorsky, Matvey Yur'yevich *NewGrD 80*
Viyel'gorsky, Mikhail Yur'yevich *NewGrD 80*
Vizard, Harold 1871- *WhoStg 1908*
Vizino, Sergey 1946- *IntWWM 80*
Vizza, Nancy J 1950- *IntWWM 77, -80*
Vlach, Josef 1923- *NewGrD 80*
Vlach, Joseph 1923- *IntWWM 77, -80*
Vlachopoulos, Yannis Gerry 1939- *CpmDNM 78, NewGrD 80*
Vlacilova, Hana 1956- *CnOxB*
Vlad, Roman 1919- *Baker 78, DcCM, NewGrD 80, WhoMus 72*
Vladigerof, Pantscho 1899- *OxMus*
Vladigerov, Alexander 1933- *Baker 78*
Vladigerov, Luben 1899- *Baker 78*
Vladigerov, Pancho 1899- *NewGrD 80*
Vladigerov, Pantcho 1899- *Baker 78*
Vladimiroff, Pierre 1893-1970 *CnOxB, DancEn 78*
Vladimirov, Yuri Kuzmich 1942- *CnOxB*
Vladimirova, Valeriya *NewGrD 80*
Vlady, Marina *MotPP, WhoHol A*
Vlady, Marina 1937- *BiDFilm, -81,*

FilmAG WE, MovMk, WorEFlm
Vlady, Marina 1938- *FilmEn, FilmgC, ForYSC, HalFC 80*
Vlahopoulos, Sotireos 1926- *ConAmC*
Vlajin, Milan 1912- *IntWWM 77, -80*
Vlasek, June *FilmEn, WhoHol A*
Vlasov, Vladimir Alexandrovich 1903- *Baker 78, NewGrD 80*
Vlassi, Christiane 1938- *CnOxB, DancEn 78*
Vlassova, Eleonora 1931- *CnOxB*
Vlatkovic, Angelo 1925- *IntWWM 77*
Vleck, Joseph V *IntMPA 77, -75, -76, -78, -79, -80*
Vlijmen, Jan Van 1935- *Baker 78, NewGrD 80*
Voces Intimae Trio *BiDAmM*
Vocht, Lodewijk De 1887-1977 *NewGrD 80*
Vockerodt, Gottfried 1665-1717 *NewGrD 80*
Vockerodt, Gottfried 1665-1727 *Baker 78*
Vockerodt, Johann Arnold *NewGrD 80*
Vockner, Josef 1842-1906 *Baker 78*
Voctuis, Michael *NewGrD 80*
Voctus, Michael *NewGrD 80*
Vodeding, Fredrik d1942 *WhoHol B*
Vodehnal, Andrea 1938- *CnOxB, DancEn 78[port]*
Vodery, Will 1885-1951 *AmSCAP 66, -80, BiDAmM, BlksBF, ConAmC*
Vodicka, Vaclav *NewGrD 80*
Vodnansky, Jan Campanus 1941- *IntWWM 77, NewGrD 80*
Vodnoy, Max 1892-1939 *WhScrn 77*
Vodopivec, Franc Marijan 1920- *IntWWM 77*
Vodorinski, Anton *NewGrD 80, OxMus*
Vodovoz, Anatoly 1936- *IntWWM 77, -80*
Vodusek, Valens 1912- *NewGrD 80*
Vodzogbe, Augustine Kofi 1924- *IntWWM 80*
Voelckel, Samuel 1560?-1617? *NewGrD 80*
Voelker, Franz 1899-1965 *CmOp*
Voelpel, Fred *WhoThe 77*
Voet, Michael *NewGrD 80*
Voetus, Michael *NewGrD 80*
Vogan, Emmet 1893-1969 *Vers B[port]*
Vogan, Emmett 1893-1969 *ForYSC, WhScrn 77, WhoHol B*
Vogeding, Fredrik 1890-1942 *WhScrn 74, -77*
Vogel, Adolf 1897-1969 *Baker 78*
Vogel, Barbara *WhoOp 76*
Vogel, Charles-Louis-Adolphe 1808-1892 *Baker 78, NewGrD 80*
Vogel, Edith *IntWWM 77, -80, WhoMus 72*
Vogel, Eleanore 1903-1973 *WhScrn 77*
Vogel, Emil 1859-1908 *Baker 78, NewGrD 80*
Vogel, Ernst 1926- *IntWWM 77, -80*
Vogel, Friedrich Wilhelm Ferdinand 1807-1892 *Baker 78*
Vogel, Henry 1865-1925 *NotNAT B, WhScrn 74, -77, WhoHol B*
Vogel, Howard 1933- *IntWWM 77, -80*
Vogel, Janet Frances 1941- *AmSCAP 66, -80*
Vogel, Jaroslav 1894-1970 *NewGrD 80*
Vogel, Jesse 1925- *IntMPA 77, -75, -76, -78, -79, -80*
Vogel, Johann Christoph 1756?-1788 *NewGrD 80*
Vogel, Johann Christoph 1758-1788 *Baker 78*
Vogel, Kajetan 1750?-1794 *NewGrD 80*
Vogel, Karsten 1943- *IntWWM 77, -80*
Vogel, Louis *NewGrD 80*
Vogel, Ludwig *NewGrD 80*
Vogel, Martin 1923- *IntWWM 77, -80, NewGrD 80*
Vogel, Michael P 1940- *IntWWM 80*
Vogel, Michael R 1940- *IntWWM 77*
Vogel, Mitch 1956- *WhoHol A*
Vogel, Patricia 1909-1941 *WhScrn 74, -77*
Vogel, Paul C 1899-1975 *FilmEn, FilmgC, HalFC 80*
Vogel, Raymond 1915- *WhoOp 76*
Vogel, Richard Friedrich Manfred 1918- *IntWWM 77, -80*
Vogel, Rudolf 1900-1967 *WhScrn 77*
Vogel, Sheldon *ConMuA 80B*
Vogel, Siegfried 1937- *WhoOp 76*
Vogel, Virgil *FilmgC, HalFC 80, WhoHrs 80*
Vogel, Vladimir 1896- *IntWWM 77, -80, OxMus*
Vogel, Wilhelm Moritz 1846-1922 *Baker 78*
Vogel, Wladimir 1896- *Baker 78, CpmDNM 80, DcCM, NewGrD 80*
Vogeleis, Martin 1861-1930 *Baker 78, NewGrD 80*
Vogelhofer, Andreas *NewGrD 80*
Vogelmaier, Andreas *NewGrD 80*
Vogelsang, Andreas *OxMus*
Vogelsang, Johann *NewGrD 80*
Vogelsang, Johannes *NewGrD 80*
Vogelsang, Judith *WomWMM A, -B*
Vogelsang, Konrad 1928- *IntWWM 77, -80*
Vogelstatter, Andreas *NewGrD 80*
Vogelweide, Walther VonDer 1170?-1230? *Baker 78, NewGrD 80*
Vogg, Herbert 1928- *IntWWM 77, -80*
Vogl, Adolf 1873-1961 *NewGrD 80*
Vogl, Caetano *NewGrD 80*
Vogl, Heinrich 1845-1900 *Baker 78, CmOp, NewEOp 71, NewGrD 80*
Vogl, Johann Michael 1768-1840 *Baker 78, NewGrD 80*
Vogl, Kajetan *NewGrD 80*
Vogl, Therese *NewGrD 80*
Vogler, Abbe 1749-1814 *NewGrD 80[port]*
Vogler, Carl 1874-1951 *NewGrD 80*
Vogler, Georg 1585-1635 *NewGrD 80*
Vogler, Georg Joseph 1749-1814 *Baker 78, NewGrD 80[port], OxMus*
Vogler, Johann Caspar 1696-1763 *NewGrD 80*
Vogler, Karl Michael 1928- *FilmgC, ForYSC, HalFC 80, WhoHol A*
Vogler, Walter A 1897-1955 *WhScrn 74, -77, WhoHol B*
Vogrich, Max William Carl 1852-1916 *Baker 78, BiDAmM*
Vogt, Augustus Stephen 1861-1926 *Baker 78, CreCan 2, NewGrD 80*
Vogt, Gustav 1781-1870 *Baker 78*
Vogt, Gustave 1781-1870 *NewGrD 80*
Vogt, Hans 1911- *NewGrD 80*
Vogt, Joannes Georgius 1669-1730 *NewGrD 80*
Vogt, Johann 1823-1888 *Baker 78*
Vogt, Mauritius 1669-1730 *NewGrD 80*
Vogt, Michael 1526-1606 *NewGrD 80*
Vogues, The *RkOn 2[port]*
Vohs, Joan 1931- *FilmEn, ForYSC, IntMPA 77, -75, -76, -78, -79, -80*
Voicius, Michael *NewGrD 80*
Voicu, Ion 1925- *NewGrD 80*
Voiculescu, Dan 1940- *IntWWM 80*
Voight, Jon *WhoHol A*
Voight, Jon 1938- *FilmEn, ForYSC, HalFC 80[port], IntMPA 77, -75, -76, -78, -79, -80, WhoThe 77*
Voight, Jon 1939- *FilmgC, MovMk[port], OxFilm*
Voigt, Henriette 1808-1839 *Baker 78*
Voigt, Johann Georg Hermann 1769-1811 *Baker 78*
Voigt, Michael *NewGrD 80*
Voigtlander, Gabriel 1596?-1643 *NewGrD 80*
Voinea, Silvia 1942- *WhoOp 76*
Voinoff, Anatole 1896-1965 *WhScrn 74, -77*
Voirin, Francois Nicolas 1833-1885 *NewGrD 80*
Voisin, Roger 1918- *NewGrD 80*
Voit, Michael *NewGrD 80*
Vojacek, Hynek 1825-1916 *NewGrD 80*
Vojnovic, Ivo 1857-1929 *CnMD*
Vojtech *NewGrD 80*
Vojtech, Ivan 1928- *NewGrD 80*
Vokes, F M T d1890 *NotNAT B*
Vokes, Frederick Mortimer 1846-1888 *NotNAT B, OxThe*
Vokes, Harry d1922 *NotNAT B*
Vokes, Howard Dean 1931- *BiDAmM*
Vokes, Jessie Catherine Biddulph 1851-1884 *OxThe*
Vokes, John Russell d1924 *NotNAT B*
Vokes, May d1957 *Film 2, NotNAT B, WhoHol B*
Vokes, Robert d1912 *NotNAT B*
Vokes, Rosina 1854-1894 *NotNAT B, OxThe*
Vokes, Victoria 1853-1894 *NotNAT B, OxThe*
Vokes, Walter Fawdon d1904 *OxThe*
Voketaitis, Arnold Mathew 1931- *WhoOp 76*
Vokkerod, Johann Arnold *NewGrD 80*
Vola, Vicki *BiE&WWA*
Voland, Herb *WhoHol A*
Volanek, Anton 1761-1817 *NewGrD 80*
Volanek, Antonin 1761-1817 *NewGrD 80*
Volare, Lorna *Film 1*
Volbach, Fritz 1861-1940 *Baker 78, NewGrD 80*
Volckaert, Edith 1949- *IntWWM 77, -80*
Volckmar, Wilhelm Valentin 1812-1887 *Baker 78, NewGrD 80*
Volcyr, Nicolas *NewGrD 80*
Volek, Jaroslav 1923- *IntWWM 77, -80, NewGrD 80*
Volek, Tomislav 1931- *NewGrD 80*
Volinine, Alexander Yemelianovich 1882-1955 *CnOxB*
Volinine, Alexandre 1882-1955 *DancEn 78*
Volk, Arno 1914- *NewGrD 80*
Volkart, Bettye Sue 1945- *AmSCAP 80*
Volkart, Hazel O 1911- *AmSCAP 80*
Volker, Franz 1899-1965 *NewGrD 80*
Volker, Wilhelm *Film 2*
Volkert, Erie T 1913- *BiE&WWA, NotNAT*
Volkert, Franz 1767-1831 *NewGrD 80*
Volkert, Franz 1767-1845 *Baker 78*
Volkert, Franz 1778-1845 *NewGrD 80*
Volkl, Walter 1929- *IntWWM 80*
Volkman, Ivan d1972 *WhScrn 77*
Volkmann, Hans 1875-1946 *Baker 78*
Volkmann, Karl-Heinz 1919- *IntWWM 77, WhoMus 72*
Volkmann, Robert 1815-1883 *Baker 78, NewGrD 80, OxMus*
Volkmann, Rudy H 1942- *AmSCAP 80*
Volkoff, Boris 1902- *CreCan 1*
Volkoff, Catherine Janet Baldwin *CreCan 2*
Volkonsky, Andrei 1933- *Baker 78, DcCM*
Volkonsky, Andrey Mikhaylovich 1933- *NewGrD 80*
Volkonsky, Prince Serge 1860-1937 *DancEn 78*
Volkov, Boris 1902- *CnOxB, CreCan 1, DancEn 78*
Volkov, Fedor Gregoryevich 1729-1763 *NotNAT B*
Volkov, Feodor Grigoryevich 1729-1763 *Baker 78, Ent, OxThe*
Volkov, Fyodor Grigoryevich 1729-1763 *NewGrD 80*
Volkov, Leonid Andreyevich 1893- *OxThe*
Volkova, Vera 1904-1975 *CnOxB, DancEn 78[port]*
Vollaerts, Jan Wilhelmus Antonius 1901-1956 *NewGrD 80*
Volland, Virginia 1909- *BiE&WWA, NotNAT*
Vollerthun, Georg 1876-1945 *Baker 78*
Vollinger, William *ConAmC A*
Vollmar, Jocelyn 1925- *CnOxB, DancEn 78[port]*
Vollmer, Lula 1898-1955 *CnMD, ModWD, NotNAT B, WhThe*
Vollmoeller, Karl Gustav 1878-1948 *CnMD, ModWD, NotNAT B*
Vollmoller, Karl Gustav 1878-1948 *McGEWD*
Vollrath, Carl Paul 1931- *CpmDNM 79, ConAmC*
Volonte, Gian Maria 1930- *FilmgC, HalFC 80, WhoHol A*
Volonte, Gian Maria 1933- *FilmAG WE, FilmEn*
Voloshinov, Victor 1905-1960 *Baker 78*
Volotskoy, Vladimir 1853-1927 *WhScrn 74, -77*
Volovini, Floretta 1938- *WhoMus 72*
Volpato, Jack Albert *AmSCAP 80*
Volpe, Alfred Michael 1936- *AmSCAP 80*
Volpe, Arnold 1869-1940 *Baker 78, BiDAmM*
Volpe, Elizabeth 1953- *IntWWM 80*
Volpe, Frederick 1865-1932 *NotNAT B, WhThe, WhoHol B*
Volpe, Frederick 1873-1932 *WhScrn 77*
Volpe, Giovanni Battista 1620?-1691 *NewGrD 80*
Volpe, Lelio Della *NewGrD 80*
Volpe, Virgilio A 1935- *AmSCAP 66, -80*
Volpi, Giacomo *NewGrD 80*
Voltaire 1694-1778 *CnThe, DcPup, EncWT, Ent, McGEWD[port], NewEOp 71, OxMus, OxThe, REnWD[port]*
Voltaire, Francois Marie Aronet De 1694-1778 *NotNAT B*
Volterra, Leon d1949 *NotNAT B*
Voltz, Hans *NewGrD 80*
Voluda, Gines De *NewGrD 80*
Volumes, The *RkOn*
Volumier, Jean Baptiste 1670?-1728 *NewGrD 80*
Volynsky, Akim Lvovich 1863-1926 *CnOxB*

Volynsky, Akim Lvovitch 1863-1926 *DancEn 78*
Vom Berg, Johann *NewGrD 80*
Vom Brandt, Jobst *NewGrD 80*
Vom Brant, Jobst *NewGrD 80*
Vom Perg, Johann *NewGrD 80*
Vomacka, Boleslav 1887-1965 *Baker 78, NewGrD 80*
VonAlbrecht, Georg 1891- *IntWWM 77, -80*
VonAlten, Ferdiand *Film 2*
VonAlten, Ferdinand 1885-1933 *WhScrn 74, -77, WhoHol B*
VonArnim, Bettina *NewGrD 80*
VonArnim, Elisabeth *NewGrD 80*
VonBartesch, Seta K 1944- *IntWWM 77, -80*
VonBerne, Eva *Film 2*
VonBetz, Matthew *WhScrn 77*
VonBlock, Bela 1889-1962 *WhScrn 74, -77, WhoHol B*
VonBlon, Franz 1861-1945 *Baker 78*
VonBolvary, Geza 1898-1961 *WhScrn 74, -77*
VonBonnhorst, Carl Franz Wilhelm 1774?-1844 *BiDAmM*
VonBrincken, Wilhelm 1882-1946 *WhoHol B*
VonBrincken, Wilhelm 1891-1946 *WhScrn 74, -77*
VonBrincken, William 1882-1946 *Film 2, Vers B[port]*
VonBulow, Fritz 1933- *IntWWM 77*
VonBulow, Gert Oluf 1946- *IntWWM 77, -80*
VonBusch-Weise, Dagmar H E 1926- *IntWWM 77, -80*
VonBusing, Fritzi d1948 *NotNAT B*
VonCollande, Gisela 1915-1960 *WhScrn 74, -77*
Vondel, Joost VanDen 1587-1679 *CnThe, EncWT, McGEWD, REnWD[port]*
VonDerGoltz, Eric 1895-1977 *AmSCAP 66, -80*
Vonderhaar, Raymond T 1919- *IntMPA 78, -79, -80*
VonDerHoya, Amadeo 1874-1922 *Baker 78*
VonDerp, Clotilde *DancEn 78*
Vondersaar, Jeanette 1951- *CnOxB*
VonDobeneck, Baron *Film 2*
VonDohnanyi, Christoph 1929- *WhoOp 76*
VonDohnanyi, Ernest 1877- *BiDAmM*
Vondrak, Paul 1939- *CnOxB, DancEn 78*
Vondruska, Petr 1943- *CnOxB*
VonEinem, Gottfried 1918- *CpmDNM 74, DancEn 78, IntWWM 77, -80, WhoMus 72*
VonEltz, Theodore d1964 *MotPP, WhoHol B*
VonEltz, Theodore 1889-1964 *Film 1, -2, TwYS*
VonEltz, Theodore 1894-1964 *FilmEn, ForYSC, MovMk, Vers A[port], WhScrn 74, -77*
VonEngleman, Andre *Film 2*
VonEsterhazy, Countess Agnes *Film 2*
VonFischer, Kurt 1913- *IntWWM 77, -80*
VonForster, Walter 1915- *IntWWM 77, -80*
VonFurstenberg, Betsy *MotPP, NotNAT, WhoHol A*
VonFurstenberg, Betsy 1931- *WhoThe 72, -77*
VonFurstenberg, Betsy 1935- *BiE&WWA*
VonGaraguly, Carl 1900- *WhoMus 72*
VonGencsy, Eva 1924- *CreCan 2, DancEn 78*
VonGerlach, Arthur 1876-1925 *WorEFlm*
VonGlatter-Gotz, Josef Karl Raimund 1914- *WhoMus 72*
VonGoertz, Harald 1924- *WhoMus 72*
VonGoth, Rolf *Film 2*
VonGunden, Heidi 1940- *ConAmC*
VonHagen *BiDAmM*
VonHagen, Egon *Film 2*
VonHagen, P A *NewGrD 80*
VonHalem, Victor 1940- *WhoOp 76*
VonHallberg, Gene 1906- *AmSCAP 66, -80*
VonHarbou, Thea 1888-1954 *FilmEn, FilmgC, HalFC 80, WhoHrs 80, WomWMM, WorEFlm*
VonHardenburg, William *Film 2*
VonHartman, Carl *Film 2, TwYS*
VonHartz, John 1933- *NatPD[port]*
VonHase, Hellmuth 1891- *IntWWM 77, -80*
VonHease, Baron *Film 2*
VonHeeringen, Ernest 1810-1855 *BiDAmM*
VonHeune, Friedrich Alexander 1929- *IntWWM 80*
VonHofmannstahl, Hugo *NotNAT B*
VonHofmannsthal *PlP&P*
VonHollay, Camilla *Film 2*
VonHuene *IntWWM 77*
VonHuy, Martin *NewGrD 80*
VonJanuschowsky, Georgine 1859-1914 *BiDAmM*
VonJordis, Eelco 1942- *WhoOp 76*
Vonk, Hans F 1942- *IntWWM 80, WhoOp 76*
VonKaltenborn, Hans 1879-1965 *WhScrn 77*
VonKarajan, Herbert 1908- *MusSN[port], WhoMus 72, WhoOp 76*
VonKlaussen, Ronald *WhoHol A*
VonKoch, Erland 1910- *IntWWM 77, -80*
VonKotschubey, Ruth 1943- *IntWWM 80*
VonKotzbue, August Friedrich Ferdinand 1761-1819 *PlP&P*
VonKunits, Luigi 1870-1931 *BiDAmM*
VonLaban, Rudolf 1879-1958 *DancEn 78[port]*
VonLaHache, Theodor 1823-1867 *BiDAmM*
VonLambeck, Frederick 1918-1950 *WhScrn 77*
VonLedebur, Leopold 1876-1955 *WhScrn 74, -77*
VonLenkeffy, Ica *Film 2*
VonLent, Lucille *Film 2*
VonLer, Sarah d1916 *NotNAT B*
VonLinnenkoff, Barbara *Film 2*
VonMagnus, Peter 1927- *WhoOp 76*
VonMatacic, Lovro 1899- *WhoOp 76*
VonMeter, Harry *Film 1, -2*
VonMeyerinck, Hubert 1897-1971 *Film 2, WhScrn 74, -77, WhoHol B*
VonMosev, Gustav *PlP&P*
Vonn, Vyola *ForYSC*
VonNagy, Kathe 1909- *FilmEn*
Vonnegut, Kurt, Jr. 1922- *ConDr 77, NatPD[port], WhoHrs 80*
Vonnegut, Marjory *PlP&P*
Vonnegut, Walter d1940 *NotNAT B*
VonOhlen, Baron 1941- *EncJzS 70*
VonOhlen, John 1941- *EncJzS 70*
VonPechy, Valerie 1947- *IntWWM 77, -80*
VonPilat, Vera *PupTheA*
VonPodewils, Torsten Hunke 1909- *IntWWM 77, -80*
VonPrauheim, Rosa *WomWMM*
VonReinhold, Calvin 1927- *BiE&WWA, NotNAT, WhoHol A*
VonRempert, Albert d1958 *WhScrn 74, -77*
VonReuter, Florizel 1890- *BiDAmM*
VonRitoy, Theodore *Film 2*
VonRitzau, Erik *Film 2*
VonRitzau, Gunther *Film 1*
VonRosen, Elsa-Marianne 1927- *DancEn 78[port]*
VonRue, Greta *Film 2*
VonSchacht, Count *Film 2*
VonScherler, Sasha 1939- *WhoHol A, WhoThe 72, -77*
VonSchiller, Carl *Film 1*
VonSchlettow, Hans *Film 2*
VonSchlippenbach, Alex 1938- *EncJzS 70*
VonSchmidt, Eric 1930- *BluesWW[port]*
VonSchwindt, Wolfgang *Film 2*
VonSeckendorff, Karl Siegmund *NewGrD 80*
VonSeyffertitz, Gustav 1863-1943 *FilmEn, Film 1, -2, FilmgC, HalFC 80, TwYS, WhScrn 74, -77, WhoHol B*
VonSeyffertitz, Gustav 1890?-1943 *MovMk[port]*
VonSeyffertitz, Gustave 1863-1943 *ForYSC*
VonSidon, Samuel Peter *NewGrD 80*
VonStade, Frederica *WhoOp 76*
VonStade, Frederica 1945- *BnBkM 80, CmOp, IntWWM 77, -80, MusSN[port], NewGrD 80*
VonSternberg, Ivanovitch Constanin 1852-1924 *BiDAmM*
VonSternberg, Josef 1894-1969 *BiDFilm, -81, DcFM, FilmEn, FilmgC, HalFC 80, MovMk[port], TwYS A, WhScrn 74, -77, WorEFlm*
VonSternberg, Joseph 1894-1969 *CmMov*
VonStroheim, Erich d1957 *MotPP, WhoHol B*
VonStroheim, Erich 1884-1957 *MovMk[port]*
VonStroheim, Erich 1885-1957 *BiDFilm, -81, DcFM, FilmAG WE, FilmEn, Film 1, -2, FilmgC, HalFC 80, TwYS[port], WhScrn 74, -77, WhoHrs 80[port], WorEFlm*
VonStroheim, Erich 1886-1957 *ForYSC, TwYS A*
VonStroheim, Erich, Jr. 1916-1968 *WhScrn 74, -77, WhoHol B*
VonStrohmer, Herbert 1924- *WhoOp 76*
VonSydow, Clas *WhoHol A*
VonSydow, Henrik *WhoHol A*
VonSydow, Max *IntMPA 75, -76, -78, -79, -80*
VonSydow, Max 1926- *ForYSC*
VonSydow, Max 1929- *BiDFilm, -81, FilmEn, FilmgC, HalFC 80, IntMPA 77, MotPP, MovMk[port], OxFilm, WhoHol A, WhoHrs 80, WorEFlm[port]*
VonSzoreghy, Julius *Film 2*
VonTilzer, Albert 1873-1956 *NewGrD 80*
VonTilzer, Albert 1878-1956 *AmPS, AmSCAP 66, -80, BiDAmM, CmpEPM, NotNAT B, PopAmC[port], Sw&Ld C*
VonTilzer, Harold 1872-1946 *NewGrD 80*
VonTilzer, Harry 1872-1946 *AmPS, AmSCAP 66, -80, BiDAmM, CmpEPM, NewGrD 80, NotNAT B, PopAmC[port], Sw&Ld B*
VonToesky, Johann Baptist *NewGrD 80*
VonTomory, Nandor 1930- *WhoOp 76*
VonTwardowski, Hans d1958 *Film 1, NotNAT B, WhScrn 74, -77, WhoHol B*
VonUllmann, Hellmuth 1913- *IntWWM 77, -80*
VonVerdo, Eldora *IntMPA 75*
VonVerdo, Elnora *IntMPA 76*
VonVolborth, Diana Danys 1941- *IntWWM 77*
VonVolborth-Danys, Diana 1941- *IntWWM 80*
VonWalther, Hertha *Film 2*
VonWangenheim, Gustav *Film 2*
VonWayditch, Gabriel Paul 1888-1969 *AmSCAP 80*
VonWinterstein, Eduard 1872-1961 *Film 2, WhScrn 74, -77, WhoHol B*
VonWurtzler, Aristid *CpmDNM 75*
VonWurtzler, Aristid 1925- *AmSCAP 66, ConAmC*
VonWurtzler, Aristid 1930- *AmSCAP 80*
VonZallinger, Meinhard 1897- *WhoMus 72*
VonZell, Harry 1906- *ForYSC, WhoHol A*
VonZemlinsky, Alexander 1872-1942 *BiDAmM*
VonZerneck, Peter *WhoHol A*
VonZinzendorf, Nikolaus Ludwig 1700-1760 *BiDAmM*
Voorberg, Marinus 1920- *NewGrD 80*
Voorhees, Don *CmpEPM*
Voorhis, Jerry 1901- *What 3[port]*
Voormolen, Alexander 1895- *DcCM, NewGrD 80*
Voormolen, Alexander Nicolaas 1895- *IntWWM 80*
Voormolen, Alexander Nicolas 1895- *Baker 78, IntWWM 77*
Voorn, Joop 1932- *Baker 78, CpmDNM 76, -80*
Voorn, Josephus Hermanus Maria 1932- *IntWWM 77, -80*
Vooss, Hanna 1916- *CnOxB*
Vopa, Giovanni Donato *NewGrD 80*
Vopelius, Gottfried 1635-1715 *Baker 78*
Vopelius, Gottfried 1645-1715 *NewGrD 80*
Vorberg, Gregor *NewGrD 80*
Vorhaus, Bernard *IntMPA 75, -76, -78, -79, -80*
Vorhaus, Bernard 1898?- *FilmEn, FilmgC, HalFC 80, IIWWBF, IntMPA 77*
Vorholz, Dieter 1932- *IntWWM 77, -80*
Vorisek, Jan Hugo 1791-1825 *Baker 78, BnBkM 80*
Vorisek, Jan Vaclav 1791-1825 *NewGrD 80[port]*
Vorkapich, Slavko 1894- *DcFM*
Vorkapich, Slavko 1895- *OxFilm, WorEFlm*
Vorkapitch, Slavko 1892-1976 *HalFC 80*
Vorkapitch, Slavko 1897- *FilmgC*
Vorkov, Zandor *WhoHrs 80*
Vorlova, Slava 1894-1973 *Baker 78, NewGrD 80*
Vorobchievici, Isidor 1836-1903 *NewGrD 80*
Vorob'yova, Anna Yakovlevna *NewGrD 80*
Voronina, Vera *Film 2*
Vos, Laurent De 1533-1580 *NewGrD 80*
Vosburgh, Alfred *Film 1, WhScrn 77*
Vosburgh, David *WhoHol A*
Vosburgh, Harold 1870-1926 *Film 1, -2, TwYS, WhScrn 77*
Voskovec, George 1905- *BiE&WWA, FilmgC, ForYSC, HalFC 80, MotPP, NotNAT, WhoHol A, WhoThe 72, -77*

Voskovec, Jiri 1905- *CnMD, EncWT*
Vosper, Frank 1899-1937 *CnThe, Film 2, HalFC 80, NotNAT B, WhThe*
Vosper, Frank O 1900-1937 *WhScrn 77*
Vosper, John d1954 *WhScrn 74, -77, WhoHol B*
Voss, Aage 1911- *IntWWM 80*
Voss, Charles 1815-1882 *Baker 78*
Voss, Frank Fatty 1888-1917 *WhScrn 77*
Voss, Friedrich 1930- *NewGrD 80*
Voss, Gerhard Johann 1577-1649 *NewGrD 80*
Voss, Isaac 1618-1689 *Baker 78, NewGrD 80*
Voss, Johann Heinrich 1751-1826 *NewGrD 80*
Voss, Peter *Film 2*
Voss, Stephanie 1936- *WhoThe 72, -77*
Vossberg, Titus Dieter 1934- *WhoOp 76*
Vosselli, Judith *Film 2*
Vossius, Gerhard Johann 1577-1649 *NewGrD 80*
Vossius, Isaac 1618-1689 *NewGrD 80*
Vostrak, Zbynek 1920- *Baker 78, DcCM, NewGrD 80*
Votapek, Ralph 1939- *Baker 78, IntWWM 77, -80, WhoMus 72*
Voteur, Ferdinand *BlkAmP, MorBAP*
Votichenko, Sacha 1888-1971 *BiDAmM*
Votrian, Peter *ForYSC*
Votrian, Ralph *ForYSC*
Votter, Romanus *NewGrD 80*
Votterle, Karl 1903-1975 *NewGrD 80*
Votto, Antonino 1896- *NewGrD 80, WhoOp 76*
Vounder-Davis, Jean 1917- *IntWWM 77, -80*
Vounderlich, Jean-Georges *NewGrD 80*
Voxman, Himie 1912- *WhoMus 72*
Voxpoppers, The *RkOn*
Voyachek, Ignaty Kasparovich *NewGrD 80*
Voynikov, Dobri 1833-1878 *NewGrD 80*
Voynow, Dick 1900-1944 *WhoJazz 72*
Voz, Laurent De *NewGrD 80*
Voznesensky, Ivan Ivanovich 1838-1910 *NewGrD 80*
Vrana, Frantisek 1914- *WhoMus 72*
Vranek, Gustav 1906- *IntWWM 77, -80*
Vrangel, Vasily Georgiyevich *NewGrD 80*
Vranicky, Anton *NewGrD 80*
Vranicky, Pavel *NewGrD 80*
Vranken, Jaap 1897-1956 *Baker 78*
Vrede, Johannes *NewGrD 80*
Vredeman *NewGrD 80*
Vredeman, Jacob 1564?-1621 *NewGrD 80*
Vredeman, Michael 1562?-1629 *NewGrD 80*
Vredeman, Sebastian 1542?- *NewGrD 80*
Vredenburg, Max 1904-1976 *Baker 78, NewGrD 80*
Vredman *NewGrD 80*
Vree, Marion F *ConAmC*
Vreede-Mees, Anna Constance Maria 1914- *IntWWM 77*
Vreedman *NewGrD 80*
Vreese, Frederic De *NewGrD 80*
Vremsak, Samo 1930- *IntWWM 77, -80*
Vrenios, Anastasios Nicholas 1940- *IntWWM 77, -80*
Vrenios, Elizabeth Kirkpatrick 1940- *IntWWM 77, -80*
Vretblad, Patrik 1876-1953 *NewGrD 80*
Vretblad, Viktor Patrik 1876-1953 *Baker 78*
Vreuls, Victor 1876-1944 *Baker 78, NewGrD 80, OxMus*
Vrhel, James J 1920- *IntWWM 77, -80*
Vrhovski, Josip 1902- *IntWWM 77, -80*
Vriderich Von Sonnenburg *NewGrD 80*
Vriderich Von Suneburg *NewGrD 80*
Vriderich Von Sunnenburg *NewGrD 80*
Vriend, Jan 1938- *Baker 78, IntWWM 77, -80*
Vries, Han De 1941- *NewGrD 80*
Vries Robbe, Willem De 1902- *NewGrD 80*
Vrieslander, Otto 1880-1950 *Baker 78, NewGrD 80*
Vrionides, Christos 1894-1961 *Baker 78*
Vroman, John 1918- *AmSCAP 66, -80*
Vroman, Mary Elizabeth 1923-1967 *BlkAmP*
Vronsky, Karel 1918- *IntWWM 77, -80*
Vronsky, Vitya 1909- *Baker 78, NewGrD 80*
Vroom, Frederic William 1858-1942 *WhScrn 74, -77*
Vroom, Frederick d1942 *Film 2, WhoHol B*
Vroom, Lodewick d1950 *NotNAT B*
Vroom, Paul 1917- *BiE&WWA, NotNAT*
Vrooman, Elizabeth *PupTheA*
Vroons, Frans 1911- *CmOp, NewGrD 80*
Vroons, Fransiscus Johannes 1911- *WhoMus 72*
Vrowenlop, Heinrich *NewGrD 80*
Vroye, Theodore-Joseph De 1804-1873 *Baker 78, NewGrD 80*
Vsevolojsky, Ivan 1835-1909 *CnOxB, DancEn 78*
Vtorushina, Olga Mikhailovna 1947- *CnOxB*
Vuataz, Roger 1898- *Baker 78, NewGrD 80*
Vuckovic, Vojislav 1910-1942 *Baker 78, NewGrD 80*
Vuert, Giaches De *NewGrD 80*
Vuillaume, J B 1798-1875 *OxMus*
Vuillaume, Jean-Baptiste 1798-1875 *Baker 78, NewGrD 80*
Vuillermoz, Emile 1878-1960 *Baker 78, NewGrD 80*
Vuillermoz, Jean 1906-1940 *Baker 78*
Vukan, George 1941- *IntWWM 80*
Vukdragovic, Mihailo 1900- *Baker 78, NewGrD 80*
Vukdragovic, Mirjana 1930- *IntWWM 80*
Vukotic, Dusan 1927- *DcFM, FilmEn, WorEFlm*
Vulchanov, Rangel 1928- *DcFM*
Vulfran *NewGrD 80*
Vulpen, Van *NewGrD 80*
Vulpius, Melchior 1570?-1615 *Baker 78, NewGrD 80*
Vuolo, Tito 1893-1962 *WhScrn 77, WhoHol B*
Vurnik, Stanko 1898-1932 *NewGrD 80*
Vycichlova, Libuse *NewGrD 80*
Vycpalek, Ladislav 1882-1969 *Baker 78, DcCM, NewGrD 80, OxMus*
Vye, Murvyn 1913-1976 *FilmEn, FilmgC, ForYSC, HalFC 80, IntMPA 77, -75, -76, -78, -79, -80, MovMk[port], Vers B[port], WhoHol A*
Vyhnalek, Ivo 1930- *IntWWM 77, -80*
Vyner, Michael Geoffrey 1943- *IntWWM 80, WhoMus 72*
Vyroubova, Nina 1921- *CnOxB, DancEn 78*
Vyshnegradsky, Ivan *Baker 78, DcCM*
Vyshnegradsky, Ivan 1893- *OxMus*
Vyslouzil, Jiri 1925- *NewGrD 80*
Vyverman, Jules 1900- *IntWWM 77, -80*
Vyvyan, Jennifer 1925-1974 *CmOp, NewGrD 80, WhoHol B, WhoMus 72*

W

Wa-Sha-Quon-Asin *CreCan 1*
Waack, Karl 1861-1922 *Baker 78*
Waart, Edo De 1941- *Baker 78, MusSN[port], NewGrD 80*
Waart, Hendrikus Aloysius Petrus De 1863-1931 *Baker 78*
Waasdorp, Nicolaas Antonius Maria 1928- *IntWWM 77, -80*
Waber, Hubert Carolus 1938- *WhoOp 76*
Wachmann, Eduard 1836-1908 *NewGrD 80*
Wachs, Paul Etienne Victor 1851-1915 *Baker 78*
Wachsmann, Franz *NewGrD 80*
Wachsmann, Klaus P 1907- *NewGrD 80*
Wachsmith, Fee *Film 2*
Wachtel, Theodor 1823-1893 *Baker 78, NewGrD 80*
Wachter, Eberhard 1929- *CmOp, IntWWM 77, -80, NewGrD 80, WhoOp 76*
Wachter, Georg d1547 *NewGrD 80*
Wachtmeister, Count Axel Raoul 1865-1947 *Baker 78*
Wackenroder, Wilhelm Heinrich 1773-1798 *NewGrD 80*
Wackernagel, Philipp 1800-1877 *Baker 78*
Wacksman, Ruth *PupTheA*
Waclaw Z Szamotul *NewGrD 80*
Wada, Yoshimasa 1943- *ConAmC*
Wadams, Golden *Film 2*
Waddams, Eric William 1913- *IntWWM 77, -80*
Waddell, James Lewis 1946- *AmSCAP 80*
Waddell, Samuel J *REnWD[port]*
Waddington, Geoffrey 1904-1966 *CreCan 2, NewGrD 80*
Waddington, Helen *PupTheA*
Waddington, Miriam 1917- *CreCan 1*
Waddington, Patrick 1901- *BiE&WWA, NotNAT, WhoHol A, WhoThe 72, -77*
Waddington, Sidney Peine 1869-1953 *Baker 78*
Wade, Adam *WhoHol A*
Wade, Adam 1935- *DrBlPA*
Wade, Adam 1937- *RkOn[port]*
Wade, Allan 1881-1954 *OxThe*
Wade, Allan 1881-1955 *NotNAT B, WhThe*
Wade, Bessie 1885-1966 *WhScrn 77, WhoHol B*
Wade, Dorothy R 1928- *IntWWM 77*
Wade, Ernestine *DrBlPA*
Wade, Frank 1908- *IntWWM 77, -80, WhoMus 72*
Wade, James *ConAmC*
Wade, Jimmy 1895?-1957 *WhoJazz 72*
Wade, John *MagIlD*
Wade, John 1876-1949 *WhoHol B*
Wade, John Francis d1786 *OxMus*
Wade, John P 1874- *Film 1, -2*
Wade, John W 1876-1949 *WhScrn 74, -77*
Wade, Joseph Augustine 1796-1845 *Baker 78*
Wade, Joseph Augustine 1801?-1845 *NewGrD 80*
Wade, Maybelle 1914- *AmSCAP 80*
Wade, Philip d1950 *NotNAT B*
Wade, Robert J, Jr. 1907- *IntMPA 75, -76*
Wade, Stuart *CmpEPM*
Wade, Walter d1963 *NotNAT B*
Wade, Walter 1926- *ConAmC*
Wade, Warren 1896-1973 *WhScrn 77*
Wadely, Betty 1911- *WhoMus 72*
Wademant, Annette 1928- *FilmEn*
Wadenius, Georg 1945- *EncJzS 70*
Wadhams, Golden 1869-1929 *WhScrn 74, -77, WhoHol B*
Wadkar, Hansa Swan 1924-1971 *WhScrn 74, -77*
Wadleigh, Michael 1941- *IntMPA 77, -75, -76, -78, -79, -80*
Wadowick, James Louis 1935- *IntWWM 77*
Wadsworth, Handel d1964 *NotNAT B*
Wadsworth, Henry 1897-1974 *FilmEn*
Wadsworth, Henry 1902-1974 *Film 2, HalFC 80, WhScrn 77, WhoHol B*
Wadsworth, James T *NewYTET*
Wadsworth, Louis *PupTheA*
Wadsworth, Lucille *PupTheA*
Wadsworth, William 1873-1950 *Film 1, -2, MotPP, WhScrn 74, -77, WhoHol B*
Wadsworth Mansion *RkOn 2A[port]*
Waechter, Eberhard 1929- *WhoMus 72*
Waefeighem, Louis Van 1840-1908 *Baker 78*
Waefelghem, Louis Van 1840-1908 *NewGrD 80*
Waehner, Karin 1926- *CnOxB*
Waelput, Hendrik 1845-1885 *Baker 78, NewGrD 80*
Waelput, Henri 1845-1885 *NewGrD 80*
Waelput, Henry 1845-1885 *NewGrD 80*
Waelrand, Hubert 1516?-1595 *NewGrD 80*
Waelrand, Huberto 1516?-1595 *NewGrD 80*
Waelrandus, Hubertus 1516?-1595 *NewGrD 80*
Waelrant, Hubert 1516?-1595 *NewGrD 80*
Waelrant, Hubert 1517?-1595 *Baker 78*
Waelrant, Hubert 1518?-1595 *OxMus*
Waelrant, Huberto 1516?-1595 *NewGrD 80*
Waeltner, Ernst Ludwig 1926-1975 *NewGrD 80*
Waesberghe, Joseph Smits Van 1901- *Baker 78, NewGrD 80*
Waganfeald, Edward James, III 1934- *AmSCAP 80*
Wagele, Antonia *NewGrD 80*
Wagemann, Rose 1940- *WhoOp 76*
Wagemans, Peter-Jan 1952- *Baker 78, IntWWM 77, -80*
Wagenaar, Bernard 1894-1971 *AmSCAP 66, -80, Baker 78, BiDAmM, ConAmC, DcCM, NewGrD 80, OxMus*
Wagenaar, Johan 1862-1941 *Baker 78, MusMk, NewGrD 80, OxMus*
Wagenaar, Nelly 1898- *IntWWM 77, -80*
Wagenaar-Nolthenius, Helene *NewGrD 80*
Wagenhals, Lincoln A 1869-1931 *NotNAT B, WhThe*
Wagenheim, Charles *ForYSC, IntMPA 77, -75, -76, -78, -79, -80, WhoHol A*
Wagenmann, Abraham 1570?-1632 *NewGrD 80*
Wagenmann, Josef Hermann 1876-1940 *Baker 78*
Wagenseil, Georg Christoph 1715-1777 *Baker 78, MusMk, NewGrD 80, OxMus*
Wagenseil, Johann Christoph 1633-1708 *Baker 78, NewGrD 80, OxMus*
Wagenseller, William H 1880-1951 *WhScrn 74, -77*
Wager, Anthony 1933- *HalFC 80, WhoHol A*
Wager, Michael 1925- *BiE&WWA, NotNAT, WhoHol A, WhoThe 72, -77*
Wagganer, Stanley Robert 1956- *AmSCAP 80*
Waggner, George 1894- *FilmEn, Film 2, FilmgC, HalFC 80, IntMPA 77, -75, -76, -78, -79, -80, WhoHrs 80*
Waggoner, Loren Richard 1923- *AmSCAP 80*
Waggoner, Lyle 1935- *IntMPA 77, -75, -76, -78, -79, -80*
Waghalter, Ignatz 1882-1949 *Baker 78*
Wagler, Frederick A d1830? *BiDAmM*
Wagner *NewGrD 80*
Wagner, Arthur 1923- *BiE&WWA, NotNAT*
Wagner, Charles L d1956 *NotNAT A, -B, WhThe*
Wagner, Christian 1924- *IntWWM 77*
Wagner, Christian Salomon *NewGrD 80*
Wagner, Cosima 1837-1930 *Baker 78, NewEOp 71*
Wagner, Douglas Edward 1952- *AmSCAP 80*
Wagner, Ed *WhoHol A*
Wagner, Edyth Elizabeth 1916- *IntWWM 77, -80*
Wagner, Elsa *Film 2, WhoHol A*
Wagner, Erika *Film 2*
Wagner, Frank 1922- *BiE&WWA, CnOxB, NotNAT*
Wagner, Fritz Arno 1889-1958 *FilmEn, FilmgC, HalFC 80, OxFilm, WorEFlm*
Wagner, Fritz Arno 1894-1958 *DcFM*
Wagner, Georg Gottfried 1698-1756 *Baker 78, NewGrD 80, OxMus*
Wagner, George *Film 2*
Wagner, George Melville 1947- *IntWWM 77*
Wagner, Gerrit Anthonie Alexander 1862-1892 *Baker 78*
Wagner, Gotthard 1678-1738 *NewGrD 80*
Wagner, Heinrich Leopold 1747-1779 *Ent, McGEWD*
Wagner, Heinrich Matusowitsch *NewGrD 80*
Wagner, J F 1856-1908 *NewGrD 80*
Wagner, Jack 1897-1965 *WhScrn 74, -77, WhoHol B*
Wagner, Jane *NewYTET*
Wagner, Jean Theophile *NewGrD 80*
Wagner, Jerry *ConMuA 80B*
Wagner, Joachim 1690?-1749 *NewGrD 80*
Wagner, Johann Gottlob 1748-1789 *NewGrD 80*
Wagner, Johann Michael 1720?-1789? *NewGrD 80*
Wagner, Johanna 1826-1894 *Baker 78, CmOp, NewEOp 71, NewGrD 80*
Wagner, John Waldorf 1937- *IntWWM 77, -80*
Wagner, Josef Franz 1856-1908 *Baker 78*
Wagner, Joseph 1678-1738 *NewGrD 80*
Wagner, Joseph 1913- *BiE&WWA*
Wagner, Joseph Frederick 1900- *DcCM*

Wagner, Joseph Frederick 1900-1974 *AmSCAP 66, -80, Baker 78, BiDAmM, ConAmC*
Wagner, Jozsef 1791-1861? *NewGrD 80*
Wagner, Karl Jacob 1772-1822 *NewGrD 80*
Wagner, Karl Jakob 1772-1822 *Baker 78*
Wagner, Kid *Film 2*
Wagner, Larry 1907- *AmSCAP 66, -80*
Wagner, Lavern John 1925- *IntWWM 77, -80*
Wagner, Leon *WhoHol A*
Wagner, Leonard *ConAmC*
Wagner, Lindsay 1949- *FilmEn, HalFC 80, IntMPA 78, -79, -80, WhoHol A*
Wagner, Ljubica 1934- *WhoOp 76*
Wagner, Lou *WhoHol A*
Wagner, Mamie *WomWMM*
Wagner, Manfred 1952- *IntWWM 77, -80*
Wagner, Manfred J 1944- *IntWWM 77, -80*
Wagner, Max 1901-1975 *WhScrn 77, WhoHol C*
Wagner, Michael J 1938- *IntWWM 77*
Wagner, Mike *WhoHol A*
Wagner, Peter 1865-1931 *Baker 78, NewGrD 80*
Wagner, Raymond James 1925- *IntMPA 78, -79, -80*
Wagner, Richard 1813-1883 *Baker 78, BnBkM 80[port], CmOp[port], -, CmpBCM, CnOxB, DancEn 78, DcCom 77[port], DcCom&M 79, GrComp[port], MusMk[port], NewEOp 71, NewGrD 80[port], OxMus, OxThe, REnWD[port]*
Wagner, Robert 1915- *WhoMus 72*
Wagner, Robert 1930- *FilmEn, FilmgC, ForYSC, HalFC 80, IntMPA 77, -75, -76, -78, -79, -80, MotPP, MovMk[port], WhoHol A, WorEFlm[port]*
Wagner, Robert F 1910- *BiE&WWA*
Wagner, Robin 1933- *BiE&WWA, NotNAT, WhoThe 72, -77*
Wagner, Roger 1914- *AmSCAP 66, -80, Baker 78, BnBkM 80, NewGrD 80*
Wagner, Rudolf *OxMus*
Wagner, Siegfried 1869-1930 *Baker 78, NewEOp 71, NewGrD 80, OxMus*
Wagner, Thomas 1931- *AmSCAP 66, ConAmC*
Wagner, Wende *WhoHol A*
Wagner, Werner S 1927- *IntWWM 77, -80*
Wagner, Wieland 1917-1966 *Baker 78, CmOp, EncWT, NewEOp 71, NewGrD 80*
Wagner, Wilhelm Richard 1813-1883 *NotNAT B*
Wagner, William 1885-1964 *NotNAT B, WhScrn 74, -77, WhoHol B*
Wagner, William Felkner 1920- *AmSCAP 80*
Wagner, Wolfgang 1919- *IntWWM 77, NewEOp 71, NewGrD 80, WhoMus 72, WhoOp 76*
Wagner-Regeny, Rudolf 1903-1969 *Baker 78, CmOp, DcCM, NewEOp 71, NewGrD 80, OxMus*
Wagoner, Dan 1932- *CmpGMD, CnOxB*
Wagoner, Porter *IntMPA 77, -75, -76, -78, -79*
Wagoner, Porter 1930- *EncFCWM 69, IlEncCM*
Wagoner, Porter Wayne 1927- *BiDAmM, CounME 74[port], -74A*
Wagoner, Ruth Diane 1954- *IntWWM 77, -80*
Wagonmasters, The *BiDAmM, EncFCWM 69*
Wahby, Youssef 1899- *DcFM*
Wahl, Walter Dare 1896-1974 *WhScrn 77, WhoHol B*
Wahlberg, Ingvar Axel 1936- *IntWWM 77*
Wahlberg, Rune 1910- *Baker 78*
Wahle, Kenneth Edward 1949- *AmSCAP 80*
Wahlte, Edgar 1930- *WhoOp 76*
Wahn, Robert Graham *IntMPA 75, -76*
Wahren, Karl Heinz 1933- *NewGrD 80*
Wahrmund *NewGrD 80*
Waidelich, Jurgen-Dieter 1931- *WhoOp 76*
Waigel *NewGrD 80*
Wailers, The *ConMuA 80A, RkOn[port]*
Wailes, Marylin 1900- *WhoMus 72*
Wailly, Paul De 1854-1933 *Baker 78*
Waimon, Seto 191-?- *DcFM*
Wain, Bea 1917- *CmpEPM, IntMPA 77, -75, -76, -78, -79*
Waine, Frederic 1911- *WhoMus 72*
Wainer, Lee *AmSCAP 66*
Wainert, Antoni *NewGrD 80*
Wainwright *NewGrD 80*
Wainwright, Gertrude May 1912- *WhoMus 72*
Wainwright, Godfrey 1879-1956 *WhScrn 74, -77*
Wainwright, Hope 1942-1972 *WhScrn 77, WhoHol B*
Wainwright, James *WhoHol A*
Wainwright, John d1911 *NotNAT B*
Wainwright, John 1723?-1768 *NewGrD 80, OxMus*
Wainwright, Jonathan Mayhew 1792-1854 *BiDAmM*
Wainwright, Loudon 1947- *IlEncR*
Wainwright, Loudon, III *ConMuA 80A*
Wainwright, Loudon, III 1946- *AmSCAP 80, RkOn 2[port]*
Wainwright, Marie d1923 *Film 2, WhoHol B, WhoStg 1906*
Wainwright, Marie 1853-1923 *NotNAT B, WhThe, WhoStg 1908*
Wainwright, Marie 1856-1923 *WhScrn 74, -77*
Wainwright, Mary Lee 1913- *AmSCAP 66, -80*
Wainwright, Richard 1757?-1825 *NewGrD 80*
Wainwright, Richard 1758-1825 *OxMus*
Wainwright, Robert 1748-1782 *NewGrD 80, OxMus*
Wainwright, Ruth 1902- *CreCan 2*
Wainwright, William d1797 *NewGrD 80*
Waissel, Matthaus 1535?-1602 *NewGrD 80*
Waisselius, Matthaus 1535?-1602 *NewGrD 80*
Waisselius, Matthaus 1540?-1602 *Baker 78*
Waissman, Kenneth 1942- *NotNAT*
Waite, Emily E *PupTheA*
Waite, Genevieve *WhoHol A*
Waite, John James 1807-1868 *NewGrD 80*
Waite, Malcolm *Film 2*
Waite, Marjorie *Film 2*
Waite, Ralph 1928- *HalFC 80, WhoHol A*
Waite, William G 1917-1980 *NewGrD 80*
Waits, Freddie 1943- *EncJzS 70*
Waits, Frederick Douglas 1943- *EncJzS 70*
Waits, Thomas Alan 1949- *AmSCAP 80*
Waits, Tom 1949- *ConMuA 80A, IlEncR*
Waitzman, Daniel Robert 1943- *IntWWM 77, -80*
Wajda, Andrzej 1926- *BiDFilm, -81, ConLC 16, DcFM, FilmEn, FilmgC, HalFC 80, MovMk[port], OxFilm, WorEFlm*
Wajnert, Antoni *NewGrD 80*
Wakabe, Michio *NewGrD 80*
Wakasugi, Hiroshi 1935- *WhoOp 76*
Wakefield, Anne *WhoHol A*
Wakefield, Douglas 1899-1951 *NotNAT B, WhThe*
Wakefield, Douglas 1900-1951 *WhScrn 74, -77*
Wakefield, Duggie 1899-1951 *FilmgC, HalFC 80, WhoHol B*
Wakefield, Frances *WhScrn 74, -77*
Wakefield, Frank *EncFCWM 69*
Wakefield, Gilbert Edward 1892-1963 *WhThe*
Wakefield, Hugh 1888- *WhThe*
Wakefield, Hugh 1888-1971 *HalFC 80, IlWWBF, WhScrn 74, -77, WhoHol B*
Wakefield, Hugh 1888-1972 *FilmgC*
Wakefield, John 1936- *IntWWM 80, WhoOp 76*
Wakefield, Mary Agnes 1853-1910 *OxMus*
Wakefield, Oliver 1909-1956 *WhScrn 74, -77, WhoHol B*
Wakeford, Kent L *HalFC 80*
Wakelkamp, Wim Antonie Johannes 1924- *IntWWM 77, -80*
Wakely, Jimmy 1914- *AmSCAP 66, -80, BiDAmM, CmpEPM, CounME 74[port], -74A, EncFCWM 69, ForYSC, IlEncCM, IntMPA 77, -75, -76, -78, -79, -80, WhoHol A*
Wakelyn, Virginia 1941- *CreCan 1*
Wakeman, Keith 1866-1933 *NotNAT B, WhThe*
Wakeman, Rick 1949- *ConMuA 80A, IlEncR*
Wakhevich, Georges 1907- *CnOxB*
Wakhevitch, George 1907- *WhoMus 72, WhoOp 76*
Wakhevitch, Georges 1907- *DancEn 78, DcFM, FilmEn, OxThe, WorEFlm*
Wakita, Kayoko 1928- *IntWWM 77*
Walacinski, Adam 1928- *Baker 78, IntWWM 77, -80, NewGrD 80*
Walbeck, Gunter 1939- *WhoOp 76*
Walberg, Betty 1921- *BiE&WWA*
Walberg, Garry *WhoHol A*
Walbrook, Anton 1896-1967 *FilmAG WE*
Walbrook, Anton 1900- *WorEFlm*
Walbrook, Anton 1900-1966 *WhThe*
Walbrook, Anton 1900-1967 *BiDFilm, -81, EncWT, FilmEn, Film 2, ForYSC, IlWWBF[port], MotPP, MovMk, NotNAT B, OxFilm, WhScrn 74, -77, WhoHol B*
Walbrook, Anton 1900-1968 *FilmgC, HalFC 80*
Walbrook, Henry Mackinnon 1863-1941 *NotNAT B, WhThe*
Walburn, Ray 1887-1969 *Film 1*
Walburn, Raymond 1887-1969 *BiE&WWA, FilmEn, Film 2, FilmgC, ForYSC, HalFC 80, HolCA[port], MotPP, NotNAT B, Vers A[port], WhScrn 74, -77, WhoHol B*
Walburn, Raymond 1897-1969 *MovMk[port]*
Walcamp, Marie 1894- *Film 1, -2, MotPP, TwYS*
Walcha, Helmut 1907- *BnBkM 80, IntWWM 77, -80, NewGrD 80, WhoMus 72*
Walcker *NewGrD 80*
Walcker, Eberhard Friedrich 1794-1872 *Baker 78, NewGrD 80*
Walcker, Johann Eberhard 1756-1843 *NewGrD 80*
Walcker, Karl 1845-1908 *NewGrD 80*
Walcker, Oscar 1869-1948 *NewGrD 80*
Walcker-Mayer, Werner 1923- *NewGrD 80*
Walcot, Charles M 1843- *WhoStg 1908*
Walcot, Charles Melton 1816-1868 *NotNAT B, OxThe*
Walcot, Charles Melton 1840-1921 *NotNAT B, OxThe*
Walcot, Isabella Nickinson 1847-1906 *OxThe*
Walcott, Arthur *Film 2*
Walcott, Brenda 1938- *BlkAmP*
Walcott, Collin 1945- *AmSCAP 80, EncJzS 70*
Walcott, Derek 1930- *BlkAmP, ConDr 73, -77, DrBlPA, MorBAP, PlP&P A*
Walcott, George *Film 2*
Walcott, Gregory *WhoHol A*
Walcott, Joe 1914- *What 1[port]*
Walcott, Ronald Harry 1939- *ConAmC*
Walcott, William *Film 2*
Walcz, Ethel *Film 2*
Wald, Jane *ForYSC, WhoHol A*
Wald, Jeff *ConMuA 80B*
Wald, Jerry *BgBands 74*
Wald, Jerry 1911-1962 *FilmEn, FilmgC, HalFC 80*
Wald, Jerry 1912-1962 *BiDFilm, -81, WorEFlm[port]*
Wald, Jerry 1918?-1973 *CmpEPM*
Wald, Jerry 1919-1973 *EncJzS 70*
Wald, Malvin D 1917- *AmSCAP 80, IntMPA 77, -75, -76, -78, -79, -80*
Wald, Max 1889-1954 *Baker 78, BiDAmM, ConAmC*
Wald, Richard C *IntMPA 77, -75, -76, -78, -79, -80, NewYTET*
Waldau, Gustav 1871-1958 *WhScrn 74, -77*
Waldbauer, Imre 1892-1953 *NewGrD 80*
Walde, Bill 1892-1959 *NewOrJ*
Walde, Henry 1902-1975 *NewOrJ*
Waldegrave, Lilias *WhThe*
Waldekranz, Rune 1911- *OxFilm*
Waldemar, Richard 1870-1947 *WhScrn 77*
Walden, Harry 1875-1921 *NotNAT B*
Walden, Herwarth 1878- *EncWT*
Walden, Lord Howard De *OxMus*
Walden, Phil *ConMuA 80B*
Walden, Robert *WhoHol A*
Walden, Stanley 1932- *ConAmC*
Walden, Stanley Eugene 1932- *AmSCAP 80*
Walden, Sylvia *WhoHol A*
Walden, William Glenn 1943- *IntWWM 77, -80*
Walder, Ernst *WhoHol A*
Walder, Herman 1905- *WhoJazz 72*

Walder, Johann Jakob 1750-1817 *NewGrD 80*
Waldersee, Paul Graf Von 1831-1906 *Baker 78*
Walderth, Ignaz *NewGrD 80*
Walderth, Joseph *NewGrD 80*
Waldis, Burkhard 1490?-1557? *NewGrD 80*
Waldis, Burkhart *OxThe*
Waldis, Otto 1906-1974 *WhScrn 77, WhoHol B*
Waldkirch, Henrik d1629 *NewGrD 80*
Waldkoenig, Mildred Dorothy 1925- *IntWWM 77*
Waldman, Robert H 1936- *AmSCAP 66, -80, ConAmC*
Waldman, Ronald 1914- *IntMPA 77, -75, -76, -78*
Waldman, Walter *IntMPA 77, -75, -76, -78, -79, -80*
Waldman, Wendy 1951- *IlEncR*
Waldmuller, Lizzi 1904-1945 *WhScrn 77*
Waldo, Elisabeth 1923- *AmSCAP 80*
Waldo, Janet *ForYSC, WhoHol A*
Waldo, Ralph Emerson, III 1944- *AmSCAP 80*
Waldorf, Wilella d1946 *NotNAT B*
Waldorff, Jerzy 1910- *NewGrD 80*
Waldow, Ernst 1894-1964 *NotNAT B, WhScrn 74, -77*
Waldridge, Harold *Film 2*
Waldridge, Herbert d1957 *WhoHol B*
Waldrige, Harold 1905-1957 *WhScrn 74, -77*
Waldron, Andrew *Film 1*
Waldron, Charles 1877-1946 *ForYSC*
Waldron, Charles D 1874-1946 *Film 1, -2, NotNAT B, WhScrn 74, -77, WhThe, WhoHol B*
Waldron, Charles K 1915-1952 *WhScrn 74, -77, WhoHol B*
Waldron, Edna 1913-1940 *WhScrn 74, -77*
Waldron, Francis Godolphin d1818 *NotNAT B*
Waldron, Gary *ConMuA 80B*
Waldron, Georgia 1872-1950 *NotNAT B*
Waldron, Isabel 1871-1950 *WhScrn 74, -77*
Waldron, Jack 1893- *BiE&WWA*
Waldron, Jack 1893-1967 *WhoHol B*
Waldron, Jack 1893-1969 *NotNAT B, WhScrn 77*
Waldron, James A d1931 *NotNAT B*
Waldron, Mal 1926- *AmSCAP 66, EncJzS 70, IlEncJ*
Waldron, Malcolm Earl 1926- *EncJzS 70*
Waldrop, Gid 1919- *Baker 78, BiE&WWA*
Waldrop, Gideon William, Jr. 1919- *AmSCAP 66, -80, ConAmC*
Waldstein, Ferdinand E J G, Count Von 1762-1823 *Baker 78, NewGrD 80*
Waldteufel, Emil 1837-1915 *Baker 78, DancEn 78, OxMus*
Waldteufel, Emile 1837-1915 *BnBkM 80, MusMk, NewGrD 80*
Wale, Reginald George 1925- *IntWWM 77, -80*
Walenn, Charles R d1948 *NotNAT B*
Walensky, Dana Grant 1948- *ConAmC*
Wales, Bert *Film 2*
Wales, Clarke H *IntMPA 75, -76*
Wales, Ethel 1881-1952 *Film 2, ForYSC, TwYS, WhScrn 74, -77, WhoHol B*
Wales, Roy Frederick 1940- *WhoMus 72*
Wales, Wally *FilmEn, Film 2, ForYSC, TwYS*
Waley, Simon 1827-1875 *Baker 78*
Walford, Ann 1928- *WhThe*
Wali, Mustafa *WomWMM*
Walk, Winfried 1931- *WhoOp 76*
Walkeley, Anthony 1672-1718 *NewGrD 80*
Walken, Christopher 1943- *FilmEn, HalFC 80, IntMPA 80, NotNAT, WhoHol A, WhoThe 77*
Walker, Aaron 1909-1975 *EncJzS 70*
Walker, Aaron Thibeaux 1910-1975 *BiDAmM, BluesWW[port], NewGrD 80*
Walker, Ada Overton 1880-1914 *DrBlPA*
Walker, Agnes T *IntWWM 77, -80, WhoMus 72*
Walker, Aida Overton 1870-1914 *BlksBF[port]*
Walker, Alan 1930- *IntWWM 80, NewGrD 80*
Walker, Allan 1906- *AmSCAP 66, -80*
Walker, Mrs. Allan *Film 1*
Walker, Antoinette *Film 1*
Walker, Arlene 1919-1973 *WhScrn 77*
Walker, Arthur Dennis 1932- *IntWWM 77, -80, WhoMus 72*
Walker, Aurora 1912-1964 *WhScrn 77*
Walker, Bee *AmSCAP 80*
Walker, Ben *Film 2*
Walker, Bertha 1908- *AmSCAP 66*
Walker, Betty *WhoHol A*
Walker, Betty Stoller 1940- *IntWWM 77, -80*
Walker, Bill *DrBlPA, WhoHol A*
Walker, Billy 1809-1875 *BiDAmM*
Walker, Billy 1891-1927 *BlksBF*
Walker, Billy 1929- *CounME 74, -74A, IlEncCM[port]*
Walker, Billy Marvin 1929- *AmSCAP 80, BiDAmM, EncFCWM 69*
Walker, Bob 1918-1951 *NotNAT B*
Walker, Bon 1894- *AmSCAP 66*
Walker, Cardon E 1916- *IntMPA 77, -75, -76, -78, -79, -80*
Walker, Catherine *Film 2*
Walker, Charles 1922-1975 *BluesWW[port]*
Walker, Charlie 1926- *BiDAmM, CounME 74[port], -74A, EncFCWM 69, IlEncCM[port]*
Walker, Charlotte 1878-1958 *FilmEn, Film 1, -2, FilmgC, ForYSC, HalFC 80, NotNAT B, TwYS, WhScrn 74, -77, WhThe, WhoHol B, WhoStg 1906, -1908*
Walker, Cheryl 1920- *ForYSC*
Walker, Cheryl 1922-1971 *MotPP, WhScrn 77, WhoHol B*
Walker, Chester W d1945 *WhScrn 77*
Walker, Christopher John Albert 1948- *IntWWM 77*
Walker, Christy 1898-1918 *WhScrn 77*
Walker, Cindy *BiDAmM, EncFCWM 69*
Walker, Clint 1927- *FilmEn, FilmgC, ForYSC, HalFC 80, IntMPA 77, -75, -76, -78, -79, -80, MotPP, WhoHol A*
Walker, Clyde Phillip 1944- *IntWWM 77, -80*
Walker, D P 1914- *NewGrD 80*
Walker, Danton d1960 *NotNAT B*
Walker, David 1934- *WhoOp 76*
Walker, David Pat 1928- *IntMPA 80*
Walker, Don 1907- *BiE&WWA, ConAmC, NotNAT*
Walker, Donald John 1907- *AmSCAP 66, -80*
Walker, Douglas Odell 1949- *AmSCAP 80*
Walker, Drake 1936- *BlkAmP*
Walker, Edward 1909- *IntWWM 77, -80, WhoMus 72*
Walker, Edyth 1867-1950 *Baker 78, CmOp, NewEOp 71, NewGrD 80*
Walker, Edyth 1870-1950 *BiDAmM*
Walker, Elbert 1921- *IntMPA 75, -76*
Walker, Eldon 1932- *IntWWM 80*
Walker, Elizabeth *WhoMus 72*
Walker, Elizabeth Tippy *WhoHol A*
Walker, Ernest 1870-1949 *Baker 78, NewGrD 80, OxMus*
Walker, Evan *BlkAmP, MorBAP*
Walker, Fiona *WhoHol A*
Walker, Frank 1907-1962 *Baker 78, NewGrD 80*
Walker, Frank Buckley 1889-1963 *EncFCWM 69*
Walker, Geoffrey Henry 1948- *IntWWM 80*
Walker, George *BlkAmP, Film 2, MorBAP, OxMus*
Walker, George 1922- *Baker 78, BiDAmM, ConAmC, NewGrD 80*
Walker, George F 1947- *ConDr 77*
Walker, George Theophilus 1922- *AmSCAP 80, BlkCS[port], DrBlPA, IntWWM 77, -80*
Walker, George W 1873-1911 *BiDAmM, DrBlPA*
Walker, Gerald Alan 1947- *IntWWM 77, -80*
Walker, Gertrude *WomWMM B*
Walker, Goodwin *WhoMus 72*
Walker, Gwyneth VanAnden 1947- *CpmDNM 80*
Walker, H M *HalFC 80*
Walker, Hal 1896-1972 *FilmEn, FilmgC, HalFC 80*
Walker, Harry H *PupTheA*
Walker, Helen 1920-1968 *FilmEn*
Walker, Helen 1921-1968 *FilmgC, ForYSC, HalFC 80, MotPP, WhScrn 74, -77, WhoHol B*
Walker, Horatio 1858-1938 *CreCan 2*
Walker, James 1905- *BluesWW[port]*
Walker, James 1929- *IntWWM 77, -80, WhoMus 72*
Walker, James 1937- *CpmDNM 72, ConAmC*
Walker, James John 1846-1922 *NewGrD 80*
Walker, James John 1881-1946 *AmSCAP 66, -80, BiDAmM*
Walker, Jeanine Ogletree 1942- *AmSCAP 80*
Walker, Jerry Jeff 1942- *ConMuA 80A, IlEncCM, IlEncR, RkOn 2[port]*
Walker, Jim Daddy James 1912?-1949 *WhoJazz 72*
Walker, Jimmie 1949- *DrBlPA, WhoHol A*
Walker, Jimmy *AmSCAP 80, JoeFr[port]*
Walker, Jo 1924- *ConMuA 80B, EncFCWM 69*
Walker, John *Film 2*
Walker, John 1732-1807 *Baker 78*
Walker, John A 1916- *BiE&WWA*
Walker, John Edward 1933- *WhoOp 76*
Walker, John Mayon 1929- *BluesWW[port]*
Walker, Johnnie 1894-1949 *FilmEn, Film 1, -2, ForYSC, TwYS*
Walker, Johnnie 1896-1949 *WhScrn 74, -77, WhoHol B*
Walker, Johnny 1894-1949 *NotNAT B*
Walker, Johnny Gordon 1947- *AmSCAP 80*
Walker, Joseph 1892- *FilmEn, FilmgC, HalFC 80, IntMPA 77, -75, -76, -78, -79, -80*
Walker, Joseph 1902- *WorEFlm*
Walker, Joseph A 1935- *BlkAmP, ConDr 77, DrBlPA, NotNAT, PlP&P A*
Walker, Joseph Cooper 1760-1810 *Baker 78*
Walker, Joseph Cooper 1761-1810 *NewGrD 80*
Walker, Joseph H 1935- *MorBAP*
Walker, Joseph William d1870 *NewGrD 80*
Walker, Joyce *WhoHol A*
Walker, Judith Ann 1946- *IntWWM 77*
Walker, June d1966 *Film 2, WhoHol B*
Walker, June 1899-1966 *BiE&WWA, NotNAT B*
Walker, June 1900-1966 *ForYSC*
Walker, June 1904-1966 *PlP&P, WhScrn 74, -77, WhThe*
Walker, Junior & The All Stars *RkOn 2[port]*
Walker, Laura d1951 *NotNAT B*
Walker, Lillian 1887-1975 *FilmEn*
Walker, Lillian 1888-1975 *Film 1, -2, MotPP, TwYS, WhScrn 77, WhoHol C*
Walker, Mallory Elton 1935- *WhoOp 76*
Walker, Mark Fesler 1918- *AmSCAP 80, ConAmC*
Walker, Martin 1901-1955 *NotNAT B, WhThe, WhoHol B*
Walker, Martin 1938- *IntMPA 77, -75, -76, -78, -79, -80*
Walker, Mary Lu 1926- *AmSCAP 80*
Walker, Michael *WhoHol A*
Walker, Michael Ernest John 1932- *IntWWM 77, WhoMus 72*
Walker, Mickey *What 2[port]*
Walker, Nancy *MotPP, NewYTET, WhoHol A*
Walker, Nancy 1921- *EncMT, HalFC 80, WhoThe 77*
Walker, Nancy 1922- *BiE&WWA, CmpEPM, ForYSC, IntMPA 78, -79, -80, MovMk, NotNAT, WhoThe 72*
Walker, Nella *ForYSC, HalFC 80*
Walker, Nella 1880?-1971 *FilmEn*
Walker, Nella 1886-1971 *Film 2, HolCA[port], ThFT[port], WhScrn 77*
Walker, Nina *WhoMus 72*
Walker, Norman 1892- *FilmEn, FilmgC, HalFC 80, IlWWBF*
Walker, Norman 1907-1963 *NewGrD 80*
Walker, Norman 1934- *CmpGMD, CnOxB, DancEn 78[port]*
Walker, Paul *Film 2*
Walker, Paul A d1965 *NewYTET*
Walker, Penelope 1956- *IntWWM 80*
Walker, Pete 1935- *HalFC 80, IlWWBF*
Walker, Peter *WhoHol A*
Walker, Phillip 1937- *BluesWW[port]*
Walker, Phyllis Mathewson *WhoMus 72*
Walker, Polly 1908- *Film 2, WhThe*
Walker, Ray *ForYSC*
Walker, Raymond 1883-1960 *AmSCAP 66*
Walker, Raymond 1935- *AmSCAP 80*

Walker, Richard 1912- *ConAmC*
Walker, Richard Link 1940- *IntWWM 77, -80*
Walker, Robert d1951 *MotPP*
Walker, Robert 1914-1951 *FilmgC, HalFC 80, MovMk[port], WhScrn 74, -77*
Walker, Robert 1918-1951 *BiDFilm, -81, FilmEn, NotNAT B, OxFilm, WorEFlm*
Walker, Robert 1919-1951 *ForYSC, MGM[port], WhoHol B*
Walker, Robert 1941- *FilmgC, HalFC 80, MotPP, WhoHol A*
Walker, Robert, Jr. 1940- *FilmEn, ForYSC*
Walker, Robert Charles 1944- *WhoOp 76*
Walker, Robert Donald 1888-1954 *Film 1, MotPP, WhScrn 77*
Walker, Robert E 1942- *AmSCAP 80*
Walker, Robert S 1935- *ConAmC*
Walker, Rose 1907-1951 *WhScrn 74, -77*
Walker, Sandra 1946- *IntWWM 80, WhoOp 76*
Walker, Sarah 1945- *IntWWM 77, -80, WhoOp 76*
Walker, Saunders *MorBAP*
Walker, Stuart 1887-1941 *FilmEn, HalFC 80*
Walker, Stuart 1888-1941 *FilmgC, NotNAT B, WhThe*
Walker, Syd d1945 *WhScrn 74, -77, WhoHol B*
Walker, Syd 1886-1945 *NotNAT B, WhThe*
Walker, Syd 1887-1945 *FilmgC, HalFC 80*
Walker, Sydney 1921- *WhoHol A, WhoThe 77*
Walker, T-Bone *BluesWW*
Walker, T-Bone 1909-1975 *EncJzS 70, IlEncJ, WhoJazz 72*
Walker, T-Bone 1910-1975 *NewGrD 80*
Walker, T-Bone, Jr. *BluesWW*
Walker, Tex 1867-1947 *WhScrn 74, -77*
Walker, Thomas 1698-1744 *NewGrD 80, NotNAT B*
Walker, Thomas 1851-1934 *NotNAT A*
Walker, Tommy 1922- *AmSCAP 66, -80*
Walker, Valerie 1928- *WhoMus 72*
Walker, Vernon 1894-1948 *FilmEn*
Walker, Virginia 1916-1946 *WhScrn 74, -77, WhoHol B*
Walker, Wally 1901-1975 *WhoHol C*
Walker, Walter 1864-1947 *WhScrn 77*
Walker, Walter 1901-1975 *WhScrn 77*
Walker, Wayne Paul 1925- *BiDAmM, EncFCWM 69*
Walker, Whimsical 1851-1934 *Ent*
Walker, William *WhoHol A*
Walker, William 1809-1875 *NewGrD 80*
Walker, William 1931- *IntWWM 80, WhoOp 76*
Walker, William A *BlkAmP*
Walker, William Jeffrie 1949- *AmSCAP 80*
Walker, William Stearns 1917- *AmSCAP 66, -80*
Walker, Willie 1896-1933 *BluesWW[port]*
Walker, Zena *WhoHol A*
Walker, Zena 1934- *WhoThe 72, -77*
Walker, Zena 1935- *FilmgC, HalFC 80*
Walker And Reedie *PupTheA*
Walker And Wood *PupTheA*
Walker Brothers, The *BiDAmM, RkOn 2[port]*
Walker-Malcoskey, Edna *AmSCAP 66, -80*
Walkes, W R d1913 *NotNAT B*
Walkin' Slim *BluesWW*
Walklett, George 1890- *WhoMus 72*
Walkley, A B 1855-1926 *EncWT*
Walkley, Alfred Bingham 1855-1926 *OxThe, PlP&P*
Walkley, Arthur Bingham 1855-1926 *NotNAT B, WhThe*
Walkov, Samuel 1917- *AmSCAP 80*
Walkowitz, Abraham 1880-1965 *DancEn 78*
Walkup, Fairfax Proudfit 1887- *BiE&WWA*
Wall, Anita *WhoHol A*
Wall, Ashley Graingér 1945- *IntWWM 77, -80, WhoMus 72*
Wall, David 1946- *CnOxB*
Wall, David V 1870-1938 *WhScrn 74, -77, WhoHol B*
Wall, Geraldine 1913-1970 *WhScrn 74, -77, WhoHol B*
Wall, Harry 1886-1966 *WhThe*
Wall, Max 1908- *Ent, WhoThe 72, -77*
Wall, Rem 1918- *BiDAmM*
Wallace, Alfred *PupTheA*
Wallace, Art *WhoHol A*
Wallace, Beryl 1910-1948 *WhScrn 74, -77, WhoHol B*
Wallace, Beulah 1898- *BluesWW[port]*
Wallace, Bill 1908-1956 *WhScrn 74, -77*
Wallace, Charles 1930- *IntMPA 77, -75, -76, -78, -79, -80*
Wallace, Chris 1934- *AmSCAP 66, -80*
Wallace, David d1955 *NotNAT B*
Wallace, Dorothy *Film 1, -2*
Wallace, Mrs. Edgar d1933 *NotNAT B*
Wallace, Edgar Horatio 1875-1932 *EncWT, Ent, FilmgC, HalFC 80, IlWWBF A, NotNAT A, -B, OxThe, WhThe, WhoHrs 80*
Wallace, Edna *WhScrn 74, -77*
Wallace, Emett Babe 1909- *AmSCAP 80*
Wallace, Ethel Lee 1888-1956 *WhScrn 74, -77, WhoHol B*
Wallace, George 1894-1960 *WhScrn 74, -77, WhoHol B*
Wallace, George 1924- *BiE&WWA, NotNAT, WhoHol A*
Wallace, Gia *PupTheA SUP*
Wallace, Grace *Film 2*
Wallace, Guy 1913-1967 *WhScrn 77*
Wallace, Hazel Vincent 1919- *WhoThe 72, -77*
Wallace, Ian 1919- *CmOp, IntWWM 77, -80, NewGrD 80, WhoMus 72*
Wallace, Inez d1966 *WhScrn 74, -77, WhoHol B*
Wallace, Irene *Film 1, MotPP*
Wallace, Irving 1916- *FilmEn, IntMPA 77, -75, -76, -78, -79, -80*
Wallace, Jack *WhoHol A*
Wallace, Jack Leslie 1909- *WhoMus 72*
Wallace, Jean *MotPP, WhoHol A*
Wallace, Jean 1923- *FilmEn, FilmgC, HalFC 80, MovMk*
Wallace, Jean 1927?- *ForYSC*
Wallace, Jean 1930- *IntMPA 77, -75, -76, -78, -79, -80*
Wallace, Jerry *AmPS A*
Wallace, Jerry 1933- *IlEncCM*
Wallace, Jerry 1938- *RkOn[port]*
Wallace, Jerry Leon 1928- *AmSCAP 80*
Wallace, John *Film 2*
Wallace, John Wesley 1914- *AmSCAP 80*
Wallace, Judy *WhoHol A*
Wallace, Katherine *Film 2*
Wallace, Kathryn 1917- *ConAmC*
Wallace, Lea *PupTheA SUP*
Wallace, Lee *WhoHol A*
Wallace, Lewis 1827-1905 *NotNAT B*
Wallace, Linda *WomWMM B*
Wallace, Louise Chapman d1962 *NotNAT B, WhoHol B*
Wallace, Lucille 1898-1977 *NewGrD 80*
Wallace, Marcia *WhoHol A*
Wallace, Maude 1894-1952 *WhScrn 74, -77, WhoHol B*
Wallace, May 1877-1938 *Film 2, WhScrn 74, -77, WhoHol B*
Wallace, Mike 1918- *IntMPA 77, -75, -76, -78, -79, -80, NewYTET*
Wallace, Mildred White *AmSCAP 66, -80*
Wallace, Milton 1888-1956 *WhScrn 74, -77, WhoHol B*
Wallace, Morgan d1953 *NotNAT B, WhoHol B*
Wallace, Morgan 1885-1953 *Film 2, ForYSC, TwYS*
Wallace, Morgan 1888-1953 *WhScrn 74, -77*
Wallace, Nellie d1933 *NotNAT B*
Wallace, Nellie 1870-1948 *EncWT, Ent, NotNAT B, OxThe*
Wallace, Nellie 1882-1948 *WhThe*
Wallace, Oliver George 1887-1963 *AmSCAP 66, -80*
Wallace, Paul 1938- *BiE&WWA, NotNAT, WhoHol A*
Wallace, Paul J 1928- *IntWWM 80*
Wallace, Ramsey *Film 2*
Wallace, Ratch *WhoHol A*
Wallace, Ray 1881- *WhThe*
Wallace, Regina *BiE&WWA, WhoHol A*
Wallace, Richard 1894-1951 *FilmEn, FilmgC, HalFC 80, TwYS A*
Wallace, Robert William 1945- *IntWWM 77, -80*
Wallace, Royce 1923?- *DrBlPA, WhoHol A*
Wallace, Rudy *BlkAmP, MorBAP*
Wallace, Sippie 1898- *WhoJazz 72*
Wallace, Vince 1939- *EncJzS 70*
Wallace, Vincent 1812-1865 *CmOp, MusMk, NewGrD 80[port]*
Wallace, William 1860-1940 *Baker 78, NewGrD 80, OxMus*
Wallace, William Vincent 1812-1865 *Baker 78, DcCom 77, OxMus*
Wallace, William Walter 1923- *AmSCAP 80*
Wallach, Allan Henry 1927- *ConAmTC*
Wallach, Edgar d1953 *NotNAT B*
Wallach, Eli 1915- *BiE&WWA, CnThe, FilmEn, FilmgC, ForYSC, HalFC 80, IntMPA 77, -75, -76, -78, -79, -80, MotPP, MovMk[port], NotNAT, OxFilm, PlP&P[port], WhoHol A, WhoThe 72, -77, WorEFlm*
Wallach, George *IntMPA 77, -75, -76, -78, -79, -80*
Wallach, Henry John 1790-1870 *PlP&P*
Wallach, Ira Jan 1913- *AmSCAP 66, -80, BiE&WWA, NotNAT*
Wallach, Lew *WhoHol A*
Wallack, Arthur J d1940 *NotNAT B*
Wallack, Edwin N *Film 2*
Wallack, Mrs. Henry J d1860 *NotNAT B*
Wallack, Henry John 1790-1870 *EncWT, FamA&A[port], NotNAT B, OxThe*
Wallack, Mrs. J W, Jr. d1879 *NotNAT B*
Wallack, James William 1791-1864 *NotNAT A, -B, PlP&P*
Wallack, James William 1794-1864 *OxThe*
Wallack, James William 1795-1864 *EncWT, FamA&A[port]*
Wallack, James William, Jr. 1818-1873 *FamA&A[port], NotNAT B, OxThe*
Wallack, Jim 1818-1873 *EncWT*
Wallack, John Johnstone 1819-1888 *OxThe*
Wallack, Lester 1819-1888 *FamA&A[port], NotNAT B*
Wallack, Lester 1820-1888 *EncWT, NotNAT A, PlP&P*
Wallack, Mrs. Lester d1909 *NotNAT B*
Wallack, Mrs. William d1850 *NotNAT B*
Wallacks, Clara *Film 2*
Wallaschek, Richard 1860-1917 *Baker 78, NewGrD 80*
Wallat, Hans *WhoOp 76*
Wallberg, Heinz 1923- *WhoOp 76*
Walleck, Anna *Film 2*
Wallek-Walewski, Boleslaw 1885-1944 *NewGrD 80*
Wallen, Martti *IntWWM 80*
Wallen, Sigurd 1884-1947 *WhScrn 74, -77*
Wallenda, Carl 1905-1978 *Ent[port]*
Wallenda, Yetta d1963 *NotNAT B*
Wallenstein, Alfred 1898- *Baker 78, BiDAmM, MusSN[port], NewGrD 80*
Wallenstein, Martin 1843-1896 *Baker 78*
Waller, Charles 1935- *BiDAmM*
Waller, Charlie *EncFCWM 69*
Waller, D W d1882 *NotNAT B*
Waller, Mrs. D W 1820-1899 *NotNAT B*
Waller, David 1920- *WhoHol A, WhoThe 72, -77*
Waller, Eddie *ForYSC*
Waller, Eddy *Vers B[port], WhoHol A*
Waller, Edmund Lewis 1884- *WhThe*
Waller, Emma 1820-1899 *FamA&A[port], OxThe*
Waller, Fats 1904-1943 *AmPS B, Baker 78, CmpEPM, DrBlPA, FilmgC, HalFC 80, IlEncJ, NewGrD 80, NotNAT B, PopAmC[port], WhoHol B, WhoJazz 72*
Waller, Florence West 1862-1912 *OxThe*
Waller, Fred 1886-1954 *DcFM, FilmEn, FilmgC, HalFC 80*
Waller, J Wallet d1951 *NotNAT B*
Waller, Jack 1885-1957 *NotNAT B, WhThe*
Waller, Juanita 1939- *WhoOp 76*
Waller, Lewis 1860-1915 *CnThe, Film 1, -2, NotNAT B, OxThe, WhThe*
Waller, Mrs. Lewis 1862-1912 *NotNAT B, WhThe*
Waller, Ronald William 1916- *IntWWM 77, -80, WhoMus 72*

Waller, Thomas 1904-1943 *AmPS, AmSCAP 66, -80, BiDAmM, MusMk[port], NewGrD 80, Sw&Ld C, WhScrn 74, -77*
Waller, Thomas 1905-1943 *BlksBF[port]*
Wallerstein *NewGrD 80*
Wallerstein, Anton 1813-1892 *Baker 78, NewGrD 80*
Wallerstein, Lothar 1882-1949 *Baker 78, CmOp, NewEOp 71*
Walleshauser, Johann Evangelist *NewGrD 80*
Walley, Deborah 1943- *ForYSC, MotPP, WhoHol A*
Wallfisch, Ernst 1920- *WhoMus 72*
Wallfisch, Peter 1924- *IntWWM 77, -80, WhoMus 72*
Wallin, Bengt-Arne 1926- *EncJzS 70*
Walling, Effie B 1879-1961 *WhScrn 74, -77*
Walling, Richard *Film 2*
Walling, Roy d1964 *NotNAT B*
Walling, Will R *Film 2*
Wallington, Billie Henry 1927- *AmSCAP 66*
Wallington, Billie June 1934- *AmSCAP 80*
Wallington, George 1923- *AmSCAP 66, -80*
Wallington, George 1924- *CmpEPM, IlEncJ*
Wallington, Jimmy 1907-1972 *WhScrn 77, WhoHol B*
Wallis, Bella d1960 *NotNAT B*
Wallis, Bertram 1874-1952 *NotNAT B, WhThe, WhoHol B*
Wallis, Delia 1946- *WhoMus 72*
Wallis, Ellen Lancaster 1856-1940 *WhThe*
Wallis, Gladys d1953 *NotNAT B*
Wallis, Hal B *IntMPA 77, -75, -76, -78, -79, -80*
Wallis, Hal B 1898- *BiDFilm, -81, FilmgC, HalFC 80, OxFilm*
Wallis, Hal B 1899- *FilmEn, WorEFlm*
Wallis, Hank *AmSCAP 80*
Wallis, John 1616-1703 *NewGrD 80*
Wallis, Shani *WhoHol A*
Wallis, Shani 1933- *WhThe, WhoThe 72*
Wallis, Shani 1938- *FilmgC, HalFC 80*
Wallis, W Allen *NewYTET*
Walliser, Christoph Thomas 1568-1648 *NewGrD 80*
Wallishauser, Johann Evangelist *NewGrD 80*
Wallisser, Christoph Thomas 1568-1648 *NewGrD 80*
Wallman, Lawrence A 1902- *BiE&WWA, NotNAT*
Wallman, Margaret *DancEn 78*
Wallmann, Margarethe 1904- *CnOxB*
Wallmann, Margarita 1914- *WhoOp 76*
Wallmann, Margherita *WhoMus 72*
Wallmann, Margherita 1904- *CmOp, NewEOp 71*
Wallner, Bertha Antonia 1876-1956 *NewGrD 80*
Wallner, Bo 1923- *NewGrD 80*
Wallnofer, Adolf 1854-1946 *Baker 78*
Wallock, Edwin N 1878-1951 *Film 1, WhScrn 77*
Wallop, Douglass 1920- *BiE&WWA, NotNAT*
Wallowitch, John 1930- *AmSCAP 80*
Walls, Betty Duke 1941- *AmSCAP 80*
Walls, Byron Robert 1937- *AmSCAP 66, -80*
Walls, Geoffrey 1925- *IntWWM 77, -80, WhoMus 72*
Walls, Robert Boen 1910- *AmSCAP 66, -80, ConAmC A, IntWWM 77, -80*
Walls, Tom 1883-1949 *FilmAG WE, FilmEn, FilmgC, HalFC 80, IlWWBF, NotNAT B, WhScrn 74, -77, WhThe, WhoHol B*
Wallschlaeger, Dean Andre 1953- *AmSCAP 80*
Wally, Gus 1904-1966 *WhScrn 74, -77, WhoHol B*
Walmer, Cassie 1888- *WhThe*
Walmisley, Thomas Attwood 1814-1856 *Baker 78, NewGrD 80, OxMus*
Walmisley, Thomas Forbes 1783-1866 *Baker 78, NewGrD 80, OxMus*
Walmsley, Dew Drop *BlkAmP*
Walmsley, Jon *WhoHol A*
Walmsley, Peter *NewGrD 80*
Waln, Ronald Lee 1931- *IntWWM 77, -80*
Walond, George *OxMus*
Walond, Richard *OxMus*
Walond, William d1836 *OxMus*
Walond, William 1725?-1770? *NewGrD 80, OxMus*
Walonis *NewGrD 80*
Walpen *NewGrD 80*
Walpen, Georg 1810- *NewGrD 80*
Walpen, Johannes Martin 1723-1787? *NewGrD 80*
Walpen, Johannes Sylvester 1767-1837 *NewGrD 80*
Walpen, Joseph Ignatius 1761-1836 *NewGrD 80*
Walpen, Sylvester 1802-1857 *NewGrD 80*
Walpen, Wendelin 1774- *NewGrD 80*
Walper, Cicely *WhoHol A*
Walpole, Sir Hugh Seymour 1884-1941 *FilmgC, HalFC 80, NotNAT B, WhScrn 74, -77, WhThe, WhoHol B, WorEFlm*
Walpole, Marjorie 1909- *IntWWM 77, WhoMus 72*
Walpole, Sir Robert 1676-1745 *OxMus, PlP&P*
Walrath, Jack Arthur 1946- *EncJzS 70*
Walrond, Winifred Olive 1919- *IntWWM 77*
Walser, Martin 1927- *CnMD, CroCD, EncWT, McGEWD, ModWD*
Walsh, Alida *WomWMM B*
Walsh, Anthony *WhoHol A*
Walsh, Arthur *WhoHol A*
Walsh, Bill *IntMPA 75*
Walsh, Bill d1975 *NewYTET*
Walsh, Bill 1913-1975 *AmSCAP 66*
Walsh, Bill 1914-1975 *FilmEn*
Walsh, Bill 1918-1975 *FilmgC*
Walsh, Bill 1918-1976 *HalFC 80*
Walsh, Billy d1952 *WhScrn 74, -77*
Walsh, Blanche d1915 *WhoHol B*
Walsh, Blanche 1873-1915 *FamA&A[port], Film 1, NotNAT B, WhThe, WhoStg 1906, -1908*
Walsh, Blanche 1874-1915 *WhScrn 77*
Walsh, Bryan *WhoHol A*
Walsh, Daniel 1948- *AmSCAP 80*
Walsh, David M *FilmEn, FilmgC, HalFC 80*
Walsh, Deirdre *WomWMM B*
Walsh, Dermot 1924- *FilmgC, HalFC 80, IlWWBF[port], IntMPA 77, -75, -76, -78, -79, -80, WhoHol A*
Walsh, Edward *WhoHol A*
Walsh, Felix *Film 1*
Walsh, Frank 1860-1932 *WhScrn 77*
Walsh, Frank 1860-1935 *Film 2*
Walsh, Frederick G 1915- *BiE&WWA, NotNAT*
Walsh, George 1892- *FilmEn, Film 1, -2, ForYSC, TwYS, WhoHol A*
Walsh, Gwenifer Ellis 1906- *WhoMus 72*
Walsh, Henry *OxMus*
Walsh, Henry H 1906- *AmSCAP 66, -80*
Walsh, J B *Film 2*
Walsh, Joe *ConMuA 80A[port], IlEncR, RkOn 2[port]*
Walsh, Joey *WhoHol A*
Walsh, John d1736 *OxMus*
Walsh, John d1766 *OxMus*
Walsh, John 1665?-1736 *NewGrD 80*
Walsh, John 1666?-1736 *Baker 78*
Walsh, John 1709-1766 *Baker 78, NewGrD 80*
Walsh, Joseph Fidler 1947- *AmSCAP 80*
Walsh, Kay 1914- *FilmAG WE, FilmEn, FilmgC, ForYSC, HalFC 80, IlWWBF, WhoHol A*
Walsh, Kay 1915- *IntMPA 77, -75, -76, -78, -79, -80, MovMk*
Walsh, Leslie Arrand 1910- *WhoMus 72*
Walsh, Lionel 1876-1916 *NotNAT B, WhoStg 1908*
Walsh, M Emmet *WhoHol A*
Walsh, Michael A 1949- *ConAmC*
Walsh, Paul 1951- *ConAmTC*
Walsh, Pauline 1906- *AmSCAP 66, -80*
Walsh, Raoul 1887- *BiDFilm, -81, FilmEn, FilmgC, HalFC 80, WhoHol A*
Walsh, Raoul 1889- *CmMov, DcFM, Film 1, -2, TwYS*
Walsh, Raoul 1892- *AmFD, CmMov, IntMPA 77, -75, -76, -78, -79, -80, MovMk[port], OxFilm, TwYS A, WorEFlm*
Walsh, Richard F 1900- *IntMPA 77, -75, -76, -78, -79, -80*
Walsh, Richard Terence 1940- *IntWWM 77*
Walsh, Sam 1877-1920 *NotNAT B, WhThe*
Walsh, Sean *WhoHol A*
Walsh, Stephen 1942- *NewGrD 80, WhoMus 72*
Walsh, Thomas 1941- *WhoMus 72*
Walsh, Thomas H 1863-1925 *NotNAT B, WhScrn 74, -77, WhoHol B*
Walsh, Thomas J d1962 *NotNAT B*
Walsh, Tom *Film 1*
Walsh, William *WhoHol A*
Walsh, William E 1922- *IntMPA 75, -76*
Walsingham, Thomas d1422? *NewGrD 80*
Walston, Ray *MotPP, WhoHol A*
Walston, Ray 1917- *FilmgC, HalFC 80, HolCA[port], WhoThe 72, -77*
Walston, Ray 1918- *BiE&WWA, FilmEn, ForYSC, IntMPA 77, -75, -76, -78, -79, -80, MovMk, NotNAT*
Walsworth, Bertha *PupTheA*
Walsworth, Ivor 1909- *WhoMus 72*
Walt, Edward John 1877-1951 *AmSCAP 66, -80*
Walta, Jaring Douwe 1941- *IntWWM 77, -80*
Waltemeyer, Jack *Film 1*
Walter *BluesWW[port]*
Walter Of Chatillon 1135?-1190? *NewGrD 80*
Walter Of Evesham *OxMus*
Walter, Anne B *WomWMM B*
Walter, Anton 1752-1826 *NewGrD 80*
Walter, Arnold 1902-1973 *Baker 78, CreCan 1, NewGrD 80*
Walter, Bruno 1876-1962 *Baker 78, BiDAmM, BnBkM 80[port], CmOp[port], ConAmC, MusMk, MusSN[port], NewEOp 71, NewGrD 80[port], NotNAT B, OxMus*
Walter, Cy 1925- *AmSCAP 66*
Walter, Cy 1925-1968 *CmpEPM*
Walter, Cy 1925-1969 *AmSCAP 80*
Walter, Cyril F 1915-1968 *BiDAmM*
Walter, Edwin d1953 *NotNAT B*
Walter, Erich 1927- *CnOxB, DancEn 78*
Walter, Eugene 1874-1941 *McGEWD, ModWD, NotNAT B, OxThe, WhThe*
Walter, Eugene Ferdinand 1923- *AmSCAP 80, PupTheA*
Walter, Franz 1907- *IntWWM 77, -80*
Walter, Fried 1907- *Baker 78, WhoMus 72*
Walter, Friedrich Wilhelm 1870-1956 *Baker 78*
Walter, Georg A 1875-1952 *Baker 78*
Walter, George William 1851-1911 *Baker 78, NewGrD 80*
Walter, Harry *Film 2*
Walter, Horst 1931- *IntWWM 77, -80*
Walter, Ignaz 1755-1822 *NewGrD 80*
Walter, Jerome *EncFCWM 69*
Walter, Jessica *IntMPA 77, -75, -76, -78, -79, -80, WhoHol A*
Walter, Jessica 1940?- *FilmEn, ForYSC*
Walter, Jessica 1944- *FilmgC, HalFC 80*
Walter, Johann 1496-1570 *Baker 78, NewGrD 80*
Walter, Johann 1527-1578 *NewGrD 80*
Walter, Johannes 1496-1570 *NewGrD 80*
Walter, John 1660?-1708? *NewGrD 80*
Walter, Joseph 1755-1822 *NewGrD 80*
Walter, Karl 1862-1929 *Baker 78*
Walter, Little *BiDAmM*
Walter, Max Donald 1910- *AmSCAP 66*
Walter, Nancy 1939- *ConDr 73, -77*
Walter, Olive 1898- *WhThe*
Walter, Rosa *Film 2*
Walter, Samuel 1916- *ConAmC, IntWWM 77*
Walter, Serge 1896-1976 *AmSCAP 66, -80*
Walter, Thomas 1696-1725 *Baker 78, BiDAmM, NewGrD 80, OxMus*
Walter, Wilfred 1882-1958 *WhoHrs 80*
Walter, Wilfrid 1882-1958 *NotNAT B, WhScrn 77, WhThe*
Walter, William Henry 1825-1893 *BiDAmM*
Walter-Briant, Fredda 1912- *BiE&WWA, NotNAT*
Walter-Ellis, Desmond 1914- *WhoHol A, WhoThe 72, -77*
Walter Jones, Elias 1921- *IntWWM 77, -80*
Walterlin, Oskar 1895-1961 *EncWT*
Walters, Albert 1905- *NewOrJ*
Walters, Barbara 1931- *IntMPA 77, -76, -78, -79, -80, NewYTET*
Walters, Bob *ConMuA 80B*
Walters, Casey *WhoHol A*

Walters, Charles 1911- *BiDFilm, -81, CmMov, DcFM, EncMT, FilmEn, FilmgC, HalFC 80, IntMPA 77, -75, -76, -78, -79, -80, MovMk[port], WorEFlm*
Walters, Charles A 1941- *AmSCAP 80*
Walters, David L *AmSCAP 80*
Walters, Derek 1936- *WhoMus 72*
Walters, Dorothy 1877-1934 *Film 2, WhScrn 77*
Walters, Easter *Film 1*
Walters, Ethel *Film 2*
Walters, Frank 1915- *IntWWM 77, -80*
Walters, Gareth 1928- *IntWWM 77, -80*
Walters, Mrs. George B d1916 *WhScrn 77*
Walters, Glen *Film 2*
Walters, Harold 1918- *AmSCAP 80*
Walters, Harold L 1918 *AmSCAP 66, ConAmC*
Walters, Irwyn Ranald 1902- *IntWWM 77, -80, WhoMus 72*
Walters, Jack 1885-1944 *WhScrn 74, -77, WhoHol B*
Walters, Jess 1908- *IntWWM 77, -80*
Walters, Jess 1912- *CmOp*
Walters, John *Film 1*
Walters, Laura 1894-1934 *WhScrn 74, -77*
Walters, Leslie 1902- *WhoMus 72*
Walters, Luana *ForYSC*
Walters, Marrian *WhoHol A*
Walters, May *Film 1*
Walters, Michael J *ConAmC*
Walters, Norby *ConMuA 80B*
Walters, Patricia W d1967 *WhScrn 74, -77, WhoHol B*
Walters, Polly 1910- *MotPP, WhThe*
Walters, Robert William 1921- *AmSCAP 66, -80*
Walters, Thorley 1913- *FilmgC, HalFC 80, WhoHol A, WhoHrs 80, WhoThe 72, -77*
Walters, Walter H 1917- *BiE&WWA, NotNAT*
Walters, Wayne D 1926- *BiDAmM*
Walters, William *Film 1*
Waltershausen, H W S Von *OxMus*
Waltershausen, Hermann Wolfgang Von 1882-1954 *NewGrD 80*
Waltershausen, Wolfgang Von 1882-1954 *Baker 78*
Walterus De Otyngton *NewGrD 80*
Walthal, Anna Mae *Film 2*
Walthal, Henry B 1880-1936 *Film 2*
Walthall, Anna Mae *Film 1*
Walthall, Henry B d1936 *MotPP, WhoHol B*
Walthall, Henry B 1870-1936 *ForYSC, TwYS*
Walthall, Henry B 1878-1936 *FilmEn, FilmgC, HalFC 80, HolCA[port], MovMk, NotNAT B, OxFilm, WhScrn 74, -77, WhoHrs 80*
Walthall, Henry B 1880-1936 *Film 1, Vers B[port]*
Walther Von Der Vogelweide *Baker 78*
Walther Von Der Vogelweide 1165?-1230? *MusMk*
Walther Von Der Vogelweide 1170?-1230? *NewGrD 80[port]*
Walther, Gretchen *WhoHol A*
Walther, Ignaz *NewGrD 80*
Walther, Johann *NewGrD 80*
Walther, Johann 1496-1570 *OxMus*
Walther, Johann Gottfried 1684-1748 *Baker 78, BnBkM 80, NewGrD 80, OxMus*
Walther, Johann Jacob 1650- *OxMus*
Walther, Johann Jakob 1650-1717 *Baker 78, NewGrD 80*
Walther, Joseph *NewGrD 80*
Walthew, Richard Henry 1872-1951 *Baker 78, OxMus*
Waltmans, Marinus Jan Hubert 1929- *IntWWM 77, -80*
Walton, Bernard 1917- *WhoMus 72*
Walton, Cedar Anthony 1934- *EncJzS 70*
Walton, Douglas 1896-1961 *ForYSC, NotNAT B, WhScrn 74, -77, WhoHol B*
Walton, Florence *Film 1*
Walton, Fred 1865-1936 *Film 2, NotNAT B, WhScrn 74, -77, WhoHol B*
Walton, Gladys 1904- *Film 2, TwYS*
Walton, Greely 1905- *WhoJazz 72*
Walton, Henry *Film 2*
Walton, Herbert C d1954 *NotNAT B, WhoHol B*
Walton, Izaak 1593-1683 *OxMus*
Walton, J K d1928 *NotNAT B*
Walton, James Monroe 1923- *AmSCAP 80*
Walton, Jess *WhoHol A*
Walton, Kenneth E 1904- *AmSCAP 66, -80, ConAmC*
Walton, Lester A *BlksBF*
Walton, Mercy Dee 1915-1962 *BluesWW[port]*
Walton, Nigel David 1944- *IntWWM 77, -80*
Walton, Paul *PupTheA*
Walton, Peggy *WhoHol A*
Walton, Punch *PupTheA*
Walton, Richard 1913- *IntWWM 77, -80, WhoMus 72*
Walton, Rosemary Jean 1944- *IntWWM 77*
Walton, Tony 1934- *BiE&WWA, NotNAT, WhoThe 72, -77*
Walton, Vera 1891-1965 *WhScrn 74, -77, WhoHol B*
Walton, Vivian Beatrice 1934- *AmSCAP 80*
Walton, Wade 1923- *BluesWW[port]*
Walton, Sir William 1902- *Baker 78, BnBkM 80, CmOp, CompSN[port], CpmDNM 73, -80, DancEn 78, DcCom 77, DcCom&M 79, DcCM, DcFM, FilmEn, FilmgC, HalFC 80, IntWWM 77, -80, MusMk, NewEOp 71, NewGrD 80[port], OxFilm, OxMus, WhoMus 72, WorEFlm*
Waltz, Gustavus d1753? *Baker 78, CmOp, NewGrD 80[port]*
Waltz, Pat d1972 *WhoHol B*
Waltzer, Neil 1944- *IntWWM 77*
Walworth, Clarence Augustus 1820-1900 *BiDAmM*
Walworth, Mead 1902- *IntMPA 75, -76*
Walworth, Theodore H, Jr. *NewYTET*
Walzel, Leopold Matthias 1902-1970 *Baker 78, IntWWM 77, WhoMus 72*
Wambach, Emile 1854-1924 *Baker 78*
Wampus Baby Stars *Film 2*
Wamsley, Peter *NewGrD 80*
Wan, Sul Te, Madame 1873-1959 *DrBlPA, WhScrn 74, -77*
Wanamaker, Sam 1919- *BiE&WWA, CnThe, FilmEn, FilmgC, ForYSC, HalFC 80, IlWWBF, IntMPA 77, -75, -76, -78, -79, -80, MotPP, MovMk, NewYTET, NotNAT, WhoHol A, WhoThe 72, -77*
Wanausek, Camillo 1906- *NewGrD 80*
Wanczura, Arnost *NewGrD 80*
Wanczura, Ernest *NewGrD 80*
Wand, Gunter 1912- *NewGrD 80*
Wanderly, Walter *RkOn 2A*
Wanderman, Dorothy 1907- *AmSCAP 66, -80*
Wandtke, Harald 1939- *CnOxB*
Wang, Alfredo 1918- *IntWWM 77, -80, WhoMus 72*
Wang, An-Ming *AmSCAP 80*
Wang, Arthur W *BiE&WWA*
Wang, James *Film 2*
Wang, Juliana *WomWMM A, -B*
Wang, Ping *WomWMM*
Wang, Shih-Fu *REnWD[port]*
Wang, Stella 1897- *WhoMus 72*
Wang, Tso-Lin *DcFM*
Wang Mak, Marion *AmSCAP 80*
Wang Yu, Jimmy *HalFC 80*
Wangberg, Eirik Wilhelm 1944- *AmSCAP 80*
Wangel, Hedwig 1875-1961 *Film 2, WhScrn 74, -77, WhoHol B*
Wangemann, Otto 1848-1914 *Baker 78*
Wangenheim, Gustav Von 1895- *CnMD, Film 2*
Wangenheim, Volker 1928- *IntWWM 77, -80, NewGrD 80, WhoMus 72*
Wanger, Walter 1894-1968 *BiDFilm, -81, CmMov, DcFM, FilmEn, FilmgC, HalFC 80, OxFilm, WorEFlm*
Wangermann, Richard *Film 2*
Wangermee, Robert 1920- *NewGrD 80*
Wangnick, Johannes *NewGrD 80*
Wanhal, Johann Baptist 1739-1813 *Baker 78, NewGrD 80*
Wanhall, J B 1739-1813 *OxMus*
Waningus Campensis *NewGrD 80*
Waniura, Ceslav *NewGrD 80*
Wanjura, Ceslav *NewGrD 80*
Wanless, John *Baker 78*
Wanless, Thomas d1712 *NewGrD 80*
Wanless, Thomas 1928- *WhoMus 72*
Wann, James Creekmore, Jr. 1948- *AmSCAP 80*
Wannenmacher, Johannes 1485?-1551 *Baker 78, NewGrD 80*
Wanner, Hughes *WhoHol A*
Wanner, Paul 1896- *CnMD*
Wanning, Johannes 1537-1603 *NewGrD 80*
Wanshel, Jeff *NatPD[port]*
Wanski *NewGrD 80*
Wanski, Jan 1762-1821? *NewGrD 80*
Wanski, Jan Nepomucen 1782-1840 *NewGrD 80*
Wanski, Jean Nepomucene 1782-1840 *NewGrD 80*
Wanski, Roch 1780-1810 *NewGrD 80*
Wanskura, Arnost *NewGrD 80*
Wanskura, Ernest *NewGrD 80*
Wansura, Arnost *NewGrD 80*
Wansura, Ernest *NewGrD 80*
Wantanabe, Akeo 1919- *IntWWM 77, -80, WhoMus 72*
Wanzer, Arthur d1949 *WhScrn 74, -77, WhoHol B*
Wanzo, Mel 1930- *EncJzS 70*
Wanzura, Ceslav *NewGrD 80*
War *ConMuA 80A, IlEncR, RkOn 2[port]*
Waram, Percy C 1881-1961 *NotNAT B, WhScrn 74, -77, WhThe, WhoHol B*
Warburg, Felix Moritz 1871-1937 *Baker 78*
Warburg, James Paul 1896-1969 *AmSCAP 66*
Warburton, Annie Osborne 1902- *IntWWM 77, -80, WhoMus 72*
Warburton, Charles M 1887-1952 *NotNAT B, WhThe*
Warburton, John 1899- *ForYSC, IntMPA 77, -75, -76, -78, -79, -80, WhoHol A*
Warchal, Bohdan 1930- *IntWWM 77, -80*
Ward, Mrs. *Film 1*
Ward, Sir A W d1924 *NotNAT B*
Ward, Aida *AmPS B*
Ward, Albert 1870-1956 *IlWWBF, NotNAT B*
Ward, Annie d1918 *NotNAT B*
Ward, Art *ConMuA 80B*
Ward, Beatrice 1890-1964 *WhScrn 74, -77, WhoHol B*
Ward, Benny *NewOrJ*
Ward, Betty *WhThe*
Ward, Beverly A *ConAmC*
Ward, Bill 1916- *IntMPA 77, -75, -76, -78, -79, -80*
Ward, Billy *AmPS A*
Ward, Billy, Dominoes *BiDAmM*
Ward, Billy And The Dominoes *RkOn*
Ward, Bradley *Film 2*
Ward, Brendan Noel *NatPD[port]*
Ward, Burt 1945- *HalFC 80, IntMPA 79, -80, What 5[port], WhoHol A, WhoHrs 80*
Ward, Carlos N 1940- *EncJzS 70*
Ward, Carrie Clarke 1862-1926 *Film 1, -2, WhScrn 74, -77, WhoHol B*
Ward, Carrie Lee *Film 2*
Ward, Charles B 1865-1917 *AmSCAP 66, -80, BiDAmM*
Ward, Christina Mary 1932- *IntWWM 77, WhoMus 72*
Ward, Clara *AmSCAP 80*
Ward, Clara 1924-1973 *BiDAmM, DrBlPA, EncJzS 70, NewGrD 80*
Ward, Clara 1927-1973 *AmSCAP 66, WhScrn 77*
Ward, Clifford T 1946- *IlEncR*
Ward, Craig *Film 2*
Ward, Dave *WhoHol A*
Ward, David 1922- *CmOp, IntWWM 77, -80, NewGrD 80, WhoOp 76*
Ward, David 1925- *WhoMus 72*
Ward, David William Bassett 1942- *IntWWM 80, WhoMus 72*
Ward, Diane 1919- *AmSCAP 66, ConAmC A*
Ward, Dorothy 1890- *OxThe, WhThe*
Ward, Douglas Turner 1930- *ConDr 73, -77, DcLB 7[port], DrBlPA, Ent, MorBAP, NotNAT, PlP&P A, WhoThe 72, -77*
Ward, Douglas Turner 1931- *BlkAmP*
Ward, Eddie *Film 2*
Ward, Edward 1667-1731 *OxMus*
Ward, Edward 1896- *AmSCAP 66, -80*
Ward, Eileen *CnOxB*

Ward, Ethel d1955 *NotNAT B*
Ward, Fannie 1872-1952 *Film 1, -2, HalFC 80, MotPP, NotNAT B, OxThe, TwYS, WhScrn 74, -77, WhThe, WhoHol B*
Ward, Fanny 1875- *WhoStg 1908*
Ward, Fleming *Film 1*
Ward, Fleming d1962 *NotNAT B*
Ward, Francis 1935- *BlkAmP, MorBAP*
Ward, Frank Edwin 1872-1953 *Baker 78, ConAmC*
Ward, Genevieve 1837-1922 *WhThe*
Ward, Genevieve Teresa 1834-1922 *NotNAT B, WhoStg 1908*
Ward, Genevieve Teresa 1838-1922 *NotNAT A, OxThe*
Ward, George *Film 2*
Ward, George, Jr. 1932- *IntWWM 77, -80*
Ward, Gerald *Film 1*
Ward, Hap, Jr. 1899-1940 *WhScrn 74, -77, WhoHol B*
Ward, Hap, Sr. 1868-1944 *NotNAT B, WhScrn 74, -77, WhoHol B*
Ward, Harry 1890-1952 *WhScrn 74, -77*
Ward, Helen 1916- *CmpEPM*
Ward, Hugh J 1871-1941 *NotNAT B, WhThe*
Ward, J C *OxMus*
Ward, James Skip *WhoHol A*
Ward, Janet *BiE&WWA, NotNAT, WhoHol A*
Ward, Jerold *Film 1*
Ward, John 1571-1638? *Baker 78, NewGrD 80, OxMus*
Ward, John Milton 1917- *Baker 78, NewGrD 80*
Ward, John Owen 1919- *IntWWM 77, -80, NewGrD 80*
Ward, Jomarie *WhoHol A*
Ward, Joseph 1942- *IntWWM 80, WhoMus 72*
Ward, Joseph S *NewGrD 80*
Ward, Judith Jones *WomWMM B*
Ward, Justine Bayard 1879- *BiDAmM*
Ward, Katherine Clare 1871-1938 *WhScrn 74, -77, WhoHol B*
Ward, Kathrin Claire *Film 2*
Ward, Larry *WhoHol A*
Ward, Lucille 1880-1952 *Film 2, WhScrn 74, -77, WhoHol B*
Ward, Mackenzie 1903- *Film 2, WhThe*
Ward, Margaret 1928- *IntWWM 80*
Ward, Marshall *WhoHol A*
Ward, Mary d1966 *BiE&WWA, NotNAT B*
Ward, Michael 1915- *FilmgC, HalFC 80, WhoHol A*
Ward, Michael Philip 1949- *AmSCAP 80*
Ward, Otto *JoeFr*
Ward, Paul Clarendon 1918- *IntWWM 77, -80, WhoMus 72*
Ward, Peggy 1878-1960 *WhScrn 74, -77*
Ward, Penelope Dudley 1914- *WhThe, WhoHol A*
Ward, Peter Garnet 1928- *IntWWM 77, WhoMus 72*
Ward, Polly 1908- *Film 2, FilmgC, HalFC 80, IlWWBF, WhoHol A*
Ward, Polly 1909- *WhThe*
Ward, Richard 1915- *DrBlPA, ForYSC, WhoHol A*
Ward, Robert *Film 2*
Ward, Robert 1917- *Baker 78, BiDAmM, BnBkM 80, CompSN[port], CpmDNM 80, ConAmC, DcCM, MusMk, NewEOp 71, NewGrD 80, OxMus*
Ward, Robin *RkOn*
Ward, Ronald 1901- *WhThe, WhoHol A*
Ward, Roscoe *Film 2*
Ward, Roy British 1929- *AmSCAP 80*
Ward, Russell *ConAmC*
Ward, S A *OxMus*
Ward, Sam 1889-1952 *WhScrn 74, -77, WhoHol B*
Ward, Sam 1906-1960 *AmSCAP 66, -80*
Ward, Samuel Augustus 1848-1903 *BiDAmM*
Ward, Sarah E 1920- *IntMPA 77, -75, -76, -78, -79, -80*
Ward, Simon 1941- *FilmgC, HalFC 80, IntMPA 77, -75, -76, -78, -79, -80, WhoHol A, WhoHrs 80, WhoThe 72, -77*
Ward, Solly 1891-1942 *NotNAT B, WhScrn 74, -77, WhoHol B*
Ward, Stuart Humphry 1923- *WhoMus 72*
Ward, Theodore 1902- *BlkAmP, DrBlPA, MorBAP*
Ward, Tiny *Film 2*
Ward, Trevor *WhoHol A*
Ward, Val Gray *MorBAP*
Ward, Valerie *Film 2*
Ward, Vera Hall *BluesWW*
Ward, Victoria 1914-1957 *WhScrn 74, -77, WhoHol B*
Ward, Warwick 1890-1967 *Film 1*
Ward, Warwick 1891-1967 *IlWWBF[port], WhScrn 77*
Ward, William Reed 1918- *AmSCAP 80, ConAmC, IntWWM 77, -80*
Ward Jones, Peter Arthur 1944- *IntWWM 80*
Ward Russell, Gillian 1953- *IntWWM 80*
Ward-Steinman, David 1936- *CpmDNM 73, ConAmC, DcCM, IntWWM 77, -80, NewGrD 80*
Warde, Anthony 1909-1975 *Vers B[port], WhScrn 77, WhoHol C*
Warde, Ernest C 1874-1923 *NotNAT B, TwYS A, WhScrn 74, -77, WhoHol B*
Warde, Frederick 1851-1935 *EncWT*
Warde, Frederick B d1935 *Film 1, -2, WhoHol B*
Warde, Frederick B 1851-1935 *NotNAT A, -B, OxThe, WhThe, WhoStg 1908*
Warde, Frederick B 1872-1935 *WhScrn 74, -77*
Warde, George *Film 2*
Warde, George d1917 *NotNAT B*
Warde, Harlan *WhoHol A*
Warde, Warwick 1898-1967 *Film 2*
Warde, Willie 1857-1943 *NotNAT B, WhThe*
Wardell, Harry 1879-1948 *WhScrn 74, -77*
Warden, Anne *IntWWM 77, -80*
Warden, Bruce Leland 1939- *AmSCAP 80*
Warden, Fred W d1929 *NotNAT B*
Warden, Jack *MotPP, WhoHol A*
Warden, Jack 1920- *BiE&WWA, FilmEn, FilmgC, ForYSC, HalFC 80, HolCA[port], NotNAT*
Warden, Jack 1925- *IntMPA 77, -75, -76, -78, -79, -80, MovMk[port]*
Warden, Judith Ann 1939- *AmSCAP 80*
Warden, William Burnand 1922- *WhoOp 76*
Wardle, Irving 1929- *WhoThe 72, -77*
Wardley, Alan John Alfred 1929- *WhoMus 72*
Wardwell, Geoffrey 1900-1955 *Film 2, NotNAT B, WhThe, WhoHol B*
Wardwell, Judith *WomWMM B*
Ware, Alice Holdslip *MorBAP*
Ware, Clifton 1937- *IntWWM 77, -80, WhoOp 76*
Ware, Eric Oesterlein 1908- *WhoMus 72*
Ware, Harriet 1877-1962 *Baker 78, BiDAmM, ConAmC*
Ware, Harriet 1878-1962 *AmSCAP 66, -80, NotNAT B*
Ware, Helen 1877-1939 *Film 1, -2, ForYSC, NotNAT B, TwYS, WhScrn 74, -77, WhThe, WhoHol B*
Ware, Helen 1887- *BiDAmM*
Ware, Henry, Jr. 1794-1843 *BiDAmM*
Ware, Irene 1911- *ForYSC*
Ware, James A *AmSCAP 66, -80*
Ware, John Marley 1942- *ConAmC, IntWWM 77, -80*
Ware, Leonard 1909-1974 *AmSCAP 66, -80, BiDAmM, WhoJazz 72*
Ware, Midge *WhoHol A*
Ware, Walter 1880-1936 *WhScrn 74, -77, WhoHol B*
Wareing, Alfred 1876-1942 *NotNAT A, -B, WhThe*
Wareing, Deryck John Highfield 1944- *IntWWM 77, -80*
Wareing, Herbert Walter 1857-1918 *Baker 78*
Wareing, Lesley 1913- *WhThe*
Warenoff, Leonard *NewGrD 80*
Warfaz, Georges De 1889?-1959 *NotNAT B*
Warfield, Charlie 1883- *BiDAmM*
Warfield, Chris *ForYSC, WhoHol A*
Warfield, David 1866-1951 *EncWT, FamA&A[port], NotNAT B, OxThe, PlP&P, WhThe, WhoStg 1906, -1908*
Warfield, Don *WhoHol A*
Warfield, Emma *PupTheA*
Warfield, Gerald Alexander 1940- *ConAmC, IntWWM 80*
Warfield, Irene 1896-1961 *Film 1, WhScrn 77*
Warfield, Marlene 1941- *DrBlPA, WhoHol A*
Warfield, Natalie *Film 2*
Warfield, Sandra 1929- *WhoOp 76*
Warfield, Theodora *Film 1*
Warfield, William *AmPS B*
Warfield, William 1920- *Baker 78, BiE&WWA, BnBkM 80, DrBlPA, NotNAT, PlP&P, WhoHol A*
Warford, Claude 1877-1950 *AmSCAP 66*
Wargo, George A *ConAmC*
Warhol, Andy *WhoHol A*
Warhol, Andy 1926- *FilmgC, HalFC 80*
Warhol, Andy 1927- *FilmEn*
Warhol, Andy 1928- *BiDFilm, -81, OxFilm, WorEFlm*
Warhol, Andy 1930- *AmFD*
Warik, Josef *WhoHol A*
Waring, Barbara 1912- *WhThe*
Waring, Dorothy *MorBAP*
Waring, Dorothy May Graham 1895- *WhThe*
Waring, Fred 1900- *AmSCAP 66, -80, Baker 78, BgBands 74[port], BiDAmM, CmpEPM, IntMPA 77, -75, -76, -78, -79, -80, WhoHol A*
Waring, Herbert 1857-1932 *NotNAT B, WhThe*
Waring, James 1922-1975 *CmpGMD[port], CnOxB*
Waring, Joh *NewGrD 80*
Waring, Mary 1892-1964 *NotNAT B, WhScrn 74, -77, WhoHol B*
Waring, Richard 1912- *WhoThe 72, -77*
Waring, Richard 1914- *BiE&WWA, NotNAT, WhoHol A*
Waring, Tom 1902-1960 *AmSCAP 66, -80, CmpEPM*
Warka, Adam *NewGrD 80*
Warkentin, Larry 1940- *ConAmC*
Warlich, Reinhold Von 1877-1939 *Baker 78*
Warlock, Peter 1894-1930 *Baker 78, BnBkM 80, DcCom&M 79, MagIlD, MusMk[port], NewGrD 80*
Warm, Hermann 1889- *DcFM, FilmEn, OxFilm, WorEFlm*
Warmell, Lennart 1927- *IntWWM 77*
Warmington, S J 1884-1941 *WhoHol B*
Warmington, Stanley J 1884-1941 *NotNAT B, WhThe*
Warmsley, Peter *NewGrD 80*
Warmuth, Carl 1811-1892 *NewGrD 80*
Warmuth, Carl 1844-1895 *NewGrD 80*
Warnas, Huibertus W Abraham Christiaan 1925- *IntWWM 80*
Warndof, Fiona McCleary *AmSCAP 80*
Warne, Katharine Mulky 1923- *ConAmC*
Warnecke, Friedrich 1856-1931 *Baker 78*
Warner, Adele *Film 2*
Warner, Albert 1884-1967 *DcFM*
Warner, Albert 1890- *NewOrJ[port]*
Warner, Anna B 1820-1915 *BiDAmM*
Warner, Anne 1869- *WhoStg 1908*
Warner, Astrid *WhoHol A*
Warner, Byron Hilbun, Jr. 1939- *AmSCAP 80*
Warner, Charles 1846-1909 *NotNAT B, OxThe*
Warner, David 1941- *CnThe, FilmAG WE, FilmEn, FilmgC, ForYSC, HalFC 80, IlWWBF, IntMPA 78, -79, -80, OxFilm, WhoHol A, WhoHrs 80, WhoThe 72, -77*
Warner, Ernest John Charles 1916- *WhoMus 72*
Warner, Frank 1903- *BiDAmM, EncFCWM 69*
Warner, Gloria 1915-1934 *WhScrn 74, -77*
Warner, Grace 1873-1925 *NotNAT B, WhThe*
Warner, H B 1876-1958 *FilmEn, Film 1, -2, FilmgC, ForYSC, HalFC 80, HolCA[port], MotPP, MovMk[port], TwYS, Vers A[port], WhScrn 74, -77, WhoHol B*
Warner, H Waldo 1874-1945 *OxMus*
Warner, Harry M 1881-1958 *DcFM*
Warner, Harry Waldo 1874-1945 *Baker 78*
Warner, Henry Byron 1876-1958 *NotNAT B, WhThe, WhoStg 1906, -1908*
Warner, J B 1895-1924 *WhScrn 77, WhoHol B*

Warner, J Wesley *Film 1*
Warner, Jack *IntMPA 77, -75, -76, -78, -79, -80*
Warner, Jack 1894- *FilmEn, FilmgC, HalFC 80, WhoHol A*
Warner, Jack 1900- *FilmAG WE, IlWWBF[port], -A*
Warner, Jack, Jr. 1916- *IntMPA 77, -75, -76, -78, -79, -80*
Warner, Jack L 1892-1978 *DcFM, FilmEn, FilmgC, HalFC 80, IntMPA 77, -75, -76, -78, TwYS B*
Warner, James B 1895-1924 *Film 2*
Warner, Josephine Queen 1910- *IntWWM 77*
Warner, Lawrence Eugene 1904- *WhoMus 72*
Warner, Pam *WhoHol A*
Warner, Philip 1901- *AmSCAP 66, -80, ConAmC A*
Warner, Richard *ConAmC, WhoHol A*
Warner, Robert *WhoHol A*
Warner, Robert A 1912- *IntWWM 80*
Warner, Sally Slade 1932- *IntWWM 77, -80*
Warner, Samuel 1888-1927 *DcFM*
Warner, Sarah Ann 1898- *AmSCAP 66, -80*
Warner, Steven *WhoHol A*
Warner, Sylvia Townsend 1893-1978 *Baker 78*
Warner, Willie 1865?-1908? *NewOrJ*
Warner Brothers *DcFM, WorEFlm[port]*
Warnes, Jennifer *RkOn 2[port]*
Warnick, Clay 1915- *AmSCAP 66, BiE&WWA, NotNAT*
Warnick, Henry Clay, Jr. 1915- *AmSCAP 80*
Warnick, Louis 1890?- *NewOrJ[port]*
Warnke, Francis Henry, Jr. 1946- *IntWWM 77*
Warnken, Rodney George 1931- *AmSCAP 80*
Warnlof, Ingela Tyra Josefina 1934- *IntWWM 77*
Warnock, Amelia Beers *CreCan 1*
Warnots, Henri 1832-1893 *Baker 78, NewGrD 80*
Warnow, Harry 1909- *AmSCAP 80*
Warnow, Helen 1926-1970 *WhScrn 74, -77*
Warnow, Mark 1902-1949 *CmpEPM*
Waronker, Lenny *ConMuA 80B*
Warr, Brian L 1946- *IntWWM 77*
Warrack, Guy 1900- *IntWWM 80, NewGrD 80*
Warrack, John 1928- *IntWWM 77, -80, NewGrD 80, WhoMus 72*
Warre, Michael 1922- *PlP&P, WhoHol A, WhoThe 72, -77*
Warrell, Ernest Herbert 1915- *WhoMus 72*
Warren, Ambrose 1656?-1730? *NewGrD 80*
Warren, Betty 1905- *WhThe*
Warren, Brett 1910- *BiE&WWA, NotNAT*
Warren, C Denier 1889-1971 *FilmgC, HalFC 80, WhScrn 74, -77, WhThe, WhoThe 72*
Warren, C Dernier 1889-1971 *WhoHol B*
Warren, Charles Marquis 1912- *FilmEn, FilmgC, HalFC 80, IntMPA 77, -75, -76, -78, -79, -80, WhoHrs 80, WorEFlm*
Warren, Dane *AmSCAP 80*
Warren, E Alyn 1875-1940 *Film 2, WhScrn 74, -77, WhoHol B*
Warren, Earl 1914- *CmpEPM*
Warren, Earle Ronald 1914- *EncJzS 70, IlEncJ, WhoJazz 72*
Warren, Ed 1924-1963 *AmSCAP 66*
Warren, Eda *WomWMM*
Warren, Edward d1930 *WhScrn 74, -77, WhoHol B*
Warren, Edward 1920-1962 *AmSCAP 80*
Warren, Edwin Brady 1910- *IntWWM 80*
Warren, Elinor Remick *IntWWM 80*
Warren, Elinor Remick 1905- *Baker 78*
Warren, Elinor Remick 1906- *AmSCAP 66, -80, ConAmC, IntWWM 77, WhoMus 72*
Warren, Eliza 1865-1935 *WhScrn 74, -77, WhoHol B*
Warren, Evelyn 1886- *IntWWM 77*
Warren, F Brooke d1950 *NotNAT B*
Warren, Fran 1926- *CmpEPM*
Warren, Frank *Film 2*
Warren, Frank 1918- *AmSCAP 66*
Warren, Frank Edward 1950- *AmSCAP 80, CpmDNM 76*
Warren, Fred H 1880-1940 *Film 1, -2, WhScrn 77*
Warren, Gary *WhoHol A*
Warren, Gene *IntMPA 79, -80, WhoHrs 80*
Warren, George William 1828-1902 *Baker 78, BiDAmM*
Warren, Gloria 1926?- *FilmEn, WhoHol A*
Warren, Guy 1923- *AmSCAP 66*
Warren, Harry *Sw&Ld C*
Warren, Harry 1893- *AmPS, AmSCAP 66, -80, Baker 78, BestMus, BiDAmM, BiE&WWA, CmpEPM, ConAmC, FilmEn, IntMPA 77, -75, -76, -78, -79, -80, NewGrD 80, NotNAT, OxFilm, PopAmC[port], PopAmC SUP*
Warren, Harry 1895- *HalFC 80*
Warren, Henry C 1855-1934 *BiDAmM*
Warren, James *ForYSC*
Warren, Jeff 1921- *BiE&WWA, NotNAT, WhoThe 72, -77*
Warren, Jennifer 1941- *HalFC 80, WhoHol A*
Warren, Jerry *WhoHrs 80*
Warren, Joseph *WhoHol A*
Warren, Joseph 1804-1881 *NewGrD 80*
Warren, Katharine *ForYSC*
Warren, Katherine 1905-1965 *WhScrn 77*
Warren, Kenneth J 1929-1973 *WhoHol A, WhoThe 72, -77*
Warren, Kenny Lee *WhoHol A*
Warren, Leonard 1911-1960 *Baker 78, BiDAmM, BnBkM 80, CmOp, MusSN[port], NewEOp 71, NewGrD 80, WhScrn 77*
Warren, Lesley Ann 1946- *ForYSC, WhoHol A*
Warren, Low *IlWWBF A*
Warren, Margie Ann 1922- *BiDAmM*
Warren, Mark 1938- *DrBlPA*
Warren, Mary *Film 2*
Warren, Mercy Otis 1728-1814 *NotNAT B*
Warren, Mike *WhoHol A*
Warren, Peter 1935- *EncJzS 70*
Warren, Raymond Henry Charles 1928- *Baker 78, IntWWM 77, -80, NewGrD 80, WhoMus 72*
Warren, Richard Henry 1859-1933 *Baker 78, BiDAmM*
Warren, Robert De 1933- *CnOxB*
Warren, Robert Henry 1919-1977 *BluesWW[port]*
Warren, Robert Penn 1905- *CnMD, Conv 1[port], FilmgC, HalFC 80, ModWD*
Warren, Rod *AmSCAP 80*
Warren, Samuel Prowse 1841-1915 *Baker 78, BiDAmM*
Warren, Samuel Russell 1815?-1882 *BiDAmM*
Warren, Smokey 1916- *BiDAmM*
Warren, T Gideon d1919 *NotNAT B*
Warren, Thomas 1730?-1794 *NewGrD 80*
Warren, Vincent 1938- *CnOxB, CreCan 2*
Warren, William 1767-1832 *EncWT, FamA&A[port], NotNAT B, OxThe, PlP&P*
Warren, William, Jr. 1812-1888 *EncWT, FamA&A[port], NotNAT A, -B, OxThe*
Warren, William A 1952- *ConAmC*
Warren, William Fairfield 1833-1929 *BiDAmM*
Warren, Wilson *WhoHol A*
Warren, Winifred Merrill *IntWWM 77, -80*
Warren-Horne, Thomas 1730?-1794 *NewGrD 80*
Warrenbrand, Jane *WomWMM B*
Warrender, Harold 1903-1953 *FilmgC, HalFC 80, IlWWBF, NotNAT B, WhScrn 74, -77, WhThe, WhoHol B*
Warrener, Warren d1961 *NotNAT B*
Warrenton, Lule 1863-1932 *Film 1, -2, WhScrn 74, -77*
Warrenton, Lulu 1863-1932 *WhoHol B*
Warrick, Carrie Repass 1903- *IntWWM 77*
Warrick, Ruth 1915- *BiE&WWA, FilmEn, FilmgC, ForYSC, HalFC 80, IntMPA 77, -75, -76, -78, -79, -80, MovMk, NotNAT, WhoHol A, WhoThe 77*
Warriner, Frederic 1916- *WhoThe 72, -77*
Warriner, Solomon 1778-1860 *BiDAmM*
Warrington, John T 1911-1978 *AmSCAP 80*
Warrock, Thomas *NewGrD 80*
Warshauer, Frank 1893-1953 *AmSCAP 66, -80*
Warshauer, Rose 1917- *AmSCAP 66, -80*
Warshaw, Mimi *WomWMM B*
Warshawsky, Ruth *WhoHol A*
Wartel *NewGrD 80*
Wartel, Atale Therese Annette 1814-1865 *NewGrD 80*
Wartel, Louis Emile 1834-1865? *NewGrD 80*
Wartel, Pierre-Francois 1806-1882 *Baker 78, NewGrD 80*
Wartenegg, Hanna 1939- *WhoOp 76*
Warwick, Bama William Carl 1917- *WhoJazz 72*
Warwick, Carl 1917- *EncJzS 70*
Warwick, Dionne *ConMuA 80A*
Warwick, Dionne 1940- *DrBlPA, RkOn*
Warwick, Dionne 1941- *BiDAmM, IlEncR[port]*
Warwick, Ethel 1882-1951 *NotNAT B, WhThe*
Warwick, Henry *Film 1*
Warwick, Jarvis *CreCan 1*
Warwick, John 1905-1972 *FilmgC, HalFC 80, IlWWBF, WhScrn 77, WhoHol A*
Warwick, Richard *WhoHol A*
Warwick, Robert d1964 *MotPP, NotNAT B, WhoHol B*
Warwick, Robert 1878-1964 *FilmEn, ForYSC, HolCA[port], NotNAT B, WhScrn 74, -77, WhThe*
Warwick, Robert 1878-1965 *FilmgC, HalFC 80, MovMk, TwYS*
Warwick, Robert 1881-1964 *Film 1, -2, Vers A[port]*
Warwick, Rose B 1934- *AmSCAP 66, -80*
Warwick, Stella Lattimore 1905-1960 *WhScrn 74, -77*
Warwick, Thomas *NewGrD 80*
Warwick, Virginia *Film 2*
Warwick, Virginia Cayce 1908- *IntWWM 77*
Warwicke, Thomas *NewGrD 80*
Warzecha, Piotr 1941- *IntWWM 77, -80, NewGrD 80*
Wascher, Aribert *Film 2*
Waschon, Pierre *NewGrD 80*
Washabaugh, Ivan J 1912- *AmSCAP 66, -80*
Washboard Sam *BluesWW*
Washboard Willie *BluesWW*
Washbourne, Mona 1903- *FilmEn, FilmgC, ForYSC, HalFC 80, WhoHol A, WhoThe 72, -77*
Washbrook, John *WhoHol A*
Washburn, Abbott M *NewYTET*
Washburn, Alice 1861-1929 *Film 1, WhScrn 74, -77, WhoHol B*
Washburn, Beverly *ForYSC, WhoHol A*
Washburn, Bryant 1889-1963 *FilmEn, Film 1, -2, ForYSC, HalFC 80, HolCA[port], MotPP, MovMk, NotNAT B, TwYS, WhScrn 74, -77, WhoHol B*
Washburn, Bryant, Jr. d1960 *WhScrn 77*
Washburn, Deric *IntMPA 80*
Washburn, Edward Abiel 1819-1881 *BiDAmM*
Washburn, Franklin Ely 1911- *IntWWM 77, -80*
Washburn, Gary Scott 1946- *AmSCAP 80, ConAmC*
Washburn, Gladys *WomWMM B*
Washburn, Henry S 1813-1903 *BiDAmM*
Washburn, Jack 1927- *BiE&WWA, NotNAT*
Washburn, John H d1917 *WhScrn 77*
Washburn, Jon Spencer 1942- *IntWWM 77, -80*
Washburn, Lalomie Marion 1941- *AmSCAP 80*
Washburn, Ralph *Film 2*
Washburn, Robert 1928- *AmSCAP 66, -80, Baker 78, CpmDNM 77, -78, -79, -80, ConAmC, IntWWM 77, -80*
Washburne, Country 1904-1974 *CmpEPM*
Washburne, Joe 1904- *AmSCAP 66, -80*
Washer, Ben 1906- *BiE&WWA, IntMPA 77, -75, -76, -78, -79*
Washington, Al 1902- *WhoJazz 72*
Washington, Albert 1935- *BluesWW[port]*
Washington, Baby *RkOn[port]*
Washington, Blue *Film 2, TwYS*
Washington, Buck Ford Lee 1903-1955 *WhoJazz 72*
Washington, D C *BluesWW*
Washington, Diamond Leon 1909- *WhoJazz 72*
Washington, Dinah *AmPS A*
Washington, Dinah 1924-1963 *BluesWW[port], CmpEPM, DrBlPA, IlEncJ, NotNAT B,*

RkOn[port], WhScrn 77, WhoHol B
Washington, Dinah 1924-1967 *BiDAmM*
Washington, Dino *WhoHol A*
Washington, Donna Day 1942- *CnOxB*
Washington, Edmond *NewOrJ*
Washington, Edward 1902-1964 *NewOrJ*
Washington, Erwin *MorBAP*
Washington, Ford Lee 1903-1955 *DrBlPA*
Washington, Fred 1888- *NewOrJ*
Washington, Freddie 1900?- *WhoJazz 72*
Washington, Fredi 1903- *DrBlPA, ThFT[port]*
Washington, Fredi 1913- *WhoHol A*
Washington, Fredie *BlksBF*
Washington, Gene *WhoHol A*
Washington, George 1732-1799 *HalFC 80*
Washington, George 1900?-1942? *NewOrJ*
Washington, George 1907- *WhoJazz 72*
Washington, Grover, Jr. 1943- *AmSCAP 80, DrBlPA, EncJzS 70*
Washington, Jack Ronald 1912-1964 *WhoJazz 72*
Washington, Judy *WhoHol A*
Washington, Kenneth Kenny *WhoHol A*
Washington, Kenny 1918-1971 *DrBlPA, WhScrn 77*
Washington, Lamont 1944?-1968 *DrBlPA*
Washington, Mack William 1908-1938 *WhoJazz 72*
Washington, Mildred *Film 2*
Washington, Ned 1901-1976 *AmPS, AmSCAP 66, -80, BiDAmM, CmpEPM, Sw&Ld C*
Washington, Paolo 1932- *WhoOp 76*
Washington, Sam *BlkAmP*
Washington, Shirley *WhoHol A*
Washington, Steve 1900?-1936 *WhoJazz 72*
Washington, Vernon *WhoHol A*
Washkill, Eddy Thomas 1921- *AmSCAP 80*
Wasielewski, Josef Wilhelm Von 1822-1896 *OxMus*
Wasielewski, Wilhelm Joseph Von 1822-1896 *Baker 78, NewGrD 80*
Wasil, Edward J 1926- *AmSCAP 66, -80*
Wasilewski, Vincent T *IntMPA 77, -75, -76, -78, -79, -80, NewYTET*
Wason, Robert Wesley 1945- *ConAmC*
Wass, Robert d1764 *NewGrD 80*
Wassenaar, Roelof 1903- *IntWWM 80*
Wasser, Arthur *PupTheA*
Wasserberger, Igor 1937- *IntWWM 77*
Wasserman, Albert *NewYTET*
Wasserman, Dale 1917- *BiE&WWA, ConDr 73, -77D, EncMT, IntMPA 77, -75, -76, -78, -79, -80, NewYTET, NotNAT*
Wasserman, Dale 1921- *BiDAmM*
Wasserman, Lew 1913- *IntMPA 77, -75, -76, -78, -79, -80*
Wasserman, Paul *ConMuA 80B*
Wasserman, Sidonie *WhoMus 72*
Wassermann, Heinrich Joseph 1791-1838 *Baker 78*
Wassmann, Hans *Film 2*
Wasson, Barbara Hickam 1918- *IntWWM 77, -80*
Wasson, D Dewitt 1921- *IntWWM 77, -80*
Wasson, George F, Jr. 1903- *IntMPA 75, -76*
Wasson, Jeffrey 1948- *IntWWM 77*
Waswo, Mary Christine 1952- *IntWWM 77*
Wata, Sussie *Film 2*
Watanabe, Akeo 1919- *Baker 78*
Watanabe, Kazumi 1953- *EncJzS 70*
Watanabe, Mamoru 1915- *IntWWM 77, -80*
Watanabe, Miwako N *IntWWM 80*
Watanabe, Ruth T 1916- *IntWWM 77, -80*
Watanabe, Sadao 1933- *EncJzS 70*
Watanabe, Sumie *WomWMM B*
Water, John *NewGrD 80*
Waterbury, Jared Bell 1799-1876 *BiDAmM*
Waterbury, Ruth *IntMPA 77, -75, -76, -78, -79, -80*
Waterhouse, David Boyer 1936- *IntWWM 77, -80*
Waterhouse, George d1601 *OxMus*
Waterhouse, George d1602 *NewGrD 80*
Waterhouse, John Charles Graeme 1939- *IntWWM 77, -80*
Waterhouse, Keith 1929- *CnThe, ConDr 73, -77, CroCD, IntMPA 77, -75, -76, -78, -79, -80, WhoThe 72, -77*
Waterhouse, William 1931- *IntWWM 77, -80, NewGrD 80, WhoMus 72*
Waterlow, Marjorie 1888-1921 *NotNAT B, WhThe*
Waterman, Denis 1948- *FilmgC, HalFC 80, WhoHol A*
Waterman, Dennis 1948- *IlWWBF, WhoThe 72, -77*
Waterman, Fanny 1920- *IntWWM 77, -80, WhoMus 72*
Waterman, George Gow 1935- *IntWWM 77, -80*
Waterman, Ida 1852-1941 *Film 1, -2, NotNAT B, WhScrn 74, -77, WhoHol B*
Waterman, Ruth Anna 1947- *IntWWM 77, -80, WhoMus 72*
Waterman, Willard *ForYSC, WhoHol A*
Waterous, Herbert d1947 *NotNAT B*
Waters, Benjamin 1902- *EncJzS 70*
Waters, Benny 1902- *EncJzS 70, WhoJazz 72*
Waters, Bunny *WhoHol A*
Waters, Charles Frederick 1895- *WhoMus 72*
Waters, David L 1940- *IntWWM 77, -80*
Waters, Edward N 1906- *Baker 78, NewGrD 80*
Waters, Emory Wallace 1947- *ConAmC*
Waters, Ethel *AmPS B, BlksB&W C*
Waters, Ethel 1886-1977 *BlksBF[port]*
Waters, Ethel 1896-1977 *Baker 78, BluesWW[port], DrBlPA, FilmEn, NewGrD 80*
Waters, Ethel 1900-1977 *BiDAmM, BiE&WWA, CmpEPM, EncJzS 70, EncMT, EncWT, Ent, FamA&A[port], Film 2, FilmgC, ForYSC, HalFC 80, IlEncJ, IntMPA 77, -75, -76, MotPP, MovMk[port], NotNAT, -A, OxThe, PlP&P, What 2[port], WhoHol A, WhoJazz 72, WhoThe 72, -77*
Waters, George W 1908- *IntMPA 77, -75, -76, -78, -79, -80*
Waters, Horace 1812-1893 *BiDAmM*
Waters, J Kevin 1933- *ConAmC, IntWWM 77, -80*
Waters, James d1923 *NotNAT B, WhThe*
Waters, James Lipscomb 1930- *AmSCAP 80, ConAmC*
Waters, Jan 1937- *WhoHol A, WhoThe 72, -77*
Waters, John *NewGrD 80*
Waters, John 1894-1962 *TwYS A*
Waters, John 1945?- *WhoHrs 80*
Waters, Marian Elizabeth *IntWWM 77, -80, WhoMus 72*
Waters, Mira *WhoHol A*
Waters, Monty 1938- *EncJzS 70*
Waters, Monville Charles 1938- *EncJzS 70*
Waters, Muddy 1915- *BiDAmM, BluesWW, ConMuA 80A[port], DrBlPA, EncFCWM 69, EncJzS 70, IlEncJ, IlEncR, RkOn*
Waters, Muddy, Jr. *BluesWW*
Waters, Patricia 1919- *AmSCAP 66*
Waters, Russell 1908- *FilmgC, HalFC 80, WhoHol A*
Waters, Ted *Film 2*
Waters, Vivian 1936- *IntWWM 77, -80*
Waters, Winslow *AmSCAP 80*
Waterson, Samuel A 1940- *WhoThe 72*
Waterston, Sam 1940- *FilmEn, HalFC 80, IntMPA 77, -75, -76, -78, -79, -80, NotNAT, PlP&P A, WhoHol A*
Waterston, Samuel A 1940- *WhoThe 77*
Watford, Gwen 1927- *WhoHol A, WhoThe 72, -77*
Wathall, Alfred G d1938 *NotNAT B*
Watkin, David 1925- *FilmEn, FilmgC, HalFC 80, WorEFlm*
Watkin, Pierre d1960 *WhScrn 74, -77, WhoHol B*
Watkin, Pierre 1889-1960 *ForYSC, HolCA[port], WhoHrs 80[port]*
Watkin, Pierre 1894?-1960 *FilmgC, HalFC 80, NotNAT B, Vers B[port]*
Watkins, Armin Johnston 1931- *WhoMus 72*
Watkins, Clifford Edward I 1940- *IntWWM 77*
Watkins, David Nigel 1938- *IntWWM 77, -80*
Watkins, Garth 1922- *IntMPA 78, -79, -80*
Watkins, Glenn 1927- *IntWWM 77, -80*
Watkins, Gordon R 1930- *BlkAmP, NatPD[port]*
Watkins, Harriette Davison 1923-1978 *BlkWAB*
Watkins, Harry d1894 *NotNAT A, -B*
Watkins, Jacqueline Elizabeth Milton 1923- *WhoMus 72*
Watkins, Jim *WhoHol A*
Watkins, Joe *NewOrJ[port]*
Watkins, Julius 1921- *CmpEPM*
Watkins, Linda 1908-1976 *FilmEn, WhThe*
Watkins, Linda 1909- *ForYSC, WhoHol A*
Watkins, Lovelace 1938- *DrBlPA*
Watkins, Mary Jane *BlksB&W C*
Watkins, Peter *WhoHol A*
Watkins, Peter 1935- *FilmEn, IntMPA 77, -75, -76, OxFilm, WorEFlm*
Watkins, Peter 1937- *FilmgC, HalFC 80, WhoHrs 80*
Watkins, R Bedford 1925- *CpmDNM 74, ConAmC*
Watkins, Reginald Jordan 1954- *AmSCAP 80*
Watkins, Sara VanHorn 1945- *IntWWM 77, -80*
Watkyn, Arthur 1907-1965 *WhThe*
Watling, Dilys 1946- *WhoThe 72, -77*
Watling, Jack 1923- *FilmgC, HalFC 80, IntMPA 77, -75, -76, -78, -79, -80, WhoHol A, WhoThe 72, -77*
Watlington, Rosalind T G 1925- *IntWWM 77, -80*
Watrous, William Russell, II 1939- *EncJzS 70*
Watson, A E T d1922 *NotNAT B*
Watson, Adele 1890-1933 *Film 2, WhScrn 74, -77, WhoHol B*
Watson, Angus James 1932- *IntWWM 77, -80, WhoMus 72*
Watson, Arthel 1923- *BiDAmM*
Watson, Audrey Lee 1934- *IntWWM 77, -80*
Watson, Benjamin T d1968 *WhScrn 77*
Watson, Betty Jane 1926- *WhThe*
Watson, Betty Jane 1928- *BiE&WWA, NotNAT*
Watson, Billy *WhoHol A*
Watson, Billy d1945 *NotNAT B*
Watson, Bobbs 1930?- *ForYSC*
Watson, Bobby 1888-1965 *FilmEn, Film 2, WhScrn 74, -77, WhoHol B*
Watson, Bobs 1930?- *FilmEn, FilmgC, HalFC 80, WhoHol A*
Watson, Caven 1904-1953 *WhScrn 74, -77, WhoHol B*
Watson, Claire 1927- *CmOp, NewGrD 80, WhoOp 76*
Watson, Coy d1968 *Film 2, WhoHol B*
Watson, Cynthia Margot 1931- *WhoMus 72*
Watson, David *WhoHol A*
Watson, Debbie *MotPP, WhoHol A*
Watson, Delmar *WhoHol A*
Watson, Doc 1923- *CounME 74[port], -74A, EncFCWM 69, IlEncCM[port]*
Watson, Douglas *WhoHol A*
Watson, Douglass 1921- *BiE&WWA, NotNAT, WhoThe 72, -77*
Watson, E Bradlee d1961 *NotNAT B*
Watson, Eddie 1904- *NewOrJ[port]*
Watson, Elizabeth d1931 *NotNAT B, WhThe*
Watson, Fanny 1886-1970 *WhScrn 74, -77, WhoHol B*
Watson, Frances Nash 1890-1971 *BiDAmM*
Watson, Fred 1927- *ConDr 73*
Watson, Gene *IlEncCM[port]*
Watson, George A 1911-1937 *WhScrn 74, -77*
Watson, Gilbert Stuart 1897-1964 *AmSCAP 66, -80*
Watson, Harmon C 1943- *BlkAmP*
Watson, Harry *Film 2*
Watson, Henrietta 1873-1964 *WhThe*
Watson, Henry *OxMus*
Watson, Henry 1846-1911 *Baker 78*
Watson, Henry, Jr. *Film 1*
Watson, Henry Cood 1818-1875 *BiDAmM*
Watson, Homer Ransford 1855-1936 *CreCan 1*
Watson, Horace 1867-1934 *NotNAT B, WhThe*
Watson, Ian Edward 1953- *IntWWM 77*
Watson, Irwin C 1934- *DrBlPA*
Watson, Ivory Deek 1909-1969 *WhScrn 77*
Watson, Jack 1921- *FilmgC, HalFC 80, WhoHol A*
Watson, Jack McLaurin 1908- *IntWWM 77, -80*
Watson, James *ConAmC*

Watson, James A, Jr. *DrBlPA, WhoHol A*
Watson, Johnny *AmSCAP 80*
Watson, Johnny 1867-1963 *BluesWW[port]*
Watson, Johnny 1935- *BluesWW[port]*
Watson, Joseph 1895?-1925? *NewOrJ*
Watson, Joseph K 1887-1942 *WhScrn 74, -77, WhoHol B*
Watson, Justice 1908-1962 *WhScrn 74, -77*
Watson, Kenneth Patrick 1929- *CreCan 1*
Watson, Kitty 1887-1967 *WhScrn 74, -77, WhoHol B*
Watson, Lee 1926- *BiE&WWA, NotNAT, WhoOp 76*
Watson, Leo 1898-1950 *CmpEPM, IlEncJ, WhoJazz 72*
Watson, Lilian *CmOp*
Watson, Lillian Barbara 1947- *IntWWM 77, -80*
Watson, Lorne 1919- *IntWWM 77, -80*
Watson, Lucile 1879-1962 *FilmEn, FilmgC, ForYSC, HalFC 80, HolCA[port], MotPP, MovMk[port], NotNAT B, ThFT[port], WhScrn 74, -77, WhThe, WhoHol B*
Watson, Lucille 1879-1962 *Vers A[port]*
Watson, Malcolm 1853-1929 *NotNAT B, WhThe*
Watson, Margaret d1940 *NotNAT B, WhThe*
Watson, Mary Baugh 1890- *IntWWM 80*
Watson, Mills *WhoHol A*
Watson, Minor d1965 *MotPP, NotNAT B, WhoHol B*
Watson, Minor 1889-1965 *FilmgC, HalFC 80, HolCA[port], MovMk, WhScrn 74, -77, WhThe*
Watson, Minor 1890-1965 *ForYSC, Vers A[port]*
Watson, Mitchell 1900-1969 *NewOrJ*
Watson, Monica Mary 1932- *IntWWM 77, -80, WhoMus 72*
Watson, Moray *WhoHol A*
Watson, Neil 1928- *WhoMus 72*
Watson, Nubra *WomWMM B*
Watson, Patricia *WomWMM*
Watson, Patrick 1929- *CreCan 1*
Watson, Robert 1888-1965 *FilmgC, ForYSC, HalFC 80*
Watson, Robert Graham 1913- *IntWWM 77, WhoMus 72*
Watson, Rosabel Grace d1959 *NotNAT B*
Watson, Roy 1876-1937 *Film 1, -2, WhScrn 74, -77, WhoHol B*
Watson, Scott *ConAmC*
Watson, Sheila 1927- *WhoMus 72*
Watson, Stuart d1956 *NotNAT B*
Watson, Susan 1938- *BiE&WWA, EncMT, NotNAT*
Watson, Sydney 1903- *NewGrD 80, WhoMus 72*
Watson, Theresa *WhoHol A*
Watson, Thomas 1557?-1592 *NewGrD 80*
Watson, Thomas M d1963 *NotNAT B*
Watson, Trevor 1942- *IntWWM 77, -80*
Watson, Vernee *WhoHol A*
Watson, Vernon 1885-1949 *WhThe*
Watson, Vernon 1895-1949 *NotNAT B*
Watson, Walter Robert 1933- *AmSCAP 80, CpmDNM 79, ConAmC, IntWWM 77, -80*
Watson, Wilfred 1911- *CreCan 2*
Watson, William *WhoHol A*
Watson, William Carl 1934- *ConAmC*
Watson, William D 1930- *NewGrD 80*
Watson, William Michael 1840-1889 *Baker 78*
Watson, Wylie 1889-1966 *FilmgC, HalFC 80, IlWWBF[port], WhScrn 74, -77, WhThe, WhoHol B*
Watt, Alan 1947- *IntWWM 80*
Watt, Douglas 1914- *AmSCAP 66, -80, ConAmTC, NotNAT*
Watt, Harry 1906- *DcFM, FilmEn, FilmgC, HalFC 80, IlWWBF, -A, IntMPA 77, -75, -76, -78, -79, -80, OxFilm, WorEFlm*
Watt, Henry Jackson 1878-1925 *NewGrD 80*
Watt, Sparky *WhoHol A*
Watt, Stan *WhoHol A*
Watt-Smith, Ian Richard 1943- *WhoOp 76*
Watters, Cyril 1907- *IntWWM 77, WhoMus 72*
Watters, Don *WhoHol A*
Watters, George Manker d1943 *NotNAT B*
Watters, Lu 1911- *BiDAmM, CmpEPM*
Watters, William *WhoHol A*
Watterson, Evelyn Lily Goddard 1916- *IntWWM 77*
Wattis, Richard 1912-1975 *FilmAG WE, FilmgC, HalFC 80, WhScrn 77, WhThe, WhoHol C, WhoThe 72*
Watts, A B 1886- *IntMPA 77, -75, -76, -78*
Watts, Alan 1915- *WomWMM*
Watts, Andre 1946- *Baker 78, BiDAmM, BnBkM 80, DrBlPA, IntWWM 77, -80, MusSN[port], NewGrD 80*
Watts, Arthur Lawrence 1914- *WhoMus 72*
Watts, Charles d1966 *WhScrn 74, -77, WhoHol B*
Watts, Charles H Cotton 1902-1968 *WhScrn 74, -77, WhoHol B*
Watts, Clem *AmSCAP 80*
Watts, Dodo 1910- *IlWWBF, WhThe*
Watts, Ernest James 1945- *EncJzS 70*
Watts, Ernie 1945- *EncJzS 70*
Watts, George 1877-1942 *WhScrn 74, -77, WhoHol B*
Watts, Grady 1908- *AmSCAP 80*
Watts, Gwendolyn *WhoHol A*
Watts, H Grady 1908- *AmSCAP 66*
Watts, Helen 1927- *BnBkM 80, IntWWM 77, -80, NewGrD 80, WhoMus 72*
Watts, Isaac 1674-1748 *OxMus*
Watts, James *Film 2*
Watts, Jeanne *WhoHol A*
Watts, John 1678-1763 *NewGrD 80*
Watts, John 1930- *ConAmC*
Watts, Jonathan 1933- *CnOxB, DancEn 78*
Watts, Lawrence 1914- *IntWWM 80*
Watts, Little Jamie *WhoHol A*
Watts, Louis Thomas 1934-1970 *BluesWW*
Watts, Marzette 1938- *ConAmC*
Watts, Mayme 1926- *AmSCAP 80*
Watts, Noble Thin Man *RkOn*
Watts, Peggy 1906-1966 *WhScrn 77*
Watts, Queenie *WhoHol A*
Watts, Richard, Jr. 1898- *BiE&WWA, ConAmTC, NotNAT, OxThe, WhoThe 72, -77*
Watts, Ruth Emmert 1922- *IntWWM 77*
Watts, Sal *WhoHol A*
Watts, Stephen 1910- *WhoThe 72, -77*
Watts, Tom *IlWWBF*
Watts, Trevor Charles 1939- *EncJzS 70, IntWWM 77, -80*
Watts, Vera 1914- *WhoMus 72*
Watts, Wintter 1884-1962 *AmSCAP 66, Baker 78, BiDAmM, ConAmC*
Watts-Phillips, John Edward 1894-1960 *WhThe*
Watts 103rd St. Rhythm Band, The *RkOn 2[port]*
Watzke, Alex 1880?-1918 *NewOrJ*
Waugh, Evelyn *WomWMM*
Waugh, Harvey Richard 1902- *ConAmC*
Waugh, Irene 1947- *WhoOp 76*
Wauters, Jozef 1939- *IntWWM 80*
Waverly, Jack 1896-1951 *AmSCAP 66, -80*
Wawerka, Anton d1937 *Film 2, WhoHol B*
Wax, Mo 1908- *IntMPA 77, -75, -76, -78, -79, -80*
Waxman, Arthur 1921- *BiE&WWA*
Waxman, Donald 1925- *AmSCAP 66, -80, CpmDNM 78, ConAmC*
Waxman, Ernest 1918- *ConAmC*
Waxman, Franz 1906-1967 *AmSCAP 66, -80, Baker 78, CmMov, CmpEPM, ConAmC, FilmEn, FilmgC, HalFC 80, NewGrD 80, WorEFlm*
Waxman, Harry 1912- *FilmEn, FilmgC, HalFC 80*
Waxman, Jon *ConMuA 80B*
Waxman, Morris D d1931 *NotNAT B*
Waxman, Stanley *WhoHol A*
Way, Bryant *BlkAmP, MorBAP*
Wayburn, Ned 1874-1942 *EncMT, Film 2, NotNAT B, WhThe*
Waycoff, Leon *FilmEn, WhoHol A*
Wayditch, Gabriel Von 1888-1969 *Baker 78, ConAmC, NewGrD 80*
Wayenberg, Daniel 1929- *IntWWM 80, NewGrD 80, WhoMus 72*
Wayland, Hank Frederic Gregson 1906- *WhoJazz 72*
Wayland, Len *IntMPA 77, -75, -76, -78, -79, -80*
Wayland, Newton Hart 1940- *ConAmC*
Wayman, Eunice 1933- *AmSCAP 80*
Waymon, Sam *DrBlPA*
Wayne, Aissa *WhoHol A*
Wayne, Alan *AmSCAP 80*
Wayne, Carol *WhoHol A*
Wayne, Chuck 1923- *CmpEPM, EncJzS 70*
Wayne, David *AmPS B, MotPP, PlP&P, WhoHol A*
Wayne, David 1914- *BiE&WWA, CmpEPM, EncMT, FilmEn, FilmgC, ForYSC, HalFC 80, MovMk, NotNAT, WhoThe 72, -77*
Wayne, David 1916- *BiDFilm, -81, IntMPA 77, -75, -76, -78, -79, -80, WorEFlm*
Wayne, Dennis 1945- *CnOxB*
Wayne, Dorothy *AmSCAP 66, -80*
Wayne, Dwight *AmSCAP 80*
Wayne, Frances 1919- *EncJzS 70*
Wayne, Frances 1924- *CmpEPM*
Wayne, Frank *WhoHol A*
Wayne, Fredd *WhoHol A*
Wayne, Gerard H 1930- *IntMPA 75, -76*
Wayne, John 1906- *ForYSC*
Wayne, John 1907-1979 *BiDFilm, -81, CmMov, FilmEn, Film 2, FilmgC, HalFC 80[port], IntMPA 77, -75, -76, -78, -79, MotPP, MovMk[port], OxFilm, WhoHol A, WhoHrs 80[port], WorEFlm[port]*
Wayne, John Ethan *WhoHol A*
Wayne, Johnny 1918- *CreCan 2*
Wayne, Justina d1951 *WhScrn 74, -77*
Wayne, Keith *WhoHol A*
Wayne, Lloyd *WhoHol A*
Wayne, Mabel 1904- *AmPS, AmSCAP 66, -80, BiDAmM, CmpEPM, Film 2*
Wayne, Marie *Film 1*
Wayne, Maude *Film 1, -2*
Wayne, Michael A 1934- *FilmgC, HalFC 80, IntMPA 77, -75, -76, -78, -79, -80*
Wayne, Naunton 1901-1970 *FilmgC, HalFC 80, IlWWBF, OxFilm, WhScrn 74, -77, WhThe, WhoHol B*
Wayne, Nina 1943- *ForYSC, WhoHol A*
Wayne, Pat 1939- *ForYSC, MotPP*
Wayne, Patricia *IlWWBF, WhScrn 77*
Wayne, Patrick 1939- *FilmEn, FilmgC, HalFC 80, IntMPA 78, -79, -80, WhoHol A, WhoHrs 80*
Wayne, Paula 1937- *BiE&WWA, NotNAT*
Wayne, Richard d1958 *Film 2, WhScrn 74, -77, WhoHol B*
Wayne, Robert 1864?-1946 *Film 2, WhScrn 77*
Wayne, Rollo 1899-1954 *NotNAT B, WhThe*
Wayne, Sid 1923- *AmSCAP 66, -80*
Wayne, Susan *WomWMM A, -B*
Wayne, Thomas 1940-1971 *BiDAmM*
Wayne, Thomas 1941- *RkOn[port]*
Wayne And Shuster *NewYTET*
We Five *RkOn 2[port]*
Wead, Frank 1895?-1947 *FilmEn*
Weadon, Percy d1939 *NotNAT B*
Weait, Christopher Robert Irving 1939- *IntWWM 77, -80*
Weakland, Rembert 1927- *NewGrD 80*
Weale, Malcolm Angus 1947- *IntWWM 77, -80*
Weales, Gerald 1925- *BiE&WWA, ConAmTC*
Wearne, Michael Collin 1942- *IntWWM 80*
Weast, Robert *ConAmC*
Weather Report *ConMuA 80A, EncJzS 70, IlEncJ, IlEncR*
Weatherburn, Robert James 1943- *IntWWM 77, -80*
Weatherford, Tazwell 1889-1917 *WhScrn 77*
Weatherford, Teddy 1903-1945 *BiDAmM, WhoJazz 72*
Weatherington, Randall L 1949- *AmSCAP 80*
Weatherly, Frederic E 1848-1933 *OxMus*
Weatherly, James Dexter 1943- *AmSCAP 80*
Weathers, Felicia 1937- *CmOp, NewEOp 71*
Weathers, Felicia 1939- *WhoOp 76*
Weathers, Roscoe 1925-1976 *AmSCAP 66, -80*
Weathers, W Keith 1943- *ConAmC*
Weathers-Bakonyi, Felicia 1937- *IntWWM 77, -80, WhoMus 72*
Weathersby, Helen d1943 *NotNAT B*

Weathersten, Nancy Lurline *IntWWM 80*
Weaver, Affie d1940 *NotNAT B*
Weaver, Carl *MorBAP*
Weaver, Charley *JoeFr, WhScrn 77*
Weaver, Curley James 1906-1962 *BluesWW*
Weaver, Dennis *MotPP, WhoHol A*
Weaver, Dennis 1924- *AmSCAP 80, FilmEn, FilmgC, ForYSC, HalFC 80, IlEncCM, MovMk*
Weaver, Dennis 1925- *IntMPA 77, -75, -76, -78, -79, -80*
Weaver, Doodles 1914- *ForYSC, JoeFr, What 4[port], WhoHol A*
Weaver, Elviry *WhoHol A*
Weaver, Emmett *ConAmTC*
Weaver, Frank *WhoHol A*
Weaver, Fritz 1926- *BiE&WWA, Ent, FilmEn, FilmgC, ForYSC, HalFC 80, NotNAT, WhoHol A, WhoThe 72, -77*
Weaver, Henry *Film 1*
Weaver, John 1673-1760 *CnOxB, DancEn 78, NewGrD 80, NotNAT B, OxMus, OxThe, PlP&P*
Weaver, John Borland 1937- *ConAmC, IntWWM 77, WhoMus 72*
Weaver, John VanAlstyn 1893-1938 *NotNAT B*
Weaver, Joseph *WhoStg 1906*
Weaver, Lee *WhoHol A*
Weaver, Leon 1883-1950 *WhScrn 77, WhoHol B*
Weaver, Marion 1902- *AmSCAP 66, -80*
Weaver, Marjorie 1913- *FilmEn, FilmgC, ForYSC, HalFC 80, IntMPA 77, -75, -76, -78, -79, -80, MovMk[port], ThFT[port], WhoHol A*
Weaver, Mary Watson 1903- *AmSCAP 66, -80, ConAmC*
Weaver, Powell 1890-1951 *AmSCAP 66, -80, Baker 78, BiDAmM, ConAmC*
Weaver, Richard A 1934- *NotNAT*
Weaver, Robert Lamar 1923- *IntWWM 77, -80*
Weaver, Sigourney 1949- *WhoHrs 80*
Weaver, Sylvester L, Jr. 1908- *IntMPA 77, -75, -76, -78, -79, -80, NewYTET*
Weaver, Thomas 1939- *ConAmC*
Weaver, Victor 1913- *IntWWM 77*
Weaver, Vivian LaVelle 1918- *BlkWAB[port]*
Weaver Brothers And Elviry, The *ForYSC*
Weavers, The *AmPS A, -B, BiDAmM, EncFCWM 69, RkOn*
Weaving, Jon Weymouth 1936- *WhoOp 76*
Webb, Alan 1906- *BiE&WWA, HalFC 80, NotNAT, WhoHol A, WhoThe 72, -77*
Webb, Alliene Brandon 1910-1965 *ConAmC*
Webb, Alyce Elizabeth 1935- *DrBlPA*
Webb, Arthur T 1950- *AmSCAP 80*
Webb, Barrie Edmund Ronald 1947- *IntWWM 77*
Webb, Bill 1926- *BluesWW[port]*
Webb, Brian Patrick 1948- *IntWWM 77, -80*
Webb, Bunyan Monroe 1935- *WhoMus 72*
Webb, Chick d1939 *BgBands 74[port]*
Webb, Chick 1902-1939 *NewGrD 80*
Webb, Chick 1907?-1939 *DrBlPA, IlEncJ*
Webb, Chick 1909?-1939 *CmpEPM, WhoJazz 72*
Webb, Clifton d1966 *AmPS B, BiE&WWA, MotPP, WhoHol B*
Webb, Clifton 1889?-1966 *WhScrn 74, -77*
Webb, Clifton 1890-1966 *Film 2, ForYSC*
Webb, Clifton 1891-1966 *CmpEPM, EncMT, FilmEn, Funs[port], WorEFlm*
Webb, Clifton 1893-1966 *BiDFilm, -81, FilmgC, HalFC 80, MovMk, NotNAT B, WhThe*
Webb, Clifton 1896-1966 *BiDAmM*
Webb, Daniel 1719?-1798 *NewGrD 80*
Webb, Daniel 1735-1815 *Baker 78*
Webb, Dean *EncFCWM 69*
Webb, Dean 1937- *BiDAmM*
Webb, Dick *Film 2*
Webb, Fay 1906-1936 *WhScrn 74, -77, WhoHol B*
Webb, Frank d1974 *WhScrn 77, WhoHol A*
Webb, Frank Rush 1851-1934 *Baker 78*
Webb, George 1887-1943 *Film 1, -2, WhScrn 77*
Webb, George James 1803-1887 *Baker 78, BiDAmM, NewGrD 80*
Webb, Harry *TwYS A*
Webb, Jack d1954 *NotNAT B*
Webb, Jack 1920- *FilmEn, FilmgC, ForYSC, HalFC 80, IntMPA 77, -75, -76, -78, -79, -80, MotPP, MovMk, NewYTET, OxFilm, WhoHol A, WorEFlm*
Webb, James R 1909-1974 *FilmEn, WorEFlm*
Webb, James R 1910-1974 *HalFC 80*
Webb, James R 1912- *CmMov, FilmgC*
Webb, Janet *WhoHol A*
Webb, Jerry *IntMPA 77, -75, -76, -78, -79, -80*
Webb, Jimmy 1942- *ConMuA 80A*
Webb, Jimmy 1946- *AmSCAP 80, IlEncR, PopAmC SUP[port]*
Webb, John d1913 *NotNAT B*
Webb, John 1611-1672 *NotNAT B, OxThe, PlP&P*
Webb, Julian Barry 1936- *IntWWM 77, -80*
Webb, June Ellen 1934- *BiDAmM*
Webb, Kenneth 1885-1966 *AmSCAP 66, -80*
Webb, Kenneth 1892- *TwYS A*
Webb, Leonard 1930- *ConDr 73, -77*
Webb, Lizbeth 1926- *WhThe*
Webb, Louis K *Film 2*
Webb, Marianne 1936- *IntWWM 77, -80*
Webb, Mildred *WomWMM*
Webb, Millard 1893-1935 *FilmEn, Film 1, TwYS A, WhScrn 74, -77, WhoHol B*
Webb, Nella d1954 *NotNAT B, WhoStg 1908*
Webb, Norma Faye 1932- *AmSCAP 80*
Webb, Percy Sergeant *Film 1*
Webb, Peter Vincent 1925- *IntWWM 77, -80*
Webb, Phyllis Jean 1927- *CreCan 1*
Webb, Richard *ForYSC, WhoHol A*
Webb, Richard 1942- *ConAmC*
Webb, Richard 1951- *IntWWM 80*
Webb, Rita *WhoHol A*
Webb, Robert *BlksB&W C*
Webb, Robert A 1911- *IntMPA 77, -75, -76, -78, -79, -80*
Webb, Robert D 1903- *FilmEn, FilmgC, HalFC 80, IntMPA 77, -75, -76, -78, -79, -80*
Webb, Roy 1888- *AmSCAP 66, -80, CmMov, HalFC 80, NewGrD 80*
Webb, Roy Dean 1937- *AmSCAP 66*
Webb, Ruth 1923- *BiE&WWA, NotNAT*
Webb, Sidney F d1956 *NotNAT B*
Webb, Speed Lawrence Arthur 1906- *WhoJazz 72*
Webb, Teena *WomWMM B*
Webb, William 1600?-1656? *NewGrD 80*
Webb, William 1902-1939 *BiDAmM, NewGrD 80*
Webbe, Samuel 1740-1816 *Baker 78, NewGrD 80, OxMus*
Webbe, Samuel 1770?-1843 *Baker 78, NewGrD 80, OxMus*
Webber, Amherst 1867-1946 *Baker 78*
Webber, Gordon McKinley 1909-1966 *CreCan 2*
Webber, Julian Lloyd 1951- *WhoMus 72*
Webber, Natalie 1942- *WhoMus 72*
Webber, Nicholas 1949- *IntWWM 77, -80*
Webber, Paul *WhoHol A*
Webber, Peggy *WhoHol A*
Webber, Robert *IntMPA 77, -75, -76, -78, -79, -80, WhoHol A*
Webber, Robert 1924- *FilmEn*
Webber, Robert 1925?- *ForYSC*
Webber, Robert 1928- *BiE&WWA, FilmgC, HalFC 80, NotNAT*
Webber, Theodore Lyman 1840-1932 *PupTheA*
Webber, William Southcombe Lloyd 1914- *IntWWM 77*
Webber, Winston 1949- *IntWWM 80*
Weber *NewGrD 80*
Weber, Adam *BlkAmP*
Weber, Adam 1854-1906 *BiDAmM*
Weber, Alain 1930- *Baker 78, NewGrD 80*
Weber, Albert 1828-1879 *BiDAmM*
Weber, Aloysia 1759?-1839 *NewGrD 80[port]*
Weber, Bedrich Divis 1766-1842 *NewGrD 80*
Weber, Ben 1916- *Baker 78, BiDAmM, BnBkM 80, ConAmC, DcCM, IntWWM 77, -80, NewGrD 80, WhoMus 72*
Weber, Bernhard Anselm 1764-1821 *Baker 78, NewGrD 80*
Weber, Bernhard Christian 1712-1758 *Baker 78, NewGrD 80, OxMus*
Weber, Bill *PupTheA*
Weber, Carl Maria Von 1786-1826 *Baker 78, BnBkM 80[port], CmOp, CmpBCM, CnOxB, DcCom 77[port], DcCom&M 79, DcPup, GrComp[port], MusMk[port], NewEOp 71, NewGrD 80[port], OxMus*
Weber, Carl Maria Von 1786-1828 *DancEn 78*
Weber, Constantia 1762-1842 *NewGrD 80*
Weber, Constanze 1762-1842 *NewGrD 80*
Weber, Diana 1945?- *CnOxB*
Weber, Eberhard 1940- *EncJzS 70*
Weber, Edith 1925- *NewGrD 80*
Weber, Edmund 1766-1828 *NewGrD 80*
Weber, Edwin J 1893- *AmSCAP 66, -80*
Weber, Franz 1805-1876 *Baker 78*
Weber, Franz Anton 1734-1812 *NewGrD 80*
Weber, Fridolin 1733-1779 *NewGrD 80*
Weber, Fridolin 1761-1833 *NewGrD 80*
Weber, Friedrich August 1753-1806 *Baker 78*
Weber, Friedrich Dionys 1766-1842 *Baker 78, NewGrD 80, OxMus*
Weber, Fritz 1761-1833 *NewGrD 80*
Weber, Georg 1540?-1599 *NewGrD 80*
Weber, Georg 1610?-1653? *NewGrD 80*
Weber, Georg Viktor 1838-1911 *Baker 78*
Weber, Gertrude Christina 1934- *IntWWM 77*
Weber, Gottfried 1779-1839 *Baker 78, NewGrD 80*
Weber, Gustav 1845-1887 *Baker 78, NewGrD 80*
Weber, Henry *PupTheA*
Weber, Henry William d1818 *NotNAT B*
Weber, Jean *Film 2*
Weber, Jean 1818-1902 *NewGrD 80*
Weber, Joan 1936- *AmPS A, -B, RkOn[port]*
Weber, Joe 1867-1942 *CmpEPM, EncMT, FilmEn, Film 1, -2, JoeFr[port], NotNAT A, WhScrn 74, -77, WhoHol B*
Weber, Mrs. Joe d1951 *NotNAT B*
Weber, Johann *NewGrD 80*
Weber, Johannes 1818-1902 *NewGrD 80*
Weber, John C 1856-1938 *BiDAmM*
Weber, Josef Miroslaw 1854-1906 *Baker 78*
Weber, Joseph 1867-1942 *BiDAmM, Ent, FamA&A[port], NotNAT B, OxThe, WhThe, WhoStg 1906, -1908*
Weber, Joseph 1937- *ConAmC*
Weber, Joseph Miroslav 1854-1906 *NewGrD 80*
Weber, Joseph W 1861-1943 *WhScrn 74, -77*
Weber, Josepha 1758?-1819 *NewGrD 80*
Weber, Kay *CmpEPM*
Weber, L Lawrence d1940 *NotNAT B, WhThe*
Weber, Lois d1939 *Film 1, MotPP, WhoHol B*
Weber, Lois 1882-1939 *FilmEn, TwYS A*
Weber, Lois 1883-1939 *WhScrn 74, -77, WomWMM*
Weber, Ludwig 1891-1947 *Baker 78, NewGrD 80*
Weber, Ludwig 1899-1974 *CmOp, NewGrD 80, WhoMus 72*
Weber, Marek *CmpEPM*
Weber, Margrit 1924- *Baker 78, NewGrD 80, WhoMus 72*
Weber, Max 1864-1920 *NewGrD 80*
Weber, Rainer 1927- *NewGrD 80*
Weber, Rex 1889-1918 *WhScrn 77*
Weber, Ruth 1943- *CnOxB*
Weber, Sophie 1763-1846 *NewGrD 80*
Weber, Stanley R 1912- *IntMPA 77, -75, -76*
Weber, Sven Fridtjof 1934- *IntWWM 80, WhoMus 72*
Weber, Wilhelm 1859-1918 *Baker 78*
Weber, Wilhelmine Frances 1916- *AmSCAP 66, -80*
Weber, Wolfgang Klaus 1935- *WhoOp 76*
Weber And Fields *CmpEPM, JoeFr[port], OxThe*
Webern, Anton 1883-1945 *Baker 78, BnBkM 80[port], CompSN[port], CnOxB, DcCom 77[port], DcCom&M 79, DcCM, DcTwCC, MusMk, NewGrD 80[port], OxMus*
Webman, Harold *AmSCAP 80*
Webster, Beatrice 1923- *IntWWM 80*
Webster, Ben 1864-1947 *Film 1, -2, HalFC 80, IlWWBF, NotNAT A, -B, WhScrn 74, -77, WhThe, WhoHol B*

Webster, Ben 1909-1973 *CmpEPM, DrBlPA, EncJzS 70, IlEncJ, NewGrD 80, WhoJazz 72*
Webster, Benjamin 1864-1947 *OxThe*
Webster, Benjamin Francis 1909-1973 *AmSCAP 66, -80, BiDAmM, EncJzS 70*
Webster, Benjamin Nottingham 1797-1882 *NotNAT B, OxThe*
Webster, Beveridge 1908- *Baker 78*
Webster, Byron *WhoHol A*
Webster, Carmen Jacqueline *ConAmTC*
Webster, Charles R 1762-1832 *BiDAmM*
Webster, Clara 1821-1844 *CnOxB*
Webster, David 1931- *IntMPA 77, -75, -76, -78, -79, -80*
Webster, Sir David 1903-1971 *DancEn 78, NewGrD 80*
Webster, Donald Frederick 1926- *IntWWM 77, -80, WhoMus 72*
Webster, Edward Mount d1976 *NewYTET*
Webster, Ernest Wesley *IntWWM 77, -80*
Webster, Ferris 1916- *HalFC 80*
Webster, Florence Ann 1860-1899 *NotNAT B*
Webster, Freddie 1916-1947 *CmpEPM, WhoJazz 72*
Webster, Freddie 1917-1947 *BiDAmM*
Webster, Frederick 1802-1878 *NotNAT B*
Webster, George 1762-1821 *BiDAmM*
Webster, Gerald B 1944- *IntWWM 77, -80*
Webster, Gilbert *WhoMus 72*
Webster, Howard *Film 2*
Webster, J P 1819-1875 *NewGrD 80*
Webster, Jean 1876-1916 *NotNAT B*
Webster, John *WhoMus 72*
Webster, John 1580?-1625? *NotNAT A*
Webster, John 1580?-1634? *CnThe, EncWT, McGEWD, NotNAT B, OxThe, PlP&P, REnWD[port]*
Webster, John 1580?-1637? *Ent*
Webster, Joseph Philbrick 1819-1875 *BiDAmM*
Webster, Katie 1939- *BluesWW*
Webster, M Coates 1906- *IntMPA 77, -75, -76, -78, -79, -80*
Webster, Mamie *BluesWW*
Webster, Margaret 1905-1972 *BiE&WWA, CnThe, NotNAT A, -B, OxThe, WhScrn 77, WhoThe 72, -77*
Webster, Maurice *NewGrD 80*
Webster, May Whitty 1865-1948 *OxThe*
Webster, Morris *NewGrD 80*
Webster, Nicholas *NewYTET*
Webster, Orpha M *PupTheA*
Webster, Paul Francis 1907- *AmPS, AmSCAP 66, -80, BiE&WWA, CmpEPM, Sw&Ld C, WhoMus 72*
Webster, Paul Francis 1907-1966 *FilmEn*
Webster, Paul Francis 1909-1966 *CmpEPM, WhoJazz 72*
Webster, Paul Francis 1910?- *FilmgC, HalFC 80*
Webster, Paul Frank 1909- *BiDAmM*
Webster, Pete *BlksB&W C*
Webster, William 1935- *WhoMus 72*
Webster-Gleason, Lucile 1888-1947 *NotNAT B, WhThe*
Wechsberg, Joseph 1907- *WhoMus 72*
Wechsler, Gil 1942- *WhoOp 76*
Wechsler, Lazar 1896- *FilmEn, IntMPA 77, -75, -76, -79, -80*
Wechter, Cecile Schroeder 1936- *AmSCAP 80*
Wechter, Julius L 1935- *AmSCAP 80*
Weck, Frederick *ConAmC*
Weck, Johann 1495?-1536 *NewGrD 80*
Wecker, Georg Caspar 1632?-1695 *NewGrD 80*
Wecker, Georg Kaspar 1632-1695 *Baker 78*
Wecker, Hans Jacob 1528-1586 *NewGrD 80*
Wecker, Johannes 1528-1586 *NewGrD 80*
Wecker, Marlene *WomWMM B*
Weckerlin, Jean-Baptiste-Theodore 1821-1910 *Baker 78, NewGrD 80, OxMus*
Weckmann, Jacob 1643-1680 *NewGrD 80*
Weckmann, Matthias 1619?-1674 *NewGrD 80*
Weckmann, Matthias 1621-1674 *Baker 78*
Weddle, Robert George 1941- *IntWWM 77, -80*
Wedekind, Frank 1864-1918 *CnMD, CnThe, EncWT, Ent, McGEWD[port], ModWD, NewEOp 71, NotNAT A, -B, OxThe, REnWD[port]*
Weder, Ulrich 1934- *WhoOp 76*
Wedge, George Anson 1890-1964 *Baker 78, OxMus*
Wedgewood, Richard B 1942- *IntWWM 77, -80*
Wedgeworth, Ann *WhoHol A*
Weed, Buddy 1918- *CmpEPM*
Weed, Frank *Film 1*
Weed, Joseph Laiten 1917- *IntWWM 77, -80*
Weed, Leland T *WhScrn 77*
Weed, Marlene *WomWMM*
Weed, Maurice James 1912- *ConAmC, IntWWM 77, -80*
Weede, Robert 1903-1972 *AmPS B, BiDAmM, BiE&WWA, EncMT, NotNAT B*
Weeden, Evelyn d1961 *WhThe*
Weeden, Paul Winston 1923- *AmSCAP 80*
Weedon, Bert 1920- *IntWWM 77, -80, WhoMus 72*
Weedon, Mary 1914- *WhoMus 72*
Weegenhuise, Johan Eduard 1910- *IntWWM 77, -80*
Weekley, Dallas Alfred 1933- *IntWWM 77, -80*
Weekley, Nancy 1936- *IntWWM 77, -80*
Weeks, Alan *WhoHol A*
Weeks, Anson 1896-1969 *AmSCAP 66, -80, BgBands 74, CmpEPM, WhoHol B*
Weeks, Barbara d1954 *NotNAT B*
Weeks, Clifford M 1938- *ConAmC*
Weeks, Harold Taylor 1893-1967 *AmSCAP 66, -80*
Weeks, John Ralph 1934- *IntWWM 77, -80, WhoMus 72*
Weeks, Marion 1887-1968 *WhScrn 74, -77, WhoHol B*
Weeks, Paul 1895- *AmSCAP 66, -80*
Weeks, Ricardo 1921- *AmSCAP 66, -80*
Weeks, Richard Harry 1949- *AmSCAP 80*
Weeks, Stephen 1948- *FilmgC, HalFC 80*
Weeks, William J 1901-1972 *AmSCAP 66, -80*
Weelkes, Thomas 1570?-1623 *BnBkM 80*
Weelkes, Thomas 1575?-1623 *Baker 78, GrComp, MusMk, OxMus*
Weelkes, Thomas 1576?-1623 *NewGrD 80*
Weems, Clinton E 1925- *AmSCAP 66, -80*
Weems, Ted 1901-1963 *AmPS A, -B, AmSCAP 66, -80, BgBands 74[port], CmpEPM, NotNAT B, WhScrn 74, -77, WhoHol B*
Weer, Helen *Film 1*
Weerbecke, Gaspar Van 1440?-1514 *MusMk*
Weerbecke, Gaspar Van 1445?- *Baker 78*
Weerbeke, Gaspar Van 1445?-1517? *NewGrD 80*
Weertz, Louis Jacob *AmSCAP 80*
Weesner, Robert D 1919- *IntMPA 75, -76*
Wegeler, Franz Gerhard 1765-1848 *Baker 78*
Wegelin, Arthur Willem 1908- *IntWWM 77, -80*
Wegelius, M 1846-1906 *OxMus*
Wegelius, Martin 1846-1906 *Baker 78, NewGrD 80*
Wegener, Else *WomWMM*
Wegener, Gottfried 1644-1709 *NewGrD 80*
Wegener, Paul 1874-1948 *BiDFilm, -81, DcFM, EncWT, FilmAG WE, FilmEn, Film 1, -2, FilmgC, HalFC 80, NotNAT B, OxFilm, WhScrn 74, -77, WhoHol B, WhoHrs 80[port], WorEFlm*
Wegener, Siegfried Karl Hermann 1916- *WhoMus 72*
Wegner, August Martin, III 1941- *CpmDNM 76, -78, ConAmC, IntWWM 77*
Wegner, Gottfried 1644-1709 *NewGrD 80*
Wegner, Sharen *WomWMM B*
Wegrzyn, Roman 1928- *WhoOp 76*
Weguelin, Thomas N 1885- *WhThe*
Wegwanowski, Paul Joseph *NewGrD 80*
Wehle, Gerhard Furchtegott 1884-1973 *Baker 78*
Wehle, Karl 1825-1883 *Baker 78*
Wehle, Peter 1914- *WhoMus 72*
Wehlen, Emmy 1887- *Film 1, WhThe*
Wehr, David A 1934- *AmSCAP 66, -80, ConAmC, IntWWM 77, -80*
Wehrle, Heinz 1921- *IntWWM 77, -80, WhoMus 72*
Wehrle, Paul 1923- *IntWWM 80*
Wehrli, Werner 1892-1944 *Baker 78, NewGrD 80*
Wei, Ch'eng-Sheng 1744-1802 *NewGrD 80*
Weichenberger, Johann Georg 1676?-1740 *NewGrD 80*
Weichert, Richard 1880-1961 *EncWT*
Weichlein, Franz 1659-1727 *NewGrD 80*
Weichlein, Romanus 1652-1706 *NewGrD 80*
Weichmann, Johann 1620-1652 *NewGrD 80*
Weichsel, Carl 1766?-1805? *NewGrD 80*
Weichsel, Charles 1766?-1805? *NewGrD 80*
Weichsel, Elizabeth *NewGrD 80*
Weichsel, Frederica 1745?-1786 *NewGrD 80*
Weichsell, Carl 1766?-1805? *NewGrD 80*
Weichsell, Charles 1766?-1805? *NewGrD 80*
Weichsell, Elizabeth *NewGrD 80*
Weichsell, Frederica 1745?-1786 *NewGrD 80*
Weideman, Carl Friedrich d1782 *NewGrD 80*
Weideman, Charles Frederick d1782 *NewGrD 80*
Weidemann, Carl Friedrich d1782 *NewGrD 80*
Weidemann, Charles Frederick d1782 *NewGrD 80*
Weidenaar, Reynold 1945- *AmSCAP 80, CpmDNM 79, -80, ConAmC*
Weidig, Adolf 1867-1931 *Baker 78, BiDAmM, OxMus*
Weidinger, Anton 1767-1852 *BnBkM 80, NewGrD 80, OxMus*
Weidinger, Christine Marie 1946- *WhoOp 76*
Weidler, Virginia 1927-1968 *FilmEn, FilmgC, ForYSC, HalFC 80, MGM[port], MotPP, ThFT[port], WhScrn 77, WhoHol B*
Weidler, Warner Alfred 1935- *AmSCAP 80*
Weidman, Charles *Film 2*
Weidman, Charles 1901-1975 *BiE&WWA, CmpGMD[port], CnOxB, DancEn 78[port]*
Weidman, Jerome 1913- *BiE&WWA, ConDr 73, -77, EncMT, NewCBMT, NotNAT, WhoThe 72, -77*
Weidman, Joan *WomWMM, -B*
Weidman, John 1946- *NatPD[port]*
Weidmann, John David 1927- *AmSCAP 80*
Weidner, Paul 1934- *NotNAT*
Weidt, A J 1866-1945 *AmSCAP 66, -80*
Weidt, Jean 1904- *CnOxB*
Weidt, Lucie 1879-1940 *CmOp*
Weidt, Lucie 1880-1940 *NewGrD 80*
Weidt, Lucy 1880-1940 *Baker 78, NewGrD 80*
Weigall, Richard 1944- *IntWWM 77, -80*
Weigand, George Alexander 1946- *IntWWM 80*
Weigand, Louis A 1856-1912 *BiDAmM*
Weigel *NewGrD 80*
Weigel, Christoph 1654?-1725 *NewGrD 80*
Weigel, Christoph 1703-1777 *NewGrD 80*
Weigel, Eugene John 1910- *Baker 78, ConAmC*
Weigel, Hans 1880- *CnMD*
Weigel, Helene 1900-1971 *CroCD, EncWT, Ent, WhThe*
Weigel, Helene 1900-1972 *CnThe*
Weigel, Johann Christoph 1661?-1726 *NewGrD 80*
Weigel, Paul 1867-1951 *Film 1, -2, TwYS, WhScrn 77*
Weight, Michael 1906- *WhThe*
Weigl *NewGrD 80*
Weigl, Bruno 1881-1938 *Baker 78*
Weigl, Johann Baptist 1783-1852 *NewGrD 80*
Weigl, Joseph 1766-1846 *Baker 78, CnOxB, NewGrD 80*
Weigl, Joseph Franz 1740-1820 *Baker 78, NewGrD 80*
Weigl, Karl 1881-1949 *Baker 78, BiDAmM, ConAmC, DcCM, NewGrD 80*
Weigl, Thaddaus 1776-1844 *Baker 78, NewGrD 80*
Weigl, Vally 1889- *CpmDNM 80, ConAmC*
Weigl, Vally 1899- *IntWWM 77*
Weigle, Charles F 1871-1966 *AmSCAP 66, -80*
Weijden, Tor *Film 2*
Weikert, Ralf 1940- *WhoOp 76*
Weikl, Bernd 1942- *WhoOp 76*
Weil, Erno S 1947- *WhoOp 76*
Weil, Grace F *PupTheA*
Weil, Harry 1878-1943 *WhScrn 74, -77*
Weil, Harry 1890-1974 *WhScrn 77*
Weil, Hermann 1877-1949 *Baker 78, BiDAmM*

Weil, Mrs. Leonard D d1963 *NotNAT B*
Weil, Max-Rene *McGEWD*
Weil, Milton 1888-1937 *AmSCAP 66, -80*
Weil, Oscar 1840-1921 *BiDAmM*
Weil, Robert *WhoHol A*
Weiland, Joyce 1931- *WomWMM B*
Weiland, Julius Johann d1663 *NewGrD 80*
Weiler, Berenice 1927- *BiE&WWA, NotNAT*
Weiler, Constance 1918-1965 *WhScrn 74, -77*
Weiler, Gerald E 1928- *IntMPA 77, -75, -76, -78, -79, -80*
Weill, Claudia 1947- *FilmEn, WomWMM, -A, -B*
Weill, Gus 1933- *NatPD[port]*
Weill, Irving 1894- *AmSCAP 66, -80*
Weill, Kurt 1900-1950 *AmPS, AmSCAP 66, -80, Baker 78, BestMus, BiDAmM, BnBkM 80, CmOp, CmpEPM, CompSN[port], ConAmC, DancEn 78, DcCom 77[port], DcCM, EncMT, EncWT, FilmgC, HalFC 80, MorBAP, MusMk, NewCBMT, NewEOp 71, NewGrD 80[port], NotNAT B, OxFilm, OxMus, PlP&P[port], PopAmC[port], PopAmC SUP, WhThe, WorEFlm*
Weille, F Blair 1930- *AmSCAP 66, -80, ConAmC*
Weiman, Rita d1954 *NotNAT B*
Weimar, Georg Peter 1734-1800 *NewGrD 80*
Wein, George 1925- *BiDAmM, CmpEPM, EncFCWM 69, EncJzS 70*
Weinbaum, Batya *WomWMM B*
Weinberg, Anton 1944- *IntWWM 77, -80*
Weinberg, Betsy L 1926- *AmSCAP 66, -80*
Weinberg, Charles 1889-1955 *AmSCAP 66, -80*
Weinberg, Gus 1866-1952 *Film 2, NotNAT B, WhScrn 74, -77, WhThe, WhoHol B*
Weinberg, Henry 1931- *AmSCAP 80, BiDAmM, ConAmC, NewGrD 80*
Weinberg, Herman G 1908- *IntMPA 77, -75, -76, -78, -79, -80*
Weinberg, Jacob 1879-1956 *Baker 78, BiDAmM, ConAmC, NewGrD 80*
Weinberg, Jacob 1883-1956 *AmSCAP 66, -80*
Weinberg, Jean *WomWMM B*
Weinberger, Jaromir 1896-1967 *AmSCAP 66, -80, Baker 78, BiDAmM, BnBkM 80, CmOp, CompSN[port], ConAmC, DcCom&M 79, IntWWM 77, -80, NewEOp 71, NewGrD 80, OxMus*
Weinberger, Josef 1855-1928 *NewGrD 80*
Weinberger-Daniels *NewYTET*
Weinblatt, Mike *IntMPA 80, NewYTET*
Weiner, Arn *WhoHol A*
Weiner, Bernard 1940- *ConAmTC*
Weiner, Dan *ConMuA 80B*
Weiner, Lawrence 1932- *AmSCAP 80, ConAmC*
Weiner, Lawrence A d1961 *NotNAT B*
Weiner, Lazar 1897- *AmSCAP 66, -80, Baker 78, BiDAmM, ConAmC, DcCM, NewGrD 80*
Weiner, Leo 1885-1960 *Baker 78, DcCM, NewGrD 80, OxMus*
Weiner, Leslie *NatPD[port]*
Weiner, Matthew 1953- *AmSCAP 80*
Weiner, Max 1920- *IntWWM 77, -80*
Weiner, Robert *BiE&WWA, NotNAT*
Weiner, Sanford William 1926- *IntMPA 75, -76*
Weiner, Stanley Milton 1925- *ConAmC, IntWWM 77, -80, WhoMus 72*
Weinert, Antoni 1751-1850 *NewGrD 80*
Weingarden, Louis 1943- *ConAmC*
Weingarten, David 1902- *AmSCAP 66, -80*
Weingarten, Joseph 1911- *WhoMus 72*
Weingarten, Laurence 1895- *FilmgC*
Weingarten, Laurence 1898-1975 *HalFC 80*
Weingarten, Lawrence *IntMPA 75*
Weingarten, Lawrence 1898-1975 *FilmEn, WhScrn 77*
Weingarten, Romain 1926- *CroCD*
Weingartner, Felix 1863-1942 *Baker 78, BnBkM 80[port], CmOp, MusMk, MusSN[port], NewEOp 71, NewGrD 80[port], OxMus*
Weinglass, Dewey 1900- *BlksBF*
Weinkoetz, Peter John *PupTheA*
Weinles, Len 1923- *AmSCAP 66*
Weinlig, Christian Ehregott 1743-1813 *Baker 78*
Weinlig, Christian Theodor 1780-1842 *NewGrD 80*
Weinlig, Christian Theodore 1780-1842 *OxMus*
Weinlig, Theodor 1780-1842 *Baker 78*
Weinmann, Alexander 1901- *NewGrD 80*
Weinmann, Johann 1477?-1542 *NewGrD 80*
Weinmann, Karl 1873-1929 *Baker 78, NewGrD 80*
Weinrauch, Ernestus 1730?-1793 *NewGrD 80*
Weinrauch, Faustinus 1730?-1793 *NewGrD 80*
Weinrib, Lennie *WhoHol A*
Weinrib, Leonard *NewYTET*
Weinrich, Carl 1904- *Baker 78, NewGrD 80, WhoMus 72*
Weinstein, Arnold 1927- *AmSCAP 80, BiE&WWA, ConDr 73, -77, NotNAT*
Weinstein, Hannah *WomWMM, -B*
Weinstein, Harvey *ConMuA 80B*
Weinstein, Henry T 1924- *IntMPA 77, -75, -76, -78, -79, -80*
Weinstein, Judy *ConMuA 80B*
Weinstein, Kit *WomWMM B*
Weinstein, Milton 1911- *AmSCAP 66, -80, ConAmC A*
Weinstein, Miriam *WomWMM A, -B*
Weinstein, Morton Neff 1927- *AmSCAP 80*
Weinstein, Sol 1928- *AmSCAP 66, -80*
Weinstein, Susan 1951- *NatPD[port]*
Weinstock, Edgar 1941- *IntWWM 77*
Weinstock, Herbert 1905-1971 *Baker 78, NewGrD 80*
Weinstock, Jack 1909- *BiE&WWA*
Weintraub, Eugene 1904- *IntWWM 80, NewGrD 80*
Weintraub, Frances d1963 *NotNAT B*
Weintraub, Fred 1928- *IntMPA 77, -75, -76, -78, -79, -80*
Weintraub, Jerry *ConMuA 80B*
Weintraub, Milton 1897-1968 *BiE&WWA, NotNAT B*
Weintraub, Sandy *WomWMM*
Weintraub, Stu *ConMuA 80B*
Weintraub, Sy 1922- *WhoHrs 80*
Weintraub, Sy 1923- *IntMPA 79, -80*
Weinwurm, Rudolf 1835-1911 *Baker 78*
Weinzierl, Max, Ritter Von 1841-1898 *Baker 78*
Weinzweig, John 1913- *Baker 78, BiDAmM, DcCM, NewGrD 80*
Weinzweig, John Jacob 1913- *CreCan 2*
Weir, Frank *RkOn*
Weir, George R d1909 *NotNAT B*
Weir, Gillian Constance 1941- *IntWWM 77, -80, NewGrD 80, WhoMus 72*
Weir, Gregg *WhoHol A*
Weir, Helen *Film 1*
Weir, Jane 1916-1937 *WhScrn 74, -77*
Weir, Mary 1783-1840 *BiDAmM*
Weir, Molly *WhoHol A*
Weir, Peter 1938?- *HalFC 80*
Weirich, Frank *ConAmTC*
Weirick, Paul 1906- *AmSCAP 66, -80*
Weis, Carl Flemming 1898- *IntWWM 77, -80, WhoMus 72*
Weis, Don 1922- *BiDFilm, -81, FilmEn, FilmgC, HalFC 80, IntMPA 77, -75, -76, -78, -79, -80, WorEFlm*
Weis, Flemming 1898- *Baker 78, NewGrD 80*
Weis, Friedrich Wilhelm 1744-1826 *NewGrD 80*
Weis, Jack 1932- *IntMPA 77, -76, -78, -79, -80*
Weis, Karel 1862-1944 *Baker 78, MusMk, NewGrD 80*
Weis, Roney 1939- *IntMPA 77, -75, -76, -78, -79*
Weisbach, Hans 1885-1961 *Baker 78*
Weisbart, David 1915-1967 *FilmEn, FilmgC, HalFC 80, WorEFlm*
Weisbeck, Nicolaus 1575?-1640? *NewGrD 80*
Weisberg, Arthur 1931- *Baker 78, NewGrD 80*
Weisberg, Brenda *IntMPA 77, -75, -76, -78, -79, -80, WhoHrs 80*
Weisberg, Julia Lazarevna *NewGrD 80*
Weisberg, Sylvia d1962 *NotNAT B*
Weisberger, Barbara 1926?- *CnOxB*
Weisbord, Sam 1911- *IntMPA 77, -75, -76, -78, -79, -80*
Weisbrod, Annette Jeanne 1937- *IntWWM 77, -80*
Weisburd, Daniel Eugene 1935- *AmSCAP 80*
Weisburd, Elaine Simone 1935- *AmSCAP 80*
Weise, Christian 1642-1708 *CnThe, EncWT, Ent, NewGrD 80, NotNAT B, OxThe, REnWD[port]*
Weise, Christian Felix Weisse 1726-1804 *OxThe*
Weisenborn, Gunther 1902-1969 *CnMD, CroCD, McGEWD, ModWD*
Weiser, Grete 1903-1970 *WhoHol B*
Weiser, Grethe 1903-1970 *WhScrn 74, -77*
Weiser, Irving 1913- *AmSCAP 66, -80*
Weiser, Martin 1916- *IntMPA 77, -75, -76, -78, -79, -80*
Weiser, Norman *ConMuA 80B*
Weisfeld, Zelma H 1931- *BiE&WWA, NotNAT*
Weisgall, Hugo 1912- *AmSCAP 66, -80, Baker 78, BiDAmM, BnBkM 80, CompSN[port], CpmDNM 79, ConAmC, DcCM, IntWWM 77, -80, NewEOp 71, NewGrD 80, WhoMus 72*
Weisgarber, Elliot 1919- *Baker 78, IntWWM 77, -80*
Weisling, Raymond 1947- *ConAmC*
Weisman, Ben 1921- *AmSCAP 66, -80*
Weisman, Benjamin 1921- *BiDAmM*
Weisman, Milton C 1895- *IntMPA 77, -75, -76, -78, -79*
Weismann, Julius 1879-1950 *Baker 78, NewGrD 80*
Weismann, Wilhelm 1900- *Baker 78, IntWWM 77, -80, NewGrD 80*
Weismuller, Johnny 1904- *CmMov, WhoHrs 80[port]*
Weiss *NewGrD 80*
Weiss, Adolph 1891-1971 *Baker 78, BiDAmM, ConAmC, DcCM, NewGrD 80, OxMus*
Weiss, Amalie *Baker 78*
Weiss, Dieter 1922- *IntWWM 77*
Weiss, Edward 1892- *ConAmC, IntWWM 77, -80*
Weiss, Elizabeth B 1940- *IntWWM 80*
Weiss, Ferdinand 1933- *IntWWM 77, -80*
Weiss, Flemming 1898- *OxMus*
Weiss, Franz 1778-1830 *Baker 78*
Weiss, Friedrich Wilhelm *NewGrD 80*
Weiss, Fritz *IntMPA 77, -75, -76, -78, -79, -80*
Weiss, George 1893-1964 *AmSCAP 66*
Weiss, George David 1921- *AmSCAP 66, -80, CmpEPM*
Weiss, George G 1922- *IntMPA 75, -76*
Weiss, Howard A 1939- *IntWWM 80*
Weiss, Jack 1932- *IntMPA 75*
Weiss, Jiri 1913- *DcFM, FilmEn, WorEFlm*
Weiss, Johann 1850-1919 *Baker 78*
Weiss, Johann Adolf Faustinus 1741-1814 *NewGrD 80*
Weiss, Johann Jacob 1662?-1754 *NewGrD 80*
Weiss, Johann Sigismund 1690?-1737 *NewGrD 80*
Weiss, Josephine 1805-1852 *CnOxB*
Weiss, Julius 1814-1898 *Baker 78*
Weiss, Karel *NewGrD 80*
Weiss, Laurence 1941- *AmSCAP 80*
Weiss, Manfred 1935- *IntWWM 77, -80*
Weiss, Marion 1923- *AmSCAP 66*
Weiss, Michael *OxMus*
Weiss, Mitchell Allen 1952- *AmSCAP 80*
Weiss, Nat *ConMuA 80B*
Weiss, Paulette *ConMuA 80B*
Weiss, Peter 1916- *CnThe, CroCD, EncWT, Ent[port], FilmEn, McGEWD[port], ModWD, NotNAT, -A, OxFilm, PlP&P, -A, REnWD[port], WhoThe 72, -77, WorEFlm*
Weiss, Piero Ernesto 1928- *IntWWM 77, -80*
Weiss, Raphael 1713-1779 *NewGrD 80*
Weiss, Robert 1949- *CnOxB*
Weiss, Robert Russell 1928- *AmSCAP 66, -80*
Weiss, Ruth *WomWMM B*
Weiss, Sam *ConMuA 80B*
Weiss, Sammy 1910- *WhoJazz 72*
Weiss, Sid 1914- *CmpEPM, WhoJazz 72*
Weiss, Silvius Leopold 1686-1750 *NewGrD 80*
Weiss, Stephan 1899- *AmSCAP 66, -80*
Weiss, Steve *ConMuA 80B*
Weiss, Sylvius Leopold 1686-1750 *Baker 78, MusMk*
Weiss, William M *IntMPA 77, -75, -76, -78,*

-79
Weiss, Willoughby Hunter 1820-1867 *OxMus*
Weissbeck, Johann Michael 1756-1808 *NewGrD 80*
Weissbeck, Nicolaus *NewGrD 80*
Weissberg, Eric *EncFCWM 69*
Weissberg, Julia Lazarevna *NewGrD 80*
Weissberg, Yulia 1878-1942 *Baker 78*
Weissberger, L Arnold 1907- *BiE&WWA, NotNAT*
Weissburg, Edward 1876-1950 *WhScrn 74, -77*
Weisse, A *Film 2*
Weisse, C F 1726-1804 *OxMus*
Weisse, Christian Felix Weisse 1726-1804 *NewGrD 80, NotNAT B*
Weisse, Hanni 1892-1967 *Film 2, WhScrn 74, -77, WhoHol B*
Weisse, Hans 1892-1940 *Baker 78*
Weissenback, Andreas 1880-1960 *Baker 78*
Weissenberg, Alexis 1929- *BiDAmM, BnBkM 80, IntWWM 77, -80, MusSN[port], NewGrD 80, WhoMus 72*
Weissenborn, Julius 1837-1888 *NewGrD 80*
Weissenburg *OxMus*
Weissenburg, Heinrich *NewGrD 80*
Weissensee, Friedrich 1560?-1622 *NewGrD 80*
Weissensteiner, Raimund 1905- *IntWWM 77, -80, WhoMus 72*
Weisshaar, Hans 1913- *NewGrD 80*
Weisshaus, Imre *NewGrD 80*
Weissheimer, Wendelin 1838-1910 *Baker 78, NewGrD 80*
Weissman, Dora d1974 *WhScrn 77, WhoHol B*
Weissman, Murray 1925- *IntMPA 77, -75, -76, -78, -79, -80*
Weissman, Richard 1935- *EncFCWM 69, IntWWM 77*
Weissman, Seymour J 1931- *IntMPA 77, -75, -76, -78, -79, -80*
Weissmann, Adolf 1873-1929 *Baker 78*
Weissmann, Janos S 1910-1980 *NewGrD 80*
Weissmann, John S 1910-1980 *Baker 78, NewGrD 80*
Weissmuller, Johnny 1904- *FilmEn, Film 2, FilmgC, ForYSC, HalFC 80[port], IntMPA 77, -75, -76, -78, -79, -80, MGM[port], MotPP, MovMk[port], OxFilm, What 1[port], WhoHol A, WorEFlm*
Weissmuller, Johnny, Jr. *WhoHol A*
Weissova, Lenka *WomWMM*
Weist-Hill, Thomas Henry 1828-1891 *NewGrD 80*
Weisz, Egon Max 1909- *WhoMus 72*
Weiter, Aisig 1878-1919 *OxThe*
Weith, Eva *BiE&WWA*
Weithaus, John Chester 1902- *AmSCAP 80*
Weitman, Norman 1927- *IntMPA 77, -75, -76*
Weitman, Robert M 1905- *IntMPA 77, -75, -76, -78, -79, -80, NewYTET*
Weitz, Emile 1883-1951 *WhScrn 74, -77*
Weitz, Ted 1907- *AmSCAP 80*
Weitzel, J Harold 1936- *IntWWM 77*
Weitzenkorn, Louis 1893-1943 *NotNAT B*
Weitzler, Morris Martin 1916- *AmSCAP 80*
Weitzmann, Carl Friedrich 1808-1880 *Baker 78, NewGrD 80*
Weitzner, David 1938- *IntMPA 77, -75, -76, -78, -79, -80*
Weiwanowski, Paul Joseph *NewGrD 80*
Wekre, Froydis Ree 1941- *IntWWM 77, -80*
Wekwerth, Manfred 1929- *CroCD, EncWT*
Welander, Karl 1943- *CnOxB*
Welch, Bob 1946- *ConMuA 80A, RkOn 2[port]*
Welch, Charles C *WhoHol A*
Welch, Constance d1976 *BiE&WWA, NotNAT B*
Welch, Deshler d1920 *NotNAT B*
Welch, Eddie 1900-1963 *WhScrn 74, -77, WhoHol B*
Welch, Elisabeth 1908- *EncMT, WhoHol A, WhoThe 72*
Welch, Elisabeth 1909- *BiE&WWA, NotNAT, WhoThe 77*
Welch, Elizabeth *FilmgC*
Welch, Elizabeth 1908- *HalFC 80*
Welch, Garth 1936- *CnOxB, DancEn 78*
Welch, Harry Foster 1899-1973 *WhScrn 77, WhoHol B*
Welch, James 1865-1917 *NotNAT B, WhThe*
Welch, James T 1869-1949 *Film 2, WhScrn 74, -77, WhoHol B*
Welch, Joseph L 1891-1960 *FilmgC, HalFC 80, WhoHol B*
Welch, Joseph N 1891-1960 *WhScrn 74, -77*
Welch, Kenneth Howard 1926- *AmSCAP 66, -80*
Welch, Lenny 1938- *RkOn*
Welch, Lew d1952 *NotNAT B*
Welch, Marilyn 1933- *AmSCAP 66, -80*
Welch, Mary 1923-1958 *NotNAT B, WhScrn 74, -77, WhoHol B*
Welch, Nelson *WhoHol A*
Welch, Niles 1888- *Film 1, -2, ForYSC, TwYS*
Welch, Norman A 1946- *AmSCAP 66, -80*
Welch, Peter 1922- *IntMPA 77, -75, -76, -78, -79, -80*
Welch, Raquel *IntMPA 77, -75, -76, -78, -79, -80, MotPP, WhoHol A*
Welch, Raquel 1940- *FilmEn, FilmgC, HalFC 80, WhoHrs 80*
Welch, Raquel 1942- *ForYSC, MovMk[port], WorEFlm*
Welch, Robert 1945- *AmSCAP 80*
Welch, Robert Gilbert d1924 *NotNAT B*
Welch, Robert L 1910- *IntMPA 77, -75, -76, -78, -79, -80*
Welch, Roy Dickinson 1885-1951 *Baker 78*
Welch, Sidney Lester, Jr. 1924- *AmSCAP 80*
Welch, William *Film 2*
Welcher, Dan Edward 1948- *AmSCAP 80, CpmDNM 77, ConAmC*
Welchman, Harry 1886-1966 *EncMT, IlWWBF, WhScrn 74, -77, WhThe, WhoHol B*
Welcker *NewGrD 80*
Welcker, Gertrude *Film 2*
Welcker, John *NewGrD 80*
Welcker, Mary d1778 *NewGrD 80*
Welcker, Peter d1775 *NewGrD 80*
Weld, Arthur Cyril Gordon 1862-1914 *Baker 78, BiDAmM*
Weld, Thomas *OxMus*
Weld, Tuesday 1943- *BiDFilm, -81, FilmEn, FilmgC, ForYSC, HalFC 80, IntMPA 77, -75, -76, -78, -79, -80, MotPP, MovMk, WhoHol A, WorEFlm[port]*
Welden, Ben 1901- *FilmgC, ForYSC, HalFC 80, IntMPA 77, -75, -76, -78, -79, -80, Vers B[port], WhThe*
Welden, Friedrich *NewGrD 80*
Welder, Philip De *NewGrD 80*
Weldon, Bunny *Film 2*
Weldon, Duncan Clark 1941- *WhoThe 77*
Weldon, Fay 1933- *ConDr 73, -77C*
Weldon, Francis 1896- *IntMPA 75, -76*
Weldon, Frank *AmSCAP 66, CmpEPM*
Weldon, Frank d1970 *AmSCAP 80*
Weldon, George 1906-1963 *Baker 78, NewGrD 80*
Weldon, Georgina 1837-1914 *Baker 78, OxMus*
Weldon, Harry 1882- *WhThe*
Weldon, Irene 1938- *IntWWM 77*
Weldon, Jess *Film 2*
Weldon, Joan 1933- *ForYSC, IntMPA 77, -75, -76, -78, -79, -80, WhoHol A, WhoHrs 80[port]*
Weldon, John *McGEWD*
Weldon, John 1676-1736 *MusMk, NewGrD 80[port], OxMus*
Weldon, Lillian 1869-1941 *WhScrn 74, -77*
Weldon, Maxine 1947- *AmSCAP 80*
Weldon, Peter *BiDAmM*
Weldon, Tim *WhoHol A*
Weldon, Will 1909- *BluesWW[port]*
Welffens, Peter 1924- *IntWWM 77, -80, WhoMus 72*
Welford, Dallas 1872-1946 *WhScrn 74, -77, WhoHol B*
Welford, Dallas 1874-1946 *Film 2, NotNAT B, WhThe, WhoStg 1908*
Welford, Nancy *Film 2*
Welin, Karl-Erik 1934- *Baker 78, DcCM, NewGrD 80*
Welisch, Walter T *PupTheA*
Welitch, Ljuba 1912- *BiDAmM*
Welitch, Ljuba 1913- *NewEOp 71*
Welitsch, Ljuba 1913- *Baker 78, CmOp, IntWWM 77, -80, MusSN[port], NewGrD 80[port], WhoMus 72*
Weliver, E Delmer 1939- *IntWWM 80*
Welk, Ehm 1884-1966 *CnMD, EncWT*
Welk, Lawrence 1903- *AmPS A, AmSCAP 66, -80, Baker 78, BgBands 74[port], BiDAmM, CmpEPM, ConMuA 80B, IntMPA 77, -75, -76, -78, -79, -80, RkOn, WhoMus 72*
Welker, Frank *WhoHol A*
Welland, Colin 1934- *ConDr 73, -77C, FilmgC, HalFC 80*
Wellejus, Henning 1919- *IntWWM 77, -80*
Wellek, Albert 1904-1972 *Baker 78, NewGrD 80, OxMus*
Weller *NewGrD 80*
Weller, Bernard 1870-1943 *NotNAT B, WhThe*
Weller, Carrie d1954 *NotNAT B*
Weller, Dieter 1937- *WhoOp 76*
Weller, Freddy 1947- *CounME 74[port], -74A, IlEncCM[port]*
Weller, Harold Leighton 1941- *IntWWM 77*
Weller, Michael 1942- *ConDr 73, -77*
Weller, Walter 1939- *IntWWM 77, -80, NewGrD 80*
Welles, Beatrice *WhoHol A*
Welles, Gwen *WhoHol A*
Welles, Jada *Film 2*
Welles, Jesse *WhoHol A*
Welles, Mel 1930?- *WhoHrs 80[port]*
Welles, Meri 1930?-1973 *WhScrn 77*
Welles, Orson *ConDr 73, -77A, IntMPA 77, -75, -76, -78, -79, -80, WhoHol A*
Welles, Orson 1915- *AmFD, BiDFilm, -81, BiE&WWA, CmMov, CnThe, DcFM, EncMT, EncWT, Ent, FamA&A[port], FilmEn, FilmgC, HalFC 80[port], MotPP, MovMk[port], NotNAT, -A, OxFilm, OxThe, WhThe, WhoHrs 80, WhoThe 72, WorEFlm[port]*
Welles, Orson 1916- *PlP&P*
Welles, Ralph *Film 2*
Welles, Rebecca *WhoHol A*
Welles, Violet *BiE&WWA, NotNAT*
Wellesley, Viscount *NewGrD 80*
Wellesley, Arthur 1890- *WhThe*
Wellesley, Charles 1875-1946 *Film 1, -2, WhScrn 74, -77, WhoHol B*
Wellesley, William *Film 2*
Wellesz, Egon 1885-1974 *Baker 78, BnBkM 80, DcCM, NewEOp 71, NewGrD 80[port], OxMus, WhoMus 72*
Wellesz, Egon 1885-1975 *CmOp*
Welling, Christopher Godfrey 1939- *WhoMus 72*
Welling, Sylvia 1901- *WhThe*
Wellington, Duke Of 1769-1852 *OxMus*
Wellington, Babe 1897-1954 *WhScrn 74, -77, WhoHol B*
Wellington, Christopher Ramsay 1930- *IntWWM 77, -80*
Wellitsch, Ljuba 1913- *IntWWM 80*
Wellman, Emily Ann d1946 *NotNAT B, WhScrn 77*
Wellman, Michael *WhoHol A*
Wellman, William, Jr. *ForYSC, WhoHol A*
Wellman, William A 1896-1975 *AmFD, BiDFilm, -81, CmMov, DcFM, FilmEn, Film 1, FilmgC, HalFC 80, IntMPA 75, -76, MovMk[port], OxFilm, TwYS A, WhScrn 77, WhoHol C, WorEFlm*
Wells, Al *BlksBF*
Wells, Amos 1934- *BluesWW[port]*
Wells, Ardis Arlee 1917- *BiDAmM*
Wells, Billy 1888-1967 *WhoHol B*
Wells, Bombadier Billy 1888-1967 *WhScrn 74*
Wells, Bombardier Billy 1888-1967 *WhScrn 77*
Wells, Bruce 1950- *CnOxB*
Wells, Bryan 1943- *AmSCAP 80*
Wells, Carole *WhoHol A*
Wells, Charles B d1924 *NotNAT B*
Wells, David John 1931- *WhoMus 72*
Wells, Dawn *WhoHol A*
Wells, Deering 1896-1961 *WhScrn 74, -77, WhThe, WhoHol B*
Wells, Dickie 1909- *CmpEPM*
Wells, Dicky 1909- *EncJzS 70, IlEncJ,*

WhoJazz 72
Wells, Doreen 1937- *CnOxB, DancEn 78*
Wells, Frank G 1932- *IntMPA 77, -75, -76, -78, -79, -80*
Wells, George *PupTheA*
Wells, George 1909- *FilmEn, FilmgC, HalFC 80, WorEFlm*
Wells, George C 1819-1873 *BiDAmM*
Wells, Guyon Russell 1931- *IntWWM 77*
Wells, H G 1866-1946 *FilmgC, HalFC 80, PlP&P, WhScrn 74, -77, WhoHol B, WhoHrs 80*
Wells, Henry James 1906- *CmpEPM, WhoJazz 72*
Wells, Herbert George 1866-1946 *NotNAT B*
Wells, Ingeborg *IIWWBF A, WhoHol A*
Wells, Jacqueline 1914- *FilmEn, Film 2, ForYSC, WhoHol A*
Wells, James Roy 1932- *IntWWM 77, -80*
Wells, Jane *Film 1*
Wells, John Barnes 1880-1935 *AmSCAP 66, -80*
Wells, John Barnes 1880-1955 *ConAmC*
Wells, Johnny 1905?- *WhoJazz 72*
Wells, Junior 1932- *BiDAmM*
Wells, Kenn 1942- *CnOxB*
Wells, Kitty 1918- *IlEncCM[port]*
Wells, Kitty 1919- *BiDAmM, CounME 74[port], -74A, EncFCWM 69*
Wells, L M 1862-1923 *Film 1, WhScrn 77*
Wells, Mai 1862-1941 *WhScrn 74, -77, WhoHol B*
Wells, Manny *ConMuA 80B*
Wells, Marcus Morris 1815-1895 *BiDAmM*
Wells, Marie 1894-1949 *Film 2, NotNAT B, WhScrn 74, -77, WhoHol B*
Wells, Marion *WhoHol A*
Wells, Mary 1943- *RkOn[port]*
Wells, Mary Ann 1896- *CnOxB*
Wells, Mary Erryl 1935- *WhoMus 72*
Wells, May *Film 1, -2*
Wells, Michael John 1946- *EncJzS 70*
Wells, Orson 1915- *ForYSC*
Wells, Patricia *WhoOp 76*
Wells, Raymond *Film 1, -2*
Wells, Rick *WhoHol A*
Wells, Robert *NewYTET*
Wells, Robert 1922- *AmSCAP 66, -80*
Wells, Robin John Andrew 1943- *IntWWM 77*
Wells, Ronald Kenneth 1926- *ConAmC*
Wells, Roxanna d1964 *NotNAT B*
Wells, Roy *AmSCAP 80*
Wells, Sheilah *WhoHol A*
Wells, Spike 1946- *EncJzS 70*
Wells, Ted *Film 2*
Wells, Thomas *ConAmC*
Wells, Veronica *WhoHol A*
Wells, Viola Gertrude 1902- *BluesWW[port]*
Wells, William d1956 *NotNAT B*
Wells, William 1909- *EncJzS 70*
Wells, William 1910- *AmSCAP 66, BiDAmM*
Wells, William Edgar 1927- *IntWWM 77*
Wells, William K *Film 2*
Wellstood, Dick 1927- *CmpEPM, EncJzS 70, IlEncJ*
Wellstood, Richard MacQueen 1927- *EncJzS 70*
Welpott, Raymond W d1973 *NewYTET*
Wels, Charles 1825-1906 *Baker 78, BiDAmM*
Welsbacher, Betty T 1925- *IntWWM 77*
Welsby, Norman 1939- *WhoOp 76*
Welsh, Alex 1929- *EncJzS 70*
Welsh, Betty *Film 2*
Welsh, Charles L 1906- *IntMPA 77, -75, -76, -78, -79, -80*
Welsh, Jane 1905- *WhThe*
Welsh, John 1905?- *FilmgC, HalFC 80, WhoHol A*
Welsh, Moray Meston 1947- *IntWWM 77, -80*
Welsh, Niles *Film 2*
Welsh, Thomas 1780?-1848 *Baker 78, NewGrD 80*
Welsh, William *Film 1, -2*
Welsh, Wilmer Haydon *ConAmC*
Welte *NewGrD 80*
Welte, Michael 1807-1880 *Baker 78*
Welter, Johann Samuel 1650?-1720 *NewGrD 80*
Welti, Albert Jakob 1894-1965 *CnMD*
Welting, Ruth Lynn 1949- *WhoOp 76*
Weltman, Philip 1908- *IntMPA 77, -75, -76, -78, -79, -80*
Weltner, George 1901- *IntMPA 77, -75, -76, -78, -79, -80*
Welton, Frederic Percy 1926- *IntWWM 80*
Weltstein, Peter 1939- *IntWWM 77*
Welty, Eudora *Conv 3[port]*
Welty, Susan Fulton *PupTheA*
Welwood, Arthur 1934- *ConAmC*
Welz, Stu *ConMuA 80B*
Wemyss, Francis Courtney 1797-1859 *FamA&A[port], NotNAT A, -B, OxThe*
Wemyss, Jean Margaret *CreCan 1*
Wen-Chung, Chou *Baker 78*
Wence, William Kenneth 1942- *AmSCAP 80*
Wences, Senor *WhoHol A*
Wenck, August Heinrich d1814? *NewGrD 80*
Wenck, Eduard 1894-1954 *WhScrn 74, -77*
Wenckel, Johann Friedrich Wilhelm *NewGrD 80*
Wend, Johannes d1608? *NewGrD 80*
Wendel, Ernst 1876-1938 *Baker 78*
Wendel, Eugen 1934- *Baker 78*
Wendel, Heinrich 1915- *CnOxB, DancEn 78, WhoOp 76*
Wendel, Paul L 1923- *AmSCAP 80*
Wendelburg, Norma Ruth 1918- *AmSCAP 80*
Wendelken-Wilson, Charles 1938- *WhoOp 76*
Wendell, Charles Wood 1910- *AmSCAP 66, -80*
Wendell, Howard D 1908-1975 *Vers A[port], WhScrn 77, WhoHol C*
Wendelstein, Johannes *NewGrD 80*
Wender, Johann Friedrich 1655?-1729 *NewGrD 80*
Wenders, Wim 1945- *BiDFilm 81, FilmEn, IntMPA 79, -80*
Wendin, Johannes d1608? *NewGrD 80*
Wendius, Johannes d1608? *NewGrD 80*
Wendkos, Paul *NewYTET*
Wendkos, Paul 1922- *BiDFilm, -81, FilmEn, FilmgC, HalFC 80*
Wendkos, Paul 1923- *WorEFlm*
Wendland, Waldemar 1873-1947 *Baker 78*
Wendler, Otto Bernhard 1895-1958? *CnMD*
Wendling *NewGrD 80*
Wendling, Dorothea 1736-1811 *NewGrD 80*
Wendling, Dorothea 1767-1839 *NewGrD 80*
Wendling, Elisabeth Augusta 1746-1786 *NewGrD 80*
Wendling, Elisabeth Augusta 1752-1794 *NewGrD 80*
Wendling, Franz 1729-1786 *NewGrD 80*
Wendling, Gustl 1752-1794 *NewGrD 80*
Wendling, Johann Baptist 1723-1797 *Baker 78, NewGrD 80*
Wendling, Karl 1750-1834 *NewGrD 80*
Wendling, Karl 1857-1918 *Baker 78*
Wendling, Pete 1888-1974 *AmSCAP 66, -80, BiDAmM, CmpEPM*
Wendorff, Laiola 1895-1966 *WhScrn 77*
Wendt, Ernst Adolf 1806-1850 *Baker 78*
Wendt, Johann *NewGrD 80*
Wendt, Stephan 1909- *CnMD*
Wendt-Walther, Ursula 1939- *IntWWM 80, WhoOp 76*
Wendtland, William Wolters 1918- *IntWWM 77*
Wengraf, John 1901- *HalFC 80*
Wengraf, John E 1897-1974 *FilmgC, ForYSC, Vers A[port], WhScrn 77, WhoHol B*
Wengren, David *Film 2*
Wenham, Jane *WhoHol A, WhoThe 72, -77*
Wenick, Georges-Henri 1718?-1760? *NewGrD 80*
Weninger, Richard 1934- *IntWWM 80*
Wenk, August Heinrich *NewGrD 80*
Wenkel, Johann Friedrich Wilhelm 1734-1792? *NewGrD 80*
Wenkel, Ortrun 1942- *WhoOp 76*
Wenkoff, Spas 1928- *IntWWM 80*
Wenman, Henry N 1875-1953 *Film 2, NotNAT B, WhThe, WhoHol B*
Wenman, T E d1892 *NotNAT B*
Wenn, Clifton *Film 2*
Wennberg, Siv Anna Margaretha 1944- *WhoOp 76*
Wenner, Gene C 1931- *IntWWM 77, -80*
Wenner, Jann *ConMuA 80B*
Wennerberg, G 1817-1901 *OxMus*
Wennerberg, Gunnar 1817-1901 *Baker 78, NewGrD 80*
Wennerberg-Reuter, Sara 1875-1959 *NewGrD 80*
Wennergren, Lena 1947- *CnOxB*
Wenning, Thomas H d1962 *NotNAT B*
Wenrich, Percy 1887-1952 *AmPS, AmSCAP 66, -80, BiDAmM, CmpEPM, NewGrD 80, NotNAT B, PopAmC[port]*
Wenstrom-Lekare, Lennart Helge 1924- *IntWWM 77, -80*
Went, Jan 1745-1801 *NewGrD 80*
Went, Johann 1745-1801 *NewGrD 80*
Wentworth, Fanny d1934 *NotNAT B*
Wentworth, John *CreCan 2*
Wentworth, Martha d1974 *Vers A[port], WhScrn 77, WhoHol B*
Wentworth, Stephen d1935 *NotNAT B*
Wentworth, W Norris *PupTheA*
Wentz, John K d1964 *NotNAT B*
Wentz-Janacek, Elisabet 1923- *IntWWM 77*
Wentzel, Nicholas Franz Xaver 1643?-1722 *NewGrD 80*
Wentzely, Mikulas Frantisek Xaver 1643?-1722 *NewGrD 80*
Wenzel, Arthur J *WhoHol A*
Wenzel, Eberhard 1896- *IntWWM 77, -80*
Wenzel, Ernst Ferdinand 1808-1880 *Baker 78*
Wenzel, Leopold 1847-1925 *Baker 78*
Wenzell *PupTheA*
Wenzinger, August 1905- *Baker 78, IntWWM 77, -80, NewGrD 80*
Werba, Erik 1918- *Baker 78, NewGrD 80, WhoMus 72*
Werba, Louis F d1942 *NotNAT B*
Werbeck, Gaspar Van *NewGrD 80*
Werbeke, Gaspar Van *NewGrD 80*
Werbesik, Gisela 1875-1956 *WhScrn 74, -77*
Werbiseck, Gisela 1875-1956 *WhoHol B*
Werckmeister, Andreas 1645-1706 *Baker 78, NewGrD 80*
Werckmeister, Vicky *Film 2*
Werder, Felix 1922- *Baker 78, DcCM, NewGrD 80*
Werder, Richard 1919- *Baker 78*
Werdier, Pierre *NewGrD 80*
Werdin, Eberhard 1911- *IntWWM 80*
Werfel, Franz 1890-1945 *BiDAmM, CnMD, CnThe, Ent, McGEWD[port], ModWD, NewEOp 71, NewGrD 80, NotNAT B, OxThe, PlP&P, REnWD[port]*
Werfel, Franz 1898-1945 *EncWT*
Werfel, Wenzel Wilhelm *NewGrD 80*
Wergeland, Henrik Arnold 1808-1845 *NotNAT B, OxThe*
Werich, Jan 1905- *CnMD, EncWT*
Werion, Rudi 1935- *IntWWM 77, -80*
Werker, Alfred Louis 1896- *FilmEn, FilmgC, HalFC 80, IntMPA 77, -75, -76, TwYS A, WhoHrs 80*
Werkmeister, Lotte 1886-1970 *WhScrn 74, -77*
Werle *IntMPA 77, -76, -78, -78, -79, -80*
Werle, Barbara *ForYSC, WhoHol A*
Werle, Floyd Edwards 1929- *AmSCAP 66, -80, ConAmC*
Werle, Frederick C *CpmDNM 79, ConAmC*
Werle, Lars 1925- *MusMk*
Werle, Lars Johan 1926- *Baker 78, DcCM, NewGrD 80*
Werlin, Johannes d1680? *NewGrD 80*
Werlin, Johannes 1588-1666 *NewGrD 80*
Werlinus, Johannes d1680? *NewGrD 80*
Werman, Tom *ConMuA 80B*
Wermann, Friedrich Oskar 1840-1906 *Baker 78*
Wermel, Benjamin 1907- *AmSCAP 66, -80*
Werndle, Anton Ignaz 1700?-1754 *NewGrD 80*
Werner, Arno 1865-1955 *Baker 78*
Werner, Bud 1936-1964 *WhScrn 77*
Werner, Christoph 1617?-1650 *NewGrD 80*
Werner, Eloise 1916- *IntWWM 77*
Werner, Ephraim *IntMPA 75, -76*
Werner, Eric 1901- *Baker 78, BiDAmM, ConAmC, NewGrD 80, OxMus*
Werner, Fred H, Jr. 1934- *AmSCAP 80*
Werner, Friedrich Ludwig Zacharias 1768-1823 *NotNAT B, OxThe*
Werner, Gosta 1908- *DcFM, FilmEn*
Werner, Gregor Joseph 1693-1766 *Baker 78, NewGrD 80*
Werner, Heinrich 1800-1833 *Baker 78*

Werner, Jean-Jacques 1935- *IntWWM 77, -80*
Werner, Johann Gottlob 1777-1822 *Baker 78*
Werner, Josef 1837-1922 *Baker 78*
Werner, Kay 1918- *AmSCAP 66, -80*
Werner, Kenneth *ConAmC*
Werner, Leszek 1937- *IntWWM 80*
Werner, Margot 1937- *CnOxB, DancEn 78*
Werner, Mort 1916- *IntMPA 75, -76, NewYTET*
Werner, Oskar 1922- *BiDFilm, -81, EncWT, FilmAG WE[port], FilmEn, FilmgC, ForYSC, HalFC 80, IntMPA 77, -75, -76, -78, -79, -80, MotPP, MovMk, OxFilm, WhoHol A, WorEFlm*
Werner, Sue 1918- *AmSCAP 66, -80*
Werner, Sven Erik 1937- *IntWWM 77, -80*
Werner, Theodor Wilhelm 1874-1957 *Baker 78*
Werner, Walter 1884-1956 *WhScrn 74, -77*
Werner, Zacharias 1768-1823 *CnThe, EncWT, Ent, McGEWD, REnWD[port]*
Werner Braun, Hermann Georg 1926- *IntWWM 77*
Werner-Kahle, Hugo 1883-1961 *WhScrn 74, -77*
Wernher, Heinrich *NewGrD 80*
Wernick, Richard 1934- *AmSCAP 66, -80, Baker 78, CpmDNM 76, -77, -79, -80, ConAmC, DcCM*
Wernicke, Enrique *PupTheA*
Wernicke, Helmuth 1909- *IntWWM 77, -80*
Wernicke, Otto 1893-1965 *WhScrn 77*
Wernik, Kazimierz 1828-1859 *NewGrD 80*
Werrecore, Mathias Hermann d1574? *NewGrD 80*
Werrecore, Matthias Hermann d1574? *NewGrD 80*
Werrekoren, Hermann Mathias *Baker 78*
Werrenrath, Reinald 1883-1953 *Baker 78, BiDAmM, Film 2*
Wershba, Joseph *NewYTET*
Wert, Giaches De 1535-1596 *Baker 78, NewGrD 80, OxMus*
Wert, Jaches De 1535-1596 *NewGrD 80*
Werth, Barbara *Film 2*
Werthner, Philip 1858-1930 *BiDAmM*
Wertimer, Ned *WhoHol A*
Wertmuller, Lina *IntMPA 78, -79, -80*
Wertmuller, Lina 1928- *ConLC 16, FilmEn, HalFC 80*
Wertmuller, Lina 1930?- *MovMk[port], WomWMM*
Wertmuller, Lina 1932- *BiDFilm 81*
Wertz, Clarence d1935 *Film 2, WhScrn 74, -77, WhoHol B*
Wertzeburc, Conrat Von *NewGrD 80*
Wery, Carl 1897-1975 *FilmAG WE*
Wery, Carl 1898-1975 *WhScrn 77, WhoHol C*
Werzlau, Joachim 1913- *NewGrD 80*
Wesch, Anthonius *NewGrD 80*
Wescott, Steven Dwight 1950- *ConAmC*
Wescourt, Gordon *WhoHol A*
Wesembeek *Baker 78*
Wesendonck, Mathilde 1828-1902 *Baker 78*
Wesendonk, Agnes 1828-1902 *NewGrD 80*
Wesendonk, Mathilde 1828-1902 *NewGrD 80*
Wesford, Susan *NotNAT B*
Weshner, David E *IntMPA 75, -76*
Wesker, Arnold 1932- *BiE&WWA, CnMD, CnThe, ConDr 73, -77, CroCD, EncWT, Ent[port], McGEWD, ModWD, NotNAT, -A, OxThe, PlP&P[port], REnWD[port], WhoThe 72, -77*
Wesley *NewGrD 80*
Wesley, Charles *OxMus*
Wesley, Charles 1707-1788 *BiDAmM, OxMus*
Wesley, Charles 1757-1834 *Baker 78, NewGrD 80, OxMus*
Wesley, Eliza 1819-1895 *OxMus*
Wesley, Francis Gwynne 1842-1921 *OxMus*
Wesley, Garret *NewGrD 80*
Wesley, Gertrude *OxMus*
Wesley, John 1703-1791 *Baker 78, BiDAmM, NewGrD 80, OxMus*
Wesley, Matthew Erasmus *OxMus*
Wesley, Norman 1921- *WhoMus 72*
Wesley, R Glenn *OxMus*
Wesley, Richard 1945- *BlkAmP, DrBlPA, MorBAP, NatPD[port], PlP&P A*
Wesley, Samuel 1766-1837 *Baker 78, BnBkM 80, MusMk, NewGrD 80[port], OxMus*
Wesley, Samuel Sebastian 1810-1876 *Baker 78, MusMk, NewGrD 80[port], OxMus*
Wesley-Smith, Martin 1945- *NewGrD 80*
Weslow, William 1925- *DancEn 78*
Weslyn, Louis 1875-1936 *AmSCAP 66, -80*
Wesolowska, Anna Krystyna 1949- *IntWWM 77, -80*
Wess, Frank Wellington 1922- *CmpEPM, EncJzS 70*
Wess, Hal 1922-1968 *AmSCAP 66, -80*
Wess, Otto Francis 1914-1969 *WhScrn 74, -77*
Wessberg, Erik Axel 1947- *IntWWM 77*
Wessel, Christian Rudolph 1797-1885 *NewGrD 80*
Wessel, Dick 1910-1965 *HalFC 80*
Wessel, Dick 1913-1965 *FilmgC, Vers B[port], WhScrn 74, -77, WhoHol B*
Wessel, Johan 1742-1785 *OxThe*
Wessel, Mark E 1894-1973 *Baker 78, BiDAmM, ConAmC*
Wessel, Richard 1913-1965 *ForYSC*
Wessel-Therhorn, Helmut 1927- *WhoOp 76*
Wesselhoeft, Eleanor 1873-1945 *WhScrn 74, -77, WhoHol B*
Wessels, Henri *BlksB&W C*
Wessely, Carl Bernhard 1768-1826 *NewGrD 80*
Wessely, Hans 1862-1926 *NewGrD 80*
Wessely, Helene 1924- *IntWWM 77, -80*
Wessely, Johann 1762-1810 *NewGrD 80*
Wessely, Othmar 1922- *IntWWM 77, -80, NewGrD 80, WhoMus 72*
Wessely, Paula 1908- *EncWT, FilmAG WE[port], FilmgC, HalFC 80, OxFilm*
Wessely-Kropik, Helene *WhoMus 72*
Wessenius, Henry 1926- *IntWWM 80*
Wesson, Alfred Frank 1901- *AmSCAP 66, -80*
Wesson, Dick 1922- *ForYSC, HalFC 80, WhoHol A*
Wesson, Eileen *WhoHol A*
Wesson, Gene 1921-1975 *WhScrn 77, WhoHol C*
Wesstrom, Anders 1720?-1781 *NewGrD 80*
West, Adam 1928- *FilmEn*
West, Adam 1929- *FilmgC, ForYSC, HalFC 80, WhoHol A, WhoHrs 80*
West, Algernon 1886- *WhThe*
West, Alvy 1915- *AmSCAP 66, -80, BgBands 74*
West, Anthonius *NewGrD 80*
West, Basil d1934 *WhoHol B*
West, Benjamin *NewGrD 80*
West, Bernard 1918- *BiE&WWA*
West, Bernie *NewYTET, WhoHol A*
West, Billie *Film 1, -2*
West, Billy 1893-1975 *FilmEn, HalFC 80, WhScrn 77, WhoHol C*
West, Bob 1937- *AmSCAP 80*
West, Brooks *WhoHol A*
West, Buster 1902-1966 *WhScrn 74, WhoHol B*
West, Charles 1886- *Film 1, -2, TwYS*
West, Charles 1914-1976 *BluesWW[port]*
West, Charles H 1885-1943 *WhScrn 77*
West, Charles Laurence 1897- *IntWWM 77*
West, Christopher *WhoHol A*
West, Claire *Film 2*
West, Con 1891- *WhThe*
West, Doc 1915-1951 *WhoJazz 72*
West, Dorothy *Film 1*
West, Dorothy Marie 1932- *BiDAmM*
West, Dottie 1932- *CounME 74[port], -74A, EncFCWM 69, IlEncCM[port]*
West, Edna Rhys 1887-1963 *Film 2, NotNAT B, WhScrn 74, -77, WhoHol B*
West, Edward Randall Kenneth 1944- *IntWWM 77, -80*
West, Eleanor *WomWMM B*
West, Elizabeth 1927-1962 *CnOxB, DancEn 78*
West, Eugene 1883-1949 *AmSCAP 66, -80*
West, Florence 1862-1913 *OxThe*
West, Ford *Film 2*
West, George *Film 2*
West, George Addison 1931- *ConAmC*
West, H E *WhoHol A*
West, H St. Barbe 1880-1935 *Film 2*
West, Harold *AmSCAP 80*
West, Hedy 1938- *BiDAmM, EncFCWM 69*
West, Henry *Film 1, -2*
West, Henry St. Barbe 1880-1935 *NotNAT B, WhThe, WhoHol B*
West, Isabel *Film 2*
West, James Buster 1902-1966 *WhScrn 77*
West, John Calvin 1938- *IntWWM 80, WhoOp 76*
West, John Ebenezer William 1863-1929 *Baker 78, NewGrD 80, OxMus*
West, Johnny *WhoHol A*
West, Joseph William *AmSCAP 80*
West, Judi *WhoHol A*
West, Katherine 1883-1936 *WhScrn 74, -77*
West, Lillian *Film 1, -2*
West, Lockwood 1905- *WhoHol A, WhoThe 72, -77*
West, Mae *GrMovC[port], IntMPA 77, -75, -76, -78, -79, -80, MotPP, WomWMM*
West, Mae 1892- *BiDAmM, BiDFilm, -81, BiE&WWA, CmpEPM, FamA&A[port], FilmEn, FilmgC, ForYSC, Funs[port], HalFC 80[port], NotNAT, OxFilm, ThFT[port], WhoHol A, WhoThe 72, -77*
West, Mae 1893- *EncWT, Ent[port], JoeFr[port], ModWD, MovMk[port], NotNAT A, WorEFlm[port]*
West, Mal 1913- *AmSCAP 66, -80*
West, Martin *AmSCAP 80, WhoHol A*
West, Melvin Kenneth 1930- *IntWWM 77*
West, Nathanael 1904-1940 *FilmgC, HalFC 80*
West, Olive *Film 1*
West, Pat 1889-1944 *WhScrn 74, -77, WhoHol B*
West, Paul 1871- *WhoStg 1906, -1908*
West, Ray 1904- *AmSCAP 66, -80*
West, Raymond B 1886-1918 *FilmEn*
West, Richard Douglas 1937- *WhoMus 72*
West, Richard M 1940- *ConAmC*
West, Robert Athow 1809-1865 *BiDAmM*
West, Roland 1887-1952 *FilmEn, FilmgC, HalFC 80, TwYS A, WhoHrs 80*
West, Steve *ConMuA 80B*
West, Thomas 1859-1932 *WhScrn 74, -77, WhoHol B*
West, Timothy 1934- *HalFC 80, WhoHol A, WhoThe 72, -77*
West, Tommy *AmSCAP 80, ConMuA 80B*
West, Wally *WhoHol A*
West, Walter *IlWWBF, WhoMus 72*
West, Wesley Webb 1924- *BiDAmM*
West, Will 1867-1922 *NotNAT B, WhThe*
West, William d1918 *WhScrn 77*
West, William 1575?-1643 *NewGrD 80*
West, William H 1888- *Film 1, -2, TwYS*
West, William Herman 1860-1915 *WhScrn 77*
West Bruce & Laing *IlEncR*
Westayer, Harry *Film 2*
Westberg, Eric 1892-1944 *NewGrD 80*
Westberry, James Kent 1939- *AmSCAP 80*
Westbrook, Francis Brotherton 1903- *WhoMus 72*
Westbrook, Helen Searles 1898-1965 *AmSCAP 66, -80, ConAmC*
Westbrook, James Earl 1938- *IntWWM 77, -80*
Westbrook, John 1922- *WhoHol A, WhoThe 72, -77*
Westbrook, Michael John David 1936- *EncJzS 70, NewGrD 80*
Westbrook, Mike 1936- *EncJzS 70, IlEncJ, NewGrD 80*
Westbrook, William Joseph 1831-1894 *Baker 78, NewGrD 80*
Westbrooks, Logan *ConMuA 80B*
Westby, Oivind 1947- *IntWWM 77, -80*
Westcote, Sebastian 1520?-1582 *NewGrD 80*
Westcott, Gordon 1903-1935 *Film 2, ForYSC, HolCA[port], WhScrn 74, -77, WhoHol B*
Westcott, Helen *IntMPA 75, -76, -78, -79, -80*
Westcott, Helen 1928- *FilmEn, ForYSC*
Westcott, Helen 1929- *FilmgC, HalFC 80, IntMPA 77, WhoHol A*
Westcott, Marcy *EncMT*
Westcott, Netta d1953 *NotNAT B, WhThe*
Westcott, Sebastian 1520?-1582 *NewGrD 80*
Westcott, Wendell J 1911- *IntWWM 77*
Westen, Lucille 1843-1877 *PlP&P*
Westen, Theo J H 1909- *IntWWM 77, -80*
Westendorf, Omer 1916- *IntWWM 77*

Westendorff, Thomas P 1848-1923 *BiDAmM*
Westenholtz *NewGrD 80*
Westenholz *NewGrD 80*
Westenholz, Barbara Lucietta Fricemelica 1725-1776 *NewGrD 80*
Westenholz, Carl August Friedrich 1736-1789 *NewGrD 80*
Westenholz, Carl Ludwig Cornelius 1788-1854 *NewGrD 80*
Westenholz, Elisabeth 1942- *IntWWM 77, -80*
Westenholz, Friedrich 1778-1840 *NewGrD 80*
Westenholz, Friedrich Carl 1756-1802 *NewGrD 80*
Westenholz, Sophia Maria 1759-1838 *NewGrD 80*
Westerberg, Stig 1918- *NewGrD 80*
Westerby, Herbert 1865-1949 *NewGrD 80*
Westerby, Robert 1909-1968 *FilmgC, HalFC 80*
Westerdijk, Lenny 1946- *CnOxB*
Westerfelt, John *Film 2*
Westerfield, James d1971 *WhoHol B*
Westerfield, James 1912-1971 *FilmgC, HalFC 80*
Westerfield, James 1913-1971 *WhScrn 74, -77*
Westerfield, James 1916- *ForYSC*
Westerfield, Rosemary Deveson *CreCan 2*
Westergaard, Peter 1931- *Baker 78, BiDAmM, ConAmC, DcCM, IntWWM 77, NewGrD 80*
Westergaard, Svend 1922- *Baker 78, CpmDNM 80, NewGrD 80*
Westerhoff, Christian Wilhelm 1763-1806 *NewGrD 80*
Westerhout, Niccolo Van 1857-1898 *Baker 78, NewGrD 80*
Westerhout, Nicola Van 1857-1898 *NewGrD 80*
Westerlinck, Wilfried 1945- *IntWWM 77, -80*
Westerlind, Ulf Hakan 1937- *IntWWM 77*
Westermeyer, Paul 1940- *IntWWM 77*
Western, Charles *WhoMus 72*
Western, Ethel *NewGrD 80*
Western, Helen 1843-1868 *NotNAT B*
Western, Helen 1844-1868 *OxThe*
Western, Johnny 1934- *BiDAmM*
Western, Kenneth d1963 *NotNAT B*
Western, Lucille 1843-1877 *NotNAT B, OxThe*
Western String Band *BiDAmM, EncFCWM 69*
Westerton, Frank H d1923 *NotNAT B, WhoHol B*
Westfalewicz, Felicja *NewGrD 80*
Westfeldt, Wallace *NewYTET*
Westfield, Catherine *PupTheA*
Westford, Lee M 1926- *AmSCAP 66, -80*
Westford, Susanne 1865-1944 *NotNAT B*
Westhoff, Johann Paul Von 1656-1705 *NewGrD 80*
Westin, Av *NewYTET*
Westin, Karl Otto 1913- *AmSCAP 80*
Westin, Philip L *ConAmC*
Westlake, Frederick 1840-1898 *Baker 78*
Westland, Henry d1906 *NotNAT B*
Westley, Helen 1875-1942 *FilmEn, HolCA[port], ThFT[port]*
Westley, Helen 1879-1942 *FilmgC, HalFC 80, MovMk, NotNAT B, PlP&P, Vers B[port], WhScrn 74, -77, WhThe, WhoHol B*
Westley, Helen 1879-1943 *ForYSC*
Westley, John d1948 *NotNAT B, WhScrn 74, -77*
Westman, Nydia 1902-1970 *BiE&WWA, FilmEn, FilmgC, ForYSC, HalFC 80, NotNAT B, WhScrn 74, -77, WhoHol B*
Westman, Nydia 1907-1970 *ThFT[port], WhThe*
Westman, Theodore *Film 2*
Westmore, Bud 1916-1973 *WhoHrs 80*
Westmore, Perc d1970 *WhoHol B*
Westmore, Percy *FilmgC*
Westmore, Wally 1906-1973 *WhoHrs 80*
Westmoreland, James *WhoHol A*
Westmoreland, Pauline 1910-1947 *WhScrn 74, -77*
Westmorland, John Fane, Earl Of 1784-1859 *Baker 78, NewGrD 80*
Westner, Lillian *WhScrn 74, -77*
Weston, Azzedin Niles 1950- *EncJzS 70*
Weston, Bill *CreCan 2*
Weston, Brad *WhoHol A*
Weston, Charles H 1917- *IlWWBF*
Weston, David 1938- *FilmgC, HalFC 80, WhoHol A*
Weston, Doris 1917-1960 *WhScrn 74, -77, WhoHol B*
Weston, Eddie 1925- *BiE&WWA*
Weston, Ellen 1939- *AmSCAP 80, BiE&WWA*
Weston, Fitz 1904?- *WhoJazz 72*
Weston, Gary *AmSCAP 80*
Weston, George d1923 *WhScrn 74, -77*
Weston, Harold *IlWWBF*
Weston, Horace 1825-1890 *BiDAmM*
Weston, Jack *ForYSC, WhoHol A, WhoThe 77*
Weston, Jack 1915- *IntMPA 77, -75, -76, -78, -79, -80*
Weston, Jack 1925- *FilmEn*
Weston, Jack 1926- *FilmgC, HalFC 80*
Weston, Jay 1929- *IntMPA 77, -75, -76, -78, -79, -80*
Weston, Joseph J 1888-1972 *WhScrn 77*
Weston, Kim 1939- *DrBlPA, RkOn, WhoHol A*
Weston, Leslie *WhoHol A*
Weston, Maggie d1926 *Film 1, WhScrn 74, -77*
Weston, Mark *WhoHol A*
Weston, Mildred *Film 1*
Weston, Pamela Theodora 1921- *IntWWM 77, -80, WhoMus 72*
Weston, Paul 1912- *AmSCAP 66, -80, BiDAmM, CmpEPM*
Weston, Randolph E 1926- *AmSCAP 66, -80, EncJzS 70*
Weston, Randy 1926- *BiDAmM, CmpEPM, DrBlPA, EncJzS 70, IlEncJ*
Weston, Robert P 1878-1936 *NotNAT B, WhThe*
Weston, Robert R *IntMPA 77, -75, -76, -78, -79, -80*
Weston, Ruth 1906-1955 *WhScrn 74, -77, WhoHol B*
Weston, Ruth 1908-1955 *NotNAT B*
Weston, Ruth 1911- *WhThe*
Weston, Sammy 1889-1951 *WhScrn 74, -77*
Weston, Thomas 1737-1776 *OxThe*
Weston, Timothy John 1952- *AmSCAP 80*
Weston, William *Film 2*
Weston, William Percy 1879-1967 *CreCan 2*
Westover, Robert d1916 *NotNAT B*
Westover, Winifred 1890- *Film 1, -2, ForYSC, MotPP, TwYS*
Westover, Wynn Earl *IntWWM 77, -80*
Westphal, Frank C 1889-1948 *AmSCAP 66, -80*
Westphal, Frederick William 1916- *IntWWM 77, -80*
Westphal, Rudolf 1826-1892 *Baker 78, NewGrD 80*
Westray *OxThe*
Westrup, Sir Jack Allan 1904-1975 *Baker 78, NewGrD 80, OxMus, WhoMus 72*
Westwood, John *Film 2*
Westwood, Martin F 1883-1928 *WhScrn 74, -77*
Wet Willie *ConMuA 80A, IlEncR, RkOn 2[port]*
Wetherall, Frances d1923 *NotNAT B, WhThe*
Wetherell, Eric David 1925- *IntWWM 77, -80, WhoMus 72*
Wetherell, Harold P 1909- *AmSCAP 66, -80*
Wetherell, Kenneth Alwyn *NewGrD 80*
Wetherell, M A 1887-1939 *Film 2, WhScrn 74, -77, WhoHol B*
Wetherell, Marmaduke Arundel 1884-1930 *IlWWBF*
Wetherell, Virginia 1943- *IlWWBF*
Wetherell, Virginia 1948?- *WhoHrs 80*
Wetherford Quartet *BiDAmM*
Wethington, Arthur Crawford 1908- *WhoJazz 72*
Wetmore, Joan 1911- *BiE&WWA, NotNAT, WhThe, WhoThe 72*
Wettergreen, Melvin Richard 1909- *AmSCAP 80*
Wettergren, Gertrud 1897- *Baker 78, NewGrD 80*
Wettling, George *IlEncJ*
Wettling, George 1906-1968 *CmpEPM*
Wettling, George Godfrey 1907-1968 *BiDAmM, EncJzS 70, WhoJazz 72*
Wettstein, Peter 1939- *IntWWM 80*
Wetz, Richard 1875-1935 *Baker 78, NewGrD 80*
Wetzel, Justus Hermann 1879-1973 *Baker 78, NewGrD 80*
Wetzel, Richard D 1935- *ConAmC*
Wetzler, Hermann Hans 1870-1943 *Baker 78, BiDAmM, ConAmC, NewGrD 80*
Wetzler, Robert Paul 1932- *AmSCAP 80, ConAmC*
Wetzstein, Frank E 1900- *IntMPA 75, -76*
Wetzsteon, Ross Duane 1932- *ConAmTC*
Weutz, Giulio *NewGrD 80*
Wever, Ned 1899- *AmSCAP 66, -80, WhoHol A*
Wever, Richard *McGEWD*
Wever, Warren *IntMPA 77, -75, -76, -78, -79, -80*
Weweler, August 1868-1952 *Baker 78*
Wewezow, Gudrun 1936- *WhoOp 76*
Wewitzer, Ralph d1825 *NotNAT B*
Wexler, Haskell 1923- *WorEFlm*
Wexler, Haskell 1926- *FilmEn, FilmgC, HalFC 80, IntMPA 77, -75, -76, -78, -79, -80, OxFilm*
Wexler, Jerry *ConMuA 80B[port]*
Wexler, Jodi *WhoHol A*
Wexler, Paul *ForYSC, WhoHol A*
Wexler, Peter 1936- *NotNAT, WhoOp 76, WhoThe 77*
Wexler, Yale *WhoHol A*
Wexley, John 1902- *WhThe*
Wexley, John 1907- *CnMD, ModWD*
Weyand, Carlton Davis 1916- *AmSCAP 80*
Weyand, Ronald *WhoHol A*
Weydahl, Hanna-Marie 1922- *IntWWM 77, -80*
Weyerhauser Baby, The *What 2[port]*
Weyers, Raymund Wolfgang 1949- *IntWWM 77, -80*
Weyher, Ruth *Film 2*
Weyl, Fernand *McGEWD*
Weyl, Roman 1921- *WhoOp 76*
Weymann, Gert 1919- *CnMD*
Weymarn, Pavel 1857-1905 *Baker 78*
Weynert, Antoni *NewGrD 80*
Weyrauch, August Heinrich Von 1788- *Baker 78, OxMus*
Weyse, C E F 1774-1842 *OxMus*
Weyse, Christoph Ernst Friedrich 1774-1842 *Baker 78, MusMk, NewGrD 80*
Weyth, John 1770-1858 *NewGrD 80*
Weyts, Nicasius *NewGrD 80*
Whale, James 1886-1957 *FilmgC, HalFC 80, WhoHrs 80*
Whale, James 1889-1957 *BiDFilm, -81, DcFM, OxFilm*
Whale, James 1896-1957 *CmMov, FilmEn, WhThe, WorEFlm*
Whale, Peter Albert 1921- *IntWWM 77*
Whale, Thomas Bernard 1778-1838 *BiDAmM*
Whalen, Michael 1899-1974 *FilmgC, ForYSC, HalFC 80*
Whalen, Michael 1902-1974 *FilmEn, What 5[port], WhScrn 77, WhoHol B*
Whalen, Michael 1907?-1974 *MovMk*
Whaley, Bert d1973 *WhScrn 77*
Whaley, George Boyd 1929- *ConAmC*
Whaley, Wade 1895- *NewOrJ[port], WhoJazz 72*
Whalley, Arthur George Cuthbert 1915- *CreCan 1*
Whalley, George 1915- *CreCan 1*
Whalley, Norma d1943 *Film 2, WhThe*
Whallon, Evan 1923- *IntWWM 77, -80*
Whalum, Hugh David, Jr. 1928- *AmSCAP 80*
Whalum, Wendell Phillips 1931- *IntWWM 77*
Whanslaw, Harry William 1883-1965 *DcPup, Ent*
Whaples, Miriam K 1929- *IntWWM 77, -80*
Wharton, Anthony P 1877-1943 *NotNAT B*
Wharton, Bessie *Film 1*
Wharton, Betty 1911- *NotNAT*
Wharton, Edith 1862-1937 *NotNAT B*
Wharton, John F 1894- *BiE&WWA, NotNAT, -A*

Wharton, Leopold 1870- *TwYS A*
Wharton, Theodore 1875- *TwYS A*
Whatham, Claude *HalFC 80*
Whatley, G Larry 1940- *ConAmC*
Whatmore, A R 1889-1960 *NotNAT B, WhThe*
Whear, Paul William 1925- *AmSCAP 80, Baker 78, ConAmC, IntWWM 77, -80*
Wheat, Gladys M *PupTheA*
Wheat, Laurence *Film 2*
Wheat, Lawrence 1876-1963 *WhScrn 77*
Wheatcroft, Adeline Stanhope d1935 *NotNAT B, WhoHol B*
Wheatcroft, Nelson 1852-1897 *NotNAT B*
Wheatcroft, Stanhope 1888-1966 *Film 1, -2, TwYS, WhScrn 77, WhoHol B*
Wheatley, Alan 1907- *FilmgC, HalFC 80, IntMPA 77, -75, -76, -78, -79, -80, WhoHol A, WhoThe 72, -77*
Wheatley, Emma 1822-1854 *NotNAT B, OxThe*
Wheatley, Francis *OxMus*
Wheatley, Frederick d1836 *NotNAT B, OxThe*
Wheatley, Jane 1881-1935 *NotNAT B, WhThe*
Wheatley, Julia 1817-1875 *BiDAmM*
Wheatley, Sarah Ross 1790-1872 *NotNAT B, OxThe*
Wheatley, William 1816-1876 *NotNAT B, OxThe*
Wheaton, Anna d1961 *NotNAT B*
Wheatstone, Charles *NewGrD 80*
Wheatstone, Sir Charles 1802-1875 *NewGrD 80, OxMus*
Wheatstone, William *NewGrD 80*
Wheatstraw, Peetie 1902-1941 *BluesWW[port]*
Whedon, Tom 1932- *AmSCAP 66, -80*
Wheeler, Andrew Carpenter d1903 *NotNAT B*
Wheeler, Benjamin F d1934 *NotNAT B*
Wheeler, Bert 1895-1968 *BiE&WWA, FilmEn, Film 2, FilmgC, ForYSC, HalFC 80, JoeFr[port], MovMk, NotNAT B, What 1[port], WhScrn 74, -77, WhoHol B*
Wheeler, Bert And Robert Woolsey *ForYSC*
Wheeler, Billy Ed 1932- *BiDAmM*
Wheeler, Billy Edd 1932- *AmSCAP 66, -80, CounME 74[port], -74A, EncFCWM 69, IlEncCM[port]*
Wheeler, Burritt 1883-1957 *WhScrn 77*
Wheeler, Burton K 1882- *What 1[port]*
Wheeler, Charles F *FilmgC, HalFC 80*
Wheeler, Clarence E 1885-1966 *AmSCAP 80*
Wheeler, Dell Hinshaw *PupTheA*
Wheeler, Douglas B 1946- *IntWWM 77, -80*
Wheeler, E B DePriest 1903- *WhoJazz 72*
Wheeler, Gayneyl Eby 1916- *IntWWM 77*
Wheeler, Gena *WhoHol A*
Wheeler, Gerald 1929- *IntWWM 77, -80*
Wheeler, Harold *DrBlPA*
Wheeler, Harold Parker, Jr. 1923- *AmSCAP 80*
Wheeler, Hugh *PlP&P A*
Wheeler, Hugh 1912- *ConDr 77, WhoThe 77*
Wheeler, Hugh 1916- *BiE&WWA, NotNAT*
Wheeler, John *WhoHol A*
Wheeler, Joseph Hugh 1927- *WhoMus 72*
Wheeler, Ken 1930- *EncJzS 70*
Wheeler, Kenneth 1930- *EncJzS 70*
Wheeler, Kenny 1930- *EncJzS 70*
Wheeler, Lois *WhoHol A*
Wheeler, Lois 1920- *BiE&WWA, NotNAT*
Wheeler, Lois 1922- *WhThe*
Wheeler, Lyle 1905- *FilmEn, FilmgC, HalFC 80, IntMPA 77, -75, -76, -78, -79, -80, WorEFlm*
Wheeler, Lyman Warren 1837-1900 *BiDAmM*
Wheeler, Margaret *WhoHol A*
Wheeler, Onie D 1921- *AmSCAP 80, BiDAmM*
Wheeler, Paul *NewGrD 80*
Wheeler, Rene 1912- *DcFM, FilmEn*
Wheeler, Richard *PupTheA*
Wheeler, Teresa d1975 *WhScrn 77*
Wheeler, William Harold 1943- *AmSCAP 80*
Wheeler And Woolsey *JoeFr[port]*
Wheelock, Donald F 1940- *AmSCAP 80, ConAmC*
Wheelock, Doris Manning *PupTheA*
Wheen, Natalie Kathleen 1947- *IntWWM 77, -80*
Wheezer *Film 2*
Wheezer 1925- *TwYS*
Whelan, Albert 1875-1961 *OxThe, WhThe*
Whelan, Arleen 1916- *FilmEn, FilmgC, ForYSC, HalFC 80, ThFT[port], WhoHol A*
Whelan, Leo M 1876-1952 *WhScrn 74, -77*
Whelan, Ron 1905-1965 *WhScrn 74, -77, WhoHol B*
Whelan, Tim 1893-1957 *FilmEn, FilmgC, HalFC 80, IlWWBF, NotNAT B, WhScrn 74, -77, WhoHol B*
Whelar, Langois M 1898-1918 *WhScrn 77*
Wheldon, Sir Huw P 1916- *IntMPA 77, -75, -76, -78, -79, -80, NewYTET*
Whelen, Christopher 1927- *IntWWM 77, -80, NewGrD 80, WhoMus 72*
Whelen, Frederick 1867- *WhThe*
Whelpton, George 1847-1930 *BiDAmM*
Whempner, Verna Huber *PupTheA*
Whetsol, Arthur 1905-1940 *IlEncJ*
Whetsol, Artie 1905-1940 *WhoJazz 72*
Whettam, Graham Dudley 1927- *IntWWM 77, -80, NewGrD 80, WhoMus 72*
Whewell, Michael 1923- *WhoMus 72*
Whichello, Abiell d1745? *NewGrD 80*
Whiffen, Mrs. *PlP&P*
Whiffen, Blanche 1845-1936 *NotNAT B, WhoHol B*
Whiffen, Thomas d1897 *NotNAT B*
Whiffen, Mrs. Thomas 1845-1936 *Film 1, NotNAT A, WhScrn 74, -77, WhoStg 1906, -1908*
Whiffin, Blanche 1845-1936 *WhThe*
Whiley, Manning 1915- *FilmgC, HalFC 80, WhThe, WhoHol A*
Whincop, Thomas d1730 *NotNAT B*
Whinyates, Seymour 1892-1978 *NewGrD 80*
Whipp, Ivy Mason *WhoMus 72*
Whipper, Leigh 1877-1975 *BlkAmP, BlksB&W, DrBlPA, MorBAP, WhScrn 77, WhoHol C*
Whipple, Guy Montrose *OxMus*
Whipple, R James 1950- *ConAmC*
Whipple, Sidney Beaumont 1888- *WhThe*
Whippo, Walter Barrows 1922- *AmSCAP 80*
Whips, Andrea *WhScrn 77*
Whistler, Harvey S 1907-1976 *AmSCAP 66, -80*
Whistler, J A McNeill 1834-1903 *OxMus*
Whistler, Margaret 1892-1939 *WhScrn 74, -77*
Whistler, Rex 1905-1944 *DancEn 78, NotNAT B, WhThe*
Whistling, Carl Friedrich 1788-1849? *NewGrD 80*
Whiston, David 1941- *IntWWM 77, -80*
Whitacre, Harold L 1901-1976 *AmSCAP 66, -80*
Whitaker *NewGrD 80*
Whitaker, Charles 1893-1960 *Film 2, ForYSC, WhScrn 77, WhoHol B*
Whitaker, Christopher Robert 1947- *IntWWM 77*
Whitaker, E E *IntMPA 77, -75, -76, -78, -79*
Whitaker, Ephraim Mallory 1816-1880 *BiDAmM*
Whitaker, Jack *NewYTET*
Whitaker, Johnny *WhoHol A*
Whitaker, Margaret Joy 1926- *IntWWM 77, -80*
Whital, Russ *Film 2*
Whitbeck, Frank 1882-1963 *NotNAT B, WhScrn 77*
Whitbread, J W d1916 *NotNAT B*
Whitbread, Samuel *PlP&P*
Whitbroke, William *NewGrD 80*
Whitby, Arthur 1869-1922 *NotNAT B, WhThe*
Whitby, Mrs. Arthur d1930 *NotNAT B*
Whitby, Gwynne 1903- *WhoHol A, WhoThe 72, -77*
Whitcomb, Ian 1941- *RkOn 2[port]*
Whitcomb, Kenneth George 1926- *AmSCAP 66, -80*
Whitcomb, Mervin W 1913- *IntWWM 77, -80*
Whitcomb, Robert B 1921- *ConAmC*
Whitcup, Leonard 1903-1979 *AmSCAP 66, -80, CmpEPM*
White, A Duane 1939- *ConAmC*
White, Alan *MotPP*
White, Alan David 1938- *IntWWM 77*
White, Alan Russell 1925- *AmSCAP 66*
White, Alfred H 1883-1972 *WhScrn 77*
White, Alice 1907- *FilmEn, Film 2, ForYSC, MotPP, ThFT[port], TwYS, WhoHol A*
White, Amos M 1889- *NewOrJ, WhoJazz 72*
White, Andrew Nathaniel, III 1942- *EncJzS 70, IntWWM 77, -80*
White, Arthur *Film 1*
White, Barbara 1924- *FilmgC, HalFC 80, WhoHol A*
White, Barry 1944- *DrBlPA, IlEncR, RkOn 2[port], WhoHol A*
White, Beatrice d1963 *NotNAT B*
White, Benjamin 1901- *NewOrJ*
White, Benjamin Franklin 1800-1879 *BiDAmM, NewGrD 80*
White, Betty *NewYTET, WhoHol A*
White, Bill 1857-1933 *WhScrn 74, -77, WhoHol B*
White, Billy *Film 1*
White, Blanche *Film 1*
White, Booker T Washington 1906-1977 *BluesWW[port]*
White, Bradford 1912- *BiE&WWA, NotNAT*
White, Carol 1941- *FilmgC, HalFC 80, IlWWBF[port], WhoHol A*
White, Carol 1942- *FilmEn*
White, Carol 1943- *FilmAG WE[port]*
White, Carol 1944- *ForYSC*
White, Carolina *Film 1*
White, Carolina 1886-1935 *BiDAmM*
White, Chappell 1920- *IntWWM 80*
White, Charles *WhoHol A*
White, Charles Albert 1830-1892 *BiDAmM, NotNAT B, PopAmC*
White, Chris 1936- *EncJzS 70*
White, Chrissie 1894- *FilmEn, FilmgC, HalFC 80, WhoHol A*
White, Chrissie 1895- *Film 1, -2*
White, Chrissie 1896- *IlWWBF[port]*
White, Christine *WhoHol A*
White, Christopher Westley 1936- *EncJzS 70*
White, Clara *BluesWW*
White, Clarence 1944-1973 *IlEncCM*
White, Clarence Cameron 1880-1960 *AmSCAP 66, -80, Baker 78, BiDAmM, ConAmC, MorBAP, NewGrD 80*
White, Cleve 1928- *BluesWW[port]*
White, Cool 1821-1891 *AmPS B, BiDAmM*
White, Dan *WhoHol A*
White, David *WhoHol A*
White, David L 1946- *AmSCAP 80*
White, Deanna *WomWMM*
White, Deloy J De 1920- *IntMPA 77, -75, -76, -78, -79*
White, Dennis *ConMuA 80B*
White, Donald Howard 1921- *AmSCAP 66, -80, Baker 78, ConAmC*
White, Drusel Burris Herbert 1954- *IntWWM 77*
White, Duane Craig 1947- *IntWWM 77, -80*
White, Edgar 1947- *BlkAmP, DrBlPA, MorBAP, NatPD[port], PlP&P A*
White, Edward J 1902-1973 *WhScrn 77*
White, Edward R 1919- *AmSCAP 66, -80*
White, Elise Fellows 1873-1933 *ConAmC*
White, Ella *BluesWW*
White, Ellerton Oswald 1917-1971 *BiDAmM, EncJzS 70*
White, Elmore d1964 *NotNAT B*
White, Elwood L 1941- *IntWWM 77, -80*
White, Eric Walter 1905- *Baker 78, NewGrD 80*
White, Erma Marceline 1925- *AmSCAP 80*
White, Ernest George *OxMus*
White, Father 1898-1962 *WhoJazz 72*
White, Felix Harold 1884-1945 *Baker 78, OxMus*
White, Fisher d1945 *WhoHol B*
White, Frances 1898-1969 *WhScrn 74, -77, WhoHol B*
White, Francis *AmPS B, MagIID*
White, Frank *NewYTET, WhoHol A*
White, Franklin 1924- *DancEn 78*
White, Fruit 1911- *WhoJazz 72*
White, Gail Ann Natterer 1936- *IntWWM 77*
White, Gary B 1940- *AmSCAP 80*
White, Gary C 1937- *AmSCAP 80, ConAmC*
White, George 1888?-1968 *CmpEPM*

White, George 1890-1968 *BiE&WWA, EncMT, Ent, NewCBMT, NotNAT B, WhScrn 74, -77, WhThe, WhoHol B*
White, George C 1935- *NotNAT*
White, George Leonard 1838-1895 *BiDAmM*
White, Georgia 1903- *BluesWW[port]*
White, Gladys *BluesWW*
White, Glen *Film 1*
White, Gloria *WomWMM*
White, Grace *BluesWW*
White, Gus *PupTheA*
White, Hilda Naomi 1892- *IntWWM 77, -80*
White, Huey d1938 *WhoHol B*
White, Hugh 1896-1938 *WhScrn 74, -77*
White, Hy 1915- *CmpEPM, WhoJazz 72*
White, Hyman 1915- *AmSCAP 66, -80*
White, Irving 1865-1944 *WhoHol B*
White, J Fisher 1865-1945 *Film 2, NotNAT B, WhThe*
White, J Irving 1865-1944 *WhScrn 74, -77*
White, Jacqueline *WhoHol A*
White, James d1862 *NotNAT B*
White, James d1927 *NotNAT B, WhThe*
White, Jane 1922- *BiE&WWA, DrBlPA, NotNAT, WhoHol A, WhoThe 72, -77*
White, Jane Douglass 1919- *AmSCAP 66, -80*
White, Jennifer *WhoHol A*
White, Jeremy 1927- *WhoMus 72*
White, Jesse *WhoHol A*
White, Jesse 1918- *FilmgC, HalFC 80, HolCA[port]*
White, Jesse 1919- *BiE&WWA, FilmEn, ForYSC, IntMPA 77, -75, -76, -78, -79, -80, MovMk, NotNAT, Vers A[port]*
White, Jim *ConMuA 80B*
White, Joan 1909- *BiE&WWA, NotNAT, WhoHol A, WhoThe 72, -77*
White, John 1779-1831 *NewGrD 80*
White, John 1855-1902 *Baker 78, BiDAmM*
White, John 1919- *ConDr 73, -77*
White, John 1936- *NewGrD 80*
White, John 1938- *IntWWM 77, -80, WhoMus 72*
White, John Albert 1935- *IntWWM 77*
White, John David 1931- *AmSCAP 66, -80, ConAmC, IntWWM 77, -80*
White, John F *NewYTET*
White, John Henry 1906- *WhoMus 72*
White, John Maurice 1940- *IntWWM 77, -80*
White, John Reeves 1924- *Baker 78*
White, John S 1910- *IntWWM 80, WhoOp 76*
White, Jose 1833-1920 *BiDAmM*
White, Joseph 1833-1920 *OxMus*
White, Joseph 1838?-1890 *BiDAmM*
White, Joseph 1933- *BlkAmP, MorBAP*
White, Joseph M 1891-1959 *AmSCAP 66, -80*
White, Josh 1908-1969 *AmSCAP 66, CmpEPM, DrBlPA, EncFCWM 69, EncJzS 70, NotNAT B*
White, Josh 1914-1969 *AmSCAP 80*
White, Joshua Daniel 1908-1969 *BiDAmM, EncJzS 70*
White, Joshua Daniel 1915-1969 *BluesWW[port]*
White, Jules J 1900- *FilmgC, HalFC 80, IntMPA 77, -75, -76, -78, -79, -80, WhoHrs 80*
White, Kay 1900- *AmSCAP 66*
White, Ken 1916- *AmSCAP 66*
White, Kevin 1952- *AmSCAP 80*
White, L Keith 1945- *CpmDNM 72*
White, Lawrence R 1925- *IntMPA 75*
White, Lawrence R 1926- *IntMPA 77, -76, -78, -79, -80, NewYTET*
White, Lee d1949 *ForYSC*
White, Lee 1886-1927 *NotNAT B, WhThe*
White, Lee Lasses 1885-1949 *Vers A[port], WhoHol B*
White, Lee Roy Lasses 1888-1949 *WhScrn 74, -77*
White, Lenny 1949- *EncJzS 70*
White, Leo *ForYSC*
White, Leo 1880-1948 *WhScrn 74, -77, WhoHol B*
White, Leo 1887-1948 *Film 1, -2, TwYS*
White, Leonard *IntMPA 77, -75, -76, -78, -79, -80*
White, Leonard, III 1949- *EncJzS 70*
White, Lesley Ann 1933- *WhoMus 72*
White, Lew *CmpEPM*
White, Louie L 1921- *ConAmC*
White, Lucy *BlkAmP*
White, Malcom *Film 2*
White, Margareta Eklund *NewYTET*
White, Marie Elizabeth Fox Warren 1908- *IntWWM 77, -80*
White, Marjorie 1908-1935 *WhScrn 74, -77, WhoHol B*
White, Marjorie 1910- *Film 2*
White, Martin John 1941- *IntWWM 77, -80*
White, Marty *AmSCAP 80*
White, Matthew *NewGrD 80, OxMus*
White, Maude Valerie 1855-1937 *Baker 78, NewGrD 80, OxMus*
White, Maurice 1944- *AmSCAP 80, ConMuA 80B*
White, May *Film 1*
White, Mrs. Meadows *OxMus*
White, Melvin R 1911- *BiE&WWA*
White, Merrill 1895?-1959 *HalFC 80*
White, Michael 1931- *AmSCAP 66, -80, Baker 78, ConAmC, DcCM*
White, Michael Simon 1936- *NotNAT, WhoThe 72, -77*
White, Michael Walter 1933- *EncJzS 70*
White, Miles 1914- *WhoThe 72, -77*
White, Miles 1920- *BiE&WWA, NotNAT*
White, Myrna *WhoHol A*
White, Nancy Elelyn 1913- *IntWWM 77*
White, Nathaniel *WhoHol A*
White, Onna 1922- *BiE&WWA, CnOxB, DancEn 78, EncMT, HalFC 80, NotNAT, WhoThe 72, -77*
White, Patricia *WhoHol A*
White, Patrick 1912- *ConDr 73, -77*
White, Paul *IntMPA 77, -75, -76, -78, -79, -80*
White, Paul d1955 *NewYTET*
White, Paul Taylor 1895-1973 *AmSCAP 66, -80, Baker 78, BiDAmM, ConAmC, WhoMus 72*
White, Pearl 1889-1938 *FilmEn, Film 1, -2, FilmgC, HalFC 80, MotPP, MovMk[port], NotNAT B, OxFilm, TwYS, WhScrn 74, -77, WhoHol B, WhoHrs 80, WorEFlm*
White, Peter *WhoHol A*
White, Peter A 1924- *WhoMus 72*
White, Peter Gilbert 1937- *IntWWM 77, -80*
White, Princess 1881-1976 *BluesWW[port]*
White, Quinten 1952- *EncJzS 70*
White, Rachel Irene 1934- *AmSCAP 80*
White, Raymond Eric 1944- *IntWWM 77, -80*
White, Richard James 1934- *IntWWM 77*
White, Robb 1909- *WhoHrs 80*
White, Robert 1530?-1574 *MusMk*
White, Robert 1534?-1574 *OxMus*
White, Robert 1535?-1574 *Baker 78*
White, Robert 1538?-1574 *NewGrD 80*
White, Rocky 1952- *EncJzS 70*
White, Roger 1913- *IntMPA 75, -76*
White, Ron 1944- *ConAmTC*
White, Ronald Anthony 1938- *AmSCAP 80*
White, Roy B *IntMPA 77, -75, -76, -78, -79, -80*
White, Russell Alan 1925- *AmSCAP 80*
White, Ruth 1914-1969 *BiE&WWA, FilmEn, HalFC 80, NotNAT B, WhScrn 74, -77, WhoHol B, WomWMM A, -B*
White, Ruth 1925- *ConAmC*
White, Ruth Eden 1928- *ConAmC*
White, Sammy 1896-1960 *NotNAT B, WhScrn 74, -77, WhoHol B*
White, Sammy 1898-1960 *Vers A[port]*
White, Samuel Driver 1938- *IntWWM 80*
White, Sheila *WhoHol A*
White, Slappy *DrBlPA, WhoHol A*
White, Sonny 1917-1971 *CmpEPM, EncJzS 70, WhoJazz 72*
White, Stanley *MorBAP*
White, Sylvia *AmSCAP 66, -80*
White, T *PupTheA*
White, Ted *AmSCAP 80*
White, Terrence Elnathan 1953- *CpmDNM 76*
White, Thelma 1911- *WhoHol A*
White, Thomas *Film 2*
White, Tony Joe 1943- *AmSCAP 80, IlEncR, RkOn 2[port]*
White, Valerie 1915-1975 *WhScrn 77, WhoHol C, WhoThe 72, -77*
White, Valerie 1916- *HalFC 80*
White, Verdine Adams 1951- *AmSCAP 80*
White, Victoria *Film 2*
White, Walter Anthony Campbell 1928- *IntWWM 77*
White, Warren *WhoHol A*
White, Washington *BluesWW*
White, Wilfrid Hyde 1903- *FilmEn, ForYSC, IlWWBF[port], IntMPA 77, -75, -76, -78, -79, -80, WhThe*
White, Wilkie *AmSCAP 80*
White, Willard Wentworth 1946- *WhoOp 76*
White, William d1660? *Baker 78*
White, William 1585?-1667? *NewGrD 80, OxMus*
White, William C 1881-1964 *Baker 78*
White, William John 1887- *AmSCAP 66*
White, William Wilfred 1894- *AmSCAP 66, -80*
White, Winifred 1906- *WhoMus 72*
White Brothers *BiDAmM*
White-Eyed Kaffir, The *OxThe*
White Lafitte, Jose 1836-1918 *NewGrD 80*
White Lafitte, Joseph 1836-1918 *NewGrD 80*
White Plains *RkOn 2A*
White Spear, Chief *Film 2*
Whitear, Sheelagh Lesley 1951- *IntWWM 77*
Whitear, Sheelagh Lesley 1959- *IntWWM 80*
Whitecotton, Shirley 1935- *ConAmC*
Whitefield, Bernard 1910- *AmSCAP 66*
Whitefield, George 1714-1770 *BiDAmM, OxMus*
Whiteford, Blackie 1873-1962 *Film 2*
Whiteford, Dick *ConMuA 80B*
Whiteford, Jock *WhThe*
Whiteford, John P Blackie 1873-1962 *WhScrn 77, WhoHol B*
Whitehall, William Henry 1908- *WhoMus 72*
Whitehead, Alfred 1887-1974 *BiDAmM, CreCan 1, NewGrD 80, WhoMus 72*
Whitehead, Allen 1921- *BiE&WWA, NotNAT*
Whitehead, Clay T *NewYTET*
Whitehead, E A 1933- *ConDr 73, -77, EncWT, WhoThe 77*
Whitehead, Geoffrey *WhoHol A*
Whitehead, Gillian 1941- *IntWWM 80, NewGrD 80*
Whitehead, James 1912- *NewGrD 80*
Whitehead, John 1873-1962 *NotNAT B, WhScrn 74, WhoHol B*
Whitehead, O Z *ForYSC, WhoHol A*
Whitehead, Omar *Film 2*
Whitehead, Paxton 1937- *NotNAT*
Whitehead, Robert 1916- *BiE&WWA, NotNAT, PlP&P, WhoThe 72, -77*
Whitehead, William d1785 *NotNAT B*
Whitehead, William J 1938- *AmSCAP 80*
Whitehill, Clarence Eugene 1871-1932 *Baker 78, BiDAmM, CmOp, MusSN[port], NewEOp 71, NewGrD 80*
Whitehill, Wayne *WhoHol A*
Whitehorse *Film 1*
Whitehouse, Esther d1946 *NotNAT B*
Whitehouse, Fred 1895-1954 *AmSCAP 66*
Whitehouse, Peter 1932- *WhoMus 72*
Whitehouse, Reginald 1898- *WhoMus 72*
Whitehouse, Richard St. Clair 1952- *IntWWM 80*
Whitehouse, William Edward 1859-1935 *Baker 78, NewGrD 80*
Whitehouse, Winifred *PupTheA*
Whitelaw, Arthur *WhoThe 77*
Whitelaw, Barrett 1897?-1947 *WhScrn 74, -77*
Whitelaw, Billie 1932- *FilmEn, FilmgC, HalFC 80, IlWWBF[port], IntMPA 77, -75, -76, -78, -79, -80, WhoHol A, WhoThe 72, -77*
Whitelaw, Reid Smith 1945- *AmSCAP 80*
Whiteley, Anne Patricia *WhoMus 72*
Whiteley, Herbert *OxMus*
Whiteley, Jon 1945- *FilmEn, FilmgC, HalFC 80, WhoHol A*
Whiteley, William 1789-1871 *NewGrD 80*
Whitelock, Kenly Wilson 1915- *IntWWM 77*
Whitelocke, Bulstrode 1605-1675 *OxMus*
Whiteman, Paul *AmPS A, -B*
Whiteman, Paul d1967 *BgBands 74[port]*
Whiteman, Paul 1890- *IlEncJ*
Whiteman, Paul 1890-1967 *Baker 78, BiDAmM, BiE&WWA, CmpEPM, EncJzS 70, ForYSC, MnPM[port],*

MusMk, NewGrD 80, OxMus, WhScrn 74, -77, WhoHol B, WhoJazz 72
Whiteman, Paul 1892-1968 *FilmgC, HalFC 80*
Whiteman, Sibyl 1937- *IntWWM 77, -80*
Whitemire, Laura G *PupTheA*
Whiten, James *BlkAmP*
Whitener, David 1944- *IntWWM 80*
Whiteside, Walker 1869-1942 *Film 1, NotNAT B, WhScrn 74, -77, WhThe, WhoHol B*
Whitespear, Greg *Film 2*
Whitfield, Anne *WhoHol A*
Whitfield, Charles 1939- *IntWWM 80*
Whitfield, David *RkOn*
Whitfield, Howard 1914- *BiE&WWA*
Whitfield, John *NewGrD 80*
Whitfield, John Brown Russell 1912- *WhoMus 72*
Whitfield, Jordan 1917-1967 *ForYSC, WhScrn 74, -77*
Whitfield, Norman *ConMuA 80B*
Whitfield, Robert Smoky d1967 *WhoHol B*
Whitfield, Vantile *BlkAmP*
Whitfield, Walter W 1888-1966 *WhScrn 74, -77*
Whitford, Annabelle d1961 *Film 1, PlP&P, WhScrn 77, WhoHol B*
Whitford, Homer 1892- *AmSCAP 66, -80, ConAmC A*
Whitford, James Keith 1917- *AmSCAP 66, -80*
Whithorne, Emerson 1884-1958 *AmSCAP 66, -80, Baker 78, BiDAmM, ConAmC, NewGrD 80, OxMus*
Whithorne, Thomas *OxMus*
Whithorne, Thomas 1528-1590? *OxMus*
Whiting, Mrs. A E *Film 1*
Whiting, Arthur Battelle 1861-1936 *Baker 78, BiDAmM, NewGrD 80, OxMus*
Whiting, Barbara *ForYSC, WhoHol A*
Whiting, Frank M 1907- *BiE&WWA, NotNAT*
Whiting, George 1884-1943 *AmSCAP 66, -80, BiDAmM*
Whiting, George Elbridge 1840-1923 *Baker 78, NewGrD 80*
Whiting, George Elbridge 1840-1924 *BiDAmM*
Whiting, Gordon *WhoHol A*
Whiting, Jack 1901-1961 *CmpEPM, EncMT, NotNAT B, WhScrn 74, -77, WhThe, WhoHol B*
Whiting, John 1915-1963 *CnThe*
Whiting, John 1917-1963 *CnMD, ConDr 77F, CroCD, EncWT, Ent, McGEWD, ModWD, NotNAT B, OxThe, WhThe*
Whiting, John 1918-1963 *REnWD[port]*
Whiting, Leonard 1950- *FilmgC, ForYSC, HalFC 80, MotPP, WhoHol A*
Whiting, Margaret 1924- *AmPS A, -B, CmpEPM, ForYSC, RkOn, WhoHol A*
Whiting, Napoleon *WhoHol A*
Whiting, Richard A 1891-1938 *AmPS, AmSCAP 66, -80, BestMus, BiDAmM, CmpEPM, NewCBMT, NewGrD 80, NotNAT B, PopAmC[port], Sw&Ld C*
Whiting, Steven Jay 1948- *AmSCAP 80*
Whiting, William 1826-1878 *BiDAmM*
Whitley, Clifford 1894- *WhThe*
Whitley, Crane d1958 *WhScrn 77*
Whitley, Ray 1901-1979 *AmSCAP 80, IlEncCM[port]*
Whitley, William Thomas 1861-1947 *OxMus*
Whitlin, Ray *WomWMM*
Whitling, Townsend 1869-1952 *NotNAT B, WhThe*
Whitlock, Mrs. 1761-1836 *NotNAT B*
Whitlock, Billy d1951 *NotNAT B*
Whitlock, Ellen Florence 1889- *IntWWM 77, WhoMus 72*
Whitlock, Lloyd 1900-1962 *Film 1, -2, ForYSC, TwYS*
Whitlock, Lloyd 1900-1966 *WhoHol B*
Whitlock, Percy 1903-1946 *NewGrD 80*
Whitlock, T Lloyd 1891-1966 *WhScrn 77*
Whitman, Alfred 1890- *Film 1, -2, TwYS*
Whitman, Ernest 1893-1954 *DrBlPA, WhScrn 74, -77, WhoHol B*
Whitman, Essie Barbara 1882-1963 *BluesWW, NotNAT B*
Whitman, Estelle d1970 *WhScrn 74, -77, WhoHol B*
Whitman, Fay 1926- *AmSCAP 66, -80*
Whitman, Gayne 1890-1958 *Film 2, ForYSC, TwYS, WhScrn 74, -77, WhoHol B*
Whitman, James K 1946- *ConAmC*
Whitman, Jerry *AmSCAP 80*
Whitman, John P d1963 *NotNAT B*
Whitman, Otis Dewey, Jr. 1924- *BiDAmM*
Whitman, Robert *ConDr 73, -77E*
Whitman, Slim 1924- *AmPS A, CounME 74[port], -74A, EncFCWM 69, IlEncCM[port]*
Whitman, Stuart *IntMPA 77, -75, -76, -78, -79, -80, MotPP, WhoHol A*
Whitman, Stuart 1926- *FilmEn, FilmgC, HalFC 80*
Whitman, Stuart 1929- *ForYSC, MovMk*
Whitman, Walt 1819-1892 *BiDAmM*
Whitman, Walt 1868-1928 *Film 1, -2, WhScrn 74, -77, WhoHol B*
Whitman, William *WhoHol A*
Whitmer, Thomas Carl 1873-1959 *Baker 78, ConAmC*
Whitmore, James *IntMPA 77, -75, -76, -78, -79, -80, MotPP, WhoHol A*
Whitmore, James 1920?- *MovMk*
Whitmore, James 1921- *BiE&WWA, FilmEn, FilmgC, ForYSC, HalFC 80, MGM[port], WhoHrs 80[port], WhoThe 77*
Whitmore, Joshua David 1949- *AmSCAP 80*
Whitmore, Keith Baden 1929- *IntWWM 77, -80, WhoMus 72*
Whitner, Edwin d1962 *NotNAT B*
Whitney, Bert C d1929 *NotNAT B*
Whitney, C C *WhoHol A*
Whitney, C Maurice 1909- *ConAmC*
Whitney, Claire 1890-1969 *Film 1, -2, TwYS, WhScrn 74, -77, WhoHol B*
Whitney, Eleanor *ForYSC*
Whitney, Eleanore 1914- *ThFT[port], WhoHol A*
Whitney, Elvie *BlkAmP*
Whitney, Fred C d1930 *NotNAT B, WhThe*
Whitney, Grace Lee 1940- *AmSCAP 80*
Whitney, James *OxFilm*
Whitney, Joan 1914- *AmSCAP 66, -80, CmpEPM*
Whitney, John *OxFilm, WorEFlm*
Whitney, John Cary 1942- *AmSCAP 80, IntWWM 77*
Whitney, Julia A 1922-1965 *AmSCAP 66, -80*
Whitney, Maurice Cary 1909- *AmSCAP 66, -80, IntWWM 77, -80*
Whitney, Mike *WhoHol A*
Whitney, Moxam 1919- *AmSCAP 66*
Whitney, Myron William 1836-1910 *Baker 78, BiDAmM*
Whitney, Peter 1916- *ForYSC*
Whitney, Peter 1916-1972 *FilmgC, HalFC 80, Vers B[port], WhScrn 77, WhoHol B*
Whitney, Ralph 1874-1928 *WhScrn 74, -77*
Whitney, Renee d1971 *Film 2, WhoHol B*
Whitney, Robert, II 1945-1969 *WhScrn 74, -77, WhoHol B*
Whitney, Robert Sutton 1904- *Baker 78, ConAmC, NewGrD 80, WhoMus 72*
Whitney, Ryan Layne 1953- *ConAmC*
Whitney, Salem Tutt d1934 *BlksB&W, -C*
Whitney, Samuel Brenton 1842-1914 *BiDAmM*
Whitrow, Benjamin 1937- *WhoThe 77*
Whitson, Beth Slater 1879-1930 *AmSCAP 66, -80, BiDAmM*
Whitson, Frank 1876-1946 *Film 1, -2, WhScrn 77*
Whitsun-Jones, Paul 1923-1974 *FilmgC, HalFC 80, WhoHol A*
Whittaker, Arthur d1914 *NotNAT B*
Whittaker, Charles *Film 2*
Whittaker, Herbert 1911- *CreCan 1, WhoThe 72, -77*
Whittaker, Howard 1922- *Baker 78, ConAmC*
Whittaker, Hudson 1900?- *BluesWW[port]*
Whittaker, James d1964 *NotNAT B*
Whittaker, William *IntMPA 77, -75, -76, -78, -79, -80*
Whittaker, William Gillies 1876-1944 *Baker 78, NewGrD 80, OxMus*
Whittall, Arnold 1935- *NewGrD 80*
Whittall, Gertrude Clarke 1867-1965 *Baker 78*
Whittell, Josephine d1961 *WhScrn 74, -77, WhoHol B*
Whitten, Delbert Emery, Jr. *Film 2*
Whitten, Margarette *BlksB&W C*
Whittenberg, Charles 1927- *Baker 78, CpmDNM 78, ConAmC, DcCM, IntWWM 77, -80, NewGrD 80*
Whitter, Henry 1892- *IlEncCM*
Whitteridge, Janet Mary 1942- *IntWWM 77, -80*
Whittier, John Greenleaf 1807-1892 *BiDAmM*
Whittingham, Jack 1910- *FilmgC, HalFC 80, IntMPA 77, -75, -76, -78, -79, -80*
Whittingham, William Rollinson 1805-1879 *BiDAmM*
Whittinghill, Dick *WhoHol A*
Whittington, Dorsey 1899- *WhoMus 72*
Whittington, Gene *WhoHol A*
Whittington, Margery 1904-1957 *Film 2, WhScrn 77*
Whittle, Charles R d1947 *NotNAT B, OxThe, WhThe*
Whittle, Daniel W 1840-1891 *BiDAmM*
Whittle, Daniel Webster 1840-1901 *NewGrD 80*
Whittle, Tommy 1926- *IntWWM 77*
Whittle, William James Bartlett 1928- *IntWWM 77, -80*
Whittlesey, Walter Rose 1861-1936 *Baker 78*
Whittlesey, White d1940 *NotNAT B, WhoStg 1908*
Whittow, Marion Frances 1947- *IntWWM 77, -80*
Whittredge, Edward B 1893- *ConAmC*
Whitty, May 1865-1948 *FilmAG WE, FilmEn, Film 1, FilmgC, ForYSC, HalFC 80, HolCA[port], MGM[port], MotPP, MovMk[port], NotNAT A, -B, OxThe, ThFT[port], Vers A[port], WhScrn 74, -77, WhThe, WhoHol B*
Whitwam, Barry *WhoHol A*
Whitwell, Craig Martin 1948- *ConAmC*
Whitwell, George Frederick 1907- *IntWWM 77, -80, WhoMus 72*
Whitworth, Geoffrey 1883-1951 *EncWT, NotNAT B, OxThe, WhThe*
Whitworth, John Anthony 1921- *IntWWM 77, -80, WhoMus 72*
Whitworth, Robert *Film 1*
Who, The *ConMuA 80A[port], IlEncR[port], NewGrD 80, RkOn 2[port]*
Who, Ziggy *AmSCAP 80*
Whone, Herbert 1925- *IntWWM 77, -80*
Whorf, Richard 1906-1966 *BiE&WWA, FilmEn, FilmgC, ForYSC, HalFC 80, MotPP, MovMk, NotNAT B, PlP&P[port], WhScrn 74, -77, WhThe, WhoHol B*
Whysall, Margaret Thirza *WhoMus 72*
Whysall, Vivienne Constance 1922- *WhoMus 72*
Whytal, A Russ 1860-1930 *NotNAT B*
Whytal, Russ 1860-1930 *WhThe*
Whytal, Mrs. Russ *WhThe*
Whytbroke, William *NewGrD 80*
Whyte, Denis Leighton 1933- *IntWWM 77*
Whyte, Frederic d1941 *NotNAT B*
Whyte, Harold d1919 *NotNAT B*
Whyte, Ian 1901-1960 *NewGrD 80*
Whyte, Patrick *WhoHol A*
Whyte, Robert *NewGrD 80*
Whyte, Robert, Jr. 1874-1916 *NotNAT B, WhThe*
Whyte, Ronny 1937- *AmSCAP 80*
Whyte, Zack 1898-1967 *WhoJazz 72*
Whythe, Jerome 1908- *BiE&WWA*
Whythorne, Thomas 1528?- *MusMk*
Whythorne, Thomas 1528-1590? *OxMus*
Whythorne, Thomas 1528?-1595 *Baker 78*
Whythorne, Thomas 1528-1596 *NewGrD 80*
Wiard, Joyce *Film 2*
Wiazemsky, Anne 1947- *FilmAG WE*
Wibaut, Frank 1945- *IntWWM 77, -80, WhoMus 72*
Wiberg, Tore 1911- *IntWWM 80*
Wicebloom, Sidney Leonard 1930- *IntWWM 77, -80, WhoMus 72*
Wicel, Georg *NewGrD 80*
Wich, Gunther 1928- *NewGrD 80, WhoOp 76*
Wich, Lorraine *AmSCAP 80*
Wichart, Lita Belle 1907-1929 *WhScrn 74, -77*
Wichello, Abiell *NewGrD 80*
Wichelow, Walter *Film 2*

Wicherek, Antoni 1929- *WhoOp 76*
Wichman, Adalin *WomWMM B*
Wichmann, Hermann 1824-1905 *Baker 78*
Wichmann, Joachim 1917- *McGEWD*
Wichmann, Russell G 1912- *ConAmC*
Wichtl, Georg 1805-1877 *Baker 78*
Wick, Bruno *WhoHol A*
Wick, Denis Gerald 1931- *IntWWM 80, WhoMus 72*
Wick, Otto 1885-1957 *AmSCAP 66, -80, ConAmC*
Wickdahl, Lillian *AmSCAP 66*
Wickede, Friedrich Von 1834-1904 *Baker 78*
Wickenhauser, Richard 1867-1936 *Baker 78*
Wickens, Dennis John 1926- *IntWWM 77, -80, WhoMus 72*
Wickens, Nigel 1937- *IntWWM 77, -80, WhoMus 72*
Wicker, Chester 1904-1970 *NewOrJ*
Wicker, Ireene *CmpEPM, What 2[port]*
Wickes, Jean Kim 1947- *IntWWM 80*
Wickes, Mary *IntMPA 75, -76, -78, -79, -80*
Wickes, Mary 1912?- *ForYSC, HolCA[port]*
Wickes, Mary 1916- *FilmEn, FilmgC, HalFC 80, IntMPA 77, NotNAT, Vers A[port], WhThe, WhoHol A*
Wickett, William Herbert 1919- *IntWWM 77, -80*
Wickham, Elmer William 1906- *AmSCAP 80*
Wickham, Florence 1880-1962 *Baker 78, ConAmC*
Wickham, Glynne 1922- *BiE&WWA, NotNAT, WhoThe 72, -77*
Wickham, Tony 1922-1948 *NotNAT B, WhThe*
Wicki, Bernard 1919- *DcFM, WhoHol A*
Wicki, Bernhard 1919- *FilmAG WE, FilmEn, FilmgC, HalFC 80, WorEFlm*
Wickland, Larry 1898-1938 *WhScrn 74, -77, WhoHol B*
Wickman, Putte 1924- *CmpEPM*
Wickman, Sally d1969 *NotNAT B*
Wicks, Allan 1923- *NewGrD 80, WhoMus 72*
Wicks, Dennis 1928- *WhoMus 72, WhoOp 76*
Wicks, Florence *Film 2*
Wickstrom, Gordon M 1926- *ConAmTC*
Wickwire, Nancy 1925-1974 *BiE&WWA, NotNAT B, WhoThe 72, -77*
Wicumbe, W De *NewGrD 80*
Widdecomb, Wallace d1969 *WhoHol B*
Widder, Roger Henry 1923- *IntWWM 77, -80*
Widdicombe, Gillian 1943- *IntWWM 77, -80*
Widdicombe, Harry d1868 *NotNAT B*
Widdicombe, Victor d1912 *NotNAT B*
Widdoes, Kathleen 1939- *BiE&WWA, FilmgC, HalFC 80, NotNAT, WhoHol A, WhoThe 72, -77*
Widdoes, Lawrence Lewis 1932- *AmSCAP 80, ConAmC*
Widdop, Walter 1892-1949 *CmOp, NewGrD 80*
Widdowson, Kenneth West 1928- *ConAmC*
Widem, Allen M 1925- *IntMPA 77, -75, -76, -78, -79, -80*
Wideman, Nena Plant 1905- *IntWWM 77, -80*
Widerberg, Bo 1930- *BiDFilm, -81, DcFM, FilmEn, FilmgC, HalFC 80, MovMk[port], OxFilm, WorEFlm*
Widerberg, Tommy 1946- *CnOxB*
Widerkehr, Jacques 1759-1823 *NewGrD 80*
Widerkehr, Philippe *NewGrD 80*
Widhalm, Leopold 1722-1776 *NewGrD 80*
Widman, Franklin Darryl 1950- *AmSCAP 80*
Widmann, Benedikt 1820-1910 *Baker 78*
Widmann, Erasmus 1572-1634 *Baker 78, NewGrD 80*
Widmann, Joseph Viktor 1842-1911 *Baker 78, NewGrD 80*
Widmanstetter, Georg d1618 *NewGrD 80*
Widmark, Richard *IntMPA 77, -75, -76, -78, -79, -80, MotPP, WhoHol A*
Widmark, Richard 1914- *FilmEn, FilmgC, ForYSC, HalFC 80, MovMk[port], WorEFlm[port]*
Widmark, Richard 1915- *BiDFilm, -81, CmMov, OxFilm*
Widmer, Ernst 1927- *IntWWM 77, NewGrD 80*
Widmer, Kurt 1940- *IntWWM 77*
Widmer, Mrs. S W *PupTheA*
Widor, Charles-Marie 1844-1937 *Baker 78, BnBkM 80, MusMk, NewGrD 80, OxMus*
Widsith *PlP&P[port]*
Widzer, Martin Ellis 1940- *AmSCAP 80*
Wiechec, M Elizabeth *WomWMM B*
Wiechowicz, Stanislaw 1893-1963 *Baker 78, NewGrD 80*
Wieck *NewGrD 80*
Wieck, Alwin 1821-1885 *Baker 78, NewGrD 80*
Wieck, Clara Josephine 1819-1896 *NewGrD 80, OxMus*
Wieck, Dorothea 1905- *FilmAG WE*
Wieck, Dorothea 1908- *FilmEn, FilmgC, ForYSC, HalFC 80, MotPP, ThFT[port], WhScrn 74*
Wieck, Dorothy 1908- *WhoHol A*
Wieck, Friedrich 1785-1873 *Baker 78, NewGrD 80, OxMus*
Wieck, Marie 1832-1916 *Baker 78, NewGrD 80*
Wieckowski, Joanna G 1943- *IntWWM 77*
Wied, Gustav 1858-1914 *CnMD, NotNAT B, OxThe, WhThe*
Wied, Karl Viktor Prinz Zu 1913- *DancEn 78*
Wiedebein, Gottlob 1779-1854 *Baker 78, NewGrD 80*
Wiedeburg, Michael Johann Friedrich 1720-1800 *NewGrD 80*
Wiedeman, Carl Friedrich *NewGrD 80*
Wiedemann, Ernst Johann 1797-1873 *Baker 78*
Wieder, Hardy 1910-1971 *AmSCAP 66, -80*
Wiederkehr, Jacob Christian Michael 1739-1823 *Baker 78*
Wiedermann, Bedrich Antonin 1883-1951 *NewGrD 80*
Wiedersheim-Paul, Annette Av *CnOxB*
Wiedmann, Ilse 1933- *CnOxB*
Wiedner, Johann Gottlieb 1714?-1783 *NewGrD 80*
Wiedner, Karl 1714?-1783 *NewGrD 80*
Wiedoeft, Rudy 1893-1940 *AmSCAP 66, -80, CmpEPM*
Wiedrich, William Walter 1957- *CpmDNM 80*
Wiegand, Heinrich 1842-1899 *Baker 78*
Wiegand, Paul Sayre *PupTheA*
Wiegold, Peter 1949- *NewGrD 80*
Wiehe, Dagmar *WhThe*
Wiehmayer, Theodor 1870-1947 *Baker 78*
Wiel, Taddeo 1849-1920 *Baker 78, NewGrD 80*
Wielakker, Gerhard 1942- *IntWWM 77*
Wieland, Christoph Martin 1733-1813 *EncWT, Ent, McGEWD[port], NewGrD 80*
Wieland, Joyce 1931- *CreCan 1, WomWMM*
Wiele, Aimee VanDe 1907- *NewGrD 80*
Wiele, Jan Pieterszoon Vander 1645-1679 *NewGrD 80*
Wielen, Jan Pieterszoon Vander 1645-1679 *NewGrD 80*
Wielepp, Kurt O d1962 *NotNAT B*
Wielhorski, Count Mateusz 1794-1866 *NewGrD 80*
Wielhorski, Count Michal 1788-1856 *NewGrD 80*
Wielhorsky, Count Mikhail 1788-1856 *Baker 78*
Wieman, Mathias 1902-1969 *FilmAG WE, WhScrn 74, -77*
Wieman, Mathias 1902-1971 *EncWT*
Wieman, Matthias 1902-1969 *Film 2*
Wiemann, Ernst 1919- *WhoOp 76*
Wiemer, Robert Ernest 1938- *AmSCAP 80*
Wienand, Karl D 1941- *IntWWM 77, -80*
Wienand, Marilyn M 1942- *IntWWM 77, -80*
Wienandt, Elwyn Arthur 1917- *IntWWM 77, -80*
Wienckowski, Jean Ellen 1947- *IntWWM 77, -80*
Wiene, Robert 1881-1938 *BiDFilm, -81, DcFM, FilmEn, FilmgC, HalFC 80, OxFilm, WhoHrs 80, WorEFlm*
Wiener, Elizabeth *WomWMM B*
Wiener, Frantz *McGEWD*
Wiener, Ivan 1933- *ConAmC*
Wiener, Jack 1926- *IntMPA 77, -75, -76, -78, -79, -80*
Wiener, Jean 1896- *DcFM, FilmEn, NewGrD 80, WorEFlm*
Wiener, Julia *WhoHol A*
Wiener, Julia 1932- *IntWWM 80*
Wiener, Sally Dixon 1926- *NatPD[port]*
Wienhorst, Richard W 1920- *ConAmC, DcCM*
Wieniawski *NewGrD 80*
Wieniawski, Adam Tadeusz 1879-1950 *Baker 78, NewGrD 80*
Wieniawski, Henri 1835-1880 *CmpBCM, GrComp[port], NewGrD 80[port], OxMus*
Wieniawski, Henryk 1835-1880 *Baker 78, BnBkM 80, MusMk, NewGrD 80[port]*
Wieniawski, Joseph 1837-1912 *Baker 78, OxMus*
Wieniawski, Jozef 1837-1912 *NewGrD 80*
Wieprecht, Friedrich Wilhelm 1802-1872 *Baker 78*
Wieprecht, Wilhelm 1802-1872 *NewGrD 80*
Wier, Albert Ernest 1879-1945 *Baker 78*
Wierbieta, Maciej *NewGrD 80*
Wiere, Harry 1908- *FilmgC, HalFC 80, JoeFr*
Wiere, Herbert 1909- *FilmgC, HalFC 80, JoeFr*
Wiere, Sylvester 1910-1970 *FilmgC, HalFC 80, JoeFr, WhScrn 74, -77, WhoHol B*
Wiere Brothers, The *FilmgC, HalFC 80, JoeFr, WhoHol A*
Wierszylowski, Jan 1927- *IntWWM 77, -80*
Wierzbicki, James Eugene 1948- *IntWWM 77*
Wierzbillowicz, Aleksander 1850-1911 *NewGrD 80*
Wierzbowski, Raymond Lawrence 1920- *AmSCAP 80*
Wiese, Henry William 1903- *BiE&WWA*
Wiesehahn, Willem 1914- *IntWWM 77, -80*
Wiesen, Bernard *IntMPA 78, -79, -80*
Wiesengrund-Adorno, Theodor *Baker 78*
Wiesengrund-Adorno, Theodore *NewGrD 80*
Wiesenthal, Berta *DancEn 78*
Wiesenthal, Bertha *CnOxB*
Wiesenthal, Elsa *CnOxB, DancEn 78*
Wiesenthal, Grete 1885-1970 *CnOxB, DancEn 78*
Wiesenthal, Martha *CnOxB*
Wiesenthal, Sam 1909- *IntMPA 77, -75, -76, -78, -79, -80*
Wiesenthal, Thomas VanDyke 1790-1833 *BiDAmM*
Wiesenthal Sisters *CnOxB*
Wieser, Gerhard 1930- *IntWWM 77, -80*
Wiest, George D 1897-1974 *AmSCAP 66, -80*
Wiest, L A 1819-1889 *OxMus*
Wiest, Paul *NewGrD 80*
Wieth, Mogens 1920-1962 *NotNAT B, OxThe, WhScrn 77, WhoHol B*
Wietor, Hieronim 1480?-1547? *NewGrD 80*
Wifstrand, Naima 1890-1968 *WhScrn 77*
Wigan, Alfred d1878 *NotNAT B*
Wigan, Mrs. Alfred d1884 *NotNAT B*
Wigan, Horace d1885 *NotNAT B*
Wigbert *NewGrD 80*
Wiggen, Knut 1927- *DcCM, NewGrD 80*
Wiggins, Arthur Montague 1920- *AmSCAP 80, ConAmC*
Wiggins, Donald Glen 1943- *ConAmC*
Wiggins, Gerald Foster 1922- *CmpEPM, EncJzS 70*
Wiggins, Gerald Foster 1956- *EncJzS 70*
Wiggins, J J 1956- *EncJzS 70*
Wiggins, John 1924- *IntWWM 77, -80, WhoMus 72*
Wiggins, Mary 1904- *ConAmC*
Wiggins, Mary L 1910-1945 *WhScrn 74, -77*
Wiggins, William Bramwell 1921- *IntWWM 77, -80, WhoMus 72*
Wigglesworth, Frank 1918- *Baker 78, ConAmC, IntWWM 77, -80, NewGrD 80*
Wiggs, Johnny 1899- *AmSCAP 66, NewOrJ[port], WhoJazz 72*
Wiggs, Sheila N 1946- *IntWWM 77, -80*
Wigham, Margaret *ConAmC*
Wight, Art F 1911- *AmSCAP 80*
Wight, Frederick Coit 1859-1933 *BiDAmM*
Wight, Ralph W 1900- *IntMPA 75, -76*
Wightman, Brian Robin 1942- *IntWWM 77, -80*
Wigley, David 1937- *WhoMus 72*
Wigman, Mary 1886-1973 *CnOxB, DancEn 78[port], NewGrD 80, OxMus*
Wigmore, Donna-Lou *WomWMM*
Wignell, Thomas 1753-1803 *BiDAmM,*

FamA&A[port], NotNAT B, OxThe, PlP&P
Wigram, Marcus Walter 1917- *WhoMus 72*
Wigston, Frederic Roland 1914- *IntWWM 77, -80, WhoMus 72*
Wigthorp, William 1579?-1610? *NewGrD 80*
Wihan, Hans 1855-1920 *Baker 78*
Wihan, Hanus 1855-1920 *NewGrD 80*
Wihlborg, Hans Ferdinand 1916- *IntWWM 77, -80*
Wihtol, Joseph 1863-1948 *Baker 78, NewGrD 80*
Wijdeveld, Wolfgang 1910- *Baker 78*
Wijk, Arnold *Baker 78*
Wiklund, Adolf 1879-1950 *Baker 78, NewGrD 80*
Wikman, Bertil 1944- *IntWWM 77, -80*
Wikman, Johan 1753-1800 *NewGrD 80*
Wikman, Johannes 1753-1800 *NewGrD 80*
Wikman, Solveig Inga-Lill 1942- *IntWWM 77, -80*
Wikmanson, Johan 1753-1800 *Baker 78, NewGrD 80*
Wikmanson, Johannes 1753-1800 *NewGrD 80*
Wikner, Stephen Charles Nevill 1948- *IntWWM 77, -80*
Wiksell, Jean Starr *PupTheA*
Wiksell, Wesley *PupTheA*
Wikstrom, Inger Elvi Margareta 1939- *IntWWM 77, -80*
Wil-Dee, Spence *WhoHol A*
Wilber, Bill *BluesWW*
Wilber, Bob 1928- *CmpEPM, EncJzS 70, IlEncJ*
Wilber, Carol Ann 1947- *IntWWM 77*
Wilber, Robert Sage 1928- *EncJzS 70*
Wilberforce, William 1759-1833 *OxMus*
Wilborn, Dave 1904- *WhoJazz 72*
Wilborn, Nelson 1907- *BluesWW*
Wilbraham, Edward 1895-1930 *NotNAT B, WhThe*
Wilbraham, John 1944- *IntWWM 77, -80, NewGrD 80, WhoMus 72*
Wilbrandt, Adolf Von 1837-1911 *EncWT*
Wilbur, Crane 1887-1973 *HalFC 80*
Wilbur, Crane 1889-1973 *FilmEn, Film 1, -2, FilmgC, ForYSC, MotPP, TwYS, WhScrn 77, WhThe, WhoHol B*
Wilbur, Lyon Perry, Jr. 1934- *AmSCAP 66, -80*
Wilbur, Richard 1921- *AmSCAP 80, BiE&WWA, NotNAT, PlP&P, WhoThe 72, -77*
Wilburn, Charles Aaron 1950- *AmSCAP 80*
Wilburn, Doyle 1930- *CounME 74, IlEncCM[port]*
Wilburn, Teddy 1931- *CounME 74, IlEncCM[port]*
Wilburn, Teddy And Doyle *EncFCWM 69*
Wilburn, Thurman Theodore 1931- *BiDAmM*
Wilburn, Virgil Doyle 1930- *BiDAmM*
Wilburn Brothers *CounME 74[port], -74A, IlEncCM[port]*
Wilburn Family *EncFCWM 69*
Wilbye, John 1574-1638 *Baker 78, BnBkM 80, CmpBCM, GrComp, MusMk, NewGrD 80, OxMus*
Wilchinski, Martha L 1897- *AmSCAP 66, -80*
Wilcke, Jodocus *NewGrD 80*
Wilckens, Friedrich 1899- *Baker 78, WhoMus 72*
Wilcox, Alexander Gordon 1909- *CpmDNM 80*
Wilcox, Barbara 1906- *WhThe*
Wilcox, Carol Ann 1945- *WhoOp 76*
Wilcox, Claire 1955- *IntMPA 77, -75, -76, -78, -79, -80*
Wilcox, Claire 1956- *ForYSC*
Wilcox, Collin 1935- *BiE&WWA, NotNAT*
Wilcox, Daniel Harris 1941- *AmSCAP 80*
Wilcox, Eddie 1907-1968 *AmSCAP 66, -80, EncJzS 70, WhoJazz 72*
Wilcox, Edwin Felix 1907-1968 *CmpEPM, EncJzS 70*
Wilcox, Frank 1907-1974 *FilmgC, ForYSC, HalFC 80, Vers A[port], WhScrn 77, WhoHol B*
Wilcox, Fred McLeod 1905?-1964 *FilmEn, FilmgC, HalFC 80, WhoHrs 80*
Wilcox, Fred McLeod 1908-1964 *BiDFilm, -81, WorEFlm*
Wilcox, Glenn C 1933- *IntWWM 77*
Wilcox, Harlow *RkOn 2A*
Wilcox, Harlow 1900-1960 *WhScrn 77*
Wilcox, Herbert *IntMPA 77, -75, -76*
Wilcox, Herbert 1890- *TwYS A*
Wilcox, Herbert 1891- *DcFM, FilmgC, HalFC 80, MovMk[port]*
Wilcox, Herbert 1892-1977 *FilmEn, IlWWBF, -A[port], OxFilm, WorEFlm*
Wilcox, Jack *HalFC 80*
Wilcox, James H 1916- *ConAmC*
Wilcox, Larry 1935- *AmSCAP 66*
Wilcox, Mary *WhoHol A*
Wilcox, R Turner 1888- *BiE&WWA*
Wilcox, Robert 1910-1955 *ForYSC, MotPP, NotNAT B, WhScrn 74, -77, WhoHol B*
Wilcox, Vivian 1912-1945 *WhScrn 74, -77*
Wilcox-Horne, Collin *WhoHol A*
Wilcoxon, Harry 1905- *IlWWBF[port]*
Wilcoxon, Henry 1905- *CmMov, FilmEn, FilmgC, ForYSC, HalFC 80, IntMPA 77, -75, -76, -78, -79, -80, MotPP, MovMk, WhThe, WhoHol A*
Wild, Brigitte 1908- *WhoMus 72*
Wild, Earl *ConAmC A*
Wild, Earl 1915- *IntWWM 77, -80*
Wild, Earl 1930?- *NewGrD 80*
Wild, Eric 1910- *CreCan 2*
Wild, George d1856 *NotNAT B*
Wild, Harrison Major 1861-1929 *BiDAmM*
Wild, Harry J *WorEFlm*
Wild, Jack 1952- *FilmgC, HalFC 80, IntMPA 77, -75, -76, -78, -79, -80, WhoHol A*
Wild, Jean Marion 1950- *IntWWM 80*
Wild, Jodocus *NewGrD 80*
Wild Cherry *RkOn 2[port]*
Wildberg, John J 1902-1959 *NotNAT B, WhThe*
Wildberger, Jacques 1922- *Baker 78, DcCM, NewGrD 80*
Wildbrunn, Helene 1882-1972 *NewGrD 80*
Wilde, Arthur L 1918- *IntMPA 77, -75, -76, -78, -79, -80*
Wilde, Brian *WhoHol A*
Wilde, Cornel *AmSCAP 66, MotPP, WhoHol A*
Wilde, Cornel 1915- *BiDFilm, -81, CmMov, FilmEn, FilmgC, ForYSC, HalFC 80, WorEFlm[port]*
Wilde, Cornel 1918- *BiE&WWA, IntMPA 77, -75, -76, -78, -79, -80*
Wilde, Cornel L 1918- *AmSCAP 80*
Wilde, Cornell 1915- *MovMk*
Wilde, Dan C 1956- *AmSCAP 80*
Wilde, David 1944- *IntWWM 80*
Wilde, David Clark 1935- *IntWWM 77, -80, WhoMus 72*
Wilde, Hagar 1904-1971 *BiE&WWA, FilmgC, HalFC 80*
Wilde, Marty 1939- *HalFC 80*
Wilde, Oscar 1854-1900 *CnMD, EncWT, Ent, HalFC 80, McGEWD[port], ModWD, NotNAT A, -B, OxFilm, OxThe, PlP&P[port], REnWD[port]*
Wilde, Oscar 1856-1900 *CnThe, CnOxB, DcPup, FilmgC, NewEOp 71, WhoHrs 80*
Wilde, Patricia 1928- *CnOxB*
Wilde, Patricia 1930- *DancEn 78[port]*
Wilde, Percival 1887-1953 *NotNAT B*
Wilde, Ran *BgBands 74*
Wilde, Ted 1889- *TwYS A*
Wilde Alexander, Der *NewGrD 80*
Wilden, Henri 1937- *WhoOp 76*
Wildenbruch, Ernst Von 1845-1909 *EncWT, McGEWD[port], ModWD, NotNAT B, OxThe*
Wilder, Alec 1907- *Baker 78, BiE&WWA, CmpEPM, CpmDNM 80, ConAmC, DcCM, NewGrD 80, NotNAT A, WhoHol A*
Wilder, Alexander 1907- *NewGrD 80*
Wilder, Arthur A 1882- *AmSCAP 66*
Wilder, Billy 1906- *AmFD, BiDFilm, -81, CmMov, ConDr 73, -77A, DcFM, FilmEn, FilmgC, HalFC 80, IntMPA 77, -75, -76, -78, -79, -80, MovMk[port], OxFilm, WorEFlm*
Wilder, Clinton 1920- *BiE&WWA, NotNAT, WhoThe 72, -77*
Wilder, Gene *ForYSC, WhoHol A*
Wilder, Gene 1934- *BiE&WWA, FilmgC, HalFC 80, MovMk, NotNAT*
Wilder, Gene 1935- *AmSCAP 80, FilmEn, IntMPA 77, -75, -76, -78, -79, -80*
Wilder, Gene 1936- *JoeFr[port]*
Wilder, Grace *PupTheA*
Wilder, Joe 1922- *CmpEPM, EncJzS 70*
Wilder, John *AmSCAP 80, WhoHol A*
Wilder, John David *WhoHol A*
Wilder, Joseph Benjamin 1922- *BiDAmM, EncJzS 70*
Wilder, Marshall P *Film 1*
Wilder, Marshall P 1859- *WhoStg 1906*
Wilder, Marshall P 1860-1915 *WhScrn 77*
Wilder, Michael David 1955- *IntWWM 80*
Wilder, Patricia Honeychile *WhoHol A*
Wilder, Philip Van 1500?-1553 *NewGrD 80*
Wilder, Robert 1901-1974 *HalFC 80*
Wilder, Stephen Gilbert 1952- *IntWWM 77, -80*
Wilder, Thornton 1897-1975 *BiDAmM, BiE&WWA, CnMD, CnThe, ConDr 73, -77, CroCD, DcLB 7[port], EncWT, Ent, FilmEn, FilmgC, HalFC 80, ModWD, NewEOp 71, NotNAT A, -B, OxThe, PlP&P[port], REnWD[port], WhThe, WhoThe 72, WorEFlm*
Wilder, Victor 1835-1892 *Baker 78, NewGrD 80*
Wilder, W Lee 1904- *FilmgC, HalFC 80, IntMPA 77, -75, -76, -78, -79, -80, WhoHrs 80*
Wilder, Warner *AmSCAP 80*
Wilderer, Johann Hugo Von 1670?-1724 *Baker 78, NewGrD 80*
Wildermann, William 1919- *WhoOp 76*
Wilderyckx, Marie-Louise 1941- *CnOxB*
Wildgans, Anton 1881-1932 *CnMD, EncWT, McGEWD[port], ModWD, OxThe*
Wildgans, Friedrich 1913-1965 *Baker 78, NewGrD 80*
Wildhack, Robert 1882-1940 *WhScrn 74, -77, WhoHol B*
Wilding, Michael 1912-1979 *FilmAG WE, FilmEn, FilmgC, ForYSC, HalFC 80, IlWWBF[port], IntMPA 77, -75, -76, -78, -79, MotPP, MovMk[port], OxFilm, What 5[port], WhThe, WhoHol A*
Wilding-White, Raymond 1922- *Baker 78, ConAmC, IntWWM 77, -80*
Wildman, John Edward, Jr. 1922- *IntWWM 77, -80*
Wile, Joan 1931- *AmSCAP 80*
Wilens, Greta *WhoMus 72*
Wiles, Margaret Jones 1911- *IntWWM 77, -80*
Wiles, Roger 1947- *AmSCAP 80*
Wiley, Darlene 1945- *WhoOp 76*
Wiley, John A 1884-1962 *NotNAT B, WhScrn 74, -77, WhoHol B*
Wiley, Lee 1915-1975 *AmSCAP 66, -80, CmpEPM, EncJzS 70, IlEncJ, WhoJazz 72*
Wiley, Millicent Yoder 1923- *IntWWM 77*
Wiley, Richard E *NewYTET*
Wilfflingseder, Ambrosius d1563 *NewGrD 80*
Wilflingseder, Ambrosius d1563 *NewGrD 80*
Wilford, Isabel *WhThe*
Wilfrid, Thomas 1888-1968 *OxMus*
Wilgus, D K 1918- *BiDAmM, EncFCWM 69*
Wilhelm Of Hirsau d1091 *NewGrD 80*
Wilhelm Von Hirsau d1091 *NewGrD 80*
Wilhelm, C 1858-1925 *NotNAT B, WhThe*
Wilhelm, Carl 1815-1873 *Baker 78, NewGrD 80, OxMus*
Wilhelm, Elsie Lee 1935- *AmSCAP 80*
Wilhelm, Franz 1945- *CnOxB*
Wilhelm, Rolf Alexander 1927- *IntWWM 77, -80, WhoMus 72*
Wilhelm, Theodore 1909-1971 *WhScrn 74, -77, WhoHol B*
Wilhelmi, Petrus *NewGrD 80*
Wilhelmj, August 1845-1908 *Baker 78, BnBkM 80, NewGrD 80, OxMus*
Wilhem, Guillaume Louis Bocquillon 1781-1842 *Baker 78, NewGrD 80, OxMus*
Wilhite, Monte 1898-1961 *AmSCAP 80*
Wilhite, Monte 1899-1961 *AmSCAP 66*
Wilhjelm, Carl Christian 1928- *IntWWM 77*
Wilhoit, Kenneth Hill 1923- *AmSCAP 66, -80*

Wilhoit, Sam T 1924- *AmSCAP 66*
Wilhoite, Donald Macrae, Jr. 1909- *AmSCAP 80*
Wilhousky, Peter J 1902-1978 *AmSCAP 66, -80*
Wilimek, Eduard 1904- *IntWWM 77, -80*
Wilk, Gerard H 1902- *ConAmTC*
Wilk, Peter Rudolph 1940- *IntWWM 80*
Wilk, Ted 1908- *IntMPA 77, -75, -76, -78, -79, -80*
Wilke, Christian Friedrich Gottlieb 1769-1848 *Baker 78*
Wilke, Hubert 1855-1940 *Film 2, NotNAT B, WhoHol B*
Wilke, Hubert, II 1921- *IntMPA 75, -76*
Wilke, Joanne Coffey 1929- *IntWWM 77*
Wilke, Lynn Hebert 1930- *IntWWM 77*
Wilke, Robert J 1911- *FilmgC, ForYSC, HalFC 80, WhoHol A*
Wilkerson, Bill d1966 *WhoHol B*
Wilkerson, Guy 1898-1971 *ForYSC, Vers B[port], WhScrn 74, -77, WhoHol B*
Wilkerson, Herbert 1881-1943 *WhScrn 74, -77*
Wilkerson, Margaret *MorBAP*
Wilkerson, William 1903-1966 *WhScrn 74, -77*
Wilkerson, William R d1962 *NotNAT B*
Wilkes, Donald E 1929- *IntWWM 77*
Wilkes, Josue Teofilo 1883-1968 *Baker 78, NewGrD 80*
Wilkes, Mattie d1927 *BlksBF*
Wilkes, Nick Emus 1907- *AmSCAP 80*
Wilkes, Sandra Ann *IntWWM 77, -80*
Wilkes, Thomas E 1935- *AmSCAP 80*
Wilkes, Thomas Egerton d1854 *NotNAT B*
Wilkey, Violet *Film 1*
Wilkie, Allan 1878-1970 *WhThe*
Wilkins, Ernest Brooks 1922- *EncJzS 70*
Wilkins, Ernie 1922- *CmpEPM, EncJzS 70*
Wilkins, George *NotNAT B*
Wilkins, Helena Judith *WhoMus 72*
Wilkins, Herbert Oscar 1889- *WhoMus 72*
Wilkins, Herve D 1848-1913 *BiDAmM*
Wilkins, Jack 1944- *EncJzS 70*
Wilkins, Joe Willie 1923- *BluesWW[port]*
Wilkins, John d1853 *NotNAT B*
Wilkins, June d1972 *WhoHol B*
Wilkins, Margaret Lucy 1939- *IntWWM 77, -80*
Wilkins, Nancy Dorothy 1923- *WhoMus 72*
Wilkins, Patricia *NatPD[port]*
Wilkins, Robert Timothy 1896- *BluesWW[port]*
Wilkins-Oppler, Nancy Dorothy 1923- *IntWWM 77, -80*
Wilkinson *NewGrD 80*
Wilkinson, Alan 1929- *IntWWM 77, -80*
Wilkinson, Anne Cochran Gibbons 1910-1961 *CreCan 2*
Wilkinson, Arthur H 1919- *WhoMus 72*
Wilkinson, Christopher 1941- *ConDr 73, -77*
Wilkinson, Constance Jane 1944- *CpmDNM 78*
Wilkinson, Dudley 1897- *AmSCAP 66, -80*
Wilkinson, Edith 1903- *IntWWM 77*
Wilkinson, Henry Spenser 1853-1937 *NotNAT B, WhThe*
Wilkinson, Jennie Gaudio *IntWWM 77, -80*
Wilkinson, John Raymond 1930- *WhoMus 72*
Wilkinson, Kenneth Roy 1933- *IntWWM 77, -80*
Wilkinson, Marc 1929- *IntWWM 77, -80, NewGrD 80, WhoMus 72, WhoThe 72, -77*
Wilkinson, Norman 1882-1934 *NotNAT B, OxThe, WhThe*
Wilkinson, Philip George 1929- *IntWWM 77, -80, WhoMus 72*
Wilkinson, Robert *IntMPA 80*
Wilkinson, Robert 1450?-1515? *NewGrD 80*
Wilkinson, Sam *Film 2*
Wilkinson, Scott 1922- *ConAmC*
Wilkinson, Tate 1734-1803 *NotNAT B*
Wilkinson, Tate 1739-1803 *NotNAT A, OxThe*
Wilkinson, Thomas Bates 1912- *WhoMus 72*
Wilkinson, Walter *DcPup, Film 2, PupTheA*
Wilkomirska, Wanda 1931- *IntWWM 77, -80, NewGrD 80*
Wilkomirski, Jozef 1926- *IntWWM 77, -80*
Wilkomirski, Kazimierz 1900- *IntWWM 77, -80, NewGrD 80*
Wilks, John 1931- *WhoMus 72*
Wilks, Peter *BlkAmP*
Wilks, Robert 1665-1732 *NotNAT A, -B, OxThe, PlP&P*
Wilkstrom, Inger E M 1939- *IntWWM 77, -80, WhoMus 72*
Willa, Suzanne d1951 *NotNAT B*
Willaden, Gene *AmSCAP 80*
Willadsen, Gene 1915- *AmSCAP 66*
Willaert, Adriaan 1490?-1562 *BnBkM 80, MusMk*
Willaert, Adrian 1480?-1562 *OxMus*
Willaert, Adrian 1490?-1562 *Baker 78, GrComp[port], NewGrD 80[port]*
Willan, Healey 1880-1968 *Baker 78, CreCan 2, DcCM, NewGrD 80[port], OxMus*
Willan, James Healey *CreCan 2*
Willander, Alfred 1947- *IntWWM 80*
Willans, Terry Jacqueline 1943- *WhoMus 72*
Willard, Catherine Livingston d1954 *NotNAT B, WhThe*
Willard, Mrs. Charles *Film 2*
Willard, Edmund 1884-1956 *NotNAT B, OxThe, WhThe, WhoHol B*
Willard, Edward Smith 1853-1915 *NotNAT B, OxThe, WhThe, WhoStg 1906, -1908*
Willard, Emma C Hart 1787-1870 *BiDAmM*
Willard, Helen Delano 1905- *BiE&WWA, DancEn 78, NotNAT*
Willard, Jess 1881-1968 *Film 1, WhScrn 77*
Willard, John 1885-1942 *Film 2, NotNAT B, WhThe*
Willard, Kelly Faye 1956- *AmSCAP 80*
Willard, Leigh *Film 2*
Willard, Samuel 1776-1859 *BiDAmM*
Willat, Irvin 1892-1976 *FilmEn, TwYS A*
Willcocks, David 1919- *BnBkM 80, IntWWM 77, -80, NewGrD 80, WhoMus 72*
Willcox, John Henry 1827-1875 *BiDAmM*
Willeke, Willem 1878-1950 *BiDAmM*
Willeke, Willem 1879-1950 *Baker 78*
Willelmus *NewGrD 80*
Willelmus De Winchecumbe *NewGrD 80*
Willems, Paul 1912- *CnMD*
Willent-Bordogni, Jean-Baptiste-Joseph 1809-1852 *Baker 78*
Willenz, Max 1888-1954 *WhScrn 74, -77, WhoHol B*
Willer *NewGrD 80*
Willer, Elias d1623 *NewGrD 80*
Willer, Georg d1632? *NewGrD 80*
Willer, Georg 1515?-1594? *NewGrD 80*
Willes, Jean *HolCA[port], MotPP, WhoHol A*
Willet, Slim 1919- *BiDAmM*
Willett, Elmer William 1911- *AmSCAP 66, -80*
Willett, Susan Mary 1954- *IntWWM 80*
Willetts, Pamela Joan 1929- *IntWWM 80, NewGrD 80*
Willey, James Henry 1939- *AmSCAP 80, ConAmC*
Willey, Leonard 1882-1964 *WhScrn 77*
William I 1027-1087 *OxMus*
William III 1650-1702 *OxMus*
William Of Hirsau *NewGrD 80*
William Of Newark *NewGrD 80*
William The Jew Of Pesaro *CnOxB, DancEn 78*
William, David 1926- *WhoThe 72, -77*
William, Joseph Ranger Bill 1878-1939 *WhScrn 77*
William, Robert d1931 *NotNAT B*
William, Warren d1948 *MotPP, WhoHol B*
William, Warren 1895-1948 *FilmEn, Film 2, FilmgC, ForYSC, HalFC 80, NotNAT B, WhScrn 74, -77, WhThe*
William, Warren 1896-1948 *MovMk*
Williams, A B d1964 *NotNAT B*
Williams, Aaron 1731-1776 *NewGrD 80*
Williams, Abby 1906- *NewOrJ[port]*
Williams, Adam 1929- *FilmgC, HalFC 80, WhoHol A*
Williams, Adrian 1956- *IntWWM 80*
Williams, Alan Robert 1910- *WhoMus 72*
Williams, Albert *Film 2*
Williams, Alberto 1862-1952 *Baker 78, MusMk, NewGrD 80, OxMus*
Williams, Alfonso *WhoHol A*
Williams, Alfred 1900-1963 *NewOrJ[port]*
Williams, Andre 1936?- *BluesWW, RkOn*
Williams, Andres 1952- *CnOxB*
Williams, Andy *AmPS A, -B*
Williams, Andy 1928- *WhoHol A*
Williams, Andy 1932- *BiDAmM*
Williams, Andy 1936- *RkOn[port]*
Williams, Ann 1935- *BiE&WWA, NotNAT*
Williams, Annabelle 1904-1967 *WhScrn 77*
Williams, Anthony 1945- *EncJzS 70*
Williams, Arnold *WhoHol A*
Williams, Arthur 1844-1915 *NotNAT B, WhThe*
Williams, Audrey M M 1936- *IntWWM 77*
Williams, Averil Myrna 1939- *IntWWM 77, WhoMus 72*
Williams, Barney 1823-1876 *FamA&A[port], OxThe*
Williams, Barney 1824-1876 *NotNAT B*
Williams, Mrs. Barney d1911 *NotNAT B*
Williams, Barry 1954- *WhoHol A*
Williams, Barry James *IntWWM 77*
Williams, Bearcat 1905- *WhoJazz 72*
Williams, Beresford 1904-1966 *WhScrn 74, -77*
Williams, Bernard Godfrey 1932- *WhoMus 72*
Williams, Bert d1922 *AmPS B, BlksB&W C, Film 1, WhoHol B*
Williams, Bert 1874-1922 *CmpEPM, DrBlPA, EncMT, Ent[port], JoeFr*
Williams, Bert 1875-1922 *AmPS*
Williams, Bert 1876-1922 *FamA&A[port], NotNAT A, -B*
Williams, Bert 1877-1922 *WhScrn 74, -77*
Williams, Bert 1878-1922 *MorBAP*
Williams, Bert 1922- *IntMPA 77, -75, -76, -78, -79, -80, WhoHol A*
Williams, Bessie *BluesWW*
Williams, Bill 1898-1973 *BluesWW[port]*
Williams, Bill 1916- *FilmEn, FilmgC, ForYSC, HalFC 80, IntMPA 77, -75, -76, -78, -79, -80, MotPP, WhoHol A*
Williams, Bill 1921-1964 *WhScrn 74, -77*
Williams, Billy *AmPS B, FilmEn, FilmgC*
Williams, Billy 1910-1972 *WhScrn 77*
Williams, Billy 1916-1972 *DrBlPA, RkOn[port]*
Williams, Billy 1929- *HalFC 80*
Williams, Billy Dee 1937- *BiE&WWA, DrBlPA, FilmEn, HalFC 80, IntMPA 77, -75, -76, -78, -79, -80, WhoHol A, WhoThe 77*
Williams, Billy Dee 1938- *WhoThe 72*
Williams, Black Benny 1890?-1924 *NewOrJ*
Williams, Blind Boy *BluesWW*
Williams, Bob 1913- *IntMPA 77, -75, -76, -78, -79, -80*
Williams, Bransby 1870-1961 *IlWWBF, NotNAT A, -B, OxThe, WhScrn 74, -77, WhThe, WhoHol B*
Williams, Bransby 1870-1964 *Film 2, FilmgC, HalFC 80*
Williams, Brinley A *PupTheA*
Williams, Brook *WhoHol A*
Williams, Bruce *PupTheA*
Williams, Buster 1942- *EncJzS 70*
Williams, Byron Olsen 1911- *AmSCAP 80*
Williams, Camella Ella *WhoMus 72*
Williams, Camilla *DrBlPA*
Williams, Campbell 1906- *WhThe*
Williams, Cara 1925- *FilmEn, FilmgC, ForYSC, HalFC 80, IntMPA 77, -75, -76, -78, -79, -80, MotPP, WhoHol A*
Williams, Carl W 1927- *IntMPA 77, -75, -76, -78, -79, -80*
Williams, Carol Hoepe 1939- *IntWWM 77*
Williams, Carol Janice 1950- *IntWWM 80*
Williams, Charles 1886-1945 *ModWD*
Williams, Charles 1893- *NewGrD 80*
Williams, Charles 1898-1958 *IntMPA 77, -75, -76, -78, -79, -80, Vers B[port], WhScrn 74, -77, WhoHol B*
Williams, Charles 1929- *BiDAmM*
Williams, Charles Anthony, Jr. 1942- *EncJzS 70*
Williams, Charles Francis Abdy 1855-1923 *Baker 78, NewGrD 80*
Williams, Charles Lee 1853-1935 *Baker 78, OxMus*
Williams, Charles Melvin 1908- *AmSCAP 66, -80, BiDAmM, EncJzS 70, NewGrD 80*
Williams, Charlie 1929- *EncFCWM 69*
Williams, Chickie 1919- *BiDAmM*
Williams, Chili *ForYSC*

Williams, Christopher A Becket 1890-1956 *Baker 78, OxMus*
Williams, Cindy *IntMPA 77, -75, -76, -78, -79, -80, WhoHol A*
Williams, Cindy 1947- *FilmEn*
Williams, Cindy 1948- *HalFC 80, MovMk*
Williams, Claiborne *NewOrJ*
Williams, Clara 1891-1928 *Film 1, WhScrn 74, -77, WhoHol B*
Williams, Clarence *BlkAmP*
Williams, Clarence 1893-1965 *AmSCAP 66, -80, BiDAmM, IlEncJ, NewOrJ*
Williams, Clarence 1898-1965 *CmpEPM, NewGrD 80, WhoJazz 72*
Williams, Clarence, III 1939- *DrBlPA, NotNAT, WhoHol A, WhoThe 77*
Williams, Claude 1908- *EncJzS 70*
Williams, Clifford 1926- *EncWT, WhoThe 72, -77*
Williams, Clifton 1923- *ConAmC*
Williams, Clyde *MorBAP*
Williams, Cootie *BgBands 74[port]*
Williams, Cootie 1908- *CmpEPM, DrBlPA, EncJzS 70, NewGrD 80*
Williams, Cootie 1910- *IlEncJ, WhoJazz 72*
Williams, Cora 1871-1927 *Film 1, -2, WhScrn 74, -77, WhoHol B*
Williams, Craig 1877-1941 *WhScrn 74, -77*
Williams, Curly *IlEncCM*
Williams, Curt *WhoHol A*
Williams, Daniel 1942- *CnOxB*
Williams, Danny *RkOn 2A*
Williams, Dave 1920- *NewOrJ*
Williams, David 1946- *EncJzS 70*
Williams, David Christmas 1871-1926 *Baker 78*
Williams, David H 1919- *AmSCAP 66, -80, CpmDNM 79, ConAmC*
Williams, David McKay 1887- *AmSCAP 66, -80, BiDAmM, ConAmC*
Williams, David Russell 1932- *AmSCAP 80, ConAmC, IntWWM 77, -80*
Williams, David Stanley 1949- *IntWWM 77*
Williams, Delbert Lee 1946- *IntWWM 77*
Williams, Derek 1910- *WhThe*
Williams, Derek Leslie 1952- *IntWWM 77*
Williams, Derick 1906- *IntMPA 77, -75, -76, -78, -79, -80*
Williams, Diahn *IntMPA 79, -80*
Williams, Dick d1962 *NotNAT B*
Williams, Dick Anthony 1938- *DrBlPA, MorBAP, WhoHol A, WhoThe 77*
Williams, Doc 1914- *BiDAmM, IlEncCM*
Williams, Don 1939- *AmSCAP 80, IlEncCM[port]*
Williams, Donald *ConAmC*
Williams, Donnie *WhoHol A*
Williams, Douglas d1968 *WhScrn 77*
Williams, Dudley 1941?- *CnOxB*
Williams, E C *MorBAP*
Williams, Earle d1927 *MotPP, WhoHol B*
Williams, Earle 1880-1927 *FilmEn, Film 1, -2, NotNAT B, TwYS*
Williams, Earle 1895-1927 *WhScrn 74, -77*
Williams, Eddie 1910?- *WhoJazz 72*
Williams, Edgar 1926- *IntWWM 77, -80, WhoMus 72*
Williams, Edgar Warren 1949- *CpmDNM 80*
Williams, Edith *PupTheA*
Williams, Edwin Lynn 1947- *IntWWM 77, -80*
Williams, Edy *WhoHol A*
Williams, Egbert Austin d1922 *BlksB&W[port]*
Williams, Egbert Austin 1876?-1922 *OxThe*
Williams, Egbert Austin 1877-1922 *BiDAmM*
Williams, Egbert Austin 1878-1922 *BlkAmP*
Williams, Elaine *WhoHol A*
Williams, Ellen Virginia *CnOxB*
Williams, Ellwoodson *BlkAmP*
Williams, Elmer A 1905-1962 *WhoJazz 72*
Williams, Elmo 1913- *FilmEn, FilmgC, HalFC 80, IntMPA 77, -75, -76, -78, -79, -80, WorEFlm*
Williams, Emery H 1931- *BluesWW[port]*
Williams, Emlyn 1905- *BiE&WWA, CnMD, CnThe, ConDr 73, -77, CroCD, EncWT, FamA&A[port], FilmAG WE, FilmEn, FilmgC, ForYSC, HalFC 80, IlWWBF[port], -A, McGEWD, ModWD, MotPP, MovMk[port], NotNAT, -A, OxThe, PlP&P[port], WhoHol A, WhoThe 72, -77, WorEFlm*
Williams, Eric *IlWWBF*
Williams, Eric Bransby 1900- *Film 2, IlWWBF*
Williams, Esther *MotPP*
Williams, Esther 1921- *CmMov, MGM[port]*
Williams, Esther 1923- *BiDFilm, -81, FilmEn, FilmgC, ForYSC, HalFC 80, IntMPA 77, -75, -76, -78, -79, -80, MovMk[port], OxFilm, What 2[port], WhoHol A, WorEFlm*
Williams, Evelyn M d1959 *NotNAT B*
Williams, Fess 1894- *CmpEPM, WhoJazz 72*
Williams, Fiddler 1908- *EncJzS 70*
Williams, Florence 1912- *WhThe*
Williams, Florian 1879-1973 *Baker 78, NewGrD 80*
Williams, Franc 1910- *EncJzS 70*
Williams, Frances *AmPS B, ConAmC*
Williams, Frances d1978 *AmSCAP 80*
Williams, Frances 1903-1959 *AmSCAP 66, CmpEPM, EncMT, NotNAT B, WhThe, WhoHol A, -B*
Williams, Frances Jennings *WhoMus 72*
Williams, Francis 1910- *EncJzS 70*
Williams, Frank Walter 1901- *BiDAmM*
Williams, Fred *WhoHol A*
Williams, Fred J 1875-1942 *WhScrn 74, -77, WhoHol B*
Williams, Freddie 1887?-1963 *NewOrJ[port]*
Williams, Frederic Arthur 1869-1942 *Baker 78*
Williams, Fritz 1865-1930 *NotNAT B, WhThe, WhoStg 1906*
Williams, G A *Film 1*
Williams, Gavin Rodney 1942- *IntWWM 77*
Williams, Gene *BgBands 74, NewGrD 80, WhoHol A*
Williams, George *ConMuA 80B, NewOrJ*
Williams, George 1854-1936 *WhScrn 74, -77, WhoHol B*
Williams, George 1910-1965 *NewOrJ*
Williams, George 1917- *CmpEPM*
Williams, George B 1866-1931 *Film 2, WhScrn 74, -77, WhoHol B*
Williams, George Ebenezer 1783-1819 *NewGrD 80*
Williams, George Emlyn 1905- *Ent, IntMPA 77, -75, -76, -78, -79, -80*
Williams, Giula 1896- *IntWWM 77*
Williams, Gloria *WhoHol A*
Williams, Grace Mary 1906-1977 *IntWWM 77, NewGrD 80, WhoMus 72*
Williams, Grant 1930- *FilmgC, ForYSC, HalFC 80, IntMPA 77, -75, -76, -78, -79, -80, MovMk, WhoHol A, WhoHrs 80[port]*
Williams, Greg *AmSCAP 80*
Williams, Griff *BgBands 74, CmpEPM*
Williams, Guinn d1962 *NotNAT B*
Williams, Guinn 1899-1962 *FilmEn, ForYSC, HolCA[port], Vers A[port]*
Williams, Guinn 1900-1962 *HalFC 80*
Williams, Guinn 1907-1962 *Film 1*
Williams, Guinn Big Boy d1962 *MotPP, WhoHol B*
Williams, Guinn Big Boy 1899-1962 *TwYS, WhScrn 74, -77*
Williams, Guinn Big Boy 1900-1962 *FilmgC, MovMk*
Williams, Guinn Big Boy 1907-1962 *Film 2*
Williams, Gus 1847-1915 *NotNAT B, WhoStg 1906*
Williams, Guy 1924- *FilmgC, HalFC 80, WhoHol A, WhoHrs 80*
Williams, Guy 1926- *ForYSC*
Williams, Gwen *Film 2*
Williams, Gwen d1962 *NotNAT B*
Williams, Hal *DrBlPA*
Williams, Hank d1953 *AmPS A, -B, ConMuA 80A*
Williams, Hank 1923-1953 *BiDAmM, CmpEPM, CounME 74[port], -74A, EncFCWM 69, IlEncCM[port], IlEncR, NewGrD 80, PopAmC SUP[port]*
Williams, Hank 1924-1953 *WhScrn 74, -77, WhoHol B*
Williams, Hank, Jr. 1949- *CounME 74[port], -74A, EncFCWM 69, IlEncCM[port], WhoHol A*
Williams, Hannah *AmPS B*
Williams, Happy 1946- *EncJzS 70*
Williams, Harcourt 1880-1957 *FilmgC, HalFC 80, NotNAT B, OxThe, PlP&P, WhScrn 74, -77, WhThe, WhoHol B*
Williams, Harold *BlkAmP*
Williams, Harry 1879-1922 *AmPS, AmSCAP 66, -80, CmpEPM, Sw&Ld B*
Williams, Harry Evan 1867-1918 *Baker 78*
Williams, Harry J *OxMus*
Williams, Hattie 1872-1942 *CmpEPM, NotNAT B, WhThe, WhoStg 1906*
Williams, Heathcote 1941- *ConDr 73, -77, EncWT*
Williams, Helen *IntWWM 77*
Williams, Henry 1907-1962 *BluesWW*
Williams, Henry F 1813-1889 *NewGrD 80*
Williams, Henry R 1813-1889 *BiDAmM*
Williams, Herb 1874-1936 *NotNAT B, WhScrn 74, -77, WhoHol B*
Williams, Herschel 1909- *BiE&WWA, NotNAT*
Williams, Hiram 1923-1952 *AmSCAP 80, NewGrD 80*
Williams, Hope 1901- *WhThe, WhoHol A*
Williams, Horace Robert 1932- *IntWWM 77, -80*
Williams, Howard *WhoHol A*
Williams, Howard 1933-1972 *ConAmC*
Williams, Hugh *AmSCAP 80, NewGrD 80*
Williams, Hugh 1904-1969 *FilmEn, FilmgC, HalFC 80, IlWWBF[port], McGEWD, MovMk[port], NotNAT B, PlP&P, WhScrn 74, -77, WhThe, WhoHol B*
Williams, Huw Tregelles 1949- *IntWWM 77, -80*
Williams, Ike 1923- *What 4[port]*
Williams, Ina d1962 *NotNAT B*
Williams, Irene *BluesWW*
Williams, Irene d1970 *WhoHol B*
Williams, Jack *WhoHol A*
Williams, Jack Eric 1944- *ConAmC*
Williams, Jacqueline Adelaide Winifred 1922- *WhoMus 72*
Williams, James Clifton 1923-1976 *AmSCAP 80*
Williams, Janice 1936- *AmSCAP 80, IntWWM 77, WhoMus 72*
Williams, Jason *WhoHol A*
Williams, Jay T 1941- *ConAmC*
Williams, Jean E *ConAmC*
Williams, Jean L *WomWMM A, -B*
Williams, Jean Sterling Mackinlay 1882-1958 *OxThe*
Williams, Jeff *MorBAP, WhoHol A*
Williams, Jeffrey 1860-1938 *Film 2, WhScrn 74, -77, WhoHol B*
Williams, Jesse Lynch 1871-1929 *CnMD, McGEWD, ModWD, NotNAT B, WhThe*
Williams, Jimmy *WhoHol A*
Williams, Jo Jo *BluesWW*
Williams, Joan Florence 1931- *AmSCAP 80*
Williams, Jody *BluesWW*
Williams, Joe *WhoHol A*
Williams, Joe 1918- *BiDAmM, BluesWW[port], CmpEPM, DrBlPA, EncJzS 70*
Williams, Joe Lee 1903- *BiDAmM, BluesWW[port]*
Williams, Joe Lee 1906- *AmSCAP 80*
Williams, John *RkOn 2A*
Williams, John d1818 *NotNAT B*
Williams, John 1817-1899 *BiDAmM*
Williams, John 1903- *BiE&WWA, FilmEn, FilmgC, ForYSC, HalFC 80, NotNAT, WhoHol A, WhoThe 72, -77*
Williams, John 1932- *FilmEn, WhoHrs 80*
Williams, John 1941- *BnBkM 80, EncJzS 70, IntWWM 77, MusSN[port], WhoMus 72*
Williams, John 1942- *NewGrD 80*
Williams, John Ajala *MorBAP*
Williams, John Alfred *BlkAmP*
Williams, John Arnold 1933- *WhoMus 72*
Williams, John D d1941 *NotNAT B, WhThe*
Williams, John Gerard 1888-1947 *OxMus*
Williams, John Gerrard 1888-1947 *Baker 78*
Williams, John J 1856-1918 *WhScrn 77*
Williams, John Lloyd *OxMus*
Williams, John M 1884-1974 *Baker 78*
Williams, John Martyn 1947- *WhoMus 72*
Williams, John Ratcliffe 1920- *IntWWM 80,*

WhoMus 72
Williams, John T 1932- Baker 78, ConAmC, IntMPA 79, -80, NewGrD 80
Williams, Johnny BluesWW
Williams, Johnny 1906- BluesWW
Williams, Johnny 1908- WhoJazz 72
Williams, Johnny 1932- HalFC 80
Williams, Jonathan WhoHol A
Williams, Joseph Baker 78, OxMus
Williams, Joseph 1920- BluesWW[port]
Williams, Joseph Benjamin 1847-1923 Baker 78, NewGrD 80
Williams, Joseph Leon 1935- BluesWW
Williams, Joseph William 1819-1883 NewGrD 80
Williams, Joyce WhoHol A
Williams, Julia 1879-1936 WhScrn 74, -77, WhoHol B
Williams, June Vanleer NatPD[port]
Williams, Kate WhoHol A
Williams, Katherine WhoHol A
Williams, Kathlyn d1960 MotPP, NotNAT B, WhoHol B
Williams, Kathlyn 1872?-1960 WhScrn 74, -77
Williams, Kathlyn 1888-1960 FilmEn, Film 1, -2, ForYSC, HalFC 80, TwYS
Williams, Katrina Sykes 1924- IntWWM 77
Williams, Kay WhoHol A
Williams, Kenneth 1926- FilmEn, FilmgC, HalFC 80, IlWWBF[port], WhoHol A, WhoThe 72, -77
Williams, Kenneth S 1920- ConAmC
Williams, Kenny WhoHol A
Williams, Kid Film 2
Williams, L C 1930-1960 BluesWW
Williams, Larry WhoHol A
Williams, Larry 1890-1956 WhoHol B
Williams, Larry 1935- RkOn[port]
Williams, Lawrence 1890-1956 WhScrn 74, -77
Williams, Lee 1938- BluesWW
Williams, Lemuel PupTheA
Williams, Leona 1943- IlEncCM
Williams, Leroy 1937- EncJzS 70
Williams, LeRoy A d1962 NotNAT B
Williams, Lester 1920- BluesWW
Williams, Lottie Film 2
Williams, Lucille Film 2
Williams, Lucy NewGrD 80
Williams, Mack 1907-1965 WhScrn 74, -77, WhoHol B
Williams, Malcolm 1870-1937 Film 2, NotNAT B, WhScrn 74, -77, WhoHol B
Williams, Margaret PlP&P
Williams, Maria Elizabeth 1952- IntWWM 80
Williams, Marie 1921-1967 Film 2, WhScrn 74, -77, WhoHol B
Williams, Marion 1927- DrBlPA, EncJzS 70
Williams, Marjorie Rose 1913-1933 WhScrn 74, -77
Williams, Marshall BlkAmP
Williams, Mary PupTheA
Williams, Mary Lou 1910- AmSCAP 66, -80, BiDAmM, BlkWAB[port], CmpEPM, ConAmC, DrBlPA, EncJzS 70, IlEncJ, **NewGrD 80, WhoJazz 72**
Williams, Mary Ruth IntWWM 77, -80, WhoOp 76
Williams, Mason 1938- BiDAmM, RkOn 2[port]
Williams, Matt 1929- AmSCAP 66, -80
Williams, Maurice And The Zodiacs RkOn
Williams, Meirion 1901- IntWWM 77, -80, WhoMus 72
Williams, Mentor 1946- AmSCAP 80
Williams, Michael 1935- WhoThe 72, -77
Williams, Midge 1908?- WhoJazz 72
Williams, Milan Bonnett 1948- AmSCAP 80
Williams, Molly d1967 WhScrn 74, -77, WhoHol B
Williams, Montagu Normington 1911-1942 NewGrD 80
Williams, Montague d1892 NotNAT B
Williams, Morgan 1907- WhoMus 72
Williams, Muriel IntMPA 77, -75, -76, -78, -79, -80
Williams, Nancy WhoOp 76
Williams, Nancy Mary 1912- WhoMus 72
Williams, Ned 1927- AmSCAP 66, -80
Williams, Nelson 1917- WhoJazz 72
Williams, Nesta CreCan 1
Williams, Nolan 1902?-1942? NewOrJ
Williams, Norwood 1880?- NewOrJ
Williams, O T Chalky d1976 WhoHol C
Williams, Oscar 1939- DrBlPA, IntMPA 79, -80
Williams, Oswald 1881-1937 MagIlD
Williams, Otis 1936- RkOn
Williams, Otis And The Charms AmPS A, RkOn
Williams, Otis Clayborn 1941- AmSCAP 80
Williams, Palmer NewYTET
Williams, Pat 1939- EncJzS 70
Williams, Patrick Joseph 1951- IntWWM 77, -80
Williams, Patrick M 1939- AmSCAP 66, ConAmC, EncJzS 70
Williams, Paul IntMPA 77, -75, -76, -78, -79, -80, WhoHol A
Williams, Paul 1940- AmSCAP 80, FilmEn, IlEncR[port], RkOn 2[port]
Williams, Paul 1944- FilmEn
Williams, Paulette MorBAP
Williams, Peggy Audrey 1920- WhoMus 72
Williams, Percy Film 2
Williams, Percy G 1857-1923 NotNAT B
Williams, Peter 1914- CnOxB, DancEn 78
Williams, Peter Fredric 1937- IntWWM 77, -80, NewGrD 80
Williams, Phyllis AmSCAP 80
Williams, Rabbit's Foot BluesWW
Williams, Ralph 1881-1948 NewGrD 80
Williams, Ralph 1904- WhoMus 72
Williams, Ralph Vaughan 1872-1958 Baker 78, DancEn 78, OxMus
Williams, Randall Hank, Jr. 1949- BiDAmM
Williams, Raymond George 1887- AmSCAP 80
Williams, Rhys 1892-1969 ForYSC, WhScrn 74, -77, WhoHol B
Williams, Rhys 1897-1969 FilmEn, FilmgC, HalFC 80, MovMk, NotNAT B, Vers A[port], WhThe
Williams, Ricardo G 1953- AmSCAP 80
Williams, Richard 1933- DcFM, FilmEn, HalFC 80, IntMPA 77, -75, -76, -78, -79, -80, OxFilm, WorEFlm
Williams, Richard 1939- IntWWM 80
Williams, Richard B 1926- AmSCAP 80
Williams, Richard Gene 1931- EncJzS 70
Williams, Robert PupTheA
Williams, Robert d1931 NotNAT B, WhoHol B
Williams, Robert 1897-1932 HalFC 80
Williams, Robert 1898?-1932 FilmgC
Williams, Robert 1899-1931 WhScrn 74, -77
Williams, Robert A 1947- IntWWM 77
Williams, Robert B IntMPA 77, -75, -76, -78, -79, -80, WhoHol A
Williams, Robert Kenneth 1921- AmSCAP 80
Williams, Robert N BiE&WWA, NotNAT
Williams, Robert Pete 1914- BluesWW[port]
Williams, Robert X, Jr. 1900- IntMPA 77, -75, -76, -78, -79, -80
Williams, Robin IntMPA 80
Williams, Robin Richey 1934- IntWWM 77
Williams, Roger 1926- AmPS A, -B, AmSCAP 66, -80, BiDAmM, ForYSC, IntMPA 77, -75, -76, -78, -79, -80, RkOn[port], WhoHol A
Williams, Roger Bevan 1943- IntWWM 80
Williams, Ronald 1947- ConAmC
Williams, Ronald Ray 1929- IntWWM 77
Williams, Rosemary Zika 1949- IntWWM 77, -80
Williams, Rubberlegs BluesWW
Williams, Rudy 1909- WhoJazz 72
Williams, Sam 1884-1961 AmSCAP 66, -80
Williams, Samm MorBAP
Williams, Sammy 1948- NotNAT
Williams, Sandra Beth 1948- BlkAmP
Williams, Sandy 1906- BiDAmM, CmpEPM, WhoJazz 72
Williams, Scott T WhScrn 74, -77
Williams, Simon WhoHol A
Williams, Sioned 1953- IntWWM 80
Williams, Skippy 1916- WhoJazz 72
Williams, Sol 1917- BiDAmM
Williams, Sonia 1926- WhThe
Williams, Spencer 1880-1965 NewOrJ[port]
Williams, Spencer 1889-1965 AmSCAP 66, -80, Baker 78, BiDAmM, CmpEPM, ConAmC, DrBlPA, WhoJazz 72
Williams, Spencer 1893-1969 BlksB&W[port], -C, BlksBF, DrBlPA, WhScrn 74, -77, WhoHol B
Williams, Stanley 1925- CnOxB, DancEn 78
Williams, Stephen 1900-1957 NotNAT B, WhThe
Williams, Sugar Boy BluesWW
Williams, Susan BluesWW
Williams, Susan Luxen 1953- AmSCAP 80
Williams, Ted 1918- Film 2, WhoHol A
Williams, Tennessee 1911- BiE&WWA, CnThe, ConDr 73, -77, CroCD, DcLB 7[port], EncWT, Ent[port], McGEWD[port], ModWD, NatPD[port], NotNAT, REnWD[port], WhoThe 72, -77
Williams, Tennessee 1914- AmSCAP 66, CnMD, FilmEn, FilmgC, HalFC 80, IntMPA 77, -75, -76, -78, -79, -80, NotNAT A, OxFilm, OxThe, PlP&P[port], WorEFlm
Williams, Tex 1917- AmPS A, CounME 74, -74A, EncFCWM 69, IlEncCM[port]
Williams, Thad WhoHol A
Williams, Thomas E OxMus
Williams, Thomas J d1874 NotNAT B
Williams, Tiger WhoHol A
Williams, Tony 1945- EncJzS 70
Williams, Treat IntMPA 80
Williams, Trevor James 1929- WhoMus 72
Williams, Van WhoHol A
Williams, Victor Monnie 1921- CpmDNM 80
Williams, Wade 1942- WhoHrs 80
Williams, Walter 1887-1940 NotNAT B, WhThe
Williams, William d1701? NewGrD 80
Williams, William A 1870-1942 WhScrn 74, -77, WhoHol B
Williams, William A 1893- BiE&WWA
Williams, William Carlos 1883-1963 BiDAmM, CnMD, ModWD, PlP&P
Williams, William John PupTheA
Williams, William Sidney Gwynn 1896- IntWWM 77, -80, OxMus, WhoMus 72
Williams, Wyndham George 1905- WhoMus 72
Williams, Zack 1888- BlksB&W[port], -C, Film 2
Williams-Jones, Pearl 1931- IntWWM 77, -80
Williamson, Alastair WhoHol A
Williamson, Albert Curtis 1867-1944 CreCan 1
Williamson, Audrey 1918- DancEn 78
Williamson, Bruce AmSCAP 66, -80
Williamson, Cecil H 1909- IlWWBF
Williamson, Claude B, Jr. 1926- AmSCAP 80, CmpEPM
Williamson, Curtis 1867-1944 CreCan 1
Williamson, David 1942- ConDr 77, WhoThe 77
Williamson, Fred 1938- DrBlPA, FilmEn, HalFC 80, IntMPA 77, -75, -76, -78, -79, -80, MovMk[port], WhoHol A
Williamson, Henry 1953- AmSCAP 80
Williamson, Hugh Ross 1901- BiE&WWA, NotNAT, WhThe
Williamson, James A 1855-1933 DcFM, FilmEn, FilmgC, HalFC 80, IlWWBF, OxFilm
Williamson, James Cassius 1845-1913 NotNAT A, -B, WhThe
Williamson, John A 1910- BluesWW[port]
Williamson, John Edward 1942- IntWWM 77
Williamson, John Finley 1887-1964 Baker 78
Williamson, John Lee 1914-1948 BiDAmM, BluesWW[port], NewGrD 80
Williamson, John Ramsden 1929- IntWWM 80
Williamson, Lambert 1907- FilmgC, HalFC 80
Williamson, Malcolm 1931- Baker 78, CmOp, CpmDNM 79, DcCom&M 79, DcCM, IntWWM 77, -80, MusMk, NewGrD 80[port], OxMus, WhoHrs 80, WhoMus 72
Williamson, Mariruth R 1932- IntWWM 77
Williamson, Melvin E 1900-1959 WhScrn 74, -77
Williamson, Mike Lee 1952- AmSCAP 80
Williamson, Muriel Coghill 1910- IntWWM 77
Williamson, Nicol PlP&P, WhoHol A
Williamson, Nicol 1938- CnThe, Ent, FilmEn, NotNAT, WhoThe 72, -77

Williamson, Nicol 1939- *FilmgC, HalFC 80, IntMPA 79, –80*
Williamson, Nicol 1940- *IlWWBF, MovMk*
Williamson, Patrick 1929- *IntMPA 77, –75, –76, –78, –79, –80*
Williamson, Paul 1947- *IntWWM 77, –80*
Williamson, Robert 1885-1949 *Film 2, WhScrn 77*
Williamson, Robin E 1889-1935 *WhScrn 77*
Williamson, Roy 1937- *IntWWM 77*
Williamson, Sonny Boy d1948 *ConMuA 80A*
Williamson, Sonny Boy 1899-1965 *BiDAmM, BluesWW[port], ConMuA 80A*
Williamson, Sonny Boy 1914-1948 *BluesWW*
Williamson, Sonny Boy 1916?-1948 *NewGrD 80*
Williamson, Stu 1933- *CmpEPM*
Williamson, Stuart Lee 1933- *BiDAmM*
Williamson, T G 1758?-1817 *NewGrD 80*
Willians, Ann *Film 2*
Willich, Jobst 1486?-1552 *NewGrD 80*
Willich, Jodocus 1486?-1552 *NewGrD 80*
Willie, Raymond *IntMPA 75, –76*
Willie B *BluesWW*
Willie C *BluesWW*
Willie The Lion *AmSCAP 80*
Willig, George 1764-1851 *BiDAmM, NewGrD 80*
Willigan, Bill *NewOrJ*
Willigan, Jim 1902?-1930? *NewOrJ*
Willing, Foy 1915- *ForYSC, IlEncCM*
Willing, James d1915 *NotNAT B*
Willingham, Calder 1922- *BiE&WWA, CnMD, NotNAT*
Willingham, Harry G 1881-1943 *WhScrn 74, –77, WhoHol B*
Willingham, Noble *WhoHol A*
Willink, George Peter John 1947- *ConAmC*
Willis, Aaron 1932- *BluesWW[port]*
Willis, Austin *WhoHol A*
Willis, Charles H *Baker 78*
Willis, Chuck 1928-1958 *BiDAmM, RkOn[port]*
Willis, Daniel Dale 1952- *AmSCAP 80*
Willis, Dave 1895-1973 *WhScrn 77*
Willis, Gladys 1902- *WhoMus 72*
Willis, Gordon *FilmEn, FilmgC, HalFC 80, IntMPA 77, –76, –78, –79, –80*
Willis, Guy 1915- *CounME 74, IlEncCM[port]*
Willis, Henry 1821-1901 *Baker 78, NewGrD 80, OxMus*
Willis, Mrs. Herbert *Film 2*
Willis, Hubert *Film 2*
Willis, James 1915- *BiDAmM*
Willis, James Douglas 1942- *CpmDNM 80*
Willis, James Frank 1909-1969 *CreCan 2*
Willis, Jerome *WhoHol A*
Willis, John 1916- *NotNAT*
Willis, John Alvin 1916- *ConAmTC*
Willis, Joshua F 1920- *NewOrJ*
Willis, Judith *CmpGMD*
Willis, Larry 1940- *EncJzS 70*
Willis, Lawrence Elliott 1940- *EncJzS 70*
Willis, Leo *Film 2*
Willis, Louise 1880-1929 *WhScrn 74, –77*
Willis, Love Maria 1824-1908 *BiDAmM*
Willis, Mary 1945- *CnOxB*
Willis, Matt *Vers B[port], WhoHrs 80*
Willis, Nat *Film 1*
Willis, Nathaniel Parker 1806-1867 *McGEWD, NotNAT B, OxThe*
Willis, Norman 1903- *Vers B[port]*
Willis, Paul *Film 1, –2*
Willis, Richard 1795?-1830 *BiDAmM*
Willis, Richard Murat, Jr. 1929- *AmSCAP 80, CpmDNM 78, ConAmC, IntWWM 77*
Willis, Richard Storrs 1819-1900 *Baker 78, BiDAmM*
Willis, Robert 1800-1875 *OxMus*
Willis, Skeeter 1907-1976 *CounME 74*
Willis, Skeeter 1917-1976 *BiDAmM, IlEncCM[port]*
Willis, Stephen Charles 1946- *IntWWM 77, –80*
Willis, Susan *WhoHol A*
Willis, Suzanne Eileen 1951- *IntWWM 77, –80*
Willis, Ted 1918- *ConDr 77, IntMPA 77, –75, –76, –78, –79, –80, WhoThe 72, –77*
Willis, Vic 1922- *CounME 74, IlEncCM[port]*
Willis, Victor *MorBAP*
Willis, Victor 1922- *BiDAmM*
Willis, William H *Baker 78*
Willis Brothers *CounME 74, –74A, EncFCWM 69, IlEncCM[port]*
Willisegger, Hansrudi 1935- *IntWWM 77*
Willisegger, Hansruedi 1935- *IntWWM 80*
Willison, David 1936- *WhoMus 72*
Willkomm, Eugen d1744 *NewGrD 80*
Willman, Allan Arthur 1909- *Baker 78, BiDAmM, ConAmC, IntWWM 77, –80*
Willman, Noel 1918- *BiE&WWA, FilmgC, HalFC 80, NotNAT, WhoHol A, WhoThe 72, –77*
Willman, Regina Hansen 1914-1965 *ConAmC*
Willman, Thomas Lindsay 1784-1840 *NewGrD 80*
Willmann *NewGrD 80*
Willmann, Caroline 1796-1860? *NewGrD 80*
Willmann, Ignaz 1739-1815 *NewGrD 80*
Willmann, Magdalena 1771-1801 *NewGrD 80*
Willmann, Max 1767-1813 *NewGrD 80*
Willmann, Walburga 1769-1835 *NewGrD 80*
Willmer, Catherine *WhoHol A*
Willmers, Rudolf 1821-1878 *Baker 78*
Willmore, Alan Charles 1935- *WhoMus 72*
Willner, A M d1929 *NotNAT B*
Willner, Arthur 1881-1959 *Baker 78*
Willock, Dave 1909- *FilmgC, ForYSC, HalFC 80, Vers A[port], WhoHol A*
Willoughby, George W *IntMPA 77, –75, –76, –78, –79, –80*
Willoughby, Hugh 1891- *WhThe*
Willoughby, Kathleen Muriel 1909- *WhoMus 72*
Willoughby, Louis Philippe Charles 1903- *IntWWM 77, –80, WhoMus 72*
Willoughby, Nancy Kiehn 1949- *IntWWM 77*
Willoughbye, John *NewGrD 80*
Willow, Ray *AmSCAP 80*
Willows, The *RkOn[port]*
Wills, Arthur 1926- *IntWWM 77, –80, NewGrD 80, WhoMus 72*
Wills, Beverly 1934-1963 *NotNAT B, WhScrn 74, –77, WhoHol B*
Wills, Billy Rufus 1934- *AmSCAP 80*
Wills, Bob 1905-1975 *AmPS A, BgBands 74, CmpEPM, EncFCWM 69, IlEncCM[port], WhScrn 77, WhoHol C*
Wills, Bob 1906- *CounME 74[port], –74A*
Wills, Brember d1948 *NotNAT B, WhThe, WhoHol B*
Wills, Chill 1903-1978 *FilmEn, FilmgC, ForYSC, HalFC 80, HolCA[port], IntMPA 77, –75, –76, –78, –79, MotPP, MovMk, Vers A[port], WhoHol A*
Wills, David 1951- *AmSCAP 80*
Wills, Drusilla 1884-1951 *NotNAT B, WhScrn 74, –77, WhThe, WhoHol B*
Wills, Edwina Wheeler *IntWWM 77*
Wills, James Robert 1905-1975 *AmSCAP 80*
Wills, Sir John Spencer 1904- *IntMPA 77, –75, –76, –78, –79, –80*
Wills, Johnnie Lee 1912- *IlEncCM*
Wills, Lou d1968 *WhoHol B*
Wills, Maury *WhoHol A*
Wills, Nat 1873-1917 *JoeFr, NotNAT B, WhScrn 77, WhoHol B*
Wills, Norma *Film 2*
Wills, Oscar 1916-1969 *BluesWW*
Wills, Robert 1905- *BiDAmM*
Wills, Tommy d1962 *NotNAT B*
Wills, W G 1828-1891 *NotNAT A, –B*
Wills, Walter 1881-1967 *WhScrn 74, –77, WhoHol B*
Willshire, James Havilland 1953- *IntWWM 80*
Willson, Joseph 1770?-1822 *BiDAmM*
Willson, Meredith 1902- *AmSCAP 66, –80, Baker 78, BestMus, BiDAmM, BiE&WWA, CmpEPM, ConAmC, ConDr 73, –77D, EncMT, HalFC 80, IntWWM 77, –80, NewCBMT, NewGrD 80, NotNAT, –A, PopAmC[port], PopAmC SUP, WhoMus 72*
Willson, Meredith 1907- *AmPS*
Willson, Osmund 1896- *WhThe*
Willson, Rini *WhScrn 74, –77*
Willy 1859-1931 *Baker 78, NotNAT B*
Willy, M 1859-1931 *WhThe*
Wilm, Nicolai Von 1834-1911 *Baker 78, NewGrD 80*
Wilma-Bagniuk, Sofia Anna 1929- *IntWWM 77, –80*
Wilmer, Douglas 1920- *FilmgC, HalFC 80, WhoHol A, WhoThe 72, –77*
Wilmer-Brown, Maisie 1893-1973 *WhScrn 77, WhoHol B*
Wilmers, Catherine Claire 1952- *IntWWM 80*
Wilmeth, Don B 1939- *NotNAT*
Wilmot, Charles d1896 *NotNAT B*
Wilmot, John, Earl 1647-1680 *Ent[port]*
Wilmot, Lee 1899-1938 *WhScrn 74, –77*
Wilmot, Robert *NotNAT B*
Wilmott, Charles d1955 *NotNAT B*
Wilmott, Gary, Jr. *PupTheA*
Wilms, Jan Willem 1772-1847 *Baker 78*
Wilms, Johann Wilhelm 1772-1847 *NewGrD 80*
Wilse, Lulee *Film 2*
Wilsey, Jay d1961 *Film 2, WhoHol B*
Wilshin, Sunday 1905- *IlWWBF, WhThe*
Wilsing, Daniel Friedrich Eduard 1809-1893 *Baker 78*
Wilsing, Joern W 1940- *WhoOp 76*
Wilson, Lady *OxMus*
Wilson, Al d1932 *WhScrn 77*
Wilson, Al 1906-1951 *AmSCAP 66, –80*
Wilson, Al 1939- *RkOn 2[port]*
Wilson, Alan C 1943-1970 *WhScrn 77*
Wilson, Albert Edward 1885-1960 *NotNAT A, –B, WhThe*
Wilson, Alex *WhoHol A*
Wilson, Alfred *NewOrJ*
Wilson, Alfred 1880?-1905 *BiDAmM*
Wilson, Alfred 1901- *IntWWM 80, WhoMus 72*
Wilson, Alice *Film 1, –2*
Wilson, Allan Harold 1949- *IntWWM 77, –80*
Wilson, Andi *MorBAP*
Wilson, Anne M *Film 2*
Wilson, Arthur d1652 *NotNAT B*
Wilson, Arthur 1885-1953 *BlksBF[port]*
Wilson, Baron *WhoHol A*
Wilson, Beatrice d1943 *NotNAT B, WhThe*
Wilson, Ben *TwYS A*
Wilson, Ben 1876-1930 *WhoHol B*
Wilson, Ben 1885- *Film 1, –2, TwYS*
Wilson, Benjamin F 1876-1930 *WhScrn 74, –77*
Wilson, Billy 1935- *CnOxB*
Wilson, Billy 1936?- *DrBlPA*
Wilson, Bob *ConMuA 80B*
Wilson, Brian 1942- *BiDAmM*
Wilson, Bruce *WhoHol A*
Wilson, Buster 1897-1949 *WhoJazz 72*
Wilson, Mrs. C Baron d1846 *NotNAT B*
Wilson, Cal *BlkAmP, WhoHol A*
Wilson, Cameron Kelly 1959- *AmSCAP 80*
Wilson, Carey 1889- *FilmEn*
Wilson, Carolyn Patricia 1954- *IntWWM 80*
Wilson, Catherine *CmOp, IntWWM 77, –80, WhoMus 72, WhoOp 76*
Wilson, Cecelia Kaye 1952- *IntWWM 77, –80*
Wilson, Cecil Frank Petch 1909- *WhThe*
Wilson, Charles d1909 *NotNAT B*
Wilson, Charles d1948 *Film 2, WhoHol B*
Wilson, Charles 1895-1948 *Vers B[port]*
Wilson, Charles C *ForYSC*
Wilson, Charles Cahill 1894-1948 *WhScrn 77*
Wilson, Charles Mills 1931- *Baker 78, IntWWM 80, NewGrD 80*
Wilson, Chris *WhoHol A*
Wilson, Chris Richard 1948- *AmSCAP 80*
Wilson, Christopher d1919 *NotNAT B*
Wilson, Christopher Robert 1952- *IntWWM 77, –80*
Wilson, Clarence H 1877-1941 *Film 2, ForYSC, WhScrn 74, –77, WhoHol B*
Wilson, Claude *WhoHol A*
Wilson, Clive 1932- *IntWWM 80*
Wilson, Clive 1942- *NewOrJ SUP[port]*
Wilson, Cronin *Film 2*
Wilson, Curtis Wayne 1941- *AmSCAP 80*
Wilson, Cynthia *WhoHol A*
Wilson, Dana *WhoHol A*
Wilson, David Chase 1951- *IntWWM 77*
Wilson, Demond 1946- *DrBlPA, WhoHol A*
Wilson, Dennis *WhoHol A*
Wilson, Diana 1897-1937 *NotNAT B, WhThe*
Wilson, Dick *WhoHol A*
Wilson, Dick 1911-1941 *CmpEPM, IlEncJ, WhoJazz 72*
Wilson, Dolores S 1926- *AmSCAP 80*

Wilson, Domingo Santa Cruz *Baker 78*
Wilson, Don *WhoHol A*
Wilson, Don 1896- *AmSCAP 66, -80*
Wilson, Donald M 1937- *CpmDNM 73, -74, -79, ConAmC, IntWWM 77, -80*
Wilson, Dooley *AmPS B*
Wilson, Dooley 1894-1953 *DrBlPA, FilmEn, FilmgC, HalFC 80, HolP 40[port], WhScrn 74, -77, WhoHol B*
Wilson, Dooley 1895- *ForYSC*
Wilson, Dorothy 1909- *FilmEn, ThFT[port], WhoHol A, WhoMus 72*
Wilson, Douglas 1935- *AmSCAP 80*
Wilson, Earl 1907- *AmSCAP 66, -80, WhoHol A*
Wilson, Earl L 1942- *AmSCAP 66, -80*
Wilson, Ed 1916-1975 *Film 2, WhScrn 77*
Wilson, Ed 1944- *EncJzS 70*
Wilson, Edith 1906- *BlksBF, BluesWW[port], WhThe*
Wilson, Edmund 1895-1972 *BiE&WWA, CnMD, ModWD, NotNAT A*
Wilson, Edna 1880-1960 *WhScrn 74, -77, WhoHol B*
Wilson, Edna May *Film 1*
Wilson, Edward John 1944- *EncJzS 70*
Wilson, Edward R 1909- *AmSCAP 66*
Wilson, Edwin 1927- *ConAmTC*
Wilson, Eleanor *WhoHol A*
Wilson, Elizabeth *WhoHol A*
Wilson, Elizabeth 1921- *NotNAT*
Wilson, Elizabeth 1925- *WhoThe 77*
Wilson, Elsie Jane *Film 1, WomWMM*
Wilson, Ethel Davis Bryant 1888- *CreCan 2*
Wilson, F Vaux *Film 2*
Wilson, Flip 1933- *DrBlPA, HalFC 80, IntMPA 77, -75, -76, -78, -79, -80, JoeFr[port], WhoHol A*
Wilson, Florence *NewGrD 80*
Wilson, Francis 1854-1935 *NotNAT A, -B, OxThe, WhScrn 74, -77, WhThe, WhoHol B, WhoStg 1906*
Wilson, Frank *BlkAmP, BlksBF, MorBAP*
Wilson, Frank 1873- *IlWWBF*
Wilson, Frank 1891-1956 *WhThe*
Wilson, Frank H 1886-1956 *DrBlPA, NotNAT B, WhScrn 74, -77, WhoHol B*
Wilson, G B L *DancEn 78*
Wilson, Galen 1926- *ConAmC*
Wilson, Garland Lorenzo 1909-1954 *BiDAmM, WhoJazz 72*
Wilson, Gene A 1920- *BiE&WWA, NotNAT*
Wilson, George 1854-1954 *WhScrn 74, -77, WhoHol B*
Wilson, George Balch 1927- *AmSCAP 80, ConAmC, DcCM*
Wilson, George Bulkeley Laird 1909?- *CnOxB*
Wilson, George H 1854-1908 *BiDAmM*
Wilson, George W 1849-1931 *NotNAT B*
Wilson, George W 1856- *WhoStg 1906*
Wilson, Georges 1921- *EncWT, Ent*
Wilson, Georgia *Film 1*
Wilson, Gerald Stanley 1918- *CmpEPM, EncJzS 70*
Wilson, Glenville Dean 1833-1897 *BiDAmM*
Wilson, Grace 1890-1962 *BiDAmM*
Wilson, Grace 1903- *WhThe*
Wilson, Grenville Dean 1833-1897 *Baker 78*
Wilson, Guy Samuel, Jr. 1942- *IntWWM 77*
Wilson, H J Lane 1870-1915 *OxMus*
Wilson, Hal 1887-1933 *Film 2, WhScrn 74, -77, WhoHol B*
Wilson, Hamilton K 1922- *BiDAmM*
Wilson, Hank *RkOn 2[port]*
Wilson, Harding 1921-1975 *BluesWW[port]*
Wilson, Harry Leon 1867-1939 *FilmgC, HalFC 80, ModWD, NotNAT B, PlP&P, WhThe*
Wilson, Harry Leon, Jr. *PupTheA*
Wilson, Harry Robert 1901-1968 *AmSCAP 66, -80, ConAmC*
Wilson, Helen M *PupTheA*
Wilson, Henry *Film 2*
Wilson, Henry 1828-1878 *BiDAmM*
Wilson, Ian *WhoHol A*
Wilson, Ilona *WhoHol A*
Wilson, Imogene Bubbles *WhScrn 74, -77*
Wilson, Ira B 1880-1950 *AmSCAP 66, -80*
Wilson, Irv *NewYTET*
Wilson, Irving M 1881-1937 *AmSCAP 66, -80*
Wilson, J Frank & The Cavaliers *RkOn 2A*
Wilson, Jack *Film 1*
Wilson, Jack 1917-1966 *WhScrn 74, -77, WhoHol B*
Wilson, Jack, Jr. 1936- *EncJzS 70*
Wilson, Jackie *AmPS A, ConMuA 80A*
Wilson, Jackie 1934- *DrBlPA, RkOn[port]*
Wilson, Jackie 1935- *BiDAmM*
Wilson, James 1922- *IntWWM 77, -80, NewGrD 80*
Wilson, James H 1843-1915 *BiDAmM*
Wilson, James Robert 1928- *IntWWM 77, -80*
Wilson, Janice *Film 2*
Wilson, Jeanna *WhoHol A*
Wilson, Jesse A 1916- *AmSCAP 80*
Wilson, Joe Lee 1935- *EncJzS 70*
Wilson, John d1696 *NotNAT B*
Wilson, John 1585-1641? *OxThe*
Wilson, John 1595-1674 *Baker 78, MusMk, NewGrD 80, OxMus*
Wilson, John 1927- *DancEn 78*
Wilson, John C 1899-1961 *EncMT, NotNAT B, WhThe*
Wilson, John Dover 1881-1969 *BiE&WWA, NotNAT B*
Wilson, John Floyd 1929- *AmSCAP 80*
Wilson, John Lawrence 1919- *WhoMus 72*
Wilson, John Newton 1909- *AmSCAP 66, -80*
Wilson, John S 1913- *BiE&WWA, NotNAT*
Wilson, John W 1910- *IntMPA 77, -75, -76, -78, -79*
Wilson, John Whitridge 1905- *WhoMus 72*
Wilson, Johnny Ancil 1935- *AmSCAP 80, NewOrJ*
Wilson, Joseph 1858-1940 *NotNAT B, WhThe*
Wilson, Joseph Lee 1935- *AmSCAP 80, EncJzS 70*
Wilson, Joseph Maria 1872-1933 *NotNAT B*
Wilson, Judy *WhoHol A*
Wilson, Juice 1904- *WhoJazz 72*
Wilson, Julie *WhoHol A*
Wilson, Karen 1942- *ConAmC*
Wilson, Katherine 1904- *Film 2, WhThe*
Wilson, Kitty 1927- *EncFCWM 69*
Wilson, Lanford 1937- *ConDr 73, -77, DcLB 7[port], NatPD[port], NotNAT, WhoThe 72, -77*
Wilson, Lee *AmSCAP 80*
Wilson, Lena 1898?-1939? *BluesWW[port]*
Wilson, Leola B *BluesWW*
Wilson, Lesley 1942- *WhoMus 72*
Wilson, Lester 1942?- *CnOxB*
Wilson, Lewis *WhoHrs 80*
Wilson, Lois *MotPP*
Wilson, Lois 1895- *HalFC 80, What 5[port]*
Wilson, Lois 1896- *FilmEn, Film 1, -2, MovMk, ThFT[port], TwYS, WhoHol A*
Wilson, Lois 1898- *BiE&WWA, ForYSC, NotNAT*
Wilson, Lola *Film 2*
Wilson, M K 1890-1933 *WhScrn 74, -77, WhoHol B*
Wilson, Mabel Elizabeth 1890- *AmSCAP 66*
Wilson, Margery *Film 1, -2, MotPP, TwYS, WomWMM*
Wilson, Marie 1916-1972 *FilmEn, FilmgC, HalFC 80, MotPP, MovMk, ThFT[port], What 3[port], WhScrn 77, WhoHol B*
Wilson, Marie 1917- *ForYSC*
Wilson, Marion T 1908- *AmSCAP 80*
Wilson, Mark *MagIlD*
Wilson, Martin 1922- *WhoMus 72*
Wilson, Mary 1944- *DrBlPA*
Wilson, Mary K 1927- *BiDAmM*
Wilson, Mattie Moultrie *MorBAP*
Wilson, Michael 1914-1978 *DcFM, FilmEn, FilmgC, HalFC 80, IntMPA 77, -75, -76, -78, WorEFlm*
Wilson, Michelle *WhoHol A*
Wilson, Millard K *Film 1*
Wilson, Mortimer 1876-1932 *AmSCAP 66, -80, Baker 78, BiDAmM, ConAmC*
Wilson, Nancy 1937- *BiDAmM, DrBlPA, EncJzS 70*
Wilson, Nancy 1940- *RkOn*
Wilson, Nancy Lamoureaux 1954- *AmSCAP 80*
Wilson, Neil *WhoHol A*
Wilson, Norman *IntMPA 77, -75, -76, -78, -79, -80*
Wilson, Olly 1937- *Baker 78, BiDAmM, BlkCS[port], ConAmC, NewGrD 80*
Wilson, Perry 1916- *WhThe*
Wilson, Peter Gardner Wotherspoon 1936- *IntWWM 77, -80*
Wilson, Phil 1937- *ConAmC, EncJzS 70*
Wilson, Philip 1886-1924 *Baker 78*
Wilson, Phillip Sanford 1941- *EncJzS 70*
Wilson, Phillips Elder, Jr. 1937- *EncJzS 70, IntWWM 77, -80*
Wilson, Quinn B 1908- *WhoJazz 72*
Wilson, R A *AmSCAP 80*
Wilson, Ray d1963 *NotNAT B*
Wilson, Rex d1951 *IlWWBF*
Wilson, Richard 1915- *FilmEn, FilmgC, HalFC 80, IntMPA 77, -75, -76, -78, -79, -80, WorEFlm*
Wilson, Richard 1941- *AmSCAP 80, Baker 78, CpmDNM 79, -80, ConAmC*
Wilson, Robert *ConDr 73, -77E*
Wilson, Robert d1610 *NotNAT B*
Wilson, Robert 1550?-1600? *Ent, NotNAT B, OxThe, PlP&P*
Wilson, Robert 1550?-1605? *EncWT*
Wilson, Robert Edward 1904-1964 *BiDAmM*
Wilson, Robert James Barclay *WhoMus 72*
Wilson, Robert M 1941- *CnOxB*
Wilson, Robert M 1944- *ConDr 77, NotNAT*
Wilson, Robert W R *WhoMus 72*
Wilson, Roberta 1904-1972 *WhScrn 77*
Wilson, Roger Cole 1912- *AmSCAP 66, -80*
Wilson, Ronald York 1907- *CreCan 1*
Wilson, Ruth Elspeth 1919- *IntWWM 77*
Wilson, Sallie 1932- *CnOxB, DancEn 78[port]*
Wilson, Sandy 1924- *BestMus, BiE&WWA, ConDr 73, -77D, EncMT, EncWT, HalFC 80, NewGrD 80, NotNAT, -A, WhoThe 72, -77*
Wilson, Sarah *WhoHol A*
Wilson, Scott 1942- *FilmgC, HalFC 80, IntMPA 77, -75, -76, -78, -79, -80, WhoHol A*
Wilson, Shadow 1919-1959 *CmpEPM, WhoJazz 72*
Wilson, Smiley 1922- *EncFCWM 69*
Wilson, Snoo 1948- *ConDr 73, -77, WhoThe 77*
Wilson, Stanley Clarence 1922- *AmSCAP 80*
Wilson, Sir Steuart 1889-1966 *NewGrD 80*
Wilson, Steven Kendall 1950- *AmSCAP 80*
Wilson, Sue *WhoHol A*
Wilson, Sydney Virginia Payne 1942- *IntWWM 77, -80*
Wilson, Teddy 1912- *BgBands 74[port], BiDAmM, CmpEPM, DrBlPA, EncJzS 70, IlEncJ, NewGrD 80, WhoJazz 72*
Wilson, Terry 1923- *ForYSC, WhoHol A*
Wilson, Theodore 1912- *AmSCAP 66, -80, EncJzS 70, NewGrD 80*
Wilson, Theodore 1943- *DrBlPA, WhoHol A*
Wilson, Thomas *NewGrD 80*
Wilson, Thomas Brendan 1927- *IntWWM 77, -80, NewGrD 80, WhoMus 72*
Wilson, Timothy 1942- *IntWWM 77, -80*
Wilson, Tom 1880-1965 *Film 1, -2, ForYSC, TwYS*
Wilson, Toni *Film 2*
Wilson, Udell *NewOrJ*
Wilson, W Cronin d1934 *NotNAT B, WhThe*
Wilson, Walter Clark 1935- *IntWWM 77*
Wilson, Walter M d1926 *NotNAT B*
Wilson, Ward 1904-1966 *WhScrn 74, -77*
Wilson, Warren 1909- *IntMPA 77, -75, -76, -78, -79, -80*
Wilson, Wayne 1899-1970 *WhScrn 74, -77*
Wilson, Wendell C 1889-1927 *WhScrn 74, -77*
Wilson, Wesley 1893-1958 *BluesWW*
Wilson, Wesley 1900- *BiDAmM*
Wilson, Whip 1915-1964 *FilmgC, HalFC 80, WhScrn 74, -77, WhoHol B*
Wilson, Whip 1919-1964 *FilmEn*
Wilson, William d1972 *WhScrn 77*
Wilson, William F 1894-1956 *WhScrn 74, -77, WhoHol B*
Wilson, William J d1936 *NotNAT B, WhThe*
Wilson, Willie 1890?- *NewOrJ[port]*
Wilson, York 1907- *CreCan 1*
Wilson, Zoey *AmSCAP 80*
Wilstach, Frank Jenners 1865-1933 *NotNAT B*

Wilstach, Paul 1870-1952 *NotNAT B, WhThe*
Wiltberger, August 1850-1928 *Baker 78*
Wiltberger, Heinrich 1841-1916 *Baker 78*
Wilton, Ann *WhoHol A*
Wilton, Augusta d1926 *NotNAT B*
Wilton, Charles Henry 1761?- *NewGrD 80*
Wilton, Eric 1883-1957 *WhScrn 77*
Wilton, Marie 1839-1921 *OxThe, PlP&P*
Wilton, Robb d1957 *NotNAT B, WhoHol B*
Wilton, Terence *WhoHol A*
Wiltshire, George *BlksB&W C*
Wiltsie, Simeon S 1853-1918 *WhScrn 77*
Wiman, Anna Deere 1924-1963 *NotNAT B, WhThe*
Wiman, Dwight Deere 1894-1951 *Film 2*
Wiman, Dwight Deere 1895-1951 *EncMT, NotNAT B, WhThe*
Wimberger, Gerhard 1923- *Baker 78, CpmDNM 78, -80, DcCM, IntWWM 77, -80, NewGrD 80, WhoMus 72, WhoOp 76*
Wimberger, Peter 1940- *WhoOp 76*
Wimberly, Anne Elizabeth Streaty 1936- *IntWWM 77, -80*
Wimberly, Warren W, Jr. 1947- *AmSCAP 80*
Wimmer, Maria 1910- *EncWT*
Wimperis, Arthur 1874-1953 *FilmEn, FilmgC, HalFC 80, IntMPA 77, -75, -76, -78, -79, NotNAT B, WhThe*
Winant, Ethel *NewYTET*
Winant, Federicus *NewGrD 80*
Winant, Forest 1888-1928 *NotNAT B*
Winant, Forrest 1888-1928 *Film 1, WhThe, WhoHol B*
Winant, W Louis 1946- *IntWWM 77*
Winbergh, Gosta Anders 1943- *IntWWM 80, WhoOp 76*
Winburn, Anna Mae Darden 1913- *BlkWAB[port]*
Wincelberg, Shimon 1924- *BiE&WWA, NatPD[port], NotNAT*
Wincenc, Joseph 1915- *IntWWM 77, -80*
Winch, Ruth Hazel 1921- *IntWWM 80, WhoMus 72*
Winchecumbe, W De *NewGrD 80*
Winchell, Charles William 1903- *IntMPA 75*
Winchell, James M 1791-1820 *BiDAmM*
Winchell, Paul 1924- *IntMPA 77, -75, -76, -78, -79, -80, WhoHol A*
Winchell, Walter 1897-1972 *AmSCAP 66, FilmgC, HalFC 80, NewYTET, NotNAT A, -B, PlP&P, WhScrn 77, WhThe, WhoHol B*
Winchester, Barbara 1895?-1968 *WhScrn 74, -77, WhoHol B*
Winchester, Caleb Thomas 1847-1920 *BiDAmM*
Winchester, Jesse 1945- *AmSCAP 80, ConMuA 80A, IlEncR*
Winchester, Sirl 1888- *AmSCAP 66, -80*
Winchester, Ted E 1952- *AmSCAP 80*
Winckel, Fritz 1907- *IntWWM 77, -80, NewGrD 80*
Winckelmann, Hermann *NewGrD 80*
Wincor, Richard 1921- *IntMPA 75, -76*
Wincott, Rosalie Avolo 1873-1951 *WhScrn 74, -77*
Wind *RkOn 2[port]*
Windeatt, George 1901-1959 *NotNAT B, WhThe*
Winderecker, Sam *PupTheA*
Windermere, Charles 1872-1955 *NotNAT B, WhThe*
Winderstein, Hans 1856-1925 *Baker 78*
Windet, John *NewGrD 80*
Windgassen, Wolfgang 1914-1974 *Baker 78, CmOp, MusSN[port], NewEOp 71, NewGrD 80[port]*
Windham, Donald 1920- *BiE&WWA, NotNAT*
Windheim, Marek 1895-1960 *ForYSC, WhScrn 74, -77, WhoHol B*
Windhurst, Johnny 1926- *CmpEPM*
Winding, August 1835-1899 *Baker 78*
Winding, Kai Chresten 1922- *AmSCAP 66, -80, BiDAmM, CmpEPM, EncJzS 70*
Winding, Kai Chresten 1929- *RkOn[port]*
Windingstad, Ole 1886-1959 *Baker 78, ConAmC*
Windom, Lawrence C 1876- *TwYS A*
Windom, W H *AmPS B*
Windom, William 1923- *BiE&WWA, FilmgC, ForYSC, HalFC 80, NotNAT, WhoHol A*
Windorf, Irene Manghir 1905- *AmSCAP 66*
Windsor, Adele *Film 2*
Windsor, Barbara 1937- *FilmgC, HalFC 80, WhoHol A, WhoThe 72, -77*
Windsor, Claire d1972 *WhoHol B*
Windsor, Claire 1897-1972 *FilmEn, Film 1, -2, ForYSC, TwYS, What 2[port], WhScrn 77*
Windsor, Claire 1898-1972 *HalFC 80, MovMk*
Windsor, George Thomas Macdonald 1900- *WhoMus 72*
Windsor, John Peter 1915- *AmSCAP 66, -80*
Windsor, Madeleine Wynne 1902- *WhoMus 72*
Windsor, Marie *MotPP, WhoHol A*
Windsor, Marie 1922- *FilmEn, ForYSC*
Windsor, Marie 1923- *FilmgC, HalFC 80, MovMk*
Windsor, Marie 1924- *IntMPA 77, -75, -76, -78, -79, -80*
Windsperger, Lothar 1885-1935 *Baker 78, NewGrD 80*
Windt, Herbert 1894-1965 *Baker 78*
Windust, Bretaigne 1906-1960 *FilmEn, FilmgC, HalFC 80, NotNAT B, WhThe, WorEFlm*
Windust, Irene *WhoHol A*
Wine-Gar, Frank 1901- *AmSCAP 66, -80*
Wineberger, Paul Anton 1758-1821 *NewGrD 80*
Winer, Linda *ConAmTC*
Winesanker, Michael Max 1913- *ConAmC*
Winestone, Benjamin 1906-1974 *EncJzS 70*
Winestone, Benny 1906-1974 *EncJzS 70*
Winfield, Joan *ForYSC*
Winfield, John Michael Tyson 1937- *IntWWM 77, -80*
Winfield, Paul 1941- *DrBlPA, HalFC 80, MovMk, WhoHol A*
Winfield, Rastus *BlksBF*
Winfield, Roger 1932- *WhoMus 72*
Winfred, Henry *BlksBF*
Winfree, Richard 1898- *AmSCAP 66, -80*
Wing, Ah *Film 2*
Wing, Dan 1923-1969 *WhScrn 74, -77, WhoHol B*
Wing, Lucie Lee 1926- *AmSCAP 80*
Wing, Toby 1913- *ForYSC, MotPP, ThFT[port], WhoHol A*
Wing, Ward *Film 2*
Wing, Winifred Gladys 1934- *IntWWM 80*
Wing, Mrs. Wong *Film 2*
Wing And A Prayer Fife And Drum Corps *RkOn 2[port]*
Wingard, James Charles 1931- *AmSCAP 80*
Wingate, Peter *CreCan 1*
Winge, Torsten *Film 1*
Wingfield, Conway d1948 *NotNAT B*
Wingfield, Lewis d1891 *NotNAT B*
Wingham, Thomas 1846-1893 *Baker 78*
Wingreen, Jason *NotNAT, WhoHol A*
Wings *ConMuA 80A, RkOn 2[port]*
Winham, Godfrey 1934-1975 *Baker 78, ConAmC*
Winick, Steven David 1944- *CpmDNM 72, IntWWM 77, -80*
Winikus, Francis Manning 1912- *IntMPA 75, -76*
Winitsky, Alex *IntMPA 79, -80*
Wink, Irma June *AmSCAP 80*
Wink, Sue Karen 1948- *AmSCAP 80*
Winkel, Diederich Niclas 1780?-1826 *NewGrD 80*
Winkel, Dietrich Nikolaus 1776?-1826 *OxMus*
Winkel, Dietrich Nikolaus 1780?-1826 *NewGrD 80*
Winkelmann, Hermann 1849-1912 *Baker 78, CmOp, NewEOp 71, NewGrD 80*
Winkle, William Allan 1940- *IntWWM 77*
Winkler, Alexander Adolfovich 1865-1935 *Baker 78, NewGrD 80*
Winkler, Carl Gottfried Theodor 1775-1856 *NewGrD 80*
Winkler, David 1948- *IntWWM 77, -80*
Winkler, David 1949- *CpmDNM 79, ConAmC*
Winkler, Edwin Theodore 1823-1883 *BiDAmM*
Winkler, Frank d1964 *NotNAT B*
Winkler, Henry *WhoHol A*
Winkler, Henry 1945- *FilmEn*
Winkler, Henry 1946- *HalFC 80, IntMPA 78, -79, -80*
Winkler, Irvin *IntMPA 77, -75, -76, -78*
Winkler, Irwin *FilmEn, IntMPA 79, -80*
Winkler, Margo *WhoHol A*
Winkler, Martin 1890?-1955? *NewOrJ*
Winkler, Marty *ConMuA 80B*
Winkler, Peter K 1943- *Baker 78, ConAmC*
Winkler, Sol 1917- *AmSCAP 80*
Winklhofer, Sharon 1947- *IntWWM 77, -80*
Winlow, Anna C *PupTheA*
Winmill, Joan *WhoHol A*
Winn, Anona *WhThe*
Winn, Godfrey *Film 2, IlWWBF A*
Winn, Godfrey 1906- *WhThe*
Winn, Godfrey 1909-1971 *WhScrn 74, -77, WhoHol B*
Winn, Godfrey 1909-1972 *FilmgC, HalFC 80*
Winn, Jack *Film 2*
Winn, Jerry 1931- *AmSCAP 66*
Winn, Jerry 1939- *AmSCAP 80*
Winn, Kitty *WhoHol A*
Winne, Jesse M 1875-1964 *AmSCAP 66, -80*
Winneberger, Paul Anton *NewGrD 80*
Winner, Joseph 1802-1878 *BiDAmM*
Winner, Joseph Eastburn 1837-1918 *BiDAmM*
Winner, Michael 1935- *FilmEn, FilmgC, HalFC 80, IntMPA 77, -75, -76, -78, -79, -80*
Winner, Michael 1936- *IlWWBF, -A*
Winner, Michael 1939- *OxFilm*
Winner, Septimus d1902 *Sw&Ld A*
Winner, Septimus 1827-1902 *Baker 78, BiDAmM, NewGrD 80, NotNAT B, PopAmC[port]*
Winner, Septimus 1847-1902 *AmPS*
Winninger, Charles 1884-1968 *MovMk[port]*
Winninger, Charles 1884-1969 *BiE&WWA, CmpEPM, EncMT, FilmEn, Film 1, -2, FilmgC, ForYSC, HalFC 80, HolCA[port], MotPP, NotNAT B, PlP&P[port], Vers A[port], WhScrn 74, -77, WhThe, WhoHol B*
Winnman, Dwight *Film 2*
Winograd, Arthur 1920- *Baker 78*
Winogradoff, Anatol *WhoHol A*
Winogron, Blanche 1911- *Baker 78*
Winold, Helga Ulsamer 1937- *IntWWM 80*
Winschermann, Helmut 1920- *NewGrD 80*
Winscott, Edwin C *WhScrn 74, -77*
Winship, Loren 1904- *BiE&WWA, NotNAT*
Winslade, Frank John 1908- *WhoMus 72*
Winslade, Richard *NewGrD 80*
Winslate, Richard *NewGrD 80*
Winsloe, Christa *WomWMM*
Winslow, Dick 1915- *AmSCAP 66, Film 2, ForYSC, TwYS, WhoHol A*
Winslow, George 1946- *FilmEn, FilmgC, ForYSC, HalFC 80, IntMPA 75, MotPP, What 5[port], WhoHol A*
Winslow, Herbert Hall 1865-1930 *NotNAT B*
Winslow, Miriam *CnOxB, DancEn 78*
Winslow, Richard 1915- *AmSCAP 80*
Winslow, Richard Kenelm 1918- *ConAmC*
Winslow, Shirley Meleese 1931- *AmSCAP 80*
Winslow, Yvonne *WhoHol A*
Winsor, J W *OxMus*
Winsor, Phil 1938- *CpmDNM 78*
Winsor, Philip Gordon 1938- *ConAmC, IntWWM 77, -80*
Winstanley, John Harold 1922- *WhoMus 72*
Winstanley, Margaret Seton 1926- *WhoMus 72*
Winstead, Kenneth C 1908- *AmSCAP 66*
Winstead, William 1942- *IntWWM 77, -80*
Winstein, Dave 1909- *NewOrJ*
Winsten, Archer 1904- *IntMPA 77, -75, -76, -78, -79, -80*
Winston, Bruce 1879-1946 *WhScrn 77, WhoHol B*
Winston, C Bruce 1879-1946 *NotNAT B, WhThe*
Winston, Charles Bruce 1879-1946 *WhScrn 74*
Winston, Hattie 1945- *DrBlPA*
Winston, Helen *WomWMM*
Winston, Helene *WhoHol A*
Winston, Irene 1920-1964 *WhScrn 74, -77, WhoHol B*
Winston, Jackie 1915-1971 *WhScrn 74, -77, WhoHol B*

Winston, James 1773-1843 *NotNAT A, –B*
Winston, Jane d1959 *NotNAT B*
Winston, Jerry *ConMuA 80B*
Winston, Julian 1941- *AmSCAP 80*
Winston, Laura *Film 1*
Winston, Robert *WhoHol A*
Winstone, Norma 1941- *EncJzS 70*
Winstons *RkOn 2A*
Winter, Banks d1936 *NotNAT B*
Winter, Charles R 1876-1952 *WhScrn 74, –77*
Winter, David *Film 2*
Winter, Donovan 1933- *IlWWBF*
Winter, Edgar 1946- *IlEncR[port]*
Winter, Edgar, Group *RkOn 2[port]*
Winter, Ethel 1924- *CnOxB, DancEn 78*
Winter, Georg Ludwig d1772? *NewGrD 80*
Winter, Gloria Frances 1938- *AmSCAP 80*
Winter, James Hamilton 1919- *IntWWM 80*
Winter, Jessie *WhThe*
Winter, Johnny 1944- *BluesWW[port], ConMuA 80A, IlEncR[port], RkOn 2[port]*
Winter, Keith 1906- *WhThe*
Winter, Laska *Film 2*
Winter, Lynette *WhoHol A*
Winter, Miriam Therese *AmSCAP 80*
Winter, Paul 1894- *ConAmC, WhoMus 72*
Winter, Paul Theodore, Jr. 1939- *EncJzS 70*
Winter, Percy Campbell 1861-1928 *NotNAT B*
Winter, Peter 1754-1825 *Baker 78, NewGrD 80*
Winter, Vincent 1947- *FilmEn, FilmgC, HalFC 80, IntMPA 75, –76, WhoHol A*
Winter, William *WhScrn 77*
Winter, William 1836-1917 *NotNAT B, OxThe, WhThe*
Winter, William 1909- *CreCan 2*
Winter, Winona 1888-1940 *NotNAT B, WhoStg 1906*
Winter, Winona 1891-1940 *WhScrn 74, –77*
Winter-Hjelm, Otto 1837-1931 *Baker 78, NewGrD 80*
Winterberger, Alexander 1834-1914 *Baker 78*
Winterbottom, Herbert Wager 1921- *IntWWM 80*
Winterfeld, Carl Georg Vivigens Von 1784-1852 *NewGrD 80*
Winterfeld, Carl Von 1784-1852 *Baker 78*
Winterfeld, Max *NewGrD 80*
Winterhalter, Hugo *AmPS A, –B*
Winterhalter, Hugo 1909-1973 *AmSCAP 66, –80, BiDAmM, CmpEPM*
Winterhalter, Hugo 1910-1973 *RkOn*
Wintermute, Harry d1938 *PupTheA*
Winternitz, Chanan 1914- *IntWWM 77*
Winternitz, Emanuel 1898- *Baker 78, NewGrD 80*
Winters, Charles *PupTheA*
Winters, David *IntMPA 77, –75, –76, –78, –79, –80, WhoHol A*
Winters, Deborah *IntMPA 77, –75, –76, –78, –79, –80, WhoHol A*
Winters, Eileene Renee 1926- *AmSCAP 80*
Winters, Geoffrey 1928- *IntWWM 77, –80, WhoMus 72*
Winters, George Archer 1950- *IntWWM 77, –80*
Winters, Grant *MotPP*
Winters, Jack *AmSCAP 80*
Winters, Janet Lewis 1899- *AmSCAP 80*
Winters, Jerry 1917- *IntMPA 77, –75, –76, –78, –79, –80*
Winters, John *AmSCAP 80*
Winters, Jonathan 1925- *FilmEn, FilmgC, ForYSC, HalFC 80, IntMPA 77, –75, –76, –78, –79, –80, JoeFr[port], MotPP, MovMk, WhoHol A*
Winters, June 1918- *AmSCAP 66, –80*
Winters, Laska *Film 2, TwYS*
Winters, Lawrence 1915-1965 *DrBlPA*
Winters, Leslie John 1923- *IntWWM 80, WhoMus 72*
Winters, Linda *FilmEn*
Winters, Marian 1924- *BiE&WWA, NatPD[port], NotNAT, WhoThe 72, –77*
Winters, Richard J 1928- *IntMPA 77, –75, –76, –78, –79, –80*
Winters, Roland 1904- *BiE&WWA, FilmEn, FilmgC, ForYSC, HalFC 80, HolCA[port], IntMPA 77, –75, –76, –78, –79, MotPP, NotNAT, Vers A[port], WhoHol A*
Winters, Roland 1905- *IntMPA 80*
Winters, Ross 1951- *IntWWM 80*
Winters, Shelley 1922- *BiDFilm, –81, BiE&WWA, FilmEn, FilmgC, ForYSC, HalFC 80, IntMPA 77, –75, –76, –78, –79, –80, MotPP, MovMk[port], NotNAT, OxFilm, WhoHol A, WhoHrs 80, WhoThe 72, –77, WorEFlm*
Wintersteen, John Schaeffer 1908- *AmSCAP 80*
Winterstein, Eduard Von 1871-1961 *EncWT*
Winterton, Bonnie Jean Moesser 1930- *IntWWM 77*
Winther, John 1933- *WhoOp 76*
Winther, Jorn H *NewYTET*
Winther, Karen *Film 2*
Winther, Lone Koppel 1938- *WhoOp 76*
Winthrop, Adelaide d1923 *NotNAT B*
Winthrop, Joy 1864-1950 *WhScrn 74, –77, WhoHol B*
Wintle, Julian 1913- *FilmgC, HalFC 80, IntMPA 77, –75, –76, –78, –79, –80*
Wintman, Melvin R 1918- *IntMPA 77, –75, –76, –78, –79, –80*
Winton, Bruce *Film 2*
Winton, Jane 1905-1959 *Film 2, MotPP, TwYS, WhScrn 74, –77, WhoHol B*
Winton, Jane 1908-1959 *ForYSC*
Wintonia, W De *NewGrD 80*
Wintzer, Richard 1866-1952 *Baker 78*
Winwood, Estelle 1883- *BiE&WWA, FamA&A[port], FilmEn, FilmgC, ForYSC, HalFC 80, MovMk, NotNAT, Vers A[port], WhThe, WhoHol A, WhoThe 72*
Winwood, Muff *ConMuA 80B*
Winwood, Steve *ConMuA 80A*
Winwood, Stevie *IlEncR*
Wiora, Walter 1906- *Baker 78*
Wiora, Walter 1907- *NewGrD 80*
Wipo 995?-1050? *NewGrD 80*
Wippel, Mary Emma 1938- *IntWWM 77*
Wiquardus *NewGrD 80*
Wircker, Johann *NewGrD 80*
Wircker, Johannes *NewGrD 80*
Wiren, Dag Ivar 1905- *Baker 78, DcCM, IntWWM 77, –80, MusMk, NewGrD 80, OxMus*
Wirges, William F 1894-1971 *AmSCAP 66, –80, BiDAmM, CmpEPM*
Wirsta, Aristide 1922- *IntWWM 77, –80*
Wirta, Nikolai 1906- *CnMD*
Wirtel, Thomas 1937- *ConAmC*
Wirth, Carl Anton 1912- *AmSCAP 66, –80, ConAmC*
Wirth, Emanuel 1842-1923 *Baker 78*
Wirth, Friedrich Moritz 1849-1917 *Baker 78*
Wirth, Helmut 1912- *Baker 78, NewGrD 80*
Wirth, Herman Felix 1885- *Baker 78*
Wirzbieta, Maciej 1523-1605 *NewGrD 80*
Wisbar, Frank 1899-1967 *HalFC 80, WhoHrs 80, WorEFlm*
Wisberg, Aubrey 1909- *FilmgC, HalFC 80, IntMPA 77, –75, –76, –78, –79, –80, NatPD[port], WhoHrs 80*
Wisdom, Norman *IntMPA 77, –75, –76, –78, –79, –80, WhoHol A*
Wisdom, Norman 1918- *FilmgC, HalFC 80*
Wisdom, Norman 1920- *EncMT, FilmAG WE, FilmEn, ForYSC, IlWWBF[port], NotNAT, WhoThe 72, –77*
Wise, Bruce 1929- *ConAmC*
Wise, Ernie *FilmgC, HalFC 80*
Wise, Fred 1915-1966 *AmSCAP 66, –80*
Wise, Herbert 1924- *WhoThe 72, –77*
Wise, Jack 1893-1954 *Film 2, WhScrn 74, –77, WhoHol B*
Wise, Joseph Edward 1939- *AmSCAP 80*
Wise, Michael 1647?-1687 *NewGrD 80*
Wise, Michael 1648?-1687 *Baker 78, OxMus*
Wise, Morna *ConAmTC*
Wise, Patricia 1944- *IntWWM 80, WhoOp 76*
Wise, Robert 1914- *BiDFilm, –81, CmMov, DcFM, FilmEn, FilmgC, HalFC 80, IntMPA 77, –75, –76, –78, –79, –80, MovMk[port], OxFilm, WhoHrs 80, WorEFlm*
Wise, Thomas A 1865-1928 *NotNAT B, WhThe*
Wise, Tom 1865-1928 *Film 2, WhScrn 74, –77, WhoHol B*
Wiseman, Adele 1928- *CreCan 2*
Wiseman, Frederic *OxFilm*
Wiseman, Frederick 1930- *BiDFilm 81, HalFC 80, NewYTET*
Wiseman, Graham Richmond 1932- *WhoMus 72*
Wiseman, Herbert 1886-1966 *NewGrD 80*
Wiseman, Joseph *IntMPA 77, –75, –76, –78, –79, –80, MotPP, WhoHol A*
Wiseman, Joseph 1918- *BiE&WWA, FilmEn, ForYSC, NotNAT, WhoThe 72, –77*
Wiseman, Joseph 1919- *FilmgC, HalFC 80, HolCA[port], Vers A[port]*
Wiseman, Mac 1925- *BiDAmM, CounME 74[port], –74A, IlEncCM[port]*
Wiseman, Scott 1909- *BiDAmM*
Wiseman, Scotty 1909- *EncFCWM 69*
Wishard, France Anne 1900- *IntWWM 80*
Wishard, Frances Anne 1900- *IntWWM 77*
Wishart, Betty Rose 1947- *CpmDNM 73, –74, –76, ConAmC, IntWWM 77, –80*
Wishart, Peter 1921- *IntWWM 77, –80, NewGrD 80, WhoMus 72*
Wishart-Hodgson, James Bentham 1930- *IntWWM 80*
Wishbone Ash *ConMuA 80A, IlEncR*
Wishengrad, Morton 1913-1963 *McGEWD, NotNAT B*
Wiske, C Mortimer 1853-1934 *BiDAmM*
Wiske, Charles Mortimer 1853-1934 *Baker 78*
Wislocki, Leszek 1931- *IntWWM 77*
Wislocki, Stanislaw 1921- *Baker 78, NewGrD 80*
Wisme, Nicholas De *NewGrD 80*
Wismer, Harry 1911-1967 *WhScrn 77, WhoHol B*
Wisner, James Joseph 1931- *AmSCAP 66, –80*
Wissema, Petronella Sophie 1921- *WhoMus 72*
Wissert, Joe *ConMuA 80B*
Wissmer, Pierre Alexandre 1915- *Baker 78, IntWWM 77, –80, NewGrD 80, WhoMus 72*
Wiswell, Andrew Muller 1905- *AmSCAP 80*
Wiszniewski, Zbigniew 1922- *Baker 78, DcCM, IntWWM 77, –80, NewGrD 80*
Wit, Antoni 1944- *IntWWM 80*
Wit, Paul De 1852-1925 *Baker 78, NewGrD 80*
Witchell, Peter James 1945- *IntWWM 77*
Witcover, Walt 1924- *BiE&WWA, NotNAT*
Witek, Anton 1872-1933 *Baker 78, BiDAmM*
Witek, Henryk 1937- *IntWWM 77*
Withee, Mable d1952 *NotNAT B*
Wither, George 1588-1667 *OxMus*
Withers *NewGrD 80*
Withers, Barbara Hildred *WhoMus 72*
Withers, Bernard Sidney 1873-1942 *NewGrD 80*
Withers, Bill 1938- *EncJzS 70, IlEncR, RkOn 2[port]*
Withers, Bill 1940?- *DrBlPA*
Withers, Charles 1889-1947 *NotNAT B, WhScrn 77, WhoHol B*
Withers, Douglas Sidney 1879-1962 *NewGrD 80*
Withers, Edward 1808-1875 *NewGrD 80*
Withers, Edward 1844-1915 *NewGrD 80*
Withers, Edward Sidney Munns 1870-1955 *NewGrD 80*
Withers, George 1850?-1920? *NewGrD 80*
Withers, Googie 1917- *FilmAG WE, FilmEn, FilmgC, HalFC 80, IlWWBF[port], IntMPA 77, –75, –76, –78, –79, –80, MovMk, OxFilm, WhoHol A, WhoThe 72, –77*
Withers, Grant 1904-1959 *FilmEn, Film 2, FilmgC, ForYSC, HalFC 80, HolCA[port], MovMk, NotNAT B, TwYS, Vers A[port], WhScrn 74, –77, WhoHol B*
Withers, Isabel 1896-1968 *WhScrn 77*
Withers, Iva 1917- *BiE&WWA, NotNAT, WhoThe 72, –77*
Withers, Jane *IntMPA 77, –75, –76, –78, –79, –80, WhoHol A*
Withers, Jane 1926- *FilmEn, FilmgC,*

HalFC 80, HolP 30[port], MotPP, MovMk[port], ThFT[port]
Withers, Jane 1927- *ForYSC*
Withers, William Harrison 1938- *EncJzS 70*
Witherspoon, Cora 1890-1957 *FilmEn, FilmgC, ForYSC, HalFC 80, MovMk, NotNAT B, ThFT[port], Vers A[port], WhScrn 74, -77, WhThe, WhoHol B*
Witherspoon, Herbert 1873-1935 *Baker 78, BiDAmM, MusSN[port], NewEOp 71, NotNAT B*
Witherspoon, James 1923- *BluesWW[port], EncJzS 70*
Witherspoon, Jimmy 1923- *EncJzS 70, IlEncJ*
Witherspoon, Matilda 1914- *BluesWW*
Withey, Chester 1887- *TwYS A*
Withington, Leonard 1789-1885 *BiDAmM*
Withrow, Scott Swain 1932- *IntWWM 77*
Withy, John d1673? *NewGrD 80*
Witkiewicz, Stanislaw Ignacy 1885-1939 *CnMD, CnThe, CroCD, EncWT, Ent[port], McGEWD[port], ModWD, REnWD[port]*
Witkin, Beatrice 1916- *AmSCAP 80, ConAmC*
Witkowski, Georges-Martin 1867-1943 *Baker 78, NewGrD 80, OxMus*
Witkowski, Leo 1908- *AmSCAP 66, -80*
Witkowski, Leon 1908- *IntWWM 77, -80*
Witlock, Lloyd *Film 2*
Witnesses, The *BiDAmM*
Witney, Michael *WhoHol A*
Witney, William 1910?- *FilmEn, FilmgC, HalFC 80, WhoHrs 80*
Witni, Monica 1928- *CpmDNM 72*
Witoszynskyj, Leo 1941- *IntWWM 77, -80*
Witsenburg, Edward 1934- *NewGrD 80*
Witt, Christian Friedrich 1660?-1716 *NewGrD 80*
Witt, Christopher 1675-1765 *BiDAmM*
Witt, Elinor *PupTheA*
Witt, Franz Xaver 1834-1888 *Baker 78, NewGrD 80, OxMus*
Witt, Friedrich 1770-1836 *Baker 78, NewGrD 80*
Witt, Ilanga *WomWMM B*
Witt, Kathy *WhoHol A*
Witt, Paul Junger *NewYTET*
Witt, Peter 1911- *BiE&WWA*
Witt, Theodor De 1823-1855 *Baker 78*
Witt, Wastl 1890-1955 *WhScrn 74, -77*
Wittaschek, Johann Matthias *NewGrD 80*
Wittassek, Johann Nepomuk August 1770-1839 *Baker 78*
Witte, Charles Dietrich 1942- *AmSCAP 80*
Witte, Christian Friedrich *NewGrD 80*
Witte, Erich 1911- *CmOp, NewEOp 71, NewGrD 80*
Witte, Georg Hendrik 1843-1929 *Baker 78*
Wittelsbach, Rudolf 1902-1972 *NewGrD 80*
Wittelshofer, Allan *PupTheA*
Witten, Dean Robert 1951- *CpmDNM 80*
Wittenberg, Philip 1895- *BiE&WWA*
Wittepers, Dirck Pieterszoon *NewGrD 80*
Wittgenstein, Count Friedrich Ernst *Baker 78*
Wittgenstein, Paul 1887-1961 *Baker 78, MusMk, NewGrD 80, OxMus*
Witthauer, Johann Georg 1751-1802 *NewGrD 80*
Wittich, Marie 1868-1931 *CmOp, NewEOp 71, NewGrD 80*
Witting, Arthur Eugene 1868-1941 *WhScrn 77*
Witting, Chris J *NewYTET*
Witting, Karl 1823-1907 *Baker 78*
Wittinger, Robert 1945- *Baker 78, NewGrD 80*
Wittlich, Kate 1935- *IntWWM 80*
Wittlinger, Karl 1922- *CnMD, CroCD, McGEWD, ModWD*
Wittman, Ellen 1939- *AmSCAP 80*
Wittop, Freddy 1921- *BiE&WWA, NotNAT, WhoThe 72, -77*
Wittstein, Ed 1929- *BiE&WWA, NotNAT, WhoThe 72, -77*
Witvogel, Gerhard Fredrik 1669?-1746 *NewGrD 80*
Witwer, H C *Film 2*
Witzel, Georg 1501-1573 *NewGrD 80*
Witzendorf, Adolph Othmar *NewGrD 80*
Witzenmann, Wolfgang 1937- *IntWWM 77, -80*
Witzthumb, Ignaz *NewGrD 80*
Wix, Florence E 1883-1956 *Film 2, WhScrn 74, -77, WhoHol B*
Wixell, Ingvar 1931- *NewGrD 80, WhoOp 76*
Wixted, Michael-James 1961- *WhoHol A*
Wizan, Joe *IntMPA 80*
Wizel, Georg *NewGrD 80*
Wizeman, Donald G, Jr. 1944- *IntMPA 77, -75, -76, -78, -79, -80*
Wizlav III Von Rugen 1265?-1325 *NewGrD 80*
Wizlaw III Von Rugen 1265?-1325 *NewGrD 80*
Wlach, Leopold 1902-1956 *NewGrD 80*
Wlaschiha, Ekkehard 1938- *WhoOp 76*
Wobisch, Helmut 1912- *NewGrD 80*
Wockenfuss, Petrus Laurentius 1675-1721 *NewGrD 80*
Woczitka, Franz Xaver *NewGrD 80*
Wodde, Michael *NewGrD 80*
Wodds, Michael *NewGrD 80*
Wode, Thomas *NewGrD 80*
Wodehouse, P G 1881- *AmPS, BiDAmM, CmpEPM*
Wodehouse, P G 1881-1975 *BiE&WWA, ConDr 73, EncMT, EncWT, HalFC 80, McGEWD, NewCBMT, PlP&P, Sw&Ld B*
Wodehouse, Pelham Granville 1881-1975 *WhThe*
Wodehouse, Pelham Grenville 1881-1975 *AmSCAP 66, -80, Ent[port], NotNAT A*
Wodehouse, Pelham Grenville 1881-1976 *BestMus*
Wodell, Frederick William 1859-1938 *Baker 78*
Wodeson, Leonard *NewGrD 80*
Wodiczka, Wenceslaus 1715?-1774 *NewGrD 80*
Wodson, Thomas *NewGrD 80*
Wodynski, Jan *CmpGMD*
Woegerer, Otto 1907-1966 *WhScrn 74, -77, WhoHol B*
Woehl, Waldemar 1902- *Baker 78*
Woeldike, Mogens 1897- *WhoMus 72*
Woelfl, Josef 1773-1812 *BnBkM 80*
Woelfl, Joseph *NewGrD 80*
Woess, Kurt 1914- *IntWWM 77, -80, WhoMus 72*
Woestijne, David VanDe 1915- *NewGrD 80*
Woffington *NewGrD 80*
Woffington, John *NewGrD 80*
Woffington, Margaret 1714?-1760 *NewGrD 80*
Woffington, Margaret 1720?-1760 *NotNAT A, -B*
Woffington, Peg 1714?-1760 *CnThe, EncWT, Ent[port], OxThe, PlP&P[port]*
Woffington, Peggy 1714?-1760 *NewGrD 80*
Woffington, Robert d1750 *NewGrD 80*
Woffington, Robert d1820? *NewGrD 80*
Wohl, Jack 1934- *AmSCAP 66, -80*
Wohl, Stanislaw *WomWMM*
Wohlafka, Louise Ann 1946- *IntWWM 77, -80*
Wohlbruck, Adolf *FilmEn*
Wohlers, Rudiger 1941- *WhoOp 76*
Wohlfahrt, Franz 1833-1884 *Baker 78*
Wohlfahrt, Heinrich 1797-1883 *Baker 78*
Wohlfart, Karl Adrian 1874-1943 *NewGrD 80*
Wohlgemuth, Gerhard 1920- *DcCM, IntWWM 77, NewGrD 80*
Wohlgemuth, Gustav 1863-1937 *Baker 78*
Wohnhaas, Theodor 1922- *IntWWM 77, -80*
Woiczynska, Maria 1945- *IntWWM 80*
Woikowski-Biedau, Viktor Hugo Von 1866-1935 *Baker 78*
Woitach, Richard 1935- *WhoOp 76*
Woizikovsky, Leon 1897- *WhThe*
Woizikovsky, Leon 1899-1975 *CnOxB*
Woizikowska, Sonia 1919- *DancEn 78*
Woizikowski, Leon 1897- *DancEn 78[port]*
Wojciech *NewGrD 80*
Wojciechowski, Cecile Cloutier *CreCan 1*
Wojtko, Donnamarie Zwolinsky 1951- *IntWWM 77, -80*
Wojzik, Anna *Film 2*
Wolanek, Anton *NewGrD 80*
Wolansky, Raymond 1926- *WhoOp 76*
Wolbert, Burton *Film 2*
Wolbert, Clarence *Film 2*
Wolbert, Dorothea 1874-1958 *WhScrn 74, -77, WhoHol B*
Wolbert, Dorothy *Film 2*
Wolbert, William 1884-1918 *TwYS A, WhScrn 77*
Wolcott, Charles Frederick 1906- *AmSCAP 66, -80*
Wolcott, James L *IntMPA 77, -75, -76, -78, -79, -80*
Wolcott, Samuel 1813-1886 *BiDAmM*
Wold, David 1890-1953 *WhScrn 74, -77*
Woldemar, Michel 1750-1815 *Baker 78, NewGrD 80*
Wolders, Robert *WhoHol A*
Woldike, Mogens 1897- *Baker 78, IntWWM 77, -80, NewGrD 80*
Wolf II d1932 *WhScrn 77*
Wolf, Alois Joseph Anton Balthasar 1775-1819? *NewGrD 80*
Wolf, Daniel 1894-1962 *AmSCAP 66, -80*
Wolf, Donald Elkan 1923- *AmSCAP 80*
Wolf, Doris 1927- *IntWWM 80*
Wolf, Emanuel L 1927- *IntMPA 77, -78, -79, -80*
Wolf, Ernst Wilhelm 1735-1792 *Baker 78, NewGrD 80*
Wolf, Ferdinand 1896- *Baker 78*
Wolf, Fred H 1897- *AmSCAP 66*
Wolf, Friedrich 1888-1953 *CnMD, CroCD, DcFM, EncWT, Ent, McGEWD, ModWD*
Wolf, Georg Friedrich 1761-1814 *NewGrD 80*
Wolf, Herbert 1917- *IntMPA 77, -75, -76, -78, -79, -80*
Wolf, Howlin' 1910- *RkOn*
Wolf, Hugo 1860-1903 *Baker 78, BnBkM 80, CmOp, CmpBCM, DcCom 77[port], DcCom&M 79, GrComp[port], MusMk, NewEOp 71, NewGrD 80[port], OxMus*
Wolf, Ilse 1921- *IntWWM 80, WhoMus 72*
Wolf, Jack 1912- *AmSCAP 66, -80*
Wolf, James Gary 1933- *IntWWM 77, -80*
Wolf, Jay 1929- *BiE&WWA, NotNAT*
Wolf, Johannes 1869-1947 *Baker 78, NewGrD 80, OxMus*
Wolf, Jurgen 1938- *IntWWM 80*
Wolf, Kenneth 1931- *ConAmC*
Wolf, Konrad 1925- *DcFM, FilmEn*
Wolf, Lawrence *WhoHol A*
Wolf, Louis Joseph Anton Balthasar 1775-1819? *NewGrD 80*
Wolf, Ludwig 1804-1859 *Baker 78*
Wolf, Manny 1927- *IntMPA 75, -76*
Wolf, Margaret Mercier *CreCan 1*
Wolf, Martin *NewGrD 80*
Wolf, Olga *AmSCAP 66, -80*
Wolf, R Peter 1942- *IntWWM 77, -80*
Wolf, Rennold 1872-1922 *NotNAT B, WhThe*
Wolf, Richard Lawrence 1950- *AmSCAP 80*
Wolf, Richard William 1928- *AmSCAP 80*
Wolf, Thomas Howard 1916- *IntMPA 77, -75, -76, -78, -79, -80*
Wolf, Thomas J, Jr. 1925- *AmSCAP 66*
Wolf, Wilhelm 1838-1913 *Baker 78*
Wolf-Ferrari, Ermanno 1876-1948 *Baker 78, BnBkM 80, CmOp, CompSN[port], DcCom&M 79, MusMk, NewEOp 71, NewGrD 80, NotNAT B, OxMus*
Wolfe, Bill *ForYSC*
Wolfe, Bud d1960 *WhScrn 77*
Wolfe, Clarence d1963 *NotNAT B*
Wolfe, David *WhoHol A*
Wolfe, Digby 1932- *AmSCAP 80*
Wolfe, Elton *MorBAP*
Wolfe, Fanny *WomWMM*
Wolfe, Harry *Film 2*
Wolfe, Humbert 1886-1940 *NotNAT B*
Wolfe, Ian 1888?- *ForYSC*
Wolfe, Ian 1896- *FilmEn, FilmgC, HalFC 80, Vers A[port], WhoHol A*
Wolfe, Jacques 1896-1973 *AmSCAP 66, -80, Baker 78, BiDAmM, ConAmC, PopAmC[port]*
Wolfe, James D *NewYTET*
Wolfe, Jane *Film 1, -2*
Wolfe, Joe 1892-1961 *NewOrJ*
Wolfe, Joel *WhoHol A*
Wolfe, Mary Louise 1953- *IntWWM 77*
Wolfe, Maurice 1887-1966 *AmSCAP 66, -80*
Wolfe, Stanley 1924- *AmSCAP 66, -80, Baker 78, ConAmC*
Wolfe, Stewart James 1920- *IntMPA 75, -76*
Wolfe, Thomas 1900-1938 *AmSCAP 66, -80, CnMD, EncWT, ModWD, PlP&P*
Wolfensberger, Rita 1928- *IntWWM 77, -80*

Wolfes, Felix 1892-1971 *Baker 78, NewGrD 80*
Wolfes, Helmuth 1901-1971 *BiDAmM*
Wolff, Albert *PupTheA*
Wolff, Albert 1884-1970 *Baker 78, CmOp, NewEOp 71, NewGrD 80*
Wolff, Arthur Sheldon 1931- *IntWWM 77, -80*
Wolff, August *NewGrD 80*
Wolff, Auguste 1821-1887 *Baker 78*
Wolff, Beverly 1928- *WhoOp 76*
Wolff, Christian 1934- *Baker 78, BiDAmM, ConAmC, DcCM, NewGrD 80*
Wolff, Christian Michael 1707-1789 *NewGrD 80*
Wolff, Christoph 1940- *Baker 78, IntWWM 77, -80, NewGrD 80*
Wolff, David *DcFM*
Wolff, Dorothy *IntWWM 77*
Wolff, Edouard 1816-1880 *Baker 78*
Wolff, Edward 1816-1880 *NewGrD 80*
Wolff, Erich 1874-1913 *Baker 78, BiDAmM*
Wolff, Ernest *PupTheA*
Wolff, Ernst Victor 1889-1960 *Baker 78*
Wolff, Esther *PupTheA*
Wolff, F Roger 1920- *AmSCAP 80*
Wolff, Frances Strupe 1911- *IntWWM 77*
Wolff, Frank 1928-1971 *WhScrn 74, -77, WhoHol B*
Wolff, Friedrich 1888-1953 *OxFilm*
Wolff, Fritz 1894-1957 *NewEOp 71, NewGrD 80*
Wolff, Hellmuth Christian 1906- *Baker 78, IntWWM 77, -80, NewGrD 80*
Wolff, Hermann 1845-1902 *Baker 78*
Wolff, Jan *Film 2*
Wolff, Konrad 1907- *IntWWM 77, -80*
Wolff, Kurt Von *NewGrD 80*
Wolff, Lothar 1909- *FilmgC, HalFC 80, IntMPA 77, -75, -76, -78, -79, -80*
Wolff, Marguerite *IntWWM 77, -80, WhoMus 72*
Wolff, Martin *NewGrD 80*
Wolff, Max 1840-1886 *Baker 78*
Wolff, Michael B 1952- *EncJzS 70*
Wolff, Mike 1952- *EncJzS 70*
Wolff, Moss Leonardus Herman 1907- *IntWWM 77, -80*
Wolff, Perry *NewYTET*
Wolff, Pierre 1863-1944 *WhThe*
Wolff, Pierre 1865-1944 *McGEWD*
Wolff, Ruth *NatPD[port], WomWMM*
Wolff, Sanford I *ConMuA 80B*
Wolff, Werner 1883-1961 *Baker 78, ConAmC*
Wolff, William 1858-1936 *NotNAT B*
Wolff, William 1861- *WhoStg 1906*
Wolffheim, Werner 1877-1930 *Baker 78, NewGrD 80*
Wolffl, Josef 1773-1812 *BnBkM 80*
Wolffl, Joseph 1773-1812 *NewGrD 80*
Wolfington, Iggie 1920- *BiE&WWA, NotNAT, WhoHol A*
Wolfit, Sir Donald 1902-1968 *CnThe, EncWT, Ent[port], FilmEn, FilmgC, ForYSC, HalFC 80, IlWWBF[port], -A, MotPP, MovMk, NotNAT A, -B, OxFilm, OxThe, WhScrn 74, -77, WhThe, WhoHol B, WhoHrs 80, WorEFlm*
Wolfl, Joseph 1773-1812 *Baker 78, NewGrD 80, OxMus*
Wolfle, Ernest Earl, Jr. 1932- *IntWWM 77*
Wolfman, Jack *WhoHol A*
Wolford, Darwin K 1936- *ConAmC, IntWWM 77, -80*
Wolfram Von Eschenbach *NewGrD 80, OxMus*
Wolfram, Joseph Maria 1789-1839 *Baker 78*
Wolfram, Victor 1920- *IntWWM 77, -80*
Wolfrum, Philipp 1854-1919 *Baker 78, NewGrD 80*
Wolfsilver, C L *AmSCAP 80*
Wolfsohn, Carl 1834-1907 *BiDAmM*
Wolfson, Billy 1898-1973 *WhScrn 77*
Wolfson, Martin 1904-1973 *BiE&WWA, NotNAT B, WhoHol B*
Wolfson, Maxwell A 1923- *AmSCAP 80*
Wolfson, Mitchell 1900- *IntMPA 77, -75, -76, -78, -79, -80*
Wolfson, P J 1903-1979 *HalFC 80*
Wolfson, Richard 1923- *IntMPA 77, -75, -76, -78, -79, -80*
Wolfson, Victor 1910- *BiE&WWA, NotNAT*
Wolfsthal, D *WhoMus 72*
Wolfurt, Kurt Von 1880-1957 *Baker 78, NewGrD 80*
Wolgast, Johannes 1891-1932 *Baker 78*
Wolgina, Lydia Borisova 1937- *CnOxB*
Wolheim, Dan *Film 2*
Wolheim, Louis 1880-1931 *FilmEn, Film 1, -2, FilmgC, HalFC 80, MotPP, MovMk, TwYS, WhScrn 74, -77, WhoHol B*
Wolheim, Louis 1883-1931 *ForYSC*
Wolheim, Louis Robert 1881-1931 *NotNAT B, OxThe*
Wolinski, David J *AmSCAP 80*
Wolkenstein, David 1534-1592 *NewGrD 80*
Wolkenstein, Oswald Von 1377?-1445 *Baker 78, BnBkM 80, MusMk[port], NewGrD 80*
Wolki, Konrad Helmuth 1904- *IntWWM 77*
Wolking, Henry Clifford, Jr. 1948- *ConAmC, IntWWM 77*
Wolkow, Fyodor Grigoryevich *NewGrD 80*
Wolkowsky, George *WhoMus 72*
Woll, Naomi *PupTheA*
Wollanck, Friedrich 1782-1831 *Baker 78*
Wollaneck, Anton *NewGrD 80*
Wollanek, Anton *NewGrD 80*
Wollank, Friedrich 1781-1831 *NewGrD 80*
Wolle, John Frederick 1863-1933 *Baker 78, BiDAmM*
Wolle, Peter 1792-1871 *Baker 78, NewGrD 80*
Wolleb, Johann Jakob 1613-1667 *NewGrD 80*
Wollenberg, Susan Lesley Freda 1949- *IntWWM 80*
Wollenhaupt, Heinrich Adolph 1827-1865 *BiDAmM*
Wollenhaupt, Hermann Adolf 1827-1863 *Baker 78*
Wollgandt, Edgar 1880-1949 *Baker 78*
Wollheim, Eric 1879-1948 *NotNAT B, WhThe*
Wollick, Nicolas 1480?-1541? *NewGrD 80*
Wollick, Nicolaus 1480?-1541? *NewGrD 80*
Wollner, Anthony A 1920- *IntMPA 75, -76*
Wollner, Gertrude Price *ConAmC*
Wollrad, Rolf 1938- *WhoOp 76*
Wolman, Dan 1941- *FilmEn*
Wolmer, Jan 1909- *IntWWM 77, -80*
Wolo *PupTheA*
Woloshin, Alex *Film 2*
Woloshin, Sidney E 1928- *AmSCAP 80*
Wolowska, Maria Agata *NewGrD 80*
Wolpa, Bertha Bee *AmSCAP 80*
Wolpe, Stefan 1902-1972 *AmSCAP 66, -80, Baker 78, BiDAmM, BnBkM 80, ConAmC, DcCM, NewGrD 80, WhoMus 72*
Wolper, David L 1928- *FilmEn, FilmgC, HalFC 80, IntMPA 77, -75, -76, -78, -79, -80, NewYTET*
Wolpert, Franz Alfons 1917- *Baker 78, IntWWM 77, -80*
Wolpert, Franz Alphons 1917-1978 *NewGrD 80*
Wolquier, Nicolas *NewGrD 80*
Wolseley-Cox, Garnet d1904 *NotNAT B*
Wolsing, Waldemar 1910- *IntWWM 77, -80*
Wolsk, Eugene V 1928- *WhoThe 77*
Wolstan Of Winchester *NewGrD 80*
Wolstenholme, Jack 1909- *WhoMus 72*
Wolstenholme, William 1865-1931 *Baker 78, OxMus*
Wolston, Henry 1877- *WhThe*
Wolter, Charlotte 1834-1897 *EncWT*
Wolter, Detlef Franz Emil 1933- *IntWWM 77, -80*
Wolters, Gottfried 1910- *NewGrD 80*
Wolters, Klaus 1926- *IntWWM 77, -80*
Woltersdorf, Joachim 1508-1554 *NewGrD 80*
Woltman, Adolf G *PupTheA*
Woltmann, Frederick 1908- *BiDAmM, ConAmC*
Woltz, Johann 1550?-1618 *NewGrD 80*
Wolveridge, Carol 1940- *WhThe*
Wolverines *BiDAmM*
Wolzanus, Nicolaus *NewGrD 80*
Wolzogen, Alfred, Freiherr Von 1823-1883 *Baker 78*
Wolzogen, Ernst, Freiherr Von 1855-1934 *Baker 78, NotNAT B*
Wolzogen, Hans Paul, Freiherr Von 1848-1938 *Baker 78, NewGrD 80, OxMus*
Womack, Bobby 1944- *ConMuA 80A, DrBlPA, IlEncR, RkOn 2[port]*
Womer, Hilda *Film 2*
Won-Sik, Lim 1919- *IntWWM 77, -80*
Wonder, Stevie *AmSCAP 80, ConMuA 80A*
Wonder, Stevie 1950- *Baker 78, DrBlPA, IlEncR[port], RkOn[port], -2[port]*
Wonder, Stevie 1951- *BiDAmM, EncJzS 70*
Wonder Who, The *RkOn 2[port]*
Wonderlich, Jean-Georges *NewGrD 80*
Wonderly, Frank *Film 2*
Wondsel, Harold E 1902- *IntMPA 75, -76*
Wong, Anna May 1902-1961 *MovMk*
Wong, Anna May 1907-1960 *Film 1, -2*
Wong, Anna May 1907-1961 *FilmEn, FilmgC, ForYSC, HalFC 80, HolP 30[port], MotPP, NotNAT B, ThFT[port], TwYS, WhScrn 74, -77, WhThe, WhoHol B*
Wong, Arthur *WhoHol A*
Wong, Betty Anne 1938- *ConAmC*
Wong, Bruce 1906-1953 *WhScrn 74, -77, WhoHol B*
Wong, Carey Gordon 1950- *WhoOp 76*
Wong, Chris *WhoHol A*
Wong, Hsiung-Zee 1947- *ConAmC*
Wong, Jadine *WhoHol A*
Wong, Linda *WhoHol A*
Wong, Mary 1915-1940 *WhScrn 77*
Wong, W Beal 1906-1962 *WhScrn 77*
Wonnacott, Olwen Elizabeth 1930- *IntWWM 77, -80*
Wonnegger, Ioannes Litavicus *NewGrD 80*
Wonnegger, Johannes Ludwig *NewGrD 80*
Wontner, Arthur 1875-1960 *CmMov, FilmEn, Film 1, -2, FilmgC, HalFC 80, IlWWBF, NotNAT B, WhScrn 74, -77, WhThe, WhoHol B*
Wood, Father *OxMus*
Wood, Abraham 1752-1804 *BiDAmM*
Wood, Allan 1892-1947 *WhScrn 77*
Wood, Anne 1907- *IntWWM 80, NewGrD 80, WhoMus 72*
Wood, Anthony 1632-1695 *NewGrD 80, OxMus*
Wood, Arthur 1875-1953 *NotNAT B, WhThe*
Wood, Arthur Augustus d1907 *NotNAT B*
Wood, Audrey 1905- *BiE&WWA, NotNAT*
Wood, Barry 1909-1970 *BgBands 74, CmpEPM*
Wood, Brenton 1941- *AmSCAP 80, RkOn 2[port]*
Wood, Britt 1885-1965 *WhScrn 74, -77*
Wood, Britt 1895-1965 *Vers A[port], WhoHol B*
Wood, Carl Buddy 1905-1948 *WhScrn 74, -77*
Wood, Charles 1866-1926 *Baker 78, NewGrD 80, OxMus*
Wood, Charles 1931?- *FilmgC, HalFC 80*
Wood, Charles 1932- *CnThe, CroCD, EncWT, REnWD[port], WhoThe 77*
Wood, Charles 1933- *ConDr 73, -77*
Wood, Charles Henry, III 1936- *IntWWM 77*
Wood, Clement 1888-1950 *AmSCAP 66, -80*
Wood, Cyrus D 1889-1942 *AmSCAP 66, -80, CmpEPM*
Wood, Daisy 1877- *WhThe*
Wood, Dale 1934- *AmSCAP 80, ConAmC*
Wood, David 1944- *WhoHol A, WhoThe 72, -77*
Wood, David Duffie 1838-1910 *Baker 78*
Wood, David Duffield 1838-1910 *BiDAmM*
Wood, Deedee 1927- *BiE&WWA, NotNAT*
Wood, Del 1920- *BiDAmM, IlEncCM*
Wood, Denis 1924- *WhoMus 72*
Wood, Donna 1918-1947 *WhScrn 74, -77, WhoHol B*
Wood, Dorothy *Film 2*
Wood, Douglas 1880-1966 *Vers B[port], WhScrn 74, -77, WhoHol B*
Wood, Douglas Albert 1950- *AmSCAP 80*
Wood, Edna 1918- *WhThe*
Wood, Edward D, Jr. 1922-1978 *WhoHrs 80*
Wood, Elizabeth M *WomWMM B*
Wood, Elizabeth Wyn 1903-1966 *CreCan 1*
Wood, Elsie Alva *WhoMus 72*
Wood, Ernest 1892-1942 *Film 2, WhScrn 74, -77, WhoHol B*
Wood, Eugene 1904-1971 *WhScrn 74, -77, WhoHol A, -B*
Wood, Evelyn *PupTheA*
Wood, Florence *WhThe*

Wood, Forrest *WhoHol A*
Wood, Frank Motley d1919 *NotNAT B*
Wood, Franker 1883-1931 *WhScrn 74, -77, WhoHol B*
Wood, Freeman N 1897-1956 *Film 2, WhScrn 74, -77, WhoHol B*
Wood, G *WhoHol A*
Wood, G 1919- *NotNAT*
Wood, G D *WhScrn 77*
Wood, Gene *WhoHol A*
Wood, George *IlWWBF A*
Wood, George 1923- *AmSCAP 66, -80*
Wood, Gloria *Film 2, WhoHol A*
Wood, Graham Edwin 1930- *IntWWM 80*
Wood, Guy B 1912- *AmSCAP 66, -80*
Wood, Harry *WhoHol A*
Wood, Haydn 1882-1959 *Baker 78, MusMk, NewGrD 80, OxMus, WhThe*
Wood, Helen E *PupTheA*
Wood, Sir Henry J 1869-1944 *Baker 78, BnBkM 80, MusMk[port], MusSN[port], NewGrD 80[port], OxMus*
Wood, Hugh 1932- *Baker 78, IntWWM 77, -80, NewGrD 80, WhoMus 72*
Wood, Irma Gaye 1945- *IntWWM 77*
Wood, J Hickory d1913 *NotNAT B*
Wood, Jane *WhoHol A*
Wood, Jane 1886- *WhThe*
Wood, Janet *WhoHol A*
Wood, John *CnThe, PlP&P A, WhoHol A, WhoThe 77*
Wood, Mrs. John 1831-1915 *NotNAT B, OxThe*
Wood, Mrs. John 1833-1915 *WhThe*
Wood, John Muir 1805-1892 *NewGrD 80*
Wood, Joseph 1915- *Baker 78, ConAmC, IntWWM 77, -80*
Wood, Judith *WhoHol A*
Wood, Judith Ellis 1945- *IntWWM 77, -80*
Wood, Kevin Joseph 1947- *CpmDNM 77, -80*
Wood, Lana 1944- *ForYSC, WhoHol A*
Wood, Lee *WhoHol A*
Wood, Leo 1882-1929 *AmSCAP 66*
Wood, Lynn *WhoHol A*
Wood, Marian Louise 1914- *AmSCAP 80*
Wood, Marjorie 1887-1955 *NotNAT B*
Wood, Marjorie 1888-1955 *WhScrn 74, -77, WhoHol B*
Wood, Mary Knight 1857-1944 *Baker 78*
Wood, Mary Laura *WhoHol A*
Wood, Maurice Albert 1914- *IntWWM 77*
Wood, Metcalfe *WhThe*
Wood, Michael 1912- *CnOxB, WhoHol A*
Wood, Mickey 1898-1963 *WhScrn 74, -77, WhoHol B*
Wood, Montgomery *FilmAG WE, WhoHol A*
Wood, Natalie 1938- *BiDFilm, -81, FilmEn, FilmgC, ForYSC, HalFC 80, IntMPA 77, -75, -76, -78, -79, -80, MotPP, MovMk[port], OxFilm, WhoHol A, WorEFlm*
Wood, Peggy *Film 1, IntMPA 77, -75, -76, -78, MotPP*
Wood, Peggy 1892-1978 *BiE&WWA, CmpEPM, EncMT, FamA&A[port], FilmEn, Film 2, FilmgC, ForYSC, HalFC 80, NotNAT, What 4[port], WhoHol A, WhoThe 72, -77*
Wood, Peggy 1894- *NotNAT A*
Wood, Peter 1927- *NotNAT, WhoThe 72, -77*
Wood, Philip 1896-1940 *WhScrn 74, -77, WhoHol B*
Wood, Ralph Walter 1902- *NewGrD 80, WhoMus 72*
Wood, Randolph C 1917- *AmSCAP 80*
Wood, Richard 1910- *IntWWM 77, -80*
Wood, Robert D *NewYTET*
Wood, Robin Laurance 1924- *WhoMus 72*
Wood, Roger *DancEn 78*
Wood, Roger 1920- *CnOxB*
Wood, Roland 1897-1967 *WhScrn 74, -77, WhoHol B*
Wood, Ron 1947- *ConMuA 80A*
Wood, Roy 1946- *ConMuA 80A, IlEncR*
Wood, Russell *ConAmC*
Wood, Ruzena Alenka Milena *IntWWM 80*
Wood, Sam *Film 1*
Wood, Sam 1883-1949 *DcFM, FilmEn, FilmgC, HalFC 80, MovMk[port], TwYS A, WhScrn 74, -77, WhoHol B, WorEFlm*
Wood, Sam 1883-1950 *OxFilm*
Wood, Sam 1885-1949 *BiDFilm, -81*
Wood, Samuel Balmforth 1896- *IntWWM 77, WhoMus 72*
Wood, Simeon 1774-1822 *BiDAmM*
Wood, Sue *AmSCAP 80*
Wood, Susan *WhoHol A*
Wood, Suzanne d1934 *WhScrn 74, -77*
Wood, Thomas *NewGrD 80*
Wood, Thomas 1892-1950 *Baker 78, NewGrD 80, OxMus*
Wood, Thor E 1932- *NewGrD 80*
Wood, Victor 1914-1958 *WhScrn 74, -77, WhoHol B*
Wood, Virginia *WhoHol A*
Wood, Vivian Poates 1928- *IntWWM 77, -80*
Wood, Wee Georgie 1897- *WhThe*
Wood, Wendell Lee 1905- *AmSCAP 66, -80*
Wood, William 1935- *ConAmC, IntWWM 77, -80*
Wood, William Burke 1779-1861 *FamA&A[port], NotNAT A, -B, OxThe, PlP&P*
Wood, William G 1859-1895 *Baker 78*
Wood, William John 1877-1954 *CreCan 2*
Wood, Woodrow Johnson 1918- *AmSCAP 66, -80*
Wood-Hill, M 1891-1954 *AmSCAP 66*
Wood-Hill, Mabel 1870-1954 *Baker 78, ConAmC*
Woodage, Wesley 1917- *IntWWM 77, -80*
Woodard, James P 1929- *ConAmC*
Woodard, Nelmatilda Ritchie 1913- *IntWWM 77*
Woodbridge, George 1907-1973 *FilmgC, HalFC 80, WhScrn 77, WhThe, WhoHol B*
Woodbridge, William C *OxMus*
Woodburn, Eric *WhoHol A*
Woodburn, James 1888-1948 *NotNAT B, WhThe, WhoHol B*
Woodbury, Albert Francis 1909- *AmSCAP 80*
Woodbury, Arthur 1930- *Baker 78, ConAmC*
Woodbury, Clare d1949 *NotNAT B*
Woodbury, Doreen 1927-1957 *WhScrn 74, -77, WhoHol B*
Woodbury, Isaac Baker 1819-1858 *Baker 78, BiDAmM, NewGrD 80*
Woodbury, Joan 1915- *FilmEn, FilmgC, ForYSC, HalFC 80, WhoHol A*
Woodbury, Lael J 1927- *BiE&WWA, NotNAT*
Woodbury, Ward 1922- *IntWWM 77, -80*
Woodchoppers, The *BiDAmM*
Woodcock, Clement *NewGrD 80*
Woodcock, Cyril 1897- *WhoMus 72*
Woodcock, Percy Franklin 1855-1936 *CreCan 1*
Woodcock, Robert d1734? *NewGrD 80*
Wooddin, Dorothy Ellen 1896- *WhoMus 72*
Woode, James Bryant 1929- *EncJzS 70*
Woode, Jimmy 1929- *EncJzS 70*
Woode, William Henri 1909- *AmSCAP 66, -80*
Woodell, Barbara *WhoHol A*
Woodell, Pat *WhoHol A*
Woodeson, Leonard 1659?-1717 *NewGrD 80*
Woodfall, William d1803 *NotNAT B*
Woodfill, Walter L 1910- *NewGrD 80*
Woodford, John 1862-1927 *Film 2, WhScrn 74, -77, WhoHol B*
Woodforde-Finden, Amy 1860-1919 *NewGrD 80*
Woodfork, Robert 1925- *BluesWW*
Woodham, Ronald 1912- *WhoMus 72*
Woodham-Smith, George Ivon 1895- *IntMPA 77, -75, -76, -78, -79, -80*
Woodhouse, Bertha O *PupTheA*
Woodhouse, Francis Michael 1944- *IntWWM 77, -80*
Woodhouse, George 1877-1954 *Baker 78*
Woodhouse, Henry W *PupTheA*
Woodhouse, Todd 1902-1958 *WhScrn 74, -77*
Woodhouse, Vernon 1874-1936 *NotNAT B, WhThe*
Woodhouse, Violet Gordon *NewGrD 80*
Woodhull, Alfred Alexander 1810-1836 *BiDAmM*
Woodin, William Hartman 1868-1934 *AmSCAP 66, -80*
Wooding, Sam 1895- *WhoJazz 72*
Woodland, Norman 1910- *IntMPA 77, -75, -76, -78, -79, -80*
Woodland, Rae *IntWWM 77, -80, WhoMus 72, WhoOp 76*
Woodland, Reginald John 1907- *WhoMus 72*
Woodlen, George Robert 1913- *AmSCAP 66, -80*
Woodley, Bruce *EncFCWM 69*
Woodley, Chris *WhoHol A*
Woodman, Britt 1920- *BiDAmM, CmpEPM, EncJzS 70*
Woodman, Jonathan Call 1813-1894 *BiDAmM*
Woodman, R Huntington 1861-1943 *AmSCAP 66*
Woodman, Raymond Huntington 1861-1942 *AmSCAP 80*
Woodman, Raymond Huntington 1861-1943 *Baker 78, BiDAmM*
Woodman, William 1932- *NotNAT*
Woodroffe, Marilyn Northcote 1947- *IntWWM 77*
Woodruff, Arthur D 1853-1934 *BiDAmM*
Woodruff, Bert 1856-1934 *Film 1, -2, TwYS, WhoHol B*
Woodruff, Edna 1874-1947 *NotNAT B, WhScrn 74, -77*
Woodruff, Eleanor *Film 1, MotPP*
Woodruff, Henry 1870-1916 *Film 1, WhScrn 77, WhThe, WhoStg 1906*
Woodruff, Henry Ingott 1869-1916 *NotNAT B*
Woodruff, John R 1909- *NotNAT*
Woodruff, William H Burt 1856-1934 *WhScrn 74, -77*
Woods, Al 1895-1946 *WhScrn 74, -77, WhoHol B*
Woods, Albert Herman 1870-1951 *NotNAT B, WhThe*
Woods, Alfred *Film 2*
Woods, Allie 1940- *DrBlPA*
Woods, Alvin 1909- *NewOrJ*
Woods, Arthur B 1904-1942 *FilmEn, Film 2, FilmgC, HalFC 80, IlWWBF*
Woods, Aubrey *ConDr 77D*
Woods, Aubrey 1928- *FilmgC, HalFC 80, WhoHol A*
Woods, Barbara Gullo 1939- *IntWWM 77*
Woods, Beryl 1934- *WhoMus 72*
Woods, Big Boy *BluesWW*
Woods, Chris 1925- *EncJzS 70*
Woods, Christopher Columbus 1925- *EncJzS 70*
Woods, Donald *BiE&WWA, IntMPA 77, -75, -76, -78, -79, -80, MotPP*
Woods, Donald 1904- *FilmEn, ForYSC, MovMk[port]*
Woods, Donald 1906- *FilmgC, HalFC 80, NotNAT*
Woods, Donald 1909- *WhoHol A*
Woods, Dorothy *Film 2*
Woods, Eddie *HalFC 80*
Woods, Elaine 1946- *IntWWM 80*
Woods, Ercell 1916-1948 *WhScrn 74, -77*
Woods, Francis Cunningham 1862-1929 *Baker 78*
Woods, Franker *Film 2*
Woods, Grant *WhoHol A*
Woods, Grant d1968 *WhScrn 77*
Woods, Harry 1889-1968 *FilmEn, Film 2, ForYSC, TwYS, WhScrn 74, -77*
Woods, Harry 1893-1968 *Vers A[port], WhoHol B*
Woods, Harry 1896-1970 *CmpEPM*
Woods, Harry MacGregor 1896-1970 *AmSCAP 66, -80, BiDAmM, PopAmC, PopAmC SUP, Sw&Ld C*
Woods, Herbert D 1943- *AmSCAP 80*
Woods, James *WhoHol A*
Woods, Johnny 1930- *EncJzS 70*
Woods, Jon 1939- *IntWWM 77*
Woods, Joseph A 1860-1926 *WhScrn 74, -77*
Woods, Lotta *WomWMM*
Woods, Mark *NewYTET*
Woods, Michael *NewGrD 80*
Woods, Milton *BlksB&W C*
Woods, Nick 1858-1936 *WhScrn 74, -77*
Woods, Oscar 1900-1956? *BluesWW*
Woods, Patricia Rudy 1946- *BiDAmM*
Woods, Phil 1931- *Conv 2[port], EncJzS 70, IlEncJ*
Woods, Philip Wells 1931- *EncJzS 70*

Woods, Richard Stanley 1952- *IntWWM 80*
Woods, Robert *BiE&WWA*
Woods, Susan *WhoHol A*
Woodson, Edgar 1927- *AmSCAP 66*
Woodson, Leonard *NewGrD 80*
Woodson, Leonard 1565?-1641? *NewGrD 80*
Woodson, Thomas d1605? *NewGrD 80*
Woodson, William *WhoHol A*
Woodstock *IlEncR*
Woodthorpe, Georgia 1859-1927 *Film 1, -2, WhoHol B*
Woodthorpe, Peter 1931- *PlP&P, WhoHol A, WhoThe 72, -77*
Woodthrope, Georgia 1859-1927 *WhScrn 74, -77*
Woodville, Kate *WhoHol A*
Woodvine, John 1929- *WhoHol A, WhoThe 72, -77*
Woodward, Betty Shaw 1932- *IntWWM 77*
Woodward, Charles d1808 *BiDAmM*
Woodward, Charles, Jr. *WhoThe 77*
Woodward, David Gilman 1949- *AmSCAP 80*
Woodward, Edward 1930- *BiE&WWA, FilmgC, HalFC 80, IlWWBF, IntMPA 77, -75, -76, -78, -79, -80, NotNAT, WhoHol A, WhoThe 72, -77*
Woodward, Enid McClure 1908- *IntWWM 77, -80*
Woodward, Eugenie *Film 1*
Woodward, Guy *Film 1*
Woodward, H Guy 1858-1919 *WhScrn 77*
Woodward, Harry 1717-1777 *OxThe*
Woodward, Henry *Film 1, -2*
Woodward, Henry Lynde 1908- *ConAmC, IntWWM 77, -80*
Woodward, James David 1932- *IntWWM 77*
Woodward, Jill *Film 1*
Woodward, Joanne 1930- *BiDFilm, -81, BiE&WWA, FilmEn, FilmgC, ForYSC, HalFC 80, IntMPA 77, -75, -76, -78, -79, -80, MotPP, MovMk[port], OxFilm, WhoHol A, WorEFlm*
Woodward, Kerry Russell 1939- *IntWWM 77, -80*
Woodward, Morgan *WhoHol A*
Woodward, Richard, Jr. 1743?-1777 *ConMuA 80B, NewGrD 80*
Woodward, Robert 1909-1972 *WhScrn 77, WhoHol B*
Woodward, Roger 1942- *NewGrD 80*
Woodward, Roger Robert 1943- *IntWWM 77*
Woodward, Roger Robert 1944- *IntWWM 80*
Woodward, Sidney 1860-1924 *BiDAmM*
Woodworth, G Wallace 1902-1969 *NewGrD 80*
Woodworth, George Wallace 1902-1969 *Baker 78*
Woodworth, Marjorie *WhoHol A*
Woodworth, Samuel 1784-1842 *BiDAmM, McGEWD*
Woodworth, Samuel 1785-1842 *NotNAT B, OxThe*
Woody, Chester F 1934- *IntMPA 77, -75, -76, -78, -79, -80*
Woodyard, Sam 1925- *EncJzS 70*
Woodyard, Samuel 1925- *EncJzS 70*
Wooland, Norman 1910- *FilmgC, ForYSC, HalFC 80, IlWWBF, WhoHol A, WhoThe 77*
Woolcott, Alexander 1887-1943 *FilmgC*
Wooldridge, David 1927- *Baker 78*
Wooldridge, David Humphry Michael 1931- *IntWWM 77, -80, WhoMus 72*
Wooldridge, Doris 1890-1921 *WhScrn 74, -77*
Wooldridge, H E 1845-1917 *NewGrD 80*
Wooldridge, Harry Ellis 1845-1917 *Baker 78*
Wooler, Alfred 1867-1937 *Baker 78, BiDAmM*
Wooler, J P d1868 *NotNAT B*
Woolett, Wilfred 1872- *BiDAmM*
Wooley, James *WhoHol A*
Wooley, Sheb *AmPS A, ForYSC*
Wooley, Sheb 1921- *AmSCAP 66, -80, CounME 74, -74A, EncFCWM 69, IlEncCM[port], RkOn, WhoHol A*
Wooley, Shelby F 1921- *BiDAmM*
Woolf, Barney 1877-1972 *WhScrn 77*
Woolf, Benjamin Edward 1836-1901 *Baker 78, BiDAmM*
Woolf, Edgar Allan d1943 *NotNAT B, WhThe*
Woolf, Gregory Buxton 1935-1971 *ConAmC*
Woolf, Henry *WhoHol A*
Woolf, James 1919-1966 *FilmEn, FilmgC, HalFC 80*
Woolf, James 1920-1966 *WorEFlm*
Woolf, John 1913- *IntMPA 77, -75, -76, -78, -79, -80, WorEFlm*
Woolf, Sir John 1913- *HalFC 80*
Woolf, Kitty d1944 *NotNAT B*
Woolf, Leslie *WhoHol A*
Woolf, Peggy *WomWMM B*
Woolf, Stanley d1959 *NotNAT B*
Woolf, Walter 1899- *AmPS B, CmpEPM, WhThe*
Woolf, Yetti 1882-1965 *WhScrn 74, -77*
Woolfe, H Bruce 1880-1965 *FilmgC, HalFC 80*
Woolfe, H Bruce 1890-1966 *IlWWBF*
Woolfenden, Guy Anthony 1937- *IntWWM 80, WhoThe 72, -77*
Woolford, Delia Osborne 1931- *IntWWM 80, WhoMus 72*
Woolgar, Sarah Jane *OxThe*
Woolhouse, Wesley S B 1809-1893 *Baker 78*
Woollam, Kenneth Geoffrey 1937- *IntWWM 77, -80, WhoOp 76*
Woollcott, Alexander 1887-1943 *EncWT, HalFC 80, ModWD, NotNAT A, -B, OxThe, PlP&P, WhScrn 74, -77, WhThe, WhoHol B*
Woollen, Russell 1923- *Baker 78, ConAmC, IntWWM 77, -80*
Woollett, Henri Edouard 1864-1936 *Baker 78*
Woolley, Clara Virginia 1938- *IntWWM 80*
Woolley, DeGraffenried *PupTheA*
Woolley, Monty *AmPS B*
Woolley, Monty 1888-1963 *EncMT, FilmEn, FilmgC, HalFC 80, MotPP, MovMk[port], NotNAT B, WhScrn 74, -77, WhThe, WhoHol B*
Woolley, Monty 1889-1963 *ForYSC*
Woolliams, Anne 1926- *CnOxB*
Woolman, Claude *WhoHol A*
Woolmore, Pamela *WhoMus 72*
Woolner, Lawrence H *IntMPA 77, -78, -79, -80*
Woolnoth, Marguerita Sainsbury 1895- *WhoMus 72*
Woolrich, Cornell 1903-1968 *HalFC 80*
Wools *PlP&P*
Wools, Stephen 1729-1799 *BiDAmM*
Woolsey, Mary Hale 1899-1969 *ConAmC*
Woolsey, Maryhale 1899-1969 *AmSCAP 66, -80*
Woolsey, Ralph *HalFC 80*
Woolsey, Robert *MovMk[port]*
Woolsey, Robert 1889-1938 *FilmEn, FilmgC, HalFC 80, JoeFr[port], MovMk, NotNAT B, WhScrn 74, -77, WhThe*
Woolsey, Robert 1889-1944 *Film 2, WhoHol B*
Woolsey, Robert 1899-1944 *ForYSC*
Wootten, Dick *ConAmTC*
Wootten, Lawrence Bernard 1921- *AmSCAP 80*
Wootwell, Tom 1865- *WhThe*
Wopmann, Alfred 1936- *WhoOp 76*
Worcester, Alec *IlWWBF*
Worch, Hugo 1855-1938 *NewGrD 80*
Worde, Wynkyn De d1534? *NewGrD 80, OxMus*
Worden, Hank 1901- *HalFC 80, WhoHol A*
Worden, Willey *AmSCAP 80*
Wordes, Smitty *WhoHol A*
Words, Sil *WhoHol A*
Wordsworth, Barry 1948- *WhoMus 72*
Wordsworth, Richard 1915- *WhoHol A, WhoHrs 80, WhoThe 72, -77*
Wordsworth, William 1770-1850 *DcPup, OxMus*
Wordsworth, William Brocklesby 1908- *Baker 78, IntWWM 77, -80, NewGrD 80, OxMus, WhoMus 72*
Wordsworth, William Derrick 1912- *WhThe*
Worgan *NewGrD 80*
Worgan, George 1802-1888 *NewGrD 80*
Worgan, James 1715-1753 *NewGrD 80*
Worgan, John 1724-1790 *NewGrD 80*
Worgan, Thomas Danvers 1774-1832 *NewGrD 80*
Work *NewGrD 80*
Work, Agnes Haynes 1876-1927 *NewGrD 80*
Work, Frederick J 1880-1942 *NewGrD 80*
Work, Henry Clay 1832-1884 *AmPS, Baker 78, BiDAmM, NewGrD 80, NotNAT B, OxMus, PopAmC[port], Sw&Ld A*
Work, John Wesley 1901-1967 *AmSCAP 66, -80, BnBkM 80, DrBlPA, NewGrD 80*
Work, John Wesley, Jr. 1901-1968 *BiDAmM, ConAmC*
Work, John Wesley, Sr. 1873-1925 *BiDAmM, NewGrD 80*
Work, Julian C 1910- *AmSCAP 66, -80, ConAmC*
Work, William 1923- *BiE&WWA, NotNAT*
Worker, Adrian 1916- *IntMPA 77, -75, -76, -78, -79, -80*
Workman, Charles Herbert 1873-1923 *NotNAT B, WhThe*
Workman, Reggie 1937- *EncJzS 70*
Workman, Reginald 1937- *EncJzS 70*
Workman, William 1940- *IntWWM 77, -80, WhoOp 76*
World's Greatest Jazzband *EncJzS 70*
Worley, Jo Anne 1937- *BiE&WWA, NotNAT*
Worley, Joanne *WhoHol A*
Worlock, Frederic 1886-1973 *BiE&WWA, WhThe, WhoThe 72*
Worlock, Frederick 1886-1973 *FilmgC, HalFC 80, NotNAT B, WhScrn 77, WhoHol B*
Worlock, Frederick 1887?- *ForYSC*
Worlthington, William d1941 *ForYSC*
Worm, A Toxen d1922 *NotNAT B*
Worm, Dieter Gerhardt 1930- *IntWWM 80*
Wormhoudt, Pearl Shinn 1915- *IntWWM 77, -80*
Worms, Gustave-Hippolyte 1836-1910 *NotNAT B, OxThe*
Worms, Jean 1884- *WhThe*
Wormser, Andre 1851-1926 *Baker 78, NotNAT B, OxMus*
Wormser, Irving 1900- *IntMPA 77, -75, -76, -78, -79, -80*
Wormser, Richard 1908- *IntMPA 77, -75, -76, -78, -79, -80*
Worne, Duke *Film 1, -2, TwYS A*
Worner, Hilda *Film 2*
Worner, Karl Heinrich 1910-1969 *Baker 78, NewGrD 80*
Wornham *NewGrD 80*
Wornum *NewGrD 80*
Wornum, A N *NewGrD 80*
Wornum, Robert *OxMus*
Wornum, Robert 1742-1815 *NewGrD 80*
Wornum, Robert 1780-1852 *NewGrD 80*
Woroniec, Antoni Arnulf *NewGrD 80*
Woronoff, Wladimir 1903- *Baker 78*
Woronov, Mary 1946- *WhoHrs 80*
Worp, Johannes 1821-1891 *Baker 78*
Worrall, Lechmere 1875- *WhThe*
Worrall, Peter Clement 1946- *IntWWM 80*
Worrall, Thomas Gary 1942- *AmSCAP 80*
Worrall, William Charles 1936- *IntWWM 77, -80*
Worschitzka, Franz Xaver *NewGrD 80*
Worsley, Bruce 1899- *WhThe*
Worsley, Wallace 1880-1944 *FilmgC, HalFC 80, TwYS A*
Worst, John William 1940- *CpmDNM 72, -79, ConAmC*
Worster, Howett 1882- *WhThe*
Wortelmann, Fritz *DcPup*
Worth, Amy 1888-1967 *AmSCAP 66, -80, ConAmC*
Worth, Barbara *Film 2, ForYSC, TwYS*
Worth, Bill 1884-1951 *WhScrn 74, -77*
Worth, Billie 1917- *BiE&WWA, NotNAT*
Worth, Bobby 1921- *AmSCAP 66, -80*
Worth, Brian *IntMPA 75, -76*
Worth, Brian 1914- *FilmgC, HalFC 80, IntMPA 77, WhoHol A*
Worth, Constance 1913-1963 *ForYSC*
Worth, Constance 1915-1963 *WhScrn 77, WhoHol B*
Worth, Edith *WomWMM B*
Worth, Faith 1938- *CnOxB*
Worth, Frank J 1903- *AmSCAP 80*
Worth, Harry *Film 2*
Worth, Irene 1916- *BiE&WWA, CnThe, EncWT, Ent, FilmgC, HalFC 80,*

NotNAT, PlP&P, WhoHol A, WhoThe 72, -77
Worth, Lillian *Film 2*
Worth, Marion *CounME 74, -74A, EncFCWM 69*
Worth, Peggy 1891-1956 *WhScrn 74, -77, WhoHol B*
Worth, Richard *Film 2*
Worth, Ted Alan 1935- *WhoMus 72*
Worthin, Helen Lee 1905-1948 *Film 2*
Worthing, Frank 1866-1910 *NotNAT A, -B, WhoStg 1906*
Worthing, Helen Lee 1905-1948 *NotNAT B, TwYS, WhScrn 74, -77, WhoHol B*
Worthington, David L 1947- *IntWWM 77*
Worthington, Roger Paul 1951- *IntWWM 77, -80*
Worthington, William J 1872-1941 *Film 1, -2, TwYS, -A, WhScrn 74, -77, WhoHol B*
Wortley, Howard S 1916- *AmSCAP 66, -80*
Wortley, Mary 1920- *WhoMus 72*
Wortman, Denis 1835-1922 *BiDAmM*
Wortman, Don A 1927- *BiE&WWA*
Worton-Steward, Andrew 1948- *IntWWM 80*
Wortzelius, Inge 1951- *IntWWM 77*
Worzischek, Johann Hugo 1791-1825 *Baker 78, NewGrD 80, OxMus*
Woschitka, Franz Xaver 1728-1796 *NewGrD 80*
Woss, Josef Venantius Von 1863-1943 *Baker 78, NewGrD 80*
Woss, Kurt 1914- *Baker 78*
Wotquenne, Alfred 1867-1939 *Baker 78, NewGrD 80*
Wotruba, Fritz 1907- *EncWT*
Wotton, William *NewGrD 80*
Wotton, William 1832-1912 *NewGrD 80*
Woudenberg, Pierre Willem Hubert 1949- *IntWWM 77, -80*
Wouk, Herman 1915- *BiE&WWA, CnMD, CroCD, EncWT, FilmgC, HalFC 80, ModWD, NotNAT*
Woulmyer, Jean Baptiste *NewGrD 80*
Wounderlich, Jean-Georges *NewGrD 80*
Wouters, Adolphe 1849-1924 *Baker 78*
Wouters, Jos 1914- *NewGrD 80*
Wowchuk, Harry N 1948- *IntMPA 77, -78, -79, -80*
Wowchuk, Nicholas *IntMPA 77, -78, -79, -80*
Woyrsch, Felix Von 1860-1944 *Baker 78, NewGrD 80*
Woytowicz, Boleslaw 1899-1980 *Baker 78, IntWWM 80, NewGrD 80*
Woytowicz, Stefania 1922- *IntWWM 77, -80, WhoMus 72*
Woytowicz, Stefania 1925- *NewGrD 80*
Wragg, Gerald 1931- *IntWWM 77, -80*
Wragg, Russell 1899- *AmSCAP 66*
Wragg, Russell 1919- *ConAmC A*
Wrancher, Elizabeth Ann 1930- *IntWWM 77, -80*
Wraneff, Vadim *Film 2*
Wrangel, Baron Vasily 1862-1901 *Baker 78*
Wrangell, Baron Vasily Georgiyevich 1862-1901 *NewGrD 80*
Wranitsky, Anton 1761-1820 *OxMus*
Wranitsky, Paul 1756-1808 *OxMus*
Wranitzky, Anton 1761-1820 *Baker 78, NewGrD 80*
Wranitzky, Antonin 1761-1820 *NewGrD 80*
Wranitzky, Paul 1756-1808 *Baker 78, CnOxB, NewGrD 80*
Wranitzky, Pavel 1756-1808 *NewGrD 80*
Wranizky, Anton 1761-1820 *NewGrD 80*
Wranizky, Antonin 1761-1820 *NewGrD 80*
Wranizky, Paul 1756-1808 *NewGrD 80*
Wranizky, Pavel 1756-1808 *NewGrD 80*
Wrastill, Florian 1717-1758 *NewGrD 80*
Wrather, Jack 1918- *IntMPA 77, -75, -78, -79, -80, NewYTET*
Wray *PupTheA*
Wray, Mrs. *PupTheA*
Wray, Aloha 1928-1968 *WhScrn 74, -77, WhoHol B*
Wray, Fay 1907- *CmMov, FilmEn, Film 2, FilmgC, ForYSC, HalFC 80[port], HolP 30[port], IntMPA 77, -75, -76, -78, -79, -80, MotPP, MovMk[port], OxFilm, ThFT[port], TwYS, What 2[port], WhoHol A, WhoHrs 80[port]*
Wray, Jane *Film 2*
Wray, John *ForYSC*
Wray, John d1940 *Film 2, WhoHol B*
Wray, John Griffith 1888-1940 *FilmEn, HolCA[port], NotNAT B, TwYS A, WhScrn 74, -77, WhThe*
Wray, John Griffith 1890-1940 *HalFC 80*
Wray, John Griffith 1895-1940 *FilmgC*
Wray, John Reginald 1915- *IntWWM 77, WhoMus 72*
Wray, Link *ConMuA 80A, IlEncR[port]*
Wray, Link 1929- *BiDAmM*
Wray, Link And The Wray Men 1935- *RkOn[port]*
Wray, Maxwell 1898- *WhThe, WhoThe 72*
Wray, Ted 1909-1950 *WhScrn 74, -77*
Wrede, Caspar 1929- *FilmgC, HalFC 80, IlWWBF*
Wrede, Ferdinand 1827-1899 *Baker 78*
Wreede, Johannes *NewGrD 80*
Wren, Sir Christopher 1631-1723 *OxThe, PlP&P*
Wren, Sir Christopher 1632-1723 *NotNAT B*
Wren, P C 1885-1941 *HalFC 80*
Wren, Sam 1897-1962 *NotNAT B, WhScrn 74, -77, WhoHol B*
Wrencher, John Thomas 1923-1977 *BluesWW[port]*
Wright, Mrs. 1705?-1750? *NewGrD 80*
Wright, Al George 1916- *AmSCAP 80*
Wright, Alfred George James 1916- *IntWWM 77, -80*
Wright, Anthony Paul 1951- *IntWWM 77, -80*
Wright, Armand Vincent Curly 1896-1965 *WhScrn 77*
Wright, Basil 1907- *BiDFilm, -81, DcFM, FilmEn, FilmgC, HalFC 80, IlWWBF, IntMPA 77, -75, -76, -78, -79, -80, OxFilm, WorEFlm*
Wright, Belinda 1927- *CnOxB*
Wright, Belinda 1929- *DancEn 78[port]*
Wright, Ben *ForYSC, WhoHol A*
Wright, Betty 1953- *RkOn 2[port]*
Wright, Bob 1911- *NotNAT, WhoHol A*
Wright, Bobby 1942- *IlEncCM[port]*
Wright, Brian James 1946- *IntWWM 77, -80*
Wright, Carter Land 1911- *AmSCAP 66, -80*
Wright, Charles Stevenson 1932- *BlkAmP*
Wright, Chris *ConMuA 80B*
Wright, Cobina, Jr. 1921- *WhoHol A*
Wright, Cowley 1889-1923 *NotNAT B, WhThe*
Wright, Cyril 1888- *IntWWM 77*
Wright, Daniel *NewGrD 80*
Wright, David 1941- *WhoThe 72, -77*
Wright, David Arthur 1934- *IntWWM 80, WhoMus 72*
Wright, Desmond Elliston 1940- *IntWWM 77, -80*
Wright, E G 1811-1871 *NewGrD 80*
Wright, Ed d1975 *WhScrn 77, WhoHol C*
Wright, Edred John 1911- *IntWWM 77, -80, WhoMus 72*
Wright, Edward A 1906- *BiE&WWA, NotNAT*
Wright, Edythe d1965 *CmpEPM*
Wright, Else Gress *WomWMM*
Wright, Ethel *Film 2*
Wright, Eugene Joseph 1923- *EncJzS 70*
Wright, Fanny d1954 *NotNAT B*
Wright, Frank A 1889- *AmSCAP 66, -80, IlEncJ*
Wright, Frank Lloyd *PlP&P*
Wright, Fred 1871-1928 *Film 2, NotNAT B, WhScrn 74, -77, WhThe, WhoHol B*
Wright, Mrs. Fred d1919 *NotNAT B*
Wright, Fred, Sr. 1826-1911 *NotNAT B*
Wright, Fred Howard 1896- *AmSCAP 80*
Wright, Frederick William, Jr. 1940- *ConAmTC*
Wright, G Harry 1901-1964 *BiE&WWA, NotNAT B*
Wright, Gary 1943- *AmSCAP 80, ConMuA 80A, IlEncR[port], RkOn 2[port]*
Wright, Gene 1923- *EncJzS 70*
Wright, Geoffrey 1912- *WhoMus 72*
Wright, Georgie d1937 *NotNAT B*
Wright, H Humberstone *Film 2*
Wright, Haidee d1943 *Film 2, WhoHol B*
Wright, Haidee 1868-1943 *NotNAT B, WhThe*
Wright, Haidee 1898-1943 *WhScrn 74, -77*
Wright, Harold 1927- *BnBkM 80*
Wright, Harry Wendell 1916-1954 *WhScrn 74, -77*
Wright, Heather *WhoHol A*
Wright, Helen *Film 1*
Wright, Henry Joseph 1935- *IntWWM 77*
Wright, Henry Otho 1892-1940 *WhScrn 74, -77*
Wright, Horace H 1914- *BiE&WWA*
Wright, Hugh E 1879-1940 *Film 1, -2, IlWWBF, NotNAT B, WhScrn 74, -77, WhThe, WhoHol B*
Wright, Huntley d1941 *WhoHol B*
Wright, Huntley 1868-1943 *NotNAT B*
Wright, Huntley 1869-1943 *WhThe*
Wright, Huntley 1870-1941 *WhScrn 74, -77*
Wright, Isobel Scott Aitken 1903 *WhoMus 72*
Wright, Jenny Lee *WhoHol A*
Wright, John *DcPup, WhoHol A*
Wright, John W 1899- *BiE&WWA*
Wright, Johnny 1914- *BiDAmM, CounME 74, -74A, EncFCWM 69, IlEncCM[port]*
Wright, K A 1899- *IntMPA 77, -75, -76, -78, -79, -80*
Wright, Kenneth Anthony 1899- *WhoMus 72*
Wright, Kenneth W 1913- *ConAmC*
Wright, Lammar 1907- *CmpEPM, WhoJazz 72*
Wright, Lammar, Sr. 1912-1973 *EncJzS 70*
Wright, Lawrence 1888-1964 *NewGrD 80, NotNAT B*
Wright, Leo Nash 1933- *EncJzS 70*
Wright, Leslie 1938- *WhoMus 72*
Wright, Lilian Cochrane 1944- *AmSCAP 80*
Wright, Lloyd, Jr. d1965 *NotNAT B*
Wright, Louis B 1899- *BiE&WWA, NotNAT*
Wright, Lyndie *DcPup*
Wright, M Searle *ConAmC*
Wright, Mack V d1965 *Film 1, -2, WhScrn 77*
Wright, Maggie *WhoHol A*
Wright, Marbeth *Film 2*
Wright, Marie d1949 *Film 2, NotNAT B, WhoHol B*
Wright, Martha *BiE&WWA, NotNAT*
Wright, Marvin M 1911- *AmSCAP 66, -80*
Wright, Mary Margaretta 1941- *IntWWM 77*
Wright, Maurice Willis 1949- *CpmDNM 76, -80, ConAmC, IntWWM 77, -80*
Wright, Nannie *Film 1*
Wright, Nathan Edward 1943- *BiDAmM*
Wright, Nicholas 1940- *WhoThe 77*
Wright, Norman Soreng 1905- *WhoMus 72*
Wright, Patrick *WhoHol A*
Wright, Peter 1926- *CnOxB, DancEn 78*
Wright, Rayburn 1922- *AmSCAP 80, ConAmC*
Wright, Rebecca 1947- *CnOxB*
Wright, Richard 1908-1960 *BlkAmP, DrBlPA, MorBAP, NotNAT A, -B, PlP&P[port]*
Wright, Robert 1911- *BiE&WWA*
Wright, Robert Craig 1914- *AmPS, AmSCAP 66, -80, BestMus, BiE&WWA, CmpEPM, EncMT, NewCBMT, NotNAT, PopAmC SUP[port]*
Wright, Rosemarie 1932- *IntWWM 77, -80, WhoMus 72*
Wright, Rowland W M 1914- *IntMPA 77, -75, -76, -78, -79, -80*
Wright, Ruby 1939- *BiDAmM*
Wright, Senator 1923- *EncJzS 70*
Wright, Shearad Hannibal 1910- *AmSCAP 80*
Wright, Stephen *WhoHol A*
Wright, Syreeta *AmSCAP 80*
Wright, Tenny *Film 2*
Wright, Teresa *MotPP, PlP&P[port]*
Wright, Teresa 1918- *BiE&WWA, FilmEn, FilmgC, ForYSC, HalFC 80[port], HolP 40[port], IntMPA 79, -80, MovMk, NotNAT, WhoHol A, WhoThe 72, -77*
Wright, Teresa 1919- *BiDFilm, -81, IntMPA 77, -75, -76, -78, WorEFlm*
Wright, Mrs. Theodore d1922 *NotNAT B, WhThe*
Wright, Thomas 1763-1829 *NewGrD 80*
Wright, Thomas Gordon 1929- *IntWWM 77, -80*
Wright, Tony 1925- *FilmgC, HalFC 80, IlWWBF[port], IntMPA 77, -75, -76, -78, -79, -80, WhoHol A*

Wright, Walter Edward 1911- *WhoMus 72*
Wright, Wayne Paul 1936- *IntWWM 77, -80*
Wright, Will 1891-1962 *ForYSC, HolCA[port], WhScrn 74, -77, WhoHol B*
Wright, Will 1894-1962 *FilmgC, HalFC 80, NotNAT B, Vers A[port]*
Wright, William 1912-1949 *ForYSC, WhScrn 74, -77, WhoHol B*
Wright, William George Currie 1936- *WhoMus 72*
Wright, William H 1902- *IntMPA 77, -75, -76, -78, -79, -80*
Wright And Forrest *BestMus*
Wrightman, Eric d1968 *WhoHol B*
Wrightsman, Stan 1910-1975 *CmpEPM, EncJzS 70*
Wrightsman, Stanley 1910-1975 *EncJzS 70*
Wrightson, Earl *CmpEPM*
Wrightson, Earl 1916- *BiDAmM*
Wrightson, Herbert James 1869-1949 *Baker 78*
Wrigley, Ben *WhoHol A*
Wrixon, Maris 1917- *ForYSC, HalFC 80, WhoHol A*
Wroblewski, Jan 1936- *EncJzS 70*
Wroblewski, Ptaszyn 1936- *EncJzS 70*
Wronowicz, Maciej *NewGrD 80*
Wronowicz, Matthia *NewGrD 80*
Wronski, Adam 1850?-1915 *NewGrD 80*
Wronski, Tadeusz 1915- *IntWWM 77, -80*
Wrubel, Allie 1905-1973 *AmSCAP 66, -80, BiDAmM, CmpEPM, Sw&Ld C*
Wrye, Donald *NewYTET*
Wrzaskala, Ryszard Jozef 1932- *IntWWM 77*
Wu, Enloc Ruth 1946- *IntWWM 77, -80, WhoMus 72*
Wu, Honorable 1903-1945 *WhScrn 74, -77, WhoHol B*
Wu, William 1935- *WhoOp 76*
Wuensch, Gerhard 1925- *Baker 78, IntWWM 80*
Wuerst, Richard 1824-1881 *Baker 78*
Wuest, Ida 1884-1958 *Film 2, WhScrn 74, -77, WhoHol B*
Wuhrer, Friedrich Anton Franz 1900-1975 *IntWWM 77, -80, NewGrD 80, WhoMus 72*
Wuhrer, Ully 1940- *CnOxB*
Wulf, Fred *Film 1*
Wulf, Jan 1735-1807 *NewGrD 80*
Wulfstan Of Winchester *NewGrD 80*
Wullner, Franz 1832-1902 *Baker 78, NewGrD 80*
Wullner, Ludwig 1858-1938 *Baker 78, NewGrD 80*
Wulstan, David 1937- *IntWWM 77, -80*
Wummer, John 1899-1977 *NewGrD 80*
Wunderer, Alexander 1877-1955 *Baker 78*
Wunderle, Carol Murphy 1943- *IntWWM 77*
Wunderlee, Frank 1875-1925 *Film 1, -2, WhScrn 74, -77, WhoHol B*
Wunderlich, Fritz d1966 *WhoMus 72*
Wunderlich, Fritz 1930-1966 *NewGrD 80*
Wunderlich, Fritz 1931-1966 *CmOp*
Wunderlich, Hans Joachim 1918- *WhoMus 72*
Wunderlich, Heinz 1919- *NewGrD 80, WhoMus 72*
Wunderlich, Jean-Georges 1755?-1819 *NewGrD 80*
Wunderlich, Johann Georg 1755?-1819 *NewGrD 80*
Wunderlich, Renner *WomWMM B*
Wunderlick, Jean-Georges 1755?-1819 *NewGrD 80*
Wunderlick, Johann Georg 1755?-1819 *NewGrD 80*
Wunsch, Hermann 1884-1954 *Baker 78*
Wunsch, Ilse Gerda 1911- *ConAmC*
Wunsch, Robert J *IntMPA 80*
Wunsch, Walther 1908- *Baker 78*
Wunsche, Konrad 1920- *CroCD*
Wuolijoki, Hella 1886-1954 *CroCD, EncWT*
Wuorinen, Charles 1938- *Baker 78, BiDAmM, BnBkM 80, CpmDNM 72, -73, ConAmC, DcCM, IntWWM 77, -80, NewGrD 80*
Wuorio, Eva-Lis 1918- *CreCan 1*
Wurfel, Vaclav Vilem 1790-1832 *NewGrD 80*
Wurfel, Wilhelm 1790-1832 *Baker 78*
Wurker, Johann *NewGrD 80*
Wurlitzer, Farny Reginald 1883-1972 *NewGrD 80*
Wurlitzer, Franz Rudolph 1831-1914 *NewGrD 80*
Wurlitzer, Howard Eugene 1871-1928 *NewGrD 80*
Wurlitzer, Rembert 1904-1963 *NewGrD 80*
Wurlitzer, Rudolph Henry 1873-1948 *Baker 78, NewGrD 80*
Wurm, Marie 1860-1938 *Baker 78, OxMus*
Wurman, Hans G 1922- *AmSCAP 80*
Wurmser, Frederic Robert Leopold *NewGrD 80*
Wurtzel, Sol M 1881-1958 *FilmEn*
Wurz, Anton 1903- *Baker 78, IntWWM 77, -80*
Wurz, Richard 1885-1965 *Baker 78, NewGrD 80*
Wurzburc, Konrad Von *NewGrD 80*
Wurzburg, Konrad Von *NewGrD 80*
Wurzel, G Friedrich *NewGrD 80*
Wurzl, Eberhard 1915- *IntWWM 77, -80*
Wussler, Robert *NewYTET*
Wust, Balthasar 1630-1704 *NewGrD 80*
Wust, Ida *Film 2*
Wust, Paul 1470?-1540? *NewGrD 80*
Wust, Paulus 1470?-1540? *NewGrD 80*
Wust, Philipp 1894-1975 *Baker 78*
Wust, Wolfgang Karl 1946- *IntWWM 77*
Wustemann, Karl 1929- *WhoOp 76*
Wusthoff, Klaus 1922- *WhoMus 72*
Wustmann, Rudolf 1872-1916 *Baker 78*
Wyands, Richard 1928- *EncJzS 70*
Wyatt, Agnes d1932 *NotNAT B*
Wyatt, Carol 1943- *WhoOp 76*
Wyatt, Doreen Marjorie 1936- *WhoMus 72*
Wyatt, Euphemia VanRensselaer 1884- *BiE&WWA*
Wyatt, Eustace 1882-1944 *WhScrn 77*
Wyatt, Frank, Jr. 1890-1933 *NotNAT B*
Wyatt, Frank Gunning 1851-1926 *WhThe*
Wyatt, Frank Gunning 1852-1926 *NotNAT B*
Wyatt, Jane *BiE&WWA, MotPP, WhoHol A*
Wyatt, Jane 1911- *FilmEn*
Wyatt, Jane 1912- *FilmgC, HalFC 80, HolP 30[port], MovMk, NotNAT, ThFT[port], WhThe, WhoThe 72*
Wyatt, Jane 1913- *ForYSC[port], IntMPA 77, -75, -76, -78, -79, -80*
Wyatt, Robert *IlEncR*
Wyble, Jimmy 1922- *EncJzS 70*
Wycherley, Margaret 1884?-1956 *PlP&P*
Wycherley, William 1640-1716 *CnThe, EncWT, Ent[port], McGEWD[port], NotNAT A, -B, OxThe, PlP&P[port], REnWD[port]*
Wycherly, Margaret d1956 *MotPP, WhoHol B*
Wycherly, Margaret 1881-1956 *FilmEn, Film 2, FilmgC, ForYSC, HalFC 80, NotNAT B, WhScrn 74, -77*
Wycherly, Margaret 1882-1956 *Vers A[port]*
Wycherly, Margaret 1884-1956 *WhThe*
Wyckham, John 1926- *WhoThe 72, -77*
Wyckoff, Bonnie 1945- *CnOxB*
Wyckoff, Evelyn 1917- *WhThe, WhoThe 72*
Wyckoff, Lou Ann *IntWWM 77, -80, WhoOp 76*
Wycombe, W De *NewGrD 80*
Wydow, Robert 1450?-1505 *NewGrD 80*
Wye, Trevor Dudley Kingsley 1935- *WhoMus 72*
Wyenn, Than *ForYSC, WhoHol A*
Wyers, Jan G 1888- *CreCan 2*
Wyes, William d1903 *NotNAT B*
Wyeth, Ann 1915- *ConAmC*
Wyeth, John 1770-1858 *BiDAmM, NewGrD 80*
Wyeth, Katya *WhoHol A*
Wyeth, Sandy Brown *WhoHol A*
Wyk, Arnold Van 1916- *Baker 78, NewGrD 80*
Wyke, Byam d1944 *NotNAT B*
Wykes, Audrey Monica 1920- *WhoMus 72*
Wykes, Louis Jane 1921- *IntWWM 77*
Wykes, Monica 1920- *IntWWM 77*
Wykes, Robert A 1926- *AmSCAP 66, -80, Baker 78, ConAmC*
Wylde, Harold Eustace 1888- *WhoMus 72*
Wylde, Henry 1822-1890 *Baker 78, NewGrD 80*
Wylde, John *NewGrD 80*
Wyldebore, John *NewGrD 80*
Wylder, Robert C 1921- *ConAmTC*
Wyle, Florence 1881-1968 *CreCan 2*
Wyle, George 1916- *AmSCAP 66, -80*
Wyler, Gretchen 1932- *BiE&WWA, NotNAT, WhoHol A*
Wyler, Richard 1934- *FilmgC, HalFC 80, WhoHol A*
Wyler, Susan *WhoHol A*
Wyler, William 1902- *AmFD, BiDFilm, -81, CmMov, DcFM, FilmEn, FilmgC, HalFC 80, IntMPA 77, -75, -76, -78, -79, -80, MovMk[port], OxFilm, TwYS A, WorEFlm*
Wylie, Austin 1893?- *BgBands 74, CmpEPM*
Wylie, Constance *Film 2*
Wylie, Frank *WhoHol A*
Wylie, James d1941 *NotNAT B*
Wylie, Julian 1878-1934 *NotNAT B, OxThe, WhThe*
Wylie, Lauri 1880- *WhThe*
Wylie, Max d1975 *NewYTET*
Wylie, Ruth Shaw 1916- *AmSCAP 80, ConAmC, IntWWM 77, -80*
Wylkynson, Robert *NewGrD 80*
Wyllie, Meg *WhoHol A*
Wyman *PupTheA*
Wyman, Addison P 1832-1872 *Baker 78*
Wyman, Dann Coriat 1923- *CpmDNM 76, ConAmC, IntWWM 77, -80*
Wyman, Eleanore 1914-1940 *WhScrn 74, -77*
Wyman, Jane 1914- *BiDFilm, -81, CmMov, FilmEn, FilmgC, ForYSC, HalFC 80, IntMPA 77, -75, -76, -78, -79, -80, MotPP, MovMk[port], ThFT[port], WhoHol A, WorEFlm[port]*
Wyman, Lilla Viles 1859-1944 *DancEn 78*
Wymark, Olwen *ConDr 73, -77*
Wymark, Patrick 1926-1970 *FilmgC, HalFC 80, IlWWBF, WhScrn 74, -77, WhThe, WhoHol B*
Wymore, Patrice *IntMPA 77, -75, -76, -78, -79, -80, MotPP*
Wymore, Patrice 1926- *FilmEn, FilmgC, HalFC 80, WhoHol A*
Wymore, Patrice 1927- *ForYSC*
Wyn, Marjery 1909- *WhThe*
Wynant, Federic 1572?-1597? *NewGrD 80*
Wynant, Federico 1572?-1597? *NewGrD 80*
Wynant, Federicus 1572?-1597? *NewGrD 80*
Wynant, H M *ForYSC, WhoHol A*
Wynants, Federic 1572?-1597? *NewGrD 80*
Wynants, Federico 1572?-1597? *NewGrD 80*
Wynants, Federicus 1572?-1597? *NewGrD 80*
Wynard, Diana 1906-1964 *WhScrn 74, -77*
Wyndham, Sir Charles 1837-1919 *NotNAT A, -B, OxThe, WhThe*
Wyndham, Dennis 1887- *WhThe*
Wyndham, Fred W d1930 *NotNAT B*
Wyndham, Gwen *WhThe*
Wyndham, Howard 1865-1947 *NotNAT B, OxThe, WhThe*
Wyndham, John 1903-1969 *FilmgC, HalFC 80, WhoHrs 80*
Wyndham, Louise Isabella d1942 *NotNAT B*
Wyndham, Mary Moore 1862-1931 *OxThe*
Wyndham, Olive 1886- *WhThe*
Wyndham, Poppy 189-?-1928 *Film 1, -2, IlWWBF*
Wyndham, R H d1894 *NotNAT B*
Wyner, Yehudi 1929- *Baker 78, BnBkM 80, ConAmC, DcCM, IntWWM 77, -80, NewGrD 80*
Wynette, Tammy 1942- *BiDAmM, CounME 74[port], -74A, EncFCWM 69, IlEncCM[port], IlEncR, RkOn 2[port]*
Wyngaerde, Antonius *NewGrD 80*
Wyngarde, Peter *WhoHol A, WhoHrs 80, WhoThe 77*
Wynkoop, Christopher *WhoHol A*
Wynn, Albert 1907-1975 *BiDAmM, CmpEPM, NewOrJ, WhoJazz 72*
Wynn, Bessie 1876-1968 *AmPS B, WhScrn 77*
Wynn, Charles *AmSCAP 80*
Wynn, Doris 1910-1925 *WhScrn 74, -77, WhoHol B*
Wynn, Ed *PupTheA*
Wynn, Ed 1886-1966 *AmSCAP 66, -80, BiE&WWA, EncMT, Ent, FamA&A[port], FilmEn, Film 2, FilmgC, Funs[port], HalFC 80[port], JoeFr[port],*

MotPP, MovMk[port], NewYTET, NotNAT B, WhScrn 74, –77, WhThe, WhoHol B
Wynn, Ed 1887-1966 *ForYSC*
Wynn, Keenan 1916- *BiE&WWA, FilmEn, FilmgC, ForYSC, HalFC 80, IntMPA 77, –75, –76, –78, –79, –80, MGM[port], MotPP, MovMk, NotNAT A, WhoHol A*
Wynn, Mae *WhoHol A*
Wynn, May *MotPP*
Wynn, May 1930- *ForYSC, IntMPA 77, –75, –76, –78, –79, –80*
Wynn, May 1931- *FilmgC, HalFC 80*
Wynn, Nan 1916-1971 *WhScrn 74, –77, WhoHol B*
Wynn, Nan 1918?- *CmpEPM*
Wynn, Ned *WhoHol A*
Wynn, Tom 1902- *WhoHol A*
Wynn, Tracy Keenan *HalFC 80, IntMPA 77, –76, –78, –79, –80, NewYTET*
Wynne, Bert 1890- *IlWWBF*
Wynne, David 1900- *IntWWM 80, NewGrD 80, WhoMus 72*
Wynne, Donald 1918- *IntMPA 77, –75, –76, –78, –79, –80*
Wynne, Owen Henry 1926- *WhoMus 72*
Wynne, Wish 1882-1931 *NotNAT B, WhThe*
Wynslate, Richard d1572 *NewGrD 80*
Wynter, Dana *IntMPA 75, –76, –78, –79, –80*
Wynter, Dana 1929- *FilmAG WE*
Wynter, Dana 1930- *FilmEn, FilmgC, ForYSC, HalFC 80, IntMPA 77, MotPP, MovMk, WhoHol A*
Wynters, Charlotte *WhoHol A*
Wynyard, Diana 1906-1964 *EncWT, FilmAG WE, FilmEn, FilmgC, ForYSC, HalFC 80, MotPP, MovMk, NotNAT B, OxFilm, OxThe, ThFT[port], WhThe, WhoHol B*
Wynyard, John 1915- *WhoThe 72, –77*
Wyrick, Barbara 1950- *AmSCAP 80*
Wyschnegradsky, Ivan Alexandrovich 1893- *Baker 78, DcCM, NewGrD 80*
Wyse, John 1904- *WhoThe 72, –77*
Wysocki, Kasper Napoleon 1810-1850 *NewGrD 80*
Wysocki, Zdzislaw 1944- *IntWWM 80*
Wysoczanska, Jadwiga 1927- *WhoOp 76*
Wyspianski, Stanislav 1869-1907 *CnMD*
Wyspianski, Stanislaw 1869-1907 *CnThe, EncWT, Ent, McGEWD[port], ModWD, NotNAT B, OxThe, REnWD[port]*
Wyss, Niklaus 1936- *Baker 78*
Wyssenbach, Rudolf 1517?-1572? *NewGrD 80*
Wytall, Mrs. Russ *Film 2*
Wyton, Alec 1921- *AmSCAP 66, –80, ConAmC, IntWWM 77, –80, NewGrD 80, WhoMus 72*
Wyttenbach, Jurg 1935- *Baker 78, DcCM, IntWWM 77, –80, NewGrD 80*
Wyvell *NewGrD 80*
Wyzewa, Teodor De 1862-1917 *NewGrD 80*
Wyzewa, Theodore De 1862-1917 *Baker 78, NewGrD 80*

X

Xanrof, Leon 1867-1953 *Baker 78, WhThe*
Xenakis, Iannis 1922- *Baker 78, BnBkM 80, CnOxB, DcCM, IntWWM 77, -80, MusMk[port], NewGrD 80[port], WhoMus 72*
Xenophon *DcPup*
Xeres, Hurtado De *NewGrD 80*
Ximenez, Jose 1601?-1672 *NewGrD 80*
Ximenez, Roberto *DancEn 78[port]*
Xinda, Spyridon *NewGrD 80*
Xindas, Spyridon *NewGrD 80*
Xinta, Spyridon *NewGrD 80*
Xiques, Ed 1939- *EncJzS 70*
Xiques, Edward F, Jr. 1939- *EncJzS 70*
Xirgu, Margarita 1888-1969 *EncWT*
Xuares, Alonso 1630?-1696 *NewGrD 80*
Xyndas, Spyridon 1812?-1896 *Baker 78, NewGrD 80*
Xyntas, Spyridon 1812?-1896 *NewGrD 80*

Y

Yablans, Frank 1935- IntMPA 77, -75, -76, -78, -79, -80
Yablans, Irwin IntMPA 77, -76, -78, -79, -80
Yablochinka, Alexandra Alexandrovna 1868-1964 EncWT
Yablochkina, Alexandra Alexandrovna 1868-1964 NotNAT B, OxThe
Yablokoff, Bella Mysell 1903- AmSCAP 66, -80
Yablokoff, Herman 1903- AmSCAP 66, -80
Yablon, Marjorie Pearl 1947- AmSCAP 80
Yablonka, Marc Phillip 1950- AmSCAP 80
Yachigusa, Kaoru WhoHol A
Yachmi, Rohangis 1940- WhoOp 76
Yacich, Chris 1901-1967 AmSCAP 80
Yacobson, Leonid 1904- CnOxB, DancEn 78
Yaconelli, Frank 1898-1965 Film 2, ForYSC, WhScrn 77, WhoHol B
Yadykh, Pavel 1922- IntWWM 77, -80
Yaffee, Ben WhoHol A
Yaged, Sol 1922- CmpEPM, Conv 2[port], EncJzS 70
Yaged, Solomon 1922- EncJzS 70
Yahya Ibn 'Ali Ibn Yahya Ibn Abi Mansur NewGrD 80
Yakima Lee AmSCAP 80
Yakimenko, Fyodor Stepanovich NewGrD 80
Yakko, Sada d1946 WhThe
Yakolev, Yuri d1970 WhoHol B
Yakovlev, Alexei Semenovich 1773-1817 OxThe
Yakovlev, Leonid Georgiyevich 1858-1919 NewGrD 80
Yakovlev, Mikhail Lukyanovich 1798-1868 NewGrD 80
Yakovlev, Yasha 1912-1970 WhScrn 74, -77
Yakovleva, K Film 2
Yakovleva, S Film 2
Yakulov, Georgi Bogdanovich 1884-1928 EncWT
Yale, Charles H d1920 NotNAT B
Yalen, Paul Edward 1954- AmSCAP 80
Yama, Conrad WhoHol A
Yamada, Isuzu 1917- FilmEn, WorEFlm
Yamada, Kosaku 1886-1965 NewGrD 80
Yamada, Koscak 1886-1965 Baker 78, NewGrD 80
Yamaguchi, Hideo 1933- IntWWM 80
Yamaguchi, Shirley MotPP, WhoHol A
Yamaha, Torakusu 1851-1916 NewGrD 80
Yamaki, Kozaburo 1931- EncJzS 70
Yamamoto, Fujiko WhoHol A
Yamamoto, Kajiro 1902-1974 FilmEn, WhScrn 77
Yamamoto, Kei WhoHol A
Yamamoto, Satsuo 1910- DcFM, FilmEn
Yamamura, So 1910- DcFM, FilmEn, WhoHol A
Yamanaka, Sadao 1907-1938 DcFM
Yamashita, Stomu 1947- NewGrD 80
Yamashita, Tsutomu 1947- NewGrD 80
Yamashita, Yosuke 1942- EncJzS 70
Yamash'ta, Stomu 1947- Baker 78, IlEncR, IntWWM 77, -80, NewGrD 80
Yamash'ta, Tsutomu 1947- NewGrD 80
Yamazaki, Tatsuo 1904- IntMPA 77, -75, -76, -78, -79, -80
Yamin, Jaime 1913- AmSCAP 66, -80
Yamins, Nathan IntMPA 75, -76
Yammamoto, Togo Film 2
Yampol'sky, Abram Il'ich 1890-1956 NewGrD 80
Yampolsky, Izrail 1905-1976 Baker 78, NewGrD 80
Yan McGEWD[port]
Yanagita, Masako 1944- IntWWM 77, -80
Yanagiya, Kingoro d1972 WhScrn 77
Yanai, Moshe WhoHol A
Yancey, Estella 1896- BluesWW[port]
Yancey, James Edward 1894?-1951 NewGrD 80
Yancey, James Edward 1898-1951 BluesWW[port]
Yancey, Jimmy 1894-1951 BiDAmM, CmpEPM, IlEncJ, NewGrD 80, WhoJazz 72
Yancey, Thomas Leland 1932- AmSCAP 80
Yanchus, Judith 1939- IntWWM 77, -80
Yancich, Milan Michael 1921- AmSCAP 80, IntWWM 77, -80
Yancy, Emily 1939- DrBlPA, WhoHol A
Yancy, Marvin ConMuA 80B
Yancy, Melvin 1922- NewOrJ SUP[port]
Yaner, Milt 1911?- CmpEPM
Yaney, Skeets IlEncCM
Yang, C K WhoHol A
Yanguas, Antonio d1753 NewGrD 80
Yaniewicz, Felix NewGrD 80
Yankee, Pat 1929- BluesWW[port]
Yankelevich, Yury Isayevich 1909-1973 NewGrD 80
Yankey, James Adumli 1942- IntWWM 80
Yankey, James Adunli 1942- IntWWM 77
Yankoff, Ventsislav 1926- WhoMus 72
Yankowitz, Susan 1941- ConDr 73, -77, NatPD[port], NotNAT
Yanks, Byron NewGrD 80
Yannai, Yehuda 1937- DcCM
Yannatos, James D 1929- CpmDNM 77, -78, -80, ConAmC
Yannay, Yehuda 1937- Baker 78, ConAmC, NewGrD 80
Yanne, Jean 1933- FilmAG WE, FilmEn, WhoHol A
Yanni, Rossanna WhoHol A
Yannicosta, Melita Elisabeth 1928- IntWWM 77, -80
Yannis, Michael 1922- WhThe
Yannopoulos, Dino WhoOp 76
Yannuzzi, William A 1933- WhoOp 76
Yano, Ben PupTheA
Yanshin, Mikhail Mikhailovich 1902- OxThe
Yantis, David M 1933- AmSCAP 80
Ya'qub Of Edessa d708 NewGrD 80
Yarborough, Barton 1900-1951 ForYSC, WhScrn 74, -77, WhoHol B
Yarborough, Bertram d1962 NotNAT B
Yarborough, Sara 1950?- CnOxB
Yarborough, Sara 1951- DrBlPA
Yarbrough, Camille WhoHol A
Yarbrough, Glenn 1930- AmSCAP 66, -80, BiDAmM, EncFCWM 69, RkOn 2[port]
Yarbrough, Harold Leroy 1934- AmSCAP 80
Yarbrough, Jean 1900- FilmEn, FilmgC, HalFC 80, IntMPA 77, -75, -76, -78, WhoHrs 80
Yardbirds, The ConMuA 80A, IlEncR, RkOn 2[port]
Yarde, Margaret 1878-1944 Film 2, NotNAT B, WhScrn 74, -77, WhThe, WhoHol B
Yarden, Elie 1923- ConAmC
Yardley, William d1900 NotNAT B
Yardumian, Richard 1917- AmSCAP 66, -80, Baker 78, CpmDNM 78, -79, ConAmC, NewGrD 80
Yarema, Neil NatPD[port]
Yarnall, Celeste WhoHol A
Yarnell, Bruce 1938-1973 WhScrn 77, WhoHol B
Yarnell, Jules ConMuA 80B
Yarnold, Benjamin d1787 BiDAmM
Yaron, Izhar 1910- IntWWM 77, -80
Yarrick, Joseph PupTheA
Yarrow, Duncan 1884- WhThe
Yarrow, Peter 1938- AmSCAP 66, -80, BiDAmM, EncFCWM 69, WhoHol A
Yarustovsky, Boris Mikhaylovich 1911-1978 Baker 78, NewGrD 80
Yarwood, A Walter Hawley CreCan 2
Yarwood, Walter 1917- CreCan 2
Yasar Kemal 1922- REnWD[port]
Yashiro, Akio 1929-1976 Baker 78, NewGrD 80
Yashvili NewGrD 80
Yashvili, Irine Luabsarbovna 1942- NewGrD 80
Yashvili, Marine Luabsarbovna 1932- NewGrD 80
Yashvili, Nana Luabsarbovna 1949- NewGrD 80
Yasser, Joseph 1893- Baker 78, IntWWM 77, -80, NewGrD 80
Yassin, Ismail 1912-1972 WhScrn 77
Yassine, Ismali d1972 WhoHol B
Yastrebitsky, A Film 2
Yastrebitsky, K Film 2
Yasui, Byron K 1940- CpmDNM 75, ConAmC
Yates PlP&P
Yates, Charles Dwight 1936- IntWWM 77
Yates, Eddy AmSCAP 80
Yates, Edmund 1832-1894 NotNAT B, OxThe
Yates, Mrs. Frederick d1860 NotNAT B
Yates, Frederick Henry 1795-1842 NotNAT B, OxThe
Yates, George Worthing WhoHrs 80
Yates, Herbert J 1880-1966 FilmEn, FilmgC, HalFC 80, WhoHrs 80, WorEFlm
Yates, Leo WhoHol A
Yates, Mary Ann Graham 1728-1787 NotNAT B, OxThe
Yates, Peter 1929- BiDFilm, -81, FilmEn, FilmgC, HalFC 80, IlWWBF, IntMPA 77, -75, -76, -78, -79, -80, MovMk[port], OxFilm, WorEFlm

Yates, Peter B 1909-1976 Baker 78
Yates, Richard 1706-1796 NotNAT B, OxThe
Yates, Ronald Lee 1947- AmSCAP 80, CpmDNM 78, -79, -80, ConAmC
Yates, Ted d1967 NewYTET
Yates, Theodosia d1904 NotNAT B
Yatsuhashi Kengyo 1614-1685 NewGrD 80
Yauger, Margaret WhoOp 76
Yavelow, Christopher Johnson 1950- ConAmC
Yavoroska, Lydia 1874-1921 NotNAT B
Yavorska, Lydia 1874-1921 WhThe
Yavorsky, Boleslav Leopol'dovich 1877-1942 Baker 78, NewGrD 80
Yawitz, Paul A 1905- IntMPA 77, -75, -76, -78, -79, -80
Yazbeck, Peter 1930- IntWWM 77
Yazvinsky, Jan 1892- CnOxB, DancEn 78
Ybarra, Ramon 1930- IntWWM 77, -80
Ybarra, Rocky 1900-1965 WhScrn 74, -77
Ybarra, Ventura Rocky 1900-1965 WhoHol B
Ycaert, Bernar NewGrD 80
Ycaert, Bernhard NewGrD 80
Ycart, Bernar NewGrD 80
Ycart, Bernhard NewGrD 80
Ydalgo, Juan NewGrD 80
Yeager, Bunny WomWMM B
Yeager, Irene Film 2
Yeamans, Annie 1835-1912 NotNAT B, WhThe
Yeamans, Jennie 1862-1906 NotNAT B
Yeamans, Lydia AmPS B
Yearsley, Claude Blakesley 1885-1961 NotNAT B, WhThe
Yearsley, Ralph 1897-1928 Film 2, WhScrn 74, -77, WhoHol B
Yeaton, Kelly 1911- BiE&WWA, NotNAT
Yeats, Jack Butler 1871-1957 CnMD
Yeats, Murray F 1910-1975 WhScrn 77, WhoHol C
Yeats, William Butler 1865-1939 CnMD, CnThe, EncWT, Ent, McGEWD, ModWD, NewEOp 71, NotNAT A, -B, OxThe, PlP&P[port], REnWD[port], WhThe
Yeaworth, Irvin Shortess, Jr. WhoHrs 80, WorEFlm
Yeazel, Robert Devon 1946- AmSCAP 80
Yeddeau, David Hugh 1918- CreCan 1
Yeend, Frances WhoMus 72
Yefremov, Oleg Nikolayevich 1927- EncWT
Yefros, Anatoly Vassilyevich 1925- EncWT
Yegorov, Vladimir Yevgenevich 1878- EncWT
Yehuda Ha-Levi d1149 NewGrD 80
Yelin, Edward M 1928- AmSCAP 66, -80
Yelina, Y Film 2
Yellen, Barry B 1935- IntMPA 75, -76
Yellen, Howard L 1928- IntMPA 75, -76
Yellen, Jack 1892- AmPS, AmSCAP 66, -80, BiDAmM, BiE&WWA, CmpEPM, NewCBMT, NotNAT, Sw&Ld C
Yellen, Salem 1906- IntMPA 75, -76
Yellin, Bob EncFCWM 69
Yellin, Gleb 1901- ConAmC A
Yellin, Gleb 1903- AmSCAP 66
Yellin, Pete 1941- EncJzS 70
Yellin, Peter 1941- EncJzS 70
Yellin, Thelma 1895-1959 NewGrD 80
Yellin, Victor 1924- NewGrD 80
Yellow Balloon RkOn 2A
Yellow Payges BiDAmM
Yelverton, Vera 1917- IntWWM 77, -80
Yen, Mou-Che 1900?- DcFM
Yenakieva, Juliana 1918?- DancEn 78
Yenne, Vernon Lee 1938- IntWWM 77
Yensen, Ula 1940-1959 WhScrn 74, -77
Yeoman, George 1869-1936 WhScrn 74, -77
Yeomans, Mary WomWMM
Yepes, Narciso 1927- BnBkM 80, IntWWM 77, -80, NewGrD 80, WhoMus 72
Yepes DeAcevedo, Fabio 1937- IntWWM 77, -80
Yerba Buena Band BiDAmM
Yermolayev, Alexei Nicolaievich 1910-1975 CnOxB, DancEn 78
Yermolov, Pyotr 1887-1953 DcFM
Yermolova, Maria Nikolaievna 1853-1928 NotNAT B, OxThe
Yermolova, Maria Nikolayevna 1853-1928 EncWT
Yerrard, Charles Film 2
Yes ConMuA 80A, IlEncR, RkOn 2[port]
Yetnikoff, Walter ConMuA 80B
Yevdokimov, Gleb 1923- CnOxB, DancEn 78
Yevreinov, Nikolai Nikolaevich 1879-1953 ModWD, OxThe
Yevreinov, Nikolai Nikolayevich 1879-1953 EncWT
Yevreinov, Nikolay Nikolayevich 1879-1953 McGEWD[port]
Yevteyeva, Yelena Victorovna 1947- CnOxB
Yffer, Louis Alexander 1925- IntWWM 77, -80
Yin, Cheng-Tsung 1941- NewGrD 80
Yip, William d1968 WhScrn 77
Yllanes, Johannes De NewGrD 80
Yllianis, Johannes NewGrD 80
Ylvisaker, John Carl 1937- AmSCAP 80
Yniguez, Richard WhoHol A
Yockey, Joann Vivian WhoOp 76
Yocom, Rachael Dunaven 1916- DancEn 78
Yoder, Dorinne Lou 1936- IntWWM 77, -80
Yoder, Paul V 1908- AmSCAP 66, -80, ConAmC
Yoell, Larry 1898- AmSCAP 66, -80
Yoffe, Shlomo 1909- Baker 78, IntWWM 77, -80
Yohe, May 1869-1938 NotNAT B, WhThe
Yokel, Alex 1889-1947 NotNAT B
Yokel, Alexander 1887-1947 WhThe
Yolen, Will H NatPD[port]
Yoltz, Greta FilmEn
Yoltz, Gretel Film 2
Yon, Pietro Alessandro 1886-1943 AmSCAP 66, -80, Baker 78, BiDAmM, ConAmC
Yonemoto, Tadashi 1908- IntMPA 75, -76
Yong, Soo WhoHol A
Yonge, Nicholas d1619 Baker 78, NewGrD 80, OxMus
Yordan, Philip IntMPA 77, -75, -76, -78, -79, -80
Yordan, Philip 1912?- DcFM
Yordan, Philip 1913?- CmMov, FilmEn, FilmgC, HalFC 80, OxFilm, WorEFlm
Yordan, Philip 1914?- NotNAT
Yordan, Phillip 1914?- BiE&WWA
Yore, Barbara PupTheA
Yoresh, Abigail WomWMM
Yorgeson, Yogy AmPS A
Yorick DcPup
York, David Stanley 1920- ConAmC
York, Dick 1928- FilmgC, ForYSC, HalFC 80, IntMPA 77, -75, -76, -78, -79, -80, MotPP, WhoHol A
York, Donald Griffith 1947- AmSCAP 80
York, Duke 1902-1952 WhScrn 74, -77, WhoHol B, WhoHrs 80
York, Elizabeth d1969 WhoHol B
York, Francine WhoHol A
York, Francine 1935?- WhoHrs 80
York, Francis Lodowick 1861-1955 Baker 78
York, Frank 1926- AmSCAP 66, -80
York, Gerald WhoHol A
York, Harley C 1944- AmSCAP 80
York, Helen Clute PupTheA
York, Jay WhoHol A
York, Jeff 1912- ForYSC, WhoHol A
York, John 1949- IntWWM 80
York, Leonard WhoHol A
York, Michael 1941- ForYSC
York, Michael 1942- FilmAG WE, FilmEn, FilmgC, HalFC 80, IlWWBF[port], IntMPA 77, -75, -76, -78, -79, -80, MotPP, MovMk[port], OxFilm, WhoHol A, WhoHrs 80[port]
York, Powell Film 2
York, Richard 1930- BiE&WWA
York, Sarah Emily Waldo 1819-1851 BiDAmM
York, Susannah MotPP, WhoHol A
York, Susannah 1939- FilmAG WE[port]
York, Susannah 1941- BiDFilm, -81, FilmEn, IlWWBF[port], MovMk[port], OxFilm
York, Susannah 1942- FilmgC, ForYSC, HalFC 80, IntMPA 77, -75, -76, -78, -79, -80, WhoHrs 80
York, Tony WhoHol A
York, W Allen WhoHol A
York, Walter Wynn 1914- ConAmC
Yorke, Alice AmPS B
Yorke, Augustus d1939 NotNAT B, WhThe
Yorke, Carol 1929-1967 WhScrn 74, -77, WhoHol B
Yorke, Colin 1941- WhoMus 72
Yorke, Dallas d1963 NotNAT B
Yorke, Edith 1872-1934 Film 2, ForYSC, TwYS, WhScrn 77
Yorke, Emerson IntMPA 75, -76
Yorke, Harold Emerson 1893-1971 AmSCAP 80
Yorke, Oswald d1943 Film 2, NotNAT B, WhScrn 77, WhThe, WhoHol B
Yorke Trotter, Thomas Henry 1854-1934 NewGrD 80
Yorkin, Bud 1926- FilmEn, FilmgC, HalFC 80, IntMPA 77, -75, -76, -78, -79, -80, MovMk[port], NewYTET
Yorkin, Bud 1929- WorEFlm
Yorkin, David Michael 1962- AmSCAP 80
Yorkney, John C 1871-1941 WhScrn 74, -77
Yorston, David WhoHol A
Yoshida, Bungoro 1869-1962 DcPup
Yoshida, Eiza 1872-1945 DcPup
Yoshida, Tsunezo 1872-1957 NewGrD 80
Yoshida, Yoshishige 1933- FilmEn
Yoshimura, Jitsuko WhoHol A
Yoshimura, Kimisaburo 1911- DcFM, OxFilm
Yoshimura, Kozaburo 1911- FilmEn, WorEFlm
Yoshinaga, Alan S 1952- AmSCAP 80
Yoshino, Riechel Morikazu 1941- IntWWM 77
Yoshioka, Emmett Gene 1944- CpmDNM 72, ConAmC
Yoshisaka, Kiyoji 1908- IntMPA 77, -75, -76, -78, -79, -80
Yoshiwara, Tomaki Film 2
Yossifov, Alexander 1940- Baker 78, NewGrD 80
Yost, Barbara ConAmTC
Yost, Dennis & The Classics IV RkOn 2[port]
Yost, Gaylord 1888-1958 Baker 78
Yost, Herbert A 1880-1945 Film 1, NotNAT B, WhScrn 74, -77, WhoHol B
Yost, Maurice PupTheA
Yost, Michel 1754-1786 Baker 78
Yost, Oliver 1924- IntWWM 77, -80
Yost, Thomas W PupTheA
Youdin, Mikhail 1893-1948 Baker 78
Youll, Henry Baker 78, NewGrD 80, OxMus
Youll, Jim d1962 NotNAT B
Youmans, Vincent d1946 WhThe
Youmans, Vincent 1898-1946 AmPS, AmSCAP 66, -80, Baker 78, BestMus, BiDAmM, CmpEPM, ConAmC, EncMT, EncWT, HalFC 80, NewCBMT, NewGrD 80, NotNAT B, PopAmC[port], PopAmC SUP, Sw&Ld C
Youmans, Vincent 1899-1946 PlP&P, -A[port]
Young NewGrD 80
Young, A S 1924- DrBlPA
Young, Alan 1919- FilmEn, FilmgC, ForYSC, HalFC 80, IntMPA 77, -75, -76, -78, -79, -80, JoeFr, WhoHol A, WhoHrs 80
Young, Alexander IntWWM 77, -80, WhoMus 72
Young, Alexander 1920- NewGrD 80, WhoOp 76
Young, Allen 1918- ConAmTC
Young, Anne Lloyd 1936- IntWWM 77, -80
Young, Anthony 1685?- Baker 78, NewGrD 80
Young, Art Film 2
Young, Arthur 1898-1959 FilmgC, HalFC 80, NotNAT B, WhScrn 74, -77, WhThe, WhoHol B
Young, Audrey WhoHol A
Young, Aurelia Norris 1915- IntWWM 77
Young, Austin 1885-1954 NewOrJ[port]
Young, Barbara Marie 1931- AmSCAP 80
Young, Barney 1911- AmSCAP 66
Young, Barry RkOn 2A
Young, Bertram Alfred 1912- WhoThe 77
Young, Bill ConMuA 80B
Young, Buck WhoHol A
Young, Buddy 1935- IntMPA 77, -75, -76, -78, -79, -80
Young, Bull d1913 WhScrn 77
Young, Burt IntMPA 79, -80, WhoHol A
Young, Captain Jack d1966 WhScrn 77
Young, Carleton d1971 WhoHol B
Young, Carleton 1906-1971 FilmgC, HalFC 80
Young, Carleton 1907-1971 FilmEn,

WhScrn 74, -77
Young, Carleton 1908?- *ForYSC*
Young, Carlton Raymond 1926- *AmSCAP 80*
Young, Carroll 1908- *IntMPA 77, -75, -76, -78, -79, -80*
Young, Cecilia *OxMus*
Young, Cecilia 1710?-1789 *Baker 78*
Young, Cecilia 1711-1789 *NewGrD 80*
Young, Charles *NewGrD 80*
Young, Charles d1874 *NotNAT B, OxThe*
Young, Sir Charles 1839-1887 *NotNAT B*
Young, Charles Chesley 1951- *AmSCAP 66, -80*
Young, Charles Mayne 1777-1856 *NotNAT A, -B, OxThe*
Young, Cheryl Lesley 1949- *AmSCAP 66, -80*
Young, Chesley Virginia 1919- *AmSCAP 66, -80*
Young, Chow *Film 2*
Young, Clara Kimball 1890-1960 *FilmEn, Film 1, -2, FilmgC, HalFC 80, MotPP, MovMk, NotNAT B, OxFilm, WhScrn 74, -77, WhoHol B, WomWMM*
Young, Clara Kimball 1891-1960 *ForYSC*
Young, Clara Kimball 1900-1960 *TwYS*
Young, Clarence, III *BlkAmP, MorBAP*
Young, Clifton 1917-1951 *WhScrn 74, -77, WhoHol B*
Young, Clint *WhoHol A*
Young, Collier 1908- *FilmgC, HalFC 80, NewYTET, WomWMM*
Young, Dalene *NatPD[port]*
Young, Dan *IIWWBF*
Young, David *WhoHol A*
Young, De De *WhoHol A*
Young, Derek 1929- *WhoMus 72*
Young, Desmond 1892-1966 *WhScrn 77, WhoHol B*
Young, Donald James 1948- *CpmDNM 78, -79*
Young, Douglas 1947- *Baker 78, NewGrD 80*
Young, Edgar Berryhill 1908- *BiE&WWA, NotNAT*
Young, Elizabeth *NewGrD 80*
Young, Eric *WhoHol A*
Young, Esther *NewGrD 80*
Young, Eugene 1919- *EncJzS 70, IlEncJ*
Young, Evelyn Marie 1928- *BlkWAB[port]*
Young, F A 1902- *OxFilm*
Young, Faron *WhoHol A*
Young, Faron 1925- *CounME 74A*
Young, Faron 1932- *BiDAmM, CounME 74[port], EncFCWM 69, IlEncCM[port], RkOn*
Young, Felicity 1937- *WhoMus 72*
Young, Florence d1920 *NotNAT B*
Young, Freddie 1902- *IntMPA 77, -75, -76, -78, -79, -80*
Young, Frederick A 1902- *FilmEn, FilmgC, HalFC 80, WorEFlm*
Young, Frederick John 1931- *IntWWM 77, -80*
Young, Gayle 1938?- *CnOxB*
Young, Georgiana *WhoHol A*
Young, Gig *MotPP, WhoHol A*
Young, Gig 1913-1978 *FilmEn, FilmgC, HalFC 80, HolP 40[port]*
Young, Gig 1915- *ForYSC*
Young, Gig 1917- *BiE&WWA, IntMPA 77, -76, -78, MovMk, WhoThe 72, -77*
Young, Gig 1943- *IntMPA 75*
Young, Gladys 1905-1975 *WhScrn 77*
Young, Gordon Ellsworth 1919- *AmSCAP 66, -80, ConAmC*
Young, Gregg Vance 1952- *AmSCAP 80*
Young, Harold 1897- *FilmEn, FilmgC, HalFC 80, IntMPA 77, -75, -76, -78, -79, -80, WhoHrs 80*
Young, Harriette *WhoHol A*
Young, Harry L 1910- *BiE&WWA, NotNAT*
Young, Heather *WhoHol A*
Young, Hester *NewGrD 80*
Young, Horace Alexander, III 1954- *AmSCAP 80*
Young, Howard Irving 1893- *WhThe*
Young, Howard L 1911- *BiE&WWA, NotNAT, WhThe*
Young, Ida 1891- *AmSCAP 66, -80*
Young, Irwin *IntMPA 77, -75, -76, -78, -79, -80*
Young, Isabella *NewGrD 80*
Young, Isabella d1791 *NewGrD 80*
Young, J Arthur d1943 *NotNAT B*
Young, J D *WhoHol A*
Young, Jack d1966 *WhScrn 77*
Young, James *Film 1*
Young, James 1878- *FilmEn, TwYS A*
Young, James Oliver 1912- *AmSCAP 66, -80, BiDAmM*
Young, James Osborne 1912- *EncJzS 70*
Young, James V *AmSCAP 80*
Young, Jane Corner 1916- *ConAmC*
Young, Janis *WhoHol A*
Young, Jeremy *WhoHol A*
Young, Jesse Colin *ConMuA 80A*
Young, Joan 1903- *WhoHol A, WhoThe 72, -77*
Young, Joe 1889-1939 *CmpEPM*
Young, Joe 1898-1946 *AmPS*
Young, John 1660?-1732? *NewGrD 80*
Young, John 1946- *IntWWM 80*
Young, John O 1918-1974 *BluesWW[port]*
Young, John Royal 1915- *Film 2*
Young, John Wray 1909- *BiE&WWA, NotNAT*
Young, Joseph *Film 2*
Young, Joseph 1889-1939 *AmSCAP 66, -80, BiDAmM, Sw&Ld C*
Young, Joseph 1927- *BluesWW[port]*
Young, Joy Marion 1906- *WhoMus 72*
Young, Kathy And The Innocents *RkOn*
Young, LaMonte 1935- *Baker 78, BiDAmM, ConAmC, ConDr 73, -77E, DcCM, NewGrD 80*
Young, Larry 1940- *EncJzS 70*
Young, Lawrance 1915- *AmSCAP 80*
Young, Lee 1917- *CmpEPM, WhoJazz 72*
Young, Lester 1909-1959 *AmSCAP 66, -80, BiDAmM, CmpEPM, DrBlPA, IlEncJ, MusMk, NewGrD 80*
Young, Loretta *MotPP*
Young, Loretta 1911- *ForYSC, WhoHol A*
Young, Loretta 1912- *BiDFilm, -81, OxFilm, ThFT[port]*
Young, Loretta 1913- *FilmEn, Film 1, -2, FilmgC, HalFC 80, IntMPA 77, -75, -76, -78, -79, -80, MovMk[port], WorEFlm[port]*
Young, Loretta 1914- *TwYS*
Young, Lucille 1892-1934 *WhScrn 74, -77, WhoHol B*
Young, Margaret Mary 1911- *BiE&WWA, NotNAT*
Young, Marilyn 1936- *CreCan 2, DancEn 78[port]*
Young, Mary 1857-1934 *WhScrn 74, -77, WhoHol B*
Young, Mary Marsden 1879-1971 *WhScrn 74, -77, WhoHol B*
Young, Maude J Fuller 1826-1882 *BiDAmM*
Young, Michael E 1939- *ConAmC*
Young, Michelle *WhoHol A*
Young, Ming *Film 2*
Young, Morris 1919- *IntMPA 78, -79, -80*
Young, Mort 1933- *ConAmTC*
Young, Ned d1968 *WhoHol B*
Young, Nedrick 1914-1968 *WhScrn 74, -77*
Young, Neil 1945- *ConMuA 80A, IlEncR[port], RkOn 2[port], WhoHol A*
Young, Nicholas *NewGrD 80, OxMus*
Young, Noah *Film 2*
Young, Norma *WhScrn 77*
Young, Norma 1928- *NotNAT*
Young, Norman Russell 1946- *AmSCAP 80*
Young, Olive 1907-1940 *WhScrn 74, -77, WhoHol B*
Young, Otis 1932- *BlkAmP, DrBlPA, FilmgC, HalFC 80, WhoHol A*
Young, Ovid 1940- *IntWWM 77*
Young, Paul *WhoHol A*
Young, Percy Marshall 1912- *Baker 78, IntWWM 77, -80, NewGrD 80, OxMus, WhoMus 72*
Young, Philip H 1937- *ConAmC*
Young, Phyllis 1925- *IntWWM 77, -80*
Young, Polly 1745?-1799 *Baker 78*
Young, Polly 1749?-1799 *NewGrD 80*
Young, Polly Ann 1908- *Film 2, ForYSC, TwYS, WhoHol A*
Young, Pres 1909-1959 *NewGrD 80*
Young, Prez 1909-1959 *NewGrD 80, WhoJazz 72*
Young, Ralph *CmpEPM*
Young, Ray *WhoHol A*
Young, Raymond *WhoHol A*
Young, Richard *WhoHol A*
Young, Rida Johnson *Sw&Ld B*
Young, Rida Johnson 1869-1926 *AmPS, AmSCAP 66, -80, CmpEPM, EncMT, NewCBMT*
Young, Rida Johnson 1875-1926 *NotNAT B, WhThe*
Young, Rita Johnson 1869-1926 *BiDAmM*
Young, Robert 1907- *BiDFilm, -81, CmMov, FilmEn, FilmgC, ForYSC, HalFC 80, IntMPA 77, -75, -76, -78, -79, -80, MGM, MotPP, MovMk[port], NewYTET, OxFilm, WhoHol A, WorEFlm[port]*
Young, Robert Floyd 1924- *IntWWM 77, -80*
Young, Robert H 1923- *ConAmC*
Young, Rod *PupTheA SUP*
Young, Roland 1887-1952 *Vers A[port]*
Young, Roland 1887-1953 *FilmEn, Film 2, FilmgC, ForYSC, HalFC 80, HolCA[port], MotPP, MovMk, NotNAT B, OxFilm, PlP&P, WhScrn 74, -77, WhThe, WhoHol B, WhoHrs 80[port]*
Young, Rolande Maxwell 1929- *AmSCAP 66, -80, ConAmC A*
Young, S D *PupTheA*
Young, Sareen Anne 1953- *IntWWM 80*
Young, Silvia *Film 2*
Young, Skip *WhoHol A*
Young, Snookie Eugene Edward 1919- *WhoJazz 72*
Young, Snooky 1919- *EncJzS 70*
Young, Sport *NewOrJ*
Young, Stanley 1906- *BiE&WWA, NotNAT*
Young, Stark 1881-1963 *EncWT, NotNAT B, OxThe, WhThe*
Young, Stephen 1931?- *HalFC 80*
Young, Stephen 1939- *FilmgC, WhoHol A*
Young, Sterling *CmpEPM*
Young, Tammany d1935 *Film 1, -2, TwYS*
Young, Tammany 1887-1936 *WhScrn 74, -77, WhoHol B*
Young, Tammy -1935 *ForYSC*
Young, Terence 1915- *BiDFilm, -81, CmMov, FilmEn, FilmgC, HalFC 80, IIWWBF, IntMPA 77, -75, -76, -78, -79, -80, MovMk[port], OxFilm, WhoHrs 80, WorEFlm*
Young, Tex *Film 2*
Young, Tommy Scott *MorBAP*
Young, Tony 1921-1966 *IIWWBF*
Young, Tony 1932?- *FilmgC, HalFC 80, WhoHol A*
Young, Trudy *WhoHol A*
Young, Trummy 1912- *CmpEPM, EncJzS 70, WhoJazz 72*
Young, Victor d1956 *Sw&Ld C*
Young, Victor 1889- *AmSCAP 80*
Young, Victor 1889-1956 *OxFilm*
Young, Victor 1889-1968 *AmSCAP 66, Baker 78, ConAmC, NotNAT B*
Young, Victor 1900-1956 *AmPS, AmSCAP 66, -80, Baker 78, BiDAmM, CmMov, CmpEPM, ConAmC, FilmEn, FilmgC, HalFC 80, NewGrD 80, NotNAT B, PopAmC, RkOn, WorEFlm*
Young, Victoria *WhoHol A*
Young, Waldemar 1890?-1938 *CmMov, FilmEn*
Young, Walter 1878-1957 *WhScrn 74, -77, WhoHol B*
Young, William d1662 *NewGrD 80*
Young, William d1671 *Baker 78, OxMus*
Young, William d1920 *NotNAT B*
Young, William Henry 1913- *IntWWM 77*
Young, Winfred d1964 *NotNAT B*
Young-Holt Unlimited *RkOn 2[port]*
Young Rascals, The *BiDAmM*
Young Roscius *OxThe, PlP&P*
Young Tuxedo Band *BiDAmM*
Young Wolf, The *BluesWW*
Youngberg, Frederick Truman 1906- *IntWWM 77*
Youngblood, Butch *WhoHol A*
Youngblood, Jessie Orian 1941- *IntWWM 77, -80*
Youngbloods, The *BiDAmM, IlEncR,*

RkOn 2[port]
Younge, Nicholas *NewGrD 80*
Younger, Beverly *WhoHol A*
Younger, Jack *WhoHol A*
Younger, Marc *AmSCAP 80*
Younger, Martin *BlkAmP*
Youngman, Donald Alexander Hay 1920- *WhoMus 72*
Youngman, Henny 1906- *JoeFr[port], NotNAT A, WhoHol A*
Youngren, Otis 1903- *AmSCAP 66*
Youngs, Alexander Basil *NewGrD 80*
Youngson, Jeannie *WomWMM A, -B*
Youngson, Robert 1917-1974 *FilmEn, FilmgC, HalFC 80*
Youngstein, Max E 1913- *IntMPA 77, -75, -76, -78, -79, -80*
Younker, M Marguerite 1900- *IntWWM 77*
Yount, Max *ConAmC*
Younts, Elizabeth Louise Mendenhall 1919- *IntWWM 77*
Youree, Charles *Film 2*
Youse, Glad Robinson 1898- *AmSCAP 66, -80, ConAmC*
Youshkevitch, Nina *DancEn 78*
Youskevitch, Igor 1912- *CnOxB, DancEn 78[port], WhoHol A*
Yousling, George E 1896- *IntMPA 75, -76*
Youssoupoff, Prince Nicolas 1827-1891 *Baker 78*
Yow, Joe d1964 *NotNAT B*
Yowlache, Chief *Film 2*
Yradier, Sebastian 1809-1865 *Baker 78, NewGrD 80, OxMus*
Yriarte, Tomas De 1750-1791 *Baker 78, NewGrD 80*
Ysac, Heinrich *NewGrD 80*
Ysac, Henricus *NewGrD 80*
Ysaguirre, Robert 1895?- *NewOrJ*
Ysaguirre, Robert 1897- *WhoJazz 72*
Ysaye, Antoine Marie Eugene 1894- *WhoMus 72*
Ysaye, Eugene 1858-1931 *Baker 78, BnBkM 80, MusSN[port], NewGrD 80[port], OxMus*
Ysaye, Jacques 1922- *WhoMus 72*
Ysaye, Theophile 1865-1918 *Baker 78, NewGrD 80, OxMus*
Yso, Pierre *NewGrD 80*
Ysore, Guillaume d1563 *NewGrD 80*
Yssandon, Jean *NewGrD 80*
Ytteseb, Peter Holling 1946- *IntWWM 77*
Yttesen, Peter Holling 1946- *IntWWM 80*
Yttrehus, Rolv 1926- *Baker 78, ConAmC, IntWWM 77, -80*
Yu, Chun Yee 1936- *IntWWM 77, -80*
Yuasa, Joji 1929- *Baker 78, DcCM, NewGrD 80*
Yudenich, Alexei 1943- *CnOxB*
Yudin, Konstantin 1896-1957 *DcFM*
Yudina, Mariya 1899-1970 *NewGrD 80*
Yuize, Shinichi 1923- *IntWWM 77, -80*
Yukio, Mishima 1925-1970 *CnThe, REnWD[port]*
Yukl, Joe 1909- *CmpEPM, WhoJazz 72*
Yule, Carol 1940- *CnOxB*
Yule, Joe 1894-1950 *FilmEn, NotNAT B, WhScrn 74, -77, WhoHol B*
Yule, Joe, Jr. 1920- *AmSCAP 80*
Yulin, Harris *HalFC 80, WhoHol A*
Yun, Isang 1917- *Baker 78, BnBkM 80, DcCM, IntWWM 77, -80, NewGrD 80*
Yung, Sen 1915- *FilmgC, HalFC 80*
Yung, Victor Sen 1916- *WhoHol A*
Yunus Al-Katib d765? *NewGrD 80*
Yuon, Paul *Baker 78, NewGrD 80*
Yuresha, Jelko 1937- *CnOxB, DancEn 78*
Yurgenson, Peter *Baker 78*
Yurgenson, Pyotr Ivanovich *NewGrD 80*
Yurgev, Yuri d1948 *NotNAT B*
Yuricich, Matthew 1923- *WhoHrs 80*
Yurieva, Maria *DancEn 78*
Yuriko 1920- *BiE&WWA, CnOxB, DancEn 78[port]*
Yurka, Blanche 1887-1974 *BiE&WWA, FilmEn, FilmgC, HalFC 80, HolCA[port], MotPP, MovMk, NotNAT B, ThFT[port], What 4, WhScrn 77, WhThe, WhoHol B, WhoThe 72*
Yurka, Blanche 1893-1974 *FamA&A[port], ForYSC, NotNAT A, Vers A[port]*
Yurlov, Alexander Alexandrovich 1927-1973 *NewGrD 80*
Yuro, Robert *WhoHol A*
Yuro, Timi 1941- *RkOn*
Yurski, Sergey Yurevich 1935- *EncWT*
Yurtis, Beverly *WomWMM B*
Yurtsev, Boris *Film 2*
Yuruk, Ali 1940- *REnWD[port]*
Yussupov, Prince Nicolas *Baker 78*
Yusupov, Prince Nikolay Borisovich 1827-1891 *NewGrD 80*
Yutkevich, Sergei 1904- *BiDFilm, -81, DcFM, FilmEn, OxFilm, WorEFlm*
Yvain, Maurice 1891-1965 *Baker 78, NewGrD 80*
Yves, Christiane *Film 2*
Yvo *NewGrD 80*
Yvoire, Claude 1913- *IntWWM 77*
Yvonne, Mimi *Film 1*
Yvonneck *Film 2*
Yzac, Heinrich *Baker 78, NewGrD 80*
Yzac, Henricus *NewGrD 80*
Yzarduy, Madame *Film 2*
Yzo, Pierre *NewGrD 80*

Z

Z Z Top *IlEncR*
Za Yemeni, Ra Twani 1946- *AmSCAP 80*
Za Zu Girl, The *BluesWW*
Zabach, Florian 1921- *AmSCAP 66, –80, CmpEPM*
Zabala, Elsa *WhoHol A*
Zabaleta, Nicanor 1907- *Baker 78, BnBkM 80, IntWWM 77, –80, MusSN[port], NewGrD 80, WhoMus 72*
Zaballos, Francisco De *NewGrD 80*
Zaballos, Rodrigo De *NewGrD 80*
Zabalza Y Olaso, Don Damaso 1833-1894 *Baker 78*
Zabel, Albert Heinrich 1834-1910 *Baker 78, NewGrD 80*
Zabelle, Flora 1880-1968 *Film 1, WhScrn 74, –77, WhThe, WhoHol B*
Zabelle, Flora 1888?-1968 *CmpEPM*
Zabern, Conrad Von *NewGrD 80, OxMus*
Zabita, Giovanni *PupTheA*
Zabka, Stanley William 1924- *AmSCAP 66, –80*
Zabludow, Michael *IntWWM 77, –80, WhoMus 72*
Zabotkina, Olga *WhoHol A*
Zabrack, Harold Allen 1928- *AmSCAP 80, ConAmC*
Zabrack, Harold Allen 1929- *Baker 78*
Zabriskie, Sherry *WomWMM B*
Zacar *NewGrD 80*
Zaccardi, Florido *NewGrD 80*
Zaccaria, Cesare De *NewGrD 80*
Zaccaria, Nicola Angelo 1923- *NewGrD 80, WhoOp 76*
Zaccaria, Nicola Angelo 1924- *WhoMus 72*
Zacchini, Giulio *NewGrD 80*
Zacchini, Hugo 1898-1975 *WhScrn 77*
Zacchini, Ildebrando d1948 *NotNAT B*
Zacchino, Giulio *NewGrD 80*
Zacchinus, Giulio *NewGrD 80*
Zacconi, Ermete 1857-1948 *EncWT, Ent, NotNAT B, OxThe, WhThe, WhoHol B*
Zacconi, Ermete 1867-1948 *CnThe*
Zacconi, Giulio Cesare 1555-1627 *NewGrD 80*
Zacconi, Lodovico 1555-1627 *Baker 78, BnBkM 80, NewGrD 80*
Zacconi, Ludovico 1555-1627 *OxMus*
Zach, Jan 1699-1773 *Baker 78, NewGrD 80*
Zach, Max Wilhelm 1864-1921 *Baker 78, BiDAmM*
Zachaeus, Michael d1698 *NewGrD 80*
Zachara *NewGrD 80*
Zachara Da Teramo *NewGrD 80*
Zachardus, Florido *NewGrD 80*
Zacharewitsch, Michael 1879-1953 *Baker 78*
Zacharia, Cesare De *NewGrD 80*
Zacharia, Friedrich Wilhelm 1726-1777 *NewGrD 80*
Zachariae, Friedrich Wilhelm 1726-1777 *NewGrD 80*
Zacharias *NewGrD 80*
Zacharias, Pope *OxMus*
Zacharias, Helmut 1920- *IntWWM 77, –80, RkOn, WhoMus 72*
Zacharias, Stephen *WhoHol A*
Zachariassen, Uffe Eilif 1935- *IntWWM 80*
Zacharie *NewGrD 80*
Zacharie Of Brindisi *NewGrD 80*
Zachariis *NewGrD 80*
Zachariis, Cesare De *NewGrD 80*
Zachary, Tony *AmSCAP 80*
Zachau, Friedrich Wilhelm 1663-1712 *Baker 78, MusMk, NewGrD 80*
Zachau, Peter 1650?-1702 *NewGrD 80*
Zachaus, Peter 1650?-1702 *NewGrD 80*
Zacher *NewGrD 80*
Zacher, Gerd 1929- *DcCM, NewGrD 80*
Zacher, Johann Michael 1651?-1712 *NewGrD 80*
Zacherle, John 1918- *RkOn*
Zacherley 1919- *JoeFr*
Zachow, Friedrich Wilhelm 1663-1712 *NewGrD 80*
Zachwatowicz-Jasienska, Katarzyna 1932- *IntWWM 77*
Zack, George 1936- *IntWWM 77, –80*
Zack, George J 1908?- *WhoJazz 72*
Zack, Jimmie 1924- *BiDAmM*
Zaconick, Dorothy *PupTheA*
Zadek, Hildegard *WhoMus 72*
Zadek, Peter 1926- *EncWT*
Zador, Eugen 1894-1977 *AmSCAP 66, –80, Baker 78, BiDAmM, OxMus*
Zador, Eugene 1894-1977 *CompSN[port], ConAmC, NewGrD 80*
Zador, Eugene 1895- *WhoMus 72*
Zador, Jeno 1894-1977 *NewGrD 80*
Zadora, Michael Von 1882-1946 *Baker 78, ConAmC, NewGrD 80*
Zadora, Michal 1882-1946 *NewGrD 80*
Zaecher, Johann Michael *NewGrD 80*
Zaentz, Saul *ConMuA 80B*
Zafransky, Dora *WhoMus 72*
Zafred, Mario 1922- *Baker 78, NewGrD 80, WhoOp 76*
Zagajewska-Szlezer, Zofia Barbara 1926- *IntWWM 77, –80*
Zager, Michael *ConMuA 80B*
Zager & Evans *RkOn 2[port]*
Zagiba, Franz 1912-1977 *Baker 78, NewGrD 80, WhoMus 72*
Zagoren, Marc Alan 1940- *NatPD[port]*
Zagorzanka, Barbara 1938- *IntWWM 77, –80*
Zagwijn, Henri 1878-1954 *Baker 78, NewGrD 80*
Zahler, Noel *ConAmC*
Zahn, Johannes 1817-1895 *Baker 78, NewGrD 80*
Zahorsky, Bohuz *WhoHol A*
Zahorsky, Philip C 1951- *IntWWM 80*
Zahortsev, Volodymyr Mikolayevich 1944- *NewGrD 80*
Zahrt, Hilda Elizabeth Bouck 1917- *IntWWM 77*
Zaiko, Thomas Joseph 1943- *IntWWM 77*
Zaimont, Judith Lang 1945- *AmSCAP 80, CpmDNM 76, –79, ConAmC, IntWWM 77, –80*
Zaitsev, Ivan Afinogenovich 1865-1930 *DcPup*
Zajaczkowski, Roman *NewGrD 80*
Zajc, Ivan 1832-1914 *Baker 78, NewGrD 80*
Zajic, Florian 1853-1926 *Baker 78*
Zajicek, Jeronym 1926- *Baker 78*
Zak, Benedikt *NewGrD 80*
Zak, Yakov 1913-1976 *Baker 78, NewGrD 80*
Zakharov, Rostislav 1907- *CnOxB, DancEn 78, NewGrD 80*
Zakharov, Vladimir Grigor'yevich 1901-1956 *Baker 78, NewGrD 80*
Zakhava, Boris Evgenevich 1896- *OxThe*
Zakotnik, Breda 1945- *IntWWM 77, –80*
Zalamella, Pandolfo 1551-1590? *NewGrD 80*
Zalanowski, Annette H 1944- *IntWWM 77*
Zalazar, Antonio De *NewGrD 80*
Zale, Tony 1914- *What 3[port]*
Zaliouk, Yuval 1939- *WhoMus 72*
Zalkind, Ronald 1949- *BiDAmM, ConMuA 80B*
Zallamella, Pandolfo 1551-1590? *NewGrD 80*
Zaltzberg, Charlotte *ConDr 77D*
Zalud, Sam d1963 *NotNAT B*
Zalzal d791 *NewGrD 80*
Zamacois, Joaquin 1894-1976 *NewGrD 80*
Zamacois, Miguel 1866- *WhThe*
Zamacola, Juan Antonio 1758-1819? *NewGrD 80*
Zamara, Antonio 1829-1901 *Baker 78, NewGrD 80*
Zamba d1964 *WhScrn 77*
Zambaldi, Silvio 1870-1932 *McGEWD*
Zambarano, Alfred P 1885-1970 *ConAmC*
Zambelli, Carlotta 1875-1968 *CnOxB*
Zambelli, Carlotta 1877- *DancEn 78*
Zambetti, John Francis 1949- *AmSCAP 80*
Zamboni, Gioseffo *NewGrD 80*
Zamboni, Giovanni *NewGrD 80*
Zamecnik, J C 1872-1953 *AmSCAP 66*
Zamecnik, J S 1872-1953 *AmSCAP 80*
Zaminer, Frieder 1927- *NewGrD 80*
Zamir, Batya *CmpGMD*
Zamissi, Lucia *Film 2*
Zammit, Angela Jemma 1949- *IntWWM 77*
Zampa, Luigi 1904- *OxFilm*
Zampa, Luigi 1905- *DcFM, FilmEn, FilmgC, HalFC 80, IntMPA 77, –75, –76, –78, –79, –80, WorEFlm*
Zampi, Giulio 1923- *IntMPA 77, –75, –76, –78, –79, –80*
Zampi, Mario 1903-1963 *FilmEn, FilmgC, HalFC 80, IlWWBF, WhScrn 77*
Zampieri, Giusto 1879-1950 *Baker 78*
Zampieri, Vittorio 1862- *WhThe*
Zamponi, Gioseffo 161-?-1662 *NewGrD 80*
Zamponi, Giuseppe 161-?-1662 *NewGrD 80*
Zamudio, Daniel 1887-1952 *NewGrD 80*
Zamyatin, Yevgeni Ivanovich 1884-1937 *CnMD, ModWD*
Zanaboni, Giuseppe 1926- *WhoMus 72*
Zanasi, Mario 1927- *WhoOp 76*
Zanata, Domenico 1665?-1748 *NewGrD 80*
Zanatta, Domenico 1665?-1748 *NewGrD 80*
Zanchi, Liberale 1570?-1621? *NewGrD 80*

Zancig, Julius MagIID
Zancigs, The MagIID
Zanckl, Narcissus NewGrD 80
Zanco, Manuel 1929- NewOrJ
Zandberg, Paul 1910- AmSCAP 66, -80
Zander, Benjamin David 1939- IntWWM 77, -80
Zander, Hans 1905- WhoMus 72
Zander, Johan David 1753-1796 NewGrD 80
Zanders, Douglas William Alfred 1918- WhoMus 72
Zandonai, Riccardo 1883-1944 Baker 78, CmOp, NewEOp 71, NewGrD 80, OxMus
Zandt, Marie Van 1861-1919 Baker 78, CmOp, NewEOp 71, NewGrD 80
Zane, Rinaldo PupTheA
Zanella, Amilcare 1873-1949 Baker 78, NewGrD 80
Zanelli, Renato 1892-1935 CmOp, NewEOp 71, NewGrD 80
Zanette, Guy 1907-1962 WhScrn 74, -77, WhoHol B
Zanetti NewGrD 80
Zanetti, Francesco NewGrD 80
Zanetti, Gasparo NewGrD 80
Zanetti, Gerolamo NewGrD 80
Zanettini, Antonio Baker 78, NewGrD 80
Zanetto Di Montichiaro 1490?-1560? NewGrD 80
Zanettovich, Renato 1921- WhoMus 72
Zanfretti, Francesca d1952 NotNAT B
Zang, Johann Heinrich 1733-1811 Baker 78, NewGrD 80
Zange, Nikolaus NewGrD 80
Zangel, Narcissus 1555?-1607? NewGrD 80
Zanger, Johann 1517?-1587 NewGrD 80
Zanger, Johannes 1517-1587 Baker 78
Zanggel, Narcissus 1555?-1607? NewGrD 80
Zangius, Nikolaus 1570?-1618? Baker 78, NewGrD 80
Zangrilli, O Film 2
Zangwill, Israel 1864-1926 ModWD, NotNAT A, OxThe, WhThe, WhoStg 1906
Zangwill, Isreal 1864-1926 NotNAT B
Zani, Andrea 1696-1757 NewGrD 80
Zani, Giacomo 1934- WhoOp 76
Zani DeFerranti, Marco Aurelio 1800-1878 NewGrD 80
Zanin, Bruno WhoHol A
Zaninelli, Luigi 1932- AmSCAP 80, ConAmC, IntWWM 77, -80
Zaninus De Peraga De Padua NewGrD 80
Zank, Ric NotNAT
Zann, Nancy Film 2
Zannatta, Domenico NewGrD 80
Zannetti NewGrD 80
Zannetti, Bartolomeo NewGrD 80
Zannetti, Francesco 1737-1788 NewGrD 80
Zannetti, Gasparo NewGrD 80
Zannetti, Luigi NewGrD 80
Zannettini, Antonio NewGrD 80
Zannini, Laura Ludovica 1937- WhoOp 76
Zannoni, Angelo NewGrD 80
Zannuck, Darryl F 1902-1979 TwYS B
Zano, Anthony AmSCAP 80
Zanolli, Silvana 1928- WhoOp 76
Zanotelli, Hans 1927- WhoOp 76
Zanotti, Camillo 1545?-1591 NewGrD 80
Zanotti, Giovanni 1738-1817 NewGrD 80
Zanten, Cornelia Van Baker 78
Zanuck, Darryl F 1902-1979 BiDFilm, -81, CmMov, DcFM, FilmEn, FilmgC, HalFC 80, IntMPA 77, -75, -76, -78, -79, -80, OxFilm, WorEFlm[port]
Zanuck, Harrison WhoHol A
Zanuck, Richard Darryl 1934- FilmEn, FilmgC, HalFC 80, IntMPA 77, -75, -76, -78, -79, -80, OxFilm
Zanussi, Krzysztof 1939- FilmEn
Zanville, Bernard FilmEn, WhoHol A
Zany, King d1939 Film 2, WhScrn 74, -77, WhoHol B
Zaparth, Jean NewGrD 80
Zapata, Carmen WhoHol A
Zapata, Joe WhoHol A
Zaphelius, Matthaus 1550?-1572? NewGrD 80
Zaphelius, Matthias 1550?-1572? NewGrD 80
Zapolska, Gabriela 1860-1921 CnMD, EncWT, McGEWD[port], ModWD
Zapor, John Randolph NatPD[port]
Zapp, Sylvia WhoHol A
Zappa, Francesco NewGrD 80
Zappa, Frank 1940- AmSCAP 80, Baker 78, BiDAmM, ConMuA 80A[port], EncJzS 70, IlEncR[port], RkOn 2[port], WhoHol A
Zappasorgo, Giovanni NewGrD 80
Zappolini, Walter 1930- CnOxB
Zara, Meredith WhoOp 76
Zaramella NewGrD 80
Zarana, Zalla Film 2
Zaraspe, Hector 1931- CnOxB
Zarate, Eliodoro Ortiz De 1865-1953 Baker 78
Zarb, George 1937- WhoMus 72
Zardi, Federicao 1912- CnMD
Zardis, Chester 1900- NewOrJ[port], WhoJazz 72
Zardt, Georg NewGrD 80
Zarebski, Juliusz 1854-1885 Baker 78, NewGrD 80
Zaremba NewGrD 80
Zaremba, John WhoHol A
Zaremba, Nikolai 1821-1879 Baker 78
Zaremba, Nikolay Ivanovich 1821-1879 NewGrD 80
Zaremba, Sigismund Vladislavovich 1861-1915 NewGrD 80
Zaremba, Vladislav Ivanovich 1833-1902 NewGrD 80
Zareska, Eugenia WhoMus 72
Zaret, Hy 1907- AmSCAP 66, -80, CmpEPM
Zaret, Peter H 1939- IntWWM 77, -80
Zarevutius, Zacharias NewGrD 80
Zarewutius, Zacharias NewGrD 80
Zarins, Margeris 1910- Baker 78, NewGrD 80
Zarins, Margers 1910- NewGrD 80
Zaritsky, Bernard 1924- AmSCAP 66, -80
Zaritsky, Libby 1925- AmSCAP 66, -80
Zarkhi, Alexander 1908- FilmEn, WorEFlm
Zarki, Alexander 1908- DcFM
Zarlino, Gioseffe 1517-1590 NewGrD 80[port]
Zarlino, Gioseffo 1517-1590 Baker 78, BnBkM 80, NewGrD 80[port], OxMus
Zarmas, Pieris 1933- WhoOp 76
Zarotus, Antonio Baker 78
Zarou, Jeannette 1936- CreCan 1, WhoOp 76
Zarova, Rini 1912-1966 WhScrn 74, -77
Zarovich, Joseph H 1890?-1971 BiDAmM
Zarrilli, Humberto PupTheA
Zarth, Georg 1708-1778? NewGrD 80
Zarzebski, Adam NewGrD 80
Zarzo, Manolo WhoHol A
Zarzo, Vicente 1938- IntWWM 77, -80
Zarzycki, Aleksander 1834-1895 NewGrD 80
Zarzycki, Alexander 1834-1895 Baker 78
Zasa, Paolo NewGrD 80
Zaslaw, Neal Alexander 1939- IntWWM 77, -80, NewGrD 80
Zaslawsky, Georges 1880-1953 Baker 78
Zastrow, Joyce Ruth 1929- IntWWM 77, -80
Zathey, Janusz Romuald 1927- IntWWM 77, -80
Zatman, Andrew Sam 1945- CpmDNM 78, -79, -80, ConAmC
Zatvrzsky, Milos NewGrD 80
Zaugg, Harry 1929- WhoMus 72
Zavadski, Yuri Alexeyevich 1894- EncWT
Zavadsky, Yuri Alexeivich 1894- OxThe
Zavaglioli, Simone NewGrD 80
Zavallos, Francisco De NewGrD 80
Zavallos, Rodrigo De NewGrD 80
Zavarsky, Ernest 1913- NewGrD 80
Zavateri, Lorenzo Gaetano 1690-1764 NewGrD 80
Zavattini, Cesare 1902- DcFM, EncWT, FilmEn, FilmgC, HalFC 80, OxFilm, WorEFlm
Zavattini, Cesare 1903- CnMD
Zavertal, Ladislao 1849-1942 Baker 78, NewGrD 80
Zavertal, Wenceslas Hugo 1821-1899 Baker 78
Zavin, Theodora ConMuA 80B
Zavrtal NewGrD 80
Zavrtal, Josef Rudolf 1819-1893 NewGrD 80
Zavrtal, Ladislav 1849-1942 NewGrD 80
Zavrtal, Vaclav Hugo 1821-1899 NewGrD 80
Zavrtal, Venceslao Hugo 1821-1899 NewGrD 80
Zavrtal, Wenceslas Hugo 1821-1899 NewGrD 80
Zavrthal NewGrD 80
Zawieyski, Jerzy 1902-1969 CroCD
Zawinul, Joe 1932- EncJzS 70, IlEncJ
Zawinul, Josef 1932- EncJzS 70
Zay, Henri 1869-1927 Baker 78
Zayas, Alfonso 1910-1961 WhScrn 74, -77
Zayas, Juana 1940- IntWWM 77, -80
Zaytz, Giovanni Von 1831-1914 Baker 78, NewGrD 80
Zazzerino NewGrD 80
Zbar, Michel 1942- Baker 78
Zbinden, Julien-Francois 1917- Baker 78, CpmDNM 80, IntWWM 77, -80, NewGrD 80
Zbruyeva, Evgeniya 1868-1936 NewGrD 80
Zbysko, Stanislaus 1879-1967 WhScrn 77
Zdravkovic, Zivojin 1914- Baker 78
Zdravkovitch, Gika 1914- IntWWM 77, -80
Zdzitowiecka, Krystyna Maria 1943- IntWWM 77, -80
Zeami, Motokiyo 1363-1443 NewGrD 80, REnWD[port]
Zeani, Virginia 1928- CmOp, NewGrD 80, WhoOp 76
Zears, Marjorie 1911-1952 WhScrn 74, -77
Zebrowski, Marcin Jozef NewGrD 80
Zecca, Ferdinand 1864-1947 DcFM, FilmEn, FilmgC, HalFC 80, OxFilm, WorEFlm
Zecchi, Adone 1904- Baker 78, NewGrD 80
Zecchi, Carlo 1903- Baker 78, NewGrD 80
Zecchillo, Giuseppe 1929- WhoOp 76
Zeccola, Vincent A 1938- AmSCAP 66, -80
Zech, Frederick 1858-1926 Baker 78
Zechlin, Dieter 1926- IntWWM 77, -80
Zechlin, Ruth 1926- Baker 78, IntWWM 77, -80, NewGrD 80
Zechner, Johann Georg 1716-1778 NewGrD 80
Zeckwer, Camille 1875-1924 Baker 78, BiDAmM, ConAmC, NewGrD 80
Zeckwer, Richard 1850-1922 Baker 78, BiDAmM, NewGrD 80
Zedda, Alberto 1928- NewGrD 80, WhoOp 76
Zee, Eleanor WhoHol A
Zeeman, Joan Javits 1928- AmSCAP 80
Zeerleder, Niklaus 1628-1691 Baker 78
Zeers, Fred C 1895-1946 WhScrn 74, -77
Zeffirelli, Franco WhoHol A
Zeffirelli, Franco 1922- FilmgC, HalFC 80, IntMPA 77, -75, -76, -78, -79, -80
Zeffirelli, Franco 1923- BiE&WWA, CmOp, EncWT, Ent, FilmEn, MovMk[port], NewEOp 71, NewGrD 80, OxFilm, OxThe, WorEFlm
Zeffirelli, Franco 1924- CnThe
Zeffirelli, Franco 1927- WhoOp 76
Zeffirelli, G Franco 1923- WhoThe 72, -77
Zegel, Ferdinand 1895-1973 WhScrn 77
Zehan, Virginia NewGrD 80
Zehm, Friedrich 1923- IntWWM 77, -80, NewGrD 80
Zehnder, Johann Peter NewGrD 80
Zehnder, Max 1901-1972 Baker 78, NewGrD 80
Zeidelman, Claire PupTheA
Zeidman, Boris 1908- Baker 78
Zeigler, Lynn Jay 1946- IntWWM 77, -80
Zeiler, Gallus 1705-1755 NewGrD 80
Zeinally, Assaf 1909-1932 Baker 78
Zeisl, Eric 1905-1959 AmSCAP 66, -80, Baker 78, BiDAmM, ConAmC, NewGrD 80
Zeisler, Fannie 1863-1927 Baker 78, NewGrD 80
Zeisler, Fanny Bloomfield BiDAmM, BnBkM 80
Zeisler, Peter 1923- BiE&WWA
Zeitlein, Lev Moiseyevich NewGrD 80
Zeitlin, Dennis Jay 1938- EncJzS 70
Zeitlin, Denny 1938- EncJzS 70
Zeitlin, Lois WhoHol A
Zeitlin, Patricia Anne 1936- AmSCAP 80
Zeitlin, Zvi 1923- IntWWM 77, -80, NewGrD 80, WhoMus 72
Zekert, Josef NewGrD 80
Zelaya, Don Alfonso 1894-1951 WhScrn 74, -77, WhoHol B
Zelechowski, Piotr NewGrD 80

Zelenka, Istvan 1936- Baker 78, IntWWM 77, -80, NewGrD 80
Zelenka, Jan 1679-1745 MusMk
Zelenka, Jan Dismas 1679-1745 Baker 78, NewGrD 80
Zelenka, Jan Lukas 1679-1745 NewGrD 80
Zelenka, Johann Dismas 1679-1745 NewGrD 80
Zelenscius, Mikolaj NewGrD 80
Zelenski, Elizabeth 1945- IntWWM 77
Zelenski, Wladislaw 1837-1921 Baker 78
Zelenski, Wladyslaw 1837-1921 NewGrD 80
Zelezny, Lubomir 1925- Baker 78
Zelinka, Jan Evangelista 1893-1969 Baker 78, NewGrD 80
Zelinka, John Evangelist 1893-1969 WhoMus 72
Zeljenka, Ilja 1932- Baker 78, DcCM, NewGrD 80
Zell, Steven Don 1948- IntWWM 77
Zellan-Smith, Georgina 1931- IntWWM 77, -80, WhoMus 72
Zellars, John MorBAP
Zellbell, Ferdinand 1689-1765 NewGrD 80
Zellbell, Ferdinand 1719-1780 NewGrD 80
Zelle, Friedrich 1845-1927 Baker 78
Zeller, Ben WhoHol A
Zeller, Carl 1842-1898 NewGrD 80
Zeller, Gary L 1940- IntWWM 77
Zeller, Karl 1842-1898 Baker 78
Zellif, Seymour Film 2
Zellman, Tollie 1887-1964 WhScrn 74, -77
Zellner, Julius 1832-1900 Baker 78
Zellner, Leopold Alexander 1823-1894 Baker 78
Zelman, Alberto 1874-1927 NewGrD 80
Zelnik, Fred 1885-1950 IlWWBF
Zeltenpferd NewGrD 80
Zelter, Carl Friedrich 1758-1832 Baker 78, MusMk[port], NewGrD 80[port], OxMus
Zemach, Nahum L 1887-1939 NotNAT B
Zemachson, Arnold 1892-1956 BiDAmM
Zeman, Anton 1937- IntWWM 80
Zeman, Jiri 1934- IntWWM 80
Zeman, Jirl 1934- IntWWM 77
Zeman, Karel 1910- DcFM, DcPup, FilmEn, FilmgC, HalFC 80, OxFilm, WhoHrs 80, WorEFlm
Zemanek, Heinz 1920- IntWWM 80
Zemeckis, Robert 1952- IntMPA 79, -80
Zemina, Valentina Film 2
Zemlinsky, Alexander Von BiDAmM
Zemlinsky, Alexander Von 1871-1942 Baker 78, NewGrD 80
Zemlinsky, Alexander Von 1872-1942 DcCM, NewEOp 71, OxMus
Zemtsovsky, Jzalij Josifovic 1936- IntWWM 77
Zemtsovsty, Jzalij Josifovic 1936- IntWWM 80
Zemtzova, Anna Film 2
Zenaro, Giulio d1590? NewGrD 80
Zenatello, Giovanni 1876-1949 Baker 78, CmOp, NewEOp 71, NewGrD 80
Zenatello, Giovanni 1879-1949 BiDAmM
Zenatti, Ariette 1931- IntWWM 77, -80
Zenck, Hermann 1898-1950 Baker 78, NewGrD 80
Zender, Hans 1936- NewGrD 80
Zender, Johannes Wolfgang Hans 1936- IntWWM 77, -80
Zenger, Max 1837-1911 Baker 78
Zengerink, Herman Joannes 1918- IntWWM 77, -80
Zenngel, Narcissus NewGrD 80
Zeno, Apostolo 1668-1750 Baker 78, BnBkM 80, NewEOp 71, NewGrD 80, NotNAT B, OxThe
Zeno, George NewGrD 80
Zeno, Henry 1880?-1918? NewOrJ
Zeno, Henry 1884?-1917 BiDAmM
Zeno, Norman 1906- AmSCAP 66
Zeno, Phyllis Williams 1926- AmSCAP 80
Zens, Will 1920- IntMPA 77, -75, -76, -78, -79, -80
Zenta, Hermann OxMus
Zenti, Girolamo d1668 NewGrD 80
Zentner, Si 1917- BgBands 74, CmpEPM
Zepler, Bogumil 1858-1918 Baker 78
Zeraschi, Helmut 1911- IntWWM 80
Zerato, Louis John 1936- AmSCAP 66, -80
Zerbe, Anthony FilmgC, HalFC 80, WhoHol A
Zerbini, Carlotta d1912 NotNAT B
Zercher, J Randall 1940- ConAmC
Zerffi, William Arthur Charles 1887- WhoMus 72
Zerga, Joseph E 1914- AmSCAP 66
Zerga, Joseph Frederick 1942- AmSCAP 66, -80
Zerga, Joseph Louis Edmund 1924- AmSCAP 80
Zeromski, Stefan 1864-1925 CnMD, ModWD
Zerr, Anna 1822-1881 BiDAmM
Zerrahn, Carl 1826-1909 Baker 78
Zerrahn, Karl 1826-1909 BiDAmM
Zerwitzky, Adam NewGrD 80
Zerzyski, Jerzy WomWMM
Zes, Tikey A 1927- ConAmC
Zesen, Philipp Von 1619-1689 NewGrD 80
Zessarskaya, Emma Film 2
Zesso, Giovanni Battista NewGrD 80
Zethelius, Gudrun 1918- IntWWM 77, -80
Zetterholm, Finn Tore 1945- IntWWM 77, -80
Zetterling, Mai 1925- BiDFilm, -81, FilmEn, FilmgC, ForYSC, HalFC 80, IlWWBF[port], IntMPA 77, -75, -76, -78, -79, -80, MotPP, MovMk[port], OxFilm, WhThe, WhoHol A, WomWMM, WorEFlm
Zetty, Claude Elias 1924- IntWWM 77, -80
Zetzer, Alfred 1916- IntWWM 77, -80
Zeugheer, Jakob 1803-1865 NewGrD 80
Zeumer, Gerti WhoOp 76
Zeuner, Charles 1795-1857 Baker 78
Zeuner, Heinrich Christopher 1795-1857 BiDAmM
Zeuner, Karl Traugott 1775-1841 Baker 78, NewGrD 80
Zeuner, Martin 1554-1619 NewGrD 80
Zeuthen, Morten 1951- IntWWM 80
Zeutschner, Tobias 1621-1675 NewGrD 80
Zganec, Vinko 1890-1976 Baker 78, NewGrD 80
Zguridi, Alexander Mikhailovich 1904- DcFM
Zhandov, Zahari 1911- DcFM
Zhdanov, Yuri 1925- CnOxB, DancEn 78
Zhdanova PlP&P
Zheljazkova, Binka WomWMM
Zhelobinsky, Valery Viktorovich 1913-1946 Baker 78, NewGrD 80
Zheutlin, Cathy WomWMM B
Zhiganov, Nazib 1911- Baker 78
Zhilin, Alexey Dmitriyevich 1766?-1848? NewGrD 80
Zhillinsky, A Film 2
Zhito, Lee ConMuA 80B
Zhitomirsky, Alexander 1881-1937 Baker 78
Zhitomirsky, Daniel' Vladimirovich 1906- NewGrD 80
Zhivotov, Alexei 1904-1964 Baker 78
Zhivotov, Alexey Semyonovich 1904-1964 NewGrD 80
Zhukov, A Film 2
Zhukov, Leonid 1892-1951 DancEn 78
Zhukovsky, German Leont'yevich 1913- NewGrD 80
Zhukovsky, Herman 1913-1976 Baker 78
Zhuraytis, Algis 1928- IntWWM 77, -80
Ziak, Benedikt NewGrD 80
Ziak, Siegbert Karl Gustav 1909- IntWWM 77, -80
Ziani, Marc'Antonio 1653?-1715 NewGrD 80
Ziani, Marco Antonio 1653?-1715 Baker 78
Ziani, Pietro Andrea 1616-16[illegible] NewGrD 80
Ziani, Pietro Andrea 1620?-16[illegible] Baker 78
Zibold, Carlos Film 2
Zich, Jaroslav 1912- Baker 78, WhoMus 72
Zich, Otakar 1879-1934 Baker 78, NewGrD 80
Zich, Ottokar 1879-1934 OxMus
Zichova, Zorka 1920- IntWWM 77, -80
Zichy, Count Geza 1849-1924 NewGrD 80
Zichy, Geza, Count Vasony-Keo 1849-1924 Baker 78
Zide-Booth, Rochelle 1938- CnOxB
Zidek, Ivo 1926- NewGrD 80, WhoOp 76
Zidek, Paulus NewGrD 80
Zidi, Claude 1934- FilmEn
Zieff, Howard HalFC 80, IntMPA 77, -78, -79, -80
Ziegel, Erich 1876-1950 EncWT
Zieger, Bruno Film 2
Ziegfeld, Flo 1869-1932 CmpEPM
Ziegfeld, Florenz DancEn 78
Ziegfeld, Florenz 1841-1923 BiDAmM
Ziegfeld, Florenz 1867-1932 EncMT, FilmgC, HalFC 80, NotNAT B, OxThe, PlP&P[port], WhThe
Ziegfeld, Florenz 1868-1932 EncWT
Ziegfeld, Florenz 1869-1932 BiDAmM, CnThe, Ent, NotNAT A
Ziegler, Anne 1910- IlWWBF A, WhThe
Ziegler, Caspar 1621-1690 NewGrD 80
Ziegler, Christian Gottlieb 1702-1760? NewGrD 80
Ziegler, Christiane Mariane Von 1695?-1760 NewGrD 80
Ziegler, Clara 1844-1909 NotNAT B, OxThe
Ziegler, Edward 1870-1947 BiDAmM, NewEOp 71, NotNAT B
Ziegler, Johann Gotthilf 1688-1747 NewGrD 80
Ziegler, Joseph Paul 1722-1767 NewGrD 80
Ziegler, Jules Morton 1900-1967 BiE&WWA, NotNAT B
Ziegler, Klara 1844-1909 EncWT
Ziegler, Richard Adam 1945- AmSCAP 80
Ziegler, William HalFC 80
Ziehn, Bernard 1845-1912 BiDAmM
Ziehn, Bernhard 1845-1912 Baker 78, NewGrD 80
Ziehrer, C M 1843-1922 NewGrD 80
Ziehrer, Karl Michael 1843-1922 Baker 78
Zielenski, Mikolaj NewGrD 80
Zielenski, Nicolas OxMus
Zielinski, Jaroslaw 1847-1922 NewGrD 80
Zielinski, Jaroslaw De 1844-1922 Baker 78
Zielinski, Tadeusz A 1931- NewGrD 80
Ziemann, Sonja WhoHol A
Ziemann, Sonja 1925- FilmAG WE
Ziemann, Sonja 1926- HalFC 80
Ziems, Harry 1907- WhoMus 72
Ziener, Bruno Film 2
Zier, Jerry Film 2
Zieritz, Grete Von 1899- IntWWM 77, -80
Zierler, Steffan NewGrD 80
Ziese, Christa-Maria 1924- WhoOp 76
Zievens, Bob ConMuA 80B
Ziffer, Felix C 1930- IntMPA 77, -75, -76, -78, -79, -80
Ziffer, Fran AmSCAP 80
Ziffer, Frances 1917- AmSCAP 66
Ziffrin, Marilyn Jane 1926- AmSCAP 80, CpmDNM 79, ConAmC
Zifkin, Walter 1936- IntMPA 77, -75, -76, -78, -79, -80
Zigmond, Jerry IntMPA 77, -75, -76, -78, -79, -80
Zigon, Marko 1929- IntWWM 80
Ziino, Ottavio 1909- WhoOp 76
Zijderlaan, Johan 1923- IntWWM 77, -80
Zika, Richard 1897-1947 Baker 78
Zikmundova, Eva 1932- IntWWM 77, -80, WhoOp 76
Zilahy, Lajos 1891- CnMD, OxThe
Zilcher, Hermann 1881-1948 Baker 78, NewGrD 80, OxMus
Zildjian NewGrD 80
Zildjian, Avedis NewGrD 80
Zilevicius, Juozas 1891- ConAmC
Zilio, Elena WhoOp 76
Zillig, Winfried 1905-1963 Baker 78, NewGrD 80
Ziloti, Alexander Il'yich 1863-1945 Baker 78, NewGrD 80
Zilzer, Wolfgang Film 2, WhoHol A
Zima, Milan Sylvester 1904-1973 AmSCAP 80
Zimbalist, Al WhoHrs 80
Zimbalist, Alfred N IntMPA 75
Zimbalist, Efrem 1889- AmSCAP 66, -80, Baker 78, BiDAmM, ConAmC, IntWWM 77, -80, MusSN[port]
Zimbalist, Efrem 1890- NewGrD 80
Zimbalist, Efrem, Jr. MotPP, WhoHol A
Zimbalist, Efrem, Jr. 1913- BiE&WWA
Zimbalist, Efrem, Jr. 1918- HalFC 80, NotNAT
Zimbalist, Efrem, Jr. 1923- FilmEn, FilmgC, ForYSC, IntMPA 77, -75, -76, -78, -79, -80, MovMk
Zimbalist, Sam 1904-1958 FilmEn, FilmgC, HalFC 80, NotNAT B
Zimina, Valentina 1899-1928 Film 2, WhScrn 74, -77, WhoHol B

Zimmer, Bernard 1893-1964 *McGEWD*
Zimmer, Friedrich 1855-1919 *Baker 78*
Zimmer, Friedrich August 1826-1899 *Baker 78*
Zimmer, Jan 1926- *Baker 78, IntWWM 77, -80, NewGrD 80*
Zimmer, Lee *WhoHol A*
Zimmer, Norma *BiDAmM*
Zimmer, Pierre *WhoHol A*
Zimmer, Toni *Film 2*
Zimmerl, Christl 1939- *DancEn 78[port]*
Zimmerl, Christl 1939-1976 *CnOxB*
Zimmerman, Charles A 1861-1916 *BiDAmM*
Zimmerman, Ed 1933-1972 *WhScrn 77*
Zimmerman, Elyn 1945- *WomWMM B*
Zimmerman, Franklin B 1923- *NewGrD 80*
Zimmerman, Gus 1887?- *NewOrJ*
Zimmerman, J Fred d1925 *NotNAT B*
Zimmerman, J Fred, Jr. d1948 *NotNAT B*
Zimmerman, James H 1938- *AmSCAP 80*
Zimmerman, Phyllis *ConAmC*
Zimmerman, Pierre-Joseph-Guillaume 1785-1853 *Baker 78, NewGrD 80*
Zimmerman, Roy 1913-1969 *NewOrJ[port]*
Zimmerman, Tom 1886?-1923 *NewOrJ*
Zimmermann, Agnes 1845-1925 *Baker 78*
Zimmermann, Agnes 1847-1925 *NewGrD 80*
Zimmermann, Anton 1741-1781 *Baker 78, NewGrD 80*
Zimmermann, Bernd Alois 1918-1970 *Baker 78, CnOxB, DcCM, NewGrD 80[port]*
Zimmermann, Don *ConMuA 80B*
Zimmermann, Ed 1933-1972 *WhoHol B*
Zimmermann, Erich 1892-1968 *NewGrD 80*
Zimmermann, Gerda 1927- *CnOxB*
Zimmermann, Heinz Werner 1930- *IntWWM 77, -80, NewGrD 80*
Zimmermann, Jorg 1933- *WhoOp 76*
Zimmermann, Louis 1873-1954 *Baker 78*
Zimmermann, Pierre-Joseph-Guillaume 1785-1853 *NewGrD 80*
Zimmermann, Udo 1943- *NewGrD 80*
Zimmerschied, Dieter 1934- *IntWWM 80*
Zimmet, Marya *WhoHol A*
Zinano, Gabriele 1560?-1635? *McGEWD*
Zinck, Bendix Friedrich 1743?-1801 *NewGrD 80*
Zinck, Benedict Friedrich 1743?-1801 *NewGrD 80*
Zinck, Benedikt Friedrich 1743-1801 *Baker 78*
Zinck, Hardenack Otto Conrad 1746-1832 *NewGrD 80*
Zinck, Harnack Otto Conrad 1746-1832 *Baker 78, NewGrD 80*
Zinck, Hartnack Otto Conrad 1746-1832 *NewGrD 80*
Zincke, Hans Friedrich August *NewGrD 80*
Zindars, Earl 1927- *ConAmC*
Zindel, Paul 1936- *CnThe, ConDr 73, -77, DcLB 7[port], McGEWD[port], NatPD[port], NotNAT, WhoThe 72, -77*
Zindel, Samuel 1650?-1703 *NewGrD 80*
Zindelin, Philipp 1750?-1622 *NewGrD 80*
Zindl, Samuel 1650?-1703 *NewGrD 80*
Zineroni, Agostino *NewGrD 80*
Zingarelli, Niccolo Antonio 1752-1837 *MusMk, NewGrD 80*
Zingarelli, Nicola Antonio 1752-1837 *Baker 78, OxMus*
Zingel, Hans J 1904-1978 *NewGrD 80*
Zingel, Rudolf Ewald 1876-1944 *Baker 78*
Zingone, Giovanni Battista *NewGrD 80*
Zingoni, Giovanni Battista *NewGrD 80*
Zink, Benedict *NewGrD 80*
Zink, Harnack Otto Conrad *NewGrD 80*
Zinkeisen, Doris Clare *DcPup, WhThe*
Zinkeisen, Konrad Ludwig Dietrich 1779-1838 *Baker 78*
Zinkler, Christiane 1947- *WhoOp 76*
Zinman, David 1936- *Baker 78*
Zinn, Michael Alan 1947- *CpmDNM 76, -79, -80, ConAmC*
Zinnegrabe, Sue *WomWMM B*
Zinneman, Fred 1907- *IntMPA 80*
Zinnemann, Fred 1907- *AmFD, BiDFilm, -81, CmMov, DcFM, FilmEn, FilmgC, HalFC 80, IntMPA 77, -75, -76, -78, -79, MovMk[port], OxFilm, WorEFlm*
Zinnen, Jean-Antoine 1827-1898 *Baker 78*
Zinner, Heda 1907- *CroCD*
Zinner, Hedda 1907- *CnMD*
Zinovieff, Joanna 1918- *IntWWM 77*
Zinsstag, Gerard 1941- *IntWWM 77, -80*
Zinzendorf, Count 1700-1760 *OxMus*
Zinzendorf, Nikolaus Ludwig Von 1700-1760 *BiDAmM, NewGrD 80*
Zionah, Levy Lirom 1929- *IntWWM 77*
Zipoli, Domenico 1688-1726 *Baker 78, MusMk, NewGrD 80*
Zipp, Friedrich 1914- *Baker 78, IntWWM 77, -80, NewGrD 80*
Zipprodt, Patricia 1925- *NotNAT, WhoOp 76, WhoThe 77*
Zirato, Bruno 1884- *WhoMus 72*
Zirler, Stephan 1518?-1568 *NewGrD 80*
Zirra, Alexandru 1883-1946 *NewGrD 80*
Ziryab d850? *NewGrD 80*
Ziskin, Victor 1937- *AmSCAP 66, -80, ConAmC A*
Zitek, Otakar 1892-1955 *Baker 78*
Zitek, Vaclav 1932- *WhoOp 76*
Zitek, Vilem 1890-1956 *NewGrD 80*
Zito, Phil 1914- *NewOrJ*
Zito, Philip Anthony 1913- *IntWWM 77*
Zito, Salvatore 1933- *AmSCAP 66*
Zito, Torrie 1933- *AmSCAP 80, ConAmC*
Ziv, Frederick W *NewYTET*
Zivkovic, Milenko 1901-1964 *Baker 78, NewGrD 80*
Zivkovic, Mirjana 1935- *IntWWM 77, -80*
Zivny, Vojtech *NewGrD 80*
Zivoni, Yossi 1939- *IntWWM 77, -80, WhoMus 72*
Ziwny, Adalbert *NewGrD 80*
Zlocha, Erika 1939- *CnOxB, DancEn 78*
Zmeskall, Nikolaus, Baron VonDomanovecz 1759-1833 *Baker 78, NewGrD 80*
Zminsky, Emanuel *NewGrD 80*
Znosko-Borovsky, Alexander 1908- *Baker 78*
Zobel, Ingeborg 1928- *WhoOp 76*
Zoebeley, Hans Rudolf 1931- *IntWWM 77, -80*
Zoeckler, Dorothy Ackerman 1915- *AmSCAP 66, -80*
Zoeller, Carl 1840-1889 *Baker 78*
Zoeller, Carli 1840-1889 *NewGrD 80*
Zoeller, Karl 1840-1889 *NewGrD 80*
Zoellner, Joseph, Sr. 1862-1950 *Baker 78*
Zoellner, Peter Lee 1919-1971 *AmSCAP 80*
Zoephel, Klaus Joachim 1929- *IntWWM 77, -80*
Zoff, Jutta 1928- *NewGrD 80*
Zoff, Otto 1890-1963 *CnMD, EncWT*
Zoffany, John 1733?-1810 *OxThe*
Zogott, Seymour S 1930- *AmSCAP 80*
Zoilo, Annibale 1537?-1592 *Baker 78, NewGrD 80*
Zoilo, Cesare 1584-1622? *NewGrD 80*
Zola, Emile 1840-1902 *CnThe, EncWT, FilmgC, HalFC 80, McGEWD, ModWD, NewEOp 71, NotNAT A, -B, OxThe, REnWD[port]*
Zola, Fred *WhThe*
Zola, Jean-Pierre *WhoHol A*
Zolan, Miro 1926- *CnOxB, DancEn 78*
Zolkowski, Alojzy 1814-1889 *EncWT*
Zolkowski, Alojzy Fortunat 1777-1822 *EncWT*
Zoll, Klaus 1944- *IntWWM 77, -80*
Zoller, Attila Cornelius 1927- *EncJzS 70*
Zoller, Bettye *AmSCAP 80*
Zoller, Karlheinz 1928- *NewGrD 80*
Zollikofer VonAltenklingen, Caspar 1707-1779 *NewGrD 80*
Zollman, Ronald 1950- *IntWWM 77, -80*
Zollner, Carl Friedrich 1800-1860 *Baker 78, NewGrD 80*
Zollner, Heinrich 1792-1836 *Baker 78*
Zollner, Heinrich 1854-1941 *Baker 78, NewGrD 80*
Zolotarev, Vasily 1872-1964 *Baker 78*
Zolotaryov, Vasily Andreyevich 1872?-1964 *NewGrD 80*
Zoltai, Denes 1928- *IntWWM 77, -80, NewGrD 80*
Zoltan, Aladar 1929- *Baker 78, NewGrD 80*
Zombies, The *ConMuA 80A, IlEncR[port], RkOn 2[port]*
Zomer, Hans 1933- *IntWWM 77, -80*
Zomerdijk, Henricus Jacobus 1918- *IntWWM 77*
Zomosa, Maximiliano 1937-1969 *CnOxB*
Zompakos, Stanley 1925- *DancEn 78*
Zonca, Giovanni Battista 1728-1809 *NewGrD 80*
Zonca, Giuseppe 1715-1772 *NewGrD 80*
Zonca, Joseph 1715-1772 *NewGrD 80*
Zonga, Giovanni Battista 1728-1809 *NewGrD 80*
Zonga, Giuseppe 1715-1772 *NewGrD 80*
Zonka, Giovanni Battista 1728-1809 *NewGrD 80*
Zonka, Giuseppe 1715-1772 *NewGrD 80*
Zonn, Paul 1938- *CpmDNM 76, ConAmC*
Zonn, Wilma Zapora 1936- *IntWWM 77, -80*
Zonni, Alexander 1931- *AmSCAP 80*
Zonta *NewGrD 80*
Zook, Mary Ann 1939- *IntWWM 77, -80*
Zoon, Gerrit 1918- *IntWWM 77, -80*
Zopff, Hermann 1826-1883 *Baker 78, NewGrD 80*
Zoppis, Francesco 1715?-1781? *NewGrD 80*
Zoras, Leonidas 1905- *Baker 78, NewGrD 80*
Zorich, Louis *WhoHol A*
Zorilla Y Moral, Jose 1817-1893 *NotNAT B*
Zorina, Vera 1917- *AmPS B, BiE&WWA, CnOxB, DancEn 78[port], EncMT, FilmEn, FilmgC, ForYSC, HalFC 80, MotPP, MovMk[port], NotNAT, ThFT[port], What 3[port], WhoHol A, WhoThe 72, -77*
Zorita, Nicasio 1545?-1593? *NewGrD 80*
Zoritch, George 1919?- *CnOxB, DancEn 78[port]*
Zorko, George Matthew 1947- *ConAmC*
Zorn, Friedrich-Albert *CnOxB, DancEn 78*
Zornicht, Jonas 1595-1629 *NewGrD 80*
Zorrilla, Francisco DeRojas *OxThe*
Zorrilla, Jose 1817-1893 *McGEWD[port]*
Zorrilla Y Moral, Jose 1817-1893 *OxThe*
Zorzor, Stefan 1932- *Baker 78*
Zosimos Of Panopolis *NewGrD 80*
Zosimus Of Panopolis *NewGrD 80*
Zoss, Joel Robert 1944- *AmSCAP 80*
Zotos, Thomas 1948- *AmSCAP 80*
Zottoviceanu, Elena 1933- *IntWWM 80*
Zou-Zou 1943- *FilmAG WE, WhoHol A*
Zouary, Maurice H 1921- *IntMPA 77, -78, -79, -80*
Zouhar, Zdenek 1927- *Baker 78, NewGrD 80*
Zousmer, Jesse d1966 *NewYTET*
Zrno, Felix 1890- *IntWWM 77*
Zsasskovszky *NewGrD 80*
Zsasskovszky, Endre 1794-1866 *NewGrD 80*
Zsasskovszky, Endre 1824-1882 *NewGrD 80*
Zsasskovszky, Ferenc 1819-1887 *NewGrD 80*
Zschau, Marilyn 1941- *WhoOp 76*
Zschocher, Johann 1821-1897 *Baker 78*
Zsigmond, Vilmos 1930- *FilmEn, HalFC 80, IntMPA 80*
Zsolt, Bende 1926- *WhoOp 76*
Zsolt, Nandor 1887-1936 *Baker 78, NewGrD 80*
Zuber, Gregor *NewGrD 80*
Zuber, Johann Friedrich d1693 *NewGrD 80*
Zuber, Ron *BlkAmP*
Zubiaurre, Valenti 1837-1914 *Baker 78*
Zubiaurre Y Unionbarrenechea, V De 1837-1914 *NewGrD 80*
Zubkovskaya, Inna 1923- *CnOxB, DancEn 78*
Zubkovsky, Nicolai 1911- *DancEn 78*
Zubler, Susan *PupTheA*
Zubrod, Paul Frederick 1949- *IntWWM 77, -80*
Zubrzycki, Boguslaw 1929- *IntWWM 77, -80*
Zucca, Mana *Baker 78*
Zuccalmaglio, Anton W Florentin Von 1803-1869 *NewGrD 80*
Zuccalmaglio, Anton Wilhelm F Von 1803-1869 *Baker 78*
Zuccari, Carlo 1704-1792 *NewGrD 80*
Zucchi, Virginia 1847-1930 *CnOxB, DancEn 78*
Zucchini, Gregorio 1540?-1616? *NewGrD 80*
Zucchino, Gregorio 1540?-1616? *NewGrD 80*
Zucco, Frances 1933-1962 *WhScrn 77, WhoHol B*
Zucco, George 1886-1960 *FilmEn, FilmgC, ForYSC, HalFC 80, HolCA[port], MovMk, NotNAT B, Vers A[port], WhScrn 74, -77, WhThe, WhoHol B, WhoHrs 80[port]*
Zuchert, Leon 1904- *Baker 78*

Zuchino, Gregorio 1540?-1616? *NewGrD 80*
Zuckerman, Irv *ConMuA 80B*
Zuckerman, Joe 1910- *IntMPA 75*
Zuckerman, Mark 1948- *ConAmC*
Zuckerman, Pinchas 1948- *IntWWM 77, -80*
Zuckermann, Wolfgang Joachim 1922- *NewGrD 80*
Zuckerova, Olga 1933- *IntWWM 77, -80*
Zuckert, Bill *WhoHol A*
Zuckmayer, Carl 1896-1977 *CnMD, CroCD, EncWT, Ent[port], FilmEn, McGEWD[port], ModWD, OxThe, REnWD[port], WhoThe 72, -77, WorEFlm*
Zuckmayer, Karl 1896- *NotNAT A*
Zuelli, Guglielmo 1859-1941 *Baker 78*
Zuffi, Pietro 1919- *WhoOp 76*
Zugler, Joseph Paul *NewGrD 80*
Zugsmith, Albert 1910- *FilmEn, FilmgC, HalFC 80, IntMPA 77, -75, -76, -78, -79, -80, NatPD[port], WhoHrs 80, WorEFlm*
Zugsmith, Alfred *WhoHol A*
Zukerman, George 1927- *NewGrD 80*
Zukerman, Pinchas 1948- *Baker 78, BnBkM 80, MusSN[port], NewGrD 80*
Zukofsky, Paul 1943- *Baker 78, ConAmC, IntWWM 77, -80, NewGrD 80, WhoMus 72*
Zukor, Adolph 1873-1976 *BiDFilm 81, DcFM, FilmEn, FilmgC, HalFC 80, IntMPA 75, -76, OxFilm, WorEFlm*
Zukor, Adolph 1874- *TwYS B*
Zukor, Eugene J 1897- *IntMPA 75, -76*
Zulaica Y Arregui, Jose Gonzalo *NewGrD 80*
Zulauf, Ernst 1876-1962 *Baker 78*
Zulauf, Max 1898- *Baker 78*
Zulawski, Wawrzyniec Jerzy 1916-1957 *NewGrD 80*
Zulehner, Carl 1770?-1830 *OxMus*
Zulema 1947?- *DrBlPA*
Zullig, Hans 1914- *CnOxB, DancEn 78*
Zulu *WhoHol A*
Zulueta, Jorge 1934- *NewGrD 80*
Zulzul *NewGrD 80*
Zumaya, Manuel De 1678?-1756 *NewGrD 80*
Zumbach, Andre 1931- *IntWWM 77, -80*
Zumbo, Francesca 1944- *CnOxB*
Zumbro, James Mark 1931- *IntWWM 77*
Zumbro, Nicholas 1935- *Baker 78*
Zumpe, Herman 1850-1903 *NewGrD 80*
Zumpe, Hermann 1850-1903 *Baker 78, CmOp*
Zumpe, Johann Christoph *NewGrD 80*
Zumpe, Johannes *NewGrD 80, OxMus*
Zumsteeg, Johann Rudolf 1760-1802 *Baker 78, MusMk, NewGrD 80, OxMus*
Zundel, John 1815-1882 *Baker 78, BiDAmM*
Zunser, Jesse 1898- *BiE&WWA, IntMPA 75, -76, NotNAT*
Zupan, Jakob 1734-1810 *NewGrD 80*
Zupancic, Oton 1878-1949 *CnMD*
Zupanovic, Lovro 1925- *IntWWM 77, -80, NewGrD 80*
Zupko, Ramon 1932- *Baker 78, ConAmC*
Zur, Menachem 1942- *CpmDNM 76, ConAmC, IntWWM 77, -80*
Zur Muhlen, Raimund Von 1854-1931 *Baker 78, NewGrD 80*
Zur Nieden, Albrecht 1819-1873 *Baker 78*
Zurawlew, George 1887- *IntWWM 77, -80*
Zurbruegg, Eva 1941- *IntWWM 77, -80*
Zurica, Pat *WhoHol A*
Zurica, Robert J *WhoHol A*
Zurke, Bob *BgBands 74*
Zurke, Bob 1912-1944 *WhoJazz 72*
Zurke, Robert 1912-1944 *BiDAmM*
Zurla, Martin *MorBAP*
Zurlini, Valerio 1926- *DcFM, FilmEn, WorEFlm*
Zusanek, Harald 1922- *CnMD, CroCD, McGEWD*
Zuschneid, Karl 1854-1926 *Baker 78*
Zuth, Josef 1879-1932 *Baker 78*
Zuvich, Dennis Michael 1942- *AmSCAP 80*
Zvereff, Nicholas 1888-1965 *CnOxB*
Zverev, Nicholas 1897?-1965 *DancEn 78*
Zverev, Nicolai 1832-1893 *Baker 78*
Zviagina, Suzanna Nicolaievna 1918- *CnOxB*
Zvirblys, Jean Ann Farrington 1923- *IntWWM 77*
Zvoboda, Andre 1910- *OxFilm*
Zvonar, Josef Leopold 1824-1865 *NewGrD 80*
Zvonar, Joseph Leopold 1824-1865 *Baker 78*
Zwar, Charles 1914- *EncMT, WhoThe 72, -77*
Zwart, Jaap 1924- *IntWWM 77, -80*
Zweers, Bernard 1854-1924 *Baker 78, NewGrD 80*
Zweig, Arnold 1887-1968 *CnMD, ModWD*
Zweig, Barry Kenneth 1942- *EncJzS 70*
Zweig, Esther Sommerstein 1906- *ConAmC, IntWWM 77*
Zweig, Fritz 1893- *Baker 78, BiDAmM*
Zweig, Stefan 1881-1942 *Ent, NewGrD 80, NotNAT A, -B, PlP&P*
Zweiller, Andreas 1545?-1582 *NewGrD 80*
Zwelinck, Jan Pieterszoon *NewGrD 80*
Zwerdling, Allen 1922- *ConAmTC*
Zwerin, Michael 1930- *EncJzS 70*
Zwertschek, Erich Sylvester 1948- *AmSCAP 80*
Zweter, Reinmar Von *NewGrD 80*
Zwetler, Johann Nepomuk Felix 1759?-1826 *NewGrD 80*
Zwetler, Theodor 1759?-1826 *NewGrD 80*
Zwettler, Johann Nepomuk Felix 1759?-1826 *NewGrD 80*
Zwettler, Theodor 1759?-1826 *NewGrD 80*
Zwibelson, Hortense *AmSCAP 80*
Zwick, Johannes 1496?-1542 *NewGrD 80*
Zwickey, Fern *PupTheA*
Zwicky, Conrad Fridolin 1946- *IntWWM 77, -80*
Zwierzchowski, Mateusz 1713?-1768 *NewGrD 80*
Zwilich, Ellen Taaffe 1939- *Baker 78, CpmDNM 80, ConAmC*
Zwingli, Huldreich 1484-1531 *NewGrD 80*
Zwingli, Ulrich 1484-1531 *NewGrD 80*
Zwintscher, Bruno 1838-1905 *Baker 78*
Zwiny, Wojciech *NewGrD 80*
Zwolinsky, Bonnie Anne 1953- *IntWWM 77*
Zwolle, Heinrich Arnold Von *NewGrD 80*
Zwolle, Henri Arnaut De *NewGrD 80*
Zwysen, Sebastian *NewGrD 80*
Zwyssig, Alberich 1808-1854 *Baker 78*
Zwyssig, Alberik 1808-1854 *NewGrD 80*
Zygmuntowski, Teodor 1740?-1800? *NewGrD 80*
Zygowicz, Julia *PupTheA*
Zykan, Otto Mathaus 1935- *Baker 78, IntWWM 77, -80*
Zylinski, Faustyn 1793?-1867 *NewGrD 80*
Zylis-Gara, Teresa 1935- *IntWWM 77, -80, MusSN[port], WhoOp 76*
Zylis-Gara, Teresa 1937- *NewEOp 71, NewGrD 80*
Zylstra, Willemina 1920- *IntWWM 77*
Zyrlerus, Stephanus *NewGrD 80*
Zytowski, Carl Byrd 1921- *IntWWM 77, -80*
Zywny, Adalbert 1756-1842 *NewGrD 80*
Zywny, Wojciech 1756-1842 *NewGrD 80*
ZZ Top *ConMuA 80A, RkOn 2[port]*